SEARS,
ROEBUCK
& CO.
CATALOGUE NO. 114

Skyhorse Publishing books may be purchased in bulk at special discounts for sales promotion, corporate gifts, fund-raising, or educational purposes. Special editions can also be created to specifications. For details, contact the Special Sales Department, Skyhorse Publishing, 307 West 36th Street, 11th Floor, New York, NY 10018 or info@skyhorsepublishing.com.

Visit our website at www.skyhorsepublishing.com.

10 9 8 7 6 5 4 3 2 1

Library of Congress Cataloging-in-Publication Data is available on file.

ISBN: 978-1-61608-873-6

Printed in Canada

Sears, Roebuck & Co.

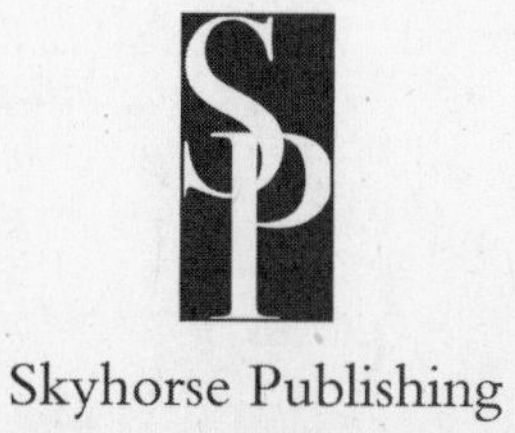

Skyhorse Publishing

Our New Home in Course of Construction.

TWENTY ACRES of our own ground in the very heart of one of the very best districts in Chicago, midway between Garfield and Douglas parks, one-half mile long and one block wide, bounded on the east by Kedzie avenue, on the south by the Chicago Terminal Railroad tracks, bounded on the west by Central Park avenue and on the north by Harvard street, and facing Spaulding, Homan and St. Louis avenues. Over 40 acres of floor space, ready July 1st, with plans for over 100 acres of floor space as it may be required from time to time to meet any growing demands. Miles of our own railroad tracks, our own railroad yards, our own motive power, engines, crews, etc., all on our own property. Our own railroad facilities to insure promptest possible shipment, lowest handling cost and the lowest possible freight rates.

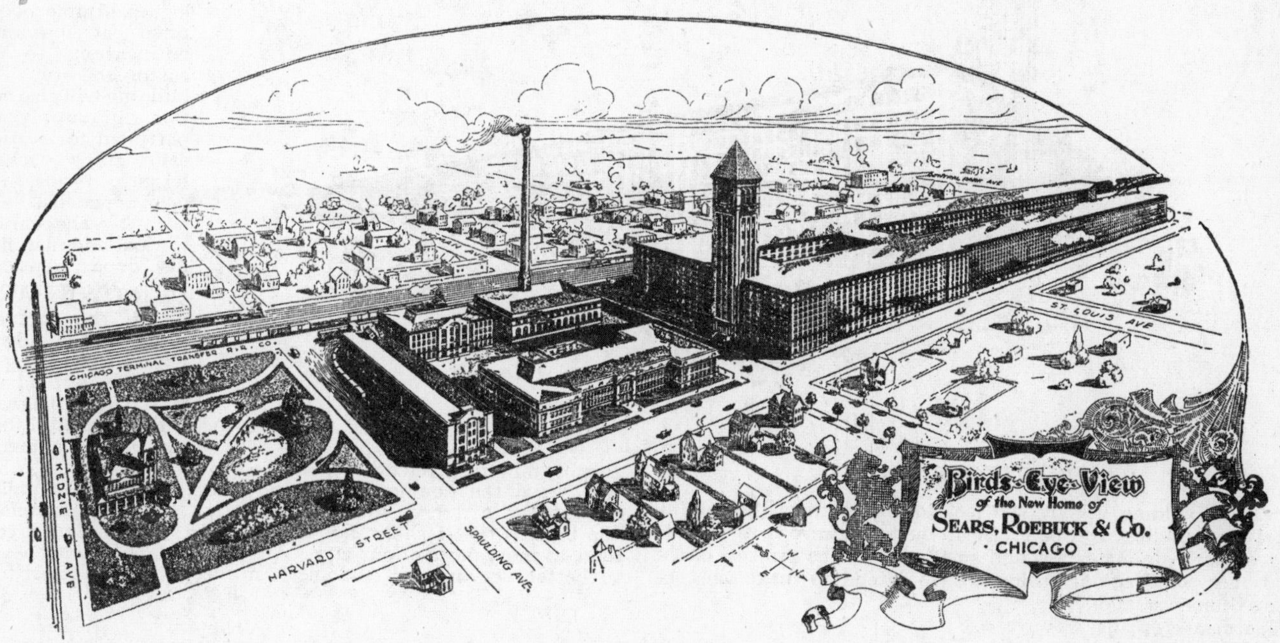

CHICAGO TERMINAL RAILROAD COMPANY.

Our own railroad connects directly with the Chicago Terminal Railroad, the great Chicago switching railroad, which connects with all the different trunk line railroads entering Chicago, and under our contract, without one penny s cost to the customer for switching, transferring or hauling in Chicago, without one penny's cost being figured in the selling price of the goods or otherwise for teaming or handling, every order will be forwarded through our railroad, the Terminal Railroad and the connecting main or trunk line railroads in Chicago with the greatest possible dispatch, and at the very lowest possible freight charge to the customer.

OUR MERCHANDISE BUILDING—THE WORKS.

The building in which we will carry the merchandise is to be known by us as the **Works,** for in this building everything is work and everything will be working, the largest single building in the world devoted to the handling of merchandise, the one building being one-fourth of a mile long (over three blocks) and one block wide. Miles of railroad tracks will run lengthwise through, in and around this building, receiving, moving and forwarding merchandise; elevators, mechanical conveyers, endless chains, moving sidewalks, gravity chutes, apparatus and conveyers, pneumatic tubes and every known mechanical appliance for reducing labor, for the working out of economy and dispatch will here be utilized in our great Works. In this building, will be employed thousands of people in the packing and filling of orders, in the packing, the shipping and the handling of merchandise.

With the facilities that we will have in this enormous building, orders sent to us will be received, filled, put onto the cars and on their way to destination in an almost incredibly short time, and the saving in cost in doing all this will all go to our customers in the shape of lower prices. In this building, every express company in Chicago will be represented by a local agent, delegated to handle our work and ours alone. The railroads and the postoffice will here be specially represented for us. The Western Union Telegraph Company and the Postal Telegraph Company will here have an office devoted exclusively to our use.

ADMINISTRATION BUILDING.

This building, immediately opposite and across Homan avenue from the Works, will be 450 feet long, 80 feet wide, three stories high and the highest type of fireproof construction, and will be devoted entirely to the administration of the business. In this building will be all the executive offices, the offices of the president, vice-president, secretary, treasurer, offices of the general manager and superintendents, offices of the Customers' Profit Sharing and Banking Departments and of the traffic manager, auditor, comptroller and bookkeepers. In this building nearly 2,000 people will be employed in opening the mail, writing the bills, answering letters and in attending to every little detail of the clerical work attached to every order that is received by us. From the building we will communicate with the Works, or main building, by tunnels, overhead bridges, pneumatic tubes, automatic carriers, telephone and telegraph, and your order, opened in this building, can be dispatched to the Works in a fraction of a minute, filled, conveyed to the railroad cars below and on the way to you in a really incredibly short time.

To promote health, efficiency and economy the building will be equipped with the most modern hygienic and health giving apparatus, including filtered warm air in winter and filtered cold air in summer, light, space and ventilation, the most sanitary plumbing and pure water from a deep artesian well, etc.

OUR OWN POWER PLANT.

In this building will be an enormously large power plant, many boilers, large, medium and small engines for their various duties, many electric dynamos, etc. The equipment will produce more than 12,000 horse power with room to later develop more than as much more. Here we will generate the electricity to run 30,000 electric lights, which will be required to light our plant by night. In this plant all heat and power will be generated for operating the network of machinery necessary to the handling of our business.

BUILDING TO HANDLE OUR ADVERTISING MATTER.

In this building, about 150 feet south of the Administration building and about 40 feet west of the printing plant, will be devoted entirely to the compiling, composition (type setting) and mailing of our catalogues, circulars and price lists of all kinds. In this building we will have a large photographing department for the making of cuts and engravings of all descriptions. This building will be 160 feet long by 90 feet wide, four stories, and will be connected to the printing plant by covered passageways. Here we expect to send out as high as fifty tons of printed matter daily, consisting of large catalogues, special catalogues, sample books, price lists, circulars, notifications to our customers, etc. This building will also contain our supply department for stationery, entry tickets, blank forms, ink, pens, pencils, etc., used by the various clerical and merchandise departments.

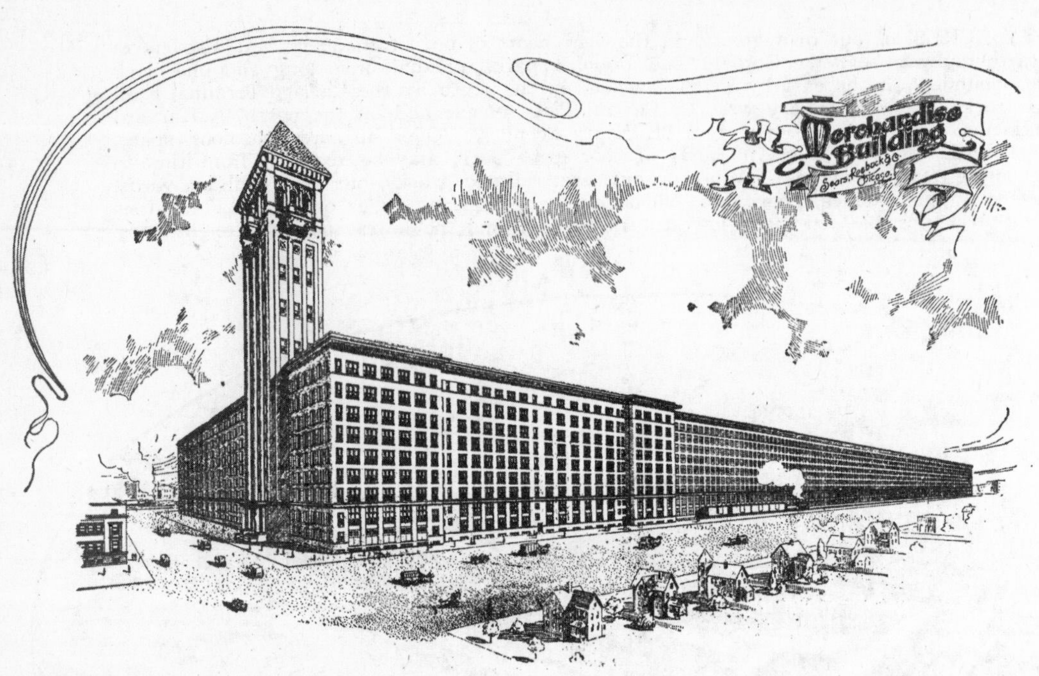

OUR OWN PARK.

To the east and south of the Administration building we shall lay out a beautiful park, with gravel walks, beautiful shade trees, ornamental shrubs, flowers, green grass and a beautiful artificial lake, which will serve the double purpose of holding millions of gallons of water as a reservoir for fire protection. Here our employes can breathe the fresh air, free from the dirt, dust and noise common to most parts of our city. All this is planned with a view to better serving our customers in every state and territory.

PRINTING PLANT.

This building, about 100 feet to the south of the Administration building, will be given up in its entirety to the printing of our catalogues, big and small, and to the printing of the stationery used in our business. We intend to make this the most modern and model printing plant possible. With perfect light, built to our own measure and requirements, railroad tracks to carry the paper leading direct to the printing presses, we look for the greatest economy. This building is being built to accommodate twenty special Cottrell rotary perfecting catalogue making printing presses, each made to our order, made especially to make our big catalogues. Add to this a large number of large, medium and small flat bed, rotary and other printing presses, plate making machines, binding, covering, gathering, trimming and other machinery and equipment, and you can form just some little idea of the extensiveness of the plans necessary to take care of the printing branch of our business. All the printing done in this building will be exclusively for our own requirements. Our own printing plant is another economy that makes for lower prices.

Everything we can do in the way of bettering the surroundings and conveniences for our employes adds to their happiness and contentment, improves their efficiency and thus tends to improve our service, quickens the dispatch of orders, lessens cost of handling and makes for lower prices.

Our City Within a Great City and How We Came to Build.

WE SAY, "our city within a great city," because it covers a tract of land one-half mile long, a fair sized **farm plat within great Chicago.** On this land great buildings are being built, more than 7,000 people will be employed within our walls, and, with the families of our employes, more than 40,000 people will seek new homes within convenient distances of our big plant.

Ten years ago this company was organized as **a house with a policy.** That policy was, is and ever shall be **quality and price.** Ten years ago we offered our catalogue to the world. Then, located in a five-story building on Adams street, we were, in less than one year, driven to seek larger quarters at Fulton and Desplaines streets, and the ten years past have been a history of build and enlarge. Covering the entire block we occupy, we were soon driven to seek large buildings in other blocks, and one by one, these buildings have been added until we now occupy in their entirety, seven enormously large buildings in Chicago, in addition to our main store.

The people's ability to judge quality and price has been shown in the unparalleled growth of our business. So accurately do they judge, that they have left their accustomed places of supply and come to us, and they tell their friends and their friends' friends and then everyone tells everyone's friends until the orders are flowing to our doors. So general and so great has been the demand from every section for the past few years, that we have been compelled at times to limit and restrict the circulation of our catalogue. Announcements of new catalogues have been withheld from many states. The past year we have not been able to supply one catalogue where three catalogues were wanted, so great has been the demand, so thoroughly do the people appreciate **quality and price. We must supply the demand** We are now in the hands of the people. It's really the people that are placing us on this broad expanse, **our city within a city.** It's the people that are causing all our factories to be enlarged. The people have come to us in such unexpected and heretofore unheard of numbers that we have been compelled to keep our catalogues from going into the additional millions of hands that wanted them. **Our policy,** the Sears, Roebuck & Co. policy, the policy of Mr. Sears and every officer, manager and director of our organization is—**quality, price, satisfaction, every facility exhausted to serve the people.**

Mere money making is far from our greatest ambition. If the principle that shapes, develops and expands our policy was not influenced and directed by a principle much higher, much greater than that of mere money making, we would have little hope for the future. If the greatest success for the future of this business was only in money making, it would not begin to pay the writer and his co-officers for directing the affairs of this institution. If the success of this institution was to be measured only by dollars gained, it would be a thousand times easier for the writer and his co-executives to retire from the multitudinous responsibilities of so great an organization and seek rest, recreation and pleasure the remainder of their lives. Dollars and cents enter into our business policy only so far as is actually necessary for the legitimate conduct and perpetuity of our business. Our ambition is to gain, merit and hold the confidence of as many of the citizens of the United States as can be made possible by the best service we can give. We have an ambition to, and we believe we will, within five years, be selling more than one hundred million dollars worth of merchandise annually, and our ambition is to see how much more we can make your dollar buy than it has ever bought before. We would rather know that in five or ten years' time we had served at least a large percentage of all the people in the United States in a way that their dollars went further, that we brought them nearer to the source of supply, thus advancing their comforts and happiness; this accomplished, we would feel much more richly repaid for all our efforts than we would if we knew we were to be repaid only by mere dollars, even riches beyond that of the richest individual or corporation in the land.

There is one policy in our house. The office boys know it as well as the officers, the managers, the assistant managers, the order pickers, the freight handlers, the clerks up and down the line, one knows it as well as the other. It's infused in every act and every thought of every individual on our payroll and will ever be inculcated in the minds of every one that is added to our force, and that is—**consider our customers, don't consider us.** Give our customers every advantage that our facilities will permit. We are the servants of the people. To serve them the very best we can, keep no advantage to ourselves, give it all to our customers. Serve every customer as it becomes an honest lawyer to serve his client with all the talent, all the ability that he may possess. Consider every customer honest. Forget yourself, remember the customer. Give the customer the highest possible quality, give him the lowest possible cost; give the customer the greatest possible facility, relieve him of any possible risk. In questions of doubt give the customer the benefit of the doubt. If we can own better goods and own them cheaper by manufacturing them ourselves, we make them ourselves, not for ourselves but for our customers. Every penny of saving, every betterment of quality, all for our customers, none for us. That's the policy of our house and our customers understand it. It's a policy for the people and by the people, organized and run for the people, and not for mere gain alone. Our own factories are building and enlarging all over the United States, all the time getting closer to the raw material and all the time working toward lower prices, not for more profit, not alone for money gain; all done through the people, by the people and for the people. If by building another factory, if by enlarging the present factory we reduce the cost of any commodity by 5 per cent, you get it, not we. Our policy says it belongs to you, therefore, we cannot take it. Our buyers know it and our sellers know it. Our policy is made, fixed and set for you.

Our work has hardly begun. You have encouraged us to do what we have, and instilled us with ambition to do more. With your support, which we already have in an overabundance, we shall continue to seek the foundation of cost in every commodity.

Many more factories will be erected, cost will yet be greatly reduced, you will yet be brought much nearer to the first cost of production. The day will come when your dollar will go much farther toward procuring for you those things which you require. You have and are furnishing us the material with which to work, and we find our pleasure, our ambition and future, working for you, the spirit of which is not mere dollar making, but comfort, pleasure and luxury building, the building of a full equivalent for the dollar of a progressive and enlightened people; and when our work is done and the time comes to hand it over to the next set of generals in line, I promise you, reader or customer, from the bottom of my heart, that if the writer and his associates have been instrumental in bringing about a condition by which the people are served and get in exchange for the dollars they earn (whether their purchases are made from us or others), a more liberal measure, a more just equivalent than would have been possible for them to have gotten had it not been for the inception, progress and development of this institution; this accomplished, if the remaining years of our application to this business do not add one penny to our present individual fortunes, I will feel abundantly repaid for all the responsibilities, all the care, all the work and effort that is yet to go into the guidance of this ship of commerce in my remaining years. This, reader, is the policy of the institution that calls your attention to the pages of this catalogue.

A Message of Good Cheer.

With malice toward none and charity for all, we extend to all mankind our sincere wishes for greater prosperity, health and happiness.

To all those who buy, to all those who build and to all those who sell, we wish you **success.** Perchance you are a competitor, retail dealer, wholesale dealer, manufacturer or a mail order house. **Great** or **small,** we wish you **well.** We believe we are all entering an era of more modern merchandising, **better values, fewer losses, greater economies,** a larger equivalent for the dollar, and therefore have a right to look for greater and grander successes than have heretofore been attained. With the almost phenomenal growth of wealth and buying power of our country, many new and modern methods in the selling of merchandise will surely develop. Retail dealers will buy closer and closer and will thus be able to give better and better values; many manufacturers, now selling to jobbers only, will begin selling to the retail dealers direct, saving him at least a good portion of the jobber's profit, while many manufacturers, now selling to jobbers or retail dealers, will offer their wares direct to the user. Jobbers will study and learn new economies so as to make lower prices; retail dealers will buy more and more for cash, growing constantly keener and keener in their buying and study of economy; catalogue houses, general and special, will continue to grow, many of the small getting large and the large getting larger, and with very few exceptions, all sellers of goods, regardless of place or method, will give **honest goods with honest representations** and an ever growing equivalent for the dollar.

Certainly this must be the method of every successful institution of every kind and place.

If every seller of merchandise in every station will constantly study how to economize in his business, carefully study values and markets, with a view of buying to the best possible advantage, get on to as near a spot cash basis as possible, and strive to give every customer the most value possible for his money, he will find plenty of room for growth and with it success.

The consumer today is buying from many catalogue houses, special and general, he is also buying from many factories direct as well as from the many thousands of retail dealers, special stores, general stores, department stores, etc. He has a right to buy where he likes and every seller has the same equal right to solicit his trade. Let us all believe as **we do,** that every **successful** dealer, retailer, catalogue house or otherwise, is **reliable.** If a grocer or clothier, let us think as well of our neighbor grocer or clothier across the street as if he were our banker. Let us rise above the petty jealousies and differences that so often grow out of competition, so that in the evening of the days' work your competitor will be as welcome to break bread at your table as would be your doctor or your banker.

We have a high regard for every honorable and reliable dealer and even though we may at times differ in **our opinions, we bear no ill will against any maker or seller in our land.**

We solicit trade from all, promising everyone the very best service which the very best facilities and organization can give. We can't do more and we never will do less.

SEARS, ROEBUCK & CO.,
By R. W. SEARS, President.

THIS BOOK

WILL BE SENT TO ANY ADDRESS

FREE

BY MAIL POSTPAID ON APPLICATION

SIMPLE RULES FOR ORDERING.

USE OUR ORDER BLANK IF YOU HAVE ONE. If you haven't one, use any plain paper.

TELL US IN YOUR OWN WAY WHAT YOU WANT, always giving the CATALOGUE NUMBER of each article. Enclose in the letter the amount of money, either a postoffice money order, which you get at the postoffice, an express money order, which you get at the express office, or a draft, which you get at any bank; or put the money in the letter, take it to the postoffice and tell the postmaster you want it registered.

IF YOU LIVE ON A RURAL MAIL ROUTE, just give the letter and the money to the mail carrier and he will get the money order at the postoffice and mail it in the letter for you.

DON'T BE AFRAID YOU WILL MAKE A MISTAKE. We receive hundreds of orders every day from young and ld who never before sent away for goods. We are accustomed to handling all kinds of orders.

TELL US WHAT YOU WANT IN YOUR OWN WAY, written in any language, no matter whether good or poor writing, and the goods will be promptly sent to you.

WE HAVE TRANSLATORS TO READ AND WRITE ALL LANGUAGES.

DON'T BE AFRAID OF THE FREIGHT OR EXPRESS CHARGES. You must pay them when you get the goods at the station, but they never amount to much compared with what we save you in cost.

IF YOU FIND IT NECESSARY TO HAVE SOME SPECIAL INFORMATION you can undoubtedly obtain it by referring to the matter contained within the first ten pages of this catalogue.

ENKLA REGLER ATT IAKTTAGA VID BESTÄLLNING.

Begagna vår beställningsblankett, om ni har en sådan. m icke, begagna vanligt rent papper.

Säg oss på edert eget sätt hvad ni önskar, alltid uppgifande katalognumret på hvarje sak. Inneslut beloppet i brefvet antingen i postoffice money order, hvilken köpes å postkontoret; express money order, hvilken köpes å expresskontoret, eller en vexel, hvilken kan köpas å hvilken bank som helst, eller också inneslut kontanta penningar i brefvet, tag det till postkontoret och säg postmästaren att ni önskar få det registrerat.

Var icke rädd för att ni gör ett misstag. Vi erhålla hundratals beställningar dagligen från unga och gamla hvilka aldrig förr sändt efter varor. Vi äro vana vid att expediera alla slags beställningar.

Säg oss på edert eget sätt hvad ni önskar. Skrif på hvilket språk som helst, bra eller dålig stafning, bra eller dålig handstil, och varorna skola blifva eder prompt tillsända.

Vi ha öfversättare som läsa och skrifva alla språk.

Det är icke nödvändigt för eder att genomläsa de första io sidorna i denna katalog, såvida ni icke önskar någon speciell upplysning. Dessa tio sidor innehålla detaljerad uppsning, så att de som i alla delar önska göra sig förtrogna med sättet att beställa och sända varor, fraktkostnader o. s. v., o. s. v., icke behöfva skrifva till oss, utan helt enkelt kunna slå upp dessa sidor och finna den upplysning de önska.

Einfache Regeln zum Bestellen.

Gebraucht unsere Bestellungszettel wenn Sie welche haben, wenn nicht nehmen Sie gewöhnliches Papier.

Im Bestellen erwähnen Sie die Catalog Numero an allen Sachen. Die Bestellung soll das Geld enthalten, entweder eine „Postoffice Money Order," (welche man gewöhnlich an der Post bekommen kann), eine "Expreß Money Order," ein Bank Certificate, das man an jeder Bank bekommen kann, oder legen Sie das Geld in den Brief mit der Bestellung, in welchem Falle Sie den Brief **Eingeschrieben** schicken sollten. Der Brief wird in der Post Eingeschrieben (Registered.)

Wir erhalten jeden Tag eine große Anzahl von Bestellungen von allen Leuten (Jung und Alt).

Sie brauchen nicht furchtsam zu sein Sachen zu bestellen, wir werden Ihr Bestellung schon verstehen.

Schreiben Sie uns in Ihrer eigener Weise, und in Ihrer eigener Sprache, was Sie wollen, einerlei ob gut oder schlecht geschrieben, und die Waare wird Ihnen sofort zugeschickt.

Wir haben Leute die alle Sprachen schreiben und übersetzen.

Die ersten zehn Seiten in diesem Catalog beziehen sich hauptsächlich an die Frachtbetrage der verschiedenen Waare und hat nur Wichtigkeit für Sie im Falle Sie in diesen Einzelheiten interessiert sind.

O NOT FAIL TO GIVE SIZE, COLOR, WEIGHT, ETC., IF REQUIRED, WHEN WRITING YOUR ORDER.

HOW WE MAKE EVERY TRANSACTION WITH US STRICTLY CONFIDENTIAL.

Why our name and address do not appear on any box, package, wrapper, tag, envelope or article of merchandise.

As many people, especially merchants, business houses, townspeople and others, do not care to have others know where or from whom they buy their goods, as many people object to having the name of the shipper spread across every box or package, so that when it is unloaded at the station or express office everyone can see what they are getting and where they buy it, to protect all those who care for this protection and make it possible for you to order your goods from us with no fear of anyone learning at the railroad station, express office or elsewhere what you bought or where you bought it, our name and address will not appear on any box, package, tag, envelope or article of merchandise.

For example: If you are a merchant and wish to buy goods to sell again, your customers will be unable to learn from any marks inside or outside where you bought the goods or what you paid for them.

If you are a professional man, or even in the employ of some merchant, who for personal reasons might object to your sending to us for goods, you need have no fear, our name will not appear on any goods or packages you get.

While we would be glad to have our name appear on every article of merchandise and on every box and package, as a valuable means of advertising, we have learned that thousands of our customers need the protection that the omitting of our name affords. This applies especially to townspeople.

NO ORDER WILL BE ACCEPTED FOR LESS THAN 50 CENTS.

PLEASE DO NOT SEND US ANY ORDER AMOUNTING TO LESS THAN 50 CENTS. If you want some article, the price of which is less than 50 cents, please include one or more other needed articles and make your order amount to 50 cents or more.

AS A MATTER OF ECONOMY, BOTH TO OUR CUSTOMERS AND OURSELVES, we do not fill orders for less than 50 cents. The postage or express charges especially make small orders under 50 cents unprofitable to the purchaser, or at least much more expensive than the orders amounting to 50 cents or more.

WE MAKE THIS EXCEPTION: In the case of needed repairs, attachments and supplies, such as needles for our sewing machines, parts of guns, etc., which can be secured only from us, we will fill the order no matter how small it may be.

TO MAKE ORDERING BY MAIL VERY PROFITABLE TO OUR CUSTOMERS we especially urge that you make your order as large as possible. Orders of from $2.00 to $5.00 or more are always very much more profitable to the purchaser than smaller orders, for the express or freight charges are in this way very greatly reduced. It always pays, even if you have to get some friend or neighbor to join with you, to make up an order of from $2.00 to $5.00 or more, and include enough heavy goods to make a profitable freight shipment of fifty to one hundred pounds. In this way you reduce the transportation charges on each item to next to nothing. You then pay the exact same freight charges that your storekeeper must pay on the goods he sells.

ON THE BASIS OF FAR GREATER VALUE FOR YOUR MONEY THAN YOU CAN POSSIBLY GET ELSEWHERE, lower prices than any other house does or can name, the best possible service, every item ordered guaranteed to reach you in perfect condition and give perfect satisfaction or your money to be immediately refunded to you; on our binding guarantee to please you in every way on every dollar sent us, wholly in your own interest we ask you to kindly conform to these terms.

OUR COMPLIMENTS TO THE RETAIL MERCHANT.

IT IS NOT OUR DESIRE TO ANTAGONIZE THE RETAIL MERCHANT (the storekeeper of the country). This is a big growing country and there is ample room for us all. Our prices are alike to all. Whether to the largest or the smallest merchant, farmer, mechanic or laborer, our price is exactly the same. Our goods are for sale at the prices plainly printed in this book, and occupation or position restricts no one from buying goods from us at our printed prices.

However, we number thousands of the best merchants of the United States among our valued customers. The prejudice which for a time existed because we would not sell to the dealer and refuse to sell to his customers, is dying out; for the shrewd, careful buying up to date merchant of today has broader business views. He buys his goods where he can get the best value for his money, and on the basis of more value for the money than is furnished by any other house we especially invite all classes of merchants to carefully compare our prices as printed in this book with the prices you have been in the habit of paying.

As explained on this page, we ship all our goods in plain boxes or packages, and our name appears on no package or article of merchandise. You can buy your goods from us at our selling prices, which are much lower than you can buy elsewhere, you can fix your profit to suit yourself and your customers will not know where you bought the goods or what you paid for them.

We want to correct the impression that may be in the minds of some merchants, that we sell exclusively to the consumer, the party who buys the goods to use. If you have this impression we are anxious to correct it. A goodly percentage of the goods we ship in all lines go direct to merchants, business houses who buy to sell again, and in some lines, especially materials and supplies, a large percentage of our goods go to manufacturers, which they use in the manufacture of their wares, which in turn they sell to dealers. Among our valued customers are the U. S. Government, state and city institutions, railroads and other large corporations, and also jobbers, brokers, retailers and consumers in all foreign lands.

WE ESPECIALLY SOLICIT THE TRADE OF THE SUCCESSFUL, SHREWD BUYING MERCHANT, who wishes to buy his wares where he can get the highest standard of quality at lower prices than he can get elsewhere.

OUR LIBERAL TERMS OF SHIPMENT.

WE HAVE NO DISCOUNTS. We sell for cash only, and the prices quoted in this catalogue are absolutely net, from which there is no discount whatever. Our prices are alike to one and all, regardless of the amount of the order, the same to the merchant as to the farmer, mechanic or laborer.

OUR TERMS OF SHIPMENT ARE VERY LIBERAL. Nearly all our customers send cash in full with their orders, thus saving the small charge the express companies always make for collecting a C. O. D. and returning the money to us, and we certainly advise sending cash in full with the order, to make this saving and as a more satisfactory way of ordering, always, of course, with the understanding that we will immediately refund your money for any goods that are not perfectly satisfactory to you.

WE ADVISE AGAINST ORDERING GOODS TO BE SHIPPED BY EXPRESS OR FREIGHT C. O. D., SUBJECT TO EXAMINATION. First, by reason of an extra express charge (as above mentioned), a charge which the express companies always make for collecting the money and returning it to us. This charge is always saved when cash in full is sent with the order. Second, where goods are shipped by freight C. O. D., subject to examination, a draft for the amount of the C. O. D. must be sent for collection either by express or to some bank in your town, and the goods must be shipped consigned to ourselves, with instructions for the railroad agent to notify you that the goods are there. The freight agent, as a rule, will allow you to examine the goods before paying for them. (Goods shipped by express, you can always examine before paying for). But on a freight shipment, before the goods can be delivered to you, you must first go to the express office or bank and pay the amount of the C. O. D. in order to have the bill of lading or order for the delivery of the goods to you. With this bill of lading or order for the goods you can then go to the railroad station and get the goods; on the other hand, if the full amount of cash is sent with your order the goods are shipped direct to you, and you only have to go to the railroad station or express office and pay the freight or express charges and take the goods; always, of course, with the understanding that if the goods are not perfectly satisfactory when received you can return them to us at our expense and we will immediately refund your money. However, to those who prefer to see and examine the goods they buy before paying for them, we offer to make shipment on C. O. D., subject to examination, pay after received liberal terms as follows:

OUR C. O. D. TERMS.

ANY GOODS QUOTED IN THIS CATALOGUE (unless otherwise specially stated, provided the order amounts to $5.00 or more), will be shipped to any address east of the Rocky Mountains by freight C. O. D., subject to examination, on receipt of a sufficient amount of cash with the order to pay all express or freight charges both ways. On receipt of such an order, the goods will go forward by express or freight C. O. D., subject to examination. You will be credited on the bill for the amount of money sent with your order. After the goods are received and examined at your nearest railroad station or express office, if they are found perfectly satisfactory you can then pay the balance of our price and freight or express charges, less the amount of money sent with the order. If, however, the goods are not perfectly satisfactory you can return them to us at our expense and we will immediately refund the cash deposit sent with your order. Our only object in requiring you to send a cash deposit sufficient to pay the freight or express charges both ways is to protect us against a class of people who might order out of curiosity, with no idea of accepting and paying for the goods when received, thus putting us to an unnecessary expense for transportation charges which our low selling prices will not warrant.

WHERE THE EXACT DEPOSIT REQUIRED IS NOT STATED, we advise that on all orders amounting to less than $10.00, one-fourth of the amount of the order be sent with the order. On orders amounting to more than $10.00 one-fifth of the amount should be sent with the order. For example, If you wish the goods shipped C. O. D., subject to examination, and your order amounts to $8.00, you should send at least $2.00 with your order. If your order amounts to $20.00, send $4.00 with your order, the balance payable after received.

NOTE—WHERE A VERY SMALL CASH DEPOSIT WILL BE ACCEPTED.

On receipt of 50 cents any watch or any item of jewelry amounting to $2.00 or more will be sent C. O. D.

On receipt of $1.00 any camera, telescope or field glass will be shipped C. O. D.

On receipt of $1.00 any graphophone or talking machine will be shipped C. O. D.

On receipt of $1.00 any organ or piano will be shipped C. O. D., to any point east of the Rocky Mountains and north of the Ohio River, or will be shipped without a deposit where the money is deposited with a reliable party in your town, as fully explained under the heading of organs and pianos.

On receipt of $1.00 any violin, guitar, mandolin, banjo, autoharp, zither or band instrument will be shipped C. O. D.

On receipt of $1.00 any bicycle, gun or revolver will be shipped C. O.

On receipt of $5.00 any buggy or carriage will be shipped to any address east of the Rocky Mountains, C. O. D.

On receipt of $1.00 any harness or saddle will be shipped to any address east of the Rocky Mountains, C. O. D.

On receipt of $1.00 any sewing machine will be shipped to any address C.O.D.

On receipt of $1.00 any stove will be shipped to any address east of the Rocky Mountains and north of Tennessee C. O. D.

On receipt of $1.00 any item of men's, boys' or children's clothing or ladies' wearing apparel amounting to $3.00 or more will be sent to any address in the United States by express C. O. D.

THE ABOVE NAMED GOODS WILL BE SENT to any address within the radius mentioned on receipt of the small cash deposit named, which deposit must accompany the order, the balance, together with the freight or express charges, to be paid after the goods are received, examined and found satisfactory. All other merchandise where deposit is not mentioned, as before stated, will, unless otherwise stated, be sent subject to examination either by freight or express where a sufficient deposit accompanies the order to pay transportation charges both ways.

IN THE INTEREST OF OUR CUSTOMERS, to save you the extra express charge for the collection and return of the money, and to save you the inconvenience attached to delivery of goods shipped by freight C. O. D., subject to examination, we specially urge that you send cash in full with your order, understanding of course that you take no risk and that we will immediately return your money if you are not perfectly satisfied. Yet, to those who prefer to see and examine the goods before they pay for them, when so requested we will make shipment C. O. D., subject to examination, to be paid for after received on the small deposit terms as above stated.

Paragraph A.

ABOUT OUR PRICES.

HOW WE CAN UNDERSELL ALL OTHER CONCERNS.

SECTION 1. BY REASON OF OUR ENORMOUS OUTPUT OF GOODS we are able to make contracts with representative manufacturers and importers for such large quantities of merchandise that we can secure the lowest possible prices, and in some lines our trade has been so large, as, for example, in vehicles, organs, stoves, cloaks, tailoring, guns, revolvers, upholstered furniture, etc., that we have been able to equip our own factories and foundries, thus saving you even the manufacturer's profit; but whether the goods are manufactured by ourselves or bought direct in large quantities, we add the smallest percentage of profit possible to the actual cost to us, and on this economic, one small profit plan, direct from manufacturer to consumer, you can buy a large percentage of the merchandise we handle, direct from us at less than your storekeeper at home can buy in quantities.

WE EMPLOY THE MOST COMPETENT BUYERS that money can obtain, men who are experts and have a life long experience in their particular lines. Our established reputation for buying everything in enormous quantities gives our buyers inside track with all the largest manufacturers, thereby giving us the benefit of first choice in the markets. Manufacturers who are overstocked often come to us and offer their goods at a big discount for cash, knowing that we have a larger outlet for merchandise than any other concern. For this reason many articles in this catalogue are quoted at less money than the actual cost to produce. No matter how cheap we buy, we give our customers the benefit, for we feel that our bargains are our customers' bargains.

SECTION 2. WE BUY AND SELL FOR CASH, and having no bad debts, no traveling men's expenses, no expenses for collecting, securing the manufacturers' lowest spot cash prices, we can sell goods at a smaller margin of profit than any other business house could do and still exist.

WE MAKE NO REDUCTIONS IN OUR PRICES. To those who are inclined to write us for a reduction from the prices quoted in this catalogue, we wish to state that we cannot make any reduction or concession, whether you order in large or small quantities. The price quoted on each and every article in this catalogue is as low as we can possibly make it, and it is out of the question to reduce these prices still further; and we earnestly believe a careful comparison of our prices with those of any other concern will convince you that we can furnish you better goods for less money than you can obtain from any other house in the United States.

ALL PRICES ARE SUBJECT TO THE FLUCTUATION OF THE MARKET. The prices quoted in this book are correct, according to market conditions at the date the catalogue is printed, and our wants have been anticipated as far as possible by contract, goods in stock, etc.; but when our stock on hand is sold or when a contract expires and the market conditions at that time are such that we are compelled to pay more money for the goods, we reserve the right to advance our prices without notice, charging you the difference the advance represents, only the difference in cost to us. The necessity for advancing prices very rarely happens, but as a protection to us, at the extremely low prices we are making, we must reserve this right, and this space is used to inform everyone of the right so reserved. If prices decline so that we are able to buy any goods to fill orders at lower prices than those printed in this catalogue, you will always get the benefit of such prices and the difference will be returned to you in cash.

AS THE TENDENCY IS FOR LARGER CONTRACTS, larger purchases, closer buying, the history of our house and our records show that **we reduce prices and return the difference in cash ten times** where we make an advance and ask more money once; but for our protection the right to recognize advances and declines must be and is reserved.

IN THIS CATALOGUE you will find only such goods listed as we can save you money on, goods that can be delivered anywhere in the United States for less money than they can be bought at your local dealer's. The amount of money that we can save you over the prices you pay at home varies from 5 to 50 per cent, according to the nature of the goods, but there is not an item quoted in this entire catalogue on which the saving is not worth taking into consideration, to say nothing of the fact that our goods are, as a rule, of higher grade than those carried by the average storekeeper or catalogue house.

THE ILLUSTRATIONS AND DESCRIPTIONS IN THIS CATALOGUE can be depended upon. We aim to illustrate and describe every article with the strictest accuracy. Most all of the illustrations are made from photographs taken direct from the article. They are such as enable you to order intelligently; in fact, with our assortment, correct illustrations and accurate descriptions, you can order from this catalogue with the same ease, confidence and security as though you were personally in our store selecting the goods yourself.

Paragraph C.

HOW TO ORDER.

Use our regular order blank if you have one; if not use any plain paper.

Always keep well supplied with our order blanks, as it is more convenient for you to make out your order on our regular order blanks than in any other way. If out of them at any time, drop us a postal card and we will be pleased to send you some.

Whether you write your order on our regular order blank or letter paper instead, **be sure to observe the following instructions:**

Always sign your full name (Christian name and surname).

Write your name in full, clearly and distinctly.

Give your postoffice, county and state, and your shipping point, if different from the postoffice.

Always give catalogue number in full (write every figure and letter in the catalogue number), description and price of each article ordered.

Always try to mention the number or name of the catalogue or circular from which your order is taken, and be sure to give the size, color, weight and measurements when required.

We must have your correct size or measurements for such goods as hats, shoes, clothing, ladies' ready made dresses, cloaks, and the size and color of everything that has size and color.

Be sure to enclose your money with your order and state plainly in your order how much money you enclose and in what form. Sending us money in one envelope and your order in another causes delay and confusion in our office, as they become separated in the mails. For instructions on how to send money see **paragraph F.**

Be sure you have followed our rules carefully about enclosing the proper amount of money with the order, including enough to pay postage if the goods are to be sent by mail, and insurance fee if to be sent by insured mail.

Be sure your name and address is written plainly and in full, that your shipping directions are plainly stated, that the exact amount of money enclosed is plainly stated, that you have given us catalogue number, price, description, correct size and measurements and you will seldom if ever have any delay or inconvenience. By carefully observing these rules you will avoid errors and loss of time by our having to write you for further information.

AFTER WRITING AN ORDER, please compare it with these rules, check it over closely and see if you have written your order correctly.

IF YOU WISH TO REFER TO ANY MATTER not concerning the order, be sure to write it on a separate sheet. Do not write about it on your order sheet, though you may enclose it in the same envelope with your order. Our orders and letters are handled in separate and distinct departments, and we ask you therefore please do not fail to observe this rule.

ALWAYS TRY TO WRITE REMARKS CONCERNING YOUR ORDER on the same sheet with the order. This will prevent the possibility of such remarks or instructions being separated from the order. Should you have occasion to write us concerning an order which you have already sent us, do not fail to mention the date on which your letter was mailed, also state the nature and value of your remittance and the name and address as given in your order. This information will enable us to promptly locate the matter you refer to.

SHOULD YOU CHANGE YOUR ADDRESS, please notify us, being sure to give old as well as new address in full.

Paragraph D.

ABOUT OMISSIONS.

ALL ORDERS FOR MERCHANDISE are accepted by us with the understanding that we will use every reasonable effort to promptly ship every item exactly as ordered, and in order to make this possible we carry in stock, constantly, merchandise to the value of more than four million dollars, and if we do not have the goods in stock we invariably buy them in Chicago if we can, even if we are compelled to pay more than we get for them, rather than delay an order or withhold shipment of any part of an order. But it sometimes happens that on an order including several items of merchandise there may be one or two items that are not in stock and cannot be had in Chicago, usually for the reason that the manufacturers are behind with their orders, have met with some accident or there has been some unusual delay in transportation.

WE THEREFORE ACCEPT ALL ORDERS with the understanding that we reserve the right when unable to ship every item, to cancel that portion of the order which we cannot ship promptly, filling the balance of the order, and returning to the customer in cash the amount for the item or items cancelled. We make this explanation so that anyone ordering merchandise from us, and receiving the goods with one or more items missing, and receiving by mail his money returned for the omitted items, will understand that the reason for omitting is that the goods are not in stock and cannot be had in Chicago at that time. Where an omission for the above reason is necessary we usually send a letter telling when we expect to have a stock of the missing goods, so that the customer may renew his order if he so desires.

UNDERSTAND, it seldom happens that we are unable to fill an order complete and exactly as given, but out of the many thousands of orders we receive every day, there are always a few (a very small number) on which items must be cancelled, and we make this explanation in our catalogue so that none of our customers need misunderstand our position.

Paragraph E.

ABOUT SUBSTITUTION.

WE ARE BITTERLY OPPOSED TO SUBSTITUTING one article for another unless instructed to do so by the customer. We believe, except in rare cases, it is very presuming on the part of any house receiving an order for one kind of goods to send another, without first having the written consent of the customer to do so. There are, however, exceptions where we take upon ourselves the responsibility of substituting, and with reference to this we make the following explanation:

IF A PARTY SENDS US AN ORDER and there is some article in that order which we have not in stock and cannot get in Chicago, but we have the same kind of an article in a higher grade, we then take the liberty of sending the higher grade at the price of the lower grade, sacrificing our profit rather than to disappoint the customer. A customer ordering a watch may call for a 7-jeweled Elgin or Waltham movement and we may not have one in stock, and there may not be one in the Chicago market, in which case we would consider ourselves justified in taking the liberty of substituting a higher grade in an 11 or 15-jeweled Elgin or Waltham movement, but always at the price of the cheaper one ordered, taking the loss ourselves for the difference in price. This is an example. The same would apply on hundreds of items in our stock, but only in cases where in our judgment the customer can only be the better pleased by reason of such action on our part. However, even this kind of substitution we admit is presuming on our part, and when such substitution is made it must be understood it is done entirely at our risk, and with the understanding that if our action is not entirely satisfactory to the customer, he is at liberty to return the goods at our expense of transportation charges both ways and his money is to be immediately returned to him.

Paragraph F.

HOW TO SEND MONEY.

SEND US A POSTOFFICE MONEY ORDER, express money order, bank draft, cash or stamps. Should you send stamps, fold them in waxed paper. We receive many orders with stamps stuck together and worthless. We do not accept revenue stamps, foreign stamps and due stamps, as they are of no value to us. Do not send them.

IF YOU LIVE ON A RURAL ROUTE you can just give the letter and the money to the mail carrier and he will get the money order at the postoffice and mail it in the letter for you.

POSTAGE STAMPS in amounts exceeding $1.00 will be accepted only at a discount of five per cent (5%), or ninety-five cents on the dollar. If you order an article priced at $2.00 and send stamps you should send $2.10. If a $3.00 article you should send $3.15 in stamps. We are compelled to dispose of all surplus stamps at a discount of from 2 per cent to 5 per cent and besides there is an extra expense in handling stamps, and our very small profit will not admit of this expense. We advise remitting by postoffice or express money order, but will accept postage stamps in any amount at 95 cents on the dollar. As an accommodation to our customers we will accept postage stamps at the face value in amounts less than $1.00.

WE RECOMMEND THE POSTOFFICE AND EXPRESS MONEY ORDER SYSTEMS, because they are inexpensive, of less trouble and safe. Besides this, if the money order should get lost or miscarry, your loss will be made good.

DO NOT UNDER ANY CIRCUMSTANCES send money or stamps in a letter except by registered mail. If sent by open mail the letter may never reach us, and in such a case a great amount of trouble and inconvenience is caused, as well as the loss you sustain. **If you prefer to remit by registered mail, we advise the use of two envelopes, one inside the other,** and the outer one carefully and securely sealed. **Do not send gold or silver coin that is defaced,** as light weight coins are worth no more than bullion and bullion is less than the face value of the coin.

TO INSURE SAFETY always register a letter containing money. Be sure to state in your order plainly how much cash you enclose and in what form. You need not be afraid of sending too much, as we always refund when too much money is sent.

Paragraph G.

METHODS OF SHIPMENT.

We can ship goods by mail (see paragraph H about mail shipments), by express (see paragraph I about express shipments), by freight (see paragraph K about freight shipments). If left to our judgment we will ship goods in the manner which will be the least expensive to our customers. **In all cases transportation charges are to be paid by the customer.**

Paragraph H.

MAIL SHIPMENTS.

The mail service affords a convenient method for the transportation of merchandise of small weight and considerable value to points that are distant from express or railroad offices. On all orders to be shipped by mail we require the full amount of cash with the order, together with sufficient money extra to pay postage and insurance or registration, when same is desired. There are three methods of shipping goods by mail:

SECTION 1. OPEN MAIL, which is so called because only the regular amount of postage, according to the classification of goods, is paid and the customer must assume all risk. We do not recommend sending goods by open mail, for if the package is lost or stolen, neither we or the customer have any recourse. In sending goods by open mail the customer must assume all risk.

SECTION 2. INSURED MAIL. This we consider the best, safest and cheapest method of shipping by mail. The following is the rate, in addition to the regular postage: For orders valued at $5.00 or under, 5 cents each. For orders valued at $10.00 or under, 10 cents each. For each additional $5.00 in value, 5 cents extra. In case of loss, we refill the order on receipt of statement certified to by your local postmaster that goods were no treceived. We advise insuring everything of value. Insurance is less than the cost of registering, because no matter how many packages the order consists of, our insurance charge would be only on the value of the order and not on the number of packages, as is the case when sent by registered mail. We guarantee for our charge the safe arrival of the entire order. If you want your mail package insured be sure to write **"Insure"** in your order, and in addition to your remittance for the order be sure to add enough money to pay postage and insurance fee. To secure adjustment it is necessary to make prompt notification of the failure to receive package.

SECTION 3. REGISTERED MAIL, so called because in such cases the postoffice authorities keep a record of the transaction and are thus enabled to trace your shipment. Registry fee per package is 8 cents in addition to the regular postage. We are not responsible for loss of registered mail.

A PACKAGE SHIPPED BY MAIL CANNOT EXCEED 4 POUNDS, but any number of packages may be sent at one time, each weighing four pounds or less. If you live at a great distance from the express office, it might be more convenient to send an order by mail in two or more packages, each weighing four pounds. **One book can be sent by mail, no matter what its weight. The rate is ½-cent per ounce.**

THE RATE ON MERCHANDISE BY MAIL IS 1 CENT PER OUNCE, on books and printed matter, ½ cent per ounce, and you should allow, in addition to the weight of an article, from one to five ounces for packing material, according to size of package shipped.

IF YOU ARE NOT SURE as to the weight of the article, be sure to enclose enough money for postage; if you send too much we will refund balance.

EXPLOSIVES, POISONOUS OR INFLAMMABLE ARTICLES cannot be mailed under any circumstances whatever.

LIQUIDS OVER 4 OUNCES CANNOT BE SENT BY MAIL, but liquids weighing 4 ounces and under can be safely shipped by mail when packed in special mailing cases. Always allow 5 cents extra for this special case.

SECTION 4. PROFITABLE MAIL SHIPMENTS. ARTICLES SUCH AS WATCHES, JEWELRY and other valuable merchandise of light weight, make profitable mail shipments. In all cases where other goods are not ordered at the same time, we advise that such articles can be sent by mail economically.

CERTAIN MEDIUM PRICED GOODS, which, being weighty, cost considerable postage for transportation, should, if possible, be ordered in connection with other needed articles, sufficient to make up express or freight shipment, thus reducing the transportation charges to one-quarter or one-eighth of the postage rate and effecting a far greater saving for you.

WITH THE EXCEPTION OF ARTICLES OF SMALL WEIGHT and of some value, sending goods by mail is by far the most expensive means of transportation, but even in cases where the postage may seem out of proportion to the value of the goods, the cost of the goods with the postage added is usually less than if purchased at the local dealer's and frequently the article wanted is not handled by them at all, while our immense stock of merchandise will supply your demands.

Paragraph I.

EXPRESS SHIPMENTS.

HOW TO FIGURE EXPRESS CHARGES. See pages 7 to 11.

SHIPPING GOODS BY EXPRESS is an absolutely safe method of transportation and offers the advantages of quick service. It is the most profitable method of shipping goods when the weight is less than 20 pounds. Frequently a customer is in a hurry for certain goods and is willing to pay the extra cost of express charges over freight, the money we save him making it profitable on such shipments instead of buying the goods at home.

IF YOU HAVE NO AGENT at your station, all express shipments will be carried to the nearest town where there is an agent. If there is no agent at your station always state in your order at what station you prefer to receive your goods.

A RECOMMENDATION THAT WILL SAVE YOU MONEY: If you live at a far distant point and wish to order some article of merchandise which would weigh about 20 pounds and amount to $6.00 or less, on which the express charges would be from $1.25 to $2.75, and you require nothing further from our catalogue at the time, show the book to your friends, let them add articles they may be in need of and the shipment can go by freight at about the same cost per 100 pounds as by express for 20 pounds, your proportion of the transportation charges being then about 60 cents. We frequently find it greatly to a customer's advantage to ship by freight instead of by express, and when we can save them money by changing the shipping directions we will often do so, unless the goods are wanted in great haste.

ALWAYS RESPOND PROMPTLY TO THE NOTIFICATION OF THE EXPRESS AGENT AS TO THE ARRIVAL OF MERCHANDISE. We are constantly in receipt of requests from them for disposition of packages by reason of the fact that consignee does not reply to postal notices promptly.

Paragraph K.

FREIGHT SHIPMENTS.

FOR FREIGHT CLASSIFICATION and freight rates see pages 7 to 11. Heavy, bulky merchandise, such as agricultural implements, household goods, furniture, groceries, hardware, etc., can be shipped most profitably by freight. When a shipment weighs 100 pounds or more, the railroad companies will charge only for the actual number of pounds.

HOW TO SAVE MONEY ON FREIGHT SHIPMENTS. Railroad companies usually charge no more for 100 pounds than they do for 20 pounds. While the extremely low prices at which we sell our merchandise would make even a small order by freight profitable, as you would certainly be getting the goods cheaper than you could possibly buy them through a dealer, at the same time it would be a considerable saving of money if you could make up a larger order, either of your own wants or club together with your neighbors, as the freight charges will amount to comparatively very little more. The saving that may be effected by anticipating your wants and sending one large order instead of five or six smaller orders at different times is quite an item, and therefore should be taken into consideration by our customers.

YOU MUST PAY THE FREIGHT OR EXPRESS CHARGES, but it will amount to very little as compared with what you will save in the price.

IF YOU HAVE NO AGENT AT YOUR SHIPPING POINT, freight charges must be prepaid. If you do not know what the freight charge will amount to be sure and allow liberally for same. If you send more than actual amount required we will immediately refund the difference. If you have an agent at your station it is not necessary to prepay charges, as they are the same whether paid by you or by us, as our system of checking rates insures for our customers almost absolute correctness in transportation charges.

WHEN WE MAKE A SHIPMENT to a railroad station where there is no agent, we guarantee safe delivery to the station. From the fact that there is no agent at the station to receive the goods the railroad company will not assume any responsibility if after they are put on the platform they are lost or damaged, and we consequently cannot hold them for such loss or damage.

CUSTOMERS WHO ORDER GOODS shipped to a station where there is no agent, must make careful arrangements for the care of the goods after they are put on the platform; otherwise, they are liable to be damaged or stolen. We would recommend that you have the goods shipped, if possible, to your nearest open station where there is an agent, thus making the railroad company entirely responsible for the goods until they are delivered to you.

OVERCHARGES IN TRANSPORTATION. Whenever a customer suspects an overcharge on the part of the transportation company, we will be pleased to give same our most prompt and careful attention in his behalf, if he will send us the expense bill received from the agent, after he has paid the charges. Complaints for overcharges are very few, as our system of checking the rates on freight and express shipments insures for our customers almost absolute correctness in transportation charges.

IF YOU HAVE REASON TO BELIEVE THAT AN ERROR HAS OCCURRED IN THE WEIGHTS, as shown on the freight expense bill, ask the agent to weigh the goods, and if it is found that the shipment is billed overweight he will correct the error and ask you to pay only for the correct weight.

Paragraph L.

INFORMATION ABOUT GOODS SHIPPED DIRECT FROM THE FACTORY.

IN ORDER TO GIVE OUR CUSTOMERS THE VERY LOW PRICES WE DO, prices based on the actual cost to manufacture, cost of material and labor only, with but our one small percentage of profit added, prices much lower than they could possibly get elsewhere, we find it necessary to ship many heavy goods direct from the factory where they are made, and in doing this we save the freight on the goods into our warehouse in Chicago, the cartage, handling and other expenses incident to merchandise passing through the store in Chicago, and we give our customers every particle of the benefit of this saving in our extremely low prices. Wherever the catalogue states the goods are shipped from the factory, the prices quoted are for these goods delivered on board the cars at the factory and the customer pays the transportation charges from the factory. In many cases, the freight from the factory will be less than from Chicago, the factory being nearer to the purchaser. In some cases the factory will be at a greater distance than Chicago, in which case there will be an additional freight beyond the Chicago rate; but even in such cases the saving to you is very great, for if we were to ship the goods to you ourselves we would be compelled to add the freight to Chicago to all the goods, and to this add the expense of handling to and from the railroad, in and out of our store and other expenses incident to general handling of merchandise in the city.

IT SOMETIMES HAPPENS that a customer orders several articles in one order that are shipped from different factories. For instance, he may order a buggy to be shipped from our factory in Southern Indiana, a stove to be shipped from our foundry in Central Ohio, a windmill that will be shipped from our factory in Southwestern Michigan. In this case we would be compelled to make three different shipments. The goods would go direct to our customer from the three different factories, but there would be no extra freight charge by reason of the three shipments, as each shipment would weigh more than 100 pounds and would therefore entitle the customer to the same freight per hundred pounds as if the shipments were all made together.

WHILE THE GREATER PART OF OUR GOODS ARE CARRIED IN STOCK IN OUR STORE AND WAREHOUSES IN CHICAGO, and this factory shipment information does not apply to small or general merchandise, we have found it necessary to make factory shipments on many heavy and bulky articles, purely in the interest of our customers, in order to give our customers the greatest possible value for their money, to enable us to deliver the goods to them at our one small percentage of profit direct from the manufacturer to the consumer, and your attention is called to the explanation that is always made in the catalogue regarding any article that is to be shipped from the factory, that you may understand that the freight is to be paid by the purchasers from the factory direct, and also that you will understand our reason for this method of handling certain merchandise.

WE FREQUENTLY RECEIVE ORDERS which include merchandise, a part of which is to be shipped direct from the factory and part direct from our store. For example: A man may order a buggy and a harness. The buggy will be shipped from the factory, the harness from the store. He may order a stove and some stove furniture, cooking utensils, etc. The stove would be shipped direct from the foundry and the cooking utensils from the store.

WHEN AN ORDER INCLUDES SUCH HEAVY GOODS as we ship direct from the factory (in order to make the low price), and other goods which we ship direct from our store, if that portion of the order which is to be shipped direct from our store is a profitable shipment (see Paragraph M about unprofitable shipments), we make two shipments; the stove, buggy or other heavy shipment going direct from the factory, the balance from our store. But it sometimes happens that that portion of the order to be shipped from our store would not be a profitable shipment. It may be for a few cooking utensils, amounting to $1.00 or $2.00, or a very low priced harness of $5.00 or $6.00, or $1.00 or $2.00 worth of miscellaneous merchandise, on which the freight charges would amount to more than the saving, or difference between our price and the price at which the customer could buy in his own town. In such cases of unprofitable shipment we use our very best judgment, and where we deem that portion of the order that is to go from our house a nonprofitable shipment, we cancel that portion of the order and return the amount to our customer in cash for the goods canceled.

AS A FURTHER EXAMPLE: The customer may order a parlor suite for $15.00 to $20.00, which we ship from the factory, and may include with his order one chair for 90 cents, which we ship from the house. This one chair (except to nearby points), would be considered an unprofitable shipment. On such an order we would take the liberty of cancelling the order for the chair, returning the 90 cents to the customer at once, and we would ship the parlor suite to him direct from the factory by freight, with a letter of full explanation for our action. This article is intended to explain our methods of treating special orders only in the interest of the customers.

Paragraph M.

ABOUT UNPROFITABLE SHIPMENTS.

WE FREQUENTLY RECEIVE ORDERS which we term "unprofitable" shipments, which means that the shipment would not be profitable to our customer. For example: A party living far distant may order a dollar's worth of sugar to go by express. The express charges would equal the cost of the sugar. We occasionally get an order for heavy hardware, the order amounting to perhaps less than $5.00. The goods weigh 100 pounds. We are asked to ship them by express. This is usually an "unprofitable" shipment. An order for a single pair of heavy cheap boots to go a great distance by express, or for very bulky woodenware or heavy and low priced merchandise, such as molasses, nails or cornmeal, might be what we term an "unprofitable" shipment for far distant points.

WE WOULD ADVISE OUR CUSTOMERS to study the freight and express rates, as given on the following pages, for we do not wish you to send us a dollar for anything unless we can save you money on the purchase.

ORDERS THAT WOULD BE UNPROFITABLE to ship by mail or express may be very profitable when sent by freight, but as one hundred pounds is usually carried by freight for the same charge as ten pounds, by adding other merchandise to your order, either for yourself or by getting your neighbors to join you in making up a large order, **you can make the shipment very profitable. Read Paragraph K before making up your order.**

Paragraph N.

CLUB ORDERS.

TO EQUALIZE OR REDUCE THE COST OF TRANSPORTATION, we advise the sending of club orders. Anyone can get up a club. Simply have your neighbors or friends send their orders in with yours and advise us to ship all to one person by freight. If each customer writes his order under his own name, it will be a very easy matter for us to keep each one's goods separate, and the freight charges will be next to nothing when shared by several persons.

IF YOU LIVE AT A FAR DISTANT POINT and wish to order some article or articles of merchandise, which, together, would weigh about twenty pounds, the value of which may be $5.00 or less, and you find that the express charges will be from $1.25 to $2.75, and there is nothing further in our catalogue that you require at the time, show this catalogue to your friends. Let your friends add twenty, thirty or forty pounds, even fifty or seventy-five pounds of goods, then the goods can go by freight and the one hundred pounds by freight will cost no more than twenty pounds by express.

Paragraph O.

HOW TO RETURN GOODS.

BEFORE RETURNING THE GOODS to us in any manner, we would ask that you communicate with us in regard to them, as we are frequently able to adjust matters in a manner that will avoid the delay occasioned by return of goods.

INVOICE NUMBER. Be sure to mention your invoice number under which goods were shipped to you by us.

NEVER RETURN GOODS BY EXPRESS if the weight is more than twenty-five pounds, as it is cheaper to send heavy packages by freight. **When you return goods by express or freight** be sure to enclose in the package your letter of instructions and particulars. **Don't forget** we must always have your invoice number. **Never write us** about a shipment and omit the invoice number. **Don't forget** that a letter containing full instructions should be in all express and freight shipments returned. **Don't forget** we must have your full name and address, exactly as given in the original shipment, in order to properly adjust any matter pertaining to an order returned.

WHEN RETURNING A PACKAGE BY MAIL, write your name, address and invoice number plainly in the upper left hand corner, providing you do not have one of the labels which we furnish when we know goods are to be returned. **Send us by separate mail** the particulars and instructions.

DO NOT ENCLOSE WRITTEN MATTER of any kind in mail packages, as by so doing you are liable to a fine of $10.00 and double letter rate postage.

DO NOT UNDER ANY CIRCUMSTANCES ENCLOSE MONEY WITH THE RETURNED GOODS.

THE UNITED STATES POSTAL LAWS AND REGULATIONS require that all packages of merchandise sent in the mails must be wrapped or enveloped in such a manner that their contents may be readily examined by the postmaster without destroying the wrapper. **Never seal packages returned by mail,** but tie them securely with twine.

DO NOT FAIL TO REGISTER MAIL PACKAGES WORTH $2.00 OR MORE. Merchandise is sometimes lost when sent by open mail. A package can be registered for 8 cents and if necessary can be traced. **Do not enclose money with returned merchandise.** We cannot be responsible for its loss.

Paragraph P.

ABOUT DELAYED SHIPMENTS.

IF YOU HAVE SENT US AN ORDER FOR GOODS and you think it is time they should have arrived, before writing us concerning the delay please consider the following:

While we are willing and glad to answer all kinds of inquiries, to make every possible kind of research, to quickly look up and trace any shipment said to have been delayed, we are daily in receipt of hundreds of letters claiming that goods have been delayed, when the orders have been filled by us with all possible promptness, and have been handled by the railroad or express companies with their usual dispatch. The investigation simply shows the customer is impatient and has not allowed sufficient time for the order to reach us, we to fill the order and the railroad or express company to deliver the goods.

WE FILL ALL ORDERS with the greatest possible dispatch consistent with proper care and safety. It requires from two to six days after your order is received for us to ship goods. Where goods are ordered that have to be made to order or finished after received, such as tailoring, upholstered furniture, vehicles, etc., additional time must be allowed. Goods shipped direct from our factory, such as stoves, sewing machines, furniture and a few other heavy items, require from five to ten days to make shipment, add to this the necessary time for the express company or railroad company to carry the goods to you and you will seldom, if ever, be disappointed in the arrival of your goods.

BEFORE WRITING us concerning goods ordered or before calling for them at your railroad station, first consider if you have allowed ample time for your order to reach Chicago, the required time for us to fill same, as above stated, and for the railroad or express company to carry it to you. If you will always do this, allowing liberal time, bearing in mind that express and railroad companies sometimes delay goods a few days after they receive them, you will seldom, if ever, have occasion to write us concerning a delay. If there is more than one freight or express agent in your town, always make inquiries at each office before writing us concerning non-arrival of goods, as it often happens that a shipment is at one office and the notification card has miscarried, while the customer has been making inquiries at another office.

IN CASE, HOWEVER, an order should be delayed beyond the time above referred to, and you write us, do not fail to mention the date on which you mailed your order, the name and address as given in the original order, the value and nature of the cash you sent, and, if possible, give us your invoice number, for if you received from us a postal card acknowledging the receipt of the order, you will find the invoice number on the card mailed you.

ABOUT MISTAKES. If we make a mistake in filling your order, kindly give us a chance to correct it. We try to fill every order absolutely correct, but errors sometimes creep in. They do in all business houses. You will always find us willing to correct ours. Do not fail to write us in case of an error; otherwise we may never know of it.

CHANGE OF ADDRESS. We would kindly request our customers to **immediately advise** us concerning any **change of address,** as we keep our records according to states and towns, and should you order from one town and then write from another, we would be compelled to send for further information before we could adjust the matter in question.

Paragraph Q.

ABOUT UNNECESSARY CORRESPONDENCE.

WHILE WE EMPLOY OVER ONE HUNDRED STENOGRAPHERS for the accommodation of our customers, and are willing and glad to answer all letters and furnish any special information that may be desired, we daily receive hundreds of letters of inquiry about things that are plainly answered in this catalogue, hundreds of letters which might be avoided, saving loss of time and unnecessary expense.

IT IS VERY SELDOM NECESSARY TO WRITE US, asking what the freight or express charge will be on any article to any point, for, from the weights given under each description and from the express and freight rates shown on pages 7 to 11, you can calculate very closely what the freight or express will amount to and save the time and trouble of writing for this information.

OUR OLD CUSTOMERS rarely ever have occasion to write us, asking what the freight or express will be on any article, and new customers will hardly ever have occasion to if they will refer to pages 7 to 11.

LETTERS CONCERNING SHIPMENTS CAN OFTEN BE AVOIDED. We receive hundreds of letters every day from parties who have ordered and have not allowed sufficient time for the order to reach us, the goods to be packed and shipped and for the goods to reach them. **(See paragraph P.)** **Never write about a shipment until ample time has been allowed for the goods to reach you.** We receive hundreds of letters asking for prices or special prices on articles on which the price is plainly printed in this catalogue. All such letters are unnecessary, for it only means an answer again referring you to the catalogue.

WE RECEIVE HUNDREDS OF LETTERS DAILY from people who ask us if we can't make changes in the goods as advertised, that they want the same thing or things with slight changes. This is all irregular and could not be furnished excepting at an advanced price, and we have found it impracticable to make any such changes, and to all such inquiries we can save you the time and trouble by saying that no changes can be made from those made plain in this catalogue. Since we answer as many as ten thousand letters a day, you will help us where a reply is necessary by answering on the back of our letter.

Paragraph R.

INSTALLMENT PLAN OR PARTIAL PAYMENT.

WE RECEIVE HUNDREDS OF LETTERS asking for prices on certain goods, especially on organs, pianos and other goods that run into money, from parties who wish to buy on the installment plan and to make settlement in notes. All these inquiries can be avoided for the reason that our only terms are cash, we never extend time, we open no accounts nor allow goods to be sold on the installment plan.

Paragraph S.

ABOUT CLAIMS FOR DAMAGE AND OVERCHARGE ON TRANSPORTATION.

WE CAREFULLY PACK AND DELIVER ALL OUR GOODS in good condition on board the cars, either in Chicago or at the factory, as made plain in this catalogue. We accept a receipt from the railroad company for the goods in good order, and it very rarely happens that any goods that we pack and ship reach their destination in bad order.

IF IT SHOULD EVER HAPPEN that any article reaches you marred, scratched, broken or in any way defective, be sure to have the railroad agent make a notation of such defect on the freight receipt (expense bill) he gives you. You can then present your claim for damage to the railroad agent from whom you received the goods, it being his duty at that end to take the matter up with the officials of that road and collect for you any damage that may have occurred.

WHILE THE PROPER PLACE FOR TAKING UP ANY CLAIMS FOR DAMAGE OR OVERCHARGE ON TRANSPORTATION on goods in transit, either by freight or express, is through the agent who delivers the goods, the trouble, delay and expense of writing us to do this can also be avoided. We, however, guarantee the goods we ship to reach you in the same perfect condition they leave us, and to be satisfactory to you in every way, and if you find them damaged in transit and you accept them and the agent hesitates to take and collect your claim for damage, you can write us enclosing your receipt (expense bill) for the freight charges paid the agent, with the agent's written notation on the expense bill, stating what the damage is, and we will take the matter up at this end, collect the damage and send the money to you. **It will be impossible for us to consider claims for damages to shipments unless the expense bill bears a notation to the effect that the shipment was received in bad condition.**

WHILE WE HAVE a large corps of stenographers and corresponding clerks **in our employ, whose duty it is to promptly and courteously answer all inquiries and give all desired information,** in order to maintain our extremely low prices the cost of conducting our business must be cut down to the very minimum, and to do this our customers are especially requested before writing us concerning freight rates, claims, delays, or before asking us for information of any kind, to carefully consult this catalogue, and if they will do this they will find in nine cases out of ten the information can be had or the adjustment of damage made, without going to the trouble of writing us or putting us to the expense of corresponding on the subject.

ON THE BASIS OF BETTER VALUE THAN YOU CAN POSSIBLY GET ELSEWHERE, the best possible service, every item you order guaranteed to reach you in perfect condition and to prove perfectly satisfactory or your money to be immediately returned to you; under our binding guarantee to please you in every way in your dealings with us, we respectfully solicit your orders.

FREIGHT AND EXPRESS RATES.

THE FOLLOWING TABLE IS TO VARIOUS POINTS IN EVERY STATE AND TERRITORY . . . . .

IT IS NOT NECESSARY to write us for freight and express rates, as the following tables and the instructions we herewith give will show just what the freight and express rates are to different points in the United States. Take the nearest town to your own in the table below, and the freight rate to your town will be almost, if not exactly, the same for 100 pounds.

YOU MUST PAY THE FREIGHT OR EXPRESS CHARGES AT THE TIME YOU GET THE GOODS FROM THE STATION.

Don't be afraid of the freight or express charges; they never amount to much compared with what we can save you in cost. In fact we guarantee that you will save money on every purchase after you pay the freight or express charges and if you do not find it so, YOU CAN RETURN THE GOODS AND WE WILL REFUND ALL YOUR MONEY AND YOU WILL NOT BE OUT ONE CENT.

NO MATTER HOW FAR AWAY you may live, we can still save you money on your purchases. **DISTANCE IS NO DRAWBACK.** Remember, your local dealer must pay the exact same rate of freight that you pay on the goods, and this cost of freight he must add to the cost of the goods when he figures his selling price. But our prices on practically everything in this catalogue are so very much lower than the same quality of goods can be had from smaller concerns, that after you pay all transportation charges, even to very distant points, we can save you money.

HOW TO FIGURE FREIGHT CHARGES.

SEE PAGE 11 for list of articles and their class, then find the weight of the desired article (which we aim to give underneath its description in this catalogue), and if not given you can estimate the weight very closely. Find the rate in following table under its class, and multiply the rate by the weight, and you have the freight charges sufficiently correct for your information.

THE RAILROADS have what is called a **MINIMUM FREIGHT CHARGE,** meaning the least amount of money they will haul a freight shipment for, no matter how little it weighs. **In the first column we quote the minimum freight charge or explain how it is made up.**

Note 3. **THE MINIMUM CHARGE,** to towns covered by Note 3 is the same as for 100 pounds at the rate under the class to which the article belongs, but not less than 50 cents.

EXPRESS CHARGES.

In the following table are given the express rates for 100 pounds, but for shipments weighing less than that see page 10. Freight is the cheapest way to ship orders weighing 20 pounds or more. Make your order for 100 pounds, if possible, and get the benefit of the minimum charge, as shipments weighing from 20 to 100 pounds usually cost no more than 20 pounds. Where two express rates are shown, add them together to figure the charges on packages weighing 7 pounds or under. For packages weighing more that 7 pounds, figure the charges at each rate separately, and then add these amounts for the total.

	Min. freight charge	1st class freight per 100 lbs	2d class freight per 100 lbs	3rd class freight per 100 lbs	4th class freight per 100 lbs	5th class freight per 100 lbs	6th class freight per 100 lbs	Express per 100 lbs
ALABAMA—								
Birmingham	Note 3	$1 19	$1 03	$0 83	$0 64	$0 55	$0 42	$ 3 75
Brewton	Note 3	1 54	1 27	1 04	85	78	71	4 00
Dadeville	Note 3	1 82	1 54	1 23	99	84	65	4 50
Decatur	Note 3	1 19	1 03	83	64	55	42	3 25
Gadsden	Note 3	1 47	1 26	1 06	85	71	58	3 75
Mobile	$1 10	1 10	90	75	58	47	41	4 00
Montgomery	Note 3	1 38	1 26	1 03	80	67	53	3 75
Ozark	Note 3	1 96	1 68	1 43	1 11	93	76	4 75
Randolph, Bibb Co	Note 3	1 67	1 42	1 21	97	88	64	4 00
Tuscaloosa	Note 3	1 48	1 28	1 04	81	70	54	4 00
ARIZONA—								
Benson	$2 79	3 44	3 01	2 66	2 10			10 75
Flagstaff	3 40	3 90	3 40	2 70	2 10			10 50
Holbrook	3 25	3 74	3 35	2 70	2 10			10 25
Phœnix	1 70	3 72	3 25	2 90	2 30			12 50
Prescott	1 70	3 72	3 25	2 90	2 30			12 00
Seligman	3 40	3 90	3 40	2 70	2 10			10 75
Solomanville	1 90	3 28	3 02	2 71	2 30			10 25
Tucson	1 45	3 52	3 05	2 70	2 10			11 00
Yucca	3 40	3 90	3 40	2 70	2 10			11 00
ARKANSAS—								
Daleville	Note 3	1 30	1 09	90	66			3 75
Fort Smith	Note 3	1 30	1 06	87	69			4 00
Fayetteville	Note 3	1 25	1 04	85	65			3 75
Knobel	Note 3	95	84	68	33			2 75
Little Rock	Note 3	1 20	1 01	77	59			3 50
Morrillton	Note 3	1 30	1 09	85	64			3 75
Newport, Jackson Co.	Note 3	1 00	83	67	55			3 25
Pine Bluff	Note 3	1 20	1 01	77	59			3 50
Texarkana	Note 3	1 30	1 15	99	90			4 00
Van Buren	Note 3	1 30	1 06	87	69			4 00
CALIFORNIA—								
Bakerfield	$2 85	3 78	3 34	2 90	2 56			11 50
Fresno	2 85	3 50	2 08	2 65	2 12			11 50
Los Angeles	2 60	3 00	2 60	2 20	1 90			11 50
Needles	3 40	3 90	3 40	2 70	2 10			11 50
Redding	2 85	3 61	3 16	2 70	2 32			12 50
Sacramento	2 60	3 00	2 60	2 20	1 90			11 50
San Bernardino	2 85	3 34	2 90	2 46	2 13			11 50
San Diego	2 60	3 00	2 60	2 20	1 90			11 50
San Francisco	2 60	3 00	2 60	2 20	1 90			11 50
Santa Cruz	2 85	3 21	2 79	2 37	2 05			12 25
Termo	3 10	5 20	4 57	3 74	3 01			13 25
COLORADO—								
Alamosa	1 65	3 05	2 55	2 02	1 56			$6 00- 2 00
Cripple Creek	1 31	2 65	2 21	1 77	1 45			7 50
Denver	75	2 05	1 65	1 25	97			6 00
Eagle	1 97	3 37	2 87	2 29	1 75			6 00- 2 75
Grand Junction	2 15	3 60	3 05	2 45	1 82			8 00
Greeley	75	2 05	1 65	1 25	97			6 00
Gunnison	1 75	3 20	2 65	2 10	1 72			8 00
Kit Carson	50	1 99	1 65	1 25	97			5 50
La Junta	50	2 05	1 65	1 25	97			6 00
Mancos	2 60	4 10	3 50	2 85	2 17			6 00- 4 00
Montrose	2 00	3 45	2 90	2 30	1 77			6 00- 3 00
Pagosa Springs	2 39	3 80	3 29	2 64	2 12			
Pueblo	75	2 05	1 65	1 25	97			6 00
Sterling	50	1 81	1 58	1 25	97			5 50
Thatcher	75	2 05	1 65	1 25	97			6 00
CONNECTICUT—								
Bridgeport	82	82	71	55	39	33		3 00
Canaan	82	82	71	55	39	33		3 00
Hartford	82	82	71	55	39	33		3 00
New Haven	82	82	71	55	39	33		3 00
New London	82	82	71	55	39	33		3 00
New Milford	82	82	71	55	39	33		3 00
Putnam	82	82	71	55	39	33		3 00
DELAWARE—								
Dover	75	75	65	50	35	30		2 90
Farmington	75	75	65	50	35	30		3 00
Middletown	75	75	65	50	35	30		2 90
Newark	73	73	63	48	33	28		2 25
DIST. OF COLUMBIA—								
Langdon	72	72	62	47	32	27		2 25
Washington	72	72	62	47	32	27		2 25
FLORIDA—								
Carrabelle	Note 3	2 31	2 00	1 73	1 51	1 31	1 09	5 75
Caryville	Note 3	1 70	1 40	1 07	94	87	80	4 50
Gainesville	Note 3	1 91	1 64	1 40	1 23	1 05	85	5 50
Jacksonville	Note 3	1 35	1 14	1 40	87	73	58	5 00
Key West	Note 3	1 93	1 64	1 48	1 23	93	86	6 00- 1 00
Pensacola	$1 10	1 10	90	75	58	47	41	4 25
Punta Gorda	Note 3	2 37	2 05	1 75	1 56	1 34	1 09	6 50
Sebastian	Note 3	2 29	1 98	1 68	1 49	1 28	1 08	6 50
Tallahassee	Note 3	2 19	1 88	1 63	1 41	1 23	1 03	5 25
Tampa (all rail)	Note 3	1 85	1 57	1 34	1 19	1 01	85	6 00
Tampa (rail and water; via Mobile)	$1 35	1 47	1 24	1 03	93	78	63	....
GEORGIA—								
Albany	Note 3	1 67	1 43	1 21	98	82	67	4 75
Atlanta	Note 3	1 47	1 26	1 06	85	71	58	3 75
Brunswick	Note 3	1 35	1 14	1 00	87	73	58	4 50
Cairo	Note 3	95	1 61	1 26	1 11	1 00	86	5 25

	Min. freight charge	1st class freight per 100 lbs	2d class freight per 100 lbs	3d class freight per 100 lbs	4th class freight per 100 lbs	5th class freight per 100 lbs	6th class freight per 100 lbs	Express per 100 lbs.
GEORGIA—Continued								
Columbus	Note 3	$1 47	$1 26	$1 06	$0 85	$0 71	$0 58	$4 50
Doerun	Note 3	2 37	2 01	1 67	1 48	1 25	1 00	5 50
Folkston	Note 3	1 67	1 43	1 26	1 11	92	72	5 25
Macon	Note 3	1 47	1 26	1 06	85	71	58	4 25
Quitman	Note 3	2 03	1 72	1 35	1 21	1 05	84	5 25
Rome	Note 3	1 47	1 26	1 06	85	71	58	3 75
Savannah	Note 3	1 35	1 14	1 00	87	73	58	5 00
Stillmore	Note 3	1 90	1 63	1 43	1 25	1 02	81	5 00
Thomasville	Note 3	1 96	1 65	1 28	1 09	93	74	5 00
Valdosta	Note 3	1 96	1 67	1 41	1 09	93	74	5 50
Warrenton	Note 3	1 77	1 53	1 31	1 07	85	71	4 50
IDAHO—								
American Falls	$2 40	3 30	2 80	2 20	1 82			8 75
Boise City	2 40	3 30	2 80	2 45	2 02			10 00
Gem	2 85	3 60	3 10	2 60	2 10			10 00
Idaho Falls	2 40	3 30	2 80	2 20	1 82			8 00
Ketchum	2 65	3 55	3 05	2 45	2 07			10 00
Moscow	2 85	3 60	3 10	2 60	2 10			10 00
Mountain Home	2 40	3 30	2 80	2 45	2 02			10 00
Pocatello	2 40	3 30	2 80	2 20	1 82			8 00
Spencer	2 40	3 30	2 80	2 20	1 82			8 00
ILLINOIS—								
Baldwin	50	77	62	49	37			2 00
Belvidere	25	35	29	24	17			75
Cairo	25	59	48	39	25			1 75
Danville	25	32	27	22	14			1 00
Freeport	25	40	32	24	18			1 00
Joliet	25	22	19	15	10			50
Litchfield	25	47	38	29	23			1 25
Milan, Rock Island Co.	25	47	37	29	22			1 25
Mt. Vernon	25	50	40	30	25			1 50
Peoria	25	40	32	24	18			1 00
Quincy	25	47	38	29	22			1 25
Springfield	25	47	38	29	22			1 00
INDIANA—								
Bedford	37	37	32	24	16	13		1 25
Connersville	39	39	33	25	17	14		1 50
Elkhart	25	25	22	20	13	09		75
Evansville	40	40	34	25	17	15		1 75
Ft. Wayne	29	29	25	20	14	11		75
Goshen	25	25	22	20	13	09		75
Indianapolis	32	32	27	22	14	12		1 25
Lafayette	30	30	25	20	13	10		90
New Albany	40	40	34	25	17	15		1 50
Terre Haute	32	32	27	22	14	12		1 25
INDIAN TERRITORY—								
Atoka	Note 3	1 50	1 29	1 07	93			3 75
Checotah	Note 3	1 35	1 16	90	70			3 25
Eufaula	Note 3	1 37	1 20	92	75			3 50
Kiowa	Note 3	1 48	1 28	1 04	85			3 75
Red Fork	Note 3	1 21	1 03	80	57			3 75
South McAllister	Note 3	1 44	1 24	92	75			3 75
Vinita	Note 3	1 25	1 03	83	60			3 25
Wagoner	Note 3	1 30	1 10	85	64			3 25
Wewoka	Note 3	1 50	1 29	1 07	95			4 00
IOWA—								
Alta	$0 25	80	65	45	32			2 00
Audubon	25	80	65	45	32			2 00
Bedford	25	80	65	45	32			2 00
Bode	25	75	63	44	31			1 75
Burlington	25	47	38	29	22			1 25
Carroll	25	79	64	44	31			2 00
Cedar Rapids	25	58	47	35	24			1 50
Centerville	25	68	57	40	29			1 75
Council Bluffs	25	80	65	45	32			2 00
Davenport	25	46	37	29	22			1 25
Des Moines	25	68	57	40	29			1 75
Hamburg	25	80	65	45	32			2 00
Ireton	25	83	67	46	33			2 40
Keokuk	25	47	38	29	22			1 25
Mason City	25	63	53	42	26			1 75
Muscatine	25	47	38	29	22			1 25
Ottumwa	25	61	50	36	26			1 75
Waterloo	25	60	50	40	25			1 75
Waukon	25	60	50	40	25			1 50
KANSAS—								
Atchison	25	80	65	45	32			2 00
Council Grove	50	1 29	1 05	80	60			3 25
Dodge City	50	1 67	1 43	1 16	92			4 50
Ft. Scott	50	97	81	55	37			2 75
Garnett	50	1 07	88	66	47			3 00
Great Bend	50	1 46	1 23	95	73			4 00
Hartland	50	1 74	1 49	1 22	97			5 00
Leavenworth	25	80	65	45	32			2 00
Leoti	50	1 70	1 46	1 18	92			4 75
Mankato	50	1 83	1 43	85	64			3 50
Meade	50	1 60	1 38	1 15	93			4 25
Norton	50	1 52	1 29	1 05	84			4 00
Sawyer	50	1 57	1 34	1 05	82			4 25
Topeka	50	1 09	89	64	47			2 75
Vesper	50	1 38	1 17	91	67			3 75
Wichita	50	1 40	1 18	91	70			3 75

	Min. freight charge	1st class freight per 100 lbs	2d class freight per 100 lbs	3d class freight per 100 lbs	4th class freight per 100 lbs	5th class freight per 100 lbs	6th class freight per 100 lbs	Express per 100 lbs
KENTUCKY—								
Alexander, Fulton Co.	Note 3	$0 80	$0 66	$0 53	$0 43	$0 34	$0 29	$2 10
Ashland	$0 45	45	39	30	21	18	15	2 00
Burnside	Note 3	93	78	66	48	43	37	2 75
Campbellsville	Note 3	97	83	69	56	49	44	2 25
Frankfort	Note 3	66	57	45	34	31	27	2 00
Henderson, Henderson County	$0 48	48	41	30	22	18	15	2 00
Hickman	60	60	50	40	33	27	24	3 25
Louisville	41	41	35	26	18	15	12	1 50
Maysville	44	44	38	29	20	17	14	2 00
Owensboro	48	48	41	30	22	18	15	2 00
Paducah	60	60	50	40	25	22	18	1 75
Paris	Note 3	68	59	46	32	29	25	2 00
LOUISIANA—								
Alexandria	Note 3	1 30	1 10	92	78	56	.....	4 75
Baton Rouge	$1 10	1 10	90	75	58	47	41	3 75
Crowley	Note 3	1 43	1 22	98	82	35	.....	5 00
Kentwood	Note 3	1 39	1 13	95	78	65	57	3 75
Lake Charles	Note 3	1 50	1 29	1 02	85	.....	.....	4 75
Many	Note 3	1 50	1 29	1 09	1 00	77	.....	5 00
Monroe	Note 3	1 30	1 10	92	78	.....	.....	4 25
Morgan City	Note 3	1 29	1 11	89	75	.....	.....	4 50
Moreauville	Note 3	1 50	1 29	1 09	1 00	77	.....	5 85
New Orleans	$1 10	1 10	90	75	58	47	41	3 75
Ponchatoula	Note 3	1 40	1 13	95	78	65	57	3 75
Shreveport	Note 3	1 30	1 10	92	78	58	.....	4 25
MAINE—								
Augusta	$1 07	94	81	64	45	38	.....	3 00
Alfred	82	82	71	55	39	33	.....	2 90
Bangor	1 07	98	85	65	47	40	.....	3 25
Brownville Junction	1 08	1 08	95	77	59	51	.....	3 75
Caribou	1 58	1 58	1 27	99	82	55	.....	4 35
Eastport	1 07	1 07	91	72	51	43	.....	4 00
Kennebunk	1 07	89	77	61	44	38	.....	2 75
Lowelltown	1 08	1 08	95	77	59	51	.....	$3 50- 60
Ludlow	1 32	1 32	1 10	86	69	50	.....	4 00
Portland and Lewiston	82	82	71	55	39	33	.....	3 00
Rockland	82	82	71	55	39	33	.....	3 25
MARYLAND—								
Annapolis	80	80	70	53	38	32	.....	2 50
Baltimore	72	72	62	47	32	27	.....	2 25
Brandywine	75	75	65	49	33	29	.....	2 75
Elkton	73	73	63	48	47	28	.....	2 75
Finksburg	72	72	62	47	32	27	.....	2 75
Frederick	72	72	62	47	32	27	.....	2 25
Germantown	72	72	62	47	32	27	.....	2 25
Hagerstown	72	72	62	47	32	27	.....	2 25
Port Tobacco	75	75	65	49	34	29	.....	2 75
MASSACHUSETTS—								
Ashley Falls	82	82	71	55	33	33	.....	3 00
Barnstable	82	82	71	55	39	33	.....	2 50- 75
Bellingham Jct	82	82	71	55	39	33	.....	2 90
Boston	82	82	71	55	39	33	.....	2 50
Graniteville	82	82	71	55	39	33	.....	2 50
Hinsdale	82	82	71	55	39	33	.....	2 50
Jefferson	82	82	71	55	39	33	.....	2 75
Lakeville	82	82	71	55	39	33	.....	2,50- 60
New Bedford	82	82	71	55	39	33	.....	3 00
Provincetown	82	82	71	55	39	33	.....	2 50- 75
Springfield	82	82	71	55	39	33	.....	2 50
Templeton	82	82	71	55	39	33	.....	2 75
MICHIGAN—								
Adrian	35	35	30	23	15	13	.....	1 25
Alba	53	53	45	34	26	20	.....	1 85
Alpena	55	55	45	35	26	20	.....	2 40
Bay City	37	37	32	24	16	13	.....	1 75
Boyne Falls	53	53	45	34	26	20	.....	2 00
Cheboygan	55	55	45	35	26	20	.....	2 50
Detroit	37	37	32	24	16	13	.....	1 25
Emmett	37	37	32	24	16	13	.....	1 50
Grand Rapids	33	33	29	22	15	12	.....	1 25
Kalamazoo	30	30	26	21	14	11	.....	75
Lansing	36	36	31	23	16	13	.....	1 25
Lake Linden	50	85	71	57	37	.....	.....	1 75- 1 10
Manistee	47	47	41	31	23	18	.....	1 75
Munising	25	75	65	48	38	.....	.....	2 00
Ishpeming	25	60	50	40	28	22	.....	1 75
Paris	42	42	36	27	19	16	.....	1 50
Petoskey	53	53	45	34	26	20	.....	2 00
MINNESOTA—								
Albert Lea	25	60	50	40	25	.....	.....	2 00
Audubon	50	1 30	1 10	85	60	.....	.....	3 75
Crookston	50	1 40	1 18	92	65	.....	.....	4 25
Duluth	25	65	55	44	28	.....	.....	2 25
Edgerton	25	86	70	49	38	.....	.....	2 50
Farris	50	1 22	1 03	81	56	.....	.....	2 00- 1 75
Hallock	50	1 45	1 22	96	68	.....	.....	2 00- 2 50
Mankato	25	65	55	43	27	.....	.....	2 00
Marshall	25	81	70	55	39	.....	.....	3 00
Menahga	50	1 16	98	77	53	.....	.....	2 00 1 75
Milan	25	90	77	64	43	.....	.....	2 75
Minneapolis	25	60	50	40	25	.....	.....	2 00
Moorhead	50	1 27	1 07	84	59	.....	.....	3 50
Redwood Falls	25	70	56	45	34	.....	.....	2 75
St. Vincent	50	1 51	1 27	1 00	71	.....	.....	2 00- 2 50
Tower	50	1 10	94	78	57	.....	.....	2 75
MISSISSIPPI—								
Ackerman	Note 3	1 25	1 02	82	70	57	51	3 50
Hazlehurst	Note 3	1 36	1 10	92	76	63	55	3 50
Holly Spring	Note 3	1 09	93	77	64	51	44	2 85
Jackson	$1 18	1 18	99	80	67	56	49	3 50
Meridian	1 18	1 18	99	80	67	56	49	4 00
Mississippi City	Note 3	1 67	1 40	1 13	90	77	68	4 25
Natchez	$1 10	1 10	90	75	58	47	41	3 75
Ocean Springs	Note 3	1 67	1 40	1 13	90	77	68	4 25
Pocahontas	Note 3	1 35	1 09	92	76	62	54	3 50
Port Gibson	$1 30	1 30	1 10	95	73	62	56	3 50
Roxie	Note 3	1 34	1 08	93	76	62	54	3 75
State Line, Wayne Co	Note 3	1 54	1 32	1 13	94	76	65	4 00
Vicksburg	$1 10	1 10	90	75	58	47	41	3 50
MISSOURI—								
Charleston	60	1 02	78	64	53	.....	.....	2 40
Chicopee	50	1 41	1 18	89	73	.....	.....	4 00
Chillicothe	25	80	65	45	32	.....	.....	2 00
Clinton	50	90	72	50	37	.....	.....	2 50
Hannibal	25	47	38	29	22	.....	.....	1 25
Independence	50	80	65	45	32	.....	.....	2 00
Jefferson City	50	71	58	42	29	.....	.....	2 00
MISSOURI—Continued.								
Kahoka	$0 25	$0 52	$0 43	$0 32	$0 23	.....	.....	$1 50
Kansas City	25	80	65	45	32	.....	.....	2 00
Kirkwood	60	66	55	43	37	.....	.....	1 90
Lincoln	75	1 01	79	57	43	.....	.....	2 50
Noel	50	1 12	91	68	49	.....	.....	3 50
Osceola	50	90	72	50	37	.....	.....	2 75
Paris	50	63	49	37	26	.....	.....	1 75
Poplar Bluff	60	1 22	1 01	84	68	.....	.....	2 50
Richards	50	97	81	55	37	.....	.....	2 75
Rolla	60	1 03	87	69	59	.....	.....	2 50
Springfield	50	90	72	50	37	.....	.....	3 00
St. Joseph	25	80	65	45	32	.....	.....	2 00
MONTANA—								
Big Timber	2 25	2 90	2 50	2 02	1 67	.....	.....	7 75
Billings	2 20	2 85	2 45	1 98	1 65	.....	.....	7 00
Butte	2 40	3 10	2 65	2 15	1 75	.....	.....	8 00
Chinook	1 98	2 54	2 23	1 79	1 53	.....	.....	$2 00- 5 25
Dillon	2 40	3 10	2 65	2 15	1 75	.....	.....	8 00
Glasgow	1 61	2 24	1 86	1 56	1 26	.....	.....	5 00- 2 00
Glendive	1 51	2 15	1 76	1 46	1 19	.....	.....	5 50
Great Falls	2 30	2 95	2 55	2 05	1 70	.....	.....	8 00
Helena	2 40	3 10	2 65	2 15	1 75	.....	.....	8 00
Iron Mountain	2 70	3 40	2 95	2 44	2 01	.....	.....	10 00
Kalispell	2 56	3 27	2 81	2 31	1 90	.....	.....	2 00- 7 00
Livingston	2 30	2 95	2 55	2 05	1 70	.....	.....	8 00
Missoula	2 50	3 20	2 75	2 25	1 85	.....	.....	9 00
NEBRASKA—								
Ainsworth	50	1 57	1 33	1 06	82	.....	.....	3 75
Alliance	50	1 81	1 58	1 25	97	.....	.....	5 00
Battle Creek	50	1 15	95	72	53	.....	.....	3 00
Beaver City	50	1 48	1 28	1 03	82	.....	.....	4 00
Chadron	50	1 90	1 64	1 34	1 03	.....	.....	4 75
Chappell	50	1 81	1 58	1 25	97	.....	.....	4 75
Cody	50	1 68	1 45	1 15	91	.....	.....	4 25
Crawford	50	2 02	1 76	1 43	1 17	.....	.....	4 75
Duncan	50	1 17	99	73	53	.....	.....	3 00
Grant	50	1 63	1 41	1 16	94	.....	.....	4 50
Hastings	50	1 31	1 11	83	62	.....	.....	3 50
Hemingford	50	1 85	1 62	1 31	1 01	.....	.....	5 00
Imperial	50	1 63	1 41	1 16	91	.....	.....	4 50
Lincoln	50	85	70	49	36	.....	.....	2 75
Loup City	50	1 45	1 23	96	75	.....	.....	3 75
Morrill	50	2 17	1 85	1 43	1 15	.....	.....	4 25
Nelson	50	1 31	1 11	83	62	.....	.....	3 50
Ogallala	50	1 63	1 41	1 16	91	.....	.....	4 50
Omaha	25	80	65	45	32	.....	.....	2 00
O'Neill	50	1 30	1 08	88	66	.....	.....	3 25
Pawnee, Pawnee Co	50	89	74	53	40	.....	.....	2 75
Thedford	50	1 58	1 36	1 10	86	.....	.....	4 25
NEVADA—								
Austin	3 75	4 80	4 30	3 60	3 00	.....	.....	13 00
Carson	3 35	4 15	3 65	2 95	2 35	.....	.....	12 25
Elko	2 85	3 90	3 40	2 70	2 10	.....	.....	11 50
Eureka, Ormsby Co	3 35	4 20	3 70	3 00	2 40	.....	.....	13 00
Hawthorne	3 35	4 90	4 40	3 70	3 10	.....	.....	13 50
Reno	2 85	3 90	3 40	2 70	2 10	.....	.....	11 50
Toana	2 85	3 90	3 40	2 70	2 10	.....	.....	11 50
NEW HAMPSHIRE—								
Berlin	82	82	71	55	39	$0 33	.....	3 50
Colebrook	82	82	71	55	39	33	.....	3 60
Conway	82	82	71	55	39	32	.....	3 00
Dover	1 07	89	71	61	44	30	.....	2 50
Enfield	82	82	71	55	39	33	.....	3 00
Keene	82	82	71	55	39	33	.....	2 75
Laconia	82	82	71	55	39	33	.....	2 90
Manchester	82	82	71	55	39	33	.....	2 50
Plymouth	82	82	71	55	39	33	.....	3 25
Portsmouth	82	82	71	55	39	33	.....	2 50
Suncook	82	82	71	55	39	33	.....	2 75
NEW JERSEY—								
Bridgeton	80	80	70	55	40	35	.....	2 50
Chatsworth	80	80	70	55	40	35	.....	2 50
Lafayette	75	75	65	50	35	30	.....	2 75
Middletown	80	80	70	55	40	35	.....	2 75
Morristown	75	75	65	50	35	30	.....	2 50
Mullica Hill	78	78	68	53	38	33	.....	2 50
Newark	75	75	65	50	35	30	.....	2 50
Oxford Furnace	75	75	65	50	35	30	.....	2 50
Pleasantville	80	80	70	55	40	35	.....	2 75
Pompton	75	75	65	50	35	30	.....	2 75
NEW MEXICO—								
Albuquerque	1 72	2 32	2 06	1 80	1 52	.....	.....	7 25
Carlsbad	1 65	2 20	1 94	1 74	1 65	.....	.....	6 75
Clayton	75	2 05	1 65	1 25	97	.....	.....	6 50
Las Vegas	1 65	2 32	2 06	1 80	1 52	.....	.....	7 25
Lordsburg	1 72	2 72	2 46	2 27	2 07	.....	.....	8 75
Raton	1 00	2 22	1 85	1 45	1 17	.....	.....	6 50
Roswell	1 65	2 20	1 94	1 74	1 65	.....	.....	6 75
Santa Fe	1 72	2 32	2 06	1 80	1 52	.....	.....	7 25
Socorro	1 72	2 32	2 06	1 80	1 52	.....	.....	7 25
NEW YORK—								
Albany	72	72	63	48	34	29	.....	2 25
Big Moose	82	82	71	55	39	33	.....	3 00
Boston Corners	82	82	71	55	39	33	.....	2 7
Buffalo	45	45	39	30	21	18	.....	1 7
Canton, St. Lawrence Co.	82	82	71	55	39	33	.....	3 00
Cortland	60	60	52	40	28	24	.....	2 25
Delhi	73	73	63	48	33	28	.....	3 00
Elmira	60	60	52	40	28	24	.....	2 25
Fort Edward	82	82	71	55	39	33	.....	2 75
Hastings, Oswego Co	68	68	59	45	32	27	.....	2 50
Lake Placid	1 52	1 52	1 34	1 05	78	63	.....	3 50
Lyons, Wayne Co	60	60	52	40	28	24	.....	2 00
Malone	82	82	71	55	39	33	.....	3 10
New York	75	75	65	50	35	30	.....	2 50
North Creek	1 10	1 10	95	75	57	50	.....	3 75
Nunda	56	56	48	37	26	22	.....	2 35
Plattsburg	1 08	1 08	92	72	52	43	.....	3 25
Poughkeepsie	75	75	65	50	35	30	.....	2 50
Rochester	56	57	48	37	26	22	.....	2 00
Saranac Lake	82	82	71	55	39	33	.....	3 10
Warsaw	56	56	48	37	26	22	.....	2 00
Watertown	75	75	65	50	35	36	.....	2 75
NORTH CAROLINA—								
Belhaven	97	1 17	1 00	80	57	47	$0 39	3 50
Charlotte	Note 3	1 40	1 20	95	70	60	47	4 00
Clinton	Note 3	1 40	1 20	95	70	60	47	4 00
Culberson	Note 3	1 82	1 55	1 33	1 10	97	72	4 50

FOR COMPLETE INDEX REFER TO PINK PAGES IN MIDDLE OF BOOK.

	Min. freight charge	1st class freight per 100 lbs	2nd class freight per 100 lbs	3d class freight per 100 lbs	4th class freight per 100 lbs	5th class freight per 100 lbs	6th class freight per 100 lbs	Express per 100 lbs
ORTH CAROLINA—Con.								
Elk Park	Note 3	$1 84	$1 62	$1 37	$1 10	$0 95	$0 80	....
Fayetteville	Note 3	1 40	1 20	95	70	58	42	$ 4 00
Goldsboro	Note 3	1 33	1 13	89	64	55	42	3 75
Goldston	Note 3	1 40	1 20	95	70	60	47	4 25
Greensboro	Note 3	1 33	1 13	89	64	55	43	3 75
Halifax	Note 3	1 32	1 12	89	64	55	43	3 50
Hertford	$0 97	1 02	87	67	47	39	32	3 25
Mount Airy	Note 3	1 43	1 22	97	71	61	48	4 25
Newbern	Note 3	1 10	93	72	54	45	36	4 25
Newport	Note 3	1 35	1 15	90	65	56	44	4 50
Raleigh	Note 3	1 33	1 13	89	64	55	43	4 00
Salisbury	Note 3	1 40	1 20	95	70	60	47	3 75
Shelby	Note 3	1 52	1 32	1 07	82	68	54	4 50
Wadesboro	Note 3	1 40	1 20	95	70	60	47	4 50
Washington	Note 3	1 10	93	74	56	48	39	3 50
Wilkesboro	Note 3	1 43	1 22	97	71	61	48	4 00
NORTH DAKOTA—								
Aneta	$0 50	1 45	1 22	96	68	....	....	$2 00- 2 40
Bismarck	50	1 60	1 35	1 07	76	....	....	4 75
Bottineau	50	1 74	1 47	1 18	88	....	....	2 00- 3 00
Carrington	50	1 58	1 34	1 06	77	....	....	4 50
Cooperstown	50	1 44	1 21	95	67	....	....	4 50
Dickinson	50	1 87	1 58	1 28	98	....	....	5 25
Ellendale	25	1 19	1 03	77	56	....	....	3 25
Fargo	25	1 17	99	77	54	....	....	3 50
Grand Forks	50	1 40	1 18	92	65	....	....	4 25
Hannah	50	1 63	1 38	1 09	78	....	....	2 00- 3 00
Jamestown	50	1 46	1 23	97	68	....	....	4 25
Lakota	50	1 48	1 25	98	69	....	....	2 00- 2 75
Maddock	50	1 62	1 37	1 09	78	....	....	5 00
Medora	50	1 94	1 64	1 34	1 05	....	....	5 50
Minot	50	1 75	1 49	1 20	89	....	....	5 00
Pembina	50	1 51	1 27	1 00	71	....	....	4 50
Stanley	50	1 88	1 57	1 28	99	....	....	2 00- 4 00
St. John	50	1 70	1 43	1 14	84	....	....	2 00- 3 00
OHIO—								
Bellefontaine	37	37	32	24	16	13	....	1 50
Bucyrus	39	39	33	25	17	14	....	1 50
Caldwell	45	45	39	30	21	18	....	2 00
Canton	41	41	35	26	18	15	....	1 50
Chillicothe	44	44	38	29	19	17	....	1.75
Cincinnati	40	40	34	25	17	15	....	1 50
Cleveland	41	41	35	26	18	15	....	1 50
Columbus	41	41	35	26	18	15	....	1 50
Coshocton	44	44	35	29	19	17	....	1 75
Eayton	40	40	34	25	17	15	....	1 50
Defiance	33	33	29	22	15	12	....	1 00
Georgetown, Brown Co.	65	60	54	41	32	26	....	....
Greenville	39	39	33	25	17	14	....	1 25
Hillsboro	44	44	38	29	19	17	....	1 50
Jobs	45	45	39	29	21	18	....	2 00
Laura	39	39	33	25	17	14	....	1 50
Lima	37	37	32	24	16	13	....	1 25
Logan, Hocking Co.	45	45	39	29	21	18	....	1 75
Marion	39	39	33	25	17	14	....	1 25
Ottawa, Putnam Co.	37	37	32	24	16	13	....	1 25
Portsmouth	45	45	39	30	21	18	....	2 00
Steubenville	45	45	39	30	21	18	....	1 75
Toledo	37	37	32	24	16	13	....	1 25
Xenia	40	40	34	25	17	15	....	1 50
OKLAHOMA TER.—								
Alva	Note 3	1 50	1 29	1 07	88	....	....	4 25
Calumet	Note 3	1 50	1 29	1 07	95	....	....	4 25
El Reno	Note 3	1 50	1 29	1 07	95	....	....	4 25
Guthrie	Note 3	1 50	1 29	1 07	95	....	....	4 00
Kingfisher	Note 3	1 50	1 29	1 07	95	....	....	4 25
Newkirk	Note 3	1 48	1 26	98	77	....	....	4 00
Oklahoma	Note 3	1 50	1 29	1 07	95	....	....	4 00
Tecumseh	Note 3	1 55	1 34	1 05	89	....	....	4 50
OREGON—								
Arlington	$2 85	3 60	3 10	2 60	2 10	....	....	11 00
Baker City	2 85	3 60	3 10	2 60	2 10	....	....	10 00
Elgin	2 85	3 60	3 10	2 60	2 10	....	....	10 00
Eugene	2 85	3 50	3 02	2 59	2 26	....	....	12 25
Heppner	2 85	3 60	3 10	2 60	2 10	....	....	11 50
Huntington	2 85	3 60	3 10	2 60	2 10	....	....	10 00
La Grande	2 85	3 60	3 10	2 60	2 10	....	....	10.00
Lebanon	2 85	3 43	2 96	2 53	2 20	....	....	12 00
Leland	2 85	3 90	3 40	2 70	2 10	....	....	13 00
Medford	2 85	3 90	3 40	2 70	2 10	....	....	13 00
Monmouth	2 85	3 38	2 92	2 48	2 15	....	....	12 00
Natron	2 85	3 52	3 03	2 60	2 27	....	....	12 25
Pendleton	2 85	3 60	3 10	2 60	2 10	....	....	10 00
Portland	2 60	3 00	2 60	2 20	1 90	....	....	11 50
Roseburg	2 85	3 76	3 24	2 80	2 45	....	....	13 00
Salem	2 85	3 33	2 88	2 44	2 10	....	....	12 00
Sheridan, Yamhill Co.	2 85	3 34	2 89	2 45	2 11	....	....	12 00
Troutdale	2 85	3 15	2 73	2 32	2 00	....	....	11 50
PENNSYLVANIA—								
Allentown, Lehigh Co.	73	73	63	48	33	28	....	2 50
Bedford	72	72	62	47	32	27	....	3 00
Blairsville	53	53	45	34	24	21	....	2 25
Driftwood	72	72	62	47	32	27	....	3 00
Erie	45	45	39	30	21	18	....	2 00
Gettysburg	72	72	62	47	32	18	....	2 25
Harrisburg	72	72	62	47	32	27	....	2 25
Huntingdon	72	72	62	47	32	27	....	2 75
Jackson Center	45	45	39	30	21	18	....	2 00
Larabee	56	56	48	37	26	22	....	2 25
Lewisburg	72	72	62	47	32	27	....	2 50
Nanticoke	73	73	63	48	33	28	....	2 50
New Castle	44	44	38	29	19	17	....	1 75
Philadelphia	73	73	63	48	33	28	....	2 25
Pittsburg	45	45	39	30	21	18	....	1 75
Pottsville	73	73	63	48	33	28	....	2 50
Reading, Berks Co.	73	73	63	48	33	28	....	2 25
Scranton	73	73	63	48	33	28	....	2 50
Sharpsville	44	44	38	29	19	17	....	1 75
Tionesta	45	45	39	30	21	17	....	2 10
Towanda	73	73	63	48	33	28	....	2 25
Uniontown	50	50	43	33	23	20	....	2 00
RHODE ISLAND—								
Bristol	82	82	71	55	39	33	....	2 50- 40
Greene	82	82	71	55	39	33	....	3 00
Pascoag	82	82	71	55	39	33	....	3 00
Providence	82	82	71	55	39	33	....	2 50
Slocum	82	82	71	55	39	33	....	3 00
Westerly	82	82	71	55	39	33	....	3 00

	Min. freight charge	1st class freight per 100 lbs	2d class freight per 100 lbs	3d class freight per 100lbs	4th class freight per 100 lbs	5th class freight per 100 lbs	6th class freight per 100 lbs	Eprxess per 100 lbs
SOUTH CAROLINA—								
Abbeville	Note 3	$1 56	$1 41	$1 11	$0 84	70	$0 62	$4 50
Aiken	Note 3	1 56	1 41	1 11	84	70	59	5 00
Beaufort	Note 3	1 35	1 14	1 00	87	73	58	5 50
Charleston	Note 3	1 35	1 14	1 00	87	73	58	4 75
Columbia	Note 3	1 47	1 26	1 06	82	68	56	4 50
Ehrhardt	Note 3	1 95	1 65	1 45	1 26	1 03	83	6 00
Florence	Note 3	1 57	1 37	1 09	82	67	54	4 50
Georgetown	Note 3	1 32	1 14	93	67	55	43	5 25
Greenville	Note 3	1 56	1 41	1 11	84	70	62	4 50
Greenwood	Note 3	1 56	1 41	1 11	84	70	62	4 50
Hampton	Note 3	1 75	1 49	1 29	1 14	94	76	5 50
Lancaster	Note 3	1 52	1 32	1 07	82	68	54	4 50
Ridgeway	Note 3	1 56	1 34	1 11	83	70	56	4 50
Spartanburg	Note 3	1 56	1 41	1 11	84	70	62	4 50
SOUTH DAKOTA—								
Aberdeen	$0 25	1 14	95	67	50	....	....	3 25
Armour	25	1 10	95	74	50	....	....	3 00
Belle Fourche	75	2 35	2 05	1 63	1 32	....	....	5 75
Canton	25	83	68	47	34	....	....	2 25
Chamberlain	25	1 25	1 08	80	55	....	....	3 00
Deadwood	75	2 25	1 95	1 60	1 32	....	....	5 75
Edgemont	75	2 04	1 78	1 43	1 19	....	....	5 50
Eureka	25	1 27	1 04	85	65	....	....	3 25
Gettysburg	25	1 27	1 04	85	65	....	....	3 25
Huron	25	1 14	95	67	47	....	....	3 25
Milbank Junction	25	94	79	65	43	....	....	3 00
Mitchell	25	1 05	94	67	47	....	....	2 75
Pierre	25	1 22	1 04	80	60	....	....	3 25
Rapid City	75	2 16	1 90	1 55	1 28	....	....	5 50
Redfield	25	1 14	95	67	50	....	....	3 25
Sisseton	25	1 01	82	65	46	....	....	3 00
Spearfish	75	2 35	2 05	1 63	1 32	....	....	6 25
Vermilion	25	89	73	51	37	....	....	2 00
Watertown	25	1 00	85	65	46	....	....	3 25
Wolsey	25	1 14	95	67	47	....	....	3 25
TENNESSEE—								
Antioch	Note 3	1 90	77	62	48	40	33	3 25
Allens Creek	Note 3	19	1 03	84	67	56	50	3 75
Bristol	$0 84	84	72	55	39	33	27	3 75
Charlestown	Note 3	1 50	1 29	1 08	86	75	57	3 50
Chattanooga	Note 3	1 16	99	82	64	55	42	3 00
Clarksville	Note 3	81	70	56	43	36	30	2 65
Clinton	Note 3	1 32	1 14	95	74	63	49	2 75
Greenfield	Note 3	91	75	60	49	37	34	3 50
Knoxville	Note 3	1 16	99	82	64	55	42	3 50
Jackson	Note 3	1 03	85	70	57	42	39	2 60
Manchester	Note 3	1 23	1 07	89	71	62	53	3 50
Memphis	$0 85	85	65	55	43	37	31	2 75
Monteagle	Note 3	1 43	1 24	1 03	85	75	67	3 50
Parson	Note 3	95	81	65	51	44	38	3 25
TEXAS—								
Abilene	Note 3	1 57	1 37	1 16	1 06	....	....	5 50
Amarillo	Note 3	1 67	1 46	1 24	1 13	....	....	5 50
Austin	Note 3	1 57	1 37	1 16	1 06	....	....	5 25
Beaumont	Note 3	1 57	1 37	1 16	1 06	....	....	5 25
Canadian	Note 3	1 62	1 42	1 20	1 10	....	....	5 25
Corpus Christi	Note 3	1 57	1 37	1 16	1 06	....	....	6 50
Dallas	Note 3	1 57	1 37	1 16	1 06	....	....	4 25
Denison	Note 3	1 57	1 37	1 16	1 06	....	....	3 75
El Paso	Note 3	1 69	1 50	1 34	1 26	....	....	7 00
Henrietta	Note 3	1 57	1 37	1 16	1 06	....	....	4 50
Houston	Note 3	1 57	1 37	1 16	1 06	....	....	5 25
Kerrville	Note 3	1 64	1 44	1 22	1 09	....	....	6 50
Laredo	Note 3	1 69	1 50	1 34	1 26	....	....	6 75
Llano	Note 3	1 57	1 37	1 16	1 06	....	....	5 75
Lufkin	Note 3	1 57	1 37	1 16	1 06	....	....	5 00
Palestine	Note 3	1 57	1 37	1 16	1 06	....	....	5 00
Pecos	Note 3	1 93	1 65	1 47	1 36	....	....	6 75
Port Lavaca	Note 3	1 57	1 37	1 16	1 06	....	....	5 75
San Angelo	Note 3	1 64	1 44	1 22	1 09	....	....	5 75
San Antonio	Note 3	1 57	1 37	1 16	1 06	....	....	5 75
Sanderson	Note 3	1 94	1 66	1 48	1 37	....	....	7 00
Seymour	Note 3	1 57	1 37	1 16	1 06	....	....	5 25
Sierra Blanca	Note 3	1 94	1 66	1 48	1 37	....	....	6 75
Spofford	Note 3	1 69	1 49	1 30	1 21	....	....	6 75
Waco	Note 3	1 57	1 37	1 16	1 06	....	....	4 75
UTAH—								
Belknap	$2 73	3 60	3 13	2 61	2 19	....	....	9 00
Bingham Jct	2 25	3 10	2 65	2 15	1 75	....	....	8 00
Cache Jct.	2 40	3 30	2 80	2 20	1 82	....	....	8 00
Colton	2 25	3 10	2 65	2 15	1 75	....	....	8 00
Dewey	2 39	3 25	2 79	2 20	1 82	....	....	8 00
Echo	2 25	3 10	2 65	2 15	1 75	....	....	8 00
Ephraim	2 50	3 30	2 83	2 31	1 89	....	....	8 25
Fairfield	2 50	3 35	2 89	2 37	1 95	....	....	8 50
Frisco	2 78	3 65	3 18	2 66	2 24	....	....	10 50
Heber	2 25	3 10	2 65	2 15	1 75	....	....	8 50
Kelton	2 85	3 90	3 40	2 70	2 10	....	....	9 25
Manti	2 50	3 30	2 83	2 31	1 89	....	....	8 25
Milford	2 73	3 60	3 13	2 61	2 19	....	....	10 25
Nephi	2 50	3 30	2 83	2 31	1 89	....	....	8 75
Ogden	2 25	3 10	2 65	2 15	1 75	....	....	8 00
Salt Lake City	2 25	3 10	2 65	2 15	1 75	....	....	8 00
Terminus	2 52	3 40	2 92	2 40	1 98	....	....	....
VERMONT—								
Bradford	82	82	71	55	39	33	....	3 25
Brattleboro	82	82	71	55	39	33	....	2 75
Burlington	82	82	71	55	39	33	....	3 25
Cavendish	82	82	71	55	39	33	....	3 00
Essex Jct.	82	82	71	55	39	33	....	3 25
Greensboro	82	82	71	55	39	33	....	3 25
Hartford	82	82	71	55	39	33	....	3 10
Leicester Jct.	82	82	71	55	39	33	....	3 25
Montpelier	82	82	71	55	39	33	....	3 25
North Bennington	82	82	71	55	39	33	....	2 75
Rutland	82	82	71	55	39	33	....	3 25
St. Albans	82	82	71	55	39	33	....	3 25
St. Johnsbury	82	82	71	55	39	33	....	3 00
VIRGINIA—								
Abingdon	84	84	72	55	39	33	....	3 75
Alexandria	72	72	62	47	32	27	....	2 25
Basic	72	72	62	47	32	27	....	3 00
Big Stone Gap	Note 3	1 20	1 03	83	70	63	56	3 25
Clarksville	Note 3	1 27	1 08	83	56	48	39	3 50
Emporia	$0 97	1 24	1 05	81	55	46	....	3 50
Farmville	72	72	62	47	32	27	....	3 50
Fredericksburg	72	72	62	47	32	27	....	2 85
Harrisonburg	72	72	62	47	32	27	....	2 50

YOUR MONEY WILL BE IMMEDIATELY RETURNED TO YOU FOR ANY GOODS NOT PERFECTLY SATISFACTORY.

	Min. freight charge	1st class freight per 100 lbs	2d class freight per 100 lbs	3d class freight per 100 lbs	4th class freight per 100 lbs	5th class freight per 100 lbs	6th class freight per 100 lbs	Express per 100 lbs
VIRGINIA—Continued.								
Lexington	$0 72	$0 72	$0 62	$0 47	$0 32	$0 27	......	$2 75
Lynchburg	72	72	62	47	32	27	......	3 25
Martinsville	Note 3	1 15	98	75	50	43	$0 35	4 00
Morley	$0 75	75	65	50	35	30	......	3 00
New Castle	84	84	72	55	38	31	......	3 25
Old Point Comfort	72	72	62	47	32	27	......	2 75
Orange, Rockingham Co.	72	72	62	47	32	27	......	3 00
Pulaski City	84	84	72	55	39	33	......	3 25
Richmond	72	72	62	47	32	27	......	3 00
Riverton	72	72	62	47	32	27	......	2 75
Salem	72	72	62	47	32	27	......	2 25
Suffolk	72	72	62	47	32	27	......	3 00
Swordscreek	84	84	72	55	39	33	......	3 25
Virginia City	84	84	72	55	39	33	......	3 25
West Point	72	72	62	47	32	27	......	3 00
WASHINGTON—								
Anacortes	2 60	3 00	2 60	2 20	1 90	......	......	11 50
Chehalis	2 60	3 00	2 60	2 20	1 90	......	......	11 50
Colfax	3 10	3 60	3 10	2 60	2 10	......	......	10 00
Connell	3 10	3 60	3 10	2 60	2 10	......	......	10 00
Coulee City	3 10	3 60	3 10	2 60	2 10	......	......	10 50
Dayton	3 10	3 60	3 10	2 60	2 10	......	......	10 00
Easton	3 10	3 60	3 10	2 60	2 10	......	......	11 00
Hoquiam	2 60	3 00	2 60	2 20	1 90	......	......	11 50
Kalama	2 60	3 00	2 60	2 20	1 90	......	......	11 50
Meyers Falls	3 39	4 14	3 62	3 09	2 55	......	......	$2 00- 9 50
Monroe	2 85	3 25	2 80	2 37	2 05	......	......	2 00- 9 00
New Whatcom	2 60	3 00	2 60	2 20	1 90	......	......	12 00
Northport	3 52	4 27	3 70	3 13	2 59	......	......	2 00- 9 50
North Yakima	3 10	3 60	3 10	2 60	2 10	......	......	11 00
Olympia	2 60	3 00	2 60	2 20	1 90	......	......	11 50
Pasco	3 10	3 60	3 10	2 60	2 10	......	......	11 50
Snohomish	2 60	3 00	2 60	2 20	1 90	......	......	11 50
South Bend	2 60	3 00	2 60	2 20	1 90	......	......	11 50
Spokane	2 85	3 60	3 10	2 60	2 10	......	......	10 00
Tacoma	2 60	3 00	2 60	2 20	1 90	......	......	11 50
Walla Walla	3 10	3 60	3 10	2 60	2 10	......	......	10 00
Wallula	3 10	3 60	3 10	2 00	2 10	......	......	10 00
Wenatchee	3 10	3 60	3 10	2 60	2 10	......	......	$2 00- 9 00
WEST VIRGINIA—								
Acme	84	84	72	55	38	$0 31	......	2 60
Beverly	97	85	72	56	40	34	......	3 25
Charleston	45	44	39	30	21	18	......	2 50
Clarksburg	57	57	49	38	26	21	......	2 25
Dingess	84	84	72	55	39	33	......	2 50
Grafton	57	57	49	38	26	21	......	2 00
Harpers Ferry	72	72	62	47	32	27	......	2 25
Hinton	72	72	62	47	32	27	......	3 00
Martinsburg	72	72	62	47	32	27	......	2 25
Parkersburg	45	45	39	30	21	18	......	2 00
Parsons	97	90	76	60	41	53	......	2 00

	Min. freight charge	1st class freight per 100 lbs	2d class freight per 100 lbs	3d class freight per 100 lbs	4th class freight per 100 lbs	5th class freight per 100 lbs	6th class freight per 100 lbs	Express per 100 lbs
WEST VIRGINIA—Con'd.								
Ripley Landing	$0 45	$0 45	$0 39	$0 30	$0 21	$0 18	......	$2 25
Romney	77	77	66	50	34	29	......	2 00
Spencer	70	63	55	46	34	27	......	2 25
Wheeling	45	45	39	30	21	18	......	1 75
WISCONSIN—								
Ashland	25	65	55	44	28	......	......	2 00
Athens	25	55	46	36	24	......	......	2 00
Beloit	25	37	30	24	18	......	......	75
Cameron	25	65	55	44	28	......	......	1 75
Chelsea	25	60	50	40	25	......	......	2 00
Chippewa Falls	25	60	50	40	25	......	......	1 75
Fond du Lac	25	40	33	28	20	......	......	1 00
Grand Rapids	25	50	42	33	23	......	......	1 50
Green Bay	25	43	36	29	20	......	......	1 25
Hudson	25	60	50	40	25	......	......	1 75
Hurley	25	65	55	44	28	......	......	2 00
Lancaster	25	50	42	33	23	......	......	1 50
Madison	25	40	35	26	18	......	......	1 00
Manitowoc	25	30	25	21	16	......	......	1 10
Milwaukee	25	25	20	15	12	......	......	60
Mineral Pt	25	46	38	30	21	......	......	1 10
Mondovi	50	60	50	40	25	......	......	1 75
Oconto	25	43	36	29	23	......	......	1 50
Pembine	25	60	50	40	25	......	......	1 50
Prairie du Chien	25	50	42	33	23	......	......	1 50
Prentice	25	60	50	40	25	......	......	2 00
Richland Center	25	50	42	33	23	......	......	1 25
Rhinelander	25	60	50	40	25	......	......	1 75
Sparta	25	50	42	33	23	......	......	1 50
Spooner	25	65	55	44	28	......	......	2 00
Sturgeon Bay	50	43	36	29	23	......	......	1 50
Wabeno	25	60	50	40	25	......	......	1 75
Wausau	25	50	42	33	23	......	......	1 75
WYOMING—								
Casper	75	2 70	2 35	1 90	1 55	......	......	6 00
Cheyenne	75	2 05	1 65	1 25	97	......	......	6 00
Cokeville	2 40	3 30	2 80	2 20	1 82	......	......	8 00
Dana	1 50	2 95	2 43	1 87	1 49	......	......	7 75
Evanston	2 00	3 10	2 65	2 15	1 75	......	......	8 00
Gillette	75	2 70	2 35	1 90	1 55	......	......	6 75
Green River	1 75	3 10	2 65	2 15	1 75	......	......	8 00
Hanna	1 50	2 91	2 40	1 85	1 47	......	......	7 50
Lander	3 65	4 00	3 65	3 20	2 85	......	......	......
Laramie	1 25	2 56	2 10	1 64	1 29	......	......	$6 75
Lusk	75	2 45	2 01	1 55	1 22	......	......	5 25
Medicine Bow	1 50	2 85	2 35	1 81	1 43	......	......	7 50
Rawlins	1 50	3 06	2 53	1 94	1 56	......	......	8 00
Sheridan	75	2 70	2 35	1 90	1 55	......	......	7 00
Wamsutter	2 25	3 10	2 65	2 06	1 68	......	......	8 00
Wheatland	1 16	2 45	2 01	1 55	1 22	......	......	6 50

HOW TO FIGURE EXPRESS CHARGES.

When rate per 100 pounds is ☞	$0.40	$0.50	$0.60	$0.75	$1.00	$1.25	$1.50	$1.75
Packages not over	1 lb. $0 25	1 lb. $0 25	1 lb. $0 25	1 lb. $0 25	1 lb. $0 25	1 lb. $0 25	1 lb. $0 25	1 lb. $0 25
Over 1 pound to	2 " 25	2 " 25	2 " 25	2 " 30	2 " 30	2 " 30	2 " 30	2 " 30
" 2 " "	3 " 25	3 " 25	3 " 25	3 " 30	3 " 30	3 " 35	3 " 35	3 " 40
" 3 " "	4 " 25	4 " 25	4 " 30	4 " 30	4 " 35	4 " 35	4 " 40	4 " 45
" 4 " "	5 " 25	5 " 25	5 " 30	5 " 35	5 " 40	5 " 40	5 " 45	5 " 50
" 5 " "	7 " 30	7 " 30	7 " 35	7 " 35	7 " 40	7 " 45	7 " 50	7 " 55
" 7 " "	10 30	10 30	10 35	10 40	10 45	10 50	10 55	10 60
" 10 " "	15 30	15 30	15 35	15 40	15 45	15 55	15 60	15 65
" 15 " "	20 30	20 30	20 35	20 40	20 50	20 60	20 70	20 75
" 20 " "	25 35	25 35	25 40	25 45	25 55	25 65	25 75	25 85
" 25 " "	30 35	30 40	30 45	30 50	30 60	30 70	30 80	30 90
" 30 " "	35 40	35 40	35 45	35 50	35 65	35 75	35 85	35 1 00
" 35 " "	40 40	40 40	40 50	40 55	40 70	40 80	40 90	40 1 00
" 40 " "	45 40	45 40	45 50	45 60	45 75	45 90	45 1 00	45 1 00
" 45 " "	50 40	50 45	50 55	50 60	50 80	50 1 00	50 1 00	50 .1 00
" 50 " "	55 40	55 50	55 60	55 65	55 85	55 1 00	55 1 10	55 1 10
" 55 " "	60 40	60 50	60 60	60 70	60 90	60 1 10	60 1 20	60 1 20
" 60 " "	65 40	65 50	65 60	65 75	65 90	65 1 15	65 1 30	65 1 30
" 65 " "	70 40	70 50	70 60	70 75	70 1 00	70 1 25	70 1 40	70 1 40
" 70 " "	75 40	75 50	75 60	75 75	75 1 00	75 1 25	75 1 50	75 1 50
" 75 " "	80 40	80 50	80 60	80 75	80 1 00	80 1 25	80 1 50	80 1 60
" 80 " "	85 40	85 50	85 60	85 75	85 1 00	85 1 25	85 1 50	85 1 70
" 85 " "	100 40	100 50	100 60	100 75	100 1 00	100 1 25	100 1 50	100 1 75

When rate per 100 pounds is ☞	$2.00	$2.50	$3.00	$3.50	$4.00	$4.50
Packages not over	1 lb. $0 25	1 lb. $0 25	1 lb. $0 25	1 lb. $0 25	1 lb. $0 25	1 lb. $0 30
Over 1 pound to	2 " 35	2 " 35	2 " 35	2 " 35	2 " 35	2 " 35
" 2 " "	3 " 45	3 " 45	3 " 45	3 " 45	3 " 45	3 " 45
" 3 " "	4 " 50	4 " 55	4 " 60	4 " 60	4 " 60	4 " 60
" 4 " "	5 " 55	5 " 60	5 " 65	5 " 70	5 " 70	5 " 75
" 5 " "	7 " 60	7 " 70	7 " 75	7 " 80	7 " 85	7 " 90
" 7 " "	10 70	10 75	10 80	10 90	10 1 00	10 1 00
" 10 " "	15 75	15 85	15 90	15 1 00	15 1 11	15 1 15
" 15 " "	20 85	20 1 00	20 1.10	20 1 20	20 1 25	20 1 30
" 20 " "	25 1 00	25 1 10	25 1 20	25 1 30	25 1 40	25 1 50
" 25 " "	30 1 00	30 1 15	30 1 30	30 1 50	30 1 60	30 1 70
" 30 " "	35 1 00	35 1 25	35 1 40	35 1 60	35 1 70	35 1 90
" 35 " "	40 1 00	40 1 25	40 1 50	40 1 75	40 1 85	40 2 00
" 40 " "	45 1 00	45 1 25	45 1 50	45 1 75	45 2 00	45 2 25
" 45 " "	50 1 00	50 1 25	50 1 50	50 1 75	50 2 00	50 2 25

This scale is the same as used by all express companies and shows how they arrive at the charges on shipments at the rates given.

Where two rates are shown in the rate tables, charges on packages weighing over 7 pounds are arrived at by adding the rates of the two different amounts given.

Where weight is 7 pounds or less, add the two amounts together and take the rate shown under the sum of the two amounts.

When the rate per 100 pounds is $2.00 or more, and the weight of the shipment is greater than 50 pounds, the express companies charge at pound rates. For example: Rate per 100 pounds, $3.00; weight of shipment, 60 pounds; charges would be $1.80.

When rate per 100 pounds is ☞	$5.00	$6.00	$7.00	$8.00	$9.00	$10.00	$11.00	$12.00
Packages not over	1 lb. $0 30	1 lb. $0 30	1 lb. $0 30	1 lb. $0 30	1 lb. $0 30	1 lb. $0 30	1 lb. $0 30	1 lb. $0 30
Over 1 pound to	2 " 35	2 " 35	2 " 35	2 " 35	2 " 35	2 " 35	2 " 35	2 " 35
" 2 " "	3 " 45	3 " 45	3 " 45	3 " 45	3 " 45	3 " 45	3 " 45	3 " 45
" 3 " "	4 " 60	4 " 60	4 " 60	4 " 60	4 " 60	4 " 60	4 " 60	4 " 60
" 4 " "	5 " 75	5 " 75	5 " 80	5 " 80	5 " 80	5 " 80	5 " 80	5 " 80
" 5 " "	7 1 00	7 1 00	7 1 00	7 1 00	7 1 00	7 1 00	7 1 00	7 1 00
" 7 " "	10 1 10	10 1 15	10 1 20	10 1 25	10 1 35	10 1 50	10 1 50	10 1 50
" 10 " "	15 1 25	15 1 35	15 1 50	15 1 60	15 1 75	15 2 00	15 2 00	15 2 15
" 15 " "	20 1 40	20 1 65	20 1 75	20 2 00	20 2 00	20 2 50	20 2 50	20 2 75
" 20 " "	25 1 60	25 1 85	25 2 00	25 2 25	25 2 50	25 3 00	25 3 25	25 3 50
" 25 " "	30 1 75	30 2 10	30 2 50	30 2 75	30 3 00	30 3 25	30 3 75	30 4 00
" 30 " "	35 2 00	35 2 50	35 2 75	35 3 25	35 3 50	35 3 75	35 4 25	35 4 75
" 35 ' "	40 2 25	40 2 75	40 3 25	40 3 50	40 4 00	40 4 25	40 4 75	40 5 25
" 40 ' "	45 2 50	45 3 00	45 3 50	45 4 00	45 4 50	45 4 75	45 5 25	45 5 75
" 45 " "	50 2 50	50 3 00	50 3 50	50 4 00	50 4 50	50 5 00	50 5 50	50 6 00

When rate per 100 pounds is ☞	$13.00	$14.00	$15.00	$16.00	$17.00	$18.00	$20.00
Packages not over	1 lb. $0 30	1 lb. $0 30	1 lb. $0 35	1 lb. $0 35	1 lb. $0 35	1 lb. $0 35	1 lb. $0 40
Over 1 pound to	2 " 35	2 " 35	2 " 40	2 " 40	2 " 45	2 " 45	2 " 50
" 2 " "	3 " 45	3 " 45	3 " 50	3 " 50	3 " 55	3 " 60	3 " 60
" 3 " "	4 " 60	4 " 60	4 " 65	4 " 65	4 " 75	4 " 75	4 " 80
" 4 " "	5 " 80	5 " 80	5 " 85	5 " 85	5 " 90	5 " 95	5 " 1 00
" 5 " "	7 1 00	7 1 10	7 1 15	7 1 15	7 1 25	7 1 40	7 1 50
" 7 " "	10 1 50	10 1 50	10 1 65	10 1 65	10 1 75	10 1 80	10 2 00
" 10 " "	15 2 15	15 2 15	15 2 35	15 2 50	15 2 60	15 2 75	15 3 00
" 15 " "	20 2 75	20 2 85	20 3 00	20 3 20	20 3 40	20 3 60	20 4 00
" 20 " "	25 3 50	25 3 50	25 3 75	25 4 00	25 4 25	25 4 50	25 5 00
" 25 " "	30 4 00	30 4 20	30 4 50	30 4 80	30 5 10	30 5 40	30 6 00
" 30 " "	35 4 75	35 4 90	35 5 25	35 5 60	35 5 95	35 6 30	35 7 00
" 35 ' "	40 5 25	40 5 60	40 6 00	40 6 40	40 6 80	40 7 20	40 8 00
" 40 ' "	45 5 85	45 6 30	45 6 75	45 7 20	45 7 65	45 8 10	45 9 00
" 45 " "	50 6 50	50 7 00	50 7 50	50 8 00	50 8 50	50 9 00	50 10 00

FREIGHT CLASSIFICATION.

1 stands for First Class.
2 stands for Second Class.
3 stands for Third Class.
4 stands for Fourth Class.
5 stands for Fifth Class.
6 stands for Sixth Class.
1¼ stands for 1¼ times First Class.
1½ stands for 1½ times First Class.
D1 stands for 2 times First Class.
2½ stands for 2½ times First Class.
3T1 stands for 3 times First Class.
4T1 stands for 4 times First Class.

THE RAILROADS CHARGE FOR FREIGHT according to its classification. For example: Stoves take 3d class rate. By referring to pages 7 to 10 you will find the 3rd class rate to the nearest town in your state. Multiply the weight of the article (which you can get from our catalogue or estimate pretty closely) by the rate, and you will be able to figure the freight charges almost to a cent. If the following list does not contain the article you want, you can, as a rule, use the rate on some article of a similar nature.

THE CLASSIFICATION ON SOME ARTICLES is different to different sections of the country. For example: Hardware takes 2nd class rate to the western and southern states, and 3rd class rate to the eastern states. Hay presses take 3rd class rate to the western states, 2nd class to the eastern states and 4th class to the southern states.

REMEMBER, We always pack and ship our goods in a manner that secures for you the LOWEST FREIGHT CHARGES.

WEST. The railroads running west, northwest and southwest from Chicago, use the western classification. Use the classification in column marked "WEST" if you live in any of the following states: Arizona, Arkansas, California, Colorado, Idaho, Illinois, Indian Territory, Iowa, Kansas, Louisiana, Minnesota, Missouri, Montana, Nebraska, Nevada, New Mexico, North Dakota, Oklahoma Territory, Oregon, South Dakota, Texas, Utah, Washington, Wisconsin, Wyoming.

EAST. The railroads running east and northeast from Chicago, use the eastern classification. Use the classification in column marked "EAST" if you live in any of the following states: Connecticut, Delaware, District of Columbia, Indiana, Maryland, Maine, Massachusetts, Michigan, New Hampshire, New Jersey, New York, Ohio, Pennsylvania, Rhode Island, Vermont, Virginia, West Virginia.

SOUTH. The railroads running south and southeast from Chicago, use the southern classification. Use the classification in column marked "SOUTH" if you live in any of the following states: Alabama, Florida, Georgia, Kentucky, Mississippi, North Carolina, South Carolina, Tennessee.

ARTICLES	CLASS WEST	EAST	SOUTH
Advertising Matter	1	1	2
Ammunition	1	2	1
Anvils	4	4	5
Asbestos Building Felt	3	3	3
Axes	2	3	3
Axles	3	4	5
Baby Carriages	1½	1½	1
Bamboo Book Racks	3T1	3T1	1½
Barb Wire	4	4	6
Bar Iron	4	4	5
Barn Door Rail	3	3	4
Baskets, Nested	D-1	D-1	1
Bath Tubs	1	1	1
Beans, Dried	3	4	2
Bed Lounges	1½	1½	1
Beds, Folding	1½	1½	1
Beds, Iron or Wood	2	2	2
Bed Slats	3	3	4
Bed Springs, Spiral	D-1	D-1	D-1
Bed Springs, Woven Wire	1	1½	1
Bedsteads, Iron or Wood	2	2	2
Bells, Iron	3	3	3
Bellows	1	1	1
Belting, Rubber, Leather or Canvas	1	2	2
Bicycles	D-1	1½	1½
Binding Twine	3	3	3
Bird Cages	3T1	3T1	D-1
Blankets	1	1	1
Blinds	3	1	4
Blowers, Rotary	1	2	2
Boards, Shoveling	3	1	
Boats, Row	4T1	4T1	4T1
Boats, Stone	2	3	
Bob Sleds	2	1	
Boilers, Steam	3	2	3
Bone, Ground	4	3	6
Bookcases	1½	1½	1½
Book Racks, Bamboo	3T1	3T1	1½
Books	1	1	1
Boots and Shoes	1	1	1
Buggies.....(See Vehicles)			
Buggy Bodies, Finished	1½	2½	1½
Buggy Bodies, Unfinished	1½	1½	2
Buggy Tops	1½	1½	1½
Buggy Wheels, Finished	1½	1	2
Buggy Wheels, Unfinished	1	1	2
Building Felt	3	3	5
Building Paper	3	3	5
Bureaus	1	1	2
Cameras	D-1	1	1½
Candles	4	3	4
Candy in Pails	2	2	4
Canned Goods	4	2	2
Cans, Milk	1	1½	1
Cant Hooks	3	2	2
Carpets	1	1	1
Carriages...(See Vehicles)			
Carts, Hand, K. D.	1	1	1
Carts, Road	1½	D-1	
Cement, Building	4	4	5
Cereals	3	4	4
Chains	2	3	5
Chairs, Bamboo, Rattan, Reed or Willow	3T1	3T1	D-1
Chairs, Cane Seat	1½	1½	1
Chairs, Invalid's Rolling	D-1	1	1
Chairs, Upholstered	D-1	1½	1½
Chairs, Wood or Leather Seat	1½	1½	1
Cheese	2	3	3
Chiffoniers	1	1	2
China Closets	D-1	1½	1½
Churns, Hand	2	1	2
Cigars and Cigarettes	1	1	1
Cloaks	1	1	1
Clocks	1	1	1
Clothes Bars	1	2	3
Clothing	1	1	1
Cobbler's Outfit	2	3	2
Cod Fish	4	5	5
Coffee	4	3	5
Coffee Mills	2	2	2
Commodes	1	1	2
Condensed Milk	4	3	3
Conductors, Pipe, not nested	D-1	1	1
Corn Cribs	4	3	5
Corn Huskers	1	2	1
Corn Planters	2	2	2
Corn Shellers, Hand, K. D.	3	2	2
Corrugated Iron	4	4	6
Cots, Folding	1	1	1
Couches	1½	1½	1
Crackers	2	2	4

ARTICLES	CLASS WEST	EAST	SOUTH
Cribs, Iron or Wood	2	2	2
Crockery	2	3	4
Crowbars	4	4	6
Cultivators, Disc, Riding, K. D.	2	2	3
Cultivators, Hand, K. D., in bundles	1	2	3
Cultivators, Walking, K.D.	3	2	3
Cupboards	1½	1½	1½
Cutters, Bone, K. D.	2	2	2
Cutters, Feed and Ensilage, K. D.	3	2	1
Cutters, Root and Vegetable, K. D.	3	2	1
Cutters (Sleighs)	2½	3T1	
Decoy Ducks	2	1	1
Desks	1	1½	1
Disc Sharpeners	2	3	2
Dishes	2	3	4
Dog Powers	1	1	1
Door Hangers	3	3	4
Door Screens	1	1	2
Doors, Common	4	3	4
Doors, Common, Glazed	4	1	3
Doubletrees, Unfinished	3	3	4
Dressers	1	1	2
Dried Fruits	3	3	2
Drills, Blacksmith's Post	2	2	2
Drills, Corn, S. U	1	1	1
Drugs	1	1	1
Drums	4T1	3T1	3T1
Dry Goods	1	1	1
Dynamite	D-1	D-1	D-1
Earthenware	2	3	4
Egg Carrier Cases	1	1	1
Electric Batteries	1	1	1
Electrical Goods	1	1	1
Emery Wheels	3	3	3
Engines, Steam or Gasoline	1	2	3
Evaporators, Fruit, S. U.	1½	1½	1
Evaporators, Sugar, K. D.	2	1	2
Explosives	D-1	D-1	D-1
Fanning Mills, K. D.	1	1	1
Feed Grinders, S. U.	2	2	4
Feed Mills, Sweep, K. D.	2	3	4
Felt, Building	3	3	5
Fence Wire, Barb and Smooth	4	4	6
Fencing	3	3	5
Fencing Machines, K. D.	1	2	3
Fertilizers	4	4	6
Firearms	1	1	1
Fish, Canned	4	3	3
Fish, Pickled or Salted	4	5	5
Flax Meal	4	5	3
Flour	4	5	6
Flower Stands, Wire	3T1	3T1	D-1
Food, Animal or Poultry	4	4	6
Food Cookers, viz.:			
Acme	3	1	1
Economy	3	1	1
Farmers' Friend	3	3	4
Handy	3	1	1
Hercules	3	2	3
Kenwood	3	1	1
Forges, Portable	2	1	2
Forks, Horse Hay	2	2	3
Freezers	1	1	2
Fruit, Canned	4	3	3
Fruit, Dried	3	3	2
Fruit Jars	3	2	3
Galvanized Iron	4	4	6
Game Traps	2	3	3
Gas Fixtures	2	2	2
Gas for Calcium Lights	1	3	1
Gas Machines	1	D-1	2
Gasoline Stoves	1	1	1
Gears, Running	1½	1	
Generators, Gas	1	D-1	2
Glassware	2	2	2
Grain Drills, K. D.	3	2	2
Granite & Enameled Ware	2	2	2
Graphophones	1½	1	1
Grease, Axle	4	3	5
Grindstone Frames	3	3	3
Grindstones	4	3	4
Grist Mills, Hand, boxed	2	2	4
Grits	4	5	5
Gunpowder	D-1	D-1	D-1
Guns, Revolvers, etc	1	1	1
Hall Trees	D-1	D-1	1½
Hammocks	1	1	1
Hardware	2	3	2
Harness and Saddles	1	1	2
Harrows, N. O. S., K. D	3	2	4

ARTICLES	CLASS WEST	EAST	SOUTH
Harrows, Disc, K. D	3	2	3
Hay Carriers	2	2	3
Hay Carrier Tracks	3	3	4
Hay Presses, Hand	3	2	4
Hay Presses, Power, loaded in box cars, actual weight	3	2	4
Hay Presses, S. U	1	1	1
Heaters, Tank	3	1	
High Explosives	D-1	D-1	D-1
Hinges, Iron	3	3	3
Hoes	2	2	3
Hollow-ware	3	3	3
Hominy	4	5	5
Horse and Mule's Shoes	4	4	6
Horse Power Jacks	3	3	2
Horse Powers	3	2	2
Hullers, Pea, Hand	1	D-1	2
Ice Cream Freezers	1	1	2
Ice Plows	1	1	
Incubators	1	1	1
Iron Beds	2	2	2
Ironing Boards	1	3	3
Iron Pipe	4	4	6
Iron Tires	3	4	6
Iron Tuyeres	3	4	2
Iron Wagon Wheels	3	2	4
Kettles	3	3	3
Kitchen Sinks, Iron	2	3	3
Ladders	1	2	1
Lamps	1	1	1
Land Rollers, K. D.	3	2	3
Lard	4	3	5
Lasts	3	2	2
Laundry Tubs, Galvanized Iron	3	1	1
Lawn Mowers	1	2	2
Lead Pipe	4	3	4
Lime	4	3	6
Linseed Meal	4	5	3
Lounges	1½	1½	1
Lye	4	3	5
Magic Lanterns	D-1	1	1
Mandrels	4	3	5
Matting	1	1	2
Mattresses, Woven Wire	1	1½	1
Meats, Cured	4	3	6
Milk Cans	1	1½	1
Mills, Cane	3	2	4
Mills, Cider and Wine Presses	2	2	
Mills, Cob and Corn	2	2	4
Millwork (see Sash, Doors, and Blinds).			
Mirrors	1	1	1
Molasses in Barrels or Kegs	4	4	5
Molasses in Cans or Kits	4	2	5
Mowers, Lawn	1	2	2
Musical Instruments	D-1	1½	1
Music Cabinets	D-1	D-1	1½
Nails	4	4	6
Notions	1	1	1
Nuts, Edible	2	2	2
Oars	1	3	3
Oat Meal	4	4	4
Oil in Barrels	3	3	3
Oil Cake Meal	4	5	3
Oil Cloth, under 13 ft. long	2	2	2
Oil Stoves	1	1	1
Organs	1	1	1
Ovens, Sheet Iron	1	1	1
Oyster Shells	4	4	6
Pails	2	1	3
Paint, in Barrel	4	3	4
Paint, in Cans or Pails	4	3	4
Paper Hangings	1	2	2
Pea Hullers, Hand	1	1	2
Phonographs	1½	1	1
Pianos	1	1	1
Pictures	1	1	1
Pipe, Lead	4	3	4
Planters, Corn, K. D.	3	2	2
Planters, Hand Corn, Bean and Potato	1	1	3
Planters, Potato, K. D.	1	2	2
Plows, Gang or Sulky, K. D.	3	2	4
Plows, Ice	1	1	
Plow Points and Shares	3	3	4
Plows, Walking, K. D	2	2	4
Plumbing Material	2	2	2
Poles, Buggy, Carriage or Wagon. Finished	1½	1	1
Unfinished	3	3	
Potato Diggers, K. D	3	2	4
Poultry Netting	3	3	5
Press Screws	3	3	3
Pulleys, Iron or Wood	2	3	4
Pumps	1	2	3
Queensware	2	3	2
Racks, Grain, Hay or Stalk, K. D.	2	2	3
Rakes, Revolving, K. D., Teeth in	1	1	3
Rakes, Sulky, K. D.	3	2	3
Range, Boilers, Iron	3	3	3
Refrigerators	2	2	2
Rice	4	4	6
Road Carts	1½	D-1	
Road Scrapers, Drag	3	1	3
Road Scrapers, Wheeled, K. D.	3	1	3
Rolled Oats	4	5	4
Roofing Paper	3	3	5
Rope	3	3	3

ARTICLES	CLASS WEST	EAST	SOUTH
Rope, Wire	3	3	4
Rubber Goods	1	1	1
Rugs, Woolen	1	1	1
Saddlery	1	1	2
Sad Irons	4	3	4
Safer, Iron	3	3	3
Salt	4	4	6
Sash, Unglazed	3	1	4
Sash Weights, Iron	4	4	6
Saw Frames, Circular, K. D	2	2	2
Saws, on Board	1	1	1
Sawing Machines, Drag, K. D.	2	1	1
Scales	2	2	3
Scientific Instruments	D-1	1	1
Screens, Door or Window	1	1	2
Seats, Carriage and Buggy	2	1	2
Seeders, Broadcast, K. D.	3	2	2
Seeders, Endgate	D-1	2	1
Seeders, Hand, Crated	1	2	1
Settees, Lawn	D-1	D-1	1
Sewing Machines	1	1	1
Sewing Machines, Drop Head	1	1	2
Shafts, Carriage and Buggy, finished	1½	D-1	1
Shot, in Boxes or Kegs	3	3	5
Shovels	2	2	3
Sideboards	1	1	2
Singletrees	3	3	
Skeins	3	4	5
Sleds, Bob	2	1	
Sleighs	2½	3T1	
Soap	4	3	6
Soap Powder	4	3	6
Sofas or Sofa Beds	D-1	D-1	1½
Sporting Goods	1	1	1
Spring Wagons............(See Vehicles)			
Stalk Cutters, K. D.	1	2	1
Stanchions, Cattle	2	3	4
Staples	4	4	6
Starch	3	3	3
Stationary	1	1	1
Stereopticons	D-1	1	1
Stove Furniture	3	3	3
Stove Pipe, Crated	1½	1½	1½
Stove Pipe, Iron	3	4	4
Stoves and Ranges	3	3	3
Stump Pullers, K. D	3	2	4
Sugar	4	3	5
Sulkies	3T1	D-1	
Surreys...........(See Vehicles)			
Swage Blocks	3	3	5
Syrup in Barrels or Kegs	4	4	5
Tables, Extension	3	2	2
Tables, Parlor	D-1	1½	1½
Tackle Blocks	3	3	5
Tanks, Galvanized Iron (Set Up)	D-1	D-1	D-1
Tanks, Galvanized Iron (Knocked Down) Sides in Rolls	1	2	2
Tank Heaters	3	1	
Tea	1	1	1
Tents	1	1	1
Tent Poles	3	3	3
Tinware	2	2	2
Tire Benders	3	3	2
Tire Shrinkers	3	2	2
Tire Upsetters	3	2	2
Tobacco	1	1	1
Tombstones	3	3	4
Tools	2	3	2
Tools in Chest	1	3	2
Tops, Buggy	1½	1½	1½
Toys	1	1	1
Traps, Animal or Bird	2	1	2
Troughs, Galvanized Steel	1	2	3
Troughs, Pig, Cast Iron	4	3	3
Trunks	1	1½	1
Tubs, Wooden	1	1	3
Twine	2	3	3
Varnish in Cans	1	2	2
Varnish in Wood	2	3	3
Vehicles (such as Buggies, Carriages, Spring Wagons, Surreys), crated under 30 inches in height and 94 inches long	1½	1¼	1
Vehicles, crated under 50 inches in height and 94 inches long	1½	D 1	1½
Vehicles, crated under 30 inches in height and over 94 inches long	1½	D-1	1
Vinegar, in Wood	4	3	6
Vises	2	3	4
Wagon Jacks	2	2	3
Wagons, Farm	1	1	4
Wall Paper	1	2	2
Wardrobes, set up	D-1	D-1	1½
Wardrobes, taken apart	2	2	2
Washing Machines	1	1	2
Washstands	1	1	2
Water Closets	1	1	3
Water Heaters	3	2	3
Weeders, K. D., in bundles	1	1	3
Wheelbarrows, K. D	2	2	2
Wheels, Buggy, finished	1½	1	2
Wheels, Buggy, unfinished	1	1	2
Wheels, Wagon, Iron	3	2	4
Wheels, Wagon, Wooden	1	1	4
White Lead, in kegs or barrels	4	4	4
Windmills and Towers	3	2	3
Window Screens	1	1	2
Wine	1	1	1
Wire, Barb or Smooth	4	4	6
Wire Fencing	3	3	5
Wire Rope	3	3	4
Woodenware	2	1	3
Wringers	2	2	2

JAMES B. FORGAN, President.
DAVID R. FORGAN, Vice President.
GEORGE D. BOULTON, Vice President.
HOWARD H. HITCHCOCK, Vice President.
RICHARD J. STREET, Cashier.
HOLMES HOGE, Assistant Cashier.
AUGUST BLUM, Assistant Cashier.
EDWARD DICKINSON, Assistant Cashier.
FRANK E. BROWN, Assistant Cashier.
CHARLES N. GILLETT, Assistant Cashier.
EMILE K. BOISOT, Manager Bond Department.
JOHN E. GARDIN, Manager Foreign Exchange Department.
MAX MAY, Assistant Manager Foreign Exchange Department.
FRANK O. WETMORE, Auditor.

ORVILLE PECKHAM, Attorney.
JAMES D. WOLEY, Assistant Attorney.

CAPITAL & SURPLUS,
$12,000,000.00.

First National Bank OF CHICAGO.

Chicago, Oct. 20, 1902.

TO WHOM IT MAY CONCERN:

It is with pleasure that we testify to our own good opinion of the integrity, responsibility and business ability of Sears, Roebuck & Company. They show a fully paid up capital and surplus of over Two Million Dollars ($2,000,000.00), and are one of the largest mercantile institutions in Chicago.

Anyone can, in our judgment, feel perfectly secure in sending money to them with their orders, as we understand that they ship their goods agreeing that anything not proving entirely satisfactory when received can be returned to them, and the money paid will be immediately returned to the purchaser.

The officers and stock holders of the company are well and favorably known to us, command our full confidence, and we believe can be relied upon to do exactly as they agree.

Yours very truly,

Jas B Forgan Prest

ERNEST A. HAMILL, PRESIDENT
CHARLES L. HUTCHINSON, VICE PRESIDENT
CHAUNCEY J. BLAIR, VICE PRESIDENT
D. A. MOULTON, VICE PRESIDENT

JOHN C. NEELY, SECRETARY
FRANK W. SMITH, CASHIER
B. C. SAMMONS, ASS'T CASHIER
J. EDWARD MAASS, ASS'T CASHIER

NO. 6106

THE CORN EXCHANGE NATIONAL BANK
OF CHICAGO.

CAPITAL $3.000.000.
SURPLUS $2.000.000.

CHICAGO, October 27, 1902.

To Whom It May Concern:

It pleases us to be able to testify to the reliability of Sears, Roebuck & Company of Chicago. The firm has a paid up capital and surplus of over Two Million Dollars ($2,000,000.00), and enjoys the highest credit with their Chicago banks, of which this bank is one.

We have no hesitancy in saying that we believe anyone who has dealings with this firm will be treated in the fairest manner possible. We can assure anyone who is thinking of placing an order with them, that, in our judgment, there is absolutely no risk in sending the money with the order.

Very truly yours,

Frank W. Smith

Cashier.

In writing to either of the above banks as to our reliability, be sure to enclose a 2 cent stamp for reply.

SAVE $50.00 TO $100.00 A YEAR ON YOUR GROCERIES.

OUR 32-PAGE GROCERY PRICE LIST SENT FREE ON APPLICATION.

DON'T PAY RETAIL PRICES FOR YOUR GROCERIES. You can buy everything you need in the grocery and meat line direct from us at the lowest Chicago wholesale prices and save all the profit your home grocery dealer makes when he sells to you. No matter how small a quantity of groceries you use, we will sell them to you at wholesale rates, at the same prices grocery dealers all over the country pay wholesale for their goods, and at the same time furnish you fresh goods as good or better in quality than you can buy elsewhere.

WE WILL SEND OUR GROCERY PRICE LIST, revised and issued every 60 days, free of charge to anyone who will fill out and send us the application blank below. We furnish a regular grocery catalogue every two months, which we mail to all of our customers, in order to follow the market and give them the benefit of the latest market quotations.

WE DO NOT CATALOGUE GROCERIES IN THIS BOOK. The prices of groceries are always fluctuating so rapidly, many articles advancing and declining from month to month, that we find it impossible to quote our line of groceries in this, our general catalogue, which holds good for one year, and we ask all who want our complete grocery price list, which shows the very latest market quotations, to write us and we will be pleased to mail it free of charge.

THIS HANDSOMELY ILLUSTRATED COMPLETE, 32-PAGE BOOK, as shown in the illustration, is our new Grocery Price List. It is 9½x12¾ inches in size, consists of 32 pages, attractively printed in colors, with hundreds of illustrations, quotations and descriptions of everything in the grocery line and is the largest, most complete and lowest priced grocery catalogue ever issued. Sign and mail the application blank below and we will send you the price list **FREE.**

This Special Grocery Catalogue names the lowest Chicago wholesale prices on

Sugar, Flour	Molasses
Tea and Coffee	Vinegar
Meats, Fish	Cheese
Spices	Crackers
Dried Fruits	Soap—Laundry and Toilet
Baking Powder	Candy
Flavoring Extracts	Stock and Poultry Food
Canned Goods	Cigars and Tobacco
Pickles	Oils, etc.
Syrups	

Tells just what the freight will be on anything to your town.

GROCERIES TAKE THE LOWEST FREIGHT RATE. Almost everything in the grocery line can go fourth class, the lowest freight rate, and in comparison to what you save, by sending your order to us, the freight charges will amount to almost nothing. Even if you do not need any groceries immediately, send this application for our big, new, handsomely illustrated, free grocery catalogue and keep it until you are ready to order groceries again. It will post you on the wholesale cost of your goods, and even if you do not send us your order, it will prevent you from paying too much for your groceries at home.

In Our Special Grocery Catalogue

YOU WILL FIND A COMPLETE LINE IN EACH OF THE FOLLOWING DEPARTMENTS AND THE MOST SURPRISING PRICES NAMED, WHICH WILL ENABLE YOU TO SAVE 15 TO 25 PER CENT ON THE GROCERIES YOU BUY.

Tea Department	Canned Goods Department	Cracker & Bakery Goods Department
Coffee Department	Jams, Jelly & Preserve Department	Candy Department
Spice Department	Fish Department	Cigar Department
Baking Powder Department	Meat Department	Tobacco Department
Extract Department	Flour and Cereal Department	Soap Department
Dried Fruit Department	Sugar and Syrup Department	Stock and Poultry Food Department

WHY YOU SHOULD HAVE OUR SPECIAL GROCERY CATALOGUE AND WHY YOU SHOULD SEND US YOUR ORDERS FOR GROCERIES.

REASON No. 1—OUR PRICES ON GROCERIES

ARE ALWAYS THE LOWEST. You will always find our prices, quality for quality and grade for grade, to be the lowest named by any grocery house. Even though (through fluctuations in the market) our printed prices are higher than the market prices, you will find when your goods are billed to you that we have billed them at the lowest market prices and refunded the difference to you in cash without notice.

REASON No. 2—PROMPT SHIPMENTS.

YOUR GROCERY ORDER IS FILLED PROMPTLY. In most cases if your order reaches us in the morning on an early morning mail, it is filled and shipped the same day, so that by anticipating your wants for only a few days you can order groceries from us with as much convenience and practically, as far as your needs are concerned, get them as promptly as if you were buying the goods from your local stores.

REASON No. 3—PURITY.

WE POINT WITH PRIDE TO THE FACT THAT OUR GROCERIES ARE STRICTLY PURE AND HIGH GRADE. In this day of adulterated goods when inferior goods masquerade as high grade, when impurities are so carefully concealed as to be unrecognizable to the non-expert, it is an important consideration to know that the goods you order and the goods you receive are pure and of the highest quality. We do not sacrifice quality to price. We could in many lines name lower prices, or, rather, prices that are apparently lower, if we were disposed to sacrifice quality and put out impure, adulterated or inferior goods; but we have a reputation to maintain, a department to continue to build up, a big trusting patronage to take care of, and we are not disposed for one moment to furnish our customers with anything but the very best qualities the market affords.

REASON No. 4—OUR PRICES

ARE UNIFORMLY LOWEST THROUGHOUT, AND CAN BE DEPENDED UPON AS BEING THE LOWEST POSSIBLE ON EACH AND EVERY ITEM. In other words, we have no leaders, baits or catches. We do not offer one item at an extremely low price to get you to make up an order of groceries, and then more than make up the difference on the various other items that you include with your order. We do not make a leader of rice, sugar, coffee, crackers, or other well known items, and depend upon the balance of your order to make the transaction profitable to us. Our prices on all of these so-called leaders are uniformly the lowest, and more than this, on all other items that enter into a grocery order, such as dried fruits, canned goods, meats, flour, cereals, syrups, molasses, etc., are just as low in proportion as on goods that are usually selected for advertising and for baits.

REASON No. 5—CLEANLINESS.

IF YOU COULD GO INTO OUR BIG GROCERY DEPARTMENT YOU WOULD REALLY BE SURPRISED WITH THE NEATNESS, ORDER AND CLEANLINESS THAT PREVAILS IN THIS DEPARTMENT. It is a source of pride and pleasure to us to take such of our customers as visit us here in Chicago through our Grocery Department, and we constantly hear comments on the commendable features. Our methods are in striking contrast to the methods of stock handling as shown and practiced by small grocery dealers throughout the country. We lay particular stress on the cleanliness and care with which our grocery stock is kept and our customers' grocery orders are handled, and we feel that this is an important reason for bespeaking your patronage.

REASON No. 6—OUR BIG VARIETY STOCK.

IN OUR GROCERY CATALOGUE, YOU WILL FIND REPRESENTED EVERYTHING THAT CAN BE FOUND IN THE LARGEST METROPOLITAN GROCERY STORES. Our lines are very large and most complete, embracing all good and recognized qualities and brands, having a variety much larger than will be found in ordinary grocery stores throughout the country. In ordering your goods from us you have the benefit of making your selection from a more varied and complete stock than if you bought the goods in your local store.

REASON No. 7—GROCERY ORDERS HELP

TO REDUCE FREIGHT CHARGES. When you are ordering goods from other of our various merchandise departments, if you do not have enough ordered to make up a profitable freight shipment, look over our grocery list, pick out what you will need in this line, and you will be enabled to make a 100-pound shipment to go by freight at likely less cost than your merchandise from the other department alone would cost you by express.

WE CAN SAVE YOU $1.00 TO $5.00 on nearly every bill of groceries, depending upon the amount, and from $50.00 to $100.00 per year on all the groceries you use. Fill out the blank lines, writing your name and address plainly, cut this application blank out and send it to us and we will send you our free Grocery Price List.

CUT OUT AND MAIL THIS BLANK TO US.

SEARS, ROEBUCK & CO., Chicago.

GENTLEMEN: — Please enter my name on your Grocery Mailing List and mail to me free, postpaid, every two months, your Grocery Price List.

NAME______________________________

POSTOFFICE______________________ STATE______________

R. F. D. No.__________ STREET AND No.______________

DEPARTMENT OF STOVES

With the largest stove foundry in the world, located in Newark, Ohio, with larger contracts than ever before for the highest grade of pig iron from the Birmingham (Alabama) district, and with larger sheet steel contracts than ever before, all purchased for spot cash at inside prices, we offer you a line of the highest grade steel and cast iron cook stoves, ranges and heating stoves, embodying all the very latest improvements, at prices very much lower than you can buy elsewhere.

THE HISTORY OF OUR OHIO STOVE FOUNDRY has been one of almost constant expansion. Season after season we have enlarged it by the addition of new buildings. We have again enlarged it, making our foundry large enough to accommodate six hundred moulders, and our mounting, polishing, finishing and storage capacity is being enlarged in proportion, making it by far the largest stove foundry in the world. In our foundry we are installing the most modern type of cast iron and steel stove and range making machinery, with a view to improving quality and reducing cost, including the highest type of stove moulding machinery, electric conveyors for taking the castings from one part of the foundry to another, automatic polishing machines, making possible a higher finish, better grade of nickeling and at a much lower cost than any other foundries, mammoth punching, cutting and shaping machines, by which the entire body of a steel range is perfectly shaped, holes punched, all parts cut out with one drop of the press, making the work perfect, and at a cost much lower than any other foundries. In every branch of the factory everything has been done to make possible the highest grade of work at the lowest possible cost. Our own railroad side tracks, connecting with several trunk lines, run into our foundry and warehouses, affording economical handling of raw material and finished stoves, doing away entirely with the expense common in most foundries.

OUR AIM has been, by having the largest stove foundry in the world, equipped with such labor saving machinery as no other foundry has, to produce a higher grade, handsomer, stronger, better fitting and a more lasting line of steel and cast iron stoves than is made by any other maker, at a lower cost to produce than any other foundry; hence we guarantee that if you order a steel or cast iron cook stove or range or heating stove from us, you will find it a better made, better finished, better fitting, handsomer and more lasting stove, one that will consume less fuel for the same amount of heat produced, than you can buy elsewhere at anything approaching our price.

WITH NO TRAVELING MEN'S EXPENSES, no handling expense from foundry to wholesale house or retail store, no bad debts, delivering the stove you order direct from our mounting room in the largest foundry in the world into the car on our own side track, the cost to us of a stove we ship to you is less than any other stove factory in America, and to this actual cost to us we add only our one small percentage of profit; hence you can buy a better stove from us at a price very much lower than you can buy elsewhere.

OUR BINDING GUARANTEE.

WE GUARANTEE any stove you order from us to reach you in the same perfect condition it leaves our foundry, and if any piece or part is cracked or broken when received, we will replace or repair such cracked or broken part free of any cost to you; but as every stove is carefully crated, it very rarely happens that a stove reaches the purchaser with even the slightest crack or injury. We further guarantee every piece and part that enters into the stove, guarantee it perfect in manufacture, perfect in operation, unequaled by any other stove or range of its class for convenience, neatness, durability, economy in consumption of fuel and in the practical results that may be obtained by its use, and if you do not find it so you can return it to us at our expense and we will immediately refund your money.

OUR 30 DAYS' FREE TRIAL OFFER.

TO CONVINCE YOU that we will furnish you a handsomer, stronger, better made, better finished, more lasting and more economical fuel consuming stove than you can buy elsewhere, and at a big saving in cost to you, we make this liberal 30 days' free trial offer:

Select any one of our stoves, send us our price, and we will send the stove to you with the understanding and agreement that you can use the stove in your own home for thirty days, during which time you can put it to every possible test, you can compare it with other stoves you have used and with stoves used by your friends and neighbors, and if you do not conclude that, size for size and kind for kind, the stove we send you is in every way better than any stove you could buy from your dealer at home or elsewhere, if you are not convinced that you have made a big saving in cost, you can return the stove to us at our expense and we will immediately refund your money, together with the freight charges you paid.

ABOUT THE FREIGHT CHARGES.

THE PRICES QUOTED are for the stoves delivered on board cars at our foundry in Newark, Ohio, from which point you must pay the freight; but stoves, as we carefully crate them, are accepted by the railroad companies at a very low freight rate (third class), and you will find the freight charges will amount to next to nothing as compared to what you will save in price. Refer to the front of this book and you will note that we quote the third class freight rate per hundred pounds to several points in your state. Take the rate quoted to the point nearest you, and then from the weight of the stove, which we give under each description, you can tell almost exactly what the freight to your town will amount to.

OUR LIBERAL C. O. D. SUBJECT TO EXAMINATION TERMS.

WHILE NEARLY ALL OUR CUSTOMERS SEND CASH IN FULL WITH THEIR ORDERS, and we advise everyone to do this in order to save the extra express charge of from 25 to 50 cents which the express companies always make for collecting the amount of the C. O. D. and returning the money to us, nevertheless, to those who wish to see and examine the stove at their railroad station before paying for it, we will, on receipt of $1.00, ship any stove to any address east of the Missouri river and north of Tennessee, or on receipt of $5.00 to any point east of the Rocky Mountains and south of Kentucky. The stove will go by freight C. O. D., subject to examination. You can examine it at your freight depot, and if found perfectly satisfactory and you are convinced that you are getting a better stove at a lower price than you could get elsewhere, you can then pay the railroad agent our price and freight charges, less the $1.00 sent with order. Understand, if you send the full amount of cash with your order you save the extra express charge of from 25 to 50 cents, and you take no risk, for the stove will be sent to you with the understanding that you are to have thirty days' free trial, and if at any time during the thirty days you become dissatisfied with your purchase, you can return the stove to us, and your money, together with any freight charges paid by you, will be immediately returned to you.

STOVE PIPE AND COOKING UTENSILS ARE EXTRA

UNDERSTAND, at the prices quoted in this catalogue we furnish only the stove as illustrated and described, and no stove pipe or cooking utensils are furnished. If you desire any stove furniture (stove pipe or cooking utensils), they should be selected from either this catalogue, or from our special catalogue, and the stove furniture will be shipped from our stock in Chicago, while the stove will be sent to you direct from our foundry; thus making two shipments, one from the foundry and one from our store. For this reason we especially urge you to make your order for cooking utensils large enough to make the purchase very profitable to you, remembering that fifty to one hundred pounds will as a rule go by freight from Chicago for as little money as ten pounds.

SPECIAL OFFER TO STOVE DEALERS.

AS WE MAKE A HIGHER GRADE OF STEEL AND CAST IRON STOVES than goes out of any other foundry in this country, and our prices as quoted in this catalogue are lower than dealers can buy in carload lots from other makers, naturally we receive a great many orders from stove dealers throughout the country who buy our stoves to sell again. And while the prices quoted in this catalogue are alike to one and all, the same whether you buy one stove or a carload, at the urgent request of many of our customers among the stove dealers we have had all our stoves branded "Newark Stove Works," after the name of our foundry. Thus the name Sears, Roebuck & Co. will not appear on any stove, so that the dealer buying one stove, one dozen stoves or a carload of stoves from us, can put them on his floor, add whatever profit he likes, sell them to the trade, and few, if any of his customers will know in buying a stove from him that he or she could buy the exact same stove from us at the same price that the dealer bought it.

HOW TO GET REPAIRS FOR OUR STOVES.

WE ALWAYS CARRY A FULL STOCK OF REPAIRS for all the stoves we catalogue or have ever sold, and can in years to come promptly supply you with any piece or part for the repair of any stove you may purchase from us, and this part will always be supplied to you at foundry cost, a mere fraction of what your dealer would charge you for a repair. If you buy a stove of your local dealer this year and two or three years hence you want a repair for the stove, your dealer may have discontinued selling the kind of stove you purchased, or the foundry may have gone out of business, and you will find yourself unable to get the needed repairs; whereas, if you buy a stove from us you may be sure we will always be ready to ship to you any part of any stove we ever sell and that at a mere fraction of what you would have to pay for the same part for a stove you would buy elsewhere.

OUR ASTONISHING VALUES IN STEEL RANGES.

AT FROM $10.30 TO $30.45, according to grade, we offer you a line of steel ranges that are not approached by anything in the range line that goes out of any other foundry in this country.

OUR $14.95 ACME HUMMER RANGE, complete with high shelf, closet and reservoir, as illustrated under Nos. 22C122 to 22C125, and furnished at $10.30 to $14.95 according to equipment, is by far the lowest price ever named for a thoroughly reliable range, and we guarantee it a stronger, better made, better finished and more lasting range than those that are so widely advertised and sold generally at $25.00 to $30.00. While we can guarantee this range to give satisfaction, we especially urge that you select the highest grade range possible to build from the heaviest of sheet steel, our Acme Regal or Acme Triumph.

OUR $18.37 ACME RENOWN STEEL RANGE, which we furnish at $18.37, complete with high shelf, closet and reservoir, as illustrated and described under No. 22C86, is superior to ranges that are being widely advertised and generally sold at prices ranging from $30.00 to $35.00, a handsomer finished, better fitting and better made range than you would be likely to buy from your dealer at home at $35.00 to $40.00. While the Acme Renown is a range we can guarantee to give satisfaction, we would especially recommend that you buy one of the highest grade ranges, our Acme Regal or Acme Triumph.

OUR ACME REGAL RANGES, which we furnish in the high shelf, closet and reservoir, as illustrated under No. 22C50, for $23.67, and our Acme Triumph, which we furnish in the high shelf, closet and reservoir style, as illustrated under No. 22C20 at $26.70, are positively the highest grade ranges made, guaranteed better than go out of any other foundry in America. We use in these ranges sheet steel that, to the best of our knowledge, is two gauges heavier than is used in any steel range manufactured by any other maker in America. There are no ranges made that will compare with the Acme Regal or Acme Triumph as to grade and weight of steel, lining, interlining, bolting, bracing, fitting, nickel trimmings, workmanship or finish. In short, an Acme Triumph or Acme Regal we guarantee to wear longer and consume less fuel than any other range made, and one of these ranges will be in better condition after five years of actual service than any range you would be likely to buy for $35.00 to $50.00 after being used one year.

OUR ACME TRIUMPH AND ACME REGAL RANGES are made with the best cast iron stove plate top, covers, centers and firebox. (And don't let anybody deceive you into the idea that any range has steel top, covers and centers, for the only top that will stand fire is made of southern cast stove plate, and all so-called steel tops and malleable castings will not last.) In our Acme Triumph and Acme Regal Ranges we use heavier steel oven plates than in any other ranges made, and they are held immovably in place by a surrounding wrought steel construction, preventing the possibility of warping or breaking from unequal expansion, and the ventilation of the oven is so perfect that we guarantee no other range will compare with these as bakers, while our system of asbestos interlining in the Regal and Triumph Ranges will prevent the heat from radiating into the room and effectually retain it in the range, thus making these two ranges the most economical ranges built in the consumption of fuel.

DUPLEX GRATE.

WITH EVERY RANGE WE BUILD we furnish a heavy duplex grate for either hard or soft coal or wood, so arranged that it can be changed to a wood grate instantly. The duplex grate can be drawn out of front of range without disturbing the fire linings. When our Acme Steel Range is used for wood only, we furnish an extension firebox, which allows a longer stick of wood to be used in the stove, so in ordering a steel range do not fail to state whether it is for wood or coal or both wood and coal.

HOT WATER FRONTS.

ALL OUR STEEL RANGES AND ALL OUR CAST IRON RANGES can be furnished with a water front to connect with a pressure boiler as shown in this illustration, and priced on each page with the ranges. For price on the pressure boiler and stand see catalogue Nos. 24C7745 to 24C7749, —see index on pink pages. Water fronts and pressure boilers are used only where there is a water supply furnished with constant pressure through pipes, which can only be obtained in towns or cities having water works, or where you have an elevated water pressure tank. The hot water front gives such ample supply of hot water that you would only require a square range as shown in illustration on the left, instead of one with the extension reservoir shown in the illustration on the right. However, water fronts can be fitted in either style of range.

$26.70 BUYS OUR ACME TRIUMPH.

THE HIGHEST GRADE

$26.70 to $30.45

BLUE POLISHED NICKEL TRIMMED STEEL RANGE MADE.

Complete with high warming closet and deep porcelain lined reservoir, exactly as illustrated. (Burns coal or wood.)

BLUE POLISHED STEEL PLATE by reason of its high cost, is only used in ranges by a very few makers and then always sold at very high prices, usually ranging from $40.00 to $60.00. Blue polished steel is the natural color of the steel as it comes in its finished state from the rolling mills, a handsome high natural polish in a soft bluish tint, and makes the handsomest steel range yet produced; blue polished steel is very hard, there is no wear out to it; it will practically wear forever.

THIS IS A SIX-HOLE RANGE exactly as illustrated, we use a thicker plate of steel than is used by any other maker. Main top, covers and centers are cast plate from Birmingham iron, and are guaranteed against fire cracks. One of the covers has two rings and a small cover in the center, being a graduated lid. The range has heavier inner lining, bracing and staying than in any other range made.

OUR FREE TRIAL OFFER. We will send you this range with the understanding that after using it 30 days, if you are not satisfied you have saved $20.00 to $30.00 in cost and have received the best range in your neighborhood, you can return it to us at our expense and we will return your money, together with the freight charges you paid.

See page 14 for our liberal $1.00 to $5.00 C. O. D. subject to examination offer.

$26.70 —TO— $30.45

WE ADVISE you to buy one of our best ranges, either our Acme Regal at $23.67 to $27.44 or this, our Acme Triumph at $26.70 to $30.45, for either range will outwear THREE of the cheaper ranges, besides saving you the whole cost in economy of fuel used.

NICKEL TRIMMING. With the heavy nickel bands all along the front edge of main top and front of the warming closet, with the large nickel closet brackets, tea shelves and trimmings, large nickel doors, heavy nickel trimmed oven door and reservoir, heavy nickel polished corners, nickel plates and panels, with the extra high finish of this range throughout, you must see, examine and compare it with other ranges to appreciate the value we are offering, for really no such a steel range goes out of any other foundry in America.

OUR SPECIAL PRICE $26.70 TO $30.45

BLUE POLISHED STEEL RANGES

We can always furnish repairs for Acmes. See page 19 about how to order repairs.

SAVED AT LEAST $20.00.

Anderson, Ind.

Sears, Roebuck & Co., Chicago, Ill.

Dear Sirs:—We are very much pleased with our blue polished steel range purchased of you. It has given satisfaction and feel that we have saved at least twenty dollars by buying of you.

H. E. WARD, M. D.

Price List of the Acme Triumph 6-Hole Polished Steel Plate Range with High Closet and Porcelain Lined Reservoir. Prices do not include pipe or cooking utensils. For Cooking Vessels see index on pink pages.

Catalogue Number	Range Number	Size of Lids	Size of Oven, Inches	Main Top Including Reservoir	Height to Main Top, Inches	Length of Fire Box for Wood, Inches	Size of Pipe to Fit Collar, Inches	Shipping Weight, Lbs.	PRICE
22C20	8-17	No. 8	16x21x14	46x29	30½	26½	7	505	$26.70
22C21	8-19	No. 8	18x21x14	48x29	30½	26½	7	520	28.29
22C22	8-21	No. 8	20x21x14	50x29	30½	26½	7	535	30.40
22C23	9-19	No. 9	18x21x14	48x29	30½	26½	7	520	28.34
22C24	9-21	No. 9	20x21x14	50x29	30½	26½	7	535	30.45

ACME TRIUMPH POLISHED STEEL PLATE RANGES

THIS STEEL PLATE IS POLISHED AND REPOLISHED by passing and repassing through ponderous rollers until a permanent beautiful blue color is obtained. It is produced by the famous Wellsville Rolling Mills, and Wellsville polished steel is the standard of the world. The sheets are handled in oil at the mills and at our steel range factory, preserving the beautiful color from all exposure to the weather in shipping.

WHEN YOU RECEIVE THE RANGE wipe off the surface of the steel with a soft cloth and observe the deep blue color of this matchless material. Does not require any further attention. Does not burn off. Does not require enameling, japanning or blacking. If you go away for a long vacation or store away the range, simply oil the surface with any common oil, like lard oil, free of salt, rub it off when ready to use again, and the beautiful blue will never be impaired.

OUR HIGH SHELF, SIX-HOLE, $24.74 ACME TRIUMPH RESERVOIR, POLISHED STEEL PLATE RANGE.

FOR COAL OR WOOD.

Delivered on board cars at our foundry in Newark, Ohio.

$24.74 TO $28.49

THIS IS EXACTLY THE SAME RANGE as illustrated on preceding page at $26.70 to $30.45, under Nos. 22C20 to 22C24, excepting with open high shelf instead of the roll front closet. This range is highly nickel plated throughout, made of the same beautiful polished steel, highly ornamented, trimmed and finished. **The main top, covers and centers are made of the very finest cast stove plate, from the purest pig iron, and not to be confused with malleable top ranges, sometimes called "steel" to deceive.** Is furnished with one graduated lid and five solid covers.

POSSESSES EVERY FEATURE of every high grade range made, all the improvements of our Acme Triumph line, guaranteed equal to any steel range on the market at any price, made of heavier steel plate than any other polished steel range; lined throughout with asbestos; **covered by binding guarantee and is furnished at $24.74 to $28.49,** in any of the following sizes as listed below. **Prices do not include pipe or cooking utensils.** For cooking utensils see index on pink pages. See page 14 for our liberal **$1.00 to $5.00 C. O. D. subject to examination offer.**

Price List of the Acme Triumph Six-Hole Polished Steel Plate Range, with High Shelf and Porcelain Lined Reservoir. Delivered on board cars at our foundry in Newark, Ohio.

Catalogue Number	Range No.	Size of Lids	Size of Oven, inches	Main Top including Reservoir, inches	Height to Main Top, inches	Fire Box for Wood, inches	Pipe, Collar	Shipping Weight, pounds	Price
22C25	8-17	No. 8	16x21x14	46x29	30½	26½	7 in.	460	$24.74
22C26	8-19	No. 8	18x21x14	48x29	30½	26½	7 in.	493	26.33
22C27	8-21	No. 8	20x21x14	50x29	30½	26½	7 in.	504	28.44
22C28	9-19	No. 9	18x21x14	48x29	30½	26½	7 in.	493	26.38
22C29	9-21	No. 9	20x21x14	50x29	30½	26½	7 in.	504	28.49

OUR BINDING GUARANTEE. With every steel range we sell we will issue a written, binding guarantee, by the terms and conditions of which if any piece or part gives out by reason of defect in material or workmanship we will replace it free of charge. Further, that it is strictly high grade, exactly as represented, and shall prove perfectly satisfactory, or we will refund all money paid to us.

OUR $22.35 ACME TRIUMPH RESERVOIR, POLISHED STEEL PLATE RANGE.

WITHOUT EITHER HIGH SHELF OR HIGH CLOSET.

FOR COAL OR WOOD. DELIVERED ON BOARD THE CARS AT OUR FOUNDRY IN NEWARK, OHIO.

THIS IS EXACTLY THE SAME RANGE as illustrated above at $24.74 to $28.49, excepting it is without the high shelf, but finished with a back guard, as shown in the illustration. It has the same highly finished nickel plating throughout, made of the same beautifully polished steel with the same ornamental cast base, highly ornamented, trimmed and finished in the same manner.

ALL THESE ELEGANT BLUE POLISHED ACME TRIUMPH STEEL PLATE RANGES are finished with an ornamental cast left end, where the heat is most excessive. The coal feed door on the left end lifts up, making a convenient opening for feeding in the coal, and is sloping so that the opening is commodious, serving equally well for inserting a broiler over the fire. The pouch coal chute connects with a convenient door in which are two nickel plated screw registers, supplying ample draft. When this door is open direct access to the duplex grate is obtained for inserting a poker. At the front of the range the nickel panel between the wood fire door and the ash door is easily removed, and the duplex grate can be drawn out and replaced at pleasure. The main top, covers and centers are made of the very finest cast stove plate from the purest Birmingham pig iron and are not to be confused with malleable top ranges sometimes called "steel" to deceive. Is furnished with one graduated lid and five solid covers.

THE ACME TRIUMPH LINE possesses every feature of every high grade range made, and is guaranteed equal to any steel range on the market, regardless of price.

OUR FREE TRIAL OFFER.

WE WILL SEND YOU ANY OF THESE RANGES with the understanding and agreement that after using it thirty days, if you are not satisfied you have saved 50 per cent, even after paying freight, and have received the best range in your neighborhood, you can return it to us at our expense, and we will return your money, together with all freight charges you paid.

SEE PAGE 14 FOR OUR LIBERAL $1.00 TO $5.00 C. O. D. SUBJECT TO EXAMINATION OFFER.

Our prices do not include pipe or cooking utensils. For cooking utensils see index on pink pages.

Price List of the Acme Triumph Six-Hole Polished Steel Plate Range, with Porcelain Lined Reservoir.

Delivered on the cars at our foundry in Newark, Ohio.

Catalogue Number	Range Number	Size of Lids	Size of Oven, inches	Main Top including Reservoir, inches	Height to Main Top, inches	Length of Fire Box for Wood, inches	Size of Pipe to Fit Collar inches	Shipping Weight, pounds	Price
22C30	8-17	No. 8	16x21x14	46x29	30½	26½	7	435	$22.35
22C31	8-19	No. 8	18x21x14	48x29	30½	26½	7	445	23.95
22C32	8-21	No. 8	20x21x14	50x29	30½	26½	7	454	26.06
22C33	9-19	No. 9	18x21x14	48x29	30½	26½	7	445	24.00
22C34	9-21	No. 9	20x21x14	50x29	30½	26½	7	454	26.11

OUR $23.57 HIGH CLOSET 6-HOLE ACME TRIUMPH POLISHED STEEL PLATE RANGE.

WITHOUT RESERVOIR. For Coal or Wood. Delivered on cars at our foundry in Newark, Ohio.

AT $23.57 TO $27.34, according to size, as listed below, we offer you this High Closet Six-Hole, Acme Triumph Polished Steel Plate Range in competition with ranges that sell at almost double the price.

THIS IS EXACTLY THE SAME RANGE as the one previously listed at $26.70 to $30.45, under Nos. 22C20 to 22C24, but without extension reservoir. As you will see by the illustration, it has the same highly ornamented high closet, with nickel bands and nickel trimmings. It has latest patent roll front, same as roll top desks are made, and at the slight difference in the cost, you will find the addition of a warming closet a very good investment.

THE MAIN TOP, COVERS AND CENTERS are made of the finest stove plate, from the purest pig iron, and not to be confused with malleable top ranges, sometimes called "steel" to deceive. Is furnished with one graduated lid and five solid covers. At the prices named we furnish this range in the sizes and dimensions below. **Prices do not include pipe or cooking utensils. For cooking utensils see index on pink pages. For our $1.00 to $5.00 C.O.D. subject to examination offer see page 14. Delivered on cars at our foundry in Newark, Ohio.**

Price List of the Acme Triumph Six-Hole Polished Steel Plate Range, without Reservoir, with High Closet:

Catalogue Number	Range No.	Size of Lids	Size of Oven, Inches	Size of Main Top, Inches	Size of End Shelf, Inches	Height to Main Top Inches	Length of Fire Box for Wood, Inches	Size of Pipe to Fit Collar, Inches	Ship'g Weight, Pounds	Price with High Closet
22C35	8-17	No. 8	16x21x14	35x29	7½x21½	30½	26½	7	435	$23.57
22C36	8-19	No. 8	18x21x14	37x29	7½x21½	30½	26½	7	450	25.15
22C37	8-21	No. 8	20x21x14	39x29	7½x21½	30½	26½	7	464	27.28
22C38	9-19	No. 9	18x21x14	37x29	7½x21½	30½	26½	7	450	25.21
22C39	9-21	No. 9	20x21x14	39x29	7½x21½	30½	26½	7	464	27.34

Water Fronts for Acme Triumph Ranges, each.............................. $2.50

Do not mistake water fronts for water reservoirs. If extension water reservoirs are wanted, see the preceding pages, showing catalogue Nos. 22C20 to 22C34.

Water fronts are used only where there is a water supply furnished with constant pressure through pipes, which can only be obtained in towns and cities having water works or from an elevated pressure tank. See page 14 about hot water fronts.

WE CAN ALWAYS FURNISH REPAIRS FOR ACMES. SEE PAGE 19 ABOUT STOVE REPAIRS.

OUR $21.63 TO $25.41 HIGH-SHELF, SIX-HOLE, ACME TRIUMPH POLISHED STEEL RANGE, WITHOUT RESERVOIR.

For coal or wood. Delivered on cars at our foundry in Newark, Ohio.

AT $21.63 TO $25.41, according to size, as listed below, we furnish this Acme Triumph six-hole polished steel range with high shelf, as illustrated, and invite the closest comparison in every little detail on this range with that of any blue polished range offered by any other dealer at within 50 per cent of the price.

THE MAIN TOP, COVERS AND CENTERS are made of the finest cast stove plate, from the purest pig iron, and not to be confused with malleable top ranges, sometimes called "steel" to deceive. Is furnished with one graduated lid and five solid covers. It is the most durable, economical and handsome polished steel range on the market.

AT THE PRICES NAMED we furnish this range in the sizes and dimensions below. Prices do not include pipe or cooking utensils. For cooking utensils see index on pink pages. See page 14 for our liberal $1.00 to $5.00 C. O. D. subject to examination offer. Delivered on cars at our foundry in Newark, Ohio.

Price List of the Acme Triumph Six-Hole Polished Steel Plate Range, without Reservoir, with High Shelf.

Catalogue Number	Range Number	Size of Lid	Size of Oven, Inches	Size of Main Top, Inches	Size of End Shelf, Inches	Height to Main Top, Inches	Length of Fire Box for Wood, Inches	Size of Pipe to Fit Collar, Inches	Ship'g Weight, Pounds.	Price with High Shelf
22C40	8-17	No. 8	16x21x14	35x29	7½x21½	30½	26½	7	410	$21.63
22C41	8-19	No. 8	18x21x14	37x29	7½x21½	30½	26½	7	423	23.21
22C42	8-21	No. 8	20x21x14	39x29	7½x21½	30½	26½	7	434	25.35
22C43	9-19	No. 9	18x21x14	37x29	7½x21½	30½	26½	7	423	23.27
22C44	9-21	No. 9	20x21x14	39x29	7½x21½	30½	26½	7	434	25.41

Water Fronts for Acme Triumphs, each.............. $2.50

Do not mistake water fronts for water reservoirs. If extension water reservoirs are wanted, see the preceding pages showing catalogue Nos. 22C20 to 22C34. Water fronts are used only where there is a water supply furnished with constant pressure through pipes, which can only be obtained in towns and cities having water works, or from an elevated pressure tank. See page 14 about hot water fronts.

OUR $19.23 ACME TRIUMPH POLISHED STEEL PLATE RANGE, WITHOUT RESERVOIR AND WITHOUT EITHER HIGH SHELF OR HIGH CLOSET.

For Coal or Wood. Delivered on board the cars at our foundry in Newark, Ohio.

THIS IS EXACTLY THE SAME RANGE as illustrated above at $21.63 to $25.41 excepting it is without the high shelf and finished with a back guard as shown in illustration. It has the same highly finished nickel plating throughout, made of the same beautifully polished steel with the same ornamental cast base, highly ornamented, trimmed and finished in the same manner. All these elegant blue polished Acme Triumph steel plate ranges are finished with an ornamental cast left end where the heat is most excessive. The coal feed door on the left end lifts up making a convenient opening for feeding in the coal, and is sloping so that the opening is commodious, serving equally well for inserting a broiler over the fire. The pouch coal chute connects with a convenient door in which are two nickel plated screw registers, supplying ample draft. When this door is open direct access to the duplex grate is obtained for inserting a poker. At the front of the range the nickel panel between the wood fire door and the ash door is easily removed and the duplex grate can be drawn out and replaced at pleasure. The main top, covers and centers are made of the very finest cast stove plate from the purest Birmingham pig iron and are not to be confused with malleable top ranges sometimes called "steel" to deceive. Is furnished with one graduated lid and five solid covers. The Acme Triumph line possesses every feature of every high grade range made and is guaranteed equal to any steel range on the market, regardless of price.

OUR FREE TRIAL OFFER. We will send you any of these ranges with the understanding and agreement that after using it thirty days if you are not satisfied you have saved 50 per cent even after paying freight, and have received the best range in your neighborhood, you can return it to us at our expense and we will return your money, together with all freight charges you paid. See page 14 for our liberal $1.00 to $5.00 C. O. D. subject to examination offer. Our prices do not include pipe or cooking utensils. For cooking utensils, see index on pink pages.

Price List of the Acme Triumph Six-Hole Polished Steel Plate Range Without Reservoir. Delivered on the cars at our foundry in Newark, Ohio.

Catalogue Number	Range Number	Size of Lid	Size of Oven, Inches	Size of Main Top, Inches	Size of End Shelf, Inches	Height to Main Top, Inches	Length of Fire Box for Wood, Inches	Size of Pipe to Fit Collar, Inches	Ship'g Weight, Pounds	Price
22C45	8-17	No. 8	16x21x14	35x29	7½x21½	30½	26½	7	365	$19.23
22C46	8-19	No. 8	18x21x14	37x29	7½x21½	30½	26½	7	375	20.82
22C47	8-21	No. 8	20x21x14	39x29	7½x21½	30½	26½	7	384	22.95
22C48	9-19	No. 9	18x21x14	37x29	7½x21½	30½	26½	7	375	20.87
22C49	9-21	No. 9	20x21x14	39x29	7½x21½	30½	26½	7	384	23.00

Water Fronts for Acme Triumphs, each.................................. $2.50

Do not mistake water fronts for water reservoirs. If extension water reservoirs are wanted, see the preceding pages showing catalogue Nos. 22C20 to 22C34.

Water fronts are used only where there is a water supply furnished with constant pressure through pipes, which can only be obtained in towns and cities having water works, or from an elevated pressure tank. See page 14 about hot water fronts.

$23.67 BUYS OUR ACME REGAL.

THE HIGHEST GRADE, BLACK ENAMELED, NICKEL TRIMMED STEEL RANGE POSSIBLE TO PRODUCE.

PRICE, $23.67

Complete with High Shelf,

WARMING CLOSET

and Deep Porcelain Lined

RESERVOIR,

Exactly as Illustrated.

HEAVIER AND THICKER steel plate than is used by any other maker; stronger, better braced, closer riveted, better fitting. Guaranteed easier operated, a better baker, will consume less fuel and outwear any other steel range on the market.

WE BUILD THIS RANGE in our own foundry using the best cold rolled range steel made. The main top, covers and centers are made of cast plate from Birmingham iron. Is furnished with one graduated lid and five solid covers. The nickeling is done in our own foundry and is not equaled by any other maker, and while we can always furnish parts for repairs, you will not be likely to ever need repairs for this range, for it will be in better condition after ten years' constant use than any of the cheap, thin steel plate ranges after one year. In fact, it is built so there is practically no wear out to it.

OUR GUARANTEE OFFER. We advise you by all means to buy this steel range in preference to any of the thinner plate and cheaper ranges, for the few dollars difference in cost will be made up many times over in the longer life and economy of fuel, and we therefore make you this offer:

ORDER THIS RANGE in the size wanted at $23.67 to $27.44 and we will send it to you with the understanding you can use it in your own home for 30 days and if you do not find it in every way the best steel range in your neighborhood and you are not satisfied you have saved $15.00 to $25.00 in price, you can return it to us at our expense and we will refund your money, together with the freight charges paid by you. See page 14 for our liberal $1.00 to $5.00 C.O.D. subject to examination offer.

THE ACME REGAL has a duplex grate for coal or wood, 6-HOLE, high warming closet and deep porcelain lined reservoir, exactly as illustrated. The light shading shows the nickel plating, such as wide bands, doors, trimmings, plates corners, etc.; the most elaboratel finished rang made.

SAVED $14.00.

Dade City, Fla.

Sears, Roebuck & Co., Chicago, Ill.

Dear Sirs:—The Acme Regal has proved quite satisfactory. After paying the freight all the way from Newark, Ohio, I saved $14.00. The same stove would cost about $50.00 here from the retail dealers.

Yours truly, THOMAS ROACH.

$23.67 barely covers the cost to build in our own foundry (the largest stove foundry in America), with but our one small profit added.

WE GUARANTEE TO FURNISH YOU IN THIS A BETTER STEEL RANGE THAN YOU CAN BUY ELSEWHERE AT ANY PRICE AND WE GUARANTEE TO SAVE YOU $15.00 TO $25.00 IN COST.

We can always furnish repairs for Acmes. See page 19 about how to order repairs.

PRICES DO NOT INCLUDE PIPE OR COOKING UTENSILS. FOR COOKING UTENSILS SEE INDEX ON PINK PAGES.

Price List of the ACME REGAL 6-HOLE STEEL RANGE with Porcelain Lined Reservoi and High Closet. Delivered on the cars at our foundry in Newark, Ohio.

Catalogue Number	Range No.	Size of Lids	Size of Oven, Inches	Main Top, Including Reservoir	Height to Main Top, Inches	Length of Fire Box for Wood	Size of Pipe to Fit Collar	Shipping Weight	PRICE
22C50	8-17	No. 8	16x21x14	46x29	30½	26½ in.	7 in.	480 lbs.	$23.67
22C51	8-19	No. 8	18x21x14	48x29	30½	26½ in.	7 in.	495 lbs.	25.26
22C52	8-21	No. 8	20x21x14	50x29	30½	26½ in.	7 in.	510 lbs.	27.39
22C53	9-19	No. 9	18x21x14	48x29	30½	26½ in.	7 in.	495 lbs.	25.31
22C54	9-21	No. 9	20x21x14	50x29	30½	26½ in.	7 in.	510 lbs.	27.44

OUR HIGH SHELF 6-HOLE $21.92 RESERVOIR STEEL RANGE

FOR COAL OR WOOD.

Delivered on Board Cars at our Foundry in Newark, Ohio.

POSSESSES EVERY FEATURE of every high grade range made, all the improvements of our Acme Regal line, guaranteed equal to any steel range on the market at any price, made of heavier steel plate than any other steel range, lined throughout with asbestos; covered by binding guarantee and is furnished at

$21.92 to $25.69

IN ANY OF THE FOLLOWING SIZES AS LISTED BELOW. PRICES DO NOT INCLUDE PIPE OR COOKING UTENSILS. FOR COOKING UTENSILS SEE INDEX ON PINK PAGES.

SEE PAGE 14 FOR OUR LIBERAL $1.00 TO $5.00 C. O. D. SUBJECT TO EXAMINATION OFFER.

PRICE LIST OF THE ACME REGAL SIX-HOLE STEEL RANGE WITH PORCELAIN LINED RESERVOIR AND HIGH SHELF.
Delivered on board cars at our foundry in Newark, Ohio.

Catalogue Number	Range No.	Size of Lids	Size of Oven, Inches	Main Top Including Reservoir	Height to Main Top	Fire Box for Wood	Pipe Collar	Shipping Weight, Lbs.	Price
22C55	8-17	No. 8	16x21x14	46x29	30½	26½	7 in.	455	$21.92
22C56	8-19	No. 8	18x21x14	48x29	30½	26½	7 in.	468	23.51
22C57	8-21	No. 8	20x21x14	50x29	30½	26½	7 in.	480	25.64
22C58	9-19	No. 9	18x21x14	48x29	30½	26½	7 in.	468	23.56
22C59	9-21	No. 9	20x21x14	50x29	30½	26½	7 in.	480	25.69

WE GUARANTEE our black enamel nickel trimmed Acme Regal Steel Ranges to be the highest grade steel ranges on the market, regardless of price, and we are perfectly willing to accept your order for an Acme Regal Steel Range, any style you may select, to be shipped to you with the understanding and agreement that after you have given it thirty days' trial in your own home, if you are not convinced it is better than any range you could buy from any dealer at any price, you can return it to us at our expense and we will immediately return your money. We guarantee the range to reach you in the same perfect condition it leaves us, and while it very rarely happens that a range is injured in transit, if the range does not reach you in perfect condition we will repair or replace it free of any cost to you.

THE ACME REGAL STEEL RANGE is made of heavier steel plate than any other range made, heavier and better interlining, better bolted, stronger braced, better fitting, will consume less fuel, wear longer and give better satisfaction than any other range made; is highly nickel trimmed, with handsome nickel doors, nickel bands around the main top and shelf, heavy nickel frame around oven door, nickel corner posts, nickel panels and nickel teapot holders. This illustration shows our Acme Regal Range with high shelf, deep porcelain lined reservoir in the various sizes, which we furnish at $21.92 to $25.69, according to size. We also show illustrations of the various equipments, including the complete range with high closet and reservoir as shown in the large illustration of the No. 22C50 on preceding page. In ordering a steel range we advise that you select the very best, the best that money can buy, our Acme Regal.

This is exactly the same Range as illustrated on the preceding page, at . . . . **$23.67 TO $27.44** under Nos. 22C50 to 22C54, with the addition of the high shelf in place of the high closet. This range is highly nickel plated throughout, enameled with the very best quality locomotive black, highly ornamented, trimmed and finished.

THE MAIN TOP, covers and centers, are made of the very finest cast stove plate from the purest pig iron, and not to be confused with malleable top ranges, sometimes called "steel" to deceive. Is furnished with one graduated lid and five solid covers.

SAVED $20.00.
Huntsville, Kan.
Sears, Roebuck & Co.,
Chicago, Ill.
Dear Sirs:—Will say we are more than pleased with the Acme Regal. It reached us in perfect order and am highly pleased with it. It is all that it is represented to be. I just saved about $20.00 on the stove. If I had bought here I would have had to pay about $45.00 for the same stove. I ordered a stove for my brother-in-law, and they say as I do about the stove. I remain, yours respectfully
JOHN WITHRODER.

$21.92 TO $25.69

OUR 6-HOLE RESERVOIR $20.03 ACME REGAL STEEL RANGE

FOR COAL OR WOOD.

Delivered on Board Cars at our Foundry in Newark, Ohio.

AT $20.03 TO $23.79 we offer this large 6-hole Acme Regal Steel Range, with porcelain lined reservoir, with all the nickel trimmings, all the improvements and the patent features, the finish, with all the guarantees that have been named on all Acme ranges previously described.

WE GUARANTEE THE SIZES WE NAME. Do not take it for granted that stoves marked the same size as ours are actually the same size. In measuring ovens, we measure the actual size of the oven bottom. When you order a range from us, you get exactly the size range that you see illustrated, exactly the same size that we specify, and if you find that any steel range you order from us differs in the slightest degree from the illustration, from the description or from the guarantee, you are at liberty to return it AND WE WILL CHEERFULLY REFUND YOUR MONEY.

$10.00 LESS THAN THE LOCAL DEALER.
Sears, Roebuck & Co., Chicago, Ill. Dow City, Iowa.
Gents:—Yours of recent date received. In reply will say that the Acme Regal Range received from you about one year ago is entirely satisfactory and everything that you claimed it to be. I think the stove cost me, placed in my home, at least $10.00 less than I could have purchased a stove of equal value from local dealers. Yours, etc., S. E. RUDD.

THIS RANGE DIFFERS FROM THOSE PREVIOUSLY DESCRIBED ONLY IN THAT THIS RANGE IS WITHOUT HIGH SHELF OR CLOSET, AS ILLUSTRATED.

THE MAIN TOP, covers and centers, are made of the very finest cast stove plate from the purest pig iron, and not to be confused with malleable top ranges, sometimes called "steel" to deceive. Is furnished with one graduated lid and five solid covers.

THIS RANGE is nickel trimmed throughout, same as those previously described, contains every good quality of every high grade range with the defects of none, and is offered at the lowest price ever before heard of for a high grade range—is the best range possible to build.

OUR SPECIAL PRICES $20.03 TO $23.79, for the sizes listed below. Prices do not include pipe or cooking utensils. For cooking utensils see index on pink pages. See page 14 for our liberal $1.00 to $5.00 C. O. D. Subject to Examination Offer.

Price List of the Acme Regal Six-hole Steel Range with Porcelain Lined Reservoir. Delivered on Board Cars at Our Foundry in Newark, Ohio.

Catalogue Number	Range No.	Size of Lids	Size of Oven, Inches	Main Top Including Reservoir	Height to Main Top	Fire Box for Wood	Pipe Collar	Shipping Weight, Lbs.	Price
22C60	8-17	No. 8	16x21x14	46x29	30½	26½	7 in.	410	$20.03
22C61	8-19	No. 8	18x21x14	48x29	30½	26½	7 in.	420	21.62
22C62	8-21	No. 8	20x21x14	50x29	30½	26½	7 in.	430	23.74
22C63	9-19	No. 9	18x21x14	48x29	30½	26½	7 in.	420	21.67
22C64	9-21	No. 9	20x21x14	50x29	30½	26½	7 in.	430	23.79

OUR RANGES are offered as the best money can buy and at prices based on the actual cost of material and labor, with but our one small percentage of profit added.

BEAR IN MIND that these prices are too low to include any cooking utensils or stove pipe. If you desire any stove furniture it must be shipped direct from our stock in Chicago, while these ranges are sent from our foundry in Newark, Ohio. This makes two shipments, one from our foundry and one from our store. For this reason we especially urge you to make your order for cooking utensils large enough to be profitable to you, remembering that 50 to 100 pounds will, as a rule, go by freight from Chicago for as low a freight charge as 0 pounds.

STOVE REPAIRS.

PLEASE NOTICE. We can always furnish repairs for Acmes. In ordering repairs for stoves, it is very important to give your purchase Invoice Number or the most complete and explicit information possible. By strictly adhering to the following rules, a great deal of annoyance, expense and delay may be averted.

1st. State whether stove is for coal only, for wood only, or a combined wood and coal burning construction.
2d. If cook stove or range, say if square top or with reservoir.
3d. The back of the stove is at the pipe collar. Stand facing the hearth on a cook stove or facing the oven door of a range.
4th. Give full number shown on outside of main top. In many instances the same size of griddle holes are placed on different stove bodies, namely, 7-18, 8-18, 8-20 or 9-20, etc., and the single No. 7, 8 or 9 in this instance would be no indication of the correct size of the stove.
5th. Be particular to furnish all dates of patents.
6th. When legs are desired, say if stove is supplied with legs only or on leg base.
7th. Give name of stove in full. A strict observance of these directions will be mutually advantageous.

OUR $20.53 HIGH CLOSET 6-HOLE ACME REGAL STEEL RANGE, FOR COAL OR WOOD.

DELIVERED ON CARS AT OUR FOUNDRY IN NEWARK, OHIO.

AT $20.53 TO $24.31 according to size, as listed below, we offer you this High Closet, Six-Hole Acme Regal Steel Range in competition with ranges that sell at almost double the price. **THIS IS EXACTLY THE SAME RANGE** as the one previously listed at $23.67 to $27.44 under Nos. 22C50 to 22C54, excepting this one is without the extension reservoir. As you will see by the illustration, it has the same highly ornamented high closet, with nickel bands and nickel trimmings. It has latest patent roll top, same as roll top desks are made, and at the slight difference in the cost, you will find the addition of a warming closet a very good investment.

THE MAIN TOP, COVERS AND CENTERS are made of the finest stove plate, from the purest pig iron, and not to be confused with malleable top ranges, sometimes called "steel" to deceive. Is furnished with one graduated lid and five solid covers. At the prices named we furnish this range in the sizes and dimensions below. **Prices do not include pipe or cooking utensils. For cooking utensils see index on pink pages. See page 14 for our $1.00 to $5.00 C. O. D. subject to examination offer.**

Price List of the Acme Regal six-hole Steel Range, without Reservoir, with High Closet:

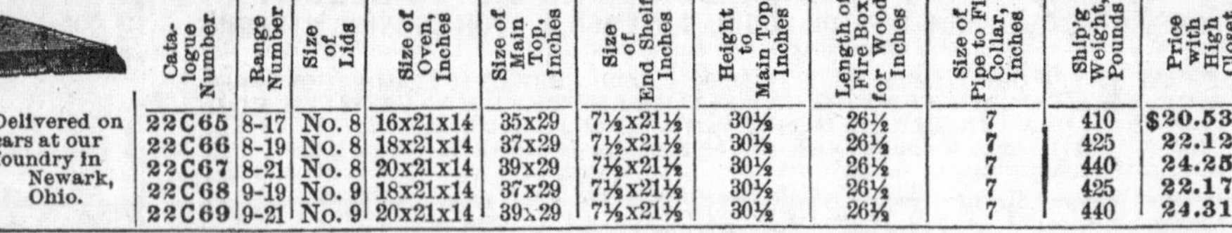

	Catalogue Number	Range Number	Size of Lids	Size of Oven, Inches	Size of Main Top, Inches	Size of End Shelf, Inches	Height to Main Top, Inches	Length of Fire Box for Wood, Inches	Size of Pipe to Fit Collar, Inches	Ship'g Weight, Pounds	Price with High Closet
Delivered on cars at our foundry in Newark, Ohio.	22C65	8-17	No. 8	16x21x14	35x29	7½x21½	30½	26½	7	410	$20.53
	22C66	8-19	No. 8	18x21x14	37x29	7½x21½	30½	26½	7	425	22.12
	22C67	8-21	No. 8	20x21x14	39x29	7½x21½	30½	26½	7	440	24.25
	22C68	9-19	No. 9	18x21x14	37x29	7½x21½	30½	26½	7	425	22.17
	22C69	9-21	No. 9	20x21x14	39x29	7½x21½	30½	26½	7	440	24.31

Water Fronts for Acme Regal Ranges. Price.......................$2.50

Do not mistake water fronts for water reservoirs. If extension water reservoirs are wanted see the preceding pages showing catalogue Nos. 22C50 to 22C64.

Water fronts are used only where there is a water supply furnished with constant pressure through pipes—which can only be obtained in towns and cities having water works, or from an elevated pressure tank. See page 14 about hot water fronts.

BEAR IN MIND that prices are without cooking utensils or stove pipe. If you desire any stove furniture it must be shipped direct from our stock in Chicago, while these ranges are sent from our foundry in Newark, Ohio. This makes two shipments, one from our foundry and one from our store. For this reason we especially urge you to make your order for cooking utensils large enough to be profitable to you, remembering that 50 to 100 pounds will, as a rule, go by freight from Chicago for as low a freight charge as 10 pounds.

FOR COAL OR WOOD.

Delivered on Cars at our Foundry in Newark, Ohio.

WE CAN ALWAYS FURNISH REPAIRS FOR ACMES. SEE PAGE 19 ABOUT STOVE REPAIRS.

OUR $18.78 TO $22.56 HIGH SHELF SIX-HOLE ACME REGAL STEEL RANGE

AT $18.78 TO $22.56 according to size, as listed below, we furnish this Acme Regal six-hole steel range with high shelf, as illustrated, and invite the closest comparison in every little detail on this range with that of any range offered by any other dealer at within 50 per cent of the price.

THE MAIN TOP, COVERS AND CENTERS are made of the finest cast stove plate, from the purest pig iron, and not to be confused with malleable top ranges, sometimes called "steel" to deceive. Is furnished with one graduated lid and five solid covers.

THIS IS EXACTLY THE SAME STOVE as one previously illustrated at $20.53 to $24.31 under Nos. 22C65 to 22C69, with the addition of the high shelf, instead of high closet. It is nickel plated throughout, exactly the same as No. 22C65 lined throughout with asbestos, made from the same extra heavy steel plate, covered by the same binding guarantee, and we offer it to you at the heretofore unheard of price of **$18.78 to $22.56.** It is the most durable, convenient, economical and handsome steel range on the market.

AT THE PRICES NAMED we furnish this range in the sizes and dimensions below. **Prices do not include pipe or cooking utensils.** For cooking utensils see index on pink pages. **SEE PAGE 14 FOR OUR LIBERAL $1.00 to 5.00 C. O. D. SUBJECT TO EXAMINATION OFFER. Delivered on cars at our foundry in Newark, Ohio. Price list of the Acme Regal Six-Hole Steel Range, without Reservoir; with High Shelf:**

Catalogue Number	Range Number	Size of Lids	Size of Oven Inches	Size of Main Top, Inches	Size of End Shelf, Inches	Height to Main Top, Inches	Length of Fire Box for Wood, Inches	Size of Pipe to Fit Coll'r Inches	Ship'g Weight Pounds	Price with high shelf
22C70	8-17	No. 8	16x21x14	35x29	7½x21½	30½	26½	7	385	$18.78
22C71	8-19	No. 8	18x21x14	37x29	7½x21½	30½	26½	7	398	20.37
22C72	8-21	No. 8	20x21x14	39x29	7½x21½	30½	26½	7	410	22.50
22C73	9-19	No. 9	18x21x14	37x29	7½x21½	30½	26½	7	398	20.43
22C74	9-21	No. 9	20x21x14	39x29	7½x21½	30½	26½	7	410	22.56

Water Fronts for Acme Regal Ranges. Price.......................**$2.50**

Do not mistake water fronts for water reservoirs. If extension water reservoirs are wanted, see the preceding pages showing catalogue Nos. 22C50 to 22C64.

Water fronts are used only where there is a water supply furnished with constant pressure through pipes, which can only be obtained in towns and cities having water works, or from an elevated pressure tank. See page 14 about hot water fronts.

OUR $16.90 SIX HOLE ACME REGAL STEEL RANGE.

FOR COAL OR WOOD. DELIVERED ON CARS AT OUR FOUNDRY IN NEWARK, OHIO.

AT $16.90 TO $20.67 according to size, as listed below, we furnish our Acme Regal, the highes grade six-hole steel range on the market, in competition with any range you can buy elsewhere at 50 per cent more money. We furnish the **Acme Regal Steel Range,** guaranteeing it to be made of heavier sheet steel than any other stove; guaranteeing it to be asbestos lined, thus insuring you economy of fuel; guaranteeing the nickel plating to be of the highest grade; guaranteeing the stove to possess all the good qualities of every strictly high grade steel range, with the defects of none.

THE RANGE IS HIGHLY NICKEL PLATED THROUGHOUT. Nickel bands on front edges of top of stove, on oven door frame, nickel panel on oven door; nickel clean out door, fire door, ash door, and nickel removable grate front, all highly finished, polished and nickeled, and we believe is the handsomest range on the market.

THE OVEN OPENING is the same size as the oven bottom, thus allowing as large a baking pan to enter as the oven will receive.

THE MAIN TOP, COVERS AND CENTERS are made of the very finest cast stove plate, from the purest pig iron, and not to be confused with malleable top ranges, sometimes called "steel," to deceive. Is furnished with one graduated lid and five solid covers.

THIS STOVE IS HIGHLY ENAMELED with the very best quality locomotive black, has highest grade removable duplex grate, for either coal or wood, or both. **We guarantee it to bake quicker, consume less fuel, give better service,** and you will find it the handsomest range on the market, regardless of price.

OUR ACME REGAL STEEL RANGES have been manufactured with a view to furnish our customers the handsomest, most economical, most durable and in every way the highest grade black enameled range possible to produce, and with a view of giving them the benefit of the reduced cost to manufacture where large quantities are turned out on a spot cash basis, and on this basis we quote our prices of **$16.90 to $20.67** on the sizes listed. If you don't find, when you get the range, that you have saved from $10.00 to $15.00 in price, you are at liberty to return range to us and we will cheerfully refund the money. **WE FURNISH THIS SIX-HOLE ACME REGAL RANGE AT $16.90 TO $20.67 in the sizes and dimensions listed below. Prices do not include pipe or cooking utensils.** For cooking utensils see index on pink pages. **SEE PAGE 14 FOR OUR LIBERAL $1.00 to $5.00 C. O. D. SUBJECT TO EXAMINATION OFFER. Price list of Acme Regal Six-Hole Steel Range, without Reservoir.**

Catalogue Number	Range Number	Size of Lids	Size of Oven, Inches	Size of Main Top, Inches	Size of End Shelf, Inches	Height to Main Top, Inches	Length of Fire Box for Wood, Inches	Size of Pipe to Fit Collar, Inches	Ship'g Weight, Pounds	Price
22C75	8-17	No. 8	16x21x14	35x29	7½x21½	30½	26½	7	340	$16.90
22C76	8-19	No. 8	18x21x14	37x29	7½x21½	30½	26½	7	350	18.49
22C77	8-21	No. 8	20x21x14	39x29	7½x21½	30½	26½	7	360	20.62
22C78	9-19	No. 9	18x21x14	37x29	7½x21½	30½	26½	7	350	18.54
22C79	9-21	No. 9	20x21x14	39x29	7½x21½	30½	26½	7	360	20.67

Delivered on cars at our foundry in Newark, Ohio.

Water Fronts for Acme Regal Ranges. Price.......................**$2.50**

Do not mistake water fronts for water reservoirs. If extension water reservoirs are wanted, see the preceding pages showing catalogue Nos. 22C50 to 22C64.

Water fronts are used only where there is a water supply furnished with a constant pressure through pipes, which can only be obtained in towns and cities having water works, or from an elevated pressure tank. See page 14 about water fronts.

$18.37 BUYS THIS HANDSOME, LARGE, FULL NICKEL TRIMMED STEEL RANGE EXACTLY AS ILLUSTRATED

Complete with high warming closet and deep porcelain lined Reservoir.

HERE'S WHERE WE CHALLENGE THE WORLD WITH THE HANDSOMEST BARGAIN RANGE EVER OFFERED

A HIGHLY ENAMELED STEEL RANGE, full nickeled and enameled with high grade locomotive black. A splendid baker, possessing all the good points of our leading lines, the Acme Regal and Acme Triumph, but not made of so heavy gauge of steel and not quite so large in the depth of the oven. Better than any of the cheap steel ranges so largely advertised and better than any offered in department stores and hardware stores at double the price. **While we always recommend our Acme Regal black enameled range and our Acme Triumph blue polished steel plate ranges as far superior to any offered by ourselves or anyone else, yet we can recommend this Acme Renown against any and all specially advertised cheap** ranges offered by anyone. We designed and constructed this range to show the world we could produce a good steel range at prices within the reach of all.

OUR FREE TRIAL GUARANTEE AND COMPARISON OFFER. Order this range at our price and we will send it to you with the understanding and agreement that you can give it 30 days' trial in your own home, and if it does not prove perfectly satisfactory and you do not find by comparison with other steel ranges it is in every way equal and in finish and beauty of design superior to any steel range advertised or sold by others for **$30.00,** you can return it to us at our expense and we will immediately refund your money, together with the freight charges you paid.

See page 14 for our liberal $1.00 to $5.00 C. O. D. subject to examination offer.

WE HAVE BUILT THIS RANGE to compete with the **many ranges now being advertised** in the papers and sold by our competitors generally at about **$30.00.** We have made it to embody every quality of any range you can buy elsewhere for **$30.00,** with many improvements over ranges sold by others around **$30.00,** such as fullness of size, asbestos lining, double bracing, extra large shelf and warming closet, wrought steel oven plates; has broiling door coal feed, duplex grate, heavy full nickel trimmings, including heavy polished nickel bands full length of main top and warming closet; nickel trimmed reservoir and oven door, full nickel doors, heavy nickel medallions, plates, etc., nickel tea shelves and closet supports; **finest trimmings throughout.**

We can always furnish repairs for Acmes. See page 19 about how to order repairs.

THIS STEEL RANGE is made in our own foundry, and at our **$18.37 price we barely cover cost of material** and labor with but our one small profit added. Every stove is branded **NEWARK STOVE WORKS, CHICAGO.** Made to burn coal or wood; come exactly as illustrated; six holes; high closet; body made from sheet steel; main top, covers and centers from very finest cast stove plate.

THE ACME RENOWN SELLS ON SIGHT.

Kirby, Rosebud Co., Mont.
Sears, Roebuck & Co., Chicago, Ill.
Gentlemen:—The Acme Renown arrived in good order. I sold it as soon as it was seen. It gave satisfaction. I shall order more early in the fall, for I consider your Acme Renown Steel Range a big bargain. Respectfully,
A. WESLEY.

EVERY ONE OF THESE RANGES is shipped with the understanding if it doesn't prove satisfactory and you do not find you have saved at least **$10.00** you can return it and get your money back; **however, we urge you to buy our highest grade ranges, the Acme Regal at $23.67 or Acme Triumph at $26.70** as shown on the preceding pages, for these two ranges at $23.67 and $26.70 are made of **heavier steel plate** than you will find in any other range built; made extra heavy, from the best material that can be procured; very best workmanship and finest finish; will consume less fuel, work better and outwear any other range on the market. While our **$18.37 Acme Renown** is as good as most steel ranges sold as highest grade, our Acme Regal or Acme Triumph cost only a few dollars more and **ARE THE VERY BEST** and really the cheapest in the end, and if you order one of these ranges and you do not find you have the best steel range **in your town** you can return it and get your money back.

At **$18.37** we offer the **Acme Renown** as the equal of steel ranges others sell at $30.00. **At $23.67 and $26.70** we offer the **Regal and Triumph Ranges** as the best steel range possible to produce, and advise you to order the best.

PRICE LIST of the ACME RENOWN BLACK ENAMELED STEEL RANGE

With High Warming Closet and Porcelain Lined Reservoir. For Coal or Wood.

Prices do not include any pipe or cooking utensils. For pipe and cooking utensils, see index on pink pages.

Prices Delivered on the Cars at our Foundry in Newark, Ohio.

Catalogue Number	Range No.	Size of Lids	Size of Oven, Inches	Main Top, including Reservoir	Height of Main Top, Inches	Length of Fire Box for Wood	Size of Pipe to Fit Collar	Shipping Weight	PRICE
22C86	8-18	No. 8	18x21x14	45x28 in.	30½	26½ in.	7 in.	420	$18.37
22C87	8-20	No. 8	20x21x14	47x28 in.	30½	26½ in.	7 in.	435	20.50
22C88	9-18	No. 9	18x21x14	45x28 in.	30½	26½ in.	7 in.	420	18.49
22C89	9-20	No. 9	20x21x14	47x28 in.	30½	26½ in.	7 in.	435	20.55

We can always furnish repairs for Acmes. See page 19 about how to order stove repairs when needed in future years.

OUR ACME RENOWN HIGH SHELF 6-HOLE $17.22 RESERVOIR STEEL RANGE.

FOR COAL OR WOOD. **DELIVERED ON BOARD CARS AT OUR FOUNDRY.**

Possesses every feature of every high grade range made.

IS AS EFFICIENT IN OPERATION, **convenience and economy of fuel, but not so heavy and durable as our Acme Regal and Acme Triumph shown on the preceding pages.** Guaranteed equal to any steel range on the market at anywhere near the price. Lined throughout with asbestos; covered by our binding guarantee and is furnished at **$17.22 to $19.39** in any of the following sizes listed below.

This is exactly the same range as illustrated on the preceding page at $18.37 to $20.55, under Nos. 22C86 to 22C89, with the addition of the high shelf instead of the high closet. This range is highly nickel plated throughout, enameled with the very best quality locomotive black, highly ornamented, trimmed and finished. **The main top, covers and centers** are made of the very finest cast stove plate, from the purest pig iron, and not to be confused with malleable top ranges, sometimes called "steel" to deceive. Prices do not include pipe or cooking utensils. For cooking utensils see index on pink pages. See page 14 for our liberal $1.00 to $5.00 C. O. D., subject to examination offer.. Delivered on board cars at our foundry.

Price List of the Acme Renown Six-Hole Steel Range with Porcelain Lined Reservoir and High Shelf:

Catalogue Number	Range Number	Size of Lids	Size of Oven, Inches	Main Top including Reservoir	Height to Main Top, Inches	Fire Box for Wood, Inches	Pipe to Fit Collar	Shipping Weight	Price
22C90	8-18	8	18x21x14	45x28	30½	26½ in.	7 inch	400 lbs.	$17.22
22C91	8-20	8	20x21x14	47x28	30½	26½ in.	7 inch	415 lbs.	19.33
22C92	9-18	9	18x21x14	45x28	30½	26½ in.	7 inch	400 lbs.	17.27
22C93	9-20	9	20x21x14	47x28	30½	26½ in.	7 inch	415 lbs.	19.39

IF DESIRED WITHOUT HIGH SHELF, DEDUCT $1.50 FROM ANY SIZE.

NEVER KNEW WHAT A GOOD RANGE WAS BEFORE.

Messrs. Sears, Roebuck & Co. Chicago, Ill. Watsontown, Pa.

Gentlemen:—Received an Acme Renown Steel range from you last fall. It was set up at once and has been in use ever since. It has given us good results, in fact, we never knew what a good range was until we tried this Steel Range. Yours, etc., WM. A. EDWARDS.

No. 22C90 TO 22C93

OUR $15.63 HIGH CLOSET SIX-HOLE ACME RENOWN STEEL RANGE.

FOR COAL OR WOOD. **DELIVERED ON CARS AT OUR FOUNDRY.**

AT $15.63 TO $17.79, ACCORDING TO SIZE, **as listed below, we offer you this High Closet Six-Hole Acme Renown Steel Range in competition with ranges that sell at almost double the price,** excepting only our Acme Regal and Acme Triumph Ranges offered in the preceding pages.

This is exactly the same range as the one previously listed at $18.37 to $20.55, under Nos. 22C86 to 22C89, excepting this one is without the reservoir. As you will see by the illustration it has the same highly ornamented high closet, with nickel bands and nickel trimmings. It has latest patent roll top, same as roll top desks are made, and at the slight difference in the cost you will find the addition of a warming closet, a very good investment. **The main top, covers and centers** are made of the finest stove plate, from the purest pig iron, and not to be confused with malleable top ranges, sometimes called "steel" to deceive. At the prices named, we furnish this range in the sizes and dimensions below. Prices do not include pipe or cooking utensils. For cooking utensils see index on pink pages. **See page 14 for our $1.00 to $5.00 C. O. D. subject to examination offer.** Delivered on cars at our foundry.

BEAR IN MIND **that prices are without cooking utensils or stove pipe.** If you desire any stove furniture it must be shipped direct from our stock in Chicago, while these ranges are sent from our foundry. This makes two shipments, one from our foundry and one from our store. For this reason we especially urge you to make your order for cooking utensils large enough to be profitable to you, remembering that 50 to 100 pounds will, as a rule, go by freight from Chicago for as low a freight charge as 10 pounds.

Price List of the Acme Renown Six-Hole Steel Range, without Reservoir, with High Closet:
If desired without high closet deduct $2.55 from any size.

Catalogue Number	Range Number	Size of Lids	Size of Oven, Inches	Main Top, including Reservoir, Inches	Height to Main Top, Inches	L'gth of Fire Box for Wood, Inches	Pipe to Fit Collar, Inches	Shipping Weight, Pounds	PRICE
22C 98	8-18	8	18x21x14	45x28	30½	26½	7	360	$15.63
22C 99	8-20	8	20x21x14	47x28	30½	26½	7	375	17.74
22C100	9-18	9	18x21x14	45x28	30½	26½	7	360	15.68
22C101	9-20	9	20x21x14	47x28	30½	26½	7	375	17.79

Water fronts for Acme Renown Ranges.......... $2.50

Do not mistake water fronts for water reservoirs. If extension reservoirs are wanted see Catalogue Nos. 22C86 to 22C89. Water fronts are used only where there is a water supply furnished with constant pressure through pipes, which can only be obtained in large towns and cities having water works, or from an elevated pressure tank. See page 14 about hot water fronts.

$15.63 TO $17.79

No. 22C98 TO 22C101

OUR $15.03 TO $17.17 HIGH SHELF SIX-HOLE ACME RENOWN STEEL RANGE.

FOR COAL OR WOOD.
Delivered on cars at foundry.

AT $15.03 TO $17.17, according to size, as listed below, we furnish this Acme Renown, the price making six-hole steel range with high shelf, as illustrated, and invite the closest comparison in every little detail of this range with that of any range offered by any other dealer at within 50 per cent of the price. We only except our Acme Regal and Acme Triumph ranges, offered on the preceding pages.

The main top, covers and centers are made of the finest cast stove plate, from the purest pig iron, and not to be confused with malleable top ranges, sometimes called "steel" to deceive. It is as handsome trimmed as all our other steel ranges; nickel plated as shown, and nickeled steel band on front edge of main top. Asbestos lined in the most approved manner, and has our binding guarantee, and we offer it to you at the heretofore unheard of price of **$15.03 to $17.17**. It is a convenient, economical and a handsome steel range, but not so heavy and durable as our Acme Regal and Acme Triumph, shown on the preceding pages.

AT THE PRICES NAMED **we furnish this range in the sizes and dimensions below. Prices do not include pipe or cooking utensils.** For cooking utensils see index on pink pages. See page 14 for our liberal $1.00 to $5.00 C. O. D., subject to examination offer. Delivered on cars at our foundry.

Price List of the Acme Renown Six-Hole Steel Range, without Reservoir, with High Shelf:
IF DESIRED WITHOUT HIGH SHELF, DEDUCT $1.50 FROM ANY SIZE.

Catalogue Number	Range Number	Size of Lids, Inches	Size of Oven, Inches	Size of Main Top, Inches	Size of End Shelf, Inches	Height to Main Top, Inches	Length of Fire Box for Wood, Inches	Pipe to Fit Collar, Inches	Shipping Weight, Pounds	PRICE
22C102	8-18	8	18x21x14	35x28	7x28	30½	26½	7	335	$15.03
22C103	8-20	8	20x21x14	37x28	7x28	30½	26½	7	350	17.11
22C104	9-18	9	18x21x14	35x28	7x28	30½	26½	7	335	15.08
22C105	9-20	9	20x21x14	37x28	7x28	30½	26½	7	350	17.17

Water fronts for Acme Renown Ranges.......... $2.50

Do not mistake water fronts for water reservoirs. If extension reservoirs are wanted see Catalogue Nos. 22C86 to 22C93.

Water fronts are used only where there is a water supply furnished with constant pressure through pipes, which can only be obtained in large towns and cities having water works, or from an elevated pressure tank.

See page 14 about hot water fronts.

No. 22C102 TO 22C105

WE CAN ALWAYS FURNISH REPAIRS FOR ACMES
See page 19 about how to ORDER STOVE REPAIRS.

PRICE AS SHOWN, DELIVERED ON THE CARS AT OUR FOUNDRY, IN NEWARK, OHIO. **$14.95**

See page 14 for our liberal $1.00 to $5.00 C. O. D. subject to examination offer.

$14.95 NEW 1905 ACME HUMMER STEEL RANGE

With Reservoir and High Closet, as Illustrated.

$12.75 for the Square Range without Reservoir, but with High Closet; **$12.50** with Reservoir, but without High Closet; **$10.30** for the Square Range without High Closet; **$14.95** for the Range exactly as illustrated hereon, complete with Porcelain Lined Reservoir and Closet. These prices are prices based on the actual cost of material and labor, with but our one small percentage of profit added, **LESS THAN SUCH A RANGE WAS EVER BEFORE SOLD**, less than any dealer can buy the same grade of steel range in carload lots. This new 1905 Acme Hummer Steel Range has been gotten out to meet the demands of people who require a thoroughly reliable range of somewhat lighter weight and lighter construction at a lower price than our highest grades, the Acme Regal and Triumph Ranges. So many high closet reservoir steel ranges have been advertised at prices ranging from $20.00 to $30.00, and we have been asked so many times to meet this competition and quote lower prices, that we have been induced to get out the **1905 Hummer** as a range infinitely better than any of these cheap advertised ranges, a range we can guarantee in every way, and yet one that can be built at a lower cost than our higher grade ranges.

OUR ACME REGAL STEEL RANGE, as illustrated and described on preceding pages, in the 8-17 size, with reservoir and high closet, has been priced at $23.67 by reason of the present market conditions of iron and steel, and the difference between our special $14.95 price for this new Acme Hummer Steel Range and our special $23.67 price for the Acme Regal, represents the exact difference in cost of material and labor. **WHILE THE ACME REGAL IS THE HIGHEST OF HIGH GRADE,** the equal of any steel range, made of extra heavy stock, highly finished and heavily nickel plated, this, our $14.95 Hummer is made of lighter steel, lighter construction throughout. We have saved by using lighter trimmings, less nickel in the finish, and still give our customers a thoroughly reliable steel range, a range large enough to give excellent service, a range we can put out under our binding guarantee as worth a dozen of the cheap so called steel ranges so widely advertised at $20.00 to $30.00, **such a range as was never before offered by us or any other house.**

THE MAIN TOP, COVERS AND CENTERS are made of the very finest cast stove plate, from the purest pig iron, and are not to be confused with malleable top ranges, sometimes called "steel" to deceive.

THE BODY OF THIS RANGE is made from carefully selected cold rolled sheet steel, strongly put together with wrought rivets and bands, reinforced at every part. Shelf and closet are also made of cold rolled sheet steel, shaped and handsomely finished. **The range is asbestos lined where necessary, nicely nickel plated bands and brackets on high closet, nickeled tea pot shelves,** nickel bands on front edge of top of stove, nickel handle and panel on oven door. **All highly polished and nickeled.**

THE OVEN OPENING IS THE SAME SIZE AS THE OVEN BOTTOM, thus allowing as large a baking pan to enter as the oven will receive. The stove is handsomely enameled with the very best quality locomotive black, and has highest grade **Duplex Grate** for burning either coal or wood. It has latest patent roll top closet, same as roll top desks are made, and at the slight difference in cost you will find the addition of a warming closet a very good investment.

THIS STOVE IS No. 8. **The oven, 18x20¾x12 inches.** Has six No. 8 cooking holes. Top cooking surface with reservoir extension is 42½x29 inches. Height from floor to main top, 29½ inches. Distance from main top to top of high closet, 26¼ inches. Total height, including closet, 54½ inches. Length of fire box for wood, 23¾ inches. **Has a spring balanced drop oven door. Operation of stove is guaranteed.**

MOST SATISFACTORY. CANNOT DUPLICATE OUR STEEL RANGE FOR $30.00.

Sears, Roebuck & Co., Chicago, Ill. Union City, Conn.

Gentlemen:—Received your Steel Range in perfect condition and it has proved most satisfactory thus far. The freight amounted to $1.71 and trucking $1.00, making a total of $2.71. There are very few like it in this place, most of them being of the heavy iron kind. As far as I have seen in regard to stoves in this place, I doubt if I could secure a stove as good for $30.00 or more. Yours truly, MRS. C. R. HARPER.

TO BE ABLE TO MAKE THESE LOW PRICES we can only offer this range delivered on cars at our foundry.

No. 22C122	Price for Square Top Range, without high closet or reservoir. Shipping weight, 285 pounds....	$10.30
No. 22C123	Price for Reservoir Range, without high closet. Shipping weight, 325 pounds....	12.50
No. 22C124	Price for Square Top Range, with high closet. Shipping weight, 359 pounds....	12.75
No. 22C125	Price for Range complete, exactly as illustrated, with high warming closet and porcelain lined reservoir. Shipping weight, 399 pounds	14.95

Water Front for Acme Hummer $2.50. See page 14 about hot water fronts. Prices do not include pipe or cooking utensils. For cooking utensils see index on pink pages.

$12.68 OUR NEW 1905 STEEL COOK STOVE

Delivered on Board the Cars at our Foundry in Newark, Ohio.

FOR $12.68 WE OFFER OUR NEW 1905 STEEL COOK STOVE,

The Acme Progress,

as the very latest and highest grade steel cook stove made, the equal of any steel cook stove you can buy elsewhere at double the price . . .

BURNS HARD COAL, SOFT COAL, COKE OR ANYTHING FOR FUEL. EVERY STOVE IS PUT OUT UNDER OUR BINDING GUARANTEE.

HOW WE MAKE THE PRICE $12.68. Operating, as we do, the largest stove foundry in the world, buying our raw material, the sheet steel and the pig iron, direct from the largest furnaces and rolling mills, equipped as we are with every modern labor saving machinery for making perfect finished work and minimizing labor, we are able to produce in this, our **$12.68 new model** steel cook stove, the Acme Progress, the highest grade steel cook stove made, a steel cook stove made of heavier plate than is used by other makers, stronger in every way, better riveted, better braced, better fitting, heavier interlining, a stove that will outwear two of the ordinary steel cook stoves and be in better condition after five years' constant use than the ordinary light steel cook stove would be after one year's use.

HIGHLY PLEASED IN EVERY WAY—SAVED $10.00.

Sears, Roebuck & Co. Chicago, Ill. Bellevue, Ohio

Dear Sirs:—I received the steel cook stove O.K. The freight was 54 cents. We saved at least $8.00 and I do not know but $10.00 would be nearer. We are highly pleased with it in every way. Yours sincerely, T. V. NORTH.

THE MAIN FRONT, MAIN TOP, COVERS AND CENTERS are made of the very finest cast stove plate, from the purest pig iron, and not to be confused with malleable top ranges, sometimes called "steel" to deceive.

THE OVEN PLATES AND BODY of the stove are made from extra heavy cut steel plate, riveted with wrought rivets, reinforced throughout, and the main front is the very finest cast stove plate.

SEE PAGE 14 FOR OUR LIBERAL $1.00 TO $5.00 C. O. D., SUBJECT TO EXAMINATION OFFER.

PRICES DO NOT INCLUDE PIPE OR COOKING UTENSILS. FOR COOKING UTENSILS SEE INDEX ON PINK PAGES.

BEAR IN MIND this price is too low to include any pipe or cooking utensils. If you want stove furniture refer to index on pink pages, remembering the stove must be shipped from our foundry in Central Ohio, and the utensils from our store in Chicago, making two shipments. Make your order for cooking vessels large enough to be a profitable shipment to you. As a rule 50 to 100 pounds will go by freight from Chicago at as low a freight charge as 10 pounds.

THIS STOVE is furnished in Nos. 8 or 9-21 size. The oven is 17½ x 20 x 12 inches; has four cooking holes and only one oven door on the right hand side as shown Size of top, including reservoir, is 42½x26 inches, height from floor to main top, 30½ inches. Has pouch feed for coal and swing door for wood, very large flue, cut top, heavy covers, heavy linings with very heavy fireback, reversible duplex grate, large ash pan, nickel plated panel on oven door, nickel reservoir panel, nickel plated oven door handle, heavy steel spring balanced drop oven door. It is furnished complete with lifter, scraper and shaker for removing the ashes from under the oven. It is fitted with a large porcelain lined reservoir, as illustrated. Length of fire box for wood is 23½ inches, pipe collar, 7 inches.

SHIPPING WEIGHT, 345 POUNDS

No. 22C126 Price, No. 8-21 with reservoir.......... $12.68 | No. 22C127 Price, No. 9-21 with reservoir.......... $13.83

If desired without reservoir, but with end shelf, deduct $2.00 from either size.

WE CAN ALWAYS FURNISH REPAIRS FOR ACMES. SEE PAGE 19 ABOUT HOW TO ORDER STOVE REPAIRS.

OUR ACME ROYAL RANGE,

WITH PORCELAIN LINED RESERVOIR AND HIGH CLOSET. FOR HARD COAL, SOFT COAL, WOOD OR ANYTHING USED FOR FUEL.

$18.13 TO $21.89

How We Trim It.

BEAUTIFULLY NICKEL PLATED MOUNTINGS THROUGHOUT,

including large, handsome **nickel plated** oven door panel, large **nickel** panel on draft door; very large **nickel** oven shelf, large, handsome, highly polished **nickel bands on main top, hearth and high closet, nickel hinge pins, nickel tea shelves; nickel plated,** patent, fancy (always cold) knobs on all doors;

FANCY NICKEL ORNAMENTATION THROUGHOUT.......

highly polished, richly ornamented and decorated, latest **rococo** design, and we believe

THE HANDSOMEST 1905 RANGE ON THE MARKET.

$18.13 to $21.89 is our price for this, our very finest, completely finished **Acme Royal Range,** delivered on the cars at our foundry in Newark, Ohio.

This $18.13 Stove is the equal of any range on the market, regardless of price; **combines every improvement** of every high grade range made, with the defects of none.

Our 20th Century Production. Full Square Oven, Duplex Grate, Cut Tops and Centers, One Graduated Lid and Five Solid Covers, Porcelain Lined Reservoir, Oven Door Kicker, Large Fire Box, Large Flues, Bailed Ash Pan, Slide Hearth Plate, Latest and Handsomest Rococo Design.

Our Gem Grate furnished **FREE,** makes it a perfect burner for all kinds of fuel, **Coal, Wood or Coke.**

Our Binding Guarantee makes you perfectly safe and insures for you such a stove as you could not buy elsewhere.

Most Stove Makers would say this oven is three or four inches wider than the size we give.

We furnish this Range just as it is shown in the various sizes at prices as listed below.

OUR BINDING GUARANTEE.

With every **Acme Royal** we issue a written, binding guarantee, by the terms of which if any piece or part gives out by reason of defect in material or workmanship, we will replace it free of charge; further, that it must be received by you in perfect condition, found exactly as represented and perfectly satisfactory, or your money will be refunded immediately.

Our New 1905 Line, Factory to Consumer Prices and Binding Guarantee, commend our line above all others.

Oven measurements do not include swell of oven door. If you do not use coal at all, order the Acme Redwood, the same range for wood only, from catalogue Nos. 22C190 to 22C195.

SAVES $10.00 ON OUR ACME ROYAL RANGE.

Malvern, O.

Sears, Roebuck & Co.,
Chicago, Ill.

Gentlemen:—I received the big Acme Royal Range in good order and hope you got the money safely. In regards to stove am very well pleased. Better than I expected. Looks better than in the list. I will recommend it wherever I can. I am satisfied that I saved $10.00 by buying of you. It burns less coal than any other stove I ever saw. I have used it nearly every day.

Yours respectfully,
LEOPOLD KEFFLER.

SEE PAGE 14 FOR OUR LIBERAL $1.00 TO $5.00 C. O. D. SUBJECT TO EXAMINATION OFFER.

SEE SUCCEEDING PAGES FOR ILLUSTRATIONS AND PRICES OF THIS ELEGANT RANGE, WITHOUT HIGH CLOSET AND WITH OR WITHOUT RESERVOIR.

PRICES DO NOT INCLUDE PIPE OR COOKING UTENSILS. FOR COOKING UTENSILS SEE INDEX ON PINK PAGES.

PRICE, DELIVERED ON THE CARS AT OUR NEWARK, OHIO, FOUNDRY.

CATALOGUE NUMBER	RANGE NUMBER	SIZE OF LIDS	SIZE OF OVEN	SIZE OF TOP, MEASURING RESERVOIR	SIZE OF FIRE BOX WHEN USED FOR WOOD	HEIGHT TO MAIN TOP	WEIGHT	PRICE
22C130	7-18	No. 7	17½x16x11½	42x25	17x8x8	28 inches	455 lbs.	$18.13
22C131	8-18	No. 8	17½x16x11½	42x25	17x8x8	28 inches	455 lbs.	18.18
22C132	7-20	No. 7	19½x18x12	45x27	19x9x9	30 inches	495 lbs.	19.72
22C133	8-20	No. 8	19½x18x12	45x27	19x9x9	30 inches	497 lbs.	19.77
22C134	8-22	No. 8	21½x20x12½	46x28	21x9x9	31 inches	538 lbs.	21.84
22C135	9-22	No. 9	21½x20x12½	46x28	21x9x9	31 inches	540 lbs.	21.89

WE CAN ALWAYS FURNISH REPAIRS FOR ACMES. SEE PAGE 19 ABOUT HOW TO ORDER STOVE REPAIRS WHEN NEEDED IN FUTURE YEARS.

OUR ACME ROYAL HIGH SHELF RESERVOIR COAL AND WOOD RANGE.

THIS IS THE EXACT SAME RANGE as the one just quoted below under No. 22C142 at $14.92, with the addition of the high shelf. This high shelf is ornamented with heavy nickel plated band, two highly polished nickel plated tea shelves, as illustrated. This range burns coal or wood, and an extra grate is furnished whereby it can be instantly changed from coal to wood, or wood to coal.

Customers are writing to us from every state in the Union that such stoves were never before seen in their sections, and when compared with the prices charged by other manufacturers, they simply wonder how it is possible to build such a stove for so little money.

ONE ACME ROYAL SELLS ANOTHER. We know if you order one of these ranges from us you will be so well pleased with it you will show it to your neighbors, tell them where you got it, what you paid for it, and in this way we will be sure to receive more orders from your neighborhood. **Nothing advertises our house more than our Acme Royal line of stoves and ranges.** Nothing has ever gone out of our house from which we have received so many letters of praise.

You will better appreciate the extraordinary values we are giving when you see and examine the stove. Prices do not include pipe or cooking utensils. See index on pink pages.

$16.80 TO $20.56

SEE PAGE 14 FOR OUR LIBERAL $1.00 TO $5.00 C. O. D. SUBJECT TO EXAMINATION OFFER.

We furnish this range in the various sizes at the prices listed, delivered on the cars at our foundry in Newark, Ohio. If you do not use coal at all, order the wood burning Acme Redwood Range from Catalogue Nos. 22C196 to 22C201.

Catalogue Number	Range Number	Size of Lids	Size of Oven, inches	Size of Top, Measuring Reservoir	Fire Box when used for wood	Height to main top	Weight, pounds	Price
22C136	7-18	No. 7	17½x16x11½	42x25	17x8x8	28	418	$16.80
22C137	8-18	No. 8	17½x16x11½	42x25	17x8x8	28	418	16.85
22C138	7-20	No. 7	19½x18x12	45x27	19x9x9	30	458	18.39
22C139	8-20	No. 8	19½x18x12	45x27	19x9x9	30	460	18.44
22C140	8-22	No. 8	21½x20x12½	46x28	21x9x9	31	500	20.51
22C141	9-22	No. 9	21½x20x12½	46x28	21x9x9	31	502	20.56

Remember our binding guarantee as to quality. Remember our binding guarantee as to delivery. Remember our binding guarantee as to price.

OUR ACME ROYAL RESERVOIR COAL AND WOOD RANGE.

Oven measurements do not include swell of oven door.

THIS RESERVOIR RANGE is offered at $14.92 to $18.70, delivered on the cars at our foundry in Newark, Ohio, and is the exact same range as No. 22C148, quoted below at $16.31, but without the high closet, and with the addition of the large porcelain lined reservoir.

If you do not use coal at all, order the wood burning Acme Redwood Range from Catalogue Nos. 22C202 to 22C201.

THE ILLUSTRATIONS we show fail to do this range justice. It must be seen to be appreciated. The handsome nickel bands around the top and around the hearth, the nickel ornamentations and trimmings throughout, the beautiful rococo pattern and the large massive castings, can only be appreciated when seen and examined. **Prices do not include pipe or cooking utensils.** See index on pink pages.

SEE PAGE 14 FOR OUR LIBERAL $1.00 TO $5.00 C. O. D. SUBJECT TO EXAMINATION OFFER.

We furnish this range in the various sizes at the prices listed, delivered on the cars at our foundry in Newark, Ohio.

Catalogue Number	Range No.	Size of Lids	Size of Oven, inches	Top, Measuring Reservoir	Fire Box When Used for Wood	Height to main top	Weight, pounds	Price
22C142	7-18	No. 7	17½x16x11½	42x25	17x8x8	28	380	$14.92
22C143	8-18	No. 8	17½x16x11½	42x25	17x8x8	28	380	14.97
22C144	7-20	No. 7	19½x18x12	45x27	19x9x9	30	420	16.51
22C145	8-20	No. 8	19½x18x12	45x27	19x9x9	30	422	16.57
22C146	8-22	No. 8	21½x20x12½	46x28	21x9x9	31	463	18.65
22C147	9-22	No. 9	21½x20x12½	46x28	21x9x9	31	465	18.70

OUR ACME ROYAL HIGH CLOSET COAL OR WOOD RANGE.

$16.31 TO $20.07

AS SHOWN IN ILLUSTRATION, this range is furnished with a large high closet with handsome double doors, ornamented with large, highly polished nickel bands around high closet, around top of stove and around hearth. The same handsome rococo pattern as is shown throughout the line, the same highly polished trimmings throughout.

UNDERSTAND, with all combination ranges for coal or wood, we furnish an extra grate free, so stove can be instantly changed from coal burner to wood burner.

ALL THE LATEST 1905 FEATURES. Large square oven, large square oven door, the manufacturers' patent features, which insures for you the most economy in the consumption of fuel. **Best baker on the market,** made from very heavy castings, with a view to furnishing our trade a range in appearance, finish, durability and style equal to anything on the market regardless of price, a range you would pay double the money for. **Oven measurements do not include swell of oven door.**

SEE PAGE 14 FOR OUR LIBERAL $1.00 TO $5.00 C. O. D. SUBJECT TO EXAMINATION OFFER.

We furnish this stove in the different styles at the prices listed, delivered on the cars at our foundry in Newark, Ohio. If you do not use coal at all, order the wood burning Acme Redwood Range, Catalogue Nos. 22C208 to 22C213. Prices do not include pipe or cooking utensils. See index on pink pages.

Catalogue Number	Range Number	Size of Lids	Size of Oven, inches	Top, not Measuring End Shelf	End Shelf	Fire Box when used for wood	Pipe to Fit Collar	Height to main top	Weight, pounds	Price
22C148	7-18	No. 7	17½x16x11½	31x25	8x25	17x8x8	7	28	405	$16.31
22C149	8-18	No. 8	17½x16x11½	31x25	8x25	17x8x8	7	28	405	16.37
22C150	7-20	No. 7	19½x18x12	33x27	9x27	19x9x9	7	30	433	17.90
22C161	8-20	No. 8	19½x18x12	33x27	9x27	19x9x9	7	30	435	17.96
22C152	8-22	No. 8	21½x20x12½	34x28	9x28	21x9x9	7	31	475	20.01
22C153	9-22	No. 9	21½x20x12½	34x28	9x28	21x9x9	7	31	477	20.07

WATER FRONTS for Royal Ranges, each, $2.00, used only where there is water supply furnished with constant pressure through pipes, which can only be obtained in towns and cities having water works or from an elevated tank.

OUR ACME ROYAL HIGH SHELF COAL OR WOOD RANGE.

AT $14.99 to $18.74 DELIVERED ON THE CARS AT OUR FOUNDRY IN NEWARK, OHIO.

WE OFFER THIS HIGH SHELF ACME ROYAL RANGE, the very latest rococo pattern, with wide, heavy, highly polished nickel plated band on top shelf, around top and hearth, nickel plated trimmings and mountings throughout; furnished with an extra grate for changing it from coal to wood, or vice versa. **Large square oven,** large square oven door; every improvement known. The finest thing on the market; the very best for 1905.

SEE PAGE 14 FOR OUR LIBERAL $1.00 TO $5.00 C. O. D. SUBJECT TO EXAMINATION OFFER.

We furnish this stove in all the different sizes listed at the prices named, delivered on the cars at our Newark, Ohio, foundry. **Oven measurements do not include swell of oven door.**

If you do not use coal at all, order the wood burning Acme Redwood Range, Catalogue Nos. 22C214 to 22C219. Prices do not include pipe or cooking utensils. See index on pink pages.

Catalogue Number	Range Number	Size of Lids	Size of Oven, inches	Top, Not Measuring End Shelf	End Shelf	Fire Box when used for wood	Pipe to fit Collar	Height to main top	Weight, pounds	Price
22C154	7-18	No. 7	17½x16x11½	31x25	8x25	17x8x8	7	28	368	$14.99
22C155	8-18	No. 8	17½x16x11½	31x25	8x25	17x8x8	7	28	368	15.04
22C156	7-20	No. 7	19½x18x12	33x27	9x27	19x9x9	7	30	396	16.58
22C157	8-20	No. 8	19½x18x12	33x27	9x27	19x9x9	7	30	398	16.63
22C158	8-22	No. 8	21½x20x12½	34x28	9x28	21x9x9	7	31	438	18.69
22C159	9-22	No. 9	21½x20x12½	34x28	9x28	21x9x9	7	31	440	18.74

If desired without high shelf deduct $1.75 from any size.

OVEN MEASUREMENTS DO NOT INCLUDE SWELL OF OVEN DOOR.

WE CAN ALWAYS FURNISH REPAIRS FOR ACMES. SEE PAGE 19 ABOUT HOW TO ORDER STOVE REPAIRS WHEN NEEDED IN FUTURE YEARS.

$14.41 FOR OUR BIG No. 8-18 ACME GRAND RANGE.

IF YOU ARE A STOVE MANUFACTURER OR DEALER and know the market price of pig iron and the relation it bears to the cost of the finished high grade stove, you will wonder how it is possible for us to produce a 400-pound square oven high shelf reservoir range and sell it for $14.41.

OUR $14.41 PRICE is made possible, first, from the fact that we operate the largest stove foundry in the world, our moulding room alone accommodating six hundred moulders. We are equipped with every known machine for reducing labor and improving quality. Our pig iron is bought direct from the furnaces in larger quantities than any other stove maker can buy. Our own railroad tracks enter our foundry and warehouses and connect with several trunk lines. Everything has been done, and on a larger scale than other stove makers, to reduce the first cost and produce the highest possible quality, and to this first cost there is none of the expense common to all other stove makers and dealers, nothing to be added except our one small percentage of profit, as the finished castings and parts come from their several places in the foundry and are assembled in the mounting room, the stove goes direct to the car tagged to the buyer. In fact, our expense stops almost where other stove makers' expense begins; hence we practically cut the price in two to the buyer and give you the highest grade of work at but little more than one-half the price you would have to pay elsewhere.

THIS BIG SQUARE OVEN, high shelf, reservoir range is the very handsomest design shown, the latest rococo pattern, mounted on a rich rococo base; has a large square oven with deep nickel plated out side oven shelf, large rococo high back shelf with nickel plated pot holders, 6-hole top with one graduated lid and five solid covers, deep porcelain lined reservoir. It is handsomely nickel trimmed, with big nickel medallion on oven door, nickel plated oven shelf, nickel plated knobs and tea shelves. The oven door is tin lined. **MAIN TOP, TOP SHELF, AND HEARTH EDGES ARE PLAIN BLACK** and easily kept clean. This stove is fitted with a duplex grate, made to burn coal only or both coal and wood and has a large ash pan. We have gotten out this, our special $14.41 Acme Grand Range, with a view of combining the good qualities of all high grade cast iron ranges, with the defects of none, giving you a range that will wear longer, bake better and consume less fuel than any cast iron range made by any other maker.

IF YOU ARE A DEALER do not order your next lot of stoves, and if a consumer, do not buy a stove until you first see and examine this, our $14.41 Acme Grand, if you are in want of a cast iron range. You will find it such a range as you could not get elsewhere, and our price will mean a big saving to you.

IF YOU ARE NOT A STOVE DEALER OR MAKER and simply want to buy a fine range for your own use, and you order this at $14.41 and then compare it with stoves that your dealer at home sells for $25.00 to $35.00 you will see that you have saved from $10.00 to $20.00 by sending your order to us for our big $14.41 Acme Grand Range.

THIS IS THE HIGHEST GRADE, newest style, most up to date, handsomest and in every way the best cast iron range possible to produce, superior to any range that goes out of any other foundry in America. We use nothing but the highest grade stove plate, Birmingham iron (no scrap iron is used); we use nothing but 72-hour coke for melting, we employ only the most skilled union moulders, our polishing and grinding is all done by automatic machinery (not accomplished by the hand work of other makers), our nickeling is higher grade than you will find on any other stove, the castings we turn out will, by reason of the iron we use and the way it is moulded, stand more strain, is less liable to warp or crack than any other stove plate made. You will find our cast iron stoves sharper and more smoothly moulded, better fitting, better bolted, better braced, heavier and stronger interlinings, better wearing and more economical in the consumption of fuel than any other stoves made.

$14.41

ACME GRAND NEWARK STOVE WORKS CHICAGO

AT OUR SPECIAL $14.41 PRICE we furnish this stove for coal or wood as desired, exactly as illustrated and described, complete with high back and shelf and porcelain lined reservoir, the same delivered on board the cars at our foundry in Newark, Ohio, from which point you must pay the freight. The stove weighs 440 pounds crated for shipping, and the freight will average for 500 miles, $1.50 to $2.00 (greater or less distances in proportion), so you can see the freight charges will amount to nothing as compared to what you will save in price.

OUR SPECIAL $14.41 PRICE is for the stove only, exactly as illustrated, and does not include pipe or cooking utensils. For prices on stove furniture, pipe, cooking utensils, etc., see index on pink pages.

ACME GRAND STOVE IS O. K., SAVED OVER $10.00.

Sears, Roebuck & Co., Chicago, Ill. Millersburg, Pa.
Dear Sirs:—Would say I am well pleased with Acme Grand stove, it is all O. K. and about the price. I saw a stove almost like mine and the party paid $27.00 for it and I would not trade him. Yours respectfully, EDWARD S. FIKE.

DEALERS CAN BUY THIS STOVE to sell again, as every stove bears the name "Newark Stove Works, Chicago." You can buy this stove from us singly, in lots of ten or in carload lots and the price is the same, $14.41. You can add $10.00 to it for your profit; sell it at $26.0[illegible] and still give much greater value than you are now giving in any stove coming from any other foundry. With the largest stove foundry in the world, material bought at the lowest possible prices, with every known labor saving machine to reduce the cost and improve the quality, we can furnish you, dealer or consumer, singly or in carloads, these and other stoves of higher grade than go out of any other foundry and at a big saving in price.

ABOUT REPAIRS. Understand, we can always furnish you repairs for any stove we sell in any of the years to come, and always at foundry cost. If any part breaks from accident or otherwise, simply write us and the repairs will be sent to you immediately at factory cost.

OUR GUARANTEE, FREE TRIAL AND REFUND OFFER.

We guarantee this stove to reach you in the same perfect condition it leaves the foundry, and if any piece or part is cracked or broken we will replace or repair it free of charge. Each stove is also covered by binding guarantee, by the terms and conditions of which if any piece or part gives out by reason of defective material or workmanship, we will replace or repair it free of charge. By our free trial offer you can order this stove, enclose our price, and we will send it to you with the understanding and agreement that you give it thirty days' trial in your own home, and if for any reason you become dissatisfied with your purchase, if you do not find, after comparing it with stoves sold by others at about double the price, that you have received a better stove than you could get elsewhere at a saving of $10.00 to $15.00, you can return the stove to us at our expense and we will return your money, together with any freight charges paid by you.

PRICES, DELIVERED ON THE CARS AT OUR NEWARK, OHIO, FOUNDRY

Catalogue No.	Range No.	Size of Lids	Size of Oven	Size of Top Measuring Reservoir.	Size of Coal Fire Box When Used for Wood	Height to Main Top	Size of Pipe Collar	Shipping Weight	PRICE
22C166	8-19	No. 8	18x18 x12	43½x26¾	19 x9½x8	29¼ in.	7 in.	417 lbs.	$14.41
22C167	8-21	No. 8	20x19¾x12½	45¾x29	20½x9½x8½	30½ in.	7 in.	463 lbs.	16.54
22C168	9-21	No. 9	20x19¾x12½	45¾x29	20½x9½x8½	30½ in.	7 in.	463 lbs.	16.59

WATER FRONTS FOR ACME GRAND RANGES, $2.00 EXTRA. SEE PAGE 14 ABOUT HOT WATER FRONTS. IF DESIRED WITHOUT HIGH SHELF DEDUCT $1.25. IF DESIRED WITHOUT RESERVOIR, BUT WITH END SHELF, DEDUCT $2.00.

$13.56 TO $15.74

OUR ACME DUCHESS FOUR-HOLE RANCE.

WITH RESERVOIR AND HIGH SHELF. FOR SOFT COAL OR WOOD.

AT $13.56 TO $15.74 with porcelain lined reservoir, we offer this new and elegant design ACME DUCHESS, for 1905, delivered on the cars at our foundry in Newark, Ohio. It is positively the most wonderful value in a new model, high grade range ever offered by any stove maker. Our binding guarantee secures you as to quality and price and is something heretofore unheard of.

IF YOU SHOULD DESIRE THIS RANGE WITHOUT THE RESERVOIR, SEE No. 22C181, SHOWN BELOW AT $10.97. THIS IS THE EXACT SAME STOVE, WITH THE RESERVOIR ADDED.

OUR $13.56 TO $15.74 PRICES are based on the actual cost of material and labor with but our one small profit added. For special features of interest to the customer, see the description below in connection with this same range without reservoir.

If you do not use coal at all, order the Acme Empress from catalogue Nos. 22C226 to 22C228, which is the same range for wood only. PRICES DO NOT INCLUDE PIPE OR COOKING UTENSILS. SEE INDEX ON PINK PAGES.

If you live south or east of Chicago make your selection from this Old Reliable Ohio line of Acme Stoves and Ranges, taking advantage of the saving in freight and saving in time on the railroad. If you live south or east of Chicago, the freight will be less than from Chicago. If you live west or north of Chicago the freight will be about 30 cents per hundred more than from Chicago. The reason we can make the price so low: We leave out the freight to Chicago and leave out the cost of hauling and handling into and out of our store, making our price direct from factory to consumer, barely covering the cost of material and labor, with but our one small percentage of profit added. A price only made possible by eliminating all the handling expenses and shipping direct from the foundry. SEE PAGE 14 FOR OUR LIBERAL $1.00 TO $5.00 C. O. D. SUBJECT TO EXAMINATION OFFER.

REMEMBER, if you require any cooking utensils or stove pipe, they go direct from our store in Chicago, making two shipments, so make your order for stove furniture large enough to be a profitable shipment for you. Bear in mind, 50 to 100 pounds will, as a rule, go by freight from Chicago at as low a freight charge as 10 pounds.

PRICES DELIVERED ON THE CARS AT OUR NEWARK, OHIO, FOUNDRY.

Catalogue Number	Range Number	Size of Lids	Size of Oven, inches	Top, including Reservoir	Height to Cooking Top	Pipe Collar	Fire Box for Wood	Weight, pounds	Price
22C178	8-18	No. 8	18x18x12	38 x26 in.	31 in.	7 in.	20 in.	412	$13.56
22C179	8-20	No. 8	20x20x12½	39½x27 in.	31½ in.	7 in.	21½ in.	445	15.69
22C180	9-20	No. 9	20x20x12½	40½x27 in.	31½ in.	7 in.	21½ in.	445	15.74

If high shelf is no desired, deduct $1.00 from any size.

OUR ACME DUCHESS FOUR-HOLE RANGE.

WITHOUT RESERVOIR AND WITH HIGH SHELF. FOR SOFT COAL OR WOOD.

$10.97 TO $13.14

AT $10.97 TO $13.14 we offer this new and elegant design ACME DUCHESS for 1905, delivered on the cars at our foundry in Newark, Ohio. It is positively the most wonderful value in a new model, high grade range ever offered by any stove-maker. Our binding guarantee secures you as to quality and price, and is something heretofore unheard of.

IF YOU PREFER THIS STOVE WITH A RESERVOIR, SEE No. 22C178, ILLUSTRATED ABOVE.

OUR $10.97 TO $13.14 PRICES are based on the actual cost of material and labor, with but our one small profit added.

THE ACME DUCHESS RANGE is designed for the burning of coal or wood, and with every Acme Duchess we furnish an extra grate and fire back, so it can be changed from coal burner to wood burner at will. THE ACME DUCHESS contains all the desirable features found in any modern range. Descriptive items of interest are a large fire box with heavy linings, extra heavy sectional fire back, outside oven shelf, oven door kicker, extra heavy covers, heavy centers, nickel plated panel on oven door, nickeled name plate, large, handsome new pattern ornamental base, heavy tin lined oven door. It has handsome nickel plated tea shelves, as illustrated; nickel plated knobs and trimmings, latest patent front feed, strictly high grade, up to date, guaranteed range at an extremely low figure.

If you do not use coal at all, order the Acme Empress from catalogue Nos. 22C229 to 22C231, which is the same range for wood only. We furnish this range in any of the sizes listed below at prices named, delivered on the cars at our Newark, Ohio, foundry.

SEE PAGE 14 FOR OUR LIBERAL $1.00 TO $5.00 C. O. D. SUBJECT TO EXAMINATION OFFER.

REMEMBER, if you require any cooking utensils or stove pipe, they go direct from our store in Chicago, making two shipments, so make your order for stove furniture large enough to be a profitable shipment for you. Bear in mind, 50 to 100 pounds will, as a rule, go by freight from Chicago at as low a freight charge as 10 pounds.

PRICE LIST OF THE ACME DUCHESS SQUARE AND HIGH SHELF.

Catalogue Number	Range Number	Size of Lids	Size of Oven, inches	Top, not including End Shelf	End Shelf	Height to Cooking Top	Pipe Collar	Fire Box for Wood	Weight, pounds	Price
22C181	8-18	No. 8	18x18x12	29x26	8x26	31	7 in.	20 in.	350	$10.97
22C182	8-20	No. 8	20x20x12½	30x27	8x27	31½	7 in.	21½ in.	383	13.09
22C183	9-20	No. 9	20x20x12½	30x27	8x27	31½	7 in	21½ in.	383	13.14

Water front to fit any size, price $2.00. If the high shelf is not desired, deduct $1.00 from any size. Prices do not include Pipe or Cooking Utensils. See index on pink pages.

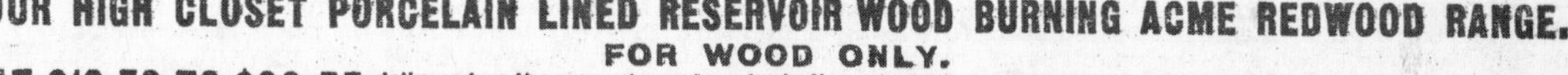

$16.78 TO $20.55

OUR HIGH CLOSET PORCELAIN LINED RESERVOIR WOOD BURNING ACME REDWOOD RANGE.

FOR WOOD ONLY.

AT $16.78 TO $20.55 delivered on the cars at our foundry in Newark, Ohio, we offer this under our binding guarantee, as the very finest thing ever before produced, the highest grade wood burning cast iron range on the market. If you will let us send you this range, we will allow you to compare it with any range ever sold in your market at any price, and if you do not find this stove not only equal but better, and the price 25 to 50 per cent lower, you are at liberty to return it at our expense, AND WE WILL CHEERFULLY REFUND YOUR MONEY.

NOTHING HAS BEEN LEFT UNDONE to make this range the finest, and nothing is omitted to make it in every way complete. This wood burning Acme Redwood Range has a large porcelain lined reservoir, a large high closet with fancy doors. The closet is ornamented with a heavy highly polished nickel band; the shelf is ornamented with two highly polished nickel plated tea shelves, the front of stove is bound with large heavy nickel plated bands, and the hearth with large nickel plated bands. It is highly nickel plated, ornamented and finished throughout.

SEE PAGE 14 FOR OUR LIBERAL $1.00 TO $5.00 C. O. D. SUBJECT TO EXAMINATION OFFER.
We believe it to be not only the handsomest, but in every detail the best cast iron range on the market.
Prices do not include Pipe or Cooking Utensils. See index on pink pages. Delivered on the cars at our Newark, Ohio, Foundry

Catalogue Number	Range Number	Size of Lids	Size of Oven, inches	Size of Top, Measuring Reservoir	Size of Fire Box	Size of Pipe to Fit Collar	Height to Main Top	Weight, pounds	Price
22C190	7-18	No. 7	17½x16½x11½	42x25	22x 9x 9	7	28	415	$16.78
22C191	8-18	No. 8	17½x16½x11½	42x25	22x 9x 9	7	28	415	16.83
22C192	7-20	No. 7	19½x18 x12	45x27	24x10x10	7	30	455	18.37
22C193	8-20	No. 8	19½x18 x12	45x27	24x10x10	7	30	455	18.42
22C194	8-22	No. 8	21½x20 x12½	46x28	26x10x10	7	31	500	20.50
22C195	9-22	No. 9	21½x20 x12½	46x28	26x10x10	7	31	500	20.55

We can always furnish repairs for Acmes. See page 19 about how to order Stove Repairs when needed in future years.

OUR

HIGH SHELF RESERVOIR WOOD BURNING ACME REDWOOD RANGE

FOR WOOD ONLY.

THIS NEW ACME REDWOOD RANGE, which is quoted at $15.48 to $19.28, according to size, delivered on the cars at our Newark, Ohio, foundry has a large porcelain lined reservoir and a large high shelf, which is handsomely trimmed and finished with a heavy, highly polished nickel band around top shelf and two fancy nickel plated teapot holders on the side. Otherwise it is exactly the same as the Acme Redwood above illustrated, as No. 22C190 at $16.78.

THIS IS A WOOD BURNING RANGE and is especially recommended to those who wish to burn wood and as a better range to buy than a combination coal and wood burner. The range has been manufactured throughout with a view of being the best wood burner possible to construct. If you order one of our Acme Redwood Ranges, if you do not find it all and even more than we claim for it, and equal to any range you can buy in your local market, regardless of price, you are at liberty to return it to us and we will cheerfully refund your money.

See page 14 for our liberal $1.00 to $5.00 C. O. D. subject to examination offer. We furnish this range in the various sizes at the prices quoted below, delivered on the cars at our Newark, Ohio, Foundry.

PRICES DO NOT INCLUDE PIPE OR COOKING UTENSILS. SEE INDEX ON PINK PAGES.

Catalogue Number	Range Number	Size of Lids	Size of Oven, inches	Size of Top, Measuring Reservoir	Size of Fire Box	Size of Pipe to Fit Collar	Height to Main Top	Weight, pounds	Price
2C196	7-18	No. 7	17½x16½x11½	42x25	22x 9x 9	7	28	378	$15.48
2C197	8-18	No. 8	17½x16½x11½	42x25	22x 9x 9	7	28	378	15.53
2C198	7-20	No. 7	19½x18 x12	45x27	24x10x10	7	30	418	17.12
2C199	8-20	No. 8	19½x18 x12	45x27	24x10x10	7	30	418	17.17
22C200	8-22	No. 8	21½x20 x12½	46x28	26x10x10	7	31	462	19.23
C201	9-22	No. 9	21½x20 x12½	46x28	26x10x10	7	31	462	19.28

$15.48

OUR ACME REDWOOD, WOOD BURNING RESERVOIR RANGE—FOR WOOD ONLY.

AT $13.57 TO $17.32 we offer this our Acme Redwood Wood Burning Range, delivered on the cars at our Newark, Ohio, foundry, complete with reservoir, and you will find it equal to ranges that retail generally at $25.00 and upward. **With large porcelain lined reservoir,** as illustrated, it combines all the late features of our Acme Redwood Line, as described below, highly nickel plated and ornamented. Has a large, highly polished nickeled steel band around top and hearth plate. It is equal to any range on the market, regardless of price, and is offered at a price far lower than inferior ranges are sold by others. It is such a range as you will find only in the very best retail stores, such ranges as are advertised by no other catalogue house; and in no department stores. This is the exact same range as No. 22C220, shown below at $12.24 and upward, with the addition of the large porcelain lined reservoir. We furnish this range in the various sizes at the prices listed below. Delivered on the cars at our Newark, Ohio, foundry. **Our measurements do not include swell of oven door.**

OUR RANGES are offered as the best money can buy and at prices based on the actual cost of material and labor, with but our one small percentage of profit added.

See page 14 for our liberal $1.00 to $5.00 C. O. D. subject to examination offer. Prices do not include pipe or cooking utensils. See index on pink pages.

Catalogue Number	Size	Size of Lids	Size of Oven, inches	Size of Top, Measuring Reservoir	Size of Fire Box	Size of Pipe to Fit Collar	Height to Main Top	Weight, pounds	Price
22C202	7-18	No. 7	17½x16½x11½	42x25	22x 9x 9	7	28	340	$13.57
22C203	8-18	No. 8	17½x16½x11½	42x25	22x 9x 9	7	28	340	13.61
22C204	7-20	No. 7	19½x18 x12	45x27	24x10x10	7	30	380	15.16
22C205	8-20	No. 8	19½x18 x12	45x27	24x10x10	7	30	380	15.21
22C206	8-22	No. 8	21½x20 x12½	46x28	26x10x10	7	31	424	17.27
22C207	9-22	No. 9	21½x20 x12½	46x28	26x10x10	7	31	424	17.32

OUR GUARANTEE. With every Acme we issue a special written binding guarantee by the terms and conditions of which, if any piece or part gives out by reason of defect in material or workmanship we will replace or repair it free of charge, excepting only the regular wear on fire box linings and grates.

DELIVERY GUARANTEE. At the prices quoted we furnish the Acme Redwood carefully crated and delivered on board the cars at our foundry in Newark, Ohio, and we guarantee the stove to reach you in the same perfect condition it leaves us, and if any piece or part is broken on arrival we will replace it free of any charge to you.

BEAR IN MIND that these prices are too low to include any cooking utensils or stove pipe. If you desire any stove furniture it must be shipped direct from our stock in Chicago, while these ranges are sent from our foundry in Newark, Ohio. This makes two shipments, one from our foundry and one from our store. For this reason we especially urge you to make your order for cooking utensils large enough to be profitable to you, remembering that 50 to 100 pounds will, as a rule, go by freight from Chicago, for as low a freight charge as 10 pounds.

$15.45 TO $19.26

OUR ACME REDWOOD, HIGH CLOSET RANGE AT $15.45 TO $19.26.

FOR WOOD ONLY; delivered on the cars at our foundry in Newark, Ohio. We offer this as the **highest grade Wood Burning Range we make.** The finest range on the market. This is the very highest grade cast iron range we have. Further on we list the same style as a coal burner, also complete with reservoir. This range contains every improvement known to high class stove making, guaranteed the very latest for 1905. The handsome pattern is the finest production shown this season. The castings in these ranges are extra heavy, making them very durable. There is practically no wear out to them. The manufacturers' several patent features insure for them economy, durability and general satisfaction not to be found in cheaper goods. This range is furnished with the high warming closet as shown in illustration; it is beautifully ornamented throughout; it has wide, heavy, highly polished nickeled steel bands on top shelf, around the top and on hearth plate. Beautifully nickel plated oven shelf and highly ornamented shields, frames, trimmings, etc. This is the exact same range as No. 22C220, quoted below at $12.24 and upward, with the addition of the high closet.

See page 14 for our liberal $1.00 to $5.00 C. O. D. subject to examination offer.

Furnished in all the different sizes listed, at the prices quoted. Delivered on the cars at our Newark, Ohio, foundry. Prices do not include pipe or cooking utensils; see index on pink pages. **Oven measurements do not include swell of oven door. We can also furnish repairs for Acmes; see page 19 for stove repairs.**

Catalogue Number	Size	Size of Lids	Size of Oven	Size of Top, not Measuring End Shelf	Size of End Shelf	Size of Fire Box	Size of Pipe to Fit Collar	Height to Main Top	Weight	Price
22C208	7-18	No. 7	17½x16½x11½	31x25	8x25	22x 9x 9	7 inch	28 inches	375 lbs.	$15.45
22C209	8-18	No. 8	17½x16½x11½	31x25	8x25	22x 9x 9	7 inch	28 inches	375 lbs.	15.50
22C210	7-20	No. 7	19½x18 x12	33x27	9x27	24x10x10	7 inch	30 inches	395 lbs.	17.04
22C211	8-20	No. 8	19½x18 x12	33x27	9x27	24x10x10	7 inch	30 inches	395 lbs.	17.09
22C212	8-22	No. 8	21½x20 x12½	34x28	9x28	26x10x10	7 inch	31 inches	435 lbs.	19.21
22C213	9-22	No. 9	21½x20 x12½	34x28	9x28	26x10x10	7 inch	31 inches	435 lbs.	19.26

OUR HIGH SHELF ACME REDWOOD RANGE, AT $14.13 TO $17.95.

FOR WOOD ONLY.

ACCORDING TO SIZE. Delivered on the cars at our foundry in Newark, Ohio. For wood only. We offer this, our **High Shelf Acme Redwood Range,** in competition with the very best ranges on the market, even at double the price. This is the exact same range as No. 22C220 quoted below at $12.24 and upward, with the addition of the high shelf. **It has the same beautiful ornamentations,** the same heavy highly polished nickeled steel bands around the top shelf, the main top, and the hearth plate. The same nickel plated mountings, trimmings, decorations, etc. The same fancy rococo pattern of design, large square oven door, large square oven, manufacturers' several patent features which insures it to be the most economical range in the consumption of fuel, the most perfect baker made. This range is for wood only, and to those who burn wood we would recommend this exclusive wood burner in preference to a combination wood and coal stove.

We furnish this range at the special prices named, and in the various sizes quoted. Delivered on the cars at our Newark, Ohio, foundry. Prices do not include pipe or cooking utensils. See index on pink pages. Oven measurements do not include swell of oven door. **We can always furnish repairs for Acmes. See page 19 about stove repairs.**

Catalogue Number	Size	Size of Lids	Size of Oven	Sizes of Top, not Measuring End Shelf	Size of End Shelf	Size of Fire Box	Size of Pipe to Fit Collar	Height to Main Top	Weight	Price
22C214	7-18	No. 7	17½x16½x11½	31x25	8x25	22x 9x 9	7 inch	28 inches	338 lbs.	$14.13
22C215	8-18	No. 8	17½x16½x11½	31x25	8x25	22x 9x 9	7 inch	28 inches	338 lbs.	14.18
22C216	7-20	No. 7	19½x18 x12	33x27	9x27	24x10x10	7 inch	30 inches	358 lbs.	15.77
22C217	8-20	No. 8	19½x18 x12	33x27	9x27	24x10x10	7 inch	30 inches	358 lbs.	15.82
22C218	8-22	No. 8	21½x20 x12½	34x28	9x28	26x10x10	7 inch	31 inches	398 lbs.	17.90
22C219	9-22	No. 9	21½x20 x12½	34x28	9x28	26x10x10	7 inch	31 inches	398 lbs.	17.95

OUR ACME REDWOOD RANGES, FOR WOOD ONLY, WITHOUT RESERVOIR.

AT $12.24 TO $16.04, according to size, for wood only, delivered on the cars at our foundry in Newark, Ohio, we offer our **Acme Redwood Range, the finest thing on the market,** regardless of price. Ranges are becoming more popular everywhere. They are more compact and in many ways more convenient, occupying less space. Our Acme Redwood Range is made with the latest and handsomest rococo pattern, as illustrated, with large square oven, with all the **latest and best improvements** known to stove making, including the very large square oven door and the large square oven. Has a handsomely ornamented tea shelf with fancy nickel plated tea pot holders, beautifully ornamented. Very highly nickeled steel bands on edges of main top and hearth, nickel plated oven shelf, door panels, door plates, hinge pin mountings, etc. **We offer this as the most economical cast iron range made** for the consumption of fuel, best baker, the most durable and highest grade range on the market, regardless of price. **The illustration does not do the range justice.** It is furnished with a heavy wide nickel band around the top and around the hearth. As fine a finished range as you will find and equal to any range made.

ABOUT THE FREIGHT. Freight amounts to nothing as compared to what you will save ir price. You will observe the stove weighs 300 to 360 pounds, according to size, and, for example stove freight rate to New Hampshire points, 800 miles, is 55 cents per hundred, or $1.43 to $1.98 for this big stove; other distances about in proportion. Don't let the question of freight deter you in sending in your order.

FOR WOOD ONLY.

This is our Wood Burning Acme Redwood Range. It is expressly for wood, having a very large fir box and taking a long stick of wood. For those who use wood only for fuel it will give much better satisfa tion than a combination range for coal and wood.

OUR RANGES are offered as the best money can buy and at prices based on the actual cost of ma rial and labor, with but our one small percentage of profit added.

Prices do not include pipe or cooking utensils. See index on pink pages. We furnish this range in any of the sizes listed at the prices quoted. Delivered on the cars at our Central Ohio foundry. Our measurements do not include swell of oven door. **See page 14 for our liberal $1.00 to $5.00 C. O. D. subject to examination offer.** We can always furnish repairs for Acmes. See page 19 about stove repairs.

Catalogue Number	Size	Size of Lids	Size of Oven	Size of Top Not Measuring End Shelf	Sizes of End Shelf	Size of Fire Box	Size Pipe to Fit Collar	Height to Main Top	Weight	Price
22C220	7-18	No. 7	17½x16½x11½	31x25	8x25	22x 9x 9	7 inch	28 inches	300 lbs.	$12.2[illegible]
22C221	8-18	No. 8	17½x16½x11½	31x25	8x25	22x 9x 9	7 inch	28 inches	300 lbs.	12.2[illegible]
22C222	7-20	No. 7	19½x18 x12	33x27	9x27	24x10x10	7 inch	30 inches	320 lbs.	13.8[illegible]
22C223	8-20	No. 8	19½x18 x12	33x27	9x27	24x10x10	7 inch	30 inches	320 lbs.	13.83
22C224	8-22	No. 8	21½x20 x12½	34x28	9x28	26x10x10	7 inch	31 inches	360 lbs.	15.9[illegible]
22C225	9-22	No. 9	21½x20 x12½	34x28	9x28	26x10x10	7 inch	31 inches	360 lbs.	16[illegible]

ACME EMPRESS FOUR HOLE RANGE

With large Porcelain Lined Reservoir and High Shelf. For Wood Only.

$13.03 TO $15.20

AT $13.03 TO $15.20 ACCORDING TO SIZE, DELIVERED ON CARS AT OUR FOUNDRY IN NEWARK, OHIO, and with porcelain lined reservoir as listed below, we offer this new and elegant design ACME EMPRESS for 1905. It is positively the most wonderful value in a new model, high grade range ever offered by any stovemaker. **OUR BINDING GUARANTEE SECURES YOU AS TO QUALITY AND PRICE.** It's something hitherto unheard of.

OUR $13.03 TO $15.20 PRICES are based on the actual cost of material and labor with but our one small profit added.

THE ACME EMPRESS IS FOR WOOD ONLY, contains all the desirable features found in any modern wood burning range. It has a large fire box with heavy linings, extra heavy fire back, outside oven shelf, oven door kicker, extra heavy covers, heavy centers, nickel plated panel on oven door, large handsome new pattern ornamental base, heavy tin lined oven door. It has handsome nickel plated tea shelves, as illustrated; nickel plated knobs and trimmings; **a strictly high grade, up to date, guaranteed range AT AN EXTREMELY LOW PRICE.**

WE CAN ALWAYS FURNISH REPAIRS FOR ACMES. See page 19 about how to order stove repairs when needed in future years.

REMEMBER, if you require any cooking utensils or stove pipe, they go direct from our store in Chicago, making two shipments; so make your order for stove furniture large enough to be a profitable shipment for you. **Bear in mind that 50 to 100 pounds will, as a rule, go by freight from Chicago at as low freight charges as 10 pounds. See page 14 for our liberal $1.00 to $5.00 C. O. D. subject to examination offer. Prices do not include pipe or cooking utensils. See index on pink pages.**

PRICES, ACME EMPRESS WITH RESERVOIR AND HIGH SHELF.

Catalogue Number	Range Number	Size of Lids	Size of Oven, Inches	Size of Top, including Reservoir	Height of Cooking Top, Inches	Size Pipe to Fit Collar, Inches	Size of Fire Box for Wood, Inches	Shipping Weight	Price
22C226	8-18	No. 8	18x18x12	38 x26	31	7	20	380	$13.03
22C227	8-20	No. 8	20x20x12½	39½x27	31½	7	21½	430	15.15
22C228	9-20	No. 9	20x20x12½	40½x27	31½	7	21½	430	15.20

If Desired without High Shelf, Deduct $1.00.

OUR ACME EMPRESS FOUR HOLE RANGE

Without Reservoir and With High Shelf.

FOR WOOD ONLY.

OUR BINDING GUARANTEE SECURES YOU AS TO QUALITY AND PRICE. IT'S SOMETHING HITHERTO UNHEARD OF.

$9.99 TO $12.15

AT $9.99 TO $12.15 according to size, as listed below, delivered on cars at our foundry in Newark, Ohio, we offer this new and elegant design **ACME EMPRESS** for 1905, as the most wonderful value in a new model, high grade range ever offered by any stovemaker.

WE HAVE EXPENDED A LARGE SUM OF MONEY to create this new model, and while we offer a heavier, handsomer and better range in our ACME EMPRESS than we were able to offer last year, the prices are lower than ever before heard of.

OUR $9.99 TO $12.15 PRICES are based on the actual cost of material and labor with but our one small profit added.

THE ACME EMPRESS IS FOR WOOD ONLY, contains all the desirable features found in any modern wood burning range. It has a large fire box with heavy linings, extra heavy fire back, outside oven shelf, oven door kicker, extra heavy covers, heavy centers, nickel plated panel on oven door, large handsome new pattern ornamental base, heavy tin lined oven door. It has handsome nickel plated tea shelves, as illustrated; nickel plated knobs and trimmings; **a strictly high grade, up to date, guaranteed range AT AN EXTREMELY LOW PRICE. See page 14 for our liberal $1.00 to $5.00 C. O. D. subject to examination offer. Prices do not include pipe or cooking utensils. See index on pink pages.**

PRICES, ACME EMPRESS WITHOUT RESERVOIR, WITH HIGH SHELF.

Catalogue Number	Range Number	Size of Lids	Size of Oven, Inches	Top, not including End Shelf	End Shelf	Height of Cooking Top, Inches	Size Pipe to Fit Collar, Inches	Size of Fire Box for Wood, Inches	Shipping Weight	Price
22C229	8-18	No. 8	18x18x12	29x26	8x26	31	7	20	323	$ 9.99
22C230	8-20	No. 8	20x20x12½	30x27	8x27	31½	7	21½	356	12.10
22C231	9-20	No. 9	20x20x12½	30x27	8x27	31½	7	21½	356	12.15

If Desired without High Shelf, Deduct $1.00.

WITH PORCELAIN LINED RESERVOIR.

OUR ACME IMPERIAL COAL COOK STOVE.

Prices do not include pipe or cooking utensils. See index on pink pages.

AT $12.64 TO $16.45 delivered on the cars at our foundry in Newark, Ohio. This stove is designed for hard coal, soft coal, wood or anything that can be burned in a stove. With every stove we furnish an extra grate, so it can be quickly changed from a coal burner to a wood burner.

THIS IS THE EXACT SAME STOVE as illustrated below under No. 22C245 at $11.06, with the addition of the large porcelain lined reservoir. Oven measurements do not include swell of oven door.

See page 14 for our liberal $1.00 to $5.00 C. O. D. subject to examination offer.

If you do not use coal at all, order the wood burning Pioneer, from catalogue Nos. 22C309 to 22C315.

Price list Acme Imperial Coal Cook Stove with reservoir, delivered on the cars at our Newark, Ohio, foundry.

Catalogue Number	Stove No.	Size of Lids	Size of Oven, inches	Top including Reservoir	Fire Box for Wood	Pipe to fit Collar	Height	Weight, pounds	Price
22C238	7-18	No. 7	17½x14½x11½	22x42	17x8x8	7	28	350	$12.64
22C239	8-18	No. 8	17½x14½x11½	22x42	17x8x8	7	28	350	12.69
22C240	7-20	No. 7	19½x16½x12	23x45	19x9x9	7	30	395	14.24
22C241	8-20	No. 8	19½x16½x12	23x45	19x9x9	7	30	395	14.29
22C242	9-20	No. 9	19½x16½x12	23x45	19x9x9	7	30	396	14.33
22C243	8-22	No. 8	21½x18½x12½	25x46	21x9x9	7	31	443	16.40
22C244	9-22	No. 9	21½x18½x12½	25x46	21x9x9	7	31	445	16.45

OUR ACME IMPERIAL COAL COOK STOVE WITHOUT RESERVOIR.

AT $11.06 TO $14.88 delivered on the cars at our foundry in Newark, Ohio. With every stove we furnish an extra grate, so it can be readily changed from coal to a wood stove.

BY CAREFUL COMPARISON of our prices with those at which the same class of goods are being offered by the best makers in the country, we are confident we are furnishing you a stove at several dollars less than anybody can buy like goods at wholesale in carload lots. Prices do not include pipe or cooking utensils. See index on pink pages. **See page 14 for our liberal $1.00 to $5.00 C. O. D. subject to examination offer.**

THIS IS THE EXACT SAME STOVE as the wood burning Acme Pioneer, illustrated and described on the following pages as Nos. 22C316 to 22C322, with the exception that it is made for burning all kinds of fuel. It has the same handsome rococo pattern, same large square oven door, same large oven, highly nickel plated trimmings throughout, beautifully ornamented and decorated, has large end shelf, large nickel plated oven shelf, large nickel plated panel on oven door, handsome nickel name plate, most expensive nickel "Alaska always cold door knobs" throughout. For an all coal stove, for a combination stove for all kinds of fuel, this is the best cook stove on the market regardless of price.

Price list Acme Imperial Coal Cook Stove without reservoir, delivered on the cars at our Newark, Ohio, foundry.

Catalogue Number	Stove No.	Size of Lids	Size of Oven, inches	Top, not measuring End Shelf	Size of End Shelf	Fire Box for Wood	Pipe to fit Collar	Height	Weight, pounds	Price
22C245	7-18	No. 7	17½x14½x11½	22x31	8x22	17x8x8	7	28	305	$11.06
22C246	8-18	No. 8	17½x14½x11½	22x31	8x22	17x8x8	7	28	305	11.11
22C247	7-20	No. 7	19½x16½x12	23x33	9x23	19x9x9	7	30	333	12.66
22C248	8-20	No. 8	19½x16½x12	23x33	9x23	19x9x9	7	30	333	12.71
22C249	9-20	No. 9	19½x16½x12	23x33	9x23	19x9x9	7	30	335	12.76
22C250	8-22	No. 8	21½x18½x12½	25x35	9x25	21x9x9	7	31	374	14.83
22C251	9-22	No. 9	21½x18½x12½	25x35	9x25	21x9x9	7	31	375	14.88

$11.06 TO $14.88

This ACME IMPERIAL COOK STOVE is designed as a combination stove for hard coal, soft coal, coke, wood, or anything that can be burned in a stove. If you do not use coal at all, order the Wood Burning Acme Pioneer, from catalogue Nos. 22C316 to 22C322.

Our measurements do not include swell of oven door.

OUR $12.23 ACME PEERLESS COOK STOVE, WITH PORCELAIN LINED RESERVOIR.

At $12.23 to $14.39 delivered on the cars at our foundry in Newark, Ohio.

AT $12.23 TO $14.39 we offer our Acme Peerless, with porcelain lined reservoir, as one of the best cook stoves on the market, regardless of price, and equal to stoves that retail at $20.00 to $30.00. Freight will amount to next to nothing as compared to what you will save in price. The Acme reservoir stove weighs from 310 to 355 pounds. It goes as third class freight, and by referring to freight classification in this catalogue, you can tell within a few cents what the freight charges will be to your place or nearest station.

This new, greatly improved pattern for 1905, is offered as one of the highest grade guaranteed soft coal or wood cook stoves, at a price even lower than anybody can buy the same goods in carload lots.

For complete detail of the points of construction, see the description of No. 22C257, given below. This is the exact same stove with the reservoir added.

Each stove is furnished with a lid lifter and shaker and scraper for removing ashes under the oven. We give you net dimensions of the stove, and all space gained by swell in doors, etc., is free. **If you do not use coal at all, order the Acme Harvest from Catalogue Nos. 22C323 to 22C326.**

See page 14 for our liberal $1.00 to $5.00 C.O.D. subject to examination offer.

We furnish the Acme Peerless at $12.23 to $14.39, delivered on the cars at our Newark, Ohio, foundry. Prices do not include pipe or cooking utensils. See index on pink pages.

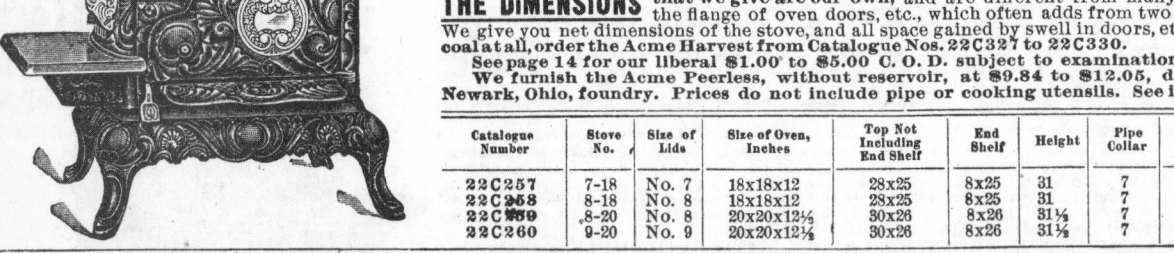

$12.23 to $14.39

Catalogue Number	Stove No.	Size of Lids	Size of Oven, Inches	Top Including Reservoir	Height	Pipe to fit Collar	Fire Box when used for Wood	Shipping Weight	Price
22C252	7-18	No. 7	18x18x12	38 x 25	31	7	20	369 lbs.	$12.23
22C253	8-18	No. 8	18x18x12	38 x 25	31	7	20	369 lbs.	12.29
22C254	8-20	No. 8	20x20x12⅓	39½ x 26	31½	7	21½	406 lbs.	14.34
22C255	9-20	No. 9	20x20x12⅓	40½ x 26	31½	7	21½	406 lbs.	14.39

We can always furnish repairs for Acmes. See page 19 about how to order stove repairs.

OUR $9.84 ACME PEERLESS COOK STOVE, WITHOUT RESERVOIR. FOR COAL OR WOOD.

THE ACME PEERLESS without reservoir is offered at $9.84 to $12.05, according to size, in competition with stoves that retail at nearly double the money. **This new 1905 pattern is a very large, heavy cook stove, well made and very artistically ornamented. It is especially recommended to those who wish to burn coal only, or coal** and wood at different times during the year. Simply changing the grates and taking out the end linings converts it from a coal to a wood burning stove, and we furnish with every stove an extra grate for this purpose.

THE ACME PEERLESS is made from very heavy castings, and we believe is one of the most durable stoves on the market, regardless of price. Has very large flues, cut top with heavy cut centers, supported by posts, heavy covers, heavy linings, with very heavy sectional fire back. Large bailed ash pan, slide hearth plate, outside oven shelf, oven door kicker, ornamented base, nickeled name plate on front door, nickel plated panels on oven door, nickel plated door knobs, tin lined oven door, swing feed. The opening for removing ashes from under the oven is in the hearth, consequently no ashes are spilled on the floor when cleaning stove.

THE DIMENSIONS that we give are our own, and are different from many manufacturers, who include the flange of oven doors, etc., which often adds from two to four inches to dimensions. We give you net dimensions of the stove, and all space gained by swell in doors, etc., is free. **If you do not use coal at all, order the Acme Harvest from Catalogue Nos. 22C327 to 22C330.**

See page 14 for our liberal $1.00 to $5.00 C. O. D. subject to examination offer.

We furnish the Acme Peerless, without reservoir, at $9.84 to $12.05, delivered on the cars at our Newark, Ohio, foundry. Prices do not include pipe or cooking utensils. See index on pink pages.

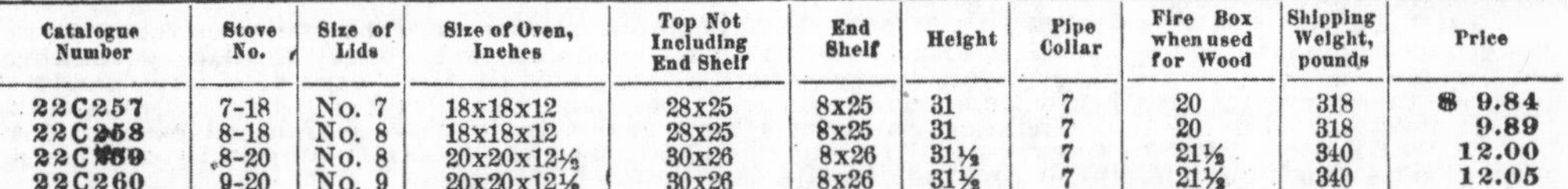

Catalogue Number	Stove No.	Size of Lids	Size of Oven, Inches	Top Not Including End Shelf	End Shelf	Height	Pipe Collar	Fire Box when used for Wood	Shipping Weight, pounds	Price
22C257	7-18	No. 7	18x18x12	28x25	8x25	31	7	20	318	$ 9.84
22C258	8-18	No. 8	18x18x12	28x25	8x25	31	7	20	318	9.89
22C259	8-20	No. 8	20x20x12⅓	30x26	8x26	31½	7	21½	340	12.00
22C260	9-20	No. 9	20x20x12⅓	30x26	8x26	31½	7	21½	340	12.05

OUR ACME DEFENDER COOK STOVE—With Reservoir.

AT $10.28 TO $13.48, delivered on the cars at our foundry in Newark, Ohio. **We offer the Acme Defender as an entirely new stove for 1905, made in our foundry from the best material that money can buy, by the most skilled mechanics that we can employ. Our prices are only the cost of the material and labor, with but our one small profit added.** The freight will amount to next to nothing as compared with what you will save in price. **The 8-18 stove weighs about 310 pounds crated ready for shipping, and the freight for 200 miles will be about 50 cents; 400 miles 75 cents; 600 miles, $1.00; 1,000 miles, $1.50.** Greater or lesser distances in proportion.

OUR BINDING GUARANTEE. **With every stove we issue a written binding guarantee,** by the terms and conditions of which, if any piece or part gives out by reason of defect in material or workmanship, we will replace it or repair it free of charge. **We guarantee safe delivery.** Every Acme Defender stove will be carefully crated, and we guarantee it to reach you in the same perfect condition it leaves us, and if upon arrival any piece or part is broken or missing, **we will replace the same free of any expense to you. We will always have a supply of parts. The Acme Defender burns hard coal, soft coal, coke, wood, or anything used for fuel.**

GENERAL DESCRIPTION. **The Acme Defender is made with very large flues,** cut tops, heavy cut centers supported by posts, heavy covers, heavy linings with heavy sectional fire back, large bailed ash pan, draw hearth, nickeled outside oven shelf, pouch feed, oven door kicker, nickel plated panel on oven door, nickel plated name plate on front door, nickel plated door knobs, heavy tin lined oven door. When ashes are removed from under the oven they are scraped into the hearth, avoiding all possibility of spilling the ashes on the floor when cleaning the stove. The Acme Defender is furnished with a lifter, shaker and scraper for removing the ashes from under the oven. **It is fitted with a large porcelain lined reservoir as shown in the illustration, and is furnished on a large, handsome rococo pattern base. If you do not burn coal at all, make your selection from the Acme Frontier, Catalogue Nos. 22C331 to 22C336. Prices do not include pipe or cooking utensils. See index on pink pages. Always state which fuel you wish to burn**

$10.28 to $13.48

SEE PAGE 14 FOR OUR LIBERAL $1.00 TO $5.00 C. O. D. SUBJECT TO EXAMINATION OFFER.

Price List Acme Defender Cook Stove, With Porcelain Lined Reservoir.
Delivered on the cars at our Newark, Ohio, Foundry.

Catalogue Number	Stove No.	Size of Lids	Size of Oven, Inches	Size of Top including Reservoir, Inches	Height, Inches	Pipe to fit Collar, Inches	Fire Box, when used for Wood, Inches	Shipping Weight, Pounds.	Price
22C261	7-16	No. 7	16x14 x10½	22x38	28½	6	18	250	$10.28
22C262	8-16	No. 8	16x14 x10½	22x38	28½	6	18	250	10.33
22C263	8-18	No. 8	18x16 x11	24x40	29	7	20	310	11.93
22C264	9-18	No. 9	18x16 x11	24x40	29	7	20	310	11 98
22C265	8-20	No. 8	20x18 x12	26x42	29½	7	22	382	13.43
22C266	9-20	No. 9	20x18 x12	26x42	29½	7	22	382	13.48

OUR ACME DEFENDER COOK STOVE—Without Reservoir.

FOR BURNING HARD COAL, SOFT COAL, COKE, WOOD, OR ANYTHING USED FOR FUEL.

DELIVERED ON THE CARS AT OUR FOUNDRY IN NEWARK, OHIO.

$7.56 to $10.75

Our Acme Defender is a coal burning **stove, but is suitable for hard coal, soft coal or wood.** We furnish with every stove an extra grate for wood, and you can use it for wood or for coal. It has very large flues, cut tops, heavy cut centers, supported by post, heavy covers, heavy lining with very heavy sectional fire back, large bailed ash pan, draw hearth, outside oven shelf, pouch feed, oven door kicker, nickel plated panels on oven door, nickel plated name plate on front door, tin lined oven door and handsome rococo leg base. **When ashes are removed from under oven they** are scraped into the hearth, thus avoiding the possibility of spilling the ashes on the floor when cleaning stove. Each stove is furnished with a lifter, shaker and scraper for removing ashes from under the oven

The Acme Defender will burn and bake as satisfactorily as the highest priced stove sold by us or any other house, and is equal in every way to any stove of equal weight and in workmanship is superior to many. **At $7.56 to $10.75 we furnish the Acme Defender in the various sizes as listed below.**

If you do not use coal at all, make your selection from the Acme Frontier, Catalogue Nos. 22C337 to 22C342. ALWAYS STATE WHICH FUEL YOU DESIRE TO USE. Prices do not include pipe or cooking utensils. See index on pink pages SEE PAGE 14 FOR OUR LIBERAL $1.00 TO $5.00 C. O. D. SUBJECT TO EXAMINATION OFFER.

PRICE LIST OF ACME DEFENDER COOK STOVE Without Reservoir.
Delivered on the cars at our Newark, Ohio, Foundry:

Catalogue Number	Stove No.	Size of Lids	Size of Oven, Inches	Top without End Shelf, Inches.	End Shelf, Inches	Height, Inches	Pipe Collar, Inches	Fire Box, when used for Wood, Inches	Shipping Weight, Pounds	Price
22C267	7-16	No. 7	16x14 x10½	22x28	8x22	28½	6	18	200	$7.56
22C268	8-16	No. 8	16x14 x10½	22x28	8x22	28½	6	18	200	7.6[illegible]
22C269	8-18	No. 8	18x16 x11	24x30	8x24	29	7	20	260	9.2[illegible]
22C270	9-18	No. 9	18x16 x11	24x30	8x24	29	7	20	260	9.2[illegible]
22C271	8-20	No. 8	20x18 x12	26x32	8x26	29½	7	22	303	10.7[illegible]
22C272	9-20	No. 9	20x18 x12	26x32	8x26	29½	7	22	303	10.7[illegible]

OUR ACME VALIANT COOK STOVE—With Reservoir.

FOR BURNING HARD COAL, SOFT COAL, COKE, WOOD, OR ANYTHING USED FOR FUEL.

$9.92 TO $13.10

AT $9.92 TO $13.10, delivered on cars at our foundry in Newark, Ohio. **This is the exact same stove as Acme Valiant,** illustrated below under No. 22C287, at **$7.37** to **$10.55**, with the addition of the large porcelain lined reservoir as shown in illustration.

One Acme Valiant sells another. If you order this stove from us, we know you will be so well pleased with the stove that you will show it to your friends, tell them where you got it, and what you paid for it, and the result will be, within a short time, there will be a dozen more Acme Valiants sold in your immediate neighborhood. Everyone who sees it is pleased with it, everyone marvels at the beauty of design, perfectness of construction, of durability, and, above all, **the heretofore unheard of figure of $9.92 to $13.10 price.**

If you do not use coal at all, make your selection from the Acme Homestead, Catalogue Nos. 22C343 to 22C348. Always state which fuel you desire to use. Prices do not include pipe or cooking utensils. See index on pink pages.

SEE PAGE 14 FOR OUR LIBERAL $1.00 TO $5.00 C. O. D. SUBJECT TO EXAMINATION OFFER.

Price List of ACME VALIANT COOK STOVE, With Porcelain Lined Reservoir.
Delivered on the cars at our Newark, Ohio, foundry.

Catalogue Number	Stove No.	Size of Lids	Size of Oven, Inches	Size of Top, including Reservoir, Inches	H'ght, Inches	Pipe to fit Collar, Inc's	Fire Box for Wood, Inches	Shipping Weight, Pounds	Price
22C281	7-16	No. 7	16x14x10½	22x38	28½	6	18	222	$9.92
22C282	8-16	No. 8	16x14x10½	22x38	28½	6	18	222	9.97
22C283	8-18	No. 8	18x16x11	24x40	29	7	20	282	11.56
22C284	9-18	No. 9	18x16x11	24x40	29	7	20	282	11.61
22C285	8-20	No. 8	20x18x12	26x42	29½	7	22	363	13.05
22C286	9-20	No. 9	20x18x12	26x42	29½	7	22	363	13.10

OUR ACME VALIANT COOK STOVE—Without Reservoir.

FOR BURNING HARD COAL, SOFT COAL, COKE, WOOD, OR ANYTHING USED FOR FUEL.

Our Acme Valiant is a coal burning stove, but is suitable for hard coal, soft coal or wood. **We furnish with every stove an extra grate for wood, and you can use it for wood or for coal.**

It has **very large flues,** cut tops, heavy cut centers supported by posts, **heavy covers,** heavy linings with very heavy sectional fire back, large bailed ash pan, draw hearth, outside oven shelf, pouch feed, oven door kicker and tin lined oven doors.

When ashes are removed from under oven they are scraped into the hearth, avoiding all possibility of spilling the ashes on the floor when cleaning stove.

Each stove is furnished with a lifter, shaker and scraper for removing the ashes from under the oven.

The Acme Valiant will burn and bake as satisfactorily as the highest priced stove sold by us or any other house, and is equal in every way to any stove of equal weight and in workmanship is superior to many.

At $7.37 to $10.55 we furnish the Acme Valiant in the various sizes as listed below. **If you do not use coal at all make your selection from the Acme Homestead, Catalogue Nos. 22C349 to 22C354. Always state which fuel you desire to use. Prices do not include pipe or cooking utensils. See index on pink pages.**

WE CAN ALWAYS FURNISH REPAIRS FOR ACMES.
SEE PAGE 19 ABOUT HOW TO ORDER STOVE REPAIRS.

$7.37 TO $10.55

SEE PAGE 14 FOR OUR LIBERAL $1.00 TO $5.00 C. O. D. SUBJECT TO EXAMINATION OFFER.

PRICE LIST OF ACME VALIANT COOK STOVE, Without Reservoir.
Delivered on the cars at our Newark, Ohio, foundry.

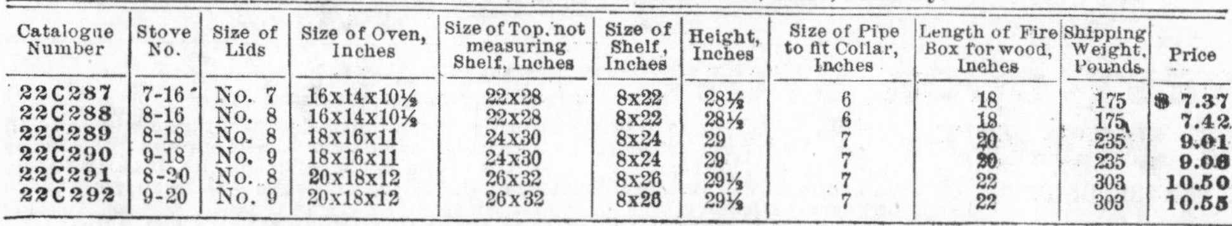

Catalogue Number	Stove No.	Size of Lids	Size of Oven, Inches	Size of Top, not measuring Shelf, Inches	Size of Shelf, Inches	Height, Inches	Size of Pipe to fit Collar, Inches	Length of Fire Box for wood, Inches	Shipping Weight, Pounds	Price
22C287	7-16	No. 7	16x14x10½	22x28	8x22	28½	6	18	175	$ 7.37
22C288	8-16	No. 8	16x14x10½	22x28	8x22	28½	6	18	175	7.42
22C289	8-18	No. 8	18x16x11	24x30	8x24	29	7	20	235	9.01
22C290	9-18	No. 9	18x16x11	24x30	8x24	29	7	20	235	9.06
22C291	8-20	No. 8	20x18x12	26x32	8x26	29½	7	22	303	10.50
22C292	9-20	No. 9	20x18x12	26x32	8x26	29½	7	22	303	10.55

OUR ACME FOREST COOK STOVE, —WITH— RESERVOIR, $16.48 AND $17.01.

FOR BURNING WOOD ONLY. Delivered on the cars at our foundry in Newark, Ohio. We furnish in this a stove weighing nearly 500 pounds, **one of the largest reservoir wood burning stoves on the market,** a stove which takes in a stick of wood 27 inches long; a stove with an oven 22x20x14 inches in size, not including the swell in oven door, and all **at less than 3¼ cents per pound.**

3¼ CENTS PER POUND means we get pay for the net cost of the **raw material and the labor,** and have for ourselves but one small percentage of profit. For a big, economical wood burning cook stove, one that is equal to any cast iron stove on the market, we **recommend the Acme Forest Reservoir Cook, and guarantee a saving to you in price of $10.00 to $15.00.**

THIS OUR ACME FOREST wood burning, **reservoir stove,** is the exact style stove as the one illustrated and listed under No. 22C307 at $12.35, with the addition of the reservoir.

IT IS A STRICTLY HIGH GRADE STOVE. Made by one of the best makers in this country, and equal to any similar stove on the market, regardless of price. Consider our very largest No. 8 Reservoir Wood Burning Stove for $16.48. Look at the size of our $17.01 No. 9 Reservoir Wood Stove. Such a big stove was never before offered for so little money. Delivered on board cars at our Newark, Ohio, Foundry. See page 14 for liberal $1.00 to $5.00 C. O. D. subject to examination offer. Prices do not include pipe or cooking utensils. See index on pink pages.

PRICES OF THE ACME FOREST COOK STOVE, WITH PORCELAIN LINED RESERVOIR.

Catalogue Number	Stove Number	Size of Lids	Size of Oven, Inches	Top, including Reservoir	Pipe to Fit Collar, Inches	Length of Fire Box, Inches	Height	Weight	Price
22C305	8-22	No. 8	22x20x14	28x42	7	27	31½	460	$16.48
22C306	9-22	No. 9	22x20x14	28x42	7	27	31½	460	17.01

REMEMBER **that we do not include the flare of oven door in giving measurements of oven, as is customary with stove dealers. Including flare of oven door, the size of oven in above stove is 23x22x14 inches.**

OUR ACME FOREST WOOD BURNING COOK STOVE AT $12.35 AND $12.88.

THIS STOVE IS MADE FROM SPECIAL PATTERNS, extra long fire box, and a very large oven, giving you an extra heavy, handsome and durable stove.

THE IMMENSE POPULARITY of these high grade cook stoves causes our foundry to work night and day in busy seasons to keep up with our orders. **Dealers will ask 50 per cent more than our direct from foundry price. Delivered on the cars at our foundry in Newark, Ohio.**

OUR ACME FOREST COOK STOVE, WITHOUT RESERVOIR, **for burning wood only. Takes wood 27 inches long. This extra large square wood burning stove, greatly improved for 1905, is offered at $12.35 and $12.88 as the greatest value ever shown in an extra large square wood burner.**

OUR ACME FOREST is such a stove as is seldom found in retail stores. It has a very large oven, very high oven, very large fire box, cut main top, cut long center, lined short center, heavy covers, tin lined oven door, wide top shelf, outside oven door shelf, large nickel plated panel on oven doors, nickeled name plate on front door, nickel plated towel rod, nickeled knobs and hinge pins. **If you live in a timber country and burn wood,** and want a large, substantial, yet economical stove, a stove that will last for 20 years, one that is covered by a binding guarantee, we would recommend the **Acme Forest Cook Stove** as the greatest value ever offered. **We furnish the Acme Forest at $12.35 and $12.88 as listed. Delivered on the cars at our foundry in Newark, Ohio. See page 14 for liberal $1.00 to $5.00 C. O. D. subject to examination offer. Prices do not include pipe or cooking utensils. See index on pink pages.**

PRICES OF THE ACME FOREST COOK STOVE, WITHOUT RESERVOIR.

Catalogue Number	Stove Number	Size of Lids	Size of Oven Inches	Top, not including Shelf	Size of Shelf Inches	Pipe to Fit Collar, Inches	Length of Fire Box, Inches	Height	Weight	Price
22C307	8-22	No. 8	22x20x14	28x32	7¼x28	7	27	31½	368	$12.35
22C308	9-22	No. 9	22x20x14	28x32	7¼x28	7	27	31½	368	12.88

OUR ACME PIONEER RESERVOIR COOK STOVE. FOR WOOD ONLY.

AT $11.65 TO $15.52 delivered on the cars at our Newark, Ohio, foundry, we offer our **Acme Pioneer Reservoir Cook Stove.** The exact same stove as No. 22C316, quoted below at $9.99, with the addition of the **heavy porcelain lined reservoir.** Has the same handsome nickel trimmings throughout; the same ornamentations and decorations, the same new 1905 rococo design, up to date in every respect, and covered by a **binding guarantee.** From the illustration you will see this stove is made with the flush top reservoir, **the very latest pattern.**

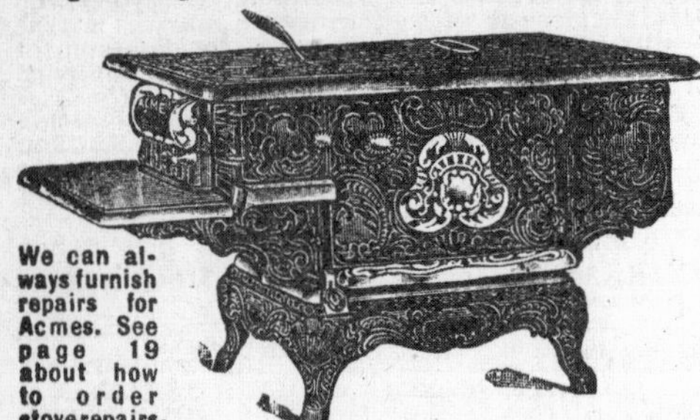

We can always furnish repairs for Acmes. See page 19 about how to order stove repairs.

OUR MEASUREMENTS DO NOT INCLUDE SWELL OF OVEN DOOR.

SEE PAGE 14 FOR LIBERAL $1.00 TO $5.00 C. O. D. SUBJECT TO EXAMINATION OFFER.

PRICES DO NOT INCLUDE PIPE OR COOKING UTENSILS. SEE INDEX ON PINK PAGES.

Prices, delivered on the cars at our foundry in Newark, Ohio.

Catalogue Number	Stove No.	Size of Lids	Size of Oven, inches	Size of Top, Measuring Reservoir	Size of Fire Box	Size of Pipe to Fit Collar	Height to Main Top	Shipping Weight, Pounds	Price
22C309	7-18	No. 7	17½x14½ x 11½	22 x 42	22x9x9	7	28	320	$11.65
22C310	8-18	No. 8	17½x14½ x 11½	22 x 42	22x9x9	7	28	320	11.70
22C311	7-20	No. 7	19½x16½ x 12	23 x 45	24x10x10	7	30	355	13.29
22C312	8-20	No. 8	19½x16½ x 12	23 x 45	24x10x10	7	30	355	13.35
22C313	9-20	No. 9	19½x16½ x 12	23 x 45	24x10x10	7	30	355	13.40
22C314	8-22	No. 8	21½x18½ x 12½	25 x 46	26x10x10	7	31	405	15.46
22C315	9-22	No. 9	21½x18½ x 12½	25 x 46	26x10x10	7	31	405	15.52

OUR ACME PIONEER WOOD COOK STOVE.

AT $9.99 TO $13.78 delivered on the cars at our Newark, Ohio, foundry, we offer our NEW 1905 MODEL, large, square oven, Rococo Acme Pioneer Cook Stove, as the handsomest, best made, highest grade stove on the market, at a price based on much closer calculation than a similar stove has ever been offered before or sold at. **This Acme Pioneer possesses the high qualities of every strictly high grade stove on the market, all the latest 1905 improvements,** everything the very best.

THIS ACME PIONEER COOK STOVE IS FOR BURNING WOOD ONLY.

THE TRIMMINGS on the Acme Pioneer are equal to anything made. It is handsomely ornamented, has fine. large nickel plated outside oven shelf, with kicker, ventilated oven door, large nickel panel on oven door, large nickel name plate on front door, nickel towel rod, teapot holder and lifter, the most expensive Alaska nickel always cold door knobs throughout. Fancy nickel plated hinge pins, vertical damper, large ash receptacle. Full ornamental base, extra heavy fire back, full cut tops and center, **the very best of trimmings throughout.**

OUR MEASUREMENTS DO NOT INCLUDE SWELL OF OVEN DOOR.

SEE PAGE 14 FOR LIBERAL $1.00 TO $5.00 C. O. D. SUBJECT TO EXAMINATION OFFER.

PRICES DO NOT INCLUDE PIPE OR COOKING UTENSILS. SEE INDEX ON PINK PAGES.

Prices, delivered on the cars at our Newark, Ohio, foundry.

Catalogue Number	Stove No.	Size of Lids	Size of Oven, inches	Size of Top, Not Measuring End Shelf	Size of End Shelf	Size of Fire Box	Size of Pipe to Fit Collar	Height to Main Top	Shipping Weight, Pounds	Price
22C316	7-18	No. 7	17½x14½x11½	22x31	8x22	22x9x9	7	28	275	$ 9.99
22C317	8-18	No. 8	17½x14½x11½	22x31	8x22	22x9x9	7	28	275	10.05
22C318	7-20	No. 7	19½x16½x12	23x33	9x23	24x10x10	7	30	300	11.59
22C319	8-20	No. 8	19½x16½x12	23x33	9x23	24x10x10	7	30	300	11.64
22C320	9-20	No. 9	19½x16½x12	23x33	9x23	24x10x10	7	30	300	11.69
22C321	8-22	No. 8	21½x18½x12½	25x35	9x25	26x10x10	7	31	335	13.73
22C322	9-22	No. 9	21½x18½x12½	25x35	9x25	26x10x10	7	31	335	13.78

FOR WOOD ONLY.

ACME HARVEST COOK STOVE. FOR WOOD ONLY.

WITH LARGE PORCELAIN LINED RESERVOIR AT..... ***$11.47 to $13.67***

DELIVERED ON CARS AT OUR FOUNDRY IN NEWARK, OHIO.

AT $11.47 TO $13.67 WE OFFER OUR ACME HARVEST WITH PORCELAIN LINED RESERVOIR, as one of the best cook stoves on the market, regardless of price, and equal to stoves that retail at $20.00 to $30.00. **You will save $10.00 to $15.00 by ordering this stove from us.**

Freight will amount to next to nothing as compared to what you will save in price. This Acme reservoir stove weighs from 361 to 386 pounds. It goes as third class freight and by referring to freight classification in this catalogue, you can tell within a few cents what the freight charges will be to your place or nearest station.

THE ACME HARVEST WITH RESERVOIR, IS OFFERED AT $11.47 TO $13.67, according to size, in competition with stoves that retail at nearly double the money. The new 1905 pattern is a very large, heavy cook stove, well made and very artistically ornamented. **It is especially recommended to those who wish to burn wood only.**

THE ACME HARVEST IS MADE FROM VERY HEAVY CASTINGS and we believe is one of the most durable stoves on the market, regardless of price. Has very large flues, cut top with heavy cut centers supported by post, heavy covers, heavy linings, with very heavy fire back. Large bailed ash pan, slide hearth plate, outside oven shelf, oven door kicker, ornamented base, nickeled name plate on front door, nickel plated panel on oven door, nickel plated door knobs, tin lined oven door. The opening for removing ashes from under the oven is in the hearth, consequently no ashes are spilled on the floor when cleaning stove. Each stove is furnished with a lid lifter and shaker, and scraper for removing ashes from under the oven.

SEE PAGE 14 FOR OUR LIBERAL $1.00 TO $5.00 C. O. D. SUBJECT TO EXAMINATION OFFER. PRICES DO NOT INCLUDE PIPE OR COOKING UTENSILS. SEE INDEX ON PINK PAGES.

PRICES, ACME HARVEST WITH RESERVOIR.

Catalogue Number	Stove No.	Size of Lids	Size of Oven, Inches	Top, including Reservoir	Height, Inches	Size Pipe to fit Collar, Inches	Length of Fire Box for Wood, Inches	Shipping Weight, Pounds	Price
22C323	7-18	No. 7	18 x 18 x 12	38 x 25	31	7	20	361	$11.47
22C324	8-18	No. 8	18 x 18 x 12	38 x 25	31	7	20	361	11.52
22C325	8-20	No. 8	20 x 20 x 12½	39½ x 26	31½	7	21½	386	13.62
22C326	9-20	No. 9	20 x 20 x 12½	40½ x 26	31½	7	21½	386	13.67

OUR NEW PATTERN 1905 ACME HARVEST COOK STOVE.

WITHOUT RESERVOIR AT..... ***$7.79 to $10.06***

DELIVERED ON CARS AT OUR FOUNDRY IN NEWARK, OHIO.

FOR WOOD ONLY.

It is especially recommended to those who wish to burn wood only.

AT $7.79 TO $10.06 WE OFFER OUR ACME HARVEST WITHOUT RESERVOIR, in competition with stoves that retail at nearly double the money. **You will save $10.00 to $15.00 by ordering this stove from us.** Freight will amount to next to nothing as compared to what you will save in price. This Acme Harvest stove without reservoir weighs from 286 to 315 pounds. It goes as third class freight, and by referring to freight classification in this catalogue, you can tell within a few cents what the freight charges will be to your place or nearest station.

THE ACME HARVEST IS MADE FROM VERY HEAVY CASTINGS and we believe is one of the most durable stoves on the market, regardless of price. Has very large flues, cut top with heavy cut centers supported by post, heavy covers, heavy linings, with very heavy fire back. Large bailed ash pan, full draw hearth, outside oven shelf, oven door kicker, ornamented base, nickeled name plate on front door, nickel plated panel on oven door, nickel plated door knobs, tin lined oven door and extension end shelf, as shown. The opening for removing ashes from under the oven is in the hearth, consequently no ashes are spilled on the floor when cleaning stove. Each stove is furnished with a lid lifter and shaker, and scraper for removing ashes from under the oven.

SEE PAGE 14 FOR OUR LIBERAL $1.00 TO $5.00 C. O. D. SUBJECT TO EXAMINATION OFFER. PRICES DO NOT INCLUDE PIPE OR COOKING UTENSILS. SEE INDEX ON PINK PAGES.

PRICES, ACME HARVEST WITHOUT RESERVOIR.

Catalogue Number	Stove Number	Size of Lids	Size of Oven, inches	Top, not including End Shelf	End Shelf	Height, Inches	Size Pipe to fit Collar, Inches	Length of Fire Box for Wood, Inches	Shipping Weight, Pounds	Price
22C327	7-18	No. 7	18 x 18 x 12	28 x 25	8x25	31	7	20	286	$ 7.79
22C328	8-18	No. 8	18 x 18 x 12	28 x 25	8x25	31	7	20	286	7.84
22C329	8-20	No. 8	20 x 20 x 12½	30 x 26	8x26	31½	7	21½	355	10.01
22C330	9-20	No. 9	20 x 20 x 12½	30 x 26	8x26	31½	7	21½	315	10.06

Our Acme Frontier Cook Stove,

WITH RESERVOIR. FOR BURNING WOOD ONLY.

$9.96 to $13.16

SEE PAGE 14 FOR OUR LIBERAL $1.00 TO $5.00 C. O. D. SUBJECT TO EXAMINATION OFFER.

At $9.96 to $13.16, according to size, delivered on the cars at our foundry in Newark, Ohio, we offer this new 1905 reservoir wood burning stove in competition with stoves that will retail at $18.00 to $20.00 and upward. This is the exact same stove as our No. 22C337 at $7.53 and upward, with addition of large porcelain lined reservoir, as illustrated. **$9.96** is a price based on the actual cost of material and labor, with but our one small percentage of profit added, and even then we are able to make this price only by reason of manufacturing them in immense numbers. Our sales in the Acme Frontier have been so large that we have been able to duplicate the moulds and enlarge our foundry and thereby reduce the cost of labor, and our customers are given the benefit of this reduction in the greatly improved stove for 1905 at **$9.96 to $13.16.**

Prices do not include pipe or cooking utensils. See index on pink pages.

Delivered on the cars at our Newark, Ohio, foundry.

PRICE LIST ACME FRONTIER COOK STOVE WITH PORCELAIN LINED RESERVOIR.

Catalogue Number	Stove Number	Size of Lids	Size of Oven, inches	Size of Top Including Reservoir, inches	Size of Pipe to Fit Collar	Height, inches	Length of Fire Box, inches	Shipping Weight, pounds	Price
22C331	7-16	No. 7	16x14x10½	22x38	6	28½	22	213	$ 9.96
22C332	8-16	No. 8	16x14x10½	22x38	6	28½	22	213	10.01
22C333	8-18	No. 8	18x16x11	24x40	7	29	24	273	11.61
22C334	9-18	No. 9	18x16x11	24x40	7	29	24	273	11.66
22C335	8-20	No. 8	20x18x12	26x42	7	29½	26	347	13.11
22C336	9-20	No. 9	20x18x12	26x42	7	29½	26	347	13.16

OUR ACME FRONTIER COOK STOVE, WITHOUT RESERVOIR.

FOR BURNING WOOD ONLY.

At $7.53 to $10.72, delivered on the cars at our foundry in Newark, Ohio, we offer the Acme Frontier as the best wood burner on the market at anything like the price. The Acme Frontier is a handsome, reliable stove of artistic design and ornamentation. Workmanship is first class; it has handsomely ornamented base, as illustrated, nickeled outside oven shelf, back top shelf, cut long centers, cut maintop, tin lined oven door, oven door kicker, nickel plated towel rod, nickel plated tea shelf, nickel plated panel on oven doors.

Our Acme Frontier at $7.53 and upward for burning wood is made at our foundry in Ohio, one of the best stove foundries in this country. Stoves that would sell in a retail way at double our price. **This stove has been greatly improved over last year,** the patterns have been carefully gone over and we can therefore offer it as the very latest thing for 1905, **which we guarantee as to quality and guarantee that our price will mean a saving to you of nearly one-half.**

See page 14 for our Liberal $1.00 to $5.00 C. O. D. Subject to Examination Offer.

Prices do not include pipe or cooking utensils. See index on pink pages. Price list, delivered on the cars at our Newark, Ohio, foundry.

$7.53 to $10.72

We can always furnish repairs for Acmes. See page 19 about how to order stove repairs.

Catalogue Number	Stove Number	Size of Lids	Size of Oven, inches	Size of Top Not Including Shelf	Size of Shelf	Size Pipe to Fit Collar	Length of Fire Box	Height inches	Shipping Weight pounds	Price
22C337	7-16	No. 7	16x14x10½	22x28	8x22	6	22	28½	178	$7.53
22C338	8-16	No. 8	16x14x10½	22x28	8x22	6	22	28½	178	7.57
22C339	8-18	No. 8	18x16x11	24x30	8x24	7	24	29	238	9.17
22C340	9-18	No. 9	18x16x11	24x30	8x24	7	24	29	238	9.22
22C341	8-20	No. 8	20x18x12	26x32	8x26	7	26	29½	287	10.67
22C342	9-20	No. 9	20x18x12	26x32	8x26	7	26	29½	287	10.72

OUR ACME HOMESTEAD COOK STOVE, WITH PORCELAIN LINED RESERVOIR.

FOR BURNING WOOD ONLY.

$8.58 to $11.75

SEE PAGE 14 FOR OUR LIBERAL $1.00 TO $5.00 C. O. D. SUBJECT TO EXAMINATION OFFER.

For a low priced wood burning reservoir stove our Acme Homestead is without an equal. The Acme Homestead for 1905 has been greatly improved. The patterns have been refinished; it will be better made than ever before, and we guarantee it equal to stoves that will sell everywhere at 33⅓ to 50 per cent more money. We are able to make this extraordinary offer price of $8.58 only by reason of manufacturing these goods in large quantities, operating our own foundry, and shipping direct to you from Newark, Ohio, saving all the intermediate expenses. **We have advertised them very extensively in** many publications, and our sales have been so enormous that the cost of production has been materially reduced, and all this reduction in cost of labor, in cost of material, we give our customers the benefit of in our heretofore unheard of **$8.58 to $11.75 price.**

Prices do not include pipe or cooking utensils. See index on pink pages.

Price list, delivered on the cars at our Newark, Ohio, foundry.

Catalogue Number	Stove Number	Size of Lids	Size of Oven, inches	Size of Top, Including Reservoir	Height, inches	Size of Pipe to Fit Collar	Length of Fire Box, inches	Shipping Weight, pounds	Price
22C343	7-16	No. 7	16x14x10½	22x38	28½	6	22	170	$ 8.58
22C344	8-16	No. 8	16x14x10½	22x38	28½	6	22	170	8.63
22C345	8-18	No. 8	18x16x11	22x40	29	7	24	230	10.22
22C346	9-18	No. 9	18x16x11	22x40	29	7	24	230	10.27
22C347	8-20	No. 8	20x18x12	22x42	29½	7	26	327	11.70
22C348	9-20	No. 9	20x18x12	22x42	29½	7	26	327	11.75

OUR ACME HOMESTEAD COOK STOVE, WITHOUT RESERVOIR.

FOR BURNING WOOD ONLY.

This wood burning cook stove without reservoir, offered at $5.94 to $9.13, according to size, as listed, is the equal of stoves that retail generally at $10.00 to $17.00. In construction it is strictly first class, has outside oven shelf, heavy covers, kicker for opening oven door. Each stove is furnished with a lifter and rake for cleaning ashes from under the oven.

This stove is widely advertised at $5.94 to $9.13, and we furnish, just as we have advertised, the greatest value in cook stoves ever offered by us or any other house at anything like the price.

Prices do not include pipe or cooking utensils. See index on pink pages.

Price list, delivered on the cars at our foundry in Newark, Ohio.

Catalogue Number	Stove Number	Size of Lids	Size of Oven, inches	Top, not including End Shelf, Inches.	Size of Shelf.	Height, inches	Size of Pipe to Fit Collar, inches	Length of Fire Box, inches	Shipping Weight, pounds	Price
22C349	7-16	No. 7	16x14x10½	22x28	8x22	28½	6	22	155	$5.94
22C350	8-16	No. 8	16x14x10½	22x28	8x22	28½	6	22	155	5.99
22C351	8-18	No. 8	18x16x11	24x30	8x24	29	7	24	215	7.58
22C352	9-18	No. 9	18x16x11	24x30	8x24	29	7	24	215	7.63
22C353	8-20	No. 8	20x18x12	26x32	8x26	29½	7	26	272	9.08
22C354	9-20	No. 9	20x18x12	26x32	8x26	29½	7	26	272	9.13

$5.94 to $9.13

SEE PAGE 14 FOR OUR LIBERAL $1.00 TO $5.00 C. O. D. SUBJECT TO EXAMINATION OFFER.

ACME ELM WOOD COOKING STOVE—WITHOUT RESERVOIR

DESIGNED AND MANUFACTURED IN OUR OWN FOUNDRY AT NEWARK, OHIO.

$4.66 TO $5.30

WE CAN ALWAYS FURNISH REPAIRS FOR ACMES. SEE PAGE 19 ABOUT HOW TO ORDER REPAIRS WHEN NEEDED IN FUTURE YEARS.

IN OFFERING this elegant specimen of a low priced, highly carved rococo design, wood cooking stove, we present an entirely new set of patterns, made only in this form, without the reservoir, for the use of those just establishing a homestead, for the use of our southern customers, who buy so frequently without the reservoir, and for the use of all wood burning districts where a low priced cooking stove is required.

ITEMS OF MERIT. MAIN TOP. The main top, covers and centers are heavy and durable. FIRE BOX. The fire box is large and exactly the length shown opposite each catalogue number and price. OVENS. The ovens are commodious and measure exactly as we state, but without including the swell of the oven doors. The oven doors are aluminine lined. ROCOCO DESIGN. The elegant modeling of this set of patterns is designed by our leading artist, and as much care and attention given to the finishing as to the highest priced stoves manufactured by us or anyone else.

ACME ELM FOUR-HOLE WOOD COOKING STOVE, WITHOUT RESERVOIR. For wood only.

Prices do not include any pipe or cooking utensils. See index on pink pages. Oven measurements do not include swell of oven doors.

PRICES, DELIVERED ON THE CARS AT OUR FOUNDRY IN NEWARK, OHIO.

Catalogue Number	Stove Number	Size of Lids	Size of Oven, Inches	Main Top, Without End Shelf	Size of End Shelf	Height, Inches	Pipe to Fit Collar	Length of Fire Box	Weight, Pounds	Price
22C360	7-15	No. 7	15x13x 9½	23x21	4x21	27	6	18	130	$4.66
22C361	7-17	No. 7	17x15x10	25x23	4x23	27½	6	20	150	5.25
22C362	8-17	No. 8	17x15x10	25x23	4x23	27½	6	20	150	5.30

ACME SUNBURST BASE BURNER, $19.87.

FOR ANTHRACITE HARD COAL.

$19.87

Made with full length, double heating, hot air flue, one of the handsomest and best heaters produced in the world. Made of the finest selected material. The body is heavily nickel plated, beautiful urn and top ornament finished in gun metal, silver nickeled dome shaped swing top, which is always cool, and which, when swung to the left, opens the magazine cover automatically, allowing the coal to be poured into the magazine. Made with tea kettle attachment at the rear of the fire chamber, where water may be kept boiling and below which is the cast smoke pipe elbow, as illustrated. Made with the hot air exit, to which a hot air pipe can be connected to heat an upper room, or is covered with an open work ornamental cap to let all the hot air into the same apartment with the stove itself. The special features of the Acme Sunburst Base Burner are self feeding magazine, large enough to run full and in the coldest weather if filled only once in the morning and once at night; mica illumination complete on either side of the stove; tea kettle attachment; return flue base heating; just beneath the tea kettle attachment is the rolling direct draft damper; hot air flue, which increases the radiating surface of the stove almost double; easily removed fire pot, which slides straight outward and can be taken out entirely without unbolting any part of the stove; duplex grate with oscillating shaking ring, the very best construction for a hard coal grate; large ash pit and ash pan which requires emtying only once a day. **This Acme Sunburst Base Burner is one of the finest products of our large Newark Ohio Stove Foundry, an entirely new 1905 design, beautifully made, most heavily nickel plated and ornamented, such a base burner as sells at retail at $10.00 to $15.00 more than we ask.** Nothing has been left undone to make the New Model Acme Sunburst Base Burner the highest of high grade burners, the best hard coal stove possible to build.

Delivery Guarantee. At the prices quoted we furnish the Acme Sunburst Base Burner, carefully crated and delivered on board the cars at our foundry, and we guarantee the stove to reach you in the same perfect condition it leaves us, and if any piece or part is broken on arrival we will replace it free of any charge to you.

Our price is based on manufacturing cost in our own foundry with only our one small profit added, and for beauty, finish, practical construction, and improvements, this Acme Sunburst Base Burner stands alone and unapproached. **See page 14 for our liberal $1.00 to $5.00 C. O. D. subject to examination offer.**

Prices delivered on the cars at our Newark, Ohio, foundry:

Catalogue Number	Stove No.	Firepot	Floor to Urn Base, inches	Floor Space, inches	Size, Pipe Collar	Weight, Pounds	Price
22C367	12	12	52	23½x23½	6 in.	300	$19.87
22C368	14	14	54	25½x25½	6 in.	335	23.19
22C369	16	16	57	27½x27½	6 in.	385	26.50

EVERY STOVE IS MADE IN OUR OWN FOUNDRY AT NEWARK, OHIO, AND PRICED ON THE BASIS OF ACTUAL FACTORY COST.

OUR $16.56 ACME CORONA BASE BURNER

WITH DOUBLE HEATING HOT AIR FLUE FOR ANTHRACITE HARD COAL.

$16.56

This new model base burning heater is built on the very latest lines, has all the new up to date features of all other heaters, every known improvement, and is made in our own stove foundry, the largest in the world, and offered on the basis of foundry cost with only one small percentage of profit added. This heater is second only to our world's finest Acme Sunburst, and is the equal of heaters that are sold generally at 50 per cent higher prices. It is a highly ornamented, heavily nickel trimmed, new 1905, up to date base burning heater. Made with silver nickeled swing cover; brass trimmed top ornament, double heating flue, by which at least 100 per cent additional heat radiation is secured; silver nickeled dome top, front corner silver nickeled ornaments, nickel name plate, mica doors, elegant nickeled foot rails, nickel leg frame, self feeding magazine with a big capacity, duplex grate, tea kettle attachment, base heating flue, screw draft register; large roomy ash pit and ash pan. The fire pots measure 13, 15 and 17 inches respectively. **See page 14 for our $1.00 to $5.00 C. O. D. Offer.**

Prices of the Acme Corona Heaters, delivered on the cars at our Newark, Ohio, foundry:

Catalogue Number	Stove No.	Size of Fire Pot	Floor to Base of Urn	Floor Space, inches	Size Pipe, Collar	Weight, pounds	Price
22C374	13	13 in.	52 in.	23½ x 23½	6 in	295	$16.56
22C375	15	15 in.	54 in.	25½ x 25½	6 in	320	19.55
22C376	17	17 in.	57 in.	27½ x 27½	6 in	370	22.53

WE CAN ALWAYS FURNISH REPAIRS FOR ACMES.

OUR $13.25 ACME SURPRISE.

A BASE HEATING, FRONT DIVING FLUE HEATING STOVE FOR BURNING COAL OR WOOD.

$13.25

One of the strongest, best made heating stoves produced in our big foundry, a stove which for heating capacity, control of fire, economy of fuel, cannot be approached by any stove made or sold today at anything like our price. A handsome stove, beautifully carved, ornamented and nickel trimmed, a stove which burns hard coal, soft coal, or wood, or anything that can be burned in any stove. Made with a beautiful ornamented urn, oval dome swing top, heavily nickel plated, main top with a griddle cover in the center, furnishing a cooking hole when dome is swung aside; and this main top can be taken out entirely to put in irregular chunks of wood which will not go in the regular fire door. The main body of the stove has elaborate rococo ornamentation, lower front has screw draft register, regulating the draft perfectly, silver nickel rail, name plate, large fire door on the right side, below which is a small nickel plated ash hearth, large ashpan, heavy durable coal fire box, standard duplex grate which can be quickly converted into a wood grate. **See page 14 for our $1.00 to $5.00 C. O. D. subject to examination offer.**

Prices of the Acme Surprise Base Heater for coal or wood, delivered on the cars at our Newark, Ohio, foundry:

Catalogue Number	Stove Number	Length of Fire Box, inches	Size of Door Opening inches	Height Without Urn, Inches	Floor Space, Inches	Size of Pipe to Fit Collar	Weight, pounds	Price
22C378	21	19	12 x 9	43	28 x23	7	250	$13.25
22C379	23	21	13 x10	43	30 x24	7	300	15.50
22C380	25	23	14 x12	48½	32 x25	7	360	19.08

The Acme Surprise cannot be furnished with a self feeding magazine.

$4.38

OUR $4.38 ACME CHIEF COAL HEATING STOVE.

FOR COAL ONLY.

A new 1905 design, strongly built, heavy, handsome cottage stove for coal only. $4.38 to $6.23, according to size. Made in our own foundry at Newark, Ohio. Greatest value ever offered in this style heater. Made with nickeled urn dome, swing top, main top fitted with two cooking holes. Main body is elaborately carved gray iron casting with nickel trimmed knobs, drop poker door, screw draft register and foot rail, all heavily silver nickeled. Basket grate fire chamber, large and roomy ash pit. Our Acme Chief is an astonishing value in heating stoves, a wonderful stove for the money, much lower in price and much better in quality than anything ever offered in this pattern of heater. Remember, we guarantee safe delivery, and that you can also always get repairs in the years to come from us for any stove we sell.

Prices of the Acme Chief Cottage Heater for coal, delivered on the cars at Newark, Ohio:

Catalogue Number	Stove Number	Length of Fire Box	Height, Without Urn	Floor Space, inches	Pipe Collar	Weight, pounds	Price
22C384	121	19 in.	33 in.	20 x 20	6	110	$4.38
22C385	123	21 in.	34 in.	22 x 20	6	125	5.09
22C386	125	23 in.	35 in.	24 x 20	6	165	6.23

ACME VENTIDUCT DOUBLE HEATER AND HOT AIR CIRCULATOR.

$10.12

At $10.12 to $15.05, delivered on the cars at our foundry in Newark, Ohio. The air enters under the middle ring, passing up between the inner and outer steel body, circulating around under the main top and passing out of the hot air collar into the room or into a pipe to an upstairs room as desired. Both inner and outer steel, bodies are of 18-gauge full cold rolled steel, and the hot air space between them extends all the way around excepting where the door is located. See page 14 for our liberal $1.00 to $5.00 C. O. D. subject to examination offer.

Items of Construction.

Highly nickeled urn, ornamental swing top, elaborately carved main top, hot air collar on top, with nickel cover, smoke collar at back, with cast elbow, nickeled steel top ring, nickeled wings each side of front, double feed doors for wood, lower feed door for coal, magazine for anthracite coal, when ordered (extra), nickeled screw check draft in doors, nickeled name panel, broad rococo middle ring, nickeled open work ring skirting, heavy single ribbed firepot, large bailed ashpan, large swing ash door, double nickeled screw supply drafts, shaker door in ash door, full nickeled base and feet. Has ball bearing draw center grate. **When ordering, always state whether you burn hard coal, soft coal or wood.** When burning anthracite or hard coal we can always supply a self feeding magazine at the extra prices quoted below.

SELF FEEDING MAGAZINES. If a self feeding magazine for burning anthracite coal is desired, add for No. 14, 92 cents; for No. 16, $1.28; for No. 18, $1.32.

Prices of the Acme Ventiduct Double Heating Hot Air Circulator, delivered on the cars at our Newark, Ohio, foundry:

Catalogue Number	Diam. Fire-pot, inches	Height, Floor to Urn Base, inches	Floor Space, inches	Weight, pounds	Price, with Wood Grate	Price, with Coal Grate	Price, with Both Grates
22C390	14	42½	23 x23	212	$10.12	$10.17	$10.60
22C391	16	45½	25½x25½	245	12.30	12.35	12.82
22C392	18	48½	28 x28	283	14.47	14.52	15.05

$9.47 TO $12.70 FOR OUR ACME CARBON DOUBLE HEATER.

$9.47

FOR COAL ONLY.

Our 16-inch Double Heater at $12.70 is large enough to heat any medium sized house. It will heat comfortably two or three down stairs rooms, and keep comfortably warm one or more up stairs sleeping rooms.

SEE PAGE 14 FOR OUR LIBERAL $1.00 TO $5.00 C. O. D. SUBJECT TO EXAMINATION OFFER.

Detailed Description—The Acme Carbon Double Heater has hot air opening, to which a pipe can be attached to heat an upper room, or is covered with an open cap to let the heat out into the lower room, as desired. The draft supply is regulated by the screw draft supply in ash door, enabling the user to give it any amount of draft or cut it off air tight, as desired. The outer casing is artistically carved open fret work. It is made with beautifully nickel plated urn, nickeled swing top, large, handsomely shaped nickeled main top, handsome nickeled front panel, nickeled door knobs, nickeled screw draft supply, large, handsome nickeled base of the new rococo design, nickeled legs to base. Has mica lights and check slide in fire door. Deep ashpan. See page 14 for our guarantee.

Prices, delivered on the cars at our Newark, Ohio, foundry:

Catalogue Number	Size of Fire-pot, inches	Height without Urn, inches	Pipe to fit Collar inches	Floor Space, inches	Weight, pounds	Price
22C393	12	42	6	20x20	195	$ 9.47
22C394	14	43	6	22x22	210	10.55
22C395	16	45	6	24x24	254	12.70

WE CAN ALWAYS FURNISH REPAIRS.

ACME OAK LEAF AT $7.25 TO $11.13.

We are still breaking records with this our new Acme Oak Leaf. Making new records every year by adding new and modern designs throughout our wonderful line of heating stoves. At $7.25 and upward for this magnificent Oak stove, delivered on the cars at our foundry at Newark, Ohio, we are offering you the most wonderful value yet extended to our customers. For coal, wood, or anything used for fuel. **The Acme Oak Leaf has a handsome nickel top ornament, a nickel steel band around the main top, as shown;** is mounted with 18-gauge smooth steel; has heavy ribbed single cast iron fire pot; the most improved shaking and draw center grate for coal; double feed doors for wood and the lower feed door is for coal. It has a nickel screw check draft in the feed door and two nickel supply screw drafts in the ash door. The broad rococo middle ring supports the beautiful nickel skirting or foot rails. The swing ash door is large and admits a large bailed ash pan. The leg base and feet are nickel, as shown. All our nickel is of the highest silver finish and is not surpassed anywhere. This Acme Oak Leaf, when desired for anthracite coal, can be furnished with self feeding magazine in any of the three sizes at a slight increase in price, as quoted below. **See page 14 for our liberal $1.00 to $5.00 C. O. D. subject to examination offer and all about our binding guarantee.**

SELF FEEDING MAGAZINES. If a self feeding magazine for burning anthracite coal is desired, add for No. 24, 92 cents; for No. 26, $1.28; for No. 28, $1.32.

Delivered on the cars at our foundry in Newark, Ohio.

Catalogue Number	Stove No.	Diameter Fire Pot	Hgt., Floor to Urn Base	Floor Space Inches	Smoke Collar	Shipping Weight, lbs.	Price with Wood Grate	Price with Coal Grate	Price with Both Grates
22C396	24	14	42½	23 x23	6	175	$7.25	$7.30	$7.99
22C397	26	16	45½	25½x25½	6	203	8.90	8.95	9.43
22C398	28	18	48½	28 x28	6	240	10.58	10.65	11.13

OUR GREAT LEADER, ACME OAK, AT $4.34 TO $9.66.

$4.34

According to size and specifications, we offer this, our Acme Oak, delivered on the cars at our foundry in Newark, Ohio, as our greatest leader for 1905—a wonder of value, the greatest achievement in stove making of the season. **The price wonder of the stove industry. Our $4.34 Acme Oak Heating Stove is the latest,** handsomest Oak pattern. It is mounted with 18-gauge smooth steel, heavy ribbed single cast iron fire pot, has shaking and draw center grate for coal, has double circular wood grate which is so constructed that the fire can be kept under complete control. Large ash pan, large feed doors. Has highly polished, heavily nickel plated foot rails, large nickel plated name plate, nickel plated top ring, handsome nickel plated fancy urn, nickel plated hinge pins and knobs, large swing top, cooking lid under swing top. Check drafts at collar and in feed door. See page 14 for our liberal $1.00 to $5.00 C. O. D. subject to examination offer. Burns anything. The Acme Oak is suitable for wood, hard coal, soft coal, coke or anything that can be burned in a stove. Height of stoves as given from floor to base of urn. We can furnish the three large sizes with self feeding magazines for anthracite coal, at 75 cents for No. 214, $1.00 for No. 216, and $1.25 for No. 218, extra. **Price list of Acme Oak Heating Stoves, delivered on the cars at our foundry in Newark, Ohio.**

Catalogue Number	Stove No.	Dia. of Fire Pot	Ht. in.	Floor Space in.	Wt. lbs.	Price with Wood Grate	Price with Coal Grate	Price with Both Grates
22C399	210	10	38	16 x16	86	$4.34	$4.39	$ 4.54
22C400	212	12	40	18½x18½	114	5.08	5.14	5.42
22C401	214	14	43	20¾x20¾	145	6.24	6.30	6.73
22C402	216	16	44	22¾x22¾	175	7.57	7.63	8.10
22C403	218	18	47	25 x25	210	9.01	9.07	9.66

We can always furnish repairs for Acmes.

THE ACME OAKDALE HEATING STOVE.

At $3.45 to $8.15, according to size and style, we furnish the Acme Oakdale, an entirely new 1905 design, a strictly high grade heater, put out under our binding guarantee for quality, and we challenge any stove foundry to duplicate it in style and quality at our astonishingly low prices. While this is a lighter stove than our Acme Oak or Acme Oak Leaf, and we recommend the better grade of heaters, still this stove is thoroughly reliable, guaranteed in every way and is far superior to heaters that are widely advertised by others at nearly double these prices. The Acme Oakdale is made in our Newark, Ohio, stove foundry, made on new lines. Body is best cold rolled steel, silver nickeled, highly polished urn with open work swing top, main top with one cooking hole. The main front is elaborately carved and has large feed door with silver finished name plate, nickeled foot rails, ribbed fire pot, large ash pit, and is altogether a good substantial heater, economical in the consumption of fuel, a better stove than you can buy elsewhere at $2.00 to $4.00 more money. See page 14 for our liberal $1.00 to $5.00 C. O. D. subject to examination offer.

SELF FEEDING MAGAZINES can be furnished with Nos. 14, 16 and 18. If a self feeding magazine for burning anthracite coal is desired, add for No. 14, 60c; for No. 16, 80c; for No. 18, $1.00.

Price List of the Acme Oakdale delivered on the cars at Newark, Ohio:

Catalogue Number	Stove No.	Dia. of Sheet Body	Ht. Floor to Urn Base	Floor Space	Smoke Collar	Shipping Wt.	Price with Wood Grate	Price with Coal Grate	Price with Both Grates
22C405	10	9	36¾	16x16	5	70	$3.45	$3.50	$3.71
22C406	12	11	37¾	17x17	6	80	4.12	4.17	4.45
22C407	14	13	38¾	18x18	6	94	4.93	4.98	5.30
22C408	16	15	40¾	21x21	6	130	6.50	6.55	6.95
22C409	18	17	41¾	21x21	6	160	7.62	7.67	8.15

OUR $5.14 TO $8.64 ACME HORNET.

$5.14

Airtight hot blast heater for hard or soft coal. At $5.14 to $8.64, according to size, delivered on the cars at our foundry in Newark, Ohio, we furnish this, the very latest, most improved and best coal burning airtight heater as a practical substitute for the regular $35.00 or $40.00 hard coal burning parlor heaters. **It is handsomely ornamented** with nickel plated foot rails, highly ornamented with nickel plated ornaments, patent double cover on top. Coal dealers claim that 1½ tons ordinary grade soft coal will last as long and give as much heat as one ton of the very best hard coal, and that it will hold fire of soft coal over night. From this it will be seen that it is one of the most economical coal burners you can buy. **The top of the stove lifts up for feeding in the fuel.** The dome swing top swings conveniently aside so the top of stove can be used for heating a kettle when desired. Has powerful central down draft smoke consumer. Mica lighted upper front door. Handsome design and finish. **A better stove for the money than ever before put on the market.** Has ornamented cast top and cast bottom. It has a nickeled ring around the top of the stove and two air inlets. It is furnished with the **draw center shaking grate.** Heavy cast fire pot and cast lining above fire pot. Has 18-gauge cold rolled steel body. Patent double cover on top. See page 14 for our liberal $1.00 to $5.00 subject to examination offer.

Prices of our Acme Hornet, delivered on the cars at our foundry in Newark, Ohio.

Catalogue Number	Diameter of Fire Pot	Height from Floor to Urn Base	Shipping Weight	Price
22C411	12 in.	39½ in.	110 lbs.	$5.14
22C412	14 in.	41¾ in.	120 lbs.	6.09
22C413	16 in.	45 in.	162 lbs.	7.10
22C314	18 in.	45¾ in.	198 lbs.	8.64

WE CAN ALWAYS FURNISH REPAIRS.

OUR $7.42 ACME FIRE KING.

$7.42

Airtight Sheet Steel Heater, Coal Burning. Our Acme Fire King Airtight Hot Blast Sheet Steel Heater, for burning hard or soft coal. Has hot blast draft and hot air circulating system. **Has ornamented cast top,** cast corrugated bottom, double jacket. It has a nickeled rim around the top of the stove and two air inlets. Is furnished with the **draw center shaking grate.** Heavy cast fire pot, cast lining above fire pot to air inlet and 20-gauge steel lining above that. Has polished steel body. **Patent double cover on top. At $7.42, $7.95 and $9.28, according to sizes, we furnish this the very latest, most improved and best coal burning airtight heater as a practical substitute for regular** $35.00 or $40.00 hard coal burning parlor heaters.

This is, without exception, the highest grade, most economical, best finished and most serviceable hot blast draft, airtight, sheet iron coal burner made. Made to burn hard coal, soft coal or coke, possesses all the very latest improvements—everything that can make it the very best stove of the kind on the market.

This hot air heater consumes 85 per cent of the smoke. Most economical stove made. **Is a** very powerful and quick acting heater.

Prices, delivered on the cars at our foundry in Newark, Ohio:

Catalogue No.	Stove No.	Size of Body, in.	Total Height	Size of Fire Pot	Weight, pounds	Price
22C416	14	16x30½	45½ in.	12 in.	140 lbs.	$7.42
22C417	16	18x31½	46½ in.	14 in.	150 lbs.	7.95
22C418	18	20x33	48 in.	16 in.	175 lbs.	9.28

OUR $4.18 ACME HOTSPUR.

Airtight Steel Heater for Hard or Soft Coal. We Can Always Furnish Repairs for ACMES.

$4.18

This is one of the latest and most modern stoves on the market. The body **is** made of smooth steel, has cast ornamented top, cast fire pot, cast lining extending up as far as draft inlet with 20-gauge steel lining above that. Furnished with the popular **draw center shaking grate and ash pan.** These stoves are claimed without any contradiction to consume 85 per cent of the smoke. All sizes use 6-inch stove pipe. **From this illustration you can form an idea of the appearance of this handsome new model airtight hot blast heater. It is handsomely ornamented with nickel plated foot rails, nickel plated hot blast dampers, screw adjustment, highly ornamented with nickel plated ornaments,** patent double cover on top. Manufacturers claim that 1¾ tons ordinary grade soft coal will last as long and give as much heat as one ton of the very best hard coal, and that it will hold fire of soft coal over night. From this it will be seen that it is one of the **most economical coal burners you can buy.**

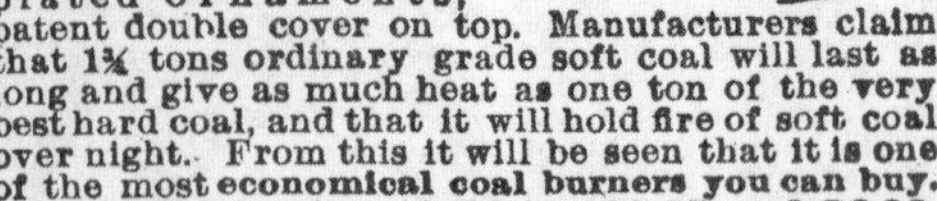

Our special price of $4.18, $5.17 and $6.38, according to size, as listed below, is so very much lower in price than these goods have ever been sold, that we believe our customers will appreciate the values we are giving. **If you favor us with your order for one of these stoves, we know you will be so well pleased, that you will send us your orders for other goods.**

Prices, delivered on the cars at our Newark, Ohio, foundry:

Catalogue No.	Stove No.	Size of Body	Total Height	Size of Fire Pot	Weight Crate	Price
22C419	12	14x27	40 in.	12 in.	90 lbs.	$4.18
22C420	14	16x29	42 in.	14 in.	110 lbs.	5.17
22C422	16	18x31	44 in.	16 in.	118 lbs.	6.38

See page 14 for our liberal $1.00 to $5.00 C. O. D., subject to examination offer.

WE GUARANTEE SAFE DELIVERY, guarantee every stove to reach our customers in the same perfect condition they leave our foundry, and if any piece or part is broken we will replace or repair it free of charge. We keep a big supply of the parts on hand, and can furnish any part on the shortest notice at factory cost. Every stove is covered by our binding guarantee.

ACME SUCCESS.

FOR WOOD ONLY.

$11.13

The highest grade, base heating, front diving flue stove made. Beautiful design, suitable for use in the parlor of the nicest home. Another great value from our Newark, Ohio, stove foundry. **A new pattern, a strictly 1905 style, made with** handsome artistic urn, beautiful nickel plated swing top, nickel base skirting leg frame, swell front, fitted with mica, main top with griddle cover in center furnishing a cooking hole, and the main top can be lifted out entirely to receive irregular chunks of wood, too large for the regular fire door; highly nickeled and polished screw draft register, regulating the draft perfectly, large ash pan running the full length of the bottom grate, automatic damper, strictly up to date in every way. **This is essentially a home stove.** It is made in three sizes, will accommodate rooms of a different size or houses of a different size. The largest size stove is amply large to heat any ordinary house, the whole downstairs to be made thoroughly comfortable, the upstairs rooms to be made comfortable for sleeping, this in the coldest weather with a less amount of fuel than with any other base heating diving flue wood burner made. All sizes use 7-inch pipe. **Furnished under our guarantee for quality, our thirty-day free trial offer, guaranteed to reach you safely, in perfect condition,** a wood burning heating stove, combining the good points of all other heaters, **a stove that will heat** more cubic feet of space than any other with the same amount of fuel. See page 14 for our C. O. D. subject to examination offer.

Prices, delivered on cars at our foundry in Newark, Ohio:

Cat. No.	Stove No.	Lgth. of Fire Box, inches	Size of Door Opening, inches	Hght. Without Urn, inches	Floor Space, inches	Weight, pounds	Price
22C440	21	21	12x 9	43	28x23	210	$11.13
22C441	23	23	13x10	43	30x24	255	13.51
22C442	25	25	14x12	48½	32x25	310	16.43

ACME IVY.

HEATING STOVE.

FOR WOOD ONLY.

$3.73

$3.73 to $5.41, according to size. Large, heavy, handsome cottage wood burning heater, made in our Newark, Ohio, foundry, and on the same general lines as the Acme Chief, with the exception that this Acme Ivy Stove is built for burning wood only, a new 1905 style, with all the practical features and improvements of our 1905 line. Made with nickeled urn, dome swing top, main top with two cooking holes; elaborately carved body free from nickel work except the two nickel draft registers and foot rail, large commodious fire chamber taking all sizes and shapes of wood. We believe **the Acme Ivy is the greatest value ever offered in a cottage wood burning heating stove. Remember, we carry a complete stock of repairs for all the stoves we make and can furnish them in the years to come.** See page 14 for our $1.00 to $5.00 subject to examination offer.

Prices, delivered on board cars at our Newark, Ohio, foundry:

Catalogue No.	Stove No.	Length of Fire Box	H'ght, in.	Floor Space, inches	Wght. lbs.	Price
22C446	21	22	33	20x20	95	$ 3.73
22C447	23	24	34	20x22	105	4.40
22C448	25	26	35	20x24	125	5.41

Ornament is not included in measuring height. All sizes take 6-inch stove pipe.

ACME WILDWOOD.

RETURN FLUE TODD STOVE.

FOR WOOD ONLY.

$6.41 TO $8.96

1905 design of wood heating stove, offered at $6.41 to $8.96, is the best Todd pattern stove made or sold anywhere. A beautiful, elaborately designed stove, with extravagant solid silver, nickel finish, unapproached in style, design, quality of material, excellence of economical construction, economical use of fuel or heating capacity of any Todd pattern stove on the market. Made with diving return flue; main body is made of blue polished steel, trimmed at the top with massive silver nickel end ornaments, nickeled urn swing top, **heavy main** top with one cooking hole, large fire door, heavy casting stove plate inner lining, hearth with draw-out center section with ash pit. All sizes use 6-inch pipe.

OUR CHALLENGE OFFER. If you want a stove of this pattern, a Todd style return flue stove for burning wood only, send us your order for this, our Acme Wildwood, and if you wish, order such a style stove from any other dealer, set them side by side when they arrive, compare them carefully in every detail, and if you and everyone else do not admit that the Acme Wildwood is by far a better stove in every way, the size and quality considered, at least 50 per cent cheaper than the stove from any other dealer, return it to us at our expense, and we will return your money and pay freight charges both ways. The Acme Wildwood must be seen to be appreciated, it is such astonishing value. See page 14 for our C. O. D. subject to examination offer.

Prices, delivered on the cars at our Newark, Ohio, foundry:

Catalogue Number	Stove Number	Length of Fire Box, inches	Size of Door Opening, inches	Floor to Urn Base, inches	Floor Space, inches	Weight, pounds	Price
22 C 450	26	25	13 x 10	30	26x19	130	$6.41
22 C 451	28	27	13 x 10	30	28x19	140	6.94
22 C 452	30	29	15 x 11	32	30x19	165	8.27
22 C 453	32	31	15 x 11	32	32x19	175	8.96

ACME NUTWOOD, BURNS WOOD ONLY, $4.82 AND UPWARD.

$4.82

Acme Nutwood is a direct draft, Todd pattern, beautifully made and finished, offered at very low prices, and while it is not a return flue Todd stove, like the Acme Wildwood, it is the very best direct draft horizontal oak stove ever offered at these prices. Has a beautiful nickeled urn and top ornament fitted to a full nickel swing top. Main top is heavily carved and when turned exposes one cooking hole. **The main body is made of cold rolled steel,** elaborately carved ends, the right end being fitted with a big wood fire door, also with a screw draft register, and below the door is a hearth shelf. The inside lining is a heavy cast stove plate lining, and the name plate, foot rail, and screw draft register are all beautifully nickel plated. All sizes use 6-inch pipe. The Acme Nutwood is covered by our binding guarantee offer, is an exceptional value in this style of stove, guaranteed to reach you in perfect condition, and we can always furnish repairs for any of our stoves in the years to come. **See page 14 for our subject to** examination offer.

Prices, delivered on the cars at our foundry at Newark, Ohio.

Catalogue No.	Stove No.	Length of Fire Box, inches	Size of Door Opening, inches	Floor to Urn Base, inches	Floor Space, inches	Weight, pounds	Price
22C455	26	25	16½x10¼	30	22 x 19	105	$4.82
22C456	28	27	16½x10¼	30	24 x 19	115	5.38
22C457	30	29	18 x11¼	32	26 x 19	135	6.30
22C458	32	31	18 x11¼	32	28 x 19	145	6.63

THE ACME CHAMPION.

FOR BURNING WOOD.

AT $2.12 TO $5.65 this is a handsome and well made box heating stove. Every plate is construted to avoid cracking. Has swing hearth, swing top and large feed door. The sizes indicate the length wood that the stove will take. Size 18 has one 6-inch cover. Size 22 has one 7-inch cover. Size 25 has two 7-inch covers. Sizes 28 and 30 have two 8-inch covers and short center. Sizes 34 and 36 have two 9-inch covers and short center in swing top.

Delivered on the the cars at our Newark, Ohio, foundry. The size indicates length of wood.

Catalogue Number	Stove No.	Height, inches	Size Pipe to Fit Collar	Weight, pounds	Price
22C460	18	19½	5 inches	51	$ 2.12
22C461	22	21½	6 inches	60	2.99
22C462	25	23	6 inches	92	3.18
22C463	28	26	6 inches	112	3.65
22C464	30	26	6 inches	115	4.01
22C465	34	29½	6 inches	159	5.29
22C466	36	29½	6 inches	165	5.65

OUR $5.94 AND $7.09 ACME GLENWOOD AIR TIGHT HOT AIR CIRCULATOR WOOD BURNER.

Delivered on the Cars at Our Foundry in Newark, Ohio.

This illustration shows our Acme Glenwood with hot blast draft and hot air circulating system. This stove burns everything (excepting coal) that is used for fuel. The feed opening is 10½ inches in diameter. The ash opening is 7 inches in diameter. Damper has screw adjustment. Ash opening is a cast drop door with a set screw fastening to make it airtight, and a screw draft opening in center to make a straight draft when desired. Takes a 6-inch stove pipe. Has nickeled foot rails and nickeled band around the top. The hot air circulating system takes the cold air from the floor and passes it up between the inner and outer jacket and out at the top, hot. By this system it will warm the farthest corner of the room, as well as the space near the stove. For burning any kind of fuel, except coal. This stove has ornamented cast iron top and corrugated cast iron bottom, polished steel body and heavy sheet steel inner walls, made of 20-gauge steel. Height of stove, 45 inches. Height of body, 26 inches.

$5 94

Our Binding Guarantee. Every one of our Airtight Hot Air Circulating Heaters is covered by our binding guarantee, covering every piece and part that enters into the stove. As a guarantee that you cannot duplicate this stove in quality of material, workmanship and finish, and that it will produce more heat for a like amount of fuel than any other airtight heater on the market, we are willing to accept your order for one of these stoves, to be sent to you with the understanding and agreement, that if after giving it ten days' trial you are not perfectly satisfied with it, and are not convinced that you have received a much better stove than you could have bought elsewhere, you are at liberty to return the stove to us at our expense, and we will immediately refund your money, together with any transportation charges you may have paid.

Size of pipe to fit collar is 6 inches on both sizes.

We can always furnish repair castings for Acmes.

Price list of the Acme Glenwood, with Hot Blast Draft and Hot Air Circulating System, delivered on the cars at our foundry in Newark, Ohio:

Catalogue Number	Stove No.	Height to Urn Base, Inches	Length, inches	Width, inches	Wg't lbs.	Price
22C467	26	37¾	26	17	100	$5.94
22C468	32	39¾	32	18	80	7.09

THE ACME BUCKEYE AIRTIGHT HOT AIR CIRCULATOR AT $5.09 AND $5.62, WOOD BURNER.

Delivered on the Cars at Our Foundry in Newark, Ohio.

The Acme Buckeye at $5.09 and $5.62 has all the features of the Acme Glenwood, shown in preceding number, excepting it is made in smaller sizes, and is of different ornamentation. It has the same hot blast draft and circulating system, and burns anything excepting coal. The screw drafts are the same, making it airtight when keeping fire. Has nickeled top band and foot rails. We guarantee that one of these hot air circulating heaters will heat more cubic feet with less fuel than any other hot air heater of the same size made, regardless of name, make or price. This is accomplished not only in the quality of material used, the heft of the steel and castings, in the careful and accurate fitting, making and finishing, but it is also accomplished through the peculiar construction which gives free circulation to the hot air, and such as is accomplished in no other hot air circulating heater made. Every stove is put out under our binding guarantee, and after giving it ten days' thorough trial if you are not convinced that you have received a better stove in every particular than you could have purchased elsewhere of the same size and style, you can return it to us at our expense, and we will immediately refund your money. Size of pipe to fit collar is 6 inches on both sizes.

Price List of the Acme Buckeye, with Hot Air Blast Draft and Hot Air Circulating System, delivered on board the cars at our Newark, Ohio, foundry:

Catalogue Number	Stove No.	Height to Urn Base, Inches	Length Inside, inches	Width Inside, inches	Top Feed Opening, Inches	Weight, pounds	Price
22C469	19	35¾	19½	13	9¾	100	$5.09
22C470	22	35¾	22	15	11¾	110	5.62

THE ACME HICKORY AIRTIGHT AT $4.03 AND $4.53.

For Wood, Hay, Cobs, Straw or Any Kind of Fuel Excepting Coal. Delivered on the cars at our Newark, Ohio, Foundry.

Our Acme Hickory, at $4.03 and $4.53 is the same stove as the Acme Buckeye, shown above, excepting it is a direct radiator, instead of a hot air circulator, and is without the nickeled top ring. It has the same hot blast down draft with screw adjustment, the same ash opening and direct draft screw adjustment, making it airtight when desired to keep fire. The same nickeled urn, foot rails and handsome finish, excepting the nickeled top ring. Not having the double cased hot air circulator, we give 1½ to 2 inches more inside measurement in the Acme Hickory.

Understand, every one of these stoves is put out under our binding guarantee, covering the workmanship and material, and we will accept your order for any one of these stoves to be sent to you with the understanding and agreement that after giving it ten days' thorough trial if you are not perfectly satisfied and are not convinced that you have received a better stove than you could have obtained elsewhere and at a big saving in cost, you can return it to us at our expense, and we will immediately refund your money together with any express charges paid by you.

Size of pipe to fit collar is 6 inches on both sizes.

We can always furnish repairs for Acmes if needed in future years. **See page 14 for our liberal $1.00 to $5.00 C. O. D., subject to examination offer.**

Price List of the Acme Hickory with Hot Blast Draft, delivered on the cars at our foundry in Newark, Ohio:

Catalogue Number	Stove No.	Height to Urn Base, Inches	Length Inside, inches	Width Inside, inches	Top Feed Opening, Inches	Weight, pounds	Price
22C471	21	36¼	21	15	9¾	85	$4.03
22C472	24	36¼	24	17	11¾	95	4.53

SHEET STEEL AIRTIGHT HEATING STOVES, 94c AND UPWARD.

OUR DOT AIRTIGHT HEATER, 94c, $1.29 AND $1.48.

Delivered on the Cars at Our Foundry in Newark, Ohio.

It will burn chunks, knots, chips, straw, cobs, hay, trash or anything used for fuel excepting coal. It is the cheapest steel airtight heater handled by us or any other house. While it is small, it is good and suitable for small rooms. It is a direct draft stove taking in the draft at the ash opening. Has oval sheet body 18, 20 and 24 inches long, and is not lined on the inside like our better airtights shown below. The small size does not require or have but three legs, equal distances apart, to support it. The two other sizes have four legs or feet, as shown in the illustration. These Dot airtight sheet steel heaters are offered in competition with the cheap airtights quoted by other houses, and are better than any of them offered at anywhere near the price, but we always recommend our Hot Blast airtight double lined heaters shown below as Catalogue No. 22C478, at $1.77, to Catalogue No. 22C489 at $3.68.

Catalogue Number	Stove No.	Length, inches	Width, inches	Pipe Collar, inches	Shipping Weight,	Price
22C475	18	17¾	14½	5	22 lbs.	$0.94
22C476	21	20½	16⅝	6	30 lbs.	1.29
22C477	25	23¾	17	6	32 lbs.	1.48

HOT BLAST SHEET STEEL AIRTIGHT HEATERS AT $1.77 TO $3.68.

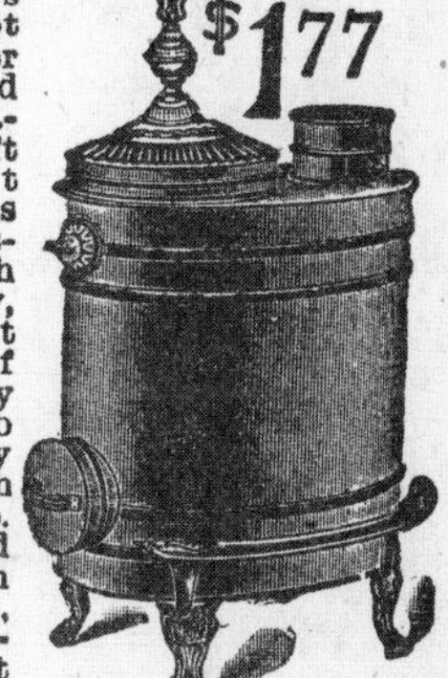

This illustration shows our better grade, with hot blast down drafts. A better stove than those quoted above, for the following reasons: The hot blast draft heats the air before it reaches the fuel, thus producing perfect combustion. The cover to ash opening is locked securely, to prevent blowing off. It is honestly constructed of good material, with heavy lining, and cannot fail to give satisfaction. The body is made of 26-gauge smooth steel, the lining is 20-gauge. Has fine nickel urn and screw draft. It will burn chunks, knots, chips, straw, cobs, hay or trash or anything used for fuel, except coal. The pipe should be provided with a damper. Put two or three inches of ashes in bottom of stove before building fire, and always leave about this quantity when cleaning the stove. Will keep fire over night. In setting up this stove, put the crimped end of stove pipe down. The feed opening is 10½ to 12½ inches in diameter; the ash opening is 6¾ inches in diameter; all sizes take 6-inch stove pipe. It has a check draft in the stove top, neat ornament on cover of fuel opening; screw draft adjuster in ash cover.

Delivered on the cars at Our Foundry in Newark, Ohio.

Price List of the Acme Airtight Smooth Steel Heater without Foot Rails:

Catalogue Number	Stove No.	Length, inches	Width, inches	Height of Body, inches	Shipping Weight	Price, Smooth Steel
22C478	20	20½	16½	19¾	37 lbs.	$1.77
22C479	24	23¾	17	23¾	41 lbs.	2.00
22C480	30	29½	17	23¾	46 lbs.	2.53

Price List of the Acme Airtight Polished Steel Heater without Foot Rails:

Catalogue Number	Stove No.	Length, inches	Width, inches	Height of Body, inches	Shipping Weight	Price, Polished Steel
22C481	120	20½	16½	19¾	38 lbs.	$2.29
22C482	124	23¾	17	23¾	42 lbs.	2.58
22C483	130	29½	17	23¾	48 lbs.	3.15

Price List of the Acme Airtight Smooth Steel Heater with Foot Rails:

Catalogue Number	Stove No.	Length, inches	Width inches	Height of Body, inches	Shipping Weight	Price, Smooth Steel
22C484	205	20½	16½	19¾	41 lbs.	$2.15
22C485	245	23¾	17	23¾	45 lbs.	2.48
22C486	305	29½	17	23¾	50 lbs.	3.05

Price List of the Acme Airtight Polished Steel Heater with Foot Rails:

Catalogue Number	Stove No.	Length, inches	Width. inches	Height of Body, inches	Shipping Weight	Price, Polished Steel
22C487	1205	20½	16½	19¾	42 lbs.	$2.67
22C488	1245	23¾	17	23¾	46 lbs.	3.06
22C489	1305	29½	17	23¾	52 lbs.	3.68

All the above airtights are for wood and will not burn coal at all.

THE ACME GIANT.

BURNS COAL ONLY.

This is a large, heavy cannon stove of extra heating power. Adapted for schools, churches, halls, stores, shops, or any place where a heavy stove is required.

MADE IN FOUR SIZES, from $4.66 to $10.79, delivered on the cars at our foundry in Newark, Ohio. Has swing feed door, large ash pit, cast foot rails, draw center and shaking grate, nickel plated knobs, extra heavy fire pot. The top is so arranged that drum can be attached at any time.

REMEMBER, OUR PRICES ON STOVES ARE LESS THAN ANYONE CAN BUY IN CARLOAD LOTS.

WE GUARANTEE SAFE DELIVERY AND ENTIRE SATISFACTION OR REFUND YOUR MONEY.

Prices, delivered on the cars at our Newark, Ohio, foundry:

Catalogue Number	Stove Number	Diameter of Fire Pot	Height, inches	Size, Pipe	Floor Space, inches	Weight, pounds	Price
22 C 423	13	13 in.	40	6	18 x 20	117	$ 4.66
22 C 424	15	15 in.	45⅛	6	20½ x 23⅛	155	6.41
22 C 425	17	17 in.	47	7	22 x 25⅛	206	8.11
22 C 426	20	20 in.	56	7	25 x 28	272	10.79

REMEMBER, the freight rates on stoves are very low. The cost of transportation on a stove need not be considered when you consider what we save for you in price. No one can compete with us in stoves.

MOOSE LAUNDRY—FOUR HOLES.

FOR COAL.

SOMETHING NEW. Our four-hole Moose laundry stove at $3.34 delivered on the cars at our Newark, Ohio, foundry, has dumping grate, four cooking holes, and with our Acme Drum Oven, shown on this page as No. 22C395 at $1.80 extra, would make a complete cooking stove. Weight, 90 pounds. Top cooking surface measures 21x22 inches. Height, 23½ inches.

No. 22C431 No. 18. Price.........................$3.34

THE ACME PRIDE, $2.96.

FOR COAL.

This is an entirely new and novel stove for the laundry. Will hold eight sad irons around the fire pot and will take a large boiler on the top at the same time. The irons lay close to the fire and heat very quickly. Has two 8-inch covers, large pouch feed and dumping grate. Made in one size only. Top surface, 14 x 21 inches. Collar takes 6-inch stove pipe. Diameter of fire pot, 12½ inches. Height, 25 inches. Weight, 90 pounds.

No. 22C432 No. 8. Price.........................$2.96

Delivered on the cars at our Newark, Ohio, foundry.

THE ACME CANNON.

AT $1.89 TO $2.97.

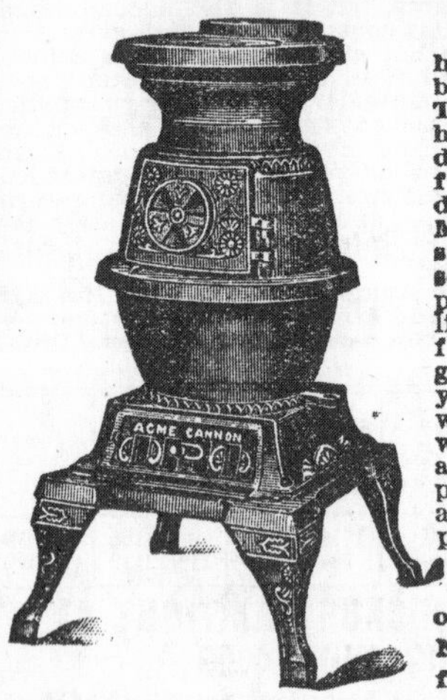

This is a cheap heating stove for burning coal only. The Acme Cannon has swing ash pit door, register and feed door and dumping grate. Made only in four sizes. You can form some idea of our prices and for how little money we are furnishing high grade stoves when you compare the weight of the stove with the price, about 4½ cents per pound. Our prices are money saving prices.

Prices, delivered on the cars at our Newark, Ohio, foundry:

Catalogue Number	Size	Diameter of Fire Pot	Height, inches	Size of Pipe to Fit Collar	Weight, pounds	Price
22C427	6	9 inches	23½	5 inches	40	$1.89
22C428	7	10 inches	27½	5 inches	46	2.22
22C429	8	11 inches	29½	6 inches	55	2.57
22C430	9	12 inches	32	6 inches	66	2.97

THE ACME PET LAUNDRY.

AT $2.54 TO $3.13.

FOR COAL.

This is a neat and desirable stove for laundry use. Has dumping grate, two covers, large front feed and takes a large boiler. It is made in three sizes. All take 6-inch stove pipe. Having succeeded in reducing our selling prices to $2.54 to $3.13 for this Acme Pet Laundry Stove, about 4 cents per pound, and guaranteeing the stove equal to any made regardless of cost, **we believe you will agree no other firm makes such prices.**

Prices, delivered on the cars at our Newark, Ohio, foundry:

Catalogue Number	Size	Size of Covers	Top Surface	Diameter of Fire Pot	Height, inches	Weight, pounds	Price
22C433	7	7 in.	14x19½	11 in	22½	64	$2.54
22C434	88	8 in.	14x19½	11 in.	22½	64	2.59
22C435	8	8 in.	14x21	12½ in.	23½	76	3.13

ACME DRUM OVEN, $1.80.

ATTACH TO ANY 6-INCH STOVE PIPE.

No. 22C395 Outside measurement, 18x14½ inches. Weight, 35 pounds. Price.........................$1.80

Quick baker, and saves the waste of heat passing up through the pipe.

KENWOOD AGRICULTURAL BOILERS.

$9.00 to $12.75.

These Boilers or Furnaces and Kettles are exceedingly popular among both farmers and butchers. They are made of cast iron throughout, have very smooth kettles and can be used for rendering lard, cooking food for stock, or other similar purposes. Price is for furnace and kettle complete with elbow, but does not include pipe. Boilers for coal have fire brick lining in furnace. Shipped knocked down from factory in Central Ohio.

No. 32C01820 30-Gallon Boiler, for wood. Weight, 275 pounds. Price.................. $ 9.00

No. 32C01821 30-Gallon Boiler, for coal and wood. Weight, 310 pounds. Price.... 10.50

No. 32C01822 45-Gallon Boiler, for wood. Weight, 355 pounds. Price.................. 11.25

No. 32C01823 45-Gallon Boiler, for coal and wood. Weight, 410 pounds. Price.... 12.75

KENWOOD FOOD COOKERS.

Can be used to cook food for stock or to heat water. The boilers are made of heavy galvanized sheet steel. Illustration shows 100-gallon size with double hinged cover. The 35 and 50-gallon sizes have single hinged cover, and the 20-gallon size has single cover to lift off. The body of the fire box is heavy sheet steel, the ends, door, hearth, etc., are cast iron. All sizes have elbow for 6-inch stove pipe, but price does not include pipe. Nos. 1, 2, 6 and 7 burn wood only. Nos. 3, 4 and 5 burn either wood or coal. Shipped knocked down from factory in Western Illinois.

Catalogue No	Size No.	Cap. gals.	Total Ht., in.	Size of Boiler L'gth in.	Width in.	Depth, in.	Wt. lbs.	Price
32C01825	1	20	29	24	17	13	60	$ 4.35
32C01826	2	35	31	30	20	15	70	5.95
32C01827	3	35	31	30	24	15	120	7.00
32C01828	4	50	39	30	24	18	130	9.15
32C01829	5	100	41	48	26	20	170	11.60
32C01830	6	50	39	30	24	18	95	7.60
32C01831	7	100	41	48	26	20	125	9.95

OUR RIVAL CAMP STOVE.

No. 6C09170 Perfect baker, good heater. This stove is made of heavy sheet steel, has heavy half-inch rolls all around bottom line of body, the corners are well mitered, are well braced inside; also has **half-inch rolls around the doors to stiffen them, strong steel latches for each door.** The cooking top is supported by strong angle braces which connect with the side of the stove, thereby preventing warpage from the weight of cooking vessels. The pipe collar is in the corner, increasing the space for top cooking. **The bake oven is corrugated to prevent warpage,** and an air space, formed by a double wall, is made between the fire and the oven; this prevents burning of food in the oven. **The stove pipe is nested in six short lengths, so as to pack inside of either the firebox or oven.** This stove burns wood; fire is placed on the ground; burns equally well inside or outside of the tent; is an excellent heater; will hold fire all night and keep the tent very comfortable; is undoubtedly the best stove of this kind on the market. The stove is not only for campers, but good for contractors, surveyors, cattlemen, people in all occupations who are compelled to stay in the open air and move from place to place. Length of stove, 29 inches; width, 16 inches; height, 14 inches. Size of oven: height, 9 inches; depth, 16 inches; width, 12 inches. Size of pot holes on top, 7 inches. Weight, crated for shipment, about 40 pounds.

Price.........................$3.15

THE ACME RADIATOR

PLAIN SIMPLE FACTS.

Anyone who has a house to heat will want an Acme Hot Air Radiator when he knows the plain, simple facts about it.

An immense proportion of heat made by the fuel burned passes out of the chimney instead of heating our rooms. "Hotter on top of the chimney than down by the stove;" yes, a good deal. The Acme Radiator is a device affixed to a stove pipe or furnace pipe to keep the heat from going up the chimney. **It does it. Your fuel bills are nearly twice as large as they would be if you used this waste heat. Don't waste it; stop it before it teaches the chimney with an Acme Radiator.** It stops the heat on its way to the chimney and makes it do double duty. You can place an **Acme Radiator** on the stove pipe in the same room with the stove. It will actually **save** from one-quarter to one-half the fuel. There is no guess work in **this** statement. Actual tests have proved it time and time again. It is a stove that throws off heat without requiring any fuel or attention at all. No dust in the room and no ashes to carry out. No gas escapes from them and they cause no obstruction at all to the draft. They can be as easily cleaned and repaired as a stove pipe. **An Acme Radiator really costs nothing.** It pays for itself in saved fuel in a very short time.

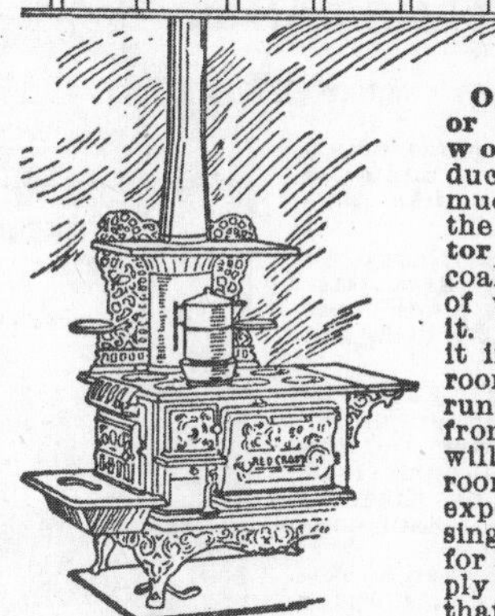

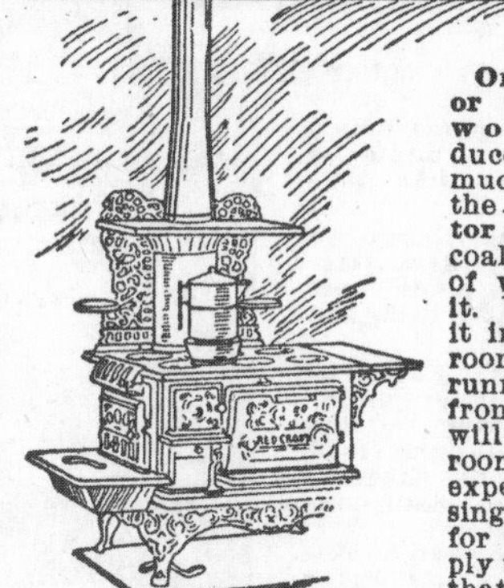

One ton of coal or one cord of wood will produce nearly as much heat with the Acme Radiator as two tons of coal or two cords of wood without it. You can place it in an upstairs room on a pipe running through from below, and it will heat that room without the expenditure of a single extra cent for fuel. It simply uses the heat that is escaping.

Round Pipe Style.

For use on stove burning anthracite coal, or wood.

To meet the demand for a cheaper radiator, this style is added. It is smaller but very efficient either on the back of a stove or to heat small upper rooms. **Cannot be used with soft coal.**

No. 22C490 For 6-inch stove pipe. Made of Woods' refined iron, with aluminum finished cast iron top and base. Diameter, 10 inches; height, 28 inches. Weight, crated, 27 pounds. Price $1.90

Square Style.

For use with stove burning anthracite coal or wood. This style is only adapted for floors above the stove. They are very handsome in design, and are bought by many who would not otherwise run a stove pipe through their house. **Cannot be used with soft coal.**

No. 22C491 For 6-inch stove pipe. Tubes made of Wood's refined iron. Aluminum finished, cast iron top and base. Size of base, 17½x13¾ inches; height, with legs, 37 inches. Weight, crated, 60 pounds. Price............................ $4.15

No. 22C492 Same as above, except the body is made of Woods' patent planished iron. Price............................ $4.75

This new style round Acme Radiator can be placed on a stove pipe in the same room with a stove, or it can be placed in an upstairs room on a stove pipe by running through from any kind of a stove below and will heat the upper room without the expenditure of a single extra cent for fuel. When used in the same room with the stove, the feet for the radiator are not required, but when you attach it to the stove pipe in the upper room it has a set of feet to support it at the floor. For use with stoves burning anthracite coal or wood. Weight, crated, 30 pounds.

No. 22C493 For 6-inch stove pipe, made of smooth cold rolled steel. Diameter, 12 inches. Height, with feet, 30½ inches. Price............ $2.70

No. 22C494 For 6-inch stove pipe, made of American patent planished iron. Diameter, 12 inches. Height, with feet, 30½ inches. Price.......... $3.30

The Original Round Style.

HARD OR SOFT COAL.

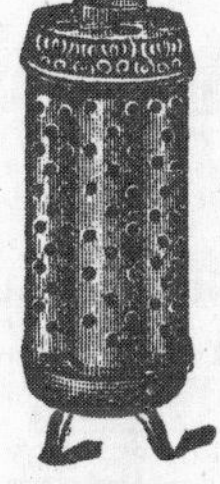

This style has been successfully sold for many years. They are adapted either for the back of stove or an upper room or hall. Furnished with inner tubes for wood and anthractic coal and without inner tubes for soft coal, for 6-inch stove pipe. Made from Woods' refined iron (sheet steel), with cast iron ends. Aluminum finish. Diameter, 12½ inches; height, with legs, 38 inches. Weight, crated, 50 pounds.

No. 22C495 For soft coal...... $3.73

No. 22C496 For hard coal or wood.................................. 3.74

No. 22C497 and No. 22C498 are the same as above, except made of Woods' patent planished iron.

No. 22C497 For hard coal or wood $4.40

No. 22C498 For soft coal.... 4.39

ACME SMOKELESS WICKLESS.

This Acme Smokeless-Wickless Blue Flame Oil Radiator Heating Stove is our latest addition to the world's wonder line of Blue Flame Oil Stoves. On another page we fully describe our Wickless Blue Flame Cooking Stoves and we here briefly say the same principle is in the Acme Smokeless Radiators. The world moves and the people reap the benefits. Heat your bath room; heat any room where other heat does not reach; heat all your rooms with the Acme Smokeless-Wickless Oil Radiators and you will find a pleasant comfortable heat. Through the tubular radiators of each stove the heated air continues to pass taking the cold air from below and passing it out into the room, constantly changing the atmosphere and giving a stronger, larger volume of hot air circulation than can be obtained from any other form of oil heater. The No. 10 will heat a small room or a bath room in the coldest weather. The No. 20 will heat a large room in the most severe weather. Order one and if not found all we claim for it or if it is not satisfactory, you can return it to us within thirty days and we will refund your money including the freight you have paid.

Reasons why our Wickless Radiators are superior to ordinary oil heaters.

1st. No wick to trim, or wick raiser to get out of order or bother with.

2d. Absolutely smokeless and odorless, others so called, are only so in name.

3d. Easily operated. Intense or slow heat, as may be desired.

4th. The radiator top is removable, leaving a most complete and effective cooking stove with a top grate nicely nickeled and finished.

5th. Have double reservoirs. Stove keeps on burning while you take upper reservoir away to refill.

6th. Have convenient bails on top to move stove around room, which also serve as handy rack on which to dry towels, etc.

Acme Wickless Radiator, No. 10, $3.80.

Has one of our powerful burners producing a most intensely hot blue flame. Radiator top contains a double row of radiator tubes—five in each row—made of planished iron, having a radiating surface equal to a cylinder over 3 feet in circumference. **Removable radiator top** especially designed to leave a lamp stove for cooking purposes. Removable reservoir holds 2½ pints, burning about seven hours. Dimensions: Total height, 25 inches; size of top, 7x12 inches; height of cooking section, 10 inches; height of radiator, 15 inches. Shipping weight, 37 pounds.

No. 22C508 Acme Wickless Radiator, No. 10. Price............ $3.80

—OIL HEATING STOVES.—

REAL HEAT MAKERS.

The entire stove is made of sheet steel. The drum tilts back for lighting. The burner is perfect, the tank of double coated steel and has outside place for filling so the tank does not require removing. Our new wick raising device raises the wick evenly and does not get out of order. **They are fine in appearance and as good as they look.**

Superb Oil Heater.

Great heat at small expense. We guarantee more heat from the amount of oil consumed than can be derived from any other heater made.

No. 22C500 Steel tank holds 4 quarts. Has registering oil indicator. Burns 10 hours with one filling. Height, to top of bail, 31 inches; wick circumference, 11 inches; diameter of drum, 8 inches. Weight, 13 pounds. Price $2.75

Ever Ready Oil Heater.

All bright parts shown are extra nickeled on steel plate, highly polished.

No. 22C501 Steel tank holds 6 quarts. Burns 10 hours with one filling. Height, to top of bail, 29 inches; wick circumference, 9 inches. Mica lighted. The handsomest, latest style, most expensively built bailed oil heater on the market. Weight, 12 pounds. Price............ $3.55

No. 22C502 Extra Wicks for either of the above heaters. Price, each.......................... 9c

No. 22C503 This stove will be found to meet all requirements of oil stove heating and keep a large room at a comfortable temperature in cold weather. The drum is made of polished steel and is perforated two-thirds of its length from the top, showing visible flame. Base and reservoir are of heavy aluminum steel, finished in black japan and tastily decorated. Is fitted with powerful control draft burner, taking wick 15 inches in circumference. Has patent wick raising device and is easily rewicked. Has convenient bail for carrying stove and top swings back on hinge allowing free access to the burner for lighting and cleaning. Tank holds 5 quarts of oil and can be refilled without removing from stove. Will burn 10 to 12 hours without refilling. Has patent central ventiduct for distributing heat by circulation as well as radiation. Is provided with floor tray which will protect carpets from damage if tank is accidentally overfilled. Height, 32½ inches. Weight, crated, 30 pounds. Price........................ $4.35

No. 22C504 Extra wicks for above. Price, each........................ .12

No. 22C507 This stove has the style and dignity and is as practical and durable as any coal stove. Entire stove is cast iron with exception of drum which is of polished steel and oil reservoir which is made of heavy aluminum steel. Has center mica section which reflects a brilliant light when stove is in use. Top swings back to allow access to burners for cleaning purposes. Has swing door in mica section for lighting. Tank holds 5 quarts and stove will burn 10 to 12 hours without refilling which can be done without removing tank from stove. Has central ventiduct which takes cold air from the floor and circulates it thoroughly heated into the room. Is provided with floor tray which will protect carpets from damage if tank is accidentally overfilled. Wick circumference, 15 inches. Height, 36 ins. Weight, crated, 70 pounds.

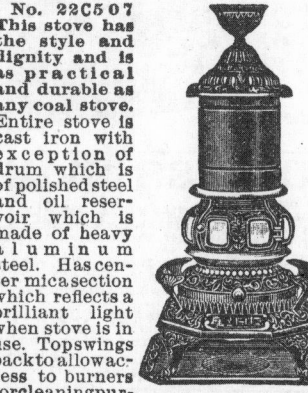

Price............................ $6.95

No. 22C506 Extra wicks for above. Price, each........................ 12c

Acme Wickless Radiator, No. 20, $6.35.

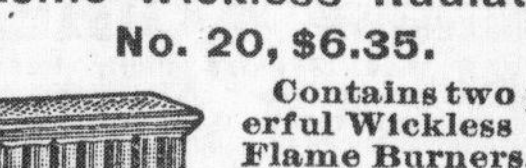

Contains two powerful Wickless Blue Flame Burners. The radiator top contains 21 radiating tubes, arranged in three rows. These are of planished iron and have a radiating surface equal to a drum cylinder 84 inches in circumference. **The radiator top is removable,** leaving a most complete and effective cooking stove. Removable reservoir holds over one gallon, permitting both burners to be operated at fair flame nearly 10 hours. Dimensions: Total height, 30 inches; size of radiator, 8x16 inches; size of cooking top, 12x16 inches. Height of cooking stove section, 10 inches; height of radiator section, 20 inches. Shipping weight, 54 pounds.

No. 22C509 Acme Wickless Radiator No. 20. Price.............. $6.35

OIL COOKING STOVES.

Our 32-Cent Lamp Stove.

Ovens cannot be used on these small stoves.

No. 22C510 One-Burner Lamp Stove. Weight, 3½ pounds. Price..32c

No. 22C511 Two-Burner Lamp Stove. Weight, 5¼ pounds. Price..64c

No. 22C512 Three-Burner Lamp Stove. Weight, 8½ pounds. Price...96c

No. 22C513 Wicks for above stoves, 4 inches wide. Price, each.........3c

Cash with order prices.

Reliance Single Oil Stoves.

Ovens cannot be used on these small stoves.

The Reliance is a well made stove in every particular, and is the cheapest well made stove on the market.

No. 22C514 No. 102¼, Single. Has two 3½-inch wicks. Weight, 6 pounds. Price.............55c

No. 22C515 No. 102½, Single. Has two 4-inch wicks. Weight, 8 pounds. Price..............75c

No. 22C516 No. 103, Single. Has three 4-inch burners. Weight, 9 pounds. Price............$1.00

Cash with order prices.

Reliance Double Oil Stoves.

Ovens cannot be used on these small stoves.

No. 22C517 No. 102¼ Double. Has four wicks 3½ inches wide. Weight, crated, 18 pounds. Price.$1.15

No. 22C518 No. 102½ Double. Has four wicks 4 inches wide. Weight, crated. 22 pounds. Price.$1.60

No. 22C519 No. 103 Double. Has six wicks 4 inches wide. Weight, crated, 25 pounds. Price..............$2.10

No. 22C520 3 -inch wicks. Price, each.......... .02

No. 22C521 4 -inch wicks. Price, each.......... .03

No. 22C522 3½-inch wicks. Price, each.......... .03

Cash with order prices.

KEROSENE OIL FOR FUEL

HAS PROVEN SO FAR SUPERIOR TO ALL OTHER FUELS that its future for cooking purposes is established. Discovery, invention and skill have developed simplicity and perfection in vaporizing kerosene oil, producing a perfect gas flame without odor, without wicks, without any smell beyond the slight flavor of artificial gas, such as is used for lighting purposes.

ACME CABINET WICKLESS KEROSENE RANGE.

Original and Only One.

THE FIRST AND ONLY WICKLESS KEROSENE RANGE WITH A CABINET OVEN EVER OFFERED TO THE PUBLIC.

WICKLESS OIL STOVES are rapidly taking the place of all other cooking apparatus, and have done more to relieve the arduous labor of the kitchen than anything ever before produced.

WE OFFER, IN OUR ACME CABINET Wickless Range, an entirely new pattern for 1905, the highest type of all cooking stoves made, and we believe, the most beautifully finished and elegantly designed stove ever offered to the public.

ITS DISTINGUISHING FEATURE IS ITS OVEN. The burners under the oven give ample heat for the most difficult baking and the flues are so constructed that it is heated evenly without products of combustion entering it, thus making it possible to bake the most delicate cake an even brown, top and bottom, without fear of contamination from the fumes of burning oil, as in other stoves.

OVEN DOOR and oven linings can be removed when so desired, thus giving use of two additional burners for cooking purposes. This is a feature which cannot be found in a range of any other kind on the market.

SPECIAL FEATURES WHICH MAKE THIS STOVE A DESIRABLE ONE TO BUY AND A PLEASURE TO USE.

ECONOMY. One gallon of coal oil (kerosene) will run one burner from 17 to 20 hours, which makes it the most economical of all summer cooking stoves.

DOUBLE RESERVOIRS. The main reservoir may be taken away for filling without extinguishing the flame, as sufficient oil remains in the lower reservoir to feed the flame.

FINISH. The entire range is highly enameled and decorated. Has handsome nickel trimmings.

FRONT VALVES. It will be noticed that the valves are at the front of the range, which overcomes the discomfort and danger of the operator's clothes catching fire from reaching over the flame.

WARMING SHELF. It is built with a warm air flue running to the top of the high shelf, enabling the user to keep anything desired thoroughly warm and is a feature not possessed by any other stove on the market.

BURNER DRUMS. Burner drums are 6 inches in diameter, giving the largest and hottest blue flame of any oil stove made.

PRICES OF OUR ACME CABINET WICKLESS KEROSENE RANGE.

Catalogue No.	Size Top, Inches	Height, Inches	Size Oven, Inches	Burners on Top	Burners Under Oven	Shipping Weight	Price
22C523	17x26⅛	36	18⅛x11½x11⅛	2	1 large	86 lbs.	$10.65
22C524	17x37½	36	18½x11½x11½	3	1 large	100 lbs.	12.80

No. 22C525 Asbestos Lighting Rings for above large burners. Price, each..........................7c

PRICES OF OUR HIGH FRAME ACME WICKLESS BLUE FLAME CABINET OIL STOVE.

No. 22C528 High Stove, No. 22. Two burners. Size of top, 22½x15½ inches; height, 24 inches. Price.........$4.65

Weight, crated, 39 pounds.

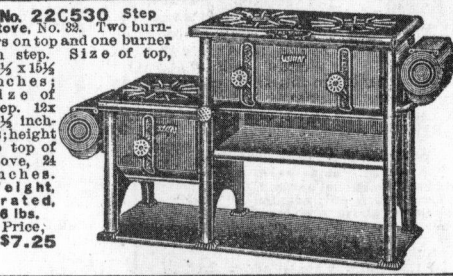

No. 22C529 High Stove, No. 23. Three burners. Size of top, 33x15½ inches; height, 24 inches. Price $5.85

Weight, crated, 49 pounds.

No. 22C530 Step Stove, No. 32. Two burners on top and one burner on step. Size of top, 22½x15½ inches; size of step, 12x15½ inches; height to top of stove, 24 inches. Weight, crated, 56 lbs. Price, $7.25

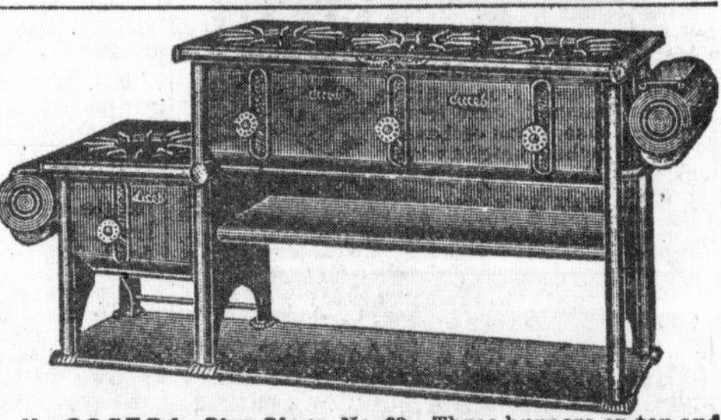

No. 22C531 Step Stove. No. 33. Three burners on top and one burner on step. Size of top, 33x15½ inches; size of step, 12x15½ inches; height to top of stove, 24 inches. Weight, crated, 66 pounds. Price..............................$8.40

"Security" Wickless Blue Flame Oil Stoves at $3.00 and $4.15.

These are well made and thoroughly reliable in every way, and are offered in competition with similar stoves sold by retail dealers at double the prices we quote. They are not as elaborately finished and do not have as large top grates and burners as our Standard Acme Wickless Stoves, and for this reason we recommend the purchase of an Acme listed under catalogue Nos. 22C523 to 22C531

No. 22C536 Two-Burner, No. 52. Size of top, 14½x22½ inches. Height, 14 inches. Weight, crated, 32 pounds. Price...$3.00

No. 22C537 Three-Burner, No. 53. Size of top, 14½x32¾ inches. Height, 14 inches. Weight, crated, 44 pounds. Price...$4.15

DESCRIPTION OF OUR CELEBRATED ACME WICKLESS BLUE FLAME OIL STOVE

FRAME made of extra quality sheet and band steel with middle brace. The supply tank containing the oil is removable and can be taken off the stove without removing troublesome bolts or screws for the purpose of filling the reservoir with oil. If these stoves are set anywhere near level the burner cannot be flooded, because the oil cannot rise any higher than the level in the lower reservoir. The flame will, therefore, always remain the same height, no matter how wide open you have the supply valve.

THE STOVE is so simple that really no directions are required. We, however, attach a card of simple instructions to each stove. You light the stove exactly as you would light a lamp, and, when combustion is started, the flame becomes a blue flame of perfect combustion.

ALWAYS A BLUE FLAME Whether you open valve too wide or remove it altogether, the flame will come to the right height and no further; but you can reduce the flame any time by partially closing the valve. Intense heat is produced by the perfect combustion given by the blue flame. Tanks hold 2¼ quarts of kerosene and will run one burner 15 hours or three burners 5 hours.

WE MAKE SPECIAL OVENS for use on these stoves, and these ovens are the most perfect made and warranted to bake satisfactorily.

See catalogue Nos. 22C534 and 22C535 for sizes and prices on ovens.

$3.70 Buys Our High Grade Acme Wickless Blue Flame Kerosene Oil Stove.

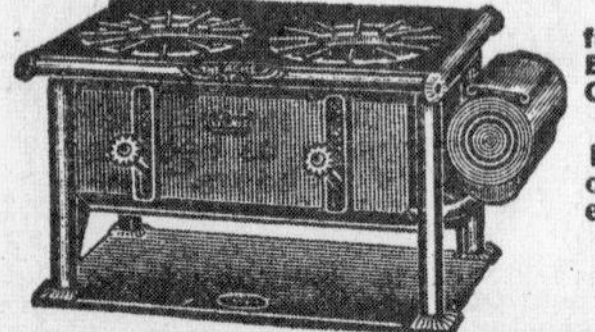

Prices of our low frame Acme Wickless Blue Flame Cabinet Oil Stove.

No. 22C526 No. 12, two-burner. Size of top, 22½x15½ inches; height 13½ inches. Price.......$3.70

Weight, crated, 31 pounds.

No. 22C527 No. 13, three-burner. Size of top, 33x15½ inches; height 13½ inches. Price, $4.95

Weight, crated, 40 pounds.

REMEMBER that the steel burner shells on all of our ACME WICKLESS STOVES give the largest and hottest blue flame of any oil stove made.

Asbestos Lighting Rings.

Asbestos Lighting Rings or Kindlers for the Acme Wickless Blue Flame Stoves are made in two sizes. All high and low frame stoves and the top burners on step stoves take the small size lighting rings. All burners on the ranges and step burners on step stoves take the large size lighting rings. We cannot furnish lighting rings for stoves not made or sold by us.

No. 22C532 Asbestos Lighting Rings, small size. Price, each..6c

No. 22C533 Asbestos Lighting Rings, large size. Price, each..7c

GAS, GASOLINE AND OIL STOVE OVENS.

We have spared no trouble or expense to produce beautiful and perfect ovens. They are larger than any other ovens on the market, lots of room inside, wide space between grates. Will do the largest loaves of bread or roasts of meat without touching upper grate. They are full flued, tin lined, ventilated perfectly, air chamber in door, tastily designed, first class in every particular. Anything done in them comes out sweet, clean and wholesome. The heat is evenly distributed, baking the tops of articles as thoroughly as the bottom without change of position. All have decorated steel tops.

Our Acme Drop Door Steel Oven at $1.49.

We show in this illustration a special oven which we have made particularly for our oil, gasoline and gas stoves. No better oven is on the market; in fact, we consider it the best oven in every respect that is manufactured. Our oven is a drop door steel oven, double cased, full flued, full tin lined, exactly as shown in illustration.

No. 22C534 Size, outside measurements, 13x20x18 inches. Weight, crated, 17 pounds. Price..........................$1.49

No. 22C535 Size, outside measurements, 13x13¾x18 inches. Weight, crated, 14 pounds. Price..........................$1.12

These ovens will not fit on the Reliance Oil Stoves.

THE ADVANCE GASOLINE STOVES AT $3.13 TO $8.13

WE ILLUSTRATE AND DESCRIBE BELOW OUR ADVANCE GASOLINE VAPOR STOVES, WHICH WE THINK WILL MEET THE DEMAND FOR MODERATE PRICED GASOLINE STOVES.

THEY ARE GUARANTEED absolutely safe and are entirely free from the serious objections of smoke and odor. In designing these stoves, the important features, safety, simplicity and durability were carefully considered and a careful reading of the descriptive points of this line will, we believe, convince anyone that we have been successful in making a stove which embodies these features.

CONSTRUCTION. All stoves have full cabinet frame, as illustrated, and are compact, neat and perfectly rigid. They are handsome in appearance, being finely japanned and tastefully decorated.

BURNERS. The Advance stove is fitted with individual generating burners scientifically constructed, and which will generate a powerful blue flame without smoke or odor in from one to one and one-half minutes. These burners are simple in construction, cannot get out of order if properly handled, and being made in a substantial manner, will last for years. All step stoves are fitted with a double burner on step, which insures thorough and uniform baking when an oven is used. The burners used on these stoves will produce more heat from a given amount of gasoline than any other burner on the market.

SAFETY All stoves are furnished with safety lay down tank, which cannot be filled while in an upright position. The tank does not have to be removed to refill, as feed pipe is connected to stove with a swivel joint, allowing the tank and pipe to drop level with stove, extinguishing the flame, thus

REMOVING ONE OF THE CHIEF CAUSES OF DANGER which, in the past, has attended the use of gasoline stoves. This is an important feature, and we offer our stoves at the same or a little lower cost than the many cheap stationary tank gasoline stoves which are sold by most dealers and which are unsafe for family use.

TAKING ALL POINTS into consideration, we believe our Advance stove will come nearer meeting the demands for a first class moderate priced stove in every particular than any yet offered to the public. It will do the work more economically and more satisfactorily. There is little or no chance for it to get out of order and if ordinary care is taken, it will last for years. If, however, by accident or otherwise, you should ever require any piece or part, we will always supply it to you at the actual factory cost. A simple card of directions is attached to every stove.

We accept every stove order to be shipped with the understanding and agreement that if it is not perfectly satisfactory after giving it **30 DAYS' TRIAL,** you can return it to us at our expense and WE WILL IMMEDIATELY RETURN YOUR MONEY, together with any freight charges paid by you.

EACH AND EVERY ONE IS GUARANTEED to be perfect in operation and workmanship, or your money will be refunded.

Below we show our **...ADVANCE STOVE...** with step attachment. This is a great convenience, as the step can be used for heating a wash boiler, or for baking with our No. 22C534 oven without interfering with the use of top burners for cooking purposes.

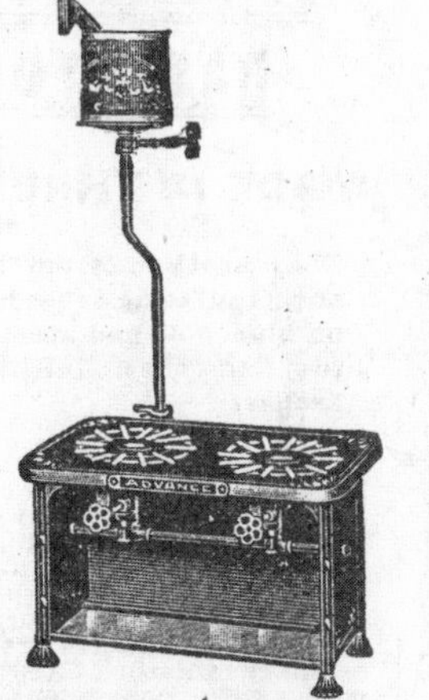

FOR PRICES —ON— Drop Door Steel Ovens for use on these stoves, see page 40, Nos. 22C534 and 22C535.

No. 22C540 Two-Burner Stove. Size of top, 14x22 inches; height, 14 inches. Shipping weight, 25 pounds. Price..........$3.13

No. 22C541 Three-Burner Stove. Same style as above. Size of top 14x32 inches; height, 14 inches. Shipping weight, 33 pounds. Price..........$4.25

No. 22C543 Three-Burner Stove with high frame. Size of top, 14x32 inches; height, 24 inches. Shipping weight, 43 pounds. Price..........$4.80

No. 22C542 Two-Burner Stove. Same style as above with high frame. Size of top, 14x22 in.; height, 24 inches. Shipping weight, 34 pounds. Price..$3.93

No. 22C545 Step Stove. Three burners on top and one double burner on step. Size of top, 14x32 inches; size of step, 14x14 inches; height, 24 inches. Shipping weight, 70 pounds. Price..........$8.13

No. 22C544 Step Stove. Same style as above with two burners on top and one double burner on step. Size of top, 14x22 inches; size of step, 14x14 inches; height, 24 inches. Shiping weight, 60 pounds. Price..........$7.00

ACME NEW METHOD GASOLINE VAPOR STOVE AT $13.30 TO $21.00.

THE SAFEST, QUICKEST AND MOST ECONOMICAL STOVES FOR GASOLINE.

IT LIGHTS LIKE GAS. A FEATURE THAT MAKES IT POPULAR, as without heat, smoke or delay, the stove can be instantly started in operation. turn the valve wheel and apply the match; the stove is ready for work.

IN OPERATION, the fluid drips drop by drop (never runs) on the perforated brass evaporator, where it is divided into fine particles, which, passing through the air, evaporate; the vapor thus made being heavier than air, passes down through the evaporator tubes mixing with and carburretting a current of air, which is lighted at the burner, producing a smokeless blue flame of great intensity and heating power.

THUS IT WILL BE SEEN that the NEW METHOD is a veritable gas machine and gas stove combined, entirely under the control of the user, who can increase or decrease the supply of fuel at will, securing the requisite amount of heat without waste; starting or stopping the fire according to requirement, thereby securing the greatest possible convenience, safety and economy of operation.

THE NEW METHOD solves the problem of economical cooking in all country homes and suburban residences where gas for fuel cannot be obtained, giving to the user every advantage, convenience and comfort which the use of gas stoves and other modern appliances affords.

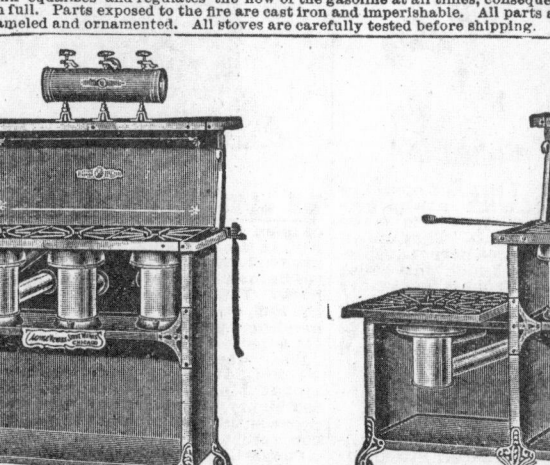

THE GENERAL CONSTRUCTION OF ALL OUR STOVES is thoroughly first class. The design is new, attractive and well planned for convenience. The frames of all NEW METHOD Stoves are made in cabinet style, and are strong and rigid. The tank or gasoline reservoir is not connected to the stove. It can be easily lifted from it and carried to an outer room for filling or cleaning, thus insuring safety. The tops are of ample width and provided with removable grates. The stove is provided with a sight feed, so that the dropping of the gasoline can at all times be seen when the stove is in operation. The valves are provided with needles, having non-corrosive points; the tank equalizes and regulates the flow of the gasoline at all times, consequently the tank works as well with a small amount of gasoline in it as it does when full. Parts exposed to the fire are cast iron and imperishable. All parts are so constructed that they can be easily cleaned; the stoves are handsomely enameled and ornamented. All stoves are carefully tested before shipping.

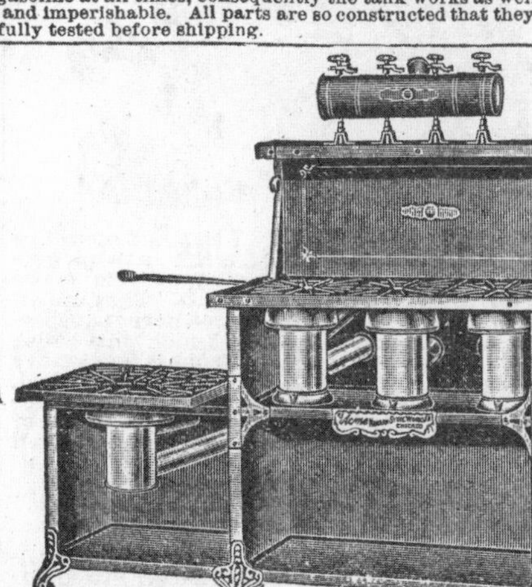

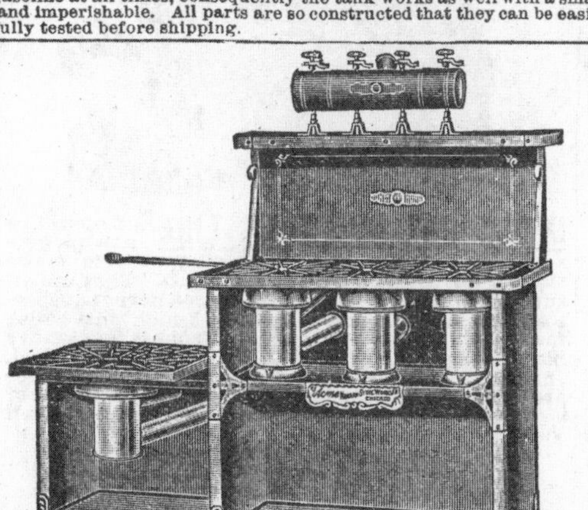

No. 22C640 Three-Burner Stove. Size of top, 35x19 inches; height to cooking top, 30 inches. Shipping weight, 90 pounds. Price, with large steel oven..........$15.40

No. 22C641 Same style of stove, with two burners. Size of top, 27x19 inches; height to cooking top 30 inches. Shipping weight, 75 pounds. Price, with large steel oven..........$13.30

If oven is not desired deduct $1.50 from above prices.

No. 22C642 Three-Burner and Step Stove. Size of main top, 35x19 inches; size of step top, 18x17 inches. Height to cooking top, 30 inches. Shipping weight, 150 pounds. Price, with large steel oven..........$18.90

No. 22C643 Same style stove, with two burners and step. Size of main top, 27x19 inches; size of step top, 18x17 inches; height to cooking top, 30 inches. Shipping weight, 135 pounds. Price with large steel oven..........$16.80

If oven is not desired deduct $1.50 from above prices.

No. 22C644 Two-Burner and Step Cabinet Oven Range. Size of main top 18¼x26¼ inches; size of step top, 12½x16¼ inches; height to cooking top, 35 inches; size of oven, 19¾x13½x11½ inches. Shipping weight, 150 pounds. Price..........$21.00

No. 22C645 Same style stove, without step attachment. Shipping weight, 130 pounds. Price..........$18.20

EXTRA LARGE BURNERS ON ALL STEP ATTACHMENTS.

STEP ATTACHMENT is a great convenience, as it can be used for heating wash boiler, or for baking with oven, without interfering with the use of the top burners for cooking purposes.

GAS HEATING STOVES

GAS HEATERS FROM $1.50 TO $5.40.

FOR EITHER NATURAL GAS OR ARTIFICIAL GAS.

EACH AND EVERY ONE IS GUARANTEED to be perfect in operation and workmanship or your money will be refunded. We use only the highest grade atmospheric burner and the highest class material in the construction of each and every stove. We challenge the world with this line of gas heaters, whether you use them for natural gas or for artifical gas. In ordering please be sure and state which kind of gas you burn, that we may send you a stove drilled properly for your gas. These stoves will not operate with gasoline gas.

In offering our customers this line of Gas Heaters we have selected the best and most efficient designs, improvements and economical attachments.

GAS RADIATORS.

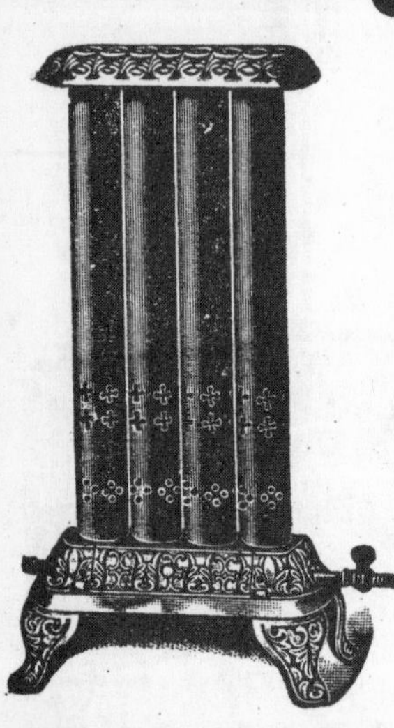

No. 22C546 Four-Tube Radiator. Height, 31 inches; length, 15 inches; width, 8 inches. Shipping weight, 35 lbs. Price..................$2.30

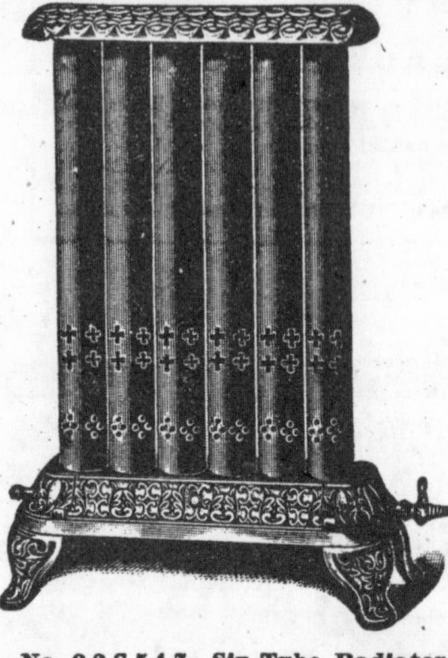

No. 22C547 Six-Tube Radiator. Height, 31 inches; length, 20 inches; width, 8 inches. Shipping weight, 45 pounds. Price..........................$3.45

No. 22C548 Eight-Tube Radiator. Height, 31 inches; length, 25 inches; width, 8 inches. Shipping weight, 53 pounds. Price..........................$4.60

WE ILLUSTRATE A LINE OF POWERFUL GAS RADIATORS.

MADE IN THREE SIZES.

They are handsome in appearance, radiating tubes being made of blue polished steel with cast top and base, finished in gold bronze.

THESE HEATERS have great radiating qualities, with the least possible consumption of gas, owing to the improved burners used. The tubes are large, each one being provided with two large Scotch tip burners, making the heating capacity greater than in ordinary radiators. Are also provided with a very convenient lighting device, so arranged that all the jets are lighted at once.

DO NOT FAIL TO STATE WHETHER YOU USE NATURAL OR MANUFACTURED GAS.

THIS ELEGANT, BUT PLAIN LITTLE ROUND HEATER AT $1.50

and upwards, burns an illuminating flame and makes a splendid little temporary heater for a large room or a permanent heater for a small room. The top and base are made of the best stove plate castings. The drum or body is made of sheet steel and the top is nickeled. Fitted with nozzle for rubber tube connection to any ordinary gaslight fixture. For prices on flexible gas stove tubing, see No. 22C563, on next page.

No. 22C549 Height, 20 inches from floor to top of ornament; diameter of drum, 6½ inches; shipping weight, 13 pounds. Price..........................$1.50

No. 22C550 Height, 24 inches from floor to top of ornament; diameter of drum, 8½ inches; shipping weight, 20 pounds. Price..........................$2.25

Do not fail to state whether you use natural or manufactured gas.

Tested and Well Satisfied.

Geneva, N. Y.

Sears, Roebuck & Co., Chicago, Ill.

Dear Sirs: I have used the gas heating stove one year and am well satisfied with it. The gas range arrived in good order, has been well tested, and will, I believe, be all you said it to be. It is just as good a stove as is sold by our local dealers for more money. I think I saved at least $5.00. I also ordered a sewing machine from you three months ago which has proved perfectly satisfactory.

Yours truly, NELS NELSON.

Has Not Seen the Stove He Would Exchange Ours For.

Goshen, Ind.

Sears, Roebuck & Co., Chicago, Ill.

Dear Sirs: Am pleased to say that the gas heating stove is the most satisfactory one I have ever had to work with. Have used it over a year, and cleaned it only once, and find it works as well today as at first. I have not yet seen the stove I would have in exchange for it. The price is such, also, that I have saved at least five or six dollars over freight expenses.

Yours respectfully, MRS. H. W. BROCKMAN.

OPEN FIRE PLACE GAS STOVES.

IN BRINGING OUT THIS LINE of open fire place gas stoves we have not spared any expense to make them THE BEST IN THE WORLD. They are all supplied with atmospheric blue flame burners, asbestos flame plate in the back and a 3-inch pipe collar for flue connections on the rear. Front is fancy stove plate casting, and outer body of blue polished steel. Inner side walls, bottom reflector and front fender are handsome polished copper finish. **This style of stove needs no recommendation as it is too well known and popular.**

WE GUARANTEE THEM TO PLEASE YOU IN EVERY PARTICULAR, OR YOUR MONEY WILL BE REFUNDED. . . .

They are made in two sizes, to heat from the smallest to the largest room in your home. Fitted for either rubber tube or iron pipe connection as desired. For prices on flexible gas stove tubing, see No. 22C563 on next page.

No. 22C552 Height, from floor to top of cast front, 23 inches; width, cast front, 16 inches; depth, 9 inches. Shipping weight, 28 pounds. Price............$3.38

No. 22C553 Height, from floor to top of cast front, 26½ inches; width, cast front, 17¼ inches; depth, 11 inches. Shipping weight, 35 pounds. Price....$4.05

Do not fail to state whether you use natural or manufactured gas.

WE ALSO OFFER AN IMPROVED STYLE of open front fire place gas heaters, made of blue polished steel, with the same blue flame atmospheric burners, the same mineral fibre asbestos flame plate and the same pipe connection in the back. The corners are nickel plated castings and the arch over opening is nickel casting. This very handsome pattern we offer at $5.40, in one size only. Its superior style is its attraction. Fitted for either rubber tube or iron pipe connection, as desired. See No. 22C563 on next page for prices on flexible gas stove tubing. We cannot recommend this pattern too highly, and when you order one, if it does not prove entirely satisfactory to you in every way, you can return it to us within thirty days, and your money will be refunded, together with all the freight you have paid.

No. 22C555 Height, 22½ inches; width, 17 inches; depth, 10 inches. Shipping weight, 25 pounds. Price..........................$5.40

Do not fail to state whether you use natural or manufactured gas.

EACH STOVE GUARANTEED AND EVERY PLATE WARRANTED.

GAS COOKING STOVES.

GAS HOT PLATES FROM 25c to $2.00. | GAS RANGES ON NEXT PAGE, $11.50 to $21.30. | Gas Cookers from $4.50 to $6.60. Gas Rangettes from $9.00 to $11.40.

IN OFFERING THIS SPLENDID LINE OF GAS COOKING STOVES AND RANGETTES AT SUCH LOW PRICES, we are endeavoring to give our gas consuming customers the benefit of the cost of material and labor with but our one small percentage of profit added. With gas hot plates at from 25 cents to $2.00, gas cookers with ovens from $4.50 to $6.60, and the little ranges or gas rangettes from $9.00 to $11.40, you will find the assortment second to none in the world. These gas stoves cannot be used with gasoline gas.

ON THE NEXT PAGE IS OUR LINE OF THE WORLD'S BEST GAS RANGES.

Nursery Gas Plate.

No. 22C556 Single Burner Gas Plate. Suitable for nursery use, warming water for shaving or cooking anything in a small vessel. Black iron. Size, 6x3½ inches. Weight, 2 pounds. Price. 25c

Gas Hot Plates.

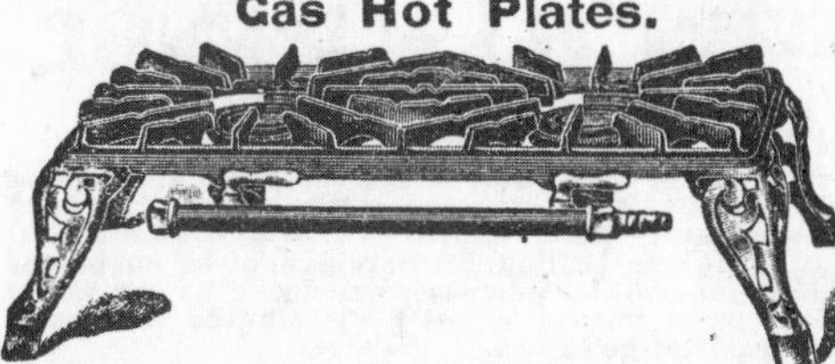

This Gas Hot Plate with two or three burners can be placed on a table or the top of your cooking stove and connected with the gas light fixture by the rubber tube quoted below as No. 22C563 and No. 22C560. It will cook over each burner just as well as over the burner on the highest priced gas range; the two-burner measures 9x18 inches and weighs 10 pounds and the three-burner measures 9x26¼ inches and weighs 16 pounds. Frame is 5¾ inches high, aluminum finished with nickel legs. A high grade stove. Material and workmanship the best. Will last a lifetime. The burners give a hot flame with two rings of jets, which are directed so as to have the most effect on the cooking utensils above.

No. 22C558 Two burners. Price.......... $1.05
No. 22C559 Three burners. Price.......... 1.60

Always state whether stoves are intended to be used for natural or artificial gas when writing your order. These gas stoves cannot be used with gasoline gas.

Gas Hot Plates.

This Gas Hot Plate is a handsomer pattern than those shown above and has a larger top. It is made with two or three burners as desired; the two-burner measures 11x20½ inches and weighs 14 pounds and the three-burner measures 11x30 inches and weighs 18 pounds. Frame is 7 inches high, black japanned, with nickel legs and levers. The top surface is large and so arranged that pots and pans can be slid over it in any direction. The burner has a loose cap and gives two rings of flame.

No. 22C561 Two burners. Price......... $1.35
No. 22C562 Three burners. Price.......... 2.00

Always state whether stoves are intended to be used for natural or artificial gas when writing your order. These gas stoves cannot be used with gasoline gas.

Gas Stove Tubing.

No. 22C563 Flexible Patent End Gas Stove Rubber Tubing. Covering is made of braided mohair; will not crack or break. Comes in 4, 5, 6, 8 and 10-foot pieces. Price, per foot.......... 3½c

No. 22C560 Pure Rubber Gas Stove Tubing. Guaranteed against leakage for two years. Inner tube is made of pure rubber, outer cover is silk finished webbing. This is the very best tubing made and will outlast the ordinary kind several years. Comes in 4, 6, 8 and 10-foot lengths. Price, per foot.......... 8c

Saves About Half the Price.

Bradford, Pa.

Sears, Roebuck & Co., Chicago, Ill.

Gentlemen: Some time ago I ordered a gas stove and got it in good order, and am pleased with it. Saved about half on the price. I could not get an inferior stove for twice the price in stores here and near by. I will always be glad to order from you in the future, Yours truly, THOMAS FISHER.

No Fault to Find.

Youngstown, O.

Sears, Roebuck & Co., Chicago, Ill.

Dear Sirs: The gas stove I purchased from you was received in good condition and is in every way just as you represented it to be. It is a beauty, a grand baker, and takes but little fuel. I have had it almost one year and have no fault to find with it. I think it is the grandest and best stove I ever saw. I could not have purchased a stove like it here for less than double the price. I am well pleased with it. I am,

Yours respectfully, MRS. MARY SMITH.

$4.50 Gas Cooker.

No. 22C564 With 2 regular cooker burners and burner under oven. The oven in this gas cooker will do as fine work as the most expensive gas range oven, as it is built on practical lines, but being made of sheet steel reduces the cost and enables you to have a two-burner gas range at $4.50. This cooker can be connected with flexible rubber tubing as described under No. 22C563 and No. 22C560, or it can be connected with gas pipe as desired. First class baking is guaranteed. STOVE No. 02. Height, 27½ inches. Top, 24x16½ inches. Oven, 16 inches wide, 12 inches high and 12 inches deep. Oven is a quick and splendid baker. Connect with rubber tubing or gas pipe as desired. Weight, crated, 49 pounds. Rubber tubing extra, see No. 22C563 and No. 22C560.

No. 22C564 Price, as shown.......... $4.50

Always state whether stoves are intended to be used for natural or artificial gas when writing your order. These gas stoves cannot be used with gasoline gas.

$5.40 to $6.60 Gas Cookers.

Regular Range Standard Star Burners, same as used in the highest priced gas ranges. The ovens are made with double flues and galvanized tops. This large gas cooker possesses all the first class features of the gas ranges and will do the work done by the best gas range ever produced. It is made with two burners, three burners or four burners on top as desired and one burner under the oven. The main top and the top burners are exactly the same—large powerful burners as those used on our world's best gas ranges. Send us your order and if you are not satisfied you can return the cooker to us at any time within 30 days and your money will be refunded, together with any freight you may have paid.

STOVE No. 2. Height, 30 inches. Top, 24½x21½ inches. Oven, 18 inches wide, 12 inches high and 12 inches deep. With two burners on top and one burner under oven. Wgt. crated 60 lbs.

No. 22C565 Price.......... $5.40

STOVE No. 3. As shown in illustration. Height, 30 inches. Top, 24½x21½ inches. Oven, 18 inches wide, 12 inches high and 12 inches deep. With three burners on top and one burner under oven. Weight, crated, 76 pounds.

No. 22C566 Price.......... $6.00

STOVE No. 4. Height, 30 inches. Top, 24½x21½ inches. Oven, 18 inches wide, 12 inches high and 12 inches deep. With four burners on top and one burner under oven. Weight, crated, 83 lbs.

No. 22C567 Price.......... $6.60

Always state whether stoves are intended to be used for natural or artificial gas when writing your order. These gas stoves cannot be used with gasoline gas.

Gas Rangettes.

For either natural gas or manufactured gas as required. With four burners on top and two-line burner under oven. In offering this gas range at $9.00 and $9.60, according to the kind of gas used, we have met a demand for a lower priced but high class small gas range which has all the good qualities of any gas range made with the defects of none. These low prices are the result of manufacturing large quantities, giving you the benefit of the cost of the material and labor with but our one small percentage of profit added. Try one and your neighbors will want one like it. If not perfectly satisfactory in every respect you can return it to us any time within 30 days and your money will be refunded, together with the freight you have paid.

Our Elegant Low Broiler Rangette.

STOVE No. 16. Has four powerful star burners, one of which is extra large, making it of double power, also simmering burner. Height from floor to main top, 31 inches. Top, 23x23 inches, with two side shelves 6 inches wide. Oven 16x16 inches and 14½ inches high. Body and oven made of cold rolled steel plate. Has nickeled oven door frame, panel and handle. Furnished with closed top for natural gas, and open grates (as shown) for artificial gas. Weight, crated, 130 pounds.

No. 22C568 For manufactured gas. Price. $9.00
No. 22C569 For natural gas. Price....... 9.60

These gas stoves cannot be used with gasoline gas.

AT $10.80 AND $11.40. For either natural or manufactured gas as ordered. In offering this little range or rangette, with a low broiler we have enabled our customers to buy a modest priced but handsome small range without being deprived of a broiling oven. The baking oven is 16x16x11 inches and the broiling oven is 16x16x5 inches. This gives ample room for baking and a splendid broiling oven also. Oven door is lined, has cast iron oven bottom and direct action oven. It is fitted with wood handled lever valves and four powerful removable star top burners, the right hand front one extra large, making it of double power, also simmering burner and a perfect broiling and baking burner. Each and every one of these rangettes have our binding guarantee the same as the big gas ranges on the next page. They have all the advantage of the full size ranges excepting in size. See page 14 for our C. O. D. subject to examination offer. If you order one of these rangettes and do not feel perfectly satisfied you can return it any time within thirty days and your money will be refunded, together with any freight you may have paid.

STOVE No. 160. Height from floor to main top, 31 inches. Top 23x23, with two side shelves 6 inches wide. Oven, 16x16 inches and 11 inches high. Broiler, 16x16 inches and 5 inches high. Body and oven made of cold rolled steel plate. Has nickeled oven door frame, panel and handle, nickeled front supply pipe. Furnished with closed top for natural gas and open grates (as shown) for artificial gas. Weight, crated, 135 pounds.

No. 22C570 For manufactured gas. Price.......... $10.80
No. 22C571 For natural gas. Price..... 11.40

These gas stoves cannot be used with gasoline gas.

SEE NEXT PAGE FOR THE WORLD'S FINEST GAS RANGES.

THE WORLD'S BEST GAS RANGES AT $8.50 TO $17.30

Furnished for either Artificial or Natural Gas and for any Pressure Desired.

THE ACME OF PERFECTION IN GAS SAVING GAS RANGES.

Only the best materials are used; the highest grade of polished steel, of beautiful color, not requiring blacking or Japan, the highest finish of smooth, strong stove plate castings, made in a factory noted for the quality of material used. Every range is guaranteed to be perfect in operation and workmanship. The illustrations do not do justice to these elegant goods; they must be seen to be appreciated. We court inspection and comparison with any gas ranges in the market. These ranges are built for economy in fuel. They can be set near an open window or door without being affected by the draft, as the sides are closed all around. Quality in construction is first with us, and the large quantities we produce enables us to sell them at these unheard of prices, $8.50 to $17.30, for the various sizes and styles described; it is the actual cost to us in large quantities with but our one small percentage of profit added.

YOUR GAS COMPANY WILL CONNECT IT FOR YOU at the same small charge

they always make when bought from them. Gas companies are always glad to connect our ranges, as they are desirous of selling their product of gas and not anxious to be dealers in gas stoves. They had to go into the gas stove business because the high prices asked by the stove and hardware dealers included so much profit the people did not buy them, thus restricting the consumption of gas, but our prices are so low and we sell so many ranges the gas companies are our friends, encouraging us to sell more and more gas ranges, connecting them for our customers for the same small fee they charge when they sell a gas range, and recommending our ranges everywhere as the most economical, durable and efficient ranges to be found.

The more ranges we sell the more gas they sell, and the consumer is the better pleased on account of the beautiful range at such a low price as $8.50 to $17.30, as described above.

SINGLE OVEN GAS RANGE.

WITH COUNTERBALANCED DROP OVEN DOOR.

AT $8.50 AND $9.65 we offer this famous single oven gas range at prices lower than the lowest, lower than any one can offer them, lower than any gas company cares to sell them, so low that gas companies are buying them from us and are proud to connect them for you at a small fee, and so low that it relieves them of the expense and trouble of trying to sell gas ranges, for we are selling them so fast they are kept busy increasing their facilities and capacity for supplying gas.

They are recommending our gas ranges for economy, good service and low prices. The range is excellence itself, and as handsome as it is good. Has three Standard Star burners, one triple capacity Giant burner with simmering burner in center and lighting separately. Four-line burner for oven, and oven lighter. The illustration shows it ready for manufactured gas. When ordered for natural gas, we furnish it with closed lids or griddle covers.

SEE PAGE 14 FOR OUR LIBERAL $1.00 TO $5.00 C. O. D. SUBJECT TO EXAMINATION OFFER.

PRICE LIST SINGLE OVEN GAS RANGE.
Do not fail to state whether you use manufactured gas or natural gas.

Catalogue Number	Stove No.	Size of Top, Including End Shelves, Inches	Size of Oven, inches	Height from Floor, inches	Shipping Weight, pounds	Price
22C572	416P	35½x22¼	16x16¼x11	29¼	162	$8.50
22C573	418P	37½x22¼	18x16¼x11	29¼	170	9.65

SINGLE OVEN GAS RANGE.

WITH WATER HEATER EXTENSION, CONTAINING WATER COIL TO BE CONNECTED TO A RANGE BOILER HAVING CITY WATER PRESSURE.

AT $12.85 AND $14.00 we offer this famous single oven and Water Heater Gas Range, with three Standard Star Burners and one triple capacity Giant Burner with one small simmering burner. These Standard Star Drilled Burners cannot be surpassed for durability and intense heat for cooking purposes excepting by our Giant burner. Our patent four-line oven burner equally distributes the heat, being the only "Bake Even" Gas Range in use.

The oven sides and bottom are flush with the oven door opening, the oven door is counter balanced and drops on a level with the oven bottom. It is smooth and free from anything to catch the pans when drawn from the oven. The top oven plate is double, forming a circulating flue for the heat, and is the best oven construction in use. The scavenger pan under the top burners catches all the grease and dirt; it is made of galvanized iron and easily removed. When ordered for natural gas, we furnish the range, with closed lids or griddle covers. Gas cocks are nickeled on brass.

SEE PAGE 14 FOR OUR LIBERAL $1.00 TO $5.00 C. O. D. SUBJECT TO EXAMINATION OFFER.

PRICE LIST SINGLE OVEN GAS RANGE.
Do not fail to state whether you use manufactured gas or natural gas.

Catalogue Number	Stove Number	Size of Top, Including Water Heater and End Shelf, Inches	Size of Oven, inches	Height from Floor	Shipping Weight	Price
22C576	416W	39½x22¼	16x16¼x11	29¼ inches	170 pounds	$12.85
22C577	418W	41½x22¼	18x16¼x11	29¼ inches	185 pounds	14.00

THESE RANGES ARE constructed of the best grade of polished steel of beautiful color. The sheet steel is lined with asbestos. The main top, main front and frame of oven doors are of the finest cast stove plate, made from the highest grades of pure pig iron, and must not be confused with the cheap mixtures of scrap iron used in so many other makes of gas ranges. The front supply pipe and cocks are nickeled.

GAS RANGE WITH LOW BROILING OVEN.

AT $11.90 AND $12.95 we offer this Drop Door Gas Range with low Broiler, in competition with the highest priced gas ranges in the world. They are gas savers and customer makers. This is the exact same range as Catalogue Nos. 22C572 and 22C573 at $8.50 and $9.65, with the addition of the low broiling oven, and is 3¼ and 4¼ inches higher. It has the exact same special points of interest to the user, as carefully described above, the same counter balanced oven door, the guarantee of efficiency and economy in the consumption of gas, and is sold at the heretofore unheard of price for such an elegant gas range of $11.90 and $12.95, according to size and attachments.

The four-line oven burner enables you to broil and bake both at the same time. This range costs a little more than the single oven range above but the difference is fully repaid by this saving. The illustration shows it ready for manufactured gas. When ordered for natural gas we furnish this range with closed lids or griddle covers.

SEE PAGE 14 FOR OUR LIBERAL $1.00 TO $5.00 C. O. D. SUBJECT TO EXAMINATION OFFER.

PRICE LIST LOW BROILER GAS RANGE.
Do not fail to state whether you use manufactured gas or natural gas.

Catalogue Number	Stove No.	Size of Top Including End Shelves, Inches	Baking Oven, inches	Broiling Oven, inches	Height from Floor	Shipping Weight	Price
22C574	116P	35½ x 22¼	16x16¼x11	16x16¼x9¼	32⅛ in.	181 lbs.	$11.90
22C575	118P	37½ x 22¼	18x16¼x11	18x16¼x9¼	33⅛ in.	193 lbs.	12.95

WE CAN ALWAYS FURNISH BURNERS AND REPAIR PARTS FOR GAS RANGES.

GAS RANGE WITH LOW BROILING OVEN.

WITH WATER HEATER EXTENSION CONTAINING WATER COIL TO BE CONNECTED TO A RANGE BOILER HAVING CITY WATER PRESSURE.

AT $16.25 AND $17.30 we offer this Drop Door Gas Range with Low Broiler, in competition with the highest priced gas ranges in the world. They are gas savers and customer makers. This is the exact same range as Catalogue Nos. 22C574 and 22C575 at $11.90 and $12.95, with the addition of the water heater extension, giving six cooking holes. It has the exact same special points of interest to the user, as carefully described above, the same spring balanced oven door, the guarantee of efficiency and economy in the consumption of gas, and is sold at the heretofore unheard of price for such an elegant gas range of $16.25 and $17.30, according to size and attachments. With four-line burner operating the baking and broiling ovens at same time.

The illustration shows it ready for manufactured gas. When ordered for natural gas we furnish this range with closed lids or griddle covers.

See page 14 for our liberal $1.00 to $5.00 C. O. D. subject to examination offer. We can always furnish Burners and Repair Parts for GAS RANGES.

PRICE LIST LOW BROILER GAS RANGE.
Do not fail to state whether you use manufactured gas or natural gas.

Catalogue Number	Stove Number	Size of Top, Including Water Heater and End Shelf, Inches	Baking Oven, inches	Broiling Oven, inches	Height from Floor	Shipping Weight	Price
22C578	116W	39½x22¼	16x16¼x11	16x16¼x9¼	32⅛ in.	205 lbs.	$16.25
22C579	118W	41½x22¼	18x16¼x11	18x16¼x9¼	33⅛ in.	225 lbs.	17.30

WOOD MANTEL DEPARTMENT.

ACME BEAUTY LINE OF GLOSS FINISH SOLID OAK MANTELS, WITH OR WITHOUT COMPLETE OUTFIT, AS DESIRED.

SEND FOR OUR FREE MANTEL CATALOGUE WHICH SHOWS LARGE FULL PAGE ILLUSTRATIONS AND FULL DESCRIPTION OF OUR COMPLETE LINE OF WOOD MANTELS, WHICH LACK OF SPACE WILL NOT PERMIT US TO ILLUSTRATE IN THIS BOOK.

AT $5.40 TO $28.85 according to shape, style and outfit selected, we offer this unsurpassed line of Solid Oak, Gloss Finished Acme Beauty Mantels in competition with the world, in quality, price and style. We do not sell imitation oak or soft wood goods. All are solid oak and gloss finished. Our prices are packed and delivered on board the cars in Chicago, and guaranteed to reach you in perfect condition and to be all we represent them to be, or you can return the shipment at our expense of freight both ways, and your money will be refunded. Acme mantels are solid oak.

Acme Beauty Outfit No. 1.

Outfit No. 1 Acme Beauty Combination Grate consists of an oxidized, bronze plated, steel grate frame, 24½ inches wide by 30¼ inches high, with an opening 20 inches wide, a 20-inch black grate basket and ash screen. The basket is very heavy and unexcelled for burning coal or wood. The steel frame has projecting canopy at the top as shown. This outfit does not include any fire brick, as same can be bought in your locality for less than the freight on them would amount to. Weight, 50 pounds.

No. 22C580 Price, outfit No. 1, when ordered separately from mantel.......................**$2.38**

Acme Beauty Outfit No. 2.

Outfit No. 2 Acme Beauty Combination, consists of this elegant bronze plated steel frame, 24½ inches wide, 30¼ inches high, with 20-inch opening, receiving 20-inch basket with a dumping bottom. This outfit includes heavy fire brick back, double draft flue dampers, and ash screen. The grate basket is 12 inches deep and the heavy fire brick back is in one piece, ready for placing. A skilled mechanic is not required to set this outfit No. 2. Anybody can set it. Handsome, durable, economical. Costs more than ordinary grates, but saves its price in one season's use. Weight, 120 pounds.

No. 22C581 Price, outfit No. 2, when ordered separately from mantel.......................**$6.84**

At $5.40 for the woodwork only; $10.15 with tile for facing and hearth; $12.53 complete with outfit No. 1 and $16.99 complete with outfit No. 2, we offer this unsurpassed mantel base packed and delivered on the cars in Chicago. Furnished 4 feet 9 inches or 5 feet wide, as desired. Total height, 4 feet 6 inches. Tile opening, 36 inches wide and 36 inches high.

BASE No. 1430.

No. 22C582 Solid oak woodwork only. Weight, 100 pounds. Price.......................**$5.40**

No. 22C583 Solid oak woodwork with tile for facing and hearth; without grate outfit. Weight, 175 pounds. Price.......................**$10.15**

No. 22C584 Solid oak, complete with outfit No. 1 and tile for facing and hearth. Weight, 225 pounds. Price....**$12.53**

No. 22C585 Solid oak, complete with outfit No. 2 and tile for facing and hearth. Weight, 275 pounds. Price....**$16.99**

If summer front is wanted, as shown on No. 22C594, add $1.25 to either outfit.

At $5.70 we offer this elegant Acme Beauty Mantel Base, woodwork only; $10.45 with tile for facing and hearth; $12.83 complete with outfit No. 1 and $17.29 complete with outfit No. 2, we offer this elegant fluted column mantel base, packed and delivered on the cars in Chicago. Furnished 4 feet 6 inches or 5 feet wide, as desired. Total height, 4 feet 4 inches. Tile opening, 36 inches wide by 36 inches high. Hearth, 18 inches deep and full width of mantel.

BASE No. 1379.

No. 22C586 Solid oak woodwork only. Weight, 100 pounds. Price.......................**$5.70**

No. 22C587 Solid oak woodwork with tile for facing and hearth; without grate outfit. Weight, 175 pounds. Price..**$10.45**

No. 22C588 Solid oak, complete with outfit No. 1 and tile for facing and hearth. Weight, 225 pounds. Price....**$12.83**

No. 22C589 Solid oak, complete with outfit No. 2 and tile for facing and hearth. Weight, 275 pounds. Price....**$17.29**

If summer front is wanted, as shown on No. 22C594, add $1.25 to either outfit.

$6.55 buys this Rich Smooth Veneered Column Acme Beauty Mantel Base, woodwork only; $11.30 gets it with tile for facing and hearth; $13.69 complete with outfit No. 1, and $18.15 complete with outfit No. 2, we offer this royal veneered column mantel base, delivered on cars in Chicago. Either 4 feet 6 inches or 5 feet wide, as desired. Total height, 4 feet 4 inches. Tile opening, 36x36 inches. Hearth, 18 inches deep, and full width of mantel.

BASE No. 1380.

No. 22C590 Solid oak woodwork only. Weight, 100 pounds. Price.......................**$6.55**

No. 22C591 Solid oak woodwork with tile for facing and hearth; without grate outfit. Weight, 175 pounds. Price.......................**$11.30**

No. 22C592 Solid oak, complete with outfit No. 1 and tile for facing and hearth. Weight, 225 pounds. Price **$13.69**

No. 22C593 Solid oak, complete with outfit No. 2 and tile for facing and hearth. Weight, 275 pounds. Price...**$18.15**

If summer front is wanted, as shown on No. 22C594, add $1.25 to either outfit.

At $13.80 for the woodwork with French beveled mirror, 28x16 inches; $18.55 with tile for facing and hearth; $20.93 complete with outfit No. 1 and $25.39 complete with outfit No. 2, we offer this beautiful mirrored mantel packed and delivered on the cars in Chicago. 4 feet 8 inches wide, Total height, 6 feet 8 inches. Tile opening, 36 inches wide and 36 inches high. Hearth, 18 inches deep and full width of mantel.

MANTEL No. 1324.

No. 22C594 Solid oak woodwork with mirror. Weight, 150 pounds. Price.......................**$13.80**

No. 22C595 Solid oak woodwork with mirror and tile for facing and hearth; without grate outfit. Weight, 225 pounds. Price.......................**$18.55**

No. 22C596 Solid oak, complete with outfit No. 1 and tile for facing and hearth. Weight, 275 pounds. Price... **$20.93**

No. 22C597 Solid oak, complete with outfit No 2 and tile for facing and hearth. Weight, 325 pounds. Price.. **$25.39**

If summer front is wanted, as shown, add $1.25 to either outfit.

For illustrations and descriptions of Grate Outfits, see Nos. 22C580 and 22C581 at top of page.

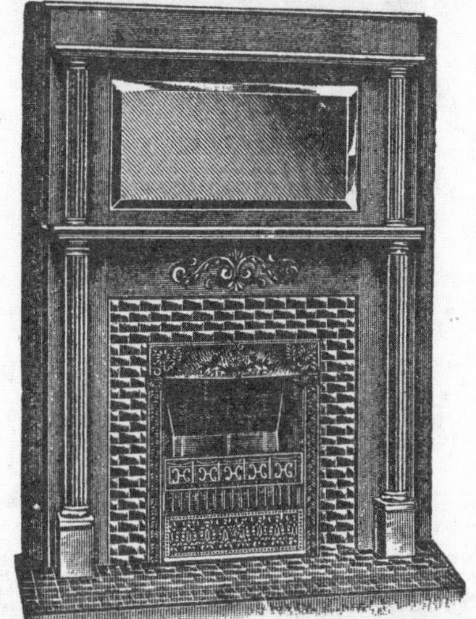

At $13.68 this fluted column Acme Beauty Mantel is offered with French beveled mirror 36x18 inches; at $13.68 for the woodwork and mirror, $18.43 with tile for facing and hearth, $20.81 complete with outfit No. 1, and $25.27 complete with outfit No. 2, we offer this unparalleled mirrored mantel packed and delivered on the cars in Chicago. Either 4 feet 6 inches or 5 feet wide as desired. Total height, 6 feet 4 inches. Tile opening, 36x36 inches. Hearth, 18 inches deep and full width of mantel.

MANTEL No. 1379.

No. 22C598 Solid oak woodwork with mirror. Weight, 150 pounds. Price.......................**$13.68**

No. 22C599 Solid oak woodwork with mirror and tile for facing and hearth, without grate outfit. Weight, 225 pounds. Price.......................**$18.43**

No. 22C600 Solid oak, complete with outfit No. 1 and tile for facing and hearth. Weight, 275 pounds. Price.....**$20.81**

No. 22C601 Solid oak, complete with outfit No. 2 and tile for facing and hearth. Weight, 325 pounds. Price.....**$25.27**

If summer front is wanted, as shown on No. 22C594, add $1.25 to either outfit.

For illustrations and descriptions of Grate Outfits, see Nos. 22C580 and 22C581 at top of page.

$12.76 buys this Acme Beauty Mantel, with French Beveled Mirror 24x16 inches; at $12.76 for the woodwork and mirror, $17.50 with tile for facing and hearth, $19.89 complete with outfit No. 1, and $24.35 complete with outfit No. 2, we offer this rich and royal mirrored mantel packed and delivered on the cars in Chicago. Either 4 feet 9 inches or 5 feet wide, as desired. Total height, 6 feet 11 inches. Tile opening, 36x36 inches. Hearth, 18 inches deep and full width of mantel.

MANTEL No. 1429.

No. 22C602 Solid oak woodwork with mirror. Weight, 150 pounds. Price.......................**$12.76**

No. 22C603 Solid oak woodwork with mirror and tile for facing and hearth; without grate outfit. Weight, 225 pounds. Price.......................**$17.50**

No. 22C604 Solid oak, complete with outfit No. 1 and tile for facing and hearth. Weight, 275 pounds. Price..**$19.89**

No. 22C605 Solid oak, complete with outfit No. 2 and tile for facing and hearth. Weight, 325 pounds. Price..**$24.35**

If summer front is wanted, as shown on No. 22C594, add $1.25 to either outfit.

For illustrations and descriptions of Grate Outfits, see Nos. 22C580 and 22C581 at top of page.

Our $13.15 Acme Beauty Mantel,

With Oval French Beveled Mirror, 28x16 inches.

$17.90 includes the tile for facing and hearth. $20.29 complete with outfit No. 1, and $24.75 complete with outfit No. 2. At these prices we pack and deliver on the cars in Chicago this stately fluted column mirrored mantel. Either 4 feet 5 inches or 5 feet wide, as desired. Total height, 6 feet 1 inch. Tile opening, 36x36 inches. Hearth, 18 inches deep and full width of mantel.

MANTEL No. 1394.

No. 22C606 Solid oak woodwork with mirror. Weight, 150 pounds. Price.... **$13.15**

No. 22C607 Solid oak woodwork with mirror and tile for facing and hearth, without grate outfit. Weight, 225 pounds. Price **$17.90**

No. 22C608 Solid oak, complete with outfit No. 1 and tile for facing and hearth. Weight, 275 pounds. Price **$20.29**

No. 22C609 Solid oak, complete with outfit No. 2 and tile for facing and hearth. Weight, 325 pounds. Price **$24.75**

If summer front, as shown on No. 22C594, is wanted, add $1.25 to either outfit.

For illustrations and descriptions of Grate Outfits, see Nos. 22C580 and 22C581 on preceding page.

Our $15.05 Favorite Acme Beauty Mantel.

$15.05 and upwards, according to outfit combination desired, for this **Favorite Acme Beauty Mantel** with elegant smooth veneered columns, French bevel plate mirror, 36x18 inches, mosaic effect in tile facing and tile hearth. Size, 6 feet 4 inches high and furnished from 4 feet 6 inches or 5 feet wide, as desired. All the preceding illustrations are equally popular and only a matter of taste in selection, but this is the people's favorite, and the price is so low our factory is kept crowded with work on this favorite mantel. **At $15.05 for the woodwork and 36x18-inch bevel edge French plate mirror; $19.80** after you add the artistic dark and light tile for the mosaic effect in the hearth and facing; **$22.18** includes all the above and adds the beautiful oxydized bronze plated steel grate outfit No. 1, as shown and described as No. 22C580, and **$26.65** gives you this magnificent mantel with the **Acme Beauty Combination Outfit No. 2**; making all the elegance one could ask in a parlor mantel. The total height of this Favorite Mantel is 6 feet 4 inches; the width will be 4 feet 6 inches or 5 feet, just as you may order it. The tile opening is 36x36 inches, and the hearth is 18 inches deep and the full width of the mantel.

MANTEL No. 1380.

No. 22C618 Solid oak woodwork and mirror, without tile or grate outfit. Weight, 125 pounds. Price........... **$15.05**

No. 22C619 Solid oak woodwork, with mirror and art tile for facing and hearth, without grate outfit. Weight, 250 pounds. Price **$19.80**

No. 22C620 Solid oak, complete with art tile and combination outfit No. 1. Weight, 300 pounds. Price........... **$22.18**

No. 22C621 Solid oak, complete with art tile and combination outfit No. 2. Weight, 350 pounds. Price........... **$26.65**

If summer front is desired, as shown on No. 22C594, add $1.25 to the price with either outfit.

For illustrations and descriptions of Acme Beauty Combination Grate Outfits, see Nos. 22C580 and 22C581 on preceding page.

At $13.39 Large French Beveled Mirror Mantel,

With Fluted Columns, 36x18-inch French Plate Mirror. Total Height, 6 feet 4 inches.

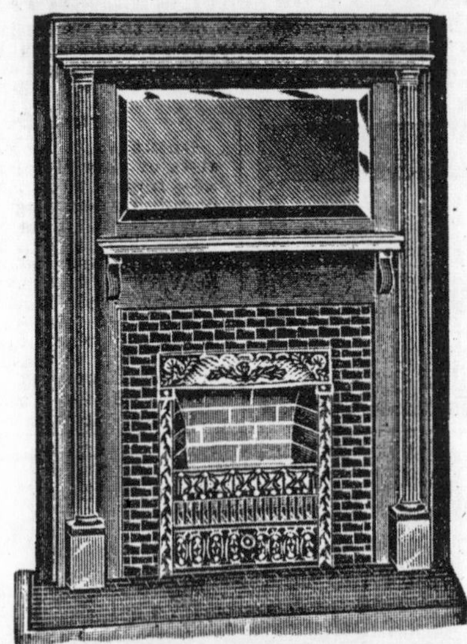

$13.39 is for the woodwork with mirror; $18.14 includes the tile for facing and hearth; $20.50 is mantel complete with outfit No. 1, tile for facing and hearth as shown, and $24.98 complete with outfit No. 2, with tile for facing and hearth. These prices are packed and delivered on the cars in Chicago. Either 4 feet 6 inches or 5 feet wide as desired. Total height, 6 feet 4 inches. Tile opening, 35½x35½ inches. Hearth, 18 inches deep and full width of mantel.

MANTEL No. 1385.

No. 22C610 Solid oak woodwork with mirror. Weight, 150 pounds. Price........................ **$13.39**

No. 22C611 Solid oak woodwork with mirror and tile for facing and hearth, without grate outfit. Weight, 225 pounds. Price **$18.14**

No. 22C612 Solid oak, complete with outfit No. 1 and tile for facing and hearth. Weight, 275 pounds. Price.................................. **$20.50**

No. 22C613 Solid oak, complete with outfit No. 2 and tile for facing and hearth. Weight, 325 pounds. Price.................................. **$24.98**

If summer front, as shown on No. 22C594, is desired, add $1.25 to either outfit.

For illustrations and descriptions of Grate Outfits, see Nos. 22C580 and 22C581 on preceding page.

Our $18.24 Acme Beauty Mantel.

At $18.24 and up, we offer this massive veneered column mantel with 18x36-inch French bevel mirror. $18.24 is for the woodwork with mirror; $24.31 includes high art encaustic tile for facing and hearth; **$26.69** adds our No. 1 Acme Beauty outfit, as shown in the illustration; and at **$31.20** we offer this beautiful massive mantel, complete with outfit No. 2 and tile for facing and hearth, all ready to install. An outfit within the reach of all and of a design and finish that adapts it to the most elegant home. The mantels are packed and delivered on board cars in Chicago. Width, 5 feet; total height, 7 feet 3 inches; mirror, 18x36 inches; tile opening, 42 inches wide by 39 inches high; hearth, 18 inches deep and full width of mantel; columns, quarter sawed, veneered and 4 inches in diameter.

MANTEL No. 135.

No. 22C626 Solid oak woodwork and mirror, without tile and grate outfit. Weight, crated, 225 pounds. Price.. **$18.24**

No. 22C627 Solid oak woodwork, with high art tile for facing and hearth, without grate outfit. Weight, crated, 300 pounds. Price.................................. **$24.31**

No. 22C628 Solid oak, complete with high art tile and outfit No. 1. Weight, crated, 350 pounds. Price........... **$26.69**

No. 22C629 Solid oak, complete with high art tile and outfit No. 2. Weight, crated, 400 pounds. Price........... **$31.20**

If summer front is desired, as shown on No. 22C594, add $1.25 to the price with either outfit.

For illustrations and descriptions of Grate Outfits, see Nos. 22C580 and 22C581 on preceding page.

$14.24 and up, Buys this Royal Acme Beauty Mantel,

With One Large Oval French Plate Beveled Mirror, 16x28 inches. Total Height, 6 feet 8 inches.

At $14.24 for the woodwork and mirror only; $18.98 including the beautiful tile for facing and hearth; $21.37 with outfit No. 1 shown as No. 22C580 and $25.83 with outfit No. 2 as shown by No. 22C581, buys this Royal Beauty, packed and delivered on the cars in Chicago. Made 4 feet 8 inches or 5 feet wide as desired. Total height, 6 feet 8 inches. Tile opening, 36 inches wide and 36 inches high. Hearth, 18 inches deep and full width of mantel.

MANTEL No. 125.

No. 22C622 Solid oak woodwork with mirror. Weight, 150 pounds. Price... .... **$14.24**

No. 22C623 Solid oak woodwork and mirror with tile for facing and hearth, without grate outfit. Weight, 225 pounds. Price. **$18.98**

No. 22C624 Solid oak, complete with outfit No. 1 and tile for facing and hearth. Weight, 275 pounds. Price.................................. **$21.37**

No. 22C625 Solid oak, complete with outfit No. 2 and tile for facing and hearth, as shown above. Weight, 325 pounds. Price.................. **$25.83**

If summer front, as shown on No. 22C594, is desired, add $1.25 to either outfit.

For illustrations and descriptions of Grate Outfits, see Nos. 22C580 and 22C581 on preceding page.

Our $19.15 Acme Beauty Mantel.

Our $19.15 Oval French Bevel Mirror Mantel, with smooth quartered oak veneered columns. $19.15 is for the woodwork and mirror alone; **$25.20** adds the beautiful high art encaustic tile for facing and hearth; at **$27.58** you have a complete outfit with our No. 1 Acme Beauty grate; and at **$32.04** we offer this unapproached, smooth column, beveled mirror Acme Beauty Mantel, complete with our outfit No. 2, making all the elegance that could be desired. Outfit No. 2 can be installed by anyone, without the aid of a mantel setter or other mechanic. These prices are packed and delivered on board cars in Chicago. Total height of this mantel is 7 feet, and is furnished 5 feet wide only; the tile opening is 42 inches wide by 39 inches high; the tile hearth is 18 inches deep and full width of mantel.

MANTEL No. 1401.

No. 22C630 Solid oak woodwork with mirror. Weight crated, 225 pounds. Price **$19.15**

No. 22C631 Solid oak woodwork, with mirror and art tile for facing and hearth, without grate outfit. Weight, crated, 300 pounds. Price **$25.20**

No. 22C632 Solid oak, complete with art tile and Acme Beauty Outfit No. 1. Weight, crated, 350 lbs. Price.. **$27.58**

No. 22C633 Solid oak, complete with art tile and Acme Beauty Outfit No. 2. Weight, crated. 400 lbs. Price.. **$32.04**

If summer front is desired, as shown on No. 22C594, add $1.25 to the price with either outfit.

OUR $20.00 ACME BEAUTY MANTEL

AT $20.00 AND UPWARD we offer this unexcelled Acme Beauty Mantel complete with 36x18-inch French plate beveled edge mirror. We show a line of mantels absolutely unsurpassed in the extent of selection offered, and in the beauty and elegance of our different designs. Among our other mantels your selection can only be governed by your own tastes, but in this, our World's Finest Acme Beauty Mantel, with large French plate beveled edge mirror, in smooth gloss finish, plain sawed golden oak with the massive quartered oak veneered columns, as shown in the illustration, we feel that we are offering a mantel that is absolutely the best upon the market, and we know that it is at a price hitherto unheard of.

THE FULL BEAUTY OF THE MANTEL cannot be shown in the illustration, as the massive proportions of the columns, mirror shelf and heavy top shelf are lost on account of the small size of the cut. The wood stock is the most carefully selected kiln dried, solid oak, and no pains are spared in the high class golden finish given it.

AT $20.00 we offer the massive woodwork with mirror only, and all we ask is that you order it, examine it at your home, and if you do not find it to be all we claim, the best bargain you ever saw, regardless of price, we will accept the return of the mantel and refund the purchase price, together with any freight charges you may have paid.

$25.22 adds the high art encaustic tile for facing and hearth.

$27.60 includes our Acme Beauty Outfit No. 1, illustrated on page 45, but we especially recommend our Outfit No. 2 as being the only one suitable with a mantel of this high quality. Furthermore, the installation of this outfit does not require the services of a brick mason as does Outfit No. 1, as we do not ship the brick with this cheaper outfit.

$32.00 owns this unexcelled mantel, complete with mirror, high art encaustic tile for facing and hearth and our Acme Beauty Outfit No. 2 as shown on page 45. This outfit is equipped with fire brick back, double dust and smoke dampers, dumping bottom grate and heavy oxidized bronze steel plated front. This high class outfit should always be used with a high grade mantel such as this one. The total height of this mantel is 7 feet and the width 5 feet only. The French plate beveled edge mirror is 36x18 inches. The tile opening is 36 inches wide by 39 inches high.

MANTEL No. 1419.

No. 22C634 Solid oak woodwork with mirror, without tile or grate outfit. Weight, crated, 225 pounds. Price.......... **$20.00**

No. 22C635 Solid oak woodwork with high art tile for facing and hearth, without grate outfit. Weight, crated, 300 pounds. Price.......... **25.22**

No. 22C636 Solid oak, complete with high art tile and Outfit No. 1. Weight, crated, 350 pounds. Price.......... **27.60**

No. 22C637 Solid oak, complete with high art tile and Acme Beauty Outfit No. 2. Weight crated, 400 pounds. Price.......... **32.00**

When summer front is desired, as shown on No. 22C594, add $1.25 to price with either outfit.

HOUSE FURNACE DEPARTMENT.

Knowing the public has been paying too much profit on Hot Air House Furnaces, we have established this department and are manufacturing the best line of hard coal, soft coal and wood furnaces, that can be had anywhere, and at prices so low as to attract orders from dealers everywhere on account of the

HIGH QUALITY, SCIENTIFIC CONSTRUCTION, DURABILITY, EFFICIENCY IN VENTILATING AND HEATING AND THE LOW PRICES WE MAKE.

Write for our question blank or information sheet, and send us a rough sketch with correct inside measurements of each floor of your house, and we will send you a perfect floor plan, showing the best method of installation, an estimate of the total cost including hot air pipes, registers, wall pipes, elbows, boots and offsets, in fact, everything needed to install your furnace in your house and at prices hitherto unheard of. Plan your work so you can order in the spring or summer, as it takes two weeks to get out your order then, but in the fall rush it would take four to six weeks.

ACME HUMMER BITUMINOUS SOFT COAL OR WOOD FURNACE.

AT $24.64 TO $66.22 without casing. **$30.10 to $74.70** with double galvanized iron casing, tee, check draft and chains, cement and bolts, we offer this Acme Hummer heating and ventilating hot air furnace with broad top fire pot for soft coal and wood. The fire pot is so broad that long sticks of wood can be put in when you desire to burn this fuel. The Acme Hummer is a dome furnace and has the largest and heaviest wrought steel combustion dome of any furnace on the market, making it a perfect soft coal burning and a thoroughly durable, quick and powerful heater.

ACME HUMMER FURNACES FOR SOFT COAL AND WOOD.

Catalogue No.	22C15	22C16
Furnace No.	34	42
Diam. base plate, in.	34	42
Diam. fire pot, inches	20	24
Size ash door, inches	11x17	13x21
Size feed door, inches	8x12	9x14½
Diam. grate, inches	16	19½
Diam. dome, inches	29	34
Size of smoke pipe, in.	7	8
Height dome, inches	24	28
Height without casing, inches	50	52
Average height with casing, inches	62	64
Shipping weight, including casing, lbs.	650	875
Heating capacity, cubic feet	7,000 to 10,000	10,000 to 14,000
Price, without casing	$24.64	$35.84
Price, with casing, as shown	30.10	41.70

Catalogue No.	22C17	22C18
Furnace No.	48	58
Diam. base plate, in.	48	58
Diam. fire pot, inches	28	30
Size ash door, inches	13x21	13x21
Size feed door, inches	12x15	12x15
Diam. grate, inches	25½	26
Diam. dome, inches	40	46
Size of smoke pipe, in.	10	10
Height dome, inches	30	30
Height without casing, inches	56	56
Average height with casing, inches	68	68
Shipping weight including casings, lbs.	1,050	1,150
Heating capacity cubic feet	14,000 to 20,000	20,000 to 26,000
Price, without casing	$55.02	$66.22
Price, with casing, as shown	62.29	74.70

ACME TROPIC FURNACE FOR ANTHRACITE HARD COAL.

AT $25.20 TO $67.20 without casing; $30.67 to $75.68 with double galvanized casing, tee, check draft and chains, we offer this popular Acme Tropic hot air furnace for anthracite hard coal, as the most desirable coal burning furnace made. The Acme Tropic is a circular radiator furnace, being equipped with a heavy, steel plate dome and radiator, giving the greatest amount of utilized radiating surface above the fire pot and insuring the most economical consumption of fuel.

ACME TROPIC FURNACE FOR ANTHRACITE HARD COAL.

Catalogue No.	22C9	22C10
Furnace No.	34	38
Diam. base plate, in.	34	38
Diam. fire pot, inches	20	22
Size ash door, inches.	11x17	13x21
Size feed door, inches	8x12	9x14½
Diam. grate, inches	16	17½
Diam. smoke pipe, in.	7	7
Height, radiator, in.	12	14
Height, without casing, inches	48	52
Average height with casing, inches	60	64
Shipping weight, including casing, lbs.	700	830
Heating capacity, cubic feet	6,000 to 8,000	8,000 to 12,000
Price, without casing	$25.20	$30.80
Price, with casing as shown	30.67	36.86

Catalogue No.	22C11	22C12
Furnace No.	42	44
Diam. base plate, in.	42	44
Diam. fire pot, inches.	24	26
Size ash door, inches.	13x21	13x23
Size feed door, inches	9x14½	10x14
Diam. grate, inches	19½	21½
Diam. smoke pipe, in.	8	8
Height radiator, in.	16	16
Height, without casing, inches	54	56
Average height with casing, inches	66	68
Shipping weight, including casing, lbs.	950	1,160
Heating capacity, cubic feet	12,000 to 16,000	16,000 to 20,000
Price, without casing	$36.40	$44.80
Price, with casing as shown	42.46	51.47

Catalogue No.	22C13	22C14
Furnace No.	48	58
Diam. base plate, in.	48	58
Diam. fire pot, inches.	28	30
Size ash door, inches.	13x21	13x21
Size feed door, inches	12x15	12x15
Diam. grate, inches	25½	26
Diam, smoke pipe, in.	10	10
Height radiator, in.	24	28
Height, without casing, inches	58	58
Average height with casing. inches	70	70
Shipping weight, including casing, lbs.	1,250	1,850
Heating capacity, cubic feet	20,000 to 30,000	30,000 to 40,000
Price, without casing	$56.00	$67.20
Price, with casing as shown	63.27	75.68

THE ACME HUMMER AND ACME TROPIC HEATING AND VENTILATING COAL FURNACES have heavy base plate and base ring, connected by three or four strong arms and the ring has high flange to receive casing. Ring is perforated at inner line to admit air between galvanized casing and its inner lining. Self packing joints where all cast parts come together. Has an extra large ash pit with dust flue, returning all light flying dust to fire chamber when shaking the revolving bar grate. Extra heavy two-section fire pot preventing cracking by fire. Large, heavy dome in Acme Hummer. Heavy dome and circular radiator in the Acme Tropic. All furnaces contain an evaporating water pan.

SEND US A ROUGH SKETCH OF THE FLOOR PLAN OF YOUR HOUSE showing points of the compass or which direction the house fronts, giving careful inside measurements of all rooms in the house, regardless of which are to be heated, showing the location of all doors, stairways, offsets, bay windows, etc., size and sketch of cellar, showing under what rooms it is located, giving location and size of chimney flue and height of cellar, and we will send you a perfect drawing of the rooms showing the proper method of installation, giving you an exact estimate of cost, including all wall pipes, basement pipes, registers and everything necessary to heat the house properly to an average of seventy degrees in the coldest weather. If you are building a new house or remodeling an old house you cannot afford to be without our prices.

SEWING MACHINE DEPARTMENT

AS THE LARGEST DEALERS IN SEWING MACHINES in the world, selling direct to the consumer, with sewing machines scattered among our customers in every neighborhood in the United States, where they can be seen in operation any day, with prices lower by half than the prices quoted by others for the same or similar grades of machines, with our liberal three months' trial proposition, our 20 years' binding guarantee, safe delivery guarantee, our pay after received terms of shipment, with an acknowledged record of having done more during the past five years to improve, perfect and simplify the manufacture of sewing machines than all other sewing machine makers combined, we especially request your attention to the following pages, which, by illustrations and descriptions, tell you what we know about sewing machines, gives you for nothing, in concise form, all that it has cost us years of toil and thousands of dollars to accumulate, and places you in a position, in the purchase of a single sewing machine, to take every advantage that we have finally gained in our years of experience in the handling and selling of sewing machines.

Why the Minnesota Sewing Machines are the Highest Grade Machines Made, and Why No Other House Can Compare in Price or Furnish a Sewing Machine That Will in Any Way Compare With the Minnesota.

THE MINNESOTA SEWING MACHINES are made for us under contract in one of the largest sewing machine factories in the world, and by the maker of the highest grades of sewing machines. This manufacturer makes sewing machines for no other catalogue or mail order house. They are made only for us under our name Minnesota. Being limited in his capacity for a long time, we were unable to buy but the one machine from the maker, our highest grade, the Minnesota Model "A," and for our cheaper machines we were compelled to go to the manufacturers that supply other catalogue houses and dealers with stenciled machines, and these we furnished under the names Burdick, Edgemere, New Queen, Howard, etc., the exact same machines that are sold by others today under various names as the highest grade machines made. But determined that even our cheaper machines should and must be in every way higher grade than any machine advertised by others, that they must be equal to machines that are sold through agents at $25.00 to $50.00, we arranged with this manufacturer to greatly enlarge his factory, and by the addition of more buildings, more automatic machinery, larger foundry and greatly increased force, to manufacture our entire line of sewing machines, building every machine, from the cheapest to the best, on the same symmetrical lines, thus giving even our cheapest machine a mechanical construction, appearance, finish, sewing mechanism, wearing quality, simplicity and ease of operation which you would not find in any sewing machine you would buy from any other house, even at two to three times our price.

Every machine will be put out under the old established name, Minnesota, and in order to give our customers a variety to select from and to make our prices very attractive, we are having the Minnesota sewing machine made in five models, namely, Models "A," "B," "C," "D" and "F," as illustrated and described on the following pages. Whether you buy the highest grade sewing machine made in the world, the Minnesota Model "A," or one of the cheaper grades, the Minnesota Models "B," "C," "D" or "F," the machine goes to you direct from the one factory and the price quoted is for the machine delivered on board cars at the factory, which is in Dayton, Ohio.

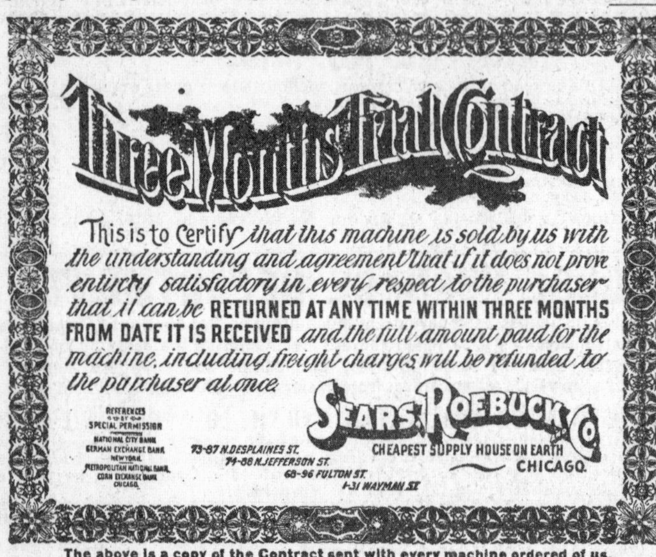

Three Months Trial Contract

This is to Certify that this machine is sold by us with the understanding and agreement that if it does not prove entirely satisfactory in every respect to the purchaser that it can be RETURNED AT ANY TIME WITHIN THREE MONTHS FROM DATE IT IS RECEIVED and the full amount paid for the machine, including freight charges will be refunded to the purchaser at once.

REFERENCES BY SPECIAL PERMISSION
NATIONAL CITY BANK,
GERMAN EXCHANGE BANK,
NEW YORK.
METROPOLITAN NATIONAL BANK,
CORN EXCHANGE BANK,
CHICAGO.

73-87 N. DESPLAINES ST.
74-88 N. JEFFERSON ST.
68-96 FULTON ST.
1-31 WAYMAN ST.

SEARS, ROEBUCK & CO.
CHEAPEST SUPPLY HOUSE ON EARTH
CHICAGO.

The above is a copy of the Contract sent with every machine ordered of us.

OUR THREE MONTHS' FREE TRIAL PROPOSITION.

AS A GUARANTEE that we will furnish you such a sewing machine as you could not get elsewhere at anything like the price, as a guarantee that if you order our Minnesota Model "A" you will get the highest grade sewing machine made, the best machine in the world, as a guarantee that if you order either the Models "B," "C" or "D" you will get a better sewing machine than you could get from any other catalogue house by ordering their highest grade machine, we make this most liberal three months' free trial proposition.

ORDER ANY MACHINE illustrated and described in this catalogue, enclosing $1.00, balance to be paid to railroad agent upon arrival of machine or send the full amount of cash with your order, and in either case the machine will go to you with the understanding and agreement that you give the machine three months free trial in your own home, during which time you can put the machine to every test and compare it with machines of any other make, and if you are not perfectly satisfied with your purchase you may return the machine to us at our expense and we will immediately refund your money, together with the freight charges paid by you.

NEEDLES, ATTACHMENTS, ACCESSORIES, SUPPLIES, ETC.

In this catalogue you will find listed all the different supplies, needles, accessories, attachments, etc., that are commonly required with these sewing machines. Of these accessories we will always carry a complete stock and can fill orders promptly and, as the prices will show, at less than one-half the prices charged by dealers generally. See page 70 for list of sewing machine supplies.

NAMES OF YOUR NEIGHBORS using our sewing machines furnished on application. If you do not happen to know of anyone in your neighborhood who has purchased from us, and you would like to know where you could see, examine and test one of our sewing machines, kindly write us for list of names and we will give you the names of the sewing machine customers we have in your neighborhood. You can learn from the purchasers how they are pleased with the sewing machine, how they think it compares with others, and how much money they feel they saved by sending their orders to us.

ABOUT THE FREIGHT.

THE FREIGHT CHARGES on a sewing machine from the factory at Dayton, Ohio, to any point in the United States will be next to nothing as compared with what you save in price. For example, the average sewing machine, crated ready for shipment, weighs about 120 pounds. Sewing machines are accepted by the railroad companies as first class freight, and the freight on a sewing machine from the factory at Dayton, Ohio, would average about as follows: 200 miles or less, 35 to 50 cents; 200 to 500 miles, 50 to 75 cents; 500 to 1,000 miles, 75 cents to $1.00. Greater or less distances in proportion.

YOU TAKE NO CHANCE of being unable to operate a Minnesota sewing machine of any model, whether you have had previous experience or not. The instruction book which is furnished free with every machine makes everything plain, and if you buy a Minnesota machine and find you cannot, by following our instructions, operate it perfectly and do all kinds of work, and, with the Model "A," if you find you cannot do any work that can be done on any sewing machine made, regardless of name, make or price, you may return it at our expense and we will immediately refund your money.

OUR LIBERAL TERMS OF SHIPMENT.

WHILE NEARLY ALL OUR CUSTOMERS send cash in full with their orders, and by sending cash in full you save an extra charge of from 25 to 40 cents, which the express companies always make for collecting the amount of the C. O. D. and returning the money to us, nevertheless, if you wish to see and examine the sewing machine before paying for it, select the sewing machine you want; fill out the enclosed order blank, or on a piece of plain paper state the machine wanted by name and catalogue number, sign your name and address plainly and give shipping directions, enclose $1.00, and we will send the sewing machine to you by freight, C. O. D., subject to examination. You can examine it at your nearest railroad station, and if found perfectly satisfactory you can then pay the railroad agent our price, less the amount sent as deposit, the freight charges and express charges on return of money, and the agent will deliver the machine to you, subject, of course, to our three months' free trial and twenty-year guarantee proposition, as explained on this page. If, however, the sewing machine is not satisfactory when received and examined, you can refuse to accept it, the railroad agent will return it to us at our expense, and we will immediately refund your $1.00.

ADVANTAGE OF SENDING CASH IN FULL WITH ORDER. As previously stated, nearly all our customers send cash in full with their orders, and the advantage of sending cash in full with your order is the saving of express charges on return of money to us. Where the machine is shipped C. O. D., subject to examination, the C. O. D. bill must be sent by express, and the express companies make a charge of from 25 to 40 cents for collecting the money and returning it to us. This is all saved where cash in full accompanies the order.

SAFE DELIVERY GUARANTEE. We guarantee every sewing machine to reach the purchaser in the exact same perfect condition it leaves us, and if any piece or part is broken by reason of rough handling in transit, or for any other reason, we will either replace or repair it or send you a new machine, all at our own expense.

REPAIRS AND SUPPLIES. We will always carry, at the factory, a full supply of all the different pieces and parts in which our various styles of sewing machines are made, and if you should meet with an accident of any kind and should want any part or parts of any sewing machine purchased from us, you can get these parts promptly and at actual factory cost.

CERTIFICATE No.______

Certificate of Guarantee.

This is to Certify that this sewing machine is warranted to be perfect in material and manufacture and to be perfect in operation if properly managed. This machine has been carefully inspected and adjusted, and there are no defects in material or workmanship. It has been delivered to the transportation company in perfect condition, carefully packed, and we guarantee it to reach your station in good order. This means that if it is damaged in transit, it may be returned to us and we will pay all expenses connected with the transaction and send a new machine without extra charge.

With fair usage we hereby agree to make good any defect in material or workmanship for a period of twenty years. Natural wear and tear on any of the parts is not considered a defect in material or workmanship.

When referring to this Guarantee please do not fail to state Certificate Number.

Dated at Chicago this ______ day of ______ 190

SEARS, ROEBUCK & CO.
CHICAGO, ILL.

OUR TWENTY YEARS' WRITTEN BINDING GUARANTEE.

WITH EVERY SEWING MACHINE (excepting our $8.25 Minnesota Model "F," which is guaranteed for five years) we issue a written binding 20 years' guarantee, by the terms and conditions of which, if any piece or part gives out at any time within twenty years by reason of defect in material or workmanship, we will replace or repair it free of charge. This is the longest, strongest and most binding guarantee furnished by any sewing machine maker or seller, and backed as it is, by our house with a capital of over two million dollars, you are made absolutely secure against any possible defect of any kind.

DESCRIPTION OF OUR MINNESOTA MODEL "D" SEWING MACHINE

FOR OUR THREE MONTHS' FREE TRIAL AGREEMENT, SEE PAGE 48.
FOR OUR TWENTY YEARS' GUARANTEE, SEE PAGE 48.
FOR DESCRIPTION OF MODEL "D" WOODWORK, SEE PAGE 50.
FOR DESCRIPTION OF MODEL "D" STAND, SEE PAGE 51.

THIS MACHINE, like our other Minnesota models, is of the lock stitch, vibrating shuttle type. Two threads are used, the upper thread from the spool on top of the arm and the lower from the bobbin in the shuttle. The threads interlock in the center of the material, thus having the same appearance on both sides of the goods.

THE MODEL "D" HEAD is very similar in construction to our Model "C" which is thoroughly described on page 52. The main differences are that our Model "D" is a smaller size head and also has smaller operating parts. The reader will note, however, from the description that the sizes of the Model "D" heads are the usual measurements for family machines, the height of the arm permits the handling of practically all household sewing.

AS A WORK DOER our Model "D" will give longer service and better satisfaction all the time than the majority of machines sold at $15.00 to $20.00. The superiority of our Minnesota models in materials, construction, workmanship and finish assures the purchaser of our Model "D" of a well built, durable and light running sewing machine at our remarkably low prices. The machine is guaranteed for a period of twenty years, during which time we agree to repair or replace, free of charge, to the purchaser any part or parts that may prove defective in material or workmanship.

DIMENSIONS OF HEAD:

Height, under arm	5 inches
Height, to top of arm	7⅛ inches
Bed Plate	6¼ in. wide by 12¼ in. long

THE FINISH OF THE HEAD is not the ordinary japanning used on many machines. A high grade of enamel is used, and the entire surface is hand rubbed, giving a smooth and high finish, after which it is varnished and baked in a high degree. The head is tastefully ornamented with colored transfers, while the face plate, balance wheel, tension plates and shuttle slides are heavily nickel plated.

THE TAKE-UP is positive in operation, being driven by the main shaft, thus insuring a perfect and regular stitch.

THE FEED is what is known as the four-motion feed, driven (indirectly) by the main shaft; fitted with four sets of teeth, which carry the goods forward evenly and firmly.

THE UPPER TENSION is a very simple arrangement and very easily understood. It is similar to the tension used on a New Home, Eldredge, Household and other standard machines, consisting of two steel plates on the upper arm through which the thread passes, the tension on the thread being regulated by a small thumb adjusting screw. These plates have a certain amount of elasticity and it is not necessary, therefore, to change the tension for a large variety of ordinary work.

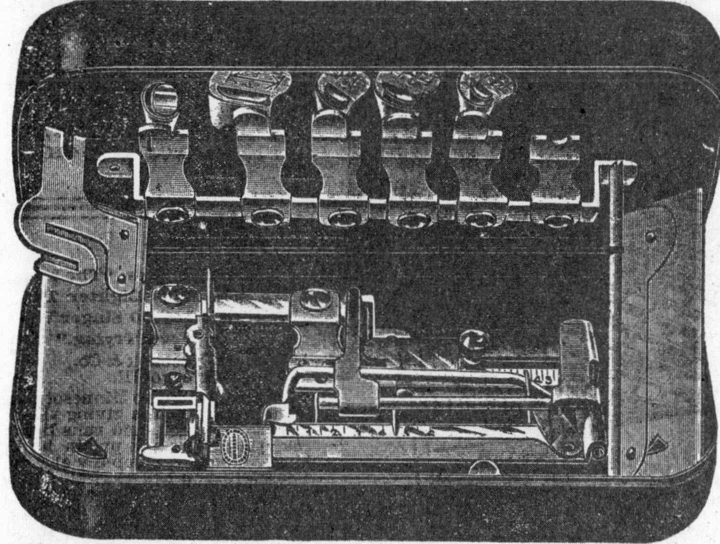

ATTACHMENTS. It has been customary with all dealers to furnish a complete set of attachments with every machine, adding not alone the cost of the attachments to the price of the machine but also the profit on the attachments, whether the customer requires them or not. We have found from our past experience that many of our customers prefer to buy the machine without attachments and we, therefore, decided to offer our Model "D" machine at the lowest possible price, which represents the actual cost of material and labor at the factory, with but our one small percentage of profit added.

THE ATTACHMENTS WILL BE FURNISHED WITH OR WITHOUT the machines and at cost price, 75 cents per set, and comprising a full set of all the latest patent foot attachments, which will be furnished by no other dealer.

WE FURNISH THE FOLLOWING SET, packed in a handsome velvet lined metal box, as shown in the illustration: One ruffler, one shirring plate, one tucker, one short foot, one under braider, one binder and one set of hemmers, different widths up to ⅝ of an inch. Our price for the full set, 75 cents. Be sure to state if you wish the attachments shipped with your machine. If ordered separately allow 17 cents extra for postage.

THE BOBBIN WINDER is the same as used on our Model "C," easy to get at and absolutely accurate in operation. Most bobbin winders are run by the belt, which on account of the slackness of the belt are generally erratic and unreliable in movement. Our Model "D" bobbin winder is driven by the upper band wheel against which the bobbin winder is pressed firmly and held in place by an adjusting screw, consequently it never slips and its action is quick and positive. When winding the bobbin it is not necessary to take the goods from under the needle, as by a special construction the upper balance wheel can be thrown out of gear and will run freely and separately from the other working parts of the head.

A DOUBLE ECCENTRIC CAM on the main shaft operates both the shuttle mechanism and the feed mechanism. This cam is made from a single piece of finest steel, and is accurately balanced to prevent any vibration when the machine is running. This construction contributes greatly to the light running and noiseless qualities of this machine, which, when compared with any other vibrating shuttle sewing machine on the market is simply remarkable.

EVERY BEARING OR WEARING POINT in the machine head is made of the finest steel that can be obtained, being thoroughly hardened by the latest and most approved process. All bearings are made adjustable, so that any slight wear that may result after many years of use can be quickly and easily taken up, and any lost motion removed by the most simple methods. This renders it practically indestructible and the most durable sewing machine ever produced.

THE SHUTTLE is the most perfect self threading cylindrical shuttle ever produced. It is made of finest steel, hardened and ground. It is absolutely self threading, being open at one end for inserting the bobbin, after which the thread is instantly drawn into place by two motions of the hand. There are no holes to thread through and the shuttle can be threaded with the eyes shut. It has a perfect tension which is practically automatic, and does not require regulating for any ordinary range of work. The bobbin carries a large amount of thread.

THE NEEDLE IS SELF SETTING, both as to height and position in needle bar, making it impossible to set a needle improperly. The machine is self threading at every point except the eye of the needle, which is the only opening through which the end of the thread must be passed.

THREAD CUTTER. To do away with the necessity of using scissors and prevent the possibility of breaking or cutting the thread too short, our Model "D" head is provided with a sharp, steel thread cutter placed on the presser bar in such a position that the thread can instantly be cut and sufficient thread remains drawn from the needle and also from the shuttle so that the machine remains threaded and ready to sew the next piece of goods.

THREAD SCALE. The front shuttle slide is stamped with a scale indicating the proper sized needles to be used with the different numbers of sewing thread.

STITCH REGULATOR. The stitch can be regulated to run from 7 to 36 stitches to the inch by means of a regulator which is located on the arm just below the bobbin winder in easy reach of the operator. The stitch regulator shortens or lengthens the movements of the feed, which, in turn, controls the size of the stitch.

FOR A MORE COMPLETE DESCRIPTION of the operating parts of our Model "D," we refer the reader to the description of our Model "C" machine, which is of the same construction. The reader will understand, however, that while the construction is the same, the parts of our Model "C" are heavier and the head larger so as to meet the requirements of such of our customers who not only need a machine for the work usually done in the household but for a very wide range of sewing from very heavy to very light.

WE CARRY IN STOCK a full supply of needles, bobbins, shuttles, attachments, etc., which are used in the operation of our machines. We can therefore fill orders for repairs promptly. An order for repairs for the Minnesota Model "D" Machines placed with us fifteen or twenty years from date would be filled as promptly as a repair order sent us today. See page 70 for prices on sewing machine supplies.

ACCESSORIES

We furnish with our Minnesota Model "D" Machine a complete set of accessories such as are usually furnished with every high grade machine, consisting of one quilter, five bobbins (and one in the machine), one cloth guide, a thread cutter, a large screwdriver, one oil can filled with oil, one screwdriver and wrench, one foot hemmer, one extra needle plate and one package of needles.

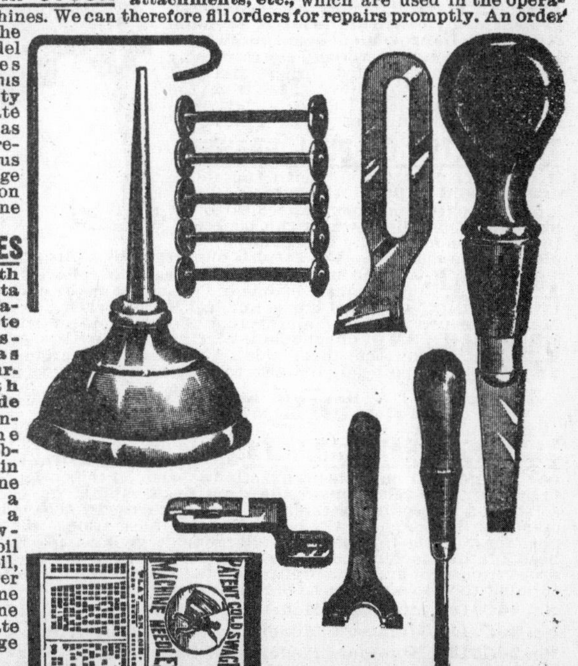

$10.85 BUYS OUR MINNESOTA MODEL "D" SEWING MACHINE

7-DRAWER UPRIGHT STYLE.

OUR MINNESOTA MODEL "D" SEWING MACHINE illustrated and described on this and the following page, even though the price may seem extremely low, is a much better machine than you can buy from any other catalogue house at $15.00, a better machine than you can buy from your dealer at home under $20.00, and that you may be the judge, we would be glad to have you order a sewing machine from any other house at $20.00, and at the same time order one of our Minnesota Model "D" Sewing Machines, with the understanding that you can set the two machines up in your own home and put them to a thorough test, and if our Minnesota Model "D" does not prove more satisfactory in every way than any machine you can buy from any other house at $20.00 or less, you can return our machine to us at our expense, and we will immediately refund your money, together with any freight or express charges you may have paid.

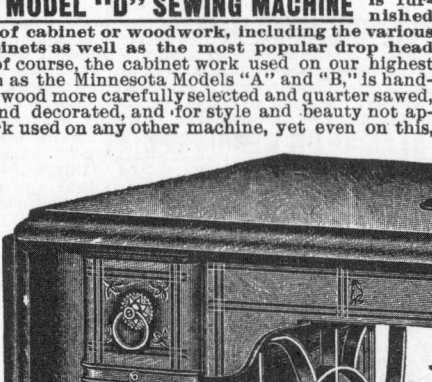

For full description of the Model "D" head, see page 49.
For full description of Model "D" stand, see page 51.
For full description of Model "D" attachments, see page 49.
For description of Model "D" accessories, see page 49.
For our liberal terms offer, see page 48.
For our three months' free trial offer, see page 48.
For our twenty years' guarantee, see page 48.
For freight rates, see column first class rates, pages 7 to 11.

DESCRIPTION OF THE MODEL "D" WOODWORK.

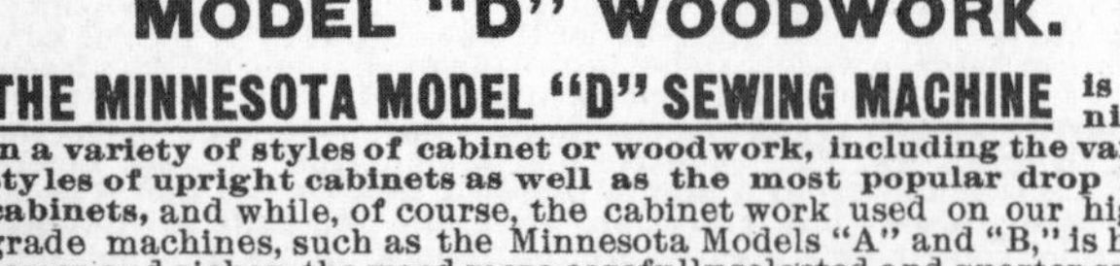

THE MINNESOTA MODEL "D" SEWING MACHINE is furnished in a variety of styles of cabinet or woodwork, including the various styles of upright cabinets as well as the most popular drop head cabinets, and while, of course, the cabinet work used on our highest grade machines, such as the Minnesota Models "A" and "B," is handsomer and richer, the wood more carefully selected and quarter sawed, elaborately carved and decorated, and for style and beauty not approached by woodwork used on any other machine, yet even on this, our Model "D" machine, we use a more substantial grade of woodwork than is usually found on machines that sell at two to three times our prices.

MATERIAL. The Model "D" cabinet is made of the best kiln dried and air seasoned oak. It is exceptionally well made, extra strong, and while it is plainer, more simple and less expensive than the cabinets shown on our Models "A" and "B," yet it is of a grade you will not find on any sewing machine you can buy elsewhere under $20.00.

FINISH. The finish is of exceptionally good quality. When the woodwork is put through the factory, it is subjected to a thorough treatment with sandpaper, which gives it a smooth surface, after which it is filled to give it the golden color which is sought after in all the best grades of oak furniture. The varnish used on this cabinet gives it a smooth, high gloss finish.

THE TABLE is made of built up stock with cross band veneers. This construction insures the table against warping, cracking and splitting.

THE SIDE DRAWERS used on both upright and drop head styles are of the latest skeleton style, a big improvement over the old fashioned boxed up drawers. They are neatly shaped, having rounded corners and just enough carving to relieve them from the severely plain effect. They are fitted with handsome nickel drawer pulls and locks.

THE CENTER OR PULL DRAWER is carved to correspond with the side drawers, and is fitted with a lock. The interior is partitioned off for needles, bobbins and other things which can be kept there more conveniently than in any other place in the machine. **We furnish one key, which fits all drawers.**

THE COVER is made of good quality bent oak, relieved from the plain with neat mouldings, veneered front and panel; the entire cover is nicely finished and polished. It is fitted with two jacket hinges and lock, so that when placed over the head of the machine it can be securely fastened and thereby affords ample protection to the machine in every way.

DRIP PAN. All of our machines are supplied with a japanned drip pan, which is fitted on the under side of the head as a protection to the operator against oil dropping from the head, and also to prevent dust getting into the working parts from the under side of the machine.

ORDER BY NUMBER.

No. 26C212

PRICE $10.85

ATTACHMENTS 75c EXTRA.

ON BOARD CARS AT DAYTON :: OHIO

Mr. Shaw Says: "The Minnesota Runs Lighter Than the $48.00 Singer We Were Trying."

Sears, Roebuck & Co., Chicago, Ill.

Gentlemen:—The Minnesota machine sent by you is giving the utmost satisfaction, and runs lighter than the one we had put in by the Singer Machine Company at $48.00. Therefore, you will see that I have saved over $28.00. I have not hesitated to show it to my neighbors, and they all seem to be very much pleased with it. You are at liberty to use this letter to the best advantage. Yours truly,

JAMES SHAW.

THE MINNESOTA MODEL "D" DROP HEAD CABINET.

THE DROP HEAD CABINETS (see following page) are the most popular styles of cabinets. They are made of solid oak, the general finish being exactly the same as the upright machines above described. **We recommend the drop head cabinet** for the reason that it serves as a protection for the head, and when closed you have in it a handsome stand or table; and, as will be seen by the illustrations, when the machine is open for work the top opens into a large table, giving ample room for goods, the head of the machine comes to place for sewing, while when closed the head drops from sight and is securely protected against dust, the table folds over, forming the top, and you have a handsome desk or table.

WE FURNISH THE MODEL "D" IN THE FIVE-DRAWER DROP CABINET AT $10.45 AND IN THE SEVEN-DRAWER DROP CABINET AT $10.95 as illustrated and described on the following page, so in selecting a Model "D" Sewing Machine, unless you have a special preference for the upright machine with cover, illustrated on this page, we would especially recommend that you order one of our five or seven drawer, drop head, cabinet machines, which we furnish at **$10.45** and **$10.95**, respectively.

No. 26C210	Minnesota Model "D," Three-Drawer, Box Cover. Price	$10.15
No. 26C211	Minnesota Model "D," Five-Drawer, Box Cover. Price	10.40
No. 26C212	Minnesota Model "D," Seven-Drawer, Box Cover. Price	10.85

The above prices do not include attachments. We furnish a complete set at 75 cents extra, as fully described on page 49.

MINNESOTA MODEL "D," SEVEN-DRAWER, DROP HEAD STYLE, $10.95

THE DROP HEAD STYLE OF MACHINE is preferable to the old style shown with the box cover; first, it is a handsomer and more compact machine, there is no cover to put on and take off, subjecting the machine to danger of scratching, marring, etc., and there is no one part of the machine removed from the other, as in the case of a covered machine when the cover is set aside. The drop head style affords a perfect protection to the head when the machine is not in use, the machine drops from sight, is completely covered and thus protected against dust, dirt or injury, and, when closed, the big leaf, which serves as a table for handling the goods at work, swings over, makes a top for the machine, and you have a handsome piece of furniture that can be used as a stand, desk or table.

WE GUARANTEE THIS MACHINE FOR TWENTY YEARS.

DESCRIPTION OF THE MINNESOTA MODEL "D" STAND.

THE MINNESOTA MODEL "D" IRON STANDS are made at the same factory that makes the heads of our sewing machines. They are made from the very best light gray Birmingham, Alabama, iron. They are moulded by automatic machines, instead of being cast by a hand process, making every piece perfectly true, smooth and of unusual strength, so that when the different parts are assembled they fit perfectly. All parts are heavily coated with black enamel by hand process. We put on a heavier, smoother, glossier, better finished and far more lasting coat of enamel than is furnished by any other sewing machine maker, and we believe we furnish a stronger, better finished and handsomer sewing machine stand than is used on any other sewing machine made.

DESIGN. The Minnesota Model "D" stand has been especially designed for us with a view of procuring a neat, graceful, open effect and, at the same time, a frame that will stand the severest tests.

THE SIDE FRAMES are made in what is popularly known as the ribbon pattern construction, which produces the best effect and the most rigid and lasting frame without being clumsy; are joined together by a full set of braces, as illustrated, bolting the side standards at the top and bottom, making the stand absolutely rigid, which is so essential in the construction of a sewing machine.

THE TREADLE is of the openwork style with full ends, pivot bearing, accurately trued, adjustable take-up between the balance wheel and the treadle, putting the entire machine under easy control of the operator.

We use the highest grade sewing machine casters made, which are carefully fitted and never come out of place.

THE BALANCE WHEEL is extra heavy, carefully adjusted, perfectly true, pivot bearing, which insures an even, easy speed to the machine, putting it at all times under perfect control of the operator.

For full description of the Model "D" head, see page 49.
For full description of the Model "D" attachments, see page 49.
For full description of the Model "D" accessories, see page 49.
For our liberal terms offer, see page 48.
For our three months' free trial offer, see page 48.
For our twenty years' guarantee, see page 48.
For freight rates, see column first class rates, pages 7 to 11.

No. 26C217
Order by Number.

On Board Cars at Dayton, Ohio.

Attachments 75c Extra.

THE DRESS GUARD to this stand is extra large, protecting the balance wheel and belt from any possible contact with the dress, at the same time substantially bracing the side frame.

THE OIL GUARD, immediately under the treadle, extends from side frame to side frame, is securely bolted, strengthens the frame and protects the working of the treadle.

INSPECTION. All parts are accurately trued, tested for strength, not a casting is allowed to be used that has a sand hole or defect or that isn't true to gauge, and as a result, for strength, beauty, design, finish, for easy running and for perfect control of the machine by the operator, we furnish a higher grade sewing machine stand than is furnished by any other maker.

Mrs. C. A. Gildea says: "I Have Been Using a Singer Machine, for Which I Paid $75.00, and I Consider the One I Have Now (the Minnesota) Equally as Good in Every Way."

Nogales, Ariz.

Sears, Roebuck & Co., Chicago, Ill.

Gentlemen:—The Minnesota Sewing Machine I ordered from you a few months ago, came to hand promptly and has, in every respect, so far proven entirely satisfactory. I have been using a Singer machine, for which I paid $75.00, and I consider the one I have now (bought of you) equally as good in every way and not costing one-third as much as I paid for the Singer.

Respectfully,
(Signed) MRS. C. A. GILDEA.

Mrs. Barnett says: "I Have Used the Wheeler & Wilson, Also the Domestic and a Number of Other Machines, But Like the Minnesota Best." Would Not Exchange the Minnesota For a $60.00 Machine.

Sheridon, Oregon.

Sears, Roebuck & Co., Chicago, Ill.

Gentlemen:—I received the sewing machine (the Minnesota) that I ordered of you in a reasonable time and I am well pleased with it in every respect. I have used the Wheeler & Wilson, also Domestic and a number of other sewing machines, but I like the Minnesota the best. One of my neighbors bought a five-drawer Singer machine in the same month I bought mine of you and my machine has seven drawers. They are both drop head machines. I would not exchange with her; she calls her machine a $60.00 machine.

Yours truly,
MRS. JAS. BARNETT.

10 95

No. 26C217
Order by Number.

No. 26C216	Model "D" Five-Drawer, Drop Head. Price..........	$10.45
No. 26C217	Model "D" Seven-Drawer, Drop Head. Price..........	10.95

The above prices do not include attachments. We furnish a full set at 75 cents extra, as fully explained on page 49.

DESCRIPTION OF THE MINNESOTA MODEL "C" HEAD

THE MINNESOTA MODEL "C" HEAD

HAS BEEN CONSTRUCTED WITH A VIEW OF FURNISHING AN EXTRA HIGH ARM MACHINE,

ONE THAT WILL GIVE UNQUALIFIED SATISFACTION,

TO MEET THE NEEDS OF OUR CUSTOMERS who desire a medium priced machine which will do a large range of work, heavy and light, equally well. While the parts are all

ABSOLUTELY GUARANTEED FIRST CLASS MATERIAL,

theyare not of as fineconstruction as our Minnesota Model "A" and "B" heads, but larger, stronger and better finished than our Minnesota Model "D" head.

DESIGN. Our Model "C" head is of the very latest design, with graceful rounded lines which give it a handsome, well proportioned and strong appearance.

SIZE. **The head is extra large size,** having as much room underneath the arm as the largest family sewing machine head. Height of arm from bed plate, 5½ inches; from needle bar to base of arm, 8⅛ inches; size of bed plate, 14⅛x7 inches.

FINISH. **The head is finished with three coats of enamel,** each coat being thoroughly baked and hardened before the next is put on and carefully rubbed down to a smooth surface, and finally treated to a coat of special varnish, which is also baked at a high degree of heat, which makes the finish practically indestructible and of a beautiful, rich black luster. Before the enamel is put on the head is treated to a coat of anti-rust preparation, which prevents the finish from cracking, checking or peeling, which so frequently occurs with other makes of machines.

DECORATION. **The arm and bed plate are decorated with handsome floral figures** in a combination of silver and gold, especially designed for this machine.

NICKEL PLATING. **The rim of the balance wheel, face plate, shuttle slides,** tension plates, needle bar, presser bar, stitch regulating plate, presser bar lifter and screw heads are all heavily nickel plated and form a handsome contrast to the black enamel finish.

OPERATING PARTS. **Our Minnesota machines are constructed with less running or operating parts than any other machine on the market,** rendering them easy to understand and operate, light running and free from vibration and noise. To do away with the liability to get out of order, common to many machines, the mechanism is so constructed that the few running parts in the Minnesota head operate entirely independent of one another and all driving power is supplied direct from the main shaft without the agency of the numerous connections, cogs and many unnecessary devices used in some machines to propel the feed, shuttle and needle bar. The operator does not have to tamper with or adjust these parts regardless of the weight of goods being sewed. The construction has made the Minnesota head famous as the most durable head ever produced.

ADJUSTMENT. **Much depends upon the adjustment of the working parts,** for should any part, for instance the shuttle, be adjusted 1-32 of an incn out of place the harmony between the parts will be destroyed and imperfect work will result. The operating parts of our Minnesota machines receive the finest and most accurate adjustment and are tested on all grades of materials and pass through numerous inspections, so that it is practically impossible for a Minnesota machine to leave our factory unless perfect in construction and adjustment.

ALL BEARINGS **are made of the best steel that can be procured,** especially selected for its durable qualities, properly tempered and case hardened so as to minimize the friction and prevent wear. All bearings are fitted with adjusting devices whereby any lost motion caused by the slight wear through years of constant use can be taken up.

RUNNING SPEED. **Every machine before being shipped from the factory is put to the severest possible test,** being set up and attached to a power pulley and run at a speed five times greater than it is possible to run any machine by foot power, and by this severe test we first learn that every machine is perfectly true in every particular and capable of the highest possible speed.

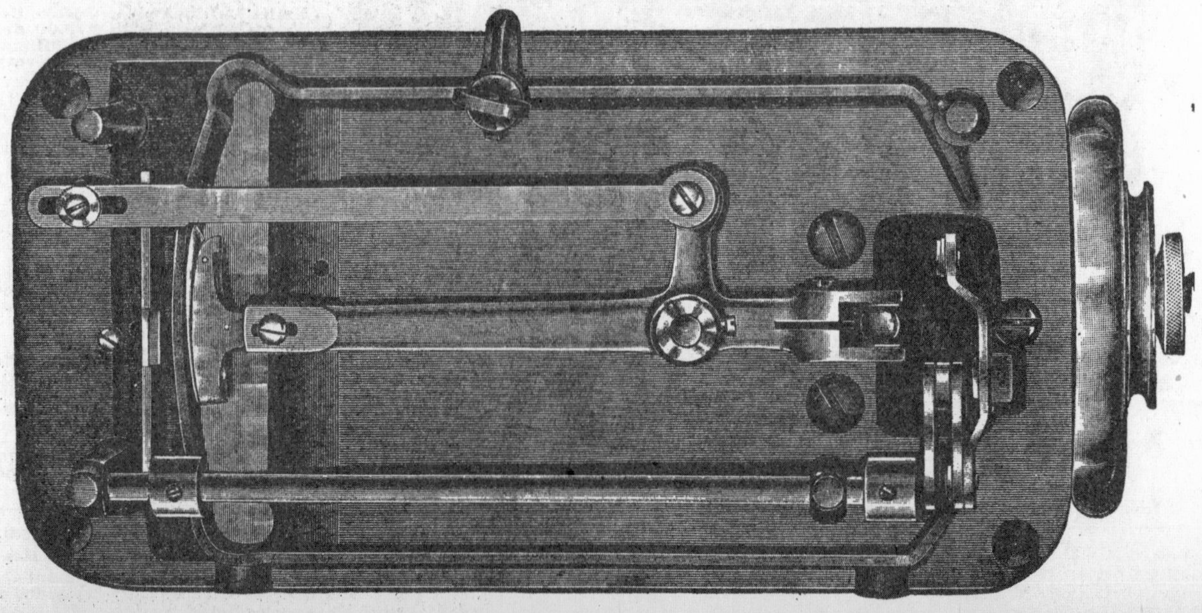

THE NEEDLE BAR is round and made of the very best quality tool steel, highly tempered. It is absolutely positive in its action, insuring even and automatic operation on materials of any weight and thickness.

THE SELF SETTING NEEDLES for this machine are the very best grade of needle it is possible to procure. Every needle is inspected and tested as to size, temper position of the eye, etc. The needle bar is constructed with a groove so that the needle can only be placed in the proper position. It is not necessary to guess at the height or position of the needle, as is the case with many other makes of machines.

THE SHUTTLE is cylindrical in shape, made of the finest hardened tool steel and ground. It is absolutely self threading, being open at one end for inserting the bobbin, after which the thread is instantly drawn into place by two motions of the hand.

THE SHUTTLE CARRIER is made of steel and is fitted with a spring lining which holds the shuttle firmly in place and prevents it from rattling when the machine is in operation. It is adjustable so that when the shuttle shows signs of wear it can be moved closer to the race, thus enabling the operator to use the same shuttle for many years with the same satisfaction as when new.

THREAD SCALE. The front shuttle slide is stamped with a scale indicating the proper size needles to be used with the different numbers of sewing thread.

THE DOUBLE FOUR-MOTION FEED is made of the very best case hardened steel, constructed with four sets of teeth, two sets on each side of the needle, which carry the goods forward firmly and evenly; as the action of the feed is entirely controlled and operated by the main shaft it is strong and certain in its movements. When you get the machine the feed will be regulated for light and medium weight materials generally used in the household, but when desiring to sew extra light goods, such as silks, dimities, lawns, etc., or extra heavy weight materials, such as skirtings, cheviots, kerseys, etc., the feed can be raised or lowered, as necessary, by means of a small screw attaching the feed to the feed rod below the bed plate. The feed can be adjusted in an instant's time, which will be highly appreciated by some of our customers who have used machines of such construction as to make it almost impossible for the operator to adjust the feed.

THE PRESSER FOOT has a very large under surface, which extends on both sides of the needle and holds any weight goods firmly in place over the feed. The forward part of the presser foot nearest the operator is curved upward so the foot will not catch in seams of fleecy materials.

THE PRESSER BAR is round and fitted with a presser bar adjuster by which the pressure on the goods is regulated. At the factory before shipping the machine this bar is regulated to give the proper pressure for most household materials and it is only necessary for you to adjust this bar when sewing on extra light or extra heavy materials. The presser bar lifter can be turned to the right and to the left, producing both the high lift and the low lift. When putting on attachments or sewing bulky materials the high lift is used.

THE TAKE-UP. Both the needle bar and take-up are driven by the shaft head at the left end of the main shaft, and therefore act simultaneously and in perfect harmony, insuring perfect stitching.

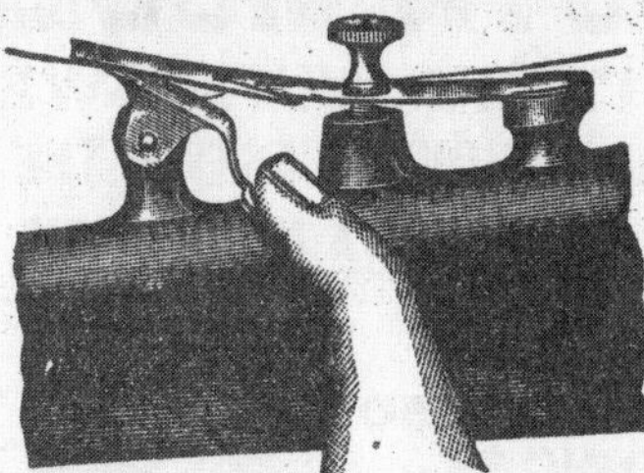

THE TENSION of our Model "C" is placed on top of the arm and consists of two flexible nickel plated steel plates, through which the thread passes. The pressure on the thread is regulated by a small thumb-screw. By pressing a small projection on the lower tension plate, called the tension release, the goods being sewed can be taken away from under the presser foot without bending the needle or breaking the thread.

STITCH REGULATOR. The stitch can be regulated to run from 7 to 24 stitches to the inch by means of a regulator which is located on the arm just below the bobbin winder in easy reach of the operator. The stitch regulator shortens or lengthens the movement of the feed, which in turn controls the size of the stitch.

THREAD CUTTER. To do away with the necessity of using scissors and to prevent the possibility of breaking or cutting the thread too short, our Model "C" head is provided with a sharp steel thread cutter placed on the presser bar in such a position that the thread can instantly be cut and sufficient thread remains drawn from the needle and also from the shuttle so that the machine remains threaded and ready to sew the next piece of goods.

BOBBIN WINDER. The bobbin winder is very neatly finished in black enamel and nickel plate. It is so simple a child can operate it. The thread is wound on the bobbin automatically and so evenly and smoothly as to make the bobbin work perfectly in the shuttle, producing an even tension and greatly improving the perfection of the stitch.

THE BOBBIN WINDER is always in position and ready to operate. It is operated by means of the belt which is placed in contact with the small pulley wheel of the bobbin winder.

MODEL "C" ATTACHMENTS.

IT HAS BEEN CUSTOMARY FOR DEALERS IN SEWING MACHINES to furnish a set of attachments with every machine, including their price of the attachments in the selling price of the machine, and also adding a margin of profit on the attachments. The purchaser is, therefore, forced to receive and pay for them whether they are required or not. From our many years' experience in selling sewing machines and carefully studying the wants of our customers, we have found that about 33⅓ per cent of sewing machine users do not need the attachments, using the machine for plain sewing only, for which are necessary only the needles, bobbin, quilter, cloth guide, foot hemmer, screwdriver and wrench, which we furnish with each machine at no additional charge. We have, therefore, deducted the cost of the attachments from our selling price and quote prices which represent only the actual cost of material and labor used in the construction of the machine alone, with our one small percentage of profit added.

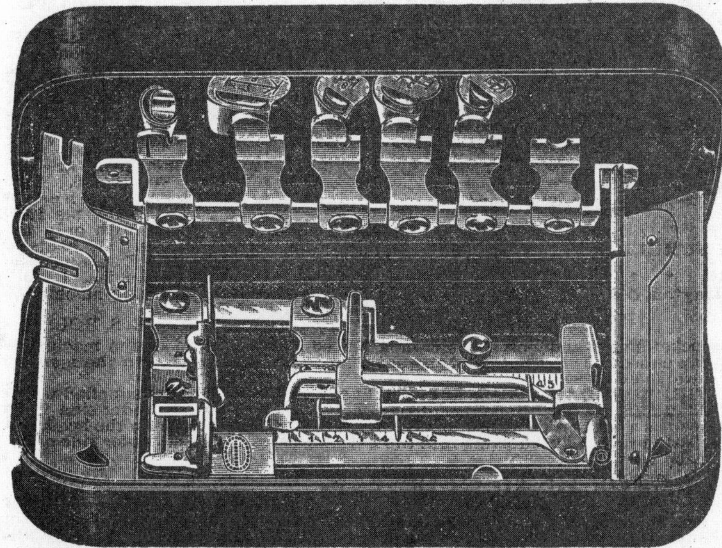

WE USE ONLY THE CELEBRATED ATTACHMENTS, made by the Greist Manufacturing Company of New Haven, Conn., whose attachments are used exclusively on high grade machines. Only the finest hardened and tempered steel is used in their construction and we guarantee to replace or repair, free of charge, any attachments that give out through defective material or workmanship. They are heavily nickel plated and polished and will last twice as long, give twice the satisfaction and service as the flimsy attachments generally used. Some firms furnish the best attachments only with their highest priced machines, and send an inferior set (usually made of tin) with their cheaper machines. Our attachments are the latest improved attachments made by the above concern, and we furnish the same set with all models of our celebrated Minnesota.

THE ATTACHMENTS WILL BE FURNISHED AT 75 CENTS PER SET. If you, the reader of this catalogue, intend to use your machine for plain sewing only, you naturally do not wish to buy attachments and will appreciate our departure from the old established custom of including a set of attachments with every machine at the customer's expense. If you require attachments you will nevertheless appreciate that it is unfair and unjust to force those who do not to receive and pay for them. If you purchase a machine without attachments and later wish to procure attachments, we can always supply you with the proper set. Some firms attempt to mislead intending purchasers by stating that they furnish their attachments "free of charge." A careful comparison of prices with a like comparison of quality, a comparison of the machines we have sold in your locality with machines furnished elsewhere, will convince anyone that not only do other firms make a charge for attachments (indirectly, because included in the price of their machines), but also ask from $5.00 to $15.00 more for their machines.

THE ATTACHMENTS are fitted on the presser bar after the sewing foot has been removed, each attachment being provided with a grooved foot which fits tightly on the presser bar and holds the attachment firmly in place and is put on and removed by hand without the aid of any tool. The set of attachments, as illustrated on the left, consists of one ruffler, one shirring plate, one tucker, one short foot, one underbraider, one binder and one set of four hemmers of different widths up to ⅞ of an inch. Price, per set....75c

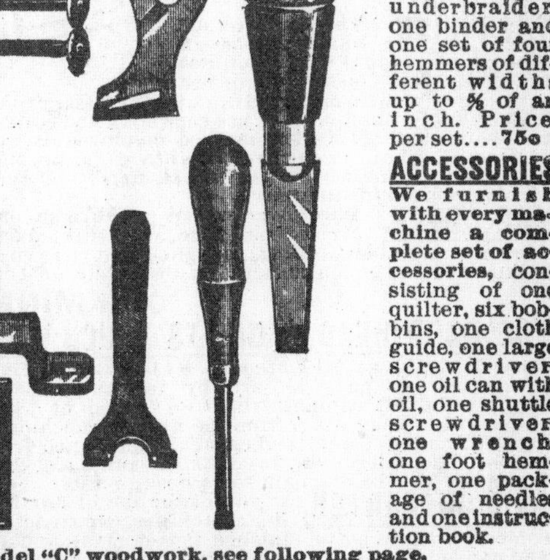

ACCESSORIES We furnish with every machine a complete set of accessories, consisting of one quilter, six bobbins, one cloth guide, one large screwdriver, one oil can with oil, one shuttle screwdriver, one wrench, one foot hemmer, one package of needles and one instruction book.

For description of Model "C" woodwork, see following page.
For description of Model "C" stand, see page 55.
For our Liberal Terms of Shipment, see page 48.
For our Three Months' Free Trial, see page 48.
For our 20 Year Written Binding Guarantee, see page 48.
For freight rates, see column first class freight rates, pages 7 to 11.

OUR MINNESOTA MODEL "C" 7-DRAWER UPRIGHT COVER STYLE AND DROP LEAF MACHINE, $11.65

FITTED WITH SWELL FRONT CABINET

OUR MINNESOTA MODEL "C" IS WITHOUT QUESTION THE BEST MEDIUM PRICED SEWING MACHINE ON THE MARKET

THIS ILLUSTRATION SHOWS OUR MINNESOTA MODEL "C" in the upright style, with drop leaf and cover, seven drawers, three on each side and one center or push drawer, affording considerable drawer space for sewing material. We can also furnish the upright style with five drawers only, two on each side and center drawer, for $11.20, and with three drawers, one on each side and push drawer, for $10.85.

For full description of Model "C" head, see pages 52 and 53.
For full description of Model "C" stand, see page 55.
For full description of Model "C" attachments, see page 53.
For our liberal terms offer, see page 48.
For our three months' free trial offer, see page 48.
For our twenty years' guarantee, see page 48.
For freight rates, see column 1st class rates, pages 7 to 11.

DESCRIPTION OF THE MINNESOTA MODEL "C" WOODWORK.

MATERIAL. All Model "C" cabinets are made from solid oak, selected stock, all thoroughly kiln dried and air seasoned to prevent possible warping, checking or cracking, and if you order a Model "C" sewing machine from us we promise that you will get a more substantial, stronger, more lasting, better made and better finished set of woodwork, no matter what style of cabinet you order, than you can get from anyone else in any sewing machine which you would buy at $25.00 or less.

DESIGN. The cabinets used on our Model "C" upright and drop head machines are built on the very latest up to date lines of high grade furniture. The top has a beautifully shaped edge, which design is followed out in the construction of the drawers and wherever appropriate.

THE TABLE. The tables of the woodwork used on our Model "C" machines are all made of built up stock with cross band veneers, which construction prevents warping, cracking or splitting. On the upright cabinets, as shown in the illustration on this page, the table has a drop leaf which, when extended, is supported by an iron bracket and affords ample table room for any kind of sewing.

THE DRAWERS. The drawers are all made to correspond in design with the table, having rounded corners. The center drawer has a double swell front and all fronts are handsomely ornamented with deep carvings. The side drawers are incased in the latest open style of frame with embossed braces, presenting a much handsomer appearance than the old boxed-in style of cabinet. They have fancy metal ring pulls and are fitted with locks, one key locking all drawers. The center drawer is unusually roomy and is partitioned off on the inside for bobbins, needles, and other supplies which are in constant use and are therefore more conveniently stored there than in any other place in the machine.

ORDER BY NUMBER.
No. 26C222 Price - - $11.65
On board cars, Dayton, Ohio.

Sent on Three Months' Trial. See page 48

ATTACHMENTS 75c EXTRA.

The 7-Drawer Minnesota cost Mr. Hollis $20.00 less than a 5-Drawer Singer and he finds Our Machine Gives Perfect Satisfaction.

Monkton, Vt.
Sears, Roebuck & Co., Chicago.
Gentlemen:—The Minnesota sewing machine I bought of you about one year ago has given perfect satisfaction. My wife would not exchange it for any other kind. It runs very easy with scarcely any noise. It is a better made machine than agents are selling here for $40.00. The seven-drawer Minnesota sewing machine cost me $20.00 less than the Singer would with only five drawers. The freight was only 77 cents to North Ferrisburgh, Vt., and I received the machine without a mark or blemish. I would advise anyone wanting a sewing machine to order of Sears, Roebuck & Co.
Yours truly, H. S. HOLLIS.

THE FINISH. The finish on all of the woodwork used on our Model "C" machines is strictly first class. In order to get a good finish on oak woodwork it is necessary to have it thoroughly sandpapered in every nook and corner when the wood is still in the white, and this is the method employed at the factory that makes our woodwork. The filler and two coats of varnish are then put on, which, together, give the machine a rich, golden oak finish and the appearance of the finest highly polished furniture.

THE COVER. The cover which we furnish on our Model "C" upright style of machine, as illustrated on this page, is made of bent veneers and solid mouldings, designed and constructed to correspond with the balance of the machine, and is absolutely dustproof. It is fitted with two socket hinges and lock so that when placed over the head of the machine it can be securely fastened and thereby afford ample protection to the machine head in every way.

THE DRIP PAN. All of our upright style of machines are supplied with a japanned drip pan, which is fitted on the under side of the head as a protection to the operator against oil dripping from the head, and also to prevent dust getting into the working parts from the under side of the machine.

OUR MINNESOTA MODEL "C" DROP HEAD CABINETS.

THE DROP HEAD CABINETS WHICH WE FURNISH in both five and seven-drawer styles at $11.25 and $11.75, respectively, and which are fully illustrated on page 55, are by far the most popular styles, excepting only the full cabinet, which we furnish at $14.45 and which is illustrated on page 56. They differ from the upright machines only in so far as the head drops from sight and is thoroughly protected from dust and dirt when not in use. The table swings over and becomes a cover so when the machine is not in use you have a handsome desk or table.

AS A GUARANTEE, if you order one of our Minnesota Model "C" Sewing Machines, that you will get a machine handsomer, stronger, better finished, better made, and a better fitting cabinet than you can get in any other machine for $25.00, we will be glad to accept your order for our Minnesota Model "C" in any of the various styles of woodwork as illustrated, to be sent to you with the understanding and agreement that if it isn't more satisfactory and in every way better than any machine you could buy elsewhere for $25.00, you may return it to us at our expense and we will immediately refund your money. While if you were to order the Minnesota Model "C" sewing machine and take it to your home and set it up on our three months' free trial proposition, we are sure you would say it is one of the best sewing machines you have ever seen, one of the handsomest oak cabinets, one of the best stands, one of the handsomest heads, one of the easiest running and most satisfactory sewing machines you have ever used, and yet, if you could compare this Minnesota Model "C" machine with our Model "A" or "B," particularly the Model "A," the highest grade sewing machine made in the world for the slight difference in cost, we are sure you would select the highest grade sewing machine made, the Minnesota Model "A," which we furnish in the five-drawer drop head cabinet at $15.20, or in the seven-drawer drop head cabinet at $15.7

No. 26C220 Minnesota Model "C" three-drawer, box cover. Price........ $10.85
No. 26C221 Minnesota Model "C" five-drawer, box cover. Price........ 11.20
No. 26C222 Minnesota Model "C" seven-drawer, box cover. Price........ 11.65

The above prices do not include attachments. We furnish a complete set at 75 cents additional, as fully explained on page 53.

OUR MINNESOTA MODEL "C" SEVEN-DRAWER DROP HEAD STYLE

...WITH SWELL FRONT CABINET...

IN ORDER TO MEET THE REQUIREMENTS of our customers who need considerable drawer space for sewing materials, we show our Minnesota Model "C" Sewing Machine in this seven-drawer, drop head style, three drawers on each side and the push drawer in the center. We can also furnish the drop head pattern with five drawers, two on each side and one center drawer for $11.25.

BY REASON OF THE FIRST CLASS MATERIALS USED in the construction of our Minnesota Model "C" head and working parts, the case hardening of every operating part subject to friction, the care with which the head parts are made and fitted together by expert workmen, and the numerous inspections and tests our machines receive before being shipped,

WE ARE ENABLED TO GUARANTEE OUR MINNESOTA MODEL "C" MACHINE to be stronger and more durable in construction, will last many years longer and give better satisfaction all the time than the sewing machines sold by other dealers, the chief merits of which are an attractive appearing stand and elaborate set of woodwork.

PRICE **$11.75**

ATTACHMENTS, 75 CENTS EXTRA.

ON BOARD CARS DAYTON, OHIO.

DESCRIPTION OF THE MINNESOTA MODEL "C" STAND.

THE MINNESOTA MODEL "C" IRON STANDS are made from the very best light gray Birmingham (Alabama) iron. They are moulded by automatic machines instead of being cast by a hand process, making every piece perfectly true, smooth and of unusual strength, so that when the different parts are assembled they fit perfectly. All parts are heavily coated with black enamel by hand process. We put on a heavier, smoother, glossier, better finished and far more lasting coat of enamel than is furnished by any other sewing machine maker, and we believe we furnish a stronger, better finished and handsomer sewing machine stand than is used on any other sewing machine made.

DESIGN. The Minnesota Model "C" Stand has been especially designed for us with a view of securing a neat, graceful, open effect, and, at the same time, a frame that will stand the severest tests.

For full description of Model "C" head, see pages 52 and 53.
For full description of Model "C" woodwork, see page 54.
For full description of Model "C" attachments, see page 53.
For our liberal terms offer, see page 48.
For our three months' free trial offer, see page 48.
For our twenty years' guarantee, see page 48.
For freight rates, see column first class rates, pages 7 to 11.

No. 26C227

ORDER BY NUMBER ONLY.

THE SIDE FRAMES are made in what is popularly known as the ribbon pattern construction, which produces the best effect and the most rigid and lasting frame, without being clumsy. They are joined together by a full set of braces, as illustrated, bolting the side standards at the top and bottom, making the stand absolutely rigid, which is so essential in the construction of a sewing machine.

THE TREADLE is of the openwork style, with full ends, pivot bearing, accurately trued, adjustable take-up between the balance wheel and the treadle, putting the entire machine under easy control of the operator.

We use the highest grade sewing machine casters made, which are carefully fitted and never come out of place.

THE BALANCE WHEEL is extra heavy, carefully adjusted, perfectly true, pivot bearing, which insures an even, easy speed to the machine, putting it at all times under perfect control of the operator.

THE DRESS GUARD to this stand is extra large, protecting the balance wheel and belt from any possible contact with the dress, at the same time substantially bracing the side frame.

THE OIL GUARD, immediately under the treadle, extends from side frame to side frame, is securely bolted, strengthens the frame and prevents the oil from dropping on the floor or carpet.

INSPECTION. All parts are accurately trued, tested for strength, not a casting is allowed to be used that has a sand hole or defect, or that isn't true to gauge, and as a result, for strength, beauty, design, finish, for easy running and for perfect control of the machine by the operator, we furnish a higher grade sewing machine stand than is furnished by any other maker.

J. E. BOTSFORD CHOSE THE MINNESOTA IN PREFERENCE TO THE WHEELER & WILSON, AND SAYS HE WOULDN'T CHANGE MACHINES TODAY.

Sears, Roebuck & Co., Chicago, Ill. Norwalk, Conn.

Gentlemen:—We are very much pleased with the Minnesota Sewing Machine. We recently had a Wheeler & Wilson, price $35.00, left at our house by an agent, but did not keep it. By sending for the Minnesota we saved about $17.50, and we wouldn't trade machines today.

Yours truly, J. E. BOTSFORD.

No. 26C226 Minnesota Model "C" Five-Drawer, Drop Head. Price........ $11.25
No. 26C227 Minnesota Model "C" Seven-Drawer, Drop Head. Price........ 11.75

The above prices do not include attachments. We can furnish a complete set at 75 cents additional, as fully explained on page 53.

OUR $14.45 FULL CABINET MINNESOTA MODEL "C" SEWING MACHINE.

DESK CABINET STYLE.

A RELIABLE, STANDARD, STRONG, HANDSOME APPEARING CABINET MACHINE FOR $14.45

WE HAVE RECEIVED so many demands for our Minnesota Model "C" Machine in the cabinet style that we have decided to catalogue the cabinet shown in these three illustrations for $14.45. While our price makes this the lowest priced cabinet machine on the market, it compares more than favorably in working qualities, durability, finish and appearance with the cabinet machines sold elsewhere at double our price.

DETAILED DESCRIPTION OF THIS HANDSOME FULL OAK CABINET.

THIS CABINET is made throughout of the very best grade of solid oak, thoroughly air and kiln dried. The door is made with panel front, ornamented with handsome design drop carvings and massive mouldings and caps. The sides are solid full panels with the same design drop carvings as appear on the door. The lid is made of built up stock with cross band sawed veneer of specially selected, handsome grain. The inside of the door is fitted with wooden pockets to hold the oil can, bobbins, screwdriver and other accessories so that they will be convenient for use when the machine is being operated. The cabinet is finished throughout in a strictly first class manner, being put together by the best cabinet makers, thoroughly sandpapered in every nook and corner, and finally given the rich golden oak finish which is in popular demand. The varnish used on this cabinet is exceptionally high grade, and gives a rich, glossy appearance similar to the finest hand polish of the highest grade furniture. The cabinet rests on four rollers so that it can be easily moved about.

Price $14.45

IN MOUNTING our Minnesota Model "C" Head in the full desk cabinet, as illustrated and in the various other cabinets, we have avoided all makes of cheap sewing machine woodwork. You will find the cabinet you get from us will not warp, check or split; you will find the sewing machine in the full cabinet or in the drop head style will be in perfect order; in the same good condition in which it left our factory, long after other cabinets, which are being sold by many at $20.00 and $25.00, have warped, cracked and given out at the joints, etc.

BALL BEARINGS. Our Model "C" Full Cabinet Machine is as light running as either the upright or the drop head style. Is fitted with our celebrated bicycle ball bearing hanger, found only on our cabinet machines, which gives the same rapidity of action and ease of operation to the machine as the ball bearing arrangement to a bicycle. All wearing parts are made of case hardened ground out steel, and the steel balls are the best in the market. Simple in construction; no getting out of order. All parts are easily accessible, so that balls or cups can be replaced at any time. All friction is eliminated and operation made a pleasure.

ORDER BY NUMBER.

BALL BEARING

AS A GUARANTEE that our Model "C" full desk cabinet sewing machine, as illustrated on this page, and offered at $14.45, will prove entirely satisfactory to you, that you will find it better than any machine you can buy from any other house at $25.00 or less, that you will find it in every way the equal of most sewing machines that are sold through agents at $35.00 to $50.00, we will gladly accept your order for one of these handsome full cabinet machines at our special $14.45 price. The machine will be sent to you with the understanding and agreement, that you can give it three months' trial, during which time you can put it to every test, compare it to any sewing machine you can buy from any other house at $25.00, and if you do not find ours in every way a handsomer, stronger and better cabinet, if it does not do better work, is not easier running, more simple to operate, less liable to get out of order; if it is not more satisfactory in every way than any machine sold by any other house at $25.00 or less, return it to us at our expense and we will immediately refund your money, together with any freight charges paid by you.

For full description of Model "C" Head, see pages 52 and 53.

For full description of Model "C" Accessories, see page 53.

For full description of Model "C" Attachments, see page 53.

For our Liberal Terms Offer, see page 48.

For our Three Months' Free Trial Offer, see page 48.

For our Twenty Years' Guarantee, see page 48.

For Freight Rates, see column "first class," pages 7 to 11.

Miss M. M. Hurlbut says: "I Have Used the New Home and Also the Singer, but I Think the Minnesota that I Got Is as Good as Either of the Other Machines."

Sears, Roebuck & Co., Chicago, Ill. Palmdale, Cal.

Gentlemen:—I am well pleased with my Minnesota Sewing Machine, and it does as good work as any other machine I ever used. I have used the New Home, and also the Singer, but I think the Minnesota I got is as good as either of the other machines. I have saved all of $20.00 by sending to you for a machine. The more I use the machine the better I like it. I have a friend and she needs a machine, so I think maybe you will get an order from her for one. She likes my machine very much.

Respectfully, MISS M. M. HURLBUT.

No. 26C229 Model "C" Full Cabinet. Furnished in Oak only..$14.45

The above price does not include attachments. We furnish a complete set at 75 cents extra, as fully explained on page 53.

ILLUSTRATED FEATURES OF THE MECHANICAL CONSTRUCTION OF OUR MINNESOTA MODEL "B" HEAD

It is impossible to devise a more perfect or more suitable sewing machine for household or domestic purposes than our MINNESOTA MODEL "B." In the matter of improvements, labor and time saving conveniences, it is second only to our Minnesota Model "A," and is built on the latest up to date principles of construction.

IT WILL DO ANY WORK, LIGHT OR HEAVY, FANCY OR PLAIN SEWING THAT CAN BE DONE ON ANY FAMILY SEWING MACHINE.

DESIGN. By reference to the illustration it will be seen that the Minnesota Model "B" Head is extremely handsome and pleasing in appearance, the general design being worked out in easy curves and rounded corners so as to avoid any suggestion of harshness or angularity.

SIZE. Our Model "B" Head is the regular standard, high arm, family style, and measures 5 inches in height under the arm, 8⅛ inches from needle to upright part of arm and 9¾ inches from bed plate to top of the needle bar. The bed plate is 6¾ inches wide by 13¾ inches long. These measurements provide sufficient space for practically any family sewing.

FINISH. The finish of the head is as fine as can be put on a sewing machine. Three coats of the highest grade of enamel are used, each coat being separately baked at a high temperature, rubbed down to a smooth surface by hand and finally beautifully decorated in an elaborate design worked out in gold and bright colors, after which it is given a coat of special varnish, also baked in a high degree of heat, which gives the machine a durable, rich and lustrous finish. Before the enamel is put on, the head is treated to a coat of anti-rust preparation which prevents the finish from cracking, checking or peeling which so frequently occurs with other makes of machines.

NICKEL PLATING. All of the bright parts, including the face plate, are first copper plated, then nickel plated and finally highly polished. This applies to the working parts underneath the bed of the machine as well as to those that are exposed to view.

LOCK STITCH. Our Model "B" is a regular lock stitch machine, which is the popular type adopted by all manufacturers of high grade machines.

SPECIAL FEATURES

High Arm. Independent, Positive Cam Take-up. Handy Tension Release. Light Running. Noiseless.

OPERATING PARTS. The operating parts of the Model "B" Head are practically the same as those of our Model "A," with the exception of the round needle bar and the shuttle and feed mechanism, which is of a slightly different construction, as will be noted by referring to the illustration of the under view of the head. All operating and working parts in this machine are made of the finest tool steel that can be obtained, and after being thoroughly hardened by the latest and most improved process, are accurately ground to a perfect fit and so constructed that any lost motion due to the slight wear that may result after many years of usage can be easily and quickly taken up. This renders it practically indestructible and one of the most durable machines ever produced.

THE INDEPENDENT TAKE-UP. The take-up is operated by a cam on the main shaft, thereby becoming absolutely positive in its action and insuring uniformity of stitch in all classes of work. In many machines, even some of the most expensive, springs are used to partly control the movement of the take-up, and the instant the spring is weakened the harmony between the take-up and other important running parts is destroyed, consequently resulting in imperfect stitches or the breaking of needles.

DOUBLE ECCENTRIC. The double eccentric on the main shaft through the arm of the head operates the shuttle, feed and needle bar mechanism. The double eccentric is made in one piece accurately balanced so as to prevent any vibration when the machine is being operated and which also contributes greatly to its light and noiseless running qualities. This construction does away with all irregular movements and produces a shuttle and feed movement which is absolutely positive in every sense of the term. A glance at the working parts of this machine shows how remarkably simple it is. There are no springs, cushions, pads or other appliances required which necessarily add to the number of parts and the liability of the machine to get out of order.

EASY TO OIL. By means of convenient oil holes and a movable metal plate on the back of the head, all bearings are easily gotten at to oil. This is a most important feature, as thorough lubrication prevents friction and wear.

THE NEEDLE CLAMP holds the needle firmly in place and permits the needle to be removed in an instant when required, even though it should break accidently in the bar where it cannot be reached by the fingers. The needles can be had from us at factory cost. See prices, page 70.

RUNNING SPEED. Every machine before being shipped from the factory is put to the severest possible test, being set up and attached to a power pulley and run at a speed five times greater than it is possible to run any machine by foot power, and by this severe test we first learn that every machine is perfectly true in every particular and capable of the highest possible speed.

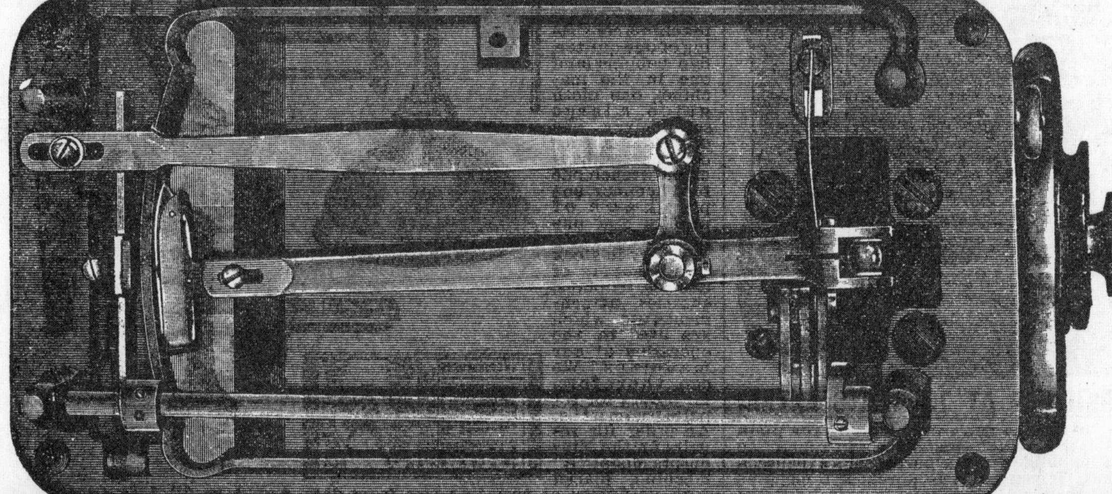

THE NEEDLE BAR is round and made of the best quality of tool steel, properly hardened and tempered. It is accurately fitted, insuring absolutely uniform wear at all points.

SELF SETTING NEEDLES for this machine are the very best grade of flank shank needle it is possible to procure. Every needle is inspected and tested as to size, temper and position of eye. The needle bar is constructed with a groove so that the needle can only be placed in the proper position. It is not necessary to guess at the height or position when setting the needle as is the case with many other makes of machines.

PRESSER FOOT. The presser foot is very large so that it will hold any weight and thickness of goods firmly in place. The edge of the foot nearest the operator is bent upward slightly so that it will not catch in fleecy materials. The presser foot can be removed from the machine in an instant without the aid of a screwdriver. The illustration shows the foot being removed after the thumbscrew has been loosened.

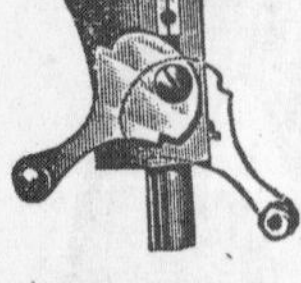

PRESSER BAR LIFTER. The presser bar is fitted with a steel, case hardened, nickel plated lifter, so constructed that it can be turned to the right or to the left, raising the bar to the desired height for heavy or light material.

NEEDLE AND THREAD SCALE. A scale indicating the proper needle to be used with the different sizes of thread is stamped on the forward shuttle slide. Breaking of thread and needles often occur if incorrect sizes of needles or thread are used.

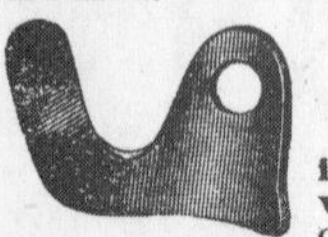

A SHARP STEEL THREAD CUTTER is placed on the presser bar, convenient to the operator, by the aid of which the thread can be easily cut, obviating the use of scissors and the danger of breaking or cutting the thread too short.

DOUBLE FEED. The feed is made of the best quality tool steel; has four sets of teeth, two on each side of the needle, and so constructed that when in operation the goods must be carried forward with absolute accuracy.

FEED MOVEMENT. (Four motion.) The feed in this machine is operated by four movements. The feed comes up, takes a firm hold on the goods, carries them forward the full length of the stitch, then it falls, releasing the goods, and comes back again toward the operator ready for the next stitch. These four movements are provided entirely by the main shaft, insuring positive action on either heavy or light work.

THE SHUTTLE. The shuttle is the most perfect, self-threading, cylindrical shuttle ever produced. It is extra large in size, made of the finest tool steel, hardened, ground and finished. It is absolutely self-threading, being open at one end for inserting the bobbin, after which the thread is instantly drawn into place by two movements of the hand. There are no holes to pass through, and the shuttle can be threaded with the eyes shut. It has a perfect tension, which is practically automatic. It does not require regulating for any ordinary work. The bobbin carries a large amount of thread. The illustration shows the shuttle being held between the thumb and forefinger while threading.

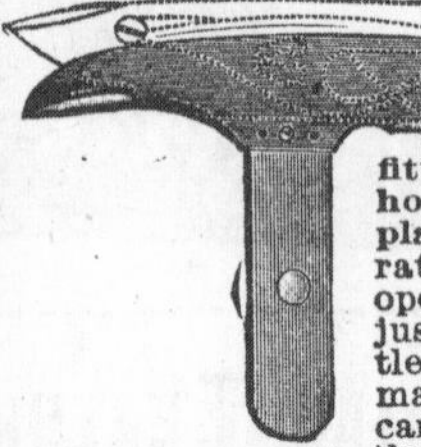

THE SHUTTLE CARRIER, the body in which the shuttle rests, is fitted with a spring which holds the bobbin firmly in place and prevents it from rattling while the machine is in operation. The carrier is adjustable, so that when the shuttle shows signs of wear, after many years of use, the carrier can be moved closer to the shuttle race, thus enabling the operator to use the same shuttle for many years, with the same satisfaction as when new.

FOR DESCRIPTION OF MODEL "B" WOODWORK
See page 59.

FOR DESCRIPTION OF MODEL "B" STAND
See page 60.

FOR DESCRIPTION OF MODEL "B" CABINET
See page 61.

FOR OUR LIBERAL TERMS OFFER
See page 48.

FOR OUR THREE MONTHS' FREE TRIAL OFFER
See page 48.

FOR OUR TWENTY YEARS' GUARANTEE
See page 48.

DISC TENSION. The upper tension of this machine is of the modern disc type and practically automatic on all classes of work. The tension and liberator are located on the side face plate toward the operator. This location of the tension is not only far more convenient, but brings the point at which the tension is applied to the thread much nearer to the eye of the needle, thus reducing the amount of thread under tension and doing away, in a large measure, with the stretch in the thread, which on the old style machines frequently caused bad stitching or skipping of stitches.

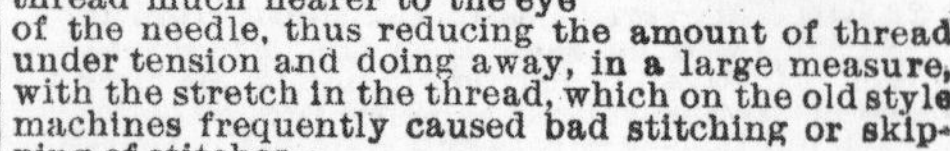

TENSION LIBERATOR. Makes it possible to remove the work from the machine by the mere touch of a finger, so that the work can be drawn from underneath the presser foot with ease. The illustration shows the extension of the tension plate, which when pressed, releases the tension on the thread.

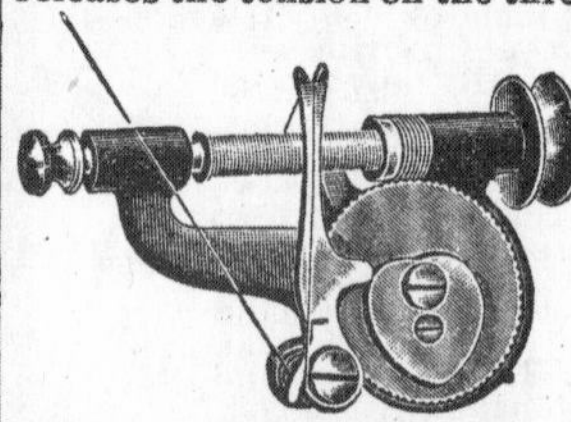

THE AUTOMATIC BOBBIN WINDER on this machine is nickel plated throughout and is the most perfect bobbin winder ever produced. It is so simple that any child can operate it, and the thread is wound on the bobbin automatically and so evenly and smoothly as to make the bobbin work perfectly in the shuttle, producing an even tension and greatly improving the perfection of the stitch. This also prevents the breaking of the lower thread, which is liable to occur with an unevenly wound bobbin.

THE BOBBIN WINDER is always in position and ready to operate. It is operated by means of the belt which is placed in contact with the small pulley wheel of the bobbin winder.

STITCH REGULATOR. The illustration shows the stitch regulator, which is fastened to the bed plate just in front of the arm in plain sight and within easy reach of the operator. The length of the stitch can be adjusted instantly by loosening the thumb nut and moving the pointer to the desired figure on the scale stamped on the stitch regulator plate. The stitch can be varied from six to thirty-two stitches to the inch, thereby affording a range from the very smallest to the largest stitch.

ATTACHMENTS FOR OUR MODEL "B" MACHINES.

OUR CUSTOMERS HAVE THE ADVANTAGE and privilege of being able to purchase a machine without attachments, and are not obliged to receive and pay for attachments which are not required. From our many years of experience in selling sewing machines we have found that about one-third of the sewing machine users do not need the attachments, using the machine for plain sewing only; the only necessary attachments being the shuttle, needles, bobbin, quilter, screwdriver, wrench and foot hemmer, which are always furnished with our machines at no additional charge. We have, therefore, deducted the cost of the attachments from the selling price and quote each machine without any extra attachments.

ATTACHMENTS WILL BE FURNISHED AT 75 CENTS EXTRA.

If you, the reader of this catalogue, intend to use your machine for plain sewing only, and do not wish to buy extra attachments, you will appreciate our departure from the old custom of including, at the purchaser's expense, a set of attachments with every machine. If you wish to purchase a machine without attachments and later on wish to secure attachments, we can always supply you at our lowest price.

WE USE THE CELEBRATED GREIST FOOT ATTACHMENTS, made by the Greist Manufacturing Co., of New Haven, Conn., on our Minnesota Model "B" machine as well as our other models. The entire set is made of the very best hardened steel of extra thickness, heavily nickel plated and consists of the following attachments, packed in a velvet lined, japanned metal box. One ruffler, one shirring plate, one tucker, one short foot, one under braider, one binder and one set of four hemmers, different widths, up to ⅝-inch. Our price for the full set, 75 cents. **Be sure to state if you wish the attachments shipped with your machine.**

ACCESSORIES

We furnish with every Minnesota model "B" Machine, a complete set of accessories such as are usually furnished with every high grade machine, consisting of one quilter, five bobbins (and one in the machine), one cloth guide, a large screwdriver, one oil can filled with oil, one screwdriver and wrench, one foot hemmer, one package of needles and one instruction book. We carry in stock a full supply of needles, bobbins, shuttles, attachments, etc., which are used in the operation of our machines. We can, therefore, fill orders for repairs promptly. An order for repairs for the Minnesota Model "B" machine, placed with us fifteen or twenty years from date, would be filled as promptly as a repair order sent us today.

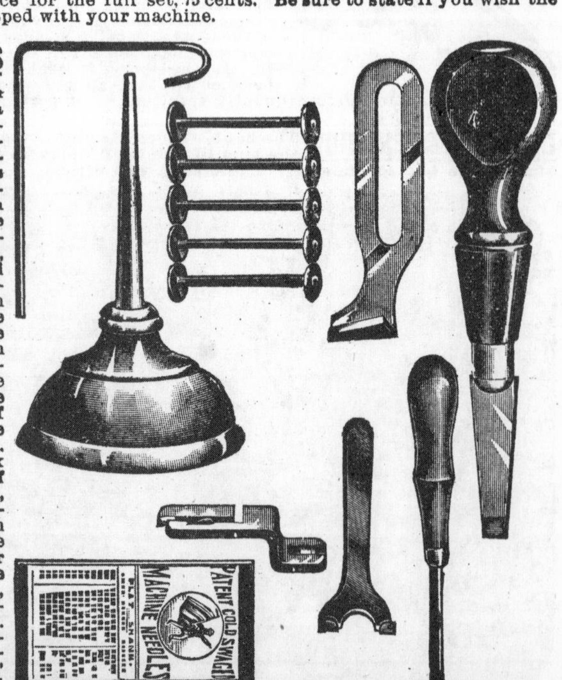

OUR 7-DRAWER DROP LEAF AND BOX COVER MINNESOTA MODEL "B" SEWING MACHINE

THIS ILLUSTRATION shows our Minnesota Model "B" Machine in the upright style with box cover. The head is stationary and cannot be lowered as in the drop head, but is protected when not in use by the bent cover furnished with the machine. The illustration shows the 7-drawer pattern at $13.20; we can also furnish the same machine with 5 drawers at $12.80 and with 3 drawers at $12.35. The mechanical construction of our Minnesota Model "B" Machine is fully described on pages 57 and 58.

For full description of Model "B" head, see pages 57 and 58.
For full description of Model "B" stand, see page 60.
For full description of Model "B" attachments, see page 58.
For our liberal terms offer, see page 48.
For three months' free trial offer, see page 48.
For our twenty years' guarantee, see page 48.
For freight rates, see column 1st class rates, pages 7 to 11.

DESCRIPTION OF WOODWORK ON OUR MINNESOTA MODEL "B" SEWING MACHINES.

THE WOODWORK on our Model "B" sewing machines is of a very much higher grade than is usually used in sewing machines. It is made especially for our machines, under contract, by the largest manufacturers of sewing machine woodwork in the world, who supply cabinets only for the highest grade sewing machines, and it cannot be in any way classed with the woodwork commonly used on machines that sell generally at $25.00 or less.

MATERIALS. Only the most select grade of solid oak is used in the construction of our Model "B" woodwork. It is carefully selected with reference to grain and color and is thoroughly aired and kiln dried to insure against warping, splitting or cracking.

DESIGN. The Minnesota Model "B" cabinet is a model of beauty and artistic design, second only to our Model "A." It is made on the lines of the high grade, up to date furniture, especially designed for us and not made for nor used on any other machines.

TABLE. The table is made of built up stock and faced with highly figured quartered oak. This construction has proven the most durable, being practically indestructible. The front edge of the table handsomely shaped. All ..les on the upright box ..r Model "B" machines, illustrated, have a drop leaf, which when raised into place, is supported by an iron brace and produces a table of ample length for any and all requirements.

DRAWER FRAMES. The drawer frames in which the side drawers are fitted are of the latest skeleton type, much handsomer in appearance and far preferable to the old fashioned solid cases.

DRAWERS. The drawers are very large and roomy, made with rounded corners to harmonize with the table. The fronts are handsomely decorated with drop carvings of floral design and fitted with brass, nickel plated and polished ring pulls. The center drawer is made of built up stock, with swell front; the interior is partitioned off for bobbins, needles and other accessories, which are in constant demand when the machine is being used. Every drawer is fitted with a lock and one key fits them all.

FINISH. In point of finish our Model "B" machine is strictly first class and of the very latest golden color, the popular finish put on high grade oak furniture. Before the finish is put on, the woodwork is most carefully sandpapered so that the varnish, which is of the very best quality, produces a hard glossy surface. The table is hand rubbed and polished.

COVER. All upright machines are provided with box cover, made of built up stock, surfaced with quartered oak and strengthened with mouldings. The front is ornamented with carved, raised panel. The cover is fitted with socket hinges and lock, so that when placed on the machine it can be locked, thereby affording full protection to the head.

Minnesota Model "B"

$13.20

BALL BEARING

DIRECTIONS
MINNESOTA MODEL 'B'
SEWING MACHINE
SILENT AND LIGHT RUNNING.

ORDER BY NUMBER.

No. 26C232

$13.20

ON BOARD CARS, DAYTON, OHIO.

ATTACHMENTS 75c EXTRA.

Mrs. Mixon says, "I have Used All the Attachments and They Worked All Right. I Saved $15.00 to $20.00 by Ordering a Minnesota."

Sears, Roebuck & Co.,
Chicago, Ill.

Gentlemen:—I received the Minnesota sewing machine, which I bought of you about four months ago, in good condition, and I am well pleased with it. I think it is as good as the machines which sell here for $30.00 and $40.00. I have used all the attachments and they worked all right, and I am well pleased with my machine. I think that I saved $15.00 to $20.00 by ordering my machine from you.

Yours truly,
MRS. MAY MIXON.

MINNESOTA MODEL "B" DROP HEAD CABINET.

THE DROP HEAD CABINET which we furnish in either five or seven-drawer, as desired, and as illustrated on the following page, the Model "B" five-drawer drop head at $12.85, seven-drawer drop head at $13.35, is built on the exact same lines as the upright or cover machine illustrated, the same grade of woodwork, the same high grade finish, the same trimming, carving, shaping, decorating and polishing; but as will be shown in the illustrations on the following page, when not in use the head drops from sight, the cover folds over and you have a perfect desk, stand or table, a handsome piece of furniture. When in use with the head raised in place, the cover forms a large leaf, giving ample room for bulky goods.

WE ESPECIALLY RECOMMEND that you select the drop head style of machine, either our five-drawer drop head Model "B" machine at $12.85, or the seven-drawer at $13.35. You get a handsome piece of furniture, the same grade of woodwork, and your machine, when not in use, is protected from dust and dirt.

WE MAKE A DIFFERENCE IN OUR SELLING PRICE between the Model "B" and Model "C" woodwork, only enough to represent the difference in cost of material and labor. It is a higher grade of material, a more carefully selected grade of wood, higher grade of finish, and in making our price we only ask the difference in the cost of manufacture, the difference in the cost of material and labor.

TO FULLY APPRECIATE the grade of woodwork we furnish in our Minnesota Model "B" machine, to understand how much better it is in every way than the woodwork generally furnished in machines at $25.00 or less, you should be able to see, examine and compare one of our Model "B" machines with machines offered by others at or about $25.00. That you may do this you are at perfect liberty to order one of our machines on our three months' free trial plan, order it shipped to your nearest railroad station by freight, C. O. D., subject to examination; at the same time order a machine from any other house at or about $25.00, compare the two machines side by side, and if you are not at once convinced that we use a higher grade of woodwork, that our upright or drop head cabinets are better made, better finished, you are at liberty to return the machine to us at our expense, and we will immediately refund your money.

No. 26C230	Model "B" Three-Drawer, Box Cover. Price	$12.35
No. 26C231	Model "B" Five-Drawer, Box Cover. Price	12.80
No. 26C232	Model "B" Seven-Drawer, Box Cover. Price	13.20

The above prices do not include attachments. We furnish a complete set at 75 cents extra, as fully explained on page 58.

OUR 7-DRAWER DROP HEAD BALL BEARING MINNESOTA MODEL "B" SEWING MACHINE

OUR MINNESOTA MODEL "B" BALL BEARING STAND.

This page describes and illustrates our Minnesota Model "B" Machine in the popular and convenient drop head style, with 7 drawers. We can also furnish this same style of machine with 5 drawers for $12.85.

OUR MINNESOTA MODEL "B" STANDS are made from the best Birmingham, Alabama, light gray iron. They are moulded by automatic machines instead of being cast by a hand process, making every piece perfectly true, smooth and of unusual strength, so that when the different parts are assembled they fit perfectly. All parts are heavily coated with black enamel by hand process. We put on a heavier, smoother, glossier, better finished and far more lasting coat of enamel than is furnished by any other sewing machine maker, and we furnish a stronger, better finished and handsomer sewing machine stand than is used on any other sewing machine made.

DESIGN. The Model "B" stand has been especially designed for us with a view of procuring a neat, graceful open effect and at the same time furnishing a frame that will stand the severest tests. The side frames or legs of the stand are made in the handsomest style open and wide ribbon pattern. This open design and the style in which the side frames are made, makes our stands the most desirable because they are so easily kept clean.

THE BRACES. The side frames or legs of the stand are joined together by a four-arm brace, bolted at the top and bottom, making the stand absolutely rigid. This is very essential, as it lessens the vibration and so causes our machines to make less noise and last longer than the machines which are built on weak and wabbly stands.

THE ARRANGEMENT OF THE BALL BEARINGS of the balance wheel is the same as that used on all high grade bicycles. The axle on which the wheel revolves passes through two steel cups, each of which contains 15 solid steel balls, which are fitted into the balance wheel, and by means of adjustable cones it is possible at all times to have the balance wheel run lightly and noiselessly. The cups and cones used on our stands are turned out of a solid bar of steel, after which they are ground out and case hardened in oil, making them impervious to wear, and with proper oiling from time to time will make them last a lifetime.

For full description of Model "B" head, see pages 57 and 58.
For full description of Model "B" woodwork, see page 59.
For full description of Model "B" attachments, see page 58.
For our liberal terms offer, see page 48.
For our three months' free trial offer, see page 48.
For our twenty years' guarantee, see page 48.
For freight rates, see pages 7 to 11.

DRESS GUARD. The dress guard to this stand is extra large, protecting the balance wheel and belt from any possible contact with the dress, at the same time substantially bracing the side frame.

OIL GUARD. The oil guard immediately under the treadle extends from side frame to side frame, is securely bolted, strengthens the frame and prevents the oil from dropping on the floor or carpet.

NO. 26C237
ORDER BY NUMBER.

$13.35 On board cars Dayton, Ohio.

Attachments, 75c extra.

THE CASTERS are of a large size, making it easy to move the machine from place to place, are carefully fitted and never break.

TREADLE. The treadle is of the open work style, with full ends, pivot bearings accurately trued, adjustable take up between the balance wheel and the treadle, putting the entire machine under easy control of the operator.

INSPECTION. All parts are accurately trued, tested for strength; not a casting is allowed to be used that has a sand hole or defect or that is not true to gauge. After the stand has been properly assembled, the balance wheel and treadle are operated by steam power at a very high rate of speed, whereby the balance wheel makes a great many more revolutions than any operator could possibly make. If there is the slightest flaw in the iron or in the construction or adjustment of the stand it becomes evident through this test and the stand is then rejected, and as a result, for strength, beauty, design, finish, for easy running and for perfect control of the machine by the operator, we furnish a higher grade sewing machine stand than is furnished by any other maker.

BALL BEARING BALANCE WHEEL. All our Model "B" machines are equipped with ball bearing hangers. The hanger is the large balance wheel and shaft fastened to the right stand leg, as shown in this illustration. As this wheel supplies the operating power to the head, the bearings on which the wheel revolves are naturally subjected to a considerable strain, but by the introduction of the ball bearings all friction is removed and the wheel revolves with the same freedom and rapidity as the ball bearing crank hanger of the bicycle. The application of the ball bearings to the balance wheel is one of the greatest improvements and the greatest aid to the light running qualities of the machine, and we have demonstrated, by actual experiments and tests, that our ball bearing hanger is at least 20 per cent lighter running than any ball bearing device or arrangement used on any other sewing machine made. By the aid of ball bearings a machine is made not only lighter running, but exceedingly easy of operation and very rapid in action.

No. 26C236 Minnesota Model "B" Five-Drawer, Drop Head. Price........ $12.85
No. 26C237 Minnesota Model "B" Seven-Drawer, Drop Head. Price........ 13.35

The above prices do not include attachments. We furnish a complete set at 75 cents additional, as fully explained on page 58.

$15.75 BUYS THE MINNESOTA MODEL "B" FULL CABINET, BALL BEARING MACHINE

OUR MINNESOTA MODEL "B" TWO-DOOR FULL DESK OAK CABINET.

ILLUSTRATION SHOWS CABINET CLOSED.

FULL DESK CABINET

To meet the requirements of our customers who prefer our Minnesota Model "B" Machine with closed cabinet, we furnish this machine with the cabinet illustrated on this page; one illustration showing the machine open for work, one illustration showing head when not in use, and the other showing the machine closed, to be used as a desk, table or other piece of furniture.

THE MODEL "B" TWO-DOOR DESK CABINET is made of selected air seasoned and kiln dried solid oak. The top is of selected quarter sawed oak, finished and hand rubbed to a mirror-like piano polish. Particular pains are taken in selecting the lumber used for the tops of our cabinets, and the special manner in which they are reinforced insures them against warping, cracking or splitting. The two doors are strongly built of solid oak, with specially selected quartered oak panels. The panels on both sides of the cabinet are also of selected quarter sawed oak. The moulding on the doors, besides being handsome and ornamental, adds materially to the strength of the cabinet. The doors are locked by means of a slip bolt and brass knob.

On board cars Dayton, Ohio.
ATTACHMENTS 75 cents extra.

THE PANELS on the two doors and sides of the cabinet are decorated with hand carved ornamental designs. There are two drawers, one of which is made to contain the attachments and accessories which are constantly in use, while the other is made especially for the bobbins, needles, thread, etc. These drawers, as shown in the illustrations on this page, are securely fastened to the upper part of the doors of the cabinet, a most convenient arrangement, because the operator will not have to move at all when wanting anything contained in either drawer.

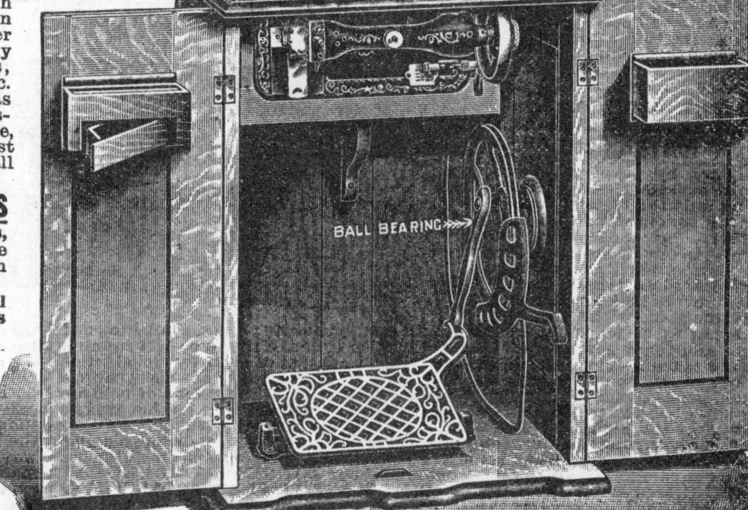

ILLUSTRATION SHOWS HEAD WHEN NOT IN USE.

ALL OUR MODEL "B" CABINETS are mounted on four large roller casters, making it easy to move the machine from place to place without any exertion whatever.

BALL BEARINGS. Our Model "B" full cabinet machine is as light running as either the upright or the drop head style; is fitted with our celebrated bicycle ball bearing hanger, found only on our cabinet machines, which gives the same rapidity of action and ease of operation to the machine as the ball bearing arrangement to a bicycle. All wearing parts made of case hardened ground out steel, and the steel balls are the best in the market. Simple in construction, no getting out of order. All parts are easily accessible, so that balls or cups can be replaced at any time. All friction eliminated and operation made a pleasure.

THIS CABINET must be seen to be appreciated. Send $1.00 as a deposit, balance to be paid upon arrival of machine and if you are not satisfied that this is the best two-door, all oak cabinet machine possible for you to procure at anything near our price of $15.75, return it to us at our expense and we will refund your money and freight charges paid by you.

DON'T order a sewing machine elsewhere. Don't buy a machine from any other dealer or agent before you see, examine and compare our machine with the machine offered by the other party, and if our machine is not better finished, lighter running, better in every way and lower in price than the best offer you can get from anyone else, when compared side by side, return our machine at our expense and we will immediately refund your money, together with all freight charges which you paid.

A full set of accessories, see page 58, free of cost, included with machine at $15.75.

For description of Model "B" head, see pages 57 and 58.
For description of Model "B" accessories, see page 58.
For description of Model "B" attachments, see page 58.
For our liberal terms offer, see page 48.
For our three months' free trial offer, see page 48.
For our twenty years' guarantee, see page 48.
For freight rates, see column 1st class freight, pages 7 to 11.

OUR WRITTEN BINDING 20-YEAR GUARANTEE SENT WITH EACH OF THESE MACHINES.

ILLUSTRATION SHOWS MACHINE OPEN AND READY FOR WORK.

Miss Ella Lytle says: "I Have Saved From $40.00 to $45.00 by Buying the Machine of You, as an Agent Would Have Charged Not Less Than $60.00."

Port Matilda, Pa.

Sears, Roebuck & Co., Chicago, Ill.

Gentlemen:—The machine came in due time and will say I could not be more pleased than I am with this machine. Everything was satisfactory about it. I am safe in saying I have saved from $40.00 to $45.00 by buying the machine of you, as an agent would have charged not less than $60.00 for any of the new machines brought through here. A great many persons who want sewing machines have been in to see mine and they all like this one. I see Mrs. J. M. Williams has received one of the same name. She examined mine and said she would have one like it. The freight was only 66 cents, less than I expected it to be. Yours truly,

MISS ELLA LYTLE.

No 26C241 Minnesota Model "B" Full Cabinet, Ball Bearing Machine. Price (furnished in oak only)........ **$15.75**

The above price does not include attachments. We furnish a complete set at 75 cents additional, as fully explained on page 58.

ILLUSTRATED FEATURES OF THE MECHANICAL CONSTRUCTION OF OUR

MODEL "A" SEWING MACHINE HEAD.

OUR MINNESOTA MODEL "A" SEWING MACHINE

On another page of this catalogue the question is asked: **CAN THE MINNESOTA MODEL "A" SEWING MACHINE, WITH ANY OUTLAY OF MONEY, BE IMPROVED IN ANY WAY?** This is followed by the statement that **WE HAVE SPENT THOUSANDS OF DOLLARS trying to find out how to make it better.**

We now take pleasure in presenting our Model "A" Sewing Machine with a number of new features which represent far greater advancement toward perfection in the sewing machine than all other changes and improvements made during the last ten or fifteen years.

THE VALUE of these improvements cannot be too highly estimated. Never before in the history of the sewing machine business have such **IMPORTANT IMPROVEMENTS**, entailing considerable expense, been added to the sewing machine without increasing the selling price.

It being an undisputed fact that a ball bearing device is the only proper arrangement to reduce friction, thereby requiring less power to operate, the superintendent of the Dayton factory has studied to apply the **BALL BEARING DEVICE** on the Minnesota Model "A" Sewing Machines, with the result that we now have the **ONLY** family sewing machine with ball bearings in the head. This makes the Minnesota Model "A" Sewing Machine the lightest, smoothest running sewing machine manufactured today.

SPECIAL FEATURES Only Ball Bearing Head Manufactured. Independent, Positive Cam Take-up. Handy Tension Release. Flat Needle Bar. Highest Arm Made. Lightest Running. Ball Bearing Stand. Double Ball Bearing Steel Pitman.

BY THE USE OF THE BEST MATERIAL that money can buy, by employing only the most skilled mechanics, by using only the highest type of sewing machine making machinery, by endeavoring to furnish in our Minnesota Model "A" Sewing Machine a machine that embodies all the good qualities of every high grade sewing machine made with the defects of none; by considering, first, strength and durability; second, all kinds of plain and fancy sewing; reducing the friction to make it the easiest running sewing machine made and nearest noiseless; by design of head, by nickel trimming and rich color ornamentation, making it by far the handsomest sewing machine on the market, we do not hesitate to say, and without fear of contradiction, when you see and try this machine you will agree with us that it is in every way the **HIGHEST GRADE SEWING MACHINE MADE IN THE WORLD.**

Since we are not on the ground we would especially request, before placing an order with your agent at home at a high price, either on time, installment or exchange plan, that you first order one of our **MINNESOTA MODEL "A" SEWING MACHINES ON OUR THREE MONTHS' FREE TRIAL PLAN,** fully explained on page 48, let it come to your nearest railroad station, take it to your home, set it up, place it side by side with any machine offered by any agent in your section, and after placing it side by side, in fairness to ourselves, we would only ask that you do not allow the agent of the other machine to be the judge, nor would we ask the right to judge his machine, but use both machines yourself, put both sewing machines to the same test, and then call in a disinterested party (best, if possible, to get a good mechanic to be the judge), and if such disinterested judge pronounces our machine in every way the better machine, and if the test to which you put the two machines in way of all kinds of plain and fancy sewing, convinces you that ours is the better machine, then keep our machine, if you like; otherwise, return it to us at our expense, and we will immediately refund your money, together with any freight charges paid by you.

NEW FEATURES EMBODIED IN THE MINNESOTA MODEL "A" SEWING MACHINES.

BALL BEARING SHUTTLE LEVER (see illustration below) which makes our Minnesota Model "A" the lightest running sewing machine on the market. The adjustment is perfect and positively will not get out of order. The cups and cones used in this construction are turned out of the best tool steel, they are ground out until the surface is as smooth as glass after which all are case hardened in oil, making them impervious to wear.

The arrangement of the two sets of ball bearings on the shuttle lever does away with practically all the friction at this important point. Instead of friction on a 2-inch axle surface of the lever we have, by the application of the ball bearings, reduced the contact surface to about one-sixteenth of an inch, the result being a machine that runs lighter, makes less noise and requires less than one-half the power to operate than any other sewing machine on the market.

NEW STYLE STITCH REGULATOR, see description under stitch regulator.

NEW BALL BEARING METAL PITMAN fully described on page 67.

OUR MINNESOTA MODEL "A" SEWING MACHINE has an extra high arm and unusually large and strong operating parts, making it especially desirable, not only for household and domestic work, but also for the use of dressmakers, tailors and all others who require sewing machines of the highest grade, capable of doing the highest range of work from extremely heavy to extremely light, both fancy and simple sewing, and which will also stand the wear and tear of constant usage. The operation of our Minnesota Model "A" head on any weight or thickness of material and with all grades of cotton and silk thread is perfect, rapid and easy. On this machine the thread will not break, even though the machine is turned in the wrong direction. Everyone who has used a sewing machine and experienced the annoyance of breaking the thread when accidentally turning the wheel the wrong way will appreciate this valuable feature.

DESIGN OF HEAD. This head is made and shaped with a view to the most perfect operation of the various parts, and yet not neglecting those perfect lines that make it the handsomest, most roomy and most shapely high arm sewing machine head possible to construct.

NICKEL PLATING. All of the bright parts of this head are heavily nickeled over copper plate, then highly polished. This insures a nickel finish that will not crack, peel, rust or wear off. This applies to the working parts underneath the bed of the machine as well as to those parts that are exposed to view. The highly polished nickel plated parts on the outside of the head, in contrast with the rich, black enamel finish, add greatly to the general handsome appearance of the machine.

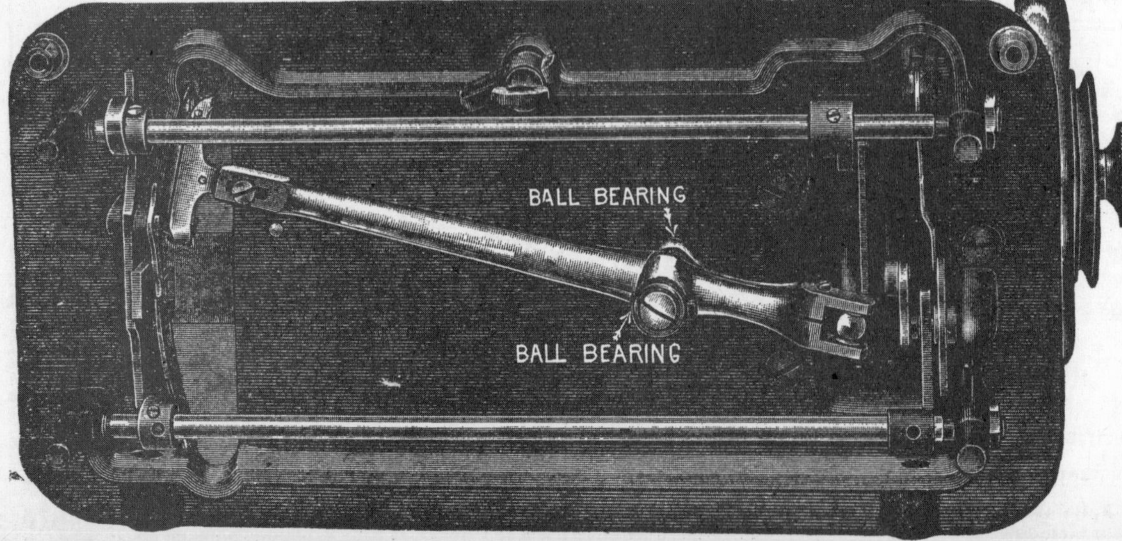

COLOR ORNAMENTATION The Model "A" head is elaborately ornamented in a special design, a combination of gold, silver, blue and orange colors, which, in contrast with the black enameling and the elaborate nickel trimmings and graceful outlines, makes it the handsomest sewing machine head possible to produce.

THE ENAMELING. All the parts that are not nickel plated are finished in black enamel. The highest grade of enamel is used, three coats being applied, each coat being separately baked on, at a high temperature, rubbed down to a smooth surface by hand and finally given a coat of special varnish, baked on at a high degree of heat, making the surface extremely hard and giving the machine a rich, heavy, lasting, fast black luster. Before the machine is enameled it is treated to one coat of special anti-rust preparation which prevents the enamel from cracking, checking or peeling, which so often occurs with other makes of machines.

LOCKSTITCH. This machine makes a perfect lockstitch, which is the popular stitch made on all high grade sewing machines.

SELF THREADING. The machine is self threading at every point except the eye of the needle, which is the only opening through which the end of the thread must be passed.

THE OPERATING PARTS. Our Minnesota Model "A" embodies all of the very latest, up to date improvements in mechanical construction. Many machines, even some of the well known makes, and practically all of the stencil machines handled by other mail order houses, retain the old time complicated construction, using many rods and bars to connect the operating parts with the main shaft, also employing springs, cushions, pads, cogs and other unnecessary devices to partly control the movements of the needle, feed and take-up. When new from the factory such machines work satisfactorily, but there is no positive assurance that the mechanism will remain in order without frequent repair. The constant aim of the best known sewing machine manufacturers throughout the world is to simplify this principle of construction in every machine by decreasing, as far as possible, the number of working parts and making each part independent of the others and thereby positive in its action. Our Minnesota Model "A" is built on the eccentric system, and all clumsy, hard working, sticky cog wheels are done away with. Less working parts are used in its make up than in any other shuttle machine, and its transmitting power construction is exceedingly simple. All running parts, even to the bobbin winder, are supplied with operating power direct from the main shaft and act absolutely independent of one another. The eccentric at the right end of the main shaft operates both the feed and shuttle, while the shaft head at the left end of the arm drives the needle bar and take-up simultaneously. By the use of this eccentric action, much less power is required to run the machine, and insures a light running, easy operating movement, harmonious action and unfailing certainty of absolute evenness in the action of the different parts, and makes it impossible for one part to be slower or quicker in movement than another. It runs nearly noiseless and smooth and will never wear loose or shaky.

BEARINGS. The bearings of this machine are of the highest mechanical type. They are either roller or ball joint bearing, according to requirement. They are automatic in their workings, have special take-up devices, doing away with all unnecessary friction, insuring an easy running and nearly noiseless machine.

ADJUSTMENT. All bearings and working parts of this machine which require adjustment are made of the finest tool steel that can be obtained, and after being thoroughly hardened by the latest and most improved process, are accurately ground to a perfect fit and so constructed that any lost motion, due to the slightest wear that may result after many years of use, can be easily and quickly taken up. This renders it practically indestructible and one of the most durable machines ever produced.

EASY TO OIL. By means of convenient oil holes and a movable metal plate on the back of the head, all bearings are easily gotten at to oil. This is a most important feature, as thorough lubrication prevents friction and wear.

RUNNING SPEED. Every machine, before being shipped from the factory, is put to the severest possible test, being set up and attached to a power pulley and run at a speed five times greater than it is possible to run any machine by foot power, and by this severe test we first learn that every machine is perfectly true in every particular and capable of the highest possible speed.

THE SHUTTLE. The shuttle is the most perfect, self threading, cylindrical shuttle ever produced. It is made of finest steel, hardened and ground. It is absolutely self threading, being open at one end for inserting the bobbin, after which the thread is instantly drawn into place by two motions of the hand. There are no holes to thread through and the shuttle can be threaded with the eyes shut. It has a perfect tension which is practically automatic and does not require regulating for any ordinary range of work. The bobbin carries a large amount of thread. The illustration shows shuttle being held between the thumb and forefinger while threading.

THE SHUTTLE CARRIER, the body in which the shuttle rests, is fitted with a spring lining which holds the shuttle firmly in place and prevents it from rattling while the machine is in operation. The carrier is adjustable so that when the shuttle shows signs of wear, after many years of use, the carrier can be moved closer to the shuttle race, thus enabling the operator to use the same shuttle for many years with the same satisfaction as when new.

THE TWO SHUTTLE SLIDES are made of steel, beveled, nickel plated and highly polished and enable the operator to get at the shuttle from the front or back.

THE SCALE, indicating the proper needles to be used with the different sizes of thread, is stamped on the forward shuttle slide.

DOUBLE FEED. The feed in this machine is made of the best quality of steel, properly tempered and equipped with four sets of teeth, two sets on each side of the needle hole. It is so constructed that when in motion the goods must be carried forward with absolute accuracy.

POSITIVE FOUR-MOTION FEED. The feed is operated with four movements. The feed comes up, takes a firm hold on the goods, carries the goods forward the length of the stitch, then it falls, releasing the goods and comes back again toward the operator, ready for the next stitch. These four movements are provided entirely by the main shaft, insuring positive action on either heavy or light goods.

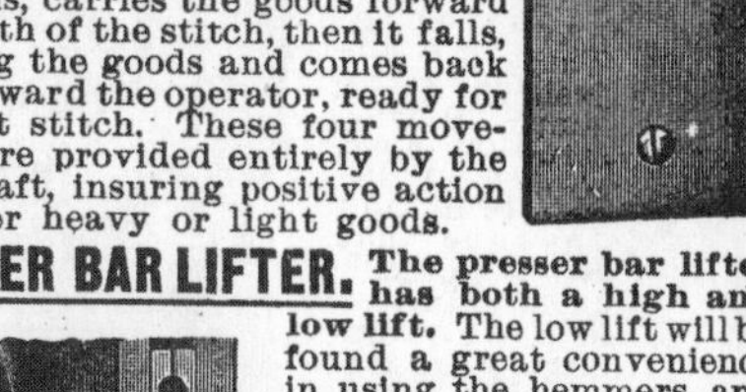

PRESSER BAR LIFTER. The presser bar lifter has both a high and low lift. The low lift will be found a great convenience in using the hemmers and other attachments, it being much easier to start the goods into the attachment properly than when the foot is raised as high from the plate as on other machines.

PRESSER FOOT. This presser foot has a large surface and the forward part, nearest the operator, is curved upward so that the feed will not catch in the seams of fleecy materials and insures for the operator thorough control at all times.

INDEPENDENT TAKE UP. The take-up in this machine is driven by a rotary cam on the end of the main shaft, making it positive in its action, insuring a perfect stitch and with no springs to get out of order or break. The positive action of this take-up makes it unnecessary to alter the tensions when the length of stitch or weight of material are changed.

DISC TENSION. The upper tension of this machine is of the modern disc type, and is practically automatic on all classes of work. The tension and liberator are located on the side of the cam house toward the operator. This location of the tension is not only far more convenient, but brings the point at which the tension is applied to the thread much nearer to the eye of the needle, thus reducing the amount of thread under tension and doing away, in a large measure, with the stretch in the thread, which, on old style machines, frequently caused bad stitching or skipping of stitches.

TENSION RELEASE. This machine is provided with a tension release, which makes it possible to remove the work from the machine by a mere touch of a finger, so that the work can be drawn from underneath the presser foot with ease.

THE STITCH REGULATOR is fastened to the bed plate just in front of the arm in plain sight and within easy reach of the operator. The length of the stitch can be adjusted instantly by loosening the thumb nut and moving the point to the desired figure on the scale stamped on the stitch regulator plate.

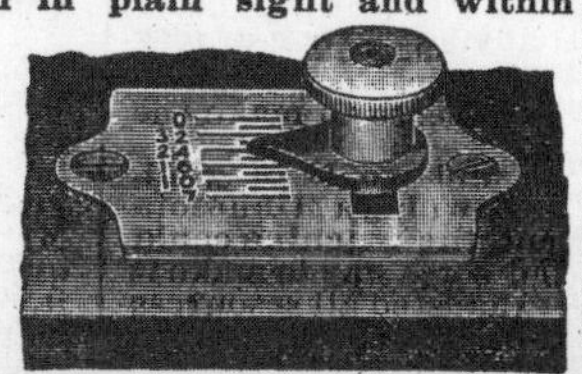

FLAT NEEDLE BAR. While far more expensive to manufacture, we use in this head a flat needle bar, made of finest steel, hardened, milled to exact size, making its bearings absolutely perfect, thus securing noiseless movement without friction. With this construction, lost motion and rattling of the needle bar is an impossibility, even after years of usage. The illustration shows the flat needle bar of our Model "A" machine, fitted with needle bar cam which connects the bar directly with the main shaft, from which it derives its operating power.

SELF-SETTING NEEDLE. The needles for this machine are the very best grade of flat shank needle it is possible to procure. Every needle is inspected and tested as to size, temper and position of eye. The needle bar is provided with a groove in which the needle shank is inserted as far as it will go, so that the operation of setting the needle is absolutely positive. It is not necessary to guess at the proper height or position of the needle.

NEEDLE CLAMP. A small clamp holds the needle firmly in place and permits the needle to be removed in an instant when required, even though it should break accidentally in the bar where it cannot be reached with the fingers. The needles can be had from us at any time at factory cost, or they can be had from any sewing machine dealer in your town.

THREAD CUTTER. This machine is supplied with a steel thread cutter, conveniently attached to the presser bar, by the aid of which the thead can be easily cut, obviating the use of scissors and the danger of breaking or cutting the thread too short.

AUTOMATIC BOBBIN WINDER. The bobbin winder on this machine is nickel plated throughout and is the most perfect bobbin winder ever produced. It is so simple that a child can operate it and the thread is wound on the bobbin automatically and so evenly and smoothly as to make the bobbin work perfectly in the shuttle, producing an even tension and greatly improving the perfection of the stitch. This also prevents the breaking of the lower thread, which is liable to occur with an unevenly wound bobbin.

THE BOBBIN WINDER is always in position and ready to operate. It is operated by means of the belt, which is placed in contact with the small pulley wheel of the bobbin winder.

THE HAND WHEEL. The hand wheel is of the very latest pattern, with handsome nickel plated and polished rim, and is so constructed that it can be easily released and made to run free in either direction for the purpose of winding the bobbin without the necessity of removing the work from the machine and without causing the working parts to operate.

LOCK NUT. The lock nut, which is located at the end of the main shaft and used to release and tighten the hand wheel, is turned out of one piece of case hardened steel, has milled edge and is heavily nickel plated and polished. The lock nut is plainly marked with arrows, showing which way it must be turned to loosen or tighten the hand wheel.

PRESSER BAR. The presser bar is made of the best quality tool steel, properly tempered and accurately fitted.

PRESSER BAR REGULATOR. A presser bar nut, made of the best grade of steel, nickel plated and polished, is provided at the top of the presser bar to regulate the pressure of the foot, more or less, as required for different weights of material.

ATTACHMENTS FOR OUR MINNESOTA MODEL "A" MACHINES

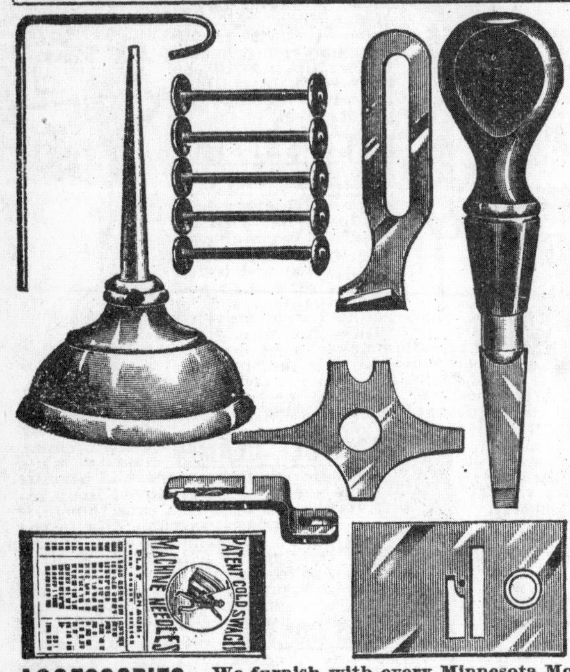

THE HIGHEST RECOMMENDATION that can be given to a set of attachments is that it is made by the Greist Manufacturing Company, the makers of the most complete, improved and expensive attachments on the market, whose attachments are used by all makers of well known standard machines, such as the Davis, Domestic, Singer, etc. Our attachments are made by this concern expressly for our machines and are made of the very best tempered steel, heavily nickel plated, and will last twice as long and do double the variety of work possible with cheaper attachments. They are adjustable, very simple in construction and so easy to understand and operate that any person can quickly learn to produce a large variety of the most beautiful work. Our instruction book, furnished free with the machine, explains fully the operation of each attachment included in the set.

ACCESSORIES. We furnish with every Minnesota Model "A" machine a complete set of accessories, such as are usually furnished with every high grade machine, consisting of one quilter, five bobbins (and one in the machine), one cloth guide, a large screwdriver, one oil can filled with oil, one combination screwdriver and wrench, one extra needle plate, one foot hemmer, one package of needles and one instruction book. We carry in stock a full supply of needles, bobbins, shuttles, attachments, etc., which are used in the operation of our machines. We can, therefore, fill orders for repairs promptly. An order for repairs for the Minnesota Model "A" machine placed with us fifteen or twenty years from date would be filled as promptly as a repair order sent today. See page 70 for prices on sewing machine supplies.

THE SET OF ATTACHMENTS, which we furnish for 75 cents, consists of one tucker, one ruffler, one shirring plate, one short foot, one under braider, one binder and one set of four hemmers of different widths up to ⅝ of an inch. These attachments are the same style as are furnished by the largest sewing machine dealers with their highest priced machines and are guaranteed to give perfect satisfaction. The attachments are handsomely nickel plated and highly polished.

ATTACHMENTS. It has been customary in the past for all dealers t furnish a set of attachments with every machine, whether the purchaser required them or not. We offer our machine with or without attachments. The prices quoted in the catalogue for the machines are all calculated without attachments, and at 75 cents we furnish a full set of the latest patent foot attachments, as shown in the illustration above, packed in a handsome velvet lined metal box arranged with a place for each particular attachment. **The attachments will be furnished at 75 cents per set.** If by mail, postage extra, 17 cents.

IF YOU, THE READER OF THIS CATALOGUE, intend to use our machines for plain sewing only, you naturally do not wish to buy attachments and will appreciate our departure from the old established custom of including a s of attachments with every machine at the customer's expense. If require attachments you will nevertheless appreciate that it is unfair a unjust to force those that do not need them to receive and pay for them If you purchase a machine without attachments and later wish to procu attachments, we can always supply you with the proper set.

SOME FIRMS ATTEMPT TO MISLEAD INTENDING PURCHASERS by stating that they furnish their attachments "free of charge." A careful comparison of prices, with a like comparison of quality, a comparison of the machines we have sold in your locality with machines furnished elsewhere, will convince anyone that not only do other firms make a charge for attachments (indirectly, because included in the price of their machines), but also ask from $5.00 to $15.00 more than the combined price of our machines and attachments

CAN THE MINNESOTA MODEL "A" SEWING MACHINE, WITH ANY OUTLAY OF MONEY, BE IMPROVED IN ANY WAY?

WE HAVE SPENT THOUSANDS OF DOLLARS and are still spending money to try to find out how to make it better. Today it is better than the best of all other makes, yet we are all the time putting it to newer and harder tests, getting professional opinions from the most skilled mechanics in the world, and, with a view to still further improving the Minnesota Model "A" Sewing Machine (if indeed, it is possible to be improved), we invite our customers to criticise. If you own a Minnesota Model "A" Sewing Machine, and you can give us any idea where it could be improved, if there is one point where you do not consider it better than any other sewing machine made in the world, we would feel very grateful for your criticism.

IF THE MINNESOTA MODEL "A" SEWING MACHINE is not the best sewing machine in the world, it is not for lack of the best material that money can buy, the most skilled mechanics that can be employed, the highest type of sewing machine machinery that can be built. Our one effort has been to make the Minnesota Model "A" Sewing Machine positively the highest grade sewing machine made in the world. To do this, we have employed expert mechanics to devote their time to studying out improvements. They have not been limited as to the cost of making improvements. On the contrary, they have been supplied with all the different high grade sewing machines made, and told to make the Minnesota Model "A" Sewing Machine so nearly perfect as to include every up to date, high grade feature of every other high grade sewing machine, with the defects of none, and with a view to more perfect sewing, ease of running and stability, to spare neither time nor expense to make any improvement that would tend to better the machine. This work of improving the Minnesota Model "A" has gone on until the most expert mechanics pronounce the machine mechanically perfect. They say there is no further room for improvement, that no outlay of money would make it sew better, run easier and make less noise or wear longer. Notwithstanding this opinion, as expressed by skilled mechanics, we are still searching for some way to make the machine better, if it is possible to better it. If any suggestion should come to us from any mechanic or from a customer, pointing out where this machine did not operate perfectly, where it did not do every part of its duty as well or better than any other sewing machine, any suggestion of any kind should come from anyone that would point the way for in any way improving this machine, we would spare neither time nor expense to make the improvement.

WHILE WE INVITE CRITICISM from everyone, and would be glad, indeed, if anyone owning a Minnesota Sewing Machine would tell us where, in their judgment, the machine could be improved, while we shall never cease trying to find some way to make it even better than it is, so far as we know today, we have exhausted all resources for bettering a family sewing machine, and we therefore have in the Minnesota Model "A" Sewing Machine the highest grade machine made in the world.

IF YOU OWN OR ARE USING A MINNESOTA MODEL "A" SEWING MACHINE, of course, you can judge for yourself. We can conclude from the thousands of testimonials we are receiving from all parts of the world, customers who have purchased these machines and tested their sewing qualities, ease of running and durability; and compared them with other makes sold at from $40.00 to $60.00, that the one universal opinion is that the Minnesota Model "A" Sewing Machine is the highest grade sewing machine made in the world, but if you have not as yet used or seen the Minnesota Model "A" Sewing Machine, and you are thinking of buying a sewing machine, we would like to give you the opportunity of judging for yourself.

JUST READ WHAT MR. DAYTON SAYS ABOUT THE MINNESOT SEWING MACHINE.

Sears, Roebuck & Co., Chicago, Ill. Fair Haven, Conn.

Gentlemen:—It is now six months since I received the sewing machine (Minnesota) and we desire to say that it is perfect in every respect. We have had Singers and Wheeler & Wilsons in our family for many years and we thought we would try another Singer. The price was, if satisfactory to us, to be $45.00. Mrs. Dayton gave it a fair trial for one month and liked it very much. I told her we were handling a great many of your machines, and asked her if she would give the Minnesota a trial, and observing your guarantee that we would be nothing out if not satisfactory, I accordingly sent for the Minnesota. She gave it a very thorough trial and pronounced it superior in every way to any machine she ever used. Here are a few of its good qualities 1st. The difference between the price of a five-drawer Singer and a seven drawer Minnesota; Singer at $45.00, the Minnesota at $15.70. 2d. The Minnesota is so easy to run. 3d. One can scarcely hear it across the room. 4th. Its beauty of style and finish. 5th. Its simplicity. We are yet looking for one fault. We pronounce it perfect in every respect, and I shall recommend it to all who want a good machine at about half the cost of others that are not any way its equal. Yours truly, J. J. DAYTON, Agent, Adams Express Co.

This Lady has Used Both the Singer and the White Machines and now has a Minnesota.

Sears, Roebuck & Co., Chicago, Ill. Halsey, Nebraska.

Gentlemen:—On March 24th I bought a Minnesota Sewing Machine of you. since that time I have used it on various kinds of work, and have found that it does perfect work, and I have given it a thorough trial. I have used the Singer and White machines, both of which cost considerably more than the Minnesota and do no better work. I think, for easy running and working qualities and workmanship, the Minnesota has but few equals, and none excel it, especially when it comes to price. I am confident that I saved $20.00 on the Minnesota above other machines that will do anything like the same work.

MRS. R. L. SPEESE.

OUR HIGHEST GRADE BALL BEARING `PECIAL DROP LEAF AND BOX COVER MINNESOTA MODEL "A" $15.45

On this page we show illustration of our MINNESOTA MODEL "A" MACHINE in the Upright Style with Seven Drawers. This is the same Machine as the Drop Head No. 26C257, but the head is stationary and cannot be lowered as in the Drop Head. We can also furnish the style illustrated on this page with 5 Drawers for $15.00 and with 3 Drawers for $14.65.

DESCRIPTION OF THE MINNESOTA MODEL "A" WOODWORK

In point of design, workmanship, finish and general appearance, the MINNESOTA MODEL "A" Machine is a beautiful piece of furniture and an ornament to any home. It should be compared only with machines that are sold generally by agents and dealers at $35.00 and $65.00. It is made at the factory which supplies the woodwork for most of the high grade machines sold exclusively through agents.

For description of Model "A" Head, see pages 62 and 63.
For description of Model "A" Stand, see page 66.
For description of Model "A" Attachments, see page 64.
For Our Liberal Terms Offer, see page 48.
For Our Three Months' Free Trial Offer, see page 48.
For Our Twenty Years' Guarantee, see page 48.
For Freight Rates, see column first class rates, pages 7 to 11.

MATERIAL. All Minnesota Model "A" Cabinets are made of carefully selected, quarter sawed, golden oak lumber, thoroughly air seasoned and kiln dried to prevent possible warping, checking or cracking, and by ordering a Model "A" -wing machine you get the most substantial, strongest and best ished set of woodwork, no matter what style of cabinet you der, that can be procured.

DESIGN. The cabinets used in all our Model "A" upright and drop head styles are made after our own patterns in the latest full swell front style with the rounded drawers, covers and tables to match.

THE TABLE. The tables of the woodwork used on our Model "A" machines are all made of built up stock; that is, there are three layers of wood, the grain of each layer unning crosswise or diagonally the other, while the upper layer highly figured, quarter sawed oak. Only the highest and most expensive grades of furniture are made in this way.

THE DRAWERS. The drawers are all made to correspond, in design, with the table. They are veneered, being made of three-ply built up ock in latest, full swell ont style, nicely decorated th raised hand carvings nd fitted with large cast rass handles. They are arge and roomy, and will easily hold the attachments, accessories and all the other supplies necessary for all kinds of sewing. The center drawer is made with a triple well front, ornamented with hand carvings to correspond with the side drawers. It is partitioned off on the inside o hold bobbins, needles and other parts which are being nstantly used by the operator. A strong lock is carey fitted on each drawer so at all can be securely ked. The key furnished h each machine fits the ocks on all the drawers.

DRAWER CASES. The drawers are tted with specially designed drawer cases, constructed so hat when the drawers are closed they have the appearance being made with unded sides.

THE FINISH. The very est grades of woodwork can be easily poiled by a poor finish; therefore, extra care is taken in the inish which is put on of our Model "A" odwork. It is ated practically n the same manner s high grade furniture, being thoroughly sandpapered while the wood is still n the white. It is impossible to procure a good polish on a piece of wood if the urface is not as smooth as it can possibly be made. All of the woodwork which used on our Model "A" machines is not only sandpapered while in the white, so after the filler and shellac are applied, so that when the varnishes are and rubbed, it gives the outer surface the highly polished finish is found only on the best grade of furniture. The drawer cases are ubbed and finished in oil, while the tops are all highly polished. Our "A" woodwork is finished in the popular dark golden oak, the color in ll high grade furniture is now being finished.

Ball Bearing Head.
Ball Bearing Stand.
Ball Bearing Steel Pitman.

PRICE $15.45
On board cars at Dayton :: Ohio.
ATTACHMENTS 75c EXTRA.

Mrs. Tanner Says the Minnesota Sewing Machine is Far Ahead of the Singer, and She Saves $40.00 on Her Purchase.

Beaver, Utah.
Sears, Roebuck & Co., Chicago, Ill.
Gentlemen:—To say that I am highly pleased with the Minnesota Sewing Machine I received from you last year does not half tell my feelings. It is so far ahead of the Singer which I have used several years past, that I feel that this truly is an age of progression.
It runs so lightly and with so little noise, the attachments are so quickly and easily adjusted, the stitch is neat and the style, workmanship and finish so excellent that too much cannot be said in its praise. I saved about $40.00, or nearly double what the machine cost. Our local agent charges $60.00 and $65.00, and yours is superior, as you give a twenty-year guarantee and they only ten years.
Yours very truly,
MRS. JOS. N. TANNER

Order by Number. No. 26C252

THE GENERAL CONSTRUCTION OF THE DROP HEAD WOODWORK described above. The lid or top of the drop head cabinet is finished and hand rubbed to a mirror like piano polish. Read complete description above, plaining how this woodwork is finished and polished. This cabinet offers a etty contrast to the brilliant black enamel of the ribbon stand and the bright lors and nickel parts of the head.

THE COVER. The cover which is used in the Model "A" upright cover machines, as illustrated above, is a full swell rounded cover, made from three-ply built up veneered stock, very elaborately carved and decorated, highly polished, nicely finished, and positively the handsomest cover made.

DROP HEAD WOODWORK. The most popular style sewing machine is the five or seven drawer drop head. In view of its great popularity, we have taken the most particular pains to furnish the neatest and most pleasing designs and the best grade of sewing machine furniture ever offered.

THE FIVE OR SEVEN DRAWER DROP HEAD CABINET STYLES are the most popular, because when closed and not in use the machine takes up much less space than any other style, and because of its excellent finish it is frequently used as a stand, writing desk or table.

No. 26C250	Minnesota Model "A" Three-Drawer, Box Cover. Price	$14.65
No. 26C251	Minnesota Model "A" Five-Drawer, Box Cover. Price	15.00
No. 26C252	Minnesota Model "A" Seven-Drawer, Box Cover. Price	15.45

The above prices do not include attachments, a complete set of which we furnish at 75 cents additional.
For complete description of Model "A" Attachments, see page 64.

OUR SEVEN-DRAWER, DROP HEAD, BALL BEARING MINNESOTA MODEL "A" $15.70

MINNESOTA Model "A" with us in sewing machines stands for the highest of high grade in everything; the best that money can buy. The words Minnesota Model "A" in a sewing machine with us, means a lighter running, nearer noiseless, more durable, handsomer and better finished sewing machine head than is made by any other maker, the best that money can buy. See illustrations and full descriptions of the Minnesota Model "A" head and all its parts on pages 62 and 63 in this book.

MINNESOTA Model "A" in sewing machines with us means for the woodwork a higher grade, better finished and handsomer cabinet than is furnished with any other sewing machine made.

This illustration shows our Minnesota Model "A" Machine in seven-drawer, drop head style, three drawers on each side and push drawer. We will furnish the same machine in the drop head style, with five drawers, for $15.20.

DESCRIPTION OF MINNESOTA MODEL "A" BALL BEARING STAND.

OUR MODEL "A" STANDS are made from the very best Birmingham, Alabama, light gray iron. These stands are moulded by automatic machines, making every piece perfectly true, smooth and of unusual strength, so that when the different parts are put together they fit perfectly. All Model "A" stand parts are filed and ground until perfectly smooth, after which they are enameled by hand process. Particular pains are taken in enameling these stands and in adjusting the different parts. This special care and attention is plainly evident when our Model "A" machines are compared side by side with machines, the selling price of which is two to three times as much as that for which you can buy the Model "A."

DESIGN. The Model "A" Stand is our own special design, made with a view of procuring a neat, graceful open effect and at the same time furnish a most rigid and solid stand. The side frames or legs are made in the handsome, open and wide ribbon pattern style. The style adopted in the side frames, besides making the stand perfectly rigid, also makes it easier to keep the stand clean and free from dust, because all parts can be reached from outside the frame.

THE BRACES. The Side Frames or Legs of the Stand are joined together by a four-arm brace, bolted at the top and bottom, making the stand absolutely rigid. This is very essential, as it lessens the vibration and so causes our machines to make less noise and last longer than those machines which are built on weak and wabbly stands.

DRESS GUARD. The Dress Guard to this Stand is extra large, protecting the balance wheel and belt from any possible contact with the dress, at the same time substantially bracing the side frame.

TREADLE. The Treadle is of the open work style, with full ends, pivot bearing accurately trued, adjustable take up between the balance wheel and the treadle, putting the entire machine under easy control of the operator.

OIL GUARD. The Oil Guard, immediately under the Treadle, extends from side frame to side frame, is securely bolted, strengthens the frame and prevents the oil from dropping on the floor or carpet.

For full description of Model "A" head, see pages 62, 63.
For full description of Model "A" woodwork, see page 65.
For full description of Model "A" attachments, see page 64.
For our liberal terms offer, see page 48.
For our three months' free trial offer, see page 48.
For our twenty years' guarantee, see page 48.
For freight rates, see column 1st class rate, pages 7 to 11.

CASTERS. We use the highest grade Sewing Machine Casters made. They are of a large size, making it easy to move the machine from place to place, are carefully fitted and never break.

ATTACHMENTS, 75c EXTRA

Ball Bearing Steel Pitman.

ORDER BY NUMBER.
No. 26C257 Price..............$15.70
On Board Cars, Dayton, Ohio.

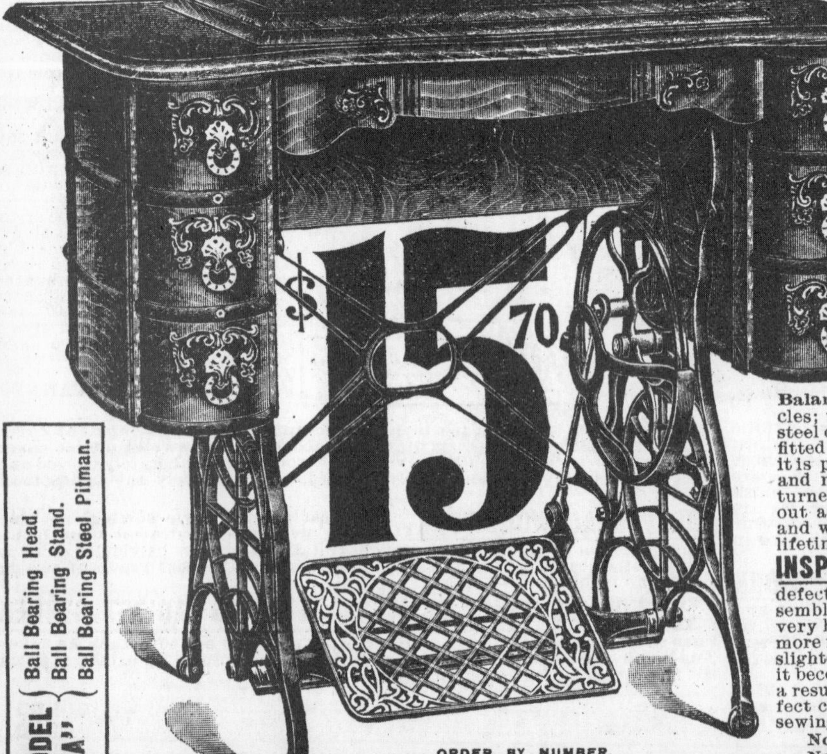

ORDER BY NUMBER.
No. 26C257 Price..............$15.70
On Board Cars, Dayton, Ohio.

BALL BEARING BALANCE WHEEL. All our Model "A" Machines are equipped with Ball Bearing Hangers. The hanger is the large balance wheel and shaft fastened to the right stand leg, as shown in the illustration. As this wheel supplies the operating power to the head, the bearings on which the wheel revolves are naturally subjected to considerable strain, but, by the introduction of the ball bearings, all friction is removed and the wheel revolves with the same freedom and rapidity as the ball bearing crank hanger of the bicycle. The application of the ball bearing to the balance wheel is one of the greatest improvements and the greatest aid to the light running qualities of the machine, and we have demonstrated by actual experiments and tests that our ball bearing hanger is at least 20 per cent lighter running than any ball bearing device or arrangement used on any other sewing machine made. By the aid of ball bearings a machine is made not only lighter running, but exceedingly easy of operation and very rapid in action.

The arrangement of the Ball Bearing of the Balance Wheel is the same as that used on all high grade bicycles; the axle on which the wheel revolves passes through two steel cups, each of which contains 15 solid steel balls, which are fitted into the balance wheels and, by means of adjustable cones, it is possible at all times to have the balance wheel run lightly and noiselessly. The cups and cones used on our stands are turned out of a solid bar of steel, after which they are ground out and case hardened in oil, making them impervious to wear, and with proper oiling from time to time will make them last a lifetime.

INSPECTION. All parts are accurately trued, tested for strength. [illegible] a casting is allowed to be used that has a sand hole, defect or that isn't true to gauge. After the stand has been properly assembled, the balance wheel and treadle are operated by steam power at very high rate of speed, whereby the balance wheel makes a great many more revolutions than any operator could possibly make. If there is the slightest flaw in the iron, or in the construction or adjustment of the stand, it becomes evident through this test and the stand is then rejected, and, as a result, for strength, beauty, design, finish, for easy running and for perfect control of the machine by the operator, we furnish a higher grade sewing machine stand than is furnished by any other maker.

No. 26C256 Model "A" Five-Drawer Drop Head. Price...$15.20
No. 26C257 Model "A" Seven-Drawer Drop Head. Price.. 15.70

The above prices do not include attachments. We furnish a complete set, as fully described on page 64, at 75 cents additional.

OUR HIGH GRADE, AUTOMATIC LIFT AND DROP HEAD, BALL BEARING MINNESOTA MODEL "A" SEWING MACHINE.

WHEN THE MACHINE is not in use and is closed, the head is protected from dust and possible injury by the lid on top and a wooden box, called the drum, which entirely encloses the head on the under side.

We guarantee the automatic lift device with which this machine is fitted to be far superior in every respect, stronger in material and construction and easier of operation than anything similar on the market.

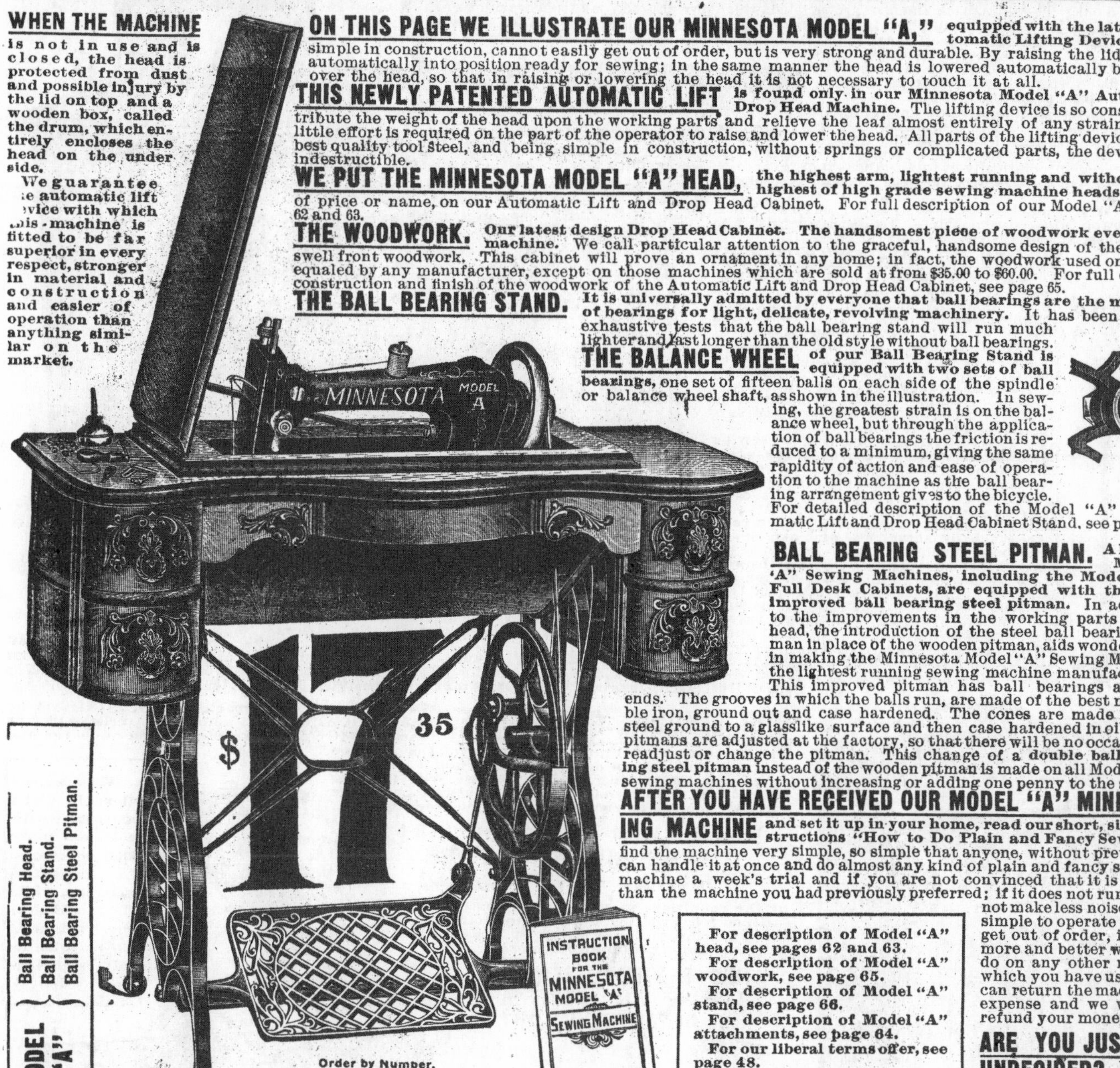

Order by Number.
No. 26C260 Price..........$17.35
On board cars at Dayton, Ohio.

ON THIS PAGE WE ILLUSTRATE OUR MINNESOTA MODEL "A," equipped with the latest improved Automatic Lifting Device. This device is simple in construction, cannot easily get out of order, but is very strong and durable. By raising the lid the head is lifted automatically into position ready for sewing; in the same manner the head is lowered automatically by folding the leaf over the head, so that in raising or lowering the head it is not necessary to touch it at all.

THIS NEWLY PATENTED AUTOMATIC LIFT is found only in our Minnesota Model "A" Automatic Lift and Drop Head Machine. The lifting device is so constructed as to distribute the weight of the head upon the working parts and relieve the leaf almost entirely of any strain. As a result but little effort is required on the part of the operator to raise and lower the head. All parts of the lifting device are made of the best quality tool steel, and being simple in construction, without springs or complicated parts, the device is practically indestructible.

WE PUT THE MINNESOTA MODEL "A" HEAD, the highest arm, lightest running and without question the highest of high grade sewing machine heads made, regardless of price or name, on our Automatic Lift and Drop Head Cabinet. For full description of our Model "A" head, see pages 62 and 63.

THE WOODWORK. Our latest design Drop Head Cabinet. The handsomest piece of woodwork ever put on a sewing machine. We call particular attention to the graceful, handsome design of the cabinet, the new swell front woodwork. This cabinet will prove an ornament in any home; in fact, the woodwork used on this model is not equaled by any manufacturer, except on those machines which are sold at from $35.00 to $60.00. For full description of the construction and finish of the woodwork of the Automatic Lift and Drop Head Cabinet, see page 65.

THE BALL BEARING STAND. It is universally admitted by everyone that ball bearings are the most perfect type of bearings for light, delicate, revolving machinery. It has been demonstrated by exhaustive tests that the ball bearing stand will run much lighter and last longer than the old style without ball bearings.

THE BALANCE WHEEL of our Ball Bearing Stand is equipped with two sets of ball bearings, one set of fifteen balls on each side of the spindle or balance wheel shaft, as shown in the illustration. In sewing, the greatest strain is on the balance wheel, but through the application of ball bearings the friction is reduced to a minimum, giving the same rapidity of action and ease of operation to the machine as the ball bearing arrangement gives to the bicycle. For detailed description of the Model "A" Automatic Lift and Drop Head Cabinet Stand, see page 69.

BALL BEARING STEEL PITMAN. All our Model "A" Sewing Machines, including the Model "A" Full Desk Cabinets, are equipped with the new improved ball bearing steel pitman. In addition to the improvements in the working parts of the head, the introduction of the steel ball bearing pitman in place of the wooden pitman, aids wonderfully in making the Minnesota Model "A" Sewing Machine the lightest running sewing machine manufactured. This improved pitman has ball bearings at both ends. The grooves in which the balls run, are made of the best malleable iron, ground out and case hardened. The cones are made of tool steel ground to a glasslike surface and then case hardened in oil. The pitmans are adjusted at the factory, so that there will be no occasion to readjust or change the pitman. This change of a double ball bearing steel pitman instead of the wooden pitman is made on all Model "A" sewing machines without increasing or adding one penny to the selling price.

AFTER YOU HAVE RECEIVED OUR MODEL "A" MINNESOTA SEWING MACHINE and set it up in your home, read our short, simple rules of instructions "How to Do Plain and Fancy Sewing." You will find the machine very simple, so simple that anyone, without previous experience, can handle it at once and do almost any kind of plain and fancy sewing. Give the machine a week's trial and if you are not convinced that it is a better machine than the machine you had previously preferred; if it does not run easier, if it does not make less noise, if it is not more simple to operate and less liable to get out of order, if you cannot do more and better work than you can do on any other make of machine which you have used or known, you can return the machine to us at our expense and we will immediately refund your money.

For description of Model "A" head, see pages 62 and 63.
For description of Model "A" woodwork, see page 65.
For description of Model "A" stand, see page 66.
For description of Model "A" attachments, see page 64.
For our liberal terms offer, see page 48.
For our three months' free trial offer, see page 48.
For our twenty years' guarantee, see page 48.
For freight rates, see column 1st class rates, pages 7 to 11.

ARE YOU JUST A LITTLE UNDECIDED? Do you question if the Minnesota Model "A" is really the very best sewing machine made in the world, and if it is, do you wonder how it is possible for us to furnish it for so little money?

Do you feel just a little uncertain as to the full length and breadth of our twenty-year guarantee? Are you just a little afraid you may have trouble in getting parts, repairs and supplies in the years to come?

Have you a preference for some particular make of sewing machine?

Have you thought when you were ready to buy a sewing machine you would get some certain make of machine, perhaps like one you have already used, like your mother's, or your sister's, or your friend's; possibly a Singer, New Home, Wheeler & Wilson, Domestic, Standard, White, or some other make of machine?

LET US CLEAR YOUR MIND. That the Minnesota Model "A" Sewing Machine is the very best machine made in the world, and that it is possible to sell it at such a very low price, you can prove for yourself without taking the slightest risk; for under our three months' free trial plan you can examine it, test it, compare it with other machines, take your time to decide, with your friends to help you decide, and if, after taking your full time, you are not satisfied that it is the best sewing machine made in the world, even though we do sell it for so little money, you may return it at our expense and we will immediately refund your money.

..r. Hillis Says He Hopes Others Needing Sewing Machines Will Buy A Minnesota and Not Make the Mistake of Buying Other Makes at Higher Prices. His Neighbors, After Seeing His Minnesota, Wish They Could Trade Their Machines for a Minnesota.

Sears, Roebuck & Co., Chicago, Ill. Moxahala, Ohio.

Gentlemen:—The sewing machine I bought of you last March is doing fine work. It works perfectly in every way. The attachments are simple and easy to learn to work. My wife, in less than half a day, could do perfect work with all attachments. Our neighbors who have other machines have come to see our machine sew. They all say the same when they leave, that they wish they could trade their machine for a Minnesota Automatic Lift, 7-drawer, drop head. ..ey won't believe we got such a machine for $17.85, and attachments 75 cents, freight 32 cents, making a total of $19.02. You are at liberty to refer anyone writing you for information from this part of the country, to me at any time. Hoping others needing a machine may buy a Minnesota, and not make a mistake by buying some other make, I remain,

Yours respectfully, W. G. HILLIS.

THE LENGTH AND BREADTH OF OUR TWENTY-YEAR GUARANTEE and your security and the certainty of your being able to get any parts, repairs or supplies in the years to come; our financial and commercial standing as evidenced by the letters from two of the largest banks in this city, shown on page 12—financial responsibility that will secure you for many thousand times the amount of your purchase—secures you absolutely in this transaction, both as to the conditions of our binding twenty-year guarantee and our promise and agreement to always keep in stock a full supply of repairs and parts which we can supply you in the years to come and at factory cost.

No. 26C260	Model "A" Five-Drawer, Drop Head, Automatic Lift	$17.35
No. 26C261	Model "A" Seven-Drawer, Drop Head, Automatic Lift	17.85

The above prices do not include attachments. We furnish a complete set, as fully described on page 64, at 75 cents additional.

OUR MINNESOTA MODEL "A" BALL BEARING MACHINE AT $17.95

WITH AUTOMATIC DROP DESK CABINET. A REGULAR $50.00 MACHINE.

A HANDSOME PIECE OF FURNITURE AS WELL AS A HIGH GRADE MACHINE.

DARK OAK ONLY.

AS MANY OF OUR CUSTOMERS have expressed a desire to purchase our Minnesota Model "A" Sewing Machine with a plainer and lighter weight cabinet than our No. 26C270, shown on page 69, we present the style shown in these illustrations, which we are confident will meet the approval of our friends who wish a tasty appearing, light weight, cabinet sewing machine. The cabinet is made of the same high grade carefully selected oak as our No. 26C270, the bottom and sides being of solid oak while the top or cover and door are made of beautifully figured quarter sawed oak. The sides, back and door are paneled, which prevents the oak from cracking or splitting.

THE DESIGN OF THE CABINET while plain, is very attractive, with heavily built, carved and ornamented mouldings. The cabinet is fitted with one large door, to which is fastened a wooden pocket for attachments, etc. Two additional drawers are placed in a drawer frame screwed to the bottom of the cabinet, which is fitted with rollers so that the machine can be easily moved from place to place.

THE CABINET is fitted with automatic device, simple in construction but very strong and durable, by which the head is raised automatically into position ready for sewing by throwing back the leaf. In the same manner the head is lowered automatically by folding the leaf or cover over the head, so that in raising or lowering the head it is not necessary to touch the head at all.

THE HEAD used in this machine is the same as is used on all of our A grade Minnesota machines. For complete description of mechanical construction, attachments, etc., see pages 62 to 64.

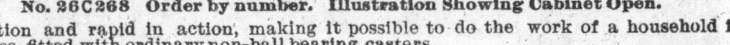

No. 26C268 Order by number. Illustration Showing Cabinet Open.

MODEL "A" { Ball Bearing Head, Ball Bearing Stand, Ball Bearing Steel Pitman.

WE FIND THE BEST ADVERTISEMENT we can possibly get is a well satisfied customer, and we have hundreds of these in every community, and among them are quite a number in every town who have bought and are now using our sewing machines, and if you will ask anyone in your neighborhood who is using one of our machines whether they have ever seen a sewing machine furnished by any other house that will compare with the machine we sold them, either in quality or price, on their answer we are sure we will receive your order.

ONE ADVANTAGE in ordering a sewing machine from us is that you can be sure of getting all kinds of sewing machine repairs and supplies in the years to come and always at the very lowest cost.

THIS MACHINE is equipped with our special ball bearing castings, which by actual use and experiment have been demonstrated to be twenty per cent lighter running than the ball bearing arrangement used in any other sewing machine. We can therefore recommend our Minnesota Model "A" cabinet sewing machine as very light running, exceedingly easy in operation and rapid in action, making it possible to do the work of a household in one-third less time than is required with machines fitted with ordinary non-ball bearing casters.

THIS TELLS JUST WHAT FREIGHT YOU WILL HAVE TO PAY. This sewing machine weighs, crated for shipment, 140 pounds. The railroad companies carry sewing machines at first class freight rates. On pages 7 to 11 you will find the first class freight rate for 100 pounds to a point nearest your town. The freight will be almost, if not exactly, the same to your town, so you can tell almost to a penny what the freight will amount to.

OUR BINDING GUARANTEE. We send with every machine OUR BINDING 20 YEARS' GUARANTEE. Should any piece or part be found defective we will replace it free of charge, and our liberal terms of shipment, allowing you the privilege of trying and examining the machine, and if not found satisfactory, returning it to us and we will pay the freight and refund your money, will at once convince you that you run no risk in sending your order to us.

WE SEND WITH EVERY MACHINE A THREE MONTHS' FREE TRIAL CERTIFICATE, by the conditions of which if you become dissatisfied with the machine at any time within three months, you may return it to us and we will immediately refund your money.

THIS BEAUTIFUL SEWING MACHINE WILL PROVE A REAL ORNAMENT IN ANY HOME. . . . .

. . The cabinet alone in this machine would cost you more than we charge for the entire machine, while the mechanical construction of the machine itself is perfection.

No. 26C268 Order by number. Illustration Showing Cabinet Closed.

NEEDLES, BOBBINS, SHUTTLES, ATTACHMENTS, and all other parts used in the construction and operation of this machine may be secured from us at any time. Our prices on parts are consistent with the low prices of our machines. We always carry a full supply of all repairs and supplies. See page 70 for prices.

THE EQUAL OF MACHINES SOLD BY OTHER DEALERS AND AGENTS AT $40.00 TO $50.00.

In ordering the machine use the following description:

No. 26C268 Minnesota Model "A" Machine, one door cabinet, automatic style (without attachments).... **$17.95**

This price does not include attachments. We can furnish a complete set, as fully described on page 64, for 75 cents additional.

The machine is delivered free on board the cars at our factory in Dayton, Ohio, from which point customer pays freight.

No. 26C268 Order by number. Illustration Showing Cabinet Half Open.

OUR HIGH GRADE BALL BEARING... MINNESOTA MODEL "A"

WITH AUTOMATIC DROP DESK CABINET $20.80

OAK $20.80

WALNUT $21.80

The Finest Sewing Machine Cabinet Made.

Highly polished panels faced with Italian veneering. Runs on rollers. Can be used as a writing desk. Handsomely ornamented and a pretty piece of furniture for every home. The HEAD, MECHANISM, ATTACHMENTS and ACCESSORIES of this machine are the same as we furnish with all of our high grade Minnesota Model "A" Machines. For beauty of design and finish this cabinet is not to be equaled.

OUR MINNESOTA MODEL "A" AUTOMATIC TWO-DOOR DROP DESK BALL BEARING CABINET.

TO PROVIDE THE BEST CABINET MADE and to outdo others we have had made for our Minnesota Model "A" a special automatic drop desk cabinet, which we furnish in solid oak or black walnut as desired. No cabinet will compare with it. When closed it has the appearance of a beautiful writing desk and can be used as such. It has a green cloth covered top and makes a nice, attractive piece of furniture for any drawing room. When so desired we can furnish the cabinet with a highly polished solid top without cloth cover. By a practical and patented device when you lift and turn the top over to the left, the sewing machine head will rise to the surface of the table ready for sewing. The machine head moves up and down and as it is counterbalanced it requires but little or no exertion to put it in place. The Two-Door Model "A" cabinet is made of solid oak or black walnut throughout as desired. Only the highest grade of material, thoroughly air seasoned and kiln dried, is used in the construction of this cabinet. The rigid inspection of the material before entering into the construction of the cabinet insures it against swelling and cracking.

Illustration Showing Cabinet Open.

THE TWO-DOOR AUTOMATIC MODEL "A" DESK CABINET when closed is 30 inches high, 21 inches deep and 25 inches wide. (See lower illustration.) When open and ready for work the table space measures 21 inches by 50 inches, more than twice the table space afforded by other machines. There is no cabinet so strongly made as our Model "A." The top or lid is made up of five layers of wood, the grain of each layer running at right angles with the layer above it, by having nothing but tops made of built up stock we do away with all possibility of warping, checking or splitting. The entire front of the cabinet, as well as the two side panels are made of especially selected quarter sawed oak. The heavy rope moulding on the doors and the beautiful hand carvings on the panels give the cabinet a massive appearance. There are two large drawers securely fastened to the lower left hand side and fitted with strong locks and handsome nickel plated drawer pulls. In these drawers may be kept all the attachments and other necessary supplies. In the upper parts of the two doors, pockets are built to hold the accessories and other parts which are in constant use. Above the pocket on each door is a small compartment conveniently arranged in which may be kept needles, bobbins, thread, etc. The doors of the cabinet, aside from their handsome design and beautiful carvings, are strongly made and can be securely locked. The cabinet is easily moved about because it is mounted on four large wooden rollers.

For full description of Model "A" head, see pages 62 and 63.
For full description of Model "A" attachments, see page 64.
For our liberal terms offer, see page 48.
For our three months' free trial offer, see page 48.
For our twenty years' guarantee, see page 48.
For freight rates, see column 1st class rates, pages 7 to 11.

Illustration Showing How Cabinet Opens.

WE PARTICULARLY RECOMMEND our Two-Door Automatic Drop Desk Model "A" Cabinet to prospective buyers because there is more value, dollar for dollar, in this cabinet than can be found in any other sewing machine manufactured.

Illustration Showing Cabinet Closed.

THE FINISH. All our Model "A" Cabinets are finished in the beautiful dark golden oak color, such as is found only on the most expensive furniture. Our Model "A" Cabinets are better, stronger and more handsomely finished than the cabinets offered by local dealers and sewing machine agents at from $50.00 to $75.00.

BALL BEARINGS. Our Minnesota Model "A" Drop Desk Cabinet Machine is as light running as either the upright or drop head styles. It is fitted with our celebrated "bicycle" ball bearing hanger, found only on our cabinet machines; which give the same rapidity of action and ease of operation to the machine as the ball bearing arrangement to a bicycle. All wearing parts are made of case hardened, ground out steel, and the steel balls are the very best in the market.

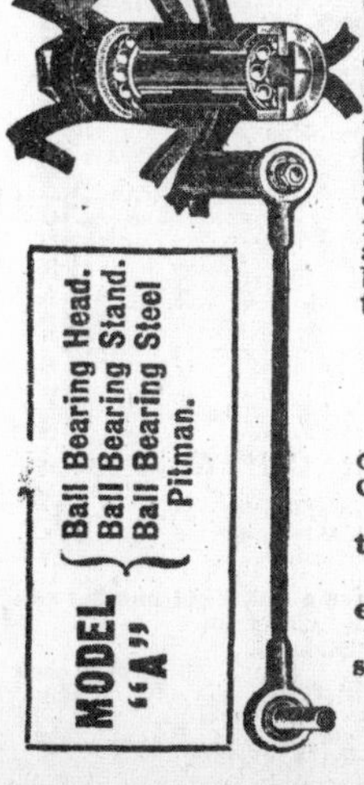

MODEL "A" { Ball Bearing Head. Ball Bearing Stand. Ball Bearing Steel Pitman.

SIMPLE IN CONSTRUCTION.
NO GETTING OUT OF ORDER.

All parts of castings are easily accessible, so that balls, cups, etc., can be replaced at any time. All friction eliminated and the operation of the machine is made a pleasure.

The extra charge which we make for walnut cabinets represents the difference in the cost of material between oak and walnut.

The prices given below are for these cabinets crated and delivered on board cars at Dayton, Ohio.

These prices do not include attachments. We furnish a complete set at 75 cents, as fully explained on page 64.

No. 26C270 Minnesota Model "A" Full Automatic Lift, Oak Cabinet Machine. Price........ $20.80
No. 26C271 Minnesota Model "A" Full Automatic Lift, Walnut Cabinet Machine. Price........ 21.80

No. 26C205 Order by Number.

OUR MINNESOTA MODEL "F" MACHINE AT $8.25.

IN LISTING OUR MINNESOTA MODEL "F" MACHINE AT $8.25, we demonstrate our ability to furnish a guaranteed 5-drawer drop head machine at the lowest price ever heard of. It is superior in every respect to machines sold elsewhere and widely advertised at $10.00 to $12.00. **While it is exceptional value for the money and we guarantee to replace any parts that might prove defective for a term of five years, we do not recommend it to give the length of service or the satisfaction of our better machines.** With care the machine will give fair service for a number of years, and we sell the Minnesota Model "F" in order to furnish the best possible machine to those who cannot afford to buy a better or more improved grade.

THE DIFFERENCE IN THE PRICE of our Minnesota Model "F" Machine and our best machines is so small that the majority of our customers purchase our higher grades, particularly the Minnesota Models "A" and "B," which are the best and most improved machines it is possible to manufacture, guaranteed for twenty years, and which will give the best of service for practically a lifetime.

DESCRIPTION OF THE MINNESOTA MODEL "F" MACHINE. The cabinet is constructed of oak, strongly made and finished very neatly, fitted with durable black enameled stand with adjustable treadle. The head has a medium arm, is neatly decorated and ornamented with nickel plated face plate, black enamel base and nickel trimmings throughout, and is fitted with many improvements not found on machines sold at such a low price. **We guarantee the machine and agree to replace or repair any defective parts free of charge for a term of five years.**

WE INCLUDE WITH THE MACHINE AT $8.25 a full set of accessories, including two screwdrivers, six bobbins, one package of needles, one cloth guide, one oil can filled with oil and one complete instruction book.

No. 26C205 MINNESOTA MODEL "F" MACHINE. Price........ **$8.25**

For terms of shipment see page 48. On board cars at Dayton, Ohio.

OUR MINNESOTA $5.95 IMPROVED HAND MACHINE.

AT $5.95 we furnish our Minnesota Hand Machine with iron base without cover, as illustrated on the left. For $7.85 we furnish the machine complete with wooden base and a fine bent wood cover. This is a very convenient machine for those that travel and for women who are unable for various reasons to operate a treadle power machine.

$5.95 AND $7.85

No. 26C290 Price, $5.95.

THIS IS A FIRST CLASS, RELIABLE MACHINE having every improvement that is found on our high grade stand sewing machines, and capable of doing the widest range of work. It has an automatic bobbin winder, self threading, vibrating steel shuttle, patent automatic take-up, self setting needle clamp, tension liberator, all the latest improvements, combining simplicity, durability and strength in construction, speed and light running qualities, unequaled for ease of management and capacity for a wide range of hemming, felling, binding, tucking, ruffling, gathering, seaming, etc., adapted to every variety of sewing, from the lightest muslin to the heaviest cloth.

THE BEARINGS are of the best hardened steel and are adjustable. We pay as much attention to the adjustment of this machine as we do to our Minnesota Model "A," and we will not admit that this machine is equaled by any hand machine on the market, regardless of price or name. One particular point of superiority lies in its feed, which is the four motion feed, the same that is used upon our high grade stand machine. This feed is absolutely positive, its movements being regulated by the eccentric lever bar, and does not require the use of coil springs to obtain the four movements of the feeding mechanism.

Wood Base and Cover. No. 26C295 Price, $7.85.

THE MAJORITY of other hand machines use the spring feed, which readily becomes weak and fails to act properly.

THE HAND ATTACHMENT can be detached and removed and the machine set on a table or stand and operated by foot power, the wheel having a groove for the belt. Other points of excellence lie in its self setting needle, positive stitch regulator, and a device by which the gearing is readily released, thus enabling the operator to wind the bobbin without operating the working parts of the machine. We furnish an instruction book and a full set of accessories free of charge with the machine. Free on board cars at Dayton, Ohio.

No. 26C290 Minnesota Hand Machine, with iron base, no cover. Price........ **$5.95**
No. 26C295 Minnesota Hand Machine, with wood base and cover. Price........ **7.85**
Full set of attachments, extra........ **.75**

SEWING MACHINE SUPPLIES.

REPAIRS OR SUPPLIES for machines listed in this catalogue, such as needles, bobbins, shuttles, attachments, etc., may be secured from us at any time at lowest possible prices.

AS WE CARRY A COMPLETE STOCK of all parts used in the construction or operation of our machines, we can fill orders for supplies without delay. The supplies furnished by us for our machines are the genuine parts, manufactured by the maker of the machines. Under the terms of our contract with the manufacturer we can furnish repairs for our machines at any time in the future. An order for repairs placed with us ten or fifteen years from date will be filled as promptly and as accurately as an order placed today. Repairs and supplies which we furnish for machines which we do not handle are purchased direct from the manufacturer, or in cases where the manufacture of the machines has been discontinued we procure the repairs and supplies from reliable sources. We guarantee all repairs to be perfect fitting.

RULES FOR ORDERING. In ordering shuttles, feeds, springs or repairs for the machines which we handle it is not necessary to send sample, simply mention name and head number of your machine. You will find the head number stamped either upon the front shuttle slide, or immediately beneath the front shuttle slide, or upon the bed plate behind the upright part of the arm. In ordering repairs for machines which we do not handle, be sure to send an illustration of the part wanted taken from your instruction book, or, if you have no illustration, it will be necessary for you to send us the old part by mail in a separate package from your order, being sure to write your full name and address on the outside wrapper of the package so we will know who it comes from and connect it quickly with your order.

WE REQUIRE CASH IN FULL, IN ADVANCE, ON ALL ORDERS FOR SUPPLIES AND REPAIRS.

Tuckers, 25 Cents Each.

We will supply tuckers at 25 cents each, for any sewing machine ever handled or sold by us, excepting Standards, Wheeler & Wilsons, Singers, New Homes, Domestics and Whites.
If by mail, postage extra, 5 cents.
When ordering, be sure to give name and head number of sewing machine.

Rufflers, 40 Cents Each.

We will supply rufflers or gatherers at 40 cents each, for any sewing machine ever handled or sold by us, excepting Standards, Wheeler & Wilsons, Singers, New Homes, Domestics and Whites.
If by mail, postage extra, 5 cents.
When ordering be sure to give name and head number of sewing machine.

Hemstitchers, 35 Cents.

When ordering hemstitchers, give name of machine and send drawing of front shuttle slide.
We will supply hemstitchers at 35 cents each, for any sewing machine ever handled or sold by us, excepting Standards, Wheeler & Wilsons, Singers, Domestics, New Homes and Whites.
If by mail, postage extra, 5 cents.

Hemstitchers for	Each	Hemstitchers for	Each
Singer	45c	Wheeler & Wilson	45c
New Home	45c	Domestic	45c
White	45c	Eldredge	45c
Standard	65c		

If by mail, postage extra, 5 cents.

Greist Tuck Folder.

Will fit any machine. Instructions sent with each folder.

It is very strong and with reasonable care is indestructible. It is made entirely of steel, heavily nickel plated, beautiful in design and finish and perfect in workmanship. It has a capacity of from pin tucks to tucks 1 inch wide and will operate equally well upon all kinds and grades of materials, whether light or heavy, starched or unstarched, or of cotton, linen, woolen or silk.
Price, each........ **45c**
If by mail, postage extra, 4c.

Feeds, 20 Cents Each.

We will supply feeds at 20 cents each, for any sewing machine ever handled or sold by us, excepting Standards, Wheeler & Wilsons, Singers, New Homes, Domestics, and Whites.
If by mail, postage extra, 3 cents.
When ordering, be sure to give name and head number of sewing machine.

Needle Plates, 15 Cents Each.

We will supply needle plates at 15 cents each, for any sewing machine ever handled or sold by us, excepting Standards, Wheeler & Wilsons, Singers, New Homes, Domestics and Whites.
If by mail, postage extra, 2 cents.
When ordering, be sure to mention name and head number of sewing machine.

Needle Clamps for Round Needle Bars, 15 Cents Each.

We will supply needle clamps at 15 cents each for any sewing machine ever handled or sold by us having a round needle bar, excepting Standards, Wheeler & Wilsons, Singers, New Homes, Domestics and Whites.
If by mail, postage extra, 1 cent.
When ordering be sure to mention name and head number of machine.

Needle Clamps for Flat Needle Bars, 22 Cents Each.

We will supply needle clamps at 22 cents each for any sewing machine ever handled or sold by us having a flat needle bar, excepting Standards, Wheeler & Wilsons, Singers, New Homes, Domestics and Whites. If by mail, postage extra, 2 cents.
When ordering, be sure to mention name and head number of machine.

SEWING MACHINE NEEDLES.

13 CENTS PER DOZEN ALWAYS SEND SAMPLE | **13 CENTS PER DOZEN ALWAYS SEND SAMPLE**

In ordering needles, **be sure to send sample, also mention name and head number of the machine.** This will insure prompt attention and the proper filling of your order for needles. No order will be filled for less than 1 dozen needles. Also send cash in full with the order and allow for postage at the rate of 2 cents per dozen.

No. 26C306 Sewing Machine Needles, for all family sewing machines regardless of name and make. Price, per doz.. **13c**
If by mail, postage extra, 2 cents.

BE SURE TO SEND SAMPLE | **No order filled for less than 1 dozen needles. Be sure to send sample.** | **BE SURE TO SEND SAMPLE**

Fellers or Small Foot Hemmers, 25 Cents Each.

We will supply hemmers and fellers at 25 cents each, for any sewing machine ever handled or sold by us, excepting Standards, Wheeler & Wilsons, Singers, New Homes, Domestics and Whites. If by mail, postage extra, 2 cents.
When ordering mention name and head number of sewing machine.

Shuttle Carriers, 15 Cents Each.

We will supply shuttle carriers at 15 cents each, for any sewing machine ever handled or sold by us, excepting Standards, Wheeler & Wilsons, Singers, New Homes, Domestics and Whites.
If by mail, postage extra, 4 cents.
When ordering, be sure to mention name and head number of machine.

Shuttle Slides, 15 Cents Each.

We will supply shuttle slides at 15 cents each, for any sewing machine ever handled or sold by us, excepting Standards, Wheeler & Wilsons, Singers, New Homes, Domestics and Whites.
If by mail, postage extra, 4 cents.
When ordering, specify whether the front or back shuttle slide is wanted, also mention name and head number of machine.

Bobbin Winders, 65 Cents.

We will supply bobbin winders at 65 cents each, for any sewing machine ever handled or sold by us, excepting Standards, Wheeler & Wilsons, Singers, New Homes, Domestics and Whites.
If by mail, packing and postage extra, 15 cents.
When ordering, be sure to mention name and head number of machine.

Bobbins.

We will supply one-half dozen bobbins at 10 cents, for any machine ever handled or sold by us and not listed below.
If by mail, postage extra, per half dozen bobbins, 2 cents.
When ordering, be sure to mention name and head number of machine.

Standard Rotary, per half dozen	50c
Wheeler & Wilson, per half dozen	50c
Singer Oscillating, per half dozen	50c
American, per half dozen	50c
White New Style Cylinder, per half dozen	25c
White Old Style, per half dozen	10c
New Home, per half dozen	10c
Domestic, per half dozen	10c
Singer V. S. No. 2, per half dozen	10c
Paragon, per half dozen	10c
Eldredge (all styles) per half dozen	10c
Davis, per half dozen	10c

We will fill no orders for less than one-half dozen bobbins.

Shuttles.

All manufacturers have made changes in the styles of shuttles used in their machines and nearly every make has several different kinds of shuttles, so that in ordering it is not only necessary to mention name of shuttle wanted, but to send picture of the shuttle or the old one as sample. In addition to remitting for cost of shuttle, include 4 cents extra to pay postage. **When ordering, do not fail to send illustration or old shuttle as a sample** to insure securing the proper duplicate, and whenever possible give head number of machine

		Price
26C400	American	$0.73
26C408	Burdick, 4 styles each	.50
26C410	Crown, any style	.65
26C418	Diamond	.99
26C420	Davis, three styles, each	.70
26C422	Demorest, each	.60
26C424	Domestic	.60
26C426	Edgemere, two styles, each	.50
26C427	Eldredge, new style	.60
26C428	Eldredge, A and B	.70
26C431	Eldredge Cylinder, old style	.97
26C436	Howard	.50
26C446	Household	.60
26C448	Helpmate	.78
26C451	Iowa	.75
26C452	Jennie June	.80
26C456	Minnesota, all styles	.50
26C458	New Home	.50
26C460	New Queen	.50
26C463	Paragon	.80
26C477	Seroco	.50
26C478	Standard, Rotary	1.00
26C481	Standard, Vibrating	.80
26C484	Singer, Old Style, Open Face	.25
26C488	Singer, High Arm	.80
26C501	White Old Style, Open Face Shuttle	.55
26C502	White, New Style Cylinder	.55

Stand Parts for Any of Our Machines.

	Price, each		Price, each
Leg, right or left	75c	Dress Guard	45c
Brace	50c	Treadle Rod	32c
Treadle	50c	Pitman	12c
Band Wheel	50c		

When ordering stand parts give name and head number and send drawing of parts wanted.

Miscellaneous.

	Price, each		Price, each
Screwdrivers	5c	Oil Cans	5c
Instruction Books	8c	Belts	8c

If by mail, postage extra, 5 cents. (Screwdrivers, Oil Cans)
If by mail, postage extra, 2 cents. (Instruction Books, Belts)

VEHICLE DEPARTMENT

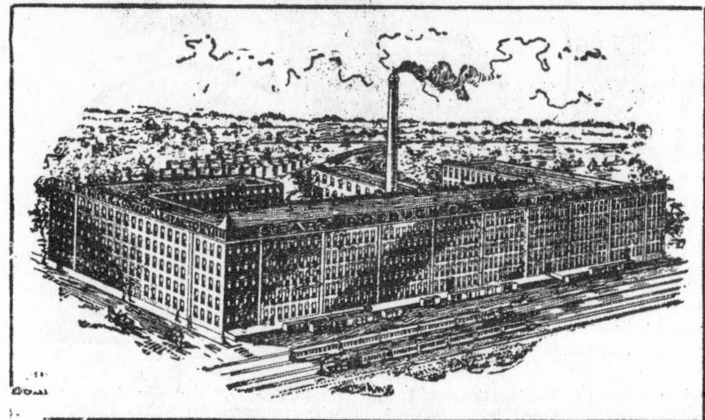

FROM THIS, OUR NEW VEHICLE FACTORY IN EVANSVILLE, IND., WE TURN OUT HANDSOMER, STRONGER, MORE LASTING, EASIER RIDING AND BETTER FINISHED VEHICLES AT LOWER PRICES THAN ANY OTHER FACTORY IN AMERICA.

CAPACITY, 35,000 FINISHED VEHICLES PER YEAR.

OUR VEHICLE FACTORY, a picture of which appears opposite, is one of the largest vehicle factories in the world, entirely new, completed in October, 1902, equipped with every modern labor saving machine that will reduce cost and improve quality. Before building this factory, the largest and best vehicle factories of all the United States were first visited with a view of getting every advantage of all other vehicle factories combined in our own new factory, and as a result this new factory is so constructed with reference to light and to the manufacture and handling of all the different parts, to the final assembling, finishing and shipping of the rig, as to keep the cost down to the lowest point, and as a result the different parts from the rough material never travel twice over the same track. On the contrary, the different rough materials are started in at the end of one of the wings where it passes on from one machine to another until it is finished, from which point the assembling of the rig begins; and as it travels on, the assembling and finishing continues, until finally the raw material that found entrance into the factory at the extreme end of one of the wings is last seen on the drying room floor as a finished vehicle of the highest grade. After the finish is set and hardened the vehicle is inspected and crated for shipment.

WHY OUR VEHICLES ARE EASIER RIDING, STRONGER, MORE DURABLE, HANDSOMER, MORE STYLISH, BETTER FINISHED AND MORE LASTING THAN ANY OTHER VEHICLE YOU CAN BUY ELSEWHERE.

"R FACTORY is located in Indiana in the very center of the greatest hardwood lumber market in the United States, so situated that we have our first pick from the best stock of the different hardwood mills, insuring us a grade of carriage wood not to be had by other makers; and for the turning of the wood in the rough into the finished parts, for the making, shaping and finishing of the wheels, gear, body, upholstering, tops, etc., we have put in the highest type of carriage making machinery that can be procured, all new, every piece of machinery as good as the best in any vehicle factory, with none of the poor, old style machinery and none that has become defective by wear; hence our gear woods, wheels, bodies, tops, irons, shafts, poles and all the different parts that go to make up a buggy or carriage come through our factory exactly alike, all interchangeable, all perfect in size and shape, all with the same high finish which you will find in no other factory. Our new automatic axle welder insures a perfect axle, our micrometer axle gauge insures perfect gather and pitch, our new patent tire welder insures a perfect weld, our automatic tire bender gives tires perfect shape; our system of putting on the tire insures a perfect dish to the wheel, while the twin wheel tire evener makes all tires true to the rims; our hydraulic press for putting the boxes in the wheels makes them everlasting, our hub boring device insures perfect track, our latest patent cushion and back machines for making upholstery produce the finest work possible to make, our patent automatic machines for the cementing of axles and axle caps produce a finish not found on any other work made.

NO OTHER FACTORY TURNS OUT A GEAR
ERE THE WHEELS TRACK AS PERFECTLY,
WHERE THE BEARINGS REST AS TRUE,
WHERE THE ADJUSTMENT IS SO ACCURATE,

and therefore where the wear is so minimized, the draft so light or the rig as easy riding. Our bodies, by our system of plugging, screwing and gluing, make a stronger, handsomer and better finished buggy or carriage body than goes out of any other factory.

TO PRODUCE A HIGHER GRADE FINISH IN THE PAINTING, a more perfect surface, better luster, a finish that will not crack, peel or blister, a painted job that will look better after two years of service than other makers' work will look in six months, we employ facilities and a system in our paint department not to be found in any other factory. Our new factory building was equipped with a view to giving us the only perfect carriage painting department in America; a room made dustproof, so high from the ground and so tight in construction and so removed from any part of the factory where dust would accumulate as to insure the entire painting of each vehicle to be done under dustproof conditions such as can be found in no other factory. The dark rooms connecting with our paint rooms are so constructed that we have absolute darkness for the drying and setting of paint. We use only the highest grade of paint that can be procured, all our oils, colors, lead, pigments and varnish are put to a chemical test before they are accepted, and in putting a buggy or carriage body through our paint department we believe it receives more coats, more and better finish under more favorable conditions than any other buggy factory in the country. Each body has the following treatment:

No. 1. Inspect.	No. 10. Rub out of filler.
No. 2. Prime.	No. 11. Reputty.
No. 3. Putty.	No. 12. Sand out of putty.
No. 4. Sand out of putty.	No. 13. Coat of color.
No. 5. Coat of lead.	No. 14. Coat of color varnish.
No. 6. First coat of filler.	No. 15. Rub out with pulverized pumice stone.
No. 7. Second coat of filler.	No. 16. Coat of rubbing varnish.
No. 8. Third coat of filler.	No. 17. Rub out with pulverized pumice stone.
No. 9. Fourth coat of filler.	No. 18. Coat of finishing varnish.

The gears have practically the same treatment, and as a result we give you a better finished, handsomer and far more lasting job of painting than you will get from any other factory.

WHY WE CAN MAKE THE PRICE BELOW ALL OTHERS. Our factory is located in the midst of the greatest hardwood lumber market in the United States. Coal mines are at our door supplying fuel for power at a little above the cost of mining. Railroad tracks run the whole length of our factory, where we load and unload direct from the cars.

WE ARE SATISFIED WITH VERY SMALL PROFITS. The vehicle department is but one branch of our immense business, therefore we can well afford to be satisfied with a very small part of the profit asked by the average vehicle house, the manufacturer or dealer who depends wholly or largely on vehicles for his profit. If we can make one dollar net on each vehicle we make and can turn out 35,000 vehicles in a year, our annual profit from the vehicle factory will be even more than satisfactory. Hence with our facilities for producing high grade work at the lowest possible cost, we can guarantee to furnish you a higher grade vehicle than you can get elsewhere and at a lower price than you could buy inferior vehicles from others.

ABOUT THE FREIGHT CHARGES. The freight charges, you will find, will amount to next to nothing as compared to what you will save in price. We located our factory in Indiana, first, with the view of being right in the midst of the best source of supply for material; second, with a view of getting the lowest possible freight rates to all points east, west, north and south, a convenient center from which we could ship to all points in the United States at the lowest possible rate of freight. We are so located that we can reach from New England to the Gulf States and to the west and southwest at a lower rate than from Chicago, and to the north and northwest our freight rate is but a shade higher than from Chicago. Our shipping facilities are such that with the sharp competition of the several roads whose tracks run into our factory, we can reach any point in the United States at a rate of freight so low that the freight charges will amount to next to nothing as compared to what you will save in price.

After you have added the freight charges to the price of any rig we quote, you will still own the rig at a much lower cost than you would have to pay others for inferior work.

IF YOU BUY A VEHICLE FROM US AND IT ISN'T SATISFACTORY AFTER YOU HAVE GIVEN IT TEN DAYS' TRIAL, SEND IT BACK TO US AND GET YOUR MONEY BACK, INCLUDING FREIGHT CHARGES PAID BY YOU.

THESE FEW LINES REALLY EXPLAIN OUR TERMS, OUR POLICY AND OUR GUARANTEE, for we leave it all with you, for after you have purchased a rig from us, whether you send cash in full with your order or have it shipped C. O. D., payable after received, after you have uncrated it, taken it home and given it ten days' trial, if it doesn't prove satisfactory in every way, if you are not convinced it is lower in price, better in quality, easier riding, stronger, more lasting, better made and a better finished rig than you could buy elsewhere, we will expect you to send it back to us at our expense, we to return your money, including the freight charges you paid.

We agree to give you a better rig at a lower price than you can buy from any other maker or dealer. When you get the rig if you don't feel we have done this we don't want you to keep it, nor do we want to put you to one penny's expense.

OUR LIBERAL TERMS OF SHIPMENT. While nearly all our customers send the full amount of cash with their order, for in doing so they save an extra charge of 25 to 50 cents, which express companies always make for collecting the amount of the C. O. D. and returning the money to us, to those who prefer to see and examine the vehicle before paying for it, we will, on receipt of $5.00, ship any vehicle (except farm wagons) to any address east of the Rocky Mountains. You can examine the vehicle at your nearest railroad station, and if found perfectly satisfactory, then pay the railroad agent our price and freight and collection charges, less the $5.00 sent with order, always, of course, with the understanding that if at any time during the first ten days you become dissatisfied with your purchase, you can return the rig to us at our expense and we will return your money, together with any freight charges paid by you.

OUR WRITTEN BINDING GUARANTEE. While every one of our vehicles are so built that they will, with proper care, last a natural lifetime, as a guarantee that everything is first class and free from the slightest defect in material or workmanship, with each rig we sell we furnish a binding one year's guarantee, covering every piece and part that enters into the construction of the vehicles, one of the strongest guarantees furnished by any vehicle factory.

SAFE DELIVERY GUARANTEED. We guarantee every vehicle we ship to reach you in the same perfect condition it leaves our factory, as we load all vehicles in the car at our shipping room door, no carting or hauling. Each vehicle is crated in the best possible manner, covered with a dustproof bag so that it will not gather dirt or dust while in transit. We aim to so wrap, cover, pack and crate our work that it can travel any distance and be sure to open up at destination in the same perfect condition as when it leaves the factory. If by chance any part should be damaged through careless or rough handling, or by accident, we agree to repair or replace the parts or furnish another rig.

REPAIRS. We can always furnish repairs at factory cost. We have a complete record of each rig we ship and will keep this record for the years to come in order to serve our customers in case of accident.

We use the celebrated Akron 2-wire rubber tires.

BE SURE TO STATE WIDTH OF TRACK

With the exception of a few special track vehicles, as noted in this catalogue, all vehicles are furnished either in the 4 feet 8 inches, narrow, or 5 feet 2 inches, wide track, as desired.

The opposite illustration shows the method of measuring track, same being distance from outside to outside of rear wheels on the ground.

OUR $22.95 ROAD WAGON.

DON'T FAIL TO STATE WIDTH OF TRACK
$22.95

No. 11C040

This vehicle, our cheapest road wagon, is built in our own factory, is fully guaranteed by us, and we use every care to see that each and every part is all good material and well put together. If we desired to reduce the quality of this rig and sell a cheaper vehicle, we could, by using cheaper wheels, upholstering, dash, body, springs, paint, etc., sell you a road wagon for about $17.00. There is no better low priced road wagon on the market today, and through the ordinary channels of trade this job would sell for much more.

BODY—23x54 inches, Corning style, made of selected material; hardwood sills, seat frame, corner posts and step strips; carefully screwed, glued and plugged.

GEAR—Axles, 15/16 inch, double collar and fantailed, hickory axle caps; reaches made of second growth hickory; axle beds cemented and clipped to axles; malleable iron full bearing fifth wheel; double reaches, braced with wrought iron stays; three and four-plate oil tempered springs, with Bailey body loops.

WHEELS—Sarven's patent, full bolted between each spoke; ⅞-inch rims, fitted with oval edge steel tires, 38 inches front and 42 inches rear.

PAINTING—Body painted black, with neat striping. Gear, Brewster gear green.

TRIMMINGS—Seat cushion and back are upholstered with imitation leather, solid panel back with springs, nicely tufted. Box spring cushion. Evans' enameled black duck dash, short carpet, anti-rattlers, wrench, etc.

TRACK—4 feet 8 inches or 5 feet 2 inches.

No. 11C040 Price, complete, with double braced shafts and steel tires. $22.95

EXTRAS.

Pole in place of shafts	$1.60
Both pole and shafts	3.75
Genuine leather cushion and back	2.00

Weight, crated under 30 inches, 380 pounds. Shipped from factory.

HANDY GOABOUT WAGON.

DON'T FAIL TO STATE WIDTH OF TRACK
$28.90

No. 11C077

BODY—29 inches wide by 76 inches long, made of carefully selected material, with a hardwood frame and seasoned panels; one seat; very handsome design, as shown in illustration.

GEAR—1 1/16-inch rear axle, 15/16-inch front axle, both fitted with double collar; selected hickory axle caps; single reach; four-plate spring in front, two three-plate springs in rear, connected to the body with our special body hanger, which is far superior to anything of its kind on the market; no wood cross-bars to break.

WHEELS—Selected grade of Sarven's patent wheels, 38 inches front and 42 inches rear; 1-inch rims, fitted with oval edge steel tires, bolted between each spoke. Can furnish 40 inches front and 44 inches rear when wanted.

PAINTING—We make a very attractive wagon of this job by painting the moulding on the body a jet black, dark green panels in between. Seat is painted black. Gear painted blood carmine, nicely striped, making a very attractive job.

TRIMMINGS—Seat and back upholstered in imitation leather, over a box spring cushion and panel back, as shown in illustration. Job comes complete with one seat, dash, double braced shafts, wrench, etc.

TRACK—4 feet 8 inches or 5 feet 2 inches wide.

No. 11C077 Price, complete with double braced shafts $28.90

EXTRAS.

Pole in place of shafts	1.60
Both pole and shafts	3.75

Weight, crated under 30 inches, 625 pounds. Shipped from factory.

THIS CUSTOMER BOUGHT OUR No. 11C139 AND SAYS HE SAVED $20.00.

Sears, Roebuck & Co., Chicago, Ill. Coonsville, Va.

Dear Sirs:—I have ordered two buggies of you besides a lot of other things. The first buggy I got of you is a dandy, and the one I ordered this summer is a very good one considering it being so cheap, only $28.95. I have saved about $40.00 on the two rigs. My top buggy can't be beaten in price or material. I have had lots of people examine it, and they say it is as good as theirs that cost them $70.00. In fact, I tried several dealers here before I ordered, so I ordered of you, and not only ordered buggies, bu[t] have ordered a lot of other things, and I have got the worth of my money. Yours truly,

W. T. LUKIN.

OUR $28.95 OPEN BUGGY.

DON'T FAIL TO STATE WIDTH OF TRACK
$28.95

No. 11C139

BODY—Piano style, 23x54 inches, made of carefully selected material. Swell body panels and convex seat panels, round corners on seat; hardwood strips gained into sills, glued, screwed and plugged. Can furnish 19-[inch] body if desired.

GEAR—Axles, 15/16 inch, dust and mud proof long distance spindles, [fan]tailed; selected hickory wood caps cemented and clipped to axles; [double] reaches, ironed and braced; three and four-plate 36-inch sweep oil tem[pered] elliptic springs, with Bailey body loops; full bearing fifth wheel. Can fu[rnish] the job on Brewster side bar springs if ordered.

WHEELS—Sarven's patent, 38 inches front and 42 inches rear, full bolted between each spoke; screwed rims, ⅞-inch, fitted with oval edge steel tires. Can furnish 40 inches front and 44 inches rear if ordered, or ¾-inch in place of ⅞-inch rims.

PAINTING—Body, plain black, with neat design on seat risers. Gear, blood carmine, with suitable striping. Can furnish New York red or Brewster green gear if ordered.

TRIMMINGS—Seat cushion and back are upholstered with dark green cloth, padded and lined seat ends; Georgia drop back, spring cushion, short carpet, boot, lined panels, leather dash, nickel plated dash rail, arm rails, seat rail and seat handles; quick shifting shaft couplers, wrench, storm apron and double braced shafts trimmed with leather. Genuine leather if ordered. See extras.

TRACK—4 feet 8 inches or 5 feet 2 inches.

No. 11C139 Complete with double braced shafts and steel tires	$28.95
Price, fitted with ¾-inch rubber tires	39.70
Price, fitted with ⅞-inch rubber tires	40.70

EXTRAS.

Pole in place of shafts	$1.60
Both pole and shafts	3.75
Genuine leather upholstering in place of cloth	1.50
Armstrong single leaf springs in place of three and four-plate springs	.

Weight, crated under 30 inches, 380 pounds. Shipped from factory.

OUR STICK SEAT OPEN BUGGY.

No. 11C136

BODY—23x54 inches, Corning style. Made of best seasoned poplar, with high panels; corner posts, seat frame and step strips made of seasoned hardwood lumber; step strips gained into sills. Body is glued, screwed and plugged. Stick seat made of bent sticks, with iron handles. 19-inch body if ordered.

GEAR—Axles, 15/16 inch, dust and mud proof bell collar long distance spindles, fantailed. All wood parts are made of selected second growth hickory. Double reach, ironed full length and securely bolted and clipped to axles. Three and four-leaf, 36-inch sweep elliptic oil tempered springs, clipped to Bailey body loops.

WHEELS—Sarven's patent, 38 inches front and 42 inches rear; screwed rims, ⅞-inch, fitted with oval edge steel tires, bolted between each spoke. Can furnish 40-inch front and 44-inch rear wheels, or compressed band hubs, if ordered.

PAINTING—Body painted black, with striping as shown in illustration; gear, blood carmine, striped to match. Can furnish New York red or Brewster green gear if ordered.

TRIMMINGS—Seat and back upholstered with light gray whipcord, spring cushion and 10-inch curved panel back, leather dash, storm apron, boot, carpet, double braced shafts, leather trimmed, quick shifting shaft couplers. Will upholster in dark green cloth if ordered. Leather furnished if ordered. See extras.

TRACK—4 feet 8 inches or 5 feet 2 inches.

No. 11C136 Complete, with double braced shafts and steel tires	$29.90
Price, fitted with ⅞-inch rubber tires	41.65

EXTRAS.

Pole in place of shafts	$1.60
Both pole and shafts	3.75
Genuine leather upholstering in place of whipcord	1.65

Weight, crated under 30 inches, 380 pounds. Shipped from factory.

PROMPT SHIPMENT. We have a large factory, a large warehouse, and we can usually ship any vehicle ordered within a few days after your order is received. We carry on hand in our warehouse at Evansville, Indiana, a large number of each style job.

OUR BOSTON BEAUTY RUNABOUT.

DON'T FAIL TO STATE WIDTH OF TRACK
$29.75

No. 11C155

BODY—Piano body, 23x54 inches; convex panels with concave seat risers; body glued, clamped, screwed and plugged, and finished hardwood seat frame, seat posts and step strips gained into sills.

GEAR—Axles, [illegible] inch, dust and mudproof, long distance, fantailed, with axle beds clipped; all wood parts are second growth hickory, sand finished. Full circle fifth wheel. Three and four-plate, 36-inch sweep, elliptic oil tempered springs, clipped to Bailey body loops. Gear ironed and braced throughout with best Norway iron.

WHEELS—Sarven's patent, screwed rims, 40 inches front and 44 inches rear; rims, ⅞ inch, fitted with oval edge steel tires, bolted between each spoke. Can furnish 38 inches front and 42 inches rear if ordered.

PAINTING—Body, jet black; gear, New York red, neatly striped with black. Can furnish blood carmine or Brewster gear green if ordered.

TRIMMINGS—Seat and back upholstered with No. 1 whipcord, light color; box spring cushion, 10-inch bent panel back, carpet, high patent leather dash; double braced shafts, leather trimmed; quick shifting shaft couplers, wrench and storm apron.

TRACK—4 feet 8 inches or 5 feet 2 inches.

No. 11C155 Price, complete, with double braced shafts and steel tires $29.75
Price, fitted with ¾-inch rubber tires 40.50
Price, fitted with ⅞-inch rubber tires 41.50

EXTRAS.

Pole in place of shafts $1.60
Both pole and shafts 3.75
Leather upholstering 1.65
Weight, crated under 30 inches, 400 pounds. Shipped from factory.

OUR PHAETON RUNABOUT.

DON'T FAIL TO STATE WIDTH OF TRACK
$31.00

No. 11C209

BODY—Bracket front, phaeton buggy body, 25x54 inches; steel rocker plates, hardwood strips gained into sills, glued, screwed and plugged. Carefully selected material used. Roomy phaeton seat.

GEAR—Axles, 1⅛ inch, bell collar, dust and mudproof; long distance spindles; wood caps, cemented and clipped to axles; double reach; fully ironed and braced; three and four-plate 36-inch sweep elliptic oil tempered springs, clipped to Bailey body loops; full bearing fifth wheel.

WHEELS—Sarven's patent, 38 inches front and 42 inches rear; ⅞-inch screwed rims, fitted with oval edge steel tires, full bolted between each spoke. Can furnish 40 inches front and 44 inches rear if ordered, also ¾-inch rims.

PAINTING—Body, plain black, with neat design on seat risers. Gear, Brewster gear green, nicely striped. Can furnish blood carmine or New York red gear if ordered. All striped to match.

TRIMMINGS—Dark green body cloth, springs in cushion and back, solid panel back, padded and lined seat ends, leather dash, carpet, storm apron, boot, quick shifting shaft couplers, wrench and double braced shafts, leather trimmed. Leather in place of cloth if ordered. See extras.

TRACK—4 feet 8 inches or 5 feet 2 inches.

No. 11C209 Complete, with double braced shafts and steel tires $31.00
Price, fitted with ¾-inch rubber tires 41.75
Price, fitted with ⅞-inch rubber tires 42.75

EXTRAS.

Pole in place of shafts $1.60
Both pole and shafts 3.75
Genuine leather upholstering in place of cloth 2.00
Weight, crated under 30 inches, 380 pounds. Shipped from factory.

THIS CUSTOMER SAVED $40.00 ON A No. 11C2400 RUNABOUT.

Whittier, Cal.

Sears, Roebuck & Co., Chicago, Ill.

Dear Sirs:—I take pleasure in giving you the following statement in regard to the Rubber Tire Runabout No. 11C2400 I ordered from you: I am well satisfied with the rig. I examined the same style of vehicle here before I ordered and obtained the lowest cash price. After paying the freight from factory to my railroad station, I saved $40.00 on my purchase.

Yours respectfully,

JOHN WOOD.

THREE-PERCH CONCORD RUNABOUT.

DON'T FAIL TO STATE WIDTH OF TRACK
$39.95

No. 11C225

BODY—27 inches wide by 56 inches long, making it very roomy. Body is extra well made of selected material, with hardwood sills, beams and seat frames, ironed and braced; seat is extra wide and deep, with a high, solid panel spring back.

GEAR—Full Concord gear, with three reaches made of carefully selected second growth hickory, ironed and braced; 1-inch long distance axles, fitted with dust and mudproof bell collars. The axle caps are selected hickory, cemented and clipped to the axles; four-plate springs, hung on equalizers, both front and rear; an extra strong gear throughout.

WHEELS—Sarven's patent, second growth hickory spokes, ⅞-inch screwed rims, fitted with oval edge steel tires, 38 inches front and 42 inches rear. If ordered, we can furnish compressed band wood hubs, also 40-inch front and 44-inch rear wheels.

PAINTING—Body and seat panels, black, nicely striped, shutter work on the seat risers being painted carmine to harmonize with the gear. Gear, blood carmine, neatly striped. Can furnish Brewster green gear if ordered, with shutter work on the seat risers to correspond.

TRIMMINGS—Seat cushion and back upholstered in dark green broadcloth over solid panel spring back and box spring cushion, nicely tufted. Can furnish whipcord upholstering if ordered. Body carpet, handsome patent leather dash, quick shifting shaft couplers, double braced shafts, leather trimmed.

TRACK—4 feet 8 inches or 5 feet 2 inches.

No. 11C225 Price, complete, with shafts and steel tires $39.95
Price, fitted with ⅞-inch rubber tires 51.70
Price, fitted with 1-inch rubber tires 53.20

EXTRAS.

Genuine leather upholstering $2.00
Pole in place of shafts 1.60
Both pole and shafts 3.75
Can furnish with a three-bow leather quarter top for 11.25
Weight, crated under 30 inches, 400 pounds. Shipped from factory.

THE POPULAR RUNABOUT.

$38.75

No. 11C2400

BODY—23x54 inches, convex panels with concave seat risers; body is glued, clamped, screwed and plugged and fitted with oval edge irons on top and at corners; hardwood step strips gained into sills; hardwood seat frame and corner posts.

GEAR—Naked axles, 1⅛ inch, best steel, swedged top and bottom; 3½-inch arch, dust and mudproof bell collars; self oiling, long distance spindles; reach heels and fifth wheel are riveted and brazed to axles; reaches are selected second growth hickory, ironed full length; open head, full bright, oil tempered springs, 36-inch sweep, clipped to Bailey body loops.

WHEELS—Sarven's patent, 36 inches front and 38 inches rear; low wheel, on account of high arch axle, makes body regulation height from the ground; screwed rims, ⅞ inch, fitted with oval edge steel tires, full bolted between each spoke.

PAINTING—Body, jet black; gear, carmine, neatly striped with black. Gear, black, New York red, Brewster gear green or canary yellow if ordered.

TRIMMINGS—Seat and back upholstered in light colored Bedford cord; box spring cushion and 10-inch bent panel back fancy stick seat; full length velvet carpet; Stanhope seat fenders, 13-inch patent leather padded dash, storm apron, wrench, and shafts trimmed with leather 36 inches from point; round shaft straps; Bradley shaft couplers.

TRACK—4 feet 6 inches only. Not built in wide track.

No. 11C2400 Price, complete, with double braced shafts and steel tires $38.75
Price, fitted with ¾-inch rubber tires 49.50
Price, fitted with ⅞-inch rubber tires 50.50

EXTRAS.

Pole in place of shafts, Bradley couplings $1.90
Both pole and shafts, Bradley couplings 4.25
Genuine leather upholstering 1.50
Weight, crated under 30 inches, 400 pounds. Shipped from factory.

OUR BOULEVARD RUNABOUT.

$41.75

No. 11C3400

BODY—23x54 inches; hardwood frame and seasoned panels, glued, screwed and plugged. Latest design double bent stick seat.

GEAR—Naked steel axles, 15/16 inch, swedged top and bottom, 3½-inch arch, with dust and mudproof bell collars, self oiling long distance spindles, drop forged reach heels and shaft shackles riveted and brazed to axle; no clips used. Fifth wheel brazed and riveted. Double reach, ironed full length. 36-inch, open head, elliptic oil tempered springs, full bright. Bradley shaft couplers. Bailey body loops.

WHEELS—Sarven's patent, 36 inches front and 38 inches rear, low wheel to counteract the high arch, makes body regulation height from ground. Hickory spokes with ⅞-inch rims, fitted with oval edge steel tires, bolted between each spoke. Rims are screwed.

PAINTING—Body plain black. Rich and handsome effect. Gear, New York red with black striping. Can furnish blood carmine gear if ordered.

TRIMMINGS—Upholstered in light colored Bedford cord, over box spring cushion and 10-inch bent panel back, full length velvet carpet; patent leather dash, wrench, storm apron, Bradley shaft couplers. Seat fenders and shafts trimmed with leather 36 inches back from point; round shaft straps.

TRACK—4 feet 6 inches only; cannot furnish in wide track.

No. 11C3400 Price, complete, with double braced shafts and steel tires........ $41.75
Price, fitted with ¾-inch rubber tires........ 52.50
Price, fitted with ⅞-inch rubber tires........ 53.50

EXTRAS.

Pole in place of shafts, Bradley couplings........ $1.90
Both pole and shafts, Bradley couplings........ 4.25
Genuine leather upholstering........ 1.50
Weight, crated under 30 inches, 400 pounds. Shipped from factory.

OUR $26.75 TOP BUGGY.

DON'T FAIL TO STATE WIDTH OF TRACK
$26.75

No. 11C01

BODY—23x54 inches, piano style, convex side panels, frame of hardwood, step strips gained into sills, panels of well seasoned poplar, glued, screwed and plugged.

GEAR—Axles, 15/16 inch, double collar, fantailed; hickory axle caps, reaches and spring bars; three and four-plate elliptic springs.

WHEELS—Selected hickory, Sarven's patent, ⅞-inch rims, fitted with ¼-inch oval edge steel tires, bolted between each spoke; 38 inches front and 42 inches rear.

TOP—Three-bow, enameled bow sockets, drill quarters, stays and roof. Dark green head lining and lined backstays; roll up back curtain with black knob fasteners; drill side curtains.

PAINTING—Body, plain black; gear, dark Brewster gear green, with two-line stripe on wheels.

TRIMMINGS—Imitation leather cushion and back, nicely upholstered on solid panel spring back and spring cushion, unlined seat ends; storm apron, drill boot, black enameled duck dash, wrench, anti-rattlers and carpet.

TRACK—4 feet 8 inches or 5 feet 2 inches.

No. 11C01 Price, complete, with double braced shafts and steel tires, $26.75

EXTRAS.

Pole in place of shafts........ $1.60
Both pole and shafts........ 3.75
Weight, crated under 30 inches, 400 pounds. Shipped from factory.

OUR MODEL TOP BUGGY.

DON'T FAIL TO STATE WIDTH OF TRACK
$30.90

No. 11C02

BODY—Piano body, 23x54 inches; convex side panels; hardwood frame, with step strips gained into sills; seasoned poplar panels, screwed, glued and plugged.

GEAR—Axles, 15/16 inch, double collar, fantailed; hickory wood parts, with axle beds cemented and clipped to axles; three and four-plate oil tempered elliptic springs.

WHEELS—Sarven's patent, ⅞-inch rims, fitted with ¼-inch oval edge steel tires, bolted between each spoke; 38 inches front and 42 inches rear. Can furnish 40 inches front and 44 inches rear if ordered.

TOP—Three-bow, rubber drill roof and quarters, with black enameled back stays, lined; dark green wool faced head lining; roll up back curtain, unlined side curtains. Can furnish four-bow top if ordered.

PAINTING—Body black, nicely striped and decorated, as shown in illustration; gear painted dark Brewster gear green, with neat striping to match body.

TRIMMINGS—Latest pattern cushion and back of Union body cloth, over solid panel back, with springs in both cushion and back; seat ends padded and lined; drill boot, carpet, storm apron, wrench, anti-rattlers, leather dash and lined panels.

TRACK—4 feet 8 inches or 5 feet 2 inches.

No. 11C02 Price, complete, with double braced shafts and steel tires, $30.90

EXTRAS.

Pole in place of shafts........ $1.60
Both pole and shafts........ 3.75
Nickel top prop nuts and dash rail........ .40
Genuine leather cushion and back........ 1.25
Weight, crated under 30 inches, 400 pounds. Shipped from factory.

OUR RIVAL LEATHER QUARTER TOP BUGGY.

DON'T FAIL TO STATE WIDTH OF TRACK
$32.95

No. 11C05

BODY—23x54 inches, piano body; hardwood frame, with step strips gained into sills; seasoned poplar panels, glued, screwed and plugged. Can furnish Corning body if ordered.

GEAR—15/16-inch double collar steel axles, fantailed; hickory reaches, ironed full length; axle beds cemented, sanded and clipped to axles; elliptic oil tempered springs, three-plate front, four-plate rear, clipped to Bailey body loops.

WHEELS—38 inches front and 42 inches rear; ⅞-inch rims, fitted with oval edge steel tires, full bolted, Sarven's patent hub. Can furnish 40-inch front and 44-inch rear wheels if ordered.

TOP—Three-bow, leather quarter top, with leather back stays; drill roof and back curtain; all wool faced head lining; roll up back curtain; drill side curtains. Can furnish four-bow top if ordered.

PAINTING—Body black, with fancy stripe and design on seat risers. Gear, carmine, striped to match. Will furnish Brewster green or New York red gear if ordered.

TRIMMINGS—Seat and back upholstered with good heavy cloth, over solid panel spring back, with springs in cushion. Seat ends padded and lined; boot, patent leather dash and lined panels, wrench, storm apron, etc.

TRACK—4 feet 8 inches or 5 feet 2 inches.

No. 11C05 Complete, with double braced shafts and steel tires.... $32.95

EXTRAS.

Pole in place of shafts........ $1.60
Both pole and shafts........ 3.75
Genuine leather cushion and back........ 1.25
Weight, crated under 30 inches, 410 pounds. Shipped from factory.

THE WONDER LEATHER QUARTER TOP BUGGY.

DON'T FAIL TO STATE WIDTH OF TRACK

No. 11C104

$35.95

Four-Bow Top same price.

BODY—Piano body, 23x54 inches, side panels, 8 inches deep. Hardwood frame with step strips mortised into sills. Corners screwed, glued and plugged. Concave risers, oval edge iron on top of panels, floor rabbeted into sills.

GEAR—Axles, 1/16 inch, long distance dust and mud proof bell collar; axle beds cemented and clipped to axles. Double reach, ironed full length. Full bearing fifth wheel, 36-inch sweep, three and four-plate oil tempered elliptic springs. Bailey body loops.

WHEELS—Sarven's patent wheels, ⅞-inch screwed rims, fitted with ¼-inch oval edge steel tires, bolted between each spoke. Made of second growth hickory, fully warranted. 38 inches front and 42 inches rear. 40-inch front and 44-inch rear if ordered.

TOP—Three-bow, leather quarters and back stays. Quarters cut deep and back stays lined and padded, with fancy needlework on lining. Roof and back curtain heavy rubber. Nickel curtain fasteners. All wool head lining and lined back curtain. Comes complete with good side curtains.

PAINTING—Body, black, with neat decoration and striping. Gear, Brewster gear green, neatly striped. Will furnish blood carmine gear.

TRIMMINGS—Seat and back upholstered with heavy, dark green body cloth, over coil spring cushion and solid panel spring back. Leather if specified, see extras. Storm apron, boot, quick shifting shaft couplers, carpet, lined panels, wrench and leather dash.

TRACK—4 feet 8 inches or 5 feet 2 inches.

No. 11C104 Complete, with double braced shafts and steel tires..... $35.95
Price, fitted with ¾-inch rubber tires..... 46.70
Price, fitted with ⅞-inch rubber tires..... 47.70

EXTRAS.

Pole in place of shafts....... $1.60 | Genuine leather upholstering... $1.50
Both pole and shafts.......... 3.75 |
Weight, crated under 30 inches, 400 pounds. Shipped from factory.

OUR WIDE BODY BUGGY.

No. 11C124

$38.95

Three-Bow Top same price.

BODY—Piano body, 25x54 inches, side panels 8 inches deep. Hardwood frame with step strips mortised into sills. Corners screwed, glued and plugged. Concave risers, oval edge iron on top of panels, floor rabbetted into sills; round seat corners; large, roomy seat.

GEAR—Axles, 1/16 inch, dust and mud proof long distance spindles; axle beds cemented and clipped to axles; double reach, ironed full length. Full bearing fifth wheel, three and four-plate oil tempered elliptic springs, 36-inch sweep. Bailey body loops.

WHEELS—Sarven's patent wheels, 1-inch screwed rims fitted with ¼-inch oval edge steel tires, bolted between each spoke; 40 inches front and 44 inches rear. Made of second growth hickory; fully warranted. 38-inch front and 42-inch rear if ordered.

TOP—Four-bow, leather quarters and back stays; quarters cut deep and back stays lined and padded, with fancy needle work on lining; roof and back curtain heavy rubber. Nickel curtain fasteners. All wool head lining and lined back curtain. Comes complete wit good side curtains.

PAINTING—Body, black, with neat decoration and striping; gear, Brewster gear green, neatly striped. Will furnish blood carmine gear.

TRIMMINGS—Upholstered with heavy dark green body cloth over coil spring cushion and solid panel spring back. Storm apron, boot, quick shifting shaft couplers, carpet, lined panels, wrench, 15-inch leather dash and shafts leather trimmed.

TRACK—4 feet 8 inches or 5 feet 2 inches. Net weight, about 315 pounds.

No. 11C124 Price, with double braced shafts..... $38.95
Price, with ⅞-inch rubber tires..... 50.70
Price, with 1-inch rubber tires..... 52.20

EXTRAS.

Pole in place of shafts....... $1.60 | Both pole and shafts..... $3.75
Genuine leather upholstering..... 1.75
Weight, crated under 30 inches, about 400 pounds. Shipped from factory.

OUR EASY RIDING SIDE SPRING BUGGY.

$36.60

Four-Bow Top same price.

DON'T FAIL TO STATE WIDTH OF TRACK

No. 11C117

BODY—Corning style body, 23x54 inches, hardwood frame, with step strips gained into sills; seasoned poplar panels, glued, screwed and plugged; convex seat panels and concave seat risers. Can furnish piano body if ordered.

GEAR—Axles, 1/16 inch, long distance with dust and mud proof bell collar; axle caps cemented, sanded and clipped to axles; long, easy riding side springs running from front to rear axle; no reaches.

WHEELS—Sarven's patent, ⅞-inch screwed rims, fitted with oval edge steel tires; 38 inches front and 42 inches rear. Can furnish 40 and 44 inches if ordered.

TOP—Three-bow, leather quarters and back stays; heavy rubber roof and back curtain; padded and lined back stays, fancy stitched; back curtain lined; good heavy side curtains, all wool head lining; nickel curtain fasteners. Can furnish four-bow if ordered.

PAINTING—Body, plain black, fancy design on seat risers; gear, Brewster gear green, neatly striped. Can furnish New York red or blood carmine gear.

TRIMMINGS—Seat and back upholstered with heavy, dark green wool dyed body cloth over solid panel spring back and spring cushion. Leather if specified, see extras. Padded and lined seat ends; short carpet and lined panels; patent leather dash, boot, storm apron, quick shifting shaft couplers, shafts leather trimmed, wrench, etc.

TRACK—4 feet 8 inches or 5 feet 2 inches.

No. 11C117 Price, with double braced shafts and steel tires.... $36.60
Price, fitted with ¾-inch rubber tires..... 47.35
Price, fitted with ⅞-inch rubber tires..... 48.35
Price, fitted with 1-inch rubber tires..... 49.85

EXTRAS.

Pole in place of shafts... $1.60 | Both pole and shafts..... $3.75
Genuine leather upholstering..... 1.50
Weight, crated under 30 inches, 400 pounds. Shipped from factory.

OUR BREWSTER SIDE BAR BUGGY.

$37.75

Three or Four-Bow Top same price.

DON'T FAIL TO STATE WIDTH OF TRACK

No. 11C160

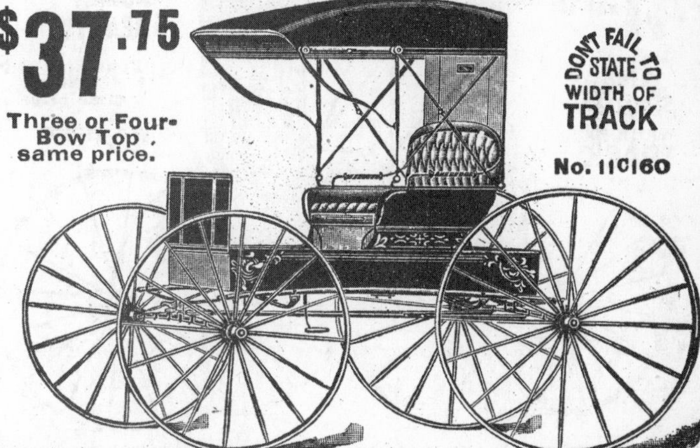

BODY—Piano box style, 19 inches wide by 54 inches long. Hardwood frame; seasoned poplar panels, screwed, glued and plugged. Steps are of hardwood, gained into sills. Can furnish 17 or 23-inch body if ordered.

GEAR—1/16-inch steel axles, fantailed; fitted with celebrated dust and mud proof bell collar long distance spindles; axle beds cemented and clipped to axles; single reach, ironed and braced; full bearing fifth wheel; combination King coil and Brewster side bar springs.

WHEELS—Sarven's patent, 38 inches front and 42 inches rear; ¾-inch screwed rims fitted with oval edge steel tires, full bolted between each spoke. Can furnish wheels 40 inches front and 44 inches rear, or 36 inches front and 40 inches rear if ordered. Can also furnish ⅞-inch rim wheels.

TOP—Two and one-half bow, leather quarters and back stays. Quarters cut deep and back stays lined and padded. Roof and back curtain, heavy rubber. All wool head lining. Comes complete with side curtains. Can furnish three or four-bow if ordered.

PAINTING—Body, black, neatly striped and decorated, as shown in illustration. Gear, blood carmine, neatly striped. Can furnish Brewster gear green if ordered.

TRIMMINGS—Seat and back upholstered with genuine leather. Lined seat ends. Georgia drop back and box spring cushion; carpet, panels lined, full leather dash, boot, storm apron, seat handles, quick shifting shaft couplers, nickel top prop nuts, rope arm rail and seat rail, wrench, and shafts leather trimmed.

TRACK—4 feet 8 inches or 5 feet 2 inches. Net weight about 290 pounds.

No. 11C160 Price, complete, with double braced shafts..... $37.75
Price, with ¾-inch rubber tires..... 48.50
Price, with ⅞-inch rubber tires..... 49.50

EXTRAS.

Pole in place of shafts..... $1.60 | Both pole and shafts..... $3.75
Weight, crated under 30 inches, about 400 pounds. Shipped from factory.

OUR AMERICAN BEAUTY.

$38.75

DON'T FAIL TO STATE WIDTH OF TRACK

Four-Bow Top if wanted same price.

No. 11C105

BODY—23x54 inches; piano body, swell panels, concave risers, convex seat panels. Hardwood frame and step strips gained into sills. Panels of well seasoned poplar, glued, screwed and plugged. Can furnish 19-inch body.

GEAR—Axles, 1 1/8 inch, long distance dust and mud proof bell collars; axle caps cemented, sanded and clipped. Double reach, thoroughly ironed and braced. 36-inch sweep three and four-plate elliptic oil tempered springs, fastened to body with Bailey body loops.

WHEELS—Sarven's patent, second growth hickory; 7/8-inch screwed rims, with full bolted, oval edge, 1/4-inch steel tires, 38 inches front and 42 inches rear. 40-inch front and 44-inch rear if ordered.

TOP—Three-bow, regular, with deep cut leather quarters, lined and padded leather back stays. All wool head lining and heavy rubber roof. Stays are fancy stitched, with scalloped edges. Rubber back curtain, lined. Heavy side curtains. Four-bow top if desired, or 2 1/2-bow Handy top.

PAINTING—Body, black, handsomely striped, with seat risers decorated. Gear, blood carmine, striped to match. Can furnish Brewster green gear if ordered.

TRIMMINGS—New style back and seat cushion, upholstered in fancy colored Keratol leather over box spring cushion and solid panel spring back. Dark green cloth cushion furnished if ordered. Padded and lined seat ends. Nickel dash rail and top prop nuts. Leather trimmed shafts. Quick shifting shaft couplers, carpet, boot, lined panels, storm apron, wrench, etc.

TRACK—4 feet 8 inches or 5 feet 2 inches. Which do you want?

No. 11C105 Price, with double braced shafts and steel tires.......$38.75
Price, fitted with 3/4-inch rubber tires.......... 49.50
Price, fitted with 7/8-inch rubber tires.......... 50.50
Price, fitted with 1-inch rubber tires.......... 52.00

EXTRAS.

Pole in place of shafts. $1.60 | Genuine leather upholstering.......... $1.50
Both pole and shafts... 3.75 | Full leather top with rubber side curtains 3.15

Weight, crated under 30 inches, 400 pounds. Shipped from factory.

OUR ACME BEAUTY.

$41.50

DON'T FAIL TO STATE WIDTH OF TRACK

Four-Bow Top if wanted same price.

No. 11C110

BODY—Piano style body, 23 inches wide by 54 inches long, bottom measurement; hardwood frame with step strips gained into sills; swell panels of well seasoned poplar; concave seat risers, convex seat panels; body is carefully clamped, glued, screwed and plugged; round corners on body and seat.

GEAR—Drop axles, 1 1/8 inch, long distance spindles fitted with dust and mud proof bell collars, axle caps cemented, sanded and clipped; 36-inch sweep three and four-plate elliptic oil tempered springs, clipped to Bailey body loops; double reach, with full bearing fifth wheel.

WHEELS—Sarven's patent, 38 inches front and 42 inches rear; spokes and rims of second growth hickory; 7/8-inch oval edge steel tires, full bolted on screwed rims. 40-inch front and 44-inch rear if ordered.

TOP—Genuine leather quarter top; three bows, with quarters cut deep; lined and padded leather back stays; heavy rubber roof, with an all wool head lining; lined rubber back curtain, heavy side curtains. Can furnish 4-bow or 2 1/2-bow Handy top if ordered.

PAINTING—Rosewood finished body, striped, and fancy design on seat risers; the gear, blood carmine, neatly striped. Can furnish New York red gear when ordered.

TRIMMINGS—Heavy, dark green body cloth, over a special new design of back, as illustrated; box spring cushion. Seat ends padded and lined; nickel dash rail, top prop nuts; comes complete with quick shifting shaft couplers, carpet, boot, lined body panels, storm apron, wrench and leather trimmed shafts.

TRACK—4 feet 8 inches or 5 feet 2 inches.

No. 11C110 Price, with double braced shafts and steel tires.......$41.50
Price, fitted with 3/4-inch rubber tires.......... 52.25
Price, fitted with 7/8-inch rubber tires.......... 53.25
Price, fitted with 1-inch rubber tires.......... 54.75

EXTRAS.

Pole in place of shafts.. $1.60 | Genuine leather upholstering.......... $1.50
Both pole and shafts.... 3.75 | Full leather top with rubber side curtains, 3.15

Weight, crated under 30 inches, 400 pounds. Shipped from factory.

OUR NEW MODEL BUGGY.

DON'T FAIL TO STATE WIDTH OF TRACK

$42.75

No. 11C206

Four-Bow Top if wanted same price.

BODY—Piano body, 23x54 inches; panels, 8 inches deep; top fitted with oval edge irons; hardwood frame with step strips gained into sills; glued, screwed and plugged; concave risers and convex seat panels.

GEAR—Axles, 1 1/8 inch, fantailed, with dust and mudproof bell collars; long distance spindles; hickory axle caps, cemented, sanded and clipped to axles; double reaches, ironed full length; 36-inch sweep three and four-plate elliptic oil tempered springs, attached to Bailey body loops.

WHEELS—Sarven's patent, made of second growth hickory; 7/8-inch rims, fitted with 1/4-inch oval edge steel tires, full bolted between each spoke; screwed rims; 38 inches front and 42 inches rear. 40-inch front and 42-inch rear if ordered.

TOP—Three-bow, leather quarters and stays; all wool head lining; padded and lined back stays, with scalloped edges; lined back curtain, good heavy side curtains, nickel curtain fasteners, stitched leather valance. Can furnish 4-bow or 2 1/2-bow Handy top if ordered.

PAINTING—Body, plain black; gear, blood carmine, neatly striped. Can furnish New York red or Brewster green gear, if ordered.

TRIMMINGS—Solid panel spring back and box spring cushion, upholstered with imported, all wool, dark green body cloth; padded and lined seat ends, leather dash, Brussels carpet, waterproof storm apron, drill fibre boot, quick shifting shaft couplers, wrench, and shafts trimmed with leather.

TRACK—4 feet 8 inches or 5 feet 2 inches.

No. 11C206 Price, with double braced shafts and steel tires.......$42.75
Price, fitted with 7/8-inch rubber tires.......... 54.50
Price, fitted with 1-inch rubber tires.......... 56.00

EXTRAS.

Pole in place of shafts. $1.60 | Genuine leather upholstering.......... $1.75
Both pole and shafts.. 3.75 | Full leather top with rubber side curtains, 3.15

Weight, crated under 30 inches, 400 pounds. Shipped from factory.

OUR CHICAGO BEAUTY.

DON'T FAIL TO STATE WIDTH OF TRACK

$41.75

Four-Bow Top if wanted same price.

No. 11C216

BODY—Latest style Corning body, 23 inches wide by 54 inches long. Hardwood body and seat frame, with seasoned poplar panels. Piano body if ordered.

GEAR—Axles, 1 1/8 inch, fantailed; long distance spindles, with dust and mud proof bell collars; hickory axle caps, cemented, sanded and clipped; double reaches, ironed full length; three and four-plate, 36-inch sweep, elliptic oil tempered springs, attached to Bailey body loops; drop axles, regular.

WHEELS—Sarven's patent, made of selected second growth hickory; 7/8-inch screwed rims, fitted with oval edge steel tires, full bolted between each spoke; 38 inches front and 42 inches rear. 40-inch front and 44-inch rear if ordered.

TOP—Three-bow, leather quarters and leather back stays; all wool head lining; padded and lined back stays; [illegible]ck curtain lined; good quality of side curtains; nickel curtain fasteners.

PAINTING—Body, black, neatly [illegible]riped and decorated with neat design on seat risers, as shown in illustration; gear, dark Brewster gear green.

TRIMMINGS—Solid panel spring back and box spring cushion, upholstered with imported, all wool, dark green body cloth; padded and lined seat ends; leather dash, Brussels carpet, waterproof storm apron, drill fibre boot, quick shifting shaft couplers, wrench, and shafts trimmed with leather.

TRACK—4 feet 8 inches or 5 feet 2 inches.

No. 11C216 Price, with double braced shafts and steel tires.....$41 75
Price, fitted with 7/8-inch rubber tires.......... 53.50
Price, fitted with 1-inch rubber tires.......... 55.00

EXTRAS.

Pole in place of shafts. $1.60 | Genuine leather upholstering.......... $2.00
Both pole and shafts.. 3.75 | Full leather top with rubber side curtains, 3.15

Weight, crated under 30 inches, about 400 pounds. Shipped from factory.

OUR NEW ACME TOP BUGGY.

DON'T FAIL TO STATE WIDTH OF TRACK

No. 11C207

$43.75

Four-Bow Top if wanted, same price.

BODY—Piano box, 23 inches wide by 54 inches long, inside bottom measurement. The frame of body and seat are of hardwood, with hardwood step strips gained into sills of body; panels are selected seasoned poplar.

GEAR—1⅛-inch fantailed steel axles; long distance spindles, fitted with dust and mudproof bell collars; hickory axle caps, cemented, sanded and clipped to the axles; 36-inch sweep; three and four-plate elliptic oil tempered springs, attached to Bailey body loops; double reach gear.

WHEELS—Sarven's patent, 38 inches front and 42 inches rear; selected second growth hickory spokes and rims; ⅞-inch screwed rims, fitted with ¼-inch oval edge steel tires, full bolted between each spoke.

TOP—Three-bow top, with deep cut genuine leather quarters and back stays; back stays padded and lined. All wool head lining, scalloped edges around skirting of top and edges of back stays. Heavy rubber roof and lined rubber back curtain. Good heavy side curtains; nickel curtain fasteners.

PAINTING—Body, black, nicely striped and decorated, as shown in the illustration; gear, blood carmine, striped with two lines of black.

TRIMMINGS—Heavy imported, all wool, dark green cloth, over fancy solid panel spring back and box spring cushion; genuine leather if wanted, see extras. Padded and lined seat ends, brussels carpet, drill fibre boot, leather dash, storm apron, quick shifting shaft couplers, wrench, and shafts trimmed with leather.

TRACK—4 feet 8 inches or 5 feet 2 inches.

No. 11C207 Complete, with double braced shafts and steel tires......$43.75
Price, fitted with ⅞-inch rubber tires........ 55.50
Price, fitted with 1-inch rubber tires........ 57.00

EXTRAS.

Pole in place of shafts............	$1.60	Full leather top with rubber side curtains..................	$3.15
Both pole and shafts..............	3.75		
Genuine leather upholstering...	2.00		

Weight, crated under 30 inches, 400 pounds. Shipped from factory.

OUR SPECIAL MODEL LIVERY BUGGY.

No. 11C222

$46.75

Three-Bow Top if wanted, same price.

BODY—Piano body, 25x54 inches, extra wide and roomy. Convex panels, concave seat risers. Top of panels fitted with oval edge irons, corners rounded. Can furnish Corning body if ordered. Roomy phaeton seat.

GEAR—Axles, 1 inch, fantailed; bell collars, dust and mudproof; long distance spindles, hickory axle caps, cemented, sanded and clipped to axles; extra heavy clips and shaft shackles. 36-inch sweep three and four-plate oil tempered elliptic springs, clipped to Bailey loops; double reach.

WHEELS—Sarven's patent, made of good second growth hickory; 1-inch rims, with screw on each side of spokes, fitted with $\frac{5}{16}$-inch oval edge steel tires, bolted between each spoke; 38 inches front and 42 inches rear.

TOP—Four-bow, leather quarters, deep cut, leather back stays, padded and lined; leather valance; all wool, heavy quality head lining; extra heavy rubber roof and back curtains, lined; heavy side curtains.

PAINTING—Body, plain black; gear, Brewster gear green.

TRIMMINGS—Seat and back upholstered with extra heavy, all wool, dark green body cloth over solid panel spring back and box spring cushion. Leather if ordered, see extras. Lined and padded seat ends; carpet, lined panels, leather dash, heavy leather strapped boot, Bradley shaft couplers, wrench, storm apron and shafts trimmed with leather.

TRACK—4 feet 8 inches or 5 feet 2 inches.

No. 11C222 Price, with double braced shafts and steel tires........ $46.75
Price, fitted with 1-inch rubber tires........ 60.00

EXTRAS.

Pole in place of shafts.....	$1.90	Full leather top with rubber side curtains....................	$3.15
Both pole and shafts...........	4.25	Genuine leather upholstering	2.00
$1\frac{1}{16}$-inch axles and 1⅛-inch wheels	2.00		

Weight, crated under 30 inches, 425 pounds. Shipped from factory.

OUR TWO IN ONE BUGGY.

No. 11C208

$43.40

The illustration shows rig without top.

BODY—Piano box, 23 inches wide by 54 inches long. Hardwood body and seat frame; step strips of hardwood, gained into sills. Top edge of panels fitted with oval edge irons. Special design seat panels, with heavy moulding, as shown in illustration. Can furnish 19-inch or 23-inch piano or Corning body if ordered.

GEAR—1⅛-inch long distance axles, with dust and mudproof bell collars; axle caps cemented, sanded and clipped. Double reach, ironed full length; 36-inch sweep three and four-plate elliptic oil tempered springs, attached to Bailey body loops. Arched axles, as shown in illustration. Can furnish drop axles if ordered.

WHEELS—Sarven's patent, made of selected second growth hickory, 38 inches front and 42 inches rear; ⅞-inch screwed rims, fitted with oval edge steel tires, full bolted between each spoke.

TOP—Three-bow, leather quarter top, with leather back stays, padded and lined, attached with a full shifting rail, so that it can be easily taken off. Heavy rubber roof and back curtain, lined with an all wool head lining. Good heavy side curtains. Can furnish four-bow top if ordered. By removing the top you will have a runabout as shown in small illustration.

PAINTING—Body and seat risers, jet black; panels of seat painted a rich carmine, which harmonizes with the gear; mouldings on panels of seat painted black, gear painted a blood carmine.

TRIMMINGS—Seat and back upholstered with a heavy, imported all wool, dark green body cloth. Padded and lined seat ends. Box spring cushion, with a three-roll bent panel back. Comes complete with drill fibre boot, quick shifting shaft couplers, leather dash, Brussels carpet, leather trimmed shafts, waterproof storm apron, wrench, etc.

TRACK—4 feet 8 inches or 5 feet 2 inches.

No. 11C208 Price with double braced shafts and steel tires........$43.40
Price, fitted with ⅞-inch rubber tires........ 55.15
Price, fitted with 1-inch rubber tires........ 56.65

EXTRAS.

Same as No. 11C207.

Weight, crated under 30 inches, 400 pounds. Shipped from factory.

THREE-QUARTER TOP BUGGY.

$47.75

DON'T FAIL TO STATE WIDTH OF TRACK

No. 11C312

BODY—Piano body, 19 inches wide and 54 inches long; hardwood frame, seat post and corner posts. Step strips gained into sills. Glued, screwed and plugged. Oval edge irons, concave risers and convex panels. Seat, 23x15 inches bottom measurement.

GEAR—Axles, 1⅛ inch, dust and mudproof bell collar, with long distance spindle. Hickory wood caps, cemented to axles, sanded and clipped. Double reach, ironed full length, with full bearing fifth wheel. Armstrong single leaf elliptic springs, connected to Bailey body loops, with additional longitudinal spring running from front to rear.

WHEELS—Sarven's patent, selected grade, ⅞-inch screwed rims, fitted with ¼-inch oval edge steel tires, full bolted between each spoke, 38 inches front and 42 inches rear. Axle boxes leaded and placed in hub by hydraulic pressure.

TOP—Three-bow, extra quality, leather quarters, cut deep. Leather back stays, padded and lined. Full leather valance, stitched front and rear. Heavy all wool head lining. Lined rubber back curtain, heavy rubber side curtains and roof. Higgins' patent fasteners. Can furnish four-bow top if ordered.

PAINTING—Body, jet black. Gear, Brewster gear green, neatly striped. Will stripe body if ordered. Can furnish New York red or blood carmine.

TRIMMINGS—Seat and back upholstered with heavy quality, imported, all wool, dark green body cloth, over solid panel spring back and box spring cushion. Leather if specified. See extras. Seat panels padded and lined. Full length velvet carpet with lined panels, 13-inch padded leather dash, drill fibre boot, storm apron, dust hood, Bradley shaft couplers, wrench, and shafts trimmed with leather 36 inches back from point.

TRACK—4 feet 8 inches or 5 feet 2 inches.

No. 11C312 Price, with double braced shafts and steel tires...$47.75
Price, fitted with ¾-inch rubber tires........ 58.50
Price, fitted with ⅞-inch rubber tires........ 59.50

EXTRAS.

Pole in place of shafts	$1.90	Genuine leather upholstering....	$1.50
Both pole and shafts...........	4.25	Full leather top with rubber side curtains........	3.50

Weight, crated under 30 inches, 400 pounds. Shipped from factory.

NEW STYLE PHAETONETTE.

DON'T FAIL TO STATE WIDTH OF TRACK

No. 11C213

$47.85

Four-Bow Top if wanted same price.

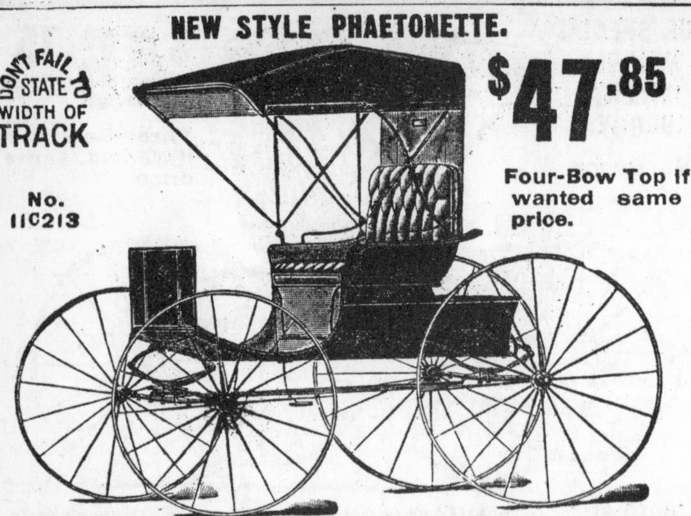

BODY—Bracket front, 25 inches wide by 54 inches long, with steel rocker plates; hardwood frame, with panels glued, screwed and plugged; step strips gained into sills; convex seat panels, concave seat risers; roomy, with plenty of leg room. Roomy phaeton seat.

GEAR—Axles, 15/16 inch, fitted with bell collar, dust and mudproof; long distance spindles, hickory axle beds, cemented to axles, sanded and clipped; 36-inch sweep, three and four-plate elliptic oil tempered springs; Bailey body loops.

WHEELS—Sarven's patent, 7/8-inch screwed rims, fitted with oval edge steel tires, bolted between each spoke; 38 inches front and 42 inches rear. Can furnish 40 inches front and 44 inches rear if ordered. Can furnish compressed band if ordered.

TOP—Three-bow, leather quarters, cut deep, lined and padded leather backstays; rubber roof and lined rubber back curtains, heavy side curtains; nickel curtain fasteners; all wool head lining; can furnish four-bow if ordered.

PAINTING—Body black, with neat design on seat risers. Gear, Brewster gear green, neatly striped. Will furnish New York red or blood carmine gear if ordered.

TRIMMINGS—Seat and back upholstered with heavy grade, all wool, dark green body cloth, over solid panel spring back and box spring cushion. Leather if ordered, **see extras**; 15-inch leather dash with nickel moulding on top edge; seat fenders, boot, storm apron, Bradley shaft couplers, carpet, seat ends padded and lined, wrench, and shafts trimmed with leather.

TRACK—4 feet 8 inches or 5 feet 2 inches.

No. 11C213 Complete, with double braced shafts and steel tires.... **$47.85**
Price, fitted with 7/8-inch rubber tires.... **59.60**
Price, fitted with 1-inch rubber tires.... **61.10**

EXTRAS.

Pole in place of shafts	**$1.90**	Genuine leather upholstering	**$2.00**
Both pole and shafts	**4.25**	Full leather top with rubber side curtains	**3.50**

Weight, crated under 30 inches, 420 pounds. Shipped from factory.

OUR FAVORITE TOP BUGGY.

DON'T FAIL TO STATE WIDTH OF TRACK

Four-Bow Top If wanted same price.

No. 11C314

$48.90

BODY—23x54 inches, piano body, top edge fitted with oval edge irons; concave seat risers; hardwood frame; step strips gained into sills.

GEAR—Axles, 15/16 inch, 1200-mile bell collar, dust and mudproof; long distance spindles; hickory axle caps, cemented, sanded and clipped to axles; double reach, ironed full length and braced; full bearing fifth wheel; three and four-plate, button head, 36-inch sweep, elliptic oil tempered springs; Bailey body loops. Drop axle if desired.

WHEELS—Sarven's patent, screwed rims, 7/8 inch, fitted with oval edge 1/4-inch steel tires; spokes and rims, selected second growth hickory; 38 inches front and 42 inches rear.

TOP—Three-bow, extra quality leather quarters and backstays, with leather valance; rubber back and side curtains and heavy rubber roof; back curtain and stays lined; all wool head lining.

PAINTING—Body, jet black; gear, Brewster gear green, neatly striped. Can furnish black, New York red or blood carmine gear if ordered.

TRIMMINGS—Seat and back upholstered with heavy, all wool dark green body cloth upholstering, over solid panel spring back and box spring cushion. Leather if ordered, see extras. Seat panels lined; full length velvet carpet and lined panels; 13-inch padded leather dash, heavy storm apron, drill fibre boot, Bradley shaft couplers and shafts trimmed with leather 36 inches from tip.

TRACK—4 feet 8 inches or 5 feet 2 inches.

No. 11C314 Price, with double braced shafts and steel tires.... **$48.90**
Price, fitted with 3/4-inch rubber tires.... **$59.65**
Price, fitted with 7/8-inch rubber tires.... **$60.65**
Price, fitted with 1-inch rubber tires.... **$62.15**

EXTRAS.

Pole in place of shafts.... **$1.90**
Both pole and shafts.... **4.25**
Extra quality leather upholstering.... **$1.50**
Full leather top, with rubber side curtains.... **$3.50**

Weight, crated under 30 inches, 400 pounds. Shipped from factory.

OUR STEEL GEAR BEAUTY.

No. 11C2310

$49.90

Four-Bow Top if wanted same price.

BODY—Piano body, 23x54 inches. Hardwood frame, seat posts and corner posts, with step strips gained into sills. Heavily convexed body and seat panels, with rounded corners. Concave seat risers.

GEAR—Naked steel gear—no axle caps—axles swedged top and bottom, high arch. Solid, drop forged perch heels, braces, shaft shackles and fifth wheel riveted and brazed to axle; no clips used. The strongest kind of gear. Bell collar, dust and mudproof; long distance spindles. Three and four-plate, 36-inch sweep, open head, oil tempered springs, connected with Bailey body loops.

WHEELS—Sarven's patent; screwed rims; 36 inches front and 38 inches rear. Low wheel used to offset the high arch of axle, bed set regulation height from ground. 7/8-inch screwed rims, fitted with 1/4-inch oval edge steel tires, full bolted. Can furnish compressed band wood hub if ordered.

TOP—Three-bow, extra quality leather quarters, cut deep; padded and lined leather back stays. Heavy rubber roof; rubber back curtain, lined; rubber side curtains. Higgins' curtain fasteners; leather valance, stitched front and rear. Light colored whipcord head lining, all wool.

PAINTING—Body, jet black, mirror finish. Gear painted regular blood carmine, striped with black.

TRIMMINGS—Seat and cushion upholstered with heavy quality Bedford cord, over solid panel spring back and box spring cushion. 13-inch padded leather dash, full length velvet carpet, seat panels padded and lined, drill fibre boot, storm apron, Bradley shaft couplers, wrench, and shafts trimmed with leather 36 inches from tip. Will furnish dark green body cloth seat and back if ordered.

TRACK—4 feet 6 inches only.

No. 11C2310 Price, with double braced shafts and steel tires... **$49.90**
Price, fitted with 3/4-inch rubber tires.... **$60.65**
Price, fitted with 7/8-inch rubber tires.... **$61.65**

EXTRAS.

Pole in place of shafts.... **$1.90**
Both pole and shafts.... **4.25**
Extra quality leather upholstering.... **$1.70**
Full leather top, with rubber side curtains.... **$3.50**

Weight, crated under 30 inches, 400 pounds. Shipped from factory.

OUR HEAVY CONCORD BUGGY.

Built on End Spring Gear, See below.

No. 11C263

$54.75

BODY—Extra large, 28 inches wide by 58 inches long; panels, 8 1/2 inches deep, hardwood frame with seasoned poplar panels, glued, screwed and plugged. Can furnish Corning style body if ordered.

GEAR—1 1/16-inch axles, fitted with heavy hickory axle caps, cemented, sanded and clipped to axles; dust and mudproof long distance spindles. Full Concord side springs, hung on equalizers and attached to body with hickory spring bar. Three-perch gear, fully ironed. Full bearing fifth wheel.

WHEELS—Sarven's patent, 1 inch, fitted with heavy oval edge steel tires, full bolted between each spoke; 38 inches front and 42 inches rear. Can furnish 40-inch front and 44-inch rear wheels if wanted.

TOP—Four-bow, leather quarters and leather backstays; lined and padded stays, lined back curtain, heavy rubber side curtains, all wool head lining, heavy rubber roof, full corded top. Can furnish three-bow if wanted.

PAINTING—Body, plain black; gear, Brewster gear green. Can furnish gear blood carmine or New York red if ordered. All neatly striped.

TRIMMINGS—Genuine leather, over high, solid panel spring back and spring cushion; leather dash and leather boot; quick shifting shaft couplers, carpet, panels lined, storm apron, wrench, etc. Can furnish cloth upholstering if wanted.

TRACK—4 feet 8 inches or 5 feet 2 inches.

No. 11C263 Complete, with double braced shafts and steel tires... **$54.75**
Price, fitted with 1-inch rubber tires.... **68.00**
No. 11C2635 Same job, only hung on elliptic springs instead of Concord, one in front and one in rear, double reach.... **52.75**

EXTRAS.

Pole in place of shafts	**$1.75**	1 1/8-inch wheels	**$1.90**
Both pole and shafts	**3.75**	Brake	**5.00**
Full leather top, with rubber side curtains			**3.75**

Weight, crated under 30 inches, 475 pounds. Shipped from factory.

ACME ROYAL TOP BUGGY, $57.75

IN THIS BUGGY, THE VERY BEST THAT WE BUILD IN OUR FACTORY, WE HAVE EMBODIED THE LATEST IMPROVEMENTS

AND OFFER YOU HEREWITH AT $57.75, A BUGGY THAT WE WOULD BE GLAD TO COMPARE WITH ANY VEHICLE SOLD THROUGH THE REGULAR CHANNELS OF TRADE FOR $85.00 TO $100.00.

Latest style arched axle, the 1200-mile long distance spindle with bell collar, making it dust and mudproof; has the best grade of Sarven's patent screwed rim wheels, Bailey body loops, 36-inch sweep open head springs, wrought iron fifth wheel, 23x54-inch body; has a high padded grain leather dash, an extra high panel back, No. 1 machine buffed leather quarters in the top, an all wool head lining, Bradley couplers, and the finish that we put on the body and gear cannot be excelled.

Saves $50.00 on Our Acme Royal Top Buggy.

Mountain View, N. J.
Sears, Roebuck & Co., Chicago, Ill.
Dear Sirs:—The No. 11C418 Buggy I bought of you last spring has proven very satisfactory, and I am very much pleased with it. I saved from $35.00 to $50.00 on the buggy by getting it from you. Yours respectfully,
J. M. DEMAREST, Jr.

Bought Five of Our Acme Royal Top Buggies. Saves 50 per cent.

Sprout, Ky.
Sears, Roebuck & Co., Chicago, Ill.
Dear Sirs;—The rigs which I received from you I was more than pleased with. Everyone says they are up to date and well built. I have saved 50 per cent on my purchase from you. The freight is next to nothing on what I saved. I have another order to send in a short time for one of my friends. I will order from you.
Yours truly,
L. N. VICE.

No. 11C418

$57.75

Four-Bow Top if wanted same price.

Detailed Description.

BODY 23x54 inches, piano style; seat, frame and step strips made of the best seasoned hardwood lumber; step strips gained into sills; panels of the best seasoned poplar lumber, fitted with oval edge irons, glued, clamped, screwed and plugged. There is no better buggy body built. If ordered we can furnish Corning style body.

GEAR Axles, 1⅛ inch, fantailed, made of the best refined steel; axle caps, cemented and primed before being clipped to the axles with wrought iron clips; has dust and mudproof bell collars, long distance axles; oil tempered elliptic three and four-plate 36-inch open head springs; reaches of the best hickory, ironed and fitted to axles with wrought iron clips; has the wrought iron full bearing fifth wheel, and Bradley shaft couplers. We can furnish drop axles if ordered.

WHEELS High grade, fully guaranteed Sarven's patent wheels, with second growth hickory spokes and screwed rims, fitted with oval edge steel tires, bolted between each spoke; ⅞-inch tread, 38 inches front and 42 inches rear. Can furnish compressed band wood hub wheels if desired, and can furnish 40 inches front and 44 inches rear, or 42 inches front and 46 inches rear if ordered.

TOP Three-bow leather quarter top with quarters cut deep, in No. 1 machine buffed black enameled leather; back stays are leather, padded and lined; raised valance front and rear, stitched by hand; heavy rubber roof and back curtain, and good rubber side curtains. We use a heavy all wool head lining in this top, and lined side and back curtains; has a bevel edge glass in the back, Peerless patent curtain fasteners on the back stays, and leather covered prop nuts. Can furnish four-bow top if ordered.

PAINTING We use nothing but the best oils and varnishes on this job, painting the body a jet black with mirror finish; gear, Brewster gear green, with glazed carmine striping. It is one of the handsomest finished vehicles on the market, and such work as will only be found on the highest grade work that sells at fancy prices in the best repositories in large cities. We can stripe the body and put a design on the seat risers if ordered. We can also furnish black, New York red or blood carmine gear if ordered, all neatly striped.

TRIMMINGS Seat and back upholstered with 16-ounce heavy all wool dark green body cloth, small biscuit cushion fitted with Staples & Handford's open coil springs, very high panel back fitted with coil springs, tufted in a small diamond pattern overstuffed; seat panels lined and padded. Job is furnished with leather covered seat handles, leather covered prop nuts, leather boot, rubber covered steps, 13-inch padded grain leather dash, double braced shafts, with 36-inch grain leather shaft trimmings and round straps, Bradley shaft couplers, full length velvet carpet, good heavy storm apron, nickel plated axle nuts, wrench, etc.

TRACK Built in either 4 feet 8 inches narrow or 5 feet 2 inches wide track, as ordered.

No. 11C418 Price, complete, fitted with double braced shafts and steel tires $57.75
Price, complete, fitted with ¾-inch rubber tires 68.50
Price, complete, fitted with ⅞-inch rubber tires 69.50
Price, complete, fitted with 1-inch rubber tires 71.00

EXTRAS.

Leather side curtains	$3.50
Machine buffed dark green leather upholstering	2.25
Leather covered bow sockets. Three-bow	2.50
Leather covered bow sockets. Four-bow	3.00
Pole in place of shafts with Bradley couplings	1.90
Both pole and shafts with Bradley couplings	4.25
Full leather top with rubber side curtains	3.50

Weight, crated under 50 inches, 420 pounds. Shipped from factory.

Our Buggy Looks Better Than Others, and $30.00 Saved.

Sears, Roebuck & Co., Chicago, Ill. Monroe, Nebraska.
Dear Sirs:—I have to tell you that the buggy was first class in every way. I have saved $30.00 by ordering from you, and I could not get such material in our town. Buggies purchased at the same time look as though they were five years old. The paint has peeled off in large places, while mine looks as good as new yet. One person said that he did not see how you could build such a buggy and put in so much leather for such a low price. Everybody that has seen your vehicles praises them. You will receive a good many orders from this locality in the future. Yours respectfully, WILLIAM HILL.

LEATHER QUARTER TOP PHAETON.

DON'T FAIL TO STATE WIDTH OF TRACK

No. 11C409

$56.95

BODY—Late design phaeton body, very roomy and comfortable, hardwood frame, seasoned panels, glued, screwed and plugged.

GEAR—Axles, 1⅛ inch, double collar, axle caps cemented and clipped; double hickory reach, ironed full length; three and four-plate oil tempered elliptic springs.

WHEELS—Sarven's patent, ⅞-inch screwed rims, fitted with full ¼-inch thick oval edge steel tires, full bolted; 36 inches front and 44 inches rear regular.

TOP—Three-bow, leather quarter top; heavy rubber roof and rubber back curtain, lined; stitched front and back valance; full corded top; rubber side curtains, patent curtain fasteners; leather back stays, padded and lined. Can furnish canopy, 2½-bow handy or 4-bow regular top if ordered, at same price.

PAINTING—Body panels, black, neatly decorated. Brewster green belt around edge, as illustrated. Gear, Brewster gear green, nicely striped.

TRIMMINGS—Heavy, dark green, all wool body cloth, upholstered over box spring cushion and high, soft panel spring back. Leather if ordered, see extras. Seat panels lined, leather dash, oil burning lamps, fenders, carpet, quick shifting shaft couplers, storm apron, shafts nicely trimmed.

TRACK—4 feet 8 inches or 5 feet 2 inches.

No. 11C409 Price, with double braced shafts and steel tires $56.95
Price, fitted with ¾-inch rubber tires 67.70
Price, fitted with ⅞-inch rubber tires 68.70

EXTRAS.

Pole in place of shafts	$1.75	Full leather top with rubber side curtains	$3.25
Both pole and shafts	3.75		
Genuine leather cushion and back	1.50		

Weight, crated under 30 inches, 475 pounds. Shipped from factory.

OUR FINEST ACME ROYAL PHAETON.

$74.95

No. 11C421

DON'T FAIL TO STATE WIDTH OF TRACK

BODY—Latest style phaeton body, large and roomy, plenty leg room, with deep padded sides and high, easy back. Made of carefully selected material, with hardwood sills and frame. Heavy raised belt and mouldings.

GEAR—Axles, 1⅛ inch, dust and mudproof, long distance; axle caps cemented, sanded and clipped to axles. Double phaeton reach, thoroughly ironed and braced. Four and five-plate elliptic oil tempered springs.

WHEELS—Sarven's patent, with ⅞-inch screwed rims, fitted with full ¼-inch thick oval edge steel tires, 36 inches front and 44 inches rear. Compressed band wood hub wheels if ordered.

TOP—Three-bow, leather quarters and leather back stays. Extra heavy rubber roof and back curtain, lined. Padded and lined back stays, full corded top, leather valance, stitched front and rear.

PAINTING—Body, black panels, with dark Brewster green belt, handsomely decorated and striped with carmine. Gear, Brewster gear green.

TRIMMINGS—Heavy dark green body cloth over high, solid panel spring back and box spring cushion, upholstered deep seat ends. Leather if ordered, see extras. Handsome leather wing dash with hand holds; best velvet carpet, serviceable storm apron, easy, Bradley shaft couplers. Shafts trimmed with leather 36 inches back from tip. Handsome oil burning lamps, square bent fenders, wrench, etc.

TRACK—4 feet 8 inches or 5 feet 2 inches.

No. 11C421 Complete with double braced shafts and steel tires $74.95
Price, fitted with ¾-inch rubber tires 85.70
Price, fitted with ⅞-inch rubber tires 86.70

EXTRAS.

Pole in place of shafts	$1.90	Full leather top with rubber side curtains	$4.00
Both pole and shafts	4.25	Three springs instead of two	2.50
Genuine leather upholstering	2.00		

Weight, crated under 50 inches, 500 pounds. Shipped from factory.

OUR CANOPY TOP PARK WAGON.

$45.95

No. 11C265

BODY—The body is 27 inches wide by 61 inches long. Hardwood frame; with well seasoned panels, screwed, glued and plugged, well ironed and braced, making a light, good appearing body, at the same time strong enough for a general purpose rig. Both seats are removable.

GEAR—1⅛-inch steel axles, fantailed, with double collar, axle beds cemented and clipped to the axles. Double reach, well ironed and braced. Four-leaf front and five-leaf rear elliptic end springs, made from good oil tempered steel, securely clipped to wood spring bar and regular body loops.

WHEELS—Sarven's patent wheels, ⅞-inch rims, fitted with oval edge steel tires. Can furnish 1-inch rim wheels if ordered. Height regular, 38 inches front and 42 inches rear. Can furnish 36 inches front and 40 inches rear or 40 inches front and 44 inches rear if specified. Compressed band wood hub wheels if wanted.

TOP—Very neat design, canopy top, well made, well finished, light and strong; good heavy head lining, with heavy fringe around edge, comes complete with full length side and back curtains.

PAINTING—Body black, neatly striped and ornamented, with fancy design on seat risers. Gear, Brewster gear green, striped to match body. Can furnish blood carmine gear if ordered.

TRIMMINGS—Both seats are upholstered in imitation leather, with full padded drop backs and box spring cushions. Comes with good quality dash; full length side and back curtains, storm apron, and shafts neatly trimmed.

TRACK—4 feet 8 inches or 5 feet 2 inches.

No. 11C265 Price, complete, with shafts $45.95

EXTRAS.

Cloth cushions and backs	$2.50
Genuine leather cushions and backs	5.00
Pole in place of shafts	1.75
Both pole and shafts	3.75

Weight, crated, under 30 inches, about 600 pounds. Shipped from factory.

OUR REGULAR JUMP SEAT BUGGY.

$49.75

No. 11C266

BODY—28 inches wide by 52 inches long, bottom measurement; made throughout of the best selected material. Hardwood frame, with selected seasoned poplar panels, glued, screwed and plugged, well ironed and braced. Both seats are roomy and comfortable, securely fastened with bolts and screws. Front seat folds down flat on bottom of body, back seat moves forward, making it the same as a one-seated buggy.

GEAR—1⅛-inch double collar, with fine steel axles, fantailed. Hickory axle caps, cemented and clipped to axles. Full circle fifth wheel. Double reach ironed full length, bolted and braced with wrought iron stay braces. Four-plate front and five-plate rear elliptic end springs.

WHEELS—Sarven's patent; selected hickory spokes and 1-inch hickory rims, fitted with oval edge steel tires. Height regular, 38 inches front and 42 inches rear. Can furnish 36 inches front and 40 inches rear, also 40 inches front and 44 inches rear, if ordered.

TOP—Four-bow; full sweep; heavy weight full rubber top. Inside of top and back stays lined with dark green cloth. Top is fastened stationary to the rear seat, can be raised and lowered like a regular top buggy. Comes complete with rubber side and back curtains.

PAINTING—Body black, neatly striped; gear, dark Brewster gear green.

TRIMMINGS—Both seats upholstered in imitation leather; regular, but all wool dark green body cloth can be had if ordered, for $1.50 extra. Comes complete with full length carpet, patent leather dash, storm apron, shafts nicely trimmed and well ironed, wrench, anti-rattlers, etc.

TRACK—4 feet 8 inches or 5 feet 2 inches.

No. 11C266 Price, complete, with two elliptic spring gear $49.75
No. 11C267 Price, complete, with Brewster side bar spring gear 50.00
No. 11C268 Price, complete, hung on three elliptic springs 51.25

EXTRAS.

Leather quarter top	$3.65	Pole in place of shafts	$1.75
Full leather top	7.25	Both pole and shafts	3.75
Cloth cushions and backs	1.50	1⅛-inch wheels	1.90
Genuine leather cushions and backs	3.50	Brake	5.00

Weight, crated under 30 inches, 650 pounds. Shipped from factory.

OUR FARMERS' CANOPY TOP SURREY.

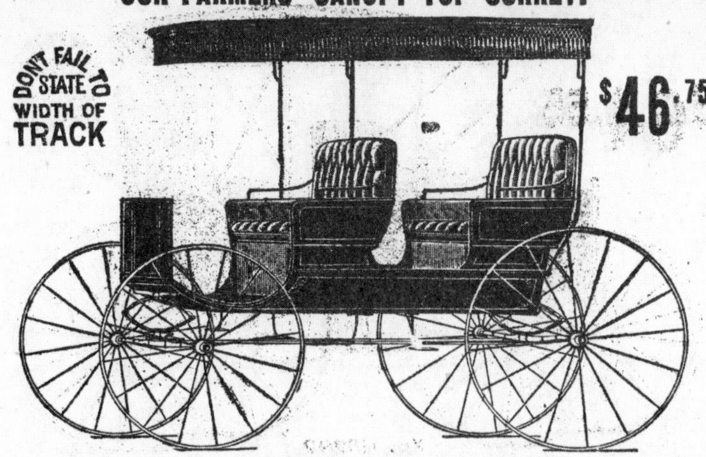
DON'T FAIL TO STATE WIDTH OF TRACK
$46.75

No. 11C080

BODY—5 feet 10 inches long by 26 inches wide, large and roomy, with plenty of space between front and rear seats; ash sills and poplar panels, well seasoned, glued, screwed and plugged; phaeton style seats, rear seat removable.

GEAR—Axles, 1 1/16 inches, double collar, fantailed; heavy axle caps, cemented, sanded and clipped to axles; double reach, well ironed and braced; full bearing fifth wheel; four and five-plate elliptic oil tempered springs, clipped to Bailey body hangers.

WHEELS—Sarven's patent; 1-inch rims, fitted with oval edge steel tires, bolted between each spoke; 38 inches front and 42 inches rear. Can furnish wheels 40 inches front and 44 inches rear if ordered.

TOP—Full size canopy top with good head lining and heavy fringe, attached with four standards, easily removed; full length side and back curtains.

PAINTING—Body black, neatly striped; fancy striping on seat risers, seat panels striped; gear, Brewster gear green, striped to match. Can furnish gear black, New York red or blood carmine if ordered.

TRIMMINGS—Dark green body cloth over solid panel spring backs and spring cushions, full buttoned; padded and lined seat ends; full length carpet, leather dash, full length side and back curtains, wrench, anti-rattlers, storm apron, etc.

TRACK—4 feet 8 inches or 5 feet 2 inches.

No. 11C080 Price, complete, with double braced shafts and steel tires....$46.75

EXTRAS.

Pole in place of shafts....$1.60
Both pole and shafts....3.75
Genuine leather cushions and backs....2.50
Weight, crated under 30 inches, 700 pounds. Shipped from factory.

OUR FARMERS' LEATHER QUARTER EXTENSION TOP SURREY.

DON'T FAIL TO STATE WIDTH OF TRACK
$52.65

No. 11C090

This Leather Quarter, Extension Top Surrey is built on the same lines of proportion, finished, upholstered and trimmed exactly like our No. 11C080, with the exception of the top.

This job has genuine leather quarter top, with leather back stays; good heavy rubber roof and back curtain, lined with a good quality of head lining. Comes complete, with full length side curtains.

No. 11C090 Price, complete, with double braced shafts and steel tires (without fenders)....$52.65

EXTRAS.

Pole in place of shafts....$1.60
Both pole and shafts....3.75
Genuine leather cushions and backs....2.50
Weight, crated under 50 inches, 750 pounds. Shipped from factory.

OUR No. 11C080 IS BETTER THAN DESCRIBED; THIS CUSTOMER SAVED $30.00.

Ty Ty, Ga.

Sears, Roebuck & Co., Chicago, Ill.

Dear Sirs:—I am well pleased with the Surrey No. 11C080 bought of you, and think your work generally surpasses the description given in your catalogue, and is superior to rigs sold in our local market. I am confident I saved from $20.00 to $30.00 on the surrey and harness, and the freight was very reasonable. I am, respectfully yours, W. H. LEWIS.

ORDERS No. 11C090 SURREY, SAVES $30.00.

Chamblee, Ga.

Sears, Roebuck & Co., Chicago, Ill.

Gentlemen:—I am well pleased with my Extension Top Surrey I ordered from you. I saved $30.00 by buying from you, and I expect to give you another order in the spring. Very truly yours, R. A. COUNCIL.

LIGHT PANEL SEAT SURREY.

DON'T FAIL TO STATE WIDTH OF TRACK
$48.55

No. 11C163

BODY—Made of seasoned hardwood, with step strips gained into sills; seasoned poplar panels, glued, screwed and plugged, panel seats 28 inches wide by 16 inches deep; body, 24 inches wide and 66 inches long.

GEAR—Axles, 1 1/16 inches, bell collar, dust and mud proof, with 1200-mile spindle; axles caps selected hickory, sanded and clipped to axles; double reach, ironed full length; full bearing fifth wheel, 36-inch sweep four and five-plate elliptic oil tempered springs, connected with Bailey body hangers.

WHEELS—Sarven's patent, 1-inch screwed rims, fitted with oval edge steel tires, full bolted; 38 inches front and 42 inches rear. Can furnish 40-inch front and 44-inch rear if ordered.

TOP—Neat canopy top, hardwood frame, mortised and screwed; covered with heavy rubber drill, lined with good quality head lining; fringe to match upholstering, with full length side and back curtains.

PAINTING—Body, black, neatly striped; Brewster body green seat panels, nicely shaded belt, very rich effect; gear, blood carmine. Can furnish Brewster gear green if ordered.

TRIMMINGS—Seats and backs upholstered with whipcord over box spring cushions and 8-inch panel backs. Can furnish Keratol leather if ordered, no extra charge. Full length fancy carpet, leather dash, storm apron, shafts trimmed with leather, quick shifting shaft couplers, wrench, etc.

TRACK—4 feet 8 inches, narrow, or 5 feet 2 inches, wide.

No. 11C163 Price, complete, with double braced shafts and steel tires....$48.55
Price, complete, with 1-inch rubber tires....61.80

EXTRAS.

Pole in place of shafts....$1.60
Both pole and shafts....3.75
Genuine leather upholstering....3.15
Weight, crated under 30 inches, 650 pounds. Shipped from factory.

LIGHT STICK SEAT SURREY.

DON'T FAIL TO STATE WIDTH OF TRACK
$49.75

No. 11C164

BODY—Made of seasoned hardwood, with step strips gained into sills; seasoned poplar panels, glued, screwed and plugged, single bend stick seats, 28 inches wide by 16 inches deep; body, 24 inches wide and 66 inches long.

GEAR—Axles, 1 1/16 inches, bell collar, dust and mud proof, with 1200-mile spindle; axles caps selected hickory, sanded and clipped to axles; double reach ironed full length; full bearing fifth wheel; 36-inch sweep four and five-plate elliptic oil tempered springs, connected with Bailey body hangers.

WHEELS—Sarven's patent, 1-inch screwed rims, fitted with oval edge steel tires, full bolted; 38 inches front and 42 inches rear.

TOP—Neat canopy top, hardwood frame, mortised and screwed; covered with heavy rubber drill, lined with good quality head lining; fringe to match upholstering, with full length side and back curtains.

PAINTING—Body, black, neatly striped; Brewster body green seat panels; nicely shaded belt, very rich effect; gear, blood carmine. Can furnish Brewster gear green if ordered.

TRIMMINGS—Seats and backs upholstered with whipcord over box spring cushions and 8-inch panel backs. Full length fancy carpet, leather dash, storm apron, shafts trimmed with leather, quick shifting shaft couplers, wrench, etc.

TRACK—4 feet 8 inches, narrow, or 5 feet 2 inches, wide.

No. 11C164 Price, complete, with double braced shafts and steel tires....$49.75
Price, complete, with 1-inch rubber tires....63.00

EXTRAS.

Pole in place of shafts....$1.60
Both pole and shafts....3.75
Genuine leather upholstering....3.15
Weight, crated under 30 inches, 650 pounds. Shipped from factory.

OUR ACME MODEL SURREY.

$58.55
DON'T FAIL TO STATE WIDTH OF TRACK

No. 11C282

BODY—Our own original design; 72 inches long by 27 inches wide; hardwood frame; seasoned poplar panels; steel rocker plates, full length, on ash sills; round corners on body and seat.

GEAR—Axles, 1 1/16-inch, dust and mudproof long distance spindles; hickory axle caps, cemented, sanded and clipped to axles; double reaches, ironed full length; full bearing fifth wheel, with king bolt in rear of axle; four and five-plate oil tempered elliptic springs, clipped to Bailey body hangers.

WHEELS—Sarven's patent, 16 spokes to the wheel; 1-inch screwed rims, fitted with oval edge steel tires, bolted between each spoke; 38 inches front and 42 inches rear. Can furnish 40 inches front and 44 inches rear if ordered.

TOP—Latest design canopy top; ash frame, mortised and screwed; covered with heavy rubber duck, with good quality head lining; all wool fringe; full length back and side curtains.

PAINTING—Body and seat panels, black; pillars and moulding on seats painted rich dark carmine, making very handsome effect; gear, Brewster gear green, neatly striped with double hairline of carmine. Can furnish black, blood carmine or New York red gear if ordered.

TRIMMINGS—Seats and backs upholstered with heavy, dark green, all wool cloth, over box spring cushions and high phaeton spring backs; double fenders, oil burning lamps, storm apron, full length carpet, leather dash, padded and lined seat ends, quick shifting shaft couplers, leather trimmed shafts, wrench, etc.

TRACK—4 feet 8 inches or 5 feet 2 inches.

No. 11C282 Price, complete, with double braced shafts and steel tires........ **$58.55**

Price, fitted with 1-inch rubber tires........ **71.80**

EXTRAS.

Pole in place of shafts........**$1.60** | Genuine leather upholstering..**$2.50**

Both pole and shafts........ **3.75**

Weight, crated under 30 inches, 700 pounds. Shipped from factory.

OUR ACME MODEL EXTENSION TOP SURREY.

No. 11C292

BODY—72 inches long by 27 inches wide; hardwood frame; seasoned poplar panels; steel rocker plates, full length, on ash sills, round corners on body and seats.

GEAR—Axles, 1 1/16-inch, dust and mudproof long distance axles, fantailed; hickory axle caps, cemented, sanded and clipped to axles; double reaches, ironed full length; full bearing fifth wheel, with king bolt in rear of axle; four and five-plate oil tempered elliptic springs, clipped to Bailey hangers.

WHEELS—Sarven's patent; 16 spokes to the wheel; 1-inch screwed rims, fitted with oval edge steel tires, bolted between each spoke; 38 inches front and 42 inches rear. Can furnish 40 inches front and 44 inches rear if ordered.

TOP—Full sweep extension top, with deep cut leather quarters and leather backstays. Backstays padded and lined. Top furnished with an all wool head lining; front valance stitched; has a heavy rubber roof; rubber back curtain, lined; full length side curtains.

PAINTING—Body and seat panels, black, pillars and moulding on seat painted blood carmine, very neat and attractive. Gear, Brewster gear green, neatly striped. Can furnish black, blood carmine or New York red gear if ordered.

TRIMMINGS—Seats and backs upholstered with heavy, dark green, all wool cloth, over box spring cushions and high phaeton spring backs; double fenders, oil burning lamps, storm apron, full length carpet, leather dash, padded and lined seat ends, quick shifting shaft couplers, shafts leather trimmed, wrench, etc.

TRACK—4 feet 8 inches or 5 feet 2 inches.

No. 11C292 Price, complete, with double braced shafts and steel tires........ **$64.55**

Price, fitted with 1-inch rubber tires........ **77.80**

EXTRAS.

Pole in place of shafts ......**$1.60** | Genuine leather upholstering, **$2.50**

Both pole and shafts........ **3.75**

Weight, crated under 30 inches, 700 pounds. Shipped from factory.

OUR ACME MODEL CUT UNDER SURREY.

$63.55
DON'T FAIL TO STATE WIDTH OF TRACK

No. 11C284

Same as No. 11C282, except the style of body and height of wheels. A cut under style body, with wheels 36 inches front and 44 inches rear.

No. 11C284 Price, complete, with double braced shafts and steel tires........ **$63.55**

Price, fitted with 1-inch rubber tires........ **76.80**

EXTRAS—Same as No. 11C282.

Weight, crated under 50 inches, 700 pounds. Shipped from factory.

OUR ACME MODEL, CUT UNDER, EXTENSION TOP SURREY.

No. 11C294

Same as No. 11C292, except the style of body and height of wheels. A cut under style body, with wheels 36 inches front and 44 inches rear.

No. 11C294 Price, complete, with double braced shafts and steel tires........ **$69.55**

Price, fitted with 1⅛-inch rubber tires........ **82.80**

EXTRAS—Same as No. 11C292.

Weight, crated under 50 inches, 750 pounds. Shipped from factory.

OUR EASY RIDING ROAD CART.

$10.35

No. 11C24

This cart is made of selected material throughout. Sarven's patent, 46-inch wheels, selected second growth hickory spokes, 1-inch rims, fitted with oval edge steel tires. Hardwood lumber used in spring block, seat frame, foot rack, etc. Shafts, selected hickory; 1⅛-inch double collar steel axles, square at shoulders, octagon shape in center, high arch. Long, easy riding springs, hung so as to balance the seat perfectly. Seat, 30 inches wide, fitted with seat rail.

TRACK—4 feet 8 inches or 5 feet 2 inches.

No. 11C24 Price, complete........ **$10.35**

EXTRAS.

Coil springs in place of regular, as shown........ **$1.00**

Tight foot rack in place of slat foot rack........ **.75**

Tight foot rack cannot be furnished when job is fitted with coil springs.

Weight, 150 pounds. Shipped from Chicago Heights, Ill.

OUR PHAETON BODY CART.

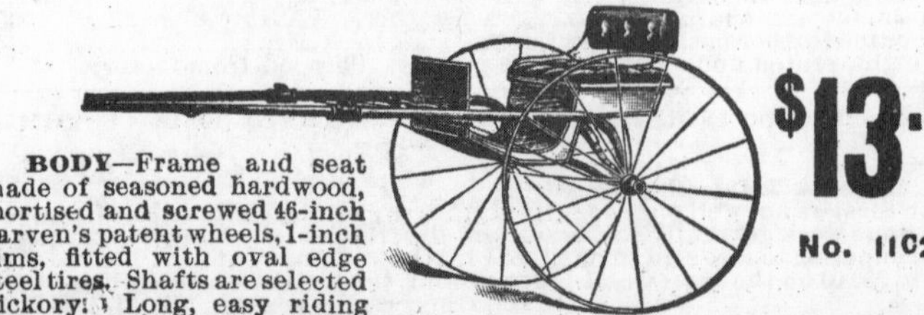

$13.60

No. 11C25

BODY—Frame and seat made of seasoned hardwood, mortised and screwed 46-inch Sarven's patent wheels, 1-inch rims, fitted with oval edge steel tires. Shafts are selected hickory. Long, easy riding springs; 1⅛-inch steel axle square in shoulder, octagon in center, high arch. Wood dash. Imitation leather upholstering, high lazy back. Body painted black; gear, Brewster gear green.

TRACK—4 feet 8 inches or 5 feet 2 inches.

No. 11C25 Price, complete........ **$13.60**

Weight, 180 pounds. Shipped from Chicago Heights, Ill.

OUR ACME ROYAL CANOPY TOP SURREY.

$78.15
DON'T FAIL TO STATE WIDTH OF TRACK

No. 11C482

BODY—73 inches long by 28 inches wide; seasoned ash sills, hardwood corner posts and uprights; sills reinforced with full length steel rocker plates; hardwood skirting back and front of seats. Panel backs are stayed with hardwood strips and corner pieces; body and seat panels are seasoned poplar with rounded corners; seat rods bolted through sills; seat panels, 12 inches deep.

GEAR—Axles, $1\frac{1}{8}$ inch, dust and mudproof bell collars; long distance spindles; axle caps are selected hickory, cemented, sanded and clipped to axles; double reaches, ironed full length; full bearing fifth wheel; four and five-plate, open head, 36-inch sweep springs, oil tempered, connected by Bailey hangers. Very comfortable and easy riding.

WHEELS—Sarven's patent; selected second growth hickory spokes, 1-inch rims, fitted with oval edge steel tires, bolted between each spoke; rims screwed on each side of spokes; 38 inches front and 42 inches rear. Can furnish compressed band wood hubs if wanted. Can furnish wheels 40 inches front and 44 inches rear if wanted.

TOP—Special design canopy top, ash frame, mortised and screwed, covered with heavy rubber duck; heavy quality all wool head lining; all wool cord and tassel fringe; rubber back stays, padded and lined; heavy rubber full length side curtains. Roll up, lined back curtain.

PAINTING—Body panels, jet black, with Brewster body green seat panels, pillars painted a dark carmine, blending nicely with seat and body panels, very rich and handsome effect; gear, a rich Brewster gear green, neatly striped, with double line of glazed carmine. Can furnish gear black, blood carmine or New York red if ordered.

TRIMMINGS—Seats and backs upholstered with all wool 16-ounce dark green body cloth, over soft coil springs in box cushions and solid panel spring backs, 22 inches high. Leather if ordered, see extras. Full length velvet carpet, grain leather double fenders, handsome oil burning lamps, leather covered seat handles, storm apron, Bradley shaft couplers, shafts trimmed with leather 36 inches back from tip, padded leather dash, upholstered seat ends, wrench, etc. Can furnish Bedford cord, with light colored head lining to match, if ordered.

TRACK—4 feet 8 inches or 5 feet 2 inches.

No. 11C482 Price, complete, with double braced shafts and steel tires $78.15
Price, fitted with 1-inch rubber tires 91.40

EXTRAS.

Pole in place of shafts $2.00
Both pole and shafts 4.25
Genuine machine buffed leather upholstering 5.00
Weight, crated under 50 inches, 800 pounds. Shipped from factory.

OUR ACME ROYAL CUT UNDER SURREY.

$84.15
DON'T FAIL TO STATE WIDTH OF TRACK

No. 11C484

This, Our Acme Royal Cut Under Surrey, is built exactly like our No. 11C482, with the exception that it has the cut under style body, with wheels 36 inches front and 44 inches rear, although we can furnish 34 inches front and 42 inches rear if wanted. The description in every particular, with the exception of the style of body and height of wheels, is like our No. 11C482.

No. 11C484 Price, complete, with double braced shafts and steel tires. $84.15
Price, fitted with 1-inch rubber tires 97.40

EXTRAS.

Pole in place of shafts $2.00
Both pole and shafts 4.25
Genuine machine buffed leather upholstering 5.00
Weight, crated under 50 inches, 800 pounds. Shipped from factory.

OUR ACME ROYAL EXTENSION TOP SURREY.

$84.65
DON'T FAIL TO STATE WIDTH OF TRACK

No. 11C492

BODY—73 inches long by 28 inches wide; seasoned ash sills; hardwood corner posts and uprights; sills reinforced with full length steel rocker plates; hardwood skirting back and front of seats; panel backs are stayed with hardwood strips and corner pieces; body and seat panels are seasoned poplar, with rounded corners; seat rods bolted through sills; seat panels, 12 inches deep.

GEAR—Axles, $1\frac{1}{16}$ inch; dust and mudproof bell collars; long distance spindles; axle caps are selected hickory, cemented, sanded and clipped to axles; double reaches, ironed full length; full bearing fifth wheel; four and five-plate, open head, 36-inch sweep springs, oil tempered, connected by Bailey hangers. Very comfortable and easy riding.

WHEELS—Sarven's patent; selected second growth hickory spokes; 1-inch rims, fitted with oval edge steel tires, bolted between each spoke; rims screwed on each side of spokes; 38 inches front and 42 inches rear. Can furnish compressed band wood hubs if wanted. Can furnish wheels 40 inches front and 44 inches rear if wanted.

TOP—Full sweep extension top, black enameled No. 1, machine buffed leather quarters, cut deep; padded and lined leather back stays; heavy leather valance; heavy rubber roof and lined rubber back curtain; all wool heavy head lining; rubber side curtains; patent curtain fasteners; black prop nuts and arm loops, as illustrated.

PAINTING—Body panels, jet black, seat panels, Brewster body green, pillars are finished in a blood carmine, blending nicely with the balance of body. Gear, Brewster gear green, striped with carmine. Can furnish gear black, New York red or blood carmine if ordered.

TRIMMINGS—Seats and backs upholstered with all wool 16-ounce dark green body cloth, over soft coil springs in box cushions and solid panel spring backs, 22 inches high. Leather if ordered, see extras. Full length velvet carpet, grain leather double fenders, handsome oil burning lamps, leather covered seat handles, storm apron, Bradley shaft couplers, shafts trimmed with leather 36 inches back from tip, padded leather dash, upholstered seat ends, wrench, etc. Can furnish Bedford cord, with light colored head lining, if ordered.

TRACK—4 feet 8 inches or 5 feet 2 inches.

No. 11C492 Price, complete, with double braced shafts and steel tires $84.65
Price, fitted with 1-inch rubber tires 97.90

EXTRAS.

Pole in place of shafts $2.00
Both pole and shafts 4.25
Genuine machine buffed dark green leather upholstering 5.00
Weight, crated under 50 inches, 800 pounds. Shipped from factory.

OUR BEST EXTENSION TOP CUT UNDER SURREY.

$90.65
DON'T FAIL TO STATE WIDTH OF TRACK

No. 11C494

This, Our Best Extension Top, Cut Under Surrey, is a companion to our No. 11C492, with the exception that it is built with the cut under style body instead of the straight sill body, and it has wheels 36 inches front and 44 inches rear, although we can furnish 34 inches front and 42 inches rear if ordered.

No. 11C494 Price, complete, with double braced shafts and steel tires .... $ 90.65
Price, fitted with 1-inch rubber tires 103.90

EXTRAS.

Pole in place of shafts $2.00
Both pole and shafts 4.25
Genuine machine buffed dark green leather upholstering 5.00
Weight, crated under 50 inches, 800 pounds. Shipped from factory.

OUR CUSTOMER SAYS No. 11C494 IS BETTER THAN A SURREY OWNED BY HIS NEIGHBOR WHICH COST $40.00 MORE.

Sears, Roebuck & Co., Chicago, Ill. Hyndman, Pa.

Gentlemen:—The Surrey, No. 11C494 I bought of you is very handsome in appearance and very substantially built. Painting is well and artistically done. The upholstering is good. The wheels and axles are just what I wanted (strong). The seats are roomy and comfortable. My family is much pleased. I would not exchange it for a vehicle a neighbor says he paid $40.00 more for.

Yours truly, JAMES M. KENNELL.

THREE-SPRING CABRIOLET.

$95.00
DON'T FAIL TO STATE WIDTH OF TRACK

No. 11C497

BODY—Made of the best seasoned hardwood, frame strongly braced 28 inches wide by 72 inches long; step strips gained into sills; steel rocker plates running full length on sills and over the cut under part, adding extra strength; seasoned poplar panels, glued, clamped, screwed and plugged.

GEAR—Axles, $1\frac{1}{16}$ inches; bell collar, long distance spindles, dust and mud proof; axle caps are selected hickory, cemented, sanded and clipped to axles; strong single reach, ironed full length and braced with wrought iron stays; full bearing fifth wheel; open head 36-inch oil tempered elliptic springs, one in front and two in rear, four-plate; body hung on Bailey hangers.

WHEELS—Sarven's patent; selected second growth hickory spokes, 1-inch screwed rims, fitted with oval edge steel tires, full bolted between each spoke, 36 inches front and 44 inches rear.

TOP—Full surrey extension top; black enameled No. 1, machine buffed; leather quarters, padded and lined, leather back stays; heavy leather valance, stitched front and rear; extra heavy quality rubber roof, lined rubber back curtain, full length rubber side curtains, patent fasteners.

PAINTING—Body painted handsomely with a blending of black body panels and rich Brewster body green seat panels; pillars neatly painted with blood carmine. Gear finished in Brewster gear green.

TRIMMINGS—Seats and backs upholstered with 16-ounce all wool dark green body cloth; solid panel spring backs and box spring cushions. Leather if ordered, see extras. Grain leather double fenders, large oil burning lamps, full length velvet carpet, storm apron, Bradley shaft couplers, padded leather dash, shafts trimmed with leather 30 inches back from tip, leather covered seat handles, wrench.

TRACK—4 feet 8 inches or 5 feet 2 inches.

No. 11C497 Price, complete, with double braced shafts and steel tires	$95.00
Price, fitted with 1-inch rubber tires	108.25
Price, fitted with canopy top and steel tires	89.00
Price, fitted with canopy top and rubber tires	102.25

EXTRAS.

Pole in place of shafts	$2.00
Both pole and shafts	4.25
Genuine No. 1 machine buffed dark green leather upholstering	5.00

Weight, crated under 50 inches, 850 pounds. Shipped from factory.

LIGHT HANDY WAGON.

No. 11C078

BODY—29 inches wide by 76 inches long; made of carefully selected material, with a hardwood frame and seasoned panels; two seats; very handsome design, as shown in illustration. Seats removable.

GEAR—$1\frac{1}{16}$-inch rear axle, $\frac{15}{16}$-inch front axle, both fitted with double collar; selected hickory axle caps; single reach; four-plate springs in front, two three-plate springs in rear, connected to the body with our special body hanger, which is far superior to anything of its kind on the market; no wood crossbars to break.

WHEELS—Selected grade of Sarven's patent wheels, 38 inches front and 42 inches rear; 1-inch rims, fitted with oval edge steel tires, bolted between each spoke. Can furnish wheels 40 inches front and 44 inches rear when wanted.

PAINTING—We make a very attractive wagon of this job, by painting the moulding on the body a jet black, very neat shade of brown panels in between. The spindles in the seat risers are painted to harmonize with the panels of the body. Seats are painted black. Gear painted New York red, nicely striped, making a very attractive but not a flashy job.

TRIMMINGS—Seat upholstered in imitation leather, over a box spring cushion and panel back, as shown in illustration. Job comes complete; two seats, dash, double braced shafts, wrench, etc.

TRACK—4 feet 8 inches, narrow, or 5 feet 2 inches, wide.

No. 11C078 Price, complete with double braced shafts	$29.55

EXTRAS.

Pole in place of shafts	$1.60
Both pole and shafts	3.75

Weight, crated under 30 inches, 600 pounds. Shipped from factory.

LIGHT PLEASURE WAGON.

No. 11C079

BODY—76 inches long by 29 inches wide; made of carefully selected material, with a hardwood frame and seasoned panels; two seats; very handsome design, as shown in illustration. Seats removable.

GEAR—$1\frac{1}{16}$-inch rear axle, $\frac{15}{16}$-inch front axle, both fitted with double collar; selected hickory axle caps; single reach; four-plate spring in front, two three-plate springs in rear; connected to the body with our special body hanger, which is far superior to anything of its kind on the market; no wood crossbars to break.

WHEELS—Selected grade of Sarven's patent wheels, 38 inches front and 42 inches rear; 1-inch rims, fitted with oval edge steel tires, bolted between each spoke. Can furnish wheels 40 inches front and 44 inches rear when wanted.

TOP—Very neat and strong canopy top, as shown in illustration, well made of selected material throughout; curtains, sides and rear, roll up and fasten at the top, as shown in illustration. Good head lining in the top, no fringe. Top is held in position by four steel standards, which hold it very rigid.

PAINTING—We make a very attractive wagon of this job, by painting the moulding on the body a jet black, dark brown panels in between. The spindles in the seat risers are painted to harmonize with the panel of the body. Seats are painted black. Gear painted New York red, nicely striped, making a very attractive job.

TRIMMINGS—Seat upholstered in imitation leather, over a box spring cushion and panel back, as shown in illustration. Job comes complete with canopy top, two seats, dash, double braced shafts, wrench, etc.

TRACK—4 feet 8 inches, narrow, or 5 feet 2 inches, wide.

No. 11C079 Price, complete with double braced shafts	$38.90

EXTRAS.

Pole in place of shafts	$1.60
Both pole and shafts	3.75

Weight, crated under 30 inches, 625 pounds. Shipped from factory.

HALF PLATFORM DELIVERY WAGON.

WITH FLARING SIDEBOARDS.

No. 11C1003

BODY—7 feet long, 34 inches wide; hardwood frame, seasoned 8-inch panel, reinforced at corners with outside corner irons; edge irons on top of side panels with flaring sideboards; drop endgate with patent fasteners; removable seat.

GEAR—Front axle, $1\frac{1}{16}$ inches, double collar; hickory axle bed, sanded and clipped; $1\frac{1}{8}$-inch rear axle, coached; four-plate elliptic spring in front, $1\frac{3}{8}$-inch platform spring in rear, four-plate sides and five-plate ends; heavy double reach, ironed and braced; capacity, 1,000 pounds. Can furnish three-spring gear if ordered.

WHEELS—Sarven's patent; 1-inch riveted rims with full bolted oval edge tires; 40 inches front and 44 inches rear, 38 inches front and 42 inches rear if ordered.

PAINTING—Body black, neatly decorated and striped; gear, blood carmine, striped. Can furnish canary yellow or dark Brewster green if ordered.

TRIMMINGS—Seats and backs upholstered with imitation leather cushion and back, box spring cushion, double roll lazy back, 12-inch leather dash, wrench, etc.

TRACK—4 feet 8 inches or 5 feet 2 inches.

No. 11C1003 Price, complete, with shafts and low seat	$38.50
Price, with high seat, as shown in small illustration	39.00

EXTRAS.

Foot Brake	$4.50
Pole in place of shafts	1.60
Both pole and shafts	3.75
Heavier $1\frac{1}{8}$-inch wheels	1.90
$1\frac{1}{4}$-inch axles, wheels with $\frac{3}{8}$-inch tires and heavier springs, making 1,800 pounds capacity	8.75

Weight, crated under 30 inches, 750 pounds. Shipped from factory.

HALF PLATFORM SPRING WAGON.

$39.75

No. 11C1015

BODY—34 inches wide by 7 feet long. Hardwood sills, well seasoned; panels, 8 inches deep, reinforced corners with outside corner irons. Edge iron on top of side panels. Drop endgate with patent fasteners. Bottom boards are crossed, adding strength to the body. Seats removable.

GEAR—Front axle, $1\frac{1}{16}$ inches, double collar with axle beds sanded and clipped, 1⅛-inch rear axle. Four-plate oil tempered elliptic spring in front. 1⅜-inch platform springs in rear, four-plate sides, five-plate ends. Heavy double reach, ironed and braced. Capacity, 1,000 pounds. Can furnish three-spring gear if wanted.

WHEELS—Sarven's patent selected hickory wheels, 1-inch riveted rims fitted with oval edge tires, 40 inches front and 44 inches rear. Can furnish 38 inches front and 42 inches rear if ordered.

PAINTING—Body black, neatly decorated and striped. Gear, Brewster gear green, nicely striped. Can furnish blood carmine or New York red gear if ordered.

TRIMMINGS—Seats and backs upholstered with imitation leather over solid panel backs and box spring cushions, 12-inch leather dash, wrench, etc.

TRACK—4 feet 8 inches or 5 feet 2 inches.

No. 11C1015 Price, complete with shafts........ **$39.75**

EXTRAS.

Canopy top with full length side and back curtains	$8.50
Foot Brake	4.50
Pole in place of shafts	1.60
Both pole and shafts	3.75
1⅛-inch wheels	1.90
Genuine leather cushions and backs	3.90
1¼-inch axles and wheels, with heavier springs	8.75

Weight, crated under 30 inches, 725 pounds. Shipped from factory.

CANOPY TOP THREE-SPRING WAGON.

$48.25

No. 11C1017

BODY—7 feet long by 34 inches wide; hardwood sills, well seasoned and braced; panels, 8 inches deep, reinforced at corner with outside corner irons; edge iron around top of side panels; drop endgate with patent fasteners; cross bottom boards; seats removable.

GEAR—Front axle, $1\frac{1}{16}$ inches, double collar with axle beds sanded and clipped; 1⅛-inch rear axle coached; four-plate elliptic oil tempered springs, one in front, two in rear; 1⅜-inch leaf; double reach, ironed and braced. Capacity, about 900 pounds. Full length body loops. Can furnish half-platform spring if ordered.

WHEELS—Sarven's patent; 1-inch riveted rims, fitted with oval edge steel tires, full bolted; 40 inches front and 44 inches rear. Can furnish 38 inches front and 42 inches rear if ordered.

TOP—Latest style wagon canopy top, ash frame, well made, covered with heavy rubber drill and lined with dark green head lining and heavy fringe; four steel standards connected to body so seats can be removed easily; full length side and back curtains.

PAINTING—Body black, neatly decorated and striped. Gear, Brewster gear green, striped to match. Can furnish New York red or blood carmine gear if ordered.

TRIMMINGS—Seats and backs upholstered with imitation leather over solid panel backs and box spring cushions; 12-inch leather dash, wrench, etc.

TRACK—4 feet 8 inches or 5 feet 2 inches.

No. 11C1017 Price, complete with shafts........ **$48.25**

EXTRAS.

Genuine leather cushions and backs	$3.90
Foot Brake	4.50
Pole in place of shafts	1.60
Both pole and shafts	3.75
1⅛-inch wheels	1.90

Weight, crated under 30 inches, 800 pounds. Shipped from factory.

OUR $58.90 IDEAL MILK WAGON.

$58.90

No. 11C1035

BODY—Body is 7 feet long by 34 inches wide, made of the best seasoned material; complete knocked down body, put together with twelve iron rods; stands only 27 inches from the ground and will turn around in a circle of 12 feet. The front panel of wagon is fitted with a swinging glass transom, 22x30 inches, the lower part being solid wood; the upper part of the front panels are fitted with glass; glass panel roller sliding doors with solid rear side and end wood panels, with a sliding window in the back, and is fitted with a portable seat with a hinge lazy back, trimmed in imitation leather.

GEAR—Axles are made of the best steel, size, 1 inch; fitted with long distance spindles; wrought fifth wheel; very strong gear, with one elliptic spring in front and two in rear, as shown in illustration. Can furnish 1⅛-inch axles and heavier gear. See list of extras.

WHEELS—Sarven's patent; 40 inches front and 44 inches rear; 1-inch tread; with screwed rims, fitted with oval edge steel tires, full bolted.

PAINTING—Body green, handsomely striped in colors; gear, standard colors to harmonize with body.

TRACK—4 feet 8 inches or 5 feet 2 inches.

No. 11C1035 Capacity, 800 pounds. Price, complete with shafts. **$58.90**

EXTRAS.

1⅛-inch axles and heavier gear throughout	$3.25	Both pole and shafts	$4.50
Pole in place of shafts	2.00	Brake	4.50
		Shaded block letters, each	.06

Weight, crated for shipment, about 750 pounds. Shipped from factory in Southern Michigan.

OUR LONG BODIED DELIVERY WAGON.

This wagon is constructed especially for rough and heavy hauling, and can be furnished with top, as shown in illustration, or without a top at prices quoted below.

$41.25 AND $58.95

No. 11C1039

BODY—The body is 9 feet long by 3 feet 2 inches wide, heavily ironed and braced, with drop endgate and furnished with seat as shown in illustration, when ordered with a top. When ordered without a top we build the seat higher, similar to small illustration under catalogue No. 11C1003.

GEAR—Double gear; axles, 1⅛ inches; 15-inch short turn full malleable circle; fitted with 38-inch duplex springs, strongly ironed, bolted and clipped. Wheels, 36 inches front and 40 inches rear, with 1¼ by $\frac{5}{16}$-inch steel tires. Riveted rims.

TRIMMINGS—The seat is furnished with a good imitation leather cushion.

PAINTING—The body is painted blue green, striped in colors, as shown in illustration. Gear, dark wine, striped with black.

TOP—The top is portable, very strongly constructed with white ash bows, standards, and sides, poplar slats on the roof, oil finished, covered with a heavy rubber duck, colored back.

Comes complete with shafts. Capacity, 1,500 pounds. Either 4 feet 8 inches narrow or 5 feet 2 inches wide track.

No. 11C1039 Price, as illustrated, with top........ **$58.95**
No. 11C1041 Price, without top........ **41.25**

EXTRAS.

Pole in place of shafts	$2.00
Both pole and shafts	4.50
1¼-inch axles, wheels and heavier springs, making 2,000 pounds capacity	3.25
Hand ratchet brake	4.50

Shipping weight, about 800 pounds with top, crated under 50 inches. Shipped from factory in Southern Michigan.

HIGH GRADE "FAMOUS" WAGONS.

WITHOUT EXCEPTION THE HIGHEST GRADE, EASIEST RUNNING, STRONGEST AND BEST FINISHED WAGONS ON THE MARKET.

THE LINE OF FAMOUS WAGONS that we have been selling in large numbers in every state in the Union are undoubtedly the strongest, easiest running and nicest appearing wagons on the market. They are manufactured from the very best thoroughly seasoned material, every piece of wood is air seasoned for not less than three years before being shaped for use, and every piece of wood before being put into the wagon is thoroughly saturated in boiling linseed oil, which protects it against climatic effects. **THE HUBS** of this line of Famous Wagons are made from the very best black birch and will never check. **THE SPOKES** are strictly second growth white oak. **THE RIMS** are bent and clipped at the joints. **THE GEAR** throughout is made of the toughest material, the box has poplar sides, with yellow pine flooring, in fact, the wagon throughout is one of the best made wagons on the market, guaranteed to outwear any two of the ordinary makes of wagons. **THE SKEINS** that we use on these wagons have a sand box that makes it absolutely sand and dust proof, the same principle as a **long distance axle** on a buggy, which alone makes our wagon far superior to others. The regular skein used by most wagon manufacturers admits the dust and sand, thus cutting out the grease, making the wagon pull hard and wearing out the skein. We have over a **dozen different improvements** on this wagon that cannot be found on any other make. **THE FRONT BOLSTER** is locked to the sand board with our patent bolster plate. The front axle, sand board, hind axle and bolster are **iron plated,** preventing the reach from wearing them. **THE REACH** has an iron ferrule in king bolt hole and chilled rub iron; reach has **two steel strips** on the bottom, running its entire length, so that it is almost impossible to wear it out. It is also fitted with two rollers on the under side, so that it will not wear the hound, has a special anti-rattler reach plate and bolt, by the means of which the reach can be extended its entire length. On the box we put a concave **cut-under rub iron** 12 inches long, so that the front wheel in turning will not wear out the box. **THE BOX** has a **self-centering** box rod nut. The sideboards have grooved **hardwood cleats,** has a **patent lever** on both sides of the box for holding the top and bottom box together, **Comstock patent endgate.** The doubletrees furnished with the wagon have our special patent **malleable evener center,** which strengthens the evener, giving it twice the life of the ordinary evener. We furnish the **best pole** that is put out by any wagon manufacturer, it is **ironed** thoroughly 34 inches on the top back from the point and **full length** on the bottom, and is furnished with the **strongest and best neckyoke** made, with a patent malleable center, and is **ironed on top** so that it cannot be gnawed by horses. Every wagon is furnished with our **celebrated truss rod axles,** ironed and braced, so that it makes it the next thing to impossible to break them under any strain; no such thing with our **special truss rod axle** construction as the skein coming off, it is impossible for the skein to come off the axle, our gears are thoroughly ironed and braced. We have **overcome every weak point.** This line of **Famous Wagons** is built by one of the **oldest and most reliable** manufacturers of farm wagons in the United States, who has an experience of building farm wagons covering a period of twenty-five years. We paint these wagons in the **best possible manner,** there is not a wagon goes out of any factory that has a finish equal to that put on our **Famous Wagons.** The body and seat are painted **green,** gear and wheels a **rich red,** striped with black. We put the word **"Famous"** on each side of the box, but our name does not appear anywhere on the wagon.

FREIGHT CHARGES. **The freight will amount to very little as compared with the amount we can save you if you order a wagon from us.** We will be pleased to advise you upon application just what the freight charges would be on any size wagon you may select.

OUR BINDING GUARANTEE. **Every piece and part entering into the construction of these wagons** is covered by our binding guarantee to be free from defect in material or workmanship.

IN ORDERING, be sure and state the **size** of skein desired, whether **wide or narrow track, size of tire** and whether **drop or stiff tongue.**

WE MANUFACTURE **a large variety of wagons, ship them to every state in the Union,** and are therefore in a position to furnish you anything that you may desire in the farm wagon line, and if there is anything not understood in this catalogue description, or if there is anything you may desire that is not shown here, it would pay you to write us, for we can save you from 25 to 40 per cent on the purchase price of anything in the wagon line.

Be sure and state whether you desire wide or narrow track.

Prices quoted include drop tongue or stiff tongue with neckyoke and doubletrees and are for the wagons free on board cars at our factory in Michigan.

STANDARD WAGON,
WITH COMSTOCK PATENT ENDGATE.

No. 11C1203

We furnish this combination Cotton Frame and Seed Box on our No. 11C1203 Wagon, if wanted at an extra charge of $5.00.

Wagon boxes are 38 inches wide on narrow track wagons and 42 inches wide on wide track wagons, but we furnish some wide track wagons with 38-inch boxes, when ordered.

Size of Skein No. 11C1203	Capacity	Size Regular Tire	Dimensions of Boxes: Lgth	Depth of Sides: Bottom	Depth of Sides: Top	Weight of Complete Wagon	Price of Gear With Pole, Whiffletrees and Neckyoke. No Brake: Cast Skein	Steel Skein	Price of Wagon, Complete, Double Box and Seat. No Brake: Cast Skein	Steel Skein	Add extra for Gear Brake	Add extra for 2-inch Tires	Add extra for 3-inch Tires
In.	Lbs.	In.	ft. in.	In.	In.	Lbs.							
2½ x 8	2000	1⅜ x ⅜	10 0	10	6	795	$30.25	$31.90	$36.90	$38.80	$3.00	$1.05	$3.20
2¾ x 8	2500	1½ x ½	10 0	12	8	875	31.90	33.60	38.15	40.10	3.50	1.35	4.00
3 x 9	3000	1½ x 9/16	10 6	13	9	1015	33.50	35.45	39.90	42.15	4.25	1.40	4.25
3¼ x 10	4000	1½ x ⅝	10 6	14	10	1080	34.75	37.25	41.75	44.20	4.50	1.60	4.80
3½ x 11	5000	1½ x ¾	10 6	16	12	1220	36.85	39.70	44.90	47.85	5.00	1.85	5.60

Regular height of wheels are 3 feet 8 inches front and 4 feet 4 inches rear, but will furnish 3 feet 4 inches front and 3 feet 8 inches rear, if ordered.

STANDARD WAGON,
WITH BOOT END BOX.

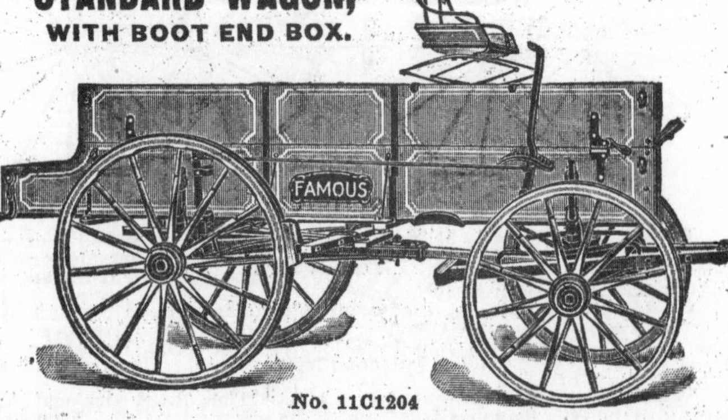

No. 11C1204

Size of Skein No. 11C1204	Capacity	Size Regular Tire	Dimensions of Boxes: Lgth	Depth of Sides: Bottom	Depth of Sides: Top	Weight of Complete Wagon	Price of Gear With Pole, Whiffletrees and Neckyoke. No Brake: Cast Skein	Steel Skein	Price of Wagon, Complete, Double Box and Seat. No Brake: Cast Skein	Steel Skein	Add extra for Gear Brake	Add extra for 2-inch Tires	Add extra for 3-inch Tires
In.	Lbs.	In.	ft. in.	In.	In.	Lbs.							
2½ x 8	2000	1⅜ x ⅜	10 0	10	6	795	$30.25	$31.90	$40.50	$42.25	$3.00	$1.05	$3.20
2¾ x 8	2500	1½ x ½	10 0	12	8	875	31.90	33.60	42.50	44.25	3.50	1.35	4.00
3 x 9	3000	1½ x 9/16	10 6	13	9	1015	33.50	35.45	43.95	46.00	4.25	1.40	4.25
3¼ x 10	4000	1½ x ⅝	10 6	14	10	1080	34.75	37.25	45.50	47.90	4.50	1.60	4.80
3½ x 11	5000	1½ x ¾	10 6	16	12	1220	36.85	39.70	48.25	51.00	5.00	1.85	5.60

Regular height of wheels are 3 feet 8 inches front and 4 feet 4 inches rear, but will furnish 3 feet 4 inches front and 3 feet 8 inches rear, if ordered.

OUR TEXAS AND SOUTH-WESTERN WAGON.

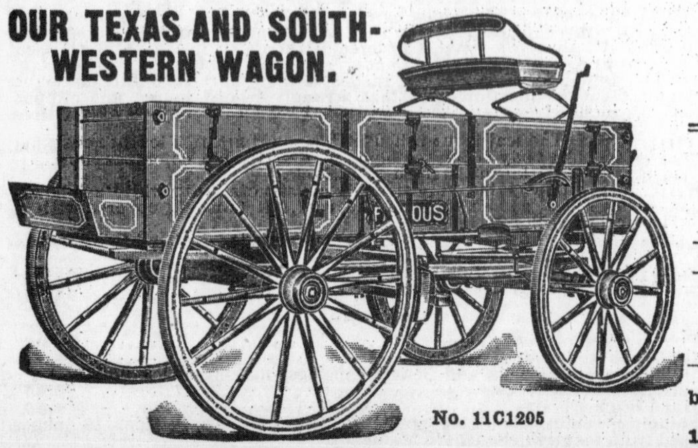

No. 11C1205

Size of Steel Skein No. 11C1205	Capacity	Size Regular Tire	Dimensions of Boxes: Lgth.	Depth of Sides: Bottom	Depth of Sides: Top	Weight of Complete Wagon	Price of Gear, With Pole, Whiffletrees and Neckyoke. No Brake	Price of Wagon, Complete, Double Box and Seat, Feed Box, Bow Staples. No Brake	Add extra for Clipped Gear Brake	Add extra for 2-inch Tires	Add extra for 3-inch Tires
In.	Lbs.	In.	ft. in.	In.	In.	Lbs.					
2½ x 8	2000	1½ x ½	10 0	12	6	900	$35.45	$44.75	$3.75	$1.05	$3.20
2¾ x 8	2500	1½ x 9/16	10 0	13	9	1000	37.60	46.80	4.25	1.35	4.00
3 x 9	3000	1½ x ⅝	10 6	14	10	1100	39.00	49.00	5.00	1.40	4.25
3¼ x 10	4000	1½ x ⅝	10 6	14	12	1200	41.25	50.50	5.00	1.60	4.80
3½ x 11	5000	1⅝ x ¾	10 6	16	12	1300	44.00	53.90	5.75	1.85	5.60

Regular height of wheels are 3 feet 8 inches front and 4 feet 4 inches rear, but will furnish 3 feet 4 inches front and 3 feet 8 inches rear, if ordered.

Tip top or 3rd boxes can be furnished on any wagon from 6 inches high to 10 inches high for $2.00 extra.

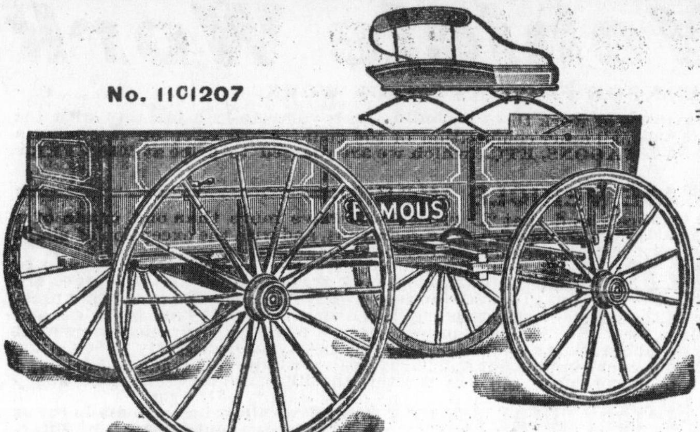

CAST SKEIN ONE-HORSE WAGON.

No. 11C1207

Cast Skein	Capacity	Steel Tire	Dimensions of Boxes: Length		Width		Bottom Sides	Top Sides	Weight of Complete Wagon	Price of Gear With Shafts Only	Price With Shafts, Double Box and Seat, Shafts Only	Add extra for Box Brake	Add extra for Gear Brake	Add extra for 2-inch Tires	Add extra for Pole in Place of Shafts
Sizes	Lbs.	Sizes	ft.	in.	ft.	in.	In.	In.	Lbs.						
2¼	1500	1¼x5/16	9	0	3	2	9	6	480	**$21.95**	**$28.35**	**$3.00**	**$3.75**	**$1.75**	**$2.50**
2½	2000	1⅜x⅜	10	0	3	2	10	6	800	**28.40**	**34.15**	**3.00**	**3.75**	**1.75**	**2.50**

WE FURNISH THIS WAGON WITH SOLID STEEL AXLES AND SARVEN'S PATENT WHEELS, IF WANTED, AT SAME PRICE.

Steel Axles are 1¼x7½ and 1⅜x8 inches, capacity of wagon the same.

Wheels on these wagons are 3 feet 6 inches front, and 4 feet rear.

LOW WHEEL FARM TRUCK.

No. 11C1208

Cast Skein	Capacity	Tire	Height of Wheels: Front		Hind		Approximate Weight	Price Without Whiffletrees, Neckyoke or Pole Spring	Add Extra for Whiffletrees and Neckyoke	Add Extra for Pole Spring
Size	Lbs.	Size	Ft.	In.	Ft.	In.	Lbs.			
3 x 9	3000	3 x⅜	3	4	3	8	650	**$29.95**	**$1.75**	**$0.90**
3 x 9	3000	3½x5/16	3	4	3	8	700	**31.25**	**1.75**	**.90**
3 x 9	3000	4 x5/16	3	4	3	8	750	**32.75**	**1.75**	**.90**
3¼x10	3000	3 x⅜	3	4	3	8	700	**30.85**	**1.75**	**.90**
3¼x10	3000	3½x5/16	3	4	3	8	750	**32.25**	**1.75**	**.90**
3¼x10	3000	4 x5/16	3	4	3	8	800	**34.05**	**1.75**	**.90**

METAL WHEEL HANDY FARM TRUCK.

No. 11C1217	Capacity	Front Wheels: Height	Front Wheels: No. of Spokes	Rear Wheels: Height	Rear Wheels: No. of Spokes	Size of Tire, inches	Weight	Price
For Farm Work	4000 pounds	28 in.	10	30 in.	10	4x⅜	590 lbs.	**$17.80**
	4000 pounds	28 in.	10	34 in.	14	4x⅜	625 lbs.	**18.85**
	4000 pounds	30 in.	10	34 in.	14	4x⅜	650 lbs.	**19.70**
For Road Use	5000 pounds	28 in.	12	30 in.	12	4x½	625 lbs.	**20.85**
	5000 pounds	28 in.	12	34 in.	14	4x½	640 lbs.	**22.05**
	5000 pounds	30 in.	12	34 in.	14	4x½	665 lbs.	**23.20**

EXTRAS:
- For neckyoke, double and singletrees................ **$1.60**
- For extra high bolsters, front wheels to turn under load................ **3.50**
- For shoe brake without chain................ **1.25**

OUR GIANT HANDY WAGON.

Our Giant Handy Wagon is furnished on any size wheel, as quoted below. When on 26-inch front and 32-inch rear wheel, the top of bolsters are only 26 inches from the ground, making it a handy wagon for loading. Axles are of best hickory; bolsters, coupling pole and tongue are best oak; stakes are oak, bound with flat iron. Coupling pole is 9 feet 4 inches long, and if wanted we can furnish 12-foot at same price. Front and rear hounds are of angle steel, almost indestructible, and the wheels are the best metal wheels made. Spokes and tires are made of the best wrought steel, guaranteed not to break on the rockiest roads. Hubs are made of superior cast iron. This wagon, with its broad tires, is handy in the field and over soft roads. Guaranteed fully by us. **Shipped** from factory in Western Illinois. Can quote prices on an all steel wagon, and can furnish this wagon fitted for log hauling, with log blocks in place of stakes.

SIZE AND PRICE OF METAL WAGONS AS SHOWN IN ILLUSTRATION.

Number	Diameter of Wheels	Tire	Carrying Capacity, 4,000 lbs.: Price	Weight	Carrying Capacity, 6,000 lbs.: Price	Weight	Carrying Capacity, 8,000 lbs.: Price	Weight
11C1215	22x28 in.	4 in.	**$20.62**	550 lbs.	**$25.39**	650 lbs.	**$30.15**	750 lbs.
	26x32 in.	4 in.	**21.43**	590 lbs.	**26.19**	700 lbs.	**31.73**	800 lbs.
Can quote prices on extra stong wheels when desired.	28x34 in.	4 in.	**21.43**	600 lbs.	**26.19**	750 lbs.	**34.03**	920 lbs.
	30x36 in.	4 in.	**22.22**	630 lbs.	**26.97**	780 lbs.	**34.92**	940 lbs.
	32x38 in.	4 in.	**23.00**	678 lbs.	**27.79**	820 lbs.	**36.50**	950 lbs.
	34x40 in.	4 in.	**23.80**	6[illegible]4 lbs.	**28.56**	850 lbs.	**38.09**	970 lbs.
	36x42 in.	4 in.	**24.60**	708 lbs.	**29.36**	870 lbs.	**39.69**	990 lbs.
	38x44 in.	4 in.	**25.40**	756 lbs.	**30.15**	900 lbs.	**41.13**	1000 lbs.

All wagons must have tires ½-inch thick when brake is ordered.

EXTRAS.

- **If tires ½-inch thick are wanted, add**................ **$1.20**
- **If tires 5 inches wide are wanted, add**................ **1.20**
- **If tires 6 inches wide are wanted, add**................ **2.50**
- **If tires 7 inches wide are wanted, add**................ **3.80**
- **If tires 8 inches wide are wanted, add**................ **$5.10**
- **If neckyoke, single and doubletree are wanted, add**................ **1.60**
- **If brake is wanted, add**................ **3.00**

All sizes obtainable are quoted in the above table. In ordering be particular to give the size of wheels required, width of tires, carrying capacity and width of track, 4 feet 6 inches or 5 feet.

This wagon comes with pole complete as shown in illustration, without whiffletree or neckyoke. If desired, we can send it fitted with shafts instead of pole at same price.

PRICE FOR EXTRAS APPLY ONLY WHEN FURNISHED IN CONNECTION WITH A REGULAR ORDER FOR WAGON, AS EXTRAS ARE NOT SOLD SEPARATELY AT THE PRICES QUOTED.

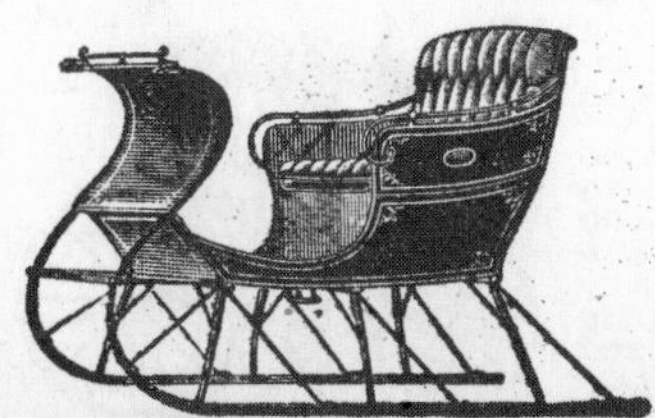

Our Free Catalogue of Cutters, Sleighs, Bob Sleds and Runner Attachments.

Our Special Free Catalogue of everything in this line will be ready October 1st, and if you expect to buy anything in the way of a cutter, sled, or runner attachments, be sure and write for the Free Cutter Catalogue. We sell cutters and sleds at much lower prices than you can get elsewhere, and beginning October 1st, we will have a large number built, ready and carried in stock for shipment on the day the order is received. If you are interested, don't fail to write for our Free Catalogue of Cutters.

Factory Grade Vehicle Work

CASH IN FULL MUST ACCOMPANY ALL ORDERS FOR FACTORY GRADE WORK.

TO ACCOMMODATE SUCH OF OUR CUSTOMERS as may want a cheaper grade of work than we build, and to compete in a fair way with the general retail, wholesale and mail order competition of the country, we offer on this page a line of regular factory grade vehicle work. OPEN AND TOP BUGGIES, CARRIAGES, WAGONS, ETC., which we are pleased to price at THE VERY LOWEST NET COST to us, with but our one small percentage of profit added.

DESCRIPTION OF FACTORY GRADE VEHICLE WORK

FACTORY GRADE is the grade of buggies sold by nearly every retail dealer in the country, every dealer in agricultural implements and vehicles. It is also the grade of work sold by nearly all mail order houses, houses that sell from catalogue. The factories making this grade of work will send out traveling salesmen at a big expense, who will go from town to town, some factories having as many as twenty-five or more salesmen on the road covering nearly all states, and these salesmen will solicit orders from buggy and implement dealers, always glad to get an order for from one rig to a carload; and when the manufacturer sells direct to the retail dealer in this way he of course pays the expenses and salary of the traveling salesman who goes to see this retail dealer, adds a big percentage for expenses, and a bigger profit than if he were selling to the larger dealer or jobber. So, in every case, the retailer pays a big price for the vehicle he buys, and he too must have a profit from the man who buys the buggy for his own use.

FROM MANY OF THESE FACTORIES the catalogue houses are supplied. The catalogue house goes to a factory, arrange for the different styles of vehicles they want, agree on the price, which of course must pay the manufacturer a profit, the manufacturer furnishes him cuts or illustrations from which he gets up his catalogue, adds his profit to the price he pays the manufacturer, and in turn he offers this factory grade buggy to the prospective buyer, and so, nine-tenths of the buggies, road wagons and surreys made are simply factory grade. Whether you buy your buggy from your local dealer at home, or you send your order elsewhere, you will be almost sure to get the plain, common factory grade work.

FACTORY GRADE VEHICLES vary very little in quality, although they may vary much in the selling price. Very few of these factories (though they may show top buggies at a variety of prices ranging from $30.00 to $50.00), will have in stock at any time more than one grade of wheels, and that "D grade," will have more than one grade of a buggy body, one grade of gear or gear irons, and with the exception of slight variations, the grade is exactly the same throughout.

WE DO NOT WISH to be understood as saying, nor do we wish you to infer, that factory grade buggies and carriages are worthless or will not give satisfaction. To say that would be to say that nine-tenths of the vehicles that are being used everywhere today are worthless and unsatisfactory. But we feel it proper that we explain to our customers what factory grade work is everywhere, why it is nearly all necessarily about alike, why nearly every implement and buggy dealer handles this grade of work, and this grade of work only; and why it is that the difference between a $30.00 buggy and a $50.00 buggy is mostly in price and not in quality of the rig.

THE FACTORY GRADE VEHICLE WORK we show below is made for us under contract by four different factories or makers; two in Southern Ohio, one in Northern Ohio and one in Michigan. This work will compare favorably with any you will be likely to be able to get from your dealer or elsewhere at even $5.00 to $15.00 more per rig than the prices we name. **Our prices are for these rigs delivered on board of cars at the factory,** from which point you must pay the freight.

WE FEEL IN JUSTICE TO OURSELVES as we are building a much higher grade of work, a line of vehicles that in quality of material, workmanship and finish stands alone, and as we are compelled to meet the retail and catalogue competition everywhere, that it is proper we show a limited line of factory grade vehicles, tell our customers just exactly what they are, offer the work at the lowest prices we can, and leave it entirely to our customers whether they buy this, the common factory grade vehicle work, or buy our own make—a special line of high grade work—as illustrated and described on the preceding pages.

$19.50 Factory Grade Rig.

For $19.50, cash in full with order, we furnish this factory grade road wagon, the exact same rig that is sold by retail dealers generally and advertised by most houses at $5.00 to $15.00 more money. The body is 22x54 inches; Sarven's patent wheels; body painted black, neatly striped; gear, green, wine or red, neatly striped; cushion and back of imitation leather.

No. 11C3642 Price, complete with shafts, $19.50
Extra for pole in place of shafts........... 1.25
Extra for factory grade rubber tires....... 9.00

Our $23.95 Factory Grade Open Buggy.

This is a factory grade open buggy, with body 22x54 inches; end springs; Sarven's patent wheels; body, painted black; gear, black, red or green, neatly striped; upholstered in imitation leather.

No. 11C3643 Price, complete with shafts..$23.95
Extra for pole in place of shafts............ 1.25
Extra for factory grade rubber tires....... 9.00

Understand, this factory grade work is not guaranteed and all orders for this work must be accompanied by cash in full, and for the slight difference in cost we especially recommend that you select a rig of our own make, a buggy that will outwear two of any factory grade work on the market.

$25.90 Factory Grade Buggy.

This factory grade rig has a body 22x54 inches, handsome stick seat, end spring, Sarven's patent wheels; body painted black; gear, green, black or red as desired; trimmed in whipcord or imitation leather as desired.

No. 11C3651 Price, complete with shafts $25.90
Extra for pole in place of shafts............ 1.25
Extra for factory grade rubber tires....... 9.00

While this is the exact same rig that is being sold by nearly all other houses and retail dealers everywhere, and as a rig of our own make will outwear two of these factory grade rigs and always look much better, we would especially recommend that you order a buggy of our own make.

Our $30.90 Factory Grade Concord Buggy.

This factory grade Concord is built on a full Concord gear, three reaches, body 56x26 inches; Sarven's patent wheels; body painted black, neatly striped; gear, black or red, neatly striped; upholstered in imitation leather.

No. 11C3653 Price, complete with shafts.$30.90
Extra for pole in place of shafts............ 1.25
Extra for factory grade rubber tires........ 9.00

Understand, all orders for factory grade work must be accompanied by cash in full. We guarantee the rigs we make in our own factory to outwear any two factory grade rigs advertised by others or sold by retail dealers generally.

Our $33.50 Factory Grade Arched Steel Gear Runabout.

This factory grade rig has a body 23x54 inches; stick seat; arched oval naked steel axles; Sarven's patent wheels; trimmed in whipcord; body painted black; gear, dark green or red, neatly striped.

No. 11C3655 Price, complete with shafts $33.50
Extra for pole in place of shafts............ 1.25
Extra for factory grade rubber tires........ 9.00

All orders for factory grade work must be accompanied by cash in full. You will get double the value by ordering a rig of our own make, which will outwear any two factory grade rigs made.

Our $24.90 Factory Grade Top Buggy.

This factory grade buggy has a body 22x54 inches; end springs, Sarven's patent wheels; body painted black; gear, dark green or red, neatly striped; upholstered in imitation leather, drill top; is furnished complete with full length side and back curtains and shafts for $24.90.

No. 11C3645 Price..............................$24.90
Extra for pole in place of shafts............ 1.25
Extra for factory grade rubber tires....... 9.00

This is the exact same buggy that is being widely advertised by many at $30.00 to $40.00, the exact same factory grade of buggy that is retailed generally by implement dealers at $35.00 to $50.00, and a buggy of our own make will outwear two of these.

$28.75 Factory Grade Leather Quarter Top Buggy.

This factory grade buggy has a leather quarter top, full length side and back curtains; piano box body 22x54 inches, end springs; Sarven's patent wheels; upholstered in imitation leather; body painted black; gear, dark green with neat striping, and at our special $28.75 price comes complete with full length side and back curtains and shafts.

No. 11C3647 Price..............................$28.75
Extra for pole in place of shafts............ 1.25
Extra for factory grade rubber tires......... 9.00

All orders for factory grade rigs must be accompanied by cash in full.

Our $30.75 Factory Grade Half Platform Spring Wagon.

This is a factory grade spring wagon. Body is 7 feet long, 32 inches wide, 8 inches deep, drop end gate, two removable seats; Sarven's patent wheels, 1-inch tread; axles, $1\frac{1}{8}$-inch; cushions and back, imitation leather. At our special $30.75 price, the wagon comes complete with two seats and shafts.

No. 11C3663 Price..............................$30.75
Extra for pole in place of shafts........... 1.25

This is a factory grade rig and is not guaranteed, and yet it is the equal of spring wagons that sell generally at $40.00 to $50.00. If you will order a wagon made in our own factory we guarantee it will outwear two factory grade rigs.

Our $42.90 Factory Grade Family Surrey.

This factory grade surrey has body 24x69 inches; canopy top, full length side and back curtains, end springs; Sarven's patent wheels, 1-inch tread; seats are upholstered in imitation leather. Our price for the rig complete with shafts, $42.90.

No. 11C3666 Price..............................$42.90
Extra for pole in place of shafts............ 1.25

All orders for factory grade rigs must be accompanied by cash in full and they are not guaranteed, and yet they are the equal of rigs that are sold by retailers generally and widely advertised at $10.00 to $20.00 more than our price. For a surrey that will outwear two factory grade rigs you should select one made in our own factory.

Our $49.75 Factory Grade Surrey.

This factory grade surrey has a body 5 feet 10 inches long by 26 inches wide; canopy top, full length side and back curtains, lamps, full size fenders and spring gear; $1\frac{1}{8}$-inch axles; 1-inch Sarven's patent wheels; trimmed in imitation leather; body painted black, gear dark green. At our special $49.75 price it comes complete with shafts.

No. 11C3665 Price..............................$49.75
Extra for pole in place of shafts........... 1.25

These factory grade rigs are not guaranteed, they are the equal of work sold by retailers generally and advertised extensively at $15.00 to $20.00 more than our price. If you want a rig that will outwear two factory grade rigs you should order work made in our own factory.

$47.00 Factory Grade Phaeton.

This phaeton has the latest style body, drill top, full length side and back curtains, fenders, lamps; is upholstered in imitation leather, has Sarven's patent wheels, and at our special $47.00 price, comes complete with shafts.

No. 11C3649 Price..............................$47.00
Extra for pole in place of shafts............ 1.25
Extra for factory grade rubber tires......... 9.00

If you want a cheap rig you will get the exact same grade of work in our factory grade that you will get in nine-tenths of the work that is sold by retail dealers generally and advertised by other houses. If you buy a rig made in our own factory you will get a rig worth two factory grade rigs and will get it at the actual cost to manufacture, with but our one small percentage of profit added.

HARNESS DEPARTMENT.

WE INVITE ATTENTION to our very complete Harness and Saddlery Department. On this line of goods we undersell the retail dealer by a big margin, as in most cases our prices to you are less than the prices at which manufacturers and jobbers sell to the ordinary retail dealer. It is no exaggeration for us to say that **we can save you from 35 to 50 per cent** on these goods, besides giving you a larger assortment and a better grade of merchandise than is found in the regular harness stores in other towns.

WE HANDLE THE VERY BEST OF HARNESS that is possible to be made. Our harness are made of the very best of high grade leather, with fine trimmings. Our single and double buggy harness are of the very latest styles, and the trimmings the very best nickel composition or Davis rubber trimmings. Our Farm, Team and Concord Harness are of the very best that can be made, and we invite the closest comparison of quality and price.

OUR $1.00 C. O. D. SUBJECT TO EXAMINATION OFFER.

While we always advise against shipping harness **C. O. D., subject to examination**, for the reason that it is usually much cheaper to ship a harness by freight than express, and when we ship harness C. O. D., subject to examination, there is an extra charge for collecting and returning the money to us of 25 to 50 cents, whereas if you send cash in full with your order the harness can be shipped direct to you by freight at the lowest rate and save you any C. O. D or collection charges; nevertheless, to those who prefer to see and examine any harness or saddle before paying for it, we will, on receipt of $1.00, ship any harness or saddle to any address, east of the Rocky Mountains, C. O. D., subject to examination. You can examine it at your nearest express office, and, if found perfectly satisfactory, exactly as represented, you can pay the agent our price and the express charges, less the $1.00 sent us.

NOTICE. **ALWAYS STATE the size of collar wanted** when ordering the harness with collars or in ordering sweat pads; if you want a harness without the collar, always state the size of hames it will require to fit your collar. **ALWAYS STATE** the kind of check wanted, whether overcheck or side check. **IF YOU DO NOT STATE** the kind of check wanted, we will send you overcheck. **ALWAYS STATE** the style of the harness you want, whether single or double, also the kind of trimmings, whether XC, nickel or imitation rubber. **ALWAYS STATE** the weight of your horse. Give us the measurement of your horse around girth, where saddle or pad work, and from gig saddle to horse's tail. The size of bridle from bit ring to bit ring over the head, and state style of horse, if long and rangy or short, chunky horse.

HARNESS DEALERS, LIVERY MEN, everyone interested in these goods are invited to compare our prices with what they have been paying for equal goods. Many goods we list, dealers can buy from us at less money than they have been paying jobbers and wholesalers. Look carefully over our very complete line of blankets, fly nets, dusters, robes, etc. **Nowhere will you find as complete an assortment, nowhere will you be able to match our low prices.**

NOTE. EXTRAS: Russet hand parts on any harness over $8.00, 25 cents extra. Extra for buckles on crupper on single harness, 15 cents; double harness, 30 cents. Add extra for old style double bellyband, 25 cents on harness over $10.00. Open or blind bridle on any harness over $8.97. We only make changes as stated in harness.

WE MAKE NO CHARGE FOR BOXING, CRATING, PACKING OR CARTAGE, BUT DELIVER ALL GOODS AT ANY EXPRESS OFFICE OR FREIGHT DEPOT IN CHICAGO FREE OF CHARGE.

Our Pan-American Single Web Harness.

This harness is made of woven web, all white or russet.

Open bridle, made of ⅝-inch web with overcheck only; **breast collar**, 2 inches wide, and traces, 1¼-inch, one solid piece; no splices in the trace; **the trace** forms a layer on the breast collar which makes it doubly strong; **pad**, 2½-inch web with 1¼-inch shaft tugs; ⅞-inch back strap; 2-inch breeching with 1-inch layer on the breeching, making a very strong breeching. The pad is hook and terret style with a good combination leather web pad, leather bound, which makes it very strong and durable; round leather crupper; **lines**, 1-inch to loop in bit; back end of traces are leather lined where the holes are punched. This is a very good cheap harness. We do not make any changes whatever in this harness. Sold only complete as listed. We do not furnish extra parts of this harness. Weight of harness, 7 pounds; shipping weight, 9 pounds.

No. 10C2 Price, per set, in white or russet.......................**$3.00**
Add extra for full russet blind bridle and overcheck....................**2.00**

Our Texas Single Harness, $4.90.

This harness is full size; a cheaper harness must be made smaller size. This harness will be large enough for a 900 to 1200-pound horse. Don't buy a cheaper single harness than this one. We don't make any changes in this harness.

Bridle, ⅝-inch check, patent leather blinds, flat winker brace and check reins, ring bit, fancy front and rosettes; overcheck or side reins, as desired; **lines**, ¾-inch, flat, all black, to loop in bit; **breast collar**, folded and stitched; **gig saddle**, 2½-inch, enameled cloth bottom, doubled and stitched bearers; **shaft tugs**, 1-inch, with ⅞-inch buckles and ¾-inch bellyband billets; **bellyband**, ⅞-inch, flat; **breeching**, folded and stitched, ⅝-inch flat hip strap, ⅝-inch turnback, lapped and stitched to crupper pieces, folded crupper, docks sewed on breeching straps, ⅝-inch; **traces**, 1-inch, doubled and stitched to breast collar. This single buggy harness comes in full XC trimmings, imitation hand sewed. Weight, about 12 pounds; shipping weight, 18 pounds.

No. 10C5 Price.................................**$4.90**
No. 10C10 Same as the description of No. 10C5, with the exception of collar and hames in place of breast collar, kip collar, any size, traces attached to hames. Weight, about 18 lbs. State size of collar wanted. Price......**$6.25**

Our Georgia Single Harness, $7.69.

This harness is large enough for 900 to 1200-pound horse.

Bridle, ⅝-inch, overcheck, box loops, round winker stay, initial letter rosettes; **breast collar**, folded, with wide layer and box loops; **traces**, 1⅛-inch, double and stitched, round edge; **breeching**, folded, with wide layer; **side straps**, ⅝-inch; **hip strap**, ⅝-inch; **turnback**, ⅝-inch, round crupper; **saddle**, 2½-inch, single strap, all leather skirts and bottom, patent leather jockey; **bellyband**, Griffith style; **lines**, ⅞x1-inch, all black, loop in bit; XC trimmings throughout. This harness will fit 900 to 1200-pound horse. Weight, boxed, about 20 pounds.

No. 10C15 Price.......................**$7.69**

Our Nebraska Single Harness, $8.45 and $9.00.

This harness will fit horse of 1250 pounds; extra large harness for 1400 or 1600-pound horse, $2.00 extra.

FULL SIZE HARNESS.

Bridle, ⅝-inch, overcheck with nose band or side rein, box loop check, round winker stay; **breast collar**, folded body, buckles and box loops, 3 feet long; **traces**, 1¼-inch, double and stitched, 6 feet long, or 1⅜-inch, 6 feet long; **breeching**, folded body with layer, 3 feet 3 inches long, **side strap**, ⅝-inch; **hip strap**, ⅝-inch; **turnback**, ⅝-inch, with round crupper sewed on; **saddle**, 3-inch strap saddle, harness leather skirt, with iron jockey or tree, leather bottom pad; **bellyband**, flat, Griffith style only; **lines**, 1⅛-inch, full length, 18 feet long, to loop in bit; **tie strap**, ⅝-inch; **trimmings**, XC only. Weight, boxed, about 20 pounds.

No. 10C36 Price, per set, 1⅛-inch traces..........................**$8.45**
No. 10C37 Price, per set, 1⅜-inch traces..........................**9.00**
Extra for buckle crupper.....................**.15**
Extra for large harness for 1400 to 1600-pound horse.......................**2.00**
Extra for russet hand parts.................**.25**
Extra for buckle and billet end lines..**.25**

Our Ashby Single Harness, With Collar and Hames, $8.97.

Bridle, ⅝-inch, box loop check, patent leather blinds, round winker brace, overcheck or side rein; **lines**, ⅞-inch, all black, to loop in bit; **traces**, 1⅛-inch, doubled and stitched, round edge finish, 3½-pound hames, iron hame, full XC plate on XC harness; **hame tugs** with box loops; **breeching**, folded, with layers, ⅝-inch single hip strap, ⅝-inch side strap and ⅝-inch back strap, with crupper sewed on; **gig saddle**, 2½-inch single strap skirt, leather bottom, with iron jockey; **bellyband**, flat, Griffith style only; **collar**, full kip. We do not make any changes in this harness, only furnish it as described above. This harness made in one size only, for 900 to 1200-pound horse. Weight, boxed, about 35 pounds.

No. 10C35 Price, with collar......**$8.97**

Our Iowa Single Harness $8.95.

Lines, a very important point about this harness is ⅞-inch by 1-inch black lines, loop in bit, **extra good stock**; **gig saddle**, extra good single strap, harness leather skirt, with heavy bearer and shaft tug; **bellyband**, folds Griffith style, ⅝-inch hip strap, ⅝-inch side strap, ⅝-inch turnback scalloped, with round crupper sewed on; **breast collar**, folded, with heavy straight layer and box loops; **breeching**, folded, with heavy straight layer double and stitched breeching brace; **traces**, the most important part of this harness, are 1⅛ inches by 6 feet long, extra good stock, well made, smooth, round edge to buckle in breast collar; **bridle**, ⅝-inch, box loops, round winker brace, patent leather blind, overcheck or side rein, fancy front and **initial letter rosettes**; **trimmings**, **fine nickel or Davis imitation rubber**. Weight, boxed, 23 pounds.

No. 10C40 Price, as illustrated....**$8.95**
Add extra for russet hand parts.......**.25**
Add extra for buckle on crupper.......**.15**
Will make this harness extra large for 1400 to 1600-pound horse, add, extra.......**2.00**

Our Maine Single Buggy Harness, $11.20.

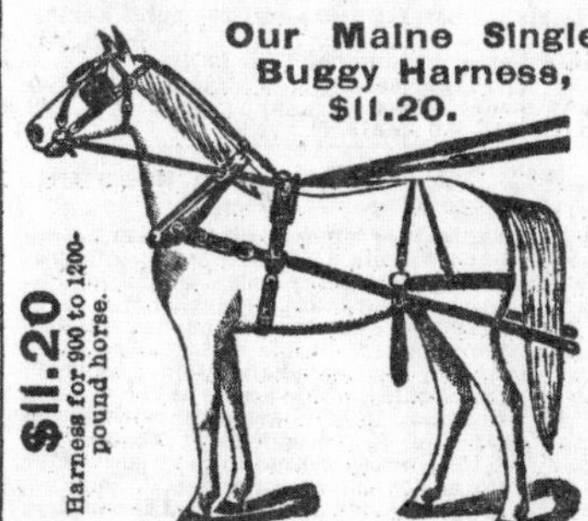

Bridle, ⅝-inch, box loop, round winker brace, (**overcheck or side rein**, blind or open bridle), patent leather blind, fancy front with **initial letter rosettes**; **lines, black**, 1-inch, to loop in bit, extra strong and well made; **gig saddle**, good single strap skirts, made of harness leather, double and stitched shaft bearer and shaft tug; **bellyband**, folded, **Griffith style only**; **breeching**, folded, with straight layers, ⅝-inch DOUBLE hip strap, ⅝-inch side strap, ⅝-inch turnback with round crupper sewed on; **traces**, the most important part of any harness, are made of selected stock, flat, round edge, 1⅛-inch by 6 feet, to buckle in hame tug; **hame and hame tug**, iron hame, japaned body and nickel terret, 1⅛-inch **hame tug**, box loop; **collar**, fine kip collar; be sure and state size wanted. Every harness we send out is carefully inspected, and when you get a harness from us you will not find any of the parts missing or mismatched. **Everything** is in order, everything is exactly as you order it and as represented and described in our catalogue, and if you do not find this to be the case, we are more than glad to make everything satisfactory by exchanging goods or refunding your money, as you desire. Weight, boxed, about 35 pounds.

No. 10C45 Price, with collar.. **$11.20**
Price, less collar.......................**10.35**
Add extra for buckles on crupper ....**.15**
Add extra for russet hand parts.......**.25**

Our Kansas Single Harness, $9.90.

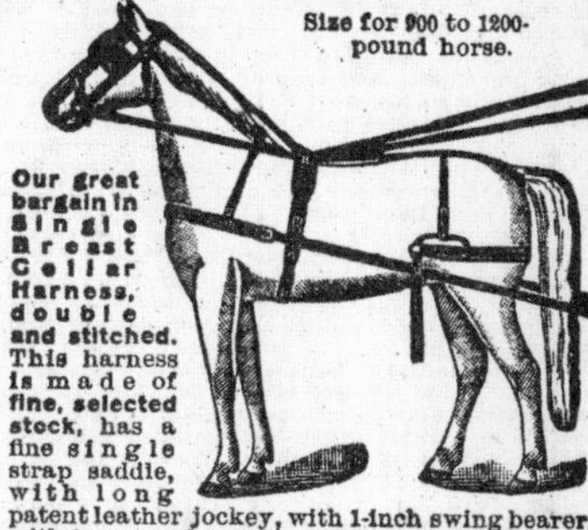

Our great bargain in Single Breast Collar Harness, double and stitched. This harness is made of **fine, selected stock**, has a fine single strap saddle, with long patent leather jockey, with 1-inch swing bearer, with terret and terret post, so you can **change the terret** and make a **low track saddle**; the bridle is made with nose band. The lines are extra fine, ⅞x1⅛-inch black hand parts, with spring billet. **Bridle**, ⅝-inch, box loop overcheck with nose band or side rein, with initial rosettes, round winker braces, fine patent leather blinds; **gig saddle**, fine single strap, with patent leather jockey, swinging bearer; **lines**, ⅞x1⅛-inch hand parts, black or russet; **breast collar, folded, with layer and box loop**, folded neck strap; **turnback**, ⅝-inch, scalloped, with round crupper sewed on; **breeching**, folded with good layer 3-ring breeching stay, ⅝-inch hip strap, ⅝-inch side strap; **bellyband**, Griffith style; **traces, one of the most important parts** about this harness, they are extra heavy, raised round edges, 1⅛-inch by 6 feet long, **extra good**. This trace is made for service; **trimmings, fine nickel** on composition or Davis imitation rubber, fancy pattern. Weight, boxed, about 24 pounds.

No. 10C55 Price............................**$9.90**
Add extra for buckles on crupper...........**.15**
Extra for double hip strap breeching.....**1.50**
Add extra for russet hand parts.............**.25**

Our New Jersey Special Harness.

Bridle, ⅝-inch, cheek, heavy patent leather blind, round winker brace, with heavy overcheck or side reins as preferred. Will always send overcheck unless side rein is ordered; **lines**, 1⅛-inch throughout, 13½ feet long, with buckle billets to buckle in the bit; **breast collar**, extra wide, folded, folded neck strap, with heavy 1¼-inch traces to buckle into the breast collar; **gig saddle**, 3½-inch, patent leather, pollywog shaft tugs and double bellyband. Extra heavy folded breeching, ⅞-inch turnback, with crupper to buckle on; ¾-inch hip strap and 1-inch side straps to wrap around the shafts. This is a very heavy, well made harness. Extra good quality leather used in this harness. Trimmed in nickel or imitation rubber. Weight, of harness, boxed for shipment, about 45 pounds.

No. 10C56 Price, per set, in nickel trimming..........................**$11.85**
No. 10C57 Price, per set, in imitation rubber..............................**11.85**

Our Bradford Single Buggy Harness.

Lace saddle, double hip strap breeching, made of extra fine quality of Dundee oak leather, nickel or Davis rubber trimmings. **Bridle**, ⅝-inch box loop cheek, round winker brace, patent leather blinds, fancy front, initial rosettes, overcheck or side rein, with tie strap; **lines**, ⅞-inch front with 1⅛-inch black hand parts and spring billets; **breast collar**, folded, with buckle and box loop, 1⅛-inch, double stitched, raised round the edge trace. **Dee** shaft tug with double bellyband or Griffith style if wanted; **gig saddle**, fine patent leather, hand laced, leather lined; **breeching**, folded, with layer, ⅝-inch double hip straps, double scallops and stitched back strap with crupper to buckle on, ⅝-inch side strap. This harness made for 900 to 1200-pound horse. Weight, 30 pounds.

No. 10C60 Nickel or Davis rubber **$10.95**
Add extra for collar and hames in place of breast collar...................**2.50**
Extra for russet hand parts on lines.....**.25**

Doctors' Heavy Single Harness, $14.95.

This harness for 900 to 1250-pound horse.

Our Best Double and Stitched Single Buggy Harness. This is a strictly new harness throughout. The call for a fine single harness of this style caused us to make it. Made of the **best of oak tanned harness leather**, well stitched throughout, we have used great care in making the bridle lines, gig saddle and traces. You will find this harness one of the best that was ever offered at this price, **$14.95. Bridle**, 5/8-inch box loop, with fine patent leather blind, round winker brace, overcheck with **nose band** or side rein, **open or blind bridle; lines**, a very important part of a good harness, are made of the **best of leather**, 1-inch, with 1⅛-inch hand parts, black; **breast collar**, heavy fold, hand finished leather, with fine scalloped, raised layer, safe under buckle, box loop, small tug box loop. Folded neck strap; **traces**, this is the finest 1⅛-inch by 6-foot raised trace made. Fine, round edge finish; **breeching**, heavy folds, hand finished leather, scalloped and raised layer, 3-ring breeching stay with box loop tug; **turnback**, ¾-inch, scalloped with round crupper, sewed on; 5/8-inch hip strap; **bellyband**, heavy fold, Griffith style; **gig saddle**, has heavy single strap harness leather skirt, extra good patent leather jockey, heavy bearer and shaft tugs; **trimmings, full nickel or Davis rubber and genuine rubber.** Weight, packed for shipment, 45 pounds.

No. 10C65 Price, per set single harness, nickel or Davis rubber $14.95
No. 10C70 Price, per set Genuine Rubber Harness 18.05
Add extra for Dee shaft tug, 25c. We do not make any other changes in this harness.

A Regular $25.00 Harness for only $11.25.

$11.25

Williams' Harness, Dundee Stock, only $11.25. This harness made for 900 to 1300-pound horses. Genuine Dundee Leather in every strap, the highest grade stock used in harness, there is no wear out to it. **You can't buy better at any price. Highest grade trimming** throughout; the harness is made by **WILLIAMS**, maker of the best single strap work on the market.

Bridle, 5/8-inch, patent leather blinds, box loops, round winker stay, layer on crown, overcheck with nose piece or round side reins, **initial rosettes; breast collar**, extra wide, V-shaped; **traces**, 1⅛-inch single strap, stitched to breast collar, with scalloped points; **breeching**, 1⅛-inch; **side straps**, ⅝-inch; **hip straps**, ⅝-inch; **turnback**, ⅝-inch, scalloped with round crupper sewed on; **saddle** 3-inch, single strap, swell padded patent leather jockey, harness leather skirt, leather bottom; **bellyband**, wide single strap, Griffith style; **lines**, ⅞x1⅛-inch black hand parts, with spring billets; **hitch rein** ⅝-inch, with snap. Made plain, smooth, round edge; **trimmings**, nickel or Davis rubber.

No. 10C150 Price, nickel trimmings or Davis rubber $11.25
No. 10C155 Price, genuine rubber trimmings 13.25
No. 10C160 **Williams' Fancy Brass Harness**, same style as No. 10C150, made with **brass trimmings throughout, yellow bridle front and yellow beaded gig saddle.** Stitching on blinds and pad is yellow. This makes a very handsome harness, trimmed in brass. **Nobby and very stylish.** Price $13.35
Add extra for double hip strap breeching 1.00
No. 10C165 **Williams' Fancy Brass Collar and Hame Harness**, made with **half patent leather collar, full plated brass hames, 1⅛-inch traces riveted to hames**, balance of trimming fine brass, same as No. 10C150, with **double hip strap breeching. This is a very handsome single strap surrey harness.** Price, with collar and hames $16.25
Russet hand parts on lines, 25 cents extra. For buckle on breast collar of this harness, add **$1.00** extra to price of harness. Open or blind bridle with this harness. Shipping weight, about 30 pounds.

Stallion Harness. Made extra large in nickel or Davis rubber, for 1400 and 1600-pound horses.
No. 10C166 Price $13.45
No. 10C167 **Williams' All Hand Made Harness**, same harness as No. 10C150, only all hand made; nickel or Davis rubber trimmed. Price, per set 15.50
No. 10C169 **Genuine Rubber, all black, hand made.** Price 17.50
Add extra for Condon safety bit, 50 cents.

Our Ohio Single Buggy Harness, $12.50. Collar and Hames.

This harness is made for 900 to 1250-pound horses.

$12.50

Bridle, ⅝-inch box loop check, patent leather blinds, round winker brace, fancy front, overcheck with **nose band or side rein**, blind or open bridle, initial rosettes, tie strap; **lines**, extra good lines, ⅞-inch front with spring billet, 1⅛-inch hand parts black; **gig saddle**, fine single strap harness leather skirts, leather bottom, double and stitched shaft bearer and shaft tug; **bellyband**, folded, Griffith style only; **breeching**, folded, with layer, ⅝-inch DOUBLE hip strap, ⅝-inch back strap with round crupper sewed on, ⅝-inch side strap; **traces**, 1⅛-inch, 6 feet long, raised round edge finish; **collar and hames**, fine kip collar, buggy size, buckle top, Dixon hame, japanned body, nickeled terret, box loop hame tug. Weight, about 35 pounds, boxed.

No. 10C171 Price of harness complete with collar $12.50
Add extra for buckle on crupper .... .15
Add extra for 3-inch full laced saddle 2.00
Add extra for russet hand parts .... .25
Add extra for Dee shaft tug .... .25

Our Lexington Single Strap Track or Buggy Harness.

This harness made for 900 to 1200-pound horses.

Bridle, ⅝-inch, overcheck, patent leather blinds, box loops, round winker stays, layer on crown, side rein or overcheck, initial rosettes, open or blind bridle; **breast collar**, 1⅛-inch; **traces**, 1⅛-inch, stitched to breast collar; **breeching**, 1⅛-inch; **side straps**, ⅝-inch; **hip straps**, ⅝-inch; **turnback**, ⅝-inch, scalloped, with round crupper sewed on; **saddle**, 2½-inch, single strap, patent leather jockey, harness leather skirt, enameled leather bottom; **bellyband**, Griffith style; **lines**, 1-inch, black, to loop in bit. **Harness all made plain, with single edge crease.** Nickel or imitation rubber trimmings throughout. Weight, boxed, about 22 pounds.

No. 10C180 Price $9.00
Add extra for buckle on crupper .... .15
Add extra for russet hand parts .... .25
We do not make any other changes in this harness.

$9.00

Our Concord Heavy Single Harness.

$13.95

Made of selected Dundee stock, well finished. Trimming, nickel or imitation rubber and genuine rubber.

Bridle, ⅝-inch, overcheck or side rein, box loop check, round winker brace, layer on crown, **open or blind bridle; breast collar**, heavy, folded body, scalloped layer, raised, box loop, safe under buckle; **traces**, 1¼-inch, double and stitched, raised round edge finish; **breeching**, folded, with scalloped raised layer, side strap 1-inch, hip strap ⅞-inch, turnback ⅞-inch scalloped, round crupper to buckle on; **saddle**, 4-inch saddle, covered seat, leather pad laced in, double bellyband, folded, with dee shaft tug; **lines**, 1-inch front with spring billets, 1⅛-inch hand parts and tie strap. Weight, packed for shipment, 50 pounds.

No. 10C86 Price, per set, nickel or imitation leather $13.95
No. 10C87 Price, per set, genuine rubber 16.60
We do not make any other changes in this harness.

Our Single Strap Buggy Harness.

$9.95

We do not make any changes in this harness.

Bridle, ⅝-inch, overcheck, box loops, round winker stay, nose band overcheck, **open or blind bridles, breast collar**, shaped extra wide; **traces**, 1⅛-inch, stitched to breast collar; **breeching**, 1⅛-inch, side strap, ⅝-inch; **hip strap**, ⅝-inch, **turnback**, ⅝-inch, scalloped, round crupper; **saddle**, 3-inch, strap, pad, patent leather jockey, harness leather skirts, leather bottom; **bellyband**, Griffith style; **lines**, 1-inch, to loop in; **trimmings**, nickel or imitation rubber. Weight, 18 pounds.

No. 10C195 Price $9.95

Our Madison Single Strap Single Harness.

$7.65

This harness made for 900 to 1200-lb. horses.

Bridle, ⅝-inch, patent leather winkers, box loop cheeks, overcheck or side reins, as desired; **breast collar**, 1⅛-inch, heavy stock; **traces**, 1⅛-inch, heavy stock; **breeching**, 1⅛-inch; **side strap**, ⅝-inch; **hip strap**, ⅝-inch; **turnback**, ⅝-inch, scalloped, with round crupper sewed on; **saddle**, 2½-inch, single strap harness leather skirts, leather bottom; **bellyband**, Griffith style; **lines**, ⅞-inch, all black, nickel or imitation rubber trimmings throughout. Weight, about 21 pounds.

No. 10C200 Price $7.65
Add extra for collar and hames in place of breast collar 2.00
Add extra for buckle on crupper .... .15
We do not make any other changes in this harness.

Our Queen Single Strap Back Harness, $10.95. Hand Made.

$10.95

Our Ohio Special Single Strap Buggy Harness, $10.60.

$10.60

We do not make any changes in this harness. This harness made for 900 to 1200-pound horses.

This harness is made by one of the best makers in America. Made by Williams, from genuine Delhi oak tanned leather; the same goods as is used by fancy city makers at very high prices. If you want a single harness don't select a cheaper number. We are anxious to sell you one of our leaders, not for the little profit, but we know you will be more than satisfied. Other orders will follow. If you buy this single harness you will wonder how it is possible to make such a harness for so little money.

Trimmings, nickel or Davis rubber; **bridle**, ⅝-inch box loop, layer on crown, round winker braces, overcheck with nose piece or round side reins, **open or blind bridle**, initial glass rosettes; **breast collar**, 1⅜-inch; **traces**, 1⅛-inch, scalloped points, stitched to breast collar; **breeching**, 1⅛-inch; **side straps**, ⅝-inch; **hip strap**, ⅝-inch; **turnback**, ⅞-inch, scalloped, with round crupper stitched on; **saddle**, 3-inch, single strap, swell padded, patent leather jockey, harness leather skirts, leather bottom; **lines**, ⅞x1⅛-inch, black hand parts, with spring billet; **bellyband**, Griffith style. Weight, boxed, about 22 pounds.

No. 10C210 Price $10.60
No. 10C220 Same style as No. 10C210, only genuine rubber trimming throughout, breast collar harness. Price $12.80

Our Pride, Single Strap Collar and Hame Single Harness.

$13.75

This harness is made in sizes only for 900 to 1250-pound horses. Be sure and state the size of collar wanted.

Bridle, ⅝-inch, box loop check, patent leather blinds, round winker stay, overcheck with nose band, layer on crown piece or side rein, **open or blind bridle**, fancy front, with initial rosettes and tie strap; **lines**, ⅞-inch front with spring billet to buckle in bit, 1⅛-inch hand parts, black; **hames**, 3½-pound iron hames, japanned body, nickel terret and draft eye, with a heavy 1⅛-inch single strap trace with swell safe attached to hame, 6 feet 4 inches long, three holes in back end; **breeching**, 1⅛-inch single strap body with scalloped and raised point, doubled and stitched breeching brace, ⅝-inch single hip strap, ⅝-inch side strap, ⅝-inch scalloped and stitched back strap with flaxseed crupper sewed on; **gig saddle**, 3-inch single strap, harness leather skirt, swell housing and patent leather jockey, leather bottom, doubled and stitched shaft bearers, box loop shaft tugs, Griffith style bellyband; **collar**, full kip collar. This harness is made in nickel, imitation rubber and genuine rubber. Shipping weight, boxed, about 30 pounds.

No. 10C250 Price, per set, for the nickel or imitation rubber harness complete, with collar $13.75
No. 10C255 Price, per set, for genuine rubber harness, with imitation rubber hames and steel bit $15.87
Add extra for full pad saddle, 3-inch 2.00
Add extra for buckle crupper .... .15
Extra for russet hand parts on lines .... .25

Hand Made Throughout. We do not make any changes in this harness. For 900 to 1250-pound horses.

Read this description carefully. Remember, this harness is hand made throughout; strictly up to date, very genteel; harness a retailer would ask $14.00 for and then consider he was giving extra good value.

Bridle, ⅝-inch, box loop check, patent leather blinds, round winker stay, overcheck with nose band or side rein, fancy front with initial rosettes, **open or blind bridle**, tie strap; **lines**, ⅞-inch front with spring billets to buckle in bit and 1⅛-inch hand parts, black; **breast collar**, 1⅝-inch single strap, with 1⅛-inch single strap traces stitched to breast collar, raised finger point, box loop tug, with ⅝-inch neck strap; **breeching**, 1⅛-inch single strap, tapered and raised point layer, ⅝-inch single hip strap, doubled and stitched breeching brace with box loop tug, ⅝-inch side straps, ⅝-inch scalloped and stitched back strap, with flaxseed crupper sewed on; **gig saddle**, 2½-inch single strap, swell housing, leather bottom, doubled and stitched shaft bearers, box loop shaft tug, single strap Griffith bellyband, one tie strap. This harness is made smooth finished throughout, very light and nobby, trimming nickel or imitation rubber and genuine rubber. Shipping weight, boxed, about 24 pounds.

No. 10C260 Price, per set, nickel or imitation rubber $10.95
No. 10C265 Price, per set, genuine rubber trimmed 12.95
Add extra for russet hand parts on lines .... .25

Single Strap Runabout Harness, $13.80.

No. 10C230 Our Special Runabout Single Strap Harness. This is something new, strictly up to date, **and is one of the big sellers. Trimmed in brass only. Bridle**, ⅝-inch, box loop check, fancy stitched blind, round winker brace, overcheck or side rein as desired, **open or blind bridle**. Will always send blind bridle, overcheck, unless ordered otherwise. **Breast collar**, 1⅞ inches wide with 1¼-inch trace attached, with scalloped points; double neck strap with brass line rings. **Breeching**, 1⅞-inch wide, single strap, with double hip strap; ⅝-inch **turnback**, scalloped, with round crupper sewed on; ⅝-inch **side strap; gig saddle**, very heavy wide single strap, **skirting extra wide, swell pad and housing; one of the latest styles single strap gig saddle**, with 1-inch swinging bearer; heavy shaft tugs, Griffith style bellyband, **lines**, 1⅛-inch throughout, with loop end to loop in bit. **This harness is only made in full brass trimming.** It is a leader, one of the latest styles in a **single strap runabout harness.**

Price for this harness **$13.80**

Shipping weight, boxed, about 30 pounds.

Our Genuine Solid Nickel German Silver Trimmed Single Buggy Harness, $14.75.

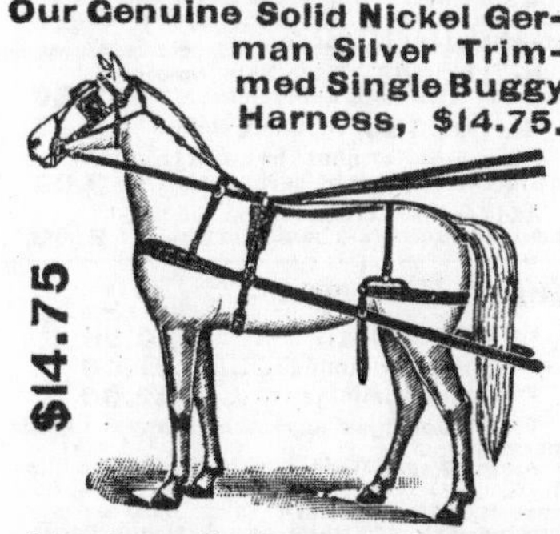

Trimming on the Harness. The trimming on this harness is the very best solid nickel German silver. The buckles, rings, hooks and terrets are all made of solid nickel. They will not tarnish, rust or wear yellow, but will hold their original finish, bright nickel forever, and the trimmings are so guaranteed by us. This is the first time that a harness at this price of **$14.75** has ever been offered with solid nickel German silver trimming, positively the best that can be made. **This harness is illustrated with our humane bridle**, the check that is easy on the horse and at the same time absolutely controls his head in the natural position. The lines work independent of the check on the bridle. The leather used in this harness is the best high grade Dundee oak tanned leather. It takes 5½ months to tan the leather that is used in this harness, which is a guarantee itself that it is the best high grade tanned leather in the country. The highest grade solid nickel German silver trimming, the very best thoroughly tanned Dundee oak leather, and the highest priced skilled workmanship combined together makes it the very highest grade harness that can be bought. If this harness is not found as represented, illustrated, and described and you are not perfectly satisfied with the harness, you can return it at our expense and we will cheerfully refund your money. It will be impossible for us to give you a higher grade or better harness regardless of what price you might pay for it. This harness is made in one kind of trimming, solid nickel, commonly known as German silver. **Bridle**, our combination bridle made with overcheck and side rein combined, ⅝-inch box loop cheeks with high grade patent leather blinds, round winker brace, ⅝-inch throat latch, layer on crown piece with solid nickel overcheck bit and a solid nickel snaffle bit. We guarantee these bits never to corrode or rust and are the highest grade bits made. **Lines**, 1-inch fronts with spring billet to buckle in the bit, 1⅛-inch hand parts, russet or black. Russet hand parts **25** cents extra. **Breast collar and traces**, breast collar is extra wide V-shaped, cut out of very heavy solid leather with 1¼-inch single strap traces stitched to the breast collar, double stitched at the back end with three holes to lengthen or shorten the pull, with neck strap to buckle on each side, made of solid leather with line rings attached to keep the lines from dropping under the shafts. **Pad or gig saddle**, long pad, leather housing, and single strap skirts trimmed with solid nickel or German silver hooks and terrets. The terrets will never wear yellow or tarnish. We guarantee them to be solid nickel through and through and the best trimming that can be made. **Bellyband**, made Griffith style, to buckle on the pad, and short straps to wrap round the shafts. Turnback, ⅝-inch, scalloped and stitched with round crupper sewed on, ⅝-inch hip strap. **Breeching**, 1⅞ inches wide with scalloped point layer, double and stitched breeching brace and ⅝-inch side straps.

No. 10C277 Price, genuine solid nickel German silver trimming **$14.75**

Add extra for old style shaft tugs with double bellyband .... **.50**

Add extra for russet hand parts .... **.25**

Notice—We do not make any other changes in this harness.

Sears' Best Hand Made Single Strap Buggy Harness, $14.32.

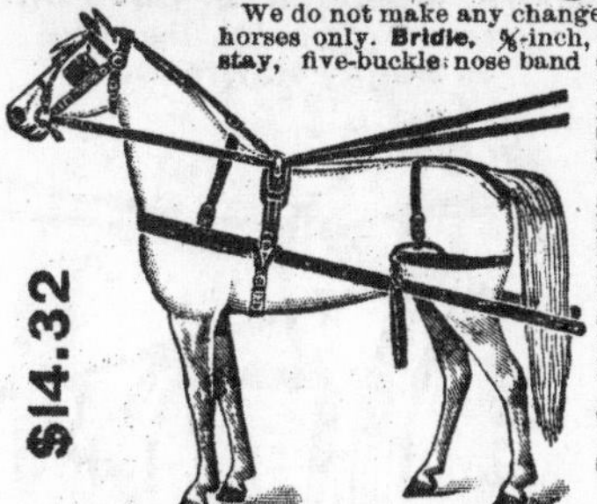

We do not make any changes in this harness. Harness made for 900 to 1250-lb. horses only. **Bridle**, ⅝-inch, box loop cheeks, patent leather winkers, round **stay**, five-buckle nose band over check, layer on crown, or side check, initial rosettes; **lines**, 1-inch fronts, 1⅛-inch black hand parts, spring billets; **breast collar**, 2-inch, single strap, box loop neck strap; **traces**, 1¼-inch, single strap, sewed to breast collar, scalloped and raised points, wave stitched; **breeching**, 1⅞-inch single strap, scalloped raised points, box loops, ⅝-inch hip strap, ⅝-inch side straps, ⅝-inch scalloped back strap, heavy flaxseed crupper; **saddle**, 3-inch single strap, swell pad and housing, patent leather jockey, leather bottom; **bellyband**, single strap, swell pattern, Griffith buckles; **trimmings**, nickel or Davis rubber and genuine rubber. Shipping weight, boxed, about 27 pounds.

No. 10C280 Price, per set for nickel or Davis rubber harness **$14.32**

No. 10C285 Price, per set, for genuine rubber harness **16.80**

Add extra for russet hand parts on lines. **.25**

All hand made, extra strong for doctors' use. Fine Dundee oak leather, smooth, round edge finish.

Our White Celluloid Trimmed Single Harness, $13.95.

This is one of the latest styles in trimming, while the style of the harness is the same as we have used for some time. This harness is much improved, made with **white celluloid hook and terret**, small buckles, nickel or Davis rubber, making a very stylish and handsome appearing harness. **Bridle**, ⅝-inch, box loop cheek, patent leather blind, round winker stay overcheck with nose band or side rein; **breast collar**, V-shape, single strap, 1⅛-inch traces stitched to breast collar, three holes in the back end; **breeching**, 1⅝-inch single strap body, ⅝-inch side straps, ⅝-inch hip strap, ⅝-inch scalloped and stitched turnback with crupper sewed on; **gig saddle or pad**, single strap skirts with patent leather jockey, fancy beaded housings; a very handsome pad or gig saddle and very durable; **bellyband**, Griffith style, box loop shaft tugs, bellyband single strap with billets to wrap around shafts; 1-inch lines throughout to loop in bit, one tie strap. This harness is made smooth, no creasing, round edge finish, the leather is good quality, well selected, and the harness is well made, with white celluloid trimmings only. This harness will weigh about 20 pounds, boxed.

No. 10C287 Price, per set, with white celluloid hook and terret, small buckles, nickel or Davis rubber **$13.95**

Add extra for Condon safety bit ..... **.50**

Our Fine Doubled and Stitched Single Buggy Harness, $23.25.

For 900 to 1200-pound horse. We do not make any changes in this harness.

This is one of the best light doubled and stitched harness that we make, the quality of the leather is of the very best, the workmanship high grade, and the trimmings and hardware used in this are the very finest, the gig saddle is of the best grade Kay saddle; **bridle**, ⅝-inch, box loop cheek with fine patent leather blind, round winker brace, folded crown piece with layer, or **open bridle; breast collar**, glove finished fold leather with narrow raised layer throughout, with 1-inch doubled and stitched traces attached to breast collar; **breeching**, glove finished fold leather body, narrow raised layer throughout, ⅝-inch side straps, ⅝-inch doubled and stitched hip strap, ⅝-inch doubled and stitched scalloped back strap, with round crupper attached; **gig saddle or pad** 2½-inch, half track, full Kay with continuous backband; this is a strictly high grade pad; **bellyband**, folded inside with layer, and outside single strap attached, with billets to wrap around shaft, box loop shaft tugs; **lines**, ⅞-inch, doubled and stitched, beaded front with spring billets to buckle in bit, 1⅛-inch black hand parts, one tie strap. This harness is made only with genuine rubber trimming, one of the best high priced single buggy harnesses in our line, and will compare with other harnesses sold throughout the country, for from $35.00 to $45.00. Weight of this harness, boxed, 29 pounds.

No. 10C289 Price of this harness, genuine rubber only **$23.25**

Single Pony Harness, $8.70 and $8.95.

For pony 300 to 750 pounds.

This Pony Harness is made in either russet or black leather, nickel or brass trimmings. Bridle, ⅝-inch cheek, box loop, with patent leather blinds, round winker brace, overcheck or flat side rein; **breast collar**, 1⅝-inch wide single strap, with 1-inch single strap traces attached or stitched to breast collar, with three holes in the back end; **breeching** is 1⅜-inch single strap body, with ⅝-inch side straps, ½-inch hip strap, ⅝-inch back strap with round crupper sewed on; **gig saddle or pad**, single strap skirts, with patent leather housing, leather bottom pad, single strap; **bellyband**, Griffith style, with billets to wrap around shafts; **lines**, ⅞-inch, to loop in bit, one tie strap. Remember, we can furnish this harness in russet or black leather, nickel or brass trimmings. Weight, 20 pounds, boxed.

No. 10C306 Price of nickel trimmed harness **$8.70**

No. 10C307 Price of brass trimmed harness **8.95**

Add extra for collar and hame harness in place of breast collar **3.15**

Our Brown Grocery Harness, $10.45.

We do not make any changes in this harness. This harness made for 900 to 1200-pound horses. **Bridle**, ⅝-inch patent leather, sensible blinds, flat rein and winker stays; **hame tugs**, with swell ends, box loops, 3½-pound iron hames; **traces**, 1¼-inch, double and stitched, round edge finish; **breeching**, folded with wide layer; **side straps**, 1-inch, double; **hip strap**, ⅝-inch; **turnback**, 1-inch, round crupper to buckle on; **saddle**, 3½ inches, patent leather, full padded; **bellyband**, folded; **lines**, 1-inch throughout to buckle in bit; **collar**, full kip.

In ordering this harness always state size of collar wanted. XC trimmings throughout. Weight, 35 pounds.

No. 10C315 Price, with collar **$10.45**

If wanted with breast collar in place of collar and hames, the price would be **9.50**

No. 10C316 Same style harness as No. 10C315, only made in brass or nickel. Price, with collar **12.50**

Price, without collar **11.50**

Our Single Express or Wagon Harness.

We do not make any changes in this harness. Trimming full japanned black. **Bridle**, ⅞-inch, box loop cheek, round rein and winker stay, sensible blind; **hames**, wood hames brass ball top, box loop hame tug with champion buckle; **traces**, 1½-inch double and stitched with clipped cockeye, 6 feet long; **breeching**, folded body with layer; 3 feet, 3 inches long, side strap: 1⅛-inch double hip strap, ⅞-inch turnback, 1⅛-inch with round crupper to buckle on; **saddle or pad**, 4½-inch harness leather skirt, cloth pad; iron jockey or tree, ring in bearer, shaft tug with dee, folded bellyband, collar strap, 1-inch; **lines**, 1-inch wide, 13½ feet long, to buckle in bit; ⅞-inch tie strap; **good collar.** Weight, 40 pounds.

No. 10C343 Price, per set, without collar **$13.50**

No. 10C344 Price, per set, with collar **15.65**

Our Fine Extra Heavy Brass Express Harness.

We do not make any changes in this harness. Harness for horses from 1,000 to 1,250 pounds.

Bridle, ⅞-inch, box loops, round rein and winker stay, face piece; **hame tugs**, box loops, red ball top, No. 6 dandy clip hame; **traces**, 1½-inch, double and stitched, round edge; **breeching**, folded with layer; ⅞-inch double hip straps; side straps, 1⅛-inch; back strap, 1⅛-inch; **saddle**, 5-inch, brass jockey, harness leather skirts, kersey pad; **shaft tugs**, with dees; **bellyband**, folded, extra heavy; **lines**, 1-inch; **choke strap**, 1-inch. Weight, 35 pounds.

No. 10C400 Price, without collar, **$18.95**

No. 10C405 Price, with collar complete **21.45**

For prices on full line of collars, see collar page 102.

Our Improved Brass and Nickel Express Harness.

1⅛-inch and 1½-inch traces.

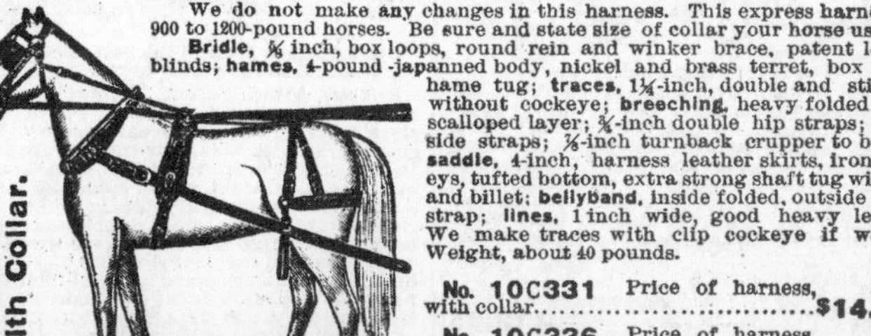

We do not make any changes in this harness. **Bridle**, ⅞-inch, box loops, round rein and winker stay; **hame tugs**, box loops, red ball top or 4-pound iron hames; **traces**, 1⅛-inch, double and stitched, round edge; **breeching**, folded with layer; ⅞-inch double hip straps; side straps, 1-inch; back strap, ⅞-inch, **saddle**, 4-inch, iron jockey, harness leather skirts, kersey pad; **shaft tugs**, with dees; **bellybands**, folded; **lines**, 1-inch; **choke strap**, 1-inch. Wt., 30 lbs.

No. 10C426 Price, without collar, **$13.50**

No. 10C431 Price, with good thong sewed collar **15.65**

No. 10C434 Same harness as No. 10C426, only made extra heavy, 1½-inch traces. Weight, 40 pounds. Price, without collar **15.50**

No. 10C439 Price, complete with collar **17.65**

Single Brass or Nickel Express Harness.

We do not make any changes in this harness. This express harness for 900 to 1200-pound horses. Be sure and state size of collar your horse uses. **Bridle**, ⅞ inch, box loops, round rein and winker brace, patent leather blinds; **hames**, 4-pound japanned body, nickel and brass terret, box loops, hame tug; **traces**, 1⅛-inch, double and stitched, without cockeye; **breeching**, heavy folded body, scalloped layer; ⅞-inch double hip straps; 1-inch side straps; ⅞-inch turnback crupper to buckle; **saddle**, 4-inch, harness leather skirts, iron jockeys, tufted bottom, extra strong shaft tug with dee and billet; **bellyband**, inside folded, outside single strap; **lines**, 1 inch wide, good heavy leather. We make traces with clip cockeye if wanted. Weight, about 40 pounds.

No. 10C331 Price of harness, with collar **$14.10**

No. 10C336 Price of harness, without collar **12.10**

No. 10C341 Price of harness, with breast collar **11.95**

Single Surrey Harness.

Nickel Trimmings, $14.65
Brass Trimmings, 15.95

This harness for 900 to 1200-pound horses.

Bridle, ⅝-inch, patent leather, round corner winkers, round side reins, round winker stays, box loops and nose band, initial glass rosettes; **hame tugs**, patent leather swell ends, full plated hames, 4 pounds; **traces**, 1¼-inch, double and stitched, round edge finish; **breeching**, folded, with scalloped raised layer, ⅝-inch double hip strap; **side straps**, ⅝-inch; **turnback**, ⅝-inch; scalloped with round crupper; **saddle**, full patent leather skirts, full padded, with enameled leather, laced in; **bellyband**, inside one folded, outside one single attached; **lines**, 1-inch hand parts, 1-inch fronts, with steel spring billets; **collar**, patent leather; either open or closed top. Weight, about 36 pounds. Nickel wire or imitation rubber trimmings. **Be sure and give size of collar wanted.**

No. 10C485 Nickel or imitation rubber. Price, with collar $14.65

No. 10C486 Brass trimmings. Price, with collar 15.95

A Surrey Harness Wonder.

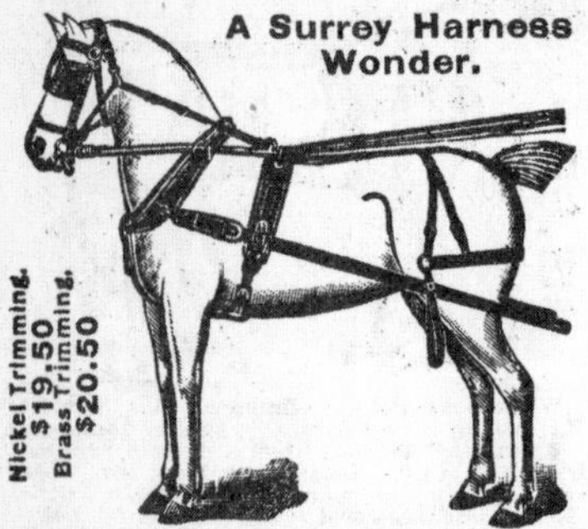

Nickel Trimming, $19.50
Brass Trimming, $20.50

They will never be so cheap again. We give you the benefit. If you don't find this the handsomest, strongest, best made, most perfect surrey harness ever seen in your section at anything like the price, return it at our expense and we will immediately refund your money. This harness is large enough for 900 or 1200-pound horses. Be sure and state size of collar wanted.

Bridle, ⅝-inch, round rein and winker stay, box loops, nose band; **hame tugs**, patent leather, box loops, safe under buckles, 4-pound full plated hames; **traces**, 1¼-inch, double and stitched, raised round edge; **breeching**, folded, with scalloped raised layer, ⅝-inch double hip straps, side straps 1 inch; **turnback**, ⅝-inch, double reversed, round crupper to buckle; **saddle**, 4-inch, covered seat, enameled leather pad, laced in; **shaft tugs**, with dees, **bellybands**, inside folded with layer, outside single attached; **lines**, ⅝-inch, 1⅛-inch hand parts; **choke straps**, 1-inch, **collar**, full patent leather, bent or buckle top, russet faced. State size of collar wanted. Weight, boxed, about 30 pounds.

No. 10C495 Nickel trimming, complete with collar. Price $19.50

No. 10C500 Same style of harness as No. 10C495, only made with full brass trimmings throughout, with the latest style swedge buckles, making one of the most stylish and fancy surrey harnesses on the market, complete with a half patent leather collar and a full brass hame; be sure and state the size of collar wanted when ordering, or size of hames to fit your collar if wanted less collar. Complete, with collar.

Price, brass trimming $20.50

Our Florida Double Buggy Harness, $13.95.

For 900 to 1200-pound horses.

Bridles, ⅝-inch, overcheck, or flat reins, box loops, round winker stays with tie strap; **hame tugs**, box loops, 7-pound iron hames; **pads**, straight leather boxings and housings, skirts single, bearers, double and stitched, **turnbacks**, ⅝-inch, round cruppers; **bellybands**, flat; **traces**, 1⅛-inch, 6 feet 4 inches, double and stitched; **lines**, ⅝-inch, 1-inch all black hand parts; **neckyoke straps**, 1⅛-inch; **choke straps**, ⅞-inch. Trimming, XC or japanned. Weight, boxed, about 40 pounds.

No. 10C521 Price of harness, without collars $13.95

Price, complete with collars 16.25

Add extra for russet hand parts .... .25

We do not make any other changes in this harness.

Freeport Double Buggy Harness.

Full nickel trimmed.

For team 900 to 1200-pound horses.

Genuine Davis imitation of rubber or full nickel double driving harness.

Bridles, ⅝-inch, patent leather blinds, box loops, over or side checks, round winker stays, fancy fronts and rosettes; **hames**, 7-pound iron, japanned body, with nickel terret; **hame tugs**, full length, heavy box loops; **pads**, straight coached, enameled leather bottoms, skirts and bearers heavy, double and stitched with layers; **turnbacks**, ⅝-inch scalloped, with crupper dock sewed on; **bellybands**, heavy, full length, finished; **traces**, 1⅛-inch, full length, 6 feet 6 inches long, double and stitched, nicely finished; **lines**, ⅝-inch, all black, cut full length, with good hand parts; **neckyoke straps**, 1⅛-inch strap with buckle; **martingales or collar straps**, ⅞-inch. Weight, boxed, about 45 pounds.

No. 10C545 Price, without collars, per set $15.95

No. 10C546 Complete with our No. 10C3415 buggy collars 18.25

Add extra for russet hand parts on lines .... .25

We make no other changes in this harness.

Our Great Bargain, $17.95.

A full nickel or Davis rubber trimmed double driving harness.

This is our leader of leaders in Double Driving Harness, and the greatest value ever offered by us or any other house. Don't buy a cheaper double buggy harness. If you order this harness you will get such a harness as was never seen in your section at anything like the price. Bridles, ⅝-inch, box loop, patent leather blinds, overcheck or side rein, round winker brace, fancy front and initial glass rosettes or open bridle; **hames**, 7-pound iron hame, japanned body, nickel terret only; **hame tugs**, patent leather, end box loop; **pads**, coach, enameled, leather bottom, single strap skirts, double and stitched bearers; **turnbacks**, ⅝-inch, scallop with round crupper sewed on; **bellybands**, folded; **traces**, 1⅛-inch, full length, 6 feet 6 inches long, double and stitched, round edge; **lines**, ⅝x1⅛-inch black hand parts. We will not make any other changes in this harness, only furnished as listed above. This harness for 900 to 1200-pound horses. Weight of set, boxed, about 40 pounds.

No. 10C576 Price, per set without collars, in nickel or Davis rubber $17.95

No. 10C581 Price, complete with collars (be sure and state size of collar wanted) $21.35

Add extra for 1¼-inch traces 2.00

Extra for russet hand parts on lines .... .25

Our Wichita Single Strap Double Buggy Harness, $20.95.

Our harness is made of the best selected stock. For team 900 to 1200-pound horses.

Bridles, ⅝-inch patent leather blinds, box loops, overcheck or side check, round winker stays, layer on crowns; **breast collars**, 2-inch, single strap with wide folded neck strap; **traces**, 1¼-inch single strap stitched to breast collars; **pads**, coach, straight, raised patent leather top, leather bottoms, beaded edge housings, skirts single strap, bearers raised, double and stitched; **turnbacks**, ⅝-inch single strap, scalloped round crupper, sewed on; **bellybands**, single strap; **lines**, 1⅛-inch black hand parts, 1-inch fronts; **neckyoke straps**, 1⅛-inch; **choke straps**, 1-inch. Made smooth round edge, not creased. Nickel or imitation rubber trimmings throughout. Weight, boxed for shipment, 45 pounds.

No. 10C560 Price $20.95

Extra for 1½-inch single strap traces 2.50

Sears, Roebuck & Co.'s Improved Special Double Buggy Harness.

This is our special harness made of the best Dundee oak leather, well selected and finished; **trimming**, fine nickel or Davis rubber. **This is one of the best double harness we handle. Bridles**, ⅝-inch box loop cheek, round winker stay, layer on crown, fine patent leather blinds, overcheck with nose band or round side checks; **hames**, 7-pound iron hame, with fancy end hame tug with box loop safe under buckle, nickel terret and draft eye on nickel hames, and Davis rubber on the other; **pads**, extra scallop housing, fine leather bottom pad, single strap skirt with heavy wide double and stitched bearer; **bellybands**, folded with layer; **traces**, the very best 1⅛-inch, 6½ feet long, or 1¼-inch 6½ feet, doubled and stitched, raised round edge finish; **lines**, a very important part of a harness, are 1-inch fronts, checks with 1⅛-inch hand parts, with buckle and billets at bit; **neckyoke straps**, 1¼-inch, extra heavy, well made, double and stitched where it goes around neckyoke, making it very strong; **martingales**, 1-inch from collar to bellyband, two tie straps. Weight, boxed, about 50 pounds.

No. 10C586 Price, 1⅛-inch traces, less collars $22.95

No. 10C587 Price, 1¼-inch traces, less collars 24.25

Extra for double hip strap breeching, 5.75

Add extra for russet hand parts. .25

Add extra for two collars No. 10C3430 4.20

Add extra for Condon safety bits 1.00

Our High Grade Double Carriage Harness for $37.30.

Trimmings, fine nickel on composition or genuine Davis rubber; **bridles**, ⅝-inch round reins and winker brace, box loops, fine coach blind, layer on crown piece, nose band on bridle, with fine initial rosettes; **8-pound hames**, full nickel plate with box loop hame tug, with fine patent leather point, safes under buckles; **pads**, **straight raised top**, fine patent leather bottom, heavy 4-inch beaded house, single skirts, double and stitched raised bearers, folded bellybands; **turnbacks**, ⅝-inch, scalloped and wave stitched with heavy round crupper; **traces**, 1¼ inches, 6½ feet, double stitched, raised round edge; **lines**, 1-inch fronts, with a buckle and billet, 1⅛-inch black hand parts sewed on; **breeching**, double hip strap, folded, with raised layer, breeching strap stitched in fold or ring, breeching strap runs up to and buckles in the hame tug buckle, with a patent leather drop or tug carrier; **neckyoke straps**, 1¼-inch collar strap, or martingale 1-inch, two hitching straps and spreader straps. Size of harness, for 900 to 1250-pound horses. Shipping weight, about 70 pounds.

No. 10C655 Price, with breeching and with collars complete $37.30

No. 10C660 Without collars. 33.40

If wanted without breeching, deduct from price of harness 3.00

Add for brass trimming on the harness with full brass hames, extra 2.40

Our Iowa Spring Wagon Harness.

XC trimming $20.95

Nickel trimming 21.98

Brass trimming 22.00

We do not make any other changes in this harness.

Spring Wagon Harness is made of extra quality Dundee oak leather, well selected; special care is taken to have them light and very strong, making a light spring wagon harness and also a light farm harness. The best is always the cheapest. Size of harness for 900 to 1200-pound horses.

Trimmings, XC, brass and nickel. Two tie and spread straps; **bridles**, ⅝-inch box loop, round rein and winker stay, sensible or square blinds (will send sensible blinds, unless ordered square); **hames**, low top wood hame with breast rings; line ring on XC harness will be XC, brass on brass harness, nickel on nickel harness; **hame tugs**, made with box loop and Champion trace buckle; **pads**, swell pad, leather bottom, single strap skirts, double and stitched bearer (will make the skirts with inside trace), loop if wanted (but must state inside loop on pad); **turnbacks**, ⅝-inch scalloped and stitched with round crupper to buckle on; ⅝-inch hip strap; **bellybands**, folded; **traces**, extra good, 1¼-inch by 6½ feet, double and stitched, raised with cockeye, made without cockeye if wanted; **lines**, a very important part of this harness, are 1 inch by 18 feet long, good and strong; **breast straps**, 1¼-inch with buckle, snap and slides 1¼-inch martingales; ⅞-inch collar snap. Weight, boxed, about 70 pounds.

No. 10C670 XC Harness, no collars $20.95

No. 10C675 Nickel Harness, no collars 21.98

No. 10C680 Brass Harness, no collars 22.00

Add extra for breeching with ⅝-inch double hip straps and ⅝-inch side straps 4.75

Be sure and state the size of hames wanted to fit collars.

OUR VERY FINEST DOUBLE DRIVING HARNESS $24.75

WITH SOLID NICKEL GERMAN SILVER TRIMMINGS.

Bridles, ⅝-inch, box loop cheek with fine grain patent leather blind; round winker brace sewed in, buckles in crown piece, layer on crown piece with overcheck loops, ⅝-inch throat latch, overcheck and side rein combined, buckling into the overcheck bit; bits are made of solid nickel German silver; the snaffle and the overcheck bits we guarantee not to rust, tarnish, or corrode, but will remain their natural color, solid nickel; **lines**, ⅝-inch cheeks with buckle and billet to buckle in the bit, and 1⅛-inch hand parts, black or russet; will always send black unless ordered russet line at 25 cents extra; **hames**, full japan body with solid nickel terret, box loop hame tugs with solid nickel buckles; **traces**, 1⅛-inch double and stitched, with raised center to buckle into the hame tug; 6½ feet long; **martingale**, ⅞ inch from bellyband to collar, 1¼-inch neckyoke strap from collar to neckyoke; **pads**, made with heavy long patent leather housing, beaded and stitched, raised bearer, folded bellyband to buckle on the skirts; **turnback**, ⅝-inch double and stitched, with crupper sewed on.

THE TRIMMING USED on this, our high grade double buggy harness, is **solid nickel**, commonly known as German silver. All the buckles, rings, the overcheck bit, the snaffle bit and the hooks and terrets on the hames are made of this high grade solid nickel German silver metal. We guarantee it not to rust, tarnish, or corrode, but will always wear the same original finish. We guarantee it to be the highest grade trimming that is used on the highest priced harness on the market.

THE LEATHER is the highest grade Dundee oak, which requires five and one-half months to tan properly, which is a guarantee in itself that it is the best leather that can be made.

THE WORKMANSHIP is the best that years of experience can produce.

COMBINING THESE THREE ESSENTIAL POINTS IN THE HARNESS, NAMELY, HIGH GRADE GERMAN SILVER TRIMMING, THE VERY BEST SELECTION OF HIGH GRADE DUNDEE OAK LEATHER, AND THE VERY BEST SKILLED WORKMANSHIP THAT CAN BE HAD IS A GUARANTEE IN ITSELF THAT IT IS THE VERY BEST DOUBLE DRIVING HARNESS THAT CAN BE MADE. We are making a leader of this harness, and at our exceptionally low price of $24.75, we guarantee it to be equal, if not superior to harness that retails throughout the country at $35.00 to $45.00.

No. 10C620 Price of double harness, without collars $24.75

No. 10C625 Price, with collars 28.95

Chain or Plow Harness.

Will fit 900 to 1000-pound horses. We do not make any changes in this harness. **Bridles,** ⅝-inch Jenny Lind or sensible blinds; **hames,** varnished, iron overtop, hook; **back bands,** 3½-inch leather with leather loops; **bellybands,** 1¼-inch with loop ends; **back straps,** 1⅛-inch, running from ring on hip to the hames with 1½-inch hip strap; **traces,** 7-foot chains with 30-inch leather piping; **lines,** ⅝-inch by 15 feet, with snaps; **breast straps,** with 1½-inch breast strap, slides and snaps. There are no hitching straps included with the harness, or pole straps. The price of the harness is without collars. For prices on collars see collar page. Weight, boxed, about 60 pounds.

No. 10C805 Double Harness, no collars. Price........................**$11.75**
Add extra for 60-inch chain pipe on No. 10C805 Harness........................**$3.75**

Our Improved Team or Plow Harness.

Full size for horses weighing 1200 pounds. We do not make any changes in this harness. **Bridles,** ⅝-inch Concord blind or Jenny Lind flat rein, flat winker brace; **hames,** black iron overtop; **pads,** flat with 1⅛-inch billets; **back straps,** 1⅛-inch; **hip straps,** 1-inch with folded crupper; **traces,** 1½-inch, 4 feet 6 inches, double and stitched with 3½-foot stage chain; **lines,** good selected stock, ⅝-inch by 18 feet, wire snap; **breast straps,** with snap and slides; **martingales,** 1½-inch, no collar strap; **tie straps.** Don't buy small size harness, as you cannot use them. Our $14.50 harness is full size. Weight boxed, about 45 pounds.

No. 10C810 Price without collars **$13.75**
Add extra for 1⅝-inch traces........ **1.00**

Our Special Farm Harness, $17.00.

Full size for 900 to 1200-pound horses. We do not make any changes in this harness. **Bridles,** ⅝-in. flat rein, round winker brace and sensible blinds; **hames,** iron overtop, clip and staple, made with breast ring; **traces,** double and stitched, 1½ inches wide and 4½ feet long, with 3½ foot stage chain; traces riveted to hames; **breeching,** folded body, 1-inch double and stitched layer, 1⅛-inch back straps running to hames, ⅝-inch double hip straps, ⅝-inch double side straps to snap to ring on trace or under horse in martingale; **pads,** flat body with 1⅛-inch **billets; lines,** 1-inch wide, 15 feet long, with snaps; **breast straps,** 1½ inches with snaps and slide. Collar straps running from collar to bellyband, 1¼ inches. Hitching reins and spread straps included with this harness. Weight, about 45 pounds.

No. 10C815 Price of harness, without collars........................**$17.00**
Add extra for 1⅝-inch traces........................**1.00**

Single Goat or Dog Harness.

Bridle, ⅜-inch with bit to snap; **breast collar,** 1¼-inch flat with plain layer point; **traces,** 1-inch, flat, sewed to breast collar; **saddle,** 2-inch flat, no tree, full lined, with loose ring terrets; **shaft tugs,** ⅝-inch; **hip strap,** ⅝-inch; **bellyband,** double with snaps; **side straps,** ⅝-inch; **turnback,** ⅝-inch, plain with safe; **breeching,** 1¼-inch, flat with plain layer point; **lines,** ⅝-inch, to snap in bit. Weight, boxed, about 3 to 5 pounds.

No. 10C830 Price, per set........**$2.70**
No. 10C835 Double Goat Harness. Price, per set for two goats........ **6.00**

Oklahoma Flat Pad Team Harness, $15.75.

For 900 to 1200-pound horses. We do not make any changes in this harness. **Bridles,** ⅝-in. sensible blinds; **hames,** black iron overtop; **pads,** flat, folded, 1⅛-inch, billets; **back straps,** 1⅛-inch, hip straps 1-inch; **traces,** 1½-inch, 5 feet 10 inches, double and stitched; **lines,** ⅝-inch, 15 feet, with snaps; **breast straps,** 1½-inch, with slides and snaps; **pole straps,** 1½-inch. **A good flat pad team harness.** Weight, about 40 pounds.

No. 10C840 Price, without collars........................**$15.75**
Add extra for 1⅝-inch traces........ **1.00**
For prices on collars, see collar page.

Our Danville Farm Harness, $22.95.

Notice—Made in sliptug, if wanted, at same price.

Weight, boxed, about 85 pounds.

Size of harness for 900 to 1200-pound horses. **Bridles,** ⅝-inch short check bridle with nose band and bit strap. Concord blind, round winker brace, round side check and tie strap; **lines,** 1 inch by 18 feet, with snaps; **traces,** 1½-inch trace, double and stitched, with cockeyes sewed in, 6 feet long; **hames,** XC iron overtop, with Hayden holdback, 1½-inch clip hame tug, Champion trace buckle, folded bellyband, breast straps, 1½ inches, with snaps and slides; pole straps, 1½ inches with collar strap; **pads,** folded body, 1⅛-inch layer with perfection tree hook and terret to buckle in hame tug; **hip straps,** 1-inch hip and back strap **with folded crupper** to buckle on.

No. 10C850 Price, complete, without collars........................**$22.95**
Add extra for 1⅝-inch traces........ **1.00**
Add extra for breeching to buckle on hip straps........................ **2.90**

No. 10C851 Same style of harness as No. 10C850, only made with **brass trimming. A fine brass trimmed team harness,** 1½-inch traces.

Price, brass trimmed harness without collars........................**$25.10**

Our Bismarck Concord Farm Harness, $25.75.

Full size harness for 900 to 1200-pound horses. **Bridles,** ⅝-inch, long check, Concord blinds, round winker brace, spotted face piece, round reins and tie strap with snap; **lines,** well selected line leather, 1-inch by 18 feet long; **traces,** fine Dundee trace leather, 6 feet long, 1½-inch double and stitched point, 2¼-inch single strap body, with cockeyes sewed in; **hame and hame tugs,** No. 6 oiled Concord bolt hame, fine **lace box loop hame tugs,** Champion trace buckle, 1¼-inch bellyband billet and heavy folded bellyband; **hip and back straps,** selected leather, 1-inch hip and back straps, sewed in. Cooper trace carrier, with trace loop to buckle on hip strap; **pads,** our special hook and terret pad, folded body, turtle bottom, with D-ring on side, with short market strap to trace buckle. One of the finest pads on the market; **breast and pole straps,** 1½-inch breast strap, with snap and roller breast snap; 1½-inch pole strap, with collar strap; spread strap and ring, tie strap. Weight, boxed for shipment, about 80 pounds.

No. 10C855 Without collars....**$25.75**
Add extra for 1⅝x2½-inch traces.. **1.50**
Extra for 1⅛-inch by 20-foot lines.. **.65**
Extra for team breeching No. 10C2490.. **2.90**
Add extra for collar No. 10C3480, each.. **2.95**

Will furnish good double and stitched traces at same price.

Our Special Single Farm Harness.

WITHOUT COLLAR, **$10.48**
WITH COLLAR... **11.70**

We make no change in this harness. Weight, boxed, about 40 lbs.

Made for plowing with double shovel plows, single cultivator, or for single spring wagon, or any work where you wish to use a single horse.

Bridle, ⅝-inch, check, sensible blinders, flat rein with round winker brace; **hames,** common iron overtop clip, and staple breast ring with hame tug riveted on; **pads,** our special flexible team pad with terret and loop; **shaft tugs,** 1½-inch, double and stitched; **breeching,** heavy folded body with layer, 1⅛-inch back strap running through loop on pad to hames, ⅝-inch double hip straps, ⅝-inch double side straps running to trace buckle; **lines,** 1 inch wide and 18 feet long; **traces,** extra strong, 1½-inch double and stitched traces, 6 feet long. Size of harness for 900 to 1200-pound horse. **Be sure and state size of collar wanted.**

No. 10C857 Without collar......**$10.48**
No. 10C858 Price, with collar.... **11.70**
NOTICE—We will make this harness with low top hames if wanted.

Dakota Team Farm Harness, $25.95, $29.95.

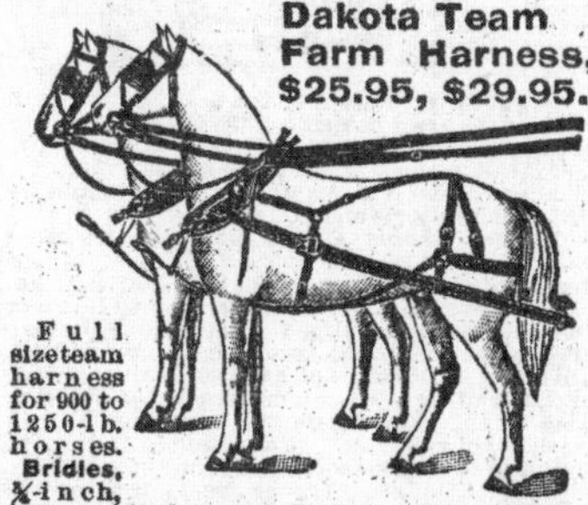

Full size team harness for 900 to 1250-lb. horses. **Bridles,** ⅝-inch, long check, spotted face piece, Concord blinds, flat rein, to throw over hame; **hames,** No. 6 oiled Concord bolt hames, 1½-inch **lace box loop hame tug,** Champion trace buckle, 1⅛-inch bellyband billets; heavy folded bellybands; **lines,** selected Dundee oak leather, 1-inch by 20 feet, with snaps; **traces,** double and stitched, 1½-inch by 6 feet long, cockeye sewed in; **breeching,** heavy folded body, wide layer, 1-inch back strap running to trace buckle and short strap running to hame, 1-inch double hip strap, ⅝-inch side strap to snap in martingale ring; **breast and pole straps,** 1½-inch breast strap with snaps and slide, 1½-inch pole strap, with collar straps; spread straps, ring and tie straps. Weight, boxed for shipment, 80 pounds.

No. 10C860 Without collars.....**$25.95**
Add extra for 1⅝-inch traces........ **1.00**

No. 10C861 Same style of harness as No. 10C860, with ⅞-inch bridle and extra heavy breeching, with 1⅛-inch double back straps, 1⅛-inch double hip straps and 1⅛-inch side straps, with 1⅝-inch traces, 6 feet long, making a heavy Dakota farm harness. Balance same as No. 10C860. Price, without collars..**$29.95**
Add extra for round reins or bridle, **.65**
Extra for brass ball hames, No. 10C3885 **1.85**
Extra for roller breast strap snaps.. **.25**
Add extra for brass ball No. 10C3880 on hames........................ **.75**
Add extra for large harness for 1400 to 1600-pound horse........................ **3.00**

Our Leader in Farm Harness for Spring Work, $16.50.

We do not make any change in this harness. This harness will fit horses from 900 to 1200 pounds. **For $16.50** we offer this leader in farm harness as the equal of harness that will be sold everywhere this year at 30 per cent more money. While $16.50 seems and is remarkably cheap, almost too cheap to be good, **we guarantee this harness to be perfect in every piece and part,** thoroughly satisfactory, and if you do not find it so and exactly as represented, return the harness to us at our expense and we will immediately refund your money.

Bridles, ⅝-inch, sensible blinds, round **reins** and winker stays; **hames,** black, iron overtop; **pads,** hook and terret or self adjusting long tug; **back straps,** 1-inch; hip straps, 1-inch; **traces,** 1½-inch, 6 feet, double and stitched; **lines,** ⅝-inch, 18 feet, with snaps; **breast straps,** 1½-inch, with slides and snaps; **pole straps,** 1½-inch; **trimmings,** XC. Shipping weight, boxed, 65 pounds.

No. 10C870 Price, without collars........................**$16.50**
Add extra for 1⅝-inch traces...... **1.00**
Add extra for team breeching...... **2.90**
Add extra for 1-inch x18-foot lines. **.50**
Add extra for harness large enough for 1500-pound horse, per set **2.75**
Add extra for collar strap on martingale........................ **.25**
For prices on collars, see collar page.

Our Fargo Hand Made Farm Team Harness. Hand Made Throughout.

We do not make any changes in this harness. **This harness is all hand made.** The very best selected Dundee oak leather, a very high class hand made team harness full japanned trimmed. You cannot make them any better.

Bridles, ⅝-inch, check, with spotted face piece, Concord blind, round winker brace, short round check, tie strap, spread strap and ring; **lines,** 1-inch by 18 feet, with snaps; **hames,** oil Concord bolt hames, breast straps 1½-inch, with snaps and slides, pole strap 1½-inch, with collar strap, ring in back end, hame tugs, 1½-inch, for bolt hame with Champion trace buckle and folded bellyband; **breeching,** heavy folded body with heavy layer, ⅝-inch double hip straps, 1-inch back strap running to trace buckle and short strap running to hame, 1-inch side straps; **traces,** heavy, 1½-inch, doubled and stitched, 6 feet long, with cockeyes sewed in. This harness for 900 to 1250-pound horses. Weight, boxed, about 86 pounds.

No. 10C895 Price for this harness complete, without collars, as listed above. Trimming, full japanned........................**$28.95**
Add extra for 1⅝-inch traces...... **1.00**

No. 10C896 Same style, brass trimmed, hames as No. 10C895, only made with brass buckle with brass ball hames and 1½-inch traces.

Price, without collars........................**$30.95**
We make only the changes stated above.

Williams' Famous Slip Tug Team Harness.

$25.90

Full size for 900 to 1250-pound horses. Don't buy a cheap team harness when you can buy our best at less money. The best is always the cheapest.

Bridles, ⅝-inch, short check, Concord blind, nose band, round winker braces, round **reins,** tie strap; **lines,** fine selected Dundee oak leather, 1 inch by 20 feet, with snap; **hames and hame tugs, No. 460XC** wood high top, with Hayden holdback, breast ring, short hame tug riveted on, Champion trace buckle; **traces,** fine heavy select stock, double and stitched, cockeye sewed in, 1½-inch by 6 feet 6 inches long; **breast and pole straps,** 1½-inch breast strap, with snap and slide, pole strap or martingale 1½-inch with collar strap; **pads,** fine perfection tree, turtle bottom, heavy skirts with round loop and inside trace loop, or hook and terret slip-tug pad with out iron tree, 1⅛-inch bellyband billet, with heavy folded bellyband; **hip and back straps,** 1-inch, with Cooper trace carrier sewed in, with trace loop; **breeching,** folded body with layer and breeching stay to buckle on hip strap, ⅝-inch side strap to snap under horse in pole strap ring. Weight, boxed for shipment, 76 pounds.

No. 10C865 Price, without collars........................**$25.90**
Add extra for 1⅝-inch x 6½-foot traces........................ **1.00**
Add extra for bolt hames and hame tugs........................ **1.75**
Add extra for 1⅛-inch by 20-foot lines........................ **.65**
Add extra for large harness for 1400 to 1600-pound horse........................ **3.00**
If wanted without breeching, deduct........................ **2.40**

For price on collars see collar page.

Our Special Brass Trimmed Slip Tug Farm Harness, $27.45.

$27.45

We do not make any changes in this harness. **This harness** is made out of the very choicest selection Dundee oak leather, full brass trimmed throughout. Trimming is of the very latest pattern, swedge buckle, high post terret and fancy post hook; **bridles**, ⅝-inch, cheeks, box loop, brass front round winker brace, round side checks, brass spotted face piece, a heavy and substantial bridle; **hames**, wood, iron bound, brass trimmed, **pads**, fine coach pad, yellow trimmed, leather bottom, single strap skirts, doubled and stitched bearer, 1¼-inch folded bellybands; **traces**, 1½-inch, 6 feet, 6 inches, raised, round edge finish; **lines**, ⅞-inch front, 1-inch hand parts, round edge finish, 18 feet long; **breast straps**, 1½-inch, round edge finish; **pole straps**, 1½ inch, with collar strap, hame strap, ⅝-inch; **back straps**, 1-inch, scalloped and stitched, with round crupper to buckle on (no hip straps), spread straps and rings and tie straps, snaps and slides. This harness can be used for farm work, carryall or hack work, a harness that is suitable for almost any kind of driving, full brass trimmed throughout, with swedge buckle. This is an entirely new harness, strictly first class in every respect. Weight, boxed, about 80 pounds.

No. 10C875 Price, without collars....$27.45
Add extra for hip straps....1.95
Add extra for double hip strap breeching....6.50
Add extra for full brass iron hames....4.00

Our Buffalo Heavy Concord Truck Harness, $27.98 and $33.40

$27.98

Bridles, ⅞-inch, long cheek, spotted face piece, Concord blinds, round winker brace, flat rein; **lines**, fine selected Dundee oak leather, 1 inch wide and 18 feet long, with snaps; **hames**, oiled Concord bolt hames **with brass balls**; **traces**, 6 feet long, 12-inch chain, heavy selected stock, double and stitched, 1½-inch, with heel chains, 1¼-inch bellyband billet and heavy folded bellyband, traces made as shown in illustration; **breeching**, heavy folded body, with 1¼-inch layer; 1-inch side strap running to hame, 1-inch double hip strap, 1-inch side strap to snap in pole strap ring under horse; **breast straps**, 1½-inch, with roller snaps; **pole straps**, made Chicago style. This harness is full size for 1000 to 1250-pound horse. Shipping weight, boxed, about 88 pounds.

No. 10C940 Price, per set, without collars....$27.98
Add extra for 1¾-inch traces on No. 10C940....1.50

No. 10C942 Extra Heavy Concord Harness, same style as No. 10C940 only made with 2-inch traces, 6 feet long, with 12-inch chains; extra heavy breeching, 1¼-inch side straps; 1¼-inch back straps; 1¼-inch double hip straps; 1¾-inch breast straps and martingale roller snaps; 1⅛-inch by 20-foot lines; ⅞-inch bridle, Dandy hame brass balls, balance of harness japanned trimmed. Price, without collars..$33.40

Add for extras to price of harness.
If wanted with 1¾-inch traces, deduct....1.40
Add extra for harness large enough for 1400 to 1600-pound horse....3.00
For No. 10C3480 curled hair face collars, each, add....2.95
For price on collars, see collar page.

Our Nebraska Team Harness, $23.25

$23.25

Bridles, ¾-inch, Concord blinds, round winker brace; **lines**, 1-inch by 18 feet long; **traces**, doubled and stitched, 6 feet long, 1½-inch, with clip cockeye riveted on; **hames, XC**, ironed overtop, with hame tugs riveted on, Champion trace buckle and bellyband billet; **folded bellyband pads**, hook and terret Perfection tree pad to buckle in trace buckle; **hip and back straps**, 1-inch, with crupper to buckle on; **breeching**, **folded body**, with heavy layer ⅝-inch side straps to snap under horse in pole strap; 1½-inch **breast straps**, with snaps and slides, two spread straps and rings, two tie straps. We will make changes in this harness. When changes are wanted be sure and allow the extra price for the parts wanted as per catalogue price. This harness for 900 to 1250-pound horses or full size. Weight, boxed, about 80 pounds.

No. 10C900 Price, without collars....$23.25
If wanted without breeching, deduct....2.40
Add extra for open halter bridle, No. 10C1937....50
Add extra for double hip strap breeching....1.50

Our Special Light Wagon or Farm Harness, $25.75 to $27.05.

We guarantee this to be the best 1½-inch farm harness that can be made, with the best quality of Dundee oak leather, the best workmanship, and if the harness is not perfectly satisfactory, you can return it to us at our expense and we will cheerfully refund your money.

The Best Short Cheek Bridles with nose band, the best kind of bridle for this style harness, and the pad patent leather housing; **adjustable skirt** so you can fit harness to large or small horse; **breeching** with double hip strap or without breeching, in which case we furnish hip strap. This style of harness is suitable for all kinds of light wagon or farm work. Leather used in this harness is the best Dundee oak leather, selected, and we guarantee it to give the best of satisfaction. **Trimming**, brass, nickel or XC plate. **Traces** are 1½-inch or 1½-inch, raised with cockeye sewed in, 6½ feet long; **hame tug** with box loop; **breast strap** and pole strap, spread strap and tie strap are included. **Lines** are 18 feet long, 1 inch wide, well made and strong. Crupper buckles on turn back. In this harness we furnish good bridles, lines, traces and pads, and this is the best harness you can buy. Weight of harness boxed, about 70 pounds.

No. 10C911 Price, per set, brass trimmed, without collars, but with breeching $27.05
No. 10C913 Price, per set, nickel trimmed, without collars, but with breeching $27.00
No. 10C914 Price, per set, XC. trimmed, without collars, but with breeching $25.75
Add extra for 1½-inch traces....1.75
If wanted without breeching and with hip strap, deduct....$2.75

Our Redwood Double Team Harness, $23.95.

This harness full size for 900 to 1250-lb. horses

Bridles, ¾-inch check, Concord blind, round rein, round winker brace, with tie straps; **hames**, common iron overtop clip hame, with back strap ring, clip hame tug, 1½-inch Champion trace buckle, folded bellyband; **traces**, 1½-inch, doubled and stitched, 6 feet long; **breeching**, folded body with layer, 1-inch side strap running to hame and to trace buckle, 1-inch back strap running to trace buckle and short strap running to hame, 1-inch double hip straps and ⅝-inch side straps; **lines**, 1-inch by 18 feet; **breast straps**, 1½-inch, with snaps and slides; **pole straps**, 1½-inch, with collar strap, ring in back end. Shipping weight, boxed, about 80 pounds.

No. 10C915 Price for this harness complete, as listed above, without collars. $23.95
Add extra for 1¾-inch traces....1.00

Montana Concord Harness, $29.97.

This harness is largely used in Montana, Oregon, Idaho, Utah and, in fact, all the western states.

How this harness is made: This harness is made with great care, with extra heavy fine Concord pad stuffed bottom; brass loop on pad with buckle and billet end to buckle into trace buckle. **Made to be used on bolt hames. Quality of leather**: Leather used in this harness is our fine **Delhi oak tanned leather. Stock is well selected, carefully cut and blacked, and we think it is equaled by none and superior to all other grades of harness leather for this particular style and grade of harness.**

Bridles, ⅞-inch, box loop, Concord blinds, spotted face piece, heavy front, round winker brace, ⅞-inch flat rein to throw over hame; **hames**, No. 6 oiled Concord bolt hame, lace box loop hame tug, Champion trace buckle, 1¼-inch bellyband billet, heavy folded bellyband; **pads**, fine Concord pad, stuffed bottom, **brass** loop on top of pad; **traces**, 6 feet long, fine selected Dundee oak leather, 1¾-inch double and stitched point, 2¼-inch single strap body with cockeye sewed on; **breeching**, heavy folded body, with wide layer, 1¼-inch back strap to run through loop on pad to hame, ⅞-inch double hip strap, ⅞-inch side strap to snap under horse in pole strap ring; **lines**, selected line leather, well made, 1-inch by 18 feet, with snap **breast straps**, 1½ inches, with roller snap, pole strap 1½ inches, with collar strap, spread strap and ring, tie strap. This harness is full size for 1000 to 1250-pound horses. Extra large harness for 1400 to 1600-pound horses will cost you $3.00 extra. Weight, about 85 pounds, boxed for shipment.

No. 10C950 Price, per set, without collars....$29.97
Add extra for brass ball hames, brass trimmed bridles, brass buckle shields, balance of harness full japanned trimmed....$3.50
Add for 1¾ inches by 2½ inches single strap body traces....$1.50
Add for 2 inches by 2¼ inches single strap body traces....$2.25
Add for toggle on traces in place of cockeye....50
For No. 10C3480 collar, each, add....2.95
For price on collars, see collar page.

Our Hercules Farm Harness, $20.50 with Breeching and $18.15 without Breeching.

$20.50

This is the best harness that $20.50 can buy. We have given careful attention to the wearing qualities of this harness, and we are sure it will give the very best of satisfaction. Understand, if this harness is not exactly as represented, and you are not perfectly satisfied that you have saved money by purchasing this harness, you are at liberty to return it to us at our expense and we will cheerfully refund your money. This is a strictly new and up to date farm harness, well made, great care being given to the parts that would get the most wear on a harness of this kind.

The harness will be furnished with blind bridle and with or without breeching, as desired. **Lines** are 1 inch wide and 20 feet long, so that they are suitable for almost any kind of work; **bridles** are made with noseband and round side reins to hook upon the pad, as shown in the illustration; **breast straps**, 1½-inch, with snaps and slides; pole straps 1½-inch, with collar strap; **hames** are long staple, iron bound, overtop, with Concord Hame Attachment riveted to the hame tug, which gives you the wearing qualities of the bolt hame and the protection of the Concord joint, which prevents the hame tug, from breaking. This is something new on a common farm harness and is sure to be appreciated by the owner; **traces**, 1½-inch wide, double and stitched, with clip cockeye riveted on, a very strong and durable trace; **pads** are self adjusting, leather bottom, blocked and sewed, and flexible back with skirts to buckle in the trace; **heavy folded bellyband**; turnback and hitch strap 1 inch wide, with Cooper trace carrier; **heavy folded crupper** buckled on; **heavy folded breeching** with straight layer, adjustable; ⅝-inch side straps to snap in the martingale. This is the best all around common farm harness ever offered by us at our exceptionally low price of $20.50, complete with breeching, as shown in the illustration, and less collars. Weight of harness, boxed, 70 pounds.

No. 10C902 Price, with breeching, but without collars....$20.50
No. 10C903 Price, without collars and without breeching....$18.15

Our Indian Territory Farm Harness, $21.95.

Shipping weight, boxed, about 75 pounds.

Full size harness for 900 to 1250-pound horses.

Bridles, ¾-inch, square or sensible blinds, round winker stay, short flat reins, with tie strap; **lines**, ⅞-inch, 18 feet, with snaps; **hames**, varnished iron overtop, with bolt; **hame tugs**, folded with layer, small 1½-inch loops, 1¼-inch bellyband billets; **traces**, 1½-inch, 6 feet, clip cockeyes; **breeching**, folded, 1-inch layer, ⅞-inch double hitch straps, ⅝-inch double back straps to buckle in market straps and hames, ⅝-inch side straps, ¾ inch lazy straps; **bellybands**, folded; **breast straps**, 1½-inch, with snaps and slides; **martingales**, 1½-inch, with collar straps; **trimming**, XC only.

No. 10C905 Price, without collars....$21.95

$27.75

We do not make any other changes in this harness. Shipping weight, boxed, about 80 lbs.

Our Famous Boston Double Truck Harness $32.35.

This harness is made of extra heavy selected stock throughout.

This harness made full size, 900 to 1250-lb. horses

Bridles, ⅞-inch, short check, spotted face piece. Concord blinds, round reins and winker stays and tie straps; **hames**, No. 10 oiled Concord bolt hames, with hame and spread strap; **traces**, 2-inch, double and stitched with three rows, front part, 1¾-inch double and stitched from loop to hook, with 24-inch heel chain; **breeching**, heavy fold with 1¾-inch layer, 1¼-inch double back straps running to hames, 1¼-inch double hip strap, 1¼-inch side strap, 1¼-inch side backers, with hook and short strap to hames; **lines**, selected stock, 1 inch wide by 18 feet long, with snap. Weight of this harness, less collars, about 85 lbs. We make no change in this harness.

No. 10C930 Without collars....$32.35
Weight, boxed for shipment, 95 pounds.

Our Superior Hand Made Team Harness, $27.75.

Bridles, ¾-inch, Concord sensible blind, flap nose band, round winker brace, round side check, double and stitched front and good heavy crown piece; **lines**, 1-inch wide by 20 feet long, buckle and billets, with snaps; **hames**, XC, ironed overtop, with folded hame tugs riveted to hame, Champion trace buckle, 1¼-inch bellyband billets, folded and stitched bellyband **pads**, heavy hook and terret, with turtle bottom to buckle in hame tug; **breast straps**, 1½-inch with snaps and slides; **pole straps**, 1½-inch with collar straps; **traces**, 1½-inch wide and 6 feet long, doubled and stitched with cockeyes sewed in; **hip straps**, 1-inch, with crupper to buckle on and trace carriers; **breeching**; heavy folded body with 1¼-inch layer, 1-inch side straps to snap under horse in martingale ring, two tie straps, two spread straps, XC or japanned trimming only. **We do not make any changes in this harness. It is strictly all hand made**, and must be ordered as described above only. This team harness is full size for 900 to 1250-pound horses.

No. 10C910 Without collars....$27.75
No. 10C3450 Collars, per pair....4.00
Add extra for 1¾-inch traces....1.00
If wanted without breeching, deduct....2.50
NOTE—Made in slip tug, if wanted, at the same price.

Our Double Express Harness.

$38.95

We do not make any changes in this harness. **This harness is made of fine Dundee leather**; full brass trimmed. **Bridles**, ⅞-inch, check; patent leather blind; round rein and winker brace; brass front and rosettes; spotted face piece. **Lines**, 1 inch by 20 feet; buckle and billet with snap. **Hames**, Concord bolt, brass dandy ball, red. **Traces**, 1¾-inch, double and stitched running to hame; 12-inch heel chain. **Pads**, Concord, with brass loop and spots. **Breeching**, 1⅝-inch, double and stitched body, 1¼-inch back strap, 1-inch double hip strap, sewed in **dee on hip**, 1⅛-inch side strap, ⅝-inch lazy strap. **Breast straps**, 1¾-inch, with roller snap. **Martingales**, 1¾-inch, with 1½-inch collar strap. This is one of the best harness we make. Brass trimmed only. Shipping weight, boxed, about 90 pounds.

No. 10C960 Price, per set, without collars....$38.95
No. 10C3480 collars are what you want with this harness. Price, each....2.95

DEPARTMENT OF SADDLES.

IN OUR SADDLE DEPARTMENT WE HAVE ENDEAVORED TO SHOW EVERYTHING IN THE SADDLE LINE, INCLUDING ALL THE VERY LATEST STYLES AND MOST DESIRABLE GOODS.

IF YOU BUY YOUR SADDLES FROM US you will be sure not only of getting lower prices than you could possibly get elsewhere, but the best grade work on the market.

OUR SADDLE TRADE HAS GROWN until we are now among the largest dealers in this line in the country. We are daily shipping saddles to almost every state and territory in the Union, as well as foreign countries. The low prices we offer, and the quality of goods we handle, commend our line to your favorable consideration.

ABOUT OUR PRICES. We advertise hand made saddles at from $1.85 upward, and we believe a careful comparison of our prices with those of any other concern will convince you that we can save you from 25 to 50 per cent in price. The freight or express charges will amount to next to nothing as compared with what you will save in price.

OUR SADDLES are all made by the largest and most reliable manufacturers in the country, concerns whose reputation for the manufacture of the highest grade work is everywhere recognized.

WE ARE EXTREMELY ANXIOUS TO RECEIVE YOUR ORDER, not so much for the little profit there is in it for us as for the good it will do us as an advertisement, and we will endeavor to send you a saddle with which you will be so well pleased that your friends will also order from us.

OUR LINE OF STOCK SADDLES we believe is the handsomest on the market, and the prices certainly are below any possible comparison. Our Western and Southwestern trade has been so very large that we have felt justified in making very extensive preparations in the stock saddle line for the coming season, and if you are in the market for this class of goods, we are sure that one trial order will convince you that you cannot afford to place your orders elsewhere.

$5.45 McClellan Saddle, $5.45.

No. 10C1321 Tree, 14-inch, yellow rawhide covered, stirrup straps, 1-inch with 2½-inch covered stirrups; 3½-inch cotton cinch with leather safe; leather skirt; a good, cheap saddle; man size only. Trimmed black leather. Shipping weight, about 10 pounds.

Price.........$5.45

Add extra for fender on stirrup strap....... 1.00

Men's $4.20 Morgan Saddle.

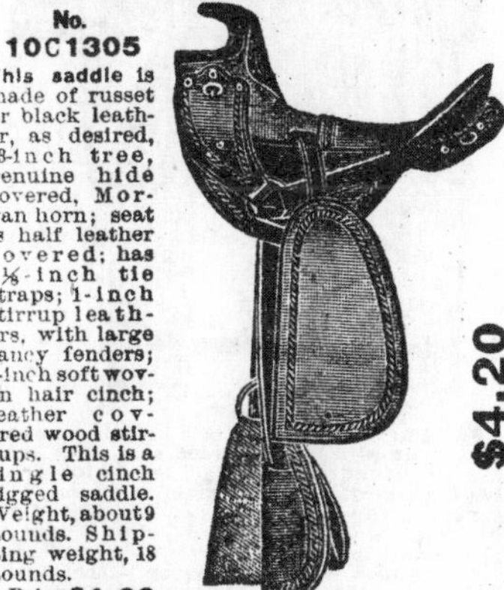

No. 10C1305 This saddle is made of russet or black leather, as desired, 13-inch tree, genuine hide covered, Morgan horn; seat is half leather covered; has 1⅛-inch tie straps; 1-inch stirrup leathers, with large fancy fenders; 4-inch soft woven hair cinch; leather covered wood stirrups. This is a single cinch rigged saddle. Weight, about 9 pounds. Shipping weight, 18 pounds.

Price $4.20

Men's $2.50 Plain English Saddle.

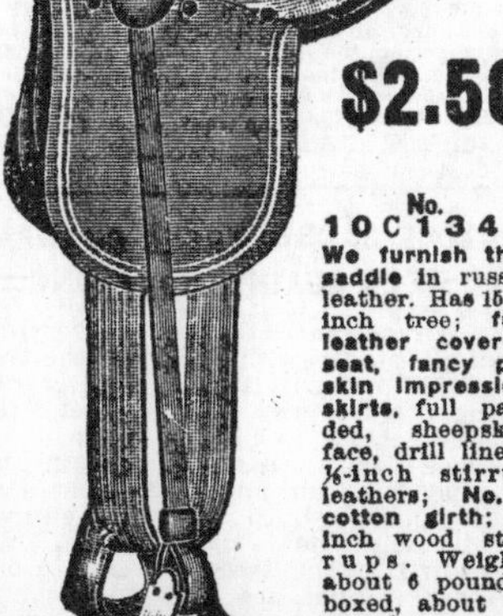

OUR $2.50 ENGLISH SADDLE.

$2.50

No. 10C1345 We furnish this saddle in russet leather. Has 15½-inch tree; full leather covered seat, fancy pig skin impression skirts, full padded, sheepskin face, drill lined; ⅞-inch stirrup leathers; No. 4 cotton girth; 3-inch wood stirrups. Weight, about 6 pounds; boxed, about 18 pounds.

Price...$2.50

Improved Kentucky Saddle, $9.20.

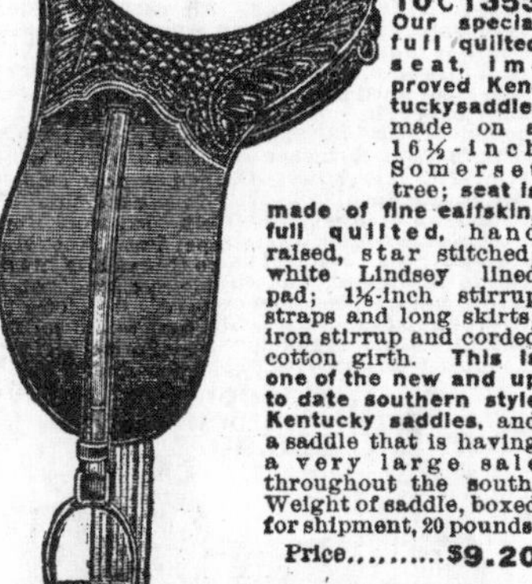

No. 10C1353 Our special full quilted seat, improved Kentucky saddle, made on a 16½-inch Somerset tree; seat is made of fine calfskin, full quilted, hand raised, star stitched; white Lindsey lined pad; 1⅛-inch stirrup straps and long skirts; iron stirrup and corded cotton girth. This is one of the new and up to date southern style Kentucky saddles, and a saddle that is having a very large sale throughout the south. Weight of saddle, boxed for shipment, 20 pounds.

Price..........$9.20

WE KNOW EVERY PIECE AND PART that enters into the construction of our saddles. We are extremely careful about the material and workmanship and we will furnish you with satisfactory goods.

Special Mosby Saddle, $9.90.

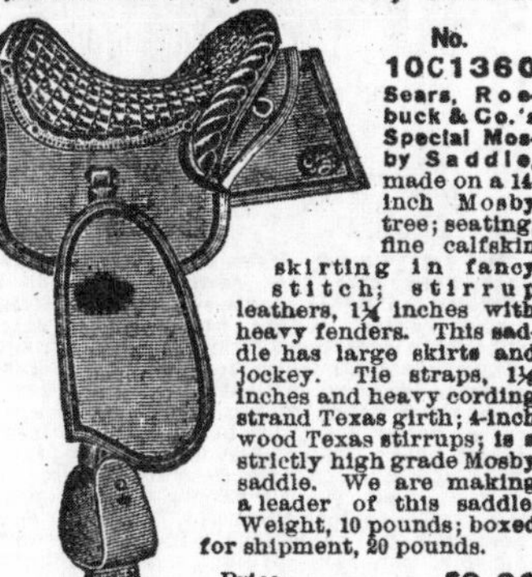

No. 10C1360 Sears, Roebuck & Co.'s Special Mosby Saddle, made on a 14-inch Mosby tree; seating, fine calfskin skirting in fancy stitch; stirrup leathers, 1¼ inches with heavy fenders. This saddle has large skirts and jockey. Tie straps, 1⅛ inches and heavy cording strand Texas girth; 4-inch wood Texas stirrups; is a strictly high grade Mosby saddle. We are making a leader of this saddle. Weight, 10 pounds; boxed for shipment, 20 pounds.

Price..............$9.90

Iron Cantle Tree, $10.60.

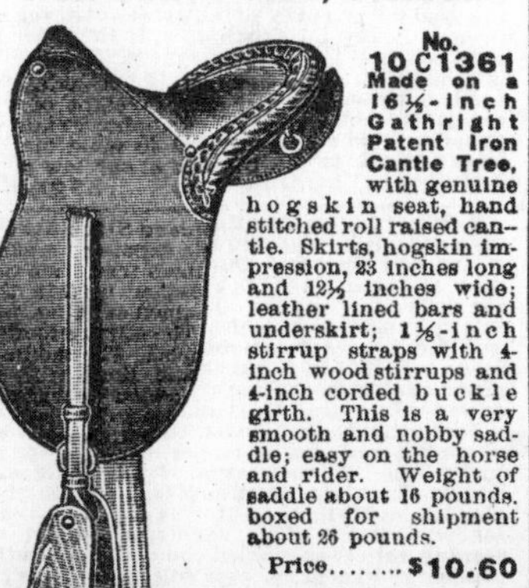

No. 10C1361 Made on a 16½-inch Gathright Patent Iron Cantle Tree, with genuine hogskin seat, hand stitched roll raised cantle. Skirts, hogskin impression, 23 inches long and 12½ inches wide; leather lined bars and underskirt; 1⅛-inch stirrup straps with 4-inch wood stirrups and 4-inch corded buckle girth. This is a very smooth and nobby saddle; easy on the horse and rider. Weight of saddle about 16 pounds, boxed for shipment about 26 pounds.

Price........$10.60

Iron Cantle Tree, $15.25.

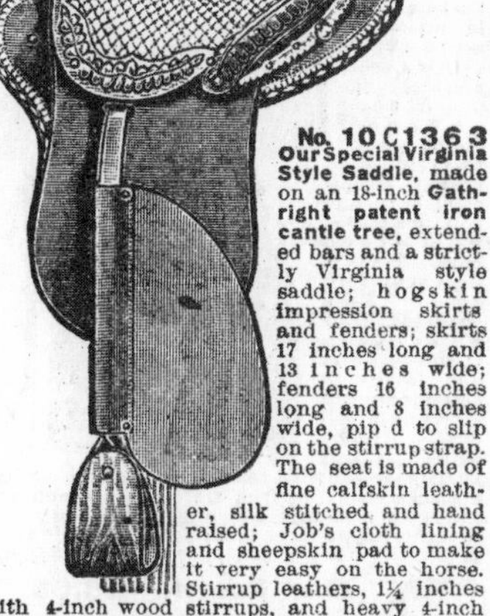

No. 10C1363 Our Special Virginia Style Saddle, made on an 18-inch Gathright patent iron cantle tree, extended bars and a strictly Virginia style saddle; hogskin impression skirts and fenders; skirts 17 inches long and 13 inches wide; fenders 16 inches long and 8 inches wide, pip d to slip on the stirrup strap. The seat is made of fine calfskin leather, silk stitched and hand raised; Job's cloth lining and sheepskin pad to make it very easy on the horse. Stirrup leathers, 1¼ inches with 4-inch wood stirrups, and heavy 4-inch corded buckle girth. This saddle is made on the Gathright patent iron cantle tree, which gives it strength and durability. Weight of saddle, 21 pounds, boxed for shipment about 30 pounds.

Price.............................$15.25

Our Lexington Spring Bar Somerset Saddle, $13.25.

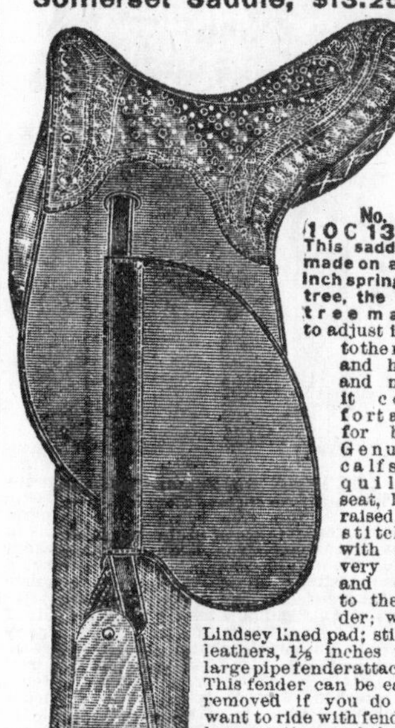

No. 10C1386 This saddle is made on a 17-inch spring bar tree, the best tree made, to adjust itself to the rider and horse and make it comfortable for both. Genuine calfskin quilted seat, hand raised, star stitched, with roll; very soft and easy to the rider; white Lindsey lined pad; stirrup leathers, 1⅛ inches with large pipe fender attached. This fender can be easily removed if you do not want to ride with fenders; heavy cotton corded girth and 4-inch Texas wood bolt stirrups. This saddle has a large sale throughout the south. A strictly first class, high grade, spring bar saddle. Weight, about 16 pounds; boxed, 26 pounds. Price...............$13.25

Men's McClellan Saddle at $7.60.

No. 10C1390 This saddle is made in russet leather only, has a genuine 14-inch McClellan tree, quilted seat, fancy long skirts, stamped and ornamented; bars padded and lined with sheepskin. Has 1-inch stirrup leathers, double super cotton girth and leather covered stirrups. Weight, about 10 pounds; packed for shipment, 21 pounds.

$7.60

Price..........$7.60

No. 10C1400 Our Special Morgan Saddle, made on 13-inch strictly high grade Morgan tree, hide covered; with 21-inch skirts, 1⅛-inch stirrup straps and three-quarter leather seat and roll cantle; fenders 14 inches long attached to stirrup straps; heavy tie straps, web cotton girths with leather chafes and connecting strap; 3-inch wood stirrups. This is one of our improved new saddles at a very moderate price, with leather roll cantle. Weight, about 12 pounds; boxed for shipment 20 pounds.

Price.......................$7.65

Black Leather Covered McClellan Saddle.

$7.50

No. 10C1391 This McClellan Saddle is made on a 14-inch tree with 12-inch seat full leather covered; 1¼-inch solid rig, over front and rear; 1¼-inch tie cinch with 4-inch solid woven hair cinch; 1-inch stirrup leathers with covered stirrups; short leather skirt. This is just the saddle you want. Weight about 10 pounds; boxed, 20 pounds. Price...............$7.50

Add for fenders, extra............ 1.50

Our Special $6.30 Stock Saddle.

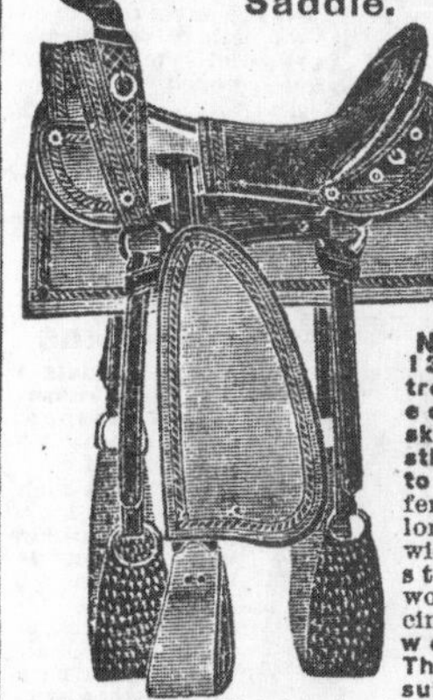

$6.30

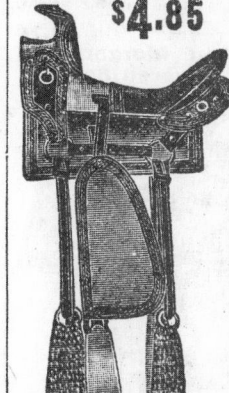

No. 10C1395 13-inch Morgan tree, hide covered; 21-inch skirts; 1⅛-inch stirrup leathers to buckle, with fenders 14 inches long, 7½ inches wide; 1⅛-inch tie straps; 4-inch woven soft hair cinches; 3-inch wood stirrups. This is a good, substantial, well made saddle. Weight, about 11 pounds; boxed for shipment, 21 pounds. Price.......$6.30

$4.85 Men's $4.85 Morgan Saddle.

No. 10C1398 This saddle is made of russet leather. It has a 13-inch hide covered Morgan tree; 1-inch stirrup leathers with fenders 13 inches long and 7 inches wide; 1-inch tie straps; solid woven hair cinches; wood stirrups. This is a double cinch rigged saddle. Weight, about 10 pounds.

Price.$4.85

Our Special Roll Cantle Morgan Saddle.

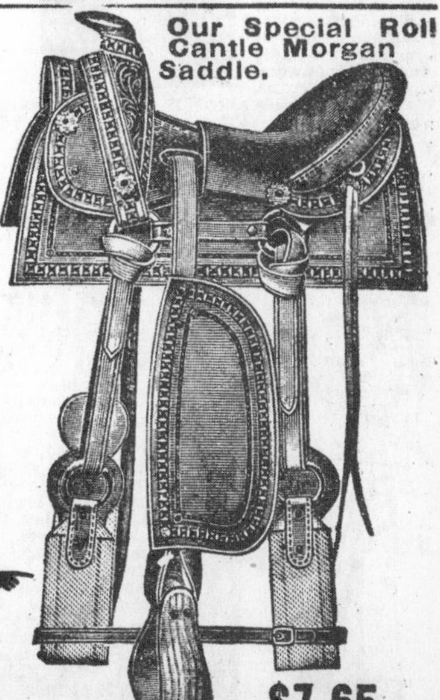

$7.65

Morgan Roll Cantle Saddle.

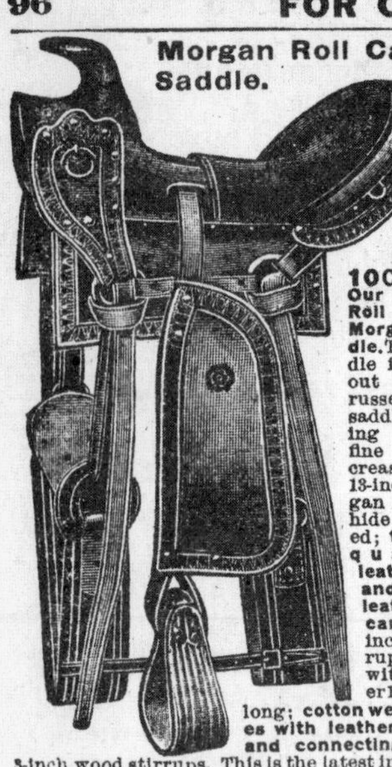

$6.15

No. 10C1402 Our Special Roll Cantle Morgan Saddle. This saddle is made out of fine russet tan saddle skirting with a fine border crease on a 13-inch Morgan tree, hide covered; three-quarter leather seat and heavy leather roll cantle; 1-inch stirrup straps with fender 13 inches long; cotton web cinches with leather chafes and connecting strap; 3-inch wood stirrups. This is the latest improved Morgan saddle, one that we believe will please a large number of boys and young men. Weight, about 12 pounds; boxed for shipment, 20 pounds. Price..................$6.15

Men's $5.75 Morgan Saddle.

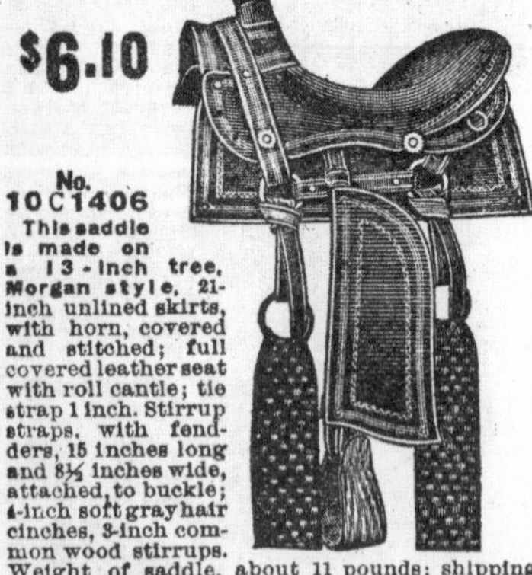

$5.75

No. 10C1405 This saddle is made of russet saddle leather; has a Morgan tree, unlined skirts, 4-inch cinches; 1-inch stirrup leathers with fenders, 14 inches long, 6½ inches wide; 1-inch tie straps; solid woven hair cinches; very strong wood stirrups. Weight, about 11 pounds; shipping weight, 22 pounds. Price..$5.75

Our Improved Morgan Full Leather Covered Seat Saddle, $6.10.

$6.10

No. 10C1406 This saddle is made on a 13-inch tree, Morgan style, 21-inch unlined skirts, with horn, covered and stitched; full covered leather seat with roll cantle; tie strap 1 inch. Stirrup straps, with fenders, 15 inches long and 8½ inches wide, attached, to buckle; 4-inch soft gray hair cinches, 3-inch common wood stirrups. Weight of saddle, about 11 pounds; shipping weight, 22 pounds. Price.............. $6.10

STOCK SADDLES.

Our Missouri Saddle, $8.60.

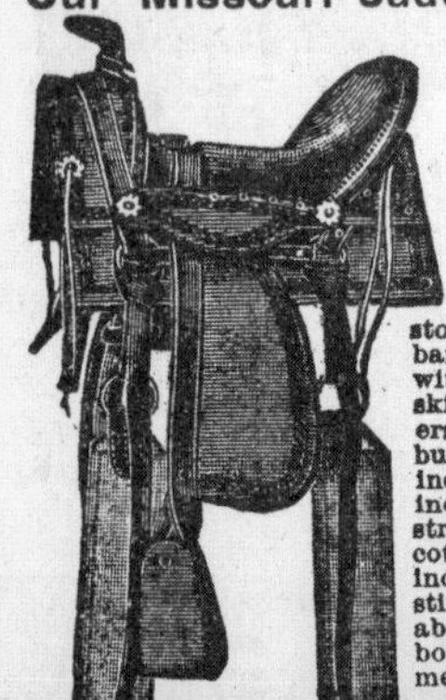

No. 10C1415 Our Special Missouri Saddle, made on 14-inch steel fork, hide covered tree. Skirts 21 inches long, good, solid stock, unlined, with bars of tree lined with wool sheepskin. Stirrup leathers, 1½ inches, to buckle; fenders, 14 inches long and 8 inches wide; tie straps, 1 inch; 4-inch cotton cinches, 4-inch Texas wood stirrups. Weight, about 15 pounds; boxed for shipment, 30 pounds.

Price.....$8.60

Our Special Kansas Runabout Saddle, $9.40.

No. 10C1416 This saddle is made of selected skirting, seat and jockey in one piece, covered rings, solid, full length stirrup straps, steel horn and roll cantle, wool lined bars. Tree, 4-inch steel fork and hide covered; bar sheepskin covered; seat and jockey in one piece; full covered roll cantle, 21-inch skirts, 1½-inch stirrup straps, with fenders 14 inches long and 8 inches wide; 1½-inch tie straps; 4-inch soft gray cinches, and 4-inch plain Texas stirrups. Weight, about 18 pounds; shipping weight, 28 pounds. Price $9.40

Our Popular $8.65 and $9.80 Saddle.

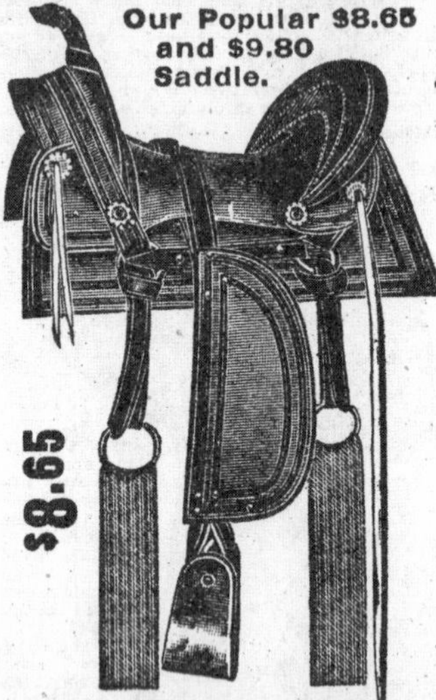

$8.65

No. 10C1420 Our Popular Saddle is made on a thoroughly first class steel fork tree, with high horn. This tree is made for general purposes, for all kinds of ordinary use, and will stand a great deal of rough work. The leather used in the making of this saddle is a fine oil tanned skirting, well selected and nicely finished. The tree is 14½ inches (this is the only size we make this saddle), with 22½-inch unlined skirts. The seating is of solid leather, fancy stamped. The saddle is made with edged creasing throughout, with steel strainer and roll cantle, 1½-inch stirrup straps, with large fenders attached. Size, 15 inches long, 7 inches wide. It is double rig to tie with 1⅜-inch tie straps, 4-inch woven cinches and 4-inch Texas wood stirrups. Weight of saddle, about 16 pounds; packed for shipment, about 30 pounds. We can highly recommend this saddle as being one of the best cheap stock saddles we handle, and is sure to give excellent service.

Price, with unlined skirts..............$8.65

No. 10C1425 The same saddle made with sheepskin wool lined skirts. Price......$9.80

Our Gunnison Stock Saddle.

We offer our $10.80 stock saddle as a low priced stock saddle, but the equal of saddles that sell generally at about $16.00. While we always urge the purchase of the better grade of goods, nevertheless at this price you will find our $10.80 Gunnison Stock Saddle such value as was never before offered.

$10.80

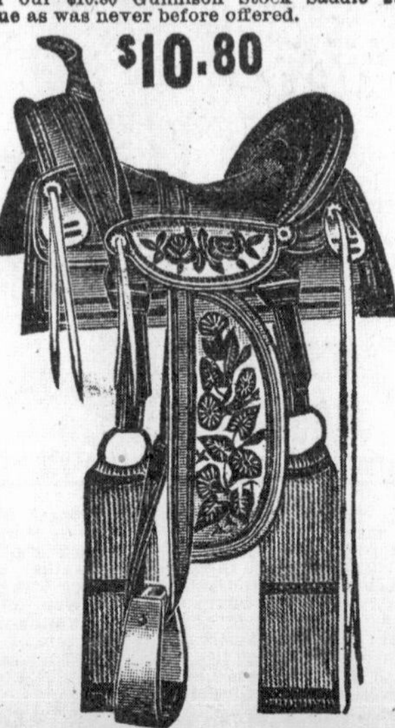

Winfield Special Stock Saddle, $17.59.

$17.59

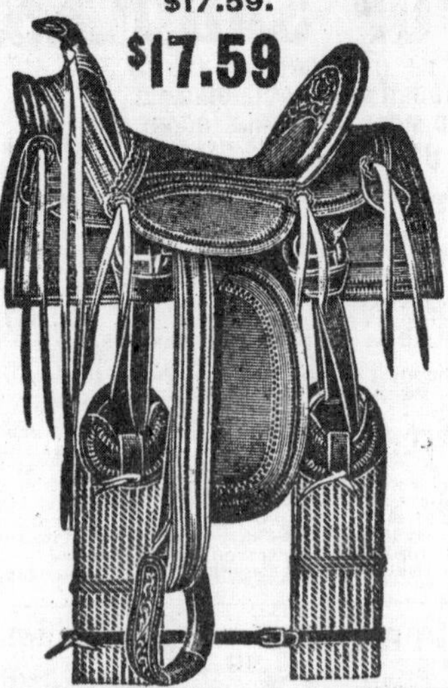

No. 10C1440 Made of selected oil tan Oregon saddle skirting. All parts of saddle are given special attention where extra heavy strain is required. Made on a 15-inch Winfield steel fork tree, hide covered, with 24-inch sheepskin wool lined skirts. Full extended seat; seat and jockey in one piece. Steel strainer and bound cantle. Stirrup leathers, 2-inch to lace, with fenders, 15 inches long and 8 inches wide, attached. Tie straps, 1½-inch on near side, to tie, and 1½-inch, to buckle, on the off side; 20-strand white Angora hair cinches; wool lined chafes and connecting straps; leather covered steel stirrups. We will make this saddle in roll cantle if wanted, but will always send bound cantle unless otherwise ordered. A strictly up to date good saddle, a saddle that would sell for $5.00 to $8.00 more than our special price. Weight, about 25 pounds; boxed, 35 pounds. Ea. $17.59

Casper Big Heavy Stock Saddle, $26.90.

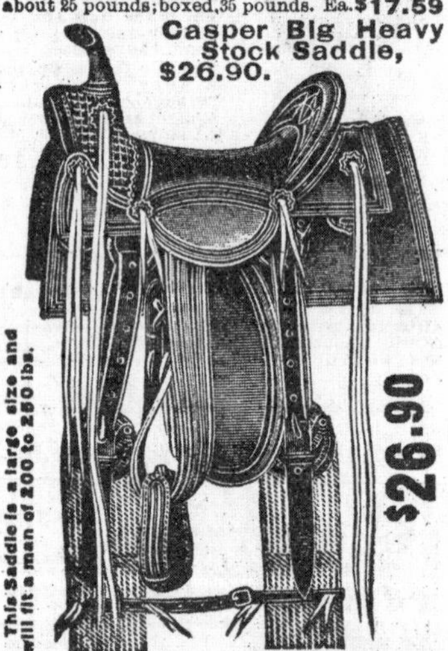

This Saddle is a large size and will fit a man of 200 to 250 lbs.

$26.90

No. 10C1442 Made on a 17-inch Visalia tree, heavy steel fork, rawhide covered. We will also make this saddle on a 17-inch Nelson tree if wanted. Large, heavy 30-inch skirts; sheepskin wool lined. Extended full seat; bound cantle; seat and jockey in one piece. This is an extra large, roomy saddle, for a big, heavy, stout rider; 3-inch stirrup leathers, to lace, with extra heavy steel leather covered stirrups. Large, heavy fender, 18 inches long, 9½ inches wide, attached. Heavy, 20-strand, white hard hair cinches; wool lined chafes and connecting straps. 1⅝-inch tie straps, 7 feet long on the near side, to buckle, and 2 inches wide on the off side, to buckle. We will make any changes in cinches wanted on this saddle; either all cotton or back band webbing cinches, but will send cinches listed regular with the saddle unless otherwise specified. We will also make this saddle in roll cantle if wanted. Remember, this saddle is made of an extra quality of fine Oregon heavy oil skirting, with full extended seat; seat and jockey in one piece. This saddle is made with lariat strap on the off side, and head string on the inner side. Weight of this saddle is about 38 pounds; shipping weight, 50 pounds. This saddle will sell in most places, from $45.00 to $65.00, and at our low price it is a special bargain. Price $26.90

No. 10C1430 Our Gunnison Stock Saddle. We have lately improved this saddle by making it on a new steel fork Gunnison tree, hide covered, 14½-inch tree. The leather used in this saddle is a fine quality oil tanned skirting, well selected and well finished. The stirrup fenders and jockey are fancy stamped. The saddle is made with 22½-inch skirts and lined with an extra quality wool sheepskin, with steel strainer and roll cantle, raised and beaded gullet, 1½-inch stirrup straps to buckle, with large fenders attached, size of fender, 16 inches long, 7 inches wide; 1¼-inch latigo straps, to tie, on a double cinch rig, genuine Mexican strong hair cinches and 3-inch California wood stirrups, leather bottom. This saddle is one of our leading sellers and, when compared with other saddles of like price, you will find it superior in quality of material and in workmanship. Weight, 20 pounds, net, and 45 pounds boxed for shipment. Price..................$10.80

Our Kit Carson Cowboy Saddle.

$20.90

No. 10C1445 This saddle is strictly new, made with full extended seat and jockey in one piece. Made on a 15-inch new San Juan tree, steel fork and hide covered. This is one of the new San Juan trees, 25-inch sheepskin lined skirts. Stirrup leathers, 2½ inches, to lace, with fenders, 16 inches long and 8½ inches wide, attached. Tie straps, 1⅝ inches wide on the near side and 1⅝ inches, to buckle, on the off side. Cinches, California strand, white Angora hair. Leather covered steel stirrups, made in bound or roll cantle. Will always send bound cantle unless ordered roll cantle. Fine quality of saddle skirting. Every part of the saddle is well selected and well finished. Strictly high grade throughout. Weight, about 28 pounds; shipping weight, 40 pounds. Price. $20.90

Our Olympia, Heavy, High Grade Cowboy Saddle.

$31.85

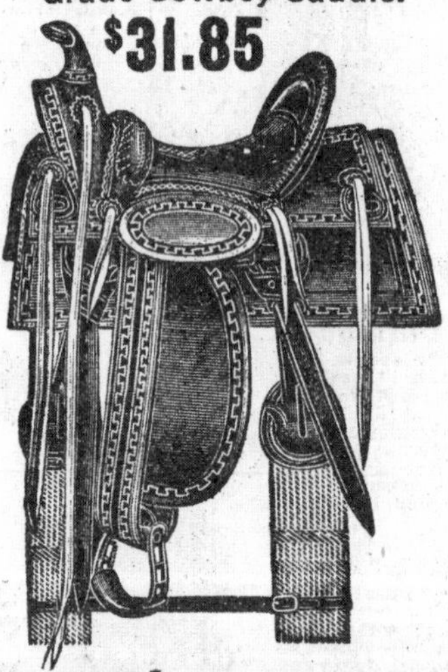

No. 10C1447 This is a strictly new saddle, made with full extended seat, with bucking roll, bound cantle. Made on a high grade 15½-inch Portland tree, steel fork, and hide covered. The Portland is new and one of the best high grade trees made, and is sure to please all who want a strictly high grade saddle. 28½-inch wool lined skirts; 3-inch stirrup leathers, to lace, with fenders, 18x9 inches, attached; 1⅝-inch tie straps on the near side and 1⅝-inch, to buckle, on the off side. Cinches, white hard hair, California strand, with leather chafes and connecting straps; XC Turner's malleable iron stirrups. Weight of this saddle about 32 pounds; shipping weight, 45 pounds. Made in bound or roll cantle. Will always send bound cantle unless order calls for roll cantle. Remember, this saddle is made of a very fine selection of oil tan skirting. Great care is taken in selecting the different straps and parts of this saddle, having them cut and highly finished. This saddle will range with all high grade stock saddles throughout the west. Price. $31.85

STOCK SADDLE TREES GUARANTEED AGAINST BREAKING

We guarantee the tree in everyone of our stock saddles, and if the tree should break in roping cattle or doing other work, you can send the saddle back to us and we will replace it with a new tree without any expense to you and pay transportation charges both ways, or else we will send you a new saddle. We know that the trees we use in our stock saddles are built to last and stand any amount of hard usage, and we therefore positively guarantee them against breaking.

Omaha Saddle, $15.50

Improved La Platte Tree. New Omaha Style.

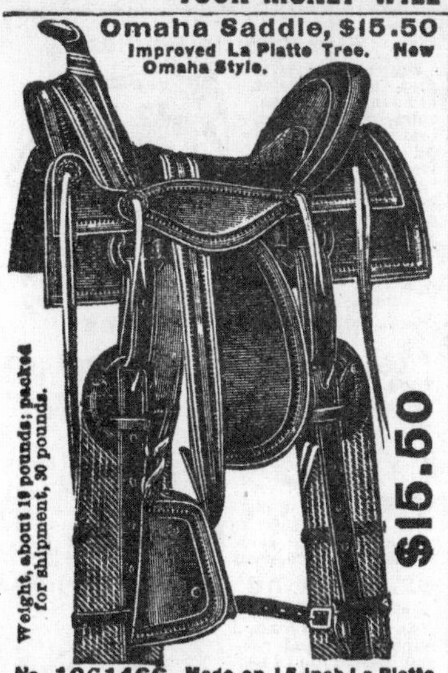

Weight, about 18 pounds; packed for shipment, 30 pounds.
$15.50

No. 10C1466 Made on 15-inch La Platte steel fork tree, hide covered, solid leather seat, roll cantle, stitched jockey; 23½-inch wool lined skirts; tie strap to buckle, 1⅜ inches on near side, 1¾ inches on off side; double rig covered rings. Cinches; 20-strand, white angora hair, with chafes and tongue and connecting strap; stirrup straps, 2 inches to lace, with fender 14½ inches long attached; 4-inch wood Texas stirrups, leather covered. Price......$15.50

Our Special Kiowa Stock Saddle.

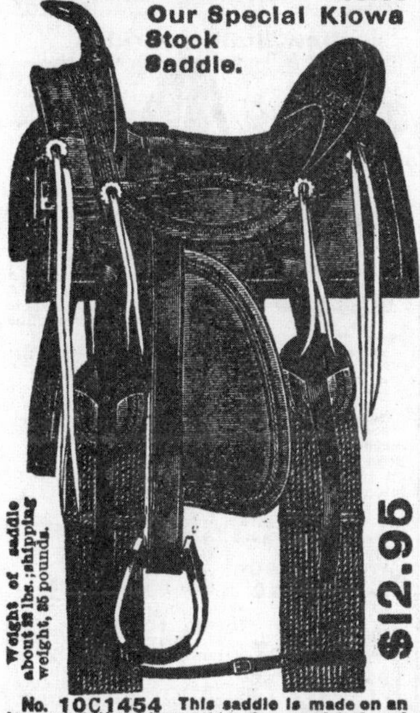

Weight of saddle about 22 lbs.; shipping weight, 35 pounds.
$12.95

No. 10C1454 This saddle is made on an improved Kiowa tree, 14½ inches, steel fork and hide covered. Has the latest improved bars and is a very good easy riding saddle tree. The saddle is made of russet tanned oiled skirting. Roll cantle. The skirts, 22 inches long and 11½ inches wide, sheepskin wool lined. Stirrup leathers, 1⅜ inches to buckle, with fender 8 inches wide and 14 inches long attached. Tie strap on the off side, 1½ inches to buckle, 1¾ inches on the near side to buckle; 15-strand soft hair cinches with leather chafes and tongues with connecting strap. Bent wood stirrups with leather bottom. This is one of the greatest bargains in our line. This saddle made in single cinch at same price. Price...........$12.95

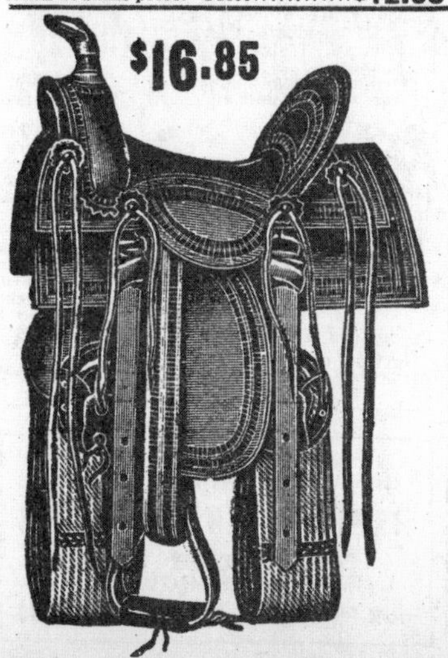

Our Special Montana Stock Saddle.

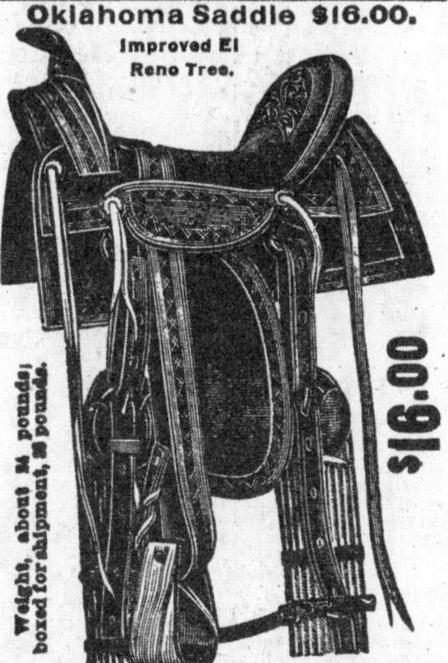

No. 10C1473 Our Special Montana Stock Saddle made on a strictly new up to date Montana swell fork tree; 15-inch full seat and jockey in one piece; rawhide trimmed, braided rawhide horn. This saddle is made in black skirting or russet skirting as desired, with white rawhide covered rings, rawhide covered bound cantle and gullet. This is a strictly new style of saddle: 27-inch wool lined skirts, 2¾-inch stirrup leathers with 9x16-inch fenders attached; iron stirrups; soft cotton front cinch, heavy belting web back cinch with connecting strap. We consider this saddle one of the greatest bargains in our line. Price.........$23.40

Oklahoma Saddle $16.00.

Improved El Reno Tree.

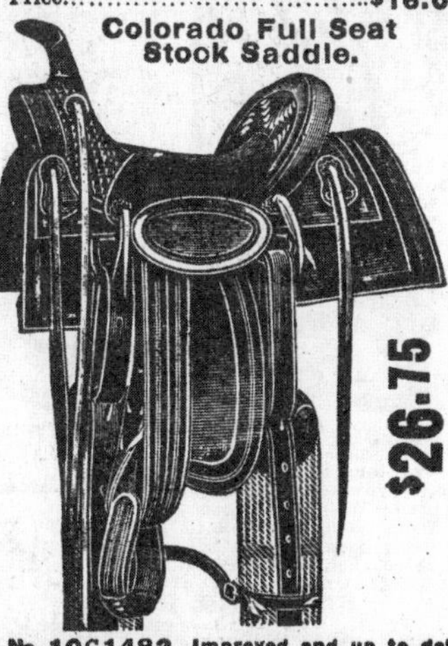

No. 10C1471 Tree, 15-inch, El Reno, steel fork, hide covered roll cantle, stitched jockey; 24-inch wool lined skirts, double rig covered rings; tie strap to buckle, 1⅜ inches on near side, 1¾ inches on off side; 20-strand hair cinches with tongue and chafes, with connecting strap; stirrup leathers to lace, 2¼ inches wide, with fenders 15 inches long attached; stirrups, 3-inch wood, California style, leather bottom. Price..............................$16.00

Colorado Full Seat Stock Saddle.

No. 10C1482 Improved and up to date Stock Saddle. Full seat and jockey tree; 16-inch Nelson steel fork, hide covered shell seat, seat and jockey in one piece, hand stitched roll cantle; 30-inch wool lined skirts; tie strap, 1¾ inches to buckle on near side, 2 inches to buckle on off side; 20-strand gray California hard hair cinches with wool lined chafes and connecting strap, 3-inch stirrup straps with fenders 18 inches long and 9 inches wide; steel leather covered stirrups; ¾-inch rope strap on off side. Weight, about 35 pounds; boxed for shipment, 55 lbs. Price..............................$26.75

Single cinch rig at same price.

Our Cherokee Stock Saddle.

No. 10C1456 This saddle is made on a strictly high grade 15-inch Cherokee steel fork tree, hide covered; bastos 24 inches long and 11½ inches wide, wool lined; full seat and jockey in one piece; bound or roll cantle (will always send bound cantle unless ordered roll); full solid back rigged saddle; 2-inch stirrup leathers to lace with fenders 15x7 inches attached; 2½-inch Texas full stirrups with leather bottom; 1¾-inch latigo on the near side and 1½-inch latigo on the off side. Covered rings and solid rigging in one piece. Cinches, California gray hair, with leather chafes and connecting strap. Weight of saddle, 20 pounds; boxed for shipment, 35 pounds. Price..............................$16.85

Our California Stock Saddle.

Improved Western Tree.

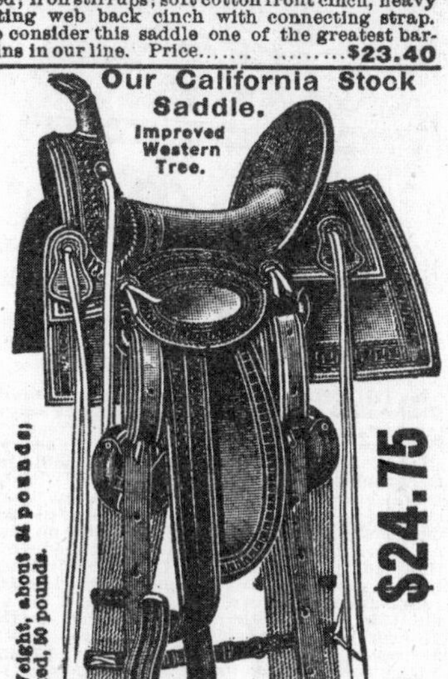

No. 10C1475 This saddle is made on a 14½-inch steel fork, beef hide covered tree, with 12-inch seat, high horn and cantle; full seat and jockey in one piece; bound or roll cantle; hand stitched 27-inch wool lined skirts; 1¾-inch tie strap on near side and 2-inch on off side to buckle; cinches, 44-strand extra hard laid fish cord with double connecting strap, wool lined chafes, 3-inch stirrup leathers with fenders 18 inches long; 7-inch wide steel leather covered stirrups. This is a very fine stock saddle, oiled skirting. Price..........$24.75

Single cinch at same price.

Our $19.73 San Juan Saddle.

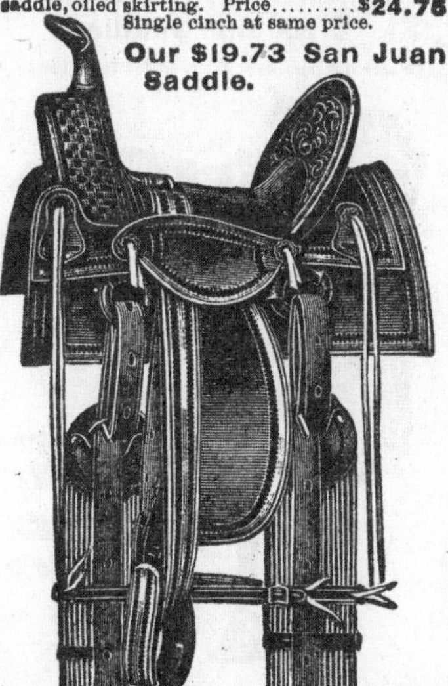

No. 10C1490 This saddle is made on 15-inch improved San Juan steel fork tree; 25-inch wool lined skirts, 2½-inch stirrup leathers to lace, with fenders 16 inches long and 8 inches wide; 1½-inch tie strap to buckle on near side, 1¾-inch on off side; Angora hair cinches with leather chafes and connecting strap with tongue; steel leather covered stirrups; roll or bound cantle. Will send bound cantle, unless order calls for roll. This is one of our big bargains in saddles. Weight, about 28 pounds; boxed, 40 pounds. Price...............$19.73

A Good $15.95 Saddle.

No. 10C1509 Our Improved Kansas Light Stock Saddle, made on the improved La Platte steel fork, hide covered tree. The best tree we can buy for a medium priced saddle. If the tree should break we will replace it free of charge and pay the transportation charges both ways. Made with one-half leather seat with leather jockey tacked and laced on. Made in roll cantle only. **Skirts**, 23½ inches long and 13 inches wide, full sheepskin lined; heavy rigging back of cantle and around the horn, with heavy leather covered ring. 1⅜-inch wide long latigo on the near side and 1¾-inch wide short latigo on the off side; stirrup leathers, 2 inches wide to lace with fenders 7½ inches wide and 14 inches long attached; 3-inch California pattern wood stirrups, bolted top and leather bottom; 18-strand California soft hair front cinch and 3½-inch belting web back cinch, with leather chafes, connecting straps and buckle tongues. **This is one of our great values in a popular saddle.** Every strap about this saddle is carefully selected, which guarantees it to be a first class article. Weight of saddle, 20 pounds; packed for shipment, about 30 pounds. Price.........$15.95

Sears' $23.95 Saddle.

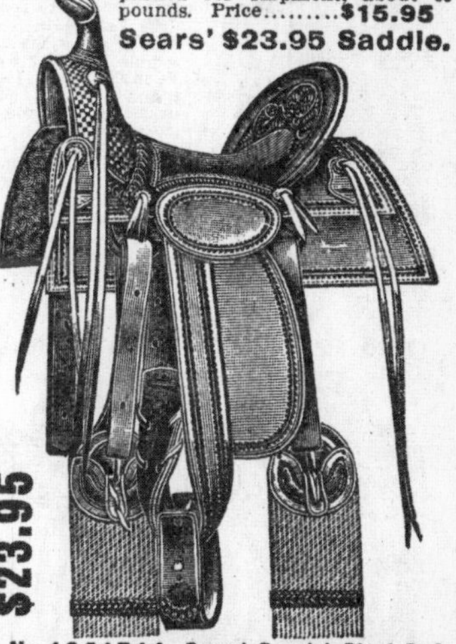

No. 10C1511 Sears' Special Stock Saddle. This is one of the latest improved saddles in our line. Made on a 15-inch Spokane steel fork hide covered tree and we guarantee it to stand all kinds of heavy work. If the tree should break we will pay the transportation charges both ways on the saddle and put in a new tree free of charge. Made with a full seat and jockey in one piece. **The saddle seat is** built up solid with heavy leather and blocked to shape so as to be easy on the rider. Made in bound or roll cantle. (Will always send bound cantle unless ordered roll.) **Skirts**, 25½ inches long, 13 inches wide, full sheepskin lined. Stirrup leathers, 3 inches wide to lace with fenders 8 inches wide and 16 inches long attached, making a very heavy, strong and substantial stirrup strap, 2½-inch Moran pattern brass bound stirrups, full leather lined and leather capped; 1½-inch wide long latigo on the near side and 1¾-inch wide short latigo on the off side. Cinches, 20-strand Angora hair with leather chafes and connecting strap and buckle tongues. Heavy leather rigging back of cantle and over and around the horn with heavy leather covered rings. Lariat strap on the off side, long head string on the near side. **This is another of our great values in a moderate priced high grade stock saddle.** Remember, we guarantee the tree and will replace it if broken. Saddles not as good as this are sold at from $36.00 to $45.00. Weight of saddle, 30 pounds; packed for shipment, about 40 pounds. Price $23.95

Our Idaho Stock Saddle, $29.65.

No. 10C1498 BigHorn Bucking Tree, Improved. Our Big Horn bucking tree, 16-inch tree, steel fork, beef hide covered. This tree takes the place of bucking roll, full seat and jockey in one piece, bound or roll cantle, hardstitched 30-inch wool lined skirts, 1¾-inch tie strap on near side, 2-inch on off side, to buckle; cinches, 30-strand white hard twisted cotton cord in front, 4-inch three-ply belting web in rear, double connecting strap, 3-inch stirrup leather with large fender attached, brass bow bound stirrups, leather bottom. Weight, about 38 pounds; boxed 50 pounds. Price............$29.65

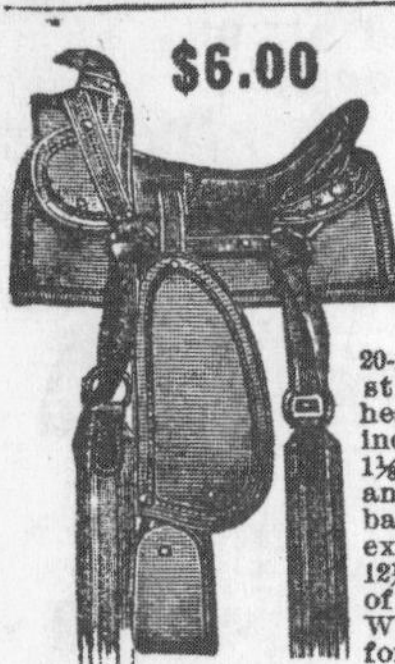

$6.00

Our Double Cinch Boys' Saddle, $6.00.

No. 10C1540 Our Double Cinch Boys' Saddle. This saddle is made in russet leather only; 20-inch skirts; 1¼-inch stirrup straps with heavy fenders, and 3½-inch wood bolt stirrups; 1⅛-inch 4-foot tie strap, and 3-inch cotton back band, web cinches; tree, extra good solid fork, 12½-inch. The rigging of this saddle is strong. Weight of saddle, packed for shipment, 12 pounds. Price $6.00

Fine Covered Stirrup Boys' Saddle.

$3.78

No. 10C1550 Fine Covered Stirrup Boys' Saddle. This saddle is made in russet or black leather, 1-inch stirrup straps with heavy fenders, covered stirrups. The boy's foot will never push through. Weight of saddle, packed for shipment, 10 pounds. Price............$3.78

Eugene Boys' Stock Saddle.

$9.65

No. 10C1557 This saddle is made on 12-inch steel fork, hide covered tree, full leather covered. Half seat, rolled cantle; skirts, 9 inches wide, 19½ inches long, unlined; stirrup straps, 1½-inch to buckle, with fenders 7x13½ inches long attached; 3-inch covered Texas stirrups; 1⅛-inch tie strap; cinches, 4-inch common gray hair. This saddle is made of oiled skirting, with jockey on the side to protect the boy's leg from stirrup straps, and is one of the best double cinch boys' saddles on the market. Weight, 13½ pounds; boxed, 24 pounds. Price....$9.65

Our Special. The Princess Side Saddle.

$9.47 AND $10.22

Tree: The tree used in the manufacture of this. Our Special Princess Side Saddle, is a strictly first class Ruwart tree, with bars of saddle padded with sheepskin so as to be soft and easy on the horse's back. Seating: The seating of this saddle is of the finest quality of buckskin, handsomely ornamental stitched, making a very soft and easy cushion. This saddle is made with large jockey on back; the skirting is handsomely stamped four pieces, pigskin impression body; extra heavy 1⅜-inch leather surcingle with ¾-inch stirrup strap; fine pigskin impression hooded stirrup; leather bottomed, lined with sheepskin, leaping horns seamed and buckskin lined; heavy double underrigging with woven hair cinches with 1⅛-inch tie straps on each side. If you order this saddle and do not find it the greatest bargain you have ever seen for the money, you can return it to us at our expense and we will refund you the money paid for this saddle. Weight, about 16 pounds; boxed for shipment, 30 pounds.

No. 10C1565 Princess Side Saddle without pocket. Price....$9.47

No. 10C1566 Princess Side Saddle with large pocket on off side, as shown in small illustration. Price....$10.22

Our Special Southwest Side Saddle, $14.00

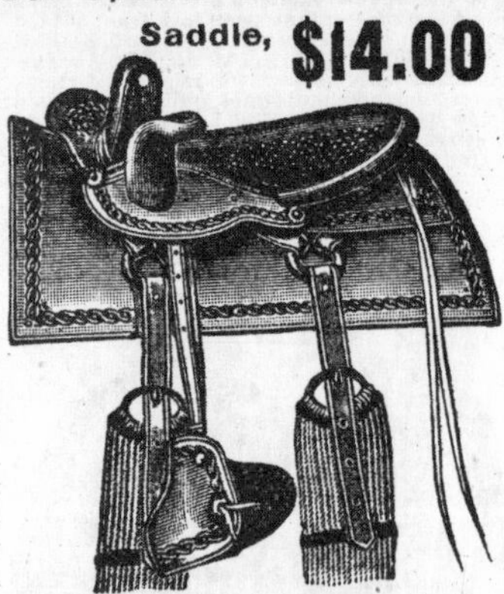

No. 10C1567 This saddle is made of oiled California skirting, double rigged seamed leaping horn, made on the Western style tree, and heavy rolled cantle, the same as men's heavy stock saddle. The tree used in this saddle is the genuine Ruwart tree; skirts, wool lined, 12½ inches wide and 28 inches long on the near side and 12½ inches wide and 23½ inches long on the off side, with pocket 5½x8½ inches on the off side. The illustrations show both sides of this saddle. The seat is all leather covered, basket stamped pattern; hand stitched solid rolled cantle. Makes a very firm, strong, durable side saddle. Stirrup strap, ⅝-inch, with 2½-inch hooded, wool lined stirrup; cinches, 20-strand white angora hair, with tongs; 1⅛-inch buckle tie straps on the off side and 1⅛-inch buckle tie straps on the near side. This is one of our special leaders for 1905. Weight, about 21 pounds; boxed, 35 pounds. Price $14.00

Sears, Roebuck & Co.'s Special Iowa Side Saddle.

Greatest Value ever Offered for the Money.

$6.95

No. 10C1580 Our Special Iowa Side Saddle, made on 18-inch Ruwart tree, skirts fancy stamped pigskin impression with fancy figured seating. Has heavy padded bars so as not to hurt the horse. 1⅛-inch tie strap on cinches; ¾-inch stirrup leather with metal shoe stirrup; 4-inch soft woven hair cinches and seamed buckskin lined leaping horn. An extra good double cinch ladies' side saddle. Weight, about 14 pounds. Price....$6.95

Ladies' $5.42 Saddle.

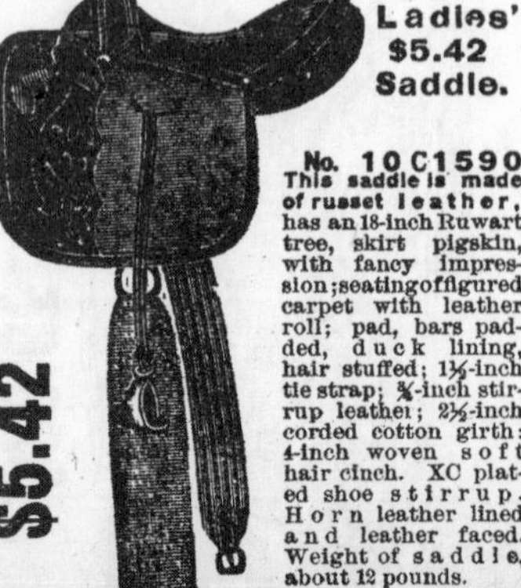

$5.42

No. 10C1590 This saddle is made of russet leather, has an 18-inch Ruwart tree, skirt pigskin, with fancy impression; seating of figured carpet with leather roll; pad, bars padded, duck lining, hair stuffed; 1⅛-inch tie strap; ¾-inch stirrup leather; 2½-inch corded cotton girth; 4-inch woven soft hair cinch. XC plated shoe stirrup. Horn leather lined and leather faced. Weight of saddle, about 12 pounds. Price....$5.42

Our Bessie Texas Side Saddle, $6.55

$6.55

No. 10C1593 Made on improved Ruwart tree, with velvet carpet seating. Roll seat and velvet carpet leg fender. A very rich and tasty side saddle. The skirt is 16½ inches wide and 13½ inches deep. Heavy cotton strand Texas girth; double cinch Texas side saddle; sheepskin padded bars. Satchel hook on off side. A strictly up to date, rich looking side saddle. Made only without leaping horn. Oiled tan California skirting throughout. Weight, boxed, about 23 pounds....$6.55

Our Special Cowboy Bridles.

No. 10C1700 Our Special Two-Ear Flat Russet Cowboy Bridle. ⅝-inch double cheeks, adjustable on both sides, with large nickel ornament. Spotted crown piece with two ear holes. Weight, about 8 ounces.

Price, as shown in illustration, without bit....$1.00
Add extra for ⅝ inch x 7 feet reins with quirt ends .65
Add extra for six-plait braided bridle reins with quirt ends.... 1.35
Add extra for bit, as shown in illustration .15
Postage extra, 12 cents.

No. 10C1701 Our Special Two-Ear Cowboy Bridle, with spotted face piece and fancy scalloped cheek, with three nickel ornament cheeks, adjustable on each side. Bridle is made out of russet oiled leather. Weight, about 16 ounces. Price, as shown in illustration, without bit, $1.50
Add extra for 1 inch x 7 feet bridle reins with quirt ends.... .65
Add extra for six-plait braided bridle reins with quirt ends.. 1.35
Add extra for bit, as shown in illustration, with bridle extra. $1.25
If by mail, postage extra, 20 cents.

No. 10C1702 Our Great Western Cowboy Bridle, made with wide pointed cheek, fancy stamped adjustable crown and throat latch. Fancy stamped brow band. One of the new, up to date Western bridles; ⅞ inch by 6 feet reins. Weight, about 24 ounces. Price of bridle, with bit, as shown in illustration....$2.85
Without bit.... 2.50
If by mail, postage extra, 30 cents.

Braided Bridle Reins.

No. 10C1709 Our Special Braided Bridle Reins, made of fine quality calfskin, extra long, with romal and quirt ends. These reins are made in three sizes, 4-plait, 6-plait and 8-plait. Weight, 10 ounces.
Price, each, for 4-plait....$1.00
Price, each, for 6-plait.... 1.35
Price, each, for 8-plait.... 2.00
If by mail, postage extra, 12 cents.

Flat Bridle Reins.

No. 10C1712 Our Special Flat Cowboy Bridle Reins. Made of ¾-inch russet leather, buckle billet ends to buckle in the bit. 7 feet long with lace string. Weight of bridle reins, 12 ounces. Price, each, for one bridle....65c
If by mail, postage extra, 14 cents.

Extra Fine Fringed Bridle Reins.

No. 10C1715 Our Extra Fine Fringed Cowboy Bridle Rein, made of russet bridle leather, buckle and billet end to buckle in the bit. Fringed solid loop and fringed quirt end. 7 feet long, 1 inch wide. Weight, 18 ounces. Price, each, for one bridle....$1.05
If by mail, postage extra, 20 cents.

Flat Snaffle Bridles.

No. 10C1800 Flat Snaffle, flat head and reins, solid crown piece, leather front. Made of good russet leather, with XC bar buckles and XC two ring port bit and ⅝-inch curb strap. Weight, about 24 ounces.
¾-inch. Price, each....$0.80
⅞-inch. Price, each.... .90
1-inch. Price, each.... 1.00

Flat Snaffle Bridles.

No. 10C1803 Flat Snaffle, flat russet leather head and reins, with XC bar buckles, head stall and reins sewed into a full cheek XC snaffle bit. Weight, about 16 ounces.
¾-inch. Price, each....$1.10
⅞-inch. Price, each.... 1.20

$2.95 Round Pelham Bridle.

No. 10C1813 Round Pelham. Superfine round russet leather bridle, round cheeks, front and two round reins, narrow loops, leather covered buckles, fine XC port bit and curb strap. Weight, about 32 ounces. Price, each. $2.95

No. 10C1815 Same style as No. 10C1813, only single reins in place of double reins. Price, each....$2.20

New Stallion Bridle.

No. 10C1818 Our Special Norman Stallion Bridle. Made of fine russet leather, brass buckles, scallop and inlaid cheeks, front and nose band, 13-foot lead rein with chain and round stopper. This is a very fine russet stallion bridle. Weight, 2½ pounds. Price of bridle, less bit....$3.85

Cowboy Bridles.

No. 10C1819 Made of oiled russet leather, with double head stall to buckle on top, reins, 5 feet long, to loop in bit, XC bar buckles, port bit and curb strap, ⅝-inch. Weight, about 33 ounces. Price, each..90c

No. 10C1820 ⅞-inch bridle with bit. Price, each....98c

No. 10C1821 Made of heavy Oregon oiled tanned leather, ¾-inch double head stall to buckle on top; ⅝-inch reins, 6 feet long to loop in bit, XC buckles, port bit and curb strap. Weight, about 1½ pounds. Price, without bit....$0.90
Price with bit, 1.00

No. 10C1822 ⅞-inch bridle with bit. Price, each....$1.10

No. 10C1823 Made extra heavy and strong, Oregon oiled tanned leather, ⅞-inch double head stall to buckle on top, ⅞-inch reins, 6 feet long, XC buckles and curb strap. Weight, 1½ pounds.
Price, without bit, each....$1.35
Price, with XC port bit.... 1.45

No. 10C1825 Extra fine and durable. Made of Oregon oiled tanned leather, ⅞-inch double head stall to buckle on top; ⅞-inch reins, 6 feet long; nickel buckles and box loops throughout. Ends of reins laced with buckskin. Weight, about 1¾ pounds. Price, without bit....$1.85

No. 10C1826 Price, with blued Texas port bit.... 2.00

No retail dealer carries a better or more satisfactory line of

HARNESS AND SADDLES

THAN ARE SHOWN IN THIS CATALOGUE

OUR PRICES ARE BELOW ALL OTHERS

Extra Heavy Cowboy Bridle.

No. 10C1827 Extra heavy Oregon oiled tanned leather, 1-inch double head stalls to buckle on top; 1-inch reins, 6 feet long, laced at ends with buckskin. Heavy fringed front, fringed slide loops on checks and throatlatch, ⅝-inch curb strap. Nickel buckles. Weight, about 2¼ pounds.
Price, without bit, each............**$2.15**
No. 10C1829 Price, with blued Texas port bit............**$2.25**

Special Mexican Diamond Braided Bridle.

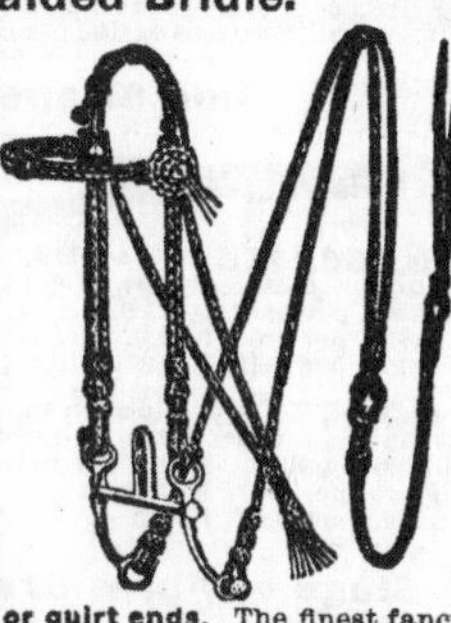

Our Special Mexican Cowboy Fine Diamond Braided Bridle, made of extra fine oil tanned calfskin, 8-plait, double head, double check and double front, with fancy rosettes; extra braided billets, self adjusting crown piece, fancy braided knots and frills, extra fine long braided reins with round loop and romal or quirt ends. The finest fancy diamond braided bridle ever offered to our many customers. Equal, if not superior, to bridles which retail at $12.00 to $15.00. Weight, 1½ pounds.
No. 10C1841 8-plait bridle, without bit. Price, each............**$4.75**
No. 10C1843 Same style of bridle as No. 10C1841, only six-plait. Without bit. Price, each............**3.75**
No. 10C1844 Same style as No. 10C1841, only four-plait. Without bit. Price, each............**3.00**

Buggy Bridles.

No. 10C1895 Our ⅝-inch Cheap Buggy Bridle (no box loop), overdraw check or side rein, patent leather blind, flat winker brace, XC buckles throughout. Weight, about 2 pounds.
Price, each............**90c**
No. 10C1896 Our ⅝-inch box loop check, patent leather blind, round winker brace, XC trimmings, over check or side rein. Weight, about 2¼ pounds.
Price, each........**$1.45**

Williams' Humane Buggy Bridle.

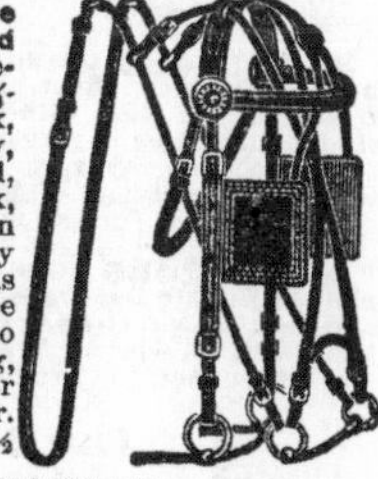

This Bridle is made with side check and over check with noseband combined; ⅝-inch box loop check, round winker stay, patent leather blind, light round sidecheck, fancy front, layer on crown; a very easy bridle on horse, holds head correct, and once used you will have no other. Trimming, nickel, Davis rubber or genuine rubber. Weight, about 2½ pounds.
No. 10C1897 Nickel bridle. Price, each............**$2.45**
No. 10C1898 Davis rubber bridle. Price, each............**$2.45**
No. 10C1900 Genuine rubber bridle. Price, each............**$2.95**

Our Fine Chicago Track Bridle.

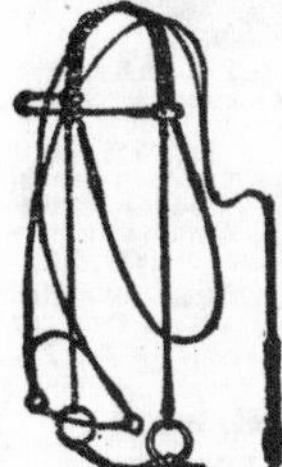

Made of selected stock, check loop in bit and buckle on crown piece, light over check with nose band, light front and rosettes. The finest grade of light driving bridle. Trimmings, nickel or Davis rubber. Weight, about 1½ pounds.
No. 10C1905 Nickel trimmings. Price, each........**$2.15**
No. 10C1909 Genuine rubber trimmings. Price, each........**$2.45**

Our $1.15 Open Bridles.

No. 10C1911 Our fine ⅝-inch Flat Check Open Bridle, over check with nose band, nickel or Davis rubber trimmings, with initial rosettes. Weight, about 1¼ pounds.
Price, each........**$1.15**

Fine Open Bridle, $1.45

No. 10C1913 Our fine Open Bridle, ⅝-inch box loop check and long layer on crown piece, over check with nose band or side rein, fancy front with initial rosettes. Weight, about 1¼ pounds.
Price, each........**$1.45**

Extra Fine Round Open Bridle.

No. 10C1915 Our Extra Fine Round Open Bridle, over check with nose band or round side rein, long layer on crown piece, round front with initial rosettes. Weight, about 1½ pounds.
Price, each........**$1.95**

Team Bridles

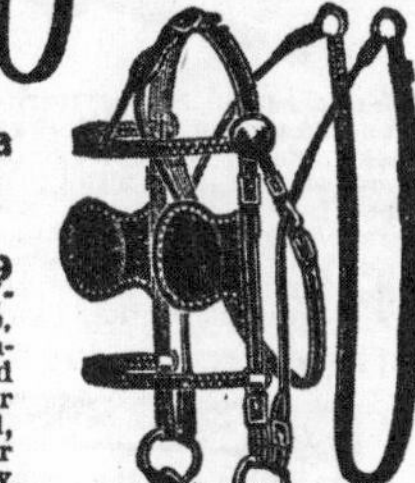

No. 10C1917 Our Fine Long Check Team Bridle, Concord blinds, round rein and winker stay, harness leather front, good bit, ⅝-inch throughout. Weight, about 3 pounds.
Price, each **$1.55**

Our Extra Fine Team Bridle.

No. 10C1919 Our Extra Fine ⅞-inch Team Bridle, short check, Concord blinds, round rein and winker stay, flat nose band, harness leather front, good heavy bit and one of the best bridles made. Weight, about 3 lbs.
Price, each. **$1.65**

Our Special Team Bridle.

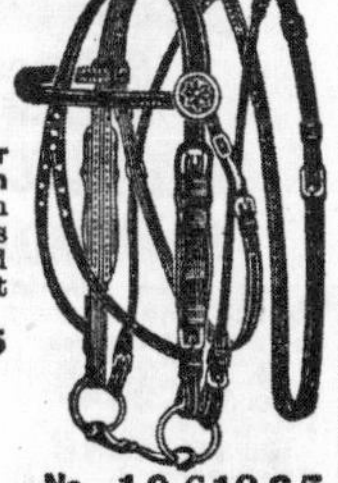

No. 10C1921 Made of fine Dundee oak leather, ⅞-inch short check. Concord blinds, round winker braces, round front, round nose band and round reins. Extra fine team bridle, Weight, 3 pounds.
Price, each....**$2.00**

No. 10C1923 Our Fine Open Round Rein XC Team Bridle, ⅞-inch scallop cheek, harness leather front and spotted face piece. Weight, about 2¾ pounds.
Price, each **$1.45**

No. 10C1925 Our Fine Round Rein, Long Check, Sensible Blind Team Bridle. Face piece with spots. Extra good team bridle for team work. Weight, 3¼ pounds.
Price, each, **$1.89**

Round Team Bridle.

No. 10C1927 Williams' Celebrated Round Team Bridle, made of Dundee oak leather with round bridle front, short round cheek, with ring and bit strap, round face piece with ring, long round rein, japan roller buckles. The best, nicest and handsomest all around heavy team open bridle on the market with japan bit. This bridle is made with japanned buckles only. Weight, about 3 pounds.
Price, each, heavy team bridle **$1.99**

Our 90-Cent Bridle.

No. 10C1929 Team Bridle, open, face short rein, fancy face piece, XC trimmings, ⅞-inch. Weight, about 1¾ pounds.
Price, each......**90c**

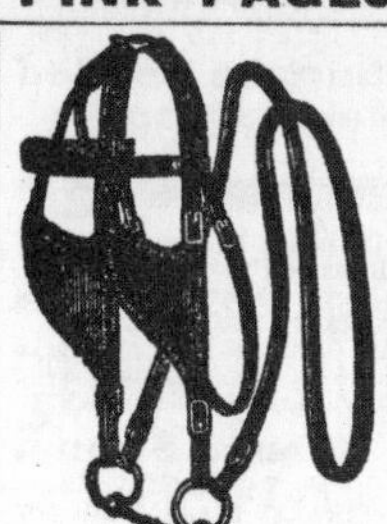

Our 53-Cent Bridle.

No. 10C1931 Our Short Flat Rein, Pigeon Wing Blind, XC trimming, ⅝-inch check and rein, harness leather front. Weight, about 1¾ lbs.
Price, each....**53c**

Our $1.75 Team Bridle.

No. 10C1933 Fine Team Bridle, made with roller buckles, four small loops on each cheek, round rein, round winker brace, sensible blinds, leather front. An extra good team bridle. XC trimmed. Weight, about 3 lbs.
Price, each, **$1.75**

No. 10C1934 Extra Heavy, Extra Strong Square Blind Bridle made 1⅛-inch check and rein, japan roller buckles, with short rein to throw over the hames, jointed bit, a very heavy durable bridle. Weight, 2½ pounds.
Price, each, **$1.27**

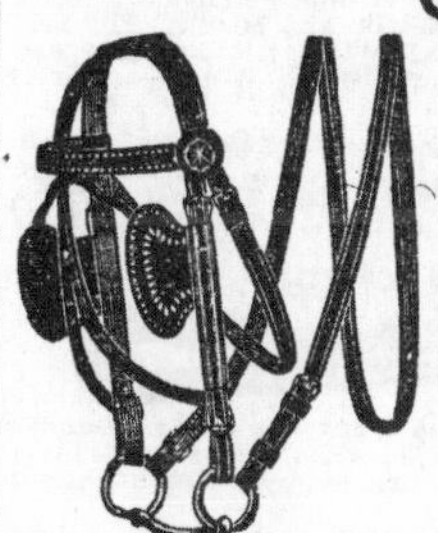

No. 10C1935 Our Jenny Lind Team Bridle, with cupped pigeon wing blind, flat winker brace, leather front, flat side rein. A farm bridle. XC trimmed. Weight, about 2¼ lbs.
Price, each....**96c**

Montana Bridle.

No. 10C1939 Sears, Roebuck & Co.'s 3¼-lb. Special Montana Team Bridle, ⅞-inch box loop check, flat rein, round winker brace and spotted face piece. Concord blinds.
Weight, 3¼ lbs.
Price, each.....**$2.00**

Dakota Bridle.

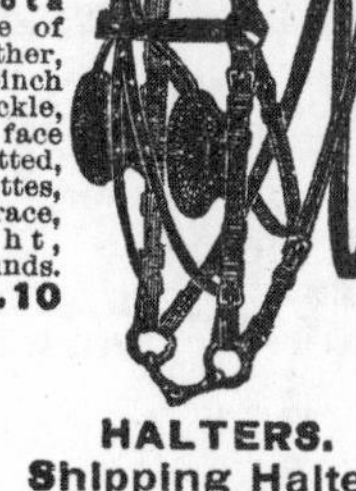

No. 10C1941 Sears, Roebuck & Co.'s Fine Dakota Team Bridle, made of fine Dundee oak leather, Concord blinds, ⅞-inch check, roller buckle, four small loops, face piece brass spotted, brass front and rosettes, round winker brace, flat rein. Weight, about 3¼ pounds.
Price, each...**$2.10**

HALTERS.

Shipping Halter.

No. 10C1975 Web Shipping Halter, 1⅛-inch web head stall, web chin strap and rope tie. Weight, about 8 ounces.
Price, each.......**$0.14**
Per dozen.......**1.50**

Special Heavy Halter.

No. 10C1985 Sears, Roebuck & Co.'s Special Heavy Assorted Color Web Halter, 1⅛-inch web, adjustable leather chin strap with rope tie, throat latch with web front. This is the best web halter you can buy. Weight, each, 16 ounces.
Price, each.........**22c**

Russet Leather Halters.

Our Russet Belting Leather Halter, made in two sizes 1-inch and 1¼-inch only.
No. 10C1988 1-inch halter. Price, each.......**$0.45**
Per dozen.......**5.00**
No. 10C1989 1¼-inch halter. Price, each.......**$0.55**
Per dozen.......**6.00**

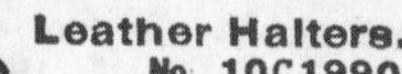

Leather Halters.

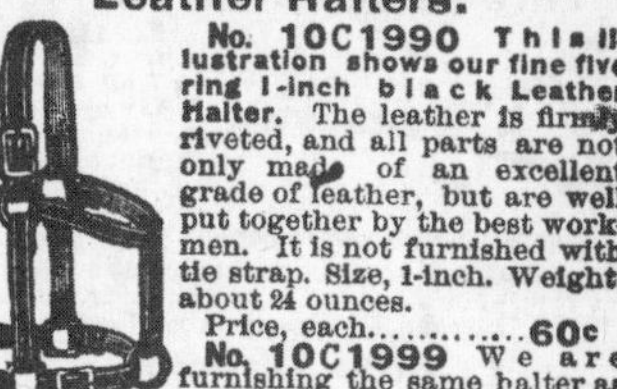

No. 10C1990 This illustration shows our fine five ring 1-inch black Leather Halter. The leather is firmly riveted, and all parts are not only made of an excellent grade of leather, but are well put together by the best workmen. It is not furnished with tie strap. Size, 1-inch. Weight, about 24 ounces.
Price, each............**60c**
No. 10C1999 We are furnishing the same halter as illustrated and described above, but extra heavy and large, being 1¼ inches in size, without tie strap. Weight, about 28 ounces. Price, each............**70c**

Colt Halter.

No. 10C2003 Our Special Colt Halter, made of black leather. Same style as No. 10C1990. Small size halter. Price, each..**50c**

A Genuine Hand Made Leather Halter for 80 Cents.

No. 10C2005 The remarkable value which we offer in this halter can only be judged fully by a personal examination. No one who buys this halter will be dissatisfied with it, but on the contrary, will be surprised at the unusual quality we are able to give them. This is a genuine hand made black leather halter, five rings, good heavy stock, furnished without tie strap. Size, 1 inch. Weight, about 1¼ pounds.
Price, each............**80c**
No. 10C2007 Hand Made Black Leather Halter, five-ring, same as above, without the strap, but heavier stock, being 1¼ inches in size. Weight, about 1¾ lbs. Price, each **96c**
No. 10C2009 Extra Fine 1½-inch Hand Made Black Leather Halter, same as illustrated and described above, but extra heavy and large size. Weight, about 2¼ pounds.
Price, each............**$1.12**
For prices on halter straps see Nos. 10C2327, 10C2329 and 10C2331, on page 100.

Our Economy Rawhide Halter, Five Rings.

No. 10C2017 This is a Special Rawhide Halter made to meet the demand for something very low in price and at the same time excellent in quality and guaranteed to be lasting and durable. Without tie strap. Size, 1 inch. Weight, about 1¼ pounds. Price, each..**39c**

83 Cents Buys a $1.50 Rawhide Halter.

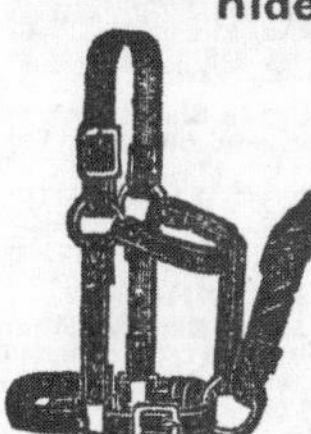

No. 10C2019 We show here an illustration of our special grade five-ring riveted Rawhide Halter. This halter is extra good quality, very heavy and well made, complete with tie strap. Size, 1 inch. Weight, about 28 ounces.
Price, each....**83c**
Price, each, without halter strap.....**50c**
No. 10C2021 Five-ring Riveted Rawhide Halter, complete with tie strap, same as illustrated and described above, but 1¼ inches wide. Weight, about 40 ounces. Price, each. **$1.08**
Price, each, without halter strap... **.70**

Our 36-Cent Cow Halter.

No. 10C2023 This is a heavy 1-inch leather cow halter, is easy on head, does not chafe around horns. The best cow halter made. Weight, about 1 pound.
Price, each.......**36c**

Halter Ropes.

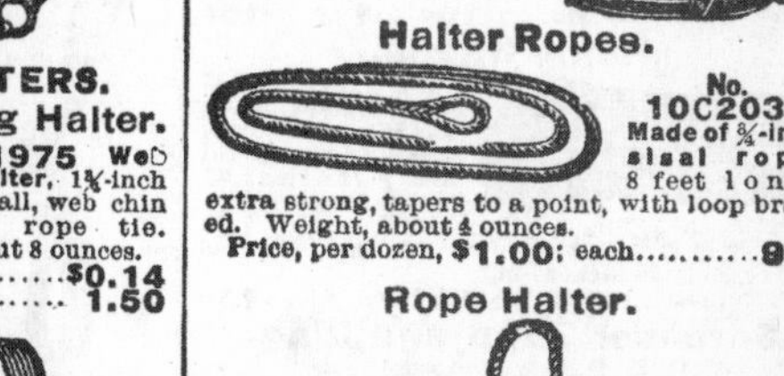

No. 10C2035 Made of ⅝-inch sisal rope. 8 feet long, extra strong, tapers to a point, with loop braided. Weight, about 4 ounces.
Price, per dozen, **$1.00**; each............**9c**

Rope Halter.

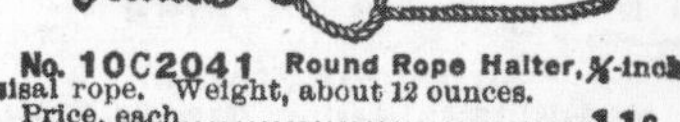

No. 10C2041 Round Rope Halter, ⅝-inch sisal rope. Weight, about 12 ounces.
Price, each............**11c**

Heavy Leather Neck Halters.

No. 10C2049 1½-inch Neck Strap, 1¼-inch stale. Weight, about 18 ounces.
Price, each............**73c**

Round Bridle Cheeks.

No. 10C2055 Our Round Bridle Cheeks, made with buckle and billet, used for making open bridle. For one horse. Weight, about 8 ounces. Price, per pair............**50c**
If by mail, postage extra, 5 cents.

Three-Buckle Overcheck.

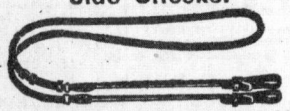

No. 10C2059 Our Special Three-Buckle Overcheck, with nose band, nickel or imitation rubber buckles and billets, good solid stock and well made. Weight, 7 ounces.
Price, each..........55c
If by mail, postage extra, 7 cents.

Side Checks.

No. 10C2062 Side Checks, ⅝-inch billets, nickel or Davis rubber buckles and rings. Weight, about 11 ounces. Price, each......57c
No. 10C2063 ⅞-inch Team Side Checks. Weight, about 12 ounces. Price, each......65c
If by mail, postage extra, 14 cents.

Single Driving Lines.

Flat for Single Buggy Harness.

No. 10C2065 Single Flat Driving Lines, ⅞-inch fronts, 1-inch russet or black leather hand parts. Length, 12 feet 6 inches. Weight, about 30 ounces. Price, per pair......$1.45
No. 10C2067 Single Flat Driving Lines, ⅞-inch fronts, with billets to buckle in bits, 1⅛-inch russet or black leather hand parts. All hand made. Weight, about 32 ounces.
Price, per pair..........$1.90
No. 10C2069 S., R. & Co.'s Special Beaded Single Driving Lines, made of fine Dundee leather, ⅞-inch beaded checks with spring billet, 1⅛-inch hand parts.
All russet. Price, per pair..........$3.65
All black. Price, per pair.......... 3.75

Double Driving Lines.

Flat for Double Buggy Harness.

No. 10C2090 Flat Double Driving Lines, ⅞-inch fronts, with 1⅛-inch russet or black leather hand parts, nickel buckles. Length, 14 feet. Price, per set for two horses......$2.60
No. 10C2093 Flat Double Driving Lines, 1-inch fronts, with 1⅛-inch russet or black leather hand parts sewed to checks. The very best double buggy line. Nickel or Davis rubber buckles. Length, 14 feet.
Price, per set for two horses..........$3.75

Double Team Lines.

No. 10C2155 Our B Grade Black Leather Team Lines made with bar rein buckles. Per set for two horses:

1 inch wide, length...	15 ft.	18 ft.	20 ft.
Weight, about, pounds	3¾	4	4½
Price, per pair......	$2.10	$2.40	$2.75

A Grade Team Lines.

No. 10C2165 Our A Grade Black Leather Team Lines, genuine hand made from selected stock, roller buckles. Per set for two horses:

1 inch wide...	15 ft.	18 ft.	20 ft.	22 ft.
Wt., about, lbs.	3¾	4	4¼	4½
Per pair...	$2.31	$2.50	$2.76	$2.90

Our AA Grade Team Lines.

No. 10C2170 Our Extra Heavy AA Grade, Hand Made Lines, from choice selected stock, with roller buckles. Per set for two horses:

1⅛ inches wide......	18 ft.	20 ft.	22 ft.
Weight, about, lbs..	4½	4¾	5½
Price, per pair......	$3.00	$3.25	$3.50

Hand Made Hame Straps.

No. 10C2300 Hame Straps. This hame strap is hand made, of fine oak stock, 21 inches long, with roller buckle and two leather loops. Weight, each, 4 ounces. Made in four sizes.

Size, inches......	¾	⅞	1	1¼
Price, each....	8c	10c	11c	18c

Hame Straps.

No. 10C2305 Hame Straps, made with twin loop, made from good heavy leather, 21 inches long.
Price, each, 1-inch, 11c; ⅞-inch..........10c
No. 10C2310 Hame Straps, same as above, only 30 inches long.
Price, each, 1-inch, 14c; ⅞-inch..........11c

Spreader Strap and Ring.

No. 10C2317 Spreader Strap and Ring for team harness, made with twin loop and one slide loop with good ring. Weight, about 2 ounces. Price, each..........14c

Spreader Straps.

No. 10C2321 Leather Spreader Straps, without rings or loops, with ⅝-inch buckle, 24 inches long, black leather. Weight, about 2 ounces. Price, each..........10c

Halter or Hitching Straps.

No. 10C2327 Black Leather Hitching Straps, 7 feet long, with German snap riveted on.

Size, inches.........	⅝	¾	⅞	1	1¼
Weight, about, ozs..	6	7	8	8	12
Price, each........	19c	23c	27c	33c	42c

No. 10C2329 With buckles.

Sizes, inches.........	⅝	¾	⅞	1	1¼
Weight, about, ounces	7	7	8	8	12
Price, each........	27c	30c	38c	45c	

Our Special Surface Tanned Rawhide Halter Strap.

No. 10C2331 This Halter Strap is made of extra fine quality of oil tanned rawhide leather, is soft and pliable, easy to tie, and is extra strong, 6 feet long, cut and twisted loop.
Size, 1 -inch; weight, 7 ounces. Each...35c
Size, 1¼-inch; weight, 8 ounces. Each...45c
Size, 1½-inch; weight, 9 ounces. Each...53c

Breast Straps.

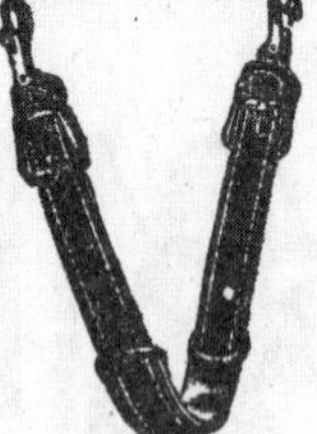

No. 10C2332 Team Breast Strap, made for a cheap team farm harness, two 1⅛-inch pieces sewed together with buckle snaps on each end, with slide. Weight, about 1½ pounds.
Price, each....$0.39
Per dozen........4.10
Add extra for Breast Strap Roller Snap on No.10C2332 Breast Strap, 11c each, or 22c per pair for two horses.

Breast Strap Made With Twin Loop.

Our Team Breast Strap, made of good heavy leather 1½ inches wide, with twin loop. Full length breast straps.
No. 10C2333 1¼ inches. Weight, about 10 ounces. Price, each..........40c
No. 10C2334 1½ inches. Weight, about 12 ounces. Price, each..........46c

Our Fine Hand Made Team Breast Strap, made with two heavy leather loops. Heavy roller buckle. 4 feet 8 inches long. Weight, each, 18 ounces.
No. 10C2335 1½-inch. Price, each..49c
No. 10C2336 1¾-inch. Price, each..53c
No. 10C2337 2 -inch. Price, each..64c

Double and Stitched Neckyoke Strap.

Our Special Double and Stitched Neckyoke Strap. This is extra strong, well made, 3 feet 4 inches long, double loop and buckle. The best kind of strap for safety to parties in buggy and carriage. Made in two sizes. Weight, about 12 ounces.
No. 10C2338 Size, 1¼-inch. Price, each..........60c
No. 10C2339 Size, 1½-inch. Price, each..........80c

Buggy Neckyoke Strap.

Our Single Strap Neckyoke Strap. Dundee oak leather, 1¼ inches wide, 3 feet 4 inches long, for neckyoke on double buggy. Weight, about ⅓ pound.
No. 10C2340 Price, each..........45c

Pole Strap or Martingale.

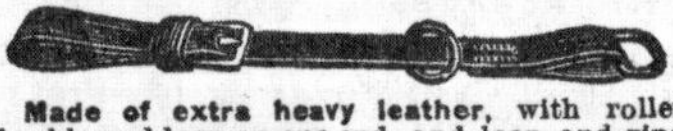

Made of extra heavy leather, with roller buckle and loop on one end, and loop and ring on the other, made in three sizes. No collar strap. Weight, each, 15 ounces.
No. 10C2345 1½-inch. Price, each..44c
No. 10C2347 1¾-inch. Price, each..49c
No. 10C2349 2 -inch. Price, each..57c

S., R. & Co.'s Chicago Truck Martingale.

This is our Heavy Martingale of fine Dundee oak leather, single strap body running from bellyband to collar, and short heavy strap running from ring on body to neckyoke, or chain, made in three sizes and the best martingale or pole strap for heavy trucking we make. 1½-inch 1¾-inch 2-inch
No. 10C2351 Each, 92c $1.08 $1.28

S., R. & Co.'s Special Heavy Team Housing.

No. 10C2375 Made of two pieces of harness leather stitched together. Leather layer on center, with curved top front, stitched around holes. The housing is left solid, so you will be able to make the hole for your hames where you want it. Size of housing, 16 inches long from center by 12¾ inches wide at bottom. This is the best solid leather team housing on the market. Weight, about 8½ pounds each. Price, each......$2.60
No. 10C2377 Price, per pair...... 5.20
We will put brass block letters on this housing for you as follows:
1¼-inch letters. Price, each..........10c
1½-inch letters. Price, each..........12c

Pole Strap or Martingale with Collar Strap.

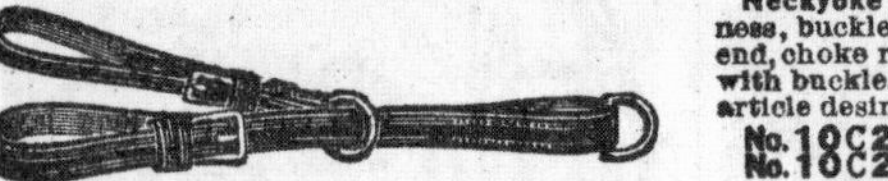

Neckyoke Martingales, for heavy team harness, buckle loop at one end, ring at the other end, choke ring stitched on; 24-inch collar strap with buckle. When ordering give number of article desired. Weight, about 18 ounces.
No. 10C2378 1½-inch. Price, each 58c
No. 10C2379 1¾-inch. Price, each 65c

Rope Traces.

No. 10C2382 Made of 1-inch Manila rope, with rope clip one end for hook hame, and clip for chain with swivel on other end. The rope part of trace is 6 feet long, the chain 18 inches. This makes an extra good plow trace, or for anything that you wish to use a pair of hook hames and traces for. A much better trace than chain. Weight, 5½ pounds.
Price, per pair..........$1.10

Crupper for Team Harness.

No. 10C2385 Our Team Crupper for Team Harness. Made with folded body, with buckle and chafe. Bent and shaped ready for use on common team harness, ¾-inch buckles. Weight, about 4 ounces.
Price, each..........17c
If by mail, postage extra, 5 cents.

Fancy Face Piece for Team Bridle.

Our Special Fancy Harness Leather Face Piece, made with loop forks for bridle checks to pass through. Zylonite center ring with chafe under ring. ¾-inch billet to buckle in the crown piece, fancy brass spots. Sold one only or in pairs. Weight, about 4 ounces.
No. 10C2389 Price, each..........39c
No. 10C2391 Price, per pair..........78c
If by mail, postage extra, each, 5 cents.

Bridle Fronts for Team Bridle.

Made with a 13-inch strip of brass and nickel with solid leather back. This bridle front is used on express or fancy team harness. Weight, about 3 ounces. Made in four sizes, as follows:
No. 10C2437 ¾-inch. Price, each...11c
No. 10C2439 ⅞-inch. Price, each...12c
No. 10C2441 1-inch. Price, each...13c
No. 10C2445 1¼-inch. Price, each...20c
If by mail, postage extra, each, 4 cents.

Brass Spotted Trimmings.

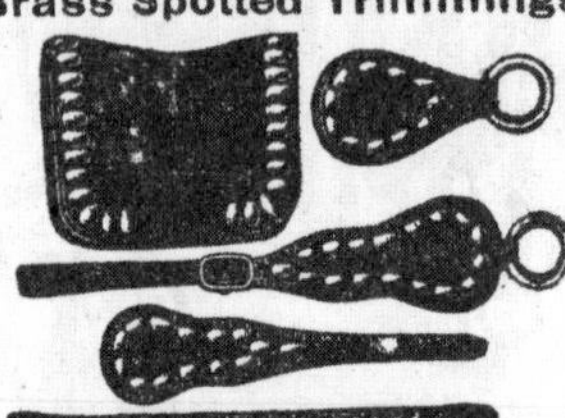

Our Brass Spotted Hame Housing, Bridle Fronts and Brass Spotted Drops Trimming for Brass Harness. Made in brass only.
No. 10C2446 Hame housing. Each...82c
No. 10C2447 1¼-inch brass fronts. Price, each..........25c
No. 10C2448 1-inch brass fronts. Price, each..........19c
No. 10C2449 Nose band. Each........28c
No. 10C2451 Face drop. Each........29c
No. 10C2452 Ring drop. Each........35c
No. 10C2453 Hip drop. Each........62c

Fine Brass or Nickel Face Drop.

No. 10C2458 Our Special Team Face Drop. Made of single Japan leather, with fancy scalloped fancy patent leather binding, billet attached ready to buckle into bridle crown. Diamond brass center star and circle or heart. When attached to bridle is very stylish and shows up the horse's head to good advantage. Weight, each, 3 ounces. Each...30c
If by mail, postage extra, 4 cents.

Our Special Brass and Nickel Harness Ornament Trimming.

Made of patent leather face with leather back. Fancy patent leather border with either a brass or nickel heart ornament or star and circle in brass or nickel, made with leather strap with snap on it to snap in the ring on the hips of the harness. These are generally used to tie the hitch line in.
No. 10C2461 The Heart Drop.
Price, each..........50c
No. 10C2462 Star and Circle.
Price, each..........50c
If you do not state nickel or brass, we will always send brass.
If by mail, postage extra, each, 5 cents.

Team Net Strings.

No. 10C2460 Our Special Upper Leather Net Strings, cut from our Dundee leather. The illustration shows one dozen net strings in bundle, cut full length. The same as we use in No. 10C9050 net.
Price, per dozen, 7-foot strings, 48c; each, 4c
Price, per dozen, 8-foot strings, 60c; each, 5c
If by mail, postage extra, per dozen, 10 cents.

Side Straps.

No. 10C2465 Side Straps for breeching on double team harness. Length, 6 feet.
Price, per pair, ⅞-inch..........59c
Price, per pair, 1-inch..........69c
Price, per pair, 1⅛-inch..........89c
No. 10C2470 Side Straps for single buggy harness, 4 feet long, either nickel or Davis rubber buckles. Price, per pair, ⅝-inch. 47c
Price, per pair, ¾-inch..........53c
Price, per pair, 1-inch..........59c

Stage or Farm Breeching.

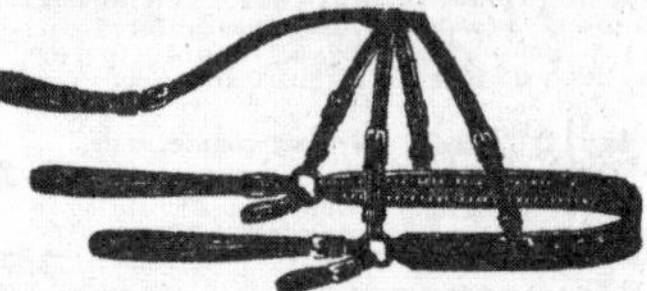

No. 10C2475 Made from the best, heavy, selected oak tan stock. Breeching folded with a 1¼-inch layer; hip strap, ⅞-inch; back strap, 1⅛-inch; double side straps, ⅞-inch; ⅞-inch lazy strap. Weight, about 8¾ pounds.
Price, per set, for two horses.......$6.75
No. 10C2480 Same Style of Breeching as No. 10C2475, only double back strap, 1-inch, running to hame. Extra strong, made of best Dundee oak leather. Weight, about 12¾ pounds.
Price, per set, for two horses.......$7.38

Dakota Team Breeching.

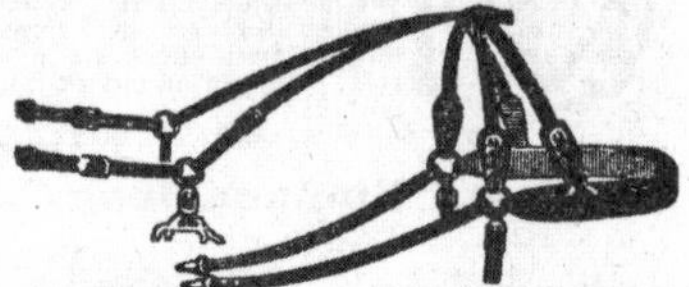

No. 10C2485 Made with 1-inch hip and back strap, with short strap to run to hame from ring on side, ⅞-inch breeching strap to snap under horse in ring on martingale. Heavy fold with wide layer, two rows stitching full length of breeching. Weight, about 12¾ pounds.
Price, per set, for two horses.......$8.35
No. 10C2486 Our Heavy, 1⅛-inch, Japanned Buckle Dakota Breeching, 1⅛-inch hip and back straps, 1⅛-inch side straps, heavy fold body with wide layer. Weight, about 15 pounds.
Price, per set, for two horses.......$9.90

Our $2.90 Team Breeching.

Made from the very best selected oak tan stock, including side straps.
No. 10C2490 ⅞-inch straps. Weight, about 5 pounds. Price, per set of two, for double harness..........$2.90
No. 10C2495 1-inch straps. Weight, about 5½ pounds. Price, per set of two, for double harness..........$3.50
No. 10C2500 1⅛-inch straps. Weight, per set, 6¾ pounds. Price, per set of two, for double harness..........$3.97

Single Strap Breast Collar and Traces.

No. 10C2550 Our Fine Single Strap Buggy Breast Collar, with single strap traces stitched to the same. Breast collar, 1⅜ inches, with 1⅛-inch traces; ⅝-inch single neck strap, nickel or Davis rubber buckles. Weight, about 2½ pounds. Price, each..........$2.15
No. 10C2555 The same style of breast collar, only made extra heavy with 1¾-inch breast collar and 1¼-inch single strap traces stitched to the breast collar and ¾-inch neck strap; suitable for harness from $12.00 to $20.00. Nickel or Davis rubber buckles. Weight, about 3½ pounds. Price, each..........$2.50

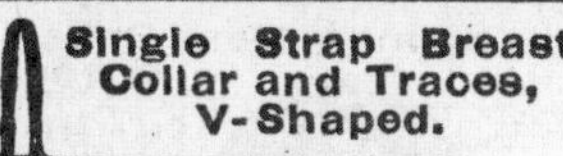

Single Strap Breast Collar and Traces, V-Shaped.

No. 10C2560 S., R. & Co.'s Special V-Shaped Breast Collar and Traces, made of extra fine Delhi oak tanned leather, with 2½-inch V-shaped body breast collar and 1⅛-inch single strap traces attached with ⅝-inch single strap neck strap. Weight, about 2½ pounds.
Price, each.......................................**$2.45**

No. 10C2565 Same style of breast collar as No. 10C2560, only made with an extra heavy 3-inch V-shaped single strap breast collar, with 1¼-inch single strap traces attached and ¾-inch single strap neck strap. Weight, about 2¾ pounds. Price, each.......................**$2.95**

Hames and Single Strap Traces Attached.

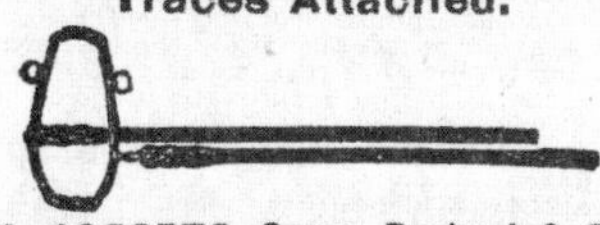

No. 10C2570 Sears, Roebuck & Co.'s Special Hames and Single Strap Traces Attached, with three holes in back end. The hames are 3½-pound wrought iron, with traces 1¼-inch riveted to the same. Be sure and state the length of hames wanted to fit your collar. Trimmings full japanned or XC. Weight, about 6 pounds. Price, per pair, for one horse, including hame straps.........................**$2.20**
Price, per pair, for one horse, with nickel terret hames, with 1⅛-inch trace........**$2.50**

No. 10C2577 Same style of hames and traces as quoted above, only fine japanned body with nickel terrets, 1⅛-inch single strap traces riveted to hames, with three holes in the back end. Weight, about 5½ pounds. Price, per pair, for one horse, including hame straps...**$2.95**

Southern Slip Harness.

Gig Saddle and Breeching Only for One Horse.

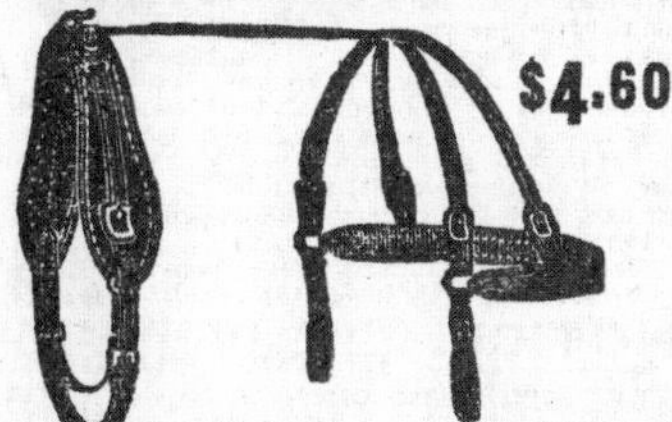

$4.60

No. 10C2580 S. R. & Co's. Special Leather Slip Harness, made with good heavy gig saddle, 5½-inch harness leather skirt, enamel duck pad, shaft tug with all double flat bellyband. Breeching, folded body with layer, ⅞-inch double hip strap, 1-inch back strap, 1-inch side strap. This harness is commonly used in the south without crupper. Weight, about 10¼ pounds. Price, per set, as shown in illustration.........................**$4.60**

Cow Bell Straps.

No. 10C2601 Our Fine Black Leather Cow Bell Strap, made with roller buckle and loop. State size of strap wanted. Weight, 8 ounces.
Size, 1½-inch. Price, each..........**29c**
Size, 2 -inch. Price, each..........**45c**
Size, 3 -inch. Price, each..........**65c**

Swiss Cow Bells.

These Swiss Cow Bells are made from Swiss bell metal. They are celebrated for their pure musical tone, which can be heard a long distance, and sound entirely different from common bells.

Catalogue No.	Diameter at mouth	Widest strap that can be used	Wt.	Price
9C06133	3 5-16 in.	1⅛-in.	¾ lb.	$0.30
9C06134	4 in.	1½-in.	1 lb.	.46
9C06135	5 in.	2⅛-in.	1½ lbs.	.80
9C06136	6½ in.	3 -in.	3 lbs.	1.30

For full line of Cow Bells, see index.

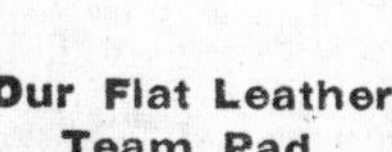

Our Flat Leather Team Pad.

No. 10C2617 Our Flat Leather Team Pad, with drop hook and terret, 1⅛-inch buckle and billet end, 3-inch solid leather body. Weight, per pair, 3½ pounds.
Price, each...........**$1.30**

Buggy Back Strap.

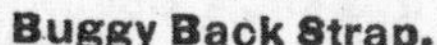

No. 10C2620 Our Special Buggy Back Strap, made of fine Dundee oak leather, scalloped and stitched, with round crupper sewed on. Made for single or double harness. Weight, about ½ pound. Price, each.......**65c**

Chain Piping.

No. 10C2625 Leather Pipes, 24 inches long, to cover trace chains for plow harness. Weight, about 3 pounds.
Price, per set of four for two horses..**$1.20**

No. 10C2630 S., R. & Co.'s Heavy Chain Piping made of fine Dundee oak leather, put up in sets of four for two horses. Bound ends, made in three sizes. This is the best chain piping made. Weight, about 4½ pounds.
Length of piping, inches 30 36 42
Price, per set of four for two horses..........**$1.80 $2.10 $2.35**

No. 10C2631 Price, per set of four for two horses, 6 feet chain piping......**$3.25**

Bellybands.

No. 10C2635 Bellyband for Chain Traces, made with loop on each end for chain to go through, with one buckle on near side. Made in three sizes. Weight, 8 to 12 ounces.

Size, inches	1⅛	1½	2
Price, each	35c	40c	49c

Team Bellybands.

No. 10C2650 Team Bellyband, folded and stitched. 18 inches long, with 1⅛-inch buckle on each end. Weight, each, ⅝ pound.
1⅛-inch team bellyband. Price, each....**44c**
1½-inch team bellyband. Price, each....**50c**

Hip and Back Straps.

No. 10C2660 Team Hip and Back Strap, made 1-inch hip and 1-inch back strap, with Cooper trace carrier sewed in with wear leather, folded crupper with buckles sewed on, trace carrier to buckle on hip strap for traces to run through. Weight, per pair, 3¾ pounds.
Price, per set, for two horses..........**$2.49**

No. 10C2670 Hip and Back Strap, for flat pad team harness, made with 1⅛-inch long back strap running through pad loop to hame, with 1-inch hip strap. Weight, per pair, 4 pounds. Price per set, for two horses...**$3.20**

Team Traces.

Our Clip Cockeye Team Trace, made of good, heavy leather, with two rows stitching and cockeye riveted on, making a very strong trace. Weight, per set, 6¾ pounds.
No. 10C2700 1⅛ inches by 6 feet.
Price, per set of four.......................**$4.50**
No. 10C2701 1¼ inches by 6 feet.
Price, per set of four.......................**5.15**

Our Fine, Light Team Trace, made of good, heavy leather, with two rows stitching, cockeye sewed in. Weight, per set, about 3 pounds.
No. 10C2705 1¼ inch by 6 feet 6 inches, flat trace. Price, per set of four traces..**$4.60**

No. 10C2710 S., R. & Co.'s Special Team Trace, made of fine Dundee oak leather, 1½-inch, 6 feet 6 inches long. This trace is used for slip tug team harness or for extra long horses. Weight, per set, about 8¾ pounds.
Price, per set of four traces for two horses.......................................**$5.50**

No. 10C2712 Price, per set, 1⅜ inches by 6 feet 6 inches, for two horses.........**$6.75**

No. 10C2715 1½ inches by 6 feet 6 inches, raised trace. Weight, per set, about 3 pounds.
Price, per set of four traces.............**$4.90**

No. 10C2720 Made from good, heavy oak tan stock, well stitched, 6 feet long, 1½ inches wide. Weight, per set, about 7¾ pounds.
Price, per set of four......................**$5.15**

No. 10C2725 1⅝-inch traces, 6 feet long. Weight, per set, about 8 pounds.
Price, per set of four.......................**$6.00**

No. 10C2730 Hand made, 6 feet long, 1½ inches wide. Weight, per set, about 7¾ pounds.
Price, per set of four.......................**$6.40**

No. 10C2735 1⅝-inch, hand made. Weight, per set, about 8 pounds.
Price, per set of four,........................**$7.30**

No. 10C2740 Single Strap Concord Trace. Made from the very best, selected, heavy cuts of oak tan stock, 1½-inch points, 2¼-inch body, 6 feet long. Weight, per set, about 8¾ pounds.
Price, per set of four traces.............**$5.67**

No. 10C2745 1⅝-inch points, 2½-inch body, 6 feet long. Weight, per set, about 8½ lbs.
Price, per set of four traces.............**$6.56**

No. 10C2746 2-inch points, 2⅝-inch body, 6 feet long. Weight, per set, about 8¾ pounds.
Price, per set of four traces.............**$7.94**
For Concord Toggles in place of cockeyes, add 50 cents.

Single Buggy Traces.

No. 10C2765 Machine Stitched Traces, 6 feet long, good, sound stock.

Size	1⅛-inch	1⅛-inch
Weight, per pair, about	33 ozs.	31 ozs.
Price, per pair	$1.56	$1.45

No. 10C2770 Best Machine Stitched Traces, 6 feet long, raised center, hand smoothed round edge, selected stock.

Size	1⅛-inch	1⅛-inch
Weight, per pair, about	33 ozs.	31 ozs.
Price, per pair	$1.73	$1.59

Double Buggy Traces.

No. 10C2775 Machine Stitched Traces, 6 feet 4 inches long, selected stock.

Size	1¼-inch	1⅛-inch
Weight, per pair, about	36 ozs.	34 ozs.
Price, per pair	$1.80	$1.60

No. 10C2780 Best Machine Stitched Traces, 6 feet 4 inches long, raised center, hand finished round edge.

Size	1¼-inch	1⅛-inch
Weight, per pair, about	36 ozs.	34 ozs.
Price, per pair	$2.00	$1.75

Our Special Single Strap Buggy Traces.

This trace is made of extra quality Dundee oak trace leather, double and stitched point and double and stitched heel; the balance of the body of trace is single strap. The trace is made in all sizes.

No. 10C2781 Size, 1⅛-inch, 6 feet. Weight, per pair, 1½ pounds. Price, per pair..**$1.35**

No. 10C2782 Size, 1¼-inch, 6 feet. Weight, per pair, 1¾ pounds. Price, per pair..**$1.41**

Our Special Single Strap Double Buggy Trace.

Made of superior quality of Dundee oak leather, single strap body, with the point double and stitched and double and stitched heel. Made 6 feet 6 inches long for double pole harness. Single strap body traces are better than the full double and stitched traces.

No. 10C2783 Size, 1⅛-inch, 6 feet 6 inches long. Weight, per pair, about 1¾ pounds.
Price, per pair...........**$1.54**

No. 10C2784 Size, 1¼-inch, 6 feet 6 inches long. Weight, per pair, about 2 lbs. Price, per pair...**$1.69**

Gig Saddles.

For Single Harness.

No. 10C2800 Gig Saddles, made of patent leather, japanned metal seat, enameled cloth pad, 2½ inches wide, with ⅞-inch shaft bearer straps and ⅝-inch bellyband straps. Japanned or XC trimmed. Wgt., about 2½ pounds.
Price, each..............**85c**

No. 10C2801 Gig Saddles, made of patent leather, japanned metal seat, enameled cloth pad, 3 inches wide, with 1-inch shaft bearer straps and ⅞-inch bellyband straps. Japanned or XC trimmed. Weight, about 3 pounds.
Price, each............**$1.05**

Single Strap Gig Saddles.

No. 10C2805 Single Strap Gig Saddle, 2½ inches wide, with harness leather skirts and enameled leather pad, ⅝-inch bellyband straps. Trimmed in nickel or imitation rubber. Weight, about 2¼ pounds. Price, each...**$1.60**

No. 10C2810 Single Strap Gig Saddle, trimmed in nickel or Davis rubber, made with swell pad, harness leather skirt, swing bearer. A gig saddle suitable for $20.00 to $25.00 harness. Weight, about 4 pounds. Price, each...**$2.29**

Iron City Team Harness Pads.

No. 10C2855 Iron City Team Pads, made with plates. Pads stuffed with housings and dee rings. This makes a good repair pad, as you can use a strap with a buckle for the skirt or flap. Japanned or XC trimmed. Weight, about 5½ pounds.
Price, per pair.............................**$1.40**

Shaft Tugs.

No. 10C2890 S., R. & Co.'s Old Style Shaft Tug, made with bent heel buckle, box loop and billet. Nickel or Davis rubber buckles. A shaft tug to be used with two bellybands. Weight, 12 ounces.
Price, per pair, ⅞-inch.......................**54c**
Price, per pair, 1-inch........................**59c**

Heavy Concord Truck Traces.

Concord Truck Traces. Made from the very best, extra heavy, selected oak tan stock, very heavy and strong, doubled and stitched, two rows of stitching, swell safe, 1½-inch bellyband, billets, 6 feet long, with 12-inch heel chains for use on a bolt hame.

No. 10C2750 Weight, about 16 pounds.
Price, 1½-inch, per set of four..........**$9.40**

No. 10C2755 Weight, about 17 pounds.
Price, 1¾-inch, per set of four..........**$10.25**

No. 10C2756 Weight, about 18 pounds.
Price, 2-inch, per set of four..........**$12.00**

Hame Tugs For Slip Tug Harness.

This is an illustration of our special Hame Tug for common slip tug farm harness. Clip hame with Champion trace buckle. A new and desirable hame tug, just introduced, and one which will be found superior to anything sold. Sold only in sets of four, in the following sizes:

No. 10C2905 Size, 1¼ inches, with box loop and Champion trace buckle, for light double harness. Weight, 2¼ pounds.
Price, per set of four for two horses.**$1.90**

No. 10C2910 Size, 1½ inches. Weight, per set, 3 lbs. Price, per set of four...**$2.05**

No. 10C2915 Size, 1¾ inches. Weight, per set, 4 lbs. Price, per set of four...**$2.30**

Our Team Harness Hame Tugs.

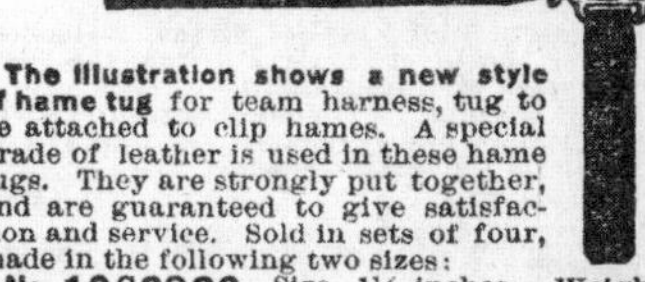

The illustration shows a new style of hame tug for team harness, tug to be attached to clip hames. A special grade of leather is used in these hame tugs. They are strongly put together, and are guaranteed to give satisfaction and service. Sold in sets of four, made in the following two sizes:

No. 10C2920 Size, 1½ inches. Weight, per set, 10 lbs. Price, per set of four...**$2.95**

No. 10C2925 Size, 1¾ inches. Weight, per set, 10 pounds. Price, per set of four.**$3.15**

Lace Box Loop Hame Tugs.

No. 10C2926 Our Fine Lace Box Loop Hame Tug, made of Dundee oak leather; to be used on bolt hame only; Champion trace buckle; 1½-inch billet for bellyband. Price, per set of four, 1½-inch.**$4.50**
Price, per set of four, 1¾-inch **4.90**

No. 10C2936 Size, 2 inches. Weight, per set, about 10 pounds. Per set of four.**$6.95**

Buggy Hame Tugs.

S., R. & Co.'s Special Buggy Hame Tug made with box loop, open eye clip. Can be used on any iron hame for single or double harness. Extra strong made in XC or japan, nickel or Davis rubber. Price is for pairs for one horse with hame strap.

No. 10C2955 XC or japanned buckles.

Size	1-inch	1⅛-inch	1¼-inch
Weight, about	20 ozs.	21 ozs.	22 ozs.
Price, per pair	80c	85c	95c

Hook and Terret Team Pad.

No. 10C2980 Our Fine Hook and Terret Team Pad, made with folded body 1¼-inch layer, three-loop and buckle and billet, turtle bottom pad fastened with pad screw and terret. Weight, about 6 pounds.
Price, per set for two horses.........**$3.40**

No. 10C2985 Same style of pad as No. 10C2980, only made with Perfection pad with skirts to buckle in hame tug buckle.
Price, per set, for two horses........**$3.25**

Flat Team Pad.

No. 10C2995 Our Flat Team Pad, made with heavy fold, with 1¼-inch layer buckle and billet, with round loop on top for back strap to run through. Weight, about 3 pounds. Price, per set, for two horses.............**$2.15**

Our Special Montana Concord Pad.

No. 10C3005 Made of Dundee oak leather, 1⅜-inch body, with 1½-inch buckle billets, 1½-inch layer with brass loop on top, leather bottom stuffed with hair, making the best all round Concord pad on the market. Weight, 2 pounds. We do not break pairs.
Price, per pair for two horses.........**$3.65**

Our Fine Slip Tug Team Pad.

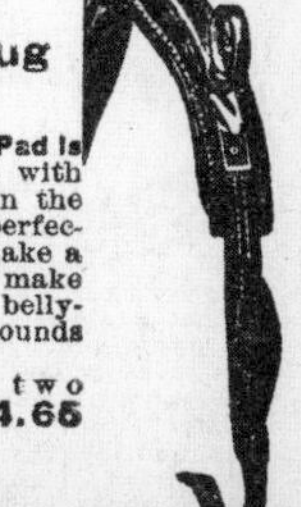

No. 10C3015 This Pad is made with heavy skirts with round loop on side to run the trace through with good perfection pad. You cannot make a pad any better than we make this; 1¼-inch billets for bellyband. Weight, about 7¼ pounds per pair.
Price, per set, for two horses...................**$4.65**

Stirrup Straps.

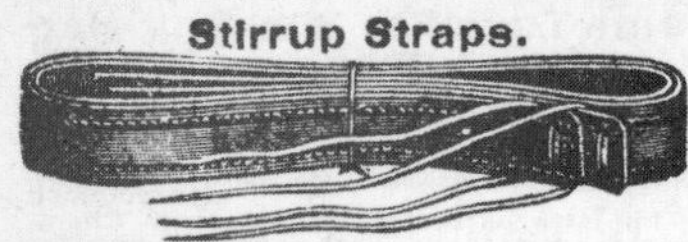

No. 10C3035 Stirrup Straps, 4 feet 6 inches long, with buckle, either black or russet leather. Weight, 1 pound.
Price, per pair, 1-inch........................**55c**
Price, per pair, 1¼-inch.....................**75c**
No. 10C3040 California Style Stirrup Straps, cut from the best Oregon oiled skirting leather, 6 feet 6 inches long, with lace strings. Weight, 2¾ pounds. 2-inch 2½-inch 3-inch
Price, per pair......**$1.30 $1.60 $2.00**
Add for fender on any California stirrup strap **$1.65** extra to price of stirrup strap.

Latigos.

No. 10C3045 Latigo Straps, 2 inches wide, for buckle cinch rig, cut from the best Oregon oiled skirting leather, with lace string to fasten. Weight, 1¾ pounds. Length for draw side, 5 feet 6 inches. Price, per pair....**$1.15**
Length for off side, 2 feet 8 inches.
Price, per pair...............................**.64**

No. 10C3050 Latigos for tie cinch rig, with lace strings to fasten to saddle rings. Weight, 10 ounces.
1¼ inches, 5 feet long. Price, per pair..**54c**
1½ inches, 5 feet long. Price, per pair..**67c**

Cowboys' Riding Pants.

No. 10C3085 Chaps, or Cowboys' Riding Pants, made of oiled chaparejos leather, stock being especially prepared for this purpose solid leather waistband, laced together, fringe on outside of each leg, two pockets. **Made for service.** Sizes, 28 to 34 inches; waist measurement not necessary. Weight, 5½ to 6½ pounds, according to length.
Price, per pair....**$7.60**

No. 10C3090 Our Special Denver Chaps or Riding Pants, made of heavy double twilled brown duck, leather waistband to lace, leather pockets, leather bottomed and leather fringe. This is an extra good strong riding chap. Weight, 2½ pounds. An ideal pair of cowboy riding pants. **Everyone likes them, because they are light and easy.** Give length of leg wanted, inside measurement, and waist measure. Price, per pair.........**$2.75**

Horse Hobbles.

No. 10C3100 Front Hobbles, two leather anklets connected by a short swivel chain, to be attached to the fore legs of a horse to prevent running or straying away when loose. Weight, 1½ pounds.
Per pair...**58c**

No. 10C3105 Side Hobbles, with chain and strap to be attached from one fore leg to one hind leg. Weight, 24 ounces.
Price, per pair..............................**65c**

Linen Lariats.

No. 10C3110 Linen Lariats, extra quality braided linen rope, ⅜-inch in diameter, with rawhide honda, have been boiled in oil, which keeps them soft and pliable and renders them waterproof; will not kink or snarl. Ends are patent grip fastened. Weight, about 3 pounds.
Price, length, 40 feet, **$1.94** 50 feet, **$2.35**
Price of ½-inch Linen Lariat, 40 feet long, heavy and strong, each...................**$3.00**

Brass Hondas for Lariats.

No. 10C3120 Our Fine Heavy Brass Hondas, made the shape of an egg and will slide the best on the rope. Weight, 3 ounces.
Price, per dozen, **$1.10**; each..........**10c**

Manila Lariat Rope.

No. 10C3125 S., R. & Co's. Special Fine Manila Lariat Rope. Made of 4 strands pure manila rope, 7-16-inch in diameter; made with our fine brass egg shaped honda. Braided on with braided tassel at the hondas and 8-inch tassel at the back end of lariat. This lariat is having a great sale throughout the country. This rope makes a very strong lariat. Weight, about 3½ pounds.

Made in lengths....	40 feet	45 feet	50 feet
Weight............	2¾ lbs.	3 lbs.	3½ lbs.
Price, each.........	**$0.70**	**$0.85**	**$0.95**
Per dozen.........	**7.90**	**9.70**	**0.90**

Texas Spur Straps.

No. 10C3135 Texas Spur Straps, oiled leather, stamped. Weight, about 5 ounces.
Price, per pair, **30c**
If by mail, postage extra, 5 cents.

Russet Leather Cuffs.

No. 10C3170 S., R. & Co.'s Special Hand Stamped Russet Leather Cuffs, made of extra fine russet leather, with three large glove buttons, which makes a fastening much better and neater and stronger than the buckle. This is one of the very finest hand stamped cuffs on the market. It is a special with us, and for our exceptionally low price we hope will meet with ready sale. Can be worn without or with coat. Length of the cuff, 7 inches. Weight, per pair, about 10 ounces. We do not break pairs. Price, per pair.........**80c**
If by mail, postage extra, 10 cents.

Double California Cinches.

No. 10C3230 Gray California Double Cinch, with chafes, tongues and connecting strap. Weight, about 2½ pounds.
Price, per pair..............................**$1.75**
No. 10C3235 White California Double Cinch, wool lined chafes, fancy stamped connecting strap, with buckle. Weight, about 2¾ pounds. Price, per pair...................**$2.00**

Tackaberry Patent Cinch Buckle.

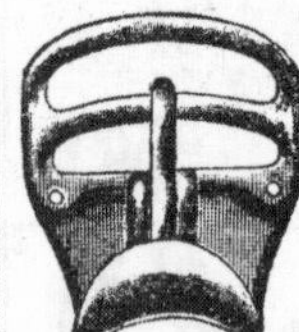

No. 10C3278 Made of malleable iron, XC plated. Size, 2-in. loops. To be used on cinches for **Cowboy saddles.**
Price each.........**15c**
If by mail, postage extra, 5 cents.

COLLARS

No. 10C3400 Plain Duck Collars, made of cotton duck with leather chafes on side, and leather pad on top and leather welt all around. Sizes, 17 to 22 inches. Weight, about 4 pounds.
Price, each..........**$0.49**
Per dozen............ **5.50**

Our 89-Cent Collar.

No. 10C3410 S., R. & Co.'s Fine Baker Face, split rim and shoulder, metal seamed rim giving extra good hame room. This is the best plow collar on the market. Marshall fasteners on top. Sizes, 17 to 22 inches. Weight, 5¼ pounds.
Price, each...**$ 0.89**
Per dozen..... **10.60**

Fine Buggy Collars.

No. 10C3415 Buggy Collar, made of the best kip leather, light and neat; will outwear three patent leather collars. Sizes, 17 to 22 inches. Weight, 3¼ pounds.
Price, each....**$ 1.15**
Per dozen...... **13.20**

No. 10C3420 Fine Buggy Collar, made of fine kip leather, turned edge, gig size. Sizes, 17 to 22 inches. Weight, 4 pounds.
Price, each....**$ 1.70**
Per dozen.... **19.75**
Be sure to state size wanted.

Patent Leather Collar.

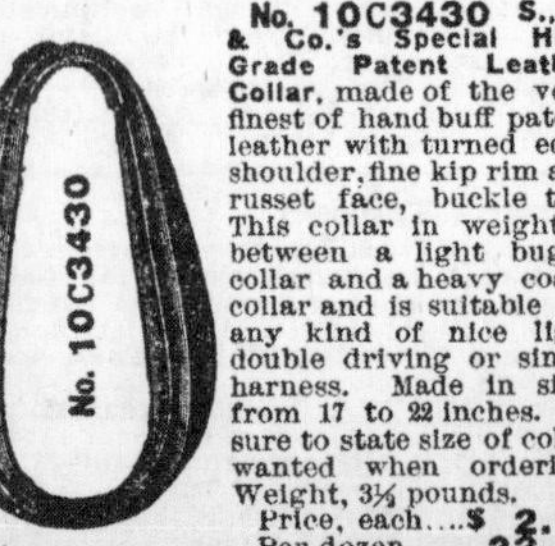

No. 10C3430 S., R. & Co.'s Special High Grade Patent Leather Collar, made of the very finest of hand buff patent leather with turned edge shoulder, fine kip rim and russet face, buckle top. This collar in weight is between a light buggy collar and a heavy coach collar and is suitable for any kind of nice light double driving or single harness. Made in sizes from 17 to 22 inches. Be sure to state size of collar wanted when ordering. Weight, 3½ pounds.
Price, each....**$ 2.10**
Per dozen..... **23.47**

Open Throat Collar.

No. 10C3435 Our Open Throat Collar is thong sewed with good cap, good kip rim and back. With this collar you can use a sweat pad that opens at bottom. Size, 17 to 22 inches. Weight, 6 pounds. Price, each....**$ 2.20**
Dozen. **25.80**

Our $1.58 Team Collar.

No. 10C3440 Good Heavy Team Collar. Black split leather back and rim, kip face, metal stitched, with Marshall's patent single top fastener. Be sure to state size wanted. Sizes, 17 to 22 inches. Weight, 6 pounds.
Price, each.**$ 1.58**
Per dozen... **18.75**

Black Leather Concord Collar.

No. 10C3450 Our Fine All Black Leather Genuine Concord Collar. Wool faced, extra heavy, with 1½-inch buckle top, one of the best collars made, and should be ordered with all of our Concord harness. Sizes, 17 to 22 inches. Weight, about 6 pounds.
Each....**$ 2.00**
Dozen .. **23.40**
Be sure to state size wanted.

Sears' Special Hair Face Team Collar.

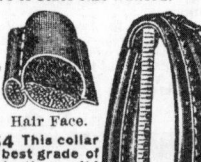

Hair Face.

No. 10C3454 This collar is made of the best grade of Dundee collar leather, solid rim, full harness leather shoulder, thong sewed, buckle top, heavy sole leather pad. The small illustration shows the hair face, the large illustration shows you how to measure collar. If you want a good collar, try this one. Sizes, 17 to 22 inches. Weight, about 6 pounds.
Price, each.............................**$ 2.15**
Per dozen................................**25.50**

Half Sweeney Collar.

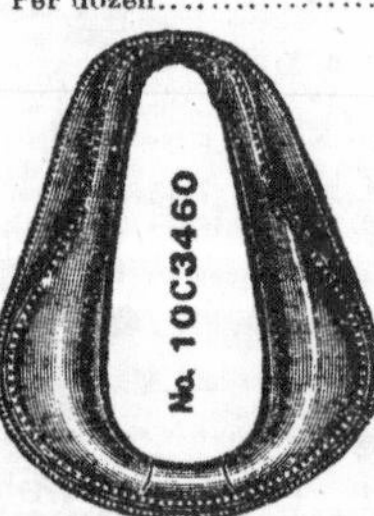

No. 10C3460 Our Fine Half Sweeney, thong sewed, wool faced team collar with Marshall's patent double top fasteners. Extra good collar for team work. Be sure to state size wanted. Sizes, 17 to 22 inches. Weight, about 5½ pounds.
Each....**$ 2.15**
Per dozen...**25.50**

NOTICE. We will make extra long collars, any style listed in our catalogue, for 50 cents per inch extra for all over 22 inches. You must send CASH IN FULL with order for extra large collars.

Our Iowa Riveted Dray Collar.

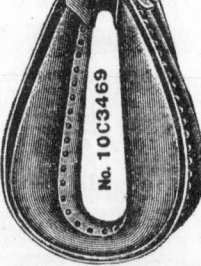

Hair Face.

No. 10C3469 Extra Heavy, All Russet Collar. Full back, genuine curled hair face, wide fender, patent riveted outseam, copper hand riveted middle seam. One of the best dray collars made. Extra heavy leather. Try this collar. Sizes, 17 to 22 inches. Weight, 8 lbs.
Price, per dozen, **$32.00**; each......**$2.95**

Lumber Case Collar.

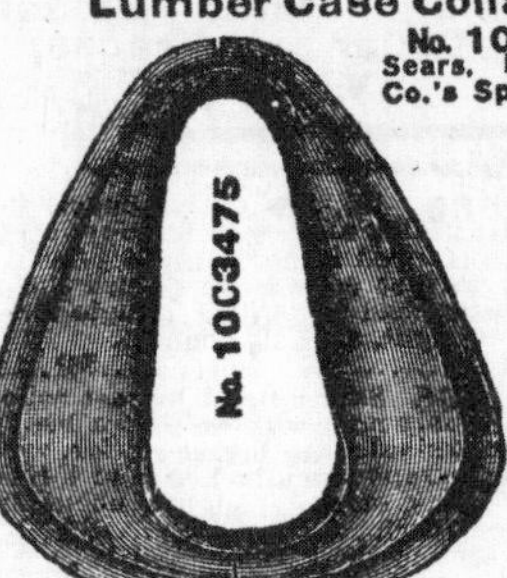

No. 10C3475 Sears, Roebuck & Co.'s Special Extra Heavy Lumber Scotch Case Collar. This collar is made of extra fine quality of Dundee oak tanned color leather, extra heavy throughout, draft of collar about 13 inches, curled hair face. This collar is used very largely in the lumber country or for extra heavy dray purposes, absolutely the best extra heavy lumber or dray case collar on the market, strictly high grade throughout. Weight about 11 pounds.
Sizes, 18 to 22 inches. Price, each. **$ 3.75**
Per dozen................................ **44.50**
Sizes, 22½ to 23 inches. Price, each. **4.45**
Sizes, 23 to 24 inches. Price, each. **4.80**

Heavy Dray Collar.

Hair Face.

No. 10C3480 Our Curled Hair Face Heavy Dray Collar, made of Dundee kip collar leather, sole leather collar pad, double Pop stitched rim, so as to give large hame room.
Draft of collar about 16 inches. This collar is made with a fine curled hair facing under leather, or same as a sweat pad. A horse will never have a sore shoulder if you use this collar. Weight, about 8½ pounds.
Sizes, 18 to 22 inches. Price, each.**$ 2.95**
Per dozen.................................. **34.40**
Sizes, 22½ to 23 inches. Price, each. **3.35**
Sizes, 23 to 24 inches. Price, each. **3.65**

NOTICE. HOW TO MEASURE HORSE COLLARS: Take a rule and place in top of collar as shown in No. 10C3454 and the inside measure will be the size you want, measuring from top to bottom on the rim or front of collar.

SWEAT PAD should be one size larger than the collar. Lay the shoulder part of your collar in about three inches of water, for 8 to 12 hours, then buckle on the horse and be sure the hames fit the collar good. Work the horse for one-half day and the collar will never make the shoulder sore; and the collar will always fit the horse

Collar Pads.

No. 10C3600 Collar Pad, made of heavy harness leather, lined with deerskin, tanned with the hair on; 9 inches long, 7 inches wide; ⅜-in. straps, 18 inches long, to buckle around collar. Weight, 12 ounces.
Price, per dozen, **$5.65**; each.......**49c**
If by mail, postage extra, each, 12 cents.

No. 10C3601 Curtis Zinc Collar Pad. Sizes, 6 to 7½ inches. Weight, 11 ounces.
Each......**$0.20**
Per dozen. **2.28**
If by mail, postage extra, each, 12 cents.

No. 10C3602 Curtis Celebrated Boss Collar Pad, made of heavy skirting leather with zinc center; double strap to buckle round the collar; very healing to horse's neck. Weight, 8 ounces.
Price, each.............................**$0.33**
Per dozen................................ **3.50**

No. 10C3603 Curtis Star Zinc Collar Pad, made of heavy galvanized zinc, with perforated top and double strap, one of the most healing pads to the neck on the market.
Weight, 12 ounces, Price, each...... **$0.23**
Per dozen.................................. **2.75**

No. 10C3604 Oscillating Top Perforated Center Collar Pad, stamped out of heavy skirting, perforated top with steel saddle, which takes the weight of the collar off the horse's neck. One of the best top collar pads on the market. Weight, 12 ounces.
Price, per dozen, **$3.50**; each........**30c**

S., R. & Co.'s Collar Pad.

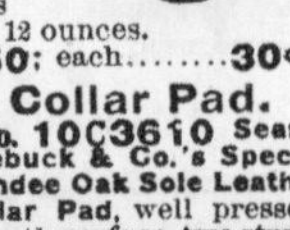

No. 10C3610 Sears, Roebuck & Co.'s Special Dundee Oak Sole Leather Collar Pad, well pressed, smooth surface, two straps with buckles, for heavy team collar pad. Weight, 4 ounces.
Price, per dozen, **$1.55**; each........**15c**
If by mail, postage extra, each, 4 cents.

Fancy Gig Sweat Pads.

No. 10C3620 Fancy Felt Gig Sweat Pad, strictly first class quality, strapped.

Size	Weight	Per doz.	Each
4½x14 inches	2 ounces	$0.80	10c
4½x18 inches	4 ounces	1.20	15c
7 x20 inches	8 ounces	2.75	27c

If by mail, postage extra, each, 8 cents.

No. 10C3645 Fancy Gig Sweat Pad, patent top, felt bottom.

Size	Weight	Per doz.	Each
4½x14 inches	4 ounces	$1.35	14c
4½x18 inches	4 ounces	2.00	20c

If by mail, postage extra, each, 4 cents.

Breast Collar Housings.

No. 10C3650 Fancy Felt Housings, fawn color. Size, 3½x36 inches, five straps on each side. Weight, about 6 ounces.
Price, per dozen, $2.15; each..........20c
If by mail, postage extra, each, 8 cents.

No. 10C3655 Fancy Felt Breast Collar Housings, pinked, patent leather covered. Weight, about 8 ounces. Price, each...$0.31
Per dozen..........3.65
If by mail, postage extra, each, 8 cents.

Felt Collar Sweat Pad.

No. 10C3677 Sears, Roebuck & Co.'s Special Fine Felt Collar Sweat Pad. Made of fine selected felt, four hooks, shaped top, 9 inches, wide draft; good thick pad, makes collar easy on horse's shoulders. Sizes, 18 to 24 inches. Open at bottom. Weight, about 12 ounces. One of the best felt pads made.
Price, each, for one collar..........30c

Genuine Fawn Stuffed Sweat Pad, 29 Cents.

No. 10C3693 Our Genuine Fawn Stuffed Sweat Pad. Made of old gold drill, well stuffed with composite stuffing, four rows of quilting, four hooks, open at bottom, 12-inch wide draft. The best Fawn Sweat Pad made. Sizes, 18 to 24 inches at same price. Weight of pad, 32 ounces. Better than the felt pad.
Price, each, for one horse..........29c
Per dozen..........$3.00

Hames.

No. 10C3800 Oiled Concord Bolt Hames. Per pair, two hames for one horse: Weight, per pair, 7 pounds.

No. 5 oil Concord, bolt combination loop. Price, per pair..........$ 0.75
Per dozen pairs..........8.40
No. 6 oil Concord, bolt combination loop. Price, per pair..........85
Per dozen pairs..........8.70
No. 8 oil Concord, bolt combination loop. Price, per pair..........90
Per dozen pairs..........9.00
No. 10 oil Concord, bolt combination loop. Price, per pair..........95
Per dozen pairs..........9.90
Size of hames, 26½ and 28 inches long.

No. 10C3830 Our Special Black No. 460 Hames. XC Plate, combination loop top Hayden hold back ring.
Price, per pair, two hames for one horse..45c
Per dozen pairs, in case lots only of 5½ dozen pairs..........$4.50

No. 10C3840 Varnished I. O. T. Hook Hames, with breast rings, to use with chain traces. Weight, per pair, 4 pounds.
Price, per pair, two hames for one horse......$0.28
Per dozen pairs, in case lots only..........$3.30

Hames and Hame Tug with Hame Strap.

Measure length of hame from top to bottom. The price is for one pair for one horse. Be sure and state size hames you want to fit your collar. Add for nickel trimmed hames and hame tug 50 cents per pair extra. Weight, about 4 pounds.

Size of buckle on hame tug..	1⅛ in.	1¼ in.
No. 10C3860 Japanned Hames and Buckle	$1.08	$1.15
No. 10C3865 XC Hames and Buckle........	1.08	1.15

Hame Tops.

No. 10C3880 Brass or Nickel Globe Ball Hame Top, can be used on any Concord hames. Made in three sizes, 1, 1⅛, 1¼.
Price, per pair, 1 -inch, weight, 12 oz....25c
Price, per pair, 1⅛-inch, weight, 13 oz....32c
Price, per pair, 1¼-inch, weight, 14 oz....37c

Brass Concord Hame Tops.

Our Chicago Dandy Brass Ball Hame Tops, 2¼ inches in diameter, can be used on all Concord bolthames. Per pair for one horse. Weight, per pair, 32 ounces.
No. 10C3886 Price, per pair, brass..84c
No. 10C3887 Price, per pair, nickel..89c

Hame Staples.

No. 10C3940 Hame Staples, with burrs, made of best quality malleable iron. Weight, per dozen, 2¼ pounds.
Price, per gross, $1.65; per dozen....15c

Hame Clips.

No. 10C3945 Hame Clips, made of the best quality wrought iron, without rivets. Weight, per dozen, 38 ounces. Price, per dozen..$0.16
Per gross..........1.75

Hame Rivets.

No. 10C3950 Hame Rivets, put up in 1-pound packages. We do not break packages.
Price, per package..........7c

Hame Loops.

No. 10C3955 Screw Hame Bottom Loops; loop will admit ⅞-inch strap. Weight, per dozen, 14 ozs. Price, per dozen....24c

Cockeyes.

No. 10C3960 Patented Clip Cockeyes, made of the best malleable iron. The cockeye is made heavy at the shoulder and the eye is large. Weight, per dozen, 70 ounces. Size, 1⅛ inch.
Price, per dozen. 35c

No. 10C3965 Japanned Screw Cockeyes.

Size, inches..........	1¼	1½	1¾	2
Weight, dozen..........	36 oz.	41 oz.	45 oz.	56 oz.
Price, per dozen..........	22c	24c	30c	38c

Bridle Rosettes.

No. 10C3990 Pflueger's Fancy Crystal Rosettes, for bridles, 1⅛ inches in diameter. Put up six pairs on a card especially for Sears, Roebuck & Co. No two pairs on the card alike, all being of different colors and different designs. All new patterns. Ornamental, strong and durable. Price, per pair..........10c
Per card of six pairs..........50c
Postage, per pair, 4 cents; per card, 20 cents.

No. 10C4002 Our Fine Solid Metal, Black Enameled Letter Rosettes, for any kind of bridle, 1½ inches in diameter, put up one pair on card, made especially for S., R. & Co. Be sure and state the letter you want. Weight, 3 ounces.
Price, per pair, 25c
If by mail, postage extra, per pair, 4 cents.

Society Emblem Rosettes.

No. 10C4003 Our Society Emblem Rosette for Buggy Bridles. This is something new and very handsome. There is nothing nicer than this new emblem rosette, made in the following emblems: Odd Fellows, Knights of Pythias, A. O. U. W., Modern Woodmen and G. A. R. Be sure and state what emblem you want. Weight, 2 ounces. Price, per pair, 20c
If by mail, postage extra, per pair, 3 cents.
We do not break pairs.

Brass or Nickel Rosettes.

No. 10C4005 S., R. & Co.'s Heavy Brass or Nickel Rosette for Dray or Express Harness. Made of solid steel back with nickel or brass polished face. The loop is extra strong and makes the best metal rosette on the market. Will match our heavy brass and nickel fronts.
Weight, 2 ounces.
Price, per pair..........21c
If by mail, postage extra, per pair, 3 cents.

Our Success Hame Fastener.

No. 10C4010 Our Success Hame Fastener. It is stronger and better than any leather hame strap. It is easily worked; place the heavy end in loop of off hame and close the hook and it will always be ready for use. These fasteners have been used for a number of years by large transfer companies and proved to be the very best. Weight, 9 ounces. Price, each..........24c

Our American Halter Chain.

This Halter Chain is cut from fine steel, and is the strongest and best chain made, there being absolutely no welds to give way. As a halter chain they have no equal; reliable, smooth and handsome, made with snap, swivel, loose ring and toggle. Weight, about 20 ounces. Made in sizes as follows:

	Medium No. 0	Heavy No. 000
No. 10C4026 4½ feet. Price, each..	$0.15	$0.19
Per dozen..........	1.50	2.10
No. 10C4031 6 feet. Price, each..	$0.18	$0.24
Per dozen..........	2.10	2.75

English Stallion Lead Chain.

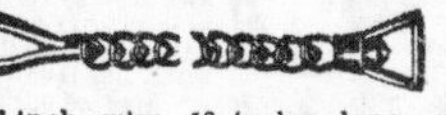

No. 10C4045 English Steel Lead Chain, 3-16-inch wire, 18 inches long, polished, with snap, swivel and D ring. Price, each..........25c
If by mail, postage extra, 12 cents.

Breast Chains.

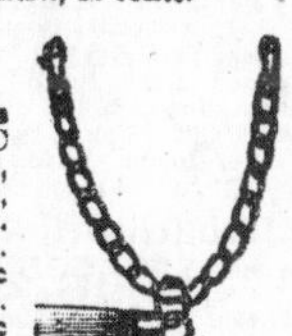

No. 10C4050 Covert's Patent Breast Chains. XC plate with snap on each end, extra strong. Weight, each, 2½ to 3 pounds. 5-16 in. wire.

Length..........	24-in.	28-in.
Price, per pair.	46c	55c
Length..........	32-in.	36-in.
Price, per pair.	57c	62c

Heel Chains.

No. 10C4075 S., R. & Co.'s Special Heel Chain. Made with screw dee and swivel; 6 links long. Can be put in any trace that you wish to use it on by using this, our special screw heel chain. 5-16-inch wire. Made in three sizes.

	Size, in.	Weight, lbs.	Price
Per set of four......	1⅛	3¼	40c
Per set of four......	1⅜	3½	41c
Per set of four......	2	4	42c

Trace Chains.

No. 10C4080 Trace Chains, made of size No. 2, ¼-inch wire, 7 feet long. Weight, per pair, 6½ pounds. Price, per pair of two chains for one horse..........38c

No. 10C4083 Sears' Special Heavy Twisted Link Trace Chain, made 7 feet long. No. 0, 5-16-inch wire, twisted links. This is the best trace chain made. Weight, per pair, 10½ pounds.
Price, per pair, for one horse..........66c

Breast Strap Roller Snap.

No. 10C4105 Our Special Breast Strap Roller Snap. XC only. Be sure and state size wanted. Made in three sizes.

Size, inches	Weight, about	Price, per doz.	Price, each
1½	8 oz.	$1.20	11c
1¾	10 oz.	1.25	12c
2	12 oz.	1.35	13c

Bristol Breast Strap Roller Snap.

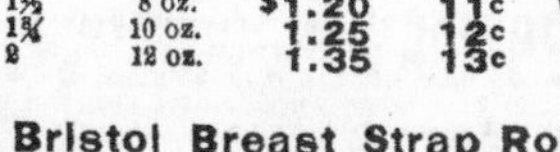

No. 10C4106 This is the best, made with extra safety guard, large, heavy roller and rivet. Made in four sizes, XC plate.

Size, inches	Weight, each	Price, per doz.	Price, each
1¼	7 oz.	$1.35	12c
1½	9 oz.	1.45	14c
1¾	11 oz.	1.55	15c
2	13 oz.	1.75	16c

Combination Neckyoke Snap.

No. 10C4110 Combination Neckyoke Snap and Breast Snap Slide. The strongest, safest and most durable snap made. It is indispensable to the farmer, as it is the only snap that can be used successfully on farm machinery. Tinned finish.

Size, inches	Weight, each	Price, per doz.	Price, each
1½	10 oz.	$1.25	13c
1¾	11 oz.	1.35	14c
2	12 oz.	1.45	15c

Breast Strap Slides.

No. 10C4115 Gray Iron Breast Strap Slide is made from our special pattern. It fits the strap, will not cut at loop and works easy on the strap. A very heavy slide, wide flange, best gray iron, fine japanned finish.

Size, inches..........	1½	1¾	2
Weight, per dozen......	4½ lbs.	6 lbs.	6¾ lbs.
Price, each..........	2c	3c	4c
Per dozen..........	20c	30c	40c

Team Terret and Pad Hooks.

Heavy Band Team Harness Terrets and Hooks, XC finish and japanned finish, style No. 215; size, 1½-inch, used for all kinds of team or farm harness.

Hooks.

Band Pattern Syracuse Bolt Pad Hook, used on team pads, with 1½-inch layer.

No. 10C4155 Japanned hook, No. 178, 1½-inch. Price, per dozen, 42c; each..........4c
No. 10C4160 XC hook, No. 178, 1½-inch. Price, per dozen, 42c; each..........5c

Terrets.

No. 10C4170 Japanned terret, No. 215, 1½-inch. Price, per dozen, 32c; each..........4c
No. 10C4175 XC terret, No. 215, 1½-inch. Price, per dozen, 32c; each..........4c

Heavy Wire Ball Hooks and Terrets.

Wire Ball Terrets and Hooks, made in three kinds of trimming, nickel on composition, solid brass, imitation rubber, gilt trimmed. Be sure and state kind of trimming you want. Order by number.

Terrets, 1½-inch.

No. 10C4196 Nickel terrets. Price, per dozen, 67c; each..........7c
No. 10C4197 Brass terrets. Price, per dozen, 67c; each..........7c
No. 10C4198 Imitation rubber. Price, per dozen, 67c; each..........7c

Bolt Hooks.

No. 10C4199 Nickel bolt hook. Price, per dozen, 67c; each..........7c
No. 10C4201 Brass bolt hook. Price, per dozen, 67c; each..........7c
No. 10C4202 Imitation rubber bolt hook, Price, per dozen, 67c; each..........7c

Post Hooks.

No. 10C4203 Nickel post hook, No. 54. Price, per dozen, $1.60; each..........14c
No. 10C4204 Brass post hook, No. 54. Price, per dozen, $1.60; each..........15c
No. 10C4206 Imitation rubber post hook, No. 54. Price, per dozen, $1.60; each..14c

Drop Hook and Terret.

S. R. & Co.'s Special Drop Hooks and Terrets. To be riveted on flat pads. A hook that will lay flat on pad. Made in XC finish only.

No. 10C4239 XC Terret No. 303. Price, per dozen, 44c; each..........4c
No. 10C4241 XC Drop Hook No. 304. Price, per dozen, 50c; each..........5c

Safety Pad Hooks.

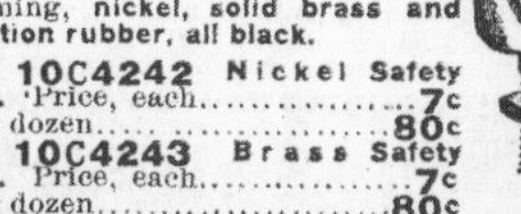

This is one of the best styles of Safety Pad Hooks. Can be used on any kind of gig saddle for single harness. Made in three kinds of trimming, nickel, solid brass and imitation rubber, all black.

No. 10C4242 Nickel Safety Hook. Price, each..........7c
Per dozen..........80c
No. 10C4243 Brass Safety Hook. Price, each..........7c
Per dozen..........80c
No. 10C4244 Imitation Rubber Safety Hook. Price, each..........5c
Per dozen..........50c

Check Hooks.

Hastings Check Hook. Can be used on either single or double harness. The best check hook on the market. Made in nickel, Davis rubber and brass. Illustrations show open and closed. The most complete check hook made.

No. 10C4246 Steel, Davis rubber. Price, per dozen, **$1.70**; each... **15c** Open. Closed.
No. 10C4247 Brass, nickel plated. Price, per dozen, **$2.25**; each........... **20c**
No. 10C4248 Solid brass, polished. Price, per dozen, **$2.00**; each........... **18c**

German Harness Snaps.

By size of snap we mean the width of strap that can be used.

No. 10C4295 German Harness Snaps, bronzed finish. We handle only the heaviest and best snaps of this style made.

Size	Weight, per dozen	Price, per dozen	Price, per gross
7/8-in.	13 oz.	12c	$1.25
1-in.	18 oz.	13c	1.30
1 1/4-in.	26 oz.	21c	2.25
1 1/2-in.	32 oz.	28c	2.95
1 3/4-in.	40 oz.	39c	4.20
2-in.	50 oz.	45c	5.00

Improved Triumph Harness Snaps.

No. 10C4300 This snap is very popular and is considered the best snap on the market today.

Size	Weight, per dozen	Price, per dozen	Price, per gross
3/4-in.	12 oz.	15c	$1.75
7/8-in.	14 oz.	16c	1.85
1-in.	16 oz.	19c	1.90
1 1/4-in.	25 oz.	29c	3.35
1 1/2-in.	28 oz.	36c	3.65
1 3/4-in.	32 oz.	40c	4.05
2-in.	46 oz.	55c	5.70

Covert's Harness Snaps.

No. 10C4305 Covert's Banner Bolt Snaps. The principal feature of the snap lies in the spring being entirely covered, shutting out all foreign substances.

Size	Weight, dozen	Price, per dozen	Price, per gross
7/8 in.	16 oz.	21c	$2.00
1 in.	18 oz.	24c	2.25
1 1/4 in.	24 oz.	37c	3.65
1 1/2 in.	26 oz.	41c	4.00
1 3/4 in.	30 oz.	45c	4.55
2 in.	44 oz.	48c	5.00

Dewey Harness Snaps.

No. 10C4310 Dewey Patent Snaps, strictly first quality. Every snap is thoroughly tested in the factory before being packed.

Size	Weight, dozen	Price, per dozen	Price, per gross
7/8 in.	14 oz.	24c	$2.60
1 in.	16 oz.	25c	2.65
1 1/4 in.	20 oz.	33c	3.60
1 1/2 in.	32 oz.	36c	3.90
1 3/4 in.	38 oz.	42c	4.55
2 in.	46 oz.	48c	5.25

Rope Snaps.

No. 10C4325 Bolt Round Eye Snaps for rope, tinned finished. Polished on the loop and milled at the nose of the hook. Every snap is thoroughly tested.

Size, inch	5/8	3/4
Weight, per dozen, ounces	15	18
Price, per dozen	25c	29c

Open Eye Bolt Snap.

No. 10C4345 Open Eye Bolt Snap, made of XC malleable iron. Can be used on chain or open eye links. Made in one size only. Weight, per dozen, 22 ounces. Price, per dozen......... **52c**

Swivel Eye Bolt Snap.

No. 10C4347 Swivel Eye Bolt Snap. Made of XC malleable iron. Round iron for rope. Snap made with swivel eye and will adjust itself to the rope. Made in three sizes. Weight, per dozen, 7/8-inch, 1 3/4 pounds.

Size, inch	3/4	7/8	1
Price, per dozen	43c	47c	78c

Loop Roller Bar and Rein Buckle.

Made same style as the common bar rein buckle, only with metal roller. This buckle never peels the strap. It is easier unbuckled than any other style of buckle of this kind without roller. Made in sizes from 1/2 to 1 1/2 inches. Japan and XC trimming. Weight, per dozen, 1-inch, 12 ounces. Known as No. 150.

No. 10C4350 XC Harness Buckle, No. 150.

Size, inch	1/2	5/8	3/4	7/8	1	1 1/4	1 1/2
Price, per doz.	6c	7c	$0.09	$0.11	$0.13	$0.19	$0.25
Per gross	62c	71c	.96	1.05	1.40	2.05	2.55

No. 10C4355 Japanned Harness Buckle, No. 150.

Size, inch	1/2	5/8	3/4	7/8	1	1 1/4	1 1/2
Price, per doz.	5c	6c	8c	$0.10	$0.12	$0.17	$0.21
Per gross	52c	60c	80c	1.00	1.15	1.80	2.30

Trace Buckles.

No. 10C4405 Three-Loop Champion Trace Buckles, made of best malleable iron, japanned finish. Size, 1 1/2 inches. Weight, 5 ounces.
Price, each......... 4c
Per dozen......... 37c
Size, 1 3/4 inches. Weight 6 ounces.
Price, per dozen, **42c**; each......... **5c**

No. 10C4410 Three-Loop Champion Trace Buckles, XC plate.
1 1/2 inches. Price, each......... 4c
1 1/2 inches. Per dozen......... 42c
1 3/4 inches. Price, each......... 5c
1 3/4 inches. Per dozen......... 48c

Heavy Roller Buckles.

This buckle is used by the leading harness makers throughout the United States, has a heavy roller on front bar, made in XC and japanned only, sold by dozen. Japanned black.

Known as No. 50 Roller Buckle.

No. 10C4445 Japanned Roller Buckles, No. 50.

Size, inch	1/2	5/8	3/4	7/8	1
Price, per doz.	4c	5c	5c	6c	8c
Per gross	42c	44c	52c	62c	73c

Size, inch	1 1/4	1 1/2	1 3/4	2
Per doz.	$0.10	$0.12	$0.15	$0.19
Per gross	1.00	1.20	1.55	1.85

No. 10C4450 XC Roller Buckle, No. 50

Size, inch	1/2	5/8	3/4	7/8	1
Per doz.	5c	5c	6c	7c	8c
Per gross	44c	52c	62c	73c	82c

Size, inch	1 1/4	1 1/2	1 3/4	2
Per doz.	$0.13	$0.15	$0.18	$0.21
Per gross	1.18	1.55	1.85	2.15

Spreader Rings.

No. 10C4520 Our Fine Celluloid Union Spreaders, made with five celluloid rings, connected together with celluloid loops; all white or assorted color rings. Size of rings from 2 inches to 1 1/4 inches. The price is for each string, not pairs. Weight, about 4 ounces.
Price, per string......... $1.05
Per dozen strings......... 12.00
If by mail, postage extra, each, 5 cents.

No. 10C4525 Union Spreader, same style as above, only three rings connected with celluloid loops; all white or fancy colors. Size of rings, 2, 1 1/2 and 1 1/4 inches. Weight, about 2 ounces.
Price, per string......... $0.59
Per dozen strings......... 6.75
If by mail, postage extra, each, 3 cents.

No. 10C4530 Celluloid Spreaders, composed of three solid celluloid rings in all white or assorted fancy colors. Weight, each, about 2 ounces. Price, per string......... $0.44
Per dozen strings......... 5.15
If by mail, postage extra, each, 3 cents.

Celluloid Rings.

No. 10C4535 S., R. & Co.'s High Grade Special Celluloid Rings. Made for us specially by the best manufacturers of this class of goods. Colors, red and blue and plain white, a ring that is used for trimming harness, such as no other concern has ever offered before. Be sure and mention color of rings wanted and the diameter. If no color is mentioned we will always send white.

Size, inches	Wt., per doz., ounces	Price, each	Price, per doz.
1 1/8	4	7c	$0.74
1 1/4	4	8c	.92
1 3/8	6	10c	1.18
1 1/2	8	13c	1.50
1 5/8	9	16c	1.70
1 3/4	10	19c	1.95
2	11	21c	2.30
2 1/4	13	22c	2.55

If by mail, postage extra, per doz., 8 to 14 cents.

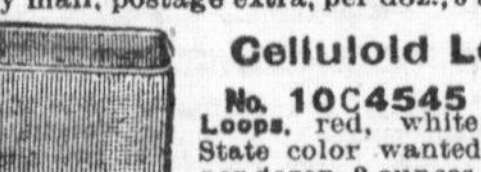

Celluloid Loops.

No. 10C4545 Celluloid Loops, red, white or blue. State color wanted. Weight, per dozen, 2 ounces.

Diameter, inch	5/8	3/4	7/8
Price, per dozen	$0.21	$0.25	$0.28
Per gross	2.35	2.67	3.00

If by mail, postage extra, per dozen, 3 cents.

Celluloid Spreaders.

No. 10C4550 Celluloid Spreaders, made of five celluloid rings and nine celluloid loops on each strap, straps are 32 inches long. Weight, 9 ounces Sold in pairs only.
Price, per pair......... **$1.90**
If by mail, postage extra, 10 cents.

Large Wood Trimming and Center Ring.

No. 10C4582 Our Special Large Wood Center Ring. Made of hard wood. Color, red white and blue. Size of ring, 2 inches in diameter. The best large wood center ring on the market. Weight, per dozen, 1 1/2 unces.
Price, per dozen, **55c**; each......... **5c**
If by mail, postage extra, per dozen, 24 cents.

Buckle Shield.

No. 10C4595 Stamped from solid brass, highly polished, edges smooth so they will not cut the straps. Made in brass or nickel. Weight, per dozen, 4 to 16 ounces.

Size, inch	1/2	5/8	3/4	7/8
Price, per dozen	18c	20c	23c	28c

Size, inches	1	1 1/8	1 1/4	1 1/2
Price, per dozen	35c	43c	50c	70c

If by mail, postage extra, per doz., 4 to 16 cents.

Harness Soap.

No. 10C4660 Frank Miller's Harness Soap. This is without question the best harness soap made. By using it your harness will wear longer and look better. Weight, per cake, 12 ounces. Price, per cake......... **11c**
If by mail, postage extra, 12 cents.

Acme Black Edge Ink.

No. 10C4685 Our Acme Edge Ink produces a jet black edge on all kinds of leather work that will not smut. This edge ink is the best permanent black. Put up in quarts and five-gallon kegs. Weight, about 2 3/4 pounds.
Price, quart bottle......... $0.15
Per dozen quart bottles......... 1.40
Per 5-gallon keg......... 1.45

Acme Gall Cure.

SHEPPARD'S
ACME
GALL CURE

No. 10C4700 Acme Gall Cure, guaranteed to cure saddle gall, collar gall, collar bunches, scratches, cuts, calks, bruised heel, speed cracks, quarter cracks, contracted feet, old sores of all kinds on horses or cattle and sure cure for sore teats on cows. No one can afford to be without a box of Acme Gall Cure.
8-oz. boxes, per dozen, **$1.18**; each..... **11c**
8-oz. boxes, per dozen, **2.31**; each..... **21c**
16-oz. boxes, per dozen, **4.28**; each..... **39c**
If by mail, postage extra, per box, 3 to 16 cents.

A Leader at 60 Cents.

No. 10C4800 The Herald. It is a new clipper and a leader. The plates are detachable and interchangeable; has two thumb nuts and tension springs; **no wrench needed to adjust this clipper.** It takes the place of the cheap clippers which we formerly imported. Weight, 14 ozs. Price..... **60c**
If by mail, postage extra, 14 cents.

The Lenox Clipper for 85c.

No. 10C4805 The Lenox. This is a standard clipper and a great favorite with horsemen; has bright red handles; **it is well finished and attractive.** Cutting plates are detachable and interchangeable. Weight, 20 ounces. Price......... **85c**
Top plates, **40c**; bottom plates......... **45c**
If by mail, postage extra, 20 cents.

The Leader Clipper for 75c.

No. 10C4815 Our 75-cent Leader Fetlock or Dog Clipper, made of extra fine tool steel plates, well ground and polished, wide mill teeth, handsomely nickel plated, fine piano steel spring. **A strictly first class clipper.** Dealers sell for $1.50. Weight, about 8 ounces.
Price......... **75c**
Top plates, **45c**; bottom plates......... **50c**
If by mail, postage extra, 10 cents.

Our $1.00 Newmarket Clipper.

No. 10C4820 The Newmarket Clipper. It is carefully constructed, handsome in appearance, has bright red handles; there is no clipper made so well known to the professional horse clippers as the Newmarket pattern, the name sells it. All parts are detachable and interchangeable. Weight, 18 ounces. Price......... **$1.00**
Top plates, **45c**; bottom plates......... **.50**
If by mail, postage extra, 20 cents.

O. K. Horse Clipper, $1.50.

No. 10C4825 The O. K. No. 62. Our old reliable; nickel plated; an excellent cutter, bright polished handles, and has had the lead of all other clippers for several seasons. Cutting plates detachable and interchangeable. Weight, 20 ounces. Price. **$1.50**
Top plates, **80c**; bottom plates......... **1.10**
If by mail, postage extra, 20 cents.

Ball Bearing Clipper.

No. 10C4830 The B. B. (Ball Bearing). New this season. Has anti-friction ball bearings, finest nickel finish, bright polished handles, and by all odds, the easiest cutting and the best clipper ever offered to the public. Cutting plates detachable and interchangeable. Weight, 21 ounces. Price.. **$1.35**
Top plates, **50c**; bottom plates......... **.70**
If by mail, postage extra, 22 cents.

Our Montana Special Sheep Shearing Machine, $12.75.

Improved 1903 Model.
Turns Easy.
Cuts fine and I get all long wool.

IMPORTANT NOTICE.

Clipper plates are packed in good order when leaving the factory. We do not furnish new plates for plates that teeth are broken out of. Be careful when using clippers. If you break the teeth you will have to buy new plates, as we do not guarantee the teeth not to break.

This machine will save time and save any injury to the sheep in shearing. It does not require a practical man to run this Special Montana Clipping Machine. A book of full instructions is shipped with every machine which shows the position that the sheep will be in.

All farmers who raise sheep and shear them should not be without one of the improved Montana Machines, or some other good sheep shearing machine, as you get longer wool and your sheep will never be injured in shearing. You will save the price of the machine in two weeks. Weight, boxed, 70 pounds.

No. 10C4850 Price of the machine, with four pair of sheep knives... **$12.75**
Top cutter......... **.20**
Bottom plates......... **.60**

ADD EXTRA for Cutting Head and Flexible Shaft for clipping horses, to attach to No. 10C4850 machine, $5.75. For price on extra Horse Knives, see No. 10C4883 at $2.50.

Our New Illinois Swing Clipper.

No. 10C4863 The very latest and best improved machine on the market. The machine suspended from ceiling by rope which passes through a screw eye free end is passed under an eccentric pulley journaled in the frame, which locks at any point desired by letting go the rope. Large balance wheel, flexible shaft, good cutting knives, turns very easy, anyone can work this machine. Complete with one cutting head. Wt., about 36 lbs. Price **$8.75**
Top plates......... **1.00**
Bottom plates......... **1.50**
Extra cutters, to attach to machine **2.50**

Our Dakota Horse Clipper, $10.75.

Turns Easy.
Cuts Fine.
I feel better.

CLIP YOUR HORSE IN SPRING.

They feel better, look better, work better and less liable to catch cold. If you value your horses don't let them stand in a barn all night with heavy damp coat of hair on, it weakens them and they lose flesh. If clipped they dry out quickly, gain flesh on less feed, and can be groomed in one fourth the time. Horses can be clipped in 30 minutes with this machine. Flexible shaft. Single nut cutters. We believe in presenting this, our latest improved Dakota Clipping Machine to our customers that we are offering them a machine that will be hard to duplicate anywhere.

No. 10C4881 Price of this machine with one set of knives complete..... **$10.75**
No. 10C4883 For extra knives to attach to the clipping head. Price, per pair **$2.50**

NOTICE—To sharpen sheep shearing knives or horse clipping plates: Take a very fine piece of emery cloth, stretch securely over a smooth surfaced board, and tack it down. Place your sheep shearing knives or clipper plates face down perfectly flat, and rub them eight or ten good quick rubs and you will sharpen the teeth very quickly. This will save you sending your plates away to be sharpened, as you can repeat this process very often during the day. Weight, boxed, 75 pounds.

Horse or Dog Clippers.

No. 10C4835 One-Handed Horse or Dog Clipper. For trimming about the ears and fetlocks requires a keen cutting one-handed clipper with strong elastic spring. You will find this is the one that is sought after. Plates detachable and interchangeable. Weight, 12 ounces. Price......... **$1.00**
No. 10C4837 Extra springs **10c**; Top plates, **45c**; Bottom plates......... **.55**
The parts of all our clippers are interchangeable and can be promptly duplicated.
If by mail, postage extra, 12 cents.

NOTE—When ordering clipper plates for an old clipper, state the name of your clipper that is stamped in plate and the number that is stamped on plate. Then we can tell if the ones we send you will fit or not; or send your old one with your order.

Lightning Belt Clipping Machine.

The most substantial, durable, light running and noiseless belt machine on the market. It has a 24-inch drive wheel which turns on roller bearings. The gear head is entirely enclosed, obviating noise and excluding dust. It is also supplied with a turned and true balance wheel, which makes machine run perfectly steady at all times. It is supplied with a 6½-foot improved flexible shaft, which insures perfect freedom of motion and an extensive range. Two sets of cutters are supplied with this machine. Weight, 100 pounds, boxed.

No. 10C4887 Price....$15.00
Extra top plates....1.00
Extra bottom plates....1.50

Special 10-Cent Open Back Curry Comb.

No. 10C4935 S., R. & Co.'s Improved Extra Fine Wire Grasp Open Back Curry Comb. Made of fine rolled steel, extra fine lacquered finish. Eight bars with riveted end pieces, wire grasp and steel shank riveted through handle.

Price $0.10
Per dozen....1.15

Our New Steel Bon Ton, Gilt Edge, Rustless and Plain Steel Curry Combs. The Best.

Made solid back, eight bars, wrought shank, running through handle and riveted, strong brace and knocker. Made in four styles finish, as follows:

No. 10C4940 Plain steel finish. Price, per dozen, $1.55; each....15c
No. 10C4941 Rustless. Galvanized steel. Price, per dozen, $1.80; each....16c
No. 10C4942 Gilt Edge. Brass plated. Price, per dozen, $1.85; each....17c
No. 10C4943 Bon Ton. Oxidized finish. Price, per dozen, $1.95; each....18c

Our Reform Curry Comb.

No. 10C4946 Our Reform Curry Comb is perfectly self cleaning, has no facilities for the storage of hair, and requires but a gentle tap on its face to rid it of all dirt. Steel comb, with leather handle. Weight, 10 ounces.
Price, per dozen, $1.55; each....15c
If by mail, postage extra, each, 10 cents.

Perfection Steel Curry Comb.

No. 10C4950 Our Perfection Back Grasp six-bar Japanned Steel Curry Comb, with mane comb riveted through handle. Weight, about 12 ounces. Price, each...$0.10
Per dozen....1.10
If by mail, postage extra, each, 12 cents.

Circular Spring Steel Curry Comb.

No. 10C4960 Circular Spring Steel Curry Comb. Three complete circles of steel, working independent of each other, attached to an iron back by a hinge joint; wood handle, a good solid comb. Weight, 10 ounces.
Price, each....$0.12
Per dozen....1.40
If by mail, postage extra, each, 10 cents.

Horse Curry Cards.

No. 10C4965 Large, 3½x8¾ inches, first quality. Weight, 8 ounces. Price, each....7c
Per dozen....84c

Horse Brushes.

We guarantee our line of Palmetto, Rice Root and Leather Back Horse Brushes strictly high grade, our bristle brushes the finest and the very best that labor and quality of material can produce. Our bristle brushes are of the very best.

No. 10C5000 Mexican Rice Root Horse Brush, wood back and strap, 3 inches wide and 7 inches long. Weight, 8 ounces.
Price, each...$0.09
Per dozen....1.00
If by mail, postage extra, each, 8 cents.

No. 10C5015 Sears, Roebuck & Co.'s India Fibre, wood back, with pointed ends horse brush. Fibre 1½ inches long. Size of brush, 2¾ by 10 inches. Weight of brush, 9 ounces. Strictly first class.
Price, per dozen, $1.72; each....15c
If by mail, postage extra, each, 10 cents.

No. 10C5050 Our Heavy Wood Back India Fibre Horse Brush, 2 inches long India fibre. Size of brush, 8½ inches long and 3½ inches wide, with leather strap. Weight of brush, 12 ounces.
Price, per dozen, $1.80; each....18c
If by mail, postage extra, each, 12 cents.

No. 10C5055 Our Extra Fine Solid Palmetto Brush. Same style as No. 10C5050. The best Pametto horse brush made. Weight, 14 ounces. Price, per dozen, $2.25; each, 20c

S., R. & Co.'s Horse Brushes.

No. 10C5090 Sears, Roebuck & Co.'s Special Quality Extra High Grade Rice Root Horse Brush. Size of brush, 10 inches long and 2¾ inches wide; double polished top, pointed ends, leather thumb and finger guards. A strictly high grade brush. Weight of brush, 12 ounces.
Price, per dozen, $3.65; each....35c
If by mail, postage extra, each, 12 cents.

No. 10C5094 Nine-Row Horse Brush, made of tampico, heavy back with patent leather strap. 8½ inches long, 4¼ inches wide. Weight, 8 ounces.
Price, per dozen, $1.50; each....15c
If by mail, postage extra, 10 cents.

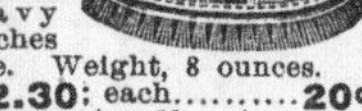

No. 10C5095 Gray Mixed Tampico Center Horse Brush with outside row of bristles. A good 11-row brush with heavy leather strap. 8½ inches long, 4¼ inches wide. Weight, 8 ounces.
Price, per dozen, $2.30; each....20c
If by mail, postage extra, 10 cents.

No. 10C5096 Our Crawford Leather Back Horse Brush. This brush is made with dark mixed tampico center, with two rows of white tampico on the outside, making a fifteen-row brush. The brush is made about 9 inches long and 4½ inches wide, with a good leather strap. Weight, 9 ounces. A good leather back horse brush.
Price....30c
If by mail, postage extra, 9 cents.

Lincoln Army Brush.

No. 10C5099 Leather Back Horse Brush. Made with flexible leather back. The back is stitched with wire. Fifteen rows of mixed tampico and bristles. Outside row of gray bristles; body of brush extra fine quality of gray tampico. Looks like an all bristle brush. A good flexible leather back army brush. Weight, 10 ounces. Size, 9 inches long and 4¼ inches wide.
Price....65c
If by mail, postage extra, 10 cents.

BACK.

FACE.

No. 10C5102 Our Improved All Bristle Brush, 15 rows, and every other tuft white and black bristles. The black bristles are long and the white bristles are short, which gives the brush a chance to penetrate the hair. Leather back and adjustable leather strap handle. This is one of the latest improved brushes, and if not found entirely satisfactory can be returned at our expense. Size, 9 inches long, 4½ inches wide. Weight, 11 ounces. We show face and back of this brush.
Price, per dozen, $12.00; each....$1.06
If by mail, postage extra, each, 12 cents.

No. 10C5109 Leather Back, Oval Shape, Tampico Center. Size of brush, 9 inches long, 4½ inches wide, with leather strap, length of tampico, 1 inch. Extra good cheap brush. Weight of brush, 12 ounces. Price....60c
If by mail, postage extra, 12 cents.

No. 10C5110 Oval Shape Horse Brush, warranted all bristles, oval face, 15 rows of sewed stub bristles. Size of brush, 9 inches long, 4 inches wide, leather strap. Same style as No. 10C5109. Weight of brush, 10 ounces.
Price....75c
If by mail, postage extra, 10 cents.

No. 10C5120 Our fine quality of Mixed Bristle Brush, flat face, fine quality of mixed black and brown bristles, flexible back, leather strap and leather back. Size of brush, 9x4½ inches. Weight of brush, 10 ounces. Same style as No. 10C5109. Price....89c
If by mail, postage extra, 10 cents.

No. 10C5130 Sears, Roebuck & Co.'s Special All Black Bristle Horse Brush. 19 rows of black bristles. Flat face. Size of brush, 9 inches long, 4½ inches wide. Weight of brush, 10 ounces.
Price....$1.35
If by mail, postage extra, 10 cents.

No. 10C5140 Sears, Roebuck & Co.'s Special Warranted All White Bristle Oval Faced Brush. 19 rows of bristle, adjustable strap, leather back. Size of brush, 9 by 4½ inches. Extra fine horse brush. Weight of brush, 12 ounces, packed in single box. Price....$1.40
If by mail, postage extra, 12 cents.

Common Sense Toe Weights

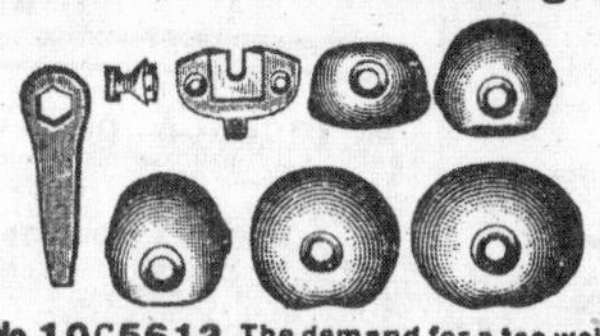

No. 10C5612 The demand for a toe weight that is easily and quickly adjusted from one ounce to six, is so great, we have had made for us this special toe weight set, consisting of a pair of spurs and five pairs of weights, 2, 3, 4, 5 and 6-ounce. The spur itself weighs 1 ounce. You will be able, therefore, to weight your horse with 1, 2, 3, 4, 5 and 6-ounce weights. The Common Sense Toe Weight is the best. We furnish as many pairs of spurs as you want at 10 cents per pair, and bolts and screws extra, per pair, 10 cents. This set of weights you can use on five horses at one time, with extra spurs. The most complete set of toe weights on the market. If not satisfactory, you can return them. Weight, 2 pounds.
Price, per set, fine nickel plated weights, 30c
Common Sense Spurs, extra per pair....10c
Bolts and screws, extra, per pair....10c
If by mail, postage extra, per set, 32 cents.

No. 10C5613 Our Solid Brass Common Sense Toe Weights. Five pairs of solid brass weights and one pair of brass spurs and flat headed brass screw bolts, the same style as No. 10C5612, only made of solid brass, highly polished. Price, per set....75c
Extra spurs, per pair....10c
Bolts and screws, extra, per pair....10c
When ordering sets of toe weights, and wanting extra spurs, bolts and screws be sure and allow the extra price for spurs, bolts and screws.

Our Improved Stallion Shield.

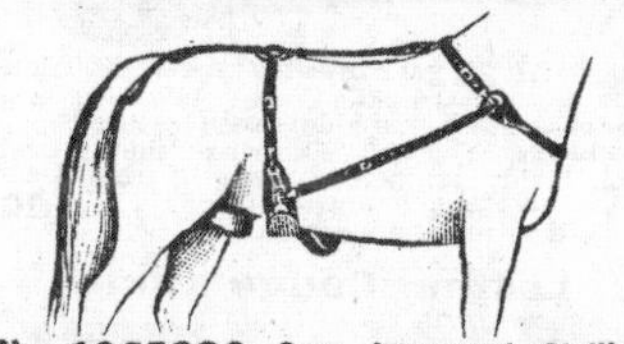

No. 10C5636 Our Improved Stallion Shield, light, clean and practical. This is the best stallion shield on the market.
Price, each....$3.65

Pacing and Trotting Hopples.

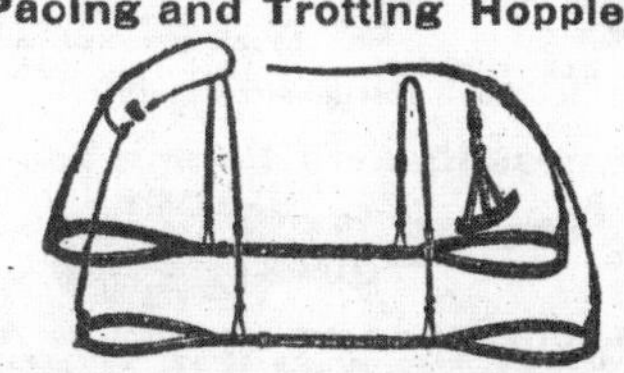

No. 10C5640 A Genuine Sears, Roebuck & Co.'s Hopple, made with lace straps, extra strong loops, covered with very fine calfskin so as not to wrinkle, made for trotting or pacing horses, strong or light weight. Finely finished, with snap adjustment, made to put on and take off the horse very quickly. This is positively the finest hopple made. Neck, hip and quarter straps complete ready for use. Medium weight hopple. Weight, about 3½ pounds.
Price, per pair, for one horse....$7.75
If by mail, postage extra, 64 cents.

Common Sense Horse Tail Clasp.

No. 10C5670 This is a simple device for holding the hair of a horse's tail. It is made of one piece of spring brass, without buckles or other contrivances. Weight, each, 2 ounces.
Price, each 10c
Per dozen....$1.20
If by mail, postage extra, each, 3 cents.

Horse Blanket Pins.

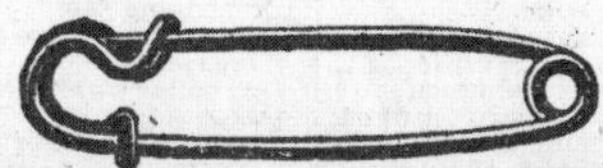

No. 10C5675 Blanket Pins, protected points. Size, 3¼ inches. Weight, per dozen, 8 ounces. Price, each....2c
Per dozen....20c
If by mail, postage extra, per dozen, 8 cents.

Our Handy Blanket Pin.

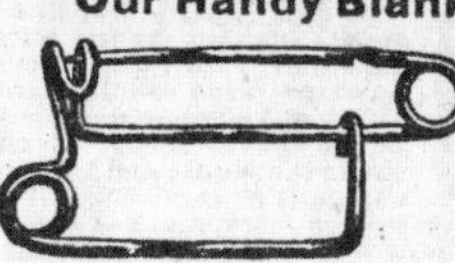

No. 10C5679 Made the same style as a blanket pin with extra safety loop to fasten around the traces, which prevents the blanket from blowing off the horse. This pin can be fastened to the blanket and when placed on the horse can be fastened around the trace which will prevent the blanket from blowing off the horse. Price, each....3c
Per dozen....25c
If by mail, postage extra, per dozen, 8 cents.

Canvas Feed Bags.

No. 10C5695 Canvas Feed Bags. Leather bottom, perforated side, with strap running over head.
Price, each....$0.36
Per dozen....4.00
If by mail, postage extra, each, 11c.

Horse Tooth Rasps.

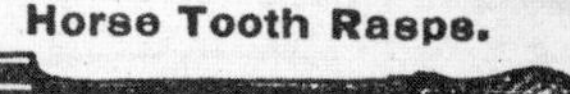

No. 10C5720 The Horse Tooth Rasp shown in this illustration is made of finely polished steel, with stiff handle; has removable file. This is one of the most desirable rasps of the kind on the market. Guaranteed first class in every respect. Weight, about 1 pound.
Price, each....$0.65
Per dozen....6.75
If by mail, postage extra, each, 16 cents.

Our 75-Cent Jointed Handle Rasp.

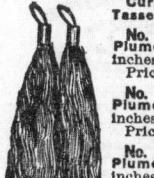

No. 10C5725 This illustration is that of House's Patent Horse Tooth Rasp. As shown in the illustration, it has a jointed handle, a very desirable feature. It is finely polished, complete with file and ready for use. Weight, about 1 pound. Price, each..$0.75
Per dozen....8.65
If by mail, postage extra, each, 16 cents.

A $2.50 Horse Tooth Rasp for $1.23.

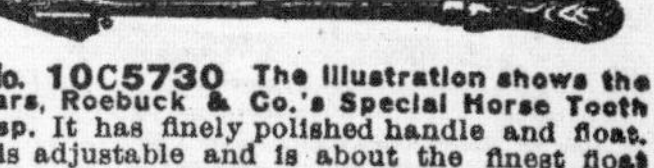

No. 10C5730 The illustration shows the Sears, Roebuck & Co.'s Special Horse Tooth Rasp. It has finely polished handle and float. It is adjustable and is about the finest float made. The file can be removed and replaced almost instantly. Complete and ready for use. Weight, about 1¼ pounds.
Price, per dozen, $13.60; each....$1.23
If by mail, postage extra, each, 24 cents.

No. 10C5735 Extra Steel Files, 3¼ inches long, for any of the above horse tooth rasps. Weight, about 4 ounces. Price, each..$0.15
Per dozen....1.50
If by mail, postage extra, each, 4 cents.

Bridle Plumes.

Curled Horse Hair Plumes or Tassels, for team harness.

No. 10C5750 Bridle Plumes, colors, red or yellow, 9 inches long.
Price, per pair....21c

No. 10C5755 Bridle Plumes, colors, red or blue, 11 inches long.
Price, per pair....25c

No. 10C5760 Bridle Plumes, colors, red or green, 13 inches long.
Price, per pair....31c
Mention color wanted. Weight, per pair, 3, 4 and 5 ounces.
If by mail, postage extra, 10 cents.

Boys' Saddle Blanket.

No. 10C5805 Our Boys' Felt Saddle Blankets, fancy pinked edge, one row of stitched braid, dark colored plain felt. Size of blanket, 24 inches long and 16 inches wide from center. Weight of blanket, 9 ounces.
Price....30c
If by mail, postage extra, 10 cents.

Gents' Saddle Blanket.

No. 10C5810 Our Gents' Felt Saddle Blanket, fancy scalloped border with star corner, plain colored body with assorted fancy braid scalloped edge. Size of blanket, 24 inches long and 16 inches wide from center. Weight of blanket, 12 ounces.
Price....50c
If by mail, postage extra, 14 cents.

Our Roosevelt Saddle Blanket.

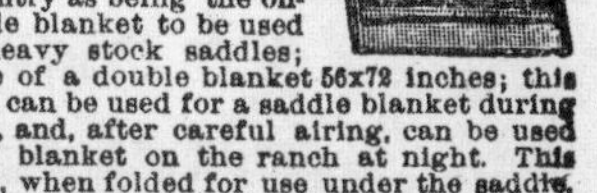

No. 10C5816 This is one of our specials, having been recommended by some of the best rough riders in the country as being the only saddle blanket to be used with heavy stock saddles; is made of a double blanket 56x72 inches; this blanket can be used for a saddle blanket during the day, and, after careful airing, can be used for bed blanket on the ranch at night. This blanket, when folded for use under the saddle, measures 30 inches; soft and easy on a horse's back.
Heavy 4-pound blanket. Price....$1.15
If by mail, postage extra, 64 cents.

Cowboy Fine Woven Hair Saddle Blanket.

No. 10C5845 Our fine heavy woven hair saddle blanket, bound ends, pure white angora hair, with light stripes on ends. This is an extra large saddle blanket, 30x40 inches. This blanket when used under a heavy stock saddle leaves plenty of air to circulate between the saddle and horse's back, preventing any galls or sore back. It is used universally throughout the western country, and has given the very best satisfaction. Weight of this blanket is 3½ pounds. Price... **$1.50**
If by mail, postage extra, 65 cents.

Our Special Feltless Saddle Blanket.

No. 10C5850 Made of heavy, old gold drill, fancy felt pinked edge, nine rows of quilting, the center being made without stuffing, the pad being stuffed with an extra heavy quality of composite stuffing. Very soft on the horse's back. A very handsome saddle blanket. Size of saddle blanket, 26 inches long, 34 inches wide. Weight, 3 pounds.
Price...**60c**
If by mail, postage extra, 48 cents.

Jumbo Express Whip.

No. 10C5893 Our Jumbo Whip is the best black and imitation gut color. The heaviest and best Jumbo whip made.
Price, per dozen, **$1.70**; each.................................**18c**

The Elk Rawhide Whip.

No. 10C5902 Full Rawhide Protruding Through Cap. Straight, black and wine, star finish, linen lined, two 4-stitch black buttons, japanned cap, Boston snap, 6 feet.
Price, per dozen, **$2.95**; each.................................**30c**

Star Finish.

No. 10C5903 Java Straight Through. Black, wine and imitation gut, star finish, loaded, linen lined, nickel and gilt spiral center; two 1½-inch chased nickel or gilt ferrules, 1½-inch head to match, rubber cushion cap, English snap, 6 feet.
Price, per dozen, **$3.50**; each.................................**35c**

Phoenix Rawhide Whip.

No. 10C5904 Rawhide. Straight, old gold and nankeen, 4 plait cover mixed. Star finish, wire wound, linen lined, two 8-stitch long old gold buttons, rubber cushion cap, English snap, 6 feet, 6½ feet. Price, per dozen, **$6.00**; each.................**85c**

Peerless Rawhide Buggy Whip.

No. 10C5940 Black Star Finish, waterproof cover, two six-stitched keeper braided buttons, japanned cap, half silk English snap. One of the best rawhide whips made, freezing will not affect this whip. Weight, about 8 ounces.

Length, feet	6	6½
Price, each	69c	74c

Our Best Full Rawhide Whip.

No. 10C5943 S., R. & Co's. Best Value Rawhide Whip, full length rawhide from point to handle, rubber lined and waterproof cover, extra quality of heavy rawhide throughout, fine black star finish, fine braided button, English snap. A handsomely finished whip, made in the one length only, 6 feet. Weight, about 6 ounces.
Price, each..$ 0.95
Per dozen..10.95

Whip Lashes.

No. 10C6000 Our 6-Plait Genuine Buck Braided Whip Lash. All hand made, well tapered, extra quality.

Length, feet	5	6	7
Price, each	26c	32c	39c

No. 10C6001 Our Special 6-Plait California Style Buck Stage Lash, with silk snap, made in two lengths.
Price, each, 10 feet.......................................**65c**
Price, each, 12 feet.......................................**75c**

No. 10C6005 Our 4-Plait Genuine Buck Braided Whip Lash. All hand braided, best quality.

Length, feet	5	6	7	8
Price, each	19c	22c	26c	50c

No. 10C6007 Our Special 8-Plait California Style Buck Lash, with silk snap. Made in two lengths.
Price, each, 10 feet.......................................**85c**
Price, each, 12 feet.......................................**97c**

No. 10C6011 Our Special 12-Plait Genuine Braided Buck Stage Lash. All hand braided plain tapered lash from loops, extra quality lash. We sell the best.

Length, feet	10	12	16
Price, each	$1.37	$1.64	$2.40

No. 10C6012 Our Special 16-Plait Genuine Braided Buck Stage Lash. The best all hand braided, well tapered. The best quality buckskin used in our high grade buck lashes.

Length, feet	10	12	16
Price, each	$1.85	$2.20	$3.10

Oklahoma Quirt.

No. 10C6260 Made of 8-plait calf, shot loaded body, fancy braided quirt, three braided knots and frills. Length of body, 20 inches; total length of quirt, 33 inches. Weight, about 16 ounces.
Price, per dozen, **$5.75**; each.................................**50c**
If by mail, postage extra, each, 16 cents.

Half Length Rawhide Center Full Leather Covered Team Whip.

No. 10C5972 Rawhide Center, Russet Covered Team Whip. 4-plait buck point. Full length of whip, 8 feet.
Price, per dozen, **$7.30**; each.................................**65c**

No. 10C5973 Our Special Heavy Rawhide Center Team Whip. Fine yellow calfskin covered, buck stitched, 6-plait braided buckskin point. Full length of whip, 8 feet.
Price, per dozen, **$9.60**; each.................................**85c**

Fancy Rawhide Whip.

No. 10C6150 Our Rawhide black German braided cover, fancy basket handle, two braided buttons, japanned cap, fancy plaited English wrist loop. Price, each...**35c**

Solid Leather Team Whips.

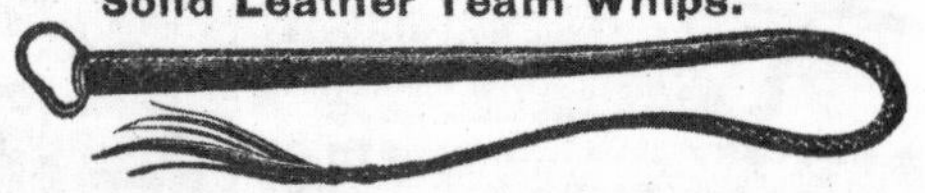

No. 10C6170 Our XX Oiled Leather Body, calf point, out seamed. The cheapest leather team whip made.

Length, feet	5	6½	7
Price, each	$0.37	$0.47	$0.57
Per dozen	4.15	4.95	5.95

If by mail, postage extra, each, 23 cents.

No. 10C6175 Our Oiled, Tanned, Covered XXXX Team Whip, buck stitched cover, fine braided buck point, two braided buttons and hand loop. Length, feet.

Length, feet	6	6½	7
Price, each	$0.54	$0.59	$0.63
Per dozen	5.95	6.50	7.10

If by mail, postage extra, each, 25 cents.

No. 10C6176 Sears' Special Extra Heavy Double XXXX Team Whip. The best leather team whip that can be made. We are making a special run on this whip. If you want the best take this whip. Length, feet.

Length, feet	6	6½	7
Price, each	$0.60	$0.69	$0.75
Per dozen	7.10	8.00	8.75

If by mail, postage extra, each, 25 cents.

Wood Creasers.

No. 10C7530 Wood Creaser, used for creasing the edge of straps, and putting a smooth edge on them. Weight, 3 ounces.
Price, double, **35c**; single.......................................**25c**
If by mail, postage extra, each, 3 cents.

Boys' Drovers' Whip.

No. 10C6180 Our Boys' Drover Whip, 6-plait, oiled kip, made with wood handle, 9 inches long, lash strongly wired on, California style. Weight, 16 ounces.

Length, feet	6	7	8
Price, each	$0.36	$0.43	$0.50
Per dozen	4.25	4.75	5.45

If by mail, postage extra, each, 20 cents.

Improved Rotary Jacksonville Drovers' Whip.

This whip is the most perfect drover whip on the market, light and easily handled, wrought iron bolt center, with maple wood revolving handle, made in three styles, as follows:

No. 10C6201 California Style, fine 8-plait latigo body, with buck point. Not shot loaded.

Length, feet	10	12	14
Price, each	$1.00	$1.25	$1.50

If by mail, postage extra, 23 cents.

No. 10C6202 Shot loaded, California style, 8-plait latigo body, buck point.

Length, feet	10	12
Price, each	$1.25	$1.40

If by mail, postage extra, 25 cents.

OUR DROVER AND QUIRT WHIPS are made of the finest whip leather. We always quote the lowest price.

S., R. & Co.'s Australian Cattle Whip.

Made with adjustable double loop fastener, revolving handle, shot loaded, warranted not to break down at handle or break the shot sack, can be easily repaired when worn out, or if you break the handle, you can put it in yourself. This is the best cattle whip made. Made in calfskin, buckskin, rawhide. Leather tanned expressly for fine cattle whips. Order by number and state number of feet long.

No. 10C6210 8-plait Calf Australian Cattle Whip.

Length, feet	10	12	14
Price	$1.35	$1.50	$1.65

No. 10C6220 8-plait Genuine Buckskin Australian Cattle Whip.

Length, feet	10	12	14
Price	$1.40	$1.55	$1.70

No. 10C6225 12-plait Genuine Buckskin Australian Cattle Whip.

Length, feet	10	12	14
Price	$1.60	$1.90	$2.05

No. 10C6235 12-plait Oiled Rawhide Australian Cattle Whip. Weight, about 24 ounces.

Length, feet	10	12	14
Price	$2.05	$2.23	$2.35

If by mail, postage extra, 28 cents.

Harness Makers' Collar Awls.

No. 10C7520 Drawing Awls or Collar Awls, as they are called, are made with large eye for sewing horse collars with leather thongs or whangs. The awl is made of the best tool steel, highly tempered. Length, from 8 to 9 inches. Weight, 4 ounces. Price..........**30c**
If by mail, postage extra, 5 cents.

Leather Gauge Knife.

No. 10C7550 This is the best hollow iron handle gauge knife in the market. Will cut from ⅛ to 4 inches in width. It is the same knife used by all practical harness makers. Price..............................**95c**
If by mail, postage extra, 18 cents.

Harness Makers' Edging Tool.

No. 10C7580 A very handy tool for removing the sharp corners of any new strap work. Made 5 inches long, nicely polished. Weight, 3 ounces. Price....................**13c**
If by mail, postage extra, 3 cents.

Harness Makers' Round Knife.

No. 10C7595 Made of the best tool steel elegantly tempered to take very sharp edge. Rosewood handles. Every one is guaranteed. Blades measure 5, 6, 6½ inches. Weight, 5 oz.
5 inches. Price.....**60c**
6 inches. Price.....**65c**
6½ inches. Price.....**75c**
If by mail, postage extra, each, 5 cents.

Square Point Trimming Knife.

No. 10C7605 Our Fine Square Point Trimming Knife. Round handle, with a fine blade made from fine tool steel. Weight, 3 ounces. Price.......**10c**
If by mail, postage extra, 3 cents.

Harness Needles.

No. 10C7685 Harness Needles, 25 in paper, assorted sizes, from 0 to 4. Price, per paper..**5c**
If by mail, postage extra, per paper, 2 cents.

No. 10C7690 Wax. Price, per ball......**1c**
If by mail, postage extra, 1 cent.

Harness Thread.

No. 10C7695 Our American Brand No. 10 Harness Thread. Natural linen color, 2-ounce balls, eight balls to pound. Will make good strong wax end.
Price, per ball, **9c**; Price, per pound...**70c**
If by mail, postage extra, per ball, 2 cents.

No. 10C7701 Our Devonshire Brand Harness Thread. Extra good, strong, smooth thread, makes very strong wax end, in 2-ounce balls, No. 10 and No. 12.
Price, per ball, No. 10 thread..........**$0.12**
Price, per pound, No. 10 thread..........**.90**
Price, per ball, No. 12 thread..........**.14**
Price, per pound, No. 12 thread..........**1.10**
If by mail, postage extra, per pound, 16 cents.

No. 10C7706 Barbour's Best Irish Flax Harness Thread. This thread is used by all the best harness makers, makes very strong wax end; 2-ounce balls, eight balls to pound; made No. 10 and No. 12.
Per ball, No. 10 thread, **13c**; per lb....**$1.04**
Per ball, No. 12 thread, **18c**; per lb.....**1.44**
If by mail, postage extra, per pound, 16 cents.

Harness Awl Blades.

No. 10C7710 Harness Awl Blades, to be used in extra handles.
Per dozen..........**20c**
If by mail, postage extra, each, 2 cents.

Wood Awl Handles.

No. 10C7715 Common Wood Awl Handles, with ferrule.
Price, each..........**2c**
Per dozen.......................................**17c**
If by mail, postage extra, each, 5 cents.

S. R., & Co.'s Special Harness Repair Kit, $3.75.

No. 10C7671 This repair kit is made up so that anyone can repair his old harness or make a new set. The following items are in this set:

One wood clamp for holding the leather to stitch
One round knife
One gauge knife
One 4-tube punch
One square point trimming knife
One paper of needles
One ball of thread
One ball of wax
Three awls and handles
One edging tool
One double wood creaser
One collar awl
One rivet set
One box of assorted rivets
One pair of pliers

This is a very complete set and sold only as listed, no parts being omitted, in a nice box so that the tools will always be in the box when you want to use them. Weight, 13 pounds.
Price, per set.......................................**$3.75**

Harness Horse.

No. 10C7740 Harness Makers' Stitching Horse. This is something every horse owner should have. Any man can do his own repairing and save his time, as well as his money. Made of good sound wood. Weight, 18 pounds. Price for stitching horse with jaw strap.......**$2.60**
Without jaw strap..........**2.35**

LEATHER.

NOTE—Owing to the uncertainty of the leather and hide market, the prices on these goods are subject to change without notice.

No. 10C7750 Union Tanned Black Harness Leather, B grade, whole side only; sides weighing from 16 to 24 pounds.
Price, per pound..........................**32c**

No. 10C7755 No. 1 Union Black Harness Leather, extra quality; weight, per side, from 16 to 24 pounds. Price, per pound..........**34c**

No. 10C7760 Pure Pittsburg Oak Harness Leather, good B grade, whole sides only; sides weigh from 16 to 24 pounds.
Price, per pound..........................**35c**

No. 10C7765 Extra Quality No. 1 Pittsburg Oak Tanned Leather, black; weight, per side, from 16 to 24 pounds. Price, per pound..**36c**

NOTE—All of our different grades of Harness Leather are selected from packers' steer hides and our weights run from 16 to 24 pounds and we will give you as near the weight as we can that you order.

CUT LEATHER FOR MAKING TEAM HARNESS.

We will furnish leather cut for team harness as follows. Same size as used in No. 10C850 harness including the following parts of harness: **Bridles**, ⅝-inch, with blinds; **lines**, 1 inch by 20 feet, 8 pieces; **hame tug folds**, billets and 1½-inch leather for making long hame tug; **four hame straps**, ⅞-inch; **two breast straps**, 1½-inch; **two martingales**; **one set traces**, 1½-inch by 6 feet, to be made up with triangular cockeye; **pad skirts**, to be made up for perfection tree; **pad bottoms**, made up to be used with perfection tree; **bellyband folds**, with 1½-inch chafer; **1-inch hip and back straps**, with folds for cruppers. This is the cut leather for a complete set of double harness same style as our No. 10C850. No hardware is included in this price. The cut leather weighs about 31 or 32 pounds.

No. 10C7766 Price, per set for cut leather as above described..........................**$16.95**

No. 10C7771 Harness leather bellies, weighing from 3½ to 7 pounds, used for repairing or making cheap strap work. Per lb. **20c**
Will send as near the weight wanted as possible.

No. 10C7772 Harness Hardware, including hames, buckles, rings, snaps, trace carriers, for a complete set of team harness, to be used in connection with No. 10C7766.
Price, per set..**$2.75**

Buckeye Safety Bit.

No. 10C8100 Made with three-ring cheek, loose bar, solid mouth or jointed, large size. This bit is one of the best team bridle bits, it will be easy on a horse or severe at the same time, providing it is necessary. Made in XC plate only. (Will always send solid mouth unless ordered jointed.) Weight, 16 ounces.
Price, per dozen, $2.75; each....24c
If by mail, postage extra, 16 cents.

Imperial Driving Bit.

No. 10C8280 Imperial Driving Bit, forged steel mouth bar. For vicious and unmanageable horses it has no equal. The tongue cannot be carried over the top of the bit. Its peculiar construction gives the driver such leverage that he is absolutely safe behind the most treacherous horse. Weight, about 11 ounces.
XC plate. Price, each....$0.35
Per dozen....4.15
Fine nickel plate. Price, each....85
Per dozen....9.50
If by mail, postage extra, each, 12 cents.

The Jay-Eye-See Bit.

No. 10C8285 For pullers and vicious horses it is unexcelled. Weight, 11 ounces.
Fine XC plate.
Price, each, $0.25
Per dozen.. 2.50
Full nickel plate.
Price, each, $0.45
Per dozen.. 5.00
If by mail, postage extra, each, 2 cents.

Success Bit.

No. 10C8290 Success Bit, the latest thing out. Most practical, humane and safest driving bit in the market. XC plate. Weight, about 10 ounces.
Each. $0.35
Per dozen....4.15
If by mail, postage extra, each, 12 cents.

Twisted Wire Bits.

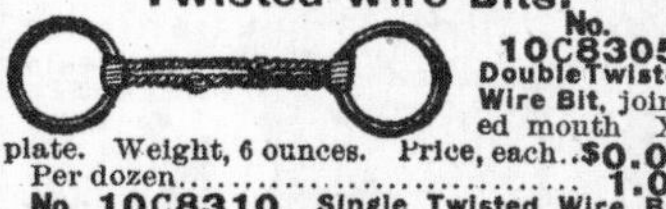

No. 10C8305 Double Twisted Wire Bit, jointed mouth XC plate. Weight, 6 ounces. Price, each..$0.09
Per dozen....1.00
No. 10C8310 Single Twisted Wire Bit. Jointed mouth, 2¼-inch ring. Weight, 5 ounces.
Price, per dozen, 80c; each....7c
If by mail, postage extra, each, 7 cents.

Stiff Ring Bit.

No. 10C8315 Solid Head Stiff Ring Bit. 3-inch ring, XC plate. Weight, about 15 ounces. Known as No. 90. Price, per dozen, $1.25; each....12c
If by mail, postage extra, each, 15 cents.

Jointed Bridle Bit.

No. 10C8320 Stiff or Jointed Bridle Bit, or 2¾-inch ring, XC plate. Weight, 9 ounces. Known as No. 47. Price, each....5c
Per dozen....56c
If by mail, postage extra, each, 10 cents.

Fine Wrought Mouth Mule Port Bit.

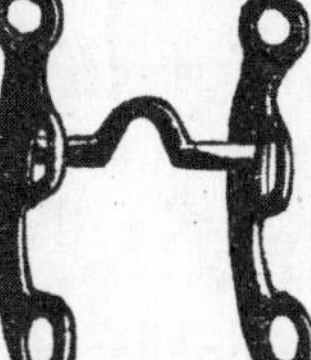

No. 10C8325 Our Fine Wrought Mouth Mule Port Bit, japanned, one of the best bits made. Weight, 14 ounces.
Price, each....$0.16
Per dozen.... 1.85
If by mail, postage extra, each, 15 cents.

Overcheck Bit.

No. 10C8330 Overcheck Bit, to be used as a separate bit on draw check reins. Weight, 2 ounces.
XC plate. Price, per dozen, 35c; each....4c
Nickel plate. Price per dozen, 45c; each..5c
If by mail, postage extra, each, 4 cents.

Our Special Overcheck Bit.

No. 10C8335 Solid bar, loop end turns up, nickel plated only. This is the latest and best nickel plated bit on the market; easy on the horse's mouth. Will not pinch the lips. Weight, 2 ounces.
Price, per dozen, 45c; each....5c
If by mail, postage extra, each, 4 cents.

Rubber Mouth Bit.

No. 10C8340 Squire's Flexible Rubber Mouth Bit, nickel, half check snaffles. Weight, 5 ounces.
Price, per dozen, $3.00; each....27c
If by mail, postage extra, each, 7 cents.

The Celebrated Humane Bit.

No. 10C8345 The Celebrated Humane Bit is made of solid leather, the strongest and best bit on the market, and cannot pull through the mouth. With this bit you do not need any overdraw bit, the overdraw buckles in small rings, and pulls from under jaw, making it very easy on horse. Weight, about 13 ounces.
Price, per dozen, $6.50; each....56c
If by mail, postage extra, each, 15 cents.

Solid Leather Bit.

No. 10C8350 This bit is made of solid leather, with steel forged rings; a very easy bit on a tender mouth horse and one that gives universal satisfaction. Weight, about 9 ounces.
Price, each....$0.27
Per dozen....3.15
If by mail, postage extra, each, 12 cents.

Our Peoria Buggy Net to Head.

No. 10C9220 Our Fine Peoria Net, body and head, with bars running to head, strings 6½ and 7 feet long, made of the same stock as No. 10C9215.
80-string, wgt., 2 lbs. Price, single net, $1.96
90-string, wgt., 2¼ lbs. Price, single net, 2.24
100-string, wgt., 2½ lbs. Price, single net, 2.40

Williams' Heavy Orange Colored Cord Team or Wagon Net.

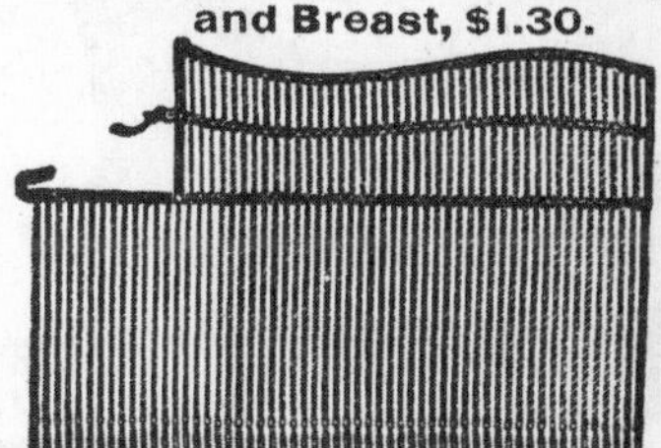

This is the best all round team or wagon net on the market this year. Made of strictly high grade material throughout; 60 orange colored strings; 8 feet in body of net; double leather bars with cord running between the bars and staple with the latest improved solid staple. We guarantee these strings not to pull through the bars. Leather hame bars in front, with breast plate with strings running around the breast snap in front. This net is made in body and breast only. We guarantee this to be the heaviest, best, well made cotton cord team net on the market and if you want something good, order Williams' Special Cord Net. Weight of net about 4 pounds.
No. 10C9035 Price, each....$ 1.45
Per dozen....17.00

Improved Wagon Net, Body and Breast, $1.30.

No. 10C9037 Our Improved Wagon Net. This net is one of the strongest team nets made. Will give as good service as the very best of leather team nets. The orange colored strings are heavy and strong with double leather bar riveted together so that the strings will not slip. It is much improved over the cheap grades of cotton cord team nets. The net is 4 feet, 8 inches from hame to tail with 60 heavy strings, with strings in the breast plate extra. Weight of this net is 4 pounds. One of the best cotton cord team nets on the market.
Price, each, for one horse....$ 1.30
Per dozen....15.00

COTTON AND LEATHER FLY NETS

WE DIRECT SPECIAL ATTENTION THIS SEASON TO OUR MOST COMPLETE AND LOWEST PRICED LINE OF COTTON AND LEATHER FLY NETS.

We have made very special and advantageous contracts for these goods, and confidently say that our prices admit of no competition. Our nets are all strictly high grade, they are full size, strong, durable, first quality, well made nets, and the prices at which we offer them are less than the same goods are sold to jobbers.

Cotton Cord Mesh Team Net, 55 Cents.

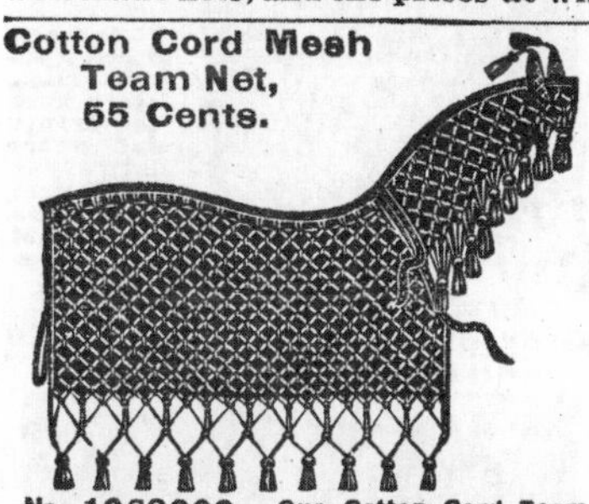

No. 10C9000 Our Cotton Cord Team Net. Body, neck and ear tips; diamond knotted mesh, woven center bar; neck part snaps to body; fancy colored body, border and tassels. An extra good cheap mesh net. Weight, 1⅞ pounds per pair.
Price, each....$0.55
Per pair, for two horses....1.10

Nelson's Special All White Buggy Net. $1.00

No. 10C9116 Our Nelson's Special Single White Mesh Buggy or Shaft Net. Made of all white cotton cord. Braided center bar; diamond mesh body, neck and ear tips. Neck snaps to body. A good, all white single net. Weight, 16 ounces. Price, each....$ 1.00
Per dozen....11.40

Our Taggart Special Fancy Single Buggy Net. $1.20

No. 10C9130 Our Taggart Special Single Buggy or Shaft Net. Apple green body, with lemon tassels, braided center bar. Small diamond mesh. Body and neck, with fancy ear tips. One of the best sellers in our line. Weight, 16 ounces.
Price, each....$ 1.20
Per dozen....13.75

Fairbanks' Special Single Buggy Net. $1.45

No. 10C9145 Our Fancy Fairbanks Special Single Cotton Mesh Shaft or Single Buggy Net. 1-inch diamond braided mesh, braided center bar, detachable neck with fancy mesh ear tips. Green body, yellow border and pink tassels. Extra row of tassels. A very handsome single buggy net. Weight, 24 ounces.
Price, each....$ 1.45
Per dozen....16.80

Our Fine Leather Express Net, Body and Breast.

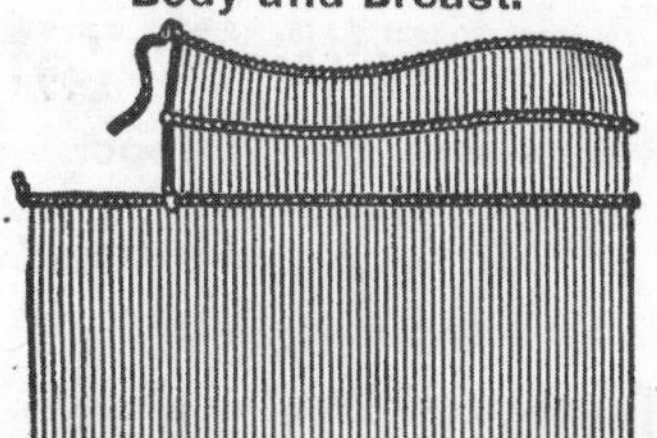

Our Farm or Express Net. Made of all black leather, ⅝-inch bar, 60-string body. Breast piece extra. Body of net, 5 feet long, with breast piece, good long strings. A fine net for spring wagon or express harness. The price is for one net for one horse.
No. 10C9212 Price, each, 60-string body and breast; weight, about 3½ pounds..$1.56

Our Best Round Leather Express Net.

This net is made out of the very best round leather strings, about 8 feet long. Made in two sizes, 60 and 70 round lashes in body, 10 lashes in breast. Bars ⅝ inch wide, rounded, punched lengthwise; strings laced through bars. The best express net made, all black leather. This makes a fine light team or express and heavy buggy or carriage net.
No. 10C9211 Price, 60-string net for one horse....$2.50
No. 10C9214 Price, 70-string net for one horse....$2.80

Our Fine Light Howard Round Leather Buggy Net.

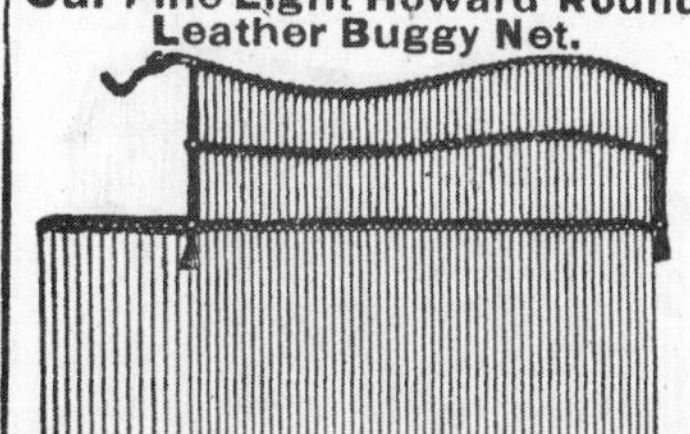

No. 10C9215 Our Fine Light Howard Round Leather Buggy Net. Made with fine round bars, improved Huston knot, strings round and 6½, 7½ and 8 feet long. This is the best light net made. The price is for one horse. Body and breast net. Well made, selected Dundee net leather, all round, black, long strings.
60-string, weight, 2 lbs. Price, each. $1.46
75-string, weight, 2¼ lbs. Price, each. 1.64
90-string, weight, 2¾ lbs. Price, each. 1.99
100-string, weight, 3 lbs. Price, each. 2.24

Burlap Fly Covers.

No. 10C9038 Plain Burlap Fly Cover. To head 90 inches long, with ear, hame and terret holes bound. Very cool on horse.
Price, per dozen, $4.45; each....38c
No. 10C9039 Fine Striped Burlap Fly Cover. To head 90 inches long, with ear, hame and terret holes bound. This is a big seller.
Price, per dozen, $5.28; each....45c

Our 35-Cent Burlap Fly Cover.

No. 10C9090 Our big value in Burlap Fly Covers. Made 40 inches deep and 90 inches long, of good open woven burlap. Plain duck trimmed. The biggest bargain you ever saw in burlap fly cover. Ventilating, light and cool on horse. Weight about 36 ounces.
Price, each....35c

Heavy Burlap Fly Cover.

53c

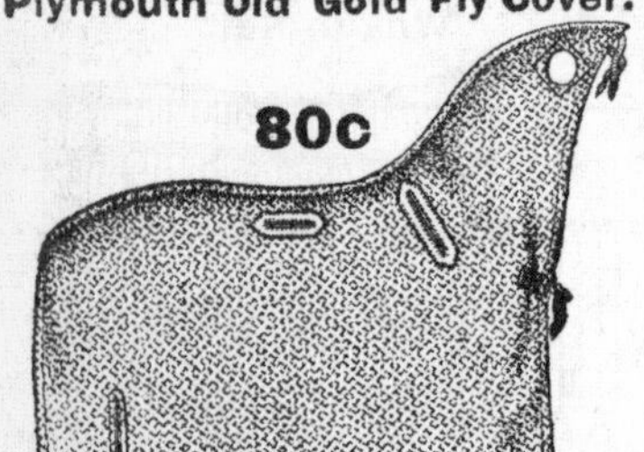

No. 10C9092 Our Plain Heavy Burlap Fly Cover. Made 40 inches deep, 100 inches long. Leather trimmed, line and terret holes. One of the best fly covers we make. Ventilating horse cover. Weight, about 40 ounces.
Price, each....................................53c

Plymouth Old Gold Fly Cover.

80c

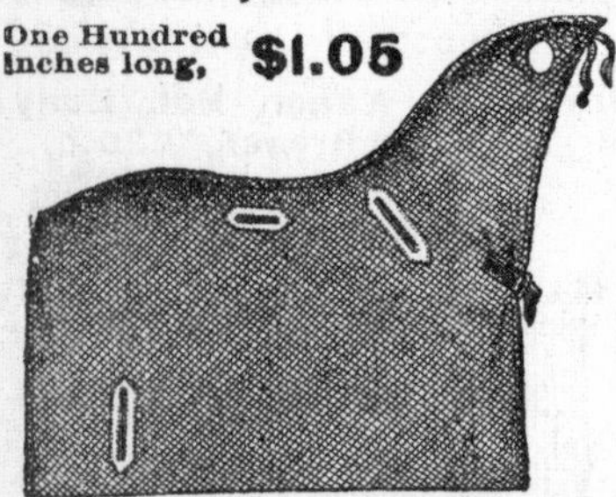

No. 10C9093 Our Plymouth Old Gold Color Fly Cover. Well made, leather trimmed, line and terret holes, leather trace holes; very strong, superior finish. Ventilating admits the air, but not the flies. Made 90 inches long. Weight, about 24 ounces.
Price, each....................................80c

The Best Fly Cover for Horses.

One Hundred inches long, $1.05

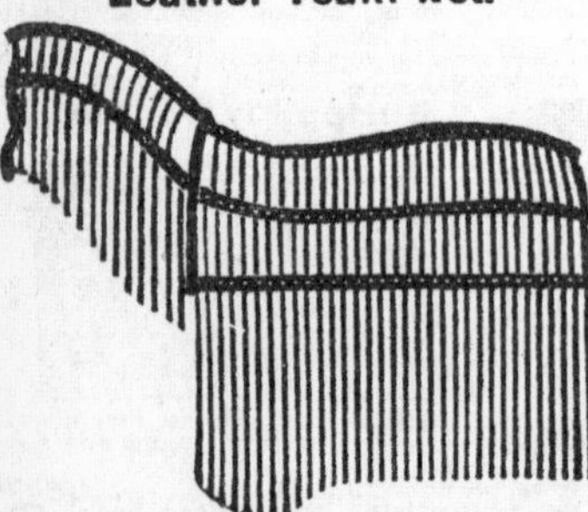

No. 10C9094 Chase's Genuine Brussels Cover, the best fly horse cover made. Leather trimmed; hame, terret and trace holes. Unexcelled for strength, durability and superior finish. Ventilating admits air but not flies. Made 100 inches long. The most perfect fly cover made. Weight, 32 ounces.
Price, each....................................$1.05

S., R. & Co.'s Fine Upper Leather Team Net.

No. 10C9043 Sears, Roebuck & Co.'s Extra Heavy Fine Upper Leather Team Net. This net is made of the finest upper leather, tanned for nets only. We have a special contract with the best net manufacturer for his entire product and we are going to give our customers the benefit of this extra bargain for a good team net; ⅞-inch harness leather bars running to head, making body and neck. No breast piece. Net with hame bars. This net is about 7¼ feet long, from head to tail, 8-foot strings over shoulders and fore legs. **The best net on the market. Made in three sizes.**
72 strings. Weight, 4 lbs. Each....$2.40
84 strings. Weight, 5 lbs. Each.... 2.70
100 strings. Weight, 5½ lbs. Each.... 3.05

For a Complete Line of
VETERINARY INSTRUMENTS, REMEDIES, ETC.
Refer to Our Drug Department.

S., R. & Co.'s Russet Belting Leather Net, $1.00.

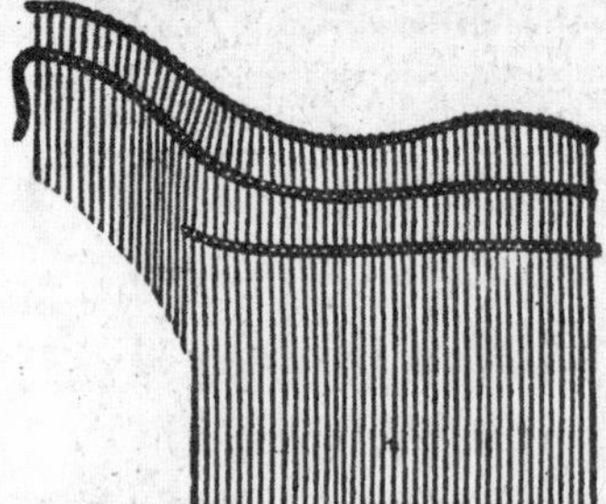

No. 10C9045 Sears, Roebuck & Co.'s Special Russet Belting Net. Made of russet belting leather, run through rollers so as to test each and every string, and no string is put into the net that is not good and strong. **This net we are making a special of this season.** It is not the cheap so called russet fly net. It is the very best that can be made of this grade of leather. Has five good heavy bars, and strings are put on with metal fasteners. Made in body and neck style. The price is for single net for one horse. Made in one size. 72 strings. Weight, 5 pounds.
Price, each....................................$1.00
Per pair, for two horses........................ 2.00

S., R. & Co.'s Light Upper Leather Team Net.

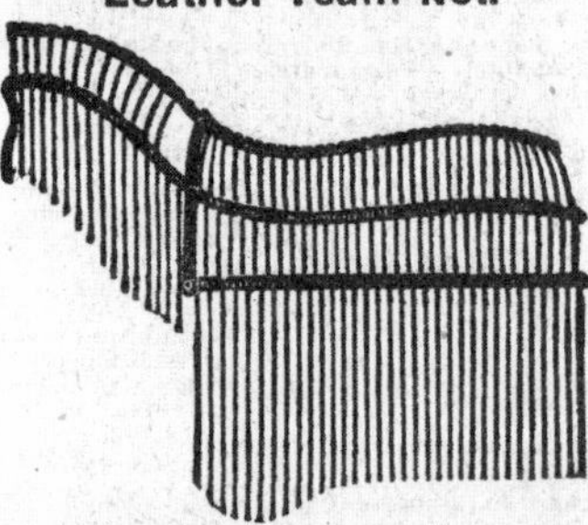

No. 10C9051 Sears, Roebuck & Co.'s Special Upper Leather Team Net. Made of extra heavy fine Dundee upper leather, with ¾-inch harness leather bars and hame leather. Body and neck net only. No breast piece. This net is about 7¼ feet long, from head to tail, with 8-foot string over shoulders and fore legs. **A better net this year than ever before, from the fact that we have our own leather tanned specially for team nets.** The price of net is for one horse. Made in three sizes.
72 strings. Weight, 3½ lbs. Each....$2.15
84 strings. Weight, 4 lbs. Each.... 2.39
100 strings. Weight, 4½ lbs. Each.... 2.74

Body and Breast Upper Leather Team Net.

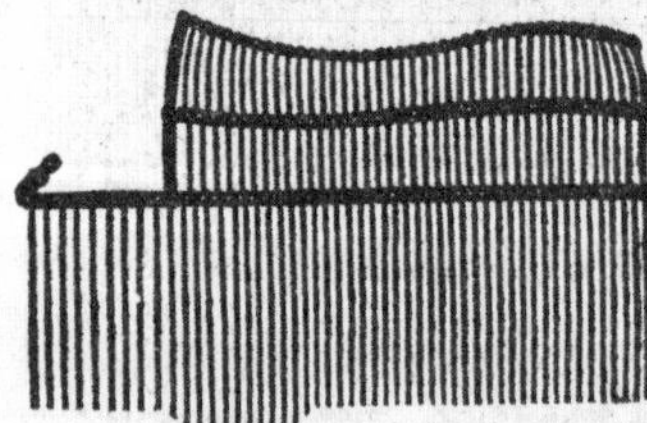

No. 10C9061 Body and Breast Upper Leather Team Net. ¾-inch harness leather bars. Dundee waxed upper leather strings, hame bar and breast piece, good long lashers. **A good body and breast upper leather net.** This net is about 5½ feet long, from hames to tail, with long string over shoulders and fore legs. Made in three sizes. Same grade as No. 10C9051.
50 strings. Weight, 2¾ lbs. Each $1.95
60 strings. Weight, 3 lbs. Each 2.30
70 strings. Weight, 3¼ lbs. Each 2.68

S., R. & Co.'s Extra Heavy Upper Leather Body and Breast Team Net.

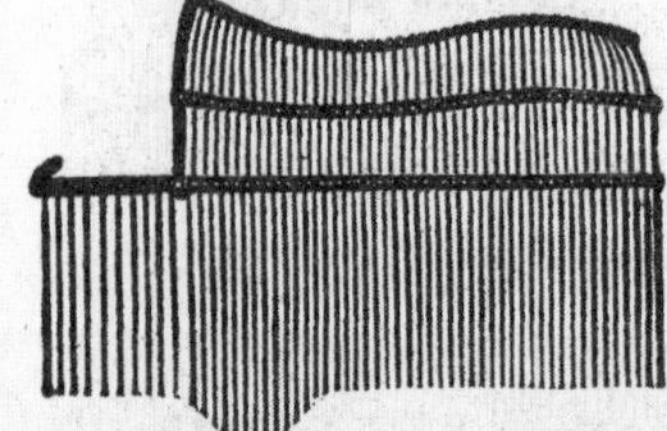

No. 10C9065 Sears, Roebuck & Co.'s Extra Heavy Body and Breast Team Net; ⅞-inch harness leather bars, long body net, hame bar, extra long strings over shoulders and fore legs, body about 5½ feet long. **The best heavy upper leather body and breast net made.** Price is for one horse.
50 strings. Weight, 3 lbs. Each....$2.25
60 strings. Weight, 3½ lbs. Each.... 2.55
70 strings. Weight, 4½ lbs. Each.... 2.90

PLAIN AND FANCY LAP ROBES.

We take great pride in the completeness of this department, as well as in the fact that we have succeeded in making lower prices for our customers than in any past season. The manager of this department has selected these goods with the greatest care to secure the best styles and qualities. Taking price and grade into consideration, these values are unapproachable. While you can get some idea of the pattern of each robe from the small illustration we show, you must see the robes in their full size, color and design to appreciate their full beauty.

Plain Linen Robe, $1.00.

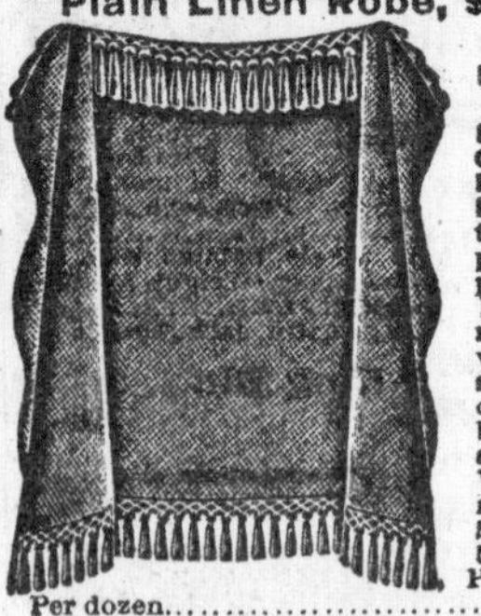

No. 10C10025 Our Plain Imported German Linen Lap Robe. Knotted fringe, perfectly plain center, large size, medium weight. A strictly high class linen buggy robe at a low price. Weight of robe, 16 ozs. Size of robe, 50x60 inches.
Price $1.00
Per dozen.................................... 11.50
If by mail, postage extra, each, 16 cents.

Our Fancy Dotted Momie Duster, 40 Cents.

No. 10C10205 Fancy border, plain fringe, with spray of flowers in center of duster. Extra Jacquard fancy woven body; a very durable lap robe and a big seller. Would retail at 75 cents. Size, 48x56 inches. Weight, 10 ozs.
Price...40c
Price, per dozen..$4.50
If by mail, postage extra, each, 10 cents.

Our Plain or Embroidered Center Momie Dusters.

No. 10C10210 Fancy plaid, double weave body, scroll border, knotted fringe on each end. A very durable buggy duster. Size, 48x56 in. Weight, about 10 ounces. Assorted fancy patterns.
Price, each, 50c
Per dozen, $5.10

No. 10C10211 Same grade robe as No. 10C10210, only fancy embroidered center. Very handsome pattern. Price, each..$0.85
Per dozen.................................... 9.60
If by mail, postage extra, each, 10 cents.

Our Special Momie Duster or Buggy Lap Robe, 65 Cents.

No. 10C10215 Fancy double weave body, handsomely dropped weave headings, with fancy border, knotted fringe and very pretty design embroidered center, with very fine blending colors, extra fine spotted weave pattern. Size, 48x56 inches. Weight, about 12 ounces. Price, per dozen, $7.50; each..65c
If by mail, postage extra, each, 12 cents.

Plain or Embroidered Center Momie Cloth Robe.

No. 10C10245 Heavy Woven Momie Cloth Lap Robe. Dark pattern, plain or embroidered center, fancy border, heavy knotted fringe. A very handsome summer duster. Weight, 14 ounces. Size, 48x55 inches.
Price, each, 55c
Per dozen, $6.00

One of Our Lap Robe Leaders, 85 Cents.

No. 10C10260 S., R. & Co.'s Special Fancy English Weave Buggy Lap Robe. Body of robe woven with fancy leaves, heavy knotted fringe and plain center. This is one of the finest high grade buggy lap robes made. Weight, 18 ounces. Size, 48x56 inches.
Price, per dozen, $9.25; each.........85c
If by mail, postage extra, each, 18 cents.

We Challenge Competition on this Number

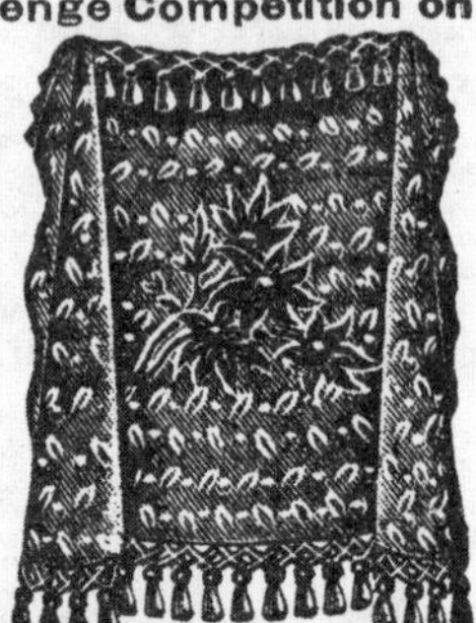

No. 10C10265 Our Fancy Embroidered Center, Fancy Woven Momie Cloth, wide border. One of the richest buggy lap robes on the market. Weight, 16 ounces. Size of robe, 48x56 inches.
Price $1.10
If by mail, postage extra, 16 cents.

The Best Robe Made for $1.65.

No. 10C10288 Our Fancy English Momie Cloth Robe. Heavy embroidered centerpiece of fancy colored zephyr. One of the finest and richest patterns made. Heavy knotted fringe and extra large lap robe. Weight, 20 ounces. Size, 48x56, inches. Price, $1.65
If by mail, postage extra, 20 cents.

Gray and Fancy Color Single and Double Plush Robes.

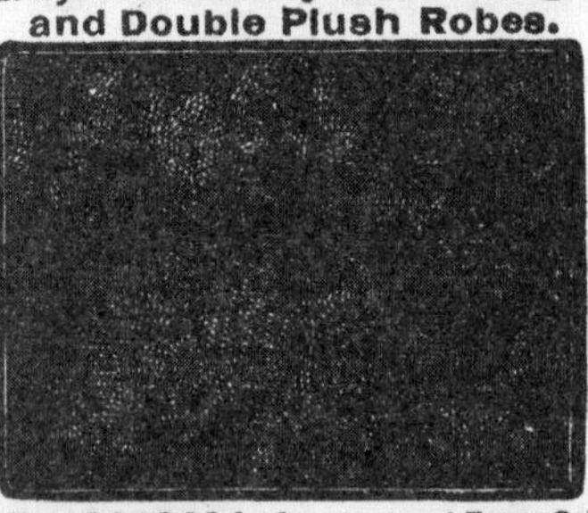

No. 10C10464 Our Gray and Fancy Color Single Plush Buggy Robe. This robe is made of soft gray and colored plush stock, bound around edges. Size, 48x60 inches. Weight, about 3 pounds. Price, gray.......$1.20
Fancy color.................................. 1.30

No. 10C10465 Our Double Plain Green Plush Carriage Robe. Plain green pattern on one side and plain black on the other side. A very handsome, stylish and well made plush robe. Size of robe, 48x60 inches. Weight of robe, about 5 pounds. Price $2.10

No. 10C10467 Sears, Roebuck & Co.'s Special, Extra Heavy, Double Green Plush Lap Robe. Plain green on one side and black on the other. This is an extra quality of fine plush robe. Size, 50x60 inches. Weight, 5½ pounds. The best kind of a robe for every day use. Always looks neat and clean. Price....$2.40

No. 10C10468 Extra Large; 54x72 inches. Same quality as No. 10C10467, very large, double, green plush robe. Weight, 7½ pounds.
Price.......................................$3.50

No. 10C10469 Sears, Roebuck & Co.'s Extra Heavy Double, Green Plush Robe. Superfine quality of plain green silk plush on one side and handsome shade of black on the other side. Double, extra large. Size, 54x72 inches. Weight, 8¾ pounds. This is the largest, handsomest and most durable double green plush robe we handle. One of the best sellers in our line. Price.................................$4.25

No. 10C10470 Sears' Special Green Plush Robe, 54x72 inches. **Rubber interlined,** making it windproof and very warm. All robes with rubber interlining **are very warm and strong.** Weight, 9½ pounds. Price...$4.50

WATERPROOF LAP ROBES.

Covert Cloth Waterproof Lap Robes.

No. 10C10472 **This lap robe is made of double texture covert cloth.** Fancy plaid lining, extra large size, 54x63 inches, 2-inch edge with four rows of stitching, made in two colors, dark oxford gray or tan color. Everyone should have one of these **Covert Cloth Rain Robes** for his buggy. Weight, 4½ pounds.
Price.................................**$2.00**

Plush Robes, Rubber Face, $1.90 and $2.30.

No. 10C10473 **Sears, Roebuck & Co.'s Special Heavy, Rubber Lined Waterproof Lap Robe.** This robe is made with a fine plush back, facing of rubber, made for all kinds of stormy weather. **Can be used with either plush or rubber side up.** Size, 48x60 inches. Weight, about 5¾ pounds.
Price.................................**$1.90**

No. 10C10475 **Sears, Roebuck & Co.'s Special Plush Lined, Rubber Faced, Storm Lap Robe.** This lap robe is made of an extra quality of rubber facing and superfine plush back. **Nothing better ever made in a storm lap robe.** Size, 50x60 inches. Weight, about 6 pounds. Price.................................**$2.30**

Our Indiana Double Plush Robes.

No. 10C10476 **This robe is made of dark colored plush body,** fancy red and yellow border, wolf head center with fancy red and green leaf effect. Size, 48x60 inches, and weight, 5 pounds. This is one of the cheap double plush robes, and yet the kind of plush robes that sell at retail for $3.50 to $4.00. Fancy pattern one side, and plain black the other. Price.......**$2.90**

No. 10C10477 Same style robe as No. 10C10476, only made with rubber interlined, making it a very warm robe and windproof.
Price.................................**$3.75**

This Robe $2.50 and $3.80.

Our Extra Double Plush Carriage Robe. The best double plush robe ever offered at our special price of $2.50 and $3.80. Red ground with black printing, black stag head in center, solid black on the other side. Why is this the best? Because it is one of the greatest values we have ever made in a plush robe. Very fine plush and made in two sizes.

No. 10C10496 Size, 48x60 inches. Weight, about 5 pounds. Price.......................**$2.50**
No. 10C10498 Size, 60x70 inches. Weight, about 7 pounds. Price.......................**$3.80**

Elk Head Plush Robe, $3.95.

No. 10C10517 **Our Special Elk Head Center with Dog Supports, Double Plush Robe**, representing the hunter's dogs guarding the elk. The colors used in this fancy medallion center are red, brown, green, white and yellow, a very handsome combination. A very beautiful robe. The pattern is something entirely new. Very rich looking. Size of this robe, 50x60 inches. Weight, about 5¾ pounds.
Price.................................**$3.95**

No. 10C10648 **Full lined with a gray mixed wool lining, two surcingles,** extra stay to front surcingle, turned and stitched binding around the neck and down the front, extra quarter stay snap front, cut to fit the horse. Made in size 26 only, and will fit 1100 to 1300-pound horse. One of the best cheap Baker plaid duck stable blankets on the market. Weight of blanket, 5 pounds. Price, each.........**$1.65**

Electric Storm Plush Robe.

No. 10C10589 **This robe is made of heavy double plush, black on one side and handsome medallion pattern on the other,** representing white and brown horses. This picture was taken as a heavy electric storm was approaching, and is considered one of the handsomest paintings before the public. This robe is a handsome reproduction of this beautiful picture, with handsome flowered border, making one of the most beautiful plush robes in the line. The equal of this handsome electric storm plush robe cannot be bought at retail for less than $8.00. It is a value that cannot be surpassed, a robe that is not only very handsome but is made of high grade material, very durable, a robe that will last season after season. You will find it pays to buy a good plush robe, and we can thoroughly recommend this number. Size, 54 x 64 inches. Weight, about 7 pounds. Price.....................**$5.00**

Brown Duck Stable Sheets.

No. 10C10619 **Our Gayton Special Brown Duck Sheet,** made with two web surcingles, snap front, cut to fit the horse. Made in sizes 24, 26, 28 and 30. The best cheap brown duck stable sheet on the market.
Price, per dozen, **$12.00**; each.......**$1.00**

No. 10C10620 **Our Albert Burlap Stable Sheet,** size 26; two surcingles, cut to fit the horse; a good burlap stable sheet. Weight, about 2¾ pounds. Price, each..............**55c**

No. 10C10621 **Our Burlap Piper Boy Stable Sheet,** made of 10-ounce burlap, two surcingles, snap front. A good sheet, cut to fit the horse. Made in sizes 24, 26, 28 and 30. The best cheap burlap sheet made. Weight, about 2¾ pounds. Price, each......................**65c**

Our Genuine Burlington Stay-on Stable Blanket, $1.35.

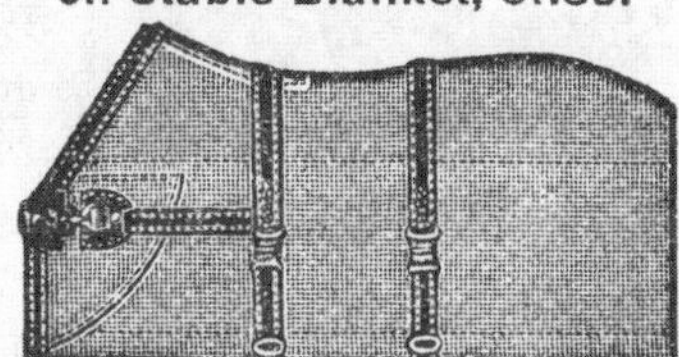

No. 10C10639 **This blanket is made out of the very best quality of mangled burlap,** gray wool mixed blanket lining, extra reinforced front, with Burlington snap attachment; two wide duck surcingles, with stay-on fasteners, extra stay to first surcingle. The biggest seller of the season. Made in one size only, size 26, and will fit a horse from 1,100 to 1,200 pounds. The greatest bargain in a genuine Burlington full lined stable blanket ever offered. Weight of blanket, 6 pounds. Price, each......**$1.35**

Our Special Wyoming Full Lined Burlap Stable Blanket.

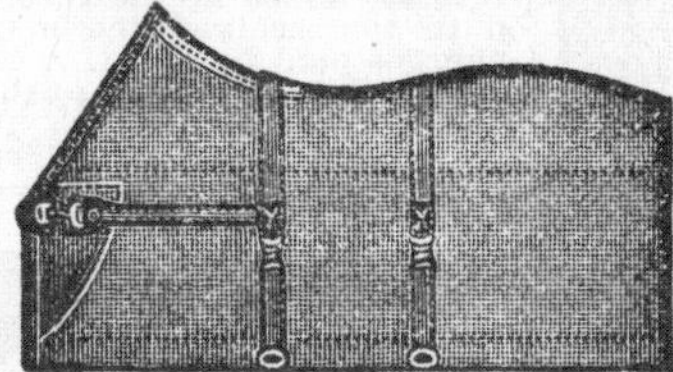

No. 10C10641 **Turned and stitched blanket edge around the neck and front.** Full lined throughout with a gray blanket lining, two corded surcingles, extra stay to first surcingle; extra reinforced front with snap fastener. A good, cheap burlap stable blanket. A horse cannot get this blanket off. Weight, 5½ pounds.
Price, each.................................**$1.25**

Our Utah Heavy Fancy Plaid Printed Duck Stable Blanket.

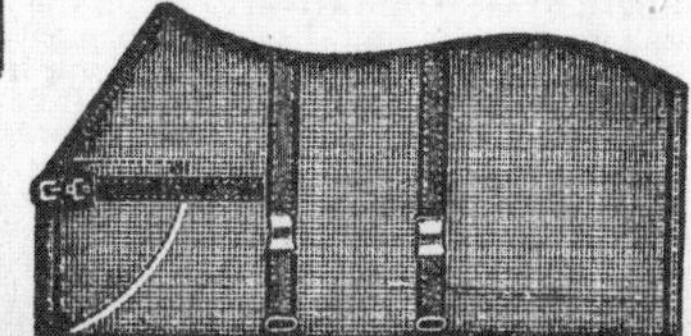

Our Buffalo Stable Blanket.

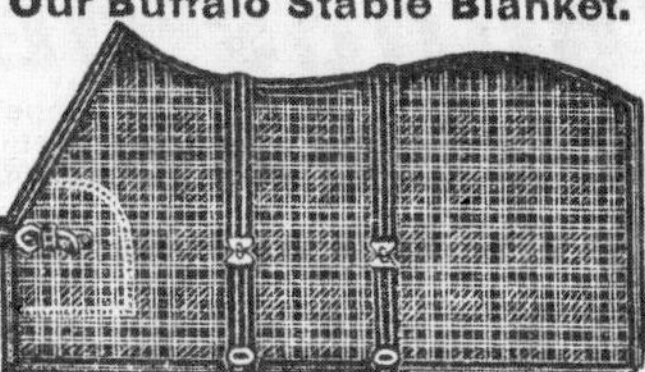

No. 10C10653 **Made of good blanket stock, heavy cotton warp, fancy block printed blanket.** This blanket has two surcingles attached. Buckle front. This is a very large seller. Good value at our low price. Size, 72 inches long. Weight, 6 pounds. Price, each..**$1.35**

Our Toledo Stable Blanket.

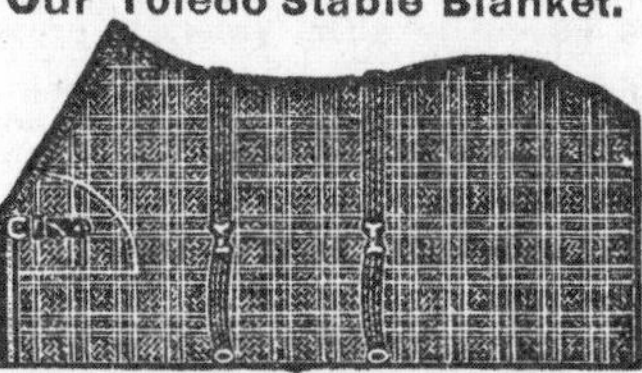

No. 10C10657 **Made of fancy printed plaid blanket stock** cut to shape of horse; **two surcingles,** buckle front; extra stayed and reinforced front. A good shaped stable blanket. Size, 72 inches. Weight, about 5½ pounds.
Price, each.................................**$1.15**

Our Special Burlington Stay-on Stable Blanket, $1.80, $1.90 $2.05.

No. 10C10665 **Made of heavy brown duck,** boot web binding, two extra heavy, wide corded surcingles with snaps and patent fasteners. **Lined with heavy fancy plaid wool lining, extra heavy reinforced front, making one of the best brown duck stable blankets on the market.** This is one of our big bargains. Made in sizes 24, 26, 28 and 30. Weight, about 5¾ lbs.
Price, size 24...............................**$1.80**
Price, size 26...............................**1.90**
Price, size 28 and 30.....................**2.05**

Our Roseburg Brown Duck Storm Blanket.

No. 10C10682 **Our Extra Large Roseburg Storm Blanket.** Made of brown duck, full fancy lined, extra large 84x90 inches with V in the neck. This is a very large, warm and exceptionally strong blanket, full quilted. Weight of this blanket, 7½ pounds. Price, each. **$2.00**

No. 10C10683 **Made of good strong duck, patent adjustable front fastening,** gray wool blanket lining, extra V-shaped gore neck to fit the horse, well hemmed all around. For a good, cheap storm blanket this is a very big seller. Size, 80x80 inches. Weight, 6 pounds.
Price, each.................................**$1.45**

Celebrated Directly Square Horse Blanket. Price, $1.45 and $1.65.

No. 10C10803 **Made of fine wool blanketing, dark snuff color, fancy stripe body and border headings.** Round sewed strap and buckle front. Extra strong double and twisted warp, making an **exceedingly strong, durable blanket**; and one wanting an extra good, strong, firm blanket will do well to order this. Made in two sizes.
Size, 76x80 inches. Weight, 5 lbs. Each, **$1.45**
Size, 84x90 inches. Weight, 7 lbs. Each, **1.65**

Dare Devil Square Horse Blanket, $1.22, $1.55 and $1.95.

No. 10C10837 **This blanket is made of fine fancy gray blanketing,** well gigged, made with firm, solid twisted warp which makes the blanket very hard to tear. Round strap and buckle front. Fine body stripes and border heading. A blanket suitable for any kind of team use. Made in three sizes.
Size, 76x80 inches, 5 lbs. Price, each **$1.22**
Size, 80x84 inches, 6 lbs. Price, each **1.55**
Size, 84x90 inches, 9 lbs. Price, each **1.95**

Our Great Eastern Fawn Square Horse Blanket, $2.00, $2.40, $2.80 and $3.60.

This blanket is made of good, clean fawn wool blanket filling, well carded with heavy double hard twisted cotton warp. Blanket firmly woven, soft and warm, with bright red heading. Looks like the best fawn blanket; the greatest bargain in a handsome fawn blanket, with bright red heading, ever offered at our price. Made in four sizes.

	Size	Weight	Price
No. 10C10862	76x80 ins.	5 lbs.	$2.00
No. 10C10863	80x84 ins.	6 lbs.	2.40
No. 10C10865	84x90 ins.	7 lbs.	2.80
No. 10C10866	90x96 ins.	9 lbs.	3.60

Nella Jay, Winner of Kentucky Futurity, Horse Blanket, $2.15, $2.49 and $2.85.

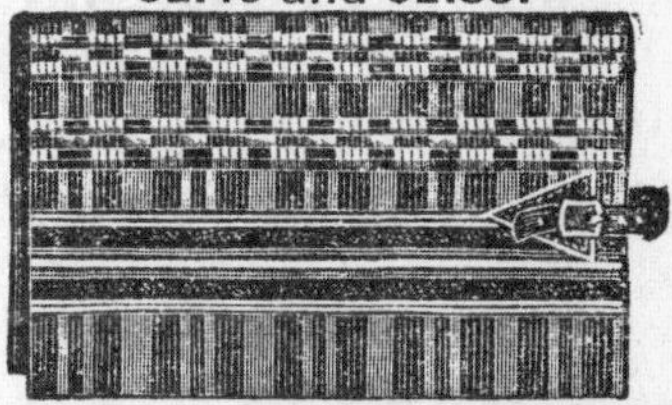

Made of block weave effect, red on one side and dark drab color on the other. Fancy block weave stripes, billet and buckle front. This blanket is made of fine, soft blanketing, with an extra heavy hard twisted warp, making a very strong, substantial blanket. Can be used either side out. Made in three sizes.

	Size	Weight	Price
No. 10C10872	76x80 ins.	5 lbs.	$2.15
No. 10C10873	80x84 ins.	6 lbs.	2.49
No. 10C10880	84x90 ins.	7 lbs.	2.85

Our Great Challenge Value Plain Black or Green Horse Blanket at $2.75 to $4.75, According to Size.

Nothing to equal this blanket sold in retail stores for less than 50 per cent higher price.

Our Special Boston Solid Black or Green Horse Blanket, made of fine all black or green blanket filling, heavy hard twisted black warp, making a very strong and serviceable blanket, one solid color. No stripes in this blanket. Plain solid black or green body, strong warp, a warm, durable and handsome blanket. Our prices, as shown below, will interest dealers everywhere, for we know they cannot buy a blanket to equal this from the jobber at as low prices as we quote. Made in four sizes.

	Size	Weight	Price
No. 10C10883	76x80 ins.	5 lbs.	$2.75
No. 10C10884	80x84 ins.	6 lbs.	3.25
No. 10C10885	84x90 ins.	7 lbs.	3.75
No. 10C10886	90x96 ins.	9 lbs.	4.75

Our Famous Nelson Square Horse Blanket. Price, $1.50 $2.10 and $2.75.

This blanket is made of dark gray and brown mixed body of the very finest of blanketing with extra strong heavy warp, with bright red stripes and bright border. This is one of **the very best standard team blankets on the market**, made for us specially and considered by us **the leader this year.**

	Size	Weight	Price
No. 10C10805	76x80 ins.	5 lbs.	$1.50
No. 10C10806	84x90 ins.	7 lbs.	2.10
No. 10C10807	90x96 ins.	9 lbs.	2.75

MUSICAL GOODS DEPARTMENT.--PIANOS.

ALL OF THE PIANOS SHOWN on the following pages are made by one of the largest and best equipped factories in the country, controlled by the Beckwith Piano Company. We have been selling these pianos for several years and their handsome appearance and beautiful tone, together with our extremely low prices have established their reputation and placed them beyond competition.

OUR LOW PRICES.

OUR LOW PRICES are the direct result of our method of sale. These pianos are shipped directly from the factory to the customer. This enables the purchaser to buy a piano at actual factory prices with only our one small margin of profit added. The actual cost of making a piano is generally less than one-half of the price which the local dealer asks you to pay. Most of this price is made up of profits added by the different dealers through whose hands the instrument passes on its way to you. Our method of sale, together with improved methods of manufacture and the advantage we possess of buying in large quantities, enables us to make prices which are far below what any other dealer can offer you. It is only necessary for you to compare our goods and prices with those offered by other dealers, to prove that this is so.

THE PRICE WHICH WE MAKE upon all of our pianos represents simply the cost of material and labor at the factory, with but one small percentage of profit added to recompense us for handling and selling the instruments. By shipping the instruments directly from the factory to the customer we are able to sell them at extremely low prices. The fact that we sell these pianos at such extremely low prices, does not prove that they are instruments of low grade, because, as stated above, the original manufacturing cost of any good piano is but a very small part of the price which the customer has to pay when he purchases in the usual way. **When you purchase a piano from us, you are paying for it exactly what it is worth,** and we do not ask you to pay us any fancy profits, and we do not find it necessary to maintain high prices as we have no dealers to protect, do not sell on the installment plan, do not take second hand instruments in exchange, and do not make any discounts in any way from our catalogue prices. We desire to impress our customers with the fact that by our liberal terms of shipment, we make it possible for them to examine and test one of our pianos in their own homes without it costing them a cent of money. Under these terms our customers do not take any risk whatever in giving us their orders for pianos, because we take all the risks, responsibilities and chances of shipment, and are prepared to receive the instruments back, refund the money, and pay freight charges both ways, where they do not prove satisfactory. **We ship every piano out with the understanding that if the customer does not find that we are saving him from $75.00 to $300.00, at least, on the purchase, he can return it to us at our expense and we will cheerfully refund the entire amount he has paid.** By our liberal terms of shipment and our extremely low prices we make it possible for every family to own a splendid concert piano. Do not make the mistake of associating our pianos with instruments sold at about the same price by other dealers. In considering the purchase of an instrument from any other dealer always bear in mind the fact stated above, that at least one-half of the price which you are asked to pay is made up of intermediate dealers' profits which do not add anything at all to the real value of the instrument.

TERMS OF SHIPMENT.—HOW TO TAKE ADVANTAGE OF OUR 30 DAYS FREE TRIAL OFFER.

We sell all of our pianos on 30 days free trial, allowing the customer to give them a thorough test and examination before requiring him to accept them. You can take advantage of our 30 days free trial offer in three ways, as follows:

OUR 25 YEARS BINDING GUARANTEE.

IN ORDER TO REMOVE ALL DOUBT from the minds of our customers and protect them fully we issue, with each piano sold, a written binding guarantee for 25 years. The fact that we can give this binding guarantee with our pianos proves that they are instruments of the very highest quality. We could not afford to do this if we did not have the greatest faith in our instruments, and this should satisfy our friends that we are prepared to protect them against loss in every way.

Sears, Roebuck and Co. Chicago

Certificate No. 96737½

Certificate of Guaranty

This Certifies that the Organ the number and name of which have been registered is made by skilled mechanics. Only thoroughly air and kiln dried lumber and other materials specially selected and prepared enter into this instrument and with fair usage we hereby agree to make good at our expense any defect in material or workmanship for a period of twenty five years.

Dated at Chicago this 1st day of August A.D. 190

Sears, Roebuck and Co.
by R. W. Sears

Reference by special permission: First National Bank, Chicago; National City Bank; Corn Exchange Nat. Bank, Chicago; Second National Bank

OUR SPECIAL PREPAID FREIGHT OFFER.

SHOULD YOU DESIRE us to send the piano by freight prepaid, you can send us your order and we will enter it at the factory and inform you immediately what the freight charges will be to your town. You can then deposit the freight charges, together with the price of the piano, in accordance with our Offer Number One, or send it to us under Offer Number Two. We will then ship the piano with all freight charges prepaid. Should you desire to know the exact freight charges upon any piano to your town we will be glad to give them to you on request, or you can figure out the charges for yourself by ascertaining from the catalogue the weight of the piano you desire, and consulting the table of freight rates given. Should your town not be given you can figure the charges to your nearest shipping point, and the additional charges, if any, will be very small. Should you deposit more than enough money to pay freight we will refund you the balance, and if you should not deposit enough we will pay the balance and send you the bill for it.

ONE YEAR FREE TRIAL OFFER.

NOT ONLY DO WE ALLOW you to try the instrument in your own home for 30 days before finally accepting it, but we also allow you to return it to us any time within one year from the time you receive it if it does not prove satisfactory, and we will refund your money and pay the freight charges both ways. We believe that you will admit that we are protecting you in every way, and that you will be taking no chances in giving us your order.

OUR SPECIAL PIANO CATALOGUE.

WE ESPECIALLY RECOMMEND that you select and purchase a piano from us as illustrated and described in this big catalogue, rather than to cause a delay by writing for our free Special Piano Catalogue, since we guarantee that any piano which you may order from these pages will reach you in perfect condition, prove in every way satisfactory, and that you will find it a much better piano than you can buy elsewhere at anything like the price we offer. We also guarantee that you will make a big saving in the cost, and if you do not find this to be so, you can return the piano to us any time within 30 days and we will immediately and cheerfully refund your money and pay the freight charges both ways. If, however, you are unable to make a selection from the illustrations and descriptions shown in this catalogue, and you feel that you would like to have better illustrations and more complete descriptions, then we will be glad to send you a copy of our Special Piano Catalogue. This catalogue will be sent to you, upon request, postage prepaid, and it will only be necessary for you to send us a postal card in order to obtain it. Simply say "Please send me your Piano Catalogue," and it will be sent by return mail.

OUR OFFER NUMBER ONE. Deposit the price of the piano you have selected with your local banker or express agent and have him fill out and sign a certificate of deposit, using the same form and words as shown in the following certificate

Town________ State________ Date________

Received from Mr.________

________Dollars in payment of Sears, Roebuck & Co.'s________

We agree to hold this money until the instrument has been received by Mr.________

________residing in________and has had 30 days trial, when we shall forward the amount to Sears, Roebuck & Co., Chicago, Ill.

If Mr.________is not perfectly satisfied with the instrument, we will refund money on surrender to us of a bill of lading showing instrument has been reconsigned to Sears, Roebuck & Co.

____
Name of bank or express Co.

____
Your banker or express agent should sign his name here.

When you have had the banker or express agent make out the receipt in the form shown above, send this receipt to us, and we will at once ship the piano which you select. We will allow you to try the instrument in your own home for 30 days. Should it prove unsatisfactory for any reason you can ship it back to us, present the shipping receipt to the banker or express agent and he will refund your money. We will also pay the freight charges both ways. Should you not return the piano at the end of 30 days the banker or express agent will send the money to us.

OUR OFFER NUMBER TWO. In case there is no banker or express agent in your town with whom you can deposit the money, you can send the price of the piano selected to us, and our banking department will issue you a certificate of deposit like the one given below.

CERTIFICATE OF DEPOSIT

No. 7634

Banking Department — Sears, Roebuck & Co.

Chicago, ... 190....

We hereby acknowledge receipt of.......................... ...., deposited in our Banking Department by ...., of..........................., and to be used in payment for one of our......................... ...., as per the following conditions: We agree to hold this money on deposit until the instrument has been received by ...., and he has had a 30 days' trial of the same in his home. If the instrument should not prove satisfactory .... is to return it to the freight depot properly packed, addressed to us and obtain a bill of lading from the freight agent to be mailed to us and upon return of the bill of lading, together with this receipt, we will immediately refund to .... the full amount of money on deposit with us with interest added at the rate of 5 per cent per annum from date we received the money together with the freight charges paid by .... We to pay the return freight charges at this end.

Signed *SEARS, ROEBUCK & CO.*

Invoice No. .... *R. W. Sears Pres.*

We will, at once ship the piano you select and allow you to try it in your home for 30 days, and if, for any reason, it should become unsatisfactory within that time you can return it to us, and we will refund your money with interest at the rate of 5 per cent per annum. We will also pay the freight charges both ways as well as cartage. Most of our customers prefer to take advantage of this offer and send the money directly to us, because we refund the money with interest at 5 per cent per annum.

OUR OFFER NUMBER THREE, C. O. D. Upon receipt of $1.00 we will send any piano for examination and approval to any point east of the Rocky Montains and north of the Ohio River. When the instrument arrives at its destination you can examine it, and if satisfactory, pay the balance of the price including freight charges, and take the piano to your home for a thorough trial. Should the instrument not prove satisfactory it can be returned to us, entirely at our expense and we will refund the $1.00 previously paid. The $1.00 deposit is simply intended as an evidence of good faith and will always be returned when the instrument does not prove satisfactory. Most of our customers prefer to send the full amount with the order because it gives them all the C. O. D. privileges and they can save the C. O. D. charges and avoid the necessity of letting their neighbors know what they paid for the instrument. By this method they can take advantage of our great 30 days free trial offer outlined above.

THE BECKWITH PIANOS.

A STANDARD LINE OF HIGH GRADE INSTRUMENTS AT PRICES LOWER THAN EVER BEFORE.

A FEW POINTERS ON THE ESSENTIALS OF A HIGH GRADE PIANO.

PIANO VALUES. **In every good piano there are two distinct values.** One is the value which the piano takes from the material and labor which enter into it and the other is the value which it takes from the genius of the man who joins these materials and makes possible its beautiful tone. When purchasing any of the so called standard pianos the customer pays from $200.00 to $400.00, simply for the reputation of the maker, and in many cases this reputation is the only good quality which the piano possesses. The tone of the piano, which it can only get from the genius of the man who makes it, is above all price and cannot be measured by the standard of dollars and cents. The Beckwith piano possesses this quality in a wonderful degree, but we do not pretend to fix any price on it and do not ask our customers to pay us for any maker's reputation or for any quality in the piano which cannot be measured according to the usual commercial standards. Both the values mentioned above are present in the Beckwith piano, but we only charge you for one, namely, the material and labor which enters into the construction of the instrument. All of our prices are based upon actual manufacturing cost.

THE MAKING OF A PIANO.

THE SCALE. **In the making of a piano** the drawing of the scale is unquestionably one of the most important points to be considered, as the scale is the foundation on which the musical construction of the piano is built. We might say that the scale of the piano is either an inspiration or it is a failure. Many piano manufacturers have redrawn the scale of their pianos and experimented with it during the entire period of their business lives and have never succeeded in securing satisfactory results. On the other hand, the scale may be perfect in its first drawing; in other words, it may be an inspiration. The scale of a piano is an exact mathematical division of its tones and depends on a good many different conditions for its success. A great object has been to cover up the two divisions in the scale known as "breaks." One of these "breaks" occurs between the over strung bass strings and that part of the scale where the three-string unison begins. Another "break" occurs in the treble where the brace is inserted in the metallic frame of the piano to give it strength and rigidity. Take one of the Beckwith pianos and run the scale from one end of the keyboard to the other and we defy any ordinary musician to find the "breaks" in the scale. While it is true that no interval on a piano is perfect, still expert musicians and piano tuners have in many instances claimed that the scale of the Beckwith piano approaches more nearly to perfection than any other piano on the market. While we do not underestimate the value of that peculiar quality which the piano maker must possess in order to produce a good instrument, still our policy has been to pay this man for his services once for all and not to follow the policy of other manufacturers and continue to charge the customers an enormous profit on each piano to compensate for the exercise of his skill. The scale of the Beckwith piano, as stated above, is as nearly perfect as it is possible to produce and the man who drew it and perfected it, has long ago been paid for his services and therefore our customers are not under the necessity of paying us any additional profit as a compensation for his skill. This value we give to our customers absolutely free. The scale of the piano being once perfected, the instrument becomes a merely mechanical affair so far as the manufacture of it is concerned and it is therefore possible to reduce its cost in the same way that any other manufacturing product is reduced. The making of the hammers, the strings, the metallic frame, the sounding board, the case and everything that enters into the construction of the instrument is a merely mechanical process, and subject to the same laws which govern all manufactured articles. This explains why we are able to furnish high grade pianos of standard quality at such ridiculously low prices. In buying a Beckwith piano you get the superior musical quality produced by the genius of the maker, but you only pay for the actual material and labor which goes into the instrument, with our one small margin of profit added.

THE ACTION. **The action plays a very important part in the tone of the piano** and although the scale may be perfect and the material which enters into the instrument excellent in every respect, if the action is poor or improperly adjusted, the instrument will not be a success in any way. A stiff, dull action will destroy the technique of the finest piano player in the world in a short time. In order to be up to the standard, the touch of the piano must be light and responsive and the action must respond promptly and work without any hesitation. In order to test this quality in a piano, strike one of the keys a number of sharp blows in quick succession. In seven out of every ten pianos you will not get a response to every note, but will simply get a succession of blurred tones. This proves that the action does not respond properly. In the Beckwith pianos great care is used to see that the action responds properly, and it makes no difference how fast the tones are struck every one will come out clear and distinct. The action of the keys is light and responsive and many eminent piano players have expressed their pleasure at playing upon these pianos for this one quality alone. **The hammers** also play an important part in the action of the piano and they must be properly constructed and adjusted in order to perform their office in producing the tone. The hammer produces the tone by striking the string and causing it to vibrate. You can observe the working of the hammers by taking off the front of the piano. But not only is it necessary that the hammers should strike the string, but it is necessary that they should strike the string at just the proper place. This is a point that is often overlooked in the manufacture of pianos. It has been shown that it is necessary for this hammer to strike the string exactly between the "nodes" or vibrations. These vibrations run along the strings in waves, and in order to produce the best results the hammer must strike the strings between these waves. In the Beckwith pianos the point where the hammer comes in contact with the strings, has been mathematically determined to the fraction of an inch. The placing of the felt on the hammers is another important point, and by examining one of the hammers on the Beckwith piano you will notice the thorough manner in which these hammers are felted. You will notice that the interior layer of felt is very hard and that the outside layer, or that part which comes in contact with the string, is of a very elastic quality of genuine piano felt of a very fine texture, especially prepared, which produces a pleasing, rich and mellow tone. The hammers of a great many pianos are carelessly felted with a poor quality of felt, which gives that hard, metallic twang which you have heard so often on cheap pianos. But it takes more than the felt to make a good hammer. It must be of an exact weight and so balanced and poised that it comes back instantly after striking the string. By striking a key of one of our Beckwith pianos and watching the hammer you will see at once that every point in its construction and adjustment has been carefully considered.

There are many fine points in the construction of a piano about which the purchaser knows nothing. One of these points is the quality of the felt which enters into the instrument. This has a great deal to do with the quality of the instrument. Many cheap pianos are made without a particle of genuine piano felt entering into their construction. Some of these instruments sound very well for a time, but the tones soon become lifeless and unresponsive. The action of a piano felted in this way will rattle after being used for a time and the keys will refuse to work with that responsiveness so much desired and the piano will be altogether a disappointment. There is no remedy for this and it is simply a bad bargain. This calamity can never happen to a Beckwith piano, as they are all thoroughly inspected before leaving the factory and are guaranteed in every way. The felts used in all of the Beckwith pianos are made of wool and are of the finest quality.

THE METAL FRAME **is another important part of the piano.** This frame must be so constructed as to give the least weight with the greatest amount of strength. As there is a strain of from 19 to 20 tons on the metal frame of the concert piano, tuned to international pitch, it is necessary that this frame should be constructed in the strongest possible manner so as to prevent its twisting or "buckling." It is on this frame that the strings are placed and it is securely bolted to the wrest plank or pin block in which the tuning pins are set. The strings of the piano must be of fine quality in order to produce a good tone. The scale of the Beckwith piano has a three-string unison in the treble and two-string unison in the overstrung bass. By "three-string unison" we mean three strings for every note. All of the bass strings are copper wound, and that part of the scale is what is known as a two-string unison.

THE SOUNDING BOARD **of the piano** mellows and increases the tone of the strings and must be made of wood which is absolutely perfect and thoroughly seasoned. The sounding board in the Beckwith pianos is made of the choicest selected Canadian spruce and ribbed with braces of the same material, which insures it against warping or splitting.

THE KEY **of the piano** is a lever used to put the action in motion, throwing the hammer against the string and producing the tone. In order to have these keys balance perfectly they are weighted with small lead weights, inserted into the key shank back of the pivot, allowing the key, when released, to rise instantly into its former position. This requires the very nicest adjustment and is one of the most famous characteristics of the Beckwith pianos. The white keys are faced on the top and ends with ivory, the black keys are made of ebony.

THE CASES **of the Beckwith pianos are perfect in every respect** and it is a fact not generally known that it takes about three months to put the finish on a good piano case. Each case is given from seven coats of varnish upwards and each coat of varnish has to set from four to six days in order to become thoroughly dry before the next coat can be applied. These different processes, when perfectly performed, will consume from 70 to 90 days. These are points which are never slighted in the cases of the Beckwith pianos. Upon the thoroughness of this process depends the extremely high glass finish for which the Beckwith piano cases are noted. In building the Beckwith piano cases the manufacturers use nothing but the best grade of richly figured sawed veneers. The case work on all these (with the exception of the Home Favorite) are double veneered inside and outside so as to provide against cracking or splitting. Anyone who is familiar with veneers and veneer work can tell by looking at the edge of either the music desk or the lower panel whether or not the piano is double veneered. If you cannot see the two layers of veneer you can rest assured that they are not there.

BUYING A PIANO.

WHEN YOU ARE READY TO PURCHASE **your piano you should use great care not only to purchase a fine instrument but also to buy it from a concern which is willing to stand behind its instruments at all times.** Many concerns are ready and willing to issue a binding guarantee with the instruments which they sell, but in nine cases out of ten the concern issuing the guarantee has not the necessary financial standing to make the guarantee good at any time. It is one thing to sell a piano at a low price and quite another to guarantee it at all times. Our low prices and our guarantee go hand in hand. We are responsible at all times for any defect which may appear in our pianos, the result of defective material or workmanship. When a local agent places a piano in your home it looks fine and the tone appears to be excellent. So far as you can see, it is a high grade piano in every way, but when the agent goes away, then the real test begins; will it be as good tomorrow, next month, and next year as it is today, and will the guarantee that the agent gives you protect you in any way? Should the instrument prove defective in any particular whom will you hold responsible and to whom will you appeal for redress? As the piano is an instrument purchased but once in a lifetime, it is certainly to your interest to use great care in selecting your piano, and as there are many points of superiority for which you have to take the word of the salesman, how necessary it is for you to purchase your piano from a house which has a standing in the business world, which will make its guarantee good at all times.

WHEN WE TELL OUR CUSTOMERS **that they can save over $200.00 on the purchase of high grade pianos, many of them refuse to believe that this is true.** People have been paying $400.00 to $500.00 for pianos for such a long time that they have grown to believe that it is necessary to pay that price in order to secure a good instrument. Many of them refuse to believe that we can sell them a strictly high grade piano, up to the musical standard in every way, with a splendid tone and beautiful finish for $165.00. Very few people know that the ordinary piano costs, to manufacture, less than one-half the price which the dealer asks the customer for it. They do not realize that the expenses of sale and the profits which the different dealers make through whose hands the instrument passes, make up more than one-half of the retail price of the instrument. These profits and selling expenses do not add anything at all to the quality of the piano after it leaves the factory. This being true, the customer can easily understand that if we ship our pianos directly from the factory, simply adding our one small percentage of profit to the manufacturing cost we can sell the piano for less than one-half the price which the local dealer and agent charges for the same grade of instrument. The dealers through whose hands the piano must pass before it reaches the customer cannot afford to handle it for nothing and a profit of $50.00 for the jobber, $50.00 for the district agent and $100.00 for the local dealer is not considered generally a large profit to make on a piano.

BUT NOT ONLY DO WE MAKE **a great saving for our customers by cutting out the intermediate dealers' profits and expenses,** but we are also able to make a great reduction in price on account of the immense buying advantage which we possess. We make contracts and purchase outright thousands of pianos at one time and this places the manufacturer in a position to buy his material at the very lowest possible figure, and all of these advantages go to the customer in low prices. Do not be afraid of the low prices which we make on our pianos. Remember, that we are taking all the chances ourselves and do not ask you to take any risk whatever. As you have to take the dealer's word for a great many qualities of the piano, why not purchase from a concern which cannot afford to sell a poor piano or ask their customers to be satisfied with an instrument which is not up to the standard in every way? That we are not exaggerating when we tell you that we can save you $250.00 on the purchase of our Special Concert Grand Piano is fully proven by the testimonials which you will find on another page of this catalogue. We do not ask you to take our word for anything we say in favor of this instrument, and when we ship you a piano we do not ask you to promise anything or assume any obligations whatever, but we do ask you to believe the statements of your friends and neighbors as found in these voluntary testimonials.

BUYING FROM THE DEALER.

IF A DEALER OFFERS YOU A PIANO which he claims is as good as the Beckwith and attempts to offer it to you at prices anywhere near as low as we are making, you can very easily ascertain what the quality of the piano is by a few judicious questions. The case of his piano may look very fine and may be highly finished, but you should always remember that in a piano, at least, a little veneer covers a multitude of sins. Ask him if the case of his piano is veneered with genuine sawed veneer. Ask him if it is cross banded and veneered both inside and out. In case he evades these questions you can easily ascertain for yourself by examining the bottom edge of the music desk or the lower front panel of the piano. If you do not find two layers of veneer plainly shown, you can make up your mind that they are not there.

Ask him if the piano is a three-string unison in the treble and two-string unison in the bass. If he tells you that it is, just simply raise the top of the piano and look inside and if you do not find each hammer in the treble striking three strings at once and each hammer in the bass striking two strings, you can make up your mind that what he has told you is not true. Ask him if the bass strings of his piano are copper wound, and if they are the best grade of imported piano strings. Ask him if all the felts in the piano are the genuine Dolge piano felts.

Ask him if the wrest plank or pin block, in which the tuning pins are set, is composed of five layers of maple running in opposite directions. If he says it is not do not buy the piano under any consideration. Ask him if the action of the piano will repeat properly. You can easily ascertain this by striking several sharp blows in quick succession on one of the keys. If the piano is fitted with repeating action you will hear every note strike clear and distinct, and if it is not fitted with this action you will get nothing but a succession of blurred tones.

Ask him if his piano is a full size concert grand, and up to the musical standard in every way. If he answers all of the above questions in the affirmative then ask him if he will put it in your home for a full thirty days trial and allow you to return it at any time within one year and receive your money back with all freight charges paid in case it should prove unsatisfactory for any reason. If he agrees to this, then ask him if he will give you a written, binding 25 years guarantee to protect you against any defect in material or workmanship which may appear in the piano at any time within that period. If he refuses to give you this guarantee or to allow you the thirty days trial or to give you permission to return the piano at any time within one year, you may be sure that he has no faith in the instrument, and as he certainly knows more about the piano than you do, you cannot afford to purchase it. If he will not guarantee the instrument, he has no right to ask you to take any chances.

If he agrees to give you the 25 years guarantee and the thirty days trial then ask him if he will sell you the piano for $195.00 cash. If he refuses to sell you the piano at this figure he is simply asking you to pay him not only his large profit, but also the profits and selling expenses of the different dealers through whose hands the piano passed before it came to him. We have had many instances where dealers have offered to sell pianos to our customers at from $165.00 to $200.00 which they claimed were equal to the Beckwith, but in every instance we have found that the piano was lacking in many of the essentials which go to make up a fine instrument. As a matter of fact it is absolutely impossible for a local dealer to sell a piano of the same high grade as the Beckwith for less than from $450.00 to $500.00. The local dealer cannot purchase a piano of this grade from his jobber or manufacturer at as low a price as we can sell it to you. No concern in this country possesses so great an advantage in buying as we do, and we are thus able to purchase these pianos at prices away below what any other concern can obtain. We give our customers all of this great advantage, as we base our prices upon the manufacturing cost with but one small margin of profit added.

A WORD ABOUT FREIGHT CHARGES.

Most of our friends hesitate to purchase pianos from us, because they believe that the freight charges will be so very high that it will make the piano too expensive. This is certainly a great mistake. In the first place the local dealer has to pay the freight upon any piano which he ships to your town, and in making up the price on the piano he has to include the freight charges which he has paid, and when you purchase the piano you not only pay the freight charges, but you pay his large profit as well. By comparing our prices on pianos with those asked you by local dealers, and then comparing the freight charges which you will have to pay with the amount which we can save you on your purchase, you will see at once that the freight charge is but a very small amount in comparison with the amount you will save on your purchase. Another advantage is, that in purchasing a piano from us you know exactly what the instrument costs you at the factory, and you know exactly what you pay in freight charges, while on the other hand, in purchasing from the local dealer you know what the piano costs you, but do not know how much of it is his profit and how much the freight charge. As a general thing the railroad companies are very reasonable in freight charges, and when you consider the fact that you have to pay the freight charges whether you buy from us or from the local dealer, we believe that you should not hesitate in giving us an opportunity to send you one of our splendid instruments under our great Thirty Days Free Trial Offer. We are always willing to tell our customers the exact cost of freight on a piano laid down at their town, and where parties wish us to do so, gladly prepay the freight where the amount of the charges is enclosed with the order. This guarantees that the freight charges will not be over the figures quoted by us. Do not let the small amount of freight charges which you will have to pay prove any obstacle to your purchasing one of these pianos, as we ship each one under our express promise to save you from $50.00 to $200.00, according to the grade of piano which you purchase.

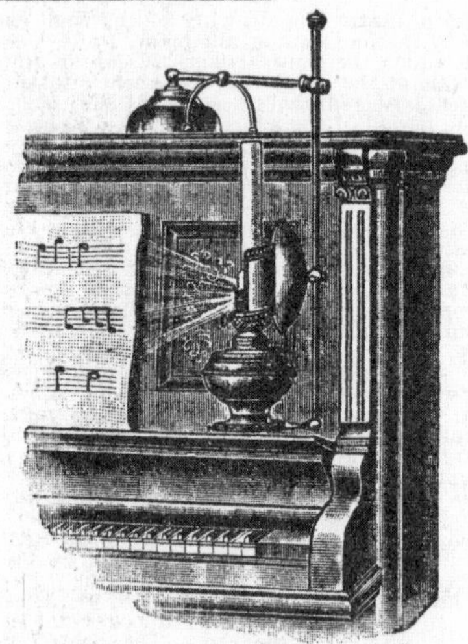

A NEW PIANO LAMP.

We are giving an illustration of a new idea in a piano lamp, which we are sure will be welcomed by all performers on the piano. This piano lamp is so constructed that the base can be set upon the top of the instrument and the lamp regulated by thumb screws and rods so that it throws the light in any direction. The illustration shows the method of placing it on the instrument. The base is weighted so as to sustain the weight of the lamp. It has adjustable shades which not only throw the light squarely upon the music page, but also screen it from the eyes of the performer. The lamp can be detached from the frame, to be filled or cleaned, and the entire outfit can be removed from the piano by simply lifting it with the hand. It is handsomely nickel plated throughout, is very ornamental and carefully and substantially made. It is fitted with a circular wick and throws a strong brilliant light.

No. 46C102 Price, complete .. **$3.25**

Weight, boxed and packed for shipment, 15 pounds.

WHAT OUR FRIENDS SAY ABOUT THE MAGNIFICENT VALUES WHICH WE ARE GIVING IN PIANOS.

Voluntary Testimonials From Just a Few of Those Who Have Purchased Pianos From Us in the Last Year.

What Our Customers Say About Our Pianos is the Best Evidence of Their Splendid Finish and Magnificent Tone.

EQUAL TO A KNABE AT $600.00.

We give below a testimonial from one of our enthusiastic customers, who is a business man in Columbus, Ohio, and not given to exaggeration in any way. We desire to call the attention of our customers to the difference in the two prices which the dealers made on the Knabe piano. $495.00 for cash and $600.00 on payments, being a difference of $105.00, which proves our assertion that dealers who sell instruments upon the installment plan must necessarily have their prices much higher than those who sell for cash. We do not know that we can add anything to this testimonial as it is complete in every respect. It is simply one of many which we receive from time to time.

Sears, Roebuck & Co., Chicago, Ill. Columbus, Ohio.

Dear Sirs:—I have already written you how well I like the Acme Cabinet Grand Piano, recently bought from you, but I would like again to state that according to my opinion the case is made and finished in the highest type of art. The tone is excellent and exquisite. I do not believe that I could have secured a better piano, no matter how much I paid or what I bought. That was my opinion the first day I received it, and it is still my opinion. In fact, the better I know the piano the better I like it. I would also add that the gentleman who selected the piano for me surely thoroughly understands pianos and piano construction. I do not believe that anyone else could have selected a piano for me that would suit me any better, and I thank him sincerely for the trouble to which he has gone. Miss Rose Lange, a young lady who is a fine pianist, has tried our piano very thoroughly. Last evening she told me that she liked my piano every bit as well as her own. She has a Knabe, which sells here for about $600.00 on payments, and for which she paid $495.00 spot cash. She says the case of my piano is much finer and more artistic than hers and that the action is easier and more responsive and the tone every bit as good as in her own piano. If you wish a recommendation at any time, refer any one to me, I will gladly tell them how much money they can save in buying a piano from you and how honorably you have treated me and of your very liberal terms of shipment. I will certainly recommend any one to get one of your pianos and thoroughly try it, knowing that you can suit them so well and save them so much money.

Respectfully yours, HENRY W. MUELLER.
662 Briggs St.

AS GOOD AS HIS NEIGHBOR'S PIANO WHICH COST $450.00.

The customer whose testimonial appears below took advantage of our great 30 Days Free Trial Offer, which gave him a splendid opportunity to compare his piano with the $450.00 instrument owned by his neighbor, and by reading the testimonial you will see that he found his piano in every way equal to the one purchased by his neighbor at $450.00.

Sears, Roebuck & Co., Chicago, Ill. Sterling, Nebraska.

Dear Sirs:—The Beckwith piano I received of you in January has given good satisfaction so far. We are well pleased with the same. We cannot see but what it is as good as our neighbor's, that cost $450.00. We are well pleased with the mandolin attachment. My neighbor's has no attachments. C. B. SMITH.

EQUAL TO PIANOS SOLD BY AGENTS AT FROM $350.00 TO $400.00.

Below we give a testimonial from another party, who after comparison and trial of our piano is willing to say that the piano we sold him is equal to those generally sold by agents at from $350.00 to $400.00. Such testimonials as these ought to convince any unprejudiced person that what we say in regard to the great saving which we can make is absolutely true in every respect.

Sears, Roebuck & Co., Chicago, Ill. Elco, Penn.

Dear Sirs:—The piano which I purchased from you reached me on June 16th, and after giving it a thorough test, both myself and friends, I am pleased to inform you that it gives satisfaction in every respect and is equal to pianos sold here by agents at $350.00 and $400.00. I would recommend it to anyone as being all that you say it is and would be pleased to have anyone who is going to purchase a piano refer to me either by letter or personally and I will gladly do what I can to aid you in making a sale. Thanking you for your past favors, I remain, yours truly, JAMES L. MOMETAIN.

EQUAL TO PIANOS SOLD BY DEALERS AT $350.00 AND BETTER TONED.

Below we give another testimonial from a customer who says that the piano we shipped him is equal to pianos sold by dealers at $350.00 and is much better in tone. Bear in mind, that the customer writes this letter entirely of his own accord and without any dictation from us in in any respect. We would be glad to have you write to the writer of any one of these testimonials and get his opinion of the merits of our instruments.

Sears, Roebuck & Co., Chicago, Ill. Three Rivers, Mich.

Dear Sirs:—I received the piano April 6th, all O. K. In appearance it is equal to a $350.00 Wellington, sold by a dealer here and better toned.

Yours respectfully, G. W. BARTO.

WOULD NOT PART WITH IT FOR ANY $300.00 PIANO IN TOWN.

It is the universal verdict of our customers as gleaned from the numerous voluntary letters which we receive that, they would not exchange the pianos which we have sold them for other pianos in the neighborhood which have cost much more in price.

Sears, Roebuck & Co., Chicago, Ill. St. Cloud, Minn.

Dear Sirs:—We received our piano and must say that we are more than pleased with it. I would not part with it for any $300.00 piano in town. In fact, we are well pleased with all our goods. I wish to thank you very much. I'll advise everybody to get their goods from Sears, Roebuck & Co.

Yours very truly, MISS M. STUCKE.

THE BECKWITH PALACE GRAND PIANO.

$115.00, A REDUCTION OF $20.00 FROM OUR LAST SEASON'S PRICE OF $135.00, is made possible by reason of our increased contract with the manufacturer, a contract which enables him to purchase his materials in much larger quantities and thus at lower prices. Under our policy of only one small profit above the actual manufacturing cost this saving all goes to the purchaser.

THE HIGHEST QUALITY OF MATERIALS only is used in this piano. The style and finish is unsurpassed, the terms most liberal, our guarantee the longest and strongest ever made. This is a $250.00 piano for $115.00.

RETAIL DEALERS easily secure $250.00 for a piano that is no better in tone, finish or quality to this, our Palace Grand at $115.00.

WE HAVE REDUCED THE PRICE on this piano to $115.00, exactly the difference in cost to us. Every advantage we gain by reason of increased sales or decreased cost of manufacture, we give our customers the benefit of. Any saving we can make by reason of economical handling goes direct to our customers in the way of lower prices.

WE SHIP THIS PIANO to any point in the United States under our great 30 days' free trial offer, which is explained in detail in the introductory pages of this department. Remember, you do not buy this, or any other Beckwith piano, until it has been thoroughly tried and tested in your own home for 30 days.

OUR...
25 Years' Binding Guarantee
which accompanies every piano, **Makes You Absolutely Safe at All Times.**

At our former price of $135.00 our beautiful **BECKWITH PALACE GRAND PIANO** represented a wonderful value, but at the new reduced price of **$115.00** it means the greatest value that can possibly be given at anywhere near our figures.

SOLD UNDER OUR GREAT 30 DAYS' FREE TRIAL OFFER, DESCRIBED ON PAGE 110.

Beckwith
Cabinet Grand.
Chicago.
$115.00
DEALERS ASK $275.00 TO $300.00 FOR THE EQUAL OF THIS INSTRUMENT.
No. 46C7
Order by Number.

The above is an illustration of our New No. 46C7 Beckwith Palace Grand Piano, $115.00, engraved from a photograph.

THE SOUNDING BOARD in this, and in all Beckwith pianos, is made of specially selected Canadian spruce of the finest quality. This is selected by experts in the business for its hardiness and closeness of grain, which, when thoroughly seasoned for years will vibrate more freely than any other wood and produce a very clear, singing tone. The sounding board of this and all Beckwith pianos is extra ribbed and reinforced, and is so constructed that it cannot crack or warp, which produces in these instruments the brilliant tone for which these pianos are noted.

THE MANDOLIN ATTACHMENT furnished free with each Beckwith piano, perfectly reproduces the tones of the mandolin, harp, zither, guitar, banjo, etc., and which is so widely advertised by other houses, who charge from $50.00 to $75.00 extra for placing it in their pianos. We make no charge for this added feature, which does not possess the metallic quality found in various other so called attachments. A very important benefit attending our attachment is the saving of the hammers from damage and wear by reason of the fact that when the attachment is in use the hammers strike against a soft surface. Many, however, do not care for the Mandolin Attachment and we will, if desired, with no extra cost, place in its stead the Muffler Attachment or Practice Pedal, an attachment of great utility as it deadens the sound at the will of the performer, a desirable feature during the hours of practice.

SIZE. 4 feet 7 inches high; 5 feet 1 inch wide; 2 feet 3 inches deep. Weight, boxed for shipment, 780 pounds.

CASE is veneered inside and outside with cross band sawed veneers, has handsome trusses and pilasters; all mouldings, trusses and pilasters in solid wood; continuous music desk with handsomely raised carved panels in very elegant and artistic designs; latest patent rolling fall board with nickel plated hinges, highly plated pedals and guards.

FINISH. We furnish these pianos in either English quarter sawed oak, French burled walnut or richly figured mahogany veneer, as desired. Very highly polished over seven coats of varnish, hand rubbed and equal in workmanship and finish to the very finest pianos made, regardless of price. When ordering be sure to state finish desired.

WREST PLANK OR PIN BLOCK to which the composition steel frame is bolted, has four thicknesses of maple veneers, the grain of each running in a different direction, making it impossible to warp or split.

SCALE. Full size, 7⅓ octaves, overstrung, three strings to each note except the wound bass strings, has ivory keys and ebony sharps, best quality of material throughout, including specially fine quality of felt in the hammers, nickel plated action rail and brackets, full length metal frame.

TONE is all that could be desired and is equal in volume and richness of quality to pianos which are retailed regularly at from $250.00 to $275.00. As the matter of tone is one of personal opinion, the instrument must be tried in order to be fully appreciated.

PRICE. At $115.00 we furnish this piano carefully boxed, including stool and instruction book, all delivered on board cars at Chicago.

WE ARE OFFERING A FINE PIANO LAMP on page 112 of this catalogue, and we would like the privilege of sending you one, as we know it will fill a long felt want in your home. The piano lamps which are now on the market are very costly, and so far as lighting up the music on a piano is concerned they are distinct failures. This lamp will set upon the top of your piano, and throw a direct light upon the music before you. We only ask $3.25 for it, and it will not only prove of great service to lighting the music page, but will also make a very nice ornament for your instrument.

..THE.. BECKWITH ARTISTS' CABINET GRAND PIANO REDUCED FROM $155.00 TO $138.00. ORDER BY No. 46C9

THE GREAT DEMAND for this piano has enabled us to reduce the price through the increase in the number manufactured, and the consequent saving effected by purchasing the materials which go to make this splendid instrument in much larger quantities, and for cash, without in the least detracting from its high standard and recognized superiority. A STRICTLY HIGH GRADE PIANO FOR

$138.00

REDUCED FROM $155.00

THIS ARTISTS' CABINET GRAND is the equal in quality of tone and construction to pianos which retail regularly at $300.00. We guarantee it to compare favorably with anything you can buy elsewhere at double the price.

Beckwith Cabinet Grand Chicago

CASE is made of the very best seasoned hardwood lumber, double cross band sawed veneers inside and outside. This is a protection against dampness, and is fully warranted not to be affected by atmospheric or climatic changes. **It is beautifully finished and decorated** with handsomely handcarved pilasters and trusses; all mouldings and trusses in solid wood.

SIZE. Our Artists' Cabinet Grand Piano is a very large piano, being 4 feet 9 inches high, 5 feet 2⅛ inches wide and 2 feet 3 inches deep, and will weigh, when boxed for shipment, 800 pounds.

No. 46C9

ORDER BY NUMBER

FINISH. We furnish this piano either in English quarter sawed oak veneer, elegant buried walnut veneer, or richly figured mahogany veneer, as desired. THE PRICE IS THE SAME, AND IN ORDERING BE SURE TO **MENTION THE VENEER WANTED.**

Sold under OUR GREAT 30-DAY FREE TRIAL OFFER described on page 110.

WREST PLANK OR PIN BLOCK to which the composition steel frame is bolted, has four thicknesses of maple veneers, the grain of each running in opposite directions, making it impossible to warp or split.

SOUNDING BOARD is made of the very best thoroughly seasoned Canadian spruce pine, especially adapted and prepared for high grade pianos, and is thoroughly braced by bars of Canadian spruce pine, which together have the most wonderful effect upon the tone of the piano.

SCALE is full size, 7⅓ octaves, overstrung bass, three strings to each note except wound bass strings, full length metal frame, and is so constructed as to produce a remarkably even quality of tone throughout.

FALL BOARD is of the Boston rolling fall pattern, the same as used on the highest grade pianos made.

TONE. This is the most important feature in a piano and can only be appreciated after a thorough test of the instrument. We guarantee our pianos to have **a rich, full and mellow tone,** considered the most desirable by all players.

MUSIC DESK is elaborately carved with finest raised carvings in the most artistic designs. The background of the carving is in dull finish, while the other space is very highly polished, producing the grand effect only found in instruments which you would pay a city dealer $300.00 to $350.00 for.

THE ACTION is made of the very best material throughout, with best quality of piano felt, nickel plated action rail and brackets, ivory keys, ebony sharps, patent repeating action, making it one of the most perfect upright piano actions it is possible to manufacture.

$138.00 IS OUR PRICE FOR OUR ARTISTS' CABINET GRAND PIANO,

including a HANDSOME PIANO SCARF, AN ELEGANT STOOL to match the piano in finish, and a FIRST CLASS INSTRUCTION BOOK, all boxed and delivered f. o. b. cars Chicago.

We have succeeded in procuring a piano lamp which fills a long felt want. You will find this lamp illustrated on page 112 of this catalogue, to which we call your attention. We only ask $3.25 for this splendid lamp, and at this price you cannot afford to be without one. Not only does it throw a direct stream of light upon the music, but it is also so arranged as to shade the light from the eyes of the performer. It is a great improvement upon the old style costly piano lamp, and we recommend it to your consideration.

OUR ARTISTS' CABINET GRAND PIANO IS FURNISHED WITH OUR PATENT MANDOLIN OR HARP ATTACHMENT.

The effect produced resembles that of a harp, mandolin or zither and does not possess the metallic quality found in various other so called attachments. A very important benefit attending our attachment is the saving of the hammers from damage and wear by reason of the fact that when the attachment is in use the hammers strike against a soft surface. We furnish the mandolin or harp attachment without extra charge. Many, however, do not care for the Mandolin Attachment, and we will, if desired, with no extra cost, place in its stead the Muffler Attachment or Practice Pedal, an attachment of great utility, as it deadens the sound at the will of the performer—a desirable feature during the hours of practice.

THE BECKWITH ACME CABINET GRAND CONCERT PIANO.

In offering this piano to our customers at $165.00, we do so with the assurance that it is equal, in every respect, to the pianos usually sold by others at from $350.00 to $400.00.

$165.00

With each one of these pianos, we send a written binding guarantee for 25 years, which fully protects the customer against any defects in material and workmanship which may appear within that period.

YOU ARE THINKING OF BUYING A PIANO, why should you go to your local dealer or agent and pay him from $350.00 to $400.00 for a piano that does not cost over $140.00 or $150.00, to manufacture. while we can sell you an instrument of the same grade at $165.00, which is the manufacturers' price with only our one small percentage of profit added? The $350.00 or $400.00, which you pay your local dealer or agent is made up mostly of the profits made by the different dealers, through whose hands the piano must pass before it reaches you. These profits are always exceedingly high, and while they more than double the price of the instrument, they do not in any way add to its musical qualities or value.

OUR GREAT THIRTY-DAY TRIAL OFFER

enables you to fully examine and test this beautiful instrument in your home before you finally decide to accept it. For the purpose of giving it a thorough trial and test, we will be glad to have you call in any musician who is unbiased and will give you his honest opinion of the instrument. If you, together with your friends, do not decide that this is the greatest bargain in a piano that you ever saw, and fully equal to instruments which are being sold at from $350.00 to $400.00 in your community, then you are at liberty to return the instrument, we will cheerfully refund your money in full and pay the entire expense of transportation both ways.

WE DO NOT ASK YOU TO SEND US ANY MONEY

Simply deposit the price of the instrument with your banker or express agent, send us a receipt like the one shown on page 110 showing that you have deposited the money, and we will immediately ship you one of these splendid pianos upon thirty days' trial. Should you have the slightest fault to find with the instrument, in any way, we do not ask you to keep it, but you can return it to us, your banker will refund your money, and we will pay the entire expense of transportation and cartage.

Beckwith Acme Cabinet Grand Concert Piano.
No. 46C11 Price, $165.00. ALWAYS ORDER BY NUMBER.

DIMENSIONS.
Our Acme Cabinet Grand Piano is extra large, being one of the largest upright pianos made. It is 4 feet 10 inches high, 5 feet 3¼ inches wide and 2 feet 3½ inches deep. The great size of this piano allows for a greater length of string and a larger sounding board, which gives the piano great volume and depth of tone. These features make this piano equal in volume to any concert grand piano on the market. This instrument is adapted as well for concerts and puplic halls as it is for parlor use, and so popular is it becoming for this purpose that it has been, up to the present time, installed in hundreds of puplic halls throughout the country. Not only does its great size make it particularly adaptable for this purpose, but the fact that it is constructed of the very best material and fully guaranteed makes it the safest piano that can possibly be bought for public purposes.

ACTION.
This piano is a three string unison in the treble and a two string unison in the bass with the exception of the 12 last bass strings. The bass strings are copper wound, and made of the very best imported piano wire. The action is the very finest that can be made. The metal frame is durably and solidly constructed, and the scale is perfection itself.

CASE.
We can furnish this piano in quarter sawed oak, burled walnut or San Domingo Mahogany. It is double veneered inside and outside and given an extremely high and durable finish. Much that is said on page 118 in regard to our Beckwith Special Concert Grand is also applicable to this instrument.

MANDOLIN ATTACHMENT.
We furnish a mandolin attachment with this piano entirely free of extra charge, or if the customer desires we can furnish as a substitute for this attachment the Beckwith Practice Pedal which muffles the tone of the instrument while the student is practicing.

WEIGHT.
Properly boxed and packed for shipment, this piano will weigh about 825 pounds.

FREE.
With each one of these pianos we send free, a very fine stool, constructed of wood, with handsome turned legs, brass claws with glass ball feet, a handsome piano scarf, and a complete instruction book.

DO NOT FAIL TO EXAMINE THE PIANO LAMP
which we are illustrating on page 112 of this catalogue, as we assure you that it is just exactly what you have been looking for for a long time. It is a vast improvement over the old style of piano lamp, which, while it was very costly, utterly failed to give the necessary light. This lamp will throw the light directly upon the music page, and is so arranged with shades that the light is shaded from the eyes of the performer. The lamp is handsomely nickel plated and finished, and is certainly a great bargain at the price.

BECKWITH SPECIAL CONCERT GRAND PIANO, $195.00

POSITIVELY THE HIGHEST GRADE PIANO MADE, ENTIRELY NEW IN DESIGN, BEAUTIFUL IN FINISH AND SPLENDID IN TONE. OFFERED IN RESPONSE TO A DEMAND FOR A PIANO OF THE HIGHEST GRADE TO BE SOLD BY OUR GREAT MONEY SAVING METHOD.

A PIANO FOR WHICH THE DEALER WILL ASK YOU FROM $450.00 TO $500.00.

WE OFFER THIS INSTRUMENT as the very highest possible attainment in the manufacture of pianos, and as an instrument which will compare favorably with the very highest class of concert pianos now on the market. As so many of our customers have requested us to furnish them a piano of extra high quality under our liberal terms of shipment, and by our great money saving method of sale we have made every effort and have at last succeeded in securing a piano which will meet every requirement of the most exact musican, both for parlor and concert use.

ONE GLANCE AT THE ENGRAVING WILL CONVINCE YOU that so far as appearance is concerned, this piano is equal in every respect to the very highest grade of concert pianos now on the market; but no engraving, however fine it may be, can give you any idea of the beautiful finish and splendid tone qualities possessed by this instrument. The great length of string and large sounding board area which this piano possesses, give it a tone at once sympathetic and mellow and of great depth and volume.

BY READING CAREFULLY THE DETAILED DESCRIPTION on the opposite page, you will see at once that every point in the manufacture of this instrument has been well considered, and that nothing but the very best materials and workmanship enter into its construction. In the manufacture of the case we use nothing but the very highest class of material. We use the very finest kind of sawed veneer and use great care to select only that wood which is the most nicely figured and has the most beautiful grain. The case of each one of these pianos is given an extremely high finish, which can only be secured by many coats of varnish, applied one upon another, allowing intervals of from two to four weeks' time between the applications of the different coats. It is a fact not generally known to our customers, that time is a great element in the manufacture of a good piano, and that it requires from 70 to 90 days to put the beautiful finish on the cases of the Beckwith Special Concert Grand Pianos. Not only is the finish and construction of the case given careful attention, but the construction of the action also is looked after with extreme care. You will find a full description of this action on the opposite page.

REMEMBER that we ship this piano under the same liberal terms of shipment that we ship all of our other pianos. We sell it under our great 30 days' free trial offer, and allow it to be returned at any time within one year, should it prove unsatisfactory for any reason. We also ship it with our 25 years' binding guarantee, which fully protects you against any defect in material or workmanship.

BECKWITH SPECIAL CONCERT GRAND PIANO **$195.00**

No. 46C13
Order by Number

Height, 4 ft. 10 in.
Length, 5 ft. 6 in.
Width, 2 ft. 4 in.
Shipping Weight, 1000 pounds.

IN PURCHASING THIS PIANO FROM US you secure two distinct and well defined values. The first is the value which the piano takes from the high class workmanship and skill, and the excellent material which enters into its construction. This is the only value for which we ask you to pay. We ask you $195.00 for this splendid piano, and this amount represents the cost of this material and labor, with but our one small profit added. Another value which you obtain is the value which the instrument takes from the genius and skill of the man who drew and perfected the scale, designed and regulated the action, and combined all these points so skillfully as to make the beautiful tone of the instrument possible. **For this value we charge you absolutely nothing.** Most piano manufacturers add a large amount to every piano they sell to pay them for this value but all we charge you for is the material and labor with a small profit added to pay us for handling the instrument. Up to the present time we are the only piano dealers who have been willing to sacrifice the profit usually made on the second of the two values above mentioned. While we do not charge our customers for this value, we absolutely guarantee that it is present in every one of these pianos and in the very highest degree.

IF YOU WILL PURCHASE ONE OF THESE PIANOS under our liberal terms of shipment, and give it a thorough and impartial trial, we believe you will agree with us that the value which we give to you absolutely free is in reality worth much more than the value for which we charge you $195.00. It is possible for a piano to be constructed of the very finest material and be made by the most skilled workmen and still be entirely deficient in that great requisite which all musical instruments should possess and which is known as "tone." In fact there are many well known pianos on the market to day made of the very best material, by the most skilled workmen, of beautiful finish and artistic appearance, which utterly fail to possess a tone of any sweetness or flexibility. You will pay from $450.00 to $700.00 for one of these instruments, simply because the maker has had in the past a high reputation for making excellent pianos. The piano for which you pay from $600.00 to $700.00 in all probability did not cost much over $160.00 to manufacture originally. Most of the additional $440.00 or $540.00 which you have paid is made up of intermediate dealers' profits and expenses, and the large profit which the manufacturer must have for his past reputation.

THE BECKWITH SPECIAL CONCERT GRAND PIANO.

THE HIGHEST ATTAINMENT IN PIANO MAKING.

No. 46C13 Price - - - - - - - - - - - - $195.00

AS ILLUSTRATED ON OPPOSITE PAGE.

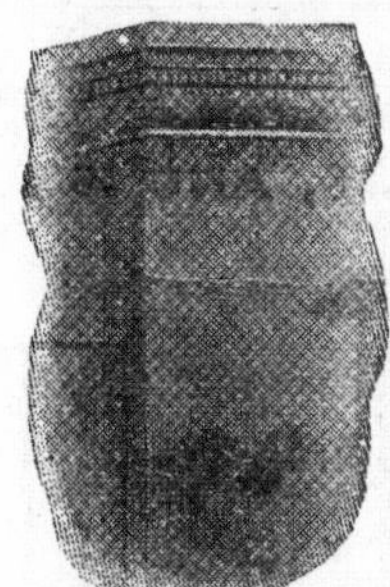

Fig. 1.

THE CASE. **The case of this piano is massive and artistic in design.** It is ornamented and tastefully decorated with handsomely executed hand carvings. The design shown on the opposite page is entirely new and was adopted only after the keenest competition on the part of several of the best piano designers in the country. It is fitted with rolling fall cover with continuous hinges and has a handsome automatic two-thirds music desk. We believe it to be the most elegant piano that has yet been offered to the public, and will be glad to have you see it and examine it for yourself. The keyboard is supported by massive double pilasters and the pedals and pedal guards are of ornamental metallic design beautifully nickel plated and polished. The panelling on the case is of the most artistic kind and combines very nicely with the tasty carvings with which the case is ornamented. Each one of these cases is given an extremely high finish which takes from 70 to 90 days to apply. Each case is double veneered inside and out, and cross banded so that it can not crack, warp or split. Cross banding means that the first or inner layer of veneer is glued to the base wood of the case under an enormous pressure, while the second or outer layer is glued in a like manner across the grain of the inner veneer, so that it will not be affected by climatic changes, no matter how severe. The engraving which accompanies this, marked Figure 1, shows how the veneer is placed on the piano case. These pianos are given a very high finish, each coat of varnish being allowed to become thoroughly dry, then being rubbed down before the next coat of varnish is applied. These successive coats of varnish give the case that smooth, glassy appearance so much admired in all fine furniture. As this varnish is perfectly transparent, the beautiful grain of the wood shows through it to good advantage. The difficulty with most cheap pianos is that the finish of the case is slighted and only about one-half the number of coats of varnish applied as will be found upon our pianos. **The design of these cases is everything that can be desired and will harmonize with the furnishings of any parlor.** We furnish them in English quarter sawed oak, French burled walnut, and San Domingo mahogany. Each case is thoroughly hand rubbed and carefully inspected before being turned out of the factory.

THE PIN BLOCK. **The pin block, which is one of the most important features of the piano, is that part of the piano which is built in the upper part of the foundation or back frame, and in which the tuning pins are set.** In this piano the pin block is made of five distinct layers of rock maple with the grain of each layer running in an opposite direction. See Figure 2. This pin block is made extra strong for the reason that in this grand piano the strain upon the tuning pins is much increased. The different layers of wood present to the tuning pin an end wood surface which holds them as tight as though they were in a vise.

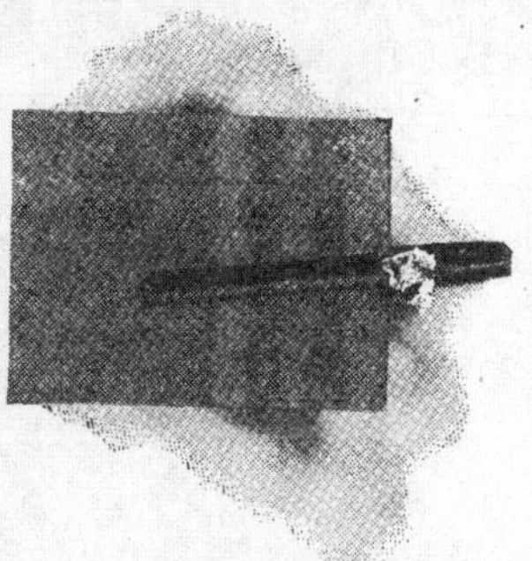

Fig. 2.

Fig. 3.

THE METAL FRAME. **As the great strain in all pianos comes upon the pin block and metal frame,** these parts have received special care at the hands of the maker. The engraving (Fig. 3) shows the metal frame of the piano and illustrates how it it is braced and reinforced to stand the strain of about 19 tons which comes upon it when the piano is tuned to international pitch. Our 25 years guarantee covers this metal frame and all other vital parts of the instrument, so you are protected at all times against any defect that might appear in the instrument.

THE SOUNDING BOARD. **A very important part of a piano is the sounding board. The piano may have a perfect scale, a fine quality of strings, good hammers, strong metal frame, the finest grade of material in every respect,** but if the sounding board is not good the piano will lack that volume and sweetness of tone which is one of the first essentials of a good instrument. The strings in all pianos are strung over the sounding board so as to take advantage of the vibrations of the wood, which amplifies and sweetens the tone of the strings. In this piano the sounding board is made of the best selected Canadian spruce pine, which is thoroughly kiln and air dried until the vegetable fibre becomes hardened and the wood becomes as resonant as the top of an old Cremona violin. In some pianos the sounding board has a great umber of ribs on it, and these are necessary to protect it against warping or splitting, but no more of these should be placed on the sounding board than are absolutely necessary to protect it against these dangers. In the Beckwith pianos there are just enough ribs placed on the sounding board, no more and no less, and the exact number of these is mathematically determined by study and experience. We guarantee that the sounding board of this piano will not become weak or cracked, as is often the case with other pianos, and if this instrument is compared with other pianos costing from $450.00 to $500.00, we know that the customer will find that in volume and sweetness of tone the Beckwith is far superior to any other piano made.

THE ACTION. **By action we mean that part of the piano which in any way assists by mechanical movements in producing the tone.** By a special contract with the manufacturers we have made arrangements to have only the very highest grade actions placed in these instruments. As a result, the Beckwith piano is famous for the evenness of its touch and the quickness with which it responds to the efforts of the performer. It has what is known as the repeating action, which brings the hammers back in position to repeat with lightning like rapidity. On most pianos it will be found that a succession of notes struck with rapidity upon one key will produce nothing more than a blur or succession of blending tones, but when struck upon a key of the Beckwith, the performer will find that each tone is distinct and marked, and that it is impossible to strike the notes with such rapidity as to cause them to blur or blend with each other. Another point that we desire to make in connection with the action in this piano, and all of our other pianos, is that the different connecting points, are so felted with the very finest kind of wool felt that they cannot come loose and rattle; a common fault with most other pianos. **Every part of this action is thoroughly inspected and tested before it leaves the factory.** We always like to have our customers examine the different parts and actions in our pianos because we know that when they have done this they will be more than satisfied that we are selling them instruments for about one-third less than they can purchase them elsewhere.

THE SCALE. **The underlying or fundamental principle upon which all pianos are built, is the scale.** This is a correct and precisely mathematical division of all the tones and semi-tones which go to make up the entire 7⅓ octaves of the instrument. This gives each particular string its proper length and determines the exact position which they shall occupy across the bridges and sounding board. The scale of this instrument is accurate and true, and we defy the most expert performer to find a break in it from the highest to the lowest tone. The scale in the Beckwith pianos has been pronounced by eminent authorities to be admirable in every respect.

THE HAMMERS. **The hammer is another important part of the piano, and the customer who would make a purchase judiciously, should see that the hammers of the piano come up to the standard fixed by experience and study.** The hammer is that part of the action which strikes the string and causes it to vibrate. But it is something more than this. It is a delicate piece of mechanical work which must be built precisely right and of just the right material and proper balance to produce the tone which is desired. The illustration (Fig. 4.) shows one of the Beckwith piano hammers. It will be noticed that the head is made of two layers of felt. The layer next to the wooden head is formed of very hard firm felt, and the outside or white layer is made of felt of softer and finer texture. If the head was all of the hard felt, it would produce a tone hard and unresponsive, but the soft outside layer of felt striking the strings causes them to vibrate in a pleasing and harmonious manner.

Fig. 4.

Fig. 5.

THE STRINGS. **This instrument has an over strung scale, and is what is known as a three string unison, each treble note having three strings, all of which are tuned in unison.** Figure 5 very nicely illustrates the way the instrument is strung. Each one of the strings placed in this piano is thoroughly guaranteed and properly tested before it is placed in position. The bass or heavier part of the scale is what is called a two string unison. All strings in the Beckwith Pianos are of the very finest quality of Poehlmann Piano Steel Wire. Each string is tested for strength, size, and perfect formation before being accepted. They must all be free from any trace of phosphorus, or sulphur, otherwise they would be brittle or liable to crack. An imperfect string produces an imperfect tone, and destroys the uniformity of tone so much desired in a fine piano. **A good string is a very important part of a piano, as the string when struck by the hammer vibrates and produces the tone.** The sounding board vibrates in harmony with the string and increases the volume of tone, therefore, if the string is poor the piano will produce a poor quality of tone. The bass strings in the Beckwith Pianos are all copper wound.

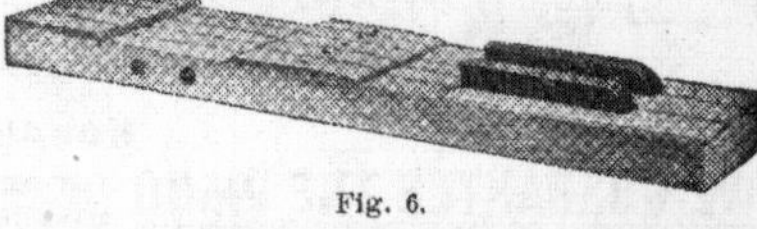

Fig. 6.

THE KEYS. **Figure 6 illustrates five Beckwith keys and shows how they are constructed.** The keys of a good piano must be constructed of thoroughly air and kiln dried material, and the ivory of the white keys must be glued to the wood under enormous pressure or they will become loose in time and fall off. This could never occur on a Beckwith piano because each one of these keys is glued separately and thoroughly tested before being placed in the piano. The keys are all so nicely balanced that they fall back to their positions instantly after being struck by the performer. To properly preserve the "balance" and insure elasticity of touch, the keys are weighted with small lead weights inserted into the key shank back of the pivot, thus allowing the key when released to rise instantly to its normal position ready for the "repeat." The white keys are covered with genuine ivory and the black keys are made of ebony, because this wood has a grain so fine that it is imperceptible to the touch.

THE MANDOLIN ATTACHMENT AND THE MUFFLER OR PRACTICE PEDAL.

WE FURNISH WITH ALL OF OUR PIANOS **without extra charge of any sort, a mandolin attachment which reproduces the tones of a harp, mandolin, guitar, etc.** This is an attachment which is so widely advertised by other manufacturers, who do not hesitate to charge from $25.00 to $50.00 extra for it. This attachment in the Beckwith pianos does not produce the metallic tone found in most other attachments of the same nature. One great advantage which this mandolin attachment possesses is that the hammers of the piano are protected from wear during its use because they strike against a soft surface, thus insuring them against damage and wear. It is so arranged that it can be used when desired and when not in use can be placed in such a position that it has no effect whatever upon the action, hammers or strings. Many piano teachers do not care for the mandolin attachment and in such cases we are always glad to place in its stead the muffler or practice pedal, a very excellent attachment and one which is very highly appreciated by music teachers from the fact that it deadens the tone when the pupil is practicing without, however, interfering with the action.

No. 46C13 **Beckwith Special Concert Grand Piano.** Price.. **$195.00**

THE BECKWITH HOME FAVORITE PIANO

A FULL SIZE GUARANTEED PIANO.

WE OFFER OUR HOME FAVORITE PIANO AT	$89.00	TO SHOW HOW GOOD A PIANO CAN BE FURNISHED AT A PRICE NEVER BEFORE HEARD OF.

IT COSTS THE REGULAR RETAIL DEALER OR AGENT MORE TO BUY ONE OF HIS PIANOS THAN WE ARE ASKING YOU TO PAY FOR THE INSTRUMENT AT THE FACTORY.....

OUR HOME FAVORITE PIANO IS A FULL SIZE INSTRUMENT, SUBSTANTIALLY BUILT, AND IS A MOST REMARKABLE INSTRUMENT AT THE PRICE.

Agents and Dealers cannot sell you an instrument the equal of this for less than $200.00.

See our Special $1.00 Deposit and 30-Day Free Trial Plan Offer on Page 110.

No. 4601 OUR $89.00 HOME FAVORITE PIANO. ORDER BY NUMBER.

WE GUARANTEE THE PIANO for only 5 years. It is the greatest value ever seen or heard of; in fact, such an instrument cannot be duplicated elsewhere at anything like the price at which we offer it; but it is not an instrument that we can guarantee as we do our other higher grade pianos, which are all guaranteed for 25 years. It will prove a serviceable instrument and should stand the test of from five to ten years' use.

THE MANDOLIN ATTACHMENT furnished in this piano enables the performer to faithfully reproduce the tones of harp, mandolin, guitar, etc., and for this patent attachment we make no extra charge. If this is not desired we will, with no extra cost, place in its stead the Muffler or Practice Pedal.

THIS PIANO IS A MOST WONDERFUL BARGAIN

But it is not so large as our other pianos, hence has not the same volume of tone. The tone is, however, very strong for the size of the piano. To enable us to offer a piano at this price, it is necessary to save wherever possible, hence the sounding board, while very strong, is not so large as in our other instruments; the metal plate is smaller, the strings are not so long, nor is the hammer so heavy, but it is EQUAL to pianos sold by MUSIC DEALERS for about $200.00.

SIZE OF PIANO. Height, 4 feet 6 inches; width, 2 feet 2 inches; length, 61 inches. Weight, boxed for shipment, 750 pounds.

THE CASE of this piano is made of solid wood, finished in mahogany or burled walnut. Extreme cold or other climatic changes are liable to cause the finish to check or peel in the course of time. We, therefore, cannot guarantee the finish on these cheaper pianos to stand, but otherwise this has no effect upon the tone or durability of the instrument.

THE ACTION is well made and a very good quality of material is used throughout. The action in this piano is as good as will be found in pianos sold by other dealers at $150.00 to $200.00.

THE SCALE is 7⅓ octaves and has overstrung bass.

THE TONE is always a matter of taste, and in this piano we endeavor to produce a tone which we believe will please most anyone. It is sweet and melodious and of ample power for all ordinary requirements.

WE SEND FREE WITH EACH PIANO a complete instruction book and a good piano stool, and if you favor us with your order and are not entirely satisfied with the instrument after you have tried it for **30 DAYS IN YOUR OWN HOME**, we will cheerfully refund your money in full. You certainly cannot afford to purchase elsewhere until you have seen and tried one of our pianos when you are assured that you will not be out one cent in the transaction if everything does not prove entirely satisfactory.

WE WISH TO CALL YOUR ATTENTION TO THE HANDSOME NEW PIANO LAMP which we are illustrating on page 112 of this catalogue. This lamp will prove a fine addition to your piano, and, at the price which we fix on it, $3.25, is certainly a bargain. It fills a long felt want, and avoids the purchase of a piano lamp, for which you will have to give from $10.00 to $25.00 at your local dealers.

OUR SPLENDID LINE OF BECKWITH ORGANS.

ON THE FOLLOWING PAGES **you will find illustrated a magnificent line of reed organs which have stood the test of time and given universal satisfaction.** Our years of experience have taught us that the Beckwith organs are the most satisfactory instruments we can offer to our customers. We could not give our customers full value for their money in any other line of organs now on the market, as in order to sell any other line it would be necessary for us to quote the same high prices that other dealers quote, and in charging our customers these high prices we would not be able to give them full value for the money they pay. **All the organs illustrated on the following pages are manufactured under our direct supervision,** so that we are absolutely certain at all times that the material and workmanship which enter into their construction are the very best that can be procured. We are thus able to guarantee each one of these instruments for a period of twenty-five years, a much longer period than other reed organs are expected to last. It will be seen from this that our customers are always sure of getting a fine instrument for their money and that they will take no chances in purchasing one of these splendid organs. By handling this line we are also able to ship the instrument direct from our factory to the customer, enabling him to purchase it at the manufacturer's price with only our one small margin of profit added to that price. In this way customers can purchase one of these organs at a lower price than his local dealer has to pay the jobber for the same grade of organ at wholesale.

THE ILLUSTRATIONS **on the following pages are wood cuts, made from photographs of the instruments, and guaranteed to be exact reproductions, so far as design of case is concerned,** but the true value of an organ consists of the action or interior arrangements, and this is something that no photograph can show. Our twenty-five-year guarantee covers everything that goes into the organ, the action as well as the case, so that you are fully protected in your purchase and need have no fear that the interior arrangement of the organ will give out with years of use. When a local agent brings an instrument to your home, you can see the case and examine it closely, but the interior arrangement of the organ is something for which you have to take his word absolutely. If you purchase the instrument and find, after a short period of use, that it fails to come up to the standard you have no redress; but, if you purchase one of our instruments, and it should prove unsatisfactory for the same reason, we stand ready to make it good and to satisfy you in every particular. **We know that we can save you from $15.00 to $25.00 upon any organ shown in this book** and all we ask is an opportunity to ship one of these instruments to you with the understanding that if you do not find that you are saving at least this much you are at liberty to return it to us, and we will refund your money and pay the freight charges both ways. You take no chances whatever in giving us an order for this instrument, because we make you the sole judge of its good qualities, and we do not compel you to keep it unless you are perfectly satisfied in every particular.

OUR LOW PRICES. **The reason why we can make such extremely low prices on these organs is very easily and simply explained.** We ship the instruments directly from the factory to you. You are thus able to purchase them at the manufacturers' price with only our one small margin of profit added. When you purchase an instrument in the regular way from a local dealer, it has already passed through the hands of several different dealers, and the price you pay for it includes the profit which every dealer must make, and also the expense which these dealers are put to in handling and selling it. You avoid the payment of all these profits and expenses when you purchase from us. It is only necessary for you to compare our organs and prices with those offered you by other dealers to prove that this is true. The organ trade of the country, until up to a recent period, has been in the hands of a few firms, who found it expedient to establish and maintain extremely high prices, because their method of handling the instruments was so expensive. The instruments after leaving the factory, were passed through the hands of several different dealers before they finally reached the customer. Each one of these dealers had to make a profit on the instruments, and all of these profits were included in the price which the purchaser finally had to pay. As a consequence the prices on organs were extremely high. **This method of sale is still in use, and the people have been paying high prices for organs for such a long time, that they have grown to believe that it is necessary to do so in order to purchase a good instrument.** We think that we have pretty thoroughly proved that we can furnish a high class organ at considerably less than the price which the ordinary dealer can afford to make on it. Our great purchasing power enables us to make the most advantageous contracts with the manufacturers, by which we are able to purchase the instruments at much lower prices than any other dealer can obtain. **We give our customers the full benefit of these low prices,** thus enabling them to purchase from us high class organs at a less price than the dealer can purchase them from his wholesaler or manufacturer. This insures an immense saving in the prices of the organs, and at the same time guarantees to the customer full value for the price he pays. The fact that we guarantee every one of our organs for twenty-five years should satisfy our customers that we have not reduced the price at the expense of the instruments themselves.

TERMS OF SHIPMENT. **We ship all of these organs on exactly the same terms that we ship our pianos,** and these terms are fully set forth on page 110, of this catalogue. We trust that you will read them carefully before selecting the instrument desired, as the knowledge of them will prevent delay in shipment and misunderstanding as well. We also give the same guarantee with our organs that we give with our pianos, and we do not ask our customers to take any chances whatever, as we assume every responsibility and take every risk involved in the sale. We have a factory in St. Paul, Minnesota, and one in Louisville, Kentucky, so that we make our shipments to the different points in the country at the least expense in freight charges. Our customers may rest assured that we will ship their organs to them by the cheapest possible route, so as to save them all unnecessary freight charges.

FREE. **We send, free, with each instrument, a fine stool,** to match the case of the organ, and a complete instruction book, by the aid of which any one can learn to play the instrument without the assistance of a teacher.

OUR NEW SPECIAL ORGAN CATALOGUE. **We would recommend especially that you make your selection of an organ from those given in this big catalogue rather than cause a delay by writing for our free special organ catalogue,** because we guarantee that any organ you may order from these pages will reach you in perfect condition and prove in every way satisfactory, and that you will find it a much better organ than you can buy elsewhere at anything like the price we offer. We also guarantee that you will make a large saving in the cost, and if you do not find this to be so, you can return the organ to us at any time, within 30 days, and we will immediately and cheerfully refund your money and pay the freight charges both ways. If, however, you are unable to make a selection from the illustrations and descriptions shown in this catalogue, and you feel that you would like to have better illustrations and more complete descriptions, then we will be glad to send you a copy of our Special Organ Catalogue. This catalogue will be sent to you upon request, postage prepaid, and it will only be necessary for you to send us a postal card in order to obtain it. Simply say: "Please send me your Catalogue of Organs," and the book will be sent by return mail.

ORGAN VALUE. **We seldom advise our customers as to which organ they should purchase.** The difference in prices which we quote for the different grades of organs, simply represents a difference in cost of the material and workmanship at the factory, and not the difference in the profit which we make on them. We add only one small margin of profit to the price of the organ no matter what it may cost us at the factory, and when we ask you to pay a higher price for one organ than for another it does not mean that we are making a larger profit on that organ, but that we are giving you a much better organ for your money. Under these circumstances we feel that we can advise our customers always to purchase the organ which represents the highest price, as they will be sure to get a much better organ and one with which they will be much better satisfied.

THE BECKWITH ACTIONS. **We are giving below a list of the different actions with which our reed organs are fitted,** and if you desire a description of any action you should always refer to this page. You will understand that the Beckwith actions are absolutely guaranteed and nothing but the best material and workmanship go into their construction. They are made of thoroughly kiln and air dried wood, felted with best quality wool felt and are high grade in every particular.

ACTION A—FIVE OCTAVES.

Four sets of reeds, two sets of two octaves and two sets of three octaves each, divided as follows:

1 set of Principal Reeds, 24 notes.
1 set of Melodia Reeds, 37 notes.
1 set of Diapason Reeds, 24 notes.
1 set of Celeste Reeds, 37 notes.
122 reeds in all.

Eleven stops, as follows:

Diapason.	Principal.
Celeste.	Cremona.
Diapason Forte.	Principal Forte.
Treble Coupler.	Bass Coupler.
Vox Humana.	Dulciana.
Melodia.	

ACTION A—SIX OCTAVES.

Same as above, except that it has one octave greater compass, the two treble sets containing four octaves each instead of three. 146 reeds in all.

ACTION B—FIVE OCTAVES.

Five sets of reeds. Two sets of two octaves each, and three sets of three octaves each, divided as follows:

1 set of Principal Reeds, 24 notes.
1 set of Melodia Reeds, 37 notes.
1 set of Diapason Reeds, 24 notes.
1 set of Celeste Reeds, 37 notes.
1 set of Flute Reeds, 37 notes.
159 reeds in all.

Thirteen stops, as follows:

Diapason.	Principal.
Dulciana.	Melodia.
Celeste.	Cremona.
Diapason Forte.	Principal Forte.
Treble Coupler.	Bass Coupler.
Vox Humana.	Viola.
Flute.	

ACTION B—SIX OCTAVES.

Same as above, except that it has one octave greater compass, the two treble sets containing four octaves each instead of three. 195 reeds in all.

ACTION C—FIVE OCTAVES.

Six sets of reeds. Three sets of two octaves each, and three sets of three octaves each, divided as follows:

1 set of Principal Reeds, 24 notes.
1 set of Melodia Reeds, 37 notes.
1 set of Diapason Reeds, 24 notes.
1 set of Celeste Reeds, 37 notes.
1 set of Flute Reeds, 37 notes.
1 set of Bourdon Reeds, 25 notes.
184 reeds in all.

Fifteen stops, as follows:

Diapason.	Principal.
Dulciana.	Melodia.
Celeste.	Cremona.
Viola.	Flute.
Diapason Forte.	Bourdon.
Treble Coupler.	Dulcet.
Vox Humana.	Principal Forte.
	Bass Coupler.

ACTION D—FIVE OCTAVES.

Eight sets of reeds. Four sets of two octaves each, four sets of three octaves each, divided as follows:

1 set of Principal Reeds, 24 notes.
1 set of Melodia Reeds, 37 notes.
1 set of Diapason Reeds, 24 notes.
1 set of Celeste Reeds, 37 notes.
1 set of Flute Reeds, 37 notes.
1 set of Bourdon Reeds, 24 notes.
1 set of Clarionet Reeds, 24 notes.
1 set of Cornet Echo Reeds, 37 notes.
244 reeds in all.

Seventeen stops, as follows:

Diapason.	Principal.
Dulciana.	Melodia.
Celeste.	Cremona.
Viola.	Flute.
Diapason Forte.	Principal Forte.
Treble Coupler.	Bass Coupler.
Clarionet.	Cornet Echo.
Bourdon.	Cornet.
Vox Humana.	

ACTION D—SIX OCTAVES.

Same as five octaves, except that it has one octave greater compass, the four treble sets containing four octaves each instead of three. 292 reeds in all.

ACTION E—FIVE OCTAVES.

Nine sets of reeds. Four sets of two octaves each, four sets of three octaves each, and one set of one octave, divided as follows:

1 set of Principal Reeds, 24 notes.
1 set of Melodia Reeds, 37 notes.
1 set of Diapason Reeds, 24 notes.
1 set of Celeste Reeds, 37 notes.
1 set of Flute Reed, 37 notes.
1 set of Bourdon Reeds, 24 notes.
1 set of Clarionet Reeds, 24 notes.
1 set of Cornet Echo Reeds, 37 notes.
1 set of Sub Bass Reeds, 13 notes.
257 reeds in all.

Eighteen stops, as follows:

Diapason.	Principal.
Dulciana.	Melodia.
Celeste.	Cremona.
Viola.	Flute.
Diapason Forte.	Principal Forte.
Treble Coupler.	Bass Coupler.
Clarionet.	Cornet Echo.
Sub Bass.	Bourdon.
Dulcet.	Cornet.

ACTION E—SIX OCTAVES.

Same as above, except that it has one octave greater compass, the four treble sets containing four octaves instead of three, 305 reeds in all.

To ascertain the number of **REEDS AND STOPS** in any of the **INSTRUMENTS** described in this catalogue,

ALWAYS REFER TO THIS PAGE.

DID YOU VISIT THE WORLD'S FAIR AT ST. LOUIS?

Thousands of visitors who attended the World's Fair at St. Louis last year will remember the beautiful exhibit of Beckwith Organs in the Liberal Arts' Building, which exhibit was in charge of the Adler Organ Company. The remarkable thing about this exhibit was not only that the booth was the handsomest in the building, the decorations the most beautiful, and that it was one of the most extensive exhibits of this character at the Fair, but that the prices placed upon the instruments were lower by half than those offered by any other exhibit of the same character on the grounds. This naturally attracted the attention of the thousands of people who were interested in organs, either as purchasers, manufacturers or dealers. This exhibit established a record in the organ trade which has never been equaled by any other concern in the organ business, and we predict that it will be a long time before any other concern will ever approach this standard, because the immense trade which we have established in organs has given us such a prestige that we have now a greater buying advantage than any other concern in the business.

But the most astonishing thing in connection with the exhibit was the high quality of the instruments there shown. Musical experts from all over the world, attracted to the exhibit by the remarkably low prices quoted and wonderfully high quality possessed by the instruments, were loud in their praise of this splendid line of reed organs. The fact that the Adler Organ Company, in charge of the exhibit, secured many diplomas and medals of honor from the judges at the fair, establishes the fact beyond dispute that the Beckwith Organs are superior to any on the market. The engraving which we show of the exhibit gives but a very poor idea of the beautiful design of the booth and its handsome trimmings. This exhibit was conducted at a great expense, with the hope that the thousands of our friends who might visit the fair could examine and see for themselves the high quality of organs which we are offering at such extremely low prices. As the judges who passed upon the merits of the different exhibits at the fair were men of discrimination and judgment, absolutely impartial and unprejudiced, the fact is established beyond any question that **the Beckwith Organs are today the very best reed organs which can be manufactured.** Of course, those who have already purchased organs from us have had this fact proven to them beyond a doubt, but to our friends who are hesitating in regard to the purchase of one of these instruments, we will simply say that the award of the judges at the fair should be sufficient to remove all of your doubts. It has always been our policy not to ask the customer to take our word for anything we say in regard to the merits of the instruments, but to give us an opportunity to prove to him by actual trial and examination that the instruments are everything that we claim for them and that we can save him from $25.00 to $40 00, according to the grade of instrument which he purchases. Following out this policy we have from time to time, printed testimonials from purchasers all over the country who have bought these organs and have expressed themselves as being more than delighted with the quality of the instruments and fully satisfied of the fact that we have saved them the amount we promised on their purchase. We now call attention, as a further proof of the quality of the instruments and the amount we can save the purchaser, to the **diplomas and medals of honor** which these organs received from the board of judges at the great world's exhibit held in St. Louis last year.

EXHIBIT OF BECKWITH ORGANS AT THE WORLD'S FAIR.

The fact that the Beckwith Organs were on exhibition at this Fair, and the fact that they occupied one of the handsomest booths in the building, proves nothing whatever as to their quality and the extremely low prices which we make on them, but the fact that they received from the board of judges, composed of eminent musicians from all over the country, the highest **diplomas of merit and medals of honor,** forever settles the fact in this country as to their extremely high quality.

If you are thinking of purchasing an organ, these are facts you should consider, as the voluntary testimonials of your friends and neighbors, and the **diplomas of merit and medals of honor** awarded by the board of judges at the World's Fair are the best evidence of the superiority of the instruments.

BECKWITH ORGAN FACTORY.

WEST VIEW OF THE BECKWITH ORGAN FACTORY AT LOUISVILLE, KENTUCKY.

The illustration above shows one of the two immense factories in which are manufactured the splendid Beckwith Organs. These two factories are devoted entirely to the manufacture of Beckwith Organs and are fitted throughout with the most modern labor saving machinery. The immense capacity of these two factories enables us to keep constantly on hand a large reserve stock of these organs, thus enabling us to make immediate shipment upon every order received. As we control the entire output of both of these factories, and guarantee to them a market for every organ they turn out, we are able to secure the very lowest possible manufacturing prices. As we place our orders with these factories for hundreds of organs at a time we enable them to purchase large quatities of lumber and other material for use in building the organs, and they are thus enabled to take advantage of every depression in the market to purchase at the lowest possible figures. The great saving which is thus made in manufacturing cost, together with the large amount which we save in selling expense, guarantees to our customers prices on our entire line of organs, which are away below what the local dealer or agent can obtain from his jobber or manufacturer upon the same grade of instruments. These organ factories are entirely new plants, which have been built with the distinct object of reducing the manufacturing cost of organs without in any way sacrificing their quality.

Another important point in this connection is that these organ factories have been established at Louisville, Ky., and St Paul, Minn., as these two points are admirably located in regard to shipping facilities. By making our northern and western shipments from our St Paul factory, and our southern and eastern shipments from our Louisville factory we can place these organs in the hands of our customers at the very least possible expense in freight charges. This is a great advantage to our customers, because it enables us to make the freight charges on each shipment from $1.00 to $5.00 lower than they would otherwise have to pay. It will pay you to consider these facts when you are ready to purchase an organ.

OUR BECKWITH PRINCESS PIANO-ORGAN, $49.45

No. 46C14 Order by Number.

ONE OF THE GREATEST BARGAINS EVER OFFERED IN A PIANO CASE ORGAN.

A MARVELOUSLY FINE INSTRUMENT AT AN EXCEEDINGLY LOW PRICE. SPLENDID IN TONE AND TUNE, AND MAGNIFICENT IN APPEARANCE.

This organ is entirely new in our line and at the price we make, $49.45, is the most wonderful value ever offered in a piano-organ.

CASE. **This is certainly one of the most attractive and unique six-octave piano organs on the market.** It is furnished in quarter sawed oak only, and is beautifully finished and hand polished. The ornamentation and mouldings throughout the entire instrument are of the latest design and neat and tasty in every particular. It has an automatic swinging fall board which, when opened, throws forward the full length duet music desk. It has two double fluted trusses and is ornamented throughout with hand carvings and embossed mouldings. It is a fine imitation of the ordinary grand piano and is fitted on each side with swinging lamp stands.

ACTION. **The different combinations in the tone of this organ are controlled by two knee swells and eleven stops.** These stops are placed the same as on an ordinary organ and are easily within reach of the player at all times. **The eleven stops are as follows:**

Celeste, Cremona, Melodia, Dulciana, Diapason, Principal, Treble Coupler, Bass Coupler, Diapason Forte, Principal Forte and Vox Humana.

By the aid of these stops the player can produce an innumerable number of harmonious and melodious combinations of tone. The instrument has 146 reeds as follows:

One Set of Celeste Reeds, one Set of Melodia Reeds, one Set of Diapason Reeds and one Set of Principal Reeds.

These are all the celebrated Newel Reeds with the tongues double riveted to the reed blocks. They are all bent, tuned and voiced by men who are expert in this line of work and are prepared especially for this organ. A feature of this instrument is the Vox Humana Stop which gives that waving, undulating effect to the music which is an exact imitation of the singing voice; hence, Vox Humana or Human Voice. These reeds have their tone amplified and qualified by the action of the different stops and knee swells.

The Action which we place in this organ is the best that we can produce and wherever connections are made, the very best of fine wool felt is used, which effectually prevents any rattling in the instrument after it has been used for a time. A great many cheap organs on the market are not felted in this way, and after the organ is used for awhile the connections will come loose and vibrate with the tones of the organ, making a rattling noise which is very unpleasant.

WE GUARANTEE THAT THIS WILL NEVER OCCUR WITH OUR

...PRINCESS... PIANO-ORGAN

The bellows with which this organ is fitted is the celebrated Beckwith Bellows which guarantees great volume of tone to the instrument. It is made of thoroughly seasoned, built up stock and covered with fine rubber cloth, which guarantees it against leaking. It is fitted with pressure valves which allow the surplus air pressure to escape and protects the bellows against being overstrained by violent pumping of the pedals.

No. 46C14
OUR BECKWITH PRINCESS PIANO-ORGAN, $49.45

THE PEDALS. **The pedals of this organ are of the regular organ pattern, bound with a beautiful metal frame handsomely nickel plated.** The pedal boards are covered with fine Brussels carpet and fitted with our new device which prevents the straps from wearing out and breaking.

DIMENSIONS. **This organ is the same size as the ordinary upright piano,** being 56 inches high, 58 inches long and 23 inches wide.

WEIGHT. **This organ weighs, properly boxed and packed for shipment, about 450 pounds.** Each instrument is properly and carefully packed so that we can guarantee that it will reach the customer in perfect condition.

THE ENGRAVING, **which we show on this page, will give you a fair idea of the style and design of the case and the general appearance and ornamentation of the instrument,** but it is impossible by a picture to give you any idea of the extreme beauty of appearance and splendid finish, together with the magnificent tone which this instrument possesses. These are things which have to be seen and heard to be appreciated.

LET US SEND YOU THIS ORGAN **on thirty days' trial, according to our offer given on page 110.** Try it in your home for this period and if you do not find that it is the greatest bargain you ever saw in a piano-organ, and superior to any piano-organ you ever saw at anywhere near the price, you can return it to us; we will cheerfully refund your money and pay the freight charges and cartage both ways. This liberal offer is made for the purpose of giving you an opportunity to examine and test this splendid instrument before finally concluding to buy it.

THE TERMS **we make on this organ are exactly the same as we make on all of our other organs,** and the same guarantees and trial offers can be taken advantage of in its purchase, all fully explained on page 110.

FREE. **WE SEND ABSOLUTELY FREE WITH THIS INSTRUMENT A FINE STOOL, made in wood to match the case of the organ and a complete instruction book,** by the aid of which any one can learn to play the instrument without the assistance of a teacher.

YOU TAKE NO RISK IN ORDERING THIS ORGAN, **because we take all the chances and responsibilities of shipment and protect you in every way against loss by OUR THIRTY DAYS and ONE YEAR TRIAL OFFERS and by OUR TWENTY-FIVE YEARS BINDING GUARANTEE.** We strive to protect our customers in every way against any loss on our goods, because we cannot afford to have any of our customers dissatisfied with the goods which we sell them. Remember that we do not ask you to keep this organ after ordering it on trial unless it is satisfactory in every particular, and we make you the sole judge of its merits. You can have the instrument in your home, call in your musical friends and get their opinions, and compare it with any instrument in your vicinity, and if you do not find that it is everything we claim for it, and a great bargain in every respect, we decidedly request that you return it to us, we will cheerfully refund your money and pay the freight charges both ways.

KINDLY READ WHAT WE HAVE TO SAY ON PAGE 120 IN REGARD TO THE EXHIBIT OF BECKWITH ORGANS AT THE WORLD'S FAIR LAST YEAR.

WHY SHOULD YOU PURCHASE A PIANO-ORGAN IN THE USUAL WAY FROM A DEALER AND PAY HIM $65.00 OR $70.00, WHEN YOU CAN PURCHASE THIS SPLENDID PIANO-ORGAN FROM US, IN EVERY WAY EQUAL AND IN MOST PARTICULARS SUPERIOR, FOR $49.45?

No. 46C14 Beckwith Princess Piano-Organ. Price $49.45

OUR BECKWITH HOME QUEEN PIANO-ORGAN

No. 46015 **$69.00** ORDER BY NUMBER

This is the same grade of organ which is usually offered throughout the country at $90.00 and $100.00, and we are only able to offer it to you at $69.00, because we ship it directly from the factory to you, charging you the manufacturer's price only, with our one small margin of profit added. We do not ask you to take our word for the merits of this splendid instrument as we make you the sole judge of its splendid qualities and you are the one to be satisfied in every respect. We furnish it in splendid mahogany, highly finished.

SEE OPPOSITE PAGE FOR DESCRIPTION.

No. 46015 ALWAYS ORDER BY NUMBER.

DIMENSIONS.

This instrument is as large as a regular concert size piano being 56½ inches high, 60 inches long and 26¼ inches wide.

WEIGHT.

Properly boxed and packed for shipment this organ weighs about 470 pounds. It is carefully packed and we guarantee it will reach you in perfect condition. We do not ask you to take any chances in this respect because we will be responsible for its safe arrival at your town. We would be glad to give you the freight charges upon request, or you can figure them up yourself by taking the weight of the instrument and consulting the table of freight rates given in the front of the catalogue.

REMEMBER,

We will ship you this organ with the understanding that if you do not find when you receive it, that you are saving from $25.00 to $30.00, at least, in comparison with the price which other dealers would ask for the same grade of organ, we will cheerfully receive it back, refund your money and pay the freight charges both ways. Our sales on these organs have been immense, owing to the extremely high qualities of the instrument, its handsome appearance and splendid tone. The piano-organ for which your dealer charges you $90.00 or $100.00, does not cost one cent more to manufacture than our Beckwith Home Queen. The difference in the price is made necessary by the profits made and the expenses incurred by the different dealers through whose hands the instrument must pass before it reaches you. This, in many cases more than doubles the original cost of the instrument, and you have to pay the extra profits and expenses. We simply charge you the original manufacturer's price with our one small margin of profit added to compensate us for our trouble in handling and selling the instrument.

ON PAGE 120 OF THIS CATALOGUE

We are showing an illustration of the exhibit of the Beckwith Organs at the World's Fair last year and also a picture of one of the immense Beckwith organ factories at Louisville, Ky. We desire to urge you to read this page carefully. Not only what we have to say in regard to the exhibits, and the diplomas of merit and medals of honor which these organs received, but also what we have to say in regard to the Beckwith organ factories.

BECKWITH HOME QUEEN PIANO-ORGAN,

No. 46015 **$69.00** ORDER BY NUMBER.

AS ILLUSTRATED ON OPPOSITE PAGE.

This Organ is unquestionably the finest instrument of its kind ever placed on the market, and at the price we offer it, $69.00, it represents a saving to the purchaser of at least $25.00 or $30.00 on the purchase.

THIS INSTRUMENT HAS BEEN STEADILY REDUCED IN PRICE

Owing to the improving and cheapening of manufacturing processes and the reduction of selling expenses, until we are able, at the present time, to offer it at this exceedingly low price. It is made in response to a demand for a reed organ which will exactly resemble a grand piano, and the engraving will show you that we have succeeded in producing an instrument which the casual observer will not be able to distinguish from a $400.00 grand piano. In making this organ we have avoided the deadening and muffling of the tone, which is so common a fault with the ordinary piano-organ. Indeed, we have taken advantage of the shape of the case to produce in the instrument a large tone qualifying chamber, which amplifies and increases the tone volume of the instrument.

BY EXAMINING THE ENGRAVING YOU WILL NOTICE THAT WE HAVE AVOIDED THE NECESSITY OF PLACING KNEE SWELLS ON THIS INSTRUMENT AND THEIR PLACE IS TAKEN BY OUR GRAND PNEUMATIC SWELL.

CASE.

The case of this organ is in every way equal to the case on an ordinary piano and can be furnished in quarter sawed oak or fine mahogany. It is veneered like any piano case and given the same high finish. The wood of this case is so treated by the finisher as to show the beautiful grain through the different coats of transparent varnish with which it is covered. The carving and ornamentations are the finest ever placed on an organ case of this variety, and the design is modeled after the most approved piano design. We have been very successful in selling this instrument as it has given such universal satisfaction. It has a full duet music desk which can be pulled forward as shown in the engraving and is fitted with a regular piano fall cover. This instrument is fitted with regular piano pedals and pedal guard of regular piano design, handsomely nickel plated and polished. While the engraving gives a very good idea of the design and ornamentations of the case it falls far short of giving you an idea of its handsome appearance and beautiful finish.

CAPACITY.

The tone, quality and power of this organ is far superior to the ordinary reed organ and it is fitted with three full sets of reeds and has a 7⅓-octave key board. It has 238 reeds in all and these can be formed into an immense number of harmonious combinations by the aid of the stops which can be seen in the engravings directly over the name of the organ. These stops are so arranged as not to be noticeable by the casual observer and do not detract from the piano effect in any way. The reeds are all the celebrated Newell reeds, are made of solid brass of the highest grade and the tongues are double riveted to the reed block. They are all tuned and bent especially for this instrument and we can guarantee their volume and sweetness of tone. The peculiar shape of the inside of the case adds to the singing quality and tone power of these reeds, and when the full power of the bellows is turned on, the effect of their different combinations is startling in its beauty.

GRAND PNEUMATIC SWELL.

This organ contains several improvements not found on any other instrument, among which is the grand pneumatic swell. This swell is placed on the organ to avoid incumbering it with knee swells. It is automatically opened by air pressure when the pedals are pumped hard and closes automatically when they are pumped lightly. When the performer desires to get more power out of the organ he naturally pumps the instrument harder and this opens the swell, allowing the full power of the organ to be heard, and when he does not desire such a volume of tone he naturally pumps the pedals with less violence and the swell closes, reducing the power of the instrument. This swell does not open suddenly, or all at once, but is opened gradually according to the power exerted on the pedals. This simple improvement will be recognized at once as being something especially fine in connection with the piano-organ, and it is not found in any other instrument on the market.

NEW PATENT OCTAVE COUPLER.

Another feature of this instrument is the new patent octave coupler operated by the middle pedal of the organ. This avoids the necessity of placing two extra stops on the organ, which would only detract from the piano effect of the case. It is an attachment whereby the tones of the instrument are coupled in both the treble and bass by pressing down the middle pedal. In order to release it, it is only necessary to press it a second time, when the coupler releases automatically. This will be recognized as a valuable addition to the instrument and will not be found on any other piano-organ on the market. The third pedal on this instrument gives the effect of a practice pedal on a grand piano, and adds to the magnificent appearance of the organ.

BELLOWS.

This organ is fitted with the celebrated Beckwith bellows and reservoir which produces a powerful and well balanced tone. These bellows are constructed of three-ply built-up stock which cannot warp or split, and covered with fine rubber cloth which guarantees them against leaking. They are so arranged that the bellows exhausts the air in the reservoir, forming a vacuum, into which the air rushes through the reeds causing them to sound. The reservoir is fitted with our Patent Automatic Pressure Valve, which relieves the surplus air pressure and prevents the bellows being over strained by violent pumping. While these bellows have an extra large capacity the pedals are so arranged that the greatest amount of leverage is taken advantage of and the smallest child can sustain the full power of the instrument for an indefinite length of time without any great effort. By the bellows and reservoir combination which we place in this instrument, and in fact, all of our organs, we insure an easy and steady supply of air to the reeds and this avoids that jerky, spasmodic effect which is so noticeable in other organs when the pedals are pumped violently.

PIPE SWELL ATTACHMENT.

This instrument has fitted over the reeds a patent pipe swell attachment which so qualifies their tone as to make them a close imitation of the pipes on the grand pipe organ. This is an improvement much sought after by organ builders, but so far it is the only invention of its kind that has ever proven successful. It has caused the sale of a good many hundreds of these organs, and has never failed to call forth the highest praise of the performer.

ACTION.

The action which we place in this organ is the very finest that can be obtained, and every bit of the material is thoroughly tested and examined before being used. Every bit of wood which enters into this action is thoroughly kiln and air dried before being worked up into the different parts for the action and so well are these things taken care of that we can guarantee our actions against defects in workmanship and material for a period of 25 years. All the different connecting parts are thoroughly felted with the best quality of wool felt, and all parts of the action intended to be air tight are covered by felt and sheepskin. In most organs the connecting parts are not felted and after they have been used for awhile they become loose and rattle. This is never found in the Beckwith organs. Every part of the action which we place in this organ is thoroughly and substantially built, so that the chances of it getting out of order are reduced to a minimum.

THE STOPS.

All of the different sets of reeds which we place in this instrument are at all times under the control of the performer and can be worked into all sorts of harmonious combinations so as to bring out the real beauty of the instrument. These stops, or rather buttons, are easily within the reach of the player's hands and enable him to change the tone combinations of the instrument at will.

OUR REDUCED PRICES.

This splendid instrument is shipped from our factory in Central Ohio directly to you. When you purchase it, you merely pay the manufacturer's price and the one small profit which we add to pay us for handling and selling the instrument. This fully explains how you can purchase this splendid organ for the extremely low price of $69.00. If this instrument was sold in the usual way through dealers it would cost you between $90.00 and $100.00 at the very lowest. We have steadily reduced the prices on our instruments and every reduction we have made in price has been the result of the improvement and cheapening of manufacturing processes, a reduction in selling expenses and not a deterioration in the quality of the goods.

OUR 25 YEARS GUARANTEE.

We are willing to stand behind our organs, and we do not ask our customers to take any chances whatever when they purchase from us. We will ship you one of these organs with the understanding and agreement that if you should discover any defect in the workmanship or material within 25 years from the time you receive it we stand ready to make the defect good and satisfy you perfectly.

OUR 30 DAYS FREE TRIAL OFFER.

We send this organ out upon the same terms that we ship all our other organs and can place it in your home for 30 days, allow you to try it thoroughly and get the opinions of your friends before finally accepting it. How you can take advantage of this trial offer is fully explained on page 110, which we trust you will read carefully. Should you take advantage of our 30 days free trial offer, and the organ proves satisfactory within that length of time, we will then allow you one year in which time you can return the instrument at our expense and have your money refunded in case it should prove unsatisfactory. This is known as **our one-year trial offer.**

FREE.

We furnish absolutely free with this instrument a splendid stool, manufactured of wood to match the case of the organ, with handsome turned legs, brass claws and glass balls on the feet. We also furnish a handsome piano scarf, and a splendid instruction book by the aid of which anyone can learn how to play the instrument without the aid of a teacher.

$19.90 FOR THIS GENUINE BECKWITH ORGAN CO.'S LARGE, HANDSOME, BEAUTIFULLY FINISHED Golden Oak Case Parlor Organ.

This is a large, handsome, well finished, golden oak case, 71 inches high, 41½ inches long, 23 inches deep. Remember, it is a large full size parlor organ, weighing, when boxed and packed for shipment, 350 pounds. It is the equal of organs that wholesale at from $25.00 to $40.00. It is a better organ than our competitors are advertising at from $25.00 to $35.00. It is an organ made in the Beckwith Organ Company's factory and fully guaranteed.

Order by Number. No. 46C19.

$19.90 GENUINE BECKWITH INSTRUMENT.

HOW IT IS POSSIBLE FOR US TO MAKE THE PRICE $19.90

WHEN YOU LOOK at the illustration of this organ and the other organs shown in this catalogue, and compare them with organs offered by other houses you will find that you can save from $5.00 to $20.00 by buying an organ from us, you will learn that in buying an organ from us you do not buy a cheap stenciled instrument, but you buy a genuine Beckwith organ, an organ bearing the name of the Beckwith Organ Company.

WE CONTROL THE ENTIRE OUTPUT OF THE BECKWITH ORGAN CO.'S TWO FACTORIES, and this gives us such an immense advantage in buying that we are able to offer you these instruments at the actual cost of material and labor with but our one small percentage of profit added. Under our contract, every organ the Beckwith Company makes comes directly to us, and therefore a Beckwith organ can be had only from us. It is the only concern which makes an organ complete from the standing timber to the finished instrument. Only the very best of lumber goes into these organs, the balance of the timber being sold generally on the market for commercial purposes. This has a great deal to do with the low cost of the instruments and their extremely high quality. Both of these immense factories are equipped with every new model labor saving machine and device for the economical manufacture of organs and every piece and part which can be manufactured to better advantage by machinery is handled in this way, and this aids materially in reducing the selling price of the organ. Nothing has been spared or left undone in our efforts to bring up the Beckwith organs to the very highest standard, and we keep the cost down so that with our small percentage of profit added our customers can buy one organ from us at a much lower price than the larger dealers can buy in carload lots.

THE ORGAN TO SELECT.

IF YOU WOULD LET US ADVISE YOU in the selection of your organ we would especially recommend that you select the highest grade organ we make, the finest parlor organ on the market, regardless of name, make or price, the Beckwith Imperial Grand, which is shown on page 128 and offered for only $39.95 to $51.95, a reduction of $5.00 from our last season's price. This is positively the richest, handsomest, best made, best finished, most powerful and sweetest toned parlor organ on the market. Therefore, in selecting an organ we would especially recommend in your interest that you select the finest instrument turned out by the Beckwith Organ Company, the Beckwith Imperial Grand, as shown in this catalogue and now offered at $39.95.

IF YOU DON'T FEEL THAT YOU CAN AFFORD TO PAY as much as $39.95 for an organ we would then recommend that you select the next organ, our Beckwith Royal Grand, which we now offer at $36.75, a reduction of $2.00 from our last season's price. This instrument is illustrated and described on the following pages and is superior to any organ you can buy elsewhere at less than double the price. If you do not feel that you can invest $39.95 and get the finest instrument the Beckwith Company makes, we would urge that you take the next to the best, the Royal Grand at $36.75 to $47.75.

IF YOU FEEL THAT YOU SHOULD MAKE A STILL SMALLER INVESTMENT we would recommend our six-octave Beckwith Cottage Organ, as shown on another page, which we now quote at $32.50, a reduction of $2.00 from last season's price. While this, our special $19.90 Beckwith Organ we guarantee equal to organs sold by others at $5.00 to $15.00 more money, and our Acme Queen, which has now been reduced to $25.95 is a thoroughly reliable instrument and better than you can buy elsewhere at less than $35.00, equal to organs that many sell at $40.00 to $50.00, we especially recommend that you select one of our higher grade instruments.

IF YOU DO NOT FEEL YOU CAN AFFORD TO BUY THE VERY BEST, the best parlor organ made, the Imperial Grand, or the next in order, the Royal Grand, then by all means order the Six-Octave Beckwith Cottage Organ at our latest cut price of $32.50, for this price of $32.50 permits of our making everything extra high grade. The difference in our selling price between a Six-octave Cottage Organ and this, our special $19.90 organ or our Cottage Favorite at the new price of $27.65, only represents the actual difference in cost of manufacture.

IF IN SELECTING AN ORGAN you will take one of the very best, the Beckwith Cottage at $32.50, the Royal Grand at $36.75 or, better still, the very best organ made, the Imperial Grand at $39.95, you will get the greatest value it is possible to turn out of the Beckwith organ factory. You will get more for your money than it is possible to give you in a cheaper instrument. The volume, the purity of tone, the lasting qualities, that special finish, the high grade features found only on the most expensive organs made, are all introduced and will be found in the three highest grade organs we make, the Beckwith Cottage Organ, the Royal Grand and the Imperial Grand; but if you do not feel that you can afford to invest from $32.50 to $39.95 for the highest grade organs made, the best instruments that ever went out of any factory, you can safely order our Cottage Favorite at the new price of $27.65 or this, our special $19.90 organ, under our binding 25 years' guarantee, with every assurance from us that it will be equal to any organ you can buy elsewhere at $10.00 to $15.00 more money, and with the privilege on your part of giving the organ a thorough trial, and if for any reason you should become dissatisfied with your purchase, you can return the organ to us at our expense, and we will immediately return your money, together with any freight charges paid by you.

IN THIS, OUR SPECIAL $19.90 ORGAN, we put a higher grade action than you will find in organs sold by others at much higher prices. It has four sets of reeds, double riveted tongues, two-octave Diapason, two-octave Principal, three-octave Melodia, three-octave Celeste. The key board is of five-octave compass, ten octaves of 122 reeds in all. The stops, by which the tone is always under perfect control, are as follows: Diapason, Echo, Piano, Celeste, Forte, Principal Celeste, Melodia, Two swells, knee and grand organ.

THE CASE, AS SHOWN IN THE ILLUSTRATION, is made of selected solid oak, finished golden. The base is of good size, affording ample room for the bellows; has neatly scalloped cheeks, finished with beaded ends and panels in front. The upper part is handsome in appearance, with heavy top rail of fancy shape, and neatly hand carved; has a good size bevel mirror, size 8x12 inches; has carved panels in sides, full length shelf underneath, ornamented with turned knobs; large music desk with carved panels and covers, large receptacle for music. Pedals are full size, covered with Brussels carpet, nickel trimmed.

REMEMBER, at $19.90 this organ does not include an organ stool nor instruction book. We furnish it delivered on board the cars at the factory. It is covered by our 25 years' binding guarantee. If you order this organ you can give it thirty days' trial, and if you are not perfectly satisfied with your purchase, you can then return it to us at our expense and we will immediately refund your money.

REMEMBER, while this is the handsomest organ ever produced and offered at anything like the price, we guarantee it the equal of instruments that are sold by others at $5.00 to $15.00 more money, we especially recommend that you select one of our three highest grade instruments, either the Imperial Grand at $39.95, the Royal Grand at $36.75, or the six-octave Beckwith Cottage at $32.50.

No. 46C19 Price, without Stool and Instruction Book........ **$19.90**

No. 46C20 Price, with Regular Action A, Five Octaves, with Stool and Instruction Book........ **25.45**

BUYS THE COTTAGE FAVORITE ORGAN

THIS ORGAN is a Valuable Addition to the **BECKWITH LINE**

THIS IS THE LATEST PRODUCTION OF THE
CELEBRATED BECKWITH ORGAN COMPANY,
AND IS ONE OF THE PRETTIEST DESIGNS ON THE MARKET.

IT IS BUILT of the same excellent material and with the same skill as all the other famous Beckwith Organs. It is offered in response to a demand for an organ with a very handsome case and artistic finish at a very moderate price. The reason why we are able to quote such an extremely low price upon it, is that our immense manufacturing facilities and enormous sales make it profitable for us to sell it at a very small increase over the manufacturing cost. We have gradually reduced the prices on our other organs, as we gained the knowledge and experience which enabled us to make and sell them at the least possible expense. We are giving our customers the advantage of this experience by quoting very low prices on this splendid new instrument.

REMEMBER, that this organ is covered by our celebrated 25 years guarantee and sold under our great 30 days and one years trial offers, which you will find fully explained on page 119 of this catalogue. We are prepared to ship you this instrument under our distinct promise to save you at least $25.00 on your purchase, and if you do not find that you have saved this amount, that it is the greatest bargain you ever saw in an organ, perfectly satisfactory in every particular and equal and in many points superior to other organs sold in your neighborhood at double the price, you can return it to us, we will refund your money and pay the entire cost of transportation both ways. So confident are we of the high quality of this instrument that we are prepared to guarantee that you cannot purchase one of the same grade from your dealer for less than $60.00.

A SPECIAL FEATURE of this instrument is the Vox Humana stop, which gives an exact imitation of the human voice in singing. You will not find any other organ on the market at anywhere near this price, which is fitted with the Vox Humana stop. This organ is also fitted with ten additional stops, which together with the 122 reeds, will form innumerable harmonious combinations. We also furnish this instrument with fifteen stops and 184 reeds at prices given below. For a description of all of these stops and reeds, see page 119. We also fit this instrument with knee swells, which place the entire power of the organ under immediate control of the performer. The pedals are so arranged as to take advantage of the greatest amount of leverage so that the immense bellows with which the organ is fitted, can be worked with perfect ease.

CASE. The case of this organ is of an absolutely new design, very handsome, massive and artistic in every respect. It is furnished in solid oak, handsomely and durably finished and is so designed as to provide for lamp stands, bric-a-brac shelves, etc. It is decorated with handsome hand carvings which are much more durable and artistic than the cheap pressed carvings usually found on organs for which your dealer charges you a much higher price. It has a handsome canopy top tastefully ornamented in keeping with the rest of the case. It is fitted with a music cabinet of new design which pulls down from the top and rests on the music desk. The front of this music cabinet is fitted with a handsome oval shape bevel French mirror. The music desk is made extra wide and will hold several pieces of music at one time. The entire front of the organ below the knee swells is so arranged that it can be taken out, thus exposing the entire front of the bellows and making it easy to remedy any defect which might appear in the valves. The entire design is original in every particular, has an appearance of quiet elegance, and an air of finish and completeness found in very few organs on the market at the present time. The case is built so as to provide for an extra large tone qualifying chamber, which increases the quality and volume of tone. The pedals are covered with handsome Brussels carpet, have neat metal frames finely nickel plated and are fitted with our patent device which prevents the pedal straps from wearing out and breaking.

THE TONE. The tone is the most important feature of any organ and this has been well provided for in the Cottage Favorite. It is fitted with the genuine Newell reeds, double riveted and of the very highest quality. These reeds are controlled at all times by the numerous stops with which the organ is fitted, thus insuring innumerable melodious combinations. It has great bellows capacity and is fitted with the Celebrated Beckwith Bellows, built on strictly scientific principles and durably constructed. The bellows is fitted with a large reservoir which forms the vacuum for the organ and guarantees a steady stream of air to the reeds, thus avoiding the jerky spasmodic effect noticed in other reed organs when the pedals are pumped violently.

YOU take no chances when you order this organ, because if it is not perfectly satisfactory in every particular, entirely suited to your wants, up to your expectations in every way and a great bargain in every respect, you can return it to us and we will send you back your money. We take all the chances and responsibility of shipment and do not ask you to promise anything or assume any obligation whatever. All we ask is that you give the organ a fair and impartial trial.

THIS IS A LARGE FULL SIZE PARLOR ORGAN.

The instrument is standard in every way. It stands 6 feet high, 42 inches long and 23 inches deep. It weighs, boxed and packed for shipment, 400 pounds.

No. 46C23 ALWAYS ORDER BY NUMBER.

No. 46C23	Action A, five octaves.........	$27.65
No. 46C24	Action C, five octaves.........	30.55

See page 119 for description of actions.

THIS ORGAN can be furnished in walnut finish without extra cost. Please note that walnut finish does not mean solid walnut, but that the case is made of hardwood and stained in a close imitation of walnut.

$32.50 FOR THE SIX-OCTAVE BECKWITH COTTAGE ORGAN

REDUCED FROM $34.50

A MOST REMARKABLE REDUCTION, MADE POSSIBLE BY AN IMMENSE INCREASE IN SALES, AN ESPECIALLY ADVANTAGEOUS CONTRACT WITH THE MANUFACTURERS, AND A GREAT REDUCTION IN SELLING EXPENSES.

No. 46C26

FOLLOWING OUR USUAL POLICY, we are giving our customers the benefit of the remarkable reduction in price, which we have been able to make on this splendid organ, and which can now be purchased at $32.50. No dealers have been able to offer a six-octave organ at anywhere near this price. Although we have been able to reduce this organ so wonderfully in price, we have not done so at the expense of the instrument itself. The same high grade of material and workmanship which has always characterized it, still enters into its construction. We issue the same written binding guarantee for twenty-five years, and sell it upon exactly the same terms which it has always been sold. This is, indeed, a splendid opportunity to purchase a six-octave organ at the ridiculously low price of $32.50.

CASE. The case of this organ is furnished in solid oak or walnut. It is handsomely finished, carved and decorated. The wood is so thoroughly seasoned that it will stand any change of climate and will not be affected by ordinary changes of temperature. The top is fitted with a handsome 10x14-inch French bevel plate mirror with pretty marquetry ornaments on each side. It has a fine music desk, lamp stand, music case and a canopy top of scroll and carved work. It is certainly one of the prettiest cases ever furnished with an organ. The illustration will give you a fair idea of the elegance of design and the general appearance of the instrument; but no illustration, however fine, can give you an idea of its fineness of finish and beauty of appearance, It is finished dark and will harmonize with the furnishings of any parlor. The case is especially constructed so as to develop the acoustic properties of the organ and forms a tone qualifying chamber which gives a pipe like quality of tone to the reeds. The bottom of the case is so constructed that there is ample room for the powerful Beckwith bellows with which it is fitted. The entire design is dignified and elegant. The pedals are covered with fine Brussels carpet and bound with handsome metal ornaments, finely nickel plated.

REMEMBER that each one of these organs is shipped out accompanied by a written, binding guarantee which provides if at any time within 25 years any defect should appear in the workmanship or material of the organ, we are bound to make it good and satisfy the customer perfectly. We also wish to call your attention to the fact that in purchasing this organ, you can take advantage of our great 30 days free trial offer, which is fully explained on page 110 of this catalogue.

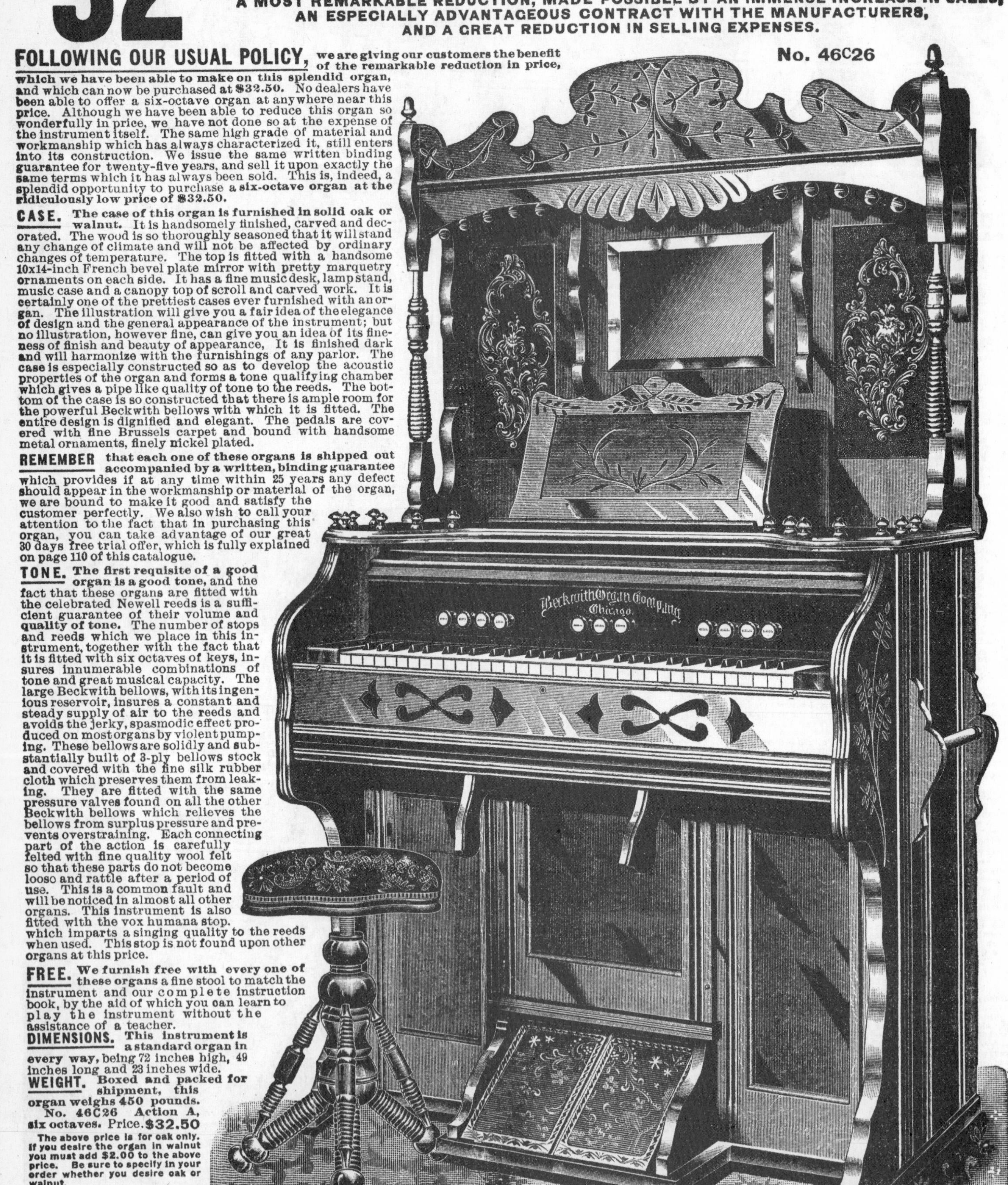

TONE. The first requisite of a good organ is a good tone, and the fact that these organs are fitted with the celebrated Newell reeds is a sufficient guarantee of their volume and quality of tone. The number of stops and reeds which we place in this instrument, together with the fact that it is fitted with six octaves of keys, insures innumerable combinations of tone and great musical capacity. The large Beckwith bellows, with its ingenious reservoir, insures a constant and steady supply of air to the reeds and avoids the jerky, spasmodic effect produced on most organs by violent pumping. These bellows are solidly and substantially built of 3-ply bellows stock and covered with the fine silk rubber cloth which preserves them from leaking. They are fitted with the same pressure valves found on all the other Beckwith bellows which relieves the bellows from surplus pressure and prevents overstraining. Each connecting part of the action is carefully felted with fine quality wool felt so that these parts do not become looso and rattle after a period of use. This is a common fault and will be noticed in almost all other organs. This instrument is also fitted with the vox humana stop. which imparts a singing quality to the reeds when used. This stop is not found upon other organs at this price.

FREE. We furnish free with every one of these organs a fine stool to match the instrument and our complete instruction book, by the aid of which you can learn to play the instrument without the assistance of a teacher.

DIMENSIONS. This instrument is a standard organ in every way, being 72 inches high, 49 inches long and 23 inches wide.

WEIGHT. Boxed and packed for shipment, this organ weighs 450 pounds.

No. 46C26 Action A, six octaves. Price. **$32.50**

The above price is for oak only. If you desire the organ in walnut you must add $2.00 to the above price. Be sure to specify in your order whether you desire oak or walnut.

ALWAYS ORDER BY NUMBER.

SEE PAGE 119 FOR DESCRIPTION OF ACTION.

See the pictures of the Beckwith Organ factory and the beautiful St. Louis World's Fair Exhibit on page 120.

$36.75 FOR THE BECKWITH ROYAL GRAND ORGAN

No. 46C40. A GRADE.

ANOTHER STARTLING REDUCTION IN PRICE.

EVERY GRADE OF THIS SPLENDID ORGAN FEELS THE EFFECT OF THIS REMARKABLE REDUCTION. A WONDERFUL OPPORTUNITY to Purchase A HIGH GRADE ORGAN at Almost Actual FACTORY COST.

OWING TO AN UNUSUALLY ADVANTAGEOUS CONTRACT which we have been able to make with the manufacturers of these organs, we are again able to offer our customers a splendid reduction in price from the highest to the lowest grade of the Royal Grand Organ. We do not seek to put the additional profit in our pockets, but follow our usual policy of giving our customers the benefit of every possible reduction which we can obtain. Examine the prices given below and compare them with the prices which we have formerly made on this organ and you will notice at once the startling reduction we have made in these prices. This is certainly a splendid opportunity for you to purchase a fine organ at a remarkably low price. We believe that the immense increase in the sales of this popular organ will fully justify us in making this remarkable reduction, and if you are figuring on purchasing an organ, you cannot afford to let this opportunity pass you. This is certainly

THE MOST SENSATIONAL REDUCTION EVER MADE IN THE PRICE OF ORGANS.

EVERY GRADE OF THIS SPLENDID ORGAN is a remarkable bargain. **Let us send you this splendid organ under our 30 days' free trial offer,** as explained on page 110 of this catalogue. Try it in your home for 30 days and if you are not fully satisfied that it is the most remarkable bargain in an organ that you ever saw in your life and fully equal and in many points superior to organs for which your neighbors pay twice the price, you can return it to us, we will cheerfully and immediately refund the entire amount you have paid and pay the freight charges both ways. You cannot afford to disregard this splendid opportunity to become the owner of one of these beautiful organs. These prices are far below what your local agent or dealer can obtain from his jobber or manufacturer on the same grade of organs, while we place you in a position to purchase one of these magnificent organs at the actual cost of material and labor at the factory with but our one small percentage of profit added.

REMEMBER, you do not take any chances in ordering this splendid instrument from us, because we take all the chances and responsibilities of shipment on our own shoulders and do not require you to accept the organ unless it is fully up to your expectations in every respect.

CASE. We can furnish the case of this organ in the finest selected walnut or oak as desired. The design is extremely handsome and whether finished in oak or walnut never fails to call for words of admiration from all who see it. The top is ornamented with a heavy 10x14-inch French bevel plate mirror and fitted with pretty bric-a-brac shelves. It has a handsome music desk, lamp stands and fall board with lock and key. The design is entirely original and can be purchased only from us. The engraving shown on this page is a wood cut, made directly from a photograph of the instrument and will give you a fair idea of the details of design and ornamentation, but it will fall far short of conveying any idea of the splendid appearance and wonderful tone which the instrument possesses. It will be necessary for you to see this instrument and try it in your own home in order to fully appreciate its many fine qualities. Our 30 days' free trial offer furnishes the opportunity for you to examine and test this organ thoroughly and you take no chances whatever in ordering the instrument, because we do not ask you to accept it unless it is perfectly satisfactory in every respect and fully up to your expectations.

PEDALS. The pedals of this organ have handsome ornamental metal frames, finely nickel plated and highly polished, and are fitted with the same ingenious arrangement for taking advantage of leverage which is found on all of our other organs. These pedals are fitted with a patent device which prevents the straps from wearing out or breaking and the pedal boards are covered with fine Brussels carpet of a handsome pattern. The pedals are so arranged as to control the full power of the bellows with a slight amount of effort and will not tire the student in any way.

FREE. We send absolutely free with each one of these organs a fine stool made in wood to match the case of the organ, with handsome turned legs, brass claws and glass balls for feet. We also send a complete instruction book, by the aid of which anyone can learn to play the instrument without the assistance of a teacher.

We Furnish This Organ in Both Five and Six Octaves, as Follows:

		PRICE
No. 46C40	Action A, Five Octaves..	$36.75
No. 46C42	Action B, Five Octaves..	39.75
No. 46C44	Action D, Five Octaves..	43.75
No. 46C46	Action A, Six Octaves....	42.75
No. 46C48	Action B, Six Octaves....	44.75
No. 46C50	Action D, Six Octaves....	47.75

(For description of actions, see page 119.)

The above prices are for oak only. If walnut is desired, add $2.00 to above prices.

DIMENSIONS: This organ is 81 inches high, 48 inches long and 24 inches deep.

WEIGHT: Properly boxed and packed for shipment this organ weighs, five octaves, 450 pounds; six octaves, 500 pounds.

WE ASK YOU to refer to page 120 of this catalogue, where you will find an illustration of the beautiful Beckwith Organ exhibit at the World's Fair last year, and also a picture of one of the two immense Beckwith organ factories. We ask you to read carefully what we have to say in regard to this factory, and also what we have to say in regard to the exhibit. The royal Grand Organ was one of the instruments which received a medal of honor.

$39.95 BUYS THE BECKWITH IMPERIAL GRAND ORGAN

REDUCED FROM $44.95 a reduction of $5.00, and guaranteed the highest grade parlor organ on the market, superior in every way to any parlor organ that goes out of any other factory in America, regardless of name, make or price. Positively the greatest organ value ever offered by any factory or dealer. Every advantage which we can possibly secure either in buying or selling we give you the full advantage of in the very low prices which we quote and enable you to buy this organ at a price which is away below all possible competition.

LOOK IN ANY MUSIC STORE, look in any organ catalogue published; whether the price another house may name is $50.00 or $100.00, you will find the organ will not compare with this our latest improved Imperial Grand. Better still, order one of these instruments on our 30-day free trial plan, compare the instruments side by side with any instrument of any other make, regardless of price, whether it be $50.00 or $100.00, and if you do not say that the Beckwith Imperial Grand which is now offered at $39.95 is handsomer, richer, better finished, stronger, better made, sweeter toned and capable of a far wider range than any other organ made, you can return the Beckwith Imperial Grand Organ to us at our expense, and we will immediately return your money, together with any freight charges paid by you.

THIS IS OUR GREATEST TRIUMPH in organ building, greatly improved over last season's Imperial Grand, an organ that combines all that is highest and best in every high grade parlor organ made, with the defects of none. Remember, not a stenciled instrument, but an instrument made by the Beckwith Organ Company and bearing their name and name plate, backed by their reputation, backed by their guarantee and again by our 25 years' written binding guarantee.

THE BECKWITH ORGAN FACTORIES are the largest and best equipped of any organ factories in the world. We control their entire output of organs, and this gives us such an immense advantage in buying that we in turn can sell you these organs at a much lower price than your local dealer has to pay his jobber or manufacturer for the same grade of instruments. In fact, we can sell you an organ at the actual cost of the material and labor which enters into it with but our one small percentage of profit added. As we have a contract with the Beckwith Organ Company by which we take every organ they manufacture, you can see that it is impossible for you to purchase a Beckwith organ from any other dealer. We give you the benefit of every advantage which we possess in selling by our inexpensive method. This is the great reason why we are able to offer these high class organs at such a ridiculously low price. Every bit of machinery contained in these great factories is of the latest design and the most improved pattern, capable of turning out work at a much less cost than is possible in other organ factories. All of these things tend to make the production of an organ very much cheaper and we give you the benefit of all of these advantages.

THE DIFFERENCE IN PRICE between this, the highest grade instrument we build, and the cheapest grade, our $19.90 and $25.95, is represented twice over in the real intrinsic value. We would advise you by all means in selecting an organ to pay a few dollars more and get the very best, since you can get for only $39.95 the highest grade organ made, a better organ than you could buy elsewhere even at two to three times the price. It's worth a dozen stenciled instruments, it's offered at less than dealers can buy in carload lots, offered at $39.95 complete with handsome stool and instruction book, offered at the actual cost to us, manufactured from the standing timber to the finished instrument, with only our one small percentage of profit added.

NOTE THE UNUSUALLY LARGE SIZE.

THIS ORGAN stands 86 inches high, or 7 feet and 2 inches, one of the highest organs ever produced. It is 48 inches wide or full 4 feet. Very few parlor organs have been made in such width. It is full 24 inches, or 2 feet in depth; giving an organ 2 feet deep, 4 feet wide and 7 feet 2 inches high. This organ weighs, five octaves, 475 pounds; six octaves, 550 pounds. In short, it is an instrument which for size, shape, for massiveness of construction, must be seen, examined and compared with other instruments to appreciate the value we are giving.

WE FURNISH IT in solid quarter sawed oak. In the case we use nothing but the most perfect and carefully selected, beautifully grained woods, taken from our own mills, where we can get a richer and better matching, better blending and an altogether handsomer selection of quarter sawed oak than makers who buy their lumber from dealers; hence we give you in this organ a case unapproached by any other maker. The case is given an extremely high finish and coated with handsome transparent varnish through which the beautiful grain of the oak shows to the very best advantage. We use only the very best grade of quarter sawed oak which makes the organ not only a splendid musical instrument but a beautiful piece of furniture as well. With the heavy, richly carved, beautifully shaped, full paneled sides, the new design of lion's head and claw foot posts, beautifully paneled base, richly shaped and elaborately finished front, a design which no picture or illustration will show the full depth of; the large, massive, rich effect produced in this, the highest grade parlor organ made, we especially urge that you order this, the best instrument the Beckwith Company makes. We can also furnish the organ in walnut.

The above engraving shows our No. 46C62 Imperial Grand Organ with 17 stops and 292 reeds. Price, $51.95
No. 46C52 Imperial Grand Organ with 11 stops. Price.................... 39.95

See opposite page for other styles.

FOR DETAILED DESCRIPTION OF THE VARIOUS PARTS, SEE FOLLOWING PAGE.

THE BECKWITH IMPERIAL GRAND ORGAN, $39.95

SEE OPPOSITE PAGE FOR ILLUSTRATION.

A SPLENDID MUSICAL INSTRUMENT.

THIS IS THE HANDSOMEST ORGAN WE HAVE TO OFFER IN A REGULAR STYLE CASE.

THE TONE is exquisitely full, round and resonant, and is susceptible of the most delicate variations. The voicing and peculiar arrangement of the reeds, the close attention to details in all processes of manufacture, and the splendid skill shown in the making and finishing of the case, has enabled us to offer in this organ an instrument which is in every way superior to organs offered by other dealers at twice the price. **We offer this organ in competition with any organ made, without the least fear as to the result.** The engraving has brought out the detail of the design very nicely, and we call your attention to the appearance of quiet beauty and refinement which it possesses. The design is the finest ever conceived by the mind of the organ designer, and the splendid way in which it has been worked out, together with the brilliant and powerful tone, makes this organ the highest achievement of the organ builder's art. The case of this organ alone could not be made in your town for the price we are asking you for the organ complete. Not only is it a splendid musical instrument, but a magnificent piece of furniture as well. The engraving on the opposite page will convince you that this is **the most beautiful organ ever brought within the reach of American homes.**

CASE. Formerly an instrument of this exquisite design and workmanship was beyond the reach of any but the most wealthy and the prices asked by others at the present time for organs which in any way approach this instrument in beauty of design and sweetness of tone, are so high as to place them beyond the reach of people of moderate means. While the engraving shows the carvings, ornamentations and general design of the case, no engraving, however excellent, can do justice to the beauty of finish and elegance of appearance for which this instrument is remarkable. We furnish this case in handsome walnut or selected quarter sawed oak, finished and hand rubbed so as to bring out to best advantage the beautiful grain of the wood. It is fitted with pretty bric-a-brac shelves, lamp stands, and fall cover with lock and key. In the top there is a music case with shelf for books, and in the front of the door a large French bevel plate glass mirror. It has a beautiful canopy top, ornamented with hand carvings and supported by two graceful pillars. Supporting the keyboard on each end of the organ are two handsomely hand carved griffins which give the design a mediaeval effect not possessed by any other organ. Every detail of the design is carefully and consistently worked out so that the organ has that finished appearance only possessed by the very highest priced instruments. When you purchase this instrument you have the assurance that you are buying the very finest specimen of the organ builder's art.

PEDALS. Pedals are arranged so that the straps cannot wear out or break, and they have handsome metal frames, nickel plated and highly polished. They are constructed so as to control the bellows with the slightest possible effort, and the full power of organ can be sustained indefinitely with slight effort on the part of the player.

OUR ONE YEAR TRIAL OFFER

WHILE YOU CAN GIVE THE ORGAN A CAREFUL EXAMINATION and thorough test inside of thirty days, yet in order to remove the doubts of our customers and make assurance doubly sure, we ship the organ with the understanding that we will receive it back at any time within one year from the date of sale if the customer is not perfectly satisfied in every respect. Under these circumstances we refund the money paid for the organ and pay all the transportation charges and other expenses exactly the same as under our 30 days trial offer. We do not believe that our friends should hesitate to give us their order for an organ, as we do not ask them to take any chances in any way, but are prepared to take every responsibility on our own shoulders.

SOLD UNDER OUR 30 DAYS FREE TRIAL OFFER
AND ALSO
UNDER OUR SPECIAL FREIGHT PREPAID OFFER
AS EXPLAINED ON PAGE 110.

MOST OF OUR FRIENDS PREFER TO SEND THE MONEY DIRECT TO US,

and more especially is this true if they have done business with us. But it is not necessary to do so by any means, as we sell these organs under our **30 days free trial offer**, which is fully explained on page 110. There are many who do not desire that their neighbors should know what they are paying for their goods, and these, of course, always send us cash with the order and take advantage of our Offers No. 1 or 2, as they may desire. They do this with the full assurance that, if the organs do not prove satisfactory, we will receive them back and cheerfully and immediately refund all the money paid, and pay the entire expense of transportation.

WITH 6 OCTAVES, 17 STOPS AND 292 REEDS AND OUR GRAND ORCHESTRAL ACTION, this is certainly the best and grandest organ ever offered to the American public. It approaches more nearly to the grandeur of a pipe organ than any organ ever made. In the hands of even an ordinary player it is susceptible to effects of indescribable and startling grandeur. We have nothing better to offer you in organs, and we know that no dealer or agent can place in your house an organ that will compare for an instant with this magnificent instrument.

FREE. We send absolutely free with each one of these organs a fine stool, made in wood to match the case of the organ, with handsome turned legs, brass claws and glass balls. Also complete instruction book, by the aid of which one can learn to play the instrument without the assistance of a teacher.

A PICTURE of the exhibit of the Beckwith Organs at the World's Fair last year is shown on page 120 of this catalogue. We are also showing a picture of one of the two immense Beckwith Organ factories, and we desire to urge you to read what we have to say in regard to the Imperial Grand Organ, illustrated on the opposite page, one of the instruments which received a medal of honor for its superior merit.

OUR 25 YEARS GUARANTEE ACCOMPANIES EVERY GRADE.

Action A, Five Octaves, Imperial Grand. $39.95

The above price is for oak only. If you desire the organ in walnut you must add $2.00 to the above price. BE SURE TO SPECIFY IN YOUR ORDER WHETHER YOU DESIRE OAK OR WALNUT.

No. 46C52

CAPACITY—This grade has four sets of reeds, as follows:

One set of Principal Reeds...24 notes
One set of Melodia Reeds.....37 notes
One set of Diapason Reeds...24 notes
One set of Celeste Reeds.......37 notes
122 reeds in all.

These reeds are all made of the finest kind of brass with tongue double riveted to reed block. They are all voiced and toned by hand and fitted by the most expert workmen.

STOPS—**This grade has 11 stops, as follows:** Diapason, Principal, Dulciana, Melodia, Celeste, Cremona, Diapason Forte, Principal Forte, Treble Coupler, Bass Coupler and Vox Humana.

Action B, Five Octaves, Imperial Grand. $42.95

The above price is for oak only. If you desire the organ in walnut you must add $2.00 to the above price. BE SURE TO SPECIFY IN YOUR ORDER WHETHER YOU DESIRE OAK OR WALNUT.

No. 46C54

CAPACITY—This grade has five sets of reeds, as follows:

One set of Principal Reeds...24 notes
One set of Melodia Reeds....37 notes
One set of Diapason Reeds...24 notes
One set of Celeste Reeds.......37 notes
One set of Flute Reeds.......37 notes
159 reeds in all.

The addition of the flute reeds adds much to the musical value of the organ, and are very useful in playing many classes of organ selections.

STOPS—**This grade has 13 stops, as follows:** Diapason, Principal, Dulciana, Melodia, Celeste, **Viola, Flute**, Cremona, Diapason Forte, Principal Forte, Treble Coupler, Bass Coupler and Vox Humana.

Action D, Five Octaves, Imperial Grand. $45.95

The above price is for oak only. If you desire the organ in walnut you must add $2.00 to the above price. BE SURE TO SPECIFY IN YOUR ORDER WHETHER YOU DESIRE OAK OR WALNUT.

No. 46C56

CAPACITY—This grade has eight sets of reeds, as follows:

One set of Principal Reeds....24 notes
One set of Melodia Reeds......37 notes
One set of Diapason Reeds....24 notes
One set of Celeste Reeds ..... 37 notes
One set of Flute Reeds.........37 notes
One set of Bourdon Reeds,...24 notes
One set of Clarionet Reeds...24 notes
One set of Cornet Echo Reeds.37 notes
244 reeds in all.

The addition of bourdon, clarionet and cornet echo reeds adds immensely to the power and volume of the organ. They also increase the number of tone combinations, and place the entire range of musical interpretation entirely within the reach of an ordinary player.

STOPS—**This grade has 17 stops, as follows:** Diapason, Principal, Dulciana, Melodia, Celeste, Viola, Flute, **Bourdon, Clarionet, Cornet, Cornet Echo**, Cremona, Diapason Forte, Principal Forte, Treble Coupler, **Bass** Coupler and Vox Humana.

Action A, Six Octaves, Imperial Grand. $44.95

The above price is for oak only. If you desire the organ in walnut you must add $2.00 to the above price. BE SURE TO SPECIFY IN YOUR ORDER WHETHER YOU DESIRE OAK OR WALNUT.

No. 46C58

This grade has the same action as No. 46C52, five octaves, with the additional reeds to complete the six octaves, making 146 reeds in all.

Action B, Six Octaves, Imperial Grand. $47.95

The above price is for oak only. If you desire the organ in walnut you must add $2.00 to the above price. BE SURE TO SPECIFY IN YOUR ORDER WHETHER YOU DESIRE OAK OR WALNUT.

No. 46C60

This grade has the same action as No. 46C54, five octaves, with the additional reeds to make the organ six octaves, making 195 reeds in all.

Action D, Six Octaves, Imperial Grand. $51.95

The above price is for oak only. If you desire the organ in walnut you must add $2.00 to the above price. BE SURE TO SPECIFY IN YOUR ORDER WHETHER YOU DESIRE OAK OR WALNUT.

No. 46C62

This grade has the same action as No. 46C56, five octaves, with the additional reeds to complete the six octaves, making 292 reeds in all.

READ OUR LIBERAL TERMS OF SHIPMENT ON PAGE 110.

ORGAN VALUE. We do not attempt to advise our customers as to which organ they should purchase. The difference in the prices which we quote on these organs simply represents the difference in the factory cost, and not the difference in the profit which we make on them. We add one small margin of profit to each order, no matter what it may cost us at the factory, and when we ask you to pay a higher price for one organ than another, it does not mean that we are making a greater profit on that organ, but that we are giving you a greater amount of organ value on the sale. Under these circumstances we feel that we can advise our customers always to purchase the organ which represents the highest price, where their financial situation will admit of it, as by so doing they will always be sure to receive more real organ value than where they purchase a cheaper style of organ.

ALWAYS ORDER BY NUMBER.

THE BECKWITH UNIVERSAL FOLDING ORGAN

FOR SCHOOLROOMS, EVANGELISTIC WORK, AND IN YOUR OWN HOME. WHEREVER MUSIC IS WANTED.

IN QUALITY THE HIGHEST. — IN PRICE THE CHEAPEST.

$27.50

THE MOST MODERN INVENTION IN PORTABLE ORGANS, combining volume and purity of tone with lightness and compactness in carrying. YOU NEED IT EVERYWHERE. Our "49-Note" (four octave) organ is rapidly supplanting more expensive instruments in churches and elsewhere.

THE BECKWITH FOLDING ORGAN is adapted for use under all circumstances and in places where there is no instrument or where portability is desired. WE CHALLENGE COMPETITION and we claim for the BECKWITH Folding Organ the maximum of durability and portability with great power and sweetness of tone.

1st—In size the smallest
2d—In appearance the neatest
3d—In traveling the handiest
4th—In shipping the strongest
5th—In carrying the lightest
6th—In wet weather the safest
7th—In folding the quickest
8th—In tone the sweetest
9th—In volume the most powerful
— BEST OF ALL. —

THE CASE—The case is made of laminated or three-ply wire wood, obviating all possibility of splitting, warping, swelling or shrinking; treated with waterproof coating inside and out and covered in beautiful seal leatherette, which is also waterproof; the corners are protected with nickel or oxidized ornaments. It folds into a compass of 10x18x29 inches and when unfolded and in a position to play is of suitable and convenient height.

THE ACTION—The action consists of two continuous sets of special scale, extra size **pipe tone** reeds; one set of double, open, 8-foot Diapason, and one set of Viola and Flute reeds, four octaves, controlled and operated by two knee levers, enabling the operator to control the varied effects from the soft, sweet Dulciana pianissimo tone to the great organ effect. The action is durably constructed, the touch very light and responsive and a volume of sound is produced, not obtained from other folding organs.

THE TONE—The tone of the Universal Folding Organ is simply marvelous and cannot be surpassed in any other make of reed organs and compares closely with the rich, mellow and sonorous tone of the pipe organ.

THE BELLOWS—The bellows is one of the latest inventions, of the inverted pattern, and in capacity equal to any parlor or chapel organ. The middle board of the bellows is securely braced, so that you do not hear that jerky, short winded effect (so characteristic in other folding organs and caused by the working of the pedals), and is made of three-ply wirewood and extra heavy gum rubber sheeting with double reinforced joints and will last indefinitely.

THE PEDALS—The pedals are neat in design and very substantial, large enough for a man's foot. Made with an improved waterproof covering and bellows webbing, connected thereto by an original device to allow for stretching.

THE FINISH—The outside covering or finish is especially deserving of attention. The handsome seal leatherette covering not only serves an ornamental purpose, but is waterproof and prevents any moisture from entering the instrument.

APPEARANCE—When folded the organ has the appearance of a neat sample case and is secure against dust, rain, snow or mice.

INSPECTION—Every organ is carefully inspected and the tone corrected before shipment so that every instrument is guaranteed to be in perfect condition and to give complete satisfaction.

The organ is endorsed by Sunday schools and leading evangelists throughout the country and will be found to adequately fill every requirement for a high grade folding organ. Size open, 10x29x30 inches. Size closed, 10x18x30 inches. Actual weight, 60 pounds; boxed for shipment, about 65 pounds.

No. 46C70 The Universal Beckwith Folding Organ.
Price.. **$27.50**

OUR QUEEN CHAPEL ORGAN, $26.45

A BEAUTIFUL INSTRUMENT at an extremely low price. **Reduced from $30.00.** This instrument is made for those who desire to purchase a Chapel style organ at a very low price, and is intended for church, Sunday school, singing society, school and home use. **We send our written, binding 25-year guarantee with each organ,** in which we agree to repair or replace, **free of charge to customers,** all parts proving defective in material or workmanship. **This is the most liberal guarantee ever offered** and proves our statement as to the instrument's fine quality. A HANDSOME STOOL AND COMPLETE INSTRUCTION BOOK, CONTAINING MANY SELECTIONS, SENT FREE WITH EACH ORGAN. **Remember, satisfaction guaranteed or money refunded.**

GENERAL DESCRIPTION.

Size of Organ—This organ is 4 feet 3 inches high, 2 feet deep and 3 feet 10 inches wide and weighs, boxed for shipment, about 380 pounds. **General Description**—This organ comes with 5 octaves, 11 stops and 2 knee swells. Contains 4 sets of reeds as follows: 1 set round pipe-like Principal reeds of 24 notes, 1 set exquisitely pure, sweet Melodia reeds of 37 notes, 1 set rich, mellow, smooth Diapason reeds of 24 notes, 1 set charmingly brilliant Celeste reeds of 37 notes; 122 in all. 11 necessary stops, as follows: Diapason, Principal, Dulciana, Melodia, Celeste, Cremona, Bass Coupler, Treble Coupler, Diapason Forte, Principal Forte, Vox Humana. Grand Organ and Knee Swell. **Description of Case**-This organ is made in solid oak, beautifully carved, decorated and ornamented, neat and tasty in design, substantially and durably constructed, elegantly finished, has upright bellows of great capacity, best steel springs, rollers, handles, safety lamp stands, sliding fall cover with lock, all the latest conveniences and improvements. The back is finished in panels and scroll work, making a very ornamental organ for a stage or platform. **The bellows** used with this action are the finest and most powerful possible to construct. The lumber is highly seasoned, the silk rubber cloth is extra heavy, and bellows cannot leak. The automatic air valve relieves all surplus pressure, so that the bellows cannot be overstrained. They are self regulating. Pedal straps are ingeniously fixed by a contrivance which will not wear and positively prevents breakage. **Tone**—This all important feature has been most carefully looked after. The reeds in this organ being especially tuned and voiced for chapel work, the tone is exceedingly brilliant and powerful, at the same time pure and melodious, a combination rarely found except in our organs. **About the Fittings**—Among the fittings of this organ will be found bevel faced celluloid stop knobs, nickel plated pedal frames with best brussels carpet, extension lamp shelves and handles. You will find every little point has been well looked after, and nothing but the very best quality of material, including wire, leather, felt, rubber cloth, etc., goes into this instrument, hence our 25-year binding guarantee. **We can also furnish this organ in walnut finish if desired.** PLEASE NOTE that walnut finish does not mean solid walnut but that the case is made of hardwood and stained in close imitation of walnut.

WE WILL GUARANTEE YOU CANNOT DUPLICATE THIS ORGAN ELSEWHERE FOR ANYWHERE NEAR THIS LOW FIGURE, AND OUR PRICE OF $26.45 SAVES YOU MONEY.

Catalogue No. 46C76 Front View.

Back View.

No. 46C76 QUEEN CHAPEL ORGAN
Order by number........ **$26.45**

REDUCED FROM OUR FORMER PRICE OF $34.00.
Catalogue No. 46C85. Order by Number.

GUARANTEED FOR 25 YEARS.
THIS IS THE LONGEST, STRONGEST AND MOST BINDING GUARANTEE ISSUED WITH ANY ORGAN.

THE BECKWITH CHOIR GEM

$32.75 No Such Bargain Was Ever Offered Before.

WE GUARANTEE this the best organ for school or church that has ever been offered at anything like the price. When you buy this organ from us at $32.75 you are buying it on the basis of the actual cost of material and labor, with only our one small percentage of profit added, buying it for less money than your local dealer can buy in quantities.

IF YOU ARE IN THE MARKET for a Chapel Organ for home, for school or for church, we are extremely anxious to receive your order, especially if the instrument is going into a public place, not for the little profit there will be in it to us, but for the opportunity to show people the value it is possible for us to furnish on our one small profit, manufacturer to consumer plan.

WE KNOW THAT ONE OF THESE ORGANS bought at $32.75 and placed in any public place, will make us friends and customers, and if favored with your order we will make it our business to see that you receive such a chapel organ as has never been shown by any other concern at anything like the price.

THIS HANDSOME ORGAN is made of solid black walnut or oak, finished in front and back. It comes complete with bench and instruction book as illustrated. The price quoted is for the organ carefully boxed and delivered free on board cars in Chicago.

SIZE OF ORGAN. This organ is 4 feet 6 inches high, 3 feet 8 inches wide and 2 feet deep, and weighs, boxed for shipment, about 400 pounds.

BY REFERRING TO THE FREIGHT RATES in front of the book, you can calculate very closely what the freight will be, but you will find it will amount to next to nothing as compared with what you will save in price.

APPEARANCE OF THE ORGAN. From the illustrations, which our artist has engraved from photographs, you can form some idea of the appearance of the instrument. We show both back and front views.

REMEMBER that the reeds in a church organ must be bent and tuned for that particular purpose, or the organ will not be suitable for church and Sunday school work. Most of the church organs now on the market are simply parlor organs in church organ cases, the reeds being bent and tuned for parlor use only. As a consequence when they are used in halls or churches they fail to develop the necessary volume of tone which alone will constitute a good church organ. There are very few men in this country today who have the ability to bend and tune reeds for church organs. One of the very best is now in the employ of the Beckwith Organ Company, and the peculiar manner in which these reeds are bent and tuned accounts for the great success which has attended our church organs. We are selling these organs almost at cost, and you cannot afford to miss this splendid opportunity to purchase a high grade church organ at an extremely low price.

DESCRIPTION OF CASE. This organ is made in solid oak or black walnut, as desired, beautifully carved, decorated and ornamented, neat and tasty in design, substantially and durably constructed, elegantly finished, has upright bellows of great capacity, **best steel springs, rollers, handles, lamp stand, sliding fall cover with lock**, all the latest conveniences and improvements.

THE BELLOWS used with this action are the finest and most powerful possible to construct. The lumber is highly seasoned, the silk rubber cloth is extra heavy, and bellows will not leak. The automatic air valve relieves all surplus pressure so that the bellows cannot be overstrained. They are self regulating. Pedal straps are ingeniously fixed by a contrivance which will not wear and positively prevents breakage.

THE TONE. The tone, as in all our organs, is remarkably pure, sweet and harmonious, combining volume and variety, while the exceedingly low price at which we offer it is alone sufficient to recommend it to those desiring a really first class organ for Sunday school, church, school or parlor use.

THIS HANDSOME CHAPEL ORGAN IS BUILT FOR THOSE WHO DESIRE PLENTY OF MUSIC AND A PLAIN, DURABLE CASE.

ABOUT THE FITTINGS. Among the fittings of this organ will be found bevel faced celluloid stop knobs, nickel plated pedal frames with best Brussels carpet, extension lamp shelf and handles. You will find every little point has been well looked after, **and nothing but the very best quality of material**, including wire, leather, felt, rubber cloth, etc., goes into this instrument, hence our **25-year binding guarantee.**

IF YOU ARE THINKING OF PURCHASING a church organ, you cannot afford to make your purchase elsewhere without giving us an opportunity to send you one of these splendid instruments on approval. We do not ask you to take any chances or to assume any risks, because we will send you the organ for trial and approval, entirely at our own expense. We ship out these organs on our great 30 days free trial offer, and if they do not prove entirely satisfactory they can be returned to us, we will refund the entire purchase price and pay the freight charges both ways. Why should you purchase an organ in the usual way and pay the extremely high prices which are always made up of intermediate dealers' profits, when you can purchase this splendid organ from us for about one-half the price you would have to pay the ordinary music dealer. These are things that you should consider when you are ready to purchase your organ. With every one of these organs we issue a binding twenty-five year guarantee, which fully protects you from loss. If you do not find when you receive the organ that it is the greatest bargain you ever saw and fully equal, if not superior to the same grade of organ offered generally for twice the price, you are at liberty to return it to us, we will refund your money and pay the entire expense of transportation.

At the top of page 120 we are showing an illustration of the splendid exhibit of Beckwith Organs at the World's Fair last year, and also a picture of one of the two immense Beckwith organ factories. We wish to urge you to read this page carefully, as we know you can do so to advantage if you desire to purchase an organ. The Choir Gem Organ is one of the instruments which received a diploma of merit awarded by the board of judges composed of eminent musicians from all over the country. It is one of the best evidences of its superior qualities.

FREE.

We send absolutely free with each one of these organs a fine bench, made in wood to match the case of the organ. Also complete instruction book, by the aid of which one can learn to play the instrument without the assistance of a teacher.

No. 46C85 Action A. Five octaves. Price.....**$32.75**
No. 46C86 Action C. Five octaves. Price......**37.75**

The above prices are for oak only. If you desire the organ in walnut you must add $2.00 to the above prices. Be sure to specify in your order whether you desire oak or walnut. See page 119 for description of actions.

You will see it is nicely finished with full panel back, elaborately decorated and ornamented and fully equal to organs which retail at more than double the price.

No. 46C85
ORDER BY NUMBER

BACK VIEW OF OUR Choir Gem Organ.

OUR HIGHEST GRADE ...THE... BECKWITH CATHEDRAL CHAPEL ORGAN

Catalogue No. 46098 **FOR $49.25**

WONDERFUL VALUE.

WE PRESENT THIS as one of the finest instruments we are able to offer, and recommend it especially for SUNDAY SCHOOL, CHURCH, LODGE, SCHOOL or PARLOR; in fact, for all audience purposes.

THIS IS AN ENTIRELY NEW DESIGN. Fitted with our patent dust-proof action, 5 octaves, 9 sets of beautifully pipe toned reeds, 257 in all, double octave couplers, 18 necessary stops, 2 knee swells; all the very latest improvements. THIS IS ONE OF THE MOST POWERFUL PUBLIC SERVICE ORGANS EVER PRODUCED.

ON THE HIGH QUALITY OF OUR INSTRUMENTS, ON THE MONEY WE CAN SAVE YOU, ON OUR ESTABLISHED REPUTATION EVERYWHERE FOR FAIR AND HONORABLE DEALING, **WE BASE OUR CLAIM FOR YOUR ORDER.**

THESE ORGANS ARE COVERED BY A WRITTEN, BINDING TWENTY-FIVE YEARS' GUARANTEE, by the terms and conditions of which, if any piece or part gives out by reason of defect in material or workmanship, we will replace it free of charge. This is the longest, strongest and most binding guarantee issued by any concern on an organ.

DESCRIPTION OF CASE. The case is 55 inches high, 58 inches long, 24 inches wide, made of the very best selected quarter sawed oak, finished golden, very elaborately carved, decorated, ornamented, finished and polished, as shown in the back and front view illustrations. It is oil finished and hand rubbed over three coats of varnish. It is finished front and back and exactly as shown in illustrations. Has lamp stand, music desk receptacle, sliding fall cover with lock, rollers for moving, and in fact has every modern improvement.

WE CAN FURNISH walnut case if desired, but recommend our quarter sawed oak, golden finish, which is a dark color, as the handsomest organ case ever made, and one which will prove more universally satisfactory than walnut. Be sure to state finish desired when ordering

Order by Number. No. 46098

The above picture, engraved from a photograph, shows the front of our Cathedral Chapel Organ.

IF YOU ARE THINKING of purchasing a church organ, you cannot afford to make your purchase elsewhere without giving us an opportunity to send you one of these splendid instruments on approval. We do not ask you to take any chances or to assume any risks, because we will send you the organ for trial and approval, entirely at our own expense. We ship out these organs on our great thirty days free trial offer, and if they do not prove entirely satisfactory, they can be returned to us, we will refund the entire purchase price and pay the freight charges both ways. Why should you purchase an organ in the usual way and pay the extremely high prices which are always made up of intermediate dealers' profits, when you can purchase this splendid organ from us for about one-half the price you would have to pay the ordinary music dealer? These are things that you should consider when you are ready to purchase your organ. With every one of these organs we issue a binding twenty-five year guarantee, which fully protects you from loss.

No. 46098
ACTION E; FIVE OCTAVES. Price - - - - - - - - **$49.25**

No. 460100
ACTION E; SIX OCTAVES. Price - - - - - - - - **$57.25**

If desired in walnut, add $2.00 to the above prices.

See page 119 for description of actions.

NAMES OF STOPS: Diapason, Principal, Dulciana, Melodia, Bourdon, Clarionet, Cornet, Cornet Echo, Cremona, Flute, Viola, Dulcet, Sub-Bass, Bass Coupler, Treble Coupler, Diapason Forte, Principal Forte, Vox Humana, Grand Organ and Knee Swell.

THE TONE. The action is the finest constructed. Built especially for the highest grade of church organ, and is peculiarly rich and full in tone and expression, and in the hands of the skilled organist, orchestral and pipe organ effects can be beautifully imitated. The voicing and peculiar arrangement of the reeds and the careful attention to the tuning have enabled us to place before our friends and the general public an action that we can pronounce to be **absolutely perfect.** It is practically dustproof and especially prepared and adapted to withstand all climatic changes. **The organ weighs, boxed for shipment, about 500 pounds.**

KINDLY REFER TO PAGE 120, on which you will find an illustration and description of the splendid exhibit of BECKWITH ORGANS at the World's Fair last year. The Cathedral Chapel Organ shown on this page received honorable mention from the judges and was awarded a diploma of merit and medal of honor for superiority in construction and finish. We ask you to read carefully what we have to say in regard to this exhibit and the Beckwith Organ factories.

FREE. We send free with every one of these organs a fine organ bench, as shown in the illustration, and a complete instruction book, by the aid of which any one can learn to play the instrument without the assistance of a teacher.

OUR GREAT VIOLIN BARGAINS.

A SPLENDID LINE OF THESE POPULAR INSTRUMENTS.

CAREFULLY TESTED AND APPROVED BY OUR VIOLIN EXPERT. EACH ONE A BARGAIN.

NO MUSICAL INSTRUMENTS are so susceptible of false valuations as violins. This is the reason why the public has been paying such high prices for such instruments in the past. No one but an expert is capable of judging the true value of a violin, and for this reason the purchaser often pays three or four times what the instrument is really worth.

IN ORDER TO PROTECT OUR CUSTOMERS against this we have engaged a violin expert who gives his whole time to the selection and purchase of violins. Each instrument is examined carefully and its true value fixed before it is purchased. We add to this value our one small margin of profit and you pay for the instrument just what it is worth and not a cent more. In this way you are always sure of getting your money's worth. Our great purchasing power gives us an immense advantage over other dealers and enables us to buy our violins at a much lower valuation than any other dealers can secure. We give our customers the full benefit of this advantage by selling the instrument to them at the actual manufacturer's price with one small percentage of profit added.

IT IS A WELL KNOWN FACT that a violin will grow better with age, provided it is properly made, so that money spent for a good violin is the very best investment you can make. Our expert examines every instrument to see if it is properly made, and the violin which you buy from us today for $5.00 may be worth many times that sum in the course of a few years. When you buy a violin in the usual way you are never sure of the future of your investment. Purchase one of the violins listed below and we will guarantee that the tone will become mellower, sweeter and more powerful with each succeeding year. We are always glad to have our customers compare the violins they purchase from us with those sold at a much higher price by other dealers, as we know that our instruments will always be found to have a sweeter tone, greater volume and be much handsomer in appearance. We give you an opportunity to make such comparison under our very liberal terms of shipment and you can fully satisfy yourself as to the merits of the instrument before we ask you to finally accept it.

No. 12C210 ORDER BY NUMBER

ALWAYS REMEMBER that a poorly made violin will never grow any better no matter how many years it is used, and when you buy a violin from us we guarantee that it is properly made, and this fact alone fully insures the future of your investment.

FREE. We send absolutely free with each violin a fine bow, a box of rosin, a set of strings and a complete instruction book.

UPON RECEIPT OF $1.00, we send any violin C. O. D. You can examine it at your express office and, if you find it perfectly satisfactory, pay the express agent the balance and the express charges. If you do not find it satisfactory it will be returned at our expense and the $1.00 will be cheerfully refunded. Most of our customers prefer to send cash in full with their orders because in that way they can save the charge which the express companies always make for collecting and returning the money. This charge will amount to from 25 to 50 cents on each shipment.

OUR TEN DAYS' TRIAL OFFER. Order one of the violins listed below, use it ten days and if you do not find it satisfactory you may return it to us. We will pay express charges both ways and refund your money in full.

OUR $1.95 STRADIVARIUS MODEL

No. 12C210

IN THIS VIOLIN we are furnishing a genuine Stradivarius model at an extremely low price. While we always recommend our customers to purchase the highest price violin their circumstances will permit, still we believe they will find no instrument at this price which will give better satisfaction. We have sold a large number of these instruments since we have begun catalogueing them and they are giving satisfaction in every case. They are made of specially selected wood, covered with beautiful transparent varnish of reddish brown color and highly finished. They possess a tone very seldom found in instruments of this price and are equal in every way to violins generally sold at twice the price. Shipping weight, 7 pounds.

No. 12C210 Price, $1.95

FRONT VIEW

BACK VIEW

No. 12C210 STRADIVARIUS VIOLIN. Price, $1.95.

OUR $3.25 CONSERVATORY MODEL.

THE GREATEST BARGAIN IN A CHEAP VIOLIN EVER OFFERED TO THE PUBLIC. GUARANTEED TO BE SATISFACTORY OR MONEY REFUNDED. USUALLY SOLD FOR FROM $6.00 TO $7.00, OUR GREAT BARGAIN PRICE, $3.25.

No. 12C214

THIS VIOLIN is a Stradivarius model, handsomely finished throughout with transparent reddish brown varnish, beautifully shaded and handsomely polished. Has a fine resonant tone and goes to the customer with the sound post accurately set, so that it is only necessary to place the strings in position and tune them up in order to use the instrument. It has a solid ebony fingerboard and tailpiece and is full size in every particular. We can recommend this instrument as a beauty in every respect and it is an exceedingly fine instrument considering the price we ask for it.

IN PURCHASING THIS VIOLIN we desire to impress you with the fact that we guarantee it, as well as our other violins, to give satisfaction. But in case you should not be fully satisfied with the instrument when you receive it, you can return it to us at our expense and we will cheerfully refund your money. We do not desire to send out violins at any time which will not give the customer perfect satisfaction. But we desire our customers to bear the fact in mind that we do not guarantee this instrument to be a $50.00 violin. We charge you $3.25 for the instrument and we will guarantee that it is as good an instrument as you can purchase anywhere else for from $5.00 to $6.00.

THE ENGRAVING which accompanies this description shows you the back and front view of this splendid instrument. This illustration is photographed from the violin so that you can get a good idea of the detail of construction and general appearance of the instrument. You cannot, however, get any idea of the handsome blending of colors, beautiful grain of the wood, or the powerful and sweet tone of the instrument from this engraving. You can only judge of these points by seeing the instrument and playing upon it. We are so well satisfied that this instrument will please you that we are prepared to send it to you upon receipt of $1.00, balance C. O. D., to give you a full opportunity to thoroughly examine and test it. Do not confound these instruments with the cheap violins usually sold by other dealers, because the price we make upon this instrument, $3.25, represents the actual cost of material and labor at the factory with only one small margin of profit added. When you buy a violin at the same price from your dealer you can safely figure that at least one-half of the price is made up of dealers' profits and selling expenses, and does not go into the construction of the violin at all. The original cost of any violin is less than one-half of the price which you pay the dealer when you purchase in the usual way. Our method of selling, directly from the factory to you, insures you purchasing the instrument at what it costs to manufacture it, with but one small percentage of profit added. These are all points that you should carefully consider when you are ready to purchase a violin; examine the violins which your dealer offers you at this price, and then order this Conservatory violin from us, and if, after a careful comparison, you do not admit that our instrument far excels them in appearance, beauty of finish, volume and sweetness of tone, we will cheerfully receive it back, refund your money and pay the express charges both ways.

No. 12C214 Conservatory Model. Price.................. $3.25

No. 12C214 ORDER BY NUMBER

CONSERVATORY

FRONT VIEW

BACK VIEW

No. 12C214 CONSERVATORY VIOLIN. Price, $3.25.

OUR GENUINE MAGGINI MODEL VIOLIN.

AN EXACT COPY OF THE WELL KNOWN MAGGINI VIOLINS, MADE BY ONE OF THE GREATEST ITALIAN VIOLIN MAKERS. $10.00 VIOLIN FOR $4.35.

FOR QUALITY AND POWER OF TONE **this is one of the best violins on the market, considering the price we ask.** The model is copied directly from the violins made by this celebrated maker, and is constructed of selected and seasoned wood, beautifully finished and covered with transparent reddish brown varnish, highly polished. It is trimmed with solid ebony fingerboard and tailpiece, and like the celebrated Maggini violin, has the characteristic, double inlaid purfling, giving it a dignified and handsome appearance. It has great purity and volume of tone and is a violin that sells at retail from $8.00 to $10.00.

THE INSTRUMENT **goes to you complete so that all it is necessary for you to do is to place the strings in position and tune it ready for playing.** We guarantee it to give satisfaction, and we are satisfied that you cannot purchase the same grade of instrument from any other dealer for less than $8.00 to $10.00. All we desire is an opportunity to send you this instrument for examination and we know that you will find that everything we say about it is true. In power, volume and sweetness of tone as well as general appearance, it is not equaled by any instrument on the market at anywhere near this price.

THE ILLUSTRATION **which accompanies this description will give you some idea of the general design and ornamentation of this violin.** You will notice the double purfling around the entire instrument, which is characteristic of the works of this celebrated Italian maker. Also the extreme bulge of both the top and back of the instrument. The engraving, however, cannot give you any adequate idea of the beautiful wood used in this instrument and the splendid finish which brings out the grain to such great advantage. **The beautiful combination of colors, made possible by the highly tinted transparent varnish with which the instrument is coated,** is a feature of these splendid violins and it is only necessary to place one of these instruments beside a violin for which you will pay the same price at your dealer's to note the great difference in appearance, beauty of finish and general construction. An expert would detect the difference instantly, by simply drawing the bow across the strings. In this instrument we are giving every musician an opportunity to purchase a very fine copy of the old and celebrated Maggini violins at a price which simply represents the cost of material and workmanship at the factory, with our well known one small margin of profit added.

No. 12C216

$4.35

SEND US ONE DOLLAR **and let us send you this instrument C. O. D. for examination and trial.** If the instrument does not prove satisfactory in every respect, it will not cost you anything to try it because you can return it at our expense and we will refund the one dollar you have deposited with us. We make these liberal terms for the purpose of giving every musician an opportunity to possess one of these beautiful instruments.

No. 12C216 Genuine Maggini Model Violin. Price.............................. **$4.35**

BEAR IN MIND **we furnish (without extra charge) with every violin, an outfit consisting of extra strings, instruction book and finger board chart, as described on page 133.**

BACK VIEW

No. 12C216 MAGGINI VIOLIN. PRICE, $4.35.

OUR STAINER VIOLIN FOR $5.15.

A Violin exactly like the famous STAINER INSTRUMENT, at the exceedingly low price of $5.15.

An instrument guaranteed to increase in value with continued use. Warranted as to tune, tone, workmanship and appearance.

No. 12C218.

ALL THE STAINER VIOLINS **are much sought after by expert violinists of today on account of their sweet and penetrating tone.** The violins that we offer are patterned carefully after the celebrated Stainer model and we do not doubt but that with a few years' use they will approach nearly to the powerful and rich tone of the original Stainer instruments. These violins are fitted with the best quality ebony trimmings, coated with handsome transparent varnish and highly polished and well finished in every respect. We are always glad to send these instruments out, because we know they will be received as satisfactory by the purchaser. They have a handsome appearance, sweet tone, and enough volume to command the applause of the listener.

No. 12C218

$5.15

WE UNHESITATINGLY RECOMMEND **this instrument to all who desire an instrument for solo or orchestra work at a moderate price.** It is an instrument that you would ordinarily pay $10.00 for and can be depended upon to be an exact copy of the violins made by this great German maker. We believe that this instrument, with proper use and care, will grow more and more valuable every day, and that it will develop into a violin of which the owner may well feel proud. The violin goes to the customer complete in every respect, with strings, rosin, bow, tuning pipe and case. **THIS INSTRUMENT is sold upon the same terms as all of our other violins, and if it does not prove satisfactory it can be returned at our expense,** and we will refund every cent of the purchase price. We desire to place one of these instruments in the hands of every player who desires to learn the instrument without investing a large amount of money, and we guarantee that he will get the worth of his money in every respect.

WE BELIEVE **it is high time for musicians to quit paying fancy prices for musical instruments.** The tone of the ordinary violin is practically an unknown quantity unless it is first thoroughly made by a maker with a reputation in this line. We guarantee that these Stainer violins, which we offer you, are made by one of the most celebrated violin makers of Germany; also, that we are not charging you any fancy price for any supposed excellence of tone, but are simply charging you a price which represents the original cost of material and labor at the factory. **While we guarantee the tone of every one of our violins we do not add anything extra to the price to cover this particular quality.** We simply desire to make a uniformly small margin of profit on everything that we sell and we are giving you a very rare opportunity to own one of these celebrated Stainer copies at a price which no other dealer can offer you. In fact, we can sell you one of these violins at a less price than your dealer will have to give the wholesaler or manufacturer for the same instrument. This is made possible by the great advantage we possess in purchasing, and the fact that we sell the instruments almost directly from manufacturer to the customer. We ask you to carefully consider the fact that you do not take any chances whatever in ordering one of these violins from us, because we are willing to take all the risk and leave you to be the judge of whether or not the instrument is exactly as we represent it. **We will ship it to you with the understanding that if you do not find that you are saving from $4.00 to $5.00 at least, you can return it to us at our expense, and we will cheerfully refund every cent you have paid.**

No. 12C218 Our Stainer Violin. Price **$5.15**

BACK VIEW

No. 12C218 STAINER VIOLIN. PRICE, $5.15.

OUR PAGANINI GUARNERIUS VIOLIN, $5.45.

An Exact Copy of the Violin Used by That Marvelous Player.

A BEAUTIFUL MODEL AND A SPLENDID TONE. ACCURATELY MADE AND FINELY FINISHED.

THIS IS A SPLENDID INSTRUMENT in every respect and is an exact copy of the Guarnerius violin used by the celebrated Paganini during his life. This model has never been offered to violinists at this price before and we are giving you an opportunity to purchase a copy of this celebrated violin at an extremely low price. The back, sides and neck are made of pieces of figured maple and the top of choice selected, seasoned silver spruce. The entire instrument is coated with beautiful transparent varnish, finely shaded and polished. The instrument is trimmed throughout with solid ebony, finely polished and its entire appearance is fine in the extreme.

THIS INSTRUMENT is especially desirable for those who desire to purchase a good violin at a low price. It has a full, sweet tone of great carrying power and has never failed to give satisfaction. We furnish this instrument, complete with bow, case, strings, etc., so that it is ready for use when you receive it. We desire to recommend it to all who desire to purchase a fine violin at a low price and upon receipt of $1.00 we will ship it C. O. D. to any part of the country. If it does not prove satisfactory it may be returned to us and the money will be cheerfully refunded.

THE ENGRAVING which accompanies this description shows the front and back of this beautiful violin, but no engraving, however good, will be adequate to carry to your mind any of the several points in beauty of appearance and excellence of workmanship which the instrument possesses. The back and sides are beautifully and evenly flamed and the varnish, with which the instrument is coated, brings out the grain of the wood in a perfect manner.

AT $5.45 we furnish the violin complete with case, fine Brazilwood bow, extra set of strings, rosin, fingerboard chart and instruction book.

THE PRICE which we ask you for this instrument represents but a very small part of its real value, as we do not charge you any fancy price for its excellent quality of tone, but the price we fix on it simply represents the cost of material and the amount paid out by the manufacturer for labor. We are selling you the instrument at the same small margin of profit at which we sell our groceries, dry goods, etc. We know it is the custom for dealers to fix fancy prices upon violins according to the excellent quality of their tone, but we are not dealing in violin tones, and we simply charge you the cost of material and labor with one small margin of profit added. We, however, wish you to remember that we fully guarantee the tone of every instrument which we sell. We are enabled to do this from the fact that all our violins are made by one of the best makers and the care and thoroughness exercised in their construction fully justifies us in guaranteeing the tone.

No. 12C219 Our Paganini Guarnerius Violin. Price..**$5.45**

BACK VIEW
No. 12C219 PAGANINI VIOLIN. Price, $5.45.

OUR $6.10 STRADIVARIUS MODEL VIOLIN.

A Violin in Which the Greatest Work of this Most Celebrated of All Makers is Accurately Copied.

ONE OF OUR BEST BARGAINS, $6.10

Complete With Brazilwood Bow, Rosin, Extra Set of Strings, Fingerboard Chart and Instruction Book.

THESE VIOLINS are made especially for us by one of the most celebrated violin makers of Europe, and are patterned accurately after the violins of the celebrated Antonious Stradivarius, who was probably the most celebrated violin maker that ever lived. The model has been strictly followed by the maker and we guarantee the instrument to possess all of the characteristics of the genuine Stradivarius violins. It has a two-piece maple back beautifully flamed, as shown in the illustration. The top is of resonant spruce, especially selected, and the entire instrument is coated with a reddish brown transparent varnish beautifully shaded in imitation of an old violin. **The neck and scroll are made of curly maple, corresponding with the back and side. The fingerboard, tailpiece and pegs are of the best quality selected ebony. As each one of these instruments is carefully examined** to see that it conforms exactly to the model after which it is patterned, the purchaser may rest assured he is getting a perfectly correct copy of the violins of this Italian violin maker. The purchase of one of these instruments will mean an investment which will increase in value with each succeeding year, as the effect of the tone vibrations and the constant hardening process through which the vegetable matter in the wood goes, will finally result in producing a resonance for which old violins are famous. We have sold many of these violins upon the recommendations of violin teachers to their pupils and we have yet to receive one complaint in regard to their quality. **May we not have an opportunity of shipping you one of these splendid instruments** with the understanding that if you do not find it equal to any $10.00 or $12.00 instrument which you can purchase in your own town you can return it to us and we will cheerfully refund your money and pay the express charges both ways?

THE ACCOMPANYING ENGRAVING is photographed directly from the instrument and shows both the front and the back view very nicely. It will give you some idea of the beautiful details of the model and the fine proportions of the instrument. Of course it can give you no idea of the beauty of appearance, fineness of finish and excellence of tone quality which is one of the characteristics of this entire line. If you desire an instrument which will give you good service, upon which it will be a pleasure to play and which will have the appearance of a $15.00 or $20.00 instrument, you cannot do better than give us an order for one of these splendid violins. When you purchase a violin at $6.10 from your dealer you are purchasing an instrument which probably costs less than $3.00 to manufacture, the balance of the price being made up of intermediate dealers' profits and selling expenses which you have to pay when you purchase the instrument.

THE PRICE which we make on this instrument, $6.10, simply represents the price we pay the manufacturer, with but one small percentage of profit added to pay us for handling and selling the instrument. We do not ask you to pay three or four different dealers' profits and we do not add anything extra to the price to pay for imaginary qualities in the instrument. All we charge you for any of these violins is exactly what the instrument is worth, no more and no less. You cannot afford to purchase an instrument elsewhere, without considering carefully our line of violins and giving us an opportunity to send you one for examination and comparison with the instruments offered by other dealers.

REMEMBER, that we allow you to return, at our expense, any instrument which does not prove satisfactory and we agree to cheerfully refund the money you have paid. Under these liberal terms of shipment you do not run any risk whatever, in giving us your order for one of these splendid violins.

No. 12C222 Our Stradivarius Model Violin. Price.... **$6.10**

BACK VIEW
No. 12C222 STRADIVARIUS VIOLIN. Price, $6.10.

OUR AMATI VIOLIN

ANOTHER SPLENDID BARGAIN $7.2

A True Copy of the Instruments of this Great Maker. An Instrument that will Grow in Value with Continued Use.

THIS INSTRUMENT is an exact copy of the celebrated violins of Nicholas Amati, who was born in Cremona, I He was one of the celebrated family of violin makers, and is considered by many the finest mak violins the family produced. His violins were noted for their beauty of shape and full, round, sweet tone. The illustrat it made from a photograph of the instrument itself and falls far short of bringing out the beautiful flame of the wood an or rich combination of color which is characteristic of this violin. This instrument has a one-piece back made of richly fl nts maple, the sides and neck of beautiful curly maple and the top is made of fine silver spruce. The entire instrument is tru- with a beautiful transparent varnish of reddish brown shade. The instrument is highly polished. **The varnish with** oice this instrument's coated, is made by a secret process and has been declared by many violin makers to very nearly ap ber the splendid varnish used by Nicholas Amati. It gives a rich, splendid appearance to the instrument and improv om- preserves the tone. **The back, tailpiece and fingerboard are made of solid ebony.** The purchaser will find in this instr arge an exact reproduction of the old Amati violins and one which will improve remarkably with age. Many violin performers test the Amati model to any other and there are many points in which they excel in beauty of appearance. We desire t this instrument in the hands of all who desire an instrument of this celebrated model and we will do so with the ass idid that the same grade of instrument cannot be purchased from any other dealer at anywhere near the price. by

WHY SHOULD YOU PURCHASE a violin in the usual way and pay a fancy price, in which is included the profi olin selling expenses of several different dealers, when you can purchase one of ish splendid instruments from us at a price which simply represents the cost of material and labor at the factory with b rth small percentage of profit added? This price is made possible by our method of selling these instruments direct from fa t- to customer. We are the first house to handle and sell musical instruments upon the same small percentage of profit th y make upon groceries, dry goods, etc. We do not ask customers to pay any fancy price for supposed fine qualities of but simply ask them to pay the manufacturer's price to which we add a small profit to pay us for handling and selling th struments. As all of our violins are well and thoroughly made, we are prepared to guarantee the tone. **We send free w every violin, a case, rosin, fine brazilwood bow, extra set of strings, fingerboard chart and instruction book.**

No. 12C223

$7.25

WHEN READY TO PURCHASE YOUR VIOLIN **you will consult your own best interests by giving us an opp tunity to correspond with you in regard to our fine line.** call your attention to the fact that a high price charged for a violin does not guarantee that it will be a fine instrument. Some of the high priced instruments on the market today are not by any means equal, either in appearance or tone, to many of the violins of our cheaper li All of our violins are hand made instruments, and are not in any way to be compared with the cheap machine m instruments usually sold at the price we make. In the general line of cheap machine made instruments the tone simply a matter of accident, but with our splendid line of hand made violins the tone is guaranteed in every respect.

THE SPLENDID AMATI MODEL INSTRUMENT **shown in the accompanying engraving is guar teed fully.** The engraving is made direct fro photograph and will give you an idea of the beautiful grain of the back and sides, but you can get no idea of the tiful blendings of color made by the combination of the wood and the transparent varnish with which it is coated. is an instrument which will grow sweeter and mellower with age, and is one of the best investments you can po make.

No. 12C223 Our Amati Violin. Price..........**$7.25**

WE CAN ALSO FURNISH **this instrument in three-quarter size in exactly the same description,** for the use of younger students, and would be glad to do so on request.

No. 12C224 Three-quarter Size. Price..........**$7.25**

WE HAVE HAD MANY CALLS **for violins for ladies,** and we are glad to announce at this time that we can furnish this instrument, seven-eighths size, of the same model and description as given above.

No. 12C226 Seven-eighths Size. Price.......**$7.25**

FRONT VIEW

BACK VIEW

No. 12C223 AMATI VIOLIN. PRICE, $7.25.

OUR

GUARNERIUS MODEL

An exact copy of the celebrated King Joseph Violins. Splendidly made by one of the best European makers. A magnificent bargain at $8.75.

No. 12C262

No. 12C262

$8.75

THE GUARNERIUS MODEL has always been a favorite with violin makers on account of its beauty of proportion. It is not quite as flat as the Stradivarius, and, as its maker was easily the peer of Stradivarius in making violins, there is little to choose between the two models. We guarantee this instrument to be a perfectly correct copy of the violins of this celebrated Italian master, and in beauty of finish and sweetness of tone it is unequaled by any violin on the market at anywhere near the price. **The back, sides and neck are made of highly seasoned, beautifully flamed maple and the top is made of the finest silver spruce.** The entire instrument is given a coat of beautiful transparent amber varnish blending into a reddish color and highly finished. The purfling is accurately and clearly inlaid and the F holes are cut accurately according to the Guarnerius pattern. **No description can give any idea of the beautiful coloring of the wood of which it is made,** and the instrument itself must be seen in order to appreciate the rich combinations and blending of color. The back is made of two pieces, accurately and evenly joined, and like all our violins the instrument is hand made throughout. The proportions of the instrument are exactly those used by Joseph Guarnerius in making his celebrated violins, and this guarantees a broad, rich, full tone.

IT IS TRIMMED THROUGHOUT **with solid ebony and goes to the customer complete with strings, genuine brazilwood bow, rosin, case, etc.,** so that it is only necessary to put the strings in place and tune them up in order to have the instrument ready to play on. These violins are made in Europe especially for us by one of the greatest makers of violins in that country who has access to some of the finest specimens of old Guarnerius violins. In this instrument the purchaser will find all of the characteristics which distinguish the Guarnerius violins from all other instruments of this character, and may feel perfectly satisfied that he has an instrument in all points resembling these famous violins. This is the same violin which the ordinary dealer will ask from $14.00 to $20.00 for, and we are able to offer it at this extremely low price, because we purchased them from the maker on a special contract and ship them with only our one small margin of profit added.

THE ACCOMPANYING ENGRAVING **shows both the front and back of this violin, and will give you a good idea of the splendid grain of the wood of which the instrument is made.** The beautiful combination of color formed by the wood and handsome amber varnish with which it is covered cannot be shown by the engraving. It will be necessary for you to see the instrument and play on it, to get any idea of its beautiful appearance and splendid mellow tone. We offer this instrument to our customers with the assurance that it will take on additional mellowness and sweetness of tone with years of use, and that the beautiful varnish will deepen and grow more beautiful in color as years go by. **You cannot afford to purchase a violin elsewhere without giving us an opportunity to send you this instrument for examination and trial.** If you desire to examine it you can take advantage of our C.O.D. offer, by which you can have the instrument sent upon receipt of $1.00, and pay the balance of the price upon the arrival of the instrument. This gives you an opportunity to test the instrument before paying balance of the price. We also allow you ten days trial upon it, as usual, before accepting the instrument. **With this instrument we give a well finished wooden case.**

No. 12C262 Guarnerius Violin. Price **$8.75**

FRONT VIEW

BACK VIEW

No. 12C262 GUARNERIUS VIOLIN. PRICE, $8.75.

ANOTHER FINE STAINER MODEL.

A FINE COPY OF THE VIOLINS OF THIS GREAT GERMAN MAKER

Beautiful in tone, tune, model and finish. Sold usually by dealers at $25.00. Our great bargain price, $11.45.

WE ARE ABLE TO OFFER in this instrument another fine violin patterned after the violins of this celebrated maker and in a somewhat higher grade than we offer on the previous page. It is an exact copy of the fine old Stainer violin and is a much finer grade than those usually sold by dealers throughout the country. It is an instrument easily sold by dealers at $25.00 and we are glad to ship it to our customers with the assurance that if they do not find it in every respect as represented, they can return it at once at our expense and have every cent of money refunded. **The back is made of a beautiful piece of maple and the top of an extra choice piece of silver spruce.** The entire instrument is covered with beautiful transparent varnish, bringing out the splendid grain of the wood in its utmost perfection. It is trimmed with solid ebony throughout and is an instrument of which any violinist may well be proud. In beauty of finish, sweetness and volume of tone and fineness of workmanship, it is not equaled by any violin on the market at twice the price.

THE INSTRUMENT goes to the customer complete with bow, strings, case, etc. We unhesitatingly recommend this instrument to all who desire a violin either for orchestra or solo use. Do not forget that we guarantee every violin we ship to be satisfactory and if it is not so it can be returned at our expense and the price cheerfully refunded.

THE ACCOMPANYING ENGRAVING will give you a fair idea of the beautiful model of this fine Stainer copy and the appearance of quiet elegance which characterizes this particular instrument. Very little attempt has been made at ornamentation in this violin, except in the extreme beauty of finish, which is made possible by the very finely grained wood and the beautiful transparent varnish which brings out the flaming on the back to great advantage. We sell this instrument at $11.45, but assure our friends that they cannot purchase an instrument of the same grade from any other dealer for less than from $8.00 to $9.00 more than we are asking. When you purchase a violin of this grade from your dealer, the price which you pay does not by any means represent the original manufacturing cost with your dealer's profit added, but it represents the profits and selling expenses of a large number of dealers through whose hands it must pass before it reaches you. **This is what makes the ordinary violin so expensive.** As a matter of fact, the original cost of a good violin is very small in proportion to the amount which the purchaser is asked to pay for it. Most of the price is made up of intermediate dealers' profits and selling expenses. By our method of sale these profits and selling expenses are entirely cut out and we can sell the instrument to you at the price which the manufacturer charges us, simply adding one small margin of profit to recompense us for handling and selling it. We make about the same percentage of profit upon these violins which we make upon our groceries, dry goods and everything else that we handle, and being the largest house in the country selling violins directly to the customer, we can afford to be contented with a very small profit, as we sell so many thousands of these violins every year.

WE GUARANTEE that the customer will get full value for every dollar that he pays us for a violin and we leave it entirely to his decision and allow him to return the instrument at our expense if everything we say in its favor is not found to be true. May we not have the opportunity of placing one of these fine Stainer copies in your hands for trial?

WITH THIS VIOLIN WE FURNISH A NICELY FINISHED WOODEN CASE.

No. 12C264 Price...$11.45

No. 12C264 $11.45

FREE OUTFIT. We furnish extra set of strings, instruction book and fingerboard chart with every violin without extra charge. See full description of this outfit on page 133.

BACK VIEW

FRONT VIEW

No. 12C264 STAINER VIOLIN. PRICE, $11.45.

GENUINE DA SALO MODEL VIOLINS

An Accurate Copy of the Famous Da Salo Violins.

A SPLENDID BARGAIN AT —$13.95—

No. 12C266 $13.95

CASPER DA SALO was a celebrated maker of violins, born in Lombardy, 1558. A characteristic of his violins is a splendid model and a tendency toward ornamentation, the purfling often being formed in scroll work on the back. The violin shown in the illustration is an exact copy of the instrument used by the celebrated Swedish artiste, Ole Bull, with the exception of the excessive ornamentation, which is a characteristic of that instrument. It has double purfling throughout and is made from old and choice wood, which insures sweetness and purity of tone. The scroll work in which the purfling is worked out on the back gives it an appearance of great value and makes it one of the handsomest violins that we sell. The back, neck and sides are made of thoroughly seasoned maple, highly figured and flamed, and the top is made of silver spruce, which is very resonant. The entire instrument is covered with beautiful transparent varnish, highly polished. This is an instrument which we guarantee will grow sweeter and mellower in tone with continued use and an instrument which will double in value in ten years. The genuine Da Salo violins which are now in existence are the handsomest ever conceived. This is not only a handsome musical instrument, but a work of art as well and one of which the owner will never tire. All we ask of you is an opportunity to ship this instrument to you and give you an opportunity to examine it and note its fine quality.

THE ENGRAVING which we show of our Da Salo violin will give you a very fair idea of the peculiar scroll work formed by the purfling on the back of the instrument; also the double purfling around the entire back and top of the instrument. This scroll work in the purfling is characteristic of the Da Salo violins and has been copied to perfection by the maker of these instruments. The engraving also shows very nicely the beautiful flame and grain of the wood, but it is necessary for you to examine the instrument and try it in order to appreciate to the fullest extent its extreme beauty and noble qualities of tone. There are few violins even among the higher priced instruments which can compare with this one either in beauty of appearance or sweetness and grandeur of tone.

DO NOT MAKE THE MISTAKE of comparing this instrument with violins sold by other dealers at this price because we desire you to always bear in mind the fact that when you purchase a violin from any other dealer you are in fact giving twice as much as it is really worth, because you are paying the large profits and selling expenses of the intermediate dealers, whereas you entirely avoid this expense by purchasing one of these splendid instruments from us. You can always be sure that the violin contains the full value of the price you pay for it and that your investment will increase in value every year. Our sales on this instrument have been remarkable, and this is due chiefly to the extreme beauty of the model and finish and the peculiar sonorous and mellow tone which the instrument possesses. Let us urge you not to place your order for a violin elsewhere until you have examined and tried this instrument thoroughly, and remember that you can always have the opportunity to try any one of our violins entirely at our expense. These Da Salo violins are used extensively by orchestral leaders and soloists throughout the country.

We recommend them particularly where a powerful and smooth tone is desired.

WITH THIS VIOLIN WE FURNISH A NICELY FINISHED WOODEN CASE.

No. 12C266 Price...$13.95

FRONT VIEW

BACK VIEW

No. 12C266 DA SALO VIOLIN. PRICE, $13.95.

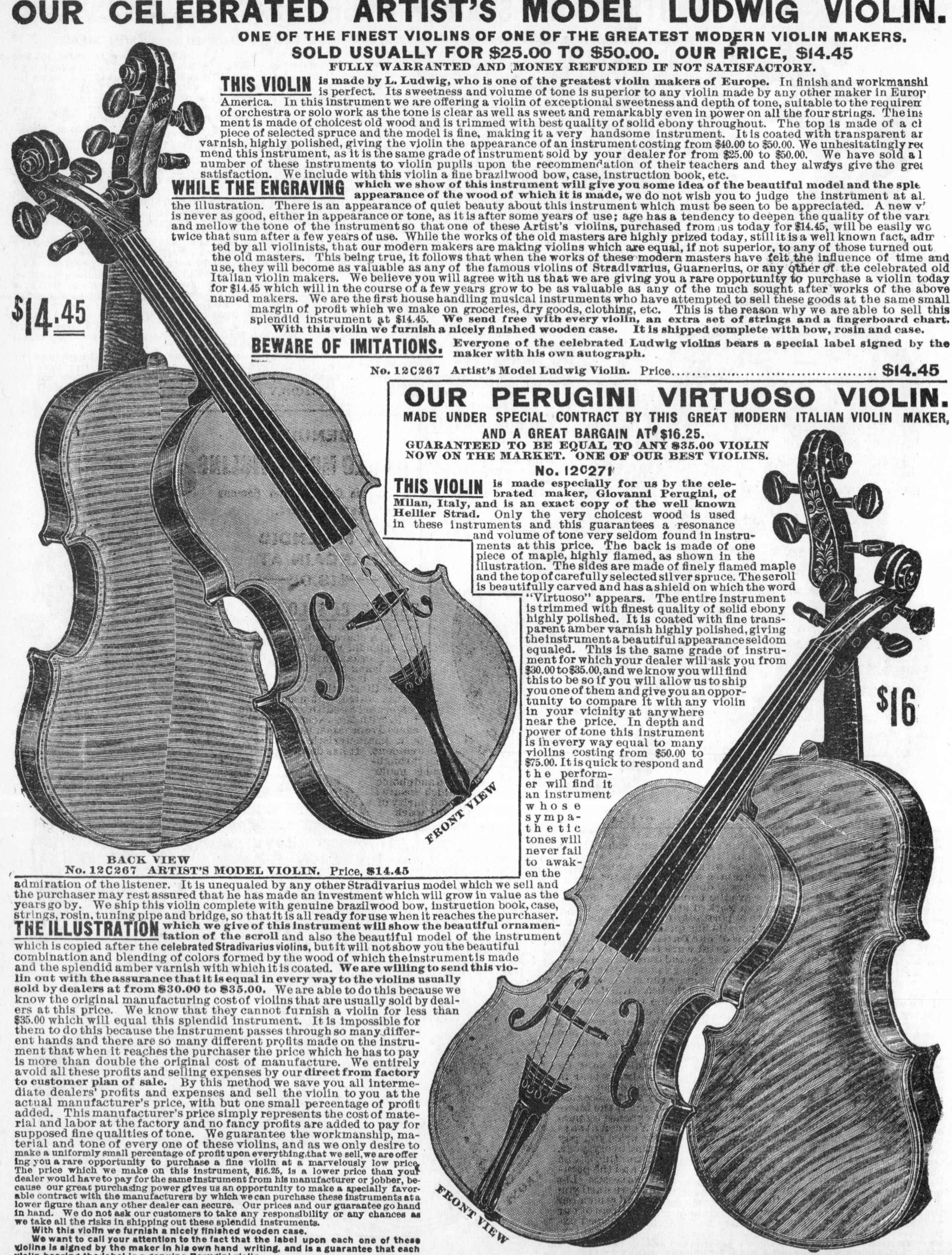

OUR CELEBRATED ARTIST'S MODEL LUDWIG VIOLIN.

ONE OF THE FINEST VIOLINS OF ONE OF THE GREATEST MODERN VIOLIN MAKERS.

SOLD USUALLY FOR $25.00 TO $50.00. OUR PRICE, $14.45

FULLY WARRANTED AND MONEY REFUNDED IF NOT SATISFACTORY.

THIS VIOLIN is made by L. Ludwig, who is one of the greatest violin makers of Europe. In finish and workmanshi is perfect. Its sweetness and volume of tone is superior to any violin made by any other maker in Europ America. In this instrument we are offering a violin of exceptional sweetness and depth of tone, suitable to the requirem of orchestra or solo work as the tone is clear as well as sweet and remarkably even in power on all the four strings. The ins ment is made of choicest old wood and is trimmed with best quality of solid ebony throughout. The top is made of a ch piece of selected spruce and the model is fine, making it a very handsome instrument. It is coated with transparent am varnish, highly polished, giving the violin the appearance of an instrument costing from $40.00 to $50.00. We unhesitatingly rec mend this instrument, as it is the same grade of instrument sold by your dealer for from $25.00 to $50.00. We have sold a l number of these instruments to violin pupils upon the recommendation of their teachers and they always give the grea satisfaction. We include with this violin a fine brazilwood bow, case, instruction book, etc.

WHILE THE ENGRAVING which we show of this instrument will give you some idea of the beautiful model and the sple appearance of the wood of which it is made, we do not wish you to judge the instrument at al the illustration. There is an appearance of quiet beauty about this instrument which must be seen to be appreciated. A new v is never as good, either in appearance or tone, as it is after some years of use; age has a tendency to deepen the quality of the vari and mellow the tone of the instrument so that one of these Artist's violins, purchased from us today for $14.45, will be easily wo twice that sum after a few years of use. While the works of the old masters are highly prized today, still it is a well known fact, adm ted by all violinists, that our modern makers are making violins which are equal, if not superior, to any of those turned out the old masters. This being true, it follows that when the works of these modern masters have felt the influence of time and use, they will become as valuable as any of the famous violins of Stradivarius, Guarnerius, or any other of the celebrated old Italian violin makers. We believe you will agree with us that we are giving you a rare opportunity to purchase a violin today for $14.45 which will in the course of a few years grow to be as valuable as any of the much sought after works of the above named makers. We are the first house handling musical instruments who have attempted to sell these goods at the same small margin of profit which we make on groceries, dry goods, clothing, etc. This is the reason why we are able to sell this splendid instrument at $14.45. **We send free with every violin, an extra set of strings and a fingerboard chart. With this violin we furnish a nicely finished wooden case. It is shipped complete with bow, rosin and case.**

BEWARE OF IMITATIONS. **Everyone of the celebrated Ludwig violins bears a special label signed by the maker with his own autograph.**

No. 12C267 Artist's Model Ludwig Violin. Price.. **$14.45**

$14.45

BACK VIEW

FRONT VIEW

No. 12C267 ARTIST'S MODEL VIOLIN. Price, $14.45

OUR PERUGINI VIRTUOSO VIOLIN.

MADE UNDER SPECIAL CONTRACT BY THIS GREAT MODERN ITALIAN VIOLIN MAKER, AND A GREAT BARGAIN AT $16.25.

GUARANTEED TO BE EQUAL TO ANY $35.00 VIOLIN NOW ON THE MARKET. ONE OF OUR BEST VIOLINS.

No. 12C271

THIS VIOLIN **is made especially for us by the celebrated maker, Giovanni Perugini, of Milan, Italy, and is an exact copy of the well known Hellier Strad.** Only the very choicest wood is used in these instruments and this guarantees a resonance and volume of tone very seldom found in instruments at this price. The back is made of one piece of maple, highly flamed, as shown in the illustration. The sides are made of finely flamed maple and the top of carefully selected silver spruce. The scroll is beautifully carved and has a shield on which the word "Virtuoso" appears. The entire instrument is trimmed with finest quality of solid ebony highly polished. It is coated with fine transparent amber varnish highly polished, giving the instrument a beautiful appearance seldom equaled. This is the same grade of instrument for which your dealer will ask you from $30.00 to $35.00, and we know you will find this to be so if you will allow us to ship you one of them and give you an opportunity to compare it with any violin in your vicinity at anywhere near the price. In depth and power of tone this instrument is in every way equal to many violins costing from $50.00 to $75.00. It is quick to respond and the performer will find it an instrument whose sympathetic tones will never fail to awaken the admiration of the listener. It is unequaled by any other Stradivarius model which we sell and the purchaser may rest assured that he has made an investment which will grow in value as the years go by. We ship this violin complete with genuine brazilwood bow, instruction book, case, strings, rosin, tuning pipe and bridge, so that it is all ready for use when it reaches the purchaser.

THE ILLUSTRATION **which we give of this instrument will show the beautiful ornamentation of the scroll and also the beautiful model of the instrument** which is copied after the **celebrated Stradivarius violins**, but it will not show you the beautiful combination and blending of colors formed by the wood of which the instrument is made and the splendid amber varnish with which it is coated. **We are willing to send this violin out with the assurance that it is equal in every way to the violins usually sold by dealers at from $30.00 to $35.00.** We are able to do this because we know the original manufacturing cost of violins that are usually sold by dealers at this price. We know that they cannot furnish a violin for less than $35.00 which will equal this splendid instrument. It is impossible for them to do this because the instrument passes through so many different hands and there are so many different profits made on the instrument that when it reaches the purchaser the price which he has to pay is more than double the original cost of manufacture. We entirely avoid all these profits and selling expenses by our **direct from factory to customer plan of sale.** By this method we save you all intermediate dealers' profits and expenses and sell the violin to you at the actual manufacturer's price, with but one small percentage of profit added. This manufacturer's price simply represents the cost of material and labor at the factory and no fancy profits are added to pay for supposed fine qualities of tone. We guarantee the workmanship, material and tone of every one of these violins, and as we only desire to make a uniformly small percentage of profit upon everything that we sell, we are offering you a rare opportunity to purchase a fine violin at a marvelously low price. The price which we make on this instrument, $16.25, is a lower price than your dealer would have to pay for the same instrument from his manufacturer or jobber, because our great purchasing power gives us an opportunity to make a specially favorable contract with the manufacturers by which we can purchase these instruments at a lower figure than any other dealer can secure. Our prices and our guarantee go hand in hand. We do not ask our customers to take any responsibility or any chances as we take all the risks in shipping out these splendid instruments.

With this violin we furnish a nicely finished wooden case.

We want to call your attention to the fact that the label upon each one of these violins is signed by the maker in his own hand writing, and is a guarantee that each violin bearing the label is a genuine Perugini violin.

No. 12C271 Perugini Virtuoso Violin. Price.......... **$16.25**

$16

FRONT VIEW

BACK VIEW

No. 12C271 PERUGINI MODEL VIOLIN. Price, $16.25

OUR LUDWIG CONCERT VIOLIN.

THE VERY BEST WORK OF THIS WELL KNOWN GERMAN MAKER. MADE ESPECIALLY FOR US ON SPECIAL CONTRACT AND FULLY WARRANTED AS TO MATERIAL, WORKMANSHIP, TONE AND TUNE.

AN INVESTMENT WHICH WILL CONSTANTLY INCREASE IN VALUE.

No. 12C275

THIS INSTRUMENT **is made by the same celebrated maker that makes our Artist's model violin and is an instrument which is recognized by all players as possessing all the qualities of the old masters.** This is our **Paginini violin** and is an exact copy of the celebrated Guarnerius instrument used by this wonderful Italian violinist and now preserved in the city of Genoa, Italy. It is made especially for us by L. Ludwig, and you cannot procure it from any other dealer. **The wood used in this instrument is of very old and choice quality and each piece is selected with great care.** The back is of very highly figured curly maple and the top is of silver spruce, especially selected for this fine instrument. They are trimmed throughout with the very finest grade of solid ebony, highly polished. The sides and neck of these instruments are made of choice curly maple, and the entire body covered with a coat of finest transparent amber varnish.

THE INSTRUMENT **is highly polished and has a decidedly distinguished appearance.** In point of material and workmanship, volume and strength of tone, this violin cannot be procured from any other dealer for less than $40.00 or $50.00. We have sold a large number of these instruments to violin soloists, and they have all been loud in their praise. We do not ask you to pay a fancy price for any supposed fine qualities which this instrument may possess, as the price we make on it, $19.85, represents only the cost of material and workmanship at the factory and the expense of shipping it from Germany to our house in Chicago. It is thoroughly examined by our expert and its true value fixed, and to this value we simply add our small margin of profit to pay us for handling and selling it. This is the reason we are charging you only $19.85 for an instrument that would otherwise cost from $40.00 to $50.00.

THIS IS A VIOLIN **which can be handed down from generation to generation and becomes more and more valuable and highly prized,** not only as an heirloom, but as a splendid musical instrument as well. You take no chances in ordering this violin, for if you do not find it satisfactory, you can return it to us and the money you paid will be cheerfully refunded. We furnish with the instrument a fine bow made of brazilwood and a finely finished wooden case. also strings, rosin, etc., so that it goes to the customer complete.

REMEMBER **that each one of these violins bears a label signed by L. Ludwig in his own hand writing.** This guarantees that every instrument bearing this label and signature has been carefully manufactured by hand and is a genuine Ludwig Violin. Do not be deceived by dealers who offer to sell you violins made by this celebrated maker, because you can purchase them from no other dealers. One glance at the label inside of the violin will show you at once that the instrument is not genuine, as it will lack the signature of this great maker.

No. 12C275 Ludwig Concert Violin. Price........................ ......**$19.85**

BACK VIEW FRONT VIEW

No. 12C275 LUDWIG CONCERT VIOLIN. PRICE, $19.85

OUR GENUINE HEBERLEIN.

A LIMITED NUMBER OF THESE GREAT INSTRUMENTS AT : : : $23.45

TAKE ADVANTAGE OF THESE BARGAINS WHILE THEY LAST.

No. 12C278

WE HAVE BEEN FORTUNATE **enough to secure a limited number of these splendid instruments and we assure you that no description that we can give will in any way suffice to do them justice.** The Stradivarius model has been closely followed and the maker has succeeded in producing a violin which is a close imitation of the celebrated Stradivarius. The back is formed of a very beautiful piece of flamed curly maple, of a handsome pattern.

THE TOP **is made of the very best quality of silver spruce,** thoroughly seasoned and accurately made. The purfling is perfectly inlaid and is the characteristic purfling of the Stradivarius violin. **The back is made of splendidly seasoned maple,** beautifully flamed, with colors handsomely blended. The instrument is made of the exact proportions of the celebrated instruments of Stradivarius, which guarantees an ever increasing volume and sweetness of tone. The sides are made of the same beautiful material as the back and the entire violin is covered with a transparent coat of amber varnish, shaded beautifully into red. It is fitted with a genuine ebony tailpiece, fingerboard and pegs, and the scroll is handsomely and cleanly cut, the points and corners being stained dark in imitation of ebony. We cannot recommend this violin too highly, as we are sure it will please every lover of this noble instrument. It has a beautiful full volume of tone, and is especially suited for orchestra work or for use on heavy solos, which require a deep and full tone. **While the engraving of the violin is made directly from a photograph of the instrument and will give you a fair idea of the model,** still nothing but an examination of the instrument itself can convey any idea of its splendid appearance or deep rich tone. The gold plated tips of the pegs and the metal harp on the tailpiece have a tendency to set off the finishing of the instrument and give it a tasty, neat appearance seldom found in other violins.

THE MOST WONDERFUL VALUE EVER OFFERED IN A VIOLIN

TO VIOLINISTS **who desire an instrument which will be an accurate copy of the famous instruments of the Italian school** we desire to say that they cannot do better than to purchase one of these splendid violins. The varnish used on these instruments is of such a quality that the colors will soften and blend with years of use and the varnish will so harden and become part of the wood that the resonance of the instrument will be wonderfully increased and the tone will become more powerful and brilliant with continued use. If the violins which the original Stradivarius made and sold for an amount that would about equal $25.00 in our money, can now be sold for from $5,000.00 to 10,000.00, is it not reasonable to suppose that the purchase of one of these violins from us at this time may mean a marvelously profitable investment for your children in the coming years? The violin differs from almost every other musical instrument from the fact that it increases in value with age and does not wear out. In a piano the action will wear and become loose and the same in an organ; but in a violin, only serves to mellow and increase the volume of tone. **We send free with this a fine brazilwood bow, rosin, fingerboard chart, instruction book,** an extra of fine Acme professional strings and everything to make the violin complete.

With each one of these violins we issue a certificate showing that the violin is a genuine Heberlein Violin, carefully made by hand by this celebrated maker. By having this certificate you will always have evidence of the fact that your violin turned out of the workshop of one of the finest violin makers in the world. No other dealers can issue a certificate of this kind, as we handle the Heberlein Violins exclusively. Should any other dealer offer to sell you a violin made by this maker it will only be necessary for you to ask for the certificate when the deception will at once be exposed.

WITH THIS VIOLIN WE FURNISH A NICELY FINISHED WOODEN CASE.

No. 12C278 Genuine Heberlein Violin. Price....... **$23.45**

FRONT VIEW BACK VIEW

No. 12C278 GENUINE HEBERLEIN VIOLIN. PRICE, $23.45.

OUR SPECIAL BARGAINS IN VIOLIN OUTFITS.

In addition to our very complete assortment of violins, shown and described on the preceding pages, we have a line of complete violin outfits, made up under the direct supervision of the manager of our musical department, who is a musician and fully acquainted with the demands of all classes of violinists.

We offer these COMPLETE OUTFITS to ARTISTS, AMATEURS and PROFESSIONALS alike.

TO CONVINCE THE PURCHASER that we are offering these outfits at an **unusually low price,** we specify exactly the articles as selected from our stock, showing at the same time the regular retail prices and also our special outfit price. To anyone who contemplates buying a violin the accessories which we offer in these outfits are always necessary.

THE OUTFITS are selected from our own stock, which is a guarantee of their high quality, and every instrument we carry is vouched for by the manufacturers of the highest grade violins in the world.

FOR THE BEGINNER ESPECIALLY we recommend these complete Violin Outfits. They include just what is necessary, and by buying the outfit together you save considerable over the prices of the separate items.

WE CHALLENGE COMPETITION ON THE QUALITY AND LOW PRICE OF OUR VIOLIN OUTFITS

OUTFIT No. 12C300

$2.85 BUYS A REGULAR $10.20 OUTFIT.

THIS OUTFIT IS THE BEST VALUE FOR THE MONEY EVER OFFERED. Anyone desiring a complete outfit for general use should not fail to see and examine our famous bargain. The outfit contains

	Regular Retail Price
one of our **Genuine Stradivarius Model Violins,** made of old wood, curly maple back and sides, top of seasoned pine, selected especially for violins, edges inlaid with purfling, **genuine ebony trimmings**	$ 8.00
1 Genuine Brazil Wood Bow, ebony frog with inlaid dots.	.75
1 Case of Marbleized Pasteboard, imported direct from Europe for our trade	.40
1 Full Set of Strings	.25
1 Piece of Rosin, good quality	.05
1 Instructor, simplest and most complete instruction book published	.50
1 Lettered Fingerboard Chart, can be adjusted to any violin without changing the instrument, a valuable guide for beginners	.25
Total value of outfit. **(Shipping weight, 7 pounds)**	**$10.20**
No. 12C300 PRICE FOR COMPLETE OUTFIT	**$2.85**

Send $2.85 with your order and we will send you this outfit by express, and if you do not find it the greatest bargain you ever saw or heard of, and entirely satisfactory in every respect, return it at our expense and we will cheerfully refund your money.

OUR CHALLENGE $13.10 VIOLIN OUTFIT FOR $5.50

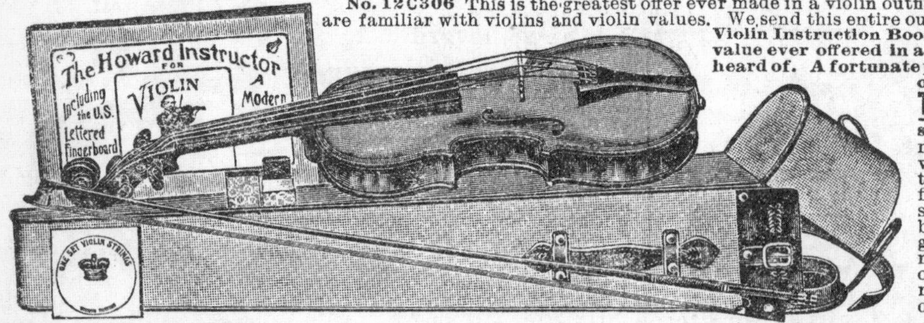

No. 12C306 This is the greatest offer ever made in a violin outfit and that this is true will be recognized at once by all who are familiar with violins and violin values. We send this entire outfit complete, consisting of **One Maggini Model Violin, Violin Instruction Book, Bow, Rosin and Case for $5.50. The most wonderful value ever offered in a violin outfit. A complete outfit at a price never before heard of. A fortunate purchase is giving us an opportunity to offer this splendid outfit to the public for the ridiculously low price of $5.50.**

THE VIOLIN. The violin which we offer with this outfit is a splendid instrument in every respect. It is a model of the celebrated Maggini violin, made by one of the most celebrated European makers of violins. It has a double purfling which is characteristic of this model, and the back and sides are made of highly flamed and figured maple, and the top of old, well seasoned silver spruce. The entire instrument is covered with a beautiful coat of transparent varnish, through which the grain of the wood shows to great advantage. The instrument has an extremely deep, powerful and rich tone and one which we can guarantee in every respect. Its trimmings are of fine quality, the fingerboard and tailpiece being of solid ebony. The neck is curly maple and finely finished.

WE SHIP THIS OUTFIT to the customer with the assurance that it cannot be purchased in the regular way for less than $13.10. We are willing to have our customers compare this outfit with anything that the local dealer has to offer in the same line at $13.10, and if he does not find that it is equal and in many points superior, he can return the entire outfit to us, we will refund the money paid and pay the express charges both ways.

SEND US $1.00 and we will ship you this entire outfit by express C.O.D. You can examine it carefully at the express office and if it is satisfactory, pay the balance of the price and take it home. If it is not satisfactory for any reason it can be returned at our expense and we will cheerfully refund the $1.00 deposited.

Regular Prices of the Different Articles of This Outfit.

One Genuine Maggini Model Violin	$10.0
One Genuine Brazil wood Bow	1.0
One Canvas, Fleece Lined, Leather Bound Case	1.0
One Set of Strings	.25
One Piece of Rosin	.10
One Complete Instruction Book	.50
One Fingerboard Chart	.25
Total regular price of Outfit	$13.10
No. 12C306 Our Great Bargain Price	**$5.50**

Shipping weight, 7 pounds.

HIGH GRADE AMATEUR OUTFIT FOR $7.25.

OUTFIT No. 12C308

THIS IS THE OUTFIT for which your dealer is asking you $15.00 and $20.00 and is one of the greatest bargains ever put on the market in the shape of a violin outfit. We are willing to ship you this outfit with the understanding and agreement that if you do not find it the greatest bargain you ever saw in a violin outfit, equal, and in many points superior, to the outfits generally sold by dealers at twice the price, you can immediately return it to us, we will cheerfully refund your money and pay the transportation charges both ways. We have so much confidence in the merits of this violin outfit that we are willing to allow you to try it entirely at our expense. If you do not accept it we pay all expenses of transportation and refund your money in full. Why should you purchase a violin outfit in the usual way, paying four or five intermediate dealers' profits, when you can order a violin from us and try it thoroughly and carefully in your home and not be under any obligations to accept it, unless it is fully satisfactory in every particular? Let us send you this violin outfit with the above understanding and agreement.

REMEMBER, you are not under any obligations to accept it unless it is fully up to your expectations and the most splendid value for the money that you ever saw in a violin outfit.

OUR 10 DAYS' TRIAL OFFER, is good in connection with this outfit, and after you receive it from the express office you can try it in your home for this period, and if within that time it should prove unsatisfactory for any reason, you can return it to us, we will pay the express charges both ways and cheerfully refund your money. We make these liberal terms for the purpose of allowing our customers to satisfy themselves fully before they finally decide on the purchase of an outfit.

THIS OUTFIT we have made up especially for the requirements of players who would like to procure a first class violin with accessories for less than $10.00. We can recommend it in every respect as being equal to outfits which could not be purchased from other dealers **at less than from $18.00 to $20.00.**

The outfit contains

	Regular Retail Price
1 Genuine **Stradivarius Model Violin,** made expressly for us by one of the best makers in Europe. It is made of specially seasoned old wood, giving the instrument an unusually mellow and sweet tone. The violin is beautifully finished throughout and fitted with the best ebony fingerboard, tailpiece and pegs. It is reddish brown in color, beautifully shaded and handsomely polished	**$12.00**
The Bow which we furnish with this outfit is a first class Brazil wood bow with ebony frog, German silver trimmed and German silver button	$1.50
The Case is of solid wood, handsomely lined, and has lock, handle and hooks	1.5
1 Set of our Acme Strings	.7
1 Piece Rosin	.7
1 Instruction Book	.5
1 Fingerboard Chart, which has proven valuable to both amateur and artist alike	.25
1 Tuning Pipe, giving the proper pitch to which the instrument should be tuned	.25
Total value of outfit **(Shipping wt. 10 lbs.)**	**$16.85**
No. 12C308 Price, for complete outfit	**$7.25**

OUR SPECIAL HIGH GRADE OUTFIT FOR $10.00.

There is no musical instrument, the value of which is so difficult for the inexperienced purchaser to determine as a violin, and that is why music dealers in general can ask an exorbitant price for the same instrument sold by us at actual cost with only our usual one small margin of profit added. The manager of our Musical Instrument Department is acknowledged as the best judge of violins in the United States, and every instrument in our line, therefore, represents the best value for the money which it is possible to procure. The violin in this outfit would readily sell at double the price we ask for the entire outfit. The entire outfit contains:

	Regular Retail Price
1 Special High Grade **Genuine Guarnerius Model Violin,** an instrument remarkably superior in every respect, made of specially selected curly maple back and sides, resonant spruce top, a rich color of varnish, beautifully shaded and handsomely polished. The trimmings are of the very best quality of solid ebony, making the instrument durable and much sought after by professionals. The tone is full and strong and suited to all requirements	$20.00
1 Vuillaume Model Bow, imitation snakewood, with carved ivory frog	4.00
1 Solid Wood Case, provided with lock, handle and spring clasps, lined throughout inside with red flannel	2.75
1 Piece Genuine Gustave Bernadel Rosin, the best manufact'd. Imported by us direct from France	.25
1 Howe's Original Violin School, complete in every respect, and teaches how to play correctly	.75
1 Set of our Acme Professional Strings, imported direct from Europe	.85
1 Fingerboard Chart, which is valuable to beginners and advanced players alike	.25
1 Set Violin Tuning Pipes, invaluable to the beginner, as it aids him in tuning his instrument accurately	.65
1 Book of Choice Violin Music	.50

OUTFIT No. 12C314

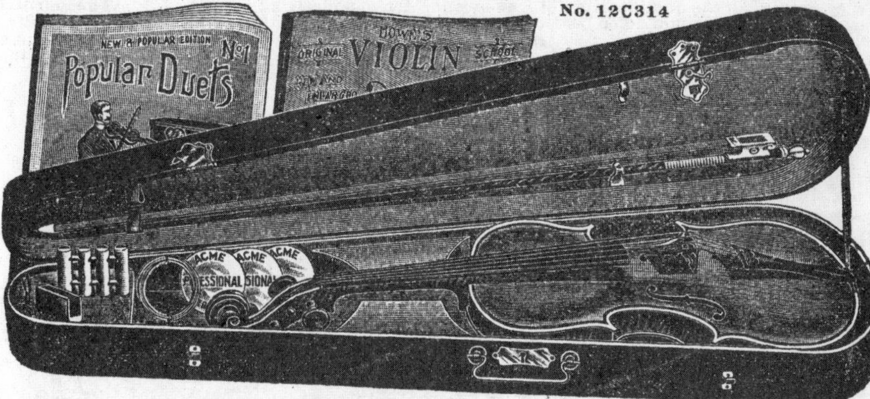

Shipping weight, 10 pounds.

Such an outfit as described above could not be purchased from your local dealer, nor, in fact, any other dealer, at less than $30.00 to $40.00.

No. 12C314 PRICE FOR COMPLETE OUTFIT $10.00

OUR SPECIAL HIGH GRADE PROFESSIONAL OUTFIT.

OUTFIT No. 12C317

A REGULAR $50.00 OUTFIT FOR $13.95.

This violin outfit is one which we have been furnishing for the past five years, and the fact of our having sold thousands of them to customers in all parts of the United States is the best evidence of the exceptional value we are offering.

THE STRADIVARIUS MODEL VIOLIN

is the best known of all the celebrated makes throughout the world. This reputation was attained only through the beautiful form of the instruments and the wonderful quality of tone which they possess. The violin in our outfit is an exceptionally fine copy of a Stradivarius and every instrument is made with great care. **The outfit includes:**

	Regular Retail Price
1 Special High Grade Stradivarius Model Violin made of selected well seasoned, curly maple back and sides. Resonant spruce top very evenly grained. The best quality solid ebony trimmings throughout. This violin is finished with pure amber varnish, which is transparent and the most desirable varnish for the finish of high grade violins. The tone is sweet and powerful	$35.00
1 Tourte Model Bow, with full German silver trimmings and best quality Brazil wood	5.00
1 Solid Wood Case, Exposition Shape, full flannel lined, provided with lock and spring clasp	3.00
1 Piece of Genuine Gustave Bernadel Rosin, the best manufactured, and imported by us direct from France	.25
1 Instruction Book, complete in every respect and teaches how to play correctly	1.00
1 Set of Acme Professional Strings, imported by us direct from Europe	.85
1 Latest Patent Violin Chin Rest, used by most players	1.50
1 Fingerboard Chart, which is valuable to beginners and advanced players	.25
1 Set of Violin Tuning Pipes, by the aid of which the instrument can be tuned accurately	.50
1 Violin Mute, required when playing soft music	.15
1 Choice Collection of violin music	.50
Total value of outfit	$48.00

SHIPPING WEIGHT, 10 POUNDS.

This outfit could not be procured from your local dealer, nor any music dealer at less than $40.00 to $50.00. **No. 12C317** Price, complete **$13.95**

A GENUINE HEBERLEIN VIOLIN.

OUTFIT No. 12C321

A HIGH GRADE SPECIAL OUTFIT FOR $17.85.

Heberlein is recognized among the well known violin makers of Europe. His instruments sell everywhere at prices ranging from $50.00 to $100.00 each. We have been able to arrange with Heberlein to make a limited number of violins for us which we can supply in an outfit at an exceptionally low price.

EVERY INSTRUMENT IS GUARANTEED

to be absolutely genuine and is accompanied by a numbered certificate countersigned by the maker. Beware of imitations. **The complete outfit listed opposite.**

	Regular Retail Price
1 Genuine Heberlein Violin, made of specially selected curly maple back and sides, resonant spruce top. The wood used in this violin is thoroughly aged, thereby insuring a mellow tone. The trimmings are of the very best quality solid ebony, well finished, which adds greatly to the appearance of the instrument. The varnish is what is known as pure amber varnish, which has been demonstrated as the best for violins. It is of rich color, beautifully shaded and highly polished. The tone is full, strong and mellow and suited to all requirements	$50.00
1 Genuine Snakewood Vuillaume Model Bow. Has handsomely carved **Genuine Ivory** frog, double pearl eye, German silver lining and ivory button	5.00
1 Violin Case, covered with a durable waterproof material, made in perfect imitation alligator skin, full lined with velvet, leather handles, nickel link clasps and nickel spring lock	5.00
1 Piece Genuine Gustave Bernadel Rosin, best manufactured, in pasteboard box. Imported by us direct from France	.25
1 Henning's School for the Violin, one of the most complete and best instruction books published. 101 pages, printed on fine paper, bound in board	1.50
1 Mammoth Collection of Violin Music, contains over 350 selections arranged by the best composers	.75
1 Set of Acme Professional Strings. Best quality in the market. Imported by us direct from Europe	.85
1 Latest Patent Violin Chin Rest, indispensable to most players	1.00
1 Violin Mute, required for playing very soft music	.15
1 Fingerboard Chart, valuable to both beginners and advanced players	.25
1 Set of Tuning Pipes, by the aid of which the Violin can be tuned accurately	.50
Total value of outfit	$65.25

No. 12C321 Price, for the complete outfit **$17.85**

SHIPPING WEIGHT, 12 POUNDS.

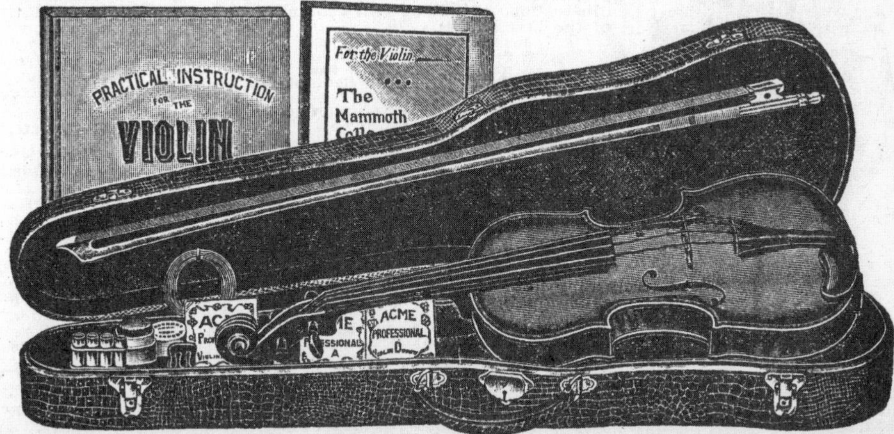

Such an outfit as here described could not be purchased from your local dealer, or, in fact, from any other dealer, at less than from $60.00 to $75.00.

GENUINE L. LUDWIG OUTFIT, $19.45.

BY SPECIAL ARRANGEMENT **with the celebrated violin maker, L. Ludwig of Leipzig, Germany,** we have been able to procure a limited number of his high grade instruments for this special outfit. His violins are sought after by the greatest players in the world, as they possess all the qualifications of a fine violin. Anyone desiring to purchase an instrument could do no better than to order one of these outfits.

IN MAKING UP THIS OUTFIT **we have endeavored to include a combination of instrument and equipment** such as has never been offered by any concern in the world and which cannot be duplicated by any music dealer at anything like the price at which we offer it.

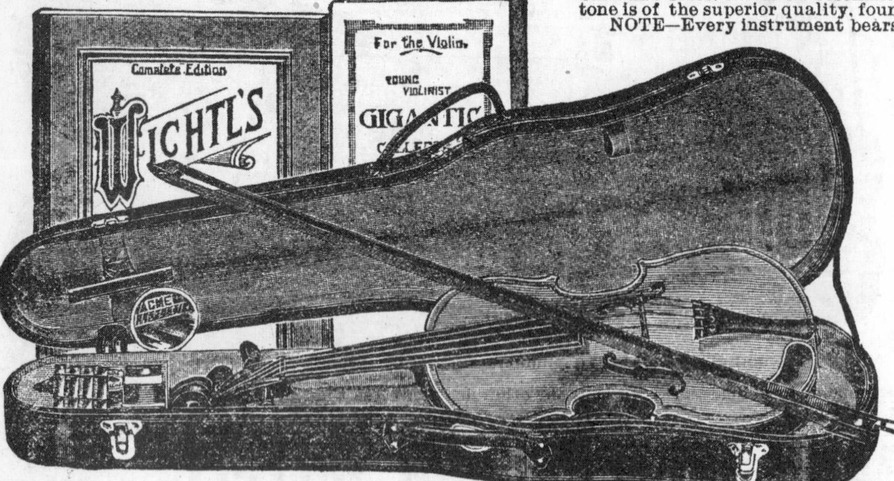

The outfit includes:	Regular Retail Price
1 Special High Grade Genuine L. Ludwig Violin, Stradivarius Model, made of specially selected curly maple, back and sides, choice old resonant spruce top, highest grade solid ebony trimmings. The tone is of the superior quality, found only in the Ludwig violins. NOTE—Every instrument bears the label, countersigned by L. Ludwig with his own autograph. (Beware of imitations.)	$50.00
1 Tourte Model Bow, with full German silver trimmings and best quality Brazil wood	5.00
1 Leather Case, Exposition Shape, full velvet lined, nickel trimmed	5.00
1 Piece of Genuine Gustave Bernadel Rosin, the best rosin manufactured, in metal box and imported by us direct from France	.25
1 "Wichtl's Young Violinist," an excellent instruction book. Contains one hundred exercises and Peerless Celebrated Violin Duets	1.00
1 Set of Acme Professional Strings, imported by us direct from Europe	.85
1 Latest Patent Violin Chin Rest, used by most players	1.00
1 Fingerboard Chart, which is valuable to beginners and advanced players	.25
1 Set of Violin Tuning Pipes, by the aid of which the instrument can be tuned accurately	.50
1 Violin Mute, required when playing soft music	.15
1 Gigantic Collection of Violin Music, a valuable book to either beginner or advanced player	.50
Total value of outfit	$64.50
No. 12C325 Price, complete	$19.45

SHIPPING WEIGHT 12 POUNDS.

The above outfit could not be procured from your local dealer, nor any music dealer at less than $50.00 to $75.00.

FINGERBOARD CHART.

With each Violoncello or Double Bass Viol we give free of charge one of these fingerboard charts. They are of great value to either beginner or professional player, for they tell at a glance the proper place to press the strings to produce the note desired. Beginners can become proficient in a very short time, with the assistance of this chart. It can be firmly gummed to the fingerboard, and in no way interferes with the tone or playing of the instrument.

VIOLONCELLOS.

Our line of Violoncellos includes only the productions of the best manufacturers. We quote the instruments both with peg head and with patent head. In tone, model and finish these violoncellos have no superior at any price. **Our liberal guarantee.** If any violoncello proves defective in workmanship or material, it may be returned to us at our expense and we will cheerfully refund your money. **Weight, packed for shipment, about 45 pounds.**

Our $9.25 Violoncello with Patent Head.

No. 12C400 This Violoncello at $9.25 is excellent value, being a good model and made of selected material, and the best care used in its construction and finish. We furnish it complete **with perfect fitting canvas bag,** violoncello bow, a piece of fine rosin in pasteboard case, **one fingerboard chart,** and a complete instruction book, and the instrument is ready to play as soon as received by you. Price..........$9.25

No. 12C406 At $11.20 we offer a violoncello which will compare very favorably with anything ordinarily carried in retail stores and for which retail dealers will ask from $15.00 to $18.00. This instrument is of excellent quality and has handsome inlaid edges which add greatly to its general appearance. It has patent head as shown in illustration. It is fitted with a complete set of the best strings,

And with it are furnished FREE,
A Perfect Fitting Canvas Bag,
A Handsome Violoncello Bow,
An Extra Large Piece of fine Rosin and
A Valuable Instructor,

by the use of which anyone can learn to play the violoncello.
Price..........$11.20

Our Highest Grade Violoncello with Peg or Patent Head, $15.45.

No. 12C420 This is an instrument which must be seen, examined and tested in order to fully appreciate all its merits. This violoncello is extra fine quality, beautifully polished. Solid ebony trimmings throughout, including the solid ebony fingerboard and solid ebony tailpiece. The peg head is the very best which is manufactured and the material used in the body is such as is found only in the highest grade instruments. It is made by expert workmen, and the construction is such that it produces a tone such as you would naturally expect only from instruments which retailers sell at from $25.00 to $30.00. We include a perfect fitting canvas bag, valuable instruction book, a violoncello bow and a large piece of our best rosin in a pasteboard box, so that the instrument is ready to play as soon as received. Price..........$15.45

No. 12C422 Same description as our No. 12C420, but fitted with best quality patent head on brass plates.
Price..........17.85

DOUBLE BASS VIOLS.

Buying as we do these desirable instruments in quantities from the leading manufacturer, we offer them with the assurance that they will compare favorably with the very finest that are made, in fact, there is no line of double bass viols manufactured which is superior in tone and workmanship to these which we quote and illustrate on this page. These instruments are furnished complete with a splendid double bass bow and complete instructor. Each instrument is packed with great care, and when ready to ship weighs 125 pounds.

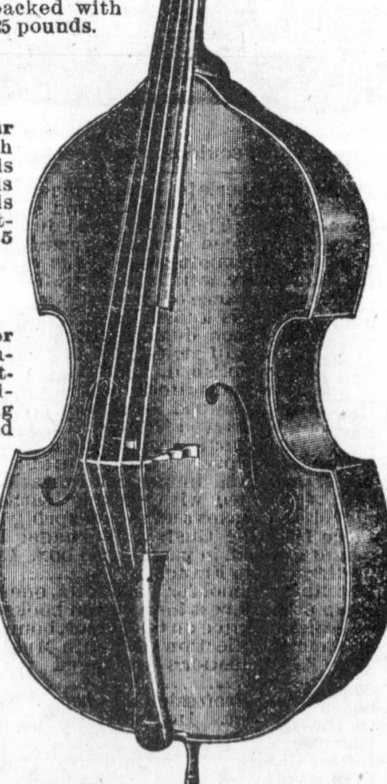

Our $18.95 One-Half Size Double Bass Viol.

No. 12C450 At $18.95 we offer a four string Double Bass Viol, one-half size, with bow, and complete instruction book. This double bass viol is of the very best model, is dark red shaded, very highly polished, and is superior quality in every respect. Best patent head. Price..........$18.95

Our Three-Quarter Size Double Bass Viol.

No. 12C462 A High Grade Three-Quarter Size Double Bass Viol for $19.50. This double bass viol has four strings, finest iron patent head and is beautifully shaded and colored. In finish it is wonderfully fine, being highly polished throughout. In model and quality it is decidedly superior and possesses a remarkably fine tone, a tone which you will ordinarily find possessed only by the most expensive instruments. Complete with excellent double bass bow and a valuable instruction book. Price..$19.50

$22.85 Double Bass Viol.

Three-Quarter Size.

No. 12C466 This Double Bass Viol has four strings, high grade iron patent head, solid ebony fingerboard. The inlaid purfling is very handsome and adds greatly to the attractiveness of the instrument, giving it the appearance of the most expensive and highest priced viols on the market. A particularly fine model and possesses a tone which is superior to the instruments ordinarily carried by retail dealers at any price. We furnish free with each instrument a good double bass bow and complete instruction book. Price.....$22.85

OUR SPECIAL $3.95 EDGEMERE CONSERVATORY VIOLIN OUTFIT.

A GENUINE STRADIVARIUS MODEL CONSERVATORY VIOLIN.

THIS VIOLIN is made for us by Albin Bauer, one of the best known makers of violins in Europe. His instruments are well known throughout the United States and other countries, and are recognized for their excellent qualities. These violins are sold by us at such a small margin of profit that in buying one of our Edgemere outfits, you get a violin which alone would cost you more than double what we ask for the entire outfit.

There is no article of merchandise that is so susceptible to false valuation as violins, and they are, therefore, sold throughout the country by other music dealers at enormous profits.

WE ARE THE FIRST CONCERN that has attempted to market musical goods in general on grocery profits, and in offering our

EDGEMERE VIOLIN OUTFIT at $3.95

we have reserved for ourselves but our usual one small margin of profit, and hope thereby to have every violin serve as an advertisement for us.

DESCRIPTION

THESE VIOLINS are made of selected, very old and thoroughly seasoned wood, especially prepared for the construction of violins. The back is made of two pieces of curly maple, beautifully flamed as shown in illustration. The top is made of spruce, selected with a view of producing the best tone. The neck and scroll are made of handsome curly maple to correspond with the back and sides.

THE FINISH of the violin is a beautiful reddish brown color, handsomely shaded and highly polished. The fingerboard, tailpiece and pegs are of genuine solid ebony, which is used only on the higher grade instruments.

THE TONE is all and even more than is usually found in violins of much higher price. Sweet in quality and amply powerful for all requirements.

ORDER ONE OF OUR $3.95 EDGEMERE VIOLIN OUTFITS and compare it with violins offered by any other dealer at from $7.00 to $10.00, and if you do not immediately recognize the superiority of our instruments you are at liberty to return it to us at our expense and we will refund your money in ful

UPON RECEIPT OF $1.00 we send this violin outfit C. O. D. subject to examination. You can examine the outfit at your express office, and if you find it perfectly satisfactory, pay the express agent the balance and the express charges. If not found entirely satisfactory the shipment will be returned to us at our expense, and we will cheerfully refund your deposit. **Most of our customers send cash in full,** thereby saving the charge which the express companies always make for collecting and returning the money, and which will amount to from 25 to 50 cents on every shipment. **We recommend sending the full amount of cash with your order.**

OUR TEN DAYS' FREE TRIAL OFFER.

ORDER ONE OF OUR $3.95 EDGEMERE VIOLIN OUTFITS, use it in your own home for TEN DAYS, and if not found to be all and even more than we claim for it, by far the greatest value you ever saw, a violin such as you could not duplicate at double the price we ask, you may return it to us at our expense of transportation charges both ways, and we will cheerfully refund your money.

No. 12C350 Price, complete outfit.......................... **$3.95**

ORDER BY NUMBER.

FRONT VIEW OF VIOLIN.

OUTFIT No. 12C350

BACK VIEW OF VIOLIN

OUR SPECIAL EDGEMERE CONSERVATORY VIOLIN OUTFIT AT $3.95.

THIS OUTFIT CONTAINS	Regular retail price
1 **Conservatory Violin,** Stradivarius Model, as described above	$10.00
1 **Genuine Brazil Wood Bow,** excellent quality	1.00
1 **Case of Solid Wood,** handsomely lined and finished	1.50
1 **Full Set of Glendon Strings**	.25
1 **Piece Rosin,** good quality	.05
1 **Winner's New American School Instruction Book**	.50
1 **Chart for Fingerboard,** can be adjusted to any violin without changing the instrument, a valuable guide for beginners	.25
1 **Tuning Pipe,** giving the pitch to which the instrument should be tuned	.10
Total value of outfit	$13.65
Our special outfit price	$3.95

Shipping weight, 10 pounds.

WE ARE THE LARGEST MUSIC DEALERS IN THE WORLD

Selling direct to the consumer, and can furnish you better goods for less money than you can buy them elsewhere.

MATCHLESS VALUES IN HIGH GRADE

GUARANTEED GUITARS.

THE GUITARS LISTED on this and the following pages are modeled after the latest and most improved shapes by a manufacturer with a reputation for making the best guitars in the United States. These instruments are all made of the very best material and by the most expert mechanics. They are made with a view of embodying the good points of all other makes of guitars, with the defects of none, made to combine in quality of selected material used, in workmanship, fitting, mounting and finishing, in the shaping and the modeling, and especially in the all important part, the sweet, pure, strong, yet soft, melodious tone, an effect not found in guitars of other makes sold generally at two to three times the special prices we ask.

OUR INCOMPARABLY LOW PRICES are made possible by reason of our taking a large part of the output of this big factory. We own these goods on the basis of the actual cost of material and labor, and the prices we name cover only the cost of material and labor, with but our one small percentage of profit added, a mere fraction of the price at which guitars of equal value are sold by others.

THE GUITAR has always been a favorite instrument upon which to play accompaniments for songs, as its light, graceful tone is sufficiently strong to support the voice and not loud enough to overcome it. The peculiar arrangement and tuning of the strings also has much to do with the popularity of this beautiful instrument.

OUR QUALITY GUARANTEE. Every guitar offered by us is sold under our binding guarantee, covering every piece and part of material and workmanship. While we could easily make a guitar to sell as low as $1.50, a guitar that would be in every way equal to guitars that are sold by others at $2.50 to $5.00, we prefer not to offer instruments that we could not guarantee to give every satisfaction, and so from the cheapest guitar we offer, the Troubadour Matchless at $2.25, to our very finest instrument, THE HARVARD, AT $21.45, EVERY GUITAR IS PUT OUT UNDER OUR BINDING GUARANTEE AND TEN DAYS' FREE TRIAL PLAN AS FOLLOWS:

OUR TEN DAYS' FREE TRIAL PLAN. Whether you send cash in full with your order or $1.00 (balance C. O. D.), we will accept your order for any guitar, the guitar to be shipped to you with the understanding and agreement that after you have given it ten days' trial and put it to every test, compared it with guitars sold by others at much higher prices, if you are not perfectly satisfied with your purchase, and if the guitar, in quality of material used, in workmanship, finish and musical qualities, isn't far superior to any guitar you could buy elsewhere at anything near the price, you can return the guitar to us at our expense and we will immediately return your money, together with any express charges paid by you.

OUR $1.00 C. O. D., SUBJECT TO EXAMINATION TERMS. While nearly all our customers send cash in full and we advise sending cash in full, however, if you prefer to see and examine the guitar before paying for it we will, on receipt of $1.00, send any guitar to any address by express, C. O. D., subject to examination, balance and express charges payable after the guitar is received. Understand, whether you send cash in full or $1.00 deposit you have the privilege of giving the guitar ten days' trial in your own home, and if it isn't perfectly satisfactory return it to us and we will return your money, including express charges paid by you.

SAFE DELIVERY GUARANTEE. We guarantee every guitar to reach you in perfect condition and if you should find the guitar scratched or damaged in any way by reason of rough handling in transit or otherwise, you can return the guitar to us at our expense and we will immediately return your money.

ABOUT THE EXPRESS CHARGES. The express charges on a guitar amount to next to nothing as compared with what we will save you in price. A guitar packed for shipment weighs about 12 pounds and the express charges for 200 miles or less will average 25 to 60 cents, and from 200 to 500 miles, from 60 cents to $1.00, or if ordered with other goods to go by freight the charges will amount to next to nothing or about 10 cents for each 500 miles.

OUR FREE OUTFIT.

We send free of any expense to the purchaser, with every guitar, from the cheapest to the best, the following complete and valuable guitar outfit.

This Book of Guckert's Chords, the most valuable book of the kind ever published, is furnished free with every guitar. This complete book contains not only instructions on the guitar and how to play chords but is a valuable book for beginners. It also contains a number of pieces of figure music which any beginner can play. It is a book that retails regularly at 50 cents.

EXTRA STRINGS—This complete set of Glendon strings, especially made for these guitars, a set of strings that will outwear two sets of any strings you can buy elsewhere, is furnished free with the outfit with every guitar we sell. This set of Glendon strings is free in addition to the set already on the guitar.

This, our latest copyrighted fingerboard chart, by the aid of which anyone can learn to play without a teacher, is furnished free with the complete outfit with every guitar, from the cheapest to the best. This chart is invaluable to beginners, for by the aid of it anyone can learn to play without a teacher, is the only self instructing chart made, can be had only from us, and remember it comes free with every guitar, from the cheapest to the best.

This genuine Capo D' Astro, as illustrated, the newest model, spring action, nickel plated, complete with cork lined clamp, a special instrument which permits you to play in flat keys, is furnished complete free with the outfit with every guitar, from the cheapest to the best.

YOU WILL RECEIVE FREE the complete outfit, **Guckert's chords, extra Glendon strings, copyrighted fingerboard chart and the celebrated magic Capo D' Astro with any guitar you order,** from the cheapest to the best, the entire outfit packed in a strong, light box, especially made with a view to safe carrying and so light as to make the express charges amount to next to nothing as compared to what you save in price.

REMEMBER, no such a free outfit is furnished by any other house with the guitar. The outfit we offer free with every guitar, from the cheapest to the best, can be had only from us.

$2.25 FOR THE NEW TROUBADOUR MATCHLESS GUITAR

FOR $2.25 we offer this, our lowest priced guitar, complete with our valuable outfit as above described. In offering this guitar at $2.25, a price that barely covers the cost of material and labor, with but our one small percentage of profit added, we especially request that you do not compare it with any of the many cheap guitars on the market, since we could easily build a guitar and sell it as low as $1.25 to $1.50 and still equal in quality guitars that are generally sold at two to three times the price. This, our special $2.25 guitar, is built on honor, of specially selected material, put out under our binding guarantee and with the special privilege of returning it at any time within ten days if you don't find it perfectly satisfactory in every way, better than any guitar you can buy elsewhere at less than $5.00.

THE BACK AND SIDES of this guitar are made of hardwood, finished in imitation mahogany, highly polished. The top is inlaid around the sound hole, the fingerboard is accurately fretted with raised frets and has inlaid position dots. The top is made of resonant spruce and the entire instrument is coated with transparent varnish and beautifully finished. The instrument has a nickel plated tailpiece which takes the strain off of the top of the guitar. It also has a genuine brass screw patent head. **While in selecting a guitar we especially recommend that you choose one of our higher grade instruments,** a guitar we offer at from $9.95 to $21.45, nevertheless if you are a beginner and you want the very best guitar that can possibly be had for the least money, we guarantee you will find this, our new Troubadour, which retails at $2.25, such a guitar as was never before offered by anyone at anything approaching the price. Remember, it comes complete with the entire outfit as described above free of extra cost.

No. 12C600 THE TROUBADOUR. Price..........$2.25

No. 12C600 Standard size. Price.......... **$2.25**

$2.35 FOR OUR NEW OAKWOOD GUITAR.

OUR SPECIAL VALUE COMPARISON OFFER.

SEND US $2.35 and we will send you this new Oakwood Guitar, exactly as illustrated and described hereon. It will go to you carefully boxed with the complete outfit free, namely: a book of Guckert's chords, an extra full set of Glendon strings, our latest copyrighted fingerboard chart and celebrated magic Capo D' Astro, such an outfit as is furnished by no other house. We will send it to you with the understanding and agreement that it must reach you in perfect condition, free from even the slightest scratch. You can take it to your own home, give it a thorough trial and you can have the further privilege of comparing it with any guitar you can buy from any other house at any price up to $5.00. If you do not find it in quality of material, workmanship and finish and tone superior to any guitar you can buy elsewhere at any price up to $5.00, you can return the guitar to us at our expense, and we will immediately return your money. **While in selecting a guitar we especially recommend that our customers select one of our higher grade instruments,** a guitar in which the price admits of our giving something unusually fine, one of the instruments shown in this catalogue that will sell at from $9.95 to $21.45, nevertheless if you are a beginner or if, for any other reason, you want to get a reliable guitar at a very low price, accept our special proposition on this, the $2.35 Oakwood, and let us prove to you by test and by comparison that we can furnish you a better guitar for $2.35 than you can buy elsewhere under $5.00, and, remember, the complete outfit which we furnish free with every guitar, from the cheapest to the best, is really indispensable to beginners, valuable to anyone and unequaled by any outfit furnished by any other house.

THIS, OUR SPECIAL $2.35 OAKWOOD GUITAR, is made of handsome imitation quarter sawed oak, **showing the broad flake of the grain.** It has a very pretty decalcomanie strip down the back and the edges are bound with white celluloid. The top is made of selected silver spruce of a beautiful golden color, finished with transparent varnish and possessing great resonance; has two handsome decalcomanie circles in colors around the sound hole and the purfling is in five different colors. The tailpiece is metal, nickel plated and highly polished. The patent head is of the best design and made of polished brass. The fingerboard and bridge are made of imitation ebony with genuine pearl position dots and frets correctly placed. The neck is made of selected birch, finished in mahogany. The entire instrument is given an extremely high finish. **Our special $2.35 price barely covers the cost of material and labor, with but our one small percentage of profit added.** Such a guitar was never before sold by manufacturer or dealer in any quantity at anything approaching the special price we name. Being the largest dealers in guitars in the world selling direct to the consumer we have been able to greatly reduce the cost of manufacture, we have been able to furnish guitars at from $2.25 to $5.00 which heretofore found a market at from $5.00 to $15.00. We have in guitars, as in everything else we sell, given our customers the benefit of every saving we made, adding only our one small percentage of profit to the actual cost to produce, so whether you are a dealer and wish to buy in quantities to sell again or you want one guitar for your own use, by taking advantage of the very low prices we are offering we guarantee to furnish you such guitar value as can be had from no other house.

No. 12C601 Standard size, complete with outfit as described. Price only.... **$2.35**

No. 12C601 THE OAKWOOD. Price..........$2.35

$2.95 BUYS OUR WONDERFUL EDGEMERE GUITAR OUTFIT.

AT $2.95 WE OFFER A GUITAR OUTFIT SUCH AS HAS NEVER BEFORE BEEN OFFERED BY ANY DEALER.

$2.95 REPRESENTS THE ACTUAL COST of every part that enters into the construction of the guitar and component parts of the outfit, with but our usual one small percentage of profit added. The guitar alone sells at from $7.00 to $8.00.

CONTRARY TO THE USUAL RUN of low priced instruments, this guitar has a sweet and beautiful tone, which, as in the case of all first class instruments, grows better from year to year.

WHEN YOU RECEIVE THIS GUITAR, we ask you to compare it with any instrument sold by any dealer at from $7.00 up. We are only able to make this price of $2.95 for the outfit by making a very large contract for these instruments, and are offering it as an advertisement for our music department,

Knowing that every purchaser of one of these instruments will be so well pleased that he will take special delight in recommending us......

No. 12C607 Order by number.

DESCRIPTION OF OUR $2.95 EDGEMERE GUITAR.

This Guitar is rosewood finish, being an exact imitation of the highest priced genuine rosewood. It has a spruce top, inlaid with variegated wood around sound hole and top edge. It is bound with celluloid and has a handsome inlaid strip in the back, as shown in the illustration. **The fingerboard** is made of genuine rosewood, with pearl position dots and raised frets. Best quality, American made **patent head, nickel plated metal tailpiece and ebony bridge.** The finish of this guitar is equal to what is put on instruments of very much higher grade, being beautifully polished throughout.

REMEMBER,

That everything we list in our line of Musical Goods is sold on the same small margin of profit which we make on this outfit.

OUR $2.95 EDGEMERE GUITAR OUTFIT

	Regular Retail Price
Consists of our EDGEMERE Guitar, as described above	$7.00
One Book of Guckert's Chords, which enables one to play without the aid of a teacher	.50
One Full Set of Glendon Strings	.50
One Lettered Fingerboard Chart, a valuable aid for beginners	.25
One Magic Capo d'Astro	.25
Total Value of Outfit	$8.50
PRICE - Shipping weight, 12 pounds.	**$2.95**

We can also furnish this guitar in quarter sawed oak, practically the same description as above. Complete with strings, Capo d'Astro, etc., all ready to use, at the following price.

No. 12C603 Price, standard size....................$2.95

UPON RECEIPT OF $1.00 we send this guitar outfit C. O. D., subject to examination. You can examine it at your express office, and, if you find it perfectly satisfactory, pay the express agent the balance and express charges. If not found entirely satisfactory, the shipment can be returned to us at our expense and we will cheerfully refund your deposit. Most of our customers send cash in full, thereby saving the charge which the express companies always make for collecting and returning the money and which amounts to from 25 to 50 cents on every shipment. We recommend sending the full amount of cash with your order.

OUR TEN DAYS' FREE TRIAL OFFER. Order one of our EDGEMERE Guitar Outfits at $2.95, try the guitar in your own home for ten days, and, if not found entirely satisfactory and all and even more than we claim for it, return it to us at our expense of transportation charges both ways and we will cheerfully refund your money in full.

$2.95 is less than any other dealer pays at wholesale for this instrument.

No. 12C607 Order by Number.

FRONT VIEW OF GUITAR

BACK VIEW OF GUITAR

ONE OF THE **BEST GUITAR VALUES** EVER OFFERED

WE ARE THE LARGEST MUSIC DEALERS IN THE WORLD

SELLING DIRECT TO THE CONSUMER, AND CAN FURNISH YOU BETTER GOODS FOR LESS MONEY THAN YOU CAN BUY ELSEWHERE.

THE STANFORD

AN ENTIRELY NEW STYLE OF GUITAR. HANDSOME IN APPEARANCE, SWEET IN TONE and FULLY WARRANTED. USUALLY SOLD FOR FROM $12.00 to $15.00.

OUR GREAT BARGAIN PRICE, $4.25.

THIS IS AN ENTIRELY NEW STYLE OF GUITAR, containing all the desirable points found in high grade instruments. It is made of the best quality of maple and finished in a perfect imitation of rosewood. This imitation is so fine that experts are not able to tell it from the genuine rosewood. **THE TOP** is made of resonant eastern spruce finished in natural wood, handsomely inlaid around the edge with different colored woods and bound with white celluloid. It has three rings of variegated wood around the sound hole. **THE BACK** is inlaid around the edge with different colored woods and bound with white celluloid. It has also a strip of colored wood running the entire length through the center of the back, as shown in the illustration. **THE FINGERBOARD** is solid rosewood fitted with raised frets and inlaid pearl position dots accurately set so as to produce a perfect scale. **THE SCREW PATENT HEAD** is of the best American make and the metal tailpiece is handsomely nickel plated. This instrument has a beautiful tone and in appearance will equal guitars that other dealers sell for from $12.00 to $15.00. This instrument we recommend for solo work, as it has a magnificent full volume of tone and the harmonics can be produced in a clear, ringing manner not usually possible upon instruments of this grade. The entire instrument is given a heavy coat of beautiful transparent varnish through which the grain of the wood can be seen plainly. It is highly polished and finished and we guarantee it to be satisfactory. It is one of the finest moderate priced guitars and you will make no mistake in purchasing one. **REMEMBER,** we offer this instrument on our famous 10-day trial plan as fully explained on page 144 and you take no risk whatever in ordering it.

WE SEND FREE WITH THIS GUITAR one Guckert Chord Book, by the aid of which anyone can learn to play upon this instrument without the assistance of a teacher. This book together with the fingerboard chart, which we send, makes it possible for anybody, without any previous knowledge of music, to acquire proficiency upon this instrument in a very short time, without paying out money for music lessons. We also include in this outfit, one extra set of strings, one fingerboard chart, before mentioned, which can be placed under the strings and which gives the position of every note on the instrument. We send also a magic capo d'astro, by the aid of which anyone can play all the chords in the different major and minor keys, by simply obtaining a knowledge of the chord of C.

No. 12C608 Standard size. Price.. **$4.25**

No. 12C608

ORDER BY NUMBER

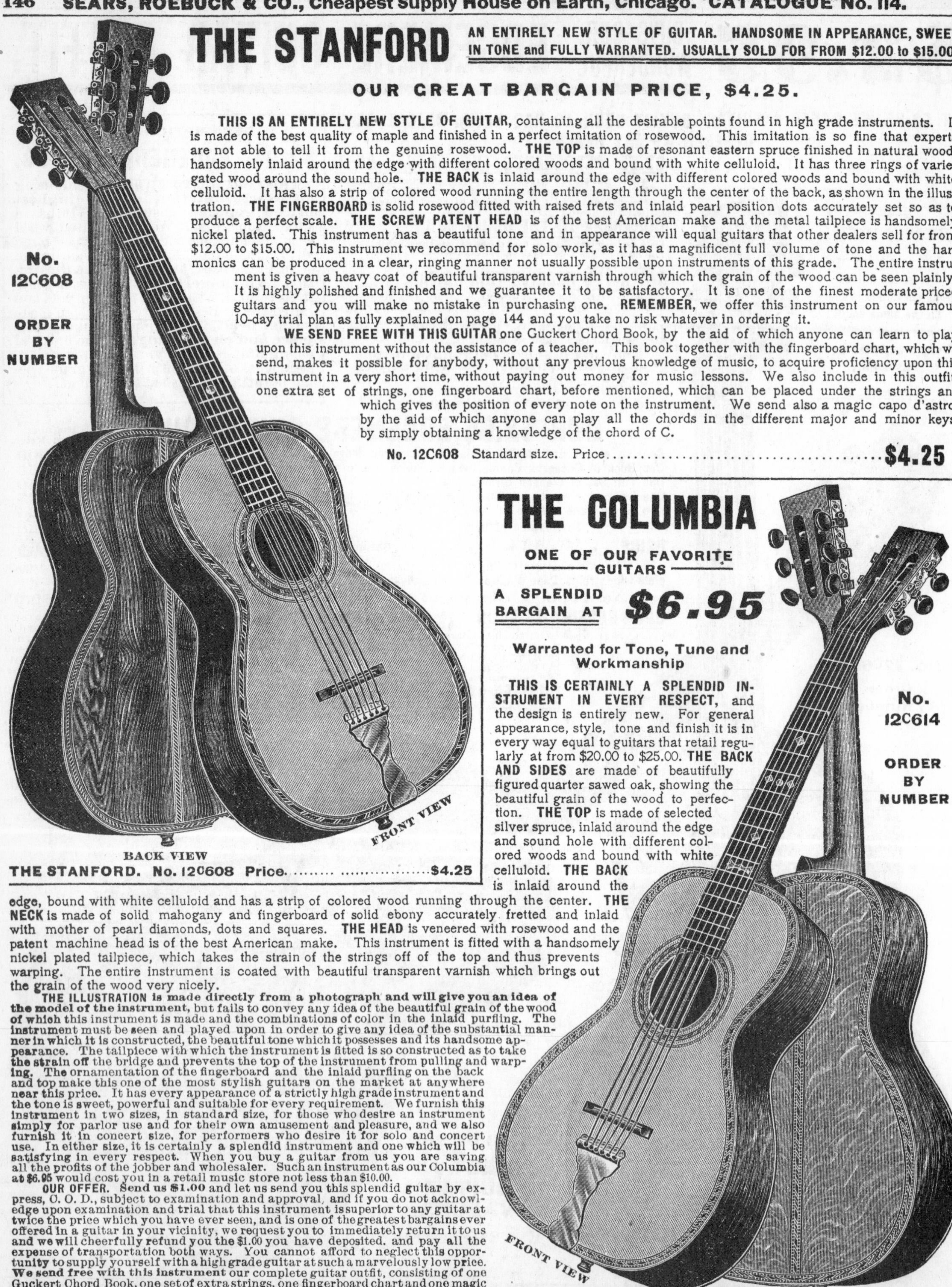

THE STANFORD. No. 12C608 Price........................$4.25

THE COLUMBIA

ONE OF OUR FAVORITE GUITARS

A SPLENDID BARGAIN AT $6.95

Warranted for Tone, Tune and Workmanship

No. 12C614

ORDER BY NUMBER

THIS IS CERTAINLY A SPLENDID INSTRUMENT IN EVERY RESPECT, and the design is entirely new. For general appearance, style, tone and finish it is in every way equal to guitars that retail regularly at from $20.00 to $25.00. **THE BACK AND SIDES** are made of beautifully figured quarter sawed oak, showing the beautiful grain of the wood to perfection. **THE TOP** is made of selected silver spruce, inlaid around the edge and sound hole with different colored woods and bound with white celluloid. **THE BACK** is inlaid around the edge, bound with white celluloid and has a strip of colored wood running through the center. **THE NECK** is made of solid mahogany and fingerboard of solid ebony accurately fretted and inlaid with mother of pearl diamonds, dots and squares. **THE HEAD** is veneered with rosewood and the patent machine head is of the best American make. This instrument is fitted with a handsomely nickel plated tailpiece, which takes the strain of the strings off of the top and thus prevents warping. The entire instrument is coated with beautiful transparent varnish which brings out the grain of the wood very nicely.

THE ILLUSTRATION is made directly from a photograph and will give you an idea of the model of the instrument, but fails to convey any idea of the beautiful grain of the wood of which this instrument is made and the combinations of color in the inlaid purfling. The instrument must be seen and played upon in order to give any idea of the substantial manner in which it is constructed, the beautiful tone which it possesses and its handsome appearance. The tailpiece with which the instrument is fitted is so constructed as to take the strain off the bridge and prevents the top of the instrument from pulling and warping. The ornamentation of the fingerboard and the inlaid purfling on the back and top make this one of the most stylish guitars on the market at anywhere near this price. It has every appearance of a strictly high grade instrument and the tone is sweet, powerful and suitable for every requirement. We furnish this instrument in two sizes, in standard size, for those who desire an instrument simply for parlor use and for their own amusement and pleasure, and we also furnish it in concert size, for performers who desire it for solo and concert use. In either size, it is certainly a splendid instrument and one which will be satisfying in every respect. When you buy a guitar from us you are saving all the profits of the jobber and wholesaler. Such an instrument as our Columbia at $6.95 would cost you in a retail music store not less than $10.00.

OUR OFFER. Send us $1.00 and let us send you this splendid guitar by express, C. O. D., subject to examination and approval, and if you do not acknowledge upon examination and trial that this instrument is superior to any guitar at twice the price which you have ever seen, and is one of the greatest bargains ever offered in a guitar in your vicinity, we request you to immediately return it to us and we will cheerfully refund you the $1.00 you have deposited. and pay all the expense of transportation both ways. You cannot afford to neglect this opportunity to supply yourself with a high grade guitar at such a marvelously low price. **We send free with this instrument** our complete guitar outfit, consisting of one Guckert Chord Book, one set of extra strings, one fingerboard chart and one magic capo d'astro. This combination makes it possible for any one, without any previous knowledge of music, to acquire proficiency on this instrument.

No. 12C614 Standard size. Price..**$6.95**
No. 12C616 Concert size. Price.. **7.65**

THE COLUMBIA. No. 12C614 Price........................$6.95

THE ARON THE BEST MEDIUM PRICED GUITAR ON THE MARKET.

BEAUTIFUL FINISH. HANDSOME APPEARANCE. SPLENDID TONE.

SOLD GENERALLY BY DEALERS FOR FROM $15.00 TO $20.00. ***SOLD BY US FOR $7.95.***

THIS GUITAR WAS FORMERLY ONE OF OUR ACME PROFESSIONAL STYLES AND NEVER SOLD FOR LESS THAN $9.95. We have succeeded, however, in reducing this price owing to a better contract which we have succeeded in making with the manufacturers and an enormous increase in our sales, which enables us to reduce selling expenses to a minimum. This also enables us to improve the guitar in many ways so we are now enabled to offer it in standard size at $7.95.

THE BACK AND SIDES are made of the best quality, especially selected highly figured mahogany. **THE TOP** is made of eastern spruce and finished in natural wood. It is inlaid around the soundhole and edge with different colored wood and bound with celluloid. **THE EDGE OF THE BACK** is inlaid the same as the top with different colored woods and bound with celluloid. **THE BACK** has also a strip of different colored woods running through the center. **THE NECK** is made of solid mahogany. **THE FINGERBOARD** is made of solid ebony accurately fretted and handsomely inlaid with mother of pearl figures and fancy designs. **THE FRONT OF THE HEAD** is veneered with rosewood and the patent head is of the best American make. **THE BRIDGE** is made of solid ebony with inlaid ivory strip, and the ornamentations throughout the entire instrument are neat and tasty. So far as tone is concerned, this instrument is the equal of any of our higher priced guitars. The price we make on this instrument includes all the extras as stated above and will represent a saving to you of at least $5.00 on your purchase. We would be glad to have you purchase this instrument and compare it with any other instrument in your town at from $15.00 to $20.00, and if you do not find that this instrument is in every way the equal of any guitar at the above mentioned price, we will cheerfully refund your money, take back the instrument and pay the express charges both ways. We believe that you will acknowledge that this is a very liberal offer and that you are taking no chances whatever in giving us your order for one of these splendid instruments. We wish you to remember the fact that we allow you full ten days trial upon this instrument and if within that time it should prove unsatisfactory for any reason it can be returned to us, we will refund your money and pay the transportation charges both ways. We sell this beautiful instrument in both standard and concert sizes and we believe that you will find either size a satisfying instrument in every way.

No. 12C650

ORDER BY NUMBER

FREE. WITH EACH ONE OF THESE GUITARS, WE SEND ABSOLUTELY FREE OUR GREAT GUITAR OUTFIT, consisting of one Guckert Chord Book, one extra set of strings, one fingerboard chart, which can be placed under the strings and gives the position of every tone. We also send one Magic capo d'astro, by the aid of which anyone can easily play accompaniments in any of the different major and minor keys.

No. 12C650 Standard size. Price.......... **$7.95**
No. 12C651 Concert size. Price.......... **8.65**

BACK VIEW FRONT VIEW

THE ARON. No. 12C650 Price...$7.95

THE CAMBRIDGE

—$8.95—

ONE OF THE BEST MODERATE PRICED GUITARS THAT WE HANDLE.

IS EQUAL IN APPEARANCE AND SWEETNESS OF TONE TO GUITARS USUALLY SOLD AT $18.00 to $20.00.

No. 12C653

ORDER BY NUMBER

THIS IS ONE OF THE PRETTIEST ROSEWOOD GUITARS THAT WE HANDLE and we can heartily recommend it to anyone who desires a medium priced instrument of handsome appearance and splendid tone. We have been handling this instrument for a long time and it has given our customers the greatest satisfaction. We furnish it in three sizes, as shown below, and will guarantee it to be perfectly satisfactory. We sell it upon the same terms that we sell all of our other guitars and we make the customer the sole judge of its merits. **THE ENGRAVING** which we show of this instrument is a wood cut made directly from a photograph of this instrument, and shows its style and model, but the beautiful combination of color formed by the wood of which the body is constructed and the inlaid purfling with which the instrument is ornamented, cannot be shown by the engraving. The varnish with which the guitar is coated is highly transparent and brings out the beautiful grain of the wood in splendid shape. This is one of the neatest and best moderate priced concert guitars on the market today. It is constructed with great care, each part being carefully and substantially made. It will last a lifetime, and will grow in sweetness and volume of tone. In buying a guitar always remember that the outside finishing of the instrument is very apt to be deceptive. It is easy to make a guitar and finish it in elegant shape, but it is quite another thing to construct such an instrument so that it will possess that broad, mellow tone which is so desirable in a guitar. We guarantee this instrument both as to appearance and tone, and if you are in the market for an instrument of this kind, we recommend it to you without hesitation.

IT IS MADE ESPECIALLY FOR US, and all the fancy profits which usually attach to a guitar of this grade are entirely cut out and the only profit you have to pay is the one small profit we add for handling and selling the instrument. This is the reason why we are able to offer at $8.95 an instrument which dealers ordinarily obtain $18.00 to $20.00 for. **IT HAS GENUINE ROSEWOOD BACK AND SIDES** and the top is made of the best quality seasoned eastern spruce, inlaid around the edge and soundhole with handsome colored wood and bound with white celluloid. **IT HAS A SOLID MAHOGANY NECK** and a genuine ebony fingerboard with inlaid mother of pearl position dots, and raised frets accurately placed so that the scale is perfect. **THE HEAD** is veneered with rosewood on the front and back and handsomely inlaid with mother of pearl. It is fitted with the best quality nickel plated American screw patent head, so adjusted as to be absolutely without any lost motion. It is a strictly high grade instrument in every respect and is covered with a coat of beautiful transparent varnish, beautifully finished and polished.

LET US SEND YOU THIS SPLENDID INSTRUMENT, together with our complete outfit consisting of Guckert Chord Book, one extra set of strings, one fingerboard chart and one Magic capo d'astro, and if you do not find when you receive it that it is a splendid bargain in every respect, and equal, if not superior, to anything that your dealer has to offer in this line, at twice the price, you can return it to us at once, and we will cheerfully refund your money and pay all the expenses of transportation both ways.

No. 12C653 Standard size. Price.......................**$8.95**
No. 12C654 Concert size. Price....................... **9.55**
No. 12C655 Grand concert size. Price.................... **10.45**

FRONT VIEW BACK VIEW

THE CAMBRIDGE. No. 12C653 Price.................. ......$8.95

THE CORNELL A REGULAR $20.00 GUITAR FOR $11.35

THIS IS A SPLENDID INSTRUMENT AND ONE WHICH WE ARE PROUD TO SHIP OUT AS IT ALWAYS GIVES SATISFACTION.

IT HAS A GENUINE ROSEWOOD BACK AND SIDES AND THE TOP IS THE BEST QUALITY EASTERN SPRUCE.

THE TOP is inlaid around the edge with a broad strip of colored wood and bound with white celluloid. **EDGE OF THE SOUNDHOLE** is inlaid with a double ring of fancy design in colored wood and bound with celluloid. **THE BACK** is handsomely inlaid around the edge and bound with celluloid the same as the top. It also has a strip in the center of the same design as the inlaying around the soundhole. **THE NECK** is genuine mahogany and the fingerboard is solid ebony, bound with white celluloid and inlaid with diamond shaped mother of pearl position dots. **THE FRONT AND BACK OF THE HEAD** are veneered with rosewood and the front is handsomely inlaid with mother of pearl stars and crescents. **THE MACHINE HEAD** on this instrument is of the best American make, and so geared as to avoid all lost motion in tuning up the strings. The entire instrument is covered with transparent varnish which brings out the grain of the wood perfectly, and the finish throughout is the finest that can possibly be put on any guitar.

THE TONE is exceedingly sweet and powerful and is splendid for accompaniment purposes as well as for solo work. We recommend this instrument highly for the use of glee clubs, and a comparison of the instrument and the price we ask, with the guitars and the prices offered by other dealers will prove to you at once that we are offering, in this guitar, an instrument which is superior to guitars offered by others at from $18.00 to $25.00. It is not necessary for you to take our word for this, as you can very easily prove it by allowing us to ship you one of these guitars on approval. We ship this guitar upon the same terms as we ship all of our other instruments and guarantee it to be satisfactory. We furnish it in three different sizes, standard size, concert size and grand concert style. The grand concert style of this guitar is truly a noble instrument and is a favorite with mandolin and guitar organizations on account of its deep profound tone.

REMEMBER, IN BUYING A GUITAR that you can tell nothing about the instrument from the appearance or the finish. There are many guitars on the market which are handsome in appearance and beautiful in finish, but which are altogether lacking in that deep, rich, mellow tone which this instrument possesses. This instrument is so accurately constructed that the most delicate harmonics are easily produced, and chords which are altogether impossible upon other guitars are easily produced upon this guitar. The instrument is so resonant in tone that the highest notes, so difficult upon ordinary guitars, become easy on this instrument. We desire to have an opportunity to send you this instrument on approval under our terms of shipment, and give you an opportunity to give it a thorough test and examination and allow you to satisfy yourself fully that it is a splendid bargain in a guitar. This is the instrument for which your dealer is asking $20.00 and upwards and we are able to make these extremely low prices because we possess such a great advantage in buying these instruments in large quantities and shipping them directly to our customers. Why should you purchase a guitar in the usual way, paying from $15.00 to $20.00 for it when you can purchase this high grade, guaranteed instrument of exactly the same grade for $11.35? Give us an opportunity to show you what a splendid instrument this is and we know you will never regret it in any way. **OUR COMPLETE OUTFIT** goes to you with this instrument, consisting of one Guckert Chord Book, one extra set of strings, one fingerboard chart and one Magic capo d'astro as fully described on page 144.

No. 12C661 Standard size. Price........ $11.35
No. 12C662 Concert size, Price........ 12.60
No. 12C663 Grand concert size. Price........ 13.75

No. 12C661

ORDER BY NUMBER

FRONT VIEW

BACK VIEW

THE CORNELL. No. 12C661 Price........ $11.35

THE PRINCETON

AN EXCEPTIONALLY FINE INSTRUMENT.

ONLY $13.75

This Beautiful Guitar Has Received the Most Careful Attention and Skill from its Makers.

THE BACK AND SIDES are made of the best quality of rosewood which has a very beautiful grain. **THE TOP** is made of selected eastern resonant spruce and is inlaid around the edge with diamond shaped and round pearl figures and bound with black and white purfling and white celluloid. **THE EDGE OF THE SOUNDHOLE** is inlaid with the same design in mother of pearl as the edge of the guitar and has also three rings of black and white wood inlaying and is bound with celluloid. **THE BACK** is bound with white celluloid and has a strip of fancy colored wood in the center. **THE NECK** is genuine mahogany, handsomely engraved. **THE FINGERBOARD** is solid ebony, bound with white celluloid, with mother of pearl squares, diamonds and stars. It has raised frets accurately placed so that the scale is perfect in every respect. **THE HEAD** is veneered in front and back with rosewood and inlaid in front with fancy mother of pearl figures. It is fitted with the highest grade of American patent head and the screws are so adjusted as to avoid all lost motion. The entire instrument is given a heavy coating of handsome transparent varnish through which the grain of the wood shows to great advantage. The general finish of the instrument is of the very best throughout, having a fine high polish which is equal in every way to the finish usually put on the most expensive guitars.

THE TONE has great breadth, volume and sweetness and the scale is so accurate that the performer finds no difficulty in making the most difficult harmonics sound loud and clear. This instrument is in every way equal to the guitars usually sold for from $20.00 to $30.00 and we will recommend it in every case where parties desire to possess a guitar of beautiful appearance and splendid tone. We sell this guitar in three different sizes and in each size it is equally desirable.

THERE IS A DISTINCT QUALITY ABOUT THIS GUITAR which is not in any sense commercial, upon which no value is fixed, but which is in itself beyond all price. This is the peculiar quality which the instrument possesses, and which it takes from the genius of the maker. Anybody with a little mechanical skill and the necessary tools and materials can make a guitar, but it requires a man with a genius for this work to make a guitar which possesses the broad, evenly balanced, rich, mellow tone which is characteristic of this instrument. This is a quality upon which we do not pretend to fix any price. We simply figure our prices upon the basis of labor and material which enters into the instrument without attempting to charge you for this quality upon which no exact value can be fixed. Neither do we charge you anything for the reputation of the maker of the instruments. We simply ask you to pay us the manufacturer's price with but one small percentage of profit added.

WE SEND A COMPLETE OUTFIT WITH THIS GUITAR consisting of one Guckert Chord Book, filled with all the major and minor chords, one extra set of high grade strings, one fingerboard chart, by the aid of which the beginner can locate every tone instantly, and one capo d'astro, by the aid of which the performer can play accompaniments in any key, by simply learning the chord of C. This makes the instrument complete in every way and a far greater bargain than can be offered you by any other dealer. See description of this free outfit on page 144.

No. 12C669 Standard size. Price........ $13.75
No. 12C670 Concert size. Price........ 14.95
No. 12C671 Grand concert size. Price........ 16.15

No. 12C669

ORDER BY NUMBER

FRONT VIEW

BACK VIEW

THE PRINCETON. No. 12C669 Price........ $13.75

THE YALE, $16.95 A SPLENDID BARGAIN — IN A GUITAR — REDUCED FROM $19.85

BEAUTIFUL IN TONE, ELEGANT IN APPEARANCE. The greatest bargain in a guitar yet offered. This is indeed a splendid instrument and in beauty of finish, elegance of appearance and sweetness of tone, is one of the best guitars ever offered to the public. It is made with the greatest care throughout and is handsomely and solidly constructed. The ornamentations are applied in an artistic manner and it has an appearance of quiet elegance which never fails to call for the admiration of all who examine it. It is certainly a work of art as well as a fine musical instrument. No pains have been spared to make this guitar a magnificent instrument in every respect, and it is the same grade of instrument for which the local dealer is asking $30.00 and $40.00. We have sold a large quantity of these guitars during the past season, and every one has given unqualified satisfaction.

THERE IS JUST ORNAMENTATION AND TRIMMING ENOUGH UPON THIS GUITAR TO MAKE IT A NEAT AND TASTY INSTRUMENT. It has an appearance and finish which very few guitars possess. Nothing has been neglected to make it a splendid instrument in every respect and for those who desire an instrument with just enough ornamentation and trimming to give it a handsome appearance will be delighted with this guitar. The engraving which we show of this instrument is made directly from the photograph of the guitar itself, and shows the design and model of the instrument and details of ornamentation and trimming, but no engraving however fine can give the customer any just idea of the beautiful finish and appearance of this guitar and its splendid tone. We sell this guitar like all the rest of our other instruments, on approval, and all we ask of the customer is to give it a fair trial and examination and we think it will demonstrate ts good qualities to him beyond a doubt. Do not purchase a guitar until you have given us an opportunity to place this magnificent instrument in your hands for a thorough test and trial. Remember, in selling you this instrument, we do not ask you to promise anything or assume any obligation in any way. We simply ask you to give us an opportunity to send it to you on approval under our terms of shipment.

No. 12C672

ORDER BY NUMBER

$16.95

MADE OF THE VERY BEST GRADE OF ROSEWOOD, with top of selected eastern spruce, inlaid around edge and sound hole with colored wood and a broad strip of pearl and bound with white celluloid. **THE BACK** has a handsome inlaid strip of fancy colored wood in the center and is bound with white celluloid. **THE NECK** is made of solid mahogany, beautifully ornamented at the heel with elaborate carvings. **THE FINGERBOARD** is solid ebony, convex in shape, and has white celluloid inlay with fancy pearl figures. The front and back of head are veneered with rosewood and the front is bound with celluloid and elaborately decorated with inlaid pearl. **THE BRIDGE PINS** are made of ivory and inlaid with pearl eyes, and are countersunk in the tailpiece so as not to interfere with the player. **THE MACHINE PATENT HEAD** is the best it is possible to procure. In point of finish and tone, this guitar is unsurpassed. It has a beautiful high polish and is in this respect the equal of the finest guitars made.

REMEMBER, WITH EVERY GUITAR WE SEND FREE OF CHARGE A LEATHER BOUND CANVAS CASE, AN EXTRA SET OF HIGH GRADE STRINGS, Guckert's book of chords, fingerboard chart, and one of our celebrated Magic Capo d'Astros. See full description of this free outfit on page 144.

No. 12C672 Price, standard size......**$16.95**
No. 12C674 Price, concert size **18.45**
No. 12C676 Price, grand concert size. **19.95**

BACK VIEW

FRONT VIEW

THE HARVARD THE VERY FINEST YET

A SUPERB INSTRUMENT SOLD REGULARLY FROM $50.00 TO $75.00

OUR GREAT BARGAIN PRICE $21.45

THE HANDSOMEST GUITAR EVER OFFERED

No. 12C681

ORDER BY NUMBER

$21.45

THIS IS THE FINEST GUITAR MADE. Not only the finest in appearance, but unquestionably the finest in tone. We furnish it in three sizes, standard, concert and grand concert size. In each size it is equally a splendid instrument. In selecting this instrument, we have instructed the manufacturers to put us up the finest instrument that could be made of its sort, and we believe you will admit when you see it, that they have succeeded in every respect. This instrument is the equal in every way of guitars that retail regularly at from $50.00 to $75.00. It is certainly a work of art in every respect, because the superb finish and the handsome inlaying which is characteristic of the instrument gives it a rich appearance possessed by no other instrument of its kind. **THE BACK AND SIDES** are made of the very finest quality of especially selected rosewood, very finely figured. **IT HAS A CHOICE, EXTRA SEASONED EASTERN SPRUCE TOP,** inlaid around the edge with a broad strip of pearl, made in alternate blocks, giving a light and dark effect which is very handsome. This strip of pearl is bound with double strips of black and white wood and the outer edge is celluloid. **THE SOUND HOLE** is ornamented in the same manner, excepting that there are three rings made of black and white fancy figured wood. There are two strips of black and white pearl around the sides of the guitar, both strips being bound with black and white purfling, making a most gorgeous effect. **THE BACK** is bound with white celluloid and has a strip of light and dark pearl down the center, the pearl being edged with black and white purfling. **THE NECK** is the very best quality of mahogany, beautifully hand carved and tipped with ivory. **THE FINGERBOARD** is of the very best quality solid ebony, convex shaped, bound with white celluloid, handsomely inlaid with mother of pearl in the shape of a vine extending from one end of the fingerboard to the other. **THE HEAD** is veneered on the front and back with three layers of wood, ebony, holly and rosewood, and shaped on the back to a point on the neck making a most beautiful effect. The front of the head is bound with celluloid and inlaid with pearl figures and fancy design.

THE PATENT HEAD is of the best American make, gold plated, tipped with ivory buttons and so adjusted that there is absolutely no lost motion. This instrument must be seen to be fully appreciated. In addition to the strings and book given with every Harvard guitar, we include with this instrument a perfect fitting canvas, leather bound case. In tone, appearance and finish, this is by far the most superb instrument we have ever seen and its sales have been immense, considering the fact that it is a high grade instrument. It is an excellent instrument for presentation purposes and will compare favorably with any $75.00 guitar that any other dealer has to offer you.

We trust that we may have an opportunity to place this magnificent instrument in your hands for examination and trial, as we are sure that you will be more than delighted with it. We furnish it in three sizes, standard, concert and grand concert size, and guarantee it to give satisfaction in every respect.

Why should you go to your dealer and pay him from $50.00 to $75.00 for a guitar when you can purchase one equally as good in tone, and far more superb in finish, from us at $21.45?

No. 12C681 Price, standard size.......................**$21.45**
No. 12C682 Price, concert size.......................... **23.45**
No. 12C683 Price, grand concert size.................. **25.25**

BACK VIEW

FRONT VIEW

OUR SPLENDID LINE OF MANDOLINS.

EACH ONE OF THESE INSTRUMENTS IS A GREAT BARGAIN. FULLY GUARANTEED AS TO FINISH, WORKMANSHIP, TONE AND DURABILITY. . . . .

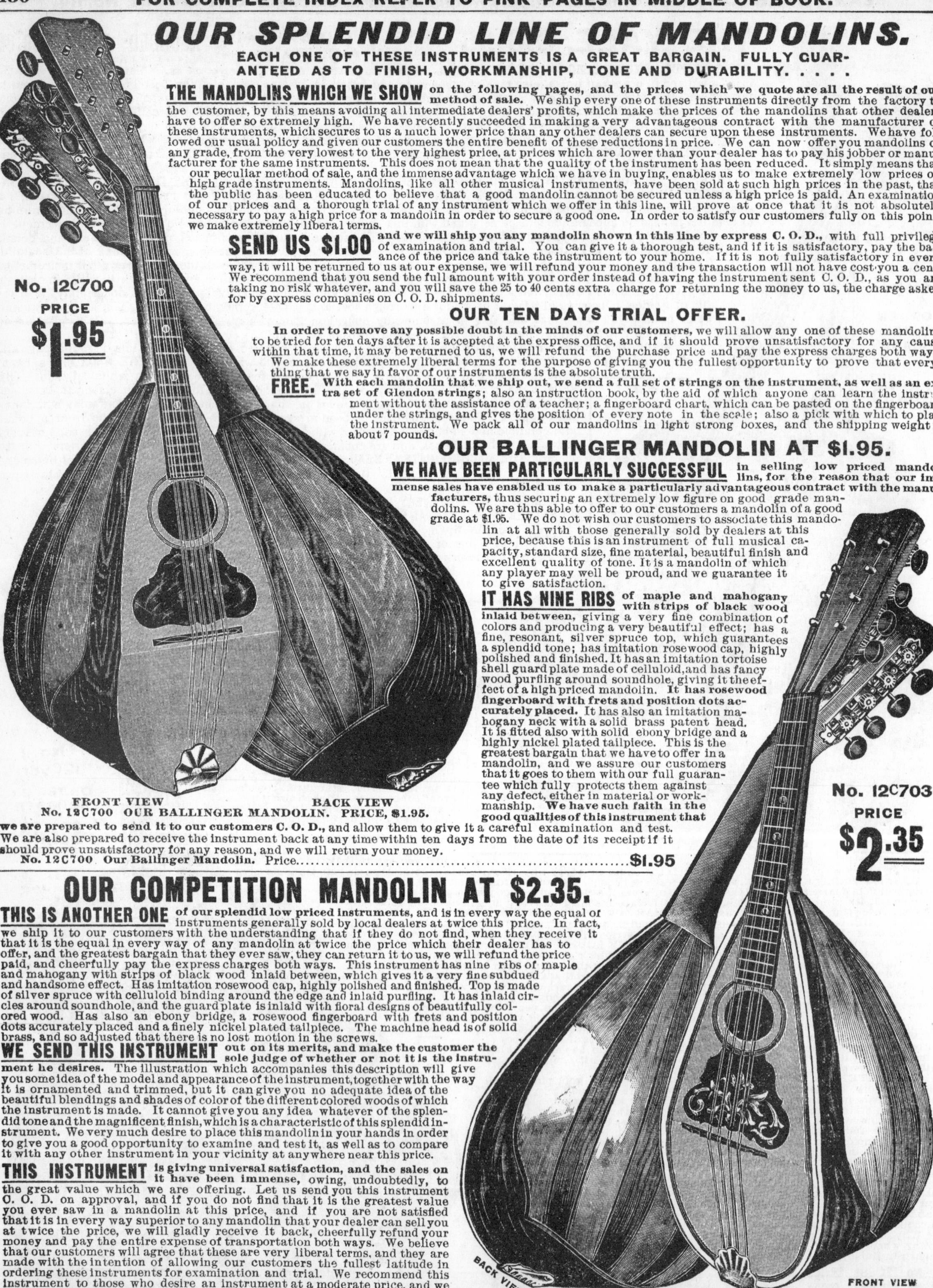

THE MANDOLINS WHICH WE SHOW on the following pages, and the prices which we quote are all the result of our method of sale. We ship every one of these instruments directly from the factory to the customer, by this means avoiding all intermediate dealers' profits, which make the prices of the mandolins that other dealers have to offer so extremely high. We have recently succeeded in making a very advantageous contract with the manufacturer of these instruments, which secures to us a much lower price than any other dealers can secure upon these instruments. We have followed our usual policy and given our customers the entire benefit of these reductions in price. We can now offer you mandolins of any grade, from the very lowest to the very highest price, at prices which are lower than your dealer has to pay his jobber or manufacturer for the same instruments. This does not mean that the quality of the instrument has been reduced. It simply means that our peculiar method of sale, and the immense advantage which we have in buying, enables us to make extremely low prices on high grade instruments. Mandolins, like all other musical instruments, have been sold at such high prices in the past, that the public has been educated to believe that a good mandolin cannot be secured unless a high price is paid. An examination of our prices and a thorough trial of any instrument which we offer in this line, will prove at once that it is not absolutely necessary to pay a high price for a mandolin in order to secure a good one. In order to satisfy our customers fully on this point, we make extremely liberal terms.

SEND US $1.00 and we will ship you any mandolin shown in this line by express C. O. D., with full privilege of examination and trial. You can give it a thorough test, and if it is satisfactory, pay the balance of the price and take the instrument to your home. If it is not fully satisfactory in every way, it will be returned to us at our expense, we will refund your money and the transaction will not have cost you a cent. We recommend that you send the full amount with your order instead of having the instrument sent C. O. D., as you are taking no risk whatever, and you will save the 25 to 40 cents extra charge for returning the money to us, the charge asked for by express companies on C. O. D. shipments.

No. 12C700
PRICE
$1.95

OUR TEN DAYS TRIAL OFFER.

In order to remove any possible doubt in the minds of our customers, we will allow any one of these mandolins to be tried for ten days after it is accepted at the express office, and if it should prove unsatisfactory for any cause within that time, it may be returned to us, we will refund the purchase price and pay the express charges both ways. We make these extremely liberal terms for the purpose of giving you the fullest opportunity to prove that everything that we say in favor of our instruments is the absolute truth.

FREE. **With each mandolin that we ship out, we send a full set of strings on the instrument, as well as an extra set of Glendon strings;** also an instruction book, by the aid of which anyone can learn the instrument without the assistance of a teacher; a fingerboard chart, which can be pasted on the fingerboard under the strings, and gives the position of every note in the scale; also a pick with which to play the instrument. We pack all of our mandolins in light strong boxes, and the shipping weight is about 7 pounds.

OUR BALLINGER MANDOLIN AT $1.95.

WE HAVE BEEN PARTICULARLY SUCCESSFUL in selling low priced mandolins, for the reason that our immense sales have enabled us to make a particularly advantageous contract with the manufacturers, thus securing an extremely low figure on good grade mandolins. We are thus able to offer to our customers a mandolin of a good grade at $1.95. We do not wish our customers to associate this mandolin at all with those generally sold by dealers at this price, because this is an instrument of full musical capacity, standard size, fine material, beautiful finish and excellent quality of tone. It is a mandolin of which any player may well be proud, and we guarantee it to give satisfaction.

IT HAS NINE RIBS of maple and mahogany with strips of black wood inlaid between, giving a very fine combination of colors and producing a very beautiful effect; has a fine, resonant, silver spruce top, which guarantees a splendid tone; has imitation rosewood cap, highly polished and finished. It has an imitation tortoise shell guard plate made of celluloid, and has fancy wood purfling around soundhole, giving it the effect of a high priced mandolin. **It has rosewood fingerboard with frets and position dots accurately placed.** It has also an imitation mahogany neck with a solid brass patent head. It is fitted also with solid ebony bridge and a highly nickel plated tailpiece. This is the greatest bargain that we have to offer in a mandolin, and we assure our customers that it goes to them with our full guarantee which fully protects them against any defect, either in material or workmanship. **We have such faith in the good qualities of this instrument that we are prepared to send it to our customers C. O. D.,** and allow them to give it a careful examination and test. We are also prepared to receive the instrument back at any time within ten days from the date of its receipt if it should prove unsatisfactory for any reason, and we will return your money.

FRONT VIEW — BACK VIEW
No. 12C700 OUR BALLINGER MANDOLIN. PRICE, $1.95.

No. 12C700 Our Ballinger Mandolin. Price....................$1.95

No. 12C703
PRICE
$2.35

OUR COMPETITION MANDOLIN AT $2.35.

THIS IS ANOTHER ONE of our splendid low priced instruments, and is in every way the equal of instruments generally sold by local dealers at twice this price. In fact, we ship it to our customers with the understanding that if they do not find, when they receive it that it is the equal in every way of any mandolin at twice the price which their dealer has to offer, and the greatest bargain that they ever saw, they can return it to us, we will refund the price paid, and cheerfully pay the express charges both ways. This instrument has nine ribs of maple and mahogany with strips of black wood inlaid between, which gives it a very fine subdued and handsome effect. Has imitation rosewood cap, highly polished and finished. Top is made of silver spruce with celluloid binding around the edge and inlaid purfling. It has inlaid circles around soundhole, and the guard plate is inlaid with floral designs of beautifully colored wood. Has also an ebony bridge, a rosewood fingerboard with frets and position dots accurately placed and a finely nickel plated tailpiece. The machine head is of solid brass, and so adjusted that there is no lost motion in the screws.

WE SEND THIS INSTRUMENT out on its merits, and make the customer the sole judge of whether or not it is the instrument he desires. The illustration which accompanies this description will give you some idea of the model and appearance of the instrument, together with the way it is ornamented and trimmed, but it can give you no adequate idea of the beautiful blendings and shades of color of the different colored woods of which the instrument is made. It cannot give you any idea whatever of the splendid tone and the magnificent finish, which is a characteristic of this splendid instrument. We very much desire to place this mandolin in your hands in order to give you a good opportunity to examine and test it, as well as to compare it with any other instrument in your vicinity at anywhere near this price.

THIS INSTRUMENT is giving universal satisfaction, and the sales on it have been immense, owing, undoubtedly, to the great value which we are offering. Let us send you this instrument C. O. D. on approval, and if you do not find that it is the greatest value you ever saw in a mandolin at this price, and if you are not satisfied that it is in every way superior to any mandolin that your dealer can sell you at twice the price, we will gladly receive it back, cheerfully refund your money and pay the entire expense of transportation both ways. We believe that our customers will agree that these are very liberal terms, and they are made with the intention of allowing our customers the fullest latitude in ordering these instruments for examination and trial. We recommend this instrument to those who desire an instrument at a moderate price, and we know that it will in every way prove satisfactory.

No. 12C703 Our Competition Mandolin. Price....................$2.35

BACK VIEW — FRONT VIEW
No. 12C703 OUR COMPETITION MANDOLIN. PRICE, $2.35

OUR EMPIRE MANDOLIN AT $3.45

A FIRST CLASS MANDOLIN AT LESS THAN DEALERS' COST.

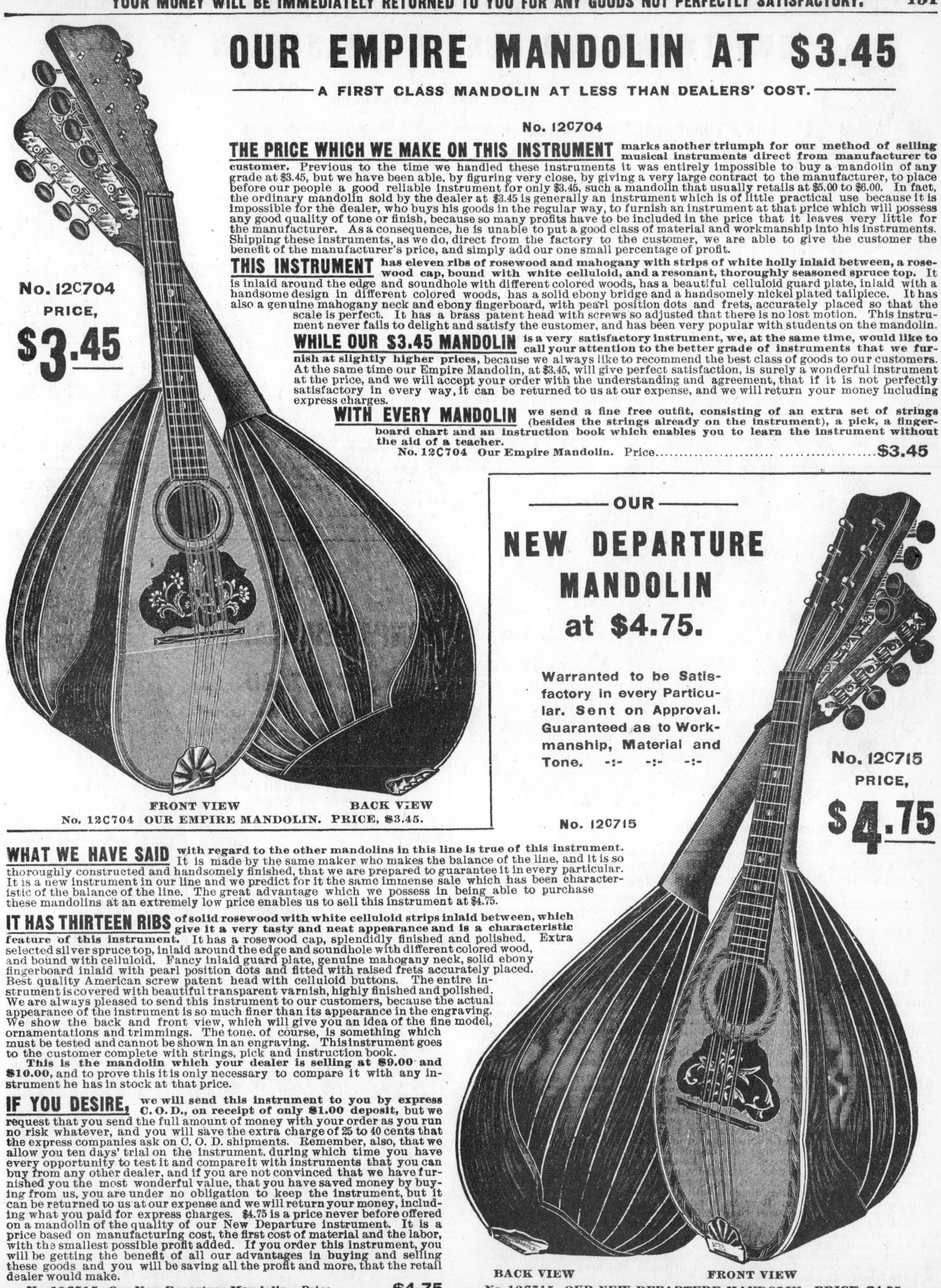

No. 12C704

No. 12C704
PRICE,
$3.45

THE PRICE WHICH WE MAKE ON THIS INSTRUMENT marks another triumph for our method of selling musical instruments direct from manufacturer to customer. Previous to the time we handled these instruments it was entirely impossible to buy a mandolin of any grade at $3.45, but we have been able, by figuring very close, by giving a very large contract to the manufacturer, to place before our people a good reliable instrument for only $3.45, such a mandolin that usually retails at $5.00 to $6.00. In fact, the ordinary mandolin sold by the dealer at $3.45 is generally an instrument which is of little practical use because it is impossible for the dealer, who buys his goods in the regular way, to furnish an instrument at that price which will possess any good quality of tone or finish, because so many profits have to be included in the price that it leaves very little for the manufacturer. As a consequence, he is unable to put a good class of material and workmanship into his instruments. Shipping these instruments, as we do, direct from the factory to the customer, we are able to give the customer the benefit of the manufacturer's price, and simply add our one small percentage of profit.

THIS INSTRUMENT has eleven ribs of rosewood and mahogany with strips of white holly inlaid between, a rosewood cap, bound with white celluloid, and a resonant, thoroughly seasoned spruce top. It is inlaid around the edge and soundhole with different colored woods, has a beautiful celluloid guard plate, inlaid with a handsome design in different colored woods, has a solid ebony bridge and a handsomely nickel plated tailpiece. It has also a genuine mahogany neck and ebony fingerboard, with pearl position dots and frets, accurately placed so that the scale is perfect. It has a brass patent head with screws so adjusted that there is no lost motion. This instrument never fails to delight and satisfy the customer, and has been very popular with students on the mandolin.

WHILE OUR $3.45 MANDOLIN is a very satisfactory instrument, we, at the same time, would like to call your attention to the better grade of instruments that we furnish at slightly higher prices, because we always like to recommend the best class of goods to our customers. At the same time our Empire Mandolin, at $3.45, will give perfect satisfaction, is surely a wonderful instrument at the price, and we will accept your order with the understanding and agreement, that if it is not perfectly satisfactory in every way, it can be returned to us at our expense, and we will return your money including express charges.

WITH EVERY MANDOLIN we send a fine free outfit, consisting of an extra set of strings (besides the strings already on the instrument), a pick, a fingerboard chart and an instruction book which enables you to learn the instrument without the aid of a teacher.

No. 12C704 Our Empire Mandolin. Price.......................................$3.45

FRONT VIEW BACK VIEW
No. 12C704 OUR EMPIRE MANDOLIN. PRICE, $3.45.

OUR
NEW DEPARTURE MANDOLIN at $4.75.

Warranted to be Satisfactory in every Particular. Sent on Approval. Guaranteed as to Workmanship, Material and Tone. -:- -:- -:-

No. 12C715
PRICE,
$4.75

No. 12C715

WHAT WE HAVE SAID with regard to the other mandolins in this line is true of this instrument. It is made by the same maker who makes the balance of the line, and it is so thoroughly constructed and handsomely finished, that we are prepared to guarantee it in every particular. It is a new instrument in our line and we predict for it the same immense sale which has been characteristic of the balance of the line. The great advantage which we possess in being able to purchase these mandolins at an extremely low price enables us to sell this instrument at $4.75.

IT HAS THIRTEEN RIBS of solid rosewood with white celluloid strips inlaid between, which give it a very tasty and neat appearance and is a characteristic feature of this instrument. It has a rosewood cap, splendidly finished and polished. Extra selected silver spruce top, inlaid around the edge and soundhole with different colored wood, and bound with celluloid. Fancy inlaid guard plate, genuine mahogany neck, solid ebony fingerboard inlaid with pearl position dots and fitted with raised frets accurately placed. Best quality American screw patent head with celluloid buttons. The entire instrument is covered with beautiful transparent varnish, highly finished and polished. We are always pleased to send this instrument to our customers, because the actual appearance of the instrument is so much finer than its appearance in the engraving. We show the back and front view, which will give you an idea of the fine model, ornamentations and trimmings. The tone, of course, is something which must be tested and cannot be shown in an engraving. This instrument goes to the customer complete with strings, pick and instruction book.

This is the mandolin which your dealer is selling at $9.00 and $10.00, and to prove this it is only necessary to compare it with any instrument he has in stock at that price.

IF YOU DESIRE, we will send this instrument to you by express C. O. D., on receipt of only $1.00 deposit, but we request that you send the full amount of money with your order as you run no risk whatever, and you will save the extra charge of 25 to 40 cents that the express companies ask on C. O. D. shipments. Remember, also, that we allow you ten days' trial on the instrument, during which time you have every opportunity to test it and compare it with instruments that you can buy from any other dealer, and if you are not convinced that we have furnished you the most wonderful value, that you have saved money by buying from us, you are under no obligation to keep the instrument, but it can be returned to us at our expense and we will return your money, including what you paid for express charges. $4.75 is a price never before offered on a mandolin of the quality of our New Departure instrument. It is a price based on manufacturing cost, the first cost of material and the labor, with the smallest possible profit added. If you order this instrument, you will be getting the benefit of all our advantages in buying and selling these goods and you will be saving all the profit and more, that the retail dealer would make.

No. 12C715 Our New Departure Mandolin. Price............$4.75

BACK VIEW FRONT VIEW
No. 12C715 OUR NEW DEPARTURE MANDOLIN. PRICE, $4.75.

OUR TWENTIETH CENTURY MANDOLIN AT $5.75.

A SPLENDID INSTRUMENT, LOW IN PRICE, THE EQUAL OF MANDOLINS THAT USUALLY RETAIL AT $10.00.

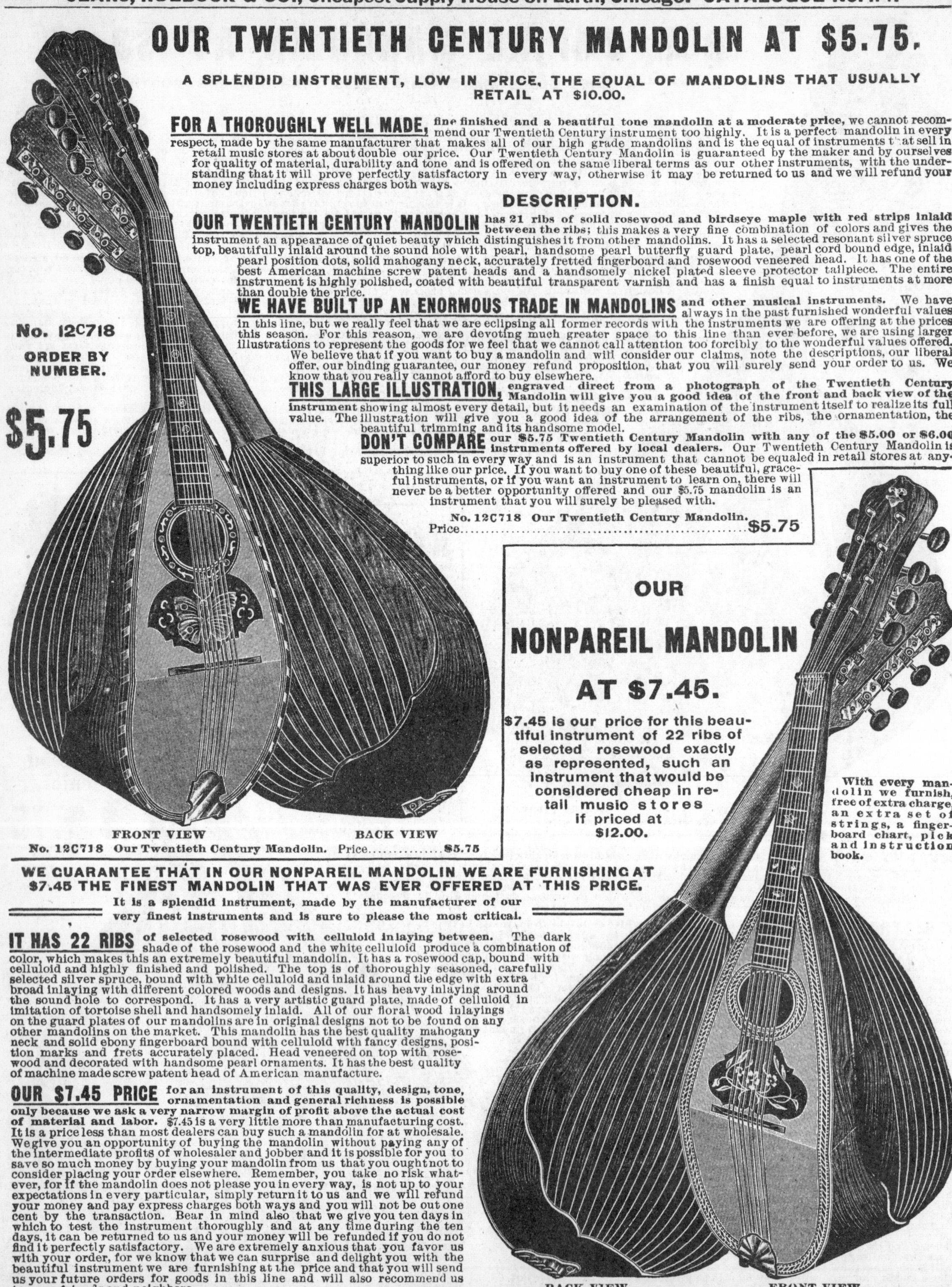

FOR A THOROUGHLY WELL MADE, fine finished and a beautiful tone mandolin at a moderate price, we cannot recommend our Twentieth Century instrument too highly. It is a perfect mandolin in every respect, made by the same manufacturer that makes all of our high grade mandolins and is the equal of instruments that sell in retail music stores at about double our price. Our Twentieth Century Mandolin is guaranteed by the maker and by ourselves for quality of material, durability and tone and is offered on the same liberal terms as our other instruments, with the understanding that it will prove perfectly satisfactory in every way, otherwise it may be returned to us and we will refund your money including express charges both ways.

DESCRIPTION.

OUR TWENTIETH CENTURY MANDOLIN has 21 ribs of solid rosewood and birdseye maple with red strips inlaid between the ribs; this makes a very fine combination of colors and gives the instrument an appearance of quiet beauty which distinguishes it from other mandolins. It has a selected resonant silver spruce top, beautifully inlaid around the sound hole with pearl, handsome pearl butterfly guard plate, pearl cord bound edge, inlaid pearl position dots, solid mahogany neck, accurately fretted fingerboard and rosewood veneered head. It has one of the best American machine screw patent heads and a handsomely nickel plated sleeve protector tailpiece. The entire instrument is highly polished, coated with beautiful transparent varnish and has a finish equal to instruments at more than double the price.

WE HAVE BUILT UP AN ENORMOUS TRADE IN MANDOLINS and other musical instruments. We have always in the past furnished wonderful values in this line, but we really feel that we are eclipsing all former records with the instruments we are offering at the prices this season. For this reason, we are devoting much greater space to this line than ever before, we are using larger illustrations to represent the goods for we feel that we cannot call attention too forcibly to the wonderful values offered. We believe that if you want to buy a mandolin and will consider our claims, note the descriptions, our liberal offer, our binding guarantee, our money refund proposition, that you will surely send your order to us. We know that you really cannot afford to buy elsewhere.

No. 12C718

ORDER BY NUMBER.

$5.75

THIS LARGE ILLUSTRATION, engraved direct from a photograph of the Twentieth Century Mandolin will give you a good idea of the front and back view of the instrument showing almost every detail, but it needs an examination of the instrument itself to realize its full value. The illustration will give you a good idea of the arrangement of the ribs, the ornamentation, the beautiful trimming and its handsome model.

DON'T COMPARE our $5.75 Twentieth Century Mandolin with any of the $5.00 or $6.00 instruments offered by local dealers. Our Twentieth Century Mandolin is superior to such in every way and is an instrument that cannot be equaled in retail stores at anything like our price. If you want to buy one of these beautiful, graceful instruments, or if you want an instrument to learn on, there will never be a better opportunity offered and our $5.75 mandolin is an instrument that you will surely be pleased with.

No. 12C718 Our Twentieth Century Mandolin. Price.......................................$5.75

FRONT VIEW BACK VIEW

No. 12C718 Our Twentieth Century Mandolin. Price..............$5.75

OUR NONPAREIL MANDOLIN AT $7.45.

$7.45 is our price for this beautiful instrument of 22 ribs of selected rosewood exactly as represented, such an instrument that would be considered cheap in retail music stores if priced at $12.00.

With every mandolin we furnish, free of extra charge, an extra set of strings, a fingerboard chart, pick and instruction book.

WE GUARANTEE THAT IN OUR NONPAREIL MANDOLIN WE ARE FURNISHING AT $7.45 THE FINEST MANDOLIN THAT WAS EVER OFFERED AT THIS PRICE.

It is a splendid instrument, made by the manufacturer of our very finest instruments and is sure to please the most critical.

IT HAS 22 RIBS of selected rosewood with celluloid inlaying between. The dark shade of the rosewood and the white celluloid produce a combination of color, which makes this an extremely beautiful mandolin. It has a rosewood cap, bound with celluloid and highly finished and polished. The top is of thoroughly seasoned, carefully selected silver spruce, bound with white celluloid and inlaid around the edge with extra broad inlaying with different colored woods and designs. It has heavy inlaying around the sound hole to correspond. It has a very artistic guard plate, made of celluloid in imitation of tortoise shell and handsomely inlaid. All of our floral wood inlayings on the guard plates of our mandolins are in original designs not to be found on any other mandolins on the market. This mandolin has the best quality mahogany neck and solid ebony fingerboard bound with celluloid with fancy designs, position marks and frets accurately placed. Head veneered on top with rosewood and decorated with handsome pearl ornaments. It has the best quality of machine made screw patent head of American manufacture.

OUR $7.45 PRICE for an instrument of this quality, design, tone, ornamentation and general richness is possible only because we ask a very narrow margin of profit above the actual cost of material and labor. $7.45 is a very little more than manufacturing cost. It is a price less than most dealers can buy such a mandolin for at wholesale. We give you an opportunity of buying the mandolin without paying any of the intermediate profits of wholesaler and jobber and it is possible for you to save so much money by buying your mandolin from us that you ought not to consider placing your order elsewhere. Remember, you take no risk whatever, for if the mandolin does not please you in every way, is not up to your expectations in every particular, simply return it to us and we will refund your money and pay express charges both ways and you will not be out one cent by the transaction. Bear in mind also that we give you ten days in which to test the instrument thoroughly and at any time during the ten days, it can be returned to us and your money will be refunded if you do not find it perfectly satisfactory. We are extremely anxious that you favor us with your order, for we know that we can surprise and delight you with the beautiful instrument we are furnishing at the price and that you will send us your future orders for goods in this line and will also recommend us to your friends and neighbors.

BACK VIEW FRONT VIEW

No. 12C724 Our Nonpareil Mandolin. Price.................. $7.45

No. 12C724 Our Nonpareil Mandolin. Price $7.45

OUR $9.95 NEAPOLITAN MANDOLIN.

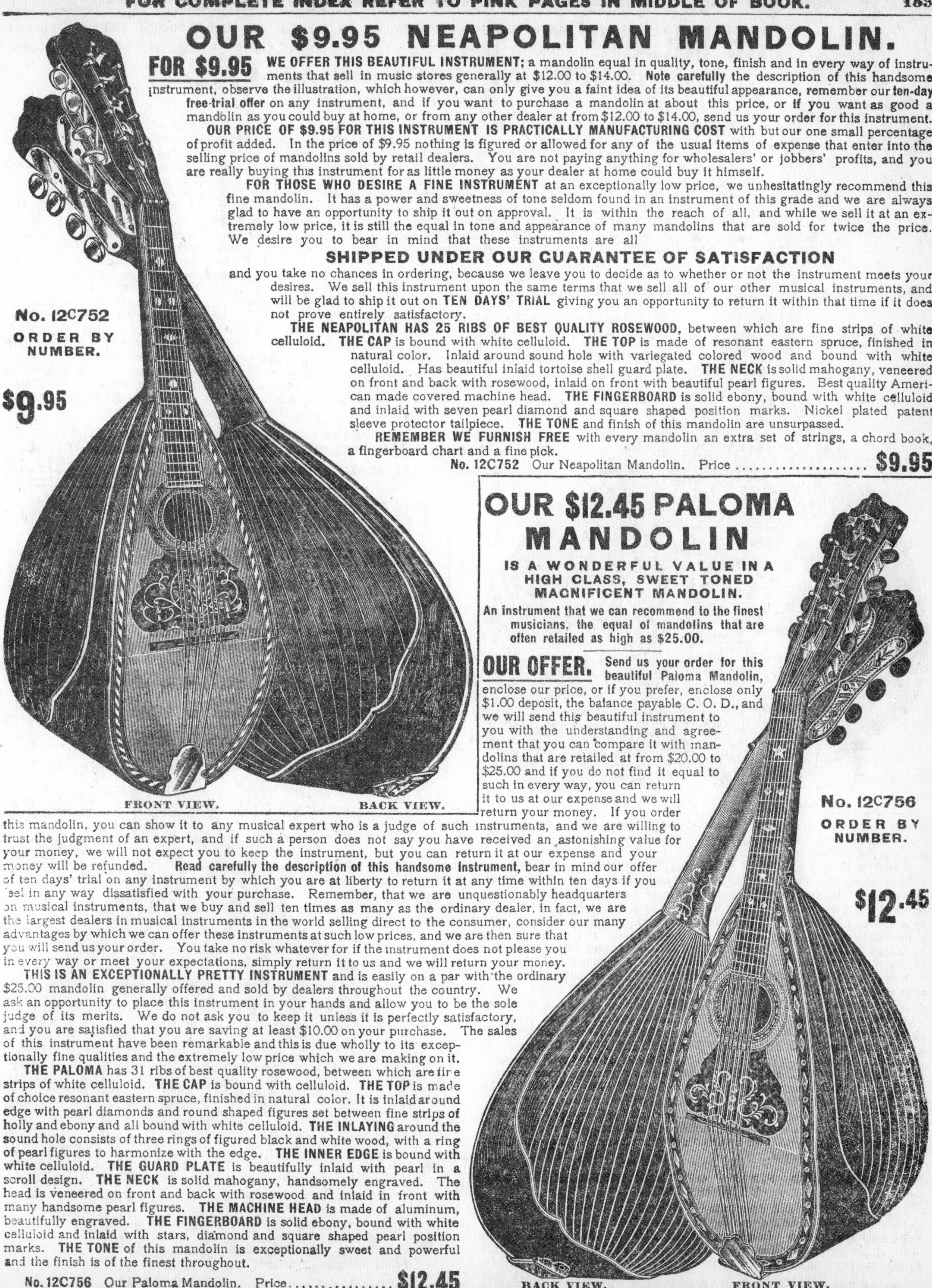

FOR $9.95 **WE OFFER THIS BEAUTIFUL INSTRUMENT;** a mandolin equal in quality, tone, finish and in every way of instruments that sell in music stores generally at $12.00 to $14.00. **Note carefully** the description of this handsome instrument, observe the illustration, which however, can only give you a faint idea of its beautiful appearance, remember our **ten-day free-trial offer** on any instrument, and if you want to purchase a mandolin at about this price, or if you want as good a mandolin as you could buy at home, or from any other dealer at from $12.00 to $14.00, send us your order for this instrument.

OUR PRICE OF $9.95 FOR THIS INSTRUMENT IS PRACTICALLY MANUFACTURING COST with but our one small percentage of profit added. In the price of $9.95 nothing is figured or allowed for any of the usual items of expense that enter into the selling price of mandolins sold by retail dealers. You are not paying anything for wholesalers' or jobbers' profits, and you are really buying this instrument for as little money as your dealer at home could buy it himself.

FOR THOSE WHO DESIRE A FINE INSTRUMENT at an exceptionally low price, we unhesitatingly recommend this fine mandolin. It has a power and sweetness of tone seldom found in an instrument of this grade and we are always glad to have an opportunity to ship it out on approval. It is within the reach of all, and while we sell it at an extremely low price, it is still the equal in tone and appearance of many mandolins that are sold for twice the price. We desire you to bear in mind that these instruments are all

SHIPPED UNDER OUR GUARANTEE OF SATISFACTION

and you take no chances in ordering, because we leave you to decide as to whether or not the instrument meets your desires. We sell this instrument upon the same terms that we sell all of our other musical instruments, and will be glad to ship it out on **TEN DAYS' TRIAL** giving you an opportunity to return it within that time if it does not prove entirely satisfactory.

No. 12C752 ORDER BY NUMBER.

$9.95

THE NEAPOLITAN HAS 25 RIBS OF BEST QUALITY ROSEWOOD, between which are fine strips of white celluloid. **THE CAP** is bound with white celluloid. **THE TOP** is made of resonant eastern spruce, finished in natural color. Inlaid around sound hole with variegated colored wood and bound with white celluloid. Has beautiful inlaid tortoise shell guard plate. **THE NECK** is solid mahogany, veneered on front and back with rosewood, inlaid on front with beautiful pearl figures. Best quality American made covered machine head. **THE FINGERBOARD** is solid ebony, bound with white celluloid and inlaid with seven pearl diamond and square shaped position marks. Nickel plated patent sleeve protector tailpiece. **THE TONE** and finish of this mandolin are unsurpassed.

REMEMBER WE FURNISH FREE with every mandolin an extra set of strings, a chord book, a fingerboard chart and a fine pick.

No. 12C752 Our Neapolitan Mandolin. Price **$9.95**

FRONT VIEW. BACK VIEW.

OUR $12.45 PALOMA MANDOLIN

IS A WONDERFUL VALUE IN A HIGH CLASS, SWEET TONED MAGNIFICENT MANDOLIN.

An instrument that we can recommend to the finest musicians, the equal of mandolins that are often retailed as high as $25.00.

OUR OFFER. **Send us your order for this beautiful Paloma Mandolin,** enclose our price, or if you prefer, enclose only $1.00 deposit, the balance payable C. O. D., and we will send this beautiful instrument to you with the understanding and agreement that you can compare it with mandolins that are retailed at from $20.00 to $25.00 and if you do not find it equal to such in every way, you can return it to us at our expense and we will return your money. If you order this mandolin, you can show it to any musical expert who is a judge of such instruments, and we are willing to trust the judgment of an expert, and if such a person does not say you have received an astonishing value for your money, we will not expect you to keep the instrument, but you can return it at our expense and your money will be refunded. **Read carefully the description of this handsome instrument,** bear in mind our offer of ten days' trial on any instrument by which you are at liberty to return it at any time within ten days if you feel in any way dissatisfied with your purchase. Remember, that we are unquestionably headquarters on musical instruments, that we buy and sell ten times as many as the ordinary dealer, in fact, we are the largest dealers in musical instruments in the world selling direct to the consumer, consider our many advantages by which we can offer these instruments at such low prices, and we are then sure that you will send us your order. You take no risk whatever for if the instrument does not please you in every way or meet your expectations, simply return it to us and we will return your money.

No. 12C756 ORDER BY NUMBER.

$12.45

THIS IS AN EXCEPTIONALLY PRETTY INSTRUMENT and is easily on a par with the ordinary $25.00 mandolin generally offered and sold by dealers throughout the country. We ask an opportunity to place this instrument in your hands and allow you to be the sole judge of its merits. We do not ask you to keep it unless it is perfectly satisfactory, and you are satisfied that you are saving at least $10.00 on your purchase. The sales of this instrument have been remarkable and this is due wholly to its exceptionally fine qualities and the extremely low price which we are making on it.

THE PALOMA has 31 ribs of best quality rosewood, between which are fine strips of white celluloid. **THE CAP** is bound with celluloid. **THE TOP** is made of choice resonant eastern spruce, finished in natural color. It is inlaid around edge with pearl diamonds and round shaped figures set between fine strips of holly and ebony and all bound with white celluloid. **THE INLAYING** around the sound hole consists of three rings of figured black and white wood, with a ring of pearl figures to harmonize with the edge. **THE INNER EDGE** is bound with white celluloid. **THE GUARD PLATE** is beautifully inlaid with pearl in a scroll design. **THE NECK** is solid mahogany, handsomely engraved. The head is veneered on front and back with rosewood and inlaid in front with many handsome pearl figures. **THE MACHINE HEAD** is made of aluminum, beautifully engraved. **THE FINGERBOARD** is solid ebony, bound with white celluloid and inlaid with stars, diamond and square shaped pearl position marks. **THE TONE** of this mandolin is exceptionally sweet and powerful and the finish is of the finest throughout.

No. 12C756 Our Paloma Mandolin. Price............... **$12.45**

BACK VIEW. FRONT VIEW.

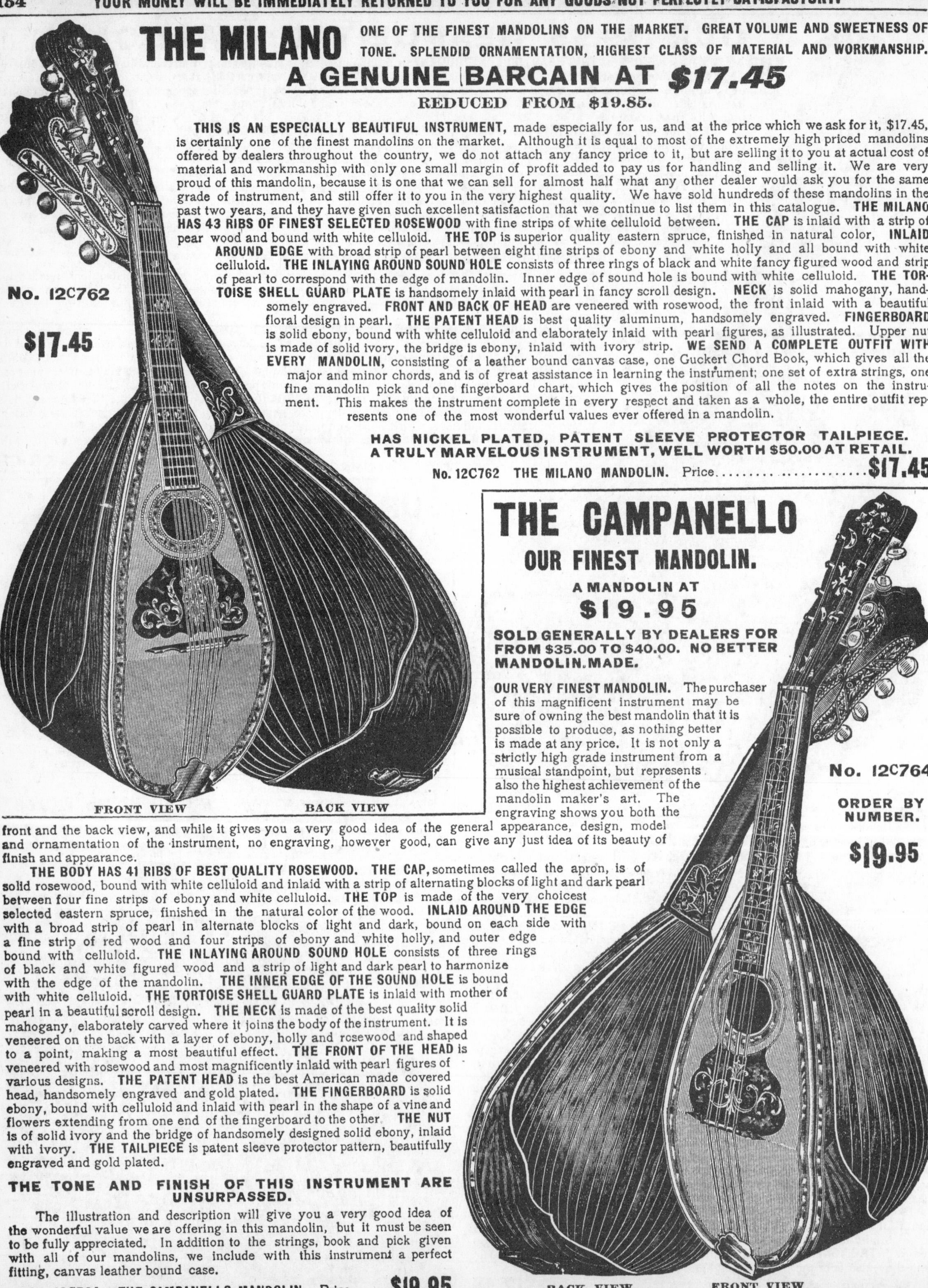

THE MILANO

ONE OF THE FINEST MANDOLINS ON THE MARKET. GREAT VOLUME AND SWEETNESS OF TONE. SPLENDID ORNAMENTATION, HIGHEST CLASS OF MATERIAL AND WORKMANSHIP.

A GENUINE BARGAIN AT $17.45

REDUCED FROM $19.85.

THIS IS AN ESPECIALLY BEAUTIFUL INSTRUMENT, made especially for us, and at the price which we ask for it, $17.45, is certainly one of the finest mandolins on the market. Although it is equal to most of the extremely high priced mandolins offered by dealers throughout the country, we do not attach any fancy price to it, but are selling it to you at actual cost of material and workmanship with only one small margin of profit added to pay us for handling and selling it. We are very proud of this mandolin, because it is one that we can sell for almost half what any other dealer would ask you for the same grade of instrument, and still offer it to you in the very highest quality. We have sold hundreds of these mandolins in the past two years, and they have given such excellent satisfaction that we continue to list them in this catalogue. **THE MILANO HAS 43 RIBS OF FINEST SELECTED ROSEWOOD** with fine strips of white celluloid between. **THE CAP** is inlaid with a strip of pear wood and bound with white celluloid. **THE TOP** is superior quality eastern spruce, finished in natural color, **INLAID AROUND EDGE** with broad strip of pearl between eight fine strips of ebony and white holly and all bound with white celluloid. **THE INLAYING AROUND SOUND HOLE** consists of three rings of black and white fancy figured wood and strip of pearl to correspond with the edge of mandolin. Inner edge of sound hole is bound with white celluloid. **THE TORTOISE SHELL GUARD PLATE** is handsomely inlaid with pearl in fancy scroll design. **NECK** is solid mahogany, handsomely engraved. **FRONT AND BACK OF HEAD** are veneered with rosewood, the front inlaid with a beautiful floral design in pearl. **THE PATENT HEAD** is best quality aluminum, handsomely engraved. **FINGERBOARD** is solid ebony, bound with white celluloid and elaborately inlaid with pearl figures, as illustrated. Upper nut is made of solid ivory, the bridge is ebony, inlaid with ivory strip. **WE SEND A COMPLETE OUTFIT WITH EVERY MANDOLIN,** consisting of a leather bound canvas case, one Guckert Chord Book, which gives all the major and minor chords, and is of great assistance in learning the instrument; one set of extra strings, one fine mandolin pick and one fingerboard chart, which gives the position of all the notes on the instrument. This makes the instrument complete in every respect and taken as a whole, the entire outfit represents one of the most wonderful values ever offered in a mandolin.

No. 12C762

$17.45

HAS NICKEL PLATED, PATENT SLEEVE PROTECTOR TAILPIECE.
A TRULY MARVELOUS INSTRUMENT, WELL WORTH $50.00 AT RETAIL.

No. 12C762 THE MILANO MANDOLIN. Price........................**$17.45**

FRONT VIEW BACK VIEW

THE CAMPANELLO

OUR FINEST MANDOLIN.

A MANDOLIN AT

$19.95

SOLD GENERALLY BY DEALERS FOR FROM $35.00 TO $40.00. NO BETTER MANDOLIN MADE.

OUR VERY FINEST MANDOLIN. The purchaser of this magnificent instrument may be sure of owning the best mandolin that it is possible to produce, as nothing better is made at any price. It is not only a strictly high grade instrument from a musical standpoint, but represents also the highest achievement of the mandolin maker's art. The engraving shows you both the front and the back view, and while it gives you a very good idea of the general appearance, design, model and ornamentation of the instrument, no engraving, however good, can give any just idea of its beauty of finish and appearance.

No. 12C764

ORDER BY NUMBER.

$19.95

THE BODY HAS 41 RIBS OF BEST QUALITY ROSEWOOD. THE CAP, sometimes called the apron, is of solid rosewood, bound with white celluloid and inlaid with a strip of alternating blocks of light and dark pearl between four fine strips of ebony and white celluloid. **THE TOP** is made of the very choicest selected eastern spruce, finished in the natural color of the wood. **INLAID AROUND THE EDGE** with a broad strip of pearl in alternate blocks of light and dark, bound on each side with a fine strip of red wood and four strips of ebony and white holly, and outer edge bound with celluloid. **THE INLAYING AROUND SOUND HOLE** consists of three rings of black and white figured wood and a strip of light and dark pearl to harmonize with the edge of the mandolin. **THE INNER EDGE OF THE SOUND HOLE** is bound with white celluloid. **THE TORTOISE SHELL GUARD PLATE** is inlaid with mother of pearl in a beautiful scroll design. **THE NECK** is made of the best quality solid mahogany, elaborately carved where it joins the body of the instrument. It is veneered on the back with a layer of ebony, holly and rosewood and shaped to a point, making a most beautiful effect. **THE FRONT OF THE HEAD** is veneered with rosewood and most magnificently inlaid with pearl figures of various designs. **THE PATENT HEAD** is the best American made covered head, handsomely engraved and gold plated. **THE FINGERBOARD** is solid ebony, bound with celluloid and inlaid with pearl in the shape of a vine and flowers extending from one end of the fingerboard to the other. **THE NUT** is of solid ivory and the bridge of handsomely designed solid ebony, inlaid with ivory. **THE TAILPIECE** is patent sleeve protector pattern, beautifully engraved and gold plated.

THE TONE AND FINISH OF THIS INSTRUMENT ARE UNSURPASSED.

The illustration and description will give you a very good idea of the wonderful value we are offering in this mandolin, but it must be seen to be fully appreciated. In addition to the strings, book and pick given with all of our mandolins, we include with this instrument a perfect fitting, canvas leather bound case.

No. 12C764 THE CAMPANELLO MANDOLIN. Price..... **$19.95**

BACK VIEW FRONT VIEW

OUR CHALLENGE MANDOLIN.

THE GREATEST OFFER EVER MADE IN A MODERATE PRICED MANDOLIN. SPLENDID IN APPEARANCE. MAGNIFICENT IN TONE AND TUNE, AND MARVELOUSLY LOW IN PRICE.

THIS MANDOLIN IS GENERALLY SOLD BY DEALERS FOR FROM $8.00 TO $10.00. OUR GREAT BARGAIN PRICE, $3.95

THE INSTRUMENT goes to the customer complete, with extra set of fine strings, a fingerboard chart, which can be pasted on the fingerboard under the strings and which is of great assistance in learning the instrument, a complete instruction book, by the aid of which anyone can learn to play without the assistance of a teacher, and a fine canvas, leather bound, flannel lined case.

THIS SPLENDID MANDOLIN OUTFIT

Consists of our Challenge Mandolin as described. Value	$10.00
One extra set of Glendon strings	.50
One lettered fingerboard chart	.25
One complete instruction book	.50
One fine canvas, flannel lined case	1.50
One mandolin pick	.05
Total value of outfit	$12.80
OUR PRICE	$3.95

$3.95

SEND US $1.00 and we will ship you this splendid outfit by express, C. O. D., subject to examination. You can try it at the express office, and if satisfactory, pay the balance of the price and take the instrument to your home. If at any time within ten days the mandolin should prove unsatisfactory for any cause you can return it to us, we will cheerfully refund you the money you have paid and we will pay the express charges both ways. Most of our customers prefer to send us the full price of the instrument with their order, for by so doing they avoid the payment of collection fees which the express companies charge and which generally amount to 25 or 50 cents on every shipment.

DESCRIPTION OF OUR CHALLENGE MANDOLIN.

THIS SPLENDID INSTRUMENT has 15 ribs of solid mahogany, between which are inlaid fine strips of black. The combination of these two colors gives a very rich effect to the body of the instrument and is always admired wherever seen. It has a genuine rosewood cap and rosewood veneered head, highly finished and polished. **The top** is made of resonant silver spruce and is bound around the edges with celluloid. It has a beautiful celluloid imitation tortoise shell guard plate with handsomely inlaid design. **The neck** is genuine mahogany with rosewood fingerboard, pearl position dots and raised frets, accurately placed, so that the scale is perfect. **It is fitted with the best quality American screw patent head,** so adjusted that there is no lost motion whatever in tuning the instrument. It is also fitted with a handsomely nickel plated tailpiece. We know that our customers will be more than satisfied with this instrument, as it has a sweet full tone and is substantially constructed and splendidly finished. In appearance and tone it is fully equal to mandolins sold at twice the price, and in shipping the instrument we make the customer the sole judge of its merits.

THE ILLUSTRATION on this page will give you a good idea of the details of the construction and ornamentation of this instrument, but can give you no idea of its beautiful finish and splendid tone. We desire to place this instrument in your hands for your approval and you take no chances in ordering it, because we take all the risk of shipment, and it is not necessary for you to accept it unless it is perfectly satisfactory in every particular.

THE ABOVE ILLUSTRATION shows the splendid case and outfit which we send with this mandolin and will give you some idea of the wonderful value which we are offering you with this mandolin. **The Guckert Chord Book** is filled with all sorts of chords in the different major and minor keys, so that anyone, without any previous knowledge of music, can learn to play this instrument without difficulty. **The fingerboard chart,** which is shown lying on the case, is intended to be cut out and pasted under the strings on the fingerboard. This shows the position of all the different notes and is of immense value to one who desires to learn to play this instrument quickly. **We also show a box of silver steel mandolin strings,** which are fine in every way for this instrument and are guaranteed to give satisfaction. **We also furnish a mandolin pick with this outfit, which is not shown in the illustration,** but which is in every way equal to the other articles of this outfit. When you purchase this mandolin from us you may be sure that you receive it complete in every way.

We are selling you this Mandolin Outfit for a much lower price than your dealer can purchase it from the wholesaler.

We would be glad to have you compare this mandolin outfit with any outfit sold by other dealers at from $6.00 up, and if you do not find that the instrument and outfit compares favorably with anything that you can buy at that price from any other dealer, we request you to return the outfit to us, and we will **refund your money and pay transportation charges both ways.**

EXAMINE THE MANDOLIN which the dealer offers you at this price and then allow us to send you this instrument on approval, and if you do not find that it is in every way superior to the instrument offered by the dealer, and in fact, to any instrument in your community at twice the price, you can return it to us and we will cheerfully refund your money and pay the express charges both ways. We make these liberal terms for the purpose of giving you an opportunity to compare this instrument with other instruments in your vicinity and also to test it thoroughly and get the opinion of your musical friends before finally accepting it.

YOU TAKE NO RISK WHATEVER in giving us your order, because we take all the chance of loss and we make you the sole judge of the merits of this instrument. If you do not find, when you receive it, that it is the greatest bargain that you ever saw in a mandolin and fully equal to any other mandolin you have ever seen at twice the price, we do not ask you to keep it, but you can return it to us at our expense and we will cheerfully refund your money.

REMEMBER that the price which we quote on this instrument is the price the manufacturer charges us, with only our small margin of profit added to pay us for handling and selling the instrument. The mandolins sold by other dealers at twice the price, do not cost any more to manufacture than does this one, but the high price which you have to pay is made up of intermediate dealers' selling expenses and profits. By our direct from factory to customer plan we avoid all of these expenses and profits and are thus able to sell you this splendid instrument at **$3.95.** The fact that we guarantee it to be satisfactory will assure you that it is a high grade instrument in every respect.

No. 12C708 Our Challenge Mandolin and complete outfit as described. Price........ **$3.95**

BE CAREFUL not to compare this instrument with mandolins offered by other dealers at the same price, as it is not by any means the same grade of instrument in any respect. We are perfectly willing that you should compare it with any other mandolin sold at this price for the purpose of proving its good quality, but we do not wish you to place it on the same level by any means as the mandolins sold by other dealers, which do not begin to represent the value in tone, material or finish which this mandolin possesses. The original manufacturing cost of any good mandolin is less than one-half the price which the ordinary dealer asks you to pay for it. The high price which you pay him is largely made up of the selling expenses and profits of intermediate dealers through whose hands the instrument passes on its way from the factory to you. All of these profits and expenses are included in the price and you have to pay them when you purchase the instrument. By our method of sale we cut out all these intermediate profits and expenses and the cost of the instrument to us is its cost to you with the addition of our small percentage of profit.

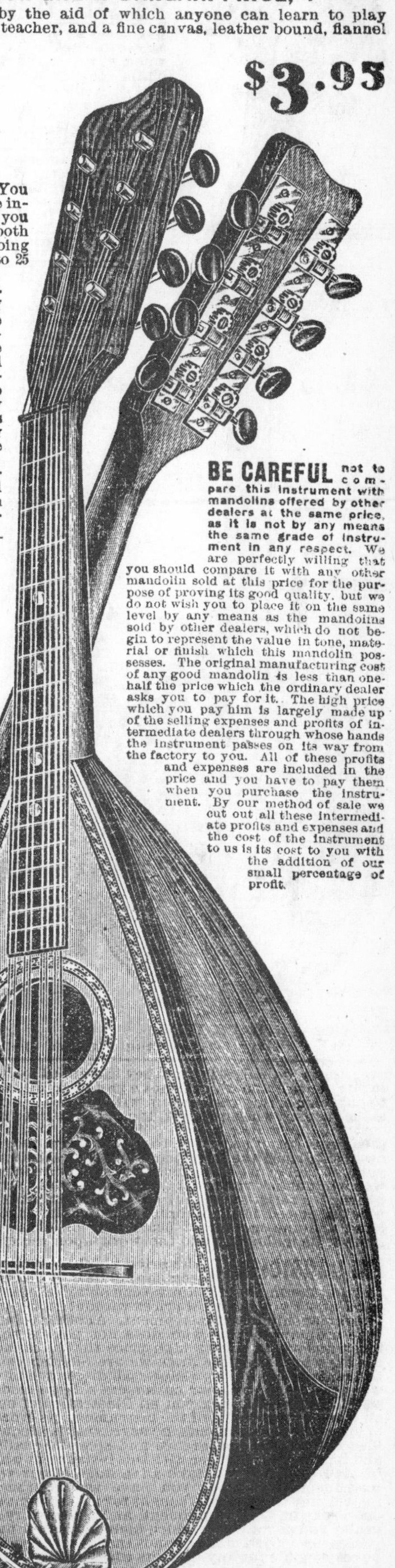

BACK VIEW FRONT VIEW

OUR SPLENDID LINE OF BANJO VALUES.

THE LARGEST AND FINEST LINE EVER OFFERED TO THE PUBLIC. EACH INSTRUMENT A SPLENDID VALUE.

It is with pleasure that we submit for your consideration the following great line of banjos. We desire to call your attention to the fact that we guarantee every instrument in this line to be perfectly satisfactory.

WE SELL THESE INSTRUMENTS the same as all of our other musical goods, directly from the factory to the customer, and by this method we guarantee the customer that he can purchase an instrument from us for less than one-half the price which he could obtain on the same grade of instrument from any other dealer. One great advantage in buying a banjo from us is that we become absolutely responsible for the instrument when we sell it and the customer always knows where to come to obtain satisfaction should the instrument not prove everything we claim for it. Where the instrument is bought in the usual way from a local dealer no one becomes responsible for its life and character, and if it turns out to be inferior the customer has to stand the loss. The great buying advantage which we possess enables us to make a very advantageous contract with the manufacturer of these instruments so that we can obtain a price which is away below what any other dealer has to pay.

UPON RECEIPT OF $1.00, we will send any banjo in this line, C. O. D., subject to examination. You can examine the instrument at your express office and if you find it perfectly satisfactory pay the express agent the balance and express charges and take the instrument home with you. If you do not find the instrument satisfactory upon examination the shipment can be returned to us at our expense and we will cheerfully refund the money deposited. Most of our customers prefer to send cash in full, thereby saving the large charge the express companies always make for collecting and returning the money, and which will amount to 25 or 50 cents on every shipment.

OUR 10-DAY TRIAL OFFER. You can order any banjo on this page, use it for ten days and if not found entirely satisfactory you can return it to us at our expense, and we will refund your money in full.

WE FURNISH FREE WITH EVERY BANJO, one set of Glendon strings, one instruction book of chords and one lettered fingerboard chart, which is invaluable to beginners.

OUR SPECIAL $1.95 BANJO.

This is an elegant low price banjo, has a genuine nickel shell, wood lined. The neck is stained in imitation cherry. It has a genuine calfskin head, 10 inches in diameter, with seven nickel plated hexagon brackets. Weight, 10 pounds.

No. 12C804 Price.. $1.95

No. 12C808

$2.45

ORDER BY NUMBER.

OUR No. 12C808 AN EXCELLENT BARGAIN. SPLENDID VALUE FOR THE PRICE.

IT HAS BEEN OUR CUSTOM in the past to quote prices on banjos as low as $1.75, but we have found that we cannot furnish a banjo which will give entire satisfaction at this price, and our No. 12C804 banjo is the lowest priced instrument of this kind that we list. We can give good value in this instrument and one that will prove satisfactory at this price, and we do not care to go into competition with other dealers who handle cheap commercial banjos at lower prices. We guarantee every one of our instruments, and cannot afford to ship out a banjo that we are not sure will be satisfactory. This instrument will be found excellent in every respect and we recommend it to those who desire a banjo of good grade at an extremely low price. It has a 10-inch head with nickel shell, wood lined. It is carefully fitted with a well made neck of imitation mahogany, has raised frets accurately placed, and the shell is fitted with nine nickel plated hexagon brackets. It also has a fine calfskin head.

WE HAVE BEEN PARTICULARLY SUCCESSFUL in selling low priced banjos and the reason for this is to be found in the fact that we are able to offer such splendid value for the money. We used to sell banjos which ran as low in price as $1.75, but experience has proven to us that we cannot give the customer a practical banjo at that figure and the lowest price that we quote on a banjo now is $1.95, and we claim the banjo at this price is superior to any banjo ever made or sold by other dealers for from $3.00 to $4.00. That this is true has been proved time and time again by customers to whom we have shipped this instrument and who have compared it with banjos offered by other dealers at more than twice the price. As we will give the same guarantee with this banjo which we give with all of our other instruments it will be evident at once, that the low price which we make on this instrument does not mean that the quality of material and labor that enters into its construction are of low grade.

No. 12C808 Banjo. Price........................ $2.45

BACK VIEW FRONT VIEW

OUR No. 12C808 BANJO. Price, $2.45

OUR EDGEMERE BANJO, AT $3.85.

One of the greatest bargains. A $6.00 banjo for $3.85. Guaranteed perfect in tune, tone and workmanship. Warranted to be satisfactory in every particular.

No. 12C812

No. 12C812

$3.85

ORDER BY NUMBER

MANY PEOPLE HESITATE to buy a banjo generally from the dealers at this price and they are perfectly right in doing so, because the banjo generally sold by dealers at this price is simply put together for the purpose of sale and will soon become absolutely useless. But we recommend this banjo to our friends because this instrument is advertised usually for from $5.00 to $6.00 by dealers generally. We do not hesitate, therefore, to advise our friends to purchase this instrument whenever they do not feel that they can afford to invest money for an instrument of a higher price. There is not a banjo in our entire line which is not a great bargain, and this instrument is equally so. We do not advise our customers to purchase this instrument without fully protecting them against any possible loss. Should the banjo not be satisfactory when received it can be returned to us, the money paid will be refunded and the transaction will not cost the customer a cent. We believe you will agree that these are very liberal terms and that this is a great opportunity for you to try this great bargain. We have sold many thousands of these banjos to people who desire to learn the instrument and they are always pronounced perfectly satisfactory in every particular. Will you not give us an opportunity to place this instrument in your hands, upon the terms given above? and we will not ask you to retain the instrument or go to expense in any way unless you find it perfectly satisfactory. It has a 11-inch, genuine nickel shell lined with wood. It has 17 nickel plated hexagon brackets, and the fingerboard is accurately fretted with raised frets and genuine mother of pearl position dots. It has a beautiful birch neck, finished in imitation mahogany and the work upon the entire instrument is thorough in the extreme.

IN CONSIDERING the price which we make on this banjo there are several points which you should bear in mind. The first is that we have such a great advantage in buying that we can obtain exceedingly low prices from the manufacturer and quote you very low prices without in any way lowering the quality of material and workmanship in the instrument. Another point which we desire you to consider is that the ordinary dealer who does not possess this advantage is compelled to buy his instruments at such a high price that he cannot afford to sell the same grade of banjo at anywhere near the price we are offering you. We buy entirely for cash and take advantage of every possible cash discount and we buy in such immense quantities that we are able to save our customers a large amount of money on every instrument we sell. We are showing you an illustration of our Edgemere Banjo, which will give you an idea of the design of the instrument, its ornamentation and trimmings. But, like all of our other instruments, no engraving is adequate to convey to the customer any just idea of its fine appearance and splendid qualities of tone. We give the same C. O. D. and ten days' trial offer with this instrument which we give with our entire line and will be glad to have you take advantage of our very liberal terms. In purchasing this instrument from us, you have the assurance that you are buying the very best instrument that can be bought for this amount of money and that you are only paying one profit on the instrument, and that a very small profit. When you buy from the dealer you pay a price which includes four or five different profits and the instrument passes through so many hands that it practically looses its identity and no one seems to be responsible for any defects which it may develop in time. When you purchase an instrument from us we become entirely responsible for it and you are always sure that we will make everything satisfactory and that the instrument will prove to be everything we claim for it.

No. 12C812 Our Edgemere Banjo. Price........................ $3.85

FRONT VIEW BACK VIEW

No. 12C812 OUR EDGEMERE BANJO. Price, $3.85

OUR $5.75 CHALLENGE BANJO.

Thirty-nine Brackets, Beautifully Made and Finished, Finest Construction Throughout, Beautiful in Tone and Tune, Offered Under Our Binding Guarantee to Prove Perfectly Satisfactory or Money Refunded, and the Equal in Every Way of Banjos that Sell Usually at Double the Price.

DESCRIPTION OF OUR CHALLENGE BANJO.

THE INSTRUMENT WE OFFER **as the leader of our banjo line, to show for how little money we can offer a strictly high grade instrument, how much value it is possible to put into a banjo at this price.** This splendid instrument has a brass shell, heavily nickel plated, lined with wood, finished in imitation mahogany and has double overspun wired edges. It has thirty-nine nickel plated hexagon brackets and a very fine quality of calfskin head. The diameter of the head is 11 inches. The neck is made of birch, highly finished in imitation of mahogany and highly polished. It has an ebony fingerboard with pearl position dots and raised frets accurately placed, making the scale perfect. It is fitted with the very latest style nickel plated tailpiece and is thoroughly and carefully constructed throughout. From the illustration you can get a very good idea of the appearance of this instrument, but you must see it to really appreciate the details of design and ornamentation and especially to get a good idea of its splendid tone.

No. 12C822

ORDER BY NUMBER

THE FREE OUTFIT WITH THE CHALLENGE BANJO

With every Challenge Banjo at $5.75 we furnish, free, an outfit consisting of an extra set of strings, instruction book, fingerboard chart, which outfit adds greatly to the value of the instrument.

FREE GLENDON STRINGS. In addition to the strings already on the banjo, we furnish in the free outfit one set of Glendon strings of fine quality, strings that would cost 25 cents at retail.

FREE INSTRUCTION BOOK. In the outfit sent free with every Challenge Banjo, we furnish a complete instruction book for the banjo by which anyone can learn to play the instrument without the assistance of a teacher. A splendid book furnished free only by us.

FREE FINGERBOARD CHART. In the outfit furnished free with every Challenge Banjo, we include a copyrighted lettered fingerboard chart which can be pasted on the fingerboard under the strings and is of the greatest assistance in finding the different positions. All of these items are furnished free with the Challenge Banjo and help to form a value that has never been equaled.

OUR QUALITY GUARANTEE.

EVERY CHALLENGE BANJO **that we ship is covered by our binding guarantee** for quality by which we guarantee each and every part that enters into the construction of the instrument, guarantee it to be perfect in every respect, in make, material, finish, tone and if the Challenge Banjo you get from us does not exhibit the best standard of quality, you can return it to us at our expense and we will return your money.

OUR $1.00 OFFER.

WHILE NEARLY EVERYONE **of our customers send the full amount of money with their order,** and we recommend this method, as it will save you the charges on the return of money to us that are always asked on a C. O. D. shipment, nevertheless, if you prefer, you need only send us $1.00 deposit, and we will send this banjo to you by express, C. O. D., subject to examination. You can examine it carefully at the express office and if you find it in every way as represented and consider it a bargain at that price, then pay the express agent the balance of $4.75 and express charges. We recommend that you send the full amount of money with your order as you run no risk whatever and will save the 25 to 40 cents extra charge on the C. O. D. shipment.

IN CONSIDERING THIS BANJO AT $5.75, **please do not compare it in your mind with the instruments offered by retail dealers at $5.00 to $6.00.** It would be a great injustice to our Challenge Banjo to look at the instrument offered by retail dealers at $5.00 or $6.00 and consider that that is what you are going to get in the Challenge Banjo. Our Challenge Banjo is far superior in quality, tone and finish to instruments sold at the same price by other dealers and if you want to get a fair idea of this instrument, you must look at the banjos sold by retailers at $8.00 and $10.00. Better still, order our Challenge Banjo at $5.75 and order any other banjo from any other dealers at the same price, let them both come together for comparison and if you do this, we are sure you will recognize the superiority of our instrument and it will be the one you buy.

OUR TEN DAYS' FREE TRIAL OFFER.

AS A FURTHER INDUCEMENT and as a further guarantee that the instrument that you get from us will prove perfectly satisfactory, and to show the great confidence that we have in this banjo, as well as all other musical instruments we show in this catalogue, we give you the further privilege of using this banjo ten days after you have received it, and if you find it in any way unsatisfactory during that time, you can return it to us and we will return your money and pay express charges both ways. Ten days will give you ample time to test the instrument, to compare the banjo with those sold by others and we are sure will only prove to you the great value we have furnished in this instrument at the price. In ordering this banjo, therefore, you are not taking the slightest risk for we stand ready to return your money immediately and pay express charges both ways if you are not perfectly satisfied in every way.

HOW WE CAN MAKE THE $5.75 PRICE ON A BANJO OF THIS QUALITY. We have **just made a special contract with one of the largest banjo manufacturers in this country.** We have contracted for an immense number of this special instrument which we call our Challenge Banjo. This manufacturer makes nothing but banjos, our order taking a large part of the product of his entire factory. All expenses for selling, such as salesmen's commission, traveling expenses, etc., are eliminated in this transaction. The manufacturer is willing to accept a very low price in consideration of this big order, as it gives him greater buying facilities in the raw materials and helps him to make his other orders to much better advantages. In other words, the prices to us from the manufacturer represents practically the bare cost of material and labor alone and to this original first cost of material and labor, we add our uniform and narrow margin of profit and we are thus able to offer this Challenge Banjo at the remarkable price of $5.75. When you buy this banjo from us at $5.75 you are paying just a little more than actual cost of material and labor and enables you to buy this instrument at about the same price that retail dealers pay in the largest quantities for such banjos. You are getting the benefit of our enormous buying facilities, the willingness of the manufacturer to accept our order at practically his cost, simply for the advantages it gives him in getting down his factory cost on other orders and our customers get the benefit of all of these advantages. When we sell the instrument to you we do not figure any middlemen's profits whatever. We need not consider salesmen's salaries, traveling expenses, any of the expenses known to wholesalers and jobbers, nor must we even consider the expense that the retail dealer must figure. Our musical goods department is only one of the fifty merchandise departments in our establishment and must stand only its one-fiftieth of our small selling expense, such as cost of catalogues, rent, light, etc.

$5.75 FOR THIS BANJO **is truly a wonder price. It will astonish dealers as well as consumers.** If you show this banjo to a dealer, he will hardly believe that you bought it at $5.75. It represents a value in banjos heretofore unheard of.

DO YOU WANT A BANJO? **If you think of buying a banjo, don't overlook this opportunity.** If you want to invest only a small amount in an instrument, you will never have a better chance. You will be getting a fine instrument at a price that, offered by any other dealer, would secure for you the cheapest kind of a banjo. Bear in mind this is an instrument that we guarantee in every respect, a high class, high grade, beautiful and full toned banjo, not a cheap, unreliable instrument, but one that you will be proud to own and play on. Remember, you get the banjo and entire outfit as described, including the extra set of strings, instruction book and fingerboard chart, all for $5.75.

WE EXPECT **every Challenge Banjo we sell to prove a big advertisement for us.** We believe that this instrument will make friends for us wherever it goes. We know it will make everyone realize the wonderful value we furnish in musical instruments. Everyone who sees the banjo will be inclined to ask the price and, learning the price, will surely write to us or look in our catalogue before buying anything in this line elsewhere. In this way we will receive the greatest possible benefit by reason of our low prices and more orders are sure to follow from every neighborhood where we send one of these instruments.

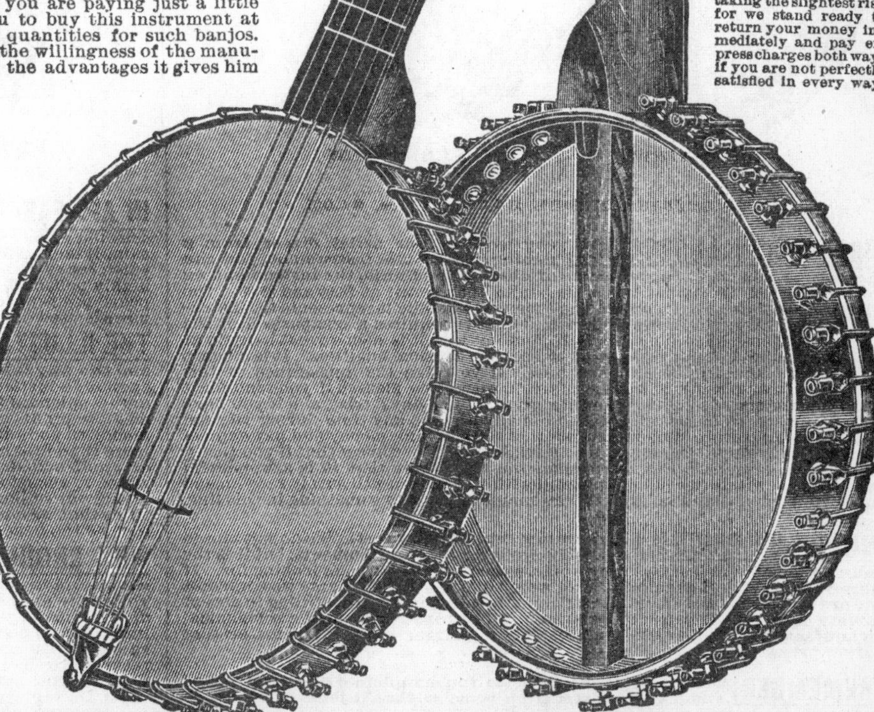

FRONT VIEW — BACK VIEW
CHALLENGE BANJO. No. 12C822 Price, $5.75.

No. 12C822 Our Challenge Banjo. Price, $5.75

OUR LEADER AT $4.95

UNQUESTIONABLY THE FINEST LOW PRICED BANJO ON THE MARKET. RETAILS GENERALLY AT FROM $8.00 TO $9.00.

OUR GREAT PRICE, $4.95

Fully warranted, and sent on ten days' trial.

No. 12C816

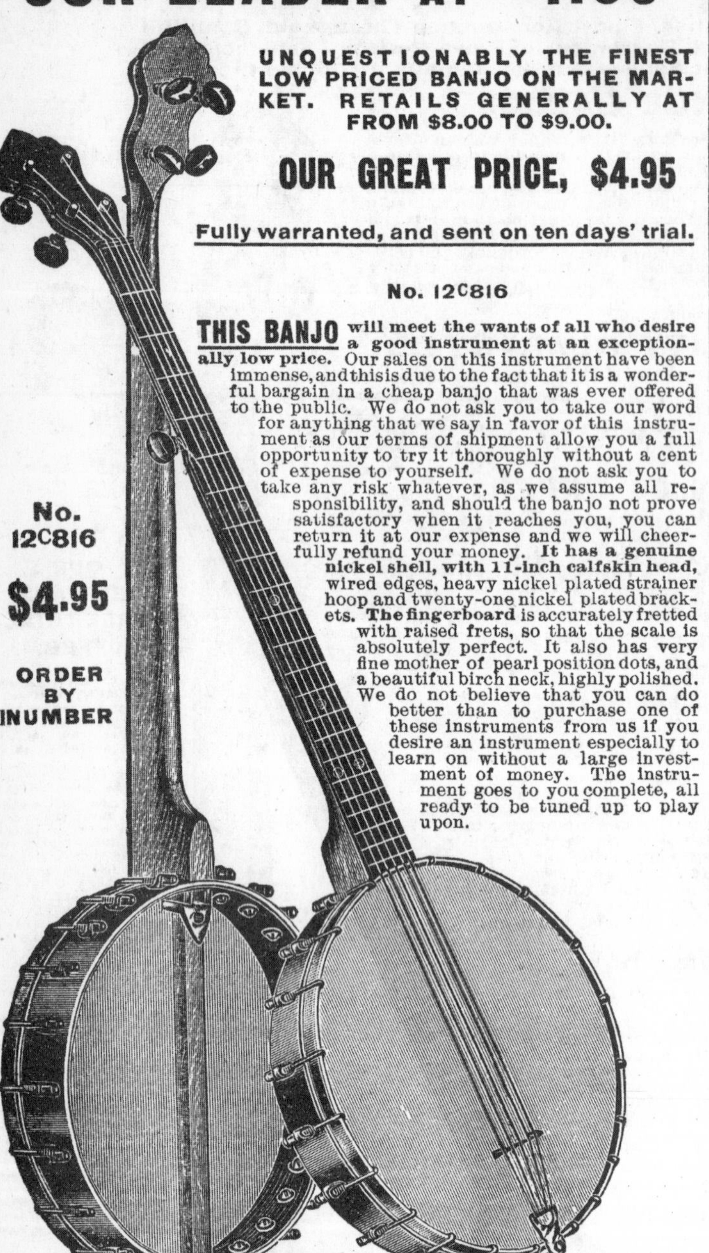

No. 12C816

$4.95

ORDER BY NUMBER

THIS BANJO **will meet the wants of all who desire a good instrument at an exceptionally low price.** Our sales on this instrument have been immense, and this is due to the fact that it is a wonderful bargain in a cheap banjo that was ever offered to the public. We do not ask you to take our word for anything that we say in favor of this instrument as our terms of shipment allow you a full opportunity to try it thoroughly without a cent of expense to yourself. We do not ask you to take any risk whatever, as we assume all responsibility, and should the banjo not prove satisfactory when it reaches you, you can return it at our expense and we will cheerfully refund your money. **It has a genuine nickel shell, with 11-inch calfskin head,** wired edges, heavy nickel plated strainer hoop and twenty-one nickel plated brackets. **The fingerboard** is accurately fretted with raised frets, so that the scale is absolutely perfect. It also has very fine mother of pearl position dots, and a beautiful birch neck, highly polished. We do not believe that you can do better than to purchase one of these instruments from us if you desire an instrument especially to learn on without a large investment of money. The instrument goes to you complete, all ready to be tuned up to play upon.

BACK VIEW FRONT VIEW

No. 12C816 LEADER BANJO. Price, $4.95.

FROM THIS ILLUSTRATION, **engraved by our artist direct from a photograph of the instrument, you can get a good idea of the appearance of our Leader Banjo, the instrument we offer at $4.95** in competition with banjos that retail at $8.00 and $9.00. The illustration shows the front and back views, and while it represents the instrument faithfully, you must understand that it requires a comparison of the banjo with those offered by others to find out why it is such a great bargain at the price, and it requires a trial to show its musical qualities. It is a banjo of splendid appearance and fine tone. If you like the appearance of this instrument, and think it will satisfy you, we will be pleased if you send for it with the understanding that you can give it a ten days' trial, and if you have any reason to be dissatisfied with it in any way, at any time during the ten days, you can return it to us and we will return your money and pay express charges both ways. We do not fear a trial or test. We know that if you really examine and compare the instrument you will admit that it is a wonderful value. You will be more than pleased with it, and you will surely recommend us to your friends and neighbors who may wish to buy something in this line.

OUR $4.95 PRICE **is a little more than factory cost.** We do not aim to make any big profit on these instruments, but it is the number of sales, and not a large profit on each sale, that we are looking for. If our contract with the manufacturer were not exceptionally large we could not afford to sell the instrument at $4.95, but the manufacturer is willing to accept a very low figure because our contract helps him greatly in the economical manufacturing of other goods and in buying larger quantities of material at lower prices.

REMEMBER, **our Leader Banjo goes to you complete with one full set of strings and instruction book, so that it is ready to tune up and play when you receive it.**

No. 12C816 Our Leader Banjo. Price........................ **$4.95**

OUR NEW CENTURY BANJO AT $6.95

A REAL ARTIST'S MODEL AND PROFESSIONAL INSTRUMENT AT THE PRICE THAT RETAIL DEALERS ASK FOR ORDINARY INSTRUMENTS.

Our New Century Banjo at $6.95 is the equal of Banjos that sell in music stores as high as $15.00.

No. 12C824

IN PAST SEASONS **Our New Century Banjo has been one of our most popular and best selling instruments.** It has always proven the finest banjo ever offered in this country at anywhere near the price. For thi season we have been able to improve the quality, to put into its manufacture just a little finer material, more carefully selected and we feel safe to say that the New Century Banjo today, the instrument we offer at $6.95, is one of the most remarkable banjo bargains ever presented to the public.

IF YOU ARE LOOKING FOR A BANJO, **which will contain all the qualities of a high grade instrument with a price which is within the reach of anyone, you should not neglect the opportunity to order one of these splendid instruments.** It will not cost you one cent to examine the instrument and test it thoroughly and you take no risks or chances whatever in ordering it. All we ask you to do is to give the instrument a conscientious and careful trial, and if you do not find that everything we have said about it is true, we are perfectly willing to have you return it, and we will refund your money. Do not place this instrument on a level with banjos sold at the same price in music stores throughout the country. No music dealer can sell this instrument at anywhere near the price we make. With each banjo we send, free, an extra set of strings, an instruction book and a finger-board chart.

No. 12C824

$6.95

ORDER BY NUMBER

FRONT VIEW BACK VIEW

No. 12C824 NEW CENTURY BANJO. Price $6.95.

IN APPEARANCE, **finish, workmanship, tone and durability, it is a regular $15.00 instrument.** It has a genuine nickel shell, selected maple rim with edges wired. The head is the best quality opaque calfskin, 11 inches in diameter and has twenty-five nickel plated brackets, with an extra heavy rabbetted strainer hoop. The neck is made of selected birch, very highly polished, and has genuine ebony fingerboard, beautifully inlaid with pearl position dots; has ebony pegs and patent tailpiece. A metal stay piece is used on the neck, which effectually prevents it from getting loose.

THE ILLUSTRATION **showing front and back views of our New Century Banjo will give you a fair idea of its construction and the way it is ornamented and trimmed,** but, of course, the illustration cannot do justice to its handsome finish and the banjo must be tried to find out its splendid tone. In buying this banjo from us you are saving all intermediate profits of wholesalers and retailers and you are getting it for as little money as your dealer could buy in quantities. The price represents a little more than first cost of material and labor with but our one small percentage of profit added, a very narrow margin of profit that no other dealer could afford to accept and continue in business, but our method of selling our goods makes our selling expenses exceedingly small, we dispose of such large quantities that we can take a very narrow margin of profit on each item and you receive the benefit of all this when you buy from us.

WHY SHOULD YOU BUY **from a dealer at home or pay some other house more money for a banjo when you can get an instrument from us for less money,** buy as fine an instrument as you desire and are protected in every way? If the instrument we send you does not meet your approval in every respect, if you don't consider, after examining it, comparing it with other instruments, and playing on it, that you have received the greatest possible value for your money, you are at liberty to return it to us at our expense and we will return your money and pay express charges both ways. We are also willing to send the instrument by express, C. O. D., subject to examination, if desired, on receipt of only $1.00 deposit, the balance and express charges to be paid after the instrument is received, examined and found perfectly satisfactory.

No. 12C824 Our New Century Banjo. Price..................... **$6.95**

THE GEM

ONE OF THE GREATEST BARGAINS EVER OFFERED IN A BANJO.

Fully Warranted as to Workmanship, Material, Tone and Tune.

Price, $9.75

No. 12C858

No. 12C858

$9.75

ORDER BY NUMBER

THIS BANJO is indeed a gem, because it is an instrument that we can sell at $9.75, and will guarantee it to be the equal of any instrument purchased elsewhere one-third higher in price. It has a heavy German silver covered rim, with double spun wired edge, thirty-one latest style brackets with protection nuts, heavy grooved top hoop, all nickel plated. It has the best quality calfskin head, full length, richly polished cherry neck; thick genuine ebony fingerboard and rosewood veneered headpiece. It is fitted with raised frets accurately set so that the scale is perfect. The fingerboard is inlaid with pearl position dots and the head is fitted with the best quality white celluloid pegs. The instrument has a clear resonant sustained tone and is splendid for either solo or accompaniment work. It is thoroughly and carefully made throughout, and is one of our best sellers. An examination and trial of this instrument will prove every assertion that we make in its favor.

BACK VIEW FRONT VIEW

No. 12C858 THE GEM BANJO. Price, $9.75.

THE ROYAL

ONE OF OUR BEST BANJO BARGAINS.

Finely Finished and Substantially Made. One of the Best Moderate Priced Banjos on the Market.

Price, $12.15

No. 12C862

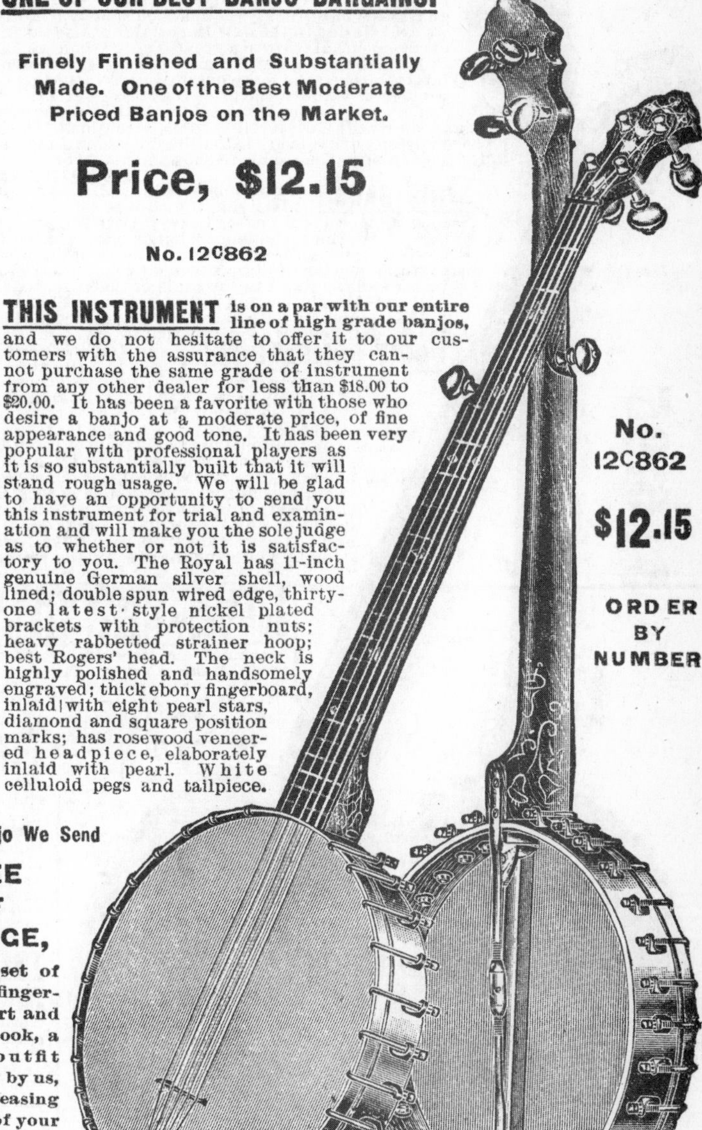

No. 12C862

$12.15

ORDER BY NUMBER

THIS INSTRUMENT is on a par with our entire line of high grade banjos, and we do not hesitate to offer it to our customers with the assurance that they cannot purchase the same grade of instrument from any other dealer for less than $18.00 to $20.00. It has been a favorite with those who desire a banjo at a moderate price, of fine appearance and good tone. It has been very popular with professional players as it is so substantially built that it will stand rough usage. We will be glad to have an opportunity to send you this instrument for trial and examination and will make you the sole judge as to whether or not it is satisfactory to you. The Royal has 11-inch genuine German silver shell, wood lined; double spun wired edge, thirty-one latest style nickel plated brackets with protection nuts; heavy rabbetted strainer hoop; best Rogers' head. The neck is highly polished and handsomely engraved; thick ebony fingerboard, inlaid with eight pearl stars, diamond and square position marks; has rosewood veneered headpiece, elaborately inlaid with pearl. White celluloid pegs and tailpiece.

FRONT VIEW BACK VIEW

No. 12C862 THE ROYAL BANJO. Price, $12.15.

With Every Banjo We Send

FREE OF CHARGE,

an extra set of strings, a fingerboard chart and a chord book, a valuable outfit given only by us, and increasing the value of your instrument. See full description of this free outfit on page 157.

WE OFFER OUR GEM BANJO on the same terms and conditions that we ship all of our musical instruments, namely, with the understanding and agreement that it will prove perfectly satisfactory in every way or it can be returned to us at our expense and we will refund your money, and also with the understanding and agreement that you will have ten days in which to try the instrument, and at any time during the ten days, if you are dissatisfied in any way, you can return it and get your money back. We are also willing to ship the banjo or any other instrument in our entire line by express C. O. D., subject to examination on receipt of only $1.00 deposit, the balance and express charges to be paid when the instrument is received, examined and found perfectly satisfactory.

AT THE SAME TIME we would like to say that nearly all of our customers send the full amount of money with their orders, and this is a much more satisfactory way of doing business, for you take no risk whatever and at the same time you will save the extra charge of 25 to 40 cents that the express companies always ask on C. O. D. shipments.

THE ILLUSTRATION showing both the front and back views of the instrument will give you a very good idea of its appearance, but it must be seen and examined, compared with other instruments of high prices to fully appreciate the value it represents at our price. It requires a critical examination to learn the beauty and value of our Gem Banjo; it is an instrument that is sure to make friends for us and to substantiate our claim for furnishing the finest musical instruments at the very lowest prices. We do not see why you should purchase a banjo in the usual way and pay a price which includes the profits of several different dealers when you can buy such a splendid banjo as this from us at actual factory cost with only one small profit added for our time and trouble in handling and selling the instrument. We believe you ought to consider this carefully before placing your order elsewhere and we trust you will give us an opportunity to demonstrate to you the peculiarly fine qualities which this instrument possesses.

No. 12C858 Our Gem Banjo. Price $9.75

NOTE. This banjo is provided with a patent steel neck adjuster, which gives greater strength to the neck and serves as a regulator to the angle of the fingerboard.

WE HAVE SO IMPROVED the quality of our musical instruments this season, we are now offering such wonderful values in every line that we have decided to devote more space to this department and to call attention to the astonishing values throughout the line by use of large illustrations. We feel that no one who has any idea of buying a banjo, mandolin, guitar or violin can afford to overlook our offers, and if the customer will consider thoroughly our liberal terms, our guarantee, our established reputation, our money refund offer, we are reasonably sure of getting the order.

BEAR IN MIND, when you purchase this instrument from us that you are buying it by an entirely new method which guarantees an immense saving to you on your purchase. We sell all of these instruments at the price which the manufacturers charge us, simply adding our one small percentage of profit to pay us for handling and selling them. In this way you are certain to procure a much better banjo for the money than you can procure from any other dealer. The price which we quote on this instrument represents the actual cost of the material and labor which enters into its construction and includes our one small percentage of profit. The illustration which we show gives you a very good back and front view of this banjo but we do not wish you to judge the instrument by the illustration, because no engraving, however good, can illustrate the splendid appearance of this banjo and its beautiful tone qualities. Our banjos are so much finer in appearance than the illustration shows them to be, that our customers are always surprised and delighted when they receive them. This is the reason why we sell such an immense quantity of them and accounts for the great advantage we possess in buying. Do not purchase a banjo elsewhere without giving us an opportunity to place this instrument in your hands for trial and examination. We know you will admit that it is the greatest bargain you ever saw in a banjo and if you do not find this to be true it will not be necessary for you to keep it, because we will receive it back, refund your money and pay the entire expense of the transaction.

No. 12C862 Our Royal Banjo. Price $12.15

THE IMPERIAL. A REGULAR $40.00 BANJO. A 3½ OCTAVE INSTRUMENT. OUR PRICE, $16.95.

AT $16.95 **we present our Imperial Banjo, a beautiful and splendid instrument in every respect, as one of the finest banjos on the market today, in every way the equal of banjos that sell in metropolitan exclusive music stores at prices ranging from $35.00 to $50.00.** This is an instrument we submit to experts, to the best banjo players, offer it to everyone who wants a really fine instrument, one of the best that money can buy and at the same time is desirous of saving all the profits that retail dealers ask on goods of this nature. Our Imperial Banjo is an instrument that we really cannot recommend too highly, cannot guarantee too strongly; it has been sold by us for years, has always given the best of satisfaction and we believe, if it is possible, that we are offering in the new Imperial for this season even a finer instrument, a handsomer banjo, better in workmanship, in tone and in every essential feature a greater value than we have ever been able to offer in a banjo at our $16.95 price. In the past the Imperial Banjo has been one of our most popular instruments, and in offering it this season to our customers, we are able to present it in a larger, clearer and more detailed illustration, as we feel that it is an instrument of such quality and a banjo that represents such wonderful value at the price that it is entitled to all the catalogue space we can possibly afford to give it. It is not so much the small profit we make on the one Imperial Banjo that we may sell to you that induces us to display it so prominently on this page, but it is because we want to bring it most forcibly to the attention of those interested in this line and we know that our greater profit will come from the pleased customer that every sale will make and from the additional orders that such a customer will send us in the future and the good his influence will do us among his friends and neighbors.

DESCRIPTION OF OUR IMPERIAL BANJO.

THIS BANJO **is not only substantially made, but is very beautifully made throughout.** It has 3¼ octaves, nickel plated German silver rim, 11 inches in diameter and 2¼ inches in depth; lined with maple; has double overspun wired edge; finest quality Roger's head; extra heavy grooved strainer hoop; 31 latest pattern brackets with protection nuts, all metal parts nickel plated. The neck is 19 inches in length, handsomely carved at base. The ebony fingerboard is extra thick and elaborately inlaid with pearl. The frets are absolutely correct. Has patent non-slipping pegs and tailpiece. The nickel plated brace, shown in the illustration, is something new and fully protected by patents, and is a great advantage, as it gives greater strength to the neck and serves as an adjuster and regulator to the angle of the fingerboard. It is difficult to give you a proper idea of the value of this banjo by means of an ordinary description and an illustration. The instrument must be seen, examined, played on and compared with the finest banjos made to appreciate its value. Every part is highly polished and finished and each instrument is carefully packed and will reach you in the same perfect condition that it leaves our hands.

DON'T COMPARE THIS, **our Imperial Banjo at $16.95, with banjos sold in retail stores at about this price. Our Imperial Banjo is the equal of instruments that sell at retail at almost three times our special price.** We make the price $16.95 because we give our customers the benefit of every advantage we have in buying and selling merchandise and we sell this banjo on the same small margin of profit above the actual cost to us as we ask on any of our most staple merchandise. We have a very large and advantageous contract with the manufacturer for this Imperial Banjo, whereby we secure them at an exceedingly low price, a price that is based on the actual cost of material and labor in the largest quantities, to which cost we add our uniform narrow margin of profit. The regular music dealer cannot buy an instrument like the Imperial at wholesale at near the price which we offer it direct to you, and at the same time you take no risks whatever in ordering from us, for our terms are most liberal, our guarantee is binding and we give you the opportunity of ten days' trial on the instrument to fully decide whether you have received the best value possible for your money. Ten days will surely allow you ample time to examine the instrument thoroughly, test it in every way, compare it, show it to your musical friends and if you decide during the ten days that it does not please you in every way, simply return it to us and we will return your money and pay express charges both ways. We could not possibly afford to make such an open and liberal offer unless we were really offering the great value we claim to give in this instrument.

No. 12C866 Our Imperial Banjo. Price.. **$16.95**

$16.95

BACK VIEW FRONT VIEW
No. 12C866 IMPERIAL BANJO. PRICE, $16.95.

THE UNIVERSITY GLEE BANJO, $19.85.

OUR VERY FINEST BANJO. **The banjo we here offer is the very best banjo made, the highest of all high grade banjos,** embodying every new and beautiful feature, the equal of any banjo on the market, regardless of name, make or price; an instrument superb in appearance and beautiful in tone. Offered to our customers on our famous ten days' trial plan, covered by our binding guarantee for quality, sold with the understanding that your money will be returned and we will pay express charges both ways if you are not delighted with your purchase. We positively state that our University Glee Banjo, which we offer at $19.85, is the equal of banjos that retail dealers sell at $50.00 to $75.00. **You may pay higher prices for a banjo, but you will not get a finer instrument than our University Glee Banjo,** for the simple reason that it is impossible to make a better instrument. You may pay a price that includes extremely large profits, for a retail dealer figures to make a very handsome profit on a sale of this kind, and in addition, when sold by the retail dealer, the price also represents the profits of several middlemen, wholesalers and jobbers. When you buy the instrument from us, you pay only one small percentage of profit above manufacturing cost and we do not figure to make a larger percentage of profit on this instrument than we do on the cheapest instrument in our line

THE UNIVERSITY GLEE BANJO **is a full 3½ octave instrument, having a 19-inch neck, accurately fretted.** The shell is full 11 inches in diameter, with nickel plated German silver rim, 2¼ inches in depth and double overspun wire edge. The rim is lined with maple and veneered with bird'seye maple, handsomely polished and finished, giving a very beautiful appearance to the inside of the banjo. It has 31 best quality shoulder brackets with protection nuts of the latest pattern and extra heavy strainer hoop; all parts handsomely nickel plated and highly polished. The head is warranted best quality genuine Joseph Roger's make. The neck in this banjo is unlike those used in other instruments, being veneered with three layers of different colored woods, on the top of which is an extra thick solid ebony fingerboard, elaborately inlaid with pearl in vine design, as illustrated. The head is veneered in the same way and inlaid with fancy pearl figures and fitted with white celluloid patent non-slipping pegs. The heel of the neck is magnificently hand carved and built up with fancy colored layers of wood to which is fastened our patent nickel plated brace, which gives greater strength to the neck and serves as an adjuster and regulator to the angle of the fingerboard. From the illustration you can get a good idea of the appearance of both the front and back of this banjo, but it must be seen to appreciate its real value. If you buy this University Glee instrument, you may be sure of owning a genuine, strictly high grade S. S. Stewart banjo and an instrument that retails usually at from $50.00 to $75.00.

SEE THE FREE OUTFIT SENT WITH EACH BANJO, DESCRIBED ON PAGE 157.

OUR QUALITY GUARANTEE.

EVERY UNIVERSITY GLEE BANJO **is covered by our binding guarantee for quality,** guaranteed perfect in every way, a strictly high class, high grade instrument, exactly as described and guaranteed to please you in every way. Our offer to return your money and pay express charges both ways if the instrument does not please you is a sufficient guarantee. Remember, also, that you have the privilege of giving the instrument a ten days' trial, during which time you will have an opportunity to test it thoroughly and at any time, during the ten days, you are at liberty to return the banjo to us and get your money back if you are not pleased with your purchase in every particular.

DO YOU WANT A FINE BANJO? **Do you hesitate about placing your order for a fine banjo with us?** If you want a fine banjo this is surely your opportunity. You cannot buy a better instrument, no matter what price you may be willing to pay. You may be a banjo expert and may feel that you cannot get an instrument good enough from us. You may feel that the price is too cheap for the instrument to be as fine as you want. To all of these doubting questions we can only refer you again to the description of this instrument, to point to our liberal offer of money refunded and ask you to simply give us the opportunity of putting this banjo in your hands for your own personal examination. If you are in doubt, send for the University Glee Banjo on our regular terms (you need only send $1.00 deposit), we will send the instrument to your express office for examination and you can write for any other fine banjo from any dealer, compare the instruments when received and if our instrument does not please you, if it isn't far better than the other instrument at the same price, or if it isn't equal in every way to the other instrument that may be offered you at double the price, simply refuse to take it and it will be returned to us at our expense and we will promptly return your dollar. We want your order for this banjo if you are looking for a fine instrument, because we know we can please you and we know that you will be a good customer of ours for all time. We are giving such values in banjos and other musical instruments as were never before offered, values that represent the best advertising we can do.

No. 12C868 Our University Banjo. Price.. **$19.85**

FRONT VIEW BACK VIEW
No. 12C868 UNIVERSITY GLEE BANJO. PRICE, $19.85.

Our $3.45 Mandolinetto.

No. 12C912 The body is 10 inches long, 7½ inches wide, made of maple, finished in imitation rosewood, light colored spruce top, with celluloid bound top edge, figured wood inlaying around sound hole, gutta percha guard plate, imitation mahogany neck, with rosewood finish and pearl position dots, brass screw patent head, nickel plated tailpiece and sleeve protector. **We include, without extra charge,** one genuine tortoise shell mandolin pick, one complete mandolin instruction book and fine canvas case, leather bound and flannel lined. Regular price, $10.00.

No. 12C912 Our price..**$3.45**
Shipping weight, about 7 pounds.

No. 12C913 Same style as No. 12C912, only made of solid rosewood with selected Eastern spruce top, celluloid bound edges, top and back, inlaying around sound hole, gutta percha guard plate, mahogany neck, solid ebony fingerboard, position dots of pearl, best quality American patent head, nickel plated tailpiece and sleeve protector combined. We include **free of charge** a genuine tortoise shell pick, complete instruction book and perfect fitting canvas case, flannel lined.

No. 12C913 Price..**$6.25**
Shipping weight, 7 pounds.

Our $7.85 Acme Professional Banjourine.

This instrument is especially built for use in banjo and mandolin clubs and is in use by all leading organizations. The Banjourine is designed for those who prefer a sharper tone and more brilliancy than is found in the ordinary banjo. Our Acme Professional Banjourine is 11 inches in diameter, has nickel plated rim with spun wire edge, 24 brackets, heavy band or strainer hoop, and best quality calfskin head; 12-inch neck, highly polished, solid ebony extension fingerboard, 20 raised frets, rosewood veneered head inlaid with pearl, ebony pegs, 6 inlaid position dots, nickel plated tailpiece, and fine canvas case, leather bound and flannel lined. **A strictly high grade instrument.**

No. 12C914 Price..**$7.85**
Shipping weight, about 15 pounds.

Our $6.85 Acme Professional Piccolo Banjo.

The Piccolo Banjo has proven an indispensable instrument in a banjo club. It is used in all leading banjo organizations. The Piccolo Banjo has 7-inch rim, 2 inches deep, neck 10 inches from nut to hoop; German silver nickel plated rim, wire edges, heavy hoop, edge or band, 16 nickel plated brackets, best quality Rogers' calfskin head, highly polished neck, solid ebony fingerboard, 17 narrow German silver raised frets, ebony veneered head, ebony pegs, pearl star inlaid in head, 6 pearl inlaid position marks, nickel plated common sense tailpiece, and fine canvas case, leather bound and flannel lined. **Shipping weight, 9 pounds.**

No. 12C915 Price..**$6.85**

N. B.—The Piccolo Banjo is tuned a full octave higher than the ordinary banjo, that is, it tunes in the high C and G.

Our $6.95 Banjo-Mandolin.

$6.95 buys this beautiful instrument. One that is seldom found in retail stores except at 50 to 75 per cent more than our direct from factory price.

No. 12C916 This instrument in appearance is just like a banjo, but is only about 22 inches long, has a 7-inch calfskin head, German silver rim, double wired edge, wood lined, 16 brackets, chased strainer hoop, mahogany neck, 14 inches long, ebony fingerboard, inlaid with pearl position dots, ebony veneered headpiece, nickel plated tailpiece and sleeve protector, and the genuine patent keys. **We furnish this instrument complete,** with a genuine tortoise shell pick, mandolin instruction book, which is the proper instructor to use, and fine canvas case, leather bound and flannel lined. Any other dealer would ask $20.00.

No. 12C916 Our price..**$6.95**
Shipping weight, 9 pounds.

THE EXTREMELY LOW PRICES which we make on the instruments shown on this page are made possible by our direct from factory to consumer plan of sale. We ship every instrument with the understanding that if it is not found to be far superior to other instruments sold by other dealers at the same price, it can be returned to us; we will cheerfully refund the money paid, and pay the express charges both ways. **WE GUARANTEE EVERY INSTRUMENT TO BE SATISFACTORY.**

MUSIC BOXES

SELF-ACTING—AUTOMATIC—CYLINDER. These boxes are made by the best manufacturer in Switzerland, the home of the music box. It is a recognized fact that the originator and best makers of musical boxes are the Swiss people. In presenting this line to our customers, we have made a very careful selection from the catalogue of one of the best known Swiss makers, and know we are offering an assortment that is unsurpassed. Every box is made with the greatest care, and the comb and mechanism being firmly attached to the bottom (the sounding board) of the beautifully finished cases, brings forth the best possible quality of tone—that sweet, delightful tone so peculiar to the Swiss box. The mechanism is simple and will not get out of order, unless tampered with. A drop of oil occasionally in the worm of the governor keeps them running nicely, and each box is furnished with a safety catch that makes serious accidents impossible.

Our $1.65, $3.15 and $3.65 Swiss Music Boxes.

No. 12C948 This box measures 4¼x3¼x2¼ inches; is a perfect little musical instrument. It plays two tunes. The case is highly finished in natural wood. The mechanism winds with a key and can be started and stopped by a small lever on the front of the box. Shipping weight, 16 ounces. Price......**$1.65**

No. 12C950 The music box as shown in illustration is 5¼ inches long, 3¼ inches wide and 2¼ inches high. The case is made of walnut, beautifully polished and highly finished. The cylinder is 2¼ inches long; the comb has 36 teeth, plays three tunes. **It is wound with a key and changes automatically.** Shipping weight, 19 ounces.
Price..**$3.15**

No. 12C952 This box is the same as No. 12C950, shown in the illustration; the same size and finish, but plays four tunes. Shipping weight, 19 ounces. Price...............**$3.65**

Our $22.95 Music Box.

No. 12C958 This box is the largest and finest box which we furnish and is the most wonderful value ever offered in this line. The case is of handsome rosewood veneer, with beautiful white wood inlaying, highly polished and finished. **The box is 24 x 9½ x 6½ inches. The cylinder is 11 inches in length and plays 12 complete and different tunes. The tone is exceptionally pleasing,** and with the new auto-zither attachment a surprising and delightful change in tune can be made. This can be used at will by the simple moving of a lever and a very pretty effect can be secured. **PLAYS 12 TUNES.**

The box is operated by a very large strong spring, which is wound up by a lever handle. There are also two levers, one to enable you to repeat any tune desired and which can be repeated as many times as you wish, the other lever to start and stop the box. **Our price on this box is considerably less than what other dealers are obliged to ask, as we import all of our Swiss boxes direct and list them at our usual one small percentage of profit.**

No. 12C958 Price......**(Shipping weight, 45 pounds)**..................**$22.95**

Our $6.25 and $7.95 Swiss Music Boxes.

No. 12C954 This box is made in imitation rosewood, highly polished and handsomely decorated. The box is 13¼ inches long, 7 inches wide, 5½ inches high. Has a 3½-inch cylinder. It plays six tunes and has a tune indicator, showing which selection is being played. **It is operated by a strong steel spring;** it is wound up by a lever handle; is also provided with two levers which enable you to have the box repeat any tune and the other lever to stop or start the music. The mechanism is covered by a glass lid to protect it from dust. **This box is a great bargain at the price at which we offer it.** Shipping weight, 12 pounds.
Price..**$6.25**

No. 12C956 This box is the same description as No. 12C954, but is somewhat larger. It has a 4½-inch cylinder and plays eight tunes; it is in every other detail the same as No. 12C954. Shipping weight, 15 pounds. Price..**$7.95**

Our Swiss Concert Music Box.

THIS BEAUTIFUL MUSIC BOX IS MADE IN SWITZERLAND, AND, AT THE PRICE WE ASK, IS ONE OF THE BEST MUSIC BOXES ON THE MARKET.

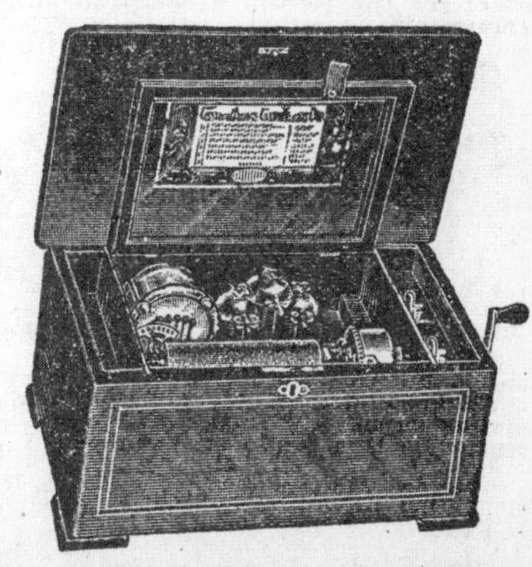

No. 12C959 The case is handsomely veneered with rosewood and has a very high piano finish. The ornaments on the case are of inlaid colored woods in handsome designs. Size, 10¼ inches wide, 17 inches long and 8 inches high. The cylinder is 6½ inches long and fitted with eight of the prettiest and most popular tunes. Besides the cylinder, this box is fitted with snare drum and orchestra bells, which can be thrown on and off at pleasure by means of a lever.

It has repeat, change, stop and start levers and winds with a handle on the side.

The action is protected from dust and dirt by an extra glass cover which can be raised so as to increase the volume of tone. The comb contains 44 resonant steel tongues and the entire mechanism of the box is well and strongly made. Shipping weight, 45 pounds.
Price..**$24.45**

THE AUTOHARP

THE AUTOHARP has become one of the **MOST POPULAR** of small instruments. This popularity is well deserved. Thousands are in use and the sale keeps on increasing at a wonderful rate. **REASONS WITHOUT NUMBER** exist for the universal demand for these high class instruments. **SIMPLICITY.** There are no complicated parts, no mechanism that requires the skilled hand to operate. Anyone—whether he has musical ability or not, can play it with very little practice, and play it well **MUSICAL QUALITY.** Thousands testify to its sweetness of tone, which equals that of the highest grade piano. The most difficult productions may be played on it, while as an accompaniment for the voice it has no superior. **CHEAPNESS.** Never before has it been possible for the house to be graced with high class music at so small an expense. The prices which we name enable the poorest to possess an instrument which will produce the sweetest music and give just as much pleasure as would a high priced piano.

Our $1.75 Autoharp.

No. 12C900 Our $1.75 Autoharp has 20 strings, 3 bars and produces 3 chords. With this instrument the simpler airs and chords may be played. **The best steel strings** are furnished and the tone is **remarkably sweet.** Without a single exception, every purchaser has been delighted with this autoharp, and would not part with it at any price if another could not be secured.

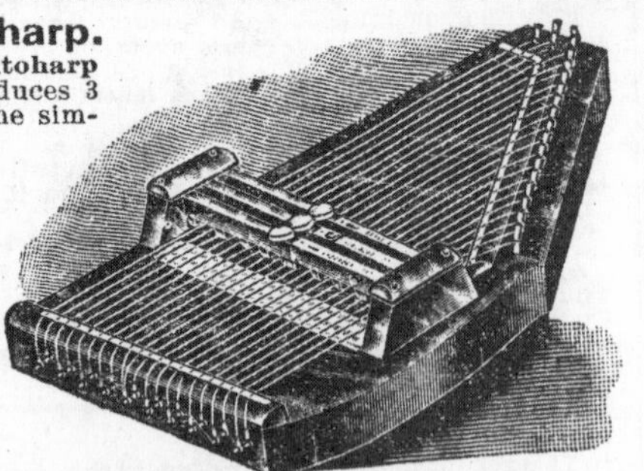

No. 12C900 Price.....**$1.75**
Weight, packed for shipment, 6 pounds.

$2.95 Buys a $5.50 Autoharp.

$2.95

No. 12C902 Our $2.95 Autoharp has 23 strings, 5 bars and produces 5 chords. The possibilities of this beautiful instrument are unbounded, and while but **little practice is needed for the beginner to play nicely,** constant practice will enable the **performer to produce very difficult music.**
No. 12C902 Price..........**$2.95**
Weight, packed for shipment, 7 pounds.

Our Special Autoharp for $4.95.

No. 12C904 For $4.95 we offer an autoharp that is entirely new, strictly first class in workmanship and susceptible to wonderful manipulation in the hands of a **musician, whether artist or amateur.** This special autoharp is **complete with 32 strings** and is fitted with **8 bars,** producing as many different chords. The range of different music is very great, and the **possibilities of the instrument are beyond that of any other** of similar construction and much higher price.

No. 12C904 Price **$4.95**
Weight, packed for shipment, 9 pounds.

$6.45 for the New Style Autoharp.

No. 12C906 This autoharp is the very latest product of the manufacturer, and is destined to become the most popular style of their entire list. **It has 37 strings and 12 chord bars;** these bars are placed closely together, making the manipulation of them exceedingly easy; they produce the major chords of C, Bb, G and F, with their relative minors. **It is strung and tuned in a perfect chromatic scale,** making it possible to pick out any tune or melody. **The finish is beautiful; highly polished ebony finish;** altogether a handsome, useful, musical **instrument.**

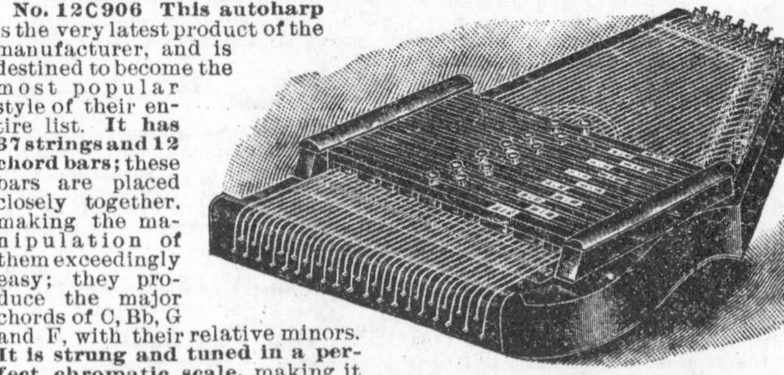

No. 12C906 Price...(**Weight, packed for shipment, 10 pounds**).**$6.45**

Our Highest Grade Concert Autoharp for $10.85.

A BEAUTIFUL INSTRUMENT

SURPASSINGLY SWEET VOLUME OF SOUND

No. 12C908 This Beautiful Concert Autoharp is one of the most desirable of all stringed instruments made. The manufacturers of the world renowned autoharp have taken **special pains with this particular style** to make it the best that high class material and expensive skilled mechanics can make. **It has 32 strings and 6 bars with shifters, producing 16 chords,** as follows: F, C, G, D major, 5 minor and 1 seventh. With this instrument, anyone with sufficient skill and practice can produce any music, however difficult. **It is** suitable for **all classes of music, sacred, classical or popular.** It is suitable **for accompaniment to the voice,** suitable to be played in connection with other musical instruments. It is unusually handsome, having the **finest inlaid edges, imitation rosewood top,** and all complete. It is polished and finished equal to the finish of a **high grade piano.** Packed in good pasteboard box.
No. 12C908 Price.(**Weight, packed for shipment, about 16 lbs.**).**$10.85**
No. 12C909 Same Autoharp as No. 12C908, but packed in fine black wood autoharp case, flannel lined. A case which would retail at $2.50.
No. 12C909 Price.......................................**$11.95**

FREE.—With each autoharp we furnish free a very complete instruction book, by the aid of which anyone can in a short time become a skillful performer on this most charming of all instruments. **WE ALSO FURNISH FREE,** a thumb ring for playing, music rack, tuning hammer and selections of autoharp music.

FOR AUTOHARP STRINGS, SEE PAGE 179. FOR CASES AND OTHER FURNISHINGS, SEE PAGE 181.

THE ZITHO-HARP

IS A NEW OVERSTRUNG INSTRUMENT OF EXTRAORDINARY BEAUTY AND ELEGANCE, PRODUCING A TO WHICH FOR SWEETNESS, PURITY AND RESONANCE FAR EXCELS ANY AND ALL INSTRUMENTS OF ITS CLASS

THIS IS A DOUBLE INSTRUMENT having two distinct parts, one for the treble or melody, played with the right hand, the other for the bass or accompaniment, arranged in harmonic groups or chords, played with the left hand. The great feature of the Zitho-Harp is the crossing at right angles of the bass and accompaniment strings over the melody strings and over the center of the sounding board and sounding hole, an entirely new arrangement found in no other instrument, making it not only easier and more convenient to play, but adding a beauty and fullness to the tone such as has never been approached on any stringed instrument. **The artistic and handsome design of the Zitho-Harp permitting of a large, deep sounding chest, accounts partly for the great volume of tone of which this instrument is capable. The beautiful and sympathetic blending of the crossed vibrations thus produced is something wonderful.**

No. 12C944 Style D. Dimensions, 19x19 inches; 33 strings; finished in ebony, handsomely decorated; 17 melody strings, with 2 sharps; 4 chords. C, D, F and G.
Price..**$1.95**
Weight, packed for shipment, 10 pounds.

THIS, TOGETHER WITH THE NATURAL AND EASY POSITION enjoyed by the performer, both hands being supported by rests, makes the Zitho-Harp truly a great favorite and "the ideal of the new century."

A MODEL SELF INSTRUCTOR with a fine variety of instrumental and vocal selections, played either by notes or figures, is given free with every instrument. The system used is so simple and easy that anyone, young or old, can learn to play without a teacher.

TO BE FULLY APPRECIATED IT MUST BE SEEN AND HEARD, AND WE PREFER TO LET THE

ZITHO-HARP

SPEAK FOR ITSELF.

No. 12C946 Style E. Dimensions, 19x19 inches; 41 strings; finished in ebony, handsomely decorated; 21 melody strings, with 6 sharps; 5 chords, C, G, F, D and A.
Price..**$3.15**
Weight, packed for shipment 12 pounds.

GUITAR ZITHERS

THE GUITAR ZITHER **is an improved and simplified German zither, upon which may be rendered the most difficult music without the aid of a teacher.** Our method of instruction is so easy that anyone can learn to play the instrument in a very short time. The bass notes are tuned in groups of chords. This is a very attractive feature because the various chords of the key are ready to be picked without effort. As an accompaniment to the voice these chords are invaluable. In connection with the violin, piano or other musical instrument, the guitar zither is especially delightful. It rewards individual skill more than any other harp in existence. These are musical instruments which charm alike the home circle and the concert audience. Every instruction book contains a list of music arranged for the instrument in figures easily comprehended. Our repertoire contains nearly everything published in the popular music of the day, besides all the standard music which has won the hearts of generation after generation.

CAUTION — Do not confuse the Guitar Zither with anything in the harp line. It is not a harp, but a zither, an instrument upon which can be played any class of music, and it is altogether without an equal.

Our Guitar Zither at $1.65.

$1.65

No. 12C921 The Guitar Zither, at $1.65 illustrated herewith, is made of maple, cherry stained and polished. It has hand rests, 31 strings and four chords, namely, C, G, F major and G minor, complete with instruction book, key and ring. Lovers of music will find this a particularly fine instrument, as it is very easily learned and is delightfully entertaining. Shipping weight, about 9 pounds.
Price..**$1.65**

A Regular $6.00 Instrument at Only $2.95.

$2.95

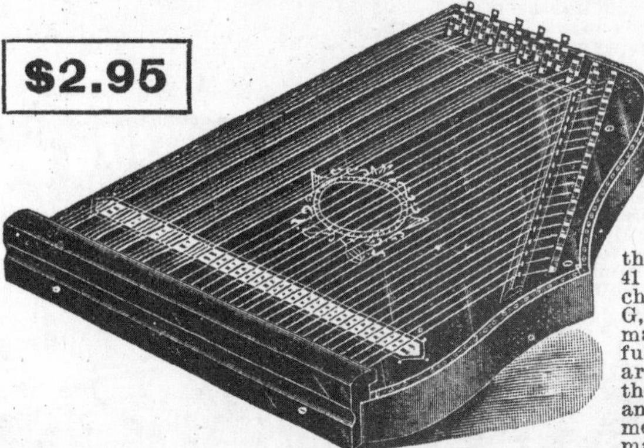

No. 12C925 This is another Guitar Zither, made of maple, ebonized, handsomely finished. It has hand rest, highly polished and is beautifully inlaid around the sound hole, has 41 strings and 5 chords, namely, C, G, F, D and A major. It is beautifully ornamented around the edge of the sounding board and is an instrument of which one may well be proud. We furnish a chart also with the instrument, which can be laid under the strings, giving the position of every note. It comes complete, with instruction book, key and ring. Shipping weight, about 9 pounds. Price...........**$2.95**

Our Guitar Zither at $1.98.

No. 12C923 This is another splendid Guitar Zither, and is made of maple, ebonized and beautifully finished. It has hand rest and is considerably larger in size than No. 12C921. It is inlaid around the sound hole with beautiful ornamentations. has 31 strings and four chords, namely, C, G, F major and G minor. Complete with instruction book, key and ring. This instrument will be found by players to be handsome in every respect. and possesses a deep, rich tone which never fails to delight the listener. It is new in our line, and we highly recommend it for its many excellent qualities. Shipping weight, about 9 pounds. Price..................**$1.98**

Our Artists' Guitar Zither at $3.95.

No. 12C927 This is a particularly fine instrument of great musical capacity. It is made of maple, ebonized, has hand rest, highly polished, and is beautifully inlaid around sound hole and the edge of the sounding board. Has nickel plated tuning pins, full chromatic scale with 51 strings and six chords, namely, C, G, F, D major, D and A minor. It has a deep, full, rich tone, and by the aid of the chart and instruction book which we send it can be very easily learned. We send it complete, with chart, instruction book, key and ring, and the purchaser will find that it will prove a never ending source of entertainment and delight. Shipping weight, about 9 pounds. Price **$3.95**

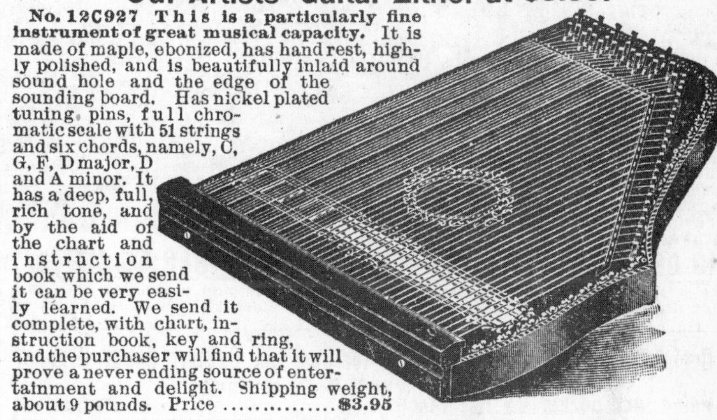

MANDOLIN-GUITAR-ZITHER.

THREE INSTRUMENTS COMBINED AT THE PRICE OF ONE.

THE WONDER OF THE AGE.

THE MANDOLIN HARP, the greatest musical instrument that has ever been placed before the public. The Mandolin, Guitar and Zither, three of the sweetest toned instruments, are combined in this Harp, which is so simply constructed that anyone may become master of it in a very short time, without the aid of a teacher. No picks or rings are required to play the instrument, a patent keyboard being used instead. As you will see in the illustration, the instrument is made after the style of the Guitar-Zither, having treble strings on which the air is played and accompaniment strings for the accompaniment. The keyboard, which is placed over the strings, is the one great feature with which the mandolin effect is produced. The keys, which are made of ebony, placed on spiral springs, extend through the cover or keyboard, which is mounted on rubber rollers actuated by springs on the ends, which, when moved rapidly, trill the strings, imitating the mandolin perfectly; in fact, a better trill can be made than with the hand. This improvement also keeps the instrument in better tune, as the strings are picked evenly at all times. The accompaniment, or guitar effect, is produced with the left hand by picking the strings, which are arranged in chords. **Any chord or chords of the key of the instruments may be made as well as thirds and sixths.** The wonderful simplicity of this instrument, together with the numbered music which is published for it, makes it the greatest novelty of the musical world. **An instruction book and a tuning hammer accompany each instrument.**

$3.45

A Bargain at $3.45.

No. 12C940 A Mandolin Harp, made of selected material, ebonized with fancy decorated hand rest, exactly as shown in the illustration. Has 31 strings, part of which are so arranged as to produce 4 chords, as follows: G, C and F major and G 7th. Packed in neat pasteboard box with instruction book and tuning key.
Weight, packed for shipment, 9 pounds.
Price......**$3.45**

A Mandolin Harp for $4.45.

No. 12C942 A Mandolin Harp, made of selected material, beautifully ebonized and decorated with decalcomanie ornamentations around the edges; has 41 strings, which are so arranged as to give 15 tones and 6 half tones on the keyboard, the balance arranged so as to produce five chords: C, G, F, D, and A major. Packed in a neat pasteboard box with instruction book and tuning key.
Weight, packed ready for shipment, 12 pounds.
Price......................**$4.45**

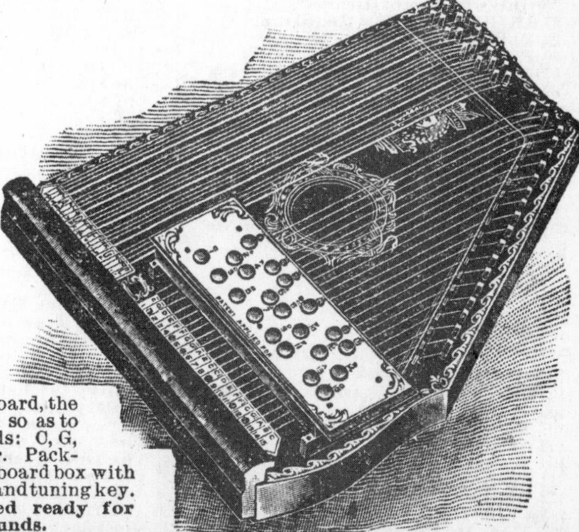

OUR GEM ROLLER ORGAN, $3.25.

OUR LEADER

THE GREATEST VALUE EVER OFFERED IN A MUSICAL INSTRUMENT. PRICE REDUCED FROM $4.20 TO $3.25. This reduction was made possible by our contracting for the entire output of the factory which makes this wonderful little instrument, AND NO DEALER IS ABLE TO FURNISH YOU A GEM ORGAN AT AS LOW A PRICE AS WE QUOTE IT.

THE CASE of the Gem Roller Organ is made of imitation dark walnut; is 16 inches long, 14 inches wide and 9 inches high.

THE GEM ORGAN is distinctly a musical instrument of excellent quality; substantially made by the best manufacturers of this class of goods in the United States. It is so simply constructed that a child can operate it. The music is obtained from a roller, which has teeth or pins like those of the cylinder of a regular Swiss music box. These pins operate on valve keys and the roller is turned by a gear which also works the bellows. The reeds used are the same as those used in regular cabinet parlor organs and the tone is therefore similar to that of a regular cabinet parlor organ.

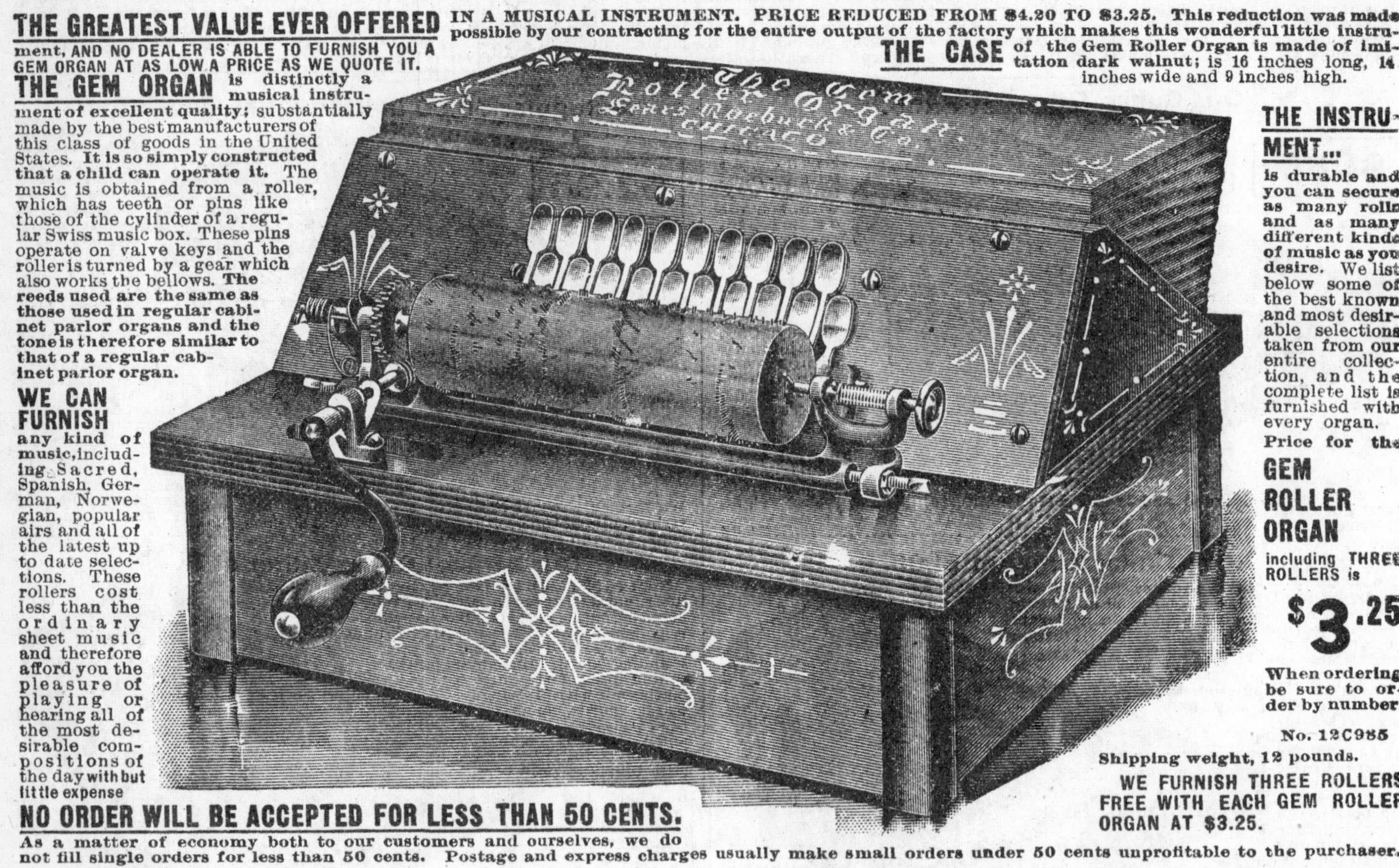

WE CAN FURNISH any kind of music, including Sacred, Spanish, German, Norwegian, popular airs and all of the latest up to date selections. These rollers cost less than the ordinary sheet music and therefore afford you the pleasure of playing or hearing all of the most desirable compositions of the day with but little expense

THE INSTRUMENT... is durable and you can secure as many rolls and as many different kinds of music as you desire. We list below some of the best known and most desirable selections taken from our entire collection, and the complete list is furnished with every organ.

Price for the **GEM ROLLER ORGAN** including THREE ROLLERS is **$3.25**

When ordering be sure to order by number.

No. 12C985

Shipping weight, 12 pounds.

WE FURNISH THREE ROLLERS FREE WITH EACH GEM ROLLER ORGAN AT $3.25.

NO ORDER WILL BE ACCEPTED FOR LESS THAN 50 CENTS.

As a matter of economy both to our customers and ourselves, we do not fill single orders for less than 50 cents. Postage and express charges usually make small orders under 50 cents unprofitable to the purchaser.

Complete List of the Best Rollers for Gem and Concert Roller Organs.

Series No. 12C986 Order by Number.

PRICE, PER DOZEN, **$2.16**; EACH............................**18 Cents.**

If by mail, postage extra, each, 6 cents.

SACRED MUSIC.

1 The Sweet Bye and Bye
2 Nearer, my God, to Thee
3 I Need Thee Every Hour
4 From Greenland's Icy Mountains
6 Onward, Christian Soldiers
12 Hold the Fort
13 Just as I Am
14 America
18 He Leadeth Me
19 I Love to Tell the Story
20 The Home Over There
21 Is My Name Written There
22 Almost Persuaded
23 Where Is My Boy Tonight
24 Bringing in the Sheaves
25 Let the Lower Lights be Burning
26 Only an Armor Bearer
27 I Will Sing of My Redeemer
29 Pull for the Shore
30 Precious Name
65 What a Friend We Have in Jesus
67 Rock of Ages
68 Sweet Hour of Prayer
72 Pass Me Not
73 Jesus, Lover of My Soul
78 Beulah Land
81 We Shall Meet Beyond the River
90 All the Way My Saviour Leads Me
91 Rescue the Perishing [There
603 Knocking, Knocking, Who is
634 Shall We Gather at the River
721 Anywhere With Jesus
726 Glory to His Name
729 The Haven of Rest
730 Everlasting Arms
734 Lead, Kindly Light

POPULAR SONGS; DANCES.

101 Waltz—Les Roses [Fly
103 When the Swallows Homeward
106 The Soldiers' Joy
107 When the Leaves Begin to Fade
108 Sweet Violets
109 Marching Through Georgia
111 Waltz, My Queen
112 Old Uncle Ned
113 Climbing Up the Golden Stairs
115 Meet Me in the Lovely Twilight
119 Vienna Polka
121 Old Folks at Home
122 Sailors' Hornpipe
123 Home, Sweet Home
124 The Marseillaise Hymn
127 Die Wacht am Rhine
132 The Dreamland Waltz
138 The Parade March
144 Nellie Gray
146 Annie Laurie
149 The Last Rose of Summer
150 Waltz—German Hearts
152 See-Saw Waltz
153 Polka—On the Wing
155 The Beautiful Blue Danube
156 Listen to the Mocking Bird
157 Then You'll Remember Me
161 The Blue Bells of Scotland
163 The Wearing of the Green
166 Little Old Log Cabin
183 The Flyaway Galop
190 Yankee Doodle
194 The Golden Slippers
195 The Quilting Party
196 Love Comes—Waltz
200 I
201 II
202 III } Gay Life Quadrilles
203 IV
204 V
205 Dixie
207 The Arkansas Traveler
209 The Kiss Waltz
212 When You and I Were Young
213 College Hornpipe
217 Medley Jig
226 Bring Back My Bonnie to Me
229 Tramp, Tramp
230 Don't Be Angry With Me, Darling
232 Johnny Get Your Hair Cut
233 Poor Old Dad
234 Waltz—Cricket on the Hearth
238 Put My Little Shoes Away
243 Money Musk
246 The Irish Washerwoman
247 The Devil's Dream
251 I'll Take You Home Again
254 Jennie, the Flower of Kildare
256 The Little Fishermaiden
262 Old Black Joe
266 Killarney
268 Comin' Thro' the Rye
270 Massa's in de Cold, Cold Ground
272 Grandfather's Clock
273 The Star Spangled Banner
275 Maryland, My Maryland
277 Hail Columbia
279 Red, White and Blue
280 Tenting on the Old Camp Ground
283 The Old Oaken Bucket
290 In Her Little Bed We Laid Her
293 You Never Miss the Water
295 The Way to be Happy—Waltz
297 St. Patrick's Day
298 Miss McLeod's Reel
301 The Girl I Left Behind Me
309 Down Went McGinty
335 Little Annie Rooney—Waltz
336 Sweetbrier Waltz
347 Good Luck Mazurka
349 Dairy Maid Waltz
351 Free as a Bird
363 Only a Dream of My Mother
368 Schottische—Little Beauty
374 Some Day I'll Wander Back Again
375 Take Me Back to Home & Mother
390 The Battle Cry of Freedom
392 Come Back to Erin
399 John Brown
406 Schottische—Always Smiling
407 Waltz—Loves' Dreamland [Deep
410 Why Did They Dig Ma's Grave so
416 Captain Jinks
420 Schottische—Happy-go-Lucky
421 My Mother's Old Red Shawl
423 Peep-O-Day—Polka
443 Oh My Darling Clementine
444 Galop—Jolly Brothers
446 Manhattan Polka
450 Clayton's Grand March
452 Fresh Life, Waltz
453 Galop—Little Fairy
456 Racquet Waltz
457 Waltz—Estudiantina
476 Silver Threads Among the Gold
480 General Grant's Grand March
517 Mary and John
527 Farewell Till We Meet Again
577 The High School Cadets' March
578 The Skirt Dance
600 After the Ball
617 God Be With You
635 Happy Day
1003 Won't You Be My Sweetheart
1004 The Bowery
1006 Two Little Girls in Blue
1009 The Washington Post March
1016 The Miner's Dream of Home
1019 Molly and I and the Baby
1020 Little Alabama Coon [Moon
1030 In Love With the Man in the
1036 Sweet Marie
1038 The Sidewalks of New York
1039 The Fatal Wedding [Yard
1050 I Don't Want to Play in Your
1053 Ben Bolt
1054 The Honeymoon March
1058 Just Tell Them That You Saw Me
1059 Only One Girl in the World for Me
1061 The Sunshine of Paradise Alley
1069 My Old Kentucky Home
1070 The Darkies' Dream
1071 Sweet Rosie O'Grady
1083 Hot Time in the Old Town
1084 Bombasto March, Two Step
1086 There'll Come a Time
1087 All Coons Look Alike to Me
1090 On the Banks of the Wabash
1096 Stars and Stripes Forever, M
1100 Sunny Side Clog
1101 She was Bred in Old Kentucky
1102 Break the News to Mother
1107 Georgia Camp Meeting
1112 Hello, Ma Baby
1113 High Born Lady
1114 Smoky Mokes
1115 Eli Green's Cake Walk
1116 Whistling Rufus
1117 Just as the Sun Went Down
1118 Just One Girl
1119 Zenda Waltzes
1120 Home to Our Mountains
1121 Narcissus
1122 Intermezzo Rusticana
1123 The Moth and the Flame
1124 Sunny Tennessee
1125 El Captain—No. 1
1126 El Captain—No. 2
1127 Soldiers in the Park
1128 Holy City
1129 Mosquito Parade
1130 Good Bye, Dolly Grey
1131 Fishers' Hornpipe
1132 Creole Belle
1133 Tale of the Kangaroo [soms Grow
1134 Down Where the Cotton Blos-
1135 I Left Because I Love You
1136 In the Good Old Summer Time
1137 Mister Dooley
1138 Bill Bailey
1139 Hiawatha
1140 By the Sycamore Tree
1141 Laughing Water

OUR $7.60 CONCERT ROLLER ORGAN.

No. 12C988

THE CONCERT ROLLER ORGAN is similar in mechanical construction to the Gem and Grand Roller Organs and operates in the same manner, the music being produced by means of a cylinder which has teeth and pins and which operate on valve keys; the roller is turned by a gear which works the bellows, and the result is a tone similar to that of a regular cabinet or parlor organ.

THE CONCERT ROLLER ORGAN is made of genuine black walnut; is 17 inches long, 16 inches wide and 13 inches high. As shown in the illustration, the mechanism is all enclosed and is visible through a door with glass panel.

THE ROLLERS for this organ are exactly the same as are used on the Gem Organ. For a complete list of tunes see preceding page.

Series No. 12C986 Price, for extra rollers, each $0.18
Per dozen 2.16

If by mail, postage extra, each, 6 cents.

Five Tunes Furnished Free With Each Concert Organ.

When packed, ready for shipment, the Concert Roller Organ weighs 30 pounds.

No. 12C988 Price $7.60

GRAND ROLLER ORGAN—A MUSICAL WONDER

No. 12C990

IN OFFERING the Grand Roller Organ we aim to furnish an instrument to fill the middle ground between the instruments of small cost and those ranging in price to several hundred dollars.

It has a compass of thirty-two notes, and thereby opens up a large field for the better class of music, such as overtures and classical selections, which could not very well be played on the small instruments. The tone is pure sweet and full, having a volume sufficient for a large hall and yet pleasing in a small apartment. The mechanism is of the first order, nothing about the whole instrument being slighted or cheapened, and is as simple as can be devised to do the

...PROPER WORK...

NOTE—Rollers or cylinders to play any of the following pieces can be obtained by indicating the number of the piece desired.

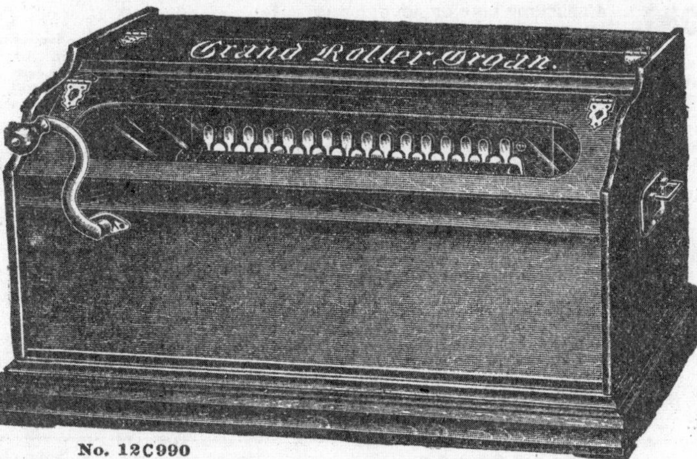

No. 12C990

THE ROLLER used in the Grand Roller Organ is a marvel of mechanical skill, each roller having from 2,500 to 4,000 separate pins which must be absolutely perfect in position. The roller is 13 inches long, 2⅛ inches in diameter and makes 8 full revolutions in completing a tune.

All wearing parts, such as keys, pins, etc., are made of steel, and all adjustments made to insure durability. The case is of oak finish, full nickel trimmed and is a handsome addition to any apartment. A complete list of music will be sent at any time upon application.

WE FURNISH FREE WITH EACH
GRAND ROLLER ORGAN
. THREE ROLLS OF MUSIC.

No. 12C990 Price, complete. $14.95
Price for extra rollers, each .. .65
Price, per dozen 7.80
If by mail, postage extra, single roller 25 cents.
Large quantities should be shipped by express or freight.

LIST OF BEST SELECTIONS:
Series No. 12C992 Order by Number.

POPULAR AIRS.

2001 Auf Wiedersehn Waltz
2002 Autograph Waltz
2003 The Thunderer March
2004 En Avant March
2008 Blooming Youth Waltz
2009 Four Little Curly Headed Coons
2010 The Nightingale's Song
2011 The Washington Post March
2015 Dramatic News Waltz
2016 After the Ball—Waltz Song
2019 Gracious Heavens—Martha
2020 The Oxford Minuet
2021 The Wedding of the Lily and the Rose
2022 The Gypsy Song—Anvil Chorus
2023 The Bowery—Waltz
2024 Par Ci Par La—Polka
2025 The High School Cadets March
2026 Mosquito Skirt Dance
2027 "Wang" Waltzes
2030 The Virginia Skedaddle
2031 Push Dem Clouds Away
2033 I Wish I Was in Dixie Land
2040 Tannhauser March
2043 Home, Sweet Home
2044 "1492" Waltzes
2046 Gondolier Waltzes
2047 I and II / 2048 IV and V } Mardi Gras Quadrilles
2050 I and II / 2051 IV and V } Palermo Quadrilles
2054 Overture—Caliph of Bagdad
2055 Sweet Marie Waltz
2059 Wedding March
2060 Overture—Tancredi
2062 Overture—William Tell
2063 The Liberty Bell March
2064 Wedding March from Lohengrin
2065 I and II / 2066 IV and V } Gondoliers Lanciers
2067 The Belle of Chicago
2070 The Fatal Wedding
2071 America, Star Spangled Banner
2073 Because I Love Thee So
2074 Skirt Dance—Faust Up to Date
2075 Coronation March—The Prophet
2080 { I. Mrs. Flarity, What Did You Mean by That / II. Do, Do, My Huckleberry
2081 Rock-a-Bye Baby
2086 { The Sidewalks of New York / I Long to See the Girl I Left Behind
2088 Overture—Poet and Peasant
2090 Yankee Doodle. My Old Kentucky Home
2091 { I Don't Want to Play in Your Yard / He Never Cares to Wander from His Fireside
2092 Military March
2097 Dream Waltz—Black Hussar
2099 Kerry Dance
2101 The Honeymoon March
2103 Old Hundred
2104 America
2107 Auld Lang Syne
2109 Beautiful Blue Danube Waltz
2112 Selection from Overture, Semiramis
2114 Sounds from the Vienna Woods
2116 Selections from Mignon
2119 Maggie Mooney. My Pearl is a Bowery Girl
2121 Slumber So Gently—Princess Bonnie
2122 Morning Leaves—Waltz
2123 Thousand and One Nights Waltz
2124 Crusaders' March—Il Talisman
2126 The Band Played On
2127 When the Swallows Homeward Fly
2129 Monastery Bells
2131 I'll Tell Papa on You. Oh, Uncle John
2132 Only One Girl in the World for Me
2134 { My Best Girl's a New Yorker / The Sunshine of Paradise Alley
2135 Yale March—Two Step
2137 { Just Tell Them That You Saw Me / I Love Only You
2138 Priest March—Opera Athalia
2139 Autophone, Melody
2140 { Battle Cry of Freedom. Tramp, Tramp / Red, White and Blue. Home, Sweet Home. Marching Through Georgia

SACRED MUSIC.

3001 O, Rest in the Lord. (Elijah)
3002 I Know that My Redeemer Liveth
3003 Come Unto Me
3004 Lead, Kindly Light
3005 Nearer, My God, to Thee
3006 Onward, Christian Soldiers
3007 Hold the Fort
3008 Jesus, Lover of My Soul
3009 Only an Armor Bearer
3010 Let the Lower Lights be Burning
3012 Sweet Hour of Prayer
3013 Beautiful Valley of Eden
3014 Sweet Bye and Bye
3015 From Greenland's Icy Mountain
3016 Portuguese Hymn
3017 Antioch

SEND FOR COMPLETE LIST OF ROLLERS.

TWO SPLENDID CONCERTINAS.

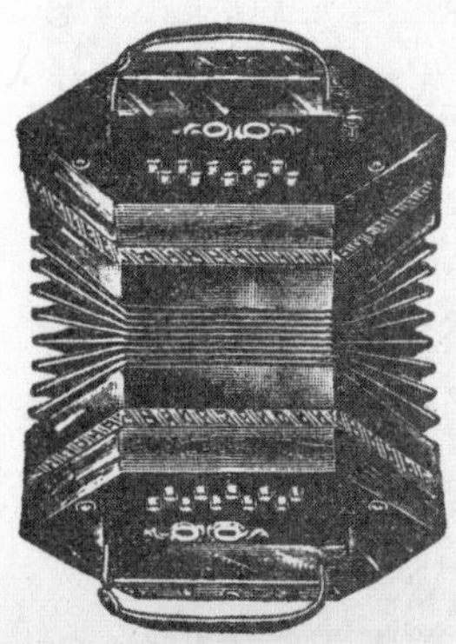

Our No. 12C1096 Concertina.

This concertina is not only a beautiful instrument in appearance, but possesses also an excellent quality of tone. It is made of solid mahogany fancy carved, bellows of eight folds, full leather bound. It has 20 bone keys and is finished splendidly throughout. The frame of the instrument is highly polished and the ornamentation throughout is in the very best of taste. We unhesitatingly recommend it to all who desire a fine concertina at an extremely low price. This is a concertina for which your dealer is asking you from $6.00 to $7.00, and you cannot buy it elsewhere for less than these prices. We buy these instruments under a special contract, and are thus able to procure the very best possible terms, and we sell you the instrument at exactly what it costs us, with but one small percentage of profit added. In this way you are able to purchase the instrument at an extremely low price. We guarantee it to be satisfactory and we assure our friends that it is a concertina of which any one may well be proud. Remember, we do not ask you to keep it unless you find it satisfactory in every respect and equal, if not superior, to concertinas sold by dealers generally at twice the price. Weight, boxed, about 8 pounds.

No. 12C1096 Price $3.45

Our S., R. & Co.'s Special Anglo-German System Concertina No. 12C1098.

This is one of the most beautiful concertinas ever manufactured and the engraving falls far short of giving any idea of its handsome appearance and splendid finish. It is made of solid mahogany, highly polished and most exquisitely carved. It has leather covered bellows of six folds, has 21 bone keys and is fitted with extra fine quality reeds. It is put up in a leather covered case with lock and key. Why should you go to the retail music dealer and purchase a concertina in the usual way when you can purchase one from us of the very same grade for one-half what the dealer asks you. You cannot buy a concertina of this grade from any local dealer for less than $12.00 or $13.00, and we are willing to ship you this instrument with the understanding that if you do not find this to be the case, you can return it to us, we will cheerfully refund your money and pay transportation charges both ways. We guarantee this concertina to be satisfactory and we assure our customers that they take no risk whatever in ordering it, because we take all the chances and responsibilities of shipment. Under our plan of sale our customers are given an opportunity to try our instruments entirely at our expense. Weight, boxed, about 10 pounds.

No. 12C1098 Price $6.65

OUR BÖHM LINE OF SOVEREIGN ACCORDIONS

A FINE LINE OF LOW PRICED ACCORDIONS.

We assure all admirers of the accordion that they will find in these instruments the greatest values ever offered in low priced accordions. They are made especially for us by a maker who has an international reputation for manufacturing these instruments. They are all well and thoroughly made throughout, and we know that we can sell them to you at a much lower price than what other dealers will ask you for the same grade of instruments. We ship them upon the same terms that we ship all of our other musical goods and allow full ten days' trial. They are all handsomely finished and ornamented and are instruments which we can conscientiously recommend to our customers. With each instrument we include a complete and comprehensive instruction book, by the aid of which anyone can learn to play on these instruments without the aid of a teacher.

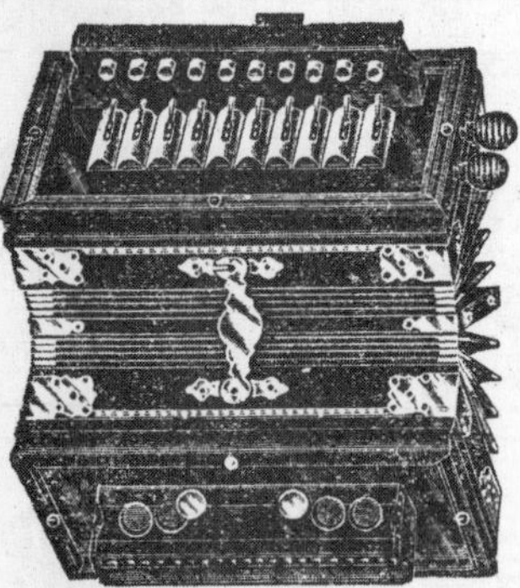

No. 12C994 **This is a very fine instrument, with ebonized highly polished frame and fancy fluted mouldings.** It has double bellows of eight folds with corner protectors. Has highly nickel plated clasps and trimmings and leather straps. Has nickel strips on the inside of the panel, is fitted with ten keys, two sets of reeds and stops. Size, 6x7x10¼ inches.
Price.....**$1.65**

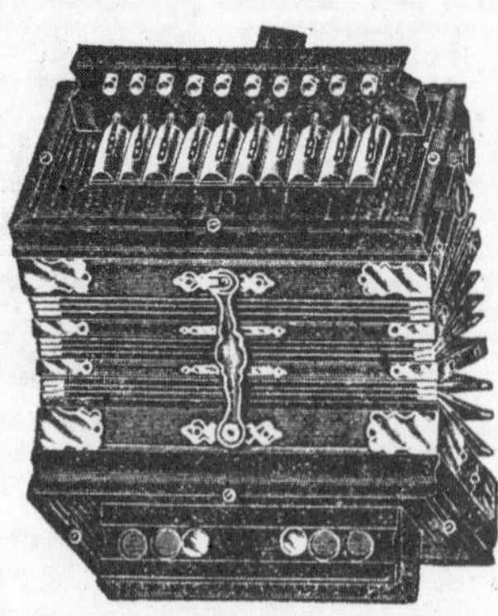

No. 12C995 This is a very fine accordion, with fluted, ebonized mouldings and dark red panels, triple bellows, eleven folds, in three alternate colors, red, black and green. Highly ornamented corner protectors, ten nickel plated keys, two sets of reeds, two stops, fancy gold paper ornamentations around the frame. Nickel plated clasps and trimmings throughout. Fitted with strips of fancy webbing. A beautiful instrument for those who desire an accordion at a medium price. Size, 5⅝x7x10¼ inches. Price **$1.95**

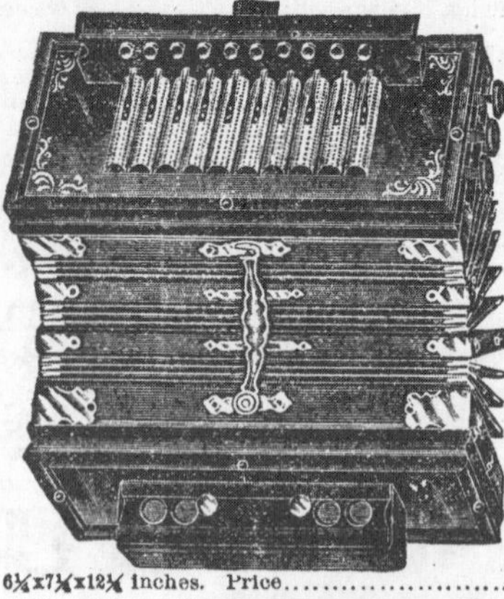

No. 12C996 Fancy fluted mouldings finished in imitation ebony. Keyboard also in imitation ebony; rich deep blue panels, with gold decorations. Triple bellows of ten folds with corner protectors, bellows and all leather work being in two colors, green and brown with rich Turkish red paper between the folds. Ten long nickel keys, nickel clasps and trimmings, three sets of steel bronzed reeds, three stops. Extra large. Size, 6¾x7¾x12¾ inches. Price..............................**$2.65**

OUR EMPRESS ACCORDIONS.—A SPLENDID LINE OF ACCORDIONS AT AN EXTREMELY LOW PRICE.

This line of accordions is manufactured by one of the best known makers of accordions in Germany, and they are all furnished for us under special contract with the manufacturers. We guarantee each instrument to be satisfactory and the purchaser has the privilege of returning any instrument he may order from us should it fail to satisfy him in any particular. These accordions are all finely finished with the metallic parts beautifully nickel plated and the frames ebonized and stained in beautiful colors. There are many imitations of these accordions on the market, but for strictly guaranteed instruments of good grade and standard reputation, our prices are far below any competition. We include, free with each instrument, a complete, valuable instruction book, by the aid of which anyone can learn the instrument without a teacher.

No. 12C1001 This is the greatest bargain in our line of accordions. It is 10¼ inches high by 6½ inches wide. The case is made of imitation mahogany, beautifully polished and finished. It has ten nickel keys, two stops and two sets of reeds. It is made with double bellows. It has nickel corners and clasps. Price.......................................**$1.90**
Weight, boxed for shipment, 7 pounds.

No. 12C997 The best double row accordion for the money yet placed on the market. Fancy fluted mouldings, ebonized keyboard, also furnished in imitation ebony. Beautiful green panels ornamented with gold pencil design, double bellows of ten folds, each fold protected by metal corner protectors, nickel clasps and trimmings in three colors, red, black and green. Four sets of reeds, nineteen keys, four stops and four basses. Size, 7¼x12 inches.
Price... ....**$4.25**

No. 12C998 The same accordion as described above, except with 21 keys.
Price..... ....**$4.65**

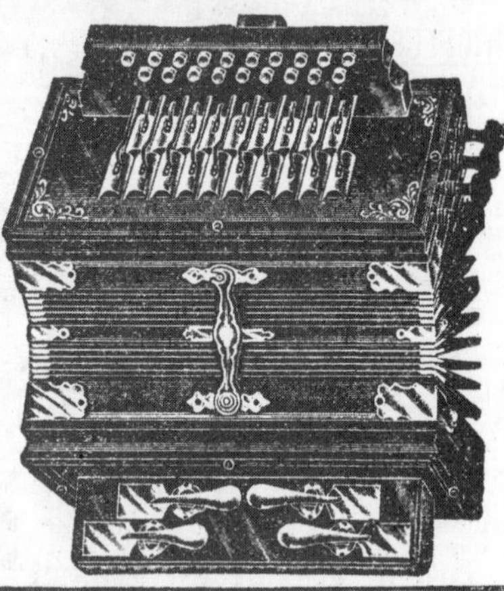

No. 12C1003 Genuine Celebrated Empress Accordion. It is 9 x 10¼ x 5⅝ inches in size. The frame is beautifully made, with highly polished ebonized mouldings with gilt lines; has nickel corners and clasps, ten nickel keys, leather straps, two ebonized stops, powerful double bellows with the center fold protected with nickel corners. Has two sets of extra broad reeds, giving it a specially strong and beautiful quality of tone. Price..............**$2.18**
Weight, boxed for shipment, about 10 pounds.

No. 12C1006 Genuine Celebrated Empress Accordion. To the lovers of this instrument we especially recommend this number as being one of the neatest and most attractive that we have in the catalogue for the price. It is 10¼ inches high and 5½ inches wide. The panels and borders are made of beautifully grained wood with ebonized keyboard and border. It has triple bellows, each bellows being alternately cream and brown color with partitions of bellows of nice marbleized green leather. It has ten keys, three sets of reeds and three stops all highly nickel plated. The bellows are protected by nickel patent corners, and the clasps and corners are also nickel plated. As to the tone of this instrument, it is far superior to many others, even of larger size, on account of the extra broad set of reeds which it contains. This accordion would regularly retail at $8.00.
Our price. (**Wt., boxed for shipment, about 8 lbs.**)....**$2.75**

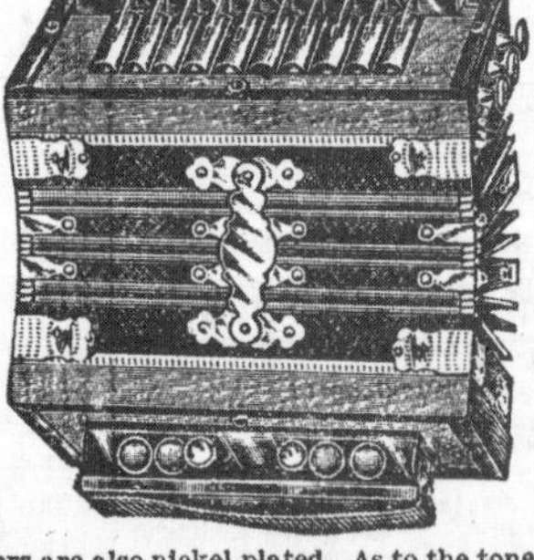

No. 12C1004 We offer this accordion in competition with any instrument you can buy elsewhere at from $6.00 to $8.00. This accordion is 13 inches in height, 6¼ inches in width, has beautiful ebonized case, fancy cut corners handsome gilt ornaments on corners and top. Beautiful gilt beading around same. Has two stops and two sets of reeds. Open action, nickel corners and clasps. Double bellows. Ea. **$2.85**
Weight, boxed, about 12 pounds.

No. 12C1016 This is a genuine Empress Double Row or Two-Key Accordion. It is an instrument of great musical capacity and volume of tone, being 11¼ inches in height and 6¾ inches in width. The case is made of beautiful ebony wood, highly polished and finished. It has eight full double bellows protected by nickel corners and clasps which contrast very nicely with the dark ebony wood of the frame. It has 19 nickel keys, two stops and two sets of extra **broad steel bronze reeds.** A better accordion than this, has never been offered by any house and we are prepared to ship this instrument to you with the understanding and agreement that if you do not find when you receive it that we are saving you at least $4.00 on your purchase and that it is a splendid bargain in every respect, you can return it to us and we will refund your money and pay the express charges both ways. Price.......................**$4.95**

No. 12C1018 Same description as No. 12C1016 but **has twenty-one keys.** Price......................**$5.85**
Weight, boxed for shipment, about 18 pounds.

No. 12C1020 The illustration opposite will give you a good idea of the details of the ornamentations and trimmings of this splendid instrument, but falls far short of giving any idea of the handsome finish and appearance, and the splendid volume of tone which it possesses. It is made of silver gray birdseye maple with ebony moulding. It has a fancy sunken keyboard with open action, fancy ebonized case and pearl buttons. It has an extra wide wood bellows perfectly protected by metal corners handsomely nickel plated, and is fitted with nickel plated clasps which can be closed when not in use. It has 10 keys, 6 stops and 3 sets of reeds. The fact that this accordion is 14½ inches in height and 9½ inches in width will convince you at once of its great musical capacity and splendid tone volume. This is one of the finest accordions in our line and at the price is one of the greatest bargains ever offered in such an instrument. All we ask is for an opportunity to send you this instrument on approval under our terms of shipment and we will take all chances of its proving satisfactory in every respect. Price.............**$5.65**
Weight, boxed for shipment, 18 pounds.

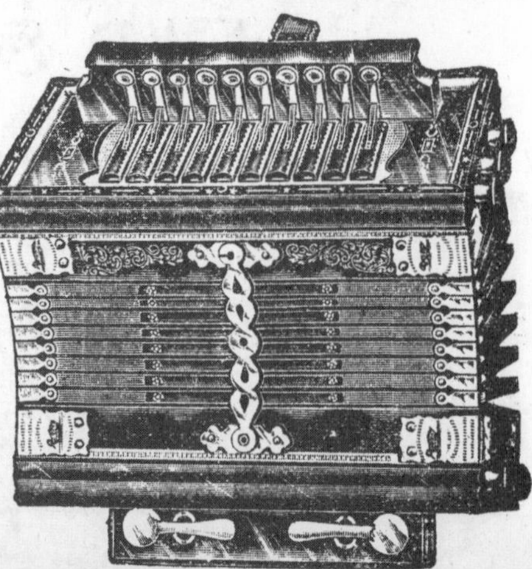

No. 12C1022 The Empress Professional Instrument. This is a large accordion, being 14½ inches high by 9 inches wide, with broad mahogany moulded frame, mahogany panels and keys. The frame and panels are ornamented with handsome gilt and nickel ornaments. Clasps and corners fully nickel plated. Sunken open keyboard, double ribbed bellows, ten keys, eight stops, four sets of reeds, tuned in chords. **Complete instruction book free.** Price.............................**$6.45**

Weight, packed for shipment, 18 pounds.

THE CELEBRATED PITZSCHLER ACCORDIONS.

Pitzschler is recognized as one of the best manufacturers of Accordions in Germany, the home of this instrument. In presenting our line of Pitzschler accordions we have selected five of the very large number of instruments made by this celebrated maker, and by special arrangement and by contracting for a large quantity, we are able to list them at prices representing **the very greatest value ever quoted in instruments of this kind.**

Anyone desiring to purchase an accordion should see and try our Pitzschler's before deciding to purchase elsewhere. Most remarkably superior in richness and purity of tone, ease of action, as well as details of construction.

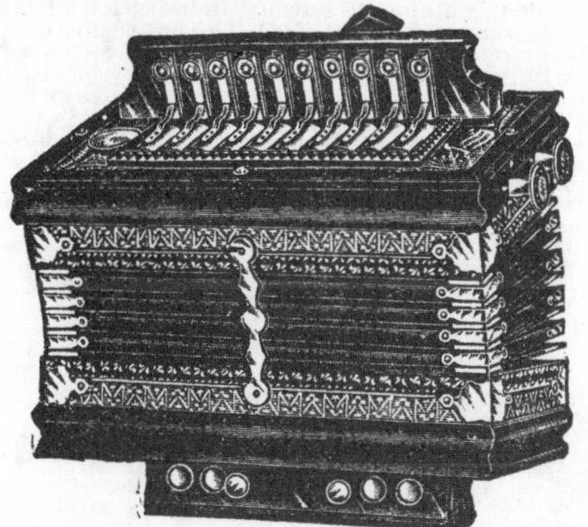

No. 12C1080 This Accordion is 6½x7½x13 inches. Is beautifully made and highly finished; has nine folds in the bellows with nickel corners; two stops and two sets of reeds; open action; two basses. The keys are mounted with mother of pearl buttons, making them easily operated and especially adapted to the touch of the fingers. This instrument is beautifully decorated and a handsomer accordion cannot be found except at a much higher price than we ask. **We include with each accordion a complete instruction book. Every instrument is carefully packed. Shipping weight, 10 pounds.**

No. 12C1080 Price.................................**$3.90**

No. 12C1082 This Accordion measures 7x8½x13½ inches; is of ebony finish, the mouldings highly polished; has 9-fold triple bellows, with metal corners; three sets of reeds and open keyboard; two basses. This is an exceptionally powerful accordion and a great bargain. **We include with each accordion a complete instruction book. Every instrument is carefully packed.**

No. 12C1082 Price.................................**$4.95**

Shipping weight, 10 pounds.

No. 12C1086 This instrument is one of the best of the Pitzschler make. It measures 7¾x7½x13¾ inches. The mouldings are all made in imitation ebony, highly polished and decorated. Has 10-fold, double, very powerful bellows protected with nickel corners; four stops, four sets of reeds and two basses. Sunken keyboard, open action. The keys are fitted with mother of pearl buttons, making the accordion easy to play. The tone of this instrument is especially powerful and of excellent quality. It is in great demand by expert accordion players. **We include with each instrument a complete instruction book. Every instrument is carefully packed.**

No. 12C1086 Price.............................**$6.45**

Shipping weight, 11 pounds.

Wonderful Value.

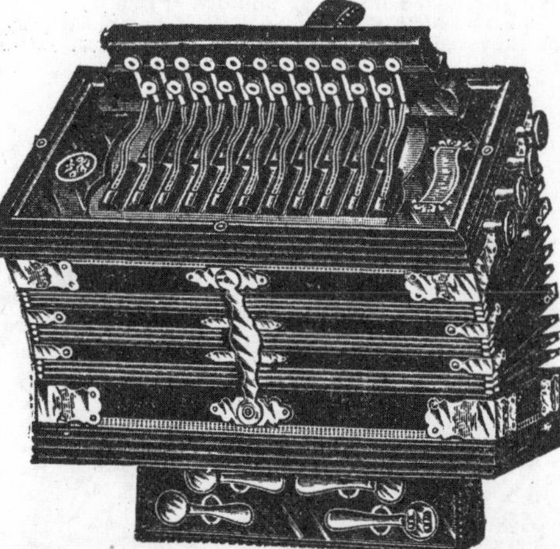

This is the finest Pitzschler Accordion we handle. It has fine fluted mouldings in imitation mahogany; panels genuine mahogany; all wood work finely polished and finished; sunken open action keyboard; double row, nineteen **nickel** keys; heavy double bellows, with **nickel protectors;** nickel plated corners and clasps; **four stops; four fine sets of reeds.** Size, 14 inches by 8 inches. A complete instruction book free.

No. 12C1088 Price.............................**$7.45**

Weight, packed, about 20 pounds.

Genuine Pitzschler Accordion, is just the same in every way as No. 12C1088, described above, but has twenty-one nickel plated keys, as shown in the illustration.

No. 12C1090 Price.............................**$7.95**

Weight, packed, about 20 pounds.

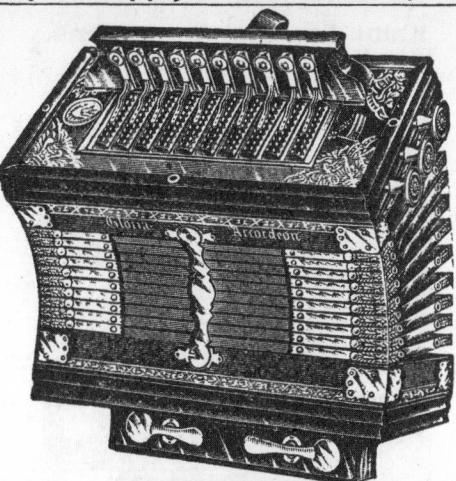

OUR $5.85 ACCORDION.

WONDERFUL VALUE.

No. 12C1084 This Accordion is one of the latest designs; measures 7x9x13½ inches. The mouldings are all finished in imitation ebony, highly polished and beautifully decorated. Has 10-fold extra broad single bellows. The ends of the bellows are entirely covered with nickel and the corners are mounted with beautiful fancy brass caps, making this one of the handsomest accordions ever offered by any music dealer. This instrument has a sunken keyboard, with open action. The keys are all mounted with mother of pearl buttons. This accordion has three sets of reeds, three stops and two basses and produces a beautiful and powerful tone. **We include with each accordion a complete instruction book. Every instrument is carefully packed.**

No. 12C1084 Price.............................**$5.85**

Shipping weight, 11 pounds.

KALBE ACCORDIONS.

The name Imperial, together with the "double anchor" trade mark, on an accordion is a guarantee of its being of the very highest grade. While the price of these goods may be a trifle higher than others, the satisfaction derived from them, on account of the perfect workmanship and wearing qualities, will amply repay for the difference in price, and they will be found much the cheapest in the end. **We guarantee every one to arrive in perfect playing condition.** You cannot make a mistake in buying a Kalbe Imperial, for you get the very best article of the kind that is made. Attention is especially called to the **patent simplex keys,** which are made of heavy metal, in one piece, and are extremely durable. All of the styles of **Imperial Accordions** that we carry are supplied with patent metal bellows corners and patent folding clasps. **Every part of these instruments is of the very best material and workmanship.**

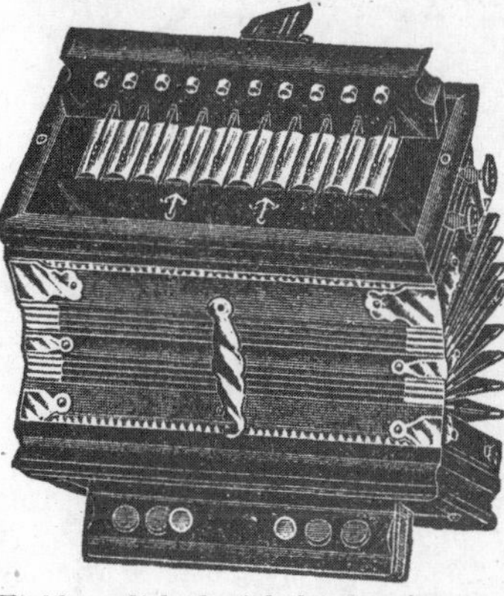

No. 12C1100 This is a splendid Kalbe instrument with an ebonized maple frame very handsomely finished. It is very highly polished and is ornamented with fluted molding. It has a powerful double bellows of nine folds with nickel plated corner protectors. Highly polished nickel trimmings and clasps, two sets of reeds and two stops. This accordion is fitted with a tremolo or vox humana attachment, which gives the tone a wavy and undulating effect in imitation of the human voice. This tremolo can be thrown in and out of action at the will of the player by means of a lever, operated by the thumb of the right hand. The instrument is splendidly fitted throughout and will be sure to satisfy all players upon the accordion. Price.....................**$3.25**

Weight, boxed for shipment, about 10 pounds.

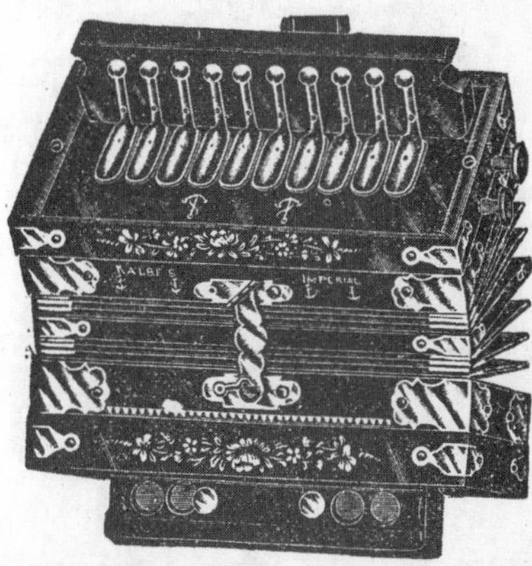

No. 12C1104 Kalbe's Imperial Miniature. Beautifully polished ebonized frame, open action, patent simplex keys, which are very durable; double bellows, with hand painted artistic design on bellows frame, patent nickel plated corners on bellows, thus proecting the weakest part of the accordion. Ten keys, two stops, two sets of reeds, and patent clasps. The size of this accordion is 10¼ inches high by 6¼ inches wide. Price.....................**$3.45**

Weight, boxed, about 10 pounds.

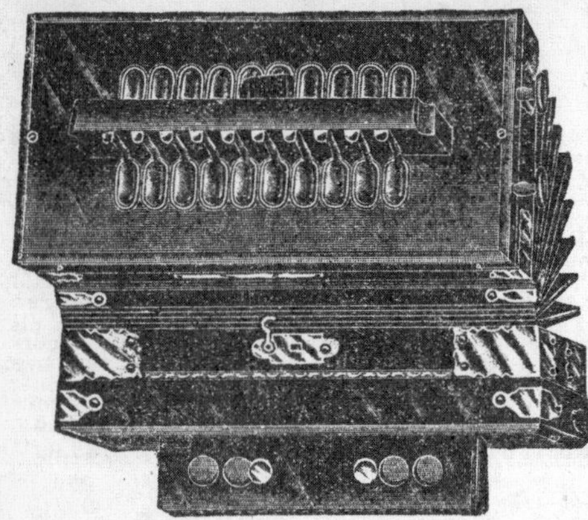

No. 12C1108 This is a Handsome Accordion with double action. This double action allows two valves to be opened by pressing one key, and this increases the volume and variety of tone. This is a special feature of this accordion and one which we recommend to all who desire an instrument of great musical capacity. The case has nickel strips around the top and bottom and large double bellows of eight folds with corner protectors. It has nickel trimmings throughout and is a splendid instrument in every respect. It is an accordion of great volume and sweetness of tone, and we recommend it to all who desire a good instrument at a moderate price. It has two sets of reeds and two stops, by the use of which a large number of tone combinations are possible. Price.......................................$3.95

Weight, boxed for shipment, 10 pounds.

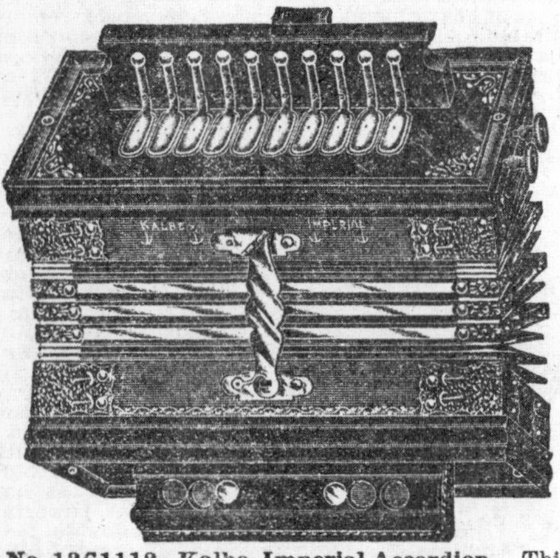

No. 12C1112 Kalbe Imperial Accordion. This is an instrument of great sweetness and volume of tone, very rich in appearance with highly polished ebonized case. The corners are protected by fancy ornamental nickel bands and the corners of the bellows panels are protected in the same way. It is handsomely ornamented and decorated throughout, has triple bellows of eight folds. The bellows folds are ornamented in gold trimming and the entire instrument is one of the handsomest on the market. It has two sets of reeds and two stops and fitted on each side with patent clasps to keep the instrument closed when not in use. Size of instrument, 6¼ inches deep and 12¼ inches wide. Price................$4.45

Weight, boxed for shipment, about 10 pounds.

No. 12C1116 Kalbe Imperial Accordion. Very fine ebonized case, highly polished, beautiful nickel plated strips around the panels. Has double bellows of ten folds, giving great volume of tone to the instrument. Has broad nickel plated corner protectors and is a handsome instrument in every respect. Three sets of reeds and three stops. This is an instrument which the purchaser will be proud to own and pleased to show to his friends. It is 6½ inches deep and 11¾ inches wide. Price...............$5.15

Weight, boxed for shipment, about 12 pounds.

Kalbe Imperial Accordions.

No. 12C1120 Kalbe Imperial. This is a splendid instrument in every respect and has a very nicely finished ebonized case; has broad nickel plated corner protectors, a handsome clasp on each side to keep it closed when not in use. Has powerful double bellows of ten folds, four sets of reeds and four stops. Is very highly ornamented throughout and we guarantee it to give satisfaction. Size, 6½ inches deep by 11¾ inches wide. Price.......................$6.55

Weight, boxed for shipment, about 12 pounds.

No. 12C1124 Kalbe's Imperial, Professional. Double row, nineteen keys, four sets of reeds tuned in octaves, thereby giving volume and strength to the tone. The cases of these accordions are very substantially made of black polished wood, open action, large nickel corners and patent clasps, substantial double bellows which are protected by patent nickel plated metal corners. These accordions are made for service and have the very best quality of tone that can be produced on any instrument of this kind. A very nice and handy size, being 11 inches high and 6¾ inches wide. **Weight, boxed, about 12 pounds.** Price......$6.95

No. 12C1128 Same as No. 12C1124, but has twenty-one keys. Price.......................................$7.45

Weight, boxed, about 15 pounds.

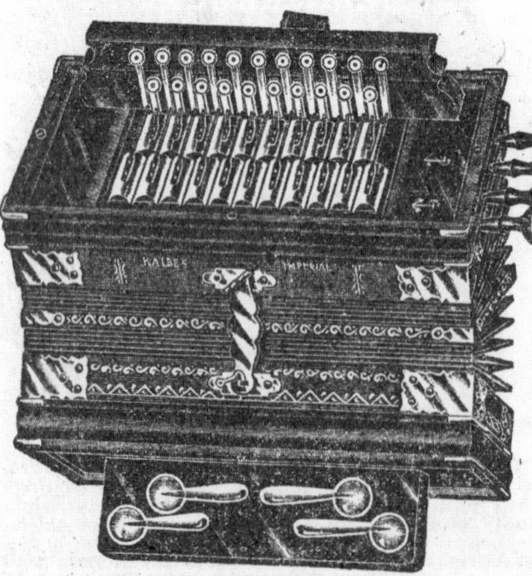

No. 12C1132 Kalbe's Imperial. Beautifully finished ebonized case, with sunken keyboard and fine nickel plated trimmings around the panels. Open action, double bellows of ten folds, nickel corner protectors and mother of pearl finger buttons, four stops and two sets of reeds. Four basses, 8 inches deep, 14¾ inches wide. This is a splendid instrument in every respect and is one of the best that we handle. Price.......................................$11.65

Weight, boxed, about 20 pounds.

Kalbe Italo-Bohemian Accordions.

THE DEMAND for Italian-Bohemian system accordions having increased very rapidly of late, we have added one of these well known accordions to our line. After careful investigation and comparison we selected the celebrated Kalbe instrument as the one to meet all requirements on account of its superior tone quality and perfect workmanship. Like all other Kalbe accordions, it speaks for itself. **Compare this accordion with other instruments of same style and ours will be found far superior in every way.**

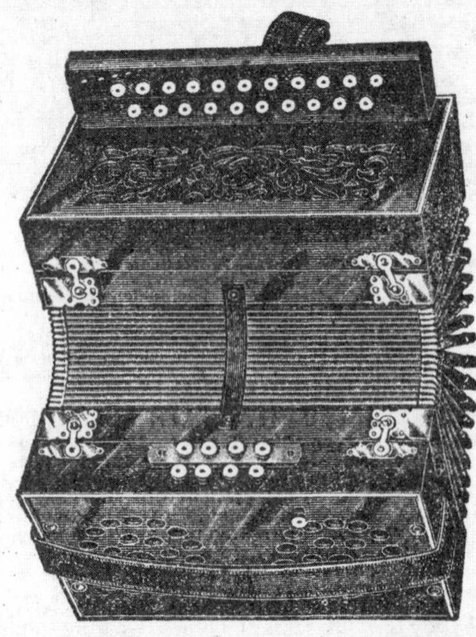

No. 12C1136 Genuine Kalbe Italian-Bohemian Accordion. It is made of a thoroughly seasoned spruce, a wood which is best known for its sonority, veneered in walnut and finished in imitation of mahogany, very highly polished. The panels are made of fancy open work of beautiful design with green cloth lining, giving the accordion a very beautiful and rich appearance. The keyboard is invisible. The keys are made of pearl, shaped like a button, making them agreeable to the touch. It has a single bellows of 16 folds, leather bound and with patent metal corner protectors. It has 21 keys, 8 basses and all trimmings are nickel plated and very highly polished. This accordion is 11½x9½x6½ inches. Weight, when packed for shipment, about 15 pounds. This celebrated accordion, for which a retail dealer would charge you $15.00, we sell for..................$9.49

BLOW ACCORDIONS.

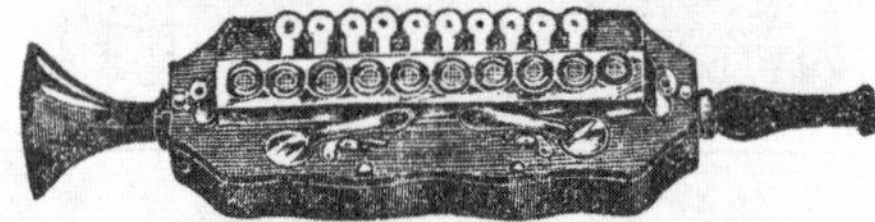

Flute Accordion. Substantially made, with 10 bone keys, 2 basses and excellent reeds. Wood case, with projecting bell. **Weight, 20 ounces.**

No. 12C2958 Price..........................70c

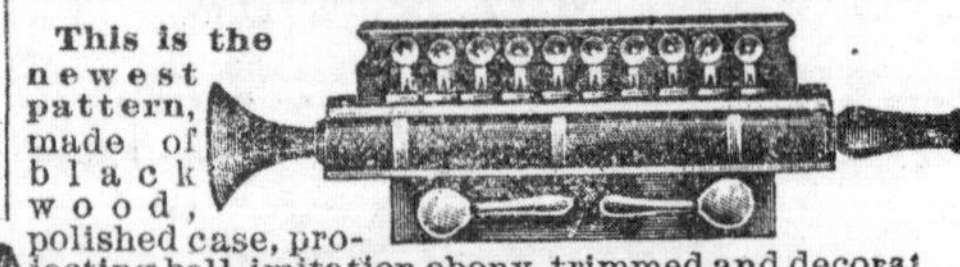

This is the newest pattern, made of black wood, polished case, projecting bell, imitation ebony, trimmed and decorated with white celluloid. Has ten keys, the same style action as our most expensive accordions and has two basses. **Weight, 24 ounces.**

No. 12C2960 Price..........................85c

The Clariophone.

A handsome little musical instrument that possesses all the necessary qualities for pleasing the ear with melodious sounds. Wood body, with fancy metal ornaments; **10 keys, 2 basses and excellent reeds.**

No. 12C2962 Price..........................90c

Weight, about 28 ounces.

Our Finest Blow Accordion; none better made; in fact this instrument is of far better quality than blow accordions usually found in retail stores. The case is made of imitation ebony, highly polished and beautifully nickel trimmed. Has projecting bell. The action is the same as used on high grade accordions, the entire key being in one piece. **Has ten keys and two basses. Weight, 30 ounces.**

No. 12C2964 Price..........................$1.05

Excelsior Harmonica Holder.

No. 12C2956 Simplicity of construction, easy and quick to adjust, durable. No hooks to tear one's clothes, no rubber to lose its elasticity, but two springs which instantly adjust themselves to any sized harmonica, thus firmly securing the same, so that the performer is at liberty to use any other instrument to accompany the harmonica at the same time. When not in use, it may be folded to a small compass. Price......................... ...30c
If by mail, postage extra, 5 cents.

HARMONICAS.

No. 12C2878 Genuine Bohm Harmonica, has ten single holes and twenty best quality brass reeds. Brass plates, nickel covers. Price...9c
If by mail, postage extra, 4 cents.

No. 12C2944 This is the David's Harp Harmonica, made by Chas. Messner & Co., and is one of our finest instruments. It has a wood frame, finished in rich red color, and the reeds are riveted solidly to heavy brass plates. It has highly nickel plated covers, beautifully polished. It is fitted with 20 holes, 20 extra broad musical reeds in perfect tune. The fancy cover is in the shape of a trumpet and so increases the tone of this instrument as to add to the brass band effect, so much desired in a harmonica. By using the hand at the bell of this trumpet the same effect can be obtained as when using a glass. On account of the shape of the harmonica the player is enabled to perform very easily, as no breath is lost through the corners of the mouth. We recommend this instrument to all who desire a complete harmonica at a very small price. Furnished in seven different keys, as follows: A, B, C, D, E, F and G.
Price...**(If by mail, postage extra, 6 cents)**...22c

No. 12C2945 This is our Empress Swan Brand Harmonica, and like the balance of our line is a fine instrument, in every respect. It is thoroughly and durably made and handsomely finished. The reeds are riveted to brass plates. It has a fancy nickel plated cover, 10 holes and 20 strong bell metal reeds in perfect tune. We ship it out in a fine telescope pasteboard case and can furnish it in seven keys, as follows: A, B, C, D, E, F and G. It is 4 inches long and 1 inch wide. In ordering harmonicas always state the key desired. Price..........12c
If by mail, postage extra, 6 cents.

No. 12C2946 This is our Empress Harp Harmonica, and is a splendid concert instrument. It has 20 holes, 40 splendidly tuned and harmonized bell metal reeds, securely riveted to brass plates. It has brass covers beautifully nickel plated and red wood frame highly polished and finished. It is a very strongly and substantially made instrument and can be furnished in seven keys, as follows: A, B, C, D, E, F and G. It goes complete in a fine pasteboard telescope case and is an instrument with which harmonica players will be more than pleased.
Price..**(If by mail, postage extra, 7 cents)**.....24c

BRASS BAND BELL HARMONICA.

No. 12C2902 The Brass Band Bell Harmonica is made by a celebrated European maker of harmonicas and is a splendidly finished and beautiful toned instrument. It is fitted with tuned bells, which can be used with wonderful effect in connection with the instrument. That it is a favorite with all harmonica players is fully proved by the enormous number which we sell. It has ten double holes, forty finely toned reeds, accurately tuned and mounted on heavy brass reed plates. The bells are of the very best quality, made of the very best bell metal and highly polished. The tone of the instrument is very powerful and possesses that broad volume so much desired in a harmonica. We recommend this instrument on account of the beautiful effect which can be produced by combining the bells with the reeds. The instrument is handsomely finished and substantially made throughout and never fails to please the purchaser. We hope you will give us an opportunity to send you one of these beautiful instruments, as we know you will admit that they are wonderful bargains.

No. 12C2902 Price...........................(If by mail, postage extra, 8 cents)...........................60c
No. 12C2903 Same as No. 12C2902, but has 1 bell, 10 holes and 20 reeds Price....(If by mail, postage extra, 8 cents)..30c

Universal Favorite Harmonica.

No. 12C2922 Universal Favorite Harmonica, made by And. Koch, whose name is a guarantee for quality. This harmonica has ten single holes, twenty bell metal reeds accurately tuned, fine tone, heavy brass reed plates, handsome nickel covers. Packed in pasteboard box with hinge cover, as illustrated. Wonderful value. Price.... ....15c
If by mail, postage extra, 6 cents.

Tremolo Concert Harmonica.

No. 12C2942 Tremolo Concert Harmonicas are made by And. Koch, sixteen double holes, 7¼ inches in length, 2 inches wide, two reeds to each hole, sixty-four reeds in all. Brass reed plates and nickel plated covers. Price.............................50c
If by mail, postage extra, 6 cents.

No. 12C2943 Same as No. 12C2942, except larger, has twenty double holes, eighty reeds in all. Price 65c
If by mail, postage extra, 7 cents.

No. 12C2948 This is our Finest Swan Brand Empress Harmonica, and is a beautiful instrument in every respect. The engraving shows it complete with case. It has 32 holes, 32 resonant and strong reeds of bell metal and heavy brass plates. It has brass covers highly nickel plated and polished. Black frame very rich. Size, 4¾ inches long by 1 inch wide. We send this instrument complete in a very fine leatherette covered pasteboard case, and we know harmonica players will be pleased with it because it is splendidly made and elegantly finished at all points. It is made of convenient size to carry in the pocket and we recommend it to all who desire a fine harmonica at a low price. We furnish this instrument in seven keys, as follows: A, B, C, D, E, F and G.
Price, complete with case........**(If by mail, postage extra, 7 cents)**.......................26c

No. 12C2947 This is an illustration of our World's Ruler Swan Brand Harmonica, and the illustration shows an entirely new model. The instrument is fitted with 12 trumpets which carry the tone from the reeds and increase them wonderfully in volume. The instrument has a black frame highly polished. The reeds are riveted solidly to brass plates and it has nickel plated covers of very fancy artistic design. It is fitted with ten holes, 20 bell metal extra sonorous reeds and goes to the customer complete in a fancy hinged cover box. It is 4½ inches long and 1½ inches wide at the top. Price....................21c
If by mail, postage extra, 6 cents.

No. 12C2890 Sousa's Band is 4 inches long, 1 inch wide; has ten holes and twenty brass reeds; heavy brass reed plates; handsome nickel covers.
Price..**(If by mail, postage extra, 6 cents)**....18c

No. 12C2916 Bohm's Jubilee Harmonica has ten single holes, twenty brass reeds, mounted on heavy brass reed plates, nickel covers. Made in imitation of organ pipes, producing an exceptionally nice quality of tone. Price. 14c
If by mail, postage extra, 5 cents.

No. 12C2918 Bohm's Sovereign Harmonica. A rare bargain in harmonicas. This harmonica is 5¼ inches long and 1¼ inches wide; has sixteen double holes and thirty-two steel bronze reeds, heavy metal reed plates and beautiful fancy nickel covers.
Price...**(If by mail, postage extra, 8 cents)**...16c

No. 12C2919 Youth's Companion. This is one of the latest ideas in harmonicas. Instead of the ordinary nickel cover the harp is made in the shape of a horn which enables the player to get the various effects which are ordinarily produced by using a tumbler. This harp has ten double holes, twenty accurately tuned brass reeds and heavy brass reed plates. It is very easy blowing and has a splendid quality of tone. Price......(Postage extra, 7 cents)......30c

The Bugle Call Harmonica.

No. 12C2935 Bugle Call. This is one of the very latest of the celebrated And. Koch's harmonicas. It is 7¾ inches long, has 24 double holes, 48 bell metal reeds, extra heavy reed plates, heavy nickel plated covers with flaring edges. By a special construction the tone of this harmonica is made to vibrate, giving it an exceptionally beautiful quality. This harmonica like all other instruments of this maker, is fully guaranteed. **Packed in handsome leatherette case, satin and velvet lined with nickel clasps.** Price...58c
If by mail, postage extra, 8 cents.

No. 12C2921 Concert Harmonica, made by And. Koch, whose name is a guarantee for quality. This harmonica has ten double holes, forty bell metal reeds, accurately tuned. Heavy brass reed plates, brass nickel plated covers. Exceptionally sweet and powerful tone. Price..................................25c
If by mail, postage extra, 7 cents

THE CELEBRATED CH. WEISS HARMONICAS.

THE HARMONICAS illustrated and described on this page are all made by Ch. Weiss, one of the most widely known makers of STRICTLY HIGH GRADE HARMONICAS.

HIS INSTRUMENTS ARE USED BY THE VERY BEST PLAYERS THROUGHOUT THE WORLD and are especially recognized for beautiful quality of tone.

THEY ARE VERY EASY BLOWING, ACCURATELY TUNED AND EXCEPTIONALLY POWERFUL IN TONE. EVERY HARMONICA IS FULLY GUARANTEED.

No. 12C2876 This illustration shows one of the brass Solo Professional Harmonicas, Band Concert Size. This instrument, like all of our harmonicas, is of very high grade and made by Ch. Weiss of Germany, one of the most celebrated harmonica makers of Europe. It is made especially for us, and is a splendid instrument in every respect. It has 20 holes, 40 reeds set on brass plates, nickel covers lapping at the ends and is highly polished and finished throughout. It comes complete in a very attractive pasteboard case and is a handy size to carry in the pocket. It is 4⅜ inches long by 1¼ inches wide. We sell this harmonica in seven keys, as follows: A, B, C, D, E, F and G. Price........(If by mail, postage extra, 8 cents)..........**45c**

No. 12C2874 This illustration gives you a fair idea of the style of the Brass Band Solo Harmonica. Like all of our other harmonicas this instrument is splendidly made and handsomely finished. The reeds are solidly fastened to brass plates and the instrument has nickel plated covers lapping over at the sides. It has 10 single holes, 20 reeds, and goes to the customer complete in a neat pasteboard case. It is 4⅛ inches long and 1 inch wide. We sell this instrument in seven different keys, as follows: A, B, C, D, E, F and G. Price..................(If by mail, postage extra, 6 cents). **19c**

No. 12C2886 Triumph Concert Harmonica. A double instrument of powerful and pleasing tone. Has ten double holes on each edge, twenty double holes in all; eighty fine bell metal reeds, brass reed plates, nickel covers.
Price......................**65c**
If by mail, postage extra, 8 cents.

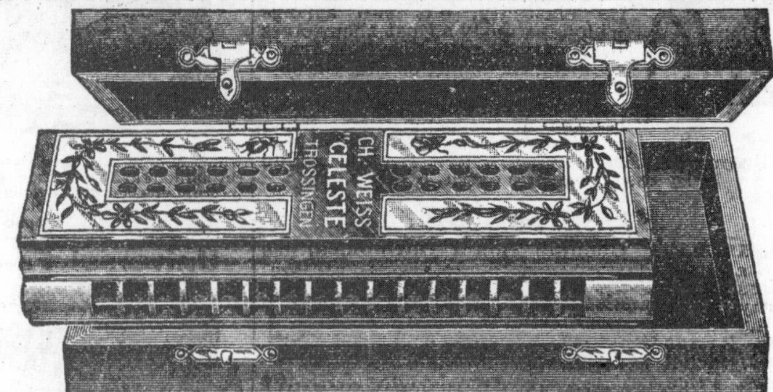

No. 12C2931 **Our Celeste Harmonica. This harmonica is made expressly for us by the celebrated maker, Ch. Weiss.** It is made of the very finest material, and is intended for those who desire an instrument of great musical capacity and splendid volume of tone. It has heavy nickel covers decorated with hand painted flowers. The panels are gold finished and give a rich appearance to the instrument. It has a wood frame, highly enameled in beautiful imitation of ivory. It is double sided, fitted with sixteen double holes, thirty-two reeds on each side, making sixty-four reeds in all. We can furnish it in all the different keys and it comes in a splendid leatherette covered, richly embossed case. This is a new instrument and one which we are prepared to recommend to all who desire something particularly fine in this line. The price which we quote on this harmonica represents simply what the harmonica costs us, with but our one small percentage of profit added, and is figured down so low that you cannot purchase a harmonica of this grade from any other dealer for less than twice the price we are making you. **The name of Ch. Weiss on the instrument is a sufficient guarantee of excellence,** and harmonica players, who purchase one of these splendid instruments, are sure to be perfectly satisfied with the service they obtain.

No. 12C2931 Price............(If by mail, postage extra, 15 cents)..............**95c**
No. 12C2932 We can furnish this instrument with eighty reeds if desired, at the following price. Price................(If by mail, postage extra, 15 cents)................**$1.15**

No. 12C2907 Brass Band Harmonica. The king of all harmonicas. The finest instrument of its kind in the world. Made by Ch. Weiss, the celebrated manufacturer. For purity and volume of tone **this harmonica has no equal. The reeds** are made of the finest bell metal and are extremely sensitive, producing a remarkably smooth tone. **The covers are flaring at the back and are made of solid brass,** heavily nickel plated and are consequently of unusual strength, thus protecting the reeds perfectly. Accurately tuned to concert pitch. **The Brass Band Harmonica** has ten double holes, forty bell metal reeds, brass reed plates and extension ends. It is in high favor with professional and amateur alike. We include a **handsomely wood lined case,** as shown in the illustration. Retails for $1.00 and is worth every cent of it. Price.......**65c**
If by mail, postage extra, 8 cents.

No. 12C2914 Same Harmonica as No. 12C2907, but has ten holes and twenty reeds, and comes packed in neat pasteboard case. Price.**19c**
If by mail, postage extra, 6 cents.

No. 12C2927 The Clarion Brass Band Harmonica, manufactured by Ch. Weiss, the celebrated manufacturer of the Brass Band Harmonica. **The wonder harmonica of the age. A new invention in harmonicas.** The brass reed plates and bell metal reeds are the same as those used in the **Celebrated Brass Band Harmonica, which has gained such a world wide reputation.** The new idea or invention is in the organ pipes, which are placed over the reeds. By means of these pipes, the performer is enabled to change the tone at will, giving imitations of the flute, church organ or trumpet calls. Its construction makes it the most powerful toned harmonica as well as the easiest blowing and most attractive that has ever been placed on the market. **Pronounced as such by professionals throughout the country.** Concert or large size harmonica has ten double holes and forty reeds. **PACKED IN HANDSOME HEAVY RED LEATHERETTE CASE HAVING SUBSTANTIAL HINGE AND NICKEL PLATED FASTENER.** Price......(If by mail, postage extra, 8 cents)...... **50c**

No. 12C2928 Clarion Brass Band Harmonica, has ten single holes and twenty reeds; packed in handsome red leatherette case. Price............**23c**
If by mail, postage extra, 6 cents.

No. 12C2926 Angel's Clarion. Manufactured by Ch. Weiss, maker of the celebrated Brass Band Harmonica. This harp resembles the brass band clarion in some respects, but is so constructed as to produce a peculiar, vibrating, organ-like tone not found in any other harmonica. It has twenty double holes, with forty brass reeds and mounted on heavy brass reed plates. Has the clarion pipe and nickel covers. Packed in neat case. Every harmonica player should own one of these harps. Price..............(If by mail, postage extra, 8 cents)... ....**60c**

THE WEISS ORGAN CONCERT HARMONICA.

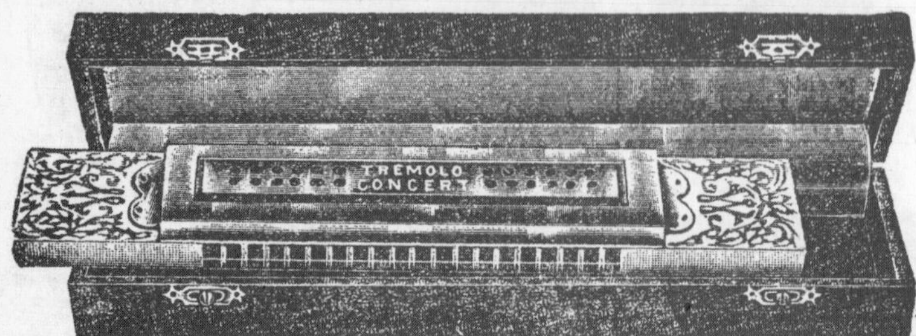

No. 12C2933 This harmonica is one of the largest, handsomest and finest toned instruments made. Coming as it does from Europe, direct from the factory of the celebrated maker, Ch. Weiss, is a guarantee as to its quality. The illustration gives but a faint idea of what an exceptionally fine harmonica it really is. The wood frame is 9¼ inches long, white enameled with gilt decorations. Has brass reed plates, highly polished nickel covers, **forty holes** on each edge, eighty best bell metal reeds accurately tuned to concert pitch, each side in a different key. The tone is deep and powerful, **with** tremolo effect, which makes it sound like a church organ. As illustrated, it is packed in a handsome wood case with leatherette covering, satin lining and nickel clasps. Price.. (**If by mail, postage extra, 14 cents**).....**90c**

No. 12C2934 This is the very latest harmonica produced by the celebrated maker, Ch. Weiss. It is made with 24 double holes on each side, 48 double holes in all, and 96 reeds, 4 heavy brass reed plates, fancy nickel plated covers. This harp is specially constructed for the vibrato tone which makes it very much finer in quality than most other harmonicas. No player should be without one. **The two sides are tuned in different keys as follows: A and E. Like all other Weiss harmonicas it is fully guaranteed.** This harmonica comes in leatherette case, handsomely lined and nickel clasp. Price...**$1.15**
If by mail, postage extra, 15 cents.

OUR BAND INSTRUMENT DEPARTMENT.

THREE SPLENDID LINES OF BRASS INSTRUMENTS FOR WHICH WE ARE SOLE AGENTS FOR THE UNITED STATES. SOLD BY OUR DIRECT FROM MANUFACTURER TO CUSTOMER PLAN, WHICH GUARANTEES AN IMMENSE SAVING TO THE PURCHASER.

EVERY INSTRUMENT WARRANTED AND SATISFACTION GUARANTEED.

WE DESIRE TO IMPRESS THE BANDMEN of this country with the fact that we are in a position to sell them all classes of band instruments equal, and, in most cases, superior in grade to the instruments generally handled by dealers throughout the country. Also that we are prepared to sell these instruments at an extremely small margin of profit, guaranteeing to the purchaser a saving of at least 30 per cent. There is no class of goods so susceptible of false valuation as musical instruments. The ordinary performer seldom possesses the technical knowledge necessary to discriminate between a good instrument and a poor one upon first trial, and the beginner is absolutely at the mercy of the dealer. It is necessary for him to take the dealer's word for the merits of the instrument, and in numerous cases he is obliged to pay two or three prices for the instrument he buys. Every one of our instruments is thoroughly examined by our buyer, who is an expert in this line, who fixes their true values before we purchase them. To this value we add our one small margin of profit, thus enabling the purchaser to buy the instruments at the manufacturers' prices with only our one small margin of profit added. Other large dealers and manufacturers find it necessary to fix very high prices upon their band instruments in order to take care of the large discounts which they make, to take old instruments in exchange, to sell upon the installment plan, and to protect their dealers in such prices as they may desire to make. We do not find it necessary to do this because we ship our goods directly to our customers, and are therefore enabled to sell these instruments at the same small profit which we make on our groceries, dry goods, etc. This explains fully how we are able to make such extremely low prices on these fine instruments, and will show the customer at once that our low prices do not mean a lack of quality in the instruments themselves.

UP TO WITHIN A RECENT PERIOD the entire trade in band instruments and supplies has been in the hands of a few firms who have found it expedient to establish and maintain high prices on account of their expensive methods of handling the goods. This method is to pass the goods from the manufacturer to the wholesaler, from the wholesaler to the retailer and finally from the retailer to the customer. Under this method it naturally follows that every dealer through whose hands the goods pass must make his profit and this profit must be included in the price which the purchaser eventually has to pay. The final result of this system is, that the price paid by the customer is generally double the original cost of manufacturing. It is thus apparent, at a glance that the cost of the goods to the purchaser, does not depend upon the cost of making them, but depends almost entirely upon the expense incurred in getting them from the factory through the hands of the different dealers to the customer. We have changed all this and are able to make extremely low prices for the following reasons:

1ST. We are in a position to buy these goods in such large quantities that we are enabled to make the most advantageous contracts with the manufacturers, thus procuring the goods at almost factory cost, and as we only add our one small margin of profit to these prices, the great saving is evident at a glance.

2ND. We ship these goods directly from our house to the purchaser and thus avoid all intermediate dealers' profits which, by the old method, made high prices necessary We are thus enabled to reduce prices to a point which was formerly thought impossible.

3RD. We do not pay anybody a commission in any form whatever on the sale of our goods, and, as agents' commissions are always added to the price of the goods sold by other dealers, our customers can see that we are saving considerable for them in this way.

4TH. We never take any second-hand instruments in exchange as part payment for new ones. Dealers who handle second-hand instruments in this way must either add the amount of the allowance which they make, to the price of the new set of instruments, or have the price already high enough to cover the possible losses in that direction. By refusing to take second-hand instruments in exchange as part payment on new ones we save our customers the amount of the allowance which other dealers would make them upon their old instruments.

5TH. We do not allow any discounts from our catalogue prices. The mere fact that a dealer can afford to allow a discount from his prices proves conclusively that his prices are higher than they ought to be. And again, if he allows you, for instance, 25 per cent discount, how much does he allow your neighbor? Are you ever quite sure that you have the very lowest prices that he can make? Did you ever think of it in that way? In buying goods from us you know that you are getting the very lowest prices, and you are absolutely sure that no one else can buy the same goods from us any cheaper.

IT HAS BEEN OUR POLICY in the past to offer our customers only goods which we can recommend and fully guarantee at all times, and this policy has been strictly adhered to in selecting the goods listed in this catalogue. Everything shown herein is fully guaranteed, and our brass instruments are all accompanied by our regular binding guarantee for one year.

WE ARE OFFERING YOU in the following pages three magnificent lines of brass instruments, and in offering these lines we have a distinct object in view. We desire to furnish instruments which will be suitable for three classes of musicians, namely—beginners, amateurs and professionals. The first line that we illustrate, made by Marceau & Co., of Paris, is exactly suited for bands, who do not wish to invest a large sum of money until they are certain that they can learn to play acceptably. These instruments are extremely low in price and are of exceptionally good quality. A comparison of our instruments and prices through our entire line will prove that we can save bands a large amount of money if they will purchase their instruments from us.

OUR DUPONT PROFESSIONAL LINE is considerably higher in grade and we offer them to advanced amateur and local concert bands. We have handled this line with great success for some years and have sold a large number of sets in this country. They have never yet failed to give satisfaction, and we recommend them for the use of amateur bands who desire to do fine concert work.

WE OFFER THE PEERLESS LINE, TOURVILLE & CO. BAND INSTRUMENTS made by Tourville & Company, of Paris, for professionals and the higher class of amateur concert bands. We are willing to place this line in competition with any line of brass instruments on the market. In beauty of appearance and grandeur of tone they are unexcelled by any band instruments now being offered to the public. Bandmen all over the country are taking advantage of the extremely low prices which we make on these instruments and the enthusiastic praise which they have everywhere received proves to us that they are destined to become as famous in this country as they are in Europe. All of our brass instruments are fitted with French light action silver piston valves and are shipped to the customer complete with mouthpiece, music rack and instruction book. They are all short concert model and fully guaranteed by us.

C. O. D. OFFER.

IN THE FIRST PLACE we guarantee every instrument to be perfectly satisfactory, and in order that the customer may satisfy himself fully before investing his money, we send every instrument, where desired, by express C.O.D., subject to examination. We always require a deposit of $1.00 in such cases as an evidence of good faith on the part of the purchaser. The instrument can be thoroughly tested at the express office, and if found satisfactory the customer can pay the balance of the price and take it to his home for further trial. Should the instrument not be found satisfactory at the express office, it can be returned to us, we will refund the $1.00 deposited and pay the express charges both ways.

OUR TEN DAYS' TRIAL OFFER.

AFTER THE CUSTOMER HAS ACCEPTED the instrument at the express office, and taken it to his home, we allow him to try it for ten days, and if at any time within that period it should prove unsatisfactory, it can be returned to us and we will refund the full price paid and pay express charges both ways. This fully protects the customer against any possible loss, and we make him the sole judge of the merits of the instruments. We ship all our band instruments and musical goods upon these terms, as we desire our customers to be perfectly satisfied before finally accepting their purchases.

WE PROTECT OUR CUSTOMERS AGAINST LOSS.

OUR CUSTOMERS will see by the above terms that we are prepared to protect them in every way against all possible loss. We desire an opportunity to demonstrate what we can do for them in the line of high grade band instruments, and we will be glad to correspond at any time with any band desiring to purchase a new set of instruments. You do not take any chances whatever in ordering from us. we take all of the risks of shipment and stand ready at all times to refund money for goods that do not prove satisfactory.

OUR SPECIAL BAND CATALOGUE.

We especially recommend that you select your band instruments from this big catalogue rather than to cause a delay by first writing for our free Special Band Catalogue, since we fully illustrate all of the principal instruments, and guarantee that any you may select from this catalogue will be in every way satisfactory. We also guarantee that you will find these instruments very much better than other instruments you can buy elsewhere at anything like the prices we offer, and that you will make a large saving in the cost to you. If you do not find this to be true, you are at liberty to return the instruments to us at any time within ten days, we will refund the price paid and pay the transportation charges both ways. If, however, you find yourself unable to make a selection from the illustrations and descriptions shown in this catalogue, and you feel that you would like to have a larger variety to select from with larger illustrations and more complete descriptions, then do not think of purchasing the instruments elsewhere until you first get our free Special Band Catalogue. This catalogue will be sent to you upon receipt of a postal card with request for it, and it will only be necessary for you to say, "Please send me your Band Catalogue."

BAND ESTIMATES.

WE ARE GIVING herewith estimates upon different sets of band instruments which we consider the very best combinations for bands of different sizes. All instruments upon which we have quoted prices are brass, highly polished. Should you desire instruments nickeled or silver plated, we will refer you to our Special Band Instrument Catalogue, or to the prices quoted on them in this catalogue.

BAND OF 8	Marceau.	Dupont.	Imperial.
2 B Flat Cornets	$11.90	$18.90	$31.90
2 E Flat Altos	19.70	26.70	33.70
1 B Flat Baritone	12.45	17.95	22.45
1 E Flat Bass	19.45	26.15	30.25
1 Bass Drum No. 12C3502	7.45	7.45	7.45
1 Snare Drum No. 12C3472	4.85	4.85	4.85
	$75.80	$102.00	$130.60

BAND OF 10	Marceau.	Dupont.	Imperial.
2 B Flat Cornets	$11.90	$18.90	$31.90
2 E Flat Altos	19.70	26.70	33.70
2 B Flat Tenors	21.90	29.70	38.50
1 B Flat Baritone	12.45	17.95	22.45
1 E Flat Bass	19.45	26.15	30.25
1 Bass Drum No. 12C3502	7.45	7.45	7.45
1 Snare Drum No. 12C3472	4.85	4.85	4.85
	$97.70	$131.70	$169.10

BAND OF 12	Marceau.	Dupont.	Imperial.
1 E Flat Cornet	$ 5.85	$8.25	$13.85
2 B Flat Cornets	11.90	18.90	31.90
2 E Flat Altos	19.70	26.70	33.70
2 B Flat Tenors	21.90	29.70	38.50
1 Tenor Slide Trombone	6.95	9.35	14.45
1 B Flat Baritone	12.45	17.95	22.45
1 E Flat Bass	19.45	26.15	30.25
1 Bass Drum No. 12C3502	7.45	7.45	7.45
1 Snare Drum No. 12C3472	4.85	4.85	4.85
	$109.50	$149.30	$197.40

BAND OF 14	Marceau.	Dupont.	Imperial.
1 E Flat Cornet	$ 5.85	$ 8.25	$13.85
2 B Flat Cornets	11.90	18.90	31.90
2 E Flat Altos	19.70	26.70	33.70
2 B Flat Tenors	21.90	29.70	38.50
2 Tenor Slide Trombones	13.90	18.70	28.90
1 B Flat Baritone	12.45	17.95	22.45
1 B Flat Bass	13.95	20.55	24.95
1 E Flat Bass	19.45	26.15	30.25
1 Bass Drum No. 12C3502	7.45	7.45	7.45
1 Snare Drum No. 12C3472	4.85	4.85	4.85
	$131.40	$179.20	$236.80

BAND OF 16	Marceau.	Dupont.	Imperial.
1 E Flat Cornet	5.85	8.25	13.85
3 B Flat Cornets	17.85	28.35	47.85
2 E Flat Altos	19.70	26.70	33.70
2 B Flat Tenors	21.90	29.70	38.50
2 Tenor Slide Trombones	13.90	18.70	28.90
1 B Flat Baritone	12.45	17.95	22.45
1 B Flat Bass	13.95	20.55	24.95
2 E Flat Basses	38.90	52.30	60.50
1 Bass Drum No. 12C3502	7.45	7.45	7.45
1 Snare Drum No. 12C3472	4.85	4.85	4.85
	$156.80	$214.80	$283.00

OUR CELEBRATED MARCEAU SOLO B FLAT CORNET.

THE MOST WONDERFUL BARGAIN EVER OFFERED IN A B FLAT CORNET, $7.95

Beautiful in tone, perfect in tune, and solidly constructed. Fitted with the best quality light action French piston valves and warranted to be satisfactory in every particular.

THIS CORNET is one of our celebrated Marceau line, and is made by one of the best known French makers of band instruments. It is the very latest model, is thoroughly constructed in every particular and we guarantee it to give satisfaction in every case. It is exceptionally fine for leaders who use a B flat cornet in their work, as its tone is exceedingly powerful and rich. It is so strongly made that it will not "blow out" with severe playing, and the valve action is so perfect that the long brilliant runs, so commonly found in street marches, can be executed with ease and rapidity. In appearance this instrument will compare favorably with cornets which are sold at twice the price and it is an excellent instrument for both solo and orchestra playing.

SEND US $1.00 and we will ship you this cornet for examination and approval. If you find it satisfactory you can pay the balance of the price to the express agent and take the instrument to your home for further trial. Should you not find it satisfactory at the express office, it will be returned at our expense and we will refund the amount deposited and it will not cost you one cent to examine and test the instrument. Should you accept it at the express office we will allow you ten days to try it in your own home and if within that time it should prove unsatisfactory you can return it to us, we will refund your money and pay the express charges both ways. We make you this liberal offer because we desire to give you an opportunity to examine and test this instrument thoroughly.

WE GUARANTEE THIS INSTRUMENT FOR ONE YEAR, and if within that period the instrument should show a defect either in material or workmanship, it can be returned to us, and we will refund the price paid and pay express charges both ways.

WHY THIS CORNET IS SUCH A WONDERFUL BARGAIN.

MANUFACTURERS AND DEALERS in this class of instruments have been charging such high prices in the past that people have been educated to think that it is necessary to give this high price for such an instrument in order to procure a good one. We have found that in order to sell such an instrument as this, at this extremely low price it is only necessary to cut off the usual enormous profits and selling expenses made by the different dealers through whose hands these instruments generally pass before they reach the purchaser. You cannot purchase an instrument of this grade from any other dealer for less than $15.00 at the very least. The cornets of this class which you purchase for $15.00 and $16.00 do not cost one cent more to manufacture than the instrument shown in the engraving. But the manufacturers and large dealers have to fix that price in order to protect the local dealer. We do not have to do this, therefore, we can offer this splendid instrument at

EXCEL ALL OTHERS IN SELLING HIGH GRADE INSTRUMENTS AT LOW PRICES.

Dale, So. Car.

Sears, Roebuck & Co.

Dear Sirs:—The instruments which I bought of you last spring give entire satisfaction; are excellent in tune, extra in grade, and I must say that you excel all others in selling high grade instruments at low prices. I advise anyone who needs high grade instruments at low cost to call on Sears, Roebuck & Co.

P. W. MAXWELL.

SURPASSED HIS EXPECTATIONS.

Allentown, Pa.

Sears, Roebuck & Co.

Dear Sirs:—In reply to your inquiry concerning band instruments I bought from you, will say that when I received them they surpassed my expectations both in workmanship and tone. We have been using them now for some time and they are still holding their own, and I can safely say that our boys care for no other make of instruments as long as you send out such instruments at such low prices. We would not sell our Dupont E Flat Bass for $25.00 more than the price we paid for it were we not to get another. We want to say further that we will recommend your instruments to whatever bandmen we meet. We had some of the best band directors to examine the Dupont Bass and they all, without exception, pronounced it an excellent instrument.

WILSON A. KICHLING.
R. F. D. No. 1. Manager Ideal Band.

THE BEST THEY HAVE EVER SEEN.

Prairieview, Kans.

Sears, Roebuck & Co.

Dear Sirs:—Some time ago I received a few Marceau Band Instruments for my band and liked them so well that we have ordered several more of your instruments, including several Dupont instruments. The old instruments in our band will soon be replaced by Duponts and Marceaus. We like the Duponts best, but both makes are far the best we have seen for the price. I do not hesitate to recommend these instruments to any and all who intend to purchase band goods.

C. A. RHOADS.

DOES NOT SEE HOW WE CAN SELL SUCH INSTRUMENTS FOR THE PRICE.

Grass Valley, Cal.

Sears, Roebuck & Co.

Dear Sirs:—I received the cornet in first class shape and consider it perfect. I don't see how you can sell such instruments for the price. Will not forget you in the future.

CLIFF H. WELDON.

MARCEAU CORNETS EQUAL TO ANY.

Loughton Lake, Mich.

Sears, Roebuck & Co.

Dear Sirs:—In answer to your letter of the 6th I can only say that I take great pleasure in playing a Marceau Cornet. I never believed that an instrument for that price would be so good as it really is. I have played cornets at the cost of $80.00, but I find that the B Flat Marceau Cornet is equal to any of them in tone or action. I would recommend the Marceau Cornet.

CHRIS HERMANN.

THE THANKS OF THE ORCHESTRA.

Plainfield, Penna.

Sears, Roebuck & Co.

Gentlemen:—As leader of the McAllister Orchestra I have the pleasure of conveying to you the thanks of the members of the orchestra who bought their instruments of you (we bought a bass horn, two clarionets and two cornets) for the high satisfaction which those instruments are giving.

A. F. WEAVER.

CLARIONET ALL RIGHT.

Fall River, Mass.

Sears, Roebuck & Co.

Gentlemen:—Replying to yours of the 8th, in regard to the clarionet I purchased from you, will say that I am well pleased with it. If you have any customers who wish to have references for your clarionets refer them to me.

LUKE MALTAIS.

HARD TO BEAT FOR THE PRICE.

Sears, Roebuck & Co. Rockwell City, Ia.

Dear Sirs:—In reply to your letter I can say that the band instruments you sent are well worth the money and hard to beat for the price.

R. R. No. 4. JOHN REYNOLDS.

TROMBONE GIVING PERFECT SATISFACTION.

Sears, Roebuck & Co. Sweden, Maine.

Gentlemen:—It is with great pleasure that I reply to your letter in regard to the slide trombone that I received of you. It is giving perfect satisfaction and is the best ever seen here for the money. It is equal to instruments sold here for $80.00. On the whole, your musical instruments are all excellent. Your organs have a deep rich tone hard to rival. The organ I bought of you is a beauty and wears well.

W. S. MANN,
Choir Singer and Musician.

LET US SEND YOU THIS INSTRUMENT ON TRIAL, and if you do not find by comparing it with any other cornet which your dealer has to offer at twice the money, that it is in every way superior, and if you do not come to the conclusion that this is the greatest bargain you ever saw and superior to any cornet ever offered at more than twice the price, we request you to immediately ship it back to us, we will refund your money in full, and pay the entire expense of shipment both ways. If you desire a splendid cornet at an exceedingly low price, you should not let this opportunity pass.

No. 12C7992 Brass, highly polished. Price........ **$7.95**
No. 12C7994 Nickel plated, highly polished. Price........ **8.95**

OUR CELEBRATED MARCEAU BAND INSTRUMENTS.

GREATEST BARGAINS IN BAND INSTRUMENTS EVER OFFERED TO THE BANDMEN OF AMERICA.

HIGH CLASS BAND INSTRUMENTS SOLD AT GROCERY PROFITS.

THIS IS ONE OF THE FINE LINES of band instruments which we have been handling for years and which have given such immense satisfaction.

WE GUARANTEE EVERY INSTRUMENT in this line and sell them on the same terms that we sell all of our other band instruments. Each horn is fitted with celebrated French piston light action valves and is splendid in model and finish. On page 171 of this catalogue you will find the terms upon which we sell these instruments fully given and also estimates of bands of different sizes, which may prove of interest to you.

Marceau E Flat Cornet.

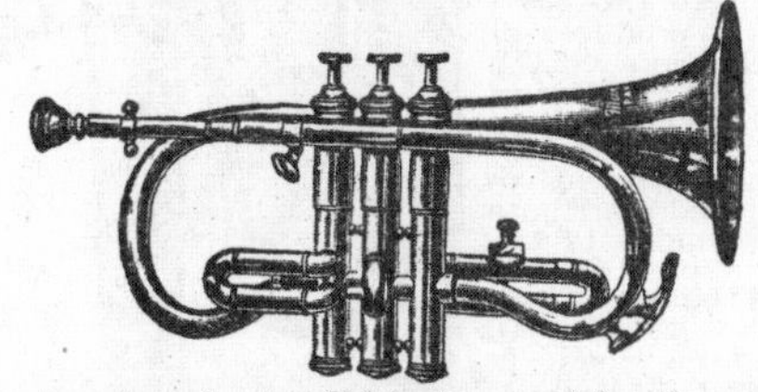

A clear toned splendid instrument for the use of leaders. Guaranteed in every way. Beautiful in model, perfect in tune and tone.
No. 12C7980 Brass, highly polished........$5.85
No. 12C7981 Nickel plated, highly polished 6.75

Marceau B Flat Cornet.
SINGLE WATER KEY.

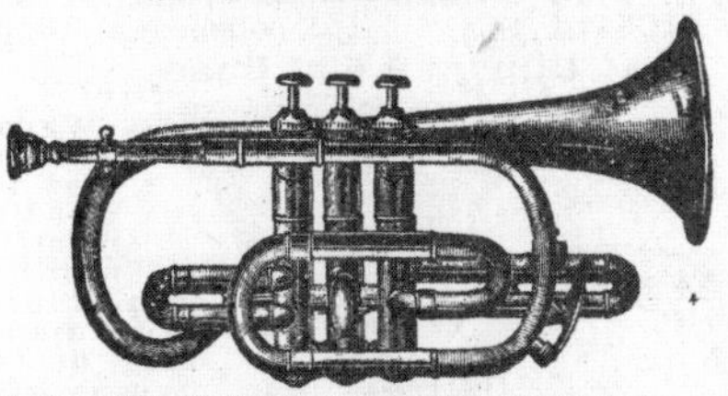

This is a fine B Flat Cornet in every way and is suitable for use in either band or orchestra. We send with it an A shank for use in orchestra, and it is a splendid instrument in every way.
No. 12C7984 Brass, highly polished $5.95
No. 12C7985 Nickel plated, highly polished 6.85

Marceau C Cornet.

We can also furnish this cornet in the key of C at the following prices:
No. 12C7988 Brass. Price..................$6.05
No. 12C7989 Nickel plated. Price.......... 6.95

Artists' Model Marceau B Flat.
DOUBLE WATER KEY CORNET.

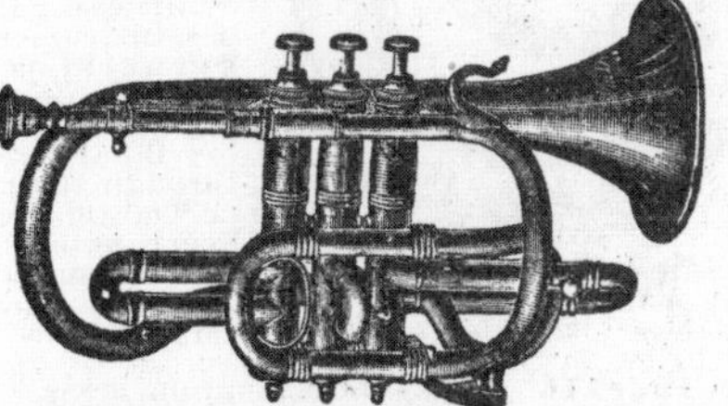

This Double Water Key Cornet has been a favorite with bandmen for a long time on account of its beautiful model and splendid tone.
No. 12C7996 Brass, polished..............$10.40
No. 12C7997 Nickel plated, highly polished........................ 11.30

Marceau E Flat Altos and B Flat Tenors.

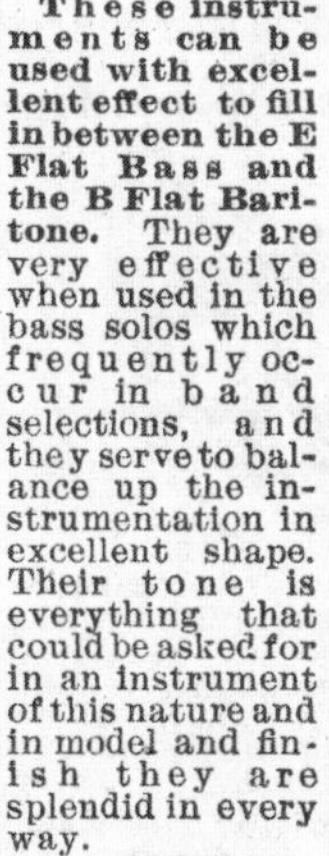

These instruments are splendid for harmony work in a band, and we recommend them highly for those who desire fine altos and tenors at extremely low prices. They have a splendid tone, a beautiful model and a handsome appearance. They are perfect in tune and tone and so well constructed that they will last a lifetime. The action of the valves is extremely light and either one of these instruments can be used very nicely for solo purposes. We guarantee them to be satisfactory, and we believe that alto and tenor players will find in these instruments just what they desire at a very small cost. We desire to place them in the hands of all who are looking for something in this line at a moderate price, and we do not ask the customer to take any chances as we assume all the risk of shipping them.
No. 12C8013 E Flat Alto, brass, highly polished......................................$ 9.85
No. 12C8014 E Flat Alto, nickel plated, highly polished............................. 11.35
No. 12C8015 B Flat Tenor, brass, highly polished.................................... 10.95
No. 12C8016 B Flat Tenor, nickel plated, highly polished......... 13.45

Marceau B Flat Baritone.

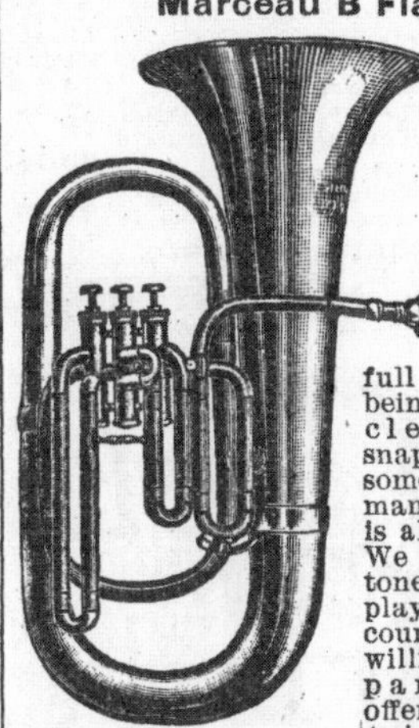

These instruments have been used with great success in all sorts of solo playing and general band work. A large number of bandmen have pronounced them the finest baritones on the market for less than double the price given below. Their tone is full and sonorous without being dull, and is light and clear without being too snappy. The model is handsome and the general workmanship on the instruments is all that can be desired. We recommend these baritones highly to baritone players throughout the country and we are always willing to have them compared with instruments offered by other dealers for twice the price.
No. 12C8017 Brass, highly polished. Price...$12.45
No. 12C8018 Nickel plated, highly polished. Price...$15.85

OUR LIBERAL C.O.D. OFFER applies to these instruments and a whole set of them can be sent C. O. D. if the customer will make a deposit with us of $1.00 for each instrument. We know we can save bands from $25.00 to $75.00 upon a set of these instruments, according to the number of horns they purchase, and all we ask is an opportunity to prove that this is true.

EACH INSTRUMENT goes to the customer complete with music rack, mouthpiece and complete instruction book. These instruction books are arranged so that they can be used together by an entire band of whatever size. May we not have an opportunity to ship you a set of these fine instruments?

Marceau B Flat Bass.

These instruments can be used with excellent effect to fill in between the E Flat Bass and the B Flat Baritone. They are very effective when used in the bass solos which frequently occur in band selections, and they serve to balance up the instrumentation in excellent shape. Their tone is everything that could be asked for in an instrument of this nature and in model and finish they are splendid in every way.
No. 12C8019 Brass, highly polished..... $13.95
No. 12C8020 Nickel plated, highly polished. Price.......................................$17.45

Marceau E Flat Bass.

We wish to call your attention particularly to this instrument and will say, without fear of contradiction, that it has never been equaled, price considered. It has a deep, rich tone and furnishes an excellent fundamental bass for any brass band. It has enough volume to answer for a large instrumentation and the tone is full and sweet enough for use, if desired, in orchestras. The model is fine and the tubing is so thoroughly braced and reinforced that it will not break down under severe use. The valves are all quick and responsive and we guarantee the instrument to be satisfactory in every particular.
No. 12C8021 Brass, highly polished $19.45
No. 12C8022 Nickel plated, highly polished, 24.45

Marceau Solo Altos.

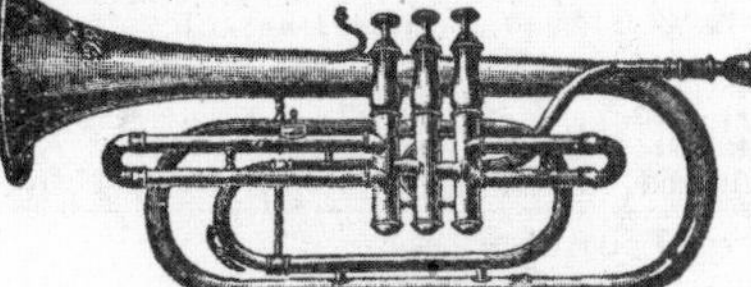

These instruments are manufactured for solo alto purposes and have been great favorites ever since their appearance. They are easy blowing, have a splendid tone and a handsome appearance.
No. 12C8011 Brass, highly polished...... ....$ 9.45
No. 12C8012 Nickel plated, highly polished........ 10.95

Marceau Valve Trombones.

These Trombones are all fine in every respect and have that deep, rich tone so peculiar to trombones. Each band should be fitted with at least two of these, as they give a coloring harmony, which could be obtained in no other way.
No. 12C8023 E Flat Alto Trombone, brass. Price... ....$ 9.75
No. 12C8024 E Flat Alto Trombone, nickel plated. Price....... 11.25
No. 12C8025 B Flat Tenor Trombone, brass. Price.............. 10.85
No. 12C8026 B Flat Tenor Trombone, nickel plated. Price.. .... 13.35
No. 12C8027 B Flat Baritone Trombone, brass. Price.......... 12.35
No. 12C8028 B Flat Baritone Trombone, nickel plated. Price... 15.25

Special Hillyard Long Model Marceau Trombones.

No. 12C8029 B Flat Tenor Trombone, brass. Price..............$11.45
No. 12C8030 B Flat Tenor Trombone, nickel plated. Price....... 13.95

FOR TERMS OF SHIPMENT, SEE PAGE 171.

Marceau Slide Trombones.

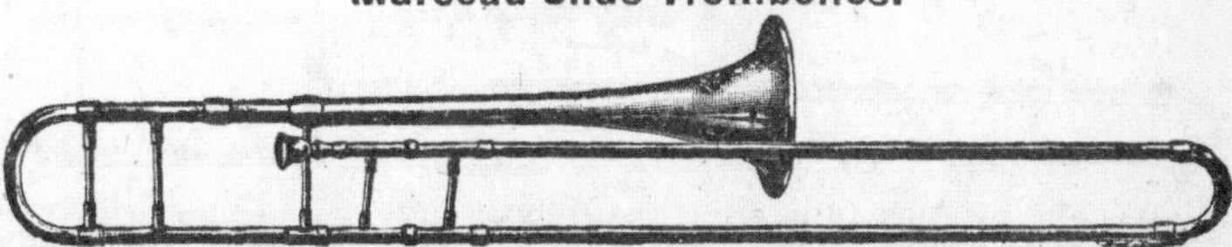

We know that these instruments will appeal to all trombone players who desire good, serviceable trombones at an extremely low price. For band and orchestra use they will be found equal to all requirements. For solo playing they have given general satisfaction. The slide works with ease and rapidity and the tone is mellow and powerful.
No. 12C8031 Brass, highly polished..................................$6.95
No. 12C8032 Nickel plated, highly polished 7.45

OUR WORLD RENOWNED DUPONT BAND INSTRUMENTS.

A High Grade Line of BAND INSTRUMENTS at extremely low prices. The greatest value ever offered in Brass Band Instruments. The entire line fitted with French light action piston valves and handsomely finished. Each Instrument complete with music rack, mouthpiece and instruction book.

Dupont E Flat Cornet.

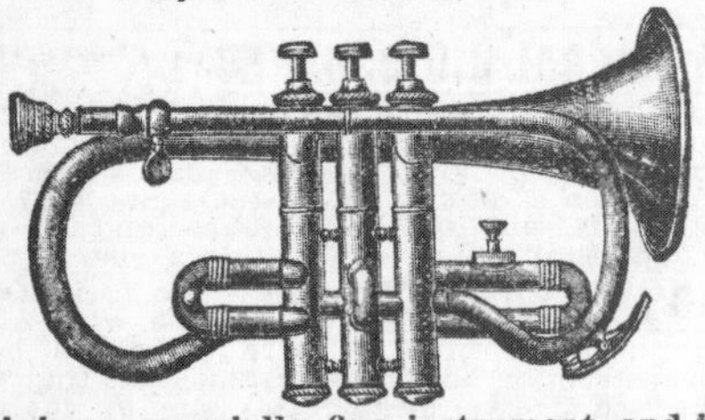

This is an especially fine instrument, and is so constructed that many of the objectionable features to be found in other E flat cornets have been entirely avoided.

No. 12C8040	Brass, polished	$ 8.25
No. 12C8042	Nickel plated	9.25
No. 12C8044	Silver plated, satin finish	13.95
No. 12C8046	Silver plated, polished	14.55

Dupont B Flat Cornet, Single Water Key.

For general band and orchestra work where steady, conscientious results are required, these cornets are particularly desirable.

No. 12C8047	Brass, polished	$ 9.45
No. 12C8048	Nickel plated	10.45
No. 12C8049	Silver plated, satin finished	15.25
No. 12C8050	Silver plated, polished	16.70

Dupont B Flat Cornet, Double Water Key.

The B Flat Cornet, illustrated above, has never been excelled in playing qualities by any band instrument ever made. The material of which it is made is of the very finest, and the skill of the maker is splendidly shown in the beautiful model and excellent finish.

No. 12C8052	Brass, polished	$11.45
No. 12C8054	Nickel plated	12.45
No. 12C8056	Silver plated, satin finish	17.65
No. 12C8058	Silver plated, polished	19.85

Dupont Solo Alto.

This instrument is intended for use as a solo alto, and while it can be used as a harmony instrument it is best adapted for use on solo alto parts in band music which have been so popular of late years.

No. 12C8076	Brass, polished	$13.30
No. 12C8078	Nickel plated	15.20
No. 12C8080	Silver plated, satin finish	22.55
No. 12C8082	Silver plated, polished	26.65

We have been very successful in handling this splendid line of band instruments because we are able to furnish them at prices away below what any other dealers can offer. We sell them upon the same terms that we sell all of our other brass instruments and make the customer the sole judge of their merits. We guarantee them to be satisfactory and know that they will meet the desires of the ordinary local concert band.

The terms upon which we ship all of our brass band instruments are fully explained on page 171, and we trust that you will give these your careful consideration.

Dupont Altos and Tenors.

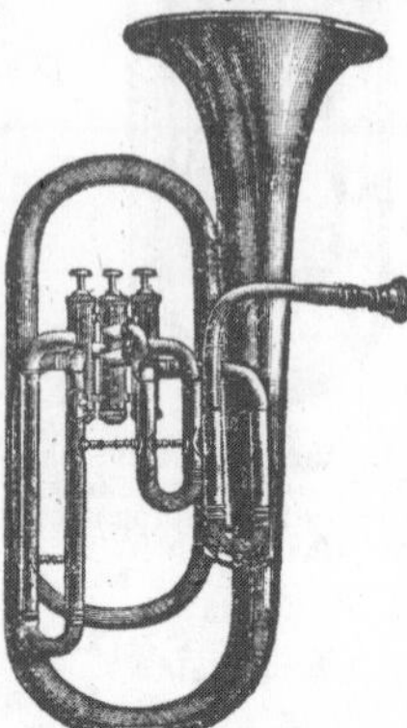

These instruments are intended for harmony purposes and for playing accompaniment parts, but they can both be used for solo work and are excellent for that purpose. The model, material and workmanship are of the highest type, they are well and strongly made, and the brass of which they are constructed is of just the right thickness and temper to produce a lasting and brilliant tone. We desire to impress upon alto and tenor players the fact that these instruments will furnish that organ like quality of tone so sought after in band music.

No. 12C8084	**E Flat Alto**, brass, polished	$13.35
No. 12C8086	**E Flat Alto**, nickel plated	15.25
No. 12C8088	**E Flat Alto**, silver plated, satin finished	19.45
No. 12C8090	**E Flat Alto**, silver plated	21.95
No. 12C8092	**B Flat Tenor**, brass	14.85
No. 12C8094	**B Flat Tenor**, nickel plated	17.35
No. 12C8096	**B Flat Tenor**, silver plated, satin finished	23.75
No. 12C8098	**B Flat Tenor**, silver plated, polished	25.95

Dupont B Flat Baritone.

We take pleasure in bringing to the notice of baritone players the magnificent instrument shown in the engraving opposite. We have supplied these instruments to a large number of bands, and in every case they have called forth the unstinted praise of the player. The tone is round, full and deep, and in solo playing it leaves nothing to be desired. Particular care has been used by the manufacturer in the production of this instrument, and we do not hesitate to say that it is certainly one of the best baritones made today.

No. 12C8100	Brass, polished	$17.95
No. 12C8102	Nickel plated	20.70
No. 12C8104	Silver plated, satin finish	27.95
No. 12C8106	Silver plated, polished	31.45

FOR TERMS OF SHIPMENT SEE PAGE 171.

Dupont B Flat Bass.

This instrument is particularly adapted for shading and blending the deep diapason tones of the tuba, and forms a connecting link in the harmony between that instrument and the baritone. It produces an excellent effect in the heavy bass solos of modern street marches and selections, and serves to blend and distribute the harmony of the bass section. It bears the stamp of M. Dupont and little more need be said in its favor. It well deserves the praise which has been bestowed upon it by those who have had an opportunity to test its merits.

No. 12C8108	Brass, polished	$20.55
No. 12C8110	Nickel plated	23.80
No. 12C8112	Silver plated, satin finished	29.45
No. 12C8114	Silver plated, polished	34.75

Dupont E Flat Bass.

We do not believe that these instruments have ever been equaled for dignity and profundity of tone by any other basses ever made, where the price is taken into consideration. They are capable, in the hands of an ordinary player, of furnishing a fundamental bass for any band, and when used in an orchestra the effect is striking and grand. They possess the quality so rare in bass instruments of being in perfect tune in the upper register, and from low B flat clear up through the entire chromatic scale, every note is full, accurate and in perfect tune. We have supplied a great many bass players throughout the country with these instruments and in every instance they have called forth the loudest praise.

No. 12C8116	**E Flat Bass**, medium, brass, polished	$26.15
No. 12C8118	**E Flat Bass**, medium, nickel plated	$29.90
No. 12C8120	**E Flat Bass**, medium, silver plated, satin finished	$38.25
No. 12C8122	**E Flat Bass**, medium, silver plated, polished	$46.95
No. 12C8124	**E Flat Contra-Bass**, brass, polished	$28.45
No. 12C8126	**E Flat Contra-Bass**, nickel plated	$31.95
No. 12C8128	**E Flat Contra-Bass**, silver plated, satin finish	$39.85
No. 12C8130	**E Flat Contra-Bass**, silver plated, polished	$47.95

Dupont Tenor Slide Trombone.

We take pleasure in offering the Dupont Slide Trombones to players because we believe that they represent the very highest possible attainments in this line, considering the extremely low prices which we are able to make. Great care and study has been given to their manufacture, and the result has been gratifying, indeed.

No. 12C8156	Brass, polished	$ 9.35
No. 12C8158	Nickel plated	11.35
No. 12C8160	Silver plated, satin finished	15.65
No. 12C8162	Silver plated, polished	17.75

Dupont Valve Trombones.

The valve trombones of this line are made after the latest approved models and are fine in every respect. Trombone players will find in them what they have been looking for for a long time.

No. 12C8132	**E Flat Alto Trombone**, brass, polished	$13.40
No. 12C8134	**E Flat Alto Trombone**, nickel plated	15.30
No. 12C8136	**E Flat Alto Trombone**, silver plated, satin finished	19.95
No. 12C8138	**E Flat Alto Trombone**, silver plated, polished	23.45
No. 12C8140	**B Flat Tenor Valve Trombone**, brass, polished	14.70
No. 12C8142	**B Flat Tenor Valve Trombone**, nickel plated	17.20
No. 12C8144	**B Flat Tenor Valve Trombone**, silver plated, satin finished	23.75
No. 12C8146	**B Flat Tenor Valve Trombone**, silver pla'd, polished	25.95
No. 12C8148	**B Flat Baritone Valve Trombone**, brass, polished	17.90
No. 12C8150	**B Flat Baritone Valve Trombone**, nickel plated	20.65
No. 12C8152	**B Flat Baritone Valve Trombone**, silver plated, satin finished	26.45
No. 12C8154	**B Flat Baritone Valve Trombone**, silv'r pla'd, polish'd	29.95

OUR SPLENDID LINE OF TOURVILLE & CO. BAND INSTRUMENTS.

Made by TOURVILLE & CO., PARIS, FRANCE.

Unquestionably the Finest Line of Brass Instruments Ever Placed on the American Market.

E Flat Cornet.

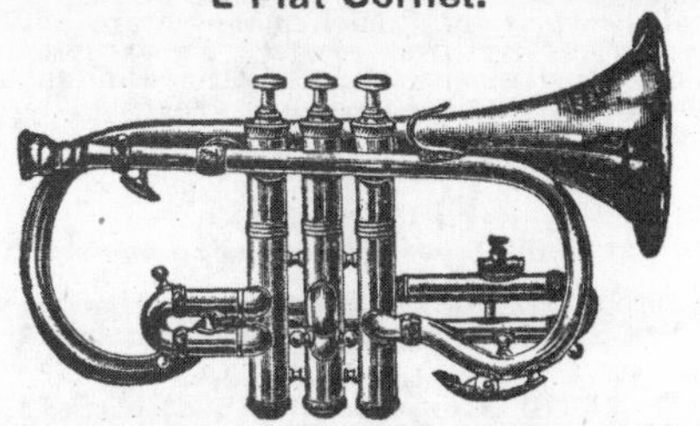

Too much cannot be said in praise of this instrument. The fact that it is made by Tourville & Co. establishes its reputation as a high grade musical instrument, but aside from this it has many points of superiority not possessed by other E flat cornets. The tone is as sweet and flexible as any B flat cornet ever made, and for ease of blowing it has never been equaled.

No. 12C8180	Brass, polished	$13.85
No. 12C8182	Nickel plated	15.10
No. 12C8184	Silver plated, satin finished	17.35
No. 12C8190	Silver plated, polished	19.35

Leaders' B Flat Cornet. Double Water Key.

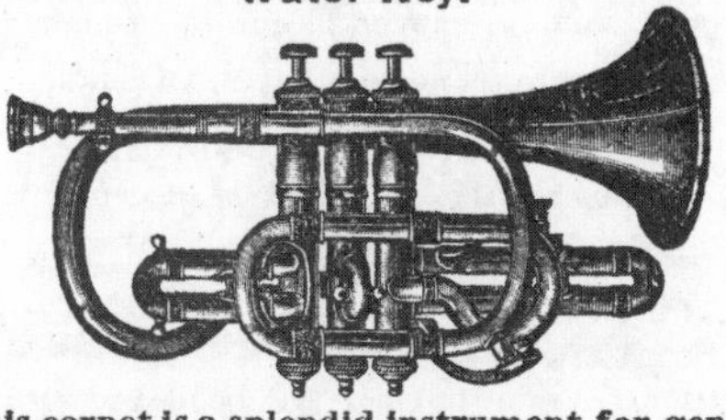

This cornet is a splendid instrument for general street and concert work, an ideal cornet for leaders who use a B flat cornet in their work. It is the handsomest cornet on the market with the exception of our Artists' cornet, and merits to the fullest extent, the great praise which has been bestowed upon it by those who are using it at the present time. Its powerful bell like tone always attracts attention, and it never fails to respond to the severest demands which can be made upon it.

No. 12C8201	Brass, polished	$15.95
No. 12C8202	Nickel plated	17.25
No. 12C8203	Silver plated, satin finished,	19.45
No. 12C8204	Silver plated, polished	21.45

Artists' B Flat Cornet.

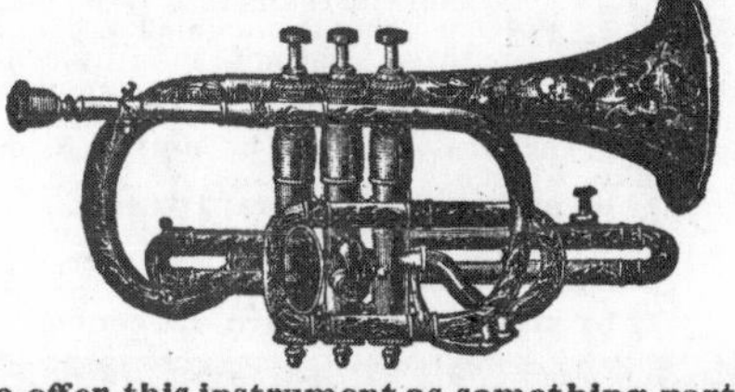

We offer this instrument as something particularly fine for soloists, and those who desire a cornet of the highest possible grade in both looks and playing qualities. It is handsomely engraved throughout, is a splendid instrument for presentation purposes, or for use on the stage, and we recommend it as a cornet which the player will take pride in using and exhibiting to his friends at all times.

No. 12C8205	Brass, polished	$18.15
No. 12C8206	Nickel plated	19.45
No. 12C8207	Silver plated, satin finished, gold lined bell	21.95
No. 12C8208	Silver plated, polished, gold lined bell	23.95

It is with pleasure that we announce to the bandmen of this country the fact that we have succeeded in making arrangements with Tourville & Co., of Paris, the most famous band instrument makers in Europe, to furnish us with their peerless line of instruments, so that we are able to offer them to the bandmen of this country by our direct from factory to customer plan, which insures an astonishing saving in every case. We will guarantee that we can save bands from $50.00 to $75.00 on the purchase of a set of these instruments. A comparison of this line and the prices we make with instruments of the same grade, and at prices made on them by other dealers, will convince you at once of the truth of our assertion. We guarantee every one of these instruments in every respect, and ship them out upon the same terms that we ship all our other musical instruments. These terms will be found fully described on page 171 of this catalogue. We are the only dealers who are handling this celebrated line of instruments in this country, and you cannot purchase them from anybody else.

Tenors and Altos.

These are by far the best harmony instruments ever turned out by any maker. Their tone is peculiarly adapted for accompaniment parts and is heavy enough for solo work. As great care has been used in their manufacture as is used in the manufacture of the finest cornets of this line, and we do not hesitate to say that they are the best instruments of their kind ever produced. Alto and tenor players will make no mistake in buying these instruments, as we guarantee that they will be perfectly satisfactory or they may be returned to us at our expense.

No. 12C8210	**E Flat Alto,** brass, polished	$16.85
No. 12C8212	**E Flat Alto,** nickel plated	18.50
No. 12C8214	**E Flat Alto,** silver plated, satin finished	22.85
No. 12C8216	**E Flat Alto,** silver plated, polished	25.85
No. 12C8218	**B Flat Tenor,** brass, polished	19.25
No. 12C8220	**B Flat Tenor,** nickel plated,	22.55
No. 12C8222	**B Flat Tenor,** silver plated, satin finished	26.75
No. 12C8224	**B Flat Tenor,** silver plated, polished	29.45

B Flat Baritone.

Of all brass instruments the baritone is perhaps the most difficult to make, for the reason that great depth and breadth of tone are required, combined with the lightest possible action. This happy combination is fully realized in this baritone. The valve action in this instrument is the result of much special thought and experiment, and the maker has succeeded in so regulating the air pressure as to produce the lightest valve action ever known.

No. 12C8226	Brass, polished	$22.45
No. 12C8228	Nickel plated	$25.95
No. 12C8230	Silver plated, satin finished	$30.95
No. 12C8232	Silver plated, polished	$35.20

Solo E Flat Alto.

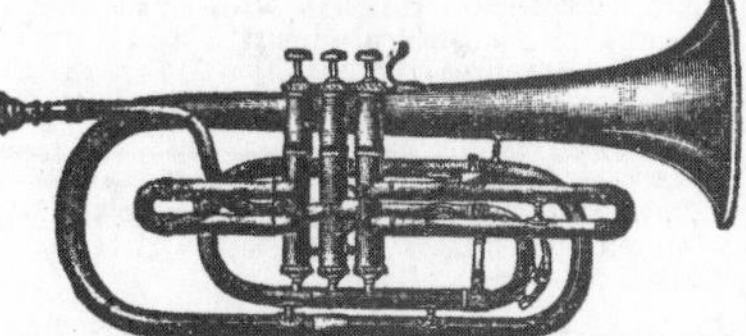

This is a favorite model with Alto players and is one which we highly recommend as handsome and durable. This instrument is easily the equal of other instruments of this line, and is very acceptable for playing solo alto parts.

No. 12C8192	Brass polished	$16.80
No. 12C8194	Nickel plated, polished	18.45
No. 12C8196	Silver plated, satin finished	22.80
No. 12C8198	Silver plated, polished	25.95

REMEMBER **that our C. O. D. offer is good in connection with this line of instruments,** and that we make you the sole judge of whether or not the instruments prove satisfactory. You can take advantage also of our ten days' trial offer in purchasing this line, and we trust you will bear in mind that you are always at liberty to return the instruments if they do not prove to your entire satisfaction.

B Flat Bass.

The merits of this instrument are on a par with the balance of the line, and the name of the maker on the bell is a guarantee of the very highest quality. It has that full, round tone so valuable in an instrument of this character, which accentuates the organ like effect of band music. It has the superb finish so characteristic of the entire line, and the same careful, conscientious skill has entered into its manufacture.

No. 12C8234	Brass, polished	$24.95
No. 12C8236	Nickel plated	28.45
No. 12C8238	Silver plated, satin finished	35.45
No. 12C8240	Silver plated, polished	39.95

E Flat Bass.

The Tuba shown in the engraving is without any question the finest E flat bass ever made in tone, tune and finish. Too much cannot be said in its praise, but we would prefer to place it in the hands of bass players and let it speak for itself. In tone, tune and valve action it is certainly a revelation, and never fails to receive the greatest praise from all who may use it. It has that grand, sonorous and at the same time mellow tone which has been the dream of both player and manufacturer for years, and only realized in this production of the master hand.

No. 12C8242	Brass, polished	$30.25
No. 12C8244	Nickel plated	33.85
No. 12C8246	Silver plated, satin finished.	43.25
No. 12C8248	Silver plated, polished	48.75

Valve Trombones.

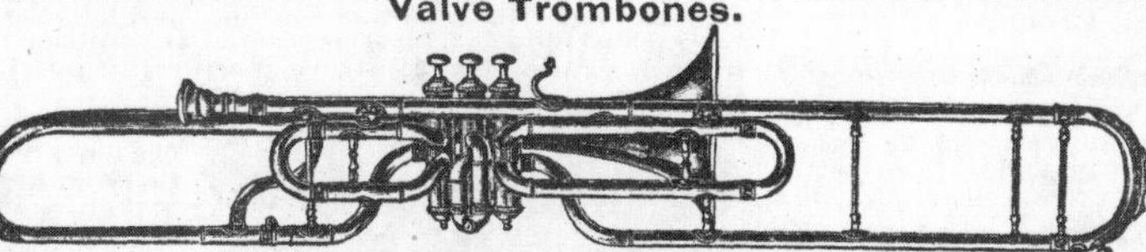

The Trombones of this line are all well balanced and easy to hold, and the model is one which has received the approval of both maker and player. Owing to the peculiarly sweet tone they possess, they are favorite instruments in all brass bands

No. 12C8266	**E Flat Alto Trombone,** brass, polished	$16.80
No. 12C8268	**E Flat Alto Trombone,** nickel plated	18.55
No. 12C8270	**E Flat Alto Trombone,** silver plated, satin finished.	22.75
No. 12C8272	**E Flat Alto Trombone,** silver plated, polished	25.80
No. 12C8274	**B Flat Tenor Trombone,** brass, polished	18.95
No. 12C8276	**B Flat Tenor Trombone,** nickel plated	21.45
No. 12C8278	**B Flat Tenor Trombone,** silver plated, satin finished	26.45
No. 12C8280	**B Flat Tenor Trombone,** silver plated, polished	28.95

Tenor Slide Trombones.

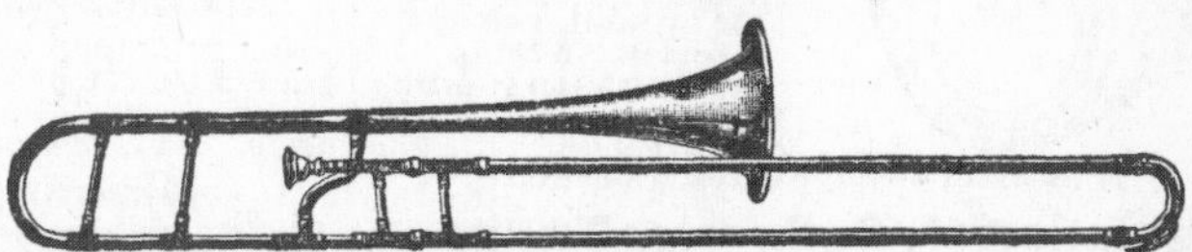

In this instrument the maker has succeeded in combining the profound tone of the old German instruments with the light, airy tones of the more recent French trombones, thus realizing a dream which has haunted both maker and player for so many years. The tone of this trombone is mellow and rich, and the style of action is perfection itself.

No. 12C8282	Brass, polished	$14.45
No. 12C8284	Nickel plated	16.25
No. 12C8286	Silver plated, satin finished	19.45
No. 12C8288	Silver plated, polished	21.85

Two Special High Grade Engraved Cornets.

We show herewith two of the greatest values in engraved cornets ever offered; strictly high grade, short model cornets.

To meet certain demands for a fancy engraved instrument, we have arranged with our manufacturers to supply two cornets of the improved short model; instruments which will compare in quality, material, tone and finish with cornets that are sold by other dealers throughout the country for at least twice what we ask.

UPON RECEIPT OF $1.00 we will ship either of these two cornets on approval according to our liberal terms, fully described on page 171.

No. 12C3300 Bb Cornet, brass, single water key, French piston valves, German silver mouthpiece, set piece, music rack and instruction book. Price.............$ 8.25

No. 12C3301 Bb Cornet, same as No. 12C3300, but nickel plated. Price.............9.25

No. 12C3302 Bb Cornet, same as No. 12C3300, but triple silver plated, satin finish. Price......12.25

No. 12C3303 Bb Cornet, same as No. 12C3300, but triple silver plated, burnished finish. Price 14.95

Our Special Engraved Double Water Key Bb Cornet.

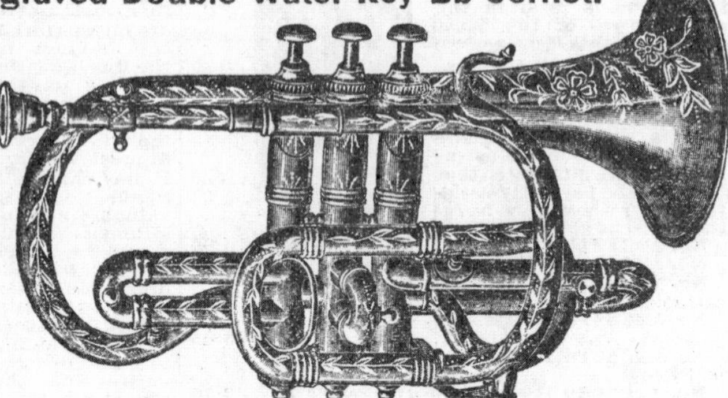

No.12C3304 Double Water Key Bb Cornet, brass, elaborately engraved artist model: reinforced chased joints and braces; light action, German silver piston valves; furnished complete with an A set piece. German silver mouthpiece, music rack and instruction book. Price.....................$12.95

No. 12C3305 Bb Cornet, same as No. 12C3304, but finely nickel plated. Price.............$13.95

No. 12C3306 Bb Cornet, same as No. 12C3305, but full triple silver plated, satin finish and gold plated bell. Price.................$17.45

No. 12C3308 Bb Cornet, same as No. 12C3304, but full triple silver plated, burnished finish, gold plated bell. Price.................$19.95

Weight of any of the above cornets, packed for shipment, 10 pounds.

BUGLES.

Officer's Bugle.

No. 12C3329 Officer's Bugle, made of brass and finely finished, key of C. Weight, boxed, about 5 pounds. Price.....$1.15

No. 12C3330 Same, finely nickel plated. Price.............$1.45

Cavalry Bugle.

No.12C3334 Cavalry Bugle, brass, key of F. Weight, boxed, 8 pounds. Price.........$1.65

No. 12C3335 Same, nickel plated..$2.05

Artillery Bugle.

No. 12C3338 Artillery Bugle, brass, key of G. Weight, boxed, 6 pounds. Price....$1.95

No. 12C3339 Same, finely nickel plated. Price....$2.45

Infantry Bugle.

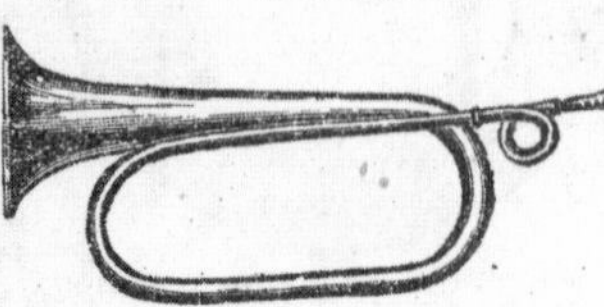

No. 12C3341 Infantry Bugle; brass; key of C with B flat crook. Weight, boxed, 6 pounds. Price....$1.70

No. 12C3342 Same, nickel plated. Price....$2.15

Hunting Horns.

No.12C3345 Hunting Horns, brass; one turn, Price.............60c

If by mail, postage extra, 15 cents.

No.12C3346 Hunting Horns, brass; three turns. Price..........95c

If by mail, postage extra, 15 cents.

Regulation U. S. Cavalry Trumpet. Key of F.

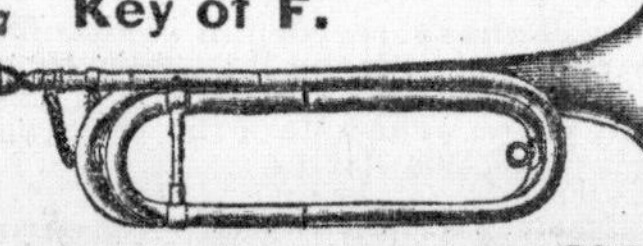

No. 12C3347 Cavalry Trumpet, key of F, made of brass, with tuning slide. Price.............................$2.25

No. 12C3348 Same, nickel plated. Price.. 2.65

Weight, boxed, 8 pounds.

OWING TO THE PECULIAR CHARACTER

of the construction of wood wind instruments, they are liable to crack at any time, and no music dealer can give a guarantee for any length of time.

WE GUARANTEE EVERY INSTRUMENT

to be in first class condition when it leaves our hands, and if properly cared for the instrument will last many years. No instrument should be put away after using without being wiped out. Dry the outside of the instrument with a rag or chamois skin, being careful to wipe the ends of the joints dry. To a new instrument or one that has been out of use for some time, a little oil should be applied daily for the first five or six days; **always oil after using, not before.**

FIFES.

Key of B Flat and C only. Instruction Book, 12c. Shipping weight, 8 ounces.

No.12C3358 Key of B Flat or C; solid rosewood; brass ferrules. Price.............25c

No. 12C3359 Key of B Flat or C; cocoa wood; German silver. Price.............27c

No. 12C3361 Key of B Flat or C; solid ebony; nickel plated ferrules. Price.............48c

No. 12C3362 Key of B Flat or C; solid ebony; long metal ferrules. **Crosby model;** extra fine quality. Price.............75c

Nickel Plated Fifes.

Shipping weight, 10 ounces.

No. 12C3363 Highly Nickel Plated Fife, for beginners with mouthpiece adjusted all ready for playing. A very fine instrument for those who desire to learn the fife. Keys of B flat or C. Price.......19c

No.12C3364 Key of B Flat or C. Nickel plated with raised finger holes, with gutta percha embouchure. Price.............55c

Our Special Acme Hand Made Fife

Shipping weight, 12 ounces.

No. 12C3365 Metal nickel plated, strictly high grade Fife for professional players. Made in two pieces. Easy blowing, perfect in scale. None better made. Keys of C or B flat. Price.............95c

Nightingale Flageolets.

No. 12C3366 Nightingale Flageolets, as shown above, made of seamless brass tubing. A reliable and well made instrument, accurately tuned, and must not be compared with cheap imitations. A sheet of instructions with each instrument. Furnished in any of the following keys: B, C, D, E, F, G. Price.............18c

No. 12C3367 Same as above, only nickel plated. Price...(If by mail, postage extra, 8 cents)....21c

BE SURE TO STATE KEY WANTED.

Atlas Fifes.

No. 12C3368 Atlas Fifes, made of cast metal, nickel plated, are of French manufacture and imported by us direct from France. An exceptionally well made instrument, accurately tuned and superior to the ordinary metal flageolets generally offered. Comes only in key of D. Price..................33c

If by mail, postage extra, 8 cents.

Flageolets.

If by mail, postage extra, 10 cents.

In Pasteboard Boxes.

No. 12C3372 Key of D, Boxwood; black; 1 key. Price.............95c

No.12C3373 Key of D, Grenadilla; German silver trimmed; 1 key. Price.............$1.15

No. 12C3375 Key of D, Grenadilla; German silver trimmed; 4 keys. Price.............$1.45

No. 12C3376 Key of D, Grenadilla; German silver trimmed; 6 keys. Price.............$1.95

Atlas Flageolets.

No. 12C3378 Atlas Flageolets, made of cast metal, nickel plated, are of French manufacture and imported by us direct from France. Is an exceptionally well made instrument, accurately tuned in key of D. Price.............49c

If by mail, postage extra, 12 cents.

Piccolo-Flageolets.

If by mail, postage extra, 12 cents.

With extra mouthpiece; can be played either as a piccolo or as a flageolet. In pasteboard boxes.

No. 12C3382 Key of D, Boxwood; German silver trimmed; 1 key. Price.............$1.25

No. 12C3383 Key of D, Grenadilla; German silver trimmed; 5 keys. Price.............$1.95

No. 12C3384 Key of D, Grenadilla; German silver trimmed; 6 keys. Price.............$2.15

Multiflutes.

No. 12C3391 Multiflute, the latest French novelty. Is a combination instrument. It is made of cast metal, nickel plated, and has three distinct mouthpieces, as shown in the illustration. The instrument is of French manufacture and imported by us direct from France. It is accurately tuned in key of F, and is easy to play. Price.............65c

If by mail, postage extra, 16 cents.

Piccolos.

If by mail, postage extra, 15 cents.

No. 12C3392 Cocoa wood, one key, German silver trimmed, in pasteboard box. Key of D or E flat. Price.............40c

No. 12C3393 Cocoa wood, with one key and tuning slide, German silver trimmed, in pasteboard box. Key of D or E flat. Price.............60c

No. 12C3394 Grenadilla wood, with tuning slide and four keys, German silver trimmed, in pasteboard box. Key of D or E flat. Price.............95c

No. 12C3395 Grenadilla wood, with tuning slide, six keys, German silver trimmed, cork joints, in pasteboard box. Key of D or E flat. Price.$1.40

Meyer Pattern Piccolo.

ANYONE KNOWING THE VALUE OF PICCOLOS will acknowledge the wonderful superiority of the MEYER PICCOLOS. The one shown in the illustration below is offered as a **select example of the highest grade Meyer pattern piccolo it is possible to make.**

No.12C3396 Grenadilla, ivory head, six keys, with slide cork joints and German silver trimmed, in fine velvet lined morocco case, as shown in illustration. Key of D or E flat. Price.............$4.10

Shipping weight, 15 ounces.

FOR FIFE AND FLUTE MOUTHPIECES, SEE PAGE 182.

OUR FINE LINE OF FLUTES.

We are illustrating on this page an exceptionally fine line of flutes, which are all of very high grade. We sell these flutes at the same small margin of profit that we sell all of our other musical instruments, and we guarantee them to be perfectly satisfactory. We do not, however, guarantee these instruments against checking or cracking, as this depends entirely upon the care given the instrument by the player. We will, however, guarantee the instruments as to tune, tone and workmanship.

All of these Flutes are made of grenadilla wood, selected stock, accurately bored and handsomely finished. They are fitted with pure German silver keys, highly polished and we guarantee them absolutely as to tone, tune and wearing qualities. These instruments are all made by one of the most celebrated European flute makers, and we take pleasure in offering them to American musicians. Remember that we send out all of these flutes with the understanding that if they do not prove satisfactory in every way, and up to your expectations in every particular, we will refund your money and pay the express charges both ways. The prices which we make on these flutes are less than one-half the prices which other dealers are asking for instruments of inferior grade, and these prices are only made possible by the fact that we ship them directly from our house to the customer. They are suitable for bands or orchestras, and can be used right along with piano or violin if the proper key is selected. Do not class these instruments with the different cheap flutes which local dealers are offering throughout the country, because these are high class instruments in every way, and when we ship them to our customers they go with our absolute guarantee of quality. If you are looking for a good flute at a very small price, we highly recommend these instruments to your consideration. We can furnish anything in this line from one-key flutes to the very finest Boehm instrument with a guarantee to sell them for lower prices than any other dealer can make.

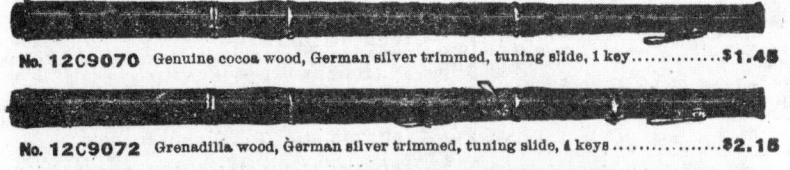

No. 12C9070 Genuine cocoa wood, German silver trimmed, tuning slide, 1 key..............**$1.45**

No. 12C9072 Grenadilla wood, German silver trimmed, tuning slide, 4 keys..................**$2.15**

No. 12C9074 Grenadilla wood, tuning slide, cork joints, 6 keys, German silver caps and trimmings..........**$2.95**

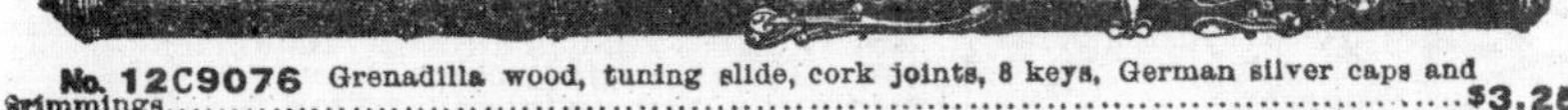

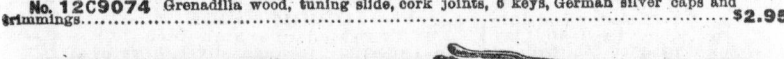

No. 12C9076 Grenadilla wood, tuning slide, cork joints, 8 keys, German silver caps and trimmings..........**$3.25**

No. 12C9078 Grenadilla wood, tuning slide, cork joints, 8 keys, German silver caps and trimmings and metal embouchure..........**$4.30**

No. 12C9079 Key of D, grenadilla wood, tuning slide, cork joints, American ivory head.... **8.85**

No. 12C9080 Genuine Meyer Model Flute. Key of D, 8 keys, grenadilla wood, tuning slide, cork joints, in fine morocco velvet lined case, with joint caps, grease box, swab, pads and screwdriver..**$5.45**

No. 12C9082 Genuine Meyer Model Flute. Key of D, 10 keys, grenadilla wood, tuning slide, cork joints, in fine morocco, velvet lined case with joint caps, grease box, swab, pads and screwdriver..**$8.45**

No. 12C9084 Genuine Meyer Model Flute. Key of D, 10 keys, grenadilla wood, tuning slide, cork joints, genuine ivory head in velvet lined morocco case, with joint caps, grease box, swab, pads and screwdriver..........**$11.45**

OUR SPLENDID LINE OF CLARIONETS.

We are now handling three fine lines of clarionets, as follows: The LaFayette & Co. Conservatoire, the celebrated J. B. Martin instruments, which we have handled so successfully for years, and the fine new line of Tourville & Co.'s Universelle clarionets.

LaFayette & Co.'s Conservatoire Clarionets.

These clarionets are certainly the finest line of low priced clarionets ever offered to the American bandmen. They are substantially made and well finished. They are made of grenadilla wood and all of the trimmings are pure German silver, highly polished. We promise to save the purchaser from $5.00 to $10.00 upon each one of these clarionets bought from us, and will ask our friends to compare them and the prices we ask, with the instruments and prices offered by other dealers. LaFayette & Co. have been manufacturing these clarionets for years. They have always given the greatest satisfaction.

No. 12C8850 13 keys, 2 rings, grenadilla wood, in A, Bb, C, or Eb..................**$9.95**
No. 12C8852 15 keys, 2 rings, grenadilla wood, in A, Bb, C, or Eb..................**11.95**
Weight, 13 keys, 20 ounces.
Weight, 15 keys, 23 ounces.

J. B. Martin Clarionets.

This is the line of favorite clarionets which we have handled for years, and which have given such universal satisfaction. We do not believe that there is a line of moderate priced clarionets on the American market today which in any way equals them in tone and finish. They are all made of genuine grenadilla wood, with trimmings of pure German silver, highly polished. They are bored through cleanly and evenly, and are accurately made throughout. We guarantee them as to tune and tone, and are prepared to take back any instrument which does not give satisfaction in every way. These clarionets, as well as the balance of our line, are fitted with the Albert system, and we can furnish them in all of the different keys. Bear in mind that you take no chances in purchasing one of these instruments, because we send them out on approval and we do not ask you to accept them unless you are perfectly satisfied in every respect. Many expert clarionet players have been surprised at the wonderful degree of superiority demonstrated by these clarionets. Bandmen desiring to furnish their reed sections with clarionets, and who are not prepared to pay a large amount for such instruments, cannot do better than purchase a set of these splendid clarionets.

No. 12C8854 13 keys, 2 rings, grenadilla wood, in A, Bb, C, or Eb.. **$11.25**
No. 12C8856 15 keys, 2 rings, grenadilla wood, in A, Bb, C, or Eb.. **13.45**
No. 12C8858 15 keys, 4 rings, grenadilla wood, in A, Bb, C, or Eb.. **15.95**
Weight, 13 keys, 20 ounces. Weight, 15 keys, 23 ounces.

Tourville & Co.'s Universelle Clarionets.

Tourville & Co.'s Universelle Clarionets are considered by experts to be the finest in the world. We are offering these instruments in response to a demand for a line of clarionets which will be as fine as can be procured. We are willing to say without question that no clarionet, however costly, can excel these instruments in tune, tone and wearing qualities. They are used by all the finest concert bands of Europe, and, are meeting with an enthusiastic reception from clarionet players in this country. They are all made of the finest selected grenadilla wood, accurately and evenly bored, with the intervals absolutely perfect. The trimmings are all pure German silver, highly polished and strongly made. Because we are offering these clarionets at such extremely low prices, we do not want you to make the mistake of classing them with the different lines of low class clarionets, which are offered throughout the country by dealers today. The reason we are able to make such extremely low prices upon these instruments is because we purchase them directly from the manufacturer in France, and sell them by our usual method directly to the customer. No clarionet should cost over $22.00, and when you pay a higher price than this you are simply paying for the name of the maker, which in many cases adds no value to the clarionet in any way.

No. 12C8860 13 keys, 2 rings, grenadilla wood, in A, Bb, C, or Eb.. **$15.45**
No. 12C8862 15 keys, 2 rings, grenadilla wood, in A, Bb, C or Eb.. **18.85**
No. 12C8864 15 keys, 4 rings, grenadilla wood, in A, Bb, C, or Eb.. **21.95**
Weight, 13 keys, 20 ounces. Weight, 15 keys, 23 ounces.

ACME PROFESSIONAL DRUMS.

THE ACME PROFESSIONAL TENOR OR SNARE DRUMS.

PRUSSIAN PATTERN.

Weight, packed, about 15 pounds.

No. 12C3470 Has 14-inch maple shell, 6 inches high; seven rods, white metal plated hooks and trimmings, six snares, one calfskin head, one pair rosewood sticks. Price..............**$4.35**

No. 12C3472 Has 16-inch maple shell, is 6 inches high with eight rods and hoops of maple, finished in imitation rosewood or ebony, with trimmings of white metal, plated, best quality calfskin head, eight rawhide snares. Price, including one pair of rosewood sticks.......**$4.85**

No. 12C3474 The same style of drum as No. 12C3472, with brass shell. Price.....**$4.95**

No. 12C3476 The same drum as No. 12C3472, but has two best quality calfskin heads. Price, including one pair of rosewood sticks..........**$5.10**

No. 12C3478 Same drum as No. 12C3472, but has brass shell, and two best quality calfskin heads. Price, including one pair rosewood sticks.......**$5.20**

No. 12C3480 Has 16-inch shell, is 6 inches high with **eight patent rods,** hoops of maple, decorated with fancy decalcomanie ornamentation, trimmings of white metal plated, best of calfskin heads, **eight rawhide snares.** Price, including one pair of rosewood sticks..........**$5.25**

No. 12C3482 Same description as No. 12C3480, with the exception of the shell, which is made of brass.
Price, including one pair of rosewood sticks..........**$5.45**

OUR ACME PROFESSIONAL TENOR OR SNARE DRUMS.

REGULATION PATTERN.

Weight, packed, about 15 pounds.

No. 12C3488 This is the regulation pattern with a shell 14 inches in diameter, made of bird's eye maple, varnish finish, 8 inches high, cord hooks, with seven braces. The hoops are of maple, finished in imitation ebony or rosewood, best of calfskin heads, **six snares,** new pattern snare strainer. Price, including one pair of sticks.**$4.85**

No. 12C3490 Regulation pattern, but with a 16-inch shell, 9½ inches high, made of bird's eye maple with maple hoops, finished in ebony or rosewood. Shell has fine varnish finish, **eight braces, best calfskin heads, new pattern snare strainers.** Price, including one pair of rosewood sticks..........**$5.55**

No. 12C3492 The same description as No. 12C3490, but has a shell made of rosewood, fine varnish finished. Price..........**$5.60**

IF YOU DO NOT FIND DESCRIBED HEREIN JUST WHAT YOU NEED, WRITE US. Additional supplies for drum corps, such as fifes, piccolos, drum major's batons, etc., will be found in this catalogue. **Many imitations of these pattern drums are now on the market.** Bear in mind that price alone does not make a bargain. Quality must be just as great a consideration. Through our factory to consumer plan we **combine quality and price** in a degree of economic perfection never before seen. We claim the best goods at the least money, and only ask a fair chance to back up every assertion.

OUR ACME PROFESSIONAL ORCHESTRA DRUMS.

No. 12C3494 Has 16-inch brass shell, 4 inches high, maple hoops finished in imitation ebony, ten rods, white metal hooks and trimmings, eight rawhide snares and two extra selected calfskin heads.
Price, including one pair rosewood sticks..........**$5.55**

No. 12C3495 Same description as No. 12C3494 but with nickel plated shell...**$5.59**

No. 12C3496 This is our best orchestra drum. It has a 16-inch diameter, nickel plated shell, 4 inches high. Hoops are made of maple, highly finished in imitation ebony and inlaid with a very fine white metal band, ½ inch wide, giving the drum a very handsome and striking appearance. It has ten nickel plated rods, nickel plated hooks and trimmings, eight rawhide snares and two calfskin heads. With this drum we include, free, a pair of genuine ebony sticks. Price..........**$6.45**

DRUMMERS' DELIGHT—SINGLE HEADED DRUMS.

No. 12C3493 This drum has been designed to meet the requirements of drummers wishing a very sharp drum. It is quick in responding to the lightest touch of the sticks. It has a bird's eye maple shell, highly polished, 14½ inches diameter, 3¾ inches high including hoops, twelve special pattern, nickel plated rods, highly polished, silk snare with special patent adjuster. Best quality transparent head. The real thing for trap drummers. **Easily** carried. Occupies little space.
Price, including a pair of genuine ebony sticks..........**$6.95**

ACME PROFESSIONAL BASS DRUMS.

Weight, packed, about 50 pounds.

Following descriptions are for the regulation pattern bass drums. **We can furnish the Prussian pattern in same size at same price.** Prussian pattern bass drums are all 9½ inches high.

No. 12C3502 Bird's Eye Maple Shell, finished in natural color, 24 inches in diameter, cord hooks 10 inches high, has eleven braces, **made of best Italian hemp cord,** strung over the improved pattern cord hook. Has one calfskin and one sheepskin head.
Price, including one buckskin head stick................**$7.45**

No. 12C3504 Same as No. 12C3502, but has two calfskin heads. Price..**$8.45**

No. 12C3510 Has a shell 28 inches in diameter, made of maple, finished in either natural color or imitation mahogany, 12 inches high, has 13| braces, **made of the best Italian hemp cord,** strung over improved pattern cord hooks, maple hoops, finished in imitation ebony or rosewood, **has one calfskin and one sheepskin head.** Price, including one buckskin head stick................**$ 8.90**

No. 12C3512 Same as No. 12C3510, but has two calfskin heads. Price................**10.25**

No. 12C3514 Has a shell 30 inches in diameter, made of maple, finished in either natural color or imitation mahogany, 12 inches high, has 14 braces, **made of the best Italian hemp,** strung over improved cord hooks, maple hoops, finished in imitation ebony or rosewood, has one calfskin and one sheepskin head. Shipping weight, boxed, 65 pounds. Price, including one buckskin head stick................**$ 9.85**

No. 12C3516 Same as No. 12C3514, but has two calfskin heads. Price................**11.95**

No. 12C3522 This is the largest bass drum we handle, and we especially recommend it to large bands on account of its deep and powerful tone. It has a shell 36 inches in diameter, 12 inches high, made of fine maple, finished in either natural color or imitation mahogany, 17 braces, nickel hooks and strung with genuine Italian hemp cord. Two extra quality calfskin heads.
Price, including one buckskin head stick................**$15.45**

Folding Drum Stand.

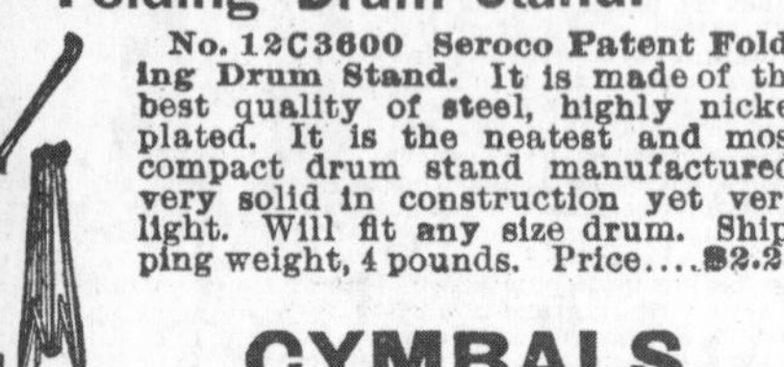

No. 12C3600 Seroco Patent Folding Drum Stand. It is made of the best quality of steel, highly nickel plated. It is the neatest and most compact drum stand manufactured, very solid in construction yet very light. Will fit any size drum. Shipping weight, 4 pounds. Price....**$2.25**

CYMBALS.

No. 12C3660 10-inch Brass Cymbals, with leather handles. Weight, 35 ounces. Price, per pair............**95c**

No. 12C3661 11-inch Brass Cymbals, with leather handles. Weight, 40 ounces. Price, per pair..........**$1.10**

No. 12C3662 12-inch Brass Cymbals, with leather handles. Weight, 45 ounces.
Price, per pair....**$1.25**

No. 12C3663 13-inch Brass Cymbals, with leather handles. Weight, 50 ounces.
Price, per pair.....**$1.45**

No. 12C3664 Turkish Cymbals, 8-inch, composition metal, with leather handles. Weight, 35 ounces.
Price, per pair................................**$3.45**

No. 12C3666 Turkish Cymbals, 12-inch, composition metal, with leather handles. Weight, 65 ounces.
Price, per pair................................**$6.95**

Drum and Cymbal Beater.

No. 12C3668 Combined Drum and Cymbal Beater. Made entirely of metal. An important advantage of this beater is being able to play with greater rapidity and accuracy than with any other make on account of its quick action and simple construction. Easy to carry, as it is easily put together and packed. Shipping weight, 5 pounds.
Price, without cymbal.........**$3.60**

Bones and Clappers.

No. 12C3670 Bones, Hardwood, 5½ inches. Weight, 5 oz. Price, per set of four........**8c**

No. 12C3672 Bones, Rosewood, 5½ inches. Weight, 5½ ounces. Price, per set of four..**11c**

No. 12C3674 Bones, Rosewood, 7 inches long. Weight, 6 ounces.
Price, per set of four................................**15c**

No. 12C3676 Bones, Solid Ebony, 5½ inches. Weight, 6 ounces. Price, per set of four........**21c**

No. 12C3678 Bones, Solid Ebony, 7 inches long. Weight, 7 ounces. Price, per set of four..........**26c**

No. 12C3680 Clappers. Made of walnut, with patent steel spring and lead clappers. Weight, 4 ounces. Price, per set of two................................**6c**

Triangles.

No. 12C3684 4-inch nickeled steel, with hammer. Weight, 7 oz. Price..**16c**

No. 12C3686 6-inch nickeled steel, with hammer. Weight, 9 oz. Price..**18c**

No. 12C3688 7-inch nickeled steel, with hammer. Weight, 12 oz. Price..**24c**

No. 12C3690 8-inch nickeled steel, with hammer. Weight, 15 ounces. Price........................**30c**

Triangle Beater.

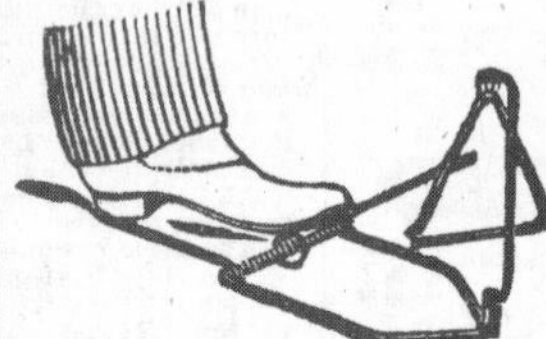

No. 12C3694 Made of nickel plated wire, very strong and durable. Used to play with foot, thus allowing both hands to be free for the use of other instruments. Shipping weight, 10 ounces.
Price, without triangle............**40c**

Tambourines.

No. 12C3696 7-inch maple rim, with tacked sheepskin head and three sets of jingles.
Weight, 10 ounces.
Price, per dozen, **$2.16; each**................**18c**

No. 12C3698 Same, with 8-inch head. Weight, 12 ounces. Price, per dozen, **$2.64;** each.........**22c**

No. 12C3700 Same, with 10-inch head. Weight, 14 ounces. Price, per dozen, **$3.24;** each..........**27c**

No. 12C3702 Maple painted rim, 8-inch tacked calfskin head, nine sets of jingles. Weight, 16 ounces.
Price................................**45c**

No. 12C3704 Maple painted rim, 10-inch tacked calfskin head, twelve sets jingles. Weight, 19 ounces.
Price................................**60c**

Salvation Army Tambourines.

No. 12C3709 10-inch Maple Hoop, fancy painted and ornamented, 28 sets brass jingles, calfskin head fastened with brass tacks. Weight, 28 ounces.
Price................................**$1.17**

No. 12C3711 Same as No. 12C3709, but with 32 sets of jingles. Weight, 32 ounces. Price.....**$1.35**

Ocarinas.

Fiehn's Vienna Make.

NO BETTER OCARINAS can be had at any price than these **genuine imported instruments.**

WE IMPORT THESE DIRECT FROM EUROPE and own them at prices enabling us to offer them to you at about what your dealer himself pays.

THESE INSTRUMENTS ARE EASILY BROKEN and must be packed with care. **We guarantee** that each Ocarina leaves our hands in perfect condition.

A sheet of instructions with each instrument showing exactly how it is played.

No.	Key of	Price	No.	Key of	Price
12C3720	C, Soprano	$0.13	12C3730	A, Alto	$0.29
12C3721	Bb, Soprano	.13	12C3732	G, Alto	.34
12C3722	A, Soprano	.13	12C3733	F, Alto	.42
12C3723	G, Soprano	.16	12C3735	Eb, Alto	.69
12C3724	F, Soprano	.16	12C3736	D, Bass	.69
12C3725	E, Soprano	.18	12C3737	C, Bass	1.00
12C3726	Eb, Soprano	.18	12C3738	Bb, Bass	1.20
12C3727	D, Alto	.22	12C3739	A, Bass	1.25
12C3728	C, Alto	.24	12C3741	G, Bass	1.85
12C3729	Bb, Alto	.27			

No. 12C3746 Quartettes: 1st and 2d Tenor, 1st and 2d Bass. Price, per set................**$2.95**

If by mail, postage extra. Sopranos, 4 cents each; Altos, 14 cents each; Basses, 26 cents each.

Jews' Harps.

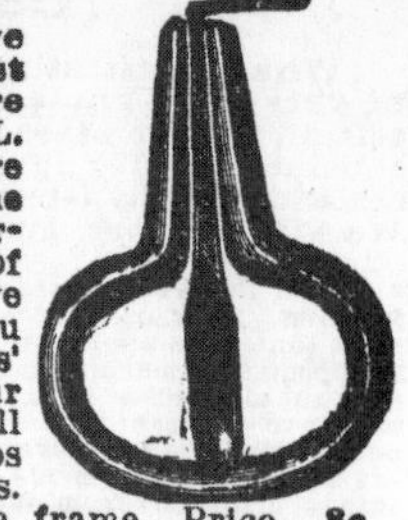

The Jews' Harps which we list below are made by the best maker in America, and are known as the genuine E. L. American Jews' Harps and are not to be compared with the many inferior harps on the market. They are all made of white metal frames and have brass tipped tongues. If you are thinking of ordering a Jews' Harp it will pay you to buy our genuine E. L. Harp. They will outlast six of the ordinary harps offered for sale by other dealers.

No. 12C3750 Has a 2-inch frame. Price...**8c**
No. 12C3751 Has a 2¼-inch frame. Price..**9c**
If by mail, postage extra, 3 cents.
No. 12C3752 Has a 2½-inch frame. Price.**12c**
No. 12C3753 Has a 2¾-inch frame. Price..**15c**
If by mail, postage extra, 4 cents.
No. 12C3754 Has a 3¼-inch frame. Price..**18c**
No. 12C3755 Has a 3½-inch frame. Price..**26c**
If by mail, postage extra, 5 cents.
No. 12C3756 Has a 3¾-inch frame. Price..**29c**
No. 12C3757 Jumbo Harp. Has a 4¼-inch frame. Price...**(If by mail, postage extra, 6 cents)**..**39c**

Tuning Forks.

New standard or low pitch.

No. 12C3780 Steel, A or C, philharmonic. Price................................**6c**

No. 12C3781 Nickel plated steel, A or C, superior quality. Price....(Postage extra, 2 cents)....**19c**

No. 12C3782 Blued steel, A or C, superior quality. Price................................**28c**

If by mail, postage extra, 2 cents.

Tuning Pipes.

New standard or high pitch.

No. 12C3790 German silver, keys of A and C combined, extra fine quality in white metal boxes. Price................**7c**

No. 12C3792 Same, keys of C and G combined. Price. **(Postage extra, 2 cents)**....**7c**

For violin, mandolin and guitar tuners, see pages containing Violin, Mandolin, Guitar and Banjo Furnishings.

Piano Tuning Hammers.

No. 12C3801 Long rosewood handle with extension rod of steel, double head with oblong holes, and single head with star holes. Extra quality, warranted. Weight, 2 pounds. Price................................**$1.35**

Metronomes.

The Metronome is used by students of music, especially of the piano, to indicate the tempo or time. The upright rod moves backward and forward like an inverted pendulum, the movement being actuated by a spring which is wound up with a key. The time is indicated both to eye and ear, the movement being in sight and ticking similar to a clock. **The time is regulated fast or slow by the sliding weight on the pendulum, while the latter has a graduated scale. This is an invaluable instrument for pupils of the piano and organ especially.** Weight, 2 pounds.

We sell both the American and French makes.

No. 12C3805 Metronome. American make, Maelzel system, imitation mahogany case. Price....................**$1.65**

No. 12C3806 Metronome. Same as above, with bell which strikes the first beat in every measure. Price..........**$2.60**

No. 12C3807 Metronome. Genuine French make, solid mahogany case. Maelzel system. Price................**$1.95**

No. 12C3808 Same as No. 12C3807, but with bell attachment. Price................................**$2.95**

NOVELTY MUSICAL INSTRUMENTS.

The Kazoo.

No. 12C3810 The Kazoo is the simplest instrument made. No trouble to learn. Place your lips to the instrument, make a noise and pleasing music is emitted. The 1902 model is all the rage. Made of metal, nickel plated. Price................**8c**

If by mail, postage extra, 2 cents.

Sonophone Brass Musical Instruments.

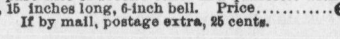

Sonophone Musical Instruments are the latest invention of the day and are rapidly becoming the most popular amusement in the novelty and musical way, as the tune is produced by singing into them. Anyone can play them without difficulty, and produce good music or many imitations if so desired. With **Sonophone Brass Band Instruments** a brass band can be organized with men or boys who have no knowledge of musical instruments whatever, but with a few rehearsals are capable of rendering brilliant music, and producing instrumental effects possible hitherto to none but the best brass bands and orchestras.

No. 12C3812 Sonophone Cornetina. Solid metal, brass finished, highly polished, 7½ inches long; 3⅝-inch bell. Price.**25c**
If by mail, postage extra, 4 cents.

No. 12C3814 Sonophone Cornet. Same as above, but much larger, being 9 inches long with a 4⅝-inch bell. Better in tone and appearance. Price................................**45c**
If by mail, postage extra, 15 cents.

No. 12C3816 Sonophone Alto. This instrument is still larger than No. 12C3814. Its tone is lower and deeper. Used to play second part alto or second tenor in a quartette with great effect. Size, 15 inches long, 6-inch bell. Price............**60c**
If by mail, postage extra, 25 cents.

STRINGS.

WE IMPORT DIRECT FROM EUROPEAN MANUFACTURERS and handle none but the best strings made. Not an inferior string sold by us at any price. We guarantee every one to be perfectly made of the best quality and material. WE DO NOT GUARANTEE THEM AGAINST BREAKING, but they will stand anything that can be expected of the best strings made. We solicit your orders on this particular line, knowing that we can please you to an eminent degree and save you from 50 to 60 per cent on every purchase.

SILVER TONED BELL BRAND STRINGS.

Without doubt the best steel strings on the market. They are carefully and accurately made of tested materials of superior quality. The steel used is especially made, giving the strings the true tone of silver like bell quality. Each string is carefully tested, heavily silver plated and polished, wrapped in anti-tarnish ribbed silver tissue paper and enclosed in an oil paper envelope, making the strings impervious to moisture and climatic changes and preserves them against tarnish and rust. We recommend the Bell Brand strings as being strictly high grade in every particular.

Silk Violin E Strings.

No.	Description	Doz.	Each
No. 12C4125	The celebrated Muller's Eternelle. Most reliable string in existence	$1.08	9c

If by mail, postage extra, 2 cents.

Excellent Quality Violin Strings.

No.	Description	Doz.	Each
No. 12C4130	E, 4 lengths, polished	$0.84	7c
No. 12C4132	E, rough finish, 4 lengths	.84	7c
No. 12C4134	A, 2½ lengths	.84	7c
No. 12C4136	D, 2½ lengths	1.08	9c
No. 12C4138	G, 1 length	.72	6c
No. 12C4139	Full set of four	Per set,	28c

If by mail, postage extra, per set, 2 cents.

No. 12C4140 G string, extra fine quality, pure silver wire wound on gut. Price, each.........40c
If by mail, postage extra, 2 cents.

Our Special Waterproof Violin Strings.

By virtue of a special preparation these are purer in tone than the ordinary strings. They are made scientifically correct and absolutely unsusceptible to climatic influences. They are especially desirable for players who are troubled with moist fingers, as they possess extraordinary durability. Every string is fully tested and warranted.

No.	Description	Doz.	Each
No. 12C4141	E, waterproof, 4 lengths	$1.56	13c
No. 12C4142	A, waterproof, 2½ lengths	1.56	13c
No. 12C4143	D, waterproof, 2½ lengths	1.92	16c
No. 12C4144	G, waterproof, 1 length	.84	7c

No. 12C4145 Full set of 4 waterproof strings. E, A, D and G. Price, per set.........49c
If by mail, postage extra, 2 cents.

Our "Verona" Brand Violin Strings.

Special attention is called to this splendid line of strings, as they are unquestionably as fine as any Italian strings made. They are made of the very best quality sheep gut, and particular attention is called to the way they are wrapped, which insures them against injury in transmission through the mails. We recommend them to all who are looking for fine violin strings at a reasonable price.

No.	Description	Doz.	Each
No. 12C4146	Violin E	$1 92	16c
No. 12C4147	Violin A	1.92	16c
No. 12C4148	Violin D	2.28	19c
No. 12C4149	Violin G	1.20	10c
No. 12C4150	Full set of above, per set		61c

Extra Quality Acme Professional Violin Gut Strings.

No.	Description	Doz.	Each
No. 12C4162	E, best quality, 4 lengths	$1.08	9c
No. 12C4164	A, best quality, 2½ lengths	1.08	9c
No. 12C4166	D, best quality, 2½ lengths	1.32	11c
No. 12C4168	G, best quality, 1 length	.84	7c
No. 12C4170	Full set of above	Per set,	36c

If by mail, postage extra, per set, 2 cents.

No. 12C4171 G string, pure silver wire wound on gut, burnished, superfine quality, each.....50c
If by mail, postage extra, 2 cents.

Glendon Violin Strings.

Silvered Steel.

No.	Description	Doz.	Each
No. 12C4172	E, 1 length	5c	
No. 12C4174	A, 1 length	5c	
No. 12C4176	D, 1 length, covered	12c	1c
No. 12C4178	G, 1 length, covered	12c	1c
No. 12C4180	Full set of four	Per set,	4c

If by mail, postage extra, per set or dozen, 2 cents.

Bell Brand Violin Strings.

Steel, triple silver plated and polished.

No.	Description	Doz.	Each
No. 12C4182	E, 1 length	24c	2c
No. 12C4184	A, 1 length	24c	2c
No. 12C4186	D, 1 length, covered steel	36c	3c
No. 12C4188	G, 1 length, covered steel	48c	4c
No. 12C4190	Full set of 4 strings	Per set,	11c

If by mail, postage extra, per set or dozen, 3 cents.

Extra Quality Acme Professional Banjo Gut Strings.

No.	Description	Doz.	Each
No. 12C4194	B or 1st and E or 5th	$0.84	7c
No. 12C4196	G or 2d	.96	8c
No. 12C4198	E or 3d	1.08	9c
No. 12C4200	A or 4th	.72	6c
No. 12C4202	Full set of five	Per set,	37c

If by mail, postage extra, per set, 2 cents.

Glendon Banjo Strings.

Silvered Steel.

No.	Description	Doz.	Each
No. 12C4220	B or 1st and E or 5th	5c	
No. 12C4222	G or 2d	5c	
No. 12C4224	E or 3d	5c	
No. 12C4226	A or 4th	24c	2c
No. 12C4228	Full set of five	Per set,	5c

If by mail, postage extra, per set, 2 cents.

Bell Brand Banjo Strings.

Steel, triple silver plated and polished.

No.	Description	Doz.	Each
No. 12C4230	B or 1st and E or 5th	24c	2c
No. 12C4232	G or 2d, 1 length	24c	2c
No. 12C4234	E or 3d, 1 length	24c	2c
No. 12C4236	A or 4th, 1 length	48c	4c
No. 12C4238	Full set of 5 strings	Per set,	12c

If by mail, postage extra, per set, 3 cents.

Professional Guitar Strings.

		Doz.	Ea.
No. 12C4240	E or 1st, sup'r quality gut	$0.96	8c
No. 12C4242	B or 2d, sup'r quality gut	.96	8c
No. 12C4244	G or 3d, sup'r quality gut	1.20	10c
No. 12C4246	D or 4th, silv'd wire on silk	.48	4c
No. 12C4248	A or 5th, silv'd wire on silk	.60	5c
No. 12C4250	E or 6th, silv'd wire on silk	.72	6c
No. 12C4252	Full set of six	Per set,	41c

If by mail, postage extra, per set, 3 cents.

Extra Quality Acme Professional Guitar Gut Strings.

No.	Description	Doz.	Each
No. 12C4260	E or 1st	$1.08	9c
No. 12C4262	B or 2d	1.08	9c
No. 12C4264	G or 3d	1.68	14c

D, A and E strings silvered wire on silk, plush knobs.

No.	Description	Doz.	Each
No. 12C4265	D or 4th	$0.96	8c
No. 12C4266	A or 5th	1.08	9c
No. 12C4267	E or 6th	1.20	10c
No. 12C4268	Full set of six	Per set,	59c

If by mail, postage extra, per set, 3 cents.

Glendon Guitar Strings.

Silvered Steel.

No.	Description	Doz.	Each
No. 12C4270	E or 1st	5c	
No. 12C4272	B or 2d	5c	

G, D, A, E strings silvered wire wound on steel.

No.	Description	Doz.	Each
No. 12C4274	G or 3d	12c	1c
No. 12C4276	D or 4th	24c	2c
No. 12C4278	A or 5th	36c	3c
No. 12C4280	E or 6th	48c	4c
No. 12C4282	Full set of six	Per set,	12c

If by mail, postage extra, per set, 2c; per doz., 4c.

Bell Brand Guitar Strings.

Steel, triple silver plated and polished.

No.	Description	Doz.	Each
No. 12C4283	E or 1st, 1 length	24c	2c
No. 12C4284	B or 2d, 1 length	24c	2c

G, D, A, E strings silvered wire wound on steel.

No.	Description	Doz.	Each
No. 12C4285	G or 3d, 1 length	48c	4c
No. 12C4286	D or 4th, 1 length	60c	5c
No. 12C4287	A or 5th, 1 length	72c	6c
No. 12C4288	E or 6th, 1 length	84c	7c
No. 12C4289	Full set of six	Per set,	26c

If by mail, postage extra, per set, 3c; per dozen, 5c.

Glendon Mandolin Strings.

Silvered Steel.

No.	Description	Doz.	Each
No. 12C4290	E or 1st, 1 length	5c	
No. 12C4292	A or 2d, 1 length	5c	
No. 12C4294	D or 3d, 1 length	12c	1c
No. 12C4296	G or 4th, 1 length	12c	1c
No. 12C4298	Full set of eight	Per set,	6c

If by mail, postage extra, per set, 2c; per doz., 4c.

Bell Brand Mandolin Strings.

Steel triple silver plated and polished.

No.	Description	Doz.	Each
No. 12C4310	E or 1st, 1 length	24c	2c
No. 12C4312	A or 2d, 1 length	24c	2c
No. 12C4316	D or 3d, 1 length	36c	3c
No. 12C4318	G or 4th, 1 length	48c	4c
No. 12C4320	Full set of eight	Per set,	22c

If by mail, postage extra, per set or dozen, 3 cents.

Best Quality Double Bass Strings.

No.	Description	Each
No. 12C4321	G or 1st, Italian gut	$0.70
No. 12C4323	D or 2d, Italian gut	90
No. 12C4325	A or 3d, Italian gut	1.15
No. 12C4327	A or 3d, silvered wire on gut	1.00
No. 12C4329	E or 4th, silvered wire on gut	1.40

Postage extra, single string, 4c; per set, 12c.

Acme Violoncello Strings.

No. 12C4340	A, best quality. Each	11c
No. 12C4342	D, best quality. Each	17c
No. 12C4344	G, best wired gut. Each	8c
No. 12C4346	C, best wired gut. Each	9c
No. 12C4348	Full set of four. Per set	45c

Postage extra, single string, 2 cents; per set, 5 cents.

Autoharp Strings.

No. 12C4350	Full set for No. 71	20c
No. 12C4352	Full set for No. 2¾	25c
No. 12C4354	Full set for No. 72⅞ or 3, 4, 5	30c
No. 12C4358	Full set for No. 6	35c
No. 12C4359	Full set for No. 73	40c
No. 12C4360	Plain steel strings. Each	3c
No. 12C4362	Bass or wound strings. Each	5c

Postage extra, single string, 1 cent; per set, 4 cents.

When ordering single strings always mention number of harp, letter of string, and whether bass, low, middle, high or highest.

Columbia Zither Strings.

No. 12C4380	Full set for Nos. 1 and 2	50c
No. 12C4382	Full set for Nos. 2½, 3 and 3½	70c
No. 12C4384	Full set for Nos. 3¾ and 4	90c

If by mail, postage extra, per set, 6 cents.

No. 12C4386	Plain steel string. Each	2c
No. 12C4387	Wound or bass string. Each	4c

If by mail, postage extra, each, 1 cent.
Postage extra, per set, 6c; single strings, 1c.

Guitar-Zither Strings.

No. 12C4390	Full set for No. 0½	48c
No. 12C4392	Full set for No. 2	48c
No. 12C4394	Full set for No. 2½	55c
No. 12C4396	Full set for No. 3½	75c
No. 12C4398	Plain strings. Each	3c
No. 12C4400	Wound or covered strings. Ea.	5c

VIOLIN CASES.

No. 12C4528 Brown Canvas. Opens at end. Leather bound edges, flannel lined, leather handle. Weight, 7 lbs. Price, 60c

No. 12C4529 Violin Case, common shape, well made of wood and half lined with flannel, complete with handle and hooks. Shipping weight, 8 pounds. Price.........68c

No. 12C4530 Same as No. 12C4529 above, with lock. Shipping weight, 8 pounds. Price.........78c

No. 12C4533 Violin Case, of select wood, American made, black varnished, full lined with flannel, complete with nickel plate lock, handle and hook clasps. Shipping weight, 8 pounds. Price.........$1.35

No. 12C4534 Violin Case, made solidly of wood, finely varnished black, exposition shape, full lined throughout with flannel; complete with lock, handle and spring clasps. Full, three-quarter or half size. Shipping weight, 8 pounds. Price.........$1.60

No. 12C4535 Violin Case, covered with a durable waterproof material made in perfect imitation alligator skin, full lined with velvet, leather handle, nickel link clasps and nickel spring lock. Shipping wgt., 8 lbs. Price $2.90

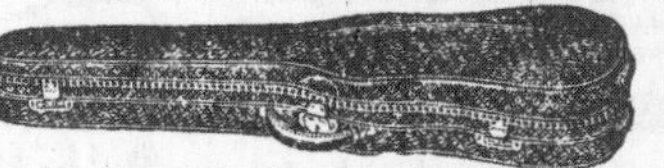

No. 12C4536 Violin Case, made of leather pulp, black finish, waterproof, fleece lined, has leather handle, nickel plated trimmings and patent spring lock. A very strong, durable and light case. Shipping weight, 8 pounds. Price.....$2.95

No. 12C4538 Violin Case, full leather covered and full lined with velvet, leather handle, nickel plated lock and hook hasps. Comes in either black or russet color. Especially good value. Shipping weight, 8 pounds. Price.........$3.50

No. 12C4540 Violin Case, seal grain leather covered, lined throughout with velvet, has hand sewed valance, leather handle and nickel plated spring clasps. This is the best case we handle and retails regularly at $7.00 to $8.00. Comes in black only. Shipping weight, 8 pounds. Price. $4.95

Violin Bows.

If by mail, postage extra, each, 15 cents.

No. 12C4543 Violin Bow, made of imitation snakewood, ebony frog, inlaid dot, pearl slide, bone button. Price.....38c

No. 12C4546 Violin Bow, ebony frog, pearl slide, pearl eye, German silver button, superior quality bow hair. Price. 50c

No. 12C4547 Violin Bow, genuine Brazil wood, ebony frog, pearl slide, pearl dot, German silver lined, German silver button. Price.........69c

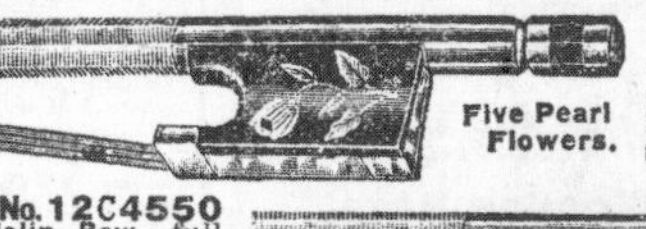

Five Pearl Flowers.

No. 12C4548 Violin Bow, iron wood, ebony frog, German silver lined, German silver button. Price.....89c

No. 12C4550 Violin Bow, full genuine Tourte model, Brazil wood, ebony frog, full German silver lined, German silver button, best quality bow hair. Price.....99c

No. 12C4552 Violin Bow, genuine Brazil wood, very carefully made, best quality ebony frog, German silver lined, extra wide frog and extra quality hair, latest style button. Price.........$1.45

No. 12C4553 Violin Bow is made of select Brazil wood, imitation of snakewood. Has imitation ivory frog and button, like No. 12C4554, double pearl eye, and is German silver lined. Best bow hair. Price.........$1.05

No. 12C4554 Violin Bow is shown in the illustration made of genuine snakewood, has genuine ivory frog, double pearl eye, German silver lined and ivory button. Only the finest quality of bow hair with this bow. Price.....$2.20

Genuine Pernambuco Wood Bows.

No. 12C4557 Genuine Pernambuco wood, best quality, ebony frog, two pearl eyes, full German silver lined, pearl slide, German silver button, full hair, best quality. Price.........$1.95

No. 12C4558 Genuine Pernambuco Wood, octagon shape, best quality ebony frog, two pearl eyes, full German silver button, full hair, best quality, a professional bow. Price.....$2.65

Pure Silver Mounted Bows.

No. 12C4560 Genuine Pernambuco wood, finest quality ebony frog, two pearl eyes, full solid silver trimmed, pearl slide, full hair, best quality. Price.........$2.95

No. 12C4561 Genuine Pernambuco wood, highly finished in natural color, best quality ebony frog, two pearl eyes, solid silver mounted pearl slide, extra full hair, best quality. Regular retail price $6.00. Our price.........$3.95

Our Finest High Grade Bow.

No. 12C4562 Genuine Pernambuco Wood Bow, octagon shape, pure silver mounted, finest ebony frog, pearl eyes and pearl slide, extra quality full hair. This bow retails regularly at $10.00. Our price.........$4.95

Violin Bow Frogs.

No. 12C4563 Violin Bow Frog, ebony, pearl dot inlaid in sides, German silver button, pearl slide. Price....17c

No. 12C4564 Violin Bow Frog, ebony, with pearl dot inlaid in sides; full German silver lined, German silver button, pearl slide. Price....27c

If by mail, postage extra, 2 cents.

Violin Bow Screws.

No. 12C4567 Bow Screw, with bone button, octagon shape, inlaying in end. Shipping weight, 1 ounce. Price....5c

No. 12C4568 Bow Screw, with ebony and German silver button, octagon shape, inlaying in end. Price....6c
If by mail, postage extra, 1 cent.

Aluminum Bow Tip.

No. 12C4569 This is a new idea and is intended for the purpose of repairing violin bows which are broken at the neck. It is so light that it does not destroy the balance or add to the weight of the bow, and makes the bow tip much stronger than if repaired in the usual way. It has a socket in the end into which the stick of the bow can be easily fitted. Price....29c
If by mail, postage extra, 2 cents.

Violin Patent Heads.

No. 12C4570 Violin Patent Head, made of solid brass, with handsome engraving on sides, bone buttons. Price, per set....19c

No. 12C4572 Violin Patent Head, handsomely nickel plated, fancy engraved sides, bone buttons. Price, per set....23c
If by mail, postage extra, 4 cents.
NOTE—Patent heads are made in one size only.

Violin Pegs.

No. 12C4580 Maple Violin Peg, imitation ebony finish, hollow shape, pearl dot in head. Price, per set of four, 7c; each....2c

No. 12C4582 Solid Ebony Violin Peg, hollow shape, pearl dot in head. Price, each, 3c
Per set of four.. 10c
By mail, postage extra each, 1 cent; per set, 2c

No. 12C4589 Solid Ebony Violin Peg, handsomely inlaid with pearl.
Price, per set of four, 64c; each....16c
By mail, postage extra, each, 1 cent; per set, 2c.

The Champion Key.

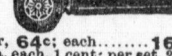

No. 12C4590 Genuine Celluloid Violin Peg, the best patent violin peg made, imitation ebony, nickel mounted.
Price, per set of four, 64c; each....16c

No. 12C4591 Same as No. 12C4590, but with white buttons.
Price, per set of four, 64c; each....16c
By mail, postage extra, each, 2 cents; per set, 6c.

Becker Friction Pegs.

No. 12C4594 These pegs are an entirely new idea, and are so arranged that they do not injure the tone of the violin whatever. They are of great value to ladies and younger scholars especially, who find difficulty in turning up the pegs of their violin. The great advantage of these pegs is that they never slip and when the string is once tuned up to the pitch it remains there.
Price, per set....58c
If by mail, postage extra, 6 cents.

Violin Chin Rests.

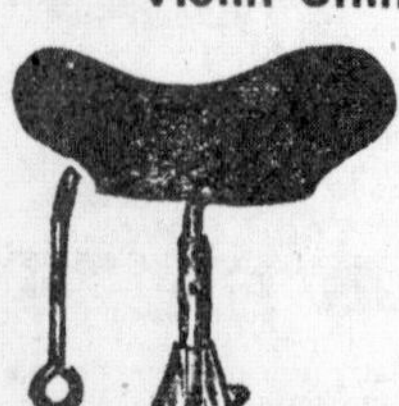

No. 12C4603 Violin Chin Rest, Gutta percha; single screw; double acting. Easily adjusted to any violin, a chin rest which has been found very satisfactory.
Price....19c

No. 12C4604 Violin Chin Rest. Becker's celebrated patent. Ebonite and nickel. Same as No. 12C4606, but without shoulder rest. Price....26c
If by mail, postage extra, each, 6 cents.

Chin and Shoulder Rest.

No. 12C4606 As shown in illustration, chin and shoulder rest combined. The most perfect and complete violin rest made.
Price....60c
If by mail, postage extra, 6 cents.

The Columbia Chin Rest.

No. 12C4607 The Columbia Chin Rest. One of the most desirable features of this chin rest is that it is adjustable to any size instrument. It is made of best gutta percha with full nickel plated mountings. It is very desirable in every respect, and we consider it one of the best chin rests on the market. Price, 55c
If by mail, postage extra, 6 cents.

Violin Tailpieces.

If by mail, postage extra, each, 2 cents.

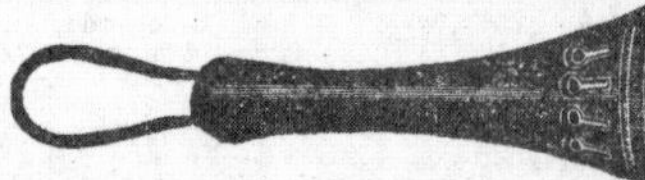

No. 12C4611 Solid Ebony Violin Tailpiece. Excellent model and finish. Fitted complete with tailpiece gut. Price....9c

No. 12C4612 Same as No. 12C4611, but without gut. Price....7c

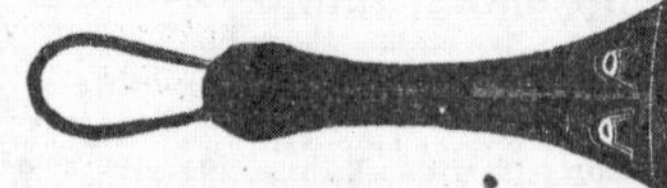

No. 12C4613 Solid Ebony New Model Tailpiece, best quality, without gut.
Price....13c

No. 12C4615 Solid Ebony Violin Tailpiece, same as No. 12C4613. Best quality. Fitted complete with tailpiece gut. Price....16c

No. 12C4617 Solid Ebony Tailpiece, highly polished, inlaid with five colored pearl flowers. Fitted complete with tailpiece gut.
Price....23c

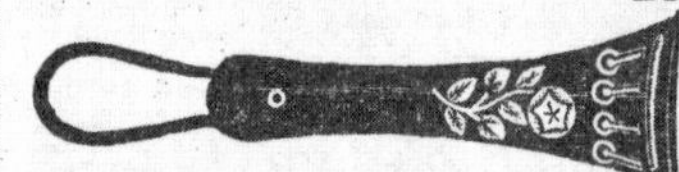

No. 12C4618 Violin Tailpiece; is made of solid ebony, inlaid with seven pearl flowers and has pearl inlay around string holes. Complete with tailpiece gut. Price....45c

No. 12C4620 Our Very Finest Violin Tailpiece, made of select solid ebony, highly polished, inlaid with 11 fancy pearl flowers and bird. Pearl inlaying around string holes. Fitted with tailpiece gut. Price....70c
If by mail, postage extra, each, 2 cents.

Violin Tailpiece Gut.

No. 12C4621 Violin Tailpiece Gut, best quality, in 12-inch lengths to fasten tailpiece to violin. Price, per length....2c
If by mail, postage extra, 1 cent.

Violin Bridges.

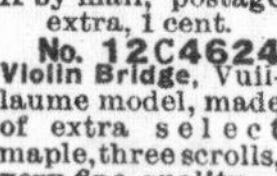

No. 12C4622 Violin Bridge, made of maple, three scrolls, good quality. Price....3c
If by mail, postage extra, 1 cent.

No. 12C4624 Violin Bridge, Vuillaume model, made of extra select maple, three scrolls, very fine quality. Price....8c
If by mail, postage extra, 1 cent.

No. 12C4626 Violin Bridge, made of selected maple. Superfine quality, three scrolls. Made for artists' use. Price....14c
If by mail, postage extra, 1 cent.

Violin Mutes.

No. 12C4630

No. 12C4630 Violin Mute, made of plain solid ebony. Price....5c
If by mail, postage extra, 1 cent.

No. 12C4632 Violin Mute, German silver.
Price....6c
If by mail, postage extra, 1 cent.

No. 12C4636

No. 12C4636 Violin Mute, as illustrated, is made of German silver, and has tuning pipe A and string gauge.
Price....16c
If by mail, postage extra, 1 cent.

Violin Fingerboards.

No. 12C4642 Solid Ebony Fingerboard, fine model, highly finished. Price....14c
If by mail, postage extra, 8 cents.

No. 12C4643 Finest Quality Ebony, French polished. Price....34c
If by mail, postage extra, 8 cents.

Chart for Violin Fingerboard.

You can learn how to play the violin without the aid of a teacher by using the patent lettered fingerboard chart. It is a great help for beginners.

No. 12C4644 This Chart is made in the shape of the fingerboard, and can be easily attached under the strings without changing the instrument, and will enable a beginner to find every note and each position readily. Retail dealers ask 25 cents for this chart. Price....4c
If by mail, postage extra, 2 cents.

Violin Nuts or Saddles.

No. 12C4646 Solid Ebony Nut for upper end of fingerboard. Price....2c
If by mail, postage extra, 1 cent.

No. 12C4648 Solid Ebony Nut, for supporting the tailpiece string. Price....3c
If by mail, postage extra, 1 cent.

Violin End Pins.

No. 12C4652 Ebony, best model, pearl dot inlaid in head. Price....3c
If by mail, postage extra, 1 cent.

Bow Hair.

No. 12C4660 Siberian, good quality, for full length bows. Price, per bunch....9c
If by mail, postage extra, 1 cent.

No. 12C4662 French, finest quality, slightly bleached. Price, per bunch....14c
If by mail, postage extra, 1 cent.

No. 12C4664 Russia, extra quality. Price, per bunch....17c
If by mail, postage extra, 1 cent.

Violin Bow Rosin.

No. 12C4672 Bow Rosin, large size cakes in oblong pasteboard box. Price....2c
If by mail, postage extra, 2 cents.

No. 12C4673 Large Size Metal Spool, in pasteboard case.
Price....5c
If by mail, postage extra, 2 cents.

No. 12C4674 Large Sized Cakes Bow Rosin, in neat wood case, to be used without removing from case. Price....6c
If by mail, postage extra, 2 cents.

No. 12C4678 Genuine Gustav Bernardel Paris Rosin, put up in convenient form. Imported direct from France. Nothing better made. Price....15c
If by mail, postage extra, 2 cents.

No. 12C4679 Same rosin as No. 12C4678, put up in fine metal box.
Price....22c
If by mail, postage extra, 2 cents.

Violin Necks.

No. 12C4680 Violin Necks, maple, unfinished, carved scroll. Price....16c
If by mail, postage extra, 8 cents.

No. 12C4682 Violin Necks, maple, unfinished, fine quality, finely carved scroll.
Price....35c
If by mail, postage extra, 8 cents.

No. 12C4684 Violin Necks, curly maple, unfinished, best quality, finely carved scroll.
Price....58c
If by mail, postage extra, 8 cents.

Sound Post Setter.

No. 12C4688 Sound Post Setter. Steel, nickel plated; can be used in adjusting sound post of any violin. Price....18c
If by mail, postage extra, 4 cents.

Violin Tuner.

No. 12C4690 Four Tuning Pipes, E, A, D, G, combined, for tuning violin. Made of German silver and tuned to concert pitch.
Price....14c
If by mail, postage extra, 3 cents.

Double Bass Bows.

No. 12C4955 Made of Maple, red painted, light wood frog, excellent quality, common model. Shipping weight, 18 ozs. Price 95c

No. 12C4957 Redwood, natural color, ebony frog, good quality, common model.
Price, (Postage extra, 18 cents)....$1.75

Double Bass and Violoncello Fingerboard Chart.

No. 12C4997 This Chart is an accurate guide, having all the notes with sharps and flats in full view, and can be adjusted on any double bass fingerboard without changing the instrument. With the use of the lettered fingerboard chart, anyone can learn how to play.
Price...(If by mail, postage extra, 2c.)..10c

No. 12C5043 This Chart is similar to the Double Bass Chart No. 12C4997, but is adapted only for the violoncello. Price....8c
If by mail, postage extra, 2 cents.

Violoncello Bags.

No. 12C5045 Perfect Fitting Canvas Bag, with button fastener. Shipping weight, 20 ounces. Price...(Postage extra, 20c.)..$1.20

Violoncello Bows.

No. 12C5064

No. 12C5062 Brazil Wood, plain ebony frog, bone button, good quality. Price..70c
If by mail, postage extra, 17 cents.

No. 12C5064 Brazil Wood, ebony frog, pearl eye, German silver button. Price...98c
If by mail, postage extra, 17 cents.

No. 12C5066 Brazil Wood, ebony frog, double pearl eye, full German silver lined, pearl slide, German silver button.
Price, (Postage extra, 17 cents.)....$1.65

Violoncello Bow Hair.

No. 12C5073 Fine Quality Siberian Bow Hair, each filling tied separately. Price. 17c
If by mail, postage extra, 2 cents.

No. 12C5101 Violoncello Patent Head. Made with separate brass plates, iron screws and maple pegs, each peg having a pearl inlaid dot in head. Shipping weight, 1 lb. Price, per set...$1.65

GUITAR FURNISHINGS.

Guitar Cases.

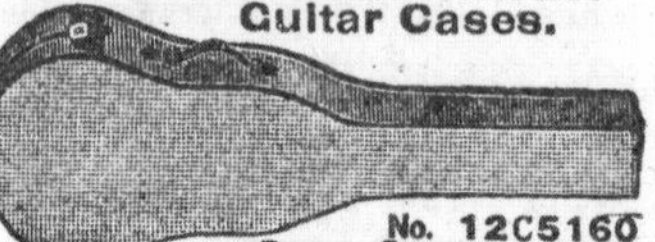

No. 12C5160 Brown Canvas, as illustrated, leather bound edges, open on end, complete with strap, buckle and handle. Standard or regular size. Weight, 5½ lbs. Price..72c

No. 12C5162 Same as No. 12C5160, for concert size. Weight, 5½ pounds. Price, 82c

No. 12C5163 Same as No. 12C5160, for grand concert size. Weight, 6 lbs. Price..92c

No. 12C5164 Hand Sewed Leather, embossed black or russet, very superior quality, for standard size guitar. Shipping weight, 10 pounds. Price....$3.80

No. 12C5166 Same as No. 12C5164, for concert size. Shipping weight, 10 pounds.
Price....$3.95

Guitar Bags.

When ordering, give size of guitar.

No. 12C5168 Fine Green Cloth, with buttons, for standard or concert guitar. Shipping wt. 1 lb. Price, (Postage 16 cents.)..50c

No. 12C5170 Green Felt, fleece lined, patent fasteners; fine quality; for standard, concert or grand concert size guitar. Shipping wt. 1 lb. Price, (Postage 16 cents.).68c

Guitar Tuners.

No. 12C5172 Six Tuning Pipes, E, B, G, D, A, E, combined, for tuning guitar. Made of German silver and tuned to concert pitch.
Price...(If by mail, postage extra, 5c)..19c

Guitar Patent Heads.

No. 12C5174 Brass, bone buttons, fine quality. Price, per set....29c
If by mail, postage extra, per set, 6 cents.

No. 12C5176 Same as No. 12C5174, nickel plated. Price, per set....38c
If by mail, postage extra, per set, 6 cents.

Guitar Tailpieces.

No. 12C5186 This is the latest novelty in the line of Guitar Tailpieces. It is made of solid brass, beautifully nickled, and of genuine American manufacture. Price 6c
If by mail, postage extra, 5 cents.

No. 12C5190 Brass, nickel plated, for any size guitar. Price....30c
If by mail, postage extra, 5 cents.

Guitar Tailpiece Bridge.

No. 12C5194 Ebony, plain with German silver fret, used in connection with metal tailpiece. Price 9c
If by mail, postage extra, 2 cents.

Guitar Bridges.

No. 12C5198 Ebony, plain, best model and finish. Price 14c
If by mail, postage extra, 4 cents.

No. 12C5200 Ebony, neat pearl inlaying at each end. Price 40c
If by mail, postage extra, 4 cents.

Guitar Bridge Pins.

No. 12C5208 Ebony, polished pearl inlaying in head. Price, per set of six......4c

No. 12C5214 Ivory, polished, pearl inlaying in head. Price, each........ 3c
If by mail, postage extra, each, 1 cent.

Guitar Fingerboards.

No. 12C5218 Ebony, with frets. Price 90c
If by mail, postage extra, 16 cents.

Guitar Fingerboard Chart.

No. 12C5220 Guitar playing made easy by using the Patent Lettered Fingerboard Chart. It is an accurate guide, having all notes, with sharps and flats, in full view, and can be easily adjusted to any guitar without changing the instrument. Price........4c
If by mail, postage extra, 2 cents.

The Magic Capo d'Astro.

No. 12C5222 Nickel plated, steel spring action, cork lined. The simplest and best Capo d'Astro made. Price..........8c
If by mail, postage extra, 3 cents.

No. 12C5225 Capo d'Astro. Another brass, highly nickel plated appliance for changing the key of the guitar. It is finely cork lined and the pressure bar fitted with rubber so as not to mar the finish of the neck of the guitar. Price........ 11c
If by mail, postage extra, 3 cents.

Guitar Capo d'Astro.

Used to clamp on fingerboard to facilitate playing in flat keys.

No. 12C5226 Capo d'Astro nickel plated, spring action, felt covered clamps. Shipping weight, 3 ounces. Price........ 19c
If by mail, postage extra, 3 cents.

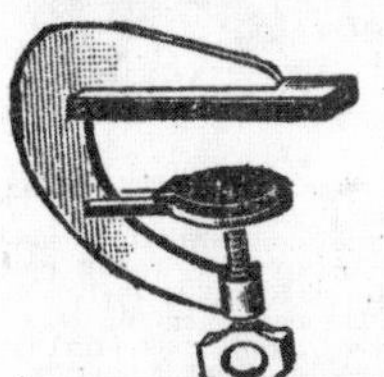

No. 12C5230 Capo d'Astro, made of brass, polished and lacquered, cork lined clamps, improved model, extra weight and strength. Weight, 3 ounces. Price........20c

No. 12C5232 Same, brass, finely nickel plated. Price........25c
If by mail, postage extra, 3 cents.

Guitar End Pins.

No. 12C5242 Ebony, plain, polished head, with pearl dot inlaid. Price..........4c
If by mail, postage extra, 1 cent.

Guitar and Banjo Frets.

No. 12C5246 German silver, in sets of eighteen. Price, per set........ 14c
NOTE—We do not break sets.
If by mail, postage extra, 3 cents.

BANJO FURNISHINGS.

Banjo Cases.

No. 12C5310 Brown canvas case, superior quality, edges bound with leather, flannel lined, with handle, for any size banjo from 7 to 13 inches. Shipping weight, 6 pounds. Price........ 82c

No. 12C5312 Extra fine black or russet leather case, embossed, flannel lined, open on end, complete as illustrated, with strap, buckle and handle, for 10 or 11-inch banjo. Shipping weight, 7 pounds. Price........$3.75

No. 12C5314 Same, for 12 or 13-inch banjo. Price........$4.55

NOTE—When ordering case for banjo, give diameter of head only.

Banjo Bags.

No. 12C5320 Fine green cloth, with buttons, for 9 to 13-inch banjo. Weight, 7 ounces. Price........36c

No. 12C5324 Green felt, box shape, fleece lined, patent fasteners, for any size banjo. Shipping weight, 12 ounces. Price........66c

Banjo Tuners.

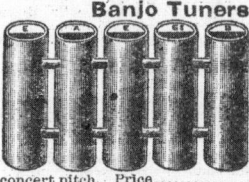

No. 12C5326 Five tuning pipes, B, G sharp, E, A and E, combined, for tuning banjos. Made from German silver and tuned to concert pitch. Price........16c
If by mail, postage extra, 4 cents.

Banjo Bridges.

No. 12C5328 Maple or rosewood; professional model. Price........2c

No. 12C5330 Solid ebony; regular model. Price........3c

No. 12C5334 Genuine Stewart; special professional; hand made. Price........6c
If by mail, postage extra, 1 cent.

Banjo Tailpieces.

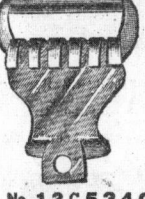

No. 12C5336 Plain solid ebony. Price....3c

No. 12C5339 A very practical tailpiece. Brass, nickel plated. Price...8c
By mail, postage extra, 2c.

No. 12C5340 Fancy design, complete with screw, bracket and nut, ready for use. Will fit any banjo. Brass, nickel plated. Price...14c
If by mail, postage, 4c.

Banjo Pegs.

No. 12C5350 Imitation ebony, hollow shape, polished, pearl dot in head. Price, each..2c

No. 12C5352 Same, but side peg. Price, each........2c

No. 12C5354 Solid Ebony, hollow shape, pearl dot in each end, regular. Price, each..4c

No. 12C5356 Same, side peg. Price, each........4c
If by mail, postage extra, each, 1c; per set, 3c.

No. 12C5362 Celluloid, imitation ebony, nickel mounted. The celebrated Champion patent. Price, per set of five, 90c; each........18c
If by mail, postage extra, per set, 3 cents.

No. 12C5364 Same as No. 12C5362, white, nickel mounted. Price, per set, 90c; each, 18c
If by mail, postage extra, per set, 4 cents.

Banjo Brackets.

No. 12C5370 Our Hexagonal Pattern Banjo Bracket is made of solid brass, highly polished, with bolt and nut. Price, per dozen, 36c; each, 3c

No. 12C5372 Same as above, but handsomely nickel plated. Price, per dozen, 48c; each, 4c

No. 12C5374 Our Ball Banjo Bracket is made of solid brass, highly polished, complete with safety nut and bolt. Price, per dozen, 48c; each, 4c

No. 12C5376 Same as above, but handsomely nickel plated. Price, per dozen, 60c; each, 5c
Weight, about 9 ounces to the dozen.
If by mail, postage extra, per dozen, 10 cents.

Banjo Thimbles.

No. 12C5386 German silver, imported pattern. Weight, 1 ounce. Price........3c
If by mail, postage extra, 1 cent.

Banjo Wrenches.

Be sure to state size of bracket nut.

No. 12C5387 Brass, key shape. Price, 4c

No. 12C5388 Brass, key shape, nickel plated. Price........7c

Banjo Fingerboard Chart.

No. 12C5392 With the aid of the fingerboard chart anyone can easily locate the notes. This chart can be adjusted to the fingerboard of any banjo and does not change the instrument in the least. Price........4c
If by mail, postage extra, 2 cents.

MANDOLIN FURNISHINGS.

Mandolin Cases.

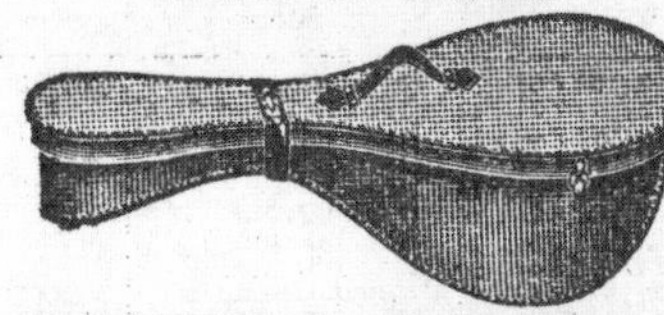

No. 12C5460 Mandolin Case, brown canvas, with leather bound edges, flannel lined, handle and patent fastenings. Shipping weight, 5 pounds. Price........60c

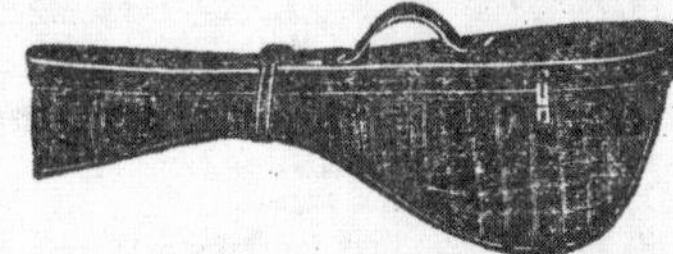

No. 12C5461 Waterproof Mandolin Case, made of rubber cloth in imitation of alligator leather, flannel lined, leather handle, patent fasteners. Shipping weight, 7 pounds. Price........$1.35

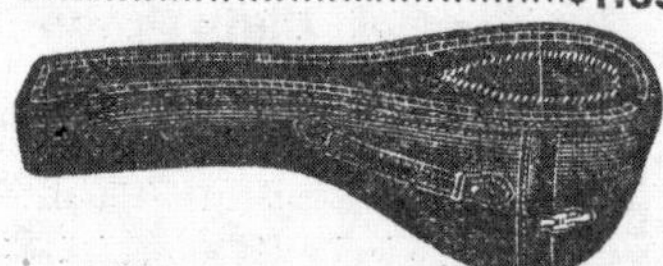

No. 12C5462 Mandolin Case, made of russet or black leather, extra quality, hand sewed, flannel lined, same as illustration. Shipping weight, 7 pounds. Price........$3.35

Mandolin Bags.

No. 12C5464 Mandolin Bag, made of green cloth with buttons, good quality. Shipping weight, 12 ounces. Price........30c

No. 12C5466 Mandolin Bag, made of green felt, full fleece lined, patent fasteners, superior quality. Shipping weight, 12 ounces. Price........45c

Mandolin Tailpieces.

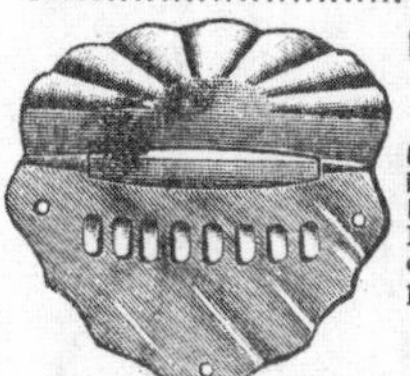

No. 12C5467 Especially attractive shell design Mandolin Tailpiece. Made of brass, nickel plated and highly polished. Price........10c
Postage extra, 3c.

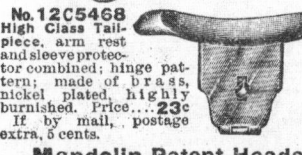

No. 12C5468 High Class Tailpiece, arm rest and sleeve protector combined; hinge pattern; made of brass, nickel plated, highly burnished. Price........23c
If by mail, postage extra, 5 cents.

Mandolin Patent Heads.

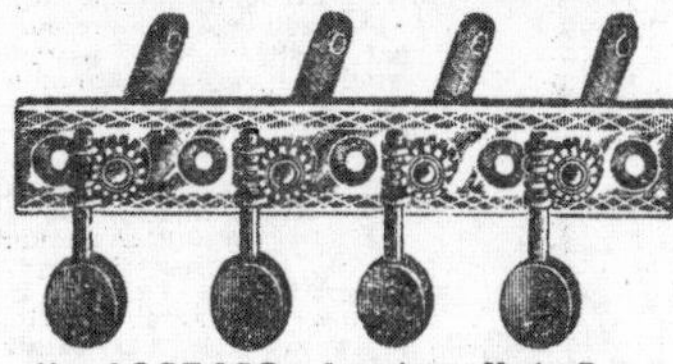

No. 12C5469 American Made Brass Patent Head, Guitar Style; bone buttons. Price, per set........32c
If by mail, postage extra, per set, 8 cents.

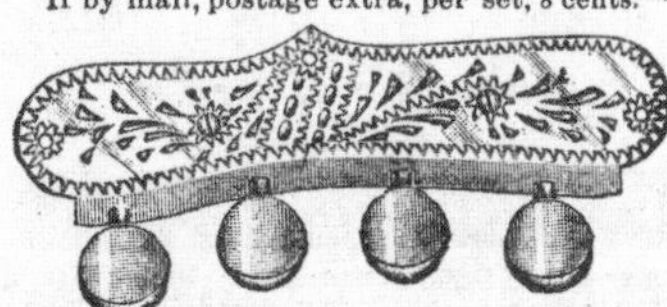

No. 12C5471 Two-piece Plate Covered Machine Head to be used on lower side of mandolin head. Made of brass, highly nickel plated and polished. Same as illustration, but not engraved. White celluloid buttons; very substantially made. Price, per set........55c

No. 12C5472 Made of solid aluminum and beautifully engraved. White celluloid buttons, as illustrated above. Price........68c
If by mail, postage extra, 8 cents.

No. 12C5473 Same as No. 12C5471, but artistically engraved, gold plated. Price......(Postage extra, 8 cents.)........78c

Mandolin Tuners.

No. 12C5477 Four tuning pipes, E, A, D, G, combined for tuning mandolin. Made of German silver and tuned to concert pitch. Price......14c
If by mail, postage extra, 3 cents.

Professional Mandolin Pick.

No. 12C5478 The Patent Mandolin Pick, fastened to the finger by steel clasp, the pick proper being held between rubber discs, it is possible for it to be held more firmly and at the same time not require the tightness of clasp which is necessary with the old pick when playing soft music. By placing the thumb and index finger lightly on the disc the player will be able to play the sweetest and softest music possible, and if necessary he can tremolo a chord with the utmost ease. Price........14c
If by mail, postage extra, 2 cents.

Mandolin Picks.

No. 12C5480 Genuine Tortoise Shell, oval shape, polished or unpolished. Price........2c
If by mail, postage extra, 1 cent.

No. 12C5482 Same, extra large, extra quality. Price........4c
If by mail, postage extra, 1 cent.

No. 12C5484 Genuine Tortoise Shell, triangular shape. Price........4c
If by mail, postage extra, 1 cent.

Mandolin Bridges.

No. 12C5486 Bridges, ebony, plain finish. Price........6c

No. 12C5490 Bridges, ebony, ivory inlaid. Price........9c
If by mail, postage extra, 2 cents.

Mandolin Fingerboard Chart.

The Latest Patent Self Instructor: the Fingerboard Chart.

No. 12C5498 With the aid of the Lettered Fingerboard Chart, anyone can easily locate the notes. The chart can be adjusted on the fingerboard of any mandolin, and does not change the instrument in the least. Our price........4c
If by mail, postage extra, 2 cents.

AUTOHARP FURNISHINGS.

Tuning Keys.

No. 12C5570 Tuning Keys, malleable iron. Price........8c
If by mail, postage extra, 2 cents.

Autoharp Picks.

No. 12C5572 Picks, celluloid. Price........2c
If by mail, postage extra, 2 cents.

No. 12C5576 Autoharp Picks, brass, spiral. Price........2c
If by mail, postage extra, 1 cent.

Autoharp Tuning Pins.

No. 12C5578 Autoharp Tuning Pins, made of blued steel. Price, per doz..8c
If by mail, postage extra, per dozen, 4 cents.

Autoharp Cases.

No. 12C5584 Autoharp Case, made of brown canvas, bound all around the edges with leather, flannel lined, superior model and quality, complete with handle, strap and name plate. To fit Nos. 71, 2¾, 72¾, 3, 4, 5 or 6 Autoharp. When ordering, be sure to give number of instrument. Shipping weight, 7 pounds. Price........90c

No. 12C5594 English Steel Wire, best quality, ¼-pound coils. Sizes from 7 to 23. Be sure to state size wanted. Price, per coil, 26c

Zither Ring.

No. 12C5627 Zither Ring, made of steel, nickel plated, new model. Sizes, 1 to 6. Price........10c
If by mail, postage extra, 2 cents.

No. 12C5650 Composition metal, adjustable with screw, for piccolo. Price...5c

No. 12C5651 Same as No. 12C5650, but for fife. Price...5c

No. 12C5655 Flute Mouthpiece, composition metal, adjustable with screw. Price...9c
If by mail, postage extra, 2 cents.

No. 12C5665 The Cleaner which we show in the illustration is made of the very best worsted in variegated colors and furnished with wire covered handle. Price...14c
If by mail, postage extra, 4 cents.

No. 12C5666 Same as No. 12C5665, but for piccolo. Price...11c
If by mail, postage extra, 4 cents.

CLARIONET FURNISHINGS.

Reed Holders and Protectors.

No. 12C5667 German Silver, with adjusting screws, for A, Bb, C, D or Eb.
Each, 23c
If by mail, postage extra, 6 cents.

No. 12C5674 Nickel Plated, for A, Bb, C, D or Eb mouthpieces.
Price...18c
If by mail, postage extra, 3 cents.

Our Clarionet Reeds are made expressly for us by a reed maker of great celebrity.

No. 12C5682 Cottereau, fine quality, for A, Bb, C, D or Eb clarionet. Price, each...5c

No. 12C5684 Barbu, superfine, for A, Bb, C, D or Eb clarionet. Price, each...7c

No. 12C5685 Genuine Martin Freres, for A, Bb, C, D or Eb clarionet. Price, each...9c

No. 12C5686 Our Special Fournier Waterproof Clarionet Reeds. These reeds are strictly waterproof, and model and quality are particularly desirable. They are made for any key clarionet. In ordering, always state for what key they are desired. Price, each...13c

No. 12C5688 Artists' Clarionet Reed, a grade of reed that is the best that can be secured at any price. Made for A, Bb, D or Eb clarionet. Price is the same. Price, each, 16c
If by mail, postage extra, 2 cents.

Clarionet Reed Case.

No. 12C5694 Leather Pocket Case, for six reeds.
Price...24c
If by mail, postage extra, 5 cents.

Give Key of Clarionet.

No. 12C5702 Solid ebony mouthpiece, without reed holder.
Price, each...28c

No. 12C5704 Grenadilla mouthpiece, with German silver reed plate, but without reed holder, any key.
Price, each...$1.45
If by mail, postage extra, 7 cents.

No. 12C5708 Clarionet Case; leather bag, lined, with handle and catch, for clarionet of any key. Shipping weight, 19 ounces. Be sure to give key of clarionet.
Price...$1.05

No. 12C5710 Clarionet Case, valise form, leather covered, flannel lined, with handle, hooks and lock. Made to carry three clarionets. Shipping weight, 4 pounds.
Price...$2.35

Cornet Cases.

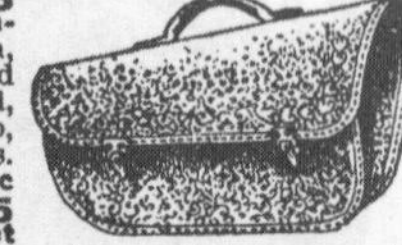

No. 12C5713 Brown or Gray Canvas, satchel form, leather bound edges, flannel lined, with shoulder strap, Shipping wgt., 6 lbs.
Price...75c

No. 12C5715 Black or Russet Pebble Leather, very fine, satchel form, as illustrated; flannel lined, nickel plated trimmings, with shoulder strap. Shipping weight, 25 ounces.
Price...98c

No. 12C5717 Cornet Case, valise form, made of wood covered with an indestructible waterproof material made in perfect imitation of pebbled leather, handsomely embossed, trimmed with nickel corners, leather handle, nickel spring lock, nickel link clasps and nickel hinges. Lined inside with velvet, partitioned off for cornet and various parts. One of the best cornet cases made. Shipping weight, 6 pounds. Price...$3.45

No. 12C5718 Our Bb Tenor Slide Trombone Cases are made of black sole leather, very artistically embossed and lined with red flannel. They have metal end protectors, strong carrying straps and handle. Suitable for either high or low pitch instruments. Furnished with extra inside pocket for low pitch slide. Shipping weight, 6 pounds. Price...$5.50

We can furnish cases for instruments of all kinds. Send for special Band Instrument Catalogue.

Calfskin Heads.

For Drums, Banjos and Tambourines.

No.	Size, inches	For	Price
12C5770	12	10-inch Shell	$0.22
12C5772	13	11-inch Drum Shell	.26
12C5774	14	11½-inch Shell	.30
12C5776	15	12-inch Shell	.39
12C5778	16	13-inch Shell	.45
12C5782	18	15-inch Drum	.65
12C5783	19	16-inch Drum	.75
12C5784	20	17-inch Drum	.85
12C5785	22	19-inch Drum	.87
12C5786	28	24-inch Bass Drum	1.30
12C5787	30	26-inch Bass Drum	1.50
12C5788	32	28-inch Bass Drum	1.75
12C5789	34	30-inch Bass Drum	2.05
12C5790	36	32-inch Bass Drum	2.55
12C5792	38	34-inch Bass Drum	2.80
12C5794	40	36-inch Bass Drum	3.25

Extra Quality Special Banjo Heads.

Genuine Rogers.

No. 12C5796 13-inch, white, for 11-inch banjo. Price...48c

No. 12C5797 14-inch, white, for 11½-inch banjo. Price...67c

No. 12C5798 16-inch, white, for 13-inch banjo. Price...94c

Our Special High Grade Transparent Heads.

No. 12C5802 13-inch for 11-inch shell. Price...48c

No. 12C5804 14-inch for 11½-inch shell. Price...59c

No. 12C5808 16-inch for 13-inch shell. Price...68c

Shipping weight, 12 to 20-inch head.. 4 ounces
Shipping weight, 20 to 28-inch head.. 9 ounces
Shipping weight, 30 to 36-inch head.. 20 ounces
Shipping weight 38 to 40-inch head.. 24 ounces

Music Stands

No. 12C5920 Our Special Umbrella Pattern Folding Music Stand, made of iron, handsomely japanned. Folds up into small compass. Shipping weight, 43 ounces.
Price...26c

No. 12C5924 Same, nickel plated. Shipping weight, 43 ounces. Price...65c

Music Stand.

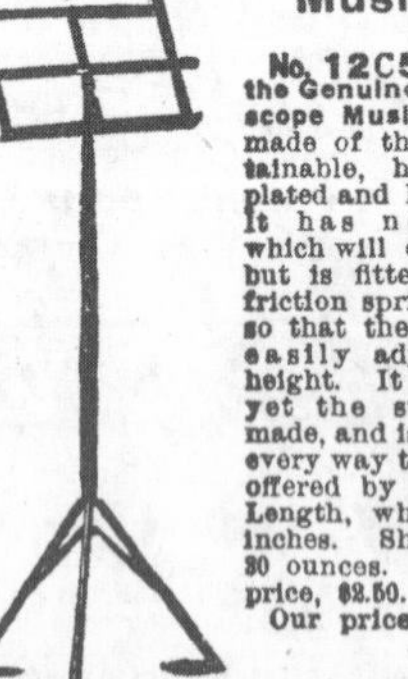

No. 12C5925 This is the Genuine "Quinn" Telescope Music Stand. It is made of the best steel obtainable, heavily nickel plated and highly polished. It has no thumbscrews which will easily wear out, but is fitted with patent friction spring adjustments so that the stand can be easily adjusted to any height. It is the lightest, yet the strongest stand made, and is far superior in every way to similar stands offered by other dealers. Length, when folded, 17 inches. Shipping weight, 30 ounces. Regular retail price, $2.50.
Our price...$1.05

Music Stand Cases.

No. 12C5926 Our Best Music Stand Case is made of sole leather and is exactly like the illustration above. It is made for folding iron stands such as we quote above. Shipping weight, 18 ounces. Price...65c

No. 12C5927 This Music Stand Case is made of black sole leather, beautifully embossed. It is 18 inches long and intended only for our stand No. 12C5925 or any other telescope stand which will not measure more than 17½ inches when closed. Shipping weight, 8 ounces.
Price...60c

Student's Music Pad.

No. 12C5930 One Hundred Sheets of Ruled Music Paper put up in the form of a pad, suitable for music students. Each sheet shows all signatures used in writing music, which serves a great aid to composers.
Price....(If by mail, postage extra, 8c)...15c

Music Blank Books.

These books are well bound and are made of good quality paper, ready ruled for writing music. Size, 7½x9½ inches.

No. 12C5940 6 staves, 40 pages...8c
No. 12C5941 8 staves, 24 pages...7c
No. 12C5942 8 staves, 40 pages...10c
No. 12C5943 8 staves, 64 pages...12c
If by mail, postage extra, per book, 4 cents.

Music Paper.

Super Royal Music Paper. Size, 10¾x13¾ inches.

No. 12C5947 10 staves, octavo.
No. 12C5948 12 staves, octavo, or oblong.
No. 12C5949 12 staves, octavo, for vocal or piano.
No. 12C5950 14 staves, octavo, or oblong.
Price, per quire (24 sheets)...21c
If by mail, postage extra, per quire, 11 cents.

Gummed Paper.

No. 12C5952 French Gummed Paper, for mending sheet music. Price, per sheet. 8c
If by mail, postage extra, 1 cent.

Ruling Pens.

No. 12C5956 Ruling Pens, with five lines for drawing staff. Price...9c
If by mail, postage extra, 1 cent.

Steel Pens.

No. 12C5962 Steel Pens, with three points, for writing music, special make.
Price, per dozen. (Postage extra, 1c)...16c

Music Rolls, Bags and Folios.

No. 12C6000 This Music Roll is made of fine black imitation monkey grain leather; heavy leather handle, strap and buckle, bound and stitched edges. It is lined throughout and has a flap at the bottom to hold music. Size, open, 14¾x15½ inches. Price...23c

No. 12C6001 This is made of beautiful imitation seal grain leather, has leather handle, strap and nickel buckle. Size, unrolled, 14½x15 inches. Price....(Postage extra, 6c)...30c

No. 12C6003 A Very Fine Imitation Seal Grain Leather Roll, has leather handle, wide strap and fancy buckle. We furnish this roll in either orange or black.
Price, (If by mail, postage extra, 6 cents) 40c

No. 12C6004 This Music Roll has beautiful double colored imitation hornback alligator skin, heavily lined, with stitched handle, wide lined and stitched strap and fine nickel buckle. It is lined throughout, and has a flap at the bottom to hold music in place. Bound and stitched all around. Size, open, 14¾x15 inches. Price....(Postage extra, 6c)...45c

No. 12C6005 This Music Roll has a fine, solid case of leather in orange and black, beautiful creased sides, and has an inside flap to keep the music in place, wide strap and finely plated harness buckle. Size, 14¾x15 inches.
Price......(Postage extra, 6 cents)...65c

No. 12C6009 This Music Roll is made of fine black buffalo grain leather, leather lined, bound and stitched edges, heavy double stitched handle, wide lined and stitched strap and fine nickel buckle. It has an inside flap at bottom to hold music in place. Size, open, 14¾x15½ inches. Price....(Postage extra, 6 cents)...80c

No. 12C6010 A Splendid Morocco Music Roll, with latest fancy leather buckle and strap, well bound with leather, not lined, making the same one of the lightest and neatest we handle. We can furnish this roll in two colors, black or brown. Price....(Postage extra, 6c)...90c

No. 12C6015 This Music Roll is made of fine seal grain leather, double stitched handle, wide lined and stitched strap and harness buckle, bound and stitched edges; leather lined throughout, and has a flap at the bottom to hold music in place. Size, open, 14¾x15½ inches.
Price......(Postage extra, 6c)...$1.05

No. 12C6016 Genuine Seal Music Roll. This would retail at from $2.50 to $3.00. A splendid roll, 15x14½ inches, especially suitable as a present. It has leather handle, strap and buckle of the latest design; leather bound.
Price....(Postage extra, 8c)...$1.45

No. 12C6018 This Music Roll is made of genuine walrus seal, double stitched strap and leather covered buckle, double stitched handle, leather bound and stitched all around; grosgrain moire lining, beautiful shades, and it has an inside flap to hold music. A fine music roll and well finished. Size, 14¾x15 inches.
Price...$2.15
If by mail, postage extra, 6 cents.

Music Bags.

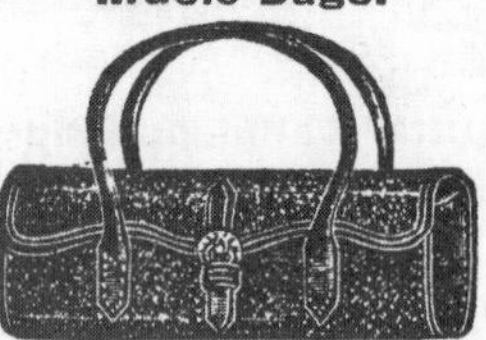

No. 12C6023 Music Bags, made in fine imitation seal grain leather. Leather handles and strap, 15 inches long and 6½ inches high. Exactly like illustration. Price...60c
If by mail, postage extra, 16 cents.

No. 12C6024 This Music Bag is made of heavy, solid, polished case leather in black or orange color, beautifully embossed around the ends in wide bands in leaf and cord design, wide stitched-in gussets at the ends. It has two round handles, and closes with a short strap and leather covered buckle. Size, closed, 6x14½ inches. Price...$1.10
State color desired when ordering.
If by mail, postage extra, 16 cents.

Imitation Alligator Music Bag.

No. 12C6025 Music Bag. Perfect imitation alligator, 15 inches wide, 12 inches high. Will hold full size sheet music without folding or rolling. Has strong strap handles, reaching entirely around the bag, which adds greatly to its strength and durability. Price...$1.35
If by mail, postage extra, 34 cents.

No. 12C6026 This Music Case and Bag is made of a waterproof and indestructible material in imitation of beautiful walrus grained leather, heavy stitched handle, bound and stitched all around, closes with fine steel catch. If a bag is desired instead of a case, all that is required is to fold it up and fasten with another catch especially put on for that purpose. The interior is muslin lined and it has four in-folding flaps to hold the music in place. When used as a case the music is carried in its full size without being folded. Comes in two colors, black and maroon. Size, open, 24½x27¼ inches. Size as a case, 1½x11¾x14¾ inches. Size as a bag, 1½x6x14¾ inches.. Price...$1.15
State color desired when ordering.

Piano and Organ Stools.

No. 12C6059 Piano or Organ Stool, made of solid oak or walnut finish, round polished top, 13½ inches in diameter; three legs; strong and well made. Shipping weight, about 20 pounds.

Price...80c

No. 12C6062 Piano or Organ Stool, made of solid oak, walnut or mahogany finish, round polished top, 12½ inches in diameter; three legs; very strong. Shipping weight, about 15 pounds.

Price...$1.15

Our $1.95 Upholstered Piano or Organ Stool.

No. 12C6064 Organ or Piano Stool, 13½x16-inch seat, covered with durable mohair plush, maroon or crimson, plain or embossed covering, dark rosewood finish legs, adjustable seat. Weight, 25 pounds, packed
Price...$1.95

Special Value at $1.45.

No. 12C6068 Piano or Organ Stool, made of solid oak or in ebony, walnut, mahogany, rosewood, burl walnut or Circassian walnut finish, nicely polished round top, 13½ inches in diameter; three legs, with brass feet and glass balls; shipping weight, about 25 pounds. Price..... **$1.45**

No. 12C6070 Same description as No. 12C6068, but with four legs. Price..... **$1.65** Solid walnut......... **2.65**

The Best Piano Stool Made for the Money.

This stool is the most massive and substantially built piano stool we have ever been able to furnish. This stool is made of solid wood, has a 15-inch round polished top with shaped edges. The top is made of two pieces of wood glued together so that it becomes doubly strong. The base has a massive center post and four legs, handsomely fluted and turned, beautiful brass claw feet with glass balls. Only the best kiln dried hardwood lumber is used throughout, and only the best quality of screws, nuts and bolts enter into the construction of this stool. We can furnish this stool in ebony, oak or walnut as desired. Weight, packed for shipment, 25 pounds.

No. 12C6072 Ebony finish. Price, **$1.95**
No. 12C6074 Solid oak. Price... **2.25**
No. 12C6076 Solid walnut. Price, **2.95**

Upright Piano Scarfs.

No. 12C6081 Special Heavy Damask Scarf, in assorted colors and patterns, with extra heavy silk fringe, draped in two places. Shipping weight, about 20 ounces. Price......................... **$1.85**

No. 12C6083 Fine Figured China Silk Scarf, in assorted colors and patterns, with heavy all silk fringe, draped in two places. Shipping weight, 5 ounces. Price..... **$1.75**

No. 12C6085 Special Fine Silk Damask Scarf, in assorted colors and patterns, with heavy silk fringe, draped in two places. Shipping weight, about 15 ounces. Price.... **$2.55**

No. 12C6087 Fine Velour Scarf, in assorted colors and patterns, with extra heavy silk fringe, draped in two places. Shipping weight, 20 ounces. Price............ **$1.65**

No. 12C6089 Extra Fine Velour Scarf, in assorted colors and patterns, with extra heavy silk fringe, draped in two places. Shipping weight, about 20 ounces. Price.... **$2.15**

Latest Popular and Sentimental Songs.

Sheet Form Only. Order by Number and Title.

No. 12C6500 Order by this number and be sure to give name of song also. Price, per dozen, **$2.28**; each......... **19c** If by mail, postage extra, each, 2 cents; per dozen, 16 cents.

We Can Furnish All Popular Songs Not Herein Listed at 23c each, and 2c for postage.

We Do Not Exchange Sheet Music.

Absence Makes the Heart Grow Fonder........
A Hundred Fathoms Deep (Bass Song)Shattuck
A Thousand Leagues Under the Sea (Bass Song)......................Petrie
Better Than Gold..............Chas. K. Harris
Bird in a Gilded Cage.........Harry Von Tilzer
Break the News to Mother.......Chas. K. Harris
Come Where the Lilies Bloom (Quartette).. ....Thompson
Coon, Coon, Coon.......................
Courage (Bass Song)......................Petrie
Every Race Has a Flag But the Coon ....Heeland and Helf
Eli Green's Cake Walk (Coon)..........Koninsky
For Old Time's Sake.........Chas. K. Harris
Hi-le, Hi-lo..................Heeland and Helf
Hello, Central..............................Harris
Honeysuckle and the Bee....................Bloom
Hot Time in the Old Town Tonight..........Metz
I'd Like to Hear That Song Again............
I'll Be There, Mary Dear..........H. Von Tilzer
In the House of Too Much Trouble.............. ....Heeland and Helf
In the Shadow of the Pines...................Lang
I've a Longing in My Heart For You, Louise.Harris
Just As Daylight Was Breaking.Kennett & Udall
Just As the Sun Went Down..................Udall
Just One Girl...............................Udall
Maizy, my Dusky Daisy.........Heeland and Helf
Mansion of Aching Hearts.........H. Von Tilzer
May Be.......................Tannehill and Rosey
Message of the Violet.................G. Luders
'Mid the Green Fields of Virginia...C. K. Harris
Moonlight Will Come Again (Quartet) Thompson
My Blushing Rose...........................Mann
My Castle on the Nile..................Johnson
My Little Georgia Rose...............Max S. Witt
My Lulu, Lulu, Loo..........................
My Old New Hampshire Home..Harry Von Tilzer
My Wild Irish Rose.........................Olcott
No One But You..............Horwitz & Bowers
One Night in June...........................Harris
On a Sunday Afternoon...........H. Von Tilzer
Put Me Off at Buffalo......................Dillon
She Was Bred in Old Kentucky..............Carter
Sing Me a Song of the South....Martin & Casey
Stay in Your Own Back Yard..................
Sweet Bunch of Daisies..................A. Owen
She's Sleeping By the Silvery Rio Grande ....Charles Kohlman
The Little Rustic Cottage by the Stream ....Heinzman
Tale of a Bumble Bee.......................
Tale of the Kangaroo..........Gustave Luders
Tale of a Sea Shell......................G. Luders
The Girl I Loved in Sunny Tennessee......Long
The Letter Edged in Black........Hattie Nevada
The Maiden with the Dreamy Eyes.......Johnson
The Moth and the Flame.......Maurice Shapiro
The Old Postmaster..........................Stern
The Spider and the Fly................Von Tilzer
The Star and the Flower.............A. Hubbel
There'll Come a Time..........Chas. K. Harris
Upon a Sunday When the Church Bells Chime...............Rosenfeld & Solman
When the Blue Skies Turn to Gold..........
When the Sunset Turns the Ocean's Blue to Gold..............................Petrie
When It's All Goin' Out and Nothing Comin' In (Coon)..............Williams and Walker
When Kate and I Were Coming Through the Rye..........................H. Von Tilzer
When Rueben Comes to Town..................Levy
When the Harvest Days Are Over.....Von Tilzer
When the Fields Are White With Cotton ....Roden and Witt
When the Lilies of the Valley Bloom Again....
When the Sweet Magnolias Bloom..............
While the Convent Bells Were Ringing........ ....Roden and Witt
You are as Welcome as the Flowers in May ....Sullivan

VOCAL MUSIC FOLIOS.

WORDS AND MUSIC.

No. 12C6540 Light Opera Music Books. The following books contain the entire music and words of the different light operas whose names are given below. The music is finely printed from splendid plates on heavy paper and the books are bound with highly ornamented covers. They give all the songs with the entire piano accompaniment. Prince of Pilsen, King Dodo, Burgomaster, When Johnny Comes Marching Home, The Fortune Teller. Price, each book......**$1.95**
If by mail, postage extra, 8 cents.
In ordering, give catalogue number, also name of book desired.

Good Old Songs Folio.

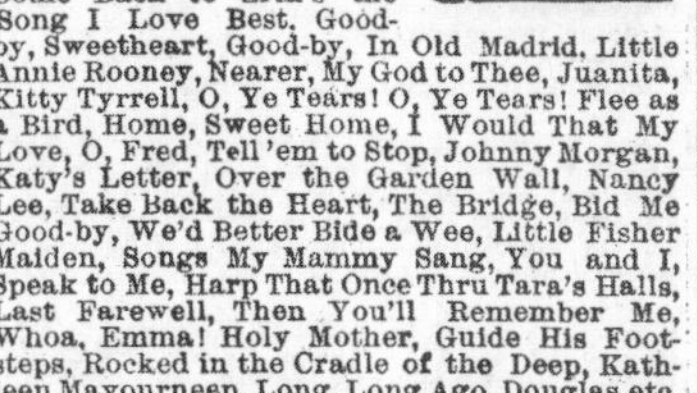

No. 12C6580 We guarantee every piece in this Folio to be the ORIGINAL and complete in every way. Please read carefully the contents: Alice, Where Art Thou, Comin' Thru the Rye, Annie Laurie, Ave Maria, Come Back to Erin's the Song I Love Best, Good-by, Sweetheart, Good-by, In Old Madrid, Little Annie Rooney, Nearer, My God to Thee, Juanita, Kitty Tyrrell, O, Ye Tears! O, Ye Tears! Flee as a Bird, Home, Sweet Home, I Would That My Love, O, Fred, Tell 'em to Stop, Johnny Morgan, Katy's Letter, Over the Garden Wall, Nancy Lee, Take Back the Heart, The Bridge, Bid Me Good-by, We'd Better Bide a Wee, Little Fisher Maiden, Songs My Mammy Sang, You and I, Speak to Me, Harp That Once Thru Tara's Halls, Last Farewell, Then You'll Remember Me, Whoa, Emma! Holy Mother, Guide His Footsteps, Rocked in the Cradle of the Deep, Kathleen Mavourneen, Long, Long Ago, Douglas, etc. Price..**20c**
If by mail, postage extra, 8 cents.

No. 12C6590 Musical Chatterbox No. 2. Contains both vocal and instrumental music. Every piece a popular favorite; choice, easy and medium piano pieces; beautiful songs for the young folks; just the collection for home; it contains, besides the music, eight beautiful illustrations. Price.............**25c**
If by mail, postage extra, 8 cents.

No. 12C6601 The Crest Collection of Popular Songs, the latest and best vocal folio published, containing the following popular songs: My Gal's a High Born Lady, Picture Turned to the Wall, God Save America, Pumpkin Pies Mother Used to Make, and 28 others, any one of which retails at 50 cents per copy. Price.........**25c**
If by mail, postage extra, 12 cents.

No. 12C6603 Crest Collection No. 2. Contains latest and more up to date pieces, such as: Always, Because, Her Memory Brings Me No Regret, and 41 selections equally as good. Price......(Postage extra, 8 cents.)......**25c**

No. 12C6606 Song Casket, a valuable collection of choice vocal music by well known authors. Contains ballads, songs with choruses, duets, quartettes, home songs, Scotch songs, etc., with piano or organ accompaniments. Price..........**30c**
If by mail, postage extra, 12 cents.

No. 12C6607 Song Offering. This is a fine collection of vocal music of the highest order of merit and is printed from fine plates on heavy paper and bound with handsome cover. It contains such pieces as: Beautiful Girl of the North, Bird, Tell Winnie I Am Waiting, Eva Darling, A Good Time Coming, and a large number of others of the same high order of merit. Price.............**30c**
If by mail, postage extra, 12 cents.

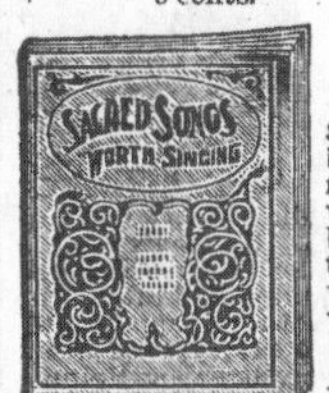

No. 12C6615 Rag Time Folio, No. 2. A splendid collection of the latest and best negro melodies of the day by favorite composers, including My Hannah Lady, Pliny, Come Kiss Your Baby, and 20 others as good. Price.........**45c**
If by mail, postage extra, 8 cents.

No. 12C6620 Sacred Songs Worth Singing. A collection of carefully selected songs which will surely please. Anybody desiring to sing something "Worth Singing" will find this book just what the title calls for. Publisher's price, 50c. Our price..........**30c**
If by mail, postage extra, 8 cents.

No. 12C6622 Portfolio of Sacred Songs. A very fine collection of sacred selections suitable for home or church. The names of the composers are a guarantee of their excellence. Chas. Gounod, J. Faure, O. King, etc. Most of the pieces herein contained are copyrighted and are not to be found in any other similar collection. Price........**30c**
If by mail, postage extra, 8 cents.

No. 12C6624 Choice Songs for High Voice, No. 2. As ideal a collection as any singer could possibly desire, each song having been selected on its merits. Singers looking for a collection of high class songs by well known composers will be highly pleased with this book. Price.................**30c**
If by mail, postage extra, 8 cents.

No. 12C6626 Choice Songs for Low Voice, No. 2. In this collection singers will find just that variety and beauty of sentiment and melody which combine to make such a book a success. Each and every song is an assured favorite. Price........**30c**
If by mail, postage extra, 8 cents.

VOCAL DUETS.

No. 12C6636 Brainard's Vocal Duet Folio. A collection of choice popular vocal duets. 100 pages. Price.........**25c**
If by mail, postage extra, 6 cents.

GRAND ARMY SONGS.

No. 12C6641 A valuable collection of war and camp songs, to which is added a selection of memorial songs and hymns for Decoration Day, etc.; choruses all arranged for male voices, organ or piano accompaniment; 100 pages; heavy paper covers. Price........**40c**
If by mail, postage extra, 5 cents.

No. 12C6642 Songs of Dixie, a collection of camp, marching and plantation songs by favorite authors. Among the selections are Dixie Land, My Old Kentucky Home, Maryland, My Maryland, Our Flag, and 40 others. The book contains 71 pages, printed on fine paper, handsomely bound with linen back. Price.......................**38c**
If by mail, postage extra, 4 cents.

DON'T FORGET POSTAGE IF YOU WANT A MUSIC BOOK SENT BY MAIL.

QUARTETTE BOOKS.

No. 12C6643 The Pan-Collegiate Collection of Songs. This is a book of songs, quartettes, etc., and is something new in its line. The selections comprise some of the latest popular songs, comic and sentimental, and are just the thing for glee clubs, colleges, etc. It is also a jolly book to have at home and will make fun anywhere; 132 pages, with handsome colored cover. Price........**25c**
If by mail, postage extra, 8 cents.

No. 12C6645 Chas. Shattuck's Beautiful Male Quartette Arrangement of Chas. K. Harris' popular publications. No. 2, in book form, 32 pages. Price........................**35c**
If by mail, postage extra, 4 cents.

No. 12C6647 The Glee Club Quartette Folio. This is the finest collection of male quartettes yet issued, suitable for all occasions and arranged by the well known musician, C. F. Shattuck. We offer this folio at the low price of........ **30c**
If by mail, postage extra, 6 cents.

MINSTREL SONGS.

No. 12C6672 The Jolly Songster. A fine collection of 200 pieces, including comic and patriotic songs, popular ballads and favorite negro melodies. Paper cover. Price.................**20c**
If by mail, postage extra, 5c.

No. 12C6678 Album of Comic Songs. This is a splendid collection of laughable songs of the highest order of merit. It contains such pieces as follows: It Tickled Me So, I Liked to Die, Johnny Morgan, Smart Young Men of Town, The Dutchman's Lament, So Nearsighted, and many others as good. Printed from fine plates on a good quality of paper and bound in paper covers. Price.........**20c**
If by mail, postage extra, 6 cents.

No. 12C6680 "They're After Me," Folio of Funny Songs for the Whole World. A new collection of the very latest comic songs by the most popular song writers of every nation; very funny; 128 pages. Price...**30c**
Postage extra, 8c.

No. 12C6684 Old and New Popular Comic Songs. 39 of the best known and most popular comic songs. Price.....................................**30c**
If by mail, postage extra, 8 cents.

No. 12C6688 Mirthful Album of Comic Songs. Containing comic, negro, Dutch, coster and Irish songs. Also a great number of comicalities by the best known comic writers of the day that have never before been published in book form. A handsome folio of 160 pages printed on fine paper and beautifully bound. Price.......**30c**
If by mail, postage extra, 8c.

GOSPEL HYMNS.

No. 12C6690 Consolidated, Nos. 1, 2, 3, 4. Large type, words and music; board cover, 400 pages. Price..**67c**
If by mail, postage extra, 10c.

No. 12C6694 Words only. Nos. 1, 2, 3, 4. Price....**17c**
If by mail, postage extra, 4c.

No. 12C6696 Gospel Hymns No. 5, with words and music; board cover. Price, **27c**
If by mail, postage extra, 6c.

No. 12C6700 Gospel Hymns No. 6. Bound in board. Price...........**25c**
If by mail, postage extra, 6 cents.

No. 12C6701 Gospel Hymns No. 6. Christian Endeavor Edition. Bound in board. Price......(Postage extra, 6 cents)......**29c**

No. 12C6704 Gospel Hymns Nos. 5 and 6, combined. Large type, board cover. Words and music. Price.................**55c**
If by mail, postage extra, 8 cents.

No. 12C6706 Gospel Hymns Nos. 5 and 6. Words only. Board cover. Price.....**18c**
If by mail, postage extra, 4 cents.

No. 12C6707 Gospel Hymns Nos. 1 to 6. Complete with words and music in one volume. We can offer this popular series of 739 hymns and tunes in one volume at an unusually low price. This edition is handsomely bound in cloth. Large type. Price...............**86c**
If by mail, postage extra, 20 cents.

No. 12C6709 Gospel Hymns Nos. 1 to 6. Complete, words only, cloth cover. Price, **17c**
If by mail, postage extra, 3 cents.

INSTRUMENTAL FOLIOS FOR PIANO.

No. 12C6714 Folio Leaves. This is a splendid collection of instrumental music for the organ or piano and every piece in it is of the very highest order of merit. It contains such selections as Christmas Bells, Clear the Track Galop, Dress Parade Polka, Florence Schottische, Idle Wild Waltz, and many others of the best composers. It is plainly printed on heavy paper and bound with a handsome paper cover. Price..........30c If by mail, postage extra, 12 cents.

No. 12C6715 Whitney Easy Piano Folio. Very fine and desirable collection of easy piano pieces, especially adapted for beginners. Nothing hard to finger or read. Waltzes, marches and everything herein contained arranged in a very easy and progressive manner. Publisher's price, 50 cents. Our price.......30c If by mail, postage extra, 8 cents.

No. 12C6718 This book contains new music of all the popular round and square dances. Plain quadrille, prairie queen quadrille, lancers, waltz-quadrille, waltz-lancers, polka, galop, schottische, gavotte, two-steps, waltzes, marches and cake-walks. Price..........30c If by mail, postage extra, 8 cents.

No. 12C6721 Musical Friends. A choice collection of piano duets, consisting of marches, waltzes, polkas, schottisches, mazurkas, galops and popular pieces by favorite authors. Price..........25c Postage extra, 8 cents.

No. 12C6728 Sacred Pianoforte Album. It is often the case that one does not care to play light, frivolous music on Sunday. In this book you will find an extremely good selection of suitable Sunday or holiday music. Price..........30c If by mail, postage extra, 8 cents.

No. 12C6732 Whitney's Folio Gems. A choice selection of recent compositions, including marches, waltzes, polkas, schottisches, etc, by popular composers; 150 pages, sheet music size. Price..........30c If by mail, postage extra, 10 cents.

No. 12C6740 The Witmark Dance Folio No. 1. This is a new folio, containing the hits of the day, such as waltzes, marches, schottisches, polkas, waltz-quadrilles, three steps, etc. Arranged for dance, and compiled from the latest popular songs. **The finest book of its kind published.** Price..........25c If by mail, postage extra, 10 cents.

No. 12C6741 Witmark Dance Folio No. 2. A later edition than Folio No. 1. Contains, When You Were Sweet Sixteen, My Wild Irish Rose, Sing Me a Song of the South, Pullman Porters' Ball, My Blushing Rose, Stay in Your Own Back Yard, Little Sallie Brown, and thirteen more equally good pieces arranged as waltzes, marches, two steps, schottisches, and lancers. Price..........25c If by mail, postage extra, 10 cents.

No. 12C6746 Pastime Dance Album. Containing thirty popular songs and instrumental hits arranged as waltzes, two steps, schottisches, polkas, marches, lancers, etc. This book includes Phrenologist Coon, The Maiden with the Dreamy Eyes, Hi-le Hi-lo, The old Postmaster, The Harlem Rag. Any one of these selections would be worth the price of the entire book. Publisher's price, 75 cents. Our price ..(Postage extra, 6c) 30c

No. 12C6752 Golden Hours. A fine collection of popular piano music, consisting of a large variety of marches and miscellaneous dance music, four-hand pieces, etc., forming a select library of elegant music. 224 pages. Price.......25c Postage extra, 12c.

No. 12C6761 The Golden Chord. A choice collection of favorite and modern pianoforte music. Gems for the home circle. 225 pages. The best folio published. Price....25c If by mail, postage extra, 10 cents.

No. 12C6769 A Collection of Easy Pieces for the Piano. By Streabog & Lichner. The best known composers of selections suitable for beginners. A folio of 119 pages, beautifully bound. Price..........30c If by mail, postage extra, 8 cents.

No. 12C6770 Easy to Play, No. 2. Another splendid collection of compositions, easily arranged. The selections in this volume are by Spindler & Behr, the celebrated composers of sparkling and interesting teaching pieces. Price...(Postage extra, 8c) 30c

No. 12C6771 Easy to Play, No. 3. In this superb collection, Lichner, Streabog, Spindler & Behr have demonstrated their skill as composers. The pieces herein contained do not only serve the best purpose of instruction, but also offer the most pleasing musical recreation. Price... 30c If by mail, postage extra, 8 cents.

No. 12C6776 Brainard's Ragtime Collection, characteristic marches, two steps, cake walks, plantation dances, etc. Price..........45c If by mail, postage extra, 8 cents.

INSTRUMENTAL FOLIOS FOR PIANO AND CABINET ORGAN.

No. 12C6784 Kinkel's Folio, Volume 1. A rare collection of bright instrumental gems for young players, arranged for piano and organ. No better books for pupils can be obtained, and we especially recommend them to teachers. Price...25c If by mail, postage extra, 10 cents.

No. 12C6796 Brainard's Collection of Marches. Suitable for use in schools and for all occasions. A book of 116 pages, printed on good paper and handsomely bound with linen back. Any piece contained in this book if bought in sheet form would cost as much as we ask for the entire book. Price..28c If by mail, postage extra, 8 cents.

No. 12C6800 Marches. Selected from the works of celebrated composers for pianoforte or organ; regular sheet music size. A large folio of the very best selections; 160 pages. Price........(Postage extra, 9 cents).... 30c

MUSIC FOR CABINET ORGANS.

No. 12C6806 Ideal Reed Organ Gems No. 1. A collection of original compositions and arrangements for the reed or cabinet organ. A splendid folio and especially adapted to the needs of beginners. 69 pages of choice music. Price..30c If by mail, postage extra, 8 cents.

No. 12C6807 Ideal Reed Organ Gems No. 2. A splendid collection of sacred, popular and operatic selections, especially arranged for the cabinet organ. Like volume No. 1, sure to please. Price........30c If by mail, postage extra, 8 cents.

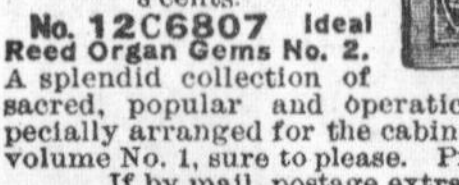

No. 12C6808 Reed Organ Folio. A new collection of the best and most popular music of the day, arranged especially for the five-octave organ. Over 60 pieces, full sheet music size; paper cover. Price.......25c If by mail, postage extra, 10 cents.

No. 12C6810 Reed Organ at Home. A collection of reed organ music, containing favorite melodies and a variety of dance music, operatic music, etc.; 128 pages. Price..........25c If by mail, postage extra, 8 cents.

INSTRUMENTAL MUSIC FOR CABINET ORGANS.

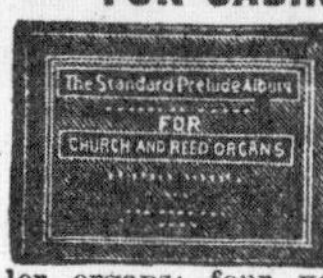

No. 12C6818 The Standard Prelude Album, for organists and amateurs. A choice collection of preludes, postludes, communion, voluntaries, marches, etc., for church and parlor organs; four volumes; sixty-four pages bound in one book. Publisher's price, $1.00. Our price..........19c If by mail, postage extra, 6 cents.

FOLIOS FOR VIOLIN AND PIANO.

No. 12C6820 Popular Duets for Violin and Piano No. 1. This is a new collection of the very latest music, including Love's Dreamland Waltzes, Mendelssohn's Wedding March, Hornpipe Polka, etc., 84 pieces; every piece a gem; 122 pages, full sheet music size; paper cover. Price..........28c If by mail, postage extra, 10 cents.

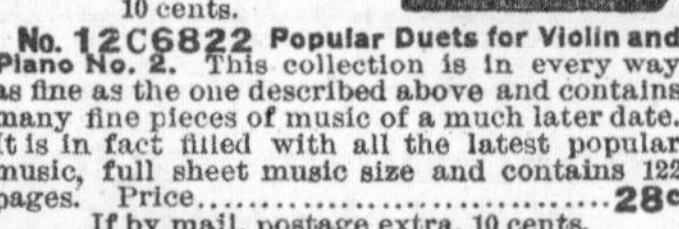

No. 12C6822 Popular Duets for Violin and Piano No. 2. This collection is in every way as fine as the one described above and contains many fine pieces of music of a much later date. It is in fact filled with all the latest popular music, full sheet music size and contains 122 pages. Price..........28c If by mail, postage extra, 10 cents.

No. 12C6824 Drawing Room Collection for the Violin and Piano. This book contains 121 pages of the best violin music by the most celebrated composers, and is a most desirable book for violin players. The pieces are arranged especially for beginners and amateurs. Price..........30c If by mail, postage extra, 10 cents.

No. 12C6835 The Witmark Violin and Piano Folio No. 5. Every violinist should have this book. The best and most popular music published is contained therein. Pretty Mollie Shannon, Stay in Your Own Back Yard, I Want a Ping Pong Man, Two steps and twenty other selections of equal beauty. No piece in this book duplicated in any other folio. The greatest value ever offered. Price.........25c If by mail, postage extra, 6 cents.

FOLIOS FOR VIOLIN.

No. 12C6838 The Young Violinist's Favorite No. 1. A collection of popular music for the violin, including overtures, quadrilles and a wide selection of dance music; 50 pages. Price..........25c If by mail, postage extra, 4 cents.

No. 12C6840 The Young Violinist's Favorite, No. 2. An entirely different edition from Folio No. 1 above, containing no duplicates. Contains 50 pages. Price ..(Postage extra, 4 cents)..25c

No. 12C6841 The Young Violinist's Gigantic Collection of standard and popular music. 350 pieces of the best music arranged in an easy manner, all in the first position. A valuable book to either beginner or experienced player, and the selections are so varied that it cannot fail to please and last a long time. Price..........25c If by mail, postage extra, 23 cents.

No. 12C6842 Musicians' Omnibus. A book containing 1,500 pieces arranged for violin, consisting of waltzes, polkas, schottisches, galops, quadrilles, jigs and clog dances, etc. Price..........68c If by mail, postage extra, 10 cents.

No. 12C6843 The Mammoth Collection for the Violin. A companion book to the Gigantic Collection. Contains over 350 selections from the operas, dances and the latest and best music published, arranged by the best composers in an artistic manner. Price..........25c If by mail, postage extra, 25 cents.

No. 12C6846 Evening Pastime. A collection of 88 popular waltzes, polkas, marches, quadrilles, also selections from favorite operas arranged in an easy and pleasing manner for the violin alone, by John Philip Sousa. Price..........55c If by mail, postage extra, 4 cents.

GUITAR FOLIOS.

No. 12C6855 Witmark's Guitar Folio No. 1. A folio of vocal and instrumental music, containing All Coons Look Alike to Me, My Gal is a High Born Lady and 26 others just as new; 72 pages, printed on fine music paper and bound in a heavy lithographed cover. Price...25c If by mail, postage extra, 5 cents.

No. 12C6856 Witmark's Guitar Folio No. 2. A folio of vocal and instrumental music, containing Just One Girl, I Love You in the Same Old Way, Because, My Coal Black Lady and about 26 more just as good. Pieces contained in this book are not duplicated in any other folio of this nature. Any single number worth the price of the entire book. Price..........25c If by mail, postage extra, 5 cents.

No. 12C6857 The Witmark's Guitar Folio No. 3. Twenty-eight pieces of exceptional merit. No number in this book contained in any other folio. Such popular pieces as Always, Just as Daylight was Breaking, Kiss Me Honey, Do, Sing Me a Song of the Sunny South, etc., are in this book. Price..........25c If by mail, postage extra, 5 cents.

No. 12C6858 The Witmark's Guitar Folio No. 4. Your guitar collection is not complete without this number. Lack of space prevents us from enumerating the wonderful amount of fine guitar music contained therein. Of the thirty numbers in this book we may mention Zamona, Absence Makes the Heart Grow Fonder, and many others just as good. There are no pieces duplicated in this series. Price..........25c If by mail, postage extra, 5 cents.

No. 12C6859 Witmark's Guitar Folio No. 5. This is the very latest number of the celebrated Witmark Guitar Folios. It contains all the latest vocal and instrumental successes of the day, 64 pages of the best music, among which are My Starlight Sue, Tale of a Sea Shell, The Donkey Laugh (instrumental), When You Were Sweet Sixteen and 27 other pieces of equal value. Price..........25c If by mail, postage extra, 6 cents.

BANJO FOLIOS.

No. 12C6866 Banjo Folio, by Brooks & Denton. This is a splendid banjo folio, filled with fine selections for that instrument and giving right along with the music an easy method of learning to play it. The following are some of the pieces: Congo Love Song, What is the Matter with the Moon To-Night, The Glow Worm and the Moth, The Colored Major and numerous others. Price..........30c If by mail, postage extra, 10 cents.

No. 12C6874 Witmark's Banjo Folio No. 2. Contains Just One Girl, Just as the Sun Went Down, Because, Honey, You'se My Lady Love and 23 others of the very latest popular hits. Pieces contained in this book are not duplicated in any other banjo folio. Any single number is worth the price of the entire book. Price..25c If by mail, postage extra 5 cents.

No. 12C6876 Witmark's Banjo Folio No. 3. This folio contains the very latest popular hits, and we think it will be sufficient that such pieces as Always, Sing Me a Song of the South, My Wild Irish Rose, etc., are in this book, any one of which is worth the price of the entire book. Pieces contained in this book are not duplicated in any other banjo folio. Price..........25c If by mail, postage extra, 5 cents.

No. 12C6878 The Witmark Banjo Folio No. 4. A later folio than No. 12C6876, and contains such great popular pieces as Absence Makes the Heart Grow Fonder, My Tiger Lily, My Blushin' Rosie, The Bridge of Sighs and thirty other vocal and instrumental selections. Your collection is not complete without this number. Pieces in this folio are not duplicated in any other banjo folio. Price..........25c If by mail, postage extra, 5 cents.

No. 12C6879 The Witmark Banjo Folio No. 5. This is the best of all collections of banjo music. The very latest book of this series. Among the pieces in this book are My Starlight Sue, My Japanese Cherry Blossom, My Sambo, The Tale of the Sea Shell. In all there are 16 vocal and 14 instrumental selections. The price for one song alone at retail would be at least 28 cents. Price..........25c If by mail, postage extra, 6 cents.

MANDOLIN and GUITAR FOLIOS.

No. 12C6884 Mark Stern's Mandolin and Guitar Folio No. 4. A collection of popular successes, such as The Maiden with the Dreamy Eyes, While the Convent Bells are Ringing, and May Be. This book is arranged in very nice and easy form so that anybody can play the contents with good effect. This book is arranged for first and second mandolin and guitar and piano. **In separate books.** Price of each book..........20c If by mail, postage extra, 3 cents.

MANDOLIN AND GUITAR FOLIOS—Cont.

No. 12C6884½ Mark Stern's Mandolin and Guitar Folio No. 5. Contains a splendid collection of popular and operatic selections. Among the twenty-five successes we shall mention: Under the Bamboo Tree, No One But You, If You'll Be Mine, Hail to The Nation—March, Summer Moon—Gavotte. Published for first and second mandolin, guitar and piano in separate parts. Price, each book 20c
If by mail, postage extra, 3 cents.

No. 12C6889 Brainard's Ragtime Collection for first and second mandolin, guitar and piano. The very latest collection of popular ragtime and characteristic selections, such as marches, cakewalks, two steps, plantation dances, etc.
Price for each instrument..................20c
If by mail, postage extra, 3 cents.

No. 12C6894 The Witmark Mandolin and Guitar Folio No. 5. Just out. No mandolin club is complete without this book. Be up to date and play the latest music. It costs no more. This book contains 23 choice selections, among which are the following: Stay in Your Own Back Yard, It's for Her, Her, Her, Sweet Maggie May, I Left My Heart in Dixie. No piece in this book is found in any other mandolin and guitar folio. Price..........25c
If by mail, postage extra, 6 cents.

CORNET AND PIANO DUETS.

No. 12C6902 Popular Duets for Cornet and Piano No. 1. A splendid collection of popular, sacred and operatic selections arranged in an easy, effective manner by the celebrated D. L. Ferrazzi. Price..........................28c
If by mail, postage extra, 11 cents.

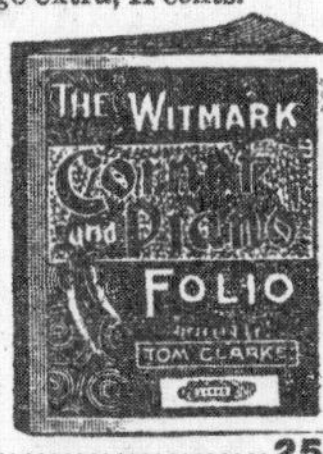

No. 12C6903 The Witmark Cornet and Piano Duets No. 1. This folio is made up of 30 cornet and piano duets, and contains such well known and popular songs as I Love You in the Same Old Way, Just One Girl, Because, When You Were Sweet Sixteen, Just As the Sun Went Down. Any one of the pieces mentioned costs the price of the book alone.
Price..........................25c
If by mail, postage extra, 6 cents.

No. 12C6904 The Witmark Cornet and Piano Duets No. 2. Contains such well known, popular pieces as Sing Me a Song of the South, Always, Absence Makes the Heart Grow Fonder, and the celebrated Victory Concert Polka, any piece alone being worth the price of the entire book. Price........25c
If by mail, postage extra, 6 cents.

No. 12C6905 The Witmark Cornet and Piano Folio No. 3. The very latest folio of this series. There is nothing better published. No effort has been spared to make this book a success. It contains the most popular selections, is printed on fine quality of paper, and is handsomely bound. Among the 20 pieces contained in this book are Stay in Your Own Back Yard, The Tale of a Bumble Bee, Mosquito Parade and the Grand American Fantasia, each of which would retail at 25 cents. Price....25c
If by mail, postage extra, 6 cents.

No. 12C6907 Cornet Players' Pastime. This is one of the most remarkable books of cornet solos ever issued. It contains 1,000 of the very best solos for B flat cornet. Printed very plainly on fine paper. Is strongly bound and contains 472 pages. It will be welcomed by every cornet player and is something very desirable in this line. Price..........25c
If by mail, postage extra, 23 cents.

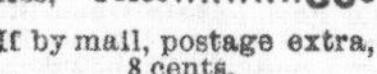

No. 12C6906 Par Excellence Cornet and Piano Selections. As light, interesting and brilliant solos, cornetists will find these selections all that can be desired. No cheap, raggy music, but all of the popular favorites. Price..........30c
If by mail, postage extra, 8 cents.

TROMBONE AND PIANO FOLIOS.

No. 12C6908 The Witmark Trombone and Piano Folio No. 3. This is the only folio of its kind on the market containing all of the latest hits of the day. The following are a few of the twenty pieces contained in this book: Good Night, Beloved, Good Night, The Tale of a Sea Shell, Mosquito Parade.
Price..........................25c
If by mail, postage extra, 6 cents.

VIOLIN, CORNET AND PIANO.

No. 12C6909 Peerless Collection No. 1. Contains all the latest songs and instrumental successes of the day. The best compositions by George Rosey and Max Witt, such as First Violin Waltzes, Belle of Granada and 46 other selections, enrich this work. Published separately for either violin, cornet or piano.
Price, each book..........20c
If by mail, postage extra, 3 cts.

VIOLIN FOLIOS—Continued.

No. 12C6911 Peerless Collection No. 2. This is another fine collection of violin solos of the same series as No. 12C6909 filled with very fine popular music for the violin, as follows: Hail to the Nation, March; The Jolly Friars, Waltzes; Selections from the Jewel of Asia, Moonlight on the Mississippi, Oh, Didn't He Ramble, and many others as good. Price, each book....20c
If by mail, postage extra, 3 cents.

DANCE JOURNAL FOR BALL ROOM ORCHESTRAS.

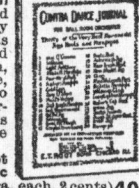

No. 12C6916 Contra Dance Journal for Ball Room Orchestras. New and good. Thirty of the very best new and old jigs, reels and hornpipes. Arranged for first and second violin, cornet, clarionet, bass, flute, trombone and piano, alto and tuba. Every dance orchestra should have this journal. Best thing of the kind ever published.
Price, each book, except piano..........................25c
Piano book. (Postage extra, each, 2 cents) 40c

Gems of the Ball Room Series.

Each number contains thirty-two or thirty-three of the very latest and best pieces of choice dance music, all kinds, strictly up to date, arranged for orchestra of eight instruments, viz., first violin, second violin, cornet, clarionet, flute, trombone (treble clef), bass viol and piano. Each part separate.

No.		Each Orchestral Part	Piano Book
12C6918	Gems No. 1	36c	70c
12C6919	Gems No. 2	36c	70c
12C6920	Gems No. 3	36c	70c
12C6921	Gems No. 4	36c	70c
12C6922	Gems No. 5	36c	70c
12C6923	Gems No. 6	36c	70c
12C6924	Gems No. 7	36c	70c
12C6925	Gems No. 8	36c	70c
12C6926	Gems No. 9	36c	70c
12C6927	Gems No. 10	36c	70c

If by mail, postage extra, each, 3 cents.
In addition to the regular parts of the Gems of the Ball Room Series, we can furnish first and second mandolin and guitar parts for Nos. 9 and 10.

Beauties of the Ball Room Series.

Choice selection of dance music, arranged for eight different orchestra instruments: First violin, second violin, cornet, flute, clarionet, trombone (treble clef), bass viol and piano. No duplicates to be found in any of the three numbers. No orchestra is complete without this series.

No. 12C6931 Beauties No. 1, orchestral parts.
Price, each, excepting piano..........36c
Piano book..........................70c
No. 12C6932 Beauties No. 2, orchestral parts. Price, each, excepting piano..........36c
Piano book..........................70c
No. 12C6933 Beauties No. 3, orchestral parts. Price, each, excepting piano..........36c
Piano book..........................70c
If by mail, postage extra, per book, 3 cents.

Pride of the Ball Room Series.

A new collection of dance music, by McCosh, Huntington and others, all well known dance writers who have given their best efforts to this work, the result of which makes this the finest collection of dance music ever issued. Every book contains entirely different selections. Arranged for the following instruments: First violin, second violin, cornet, flute, clarionet, trombone (treble clef), bass viol and piano.

No. 12C6937 Pride No. 1, orchestral parts. Price, each, excepting piano..........36c
Piano book..........................70c
No. 12C6938 Pride No. 2, orchestral parts. Price, each, excepting piano..........36c
Piano book..........................70c
If by mail, postage extra, per book, 3 cents.

CONCERT AND PARLOR GEMS.

No. 12C6939 Concert and Parlor Gems. For concerts, entertainments and home amusements. Beautiful music. Easy, not over grade two. Particularly good for young orchestras. Books for first and second violin, cornet, clarionet, bass and cello, flute, viola, trombone and piano. Also books for first and second mandolin and guitar, making a splendid set for these instruments.

Price, each book, excepting piano..........32c
Piano book..........................47c
If by mail, postage extra, per book, 2 cents.

No. 12C6942 Root's Beginners' Orchestra. A collection of easy overtures, waltzes, schottisches, etc., selected and arranged by the celebrated Professor D. S. McCosh. This is an exceptionally fine orchestral book, and is arranged for the following instruments: First violin, second violin, cornet, clarionet, bass and cello, flute, viola, trombone, first mandolin, second mandolin, guitar and piano.
Price, each book, excepting piano..........32c
Piano book..........................47c
If by mail, postage extra, per book, 2 cents.

ORCHESTRA SELECTIONS.

No. 12C6948 Order by number and title. The best and newest popular pieces, arranged for full orchestra, 10 parts and piano. Price, each..........................50c
If by mail, postage extra, 3 cents.

A Bird in a Gilded Cage (Waltz)..........Von Tilzer
Alagazam (Characteristic Two Step)
All Hands 'Round (Lancers). Very easy........J. Zimmerman
Anona, Intermezzo (Two Step)
Because (Waltz)..........Mackie
Blaze Away (Two Step)..........Holtzman
Creole Belles (Rag Time March)
Darktown Is Out Tonight (Two Step). Intro. Hottest Coon in Dixie. Arr. by......R. Recker
Golden Echoes (Waltzes)
Hiawatha, Intermezzo (Two Step)
Huckleberry Cross Roads (A Country Cake Walk)..........Robert Cone
Hunky Dory (Two Step)..........Holtzman
I Want a Real Coon (Cake Walk)..........Adler
Just as the Sun Went Down.....Arr. by Mackie
Just One Girl (Waltz)..........Mackie
Ma Tiger Lily (Cake Walk)..........A. B. Sloane
Mosquito Parade (Two Step)
My Mose Babe (Cake Walk)
On a Sunday Afternoon
Rambling Mose (Two Step)
The Gondolier (Two Step)
The Latest Fad (Three Step)..........Nat. D. Maine
The Steel King (March, Two Step)
The Tale of the Kangaroo (Polka).....G. Luders
Virginia Beauties (Two Step)
When the Harvest Days Are Over, My Jersey Lily (Waltz)..........Von Tilzer

MUSIC FOR MILITARY BANDS.

No. 12C6950 Order by number and title. The latest up to date selections of military band music, complete with 26 parts, but so arranged that they can be used for small or large bands. Price, each..........35c
If by mail, postage extra, 3 cents.

A Bird in a Gilded Cage (Waltz)..........Von Tilzer
Alagazam (Characteristic Two Step)
Blaze Away (Two Step)..........Holtzman
Calanthe (Waltzes)
Creole Belles (Rag Time March)
Golden Echoes (Waltzes)
Hiawatha, Intermezzo (Two Step)
Hunky Dory (Two Step)..........Holtzman
Just As the Sun Went Down (Waltz) Intro. Nobody Wants Me Now. Arr. by W. H Mackie
Just One Girl (Waltz) Arr by..... W. H. Mackie
On a Sunday Afternoon
Rambling Mose (Two Step)
Sing Me a Song of the South (Waltz). Intro. A Song That Would Last Evermore. Arr. by..........W. H. Mackie
The Mosquitoes' Parade (March and Two Step)..........Howard Whitney
The Steel King (March, Two Step)
The Tale of the Kangaroo (Polka) Gustav Luders
When the Harvest Days Are Over, My Jersey Lily (Waltz)..........Von Tilzer

ROOT'S GEM BAND BOOK.

No. 12C6954 Root's Gem Band Book. This book contains sixteen easy and attractive pieces of medium grade, arranged for the following instruments: Piccolo, Eb clarionet, clarionets, solo Bb cornet, 1st Bb cornet, 2d and 3d Bb cornets, Eb cornet, solo alto, 1st and 3d altos, tenors (treble), tenors (bass), baritone (treble), baritone (bass), Bb bass (treble), tubas, drums.
Price, each book..........................15c
If by mail, postage extra, per book, 2 cents.

PIANO INSTRUCTION BOOKS.

No. 12C6955 Brainard's New, Easy Method for Piano. Containing complete and thorough instructions; also a choice selection of vocal and instrumental music. Regular retail price, $1.00.
Our price...40c
If by mail, postage extra, 8 cents.

No. 12C6958 Root's New Musical Curriculum for Pianoforte Playing, Singing and Harmony. Bound in board. Publishers' price, $3.00.
Our price...$1.95
If by mail, postage extra, 28 cents.

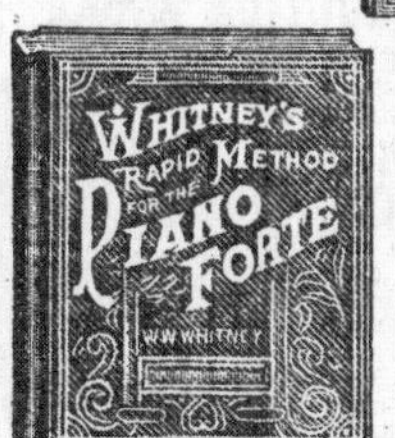

No. 12C6959 Whitney's Rapid Method for the Pianoforte. A thorough, progressive course of lessons presented in an easy and attractive form; with illustrations showing proper position of the hands and fingers on the keyboard. Also contains a great variety of instrumental pieces by distinguished authors. Bound in board. Regular retail price, $2.00. Our price..........80c
If by mail, postage extra, 20 cents.

WE WILL SATISFY YOU WITH OUR GOODS IN EVERY WAY OR ELSE RETURN YOUR MONEY.

THE RAPID PIANO INSTRUCTOR.

No. 12C6961 Chord Book for Piano. This book was especially compiled for us by the celebrated instructor and composer, E. H. Guckert. It contains illustrations of the piano keyboard showing the fingers to be used in each chord, besides many other valuable illustrations and instructions for the beginner or advanced pupil. This book will teach any one how to play chords and accompaniments without the aid of a teacher. Price..........$1.00
If by mail, postage extra, 12 cents.

The Witmark Progressive Method for the Piano.

A distinctly modern book, especially desirable, as it contains a series of up to date instructive compositions instead of the old fashioned studies. It is arranged in a melodious form, making it more interesting for the pupil—a book of exceptional merit, as it starts at the first rudiments and instructs by easy stages.

No. 12C6966 Board cover.
Price........80c
No. 12C6967 Paper cover. Price. 65c
If by mail, postage extra, boards, 12 cents; paper, 10 cents.

ORGAN INSTRUCTION BOOKS.

No. 12C6968 Chord Book for Organ. This book was especially compiled for us by E. N. Guckert, the celebrated instructor and composer. It contains 24 illustrations of the keyboard of the organ, showing the fingers used in each chord, besides other valuable instructions for the beginner or advanced pupil. This book will teach any one how to play chords and accompaniments without the aid of a teacher.
Price..........$1.00
If by mail, postage extra, 16 cents.

No. 12C6982 White's School for the Reed Organ. One of the best methods ever offered. Contains a full and comprehensive method of instruction, also scales, studies, exercises, voluntaries, songs, marches, waltzes, polkas, opera melodies, hymns, tunes, etc., arranged expressly for the reed organ, melodeon or harmonium, by C. A. White and Charles C. Blake. Contains 152 pages. Bound in board. Price..........65c
If by mail, postage extra, 12 cents.

No. 12C6984 Karl Merz's Improved and Modern Method for the Parlor Organ. Contains complete elementary department, exercises in all keys, hints to pupils and teachers, voluntaries, preludes, popular airs and beautiful songs, to which is added a complete course of thorough bass instruction. This book retails at $2.00. Our price (Postage extra, 18 cents) 55c

Easy Method for the Parlor Organ.

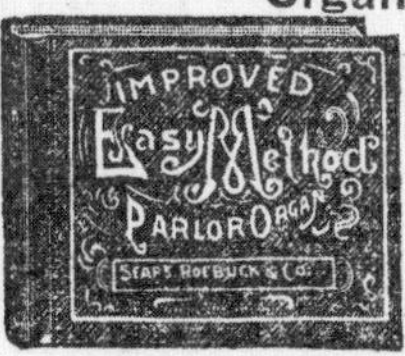

No. 12C6988 Whitney's Improved Easy Method for the Parlor Organ. New and enlarged edition. This is a new and attractive system by which the pupil may rapidly learn to play the organ. Besides a thorough course in music, this book contains a choice collection of vocal and instrumental pieces, progressively arranged. Publisher's price, $1.50. Our price..........50c
If by mail, postage extra, 13 cents.

No. 12C6989 Whitney's Complete Instructor for the Parlor Organ. Contains a complete graded system with pleasing exercises, easy waltzes, marches, polkas, quicksteps, schottisches, operatic airs, songs and ballads; in fact, selections from the best European and American composers. All directions for the caring of organ, explanation of stops, technical studies and transposition are herein contained. Publisher's price, $2.50.
Our price, heavy board covers.......$1.20
If by mail, postage extra, 19 cents.

Organ and Piano Charts.

No. 12C6995 Mason's Organ Chart. This chart is the most wonderful invention of the age, for with the use of Mason's Indicator, piano and organ playing can be learned in one day. A child ten years old can understand it perfectly. Mason's Indicator is a machine which fits over the keys of a piano or organ, indicating where and how the hands are to be placed and the proper keys to strike, changing the position and the arrangement to suit the different keys. Price 75c
If by mail, postage extra, 3 cents.

VIOLIN INSTRUCTION BOOKS.

No. 12C6996 Howe's Violin Without a Master. Containing new and complete rules and exercises, with full directions in bowing and all necessary instructions to perfect the learner in the art of playing the violin; to which is added a large selection of popular airs and dance music, as well as operatic airs, with several pieces arranged as duets. Price... 22c
If by mail, postage extra, 3 cents.

Howard Violin Instructor.

No. 12C6997 A very fine instructor for this splendid instrument filled with scales and exercises in all the minor and major keys, and explains all the different parts of a violin and the best methods of studying it. It is filled with many fine musical selections of particular advantage to the student and easy to learn to play. It has a complete musical dictionary, giving an explanation of the different musical terms and also contains a fingerboard chart which will be of great assistance in learning the instrument. Price........ 20c
If by mail, postage extra, 4 cents

No. 12C7004 Henning's School for the Violin. Specially revised, with bow and finger marks added. In three parts, complete in one book; 101 pages, printed on fine paper, bound in board.
Price, complete... 80c
If by mail, postage extra, 15 cents.

No. 12C7012 Maza's Complete Violin Instructor. Contains besides a dictionary of musical terms and exercises in all positions, several of Pleyel's celebrated duets.
Price 30c
If by mail, postage extra, 8 cents.

No. 12C7014 Benjamin's Illustrated Violin Method. This is the latest publication in the way of a violin instructor and is the best work for the beginner ever put upon the market. It contains the complete elementary course; is profusely illustrated; also contains a collection of popular music; 79 pages, sheet music size. Price.... 37c
If by mail, postage extra, 5 cents.

No. 12C7016 Wichtl's Young Violinist. An excellent book for beginners, as it contains the first instructions in the violin line, including one hundred progressive exercises in the first position through all intervals and keys, with the second violin part for the teacher. It contains also Pleyel's celebrated violin duets.
Price 38c
If by mail, postage extra, 10 cents.

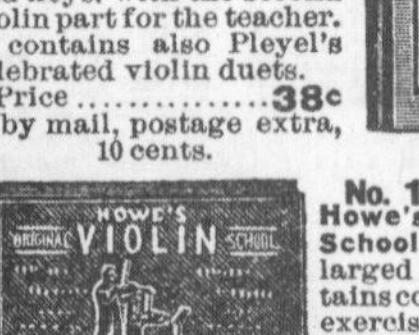

No. 12C7018 Howe's Original Violin School, new and enlarged edition. Contains complete rules and exercises, together with a collection of over 450 pieces of every variety. Hundreds of old familiar airs, never before published, for the violin. Extra large type and fine paper. Price........ 20c
If by mail, postage extra, 4 cents.

No. 12C7020 Howe's Diamond School for the Violin, contains complete instructions, full directions for bowing and 558 pieces of dance music.
Price........ 20c
If by mail, postage extra, 4 cents.

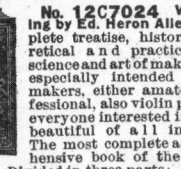

No. 12C7021 The Violin; How to Master It. This little book is a treatise on the violin itself. It gives all the points in the art of playing the violin besides all the special instructions on position and bowing. It is also furnished with a complete fingerboard chart showing the different positions in which the violin can be played. A great help to teacher and pupil. Price........ 15c
If by mail, postage extra, 3 cents.

No. 12C7024 Violin Making by Ed. Heron Allen. A complete treatise, historical, theoretical and practical on the science and art of making violins, especially intended for violin makers, either amateur or professional, also violin players and everyone interested in this most beautiful of all instruments. The most complete and comprehensive book of the kind ever published. Divided in three parts: Historical, which relates to the ancestry of the violin, its origin, its famous makers; theoretical, the woods, models and parts entering into the construction of a violin; practical, instructing you as to the tools, varnish, moulds and everything connected with the building of a violin, so that by following the instructions carefully one may be able to build a violin or, at least, to detect its good or bad qualities. This book also contains more than 200 illustrations and charts.
Price, handsomely bound in cloth, with gold lettering........ $1.60
If by mail, postage extra, 15 cents.

GUITAR INSTRUCTION BOOKS.

No. 12C7030 Bowers' Standard Method for the Guitar. Positively the most popular instruction book for the guitar ever published; bound in paper. Price........ 25c
If by mail, postage extra, 4 cents.

No. 12C7033 New and Improved Method for the Guitar. By Carcassi, the celebrated guitarist, embracing much valuable matter not contained in other books. The number of popular songs in each of the different keys, together with the masterly instructions of Carcassi, make this a desirable method to both teacher and scholar.
Price........ 50c
If by mail, postage extra, 12 cents.

No. 12C7039 Guckert's Complete Rapid Diagram Chord Book for the Guitar. The best book of its kind published, written expressly for us by E. N. Guckert and published and copyrighted by us. Mr. Guckert claims it to be the most complete diagram self instructor published. The book contains popular guitar solos that can be played by anyone at sight, a feature not to be found in other chord books. List price, 50 cents. Our price........ 18c
If by mail, postage extra, 2 cents.

Howard Guitar Instructor.

No. 12C7040 This is one of the best guitar instructors yet issued for this instrument, and we recommend it to all who desire to play upon the guitar without the aid of a teacher. It is filled with all sorts of exercises and plain explanations, has a splendid musical dictionary, chords in all the minor and major keys, as well as a complete set of scales. It is filled with many fine musical selections among which are the following: Sweet Hour of Prayer, Blue Bells of Scotland, Robin Adair and many fine marches and waltzes. We also enclose in this instructor a very fine fingerboard chart which will prove of great assistance in learning to play the instrument. Price........ 20c
If by mail, postage extra, 4 cents.

BANJO INSTRUCTION BOOKS.

No. 12C7053 Witmark's Progressive Banjo Method, written and compiled by G. L. Lancing. Complete, progressive, practical, thoroughly up to date method. A great aid to the teacher. The elementary or first part will enable the pupil to progress so as to play the popular selections of today within a short time. The entire work is arranged in a most progressive and systematic manner. The book contains 88 pages. Has superior quality paper flexible cover and linen back. Publisher's retail price, $1.00.
Our price......(Postage extra, 10c)........ 65c

No. 12C7055 Guckert's Complete Rapid Diagram Chord Book for the Banjo. The best book of its kind published, written expressly for us by E. N. Guckert and published and copyrighted by us. Mr. Guckert claims it to be the most complete diagram self instructor published. The book contains popular banjo solos that can be played by anyone at sight, a feature not found in other chord books. List price, 50 cents. Our price..... 18c
If by mail, postage extra, 2 cents.

The Howard Banjo Instructor.

No. 12C7056 A very fine instructor for this instrument, with all sorts of exercises, plates and descriptions, so that the beginner can learn the instrument without the aid of a teacher. Diagrams of all the principal minor and major chords, scales and many splendid pieces of music, among which are the following: Sailor's Horn Pipe, Dixie, Irish Washwoman, Wedding March, Waltzes, etc., plainly printed on heavy paper with a fine cover. Also includes fingerboard chart for the banjo.
Price........ 20c
If by mail, postage extra, 4 cents.

MANDOLIN INSTRUCTION BOOKS.

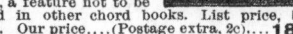

No. 12C7069 Guckert's Complete Rapid Diagram Chord Book for the Mandolin. The best book of its kind published, written expressly for us by E. N. Guckert and published and copyrighted by us. Mr. Guckert claims it to be the most complete diagram self instructor published. The book contains popular mandolin solos that can be played by anyone at sight, a feature not to be found in other chord books. List price, 50 cents. Our price....(Postage extra, 2c).... 18c

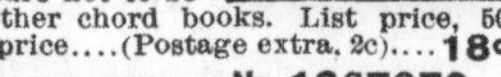

No. 12C7070 Howe's Original Mandolin Collection and School. A very easy and comprehensive method for this beautiful instrument, containing complete theory of music, also splendid collection of 450 selections, arranged in an easy and effective manner. New and enlarged edition.
Price........ 25c
If by mail, postage extra, 4 cents.

No. 12C7071 Howard Mandolin Instructor. A fine instructor for the mandolin filled with all sorts of plain instructions, exercises, scales and chords in all of the principal minor and major keys. With the aid of this instructor the beginner can learn to play the mandolin without the aid of a teacher. It has a very fine musical dictionary and contains many splendid pieces of music among which are the following: I Dreamt I Dwelt in Marble Halls, La Paloma and many fine marches and waltzes. Printed on heavy paper with a handsome cover. Price........ 20c
If by mail, postage extra, 4 cents.

No. 12C7072 Witmark's Progressive Mandolin Method. A distinctively modern book, written and compiled by T. P. Trinkaus, the mandolin expert. Especially desirable, as it contains a series of simple melodies and exercises as well as a number of very fine pieces. It starts at the very first rudiments and instructs by easy stages so that by a slight effort any person using the book can become a good player without a teacher. The book contains 105 pages, printed on a superior quality of paper, flexible cover and linen back. Publisher's retail price, $1.00. Our price........ 65c
If by mail, postage extra, 10 cents.

No. 12C7077 Hamilton's Imperial Mandolin Instructor. A wonderfully simple method for the mandolin. Adapted especially for the use of beginners without a teacher; one of the most up to date and easiest methods to learn from published. In addition to its elementary department, the book contains nearly 50 pages of easy and beautiful music for mandolin with guitar accompaniment.
Price........(Postage extra, 6c)........ 35c

MISCELLANEOUS INSTRUCTION BOOKS.

NOTE, IMPORTANT—When ordering any of the instruction books listed be sure to state for which instrument.

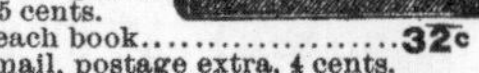

No. 12C7080 Winner's Eureka Method. Exactly suited to the needs of the beginner and especially adapted to the growing wants of the pupil. One of the latest and best instruction books published for piano, organ, violin, guitar, mandolin, banjo, accordion, flute, fife, cornet, piccolo, zither, violoncello, clarionet and flageolet. Regular retail price, 75 cents.
Our price, each book........ 32c
If by mail, postage extra, 4 cents.

No. 12C7082 Ryan's True Instructor for harmonica, double bass, ocarina, E flat alto, trombone, concertina, drum, fife, clarionet, violin, guitar, mandolin, violoncello, flute, bugle, cornet and banjo. Publisher's price, 50 cents. Our price, each book..... 18c
If by mail, postage extra, 3 cents.

No. 12C7098 Winner's Primary School for accordion, organ, violin, mandolin, guitar, banjo, flute, fife, violoncello, clarionet and cornet. Not condensed; unabridged. Specify for which instrument book is wanted.
Price, each book........ 13c
If by mail, postage extra, 3 cents.

No. 12C7119 Otto Langey's Celebrated Instructors for any instrument. These books have a world wide reputation as being among the finest instructors ever published, being easily understood, yet complete in every detail, so that a beginner using one of these books with practice, can easily master any instrument. Published for cornet, Eb alto, Bb tenor, bass clef; Bb tenor, treble clef; Bb tenor slide trombone, bass clef; Bb tenor slide trombone, treble clef; Bb baritone, bass clef; Bb baritone, treble clef; Bb bass, bass clef; Bb bass, treble clef; Eb bass, clarionet, flute, piccolo, violin, viola, violoncello, double bass, guitar, mandolin, banjo, saxophone, oboe, bassoon, French horn, drums, fife, tympany, orchestra bells, xylophone and piano. Coleman's edition. Regular retail price, $1.00. Our price, each book........ 38c
If by mail, postage extra, 7 cents.

No. 12C7121 Autoharp Instructor. By C. F. Zimmerman, containing full instructions, besides a great number of easy selections for the beginner. Price........ 19c
If by mail, postage extra, 6 cents.

No. 12C7123 Howe's Army and Navy Fife Instructor, containing complete course of instructions, also calls, signals and the complete camp and garrison duties as practiced in the United States army and navy, besides marches, quicksteps, waltzes, etc. Paper cover.
Price........ 20c
If by mail, postage extra, 4 cents.

No. 12C7140 Rudiments of Music. A concise and thoroughly practical course of instruction on the art of singing by note; prepared by J. R. Murray. Price........ 9c
If by mail, postage extra, 2 cents.

No. 12C7146 Pronouncing Pocket Dictionary of over 500 musical terms. Price.. 12c
If by mail, postage extra, 1 cent.

BALL ROOM GUIDE AND CALL BOOKS.

No. 12C7150 Prof. Clendenen's Fashionable Quadrille Book and Guide to Etiquette. This book contains all the necessary instructions, both with reference to etiquette on the ball room floor, as well as description of figures and calling. New and revised edition contains the Trilby Two-Step Quadrille, Oxford Minuet, Aurora, La Veta, Chicago Glide, the latest German and 50 other popular dances; 89 pages. Price........ 20c
If by mail, postage extra, 2 cents.

No. 12C7152 Howe's New American Dancing Master, containing 400 dances and including 100 figures of the German. The latest and most fashionable dances are included, with full explanation of the latest and most approved figures and calls for the different changes, as well as rules on deportment, toilet and etiquette of dancing; 140 pages.
Price........ 30c

No. 12C7158 Gems of the Ball Room Call Book. Contains 100 pages of calls that every dance orchestra should have; 25 Plain Quadrilles, several Prairie Queens, Lancers, Waltz Quadrilles, etc. Price........ 25c
By mail, postage extra, 3 cents.

For other Dancing and Call Books, see our BOOK DEPARTMENT.

THE MUSIC FOLIOS WE LIST ARE STANDARD
AND THE VERY BEST IN EACH PARTICULAR LINE.
WE HAVE MADE A CAREFUL STUDY OF THIS DEPARTMENT.

WATCH, DIAMOND AND JEWELRY DEPARTMENTS.

SEARS, ROEBUCK & CO.'S Special Watch Movements are the perfection of mechanical skill, made especially for us after our own original designs and in such large quantities that we get them at a price which enables us to sell them to you at what other dealers very often ask for cheap and unreliable watches.

WHEN YOU BUY A GOLD FILLED CASE bear in mind that the Sears' gold filled case is recommended above all others, being made of two extra heavy plates of solid gold over a hard composition metal. Will wear longer than any other gold filled case made and is the handsomest, best finished and best fitting gold filled watch case made. **If you select a Sears' case you will have the best gold filled watch case ever made.**

NOTICE. **We sell our watches only in the combinations quoted in our catalogue and will only supply the case and movements as quoted under each watch.**

MAIL AND EXPRESS SHIPMENTS. **We recommend sending watches by express, as they do not receive the hard usage as when sent by mail. Our statistics show that 90 per cent of breakages in watches happen while in transit through the mails; therefore, we again advise you to have watches shipped by express, and all other small jewelry by mail, as it is perfectly safe and far the cheapest.** Postage is 1 cent per ounce. A watch packed for shipment weighs from 6 to 8 ounces; chains, rings and other small articles of jewelry about 2 ounces. Packages amounting to $1.00 or over should be registered, which costs 8 cents extra, as this is the safest method. **25 cents will carry any watch to any part of the United States by express.**

ENGRAVING. **Cash in full must accompany all orders when goods are marked with engraving. We charge for engraving in script on jewelry, watches, etc.,** 2½ cents per letter; in old English, small, 5 cents per letter.

Monograms on silverware and jewelry are all the rage. Prices for two or three-letter combination, script or ribbon style, as follows:

	Script	Ribbon
½-inch size	20c	25c
¾-inch size	30c	35c
1 -inch size	40c	47c
1½-inch size	55c	65c

In writing orders when goods are to be engraved, write or draw plain letters, so as to avoid mistakes. **We cannot exchange goods after they have been engraved.**

REGARDING ENGRAVINGS ON WATCH CASES. **It sometimes happens that we are out of the exact engraving on watch case ordered,** but we aim to carry exact designs. When the exact engraving cannot be had, we always have a very similar one, which we will take the liberty of sending rather than delay your order, **it being understood you can return same if not perfectly satisfactory.**

WATCH REPAIRING. **We have a thoroughly equipped mechanical department, which is fitted with all of the latest tools and appliances for** the repairing of all kinds of watches. Our charges are about one-half what is usually charged by the retail dealers, and the work will be done in a very superior manner. We cannot give an accurate estimate of the cost of repairs without a thorough examination of the work. Our charges are merely enough to cover cost of material and labor. In sending a watch for repairing be sure to send it by registered mail; mark on the outside of the package your name and address, and write us at the same time that you have done so, giving full explanation regarding trouble with watch.

Illustrations show exact size of Watches and Jewelry except when otherwise stated.

OUR BINDING GUARANTEES.

WATCH CASE GUARANTEE. **Where a watch case in this catalogue is described as guaranteed for life, 25, 20, 10, 5 or 2 years,** it applies to gold filled watch cases, and means that the case is covered by two plates of solid gold over an inner plate of hard composition metal, and the gold is guaranteed to wear and retain its perfect color for the time stated, and if the gold in any piece or part of the case wears through within the stipulated time mentioned in the description and in the guarantee, the case will be replaced by a new case free of cost to you.

MOVEMENT GUARANTEE. **Where we guarantee a watch movement for five years,** the guarantee is absolute and binding upon us to replace or repair, free of cost to you, any piece or part of the watch movement that may become defective by reason of imperfect material or workmanship at any time within five years; and while this guarantee does not include removing dirt, cleaning of movement or repairing, free of cost, any piece or part that may be broken or damaged through careless or improper handling, it is the widest, longest and strongest watch movement guarantee ever issued, and if you buy any movement from us and on the last day of the fifth year the watch stops or fails to keep accurate time, and this failure is in any way due to imperfect material or workmanship, it will be repaired by us or replaced with a new movement free of any cost to you. **Our written guarantees which accompany every watch and movement** are so written over our own signature that there can be no question of your absolute security in the purchase of any watch case, watch movement or complete watch from us.

DIAMOND GUARANTEE. **Our Refund, Exchange and Guarantee Certificate. With every diamond we issue a written, binding guarantee,** with a further agreement that you can at any time return any diamond you may select, where weight and quality are quoted, and exchange it for any other diamond or other article of jewelry at the same or higher price.

We further agree on the return of any diamond purchased from us within 60 days of purchase, when so requested, to refund in cash your full purchase price, and we further agree at any time after 60 days, on return of any diamond to us, when requested to do so, to refund your full purchase price less 10 per cent.

JEWELRY GUARANTEE. **Where we describe any article of jewelry as solid gold, gold filled or gold plated,** where we describe it as 18, 14 or 10-karat or solid silver, silver filled or silver plated, the article of jewelry is covered by our binding guarantee, guaranteeing it to be in every way exactly as represented by us, and if after received, examined and put to any kind of test, acid or otherwise, it should prove any different, should fall short in the slightest degree of the representation made in this catalogue, we will replace the article purchased with a new article or refund your money, as you may direct. However, this will never be necessary, for every article shown in this catalogue is in quality, finish and in every way up to the full standard of the description given and so guaranteed by our binding guarantee.

OUR SEARS LIFE GUARANTEE.

Where we describe any gold filled case or article of jewelry or silverware as carrying our SEARS LIFE GUARANTEE, we mean that should any of these articles fail in any part to be exactly as warranted, we will exchange same at any time within your natural life, whether you have owned the article five years, twenty years or fifty years. Return it to us, and we will upon receipt of it send another one of the same quality FREE OF CHARGE.

TECHNICAL TERMS USED IN DESCRIBING JEWELRY AND SILVERWARE.

BRIGHT POLISH is a finish on silver and gold showing the bright polished surface of the metal itself without coloring, and always has a bright and shining surface.

SATIN FINISH. The finishing of jewelry and silverware by sand blasting or a scratch brush, which dulls the surface and gives it a peculiar satiny effect, and shows the dull color of the metal without any other coloring.

ROMAN COLOR is the absolutely pure color of virgin gold. It is pure gold plated upon a lower karat of gold and is of a rich, bright yellow or canary color, the same color as nuggets or pure 24-karat gold. Two methods are used in putting this color on, the electro plating process and the acid process. The acid process is used only on 14 and 18-karat jewelry. When Roman color is used, the article is generally satin finished after.

HAND ENGRAVING. When stated that the article is hand engraved, we mean that the article is beautified, as the illustration of the article shows, by bright cutting done by hand with an engraving tool.

GOLD FILLED STOCK. Gold filled stock is made of stock that is gold filled, the outside or visible surface being a sheet of solid gold of substantial thickness, hard soldered on a plate of base metal.

ROLLED PLATE. Rolled plate is made very similarly to gold filled stock, with the exception that the plate is rolled to a thinner degree and has not the wearing ability of gold filled stock.

ELECTRO PLATE. Electro plate is a process of gold plating by electricity. This is the cheapest and quickest method of gold plating. Electro plated jewelry cannot be guaranteed, and will wear but a short time. It is very difficult to recognize electro plated jewelry from rolled plate or gold filled. Only one well versed and educated in the jewelry business can recognize the difference.

TECHNICAL TERMS USED IN DESCRIBING WATCHES.

FULL ADJUSTMENT. A high grade watch is fully adjusted when it is adjusted to heat, cold, isochronism and to six positions.

Our 17-jeweled **Sears, Roebuck & Co.** special line of movements in 18, 16 and 6 size are all fully adjusted.

ADJUSTED TO TEMPERATURE. As a watch is only as perfect as the balance wheel and hairspring is perfect, and as these parts are made of metal, and metal contracts and expands with variations in temperature, a watch to be adjusted to temperature must have the balance wheel so constructed as to allow for extreme cold or extreme heat. In other words, the balance wheel must be so constructed that one metal will expand to such an amount as can be taken up by the other metal used in its make-up. When the balance wheel is so constructed that this variation does not affect it, it is known then to be adjusted to temperature.

ADJUSTED TO ISOCHRONISM is an adjustment of the hairspring by which it vibrates with the balance wheel in perfect uniformity; that is, when the long and short arcs of a balance wheel are caused to perform in the same time by means of the hairspring. This assures accuracy in time keeping.

ADJUSTED TO POSITION. This adjustment can only be brought about by having the balance wheel in perfect poise and absolutely trued. The watch is run and timed in six different positions and corrections are made from time to time until the watch runs in each position without any variation in time.

Our 15-jeweled **Sears, Roebuck & Co.** special line of movements in 18, 16 and 6 size, also the **Edgemere** line of movements made especially for us, are all adjusted to position.

BREGUET HAIRSPRINGS. This hairspring differs from the old style flat hairspring in having the outer coil adjusted above the other coil and tempered in this position. This arrangement insures a condition for perfect adjustment of the hairspring in all positions, thus obviating all chances of its becoming misplaced and entangled, as has always been the case with flat hairsprings.

Our **Sears, Roebuck & Co.** special movements and the **Edgemere** line of movements made expressly for us all have Breguet hairsprings.

PATENT REGULATOR is a device for controlling the vibrations of the hairspring, and by its use a watch can be regulated to the smallest fraction of time.

Our 17 and 15-jeweled **Sears, Roebuck & Co.** special full adjusted movements, also the **Edgemere** movements in 18 and 0 size, have patent regulators.

STEM WIND AND STEM SET. All watches that are set by turning the winding crown, whether they are set by pulling out a setting lever or by pressing in a push pin, are known as stem set and stem wind watches.

PENDANT SET. All watches that are set without setting lever or push pin are known as pendant set watches, being set by pulling out the winding crown which is located at top of pendant or neck, as it is sometimes called; the hands may be set by simply turning the crown, which is pushed back into place when hands are in desired position.

TIMING SCREWS. With the use of these screws a watch can be brought down to accurate time without in any way changing the position of the hairspring. Only a watchmaker can manipulate these screws. Care must be taken in the use of them in timing a watch, together with great skill, as a well poised balance wheel is very delicate and easily put out of true and is often spoiled by incompetent workmen.

Our **Sears, Roebuck & Co.** special movements and the **Edgemere** line of movements made expressly for us all have timing screws.

CUT BALANCE. The cut or expansion balance is the most reliable for accurate time. They are constructed so that there can be only a minimum amount of variation by any climatic change, whereas the solid balance wheel, by contraction or expansion, will vary when used where variations of temperature are met with.

Our **Sears, Roebuck & Co.** special movements and the **Edgemere** line of movements made expressly for us all have cut balance.

RUBY JEWELS are used in the high priced, fine finished watches. By ruby jewels, we mean the jewels are of genuine ruby. **Garnet jewels** are mostly used in the average middle priced watches and are made of garnet, and cheap imported watches are sometimes fitted with glass jewels.

Our **Sears, Roebuck & Co.** special movements and the **Edgemere** line of movements made expressly for us all have ruby jewels.

DOUBLE SUNK DIALS are made of three pieces: The outer part on which the numerals are placed, the center or plain field, and the small circular disc for registering the seconds. This construction is a great advantage over the plain dials, as a preventive of the hands catching, thereby causing the watch to stop.

Our **Sears, Roebuck & Co.** special movements in 18 and 16 size have double sunk dials.

SAFETY PINION is a patent device on the center wheel arbor of a watch, the purpose of which is to protect the train wheels and mainspring barrel from damage in cases where the mainspring breaks.

Our **Sears, Roebuck & Co.** special movements and the **Edgemere** line of movements made expressly for us all have patent pinions.

OUR TROPHY AND PRIZE BADGES ARE THE VERY LATEST DESIGNED.

THE ILLUSTRATIONS show the exact sizes. We engrave any inscription wanted at the rate of 1½ cents per letter for script, 3½ cents per letter for old English, or 3 cents per letter for block. This price for engraving is for badge work only. In engraving badges two kinds of lettering are usually used, script and block, or script and old English.

OUR STERLING SILVER BADGES are made of solid sterling silver through and through, every piece being solid sterling silver, which is 925-1000 fine. Our gold filled badges give general good satisfaction. The same method used in gold filled cases was adopted for the manufacture of these badges.

TIME FOR MAKING. You must anticipate in ordering these goods as we cannot possibly turn them out and give well finished goods in less time than fifteen to twenty days from date of receiving the order. It must be understood that under no consideration whatever can we deviate from our prices.

CASH IN FULL must accompany all orders for class pins and badges and we sell them with the understanding only that they are not exchangeable or returnable, but we guarantee them to be exactly as described in every particular.

If by mail, postage extra, each, 3c.; insurance or registry extra.

No. 4C1925 Solid Gold. Price......$3.30
No. 4C1927 Solid Silver. Price......$1.00
No. 4C1929 Gold Filled. Price......$1.25

No. 4C1931 Solid Gold. Price......$4.12
No. 4C1933 Solid Silver. Price......$1.50
No. 4C1936 Gold Filled. Price......$1.90

No. 4C1938 Solid Gold. Price......$8.75
No. 4C1941 Solid Silver. Price......3.75
No. 4C1943 Gold Filled. Price......4.50

No. 4C1951 Solid Gold. Price......$2.25
No. 4C1953 Solid Silver. Price......65c
No. 4C1955 Gold Filled. Price......75c

No. 4C1963 Solid Gold. Price......$1.00
No. 4C1964 Solid Silver. Price......32c
No. 4C1965 Gold Filled. Price......37c

No. 4C1957 Solid Gold. Price....$3.00
No. 4C1959 Solid Silver. Price....$1.00
No. 4C1961 Gold Filled. Price...$1.25

No. 4C1966 Solid Gold. Price..........$1.00
No. 4C1967 Solid Silver. Price..........37c
No. 4C1968 Gold Filled. Price..........50c

PRICES CUT AGAIN! We can buy them cheaper now, was $1.65 NOW $1.35

SEND US $1.35 and we will ship you by express our entire Wire Workers' Outfit, exactly as illustrated, and if after you have carefully examined it you do not find it equal or better than sets offered for $1.95 and $2.25, return it and we will refund your money, together with the express charges. This outfit consists of the following items:

1 pair snipe nose pliers, 1 pair round nose pliers, 1 pair side cutting pliers, 1 file with handle, 1 ounce gold plated wire (⅛-ounce round and ⅛-ounce square), ½-gross plated washers, assorted, 1 lot assorted shells, 1 drill (not shown in illustration), 2 sample names. Follow the principle used in making these names and you will know the entire art.

No. 4C2004 Price..........(Shipping weight, about 1¾ pounds)..........**$1.35**
Order by Number. If by mail, postage extra, 27 cents.

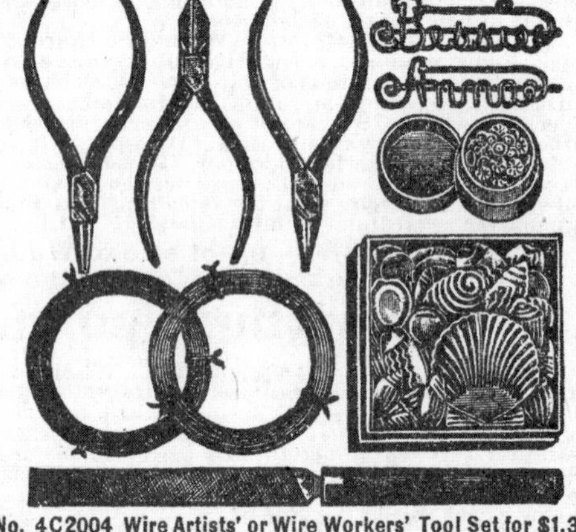

No. 4C2004 Wire Artists' or Wire Workers' Tool Set for $1.35

PRICES OF GOLD PLATED WIRE AND WIRE WORKERS' MATERIAL.

WE CANNOT SELL ANY OF THIS MATERIAL IN SMALLER QUANTITIES THAN QUOTED.

No. 4C2006 1st quality round wire. Sizes, 16 to 21 gauge. Price, per ounce..........65c
No. 4C2008 2d quality round wire. Sizes, 16 to 21 gauge. Price, per ounce..........45c
No. 4C2010 3d quality round wire. Sizes, 16 to 21 gauge. Price, per ounce..........20c
No. 4C2012 1st quality square wire. Sizes, 18 to 22 gauge. Price, per ounce..........65c
No. 4C2014 2d quality square wire. Sizes, 18 to 22 gauge. Price, per ounce..........45c
No. 4C2016 3d quality square wire. Sizes, 18 to 22 gauge. Price, per ounce..........20c
No. 4C2019 Solid Silver Wire. Sizes, 16 to 21 gauge. Price, per ounce..........78c
No. 4C2020 Solid Gold Wire, 8-karat. Sizes, 16 to 21 gauge. Price, per pennyweight..........50c
No. 4C2022 Solid Gold Wire, 10-karat. Sizes, 16 to 21 gauge. Price, per pennyweight..........60c
No. 4C2024 Solid Gold Wire, 14-karat. Sizes, 16 to 21 gauge. Price, per pennyweight..........80c
No. 4C2026 Jump Rings. 1 gross assorted sizes. Gold Plated. Price, per gross..........13c

Wire.
No. 4C2006 to No. 4C2024.

No. 4C2028 Scarf Pin Backs, Rolled Gold Plated, for mounting quartz, etc. Price, per dozen..........45c
No. 4C2030 Pin Tongs, Rolled Gold Plated, for repairing brooches, assorted. Price, per gross..........60c
No. 4C2032 Gold Plated Swivels. Gents' size. Per doz. 45c
No. 4C2034 Gold Filled Swivels. Gents' size. Price, per dozen, $1.44; each..........12c
No. 4C2036 Gold Plated Swivels. Ladies' size. Per doz. 45c
No. 4C2038 Gold Filled Swivels. Ladies' size. Price, per dozen, $1.44; each..........12c
No. 4C2040 Gold Filled Bars. Gents' size. Per doz. $1.00
No. 4C2042 Gold Filled Bars. Ladies' size. Per doz. 75c
No. 4C2044 Gold Plated Bars. Gents' size. Per doz. 35c
No. 4C2046 Gold Plated Bars. Ladies' size. Per doz. 35c
No. 4C2048 Gold Plated Toggles. Ladies' or Gents' size. Price, per dozen..........30c
No. 4C2050 Gold Filled Toggles. Ladies' or Gents' size. Price, per dozen..........$1.00
No. 4C2052 Gold Filled Dumbbell Pattern Button Backs. Price, per dozen..........75c
No. 4C2054 Gold Plated Button Backs. Price, per dozen..........35c
No. 4C2056 Gold Filled Button Backs. Price, per dozen..........50c
No. 4C2058 Gold Plated Stud Backs. Price, per dozen..........20c
No. 4C2060 Gold Filled Stud Backs. Price, per dozen..........35c
No. 4C2062 Gold Plated Scarf Pin Backs. Price, per dozen..........20c
No. 4C2063 Gold Plated Hat Pin Stems for Mounting Quartz, Etc., Price, per dozen..........40c
No. 4C2064 Gold Filled Scarf Pin Backs. Price, per dozen..........70c
No. 4C2066 Gold Solder. Price, per pennyweight..........20c
No. 4C2068 Silver Solder. In ¼-ounce sheets. Price, per ounce..........80c

No. 4C2070 Soft Solder. Price, per bundle..........5c
No. 4C2072 Catches for Brooches. Gold Plated. Per gross..........45c
No. 4C2074 Joints for Brooches. Gold Plated. Per gross..........45c
No. 4C2076 Ear Wire Drops. Gold Filled. Price, per dozen..........25c
No. 4C2078 Ear Wire Screws. Gold Filled. Price, per dozen..........50c
No. 4C2080 Brass Riveting Wire, assorted sizes. Per bundle..........5c
No. 4C2082 Brass Blow Pipe. Price, each..........10c
No. 4C2084 Soldering Coppers. Price, each..........20c
No. 4C2086 Soldering Fluid. Price, per bottle..........15c
No. 4C2088 Soldering Tweezers. Price, each..........15c
No. 4C2090 Binding Wire. Price, per spool..........10c
No. 4C2092 Gold Plated Jobbing Plate. Price, per ounce..........75c
No. 4C2094 Jobbing Stones, assorted. Containing all colors and sizes in imitation of genuine. Price, per gross..........75c
No. 4C2095 Fine Eye Shells for Hat Pins. Price, per dozen..........30c
No. 4C2096 Shells Assortment. In box as in No. 4C2004..........15c
No. 4C2097 Money Cowrie Shells for Cuff Buttons. Per 100..........42c
No. 4C2098 Coffee Shells. Price. per 100..........30c
No. 4C2101 Rice Shells. Price, per 100..........22c
No. 4C2102 Panama Shells. Price, per 100..........$1.00
No. 4C2104 Cat's Eyes. One hole. Price, per dozen..........28c
No. 4C2106 Cat's Eyes. Two hole. Price, per dozen..........28c
No. 4C2107 Spar Balls. 10 millimeters. Price, per gross..........20c
No. 4C2109 Faceted Beads. Assorted colors. Per gross..........35c
No. 4C2112 Round Bracelet Beads. Blue and pink. Per 1,000..........50c
No. 4C2114 Rolled Plated Heart Bangles. Price, per gross..........$1.15
No. 4C2115 Large Brown Sea Beans. Price, per dozen..........20c
No. 4C2117 Large Red Sea Beans. Price, per dozen..........5c

OUR SPECIAL DRIVE IN TOOLS. WATCHMAKERS' JEWELERS' AND SILVERSMITHS' OUTFITS FOR... $3.65

No. 4C2120 **Our Special Drive in Tools. A Watchmakers', Jewelers' and Silversmiths' Outfit for $3.65,** consisting of twenty-four distinct tools, each one being used to perform certain important duties. This set can be used not only by beginners, but by anyone wishing to repair watches, clocks or silverware. A splendid set to practice with. You can always add from time to time necessary tools from our long and varied list of watchmakers' tools printed on the next page. This set consists of twenty-four separate and distinct tools and appliances, as follows: 1 jewelers' flat file with handle, 1 watchmakers' hammer with handle, 1 watchmakers' rubber magnifying eyeglass, 1 pair jewelers' cutting pliers, 1 pair calipers, 1 watchmakers' riveting stake, 1 small bench vise, 1 pair soldering tweezers, 1 pair watchmakers' tweezers, 1 pair jewelers' flat pliers, 1 watchmakers' or jewelers' pin vise, 3 watchmakers' screwdrivers (each being a different size, 1 jewelers' soldering copper, 1 watchmakers' or clockmakers' brush, 4 needle files, very important for watchmakers and jewelers), 1 bundle peg wood, 3 pivot broaches; to this complete set of twenty-four distinct and separate tools is likewise added, 1 cube of refined jewelers' chalk, one bottle of watchmakers' oil, 1 bundle of watchmakers' pith wood, 1 bundle of brass wire, 1 text book. This book gives receipts, new methods, and much valuable information regarding watch repairing, stone setting and other valuable pointers.

No. 4C2120 Price, complete, with all above mentioned additions, and boxed in a neat wooden box..........(Weight, complete, about 5 pounds.)..........**$3.65**

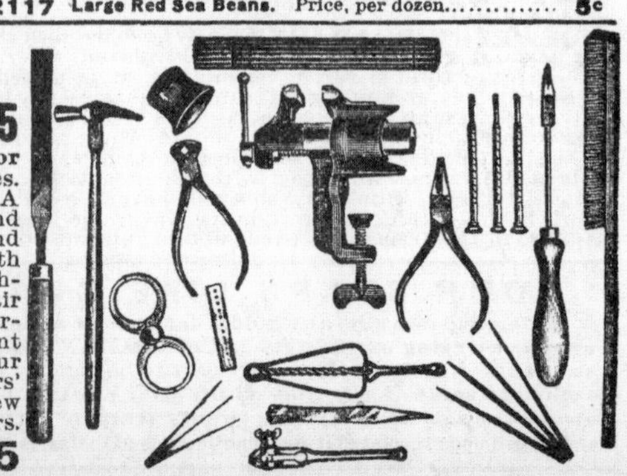

WATCHMAKERS' TOOLS ....AND MATERIALS

For want of space we can illustrate only the most useful and desirable, and we have been compelled to reduce the illustrations in order to illustrate what we do. The goods, however, are all of standard make and size, **and of the best quality. We will be glad to quote prices on watchmakers' lathes, chucks, etc.** If there is anything you want that you do not find illustrated, send us your order, enclosing market price for same, and give an accurate description. If you do not know what the cost is, be sure to enclose enough, and we will return what is left. We will be glad, however, to quote prices, if you desire, before ordering. **When ordering material for repairs, always send a sample if possible.** If not, fully describe the size and make of watch or clock for which parts are intended.

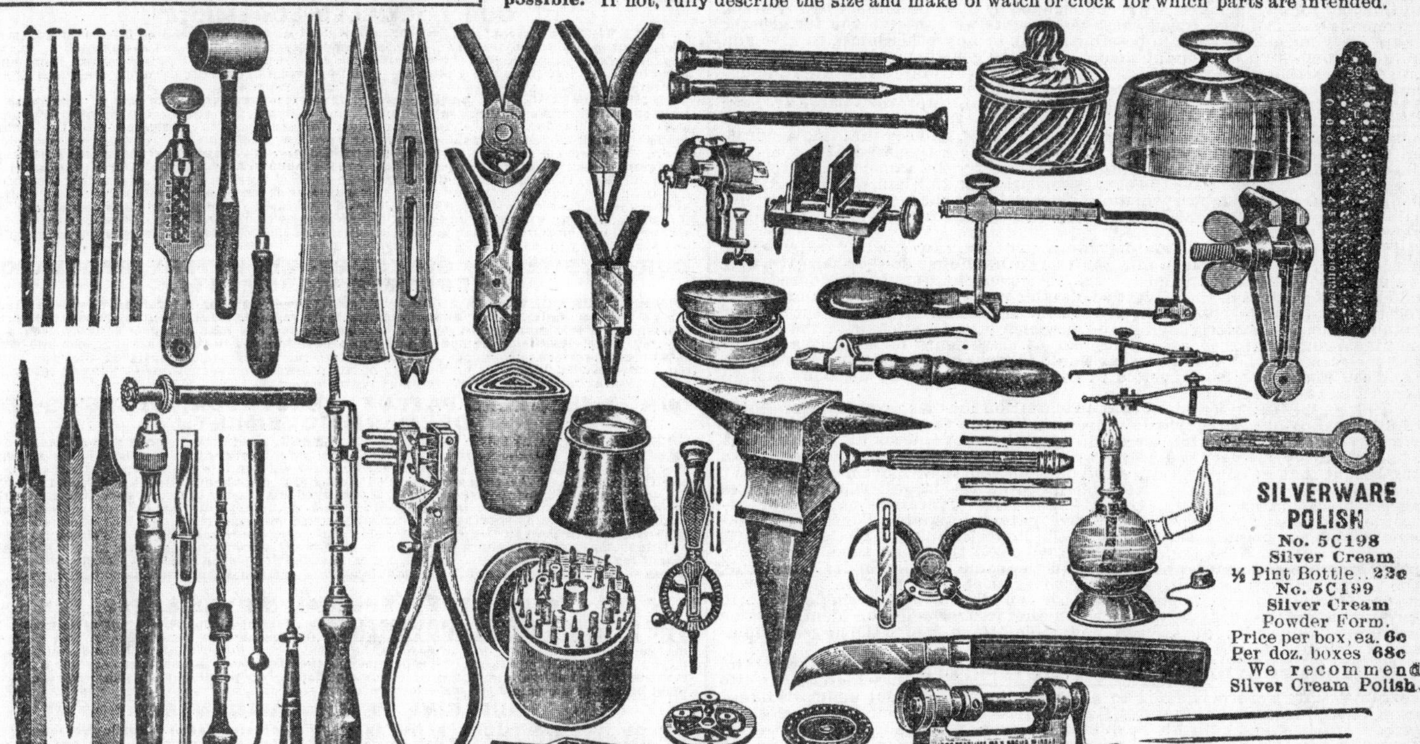

SILVERWARE POLISH

No. 5C198 Silver Cream ½ Pint Bottle.. 23c
No. 5C199 Silver Cream Powder Form. Price per box, ea. 6c
Per doz. boxes 68c
We recommend Silver Cream Polish.

No.		
4C2200	Alcohol Cups....................each	$0.35
4C2202	Anvil (jewelers')....................each	.75
4C2203	Blow Pipes, common brass..........each	.10
4C2206	Blow Pipes, with balls..........each	.30
4C2208	Blow Pipes, nickel plated, with ball, each	.50
4C2212	Buffs, Leather Flat..........each	.05
4C2214	Buffs, Felt Flat..........each	.10
4C2216	Brushes, watch or clock..........each	.30
4C2217	Brushes, wheel for polishing lathe, 3 row, 2¼-inch..........each	.25
4C2219	Burnisher, for polishing pivots....each	.20
4C2222	Broach Handle, adjustable..........each	.25
4C2224	Broaches, Pivot, Swiss make, no less than 1 dozen sold..........per dozen	.15
4C2226	Caliper, pinion, plain..........each	.25
4C2228	Caliper, regular..........each	.30
4C2230	Caliper, nickel plated, with bar and screw..........each	.35
4C2232	Clock Screwdriver..........each	.28
4C2234	Clock wire bender..........each	.20
4C2236	Countersinks, per set of three..........	.45
4C2238	Countersinks, adjustable handle, per set	.60
4C2240	Crucibles, per set of four..........	.10
4C2242	Cups, Oil, for watch or clock......each	.20
4C2244	Drills, common, no less than 1 dozen sold..........per dozen	.36
4C2246	Drills, Stock, common..........each	.35
4C2248	Drill Bow, to use with above stock each	.20
4C2250	Drill Stock, patent spiral, small size..........each	.25
4C2252	Drill Stock, patent guard..........each	.85
4C2256	Eyeglass, Watchmakers', common each	.19
4C2258	Eyeglass, Watchmakers', with coil spring..........each	.35
4C2260	Files, round or square, small..each	.18
4C2262	File, knife..........each	.35
4C2264	Files, needle, three-cornered..........each	.15
4C2266	Files, needle, knife..........each	.15
4C2268	Files, needle, oblong..........each	.15
4C2270	Files, needle, one-half round ....each	.15
2272	Files, needle, square..........each	.15
2274	Files, needle round..........each	.15
2278	Files, flat, regular..........each	.35
2280	Files, screw head..........each	.25
2281	Files, pivot, right or left..........each	.20
2283	Gauge, for measuring mainspring, each	.45
2285	Gravers, square, any size..........each	.15
2286	Hammer Handles, ebony..........each	.10
2288	Hammer Handles, maple..........each	.05
2290	Hammers, Stubb's, according to size. ....40c to	.75
2292	Hammers, Swiss..........each, 15c to	.40
2294	Hands, Watch, per dozen pair..........	.50
2296	Hands, Second, per dozen..........	.30
2298	Hands, Clock, per dozen..........	.30
2300	Handles, adjustable, for graver or small files..........each	.15
2302	Handles, adjustable, for medium files..........each	.25
4	Jeweling Tool, bezel opener and closer..........each	1.75
	Jewelers' Cement, per bottle......each	.25
	ewel Pin Setter..........each	.88
	weling Tool, Crosby's patent, complete..........each	1.25

No.		
4C2312	Keys, Watch, no less than 1 dozen sold per dozen..........	$0.25
4C2314	Keys, Watch, wind any watch.....each	.10
4C2316	Keys, Watch, for bench use..........each	.25
4C2318	Keys, iron or brass, for clocks....each	.05
4C2320	Lamps, Alcohol, patented, large ..each	1.00
4C2322	Lamps, Alcohol, faceted glass, medium..........each	.60
4C2324	Mainsprings, Watch, each, 8c; per doz.	.96
4C2326	Mainsprings, Clock, 1-day..........each	.15
4C2328	Mainsprings, Clock, 8-day..........each	.45
4C2330	Mainspring Punch, improved......each	1.25
4C2332	Mainspring Winder..........	1.50
4C2334	Mainspring Winder, Swiss make ..each	.35
4C2336	Mallet, Jewelers'..........each	.20
4C2338	Movement Holder..........each	.75
4C2340	Oil, Watch or Clock..........per bottle	.20
4C2342	Oiler, Watch..........each	.15
4C2346	Pin Slide, common medium........each	.35
4C2349	Pin Vise, nickel plated, adjustable..........each	.25
4C2350	Punch, Mainspring, English........each	.45
4C2352	Punch, Mainspring (3 punches)..per set	1.00
4C2354	Punches, set of 24, with hollow stake, in hardwood box........complete set	1.25
4C2355	Pliers, case spring..........each	.30
4C2356	Pliers, round..........each	.35
4C2357	Pliers, for holding watch hands, 2 hole..........each	.35
4C2358	Pliers, flat..........each	.35
4C2362	Pliers, cutting, regular Swiss.....each	.60
4C2363	Peg and Pith Wood, per bundle, 5c; ....per dozen	.50

No.		
4C2366	Roller Remover..........each	$0.75
4C2368	Ruby Pin Setter..........each	.25
4C2370	Screw Holder and Driver combined, each	.50
4C2372	Screw Holder..........each	.15
4C2374	Screw Plate, 36 holes..........	.75
4C2376	Screwdriver, Watch, large..........each	.15
4C2378	Screwdriver, Watch, medium......each	.15
4C2380	Screwdriver, Watch, small..........each	.15
4C2382	Screwdriver, Watch, adjustable, 4 sizes..........each	.25
4C2388	Stake, Riveting, hard steel.......each	.25
4C2389	Stake, for straightening watch cases..........each	.25
4C2390	Saw Frame, Swiss, extra quality, nickel plated, ea.,	.85
4C2392	Saws for above, no less than 1 dozen sold. ....Per dozen	.10
4C2394	Soldering copper..........each	.20
4C2396	Soldering fluid, per bottle..........	.15
4C2398	Solder, silver, no less than ½ ounce sold. ....per ounce,	.80
4C2400	Solder, gold 14k, no less than 1 dwt. sold, per dwt.,	.75
4C2402	Screw Stock and Dies..........per set	2.00
4C2404	Tweezers, fine..........each	.35
4C2406	Tweezers, hand removing..........each	.25
4C2407	Tweezers, hairspring collet removing ......each	.30
4C2408	Tweezers, medium..........each	.35
4C2409	Tweezer, for adjusting clock pinions..........each	.40
4C2410	Tweezers and Hand Raiser combined..........each	.45
4C2411	Hairspring stud remover..........each	.30
4C2412	Vise, Bench..........each	.70
4C2414	Vise, Hand..........each	.75
4C2416	Watch Cover Glass..........each	.35
4C2418	Watch Glasses, hunting style, fitted..........each	.10
4C2420	Watch Glasses, assorted hunting..........per gross	2.75
4C2422	Watch Glasses, thick, open face, fitted..........each	.20
4C2424	Watch Glasses, thick, open face..........per dozen	.50
4C2426	Watch Keys, Birch's..........each	.20

A Big Cut in Watchmakers' Tool Sets. Our Complete Watchmakers' Tool Set, Price $7.50.

THE TOOLS AND IMPLEMENTS **we herewith illustrate are the most necessary in the equipment of a watchmaker's kit.** Every one of them performs important work, making it absolutely necessary to have at least as great a selection as we illustrate in our complete set. The material of our tools is made of the very finest procurable; the most expert toolmakers, skilled in their art, the only ones employed in the production of this merchandise.

EACH TOOL **goes through a rigid inspection before leaving our establishment,** so that we are assured of them being received by our customers in perfect condition. Our mechanics here who do our watch work use our own manufacture of tools and the work done by us is excelled by none. **This set for $7.50 consists of 36 separate and distinct pieces.** Any man of average mechanical skill can learn to rectify the majority of causes that make a watch stop. The set not alone includes tools necessary for watch repairing, but likewise includes a complete set of tools for silverware, jewelry and clock repairing. **We know that you would not fail to be pleased with your purchase if you conclude to favor us with an order for one of these wonderful watchmakers' and jewelers' sets.**

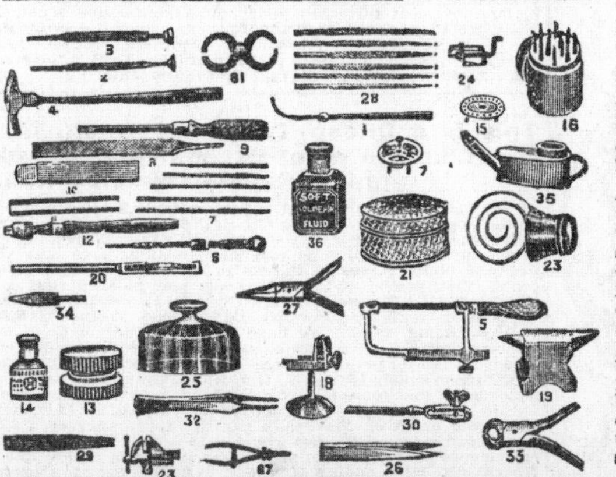

No. 4C2201 Complete Tool Set, $7.50.

No. 4C2201 Price for complete set, including text book...... **$7.50**

DESCRIPTION OF OUR OWN WATCH MOVEMENTS.

OUR OWN MOVEMENTS as listed through our Watch Department, complete with the various cases, movements that are made especially for us under contract and as illustrated and described on this and following pages, are recommended by us in preference to any other movement you can buy, for in these movements we can give you far greater value for your money than is possible for us or any other house to give you in any other watch movement made. Why you get almost double the watch movement value when you select one of our movements, illustrated and described on this page, as compared with any other movement made.

ALL WATCH MOVEMENTS bearing the manufacturer's name are sold by the manufacturer to the wholesaler at a fixed list price, subject to certain fixed discounts, and for these movements, no matter whether the wholesaler buys a dozen or a thousand at a time, the fixed list price and the fixed list discount is exactly the same, and as a result the very largest buyer pays the exact same price for an Elgin, Waltham, Hampden, Illinois or other factory made movement that the very smallest wholesale buyer pays. Everyone pays a price that means for the manufacturer a very handsome profit.

DETERMINED that we should give our customers far greater watch value for their money than any other house does or can give, that we should sell direct to our customer one movement, quality considered, at a much lower price than the largest wholesaler can buy from the regular manufacturer even in thousand lots, we took the matter up with one of the largest manufacturers of strictly high grade movements in America, with the idea of making a contract for so large a number of movements, for so large a part of the entire capacity of his factory as would induce this manufacturer to depart from the long established custom of one list price and one discount, and we succeeded to this extent:

THIS MANUFACTURER agreed that on condition that we would take one-half of all the movements they would produce in their factory they would agree with us on a plan by which we could own the movements at a cost to us approximately the very same as if we owned the factory ourselves, but as this meant that we could produce and offer for sale their movements at about one-half the price which they were getting from the largest wholesalers, the agreement made restricted us from using the manufacturer's name. For example, take the gents' 18-size, 17-jeweled, patent regulator Edgemere movement which the manufacturer sells to the largest wholesale dealers at $14.00, less 50 per cent (or $7.00), under his name. We sell the exact same movement, piece for piece and part for part, made in the same factory under our name, the Edgemere, complete with a 3-ounce silverine case for $6.55; in other words, we sell this movement complete with case and all, selling one single watch to any customer for 45 cents less than the manufacturer sells the identical same movement alone without the case, under his own name, to the largest wholesale watch dealers.

THE MANUFACTURER OF OUR MOVEMENTS takes this position, in which he is quite correct: If we were permitted to put these movements out under his name, mentioning his (the manufacturer's) grade, and sell them, including cases, at the price we do, it would ruin his business with every wholesale and retail watch dealer in America, since we sell the complete watch, movement, case and all, for less than the wholesale dealers buy the movement alone from the manufacturer, or the complete watch for about one-half the price the little retail dealer must pay the wholesale dealer for the movement alone.

THESE, OUR SPECIAL EDGEMERE AND SEARS, ROEBUCK & CO.'S MOVEMENTS as illustrated and described on this and following pages, and as priced complete with the different cases on the following pages, are made by one of the largest, most reliable and best known watch movement manufacturers in America, a watch company whose name is almost a household word, a movement maker whose name appears on the dial and plate of hundreds of thousands of watches that are now in the pockets of users all over the world, and our contracts permit us to sell you the identical same movements, the same high grade work everything exactly alike, piece for piece and part for part, under our own name, at about one-half the lowest price at which you can buy the identical same movement from almost any retail jeweler in the country; for this company's movement's will be found in almost every jewelry store in the land.

OUR 7-JEWELED EDGEMERE.

NOTE THE ILLUSTRATION AND DESCRIPTION of our gents' 18-size 7-jeweled Edgemere movement as shown on this page, and note, especially, the very low prices at which we furnish this movement complete, with the various cases, as shown on the following pages. Remember, in spite of the low price, we guarantee this 7-jeweled Edgemere movement the equal of any 7-jeweled movement made, regardless of name, make or price.

DON'T COMPARE THIS, our 7-jeweled Edgemere movement, with any of the cheap 7-jeweled movements on the market. We have discontinued the sale of the Trenton, Standard and Century 7-jeweled movements, since our contract enables us to offer you one of the highest grade 7-jeweled movements made at a lower price than other houses can sell even the cheap grade of 7-jeweled movements. **Our 7-jeweled Edgemere is put out under our binding five year guarantee as the equal of any 7-jeweled movement made in America,** and in running and lasting qualities worth more than double any of the cheap 7-jeweled movements, and if you order one and do not find it so, you may return it to us at our expense and we will immediately refund your money. Therefore, if you want a 7-jeweled movement you will get double the value in our Edgemere that you will get in any one of the cheap 7-jeweled movements, and we guarantee you will get all and more value than you will get in any of the 7-jeweled movements you can buy of any make at any price.

OUR 12-JEWELED, GENTS' 18-SIZE, PATENT REGULATOR EDGEMERE MOVEMENT.

WHILE OUR CONTRACTS FOR MOVEMENTS permit of our furnishing this high grade, full 12-jeweled, fancy nickel damaskeened, patent regulator, cut balance, Breguet hairspring movement for less money than we could sell you under the manufacturer's name even a 7-jeweled Elgin, Waltham, Hampden or Illinois movement, if you order a watch with one of our 12-jeweled Edgemere movements, and if after receiving it you are not satisfied that the movement intrinsically is worth double that of any 7-jeweled movement made, you can return the watch to us at our expense, we to refund your money.

OUR 17-JEWELED, PATENT REGULATOR, GENTS' 18-SIZE EDGEMERE MOVEMENT.

WHILE THIS MOVEMENT HAS FULL 17 JEWELS, solid nickel, fancy gold damaskeened patent regulator, Breguet hairspring, cut balance, patent pendant, all jewels in screw settings, everything the highest grade, yet under our contract we own this movement at a price, and we can furnish you even this, our 17-jeweled Edgemere movement, fitted complete in any case shown on the following pages at from $3.00 to $5.00 less money than it would be possible to furnish you the exact same movement under the manufacturer's name, or any other movement of equal grade; in short, we can furnish you this movement for only 25 cents more than it is possible to furnish you the plain 15-jeweled non patent regulator Elgin, Waltham, Hampden or Illinois movement; in short, for a strictly high grade watch, by selecting this, our 17-jeweled patent regulator Edgemere movement, we can almost double the value we can give you in a watch with a movement bearing the manufacturer's name and therefore also bearing the manufacturer's long profit.

OUR OTHER SPECIAL MOVEMENTS.

THE OTHER SPECIAL MOVEMENTS we furnish in the different sizes and grades illustrated and described on this page are movements that we own on the basis of the actual cost of material and labor, to which we add but our one small percentage of profit, and can therefore furnish you almost double the movement value in any one of these movements that we can possibly furnish you in any movement bearing the name of the manufacturer.

OUR FIVE YEARS' GUARANTEE.

EVERY ONE OF THESE MOVEMENTS is covered by our binding five years' guarantee, covering every piece and part that enters into the movement, and if any part should fail to perform its duty within five years through defective material or workmanship, it will be replaced or repaired by us free of any charge.

WE WOULD ESPECIALLY RECOMMEND in selecting a watch from the following pages, to get the greatest possible value for your money, to avoid paying unnecessary profit to any manufacturer for name only, that you select one of our special movements fitted in any case you may choose. **Remember, the movement goes to you under our binding five years' guarantee** and with the understanding and agreement that if it isn't perfectly satisfactory to you, if you are not convinced you have made a big saving by buying one of our special movements rather than buying an Elgin, Waltham, Hampden or any other make of movement, you can return the watch to us at our expense and we will immediately refund your money.

Gents' 18-size, Open Face or Hunting Case, 7-Jeweled Edgemere Movement.

Gents' 18-size Edgemere, open face or hunting case, full nickel, 7-jeweled, neatly damaskeened, expansion balance, hairspring hardened and tempered, highly finished regulator, patent pinion, polished screws, marginal figures on dial, true timing screws, quick train, worth double any of the cheap 7-jeweled movements and guaranteed the equal of any 7-jeweled movement made.

NOTE—We sell this high grade 7-jeweled movement complete in any case for less than others sell the cheap grades of 7-jeweled movements.

Gents' 18-Size, Stem Wind, Open Face or Hunting Case, 12-Jeweled Edgemere Movement.

This movement is solid nickel, fancy gold damaskeened and ornamented, patent regulator, upper plate full jeweled, all jewels are set in screw settings, cut expansion balance, true timing screws, Breguet hairspring. You will note from the prices as shown on the following pages that we can furnish you a case fitted with this 12-jeweled patent regulator Edgemere movement complete for less than we can furnish the same case with a 7-jeweled movement bearing the manufacturer's name. If you order a watch with this 12-jeweled patent regulator Edgemere movement and do not consider the movement double the value of any 7-jeweled movement made, you can return it to us at our expense and we will immediately refund your money.

Gents' 18-Size, Open Face or Hunting Case, 17-Jeweled Edgemere Movement.

This movement is regular 18-size; it is solid nickeled, beautifully gold and nickel damaskeened and finished; it has 17 jewels, all set in screw settings, patent regulator, Breguet overstrung hairspring, cut expansion balance, true timing screws, quick train, safety pinion, compensating balance, exposed winding wheel, fine sunk enamel dial.

You will note from the prices on the following pages that we furnish this 17-jeweled patent regulator movement at a few cents more than the plain 15-jeweled movement without patent regulator furnished under manufacturers' names, and at from $3.00 to $5.00 less than the identical same grade 17-jeweled patent regulator movement furnished under the manufacturer's name. Therefore, to get double the value for your money in a gent's 18-size watch, we especially recommend, in preference to all other movements, that you select a case and order us to fit in the case one of these 17-jeweled patent regulator movements.

This gents' 18-size, open face or hunting case, full 15-jeweled movement bears the name "Sears, Roebuck & Co.'s Special, Chicago, Ill." It is gotten out for us by the manufacturer with a view of making it in every way a higher grade 15-jeweled movement than is made by any other manufacturer an improvement over any other 15-jeweled movement on the market; full plate, solid nickel, richly damaskeened, full 15-jeweled, jewels have screw settings, micrometer patent regulator, cut expansion balance, overstrung Breguet hairspring, patent pinion and escapement. In quality of material and fine mechanical lines, in workmanship, finish, in lasting qualities, in accurate time keeping, nothing is spared to make this positively the highest grade 15-jeweled movement on the market, and while, as shown in the following pages, we furnish it for less than we sell 15-jeweled movements bearing the manufacturer's name, if you buy this movement and after giving it a reasonable test as to time, if you do not consider it better than any other 15-jeweled movement on the market, you can return it to us at our expense and we will immediately refund your money.

NOTE, that different from any of the 15-jeweled movement of other makes, this, our 15-jeweled movement, is accurately adjusted to all positions, and you get in this the only accurately adjusted 15-jeweled movement made.

This is a Cheap Traveling Watch, Made to Look Like the Most Expensive 21-Jeweled Adjusted Railway Watch Made.

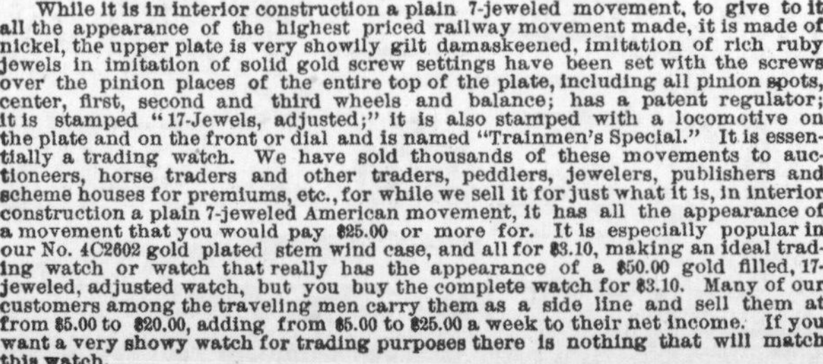

While it is in interior construction a plain 7-jeweled movement, to give to it all the appearance of the highest priced railway movement made, it is made of nickel, the upper plate is very showily gilt damaskeened, imitation of rich ruby jewels in imitation of solid gold screw settings have been set with the screws over the pinion places of the entire top of the plate, including all pinion spots, center, first, second and third wheels and balance; has a patent regulator; it is stamped "17-Jewels, adjusted;" it is also stamped with a locomotive on the plate and on the front or dial and is named "Trainmen's Special." It is essentially a trading watch. We have sold thousands of these movements to auctioneers, horse traders and other traders, peddlers, jewelers, publishers and scheme houses for premiums, etc., for while we sell it for just what it is, in interior construction a plain 7-jeweled American movement, it has all the appearance of a movement that you would pay $25.00 or more for. It is especially popular in our No. 4C2602 gold plated stem wind case, and all for $3.10, making an ideal trading watch or watch that really has the appearance of a $50.00 gold filled, 17-jeweled, adjusted watch, but you buy the complete watch for $3.10. Many of our customers among the traveling men carry them as a side line and sell them at from $8.00 to $20.00, adding from $5.00 to $25.00 a week to their net income. If you want a very showy watch for trading purposes there is nothing that will match this watch.

Gents' 18 Size, Open Face or Hunting Case, Stem Wind, 17-Jeweled, Adjusted S., R. & Co. Special Movement.

This movement is marked "Sears, Roebuck & Co. Special," is solid nickel, richly damaskeened and finished, has 17 ruby jewels, raised gold settings with screws, accurately and especially adjusted to heat, cold, isochronism and all positions, the most accurate and complete adjustment lines on any watch made; quick train, hand finished escape wheel, compensating balance, Breguet overstrung tempered hairspring, new improved patent micrometer regulator barrel arbor pivots, double sunk glass enamel dial, with marginal figures. This 17-jeweled, full adjusted, full plate movement is gotten out for us with a view to furnishing a higher grade adjusted movement than is made and sold by any watch company in America. While we furnish it at a much lower price than you can buy a 17-jeweled adjusted movement bearing the manufacturer's name, if you order this movement and do not find, after giving it a thorough trial, that it gives better satisfaction than any other 17-jeweled movement made, you can return it to us at our expense and we will immediately refund your money.

NOTE the difference between this 17-jeweled Sears, Roebuck & Co. Special and our 17-jeweled Edgemere. It is the very fine adjustment of this movement, the adjustment to all positions, temperature and isochronism, which accounts for the difference in cost to manufacture.

Gents' 16-Size, Open Face or Hunting Case, 12-Jeweled, Nickel, Patent Regulator Edgemere Movement.

This movement is made for us under contract, and at our price, fitted with any 16-size case as shown on the following pages, we can give you double the value in this movement that you can get in any 16-size movement bearing the manufacturer's name. It is a handsome movement, full 12-jeweled, has micrometer patent regulator, richly damaskeened and ornamented in gold. For accurate time keeping qualities and long service there is no movement made within several dollars of the price we name that will compare with this movement.

Gents' 16-Size, Open Face or Hunting Case, Stem Wind Movement.

This is positively the highest grade 15-jeweled 16 size movement made, each movement stamped "Sears, Roebuck & Co.'s Special." It is full 15-jeweled, all jewels in screwed settings and it is accurately adjusted to positions; has cut expansion balance, overstrung Breguet hairspring, gotten out with a view of giving our customers in every respect a better 15-jeweled 16-size movement than is made or sold by any watch company in the country. This movement has the latest exposed winding wheel, every up to date feature found in any other 16-size movement, and still we furnish it at as low a price as any other 16-size movement made.

Gents' 16-Size Open Face or Hunting Case, 17-Jeweled Adjusted Movement.

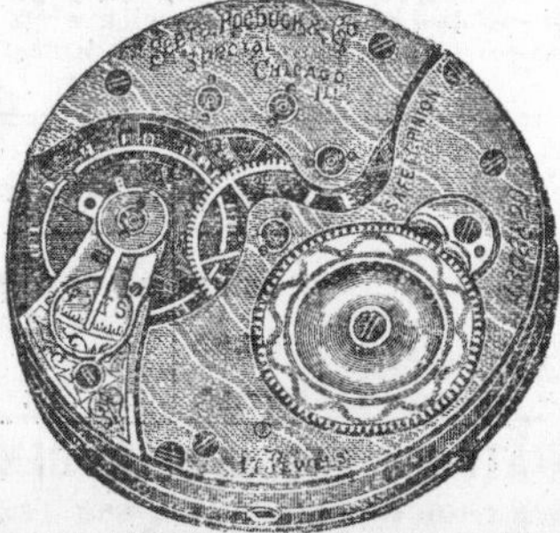

This is our gents' 17-jeweled adjusted 16-size movement, each movement stamped "Sears, Roebuck & Co.'s Special." It is 17-jeweled, all jewels in screwed settings, accurately adjusted to heat, cold, position and isochronism; has the latest patent micrometer regulator, patent pinion and escapement, exposed winding wheel, has every new and up to date improvement, combines all the best in all the highest grade 17-jeweled 16-size movements made, and yet we offer it at a lower price than we can offer any other 17-jeweled movement.

Gents' 12-Size, Open Face or Hunting Case, Solid Nickel, 10-Jeweled, Stem Wind and Stem Set Movement.

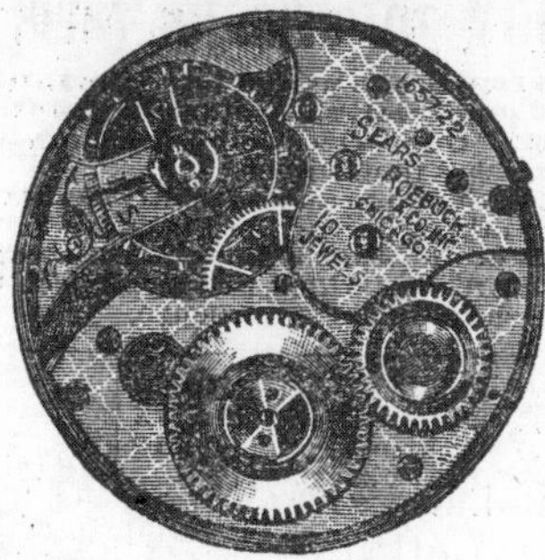

These movements are stamped "Edgemere, Sears, Roebuck & Co." They are 10-jeweled, exposed winding wheel, cut expansion balance, Breguet hairspring, true timing screws. This is a movement made especially for us. It is extra high grade, and under our contract we can furnish it for less money than we can furnish 7-jeweled 12-size movements of other makes, and in buying a 12-size gents' watch, we especially recommend that you select this movement.

Ladies' 6-Size, Hunting Case, Stem Wind and Stem Set, 7-Jeweled Edgemere Movement.

Like the gents' 18-size movement, we guarantee this 7-jeweled movement the equal of any 7-jeweled 6-size movement made, and worth two of any of the cheap 7-jeweled movements on the market. It is the highest grade 7-jeweled movement made, and in selecting a ladies' watch, we would especially recommend that you select our 7-jeweled Edgemere; has gold damaskeening, cut expansion balance, sunk second enamel dial, a great improvement over any other 7-jeweled 6-size movement on the market.

Ladies' 6-Size, Hunting Case, Stem Wind and Stem Set, Solid Nickel, 12-Jeweled Edgemere Movement.

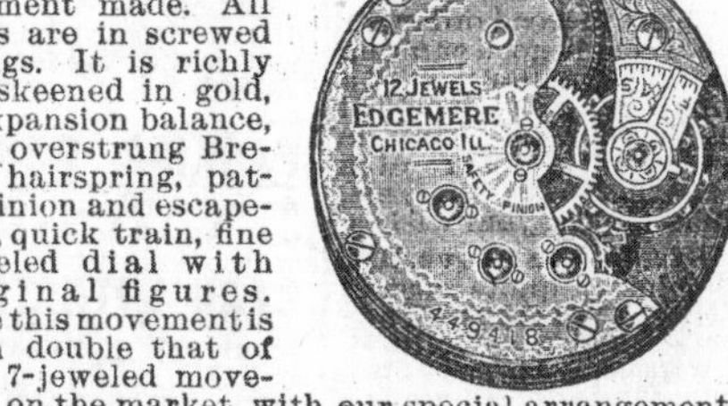

This is the highest grade 12-jeweled 6-size movement made. All jewels are in screwed settings. It is richly damaskeened in gold, cut expansion balance, finest overstrung Breguet hairspring, patent pinion and escapement, quick train, fine enameled dial with marginal figures. While this movement is worth double that of any 7-jeweled movement on the market, with our special arrangements we furnish this movement as shown on the following pages at even less than the regular grade 7-jeweled movements.

Ladies' 6-Size, Stem Wind and Stem Set, Hunting Style, 17-Jeweled Edgemere Movement.

This movement is full 17-jeweled, all jewels in screwed settings, solid nickel, richly damaskeened and ornamented in gold, has cut expansion balance, true timing screws, finest overstrung Breguet hairspring, and yet, under our special arrangements, we can furnish this movement at about one-half the price charged by manufacturers for identically the same movement under their name. **Rather than buy a 7 or 15-jeweled movement of any other make we especially recommend that in selecting a ladies' 6-size watch you choose this, our 17-jeweled Edgemere.**

Ladies' 6-Size, Hunting Case, Stem Wind and Stem Set, Solid Nickel, Ruby Jeweled S., R. & Co.'s Special.

These movements are the Sears, Roebuck & Co. Special, and they are gotten out with a view of giving our customers a higher grade 15-jeweled 6-size movement than is made by any watch company in America. This movement is accurately adjusted to position, the 15 jewels are the highest grade rubies, perfect settings, set with screws, has the latest compensating cut balance, true timing screws, has the finest overstrung Breguet hairspring, is richly damaskeened in gold, has sunk second dial, patent pinion and escapement, quick train, guaranteed the highest grade 6-size 15-jeweled movement on the market.

Ladies' 6-Size, Hunting Case, Stem Wind, 17-Jeweled, Adjusted Movement.

These movements are marked "Sears, Roebuck & Co.'s Special." They are positively the highest grade 17-jeweled 6-size movements made. Solid nickel, richly damaskeened in gold, full 17 jewels, finest ruby jewels in gold settings, settings set with screws, compensating cut balance, balance adjusted with true timing screws, finest overstrung patent Breguet hairspring, polished center wheel, quick train, patent pinion. Movement is accurately adjusted to heat, cold, position and isochronism, combining everything that you could get in any movement that you would pay three times the price for if sold by any manufacturer under the manufacturer's name and number, so in selecting the very finest thing in a ladies' 6-size watch, we would especially recommend that you select this movement, and we will furnish it to you, quality for quality, at one-half the price you could buy any other make.

Ladies' 0-Size, 7-Jeweled, Swiss Stem Wind and Stem Set Movement.

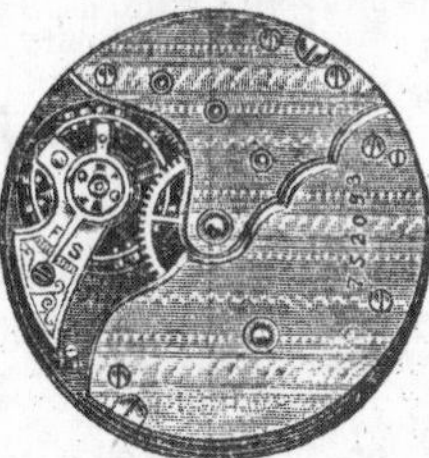

This movement is made for us under contract. It is full nickel, quick train, 7 jewels patent pinion and patent lever escapement, and we guarantee it the highest grade 7-jewel, small 0-size movement made. You will find this movement will keep better time and last twice as long as any other 7-jeweled 0-size movement on the market, and yet, under our special arrangements with the manufacturer, we can furnish this in a much higher grade 7-jeweled movement than you could get elsewhere at less than the ordinary 7-jeweled movements are sold by others. In selecting a very small watch for a lady in an 0-size, unless you want to get our high grade Edgemere 0-size movement, we would especially advise that you select this in preference to any other 7-jeweled 0-size movement made.

Ladies' 0-Size 15-Jeweled Patent Regulator Edgemere Movement.

This small 0-size ladies' movement is solid nickel, richly finished, full 15-jeweled, jewels in beautiful settings, full screwed. It is very elaborately finished, has the latest patent micrometer regulator, cut expansion balance, finest patent straight line lever escapement, quick train, patent pinion; in short, it is the highest grade 15-jeweled 0-size movement made and will outwear two of the ordinary 0-size 15-jeweled movements, and yet, under our special arrangements with the manufacturer, owning this movement as we do on the basis of the actual cost of material and labor, we can, after adding our one small percentage of profit, furnish it to you at a much lower price than we can furnish a 15-jeweled movement of other make bearing the manufacturer's name and grade.

If you want a small watch for a lady, select this, our highest grade 15-jeweled Edgemere movement, fit it in any 0-size case, and if, after giving it a fair trial, you are not convinced that it is the highest grade 15-jeweled 0-size movement made, you can return the watch to us at our expense and we will immediately refund your money.

ON THE DIFFERENT PAGES in this catalogue in which the various watches are illustrated and described, together with the different cases we furnish in the various sizes, you will find listed various makes of movements and various styles of cases. You will find the Elgin, Waltham and Hampden. You will also find listed and priced our various grades of special Edgemere and Sears, Roebuck & Co.'s Special Movements. You will observe, if you will follow these prices, that grade for grade, jeweling for jeweling, our Edgemere and Sears, Roebuck & Company movements are quoted at prices much lower than the Elgin, Waltham, Hampden and others. The reason for this marked difference in price is accounted for by the difference in cost to us.

THESE SPECIAL MOVEMENTS as illustrated and described on this page, as before explained, we own under contract at the actual cost of material and labor, with but our one small percentage of profit added. As a result they cost you very much less than any other movement we can offer, and if you will send us your order for any watch fitted with any one of our special movements it will go to you under our binding five years' guarantee, and with the understanding and agreement that if you do not find it, grade for grade, jeweling for jeweling, as good, if not better than any movement made by any maker in America, regardless of name, make or price, you can return the watch (movement and case) to us at our expense and we will refund your money.

WE WANT JEWELERS, GENERAL MERCHANTS WHO HANDLE WATCHES, AND EVERYBODY TO SEND US THEIR WATCH REPAIRS

IT WILL PAY THE JEWELER better to send his repairs to us and have the work properly done, with new material of the right kind, than to pa up the job with old material, soft solder or material which does not fit, as is the custom where there is not a large stock well selected material and a good outfit of tools at hand. **Our prices being from one-half to one-fourth the regular prices,** there is a large profit left for th dealer or an equal saving to those who send their watches to us direct.

REMEMBER, that a watch should not run longer than one and one-half years without having the oil cleaned off and fresh oil applied. An engine or sewing machine will be oiled several times per day, but we have known people to carry a watch for ten years without having it cleaned or fresh oil applied. Usually, a movement thus treated **is of no value, being entirely worn out.** Our charge for cleaning and oiling is **50 cents.** The regular retail price is **$1.50.** We give below a list of charges for repairs which will be subject to change in some cases. For example: Old fusee watches, made some fifty or sixty years ago in England, the material of which is difficult to procure.

Balances, American Expansion	$1.50 to $2.75
Balances, Am. Steel or Nickel	.50
Balances, English, Steel or Composition	1.00
Balances, Swiss, Composition	.75
Balances, Swiss, with screw	1.25
Balances, Swiss, Expansion, cut	3.00
Cleaning, ordinary Swiss, Duplex or American	.50
Cleaning, ordinary English	1.00
Demagnetizing Watch Movements, ordinary	1.50
Demagnetizing Watch Movements, finer grades	$2.00 to 4.00
Dials, Swiss, without seconds	1.00
Dials, Swiss, with seconds	1.50
Dust Bands, American	.25
Hairsprings, ordinary flat	.75
Hairsprings, Breguet	1.50
Hands, common	each .10
Hands, fine	each .20
Jewels, American, Cock or Foot (with settings)	.50
Jewels, American, 3d, 4th or 'Scape	50c to .75
Jewels, Endstone, in setting	.50
Jewels, Cap, Swiss (with plate)	.25
Jewels, Swiss, 3d, 4th, 'Scape or Balance, set in plate	.50
Jewels, Swiss, 3d, 4th, 'Scape or Balance, Fine Ruby	1.50
Jewels, Swiss, Center, Fine Ruby in Gold Set	3.00
Jewels, Roller	.35
Jewels, Pallet, Set in old Settings, American	.75
Mainsprings, Swiss	$0.50
Mainsprings, English, with hook	.75
Mainsprings, American	.50
Mainsprings, Repeaters, etc.	$1.00 to 1.50
Pallets, Fork and Arbor, complete, ordinary	3.00
Pallets, Fork and Arbor, complete, American	$1.25 to 2.50
Pinions, American, 3d, 4th or 'Scape	.75
Pinions, American, Center	1.00
Pinions, American, Center, Patent, complete with Wheel	2.00
Pinions, Cannon	.50
Pinions, Swiss, 3d, 4th or 'Scape, ordinary	1.00
Pinions, Swiss, 3d, 4th or 'Scape, fine	$1.75 to 2.00
Pinions, Swiss, Center, ordinary	1.50
Pinions, Swiss, Center, fine	2.00
Pinions, Swiss, Cannon	.50
Ratchets, English, Swiss or American	.50
Staffs Balance, American	75c to $1.25
Staffs Balance, Howard, etc.	2.50
Staffs Balance, English, ordinary	1.25
Staffs Balance, English, fine	$1.50 to 2.50
Staffs Balance, Swiss, ordinary	1.25
Staffs Balance, Swiss, fine	2.50

Changing Key Wind Cases to Stem Wind.

Silver Cases	$1.50
Gold Cases	2.50

WHEN WATCHES are sent with instructions to put them in good order we will do everything necessary to put them in good running condition, but when the instructions are to repair a certain particular part of a watch, the repairs will be strictly confined only to the part or parts specified and we cannot hold ourselves responsible for anything further that may be necessary to insure correct running of the watch. In sending any part of a watch, if your intention is to fit same yourself, do not instruct us to fit same, but kindly use the word "select." This prevents misunderstanding your wishes.

If an idea of the cost of repairs cannot be obtained from the above list, send the watch to us and on receipt of same we will examine it, quote cost of repairing and hold for instructions. **SHIPPING DIRECTIONS**—When shipping watches or jewelry for repairs or exchange, mark plainly as follows: **SEARS, ROEBUCK & CO., Watch Repair Dep't, Fulton, Desplaines, Wayman and Jefferson Sts., Chicago, Ill.,** and in upper left hand corner put your own name and address, prefixing the word "From." Also inclose a card **in the package with your name and address** and state that the watch is for repairs. At the same time write us a letter stating that you have sent a watch (by mail or express) for repairs, what repairs you want made, or that you wish us to quote cost of repairing.

Our New Swiss Imported 12-Size Thin Model Jeweled Movement.

It has 17 fine ruby jewels, cut expansion balance wheel, patent high polished whip lash patent regulator, Brequet hairspring, plate jewels all in screw settings, has exposed winding wheels, full dust protecting side bands, is stem wind and pendant set. The dial has plain Arabic figures, with red marginal minute figures. Remember, this movement is not American make. However, it is offered and sold by many as a product of American manufacture. We sell them for what they are, a very fine Swiss imported movement, a movement that we can recommend and warrant to you for a term of five years. Each one carries our binding guarantee.

Prices in the various cases for the watch complete are as follows:

No. 4C1000 Fitted in Alaska silver open face case, screw back and bezel....................$ 8.75
No. 4C1010 Fitted in solid silver Hunting case....................11.00
No. 4C1020 Fitted in a 20-year gold filled case, open face, screw back and bezel, beautifully engraved....................$11.27
No. 4C1030 Fitted in a 20-year gold filled case, Hunting style, beautifully engraved....................$14.27

This Fine Watch Box for 20c.

No. 4C2000 This picture, made from a photograph, shows one of our fine silk plush lined and covered watch boxes that we supply for 20 cents extra with any watch purchased of us. In ordering, state what size watch the case is intended for.
Price....................20c

CUT PRICE, 18 CENTS.

The Ajax Watch Insulator or Protector protects your watch. It is made of a secret compounded metal, beautifully enameled and lined with velvet. **Order by number.** The maker guarantees that this insulator protects the watch case from wear and the movement from all ordinary magnetic influence. It fits all size watches, open face or hunting style of all makes. **When ordering don't fail to give size and make of case and whether open face or hunting style is wanted.**
No. 4C2002 Price....................18c

PACKING FOR SHIPMENT. Watches should be wrapped in some soft material (cotton batting is good), and packed in a strong box, about 2x3x3 inches. **Do not try and ship more than one watch in a box of this size, as it requires considerable packing about each watch to insure safe shipment.**

CASH WITH THE ORDER must be sent for all repair work. If you do not know what the cost will be, send what you think will more than cover it and we will refund the balance. If to be returned by mail, send 7 cents for each watch for postage and 8 cents extra for regis

WE BUY OLD GOLD AND SILVER and pay the highest ma price, namely, 18-karat g 72c; 14-karat gold, 56c, and 10-karat gold, 40c per pennyweight. Silver fluctuates in value, but at the present time is worth 50c per ounce. In all cases w hold old metal until we are advised by customers that estimate of value is satisfactory.

Watch Repairing.

By N. B. Sherwood.

A practical book, written in a practical manner, by a practical man. Informs about the bench and its accessories, the vise and the oilstone, lathe appliances, the jacot lathe, depthing tool, expanding the web of a wheel, the spreading tool and its use, the rounding-up tool, stud remover, opening the regulator, roller remover, replacing broken teeth, graining, polishing blocks, polishing steel work, pivots, hardening, stamping, etc. Illustrated. Size, 5¼x7¾ inches.
No. 3C059330 Price....................25c
If by mail, postage extra, 5 cents.

American Watchmaker and Jeweler.

By Henry G. Abbott.

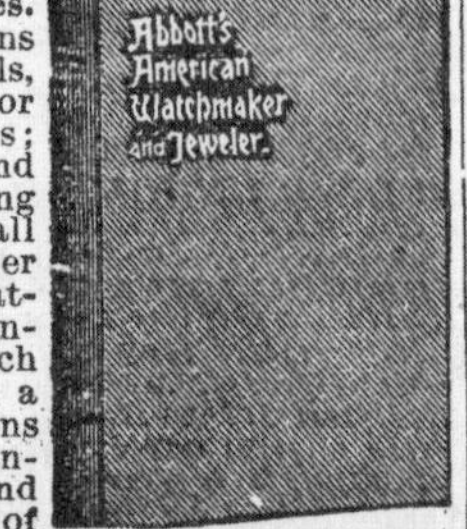

Compiled from the best and most reliable sources. Contains complete directions for using all the latest tools, attachments and devices for watchmakers and jewelers; electroplating, bronzing and staining all metals; soldering and directions for making all kinds of hard and soft solder and fluxes; steel, its treatment in annealing, hardening, tempering, etc.; watch cleaning, repairing, etc.; a treatise on wheels and pinions and hundreds of miscellaneous recipes, formulas and hints on all kinds of work, of great value to every workman. 367 pages. Illustrated with 288 engravings. Size, 5½x7½ inches. Retail price, $1.25.
No. 3C059312 Cloth. Our price....................98c
If by mail, postage extra, 10 cents.

$15.23 $15.23

NEW THIN MODEL OPEN FACE AND HUNTING STYLE DUEBER-HAMPDEI

16-SIZE 25-YEAR WARRANTED GOLD FILLED AN 14-KARAT SOLID GOLD COMPLETE WATCHE

These cases are made by the Dueber Watch Company. They are the correct thing, the right size and shape, han engraved and in every respect perfect. The movements ar all new models manufactured by the Hampden Watch Company each one guaranteed an accurate time piece for five years Note the prices and compare them with what others ask for the same watch. We fit these movements into case as number shows.

The engraving will be similar to the illustration.
No. 4C2450 25-year gold filled open face.
No. 4C2452 25-year gold filled hunting.
No. 4C2454 14-karat solid gold open face.
No. 4C2456 14-karat solid gold hunting.

	No. 4C2450	No. 4C2452	No. 4C2454	No. 4C2456
Full 17 jeweled General Stark movement	$15.23	$16.07	$30.00	$33.00
Full 17 jeweled William McKinley movement	16.93	17.77	31.70	34.70
Full 21 jeweled William McKinley movement	27.93	28.77	42.70	46.70

DEALERS AND ALL MERCHANTS WHO SELL WATCHES AND JEWELRY CAN MAKE MON by buying from us. We can furnish them any goods from our big Watch and Jewelry Departme for much less than they can buy elsewhere. Our Watch and Jewelry Department offers a gre opportunity for money making.

77c AND UPWARDS FOR AMERICAN WATCHES

Nickel, Metal, Electro Plate, Silver, Gold Filled and Solid Gold Watches at prices heretofore unknown. SWEEPING REDUCTIONS ON EVERYTHING IN THIS DEPARTMENT made possible by larger purchases and larger contracts than ever before, means lowest prices ever quoted by us or any other house. Our prices are prices unknown to others. A great saving to buyers. Remember, we are always ready to refund your money if our goods are not found at all times as represented.

77c

No. 4C2500

CUT AGAIN
No. 4C2500

77-CENT AMERICAN WATCH.

Far better than ever and yet only 77 cents.

A gentleman's stem wind watch for 77 cents.

This is a **nickel plated** metal watch, stem wind and pendant set, regular 18-size, **open face case. A patent lever** movement, and runs 30 to 36 hours with one winding.

Guaranteed American made and a very good timekeeper; movement is strong in construction, and will stand much rougher usage than a finer and higher priced watch.

Remember your boy with one of these 77-cent watches. Nothing will please him better. **77 cents** is little money and **far less money** than the watch can be bought for elsewhere.

No. 4C2500 Price........ ......77c

ALASKA SILVER ALL AMERICAN OPEN FACE WATCH

$1.98 FOR AN AMERICAN STEM WIND AND STEM SET nickel movement and American case.

With Every Watch Sold We Send Our Signed Five-year Written Binding GUARANTEE.

ALASKA SILVER CASE. THIS HANDSOME CASE, AS ILLUSTRATED, is what is known as ALASKA SILVER. It is a composition of several metals, giving the watch the appearance of coin silver; and in fact, it is in appearance and in every way, except intrinsic value, the equal of coin silver. **It will wear and retain its coin silver color for a lifetime.** It is handsomely finished, as shown in illustration, in a **CORRUGATED PATTERN** with fancy heavy beaded edge. It is open face, full 18-size, stem wind and stem set, and is fitted with a heavy bevel edge crystal.

AT $1.98 WE FURNISH THIS CASE COMPLETE WITH MOVEMENT in what we call snap back and snap bezel. The front and back snap on.

MOVEMENT. WE FURNISH IN THIS WATCH OUR SPECIAL PRICE OF $1.98 a jeweled solid nickel stem wind and stem set movement. These movements are made expressly for us by one of the largest makers of American watches.

$1.98

No. 4C2502 Snap back and snap bezel.

OUR SPECIAL AND HERETOFORE UNHEARD OF PRICE OF $1.98 COMMENDS THIS WATCH to all those who require a reliable timepiece and American case that will not tarnish, for very little money, and **$1.98** is a price based on the actual cost to produce, with but our one small profit added.

No. 4C2504 Same Watch as above, with the case hinged in front and snap back, $2.08. We recommend this hinged or jointed front case at $2.08. The 10 cents additional which we charge you is the exact difference in the cost to us, and we believe the watch is well worth the difference.

No. 4C2504 Price................**$2.08**

No. 4C2506

$1.23

No. 4C2506
THE PADISHA.

Manufactured by the New England Watch Company.

AT THE SAME PRICE QUOTED BY US LAST YEAR.

AT $1.23 THIS NEW ENGLAND WONDER. **A genuine American made watch.** It runs thirty to thirty-six hours with **one winding and keeps good time.** It is stem wind and stem set. If properly handled and cared for it will last for years. **The case is plain polished, nickel plated.** The movement is one of the most simple known. It comes in both nickel and gilt, has the duplex escapement, both pivots fitted with genuine jewels. While we do not guarantee this watch for the price, **$1.23**, we know you will be entirely satisfied.

No. 4C2506 Price...**$1.23**

No. 4C2508
SILVER,
$9.50

No. 4C2510
NICKEL,
$8.00

PRICES CUT ON 8-DAY WATCHES

$9.50 for an 8-day, 15-jeweled solid silver open face watch.

$8.00 for an 8-day, 15-jeweled solid nickel open face watch.

An 8-Day Watch now perfected. Why be bothered winding your watch every night! Each one carries with it our written, binding, five-year guarantee, we warrant it to run accurately and give entire satisfaction for a term of five years. Remember, you need wind it but once every eight days. Never before, at anything like the price, has such a marvel of mechanical skill been offered; never before has an 8-day watch been successfully constructed. At **$9.50** we have to offer a solid silver, 8-day, full fifteen-jeweled Swiss lever, stem wind and stem set watch warranted for five years. The case is heavy solid silver, plain polished, open face, jointed front and back. The movement has fifteen fine ruby jewels, finely gilded plates, has lever escapement, cut balance wheel, true timing screws, polished safety pinions, breguet hair spring, and is manufactured by one of the largest and most reliable concerns in Switzerland.

No. 4C2508 Fifteen-jeweled, solid silver, 8-day watch. Price...**$9.50**

At $8.00 we offer a fine solid nickel case, open face, plain polished, stem wind and set, fitted with a fine 8-day, fifteen-jeweled, gilded movement, made in Switzerland. This movement has fifteen fine ruby jewels, plates beautifully gilded, breguet hair spring, true timing screws, polished safety pinions and is **guaranteed for a term of five years.**

No. 4C2510 Fifteen-jeweled, solid nickel, 8-day watch. Price **$8.00**

SWISS CALENDAR WATCH
No. 4C2512

If you own one of these watches you will not find it necessary to consult an almanac or ask anyone to tell you the day of the month. The case is nickel plated, and fitted with a heavy beveled edge glass. **The movement** is imported, stem wind and stem set, jeweled, cylinder escapement, hard enameled dial, and in addition to being complete in every respect as a timekeeper, it has **a complete calendar, which works automatically, always indicating correctly the day of the month.**

No. 4C2512 Price......**$3.60**

No. 4C2513

$3.60

Solid Silver, Gold Filled and Gun Metal

MOON CALENDAR WATCHES
AT PRICES CUT AGAIN.

This watch is made in Switzerland and is a mechanical wonder, but at the same time is offered at a price which is within the reach of all. The case is **solid silver,** beautifully engraved, and fitted with heavy beveled edge glass.

No. 4C2514

$6.30

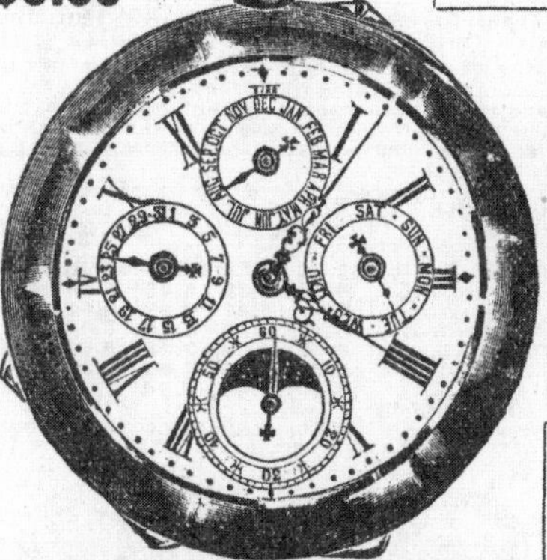

The movement is stem wind and stem set, patent lever escapement, full jeweled, and in addition to being a complete timepiece, it is also a **COMPLETE CALENDAR, indicating the day of the week, day of the month, month of the year, and the changes of the moon.** At the same time it is so simple that it is not more liable to get out of order than an ordinary watch. **It is fully guaranteed by both the manufacturers and ourselves.**

We can furnish it in open face only.

No. 4C2514 Price, solid silver, each..................................**$6.30**

No. 4C2516 Price, gun metal, same as above..................................**$4.87**

No. 4C2518 Price, gold filled, 20 years guaranteed..........................**$16.50**

A BOY'S GOOD WATCH FOR $2.18.

This watch, as illustration shows, is the very latest twelve size, extra thin model. The case is snap bezel and back, dustproof, made of solid nickel, not plated as most of these watch cases on the market are, but solid nickel through and through. It looks like solid silver. It will never rust; it will never tarnish; it will always be bright. The movement will keep good time, it is jeweled, it is stem wind and pendant set, the balance wheel is compensated, plates frosted, in fact, a watch such as any boy would be proud to own, and one that will give good satisfaction. This watch is imported by us from Switzerland, the home of watchmaking. While we guarantee it to be the best $2.18 can buy, and sold by others for at least $5.00, we cannot warrant it, but we will guarantee it being received in perfect going order, and if properly taken care of, should last as long as any other watch.

No. 4C2521 Price..............................**$2.18**

No. 4C2521
$2.18

Elgin and Waltham Watches Quoted on Pages 216 to 218.

GENTLEMEN'S 18-SIZE AND LADIES' 6-SIZE WATCHES.

OPEN FACE AND HUNTING STYLE, MADE IN ELECTRO PLATE, SILVER PLATE, GOLD FILLED AND SOLID SILVER.

$2.39 TO $5.68

OUR GOLD FILLED WATCHES. The cases on these watches are made of gold filled stock, two solid gold plates soldered over a plate of composition metal, thus making the case solid gold on the outside and solid gold on the inside. They are manufactured by the Illinois Watch Co. of Elgin, Ill. They are warranted by the maker for the term of two, five or ten years, according to the thickness of the gold used.

We give with each watch sold our own guarantee, to substantiate and verify the manufacturers.

Electro Plated, 18-Size.
No. 4C2632 Open Face, Screw Back and Bezel.
No. 4C2634 Hunting Style.

OUR SOLID SILVER CASES

We guarantee to be pure coin silver through and through, and give our written guarantee to that effect.

We can furnish a fine Plush Presentation Case to fit any watch. See page 192.

Gold Filled, 18-Size. Guaranteed for 2 years.
No. 4C2636 Open Face, Screw Back and Bezel.
No. 4C2638 Hunting Style.

ELECTRO PLATED AND SILVER PLATED CASES. These cases are made by the electro plating process. This is the cheapest known process of plating and we do not guarantee the wearing ability of them. They may wear for one month or six. We offer these electro plated and silver plated cases for just what they are.

These cases are often used by unscrupulous merchants and fake concerns and offered as "high grade gold filled and solid silver," but we tell you plainly just what they represent.

Gold Filled, 18-Size. Guaranteed for 5 years.
No. 4C2640 Open Face, Screw Back and Bezel.
No. 4C2642 Hunting Style.

For **$1.25** extra we can furnish a fancy dial and gold hands on any watch on this page.

Gold Filled, 18-Size. Guaranteed for 10 years.
No. 4C2644 Open Face, Screw Back and Bezel.
No. 4C2646 Hunting Style.

THE MOVEMENTS quoted on this page are all of representative makes. They are all well known throughout the country. We warrant each one of them for a term of five years against defective material or workmanship.

We Fit These Cases With the Following Movements.	No. 4C2632	No. 4C2634	No. 4C2648	No. 4C2650	No. 4C2636	No. 4C2638	No. 4C2640	No. 4C2642	No. 4C2652	No. 4C2654	No. 4C2644	No. 4C2646
7 Jeweled EDGEMERE, S. R. & Co.'s Special Make.....	$2.39	$2.44	$2.59	$2.84	$3.34	$3.94	$3.64	$4.04	$3.84	$4.14	$4.39	$5.04
7 Jeweled Hampden, Gilt...	4.00	4.10	4.20	4.45	4.95	5.55	5.25	5.65	5.45	5.75	6.00	6.65
11 Jeweled Hampden	4.35	4.45	4.55	4.80	5.30	5.90	5.60	6.00	5.80	6.10	6.35	7.00
Full 12 Jeweled EDGEMERE, S. R. & Co.'s Special Make..	4.15	4.25	4.35	4.60	5.10	5.70	5.40	5.80	5.60	5.90	6.15	6.80
Full 15 Jeweled SEARS, ROEBUCK & CO.'S Special....	5.25	5.35	5.45	5.70	6.20	6.80	6.50	6.90	6.70	7.00	7.25	7.90
Full 15 Jeweled Hampden	5.43	5.53	5.63	5.88	6.38	6.98	6.68	7.08	6.88	7.18	7.43	8.08
Full 17 Jeweled EDGEMERE, S. R. & Co.'s Special Make..	5.68	5.78	5.88	6.13	6.63	7.23	6.93	7.33	7.13	7.43	7.68	8.33
Trainmen's Special, marked, 17 Jeweled adjusted	3.10	3.15	3.30	3.55	4.05	4.65	4.35	4.75	4.55	4.85	5.10	5.75

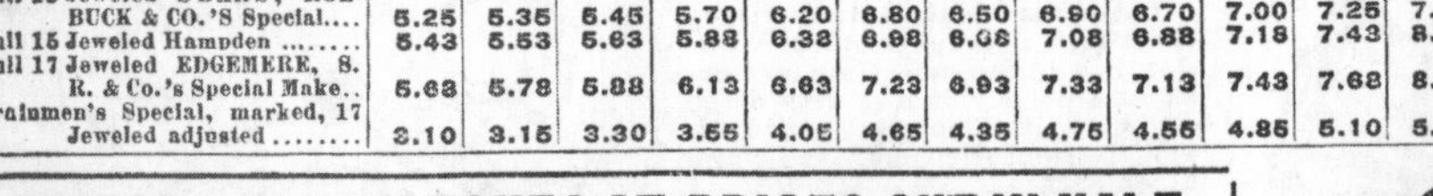

LADIES' 6-SIZE WATCHES AT PRICES CUT IN HALF.

MERCHANTS AND DEALERS CAN BUY CHEAPER FROM US THAN ELSEWHERE.

AT $2.90 FOR LADIES' ELECTRO PLATED CASES. We do not guarantee them. They will not wear over two to three months; great sellers at $4.95. You can make $2.05 on each one sold and offer a bargain.

SOME LADIES LIKE SILVER WATCHES. These cases are solid silver through and through, hand engraved and perfectly finished in every detail. We warrant them. Our guarantee goes with each watch sold. Open face solid silver at $3.80; Hunting style, $4.30. **AT $3.80** for Ladies' 6-size Gold Filled Watches complete with movement. They are guaranteed gold filled, perfect in every respect; we warrant them to wear and retain their gold appearance for a term of two years.

AT $3.95 for a 5-year Gold Filled Case and an American made movement, complete watch. This case is made by one of the most representative case makers; his guarantee accompanies each case and our own special written binding guarantee likewise, covering a period of five years on both case and movement.

WE FIT THE CASES BELOW WITH THE FOLLOWING 6-SIZE MOVEMENTS.	No. 4C2656	4C2658 4C2664	No. 4C2660	No. 4C2662	No. 4C2666
7 Jeweled EDGEMERE, S. R. & Co.'s Special Make.....	$2.90	$3.80	$4.30	$3.95	$4.70
7 Jeweled No. 200 Grade Hampden, Gilt..	4.49	5.39	5.89	5.54	6.29
11 Jeweled No. 206 Grade Hampden..........................	5.57	6.47	6.97	6.62	7.37
12 Jeweled EDGEMERE, S. R. & Co.'s Special Make...........	4.39	5.29	5.79	5.44	6.19
Full 15 Jeweled SEARS, ROEBUCK & CO.'S SPECIAL.............	5.75	6.65	7.15	6.80	7.55
Full 15 Jeweled No. 213 Grade Hampden......................	6.25	7.15	7.65	7.30	8.05
Full 17 Jeweled EDGEMERE, S. R. & Co.'s Special Make..........	6.50	7.40	7.90	7.55	8.30
Full 17 Jeweled SEARS, ROEBUCK & CO.'S SPECIAL. Especially made. This is the greatest watch value ever offered	8.60	9.50	10.00	9.65	10.40

YOU NEED NOT LOOK FURTHER

YOU CANNOT GET THESE VALUES FROM ANY OTHER HOUSE FOR ONE-THIRD MORE MONEY.

Silver Plated, 18-Size.
No. 4C2648 Open Face, Screw Back and Bezel.
No. 4C2650 Hunting Style.

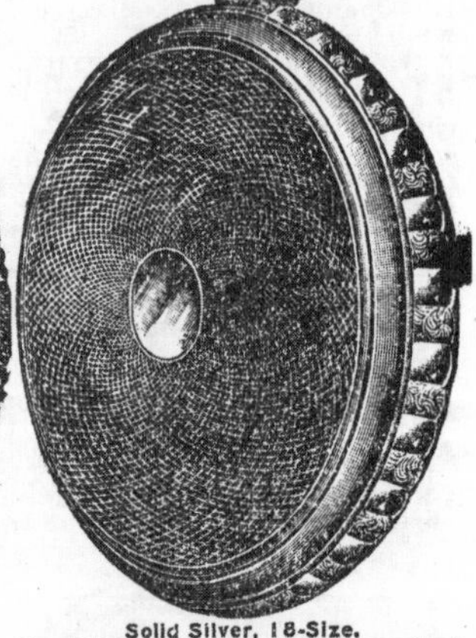

Solid Silver, 18-Size.
No. 4C2652 Open Face, Screw Back and Bezel.
No. 4C2654 Hunting Style.

2.90

For **$1.25** extra we can furnish a fancy dial and gold hands on any watch on this page.

Electro Plated, 6-Size.
No. 4C2656 Hunting Style.

Solid Silver, 6-Size.
No. 4C2658 Open Face.
No. 4C2660 Hunting Style.

This is an exact picture of the 15-Jeweled Sears, Roebuck & Co.'s Special Movement.

AT $5.75.

This high grade 15-jeweled movement fitted in any one of these cases at $5.75 to $7.55, according to case.

YOU cannot imagine the excellent values we are offering unless you see and compare the goods and prices with others.

Gold Filled, 6-Size.
Guaranteed for 5 Years.
No. 4C2662 Hunting Style.

REGARDING the engravings, we generally have the exact pattern, if not we will send very similar design.

Gold Filled, 6-Size.
Guaranteed for 2 Years.
No. 4C2664 Hunting Style.

$4.70

Gold Filled, 6-Size.
Guaranteed for 10 Years.
No. 4C2666 Hunting Style.

THE WORLD RENOWNED DUEBER SILVERINE AND ALASKA SILVER, 18-SIZE WATCHES AT PRICES NEVER HEARD OF BEFORE.

PLAIN OPEN FACE **$2.20** AND UP.

FOR 20 CENTS WE FURNISH A BEAUTIFUL PLUSH **Presentation Case** TO FIT ANY WATCH.

SEE No. 4C2000 ON PAGE 192.

No charges for repairs on watches or clocks will be allowed unless our written consent is first secured in advance.

For $1.25 extra, we can furnish a fancy dial and gold hands on any watch on this page.

PROTECT YOUR WATCH WITH AN AJAX WATCH INSULATOR.

See page 192

No. 4C2002

PRICE, 18c

18 SIZE

No. 4C2700 Open Face, Jointed Case.
No. 4C2702 Open Face, 3 oz., Screw Back & Bezel.

18 SIZE

No. 4C2704 Hunting, Engraved Case.

18 SIZE

No. 4C2706 Screw Bezel and Solid Back

18 SIZE

No. 4C2708 Hunting, Plain Case.

This illustration shows our **18-SIZE SEARS, ROEBUCK & CO.'S SPECIAL 17 JEWELED MOVEMENT.** We recommend it as the greatest movement offer ever made for perfection of make and accuracy of time.

WE FIT THESE CASES WITH THE FOLLOWING 18-SIZE MOVEMENTS.	4C2700 4C2702	4C2706	4C2704 4C2708	4C2710 4C2712
7 JEWELED EDGEMERE, SEARS, ROEBUCK & CO.'S SPECIAL MAKE..	$2.20	$2.55	$2.65	$2.90
Trainmen's Special, Marked 17 Jeweled, Adjusted	3.00	3.35	3.45	3.70
7 Jeweled Hampden, Gilt	3.80	4.15	4.25	4.50
11 Jeweled Hampden	4.38	4.60	4.70	5.10
FULL 12 JEWELED EDGEMERE, SEARS, ROEBUCK & CO.'S SPECIAL MAKE..	4.10	4.45	4.55	4.80
Full 15 Jeweled Hampden	5.48	5.71	5.80	6.18
FULL 15 JEWELED SEARS, ROEBUCK & CO.'S SPECIAL	5.28	5.51	5.60	5.98
FULL 17 JEWELED EDGEMERE, SEARS, ROEBUCK & CO.'S SPECIAL MAKE..	5.63	5.86	5.95	6.33
Full 17 Jeweled Dueber Grand Hampden, Adjusted	9.80	10.03	10.12	10.50
Full 17 Jeweled New Railway Hampden, Adjusted	16.80	17.03	17.12	17.50
Full 21 Jeweled John Hancock Hampden, Adjusted	19.23	19.46	19.55	19.93
Full 21 Jeweled Special Railway Hampden, Adjusted	20.85	21.08	21.17	21.55
Full 23 Jeweled New Railway Hampden, Adjusted	23.30	23.53	23.62	24.00
Full 23 Jeweled Special Railway Hampden, Adjusted	28.95	29.18	29.27	29.65
FULL 17 JEWELED SEARS, ROEBUCK & CO.'S SPECIAL, ADJUSTED. THE GREATEST WATCH VALUE EVER OFFERED	9.60	9.83	9.92	10.30

THE ONLY 4½-OUNCE ALASKA SILVER CASE MANUFACTURED IN THE WORLD.

WE HAVE THEM. YOU CANNOT BUY THEM ELSEWHERE.

No. 4C2714

$2.65

WE GUARANTEE this case to weigh 4½ ounces without the movement. An extra heavy watch is often called for by men who are engaged in heavy work, and to supply this demand we have had made this extra heavy 4½-ounce dust and damp proof Alaska silver case. This case is made to stand 800 pounds strain; in other words, your movement is safe in this case, no matter what might happen. The composition of this watch is of the best grade of Alaska silver composition metal, in every way except in intrinsic value the equal of coin silver. It is guaranteed to wear and retain its perfect coin silver color for a lifetime. This case is open face, screw back and bezel, dust and damp proof. Our special price, **$2.65**, includes this case and a 7 jeweled stem wind and stem set quick train movement.

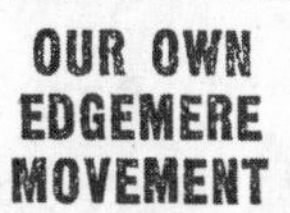

OUR OWN EDGEMERE MOVEMENT

Guaranteed by a written guarantee for five years, but with care will last a lifetime.

18 SIZE

AT $3.45 fitted with the 17 jeweled Trainmen's Special, exactly as illustrated and described.

TRAINMEN'S SPECIAL. American manufactured movement, 18-size, elaborately damaskeened nickel and gilt movement; ruby jewels in raised settings, train, straight line escapement, exposed pallets, compensation quick balance, stem wind and set, hard enameled dial, locomotive on movement and dial and movement stamped "17 jewels adjusted." Has the appearance of a $25.00 railroad movement.

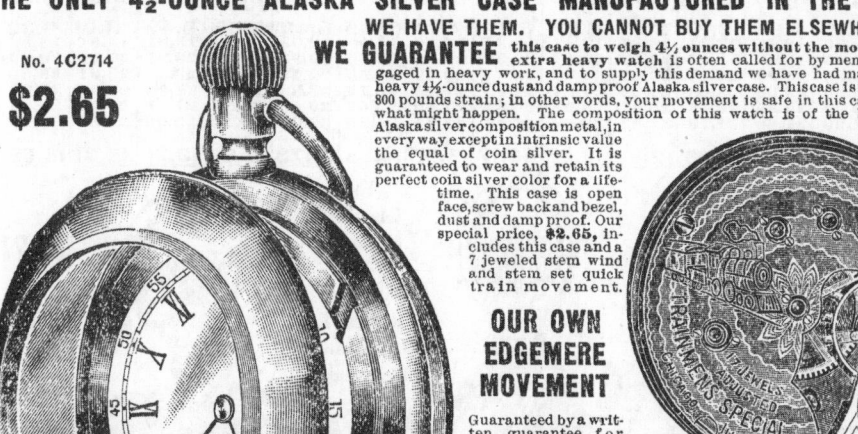

ORDER ONE OF THESE WATCHES and if you don't find it in every way as described, return it and we will refund your money. We can fit in this case any movement you desire as quoted below:

WITH THE 7 JEWELED EDGEMERE, SEARS, ROEBUCK & CO.'S SPECIAL MAKE	$ 2.65
With the Trainmen's Special	3.45
With the 7 Jeweled Elgin or Waltham, Gilt	4.55
With the 7 Jeweled Elgin or Waltham, Nickel	5.07
WITH THE 12 JEWELED EDGEMERE, SEARS, ROEBUCK & CO.'S SPECIAL MAKE	4.30
WITH THE FULL 15 JEWELED SEARS, ROEBUCK & CO.'S SPECIAL MAKE	6.10
With the Full 17 Jeweled New Railway Hampden, Adjusted	17.20
WITH THE FULL 17 JEWELED EDGEMERE, SEARS, ROEBUCK & CO.'S SPECIAL MAKE	6.55
With the Full 21 Jeweled Special Railway Hampden, Adjusted	21.25
With the Full 23 Jeweled New Railway Hampden, Adjusted	23.70
With the Full 23 Jeweled Special Railway Hampden, Adjusted	29.35
WITH THE 17 JEWELED SEARS, ROEBUCK & CO.'S SPECIAL, SPECIALLY ADJUSTED, NICKEL	10.00

This watch case fitted with our special Sears, Roebuck & Co.'s 17-jeweled movement is such a watch as cannot be procured elsewhere as to quality, for both durability and time keeping, at three times the amount we ask. **$10.00** is our price for a specially adjusted, solid nickel, 17-jeweled high grade movement.

SOLID GOLD ONLAID

ALASKA SILVER CASES.

Prices Quoted Above, $2.90 and Up.

No. 4C2710 Stag Onlaid.

No. 4C2712 Engine Onlaid.

18 SIZE

No. 4C2710 Open Face, Screw Back and Bezel, Solid Gold Stag Onlaid.

No. 4C2712 Same style case as above, Solid Gold Engine Onlaid.

ELGIN AND WALTHAM WATCHES QUOTED ON PAGES 216 TO 218.

18-SIZE SOLID SILVER WATCHES.

PLAIN POLISHED, HAND ENGRAVED OR SOLID GOLD INLAID. OPEN FACE AND HUNTING STYLES IN ALL WEIGHTS.

GENTLEMEN'S OR LADIES' SIZE GERMAN SILVER OPEN FACE NOVELTY WATCH.

No. 4C2798 Our New Gentlemen's Thin 15-size German Silver, Gray Oxidized Finish, Antique Pattern Open Face Novelty Watch. The illustration shows the back and front of the watch. The case is artistically designed, engraving in bas-relief, similar in design as shown. The movement is imported from Switzerland, has jeweled escapement, damaskeened nickel plates. Price........$3.15

No. 4C2799 Same as No. 4C2798 but ladies' 0-size. Price........$3.15

FOR A HEAVY, STRONG, SUBSTANTIAL WATCH CASE, to thoroughly protect the watch movement, there is nothing superior to a solid silver watch case properly constructed. These cases, of solid coin silver, are made under a written signed contract, every detail in the specifications is carried out to the very letter. We offer you an absolutely perfect case at prices that speak for themselves. The quality of these goods, the prices we ask, are the best argument to convince you that competitors can not buy at our selling price.

FOR $1.25 extra we will furnish a fancy dial and gold hands on these silver watches on this page.

See Pages 190 and 191 for the Descriptions and Beautiful Illustrations of : : Our Special Sears, Roebuck & Co. EDGEMERE LINE OF WATCH MOVEMENTS.

NO CHARGES for REPAIRS ON WATCHES OR CLOCKS WILL BE ALLOWED UNLESS OUR WRITTEN CONSENT IS FIRST SECURED IN ADVANCE.

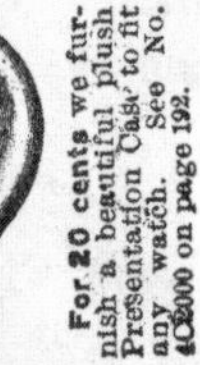

For 20 cents we furnish a beautiful plush Presentation Case to fit any watch. See No. 4C8000 on page 192.

OPEN FACE, SCREW BACK AND BEZEL.
No. 4C2800 3-ounce Plain Polished Case.
No. 4C2802 As above. Hand engraved.
No. 4C2804 4-ounce Plain Polished Case.
No. 4C2806 As above. Hand engraved.

OPEN FACE, JOINTED FRONT AND BACK.
No. 4C2808 3-ounce Plain Polished Case.
No. 4C2810 As above. Hand engraved.
No. 4C2812 4-ounce Plain Polished Case.
No. 4C2814 As above. Hand engraved.

HUNTING STYLE.
No. 4C2816 3-ounce Plain Polished Case.
No. 4C2818 As above. Hand engraved.
No. 4C2820 4-ounce Plain Polished Case.
No. 4C2822 As above. Hand engraved.
No. 4C2824 5-ounce Plain Polished Case.
No. 4C2826 As above. Hand engraved.

We Fit These Cases with the Following 18-Size Movements:	4C2802 4C2810	4C2800 4C2808	4C2816 4C2829	4C2804 4C2812	4C2806 4C2814 4C2820	4C2832 4C2834	4C2836 4C2838	4C2824	4C2830	4C2818	4C2822	4C2826	4C2831
7 JEWELED EDGEMERE, SEARS, ROEBUCK & CO.'S SPECIAL MAKE	$5.39	$5.09	$5.27	$5.81	$6.11	$6.01	$6.74	$7.69	$5.57	$5.73	$6.55	$8.15	$6.52
Trainmen's Special, Stamped 17 Jeweled Adjusted.	6.19	5.89	6.07	6.61	6.91	6.81	7.54	8.49	6.37	6.53	7.35	8.95	7.32
7 Jeweled Hampden, Gilt	6.93	6.63	6.80	7.35	7.65	7.55	8.28	9.23	7.10	7.27	8.09	9.69	8.06
11 Jeweled Hampden	7.33	7.03	7.20	7.75	8.05	7.95	8.68	9.63	7.51	7.67	8.50	10.09	8.46
FULL 12 JEWELED EDGEMERE, SEARS, ROEBUCK & CO.'S SPECIAL MAKE	6.73	6.43	6.60	7.15	7.45	7.35	8.08	9.03	6.91	7.07	7.90	9.49	7.86
Full 15 Jeweled Hampden	8.43	8.13	8.31	8.85	9.15	9.05	9.78	10.73	8.61	8.77	9.59	11.19	9.56
FULL 15 JEWELED SEARS, ROEBUCK & CO.'S SPECIAL	7.80	7.50	7.77	8.32	8.62	8.52	9.25	10.20	8.08	8.24	9.07	10.66	8.97
FULL 17 JEWELED EDGEMERE, SEARS, ROEBUCK & CO.'S SPECIAL MAKE	8.15	7.85	8.12	8.67	8.97	8.87	9.60	10.55	8.43	8.59	9.42	11.01	9.32
Full 17 Jeweled Dueber Grand Hampden, Adjusted	12.75	12.45	12.63	13.17	13.47	13.37	14.10	15.05	12.93	13.09	13.91	15.51	13.88
Full 17 Jeweled New Railway Hampden, Adjusted	19.75	19.45	19.63	20.17	20.47	20.37	21.10	22.05	19.93	20.09	20.91	22.51	20.88
Full 21 Jeweled John Hancock, Hampden, Adjusted	22.25	21.95	22.13	22.67	22.97	22.87	23.60	24.55	22.43	22.59	23.41	25.01	23.38
Full 21 Jeweled Special Railway Hampden, Adjusted	23.80	23.50	23.68	24.22	24.57	24.42	25.15	26.10	23.98	24.14	24.96	26.56	24.93
Full 23 Jeweled New Railway Hampden, Adjusted	26.25	25.95	26.13	26.67	26.97	26.87	27.60	28.55	26.43	26.59	27.41	29.01	27.38
Full 23 Jeweled Special Railway Hampden, Adjusted	31.90	31.60	31.78	32.32	32.62	32.52	33.25	34.20	32.08	32.24	33.06	34.66	33.03
FULL 17 JEWELED SEARS, ROEBUCK & CO.'S SPECIAL. Especially Adjusted. This is the greatest watch value ever offered.	12.55	12.25	12.43	12.97	13.27	13.17	13.90	14.85	12.73	12.89	13.71	15.31	13.68

REPEATING WATCHES

16-SIZE SOLID SILVER.

GOLD FILLED AND GUN METAL.

OPEN FACE 1-4 HOUR REPEATER.

Own one of these watches and you will be able to know the time at any hour of the night without seeing. This style of watch not alone registers perfect time, but also when you desire it strikes the hours and quarter hours on a soft toned bell. This is done by simply pushing the lever on side of watch upward toward the crown or winding stem, which starts the striking arrangement. Each stroke of the single bell counts the hour, each stroke of the double bell counts the quarters.

WE CAN RECOMMEND THIS WATCH being particularly perfect in time keeping, as it is manufactured in Switzerland by one of the largest manufacturers there, and without doubt represents, for the price, one of the most perfect of Swiss watches. The movement contains seventeen fine genuine garnet jewels, has the latest straight line jeweled lever escapement, cut expansion balance, with Breguet hair spring. The movement itself is of solid nickel, beautifully finished and polished. It is adjusted to position and isochronism. It is stem wind and stem set and is just such a watch that heretofore has beensold to only the wealthiest people at most extravagant prices. On account of a new arrangement with the factory in Switzerland, we have been able to have made for our

No. 4C2839 to No. 4C2843 express use and benefit these watches at prices so low that we are able to sell them to you at less than one-third of what similar watches are offered by big wholesale dealers. Remember when you own a repeater you own not alone an accurate timepiece but one of the most useful and interesting novel watches ever made.

No. 4C2839 Fitted in a genuine gun metal tight closing case with gold filled crown, stem and repeater slide. Price....$16.75

No. 4C2841 Same movement as described above, fitted in a solid silver case. Price........22.00

No. 4C2843 Fitted in a gold filled case, guaranteed to wear and retain its solid gold appearance for a term of 20 years. Price........27.50

The Edgemere Movement Is Made in Four Grades, 7, 12, 15 and 17 Jeweled.

$5.27 TO $33.25

No. 4C2829 2-ounce Plain Polished Case, dust and damp proof, screw bezel, solid back.
No. 4C2830 As above. Hand engraved.
No. 4C2831 3-ounce Heavy Plain Polished Screw Bezel and Solid Back Case, has gold reflector and damp proof crown.

No. 4C2832 3-ounce Case, Open Face, screw back and bezel, gold inlaid Stag. Prices of watch listed above.
No. 4C2834 3-ounce Case, Open Face, screw back and bezel, gold inlaid Engine.
No. 4C2836 4-ounce Case, Stag inlaid.
No. 4C2838 4-ounce Case, Engine inlaid.

ELGIN AND WALTHAM WATCHES QUOTED ON PAGES 216 TO 218.

HORSE TIMERS.

OUR.... **$4.20** Horse Timer

No. 4C2900

HORSE TIMER ONLY.

It has start, stop and fly back arrangement, operated from the crown. It is also provided with minute register. It has a metal case, heavily nickel plated, plain polished, and fitted with cylinder escapement, imported movement. Just the thing for those who do not care to invest much money in a timepiece for races of any kind.

No. 4C2900 Price.........$4.20

No. 4C2901 Same style as above but with fine jeweled lever escapement movement. Price, $5.95

LUGRIN'S PATENT OPEN FACE CHRONOGRAPHS

With Split Seconds, With or Without Minute Register.

ILLUSTRATION SHOWS MINUTE REGISTER.

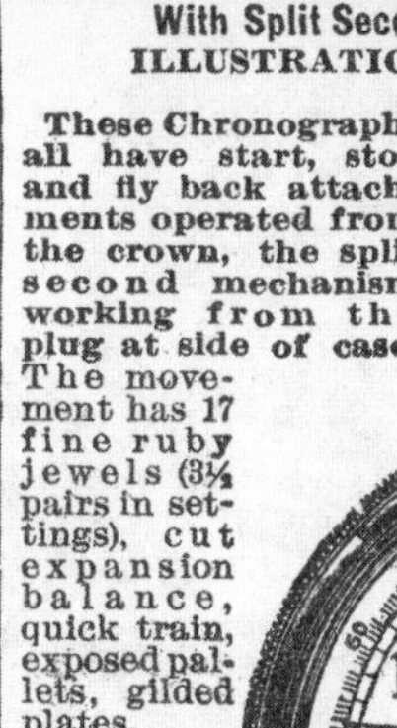

These Chronographs all have start, stop and fly back attachments operated from the crown, the split second mechanism working from the plug at side of case. The movement has 17 fine ruby jewels (3½ pairs in settings), cut expansion balance, quick train, exposed pallets, gilded plates.

$27.50 TO $96.00

The Chronograph with minute register has the addition of three more jewels and the independent minute fly back register. We can recommend any one of these chronographs, as we know that they represent the very latest improvements, and are warranted to be accurate in every detail. You cannot get their equal anywhere for twice what we ask.

No. 4C2902 TO No. 4C2916

Chronograph with Split Seconds.

No. 4C2902	17 Jeweled, in Nickel Case	$27.50
No. 4C2904	17 Jeweled, in Silver Case	47.00
No. 4C2906	17 Jeweled, in 20-Year Gold Filled Case	57.00
No. 4C2908	17 Jeweled, in 14-Karat Solid Gold Case	91.00

Chronograph with Split Seconds and Minute Register.

No. 4C2910	20 Jeweled, in Nickel Case	$32.50
No. 4C2912	20 Jeweled, in Silver Case	52.00
No. 4C2914	20 Jeweled, in 20-Year Gold Filled Case	62.00
No. 4C2916	20 Jeweled, in 14-Karat Solid Gold Case	96.00

A WATCH WITHOUT HANDS.

No. 4C2919 **$8.15**

ORDER BY NUMBER

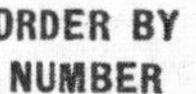

Our new solid silver small 18-size open face novelty watch. The center circle shows the hour and the oval the minute. It is wound and set the same as any other watch, but is less complicated and less liable to get out of order. You will never be bothered on account of the hands catching or dropping off, or finding that your watch does not keep accurate time on account of the hands being too loose. This watch comes in a size smaller than the regular 18-size. The case is solid silver, $\frac{935}{1000}$ fine, in other words, solid sterling silver, stem wind and stem set, comes in open face only. The dial is a beautiful silver dial with rich raised gold ornamentation, exactly as illustration shows. The movement is imported from Switzerland. It has 15 fine ruby jewels, straight line lever escapement, and is perfectly finished in every detail, a watch that we can recommend, being an accurate timekeeper.

No. 4C2919 Price.......$8.15

No. 4C2921 Same as No. 4C2919 but with black oxidized steel gun metal case. Price.......$6.90

20-YEAR GOLD FILLED **$9.13** 25-YEAR GOLD FILLED **$11.15**

No. 4C2926 Gold Filled. Guaranteed for 20 years. Plain polished or engine turned.
No. 4C2928 Gold Filled. Guaranteed for 25 years. Plain polished or engine turned.

$9.13 AND $11.15

18-SIZE, OPEN FACE, SOLID BACK, SWING RING, GOLD FILLED WATCHES.

Guaranteed for 20 and 25 years' continuous wear. The Illinois Watch Case Co., of Elgin, Ill., manufacturers of these cases, agree to replace with a brand new gold filled case of same style and grade, any one of their cases worn through to the base metal within 20 or 25 years.

The swing ring, a new improvement on gold filled cases, makes it possible to produce an absolutely dust and damp proof watch case. You can examine the movement in a swing ring case without difficulty. See illustration. The front or bezel screws off. The back is solid, made of one piece. The movement is fastened in the center ring which is securely joined to the case by a strong hinge. To examine the works, lift up the swing ring (illustration shows the ring partially lifted); to replace in case, let ring drop back in first position and screw on bezel.

$9.13 FOR THE COMPLETE WATCH.

This beautifully finished and new perfected case with our 12-jeweled Edgemere movement, exactly as described, for $9.13. To railway men, train starters and all others wanting a reliable timepiece, one that can be depended upon, we can recommend the 23-jeweled Special Railway, fitted in one of these new dust proof swing ring cases as an absolute protection against dust and damp.

No. 4C2930 Gold Filled. Guaranteed for 25 years. Hand engraved.
No. 4C2932 Gold Filled. Guaranteed for 20 years. Hand engraved.

THIS IS THE ILLUSTRATION OF OUR EDGEMERE

full 17-jeweled movement, engraved by our artist direct from the movement. The Edgemere is solid nickel through and through. The top plate is beautifully damaskeened in gold and nickel.

IT HAS 17 RUBY JEWELS,

each jewel set in finely polished setting, fitted by screws. Bright polished patent regulator, double cut expansion balance wheel, genuine Breguet hairspring, safety barrel, patent safety pinions and goldine timing screws.

THE ENTIRE MOVEMENT IS PERFECTLY FINISHED IN EVERY DETAIL, TIMED AND REGULATED.

See the list of movements we offer. Each one at the price quoted is a bargain and represents a standard of excellence.	No. 4C2930 25 Year Engraved	No. 4C2926 20 Year	No. 4C2928 25 Year	No. 4C2932 20 Year Engraved
Full 12 jeweled Edgemere	$11.65	$ 9.13	$11.15	$ 9.63
Full 15 jeweled Sears, Roebuck & Co.'s Special	13.20	10.68	12.70	11.18
Full 17 jeweled Edgemere, S., R. & Co.'s Special make	14.02	11.50	13.52	12.00
Full 17 jeweled Sears, Roebuck & Co.'s Special	16.70	14.18	16.20	14.68
Full 21 jeweled Special Railway Hampden	27.95	25.43	27.45	25.93
Full 23 jeweled Special Railway Hampden	36.05	33.53	35.55	34.03

ANOTHER CUT. YOUR CHOICE, $4.85.

We give you the advantage of it. The manufacturer has again reduced the price to us. Last season we sold this watch for $5.25. Either Ladies' 0-size Hunting or Gents' 16-size hunting or open face, screw back and screw bezel. Order whichever you want, 5-year guaranteed gold filled hunting case in ladies' 0-size or gentlemen's 16-size hunting or open face, fitted with 7 jeweled movement.

No. 4C2936 No. 4C2938 **$4.85**

No. 4C2936 Gents' 16-size Hunting Style.
No. 4C2938 Gents' 16-size Open Face Style.

$4.85 MONITOR ELGIN

No. 4C2935 Ladies' 0-size.

Description of the 16-size American made movement called "The Reliance," fitted in the gentlemen's size, 5-year guaranteed gold filled case. This movement has 7 ruby jewels, cut balance, patent safety pinion and barrel and double sunk second dial. **We give our written binding guarantee with every one sold, protecting you for a term of five years against defective material or workmanship.**

Description of Cases: These cases are manufactured by the celebrated Illinois Watch Case Co. Each case is accompanied by their personal guarantee. These cases are made of two plates of solid 10-karat gold, covering an inner composition of base metal, and are guaranteed to wear and retain their gold appearance for a term of five years. They are engraved and chased after the very latest gold designs. They have the antique bow; they both are stem wind and stem set; in fact, for $4.85 you have a watch that could not possibly be purchased by any retail jeweler for twice this amount.

You can sell them at $10.00 each and still offer a bargain.

Description of the movement used in the ladies' 0-size watch. This movement has 7 fine jewels, lever escapement, cut balance wheel, fine cut polished pinions. They are imported from Switzerland, the home of watches, and we give our 5-year guarantee with every one sold. We know they will give entire satisfaction. See the illustration of movement.

This is an illustration of the Ladies' 0-size movement.

This is an illustration of the movement we fit in the gents' case, complete watch, $4.85.

For $1.25 extra we can furnish a fancy dial and gold hands on any watch on this page.

18-SIZE HUNTING STYLE AND OPEN FACE SCREW BACK AND SCREW BEZEL CASES.

WARRANTED TO WEAR FOR 20 YEARS.

The SEARS Gold Filled Case is recommended above all others, being made of two extra heavy plates of solid gold over a hard composition metal. Will wear longer than any other gold filled watch case made, and is the handsomest, best finished and best fitting gold filled watch case made. If you select a SEARS case you will have the best gold filled watch case ever made.

$5.87 to $35.15

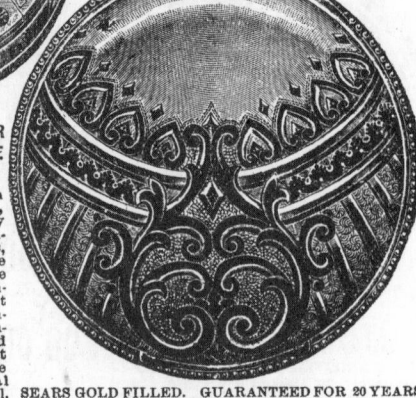

This movement is fitted in a Sears Case.

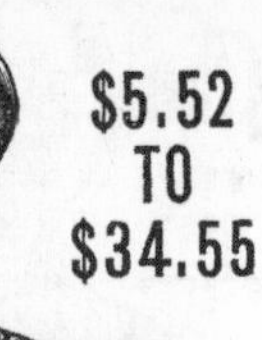

$5.52 TO $34.55

JOHN C. DUEBER GOLD FILLED.
GUARANTEED FOR 20 YEARS.

No. 4C3000 Open Face, Screw Back and Bezel. Engraved.
No. 4C3002 Open Face, Screw Back and Bezel. Plain Polished.
No. 4C3004 Open Face, Screw Back and Bezel. Engine Turned.
No. 4C3006 Hunting Style. Engraved.
No. 4C3008 Hunting Style. Plain Polished.
No. 4C3010 Hunting Style. Engine Turned.

FAHY'S GOLD FILLED. GUARANTEED FOR 20 YEARS.

No. 4C3013 Open Face, Screw Back and Bezel. Engraved.
No. 4C3015 Open Face, Screw Back and Bezel. Plain Polished.
No. 4C3017 Open Face, Screw Back and Bezel. Engine Turned.
No. 4C3019 Hunting Style. Engraved.
No. 4C3021 Hunting Style. Plain Polished.
No. 4C3023 Hunting Style. Engine Turned.

DESCRIPTION OF OUR 17-JEWELED EDGEMERE MOVEMENT.

Solid nickel through and through, 17 jewels, adjusted. Full plate, fancy solid gold damaskeened finish, five pair gold settings, compensation full double cut expansion balance wheel, adjusted to isochronism and position, patent micrometer regulator, genuine ruby jeweled pin, highly polished beveled edged screws, fully protecting dust band, safety pinion, double sunk white enameled dial and sunk second hand dial. **The superior construction of this movement adapts it to the most exacting service.**

SEARS GOLD FILLED. GUARANTEED FOR 20 YEARS

No. 4C3025 Open Face, Screw Back and Bezel.
No. 4C3027 Hunting Style.

ELGIN AND WALTHAM WATCHES QUOTED ON PAGES 216 TO 218.

Protect your watch with an Ajax Watch Insulator. See page 192

No. 4C2002
Price, 18c

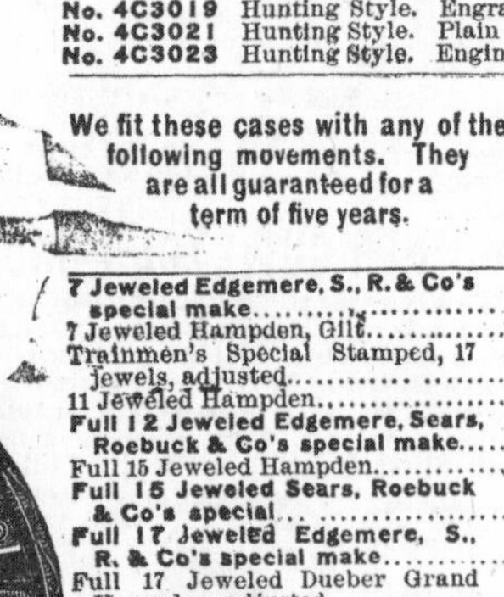

We fit these cases with any of the following movements. They are all guaranteed for a term of five years.	4C3000 4C3033 4C3002 4C3037 4C3004 4C3041 4C3025 4C3043 4C3028 4C3045	4C3013 4C3015 4C3017 4C3053	4C3006 4C3035 4C3008 4C3039 4C3010 4C3047 4C3027 4C3049 4C3030 4C3051	4C3019 4C3021 4C3023 4C3055
7 Jeweled Edgemere, S., R. & Co's special make	$ 5.52	$ 5.87	$ 8.04	$ 8.64
7 Jeweled Hampden, Gilt	7.11	7.46	9.63	10.23
Trainmen's Special Stamped, 17 jewels, adjusted	6.32	6.67	8.84	9.44
11 Jeweled Hampden	7.48	7.83	10.00	10.60
Full 12 Jeweled Edgemere, Sears, Roebuck & Co's special make	6.90	7.60	8.90	10.50
Full 15 Jeweled Hampden	9.56	9.90	11.08	11.68
Full 15 Jeweled Sears, Roebuck & Co's special	7.95	9.65	10.00	11.90
Full 17 Jeweled Edgemere, S., R. & Co's special make	8.25	9.95	10.30	12.20
Full 17 Jeweled Dueber Grand Hampden, adjusted	12.88	13.23	15.40	16.00
Full 17 Jeweled New Railway Hampden, adjusted	19.88	20.23	22.40	23.00
Full 21 Jeweled John Hancock Hampden, adjusted	22.31	22.66	24.83	25.43
Full 21 Jeweled Special Railway Hampden, adjusted	23.93	24.28	26.45	27.05
Full 23 Jeweled New Railway Hampden, adjusted	26.38	26.73	Not Made	Not Made
Full 23 Jeweled Special Railway Hampden, adjusted	32.03	32.38	34.55	35.15
Full 17 Jeweled Sears, Roebuck & Co's Special, especially adjusted. This is the greatest watch value ever offered	12.68	13.00	16.20	16.80

$5.52 TO $34.55

SEARS GOLD FILLED. GUARANTEED FOR 20 YEARS.

No. 4C3033 Open Face, Screw Back and Bezel.
No. 4C3035 Hunting Style.

JOHN C. DUEBER GOLD FILLED.
GUARANTEED FOR 20 YEARS.

No. 4C3028 Open Face, Screw Back and Bezel.
No. 4C3030 Hunting Style.

$5.52 TO $34.55

This illustration shows how our **12 Jeweled Edgemere** looks; see description on page 190. We fit it in any case on this page for $6.90 to $10.50 according to make.

Regarding Engravings

We generally have exact patterns; when not procurable we will send a very similar new design.

$5.52 TO $34.55

FOR 20 CENTS

We furnish a beautiful plush Presentation Case to fit any watch.

See No. 4C2000, on page 192.

ILLINOIS WATCH CASE CO. GOLD FILLED.
GUARANTEED FOR 20 YEARS.

No. 4C3037 Open Face, Screw Back and Bezel.
No. 4C3039 Hunting Style.

ILLINOIS WATCH CASE CO. GOLD FILLED.
GUARANTEED FOR 20 YEARS.

No. 4C3041 Open Face, Screw Back and Bezel. Engraved as illustrated.
No. 4C3043 Open Face. Plain Polished.
No. 4C3045 Open Face. Engine Turned.
No. 4C3047 Hunting Style. Engraved as illustrated.
No. 4C3049 Hunting Style. Plain Polished.
No. 4C3051 Hunting Style. Engine Turned.

FAHY'S GOLD FILLED.
GUARANTEED FOR 20 YEARS.

No. 4C3053 Open Face, Screw Back and Bezel.
No. 4C3055 Hunting Style.

GOLD FILLED 18 SIZE Open Face and Hunting Cases

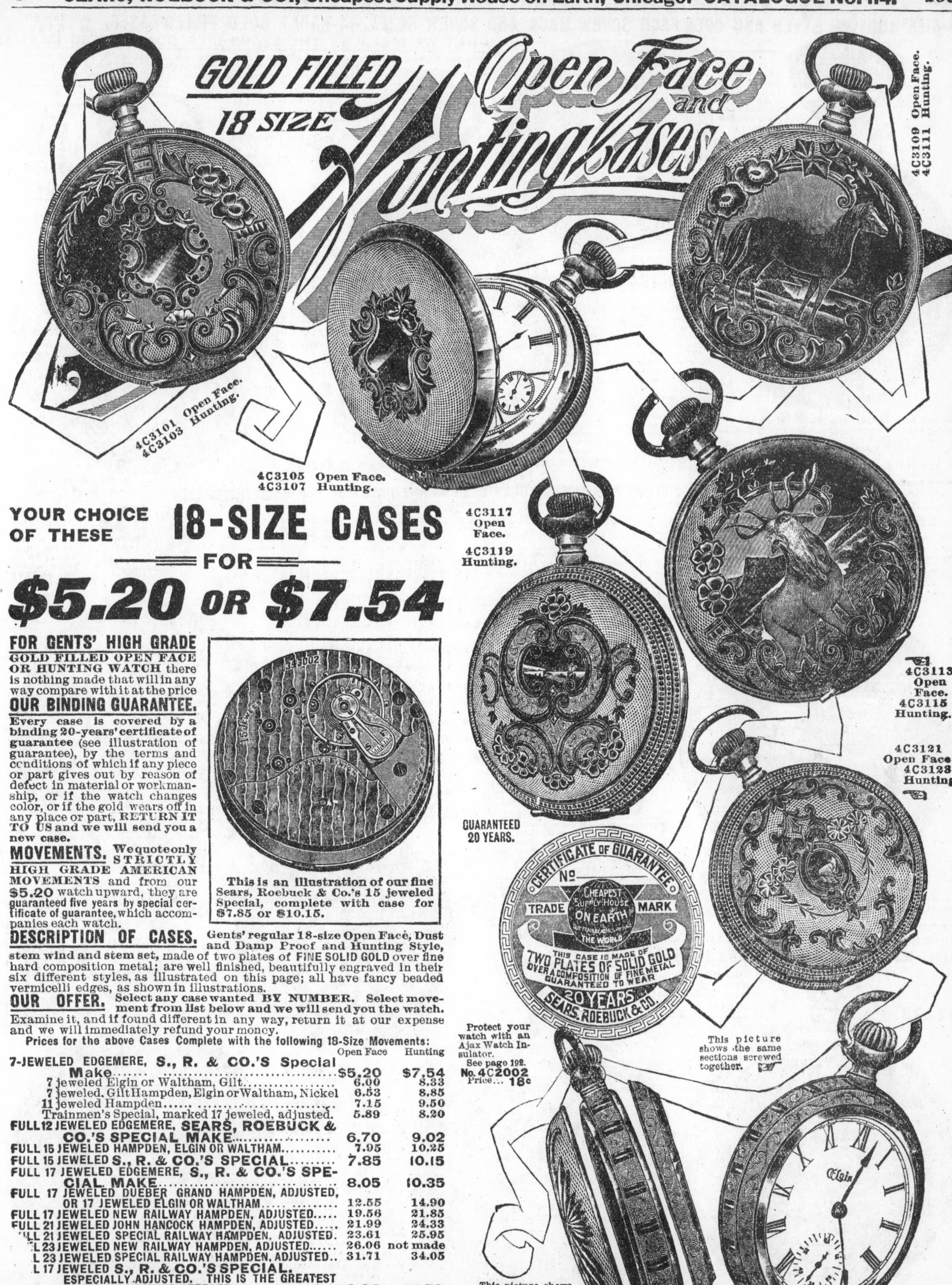

This is an illustration of our fine Sears, Roebuck & Co.'s 15 jeweled Special, complete with case for $7.85 or $10.15.

Protect your watch with an Ajax Watch Insulator. See page 192. No. 4C2002 Price... 18c

This picture shows the same sections screwed together.

This picture shows the three sections of our Open Face, Screw Back and Screw Bezel Cases.

YOUR CHOICE OF THESE 18-SIZE CASES FOR $5.20 OR $7.54

FOR GENTS' HIGH GRADE GOLD FILLED OPEN FACE OR HUNTING WATCH there is nothing made that will in any way compare with it at the price

OUR BINDING GUARANTEE. Every case is covered by a binding 20-years' certificate of guarantee (see illustration of guarantee), by the terms and conditions of which if any piece or part gives out by reason of defect in material or workmanship, or if the watch changes color, or if the gold wears off in any place or part, RETURN IT TO US and we will send you a new case.

MOVEMENTS. We quote only STRICTLY HIGH GRADE AMERICAN MOVEMENTS and from our $5.20 watch upward, they are guaranteed five years by special certificate of guarantee, which accompanies each watch.

DESCRIPTION OF CASES. Gents' regular 18-size Open Face, Dust and Damp Proof and Hunting Style, stem wind and stem set, made of two plates of FINE SOLID GOLD over fine hard composition metal; are well finished, beautifully engraved in their six different styles, as illustrated on this page; all have fancy beaded vermicelli edges, as shown in illustrations.

OUR OFFER. Select any case wanted BY NUMBER. Select movement from list below and we will send you the watch. Examine it, and if found different in any way, return it at our expense and we will immediately refund your money.

Prices for the above Cases Complete with the following 18-Size Movements:

	Open Face	Hunting
7-JEWELED EDGEMERE, S., R. & CO.'S Special Make	$5.20	$7.54
7 jeweled Elgin or Waltham, Gilt	6.00	8.33
7 jeweled, Gilt Hampden, Elgin or Waltham, Nickel	6.53	8.85
11 jeweled Hampden	7.15	9.50
Trainmen's Special, marked 17 jeweled, adjusted.	5.89	8.20
FULL 12 JEWELED EDGEMERE, SEARS, ROEBUCK & CO.'S SPECIAL MAKE	6.70	9.02
FULL 15 JEWELED HAMPDEN, ELGIN OR WALTHAM	7.95	10.25
FULL 15 JEWELED S., R. & CO.'S SPECIAL	7.85	10.15
FULL 17 JEWELED EDGEMERE, S., R. & CO.'S SPECIAL MAKE	8.05	10.35
FULL 17 JEWELED DUEBER GRAND HAMPDEN, ADJUSTED, OR 17 JEWELED ELGIN OR WALTHAM	12.55	14.90
FULL 17 JEWELED NEW RAILWAY HAMPDEN, ADJUSTED	19.56	21.85
FULL 21 JEWELED JOHN HANCOCK HAMPDEN, ADJUSTED	21.99	24.33
ᐧLL 21 JEWELED SPECIAL RAILWAY HAMPDEN, ADJUSTED.	23.61	25.95
L 23 JEWELED NEW RAILWAY HAMPDEN, ADJUSTED	26.06	not made
L 23 JEWELED SPECIAL RAILWAY HAMPDEN, ADJUSTED	31.71	34.05
L 17 JEWELED S., R. & CO.'S SPECIAL. ESPECIALLY ADJUSTED. THIS IS THE GREATEST WATCH VALUE EVER OFFERED	12.36	14.70

r Full Description of above Movements, see introductory pages to this Department

FOR $1.25 EXTRA we can furnish a fancy dial and gold hands on any watch on this page.

18-SIZE HUNTING STYLE AND OPEN FACE SCREW BACK AND SCREW BEZEL, 14-KARAT GOLD FILLED CASES, WARRANTED 25 YEARS.

WHAT WE MEAN BY THE SEARS LIFE GUARANTEED CASE.

The Sears Life Guaranteed Case is a gold filled case of the very highest quality and the nearest approach to a solid gold case manufactured. The Sears Life Guaranteed Case means that should any one of these cases wear down to the inner composition metal any time within your natural life, whether you have owned the case five years, twenty years or fifty years, return it to us, and we will, upon the receipt of same, exchange it for a brand new case of same quality, free of charge.

We recommend the **SEARS LIFE GUARANTEED CASE.**

For **$1.25** extra we can furnish a fancy dial and gold hands on any watch on this page. . . .

Fahys Gold Filled. Warranted for 25 Years.
No. 4C3240 Open Face, Screw Back and Bezel, Engraved as Illustration.
No. 4C3242 Hunting Style, Engraved as Illustration.
No. 4C3244 Open Face. Plain Polished or Engine Turned.
No. 4C3246 Hunting Style. Plain Polished or Engine Turned.

Description of Sears, Roebuck & Co.'s 17-Jeweled, 18-Size, Specially Made Movement.

Solid nickel through and through, 17 jewels, adjusted. Full plate, fancy solid gold damaskeened finish, lever escapement, five pair gold settings, full compensation double cut expansion balance wheel, adjusted to isochronism and position, patent micrometer regulator, genuine ruby jeweled pin, highly polished bevel edge screws, fully protecting dust band, safety pinion, double sunk, white enameled dial and sunk second hand dial. The superior construction of this movement adapts it to the most exacting service.

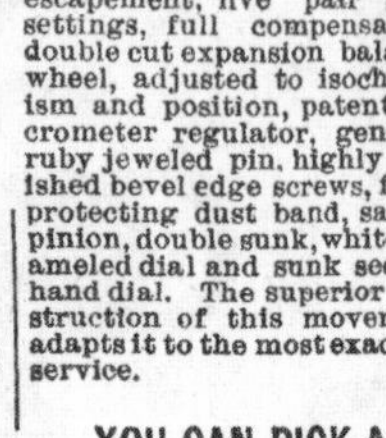

John C. Dueber Gold Filled. Warranted for 25 Years
No. 4C3248 Open Face, Screw Back and Bezel.
No. 4C3250 Hunting Style.

Sears Gold Filled. Life Guarantee.
No. 4C3252 Open Face, Screw Back and Bezel.
No. 4C3254 Hunting Style.

YOU CAN PICK ANY OF THESE DESIGNS AND HAVE THE BEST.

$9.85 complete with the EDGEMERE MOVEMENT

ELGIN AND WALTHAM WATCHES QUOTED ON PAGES 216 TO 218.

WE FIT THESE CASES WITH THE FOLLOWING 18-SIZE MOVEMENTS	4C3248 4C3264 4C3272	4C3240 4C3244 4C3260	4C3250 4C3266 4C3274	4C3242 4C3246 4C3262	4C3252 4C3256 4C3268	4C3254 4C3258 4C3270
7 Jeweled Edgemere, Sears, Roebuck & Co.'s Special Make	$7.59	$9.20	$9.89	10.55	$9.85	11.55
7 Jeweled Hampden. Gilt	9.18	10.80	11.48	12.15	11.45	13.15
11 Jeweled Hampden	9.55	11.17	11.85	12.52	11.82	13.52
Full 12 Jeweled Edgemere, Sears, Roebuck & Co.'s Special Make	9.38	11.00	11.68	12.35	11.65	13.35
Full 15 Jeweled Hampden	10.63	11.90	12.93	13.25	12.55	14.25
Full 15 Jeweled Sears, Roebuck & Co.'s Special	9.80	11.85	[illegible]	13.20	12.45	14.15
Full 17 Jeweled Edgemere, Sears, Roebuck & Co.'s Special Make	10.73	12.00	[illegible]	13.38	12.80	14.40
Full 17 Jeweled Dueber Grand Hampden, adjusted	14.95	16.60	17.25	17.95	17.25	18.95
Full 17 Jeweled New Railway Hampden, adjusted	21.95	23.60	24.25	24.90	24.25	25.90
Full 21 Jeweled John Hancock Hampden, adjusted	24.38	26.00	26.68	27.35	26.65	28.35
Full 21 Jeweled Special Railway Hampden, adjusted	26.00	27.62	[illegible]	29.00	28.27	30.00
Full 23 Jeweled New Railway Hampden, adjusted	28.45	30.07	Not made	Not made	30.72	Not made
Full 23 Jeweled Special Railway Hampden, adjusted	34.10	35.72	36.40	37.10	36.37	38.10
Full 17 Jeweled Sears, Roebuck & Co.'s Special. Especially adjusted. This is the greatest watch value ever offered.	14.65	16.37	16.90	17.75	17.02	18.75
Trainmen's Special, Stamped 17 Jewels, adjusted	8.39	10.00	10.69	11.35	10.65	12.35

Protect your watch with an Ajax Watch Insulator. See page 192. No. 4C2002 Price, 18c.

Sears Gold Filled. Life Guarantee.
No. 4C3256 Open Face, Screw Back and Bezel.
No. 4C3258 Hunting Style.

THE manufacturer's guarantee goes with each case sold, together with our own special written, binding guarantee. We doubly protect you. Select any one of these watches, send us your order with the distinct understanding that after the watch is received, if it is not in every way exactly as represented, perfectly satisfactory and most excellent value for the money, you can return it to us and we will refund your money.

Fahy's Co. Gold Filled. Warranted for 25 Years.
No. 4C3260 Open Face, Screw Back and Bezel.
No. 4C3262 Hunting Style.

You can buy one watch from us cheaper than your local dealer does when he buys ten elsewhere.

IF NOT SATISFIED with Your Watch try a SEARS.

FOR $1.25 extra we can furnish a fancy dial and gold hands on any watch on this page.

Ill. Watch Co. Gold Filled. Warranted for 25 Years.
No. 4C3264 Open Face, Screw Back and Bezel.
No. 4C3266 Hunting Style.

Sears Gold Filled. Life Guarantee.
No. 4C3268 Open Face, Screw Back and Bezel.
No. 4C3270 Hunting Style.

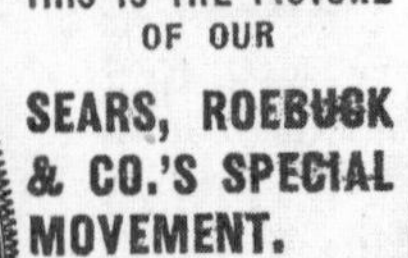

THIS IS THE PICTURE OF OUR

SEARS, ROEBUCK & CO.'S SPECIAL MOVEMENT.

IT IS A FULL 15-JEWELED

Handsomely damaskeened, patent regulator and escapement, safety pinion, jewels set in settings, guaranteed for five years and one of the best high grade movements on the market. We fit in any of these cases at $9.80 to $14.15.

Ill. Watch Co. Gold Filled. Warranted for 25 Year
No. 4C3272 Open Face, Screw Back and Bezel.
No. 4C3274 Hunting Style.

THIN MODEL 16-SIZE OPEN FACE AND HUNTING GOLD FILLED CASES.

WHAT WE MEAN BY THE SEARS LIFE GUARANTEED CASE.

The Sears Life Guaranteed Case is a **gold filled case** of the very highest quality and the nearest approach to a solid gold case manufactured. The Sears Life Guaranteed Case means that should any one of these cases wear down to the inner composition metal any time within your natural life, whether you have owned the case five years, twenty years or fifty years, return it to us and we will upon the receipt of same exchange it for a brand new case of same quality, free of charge.

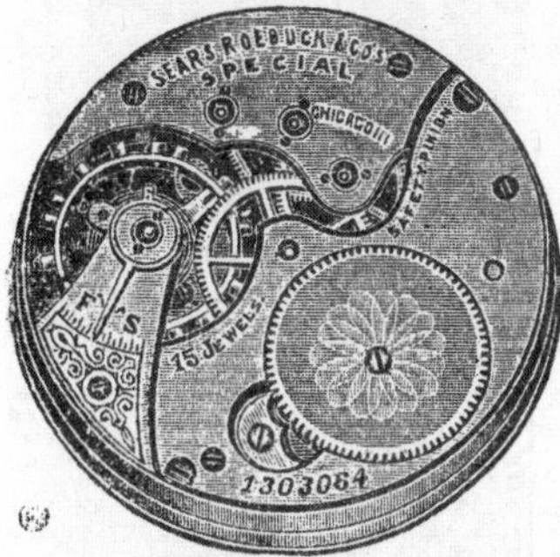

This is the picture of our Special Full 15-Jeweled Movement. Each jewel is in setting. The plates are gilded a fine Roman color. Cut expansion balance wheel. Patent pinions and we guarantee it to give entire satisfaction.

$9.20 to $19.05

GUARANTEED FOR 25 YEARS.
No. 4C3348 Fahys Open Face, Screw Back and Bezel, Engraved.
No. 4C3350 Fahys as above, Plain Polished or Engine Turned.
No. 4C3352 Fahys Hunting Style, Engraved.
No. 4C3354 Fahys as above, Plain Polished or Engine Turned.

Regarding Engravings, we generally have exact pattern. When not, we will send a very similar design.

GUARANTEED FOR 25 YEARS.
No. 4C3356 John C. Dueber Open Face, Screw Back and Bezel.
No. 4C3358 John C. Dueber Hunting Style.

"They keep time to the second," is what the inspector said of our SEARS, ROEBUCK & CO.'S Special Movement. It is specially adjusted.

$9.20 to $19.05

GUARANTEED FOR 25 YEARS.
No. 4C3360 Fahys Open Face, Screw Back and Bezel.
No. 4C3362 Fahys Hunting Style.

OUR SEARS LIFE GUARANTEED CASE IS THE BEST. See the prices **$9.80 TO $19.80** for any one of these high grade Life Guarantee Sears Cases, according to movement.

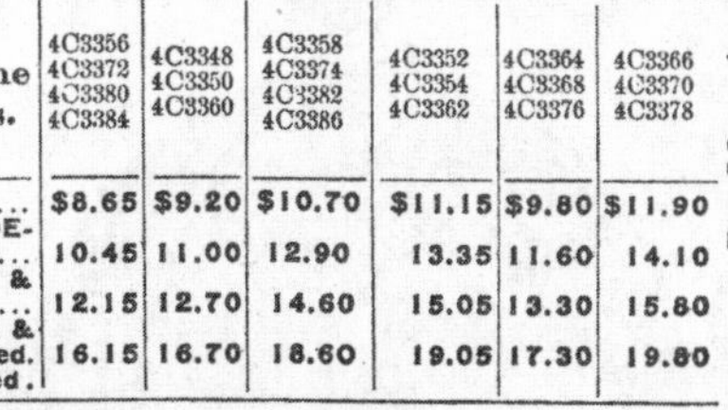

We Fit These Cases With The Following 16-Size Movements.	4C3356 4C3372 4C3380 4C3384	4C3348 4C3350 4C3360	4C3358 4C3374 4C3382 4C3386	4C3352 4C3354 4C3362	4C3364 4C3368 4C3376	4C3366 4C3370 4C3378
7 Jeweled Reliance Movement	$8.65	$9.20	$10.70	$11.15	$9.80	$11.90
Full 12 Jeweled Edgemere, SEARS, ROEBUCK & CO.'S SPECIAL MAKE	10.45	11.00	12.90	13.35	11.60	14.10
Full 15 Jeweled SEARS, ROEBUCK & CO.'S SPECIAL	12.15	12.70	14.60	15.05	13.30	15.80
Full 17 Jeweled SEARS, ROEBUCK & CO.'S SPECIAL. Especially Adjusted. Greatest Watch Movement Ever Offered.	16.15	16.70	18.60	19.05	17.30	19.80

For 20 cents we furnish a beautiful plush Presentation Case to fit any watch. See No. 4C2000, on page 192.

$9.80 to $19.80

GUARANTEED FOR LIFE.
No. 4C3364 Sears Open Face, Screw Back and Bezel.
No. 4C3366 Sears Hunting Style.

PROTECT YOUR WATCH WITH AN AJAX WATCH INSULATOR. See page 192, No. 4C2002. PRICE....18c

FOR $1.25 EXTRA WE CAN FURNISH A FANCY DIAL AND GOLD HANDS ON ANY WATCH ON THIS PAGE.

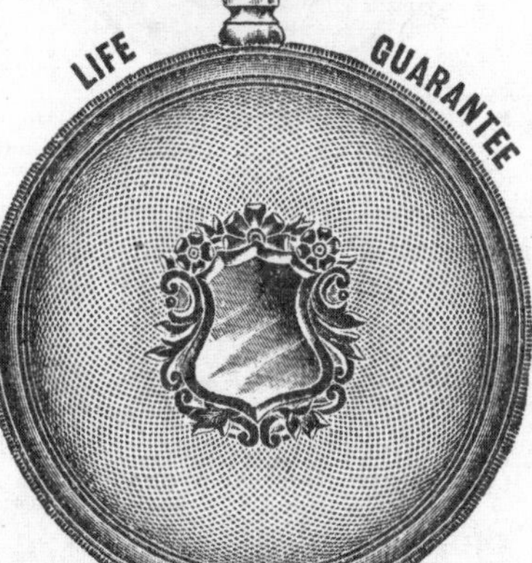

GUARANTEED FOR LIFE.
No. 4C3368 Sears Open Face, Screw Back and Bezel.
No. 4C3370 Sears Hunting Style.

$16.15 OR $18.60 Fitted with our 17 jeweled adjusted movement.

GUARANTEED FOR 25 YEARS.
No. 4C3372 Illinois Watch Case Co. Open Face, Screw Back and Bezel.
No. 4C3374 Illinois Watch Case Co. Hunting Style.

THE BEST IS THE CHEAPEST. BUY THE **SEARS LIFE** CASE.

Our New **Sears Case** is perfect in every detail.

GUARANTEED FOR LIFE.
No. 4C3376 Sears Open Face, Screw Back and Bezel.
No. 4C3378 Sears Hunting Style.

GUARANTEED FOR 25 YEARS.
No. 4C3380 Illinois Watch Case Co. Open Face, Screw Back and Bezel.
No. 4C3382 Illinois Watch Case Co. Hunting Style.

ELGIN AND WALTHAM WATCHES QUOTED ON PAGES 216 TO 218.

No charges for repairs on watches or clocks will be allowed unless our written consent is first secured in advance.

$8.65 to $18.60

GUARANTEED FOR 25 YEARS.
No. 4C3384 John C. Dueber Open Face, Screw Back and Bezel.
No. 4C3386 John C. Dueber Hunting Style.

12-SIZE THIN MODEL GOLD FILLED COMPLETE WATCHES, WARRANTED FOR 20 YEARS, AT $8.31 TO $13.95

ACCORDING TO STYLE OF CASE AND GRADE OF MOVEMENT. OPEN FACE, SCREW BACK AND BEZEL OR HUNTING STYLE CASES.

HOW OUR GOLD FILLED WARRANTED 20-YEAR CASES are made. Two thick sheets of solid gold, heavy enough to wear for the given time, are soldered over a layer of extra stiffened composition metal, making a case equal in wearing ability to that of solid gold. By this method of manufacturing we offer you a case solid gold outside and solid gold inside.

$8.31 to $13.95 for complete Watch.

TAKE YOUR CHOICE OF CASES

For $1.25 extra we can furnish a fancy dial and gold hands on any watch on this page.

This is the picture of our **12-size Edgemere movement,** fitted in any of these 12-size cases at **$9.25** for Open Face and **$11.55** for Hunting style. Prices quoted for complete watch.

No. 4C3401 Hunting Style.
No. 4C3403 Open Face, Screw Back and Bezel

No. 4C3405 Hunting Style.
No. 4C3407 Open Face, Screw Back and Bezel

No. 4C3409 Hunting Style.
No. 4C3411 Open Face, Screw Back and Beze

$9.25 and $11.55 For the COMPLETE WATCH fitted with the EDGEMERE

REGARDING THE ENGRAVINGS, we generally have the exact pattern as illustrated; if not, we send a very similar design.

Protect your watch with an Ajax Watch Insulator. See page 192, No. 4C2002. Price..........18c

OUR 12-SIZE 10-Jeweled EDGEMERE will give CORRECT TIME.

No. 4C3413 Hunting Style.
No. 4C3415 Open Face, Screw Back and Bezel

No. 4C3417 Hunting Style.
No. 4C3419 Open Face, Screw Back and Bezel

No. 4C3421 Hunting Style.
No. 4C3429 Open Face, Screw Back and Bezel

	Open Face	Hunting Style
7 Jeweled Fine Swiss Lever	$ 8.31	$10.61
7 Jeweled Elgin or Waltham	9.81	12.11
10 Jeweled EDGEMERE, SEARS, ROEBUCK & CO.'S SPECIAL MAKE	9.25	11.55
15 Jeweled Elgin or Waltham	11.65	13.95

No. 4C3423 The very latest 16-Size extra thin oxidized polished gun metal watch with illuminated dial. Send us $5.10 and 14 cents for mail charges, $5.24 in all, and we will at once ship you this newest gentlemen's watch.

The case is made with a solid back and snap front, and is absolutely dustproof; it is stem wind and stem set, is full jeweled, has exposed balance wheel, illustration shows a new mechanical construction. This watch is imported by us from Switzerland; each one is guaranteed for a term of five years. It will please you and everybody else who sees it. At $5.10, we are selling this watch at 30 per cent less than similar inferior watches are being sold for. Ea., **$5.10**

No. 4C3425 Same style as No. 4C3423, but case of solid silver, engine turned. Price.......... **$6.85**

No. 4C3427 Same style as No. 4C3423, but gold filled case guaranteed 20 years. Price.......... **$8.25**

GENTS' 16-SIZE Hunting and Open Face, 20-YEAR GOLD FILLED WATCHES.

$6.20 TO $16.25

$10.55 for the highest grade 16-size hunting, 20-year guaranteed gold filled case, complete with a 12-jeweled Edgemere Movement means a great saving to you—a price much lower than is made by any other house.

$8.00 for your choice of cases in open face, fitted with a genuine 12-jeweled Edgemere Movement.

NO CHARGES FOR REPAIRS ON WATCHES OR CLOCKS will be allowed unless our written consent is first secured in advance.

GUARANTEED Highest Grade Gold Filled Case and accompanying each case is a binding 20-year guarantee, by the terms and conditions of which, if the case wears through or changes its color within 20 years we will replace it free of charge.

$6.20 TO $16.25

ALL OPEN FACE CASES on this page are Screw Back and Screw Bezel, dust and damp proof style.

NEVER BEFORE in the history of the watch case business has the small or 16-size case sold so well as at the present time.

WE CONTROL The product of the factory on these 16-size Hunting, 20-year Gold Filled Cases, which alone makes it possible for us to make this incomparably low price.

No. 4C3431 Hunting Style. Gold Filled.
No. 4C3433 Open Face, Screw Back and Bezel. Gold Filled.

No. 4C3435 Hunting Style. Gold Filled.
No. 4C3437 Open Face, Screw Back and Bezel. Gold Filled.

No. 4C3439 Hunting Style. Gold Filled.
No. 4C3441 Open Face, Screw Back and Bezel. Gold Filled.

	Open Face	Hunting
7 jeweled Reliance Movement	$ 6.20	$ 8.75
7 jeweled Elgin or Waltham	8.20	10.75
Full 12 jeweled EDGEMERE, SEARS, ROEBUCK & CO.'S SPECIAL MAKE	8.00	10.55

	Open Face	Hunting
15 jeweled Elgin or Waltham	$11.70	$14.25
Full 15 jeweled SEARS, ROEBUCK & CO.'S SPECIAL	9.70	12.25
Full 17 jeweled SEARS, ROEBUCK & CO.'S SPECIAL, especially made. The greatest watch value ever offered	13.70	16.25

ELGIN AND WALTHAM WATCHES QUOTED ON PAGES 216 to 218.

OUR 16-SIZE THIN MODEL, SOLID SILVER AND SILVERINE WATCHES

A SOLID SILVER CASE fitted with an American made movement for $4.50. You can save 25 to 35 per cent by buying your watches from us. Why not get a watch that is reliable in every respect. We give you our written, binding guarantee with every watch we sell to be as represented. The 16-size watch is a size smaller than the popular 18-size. It does not weigh down your vest; it fits the pocket; it's the gentleman's size. The correct size for your young son. It's the doctor's size watch; in fact, it pleases all and is adapted for all.

$3.05 TO $12.00

PROTECT YOUR WATCH with an AJAX WATCH INSULATOR. See page 192. No. 4C2002 Price...18c

No. 4C3500 Silverine. Screw Back and Screw Bezel.
No. 4C3502 Solid Silver, same as above.

No. 4C3504 Solid Silver Hunting Style, gold ornamented, hand engraved, gold filled, fancy center.

No. 4C3506 Silverine, Jointed Back and Front.
No. 4C3508 Solid Silver, same as above.

16-SIZE SILVER AND SILVERINE CASES.

THE NEW OPEN FACE

New Model Dust Proof Swing Ring Case, now made in the popular 16-size. It has a screw bezel and solid back. The movement fits in a swinging inside ring. We show and quote them in solid silver and in solid nickel. Guaranteed not to tarnish.

WE HAVE REDUCED THE PRICES so that we will sell thousands of them. You need not buy until you have investigated. Price these watches at the jewelry store; don't buy unless you find what we say is true; 35 to 50 per cent cheaper than what they ask. Order one of these watches, we will ship to you by express or mail, mail is the cheaper way, and if not as described and not as you expected, return it and we will refund you your money. You take no risk in ordering goods from us.

FOR $1.25 EXTRA we can furnish a fancy dial and gold hands on any watch on this page.

FOR 20c We furnish a beautiful plush Presentation Case to fit any watch. No. 4C2000 on page 192.

$3.40 TO $12.50

OPEN FACE SWING RING.
No. 4C3509 Solid Silver.
No. 4C3511 Solid Nickel.

No. 4C3510 Silverine Hunting Style Case.
No. 4C3512 Solid Silver.
No. 4C3514 Solid Silver, engine turned.

SEARS, ROEBUCK & CO. SPECIAL 16-SIZE

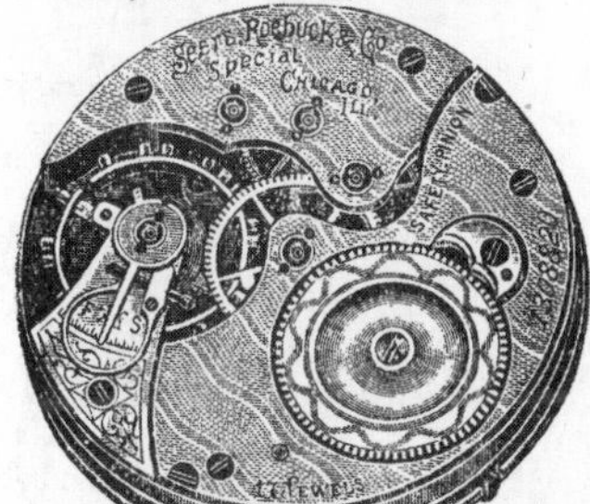

We fit these cases with the following 16-Size Movements.	4C3500 4C3506	4C3510 4C3511	4C3502	4C3508	4C3512 4C3514	4C3504	4C3509
7 Jeweled Reliance Movement	$3.05	$3.40	$4.50	$4.90	$5.00	$7.25	$5.20
Full 12 Jeweled EDGEMERE, SEARS, ROEBUCK & CO.'S SPECIAL MAKE	4.80	5.15	6.25	6.65	6.75	9.00	6.95
Full 15 Jeweled SEARS, ROEBUCK & CO.'S SPECIAL	8.55	8.90	10.00	10.40	10.50	12.75	10.70
Full 17 Jeweled SEARS, ROEBUCK & CO.'S SPECIAL. Especially Made. The Greatest Watch Value Ever Offered	10.55	10.90	12.00	12.40	12.50	14.75	12.70

LADIES' 0-SIZE DIAMOND SET GOLD FILLED WATCH FOR $8.00

A DIAMOND SET WATCH SUCH AS YOU PAY DOUBLE THE MONEY FOR ELSEWHERE. Order No. 4C3516

A DIAMOND SET, GOLD FILLED CASE with movement like this was never before offered even at wholesale in quantities at anything like **$8.00. WE TAKE ALL THESE CASES the factory makes** in order to get the price, and **$8.00** is actual cost to us under season contract with only our one small profit added. **THE DIAMOND ALONE** which is set in the case would retail in many jewelry stores for more than we ask for the complete watch.

IF YOU CONTEMPLATE MAKING A PRESENT to your wife, your sister or sweetheart, nothing can be more appropriate. $8.00 is our price, you could not with twice as much expended make a grander showing.

THINK OF IT AT $8.00 A GENUINE 20-YEAR GUARANTEED FILLED CASE, SET WITH A GENUINE DIAMOND. Fitted with a fine 7-jeweled lever movement, imported from Switzerland. $8.00 is the price.

DESCRIPTION OF CASE. Case is ladies' 0-size, one size smaller than the regular ladies' 6-size and the **most popular, handsomest and neatest size ladies' watch** made. **A genuine diamond** which is handsomely cut and polished is set in back of watch, case is **HIGHEST GRADE GOLD FILLED**, made from two plates of solid gold over an inner plate of hard composition metal, and is guaranteed by special certificate of guarantee to wear and hold its **solid gold color for twenty years**; case is hunting style, has handsome antique bow, and is one of the **VERY BEST LADIES' 0-SIZE DIAMOND SET GOLD FILLED CASES MADE.**

THE MOVEMENT is made by a celebrated watch factory in Switzerland, under special contract, so as to be able to make a lower price than on their regular high grade exporting line. It is 7-jeweled, 0-size, patent pinion, stem wind and stem set, quick train, lever escapement, and is guaranteed an accurate timekeeper for five years, and with care will last a lifetime.

No. 4C3516
The illustration shows the Diamond Set Watch.

Illustration shows movement.

BOYS' OR GENTLEMEN'S GENTEEL THIN, 12-SIZE, GOLD FILLED WATCHES.

$7.30 No. 4C3520 12-Size Hunting Style.

A small, thin, genteel, high grade, twenty-year gold filled watch, the coming size, thickness, shape and style for boy or gentleman, the neatest, most perfect watch made.

Price, $7.30 and upward, according to grade of movement. All the movements we fit in this case are 6-size. The case is made especially for that size movement.

No. 4C3520

THIS 12-SIZE GOLD FILLED CASE is gotten up in imitation of the very finest **14-karat solid gold case, extra thin model,** 12-size, two sizes smaller than the regular 16-size and three sizes smaller than the regular 18-size. **Plenty large enough for any gentleman,** not a load in the pocket, but a thin, light, neat watch and far more sensible than a heavy watch, also a **VERY POPULAR SIZE for boys.**

THIS CASE IS THE HIGHEST GRADE GOLD FILLED warranted for twenty years, a certificate of guarantee accompanying each case. It is hunting style, fine engine turned in perfect imitation of **solid gold, has solid gold antique bow and crown.**

We fit in this case the following 6-size movements:

7 Jeweled EDGEMERE, SEARS, ROEBUCK & CO.'S SPECIAL MAKE	$7.30
7 Jeweled Elgin or Waltham, Gilt	8.09
7 Jeweled No. 200 Grade Gilt Hampden, Elgin or Waltham, Nickel	8.62
12 Jeweled EDGEMERE, SEARS, ROEBUCK & CO.'S SPECIAL MAKE	8.50
11 Jeweled No. 206 Grade Hampden	10.00
Full 15 Jeweled SEARS, ROEBUCK & CO.'S SPECIAL	10.50
Full 15 Jeweled No. 213 Grade Hampden, Elgin or Waltham	10.65
Full 17 Jeweled EDGEMERE, SEARS, ROEBUCK & CO.'S SPECIAL MAKE	10.90
Full 17 Jeweled SEARS, ROEBUCK & CO.'S SPECIAL. Especially made. This is the greatest watch value ever offered	13.00

Our $1.58 Ladies' 6-Size Open Face Nickel Watch

SEND US $1.58 and mail charges, 12 cents, $1.70 in all, and we will send you this watch exactly as pictured, exactly as described.

THIS WATCH is solid nickel through and through and the case will wear forever. **The movement** is made by one of the largest companies. It is stem wind and stem set. You need not open the watch to wind or set it. **The size** is same as illustration, the ideal size for any young lady wishing an inexpensive watch for everyday use. It is a good timekeeper and while we do not guarantee it, we know it will give entire satisfaction.

12 CENTS EXTRA IF SENT BY MAIL.

The watch will reach you in perfect order and with ordinary care will wear and prove satisfactory for years.

$1.58 is our price. The best watch for the money ever offered in a Ladies' 6-Size, Nickel American Made Watch.

No. 4C3518 Order by Number

THIN MODEL 16-SIZE

SEARS, DUEBER, ELGIN GIANT AND FAHYS

GOLD FILLED, HUNTING AND OPEN FACE SCREW BACK and BEZEL, DUST and DAMP PROOF CASES.

$6.65 TO $16.95

THE SEARS GOLD FILLED CASE IS RECOMMENDED ABOVE ALL OTHERS.

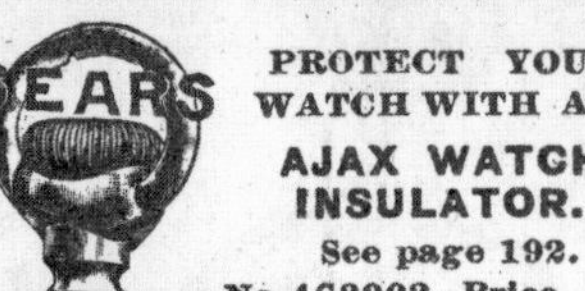

PROTECT YOUR WATCH WITH AN AJAX WATCH INSULATOR.

See page 192.

No. 4C2002 Price..18c

Picture of our 12-Jeweled EDGEMERE fitted in our SEARS CASE for $8.25.

GUARANTEED FOR 20 YEARS.
No. 4C3600 Open Face, Screw Back and Bezel, Engraved as Picture.
No. 4C3602 As above, Engine Turned or Plain Polished.
No. 4C3604 Hunting Style, Engraved as Picture.
No. 4C3606 As above, Engine Turned or Plain Polished.

GUARANTEED FOR 20 YEARS.
No. 4C3607 Open Face, Screw Back and Bezel.
No. 4C3608 Hunting Style.

$6.05 TO $16.50

GUARANTEED FOR 20 YEARS.
No. 4C3613 Open Face, Screw Back and Bezel.
No. 4C3615 Hunting Style.

GUARANTEED FOR 20 YEARS.
No. 4C3609 Open Face, Screw Back Bezel.
No. 4C3611 Hunting Style.

$8.25 fitted with the 12-Jeweled Edgemere.

THE OPEN FACE CASES SHOWN ON THIS PAGE ARE ALL SCREW BEZEL AND SCREW BACK.

THE SEARS is the latest and best made

GUARANTEED FOR 20 YEARS.
No. 4C3621 Open Face, Screw Back and Bezel.
No. 4C3623 Hunting Style.

WE FIT THESE CASES WITH THE FOLLOWING 16-SIZE MOVEMENTS:	No. 4C3607 4C3613 4C3616 4C3621 4C3624 4C3629 4C3633	No. 4C3600 4C3602 4C3609	No. 4C3608 4C3615 4C3618 4C3623 4C3626 4C3631 4C3635	No. 4C3604 4C3606 4C3611
7 Jeweled Reliance Movement	$ 6.05	$ 6.65	$ 8.60	$ 9.05
Full 12 Jeweled Edgemere, Sears, Roebuck & Co.'s Special make	8.25	8.85	10.80	11.25
Full 15 Jeweled Sears, Roebuck & Co.'s Special	9.95	10.55	12.50	12.95
Full 17 Jeweled Sears, Roebuck & Co.'s Special. Especially made	13.95	14.55	16.50	16.95
The Greatest Watch Value Ever Offered.				

ELGIN AND WALTHAM WATCHES QUOTED ON PAGES 216 TO 218.

GUARANTEED FOR 20 YEARS.
No. 4C3616 Open Face, Screw Back and Bezel.
No. 4C3618 Hunting Style.

$13.95 fitted with our 17 Jeweled Adjusted Movement.

$6.05 TO $16.50

GUARANTEED FOR 20 YEARS.
No. 4C3624 Open Face, Screw Back and Bezel.
No. 4C3626 Hunting Style.

14 CENTS Will carry any of these watches by registered mail to any part of the United States.

GUARANTEED FOR 20 YEARS.
No. 4C3629 Open Face, Screw Back and Bezel.
No. 4C3631 Hunting Style.

GUARANTEED FOR 20 YEARS.
No. 4C3633 Open Face, Screw Back and Bezel
No. 4C3635 Hunting Style.

FOR 20 CENTS we furnish a beautiful plush Presentation Case to fit any watch. See No. 4C2000 on page 192.

No. 4C3636

An 18-Size Open Face Alarm Watch, the very latest invention out. You can set this watch to alarm any time you desire. The alarm is loud enough to awake the average sleeper. Full directions on a printed slip accompany every watch shipped. Price, $6.35. This watch is imported from Switzerland. It is stem wind and stem set, lever escapement, all important bearings are jeweled. It is guaranteed an accurate timekeeper. The case is gun metal, oxidized black. The illustration shows the exact size of the watch. Bear in mind this watch is not an intricate affair, but it is a simple practical device. It is a novelty wanted by many, but never until now has a practical one been placed on the market. We guarantee them to be perfect in every detail, and our five-year written guarantee goes with every one sold.

No. 4C3636 Price $6.35

12-SIZE OPEN FACE OR HUNTING STYLE DUEBER HAMPDEN COMPLETE WATCHES

SOLID GOLD AND GOLD FILLED CASES.

WE OFFER AT $14.62 THE 12-SIZE HAMPDEN WATCH CO.'S COMPLETE WATCH. The case is guaranteed 14-karat gold filled and warranted for a term of 25 years' wear. The movement is the General Stark, 15 jeweled, exactly as described. Never before in the history of the watch business have such values been offered for the money.

THE MOVEMENTS. We can recommend any one of the movements quoted as being an accurate timekeeper, perfectly finished in every detail, stem wind and lever set, all the latest modern improvements being employed. They positively are up to date in every respect.

Protect your watch with an AJAX WATCH INSULATOR See page 192. No. 4C2002 Price, 18c

$14.62 TO $44.50

FOR $1.25 EXTRA we can furnish a fancy dial and gold hands on any watch on this page.

FOR 20 CENTS EXTRA we can supply a PLUSH PRESENTATION CASE for any watch we sell. See page 192.

25 CENTS will carry any watch to any part of the United States by express.

No. 4C3700 Open Face Jointed Case, 14-karat gold filled, warranted 25 years.
No. 4C3702 Hunting Style Case, same make and quality as above.
No. 4C3704 Hunting Style Case, 14-karat solid gold.
No. 4C3706 Open Face Style, 14-karat solid gold.

No. 4C3707 Open Face Jointed Case, 14 karat gold filled, warranted 25 years.
No. 4C3709 Hunting Style Case, same make and quality as above.
No. 4C3711 Hunting Style Case, 14-karat solid gold.
No. 4C3713 Open Face Style, 14-karat solid gold.

No. 4C3715 Open Face Jointed Case, 14-karat gold filled, warranted 25 years.
No. 4C3717 Hunting Style Case, same make and quality as above.
No. 4C3719 Hunting Style Case, 14-karat solid gold.
No. 4C3721 Open Face Style, 14-karat solid gold.

No. 4C3723 Open Face Jointed Case, warranted 25 years.
No. 4C3725 Hunting Style Case, same make and quality as above.
No. 4C3727 Hunting Style Case, 14-karat solid gold.
No. 4C3729 Open Face Style, 14-karat solid gold.

Description of the Dueber Grand Movement.

Nickel, 17 ruby and sapphire jewels in composition settings, adjusted Breguet hair spring, patent regulator, mean time screws, bright flat screws, elegantly engraved and damaskeened, gold lettering, Arabic and Roman dial, red marginal figures.

Compare our prices with those of others and be convinced that we are the cheapest.	No. 4C3707 Open Face Gold Filled	No. 4C3700 No. 4C3715 No. 4C3723 Open Face Gold Filled	No. 4C3702 No. 4C3717 No. 4C3725 Hunting Gold Filled	No. 4C3709 Hunting Gold Filled	No. 4C3704 No. 4C3719 No. 4C3727 Hunting Solid Gold	No. 4C3711 Hunting Solid Gold	No. 4C3706 No. 4C3721 No. 4C3729 Open Face Solid Gold	No. 4C3713 Open Face Solid Gold
With 15 jeweled General Stark	$14.40	$14.62	$15.08	$14.85	$30.15	$27.00	$27.45	$24.30
With 17 jeweled Dueber Grand	17.10	17.38	17.85	17.55	32.85	30.00	30.00	27.00
With 21 jeweled John Hancock	28.80	29.35	29.80	29.25	44.50	41.40	41.85	38.70

$2.50 16-SIZE GUN METAL

No. 4C3698 Gentlemen's 16-size, thin model, open face, plain polished, gun metal watch. Has beautiful fancy dial as illustration shows. The movement is imported from Switzerland, has jeweled cylinder escapement and damaskeened nickeled plates. It is recommended to all who desire a cheap and durable watch. Sold for twice what we ask for by all the leading jewelers in the country. Price..........$2.50

6-SIZE SILVERINE. SOMETHING NEW.

$2.90 TO $8.92

OUR 6-SIZE SILVERINE WATCHES in hunting and open face style. Silverine is one of the newly compounded metals. It looks like silver, wears like silver, has the same color and appearance as silver but is very much tougher, and costs less. At $2.90 to $8.92 we are offering these silverine ladies' watches.

THE MOVEMENTS are all representative makes, each one of them is guaranteed an accurate timekeeper and **WE FULLY WARRANT THEM FOR A TERM OF 5 YEARS** against defective material or workmanship.

No. 4C3741 Open Face Style.
No. 4C3743 Hunting Style.

6-SIZE SILVERINE.	No. 4C3741	No. 4C3743
7 jeweled EDGEMERE, SEARS, ROEBUCK & CO.'S SPECIAL MAKE	$2.90	$3.22
7 jeweled No. 200 Grade Hampden, Gilt	4.49	6.81
12 jeweled EDGEMERE, SEARS, ROEBUCK & CO.'S SPECIAL MAKE	4.70	7.00
11 jeweled No. 206 Grade Hampden	5.62	5.94
Full 15 jeweled SEARS, ROEBUCK & CO.'S SPECIAL	5.92	6.24
Full 15 jeweled No. 213 Grade Hampden	6.25	6.57
Full 17 jeweled EDGEMERE, SEARS, ROEBUCK & CO.'S SPECIAL MAKE	6.40	6.72
Full 17 jeweled SEARS, ROEBUCK & CO.'S SPECIAL	8.60	8.92
Especially made. This is the greatest watch value ever offered.		

12-SIZE SILVER AND SOLID NICKEL WATCHES

LATEST STYLE. NEWEST MODEL. HUNTING CASE OR OPEN FACE.

THESE WATCH CASES are solid silver or solid nickel through and through, fitted with the

10-JEWELED EDGEMERE MOVEMENT,

manufactured for our especial use and guaranteed for a term of five years, makes an ideal watch. It is large enough for time keeping, yet small enough not to bulge or weigh down the pocket. This size watch is recognized by all experts as being perfect.

$5.90 TO $8.05

Description of the Edgemere Movement.

12-SIZE open face or hunting; nickel bright polished damaskeened plates; 10 fine ruby jewels, Breguet hair spring, cut balance, patent pinions, beveled screw heads, exposed winding arrangement, double sunk dial, moon hands and red marginal figures.

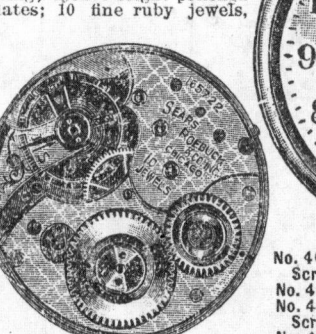

No. 4C3744 Nickel, Open Face Screw Back and Bezel......$5.90
No. 4C3746 Nickel, Hunting. 6.22
No. 4C3748 Silver, Open Face Screw Back and Bezel...... 7.22
No. 4C3750 Silver, Hunting.. 8.05

ILLUSTRATION SHOWS the Edgemere Movement fitted in any one of the above cases at $5.90 to $8.05, according to style and kind of case.

$3.30 AND $4.05

Boys' Size. Solid Silver.

AT $3.30 AND $4.05 WE OFFER A

BOYS' SOLID SILVER WATCH

Either style, open face at $3.30 or Hunting at $4.05 each. These watches are the ideal size for a boy. The exact size as illustration. They are solid silver through and through, stem wind and stem set, beautifully hand engraved, perfect joints, close fitting lids, heavy and durable. Just the kind of watch your boy should have. The movements of these watches are imported Swiss ones. They have 7 jewels, the bridging beautifully damaskeened, perfectly finished throughout and will keep very good time. Never before has such a splendid watch been offered for any thing like the price. $3.30 in Open Face or $4.05 in Hunting. ORDER BY NUMBER. Please your boy, order one and let him have a genuine Solid Silver Watch.

No. 4C3752 Hunting Style. Price....................$4.05
No. 4C3754 Open Face, Price.................... 3.30

ELGIN and WALTHAM WATCHES quoted on pages 216 to 218.

$6.40 TO $12.30

LADIES' 6-SIZE GOLD FILLED CASES, GUARANTEED FOR 25 YEARS.

WHAT WE MEAN BY THE SEARS LIFE GUARANTEED CASE. The Sears Life Guaranteed case is a gold filled case of the very highest quality and the nearest approach to a solid gold case manufactured. The Sears Life Guaranteed Case means that should any one of these cases wear down to the inner composition metal any time within your natural life, whether you have owned the case five years, twenty years or fifty years, return it to us, and we will upon the receipt of same exchange it for a brand new case of same quality, free of charge.

$8.05 TO $13.75

At $12.07 our Sears Case, fitted with our 12-Jeweled 6-size Edgemere movement gives you the best case made and 5-year guaranteed movement.

You will be better satisfied if you have your watch shipped by express.

For $1.25 extra we can furnish a fancy dial and gold hands on any watch on this page.

$9.05 TO $14.75

No. 4C3836 6-size, solid silver case, inlaid with solid gold ornaments and gold shield on back.
Fitted with 7-jeweled Edgemere. Price..........$6.40
Fitted with 12-jeweled Edgemere. Price..........$8.45
Fitted with 17-jeweled Edgemere. Price..........$10.50
Fitted with 15-jeweled Sears, Roebuck & Co.'s Special. Price..........$9.75
Fitted with 17-jeweled Sears, Roebuck & Co.'s Special. Price..........$12.30

Illinois Watch Case Co. No. 4C3838 14-K. Filled. Warranted 25 years.

Illinois Watch Case Co. No. 4C3842 14-K. Filled. Warranted 25 years.

No. 4C3844 Sears' 14-K. Filled. Warranted for life.

BEAR IN MIND YOU CAN BUY NOTHING BETTER IN 17-JEWELED GRADE THAN THE SEARS, ROEBUCK & CO. MOVEMENT.

$11.40 TO $17.10

Protect your watch with an AJAX WATCH INSULATOR. See page 192, No. 4C2002. Price........ 18c

Illinois Watch Case Co. No. 4C3840 Raised Gold Ornamentation, 14-K. filled. Warranted 25 years.

For 20 Cents we furnish a beautiful Plush Presentation Case to fit any watch. See No. 4C2000 on page 192.

$9.05 AND UP.

Regarding the engravings: We generally have the exact pattern; if not, we will send a very similar design.

No 4C3850 Fahys' 14-K. Filled. Warranted 25 years.

No. 4C3852 Fahys' 14-K. Filled. Warranted 25 years.
No. 4C3854 Same make. Engine turned.

No. 4C3856 Sears' 14-K. Filled Warranted for life.

No. 4C3846 Raised Gold Ornamentation, Fahys' 14-K. Filled. Warranted 25 years.
No. 4C3848 Same as above. Diamond set.

All Watches shown on this page are Hunting Style.

These cases are all hand engraved and hand chased.

$9.05 AND UP.

$10.35 TO $16.05

SEARS, ROEBUCK & CO

Special 6-Size Movement.

Nickel, very elaborately designed, damaskeened finish, 17 jeweled, full compensation balance wheel, patent safety center pinion, ruby roller and pallet escapement, blued beveled edge, highly polished screws.

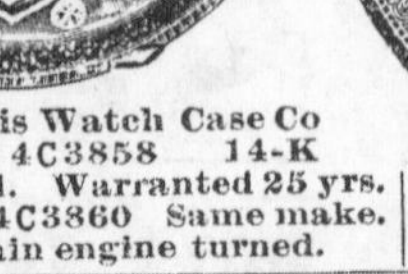

Illinois Watch Case Co No. 4C3858 14-K Filled. Warranted 25 yrs. No. 4C3860 Same make. Plain engine turned.

No. 4C3862 Dueber 14-K. Filled. Warranted 25 years.
No. 4C3864 Same make. Plain engine turned.

No. 4C3866 Sears' 14-K. Filled. Warranted for life.

Illinois Watch Case Co. No. 4C3868 14-K. Filled. Warranted 25 years. Plain polished, set with 5 genuine rose diamonds.

Movement consists of three separate bridges, artistically arranged, plain white, hard enameled dial and fancy blued steel hands. We absolutely guarantee it to give perfect satisfaction.

WE FIT THESE CASES WITH THE FOLLOWING 6-SIZE MOVEMENTS:	No. 4C3850 No. 4C3852 No. 4C3854	4C3838, 4C3860 4C3842, 4C3862 4C3858, 4C3864	No. 4C3840	No. 4C3846	No. 4C3848	No. 4C3844 No. 4C3856 No. 4C3866	No. 4C3868
7 Jeweled Edgemere, SEARS, ROEBUCK & CO.'S SPECIAL MAKE	$ 8.55	$ 8.05	$10.80	$11.40	$15.20	$9.05	$10.35
7 Jeweled Hampden. Gilt	9.62	9.12	12.37	12.97	16.27	10.12	11.92
11 Jeweled Hampden	11.27	10.77	13.52	14.12	17.92	11.77	13.07
Full 12 Jeweled Edgemere, SEARS, ROEBUCK & CO.'S SPECIAL MAKE	11.57	9.22	12.57	13.17	16.47	12.07	12.12
Full 15 Jeweled Hampden	11.90	11.40	14.15	14.75	18.55	12.40	13.70
Full 15 Jeweled SEARS, ROEBUCK & CO.'S SPECIAL	12.66	10.24	14.00	14.60	18.40	13.13	13.55
Full 17 Jeweled Edgemere, SEARS, ROEBUCK & CO.'S SPECIAL MAKE	13.00	10.59	14.35	14.95	18.75	13.48	13.90
Full 17 Jeweled SEARS, ROEBUCK & CO.'S SPECIAL. The Greatest Watch Value ever offered	14.25	13.75	16.50	17.10	20.90	14.75	16.05

ELGIN AND WALTHAM WATCHES QUOTED ON PAGES 216 TO 218.

PROTECT YOUR WATCH WITH AN AJAX WATCH INSULATOR. SEE PAGE 192, No. 4C2002. Price, 18 CENTS.

OUR SPECIAL Ladies' GOLD FILLED Watches 6 SIZE GUARANTEED 20 years

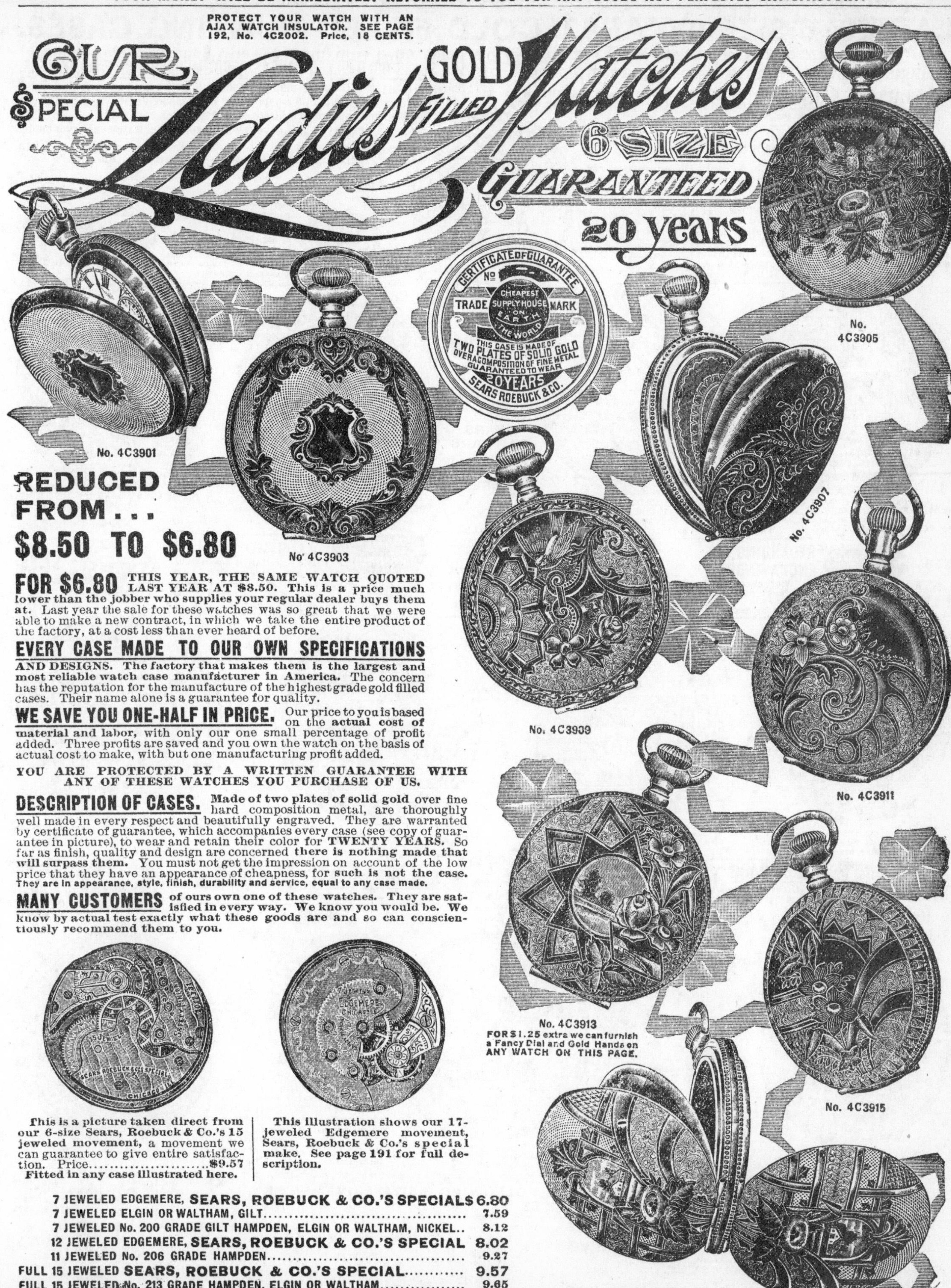
CERTIFICATE OF GUARANTEE
No
TRADE CHEAPEST SUPPLY HOUSE ON EARTH THE WORLD MARK
THIS CASE IS MADE OF TWO PLATES OF SOLID GOLD OVER A COMPOSITION OF FINE METAL GUARANTEED TO WEAR 20 YEARS
SEARS ROEBUCK & CO.

No. 4C3901

No. 4C3903

No. 4C3905

No. 4C3907

No. 4C3909

No. 4C3911

No. 4C3913

FOR $1.25 extra we can furnish a Fancy Dial and Gold Hands on ANY WATCH ON THIS PAGE.

No. 4C3915

No. 4C3917

REDUCED FROM... $8.50 TO $6.80

FOR $6.80 THIS YEAR, THE SAME WATCH QUOTED LAST YEAR AT $8.50. This is a price much lower than the jobber who supplies your regular dealer buys them at. Last year the sale for these watches was so great that we were able to make a new contract, in which we take the entire product of the factory, at a cost less than ever heard of before.

EVERY CASE MADE TO OUR OWN SPECIFICATIONS AND DESIGNS. The factory that makes them is the largest and most reliable watch case manufacturer in America. The concern has the reputation for the manufacture of the highest grade gold filled cases. Their name alone is a guarantee for quality.

WE SAVE YOU ONE-HALF IN PRICE. Our price to you is based on the actual cost of material and labor, with only our one small percentage of profit added. Three profits are saved and you own the watch on the basis of actual cost to make, with but one manufacturing profit added.

YOU ARE PROTECTED BY A WRITTEN GUARANTEE WITH ANY OF THESE WATCHES YOU PURCHASE OF US.

DESCRIPTION OF CASES. Made of two plates of solid gold over fine hard composition metal, are thoroughly well made in every respect and beautifully engraved. They are warranted by certificate of guarantee, which accompanies every case (see copy of guarantee in picture), to wear and retain their color for TWENTY YEARS. So far as finish, quality and design are concerned there is nothing made that will surpass them. You must not get the impression on account of the low price that they have an appearance of cheapness, for such is not the case. They are in appearance, style, finish, durability and service, equal to any case made.

MANY CUSTOMERS of ours own one of these watches. They are satisfied in every way. We know you would be. We know by actual test exactly what these goods are and so can conscientiously recommend them to you.

This is a picture taken direct from our 6-size Sears, Roebuck & Co.'s 15 jeweled movement, a movement we can guarantee to give entire satisfaction. Price........................$9.57 Fitted in any case illustrated here.

This illustration shows our 17-jeweled Edgemere movement, Sears, Roebuck & Co.'s special make. See page 191 for full description.

7 JEWELED EDGEMERE, SEARS, ROEBUCK & CO.'S SPECIAL	$6.80
7 JEWELED ELGIN OR WALTHAM, GILT	7.59
7 JEWELED No. 200 GRADE GILT HAMPDEN, ELGIN OR WALTHAM, NICKEL	8.12
12 JEWELED EDGEMERE, SEARS, ROEBUCK & CO.'S SPECIAL	8.02
11 JEWELED No. 206 GRADE HAMPDEN	9.27
FULL 15 JEWELED SEARS, ROEBUCK & CO.'S SPECIAL	9.57
FULL 15 JEWELED No. 213 GRADE HAMPDEN, ELGIN OR WALTHAM	9.65
FULL 17 JEWELED EDGEMERE, SEARS, ROEBUCK & CO.'S SPECIAL	9.90
FULL 17 JEWELED SEARS, ROEBUCK & CO.'S SPECIAL	12.50

LADIES' 6-SIZE 10-KARAT GOLD FILLED HUNTING CASES.

At $7.35 or $7.85 your choice of cases, any one on this page, fitted with the 7-Jeweled Edgemere Movement.

GUARANTEED BY THE MAKER FOR A TERM OF TWENTY YEARS.

AT $8.62 OR $10.12 we offer you the choice of any case shown on this page fitted with our 12-Jeweled, 6-Size Edgemere, illustrated on page 191.

THE SEARS GOLD FILLED CASE IS RECOMMENDED ABOVE ALL OTHERS.

Being made of two extra heavy plates of solid gold over a hard composition metal, will wear longer than any other gold filled case made, and is the handsomest, best finished and best fitting gold filled watch case made. If you select a Sears case you will have the best gold filled watch case ever made.

FOR $1.25 EXTRA we can furnish fancy dial and gold hands on any watch on this page.

OUR WRITTEN BINDING GUARANTEE

goes with each and every watch we sell; the manufacturer likewise warrants them to be exactly as represented.

$7.35 to $13.05

12 cents will carry a ladies' watch to any point in the United States by registered mail; 25 cents to any point by express.

Illustration of our 17-Jeweled, 6-Size Edgemere.

FOR **$10.80** we fit the ABOVE MOVEMENT in our SEARS 20 YEARS GOLD FILLED CASE.

OUR 6-SIZE 17-JEWEL SEARS, ROEBUCK & CO. movement is the most reliable ladies' size movement made.

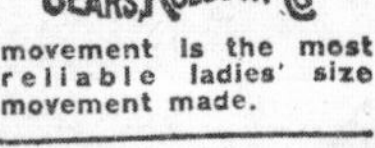

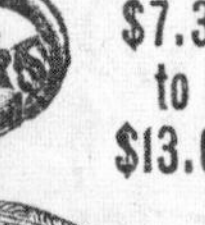

$7.35 to $13.05

ILLINOIS WATCH CASE CO.
No. 4C4001 10-K. Gold Filled, 20 years guaranteed.
No. 4C4002 Engine Turned.

ILLINOIS WATCH CASE CO.
No. 4C4005 10-K. Gold Filled, 20 years guaranteed.

ILLINOIS WATCH CASE CO.
No. 4C4007 10-K. Gold Filled, 20 years guaranteed.

No. 4C4009 SEARS' 10K. Gold Filled 20 years guaranteed.

$7.85 to $13.55

REGARDING THE ENGRAVINGS

We generally have the exact pattern. If not, we will send a very similar design.

You will not be disappointed in the Timekeeping Qualities of the SEARS, ROEBUCK & CO. Special Movement.

FOR 20 CENTS

We furnish a beautiful Plush Presentation Case to fit any watch. See No. 4C2000 on page 192.

$7.35 to $13.05

FAHYS.
No. 4C4010 10-K. Gold Filled, 20 years guaranteed.

ILLINOIS WATCH CASE CO.
No. 4C4012 10-K. Gold Filled, 20 years guaranteed.

FAHYS.
No. 4C4014 10-K. Gold Filled, 20 years guaranteed.
No. 4C4016 Engine turned.

No. 4C4019 SEARS' 10-K. Gold Filled, 20 years guaranteed.

$7.35 to $13.05

COMPARE our watch prices with those quoted by others and note the difference in our favor.

This is an illustration of our 6-Size Sears, Roebuck & Co. 15-Jeweled Movement. A movement we can recommend as an accurate timekeeper. This movement fitted in a Sears case at $9.64 is a bargain.

SEE OUR PRICES; make no mistake. Any one of these watches from $7.35 to $13.55.

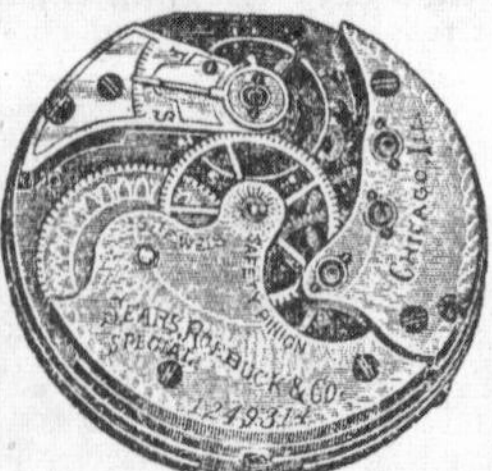

This is an illustration of our 6-Size Sears, Roebuck & Co. Special 17-Jeweled Movement. We guarantee this movement to give you absolute satisfaction. Fitted in the Sears case at $13.05 makes it a rare bargain.

$7.35 to $13.05

DUEBER.
No. C4020 10-K. Gold Filled, 20 years guaranteed.

ILLINOIS WATCH CASE CO.
No. 4C4022 10-K. Gold Filled, 20 years guaranteed.

No. 4C4025 SEARS' 10-K. Gold Filled, 20 years guaranteed.

WE FIT ANY ONE OF THESE CASES WITH THE FOLLOWING 6-SIZE MOVEMENTS AT $7.35 TO $13.55.

	No. 4C4010, No. 4C4014, No. 4C4016	No. 4C4001, No. 4C4002, No. 4C4005, No. 4C4007, No. 4C4009, No. 4C4012, No. 4C4019, No. 4C4020, No. 4C4022, No. 4C4025
7 jeweled EDGEMERE, SEARS, ROEBUCK & CO.'S SPECIAL MAKE	$7.85	$ 7.35
7 jeweled No. 200 Grade Hampden, Gilt	9.40	8.94
12 jeweled EDGEMERE, SEARS, ROEBUCK & CO.'S SPECIAL MAKE	10.12	8.62
11 jeweled No. 206 Grade Hampden	10.57	10.07
Full 15 jeweled SEARS, ROEBUCK & CO.'S SPECIAL	11.15	9.64
Full 15 jeweled No. 213 Grade Hampden	11.20	10.70
Full 17 jeweled EDGEMERE, SEARS, ROEBUCK & CO.'S SPECIAL MAKE	11.30	10.80
Full 17 jeweled SEARS, ROEBUCK & CO.'S SPECIAL. ESPECIALLY MADE. This is the greatest watch value ever offered	13.55	13.05

ELGIN AND WALTHAM WATCHES QUOTED ON PAGES 216 to 218.

LADIES' 0-SIZE 25-YEAR GOLD FILLED WATCHES

AND SEARS GOLD FILLED CASES GUARANTEED FOR LIFE.

MANUFACTURED BY THE MOST REPRESENTATIVE GOLD FILLED CASE MANUFACTURERS IN THE WORLD.

THE QUALITY OF THESE CASES is the highest. They are 14-karat gold filled, guaranteed to wear for a term of 25 years. Nothing superior made. No case better in the market. They lead them all. The size is the very latest and best adapted for ladies' use. The designs are artistic copies of the highest grade solid gold patterns. The general finish is the same as in solid gold. They are hand engraved throughout. The antique bow and crown, lips and joints are perfect in every detail.

THE GUARANTEE GIVEN: Each case is warranted by the maker, and we send, together with this, our own special binding guarantee.

WHAT WE MEAN BY THE SEARS LIFE GUARANTEED CASE. The Sears Life Guaranteed Case is a gold filled case of the very highest quality and the nearest approach to a solid gold case manufactured. The Sears Life Guaranteed Case means that should any one of these cases wear down to the inner composition metal any time within your natural life, whether you have owned the case five years, twenty years or fifty years, return it to us, and we will upon the receipt of same exchange it for a brand new case of same quality, free of charge.

DESCRIPTION OF OUR 0-SIZE, 15-JEWELED EDGEMERE MOVEMENT. Solid nickel plates through and through, 15 finely polished ruby jewels, cut balance, lever escapement, patent pinion, perfect in finish and detail, and warranted for 5 years.

$8.30 TO $11.60

For $1.25 Extra WE CAN FURNISH FANCY DIAL AND GOLD HANDS ON ANY WATCH ON THIS PAGE.

No. 4C4132
14-karat. Guaranteed for 25 years' wear. Made by the Illinois Watch Case Co.

No. 4C4134
14-karat. Guaranteed for 25 years' wear. Made by the Illinois Watch Case Co.

REGARDING THE ENGRAVINGS, WE GENERALLY HAVE THE EXACT PATTERN; IF NOT, WE WILL SEND A VERY SIMILAR DESIGN.

This is a picture taken direct from our 15-jeweled Edgemere, the only and best 15 jeweled movement on the market. We warrant it for five years.

The higher the grade the better the time. We advocate higher jeweling than the 7-jewel grades.

No. 4C4136 Gold Ornamented. 14-karat. Guaranteed for 25 years' wear. Made by the Illinois Watch Case Co.

$14.75 TO $18.05

No. 4C4138 Gold Ornamented and Diamond Set. 14-karat. Guaranteed for 25 years' wear. Made by the Illinois Watch Case Co.

25 cents will carry a ladies' watch by express.

No. 4C4140
14-karat. Guaranteed for 25 years' wear.
No. 4C4142 Above make. Plain Engine Turned. Made by Joseph Fahys.

No. 4C4144
14-karat. Guaranteed for 25 years' wear. Made by Joseph Fahys.

No. 4C4146
14-karat. Guaranteed for Life. THE SEARS CASE.

For $1.25 Extra We can furnish fancy dial and gold hands on any watch on this page.

No. 4C4148
Set with 4 Genuine Diamonds. 14-karat. Guaranteed for 25 years' wear. Made by Joseph Fahys.

No. 4C4150
14-karat. Guaranteed for 25 years' wear.
No. 4C4152 Above make. Plain Polished or Engine Turned. Made by John C. Dueber.

$8.30 TO $11.60

Try our Edgemere Movement and be satisfied.

No. 4C4154
14-karat. Guaranteed for 25 years' wear.
No. 4C4156 Plain Polished or Engine Turned. Same quality. Made by the Illinois Watch Case Co.

The Sears cases we can recommend for elegant finish and durability.

No. 4C4158
14-karat. Guaranteed for Life. THE SEARS CASE.

For 20 cents we furnish a beautiful plush Presentation Case to fit any watch. See No. 4C2000 on page 192.

No. 4C4160
14-karat. Guaranteed for Life. THE SEARS CASE.

We carry only the most celebrated standard goods made.

No. 4C4162
14-karat. Guaranteed for 25 years. Made by the Illinois Watch Case Co.

$9.15 TO $12.45

No. 4C4164
14-karat. Guaranteed for Life. THE SEARS CASE.

WE FIT THESE CASES WITH THE FOLLOWING 0-SIZE MOVEMENTS AT $8.30 TO $18.05. WE RECOMMEND THE 15-JEWELED EDGEMERE MOVEMENT AND SEARS CASE AT $12.45.	No. 4C4140 No. 4C4142 No. 4C4144	No. 4C4132 No. 4C4134 No. 4C4150 No. 4C4152 No. 4C4154 No. 4C4156 No. 4C4162	No. 4C4136	No. 4C4138	No. 4C4148	No. 4C4146 No. 4C4158 No. 4C4160 No. 4C4164
7 jeweled Bijou Swiss Lever	$ 8.80	$ 8.30	$11.05	$14.75	$11.55	$ 9.15
11 jeweled Fine Swiss Lever	11.10	10.60	13.35	17.05	13.85	11.45
Full 15 jeweled EDGEMERE, SEARS, ROEBUCK & CO.'S SPECIAL MAKE	12.10	11.60	14.35	18.05	14.85	12.45

ELGIN AND WALTHAM WATCHES QUOTED ON PAGES 216 TO 218.

$10.40 Buys our 15 jeweled Edgemere, fitted in any of these high grade cases you may select.

ANOTHER CUT IN PRICES ON
LADIES' HIGHEST GRADE O-SIZE HUNTING STYLE GOLD FILLED WATCHES

ONLY $7.10 for your choice of these beautifully engraved, high grade cases, as shown below, fitted with the genuine 7-jeweled SWISS LEVER MOVEMENT.

The Latest Styles. All Selected from Newest Designs. Never Before Shown. We Own the Exclusive Right to These Patterns. You Cannot See Them Elsewhere.

TWELVE DIFFERENT PATTERNS OF CASES to select from and all the latest designs. We earnestly believe that such a handsome, high grade, gold filled watch was never before offered for as little money as $7.10. It is a price that others would find impossible to duplicate, a price that is made possible only by reason of our immense outlet for high grade watches.

THESE LADIES', HANDSOME, O-SIZE CASES, as illustrated below, are the best on the market. They are made by the most reputable watch case manufacturer in America, made by the highest grade method there is, on heavy plates of solid gold over an inner plate of hard composition metal, and are guaranteed by our special certificate to wear for twenty years. They come in the 0-size, one size smaller than the regular 6-size, the most popular, stylish and handsome size for ladies' wear made. They are beautifully engraved and decorated and the latest style antique bow and winding crown or stem wind and stem set hunting case style.

GUARANTEED FOR TWENTY YEARS.

OUR PROTECTIVE OFFER: IF, AFTER YOU EXAMINE THE WATCH YOU GET, you do not find it in EVERY WAY just as represented and warranted, return it to us, and we will REFUND YOU THE PURCHASE PRICE.

NO CHARGES FOR REPAIRS on watches or clocks will be allowed unless our written consent is first secured in advance.

$7.10 is the LOWEST price ever known on any case fitted with the 7-jeweled Swiss Lever movement.

THE EDGEMERE IS OUR LATEST MOVEMENT BARGAIN.

No. 4C4199 No. 4C4201

No. 4C4203 Special bargain in a ladies' O-size gold plated trading watch. This watch is the exact counter part of the finest grade gold filled watch manufactured. It is not guaranteed; will wear six months to a year if very carefully handled. It is a great watch to use for trading purposes. It is stem wind and stem set and the movement we fit in this watch is an imported 7 jeweled Swiss lever movement, and will give excellent satisfaction as a time-keeper. We warrant it being received in a perfect going order. At $3.65 these watches are rare bargains. They are being offered by premium houses in newspaper advertisements at twice this amount and sold as gold filled. Remember our price is but $3.65. Order by number.

No. 4C4203 Price, for complete watch........**$3.65**

YOU HAVE YOUR CHOICE OF CASES.

No. 4C4205 No. 4C4207

YOU CAN MAKE MONEY SELLING THESE WATCHES.

No. 4C4209 No. 4C4211

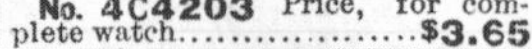

No. 4C4219 Our special O-size solid silver case, with solid gold ornamentation. This case is one of the most beautiful productions this year in the watch market. The contrast between the different colored gold onlaid on the white silver surface makes an effect unequalled. This watch is stem wind and stem set, hunting style.

Fitted with the 7 jeweled Swiss lever movement. Price.....**$6.60**

Fitted with the 11 jeweled Swiss lever movement. Price.....**$7.35**

Fitted with the 7 jeweled Elgin or Waltham movement. Price, **$9.75**

Fitted with the celebrated 15 jeweled Edgemere, Sears, Roebuck & Co.'s special movement. Price..........**$8.85**

For 20 cents we furnish a beautiful Plush Presentation Case to fit any watch. See No. 4C2000, on page 192.

No. 4C4213 No. 4C4215

OUR O-SIZE EDGEMERE MOVEMENT HAS 15 FINE RUBY JEWELS.

No. 4C4217 No. 4C4221

JEWELERS ASK 50 PER CENT MORE FOR WATCHES OF SAME GRADE.

No. 4C4223 No. 4C4225

WE CAN FIT THESE MOVEMENTS IN ANY OF THE ABOVE CASES.

7 Jeweled Swiss Lever Movement	$ 7.10
11 Jeweled Lever	9.40
7 Jeweled Elgin or Waltham	10.30
Full 15 Jeweled EDGEMERE, SEARS, ROEBUCK & CO.'S Special Make	$10.40
Full 15 Jeweled Elgin or Waltham	14.00

WE GUARANTEE ANY OF THE ABOVE MOVEMENTS FOR FIVE YEARS.

ELGIN AND WALTHAM WATCHES QUOTED ON PAGES 216 TO 218.

$7.60 TO $12.75 LADIES' HUNTING STYLE O-SIZE 10-KARAT GOLD FILLED WATCHES $7.60 TO $12.75

GUARANTEED FOR 20 YEARS.

AT $7.60 TO $12.75 according to the prices listed below, we offer these handsome, beautifully engraved, guaranteed watches, made by the most responsible and representative manufacturers, at prices that are below any kind of competition. At $7.60 to $12.75, according to the movement selected, you can buy from us a ladies' 0-size, 10-karat case, 20-year guaranteed watch, the equal of what would cost you elsewhere 20 to 30 per cent more money.

EVERY MOVEMENT WE OFFER IS HIGH GRADE. Our Edgemere movement cannot be excelled. It is the very latest design and highest grade, and perfect in every way.

EVERY CASE IS A GEM OF THE ENGRAVER'S ART, and we call special attention to the handsome SEARS' CASE, as shown below. Every case represents a standard for quality. Whether you select a Dueber, Fahys, Sears or Giant case, you cannot make a mistake.

Edgemere Movement.

THE SEARS GOLD FILLED CASE is recommended above all others, being made of two extra heavy plates of solid gold over a hard composition metal. Will wear longer than any other gold filled case made, and is the handsomest, best finished and best fitting gold filled watch case made. IF YOU SELECT A SEARS CASE YOU WILL HAVE THE BEST GOLD FILLED WATCH CASE EVER MADE.

TRY OUR 15-JEWELED EDGEMERE Movement at $10.90 to $12.75, fitted in any one of these cases ☞ This is the picture of the 15-Jeweled Edgemere Movement. We advocate 15-jeweled movements.

12 CENTS WILL CARRY ANY ONE OF THESE WATCHES TO ANY PART OF THE UNITED STATES BY MAIL. 25 CENTS BY EXPRESS.

$7.60 TO $10.90

We will treat you as we would like to be treated were we in your place.

No. 4C4301
Guaranteed for 20 Years.
Illinois Watch Case Co. Make.

No. 4C4303
Guaranteed for 20 Years.
Illinois Watch Case Co. Make.

Regarding the engravings. We generally have the exact pattern. If not, we will send a very similar design.

No. 4C4305
Guaranteed for 20 Years.
Illinois Watch Case Co. Make.

Pictures show the exact size of watch.

No. 4C4306 Colored Gold Ornamented.
Guaranteed for 20 Years.
Illinois Watch Case Co. Make

We know that you would be a steady customer if you bought once.

$7.60 TO $10.90

No. 4C4309
Guaranteed for 20 Years.
Sears' Make.

FOR PRICES SEE LIST AT BOTTOM OF PAGE.

$7.90 TO $11.20

THESE PICTURES SHOW THE EXACT SIZE OF THE WATCHES.

No. 4C4311
Guaranteed for 20 Years.
Joseph Fahys' Make.

No. 4C4313 Engraved.
Guaranteed for 20 Years.
Joseph Fahys' Make.

No. 4C4317
Guaranteed for 20 Years.
Illinois Watch Case Co. Make.

These cases come with assorted engravings, all the new designs.

No. 4C4318
Guaranteed for 20 Years.
Joseph Fahys' Make.

$7.60 TO $10.90

No. 4C4321
Guaranteed for 20 Years.
Sears' Make.

$7.60 TO $10.90

We fill orders with promptness and care.

No. 4C4322
Guaranteed for 20 Years.
Illinois Watch Case Co. Make.
No. 4C4323 Same make, but Plain Engine Turned.

No. 4C4325
Guaranteed for 20 Years.
Illinois Watch Case Co. Make.

For prices on these cases with different movements, see price list below.

No. 4C4326
Guaranteed for 20 Years.
John C. Dueber's Make.

For 20 cents we furnish a beautiful plush Presentation Case, to fit any watch. See No. 4C2000 on page 192.

No. 4C4329
Guaranteed for 20 Years.
Sears' Make.

$7.90 TO $11.20

No. 4C4330
Guaranteed for 20 Years.
Joseph Fahys' Make.

WE FIT THESE CASES WITH THE FOLLOWING O-SIZE MOVEMENTS:

WE RECOMMEND 15 JEWELED MOVEMENTS.

	PRICES OF COMPLETE WATCH.		
	Nos. 4C4301, 4C4303, 4C4305, 4C4309, 4C4317, 4C4321, 4C4322, 4C4323, 4C4325, 4C4326, 4C4329	No. 4C4306	No. 4C4311, No. 4C4313, No. 4C4318, No. 4C4330
7 Jeweled Fine Swiss Lever	$ 7.60	$ 9.45	$ 7.90
11 Jeweled Fine Swiss Lever	9.90	11.75	10.20
FULL 15 JEWELED EDGEMERE, SEARS, ROEBUCK & CO.'S SPECIAL MAKE	10.90	12.75	11.20

"THE FOUR HUNDRED"

SMALLEST AMERICAN WATCH MADE. HANDSOMEST LADIES' WATCH MADE. OPEN FACE OR HUNTING STYLE IN 14K SOLID GOLD AND 14K GOLD FILLED. GUARANTEED FOR 25 YEARS' WEAR. PRICES REDUCED AGAIN.

"MOLLY STARK" IS THE NAME OF THE 7-JEWELED HAMPDEN MOVEMENT. "DIADEM" IS THE NAME OF THE 15-JEWELED HAMPDEN MOVEMENT.

$16.48 AND $19.25 for 14-karat Solid Gold Cases, according to movement. **$10.65 TO $13.75** is our special offer, according to grade of movement for gold filled. **IN 14-KARAT SOLID GOLD** you have a watch second to none. They have just been put on the market and are meeting with great success.

WE WARRANT THESE GOOOS BEING EXACTLY AS REPRESENTED.

THE DUEBER "400"-SIZE is the exact size as illustrated: all the rage in large cities; very dainty, very handsome and just as durable, just as accurate as the largest sizes. **THESE "400"-SIZE CASES** are stem wind and stem set hunting cases, elaborately engraved, decorated and ornamented as shown in illustrations, made with the latest style handsome antique bow.

No charges for repairs on watches or clocks will be allowed unless our written consent is first secured in advance.

ANY NAME ENGRAVED on THESE CASES AT THE RATE OF 2½ CTS. PER LETTER.

WE ADVOCATE THE 15 JEWELED GRADE MOVEMENT.

12 CENTS will carry one of these watches anywhere in the United States by registered mail.

No. 4C4400 14-K. Filled, Hunting.
No. 4C4402 As above, Open Face.
No. 4C4404 14-K. Solid Gold, Hunting.
No. 4C4406 As above, Open Face.

No. 4C4416 14-K. Filled, Hunting.
No. 4C4418 As above, Open Face.
No. 4C4420 14-K. Solid Gold, Hunting.
No. 4C4422 As above, Open Face.

No. 4C4424 14-K. Filled, Hunting.
No. 4C4426 As above, Open Face.
No. 4C4428 14-K. Solid Gold, Hunting.
No. 4C4430 As above, Open Face.

No. 4C4432 14-K. Filled, Hunting.
No. 4C4434 As above, Open Face.
No. 4C4436 14-K. Solid Gold, Hunting.
No. 4C4438 As above, Open Face.

No. 4C4474 14-K. Filled, Hunting.
No. 4C4476 As above, Open Face.
No. 4C4478 14-K. Solid Gold, Hunting.
No. 4C4480 As above, Open Face.

HIGHEST GRADE GOLD FILLED MODEL. Made by the Great Dueber Watch Case Co., at Canton, Ohio, from extra heavy plates of 14-karat solid gold over an inner plate of hard composition metal, and is guaranteed to wear for 25 years. A written binding 25 years' certificate of guarantee signed by John C. Dueber accompanies each case, by the terms and conditions of which if the case wears through or changes color within 25 years it will be replaced with a new one FREE OF CHARGE.

WE FIT THESE CASES WITH THE FOLLOWING MOVEMENTS:	Hunting, Solid Gold	Open Face, Solid Gold	Hunting, Gold Filled	Open Face, Gold Filled
	Nos. 4C4404, 4C4428, 4C4420, 4C4436, 4C4478	Nos. 4C4408, 4C4430, 4C4422, 4C4438, 4C4480	Nos. 4C4400, 4C4424, 4C4416, 4C4432, 4C4474	Nos. 4C4402, 4C4426, 4C4418, 4C4434, 4C4476
Full 7-Jeweled Molly Stark Hampden.	$16.48	$16.48	$10.90	$10.65
Full 15-Jeweled Diadem Hampden....	19.25	19.25	13.75	13.50

ALL OF THE ABOVE MOVEMENTS WE GUARANTEE FOR A TERM OF FIVE YEARS.

16-SIZE, 12-SIZE AND 0-SIZE NAPOLEON GOLD FILLED CASES.

GUARANTEED FOR A TERM OF TEN YEARS.

Prices Cut to Less Than Wholesale.

$5.60 TO $7.90

$8.85 TO $11.15

ELGIN WATCHES QUOTED ON PAGES 216 TO 218.

$5.65 AND $8.24

NEVER BEFORE has a 10-year gold filled case been offered at the price we are asking. The very latest sizes shown here. 16-size, 12-size in Open Face or Hunting style and 0-size, the latest gentlemen's size, boys' size and ladies' size. The Napoleon Case is manufactured by the celebrated Illinois Watch Case Company, of Elgin, Ill., manufacturers of the Elgin Giant and Elgin Commander gold filled cases.

$5.90 for a gentlemen's 16-size gold filled watch, hunting style, fitted with the Reliance movement, is a price unheard of before. Our $5.65 price for this 0-size 10-karat 10-year gold filled case fitted with a fine 7-jeweled Swiss lever movement, means a saving to you of no less than 50 per cent.

REMEMBER our liberal offer holds good with any of the watches you may select. If goods are not found as represented, return them and we will refund your money.

THE MOVEMENTS. We guarantee any of these movements for a term of five years against defect in material or workmanship.

No. 4C4483 16-Size Hunting Style.
No. 4C4485 16-Size Open Face, Screw Back and Bezel.

	4C4483	4C4485
With 7-Jeweled Reliance Movement	$5.90	$5.60
With 12-Jeweled Edgemere Movement	7.90	7.60

No. 4C4486 12-Size Hunting Style.
No. 4C4488 12-Size Open Face, Screw Back and Screw Bezel.

	4C4486	4C4488
With 10-Jeweled Edgemere Movement	$9.15	$8.85
With 15-Jeweled Fine Swiss Lever Movement	11.15	10.85

No. 4C4490 0-Size.
With 7-Jeweled Fine Swiss Lever Movement.........$5.65
With 15-Jeweled Edgemere Movement.......... 8.24

LADIES' SOLID GOLD EXTRA SMALL SIZE SWISS CHATELAINE WATCHES.

A NEW IMPORTATION WITH US. Many ladies want very small watches, and to fill this demand we have imported five extra small watches. The movements fitted in these cases are all fine jeweled cylinder movements, and while we cannot guarantee them to run accurately, that is to run to the minute, we do warrant them to give entire satisfaction. It is impossible for a watch of this very small size to run as accurately as the larger sizes, but for all practical uses will give satisfaction.

The higher the grade the more accurate the time.

LATEST DESIGNS and PRETTIEST PATTERNS are the only ones we carry in stock.

REGARDING ENGRAVINGS. We generally have exact patterns, when not procurable we will send a very similar new design.

For 20c we furnish a beautiful plush Presentation Case, to fit any watch. Order by number and give size of watch. No. 4C2000 Price..20c

$10.75

$12.50

No. 4C4491 Open Face Chatelaine. Yellow Roman color, satin finished solid gold case, stem wind and stem set, raised floral ornamentation. Price for complete watch in beautiful plush case..................$10.75

No. 4C4492 Open Face Chatelaine. Solid gold case, stem wind and stem set, fancy enameled subjects in appropriate colors, similar to illustration. Price for complete watch in beautiful plush case..................$7.85

No. 4C4493 Open Face Chatelaine. Solid gold case, stem wind and stem set, fancy enameled subjects in appropriate colors, similar to illustration, with fancy enameled dial. Price for complete watch in beautiful plush case..................$10.75

No. 4C4494 Open Face Chatelaine. Solid gold case, perfectly plain polished throughout, stem wind and stem set, with handsome fancy illuminated dial. Price for complete watch in beautiful plush case..................$7.00

No. 4C4495 Open Face Chatelaine. Solid gold with beautiful solid gold Arabic dial. This is the smallest watch of the five shown here, and is fitted with the finest movement of them all. Price for complete watch in beautiful plush case..................$12.50

LADIES' IMPORTED CHATELAINE WATCHES AND GENTLEMEN'S No. 4C4531 SPECIAL GUN METAL WATCH AT $2.25.

IN GUN METAL, SILVER INLAID, SOLID SILVER, GOLD FILLED, SOLID GOLD AND ENAMELED. The illustrations show exact size. Every one of our silver chatelaine watches is $\frac{925}{1000}$ fine, and guaranteed not to turn yellow. Some firms are offering silver watches only $\frac{825}{1000}$ fine, but we caution you that they will invariably turn in color. They cost to import less money by quite a percentage, but we do not desire to place on the market inferior goods.

Engraving can be done on any one of our plain polished cases. A monogram on the back on one of these watches increases its beauty materially. For 35 cents extra we can engrave a two or three letter monogram on any plain watch illustrated here.

$2.00

No. 4C4532 Ladies' gun metal open face chatelaine watch. The case is plain polished, black gun metal. The movement is the celebrated full jeweled Leonore, manufactured in Switzerland. Has cut expansion balance, lever escapement and nickel plates, is stem wind and pendant set. Warranted for a term of five years. Price.......... $6.00

$3.60

No. 4C4536 Ladies' solid silver open face stem wind and pendant set chatelaine watch. Case is solid silver, beautifully engraved. The illustration shows back and front of the watch. The movement is called the Lady Rose, imported from Switzerland, has cylinder escapement, damaskeened nickel plates, 10 fine ruby jewels, and is an excellent timekeeper. Price.......... $4.90

$6.75

No. 4C4530 Ladies' gun metal open face stem wind and stem set chatelaine watch. Case is black, plain polished gun metal. The movement is Swiss imported, has 2 jewels. Will give very good satisfaction. A wonderful bargain for the price. Price, $2.00

No. 4C4531 Gentlemen's size. Price.......... $2.25

$6.00

No. 4C4534 Ladies' solid silver open face stem wind and pendant set chatelaine watch. Case is solid silver, beautifully engraved. Illustration shows back and front of watch. The movement is Swiss imported, has cylinder escapement, 7 jewels. Price....... $3.60

$4.90

No. 4C4538 Ladies' solid silver open face stem wind and pendant set chatelaine watch. The case is handsomely engraved. The illustration shows the back as well as the front of watch. The movement is the celebrated full jeweled Leonore, manufactured in Switzerland, has cut expansion balance, straight line escapement, with damaskeened nickel plates. This watch is warranted for five years. Price.......... $6.75

Ladies' Solid Silver Watch, $4.20.

No. 4C4540 Ladies' solid silver hunting chatelaine watch, stem wind and stem set, with second hand. The case is handsomely engraved. The movement is imported from Switzerland, has 7 jewels, cylinder escapement and nickel plates. Price.... $4.20

$4.20

$5.60

No. 4C4544 Ladies' silver inlaid open face stem wind and pendant set chatelaine watch. The case is gun metal with silver inlaid, called Niello. The movement is imported from Switzerland, has cylinder escapement, 7 jewels, plates of nickel. Price.......... $4.00

$3.82

No. 4C4548 Ladies' enameled open face stem wind and stem set chatelaine watch. The case is beautifully enameled in colors with similar subjects, as illustration shows. The illustration shows both the back and front of the watch. The movement has 7 fine ruby jewels, gold plated lever escapement, and is a good timekeeper. Price.......... $4.65

$6.50

No. 4C4552 Ladies' gold filled open face plain polished screw back and bezel chatelaine watch. The case is warranted for twenty years wear. Is stem wind and pendant set, fitted with the celebrated full jeweled Leonore movement, manufactured in Switzerland. It has cut expansion balance, lever escapement and nickel plates. The movement is warranted for a term of five years. Price.......... $8.50

No. 4C4542 Ladies' solid silver hunting style stem wind and stem set chatelaine watch. The case is beautifully engraved as illustration shows. The movement is Swiss imported, called Lady Rose, has cylinder escapement, damaskeened nickel plates and 10 fine ruby jewels and is an excellent timekeeper. Price.......... $5.60

$4.00

No. 4C4546 Ladies' silver inlaid open face novelty chatelaine watch. The case is gun metal with silver inlaid, called Niello. Illustration shows the back and front of watch. The movement is a Swiss imported, has cylinder escapement and 7 jewels. Price.......... $3.82

$4.65

We can supply Chatelette Pin and Box similar to No. 4C4556 at $1.00 extra.

No. 4C4550 Ladies' solid gold 10 karat plain polished stem wind and pendant set chatelaine watch. The movement has cylinder escapement, 7 jewels, beautiful damaskeening on nickel plates, fancy dial, as illustration shows. Price.......... $6.50

$8.50

$11.00

Ladies' Solid Gold Watch $11.00.

No. 4C4554 14 karat solid gold open face stem wind and stem set chatelaine watch. The case is plain polished. The movement is called the Rosalind, has 7 fine ruby jewels, cylinder escapement, with damaskeened nickel plates. Price.. $11.00

No. 4C4556 Less money than before and better than ever. Genuine French Enameled Chatelaine Watch for $5.00. The case is gold filled, beautifully enameled in either blue, ruby red or green. The chatelaine matches the watch. The movement is an imported one, made in Switzerland, perfectly trued and adjusted; we guarantee it to give entire satisfaction. The picture is two-thirds size of watch. It is the exact size of watch No. 4C4548.

At $5.00 for the complete outfit, case, chatelaine and watch, you have a bargain at least 50 per cent cheaper than any local jeweler could possibly sell it. Price.......... $5.00

If by mail, postage extra, 16 cents.

Ladies' Solid Silver O-Size Watches.

$5.25

OPEN FACE OR HUNTING STYLE AT THE SAME PRICE.

AN AMERICAN MADE WATCH in this small size, made of silver, has been wanted by thousands of ladies. So as to make our catalogue complete, so as to positively quote all kinds and styles of watches, we show here the smallest silver American watch made. These cases are solid sterling silver through and through, hand engraved; they have the antique bow; the entire case is perfectly finished in every respect. They are stem wind and pendant set. **We guarantee the movement for a term of five years, and the case will last your natural lifetime.** We fit these cases with the following movements at prices quoted:

No. 4C4558 Open Face.
No. 4C4560 Hunting Style.

PRICES QUOTED HERE ARE FOR THE COMPLETE WATCH, OPEN FACE OR HUNTING STYLE.	4C4558 4C4560
7 Jeweled Swiss Lever	$5.25
7 Jeweled Elgin or Waltham	8.70
Full 15 Jeweled EDGEMERE, Sears, Roebuck & Co.'s Special	8.55

FOR $1.25 EXTRA we can furnish a fancy dial and gold hands on any watch on this page.

18 AND 16-SIZE BOSS AND CRESCENT GOLD FILLED WATCHES

IN 10 AND 14-KARAT QUALITY. OPEN FACE OR HUNTING STYLE.

PROTECT YOUR WATCH WITH AN AJAX WATCH INSULATOR. See page 192, No. 4C2002 Price **18** cents

$7.65 TO $39.15

This illustration shows how our 17 Jeweled Edgemere looks. The greatest watch value ever offered for the money.

$7.65 TO $39.15

REGARDING THE ENGRAVINGS, we generally have the exact pattern as illustrated. If not, we send a very similar design.

18-SIZE BOSS GOLD FILLED.
No. 4C4600 Open Face, Screw Back and Bezel, 20-Year. 10 karat.
No. 4C4602 Hunting, 20-Year. 10 karat.
No. 4C4604 Open Face, Screw Back and Bezel, 25-Year. 14 karat.
No. 4C4606 Hunting, 25-Year. 14 karat.

SEND 50 CENTS and we will send you any watch by express, C. O. D., the balance payable after watch is received and found satisfactory.

18-SIZE. CRESCENT GOLD FILLED.
No. 4C4608 Open Face, Screw Back and Bezel, 20-Year. 10 karat.
No. 4C4610 Hunting, 20-Year. 10 karat.
No. 4C4612 Open Face, Screw Back and Bezel, 25-Year. 14 karat.
No. 4C4614 Hunting, 25-Year. 14 karat.

18-SIZE. BOSS GOLD FILLED.
No. 4C4616 Open Face, Screw Back and Bezel, 20-Year. 10 karat.
No. 4C4618 Hunting, 20-Year. 10 karat.
No. 4C4620 Open Face, Screw Back and Bezel, 25-Year. 14 karat.
No. 4C4622 Hunting, 25-Year. 14 karat.

18-size, solid nickel, 17 jewels, straight line lever escapement, adjusted. Full plate, fancy solid gold damaskeened finish, five pairs gold settings, compensation full double cut expansion balance wheel, adjusted to isochronism and position, patent micrometer regulator, genuine ruby jeweled pin, highly polished beveled edged screws, fully protecting dust band, safety pinion, double sunk, white enameled dial and sunk second hand dial. The superior construction of this movement adapts it to the most exacting service.

THE SEARS GOLD FILLED CASE IS RECOMMENDED ABOVE ALL OTHERS,

being made of two extra heavy plates of solid gold over a hard composition metal. Will wear longer than any other gold filled case made, and is the handsomest, best finished and best fitting gold filled watch case made. If you select a Sears case you will have the best gold filled watch case ever made.

We fit these movements in any of the 18-size cases. Prices are for complete watches.	Nos. 4C4600 4C4608 4C4616	Nos. 4C4602 4C4610 4C4618	Nos. 4C4604 4C4612 4C4620	Nos. 4C4606 4C4614 4C4622
7 Jeweled Edgemere, SEARS, ROEBUCK & CO.'S special make	$ 7.65	$10.00	$10.55	$12.90
7 Jeweled Hampden, Gilt	9.25	11.60	12.15	14.50
Trainmen's Special, Stamped, 17 Jewels, adjusted	8.45	10.80	11.35	13.70
11 Jeweled Hampden	9.43	11.78	12.33	14.68
Full 12 Jeweled EDGEMERE, especially made for SEARS, ROEBUCK & CO.	9.15	11.50	12.05	14.40
Full 15 Jeweled Hampden	10.20	12.55	13.10	15.45
Full 15 Jeweled SEARS, ROEBUCK & CO.'S especially made	10.05	12.40	12.95	15.30
Full 17 Jeweled Edgemere, SEARS, ROEBUCK & CO.'S special make	10.30	12.65	13.20	15.55
Full 17 Jeweled Dueber Grand Hampden	13.95	16.30	16.85	19.20
Full 17 Jeweled New Railway Hampden	22.90	25.25	25.80	28.15
Full 21 Jeweled John Hancock Hampden	24.70	27.05	28.00	30.35
Full 21 Jeweled Special Railway Hampden	26.30	28.65	29.20	31.25
Full 23 Jeweled New Railway Hampden	Not made	30.65	31.20	Not made
Full 23 Jeweled Special Railway Hampden	32.90	36.25	36.80	39.15
Full 17 Jeweled SEARS, ROEBUCK & CO.'S SPECIAL, especially made. The greatest watch bargain ever offered	15.00	17.35	17.90	20.25

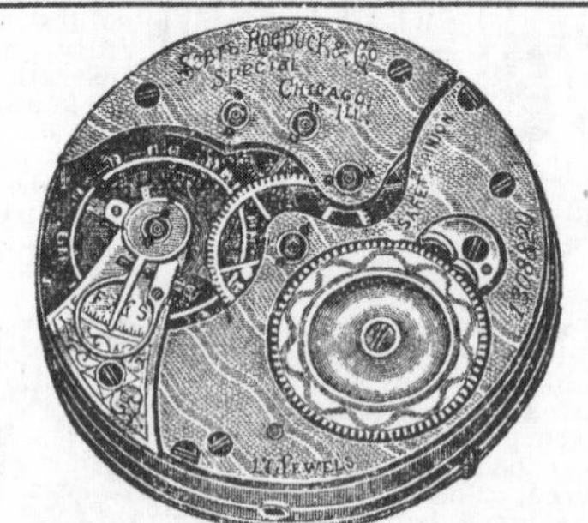

16-size, solid nickel, fancy gold damaskeened finish. 17 genuine ruby jewels in solid gold settings, straight line lever escapement, exposed to view winding apparatus, the steel parts of which are highly polished and chamfered; patent micrometer regulator, five pairs of extra solid gold settings and gold train, genuine ruby pallette jewels visible to view, and ruby roller jewel, patent safety center pinion and barrel. Compensation double cut, full expansion balance wheel, adjusted in accordance to variations of the temperature, fully protecting dust band, double sunk, genuine hard French enamel dial. This movement will excel the highest grade movements on the market.

$8.51 TO $21.00

16-SIZE BOSS AND CRESCENT WATCHES.

$8.51 TO $21.00

WE OFFER MOVEMENTS OF ESTABLISHED REPUTATION ONLY.

MOVEMENTS THAT HAVE STOOD THE TEST OF TIME and are known to be RELIABLE and ACCURATE. We have sold our watches in every locality, some of them can surely be found right in your own neighborhood. Ask your friend or neighbor what he thinks of the SEARS, ROEBUCK & CO.'S SPECIAL MOVEMENT, for we are willing to accept his judgment.

DON'T BUY A WATCH UNTIL YOU HAVE INVESTIGATED THE MOVEMENTS WE ILLUSTRATE ABOVE.

We fit the following movements in the 16-size cases at prices quoted. Prices are for the complete watch.	Nos. 4C4624 4C4632	Nos. 4C4626 4C4634	Nos. 4C4628 4C4636	Nos. 4C4630 4C4638
7 Jeweled Reliance	$ 8.51	$11.05	$11.61	$13.86
Full 12 Jeweled EDGEMERE, OUR SPECIAL MAKE	10.55	12.80	13.30	15.30
Full 15 Jeweled SEARS, ROEBUCK & CO.'S SPECIAL	12.25	14.50	15.00	17.00
Full 17 Jeweled SEARS, ROEBUCK & CO.'S SPECIAL, especially made, the greatest watch offer ever made	16.25	18.50	19.00	21.00

16-SIZE. BOSS GOLD FILLED.
No. 4C4624 Open Face, Screw Back and Bezel, 20-Year. 10 karat.
No. 4C4626 Hunting, 20-Year. 10 karat.
No. 4C4628 Open Face, Screw Back and Bezel, 25-Year. 14 karat.
No. 4C4630 Hunting, 25-Year. 14 karat.

16-SIZE. CRESCENT GOLD FILLED.
No. 4C4632 Open Face, Screw Back and Bezel, 20-Year. 10 karat.
No. 4C4634 Hunting, 20-Year. 10 karat.
No. 4C4636 Open Face, Screw Back and Bezel, 25-Year. 14 karat.
No. 4C4638 Hunting, 25-Year. 14 karat.

LADIES' GOLD FILLED WATCHES, O-SIZE AND 6-SIZE, HUNTING STYLE ONLY, FOR $8.75 AND UPWARDS.

FOR $1.25 extra we can furnish fancy dial and gold hands on any watch on this page.

GUARANTEED TO WEAR FOR 20 AND 25 YEARS, ACCORDING TO GRADE OF CASE.

We engrave your name in script at 2½ cents per letter on any watch.

12 cents will carry any one of these watches to any part of the United States.

No charges for repairs on watches or clocks will be allowed unless our written consent is first secured in advance.

Protect your watch with an Ajax Watch Insulator. See Page 192. No. 4C2002. Price..................18c

BOSS-14K

$10.02 and up.

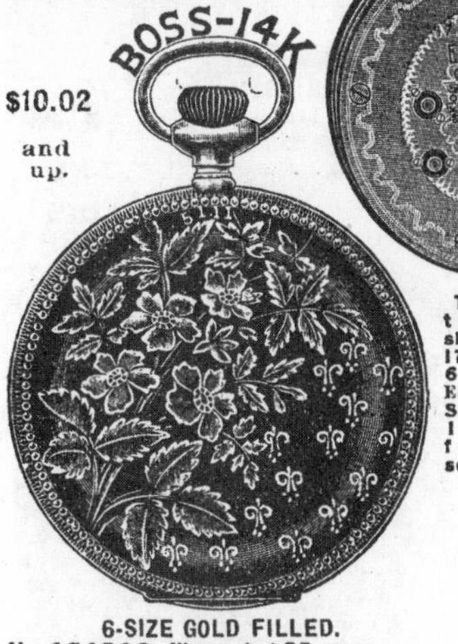

This illustration shows our 17-jeweled 6 size Edgemere. See page 190 for full description.

BOSS-10K

CRESCENT 6 SIZE

This illustration shows our 12-jeweled 6 size Edgemere. See page 190 for full description.

CRESCENT 6 SIZE $10.02 and up.

6-SIZE GOLD FILLED.
No. 4C4800 Warranted 25 years.
No. 4C4802 Same make. Plain engine turned.

6-SIZE GOLD FILLED.
No. 4C4804 Warranted 20 years.
No. 4C4806 Same make. Plain engine turned.

6-SIZE GOLD FILLED.
No. 4C4808 Warranted 25 years.
No. 4C4810 Same make. Plain engine turned.

6-SIZE GOLD FILLED.
No. 4C4812 Warranted 25 years.

BOSS-14K $10.02 and up.

CRESCENT $8.75 and up.

BOSS AND CRESCENT GOLD FILLED CASES we can recommend to our customers and know that none better can be bought. The method of making, finish and wearing ability can not be excelled. They are exact counterparts of solid gold 14-karat cases, worth four times the price we ask. None but an expert or a well informed jeweler can tell the Boss and Crescent Gold Filled Cases from the highest grade solid gold ones.

Remember the Manufacturers Guarantee Every One of These Cases.

THE MOVEMENTS QUOTED BELOW we guarantee for a term of five years against defective material or workmanship. Each one is regulated and thoroughly oiled before leaving our establishment. The make of a movement means much. We only carry such makes that by long experience we know are accurate and reliable timekeepers.

THESE PRICES ARE FOR THE 6-SIZE COMPLETE WATCH CASE AND MOVEMENT.	20-YEAR	25-YEAR
	4C4804 4C4806 4C4816 4C4818	4C4800 4C4802 4C4808 4C4810 4C4812 4C4814
7 Jeweled EDGEMERE, SEARS, ROEBUCK & CO.'S SPECIAL MAKE......	$ 8.75	$10.02
7 Jeweled Hampden Gilt..............	10.00	11.42
11 Jeweled Hampden..............	11.24	12.59
Full 12 Jeweled EDGEMERE, SEARS, ROEBUCK & CO.'S SPECIAL MAKE.......	9.90	11.32
Full 15 Jeweled SEARS, ROEBUCK & CO.'S SPECIAL..............	11.18	12.53
Full 15 Jeweled Hampden..............	11.28	12.63
Full 17 Jeweled EDGEMERE, SEARS, ROEBUCK & CO.'S SPECIAL MAKE......	11.38	12.73
Full 17 Jeweled SEARS, ROEBUCK & CO.'S SPECIAL. Especially made. This is the greatest watch offer ever made..............	14.50	15.85

6-SIZE GOLD FILLED.
No. 4C4814 Warranted 25 years.

6-SIZE GOLD FILLED.
No. 4C4816 Warranted 20 years.
No. 4C4818 Same make. Plain engine turned.

BOSS-14K $10.40 and up.

The higher the grade the better the time. We advocate higher jeweling than 7-jewel grades.

BOSS-14K

Try our Edgemere Movement and be satisfied. We carry only the most celebrated and standard goods made.

BOSS-10K

For 20 cents we furnish a beautiful plush Presentation Case, to fit any watch. Order by number and give size of watch. No. 4C2000 Price............20c

CRESCENT O SIZE

WE FILL ORDERS WITH PROMPTNESS AND CARE.

CRESCENT O SIZE $10.40 and up.

O-SIZE GOLD FILLED.
No. 4C4820
Warranted 25 years.

O-SIZE GOLD FILLED.
No. 4C4822
Warranted 25 years.
No. 4C4824 Same make and grade. Plain engine turned.

O-SIZE GOLD FILLED.
No. 4C4826
Warranted 20 years.
No. 4C4828 Same make and grade. Plain engine turned.

O-SIZE GOLD FILLED.
No. 4C4830
Warranted 25 years.
No. 4C4832 Same make and grade. Plain engine turned.

O-SIZE GOLD FILLED.
No. 4C4834
Warranted 25 years.

BOSS-10K $9.00 and up.

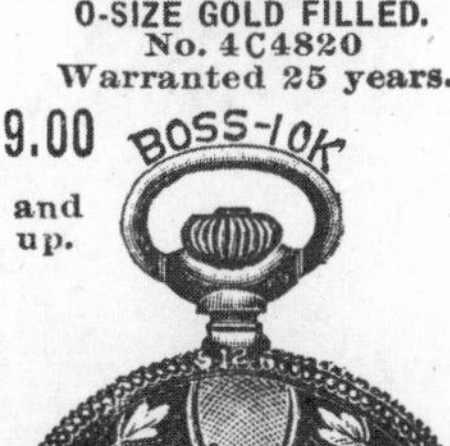

AT $12.30 FOR OUR O-SIZE 15-JEWELED ....EDGEMERE....

FITTED IN EITHER A BOSS OR CRESCENT 10-KARAT GOLD FILLED CASE : : : : : : :

means offering a reliable timekeeper and a representative case for less than trash is usually sold for. Our own written, binding guarantee together with that of the maker of these cases goes with every one we sell. You are doubly protected.

THESE PRICES ARE FOR THE O-SIZE COMPLETE WATCH, CASE AND MOVEMENT.	20-YEAR	25-YEAR
	Nos. 4C4826 4C4828 4C4836 4C4838 4C4840	Nos. 4C4820 4C4822 4C4824 4C4830 4C4832 4C4834
7 Jeweled fine Swiss Lever..............	$ 9.00	$10.40
11 Jeweled Fine Swiss Lever..............	11.30	12.70
Full 15 Jeweled EDGEMERE, SEARS, ROEBUCK & CO.'S SPECIAL MAKE.....	12.30	13.55

O-SIZE GOLD FILLED.
No. 4C4836 Warranted 20 yrs.

This is an illustration of our new 15-jeweled, O-size, Edgemere Movement. We warrant it an accurate timekeeper for five years.

FOR $12.30 OR $13.55,
According to grade of case.

CRESCENT O SIZE $9.00 and up.

O-SIZE GOLD FILLED.
No. 4C4838 Warranted 20 years.
No. 4C4840 Same make and grade. Plain engine turned.

Gentlemen's Elgin and Waltham 18-Size Gold Filled, Solid Silver and Silverine Watches for $4.55 and Upwards

OPEN FACE AND HUNTING STYLE.

ALL OPEN FACE CASES SHOWN HERE ARE SCREW BACK AND SCREW BEZEL, DUST AND DAMP PROOF.

Protect your Watch with an Ajax Watch Insulator. See page 192. Price, 8c.

SILVER

FOR 20 CENTS we furnish a beautiful plush PRESENTATION CASE to fit any watch. Order by number and give size of watch. No. 4C2000 Price, 20c

SEARS LIFE GUARANTEE

WHAT WE MEAN BY THE SEARS LIFE GUARANTEED CASE.

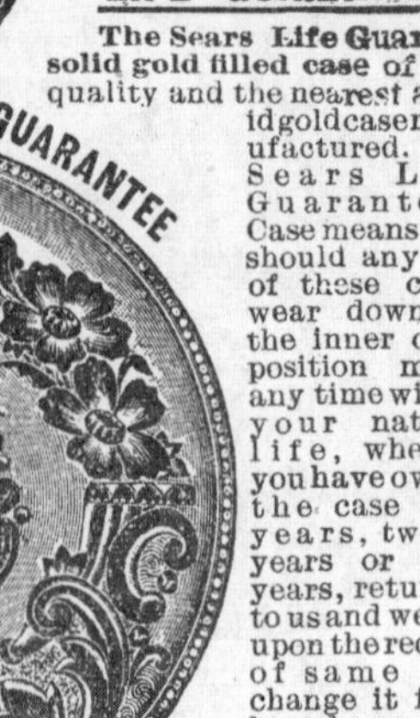

The Sears Life Guaranteed Case is a solid gold filled case of the very highest quality and the nearest approach to a solid gold case manufactured. The Sears Life Guaranteed Case means that should any one of these cases wear down to the inner composition metal any time within your natural life, whether you have owned the case five years, twenty years or fifty years, return it to us and we will upon the receipt of same exchange it for a brand new case of same quality, free of charge.

$6.43 AND UP.

SOLID SILVER.—3 and 4-ounce.
No. 4C4900 Open Face, Screw Back and Bezel, 3-ounce.
No. 4C4902 Hunting, 3-ounce.
No. 4C4904 Open Face, Screw Back and Bezel, 4-ounce.
No. 4C4906 Hunting, 4-ounce.
No. 4C4908 Open Face, Solid Back, Screw Front. Dust and damp proof.

SEARS.
GOLD FILLED.
No. 4C4907 Open Face, Screw Back and Bezel, 20-year.
No. 4C4909 Hunting. 20-year.
No. 4C4911 Open Face, Screw Back and Bezel, Life Guarantee.
No. 4C4912 Hunting, Life Guarantee.

ILLINOIS WATCH CASE CO.
GOLD FILLED.
No. 4C4919 Open Face, Screw Back and Bezel, 20-year.
No. 4C4921 Hunting, 20-year.
No. 4C4923 Open Face, Screw Back and Bezel, 25-year.
No. 4C4925 Hunting, 25-year.

WE FIT THESE CASES WITH THE FOLLOWING 18-SIZE MOVEMENTS:	Nos. 4C4900 4C4908 4C4907 4C4919 4C4926	No. 4C4934	No. 4C4902	Nos. 4C4946 4C4948	Nos. 4C4904 4C4906	Nos. 4C4909 4C4921 4C4928	No. 4C4936	Nos. 4C4923 4C4930	No. 4C4938	Nos. 4C4925 4C4932	No. 4C4940	No. 4C4911	No. 4C4913
7 Jeweled Grade Elgin or Waltham Gilt	$ 6.43	$ 8.12	$ 6.53	$ 6.83	$ 7.18	$ 8.48	10.42	$ 8.43	10.67	10.68	13.42	11.32	14.42
7 Jeweled Grade Elgin or Waltham Nickel	6.95	8.64	7.05	7.35	7.70	9.00	10.94	8.95	11.20	11.20	13.94	11.84	14.94
Full 15 Jeweled Grade Elgin or Waltham Nickel	8.00	9.70	8.10	8.50	8.73	10.05	12.00	10.00	12.25	12.25	15.00	12.90	16.00
Full 17 Jeweled Grade Elgin or Waltham	10.90	12.58	11.00	11.40	11.58	12.95	14.88	12.90	15.13	15.13	17.88	15.77	18.87
Full 17 Jeweled G. M. Wheeler, Elgin or P.S. Bartlett Waltham, adjusted	13.25	14.95	13.35	13.75	13.90	15.30	17.25	15.25	17.50	17.50	20.25	18.15	21.25
Full 17 Jeweled B. W. Raymond Elgin, or Appleton Tracy Premier Grade Waltham, adjusted	22.17	23.87	22.27	22.67	22.92	24.22	26.17	24.22	26.42	26.42	29.15	27.07	30.15
Full 21 Jeweled "Father Time" Elgin or Crescent St. Waltham, adjusted	26.37	28.07	26.47	26.87	Not furnished	28.42	30.37	28.37	30.62	30.62	33.37	31.27	34.37
Full 21 Jeweled Vanguard Waltham, adjusted	31.62	33.32	31.72	32.12		33.67	35.62	33.62	35.87	35.87	38.62	36.52	39.62
Full 19 Jeweled B. W. Raymond Elgin, or Crescent St. Waltham. Made in Open Face Only	Not furnished	Not Made	Not Made	Not furnished	Not Made	Not Made	Not Made	25.75	28.00	Not Made	Not Made	28.65	Not Made 37.00
Full 19 Jeweled Vanguard Waltham	29.00	30.70	29.10	29.50	Not furnished	31.05	33.01	31.00	33.26	33.25	36.00	33.91	Not Made
Full 21 Jeweled Veritas Elgin, Made in Open Face Only	Not furnished	Not Made	Not Made	Not furnished	Not Made	Not Made	Not Made	33.62	35.87	Not Made	Not Made	36.52	
Full 23 Jeweled Veritas Elgin, Made in Open Face Only		Not Made	Not Made		Not Made	Not Made	Not Made	36.25	38.50	Not Made	Not Made	39.15	Not Made

DUEBER

$6.43 AND UP.

FOR $1.25 EXTRA WE CAN FURNISH FANCY DIAL AND GOLD HANDS ON ANY WATCH ON THIS PAGE.

FOR $6.43 THE SEARS 20-year Open Face Gold Filled Case and an Elgin or Waltham movement or $8.48 for the same movement fitted in the SEARS HUNTING STYLE CASE means you can own the best for LITTLE MONEY

$6.83 AND UP.

DUEBER.
GOLD FILLED.
No. 4C4926 Open Face, Screw Back and Bezel, 20-year.
No. 4C4928 Hunting, 20-year.
No. 4C4930 Open Face, Screw Back and Bezel, 25-year.
No. 4C4932 Hunting, 25-year.

WARRANTED 14FK 25 YEARS

$8.12 AND UP.

FAHYS.
GOLD FILLED.
No. 4C4934 Open Face, Screw Back and Bezel, warranted 20 years.
No. 4C4936 Hunting, warranted 20 years.
No. 4C4938 Open Face, Screw Back and Bezel, warranted 25 years.
No. 4C4940 Hunting, warranted 25 years.

SILVERINE.
No. 4C4942 Open Face, Screw Back and Bezel. Fitted with 7-jeweled nickel Elgin or Waltham movement. Price.......... $4.55
No. 4C4943 Same as No. 4C4942, but with gilt Elgin or Waltham movement. Price..... $4.13
Not furnished with any other movements.
No. 4C4944 Hunting. Fitted with 7-jeweled Elgin or Waltham movement. Price $4.90
No. 4C4945 Same as No. 4C4944, but with gilt Elgin or Waltham movement. Price....... $4.38
Not furnished with any other Elgin or Waltham movements. SEE PAGE 195.

SOLID SILVER. 3-ounce Solid Silver Open Face, Screw Back and Bezel, Gold Inlaid Subjects.
No. 4C4946 Engine Inlaid.
No. 4C4948 Stag Inlaid.

12 AND 16-SIZE GENTLEMEN'S ELGIN AND WALTHAM WATCHES

Protect your Watch with an AJAX WATCH INSULATOR. See page 192. No. 4C2002 Price.. 18c

12 and 16-SIZE.
Open Face and Hunting Style.

REMEMBER, all of our Open Face Watches are screw bezel and screw back. This model of case is dust and damp proof, the best kind of a case to protect the movement with. All employes of railroads, occupying responsible positions, use the **Open Face Screw Back and Screw Bezel Dust and Damp Proof Cases.** They know it is the best case made to protect valuable movements.

OUR GUARANTEE GOES WITH EVERY ONE SOLD.

We will replace with a brand new case any **Sears Gold Filled Case** that shows the gold worn down to the composition metal within 20 years or any time in your entire lifetime, according to grade of case.

SILVER, SILVERODE AND GOLD FILLED.
20, 25 YEARS AND LIFE GUARANTEE.

WHAT WE MEAN BY THE SEARS LIFE GUARANTEE CASE. The Sears Life Guaranteed Case is a gold filled case of the very highest quality and the nearest approach to a solid gold case manufactured. The Sears Life Guaranteed Case means that should any one of these cases wear down to the inner composition metal any time within your natural life, whether you have owned the case five years, twenty years or fifty years, return it to us and we will upon the receipt of same exchange it for a brand new case of the same quality, free of charge.

The Sears Case comes in open face or hunting style, as desired. We always carry a complete line of them. **Some people** prefer the hunting style case.

Warranted for 20 and 25 years.

16-Size. Illinois Watch Case Co. Gold Filled.
No. 4C5063 Open Face, Screw Back and Bezel, 20-Year.
No. 4C5064 Hunting, 20-Year.
No. 4C5065 Open Face, Screw Back and Bezel, 25-Year.
No. 4C5066 Hunting, 25-Year.

16-SIZE. SEARS. GOLD FILLED.
No. 4C5067 Open Face, Screw Back and Bezel, 20-Year.
No. 4C5068 Hunting, 20-Year.
No. 4C5069 Open Face, Screw Back and Bezel, Life Guarantee.
No. 4C5070 Hunting, Life Guarantee.

16-SIZE. FAHYS. GOLD FILLED.
No. 4C5071 Open Face, Screw Back and Bezel, 20-Year.
No. 4C5072 Hunting, 20-Year.
No. 4C5073 Open Face, Screw Back and Bezel, 25-Year.
No. 4C5074 Hunting, 25-Year.

20-year Warranted, Gold Filled Open Face, 16-size Elgin or Waltham Watches...... **$7.99** | 20-year Warranted, Gold Filled Hunting, 16-size Elgin or Waltham Watches...... **$9.95**

PRICES QUOTED ARE FOR THE WATCHES COMPLETE.

WE FIT THE FOLLOWING MOVEMENTS IN ANY OF THESE 16-SIZE CASES, AS ILLUSTRATED.	4C5075 Open Face Silverode	4C5076 Hunting Silverode	No. 4C5077 Open Face Silver	No. 4C5078 Hunting Silver	Nos. 4C5063 4C5067	No. 4C5071	No. 4C5065	No. 4C5069	No. 4C5073	Nos. 4C5064 4C5068	No. 4C5072	No. 4C5066	No. 4C5070	No. 4C5074
7 Jeweled Grade Elgin or Waltham	$5.74	$6.09	$6.75	$7.25	$7.99	$9.15	$9.85	14.35	13.75	$9.95	11.75	11.55	15.50	$14.75
Full 15 Jeweled Grade Elgin or Waltham	Not Furnished.	Not Furnished.	10.40	10.90	11.60	12.80	13.50	18.00	17.40	13.65	15.40	15.15	19.15	18.40
Full 17 Jeweled Grade Elgin or Waltham			Not Furnished.	Not Furnished.	14.85	15.95	16.68	21.15	20.55	16.75	18.55	18.25	22.30	21.55
Full 17 Jeweled Royal Grade Waltham, Adjusted					17.15	18.35	19.03	23.55	22.95	19.05	20.95	20.55	24.70	23.95
Full 17 Jeweled No. 242 Grade Elgin, Adjusted					21.02	22.25	22.97	27.45	26.85	23.00	24.85	24.42	28.60	27.85
Full 17 Jeweled Riverside Grade Waltham, Adjusted					24.10	25.40	26.10	30.60	30.00	26.20	28.00	27.52	31.75	31.00
Full 17 Jeweled No. 243 Grade Elgin, Adjusted					25.80	27.00	27.70	32.20	31.60	27.80	29.60	29.06	33.35	32.60
Full 23 Jeweled Vanguard Grade Waltham, Adjusted					34.20	35.40	36.10	40.60	40.00	36.20	38.00	37.30	41.75	41.00
Full 21 Jeweled No. 156 Grade Elgin or Riverside Maximus Grade Waltham, Adjusted.					55.20	56.40	57.01	61.60	61.00	57.20	59.00	58.65	62.75	62.00

$5.74 AND UP.

16-SIZE. SOLID SILVER AND SILVERODE.
No. 4C5075 Open Face, Screw Back and Bezel, Silverode.
No. 4C5076 Hunting, Silverode.
No. 4C5077 Open Face, Screw Back and Bezel, Solid Silver.
No. 4C5078 Hunting, Solid Silver.

20-year Warranted, Gold Filled Open Face, 12-size Elgin or Waltham Watches........ **$9.25** | 20-year Warranted Gold Filled Hunting, 12-size Elgin or Waltham Watches....... **$11.05**

PRICES QUOTED ARE FOR THE WATCHES COMPLETE.

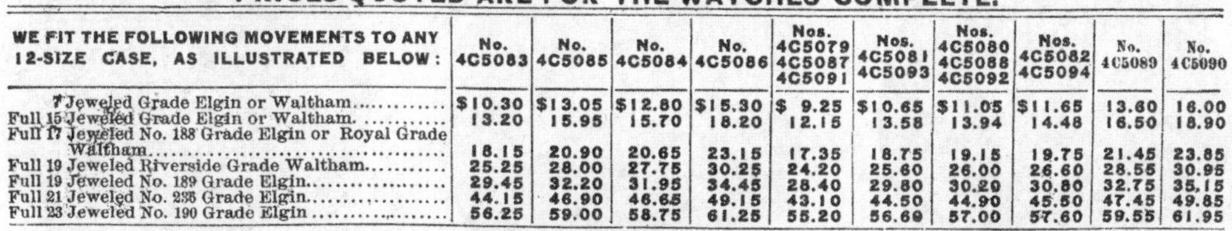

WE FIT THE FOLLOWING MOVEMENTS TO ANY 12-SIZE CASE, AS ILLUSTRATED BELOW:	No. 4C5083	No. 4C5085	No. 4C5084	No. 4C5086	Nos. 4C5079 4C5087 4C5091	Nos. 4C5081 4C5093	Nos. 4C5080 4C5088 4C5092	Nos. 4C5082 4C5094	No. 4C5089	No. 4C5090
7 Jeweled Grade Elgin or Waltham	$10.30	$13.05	$12.80	$15.30	$9.25	$10.65	$11.05	$11.65	13.60	16.00
Full 15 Jeweled Grade Elgin or Waltham.	13.20	15.95	15.70	18.20	12.15	13.58	13.94	14.48	16.50	18.90
Full 17 Jeweled No. 188 Grade Elgin or Royal Grade Waltham	18.15	20.90	20.65	23.15	17.35	18.75	19.15	19.75	21.45	23.85
Full 19 Jeweled Riverside Grade Waltham	25.25	28.00	27.75	30.25	24.20	25.60	26.00	26.60	28.55	30.95
Full 19 Jeweled No. 189 Grade Elgin	29.45	32.20	31.95	34.45	28.40	29.80	30.20	30.80	32.75	35.15
Full 21 Jeweled No. 235 Grade Elgin	44.15	46.90	46.65	49.15	43.10	44.50	44.90	45.50	47.45	49.85
Full 23 Jeweled No. 190 Grade Elgin	56.25	59.00	58.75	61.25	55.20	56.69	57.00	57.60	59.55	61.95

$9.25 TO $57.60

THE ENGRAVING.

Regarding the engravings, we generally have the exact pattern; if not, we will send a very similar design.

FOR $1.25 EXTRA WE FURNISH FANCY DIAL AND GOLD HANDS ON ANY WATCH ON THIS PAGE.

25 CENTS will carry any Watch to any part of the United States by Express.

$9.25 TO $57.60

12-Size. Illinois Watch Case Co. Gold Filled.
No. 4C5079 Open Face, Screw Back and Bezel, 20-Year.
No. 4C5080 Hunting, 20-Year.
No. 4C5081 Open Face, Screw Back and Bezel, 25-Year.
No. 4C5082 Hunting, 25-Year.

12-SIZE. FAHYS. GOLD FILLED.
No. 4C5083 Open Face, Screw Back and Bezel, 20-Year.
No. 4C5084 Hunting, 20-Year.
No. 4C5085 Open Face, Screw Back and Bezel, 25-Year.
No. 4C5086 Hunting, 25-Year.

12-SIZE. SEARS. GOLD FILLED.
No. 4C5087 Open Face, Screw Back and Bezel, 20-Year.
No. 4C5088 Hunting, 20-Year.
No. 4C5089 Open Face, Screw Back and Bezel, Life Guarantee.
No. 4C5090 Hunting, Life Guarantee.

12-Size. Illinois Watch Case Co. Gold Filled.
No. 4C5091 Open Face, Screw Back and Bezel, 20-Year.
No. 4C5092 Hunting 20-Year.
No. 4C5093 Open Face, Screw Back and Bezel, 25-Year.
No. 4C5094 Hunting, 25-Year.

LADIES' O-SIZE AND 6-SIZE GOLD FILLED, HUNTING STYLE ELGIN AND WALTHAM WATCHES FOR $9.25 AND UPWARDS.

GUARANTEED FOR 20 AND 25 YEARS AND FOR LIFE, ACCORDING TO GRADE OF CASE.

$10.52 AND UP

Illinois Watch Case Co.
GOLD FILLED—O-SIZE.
No. 4C5100 Warranted 20 yrs.
No. 4C5102 Warranted 25 yrs.

No charges for repairs on watches or clocks will be allowed unless our written consent is first secured in advance.

THE LATEST DESIGNS IN CHASING AND ENGRAVING

Illinois Watch Case Co.
GOLD FILLED—O-SIZE.
No. 4C5104 Warranted 25 yrs.
Genuine Rose Diamond.

LIFE GUARANTEE

Sears.
GOLD FILLED—O-SIZE.
No. 4C5105 Warranted 20 yrs.
No. 4C5107 Warranted for life

If our goods are not exactly as represented and described, return them and we will cheerfully refund the money.

Fahys.
GOLD FILLED—O-SIZE.
No. 4C5110 Warranted 20 yrs.
No. 4C5112 Warranted 25 yrs.

FOR $1.25 Extra we can furnish fancy dial and gold hands on any watch on this page.

$10.52 AND UP

Dueber.
GOLD FILLED—O-SIZE.
No. 4C5114 Warranted 20 yrs.
No. 4C5116 Warranted 25 yrs.

$12.15 AND UP

Illinois Watch Case Co.
GOLD FILLED—O-SIZE.
No. 4C5118 Warranted 25 yrs.
Three Genuine Rose Diamonds.

ALL OF THE CASES SHOWN ON THIS PAGE ARE HUNTING STYLE ONLY.

THE SEARS GOLD FILLED CASE IS RECOMMENDED ABOVE ALL OTHERS.

Being made of two extra heavy plates of solid gold over a hard composition metal, will wear longer than any other gold filled case made, and is the handsomest, best finished and best fitting gold filled watch case made. If you select a Sears case you will have the best gold filled watch case ever made.

WE FIT THE FOLLOWING MOVEMENTS IN ANY OF THESE O-SIZE CASES. THE PRICES QUOTED ARE FOR THE WATCHES COMPLETE.	Nos. 4C5100 4C5105 4C5114 4C5120	No. 4C5110	Nos. 4C5102 4C5116 4C5122	No. 4C5107	No. 4C5112	No. 4C5104	No. 4C5118
7 Jeweled Grade Elgin or Waltham	$10.52	$11.50	$11.22	$13.65	$13.30	$11.82	$12.15
Full 15 Jeweled Grade Elgin or Waltham	14.20	15.50	14.90	17.35	17.00	15.50	15.75
Full 16 Jeweled Lady Waltham Grade Waltham	15.25	18.12	15.95	19.97	19.62	16.55	16.78
Full 17 Jeweled Riverside Waltham	25.22	26.55	25.92	28.40	28.05	26.52	26.57
Full 18 Jeweled No. 201 Grade Elgin	26.80	28.10	27.50	29.95	29.60	27.10	28.11
Full 19 Jeweled Riverside Maximus Grade Waltham	35.20	36.50	35.90	38.35	38.00	36.50	36.35

$10.52 AND UP

Illinois Watch Case Co.
GOLD FILLED—O-SIZE.
No. 4C5120 Warranted 20 yrs.
No. 4C5122 Warranted 25 yrs.

$8.20 AND UP

Illinois Watch Case Co.
GOLD FILLED—6-SIZE.
No. 4C5125 Warranted 20 years.
No. 4C5127 Warranted 25 years.

REGARDING THE ENGRAVINGS We generally have the exact pattern. If not, we send a very similar design.

Illinois Watch Case Co.
GOLD FILLED—6-SIZE.
No. 4C5128 Warranted 25 years.
Set with Genuine Brilliant Cut Diamond. Raised Ornamentation

For 20 cents we furnish a beautiful plush Presentation Case, to fit any watch. Order by number and give size of watch.
No. 4C2000 Price...20c

Sears.
GOLD FILLED—6-SIZE.
No. 4C5129 Warranted 20 years.
No. 4C5131 Warranted for life.

25 cents will carry a ladies' watch to any point in the United States by express.

$9.70 AND UP

Fahys.
GOLD FILLED—6-SIZE.
No. 4C5134 Warranted 20 years.
No. 4C5136 Warranted 25 years.

$8.20 AND UP

Dueber.
GOLD FILLED—6-SIZE.
No. 4C5138 Warranted 20 years.
No. 4C5140 Warranted 25 years.

BUY THE BEST and you will select the SEARS case as the best gold filled case manufactured. The SEARS case being the latest gold filled case on the market, it has all the modern improvements. The designs are copied from the newest designs in solid gold cases by skilled engravers. The method of making the Sears case is up to date and only modern machinery is used. The amount of gold used on the Sears case is greater than on any other case made.

THE BEST CRITERION. We have sold thousands of SEARS cases and no doubt some friend or neighbor in your community owns one. Ask him or her what they think of the SEARS case. Judge from what is said. We are willing to accept the decree, we know it can mean nothing else but an order from you for a Sears case.

25 CENTS WILL CARRY ANY ONE OF THESE WATCHES TO ANY PART OF THE UNITED STATES BY EXPRESS.

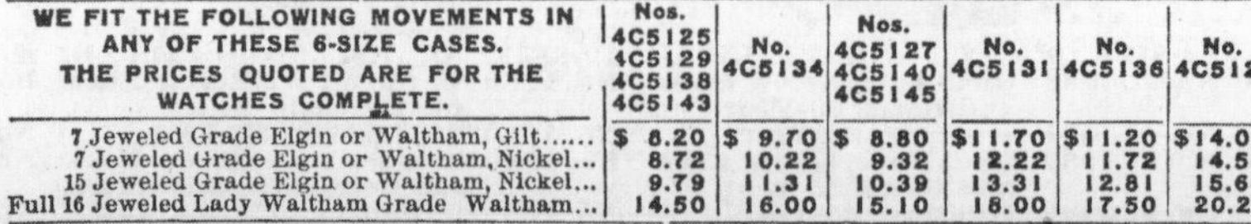

WE FIT THE FOLLOWING MOVEMENTS IN ANY OF THESE 6-SIZE CASES. THE PRICES QUOTED ARE FOR THE WATCHES COMPLETE.	Nos. 4C5125 4C5129 4C5138 4C5143	No. 4C5134	Nos. 4C5127 4C5140 4C5145	No. 4C5131	No. 4C5136	No. 4C5128
7 Jeweled Grade Elgin or Waltham, Gilt	$ 8.20	$ 9.70	$ 8.80	$11.70	$11.20	$14.06
7 Jeweled Grade Elgin or Waltham, Nickel	8.72	10.22	9.32	12.22	11.72	14.58
15 Jeweled Grade Elgin or Waltham, Nickel	9.79	11.31	10.39	13.31	12.81	15.60
Full 16 Jeweled Lady Waltham Grade Waltham	14.50	16.00	15.10	18.00	17.50	20.26

$8.20 AND UP

Illinois Watch Case Co
GOLD FILLED—6-SIZE.
No. 4C5143 Warranted 20 years.
No. 4C5145 Warranted 25 years.

18-SIZE HUNTING STYLE SOLID 14-KARAT GOLD WATCHES.

IN ARTISTIC DESIGN, WORKMANSHIP AND FINISH

OUR GOLD WATCHES EXCEL THE MARKET; our efforts in purchasing not being entirely for securing low prices, but to secure the finest quality of a gold case in addition. OUR WATCHES ARE SOLID, 14-KARAT GOLD THROUGHOUT, GUARANTEED UNITED STATES MINT ASSAY. We do not handle any lower quality of gold case than 14-karat.

IN BUYING A SOLID GOLD WATCH

YOU HAVE AN ARTICLE OF INTRINSIC VALUE on which money can be realized much easier than on any other article of merchandise; and when you consider our very low price on our one small profit plan, direct from manufacturer to consumer, we know you can always obtain very near the full value of your watch when disposing of it.

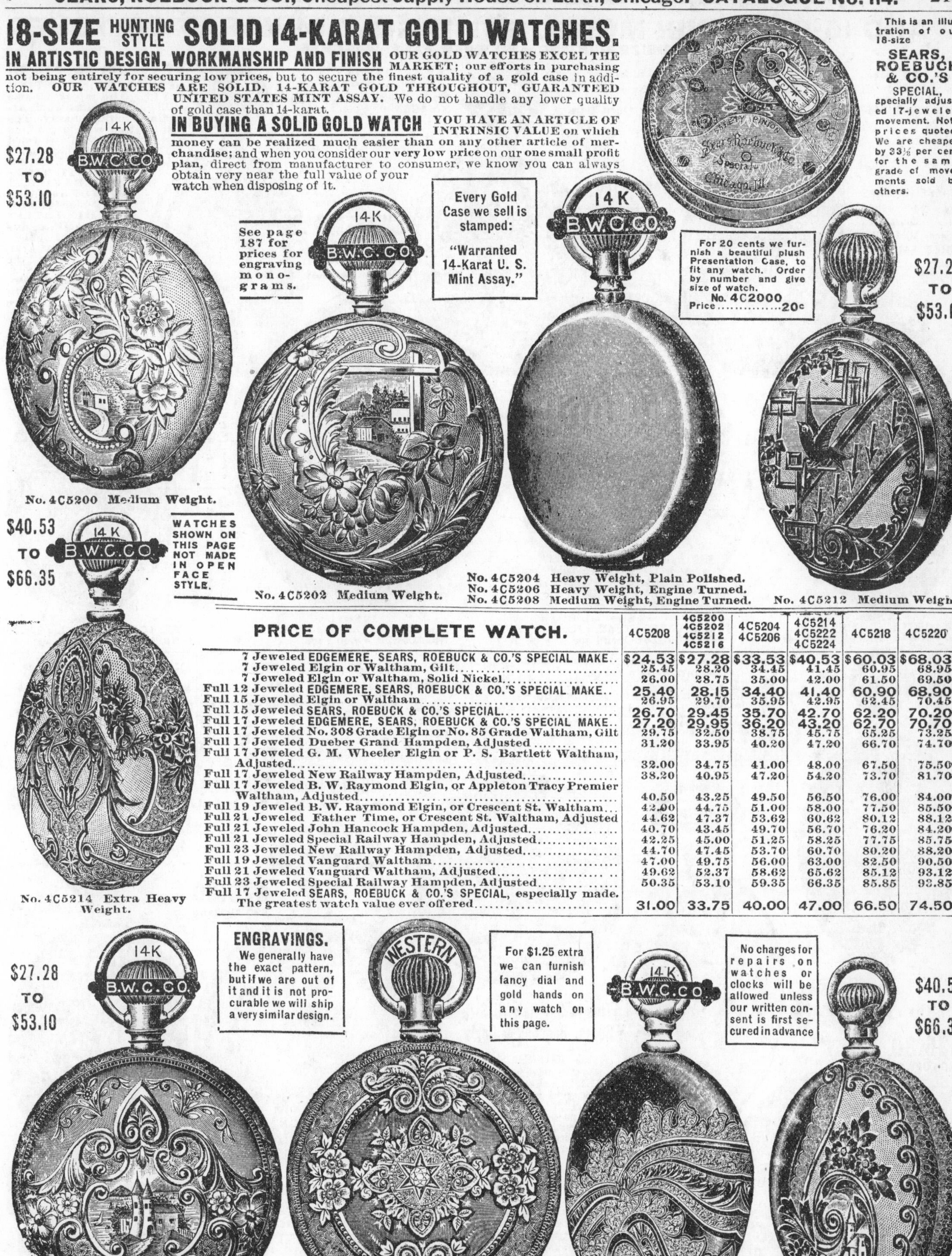

This is an illustration of our 18-size SEARS, ROEBUCK & CO.'S SPECIAL, specially adjusted 17-jeweled movement. Note prices quoted. We are cheaper by 33⅓ per cent for the same grade of movements sold by others.

$27.28 TO $53.10

No. 4C5200 Medium Weight.

See page 187 for prices for engraving monograms.

Every Gold Case we sell is stamped: "Warranted 14-Karat U. S. Mint Assay."

For 20 cents we furnish a beautiful plush Presentation Case, to fit any watch. Order by number and give size of watch.
No. 4C2000
Price..............20c

No. 4C5202 Medium Weight.

No. 4C5204 Heavy Weight, Plain Polished.
No. 4C5206 Heavy Weight, Engine Turned.
No. 4C5208 Medium Weight, Engine Turned.

$27.28 TO $53.10

No. 4C5212 Medium Weight.

$40.53 TO $66.35

WATCHES SHOWN ON THIS PAGE NOT MADE IN OPEN FACE STYLE.

No. 4C5214 Extra Heavy Weight.

PRICE OF COMPLETE WATCH.	4C5208	4C5200 4C5202 4C5212 4C5216	4C5204 4C5206	4C5214 4C5222 4C5224	4C5218	4C5220
7 Jeweled EDGEMERE, SEARS, ROEBUCK & CO.'S SPECIAL MAKE..	$24.53	$27.28	$33.53	$40.53	$60.03	$68.03
7 Jeweled Elgin or Waltham, Gilt..........	25.45	28.20	34.45	41.45	60.95	68.95
7 Jeweled Elgin or Waltham, Solid Nickel..........	26.00	28.75	35.00	42.00	61.50	69.50
Full 12 Jeweled EDGEMERE, SEARS, ROEBUCK & CO.'S SPECIAL MAKE..	25.40	28.15	34.40	41.40	60.90	68.90
Full 15 Jeweled Elgin or Waltham..........	26.95	29.70	35.95	42.95	62.45	70.45
Full 15 Jeweled SEARS, ROEBUCK & CO.'S SPECIAL..........	26.70	29.45	35.70	42.70	62.20	70.20
Full 17 Jeweled EDGEMERE, SEARS, ROEBUCK & CO.'S SPECIAL MAKE..	27.20	29.95	36.20	43.20	62.70	70.70
Full 17 Jeweled No. 308 Grade Elgin or No. 85 Grade Waltham, Gilt	29.75	32.50	38.75	45.75	65.25	73.25
Full 17 Jeweled Dueber Grand Hampden, Adjusted..........	31.20	33.95	40.20	47.20	66.70	74.70
Full 17 Jeweled G. M. Wheeler Elgin or P. S. Bartlett Waltham, Adjusted..........	32.00	34.75	41.00	48.00	67.50	75.50
Full 17 Jeweled New Railway Hampden, Adjusted..........	38.20	40.95	47.20	54.20	73.70	81.70
Full 17 Jeweled B. W. Raymond Elgin, or Appleton Tracy Premier Waltham, Adjusted..........	40.50	43.25	49.50	56.50	76.00	84.00
Full 19 Jeweled B. W. Raymond Elgin, or Crescent St. Waltham...	42.00	44.75	51.00	58.00	77.50	85.50
Full 21 Jeweled Father Time, or Crescent St. Waltham, Adjusted	44.62	47.37	53.62	60.62	80.12	88.12
Full 21 Jeweled John Hancock Hampden, Adjusted..........	40.70	43.45	49.70	56.70	76.20	84.20
Full 21 Jeweled Special Railway Hampden, Adjusted..........	42.25	45.00	51.25	58.25	77.75	85.75
Full 23 Jeweled New Railway Hampden, Adjusted..........	44.70	47.45	53.70	60.70	80.20	88.20
Full 19 Jeweled Vanguard Waltham..........	47.00	49.75	56.00	63.00	82.50	90.50
Full 21 Jeweled Vanguard Waltham, Adjusted..........	49.62	52.37	58.62	65.62	85.12	93.12
Full 23 Jeweled Special Railway Hampden, Adjusted..........	50.35	53.10	59.35	66.35	85.85	93.85
Full 17 Jeweled SEARS, ROEBUCK & CO.'S SPECIAL, especially made. The greatest watch value ever offered..........	31.00	33.75	40.00	47.00	66.50	74.50

$27.28 TO $53.10

ENGRAVINGS. We generally have the exact pattern, but if we are out of it and it is not procurable we will ship a very similar design.

For $1.25 extra we can furnish fancy dial and gold hands on any watch on this page.

No charges for repairs on watches or clocks will be allowed unless our written consent is first secured in advance

$40.53 TO $66.35

No. 4C5216 Medium Weight.

No. 4C5218 Extra Heavy Weight, Colored Gold Ornamentation.
No. 4C5220 Colored Gold Ornamentation, set with Fine Large Diamond.

No. 4C5222 Extra Heavy Weight.

No. 4C5224 Extra Heavy Weight.

12 AND 16-SIZE THIN MODEL SOLID GOLD 14-KARAT WATCHES

12-SIZE HUNTING AND OPEN FACE WATCHES.

12 Size.
No. 4C5300 Hunting Style.
No. 4C5302 Open Face.

12 Size.
No. 4C5304 Hunting Style.
No. 4C5306 Open Face.

12 Size.
Plain Polished.
No. 4C5308 Hunting Style.
No. 4C5310 Open Face.

AT $24.50 OR $25.75

OPEN FACE OR HUNTING STYLE. The latest 12-size solid gold 14-karat, warranted United States Assay. The case is fitted with a genuine Elgin or Waltham 7-jeweled grade movement; **GUARANTEED AN ACCURATE TIMEKEEPER FOR A TERM OF 5 YEARS. The 12-Size WATCH IS THE LATEST SIZE MADE,** and is the smallest gentlemen's size, a size larger than the largest ladies' size, **the most popular size used in large cities.**

THESE WATCHES have good weight cases, guaranteed to wear and GIVE ENTIRE SATISFACTION.

WARRANTED FINE 14-KARAT U. S. ASSAY.

The two Western Cases are extra heavy, the BEST Solid Gold Case manufactured, with no exception.

For $1.25 extra we can furnish fancy dial and gold hands on any watch on this page.

12 Size.
No. 4C5312 Hunting Style.
No. 4C5314 Open Face.

12 Size.
No. 4C5316 Hunting Style.
No. 4C5318 Open Face.

12 Size.
No. 4C5320 Hunting Style.
No. 4C5322 Open Face.

12 Size.
No. 4C5324 Hunting Style.
No. 4C5326 Open Face.

No. 4C5328 Hunting Style.
No. 4C5330 Open Face.

12 Size.

We Fit these Cases with the following 12-Size Movements. WARRANTED FOR 5 YEARS.	No. 4C5302 4C5310	No. 4C5314	No. 4C5300 4C5308	No. 4C5306	No. 4C5312	No. 4C5304 4C5326	No. 4C5318	No. 4C5324	No. 4C5322 4C5330	No. 4C5316	No. 4C5320 4C5328
7 Jeweled Grade Elgin or Waltham	$24.50	$26.25	$25.75	$26.75	$27.25	$29.75	$31.75	$32.75	$34.45	$36.25	$38.25
Full 10 Jeweled **EDGEMERE, SEARS, ROEBUCK & CO.'S SPECIAL MAKE**	24.30	26.05	25.55	26.55	27.05	29.50	31.55	32.55	34.25	36.05	38.05
Full 15 Jeweled Grade Elgin or Waltham	27.25	29.00	28.50	29.50	30.00	32.50	34.50	35.50	37.20	39.00	41.00
Full 17 Jeweled No. 275 Grade Elgin or Royal Grade Waltham	32.00	33.75	33.25	34.25	34.75	37.25	39.25	40.25	41.95	43.75	45.75
Full 19 Jeweled Riverside Grade Waltham	38.75	40.50	40.00	41.00	41.50	44.00	46.00	47.00	48.70	50.50	52.50
Full 19 Jeweled No. 189 Grade Elgin	42.75	44.50	44.00	45.00	45.50	48.00	50.00	51.00	52.70	54.50	56.50
Full 21 Jeweled No. 236 Grade Elgin	56.75	58.50	58.00	59.00	59.50	62.00	64.00	65.00	66.70	68.50	70.50
Full 23 Jeweled No. 190 Grade Elgin	68.25	70.00	69.50	70.50	71.00	73.50	75.50	76.50	78.20	80.00	82.00

16-Size Hunting Thin Model 14-Karat Solid Gold Case.

REMEMBER: We carry nothing but 14-karat quality in our solid gold cases.

$26.80 AND UPWARD

$36.30 TO **$81.50**

$36.30 AND UPWARD

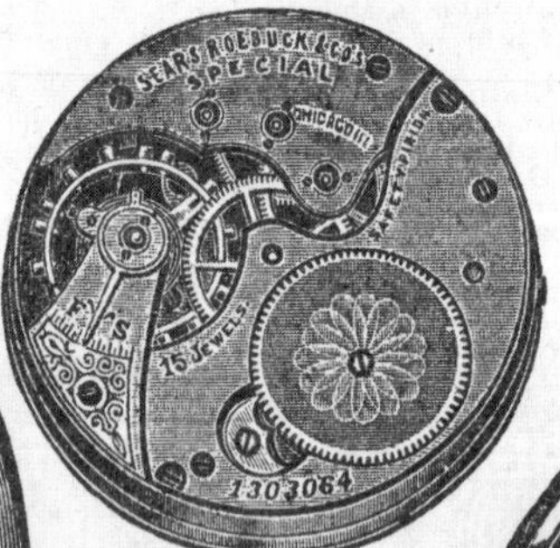

This Is Our New 16-Size Sears, Roebuck & Co.'s

Special 15-Jeweled Movement.

See the description. It is full 15-jeweled, set in settings, solid gold plated, Roman color, beautifully finished, patent pinion and escapement, high grade finish throughout, guaranteed for five years.

16 Size.
No. 4C5331 Hunting Style. Plain or Engine Turned. Medium Weight.
No. 4C5332 Same as No. 4C5331. Heavy Weight.

16 Size.
No. 4C5336 Hunting Style. Medium Weight.

16 Size.
No. 4C5338 Hunting Style. Extra Heavy Weight.

16 Size.
No. 4C5340 Hunting Style. Heavy Weight.

WE FIT THESE CASES WITH THE FOLLOWING 16-SIZE MOVEMENTS.	No. 4C5336	No. 4C5331	4C5338 4C5340	No. 4C5332
7 Jeweled Grade Elgin or Waltham	$27.00	$29.00	$36.50	$32.50
Full 12 Jeweled **EDGEMERE, SEARS, ROEBUCK & CO.'S SPECIAL MAKE**	26.80	28.80	36.30	32.30
Full 15 Jeweled Grade Elgin or Waltham	30.50	32.50	40.00	36.00
Full 15 Jeweled **SEARS, ROEBUCK & CO.'S SPECIAL**, especially made	28.50	30.50	38.00	34.00
Full 17 Jeweled No. 241 Grade Elgin or No. 630 Grade Waltham	33.50	35.50	42.00	38.00
Full 17 Jeweled Royal Grade Waltham	35.75	37.75	45.25	41.25
Full 17 Jeweled No 242 Grade Elgin	39.50	41.50	49.00	45.00
Full 17 Jeweled Riverside Grade Waltham	42.50	44.50	52.00	48.00
Full 17 Jeweled No. 243 Grade Elgin	44.00	46.00	53.50	49.50
Full 23 Jeweled Vanguard Grade Waltham	52.00	54.00	61.50	57.50
Full 21 Jeweled No. 156 Grade Elgin or Riverside Maximus Grade Waltham	72.00	74.00	81.50	77.50
Full 17 Jeweled **SEARS, ROEBUCK & CO.'S SPECIAL**, especially made. The greatest watch value ever offered	32.50	34.50	42.00	38.00

LADIES' SOLID 14-KARAT GOLD 6-SIZE, HUNTING STYLE WATCH FOR $14.30.

JOBBERS AND DEALERS CANNOT UNDERSTAND how we areable to make the price on solid gold watches. We are positively selling for less than what they pay for them. Order one and be convinced. The goods are exactly as represented in every detail. None but the genuine article. See the prices quoted below. HOW WE DO IT AT THE PRICE.—The story is easily told. We buy cheaper, our expenses for handling are less, and we are satisfied with smaller profits than other wholesalers. REMEMBER, $14.30 to $35.00 are the prices on these watches, according to grade of movements.

$14.30 to $20.00

REGARDING ENGRAVINGS. We generally have the exact pattern. If not, we will send a very similar design.

DESCRIPTION OF CASES. These cases are stamped as follows: "Warranted 14-karat U. S. Assay." They are solid gold through and through.

Our 6-Size 17-Jewel Sears, Roebuck & Co. Movement is the most reliable ladies' size movement made.

25 cents will carry a ladies' watch to any point in the United States by express.

$14.30 to $20.00

No. 4C5400 Solid Gold.

No. 4C5403 Solid Gold.

No. 4C5404 Solid Gold.

No. 4C5407 Solid Gold.

No. 4C5409 Solid Gold.

$21.30 TO $26.50

No charges for repairs on watches or clocks will be allowed unless our written consent is first secured in advance.

This is a picture of our 17-jeweled Sears, Roebuck & Co. Special 6-size movement. We warrant it an accurate timekeeper.

For 20 cents we furnish a beautiful Plush Presentation Case to fit any watch. See No. 4C2000, on page 192.

The 17-Jeweled Edgemere Movement is recommended by us. For the price nothing equals the 7 and 12-Jeweled grades of same make.

$21.30 TO $26.50

No. 4C5410 Solid Gold.

No. 4C5412 Solid Gold.

No. 4C5414 Solid Gold. Colored Gold Ornamented.

No. 4C5417 Solid Gold.

$17.30 to $23.00

For a good cheap watch buy our Edgemere.

No. 4C5419 Solid Gold. Colored Gold Ornamented.

No. 4C5420 Solid Gold. Genuine Diamond Set and Colored Gold Ornamented.

SEARS, ROEBUCK & CO.'S SPECIAL.

This is a picture of our 15-jeweled Sears, Roebuck & Co. Special 6-size movement. We recommend it.

WE CAN ENGRAVE your name in script at 2½ cents per letter upon any watch.

We can conscientiously recommend our Sears, Roebuck & Co.'s Special Movements.

No. 4C5423 Solid Gold. Genuine Diamond Set and Colored Gold Ornamented.

$27.30 to $33.00

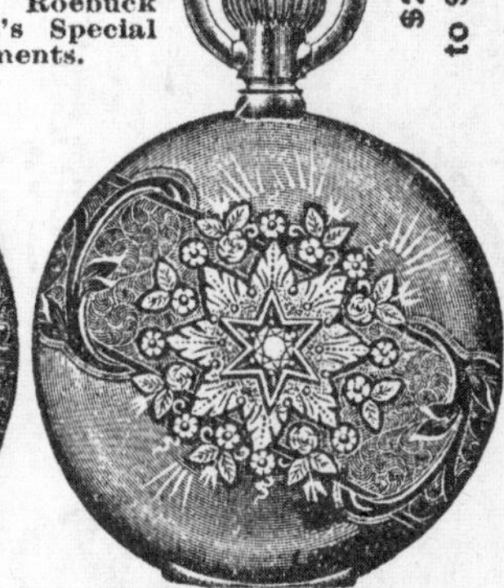

No. 4C5424 Solid Gold. Genuine Diamond Set and Colored Gold Ornamented.

$29.30 to $35.00

WE FIT THESE CASES WITH THE FOLLOWING 6-SIZE MOVEMENTS.	4C5400 4C5403 4C5404 4C5407 4C5409	No. 4C5419	No. 4C5414	Nos. 4C5410 4C5417	No. 4C5412	No. 4C5420	No. 4C5423	No. 4C5424	Nos. 4C5427 4C5428
7 Jeweled Edgemere, Sears, Roebuck & Co.'s Special Make	$14.30	$17.30	$19.80	$21.30	$22.05	$24.80	$26.30	$27.30	$29.30
7 Jeweled No. 200 Grade Hampden, Gilt	15.89	18.89	21.39	22.89	23.64	26.39	27.89	28.89	30.89
7 Jeweled Grade Elgin or Waltham, Gilt	15.95	18.95	21.45	22.95	23.70	26.45	27.95	28.95	30.95
7 Jeweled Grade Elgin or Waltham, Nickel	16.50	19.50	22.00	23.50	24.25	27.00	28.50	29.50	31.50
11 Jeweled No. 206 Grade Hampden	17.00	20.00	22.50	24.00	24.75	27.50	29.00	30.00	32.00
Full 12 Jeweled Edgemere, Sears, Roebuck & Co.'s Special Make	15.90	18.90	21.40	22.90	23.65	26.40	27.90	28.90	30.90
Full 15 Jeweled No. 213 Grade Hampden	17.65	20.65	23.15	24.65	25.40	28.15	29.85	30.65	32.65
Full 15 Jeweled Grade Elgin or Waltham	17.45	20.45	22.95	24.45	25.20	27.95	29.45	30.45	32.45
Full 15 Jeweled Sears, Roebuck & Co.'s Special	16.95	19.95	22.45	23.95	24.70	27.45	28.95	29.95	31.95
Full 17 Jeweled Edgemere, Sears, Roebuck & Co.'s Special Make	17.70	20.70	23.20	24.70	25.45	28.20	29.70	30.70	32.70
Full 17 Jeweled Sears, Roebuck & Co.'s Special. Especially made. This is the greatest watch value ever offered	20.00	23.00	25.50	26.50	27.75	30.50	32.00	33.00	35.00

This same case but without stones set in name $3.00 less than prices quoted.

No. 4C5427 Solid Gold. Genuine Diamond Set and Colored Gold Ornamented.

No. 4C5428 Solid Gold.

OUR 12-JEWELED EDGEMERE MOVEMENT, manufactured expressly for us and fitted in any one of these cases at from $15.90 to $30.90, enables you to purchase a high grade, excellent timekeeper at prices less than trash is offered by others.

No. 4C5428 This case is set with two genuine diamonds and three rubies, plain or satin finish, made with any name. This case is made to order and takes about eight to ten days. We can supply no other combination of stones than the ones mentioned. Furnished in plain polished or satin finish.

LADIES' 0-SIZE SOLID 14-KARAT GOLD WATCHES

Guaranteed Exactly as Represented and Described.

QUALITY. These cases are solid gold 14-karat fine. Each case is stamped as follows: "Warranted 14-K. U. S. Assay." You are positively protected and need have no hesitancy in buying.

The illustrations of all watches in this catalogue show exact size of the watch.

☞ THIS ILLUSTRATION shows a three-letter monogram. Price quoted includes engraving.

FOR A CASE THAT WILL WEAR YOUR NATURAL LIFETIME BUY A WESTERN.

No. 4C5500 Any one, two or three letters, ribbon monogram. Plain or satin finished case.

No. 4C5502 Plain polished or satin finished case, set with genuine diamond.

No. 4C5503 Plain Case Set with Five Genuine Cut Diamonds.

$12.50 and upwards

SEE PRICE LIST ..AT.. BOTTOM OF PAGE.

$18.00 and upwards

Movements are guaranteed for five years.

No. 4C5505

No. 4C5507

No. 4C5509

No. 4C5510

No. 4C5512

WORKMANSHIP AND FINISH second to none. The engraving is hand work. The designing the very latest and up to date. The entire case is finished in an absolutely perfect manner. No rough edges and no loose joints. The lids fit snug and securely, making the case practically dust proof.

A good graduation present. None better.

12c will carry any of these watches anywhere by mail.

Our 15 jeweled Edgemere will give correct time.

EVERY SOLID GOLD CASE WE SELL IS STAMPED "14-KARAT GOLD, WARRANTED, U. S. MINT ASSAY."

No. 4C5514

No. 4C5516

No. 4C5518

No. 4C5521

$24.00 and upwards

Regarding the engravings, we generally have the exact pattern. If not, we will send a very similar design.

These cases are all hand engraved and hand chased.

The cases on this page are the best made.

THEY WILL WEAR A LIFETIME.

See Price List at Bottom of Page.

No. 4C5523 Plain Case set with three Genuine Diamonds

No. 4C5524 Set with one Genuine Diamond

No. 4C5526 Colored Gold Ornamented

No. 4C5529 Raised Gold Applique

No. 4C5530 Colored Gold Ornamented

For 20 cents we furnish a beautiful Plush Presentation Case to fit any watch. Order by number and give size of watch. No. 4C2000 Price ... 20c

WE GUARANTEE ANY OF THE MOVEMENTS BELOW FOR A TERM OF FIVE YEARS.

A FINE BIRTHDAY GIFT.

☞ No. 4C5538 This illustration shows case set with two genuine diamonds and three rubies, plain or satin finish, made with any name. This case is made to order and takes about 8 to 10 days. We can supply no other combination of stones than the ones mentioned. Without stone setting, price is $2.50 less than quoted for No. 4C5538.

No. 4C5533 Colored Gold Ornamented, Set with Genuine Diamond

No. 4C5534 Plain Case, set with three Genuine Diamonds

No. 4C5536 Colored Gold Ornamented, Set with Genuine Diamond

WE FIT THESE CASES WITH THE FOLLOWING 0-SIZE MOVEMENTS: PRICE OF COMPLETE WATCH.	4C5505 4C5507	4C5509 4C5510	4C5512 4C5514	4C5500	4C5516 4C5521	4C5518	4C5530	4C5526 4C5502	4C5524	4C5523 4C5529 4C5533	4C5536	4C5534	4C5503 4C5538
7 jeweled Fine Swiss Lever	$12.50	$15.00	$18.00	$18.75	$18.60	$19.20	$20.40	$21.00	$22.20	$24.00	$23.75	$23.40	$27.00
11 jeweled Fine Swiss Lever	14.80	17.30	20.30	21.05	20.90	21.50	22.70	23.30	24.50	26.30	26.05	25.70	29.30
7 jeweled Grade Elgin or Waltham	16.00	18.50	21.50	22.25	22.10	22.70	23.90	24.50	25.70	27.50	27.25	26.90	30.50
Full 15 jeweled **EDGEMERE, SEARS, ROEBUCK & CO.'S SPECIAL MAKE**	**15.80**	**18.30**	**21.30**	**22.05**	**21.90**	**22.50**	**23.70**	**24.30**	**25.50**	**27.30**	**27.05**	**26.70**	**30.30**
Full 15 jeweled Grade Elgin or Waltham	19.50	21.20	25.00	25.75	25.60	26.20	27.40	28.00	29.20	31.00	30.75	30.40	34.00
Full 16 jeweled Lady Waltham or Grade Waltham	20.50	23.00	26.00	26.75	26.60	27.20	28.40	29.00	30.20	32.00	31.75	31.40	35.00
Full 16 jeweled No. 68 Grade Waltham	21.50	24.00	27.00	27.75	27.60	28.20	29.40	30.00	31.20	33.00	32.75	32.40	36.[illegible]
Full 17 jeweled No. 200 Grade Elgin	22.50	25.00	28.00	28.75	28.60	29.20	30.40	31.00	32.20	34.00	33.75	33.40	[illegible]
Full 17 jeweled Riverside Waltham	30.00	32.50	35.50	36.25	36.10	36.70	37.90	38.50	39.70	41.50	41.25	40.90	44.50
Full 19 jeweled No. 201 Grade Elgin	31.50	34.00	37.00	37.75	37.60	38.20	39.40	40.00	41.20	43.00	42.75	42.40	46.00
Full 17 jeweled No. 70 Grade Waltham	34.00	36.50	39.50	40.25	40.10	40.70	41.90	42.50	43.70	45.50	45.25	44.90	48.50
Full 19 jeweled Riverside Maximus Grade Waltham	39.50	42.00	45.00	45.75	45.60	46.20	74.04	48.00	49.20	51.00	50.75	50.40	54.00

GENTLEMEN'S FINEST QUALITY GOLD FILLED, ROLLED GOLD PLATE, GOLD ELECTRO PLATE, WHITE METAL, NICKEL and SOLID SILVER VEST CHAINS

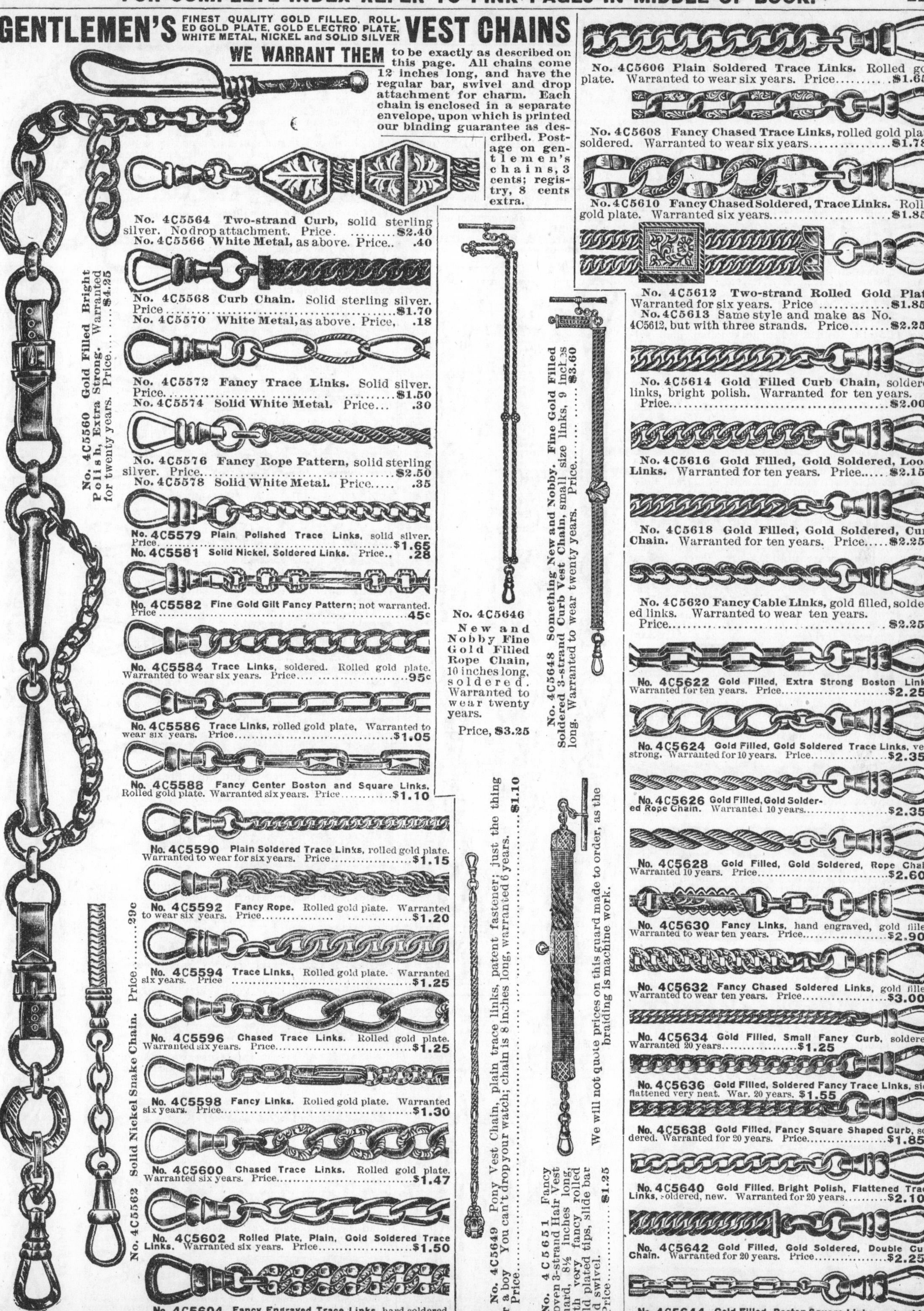

WE WARRANT THEM to be exactly as described on this page. All chains come 12 inches long, and have the regular bar, swivel and drop attachment for charm. Each chain is enclosed in a separate envelope, upon which is printed our binding guarantee as described. Postage on gentlemen's chains, 3 cents; registry, 8 cents extra.

No. 4C5560 Gold Filled Bright Polish, Extra Strong. Warranted for twenty years. Price.......$4.25

No. 4C5564 **Two-strand Curb,** solid sterling silver. No drop attachment. Price. $2.40
No. 4C5566 **White Metal,** as above. Price.. .40

No. 4C5568 **Curb Chain.** Solid sterling silver. Price.............$1.70
No. 4C5570 **White Metal,** as above. Price, .18

No. 4C5572 **Fancy Trace Links.** Solid silver. Price.............$1.50
No. 4C5574 **Solid White Metal.** Price... .30

No. 4C5576 **Fancy Rope Pattern,** solid sterling silver. Price.............$2.50
No. 4C5578 **Solid White Metal.** Price..... .35

No. 4C5579 **Plain Polished Trace Links,** solid silver. Price.............$1.65
No. 4C5581 **Solid Nickel, Soldered Links.** Price., .28

No. 4C5582 **Fine Gold Gilt Fancy Pattern;** not warranted. Price.............45c

No. 4C5584 **Trace Links,** soldered. Rolled gold plate. Warranted to wear six years. Price.... ....95c

No. 4C5586 **Trace Links,** rolled gold plate. Warranted to wear six years. Price.............$1.05

No. 4C5588 **Fancy Center Boston and Square Links.** Rolled gold plate. Warranted six years. Price...........$1.10

No. 4C5590 **Plain Soldered Trace Links,** rolled gold plate. Warranted to wear for six years. Price.............$1.15

No. 4C5592 **Fancy Rope.** Rolled gold plate. Warranted to wear six years. Price.............$1.20

No. 4C5594 **Trace Links.** Rolled gold plate. Warranted six years. Price.............$1.25

No. 4C5596 **Chased Trace Links.** Rolled gold plate. Warranted six years. Price.............$1.25

No. 4C5598 **Fancy Links.** Rolled gold plate. Warranted six years. Price.............$1.30

No. 4C5600 **Chased Trace Links.** Rolled gold plate. Warranted six years. Price.............$1.47

No. 4C5602 **Rolled Plate, Plain, Gold Soldered Trace Links.** Warranted six years. Price.............$1.50

No. 4C5604 **Fancy Engraved Trace Links,** hard soldered. Rolled gold plate. Warranted to wear six years. Price..$1.55

No. 4C5562 Solid Nickel Snake Chain. Price.........29c

No. 4C5646 New and Nobby Fine Gold Filled Rope Chain, 10 inches long, soldered. Warranted to wear twenty years.

Price, $3.25

No. 4C5648 Something New and Nobby. Fine Gold Filled Soldered 3-strand Curb Vest Chain, small size links, 9 inches long. Warranted to wear twenty years. Price.......$3.60

No. 4C5649 Pony Vest Chain, plain trace links, patent fastener; just the thing for a boy. You can't drop your watch; chain is 8 inches long, warranted 6 years. Price.............$1.10

No. 4C5651 Fancy Woven 3-strand Hair Vest Guard, 8½ inches long, with very fancy rolled gold plated tips, slide bar and swivel. Price.............$1.25

We will not quote prices on this guard made to order, as the braiding is machine work.

No. 4C5606 **Plain Soldered Trace Links.** Rolled gold plate. Warranted to wear six years. Price..........$1.65

No. 4C5608 **Fancy Chased Trace Links,** rolled gold plate, soldered. Warranted to wear six years.............$1.78

No. 4C5610 **Fancy Chased Soldered, Trace Links.** Rolled gold plate. Warranted six years.............$1.85

No. 4C5612 **Two-strand Rolled Gold Plate.** Warranted for six years. Price.............$1.85
No. 4C5613 Same style and make as No. 4C5612, but with three strands. Price........$2.25

No. 4C5614 **Gold Filled Curb Chain,** soldered links, bright polish. Warranted for ten years. Price.............$2.00

No. 4C5616 **Gold Filled, Gold Soldered, Loose Links.** Warranted for ten years. Price..... $2.15

No. 4C5618 **Gold Filled, Gold Soldered, Curb Chain.** Warranted for ten years. Price.....$2.25

No. 4C5620 **Fancy Cable Links,** gold filled, soldered links. Warranted to wear ten years. Price.............$2.25

No. 4C5622 **Gold Filled, Extra Strong Boston Links.** Warranted for ten years. Price.............$2.25

No. 4C5624 **Gold Filled, Gold Soldered Trace Links,** very strong. Warranted for 10 years. Price.............$2.35

No. 4C5626 **Gold Filled, Gold Soldered Rope Chain.** Warranted 10 years.............$2.35

No. 4C5628 **Gold Filled, Gold Soldered, Rope Chain.** Warranted 10 years. Price.............$2.60

No. 4C5630 **Fancy Links,** hand engraved, gold filled. Warranted to wear ten years. Price.............$2.90

No. 4C5632 **Fancy Chased Soldered Links,** gold filled. Warranted to wear ten years. Price.............$3.00

No. 4C5634 **Gold Filled, Small Fancy Curb,** soldered. Warranted 20 years.............$1.25

No. 4C5636 **Gold Filled, Soldered Fancy Trace Links,** side flattened very neat. War. 20 years. $1.55

No. 4C5638 **Gold Filled, Fancy Square Shaped Curb,** soldered. Warranted for 20 years. Price.............$1.85

No. 4C5640 **Gold Filled, Bright Polish, Flattened Trace Links,** soldered, new. Warranted for 20 years.............$2.10

No. 4C5642 **Gold Filled, Gold Soldered, Double Curb Chain.** Warranted for 20 years. Price.............$2.25

No. 4C5644 **Gold Filled, Boston Square Links,** not soldered. Warranted for 20 years. Price.............$2.35

SOMETHING NEW IN HIGH GRADE GOLD FILLED CHAINS.

OUR SEARS' LIFE GUARANTEE GOLD FILLED CHAINS.

ON THIS PAGE we show our very latest addition in the chain department. Our Sears' Life Guarantee Chain is the highest grade gold filled chain on the market.

We guarantee it to wear for the term of your natural life. By this we mean, should any one of our Sears' Life Guarantee gold filled chains wear down to the inner composition metal, although you owned it for 50 years, 25 years, 10 years or any time within your natural life, you can return it to us, and upon its receipt, we will forward at once a brand new Sears' Life Guarantee gold filled chain free of all charge. Every chain shown on this page, unless otherwise stated, has soldered links. They are all 12 inches long and have the bar, swivel and drop attachment for charm. The gold filled chains, warranted for 10 and 20 years, shown on this page, are all simple and practical in design and exact counterparts of solid gold chains. Each one carries our guarantee for time stated continuous wear.

No 4C5652 Gold filled, bright polish, gold soldered double curb chain, warranted 20 years..$2.50

No. 4C5654 Gold filled, bright polish, lapped side links, gold soldered, warranted 20 years........$2.55

No. 4C5656 Gold filled, bright polish, fancy swedged trace links, gold soldered, warranted for 20 years. Price..........$2.65

No. 4C5658 Gold filled, bright polish, gold soldered double curb chain, warranted 20 years..$2.75

No. 4C5660 Gold filled, bright polish, chased loose trace links, gold soldered, warranted 20 years. Price..........$2.75

No. 4C5662 Gold filled, gold soldered, double strand, double curb chain, with solid gold front slide, bright polish, warranted 20 years. Price......$2.85

No. 4C5664 Gold filled, soldered, bright finish cable link chain, warranted 20 years. Price....$3.00

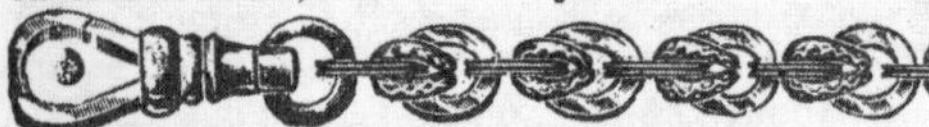

No. 4C5666 Gold filled, California pattern, Roman and bright finish, links not soldered, warranted 20 years. Price..........$3.05

No. 4C5668 Gold filled, gold soldered, double strand, double curb chain, with solid gold front slide, bright polish, warranted 20 years. Price.....$3.25

No. 4C5670 Same as No. 4C5668, but with large tips. Price..........$3.75

No. 4C5672 Gold filled, ship's cable soldered links, bright polish, warranted 20 years. Price......$3.40

No. 4C5674 Gold filled, finest chain on the market, ornamented square link Boston chain, our own design; links are not soldered; warranted for 20 years. Price..........$3.48

No. 4C5676 Gold filled, extra strong Boston square links, not soldered, bright polish, warranted for 20 years. Price..........$3.50

No. 4C5678 Gold filled, bright polish, gold soldered double curb chain, warranted 20 years..$3.50

No. 4C5680 Gold filled, gold soldered, bright finish loose curb links, warranted 20 years. Price, $3.50

No. 4C5682 Gold filled, fancy double trace links, gold soldered and bright finish throughout, very substantially made, warranted 20 years. Price...$3.56

No. 4C5684 Gold filled, bright finish Boston links, warranted for 20 years. Price..........$3.58

No. 4C5686 Gold filled, gold soldered, hand engraved loose curb links, warranted 20 years...$3.80

No. 4C5718 Solid gold front, bright polish, hand engraved fancy links, not soldered, warranted 20 years...$4.35

No. 4C5720 Two-strand rope chain, gold filled, engraved slide, warranted for 20 years. Price..........$3.45

No. 4C5722 Sears' Life Guarantee Chain, gold filled bright polish, gold soldered loose curb links. Price..........$4.65

No. 4C5724 Sears' Life Guarantee Chain, gold filled, bright polish, gold soldered trace links. $5.00

No. 4C5726 Sears' Life Guarantee Chain, gold filled, bright polish, gold soldered double curb links. Price..........$5.25

No. 4C5728 Sears' Life Guarantee Chain, gold filled, bright polish, gold soldered extra heavy loose curb links. Price..........$5.50

No. 4C5730 Sears' Life Guarantee Chain, gold filled, bright polish, gold soldered plain square links. Price..........$5.75

No. 4C5732 Sears' Life Guarantee Chain, gold filled, bright polish, gold soldered Boston square links. Price..........$6.00

No. 4C5734 Sears' Life Guarantee Chain, gold filled, bright polish, gold soldered fancy double wire trace links. Price..........$6.40

No. 4C5688 Gold filled, soldered, fancy square link cable, bright finish, warranted for 20 years.....$3.95

No. 4C5690 Gold filled, lapped, bright, soldered, extra heavy and strong curb links, warranted for 20 years. Price..........$4.00

No. 4C5692 Gold filled, soldered, fancy square link cable, bright finish, warranted 20 years........$4.00

No. 4C5694 Gold filled, fancy bright polish, soldered trace links, warranted 20 years. Price..$4.15

No. 4C5696 Gold filled, bright polish, chased, soldered trace links, very durable, warranted for 20 years. Price..........$4.20

No. 4C5698 Gold filled, gold soldered, double strand, double curb chain, with solid gold front slide, bright polish, warranted 20 years. Price....$3.65

No. 4C5700 Gold filled, gold soldered, triple strand, double curb chain, with solid gold front slide, bright polish, warranted 20 years. Price.......$4.12

No. 4C5702 Three-strand curb chain, hand engraved slide and tips, gold filled, warranted 20 years. Price..........$4.50

No. 4C5704 Gold filled, gold soldered, triple strand, double curb chain, with solid gold front slide, bright polish, warranted 20 years. Price....$4.65

No. 4C5706 Same as No. 4C5704, but with large square tips. Price..........$5.15

No. 4C5708 Gold filled, bright polish, hand engraved loose curb links, gold soldered, warranted 20 years. Price..........$5.75

No. 4C5710 Sears' Life Guarantee Chain, gold filled, bright polish, gold soldered loose curb links. Price..........$3.50

No. 4C5712 Sears' Life Guarantee Chain, gold filled, bright polish, gold soldered flattened trace links. Price..........$4.00

No. 4C5714 Sears' Life Guarantee Chain, gold filled, bright polish, gold soldered flattened trace links. Price..........$4.25

No. 4C5716 Sears' Life Guarantee Chain, gold filled, bright polish, gold soldered long loose trace links. Price..........$4.65

No. 4C5650 Gold filled, extra specially made for customers wanting a strong chain for heavy work, soldered throughout, warranted for 20 years. Price..........$4.00

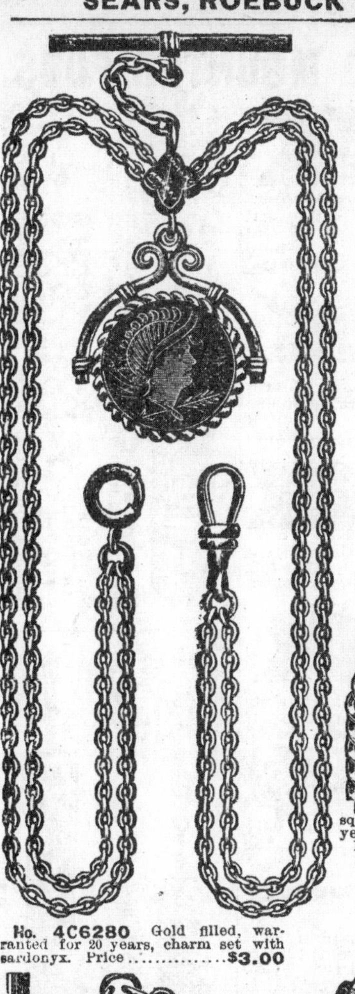

No. 4C6280 Gold filled, warranted for 20 years, charm set with sardonyx. Price $3.00

No. 4C6282 The new safety fob with Washburn patent fastener, gold filled mountings, signet seal. You cannot drop your watch if you own one of these fobs. Bright polish, warranted for 20 years. Width, ⅜ inches; length, 4½ inches. Price $2.15
Two-letter monogram, 20 cents extra.

No. 4C6284 The new safety fob with Washburn patent fastener. Gold filled mountings, signet seal. You cannot drop your watch if you own one of these fobs. Bright polish, warranted for 20 years. Width, 1 inch; length, 4⅜ inches.... $3.00
Two-letter monogram, 20 cents extra.

No. 4C6286 New patent Bigney vest watch fob. You cannot drop your watch if you own one of these fobs. Gold filled mountings and gold filled woven wire fob, warranted for 20 years, bright polish; handsome stone set charm. Width, 1 inch; length, 4½ inches. Price........ $3.15

No. 4C6288 New patent Bigney vest fob combined. You can't drop your watch if you own one of these fobs. Gold filled, bright and Roman finish, warranted for 20 years. Length of fob, 6 inches; width, 1 inch. Price $3.60

No. 4C6290 The new safety fob with Washburn patent fastener. Gold filled mountings, signet seal. You cannot drop your watch if you own one of these fobs. Bright polish, warranted for 20 years. Width, 1 inch; length, 5 inches...... $3.75
Two-letter monogram, 20 cents extra.

No. 4C6292 New patent Bigney vest watch fob. You cannot drop your watch if you own one of these fobs. Gold filled mountings and gold filled woven wire fob; warranted for 20 years, bright polish, signet charm, made to engrave. Width, 1⅛ inches; length 4½ in. Price, $3.85

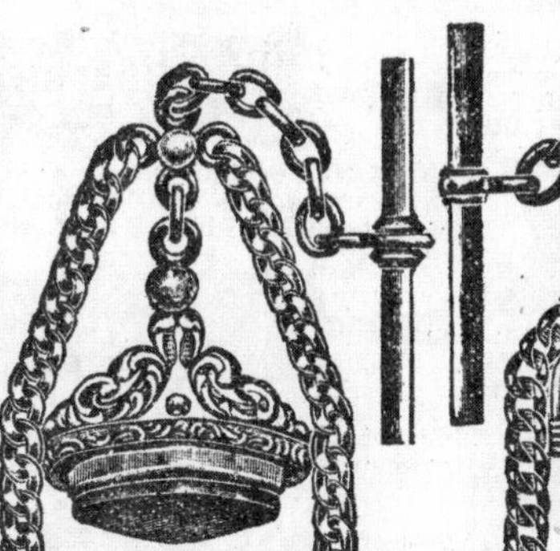

No. 4C6294 Gold filled, soldered square curb links, warranted for 20 years. Price $2.70

No. 4C6296 Fancy chain, gold filled, warranted for 20 years, engraved, intaglio cut onyx charm. Price $3.10

No. 4C6298 Polished double links, gold filled, warranted for 20 years, head engraved stone charm. Price $3.25

No. 4C6300 Boston links chain, gold filled, warranted for 20 years. engraved, intaglio cut charm. Price........... $3.00

If by mail, postage, 3 cents; insurance or registry, 8c extra.

No. 4C6302 Durable, polished links, gold filled, warranted 20 years, engraved red cornelian charm. Price $1.75

No. 4C6304 Gold filled, soldered cable, warranted for 20 years, amethyst set charm. Price $2.80

No. 4C6306 Fancy chased links, gold filled, warranted 20 years, cameo cut, red onyx stone charm. Price $1.60

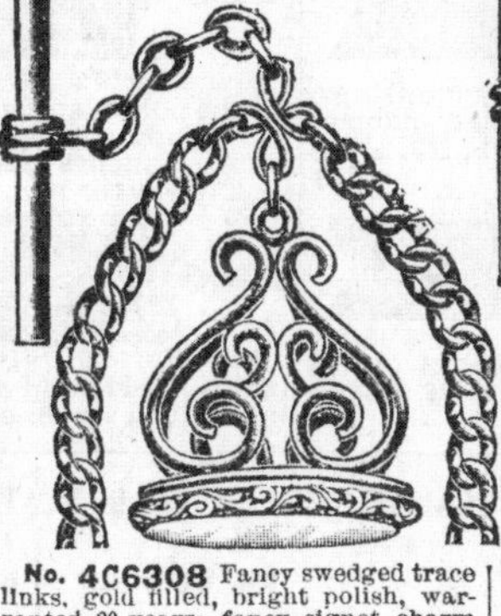

No. 4C6308 Fancy swedged trace links, gold filled, bright polish, warranted 20 years; fancy signet charm for monogram. Price........ $3.00
Two-letter monogram, 25 cents extra.

No. 4C6310 Chased links, gold filled, warranted 20 years, engraved border, charm set with red cornelian stone. Price $1.90

No. 4C6312 Gold filled, soldered, double rope, warranted for 20 years, pearl set charm. Price $3.75

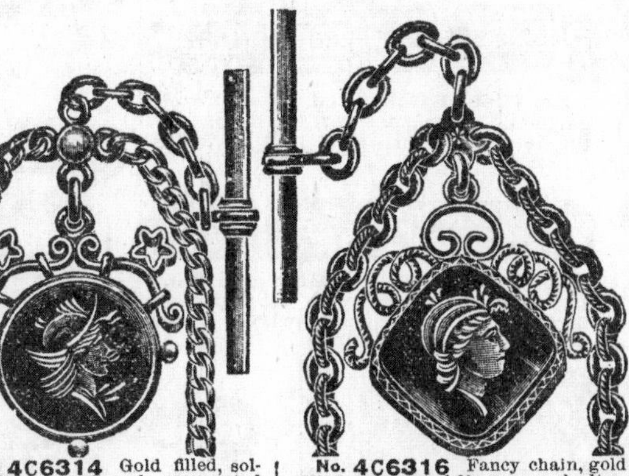

No. 4C6314 Gold filled, soldered, engraved curb, warranted for 20 years, green onyx set charm. Price $3.00

No. 4C6316 Fancy chain, gold filled, warranted 20 years, each alternate link twisted, fancy stone charm. Price $1.88

No. 4C6318 Plain polished lapped side trace links, gold filled, bright polish, warranted 20 years, fancy stone set charm. Price, $2.25

No. 4C6320 Plain polished cable links, gold filled, bright polish, warranted 20 years, stone set charm. Price $2.20

No. 4C6322 Gold filled pony vest chain, warranted 20 years, brown onyx set charm.... $2.15

No. 4C6324 Rolled gold plate pony vest chain, warranted for 5 years, plain polish, sardonyx charm. Price............ $1.00

No. 4C6326 Gold filled pony vest chain, warranted for 10 years, bright polish, sardonyx charm. Price $1.25

GOLD FILLED, ROLLED PLATE, NICKEL AND SOLID GOLD MOUNTED FOBS.

Three cents will carry any one of these fobs, hair chains or silk vest chains to any part of the United States. Insured or registered mail 8 cents extra.

BE IN LINE. EVERYBODY IS WEARING A FOB.

No. 4C6451 **Silk Fob,** silver filled initial, any letter; 6¼ inches long; patent fastener to attach watch. Price....................42c

No. 4C6452 Rolled plate mountings, stone charm; silk fob, 1½ inches wide, 6¼ inches long. Price....................60c

No. 4C6454 Gold plate mountings, bright polished, stone set charm, silk fob, 1⅜ inches wide, 7 inches long. Price....75c

No. 4C6456 **Pendant and Slide,** Roman finish, pendant set with 2 emeralds and 2 opals; silk fob, 7 inches long, 1¼ inches wide. Price....................85c

No. 4C6458 Gold filled mountings, bright polish, fancy gold filled charm, roman rose satin finish; silk fob, 1⅜ inches wide, 7 inches long. Price....................95c

No. 4C6460 Gold filled mountings, bright polish, hand engraved, silk fob, 1⅛ inches wide, 7 inches long. Price....................90c

No. 4C6462 Gold front mountings, bright polish, hand engraved, silk fob, 1⅜ inches wide, 7 inches long. Price....................$1.00

No. 4C6464 Gold filled mountings, bright polish, stone set seal charm; silk fob, 1⅜ inches wide, 7 inches long. Price..$1.11

No. 4C6466 Gold filled mountings, bright polish, gold filled charm, set with genuine stone; silk fob, 1⅜ inches wide, 6½ inches long. Price....................$1.90

No. 4C6468 Gold filled, hand chased, strong, amethyst set charm; silk fob, 1⅜ inches wide, 7 inches long. Price.....$2.00

No. 4C6470 Gold filled mountings, bright polish, solid gold front charm, made to be engraved; silk fob, 1¼ inches wide, 6½ inches long. Price....................$2.00
Two-letter monogram, 20 cents extra.

No. 4C6472 Gold filled mountings, bright polish, gold filled signet charm, made for monogram work; silk fob, 1⅜ inches wide, 6½ inches long. Price..........$2.25
Two-letter monogram, 20 cents extra.

No. 4C6476 **Silk Fob,** 1⅜ inches wide, 7 inches long, solid gold charm and mountings, blood stone set charm. Price....$6.90

No. 4C6474 **Silk Fob,** 1¼ inches wide, 7 inches long, gold filled mountings, fine seal locket for two pictures; bottom of seal plain, for monogram. Price..........$3.00
Monogram of two or three letters, 35c extra.

No. 4C6478 **Roman Finished Secret Locket Pendant,** set with 4 rhinestones; fine black leather fob, 7 inches long, 1¼ inches wide. Price....................$1.20

No. 4C6480 Gold filled mountings, bright polish, extra fine quality seal leather fob, 1¼ inches wide, 7 inches long. Price..$1.25

No. 4C6482 Extra fine gold filled mountings, bright polish; fine leather fob, 1¼ inches wide, 6½ inches long. Price...$1.45

No. 4C6484 **Solid Nickel Fob,** very strong and durable. Price....................45c

No. 4C6486 Gold filled, warranted 6 years, plain links, not soldered; entire length, 5½ inches, ¾ inch wide. Price..$1.50

No. 4C6492 Gold filled mountings, gold filled, bright polish, woven wire fob, 1¼ inches wide, 5½ inches long. Price...$2.30

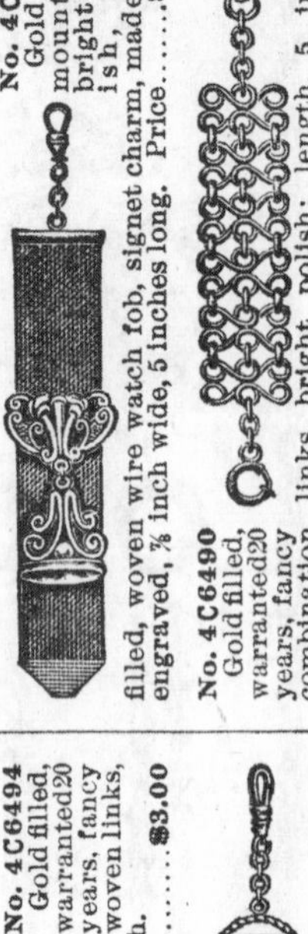

No. 4C6488 Gold filled mountings, bright polish, gold filled, woven wire watch fob, signet charm, made to be engraved, ⅞ inch wide, 5 inches long. Price......$2.10

No. 4C6490 Gold filled, warranted 20 years, fancy combination links, bright polish; length, 5 inches, width, ¾ inch. Price....................$2.25

No. 4C6494 Gold filled, warranted 20 years, fancy woven links, bright polish; length, 6 inches, width, ¾ inch. Price....................$3.00

No. 4C6496 Gold filled, soldered links, red sardonyx charm; 6 inches long, ⅞ inch wide. Price..........$3.00

BEST QUALITY ROLLED GOLD PLATE, GOLD FILLED AND SOLID GOLD MOUNTINGS, FOR GENTS' AND LADIES' HAIR AND SILK VEST CHAINS.

No. 4C6512 Shows bar, toggle and swivel.

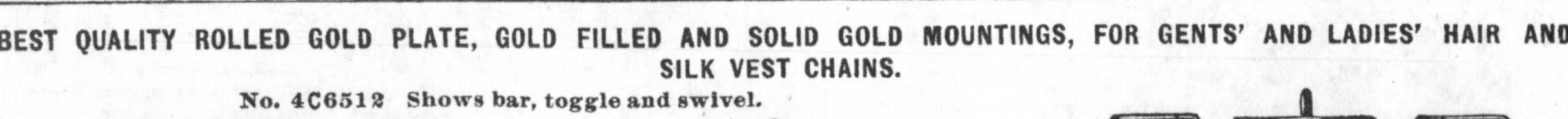

No. 4C6501 Gold filled, set with pearl and two garnets. Price, per set, including bar, toggle and swivel.....95c

No. 4C6511 Gold filled, pearl and two garnets. Price, per set, including bar, toggle and swivel....................95c

No. 4C6506 Gold filled, hand engraved. Price, complete, including bar, toggle and swivel....................80c

No. 4C6505 Gold filled, hand engraved, made for double hair chain. Price, per set, including bar, toggle and swivel.$1.15

No. 4C6509 Best quality gold filled fluted pattern, engraved. Price, per set, including bar, toggle and swivel.....80c

No. 4C6512 Fine solid gold. Price, per set, including bar, toggle and swivel....$5.00

HAIR CHAINS.

No. 4C6498 Hair chain braided to order, like above. Price......$1.00

No. 4C6500 Same as above; 2 strands. For mounting No. 4C6505. Price..........$1.50

Requires about 1½ ounces haircombings to braid a chain. Is made in two pieces, and together with mountings is 12½ inches long. When you send in your hair to be braided be sure and write us when you do so and put your name and address on package.

No extra charge for mounting the hair when the mountings are purchased from us.

No. 4C6514 **Silk Vest Chain,** gold filled mountings. Length, 12 inches. Price....................75c

No. 4C6516 **Silk Vest Chain,** three strands, gold filled mountings. Length, 9 inches. Price....................85c

No. 4C6518 **Silk Vest Chain,** gold filled mountings. Length, 11 inches. Price....................70c

No. 4C6520 **Silk Vest Chain,** fancy braided, gold filled mountings. Length, 7 inches. Price....................85c

No. 4C6522 **Silk Vest Chain,** gold filled mountings. Length, 9 inches. Price....................$1.25

No. 4C6524 **Silk Vest Chain,** gold filled mountings. Length, 9 inches. Price....................$1.20

LADIES' GOLD FILLED, SOLID SILVER AND ROLLED PLATE GUARD CHAINS

REGULAR LENGTH, 48 INCHES.

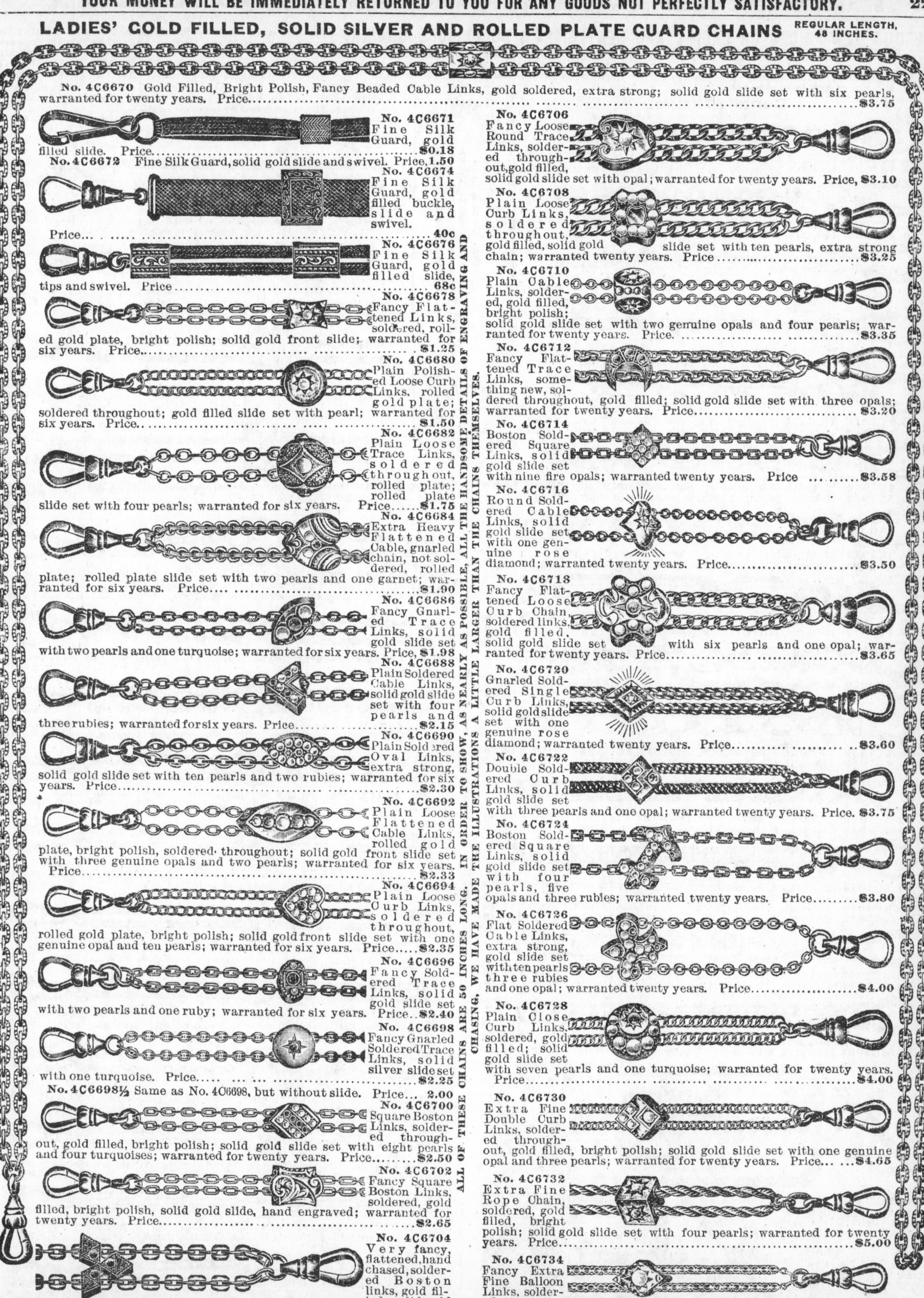

No. 4C6670 Gold Filled, Bright Polish, Fancy Beaded Cable Links, gold soldered, extra strong; solid gold slide set with six pearls, warranted for twenty years. Price........ $3.75

No. 4C6671 Fine Silk Guard, gold filled slide. Price........ $0.18

No. 4C6672 Fine Silk Guard, solid gold slide and swivel. Price, 1.50

No. 4C6674 Fine Silk Guard, gold filled buckle, slide and swivel. Price........ 40c

No. 4C6676 Fine Silk Guard, gold filled slide, tips and swivel. Price........ 68c

No. 4C6678 Fancy Flattened Links, soldered, rolled gold plate, bright polish; solid gold front slide; warranted for six years. Price........ $1.25

No. 4C6680 Plain Polished Loose Curb Links, rolled gold plate; soldered throughout; gold filled slide set with pearl; warranted for six years. Price........ $1.50

No. 4C6682 Plain Loose Trace Links, soldered throughout, rolled plate; rolled plate slide set with four pearls; warranted for six years. Price...... $1.75

No. 4C6684 Extra Heavy Flattened Cable, gnarled chain, not soldered, rolled plate; rolled plate slide set with two pearls and one garnet; warranted for six years. Price........ $1.90

No. 4C6686 Fancy Gnarled Trace Links, solid gold slide set with two pearls and one turquoise; warranted for six years. Price, $1.98

No. 4C6688 Plain Soldered Cable Links, solid gold slide set with four pearls and three rubies; warranted for six years. Price........ $2.15

No. 4C6690 Plain Soldered Oval Links, extra strong, solid gold slide set with ten pearls and two rubies; warranted for six years. Price........ $2.30

No. 4C6692 Plain Loose Flattened Cable Links, rolled gold plate, bright polish, soldered throughout; solid gold front slide set with three genuine opals and two pearls; warranted for six years. Price........ $2.33

No. 4C6694 Plain Loose Curb Links, soldered throughout, rolled gold plate, bright polish; solid gold front slide set with one genuine opal and ten pearls; warranted for six years. Price..... $2.35

No. 4C6696 Fancy Soldered Trace Links, solid gold slide set with two pearls and one ruby; warranted for six years. Price.. $2.40

No. 4C6698 Fancy Gnarled Soldered Trace Links, solid silver slide set with one turquoise. Price........ $2.25

No. 4C6698½ Same as No. 4C6698, but without slide. Price... 2.00

No. 4C6700 Square Boston Links, soldered throughout, gold filled, bright polish; solid gold slide set with eight pearls and four turquoises; warranted for twenty years. Price........ $2.50

No. 4C6702 Fancy Square Boston Links, soldered, gold filled, bright polish, solid gold slide, hand engraved; warranted for twenty years. Price........ $2.65

No. 4C6704 Very fancy, flattened, hand chased, soldered Boston links, gold filled, solid gold slide set with three pearls; warranted for twenty years. Price, $3.00

ALL OF THESE CHAINS ARE 50 INCHES LONG. IN ORDER TO SHOW, AS NEARLY AS POSSIBLE, ALL THE HANDSOME DETAILS OF ENGRAVING AND CHASING, WE HAVE MADE THE ILLUSTRATIONS A LITTLE LARGER THAN THE CHAINS THEMSELVES.

No. 4C6706 Fancy Loose Round Trace Links, soldered throughout, gold filled, solid gold slide set with opal; warranted for twenty years. Price, $3.10

No. 4C6708 Plain Loose Curb Links, soldered throughout, gold filled, solid gold slide set with ten pearls, extra strong chain; warranted twenty years. Price........ $3.25

No. 4C6710 Plain Cable Links, soldered, gold filled, bright polish; solid gold slide set with two genuine opals and four pearls; warranted for twenty years. Price........ $3.35

No. 4C6712 Fancy Flattened Trace Links, something new, soldered throughout, gold filled; solid gold slide set with three opals; warranted for twenty years. Price........ $3.20

No. 4C6714 Boston Soldered Square Links, solid gold slide set with nine fire opals; warranted twenty years. Price........ $3.58

No. 4C6716 Round Soldered Cable Links, solid gold slide set with one genuine rose diamond; warranted twenty years. Price........ $3.50

No. 4C6718 Fancy Flattened Loose Curb Chain, soldered links, gold filled, solid gold slide set with six pearls and one opal; warranted for twenty years. Price........ $3.65

No. 4C6720 Gnarled Soldered Single Curb Links, solid gold slide set with one genuine rose diamond; warranted twenty years. Price........ $3.60

No. 4C6722 Double Soldered Curb Links, solid gold slide set with three pearls and one opal; warranted twenty years. Price. $3.75

No. 4C6724 Boston Soldered Square Links, solid gold slide set with four pearls, five opals and three rubies; warranted twenty years. Price........ $3.80

No. 4C6726 Flat Soldered Cable Links, extra strong, gold slide set with ten pearls three rubies and one opal; warranted twenty years. Price........ $4.00

No. 4C6728 Plain Close Curb Links, soldered, gold filled; solid gold slide set with seven pearls and one turquoise; warranted for twenty years. Price........ $4.00

No. 4C6730 Extra Fine Double Curb Links, soldered throughout, gold filled, bright polish; solid gold slide set with one genuine opal and three pearls; warranted for twenty years. Price........ $4.65

No. 4C6732 Extra Fine Rope Chain, soldered, gold filled, bright polish; solid gold slide set with four pearls; warranted for twenty years. Price........ $5.00

No. 4C6734 Fancy Extra Fine Balloon Links, soldered throughout, gold filled, bright polish; solid gold slide set with genuine opal; warranted for twenty years. Price........ $5.70

SEE OUR NEW PRICES ON LADIES' AND GENTLEMEN'S SOLID GOLD CHAINS.

You can wear any one of these Solid Gold Chains for your natural lifetime and keep it in the family forever.

The ladies' guard chains are all regular standard length, 48 inches. Also please note that we give the weight on every gentlemen's solid gold chain we illustrate. You know exactly what you are buying; 5 to 6 pwt. chain is considered light weight; 21 pwt. is considered extra heavy weight. **THE PRICES ON LADIES' SOLID GOLD GUARD CHIANS VARY on account of the weight of gold in them.** The lighter the chain the less it costs, although the cheapest chain shown is strong enough to protect any ladies' watch.

Postage extra on gentlemen's chains, 3 cents; 8 cents extra for registered or insured mail. Postage on ladies' guards, 4 cents; 8 cents extra for registered or insured mail.

Gents' Chains.

No. 4C7000 10-karat, 10 inches long, between 5 and 6 pwt... $4.20
No. 4C7002 14-karat, 10 inches long, between 5 and 6 pwt... 5.46

No. 4C7004 10-karat, 10 inches long, between 5 and 6 pwt.. $4.56
No. 4C7006 14-karat, 10 inches long, between 6 and 7 pwt... 6.79

No. 4C7008 10-karat, 10 inches long, between 7 and 8 pwt.. $6.08
No. 4C7010 14-karat, 10 inches long, between 8 and 9 pwt.. 8.73

No. 4C7012 10-karat, 10 inches long, between 7 and 8 pwt... $5.60
No. 4C7014 14-karat, 10 inches long, between 7 and 8 pwt... 7.28

No. 4C7016 10-karat, 10 inches long, between 6 and 7 pwt... $4.90
No. 4C7018 14-karat, 10 inches long, between 7 and 8 pwt... 7.28

No. 4C7020 10-karat, 10 inches long, between 8 and 9 pwt. Price.. $6.30
No. 4C7022 14-karat, 10 inches long, between 9 and 10 pwt. Price.. 9.10

No. 4C7024 10-karat, 12 inches long, between 19 and 20 pwt. Price.. $14.00
No. 4C7026 14-karat, 12 inches long, between 21 and 22 pwt. Price.. 20.02

No. 4C7028 10-karat, 10 inches long, between 12 and 13 pwt. Price. $ 9.10
No. 4C7030 14-karat, 12 inches long, between 15 and 16 pwt. Price. 14.56

No. 4C7032 10-karat, 12 inches long, between 13 and 14 pwt. Price. $ 9.80
No. 4C7034 14-karat, 12 inches long, between 14 and 15 pwt. Price. 13.65

No. 4C7036 10-karat, 12 inches long, between 14 and 15 pwt. Price. $10.50
No. 4C7038 14-karat, 12 inches long, between 16 and 17 pwt. Price. 15.47

No. 4C7040 10-karat, 10 inches long, between 6 and 7 pwt. Price.. $4.90
No. 4C7042 14-karat, 10 inches long, between 7 and 8 pwt. Price.. 7.28

No. 4C7044 10-karat, 12 inches long, between 23 and 24 pwt. Price. $16.80
No. 4C7046 14-karat, 12 inches long, between 25 and 26 pwt. Price. 23.66
No. 4C7048 10-karat, 12 inches long, between 15 and 16 pwt. Price. 11.20
No. 4C7050 14-karat, 12 inches long, between 17 and 18 pwt. Price. 16.38

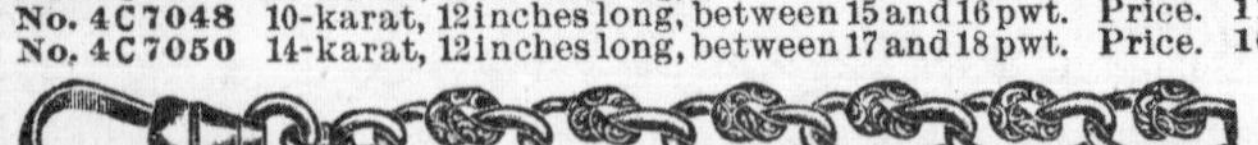

No. 4C7052 10-karat, 12 inches long, between 15 and 16 pwt. Price. $11.28
No. 4C7054 14-karat, 12 inches long, between 17 and 18 pwt. Price. 16.38

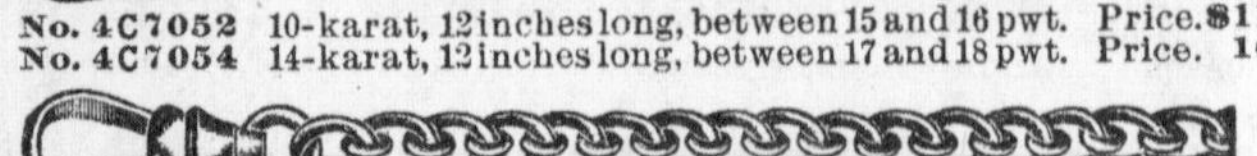

No. 4C7056 10-karat, 12 inches long, between 14 and 15 pwt. Price. $10.50
No. 4C7058 14-karat, 12 inches long, between 16 and 17 pwt. Price. 15.47

No. 4C7060 10-karat, regulation length. Price, $7.35
No. 4C7062 Without charm. Price......... $5.60
No. 4C7064 14-karat, regulation length. Price, $10.75
No. 4C7066 Without charm. Price......... $8.75

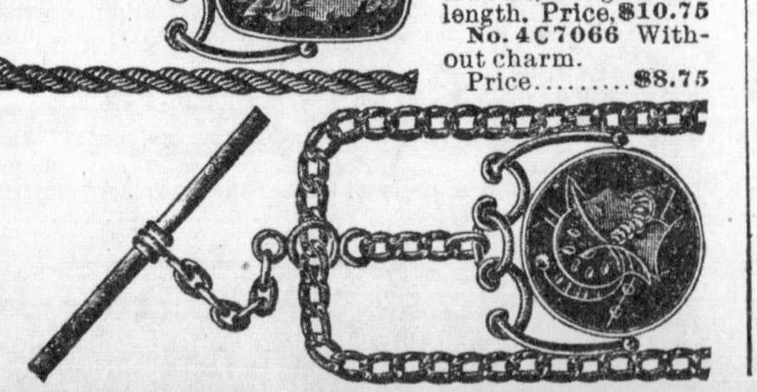

No. 4C7068 10-karat, regulation length. Price, $7.83
No. 4C7070 Without charm. Price......... $6.08
No. 4C7072 14-karat, regulation length. Price, $10.00
No. 4C7074 Without charm. Price......... $7.75

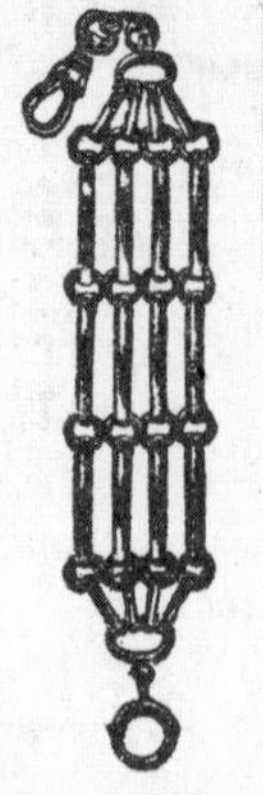

No. 4C7077 Fine fob solid 14-karat gold, something new and nobby, 5¼ inches long, 11 to 12 pwt. in weight. Price, $16.50

Ladies' Chains.

No. 4C7100 Fine solid gold, 14-karat, bright polish, soldered trace links, Roman color slide set with three pearls. Price, $8.33
No. 4C7102 10-karat, same style as above. Price...... 6.75

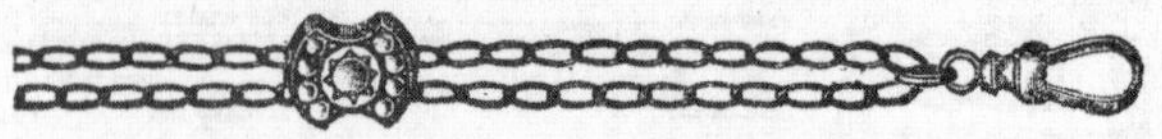

No. 4C7104 Fine solid gold, 14-karat, bright polish, soldered trace links, slide set with eight pearls and one opal. Price... $6.75
No. 4C7106 10-karat, same style as above. Price....... 4.95

No. 4C7108 Fine solid gold, 14-karat, polished lapped cable links, soldered throughout, slide set with four pearls and one opal, $11.50
No. 4C7110 10-karat, same style as above. Price..... 8.85

No. 4C7112 Fine solid gold, 14-karat, soldered rope pattern, slide very fancy, set with one diamond. Price.............................. $16.50
No. 4C7114 10-karat, same style as above. Price.............. 13.00

No. 4C7116 Fine solid gold, 14-karat, bright polish, soldered, lapped cable links, slide set with two pearls and one opal. Price............ $17.40
No. 4C7118 10-karat, same style as above. Price.............. 13.00

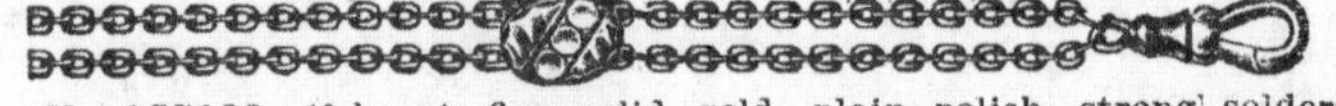

No. 4C7120 10-karat, fine solid gold, plain polished links, ruby set slide. Not made in 14-karat. Price... .... $4.65

No. 4C7122 10-karat, fine solid gold, plain polish, strong soldered trace links, three pearls set in slide. Not made in 14-karat. Price.. $6.50

No. 4C7124 10-karat, fine solid gold, fancy bright polish, soldered links, heavy weight, opal set slide. Not made in 14-karat. Price..... $7.00

No. 4C7126 10-karat, fine solid gold, Roman color, chased soldered links, pearl set slide. Not made in 14-karat. Price..... .... $5.85

No. 4C7128 10-karat, fine solid gold, bright polish, soldered links three pearls in slide. Not made in 14-karat. Price............. .. $6.50

No. 4C7130 10-karat, fine solid gold, bright polish, soldered links, two pearls and one turquoise set in slide. Not made in 14-karat. Price.... $7.10

No. 4C7132 10-karat, fine solid gold, bright polish, soldered chased links, genuine rose diamond set slide. Not made in 14-karat. Price.. $6.70

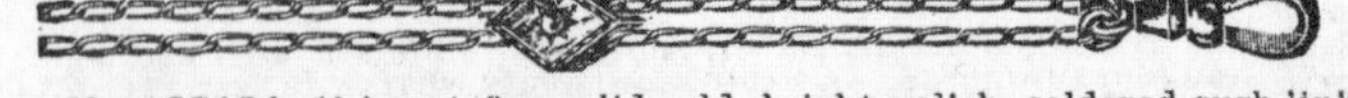

No. 4C7134 10-karat, fine solid gold, bright polish, soldered curb links, opal set slide. Not made in 14-karat. Price......... .... $4.50

No. 4C7136 10-karat, fine solid gold, bright polish, soldered trace links, ruby set slide. Not made in 14-karat. Price..................... $5.15

No. 4C7138 10-karat, fine solid gold, heavy, bright polish, soldered ornamented trace links. Not made in 14-karat. Price.................. $8.75

BEST QUALITY NECK CHAINS, SOLID GOLD, GOLD FILLED AND GENUINE AMBER

OUR NECK CHAINS ARE THE NEWEST AND BEST ON THE MARKET. Our Solid Gold Chains are warranted solid gold through and through. Postage on neck chains, 3 cents. Insurance or registry, extra.

Our gold filled chains are warranted to wear and give the very best satisfaction.

Only tasty designs carried in our stock. We show the two popular lengths, the regular 13-inch chain and the new 22-inch chain. All chains illustrated on this page have soldered links. They are strong and durable.

No. 4C7201 Gold filled 14-inch chain, soldered links, bright polish, heart shaped locket to hold 2 pictures, set with turquoise. Price..**$1.40**

No. 4C7202 Gold filled 13-inch chain, Roman colored heart, set with turquoise. Price..**$1.10**

No. 4C7204 Gold filled 13-inch chain, fancy Roman colored gold pendant, set with ruby doublet stone. Price..**$1.50**

No. 4C7206 Gold filled 13-inch chain, fancy Roman colored gold pendant, set with almandine stone. Price..**$1.40**

No. 4C7208 Gold filled 13-inch chain, fancy heart pendant, set with genuine opal. Price..**$1.60**

No. 4C7209 Gold filled rope pattern chain, 14 inches long, bright polish, hand engraved locket, holds two pictures. Price..**$1.95**

No. 4C7212 Gold filled 13-inch chain. Roman colored pendant, set with four pearls and one turquoise. Price..**$1.60**

No. 4C7215 Gold filled 22-inch chain, soldered links, bright polish, heart shaped locket, to hold two pictures, set with 1 genuine opal and 4 ruby doublets. Price,**$2.25**

No. 4C7216 Gold filled 13-inch chain, bright, chain satin finish, locket holds two pictures, set with pearls and ruby. Price..**$1.85**

No. 4C7218 Gold filled 13-inch chain, plain polish, locket holds two pictures. Each....**$1.75**

No. 4C7219 Same as No. 4C7218. **Solid gold.** Price....**$6.25**

No. 4C7220 Gold filled, chain 13 inches, fancy pendant, set with pearls and turquoise. Price **$1.75**

No. 4C7222 Solid gold 13-inch chain, Roman finish, fancy links. Price..**$2.00**

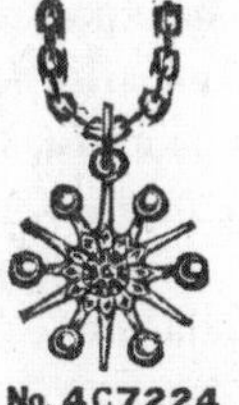

No. 4C7224 Solid gold 13-inch chain, plain trace links, six pearls and one ruby center. Price..**$3.50**

No. 4C7226 Solid gold 13-inch woven wire chain, set with pearls and one real diamond. Price..**$5.40**

No. 4C7228 Solid gold 13-inch, plain trace links, thirteen turquoise and fifteen pearls. Price..**$4.50**

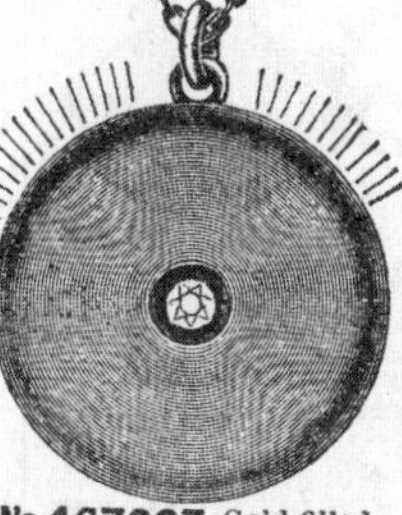

No. 4C7227 Gold filled, 22-inch chain, soldered throughout, bright polish, round locket to hold two pictures, set with 1 rhinestone. Price........**$2.40**

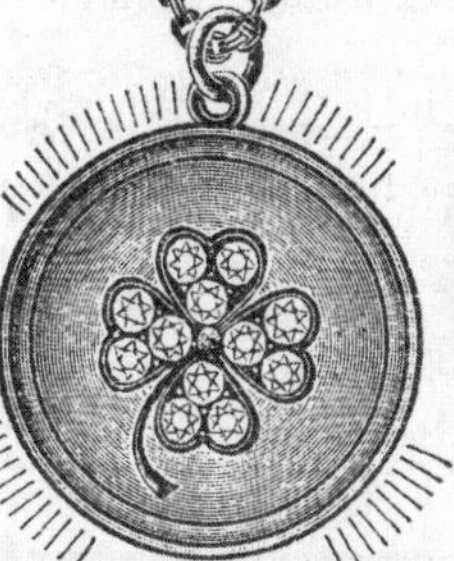

No. 4C7229 Gold filled chain, 22 inches long, soldered links, bright polish, locket to hold two pictures, set with rhinestones. Price..**$2.87**

No. 4C7236 Gold filled, 22-inch chain, plain satin finish, secret locket, holds two pictures. Price **$2.25**

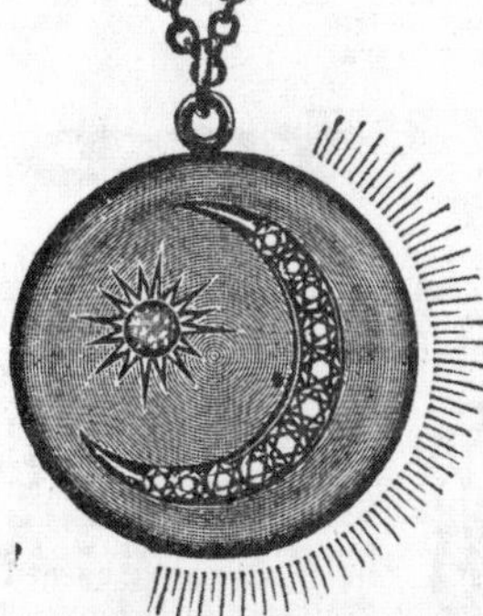

No. 4C7238 Gold filled, bright finish, 22-inch chain, satin finish, secret locket, holds two pictures. Set with rhinestones and one fire opal. Price...............**$2.50**

No. 4C7240 Gold filled 22-inch chain, plain satin finish, secret locket. Holds two pictures. Price..**$2.40**

No. 4C7242 Gold filled 22-inch chain, satin finish, two pictures, secret locket; set with rhinestones and 1 opal. Price..........**$2.75**

No. 4C7244 Gold filled, bright finished chain, soldered links, bright finish, locket holds two pictures. Set with rhinestones and 1 ruby. Price.....................**$3.15**

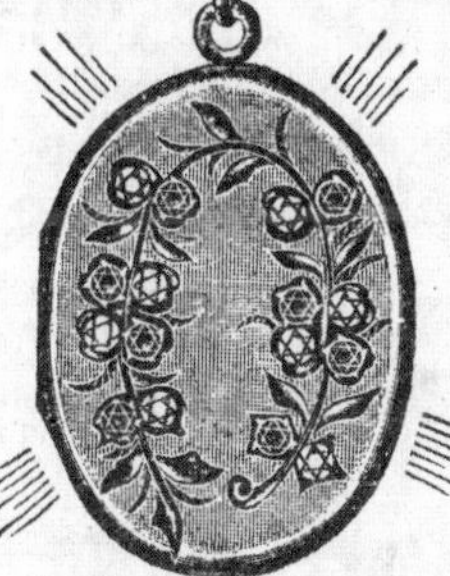

No. 4C7246 Gold filled, bright finished chain, 22 inches, soldered links, satin finish, locket set with rhinestones and eight rubies; holds two pictures. Price.............**$2.68**

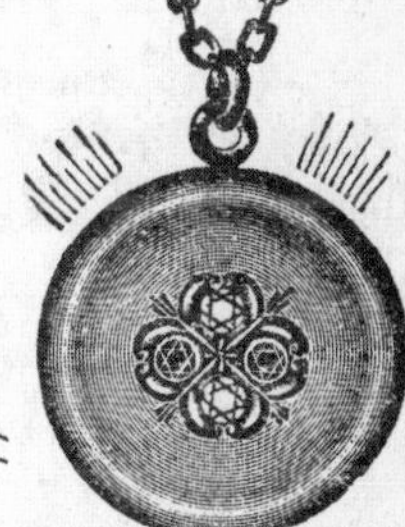

No. 4C7248 Gold filled, bright finished chain, 22 inches, soldered links, satin finish, locket holds two pictures set with two rhinestones and two rubies. Ea...**$2.35**

No. 4C7250 Solid gold, 13-inch Roman finish, soldered trace links, three heart pendants, each set with turquoise. This chain is particularly adapted for babies and children. Price **$2.50**

No. 4C7251 First Quality Genuine Amber Bead Necklace. Beads with hand cut facets, strung on linen cord with screw clasp. Length, 12 inches. Price..**$1.00**

No. 4C7252 First Quality Genuine Amber Bead Necklace. Same style as No. 4C7251, 14 inches long. Price..........................**$1.20**

No. 4C7253 First Quality Genuine Amber Bead Necklace. Hand cut facets. Same style as No. 4C7251, but 15 to 16 inches long. Price..........................**$1.40**

It is said by some that genuine amber beads prevent croup and other throat troubles in children.

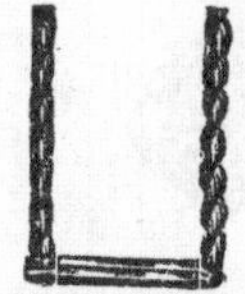

No. 4C7254 Solid gold, 13-inch, soldered rope chain, no pendant. Price..**$2.75**

No. 4C7256 Same style as No. 4C7254, 22-inch. Price..**$4.25**

No. 4C7258 Gold filled, 22-inch soldered rope chain, no pendant. Price..**$2.15**

No. 4C7260 Same style as No. 4C7258, solid gold. Price..**$5.25**

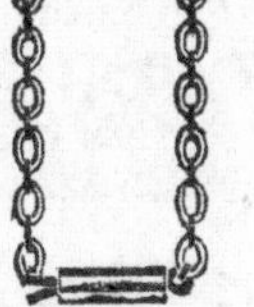

No. 4C7262 Gold filled, 22-inch chain, no pendant. Price..**$1.10**

No. 4C7264 Same style as No. 4C7262, solid gold. Price..**$2.25**

No. 4C7266 Gold filled, 22-inch chain, no pendant. Price. **$1.20**

No. 4C7268 Same style as No. 4C7266 solid gold. Price..**$4.25**

No. 4C7270 Gold filled, 22-inch chain, no pendant. Price**$1.50**

No. 4C7272 Same style as No. 4C7270, solid gold. Price **$5.25**

No. 4C7274 Gold filled 22-inch chain, bright polish, secret locket; holds two pictures. Set with pearls and 1 ruby. Price.........**$3.20**

No. 4C7276 Gold filled 22-inch chain, Roman color, secret locket; holds two pictures. Set with pearls and 1 turquoise. Price....**$2.60**

Bead necklaces are again in the height of fashion. We illustrate and quote here only the three appropriate sizes. Our gold filled bead necklaces are made from 14-karat gold filled stock. Our solid gold necklaces are made from absolutely 14-karat pure gold. We wish to caution and advise you of the fact that unless a bead necklace is 14-karat pure gold, it will invariably discolor the neck. Therefore, we quote and illustrate only 14-karat goods here. Mail charges on any one of these necklaces to any part of the United States, about 3 cents. Registry, 8 cents extra.

No. 4C7281 Gold Filled Bead Necklace, bright polish, same size bead as illustration shows. 13½ inches long. Price.....................**$2.25**

No. 4C7283 Solid Gold 14-karat Warranted Bead Necklace, satin Roman finish, same style as No. 4C7281, but slightly smaller sized beads. Length, 14 inches. Price.....................**$6.28**

No. 4C7285 Gold Filled Bead Necklace, bright polish, same size bead as illustration shows. 13½ inches long. Price.....................**$2.50**

No. 4C7290 Solid Gold 14-karat Bead Necklace, satin Roman finish, same style and size exactly as No. 4C7285. Length, 14 inches. Price.....................**$12.10**

No. 4C7292 Gold Filled Bead Necklace, bright polish, same size bead as illustration shows. 13½ inches long. Price.....................**$2.65**

No. 4C7294 Solid Gold 14-karat Bead Necklace, satin Roman finish, same size and style as No. 4C7292. Length, 14 inches. Price.....................**$15.00**

SOLID GOLD, GOLD FILLED AND SOLID STERLING SILVER BRACELETS.

If by mail, postage extra, each, 3 cents.
Insurance or registry, 8 cents extra.

No. 4C7400 Child's or Baby Bracelet, gold filled, bright finish, the very latest engraved bangles, soldered links. Price........ **$1.60**

No. 4C7402 Child's or Baby Bracelet, sterling silver, same style as No. 4C7400, bright finish. Price.......................... **$1.20**

No. 4C7404 Misses' Gold Filled Signet Bracelet, hand chased and engraved, soldered links. Price......... **$2.35**
Monogram of three letters, 20 cents extra.

No. 4C7406 Misses' Gold Filled Bracelet, plain polished links, length, 5 inches. Price... **48c**
No. 4C7408 Solid Sterling Silver, same style as No. 4C7406. Price **48c**

No. 4C7410 Solid Gold, Roman color, same style as No. 4C7406. Price **$3.00**

No. 4C7412 Best Rolled Gold Plate Bracelet, fancy chased, soldered links, 7½ inches long. Price.............. **$1.08**

No. 4C7414 Gold Filled Bracelet, best quality, fancy chased links. Price.............. **$2.00**
No. 4C7416 Same style as No. 4C7414. Solid gold. Price **$15.00**

No. 4C7418 Gold Filled Bracelet, best quality with fancy chased links. Price **$2.45**
No. 4C7420 Solid Sterling Silver, same style as No. 4C7418. Price **$1.75**
No. 4C7422 Same style as No. 4C7418, solid gold. Price, **$6.60**

No. 4C7424 Gold Filled Bracelet, bright polish, square hand chased links, something novel. Price.............................. **$2.00**
No. 4C7426 Solid Silver Bracelet. Same style No. 4C7424, but not chased links; plain satin finished lock. Price....... **$2.25**

No. 4C7428 Best Gold Filled Bracelet, plain and fancy soldered links, 7½ inches long. Price............................ **$2.20**

No. 4C7430 Best Gold Filled Bracelet, hand chased and hand engraved, soldered fancy links, 7¾ inches long. Price.... .... **$3.15**

No. 4C7432 Best Gold Filled Signet Bracelet, for monogram, fancy soldered links. Price.......................... **$3.35**
Monogram of three letters, 35 cents extra.

No. 4C7434 Gold Filled Locket Bracelet, holds two pictures, fancy hand chased and engraved, soldered links. Price.............................. **$3.20**
Monogram of three letters, 35 cents extra.

No. 4C7436 Gold Filled Locket Bracelet, holds two pictures, fancy hand chased, soldered links. Price.............................. **$3.28**
Monogram of three letters, 35 cents extra.

No. 4C7438 Best Rolled Gold Plate Bracelet, plain and fancy soldered links, 7½ inches long. Price.............................. **$1.60**

No. 4C7440 Solid Silver Bracelet, hand engraved and hand chased six solid silver heart pendants, each set with turquoise and opal. Price for complete bracelet........... **$2.50**

LOCK AND KEY FOR BRACELET.

No. 4C7448 Gold Filled Lock for Bracelets, small size. Price.. **37c**
No. 4C7449 Solid Silver, same style and size as No. 4C7448. Price.. **34c**
No. 4C7450 Gold Filled, medium size. Price.. **42c**
No. 4C7451 Solid Silver, same style and size as No. 4C7450. Price.. **42c**
No. 4C7452 Gold Filled, large size. Price.. **50c**
No. 4C7453 Solid Silver, same style and size as No. 4C7452. Price.. **50c**

No. 4C7448 to 4C7453. Illustration shows large size No. 4C7452.

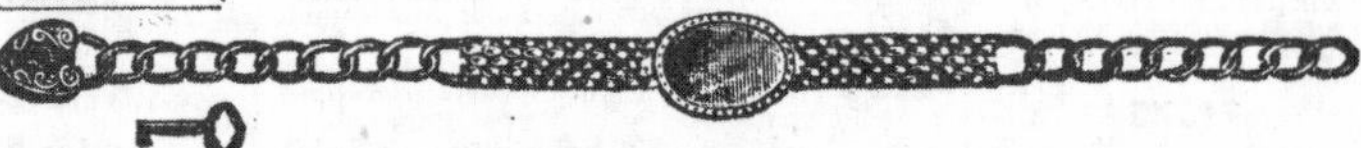

No. 4C7455 Gold Filled Bracelet, plain polish, 7¼ inches long, ¼ inch wide, with signet locket center, to hold one picture. Price.............. **$2.85**
Monogram engraved for 25 cents extra.

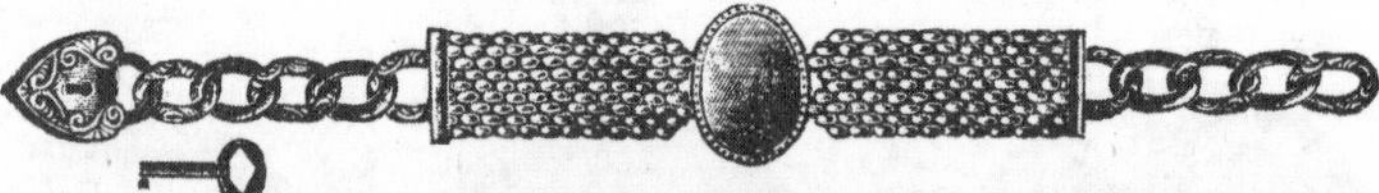

No. 4C7457 Gold Filled Bracelet, plain polish, 7¼ inches long, ⅜ inch wide, with signet locket center, to hold one picture. Price.............. **$3.40**
Monogram engraved for 25 cents extra.

No. 4C7461 Gold Filled Spring Seal Bracelet. Plain and hand chased links, fits any size wrist; with handsome engraved seal. Price.......... **$3.75**
Monogram of 3 letters, 35 cents extra.

No. 4C7463 Gold Filled Spring Bracelet. Plain and hand chased links, fits any size wrist; the newest up to date bracelet on the market. Price........... **$2.95**

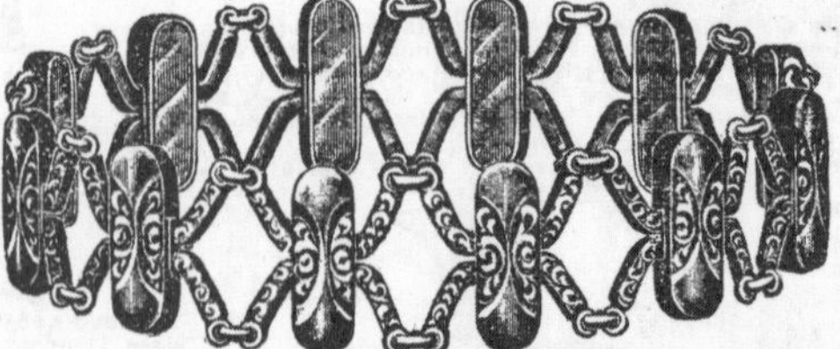

No. 4C7465 Gold Filled Bright Polished Fancy Hand Carved Spring Bracelet, fits any size wrist. Illustration shows bracelet stretched ¾ size. Price........... **$2.35**
No. 4C7466 Same style as No. 4C7465, but solid silver. Price........... **$2.25**

No. 4C7467 Gold Filled Bright Polished Seal Bracelet, fits any size wrist, has hand carved links and seal. Price............ **$3.00**
Monogram of 3 letters, 35 cents extra.

No. 4C7469 Best Gold Filled Bracelet, hand chased, fancy soldered links. Length, 7¼ inches. Price.............................. **$1.95**

CRYSTALLINE DIAMOND JEWELRY.

RINGS, SCARF PINS, STUDS, EARRINGS AND BROOCHES IN SOLID GOLD, SOLID SILVER AND GOLD FILLED MOUNTINGS, SET WITH CRYSTALLINE DIAMONDS. YOU MUST SEE THEM TO APPRECIATE THEM.

Crystalline Diamonds are worn by actors and actresses and those wanting the most perfect imitation diamond known. We have thousands of professional people, actors and actresses throughout the United States, who buy our Crystalline diamonds to wear instead of using the genuine article. Experience has taught them that only the judgment of experts can detect the difference between our Crystalline diamonds and the highest grade genuine diamond worth fifty times as much.

No. 4C7490 Solid gold. Price.......**$2.25**

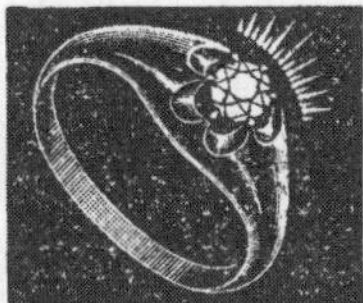

No. 4C7491 Solid gold. Price....**$3.75**
No. 4C7492 Rolled plate. Price.....**50c**

No. 4C7493 Solid gold. Price.......**$2.50**

No. 4C7494 Solid gold. Price.......**$4.00**

No. 4C7495 Solid gold. Price...**$3.25**
No. 4C7496 Rolled plate. Price... **.50c**

No. 4C7497 Solid gold. Price......**$3.00**
No. 4C7498 Rolled plate. Price.........**60c**

No. 4C7499 Solid gold. Price.........**$3.00**
No. 4C7500 Rolled plate. Price...........**60c**

No. 4C7501 Solid gold. Price......**$3.75**
No. 4C7502 Rolled plate. Price.........**68c**

DON'T FAIL TO GIVE SIZE OF RING WANTED.

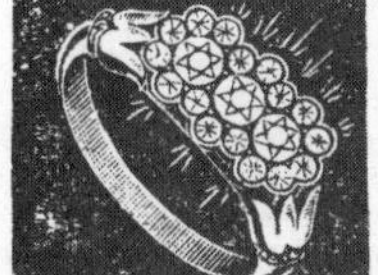

No. 4C7503 Solid gold. Price.... .... **$3.50**

No. 4C7504 Solid gold. Price.........**$2.85**

No. 4C7505 Gold filled scarf pin, 1 Parisian pearl. Price...**$1.20**

No. 4C7506 Gold filled scarf pin. Price...**$1.60**

No. 4C7508 Gold filled scarf pin. Price...**$1.08**

No. 4C7509 Solid gold studs, plain mounting. Price.....**90c**
No. 4C7510 Same style, gold filled. Price.....**35c**

No. 4C7511 Solid gold studs, plain mounting. Price**$1.25**
No. 4C7512 Same style, gold filled. Price..**50c**

No. 4C7513 Solid gold studs, plain mounting. Price.. **$2.00**
No. 4C7514 Same style, gold filled. Price.**60c**

No. 4C7515 Solid gold Ear knobs. Per pair, **$1.60**

No. 4C7516 Solid gold. Per pair, **$1.85**

No. 4C7517 Solid gold. Per pair, **$2.50**

No. 4C7518 Solid gold. Per pair. **$2.00**

No. 4C7520 Solid gold. Per pair, **$3.75**

No. 4C7521 Gold filled. Per pair...**60c**

No. 4C7522 Gold filled. Per pair...**80c**

No. 4C7523 Gold filled. Per pair...**50c**

No. 4C7524 Gold filled. Per pair...**75c**

No. 4C7525 Gold filled. Per pair..**75c**

No. 4C7526 Solid gold, Price........... ...**$3.75**

POSTAGE ON EARRINGS, 2 CENTS EXTRA.

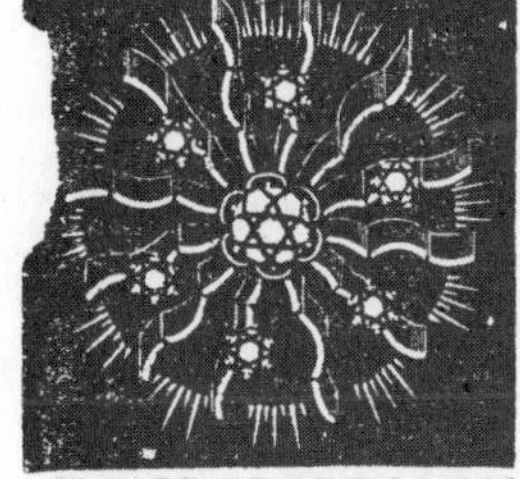

No. 4C7527 Solid gold. Price.................**$6.00**

No. 4C7528 Solid gold. Price.................**$7.25**

No. 4C7529 Gold filled. Price.......................**$3.00**

No. 4C7530 Gold filled. Price.................**$1.87**

No. 4C7531 Gold filled Price....... ....**$1.90**

No. 4C7532 Solid silver, one fine Egyptian pink pearl. Price.... .... **$4.00**
No. 4C7533 Similar style, but gold filled mounting. Price...**$4.50**

No. 4C7534 Solid silver. Can be used as a neck pendant or chatelette for watch. Price.................**$2.50**
No. 4C7535 Similar style, but gold filled mounting. Price.........**$2.85**

No. 4C7536 Gold filled. Price... **.68c**

No. 4C7537 Gold filled. Price.....**75c**

No. 4C7538 Gold filled. Price..**$1.15**

No. 4C7539 Solid silver. Price....................**$1.70**
No. 4C7540 Gold filled. Price....................**$1.30**

No. 4C7541 Gold filled. Price, **$1.30**

No. 4C7544 Solid silver. Price............ ....**$3.20**
No. 4C7545 Similar style, but gold filled mounting. Price....... ...**$3.65**

No. 4C7546 Solid silver. Price.......... ....**$2.60**
No. 4C7547 Gold filled. Price..................... 2.10

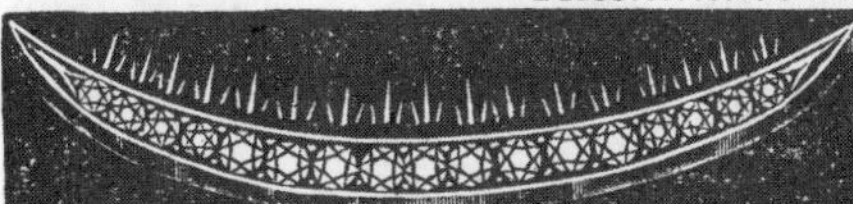

No. 4C7542 Solid silver. Price..... ..**$2.00**
No. 4C7543 Gold filled. Price 1.65

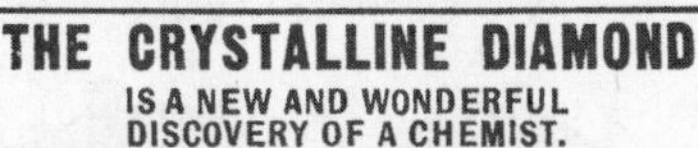

THE CRYSTALLINE DIAMOND
IS A NEW AND WONDERFUL DISCOVERY OF A CHEMIST.
It is the nearest approach to the genuine diamond ever discovered.

: : : BRILLIANCY : : :
Our Crystalline Diamond looks like a diamond and wears like a diamond, and is as brilliant as a diamond. At night it gives out a peculiar phosphorescent light but few GENUINE DIAMONDS have at all.

No. 4C7548 Solid silver. Price...**$2.50**

No. 4C7549 Gold filled. Price............. **$2.60**

No. 4C7550 Gold filled. Price..................**$2.68**

No. 4C7551 Gold filled. Price.................**$2.40**

GOLD FILLED, GOLD PLATED AND SOLID SILVER RINGS.

HOW GOLD FILLED RINGS ARE MADE.

WE offer you here a line of gold filled rings. It will be interesting to you and much more satisfactory before making a purchase of a gold filled ring to know just how they are made. The operation is very easy when it is understood. To start with, a piece of solid gold tube from 1½ to 2 inches in diameter is taken and the hole on the inside made perfectly smooth, after which a piece of hard, fine composition metal is placed on the inside of the tube so as to fit the opening perfectly. Some fine gold solder is now placed in the crevice and the whole is inserted in the furnace. As soon as the two pieces are heated sufficiently the solder flows into the crevice, after which it is removed from the furnace, and after it is cold the two original pieces are one. One end of this piece is then hammered and drawn out, so as to make it a little smaller, after which it is inserted in what is called the draw plate, which is a long steel plate with a number of holes in it of such shape as the pieces which it is desired to make. These holes are graduated in size, at one end being very large and at the other end small. The piece of material to be worked on is inserted in the large hole first, and with a pair of tongs it is drawn through; this reduces the piece, when it is again hammered at the end to make it small enough to be inserted in the next smaller hole and in turn drawn through this.

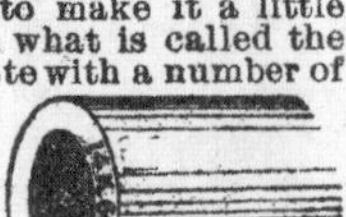

THE edges of the holes are all polished so as not to scrape, but to press the metal. This drawing hardens the metal to such an extent that after drawing it through several times it would break easily. It is then annealed by inserting it in the fire and allowing it to cool gradually. After the piece has been drawn out to the required shape and size, one end is bent around a steel mandrel until it has formed a circle of the size the ring is to be made. It is then cut off at the proper place and both ends are carefully surfaced in order to bring them together and make a perfect joint, and on this joint is placed some fine gold solder and the ring inserted in a furnace sufficiently heated to cause the solder to flow into the joint. The ring is then polished carefully on a cotton buff wheel with tripoli and rouge, after which it is ready for the market. Solid gold rings are made in the same manner with the exception of the composition metal on inside.

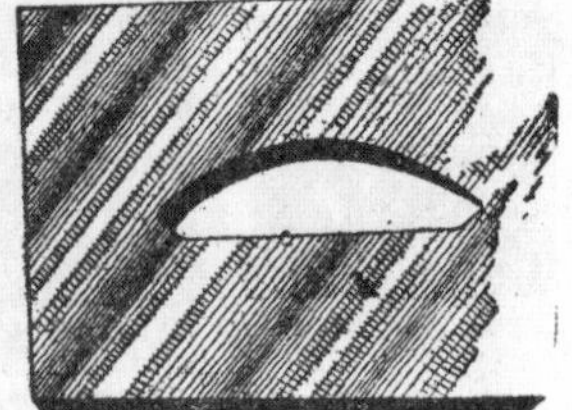

The market is flooded with cheap brass rings which are electro gold plated, and are called rolled plate or rolled gold plate, and which are utterly worthless. In gold filled rings we handle nothing but the very best.

SEE OUR PRICES ON BEST QUALITY 14-KARAT GOLD FILLED RINGS.

WILL BE FURNISHED IN SIZES 5 TO 13.

If by mail, postage on rings, 2 cents.

No. 4C7600 Plain oval band. Price......60c

No. 4C7602 Plain oval band. Price......95c

No. 4C7604 Plain oval band. Price ...$1.30

No. 4C7606 Plain oval band. Price....$1.65

No. 4C7608 Plain flat band. Price....$1.30

No. 4C7610 Plain flat band. Price....$1.70

No. 4C7612 Flat band chased. Price..80c

No. 4C7614 Flat band chased. Price....75c

No. 4C7616 Flat band chased. Price....80c

No. 4C7618 Flat band, fancy engraved and embossed. Ea..$1.00

No. 4C7620 Flat band, fancy engraved and embossed. Ea..$1.30

No. 4C7622 Flat band, engraved and embossed. Price..$1.40

No. 4C7624 Flat band, fancy engraved and embossed. Ea..$1.55

No. 4C7626 Flat band, fancy engraved and embossed. Ea. $1.70

Don't fail to give size of ring wanted.

SECOND QUALITY GOLD FILLED RINGS.

FOR THE PRICE NOTHING BETTER ON THE MARKET.

No. 4C7628 Plain oval band. Price......45c

No. 4C7630 Plain oval band. Price......60c

No. 4C7632 Plain oval band. Price......80c

No. 4C7634 Plain oval band. Price....$1.00

No. 4C7636 Plain flat band. Price... ..90c

No. 4C7638 Plain flat band. Price....$1.00

No. 4C7640 Flat band chased. Price..60c

No. 4C7642 Flat band chased. Price....55c

No. 4C7644 Flat band chased. Price....60c

No. 4C7646 Flat band chased. Price....55c

No. 4C7648 Flat band chased. Price....70c

No. 4C7650 Flat band chased. Price....75c

No. 4C7652 Flat band chased. Price....85c

No. 4C7654 Flat band chased. Price..95c

GOLD FILLED AND SOLID SILVER SET RINGS, GUARANTEED TO GIVE ENTIRE SATISFACTION.

No. 4C7656 Gold filled. 8 rhinestones, 1 turquoise. Ea. 65c

No. 4C7658 Gold filled. 1 rhinestone. Price 50c

No. 4C7660 Gold filled. 1 emerald. Ea...68c

No. 4C7662 Gold filled. 3 rubies. Ea...70c

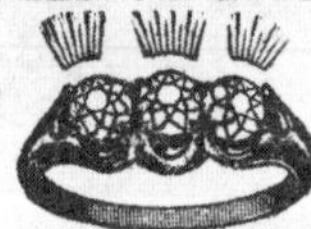

No. 4C7664 Gold filled. 3 rhinestones. Price.... 50c

HOW TO DETERMINE THE SIZE OF RING WANTED.

Cut a strip of thick paper so that the ends will exactly meet, when drawn tightly around the second joint of the finger. Lay one end on the diagram at O and order the size the other end indicates.

RING SIZES.

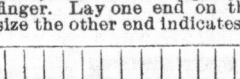

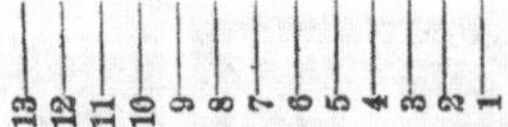

No. 4C7666 Gold filled. 1 almandine Price..........25c

No. 4C7668 1 ruby. Price. 25c

No. 4C7670 1 emerald. Ea..25c

No. 4C7673 Gold filled, 9 rhinestones, 1 emerald. Price..........95c

No. 4C7676 1 fine brilliant. Price...45c

No. 4C7678 1 ruby Price.............45c

No. 4C7680 1 emerald. Price.......45c

No. 4C7682 Gold filled. 1 rhinestone, extra fine. Price, ...50c

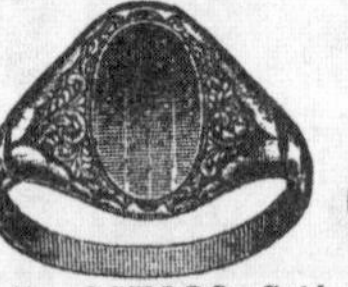

No. 4C7683 Gold Filled Seal Ring...67c Engraving, 5c per letter extra for Old English.

No. 4C7685 Gold Filled Seal Ring. Price..........30c Monogram 10c extra.

No. 4C7687 Gold filled. 1 fine imitation ruby. Price.......18c

No. 4C7689 Gold filled. Carbuncle. Price..... 60c

No. 4C7692 Gold filled. Fine ruby doublet. Price.... ....40c

No. 4C7693 Gold filled. Fine imitation ruby Price..........85c

No. 4C7695 Gold filled. Carbuncle. Price..........40c

No. 4C7697 Gold filled. 1 genuine tiger eye cameo. Price...48c

No. 4C7698 Gold filled. Brilliant and 2 garnets. Price....60c

No. 4C7699 Gold filled. Fine imitation opal. Price..........72c

No. 4C7701 Gold filled. 2 imitation rubies, 1 imitation diamond. Ea. 80c

No. 4C7702 Gold filled. Carbuncle. Price..........70c

SOLID SILVER RINGS.

No. 4C7703 Gold filled. Rubies and pearls Price..........40c

No. 4C7708 Gold filled. Emerald set. Price........38c

No. 4C7706 Solid silver, extra heavy; set with ruby doublet. Price $1.50

No. 4C7707 Solid silver, extra heavy; seal ring. Price..........$1.65 3 letter monogram 25c extra.

No. 4C7709 Solid silver seal ring. Price..........50c Monogram, 10c extra.

No. 4C7710 Solid silver, plain polish, set with imitation ruby. Price.....65c

No. 4C7715 Solid silver, engraved, set with imitation turquoise. Price.....68c

No. 4C7720 Solid silver, snake pattern, set with 1 fine ruby, 2 emerald eyes. 88c

SOLID GOLD AND SOLID SILVER SEAL, PLAIN AND ENGRAVED RINGS.

No. 4C7995 Seal Ring. Price.....$1.50 Monogram 20 cents extra.

No. 4C7996 Ladies' Seal Ring, light weight. Price ....$1.60 Monogram 20 cents extra.

No. 4C7997 Ladies' Seal Ring, hand carved fancy heads. Roman finish. Price...$2.15 Monogram 25 cents extra.

No. 4C7998 Ladies' Seal Ring. Price.....$2.00 Monogram 25 cents extra.

No. 4C7999 Ladies' Seal Ring. Price.....$2.25 Monogram 25 cents extra.

No. 4C8001 Ladies' Seal Ring, set with 6 pearls. Price.....$2.25 Monogram 20 cents extra.

No. 4C8003 Ladies' Seal Ring, hand carved, Roman satin finish. Price...$2.85 Monogram 25 cents extra.

No. 4C8005 Seal Ring. Price...$3.00 Monogram 25 cents extra.

No. 4C8007 Seal Ring. Price...$4.25 Monogram 25 cents extra.

No. 4C8009 Seal Ring, Ladies' or Gentlemen's, Roman satin finish. Hand carved. Price.........$4.50 Monogram 25c extra.

No. 4C8011 Seal Ring. Price.$4.50 Monogram 25c extra.

No. 4C8013 Seal Ring, Ladies' or Gentlemen's. Hand carved mermaids......$5.10 Monogram 25 cents extra.

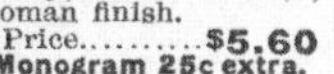
No. 4C8015 Seal Ring, Gentlemen's. Very heavy, hand carved, Roman finish. Price.........$5.60 Monogram 25c extra.

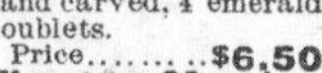
No. 4C8017 Gentlemen's Seal Ring, hand carved, 4 emerald doublets. Price.........$6.50 Monogram 30c extra.

No. 4C8019 Gentlemen's Seal Ring, extra heavy, hand carved, Roman satin finish. Price..........$8.00 Monogram 30c extra.

No. 4C8027 Seal Ring. Extra finely carved and extra heavy. Price......$9.75 Monogram 30c extra.

No. 4C8029 Extra Heavy Engraved, set with Ruby Doublet. Price...........$6.00

No. 4C8032 Gypsy Ring. Set with 3 Ruby Doublets. Price.......$3.98
No. 4C8031 Same style as No. 3C8032, set with Emerald Doublet. Price..$3.98
No. 4C8033 Same style as above, but set with genuine Opals. Price.......$5.98

No. 4C8034 Flat Belcher, set with Ruby Doublet. Price, $3.50
No. 4C8036 Same as No. 4C8034, set with Emerald Doublet. Price $3.50

No. 4C8037 Extra Heavy, Large Genuine Opal Set. Price..$5.98

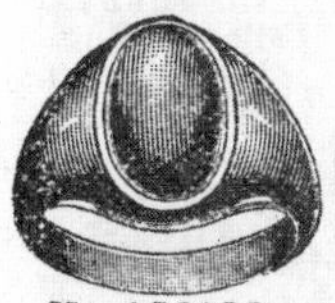
No. 4C8038 Carbuncle. Price....$2.75

No. 4C8040 Set with Ruby or Emerald Doublet. Price.....$3.50

No. 4C8042 Tiger Eye Cameo. Price..$1.48

No. 4C8044 Onyx Intaglio. Price...$2.05

No. 4C8046 Tiger Eye Cameo. Price....$3.00

SOLID SILVER RINGS.

No. 4C8048 Solid silver. Ea..60c
No. 4C8050 Gold Topped Shield...80c

No. 4C8052 Solid silver. Ea..50c
No. 4C8054 Gold Topped Hearts...70c

No. 4C8056 Solid silver. Each............40c

No. 4C8058 Solid silver. Ea. 23c

No. 4C8060 Solid silver. Ea. 38c

No. 4C8062 Solid silver. Ea. 45c

No. 4C8064 Solid silver. Ea. 65c

FINEST QUALITY SOLID GOLD PLAIN AND ENGRAVED BAND RINGS.

2 dwt.
No. 4C8066 10-karat..$1.16
No. 4C8068 14-karat.. 1.56
No. 4C8070 18-karat.. 1.96

3 dwt.
No. 4C8072 10-karat..$1.74
No. 4C8074 14-karat.. 2.34
No. 4C8076 18-karat.. 2.94

5 dwt.
No. 4C8078 10-karat..$2.90
No. 4C8080 14-karat.. 3.90
No. 4C8082 18-karat.. 4.90

6 dwt.
No. 4C8084 10-karat... .....$3.48
No. 4C8086 14-karat......... 4.68
No. 4C8088 18-karat......... 5.88

3 dwt. Tiffany style.
No. 4C8090 10-karat..$1.74
No. 4C8092 14-karat.. 2.34
No. 4C8094 18-karat.. 2.94

4 dwt. Tiffany style.
No. 4C8096 10-karat..$2.32
No. 4C8098 14-karat.. 3.12
No. 4C8100 18-karat.. 3.92

5 dwt. Tiffany style.
No. 4C8102 10-karat..$2.90
No. 4C8104 14-karat.. 3.90
No. 4C8106 18-karat.. 4.90

2 dwt.
No. 4C8108 10-karat $1.16
No. 4C8110 14-karat 1.56
No. 4C8112 18-karat 1.96

4 dwt.
No. 4C8114 10-karat..$2.32
No. 4C8116 14-karat.. 3.12
No. 4C8118 18-karat.. 3.92

6 dwt.
No. 4C8120 10-karat..$3.48
No. 4C8122 14-karat.. 4.68
No. 4C8124 18-karat.. 5.88

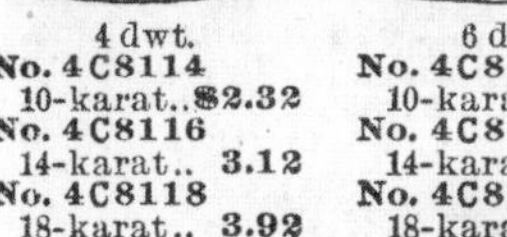
No. 4C8127 Very Light Weight. Price................90c

No. 4C8129 Very Light Weight. Price.........$1.05

No. 4C8131 Light Weight. Price............$1.12

No. 4C8133 Light Weight. Price..........$1.16

No. 4C8135 Light Medium Weight. Price............$1.24

No. 4C8137 Light Medium Weight. Price............$1.32

No. 4C8139 Light Medium Weight. Price............$1.32

No. 4C8141 Light Medium Weight. Price............$1.32

No. 4C8143 Medium Weight. Price............$1.40

No. 4C8145 Medium Weight. Price........... $1.50

No. 4C8147 Medium Weight. Price............$1.50

No. 4C8149 Medium Weight. Price............$1.60

No. 4C8151 Medium Weight. Price............$1.66

No. 4C8153 Heavy Medium Weight. Price............$1.72

No. 4C8155 Heavy Medium Weight. Price............$1.85

No. 4C8157 Heavy Medium Weight. Price............$1.94

No. 4C8159 Heavy Medium Weight. Price............$1.98

No. 4C8161 Heavy Weight. Price............$2.10

No. 4C8163 Heavy Weight. Price............$2.10

No. 4C8165 Heavy Weight. Price............$2.14

No. 4C8167 Very Heavy Weight. Price............$2.45

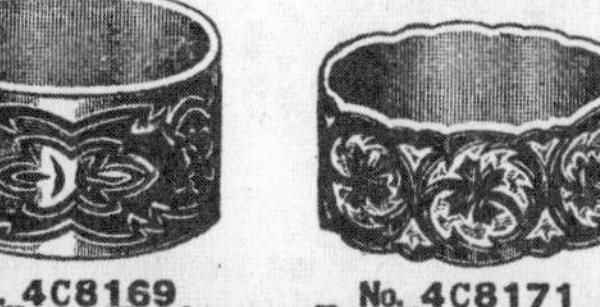

No. 4C8169 Very Heavy Weight. Price............$2.50

No. 4C8171 Very Heavy Weight. Price............$2.60

DON'T FAIL TO GIVE SIZE OF RING.

No. 4C8173 Extra Heavy Weight. Price............$3.20

No. 4C8175 Extra Heavy Weight. Price............$3.35

No. 4C8177 Heavy Medium Weight. Colored Gold Inlaid. Price, $2.40

No. 4C8179 Heavy Weight. Colored Gold Inlaid. Price......$2.85

BABIES' AND CHILDREN'S SOLID GOLD SET AND BAND RINGS.

BABY RINGS ARE MADE IN SIZES FROM 0 TO 3. MISSES' RINGS TO FIT MISSES' AND BOYS', AGES 14 TO 16 YEARS, IN SIZES FROM 5 TO 8 ONLY.

For full instructions for measurement of ring size, see table below. When cash in full is sent with order the rings can be sent by mail, postage, 3 cents; registered mail, 8 cents extra.

No. 4C8505 Baby Ring, 1 turquoise. Price....42c

No. 4C8506 Baby Ring, 1 fire opal. Price....50c

No. 4C8507 Baby Ring, 3 garnets. Price......50c

No. 4C8508 Baby Ring, 1 garnet. Price......58c

No. 4C8509 Baby Ring, 1 emerald doublet. Price......63c

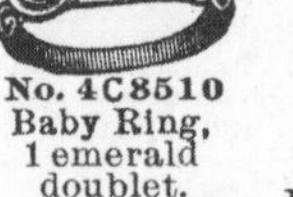
No. 4C8510 Baby Ring, 1 emerald doublet. Price......65c

No. 4C8511 Baby Ring, 1 garnet. Price.... 65c

No. 4C8512 Baby Ring, 1 turquoise. Price... ..65c

No. 4C8513 Baby Ring, 1 ruby doublet, 2 pearls. Price..... 68c

No. 4C8514 Baby Ring, 1 garnet. Price....68c

No. 4C8515 Baby Ring, 2 turquoise, 1 pearl. Price......78c

No. 4C8516 Baby Ring, 1 turquoise. Price......80c

No. 4C8517 Baby Ring, 1 garnet. Price......80c

No. 4C8518 Baby Ring, 1 opal, 2 pearls. Price......85c

No. 4C8519 Baby Ring, Rose finish, hand carved, for initial. Price......85c

No. 4C8520 Baby Ring, Roman rose color, for initial. Price...$1.00

No. 4C8521 Baby Ring, 1 emerald doublet, 8 pearls. Price...$1.00

No. 4C8522 Baby Ring, Roman rose color, for engraving initial. Price... $1.04

No. 4C8523 Baby Ring, hand carved, 1 pearl. Price...$1.08

No. 4C8524 Baby Ring, 3 olivines. Price. $1.10

DON'T FAIL TO GIVE SIZE OF RING WANTED.

No. 4C8525 Baby Ring, hand carved, 1 pearl. Price...$1.15

No. 4C8526 Baby Ring, 1 rose diamond. Price...$1.15

No. 4C8527 Baby Ring, 1 genuine rose diamond, 2 garnets. Price...$1.15

No. 4C8528 Baby Ring, 1 genuine rose diamond. Price... $1.50

No. 4C8529 Baby Ring, Extra heavy, 1 genuine cut diamond. Price...$2.25

No. 4C8530 Baby Ring. Price......30c

No. 4C8531 Baby Ring. Price 39c

No. 4C8532 Baby Ring. Price......40c

No. 4C8533 Baby Ring. Price......54c

No. 4C8534 Baby Ring. Price....58c

No. 4C8535 Baby Ring. Price......58c

No. 4C8536 Baby Ring. Price......65c

No. 4C8537 Misses' Ring, 1 carbuncle. Price.......80c

No. 4C8538 Misses' Ring, 1 almandine, 2 pearls. Price..........88c

No. 4C8539 Misses' Ring, 1 pearl, 2 turquoise. Price......88c

No. 4C8540 Misses' Ring, engraved, set with pearl. Price........ 90c

No. 4C8541 Misses' Ring, 1 turquoise. Price..........95c

No. 4C8542 Misses' Ring, 6 pearls, 1 turquoise. Price......... $1.00

No. 4C8543 Misses' Ring, 1 carbuncle. Price.... $1.00

No. 4C8544 Misses' Ring, 1 opal. Price...... $1.06

No. 4C8545 Misses' Ring, 1 fire opal. Price..... $1.10

No. 4C8546 Misses' Ring, 1 large turquoise. Price.......$1.25

No. 4C8547 Misses' Ring, 1 pearl. Price.........$1.25

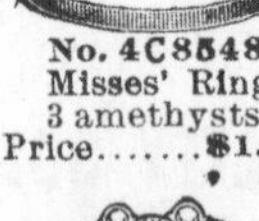
No. 4C8548 Misses' Ring, 3 amethysts. Price.......$1.30

No. 4C8549 Misses' Ring, seal ring, Roman satin finish. Price............$1.30
2-letter monogram, engraved, 15c extra.

No. 4C8550 Misses' Ring, 3 turquoise. Price.........$1.32

No. 4C8551 Misses' Ring, 1 genuine fire opal. Price.....$1.35

No. 4C8552 Misses' Seal Ring, Roman finish. Pr.. $1.37
2-letter monogram, engraved, 15c extra.

No. 4C8553 Misses' Ring, 1 genuine pearl, 1 sapphire. Price.......$1.38

No. 4C8554 Misses' Ring, 1 almandine. Price.... ..$1.50

No. 4C8555 Misses' Ring, 3 turquoise, 4 pearls. Price.......$1.50

No. 4C8556 Misses' Ring, 3 ruby doublets, 4 pearls. Price.......$1.50

No. 4C8557 Misses' Ring, 1 fire opal, 2 pearls. Price...........$1.60

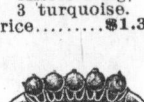

No. 4C8558 Misses' Ring. 5 genuine fire opals. Price.......$1.60

No. 4C8559 Misses' Ring, 1 opal. Price.....$1.60

No. 4C8560 Misses' Ring, 1 almandine. Price.......$1.60

No. 4C8561 Misses' Ring, 1 large genuine fire opal. Price.......$1.62

No. 4C8562 Misses' Ring, 1 ruby doublet, 2 pearls. Price.......$1.75

No. 4C8563 Misses' Ring, 2 almandines, 2 pearls. Price.......$1.75

No. 4C8564 Misses' Ring, 4 genuine fire opals, 1 emerald. Price.......$1.80

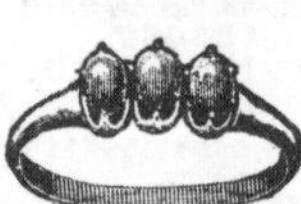
No. 4C8565 Misses' Ring, 3 genuine fire opals. Price...........$1.80

No. 4C8566 Misses' Ring, 1 genuine fire opal. Price.........$1.85

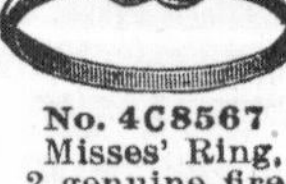
No. 4C8567 Misses' Ring, 2 genuine fire opals, 2 pearls. Price.....$2.00

No. 4C8568 Misses' Seal Ring, 2 garnets. Price.. ....$2.40
2-letter monogram, engraved, 20c extra.

No. 4C8569 Misses' Ring, engraved band. Price. 62c

No. 4C8570 Misses' Ring, engraved band. Price..........65c

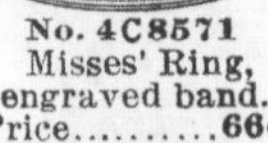
No. 4C8571 Misses' Ring, engraved band. Price..........66c

No. 4C8572 Misses' Ring, engraved band. Price 68c

No. 4C8573 Misses' Ring, engraved band. Price........ ..69c

No. 4C8574 Misses' Ring, engraved band. Price...........70c

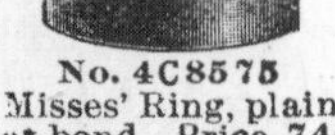
No. 4C8575 Misses' Ring, plain flat bond. Price, 74c

No. 4C8576 Misses' Ring, engraved band. Price.... ..76c

No. 4C8577 Misses' Ring, engraved band. Price..........81c

No. 4C8578 Misses' Ring, engraved band. Price........ .90c

No. 4C8579 Misses' Ring, engraved band. Price..........90c

No. 4C8580 Misses' Ring, engraved band. Price......... 92c

No. 4C8581 Misses' Ring, oval band. Price..........98c

BE SURE AND GIVE US THE SIZE.
HOW TO DETERMINE THE SIZE.
Cut a strip of thick paper so that the ends will exactly meet, when drawn tightly around the second joint of the finger. Lay one end on the diagram at O and order the size the other end indicates.

RING SIZES.

13, 12, 11, 10, 9, 8, 7, 6, 5, 4, 3, 2, 1, O

FINEST QUALITY SOLID GOLD GENTS' INITIAL RINGS.

POSTAGE ON RINGS, EXTRA, 2 CENTS.
By Registered Mail, 10c.

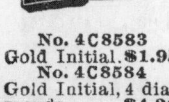

No. 4C8583 Gold Initial. $1.95
No. 4C8584 Gold Initial, 4 diamonds....... $4.20

No. 4C8585 Gold Initial.. $2.00
No. 4C8586 Gold Initial, 5 diamonds........ $4.60

No. 4C8587 Gold Initial........... $2.90
No. 4C8588 Gold Initial, 6 diamonds... $6.15

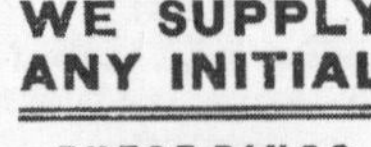
WE SUPPLY ANY INITIAL

THESE RINGS FURNISHED WITH
Odd Fellow, Masonic or Knights of Pythias
Emblems at same price as quoted for initials.

No. 4C8589 Gold Initial....... $6.75
No. 4C8590 Gold Initial, 6 diamonds... $9.50

No. 4C8591 Gold Initial.. ....$4.95
No. 4C8592 Gold Initial, 6 diamonds... $7.65

LADIES' FINE SOLID GOLD STONE SET RINGS.

Compare any ring illustrated on the following pages with any ring owned by your friends, or shown in your local store, and compare prices. If ours is not the best, and you are not saving money, don't buy. Remember, postage on rings is only 2 cents; insurance, 5 cents extra, up to $5.00 purchase.

Get a Birthday Ring. We particularly direct your attention to ring No. 4C8718. This is the ideal birthday ring. Price, **$1.68**, the best value ever offered. The stones used according to month are as follows: January, garnet; February, amethyst; March, bloodstone; April, diamond doublet; May, emerald; June, agate; July, ruby; August, sardonyx; September, sapphire; October, opal; November, topaz; December, turquoise. **Don't fail to give exact size of ring wanted.**

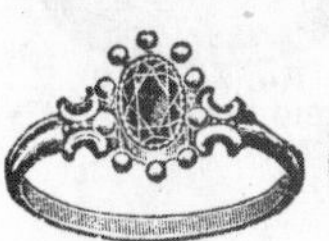

No. 4C8602 Fancy mounting, 1 large ruby doublet. Price.. **$1.30**

No. 4C8604 Fancy mounting, 2 ruby doublets. Price..... **$1.35**

No. 4C8606 Light weight mounting, 3 rubies, 6 pearls. Price... **$1.60**

No. 4C8608 1 ruby doublet, 8 pearls. Price... **$1.85**

No. 4C8610 1 ruby doublet. Price..... **$1.90**
No. 4C8612 Emerald doublet. Price..... **$1.90**

No. 4C8614 Fancy mounting, 1 large ruby doublet. Price... **$1.95**

No. 4C8616 Ruby doublet set. Price, **$2.00**
No. 4C8618 Emerald doublet. Price, **$2.00**

No. 4C8620 1 ruby doublet, 12 rhinestones. Price... **$2.00**

No. 4C8622 1 large ruby. Price... **$2.25**

No. 4C8624 2 ruby doublets, 2 pearls. Price..... **$2.50**

No. 4C8626 Ruby set. Price... **$2.60**

No. 4C8628 2 rubies, 1 emerald, 2 pearls. Price... **$2.60**

No. 4C8630 1 ruby, 12 brilliants. Price... **$2.75**

No. 4C8632 4 rubies, 1 pearl. Price..... **$2.75**

No. 4C8634 2 rubies and 2 whole pearls. Price... **$2.75**

No. 4C8636 5 ruby doublets. Price... **$3.05**

No. 4C8638 Plain polished mounting, 2 ruby doublets, 2 genuine whole pearls. Price......... **$3.05**

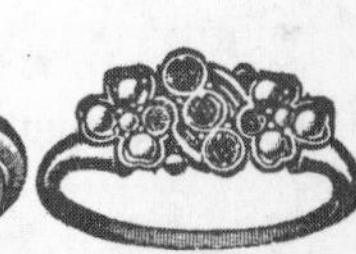

No. 4C8640 3 emeralds, 2 rubies, 8 pearls. Price. **$3.15**

No. 4C8642 Extra heavy, ruby set. Price..... **$3.25**

No. 4C8644 Plain polished mounting, 2 ruby doublets, 4 genuine whole pearls. Price......... **$3.55**

No. 4C8646 1 ruby doublet. Price..... **$3.65**

No. 4C8648 12 rubies, 5 pearls. Price..... **$3.75**

No. 4C8650 1 ruby doublet, 4 genuine half pearls. Price..... **$4.00**

No. 4C8652 2 rubies, 2 genuine whole pearls. Price..... **$4.00**

No. 4C8654 Plain mounting, 3 large ruby doublets. Price..... **$2.65**

No. 4C8656 Fancy mounting, 1 large ruby doublet. Price... **$2.00**

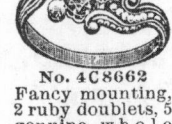

No. 4C8658 4 rubies, 5 whole pearls. Price **$4.00**

No. 4C8660 Fancy mounting, 6 ruby doublets, 1 genuine whole pearl. Ea.. **$4.05**

No. 4C8662 Fancy mounting, 2 ruby doublets, 5 genuine whole pearls. Ea. **$4.05**

No. 4C8664 Fancy mounting, 3 ruby doublets, 6 genuine whole pearls. Ea. **$4.20**

No. 4C8666 10 rubies, 5 real pearls. Price..... **$4.45**

No. 4C8668 4 ruby doublets, 6 genuine pearls. Price..... **$4.80**

No. 4C8670 2 emerald sets. Ea.. **$1.35**
No. 4C8672 Turquoise set. Ea. **$1.35**
No. 4C8674 Ruby set. Price..... **$1.85**

No. 4C8676 Emerald and ruby. Price, **$1.58**

No. 4C8678 3 imitation emeralds, 4 pearls. Price..... **$1.67**

No. 4C8680 Fancy mounting, 1 large emerald doublet. Ea. **$1.80**

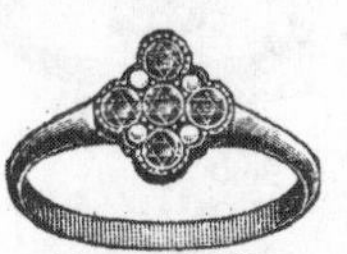

No. 4C8682 5 emerald doublets, 4 pearls. Price..... **$1.88**

No. 4C8684 1 fine emerald doublet. Price..... **$2.30**

No. 4C8686 1 emerald, 6 pearls. Price..... **$2.50**

No. 4C8688 7 emerald doublets, 6 pearls. Price..... **$2.50**

No. 4C8690 5 emeralds, 8 pearls. Price..... **$2.75**

No. 4C8692 Fancy mounting. 1 large emerald doublet, 2 genuine pearls. Price... **$2.75**

No. 4C8694 1 emerald, 12 pearls. Price..... **$2.75**

No. 4C8696 1 large emerald doublet, 2 genuine pearls. Price **$3.20**

No. 4C8698 11 emeralds, 10 pearls. Price..... **$3.50**

No. 4C8700 4 emerald doublets. Price..... **$3.60**

No. 4C8702 Plain polished mounting, 4 emerald doublets, 10 genuine pearls. Price......... **$3.65**

No. 4C8704 6 fine emerald doublets. Price..... **$3.80**

No. 4C8706 1 emerald doublet, 6 genuine pearls. Price..... **$4.75**

No. 4C8708 4 emeralds, 8 genuine pearls. Price... **$4.88**

No. 4C8710 2 ruby doublets, 1 emerald doublet. Price..... **$8.00**

No. 4C8712 Light weight, 3 genuine opals, 4 pearls. Price..... **$1.60**

No. 4C8714 Light weight, 6 genuine opals, 3 pearls. Price..... **$1.60**

No. 4C8716 Light weight, 4 genuine opals, 5 pearls. Price..... **$1.60**

No. 4C8718 Special Bargain Birthday Ring, plain Tiffany. See description at top of page. Price **$1.68**

No. 4C8720 1 genuine opal, 2 pearls. Price..... **$1.85**

No. 4C8722 2 genuine opals, 4 pearls. Price..... **$1.90**

No. 4C8724 2 genuine opals. Price... **$2.00**

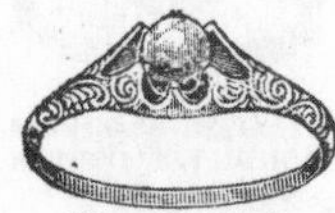

No. 4C8726 1 genuine opal. Price..... **$2.00**

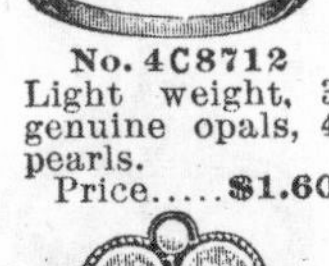

No. 4C8728 2 large genuine opals, 2 pearls. Price..... **$1.80**

No. 4C8730 Tiffany mounting, 5 genuine opals. Ea.. **$2.30**

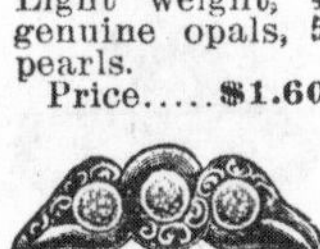

No. 4C8732 3 genuine opals. Price..... **$2.50**

No. 4C8734 7 genuine opals. Price..... **$2.70**

No. 4C8736 1 large genuine opal. Price, **$2.75**

No. 4C8738 3 genuine opals. Price..... **$2.85**

No. 4C8740 6 pearls and 3 turquoise. Each.. **$2.90**

No. 4C8742 5 genuine opals, 5 pearls. Price..... **$2.98**

No. 4C8744 4 opals, 1 olivine. Price..... **$3.00**

No. 4C8746 1 large opal. Price..... **$2.40**

No. 4C8748 Large genuine opal. Price..... **$3.10**

No. 4C8750 2 genuine opals, 8 pearls. Price **$3.55**

No. 4C8752 1 opal, 1 almandine, 6 pearls. Price..... **$3.80**

No. 4C8754 4 genuine opals, 10 emerald doublets. Price..... **$3.80**

No. 4C8755 1 large genuine opal. Price..... **$3.90**

LADIES' SOLID GOLD FANCY STONE SET RINGS.

No. 4C8756
3 opals, 4 rubies. Price.....$4.00

No. 4C8758
3 genuine fire opals, 12 pearls. Price.......$4.10

No. 4C8760
6 genuine opals, 6 pearls, 1 ruby. Price. ...$4.15

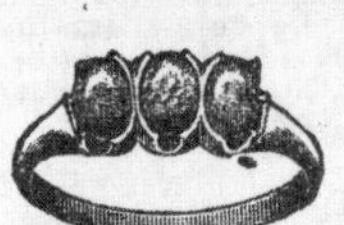
No. 4C8762
3 genuine opals. Price.......$4.00

No. 4C8764
4 genuine opals, 12 pearls. Price.......$4.50

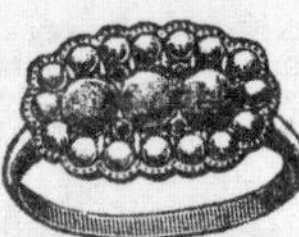
No. 4C8766
3 genuine opals, 4 garnets, 16 pearls. Price.......$4.50

No. 4C8768
4 genuine opals and 20 olivines. Price.....$4.50

No. 4C8770
1 genuine opal. Price.....$4.75

No. 4C8772
1 genuine opal, 26 pearls. Price.......$5.00

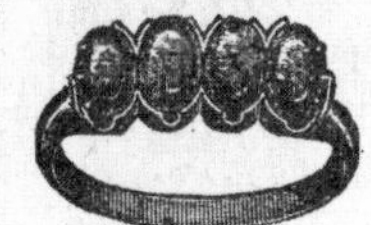
No. 4C8774
Extra heavy, 4 genuine opals. Price.......$5.25

No. 4C8776
1 genuine opal, 6 emerald doublets. Price.......$5.80

No. 4C8778
3 large genuine opals. Price.......$5.65

No. 4C8780
1 fine genuine opal. Price.......$7.50

No. 4C8782
1 amethyst doublet. Price.......$1.50

No. 4C8784
1 amethyst, 2 pearls. Price.....$1.65

No. 4C8786
2 amethysts, 3 pearls. Price.....$1.95

No. 4C8788
3 amethysts. Price.....$2.25

No. 4C8790
1 large amethyst. Price.......$2.25

No. 4C8792
Fancy mounting, amethyst doublet. Price.......$2.50

No. 4C8794
3 amethysts, 8 pearls. Price $2.50

No. 4C8796
1 amethyst, 2 genuine pearls. Price. $3.00

No. 4C8798
1 large amethyst, 12 genuine pearls. Price.......$5.50

No. 4C8800
Light weight, 12 pearls, 2 rubies. Price...$1.60

No. 4C8802
5 pearls, 4 emeralds. Price.....$1.68

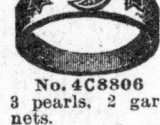

No. 4C8804
4 pearls, 4 sapphires. Price.........$1.90

No. 4C8806
3 pearls, 2 garnets. Price.....$1.98

No. 4C8808
1 fine Egyptian pearl. Price.......$2.00

No. 4C8810
1 pearl. Price.......$3.60

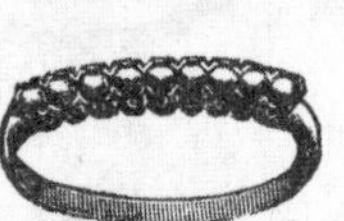
No. 4C8812
9 genuine whole pearls. Price.......$3.95

No. 4C8814
2 turquoise, 2 pearls. Price.....$1.60

No. 4C8818
1 turquoise, 4 pearls. Price.....$1.65

No. 4C8820
1 turquoise, 6 pearls. Price.....$2.25

DON'T FAIL TO GIVE SIZE OF RING WANTED.

No. 4C8824
6 rhinestones, 1 turquoise. Price.....$2.30

No. 4C8826
2 turquoise, 1 pearl. Price.......$2.50

No. 4C8828
1 turquoise, 4 genuine pearls. Price.......$2.75

No. 4C8830
4 turquoise, 6 pearls. Price.......$2.75

No. 4C8832
4 turquoise, 5 pearls. Price.......$2.90

No. 4C8834
1 large turquoise, 20 pearls. Price $3.25

No. 4C8836
1 turquoise set. Price. $3.35

No. 4C8838
5 turquoise, 6 pearls. Price...$3.40

No. 4C8840
Fancy mounting, 3 turquoise, 5 genuine pearls. Price.....$3.45

No. 4C8842
4 turquoise, 7 pearls. Price.....$3.75

No. 4C8844
2 turquoise, 8 genuine pearls. Price.....$3.98

No. 4C8846
1 turquoise, 6 genuine pearls. Price.......$4.25

No. 4C8848
1 fine garnet doublet. Price.....$1.75

No. 4C8850
3 garnets. Price.......$1.78

No. 4C8852
1 garnet, 12 pearls. Price.......$2.20

No. 4C8856
7 garnet doublets, 6 pearls. Price.....$2.85

No. 4C8858
7 garnets, 12 pearls. Price.......$3.25

No. 4C8860
1 garnet. Price.......$3.50

No. 4C8862
Plain mounting, 1 garnet and 12 genuine pearls. Price.......$4.60

No. 4C8864
3 almandines. Price.....$1.45
No. 4C8865
3 Ruby doublets. Price.....$1.45

No. 4C8866
3 almandines, 10 pearls. Price.......$2.90

No. 4C8868
4 almandines, 10 pearls. Price.......$3.00

No. 4C8872
2 almandines, 2 genuine pearls. Price.....$2.85

No. 4C8874
1 topaz. Price.....$1.45

No. 4C8876
1 topaz, 2 genuine pearls. Price.......$2.40

No. 4C8878
1 topaz, 8 pearls. Price.......$4.75

No. 4C8880
3 sapphire doublets. Price.......$1.48

No. 4C8882
Fancy mounting, 1 large sapphire doublet. Price.....$1.95

No. 4C8884
Sapphire doublet, 6 pearls. Price.......$2.25

No. 4C8888
1 sapphire, 6 genuine pearls. Price.......$3.00

No. 4C8890
Plain polished mounting, sapphire doublet and 2 whole genuine pearls. Price.......$3.25

No. 4C8892
1 large sapphire doublet, 6 pearls. Price...$3.20

No. 4C8894
4 sapphire doublets, 2 genuine pearls. Price.......$3.40

No. 4C8896
Plain polished mounting, 3 sapphire doublets, 4 genuine whole pearls. Price.....$3.65

No. 4C8898
4 sapphire doublets, 1 genuine pearl. Price.......$3.75

No. 4C8900
1 rhinestone. Price.......$1.50

No. 4C8902
7 rhinestones. Price.......$1.85

No. 4C8904
1 rhinestone, 2 rubies, 10 pearls. Price.......$3.25

No. 4C8906
1 rhinestone, 4 genuine pearls. Price.....$3.90

No. 4C8908
Fancy mounting, 1 genuine rose diamond. Price, $3.15

GENUINE DIAMONDS AND SOLID GOLD 14-KARAT MOUNTINGS.

WITH EVERY DIAMOND we issue a written, binding guarantee, with a further agreement that you can at any time return any diamond you may select from this catalogue, and exchange it for any other diamond or other article of jewelry at the same or a higher price.

WE FURTHER AGREE on the return of any diamond purchased from us within 60 days of purchase, when so requested, to refund in cash your full purchase price, and we further agree, at any time after 60 days, on return of any diamond to us, when requested to do so, to refund your full purchase price, less 10 per cent.

YOU CAN BUY A DIAMOND from us today at $3.66 to $276.00 and you can keep it for three months or three years or longer, and if you so desire return it to us and we will refund you in cash the full amount of money you paid us for it, less 10 per cent. But we must caution you that we positively will not exchange, refund, or allow credit for any diamond purchased from us unless it is in or with the original setting and is accompanied by our guarantee and refund certificate that was sent with the diamond.

EXCEPTIONS WHERE WE DO NOT GIVE OUR REFUND AND EXCHANGE CERTIFICATE WITH A PURCHASE. This ruling applies to such items plainly marked "no refund certificate," and is made necessary for the reason that where we allow a refund certificate, the cost of making the mounting is but a small item of cost and the gold value is the principal one. Where we do not give our refund certificate, the actual gold value amounts to but little and the principal cost is in the making and the cost of the pearls, fancy stones, etc., and as we melt up all returned mountings, our loss would be too great where the cost of making the article is the principal expense. However, we will allow for the diamond without the mounting. On most of our diamond mounted jewelry we quote quality and weight. Where quality and weight are not given we do not allow refunds or exchange after goods have been worn.

GRADES OF DIAMONDS.

FIRST QUALITY. These stones are perfect in color, proportion, brilliancy, shape and are free from all flaws.

SECOND QUALITY (sometimes called "Commercial White"). A second quality diamond is in every particular the same as a first, except for the color. The second quality has a slight shade of yellow. This yellow sometimes increases the brilliancy of the stone. At night it is often more fiery than the best grade in the first quality. To the inexperienced it is difficult to see the yellow tinge. This can be discovered by holding the diamond sidewise to the sunlight.

THIRD QUALITY. A third quality diamond is one that is brilliant and well cut, but has some imperfection or blemish, generally so small and so slight that it requires one high in the knowledge of diamonds to be able to detect the imperfection at all. Our own third quality diamonds are practically perfect in cut and shape. The color may be the same as in our first or second quality, but by close examination it is possible to detect a blemish of some sort. Our third quality diamonds never have cracks in them or large, unsightly chunks or pieces knocked out of them. The same quality that we sell for third quality is sold by some monthly payment houses and by small dealers as first quality stones. These people either buy and sell them as first quality because they are unable to judge diamonds, or they are fully aware of the imperfections and are simply misrepresenting the goods.

TIME PAYMENT CONCERNS sometimes sell diamonds to people who do not care what they pay for them. Some of their customers never pay. Still these concerns are making money. The selling price on any merchandise is based on the actual cost of the item with the expense of advertising, marketing and collecting, to which sum a regular profit is added. We, therefore, caution and point out to you the fact that marketing diamonds by the partial payment system is known to be the most costly of all.

WE ASK A CAREFUL COMPARISON of our goods with those shown by other concerns, which will do more toward showing the value we give than any other argument.

FINE SOLID GOLD FINGER RINGS. SET WITH FINE SELECTED GENUINE DIAMONDS.

Our binding guarantee and refund certificate goes with every ring.

Flat Belcher Mounting, set with 1/8-carat diamond.
No. 44C10002 Third quality diamond. Price...$8.88
No. 44C10004 Second quality diamond. Price, $11.38
No. 44C10006 First quality diamond. Price, $13.50
No. 44C10008 Mounting only, without stone. Ea. $2.25

Flat Belcher Mounting, set with 1/4-carat diamond.
No. 44C10010 Third quality diamond. Price, $17.50
No. 44C10012 Second quality diamond. Price, $23.50
No. 44C10014 First quality diamond. Price, $27.50
No. 44C10016 Mounting only, without stone. Ea. $2.50

Flat Belcher Mounting, set with 1/2-carat diamond.
No. 44C10026 Third quality diamond. Price, $47.00
No. 44C10028 Second quality diamond. Price, $55.50
No. 44C10030 First quality diamond. Price, $66.50
No. 44C10032 Mounting only, without stone. Ea. $4.00

Flat Belcher Mounting, set with 7/8-carat diamond.
No. 44C10034 Third quality diamond. Price, $87.88
No. 44C10036 Second quality diamond. Price, $101.87
No. 44C10038 First quality diamond. Price, $125.50
No. 44C10040 Mounting only, without stone. Ea. $4.75

Flat Belcher Mounting, set with 1 1/4-carat diamond.
No. 44C10042 Third quality diamond. Price, $135.50
No. 44C10044 Second quality diamond. Price, $155.50
No. 44C10046 First quality diamond. Price, $193.00
No. 44C10048 Mounting only, without stone. Ea. $5.50

Round Belcher Mounting, set with 3/4-carat diamond.
No. 44C10074 Third quality diamond. Price, $75.50
No. 44C10076 Second quality diamond. Price, $87.50
No. 44C10078 First quality diamond. Price, $107.75
No. 44C10080 Mounting only, without stone. Ea. $4.25

Round Belcher Mounting, set with 1-carat diamond.
No. 44C10082 Third quality diamond. Ea.. $104.75
No. 44C10084 Second quality diamond. Ea.. $123.25
No. 44C10086 First quality diamond. Ea.. $147.75
No. 44C10088 Mounting only, without stone. Ea. $5.00

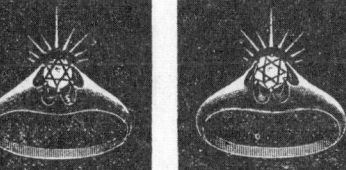

Round Belcher Mounting, set with 1 1/2-carat diamond.
No. 44C10090 Third quality diamond. Price, $122.50
No. 44C10092 Second quality diamond. Price, $138.31
No. 44C10094 First quality diamond. Price, $166.38
No. 44C10096 Mounting only, without stone. Ea. $5.50

Tiffany Belcher Mounting, set with 3/16-carat diamond.
No. 44C10106 Third quality diamond. Price, $12.69
No. 44C10108 Second quality diamond. Price, $16.44
No. 44C10110 First quality diamond. Price, $19.63
No. 44C10112 Mounting only, without stone. Ea. $2.75

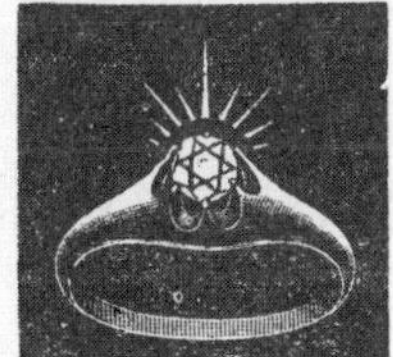

Tiffany Belcher Mounting, set with 1/4-carat diamond.
No. 44C10114 Third quality diamond. Price, $18.00
No. 44C10116 Second quality diamond. Price, $24.00
No. 44C10118 First quality diamond. Price, $28.00
No. 44C10120 Mounting only, with out stone. Ea. $3.00

Tiffany Belcher Mounting, set with 5/16-carat diamond.
No. 44C10122 Third quality diamond. Price, $22.25
No. 44C10124 Second quality diamond. Price, $29.75
No. 44C10126 First quality diamond. Price, $34.75
No. 44C10128 Mounting only, without stone. Ea. $3.50

Six-Pronged Tooth Mounting, set with 1/4-carat diamond.
No. 44C10146 Third quality diamond. Price, $18.75
No. 44C10148 Second quality diamond. Price, $24.75
No. 44C10150 First quality diamond. Price, $28.75
No. 44C10152 Mounting only, without stone. Ea. $3.75

Six-Pronged Tooth Mounting, set with 1/2-carat diamond.
No. 44C10162 Third quality diamond. Price, $47.75
No. 44C10164 Second quality diamond. Price, $56.25
No. 44C10166 First quality diamond. Price, $67.25
No. 44C10168 Mounting only, without stone. Ea. $4.75

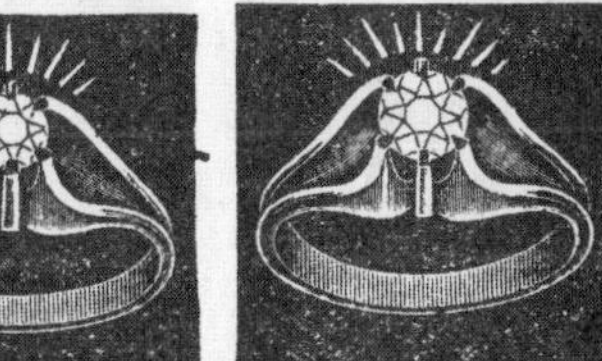

Six-Pronged Tooth Mounting, set with 3/4-carat diamond.
No. 44C10178 Third quality diamond. Ea.. $76.75
No. 44C10180 Second quality diamond. Ea.. $88.75
No. 44C10182 First quality diamond. Ea., $109.00
No. 44C10184 Mounting only, without stone. Ea. $5.50

Security Crown Flat Belcher Mounting, set with 1/2-carat diamond.
No. 44C10209 Third quality diamond. Price. $48.50
No. 44C10211 Second quality diamond. Price. $57.00
No. 44C10213 First quality diamond. Price. $68.00
No. 44C10215 Mounting only, without stone. Ea. $5.50

Security Crown Flat Belcher Mounting, set with 5/8-carat diamond.
No. 44C10217 Third quality diamond. Price. $63.25
No. 44C10219 Second quality diamond. Price. $71.38
No. 44C10221 First quality diamond. Price. $88.25
No. 44C10223 Mounting only, without stone. Ea. $5.75

Security Crown Tiffany Mounting, set with 7/16-carat diamond.
No. 44C10264 Third quality diamond. Price, $37.78
No. 44C10266 Second quality diamond. Price, $46.53
No. 44C10268 First quality diamond. Price, $53.53
No. 44C10270 Mounting only, without stone. Ea. $2.38

Security Crown Tiffany Mounting, set with 1/2-carat diamond.
No. 44C10272 Third quality diamond. Price, $45.50
No. 44C10274 Second quality diamond. Price, $54.00
No. 44C10276 First quality diamond. Price, $65.00
No. 44C10278 Mounting only, without stone. Ea. $2.50

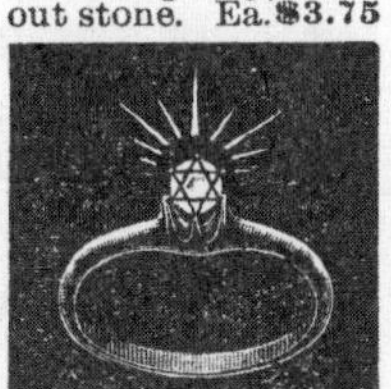

Tiffany Mounting, set with 1/8-carat diamond.
No. 44C10300 Third quality diamond. Price, $8.63
No. 44C10302 Second quality diamond. Price...... $11.13
No. 44C10304 First quality diamond. Price, $13.25
No. 44C10306 Mounting only, without stone. Ea. $2.00

Tiffany Mounting, set with 1/4-carat diamond.
No. 44C10316 Third quality diamond. Price, $17.25
No. 44C10318 Second quality diamond. Price....... $23.25
No. 44C10320 First quality diamond. Price, $27.25
No. 44C10322 Mounting only, without stone. Ea. $2.25

Tiffany Mounting, set with 3/8-carat diamond.
No. 44C10326 Third quality diamond. Ea.. $27.63
No. 44C10328 Second quality diamond. Price..... $37.38
No. 44C10330 First quality diamond. Ea.. $43.75
No. 44C10332 Mounting only, without stone. Ea. $2.50

FINE SOLID GOLD FINGER RINGS, SET WITH FINE SELECTED GENUINE DIAMONDS.

OUR BINDING GUARANTEE AND REFUND CERTIFICATE GOES WITH EVERY RING SHOWN ON THIS PAGE

PRICE QUOTED IS FOR COMPLETE RING, THAT IS STONE AND MOUNTING.

Tiffany Mounting, set with 1/2-carat diamond.
No. 44C10334 Third quality diamond. Price, $45.60
No. 44C10336 Second quality diamond. Price, $54.10
No. 44C10338 First quality diamond. Price, $65.10
No. 44C10340 Mounting only, without stone. Ea..$2.60

Tiffany Mounting, set with 5/8-carat diamond.
No. 44C10342 Third quality diamond. Price, $60.25
No. 44C10344 Second quality diamond. Price, $68.38
No. 44C10346 First quality diamond. Price, $85.25
No. 44C10348 Mounting only, without stone. Ea..$2.75

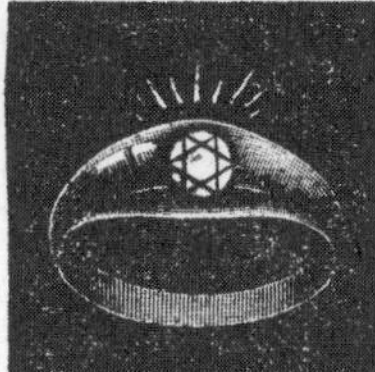

Plain Gypsy Mounting, set with 1/4-carat diamond.
No. 44C10350 Third quality diamond. Price, $19.50
No. 44C10352 Second quality diamond. Price, $25.50
No. 44C10354 First quality diamond. Price. $29.50
No. 44C10356 Mounting only, without stone. Ea..$4.50

Plain Gypsy Mounting, set with 3/8-carat diamond.
No. 44C10358 Third quality diamond. Price, $30.63
No. 44C10360 Second quality diamond. Price, $40.30
No. 44C10362 First quality diamond. Price, $46.75
No. 44C10364 Mounting only, without stone. Ea..$5.50

Fancy Flat Belcher Mounting, set with 3/8-carat diamond.
No. 44C10382 Third quality diamond. Price, $28.63
No. 44C10384 Second quality diamond. Price, $38.38
No. 44C10386 First quality diamond. Price, $44.75
No. 44C10388 Mounting only, without stone. Ea..$3.50

Fancy Flat Belcher Mounting, set with 7/16-carat diamond.
No. 44C10390 Third quality diamond. Price, $41.63
No. 44C10392 Second quality diamond. Price, $49.06
No. 44C10394 First quality diamond. Price, $58.68
No. 44C10396 Mounting only, without stone. Ea..$4.00

Security Crown Lion's Claw Mounting, set with 1/4-carat diamond.
No. 44C10398 Third quality diamond. Ea. $20.50
No. 44C10400 Second quality diamond. Ea. $26.50
No. 44C10402 First quality diamond. Ea. $30.50
No. 44C10404 Mounting only, without stone. Ea. $5.50

Perforated Fancy Flat Belcher Mounting set with 3/8-karat diamond.
No. 44C10406 Third quality diamond. Price. $29.38
No. 44C10408 Second quality diamond. Price. $39.13
No. 44C10410 First quality diamond. Price. $45.50
No. 44C10412 Mounting only, without stone. Ea..$4.25

Security Crown Hand Carved Belcher Mounting, set with 1/2-carat diamond.
No. 44C10423 Third quality diamond. Price. $50.25
No. 44C10425 Second quality diamond. Price. $58.75
No. 44C10427 First quality diamond. Price. $69.75
No. 44C10429 Mounting only, without stone. Ea..$7.25

Security Crown Round Belcher Mounting, set with 3/4-carat diamond.
No. 44C10430 Third quality diamond. Price. $77.25
No. 44C10432 Second quality diamond. Price. $89.25
No. 44C10434 First quality diamond. Price, $109.50
No. 44C10436 Mounting only, without stone. Ea..$6.00

Security Crown Hand Carved Belcher Mounting, set with 3/4-carat diamond.
No. 44C10438 Third quality diamond. Price. $78.75
No. 44C10440 Second quality diamond. Price. $90.75
No. 44C10442 First quality diamond. Price, $111.00
No. 44C10444 Mounting only, without stone. Ea..$7.50

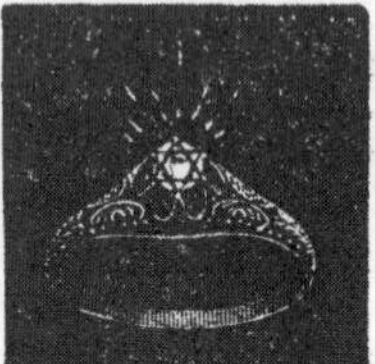

Carved Belcher Mounting, set with 1/8-carat diamond.
No. 44C10446 Third quality diamond. Price.. $9.88
No. 44C10448 Second quality diamond. Price. $12.38
No. 44C10450 First quality diamond. Price. $14.50
No. 44C10452 Mounting only, without stone. Ea..$3.25

Carved Belcher Mounting, set with 1/4-carat diamond.
No. 44C10454 Third quality diamond. Price. $18.75
No. 44C10456 Second quality diamond. Price. $24.75
No. 44C10458 First quality diamond. Price. $28.75
No. 44C10460 Mounting only, without stone. Ea..$3.75

Carved Belcher Mounting, set with 3/8-carat diamond.
No. 44C10462 Third quality diamond. Ea. $29.13
No. 44C10464 Second quality diamond. Ea. $38.88
No. 44C10468 First quality diamond. Ea. $45.25
No. 44C10470 Mounting only, without stone. Ea. $4.00

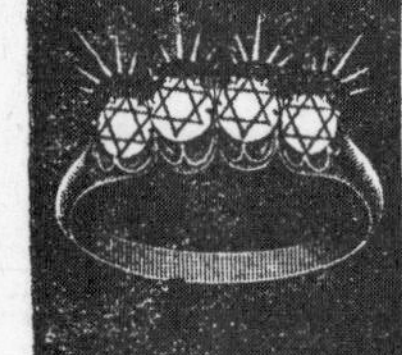

Four-Stone Plain Tiffany Mounting, total weight of diamonds, 7/8-carat.
No. 44C10524 Third quality diamonds. Price, $54.13
No. 44C10526 Second quality diamonds. Price, $73.63
No. 44C10528 First quality diamonds. Price, $88.01
No. 44C10530 Mounting only, without stone. Ea..$4.25

Fancy 2-Stone Mounting, total weight of diamonds, 1 carat.
No. 44C10532 Third quality diamonds. Price, $89.50
No. 44C10534 Second quality diamonds.
Price $106.50
No. 44C10536 First quality diamonds.
Price...... $128.50
No. 44C10538 Mounting only, without stone. Ea..$3.50

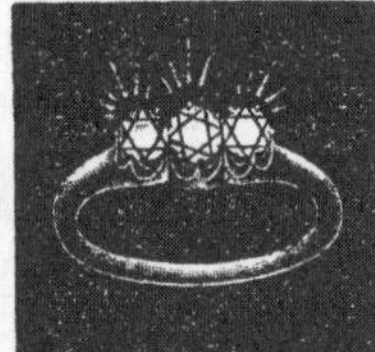

Three-Stone Plain Tiffany Mounting, total weight of diamonds, 5/8-carat.
No. 44C10540 Third quality diamonds. Price, $38.73
No. 44C10542 Second quality diamonds. Price, $52.23
No. 44C10544 First quality diamonds. Price, $62.61
No. 44C10546 Mounting only, without stone. Ea..$3.85

Fancy Belcher Mounting, set with 5/16-carat diamond.
No. 44C10558 Third quality diamond. Price. $21.75
No. 44C10560 Second quality diamond. Price. $29.25
No. 44C10562 First quality diamond. Price. $34.25
No. 44C10564 Mounting only, without stone. Ea..$3.00

Fancy Twist Belcher Mounting, set with 3/16-carat diamond.
No. 44C10566 Third quality diamond. Price. $12.69
No. 44C10568 Second quality diamond. Price. $16.44
No. 44C10570 First quality diamond. Price. $19.63
No. 44C10572 Mounting only, without stone. Ea..$2.75

Fancy Flat Belcher Mounting, set with 3/16-carat diamond,
No. 44C10574 Third quality diamond. Price. $12.44
No. 44C10576 Second quality diamond. Price. $16.19
No. 44C10578 First quality diamond. Price. $19.38
No. 44C10580 Mounting only, without stone. Ea..$2.50

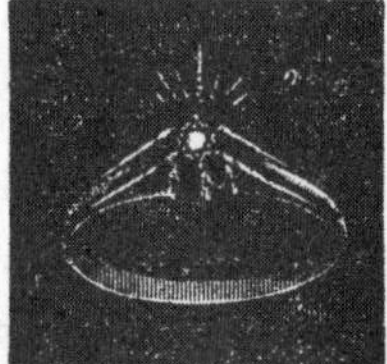

Fancy Belcher Mounting, set with 3/32 carat diamond.
No. 44C10582 Third quality diamond. Price. $7.22
No. 44C10584 Second quality diamond. Price. $9.09
No. 44C10586 First quality diamond. Ea. $10.69
No. 44C10588 Mounting only, without stone. Ea. $2.25

DON'T FAIL TO GIVE SIZE OF RING WANTED.

Engraved Belcher Mounting, set with 3/32 carat diamond.
No. 44C10590 Third quality diamond. Price..$7.47
No. 44C10592 Second quality diamond. Price..$9.34
No. 44C10594 First quality diamond. Price..$10.94
No. 44C10596 Mounting only, without stone. Ea..$2.50

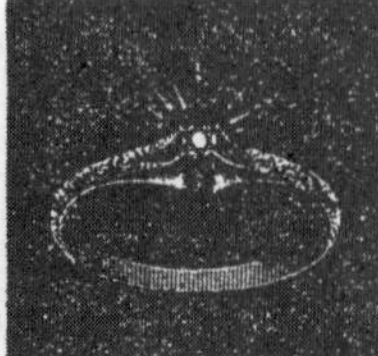

Fancy Belcher Mounting, set with 5/64-carat diamond.
No. 44C10600 Third quality diamond. Price..$6.39
No. 44C10602 Second quality diamond. Price..$7.95
No. 44C10604 First quality diamond. Price..$9.28
No. 44C10606 Mounting only, without stone. Ea..$2.25

Fancy Belcher Mounting, set with 5/64-carat diamond.
No. 44C10608 Third quality diamond. Price..$6.74
No. 44C10610 Second quality diamond. Price..$8.30
No. 44C10612 First quality diamond. Price..$9.63
No. 44C10614 Mounting only, without stone. Ea..$2.60

Engraved Round Belcher Mounting, set with 1/16-carat diamond.
No. 44C10616 Third quality diamond. Price..$5.81
No. 44C10618 Second quality diamond. Price..$7.06
No. 44C10620 First quality diamond. Price..$8.13
No. 44C10622 Mounting only, without stone. Ea..$2.50

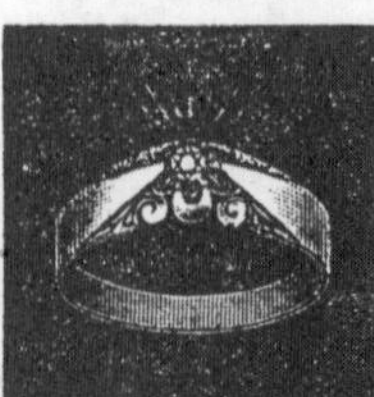

Engraved Flat Belcher Mounting, set with 1/16-carat diamond.
No. 44C10624 Third quality diamond. Price..$5.81
No. 44C10626 Second quality diamond. Price..$7.06
No. 44C10628 First quality diamond. Price. $8.13
No. 44C10630 Mounting only, without stone. Ea..$2.50

Fancy Belcher Mounting, set with 1/32-carat diamond.
No. 44C10632 Third quality diamond. Price..$3.66
No. 44C10634 Second quality diamond. Price..$4.28
No. 44C10636 First quality diamond. Price..$4.81
No. 44C10638 Mounting only, without stone. Ea..$2.00

Fancy Belcher Mounting, set with 1/32-carat diamond.
No. 44C10640 Third quality diamond. Price. $3.66
No. 44C10642 Second quality diamond. Price. $4.28
No. 44C10644 First quality diamond. Price. $4.81
No. 44C10646 Mounting only, without stone. Ea. $2.00

DIAMOND BROOCHES, SET WITH FINE SELECTED DIAMONDS.

EACH ONE CARRIES OUR BINDING GUARANTEE AND REFUND CERTIFICATE, UNLESS "NO REFUND CERTIFICATE" IS PRINTED UNDER THE QUOTATION.

PRICE QUOTED IS FOR BROOCH COMPLETE, STONE AND MOUNTING.

No. 44C11000 Fancy brooch, Roman color, set with 1 small diamond. Price........$3.75
No refund certificate.

No. 44C11004 Fancy brooch, Roman color, set with 1 small diamond. Price........$4.25
No refund certificate.

No. 44C11012 Fancy brooch or pendant, Roman color, set with 1 small diamond. Price......$4.75
No refund certificate.

No. 44C11018 Fancy pearl brooch, set with 1 small diamond. Price........$6.25
No refund certificate.

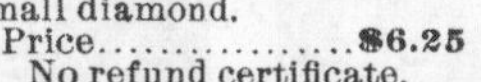

No. 44C11026 Rose finish, 1 fine diamond. Price........$8.50
No refund certificate.

No. 44C11028 Fancy pearl brooch or pendant, set with 1 small diamond. Price........$8.75
No refund certificate.

No. 44C11034 Fancy pearl brooch or pendant, likewise can be used as watch chatelette. Set with 1 fine diamond. Price, $12.00
No refund certificate.

No. 44C11044 Rose finish, 3 fine diamonds. Price........$15.00
No refund certificate.

No. 44C11046 Fancy pearl brooch or pendant, set with 1 small diamond. Price, $16.50
No refund certificate.

No. 44C11048 Fancy pearl brooch or pendant, set with 1 small fine diamond. Price, $21.00
No refund certificate.

Brooch or pendant, bright finish, set with 9 stones, $\frac{3}{8}$ carat of diamonds in all.

No. 44C11084 Third quality diamonds. Price........$24.88

No. 44C11086 Second quality diamonds. Price........$32.38

No. 44C11088 First quality diamonds. Price........$38.75

No. 44C11090 Mounting only, without stone. Price........$5.00

Fancy brooch or pendant, set with 7 diamonds, weighing $\frac{5}{16}$ carat, and genuine pearls.

No. 44C11092 Third quality diamonds. Price........$30.56

No. 44C11094 Second quality diamonds. Price........$36.81

No. 44C11096 First quality diamonds. Price........$42.13

No. 44C11098 Mounting only, without stone. Price........$14.00
No refund certificate.

Brooch or pendant, bright polish, set with 6 diamonds. Weight, $\frac{1}{4}$ carat.

No. 44C11100 Third quality diamonds. Price........$37.00

No. 44C11102 Second quality diamonds. Price........$47.00

No. 44C11104 First quality diamonds. Price........$55.50

No. 44C11106 Mounting only, without stone. Price........$10.50

Fancy brooch or pendant, bright finish, set with 11 diamonds weighing $\frac{3}{4}$ carat.

No. 44C11124 Third quality diamonds. Price. $51.85

No. 44C11126 Second quality diamonds. Price........$67.20

No. 44C11128 First quality diamonds. Price........$79.15

No. 44C11130 Mounting only, without stone. Price........$12.00

Brooch or pendant, bright polish, set with $\frac{5}{8}$-carat diamonds, 9 stones.

No. 44C11140 Third quality diamonds. Price........$62.29

No. 44C11142 Second quality diamonds. Price........$82.04

No. 44C11144 First quality diamonds. Price........$99.54

No. 44C11146 Mounting only, without stone. Price........$10.66
No refund certificate.

Fancy brooch, rose gold finish, set with 1 diamond weighing $\frac{1}{32}$ carat.

No. 44C11156 Third quality diamond. Price........$7.16

No. 44C11158 Second quality diamond. Price........$7.78

No. 44C11160 First quality diamond. Price........$8.31

No. 44C11162 Mounting only, without stone. Price........$5.50

Brooch or pendant, bright polish, set with $\frac{1}{4}$-carat diamond; one stone only.

No. 44C11230 Third quality diamond. Price........$21.00

No. 44C11232 Second quality diamond. Price........$27.00

No. 44C11234 First quality diamond. Price........$31.00

No. 44C11236 Mounting only, without stone. Price........$6.00

Fancy pearl brooch or pendant, set with $\frac{1}{4}$-carat diamond and genuine pearls.

No. 44C11238 Third quality diamond. Price........$27.75

No. 44C11240 Second quality diamond. Price........$33.75

No. 44C11242 First quality diamond. Price........$37.75

No. 44C11244 Mounting only, without stone. Price........$12.75
No refund certificate.

Fancy brooch or pendant, bright finish, set with $\frac{3}{8}$-carat diamond.

No. 44C11246 Third quality diamond. Price........$34.63

No. 44C11248 Second quality diamond. Price........$44.38

No. 44C11250 First quality diamond. Price........$50.95

No. 44C11252 Mounting only, without stone. Price........$9.50
No refund certificate.

Fancy brooch or pendant, bright polish, set with one diamond weighing $\frac{1}{8}$ carat.

No. 44C11254 Third quality diamond. Price........$52.50

No. 44C11256 Second quality diamond. Price........$61.00

No. 44C11258 First quality diamond. Price........$72.00

No. 44C11260 Mounting only, without stone. Price........$9.50

FINE SOLID GOLD FANCY FINGER RINGS, SET WITH GENUINE ROSE AND SELECTED DIAMONDS AND IN COMBINATION WITH OTHER GEMS

No. 44C11273 Hand engraved mounting, set with fine rose diamond. Price.........$2.00

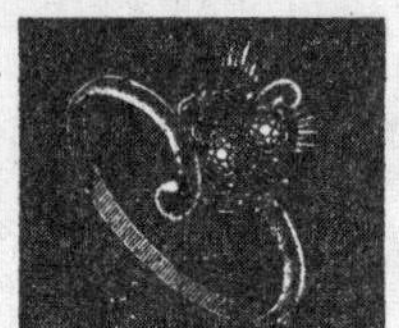

No. 44C11274 Fancy mounting, set with 2 almandine doublets and 2 rose diamonds. Price.........$2.25

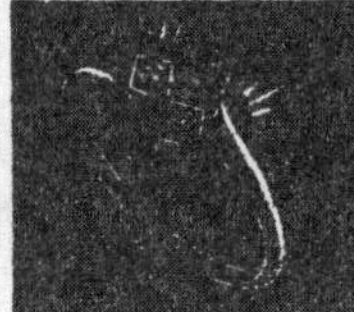

No. 44C11275 Two rose diamonds and 2 garnets. Price.........$2.75

We issue no refund certificate with these rings, but IF THEY ARE NOT EXACTLY AS REPRESENTED RETURN THEM AT ONCE, and we will refund your money together with transportation charges.

No. 44C11276 One rose diamond and 4 ruby doublets. Price........$3.25

No. 44C11277 Hand engraved mounting, set with 1 fine rose diamond. Price $3.25

No. 44C11278 Two fine rose diamonds and 2 emeralds. Price..$4.10

No. 44C11279 Hand carved and chased. Extra heavy ring, set with 1 fine rose diamond..$3.60

No. 44C11280 Two very fine rose diamonds and 2 fire opals. Price..$4.25

No. 44C11281 Two rose diamonds and 2 turquoise. Price.........$4.50

No. 44C11282 Fancy shank, set with 1 fire opal and 6 rose diamonds. Price.........$4.90

No. 44C11284 Two fine rose diamonds and 1 almandine. Price.........$4.95

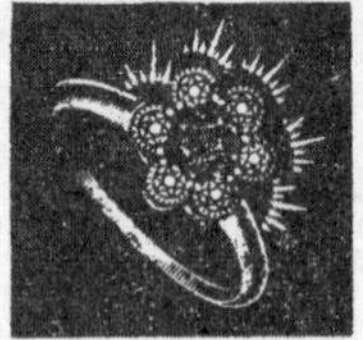

No. 44C11286 Six rose diamonds, 1 ruby doublet. Price.........$5.60

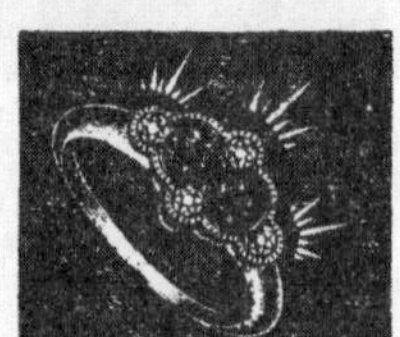

No. 44C11292 Four rose diamonds, 2 emerald doublets. Price.......$6.25

No. 44C11296 Four fine rose diamonds and 3 fine opals. Price...$6.85

No. 44C11300 Six fine rose diamonds and 1 emerald doublet. Price.........$7.50

No. 44C11304 Six very fine rose diamonds and 1 fire opal. Price.........$8.25

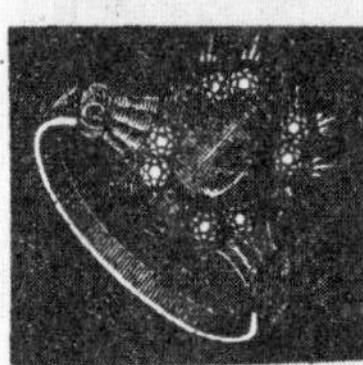

No. 44C11308 Set with 5 fire opals and 8 rose diamonds. Price.........$9.75

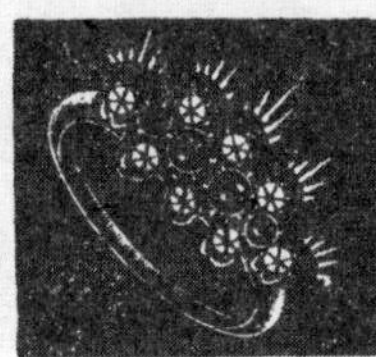

No. 44C11310 Eight fine rose diamonds and 4 almandines. Price.........$9.95

No. 44C11320 One diamond. Price.........$3.25

No. 44C11326 One diamond, 1 emerald and 1 ruby doublet. Price.......$4.25

No. 44C11330 One diamond, 2 opals. Price.........$5.45

No. 44C11332 One diamond. Price.........$6.00

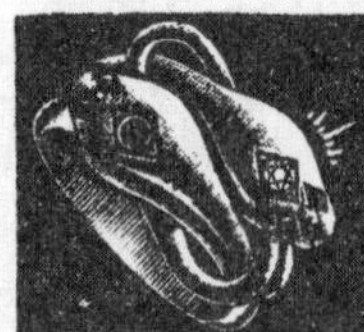

No. 44C11334 One diamond, emerald and ruby eyes. Price.........$6.50

No. 44C11360 Two diamonds, 2 ruby doublets. Price.........$9.00

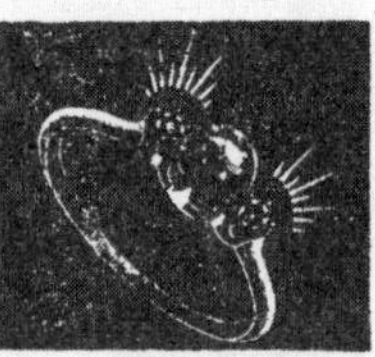

No. 44C11378 Two diamonds and 1 large fire opal. Price........$11.50

No. 44C11382 Three diamonds. Price.........$12.00

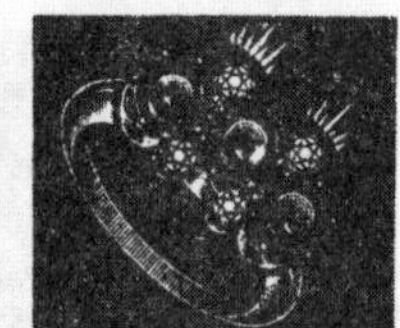

No. 44C11386 Three imitation turquoise and 4 diamonds. Price $12.00

No. 44C11395 Two garnet eyes, 1 fine cut diamond, Roman rose finish. Price $11.00

No. 44C11400 Two diamonds, 1 garnet. Price........$15.00

No. 44C11404 Four diamonds and 3 bright cut oriental garnets. Pr..$15.00

No. 44C11406 One fire opal and 6 diamonds. Price........$15.00

No. 44C11408 1 large diamond and 2 imitation turquoise. Price......$15.75

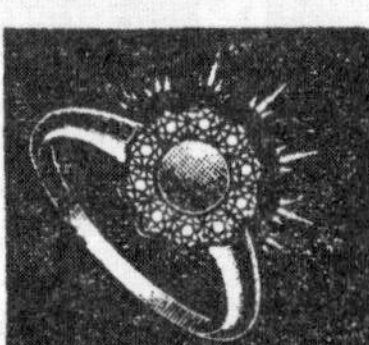

No. 44C11412 Ten diamonds, 1 fire opal. Price.........$16.78

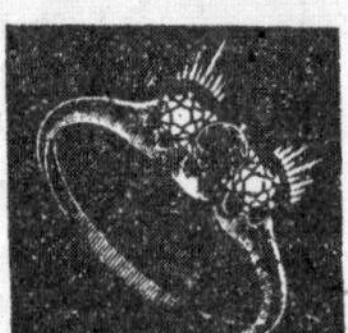

No. 44C11418 Plain mounting, set with 1 sapphire and 2 genuine diamonds. Price......$17.50

DON'T FAIL TO GIVE SIZE OF RING WANTED.

No. 44C11420 One oriental topaz and 2 diamonds. Price........$17.50

No. 44C11424 Plain shank, set with 5 genuine oriental pearls and 4 diamonds. Price, $18.00

No. 44C11426 Eight diamonds, 4 fire opals. Price........$20.00

No. 44C11428 Plain shank, set with 3 imitation turquoise and 4 diamonds. Price........$20.75

No. 44C11434 Plain shank, set with 7 fine diamonds and 6 fire opals. Price........$22.00

No. 44C11436 Snake ring, set with 1 genuine ruby and 1 diamond. Price........$22.00

No. 44C11438 Plain shank, set with 3 fire opals and 10 diamonds. Price..... $22.00

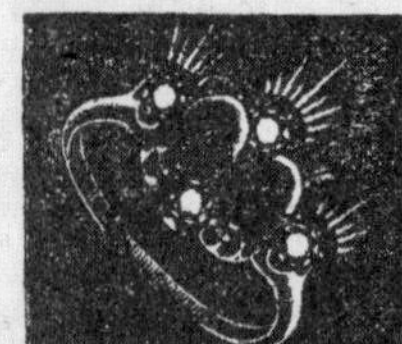

No. 44C11444 Four diamonds, 2 imitation turquoise. Price....... $23.00

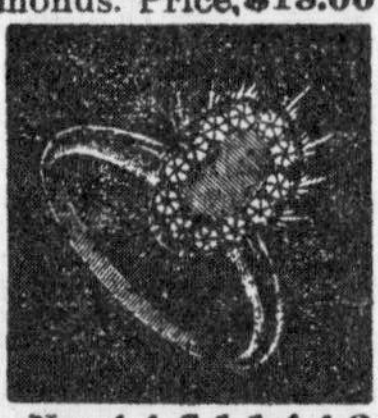

No. 44C11448 Twelve fine diamonds and 1 large Hungarian opal. Price....... $23.75

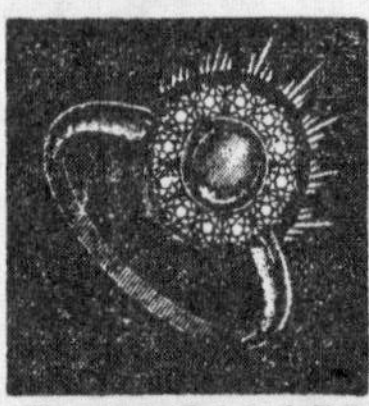

No. 44C11450 Plain shank, set with 1 large Hungarian opal and 14 diamonds. Price........$25.00

No. 44C11454 Six fine diamonds and 1 large Hungarian opal. Price...$26.50

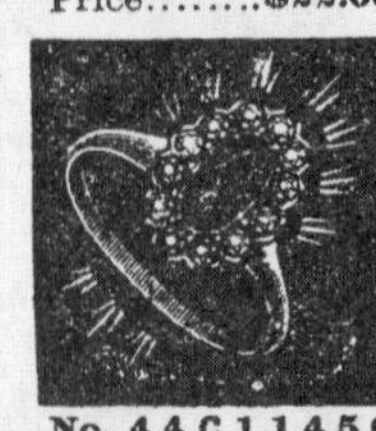

No. 44C11456 Twelve diamonds and 1 sapphire doublet. Price.....$28.50

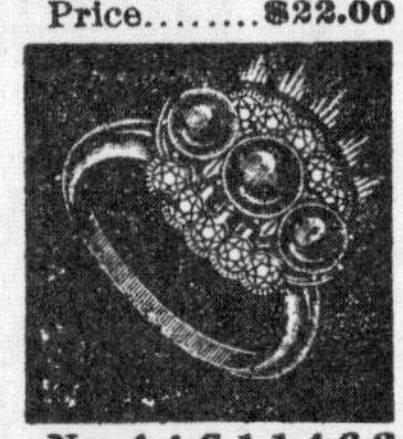

No. 44C11468 Plain shank, set with 3 imitation turquoise and 10 diamonds. Price, $34.00

No. 44C11480 Extra Heavy Snake Ring, set with 2 genuine rubies and 4 diamonds. Ea. $36.00

FINE SOLID GOLD FANCY LOCKETS, TIE CLASPS, CUFF LINKS, BRACELETS AND PINS, SET WITH ROSE AND REGULAR CUT GENUINE SELECTED DIAMONDS.

We do not give a refund certificate with any of these diamonds, but if they are not found exactly as represented and described, return them at once and we will immediately refund the purchase price, together with transportation charges.

PRICE QUOTED IS FOR ARTICLE COMPLETE, INCLUDING STONE AND MOUNTING.

No. 44C11850 One rose diamond, solid gold. Holds one picture. Price........$6.00

No. 44C11852 One rose diamond, solid gold. Holds one picture. Price.....$6.75

No. 44C11854 One diamond, solid gold. Holds one picture. Price............$9.00

No. 44C11856 Six rose diamonds, solid gold. Holds one picture. Price..........$12.50

No. 44C11858 One diamond, two emeralds, solid gold. Holds one picture. Price......$12.50

No. 44C11860 One diamond, solid gold. Holds two pictures. Price....$14.00

No. 44C11862 One diamond, solid gold. Holds two pictures. Price............$7.00

No. 44C11864 One diamond, solid gold. Holds two pictures. Price............$7.00

No. 44C11866 One diamond, solid gold. Holds one picture. Price............$8.50

No. 44C11868 Four large rose diamonds, solid gold. Holds one picture. Price.........$8.50

No. 44C11870 One diamond, solid gold. Holds two pictures. Price............$6.95

No. 44C11872 Five large rose diamonds and one emerald, solid gold. Holds two pictures. Price........$11.90

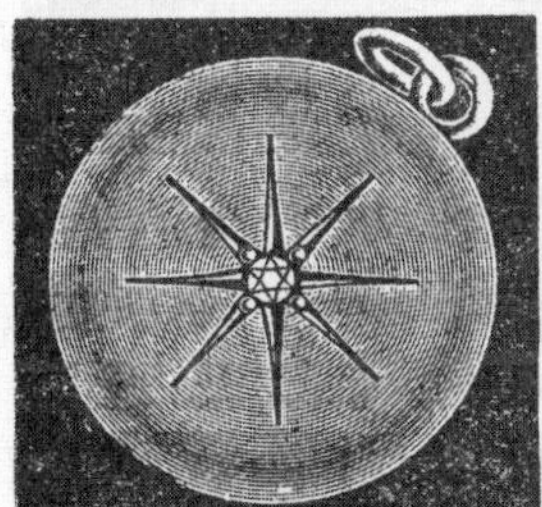
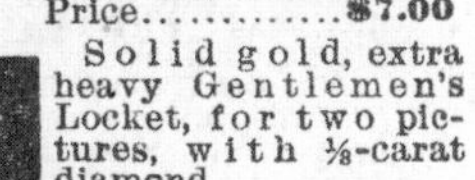
Solid gold, extra heavy Gentlemen's Locket, for two pictures, with ⅛-carat diamond.
No. 44C11874 Third quality diamond. Price.........$14.63
No. 44C11876 Second quality diamond. Price.........$17.13
No. 44C11878 First quality diamond. Price.........$19.25
No. 44C11880 Mounting only. Price..........$8.00

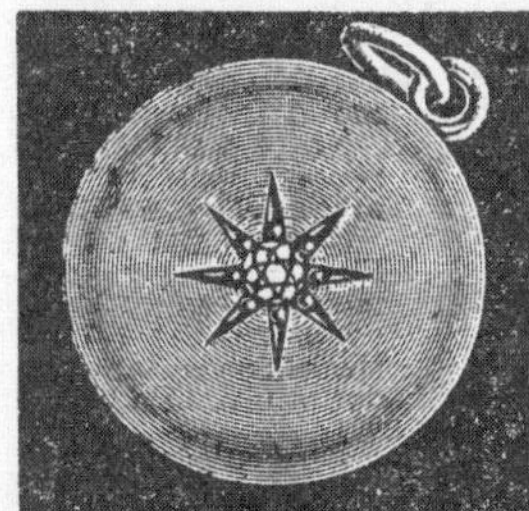
Solid gold, extra heavy Gentlemen's Locket, for two pictures, with ⅛-carat diamond.
No. 44C11882 Third quality diamond. Price.........$18.94
No. 44C11884 Second quality diamond. Price.........$22.69
No. 44C11886 First quality diamond. Price.........$25.88
No. 44C11888 Mounting only. Price..........$9.00

No. 44C11897 Solid gold; 1 diamond. Per pair......$5.25

No. 44C11898 Solid gold; 1 diamond. Per pair......$5.50

No. 46C11899 Solid gold, Roman satin finish, set with 1 fine cut diamond. Per pair..........$6.00

No. 44C11900 Solid gold; 1 diamond. Per pair.....$6.00

No. 44C11901 Solid gold, Roman yellow finish, set with 1 fine cut diamond. Per pair...$6.35

No. 44C11902 Solid gold; 1 diamond. Per pair......$6.25

No. 44C11903 Solid gold, Roman yellow finish, set with 1 genuine diamond and 1 genuine Oriental ruby. Per pair, $6.85

No. 44C11904 Solid gold; 1 diamond, 1 ruby and 1 sapphire. Per pair......$8.50

No. 44C11905 Solid gold, Roman yellow finish, set with 1 fine cut diamond. Per pair. $8.50

No. 44C11906 Solid gold; 1 diamond. Per pair........$7.50

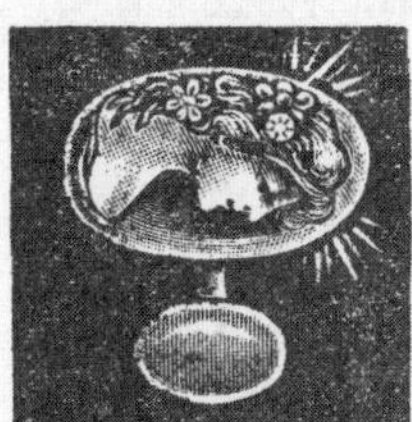
No. 44C11907 Solid gold, red rose and green gold satin finish, set with 1 fine cut diamond. This is one of the most artistic buttons put on the market this year. Per pair.....$8.75

No. 44C11908 Solid gold; set with diamonds. Per pair........$13.25

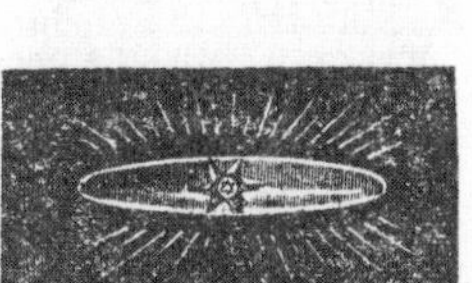
No. 44C11909 Solid Gold Baby or Cuff Pins. Roman finish, set with 1 small fine cut diamond. Price, per pair....$4.50

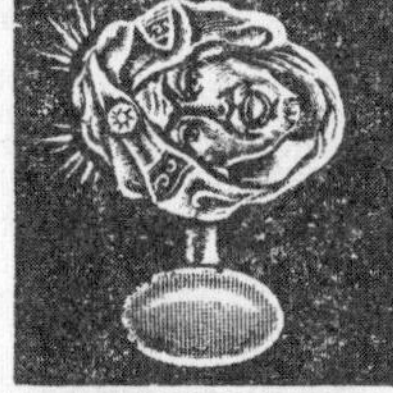
No. 44C11911 Solid gold, Roman yellow finish, set with 1 fine cut diamond. Per pair........$10.00

No. 44C11913 Solid gold, Roman yellow satin finish, set with 1 fine cut diamond. Per pair......$10.50

No. 44C11912 Solid Gold Necktie Clasp, set with 1 fine small diamond. Price..$4.00

No. 44C11526 Roman finish Crescent, 1 rose diamond. Price.....$1.75 No refund certificate.

No. 44C11530 Roman finish, set with 1 fine small diamond. Price.....$2.35 No refund certificate.

No. 44C11538 Roman finish, set with 1 fine small diamond. Price.....$3.50 No refund certificate.

No. 44C11542 Roman finish, Tiger Head, set with 1 small fine diamond...$3.50 No refund certificate.

No. 44C11550 Roman finish, 1 fine diamond. Price.....$3.90 No refund certificate.

No. 44C11552 Roman finish, bright cut, with pearls and 1 small diamond...$4.50 No refund certificate.

No. 44C11566 Bright finish, set with pearls and 1 fine small diamond. Price, $4.50 No refund certificate.

No. 44C11580 Roman finish, set with 1 fine small diamond. Price...$6.00 No refund certificate.

FINE SOLID GOLD STUD AND EARRING MOUNTINGS

SET WITH GENUINE SELECTED DIAMONDS.

Our Binding Guarantee and Refund Certificate Goes with Every Stud or Pair of Earrings Shown on This Page.

PRICE QUOTED IS FOR COMPLETE ITEM, INCLUDES DIAMOND AND MOUNTING.

Fancy Stud Mounting, set with 1/32-carat diamond.
No. 44C11600 Third quality diamond. Price..**$3.66**
No. 44C11602 Second quality diamond. Price..**$4.28**
No. 44C11604 First quality diamond. Price..**$4.81**
No. 44C11606 Mounting only, without stone. Ea.**$2.00**

Fancy Stud Mounting, set with 1/16-carat diamond.
No. 44C11610 Third quality diamond. Price..**$5.31**
No. 44C11612 Second quality diamond. Price..**$6.56**
No. 44C11614 First quality diamond. Price..**$7.63**
No. 44C11616 Mounting only, without stone. Ea.**$2.00**

Fancy Stud Mounting, set with ⅛-carat diamond.
No. 44C11626 Third quality diamond. Price..**$8.88**
No. 44C11628 Second quality diamond. Price, **$11.38**
No. 44C11630 First quality diamond. Price, **$13.50**
No. 44C11632 Mounting only, without stone. Ea.**$2.25**

Plain Stud Mounting, set with ¼-carat diamond.
No. 44C11642 Third quality diamond. Price, **$17.00**
No. 44C11644 Second quality diamond. Price, **$23.00**
No. 44C11646 First quality diamond. Price, **$27.00**
No. 44C11647 Mounting only, without stone. Ea.**$2.00**

Fancy Stud Mounting, set with ⅜-carat diamond.
No. 44C11656 Third quality diamond. Price, **$27.38**
No. 44C11658 Second quality diamond. Price, **$37.13**
No. 44C11660 First quality diamond. Price, **$43.50**
No. 44C11662 Mounting only, without stone. Ea.**$2.25**

Plain Stud Mounting, set with ½-carat diamond.
No. 44C11672 Third quality diamond. Price, **$45.25**
No. 44C11674 Second quality diamond. Price, **$53.75**
No. 44C11676 First quality diamond. Price, **$64.75**
No. 44C11678 Mounting only, without stone. Ea.**$2.25**

Plain Stud Mounting, set with ⅝-carat diamond.
No. 44C11680 Third quality diamond. Ea..**$59.75**
No. 44C11682 Second quality diamond. Ea..**$67.88**
No. 44C11684 First quality diamond. Ea..**$84.75**
No. 44C11686 Mounting only, without stone. Ea.**$2.25**

Plain Stud Mounting, set with ¾-carat diamond.
No. 44C11688 Third quality diamond. Price, **$73.75**
No. 44C11690 Second quality diamond. Price, **$85.75**
No. 44C11692 First quality diamond. Price, **$106.00**
No. 44C11694 Mounting only, without stone. Ea.**$2.50**

Plain Stud Mounting, set with 1-carat diamond.
No. 44C11704 Third quality diamond. Price, **$102.60**
No. 44C11706 Second quality diamond. Price **$121.10**
No. 44C11708 First quality diamond. Price, **$145.60**
No. 44C11710 Mounting only, without stone. Ea.**$2.60**

Plain Stud Mounting, set with 1⅛-carat diamond.
No. 44C11712 Third quality diamond. Price, **$119.75**
No. 44C11714 Second quality diamond. Price, **$135.56**
No. 44C11716 First quality diamond. Price, **$163.63**
No. 44C11718 Mounting only, without stone. Ea.**$2.75**

Plain Stud Mounting, set with 1¼-carat diamond.
No. 44C11720 First quality diamond. Price, **$132.75**
No. 44C11722 Second quality diamond. Price, **$152.75**
No. 44C11724 First quality diamond. Price, **$190.25**
No. 44C11726 Mounting only, without stone. Ea.**$2.75**

Plain Stud Mounting, set with 1½-carat diamond.
No. 44C11728 Third quality diamond. Price, **$175.25**
No. 44C11730 Second quality diamond. Price, **$191.75**
No. 44C11732 First quality diamond. Price, **$227.75**
No. 44C11734 Mounting only without stone. Ea.**$2.75**

Plain Stud Mounting, set with 2-carat diamond.
No. 44C11736 Third quality diamond. Ea..**$232.75**
No. 44C11738 Second quality diamond. Ea..**$254.75**
No. 44C11740 First quality diamond. Ea..**$302.75**
No. 44C11742 Mounting only, without stone. Ea.**$2.75**

Fancy, regular, bright polished earrings. Total weight of diamonds, 1/16 carat in pair.
No. 44C11750 Third quality diamonds. Price............**$6.32**
No. 44C11752 Second quality diamonds. Price............**$7.56**
No. 44C11754 First quality diamonds. Price............**$8.62**
No. 44C11756 Mountings only, without stone Price............**$3.00**

Fancy, regular, bright polished earrings. Total weight of diamonds, ⅛ carat in pair.
No. 44C11758 Third quality diamonds. Price............**$9.87**
No. 44C11760 Second quality diamonds. Price............**$12.37**
No. 44C11762 First quality diamonds. Price............**$14.51**
No. 44C11764 Mountings only, without stone. Price............**$3.25**

Fancy, regular, bright polished earrings. Total weight of diamonds, ¼ carat in pair.
No. 44C11766 Third quality diamonds. Price............**$17.01**
No. 44C11768 Second quality diamonds. Price............**$22.01**
No. 44C11770 First quality diamonds. Price............**$26.25**
No. 44C11772 Mountings only, without stone. Price............**$3.75**

Fancy, regular, bright polished earrings. Total weight of diamonds, ⅜ carat in pair.
No. 44C11774 Third quality diamonds. Price............**$41.75**
No. 44C11776 Second quality diamonds. Price............**$56.75**
No. 44C11778 First quality diamonds. Price............**$66.75**
No. 44C11780 Mountings only, without stone. Price............**$4.25**

Fancy, regular, bright polished earrings. Total weight of diamonds, ¾ carat in pair.
No. 44C11782 Third quality diamonds. Price............**$54.51**
No. 44C11784 Second quality diamonds. Price............**$74.01**
No. 44C11786 First quality diamonds. Price............**$86.75**
No. 44C11788 Mountings only, without stone. Price............**$4.25**

Plain, regular, bright polished earrings. Total weight of diamonds, ⅞ carat in pair.
No. 44C11790 Third quality diamonds. Price............**$79.01**
No. 44C11792 Second quality diamonds. Price............**$93.87**
No. 44C11794 First quality diamonds. Price............**$113.11**
No. 44C11796 Mountings only, without stone. Price............**$3.75**

Plain, regular, bright polished earrings. Total weight of diamonds, 1 carat in pair.
No. 44C11798 Third quality diamonds. Price............**$90.00**
No. 44C11800 Second quality diamonds. Price............**$107.00**
No. 44C11802 First quality diamonds. Price............**$129.00**
No. 44C11804 Mountings only, without stone Price............**$4.00**

Plain, regular, bright polished earrings. Total weight of diamonds, 3 carats in pair.
No. 44C11806 Third quality diamonds. Price............**$351.00**
No. 44C11808 Second quality diamonds. Price............**$384.00**
No. 44C11810 First quality diamonds. Price............**$456.00**
No. 44C11812 Mountings only, without stone. Price............**$6.00**

Plain, polished, screw earrings. Total weight of diamonds, ½ carat in pair.
No. 44C11814 Third quality diamonds. Price............**$33.00**
No. 44C11816 Second quality diamonds. Price............**$45.00**
No. 44C11818 First quality diamonds. Price............**$53.00**
No. 44C11820 Mountings only, without stone. Price............**$3.00**

Plain, polished, screw earrings. Total weight of diamonds, ¾ carat in pair.
No. 44C11822 Third quality diamonds. Price............**$53.76**
No. 44C11824 Second quality diamonds. Price............**$73.26**
No. 44C11826 First quality diamonds. Price............**$86.00**
No. 44C11828 Mountings only, without stone. Price............**$3.50**

Plain, polished, screw earrings. Total weight of diamonds, 1¼ carats in pair.
No. 44C11830 Third quality diamonds. Price............**$119.50**
No. 44C11832 Second quality diamonds. Price............**$135.76**
No. 44C11834 First quality diamonds. Price............**$169.50**
No. 44C11836 Mountings only, without stone. Price............**$4.50**

Plain, polished, screw earrings. Total weight of diamonds, 1½ carats in pair.
No. 44C11838 Third quality diamonds. Price............**$148.00**
No. 44C11840 Second quality diamonds. Price............**$172.00**
No. 44C11842 First quality diamonds. Price............**$212.50**
No. 44C11844 Mountings only, without stone. Price............**$5.50**

FINE ROLLED GOLD PLATE AND GOLD FILLED GENTS' CHARMS, SET WITH POPULAR COLORED STONES.

No. 4C8910 Rolled gold plate, fancy swinging bale, topaz set. Price....... 30c

No. 4C8912 Gold filled, bright polish, two brilliants and two emeralds, hand engraved. Price........ $1.00

No. 4C8914 Gold Filled Compass, fancy mounting, no toy, but scientifically accurate. Price........ $1.50

No. 4C8916 Lantern charm, ruby glass. Price........ 46c

No. 4C8920 Rolled gold plate, fancy mounting, engraved stone setting. Price........ 45c

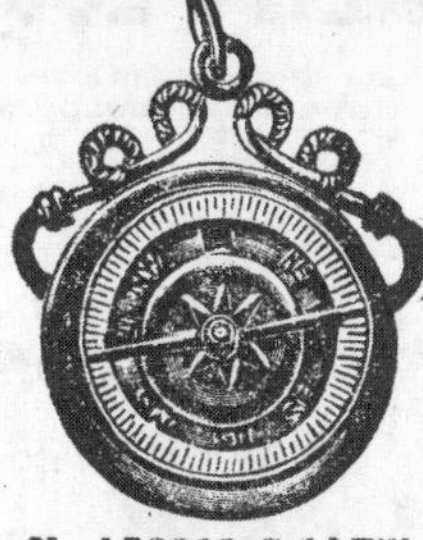
No. 4C8922 Gold Filled Compass, extra fine, fancy mounting. Price........ $1.45

No. 4C8923 Gold filled, bright finish, stone intaglio base. Price.... ....75c

If by mail, postage extra, 3 cents. Insurance or Registry extra.

No. 4C8924 Gold filled, Roman color, bull heavily gold plate, ruby eyes. Price....65c

No. 4C8925 Gold filled, fancy mounting, bright finish, swinging crystal bale. Price.....52c

No. 4C8926 Rolled gold plate, bright polish, fancy views. Price.... 30c

No. 4C8927 Rolled gold plate, bright polish, garnet eyes. Price....35c

No. 4C8928 Rolled gold plate, fine Compass. Price........45c

No. 4C8929 Gold filled, fancy Horseshoe and Horse. Price..90c

No. 4C8930 Rolled Gold Plated Mail Pouch....40c

No. 4C8931 Gold filled, fancy engraved, genuine stone set. Price...85c

No. 4C8932 Rolled gold plate, bright finish, exact counterpart of a fish. Price.....30c

No. 4C8933 Gold Filled Compass, fancy mounting, very accurate. Price........ 85c

No. 4C8934 Rolled Gold Plated Bicycle Charm. Price........50c

No. 4C8935 Rolled gold plate, bright finish. Faith, Hope and Charity. Price........46c

No. 4C8936 Rolled gold plate, chased Roman center Heart. Price...30c

No. 4C8937 Rolled gold plate, engraved, with brilliant setting. Price..35c

No. 4C8938 Gold filled, hand carved Horse, heavy gold plate, with ruby eyes. Price........ $1.35

No. 4C8939 Gold filled, fancy engraved, with three stones. Price..55c

SOLID GOLD AND SOLID GOLD SIDE LOCKETS,

made to hold one and two pictures according to description. Postage on lockets 3 cents extra, and 5 cents extra for insured mail. Monograms engraved for 20 to 35 cents extra. Our Solid Gold Side Lockets are practical and positively will wear your natural lifetime. They have solid gold sides; all that part which the illustration shows is solid gold through and through. Our Solid Gold Lockets are solid gold, every piece and particle of them.

No. 4C8956 Solid gold, extra heavy, satin finish, for 2 pictures. Price.......$4.12
Two or three letter monogram, engraved, 20c extra.

No. 4C8940 Solid gold sides, satin finish, for two pictures. Price........ $1.35

No. 4C8944 Solid gold sides, satin finish, hand engraved, star set with opal, for one picture. Price........ $2.75

No. 4C8946 Solid gold sides, satin finish, hand engraved, for two pictures. Price........ $2.50

No. 4C8948 Solid gold sides, bright polish, hand engraved, fancy baled, for two pictures. Price.......$3.30

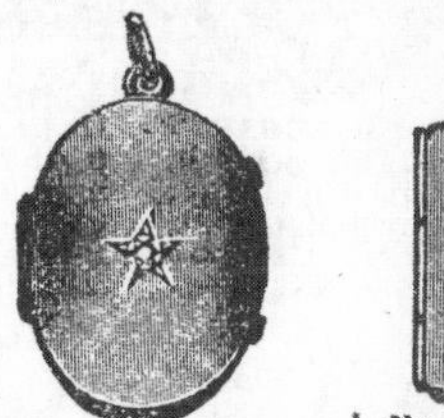
No. 4C8950 Solid gold sides, satin finish, star with diamond spark, for one picture. Price........ $3.45

No. 4C8952 Solid gold sides, satin finish, hand engraved star, set with 5 pearls and 1 ruby doublet, for one picture. Price........ $3.65

4C8954 is adapted for a monogram. Price........ 20c

No. 4C8954 Solid gold, satin finish, plain, for one picture. This locket is beautified by a monogram. Price........ $4.00

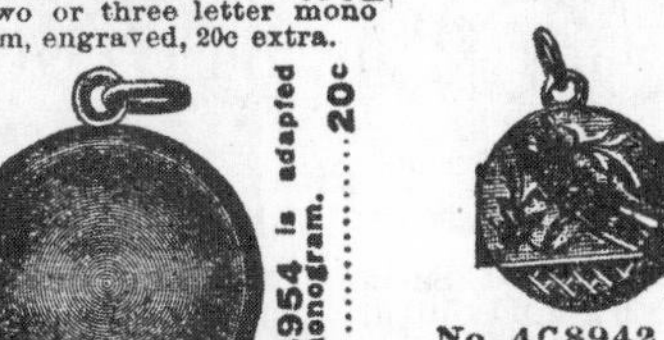
No. 4C8942 Solid gold sides, satin finish, for two pictures. Price........ $1.50

No. 4C8958 Solid gold, satin finish, hand engraved, raised colored gold ornamentation, for 2 pictures. Price...$4.25

No. 4C8960 Solid gold, bright polish, hand engraved, raised colored gold ornamentation, for 1 pictures. Price...$4.50

No. 4C8962 Solid gold, satin finish, raised rococo border, for one picture. Price........ $4.50

4C8962 is adapted for a monogram.

No. 4C8964 Solid gold, roman yellow finish, very new and artistic, for one picture. Price........ $4.87

No. 4C8966 Solid gold, satin finish, with raised colored gold ornamentation, for two pictures. Price........ $4.90

No. 4C8968 is adapted for a monogram. Price..20c

No. 4C8968 Solid gold, Roman satin finish, plain, for one picture. This locket is beautified by a monogram. Price........ $5.00

No. 4C8970 Solid gold, yellow satin finish, raised bright gold Masonic emblem, for 2 pictures. Price, $5.60
No. 4C8972 Same style as No. 4C8970, Odd Fellows emblem. Price........ $5.60
No. 4C8974 Same style as No. 4C8970, Knights of Pythias emblem. Price....$5.60

No. 4C8976 Solid gold, satin finish, raised colored gold ornamentation, for two pictures. Price........ $5.65

4C8978 is adapted for a monogram. Price........ 35c

No. 4C8978 Solid gold, satin finish, plain, extra heavy, for two pictures. Price........ $5.65

No. 4C8969 Solid gold, satin finish, raised colored gold ornamentation, for two pictures. Price.....$6.10

No. 4C8980 Solid gold, satin finish, raised rococo border, for one picture. Price........ $5.65
Two or three letter monogram, engraved, 20c extra.

No. 4C8982 Solid gold, satin finish, raised colored gold ornamentation, for two pictures. Price........ $6.75

FINEST QUALITY LOCKETS IN ROLLED GOLD PLATE, GOLD FILLED AND GOLD FRONT. MADE TO HOLD ONE AND TWO PICTURES.

Illustrations show exact size. We can engrave a monogram on any of these lockets at the rate of 20 to 35 cents each for a two or three letter monogram, according to size. Postage on lockets 3 cents extra, 5 cents extra if sent by insured mail.

No. 4C9100 Gold front, hand engraved. Price..40c

No. 4C9102 Rolled gold plate, bright polish; for 2 pictures. Price..42c

No. 4C9104 Bright polish, rolled gold plate, 1 rhinestone. Price....48c

No. 4C9106 Gold front, hand engraved, 3 stone settings. Price..55c

No. 4C9108 Rolled gold plate, bright polish, 1 rhinestone; holds 2 pictures. Price..56c

No. 4C9110 Gold filled, Roman color, ornamented. Price..56c

No. 4C9112 Gold front, hand engraved, four stone settings. Price............60c

No. 4C9114 Rolled gold plate, bright polish; holds 1 picture. Price......62c

No. 4C9116 Rolled gold plate, bright polish; for 2 pictures. Price....64c

No. 4C9118 Rolled gold plate, bright polish, 1 rhinestone; holds 2 pictures. Price..66c

No. 4C9120 Rolled gold plate, bright polish; holds 2 pictures. Price....68c

No. 4C9122 Plain satin finish, brilliant center. Price........68c

No. 4C9124 Locket, engraved, brilliant setting. Price....75c

No. 4C9126 Rolled gold plate, 1 ruby doublet; holds 2 pictures. Price........76c

No. 4C9128 Solid gold front, hand engraved. Price....89c

No. 4C9130 Rolled gold plate, bright polish, 1 emerald doublet; holds 1 picture. Price........89c

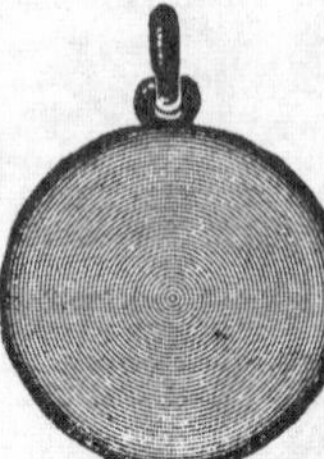

No. 4C9132 Gold filled, plain polish. Price.....$1.00

No. 4C9134 Gold filled, bright polish, set with opal. Price..$1.20

No. 4C9136 Gold front, fancy mounting, hand engraved. Price....75c

No. 4C9138 Plain polish, gold filled; for 2 pictures. Price. $1.30

No. 4C9140 Solid gold front, bright polish; holds 2 pictures. Price. $1.30

No. 4C9142 Solid gold front, bright polish, 8 rhinestones; holds 2 pictures. Price.....$1.30

No. 4C9144 Solid gold front, hand engraved, set with opal. Price.........$1.35

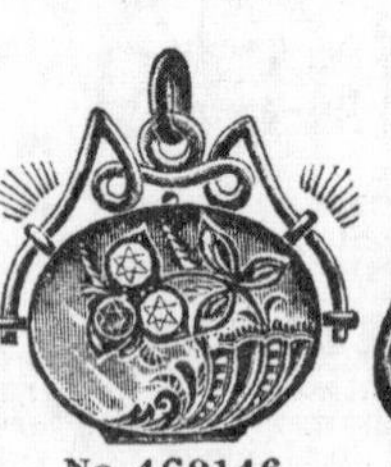

No. 4C9146 Solid gold front, 2 rhinestones, 1 ruby doublet; holds 2 pictures. Price.....$1.40

No. 4C9148 Satin finish, gold filled, 1 rhinestone; for 2 pictures. Price. ...$1.40

No. 4C9150 Satin finish, gold filled; for 2 pictures. Price.....$1.75

No. 4C9152 Roman satin finish, gold filled, 1 rhinestone, 1 emerald doublet, holds 2 pictures. Price.............$1.40

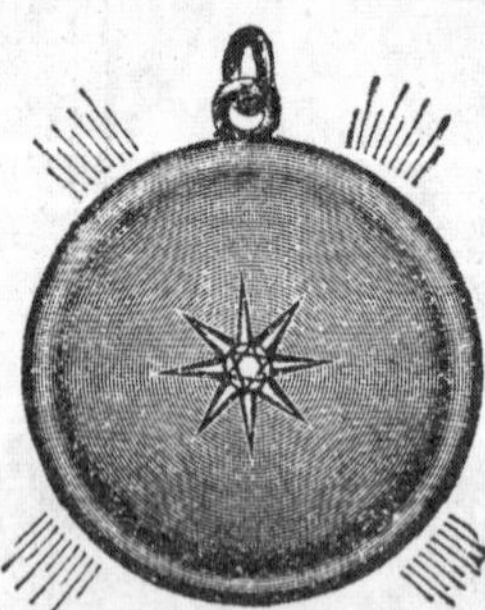

No. 4C9154 Gold filled, bright polish, holds two pictures; set with 1 rhinestone. Price..........$1.50

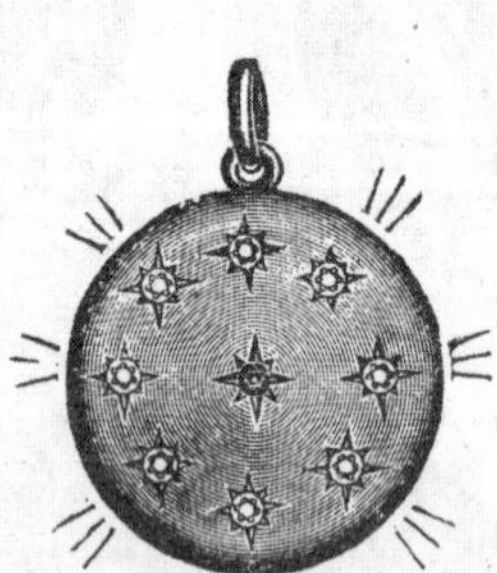

No. 4C9156 Gold filled, 8 rhinestones and 1 ruby. Price............$1.50

No. 4C9158 Plain polish, gold filled, 8 rhinestones; for 2 pictures. Price.............$1.65

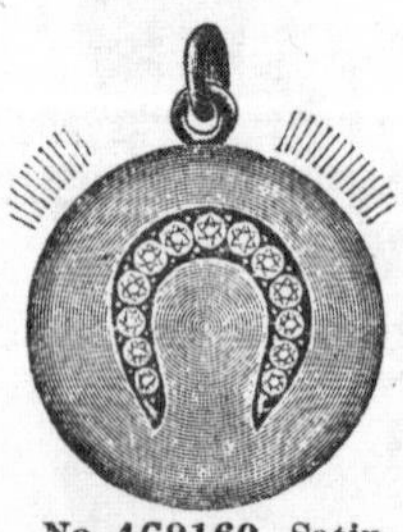

No. 4C9160 Satin finish, gold filled, 13 rhinestones; holds 2 pictures. Price.........$1.60

No. 4C9162 Solid gold front, plain polish, 1 fire. opal, 16 pearls; holds 2 pictures. Price..$1.75

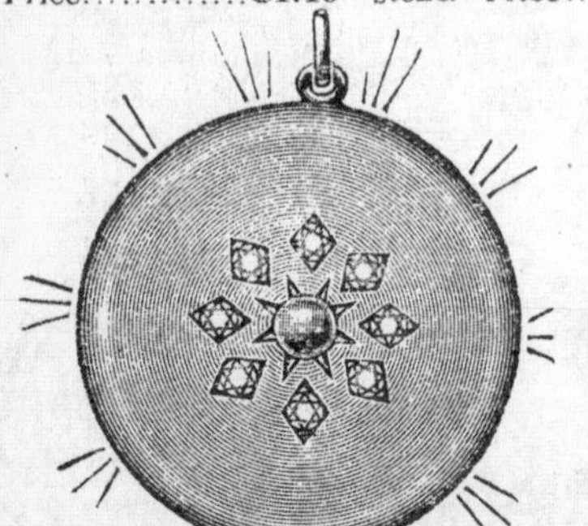

No. 4C9164 Gold filled, 8 rhinestones, 1 turquoise; diameter, 1⅜ in. Price..$2.00
No. 4C9168 As above, diameter, 1¼ inches. Price.........................$1.60
No. 4C9170 As above, diameter, 1 inch. Price.....................$1.40

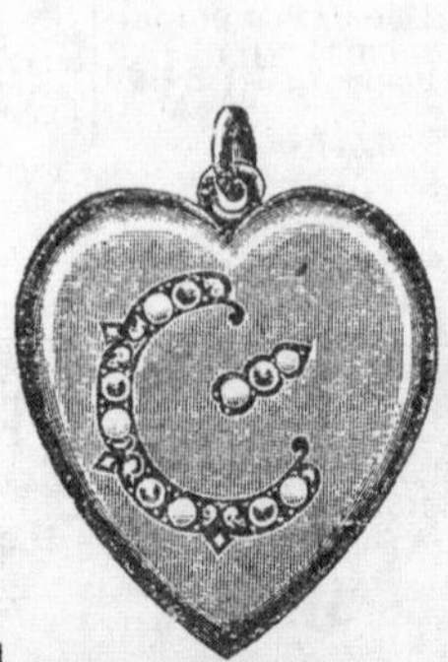

No. 4C9172 Satin finish, gold filled, 5 turquoise, 6 pearls; holds 2 pictures. Price.........$2.00

No. 4C9174 Gold filled, rose color finish, holds 2 pictures, set with 2 rubies and 1 rhinestone. Price.............$2.10

No. 4C9176 Plain polish, gold filled, 1⅝ inches long. Price. $2.50
No. 4C9178 As above, 1 inch long. Price..................$1.25

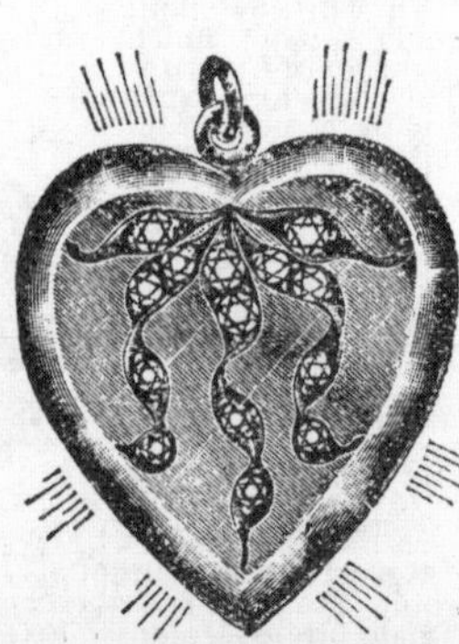

No. 4C9180 Gold filled, bright polish, set with 14 rhinestones, holds two pictures. Price. $2.65

SOCIETY EMBLEM CHARMS AND RINGS, GOLD AND GOLD FILLED.

These Charms are Warranted to give Absolute Satisfaction in every Particular. Illustrations Show Exact Size and Design.
WE CAN SUPPLY ANY ORDER QUOTED UNDER ILLUSTRATIONS. TO AVOID MISTAKES, GIVE CATALOGUE NUMBER AND STATE THE EMBLEM WANTED.

Gold filled trimmings, set with black onyx center, emblem in colored enamel. Order by number.
Price $1.00
No. 4C9292 Odd Fellows.
No. 4C9294 Masonic.
No. 4C9296 Knights of Pythias.
No. 4C9298 G. A. R.
No. 4C9300 Modern Woodmen of America.
No. 4C9302 Woodmen of the World.
No. 4C9304 Red Men.

Gold filled, bright polish, hard enameled emblem. Order by number. Price.......... $1.90
No. 4C9306 Modern Woodmen of America
No. 4C9308 Woodmen of the World.
No. 4C9310 Masonic
No. 4C9312 K. of P.
No. 4C9314 Odd Fellows.
No. 4C9316 United Workmen.
No. 4C9318 Knights of Columbus.

Gold filled, hard enameled, bright finish. Order by number. Price....... 60c
No. 4C9320 Ancient Order United Workmen.
No. 4C9322 Redmen.
No. 4C9324 Modern Woodmen.
No. 4C9326 Woodmen of the World.
No. 4C9328 Independent Order of Foresters.
No. 4C9330 Odd Fellows.
No. 4C9332 K. of P.
No. 4C9334 G.A.R.

Solid gold mounting, black onyx center, hard enameled. Order by number.
Price.......... $4.25
No. 4C9336 Knights of Maccabees.
No. 4C9338 K. of P.
No. 4C9340 Modern Woodmen of America
No. 4C9342 Redmen.
No. 4C9344 Woodmen of the World.
No. 4C9346 Odd Fellows.

Solid gold, hard enameled emblem, bright mounting. Order by number.
Price....... $3.40
No. 4C9348 Woodmen of America.
No. 4C9350 Woodmen of the World.
No. 4C9352 Masonic.
No. 4C9354 Odd Fellows.
No. 4C9356 K. of P.
No. 4C9358 Knights of Maccabees.

Pearl, emblem onlaid, gold plate, filled mounting. Order by number.
Price 40c
No. 4C9360 Independent Order of Foresters.
No. 4C9362 Woodmen of America.
No. 4C9364 Maccabees.
No. 4C9366 Ancient Order United Workmen.
No. 4C9368 Woodmen of the World.
No. 4C9370 K. of P.
No. 4C9371 G. A. R.
No. 4C9372 Redmen.
No. 4C9373 Odd Fellows.

Gold filled, bright polish, hard enameled emblem. Order by number.
Price.......... 85c
No. 4C9374 Masonic.
No. 4C9376 Odd Fellows.
No. 4C9378 K. of P.
No. 4C9380 Knights of Maccabees.
No. 4C9382 Knights of Columbus.

Solid gold ring, heavy weight, any emblem, fine hard enameled. Order by number. Ea.. $5.50
No. 4C9433 Masonic
No. 4C9435 Odd Fellows.
No. 4C9437 Knights of Pythias.
No. 4C9439 Modern Woodmen.
No. 4C9441 Woodmen of the World.
No. 4C9443 Red Men.
No. 4C9445 United Workmen.
No. 4C9447 Knights of Maccabees.
No. 4C9449 Knights of Columbus.
No. 4C9451 Elks.

No. 4C9384 Gold filled, Masonic and Odd Fellows, combined. Price.. $1.15
No. 4C9386 Same as above, solid gold.
Price. $3.75
No. 4C9388 Solid gold, Masonic only.
Price......... $2.50

No. 4C9390 Solid gold, Knight Templars. Extra heavy black onyx, 9 rubies and 4 genuine rose diamonds.
Price....... $15.00

No. 4C9392 Knights of Pythias, solid gold, hard enameled. Price, $6.98
No. 4C9394 Same as No. 4C9392, but gold filled.
Price.......... $1.15
No. 4C9396 Same as No. 4C9392, but uniform rank. Price...... $1.25

Rolled plate, hard enameled. Order by number.
Price. 35c
No. 4C9398 Ancient Order United Workmen.
No. 4C9401 Masonic.
No. 4C9403 Odd Fellows.
No. 4C9405 K. of P.
No. 4C9407 K.O.T.M.
No. 4C9409 Modern Woodmen of America.
No. 4C9411 Woodmen of the World.
No. 4C9415 G. A. R.
No. 4C9417 United Workmen.
No. 4C9419 Redmen.

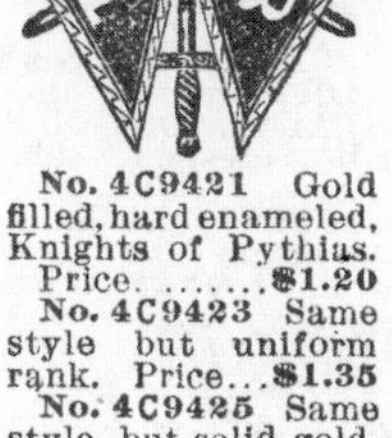

No. 4C9421 Gold filled, hard enameled, Knights of Pythias.
Price. $1.20
No. 4C9423 Same style but uniform rank. Price... $1.35
No. 4C9425 Same style, but solid gold.
Price......... $8.75

No. 4C9427 Solid gold, stone center, Masonic.
Price.... $3.90
No. 4C9429 Same style, but gold filled mounting. Price, $1.10
No. 4C9431 Same style, but not stone center.
Price $1.50

PLEASE NOTE WE CARRY MANY DIFFERENT EMBLEMS QUOTED UNDER EACH DESIGN SHOWN.
POSTAGE ON CHARMS, 3 CENTS EXTRA.

No. 4C9483 Gold filled, enameled, Woodmen of America. Price... $1.00
No. 4C9485 Gold filled, Woodmen of the World. Ea... $1.00

No. 4C9453 Gold filled, enameled and engraved, Independent Order of Odd Fellows. Price... $1.25
No. 4C9455 Same as above, solid gold.
Price.......... $8.00

Solid gold, hard enameled, engraved. Order by number.
Price. ... $2.75
No. 4C9457 Odd Fellows.
No. 4C9459 Masonic.
No. 4C9461 Knights of Pythias.

No. 4C9463 Solid gold, extra heavy, enameled colors, hand engraved.
Price....... $12.00

No. 4C9465 Gold filled, hard enameled, G.A.R.
Price.......... 75c
No. 4C9467 Solid gold.
Price.... $4.00

No. 4C9469 Solid gold, Masonic, enameled letter. Price.. $3.60

No. 4C9473 Blue enameled, gold filled, Masonic.
Price.... $1.25
No. 4C9475 Same as above, solid gold.
Price..... $3.75

No. 4C9477 Gold filled, enameled and engraved, Sons of Veterans.
Price.......... 85c
No. 4C9481 Same as above, solid gold. Price. $4.50

No. 4C9487 Daughters of Rebekah, solid gold. Ea. $3.00

No. 4C9489 Solid gold, hard enameled and engraved, Ancient Order United Workmen.
Price..... $3.75

No. 4C9491 Solid gold, enameled, Knights of Pythias.
Price. $1.98

No. 4C9493 Gold filled, hard enameled, Eastern Star.
Price.... ..... 98c
No. 4C9495 Solid gold, larger than No. 4C9493, with 10-point star.
Price..... $3.30

No. 4C9497 Solid gold, Independent Order of Foresters.
Price......... $3.85
No. 4C9499 Same style, but gold filled.
Price.......... $1.10

No. 4C9501 Gold filled, Improved Order of Red Men.
Price....... 75c

No. 4C9503 Gold filled, Woodmen of America.
Price... ..... 96c
No. 4C9505 Woodmen of the World. Price. 96c

No. 4C9507 Gold filled, enameled and engraved, G. A. R.
Price 75c
No. 4C9509 Same style, but solid gold.
Price $4.00

No. 4C9511 Gold filled, Elks.
Price.. $1.20
No. 4C9513 Solid gold, Elks.
Price. $10.00

No. 4C9515 Solid gold, enameled, Odd Fellows.
Price... $2.00

SOLID GOLD AND GOLD FILLED EMBLEM PINS AND BUTTONS.

THESE GOODS ARE IN EVERY PARTICULAR EXACTLY AS DESCRIBED. We warrant them to give entire satisfaction. To avoid mistakes please give number and state emblem wanted. Order from us and if after you examine the goods you do not find them better than others are offering at 25 to 40 per cent more, return them and we will refund your money.

TWO CENTS WILL CARRY ANY ONE OF THESE PINS TO ANY PART OF THE UNITED STATES OF AMERICA BY MAIL, INSURANCE OR REGISTRY EXTRA.

WOODMEN OF THE WORLD QUOTED UNDER WOODMEN OF AMERICA.

No. 4C9601 Gold filled, Masonic, engraved. Price......34c
No. 4C9602 Solid gold, same as above. Price........60c

No. 4C9604 Gold filled, Masonic, enameled and engraved. Price........45c
No. 4C9606 Solid gold. Same as above. Each..75c

No. 4C9608 Gold filled, Masonic, enameled. Price........50c
No. 4C9610 Solid gold, same as above. Price........88c

No. 4C9612 Gold filled, Masonic and Odd Fellows, enameled. Price........40c
No. 4C9613 Solid gold, same as above. Price.60c

No. 4C9615 Gold filled, Odd Fellows, enameled. Price........36c
No. 4C9617 Solid gold, same as above. Price........64c

No. 4C9620 Gold filled. Odd Fellows, enameled. Price........40c
No. 4C9621 Solid gold, same as above. Price........68c

No. 4C9624 Gold filled, Odd Fellows. Engraved. Pr..40c
No. 4C9625 Solid gold, same as above. Price...$1.08

No. 4C9628 Gold filled, Odd Fellows. Price......25c
No. 4C9630 Solid gold, same as above. Price......50c

No. 4C9632 Gold filled, Ladies of Maccabees 65c
No. 4C9634 Solid gold. Same as above. Price...$1.20

No. 4C9636 Gold filled, Knights of Pythias. Price........55c
No. 4C9638 Solid gold. Same as above. Pr.$1.15

No. 4C9640 Gold filled, Knights of Pythias. Price........50c
No. 4C9642 Solid gold, same as above. Price........88c

No. 4C9644 Gold filled, G. A. R. enameled. Price..50c
No. 4C9646 Solid gold, same as above. Price.....$1.00

No. 4C9648 Gold filled, Modern Woodmen. Price......40c
No. 4C9650 Solid gold, same as above. Price.75c
No. 4C9652 Same style, Woodmen of the World, solid gold. Price..75c

No. 4C9654 Gold filled, Modern Woodmen. Pr.40c
No. 4C9656 Solid gold. same as above. Price..88c
No. 4C9658 Same style, Woodmen of the World, solid gold. Price...88c

No. 4C9661 Gold filled, Woodmen of America. Price........48c
No. 4C9662 Solid gold. Same as above. Price..70c

No. 4C9664 Gold filled, Ancient Order United Workmen. Price.....50c
No. 4C9666 Solid gold, same as above. Price........90c

No. 4C9668 Gold filled, Red Men. Price.....50c
No. 4C9670 Solid gold, same as above. Price......90c

No. 4C9672 Gold filled, Catholic Order of Foresters. Pr..75c
No. 4C9674 Solid gold, same as above. Price........$1.25

No. 4C9676 Gold filled, Independent Order of Foresters. Price......50c
No. 4C9678 Solid gold, same as above. Price......88c

No. 4C9680 Gold filled, Ancient Order of Foresters. Price........50c
No. 4C9682 Solid gold, same as above. Pr.$1.25

No. 4C9684 Gold filled, Catholic M. B. Association. Price..50c
No. 4C9686 Solid gold, same as above. Price........88c

No. 4C9688 Gold filled, Elks. Price........65c
No. 4C9690 Solid gold, same as above. Price........$1.40

No. 4C9692 Gold filled, Maccabees. Price........50c
No. 4C9694 Solid gold, same as above. Price. 88c

No. 4C9696 Gold filled, Christian Endeavor. Price....... 50c
No. 4C9698 Solid gold, same as above. Price...... 95c

No. 4C9700 Gold filled, Epworth League. Price.....45c
No. 4C9702 Solid gold, same as above. Price.....75c

No. 4C9703 Gold filled, Rathbone Sisters. Price........64c
No. 4C9706 Solid gold. As above. Price.....$1.40

No. 4C9708 Gold filled, Daughters of Rebekah. Price........50c
No. 4C9710 Solid gold, same as above. Price.....$1.00

No. 4C9712 Gold filled, Daughters of Rebekah. Price........75c
No. 4C9714 Solid gold. As above. Price...$1.40

No. 4C9716 Gold filled, Degree of Honor. Price........45c
No. 4C9718 Solid gold, same as above. Price.88c

No. 4C9720 Gold filled, Eastern Star. Price........50c
No. 4C9722 Solid gold. Same as above. Price........$1.15

No. 4C9724 Gold filled, Eastern Star. Price........75c
No. 4C9726 Solid gold. Same as above. Price........$1.75

No. 4C9728 Gold filled, Royal Neighbors. Price......75c
No. 4C9730 Solid gold. Same as above. Price...$1.50

No. 4C9733 Gold filled, Epworth League. Price.75c
No. 4C9735 Solid gold, same as above. Price.......$1.30

SOLID GOLD AND GOLD FILLED EMBLEM BUTTONS Solid Gold, 60c each Gold Filled, 28c each Half Size, 55c each HALF SIZE BUTTONS MADE IN SOLID GOLD ONLY.

ORDER BY NUMBER. ORDER BY NUMBER.

No. 4C9736 Gold filled, Masonic. No. 4C9738 Solid gold. No. 4C9740 Half size.

No. 4C9742 Gold filled, Odd Fellows. No. 4C9744 Solid gold. No. 4C9746 Half size.

No. 4C9748 Gold filled, Knights of Pythias. No. 4C9750 Solid gold. No. 4C9752 Half size.

No. 4C9754 Gold filled, Ancient Order U'ted Wkm'n. No. 4C9756 Solid gold. No. 4C9758 Half size.

No. 4C9755 Gold filled, International Association of Machinists. No. 4C9757 Solid gold. Half size not made.

No. 4C9759 Gold filled, Order of Eagles. No. 4C9761 Solid gold. Half size not made.

No. 4C9760 Gold filled, Maccabees. No. 4C9762 Solid gold. No. 4C9764 Half size.

No. 4C9766 Gold filled, Red Men. No. 4C9768 Solid gold. No. 4C9770 Half size.

No. 4C9772 Gold filled, Woodmen. No. 4C9774 Solid gold. Half size not made.

No. 4C9776 Gold filled, Elks. No. 4C9778 Solid gold. No. 4C9780 Half size.

No. 4C9782 Gold filled, Foresters. No. 4C9784 Solid gold. No. 4C9786 Half size.

No. 4C9788 Gold filled, Foresters of America. No. 4C9790 Solid gold. Half size not made.

No. 4C9792 Gold filled, Catholic Or'er of Foresters. No. 4C9794 Solid gold. No. 4C9796 Half size.

No. 4C9763 Gold filled, Royal Arcanum. No. 4C9765 Solid gold. No. 4C9767 Half size.

No. 4C9773 Gold filled, Railroad Conductors. No. 4C9775 Solid gold. Half size not made.

No. 4C9777 Gold filled, Knights of Columbus. No. 4C9779 Solid gold. Half size not made.

No. 4C9781 Gold filled, Royal League. No. 4C9783 Solid gold. No. 4C9785 Half size.

No. 4C9787 Gold filled, G. A. R. No. 4C9789 Solid gold. Half size not made.

No. 4C9791 Gold filled, Sons of Veterans. No. 4C9793 Solid gold. Half size not made.

No. 4C9797 Gold filled, Patriotic Sons of America. No. 4C9799 Solid gold. Half size not made.

GENTLEMEN'S SOLID GOLD AND GOLD FILLED CUFF BUTTONS.

POSTAGE ON CUFF BUTTONS, 3 CENTS EXTRA. REGISTRATION, 8 CENTS EXTRA.

No. 4C9801 Rolled gold plate, bright polish, with carved pearl center. Price, per pair, 22c

No. 4C9803 Rolled gold plate, bright polish, raised ornamentation. Price, per pair, 28c

No. 4C9805 Rolled gold plate, fancy colored gold, hand chased. Price, per pair, 35c

No. 4C9807 Rolled gold plate, bright polish, raised ornamentation. Price, per pair, 36c

No. 4C9809 Rolled gold plate, bright finish, fancy raised ornamentation, colored gold effect with fancy stone center. Price, per pair.....36c

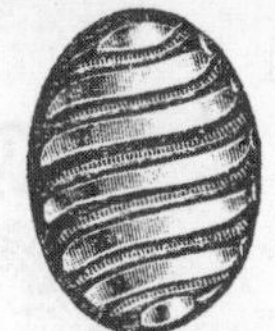

No. 4C9811 Rolled gold plate, raised ornamentation, bright polished. Price, per pair, 42c

No. 4C9813 Rolled gold plate, bright polish, imitation hand engraving, imitation gold front. Price, per pair, 45c

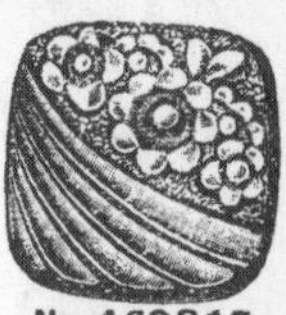

No. 4C9815 Rolled gold plate, bright gold and Roman satin finish, raised ornamentation. Per pair.....50c

No. 4C9820 Gold front, hand engraved. Per pair........70c

No. 4C9822 Rolled gold plate, raised ornamentation and engraved. Per pair........75c

No. 4C9824 Gold front, hand engraved. Per pair....70c

No. 4C9828 Gold front, hand engraved, fancy border, bright finish. Per pair.....88c

No. 4C9830 Solid gold front, hand engraved, bright finish, very fine. Per pair..$1.15

No. 4C9832 Solid gold front, bright and Roman finish, hand engraved, very elegant. Pair. $1.35

No. 4C9834 Solid gold front, bright and Roman finish, hand engraved, very elegant. Pair. $1.25

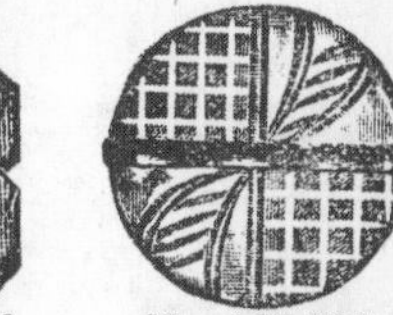

No. 4C9836 Pearl, gold band ornamentation. Per pair...31c

No. 4C9838 Solid gold front, bright and Roman finish, hand engraved, very elegant. Pair. $1.55

No. 4C9840 Pearl, gold band ornamentation. Per pair.....28c

No. 4C9844 Ladies' or boys', solid gold front, hand engraved. Per pair.....75c

No. 4C9846 Ladies' or boys', solid gold front, hand engraved. Per pair.....75c

No. 4C9848 Solid gold front, satin finish, hand engraved. Per pair.......$1.50

½-inch 2 or 3-letter monogram, 40 cents extra.

No. 4C9852 Solid gold, satin finish. Per pair......$2.50

Engraving 5c per letter, Old English.

No. 4C9853 Solid gold, hand engraved, bright cut initial; any letter furnished. Per pair... $2.65

SOLID GOLD DUMB BELL PATTERN CUFF LINKS.

No. 4C9858 Roman yellow color, raised ornamentation, extra strong. Per pair......$3.70

No. 4C9859 Plain bright polish. Per pair......$1.40 40c extra for 2 or 3-letter monogram.

No. 4C9860 Raised ornamentation, bright finish. Per pair......$2.75

No. 4C9861 Bright finish throughout, fancy rococo border. Per pair......$2.85

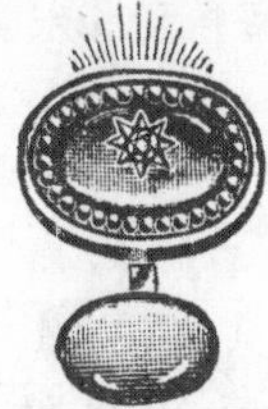

No. 4C9862 Roman yellow color, set with genuine rose diamond. Per pair......$3.40

No. 4C9863 Roman yellow, satin finish, with bright cut hand engraving. Per pair......$3.50

No. 4C9864 Roman yellow color, set with fire opal. Per pair... $2.20

No. 4C9865 Bright finish, with fancy raised design. Per pair....$3.60

Engraving 5c per letter for large script.

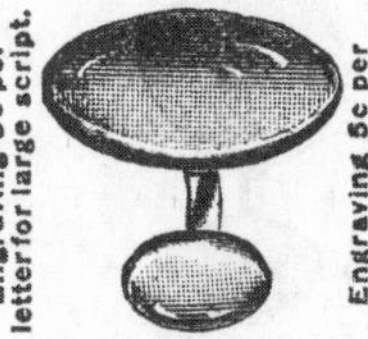

No. 4C9866 Roman yellow color. Made heavy. Per pair.....$2.40

Engraving 5c per letter for Old English.

No. 4C9867 Roman yellow and rose gold, satin finish, very artistic. Per pair....$4.50

No. 4C9868 Roman yellow color, raised ornamentation, set with fire opal. Per pair, $2.50

No. 4C9869 Plain polish, extra heavy, with beautiful small bead border. Price, per pair...... $4.68 40c extra for 2 or 3-letter monogram

No. 4C9870 Roman yellow color, raised ornamentation, extra strong. Per pair, $2.50

No. 4C9871 Roman yellow, satin finish, extra heavy. Nothing can be finer in solid gold buttons than these. Per pair...$5.75

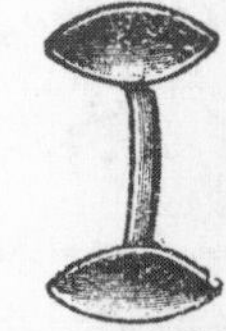

No. 4C9872 Plain polish. Price, per pair, $1.80

No. 4C9873 Roman yellow, satin finish, made extra heavy, raised artistic design, Roman gladiator. Price, per pair, $4.95

No. 4C9874 Plain polish, Roman yellow color. Per pair.....$2.00

No. 4C9876 Plain polish. Per pair......$1.60

No. 4C9878 Plain polish. Per pair....$1.75

No. 4C9882 Plain polish. Per pair......$2.70 40c extra for 2 or 3-letter monogram.

No. 4C9884 Extra heavy, rose color. Per pr., $2.75

No. 4C9886 Extra heavy, rose finish, set with sapphires. Per pair....$7.00

No. 4C9888 Very artistic, Roman finish. Per pair $2.85

No. 4C9890 Bright and Roman yellow finish. Per pair......$2.75

No. 4C9892 Plain, Roman yellow, satin finish. Per pr.. $2.50 40c extra for 2 or 3-letter monogram.

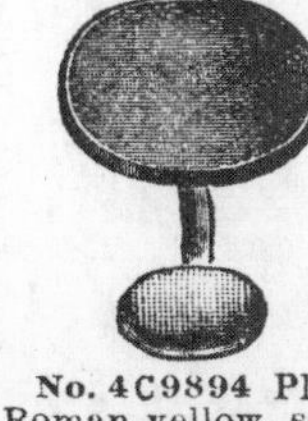

No. 4C9894 Plain, Roman yellow, satin finish. Per pr.. $2.50 40c extra for 2 or 3-letter monogram.

No. 4C9896 Bright and Roman yellow finish. Per pr., $3.25

No. 4C9898 Bright and Roman yellow finish, set with rhinestone. Per pr.. $3.50

No. 4C9900 Roman yellow color, with bright onlaid emblem. Masonic. Per pair.......$3.50

No. 4C9902 Odd Fellows. Per pair $3.50

No. 4C9904 K. of P. Per pair.......$3.50

GENTS' DUMB BELL PATTERN CUFF LINKS

In Rolled Gold Plate, Solid Gold Front, and Gold Filled Stock. If by mail, postage on cuff links, extra, 3 cents.

No. 4C10001 Rolled gold plate, imitation gold front, set with three fancy stones. Per pair......25c

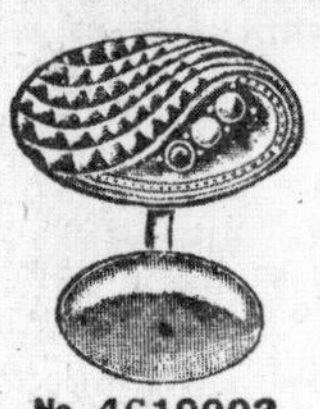

No. 4C10003 Rolled gold plate, bright polish, raised ornamentation, fancy stone sets. Price, per pair.....26c

No. 4C10007 Rolled gold plate, imitation gold front, imitation hand engraved, bright polish. Price, per pair, 28c

No. 4C10009 Rolled gold plate, bright polish, raised ornamentation, imitation diamond. Price, per pair.....30c

No. 4C10011 Rolled gold plate, bright polish, raised ornamentation. Price, per pair.....30c

No. 4C10013 Rolled gold plate, bright polish, colored gold effect, fancy stone set. Price, per pair..... 32c

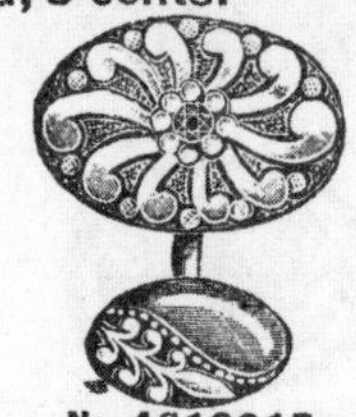

No. 4C10015 Rolled gold plate, raised ornamentation, fancy stone center. Price, per pair...35c

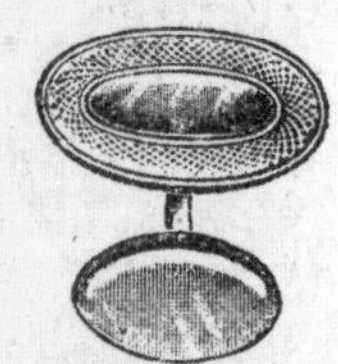

No. 4C10017 Rolled gold plate, imitation gold front. Price, per pair.....35c

No. 4C10019 Rolled gold plate, bright polish, fancy gold color. Price, per pair.....38c

No. 4C10023 Rolled gold plate, bright polish. Price, per pair.....40c

No. 4C10025 Rolled gold plate mountings, pearl button effect. Per pair.....40c

No. 4C10027 Rolled gold plate, bright polish, raised ornamentation. Per pair.......42c

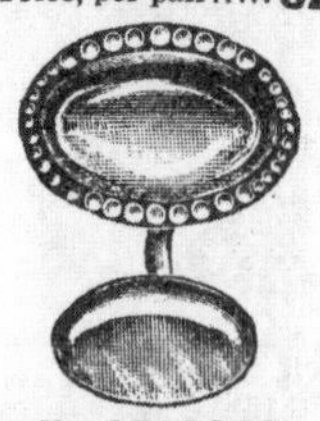

No. 4C10029 Rolled gold plate, bright polish, raised bead ornamentation. Per pair 42c

No. 4C10031 Rolled gold plate, bright polish, raised ornamentation. Per pair.......45c

No. 4C10033 Rolled gold plate, bright polish, raised ornamentation, various colored gold. Price, per pair.....48c

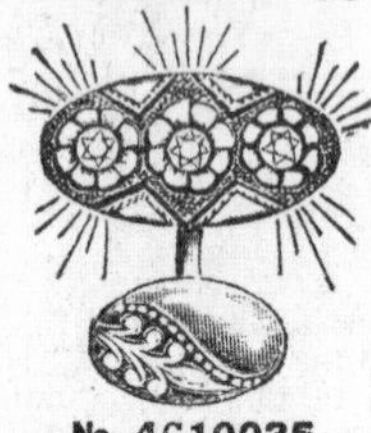

No. 4C10035 Rolled gold plate, bright polish, raised ornamentation, three fine imitation diamonds. Price, per pair.....48c

No. 4C10037 Rolled gold plate, bright polish, raised ornamentation. Price, per pair.....48c

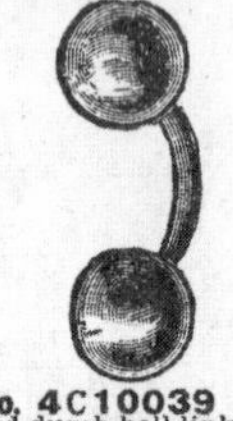

No. 4C10039 Gold filled dumb bell links. Price, per pair.....50c
No. 4C10041 Solid gold. Per pair.....$2.25
No. 4C10043 Solid silver. Per pair.....50c

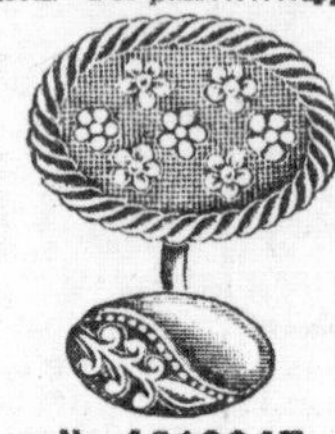

No. 4C10047 Rolled gold plate, bright polish and Roman yellow finish; applied ornamentation. Price, per pair..... 50c

No. 4C10049 Rolled gold plate. Imitation solid gold front, bright polish. Price, per pair.... 56c

No. 4C10051 Rolled gold plate, bright polish, raised ornamentation, set with two fancy stones. Price, per pair.... 58c

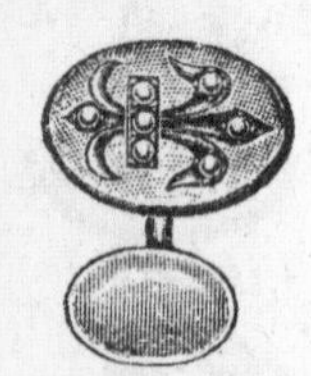

No. 4C10053 Rolled gold plate, Roman yellow satin finish, set with imitation opals. Per pair......58c

No. 4C10055 Rolled gold plate, bright polish, fancy knot effect. Price, per pair.....60c

No. 4C10057 Gold filled, hand engraved, brilliant set. Price, per pair.....65c

No. 4C10059 Gold filled, bright polish, raised ornamentation. Price, per pair.....69c

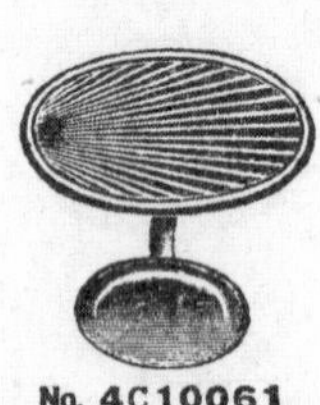

No. 4C10061 Solid gold front, hand engraved, sun ray pattern. Price, per pair.....72c

No. 4C10063 Gold filled, bright polish, raised ornamentation. Price, per pair, 72c

No. 4C10065 Solid gold front, hand engraved, bright polish. Price, per pair...74c

No. 4C10067 Gold filled, Roman yellow satin finish, set with two imitation diamonds and two fancy stones. Price, per pair 75c

No. 4C10073 Gold filled, Roman yellow satin finish, set with two rhinestones and one fancy stone. Price, per pair.....80c

No. 4C10075 Solid gold front, hand engraved. Price, per pair.....85c

No. 4C10077 Gold filled, bright polish, raised ornamentation. Price, per pair.....85c

No. 4C10079 Gold filled, bright polish and Roman yellow color, very artistic. Price, per pair.....90c

No. 4C10081 Solid gold front, bright polish, hand engraved. Price, per pair.....98c

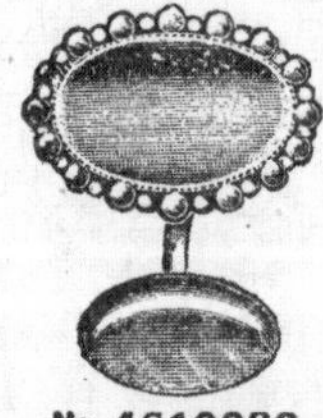

No. 4C10083 Gold filled, bright polish, fancy beaded border. Price, per pair...98c Two or three-letter monogram, 40 cents extra.

No. 4C10085 Solid gold front, bright finish, hand engraved. Price, per pair..$1.00

No. 4C10087 Gold filled, bright polish and Roman yellow satin finish. Price, per pair..$1.00

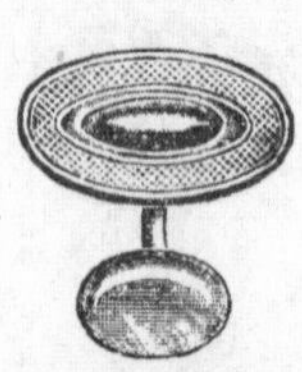

No. 4C10089 Gold filled, bright polish, fancy turquoise center. Price, per pair..$1.05

No. 4C10093 Solid gold front, bright polish, hand engraved. Price, per pair..$1.12

No. 4C10095 Solid gold front, Roman yellow satin finish, bright cut, hand engraved. Price, per pair..$1.15

No. 4C10097 Solid gold front, bright polish, hand carved. Price, per pair..$1.20

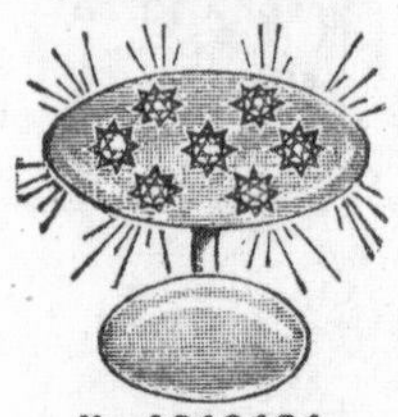

No. 4C10101 Gold filled, Roman yellow finish, set with very fine imitation diamonds. Price, per pair $1.25

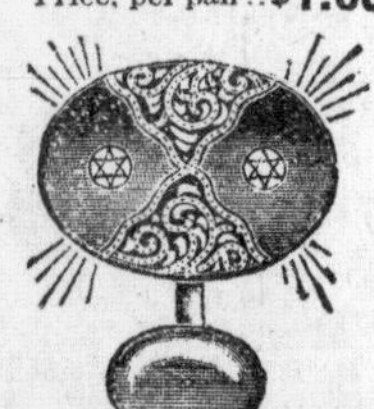

No. 4C10103 Solid gold front, hand engraved, bright polish, two imitation diamonds. Price, per pair..$1.35

No. 4C10105 Solid gold front, hand engraved. Price, per pair..$1.40

No. 4C10107 Solid gold front, bright polish, hand engraved. Price, per pair..$1.45

Note the 6 varieties of Emblem Buttons we carry.

Order by number, and state Emblem wanted.

No. 4C10109 Masonic.
No. 4C10111 Odd Fellows.
No. 4C10113 Knights of Pythias.
No. 4C10115 Redmen.
No. 4C10117 Woodmen of America.
No. 4C10119 Woodmen of the World.

Solid gold front, hand engraved, your choice. Price, per pair.............$1.45
ORDER BY NUMBER.

No. 4C10121 Solid gold front, hand engraved, bright. Per pair.......$1.45

This shows the pipe stem stud closed.

BEST QUALITY STUDS, COLLAR BUTTONS AND LADIES' WATCH CHATELETTE PINS.

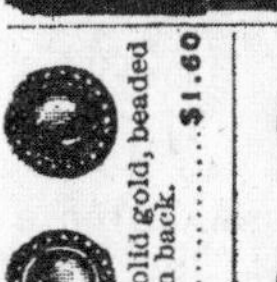

No. 4C10202 Solid gold, beaded border, pipe stem back. Price, per set......$1.60

No. 4C10208 Solid gold, pearl set, pipe stem back. Price, per set..........$2.00

No. 4C10214 Solid gold, genuine opal. Price..$1.60

No. 4C10216 Solid gold, Egyptian pearl. Price. $1.65

No. 4C10218 Solid gold, emerald doublet. Price....$1.60
No. 4C10220 Ruby doublet. Price....$1.60

No. 4C10222 Solid gold, Emerald doublet. Price....$1.25
No. 4C10224 Ruby doublet. Price....$1.25
No. 4C10228 Genuine opal. Price... $1.35

No. 4C10226 Solid gold, ruby doublet. Price... $1.95
No. 4C10229 Emerald doublet. Price$1.95

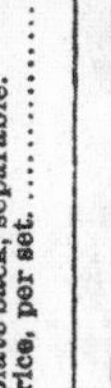

No. 4C10230 Pearl front, rolled plate back, separable. Price, per set. 20c

No. 4C10234 Gold front, gold filled back, separable, Price, per set..........50c

Separable. No. 4C10274 Gold filled. Price.... 9c

Separable. No. 4C10276 Solid g'ld fr'nt Price....23c

SOLID GOLD COLLAR BUTTONS.

No. 4C10258 Ball top, medium. Price......90c

No. 4C10260 Ball top, high. Price....$1.00

No. 4C10262 Flat top, low. Price. 90c
No. 4C10264 Flat top, medium. Price...... 95c

No. 4C10266 Flat top, high. Price....$1.00

No. 4C10268 Lever top, medium..80c
No. 4C10270 Lever top, large..$1.10

No. 4C10272 Lever pointer. Price...$1.10

IT-SO-EZIE.

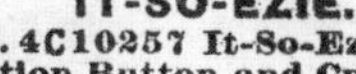

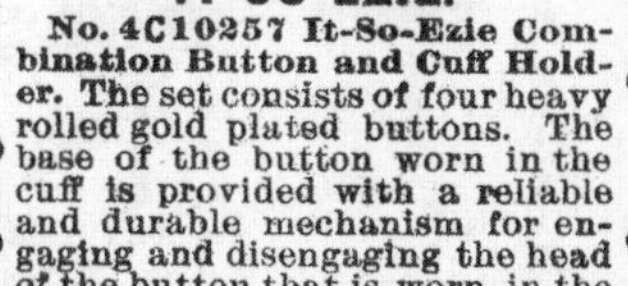

No. 4C10257 It-So-Ezie Combination Button and Cuff Holder. The set consists of four heavy rolled gold plated buttons. The base of the button worn in the cuff is provided with a reliable and durable mechanism for engaging and disengaging the head of the button that is worn in the wrist band. The illustration shows the button attached and detached. To release them, tip the top button and they will separate.

Price, per set	$0.21
Six sets	1.10
Twelve sets	2.00

GOLD FILLED COLLAR BUTTONS.

Ball Top.	Flat Top.	LeverPearlBack	Lever Medium.	Lever High.	Lever Pointer.
No. 4C10280 Rolled gold plate. Price. 8c	No. 4C10286 Rolled gold plate. Price. .. 8c	No. 4C10292 Rolled gold plate. Price.. .....10c	No. 4C10298 Rolled gold plate. Price... 8c	No. 4C10304 Rolled gold plate. Price....... 8c	No. 4C10310 Rolled gold plate. Price..... 8c
No. 4C10282 Gold filled. Price......20c	No. 4C10288 Gold filled. Price ...20c	No. 4C10294 Gold filled. Price.......20c	No. 4C10300 Gold filled. Price.......20c	No. 4C10306 Gold filled. Price......20c	No. 4C10312 Gold filled. Price...... 20c
No. 4C10284 Gold plate. Per dozen.38c	No. 4C10290 Gold plate. Per dozen.38c	No. 4C10296 Gold plate. Per dozen...38c	No. 4C10302 Gold plate. Per dozen...38c	No. 4C10308 Gold plate. Per dozen...38c	No. 4C10314 Gold plate. Per dozen... 38c

LADIES' WATCH CHATELETTES.

You can improve the appearance of your costume by wearing one of our swell chatelettes to hang your watch on, or, if you desire, you can use one of these nobby pins as a brooch. Illustrations show the exact size. Each one comes with a swivel attached as on No. 4C10372.

If by mail, postage extra, 8 cents.

No. 4C10350 Solid gold Roman finish, set with 4 turquoise. Price.....$3.00

No. 4C10352 Solid gold, Roman finish, beaded border, 20 pearl sets. Price..... $3.25

No. 4C10354 Solid gold, plain polish. Price.....$1.88
No. 4C10355 Solid silver, same style as No. 4C10354. Price.... ...72c

No. 4C10340 Rolled gold plate, blue enameled, bright polish. Price.........38c

No. 4C10341 Gold filled, bright polish, hand chased and engraved. Price........80c

No. 4C10342 Rolled gold plate, bright polish, set with 7 pearls. Price........40c

No. 4C10343 Gold filled, bright polish, set with six fine imitation diamonds and five rubies. Price................$1.05

No. 4C10344 Solid gold front, bright polish, hand engraved. Price........50c

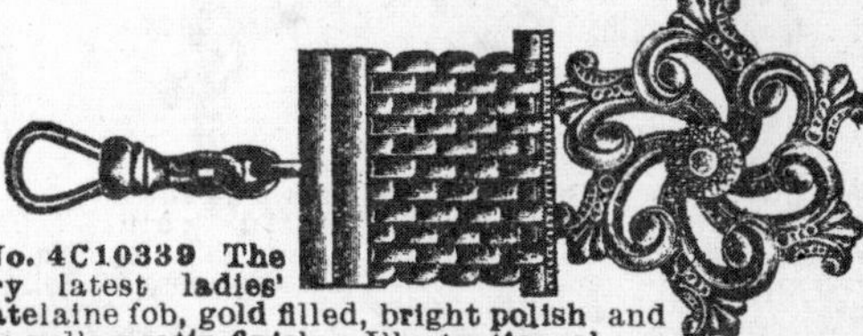

No. 4C10339 The very latest ladies' chatelaine fob, gold filled, bright polish and rose yellow satin finish. Illustration shows exact size. Price..$2.25

No. 4C10345 Gold filled, bright polish, set with fine imitation diamond and 21 pearls. Price.... $1.10

No. 4C10346 Solid gold front, hand engraved, bright polish. Price........60c

No. 4C10356 Gold filled, Roman color, hard enameled. Price......50c

No. 4C10358 Gold filled, bright finish, beaded edge. Price..........60c

No. 4C10360 Gold filled, bright finish, set with four pearls. Price..........75c

No. 4C10362 Gold filled, rose finish, raised ornamentation, four amethysts. Price, $1.25

No. 4C10364 Gold filled, bright finish, chased, beaded border. Price.....98c

No. 4C10366 Gold filled, bright finish, ornamented, engraved, pearl and turquoise sets. Price...$1.06

No. 4C10368 Gold filled, rose finish, burnished opal and seven emerald doublet sets. Price...$1.20

No. 4C10370 Gold filled over sterling silver; set with 36 crystalline diamonds. Price.......$2.25

No. 4C10371 Gold filled, bright polish, set with fine imitation diamonds. One of the most attractive chatelettes on the market. Price..........................$3.25

No. 4C10372 Rolled gold plate, Roman finish. Price..........48c
No. 4C10374 Solid silver, satin finish. Price...65c

No. 4C10376 Gold filled, bright finish. Price..........58c

No. 4C10378 Gold filled, bright finish. Price......... 70c

No. 4C10380 Gold filled, bright finish. Price........78c

SCARF AND STICK PINS, THIMBLES AND HAIR COMBS,

All scarf pins shown on this page have the regular 2-inch pin stems. Postage extra on scarf pins, stick pins and thimbles, 2c extra; 5c extra if by insured mail.

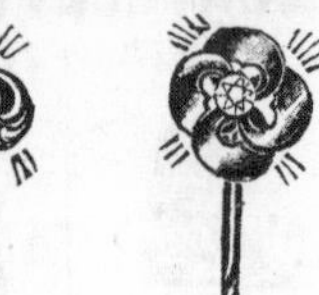

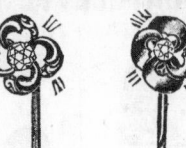

No. 4C10601 Rolled gold plate, 1 rhinestone Ea. 16c

No. 4C10603 Rolled gold plate, 1 rhinestone. Ea. 18c

No. 4C10605 Rolled gold plate, 1 ruby doublet set. Price.....20c

No. 4C10607 Rolled gold plate, 1 rhinestone. Ea. 23c

No. 4C10609 Rolled gold plate, 1 rhinestone set..25c

No. 4C10610 Gold filled, bright finish, chased, opal set........45c

No. 4C10611 Rolled gold plate, 2 pearls and 1 turquoise. Ea. 21c

No. 4C10614 Gold filled, bright finish, opal set. Price... 40c

No. 4C10616 Gold filled, Tiffany setting, white stone. Pr. 27c

No. 4C10618 Gold filled, Tiffany setting, white stone. Price..40c

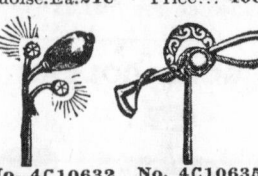

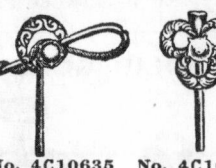

No. 4C10621 Gold filled, 1 large imitation emerald. Price....28c

No. 4C10622 Rolled plate, cluster, 4 rubies, 4 white stones, 1 pearl. Price....40c

No. 4C10623 Gold filled, emerald doublet, 4 rhinestones. Pr. 29c

No. 4C10625 Gold filled, emerald set, 2 rhinestones and 3 pearls. Price....35c

No. 4C10627 Gold filled head, 3 pearls, gold filled pin. Price....40c

No. 4C10629 Solid gold head, gold filled pin. Price....34c

No. 4C10632 Rolled plate, pearl, 2 brilliants. Price....25c

No. 4C10635 Solid gold head, pearl set, gold filled pin. Price. 38c

No. 4C10637 Solid gold head, 1 pearl, gold filled pin. Price. ..38c

No. 4C10638 Rolled plate, fancy, 5 brilliants, 1 sapphire. Price..50c

No. 4C10641 Solid gold head, 3 pearls, gold filled pin. Price....40c

No. 4C10643 Solid gold head, 1 large ruby doublet, gold filled pin. Price....45c

No. 4C10645 Solid gold head, 1 ruby doublet set, gold filled pin. Price....45c

No. 4C10646 Rolled plate, horseshoe, 9 brilliants. Price....50c

No. 4C10648 Rolled plate, horseshoe, 7 rubies, 8 brilliants. $1.00

No. 4C10650 Rolled plate, cluster, 14 brilliants, 8 rubies, 1 pearl Price....85c

No. 4C10653 Solid gold head, 1 pearl set, gold filled pin. Price. 50c

No. 4C10654 Gold filled, horseshoe and arrow, 9 pearls. 75c

No. 4C10657 Solid gold head, 3 pearls, gold filled pin. Price....50c

No. 4C10658 Solid gold, fancy finished elephant. Price. $2.50

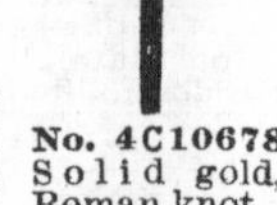

No. 4C10660 Solid gold hearts. Price....75c

No. 4C10662 Solid gold, bright polish, emerald setting. Price....85c

No. 4C10664 Solid gold, hand eng'ved, genuine opal. Price, $1.10

No. 4C10666 Solid gold, ruby and emerald setting. Price, $1.30

No. 4C10669 Solid gold head, 1 genuine opal. Price....60c

No. 4C10670 Solid gold, fancy flower, 1 opal. Price... $1.25

No. 4C10672 Solid gold, 13 brilliants, ruby center. Price. $1.50

No. 4C10674 Solid gold, any initial. Price, $1.00

No. 4C10677 Solid gold head, 1 genuine opal, gold filled pin. Price. $1.15

No. 4C10678 Solid gold, Roman knot. Price..80c

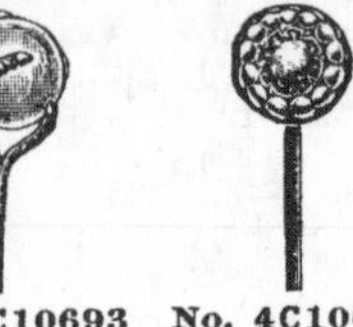

No. 4C10680 Solid gold, Roman color. Price....70c

No. 4C10682 Solid gold, Roman color, engraved, almandine center. Pr. $1.90

No. 4C10684 Solid gold fancy sickle, 2 turquoise, 2 pearls. Price. $2.00

No. 4C10687 Solid gold, 2 genuine opals. Price. $1.22

No. 4C10688 Solid gold, bright finish, knot, emerald set. Price, $1.10

No. 4C10690 Solid gold, bright finish, Roman colored rope. Price, $1.15

No. 4C10693 Solid gold, 1 large Egyptian pearl. Price. $1.30

No. 4C10695 Solid gold, 14 pearls, 1 genuine opal. Price. $1.40

No. 4C10697 Solid gold, 8 rhinestones. Price. $1.80

No. 4C10699 Solid gold, bright polish, large genuine opal. Price. $3.00

SILVER, GOLD FILLED AND SOLID GOLD THIMBLES.

If by mail, postage extra, 2 cents. DON'T FAIL TO GIVE SIZE OF THIMBLES WANTED.

Don't fail to give size of thimble wanted

No. 4C10701 Solid silver. Price........12c

No. 4C10703 Solid silver, heavy. Price........22c

No. 4C10705 Solid silver, beautifully engraved. Price........42c

No. 4C10707 Solid silver, octagon shape, hand engraved. Price........33c

No. 4C10709 Solid silver, open top. Price........25c

No. 4C10711 Gold filled, engraved, warranted. Price........95c

No. 4C10713 Solid 10-karat gold. Price..... $1.85

No. 4C10715 Solid 14-karat gold. Price... $3.70

LADIES' SIDE AND BACK COMBS.

The settings are securely fastened so as to prevent loss; in fact, we believe the finest hair ornaments ever made, considering the wonderfully low figures we are quoting for this high grade of merchandise. We can send by mail any one of these combs for 3 cents; insured mail would cost extra, 5 cents.

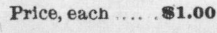

No. 4C10719 Back Comb, 4½ inches wide, imitation shell with rich Roman colored, gold filled trimming. Price, each $1.00

No. 4C10721 Back Comb, 4½ inches wide, fine imitation shell, gold filled Roman colored trimmings; set with 5 turquoise. Price, each $1.58

No. 4C10723 Back Comb, 4½ inches wide, fine imitation shell, trimmed with gold filled Roman colored ornament; set with 3 turquoise. Price, each $1.70

No. 4C10725 Back Comb, 4½ inches wide, imitation shell, gold filled Roman colored trimmings; set with 25 pearls. Price, each $1.90

No. 4C10727 Side Combs, 4 inches wide, fine imitation shell, gold filled Roman colored trimmings; each comb set with 9 turquoise. Price, per pair... $3.00

No. 4C10729 Side Combs, nothing finer on the market, 4 inches wide, fine imitation shell, with gold filled Roman colored trimmings; each comb set with 6 amethysts and 3 pearls. Pr. pair. $3.10

LADIES' LACE PINS, CUFF PINS, BABY PINS AND PIN SETS.

MAIL CHARGES on Lace Pins, Brooches, Cuff Pins, Baby Pins and Sets, 2 cents extra. 8 cents extra by insured or registered mail.

No. 4C10804 Lace Pin, gold front, engraved, set with 3 fancy stones. Price.......... 60c

No. 4C10812 Lace or Belt Pin. Gold filled; the newest out, 25 pearls and 25 turquoise. Price $2.10

No. 4C10814 Lace or Belt Pin, gold filled, the very latest, 10 pearls and 10 turquoise. Price........ 95c

No. 4C10816 Lace or Belt Pin, gold filled, set with 26 crystalline diamonds. Ea... $1.50

No. 4C10818 Lace or Belt Pin, gold filled, set with 11 crystalline diamonds. Price.. $1.05

CUFF PINS AND CHILD'S BIB AND BABY PINS, ETC.

No. 4C10820 Baby Pin, gold filled, Roman and bright finish. Price........ 48c Engraving 2½ cents per letter extra if desired.

No. 4C10822 Baby Pin, gold filled, Roman and bright finish. Price........ 42c Engraving 2½ cents per letter extra if desired.

No. 4C10826 Solid gold front, engraved. Price, per pair......... 40c

No. 4C10832 Solid gold front, engraved. Price, per pair......... 60c

No. 4C10828 Gold front, raised ornamented ends. Per pair...... 38c

No. 4C10834 Solid gold front, 1 garnet, 1 pearl and 1 sapphire. Price, per pair 70c

No. 4C10838 Solid gold, Roman color, raised ornamentation. Price, per pair... $1.58

WE CHARGE 2½ CENTS PER LETTER FOR SCRIPT ENGRAVING; 5 CENT FOR OLD ENGLISH.

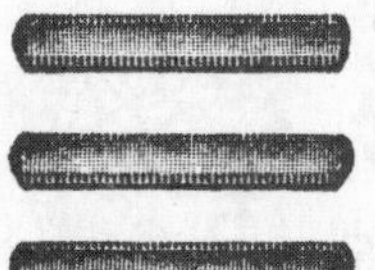

No. 4C10856 Solid gold front, Roman color, hand engraved. Price, per set of 3, 95c

No. 4C10858 Solid gold front, bright finish, set with pearls and turquoise. Per set of 3....... $1.20

No. 4C10860 Gold filled, hand engraved, bright finish, soldered chain. Price............................... 60c

No. 4C10862 Solid gold front, Roman finish, bright engraved, soldered chain. Price.................. $1.20

No. 4C10864 Solid gold front, bright finish, soldered chain, set with turquoise. Price.................. $1.20

No. 4C10866 Gold front, bright finish, hand engraved, soldered chain. Price 80c

No. 4C10868 Solid gold front, Roman finish, bright hand engraving, soldered chain. Price. 98c

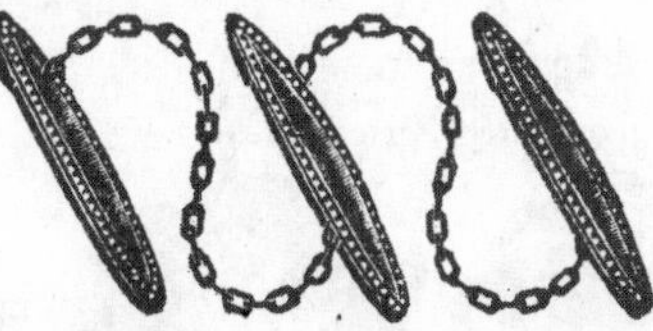

No. 4C10870 Solid gold, Roman color, beaded edge, soldered links. Price................................ $1.75

No. 4C10874 Solid gold, Roman color, hand engraved, soldered links. Price $2.60

No. 4C10876 Button Sets, solid gold, soldered links, Roman finish. Price, per set................ $2.15

No. 4C10877 Same as above, gold filled. Price, per set............ 48c

ROLLED GOLD PLATE AND GOLD FRONT BROOCHES.

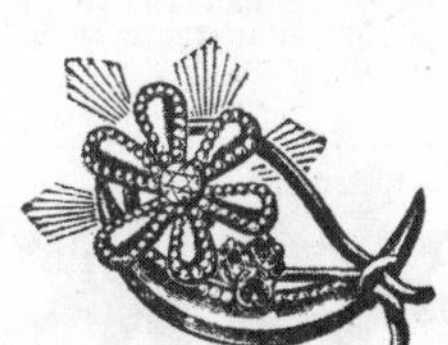

No. 4C10878 Gold filled, bright polish, 3 amethysts and 1 rhinestone. Price... ...... 32c

No. 4C10882 Gold front, bright polish, 4 imitation opals..... 35c

No. 4C10884 Gold filled, bright plain polish. Price.. 36c

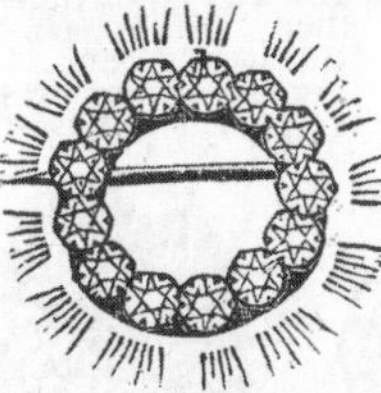

No. 4C10886 Rolled gold plate, bright polish, 13 rhinestones. Price............ 37c

No. 4C10888 Gold filled, bright polish, enameled in black, 38c

No. 4C10890 Gold filled, Roman and bright polish, 1 amethyst. Price, 38c

No. 4C10892 Gold filled, Roman and bright polish, 1 emerald doublet. Price.......... 38c

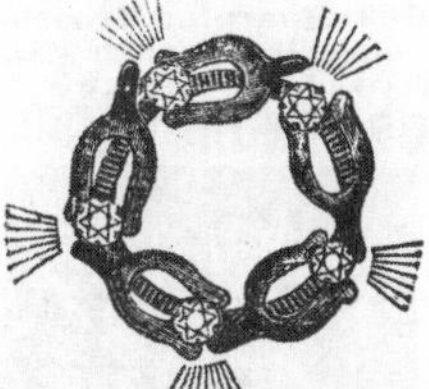

No. 4C10894 Gold front, bright polish, 5 rhinestones. Price, 40c

No. 4C10898 Gold filled, bright polish, 3 rhinestones and 1 ruby. Price. ... 42c

No. 4C10900 Hard enameled in black, 6 pearls. Price..... 44c

No. 4C10904 Gold filled, bright polish, 9 pearls and 1 rhinestone...... 45c

No. 4C10906 Gold front, bright polish, 5 rhinestones and 1 ruby doublet. Price...... 46c

No. 4C10908 Gold front, bright polish, 1 turquoise. Price, 50c

No. 4C10910 Gold filled, bright polish, 1 amethyst. Ea. 50c

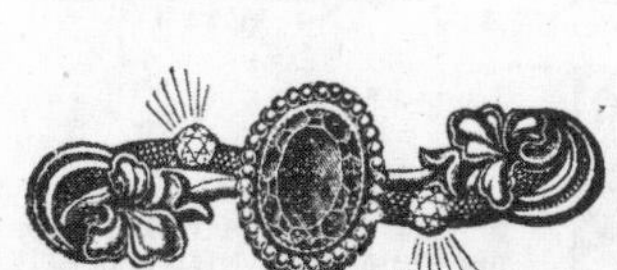

No. 4C10914 Rolled gold plate, bright and Roman finish, one amethyst and 2 rhinestones. Price............................ 32c

No. 4C10916 Gold front, bright polish, 7 rhinestones. Price........... 40c

No. 4C10918 Gold front, hand engraved, bright polish. Price.. .... 45c

No. 4C10920 Gold front, bright polish and Roman finish, 1 ruby doublet.... 55c

No. 4C10922 Gold filled, bright and Roman finish, for initial. Price............ 52c
Extra for engraving 2½ cents per letter for script, 5c for Old English.

LADIES' ROLLED PLATE AND GOLD FILLED FANCY PINS, MOURNING PINS AND GOLD FILLED BROOCHES.

No. 4C11000 Gold filled; 1 genuine opal. Price.........$1.30

No. 4C11002 Rolled plate; bright finish, garnets and pearls. Price...........68c

No. 4C11003 Hard enameled in appropriate colors; 1 rhinestone.....56c

No. 4C11005 Gold front; 7 almandines. Price...55c

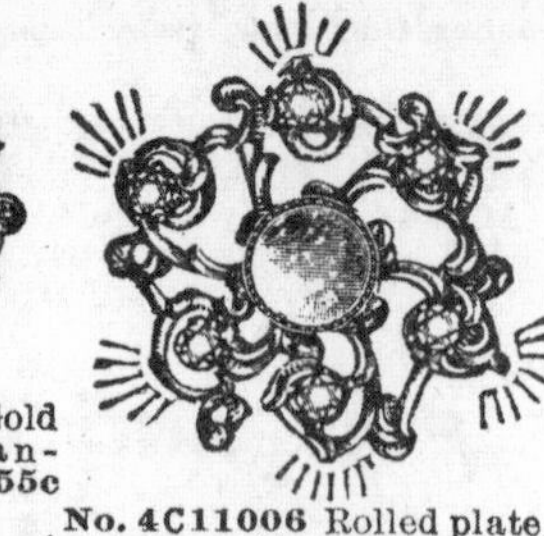

No. 4C11006 Rolled plate; imitation diamonds and 1 imitation opal. Price...40c

No. 4C11008 Gold filled; bright polished. Price.....69c

No. 4C11010 Gold filled; Roman finish; 6 brilliants and 1 almandine. Price.68c

No. 4C11012 Gold filled; enameled in colors; 1 genuine opal. Price......85c

No. 4C11014 Gold filled; Roman finish; 4 brilliants and 5 pearls. Price....75c

No. 4C11016 Gold filled; bright polish; 8 ruby doublets. Price......75c

No. 4C11018 Gold filled; Roman and enameled, 5 pearls. Price...........58c

No. 4C11020 Gold filled; Roman finish; brilliants and olivines Price.............$1.15

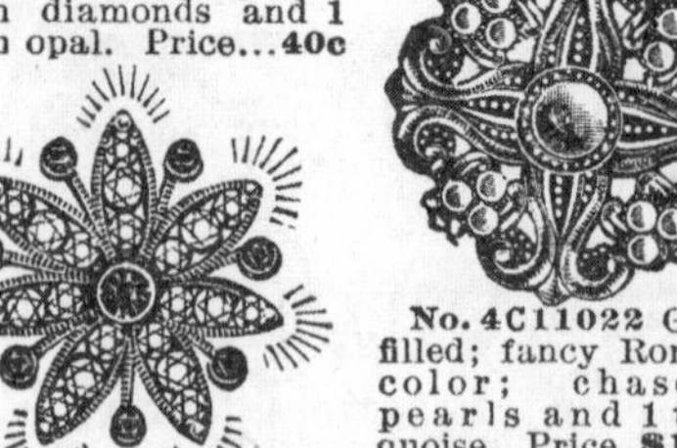

No. 4C11022 Gold filled; fancy Roman color; chased; pearls and 1 turquoise. Price..$1.36

No. 4C11025 Gold filled, bright polish; 1 emerald and pearls. Price............75c

No. 4C11027 Gold filled, bright polish; rhinestones, 1 amethyst. Price,75c

No. 4C11028 Gold filled; Roman finish; enameled; 3 pearls. Price...........68c

No. 4C11031 Gold filled, bright polished; 1 genuine opal. Price...........76c

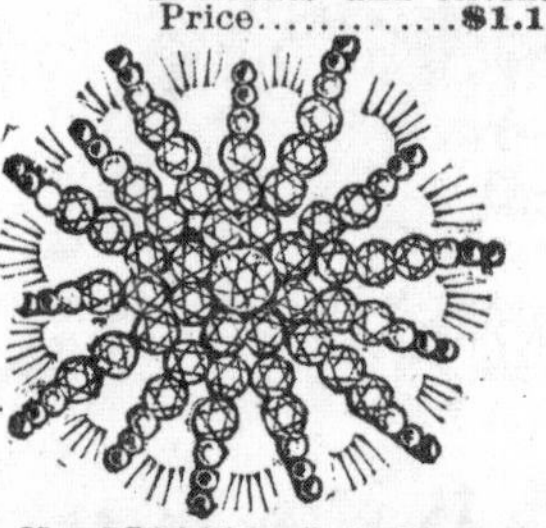

No. 4C11032 Gold filed; bright finish; brilliants; gorgeous effect. Price..$1.80

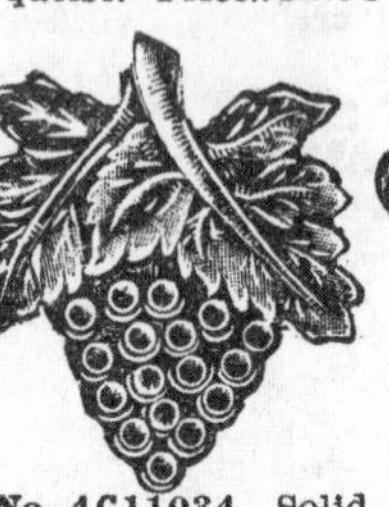

No. 4C11034 Solid gold front; bright polish; set with 17 garnets. Price......$1.25

No. 4C11036 Gold filled monogram brooch, bright and Roman finish. Price...........80c
2½c extra per letter for engraving or 35c for monogram if desired.

No. 4C11039 Gold filled, bright polish; 3 amethysts, 3 pearls and 2 rhinestones. Price.......... 63c

POSTAGE ON BROOCH PINS 2 CENTS EXTRA. INSURANCE OR REGISTRY EXTRA.
SEE INTRODUCTORY PAGE IN THIS DEPARTMENT FOR INSTRUCTIONS.

No. 4C11042 Solid gold front; Roman finish; 1 turquoise, 1 pearl and 1 garnet. Price $1.00

No. 4C11044 Solid gold front; Roman finish; set with 3 garnets. Price....$1.00

No. 4C11040 Solid gold front; Roman and bright finish; engraved. Price..$1.00

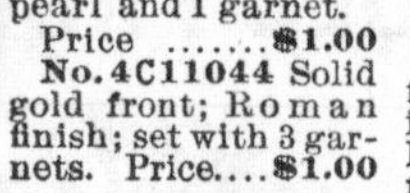

No. 4C11044

No. 4C11046 Gold filled; bright polish; pearls and 1 large turquoise matrix. Price...$1.50

No. 4C11048 Gold filled; hand chased; Roman color; 7 fine amethysts. Price.........$1.45

No. 4C11049 Gold front; rhinestones and almandines. Price.............65c

No. 4C11050 Gold filled monogram brooch; bright and Roman finish. Price.......$1.15
2½c extra per letter for engraving or 35c for monogram if desired.

No. 4C11052 Gold filled; raised ornamentation; 1 genuine opal. Price.............$1.35

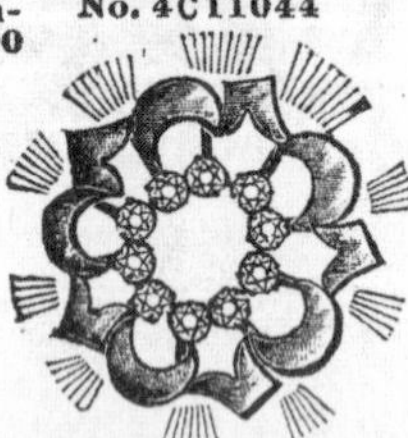

No. 4C11055 Gold front, bright polish; 10 rhinestones. Price.........62c

No. 4C11057 Gold front, bright polish, hand engraved. Price.............60c

No. 4C11059 Gold front, bright polish and Roman finish; 1 emerald. Price............58c

No. 4C11060 Gold filled; Roman finish; 1 rhinestone. Price...............98c

No. 4C11062 **Mourning Brooch Pin,** black enameled branch with fine jet flowers. Price........90c

No. 4C11065 Gold filled, bright polish; rhinestones. Price..........50c

No. 4C11067 Gold front, bright polish; rhinestones and 1 ruby. Price....74c

No. 4C11068 Roman and enameled; brilliants and pearls. Price..............40c

No. 4C11072 **Mourning Brooch Pin,** black enamel and jet ornaments. Price......35c

GOLD FILLED BROOCHES OR PENDANTS.

No. 4C11074

No. 4C11074 Gold filled; brooch or pendant, pearls and 1 fine opal. Price..$2.25

No. 4C11076 Gold filled; brooch or pendant, fine rhinestones. Price..$2.10

No. 4C11076

No. 4C11078 Gold filled; bright finish; brooch or pendant, set with pearls and 1 fine fire opal. Price......... ......$2.00

No. 4C11080 Gold filled; bright finish; brooch or pendant, set with fine rhinestones. Price. $1.90

No. 4C11082 Gold filled; bright finish; brooch or pendant, set with pearls and 1 fine opal. Price............ $1.50

FANCY SOLID GOLD PENDANTS OR BROOCHES.

For the price, you cannot duplicate these goods anywhere. They are solid gold through and through, guaranteed, and if not as described, money will be refunded on return of goods. If by mail, postage extra, 2 cents. Registered mail, 8 cents extra.

No. 4C11200 One large amethyst, rose finish. Price...... $5.25

No. 4C11202 Bright finish, 7 rhinestone sets. Price...$4.50

No. 4C11204 Color'd gold leaves, set with 4 pearls, 1 ruby doublet. Price...... $2.40

No. 4C11206 Set with 7 pearls. Price....$3.50

No. 4C11208 New rose gold finish, set with 5 pearls. Price..........$3.00

No. 4C11210 Set with ruby center. Price... $3.65

No. 4C11212 Colored gold pansy, set with pearl. Price.......... $4.15

No. 4C11214 Three pearls and 3 ruby doublets. Price.... $2.05

No. 4C11216 Roman finish, one fine genuine rose diamond. Price...$3.25

No. 4C11218 Roman finish, pearl set. Price $1.75

No. 4C11220 Bright finish, ruby set. Price... $2.75

No. 4C11222 Rose finish, pearl set. Price...$4.10

No. 4C11224 Bright finish, 6 emeralds and 1 fire opal. Price...... $3.50

No. 4C11226 Roman finish, 6 pearls and 1 fire opal. Price.........$4.25

No. 4C11228 Roman finish, hand chased. Price....... $1.90

No. 4C11230 Roman finish, set with 45 pearls and 1 fire opal. Price........ $6.00

No. 4C11232 Roman finish, fifty pearls, 1 fire opal. Price...........$5.00

No. 4C11234 Green enameled, set with one pearl. Price...$3.75

No. 4C11236 Bright finish, 24 pearls, 6 rubies and 1 fire opal. Price $4.15

No. 4C11238 Rose finish, very new. Price..$4.50

No. 4C11240 Bright finish, set with 6 pearls and 1 ruby. Price, $4.25

No. 4C11242 Absolutely new in design, set with 58 pearls and 1 ruby doublet for the eye. Price..$8.25

No. 4C11244 Roman colored flowers, pearl and almandine centers. Ea., $3.33

No. 4C11246 Bright and Roman, set with 3 pearls. Price.........$2.75

No. 4C11248 Roman satin finish, engraved, set with genuine diamond. Price, $3.25

No. 4C11250 Roman satin finish, set with genuine diamond. Price....$3.25

No. 4C11252 Bright and colored gold, 4 pearls. 1 ruby. Price.......$4.00

No. 4C11254 Rose finish, set with turquoise. Price,.... $3.90

No. 4C11256 Bright finish, set with one turquoise. Price....$2.25

No. 4C11258 Bright finish, set with one fire opal. Price...... $2.50

No. 4C11260 Bright finish, set with emerald. Price... $2.15

No. 4C11262 Bright and colored gold, set with amethyst. Price............$2.15

No. 4C11264 Bright finish. Price....$1.75

No. 4C11266 Roman color, satin finish. Price............$1.60

No. 4C11268 Bright finish, set with ruby. Price $2.75

No. 4C11270 Bright finish, set with sapphire. Price..... ..$2.25

No. 4C11272 Satin and Roman finish, center plain for monogram. Price..............$4.75 Two or three letter monogram, 35 cents extra.

No. 4C11274 Bright finish, set with pearl. Price..$2.15

No. 4C11276 Roman finish, hand engraved, hand chased; set with 1 fire opal, extra heavy. Price.....$6.50

No. 4C11278 Bright finish, set with 77 genuine pearls and 1 ruby doublet eye. Price...............$9.00

No. 4C11280 Bright finish, set with 40 pearls and 1 fire opal. Price.......... $4.00

No. 4C11281 Roman finish, hand engraved and hand chased; set with 18 pearls and 1 large fire opal. Ea...$6.75

No. 4C11284 Bright finish, set with 18 pearls and 1 fire opal. Price................$3.00

No. 4C11286 Bright finish, set with 24 pearls and 1 large fire opal. Price..... $9.00

No. 4C11287 Roman finish, hand engraved and hand chased; set with 6 whole pearls and 1 large fire opal. Price, $7.50

No. 4C11290 Roman Finish Sunburst Brooch; set with 9 very fine fire opals. Price............$10.50

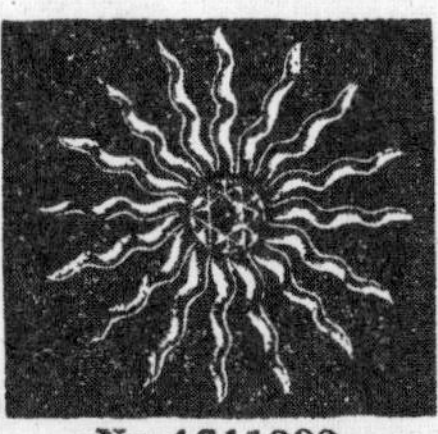

No. 4C11292 Bright finish, set with ruby doublet. Price............$3.75

No. 4C11294 Roman finish, hand engraved and hand chased; bright cut throughout; set with 48 genuine pearls and 1 large fire opal. Price $16.50

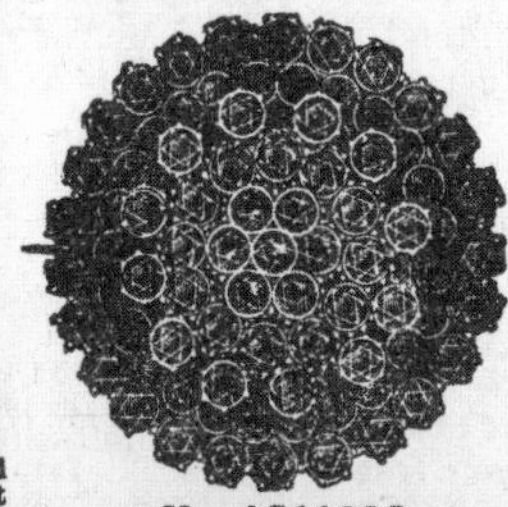

No. 4C11296 Bright finish, set with genuine Bohemian garnets. Price.$2.50

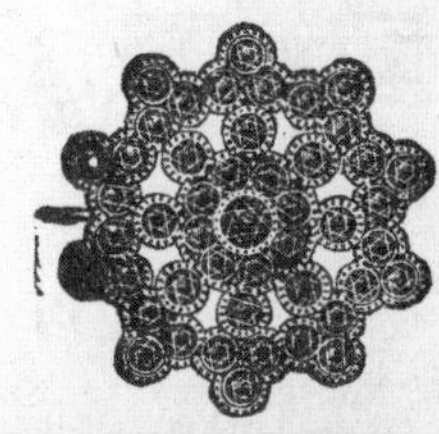

No. 4C11298 Bright finish, set with genuine Bohemian garnets. Price...............$1.25

FINEST QUALITY

GOLD FILLED, ROLLED GOLD PLATE AND SOLID GOLD EARRINGS AND DROPS.

POSTAGE EXTRA, 2 CENTS. REGISTERED MAIL, 8 CENTS EXTRA.

No. 4C11400 Rolled gold plate hoop rings, engraved, solid gold wires. Per pair, 35c.

No. 4C11402 Rolled gold plate hoop rings, engraved, solid gold wires. Per pair, 45c.

No. 4C11404 Solid gold fronts, hand engraved, ball pendants. Per pair, 50c.

No. 4C11406 Solid gold fronts, hand engraved, ball pendants. Per pair, 50c.

No. 4C11408 Solid gold fronts, hand engraved, ball pendants. Per pair, 65c.

No. 4C11410 Solid gold fronts, engraved, ball pendants. Per pair, 65c.

No. 4C11412 Solid gold fronts, rhinestone, solid gold wires. Per pair, $1.15.

No. 4C11414 Solid gold fronts, engraved, ball pendants. Per pair, 35c.

No. 4C11416 Solid gold fronts, hand engraved, ball pendants. Per pair, 65c.

No. 4C11420 Solid gold fronts, engraved, ball pendants. Per pair, 92c.

No. 4C11422 Solid gold fronts, engraved, with garnets. Per pair, $1.00.

No. 4C11424 Solid gold fronts, escalloped, set with garnets. Per pair, 75c.

No. 4C11426 Solid gold fronts, hand engraved, ball pendants. Per pair, 75c.

No. 4C11434 Solid gold fronts, hand engraved. Per pair, 50c.

No. 4C11436 Solid gold fronts, hand engraved, set with turquoise. Pr. 65c

No. 4C11438 Solid gold fronts, hand engraved, set with ruby. Per pair, 65c

14-KARAT SOLID GOLD EARRINGS, DROPS AND SETS.

No. 4C11440 Solid gold earrings, bright polish. Per pair.......65c

No. 4C11442 Solid gold hoop rings, faceted and polished. Per pair.......98c

No. 4C11444 Solid gold, plain hoop earrings. Per pair.....$1.00

No. 4C11446 Solid gold, with real pearls, ball pendants. Per pair...$1.00

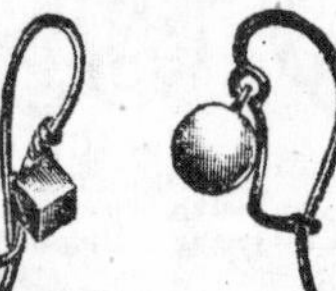
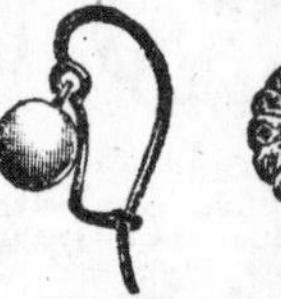

No. 4C11448 Solid gold, pearl center, ball pendants. Per pair $1.00

No. 4C11450 Solid gold, fancy turquoise center, ball pendants. Per pair $1.00

No. 4C11452 Solid gold, hand chased, ball pendants. Per pair $1.48

No. 4C11454 Solid gold, polished cube. Per pair $1.00

No. 4C11456 Solid gold, plain polished ball. Per pair.....$1.25

No. 4C11458 Solid gold, enameled, garnet center. Per pair.....$1.45

No. 4C11460 Solid gold, fancy setting, rhinestone set. Per pair.....$1.25

No. 4C11461 Solid gold, set with 7 genuine Bohemian garnets. Per pair.......96c

No. 4C11464 Solid gold, fancy setting, rhinestone set. Per pair.....$1.50

No. 4C11466 Solid gold setting, fancy top, rhinestone. Per pair.....$1.65

No. 4C11468 Solid gold, fancy setting, rhinestone. Per pair $2.00

No. 4C11470 Solid gold, engraved, very heavy rhinestone. Per pair...$4.50

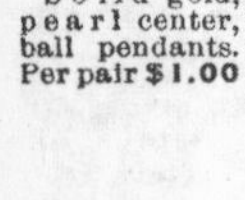

No. 4C11472 Solid gold, fancy cup setting, genuine pearl set. Per pair.....$1.60

No. 4C11474 Solid gold, fancy engrav'd garnet center. Per pair.....$1.48

No. 4C11476 Solid gold, fancy mounting, ruby set. Per pair $2.00

No. 4C11478 Solid gold, chased, Roman color, ruby set. Per pair $2.25

No. 4C11480 Solid gold, plain polished ball. Per pair.....$1.25

No. 4C11482 Solid gold, Roman knot, pearl center. Per pair $1.60

No. 4C11484 Solid gold, fancy setting, rhinestone. Per pair $2.00

No. 4C11486 Solid gold, three leaf clover, almandine set. Per pair.....$2.35

No. 4C11488 Solid gold, engraved, almandine set. Per pair $2.55

No. 4C11490 Solid gold, set with 12 rhinestones, one turquoise. Per pair $3.50

No. 4C11492 Solid gold, Roman knot, set with almandines. Per pair.....$1.30

No. 4C11494 Solid gold, fancy setting, set with rubies, Per pair $2.70

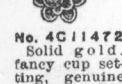

No. 4C11496 Solid gold, plain setting, set with pearls. Per pair $1.20

No. 4C11498 Solid gold, fancy Roman colored knot, set with opals. Per pair $2.35

MOURNING OR JET EAR DROPS, WITH SOLID GOLD WIRES.

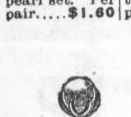

No. 4C11500 Ear Drops, jet balls, solid gold wires. Per pair...50c

No. 4C11502 Ear Drops, jet flowers, solid gold wires. Per pair.......65c

No. 4C11504 Ear Drops, jet flowers, gold ear wires. Per pair...75c

No. 4C11506 Ear Drops, jet flowers, gold wires. Per pair...70c

No. 4C11508 Ear Drops, jet cube, gold wires. Per pair.......45c

No. 4C11510 Jet Ear Drops. Per pair...50c

Illustrations Show Exact Size.

SOLID SILVER, GOLD FILLED, ROLLED GOLD PLATE AND SOLID GOLD CROSSES.

POSTAGE ON CROSSES, 3 CENTS EXTRA; INSURANCE OR REGISTRY EXTRA.

No. 4C11512 Rolled plate, engraved. Price.......25c

No. 4C11513 Gold filled cross, set with imitation pearls and ruby center. The latest idea, very fashionable. Price, 95c

No. 4C11514 Gold filled, set with almandines and 1 brilliant. Price..90c

No. 4C11516 Solid gold front, fancy engraved, satin finish. Price........80c

No. 4C11517 Gold filled cross, set with imitation rubies. The latest idea, very fashionable. Price. ...$1.15

No. 4C11518 Fine solid gold, fancy engraved, satin finish. Price.....$1.48

No. 4C11519 Solid silver. Price.. ...22c
No. 4C11521 Gold filled, bright burnished. Price. 28c
No. 4C11523 Solid gold. Price.. .....$1.20

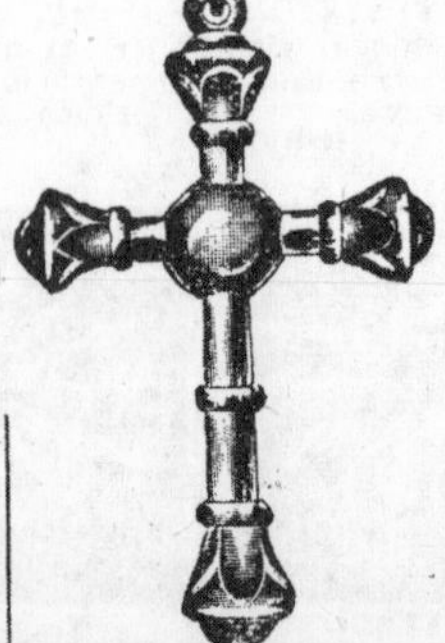

No. 4C11524 Gold filled, bright burnished. Price, 80c

No. 4C11525 Solid Silver. Price........32c
No. 4C11527 Gold filled, set with turquoise. Price........35c
No. 4C11529 Solid gold. Price......$1.45

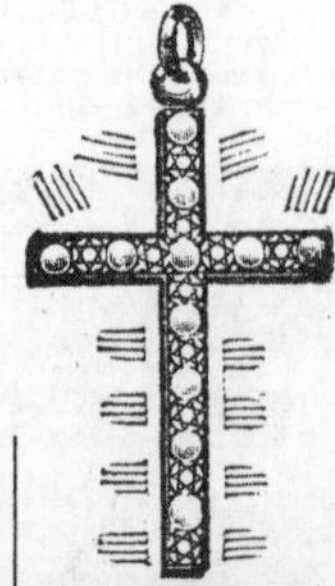

No. 4C11530 God front, set with pearls and rhinestones. Price...$1.65

SPECIAL VALUES IN GOLD PLATED JEWELRY.

A GROWING DEMAND from clothing stores, furnishing goods stores, dry goods stores, traders and others for a grade of gold plated jewelry such as is commonly sold by retail clothiers and dry goods merchants, has induced us to add the following special lines of gold plated jewelry, to our already big line of the highest grade gold plated, gold filled and solid gold jewelry.

THERE IS A GREAT DEMAND among our millions of customers, those who buy for their own use, as well as those who buy to sell again, for a dependable quality of gold plated jewelry that can be sold at a fraction of the price we are compelled to ask for the highest grades of gold plated and gold filled and solid gold jewelry, such as is shown in the other pages of this catalogue.

TO SUPPLY THIS DEMAND, on the following pages we show a variety of jewelry in the very latest styles and patterns which we offer at the lowest price at which any dependable grade of gold plated jewelry can possibly be offered, and at prices very much lower than the same grade of jewelry is or has ever been offered by any other house in any quantity.

THE SPECIAL GOLD PLATED JEWELRY which we offer on the following pages is not to be compared with any of the cheap electro plated jewelry that is so widely advertised and sold by cheap jewelry houses, peddlers, etc. Every piece of jewelry illustrated is well made and beautifully finished, all nicely gold plated, highly polished and finished, and has all the appearance of the higher grade of gold plated and gold filled jewelry which sells at several times the price we ask.

THIS IS THE EXACT SAME GRADE of gold plated jewelry as you will find in the best dry goods stores as well as in many of the most representative retail jewelry stores. For example, the cuff buttons and cuff links which we offer at from 10 to 20 cents each (special prices in dozen lots), are the exact same links and buttons that retail generally at from 25 to 50 cents per pair. The handsome, new style brooches which we offer at 10 to 25 cents are the exact same style and grade of gold plated goods that retail generally at 25 cents to $1.00. The stick pins, scarf pins and other pieces of gold plated jewelry shown in this line, which we offer at 10 to 20 cents (special prices per dozen quantities), are the exact same goods that retail everywhere at from 25 to 50 cents each. The chains which we show in a big variety, at prices ranging from 10 to 50 cents each (special prices in dozen quantities), are the exact same new, late style goods that are retailed generally at from 50 cents to $1.50.

WHILE WE DO NOT GUARANTEE THE WEARING QUALITIES of this grade of jewelry, as before stated, it is the exact same grade of gold plated jewelry that is sold largely by dealers under one, two and three year guarantees at from two to ten times the price we ask. The length of time any piece of this jewelry will wear without the gold wearing off and without tarnishing or discoloring depends on the kind of wear the piece of jewelry gets. For example, a scarf pin, brooch, charm or cuff button will wear much longer than a ring. Every piece we offer will give the best of satisfaction and we guarantee it the equal of any gold plated jewelry retailed generally at from two to five times the price we ask.

SPECIAL OPPORTUNITY FOR DEALERS, JEWELERS, CLOTHIERS, GENERAL STORES, TRADERS AND OTHERS TO BUY IN QUANTITIES AT HERETOFORE UNHEARD OF LOW PRICES.

WE ARE SELLING THIS JEWELRY AT PRICES MUCH LOWER than the same grade of jewelry was ever sold by any manufacturer or wholesale dealer. At our special prices you can supply your wants at a much lower cost than you have ever before been able to buy. If you have a general store or are engaged in the clothing, dry goods or furnishing goods business and do not carry a stock of jewelry, we especially urge that you order a small assortment selected from the following pages. We will guarantee you will find the goods the very latest style, gold plated goods that will give satisfaction, an assortment of gold plated jewelry that will find ready sale with your trade and at prices from three to five times the price you pay us. If you don't carry jewelry, put in a little stock, if only an assortment of $5.00 or $10.00, and you will be surprised how rapidly these goods will sell. A $10.00 assortment at our prices, as selected from these pages, would, at average retail prices, bring $50.00 to $75.00, and we are sure if you make the start you will in time carry a liberal stock and add greatly to your profit by the small investment made.

DEALERS AND TRADERS are especially urged to make up a small order of this popular priced gold plated jewelry as selected from these pages. Make up a $5.00 assortment, if you please, and the shrewd peddler or trader will be able to sell the lot for at least $25.00.

WHILE THE VERY LOW PRICES at which we sell this popular grade of gold plated jewelry will attract thousands of our customers, who may wish to buy one item for their own use, the prices we offer enable you to buy for 10 or 15 cents, one article for which you would have to pay at retail from 25 cents to $1.00. This grade of gold plated jewelry is offered especially to supply the retail jeweler, the peddler and the trader who wishes to buy in dozen lots and take advantage of our very low prices, prices much lower than were ever before quoted on this grade of goods.

YOU WILL NOTE UNDER EACH ARTICLE OF JEWELRY we quote the single price, also the price per one-half dozen and the price per dozen, making a special price where orders are placed for dozen lots, and in ordering a dozen you are at liberty to assort the dozen. For example, if you are selecting cuff buttons and wish to take advantage of our dozen price you can make up the dozen by selecting one or two of each number at the same price. For instance, there may be one-half dozen numbers that sell at $1.50 a dozen, in which case you are at liberty to select two of each number and get the benefit of the dozen price. In this way it gives the dealer, the peddler or the trader an opportunity to get together a very attractive assortment of the showiest cheap gold plated jewelry made for a very small investment. Just a few dollars, $5.00 to $10.00, would make up an assortment of jewelry that would prove very attractive in any clothing store, dry goods store, general store or in the stock of any peddler or trader.

REMEMBER, THESE ARE BEAUTIFUL GOODS, handsomely finished and highly polished, all gold plated, the same grade of latest style goods as is handled usually by the retail clothing trade and dry goods trade, but none of this jewelry is guaranteed by us, nor will it be replaced or repaired by us after being worn except when otherwise specified. We will fill any order for this jewelry, sending it to anyone with the understanding and agreement that if it isn't perfectly satisfactory when received, it can be returned to us at our expense, and the money sent us will be immediately refunded, together with any express charges paid by the customer, but after the jewelry has been worn, used or carried in stock, or offered for sale, it is not returnable to us and no repairs will be made on it by us. If you wish to buy jewelry which is guaranteed to wear for years you should select the higher grade gold plated, gold filled and solid gold jewelry shown in this catalogue.

REMEMBER, WE ACCEPT NO ORDER FOR LESS THAN 50 CENTS. If you wish to buy an item of jewelry for your own use, the price of which is less than 50 cents, select enough more needed jewelry or other merchandise to make your order amount to 50 cents or more.

Collar Button Price List, No. 4C15000 to No. 4C15100.

To order correctly, give catalogue number for shape wanted and letter as shown for quality and style desired.

		Price for 1 Dozen only	Price for ½ Gross only	Price per Gross, for 1 Gross or more
A	Gold plated top, post and bottom	$0.18	$1.05	$2.00
B	Gold plated, with pearl bottom	.28	1.58	3.00
C	Gold plated, with celluloid bottom	.18	1.05	2.00
D	Second quality, rolled gold plated top, post and bottom	.36	2.10	4.00
E	Second quality, rolled gold plated, with pearl bottom	.39	2.23	4.25
F	Second quality, rolled gold plated, with celluloid bottom	.36	2.10	4.00
G	First quality, rolled gold plated top, post and bottom	.69	3.94	7.50
H	First quality, rolled gold plated, with pearl bottom	.73	4.20	8.00
I	First quality, rolled gold plated, with celluloid bottom	.69	3.94	7.50

No. 4C15000 Large size pointer.

No. 4C15010 Narrow shape pointer.

No. 4C15020 Small size pointer.

No. 4C15030 Large size lever.

No. 4C15040 Medium size lever.

No. 4C15050 Tall flat top post.

No. 4C15060 Medium flat top post.

No. 4C15070 Medium size ball top.

No 4C15080 Large size ball top.

No. 4C15090 Wedge shape, large size, solid post.

No. 4C15100 Wedge shape, small size, solid post.

No. 4C15120 Separable, engraved top, solid silver bottom.
One dozen.. $0.69
Half gross.. 3.94
One gross.. 7.50

No. 4C15130 Separable, celluloid bottom, fancy stone set.
One dozen.. $0.48
Half gross.. 2.76
One gross.. 5.25

No. 4C15140 Separable, pearl setting, celluloid bottom.
One dozen, $0.58
Half gross, 3.35
One gross.. 6.38

Collar Button Sets, Consisting of Two Lever, One Ball Top and One Pointer.

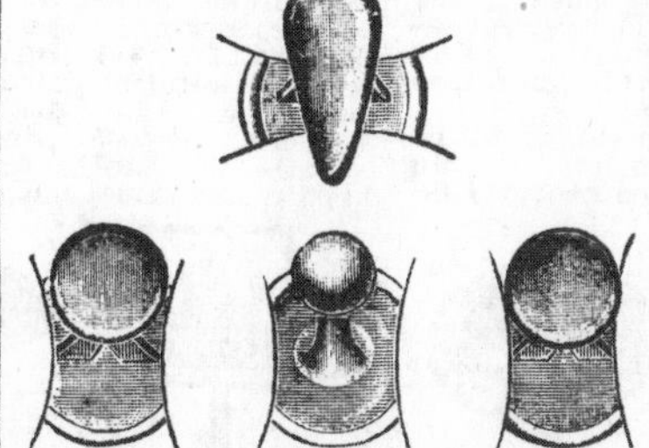

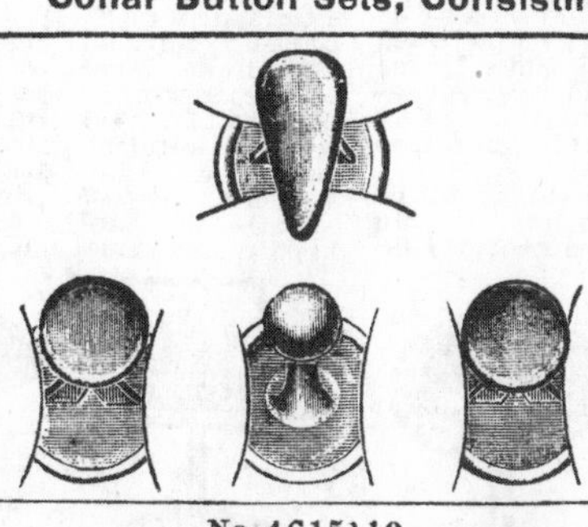

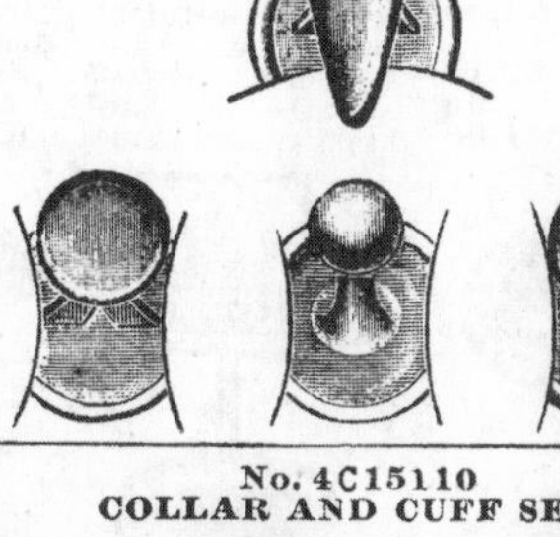

No. 4C15110
COLLAR AND CUFF SETS.

No. 4C15110
Collar Button Set Price List.
To order correctly, give catalogue number of set and letter for quality desired.

		Price for 1 Dozen Sets only	Price for ½ Gross Sets only	Price for 1 Gross Sets or more
A	Gold plated top post and bottom	$0.72	$4.20	$8.00
B	Gold plated top post, pearl bottom	1.12	6.32	12.00
C	Gold plated top post, celluloid bottom	.72	4.20	8.00
D	Second quality rolled gold plated top post and bottom	1.44	8.40	16.00
E	Second quality rolled gold plated top post with pearl bottom	1.56	8.92	17.00
F	Second quality rolled gold plated top post with celluloid bottom	1.44	8.40	16.00
G	First quality rolled gold plated top post and bottom	2.76	15.76	30.00
H	First quality rolled gold plated top post with pearl bottom	2.93	16.80	32.00
I	First quality rolled gold plated top post with celluloid bottom	2.76	15.76	30.00

No. 4C15150 Separable, rhinestone, pearl set top, celluloid bottom.
One dozen.. $0.58
Half gross.. 3.35
One gross.. 6.38

No. 4C15160 Separable, rhinestone, pearl set top, celluloid bottom.
One dozen.. $0.48
Half gross.. 2.76
One gross.. 5.25

No. 4C15170 Separable, fancy stone set, pearl bottom.
One dozen.. $0.58
Half gross.. 3.35
One gross.. 6.38

No. 4C15180 Bone collar button, one piece.
One dozen...... 5c
One gross... 50c

No. 4C15190 Bone collar button, one piece.
One dozen...... 6c
One gross.... 65c

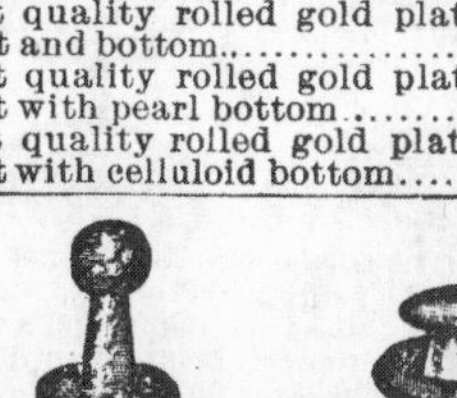

No. 4C15200 Pearl collar button, one piece.
One dozen.... 46c

No. 4C15210 Pearl collar button, one piece.
One dozen.... 42c

No. 4C15220 Pearl collar button, one piece.
One dozen.. 52c

No. 4C15230 Gold plated, bright finished lever end cuff links, set with assorted fancy stones.
Per pair....$0.10
6 pairs..... .53
12 pairs..... 1.00

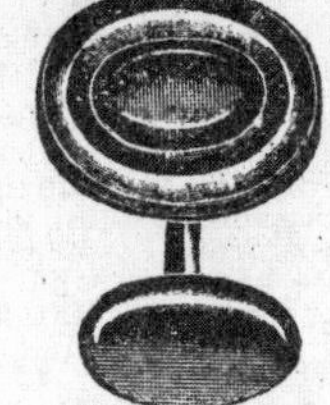

No. 4C15235 Gold plated, bright polished cuff links, lever ends, set with large imitation garnet carbuncle.
Per pair....$0.10
6 pairs..... .53
12 pairs..... 1.00

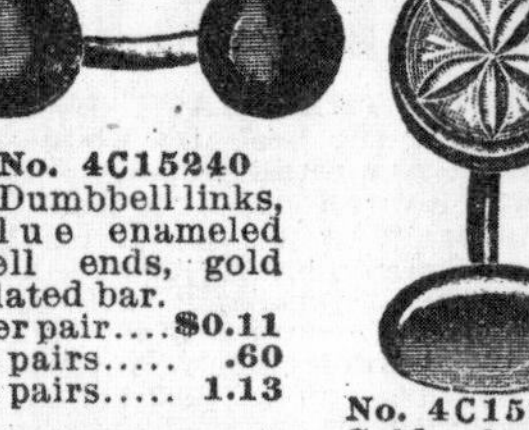

No. 4C15240 Dumbbell links, blue enameled bell ends, gold plated bar.
Per pair....$0.11
6 pairs..... .60
12 pairs..... 1.13

No. 4C15245 Dumbbell links, white enameled bell ends, gold plated bar mountings.
Per pair....$0.11
6 pairs..... .60
12 pairs..... 1.13

No. 4C15250 Gold plated, bright polished cuff links, lever ends, hand carved mother of pearl setting.
Per pair....$0.11
6 pairs..... .60
12 pairs..... 1.13

No. 4C15255 Gold plated, bean end cuff links, bright polish, raised ornamentation, hard soldered throughout.
Per pair....$0.14
6 pairs..... .79
12 pairs..... 1.50

No. 4C15260 Gold plated, bright polished cuff links, lever ends, raised ornamentation.
Per pair....$0.14
6 pairs..... .79
12 pairs..... 1.50

No. 4C15265 Gold plated, bright polished cuff links, lever ends, raised ornamentation.
Per pair....$0.14
6 pairs..... .79
12 pairs..... 1.50

No. 4C15270 Gold plated, bright polished cuff links, raised ornamentation, lever ends.
Per pair..$0.14
6 pairs.. .79
12 pairs... 1.50

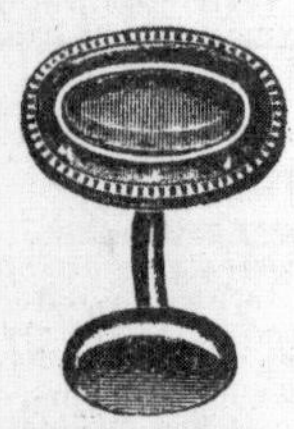

No. 4C15275 Gold plated, bright finished cuff links, bean ends, set with large imitation opal.
Per pair....$0.14
6 pairs..... .79
12 pairs..... 1.50

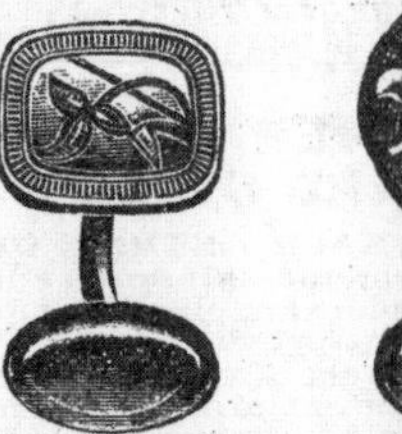

No. 4C15280 Gold plated, bright polished cuff links, lever ends, engraved ornamentation, hard soldered.
Per pair....$0.16
6 pairs..... .89
12 pairs.... 1.69

No. 4C15285 Gold plated, bright finished cuff links, lever ends, raised ornamentation.
Per pair....$0.16
6 pairs..... .89
12 pairs..... 1.69

No. 4C15290 Pearl cuff links, gold plated, lever ends.
Per pair....$0.16
6 pairs..... .89
12 pairs..... 1.69

No. 4C15295 Gold plated, bright polished cuff links, lever ends, raised ornamentation.
Per pair....$0.16
6 pairs..... .89
12 pairs..... 1.69

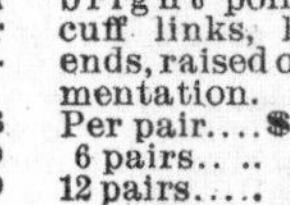

No. 4C15300 Gold plated, bright polished cuff links, lever ends, raised ornamentation.
Per pair....$0.16
6 pairs..... .89
12 pairs..... 1.69

No. 4C15305 Gold plated, bright polished cuff links, lever ends, perfectly plain finished.
Per pair....$0.16
6 pairs... .89
12 pairs... 1.69

No. 4C15310 Gold plated, bright polished cuff links, bean ends, hard soldered throughout.
Per pair..$0.17
6 pairs... .99
12 pairs... 1.88

No. 4C15315 Gold plated, bright polished cuff links, lever ends, hard enameled in various colors.
Per pair....$0.17
6 pairs..... .99
12 pairs..... 1.88

No. 4C15320 Gold plated, bright polished cuff links, bean ends, hard soldered throughout, raised ornamentation of horse's head.
Per pair....$0.17
6 pairs..... .99
12 pairs.... 1.88

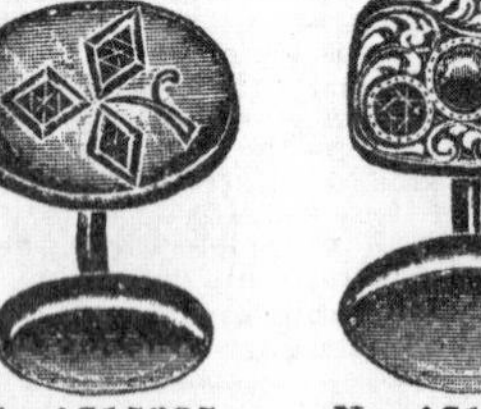

No. 4C15325 Gold plated, bright polished cuff links, lever ends, set with assorted stones.
Per pair....$0.17
6 pairs... .99
12 pairs..... 1.88

No. 4C15330 Gold plated, bright polished cuff links, lever ends, raised ornamentation, set with fancy stones.
Per pair....$0.17
6 pairs..... .99
12 pairs..... 1.88

No. 4C15335 Gold plated, bright polished cuff links, lever ends, raised ornamentation.
Per pair....$0.17
6 pairs.... .99
12 pairs..... 1.88

No. 4C15340 Gold plated, bright polished cuff links, lever ends, raised ornamentation, set with mother of pearl.
Per pair....$0.17
6 pairs..... .99
12 pairs..... 1.88

No. 4C15345 Gold plated, bright polished cuff links, lever ends, set with imitation opal.
Per pair....$0.17
6 pairs..... .99
12 pairs..... 1.88

No. 4C15350 Gold plated, bright polished cuff links, bean ends, raised ornamentation, set with imitation opal.
Per pair..$0.17
6 pairs.. .99
12 pairs.. 1.88

No. 4C15355 Gold plated, bright polished cuff links, bean ends, imitation gold front, hand engraved ornamentation.
Per pair....$0.17
6 pairs..... .99
12 pairs..... 1.88

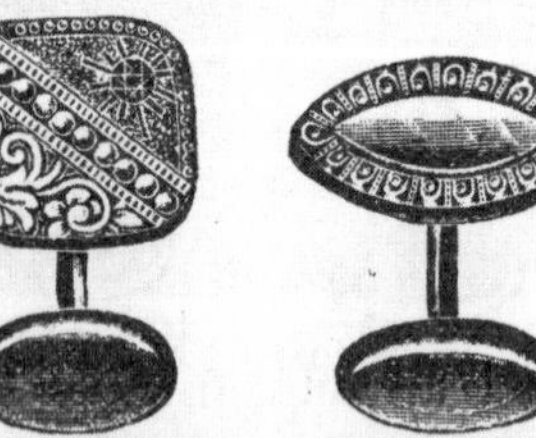

No. 4C15360 Gold plated, bright polished cuff links, lever ends, raised ornamentation, set with imitation amethyst.
Per pair....$0.17
6 pairs..... .99
12 pairs..... 1.88

No. 4C15365 Gold plated, bright polished cuff links, lever ends, raised ornamentation.
Per pair....$0.17
6 pairs..... .99
12 pairs..... 1.88

No. 4C15370 Gold plated, bright polished cuff links, lever ends, raised ornamentation, set with imitation opal.
Per pair....$0.17
6 pairs..... .99
12 pairs..... 1.88

No. 4C15375 Gold plated, bright polished cuff links, lever ends, raised ornamentation, set with imitation turquoise.
Per pair....$0.17
6 pairs..... .99
12 pairs..... 1.88

No. 4C15380 Gold plated, bright polished cuff links, bean ends, raised ornamentation, set with imitation turquoise.
Per pair....$0.17
6 pairs..... .99
12 pairs..... 1.88

No. 4C15385 Gold plated, bright polished cuff links, bean ends, hard soldered, enameled in fancy colors.
Per pair....$0.17
6 pairs..... .99
12 pairs..... 1.88

No. 4C15390 Gold plated, roman satin finished cuff links, set with imitation pearl.
Per pair..$0.17
6 pairs.. .99
12 pairs.. 1.88

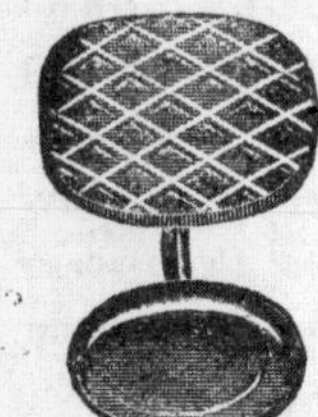

No. 4C15395 Pearl cuff links, gold plated, lever ends, hand carved.
Per pair....$0.17
6 pairs.... .99
12 pairs.... 1.88

No. 4C15400 Gold plated, bright polished cuff links, lever ends, set with imitation emerald, engraved ornamentation.
Per pair....$0.17
6 pairs.... .99
12 pairs.... 1.88

No. 4C15405 Gold plated, bright polished cuff links, lever ends, set with imitation sapphire.
Per pair....$0.17
6 pairs..... .99
12 pairs..... 1.88

No. 4C15410 Gold plated, bright polished cuff links, bean ends, set with large carbuncle.
Per pair....$0.17
6 pairs..... .99
12 pairs..... 1.88

No. 4C15415 Gold plated, bright polished cuff links, lever ends, engraved ornamentation, imitation gold front.
Per pair....$0.17
6 pairs..... .99
12 pairs..... 1.88

No. 4C15420 Gold plated, bright polished cuff links, lever ends, raised ornamentation, set with fancy stones.
Per pair....$0.17
6 pairs..... .99
12 pairs..... 1.88

No. 4C15425 Gold plated, bright polished cuff links, lever ends, set with imitation rubies.
Per pair....$0.17
6 pairs..... .99
12 pairs..... 1.88

No. 4C15430 Gold plated, bright polished cuff links, lever ends, raised ornamentation, set with imitation rubies.
Per pair..$0.17
6 pairs.. .99
12 pairs.. 1.88

No. 4C15435 Gold plated, bright polished cuff links, lever end, raised ornamentation.
Per pair....$0.17
6 pairs..... .99
12 pairs..... 1.88

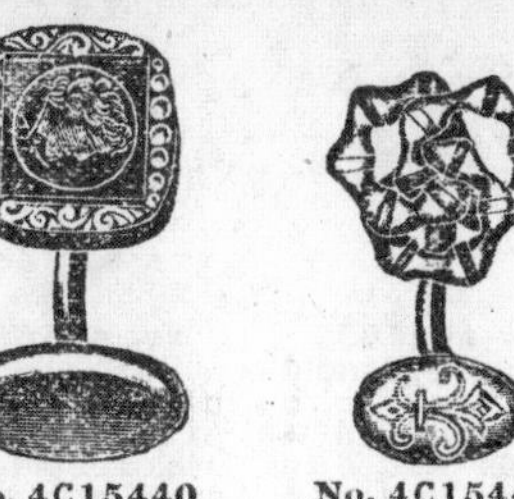

No. 4C15440 Gold plated, bright polished cuff links, lever end, set with imitation intaglio.
Per pair....$0.17
6 pairs..... .99
12 pairs..... 1.88

No. 4C15445 Gold plated, bright polished cuff links, bean end, fancy colors, hard enameled ornamentation.
Per pair....$0.17
6 pairs..... .99
12 pairs..... 1.88

No. 4C15450 Gold plated, bright polished cuff links, bean end, set with large gold stone.
Per pair....$0.17
6 pairs..... .99
12 pairs..... 1.88

No. 4C15455 Gold plated, bright polished cuff links, lever end, set with imitation opal.
Per pair....$0.17
6 pairs..... .99
12 pairs..... 1.88

No. 4C15460 Gold plated, bright polished cuff links, lever end, set with imitation sapphire.
Per pair....$0.17
6 pairs..... .99
12 pairs..... 1.88

No. 4C15465 Gold plated, bright polished cuff links, lever end, set with imitation turquoise.
Per pair....$0.17
6 pairs..... .99
12 pairs..... 1.88

No. 4C15470 Gold plated, bright polished cuff links, lever end, raised ornamentation.
Per pair..$0.17
6 pairs... .99
12 pairs... 1.88

No. 4C15475 Gold plated, bright polished cuff links, lever end, raised ornamentation, set with imitation amethyst.
Per pair....$0.17
6 pairs..... .99
12 pairs..... 1.88

No. 4C15480 Gold plated, bright polished cuff buttons, set with imitation sardonyx intaglio
Per pair....$0.06
6 pairs..... .30
12 pairs..... .56

No. 4C15485 Gold plated, bright polished cuff buttons, fancy stone setting.
Per pair....$0.06
6 pairs..... .30
12 pairs..... .56

No. 4C15490 Gold plated, bright polished cuff buttons, set with fancy stone.
Per pair....$0.06
6 pairs..... .30
12 pairs..... .56

No. 4C15495 Gold plated, bright polished cuff buttons, set with imitation cameo.
Per pair....$0.06
6 pairs..... .30
12 pairs..... .56

No. 4C15500 Gold plated, bright polished cuff buttons, ornamented with imitation tortoise shell.
Per pair....$0.06
6 pairs..... .30
12 pairs..... .56

No. 4C15505 Gold plated, bright polished cuff buttons, for ladies, mother of pearl setting.
Per pair....$0.11
6 pairs..... .60
12 pairs..... 1.13

No. 4C15510 Gold plated, bright polished cuff buttons, raised ornamentation, set with mother of pearl.
Per pair..$0.11
6 pairs... .60
12 pairs... 1.13

No. 4C15515 Mother of pearl plain polished cuff buttons.
Per pair....$0.12
6 pairs..... .70
12 pairs..... 1.32

No. 4C15520 Gold plated, bright polished cuff buttons, set with large imitation emerald.
Per pair....$0.11
6 pairs..... .60
12 pairs..... 1.13

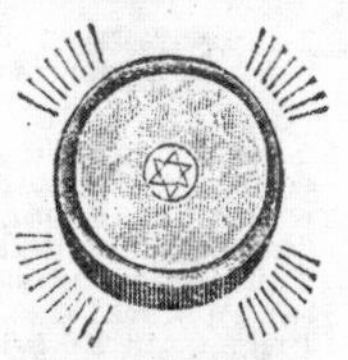

No. 4C15525 Gold plated, bright polished cuff buttons, set with mother of pearl with rhinestone center.
Per pair....$0.12
6 pairs..... .70
12 pairs..... 1.32

No. 4C15530 Gold plated, bright polished cuff buttons, set with fancy stones.
Per pair....$0.16
6 pairs..... .89
12 pairs..... 1.69

No. 4C15535 Gold plated, bright polished cuff buttons, raised ornamentation.
Per pair....$0.16
6 pairs..... .89
12 pairs..... 1.69

No. 4C15540 Gold plated, bright polished cuff buttons, raised ornamentation.
Per pair....$0.16
6 pairs..... .89
12 pairs..... 1.69

No. 4C15545 Mother of pearl cuff buttons, plain polished.
Per pair....$0.16
6 pairs..... .89
12 pairs..... 1.69

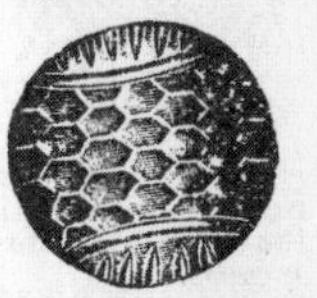

No. 4C15550 Mother of pearl cuff buttons, hand carved.
Per pair..$0.16
6 pairs... .89
12 pairs... 1.69

No. 4C15555 Gold plated, bright polished cuff buttons, raised ornamented border.
Per pair....$0.17
6 pairs..... .99
12 pairs..... 1.88

No. 4C15560 Gold plated, bright polished cuff buttons, raised ornamentation, imitation hand carving.
Per pair....$0.17
6 pairs..... .99
12 pairs..... 1.88

No. 4C15565 Gold plated, bright polished cuff buttons, imitation hand carving.
Per pair....$0.17
6 pairs..... .99
12 pairs..... 1.88

No. 4C15570 Gold plated, bright polished cuff buttons, set with imitation opals.
Per pair....$0.17
6 pairs..... .99
12 pairs..... 1.88

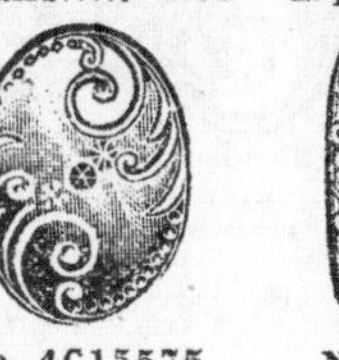

No. 4C15575 Gold plated, bright polished cuff buttons, raised oramentation, set with imitation emerald.
Per pair....$0.17
6 pairs..... .99
12 pairs..... 1.88

No. 4C15580 Gold plated, bright polished cuff buttons, raised ornamentation, fancy border.
Per pair...$0.17
6 pairs..... .99
12 pairs..... 1.88

No. 4C15585 Gold plated, bright and roman satin finished cuff buttons, raised ornamentation, set with imitation ruby.
Per pair....$0.17
6 pairs..... .99
12 pairs..... 1.88

No. 4C15590 Gold plated, bright polished cuff buttons, richly ornamented with engraving, imitation gold front.
Per pair..$0.17
6 pairs.. .99
12 pairs... 1.88

No. 4C15595 Gold plated, bright polished cuff buttons, ornamented with engraving, imitation gold front.
Per pair....$0.17
6 pairs..... .99
12 pairs..... 1.88

No. 4C15600 Gold plated, bright finished cuff buttons, raised ornamentation, set with imitation diamonds.
Per pair....$0.17
6 pairs..... .99
12 pairs..... 1.88

No. 4C15605 Mother of pearl cuff buttons, hand carved, with gold strip ornamentation.
Per pair....$0.19
6 pairs..... 1.08
12 pairs..... 2.00

No. 4C15610 Gold plated, bright polished cuff buttons, set with imitation diamonds.
Per pair....$0.19
6 pairs..... 1.08
12 pairs..... 2.00

No. 4C15615 Gold plated, bright polished cuff buttons, set with gold stone center.
Per pair....$0.19
6 pairs..... 1.08
12 pairs..... 2.00

REMEMBER

WE GUARANTEE TO SATISFY YOU
in every way and give you
MUCH BETTER VALUES
than you could secure elsewhere, otherwise, you can return the goods to us and we will immediately return your money.

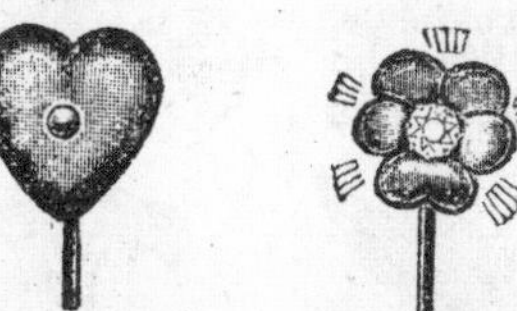

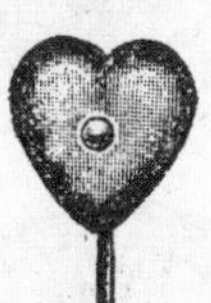

No. 4C15620 Scarf pin, gold plate, roman finish, set with one imitation pearl.
Price, each.$0.05
6 for....... .24
12 for....... .44

No. 4C15625 Scarf pin, gold plate, roman finish, fancy enameled, set with 1 imitation diamond.
Price, each.$0.05
6 for....... .24
12 for.... .44

No. 4C15630 Scarf pin, gold plate, bright finish, set with one large imitation opal.
Price, each.$0.06
6 for....... .30
12 for....... .56

No. 4C15635 Scarf pin, gold plate, one large imitation diamond.
Price, each.$0.06
6 for....... .30
12 for....... .56

No. 4C15640 Scarf pin, gold plate, set with one imitation diamond.
Price, each.$0.06
6 for....... .30
12 for....... .56

No. 4C15645 Scarf pin, gold plate, set with one imitation diamond.
Price, each.$0.06
6 for....... .30
12 for....... .56

No. 4C15650 Scarf pin, gold plate, roman color, fancy enameled, set with one imitation pearl.
Price, each.$0.06
6 for....... .30
12 for....... .56

No. 4C15655 Scarf pin, gold plate, bright polish, set with one large Egyptian pearl.
Price, ea..$0.07
6 for..... .40
12 for..... .75

No. 4C15660 Scarf pin, gold plate, bright finish, set with imitation pearls.
Price, each, $0.07
6 for ... .40
12 for ... .75

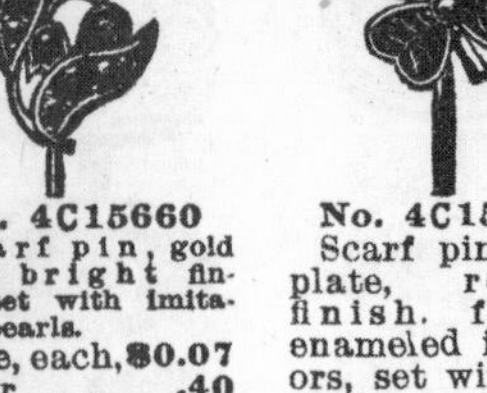

No. 4C15665 Scarf pin, gold plate, roman finish, fancy enameled in colors, set with imitation opal.
Price, each, $0.09
6 for ... .53
12 for ... 1.00

No. 4C15670 Scarf pin, gold plate, roman finish, fancy enameled in colors, set with imitation turquoise.
Price, each, $0.09
6 for ... .53
12 for ... 1.00

No. 4C15675 Scarf pin, gold plate, fancy enameled in colors, set with imitation turquoise.
Price, each, $0.09
6 for ... .53
12 for ... 1.00

No. 4C15680 Scarf pin, gold plate, roman color, enameled, set with one imitation diamond.
Price, each, $0.09
6 for ... .53
12 for ... 1.00

No. 4C15685 Scarf pin, gold plate, set with imitation diamonds and one large imitation opal.
Price, each, $0.09
6 for ... .53
12 for ... 1.00

No. 4C15690 Scarf pin, gold plate, bright plain polish, ornamented by engraving.
Price, each, $0.09
6 for ... .53
12 for ... 1.00

No. 4C15695 Scarf pin, roman color, set with three Egyptian pearls.
Price, ea., $0.10
6 for ... .58
12 for ... 1.12

No. 4C15700 Scarf pin, gold plate, bright finish, ornamented with engraving.
Price, each, $0.10
6 for ... .58
12 for ... 1.12

No. 4C15705 Scarf pin, gold plate, bright finish, fancy enameled.
Price, each, $0.10
6 for ... .58
12 for ... 1.12

No. 4C15710 Scarf pin, gold plate, bright polish, raised ornamentation, set with imitation opal.
Price, each, $0.10
6 for ... .58
12 for ... 1.12

No. 4C15715 Scarf pin, gold plate, bright finish, set with four imitation diamonds and one large Egyptian pearl.
Price, each, $0.17
6 for ... .92
12 for ... 1.75

No. 4C15720 Scarf pin, gold plate, bright finish, set with imitation diamonds.
Price, each, $0.17
6 for ... .92
12 for ... 1.75

No. 4C15725 Scarf pin, gold plate, set with imitation diamonds.
Price, each, $0.17
6 for ... .92
12 for ... 1.75

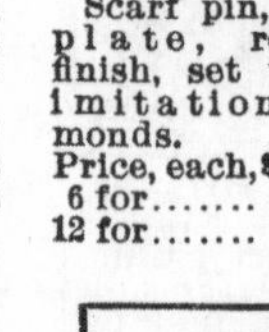

No. 4C15730 Scarf pin, gold plate, roman finish, set with imitation diamonds.
Price, each, $0.17
6 for ... .92
12 for ... 1.75

No. 4C15735 Scarf pin, gold plate, roman finish, set with imitation diamonds.
Price, ea., $0.18
6 for ... 1.05
12 for ... 2.00

No. 4C15740 Scarf pin, gold plate, roman color, set with imitation diamonds.
Price, each, $0.18
6 for ... 1.05
12 for ... 2.00

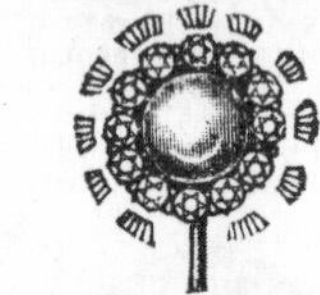

No. 4C15745 Scarf pin, gold plate, bright finish, set with four imitation diamonds.
Price, each, $0.18
6 for ... 1.05
12 for ... 2.00

No. 4C15750 Scarf pin, gold plate, set with imitation diamonds and one large Egyptian pearl.
Price, each, $0.24
6 for ... 1.38
12 for ... 2.63

No. 4C15755 Shirt stud, gold plate, set with imitation diamond called Venezuelan crystal, ¼-karat size.
Price, each, $0.06
6 for ... .30
12 for ... .56

No. 4C15760 Shirt stud, gold plate, set with imitation diamond, called Venezuelan crystal, ¾-karat size.
Price, each, $0.06
6 for ... .30
12 for ... .56

No. 4C15765 Shirt stud, gold plate, set with imitation diamond, called Venezuelan crystal, 1¼-karat size.
Price, each, $0.06
6 for ... .30
12 for ... .56

REMEMBER

WE ACCEPT NO ORDER FOR LESS THAN 50 CENTS.

— ALSO THAT —

WE WILL NOT REPAIR OR EXCHANGE ANY OF THESE GOODS AFTER THEY HAVE BEEN WORN.

No. 4C15770 Fancy brooch, gold plate, roman finish, ornamented with enamel, imitation ruby in center.
Price, each ... $0.09
6 for ... .50
12 for ... .94

No. 4C15775 Brooch, gold plate, bright polish, raised ornamentation.
Price, each ... $0.09
6 for ... .50
12 for ... .94

No. 4C15780 Fancy lace pin, gold plate, bright finish, raised ornamentation.
Price, each ... $0.11
6 for ... .60
12 for ... 1.13

No. 4C15785 Fancy lace pin, gold plate, bright polish, raised ornamentation.
Price, each ... $0.11
6 for ... .60
12 for ... 1.13

No. 4C15790 Fancy brooch, gold plate, bright polish, raised ornamentation, set with imitation turquoise.
Price, each ... $0.11
6 for ... .60
12 for ... 1.13

No. 4C15795 Fancy brooch, gold plate bright polish, set with one imitation diamond in center.
Price, each ... $0.12
6 for ... .70
12 for ... 1.32

No. 4C15800 Fancy brooch, black enameled, for mourners.
Price, each ... $0.12
6 for ... .70
12 for ... 1.32

No. 4C15805 Fancy chatelette, gold plate, bright polish, raised ornamentation. Hook to suspend watch on.
Price, each ... $0.14
6 for ... .79
12 for ... 1.50

No. 4C15810 Fancy brooch, roman finish, gold plate, fancy enameled, set with 1 large imitation opal.
Price, each ... $0.16
6 for ... .89
12 for ... 1.69

No. 4C15815 Fancy brooch, gold plate, bright polish, set with 7 imitation diamonds.
Price, each ... $0.16
6 for ... .89
12 for ... 1.69

No. 4C15820 Black enameled brooch for mourners.
Price, each ... $0.12
6 for ... .70
12 for ... 1.32

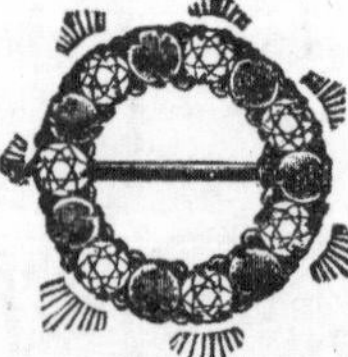

No. 4C15825 Fancy brooch, gold plate, roman finish, set with imitation diamonds and 7 turquoise.
Price, each ... $0.14
6 for ... .79
12 for ... 1.50

No. 4C15830 Fancy brooch, gold plate, roman finish, set with imitation diamonds.
Price, each ... $0.14
6 for ... .79
12 for ... 1.50

No. 4C15835 Fancy brooch, gold plate, bright polish, set with seven imitation diamonds.
Price, each ... $0.16
6 for ... .89
12 for ... 1.69

No. 4C15840 Fancy brooch, gold plate, bright finish, blue enameled, set with imitation pearl.
Price, each ... $0.16
6 for ... .89
12 for ... 1.69

No. 4C15845 Fancy brooch, gold plate, bright finish, black enameled, set with imitation pearl.
Price, each ... $0.16
6 for ... .89
12 for ... 1.69

No. 4C15850 Fancy chatelette, gold plate, roman finish, enameled in blue and white. Hook to suspend watch on.
Price, each ... $0.17
6 for ... .99
12 for ... 1.88

No. 4C15855 Fancy bar pin, gold plate, roman finish, set with imitation diamonds. Price, each ... $0.17
6 for ... $0.99 12 for ... 1.88

No. 4C15865

Fancy brooch, gold plate, bright finish, set with imitation diamonds.
Price, each ... $0.19
6 for ... 1.08
12 for ... 2.06

No. 4C15860 Fancy chatelette, roman finish, gold plate, enameled in green and white. Hook to suspend watch on.
Price, each ... $0.17
6 for ... .99
12 for ... 1.89

No. 4C15870
Black enameled brooch, for mourners.
Price, each........$0.19
6 for.............. 1.08
12 for.............. 2.06

No. 4C15875
Fancy brooch, gold plate, bright finish, black enameled, set with imitation pearls.
Price, each.....$0.21
6 for.......... 1.18
12 for.......... 2.25

No. 4C15880
Fancy brooch, gold plate, roman finish, enameled in colors, set with one imitation diamond.
Price, each....$0.19
6 for.......... 1.08
12 for.......... 2.06

No. 4C15885
Fancy chatelette, gold plate, roman finish, enameled in colors; hook to suspend watch on.
Price, each......$0.19
6 for............ 1.08
12 for............ 2.06

No. 4C15890
Fancy brooch, black enameled, bright polish, set with pearls, for mourners.
Price, each.....$0.21
6 for.......... 1.18
12 for.......... 2.25

No. 4C15895
Fancy brooch, roman finish, gold plate, fancy enameled, set with imitation pearls.
Price, each...$0.21
6 for.......... 1.18
12 for.......... 2.25

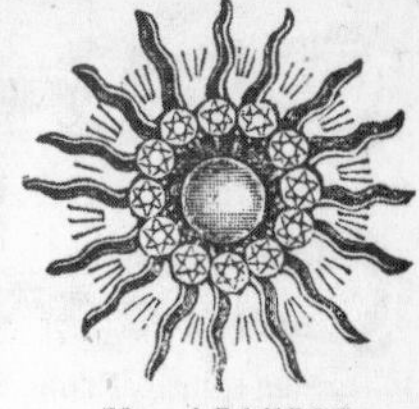

No. 4C15900
Fancy brooch, gold plate, bright polish, set with imitation diamonds and one large imitation pearl.
Price, each..$0.21
6 for........ 1.18
12 for........ 2.25

No. 4C15905
Fancy bar pin, gold plate, roman finish, set with nine imitation diamonds.
Price, each............$0.21
6 for.................. 1.18
12 for.................. 2.25

No. 4C15910
Fancy lace pin, gold plate, bright polish, set with imitation diamonds.
Price, each..................$0.21
6 for.......................... 1.18
12 for.......................... 2.25

No. 4C15915
Fancy brooch, gold plate, bright polish, set with imitation diamonds.
Price, each.........$0.21
6 for.............. 1.18
12 for.............. 2.25

No. 4C15920
Black enameled brooch, for mourners.
Price, each........$0.19
6 for.............. 1.08
12 for.............. 2.06

No. 4C15925
Fancy bar pin, gold plate, fancy black enamel, set with imitation pearls.
Price, each.........$0.21
6 for.............. 1.18
12 for.............. 2.25

No. 4C15930
Fancy bar pin, black enameled, set with imitation pearls.
Price, each............$0.21
6 for.............. 1.18
12 for.............. 2.25

No. 4C15935
Gold plated baby pin set, bright polish, raised ornamentation with fancy enameling.
Price, per set..$0.11 12 for........ $1.13
6 for........................ .60

No. 4C15940
Gold plated cuff pins, bright finish, enameled in blue.
Per pair....... $0.11
6 for.......... .60
12 for.......... 1.13

No. 4C15950
Gold plated cuff pins, roman color, satin finish, ornamented by hand engraving.
Per pair..........$0.14
6 for.............. .79
12 for.............. 1.50

No. 4C15945
Gold plated cuff pins, bright polish, ornamented by hand engraving.
Per pair..........$0.12
6 for.............. .70
12 for.............. 1.32

No. 4C15955
Gold plated cuff pins, plain bright polish.
Per pair...........$0.11
6 for.............. .60
12 for.............. 1.13

No. 4C15960
Gold plated cross, bright polish, red enameled heart.
Price, each....... $0.09
6 for.............. .50
12 for.............. .94

No. 4C15965
Gold plated secret locket, bright polish, raised ornamentation.
Price, each........$0.14
6 for.............. .79
12 for.............. 1.50

No. 4C15970
Gold plated secret locket, bright polish, raised ornamentation.
Price, each....... $0.16
6 for.............. .89
12 for.............. 1.69

No. 4C15975
Gold plated love locket, bright polish, set with pearls and turquoise.
Price, each......$0.19
6 for.......... 1.08
12 for.......... 2.06

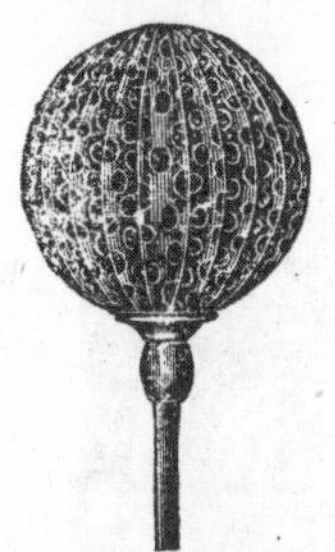

No. 4C15980
Hat pin, black enamel finish. Pin stem 7 inches long.
Price, each,$0.07
6 for....... .40
12 for....... .75

No. 4C15985
Hat pin, gold plate, roman finish, fancy stone setting. Pin stem 7 inches long
Price, each,$0.07
6 for....... .40
12 for....... .75

No. 4C15990
Hat pin, gold plate, roman gold finish, set with imitation turquoise. Pin stem 7 inches long.
Price, each,$0.07
6 for....... .40
12 for....... .75

No. 4C15995
Hat pin, oxidized silver finish, repousse flower. Pin stem 7 inches long.
Price, each,$0.11
6 for....... .60
12 for....... 1.13

No. 4C16000
Hat pin, gold plate, roman finish. Pin stem 7 inches long.
Price, each,$0.12
6 for....... .70
12 for....... 1.32

No. 4C16005
Hat pin, silver oxidized finish. Pin stem 7 inches long.
Price, each,$0.12
6 for....... .70
12 for....... 1.32

No. 4C16010
Hat pin, mother of pearl. Pin stem 7 inches long.
Price, each,$0.14
6 for....... .79
12 for....... 1.50

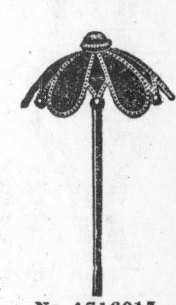

No. 4C16015
Hat pin, gold plate, fancy enameled in black, set with imitation pearl. Pin stem 7 inches long.
Price, ea.,$0.16
6 for....... .89
12 for....... 1.69

No. 4C16020
Hat pin, gold plate, roman gold finish, set with one imitation diamond. Pin stem 7 inches long.
Price, each..$0.16
6 for....... .89
12 for........ 1.69

No. 4C16025
Hat pin, black finish. Pin stem 7 inches long.
Price, each........$0.17
6 for.............. .99
12 for.............. 1.88

No. 4C16030
Hat pin, gold plate, roman finish, set with imitation ruby. Pin stem 7 inches long.
Price, each.$0.19
6 for........ 1.08
12 for........ 2.06

No. 4C16035
Hat pin, black finish. Pin stem 7 inches long.
Price, each........$0.19
6 for.............. 1.08
12 for.............. 2.06

No. 4C16040
Hat pin, mother of pearl. Pin stem 7 inches long.
Price, each.$0.19
6 for....... 1.08
12 for....... 2.06

No. 4C16045
Hat pin, oxidized silver finish, set with imitation pearls. Pin stem 7 inches long.
Price, each.$0.19
6 for....... 1.08
12 for....... 2.06

No. 4C16050
Hat pin, gold plate, roman color, set with imitation diamonds and amethyst center. Pin stem 7 inches long.
Price, each $0.21
6 for....... 1.18
12 for....... 2.25

No. 4C16055 Gold plated gentlemen's vest chain, bright polish; 12 inches long. Price, 12 for **94c**; 6 for **50c**; each......9c

No. 4C16060 Gold plated gentlemen's vest chain, bright polish; 12 inches long. Price, 12 for **94c**; 6 for **50c**; each......9c

No. 4C16065 Gold plated gentlemen's vest chain, bright polish; 12 inches long. Price, 12 for **$1.12**; 6 for **59c**; each......10c

No. 4C16070 Gold plated gentlemen's vest chain, bright polished; 12 inches long. Price, 12 for **$1.12**; 6 for **59c**; each......10c

No. 4C16075 Gold plated gentlemen's vest chain, bright polish; 12 inches long. Price, 12 for **$1.12**; 6 for **59c**; each......10c

No. 4C16080 Gold plated gentlemen's vest chain, bright polish; 12 inches long. Price, 12 for **$1.12**; 6 for **59c**; each......10c

No. 4C16085 Gold plated gentlemen's vest chain, bright polish; 12 inches long. Price, 12 for **$1.12**; 6 for **59c**; each......10c

No. 4C16090 Gold plated gentlemen's vest chain, bright polish; 12 inches long. Price, 12 for **$1.12**; 6 for **59c**; each......10c

No. 4C16095 Gold plated gentlemen's vest chain, bright polish; 12 inches long. Price, 12 for **$1.12**; 6 for **59c**; each......10c

No. 4C16100 Gold plated gentlemen's vest chain, bright polish; 12 inches long. Price, 12 for **$1.50**; 6 for **79c**; each......14c

No. 4C16105 Gold plated gentlemen's vest chain, bright polish; 12 inches long. Price, 12 for **$1.50**; 6 for **79c**; each......14c

No. 4C16110 Gold plated gentlemen's double vest chain, bright polish, 12 inches long.

Price, 12 for **$2.62**; 6 for **$1.37**; each......24c

No. 4C16115 Fine gold plated gentlemen's vest chain, bright polish throughout; length, 12 inches; warranted for one year.

Price, 12 for **$4.50**; 6 for **$2.37**; each......42c

No. 4C16120 Fine gold plated gentlemen's vest chain, bright polish throughout; length, 12 inches; soldered links; warranted for one year.

Price, 12 for **$4.50**; 6 for **$2.37**; each......42c

No. 4C16125 Fine gold plated gentlemen's vest chain, bright polish throughout, soldered links; length, 12 inches; warranted for one year.

Price. 12 for **$4.50**; 6 for **$2.37**; each......42c

No. 4C16130 Fine gold plated gentlemen's vest chain, bright polish throughout, soldered links; length, 12 inches; warranted for one year.

Price, 12 for **$4.50**; 6 for **$2.37**; each......42c

No. 4C16135 Fine gold plated gentlemen's vest chain, bright polish throughout, soldered links; length, 12 inches; warranted for one year.

Price, 12 for **$4.50**; 6 for **$2.37**; each......42c

No. 4C16140 Fine gold plated gentlemen's vest chain, bright polish throughout, soldered links; length, 12 inches; warranted for one year.

Price, 12 for **$4.50**; 6 for **$2.37**; each......42c

No. 4C16145 Fine gold plated gentlemen's vest chain, bright polish throughout; length, 12 inches; warranted for one year.

Price, 12 for **$4.50**; 6 for **$2.37**; each......42c

No. 4C16150 Gold plated, bright polish, double sided royalty chain, with charm, 14 inches long. Price, each......$0.21
6 for......1.18
12 for......2.25

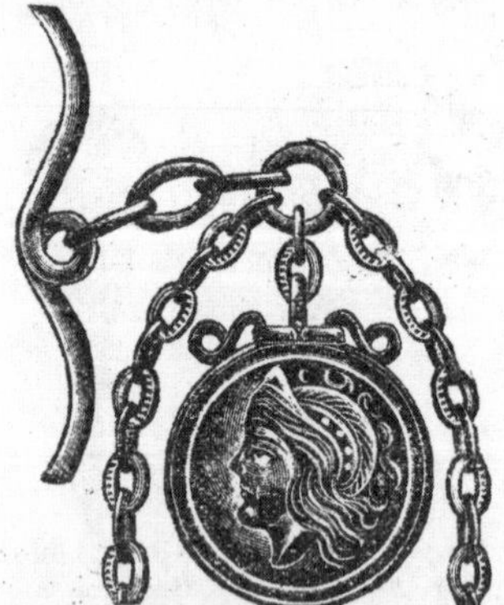

No. 4C16155 Gold plated, bright polish, double sided royalty chain, with charm, 14 inches long. Price, each......$0.21
6 for......1.18
12 for......2.25

No. 4C16160 Gold plated, bright polish, double sided royalty chain, with charm, 14 inches long. Price, each......$0.21
6 for......1.18
12 for......2.25

No. 4C16165 Gold plated, bright polish, double sided royalty chain, with charm, 14 inches long. Price, each......$0.21
6 for......1.18
12 for......2.25

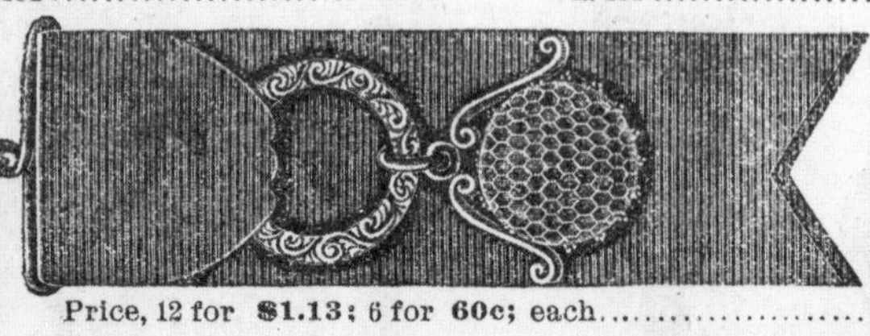

No. 4C16170 Gentlemen's silk fob, with bright polish, gold plated trimmings, fancy stone charm; entire length of fob, 6½ inches.

Price, 12 for **$1.13**; 6 for **60c**; each......11c

No. 4C16175 Gold plated gentlemen's fob, bright finish, with fancy bead centers and mother of pearl charm. Entire length of fob, 5 inches.

Price, 12 for **$1.32**; 6 for **70c**; each......12c

No. 4C16180 Gold plated, bright finish, gentlemen's fob, with stone set charm. Entire length, 6 inches. Price, 12 for **$1.50**; 6 for **79c**; each......14c

No. 4C16185 Gentlemen's fob, nickel plated, with fancy stone charm. Entire length of fob, 6½ inches.

Price, 12 for **$1.50**; 6 for **79c**; each......14c

No. 4C16186 The latest craze. Gentlemen's fob, imitation ancient Egyptian design, silver plated, oxidized finish on German silver. Length 5½ inches.

No. 4C16187 Same as No. 4C16186, but gilt finish.

Price, each........................ $0.12
6 for........................ .66
12 for........................ 1.25

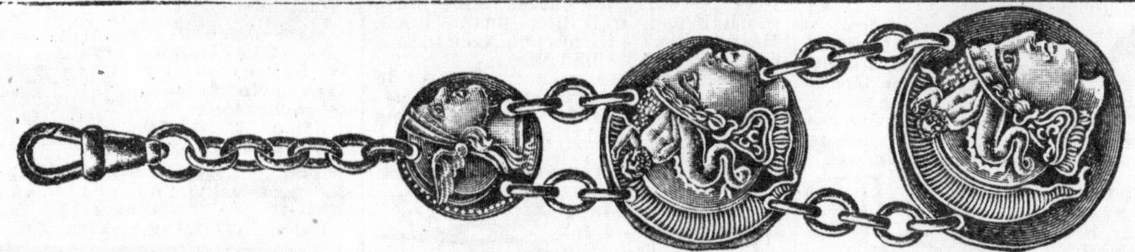

No. 4C16188 The latest craze. Gentlemen's fob, imitation ancient Roman coin design, silver plated, oxidized finish on German silver. Length 5 inches.

No. 4C16189 Same as No. 4C16188, but gilt finish.

Price, each........................ $0.19
6 for........................ 1.07
12 for........................ 2.05

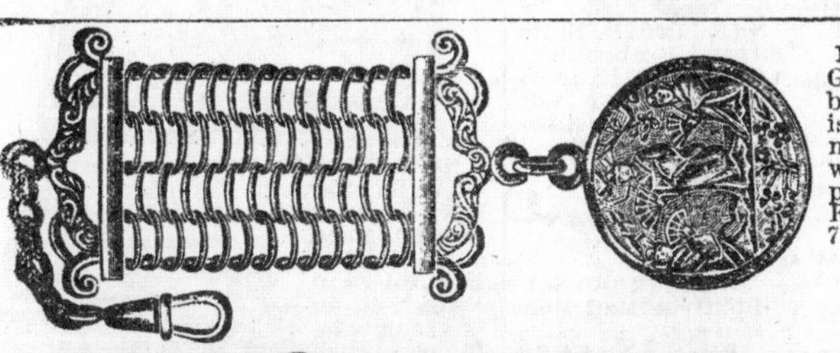

No. 4C16190 Gold plated, bright finished, gentlemen's fob, with gold plated charm. Entire length, 7 inches.
Each.. $0.21
6 for.. 1.18
12 for.. 2.25

No. 4C16195 Gentlemen's silk fob, with rolled plated mountings, warranted to give satisfaction. Entire length of chain 6 inches.
Each.. $0.31
6 for.. 1.75
12 for.. 3.37

No. 4C16200 Gentlemen's silk fob, with rolled plated mountings, warranted to give satisfaction. Entire length of chain, 6 inches. Price, 12 for $3.37; 6 for $1.75; each...31c

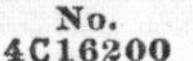

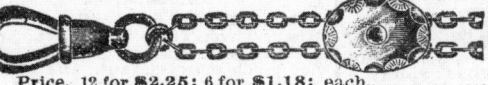

No. 4C16205 Gold plated guard chain, bright polish, Chain 48 inches long. Price, 12 for $2.25; 6 for $1.18; each........ 21c

No. 4C16210 Gold plated guard chain, bright polish, slide set with imitation stone, 48 inches long. Price, 12 for $2.25; 6 for $1.18; each........ 21c

No. 4C16215 Rolled gold plated guard chain, guaranteed for two years, soldered links. Length 48 inches, slide set with imitation pearl. Price.. 94c

No. 4C16220 Rolled gold plated guard chain, guaranteed for two years, soldered links. Length, 48 inches; slide set with imitation pearls. Price...94c

No. 4C16225 Rolled gold plated guard chain, guaranteed for two years, soldered links. Length, 48 inches; slide set with imitation pearls. Price........ 94c

No. 4C16230 Rolled gold plated guard chain, guaranteed for two years, soldered links. Length, 48 inches; slide set with imitation pearls. Price.... 94c

No. 4C16235 Rolled gold plated guard chain, guaranteed for two years, soldered links. Length 48 inches; slide set with imitation ruby and pearls. Price........ 94c

No. 4C16240 Rolled gold plated guard chain, guaranteed for two years, soldered links. Length, 48 inches; slide set with imitation pearls. Price.... 94c

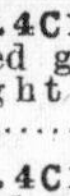

No. 4C16245 Gold plated neck chain and charm. Chain, 19 inches long. Charm is set with imitation turquoise.
Price, each....... $0.17
6 for........ .99
12 for........ 1.87

No. 4C16250 Gold plated neck chain, bright polish, chain 19 inches long, charm is perfectly plain polish, secret locket.
Price, each... $0.21
6 for........ 1.18
12 for........ 2.25

BE SURE AND GIVE US THE SIZE OF RING DESIRED.

HOW TO DETERMINE THE SIZE.

Cut a strip of thick paper so that the ends will exactly meet when drawn tightly around the second joint of the finger. Lay one end on the diagram at O and order the size the other end indicates.

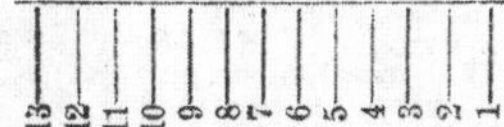

No. 4C16255 Gold plated, bright finished, plain ring. Sizes, 6 to 13.
Price, each... $0.14
6 for........ .79
12 for........ 1.50

No. 4C16260 Gold plated, bright finished, plain ring. Sizes, 6 to 13.
Price, each.. 6c
6 for........ 33c
12 for........ 63c

No. 4C16270 Gold plated, bright finished, plain ring. Sizes, 6 to 13.
Price, each.. 4c
6 for........ 20c
12 for........ 38c

No. 4C16275 Gold plated, bright finished, flat band ring. Sizes, 6 to 13.
Price, ea.. 6c
6 for..... 36c
12 for..... 69c

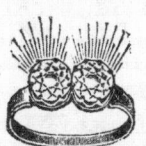

No. 4C16280 Gold plated, bright finished, flat band ring. Sizes, 6 to 13.
Price, each.. 5c
6 for....... 27c
12 for....... 50c

No. 4C16285 Gold plated, bright finished, gentleman's fancy engraved band ring. Sizes, 6 to 13.
Price, each.. 9c
6 for........ 43c
12 for........ 81c

No. 4C16290 Gold plated, bright finished, ladies' fancy finger ring, set with 2 pearls and 2 rubies. Sizes, 6 to 13.
Price, ea.. $0.14
6 for..... .79
12 for..... 1.50

No. 4C16295 Gold plated, bright finished, ladies' finger ring, set with 1 imitation diamond and 1 imitation emerald. Sizes, 6 to 13.
Price, ea.. $0.17
6 for..... .98
12 for..... 1.87

No. 4C16300 Gold plated, bright finished, ladies' finger ring, set with 2 imitation diamonds. Sizes, 6 to 13.
Price, ea.. $0.17
6 for..... .98
12 for..... 1.87

No. 4C16305 Gold plated, bright finished, ladies' finger ring, set with 1 imitation diamond and 1 imitation ruby. Sizes, 6 to 13.
Price, ea.. $0.17
6 for..... .98
12 for..... 1.87

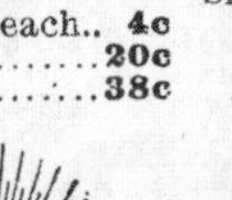

No. 4C16310 Gold plated, bright finished, finger ring, fancy shank, set with 1 large imitation diamond. Sizes, 6 to 13.
Price, ea.. $0.19
6 for..... 1.07
12 for..... 2.05

No. 4C16315 Gold plated, bright finished, gentlemen's gypsy ring, set with 3 rubies. Sizes, 6 to 13.
Price, ea. $0.37
6 for.... 2.16
12 for.... 4.00

STERLING SILVER NOVELTIES.

MOST APPROPRIATE FOR A GIFT OR PERSONAL USE.

These goods are made of the finest sterling silver. They are sufficiently heavy to be well able to stand continual usage. Our amethyst set novelties have a beautiful amethyst set in the end of each handle, finishing the article in most exquisite style.

No.4C12600 Solid Silver Manicure File, amethyst set, 6 inches. Price.....68c
If by mail, postage extra, 4 cents.

No.4C12602 Solid Silver Manicure File, 6 inches. Price.....48c
If by mail, postage extra, 4 cents.

No.4C12604 Solid Silver Nail Clip, amethyst set, 5¾ inches. Price.....75c
If by mail, postage extra, 5 cents.

No.4C12606 Solid Silver Nail Clip, 5¾ inches. Price.....65c
If by mail, postage extra, 5 cents.

No.4C12608 olid Silver Nail Knife, amethyst set, 5¼ inches. Price.....68c
If by mail, postage extra, 4 cents.

No. 4C12610 Solid Silver Nail Knife, 5½ inches. Price.....50c
If by mail, postage extra, 4 cents.

No. 4C12612 Solid Silver Cuticle Knife, amethyst set, 5 inches. Price.....68c
If by mail, postage extra, 4 cents.

No.4C12614 Solid Silver Cuticle Knife, 4¾ inches. Price.....50c
If by mail, postage extra, 4 cents.

No. 4C12616 Solid Silver Hair Curler, amethyst set, 7½ inches. Price.....80c
If by mail, postage extra, 5 cents.

No. 4C12618 Solid Silver Hair Curler, 7½ inches. Price.....50c
If by mail, postage extra, 5 cents.

No. 4C12620 Solid Silver Tooth Brush, amethyst set, 6½ inches. Price.....68c
If by mail, postage extra, 4 cents.

No. 4C12622 Solid Silver Tooth Brush, 6½ inches. Price.....55c
If by mail, postage extra, 4 cents.

No. 4C12624 Solid Silver Hand Brush, amethyst set, 7 inches. Price.....70c

No. 4C12626 Solid Silver Hand Brush, 6½ inches. Price.....60c
If by mail, postage extra, 4 cents.

No. 4C12628 Solid Silver Shoe Button Hook, amethyst set, 7½ inches. Price.....64c
If by mail, postage extra, 4 cents.

No.4C12630 Solid Silver Shoe Button Hook, 7½ inches. Price.....48c
If by mail, postage extra, 4 cents.

No.4C12632 Solid Silver Shoe Horn, amethyst set, 7 inches. Price.....74c
If by mail, postage extra, 6 cents.

No. 4C12634 Solid Silver Stocking Darner, amethyst set, 6¼ inches. Price.....68c
If by mail, postage extra, 5 cents.

No. 4C12636 Solid Silver Stocking Darner, 6¼ inches. Price.....48c
If by mail, postage extra, 6 cents.

No. 4C12638 Solid Silver Baby Rattle, amethyst set, 5¼ in. Price 95c
If by mail, postage extra, 5 cents.

No.4C12640 Solid Silver Table Bell, 5 inches. Price.....50c
If by mail, postage extra, 5 cents.

No. 4C12642 Solid Silver Table Bell, amethyst set, 5 inches. Price 64c

No. 4C12644 Solid Silver Reading Glass, amethyst set. 7 inches. Price.....$1.40
If by mail, postage extra, 8 cents.

No. 4C12646 Solid Silver Writing Blotter, amethyst set, 5½ inches. Price.....68c
If by mail, postage extra, 5 cents.

No. 4C12648 Solid Silver Writing Blotter, 5¼ inches. Price.....48c
If by mail, postage extra, 5 cents.

No. 4C12650 Solid Silver Paper Knife, amethyst set, 7½ inches. Price.....72c
If by mail, postage extra, 5 cents.

No. 4C12652 Solid Silver Letter Opener. 7½ inches. Price.....60c
If by mail, postage extra, 5 cents.

No. 4C12653 Solid Silver Letter Opener. 4¼ inches. Price.....75c
If by mail, postage extra, 3 cents.

No. 4C12654 Solid Silver Paper Knife. Pearl blade; 7 inches. Price.....73c
If by mail, postage extra, 5 cents.

No. 4C12656 Solid Silver Paper Knife. Pearl blade; 5½ inches. Price.....60c
If by mail, postage extra, 4 cents.

No. 4C12658 Solid Silver Letter Seal, amethyst set, 4 inches, with any letter engraved. Price.....68c
If by mail, postage extra, 4 cents.

No.4C12660 Solid Silver Letter Seal. 4 inches, with any letter engraved. Price.....58c
If by mail, postage extra, 4 cents.

No. 4C12662 Solid Silver Ink Eraser, amethyst set, 5 inches. Price.....64c
If by mail, postage extra, 4 cents.

No. 4C12664 Solid Silver Ink Eraser. 4½ inches. Price.....50c
If by mail, postage extra, 4 cents.

No. 4C12666 Silver Book Mark. Silk ribbon, sterling silver mounted book mark. Price.....25c
If by mail, postage extra, 2 cents.

No. 4C12668 Solid Silver Crocheting Set. Needle, seven inches; scissors, 3½ inches. Price.....$1.00
If by mail, postage extra, 10 cents.

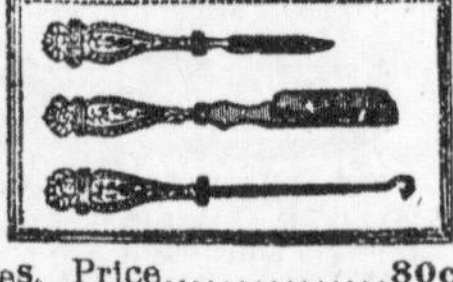

No. 4C12670 Solid Silver Toilet Set. Button hook, 6 in.; tooth brush, 6 inches; nail file, 4¼ inches. Price.....80c
If by mail, postage extra, 10 cents.

No. 4C12671 Needle Emery. 1½ inches. Price.....25c
If by mail, postage extra, 5 cents.

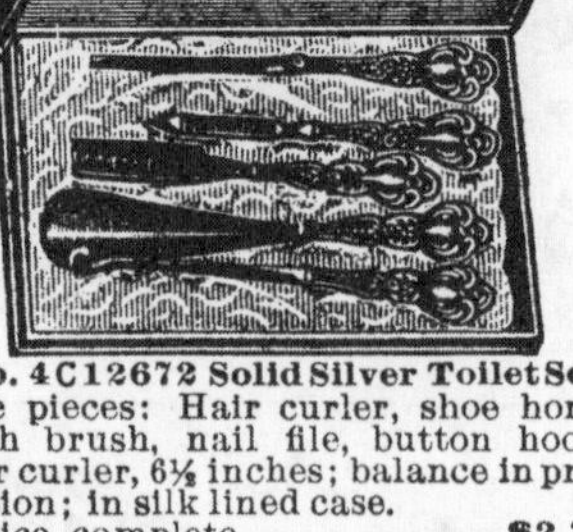

No. 4C12672 Solid Silver Toilet Set. Five pieces: Hair curler, shoe horn, tooth brush, nail file, button hook. Hair curler, 6½ inches; balance in proportion; in silk lined case.
Price, complete.....$2.35
If by mail, postage extra, 20 cents.

No.4C12674 Pearl Teething Ring, solid silver bells. Price.....75c
If by mail, postage extra, 3c.

No.4C12676 Solid Silver Manicure Scissors, 4 in. Price.....68c
Postage extra, 3c.

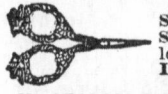

No.4C12678 Solid Silver Embroidery Scissors, 4 inches long. Price.....68c
If by mail, postage extra, 3 cents.

No.4C12680 Solid Silver Sewing Scissors, 4½ inches. Price.....75c
If by mail, postage extra, 4 cents.

No. 4C12682 Solid Silver Nail Polisher, 4½ inches. Price.....$1.20
If by mail, postage extra, 4 cents.

No.4C12684 Solid Silver Nail Polisher, 3¼ inches. Price.....65c
If by mail, postage extra, 3 cents.

No.4C12686 Solid Silver Hat Brush, 5½ in. Price.....98c
If by mail, postage extra, 4 cents.

No. 4C12688 Solid Silver Clothes Brush, 7 inches. Price.....$2.25
If by mail, postage extra, 10 cents.

No. 4C12690 Solid Silver Velvet Brush, 6¼ inches. Price.....$1.75
If by mail, postage extra, 8 cents.

No. 4C12692 Solid Silver Shaving Brush, 4¼ inches. Price.....(Postage extra, 3c.).....80c

No. 4C12694 Solid Silver Cigar Cutter, 2¾ in. Price.....75c
Postage extra, 3 cents.

No.4C12696 Solid Silver Cigar Cutter, 1½ inches. Price.....65c
If by mail, postage extra, 3 cents.

No. 4C12698 Solid Silver Pocket Knife, 2 blades and scissors, 3 inches. Price.....(Postage extra, 8c.).....$2.00

No.4C12700 Ladies' Solid Silver Pocket Knife, 1½ inches. Price.....65c
If by mail, postage extra, 3 cents.

No. 4C12702 Solid Silver Stamp Box. 1¼ inches. Price.....50c
If by mail, postage extra, 2c.

No. 4C12704 Solid Silver Stamp Box. 1⅛ inches. Heavy. Price.....72c
If by mail, postage extra, 3 cents.

No.4C12706 Solid Silver Match Box. 2 inches long. Price.....68c
If by mail, postage extra, 3 cents.

No.4C12708 Solid Silver Match Box. 2¾ inches long. Price.....$1.35
If by mail, postage extra, 4 cents.

No. 4C12710 Solid Silver Match Box. 2¾ inches long. Price, $1.75
If by mail, postage extra, 4 cents.

No. 4C12712 Solid Silver, Heavy Match Box. 2½ inches. Price.....$2.15
If by mail, postage extra, 5 cents.

No. 4C12714 Solid Silver, Heavy Match Box. 2½ inches long. Price.....$2.25
If by mail, postage extra, 5 cents.

No. 4C12716 Solid Silver, Very Heavy Match Box. 2½ inches long. Price.....$2.40
Postage extra, 5c.

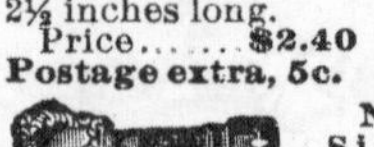

No.4C12718 Solid Silver Baggage Check. 3½ inches. Price .....(Postage extra, 3c).....58c

No. 4C12724 Silk Suspenders, solid silver buckles, in fine glass covered box. Price..(Postage extra, 25c). $1.65

No.4C12726 Solid Silver Handled Baby Set, in box; comb, 4¾ inches, brush 5½ inches. Price...(Postage extra, 6c.).....75c

No. 4C12728 Solid Silver Baby Set, in box; comb 5 inches, brush 5¾ inches. Ea., $2.25
Postage extra, 6 cents.

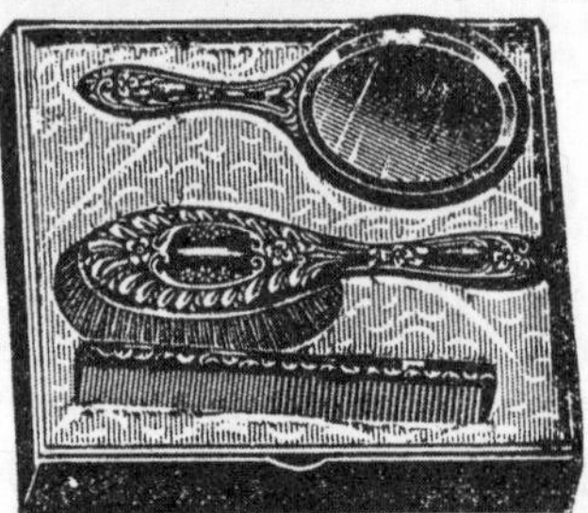

No. 4C12731 Solid Silver Toilet Set, complete in box. Price.....$6.00
Not mailable.

No. 4C12747 Solid Silver Extra Heavy Three-Piece Toilet Set, complete in box; similar to No. 4C12731 but much more elegant. We advise you to select this heavy set for all practical purposes.
Price.....$8.90
Not mailable.

No. 4C12733 Mirror, 7½ inches. Price. (Not mailable.).....$3.63
No. 4C12735 Comb, 7 inches. Price. .(Postage extra, 3c.)..$0.38
No. 4C12737 Brush, 7¾ inches. Price...(Postage extra, 4c.)..$2.00

No.4C12738 Solid Silver Glove Set, 5 pieces, box 5x4 inches, complete. Price.....$1.58
If by mail, postage extra, 10 cents.

No. 4C12740 Solid Silver Embroidery Set, 3 pieces Price,(Postage, 6c) $1.20

No. 4C12743 Garters, Solid Silver mountings, set with fancy stone, fine silk web; in box. Price, per pr, $1.90
If by mail, postage extra, 6 cents.

No. 4C12745 Garters, Solid Silver mountings, fine silk web. Price, per pr, $1.27
Postage extra, 6 cents.

SOLID GOLD PENS AND PEARL HOLDERS.

MADE UNDER CONTRACT FOR US. THE SPECIFICATIONS ARE CARRIED OUT IN EVERY DETAIL.

OUR PENS AND HOLDERS.

THE BEST ON THE MARKET. The manufacturer, following the exact details of our contract, produces for us, at a price cheaper by 25 per cent, pens that are worth 50 per cent more than the best pen sold by others. We have them made of solid gold through and through, heavy and well tempered. The points of every one of them are tipped with genuine iridium (sometimes called diamond pointed). Iridium, a very hard metal, being applied at the writing point of a pen, gives it a wearing period of practically a lifetime. The pearl sticks, gold filled holders and noses are made and selected from the best stock to be purchased. Illustrations are reduced size. The actual size of pens and holders are from 6 to 7¾ inches long. No. 1 pen and holder is 6 inches long, balance of sizes in proportion.

Don't be misled by fancy prices asked by others. We warrant our pens and holders the equal of any and better than the most.

AT 15 OR 25 CENTS EXTRA WE WILL FURNISH A FINE PEN BOX.

No. 4C12872 Moroccoine covered....15c
No. 4C12874 Genuine silk plush covered, plush lined....25c
With any pen you select.

BEST QUALITY SOLID GOLD PEN IN GOLD FILLED AND EBONY DESK HOLDER.

		No. 1 Pen.	No. 2 Pen.	No. 3 Pen.	No. 4 Pen.	No. 5 Pen.	No. 6 Pen.	No. 7 Pen.
No. 4C12800	10-karat gold Pen with Holder.	$0.60	$0.65	$0.70	$0.75	$0.90	$1.00	$1.20
No. 4C12802	16-karat gold Pen with Holder.	.70	.75	.90	1.00	1.15	1.25	1.50

BEST QUALITY SOLID GOLD PEN IN GOLD PLATED AND EBONY SLIDE HOLDER.

		No. 1 Pen.	No. 2 Pen.	No. 3 Pen.	No. 4 Pen.	No. 5 Pen.	No. 6 Pen.	No. 7 Pen.
No. 4C12804	10-karat gold Pen with Holder.	$0.80	$0.85	$0.95	$1.00	$1.15	$1.35	$1.50
No. 4C12806	16-karat gold Pen with Holder.	.90	.95	1.15	1.25	1.40	1.60	1.80

BEST QUALITY GOLD PEN IN GOLD FILLED AND PLAIN PEARL DESK HOLDER.

		No. 1 Pen.	No. 2 Pen.	No. 3 Pen.	No. 4 Pen.	No. 5 Pen.	No. 6 Pen.
No. 4C12808	10-karat gold Pen with Holder.	$0.62	$0.90	$0.95	$1.10	$1.35	$1.55
No. 4C12830	16-karat gold Pen with Holder.	.85	1.00	1.15	1.35	1.60	1.80

SOLID GOLD PEN IN BEST QUALITY GOLD FILLED AND PLAIN PEARL SLIDE HOLDER.

		No. 1 Pen.	No. 2 Pen.	No. 3 Pen.	No. 4 Pen.	No. 5 Pen.	No. 6 Pen.
No. 4C12832	10-karat gold Pen with Holder.	$1.00	$1.15	$1.20	$1.40	$1.50	$1.70
No. 4C12834	16-karat gold Pen with Holder.	1.10	1.25	1.40	1.65	1.75	2.00

SOLID GOLD PEN IN BEST QUALITY GOLD FILLED AND FANCY FULL TWIST PEARL DESK HOLDER.

		No. 1 Pen.	No. 2 Pen.	No. 3 Pen.	No. 4 Pen.	No. 5 Pen.	No. 6 Pen.
No. 4C12837	10-karat gold Pen with Holder.	$0.95	$1.10	$1.25	$1.40	$1.60	$1.80
No. 4C12839	16-karat gold Pen with Holder.	1.05	1.25	1.45	1.65	1.85	2.05

SOLID GOLD PEN IN BEST QUALITY GOLD FILLED AND FANCY THREE-QUARTER TWIST CUT PEARL DESK HOLDER.

		No. 1 Pen.	No. 2 Pen.	No. 3 Pen.	No. 4 Pen.	No. 5 Pen.	No. 6 Pen.
No. 4C12843	10-karat gold Pen with Holder.	$0.95	$1.10	$1.25	$1.40	$1.60	$1.80
No. 4C12845	16-karat gold Pen with Holder.	1.05	1.25	1.45	1.65	1.85	2.05

SOLID GOLD PEN IN BEST QUALITY GOLD FILLED AND FANCY HAND TURNED PEARL DESK HOLDER.

		No. 1 Pen.	No. 2 Pen.	No. 3 Pen.	No. 4 Pen.	No. 5 Pen.	No. 6 Pen.
No. 4C12847	10-karat gold Pen with Holder.	$1.00	$1.15	$1.30	$1.45	$1.65	$1.85
No. 4C12849	16-karat gold Pen with Holder.	1.10	1.30	1.50	1.70	1.90	2.10

SOLID GOLD PEN IN BEST QUALITY GOLD FILLED AND TWIST PEARL SLIDE HOLDER.

		No. 1 Pen.	No. 2 Pen.	No. 3 Pen.	No. 4 Pen.	No. 5 Pen.	No. 6 Pen.
No. 4C12850	10-karat gold Pen with Holder.	$1.20	$1.40	$1.50	$1.60	$1.85	$1.95
No. 4C12852	16-karat gold Pen with Holder.	1.30	1.50	1.75	1.85	2.10	2.20

SOLID GOLD PEN IN BEST QUALITY GOLD FILLED AND RUSTIC CUT PEARL DESK HOLDER.

		No. 1 Pen.	No. 2 Pen.	No. 3 Pen.	No. 4 Pen.	No. 5 Pen.	No. 6 Pen.
No. 4C12854	10-karat gold Pen with Holder.	$0.95	$1.10	$1.25	$1.40	$1.60	$1.80
No. 4C12856	16-karat gold Pen with Holder.	1.05	1.25	1.45	1.65	1.85	2.05

If by mail, postage extra, 3 cents; registry or insurance extra. Be sure to state how much is inclosed for postage, and follow instructions in front of book.

Sterling Silver Desk Set.

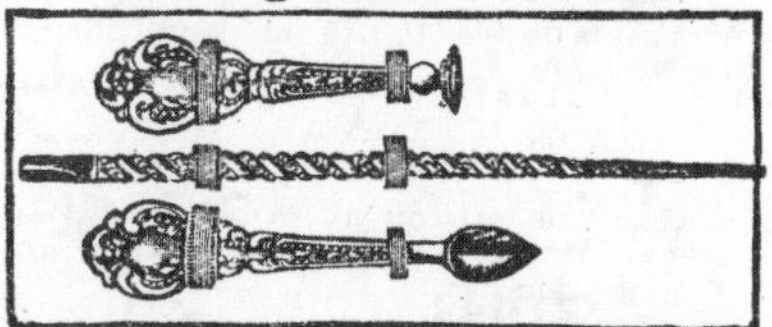

No. 4C12913 Sterling Silver Desk Set on card. Set consists of silver penholder, 6 inches long; silver handled ink eraser, 3¾ inches long; silver handled letter seal, 3 inches long.

Price, complete set....$1.25

If by mail, postage extra, 6 cents.

Combination Desk Set.

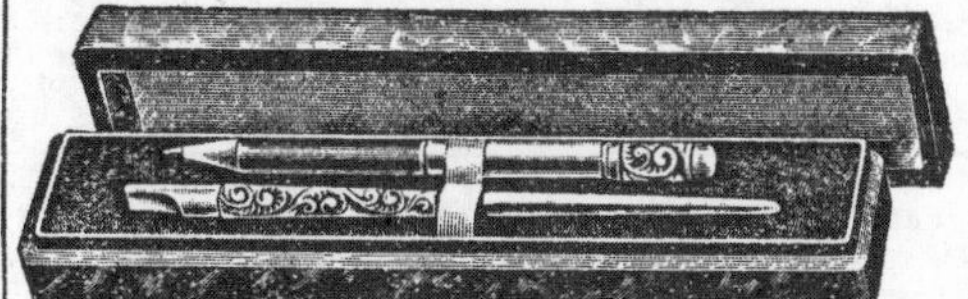

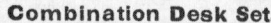

No. 4C12915 Combination Desk Set, consisting of one solid silver penholder, 6¼ inches long, and one solid silver lead pencil holder with rubber eraser attached, 2¾ inches long; entire length, with pencil, 5 inches. Complete in hardwood polished oak box, silk plush lined. Price, per set....$1.95

If by mail, postage extra, 6 cents.

Our $1.85 Desk Set.

No. 4C12917 Combination Desk Set, with the best gold filled mountings, consisting of one pearl letter opener, 4¼ inches long; one pen and penholder, pen, solid gold; entire length, 6¼ inches; one fancy screw toothpick, full extended length, 2¾ inches; and one screw pencil, full extended length, 3 inches.

Price, complete in enameled paper velvet lined box....$1.85

If by mail, postage extra, 4 cents.

Combination Desk Sets.

No. 4C12919 Desk Set, consisting of pearl paper cutter and pearl handled penholder and solid gold 16-K No. 1 pen. Cutter and penholder made to match, ornamented with gold filled wire work.

Price, with box complete....$2.00

If by mail, postage extra, 3 cents.

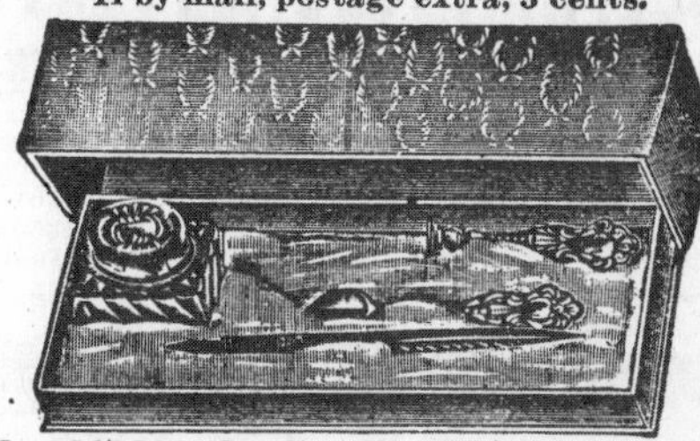

No. 4C12921 Sterling Silver Desk Set, in fine silk lined paper box. Set consists of silver covered fluted square ink well, 1½x1½x1½ inches; silver handled letter seal, 2½ inches long; pearl penholder with solid No. 1 gold pen, 5 inches long; silver handled ink eraser, 3¼ inches long.

Price, for complete set....$2.25

If by mail, postage extra, 20 cents.

No. 4C12923 Desk Set, consisting of pearl pen and pearl pencil and plush covered and lined box. Pen is solid gold, 16-karat, No. 1 size; pencil is pearl with gold filled trimmings.

Price, for complete set....$2.50

If by mail, postage extra, 4 cents.

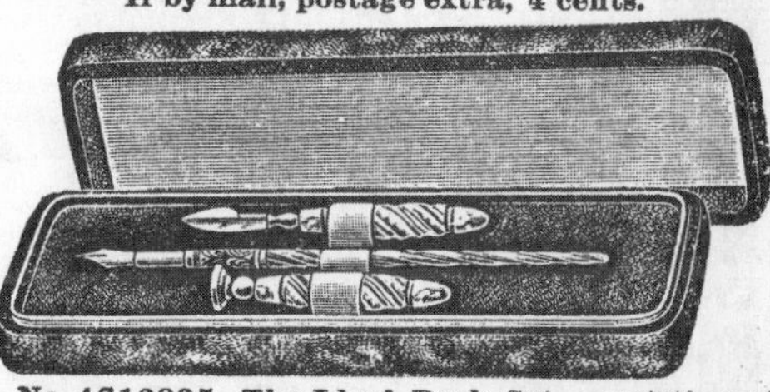

No. 4C12925 The Ideal Desk Set, consisting of one fine pearl letter seal, 2½ inches long; one fine pearl hand turned penholder with solid silver nose, fitted with a solid gold pen; full length of penholder and pen, 6¼ inches, and one pearl handled steel eraser; full length, 3¾ inches. Price, complete in beautiful silk plush box, velvet lined....$3.15

If by mail, postage extra, 4 cents.

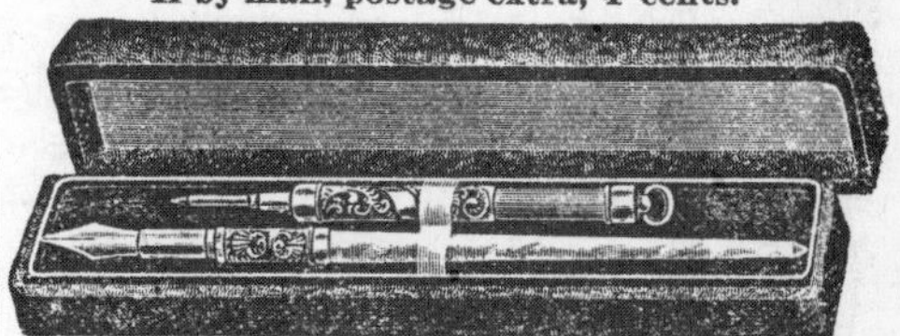

No. 4C12927 Combination Desk Set, consisting of one gold filled magic pencil, full extended length, 5 inches; one pearl penholder with gold filled nose, fitted with large size solid gold pen; full length of pen holder, including pen, 7½ inches. Price, complete in beautiful silk plush box, velvet lined....$3.25

If by mail, postage extra, 4 cents.

Screw Pencils.

No. 4C12929 Rolled Gold Plate Screw Pencil; full extended length, 2¾ inches. Price....18c

If by mail, postage extra, 2 cents.

No. 4C12931 Rolled Gold Plate Screw Pencil, handsomely engraved; full extended length, 4 inches. Price....55c

If by mail, postage extra, 2 cents.

No. 4C12933 Rolled Gold Plate, Bright Polish, Fancy Screw Pencil; full extended length, 4 inches. Price....58c

If by mail, postage extra, 2 cents.

No. 4C12935 Gold Filled, Bright Polish, Handsomely Engraved Magic Pencil; full extended length, 3¾ inches. Price....75c

If by mail, postage extra, 2 cents.

No. 4C12937 Rolled Gold Plate, Bright Polish, Handsomely Engraved Magic Pencil; full extended length, 4¾ inches. Price........................ **80c**
If by mail, postage extra, 3 cents.

No. 4C12939 Rolled Gold Plate, Bright Polish, Perfectly Plain Magic Pencil; full extended length, 4¾ inches. Price........................ **90c**
If by mail, postage extra, 3 cents.

No. 4C12941 Gold Filled, Bright Polish, Handsomely Chased Magic Pencil; full extended length, 4¾ inches. Price........................ **$1.15**
If by mail, postage extra, 3 cents.

No. 4C12943 Gold Filled, Bright Polish, Fancy Magic Pencil; full extended length, 6 inches. Price........................ **$1.50**
If by mail, postage extra, 3 cents.

PAUL E. WIRT FOUNTAIN PENS AND OUR OWN SPECIAL MAKE, THE NEW WABASH MADE ONLY FOR US.

BEFORE LISTING A LINE OF FOUNTAIN PENS we have thoroughly investigated the mechanism of all makes, and have spared no pains to place at the disposal of our customers, **the finest fountain pens manufactured.** The construction of these pens is of such a simple and practical kind that it is utterly impossible for one of them to become out of order, and cause more trouble to the writer and destroy more copy than the entire thing is worth, instead of being a convenience, making it in reality an absolute inconvenience.

THE PAUL E. WIRT FOUNTAIN PEN stands at the head without a peer. **It is most simple and practical in construction as to operation and beauty of workmanship.** Their popularity rests upon the fact that their ink feed device is the most perfect and simplest ever discovered. Do not buy inferior imitations, but get the original, genuine article. They are elegant, simple, clean and durable; every fountain is fitted with a 14-karat solid gold pen. Each one is warranted by the manufacturers, **and we guarantee them to you personally to be the finest and most practical pen made.**

No. 4C12999 Our New Wabash, with patent, non-breakable cap, something bran new in the fountain pen line. The cap has a ferrule of rolled gold plate, as illustration shows, which makes it practically non-breakable. The cap is the weak point on the fountain pen. The case is perfectly plain and has non-leakable screw nozzle, medium length and fitted with a No. 2 solid gold pen. Comes only medium pointed, a pen well selected for general work. Price........................ **$1.20**

No. 4C13000 The Wabash. Plain case, screw nozzle, medium length, fitted with No. 2 medium 14-karat solid gold pen; medium pen only furnished. Price........................ **65c**

We guarantee this pen to be equal to any sold by others for $1.00 to $1.25.

No. 4C13038 Fine Gold Filled, Fancy Chased Toothpick and Ear Spoon. Entire length, 4 inches. Pick and spoon can be shoved back in case when not in use. Price.... **$1.25**

No. 4C13040 Fancy Gold Filled Beautifully Engraved Toothpick, has fancy stone set on end; entire length, 3 inches. Toothpick can be slid back into case. Illustration shows pick ready for use. Price.... **72c**

No. 4C13002 Chased case, slip nozzle, medium length, fitted with No. 2 fine, medium or stub gold pen. Price.. **$1.10**
No. 4C13004 Chased case, medium length, regular nozzle, fitted with No. 2 fine, medium or stub gold pen. Price.. **$1.20**

No. 4C13006 Taper case, regular size, chased, fitted with No. 3 fine, medium or stub gold pen. Price. **$1.95**
No. 4C13008 Taper case, chased, regular size, gold mounted, fitted with No. 3 fine, medium or stub gold pen. Price........................ **$2.75**

No. 4C13010 Hexagon, regular plain case, fitted with No. 3 fine, medium gold or stub pen. Price........ **$2.50**
No. 4C13012 Regular hexagon, special size case, fitted with No. 4 fine, medium or stub gold pen. Price.. **$2.75**
No. 4C13014 Regular hexagon, special size thick case, fitted with No. 5 fine, medium or stub gold pen. Price........................ **$3.00**

No. 4C13016 Regular size case, gold mounted, fitted with No. 3 fine, medium or stub gold pen. Price........................ **$2.25**
No. 4C13018 Extra size case, gold mounted, fitted with No. 4 size pen. Price.......... **$2.40**

No. 4C13020 Ladies' pen, gold mounted, fine chased taper case, fitted with No. 2 fine, medium or stub gold pen. Price........ **$3.00**
No. 4C13022 Ladies' pen, full gold and silver mounted, thin taper case, fitted with fine, medium or stub gold pen. Price........................ **$3.75**

No. 4C13024 Hexagon case, regular size, gold trimmed, fitted with No. 3 fine, medium or stub gold pen. Price........................ **$3.00**
No. 4C13026 Hexagon case, gold mounted, special size thick case, fitted with No. 4 fine, medium or stub gold pen. Price........................ **$3.50**
No. 4C13028 Hexagon case, gold mounted, extra special size thick case, fitted with No. 5 fine, medium or stub gold pen. Price.... **4.00**

No. 4C13030 Solid Sterling Silver Holder, beautifully chased and tapered, very pretty and stylish. Price........................ **$1.15**

Gold Filled and Ebony Telescopic Holder, with best quality iridium pointed pens.
No. 4C13032 10 karat Pen with Holder. Price, No. 3 Pen, **$0.95**; No. 4 Pen, **$1.00**; No. 5 Pen, **$1.20**; No. 6 Pen, **$1.40**; No. 7 Pen.. **$1.55**
No. 4C13034 16-karat Pen with Holder. Price, No. 3 Pen, **1.15**; No. 4 Pen, **1.25**; No. 5 Pen, **1.45**; No. 6 Pen, **1.65**; No. 7 Pen.. **1.85**

No. 4C13036 Gold Filled, Improved Telescopic Penholder and Combined Screw Pencil. When it is desired to use the pencil the pen can be slid back into the holder by means of a band on the outside, and the pencil can be brought into position.
16-karat Pen with Holder. Price, No. 3 Pen, **$1.70**; No. 4 Pen, **$1.95**; No. 5 Pen, **$2.10**; No. 6 Pen........................ **$2.45**

GOLD PENS REPOINTED

for 22 cents each. 2 cents extra for mail charges.

Don't be misled by fancy prices on gold pens. We will match ours against any.

Finest Quality Solid Gold Pens.

LONG NIBS.

Catalogue No.		10-karat	16-karat
4C13080	No. 1	$0.35	$0.45
4C13082	No. 2	.40	.50
4C13084	No. 3	.45	.65
4C13086	No. 4	.50	.75
4C13088	No. 5	.65	.90
4C13090	No. 6	.75	1.00
4C13092	No. 7	.90	1.20
4C13094	No. 8	1.10	1.45

STUB.

MADE IN 16-KARAT ONLY.

Cat. No.	No.		Cat. No.	No.	
4C13096	4	$0.75	4C13100	6	$1.00
4C13098	5	.90	4C13101	7	1.20

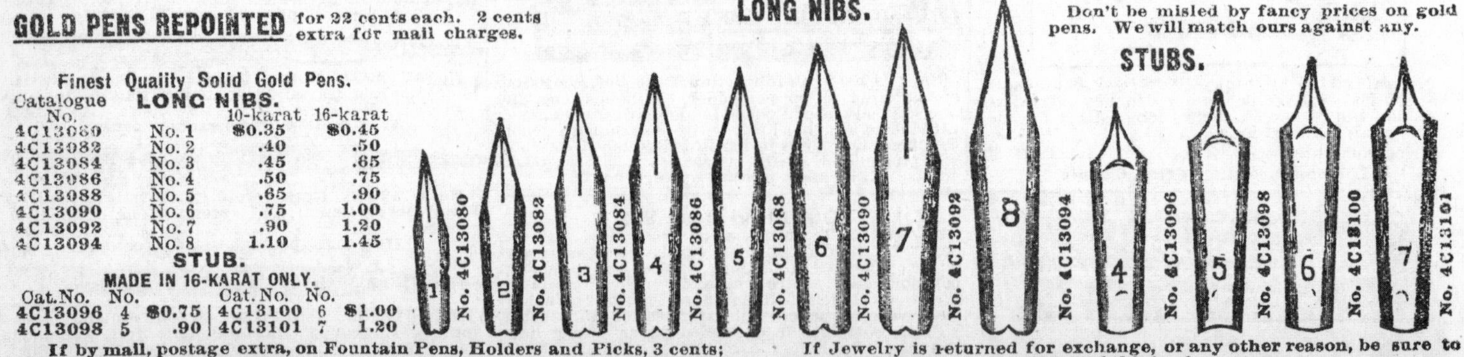

If by mail, postage extra, on Fountain Pens, Holders and Picks, 3 cents; registry or insurance extra.

If Jewelry is returned for exchange, or any other reason, be sure to follow instructions in front part of this book.

OUR SILVERWARE DEPARTMENT.

IN SILVERWARE WHERE DOZEN PRICES ARE QUOTED, THE MARGIN OF PROFIT BEING SO SMALL, WE CANNOT SELL LESS THAN ONE-HALF DOZEN OF A KIND.

THE REASON WHY WE ARE SUCCESSFUL.

We have only carried such makes as we know to be of such honest material and workmanship that there could be no question as to its wearing ability. When we sold an item we sold it on honor and we knew that it was going to give entire satisfaction in every particular.

OUR SEARS, ROEBUCK & CO.'S FLAT WARE, stamped "Paragon" and the Seroco Brand Silver Plated Cutlery is made under special contract. We can recommend them above all other makes. A full description and prices are quoted on page 267. We can not engrave knives as they are made of steel.

THE SEROCO BRAND KNIVES AND FORKS, another brand of our own, the equal of all other brands offered by others as being the best. This brand equals any manufactured, with the exception of our Paragon brand, which positively has no equals. See the prices on knives and forks below. You can not buy the equal of our 16-dwt. knives and forks anywhere. They positively are the best manufactured.

Mail Charges on Knives and Forks, About 48 Cents Per Dozen. | All Medium Knives are 9¼ inches long. Forks are 7½ inches long.

Sears, Roebuck & Co.'s Special Brand 12 and 16-dwt. Knives and Forks.—Stamped Paragon.

No. 5C100 Medium Shell Pattern Knives, 12 dwt. Price, per dozen. $2.70 | No. 5C102 Medium Shell Pattern Forks, 12 dwt. Price, per dozen. $2.70

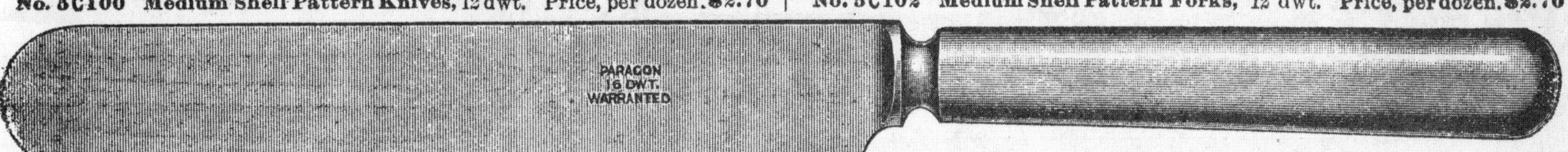

No. 5C104 Medium Plain Pattern Knives, 12 dwt. Price, per dozen. $2.60
No. 5C106 Medium Plain Pattern Forks, 12 dwt. Price, per dozen. 2.60
No. 5C108 Medium Plain Pattern Knives, 16 dwt. Price, per dozen. $3.50
No. 5C110 Medium Plain Pattern Forks, 16 dwt. Price, per dozen. 3.50

Seroco Brand Knives and Forks. Made Especially for Sears, Roebuck & Co.

All Medium Knives shown on this page are 9¼ inches long. Forks are 7½ inches long.

No. 5C166 Plain Medium Knives, 6-dwt. plate. Price, per dozen. $1.80
No. 5C168 Plain Medium Forks, 6-dwt. plate. Price, per dozen.. 1.80
No. 5C170 Plain Medium Knives, 8-dwt. plate. Price, per dozen.. 2.00
No. 5C172 Plain Medium Forks, 8-dwt. plate. Price, per dozen.. 2.00
No. 5C174 Plain Medium Knives, 12-dwt. plate. Price, per dozen. $2.50
No. 5C176 Plain Medium Forks, 12-dwt. plate. Price, per dozen.. 2.50
No. 5C178 Plain Medium Knives, 16-dwt. plate. Price, per dozen.. 3.15
No. 5C180 Plain Medium Forks, 16-dwt. plate. Price, per dozen.. 3.15

A POINT OF INFORMATION.

Pure solid silver will tarnish. Coal gas, smoke, even the atmosphere will cause silver to oxidize, that is, turn dark. This does not denote that it is of inferior grade or poor manufacture. Silverware, to be kept bright and clean, should be polished from time to time.

No. 5C198 Silver Cream is unquestionably the purest and best silver polish made, contains no acid and will not scratch. Price, ½ pint, 22c

No. 5C199 Silver Cream, powder form. Price, per box 6c

If by mail, postage extra, 4 cents.

Wm. A. Rogers' 12-dwt. Knives and Forks.

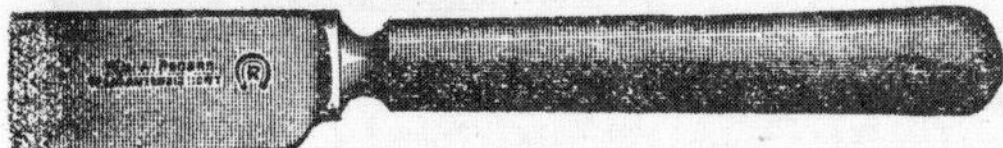

No. 5C112 Medium Knives, plain. Per dozen. $2.40
No. 5C114 Medium Forks, plain. Per dozen. 2.40
No. 5C116 Dessert Knives, plain. Per dozen. 2.35

No. 5C120 Medium Knives, shell. Per dozen.. $2.50
No. 5C122 Medium Forks, shell. Per dozen.. 2.50
No. 5C124 Dessert Knives, shell. Per dozen.. 2.45

No. 5C128 Medium Knives, fancy. Per dozen. $3.00
No. 5C130 Medium Forks, fancy. Per dozen. 3.00
No. 5C132 Dessert Knives, fancy. Per dozen. 2.90

No. 5C138 Medium Knives, hollow handle, Marcella pattern. Price, per dozen $7.00

No. 5C140 Medium Knives, hollow handle, Warwick pattern. Price, per dozen $7.00

Hollow handle forks not made. See page 268 for forks to match.

Rogers' 1847 Brand 12-dwt. Knives and Forks.

No. 5C142 Medium Knives, plain. Per dozen. $2.98
No. 5C144 Medium Forks, plain. Per dozen. 2.98
No. 5C146 Three-Piece Carving Set, same style. Price, per set........ 3.15
No. 5C148 Dessert Knives, plain. Per dozen.... 3.15
No. 5C150 Dessert Forks, plain. Per dozen..... 3.15
No. 5C152 Fruit Knives, same style. Per doz... 2.25

No. 5C154 Medium Knives, shell. Per dozen.... $3.15
No. 5C156 Medium Forks, shell. Per dozen... 3.15
No. 5C158 Three-Piece Carving Set, same style. Price, per set........ 3.25
No. 5C160 Dessert Knives, shell. Per dozen. 3.25
No. 5C162 Dessert Forks, shell. Per dozen... 3.25
No. 5C164 Fruit Knives, same style. Per doz. 3.25

Sterling Plate Knife and Fork Set.

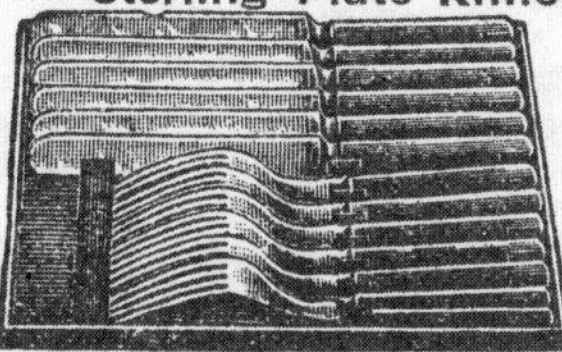

No. 5C182 Plain Pattern Knife and Fork Set, regular size, plated with 4 dwt. of silver; excellent value. Price for complete set $1.25

No. 5C184 As above, 6 dwt. silver to the dozen. Price........ $1.80

Our $1.22 Silver Plated Knife and Fork Set.

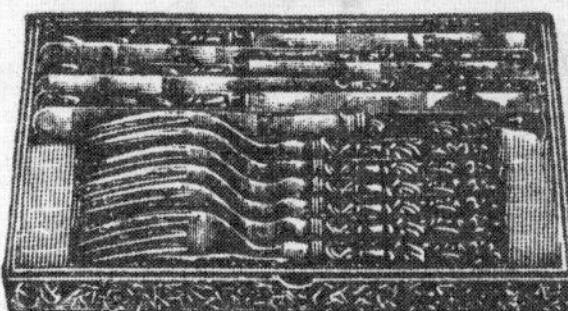

No. 5C187 Knife and Fork Set, the knives are plain handles, but the forks are engraved like the flat fancy patterns; six knives and six forks in box, complete. Price, per set........ $1.22

If by mail, postage extra, 35 cents.

Our $1.95 Knife and Fork Set.

No. 5C188 Set of six each, Fancy Knives and Forks, engraved handles. Both the knives and forks are made of solid steel and finished in a very thorough manner. Price, per set..... $1.95

If by mail, postage extra, 35 cents.

We engrave script letters for 2½ cents each.

Shipping Weight, 4 lbs.

No. 5C2110 Crumb Set, satin finish, bright hand engraved, fancy rococo border, ebony handle on scraper. Dimensions of tray, 7x9 inches; scraper in proportion. Price, per set........ $1.68

No. 5C2114 Bread Tray, hand burnished finish; fancy rococo border, hand engraved. Length, 12 inches; width, 6½ inches. Price........ $1.40

Shipping weight, 4 pounds.

No. 5C2118 Cake Basket, full hand burnished, with rococo border center; is handsomely ornamented. Extreme height, 9⅞ inches; diameter, 9 inches. Price........ $1.55

Shipping weight, 7 pounds.

No. 5C1622 Cracker Jar, fancy engraved, satin finish; height, 9½ inches. Price.. $1.50

Shipping weight, about 7½ lbs.

No. 5C2124 Cake Basket, satin finish, ornamented border; height, 9¼ inches; length, 10¾ inches. Price........ $2.75

Shipping weight, 7 pounds.

ALASKA SILVERWARE—A NEW DISCOVERY

THE CHEAPEST AND BEST FLAT WARE MADE The Alaska silverware is not plated, but is the same solid metal through and through, and will hold the same color as long as there is any portion of the goods left. Do not be deceived by any dealer who undertakes to sell you any of the numerous imitations of this ware, that are sold on the market for more money than we ask for the genuine. **The genuine Alaska Silverware can be had only of us.**

BEFORE TAKING HOLD OF THIS NEW DISCOVERY we left nothing undone to thoroughly investigate the properties of this metal, and to test the same in every conceivable manner, to satisfy ourselves that it was all that it was represented to be. After having made all sorts of experiments, and it stood all tests, we made a contract with the factory to handle the goods. It has now been about seven years since we began to handle this line, and it has not only proved from experiment to be as represented, but with seven years of actual service in the hands of many thousands of our customers, who send us the most flattering recommendations in praise of these goods, and with the rapidly increasing sales, we feel that we cannot recommend it too highly.

THE METAL IS VERY DENSE AND TOUGH, is almost as white as genuine silver, takes a beautiful polish and requires much less care than does silver plated ware. You can scrape kettles or pots, or subject it to any kind of service without fear of damage.

THE FANCY PATTERN is equal in appearance and artistic finish to any of the best silver plated or solid silver goods on the market. The immense quantities of these goods we handle, and the condition of our contract direct with the factory, puts us in a position to furnish this genuine Alaska Silverware at a slight advance over cost to manufacture.

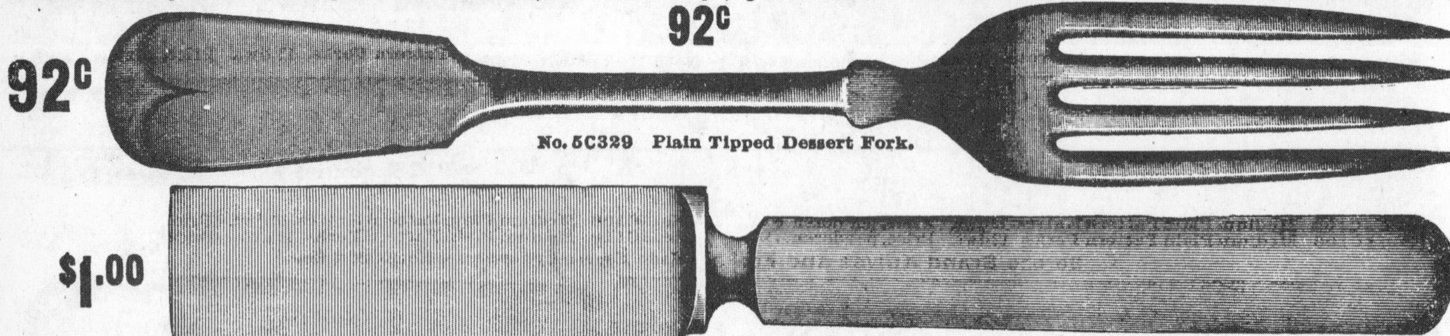

92c

No. 5C329 Plain Tipped Dessert Fork.

$1.00

No. 5C332 Medium Alaska Silverware Knife.

Relative Lengths: Tea spoons, 5¾ inches; dessert spoons, 7½ inches; table spoons, 8¼ inches; dessert forks, 7 inches; medium forks, 7⅝ inches; medium knives, 9 inches; sugar shells, 5¾ inches; butter knives, 7 inches.

OUR GUARANTEE.

ALASKA SILVERWARE KNIVES are not plated. They are the same metal and color through and through. They are proof against all table and fruit acids. They will not rust. They will not tarnish. They will cut and cut well. They can be ground and sharpened like a steel knife, and we guarantee them for the term of your natural lifetime.

46c

Tipped Pattern Tea Spoon.

We can supply leatherette cases, fancy lined, to hold twelve tea spoons for 25 cents, to hold six knives and six forks, for 25 cents, to hold twelve tea spoons, butter knife, sugar shell and pickle fork, at 25 cents, to hold twelve tea spoons and six table spoons, at 38 cents, to hold one dozen table spoons, at 25 cents. Cases only supplied when goods are ordered to fill same from us.

50c

Fancy Pattern Tea Spoon.

46c

Shell Pattern Tea Spoon.

50c

Beaded Pattern Tea Spoon.

Silverware and Jewelry Cleaning Outfits.

No. 5C300 Our Silverware and Jewelry Cleaning Outfit, consisting of one cleaning brush, one box of fine sifted drying sawdust, one fine India sponge, one piece chamois skin, one box silver cream powder, with full directions; one ¼-pint bottle silver cream polish, with full directions. This complete cleaning outfit in wooden case, made especially for the purpose. Price....85c
Weight, packed for shipment, 2½ pounds.

No. 5C302 Our Cleaning Outfit, similar to above described outfit, but consisting of one cleaning brush, drying sawdust, sponge, chamois, and silver cream in powder form, in fine pasteboard leatherette case made for the purpose, durable and strong. Price.....65c
If by mail, postage extra, 16 cents.

OUR SPECIAL PRICES.

Any of these goods can be sent by mail on receipt of price and additional amount named to pay postage.

Postage on the above goods, if to go by mail, will be extra per half dozen as follows: On tea spoons, 6 cents; dessert spoons or forks, 12 cents; table spoons or medium forks, 15 cents; medium knives, 20 cents; and sugar shells or butter knives, 2 cents each. It is cheaper to send them by express, if you have an express office near by.

No.	Article		Tipped Pattern, per Set of Six	Shell Pattern, per Set of Six	Fancy Pattern, per Set of Six	Beaded Pattern, per Set of Six
No. 5C326	Tea Spoons	set of ½ dozen,	$0.46	$0.46	$0.50	$0.50
No. 5C327	Dessert Spoons	set of ½ dozen,	.76	.76	.80	.80
No. 5C328	Table Spoons	set of ½ dozen,	.92	.92	1.00	1.00
No. 5C329	Medium Forks (regular size)	set of ½ dozen,	.92	.92	1.00	1.00
No. 5C330	Dessert Forks	set of ½ dozen,	.76	.76	.80	.80
No. 5C332	Plain Handle Alaska Silverware Medium Knives,	set of ½ dozen,	1.00	Not made	Not made	Not made
No. 5C333	Sugar Shells	each,	.15	.15	.16	.16
No. 5C334	Butter Knives	each,	.15	.15	.16	.16

The standard of quality and finish of the above goods are guaranteed by the manufacturer to us, and we guarantee them to our customers. You run no risk whatever in purchasing this ware, for if you do not find them to be exactly as represented, they can be returned to us and your money will be refunded. Be sure to state catalogue number and pattern wanted when you order.

WE DO NOT MAKE ANY OTHER PIECES THAN THOSE MENTIONED ABOVE OF ALASKA SILVERWARE.

OUR OWN SPECIAL HIGH GRADE TRIPLE SILVER PLATED TABLEWARE.

OUR SUPERIOR LINE OF FANCY PIECES ILLUSTRATED BELOW ARE UNEQUALED.

OUR OWN SPECIAL HIGH GRADE SILVER PLATED TABLEWARE. To be able to give our customers the best value in strictly high grade silverware, we have had manufactured expressly for us an entirely new brand called the Paragon, by one of the largest and most reliable manufacturers in America. Our new Paragon brand is made after our own specifications. Each piece contains a greater amount of silver than any other brand of standard plated ware on the market. We have investigated the weights offered by other makers and our Paragon brand of silverware positively is the heaviest. This year we have changed the pattern, and instead of marking it with our own name, we have had it stamped Paragon, together with the quality whether extra plate or triple plate. We control both the pattern and the brand.

THE DISPOSITION OF MANUFACTURERS has been to cheapen this class of goods and yet hold it at a higher price, and in order that our customers might have the very best, we have gotten these goods out under our own specifications; we know just the amount of silver that goes on every piece, we know we are perfectly safe in issuing a binding guarantee and we are able to make the price based on the actual cost of material and labor, with but our one small percentage of profit added, which will mean a great saving to our customers.

EACH PIECE IS STAMPED "PARAGON."

Rose Pattern Table Spoon Handle.

WE CAN SUPPLY LEATHERETTE CASES, fancy lined, to hold twelve tea spoons for 25 cents, to hold six knives and six forks for 25 cents, to hold twelve tea spoons, butter knife, sugar shell, and pickle fork at 25 cents, to hold twelve tea spoons and six table spoons at 38 cents, to hold twelve table spoons at 25 cents. Cases only supplied when goods are ordered to fill same from us.

IF YOU BUY OUR SPECIAL BRAND WARE you will get the best plated ware that money can buy. The silver that goes into the plating of these goods is $\frac{999}{1000}$ fine and is the highest grade used in silverware.

DIFFERENT FROM ALMOST ALL OTHER SILVERWARE, our silverware is made by a manufacturer of long experience in the manufacture of gold filled watch cases and is made on the same principle as gold filled watch cases are made, and while we term it silver triple plated it is really silver filled. It is made from two heavy plates of sterling silver over a base of hard metal, and is a goods there is practically no wear out to.

THOUGH WE HAVE BETTERED THE QUALITY AND WEIGHT CONSIDERABLY, on account of the immense contract we are able to place same at a price more advantageous than last year. According to our usual method we therefore give you the advantage of our better purchase and reduced our prices accordingly. The word "plate" does not appear on the goods. It would require an expert to know that they were not solid sterling silver.

Six Paragon Brand Rose Pattern Tea Spoons, in fancy lined box complete as illustration shows. Box is cloth covered, hinged top and lined.

No. 5C582 Six Tea Spoons, Rose pattern, extra plate. Price........................**$1.19**
No. 5C584 Six Tea Spoons, Rose pattern, triple plate. Price **$1.50**
No. 5C586 Six Table Spoons, Rose pattern, extra plate. Price.........................**$2.10**
No. 5C588 Six Table Spoons, Rose pattern, triple plate. Price.........................**$2.72**

No.	Article	Plate	Tipped Pattern Per doz.	Shell Pattern Per doz.	Rose Pattern Per doz.
No. 5C550	Tea Spoons	Extra Plate	$1.58	$1.58	$1.67
No. 5C552	Tea Spoons	Triple Plate	2.16	2.16	2.30
No. 5C554	Dessert Spoons	Extra Plate	2.80	2.80	3.10
No. 5C556	Dessert Spoons	Triple Plate	3.60	3.60	4.15
No. 5C558	Table Spoons	Extra Plate	3.16	3.16	3.34
No. 5C560	Table Spoons	Triple Plate	4.32	4.32	4.60
No. 5C562	Medium Forks	Extra Plate	3.16	3.16	3.34
No. 5C564	Medium Forks	Triple Plate	4.32	4.32	4.60
No. 5C566	Dessert Forks	Extra Plate	2.80	2.80	3.10
No. 5C568	Dessert Forks	Triple Plate	3.60	3.60	4.15
No. 5C570	Sugar Shell	Triple Plate, each	.30	.30	.32
No. 5C572	Butter Knives	Triple Plate, each	.35	.35	.40

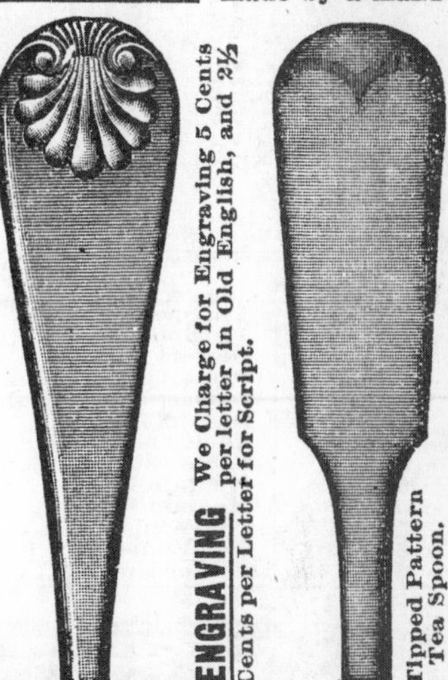

ENGRAVING
We Charge for Engraving 5 Cents per letter in Old English, and 2½ Cents per Letter for Script.

Shell Pattern.

Tipped Pattern Tea Spoon.

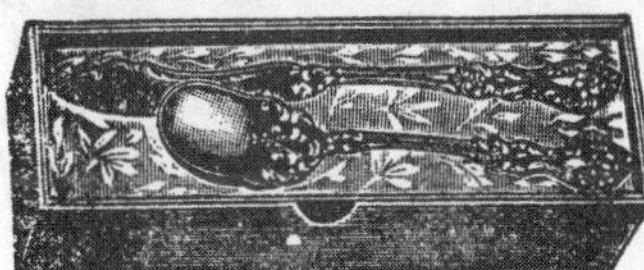

No. 5C403 Sugar Shell and Butter Knife Combination. Paragon brand, triple plate, rose pattern. Length of butter knife, 7 inches; length of sugar shell, 6 inches; in fine lined box. Price, per set....**76c**
No. 5C405 Same as above, gilt blade and bowl. Price, per set................................**$1.04**
If by mail, postage extra, 7 cents.

No. 5C410 Berry Spoon, Paragon brand, triple plate, rose pattern; 8½ inches long; in fine lined box. Price..**60c**
No. 5C412 Same as above, with gilt bowl...**85c**
If by mail, postage extra, 8 cents.

No. 5C415 Butter Knife. Paragon brand, triple plate, rose pattern, 7¼ inches long; in fine lined box. Price....................................**42c**
No. 5C417 Same as above, with gilt blade....**57c**
If by mail, postage extra, 4 cents.

No. 5C419 Pickle Fork. Paragon brand, triple plate, rose pattern, 7¼ inches long; in fine lined box. Price **38c**
No. 5C421 Same as above, gilt tines. Price, **48c**
If by mail, postage extra, 4 cents.

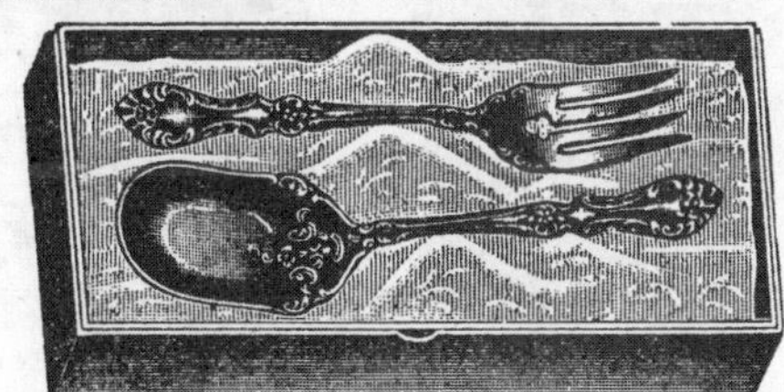

No. 5C422 Salad Set, Paragon brand, triple plate, rose pattern. Length of spoon, 8½ inches; length of fork, 8 inches; in fine lined box. Price, per set..**$1.20**
No. 5C424 Same as above, gilt bowl and tines. Price, per set...(Postage extra, 11c).... **1.60**

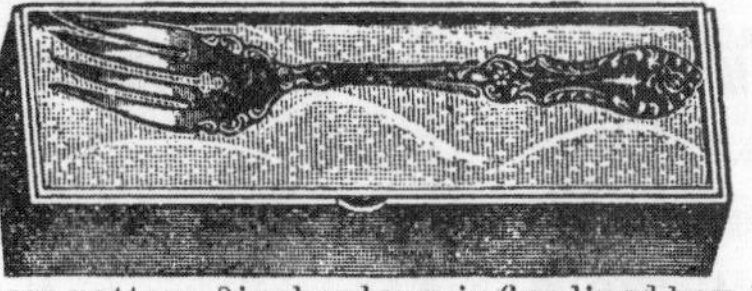

No. 5C426 Cold Meat Fork, Paragon brand, triple plate, rose pattern, 8 inches long; in fine lined box. Price.**60c**
No. 5C428 Same as above, gilt tines. Price, **75c**
If by mail, postage extra, 8 cents.

No. 5C430 Pie Server, Paragon brand, triple plate, rose pattern, 9 inches long; in fine lined box. Price.............**70c**
No. 5C432 Same as above, gilt blade. Price, **95c**
If by mail, postage extra, 8 cents.

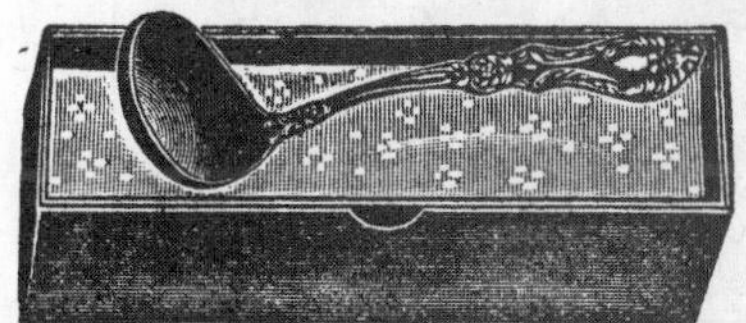

No. 5C436 Gravy Ladle, Paragon brand, triple plate, rose pattern, 8 inches long; in fine lined box. Price **70c**
No. 5C438 Same as above, gilt bowl. Price, **84c**
If by mail, postage extra, 8 cents.

No. 5C443 Sugar Shell, Paragon brand, triple plate, rose pattern, 6 inches long; in fine lined box. Price. **34c**
No. 5C445 Same as above, with gilt bowl.......................**47c**
If by mail, postage extra, 4 cents.

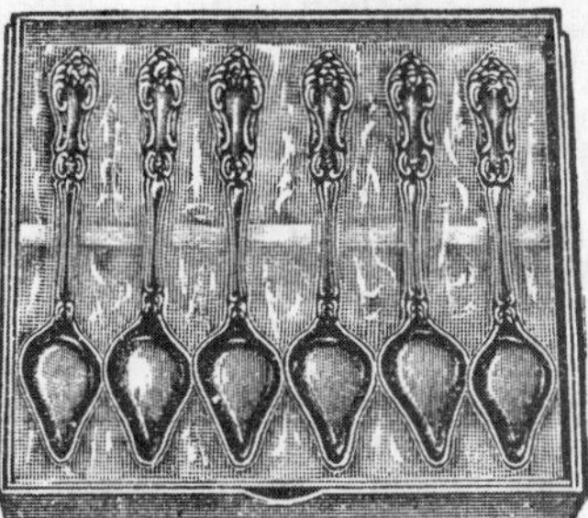

Orange Spoons. Paragon brand, triple plate, rose pattern. Length, 6¼ inches; in fine lined box.
No. 5C448 Price, per set of six, plain, **$1.05**
No. 5C450 Price, per set of six, gilt bowls. **$1.45**
If by mail, postage extra, 6 cents.

OUR $5.70 FOUR-PIECE TEA SET.

No. 5C2631 Four-Piece Tea Set, consisting of tea pot, sugar bowl, cream pitche and spoon holder; spoon holder and cream pitcher gold lined. This set is satin finished and has latest applied trimmings, as illustration shows. The pattern is the very latest idea in this kind of ware. Tea pot holds 5½ half pints, height, 7½ inches, sugar bowl is 6 inches high, cream pitcher, 3½ inches high, and spoon holder 3¼ inches high. Cream pitcher and spoon holder are gold lined. We guarantee it to be quadruple plated. While we do not generally advocate buying cheap sets, we can conscientiously recommend this cheap set as being serviceable and will in every way prove entirely satisfactory. Price, per set.......... **$5.70**
Weight of set, packed for shipment, about 20 pounds.

THE CELEBRATED WM. A. ROGERS LATEST PATTERNS.

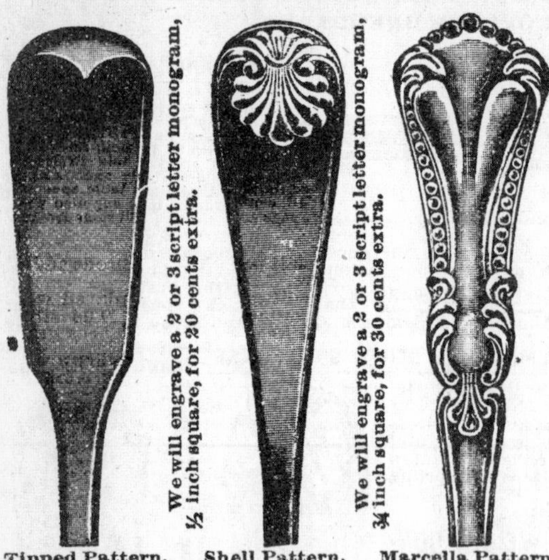

Tipped Pattern. Shell Pattern. Marcella Pattern.

WE DEFY COMPETITION in this line of silverware. Our prices are based on one small per cent of profit and we do not gauge our prices on quotations made by others. Therefore our prices usually show at least 20 to 25 per cent less than others are asking, and sometimes a greater saving.

The Arundel pattern has been discontinued by us, except on fancy pieces, as we have procured the very latest pattern this company has just placed on the market, called the Hanover Pattern. It is a very beautiful design and more massive in appearance, and in every way better than the pattern discontinued by us. The blanks are of 21 per cent nickel silver, the highest grade used, plated with pure sterling silver of substantial thickness. Every piece of Wm. A. Rogers silverware will give entire satisfaction. We quote two qualities on this page: the A1 extra plate and the triple plate. **A1 plate is marked on each piece thus, A1—X, on triple plate thus, A1—XXX.** We recommend the triple plate, as more silver is used and so will wear longer.

THE TIPPED, SHELL AND CARLTON PATTERNS are not as heavy in weight, in fact, much lighter; we refer to the blanks used for them, as the balance of the goods shown here, but the same amount of silver is plated upon them. We charge for engraving, 2½ cents per letter for script; 5 cents per letter for Old English.

We will engrave a 2 or 3 letter, ribbon style, monogram, ½ inch square, for 25 cents extra.

We can supply leatherette cases, fancy lined, to hold twelve tea spoons, for 25 cents; to hold six knives and six forks, for 25 cents; to hold twelve tea spoons, butter knife, sugar shell and pickle fork, at 25 cents; to hold twelve tea spoons and six table spoons, at 38 cents; to hold one dozen table spoons, at 25 cents. Cases only supplied when goods are ordered to fill same from us.

Warwick Pattern. Hanover Pattern. Carlton Pattern.

Catalogue No.	Prices Quoted Per Dozen		Tipped	Shell	Marcella	Warwick	Hanover	Carlton
5C601	**Tea Spoons**	A 1 Extra Plate	$0.82	$0.82	$1.70	$1.70	$1.70	$0.82
5C603	**Tea Spoons**	Triple Plate	1.52	1.52	2.40	2.40	2.40	1.52
5C605	**Dessert Spoons**	A 1 Extra Plate	1.52	1.52	3.24	3.24	3.24	1.52
5C607	**Dessert Spoons**	Triple Plate	2.84	2.84	4.12	4.12	4.12	2.84
5C609	**Dessert Forks**	A 1 Extra Plate	1.52	1.52	3.24	3.24	3.24	1.52
5C611	**Dessert Forks**	Triple Plate	2.84	2.84	4.12	4.12	4.12	2.84
5C613	**Table Spoons**	A 1 Extra Plate	1.64	1.64	3.42	3.42	3.42	1.64
5C615	**Table Spoons**	Triple Plate	3.04	3.04	4.82	4.82	4.82	3.04
5C617	**Medium Forks**	A 1 Extra Plate	1.64	1.64	3.42	3.42	3.42	1.64
5C619	**Medium Forks**	Triple Plate	3.04	3.04	4.82	4.82	4.82	3.04
5C621	**Coffee Spoons**	Small 4¼-inch	not made	.82	1.70	1.70	1.70	.82
5C623	**Sugar Shells**	A 1 Extra Plate only	.13	.13	.27	.27	.27	.13
5C625	**Butter Knives**	A 1 Extra Plate only	.15	.15	.30	.30	.30	.15

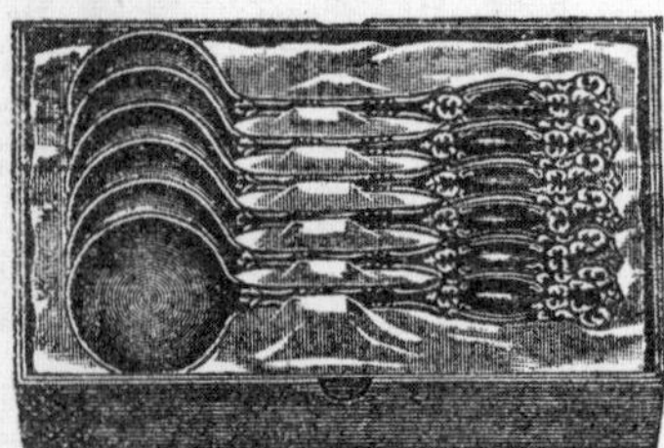

No. 5C630 **Soup Spoon Set,** Warwick pattern. The latest round pattern bowl; 7 inches long. Price, per set of 6 .... $2.10
If by mail, postage extra, 16 cents.

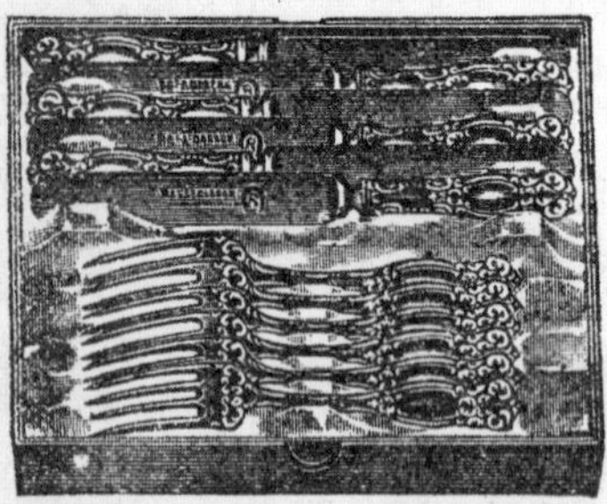

No. 5C634 **Knife and Fork Set,** Warwick pattern. The knives are hollow handled, finest made, guaranteed 12-pennyweight plate, and the forks are triple plated. Knives, 9 inches; forks, 7½ inches. Price, complete in silk lined box $6.15
Shipping weight, 2¼ pounds.

No. 5C646 **Dinner Set,** Carlton pattern, 16 pieces, 6 table spoons, 6 tea spoons, butter knife, sugar shell, and salt and pepper shaker.
Price, per set $2.75
If by mail, postage extra, 34 cents.

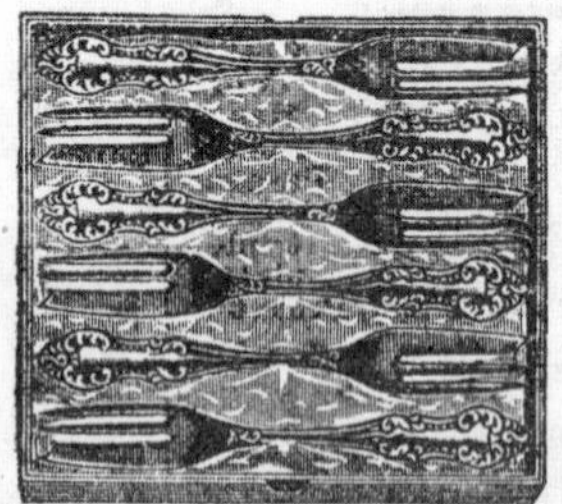

No. 5C648 **Pie Forks,** Carlton pattern, set of 6; 7½ inches long.
Price, per set $2.00
If by mail, postage extra, 13 cents.

No. 5C650 **Tea Set,** 8 pieces, Carlton pattern, 6 tea spoons, butter knife and sugar shell. Price, per set.. $1.19
If by mail, postage extra, 14 cents.

No. 5C718 **Cold Meat Fork,** Arundel pattern, 8¼ in. long. Price...... 48c
No. 5C719 Same, but with gilt tines. Price 72c
If by mail, postage extra, 6 cents.

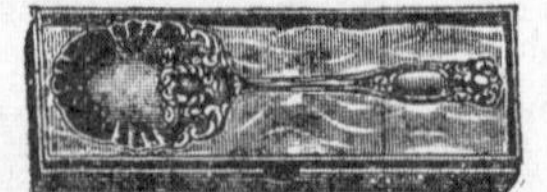

No. 5C726 **Berry Spoon,** Warwick pattern, gilt bowl, 9 inches long.
Price $1.15
No. 5C727 **Berry Spoon,** Arundel pattern, plain silver bowl. Price.. 80c
If by mail, postage extra, 8 cents.

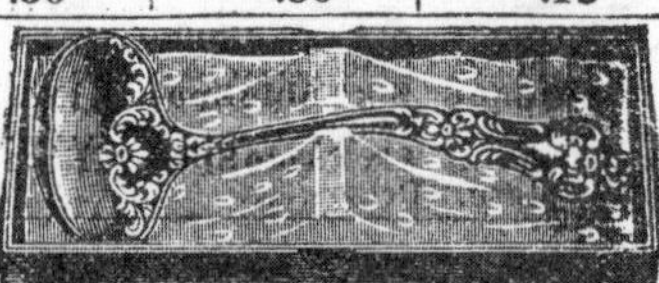

No. 5C730 **Cream Ladle,** Arundel pattern, 6 inches long. Price.... 42c
No. 5C732 **Gravy Ladle,** Arundel pattern, 7 inches long. Price.. 58c
No. 5C736 **Soup Ladle,** Arundel pattern, 10½ in. long. Price... $1.58
If by mail, postage extra, each, 10c.

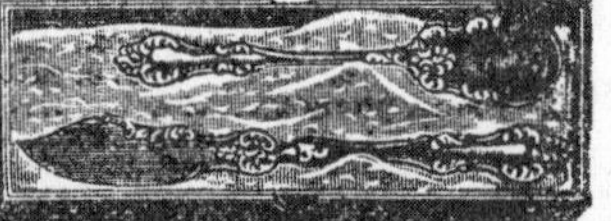

No. 5C748 **Butter and Sugar Sets,** Carlton pattern, gilt bowl. Knife, 7 inches long. Price, per set... 62c
If by mail, postage extra, 8 cents.

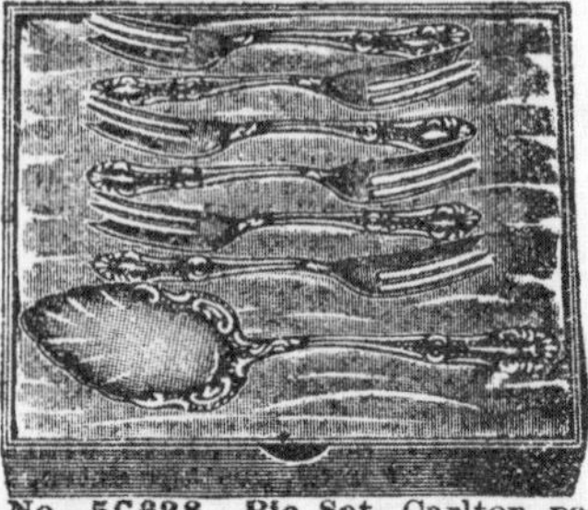

No. 5C828 **Pie Set,** Carlton pattern. 6 forks, 7½ inches, and pie knife, 9 inches. Price, per set $2.62
Shipping weight, 1½ pounds.

ORDER OUR No. 5C2602 FOUR-PIECE, QUADRUPLE SILVER PLATE, HAND ENGRAVED, SATIN FINISHED TEA SET for $9.50 and compare it with the finest silver tea set that you know of, costing $15.00 to $20.00, and if ours is not its superior return it and we will refund your money.

OUR $9.50 QUADRUPLE SILVER PLATED TEA SET.

No. 5C2602 **For $9.50 we will sell you this Quadruple Silver Plated Tea Set.** Quadruple plate is one plate heavier than triple plate, and we guarantee it to wear and give entire satisfaction. You cannot buy a better quality set even though you paid $15.00 or $20.00. **This set is hand engraved, satin finish, has fancy feet and made extra heavy throughout. The set consists of a coffee or tea pot, capacity, about two quarts, 8¼ inches high; sugar bowl, 6¼ inches high; cream pitcher, 3¾ inches high, and spoon holder, 3½ inches high. These pieces made in proportion to the coffee pot.**

No. 5C2602 Four-piece set.... $9.50
No. 5C2604 Syrup Pitcher to match, extra 2.65
No. 5C2606 Butter Dish, extra 2.85
No. 5C2608 Tray, 15x11 inches, extra 2.65

Weight of set, packed for shipment, about 20 pounds.

LATEST AND BEST PATTERNS OF FANCY SILVER PLATED TABLEWARE.

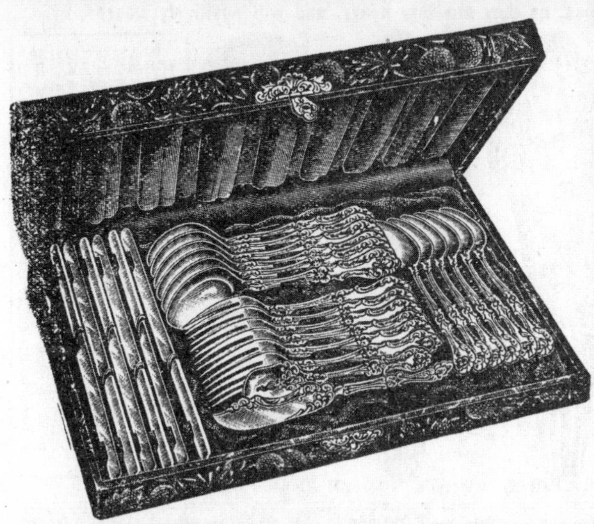

OUR 26-PIECE COMBINATION SET,

in silk lined, plush covered or leatherette case, consisting of 6 tea spoons, 6 table spoons, 6 dinner forks, 6 dinner knives, butter knife and sugar shell, a splendid wedding gift; complete dinner set for 6 people. Prices quoted include case. Weight, 6 pounds. We supply the following brands:

	Price per Set in Leatherette Case.	Price per Set in Plush Case.
No. 5C757 Extra Plate Paragon Brand, Shell pattern, with Paragon 12 pennyweight knives	$6.30	$6.70
No. 5C759 Triple Plate Paragon Brand, Shell pattern. Complete set with Paragon 12 pennyweight knives	7.75	8.15
No. 5C761 Extra Plate Paragon Brand, Rose pattern. We recommend this brand if you want the finest pattern on the market. See illustration of the Rose pattern. Price, for complete set, 12 pennyweight plain Paragon knives	6.55	6.95
No. 5C769 Triple Plate Paragon Brand, Rose pattern. The finest pattern and the highest quality. Price, complete, with 12 pennyweight plain Paragon knives	8.12	8.52
No. 5C771 Triple Plate Paragon Brand, Rose pattern. This brand is without question the best manufactured, the newest pattern and the highest quality. Plain Paragon knives, 16 pennyweight. We give our written binding guarantee for 15 years with this set. Price	8.57	8.98
No. 5C773 Rogers Bros.' A1 Plate, 1847 Brand, Berkshire pattern (see illustration of pattern), plain handle knives and forks. Price, for complete set	7.59	7.99
No. 5C775 Rogers' 1847 Brand, Triple Plate, Berkshire pattern plain handle knives and forks. Price, for complete set	8.88	9.29
No. 5C779 Wm. A. Rogers' A1 Extra Plate, Shell pattern. Price for complete set	3.96	4.36
No. 5C781 Wm. A. Rogers' Triple Plate, Shell pattern. Price for complete set	5.72	6.12

1847 Rogers. Berkshire Pattern. — Paragon. Rose Pattern. — W. A. Rogers. Shell Pattern.

ROGERS BROTHERS' 1847 GOODS.

OUR SPACE WILL NOT PERMIT US TO LIST MORE THAN A PORTION OF THE SAME. WE, HOWEVER, HAVE REPRESENTED ONE OF EACH STYLE OF NEARLY ALL THE STYLES IN WHICH THESE GOODS ARE MADE, WHICH INCLUDES THEIR VERY LATEST AND BEST PATTERNS. SEE PAGE 266 FOR KNIVES.

We list the goods in two grades, namely, what is known as the A1 plate and the triple plate; the latter of which is the better of the two.

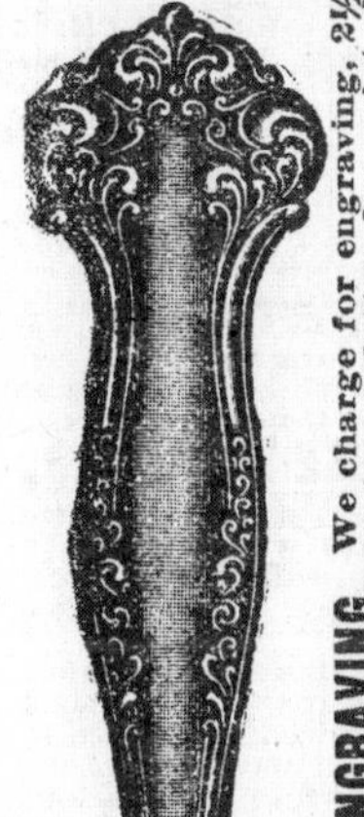

Avon Pattern

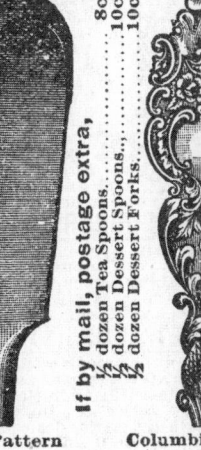

ENGRAVING. We charge for engraving, 2½ cents per letter for script, 5 cents per letter for Old English.

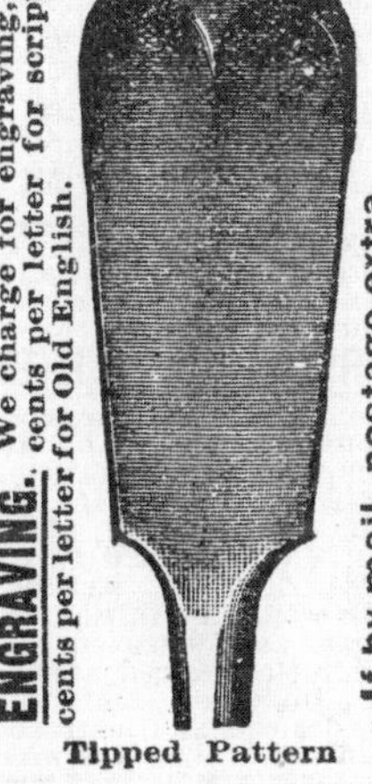

Tipped Pattern

If by mail, postage extra,
½ dozen Tea Spoons.....8c
½ dozen Dessert Spoons.....10c
½ dozen Dessert Forks.....10c

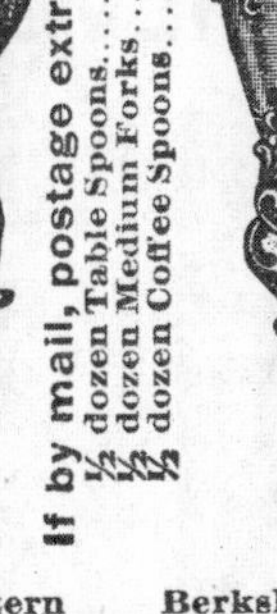

Columbia Pattern

If by mail, postage extra,
½ dozen Table Spoons.....15c
½ dozen Medium Forks.....12c
½ dozen Coffee Spoons.....5c

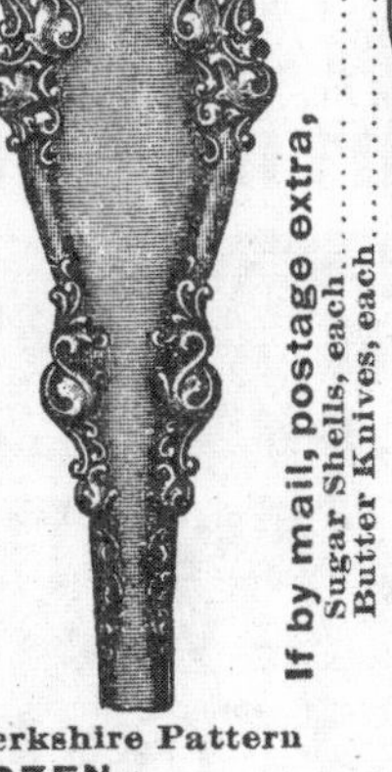

Berkshire Pattern

If by mail, postage extra,
Sugar Shells, each.....3c
Butter Knives, each.....3c

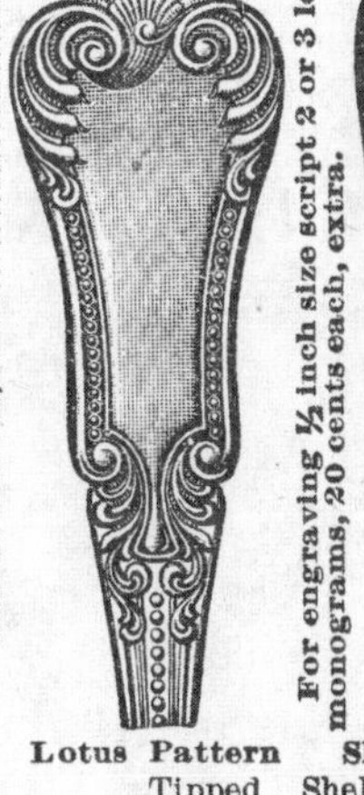

Lotus Pattern

For engraving ½ inch size script 2 or 3 letter monograms, 20 cents each, extra.

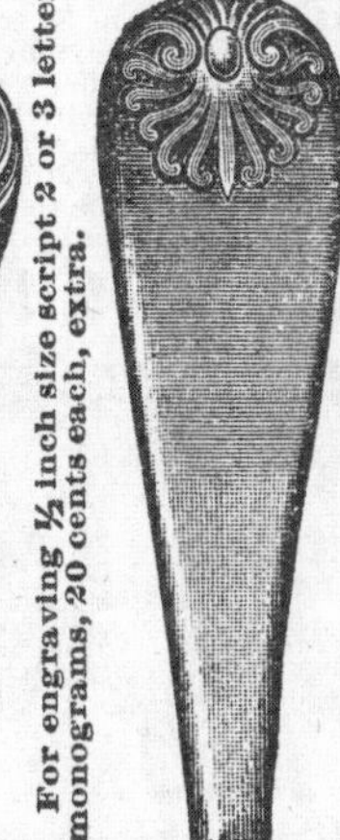

Shell Pattern

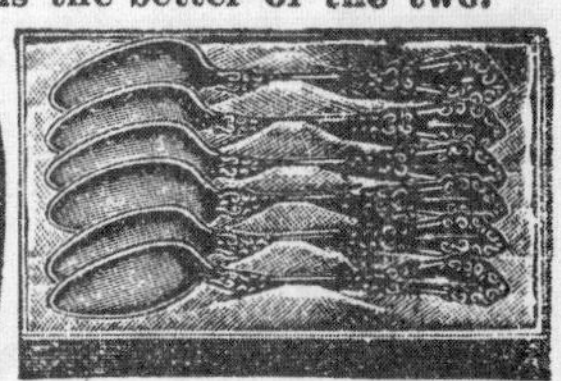

This illustration shows our white enameled white paper lined box that we can supply with any order at the following prices extra.

No. 5C974 Box to hold 6 tea spoons only. Price...6c
No. 5C976 Box to hold 12 tea spoons only. Price.10c
No. 5C978 Box to hold 6 table spoons only. Price.10c
No. 5C980 Box to hold 12 table spoons only. Price.12c
No. 5C982 Box to hold 6 table forks only. Price.10c
No. 5C984 Box to hold 12 table forks only. Price.12c

PRICE PER DOZEN.

No.	Article	Plate	Description	Tipped	Shell	Avon	Columbia	Berkshire	Lotus
No. 5C902	Tea Spoons.	A1 Plate	Tea Spoons are 6 inches long	$2.04	$2.04	$2 28	$2.28	$2.28	$2.28
No. 5C904	Tea Spoons.	Triple Plate.	Tea Spoons are 6 inches long	2.90	2.90	3.14	3.14	3.14	3.14
No. 5C906	Dessert Spoons.	A1 Plate	Dessert Spoons are 7 inches long	3.62	3.62	4.12	4.12	4.12	4.12
No. 5C908	Dessert Spoons.	Triple Plate	Dessert Spoons are 7 inches long	4.83	4.83	5.32	5.32	5.32	5.32
No. 5C914	Table Spoons.	A1 Plate	Table Spoons are 8 inches long	4.12	4.12	4.56	4.56	4.56	4.56
No. 5C916	Table Spoons.	Triple Plate	Table Spoons are 8 inches long	5.80	5.80	6.28	6.28	6.28	6.28
No. 5C918	Medium Forks.	A1 Plate	Medium Forks are 7½ inches long	4.12	4.12	4.56	4.56	4.56	4.56
No. 5C920	Medium Forks.	Triple Plate	Medium Forks are 7½ inches long	5.80	5.80	6.28	6.28	6.28	6.28
No. 5C922	Coffee Spoons.	A1 Plate	Small, 4¼ inches long	not made	2.20	2.28	2.28	2.28	2.28
No. 5C924	Sugar Shells.	A1 Plate only.	6 inches long. Price, each	.36	.36	.38	.38	.38	.38
No. 5C926	Butter Knife.	A1 Plate only.	7½ inches long. Price, each	.43	.43	.46	.46	.46	.46

CASTORS, BERRY OR FRUIT DISHES.

No. 5C1632 Castor, five bottles, bright finish; height, 14 inches.
Price.....96c
Shipping weight, 7½ lbs.

No. 5C1636 Castor, five bottles, satin finish, with bright hand engraving; height, 14 inches. Price.....$1.65
Shipping weight, 7½ lbs.

No. 5C1642 Castor, five fancy glass bottles, fancy handle and frame satin finish, with bright hand engraving; height, 16 inches.
Price.....$3.50
Shipping weight, 7½ pounds.

No. 5C2342 Berry or Fruit Dish, fancy handle, raised ornamentation, beautifully scalloped china dish, white on the outside and pink on the inside and beautifully ornamented in raised gold work. Price.....$5.65
Shipping weight, 9 pounds.
We cannot give you a description that will fully describe the beauties of this dish nor does the illustration give more than an idea of it.

No. 5C2344 Fruit Dish, pink opal bowl, raised ornamentations, bright base, fancy feet, ornamented border. Height, 10 inches.
Price.....$3.00
Shipping weight, 9 pounds.

For Complete Line of Castors, Fruit Dishes, Cake Baskets, etc., send for our Special Watch, Jewelry and Silverware Catalogue.

SOLID $\frac{925}{1000}$ PER CENT FINE STERLING SILVER FLATWARE.

We give weights on sterling silver flatware, but we recommend the 8 or 10-ounce tea spoons, as they are very heavy, and will positively wear forever.

REMEMBER, that our Solid Silver Flatware is solid silver through and through, every grain of it being of the same quality, $\frac{925}{1000}$ fine silver. We merely show the tops of the handles so as to give you a correct idea of the patterns. We carry all the fancy pieces. Please note that we quote in the price list butter knives, sugar shells, berry spoons, cream ladles, gravy ladles, cold meat forks, etc. All of the fancy pieces come in a beautiful silk lined box, for which there is no extra charge. Our solid silverware is stamped Sterling Silver, not coin, which is only $\frac{800}{1000}$ to $\frac{850}{1000}$ fine but Sterling silver $\frac{925}{1000}$ fine. When you see this mark you are positive that you are getting honest goods. WE BAR NONE whether retailer or wholesaler. Our prices are 10 to 15 per cent cheaper than the cheapest and the WARE IS POSITIVELY THE BEST.

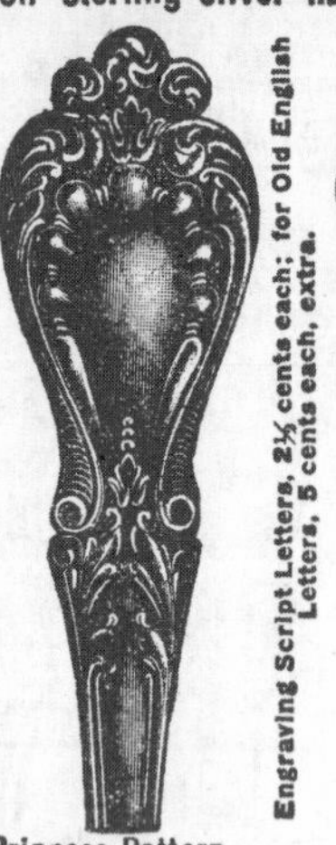

Princess Pattern.

Engraving Script Letters, 2½ cents each; for Old English Letters, 5 cents each, extra.

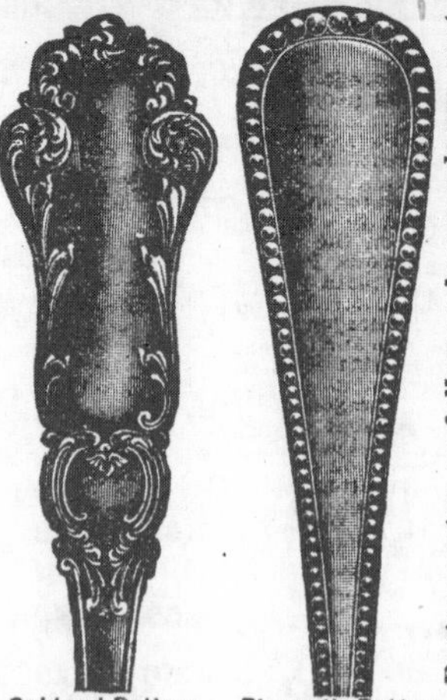
Oakland Pattern. Plymouth Pattern.

Postage extra, as follows, when goods are sent by mail.

Registered mail, 8 cents extra.

Sugar Shells.......3 cents.
Cold Meat Forks and Cream Ladles.......5 cents.
Tea Spoons.......6 cents.
Table Spoons and Forks.......12 cents.
Butter Knives.......3 cents.

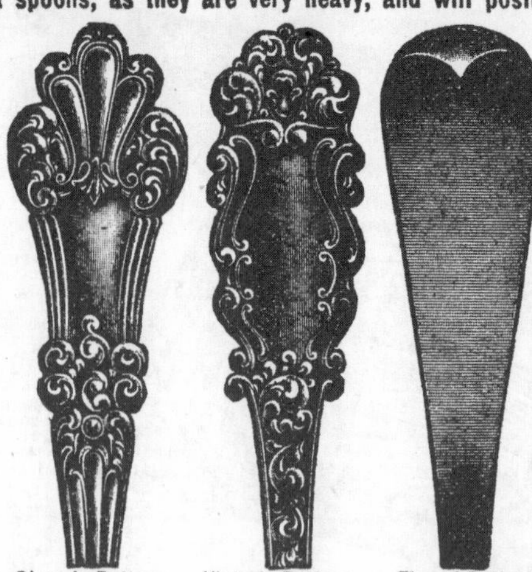
Olympia Pattern. Victoria Pattern. Tipped Pattern.

WE SUPPLY LEATHERETTE CASES, fancy lined, to hold twelve tea spoons for 25 cents; to hold six knives and six forks for 25 cents; to hold twelve tea spoons, butter knife, sugar shell, and pickle fork at 25 cents; to hold twelve tea spoons and six table spoons at 38 cents; to hold one dozen table spoons at 25 cents. Cases only supplied when goods are ordered to fill same from us.

Catalogue Number		Princess Pattern	Oakland Pattern	Plymouth Pattern	Olympia Pattern	Victoria Pattern	Tipped Pattern
5C1201	Tea Spoons, 6 ounces to the dozen. Price, per set of six..........	$2.84	$2.68	$2.52	$2.84	$2.84	$2.68
5C1203	Tea Spoons, 8 ounces to the dozen. Price, per set of six..........	3.78	3.58	3.36	3.78	3.78	3.58
5C1205	Tea Spoons, 10 ounces to the dozen. Price, per set of six..........	4.72	4.46	4.20	4.72	4.72	4.46
5C1207	Table Spoons, 18 ounces to the dozen. Price, per set of six..........	Not Made	8.04	7.56	Not Made	Not Made	Not Made
5C1209	Table Spoons, 20 ounces to the dozen. Price, per set of six..........	9.45	8.92	8.42	9.45	9.45	8.92
5C1211	Medium Forks, 21 ounces to the dozen. Price, per set of six..........	9.92	9.40	8.82	9.92	9.92	9.40
5C1213	Dessert Spoons, 15 ounces to the dozen. Price, per set of six..........	7.08	6.72	6.30	7.08	7.08	6.72
5C1217	Medium Knives, hollow handles, in box. Price, per set of six..........	8.66	Not Made	Not Made	8.66	8.66	Not Made
5C1219	Coffee Spoons, gilt bowl. Price, per set of six..........	2.50	2.50	2.50	2.50	2.50	Not Made
5C1221	Sugar Shells, gilt bowl, in silk lined box. Price, each..........	1.20	1.20	1.20	1.20	1.20	Not Made
5C1223	Butter Knives, plain blades, in silk lined box. Price, each..........	1.50	1.50	1.50	1.50	1.50	Not Made
5C1231	Berry Spoons, gilt bowl, large size, in silk lined box. Price, each..........	3.75	3.75	3.75	3.75	3.75	Not Made
5C1235	Cream Ladles, gilt bowl, large size, in silk lined box. Price, each..........	1.85	Not Made	1.85	1.85	1.85	Not Made
5C1237	Gravy Ladles, gilt bowl, in silk lined box. Price, each..........	2.50	2.50	2.50	2.50	2.50	Not Made
5C1243	Cold Meat Forks, large size, in silk lined box. Price, each..........	3.10	3.10	3.10	3.10	3.10	Not Made

OUR $4.44 INITIAL SILVERWARE SET.

FOR $4.44 we offer a 26-piece set of silverware, engraved with any initial, complete with case, the equal of anything you can buy anywhere at three times the price.

NO RISK IN ORDERING ONE OF THESE SETS. Examine and compare it. If you have not a bargain, return it and we will refund your money. Express charges will amount to next to nothing as compared with what you will save in price. The express charges will average for 500 miles, 35 cents; 1,000 miles, 50 cents. Greater distances in proportion.

THIS SET CONSISTS OF 6 full size table spoons as illustrated, each spoon engraved on the handle with any initial desired, as shown in illustration; 6 tea spoons as illustrated, each spoon engraved on the handle with any initial desired, as shown in illustration; 6 full size forks as illustrated, each fork engraved on the handle with any initial desired, as illustrated; 1 sugar shell, 1 butter knife and 6 knives, the knives we cannot engrave.

ALASKA SILVERWARE KNIVES ARE NOT PLATED. They are the same metal and color through and through. They are proof against all table and fruit acids. They will not rust. They will not tarnish. They will cut and cut well. They can be ground and sharpened like a steel knife and we guarantee them for the term of your natural lifetime.

IN ADDITION TO THE 26 PIECES of silverware as illustrated, we furnish this handsome plush covered and fancy blue lined case. Case is 12 inches long, 10 inches wide and 2 inches deep, nicely finished with a fancy metal clasp and so divided as to just hold the 26 pieces in position, as shown in illustration, so that when the tableware is not in use it can be kept in perfect condition in the case, as illustrated.

THIS SOLID SILVER METAL is the nearest approach in composition metal for tableware to the pure coin silver that has ever been attained. This composition silver is one solid metal through and through, guaranteed to retain its perfect silver color and wear forever. Each piece is stamped "Alaska Silverware."

IT WILL NEVER TARNISH. It is stronger than silver; more springy; you can scour it with a brick; you cannot harm it.

THIS SILVER COMPOSITION METAL is made by a process known only to the manufacturer of these sets, who supplies them to us in immense quantities; is in appearance, finish and every way (except intrinsic value) equal to coin silver. In appearance it cannot be told from solid coin silver, it must be examined by an expert to detect the difference. We can furnish the pieces separately, engraved with any letter, at the prices quoted here.

No. 5C1472	Tea Spoons. Price, per set of six..........	$0.60
No. 5C1473	Table Spoons. Price, per set of six..........	1.20
No. 5C1474	Medium Forks. Price, per set of six..........	1.20
No. 5C1476	Dessert Spoons. Price, per set of six..........	1.06
No. 5C1477	Dessert Forks. Price, per set of six..........	1.06
No. 5C1478	Sugar Shells. Price, each..........	.18
No. 5C1479	Butter Knives. Price, each..........	.25
No. 5C332	Plain Medium Knives. Price, per set of six..........	1.00

No. 5C1470 COMPLETE SET, WITH CASE. $4.44.

AT $4.44 WE FURNISH THIS 26-PIECE SET of initial silverware complete with case as the greatest value ever offered in this class of goods; in fact, our $4.44 price is based on the actual cost to us in immense quantities for cash, with but our one small percentage of profit added.

Postage on these goods, if to go by mail, will be extra per half dozen as follows: Tea spoons, 6 cents; dessert spoons or forks, 12 cents; table spoons or medium forks, 15 cents; and sugar shells or butter knives, 3 cents each. It is cheaper to send by express, if you have an express office near by.

DO NOT COMPARE THIS, our composition silver initial ware, with any of the cheap plated ware that is offered in cases. We could furnish a 26-piece set of cheap silver plated ware with a cheap case similar to the cases that are being furnished by some houses at $1.50 to $2.00, but we believe our customers want a higher grade of goods and we have received so many letters of commendation for this class of goods the past two seasons that we have decided to increase our contracts and offer the goods in sets of twenty-six pieces at even a lower price than we have ever before been able to sell the same class of goods without the case.

IN OUR CLOCK DEPARTMENT

Our customers will note that we have illustrated only the most beautiful and up to date designs on the market. The best clock makers in the United States are represented throughout these pages. They are the oldest and most reliable makers. The Waterbury Clock Co., the Seth Thomas Clock Co., the New Haven Clock Co., and the Ansonia Clock Co., stand preeminent in the United States. Every clock we sell is guaranteed by the manufacturers, and we personally warrant every clock sold to give entire and absolute satisfaction; and for extra special bargains, for the biggest value for the money, for clocks that we can and do give our written binding guarantee with every one sold, we would respectfully direct your attention to the following clocks: Each one is made under special contract for us. They are manufactured by one of the makers named, but on account of the particularly low price we name, we cannot print the maker's name. However, each one of these clocks carries our binding guarantee for a term of five years. For an alarm clock we recommend our Sears, Roebuck & Co. Special, No. 5C2916 at 76 cents. For a cabinet clock, we would recommend our No. 5C3096, price, $2.20, or if this design does not suit you and you wish a calendar attachment together with a thermometer and barometer, we would direct your attention to our No. 5C3099, price, $2.64. If you want a mantel clock, something very fine, the greatest value for the money, you can surely make a selection from the following clocks: The movements are of the highest standard. It is only a question of design in the case. Our Acme Queen Cathedral Gong Clock at $5.55, No. 5C3301, our Prince Elias, No. 5C3302, our Queen Clyde, No. 5C3305, Our American Lady, No. 5C3917, price, $4.20, our Countess Janet, No. 5C3711, price, $3.75, or the Empress, No. 5C3901, price, $4.60.

ALARM CLOCKS.

Nickel Alarm Clock. Made at LaSalle, Ill. 4-inch dial. Height, 6½ inches, width, 4¼ inches; a good timekeeper.
No. 5C2900
Price..............56c
Shipping weight, 2 pounds.

No. 5C2906 Mauser, Luminous. Nickel Alarm Clock with luminous dial; height, 6½ inches; width, 4¼ inches; 4-inch dial; manufactured by the New Haven Clock Company. The dial on this clock is luminous and will show distinctly the time in the dark.
No. 5C2906 Price..............78c
Shipping weight, 2 pounds.

No. 5C2908 Luminous Pirate Alarm Clock, made by the Ansonia Clock Company, height, 6½ inches; width, 4¼ inches; dial, 4 inches. This dial is luminous. You can tell the time in the darkest night, the darker it is the brighter it glows.
No. 5C2908 Price..............80c
Shipping weight, about 2 pounds.

No. 5C2910 "Must Get Up." Nickel Alarm Clock; height, 5⅞ inches; dial, 4½ inches; made by the Waterbury Clock Co. This clock has very large bell on the back of the clock; the alarm runs five minutes with one winding; can be made to run a short, medium, long, or extra long time, and can be stopped at pleasure.
No. 5C2910 Price..............$1.16
Shipping weight, 2 pounds.

No. 5C2912 Spasmodic Alarm Clock, made by the Waterbury Clock Co. Dial, 4½ inches. Has a very large bell on back. Alarms for 15 minutes at intervals of one-half minute.
Price..............$1.16
Shipping weight, about 2 pounds.

No. 5C2914 The Fly Alarm Calendar Clock. Height, about 6½ inches; dial, 4 inches; one-day clock with calendar and alarm, manufactured by the New Haven Clock Company. Movement, very fine grade lever; a clock that we know will give entire satisfaction in every respect; has fine large nickel alarm bell on top, entire clock beautifully burnished, the calendar very finely adjusted, and thoroughly inspected before leaving our establishment. Has extra long alarm ring or can be regulated by winding apparatus for short ring.
No. 5C2914 Price..............88c
Shipping weight, 2 pounds.

Sears, Roebuck & Co.'s Special.

Sears, Roebuck's Special. Nickel Alarm Clock. Height, 6¼ inches; dial, 4 inches; made expressly for us by one of the largest clock companies in the United States. It goes through a thorough inspection before leaving our establishment by one of our expert watchmakers; a clock we can conscientiously recommend to you as being everything an alarm clock should be.
No. 5C2916 Price..............76c
Shipping weight, 2 pounds.

Beautiful Oxidized Alarm Clock for $2.28.

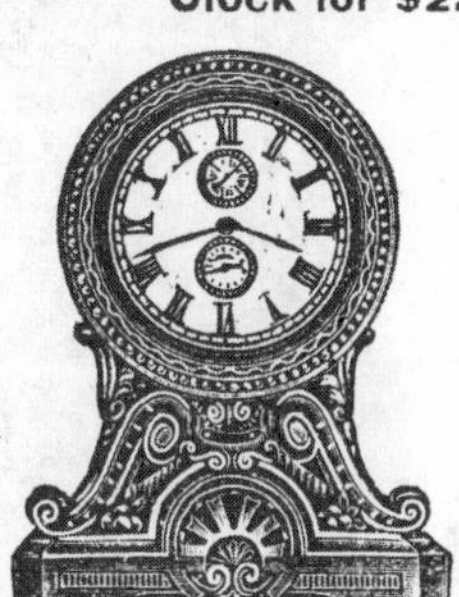

The New Long Alarm Clock, rings from 10 to 15 minutes, but can be switched off any minute desired. This clock will not tip over; no battery necessary; absolutely no trouble. **The case is finished in oxidized copper,** beautifully finished, in fact, making an ornament that would grace any parlor mantelpiece. Height, 9 inches; dial, 4½ inches; movement manufactured by the celebrated **Seth Thomas Clock Company,** and is **guaranteed to give absolute satisfaction in every respect. Runs 30 hours with one winding.** The steel parts are fish oil hardened, brass parts wrought by hand, full conical pivots, patent pinions, agate drawn hairspring, agate drawn mainspring, thoroughly timed and adjusted. **It is a clock longed for by thousands.** It fills a long felt want. If not exactly as described in every particular return it and we will refund your money. **We guarantee it to reach our customers in perfect condition.**
No. 5C2922 Price..............$2.28
Shipping weight, 7 pounds.

No. 5C2919 The Racket Strike Alarm Clock, made by the Ansonia Clock Co. Height, 6⅛ inches; width, 4¾ inches; dial, 4½ inches. Strikes the hours and half hours on bell. A good timekeeper, guaranteed to give entire satisfaction.
No. 5C2919 Price..............$1.48

No. 5C2929 The Repeater Intermitting Alarm Clock, manufactured by the Ansonia Clock Co.; runs thirty-six hours with one winding; dial, 5 inches in diameter. Alarms for twenty-five minutes at intervals; twenty seconds of alarm, then fifteen seconds of silence.
No. 5C2929 Price..............$1.20
Shipping weight, 2 pounds.

No. 5C2931 Wasp Alarm Clock, lever escapement, runs one day with one winding; stands 3¼ inches high; dial, 2 inches in diameter; is manufactured by the Waterbury Clock Company and is guaranteed to keep correct time.
No. 5C2931 Price..............$1.06
Shipping weight, 1½ pounds.

No. 5C2933 Wasp One-Day Time, lever escapement. Dial, 2 inches in diameter; runs thirty-six hours with one winding; manufactured by the Waterbury Clock Company; is guaranteed to give correct time.

No. 5C2933 Price, 78c
Shipping weight, 1½ pounds.

Our $2.20 Cabinet Clock.

No. 5C3096 THE AMSTERDAM Cabinet Clock. This clock stands 22 inches high and is 15 inches wide. Made exclusively for us by one of the four big clock manufacturers. The case is made of solid oak only, not veneered or grained to imitate oak, but solid oak through and through. The illustration shows you, but in a very faint way, the beautiful floral design worked out in the wood. The movement is manufactured by one of the most representative clock companies and carries with it our own special written binding guarantee for a term of five years. It runs 8 days with one winding, strikes the hours and half-hours. Dial, 6 inches in diameter. We would particularly advise purchasing this clock, as we know that it is, without the shadow of a doubt, the greatest clock value ever offered. You positively will be more than pleased with our purchase should you favor us. Weight of clock, boxed ready for shipment, about 10 lbs. Price....$2.20
No. 5C3098 With alarm attachment.
Price.......$2.40

No. 5C3099 THE NETHERLANDS. We cannot tell you the maker's name on account of the special cut price, but we can tell you that it is manufactured by one of the four big clock companies in the United States, and we guarantee it to give entire and absolute satisfaction. Our written, binding guarantee goes with every clock sold. This clock is made of solid oak only, guaranteed not veneered or stained to represent oak, but is solid oak through and through. The clock stands 22 inches high and is 15 inches wide. The illustration does not, by any means, give you any idea of the beautiful effect this clock has. The movement runs 8 days with one winding, strikes the hours and half-hours, and has calendar attachment, showing the days of the month, likewise has barometer and thermometer indicating at all times the temperature and enabling you to anticipate the changes in the weather. Dial, 6 inches in diameter. Our price for this specially made clock is $2.64. Don't think that because we have named such a wonderfully low price on this clock that it is not the best on the market. Money cannot buy a better clock no matter what price you pay for this style of clock. This price is possible only for the reason that we maintain our one small per cent profit policy and on account of a special arrangement with the factory for an immense quantity at a remarkably low price, as always, we give you the benefit of this remarkable purchase. Clock boxed ready for shipment, 20 pounds. Price..............$2.64

This 8-Day Clock for $1.94.

THE ALDRICH is made by the Waterbury Clock Co., in either oak or walnut, as desired. It runs eight days with one winding, it stands 22 inches high, has 6-inch dial, strikes the hours and half-hours on a wire bell. Case is beautifully carved and perfectly made in every detail. Weight, boxed ready for shipment, about 20 pounds.

No. 5C3102 Price, **$1.94**
No. 5C3104 With alarm. Price..............$2.25
No. 5C3106 With cathedral gong, no alarm. Price..............$2.15
No. 5C3108 With cathedral gong and alarm. Price..............$2.50

Nothing Finer for $4.00. Our Price, $2.12.

No. 5C3115 THE LAYTON. Fancy Cabinet Clock; 22½ inches high; dial, 6 inches; made in oak only; beautifully carved and ornamented; fine eight-day movement; made by the Ansonia Clock Company; strikes the hours and half-hours on wire bell. Weight, boxed ready for shipment, about 20 lbs.
No. 5C3115
Price..............$2.12
No. 5C3117 With alarm. Price, **$2.42**
No. 5C3119 With gong. Price..............$2.38

The Stanton, $2.46.

A new pattern eight-day clock, made by the Waterbury Clock Company and is guaranteed to give entire satisfaction. The case is made of solid oak, stands 22 inches high, embellished with beautiful gilt ornaments, which lend a beauty to this style of a clock, unequaled by any other style of ornamentation. The dial is 6 inches in diameter. The pendulum is of corrugated brass. The clock runs 8 days at one winding, strikes the hours and half-hours on a wire bell. Weight, boxed ready for shipment, about 20 pounds.

No. 5C3121 Price..............$2.46
No. 5C3123 With alarm. Price.............. 2.72
No. 5C3125 With gong and alarm. Price, 2.92

This Choice Bargain at $3.12.

Another rare specimen of clock perfection manufactured by the Celebrated Waterbury Clock Co., in oak or walnut.

No. 5C3127 CLIMAX. This clock not alone gives you the time for eight days with one winding, but likewise gives you the date of the month, the temperature of the weather and the condition of the atmosphere, having barometer and thermometer attachments, strikes the hours and half-hours. It stands 26¾ inches high; fancy rococo 6-inch dial. The movement, one of the best manufactured, is warranted an accurate timekeeper. The pendulum is exposed, the glass is beautifully decorated, and we believe it is one of the choicest of choice bargains we are offering this season. Weight, boxed ready for shipment, about 20 pounds.

No. 5C3127 Price of clock complete........ $3.12

A Special Value for $2.45.

THE FELIX Eight-Day Clock, suitable for the office, workshop or the house. It has a complete calendar attachment, showing the days of the month. It strikes the hours and half-hours on a wire bell. Stands 22 inches high, has 6-inch dial, beautifully embossed, made in oak or walnut by the Waterbury Clock Co., guaranteed an accurate timepiece. Weight, boxed ready for shipment, about 20 pounds.

No. 5C3128 Price.......... $2.45

No. 5C3130 Same with cathedral gong. Price.......$2.60

Our $2.60 Cabinet Clock.

No. 5C3144 THE DABURY. One of the most complete clocks ever offered to the public. It has an eight-day movement, guaranteed by the Waterbury Clock Company. Oak or walnut case, beautifully carved and decorated, glass door. Strikes the hours and half-hours on a wire bell. It also has thermometer and barometer attachment. The pendulum is ornamented and very fancy. Entire clock stands 22 inches high and has a 6-inch fancy rococo dial. Weight, boxed ready for shipment, about 20 pounds.

No. 5C3144 Price........................ $2.60
No. 5C3146 With alarm. Price............ 2.90
No. 5C3148 With cathedral gong. Price... 2.80

A Bargain for $3.60.

No. 5C3151 THE ROCHESTER. Fancy Cabinet Clock in solid black walnut only; very fancy ornamented and carved case; height, 26¾ inches; dial, 6 inches; fitted with eight-day movement; made by the Waterbury Clock Company; strikes hours and halves on wire bell; with calendar. Weight, boxed ready for shipment, about 20 pounds.

No. 5C3151 Price.....$3.60

No. 5C3153 With cathedral gong. Price, $3.90

Our New ACME QUEEN CATHEDRAL GONG CLOCK Price Cut to $5.55

QUANTITY COUNTS: WE EXPECT TO SELL THOUSANDS AT THIS PRICE.

FROM this large illustration, which is engraved by our artist direct from a photograph, you can form some idea of the appearance of this clock and figure, but it must be seen to be appreciated.

No. 5C3301

AT $5.55 we furnish this clock complete with handsome bronze figure, exactly as illustrated. At $4.70 we furnish the clock only, without the bronze figure. Order this clock and if you do not find it all and even more than we claim for it, such a clock as you could not buy elsewhere even at double the price, you can return it to us at our expense and we will cheerfully refund your money. At $5.55 we offer this big, handsome clock complete, with large bronze figure as illustrated, as the greatest value we have ever offered in a high grade cathedral gong 8-day clock.

THIS OUR SPECIAL $5.55 CLOCK complete with figure, is a clock that we believe combines the good qualities of all high grade Waterbury mantel clocks, with the defects of none. This clock is covered by a binding guarantee, and if any piece or part gives out by reason of defect in material or workmanship or for some reason the clock fails to run accurately, it can be returned at our expense and we will cheerfully refund your money.

AS A GIFT, A WEDDING OR A BIRTHDAY PRESENT you cannot select anything more appropriate. One of these clocks will be useful as well as ornamental, and will last a generation. Nothing handsomer for mantel ornamentation; nothing more useful than our $5.55 Acme Queen Parlor Clock.

WHILE WE OFFER MANY RARE BARGAINS in our clock department, offer them at the manufacturers' lowest prices, prices as low, and in many cases even lower than dealers can buy in quantities, this our Special Acme Queen Cathedral Gong 8-day clock, complete with figure, at $5.55 is the greatest clock value in our catalogue, and we recommend this clock in preference to all others. It is a handsome clock for mantel or shelf; for an ornament for the home there is no clock made that will compare with it at anything like the price; as a timekeeper there is nothing better.

GENERAL DESCRIPTION. SIZE—Height of clock, including figure, 20 inches; clock only, 11½ inches; figure only, 8½ inches. Length of clock at base, 17½ inches; length of clock at top, 15 inches. Diameter of dial, 5½ inches. Length of bronze figure, 9 inches.

This large, handsome bronze figure and marbleized clock is made in two colors, black and green, in imitation of black and Mexican onyx, and it so closely resembles the genuine Mexican onyx that it cannot be detected except by an expert. Better than the genuine onyx, it can be cleaned with a damp cloth without injury and is guaranteed never to warp or crack. This is an eight-day clock—runs eight days with one winding—and strikes the hours upon a perfect cathedral gong and half hours on a cup bell.

This clock stands on large handsome bronze feet. It is ornamented with lion head bronze side ornaments, heavy bronze panel ornaments and bronze center ornaments. It is furnished with a handsome mosaic dial in heavy gilt, 5½ inches in diameter. This clock is one of the highest grade made by the Waterbury Company. It has blued steel hands, the movement is highly polished wrought brass. All steel parts are oil tempered. Has the latest improved regulator and pinions, safety barrel and escapement. Weight, boxed ready for shipment, 25 pounds.

No. 5C3299 Price of clock only, without bronze figure.............$4.70
No. 5C3301 Price, Acme Queen Cathedral Gong Clock, as illustrated......... 5.55

$3.65 for Our Prince Elias.

$3.65

OUR PRINCE ELIAS, the newest clock out of the factory, exactly in every particular as illustration shows, for $3.65. Don't think that you will not get or cannot buy from us a fine clock for this price. In fact, this price is no criterion. The clock is really worth twice as much. Your local dealer or the jobber he buys it from would pay 25 to 45 per cent more than we ask you for it, in other words, you would have to pay your local dealer for a clock as good as this and as handsome as this one, from $5.00 to $6.00. This clock is made expressly for us by the Waterbury Clock Co., of Waterbury, Conn. Each one of them is thoroughly guaranteed and we warrant them to give entire satisfaction.

DESCRIPTION OF CASE. The case is made of wood, covered with a secret prepared enamel, imitating black marble. It is guaranteed not to chip or wear off and always retains its deep black marble-like appearance. It has handsome gilt feet, marbleized gilt metal capped and gilt metal based columns, beautiful gilt scroll metal work at top and base. The sides are also ornamented by two gilt metal designs, exactly as the illustration shows. The dial is very pretentious, made of metal fancy work and is 5 inches in diameter.

DESCRIPTION OF MOVEMENT. The movement fitted in this case is one of the Waterbury guaranteed movements, runs eight days with one winding. It is made of the finest tempered steel and hand wrought brass; it strikes the hours on a cathedral gong and the half hours on a brass bell. You can always know the time without seeing the clock. The hands are very fine hand sawed blue steel of the fleur de lis pattern.

No. 5C3302 Price.............................$3.65

Our Queen Clyde Mantel Clock for $3.12.

$3.12

Never before in the history of the clock business was ever such a fine clock offered for this price, $3.12. The wholesale clock dealers cannot buy a clock anywhere as fine as this one for 30 per cent more than we ask. We are able to offer this clock at the price, because of a special concession from the manufacturers, on account of our great purchase from them of other goods. They do not make a cent profit when selling this particular clock to us.

Description of case. The clock case is of wood, well seasoned and guaranteed not to warp or crack, it is enameled in black, then polished to a high gloss.

The ornamentation. A beautiful gilt border of the rococo pattern made of metal sets off the top. This is entirely a new idea in clock ornamentation, no other clock has it. The front of the clock on the base is ornamented by three beautiful gilt metal scrolls, two fine columns, one on each side of the dial, made in exact imitation of marble, lend a rich appearance to the clock; the dial is 5½ inches in diameter with ornamented sash.

This clock stands 10½ inches high and is 12½ inches wide at the base.

The movement is manufactured by one of the most representative clock makers in the United States. On account of the cut price we cannot give name. It runs eight days with one winding, strikes the hours and half hours on a soft toned gong. Weight, packed ready for shipment, about 16 pounds.

No. 5C3305 Price.............................$3.12

Regular Eight-Day Clock with Perpetual Calendar Attachment for $6.40.

No. 5C3310 This clock is manufactured by the Waterbury Clock Company in either oak or walnut. Stands 28¼ inches high. It runs 8 days with one winding, strikes the hours and half hours on a cathedral gong. **It has the calendar attachment,** as shown on the lower dial, which is a perpetual one, marking even the leap years without having to be reset. The dials are 8 inches in diameter. This clock is particularly adapted for dining rooms, libraries and offices. We warrant it to be an accurate timekeeper. The parts are made of finely wrought brass and oil tempered steel, most accurate for timekeeping, and giving it great durability. **The case is beautifully hand engraved and embossed.** The glass in the door is decorated in black and gold. See our price, **$6.40. We absolutely guarantee it to give satisfaction.** Weight, boxed for shipment, about 25 pounds.

No. 5C3310 Price..**$6.40**

$2.94 Buys a Calendar Clock with Barometer and Thermometer.

No. 5C3516 THE GIBSON Calendar 8-Day Clock with thermometer and barometer. This clock is one of the greatest bargains that we have ever been able to offer to our customers. It can be furnished in solid black walnut or antique oak case, as desired. The height is 24 inches, dial, 6 inches. The movement is one of the **best made** by the Waterbury Clock Co. Runs eight days with one winding and strikes the hours and half hours. **It is warranted to be an accurate timekeeper.** Has a complete calendar attachment which works automatically and always indicates correctly the day of the month. It has a perfect thermometer on one side and on the other a barometer. We cannot furnish it with alarm. Weight of clock, boxed ready for shipment, 17 pounds.

No. 5C3516 Price, **$2.94**

DROP OCTAGON. Has solid oak or fine veneered case. Made by the Waterbury Clock Company and is thoroughly reliable. Is designed for offices, schools or churches. Weight, boxed, 25 pounds.

No. 5C3518 Eight-day, 10-in. dial, time only. Price............**$2.80**

No. 5C3520 Eight-day, 10-in. dial; time only, with calendar. Price......**$3.10**

No. 5C3522 Eight-day, 10-in. dial; strikes hours and halves. Price..................**$3.40**

No. 5C3524 Eight-day, 12-in. dial; time only. Price....**$3.10**

No. 5C3526 Eight-day, 12-in. dial; strikes hours and half hours. Price..................**$3.50**

No. 5C3528 Eight-day, 12-in. dial; time only, with calendar. Price..................**$3.30**

NOTE—The height of the clocks with 10-inch dial is 21 inches; 12-inch dial, 23½ inches.

$4.78

No. 5C3555 CUCKOO CLOCK. Case is made of German oak or walnut ornamented with inlaid ash, ebony and mahogany. Beautifully hand carved throughout, strikes the hours and half hours on a wire bell, the cuckoo appears and calls at the same time. Height of clock, 21 inches; width, 14 inches. The movement is made in the Black Forest, Germany, of the finest tempered steel and polished brass, finely finished and adjusted, guaranteed to be a good timekeeper. One of the most artistic ornaments for a parlor ever made. Weight, boxed, 25 pounds.

No. 5C3555 Price..**$4.78**

German Cuckoo Clock, $6.75.

It strikes the hours and half hours on a wire bell, a cuckoo appears and calls at the same time.

$6.75

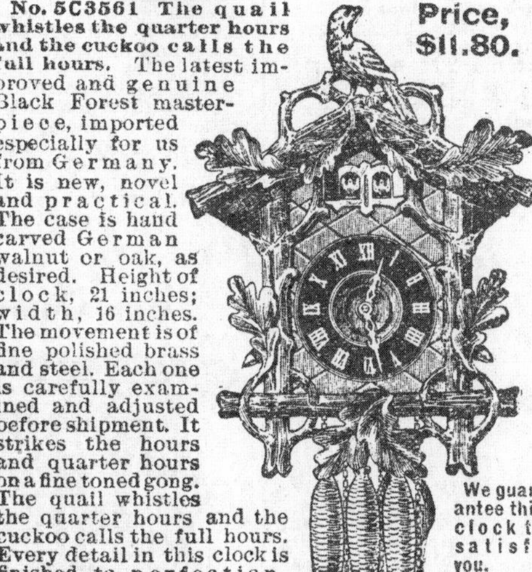

No. 5C3557 CUCKOO. Case made of German oak or walnut, hand carved bird top, hand carved oak leaves. The entire carving on this clock is done by hand by the natives of the Schwarzwald, Germany, and is especially fine and artistic. The figures are accurate and lifelike. **The movement is made of the very finest tempered steel and highly wrought brass.** It is finely finished and perfectly adjusted. Height, 18 inches; width, 14 inches. Weight, boxed, 20 lbs.

No. 5C3557 Price..........**$6.75**

Quail and Cuckoo Clock.

Price, $11.80.

No. 5C3561 The quail whistles the quarter hours and the cuckoo calls the full hours. The latest improved and genuine Black Forest masterpiece, imported especially for us from Germany. It is new, novel and practical. The case is hand carved German walnut or oak, as desired. Height of clock, 21 inches; width, 16 inches. The movement is of fine polished brass and steel. Each one is carefully examined and adjusted before shipment. It strikes the hours and quarter hours on a fine toned gong. The quail whistles the quarter hours and the cuckoo calls the full hours. Every detail in this clock is finished to perfection. Weight, boxed ready for shipment, about 25 pounds

We guarantee this clock to satisfy you.

No. 5C3561 Price....................................**$11.80**

Our $3.65 Eight-Day Clock.

No. 5C3706 The Dupont Mantel Clock runs eight days with one winding. It is manufactured by the celebrated Waterbury Clock Co., of Waterbury, Conn., and is guaranteed to give entire satisfaction. The case is 10¾ inches high, 13⅞ inches wide, made of black hand polished wood with gilt engraving on base. It has gilt feet, side and front ornaments. The dial is 5½ inches in diameter. Strikes the hours on a gong and the half-hours on a cup bell. Weight of clock, boxed ready for shipment, 14 pounds.

Price..**$3.65**

$4.40 Buys an $8.00 Clock.

$4.40  **$4.40**

No. 5C3722 The Dawson. A polished wood, eight-day clock, strikes the hours on a gong and the half-hours on a cup bell. Clock stands 11 inches high; width, 16⅝ inches; dial, 5¼ inches. The combination of two colors, black and marble, together with the gilt front, side ornaments and gilt feet, lends a beauty to this clock that cannot be described. You must see the clock to appreciate it. Remember, this clock is not made by a cheap manufacturer, but is the creation of the celebrated Waterbury Clock Co., Waterbury, Conn., and warranted in every respect. Weight, boxed ready for shipment, about 18 pounds.

Price,..**$4.40**

Beautiful Mantel Clock for $5.00.

$5.00

Our $3.75 Mantel Clock.

$3.75

No. 5C3711 OUR COUNTESS JANET Mantel Clock. The most wonderful bargain ever offered in the United States. This mantel clock is made of wood, then hard enameled in black with marbleized ornamentation, exactly as illustration shows. Stands 10¾ inches high, 7⅛ inches deep, 16⅛ inches wide. Has gilt metal feet, side ornaments and tops and bases of the two columns on front of clock. It has an eight-day movement, strikes the half-hours on a bell, and the hours on a gong. The dial is 5½ inches in diameter, with plain numerals; the dial sash is the latest Parisian pattern. This is one of the most wonderful values offered. It was made especially for us, and carries our five-year binding guarantee. We cannot divulge the maker's name on account of the low price quoted. The movement will give particular good satisfaction, it is of hard rolled brass and oil tempered steel parts. All friction in the train and delicate running parts has been reduced to a minimum, thereby giving it a life of accurate time keeping not possible in other clocks. Weight, 20 pounds. Price...........................**$3.75**

No. 5C3723 THE PATMOS. A very handsome mantel clock, a most excellent imitation of Mexican onyx, and unless it is examined very closely no one would believe that it was not a real onyx clock. **It holds a beautiful polish and with proper care will last a lifetime.** If the case gets soiled or dirty it can be wiped off with a damp cloth. Has fancy bronze feet in artistic design and side dragon head metal ornaments. The base is of the Corinthian style. Length of clock, 17 inches; height, 11¼ inches. **Has an eight-day movement, made by Seth Thomas Clock Company.** Strikes hours on a cathedral gong and half hours on a cup bell; regulated by patent regulator without touching the pendulum. Weight, boxed, about 20 pounds.

Price..**$5.00**

NO CHARGES FOR REPAIRS

on Watches and Clocks will be allowed unless our written consent is first secured in advance.

The Harvey Mantel Clock for $5.58.

No. 5C3728 THE HARVEY, eight-day, enameled iron, made by the Waterbury Clock Co.; height, 10¾ inches; width, 16⅝ inches; dial, 5¼ inches in diameter, fitted with the new rococo pattern sash and ornamented bezel. This clock strikes the hours on a gong and the half-hours on a cup bell. **The ornamentation on this clock is exceptional, the gilt feet, front and side metal trimmings contrasting with the black enamel gives it a very rich appearance.** You cannot wear this clock out, all the parts are of rolled brass and tempered steel, the case is of black iron heavily black enameled and then kiln baked. Weight of clock, boxed for shipment, 35 pounds. Price.....$5.58

Our Empress Mantel Clock, $4.60.

No. 5C3901 OUR EMPRESS MANTEL CLOCK, exactly as illustration shows in every detail. It stands 10¾ inches high, 7 inches deep, 17½ inches wide. It has solid gilt bronze feet, gilt bronze side ornaments, gilt bronze caps and base of the six columns that ornament the front of the clock. Clock is made of wood, enameled in black, with marbleized trimmings. This enameling is guaranteed not to warp or chip off. A woolen cloth, slightly sprinkled with sweet oil, lightly rubbed over this clock, will keep it in perfect condition for practically a lifetime. The dial is plain, 5¾ inches in diameter. The sash which surrounds it is the very latest rococo design. The movement runs for eight days with one winding, strikes the half hours on a metal bell and the hours on a sweet toned gong. Each piece and part of this clock goes through a rigid inspection. It is manufactured by one of the most celebrated clock companies in the United States, but on account of the low price quoted here, we cannot print the maker's name. The movement in this clock, as in all of our own special clocks, we are particularly proud of, as it is made of hardened rolled brass and oil tempered steel parts. The bearings and all intricate and delicate parts, where friction reduces the wearing ability, are so constructed that it is reduced to a minimum, therefore we know our special line of clocks will outwear any on the market and give accurate time. **This clock is the most massive and most pretentious and biggest value for the money ever before offered.** Clocks sold by the makers of this clock, of similar design but not so massive or eleborate bring from the retail jewelers and from the jobbers from 25 to 30 per cent more than the price we ask. Seeing is believing. Don't buy this clock from us unless you find our statements are true. Just compare this clock with others, and we are satisfied that we will get your order. Weight, boxed for shipment, 22 pounds.

Price..........$4.60

The Hollis. Rare Value for $4.68.

No. 5C3905 THE HOLLIS. Beautiful adamantine finished clock, manufactured by the Seth Thomas Clock Co. The movement of this clock is a very fine handwrought brass movement, oil tempered steel parts, agate drawn hairspring and mainspring, conical pivots, patent pinions, **adamantine finish, which never dulls but is always beautiful as if newly polished, covers this case; it is guaranteed not to wear or chip off.** A beautiful head of a lion in solid bronze ornaments the sides. Handsome bronze feet. **Hand engraved scrolls of various designs ornament the front.** The dial is 5 inches, with Roman figures. This clock stands 11 inches high and 14 inches long, **goes eight days with one winding; strikes the hours and half hours upon a cathedral gong.** Warranted to keep accurate time, with care will last a natural lifetime. Weight of clock when boxed is about 20 pounds. Price..........$4.68

A Beautiful Gilt Mantel, Desk or Bureau Clock, $1.06.

No. 5C3705 Mantel, Desk or Bureau Clock. Runs 36 hours with one winding. Has 2-inch dial, with fine French beveled glass. Clock stands 6 inches high, and is manufactured by the Waterbury Clock Co. We guarantee this clock to give entire satisfaction. Weight, boxed, ready for shipment, about 2¼ pounds.

No. 5C3705 Price..........$1.06

The Beauty Mantel Clock for $5.95.

No. 5C3908 THE BEAUTY. One of the finest and most artistic clocks ever manufactured. We contracted with the factory to use an immense quantity at an unheard of price. **We quote a selling price unheard of before for a clock of this high standard of make.** Height, without ornament, 11 inches; base, 17 inches; with ornament, clock stands 19 inches high. **The movement is manufactured by the Seth Thomas Clock Company,** and is guaranteed to keep accurate time. It runs for eight days with one winding. The parts are made of fine wrought polished brass and oil tempered steel. It strikes the half hours on a cup bell and the hours on a cathedral gong that is toned with the church bells. **The case** is adamantine finished and highly polished, therefore can be cleaned without injury with a damp cloth. **Foot and side ornaments are of highly burnished bronze.** It is a clock such as you have never seen before for the price. Clock and ornament, boxed ready for shipment, weighs 25 pounds.

No. 5C3908 Price, complete with figure ...$5.95

No. 5C3910 Price, without figure..........$4.95

No. 5C3912 Figure alone. Price..........$1.00

Our Edgemere Queen Mantel Clock at $5.15.

No. 5C3915 OUR EDGEMERE QUEEN MANTEL CLOCK. The latest and newest design in clocks. This is one of the Seth Thomas Clock Co.'s latest productions. The case is mahogany, covered with a transparent material called adamantine, guaranteed impervious to dust, damp and age. A damp cloth keeps it new and polished forever. It is always glossy, always new and one of the richest appearing clocks ever placed on the market.

Dimensions of clock—Height, 11⅛ inches; length, 16¼ inches; depth, 6¼ inches. **The movement is one of the latest improved Seth Thomas clock movements.** It runs eight days with one winding, the parts are guaranteed fine wrought polished brass and oil tempered steel. It strikes the hours on a cathedral gong and half hours on a cup bell. **The case** is ornamented with two gilt lion heads, one on each end. The front is ornamented by four columns, topped and based with fine gilded metal ornaments. The entire clock rests upon four gilded feet, exactly as shown in illustration. **The dial is one of the latest Parisian patterns, gilded and beautifully executed;** the design is brought out most elaborately. Dial is 5¾ inches in diameter, making it possible for you to see the time from quite a distance. We consider this one of the most artistic, one of the most beautiful clocks on the market. It embodies the perfections of all and the faults of none. Weight, boxed for shipment, about 20 pounds.

Price..........$5.15

Our American Lady Mantel Clock, $4.20.

No. 5C3917 OUR AMERICAN LADY MANTEL CLOCK, manufactured by one of the biggest and most representative makers in the United States, but on account of the very low price quoted, we dare not print the maker's name. However, it carries our five-year written binding guarantee, and we know you will be entirely satisfied with it. This clock stands 10¾ inches high, 7 inches deep and 17 inches wide. It has solid gilt bronze feet and side ornaments, also metal top and base on the four columns, as illustration shows. The dial is 5¾ inches in diameter, the very latest pattern of fancy fret work, with a beautiful rococo sash. The case is of wood, black enameled, warranted not to peel, chip or crack off. A soft woolen cloth, sprinkled with sweet oil, will keep it as new, practically, for a lifetime. The movement runs eight days with one winding; strikes the half hours on a metal bell and the hours on a soft toned gong. **This, our American Lady mantel clock, is one of the special bargains we have referred you to in our description on page 270.** If this clock suits your taste, we refer to the design, we know that a better clock or a greater value for the money cannot be had for twice what we ask. We are particularly proud of the movement used in this clock, as it is made of solid hardened rolled brass and oil tempered steel parts. The bearings and other delicate parts are so constructed that the friction is reduced to a minimum, therefore the life of the clock is greater than any other. Weight, boxed for shipment, 20 pounds.

Price..........$4.20

WALL PAPER DEPARTMENT.

DIRECT FROM OUR OWN WALL PAPER MILL WE OFFER YOU SUCH GREAT VALUES IN NEW, STYLISH, DEPENDABLE 1905 PATTERNS OF WALL PAPER AS WERE NEVER BEFORE HEARD OF. NEW AND EXCLUSIVE DESIGNS. ASTONISHINGLY LOW PRICES.

SINCE WE HAVE ESTABLISHED our own wall paper mill, in which we manufacture every roll of wall paper we sell, we are prepared to eclipse all former offers in the way of value giving in this department. We are prepared to offer to our customers for the season of 1905, such a beautiful line of new designs and patterns; such a high quality of wall paper throughout and at prices that are simply wonderful, they are so very low. We know that dealers, wholesalers, jobbers, retailers and customers alike will be surprised and wonder how we can furnish such wall paper for so little money.

WE ARE PREPARED for an enormous wall paper business this season. We have enlarged our factory, equipped ourselves with an entirely new and most carefully considered and carefully selected line of designs, and we can confidently state that we are in a position to sell you wall paper such as no other house can rival. You can buy your wall paper from us and be sure of the latest and most exclusive designs and at the same time buy your wall paper for less money than your local dealer could possibly buy at wholesale.

OUR FREE SAMPLE BOOK OF WALL PAPER. In this catalogue we illustrate and describe some of our great leaders in wall paper for 1905, some of the best values we have to offer in our entire line. If you desire, you can send us your order direct from this catalogue, selecting the paper from the patterns described herein and with the assurance that you will be pleased and satisfied with your purchase. At the same time, if you would like to see samples of our entire line of side wall paper, simply write and ask for our free Wall Paper Sample Book and the complete book of thirty-nine samples will be sent you immediately by mail, postpaid. This free wall paper sample book shows a fair sized sample of all our wall paper (with the exception of the border and ceiling paper) and from this small sample book you can see the exact pattern, coloring, design, etc. The wall paper sample book is free, and if you write for it, we will at the same time send you our plain and complete instructions how to hang your own wall paper, enabling you to do the job without employing a professional paperhanger. If you are interested in wall paper and do not send your order direct from this catalogue, don't fail to write for the free Sample Book of Wall Paper.

AT 3 CENTS TO 25 CENTS per double roll of 16 yards, we show in this catalogue a wonderful range of styles and designs in wall paper, all strictly new and up to date for this season, all made up in our own factory (one of the largest wall paper factories in the world), under the very greatest economical conditions for manufacturing, and under our policy of making our selling price represent only the cost of manufacture with but our one uniform small percentage of profit added, we are able to name prices in this department which mean a very substantial saving for everyone who favors us with an order. Considering for how little money it is possible to buy the very best grades of wall paper, as shown in this catalogue, and considering how great an improvement is possible in the home by the use of new papering, also how easily, from our instructions and illustrations on the following pages, a good job of papering can be done, it would seem that our sales of wall paper are bound to increase very materially and that we can look for orders from practically everyone receiving this catalogue. So much is added to every room in beauty, cleanliness and utility by the use of wall paper (there is no method of treating the walls that pleases so constantly), that we ask you to consider our samples and prices carefully, to note for how little money you can paper a room or an entire house in very good taste, and then if you are fully satisfied with our values, send us an order.

REMEMBER, we accept your order and your money with the understanding and agreement that if the paper we send you does not prove perfectly satisfactory in every way, if you are not convinced when received that we have furnished you the very best value in wall paper it is possible to secure, if you do not feel satisfied that we have saved you money, you are at liberty to return the paper to us at our expense and we will immediately refund your money, together with any transportation charges you may have paid.

OUR LINE includes plain colorings, two-tone effects, glimmers, embosses, gilts, silks and ingrains and plain blank paper. The quality of stock ranges from 10 to 16 ounces.

WE GIVE YOU THE BENEFIT of exclusive patterns. Our stock is large and up to date, and our prices are just one-half of what you would have to pay for goods of a similar character purchased at retail or through agents; in fact, it is doubtful whether such styles, patterns and designs as these shown can be secured in small retail stores, from paperhangers, or traveling agents at any price.

WE ARE NOT IN THE TRUST. You may not be aware of it, but almost every roll of wall paper sold throughout the country is controlled by the wall paper trust. Almost all of the dealers and agents are compelled to buy their wall paper from factories controlled by the trust.

OUR FACTORY IS NOT IN THE TRUST. Our prices are based on the actual cost of material and labor, with our one small profit added, and in buying these goods from us you secure them at factory prices, and save all the jobbers', retailers' and agents' profits. In addition, we furnish you with a better quality of goods, and the advantage of buying your wall paper from us is not only in the money we can save you, but in the general superiority of the papers we offer.

YOU WILL FIND THE PRICES, NAME AND NUMBER printed in plain figures; you will find the price of the wall paper, the price and width of the border and ceiling to match; hence, in ordering, you can select any pattern contained in this book, and the proper ceiling and border (if any ordered), matching in color and pattern, will be sent. Any part of a combination can be purchased separately. Thus you can order side wall only, ceiling only, or as many yards of border as you wish.

WE QUOTE PRICES BY THE DOUBLE ROLL. Remember that a double roll contains 16 yards, and in comparing our prices with those of others, do not be deceived by the prices which dealers and agents often offer wall paper at in single rolls, which contain but 8 yards of paper, or only one-half as much as a double roll of our paper. Read the full instructions, "How to Order." Read the instructions on "Hanging Wall Paper," on the following pages.

OUR GUARANTEE. We guarantee every roll of paper we put out to be strictly first class, the very best quality of its kind, and should any wall paper not prove satisfactory when received, you are at liberty to return it and we will refund your money, including transportation charges. We also guarantee that our prices are the very lowest possible for equal qualities. Every order will be filled very carefully, and you may send us your order with every assurance that you will be well satisfied in every respect.

OUR BIG WALL PAPER BOOK for dealers and agents will be sent on receipt of 25 cents. In addition to the small Sample Book of Wall Paper, which is sent free, postpaid on application, we also issue a much larger and complete sample book which measures 15x18 inches closed, intended for the use of agents, dealers, paperhangers, painters, contractors, canvassers, etc. We get up this large sample book for the benefit of people who deal in wall paper and also for such of our customers as wish a line of large sized samples to select from; a book which shows ceiling and border paper as well as the side wall paper. This large book is about 15x18 inches square and about 1¼-inch thick; shows all of our wall paper patterns, all fully described and priced. As this book is a very large and expensive book to get up; one that is made especially to interest careful, close buying dealers, paperhangers, contractors, etc., we require all applications for this book of wall paper to be accompanied by 25 cents. We ask 25 cents from each applicant as an evidence of good faith and to help pay for the cost of the book. We prepay express on the book.

TO PAPERHANGERS. If you are a paperhanger you cannot afford to be without this big sample book. It shows the handsomest line of wall papers for this season and at prices much lower than you are now paying. With this big book of samples you can make closer prices on your work and bigger profits for yourself, for you will find our prices much lower than the prices you are now paying. This big book is issued especially in the interest of wall paper hangers.

TO WALL PAPER DEALERS. If you are a dealer in wall paper you cannot afford to be without our dealers' big book, for the line of samples cannot be equaled by any line you are now carrying. You will find our prices so much lower than the prices you are now paying that you can control the sale of wall paper in your section and still make more profit than you are now making.

TO AGENTS AND CANVASSERS. If you are now soliciting orders for wall paper in your section, do not fail to send 25 cents for this dealers' big book. You will find the line handsomer and better than the line you are showing and the prices are very much lower. From our big book you can no doubt sell wall paper at what your paper now costs you and still make a handsome profit.

TO CONTRACTORS, RENTAL AGENTS, PAINTERS AND OTHERS who buy wall paper in quantities, we especially urge that you send 25 cents for the dealers' big book. You will be surprised at the prices and at the big line we show. You will find that at our prices you can afford to repaper rooms that otherwise would not be papered. You will find the expense of repapering will be very different from what it would be at the price you are now paying.

THIS BIG BOOK closed measures 15x18 inches. The book weighs about five pounds, is one of the largest and handsomest and most complete books of wall paper samples published. The book contains an immense line of all the very latest designs in handsome colorings for this season; large samples of wall, border and ceiling papers for all purposes, for homes, bedrooms, dining rooms, halls, kitchens, etc., for public buildings, churches, schools, halls, etc. Everything very complete and at prices heretofore unknown, prices much lower than ever before, prices less than dealers can buy elsewhere in any quantity.

IF YOU WANT TO KNOW just exactly the design, just the size of the pattern, all the colorings, etc., if you wish to know just what kind of border and ceiling paper will be furnished to match the wall paper, we recommend by all means that you send 25 cents for the big book.

TO REDUCE THE COST of our 25-cent dealers' wall paper book to next to nothing, we advise getting your neighbors interested, one, two or even four or five, thus reducing the cost of the book to each one of you to but a few cents, 5 to 10 cents, and you will find you will save the cost of the book many times over on your first order for wall paper; besides you will have the satisfaction of selecting from one of the largest books published, from an immense line of samples including samples of border and ceiling as well as side wall paper, samples 15 x 18 inches square, from which you can see just what the patterns and colorings are.

SAMPLES NOT NECESSARY WHEN ORDERING. Our Wall Paper Department is in charge of an experienced wall paper man, an expert in the selecting of harmonizing shades and designs, and without sending for samples, if you will select the paper wanted from the following illustrations and descriptions, and will tell us for what kind of rooms the paper is wanted, give us an idea of color and pattern, let us know the color of the carpet, furniture or other decorations of the room, we will give you the service of an expert designer and wall paper maker in selecting the most harmonizing wall paper for your wants. He will give you the best values in our house, and you will, we are sure, be better pleased with his selection than if you yourself were selecting it from samples. All our old customers who have bought wall paper from us almost invariably leave the selecting of harmonizing shades and colorings to the expert in this department, and they tell us they get much better effects, and better satisfaction than when they themselves make the selection from samples.

RULES FOR MEASURING A ROOM.

Measure the length in feet of the four walls, add together, then multiply by the height in feet, the result will give the total number of square feet of wall surface; now deduct for windows and doors. Multiply the height by the width of each door and window, add together the square feet of each and deduct from the amount; now you have the net total amount of wall surface to be papered, divide this total by 60, the result is the number of rolls required for the walls.

FOR SIDE WALL.

Example: Room 15 feet long, 12 feet wide, 9 feet high. One window, 6x4 feet; one door, 7x4 feet; one window, 3½x4 feet.

15
15
12
12
―
54
9 Multiply.
―
486
66 Deduct.
―
60)420
―
7 Rolls.

1 window, 6 x4=24 square feet.
1 door, 7 x4=28 square feet.
1 window, 3½x4=14 square feet.
66 square feet.

FOR CEILING.

The number of rolls required for ceiling is ascertained the same way, dividing the number of square feet by 60.
Example: Room 15 feet long, 12 feet wide.
15x12=180
60)180
Double rolls.... 3

Wall paper weighs about 1¼ pounds per double roll. We do not trim wall paper because the edges being exposed, if damaged in transit, would render perfect matching impossible.

INSTRUCTIONS HOW TO HANG YOUR OWN WALL PAPER.

No Experience Necessary. Our Illustrations Tell the Story.

Heretofore we have given our friends printed instructions only, which, while simple, did not convey the correct idea. We now show several illustrations which will assist our customers materially and anybody can do as good a job of paperhanging as any professional paperhanger.

Illustration No. 1.

PREPARATION.

Secure two boards about 8 feet long and 10 or 12 inches wide, lay side by side, having the ends rest on a table or box at each end. The height should not exceed 3 feet. This will be your table. Now secure some plank for the platform on which to stand, which should be nearly as long as the width of the room you wish to paper. Make your platform sufficiently high so your head will be about 6 inches from the ceiling. This platform can be made by placing a board on two ordinary chairs or boxes. Secure the other necessary articles needed for your work. To apply the paste you will require a paste brush from 6 to 10 inches wide (a whitewash or calcimine brush will answer). A long pair of shears to secure a straight cut to trim the edges. **A smoothing brush** to smooth down the paper with after the same is hung and perfectly matched. If no smoothing brush is at hand, use a clothes brush or whisk broom. **A seam roller is required** to press down and smooth down the edges where each strip of paper laps over or is joined together. (You will note on the following pages that we offer all paperhangers' tools at actual cost). If you have no seam roller use a bed caster.

CAUTION—Do not use the seam roller until your paste on paper that is hung is partially dry—see further instructions. **Paper your ceiling first,** for in doing this work you are apt to touch the side walls with paper that has paste on, or with soiled hands, and your work will not look neat.

HOW TO TRIM WALL PAPER.

After you have ascertained the length of your room, unroll the paper face up on your work table, then match and cut same. Be sure that you have at least 3 or 4 inches at each end to come down on side wall (see illustration No. 3). It is absolutely necessary to have your ceiling paper come down on the side wall a trifle so as to cover any space left blank after border is put on, caused by ceiling not always being perfectly level. The larger the design the more surplus is required for matching; this surplus will be covered by the border or side wall paper. Before starting to hang, cut sufficient lengths of paper to cover the entire ceiling. Turn all the paper face down and you are now ready to apply the paste on the first or top length.

Illustration No 2.

PASTING AND TRIMMING.

The bucket of paste should be placed on the right hand side of the operator. Now apply the paste evenly on the top strip of paper, beginning on the left hand end of the table as you face same. After you have applied the paste on about one-half of the length, lay aside your brush and fold over the part of the paper that is pasted, using extra care that the sides are exactly even (see illustration No. 1). Now apply the paste to the other half and fold that over towards the center, same as first half. If the strip of paper is longer than your table, paste the left half; after folding allow the folded end to hang over the end of the table and rest on the floor while you are pasting and folding the other half. You now have an entire strip of paper before you, all pasted and folded, and the sides of the paper perfectly even and ready for trimming. Draw the strip of paper towards you about 3 inches from the edge of the table and proceed to trim, commencing at the right (see illustration No. 2). The great advantage in trimming paper after pasting is that the paste will then be more evenly distributed on the edges. It also takes less time, as you trim two thicknesses at once. **Always be sure to paper ceiling first.**

HOW TO HANG THE CEILING PAPER.

After the selvage is trimmed off your paper will be 18 inches wide. We have already explained when papering ceiling why the ends should come down a few inches on the side wall. For the same reason the first strip put up and also the last strip of ceiling should lap 2 inches on the side wall. As a guide for hanging the first length of ceiling paper properly, draw a line with chalk or charcoal 16 inches from the side wall. This is best done by driving a small nail in ceiling 16 inches from the side wall at each end of the room before starting to paper. Chalk a piece of cord, tie same to the nails, draw it tight, then take hold of the cord in the center, pull down and let go; the cord will strike the ceiling and leave a straight line. (We show this line in illustration No. 3.) Next you take the first piece of ceiling paper (which you have already pasted, folded and trimmed). Mount your raised platform, unfold the end to your right (as you start in the right hand corner of the room), let the other end, which is still folded, hang over a roll of paper which you hold in your left hand (see illustration No. 3). Commence in corner of ceiling, having the first strip come between the chalk line and the wall you face, allowing both the end and side of the paper to come down on the side wall 2 inches as explained. Now guide your paper with your right hand along the chalk line, at the same time pressing the paper to the ceiling with the flat of your hand as you move along and smoothing same with brush or whisk broom. When half of the first ceiling strip is put on, then unfold the other half and continue to the end of the first strip. When hanging the second length, you are guided by the edge of the first strip, and so on until the last strip of ceiling is put up. The edge of the last strip should also lap on the side wall. Care must be taken to have your patterns match.

Illustration No. 3.

HANGING SIDE WALL PAPER.

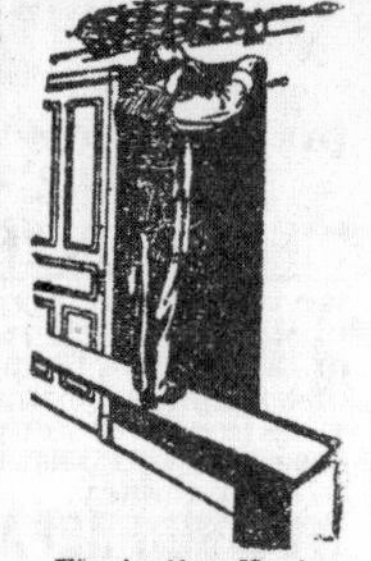

Illustration No. 4.

Always hang the side wall paper before hanging border. Follow the same instructions for cutting paper for side wall as previously outlined for ceiling. Paper should be cut from 4 to 5 inches longer than the length required for the side wall that is to be papered. In cutting your side wall paper, you can allow for the space of wall that the border will cover. All borders are either 9 or 18 inches wide. Be sure to match the pattern (which is very simple) as you have allowed from 4 to 6 inches in cutting, you can raise or lower each strip or length of paper as the pattern may require. In matching your side wall paper on the work table you will find when a large pattern is selected that there will be at times a waste of 8 or 10 inches which will have to be cut off. The upper end of the side wall paper will be uneven but the border will cover same. The lower end which stops at the base board is either trimmed with a base trimmer (see wall paper tools) or a pair of shears. When using shears, paste your paper in place close down to the base board, use the back of the shears to mark with, running same over top of paper where top of base board and plaster meet, then lift your paper a little (the paste still being fresh will permit of this), then cut where you have marked with shears and smooth down with brush or whisk broom. To hang side wall paper, arrange your platform or step ladder so it is about 12 inches from the wall, commence at any door, this will be of great assistance to you in hanging the first piece of side wall paper straight, then continue around the room until finished. All short pieces can be used over doors and windows. Take your first length of paper that has been pasted, folded and trimmed, mount the platform or ladder, unfold both ends and the entire strip hangs perpendicular (see illustration No. 4), lean forward, looking down along the edge and when the pattern is properly matched, allow the paper to touch the wall and smooth down with a brush or whisk broom. **About ten minutes should elapse before using the seam roller** as the paste is still wet and will squeeze out at the edges. Occasionally it will happen that a strip is not properly matched after being hung, in such cases remove the strip at once and proceed over again.

Illustration No. 5.

HANGING THE BORDER.

The border should be hung last and can be cut in five or six pieces should it be easier to hang in that way. Do not commence in the corner, but have the end lap over on the other wall about 4 inches. Cut the border through the center of the largest figure as a joint cannot be noticed after it is hung. Paste, fold and trim the border, same as you did in the side wall and ceiling. Take the folded strip of border, mount your platform or ladder, unfold the right end and proceed as shown in illustration No. 5. Should the ceiling be uneven it is best to draw a chalk line on the wall immediately under the ceiling. Make your chalk line in same manner as explained in our instructions for hanging first strip of ceiling (see line in illustration No. 5). This should be done on a line with the lowest part of the ceiling. This will leave the ceiling paper exposed above the border on the wall in some places. For this reason we recommend in our instructions on hanging ceiling paper to allow same to come down on side wall 2 inches. We trust the foregoing instructions are plain and that they will be of assistance to those who hang their own paper.

ABOUT ORDERING WALL PAPER.

After you have figured and ascertained the exact number of rolls required to paper your rooms, it is advisable to add an extra roll of each wall and ceiling and several yards of border. We do not want you to buy more paper than is actually needed, but we make above suggestion, having our customers' interest in mind. You may accidentally spoil a strip or when figuring you may overlook projections, such as chimneys, etc. Often an extra roll, worth a few cents, may avoid a great deal of inconvenience caused by waiting for additional paper to come on account of shortage.

HOW TO MAKE PASTE.

Enough to paper a good sized room: Take 2 pints of flour, rub smooth in 2 quarts of cold water, add 8 quarts of boiling water and let this boil slowly. Stir constantly for 10 minutes. When cold, stir in two tablespoonsful of powdered alum. Use about as thick as will run off the brush.

Starch Paste, which is considered very satisfactory, is made in the following manner: Dissolve 1 pound of best gloss starch in a quart of cold water. Use a large pail or dish pan. Boil a kettle of water and add same to starch gradually, stirring constantly until starch is cooked. When paste cools and is too thick, same can be reduced with cold water.

OUR PLAIN FLORAL PAPER WITHOUT BACKGROUND.

EXACTLY AS ADVERTISED, 1½c PER SINGLE ROLL, 3c PER DOUBLE ROLL.

This, our lowest priced paper, made in a neat floral design, is finished without background, and while it will compare favorably with papers that sell generally at double the price, and is suitable for papering bedrooms, closets, kitchens, etc., but since it costs just as much to hang this paper as the richest, heavy background paper that will wear very much longer, be less susceptible to dust and dirt and look very much richer, we would especially recommend, that in selecting a paper, that you select one of our rich, heavy background papers at from 10 cents per roll upwards. For example, while 26 cents will supply enough of this paper to cover a room 11x11, 9 feet high, side wall, border and ceiling, less than $1.00 will supply the same amount of a rich, heavy background 10-cent paper, paper that will last twice as long, always look rich and beautiful; besides, the labor of hanging is exactly the same, so we always advise our customers, since the difference in the cost between this, our cheapest paper, and a rich, heavy background paper at 10 to 15 cents a roll, is only about $1.00 to a room, that in their own interest, as a matter of real economy, they select one of the richest patterns we have to offer,

No. 53C191 Wall. Price, per double roll, 3c
No. 53C1191 Border, 9 inches wide. Price, per yard, ⅛c; 8 yards for........1c
No. 53C192 Ceiling. Per double roll.....3c

Cost of this paper for a room, size 11x11 feet, height of ceiling 9 feet, will be as follows:
For side wall and border.................. **20c**
For ceiling.............................. **6c**
Or total cost of wall, border and ceiling, **26c**

On the price of 26 cents for the above sized room, we allow for four ordinary size openings, namely, two doors and two windows.

THE ROMAN TILE.

7 CENTS PER DOUBLE ROLL.

A very pretty tile or block effect in green, red and silver on a medium green background. The illustration is a good likeness of the pattern. We consider the pattern one of the best and neatest tile patterns on the market. Adapted for kitchens, halls, bathrooms and closets.

For a low priced, durable, attractive, bright and cheerful wall paper we can highly recommend this, our Roman Tile, at 7 cents per double roll. It is one of the best patterns we have ever seen produced in a low priced paper; one that will wear well and prove durable, and yet ornament any room. As far as the quality is concerned, it is positively equal to papers that retail at 10 and 14 cents. The Roman Tile is shown by a small sample in our free Wall Paper Sample Book, sent to anyone on application, but if you desire, you can send us your order direct from this catalogue with every assurance of receiving satisfactory goods.

Made with a 9-inch border, blending into a light green ceiling.

No. 53C197 Wall. Price, per double roll........ 7c
No. 53C1197 Border. Price, per yard.. ½c
No. 53C198 Ceiling. Price, per double roll........ 7c

The same pattern as above described, produced in red, cream, green and black on a medium brown background. This is also a pleasing combination of colors and only a matter of preference as to the background. Made with a 9-inch border, blending into a light buff ceiling. The brown background wall paper will be sent, when ordered, under the following numbers:

No. 53C207 Wall. Price, per double roll........ 7c
No. 53C1207 Border. Price, per yard. ½c
No. 53C208 Ceiling. Price, per double roll........ 7c

THE GLENMORE.

8 CENTS PER DOUBLE ROLL.

A very neat wall hanging produced in colors that cannot but please everyone. For small parlors or bedrooms we can recommend this pattern as one that will give entire satisfaction. A low priced paper, nevertheless artistic. Flowers in red, pink, green and blue on a gray background. At 8 cents per double roll, this well covered, handsome wall paper is a bargain and cannot be equaled. This paper can be used for high class decorating, as it is up to date in pattern and colorings.

When you consider for how little money you can get a nice appearing, good quality wall paper and how much new paper adds to the appearance of any room, and also how little trouble it is to hang your own wall paper, you will admit that there is no excuse for any rooms in your house looking old, or dingy. This Glenmore paper is one of the big values in our line of cheap papers; a pattern that we offer in competition with wall paper that retails generally at 15 cents per double roll. The Glenmore and our entire line of wall paper is shown by means of samples in our free Wall Paper Sample Book, sent to anyone on application. Made with a 9-inch border, blending to a lighter gray ceiling.

No. 53C175 Wall. Price, per double roll........ 8c
No. 53C1175 Border. Price, per yard.. 1c
No. 53C176 Ceiling. Price, per double roll........ 8c

GOOD PAPERING CAN BE DONE WITHOUT EXPENSIVE TOOLS.

All that is required to do ordinary papering is a pair of shears, a paste brush, a smoothing brush and a seam roller. No household is without a pair of shears. For applying the paste any whitewash or calcimine brush will do. If none is at hand we can supply one for 21 cents (see Paperhangers' Tools), a smoothing brush for 12 cents and a seam roller for 10 cents, making a total of 43 cents for tools which will enable you to hang paper. Of course we have other tools to facilitate paper hanging, but good work can be done with the few inexpensive tools mentioned above.

THE LORAINE.

A BEAUTIFUL DESIGN, ONLY 10 CENTS PER DOUBLE ROLL.

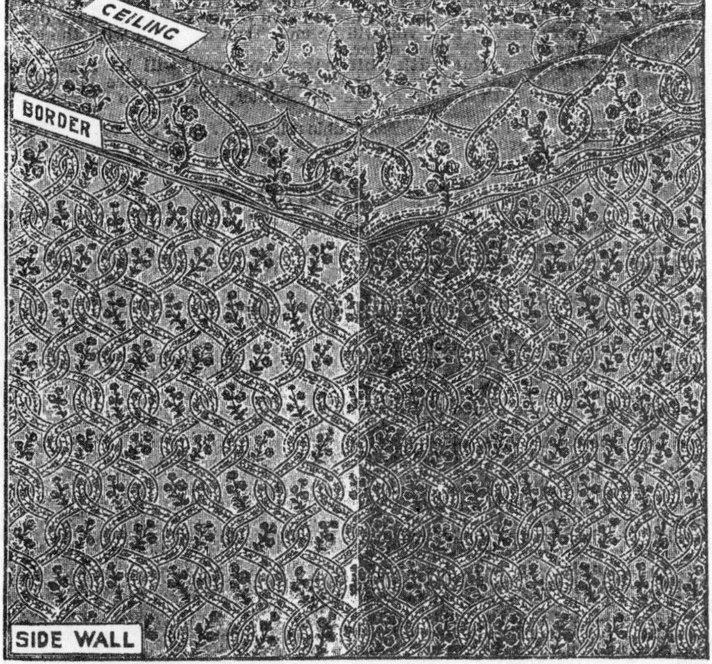

For beauty and style at 10 cents per double roll there is nothing on the market equally as good. The illustration will give an idea as to the appearance of this beautiful paper, but we assure you that you will be more than pleased when you see the paper. The background is a soft cream, nearly white, flowers in red and pink. Narrow ribbons interlaced, followed by a vine in green with gold decorations continues the entire length. The border is 9 inches wide and blends into a pure white ceiling.

It is difficult to give you an accurate idea of the appearance and beauty of the Loraine design by means of a description and illustration. The illustration will show the pattern effect, but it will, of course, be impossible to reproduce the beautiful combination of colors. Our free Wall Paper Sample Book, sent to anyone on application, shows an actual sample of this paper, but at the same time, if you do not wish to wait for samples, you can order the Loraine direct from this description and we guarantee to please you in every way or immediately return your money. At 10 cents per double roll we offer the Loraine as the pick and choice of the 10 cent papers in our line and the equal of wall paper that will sell in all other stores at 20 and 25 cents per roll. It is a beautiful pattern and a thoroughly dependable and durable paper and of a quality that is unsurpassed.

No. 53C173 Wall. Price, per double roll........ 10c
No. 53C1173 Border. Price, per yard........ 1c
No. 53C174 Ceiling. Price, per double roll........ 10c

THE NEWPORT.

A SWELL DESIGN AT 16 CENTS PER DOUBLE ROLL.

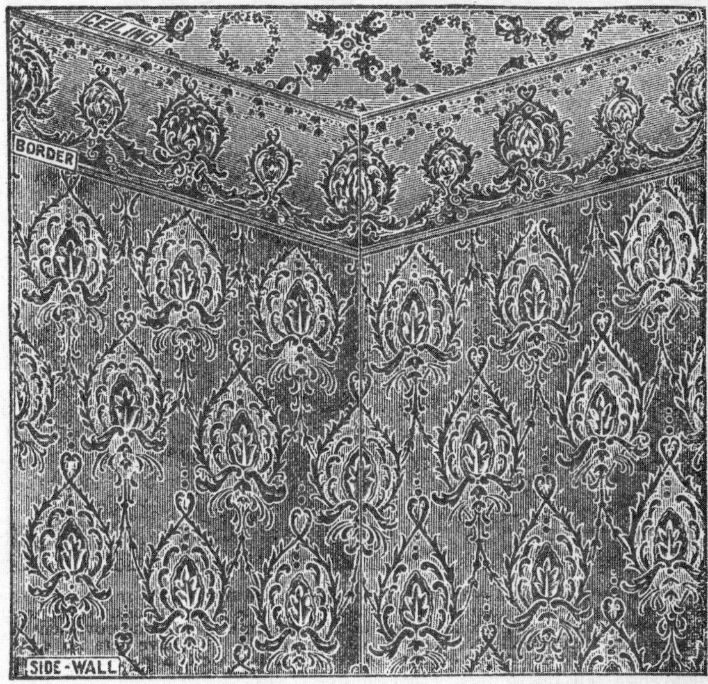

A very attractive wall decoration; a set figure design in dark red, light red and gold. One of the prettiest effects in red ever shown and a cheerful paper for parlors, dining rooms and halls. A sparkling wall decoration, rich in gold and colors. The price quoted is fully 50 per cent lower than a similar design can be purchased for elsewhere.

We doubt whether any other wall paper concern can show as rich a wall paper at the price that we are asking for this artistic design. We show it here because it is one of our leaders for 1905; a pattern that we have selected to emphasize for how little money we can furnish a beautiful high class wall paper, and at 16 cents per double roll we claim that it is a wonder of value. Read what we say about how to measure a room and how to order; also instructions how to hang your own wall paper, on page 276, and then send us your order direct from this catalogue and if you are not more than pleased with the paper we send you, you are at liberty to return it to us at our expense and we will promptly return your money. Our free Wall Paper Sample Book, sent on application, show samples of our entire line of wall paper.

Made with an 18-inch border, blending to a buff ceiling.

No. 53C189 Wall. Price, per double roll........ 16c
No. 53C1189 Border. Price, per yard........ 2c
No. 53C190 Ceiling. Price, per double roll........ 16c

THE ESMOND.

A POPULAR STYLE WALL PAPER AT 14 CENTS.

The background of this paper is a soft French gray and one of the most popular tints now used by high class decorators. The design is a combination set and floral; a bouquet of flowers in pink, red and white is inclosed by scroll figures in gold, with a choke in a darker gray. The figure is also crowned with a spray of flowers in pink, red and white. The stripe in a darker gray is broken by the figure.

The Esmond is another of our beautiful exclusive designs in wall paper for this season. The illustration will give you some idea as to the design, but the paper must be seen to be appreciated. It is rich in effect and has all the style and appearance and, in fact, is equal in every way to papers that sell at 30 to 35 cents per roll. If you will favor us with your order for this, our special 14-cent Esmond paper, we will accept your order with the positive understanding that if you are not more than pleased with the wall paper when it is received, you can return it to us at our expense and we will promptly return your money. While you can send your order immediately, we will gladly send you our free Sample Book of Wall Paper on application, which shows a sample of the Esmond as well as our entire line of 1905 designs.

In all it is a handsome design, harmoniously colored and one of the prettiest wall hangings made.

No. 53C231 Wall. Price, per double roll........14c
No. 53C1231 Border. Price, per yard. 2c
No. 53C232 Ceiling. Price, per double roll........14c

THE BLENHEIM.

ONE OF OUR 1905 PRIZE DESIGNS AT 16 CENTS.

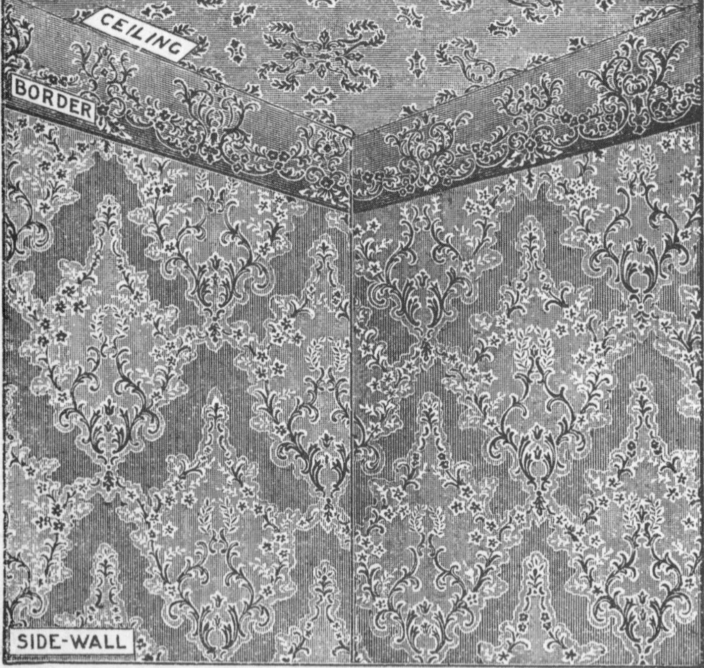

The most artistic wall decoration ever produced. It is really unnecessary to describe this beautiful wall hanging; the design is sufficient to impress upon you that the color combination in this pattern is beyond improvement; it was copied from a wall decoration of a famous castle. We have here an exact reproduction of a decoration of the most skilled artists' work, a perfect harmony of colors, a design beautiful in every respect. The design is a combination floral and scroll; the figure as above illustrated is produced by means of scroll outlines in gold and small red and white flowers. The background of the figure is a beautiful green, the darker portions shown in the illustration are a deep red. The contrast is something beautiful which it would be impossible to describe. The Blenheim is without question the neatest combination red and green paper on the market.

The illustration will give you some idea of the Blenheim pattern, but the paper must be seen to be appreciated. If you order the Blenheim you can feel that you are getting a paper superior to most papers that retail as high as 35 cents per roll. Bear in mind that the Blenheim, as well as all of our wall paper, is made in our own mill and is offered to you direct on the basis of actual manufacturing cost with just our one small percentage of profit added. Our free Wall Paper Sample Book, sent on request, shows the actual samples of our entire line of wall paper, although you can send us your order direct from this catalogue and be sure of receiving perfect and satisfactory goods.

Made with an 18-inch border which blends to a ceiling in light green, decorated in red and gold. At only 16 cents per double roll you can secure this artistic wall hanging, a paper which is worth double the price, a design and color combination which you cannot secure elsewhere.

No. 53C57 Wall. Price, per double roll........16c
No. 53C157 Border. 18 inches wide. Price, per yard........2c
No. 53C58 Ceiling. Price, per double roll........16c

THE PALAIS.

A HANDSOME NEW PAPER AT 17 CENTS.

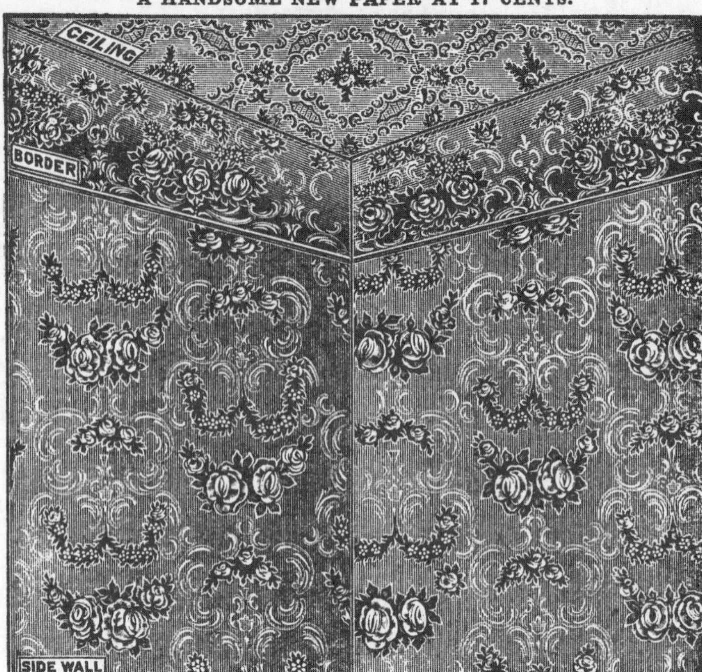

This is another of the high class decorative papers, and modern in every respect. Dark greens are very popular, the one represented here is very prettily colored and a charming wall hanging. The design is a floral and scroll; the scroll in green, bronze and gold, the floral, which consists of beautiful roses, are reproduced in red and pink, their natural colors.

READ THIS IT COSTS VERY LITTLE TO PAPER A ROOM WITH HIGH GRADE PAPER.

A large parlor 14x16 feet, 10 feet high, will require 9 rolls for the side wall, 4 rolls for the ceiling and 20 yards of border, papered with this high grade wall paper will cost the small sum of $2.71, allowing for four ordinary openings. This is the total cost of the paper, side wall, border and ceiling. Do the work yourself, our complete instructions will help you to do a perfect job and make it a pleasure to hang wall paper.

The Palais is another one of our prize designs; a real triumph in decorative wall covering. The picture will give you some idea as to the design, and all that we can say is that you will be more than delighted with the actual paper if you favor us with your order.

Decorate your parlor with this paper and you will be more than pleased. An up to date wall paper at less than one-half the price charged by others. It is made with a beautiful 18-inch border, blending to a light green ceiling, the ceiling is also nicely decorated.

No. 53C205 Wall. Price, per double roll........17c
No. 53C1205 Border. Price, per yard........2c
No. 53C206 Ceiling. Price, per double roll........17c

THE ABINGTON.

A SILK WALL PAPER AT 20 CENTS.

This is our high class silk wall paper; the design is modern and artistic in every respect. Silk wall hangings are in demand everywhere and the one represented here is the finest we have seen. The illustration is an exact reproduction of the design but it would be impossible to describe the attractiveness of the design and colorings. It is without question one of the finest silk wall hangings produced. The background is a yellow green tint, the design is a combination set and floral, a wreath of small roses in pink and red incloses small scroll figures in blue and white, the broken stripe being nearly all white. The figures, which measure 6x8 inches, are connected by a festoon of leaves and flowers, a flowing ribbon in pink and white is above every figure. Made with an 18-inch border, blending into a lighter ceiling. Sidewall and border are heavily embossed.

The Abington is a pattern which we show with particular pride as there is nothing that can approach it in wall paper sold at retail for less than 50 cents per roll. It is really an exclusive design; a paper that will ornament parlor, library or sitting room; as rich in effect as any of the most high priced papers that you will find in large city stores. Remember, if you do not care to wait for samples, you can order direct from the wall paper illustrated and described in this catalogue with the assurance of receiving the most satisfactory goods. In fact, we have taken particular pains to show herein only our best values and greatest leaders for 1905. However, if you would like to see samples of the actual papers themselves, don't fail to write for our free Wall Paper Sample Book. In sending us your order for wall paper you not only get the advantage of saving at least one-half in the cost as compared with what you would pay for paper of equal quality in retail stores or from any other dealer, but you also get the advantage of a selection from positively the most complete and up to date line of papers ever placed on the market.

No. 53C211 Wall. Price, per double roll........20c
No. 53C1211 Border. Price, per yard........2c
No. 53C212 Ceiling. Price, per double roll........20c

THE AMEER.

ONE OF OUR VERY FINEST WALL PAPER PATTERNS.

A modern floral tapestry in a design which we claim to be the prettiest on the market. The colorings are beautiful and harmonize perfectly. The background in dark red with an overprint consisting of narrow dark lines. The floral is produced in brown, green, blue and yellow, a perfect harmony of colors; the overprint, consisting of narrow black lines, cover the flowers as well, which produces a remarkable effect, bringing out the real tapestry effect. The border is 9 inches wide. The ceiling is a light terra cotta. Tapestry wall hangings are increasing in popularity and used extensively for high class decorating. The border, while only 9 inches wide, can be put in rooms with a high ceiling by allowing the ceiling paper to come down on the wall about 8 inches, then put the border where you left off with the ceiling—that is 8 inches from the ceiling. This will look very pretty; it is the latest style of hanging a narrow border in rooms with high ceiling.

If you want one of the prettiest wall papers ever produced, a new 1905 design, something exclusive and out of the ordinary, a paper that is suitable for the nicest parlors or other rooms, let us induce you to send us your order for this particular Ameer pattern, and if you do not agree with us and do not find the paper all and more than we claim for it, you are at liberty to return it to us at our expense and we will return your money. At 25 cents per double roll we offer the Ameer as the equal of any paper on the market, regardless of price. It is a paper that would retail in fine city stores at 50 and 60 cents per double roll. It is one of our very finest papers; one of the best we have to offer; a wall paper that is much richer in effect and much better in quality than any wall paper that you can buy in the ordinary wall paper stores in small cities. You can freely send us your order direct from this catalogue without waiting for further samples or descriptions, but if you desire we will gladly send you our free Sample Book of Wall Paper, showing a sample of the Ameer, as well as our entire line of other wall paper.

No. 53C223 Wall. Price, per double roll........25c
No. 53C1223 Border. Price, per yard........1c
No. 53C224 Ceiling. Price, per double roll........25c

DESCRIPTION AND PRICE LIST OF INGRAIN WALL PAPERS.

The term "Ingrain," as applied to wall decoration, means a plain paper without figure decoration of any kind or description. Ingrains are made in various colors on plain, heavy stock, 30 inches wide. Ingrains are used in parlors, dining rooms, stores, art galleries, drawing rooms, etc. Where pictures are to be hung, ingrains are generally preferred because there is no figure or decoration to detract from the picture itself.

Green is a popular color when a background for richly framed pictures is desired. The deep red ingrain is preferred for dining rooms and, when used in this manner, forms an excellent background for plate rails, with an attractive arrangement of china and glassware. The lighter colors of ingrains, old rose, blue, light green, terra cotta and Vermont stone gray can be used in almost any room where furnishings are such that highly colored or rich gold wall hangings might prove too strong a contrast.

The borders for the ingrain papers are 18 inches wide, the pattern is the same on all of the ingrains, but is made in different colors to harmonize with the ingrain wall paper. The design is a beautiful one, a festoon of large roses with gold decorations, one of the prettiest borders made. The ceilings are likewise made in different tints to harmonize with the borders and ingrain wall paper, but the pattern is the same on all of the ingrains. The decorations on the ceilings are very pretty, produced in gold and colors.

No. 53C1 Vermont Stone Ingrain. Price, per double roll of 16 yards........18c
No. 53C15001 Border, 18 inches wide, to match sidewall and ceiling. Price, per yd. 2c
No. 53C5001 Ceiling, to match sidewall and border. Price, per double roll......18c

No. 53C3 Light Green Ingrain. Price, per double roll........20c
No. 53C15003 Border, 18 inches wide, to match sidewall and ceiling. Price, per yd. 2c
No. 53C5003 Ceiling, to match sidewall and border. Price, per double roll......20c

No. 53C4 Light Blue Ingrain. Price, per double roll........20c
No. 53C15004 Border, 18 inches wide, to match sidewall and ceiling. Price, per yard........2c
No. 53C5004 Ceiling, to match sidewall and border. Price, per double roll..20c

No. 53C5 Terra Cotta Ingrain. Price, per double roll........20c
No. 53C15005 Border, 18 inches wide, to match sidewall and ceiling. Price, per yard........2c
No. 53C5005 Ceiling, to match sidewall and border. Price, per double roll..20c

No. 53C9 Dark Green Ingrain. Price, per double roll........22c
No. 53C15009 Border, 18 inches wide, to match sidewall and ceiling. Price, per yard........2c
No. 53C5009 Ceiling, to match sidewall and border. Price, per double roll.22c

No. 53C10 Pure Dark Red Ingrain. Price, per double roll........22c
No. 53C15010 Border, 18 inches wide, to match sidewall and ceiling. Price, per yard........2c
No. 53C5010 Ceiling, to match sidewall and border. Price, per double roll..22c

No. 53C12 Old Rose Color Ingrain. Price, per double roll........20c
No. 53C15012 Border, 18 inches wide, to match sidewall and ceiling. Price, per yard........2c
No. 53C5012 Ceiling, to match sidewall and border. Price, per double roll..20c

ROOM MOULDINGS

ENHANCE THE BEAUTY OF THE WALL DECORATION, and are the most convenient method for hanging pictures. They are placed from 9 to 18 inches from the ceiling, where the lower part of the border connects with the side walls.

THIS MOULDING CANNOT BE USED FOR FRAMING PICTURES.

No. 53C50 Fancy Figured Moulding, 2 inches wide. Green top, red bottom, gilt tipped ornaments. Used with any red, green or gilt wall decoration. Price, per foot........3c

No. 53C124 Fancy figured, 1½ inches wide, finished in two shades of green delicately blended, gilt tipped ornaments. Will harmonize with any green wall decoration. Price, per foot........2c

No. 53C165 Fancy figured, 1½ inches wide, two shades rich red blended, tips of ornaments gold. Used with wall paper or decorations where the general color effect is red. Price, per foot........2c

No. 53C66 Polished White Enameled Moulding. Will look well with any light color wall decoration. 1½ inches wide. Price, per foot........2c

No. 53C43 Imitation Oak Moulding, 1½ inches wide, nicely finished. Can be used with any kind of decoration. Price, per foot........1½c

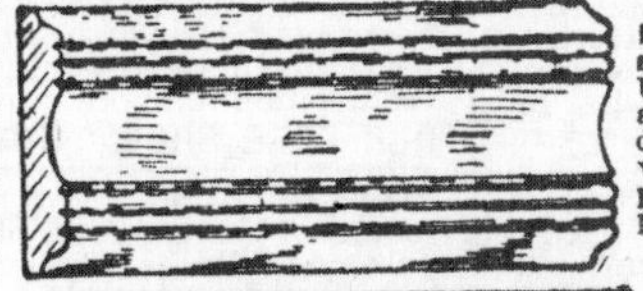

No. 53C72 Chair Rail, 2½ inches wide, solid polished oak. Used as chair rail, or as dado rail or divider. The finish is the very finest French polish that can be produced. Price, per foot...4c

No. 53C29 Ornamented Gilt Beading, ½ inch wide. Used for paneling on ceiling and side wall. Price, per foot........1½c

No. 53C157 Fancy figured, 1½ inches wide. Color, light green, blending into white, gilt tipped ornaments. Used with wall decorations of a light green shade. Price, per foot........2c

No. 53C123 Fancy figured, all gilt. 1½ inches wide. A beautiful moulding. Can be used with any shade or color of wall paper or decoration. Price, per foot........2c

No. 53C93 Burnished Gilt Moulding. The very best quality of gilt, will last for years. Lower part finished in mat gold and upper part highly burnished. 1½ inches wide. No better on the market. Can be used in any room with any color wall decoration. Price, per foot........3½c

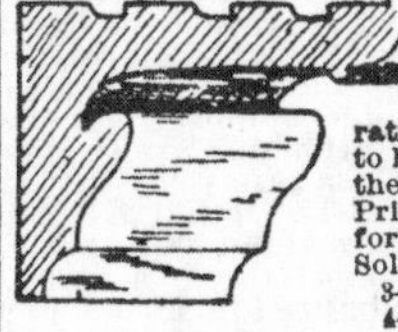

No. 53C140 Plate Rail. Extensively used to complete parlor, library and dining room decorations. It is a narrow shelf with grooves to hold photos, plates, etc. The finish is the very finest that can be produced. Printed directions with nails and screws for putting up sent with every shipment. Solid polished oak.

3-inch shelf. Price, per foot...9c
4-inch shelf. Price, per foot...11c

Plate Rail Ends or Brackets.

In order to enable our customers to put up plate rails with ease, we have especially made up our new plate rail ends or brackets. They are used to finish ends at doors and windows. Highly polished to match the plate rails.

No. 53C142 Price, each........9c

A WORD ABOUT OUR ROOM MOULDINGS, PLATE AND CHAIR RAILS.

We handle the best mouldings, made from the best material by careful workmen and we challenge any dealer to produce a better grade. The gilt on our mouldings will not tarnish, this we guarantee and the gilt will look as well after several years as when first put up. Our plate and chair rails are made from genuine first grade seasoned oak, the polish is the fine t that can be produced and equal to the finish on a piano, still we are quoting lower prices for better goods than others ask for cheaper qualities.

THE GILT ON OUR MOULDINGS IS WARRANTED NOT TO TARNISH.

READY MIXED PAINTS

FROM OUR OWN FACTORY

WE ARE NOW MANUFACTURERS OF READY MIXED PAINTS. EVERY GALLON OF MIXED PAINT WE SELL IS MADE IN OUR OWN FACTORY, HENCE WE ARE ABLE TO CONTROL THE QUALITY AND GIVE OUR CUSTOMERS A HIGHER GRADE OF READY MIXED PAINT AT MUCH LOWER PRICES THAN THEY COULD POSSIBLY BUY ELSEWHERE.

AS MANUFACTURERS WE OFFER YOU MANY ADVANTAGES.

OUR READY MIXED PAINT DEPARTMENT having grown until for the past two seasons we have been taking the greater part of the output of a large paint factory, we concluded to make a thorough investigation into the cost of producing strictly high grade ready mixed paints, with a view of establishing our own factory, where we could get out the very highest grade of work, and be in a position at the same time to give our customers the benefit of any saving we might make by making the paint ourselves. As a result we first secured the services of one of the best paint makers in America, a man who has had years of experience in the manufacture of all the highest grades of ready mixed paints, as well as varnishes, pigments, colors, etc., and especially in paint making, and one of the best paint and color chemists in the country.

THE RESULT of our investigation proved that better paints could be produced than those now on the market, and yet when figured at the actual cost to produce, with but one small percentage of profit added, could be offered our customers at prices very much lower than inferior grades are sold.

OUR PAINT FACTORY, located directly across the street from our main building, as shown in the above illustration, has been equipped with the most modern paint making machinery, with a view to producing the very highest grades and by the use of the most modern machinery at the minimum of cost. Our contracts for materials are all for especially high grade goods, hence we can today offer you from our own paint factory, made by ourselves under the direct supervision of our own master paint maker, such grades of ready mixed paint as you could not get elsewhere, and at prices lower than were ever before known.

AS A GUARANTEE that we will furnish you better paint at lower prices than you can buy elsewhere, we will be very glad to accept your order for any quantity or grade of our ready mixed paint and ship it to you with the understanding that if after received, examined and compared with any other paint that you can buy at within 25 to 50 cents per gallon of our price, if you are not convinced that our paint is the equal or better, you can return the paint to us at our expense and we will immediately refund your money, making no charge for the paint used in the test.

SPECIAL TO CONTRACTORS, carpenters, builders, manufacturers, railroads and large users of paint. While our price is alike to all (it is already figured so low, reduced to the actual cost to produce in our own factory with but our one small percentage of profit added), the same whether you order one barrel or one hundred barrels, by comparison you will find our prices much lower than you are now paying, and if you will give us one trial order we know you will give us your entire paint business ever after. We already have the exclusive trade in this line of many of the largest paint users in the country, and we especially urge a trial order from all large users of ready mixed paint.

AT 85 CENTS TO 98 CENTS PER GALLON we furnish the highest grade ready mixed house paint, our celebrated Seroco brand.

WE OFFER OUR SEROCO READY MIXED HOUSE PAINT, every gallon of which is made in our own paint factory directly under our own supervision, as positively the very highest grade ready mixed house paint made, the equal of paint that is sold generally throughout the country at 50 per cent higher prices. On the following pages we list the different shades that we furnish in the Seroco Ready Mixed House Paint at 85 cents to 98 cents a gallon, according to quantity.

OUR SEROCO READY MIXED HOUSE PAINT has been on the market for years, it has been for years the highest grade ready mixed paint it was possible for the largest and oldest paint manufacturer in the country to make for us under contract. Since the establishment of our own paint factory we have endeavored to improve the quality in every way. We have raised the standard of the raw materials and ingredients that enter into its manufacture, we have tried to get a uniformly higher grade of white lead and linseed oil, we are putting every gallon of Seroco grade house paint under a most rigid inspection before shipment, and even considering the reputation our Seroco Ready Mixed House Paint has had in the past for quality, we can safely say that from now on, this grade of paint will be better than ever, will be found to be higher grade, will go further, cover more surface, last longer, will not chip, peel, crack or blister and has absolutely no equal on the market today in a ready mixed, high grade paint. We know that our Seroco brand of ready mixed house paint, the quality we are today putting out, will look better and brighter after five years' service than the ordinary ready mixed house paint looks after six months of wear. There are higher priced ready mixed house paints on the market, paints that are sold by manufacturers and dealers, at prices ranging from $1.00 to $2.00 per gallon, but our Seroco brand of ready mixed paint is equal, if not superior, to such of the highest priced paints made today. We are willing that you should compare our Seroco grade of paint that we furnish at **85 cents to 98 cents per gallon**, according to quantity, with any ready mixed paint that you can buy elsewhere even at double the price, and if you do not find that the Seroco ready mixed paint is equal to such other paints in every particular you need not keep the paint you get from us, but it can be returned to us at our expense, and your money will be promptly refunded.

Seroco Weatherproof Mineral Roof, Barn and Fence Paint at 50 cents to 65 cents per Gallon, According to Quantity.

FOR ALL OUTSIDE WORK, out buildings of all kinds, roofs, barns, fences, metallic work, structural iron work, etc., there is just one paint to use, namely, our Seroco Weatherproof Mineral Barn, Roof and Fence Paint that we furnish in the six shades as described on the following pages at **50 cents to 65 cents per gallon**, according to quantity. Cheaper barn paints are on the market. It would be possible for us, if we sacrificed quality to price, to furnish a so called barn paint as cheap as 35 cents per gallon in large quantities, but we have experimented carefully, we have made many tests of grades of paint for outdoor work, and in this, our Seroco Weatherproof Mineral Roof, Barn and Fence Paint, we believe we have the ideal paint for the purposes for which it is intended.

OUR TWO BIG FREE PAINT BOOKS.

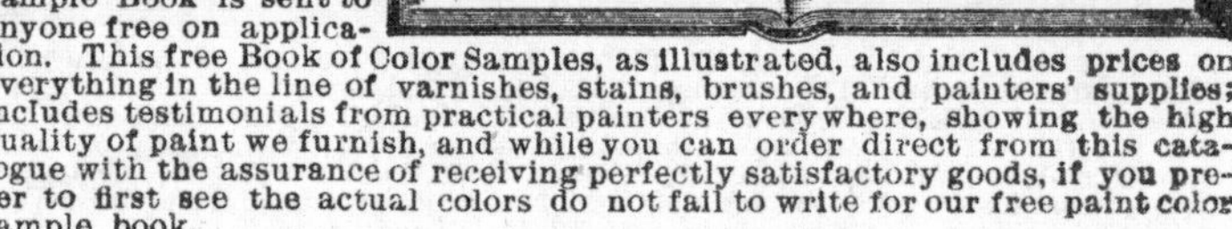

We furnish two books on the subject of painting absolutely free. One is our **PAINT COLOR SAMPLE BOOK,** showing the actual shades of all the paints we make, 85 different color samples, showing the exact shade and color, together with full information about prices on all our paints, full information how to select the colors of all the different makes and grades of paints we handle, and this Paint Color Sample Book is sent to anyone free on application. This free Book of Color Samples, as illustrated, also includes prices on everything in the line of varnishes, stains, brushes, and painters' supplies; includes testimonials from practical painters everywhere, showing the high quality of paint we furnish, and while you can order direct from this catalogue with the assurance of receiving perfectly satisfactory goods, if you prefer to first see the actual colors do not fail to write for our free paint color sample book.

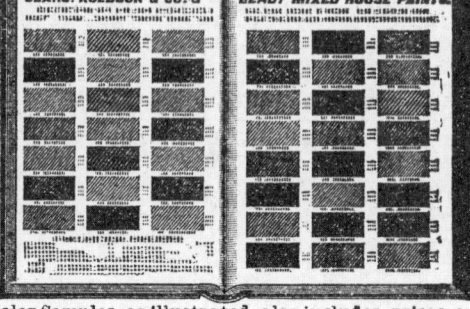

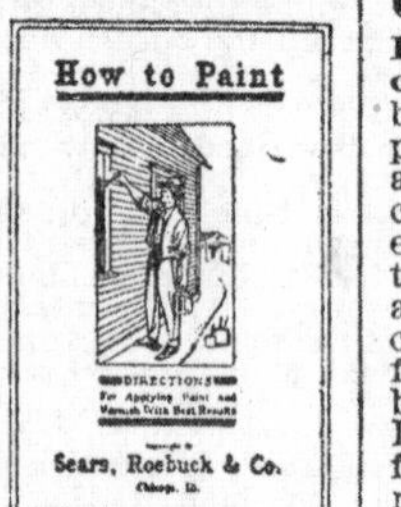

OUR FREE BOOK, "HOW TO PAINT." With every Paint Color Sample Book we also send out free of charge, our free book "HOW TO PAINT." This is a book carefully compiled by us, showing by means of plain pictures and simple directions just how to apply any kind of paint, how to do any job of painting successfully. This book makes everything so plain and explicit, the instructions are so simple, the illustrations are so easy to understand that anyone, without any previous experience, can do any job of painting successfully. Understand, when you write and ask for a free sample book of paints, with the free color sample book, we will also send you this book, "How to Paint." It contains a world of information about painting, a big fund of valuable instructions and directions, worth more than a dozen of the textbooks on the subject of painting which sell at various prices.

WITH THE AID OF OUR FREE BOOK, "HOW TO PAINT," you can do the job yourself even though you have never done any painting before. You need not hire a practical painter to do the work. We guarantee success. **Everything is made so plain that you cannot make a mistake.** Remember, the free book, "How to Paint," goes with every sample book, and these two valuable books are sent to anyone on application. If you will mail us a postal card, simply ask for the Free Paint Sample Book, the Book of Color Samples, and the free book, "How to Paint," together with order blanks, etc., all the samples, all the valuable information, will be sent to you by return mail, postpaid.

HOW TO ORDER PAINT.

While we will send our book of color samples free to any address on application, and the book shows all the different shades in natural colors of all the different paints we make, and also includes a fund of useful information as to how to paint, how to select colors, etc., it isn't really necessary to delay to write for this free sample book, for it is not necessary to have this sample book from which to make selections.

OUR FREE BOOK, "HOW TO PAINT." With every order for paint we will include, free of charge, our book, "How to Paint." This is a valuable book, carefully compiled, showing by means of pictures and plain directions just how anyone can do any job of painting. No experience required. Remember, the book, "How to Paint," is included absolutely free of charge with every order for paint.

YOU CAN ORDER FROM THIS CATALOGUE, select the paint wanted, select the shades desired, always ordering by number, and if by chance the shade you select by name from this catalogue is not satisfactory to you after received, you can return it to us at our expense, and we will exchange it for any other shade you may want, or refund your money, as you see fit.

To Ascertain the Quantity of Paint Required.

Add together the length in feet of the sides and ends of a building, then multiply by the height, and divide the product by 250, the result will give the number of gallons of paint required for two coats.

For example:

Front,	20 feet
Rear,	20 feet
Side,	30 feet
Side,	30 feet
Total,	100 feet
Multiply height,	20 feet
Total,	2,000 feet

Divide by 250, the number of square feet a gallon of our paint will cover two coats, and you will find it will require 8 gallons to cover the surface, two coats.

ABOUT THE FREIGHT.

The freight charges on ready mixed paint will amount to next to nothing as compared with what you will save in price. Paint in tin cans is accepted by the railroad companies at next to the lowest freight rate (or third class), while in pails, kegs, half barrels and barrels it is taken at the lowest freight rate (or fourth class). Our paint weighs about 13¼ pounds to the gallon, 8 gallons to 100 pounds; so when ordered in quantities of 8 gallons or more, the freight per gallon for two hundred miles amounts to about 3 cents; four to six hundred miles, 4 to 5 cents; greater distances in proportion. The freight is a mere trifle compared to what you will save in price.

Seroco Ready Mixed House Paint.

FOR A READY MIXED PAINT for houses, for interior or exterior work, or even for barns, fences, for wood or iron where an extra grade, an extra durable and handsome, easy working and fine finish paint is desired, the very best ready mixed paint made, we especially recommend this, our own Seroco Ready Mixed Paint.

REMEMBER, Seroco Ready Mixed Paint is made in our own factory, we guarantee every gallon to be full weight and full measure, to give perfect satisfaction or we will refund your money. At 85 cents to 98 cents per gallon, according to quantity ordered, we furnish this, our Seroco Ready Mixed Paint, made in our own paint factory, at prices that are based on the actual manufacturing cost, the cost of the raw material and labor, with but our one small percentage of profit added, and you can buy this, the highest grade ready mixed house paint from us at a lower price than dealers can buy their paint from other sources in any quantity.

YOU CAN ORDER DIRECT from this catalogue, selecting the color wanted from the colors listed below, with our guarantee that the color and quality will please you, or we will immediately return your money; but if you prefer to see the exact colors before ordering, write us and we will mail you our special Paint Color Sample Booklet free, with our compliments. This booklet shows samples of the actual colors of all the different paints we handle.

WE FURNISH our Seroco Ready Mixed House Paint, the highest grade house paint on the market, at prices ranging from 85 cents to 98 cents per gallon, according to package, as follows:

Our 98-Cent Seroco House Paint.

At 98 cents per gallon we furnish the Seroco Ready Mixed Paint put up in 1-gallon tin pails, exactly as illustrated. The difference in price between 85 and 98 cents per gallon only represents the difference in cost of the package to us. If you require five gallons or more it will pay you to order this paint in buckets or barrels. Understand, it is put out under our binding guarantee that if it does not please you, if you don't find it better than any ready mixed paint made, regardless of price, you can return it to us at our expense, and we will immediately return your money.

AT 95 CENTS PER GALLON we furnish our Seroco, the highest grade ready mixed paint made, in 5-gallon buckets, exactly as illustrated.

In this package, in a 5-gallon wooden baled bucket, we can furnish our Seroco Paint at 95 cents per gallon. 95 cents barely covers the actual cost of material and labor; made, ground and put up in our own factory, with but our one small percentage of profit added. If you buy this paint from us you will get such value as you could not get from any other house.

93 CENTS PER GALLON for our Seroco Ready Mixed House Paint in 10-gallon buckets.

At 93 cents per gallon we are able to produce this paint in our own factory, at a price that barely covers the cost of material and labor, with but our one small percentage of profit added. Understand, we guarantee this paint superior to any paint you can possibly mix by hand.

88 Cents per Gallon for Seroco Mixed Paint, in 25-Gallon Half Barrels.

88 cents per gallon buys our highest grade Seroco Ready Mixed House Paint, put up in 25-gallon half barrels, exactly as illustrated.

This shows the style in which we put up Seroco paint in half-barrel lots and are able to offer it at 88 cents per gallon, just enough to cover cost of manufacture, with but our one small profit added.

85 Cents per Gallon for Seroco Paint in Full 50-Gallon Barrels.

At 85 cents per gallon, made in our own factory.

In 50-gallon barrels this excellent Seroco Ready Mixed Paint is offered at 85 cents per gallon. Remember, every gallon of Seroco Ready Mixed Paint is guaranteed to give satisfaction in wearing qualities and covering capacity. This means you are absolutely safe when purchasing a barrel of this paint. The money paid will be promptly refunded if for any reason you should think that the paint is not as represented.

Prices and List of Colors of Seroco Ready Mixed House Paint.

No. 30C100 Always order by color number as well as catalogue number.

201 French Gray	224 Maroon
202 Lavender	225 Bronze
203 Straw	226 Willow Green
204 Pea Green	227 Drab
205 Light Drab	229 Red
206 Canary	230 Brown
207 Lemont Stone	231 French Yellow
208 Pearl	233 Slate
209 Beaver	235 Light Stone
210 Pink	237 Dark Gray
211 Milwaukee Brick	240 Yellow Stone
213 Nile Green	241 Green Tint
214 Olive Drab	242 Light Slate
215 Cream	244 Sky Blue
216 Fawn	246 Colonial Yellow
217 Pure Blue	250 Azure Blue
218 Buff	251 Orange
219 Terra Cotta	252 Oakwood
220 Apple Green	IW Inside White
221 Leather Brown	OW Outside White
223 Light Blue	Blk Black

Prices for above colors.	Each	Gallon
1-quart cans	28c	
2-quart cans	53c	
1-gallon cans	98c	
5-gallon buckets		95c
10-gallon buckets		93c
25-gallon half barrels		88c
50-gallon barrels		85c

Special Colors.

No. 30C102	1 gal.	2 qts.	1 qt
232 Myrtle Green	$1.30	70c	40c
234 Vermilion	1.80	95c	50c
236 Emerald Green	1.30	70c	40c
247 Carmine	1.80	95c	50c
253 Golden Green	1.30	70c	40c

Brushes to Use With Seroco Ready Mixed House Paint.

For inside wall painting, use a No. 30C551 or No. 30C552 wall brush, any size, 3½ or 4-inch recommended. For interior wood work use a round paint brush, No. 30C545 or No. 30C546, any size, 3-0 or 4-0 recommended. For windows use a sash tool, No. 30C543 or No. 30C544; sizes 4 to 8 are best adapted for this work.

For outside house painting the following brushes are required: Wall brush, round paint brush, two or three sash tools. No. 30C551 or No. 30C552 wall brush, sizes 3½, 4 or 4½ inches in width are recommended for the walls. No. 30C545 or No. 30C546 round paint brushes, sizes 3-0 to 5-0, for applying the trimming colors. No. 30C543 or No. 30C544 sash tools, one each, sizes 4 and 8, for general trimming and used where the round paint brush will be found too large.

Seroco Ready Mixed Floor Paints.

No. 30C104 Made from the very best pigments, by the latest and most improved machinery. **Absolutely the best floor paint made;** guaranteed to please or can be returned at our expense. **Paint will dry in one night.**

	540 Lead
	550 Maroon
	560 Oxide Red
	570 French Gray
510 Yellow	580 Floor Yellow
530 Drab	590 Floor Green

Price, 1-quart cans 28c
Price, 2-quart cans 53c
Price, 1-gallon cans 98c

Price for larger quantities same as Seroco House Paints.

Use a No. 30C551 or No. 30C552 wall brush for applying above Seroco Floor Paint, 3, 3½ or 4 inches in width recommended.

Seroco Weatherproof Mineral Barn, Roof and Fence Paint.

Seroco Weatherproof Mineral Barn, Roof and Fence Paint, the most durable mineral paint, finely ground and thinned with linseed oil, the very best barn, roof and fence paint that we handle, is especially recommended for these purposes and for all purposes where the paint is especially exposed to the weather.

As a preservative this paint cannot be excelled, and we recommend it in every way for shingles, tin or iron roofs, structural iron work, barns, elevators and posts or timbers to be put under the ground. This mineral and weatherproof paint is acknowledged to be the best preserver of wood and the most durable. It is also water and rustproof, will stop leaks, prevent corrosion and is free from acids. One gallon covers about 300 square feet of surface two coats. We know that our Seroco Weatherproof Mineral Barn, Roof and Fence Paint will cover more surface, last longer, will give better satisfaction and is altogether the most desirable and durable paint for these purposes ever manufactured, and considering the covering surface and wearing qualities, it is worth double the price of any ordinary roof, fence or barn paint.

While our Free Color Sample Booklet shows the six different colors of this special weatherproof mineral barn, roof and fence paint and will be sent to any address on application, we would advise you to send your order direct from the catalogue, stating which of the six colors you desire; we will send the paint to you, guaranteeing the color to please you and the paint to prove satisfactory, or you can return it to us at our expense and we will immediately refund your money. Put up in 1-gallon cans, 5-gallon buckets, one-half barrels containing 25 gallons, and barrels containing 50 gallons. Made in six shades.

Prices and List of Colors of Seroco Weatherproof Mineral Barn, Roof and Fence Paint.

No. 30C108 Give catalogue number as well as name and number of color when ordering. Colors:

800 Oxide Red	830 Yellow
810 Lead Color	850 Maroon
820 Dark Gray	860 Natural Green

	Gallon
Price, 1-gallon can	65c
Price, 5-gallon bucket	60c
Price, 25-gallon barrel	55c
Price, 50-gallon barrel	50c

The Kind of Brushes to Use with Seroco Barn, Roof and Fence Paint.

For painting roofs and the walls of barns, sheds, etc., use a No. 30C551 or No. 30C552 wall brush, 4 or 4½ inches in width. For fences use the same brush but narrower, 3 or 3½ inches in width, or No. 30C545 or No. 30C546 round paint brush, size 3-0. For trimming use a round paint brush, No. 30C545 or No. 30C546, size 3-0.

Seroco Graphite-Creosote Paint.

No. 30C110 For barns, roofs, iron work, etc. Some prefer a Graphite Paint for painting barns, roofs, etc., for this reason we have made a paint which consists of pure air-floated graphite, sufficient mineral to give it the proper color, creosote and linseed oil. While it makes an excellent barn paint, it is especially recommended for surfaces under water, such as posts and timbers to be put under ground.

360 Dark Red	363 Dark Lead
361 Brown	364 Black
362 Willow Green	

Price, 1-gallon cans, per gallon 70c
5-gallon buckets, per gallon 65c
½-barrel, 30 gallons, per gallon 58c
1-barrel, 50 gallons, per gallon 53c

Seroco Graphite-Creosote Paint is applied with the same brushes recommended for our Seroco Weatherproof Mineral Barn, Roof and Fence Paint.

Seroco Shingle Stain and Preservative.

No. 30C112 While our Mineral Paint is highly recommended for shingled roofs, still some prefer a shingle stain. These stains are the best manufactured, the shingles can be dipped in same or applied with a brush. A shingled roof coated with these stains will last twice as long.

Furnished in the following shades: Red, Moss Green, Dark Green, Brown, Light Slate, Dark Slate, and Black.

Price, 1-gallon cans, per gallon 60c
Price, 5-gallon jacket cans, per gallon 55c
Price, 25-gallon barrels, per gallon 50c
Price, 50-gallon barrels, per gallon 45c

Apply above Seroco Shingle Stain with a No. 30C551 or No. 30C552 wall brush, the largest size recommended.

READ WHAT A FEW OF OUR CUSTOMERS SAY ABOUT SEROCO READY MIXED PAINT. THOUSANDS WRITE THE SAME WAY.

Experienced Painter's Verdict.

Carlton Center, Mich.

Sears, Roebuck & Co., Chicago, Ill.

Gentlemen:—I am very much pleased with your paint. The man that did my painting says it is the best ready mixed paint he ever used, and he is an experienced painter. It holds its color well and will not peel off as I have seen some other brands. I think I saved 30 per cent in buying my paint of you.

Yours truly,
JOHN USBORNE, SR.

Really Better Than He Expected.

Benton, Ill., R. R. No. 3.

Sears, Roebuck & Co., Chicago, Ill.

Gentlemen:—Gives the best of satisfaction. It was really better than I expected. It holds its color well, and I saved 32 cents per quart. I have to pay 60 cents per quart for paint from my home dealer, so I save 32 cents, less freight charges, which is a very small item. You can count me as one that is well satisfied. Your paint is as good as any that I can get here.

Yours truly,
HOSEA HILL.

Saved 52 Cents a Gallon.

Boyden, Iowa.

Sears, Roebuck & Co., Chicago, Ill.

Gentlemen:—Seroco Ready Mixed is as good a paint as I ever used; was well pleased with it. The same paint I would have to pay $1.50 per gallon here I got of you for 98 cents; so you see I have saved 52 cents per gallon.

Yours truly, ALBERT DEAN.

Seroco Buggy Paints.

No. 30C115 Our buggy paints are ground in the best coach varnish. The colors are guaranteed not to fade. It is prepared especially for buggies and carriages, but can be used on chairs, settees, benches, or any article exposed to the weather. One coat makes a beautiful and durable finish. Ready for use and no varnish required.

Colors:

600	Yellow	640	Dark Green
610	Vermilion	650	Blue
620	Light Wine	660	Dark Wine
630	Coach Green	670	Coach Black

Price, ½ pint, per can.......... $0.20
Price, 1 pint, per can.......... .30
Price, 1 quart, per can.......... .50
Price, 1 gallon, per can.......... 1.85
Do not fail to state color wanted.

Apply Seroco Buggy Paint with a varnish brush, we recommend No. 30C516 or No. 30C520 for fine work, A 2-inch brush is the best size.

Wagon Paint.

No. 30C116 Wagon Paint, ground in pure linseed oil and the best coach varnish. It is the best wagon paint, extremely tough and will not crack. The colors are permanent and will not fade. One coat of Seroco wagon paint, at a small expense, will preserve your wagon or implement and make it look like new. Dries hard with a high gloss. Colors: red, green, blue, vermilion, yellow and black. Apply with a No. 30C516, 30C518 or 30C520 varnish brush, 1, 2 or 2½ inches in width.

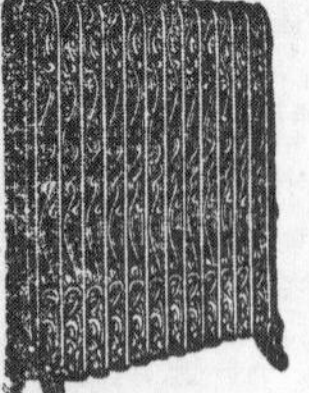

Price, 1-quart can.......... $0.45
Price, ½-gallon can.......... .80
Price, 1-gallon can.......... 1.50

Radiator Enamel.

No. 30C118 This enamel is especially made for radiators, steam pipes and other steam heated surfaces. It is ready for use and dries with a fine glossy finish, very durable and tough. Apply with a No. 30C544 Sash Tool, size 6 or 8.

	Gallon	Quart	Pint
Maroon..........	$1.05	$0.30	18c
Pea Green..........	1.25	.35	20c
Terra Cotta..........	1.25	.35	20c
Bronze Green..........	1.25	.35	20c
Aluminum..........	2.60	.75	45c
Gold..........	4.00	1.15	60c

Seroco Decorative Enamel.

No. 30C120 For all decorative work; is ready mixed, can be applied on anything and everything, any kind of furniture, iron beds, shelves, wicker work, baby carriages, clocks, etc. One half pint can is sufficient for an ordinary iron bed and will make it look like new. When ordering, be sure and mention color wanted: White, pink, light blue, light green, yellow, vermilion, red, brown, maroon, chrome green and black. Apply with a varnish brush, 1 or 1½ inches in width. No. 30C518 and No. 30C520 will do good work. For painting very small articles use a Sash Tool, No. 30C543 or 30C544, size 2 or 4.

Price, ½-pint can.......... 20c
Price, 1-pint can.......... 35c

Aluminum Enamel.

No. 30C122 Can be applied to anything, any kind of metal or wood, picture frames, furniture, shelves, clocks, stoves, mantels, etc.; it dries in a few hours with a silver finish and will not rub off. Water and heat will not affect it. Apply with a Camel's Hair brush, No. 30C507, size ¼, ⅝ or ¾ recommended for small work. No. 30C508 or 30C509, size 1 or 1¼ recommended for flat surfaces.

	Dozen	Each
Price, ⅛-pint can..........	$1.15	11c
Price, ¼-pint can..........	1.90	18c
Price, ½-pint can..........	2.90	28c
Price, 1-pint can..........	4.75	42c

Seroco Gloss Enamel for Interior Use.

No. 30C125 This enamel produces a beautiful luster on walls, plastered or wood, and is a desirable article for kitchens, dining rooms, bedrooms and hospital wards, as it is easily cleaned. We furnish it in twelve shades, as follows: Pearl, light slate, cream, apple green, pea green, nile green, light blue, dark blue, lavender, pink, lilac, carmine, also white, ivory and black. Apply with a Wall Brush No. 30C551 or 30C552, size 3, 3½ or 4 inches.

Price, ¼-pint can.......... $0.13
Price, 1-pint can.......... .24
Price, 1-quart can.......... .45
Price, ½-gallon can.......... .78
Price, 1-gallon can.......... 1.48

Bath Tub Enamel.

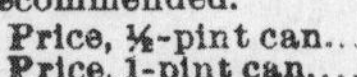

No. 30C126 White Bath Tub Enamel, Liquid Porcelain. A common iron tub coated with this preparation will have a beautiful appearance. Apply with a good varnish brush. No. 30C520, 1½ inches in width is recommended.

Price, ½-pint can.......... 25c
Price, 1-pint can.......... 45c

Wire Screen Enamel.

No. 30C128 Green or Black Wire Screen Enamel. Ready for use and easily applied; does not clog meshes of screens, and one coat gives to old, rusty screens a rich, brilliant and lasting finish. Apply with a varnish brush, 1 or 1½ in. wide.

Price, ½-pint can.......... 15c
Price, 1-pint can.......... 30c
State color wanted.

Black Iron and Roof Paint.

No. 30C130 Black Iron and Roof Paint cannot be excelled for general durability and preservative qualities. It is made especially for covering all kinds of metal work, dries rapidly with a hard, glossy black finish, and is absolutely water and acid proof. This is a paint universally used by railroads and steamboat companies for smoke stacks, bridges, etc., and should not be confounded with cheap mineral or black paints. **The best paint for iron work, all purposes.** In black only. Will cover from 900 to 1,000 square feet of smooth, metal surface per gallon, making it an economical paint to use. Apply with a Wall Brush, No. 30C551 or 30C552, the largest size recommended.

Price, 1-gallon can.......... 85c
Price, 5-gallon jacket can, per gallon.......... 75c
Price, 10-gallon jacket can, per gallon.......... 70c
Price, 50-gallon barrel, per gallon.......... 65c

G Stove Pipe Enamel.

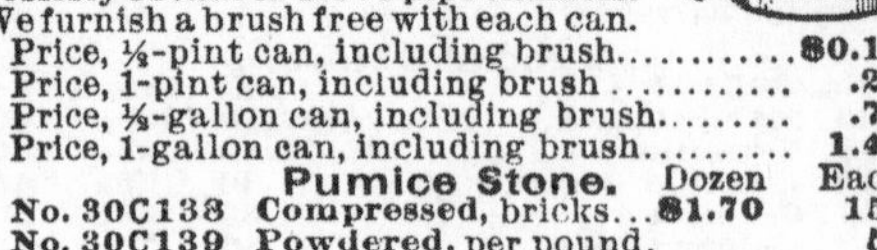

No. 30C132 G Stove Pipe Enamel. Especially prepared for use on stove pipes, stoves, furnaces, grates, steam and water pipes, boilers, smokestacks, garden tools, iron fences, brackets, etc. **One coat produces a brilliant black finish;** very elastic. Will not crack, chip, peel or burn off. Ready for instant use. Apply with a varnish brush. No. 30C517 or 30C518, size 1 or 1½ inches.

Price, ½-pint can. Weight, ⅝ pound.......... $0.15
Price, 1-pint can. Weight, 1⅛ pounds.......... .26
Price, 1-gallon can.......... 1.60

Egyptian Stove Pipe Enamel.

No. 30C133 The most satisfactory stove pipe and iron enamel ever put on the market. It is not so extensively advertised as some brands, but it will wear longer and produce a better finish than anything you can possibly obtain in stove pipe enamels. We furnish a brush free with each can.

Price, ½-pint can, including brush.......... $0.15
Price, 1-pint can, including brush.......... .25
Price, ½-gallon can, including brush.......... .75
Price, 1-gallon can, including brush.......... 1.45

Pumice Stone.

		Dozen	Each
No. 30C138	Compressed, bricks...	$1.70	15c
No. 30C139	Powdered, per pound.		5c

Plaster Paris.

No. 30C140 Price, per barrel of about 250 pounds.......... $2.00
Less quantity, per pound.......... .02

Pure French Ochre in Oil.

No. 30C150 Pure French Ochre in oil, in 12½, 25 and 100-pound kegs. Price, per lb.......... 4c

English Venetian Red in Oil.

No. 30C151 English Venetian Red, especially adapted for painting brick buildings. In 12½, 25 and 100-pound kegs. Price, per pound.......... 4c

White Ochre in Oil.

No. 30C152 White Ochre Ground in Oil. Ground in pure linseed oil and used as primer only. 12½, 25, 50 and 100-lb. kegs, per pound.......... 4c

Zinc in Oil.

No. 30C158 Pure Green Seal French Zinc, in oil, 12½ and 25-lb. cans. Price, per pound.......... 12½
No. 30C159 Pure Green Seal French Zinc, in oil, 1 to 5-lb. cans. Price, per pound.......... 15c
No. 30C160 Zinc in Oil, American Snow White, 12½ and 25-lb. pails. Price, per pound.......... 7c

Putty.

No. 30C165 Putty in bladders, 10 to 25 pounds. Price, per pound.......... 2½c

Glaziers' Points.

No. 30C166 Zinc Glaziers' Points, for fastening glass in sash; put up in ¼-pound papers. Price, per paper.......... 3c

White Lead.

No. 30C171 Great Western White Lead in Oil; a special grade. Kegs of 12½, 25, 50 or 100 pounds.
Price, per pound.......... 4½c

Seroco Brand Painters' White Lead.

No. 30C172 A combination of absolutely pure white lead and zinc ground in pure linseed oil. A lead that will wear longer and work better than strictly pure white lead. We guarantee it. Kegs of 12½, 25, 50 and 100 pounds. Price, per pound... 5c

National Lead Co.'s Brands White Lead.

No. 30C176 The following brands of white lead are controlled by the National Lead Co., for this reason we cannot guarantee a price. We will be pleased to quote prices at any time, but you can send in your orders with every assurance that we will give you the benefit of the lowest market price. We handle the following brands: Red Seal, Shipman, Southern, Collier, and Eckstein.

Put up in 12½, 25, 50 and 100-pound kegs.

The Seroco Colors in Oil.

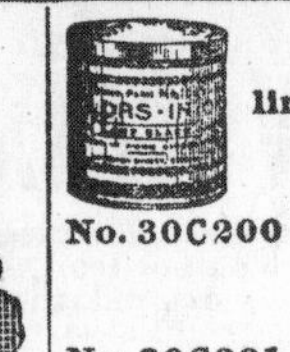

For tinting paints. Ground in pure linseed oil, strong and permanent.

		1, 2 & 5-lb. cans. Price, per lb.
No. 30C200	**Blacks.** Refined Lamp Black..........	15c
	Coach Black..........	14c
	Ivory Black..........	13c
	Drop Black..........	12c
No. 30C201	**Blues.** Prussian Blue..........	36c
	Ultramarine Blue..........	17c
	Cobalt Blue..........	28c
No. 30C202	**Browns.** Raw and Burnt Umber	12c
	Raw and Burnt Sienna..........	11c
	Vandyke Brown..........	12c
No. 30C203	**Greens.** Blind Green..........	16c
	Chrome Green..........	13c
No. 30C204	**Reds.** English Venetian..........	8c
	Indian Red..........	14c
	Tuscan Red..........	16c
	Unfading Red..........	28c
	English Rose Pink..........	17c
	English Rose Lake..........	26c
	Scarlet Vermilion..........	18c
No. 30C205	**Yellows.** Chrome, L. M. & O.,	16c
	Yellow Ochre..........	8c
No. 30C206	**Graining Colors.** Light Oak, Dark Oak, Antique Oak, Walnut, Cherry, Mahogany..........	12c

All of the above colors furnished in 25-pound cans, at 2 cents per pound less.

Oil Stain.

No. 30C215 Perfect imitations of natural wood, cherry, rosewood, mahogany, walnut, light oak, dark oak, antique oak. For staining interior woodwork or any work not finished. This stain cannot be applied over varnished or painted surfaces. One or two coats of varnish applied over it will produce a fine finish. Nos. 300, 302 and 298 or 299 varnishes can be used in connection with these stains. Apply with a varnish brush. Price, ½ pint, per can.......... $0.17

Price, 1 pint, per can.......... .24
Price, 1 quart, per can.......... .43
Price, ½ gallon, per can.......... .77
Price, 1 gallon, per can.......... 1.40

Varnish Stain.

No. 30C216 Stain and varnish used separately, on new work, produce a better finish than varnish stain, but for refinishing painted or varnished surfaces, such as old furniture or painted or varnished woodwork, this varnish stain is recommended. It stains and varnishes in one operation. Dries hard with a fine luster. Furnished in the following natural wood colors: cherry, rosewood, mahogany, walnut, light oak, dark oak, antique oak. Do not fail to mention color wanted. Apply with a varnish brush, 2-inch brush recommended.

Price, ½ pint, per can.......... $0.17
Price, 1 pint, per can.......... .24
Price, 1 quart, per can.......... .43
Price, ½ gallon, per can.......... .77
Price, 1 gallon, per can.......... 1.40

Whiting.

No. 30C218 Extra Gilders' Whiting, fine quality, bolted. Barrels about 400 pounds, per pound.......... 1c
Less quantity, per pound.......... 2c

Dry Colors.

The following dry colors are used for tinting calcimines, making graining colors and other purposes. Some use these dry colors for painting purposes by mixing them with linseed oil. This we do not recommend unless the mixture is put through a paint mill as you will have nothing but a coarse mixture which is not fit for anything. If a mineral paint is desired at a low price you will profit by purchasing the Seroco Weatherproof Mineral, Barn, Roof and Fence Paint as then you will have a substantial paint, a paint that will wear three times as long therefore cheapest in the end.

We handle only best qualities.	Bbl., per lb.	Per lb.
No. 30C220 Yellow Rochelle Ochre, 400 pounds in barrel..........	1c	2c
No. 30C221 Imported Marseilles Yellow Ochre, strong in color, 100-pound drums..........	3½c	4c
No. 30C222 Italian Buff (light), 500 pounds..........	1c	2c
No. 30C223 American Venetian Red, 350 pounds..........	1c	2c
No. 30C224 Imperial English Venetian Red, 336 pounds..........	2c	2½c
No. 30C225 Snow White Wood Filler, 400 pounds..........	1½c	2c
No. 30C226 Prince's Brown Mineral, 350 pounds..........	1c	2c
No. 30C227 White Ochre, 400 pounds..........	1½c	2c
No. 30C228 Lampblack, Germantown, 80 pounds..........	9c	10c
No. 30C229 Burnt Turkey Umber, 350 pounds..........	3½c	6c
No. 30C230 Raw Turkey Umber, 350 pounds..........	3½c	6c
No. 30C231 Burnt Italian Sienna, 350 pounds..........	4½c	7c
No. 30C232 Red Lead, 100 lbs..........	7c	8c
No. 30C233 Raw Italian Sienna, 350 pounds..........	4½c	7c
No. 30C234 Chrome Green, best..........		8c
No. 30C235 Chrome Yellow Lemon..........		10c
No. 30C236 French Gray or Slate, 400 pounds in barrel..........	1c	2c
No. 30C237 Ultramarine Blue..........		7c

Seroco Water Paint.

No. 30C250 Only requires mixing with water. Weatherproof, sanitary, fireproof. A dry powder. In white and various colors.

A water paint for the interior painting of residences, and on account of its sanitary nature and fireproof qualities, it is admirably adapted for the interior painting of factories, warehouses, docks, public buildings, breweries, stables, air shafts and court yards, and can be applied on sand finished walls, stone, brick or any solid surface. The average covering power of this paint is from 20 to 30 square feet to the pound, according to the surface to be painted. **Full directions with each package.**

Seroco Water Paint Price List.

		400-lb. bbls., per lb.	100-50-25 lb. kegs, per lb.	5-lb. package, per lb.
No. 10	White	5c	6c	7c
No. 20	Slate	7c	8c	9c
No. 30	Buff	7c	8c	9c
No. 40	Canary	7c	8c	9c
No. 50	Nile Green	7c	8c	9c
No. 60	Red	7c	8c	9c
No. 70	Dark Gray	7c	8c	9c
No. 80	Dark Blue	7c	8c	9c
No. 90	Light Blue	7c	8c	9c
No. 100	Pink	7c	8c	9c
No. 120	Blind Green	10c	11c	12c

Seroco Sanitary Calcimine.

Durable wall finish; absolutely healthful; mixed with water only; will not rub off; cannot fade. Made in 12 colors and white.

The Sanitary Wall Finish is ready for use when it is mixed with water and is unequaled for plain or high class decorative work on walls and ceilings. It covers well and one coat will generally be found sufficient. It can be recoated at any time when necessary, it forms a durable coating which will not decay, peel away or rub off if applied to a solid surface. One pound properly mixed and applied, covers from 60 to 100 square feet, according to the surface. To obtain good results, all surfaces that have been calcimined should be thoroughly cleaned, and all lime and whitewashed walls should be well scraped and sized before applying.

In ordering, be sure to give number and color.

No. 100	White	No. 107	Cream
No. 101	Pearl	No. 108	Lavender
No. 102	Pink	No. 109	Buff
No. 103	Lilac	No. 110	Light Stone
No. 104	Nile Green	No. 111	Blue Tint
No. 105	Straw	No. 112	Canary
No. 106	French Gray		

No. 30C252 White, per 5-pound package.....26c
Tints, per 5-pound package.....28c

Pure Graphite Paint Paste.

No. 30C262 To 12½ pounds (1 gallon) paste, add 3 gallons boiled oil, making 4 gallons of Pure Graphite Paint, ready for use. Will cover 1,000 square feet smooth metal per gallon. Will not crack, blister or peel off; is not affected by heat or cold, smoke, steam, moisture, acids, alkali or brine, or by climatic changes. **For use on roofs, stacks, boilers, bridges, structural iron work of any kind.** This paint is manufactured from pure graphite and absolutely pure linseed oil. Is a dark slate color.

Price, per 5 -pound can.....$0.40
Price, per 12½-pound can.....85
Price, per 25 -pound can.....1.60

Seroco Floor Oil.

No. 30C275 Seroco Floor Oil. A special preparation for floors of residences and stores. A very small quantity applied with a cloth will bring out a rich color; also, it will do away with scrubbing, as floors oiled with Seroco Floor Oil are easily cleaned by simply washing them with soap and water.

Price, per pint can.....$0.20
Price, per quart can.....30
Price, per ½-gallon can.....52
Price, per 1-gallon can.....90
Price, per 5-gallon jacket can.....4.00

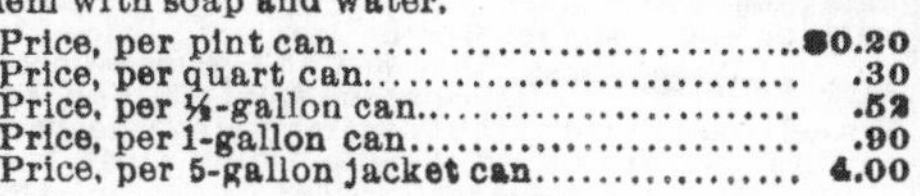

Seroco Floor Wax.

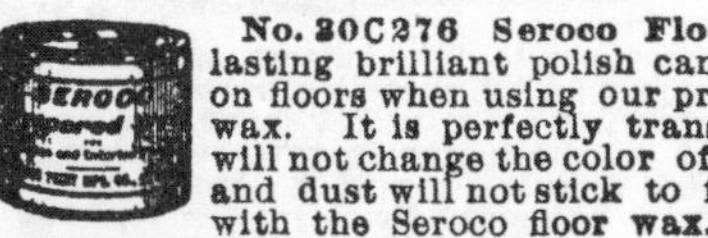

No. 30C276 Seroco Floor Wax. A lasting brilliant polish can be obtained on floors when using our prepared floor wax. It is perfectly transparent and will not change the color of wood. Dirt and dust will not stick to floors waxed with the Seroco floor wax. One pound will cover about 300 square feet. Directions are simple and plainly printed on every can. Put up in 1-pound cans.

Price, per can.....28c

Dancing Floor Wax.

No. 30C277 Dancing Floor Wax. (Powdered.) This is the best preparation for dancing floors, easily applied and can be used on new, old or canvas covered floors. Guaranteed not to soil the most delicate fabric. Sprinkle it on the floors and the dancers will do the rest. Put up in 1-pound cans. Price, per can...33c

Seroco Floor Color Varnish in Natural Wood Colors.

No. 30C278 Softwood floors can be made to look like hardwood by applying this wonderful Color Varnish. The most artistic finish can be put on any kind of floors with very little labor or expense. It can be applied over painted floors and hardwood imitated to perfection. It is made from an elastic, hard drying varnish, combined with chemically pure, soluble oil colors. It cannot be surpassed for finishing floors of all kinds, as well as furniture and woodwork of every description. It is translucent, free from sediment and non-fading. Dries hard over night with a fine tone and luster and will not scratch or mar white. Made in five shades—dark oak, light oak, mahogany, cherry and walnut.

5 Gallons	1 Gallon	½ Gallon	Quart	Pint
$8.25	$1.75	98c	53c	29c

Seroco Filler.

No. 30C279 Seroco Filler for Cracks in Floors. A specially prepared, elastic, non-shrinkable compound for filling cracks of floors or furniture before applying paint or varnish; also adapted for smoothing rough surfaces.

Price, 1-pound can.....15c
Price, 5-pound can.....65c

Seroco Paste Wood Filler.

No. 30C285 All open grained hardwoods, such as oak, ash, etc., must be filled in order to produce a perfect varnish finish. This filler is the best made, easily applied and dries very hard. Made in two shades, light oak and dark oak.

Price, 1-pound can.....$0.08
Price, 5-pound can.....35
Price, 25-pound can.....1.50

Seroco Liquid Wood Filler.

No. 30C286 For filling or first coating all kinds of close grained natural woods, such as pine, poplar, etc., that have not been previously finished. It thoroughly seals up the wood pores and effectually prevents suction or the absorption of moisture. This material is transparent and does not need to be rubbed off or sandpapered before applying the varnish coats. It does not sink away like varnish, but dries on the surface, thus equaling, for work of this nature, two coats of varnish. A coat or two of varnish applied over this material produces a really remarkable finish.

5 Gallons	1 Gallon	½ Gallon	Quart	Pint
$5.25	$1.15	65c	35c	20c

Steel Wool and Shavings.

No. 30C288 Steel Wool is a mass of fine fibres of steel resembling curled hair, which, while sharp, does not scratch but will cut as smoothly as the finest sandpaper, emery or pumice stone. For many purposes it is superior to sandpaper, etc. Used for rubbing down fillers and varnishes; in fact, it takes the place of sandpaper or pumice stone and will be found a much better article to use. Steel shavings is a coarse grade and is used for removing rust from iron preparatory to painting, also for cleaning floors or any surface of old varnish.

No. 0. Very fine. Price, per pound.....45c
No. 1. Fine. Price, per pound.....35c
No. 3. Fine. Price, per pound.....30c
Steel shavings, coarse. Price, per pound.....25c

VARNISH DEPARTMENT.

SEROCO HOUSE VARNISHES.

The following varnishes are made by one of the largest and best varnish manufacturers in the country. The very same varnishes are sold under the manufacturers' brands at from 50 cents to $1.50 per gallon higher than the prices we are quoting. We guarantee every ounce of our varnishes and no matter how costly the job, we guarantee satisfaction or money refunded. **Let us have a trial order, it will cost you nothing should it fail to give satisfaction.**

Seroco Extra Light Hard Oil Finish.

No. 30C298 Especially designed for finishing all kinds of natural wood surfaces where the grain and color are to be preserved. Works freely and dries in about 24 hours with an elegant gloss. This material may also be used with marked satisfaction on wainscoting, baseboards and inside doors.

5 Gallons	1 Gallon	½ Gallon	Quart	Pint
$6.00	$1.30	75c	42c	23c

Seroco No. 1 Hard Oil Finish.

No. 30C299 Splendidly adapted for general interior woodwork. Is pale, free flowing and durable and possesses a full and substantial body. Dries free from dust in 2 to 3 hours.

5 Gallons	1 Gallon	½ Gallon	Quart	Pint
$4.75	$1.05	63c	35c	20c

Seroco Furniture Varnish.

No. 30C300 This varnish may be used to brighten up worn and lusterless furniture of every description. It dries over night and imparts a fine gloss finish. For general repair work in the household on articles in daily use that must be finished hurriedly, this material is recommended.

5 Gallons	1 Gallon	½ Gallon	Quart	Pint
$4.00	90c	55c	32c	18c

Seroco Cabinet Finish.

No. 30C301 This varnish is designed for highest grade interior woodwork that is to be rubbed and polished; also gives a beautiful finish when left in the gloss. Is exceptionally rich and lustrous and on account of its elasticity, is extremely durable. Dries dust free in 3 to 4 hours and sufficiently hard for rubbing in 60 hours.

5 Gallons	1 Gallon	½ Gallon	Quart	Pint
$7.00	$1.50	85c	47c	25c

Seroco Interior Varnish.

No. 30C302 A high grade varnish, especially adapted for first class interior woodwork finishing and fine furniture. This varnish is of substantial body, light in color and works with great freedom. It gives a lasting and elegant finish and dries in from 10 to 12 hours.

5 Gallons	1 Gallon	½ Gallon	Quart	Pint
$5.00	$1.10	65c	37c	20c

Seroco Interior Spar Finish.

No. 30C303 For high class interior wood work. Exceedingly pale, free working and very durable. It dries free from dust in 4 to 6 hours. Can be safely rubbed in from 2 to 3 days and polished to a high and permanent luster in 4 days.

5 Gallons	1 Gallon	½ Gallon	Quart	Pint
$8.00	$1.70	95c	52c	28c

Seroco Durable Floor Varnish.

No. 30C304 Unequaled for finishing floors of all kinds, natural wood, painted or oil cloth. Will not turn white under repeated washing or foot friction, and dries to walk on over night. It is easily applied and gives an elegant and durable finish. This is undoubtedly the best floor varnish on the market.

5 Gallons	1 Gallon	½ Gallon	Quart	Pint
$8.25	$1.75	98c	53c	29c

Seroco Outside Spar Varnish.

No. 30C305 For finishing all kinds of exposed surfaces, such as outside doors, vestibules and store fronts. It is also especially recommended for finishing inside blinds and the woodwork in bath rooms and on sinks, where a very elastic and durable varnish should be employed.

5 Gallons	1 Gallon	½ Gallon	Quart	Pint
$10.75	$2.25	$1.25	65c	35c

Seroco White Damar Varnish.

No. 30C307 Made from imported Batavia gum. For finishing over any enameled surfaces, white or ivory, without producing discoloration. It may also be used with excellent satisfaction on fine wall paper hangings or on delicately tinted painted walls. Is of good body and dries well.

5 Gallons	1 Gallon	½ Gallon	Quart	Pint
$7.00	$1.50	85c	47c	25c

Seroco Black Asphaltum.

No. 30C309 For finishing all kinds of castings, smoke stacks, stove pipes, fenders, coal hods, iron work of agricultural implements, etc. It produces a jet black, brilliant finish and absolutely prevents rust or corrosion. It is heavy in body and quick drying.

5 Gallons	1 Gallon	½ Gallon	Quart	Pint
$2.50	60c	33c	22c	13c

Seroco Turpentine Japan Dryer.

No. 30C310 A first class house painters' japan, dependable in all kinds of weather. A good binder and a sure and quick dryer. It contains no acids and will not cause the paint with which it is mixed to burn, blister, crack, chalk or peel. It mixes readily with oil and does not detract from the elasticity of the paint.

5 Gallons	1 Gallon	½ Gallon	Quart	Pint
$3.50	80c	50c	30c	18c

Seroco Oil Shellac.

No. 30C312 This is a clear first coater or filler for new woods that have not been previously finished. It has a good body and produces a substantial and safe surface or base coat. It dries to sandpaper in 6 to 8 hours.

5 Gallons	1 Gallon	½ Gallon	Quart	Pint
$6.50	$1.40	80c	45c	25c

FINE CARRIAGE VARNISHES.

Seroco Wearing Body Varnish.

No. 30C313 A brilliant, durable and elastic varnish for finishing carriage and buggy bodies. It works and flows with surprising freedom and may be used on the largest surfaces, such as carriage bodies, with the greatest safety and satisfaction. It is very pale and will not darken or injure the lightest shades of body color. It dries free from dust in 12 to 16 hours and hardens properly in from 2 to 3 days.

1 Gallon	½ Gallon	Quart	Pint
$3.00	$1.60	85c	45c

Seroco Medium Drying Body.

No. 30C314 For finishing carriage bodies when time will not permit the use of our best Wearing Body. Is pale, elastic and very durable. Works and flows with freedom and may be used with safety on larger panels. It dries hard in from 36 to 48 hours.

1 Gallon	½ Gallon	Quart	Pint
$2.75	$1.48	78c	42c

Seroco Elastic Gear.

No. 30C315 Used for finishing gear parts and wheels. Is free working, brilliant and durable. It sets in 6 to 8 hours and dries hard in 36 to 48 hours. This varnish may also be used for body finishing when drying despatch is an important consideration. This is a superior all around varnish for carriage finishing.

1 Gallon	½ Gallon	Quart	Pint
$2.85	$1.55	80c	43c

Seroco Quick Rubbing Varnish.

No. 30C316 This is an excellent material intended for undercoats of gears and bodies where time is a matter of consideration. Dries inside of 2 days to admit of being rubbed without sweating.

1 Gallon	½ Gallon	Quart	Pint
$2.50	$1.35	72c	38c

Seroco Hard Rubbing Body.

No. 30C317 For undercoats of gears or bodies. This is a magnificent material of light color and good body. It rubs without sweating in about 4 days and sets free from dust in from 8 to 12 hours.

1 Gallon	½ Gallon	Quart	Pint
$2.60	$1.40	75c	40c

Seroco Quick Black Rubbing.

No. 30C319 Made from our Medium Rubbing Varnish and the best Drop Black. Will rub without sweating in about 2 days.

1 Gallon	½ Gallon	Quart	Pint
$3.10	$1.65	87c	45c

Seroco One Coat Coach.

No. 30C320 A splendid varnish for general repair work. On carriages when work is simply dull or lusterless, otherwise in good condition, one coat of this varnish on the entire vehicle will produce a finish practically equal to a new job. It is light in color, elastic, brilliant and durable. Dries free from dust in about 12 hours and hardens to admit the use of the vehicle in about 3 days.

1 Gallon	½ Gallon	Quart	Pint
$2.70	$1.45	77c	40c

Seroco Wagon and Implement Varnish.

No. 30C321 For agricultural implements, wagons, etc. A good varnish for general outside work. Has a good body, a fine luster and is light in color and wears well. Dries in about 10 to 14 hours.

1 Gallon	½ Gallon	Quart	Pint
$1.65	93c	50c	27c

Seroco Gold Size.

No. 30C322 Especially adapted for use in binding colors and for rough stuff; it is also a reliable gold leaf sizing.

1 Gallon	½ Gallon	Quart	Pint
$2.25	$1.25	65c	35c

Seroco Coach Japan.

No. 30C323 A reliable japan for binding and drying colors and rough stuff.

1 Gallon	½ Gallon	Quart	Pint
$1.75	98c	53c	30c

Orange Shellac.

No. 30C326 Orange Shellac.

1 Gallon	½ Gallon	Quart	Pint
$2.25	$1.20	65c	35c

Seroco W. A. White Shellac.

No. 30C327 Seroco W. A. White Shellac.

1 Gallon	½ Gallon	Quart	Pint
$2.25	$1.20	65c	35c

Seroco Varnish and Paint Remover.

No. 30C328 Guaranteed to remove paints, varnish or oil from wood, iron or bath tubs without damage to the wood, veneer, glue or filler. Nor does it injure the hands of the operator in any way.

1 Gallon	Quart	Pint
$1.40	40c	23c

Seroco Furniture Polish.

No. 30C330 Adapted for use on old as well as new furniture. It has the advantage over other polishes of not gumming up in the corners, and therefore will not collect dust or dirt. It is perfectly harmless and will not affect the varnish in any way. It can be used as well on ordinary furniture as on the finest piano, organ and other highly finished work. This is without question the finest and safest polish on the market.

Price, per pint can........................ $0.25
Per quart can........................ .45
Per gallon can........................ 1.70

Seroco Paint and Varnish Reviver.

No. 30C332 This reviver combines the properties of a cleanser as well as a renewer for any painted or varnished surface. Where the paint or varnish is in good condition but very dirty or greasy, a small quantity of this Reviver with a little rubbing will produce a surface equal to new. Guaranteed not to injure the paint or varnish. Convince yourself of its value by giving it a trial.

Price, per pint can........................ $0.23
Per quart can........................ .42
Per gallon can........................ 1.50

Seroco Liquid Metal Polish.

No. 30C342 For polishing brass, zinc, tin, nickel, copper or silver. Can be used on anything made of metal, and is especially recommended for outdoor metal work, such as brass and zinc signs, show cases, railings, metal parts of harness, etc. Warranted not to injure the finest metals. No other polish will give the brilliant and lasting luster obtained when using Seroco Liquid Metal Polish.

Price, per ½-pint can........................ 10c
Price, per pint can........................ 18c
Price, per quart can........................ 30c
Price, per gallon can........................ 95c

For Prices on Oils Write for Our FREE GROCERY CATALOGUE.

REVISED AND ISSUED EVERY SIXTY DAYS.

Prices on oils fluctuate so rapidly that we do not find it satisfactory to quote the prices in this catalogue, but ask all who are interested in oils to write for our Free Grocery Price List which will be sent on application. You will not only find the latest market prices on oils, but you will also find very low prices on the entire line of groceries and will find that we can save you a great deal of money on the groceries you use.

Flitters.

No. 55C02725 Bronze Flitters or Leaf Brocades, for sign work. Highest grade flitters made. Used everywhere by professional sign painters and decorators.

Color.	Price, per lb.	Price, per oz.
Pale gold and rich gold	$0.68	6c
Copper and crimson	.72	7c
Blue, orange, fire, green and lemon	.83	8c
Silver and aluminum	1.10	9c

One-half pound lots furnished at pound rates. Less than one-half pound lots at ounce rates only.

No. 55C02730 Best Gold Bronze Powder, for ornamental and decorative purposes. Furnished in three shades, light or rich gold, medium or pale gold and deep gold.

Price, per pound, 72c; per ounce........................ 7c

No. 55C02735 Liquid for Mixing Bronze Powder.

Price, per 4-oz. bottle	Price, per 1-pint can	Price, per 1-quart can	Price, per 1-gallon can	Price, per 5-gallon can
8c	14c	25c	90c	$3.50

Fuller's Wall Paper Cleaner.

No. 30C351 Used by the best paperhangers throughout the country. A dry powder to be mixed with cold water.

Price, per 1-lb. box........................ $0.15
Per dozen........ 1.50

Seroco Wall Paper Cleaner.

No. 30C352 Put up in a tin box, prepared ready for use, no mixing required. No experience necessary, anyone can clean wall paper with the Seroco Wall Paper Cleaner. It will remove smoke and dust from wall paper, window shades and fresco and bring out the original color. Price, per 1 pound can, sufficient for one room........................ 10c

Paperhangers' Seam and Smoothing Rollers.

Our seam rollers are guaranteed the very best and with ordinary care will last a lifetime. A seam roller is necessary to do good work, and as our prices are very low, it will pay you to include a roller with your order for wall paper.

No. 30C400 Seam Roller, 1¼ inches wide, flat face, rubber covered. Shipping weight, 5 ounces. Price........ 15c

No. 30C401 Seam Roller, 1 inch wide, oval face, maple roller, as illustrated. Shipping weight, 4 ounces. Price... 10c

No. 30C402 Side Arm Seam Roller, bevel face, celluloid covered, 1 inch wide. The handiest roller manufactured. Indispensable for ceilings, door casings and frames. Shipping weight, 5 ounces. Price........ 30c

Smoothing Roller.

No. 30C403 Smoothing Roller, 8 inches wide, felt covered. The most satisfactory smoothing roller made. Shipping weight, 12 ounces. Price........ 60c

No. 30C404 Smoothing Roller, same as above, but without covering; maple roller. Shipping weight, 12 ozs. Price.. 40c

No. 30C405 The Zylonite Ivory Seam Roller, oval face. For the professional paperhanger; will never wear out. Shipping weight, 7 ounces. Price........ 65c

Wheel Knives, Base Trimmers, Etc.

We deal direct with the manufacturer of Paperhangers' Tools. Should a blade or other parts break, caused by any defect, we will cheerfully replace the tool absolutely free of charge.

No. 30C410 Wheel Knife for Trimming Wall Paper. Shoulder on both sides. Blade 2 inches in diameter. Shipping weight, 5 ounces. Price... 28c

No. 30C411 Base Trimmer. Serrated edge, iron handle. A handy tool for trimming around casings, frames, etc. Shipping weight, 5 ounces. Price........ 24c

No. 30C412 Wheel Knife, with patent device for keeping the paste off the blade, always clean and sharp. Shipping weight, 5 ounces. Price........................ 48c

No. 30C413 Combination Base Trimmer and Paper Knife. No paperhanger should be without this handy tool. Shipping weight, 5 ounces. Price........................ 40c

No. 30C414 Wheel Knife. Offset handle, a very handy tool, 2-inch blade. Nickel plated frame. Shipping weight, 6 ounces. Price........................ 45c

Paperhangers' Shears.

No. 28C0742 Keene Cutlery Co.'s Paperhangers' or Bankers' Shears. Nickel plated steel laid blades and enameled handles. Fully warranted. Shipping weight, 10 to 14 ounces.

Size, inches	10	12	14	16
Length of cut, inches	5½	7	8½	10
Price	57c	72c	95c	$1.20

Folding Paste Table.

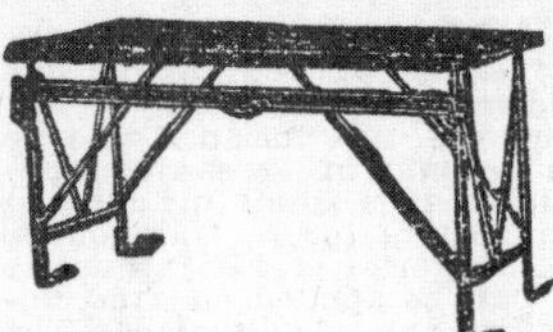

No. 30C420 Folding Paste Table. The best on the market. Made of the very best material. Strong and light in weight, with space and hooks for carrying straight edge and tools. 23 inches wide, open, 11½ inches closed.

7 feet long. Price........................ $3.10
8 feet long. Price........................ 3.35

Paste Boards.

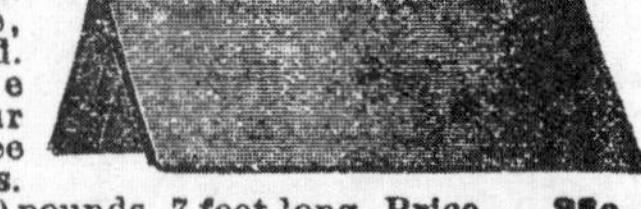

No. 30C421 Paste Boards, 23 inches wide, 11½ inches closed. Made of white wood, with four battings and three brass hinges. Weight, about 10 pounds. 7 feet long. Price..... 98c

7 feet long, with 4-inch zinc strip. Weight, about 20 pounds. Price........................ $1.25

Ridgely's Trimmer.

No. 30C425 Genuine Ridgely's Model "A" Trimmer. Furnished only with complete outfit, consisting of trimmer, straight edge and zinc.

6-foot outfit, complete. Price. $3.75
7-foot outfit, complete. Price........ 4.00
8-foot outfit, complete. Price........ 4.25

Ridgely's Newest Trimmer.

No. 30C426 Model "B" Ideal Trimmer. This new trimmer is designed for a whole hand rest, therefore, the leverage obtained is enormous and will cut anything in the way of paper or burlap for decorations. The Straight Edge furnished with the above trimmer is a three-piece brass bound edge.

6-foot outfit complete. Price........ $3.75
7-foot outfit complete. Price........ 4.00
8-foot outfit complete. Price........ 4.25

Ridgely's Three-Piece Straight Edge.

No. 30C432 The best Straight Edge made, cannot warp or twist. Made of the best seasoned wood and with proper care it will remain true and last a lifetime. Bound on both sides with angle and channel brass. This is the regular Ridgely Model "B" Trimmer Straight Edge but can be used for knife work. The best all around Straight Edge.

7 feet long. Price........................ $2.00
8 feet long. Price........................ 2.25

Glass Cutters.

No. 30C450 Revolving Steel Wheel Glass Cutter, metal handle, polished and bronzed, extra quality cutting wheel. Shipping weight, 3 ounces. Price........ 3c

No. 30C451 Revolving Steel Wheel Glass Cutter, bronzed, with knife sharpener, corkscrew and can opener combined. Shipping weight, 4 ounces. Price........................ 4c

No. 30C452 A fine durable Glass Cutter, with putty knife on end. Shipping weight, 4 ounces. Price.. 7c

No. 30C453 Glass Cutter. Damascus Coal Carbon Disc Wheel Glass Cutter. The finest revolving wheel glass cutter made, rosewood handle, solid steel head. Shipping weight, 3 ounces. Price........ 15c

No. 30C454 Goodell's Improved Glass Cutter with turret head. The cutters are carefully hardened and ground by special process. Polished and nickel plated frame; turret head, six cutter wheels, which can be instantly revolved to place. Nickel plated ferrule, rosewood finish handle. Shipping weight, 3 ounces. Price........................ 23c

OUR FREE BOOK, "HOW TO PAINT,"

is included with every order for goods from this department. We have felt that our customers needed a book written in plain language, giving full instructions how to apply any kind of paint, and we have gotten up this book in answer to this need. It is a valuable instruction book and is given absolutely free with the paint sample book or with an order for paints from the catalogue. You need not be an expert painter to apply our paint, varnish, enamel, etc. With every item we furnish plain and simple instructions by which any one can do the work successfully. In addition to these plain and simple instructions which are set forth on each package we also send our book, "How to Paint," free. This book explains everything in detail and tells it all in plain language that anyone can understand. You will find there is nothing difficult about doing a job of painting, and with the aid of the free book, "How to Paint," any man or boy can do the work successfully.

Glaziers' Diamonds.

Our Glaziers' Diamonds are made of the best quality genuine diamonds. The mountings are made in the very best possible manner, highly finished and heavily nickel plated. We guarantee our diamonds to reset not less than four times and give good satisfaction, provided they are sent to us to reset. NEVER CUT TWICE IN THE SAME PLACE.

No. 30C458 The Standard Keyed Diamond, for single thick glass. A good diamond for ordinary use. Shipping weight, 4 ounces. Price..........**$2.90**

No. 30C459 Keyed Diamond, for single thick glass. A very cheap diamond when quality is considered. Shipping weight, 4 ounces. Price....**$3.25**

No. 30C460 Superior Keyed Diamond. A very fine diamond for general use. Will cut double strength glass. Shipping weight, 4 ounces. Price..........**$4.35**

No. 30C461 Extra Superior Keyed Diamond. Cuts anything except plate glass. Shipping weight, 4 ounces. Price..........**$5.95**

No. 30C462 Superior Keyed Plate Glass Diamond. A very superior cutter for general use, and will cut plate glass. Shipping weight, 5 ounces. Price..........**$9.00**

No. 30C463 Extra Superior Keyed Plate Glass Diamond. Cuts any kind of rough or polished plate glass. **Dealers have always charged an exorbitant profit on this class of diamonds, selling them as high as $20.00.** By contracting for a large number and selling them at our usual one small profit, we are able to make the price only..........**$10.95**
Shipping weight, 5 ounces.

Superior Diamond Glass Cutter.

Anyone can cut glass with this tool successfully. Genuine diamond, finished in the best manner and metal parts nickel plated. Hold the diamond, as shown in illustration, against the ruler. Place it perpendicularly on the glass, so it rests on the diamond and guide wheel, the wheel towards you. Press on it gradually, until it makes a singing sound, not a harsh noise. Draw over the glass slowly and uniformly. **Never cut twice in the same place.**

No. 30C464 Sure cut. Will cut single strength glass. Price..........**$2.95**

No. 30C465 Sure cut, superior diamond. A very fine diamond for general use, will cut double strength glass. Price..........**$4.35**

No. 30C466 Sure cut, extra superior diamond. Will cut anything excepting plate glass. Price..........**$5.95**

Putty Knives.

No. 30C470 Putty Knife, with stiff blade square point, a substantial tool. Price..........**5c**

No. 30C471 Putty Knife, same as above, but with spring blade. Price..........**5c**

No. 30C472 Putty Knife, with stiff blade, square point, cocobolo handle, lap bolster, strongly riveted. A superior tool. Weight, 4 ounces. Price..........**12c**

No. 30C473 Putty Knife, with spring blade, square point, cocobolo handle, lap bolster. Strongly riveted. Weight, 4 ounces. Price..........**12c**

No. 30C474 Putty Knife, with stiff blade, bevel point, cocobolo handle, lap bolster. A high grade knife. Weight, 4 ounces. Price....**15c**

No. 30C475 Putty Knife, with spring blade, bevel point, cocobolo handle, lap bolster. Weight, 4 ounces. Price..........**15c**

Scraping Knives.

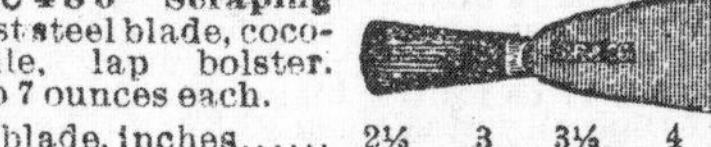

No. 30C480 Scraping Knife. Best steel blade, cocobolo handle, lap bolster. Weight, 5 to 7 ounces each.

Width of blade, inches	2½	3	3½	4
Price	30c	35c	43c	50c

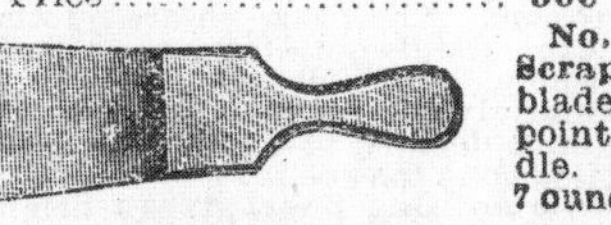

No. 30C482 Wall Scraping Knife, stiff blade, 5-inch square point, beechwood handle. Shipping weight, 7 ounces. Price......**8c**

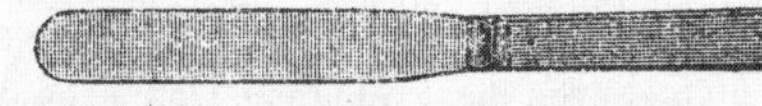

No. 30C485 Spatulas or Painters' Pallette Knife, lap bolster, cocoa handle.

Length of blade, inches	4	6	8	10
Price	16c	22c	35c	58c

Paperhangers' Knives.

No. 30C486 Paperhangers' Square Point Knife, extra quality steel, wood handle. Shipping weight, 3 ounces. Price..........**12c**

No. 30C487 Paperhangers' Round Point Butting Knife, best of steel, blade 8 inches long. Price..........**12c**

YOU WILL FIND OUR PRICES ON BRUSHES TO BE BELOW ANY KIND OF COMPETITION.

These goods are usually sold at a very large margin of profit, but we price them at the lowest possible prices, the same as we figure on other merchandise.

BRUSHES.

In our line of brushes listed below, we aim to quote such as are more commonly used. These goods are all of durable quality.

Camel's Hair Brushes.

The following brushes are used by carriage painters for striping, lettering and other carriage work.

No. 30C500 Camel's Hair Lettering Pencils, rose bound, fine quality. Hair, 1 inch long.

Sizes	1	2	3	4	5	6	7	8
Price, each	2c	2c	3c	3c	3c	3c	4c	4c
Per dozen	16c	19c	21c	23c	25c	28c	34c	38c

No. 30C501 Camel's Hair Striping Pencils. Rose bound, fine quality. Hair, 2 inches long.

Sizes	1	2	3	4	5	6	7	8
Price, each	2c	3c	3c	3c	4c	4c	5c	6c
Per dozen	19c	22c	26c	31c	38c	44c	50c	56c

No. 30C502 Camel's Hair Swan Quill Pencils, for lettering and striping.

Sizes, inches	⅛	¾	1	1¼	1½	1¾	2	2¼
Price, each	4c	4c	5c	5c	6c	7c	7c	8c
Per dozen	41c	44c	50c	56c	63c	69c	75c	81c

No. 30C503 Camel's Hair Flat or Sword Stripers. Square ends, tin ferrules, without handle, for carriage work. Hair, 1⅛ to 2¼ inches long.

Sizes	1	2	3	4
Price, each	5c	6c	7c	8c
Per dozen	59c	64c	75c	88c

No. 30C504 Camel's Hair Dagger Stripers. Diagonal ends, copper wire bound, small cedar handle; for carriage work. Hair, 1⅛ to 2¼ inches long.

Sizes	1	2	3	4
Price, each	$0.09	$0.10	$0.11	$0.12
Per dozen	1.05	1.15	1.20	1.25

No. 30C505 Camel's Hair Marking Brushes. Polished handles.

Sizes	1	2	3	4
Price, each	3c	3c	4c	5c
Per dozen	32c	35c	40c	50c

No. 30C506 Camel's Hair Lacquering Brushes. Polished handles; fine quality; round.

Sizes	1	2	3	4	5	6
Price, each	4c	4c	4c	5c	7c	9c

No. 30C507 Camel's Hair Lacquering Brushes. Polished handles; fine quality; flat.

Sizes	⅜	½	⅝	¾	⅞	1
Price, each	5c	6c	7c	9c	11c	13c

Flat Camel's Hair Brushes.

Flat Camel's Hair Brushes are used for high class carriage work in putting on color and should not be used as a varnish brush. Very thin paints such as gold, silver or aluminum should be put on with this brush.

Mottling Brushes.

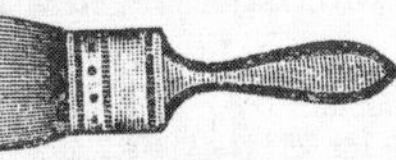

No. 30C508 Pure Camel's Hair Mottling Brushes or Spalters. Short cedar handles, tin ferrules, fine quality.

Size, inches	1	1½	2	2½	3
Price, each	12c	15c	21c	29c	37c

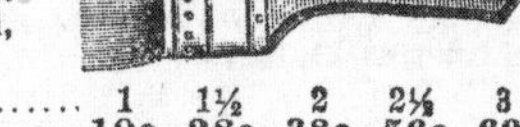

No. 30C509 Color Brush, same as No. 30C508, brass bound, a thicker brush.

Size, inches	1	1½	2	2½	3
Price, each	19c	28c	38c	56c	69c

Blenders.

No. 30C512 Round Badger Hair Blenders or Softeners, for graining and oil painting; polished handles.

Sizes	1	2	3	4	5	6
Price, each	10c	15c	18c	21c	26c	32c
Sizes	7	8	9	10	11	12
Price, each	36c	43c	50c	59c	72c	84c

No. 30C513 Flat Knotted Badger Hair Blenders, polished handles, set in bone.

Size, inches	2	2½	3	3½	4	4½
Price, each	51c	65c	76c	90c	$1.00	$1.40

Varnish Brushes.

For fine carriage and piano work, No. 30C515 is recommended, but for varnishing woodwork, wagons and implements, any of the other brushes will give excellent satisfaction. Where a little varnishing is to be done a cheap brush will answer, but No. 30C516 or No. 30C520 are recommended where particular work is required.

No. 30C515 Badger Hair Flowing Varnish Brushes, for fine varnishing, carriages, pianos, etc. Single thick, chiseled, tin ferrules.

Size, inches	1	1½	2	2½	3
Price, each	23c	33c	45c	55c	60c

No. 30C516 Fitch Flowing Varnish Brushes, superfine quality, single thick. Tin ferrules.

Size, inches	1	1½	2	2½	3
Price, each	13c	19c	25c	31c	38c

No. 30C517 Extra Flat Bristle Varnish Brushes, double thick, Chinese bristles, stained handles, tin ferrules.

Size, inches	1	1½	2	2½	3
Price, each	4c	6c	8c	10c	14c

No. 30C518 Bristle Flowing Varnish Brushes, stained handles, tin ferrules, black Chinese bristles, chiseled.

Size, inches	1	1½	2	2½	3
Price, each	6c	9c	12c	14c	20c

No. 30C520 An extra fine, extra thick, soft elastic Chinese Bristle Flowing Varnish Brush. Something for the painter who does good work.

Size, inches	1	1½	2	2½	3
Price, each	14c	20c	25c	36c	46c

Improved Davis Wood Grainers.

No. 30C525 The Improved Davis Wood Grainers are composed of three rubber rolls, 5 inches in length. With the corrugated roll any known growth of wood can be imitated. Quarter sawed oak grain is produced with roll No. 2, the one with the irregular grooves. Roll No. 3 is used in place of combs for straight line work in connection with the other two rolls; this roll is made with three sizes of combs. Anyone possessing a set of our improved graining rolls can with a few minutes practice do a perfect job of graining and natural wood imitated that it would be impossible to distinguish the natural grain of any wood from the grain made by our improved wood grainers. Complete instructions packed with every set. Weight, 14 oz. Price, per set of three rolls, **$1.50**

Steel Grainers.

No. 30C526 Best English Graining Combs. Best quality steel, in sets of 12 assorted, 1 to 4 inches, in tin compartment case. Weight, 14 oz. Price, per set..**85c**

Wall Stippler.

No. 30C527 This brush is used to produce the rough effect on painted interior walls. Made of best gray Russia bristles, 3⅜ inches long. Price..........**$1.75**

Walnut Stippler or Grainer.

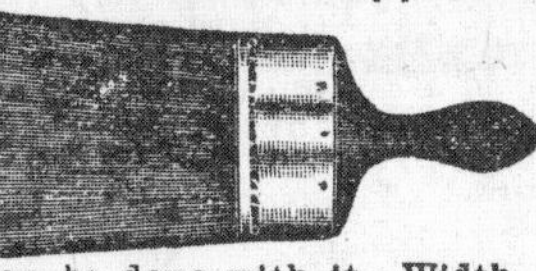

No. 30C528 Used for the same work mentioned above, but produces an entirely different grain. This is a well made brush and the best work can be done with it. Width, 3½ inches, length of bristles, 6½ inches. Price..........**90c**
Width, 4 inches, length of bristles, 6½ inches. Price..........**$1.00**

Marking Brushes.

No. 30C540 Bristle Marking Brushes, round polished handles.

Size	1	2	3	4	5	6
Price, each	3c	3c	3c	3c	4c	4c
Price, per dozen	20c	22c	25c	26c	28c	31c

Artists' Brushes.

No. 30C542 Extra Quality Flat Bristle Artists' Brushes or Fitch Tools, white bristles, black handles, tin ferrules.

Size, inches	⅛	¾	1	1¼	1½
Price, each	5c	7c	$0.10	$0.14	$0.17
Per dozen	45c	75c	1.05	1.50	1.87

Sash Tools.

Generally used by painters for painting window sash and moulding, also used for trimming and painting around corners. Can be used as a general family brush where a small brush is wanted.

No. 30C543 Extra Fine Black Sash Tool, black Chinese bristles, oval shape, warranted not to twist; a brush for particular people.

Size	1	2	4	6	8	10
Price, each	6c	7c	9c	12c	16c	22c

No. 30C544 Ex. Ex. French Sash Tools. All fine white bristles, wire bound.

Size	1	2	3	4	5	6	7	8	9	10
Price, ea.	3c	3c	4c	5c	6c	7c	8c	9c	$0.10	$0.12
Per doz...	30c	31c	42c	48c	60c	72c	79c	85c	1.04	1.30

Round Paint Brushes.

For general house painting. Length given is length of bristles clear of binding or ferrule.

No. 30C545 Round Paint Brushes, wire bound, white bristles outside, mixed center.

Sizes	1-0	2-0	3-0	4-0	5-0	6-0
Length, inches	3	3⅛	3½	3¾	4	4¼
Price, each	18c	20c	23c	25c	31c	33c

Paint Brushes.

No. 30C546 Round Paint Brushes, wire bound. All best selected Russian bristles.

Sizes	1-0	2-0	3-0	4-0	5-0	6-0
Length, inches	3⅜	3⅞	4⅛	4⅜	4⅝	4⅞
Price, each	40c	50c	63c	85c	$1.05	$1.20

No. 30C547 Oval Paint Brushes, all white Russia bristles; wire bound. A brush that will do a good job and wear well.

Sizes	1-0	2-0	3-0	4-0	5-0	6-0
Length	3⅜	3⅞	4⅛	4⅜	4⅝	4⅞
Price	42c	55c	65c	92c	$1.10	$1.30

Oval Varnish Brushes.

Length given is length of bristles clear of binding or ferrule.

No. 30C550 Chiseled Oval Varnish Brushes, very elastic; best selected black Chinese bristles; nickel plated rings.

Sizes	1-0	2-0	3-0	4-0	5-0	6-0
Length, inches	2⅛	2¾	3	3	3¼	3½
Price, each	28c	36c	42c	48c	55c	67c

Flat Paint or Wall Brushes.

Wall brushes are generally used for painting large surfaces, such as roofs, interior and exterior walls, floors, etc. Extension Wall Brushes and Stucco Paint Brushes are better grades and have longer bristles.

Length given is length of bristles clear of binding or ferrule.

No. 30C551 Wall Brush. A good working brush, all Chinese bristles, tin ferrules.

Width, inches	2½	3	3½	4	4½
Length, inches	2	2⅛	2¼	2½	2⅞
Price, each	10c	12c	15c	20c	23c

No. 30C552 Wall Brush. All black Chinese bristles, solid center. This brush will do good work, metal bound.

Width, inches	3	3½	4	4½	5
Length, inches	2¾	3	3¼	3½	3¾
Price, each	28c	36c	44c	56c	72c

No. 30C555 Extension Wall Brush, brass bound, white Okatka bristles, full, stiff, springy stock. **Our standard brush for painters' use.**

Size	6	7	8	9	10
Width, inches	3	3½	4	4½	5
Length, bristles	3⅞	4⅛	4⅜	4⅝	4⅞
Price, each	58c	78c	$1.05	$1.40	$1.65

Stucco Paint Brush.

No. 30C560 Stucco Paint Brush. Full stock, very full and stiff, extra long, and very best selected white Russian bristles, leather bound. Used mostly by frescoers and for stucco work.

Sizes, inches	3½	4	4½
Length, inches	4⅛	4⅜	4⅝
Price, each	$1.00	$1.25	$1.45

Black Stucco Paint Brush.

No. 30C561 Stucco Paint Brush. Best black Chinese bristles. First class in every respect and guaranteed to give good satisfaction.

No	25	30	35	40
Width, inches	3	3½	4	4½
Length, inches	4¼	4½	4¾	5
Price, each	68c	80c	$1.05	$1.20

Calcimine Brushes.

Length given is length of bristles clear of binding or ferrule.

No. 30C565 Calcimine Brush for common work, white casing, with gray center. Metal bound.

Width, inches	6	7	8
Length, inches	3½	3¾	4¼
Price, each	22c	25c	31c

No. 30C566 Calcimine Brush. White bristles. Metal bound. Excellent quality.

Size, inches	6	7	8
Length, inches	3⅝	3¾	3⅞
Price, each	60c	71c	88c

No. 30C567 Selected Russian White Bristle Calcimine Brush. Brass bound.
Size, inches, 7; length, 4⅝. Price, each........$1.56
Size, inches, 8; length, 4⅝. Price, each........1.88

No. 30C568 New York Style Calcimine Brushes. Extra heavy. Specially selected Russian bristles, finest workmanship. **Metal bound. Will last a lifetime.**
Size, inches, 7; length, 5⅜. Price, each........$2.75
Size, inches, 8; length, 5⅜. Price, each........3.00

Whitewash Brushes.

No. 30C570 Whitewash Brush. White tampico stock (not a bristle in it). The stock is soft and white. Metal bound. Used for whitewashing fences, outbuildings, etc.

Width, inches	6	7	8
Length, inches	2¾	3	3
Price, each	8c	9c	12c

No. 30C571 Whitewash Brush, all American bristles, white outside. A fair quality brush for common work. Leather bound. Width, 7½ inches; length of bristles, 2⅝ inches.
Price, each........25c

No. 30C572 Whitewash Brush, all white bristles; looks well and works well. Metal bound.

Width, inches	8	9
Length, inches	3	3¼
Price, each	43c	55c

No. 30C573 Extension Whitewash Brush, all white bristles. Metal bound. Exceedingly good value at the price.
Width, inches, 8; length, inches, 3⅝. Each...$0.88
Width, inches, 9; length, inches, 3⅞. Each...1.08

No. 30C574 Whitewash Brush, all white Russian bristles; extension style. Metal bound. A brush that's used by many calciminers and whitewashers.

Width, inches	8	8½
Length, inches	4¼	4⅝
Price, each	$1.57	$1.87

Stucco Whitewash Brush.

No. 30C580 Stucco Whitewash Brush. Wide and heavy, for whitewashers and plasterers' use. Made of the finest white Okatka bristles. Leather bound.

Width, inches	9	9
Length, inches	4⅝	5⅛
Price, each	$2.28	$3.00

Plasterers' Brush.

No. 30C581 Plasterers' Brush. All gray, stiff bristles. Will hold lots of water, wear well and give satisfaction. Leather bound.

Sizes	1	2
Width, inches	7½	8½
Length, inches	3¾	4
Price, each	$1.56	$1.95

Painters' Duster.

No. 30C583 Painters' Duster. Gray bristles, black outside. Raised center.

Sizes	1	4
Length, inches	4	4¼
Price, each	30c	45c

Paperhangers' Smoothing Brushes.

No. 30C585 Paperhangers' Smoothing Brush. Two rows white fibre, wire drawn. Width, 10 inches. A good brush for the householder who wishes to paper several rooms. Price, each........12c

No. 30C586 Paperhangers' Smoothing Brush. Two rows stiff Chinese bristles, 2⅛ inches long, wire bound.

Width, inches	10	12
Price, each	58c	80c

Paperhangers' Paste Brushes.

No. 30C590 Paperhangers' Paste Brush. White hair casings. Imitation white bristle center. Double nailed, leather bound. Width, 7½ inches; length of bristles, 3¾ inches.
Price........55c

Brick Liner.

No. 30C595 Brick Liner, white bristles.

Size, inches	2	2½	3
Price, each	5c	6c	9c

Glue Brushes.

No. 30C598 Glue Brush. Made entirely of metal and bristles and will stand the constant shrinking and swelling that glue brushes are subjected to. Iron handle, brass ferrule and all white bristles.

Sizes	2	4	6
Length, inches	2¾	3	3½
Price, each	18c	25c	38c

Steel Wire Brushes.

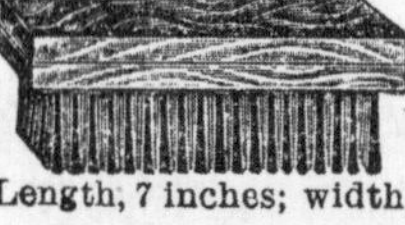

No. 30C599 Steel Wire Brush. For removing old paint, rust and dirt from iron, stone, brick and woodwork. Made of the best steel wire, hard wood block, 6 rows. Length, 7 inches; width, 2⅜ inches. Price, each..33c

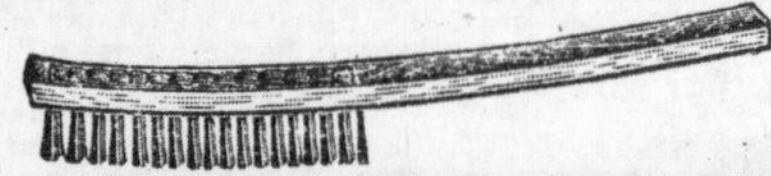

No. 30C600 Steel Wire Brush with Handle. Narrow steel wire brush, suited for cleaning ornamental iron work, corners, etc. 3 rows wire. Width, 1 inch, length of brush, 5¾ inches; entire length with handle, 13 inches. Price, each........22c

GLUE.

No. 30C650 High Grade Flake Glue. Suited to the requirements of the most exact woodworker. Can be used on all woods, even the hardest, and is especially adapted for furniture repairing. May also be used for making printers' rollers, white mouldings, emery wheels and belts, chipping glass and for every other purpose where strength and flexibility are requisites. Price, per pound....17c
In 100-pound kegs, per pound........16c
In 200-pound barrels, per pound........15c

No. 30C651 Flake Carpenters' Glue. A splendid glue for cabinetmakers, carpenters and for general repairing. Price, per pound........15c
In 100-pound kegs, per pound........14c
In 200-pound barrels, per pound........12c

No. 30C652 Calciminers' Glue. A thin cut white glue, especially prepared for calciminers, and the best in the market for that purpose.
Price, per pound........18c
In 100-pound kegs, per pound........17c
In 200-pound barrels, per pound........16c

No. 30C653 Special Flake Glue. Unsurpassed for soft wood joining and veneering, bookbinding, paper boxes, wood boxes, sizing barrels and pails, composition mouldings, picture frame joining, lining trunks and coffins, medium grade calcimining and wall sizing, and for all other purposes where the highest grade glue is not required.
Price, per pound........10c
In 100-pound kegs, per pound........9½c
In 200-pound barrels, per pound........9c

No. 30C654 Ground Glue, same as No. 30C653. Ground glue is quickly prepared and does not require more than 30 minutes' soaking.
Price, per pound........11c
In 100-pound kegs, per pound........10c
In 200-pound barrels, per pound........9½c

No. 30C657 Flake Gelatine. To be used for high grade joining, repairing leather belts, sizing straw hats and sizing walls. Price, per pound..28c
In 100-pound kegs, per pound........27c
In 200-pound barrels, per pound........26c

Army and Navy Liquid Glue.

No. 30C660 The strongest glue made; if you do not find it so, we will refund the full price paid for same. It will cement together all known substances, such as wood, leather, ivory, cork, cloth, marble, glass, iron, china, crockery, pearl, metals, porcelain, etc. Used and endorsed by the U. S. Government. This is not a fish glue but a pure hide and sinew glue in liquid form and has no offensive odor. It will keep indefinitely. Put up in self-sealing tubes, bottles and cans. The tubes are expressly put up for family use.
Price, small tube........4c
Price, large tube........9c
Price, 2-oz. bottle with cap and brush........9c
Price, ¼-pint can........18c
Price, 1-pint can........28c
Price, 1-quart can........52c

Porcelain Enameled Glue Pots.

No. 30C665 The best glue pot on the market.
Capacity, ½ pint. Price, each........39c
Capacity, 1 pint. Price, each........46c
Capacity, 1 quart. Price, each........54c

SEROCO SAFETY KEROSENE.

This is the very finest Pennsylvania kerosene and should not be compared with the common Ohio and Indiana oils. You may not know it, but Pennsylvania kerosene is the very best on the market and very few dealers in the country handle it. Our price may be a little higher than you can purchase the Ohio oil for, but you will find that it is cheaper and more satisfactory in the end to use the very best Pennsylvania kerosene. The price we are quoting is lower than you can possibly obtain the same grade of goods for elsewhere. This oil is shipped to us direct from the Pennsylvania oil wells independent of any trust. We have decided to handle one grade only, as the best oil is none too good.

For lamps there is nothing finer; gives a bright, white light, absolutely odorless, and a clean ash will be found on the wick instead of a heavy black crust.

Especially recommended for incubators. The best, reliable, even heat producing oil should be used in incubators, and we have it in the Seroco Safety Kerosene, a pure Pennsylvania product.

Price of above oil will be found in our Special Grocery Price List. Mailed free on request. Price quoted promptly on application.

Home Oil Tank.

No. 30C704 Capacity, 60 gallons; diameter, 25¼ inches; height, 40¾ inches. Force pump diameter, 1¼ inches. Will hold full barrel of oil and 10 gallons to spare. **Made of best galvanized iron in body and bottom.** Wood bottom under metal, tin hood, portable, steady stream pump, which can be taken out and used for pumping oil from barrel into tank. Painted. Weight, crated for shipment, 50 pounds.
Price, with pump complete........$3.50

No. 30C703 Extra pumps, each........ .90

Gasoline Tanks.

No. 30C706 Gasoline Tanks, holding 60 gallons, 4-inch screw top, ½-inch brass faucet, each..$3.25

SPECIAL NOTICE No. 30C705.

We do not sell less than one gallon of such oils where reference is made to this notice, and the following extra charges are made for the cans and half barrels, which do not fail to include in your remittance:

Half barrel, extra	$1.00
10-gallon wood jacket tin can, extra	.55
5-gallon wood jacket tin can, extra	.30
3-gallon wood jacket tin can, extra	.25
2-gallon wood jacket tin can, extra	.25
1-gallon plain tin can, extra	.10

No extra charge when purchased in original barrels, containing about 52 gallons.

Lard Oils.

Cans and Half Barrels Extra. See Special Notice No. 30C705.

No. 30C708 Extra Winter Strained Lard Oil, used extensively by plumbers, brass spinners, etc. For all kinds of lubricating and for miners' lamps, railroad lanterns, etc. Price, per gallon...67c

No. 30C709 No. 1 Lard Oil, used for lubricating and mixing, a very good oil, but not so white and clear as the winter strained. Price, per gallon...42c

Neatsfoot Oils.

Cans and Half Barrels Extra. See Special Notice No. 30C705.

No. 30C710 Pure Neatsfoot Oil, used in dressing leather, oiling guns, etc. We are headquarters and sell at right prices. Price, per gallon...80c

No. 30C711 Extra Neatsfoot Oil, commonly sold for purest. Price, per gallon...60c

No. 30C712 No. 1 Neatsfoot Oil, commonly sold for extra. Price, per gallon...43c

Cylinder Oils.

Cans and Half Barrels Extra. See Special Notice No. 30C705.

No. 30C714 High Test Cylinder Oil. This oil comes from the finest wells in Pennsylvania, and, although high in price, we consider this the cheapest cylinder oil in the end, as it goes farther. Light in color and absolutely pure. Price, per gallon...38c

No. 30C715 Eclipse Cylinder Oil. A compounded cylinder oil, especially adapted for low steam pressure. Price, per gallon...34c

No. 30C716 Extra Cylinder Oil. Compounded oil, especially adapted for high steam pressure. Price, per gallon...30c

Gasoline Engine Cylinder Oil.

No. 30C717 Special Compounded Cylinder Oil for stationary, gas and gasoline engines and automobiles. This is strictly high grade oil and guaranteed. Do not experiment with cheap oils and ruin the cylinder of your engine.

Price, 1-gallon can, including can	$0.38
Price, 5-gallon can, including can	1.70
Price, 10-gallon can, including can	3.20

Engine Oils.

Cans and Half Barrels Extra. See Special Notice No. 30C705.

No. 30C718 Dynamo Engine Oil. Price, per gallon...28c

No. 30C719 No. 1 Red Engine Oil. Price, per gallon...22c

No. 30C720 No. 2 Engine Oil. Price, per gallon...18c

Cream Separator Oil for Hand Power Separators.

Cans and half barrels extra. See special notice No. 30C705.

A very fine light oil for lubricating Separators operated by hand. Warranted not to gum or cause the machine to run hard even in the coldest weather.

No. 30C721 Hand Power Separator Oil. Price, per gallon...27c

Cream Separator Oil for Power Machines.

Cans and half barrels extra. See special notice No. 30C705.

A heavier oil for Separators operated by power, strictly high grade and the best lubricant on the market. Give it a trial and if not found to lubricate perfectly, we will refund your money and make no charge for oil used.

No. 30C722 Separator Oil for Power Machines. Price, per gallon...25c

S., R. & Co.'s Harness Oil.

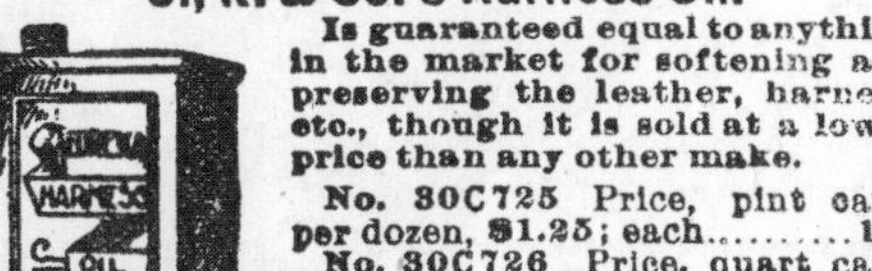

Is guaranteed equal to anything in the market for softening and preserving the leather, harness, etc., though it is sold at a lower price than any other make.

No. 30C725 Price, pint cans, per dozen, $1.25; each...12c

No. 30C726 Price, quart cans, per dozen, $2.25; each...20c

No. 30C727 Price, gallon cans, per dozen, $5.00; each...50c

No. 30C728 Price, 5-gallon cans, per can...$2.00

No. 30C729 Price, 10-gallon cans, per can, 3.30

OUR NEW AND VALUABLE BOOK "HOW TO PAINT" is sent absolutely FREE OF CHARGE with every order from this department. It is also sent with every request for paint color samples. By means of this instruction book you can do any job of painting, even though you have not done any of the work before. Everything is made plain by means of illustrations and simple instructions.

Harness Dressing.

No. 30C732 Frank Miller's Harness Dressing, for harness, saddles, fly nets, etc. **Gives a beautiful finish, does not lose its luster.** Directions for using on every package.

Price, per pint can...19c
Price, per quart can...34c

Weight about, pints, 1 pound; quarts, 2¼ pounds.

Carriage Top Dressing.

No. 30C734 Frank Miller's Dressing for buggy and carriage tops. **Gives an elastic, durable, jet black waterproof gloss.** Can be easily used on the finest stock. Directions on each can.

Price, per ½ pint can...25c
Price, per pint can...39c

Acme Red Seal Carriage Top Dressing.

No. 30C735 The best ever used for preserving tops of buggies and carriages. Gives an elegant gloss and makes the leather waterproof.

Price, per ½-pint can...17c
Weight, about ¾ pound.
Price, per pint can...25c
Weight, about 1¼ pounds.
Price, per quart can...42c
Weight, about 2¼ pounds.

Seroco Waterproof Carriage Top Dressing.

No. 30C736 Made in our own factory and we know exactly the material used in preparing this dressing. Guaranteed not to injure the finest leather or rubber. You can preserve your buggy top and make it look like new for just a trifle.

Price, ½-pint can...15c
Price, pint can...23c
Price, quart can...40c

Weights same as No. 30C735

Machine Oils.

Cans and Half Barrels Extra. See Special Notice No. 30C705.

	Per gallon
No. 30C745 Excelsior Machine Oil	20c
No. 30C746 Summer Black Oil	13c
No. 30C747 15 degrees	14c
No. 30C748 Zero	15c

No. 30C749 Pure Natural W. Va. Lubricating Oil; the best below zero. will flow in cold weather. Price, per gallon...26c

No. 30C750 XXXX Castor, lubricating, etc.	85c
No. 30C751 Castor, machine No. 2	22c
No. 30C752 Castor, machine No. 1	20c

Spirits Turpentine.

Cans and Half Barrels Extra. See Special Notice No. 30C705.

No. 30C755 Spirits Turpentine. Price on application.

Cup Grease.

	Per pail
No. 30C758 Price, 10-lb. pail	$0.70
Price, 25-lb. pail, hard or soft	1.60
Price, 50-lb. pail, hard or soft	3.00

Sewing Machine Oil.

	Per Dozen	Each
No. 30C760 Sewing Machine Oil.		
Price, per 2-ounce bottle	50c	5c
Price, per 4-ounce bottle	85c	8c
No. 30C762 Pure Sperm Sewing Machine Oil, best quality oil.		
Price, 4-oz. tin cans, with oiler spout	90c	10c

Harvester Oil.

Cans and Half Barrels Extra. See Special Notice No. 30C705.

No. 30C765 For threshing machines, windmills, harvesters, mowers and heavy farm machinery of all kinds, is highly recommended by those who have used it. Price, per gallon...26c

Mexican Plumbago Axle Grease.

No. 30C775 Made from pure Mexican plumbago (graphite) combined with the best lubricating oil, and chemically solidified. Can be used on the lightest carriages or the heaviest trucks. Order a box and try this experiment, which will prove that it is the best and cheapest axle grease manufactured. Grease one side of your vehicle with our Mexican Plumbago Axle Grease and the other side with some other grease (the best you can buy), being sure to use much less of ours than of the other. Ours will wear longest, even though less of it is used. This grease will be found a fine article for lubricating all kinds of farm machinery, windmills, etc.

Price, per 10-pound can, 70c; per 1-pound can, 8c

Mather Thousand Mile Axle Oil.

A pure lubricant, free from rosin or grit, especially prepared for carriage and wagon axles. Especially adapted to our Mather 1,000-Mile Axle. Guaranteed to run longer than any other oil or grease made.

No. 30C800 Price, per pint	$0.20
No. 30C801 Price, per quart	.30
No. 30C802 Price, per gallon	1.00

Strictly Pure Linseed Oil.

The price of linseed oil is constantly changing. Were we to quote prices in this catalogue it would very likely not be correct by the time our customers receive same. Mail us a postal at any time and we will immediately, on receipt of same, quote you a price which will be guaranteed for 15 days.

We sell any quantity from one gallon up.

Sperm Oil for Burning.

No. 30C812 Sperm Oil. Price, quart can 25c
Price, per ½-gallon can...45c
Price, per 1-gallon can...85c

Signal Oil.

No. 30C813 Signal Oil. Expressly for lantern use. No charge for can.

Price, per ¼ gallon can...15c
Price, per ½ gallon can...28c
Price, per 1 gallon can...52c

Pine Tar.

No. 30C820 Genuine North Carolina Pine Tar. We furnish pine tar in barrels of 50 gallons each and in sealed tins as quoted below. **We buy this tar direct, and you will find our prices the lowest.**

50-gallon barrels, each	$6.00
Quart cans, per dozen	1.00
Quart cans, each	.10
Half gallons, per dozen	2.00
Half gallons, each	.20
Gallons, per dozen	3.00
Gallons, each	.32

Coal Tar.

Distilled Liquid Coal Tar.

No. 30C821 Price, per 50-gallon barrel	$5.00
Price, per 25-gallon barrel	3.50
Price, per 10-gallon can	1.75
Price, per 5-gallon can	1.00
Price, per 1-gallon can	.28

Graphite Roof Cement.

No. 30C824 For repairing any kind of leak, roofs, chimneys, gutters, porch floors, etc. Easily applied with a putty knife or wood paddle. Guaranteed to stop any leak. Strictly elastic and will not crack; the severest exposure will not affect it.

Price, per 2-pound can...20c
Price, per 5-pound can...40c

Washed Hair for Plastering.

At 20 cents per bushel we offer the very highest grade of washed hair for plastering. This is the very best hair on the market; we can guarantee the goods.

No. 30C830 Price, per bushel package, compressed...20c

GRAPHITE (PLUMBAGO) AND GRAPHITE PREPARATIONS.

Dry Graphite Plumbago.

No. 30C850 For lubricating and painting purposes. Air floated plumbago. Price, per pound, 7c

Mexican Graphite Plumbago.

No. 30C852 For foundries, stove polish and paints. Price, per pound...4c

Mexican Graphite Pipe Cement.

Pipe Joint Compound.

No. 30C855 For use in joints of radiators, steam and hot water apparatus, gas pipes in streets and buildings, for bolts and screws, and for general use of gas fitters, plumbers, engineers and machinists. Mexican Pipe Joint Compound does not "set," and joints can remain for months and years and can then be easily removed, rendering unnecessary the breaking of joints, couplings or tools.

Price, per 1 -pound can	$0.18
Price, per 5 -pound can	.75
Price, per 12½-pound can	1.85
Price, per 25-pound can	3.60

No. 205 Lubricating Graphite.

No. 30C857 Guaranteed absolutely pure and the best graphite on the market. No engineer should be without it.

Price, per 1-pound can	$0.18
Price, per 5-pound can	.80
Price, per 10-pound box	1.40
Price, per 25-pound box	2.75
Price, per 100-pound keg	9.75

WHILE WE GLADLY SEND THE TWO FREE PAINT BOOKS TO ANYONE, that is the Book of Paint Color Samples, showing 85 different shades, and the Free Book of Instructions "HOW TO PAINT", nevertheless we recommend that you order your paint direct from this catalogue with the understanding that everything will turn out perfectly satisfactory or we will immediately return your money. You can do this because you will get the **Free Book, "How to Paint"**, with the goods we send you. **Still, if you prefer to see the actual shades, do not hesitate to write for the TWO FREE PAINT BOOKS.**

SPORTING GOODS DEPARTMENT.

ON RECEIPT OF $1.00 we will ship any gun or revolver by express C. O. D., subject to examination, the balance to be paid upon receipt of the goods, if found entirely satisfactory; but we recommend that you send cash in full with your order, thereby saving the extra charge on a C. O. D. shipment. Nearly all of our customers send cash in full with their orders, as we agree to promptly refund your money for anything not entirely satisfactory. All we ask is that you keep goods in perfect condition. Ammunition, Tents and Seines will not be shipped C. O. D.

ENGRAVED, SPECIALLY FINISHED HAMMERLESS GUN, $13.40.

FOR $13.40

WE OFFER THIS SPECIALLY FINISHED, EXTRA WELL MADE, ELABORATELY ENGRAVED AND DECORATED, DOUBLE BARREL, HAMMERLESS, BREECH LOADING, 12-GAUGE SHOTGUN UNDER OUR GUARANTEE FOR QUALITY, WORKMANSHIP, MATERIAL, FINISH, SHOOTING QUALITIES, PATTERN, PENETRATION. YOUR MONEY BACK IF IT ISN'T IN EVERY WAY SUPERIOR TO ANY DOUBLE BARREL HAMMERLESS SHOTGUN YOU CAN BUY ELSEWHERE AT LESS THAN $25.00.

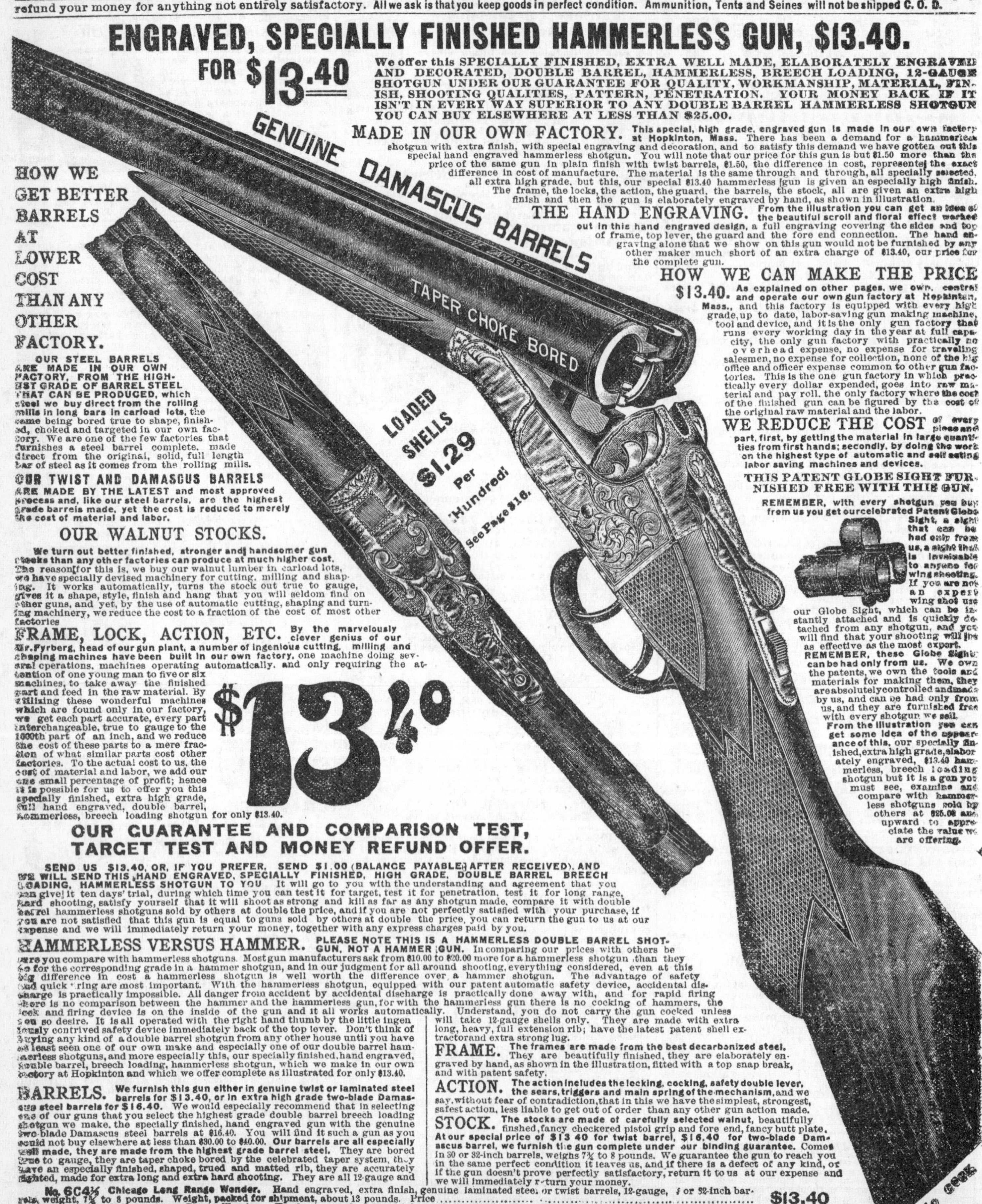

MADE IN OUR OWN FACTORY. This special, high grade, engraved gun is made in our own factory at Hopkinton, Mass. There has been a demand for a hammerless shotgun with extra finish, with special engraving and decoration, and to satisfy this demand we have gotten out this special hand engraved hammerless shotgun. You will note that our price for this gun is but $1.50 more than the price of the same gun in plain finish with twist barrels, $1.50, the difference in cost, represents the exact difference in cost of manufacture. The material is the same through and through, all specially selected, all extra high grade, but this, our special $13.40 hammerless gun is given an especially high finish. The frame, the locks, the action, the guard, the barrels, the stock, all are given an extra high finish and then the gun is elaborately engraved by hand, as shown in illustration.

THE HAND ENGRAVING. From the illustration you can get an idea of the beautiful scroll and floral effect worked out in this hand engraved design, a full engraving covering the sides and top of frame, top lever, the guard and the fore end connection. The hand engraving alone that we show on this gun would not be furnished by any other maker much short of an extra charge of $13.40, our price for the complete gun.

HOW WE CAN MAKE THE PRICE $13.40. As explained on other pages, we own, control and operate our own gun factory at Hopkinton, Mass., and this factory is equipped with every high grade, up to date, labor-saving gun making machine, tool and device, and it is the only gun factory that runs every working day in the year at full capacity, the only gun factory with practically no overhead expense, no expense for traveling salesmen, no expense for collection, none of the big office and officer expense common to other gun factories. This is the one gun factory in which practically every dollar expended, goes into raw material and pay roll, the only factory where the cost of the finished gun can be figured by the cost of the original raw material and the labor.

WE REDUCE THE COST of every piece and part, first, by getting the material in large quantities from first hands; secondly, by doing the work on the highest type of automatic and self acting labor saving machines and devices.

THIS PATENT GLOBE SIGHT FURNISHED FREE WITH THIS GUN.

REMEMBER, with every shotgun you buy from us you get our celebrated Patent Globe Sight, a sight that can be had only from us, a sight that is invaluable to anyone for wing shooting. If you are not an expert wing shot use our Globe Sight, which can be instantly attached and is quickly detached from any shotgun, and you will find that your shooting will be as effective as the most expert. REMEMBER, these Globe Sights can be had only from us. We own the patents, we own the tools and materials for making them, they are absolutely controlled and made by us, and can be had only from us, and they are furnished free with every shotgun we sell.

From the illustration you can get some idea of the appearance of this, our specially finished, extra high grade, elaborately engraved, $13.40 hammerless, breech loading shotgun but it is a gun you must see, examine and compare with hammerless shotguns sold by others at $25.00 and upward to appreciate the value we are offering.

HOW WE GET BETTER BARRELS AT LOWER COST THAN ANY OTHER FACTORY.

OUR STEEL BARRELS ARE MADE IN OUR OWN FACTORY, FROM THE HIGHEST GRADE OF BARREL STEEL THAT CAN BE PRODUCED, which steel we buy direct from the rolling mills in long bars in carload lots, the same being bored true to shape, finished, choked and targeted in our own factory. We are one of the few factories that furnishes a steel barrel complete, made direct from the original, solid, full length bar of steel as it comes from the rolling mills.

OUR TWIST AND DAMASCUS BARRELS ARE MADE BY THE LATEST and most approved process and, like our steel barrels, are the highest grade barrels made, yet the cost is reduced to merely the cost of material and labor.

OUR WALNUT STOCKS.

We turn out better finished, stronger and handsomer gun stocks than any other factories can produce at much higher cost. The reason for this is, we buy our walnut lumber in carload lots, we have specially devised machinery for cutting, milling and shaping. It works automatically, turns the stock out true to gauge, gives it a shape, style, finish and hang that you will seldom find on other guns, and yet, by the use of automatic cutting, shaping and turning machinery, we reduce the cost to a fraction of the cost of most other factories.

FRAME, LOCK, ACTION, ETC. By the marvelously clever genius of our Mr. Fyrberg, head of our gun plant, a number of ingenious cutting, milling and shaping machines have been built in our own factory, one machine doing several operations, machines operating automatically, and only requiring the attention of one young man to five or six machines, to take away the finished part and feed in the raw material. By utilizing these wonderful machines which are found only in our factory, we get each part accurate, every part interchangeable, true to gauge to the 1000th part of an inch, and we reduce the cost of these parts to a mere fraction of what similar parts cost other factories. To the actual cost to us, the cost of material and labor, we add our one small percentage of profit; hence it is possible for us to offer you this specially finished, extra high grade, full hand engraved, double barrel, hammerless, breech loading shotgun for only $13.40.

$13.40

OUR GUARANTEE AND COMPARISON TEST, TARGET TEST AND MONEY REFUND OFFER.

SEND US $13.40, OR, IF YOU PREFER, SEND $1.00 (BALANCE PAYABLE AFTER RECEIVED), AND WE WILL SEND THIS HAND ENGRAVED, SPECIALLY FINISHED, HIGH GRADE, DOUBLE BARREL BREECH LOADING, HAMMERLESS SHOTGUN TO YOU. It will go to you with the understanding and agreement that you can give it ten days' trial, during which time you can test it for target, test it for penetration, test it for long range, hard shooting, satisfy yourself that it will shoot as strong and kill as far as any shotgun made, compare it with double barrel hammerless shotguns sold by others at double the price, and if you are not perfectly satisfied with your purchase, if you are not satisfied that this gun is equal to guns sold by others at double the price, you can return the gun to us at our expense and we will immediately return your money, together with any express charges paid by you.

HAMMERLESS VERSUS HAMMER. PLEASE NOTE THIS IS A HAMMERLESS DOUBLE BARREL SHOTGUN, NOT A HAMMER GUN. In comparing our prices with others be sure you compare with hammerless shotguns. Most gun manufacturers ask from $10.00 to $20.00 more for a hammerless shotgun than they do for the corresponding grade in a hammer shotgun, and in our judgment for all around shooting, everything considered, even at this big difference in cost a hammerless shotgun is well worth the difference over a hammer shotgun. The advantage of safety and quick firing are most important. With the hammerless shotgun, equipped with our patent automatic safety device, accidental discharge is practically impossible. All danger from accident by accidental discharge is practically done away with, and for rapid firing there is no comparison between the hammer and the hammerless gun, for with the hammerless gun there is no cocking of hammers, the lock and firing device is on the inside of the gun and it all works automatically. Understand, you do not carry the gun cocked unless you so desire. It is all operated with the right hand thumb by the little ingeniously contrived safety device immediately back of the top lever. Don't think of buying any kind of a double barrel shotgun from any other house until you have at least seen one of our own make and especially one of our double barrel hammerless shotguns, and more especially this, our specially finished, hand engraved, double barrel, breech loading, hammerless shotgun, which we make in our own factory at Hopkinton and which we offer complete as illustrated for only $13.40.

BARRELS. We furnish this gun either in genuine twist or laminated steel barrels for $13.40, or in extra high grade two-blade Damascus steel barrels for $16.40. We would especially recommend that in selecting one of our guns that you select the highest grade double barrel breech loading shotgun we make, the specially finished, hand engraved gun with the genuine two-blade Damascus steel barrels at $16.40. You will find it such a gun as you could not buy elsewhere at less than $30.00 to $40.00. Our barrels are all especially well made, they are made from the highest grade barrel steel. They are bored true to gauge, they are taper choke bored by the celebrated taper system, they have an especially finished, shaped, trued and matted rib, they are accurately sighted, made for extra long and extra hard shooting. They are all 12-gauge and will take 12-gauge shells only. They are made with extra long, heavy, full extension rib; have the latest patent shell extractor and extra strong lug.

FRAME. The frames are made from the best decarbonized steel. They are beautifully finished, they are elaborately engraved by hand, as shown in the illustration, fitted with a top snap break, and with patent safety.

ACTION. The action includes the locking, cocking, safety double lever, the sears, triggers and main spring of the mechanism, and we say, without fear of contradiction, that in this we have the simplest, strongest, safest action, less liable to get out of order than any other gun action made.

STOCK. The stocks are made of carefully selected walnut, beautifully finished, fancy checkered pistol grip and fore end, fancy butt plate.

At our special price of $13 40 for twist barrel, $16.40 for two-blade Damascus barrel, we furnish the gun complete under our binding guarantee. Comes in 30 or 32-inch barrels, weighs 7½ to 8 pounds. We guarantee the gun to reach you in the same perfect condition it leaves us, and if there is a defect of any kind, or if the gun doesn't prove perfectly satisfactory, return it to us at our expense and we will immediately return your money.

No. 6C4½ Chicago Long Range Wonder. Hand engraved, extra finish, genuine laminated steel or twist barrels, 12-gauge, 30 or 32-inch barrels, weight, 7½ to 8 pounds. Weight, packed for shipment, about 13 pounds. Price ... $13.40

No. 6C6½ Chicago Long Range Wonder. Hand engraved, extra high grade two-blade Damascus steel barrels, 12-gauge, 30 or 32-inch barrels; weight, 7½ to 8 pounds. Weight, packed for shipment, about 13 pounds. Price ... 16.40

THIS HAMMERLESS DOUBLE BARREL BREECH LOADING SHOTGUN ONLY.... $10.90

FOR $10.90 we furnish this strictly high grade, new improved model Hammerless Double Barrel Breech Loading Shotgun, made by the Hopkinton Fire Arms Company, of Hopkinton, Mass. We own this factory and control the manufacture of these guns and the cost to manufacture is based on the actual cost of material and labor, which alone makes possible a $10.90 price on a double barrel hammerless breech loading shotgun, which is superior in every way to any other hammerless gun you can buy at less than $25.00.

WHY WE CAN SELL you a better gun for $10.90 than you could buy elsewhere for $25.00. No other gun factory in the world is equipped with such facilities for turning out high grade hammerless guns at so small a cost. First, as an inducement for us to locate our factory at Hopkinton, Mass., we received such liberal concessions from the city of Hopkinton that we were placed in possession of one of the best constructed gun factories in the country, practically without cost to ourselves. The factory site which we secured covers large and beautiful grounds on the handsomest residence street in the city, on which is erected one building 180 feet long, three stories and basement, with two large projecting L's; another long division, three stories and basement, 40 feet wide by 212 feet long, and, excepting for the frame, the exterior of these buildings is practically glass, making it one of the lightest factories in America. The concessions we received from the city were such that the entire factory plant, ground, power and power equipment were virtually donated to us, thus practically eliminating all rent or storage charge. It is the only gun factory that runs at full capacity every working day in the year, thus reducing the cost by getting the greatest amount of product out of the equipment and the most economical distribution of labor or pay roll. Being located in a New England city and being the only manufacturing industry in the city, we have been able to secure an ample supply of skilled labor at a moderate wage scale.

No. 6C10

Detailed description of our $10.90 Hammerless Double Barrel Breech Loading Shotgun, made by the Hopkinton Fire Arms Company, at Hopkinton, Mass.

FROM THE ABOVE ILLUSTRATION, carefully engraved by our artist direct from a photograph of the gun, you can get a general idea of the outline appearance and construction of the gun. For detailed description see the first following page describing our $11.90 hammerless shotgun. Our own patent Globe Sight is free with this gun.

$10.90

OUR $1.00 OFFER AND 10 DAYS' FREE TRIAL PROPOSITION.

AS A GUARANTEE that any one of our Hopkinton Fire Arms Co.'s guns, which we offer at $10.90 to $14.90, are superior to any hammerless gun you can buy elsewhere at $25.00, we will, on receipt of $1.00, send any gun to any address by express, C. O. D., subject to examination. You can examine it at your express office and if found perfectly satisfactory then pay the express agent our price and express charges, less the $1.00 sent with order; and whether you send $1.00 with your order or cash in full, the gun will go to you with the understanding and agreement that you can give the gun ten days' trial, during which time you can put it to every test, a test as to target, penetration, long range and hard shooting, and, **if you do not find it the equal of any gun on the market, a better gun than you could buy elsewhere at $25.00, you can return the gun to us at our expense and we will immediately refund your money.** We advise sending cash in full with your order, since you save an extra express charge of 25 to 50 cents.

WITH THE EXCEPTION OF THE BARRELS this $10.90 hammerless gun is identically the same as the $11.90 gun, illustrated and described on the following page. The frame, action, stock, fore end, general finish, the entire mechanism is identical. On the following page we have illustrated and described the working parts; everything is described in detail, and from this description you can tell exactly what this, our $10.90 gun is.

THIS, OUR $10.90 GUN, has genuine blued armory steel barrels, both barrels bored from a solid bar of genuine armory steel, beautifully blued and finished, choke bored by the celebrated taper system; otherwise the gun is exactly the same as the gun illustrated and described on the full page following. This, our $10.90 gun, has genuine blued armory steel barrels, our $11.90 gun has genuine laminated steel barrels, and our $14.90 gun has genuine Damascus steel barrels. In determining whether you wish this gun at $10.90, $11.90 or the $14.90 Hopkinton breech loading hammerless shotgun, you have only to determine whether you want armory steel barrels, laminated steel barrels or genuine Damascus steel barrels. These guns come in 12-gauge, 30 or 32-inch barrels; weight, 7¾ to 8 pounds. **Every gun is guaranteed, bored for smokeless or black powder, and combines every up to date feature of all other hammerless guns that sell at four to five times the price.** If you buy one of these guns and give it ten days' trial and are not perfectly satisfied, you can return it to us at our expense and we will immediately refund your money.

THIS FACTORY is equipped with every known labor saving gun making automatic machine. The material comes into our factory in the rough—the steel barrel stock is received by the carload direct from the rolling mills in solid bars of steel, the walnut for stocks and fore ends comes to us direct from the saw mills in rough lumber in carload lots. Thus different from nearly all manufacturers who buy nearly all their parts in a finished or semi-finished state and pay several manufacturers' profits, every piece that goes into one of our guns goes into our factory in the original rough state, and through our hundreds of automatic machines is made, shaped and finished as you see it in the finished gun. **Large as our Hopkinton factory is (one of the largest in the United States), we have there practically no office expense,** since the entire output comes to us here, no traveling salesmen, no bad accounts, no advertising or exhibition expenses, no high salaried officers. Every employe in our factory is a producer. The cost of the gun to us in our factory is actually reduced to the cost of a certain number of pounds of steel in the rough at so much per pound, a certain amount of lumber for stocks and fore ends based on so much per thousand feet, with our pay roll expense added, a pay roll simplified and reduced by the aid of every known gun making automatic machine, and as a result, **we furnish you our Hopkinton Fire Arms Company line of Hammerless Double Barrel Breech Loading Shotguns at $10.90, $11.90 and $14.90, according to grade of barrels,** guaranteeing the guns in every way superior to any hammerless double barrel gun you can buy elsewhere at $25.00 or less.

You really cannot afford to buy a hammer breech loading shotgun when you can get all the advantages, all the additional safety, the advantage of rapid firing (every time you open the gun you cock the hammers), and all modern perfection in the hammerless gun for only $10.90.

LOOK AT ANY OTHER LINE OF GUNS, examine any other catalogue, go to any gun store in America, and for like quality you will find they will ask you at least $10.00 more for a hammerless gun than for a hammer gun; but with our facilities in our Hopkinton factory we eliminate all this $10.00 difference and more and give you for $10.90, under our guarantee, a better hammerless shotgun than you can buy elsewhere for $25.00.

No. 6C10 Made in 12-gauge only, 30 or 32-inch barrels, 7¾ to 8 pounds weight. Price, including our Globe Sight..**$10.90**
Weight, packed for shipment, 14 pounds.

LOADED SHELLS, $1.29 PER 100. SEE PAGE 316.

$14.90 BUYS OUR GENUINE TWO-BLADE DAMASCUS STEEL BARREL HAMMERLESS DOUBLE BARREL BREECH LOADING SHOTGUN.

THIS HAMMERLESS DOUBLE BARREL BREECH LOADING SHOTGUN, made by the Hopkinton Fire Arms Company, of Hopkinton, Mass., furnished complete with our highest grade genuine Damascus steel barrels for only $14.90, we guarantee the equal of any hammerless double barrel breech loading shotgun you can buy elsewhere at $30.00 to $40.00.

$14.90 barely covers the cost of material and labor in our own factory at Hopkinton, Mass., a factory where, as before explained, all overhead expenses, common to other manufacturers, have been eliminated, a factory where only the raw material and labor enters into the cost of the gun, and to this cost only our one small percentage of profit is added, which makes the price $14.90.

THIS SPECIAL $14.90 PRICE for a Damascus steel barrel hammerless shotgun is made possible only by running our factory to its fullest capacity every working day in the year and turning out the largest number of guns possible to build in every one of the 300 days of the year, and all the advantages we have at this factory are given to you at these special prices.

YOU CANNOT AFFORD to pay $8.00 to $20.00 for a hammer breech loading shotgun when you can buy this line of high grade guaranteed hammerless shotguns for only $10.90 to $14.90, according to grade of barrels used, for in the hammerless gun you have safety of action, rapidity of firing (every time you open the gun you cock the hammers), freedom from projecting hammers and modern construction that you can get in no other hammerless GUN AT LESS THAN TWO OR THREE TIMES THE PRICE.

No. 6C14

For detailed description as to construction, working parts, safety brake, frame, stock, finish and everything, see following page. The guns are identical excepting as to barrels.

THE ABOVE ILLUSTRATION, engraved from a photograph, gives you a general idea of the appearance of this, our highest grade genuine Damascus steel barrel hammerless breech loading shotgun, of the Hopkinton Fire Arms Co.'s make, of Hopkinton, Mass., a factory we own, control and operate.

OUR 10 DAYS' FREE TRIAL OFFER.

AS A GUARANTEE that this gun will please you and that you will find it better than any hammerless gun you could buy elsewhere at two to three times the price, as a guarantee that you would not trade it for any two hammer breech loading shotguns that you could buy elsewhere at the same price, as a guarantee that you will find it in quality of material, workmanship and finish, in long range killing quality and penetration, pattern and outline, in all the new, up to date features and in every way entirely satisfactory, you can send us your order for this gun—either enclose our price, or $1.00, balance payable after received—**you can take the gun home, you can give it ten days' trial, and if you are not satisfied in every way you can return the gun to us at our expense, and we will immediately refund your money, together with any express charges paid by you.**

THE DAMASCUS BARRELS used on this, our $14.90 gun, are the highest grade Damascus steel barrels used in our factory. They are beautifully finished, as the illustration will give you some idea, they are taper choke bored by the celebrated taper system, bored for smokeless or black powder; they are in quality of material, workmanship, finish and in every way equal to Damascus barrels that are used in many factories on hammerless shotguns that sell at from $50.00 to $100.00. These barrels are the finest Damascus steel barrels we make, made on the basis of the actual cost of material and labor, and we give you the benefit of this cost to us in our special $14.90 price for this gun.

THIS GUN is identically the same as the gun illustrated and described on the following page and the one illustrated and described at the top of this page, excepting only in the barrels, this gun having our highest grade genuine Damascus steel barrels, while our $10.90 gun has blued armory steel barrels and our $11.90 has our highest grade laminated steel barrels.

WHILE WE ARE HEADQUARTERS for double barrel breech loading hammer shotguns and can give you greater value in a hammer shotgun than you can get elsewhere, and while we make thousands of single barrel hammer and hammerless breech loading shotguns in our own factory, and notwithstanding we are the only importers of Belgian guns in America, selling direct to the consumer, one of the largest buyers in America of Belgian guns and can furnish you a foreign made gun at a very much lower price than you could buy elsewhere, if you are in want of a shotgun we would especially recommend **that you buy either our $10.90, $11.90 or $14.90 Hopkinton Fire Arms Co.'s Hammerless Double Barrel Breech Loading Shotgun,** as illustrated and described on these two pages, for in any one of these three guns you get the greatest gun value possible to give, you get a gun that we guarantee in every way better than any hammerless gun you can buy elsewhere at two or three times the price, and if you do not find it so after giving it ten days' thorough trial, comparing it with guns made and sold by others at two to three times our price, you are at liberty to return the gun to us at our expense and we will immediately refund your money.

These guns come in 12-gauge only, 30 or 32-inch Damascus steel barrels, weight, 7¾ to 8 pounds; perfect in outline, perfect in finish, superior to any Damascus barrel hammerless gun on the market sold at $30.00 to $40.00. Weight, packed for shipment, about 14 pounds.

No. 6C14 Price, 12-gauge, 30 or 32-inch barrels; weight, 7¾ to 8 pounds, including our Globe Sight..**$14.90**

OUR STRICTLY AMERICAN HAMMERLESS SHOTGUN, MANUFACTURED FOR US BY HOPKINTON FIRE ARMS CO., HOPKINTON, MASS.

AT $11.90 IT IS THE WORLD'S WONDER.

$11.90 buys the now justly celebrated, high grade, 12-gauge, Chicago Long Range Wonder, Double Barrel Breech Loading Hammerless Shotgun, as illustrated hereon, a double barrel, hammerless gun, which in gun making is indeed the "World's Wonder."

OUR OWN PATENT GLOBE SIGHT FURNISHED FREE WITH THIS SHOTGUN.

OUR GLOBE SIGHT is a wonderful invention, for it makes possible more accurate and far more rapid wing shooting than would otherwise be possible. Can be quickly put on or taken off from any gun. When aimed at a bird on the wing (flying ever so fast) it defines a big circle, and when the bird appears within that circle (as it will, even if you are a very poor shot), pull the trigger and you kill the bird every time. THIS SIGHT DOUBLES THE VALUE OF ANY SHOTGUN, but we furnish it free with this gun and all other shotguns.

YOU CANNOT ESTIMATE THE VALUE OF OUR PATENT GLOBE SIGHT.

We do not sell this Sight. We give it free with our guns.

Don't Buy a Gun Without It.

HOW A $11.90 PRICE IS MADE POSSIBLE.

The manager of our gun department being convinced that high grade hammerless shotguns, such as are usually offered, were being sold at prices unreasonably high, conceived the idea of establishing a strictly up to date modernized gun factory of our own, where a high grade gun, embodying all the good points of other high grade guns could be made and offered to our customers at a price that would barely cover the cost to make and leave us our one small percentage of profit. To accomplish this we secured as manager of our gun factory one of the best gun makers in America, a gentleman who has for years been in charge of several of the best gun and revolver factories in this country We also secured the services of his two sons, expert gun machinists, gun and gun toolmakers. These three gentlemen, the father and two sons in charge, selected and had built for our factory the very highest types of gun making machinery, machines built, with marked improvements of their own over the machines employed by other gun factories. Ample time was taken for the making of all special tools, dies, patterns, jigs, chucks, gauges, etc., everything essential to the accurate making and finishing of every part of the gun was completed and perfected before any start was made to get out guns. All this machinery, all necessary tools and appliances were perfectly placed in one of the most modern gun plants in this country. A competent corps of selected mechanics, the best men picked from the best factories, where the father and two sons had formerly been in charge, were engaged and detailed to take charge of, operate and make the different parts that go into our $11.90 LONG RANGE WONDER so that when the factory was opened for the production of the Long Range Wonder, every piece came out with a nicety and perfectness of shape and finish to be found only on the highest grades of guns made, a gun with a general outline, weight, shape, proportion, dimensions, style, finish, fit, strength, durability, long and hard range shooting, simplicity of action such as can be equaled only by the most expensive guns on the market.

TAPER CHOKE BORED.

$11.90

ABOUT THE SAFETY OF HAMMERLESS GUNS.

Many hunters who have always used hammer guns are under the impression that hammerless guns are dangerous. We would like to say in regard to this that hammerless guns are just as safe as hammer guns, in fact they may be considered safer for it is possible to lock a hammerless gun by the safety slide so that it is absolutely impossible to pull off the hammers, whereas with a hammer gun it has often happened that when the hammer was at half cock something coming in contact with the hammer has discharged a shell accidently. This is not possible with a hammerless gun, for the hammer is concealed within the frame, and it is impossible for it to come in contact with anything. Remember every time you open a hammerless gun you cock it and it is ready to shoot.

Illustration showing the action of our Chicago Long Range Wonder.

E	is the safety slide.	M	is the left trigger.
F	is the top lever.	N	is the right trigger.
G	is the top lever spring.	O	is the guard.
H	is the main spring.	P	is the sear.
I	is the safety guide.	Q	is the hammer.
K	is the safety rocker.	R	is the cocking lever.
J	is the sear spring.	S	is the stock.
L	is the trigger spring screw.		

AT $11.90 we know we are offering a hammerless gun that once seen, you would have no other. If you are about to select a cheap foreign made gun at $10.00 to $20.00, a single barrel gun at $5.00 to $15.00 or a high priced gun at $30.00 to $50.00, and could first see our Hammerless Long Range Wonder at $11.90, you would instantly accept this gun in preference to any other gun made.

BUILT IN OUR OWN FACTORY

under the direct supervision of one of the most skilled gun makers in America, utilizing the highest types of automatic gun making machinery, buying only the highest grades of raw gun material, we produce the finished hammerless, double barrel shotgun as illustrated, at a net shop or factory cost that enables us to undersell almost any other maker by half, and quote the astonishingly low price of $11.90.

The $11.90 LONG RANGE WONDER

is a hammerless gun that must be seen to be appreciated, a gun that is seldom equaled even by the most expensive guns, in its perfect proportion, in its beautiful case hardened finish, in all those lines so much appreciated by the lover of a fine hammerless shotgun.

ON RECEIPT OF $1.00 we will send this gun to any address by express C. O. D., subject to examination, balance of $10.90 and express charges to be paid after the gun is received and found in every way satisfactory. We, however, recommend that you send cash in full with your order and save the small extra charge on a C. O. D. shipment. Nearly all of our customers send cash in full with their orders, as every gun goes out under our binding guarantee for quality, and if you do not find it the greatest gun value you have ever seen, return it to us at our expense of express charges both ways and we will return your money.

THIS ILLUSTRATION which is engraved from a photograph taken direct from our $11.90 Chicago Long Range Wonder, will give you some idea of the appearance of this handsome gun, but it must be seen and compared with other hammerless shotguns to appreciate the value we are giving.

DETAILED DESCRIPTION.

BARRELS. We furnish this gun with either blued steel at $10.90, genuine twist or laminated steel barrels at $11.90, or genuine Damascus barrels at $14.90, as desired. See the preceeding page for description and prices of blued steel and Damascus.

THE TWIST OR LAMINATED STEEL BARRELS we use in these guns are the highest grade of genuine laminated steel, and should not be compared with the many imitations and so called laminated steel barrels that are not safe for high explosive powders. Our barrels are made for the highest explosive gun powders used, such as white or nitro powder. The Damascus barrels are extra high grade, beautifully finished. The method of making Damascus barrels is illustrated and described on another page. These barrels are all beautifully browned and given an extra high finish. They are the highest strength barrels of the kind made, and are made with handsome heavy matted rib, tapering from breech to muzzle, as found only on the most expensive guns made. The matting is especially fine, of neat design. The rib is extra heavy, and beautifully finished. The barrels are made with a strong Edwards extension rib. They are taper choke bored, by the celebrated Taper system, to insure the strongest long range shooting qualities, the best possible target, the highest possible penetration, and being made in the proper proportion of heft at the butt, the minimum of recoil is obtained. The barrels are flatted at the breech with a genuine flat water table, found only on the most expensive guns made. They have a very heavy self locking steel lug, the strongest fore end lug used on any gun made.

FRAME. The frame is made of the best quality of decarbonized steel. It is thoroughly machined and accurately fitted, beautifully case hardened, and made especially strong at the points where the recoil acts in order to insure perfect safety. In design it is one of the handsomest hammerless shotgun frames made, smooth, symmetrical, strong at every part, perfect fitting and highly polished.

ACTION. This includes the locking, cocking safety double lever, the concealed hammers, sears, triggers and main spring of the mechanism with which the gun is operated, and these parts are made from the very best material procurable. Positive, accurate, yet simple in construction, made interchangeable so that if the parts should break (which rarely happens) they can be immediately replaced at a very slight expense. The action will, in simplicity of construction, strength, durability, in finish and every essential feature, compare favorably with the action furnished on the highest priced hammerless shotguns made.

STOCK. The stock is handsomely shaped, pistol grip, handsomely checkered in a neat design, fancy checkered butt plate. The stock is made from carefully seasoned selected walnut, hand finished and hand polished, and fitted to the gun by one of the best gun stock fitters in the country.

FORE END. The fore end is made from carefully selected walnut, handsomely finished and polished, beautifully checkered in a neat design, made with a special patent spring fastener.

SAFETY. We offer in our $11.90 Long Range Wonder Hammerless Gun one of the best safety devices used on any gun. It is positive and automatic in its action and renders an accident next to impossible, as the gun always stands on safe when loaded, unless pushed forward ready to shoot. Standing on safe the triggers are locked and the gun cannot be discharged. By a very ingenious mechanical device, we feel we have the best automatic safety made.

GENERAL FINISH. This gun is not only honestly built from the best material procurable, by skilled makers, but in finish you will find it has none of the ear marks of cheapness common to hammerless guns that sell for from $20.00 to $30.00, on the contrary, in finish it is given all the appearance of a high priced hammerless gun such as sells at $50.00 and upwards. The beautiful browning effected on the barrel, the case hardening of the frame and trigger guards, bringing out a clear handsome mottled effect unequaled by any other maker; the high finish given to stock and fore end, the artistically finished checkering, the taper extension rib (a special mark of high grade) and the generally well proportioned outlines of the gun throughout gives you in this gun at $11.90 all the show and style, as well as all the essential features, everything that you would get in a hammerless shotgun that cost three times the money.

SHOOTING QUALITIES. This all essential point has been the foundation from which the manufacturer has built this gun up, to furnish a gun that would not shoot loose, that would be the equal of any gun made for durability and a gun that could be relied upon for close, hard shooting at long range, and one in which white or nitro powder could be used as safely as the regular black powder. This gun has been built on lines to insure all this in the highest degree. The barrels are made gauged and bored (choke bored by the celebrated Taper system) to effect the best possible target, the longest range that it is possible for white or black powder to throw shot, and no matter what make or what price you may pay for a gun you will get no gun that will shoot stronger or better.

WEIGHT, LENGTH, GAUGE, ETC. These guns are MADE IN 12-GAUGE ONLY. They can be furnished in no other gauge. They are made in 30 or 32-inch barrels as desired, and can be furnished in weights ranging from 7¾ to 8 pounds, as desired. In ordering be sure to state length of barrel and weight wanted.

ABOUT BROKEN PARTS OR REPAIRS. While this gun is built with a view of making repairs or replacements unnecessary, in case by accident or otherwise, any piece or part should get broken or lost, we wish to say that from our factory we can at any time to come furnish at a comparatively small expense to the purchaser any piece or part to replace any part that may break or get lost. This should be quite an object to the purchaser of a gun, for it may mean the saving to you of quite an expense at some future date.

AN ALL PURPOSE GUN. We are manufacturing this gun to meet the general demand throughout the country for a thoroughly reliable, high grade hammerless all purpose double barrel breech loading shotgun, and it is suitable for all kinds of game that can be hunted with any shotgun—geese, ducks, prairie chickens, partridges, squirrels, quails, snipe, rabbits—in fact it is an all around general purpose, high grade, up to date guaranteed, double barrel, hammerless, breech loading shotgun.

We make the price, $11.90, a very small percentage above the actual cost to produce in our own factory, the cost of material and labor, for we must depend upon our customers, upon the illustrations and descriptions given on this page to consume the entire output of our factory.

We have at present a capacity of about 35 guns a day, or 10,500 a year, and to insure our selling every gun we make we have really made the price ridiculously low, namely, $11.90. Understand, you send us your order, we taking all the risk, guaranteeing the gun to you in every respect, guaranteeing it to reach you in the same perfect condition it leaves us, and further, if not found perfectly satisfactory to you, to be returned to us at our expense of express charges both ways, we to return your money at once.

EVERY LITTLE POINT is studied in this gun to make it in all essential points the equal of any gun made, regardless of price, a shotgun we can recommend above all others.

No. 6C16 Chicago Long Range Wonder, genuine laminated steel barrels, 12-gauge, 30 or 32-inch barrels, 7¾ to 8 pounds.
Price.. $11.90

$1.29 PER HUNDRED BUYS HIGHEST GRADE BLACK POWDER LOADED SHELLS MADE. SEE PAGE 316.

L. C. SMITH HAMMERLESS BREECH LOADING SHOTGUNS.

MADE BY THE HUNTER ARMS CO., FULTON, N. Y.

OUR BINDING GUARANTEE. Every gun which we sell is covered by our binding guarantee, which means that if any piece or part gives out by reason of defective material or workmanship, within one year, we will replace it free of charge. You may order any gun of us and if you do not find it satisfactory or as represented, you may return it to us at our expense of transportation charges both ways and we will immediately refund your money.

PRICES—The manufacturer fixes the selling price of these guns and will not allow us or any other house to sell them lower.

GENERAL DESCRIPTION. All L. C. Smith Hammerless Guns are full choke bored, have English walnut pistol grip stock, tapered matted rib, case hardened locks and frame, rubber butt plate, compensating extension rib and fore end and patent safety slide. OUR PATENT GLOBE SIGHT is furnished free with all Smith guns.

ARMOR STEEL BARRELS.

GLOBE SIGHT free with this gun.

BORED FOR NITRO POWDER.

This grade is fitted with armor steel barrels, full choke bored, no engraving.

No. 6C26 No. 00 grade, 12-gauge, 30 or 32-inch barrels; weight, 7½ to 8 pounds. Price........................$25.00

Weight, packed for shipment, about 15 pounds.

DAMASCUS BARRELS.

GLOBE SIGHT free with this gun.

BORED FOR NITRO POWDER.

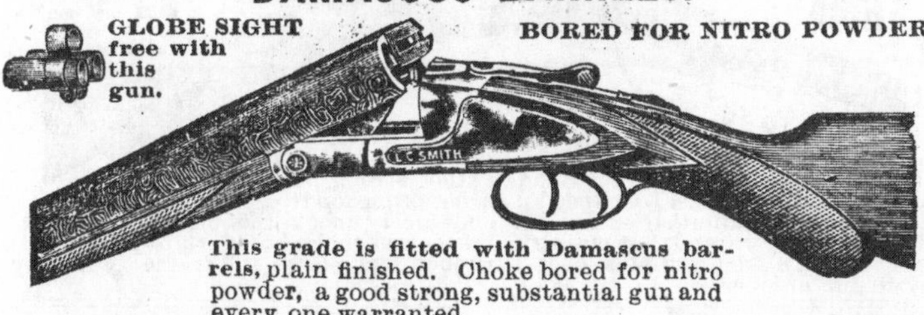

This grade is fitted with Damascus barrels, plain finished. Choke bored for nitro powder, a good strong, substantial gun and every one warranted.

No. 6C32 No. 0 grade, plain finish, not engraved, 12-gauge, 30 or 32-inch barrels; weight, 7½ to 8 pounds. Price........................$32.90

No. 6C36 No. 1 grade, plain finish, line engraving, 12-gauge, 30 or 32-inch barrels; weight, 7½ to 8 pounds. Price........................$42.00

Weight, packed for shipment, about 15 pounds.

OUR L. C. SMITH HAMMER GUNS.

We have had numerous inquiries within the last year for the celebrated L. C. Smith Hammer Guns, and are now prepared to furnish them in the following specified grades.

The L. C. Smith Hammer Guns have the patent cross bolt locks, top snap action, compensating fore end, rebounding bar locks, circular hammers, best American walnut stock and fore end, checkered pistol grip, fancy butt plate, case hardened frame, and are choke bored for black or smokeless powder.

These guns are too well known and too popular to require an exhaustive description, for you probably know the L. C. Smith guns have as many friends among the shooters as any guns made.

Globe Sight free with this gun.

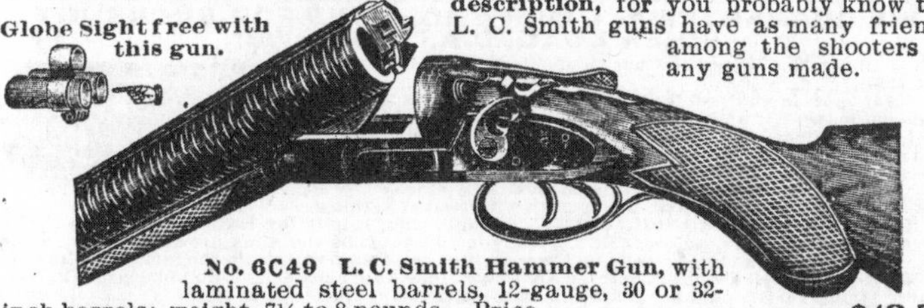

No. 6C49 L. C. Smith Hammer Gun, with laminated steel barrels, 12-gauge, 30 or 32-inch barrels; weight, 7½ to 8 pounds. Price........................$18.50

No. 6C51 L. C. Smith Hammer Gun, with two-blade Damascus barrels, 12-gauge, 30 or 32-inch barrels; weight, 7½ to 8 pounds. Price............$23.00

Weight, packed for shipment, about 15 pounds.

REMINGTON NEW MODEL DOUBLE BARREL SHOTGUNS.

MANUFACTURED BY THE REMINGTON ARMS CO., ILION, N. Y.

WE GUARANTEE EVERY REMINGTON GUN to be free from defective material and workmanship and if any piece or part gives out by reason of defect within one year we will replace it free of charge. Order one of these guns and if you do not find it satisfactory and exactly as represented, return it to us at our expense and we will refund your money.

No. 3 GRADE REMINGTON DOUBLE BARREL SHOTGUN.

GLOBE SIGHT free with this Gun.

$23.00

DESCRIPTION. All No. 3 grade Remington double barrel shotguns have two-blade Damascus barrels, matted rib, double bolt locks, extension rib, rebounding hammers, checkered pistol grip stock and fore end, top snap action, choke bored on the latest improved system for nitro or black powder, frame beautifully case hardened. All parts are interchangeable. All hammer guns have Deeley & Edge patent fore end.

Catalogue Number	Grade	Style of Barrels	Gauge	Length Barrels	Weight	Price
6C67	No. 3	Damascus	12	30 or 32 in.	7½ to 8 lbs.	$23.00
6C67½	No. 3	Damascus	10	32 in.	9 to 9¾ lbs.	

Shipping weight, about 14 pounds.

REMINGTON DOUBLE BARREL HAMMERLESS SHOTGUNS.

Our Patent Globe Sight is furnished FREE with this Gun.

The K grade has patent snap fore end. All the other grades have Purdy fore end.

The frames of K, A and AE grades are plain finished and case hardened. Made from best quality drop forgings and possess high class workmanship. All Hammerless Guns have the nitro bite extension rib, handsomely matted.

Cat. No.	Grade	Style of Barrels	Style of Extractor	Gauge	Length Barrels	Weight, Lbs.	Price
6C66	K	Blued Steel	Regular	12	30 inch	7¼ to 8	$21.50
6C68	A	2-Blade Damascus	Regular	12	30 or 32	7½ to 8	30.00

Shipping weight, about 14 pounds when packed.

Allow two to four weeks' time on guns made to special order. If made according to your order they cannot be returned under any circumstances. We do not charge for boxing guns.

ITHACA NEW MODEL HAMMER SHOTGUNS.

MANUFACTURED BY THE ITHACA GUN CO., ITHACA, N. Y.

OUR BINDING GUARANTEE. Every Ithaca gun is covered by a binding guarantee, by the terms and conditions of which if any piece or part gives out by reason of defect in material or workmanship within one year, we will replace or repair it free of charge. You may order one of these guns and if you do not find it satisfactory or as represented, return it to us at our expense of transportation charges and we will refund your money.

THE MANUFACTURER fixes the selling price of these guns and will not allow us or any other house to sell them lower.

ILLUSTRATION SHOWING THE HEAVY BREECH OF ITHACA GUNS.

This illustration is intended to show our customers the double thick breech of Ithaca Guns. All guns made for us by the Ithaca Gun Co. have this reinforced breech and are made extra strong for any proper load of black or nitro powder. We charge you nothing for boxing guns for shipping.

ITHACA HAMMER GUN.

OUR GLOBE SIGHT free with every Ithaca Gun.

Illustration of No. 6C75.

GENERAL DESCRIPTION. All of our Ithaca guns are made from the best grade of selected barrels, nicely case hardened breech, beautiful matted rib, top snap action, selected walnut stock, extension rib, blued mountings, compensating patent fore end, and choke bored for trap and long range shooting. The shooting qualities of the Ithaca guns cannot be surpassed and for penetration and long range shooting are equal to any guns regardless of price. All are bored for black and nitro powder and all barrels have heavy breech.

Our Patent Globe Sight is furnished free with all Ithaca guns.

Catalogue Number	Grade	Style of Barrels	Gauge	Length Barrels	Weight	Price
6C75	A	Stub Twist	12	30 or 32 in.	7½ to 8 lbs.	$19.00
6C75½	A	Stub Twist	10	32 in.	9 to 9¾ lbs.	
6C77	AA	Damascus	12	30 or 32 in.	7½ to 8 lbs.	21.00
6C77½	AA	Damascus	10	32 in.	9 to 9¾ lbs.	

Shipping weight, when packed, about 14 pounds.

No. 1 AND 2 GRADE REMINGTON DOUBLE BARREL SHOTGUNS.

GLOBE SIGHT free with this Gun.

$17.50

Illustration of No. 1 Grade.

Our Patent Globe Sight is furnished free with every Remington gun. This sight can be instantly adjusted to or taken from any gun and is a remarkable help in getting game if you are not an expert shot.

DESCRIPTION All No. 1 and No. 2 Grade Remington Double Barrel Shotguns have genuine armory steel barrels, or genuine twist barrels at the following prices, matted rib, rebounding hammers, checkered pistol grip stock and fore end, top snap action, choke bored on the latest improved system for nitro or black powder, frame beautifully case hardened. All parts are interchangeable and Deeley & Edge patent fore end.

Always state the length of barrels wanted.

Catalogue Number	Grade	Style of Barrels	Gauge	Length of Barrels	Weight	Price
6C63	No. 1	Armory Steel	12	30 inches	7½ to 8 lbs.	$17.50
6C63¼	No. 1	Armory Steel	10	32 inches	9 to 9¾ lbs.	18.50
6C65	No. 2	Twist	12	30 inches	7¼ to 8 lbs.	21.50

Weight, packed for shipment, about 14 pounds.

ITHACA HAMMERLESS SHOTGUNS.

Globe Sight free with this gun.

ALL BORED FOR NITRO OR BLACK POWDER.

$18.00 TO $29.50

No. 6C76

THIS GRADE has fine English stub twist barrels American walnut stock, with checkered pistol grip, checkered compensating fore end, nitro locking extension rib. Top snap break, the strongest break made, choke bored for black or nitro powder and long range shooting, fancy tapered and matted rib. A good, strong, honest gun in every way. The Field gun is practically the same gun in every way, except it is fitted with smokeless steel barrels instead of twist barrels and has a half pistol grip. The smokeless steel barrels are bored and guaranteed for all proper loads of smokeless powder. The No. 1¼ grade is the same as the No. 1 grade, but fitted with Damascus barrels.

Catalogue Number	Grade	Style of Barrels	Gauge	Length Barrels	Weight	Price
6C74	Field	Smokeless Steel	12	30 or 32 in.	7¼ to 8 lbs.	$18.00
6C74½	Field	Smokeless Steel	10	32 in.	9 to 9¾ lbs.	
6C76	No. 1	Stub Twist	12	30 or 32 in.	7¼ to 8 lbs.	24.00
6C78	No. 1½	Damascus	12	30 or 32 in.	7¼ to 8 lbs.	29.50

Weight, packed for shipment, about 14 pounds.

ABOUT SAFETY OF HAMMERLESS GUNS. Many hunters who have always used hammer guns are under the impression that hammerless guns are dangerous. We would like to say in regard to this, that hammerless guns are just as safe as hammer guns; in fact, they may be considered safer, for it is possible to lock a hammerless gun by the safety slide so that it is absolutely impossible to pull off the hammers; whereas, with a hammer gun, it has often happened that when the hammer was at half cock, something coming in contact with the hammer has discharged a shell accidentally. This is not possible with a hammerless gun, for the hammer is concealed within the frame, and it is impossible for it to come in contact with anything.

NEW IMPROVED BAKER BREECH LOADING SHOTGUNS.

MADE BY THE BAKER GUN AND FORGING CO., BATAVIA, N. Y.

OUR GUARANTEE. We guarantee these guns to be free from defects in material and workmanship, and if any piece or part gives out by reason of defective material or workmanship, we will replace it free of charge within one year. Our patent Globe Sight is furnished free with every Baker gun.

SHOULD YOU ORDER one of these guns you do so with the understanding that if it is not perfectly satisfactory you may return it at our expense and we will refund your money.

PRICES—The manufacturer makes the selling price of these guns and will not allow us nor any other house to sell them lower.

Our patent Globe Sight free with this gun.

$22.00

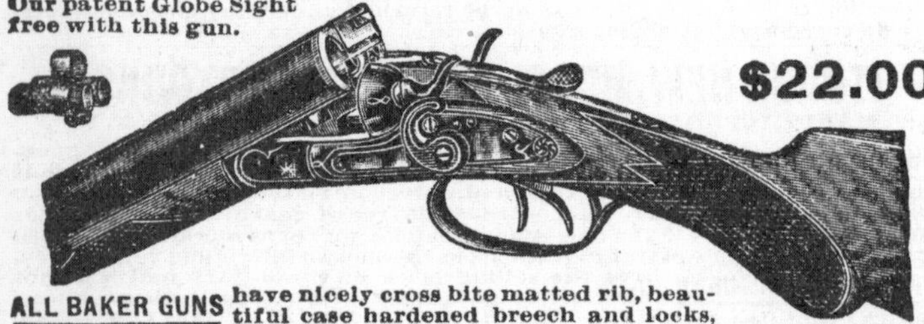

ALL BAKER GUNS have nicely cross bite matted rib, beautiful case hardened breech and locks, selected walnut pistol grip stocks, top snap action, compensating patent fore end, and each and every gun is choke bored and thoroughly tested before leaving the works, and no gun is allowed to go out that will not make a good target. All are bored for black or nitro powder, and the hammerless guns have a patent safety slide.

Catalogue Number	Grade	Style of Barrel	Gauge	Length of Barrels	Weight of Guns	Price
6C83	Hammer	Twist	12	30 or 32 in.	7⅛ to 8 lbs.	$22.00
6C83¼	Hammer	Twist	10	32 inches	9 to 9¾ lbs.	

NEW BAKER HAMMERLESS GUNS.

Catalogue Number	Grade	Style of Barrel	Gauge	Length of Barrels	Weight of Guns	Finish	Price
6C86	Leader	Twist	12	30 inch	7¼ to 8 lbs.	Plain	$22.00
6C88	Model B	Twist	12	30 inch	7¼ to 8 lbs.	Engr'd	31.00
6C90	Model A	Damascus	12	30 inch	7¼ to 8 lbs.	Engr'd	36.50

Weight, packed for shipment, about 14 pounds.

KNICKERBOCKER HAMMERLESS GUN, $16.75.

Made by the American Gun Co. of New York, factory in Connecticut.

12-Gauge Only.

Bored for Nitro or Black Powder.

Our Patent Globe Sight is FREE with this GUN.

THIS IS THE LATEST HAMMERLESS SHOTGUN ON THE MARKET. It is made from the best material that money can buy—made on fine lines, balances perfectly and is a neat, attractive, serviceable gun.

DESCRIPTION. The Knickerbocker is fitted with top snap break, laminated steel barrels, strong bar locks, beautifully matted L-shape Edwards' extension rib, double bolt locks, straight grained walnut stock and fore end handsomely checkered, Deeley & Edge patent fore end, full pistol grip capped with ornamental rosette, choke bored for close shooting; a good, sound, honest, hammerless gun. Weight, packed for shipment, about 14 pounds.

No. 6C100 Fitted with Laminated steel barrels, in 12-gauge, 30 or 32-inch barrels. 7¼ to 7¾ pounds. Price........................**$16.75**

No. 6C102 The same Gun fitted with genuine two-blade Damascus barrels, 12-gauge, 30 or 32-inch barrels, 7½ to 7¾ pounds. Price........**$18.25**

LOADED SHELLS $1.29 PER 100. SEE PAGE 316.

BARGAINS IN PARKER HAMMERLESS GUNS.

Catalogue Number	Grade	Style of Barrel	Gauge	Length of Barrels	Weight of Guns	Price
6C114	G. H.	Damascus	12 12	30 in. 32 in.	7½ to 7¾ lbs. 7¾ lbs.	$48.75
6C116	P. H.	Twist	12 12	30 in. 32 in.	7½ to 8 lbs. 8¼ lbs.	39.75
6C118	V. H.	Steel	16	30 in.	7 lbs.	30.75

OUR LINE OF IMPORTED DOUBLE BARREL SHOTGUNS.

OUR LINE OF IMPORTED GUNS is very extensive and embraces the products of some of the best European makers. We recognize no competition in this line, and a comparison of our prices with those of other houses will convince you that we have none. We aim to handle only thoroughly first class goods, guns that will stand service and give the best satisfaction, and every gun we offer is warranted in every respect.

In our line of imported guns we would call your attention to our Double Barrel Breech Loader, our T. Barker, our Special Greener Action Guns, and our high grade machine guns. We are in a position to make you prices on this class of goods at least 25 per cent below any competition, and if you will favor us with your order we know you will be so well pleased that you will not only give us your future orders, but recommend our house to your friends.

HOW OUR IMPORTED GUNS ARE TESTED BY THE BELGIAN GOVERNMENT.

All our imported guns are tested by the government of Belgium in the following manner: After the barrels are first made and before they are brazed together, reamed or chambered, they are sent to the government proof house where a plug is screwed into the breech of the barrel and it is loaded with 11 drams of good quality black powder and a bullet weighing 1 ounce. After this test they are brazed together and tested again with 7 drams of good black powder and a bullet weighing 1 ounce. After this second test is made, the frame, or breech, is fitted to the barrels and they are tested for the third time with 6½ drams of powder and 1⅛ ounces of shot. You will see that the test is very severe and each and every Belgian gun which we sell, from the cheapest to the best, is put through this same test, so if you buy a Belgian gun of us you are assured that you are getting a gun which has been thoroughly tested for Sears, Roebuck & Co. with more powder and more shot than you can possibly put into a shell. In order to put such a heavy charge into the barrels the government must load from the muzzle and any gun you buy from us is safe, as you will see by the foregoing rigid tests.

OUR $6.35 BACK ACTION GUN.

AN IMPORTED EXTENSION RIB GUN.

10, 12 and 16-Gauge.

$6.35

Our Patent Globe Sight is FREE with this gun. We do not sell this SIGHT. We give it FREE with our guns.

GENERAL DESCRIPTION. This gun is fitted with top snap break, laminated steel finished barrels, made of best Raleigh steel, strong back action rebounding locks, L-shaped Edwards' extension rib, rebounding hammers, straight grain walnut stock and fore end nicely checkered, pistol grip stock, patent snap fore end, flat plain rib, left barrel choke bored, right barrel cylinder bored, nitro firing pins, case hardened lock plates and frame. Order by catalogue number.

Catalogue No.	Grade	Style of Barrels	Gauge	Length of Barrels	Weight	Price
6C237	No. 559	Laminat'd	12	30 or 32 in.	7¼ to 8 lbs.	$6.35
6C237¼	No. 559	steel	16	30 inches	6¾ to 7 lbs.	6.60
6C237½	No. 559	finished	10	32 inches	8¼ to 9¾ lbs.	6.85

Weight, packed for shipment, about 14 pounds.

RUSTED AND DAMAGED GUNS OR RIFLES. Do not return to us a gun, revolver or rifle which is rusted, pitted or has the finish worn off, for we have no way of selling these guns. If you have a gun, rifle or revolver which needs repairing first write us, fully describing the article and what is broken and we may be able to send you the part necessary, thus saving the express charges on the gun both ways.

OUR 10-CENT BOOKLET tells how to care for guns and rifles, how to prevent barrels from bursting, explains trajectory of rifles and gives much useful information to shooters. Send 10 cents and ask for our Booklet of Information to Shooters.

WE GUARANTEE ALL OUR SHOTGUNS FOR BUCKSHOT WHEN LOADED AS FOLLOWS:

This illustration shows how buckshot should be loaded in a shell.

1st—put in the powder; 2d—put in a card wad; 3rd—put in two felt wads; 4th—put in a layer of buckshot; 5th—a card wad, then another layer of buckshot and a card wad. Always put a card wad between each layer of buckshot and if you wish you may sprinkle sawdust around the buckshot or in cold weather you may use lard or paraffine around the buckshot instead of sawdust.

RULE FOR LOADING BUCKSHOT. The following rule is for Raymond shot which we have tested. You may use other shot, but if you do it must be the same size as Raymond, so the pellets will lie flat and not pile up on the wad, otherwise they will strain the muzzle of the gun.

A 12-gauge shell should take three No. 4 buck, four No. 6 buck or five No. 8 buckshot in each layer. Don't vary from this. Notice, these are all even numbers of buckshot.

A 10-gauge shell should take three No. 3 buck, four No. 5 buck or five No. 7 buckshot in each layer. Notice, they are all uneven numbers.

A 16-gauge shell should take three No. 5 buck or four No. 7 buckshot in each layer.

Don't try to use larger sizes or you may injure the barrel and we will not be responsible for same.

OUR HIGHLY ENGRAVED DIANA STYLE BREECH SHOTGUN. 30, 32 or 38-inch barrels.

30 or 32-inch barrels, **$7.95**

38-inch barrels, **$9.92**

We furnish our patent Globe Sight free with every shotgun. Doubles the value of any shotgun.

DESCRIPTION. This gun is fitted with top snap break, back action locks, two-blade Damascus finished barrels, Edwards' L-shaped extension rib, handsomely matted, rebounding circulars hammers, straight grained seasoned walnut stock and fore end nicely checkered, pistol grip stock, nitro firing pins, patent snap fore end, case hardened frame and lock plates, Diana style breech, the frame and locks being highly engraved, and the barrels are bored smooth and true to gauge for black or smokeless powder. The left barrel is choke bored and the right barrel cylinder bored. Always state length of barrel when you order.

Catalogue Number	Grade	Style of Barrels	Gauge	Length Barrels	Weight	Price
6C238	No. 569	Two-blade Da-	12	30 or 32 in.	7¼ to 8 lbs.	$7.95
6C239	No. 569	mascus finish	12	38 inches	8 to 8¼ lbs.	9.32

Weight, packed for shipment, about 14 pounds.

OUR CELEBRATED SAM HOLT GUNS, 10-GAUGE FOR $9.20, OR 12-GAUGE FOR $8.95.

Our patent Globe Sight furnished free with this gun.

For **$8.95** we offer you a 12-gauge genuine bar lock double barrel breech loader.

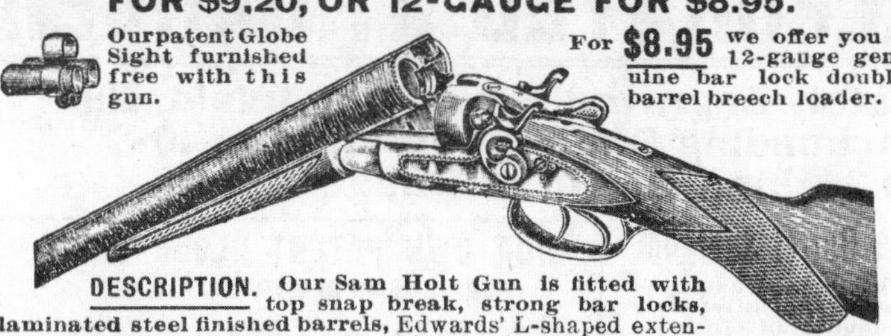

DESCRIPTION. Our Sam Holt Gun is fitted with top snap break, strong bar locks, laminated steel finished barrels, Edwards' L-shaped extension rib nicely fitted, rebounding circular hammers, straight grain well seasoned checkered stock and fore end, pistol grip stock, nitro firing pins, patent snap fore end, chase engraving on the locks, case hardened frame and lock plates, bored smooth and true to gauge for black or smokeless powder. The left barrel is choke bored and the right barrel is cylinder bored for field shooting. Always state length of barrel wanted in your order.

Catalogue Number	Grade	Style of Barrels	Gauge	Length Barrels	Weight	Price
6C247	No. 659	Laminated	12	30 or 32 in.	7½ to 8 lbs.	$8.95
6C247½	No. 659	Steel Finish	10	32 inches	8¾ to 9½ lbs.	9.20

Weight, packed for shipment, about 14 pounds.

THE CELEBRATED THOMAS BARKER DOUBLE BARREL BREECH LOADING SHOTGUN FOR $9.85.

10, 12, 16 AND 20-GAUGE.

Left Barrel Choke Bored.

Our Patent Globe Sight furnished free with this gun. Doubles the value of any shotgun for wing shooting.

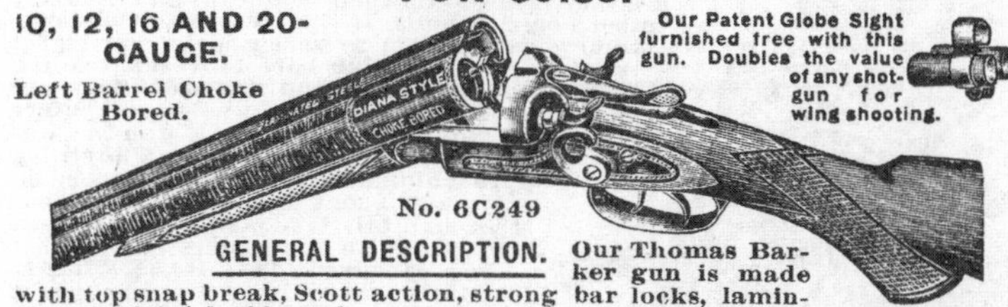

No. 6C249

GENERAL DESCRIPTION. Our Thomas Barker gun is made with top snap break, Scott action, strong bar locks, laminated steel finished barrels, extension rib beautifully matted, rebounding circular hammers, straight grained walnut stock and fore end nicely checkered, full pistol grip stock with shield inlaid, nitro firing pins, patent snap fore end, chased engraving on locks, case hardened frame and lock plates, left barrel full choke bored, right barrel cylinder bored; all barrels bored smooth and true to gauge. A wonder for the money and a gun that will shoot black or smokeless powder. Always state length of barrel wanted.

Catalogue No.	Grade	Style of Barrels	Gauge	Length of Barrels	Weight of Gun	Price
6C249	No. 659 MD	Lami-	12	30 or 32 in.	7½ to 8 lbs.	$ 9.85
6C249¼	No. 659 MD	nated	16	30 in.	6¾ to 7 lbs.	9.90
6C249½	No. 659 MD	Steel	20	30 in.	6¼ to 6¾ lbs.	9.95
6C249¾	No. 659 MD	Finish	10	32 in.	8¾ to 9¼ lbs.	10.15

Weight, packed for shipment, about 14 pounds.

OUR $10.65 IMPORTED DOUBLE BARREL BREECH LOADER, WITH ENGRAVED LOCKS.

OUR PATENT GLOBE SIGHT FURNISHED FREE WITH THIS GUN. Our sight adds many dollars value to the gun.

LOADED SHELLS $1.29 PER 100.

SEE PAGE 316.

No. 6C250

DETAILED DESCRIPTION. Our engraved lock gun is fitted with Scott action, top snap break, strong bar locks, two-blade Damascus finished barrels, rebounding circular hammers, straight grained well seasoned walnut stock and fore end nicely checkered, full pistol grip stock with inlaid shield, patent snap fore end, nitro firing pins, scroll engraving on the lock plates, case hardened frame and lock plates, bored smooth and true to gauge for black and smokeless powder, left barrel choke bored, right barrel cylinder bored, suitable for black or smokeless powder. Always mention length of barrel wanted.

Catalogue No.	Grade	Style of Barrels	Gauge	Length of Barrels	Weight of Gun	Price
6C250	No. 639 ME	2-Blade Damascus Finish	12	30 or 32 in.	7½ to 8 lbs.	$10.65

Weight, packed for shipment, about 14 pounds.

OUR COMBINATION SHOTGUN AND RIFLE, $15.00.

Our Globe Sight FREE with this gun.

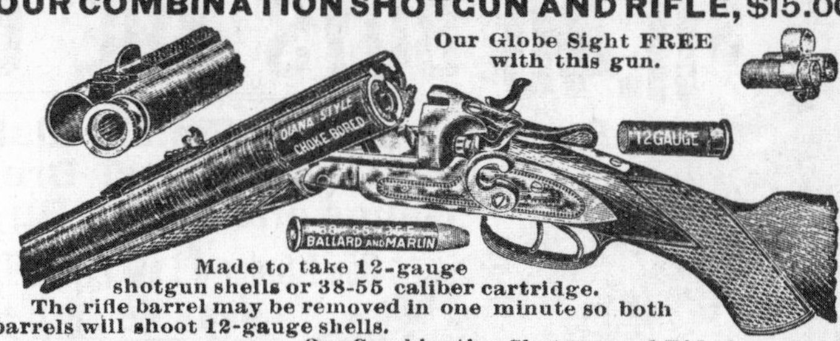

Made to take 12-gauge shotgun shells or 38-55 caliber cartridge. The rifle barrel may be removed in one minute so both barrels will shoot 12-gauge shells.

DETAILED DESCRIPTION. Our Combination Shotgun and Rifle is a new departure in this line, in that the rifle barrel is auxiliary and may be removed in a minute and both barrels may be used for shotgun shells. It is fitted with Scott action, top snap break, laminated steel finished barrels with Diana style breech. Strong bar rebounding locks, elevated matted and engine turned rib fitted with sporting rear and sporting front sight, Edwards' L-shape extension rib; rebounding circular hammers, straight grained walnut stock and fore end nicely checkered, full pistol grip with shield inlaid, patent snap fore end, nitro firing pins, left barrel choke bored, right barrel cylinder bored, case hardened forged frame and lock plates, suitable for birds and heavy game. The 38-55 cartridge is suitable for heavy game such as deer, moose, etc.

Catalogue No.	Caliber	Style of Barrels	Gauge	Length of Barrels	Weight of Gun	Price
6C259	38-55 C. F.	Laminat'd Steel Finish	12	30 in.	9 to 9¼ lbs.	$15.00

Weight, packed for shipment, about 14 pounds.

OUR HIGHLY ENGRAVED DIANA STYLE, DOUBLE BARREL BREECH LOADER FOR ONLY $9.98.

MADE IN 12-GAUGE ONLY.

12-GAUGE LOADED SHELLS. $1.29 per 100. See page 316.

Our Patent Globe Sight furnished free with this gun. Doubles the value of any shotgun for wing shooting.

No. 6C270

MINUTE DESCRIPTION. Our Diana Style Breech Gun is fitted with top snap break, laminated steel finished barrels, strong bar rebounding locks, L-shape Edwards' extension rib, rebounding circular hammers, imported walnut stock and fore end nicely checkered; full pistol grip with inlaid shield, patent snap fore end, nitro firing pins, flat matted rib, left barrel choke bored, right barrel cylinder bored; both barrels bored smooth and true to gauge for black and smokeless powder; case hardened forged frame and lock plates. A beautiful gun at a low price. Order by catalogue number and state length of barrels wanted.

Catalogue Number	Grade	Style of Barrels	Gauge	Length Barrels	Weight	Price
6C270	No. 839N	Damascus Finish	12	30 or 32 in.	7½ to 8 lbs.	$9.98

Weight, packed for shipment, about 14 pounds.

CELEBRATED GREENER ACTION BREECH LOADING SHOTGUN, $12.06.

12-GAUGE ONLY.

$12.06 BUYS A GREENER BOLT GUN

The barrels of this gun are made of Wilson's best steel.

Our Patent Globe Sight furnished free with this gun.

No. 6C271

DESCRIPTION of our Greener Action Cross Bolt Shotgun. It is fitted with Scott action top snap break, Damascus finished barrels, strongest bar action locks, with rebounding circular hammers, nicely matted extension rib with Greener action cross bolt in the extension; straight grained walnut stock and fore end nicely checkered; full pistol grip with inlaid shield, giving the grip a handsome appearance; patent snap fore end, scroll engraving on the lock plates, left barrel choke bored, right barrel cylinder bored for field shooting; bored smooth and true to gauge for black and smokeless powder. Order by catalogue number and state length of barrel wanted.

Catalogue Number	Grade	Style of Barrels	Gauge	Length Barrels	Weight	Price
6C271	No. 365	Damascus Finish	12	30 or 32 in.	7½ to 8 lbs.	$12.06

Weight, packed for shipment, about 14 pounds.

OUR CARVED STOCK IMPORTED DOUBLE BARREL BREECH LOADING SHOTGUN, $11.10.

Our Patent Globe Sight furnished free with this gun. Worth the price of the gun for wing shooting.

No. 6C257

Weight, packed for shipment, about 14 pounds.

DESCRIPTION. Our Carved Stock Shotgun is fitted with Scott action top snap break, bar locks. Damascus finished barrels with matted hexagon breech beautifully matted as shown in the illustration. Extension rib, Edwards' patent, rebounding circular hammers, straight grained walnut stock and fore end beautifully carved in leaf design, pistol grip stock, nitro firing pins, patent snap fore end, case hardened frame and lock plates, left barrel choke bored, right barrel cylinder bored, bored true to gauge for black or smokeless powder. Always mention length of barrels wanted.

Catalogue No.	Grade	Style of Barrels	Gauge	Length of Barrels	Weight of Gun	Price
6C257	669C	Damascus Finish	12	30 or 32 in.	7¼ to 7¾ lbs.	$11.10

$11.40 BUYS THE CELEBRATED T. BARKER

Royal Damascus Finish, Elaborately Engraved, Silver Dog Inlaid, Bar Lock, Double Barrel Breech Loading Shotgun, in 10, 12 or 16-Gauge and $13.35 Buys a 36-inch Barrel 12-Gauge Gun.

Loaded Shells $1.29 per 100. See page 316.

THIS HANDSOME GUN is gotten out especially for us, following our own detailed specifications, with a view of giving our customers a higher grade, handsomer and better finished shotgun than can possibly be had elsewhere at anything approaching the price.

A NUMBER OF GUNS have been gotten out by various makers in imitation of this, our celebrated T. Barker gun, but you will find any gun offered by any other house bearing the appearance of this our T. Barker Special, will suffer by comparison; in other words, if you will order this gun from us and then order any of the imitations offered by others, and will compare them side by side, you will find that they do not in any way compare with this

OUR SPECIAL T. BARKER GUN AT

$11.40

THE ROYAL DAMASCUS FINISHED BARRELS

are thoroughly reliable as to quality and have all the handsome appearance of the most expensive barrels made, and each barrel is branded on the rib, Royal Damascus. These barrels are made and bored especially for field shooting, the right barrel being cylinder bored for an open target, and the left barrel choke bored for a close target. The locks and frame are elaborately engraved; **the gun is pistol grip, the grip and fore end neatly checkered.** It is finished with a handsome German silver shield or medallion in the full pistol grip. In short, **the gun has been gotten out according to our own specifications on lines more up to date, handsomer, more modern and in every way better than anything shown by any maker.**

AT ANY PRICE APPROACHING OUR $11.40 PRICE.

Don't Order a Low Priced Double Barrel Shotgun.

WHILE WE SELL double barrel breech loading shotguns of the latest style as low as $6.25, and a number of others at prices lower than this **our celebrated T. Barker Royal Damascus finished gun,** we especially urge that you order one of our higher grade guns, either this, **our highest grade T. Barker Royal Damascus finish double barrel breech loader,** or one of our American Gun Company's high grade, double barrel, breech loading shotguns. You will be much better satisfied by selecting this or a higher grade gun. You will find such a selection much cheaper in the end. In the shooting qualities, wearing qualities and general satisfaction it pays to select one of our double barrel guns at from $11.40 and upward.

OUR OWN PATENT GLOBE SIGHT

FURNISHED FREE WITH THIS GUN.

This Globe Sight, which makes wing and fast shooting easy, a sight which can be quickly put on or taken off the gun, is furnished free with every T. Barker gun at $11.40. If you order this gun at $11.40 you will get with the gun, free of any cost, our own special patent Globe Sight as illustrated.

WHILE THE PROFIT IS THE SAME TO US, just our one small percentage of profit above the actual cost of material and labor, and the prices on all our guns are very much lower than you can buy from any other house, **wholly in the interest of our customers we urge you to select one of our higher grade guns, a double barrel breech loading shotgun at $11.40 and upward. You will get such gun value as was never before given, you will get such a gun as was never seen in your section at anything approaching the price,** and, remember, every gun is sent to you subject to your thorough test trial and approval, sent to you with the understanding that you can give it **TEN DAYS' TRIAL,** during which time you can put it to every test; you can compare it with guns made and sold by others, and **if you are not convinced that we are giving you a better gun at a lower price than you can buy elsewhere, you can return the gun to us at our expense, and we will immediately**

RETURN YOUR MONEY

together with any express charges you may have paid.

REMEMBER, with this and all our high grade guns

We Furnish Free

OUR PATENT GLOBE SIGHT,

which really doubles the efficiency of any gun. We do not sell these sights. **WE FURNISH THEM FREE WITH OUR GUNS.** Remember, we sell these guns subject to your decision that you are

GETTING BETTER VALUE IN EVERY WAY THAN YOU COULD GET IF YOU BOUGHT YOUR GUN FROM ANY OTHER HOUSE.

ILLUSTRATION SHOWING THE PATENT FORE END, FRAME AND INLAID FULL PISTOL GRIP.

FROM THE LARGE ILLUSTRATION, engraved by our artist from a photograph, we have endeavored to give you just a little idea of the beautiful finish, the elaborate appearance and the new up to date lines produced in this gun and **OFFERED AT ONLY............ $11.40**

OUR SPECIAL PRICE,

$11.40

for 30 or 32-inch barrels or

$13.35

for 12-gauge gun with 36-inch barrels.

LOADED SHELLS, $1.29 per 100. See page 316.

DETAILED DESCRIPTION.

BARRELS—The Royal Damascus finished barrels. Each pair of barrels is branded on the rib "Royal Damascus." The right barrel is cylinder bored and the left barrel choke bored. The barrels have all the beautiful finish effect of the most expensive Damascus barrels made. They are finished with shell extractor, "L" shaped extension rib, making a strong locking device. They are fitted with heavy lugs, locking securely into the frame; they are nicely shaped and finished, have a neat, handsome matted rib and they are bored for either black, nitro or smokeless powder.

FRAME—The frame is solid steel, strong, beautifully finished, elaborately engraved, handsomely case hardened, made extra strong and of the latest model.

MOUNTINGS—The gun is mounted with neat low circular hammers, adjusted so that they are out of the line of sight; handsome top snap break; the locks are the latest type of bar lock, each lock branded "T. Barker," and the left lock inlaid with a handsome solid silver hunting dog, which in connection with the hand engraving on the lock represents a strikingly beautiful appearance; has the latest style trigger guard, elaborately engraved; neatly shaped triggers; strong, heavy nitro firing pins; locks are rebounding and come back automatically to half cock on being fired.

STOCK—Stock is made from carefully selected and well seasoned black walnut, beautifully finished, made full pistol grip. The pistol grip is finished with a handsome German silver shield, grip is handsomely decorated as illustrated, fancy butt plate to stock; stock is beautifully shaped, giving the gun an even balance. Comes complete with handsome selected black walnut patent fore end, **which is handsomely checkered and beautifully finished.**

GAUGE—Our T. Barker gun is furnished in 10, 12 or 16-gauge as desired.

Our $11.40 price barely covers the cost of material and labor, with but our one small percentage of profit added. It is the greatest value ever shown in a gun at the price; **it is such a gun as can be had from no other house for only $11.40.**

OUR FREE TRIAL GUARANTEE AND C. O. D. OFFER.

As a guarantee that this is in every way a better gun than any gun you can buy elsewhere at the price, we will accept your order and ship the gun to you with the understanding and agreement that you can give it ten days trial, during which time you can put it to any test and if for any reason you become dissatisfied with your purchase, you can return it to us at our expense and we will return your money, together with any express charges paid by you.

Further, if you do not wish to send the full amount with your order, we will on receipt of $1.00 send this gun to any address by express C. O. D.

You can examine it at your express office, and if found perfectly satisfactory and exactly as represented; if you are convinced you are getting in this our special **$11.40 T. Barker Gun,** a handsomer and better gun than you could get elsewhere at anything like the price you can then pay the express agent the balance, $10.40, and express charges. Otherwise the agent will return the gun to us at our expense and we will immediately return to you the $1.00 sent to us.

FROM THE ILLUSTRATION engraved by our artist direct from a photograph, **you can get just a little idea of the appearance of the gun,** although you must see and examine this gun and compare it with guns sold by others at higher prices to appreciate the real value we are offering, yet the picture will give you just a little idea of the **HANDSOME EFFECT WORKED OUT IN THESE ROYAL DAMASCUS FINISHED BARRELS,** in the elaborate engraving of the frame and locks, of the solid silver dog inlaid in the lock, of the general handsome outlines of this

NEW, UP TO DATE, BEAUTIFULLY FINISHED SHOTGUN.

No. 6C272	12-gauge, 30 or 32-inch barrels; state length of barrels wanted. Weight, 7¼ to 8 lbs. Price	$11.40
No. 6C272½	16-gauge, 30-inch barrels. Weight, 6¾ to 7 pounds. Price	11.45
No. 6C272¾	10-gauge, 32-inch barrels. Weight, 8¾ or 9¼ pounds. Price	11.65
No. 6C273	12-gauge, 36-inch barrels. Weight, 8 to 8¼ pounds. Price	13.35

Weight, packed for shipping, about 14 pounds.

No. 6C272 ORDER BY NUMBER Price, $11.40.

GIANT 8-GAUGE GOOSE GUN, 36-INCH BARRELS.

$21.40

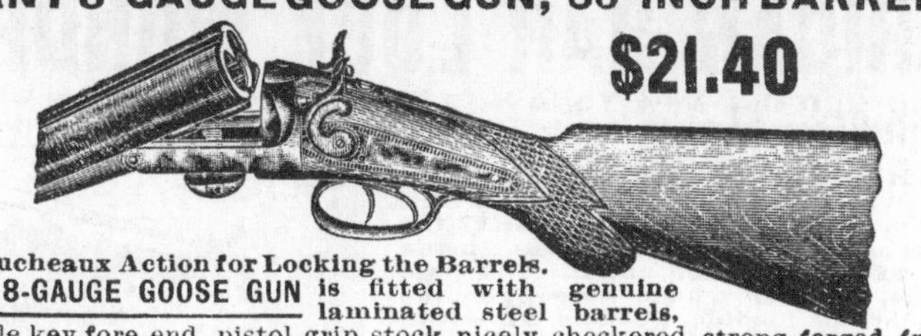

Lefaucheaux Action for Locking the Barrels.

OUR 8-GAUGE GOOSE GUN is fitted with genuine laminated steel barrels, double key fore end, pistol grip stock nicely checkered, strong forged frame nicely case hardened, bored smooth and true to gauge for long range shooting with buckshot. Order by catalogue number.

Catalogue Number	Grade	Style of Barrels	Gauge	Length Barrels	Weight Gun	Price
6C282	No. 5801	Laminated Steel	8	36 inches	12 to 14 lbs.	$21.40

Weight, packed for shipment, about 18 pounds.

ON THIS PAGE WE SHOW THREE STRICTLY HIGH GRADE GUARANTEED AMERICAN GUNS.

THESE GUNS ARE MANUFACTURED BY THE AMERICAN GUN CO. OF NEW YORK, AND THE FACTORY IS LOCATED IN NEW ENGLAND.

THERE ARE MORE THAN 120,000 of these guns now in use and all have been sold within the past 9 years. You cannot afford to buy a cheap gun when you can get a strictly high grade, genuine American machine made, double barrel breech loading gun, with long range shooting qualities, strong penetration and good workmanship.

BARRELS. The three guns which we describe and illustrate on this page are fitted with genuine Armory Steel Barrels, Genuine Twist or Laminated Steel Barrels and Genuine Damascus Barrels, and we guarantee these guns to be genuine or money refunded. These barrels should not be confused with the many imitation twist or laminated steel and imitation Damascus barrels as sold by some houses. We guarantee them to be the genuine barrels or money refunded. No other house will give you such a guarantee. CHOKE BORED—All are taper choke bored for long range shooting.

OUR NEW $8.93 AMERICAN GUN.

No. 6C361

OUR PATENT GLOBE SIGHT FREE WITH THIS GUN. You would not take $10.00 for the sight alone after you had used it; can be instantly put on or taken off.

DESCRIPTION of our $8.93 New American Gun. This gun is fitted with genuine Armory steel barrels, decarbonized and blued finish, crescent top snap break, strong steel rebounding locks, all parts hardened, rebounding circular hammers, crescent style extension rib beautifully matted and engine turned, straight grained, well seasoned walnut stock and fore end nicely checkered, full pistol grip capped with ornamental rosette, double bolt locks, a feature seldom found on a gun at this price; nitro firing pins, flat top rib, left barrel full choke bored, right barrel modified choke bored for field shooting. All barrels are bored true to gauge for black or smokeless powder, the locks and frame are made of best steel and beautifully case hardened and lock plates are hand engraved with chased line engraving, the only gun of this price on the market fitted with Deeley & Edge patent fore end. Order by catalogue number and state length of barrel wanted.

Catalogue Number	Grade	Style of Barrels	Gauge	Length Barrels	Weight Gun	Price
6C361	No. 1	Armory Steel	12	30 or 32 in.	7¾ to 8 lbs.	$8.93

Weight, packed for shipment, about 14 pounds.

LOADED SHELLS $1.29 PER HUNDRED. SEE PAGE 316.

THE NEW AMERICAN DOUBLE BARREL BREECH LOADER, $11.95.

This Gun has Genuine Two-Blade Damascus Barrels, and is Strictly of American Make. Made by the American Gun Company, New York.

OUR GLOBE SIGHT free with this Gun.

Made in 12-Gauge Only. 30 or 32-inch Barrels.

$11.95

No. 6C363

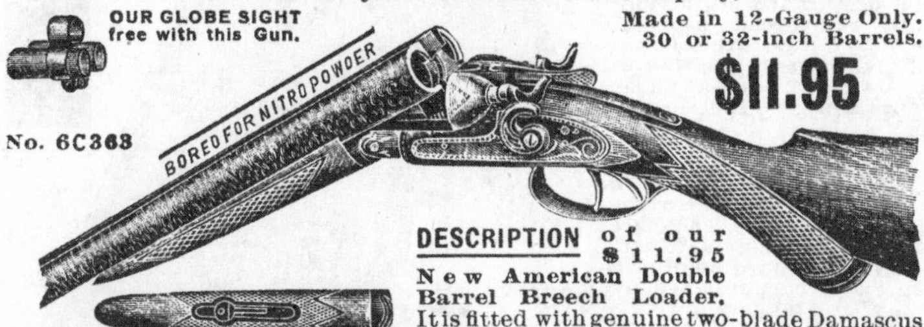

DESCRIPTION of our $11.95 New American Double Barrel Breech Loader. It is fitted with genuine two-blade Damascus barrels, the celebrated Crescent top snap break, strong steel bar rebounding locks, with hardened parts well made and well fitted, rebounding circular hammers, Crescent style extension rib beautifully engine turned and matted, straight grained and well seasoned walnut stock and fore end handsomely checkered, full pistol grip with ornamental rosette, double bolt locks for locking the barrels to the frame, nitro firing pins, flat top rib, left barrel full choke bored and right barrel modified choke for field shooting, all barrels bored smooth and true to gauge for black or smokeless powder, frame and lock plates of best steel and beautifully case hardened, and the lock plates hand engraved with chased line engraving, fitted with Deeley & Edge patent fore end. **Order by catalogue number and state length of barrel wanted.**

Catalogue No.	Grade	Style of Barrels	Gauge	Length of Barrels	Weight, pounds	Price
6C363	No. 3	Genuine Damascus	12	30 or 32 in.	7¾ to 8	$11.95

Weight, packed for shipment, about 14 pounds.

OUR SPECIAL HIGH GRADE, HAND ENGRAVED, AMERICAN DOUBLE GUN.

Made by the American Gun Company, New York.

OUR GLOBE SIGHT free with this Gun.

$12.98

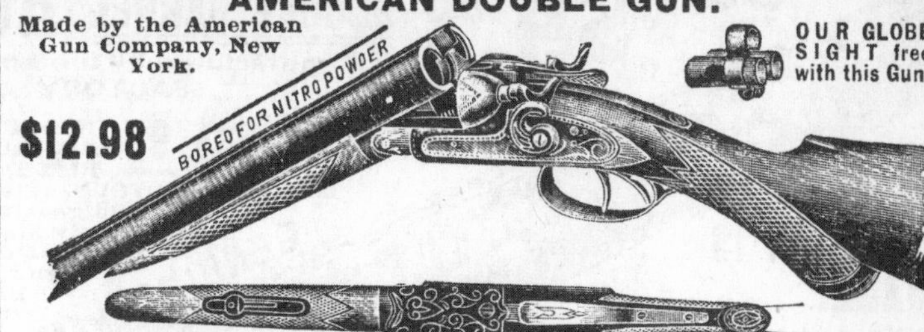

DESCRIPTION of our $12.98 New American Double Barrel Breech Loader. It is fitted with genuine laminated steel barrels, celebrated Crescent top snap break, strong bar rebounding locks with hardened parts well made and well fitted. Crescent style extension rib, engine turned and handsomely matted, rebounding shapely circular hammers, straight grained and well seasoned walnut stock and fore end handsomely checkered, full pistol grip with ornamental rosette, double bolt locks (the strongest made, and seldom found on guns at this price), nitro firing pins, flat top rib, left barrel full choke bored and right barrel modified choke bored for field shooting, all barrels bored smooth and true to gauge for black or smokeless powder. The frame locks, guard and fore end iron are handsomely hand engraved; the design is laid out in scroll pattern, and this pattern is fitted with **the celebrated Deeley & Edge patent fore end**, as shown in illustration. **Order by number and state length of barrel wanted.**

Catalogue No.	Grade	Style of Barrels	Gauge	Length of Barrels, inches	Weight, pounds	Price
6C364	No. 4	Laminated Steel	12	30 or 32	7¾ to 8	$12.98

Weight, packed for shipment, about 14 pounds.

OUR YOUNG REPEATING TWO-SHOT SINGLE BARREL SHOTGUN, $15.00.

We have purchased the factory, machinery, patents and stock of the Young Repeating Arms Co., of Columbus, Ohio, and are offering these handsome, well made two-shot repeating single barrel shotguns at only $15.00 each. The actual factory cost for materials and labor of these guns is considerably over $19.00 and these guns were calculated to list at $75.00 to $250.00, with regular trade discounts to the dealer.

This gun was invented by Mr. C. A. Young, an expert trap shooter and was calculated to take the place of a double barrel gun at the trap. In order to operate the gun, you place one shell in the magazine and one in the barrel. After firing one shot, you push the fore end forward, which ejects the empty shell and by pulling the fore end back, the barrel receives the second loaded shell ready to fire, the movement being very similar to the magazine movement of repeating shotguns such as Marlin and Winchester.

These guns are made from the best material that money can buy, no expense has been spared to make a thoroughly first class two-shot repeating single barrel shotgun. The frame is made of the very best forging, beautifully hand engraved and case hardened, with barrel from the very best quality of steel; all have straight grained, well seasoned walnut stock and fore end, beautiful matted rib on the top of the barrel which can be had only in very high priced single barrel guns, choke bored for close, hard, long range shooting and full directions for operating and taking the gun down accompanies each gun.

They are made in 12-gauge only, 32-inch barrel, weighing about 7¾ pounds. This is a rare opportunity to get a high priced gun, one that was built and designed for trap shooting trade only, at a popular price.

No. 6C387 Young Repeating Two-Shot Single Barrel Breech Loading Shotguns, 12-gauge, 32-inch barrel, weight about 7¾ pounds, hand engraved frame. Price........ **$15.00**

Weight, packed for shipment, about 14 pounds.

OUR AUXILIARY RIFLE BARREL, CALIBER 38-55, FOR 12-GAUGE SHOTGUNS, $5.00.

No. 6C388 38-55 caliber Auxiliary Rifle Barrel, to fit a 30 or 32-inch 12-gauge shotgun. State which length is wanted. Weight, 1¾ to 2 pounds. Price........ **$5.00**

If by registered mail, postage extra, 40 cents.

OUR WILDWOOD SINGLE BARREL BREECH LOADING SHOTGUN.

$2.25

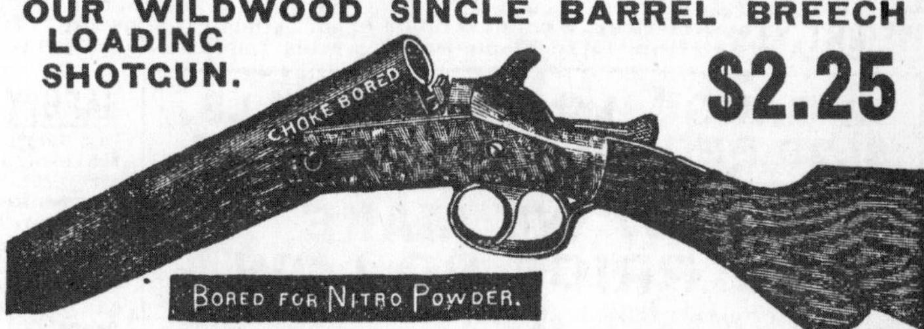

This is the lowest price ever made by any house in the world, on a top snap single barrel breech loading shotgun a price lower than any dealer can buy, and a price that is unprecedented in the history of gun selling.

For $2.25 we offer our customers a first class single barrel shotgun made from the best material that money can buy, and for finish, shooting qualities and general appearance no other house can approach us at 25 per cent more money.

Our $2.25 Wildwood Single Barrel Breech Loading Shotgun is fitted with a decarbonized blued steel barrel, taper choke bored for black, white or nitro powder, strong steel frame and breech, top snap break, the best break ever invented, straight grained well seasoned black walnut pistol grip stock and black walnut fore end, ornamented fancy butt plate, finished and fitted with the same care and skill as our higher priced shotguns, beautiful case hardened frame, the barrel is bored smooth and true to gauge, rebounding hammer which is hung in the center so it strikes the primer squarely, and our heretofore unheard of price of $2.25 makes this the best gun value ever offered and probably that ever will be offered. This gun is the equal in strength, durability and construction to any single barrel gun on the market.

No. 6C389 Our Wildwood Single Barrel Breech Loading Shotgun, 12-gauge, 30-inch barrel only, case hardened frame. Price........ **$2.25**

No. 6C390 Our Wildwood Single Barrel Breech Loading Shotgun, 12-gauge, 30-inch barrel, with nickel plated frame. Price........ **2.35**

No. 6C391 Our Wildwood, in 16-gauge, 30-inch barrel. Price........ **2.75**

Weight, packed for shipment, about 10 pounds.

GUNS REPAIRED. If you have a gun, rifle or revolver that needs repairing or refinishing, we are able to do the work in a very satisfactory manner. We have one of the best appointed gun shops in the country, complete with all necessary machinery to do repair work of all kinds and employ only expert gunsmiths who have had years of experience.

We will be glad to quote prices on repair work and you will find, quality of work considered, we are able to do your repair work for less money than you could possibly have it done for elsewhere.

SEND 10 CENTS FOR OUR BOOKLET OF USEFUL INFORMATION TO SHOOTERS.

SEND GOODS BY FREIGHT. We advise sending goods by freight, as it is cheaper than by express. If you order a gun or a rifle, and you include enough needed goods from our big catalogue to make a shipment of 50 to 100 pounds, the entire shipment will be very near as cheap by freight as the gun alone would cost you by express. When shipping 50 to 100 pounds or more by freight, it makes the cost practically next to nothing on each item.

OUR $9.95 DOUBLE BARREL AMERICAN BAR LOCK WONDER

Manufactured by the American Gun Co., New York, N. Y.
FACTORY AT NORWICH, CONN.

FOR $9.95 WE OFFER THIS STRICTLY HIGH GRADE, A1, AMERICAN MADE, EXTRA STRONG, FULL PISTOL GRIP, DOUBLE BARREL BREECH LOADING SHOTGUN, as the superior of any imported machine made gun sold generally at $20.00 to $30.00, and the first time a strictly high grade, bar lock, choke bored, genuine laminated steel, breech loading, genuine American gun WAS EVER OFFERED AT ANYTHING LIKE THE PRICE.

How the bird appears when using our Globe Sight.

GENUINE LAMINATED STEEL.

TAPER CHOKE BORED

WHERE THE GUN IS MADE.

THIS GUN is made for us under contract by a large manufacturer who has gained the reputation for the manufacture of strictly high grade breech loading shotguns, guns that are made and offered in competition with other American guns that sell at double the price. Only skilled mechanics are employed.

Every piece and part that enters into this gun is made true to gauge and is interchangeable. The locks are rebounding and all have double locking bolts.

$9.95

OUR PATENT GLOBE SIGHT FURNISHED FREE WITH THIS GUN.

This sight can be instantly adjusted to, or taken off from any shotgun without in any way marring or scratching the gun barrel. When the gun is aimed at a bird on the wing, no matter how swiftly it flies or how inexperienced the marksman, it describes a large circle around the bird, and once the bird is within the circle and you fire you are sure of hitting the mark. It makes possible the most effective and accurate wing shooting, even in the hands of an inexperienced hunter. This sight really doubles the value of any shotgun for actual service. Once you have used our sight, you would not be without it even at the cost of the gun, and yet we furnish it free with this and all other shotguns.

While our prices on the guns, including the sight, are very much lower than you can buy the gun, without the sight, elsewhere, for a gun for wing shooting, one fitted with our patent sight would be really cheaper than you could buy elsewhere, even if our price were double.

Understand, we own and control the patent. The sight can only be had from us. It is free with this gun.

GENERAL DESCRIPTION.

BARRELS. The barrels are genuine laminated steel. They are made on the most approved process. Every barrel, before leaving the factory, is thoroughly tested with nitro (white and black) powder, tested to the greatest possible strain. These barrels are choke bored on the latest taper system, with a view to giving the most perfect target, the greatest possible penetration, to insure long range effect such as can be had only from the highest grade American guns made.

FINISH OF BARRELS. These barrels are given an extra fine finish and polish. The illustration will give you some idea of the effect worked out on the coloring process, the barrels being browned, colored and decorated by the latest barrel coloring process.

RIB. The rib to these barrels is handsomely finished, beautifully matted, perfectly leveled and comes with a heavy genuine Edwards' lock extension rib.

EXTRACTOR. These barrels are fitted with the very latest shell extractor, as illustrated; positive in its action.

EXTRA HEAVY BOLTS. These barrels are fitted with extra heavy double bolts, made very strong, thus insuring perfect lock and a strength from which the gun, even with the use of white or black powder, cannot give out or wear loose or shaky.

LENGTH OF BARREL. The American Wonder comes with either 30 or 32-inch barrels, as desired. In ordering, be sure to state whether you wish 30 or 32-inch barrels.

WEIGHT. The American Wonder is made to weigh from 7¾ to 8 pounds.

AMERICAN WONDER FRAME. This gun is made with one of the heaviest, strongest and most durable steel gun frames made. The frames are extra heavy, strong in every part, extra well finished, case hardened and handsomely colored. They have the latest nitro firing pins, handsomely shaped; perfect acting top snap break, neat circular rebounding hammers, very strong genuine bar lock, with steel hardened interchangeable parts, perfectly finished.

STOCK. The stock is made from carefully selected straight grained walnut, thoroughly seasoned. It is perfectly shaped. The maker of these guns employs only the most expert stock makers. The stock is fitted to the frame by an automatic stock fitting machine that insures a perfect fit and the frame and stock are so constructed at the point of construction as to insure the strongest kind of a stock where many guns are weakened. This stock is full pistol grip with a handsome fancy cap on grip. The grip is handsomely checkered, as illustrated. Stock comes with handsomely ornamented butt plate.

FORE END. Our $9.95 American Wonder is fitted with the Edwards' automatic fore end, made of selected walnut, handsomely checkered as illustrated, beautifully finished, self locking in its application.

GAUGE. These guns come in 12-gauge only, but in shooting qualities, penetration, pattern and for long range work they are the equal of any ordinary 10-gauge American gun. For all kinds of game for which a shotgun is used this American Wonder is perfectly suited.

$9.95

BORED FOR NITRO POWDER

12-GAUGE LOADED SHELLS, $1.29 PER 100. SEE PAGE 316.

HOW WE MAKE THE PRICE SO LOW.

While a thoroughly reliable genuine American Double Barrel Breech Loading gun has never been sold at anything beginning to approach our special $9.95 price, determined that we would get out a genuine American gun at as low or a lower price than the very inferior machine made foreign or Belgian gun could be sold, we took the matter of manufacturing this high grade gun up with a celebrated New England gun maker, figuring how, by running a certain branch of his factory at its utmost capacity, the price of a reliable gun might be greatly reduced. We found by employing the very highest type of automatic working machinery for making the different parts, by buying the raw material, including the drop forgings, steel, walnut, etc., in large quantities, and by running the factory to its utmost capacity, the actual factory cost, the cost of material and labor, could be reduced even below what we ourselves or the manufacturer had any idea of reaching, and to this net factory cost, the cost of material and labor, we add our one small percentage of profit and name you the heretofore unheard of price of $9.95.

THE BARRELS ON THESE GUNS are all Genuine Laminated Steel, and not imitation Laminated Steel as sold by some houses. We guarantee them just as represented or money refunded.

NO OTHER HOUSE will give you such a guarantee on a gun at the price which we offer you this gun, and it is certainly the best gun value offered by any house in the United States.

SAFETY AND DURABILITY. First, in considering hard, long range shooting, extra penetration, extra target, the question of strength, durability and safety has not been overlooked, and while it is not safe to use white or nitro powder in any cheap foreign made guns or many of the cheap American guns manufactured, this gun is built for shooting any white powder of proper load that can be safely used in any of the highest priced American guns made. It has been built extra strong, of the best material, strongly locked, strongly reinforced, especially strong where many guns are weak, all with a view of giving you a gun that will be always safe, always reliable; a gun that will last for years and give the very best of satisfaction.

SHOOTING QUALITIES. Too much cannot be said for the shooting qualities of our $9.95 Wonder. Nothing has been spared to make this gun in shooting quality the equal of any gun made, regardless of price. The gun was in every part designed by one of the best and most practical gun makers in this country. It was designed after considering all the strong points for shooting work of all other American guns, and has been built with a view of embodying the strong features of other double barrel breech loading American guns with the defects of none. If a strong point, one that would add to the target or penetration, anything that would help for long range shooting, was found in another American gun, it has been applied in this, so that we feel perfectly safe in assuring the purchaser that he will find in this gun a gun that will equal if not outdo in strength and shooting qualities any other gun he has ever used.

No. 6C366 Our American Bar Lock Wonder, 12-gauge, 30 or 32-inch barrels; weight, 7¾ to 8 pounds. State length wanted. Price........ **$9.95**

WHEN ORDERING PARTS for guns, rifles or revolvers, always give catalogue number in full, also give the name, caliber, gauge of the gun, rifle or revolver. This will save us from writing you for this information.

NOTICE. The Canadian government charges 30 per cent duty on guns shipped into Canada from this country.

$14.87 BUYS THE AMERICAN GUN CO.'S HIGHEST GRADE,

GENUINE DAMASCUS BARRELS, Elaborately Engraved, Deeley & Edge Patent Fore End, Top Break, Bar Lock, Double Bolt Pistol Grip, Low Circular Hammers, **REINFORCED DOUBLE BARREL BREECH LOADING SHOTGUN.**

A genuine American made gun from the American Gun Company of New England, the highest grade double barrel breech loading shotgun made by these American makers; superior to double barrel breech loading shotguns made and sold by other makers at $20.00 to $25.00.

GENUINE DAMASCUS BARRELS

TAPER CHOKE BORED

OUR FREE TRIAL, FREE COMPARISON and BINDING GUARANTEE OFFER.

Order this gun at our special price of $14.87, we will send the gun to you with the understanding and agreement that you can give it 10 days' trial, during which time you can put it to every test, the test of hard, long range shooting, target and penetration; you can compare it with double barrel breech loading shotguns made and sold by other makers at $20.00 to $30.00, and if you are not convinced that you have a better gun at a much lower price than you could buy elsewhere, you can return the gun to us at our expense, at any time within ten days, and we will immediately refund your money, together with any express charges you may have paid; further, every piece and part of material that enters into the construction of this gun is covered by our binding guarantee, and any part proving defective within one year can be returned to us at our expense, and we will replace it free of charge.

WHILE NEARLY ALL OUR CUSTOMERS SEND CASH IN FULL WITH THEIR ORDERS,

and we advise you to send cash in full, for you will save the extra charge of from 25 to 50 cents which express companies always make for collecting the amount of the C. O. D. and returning to us, we, of course, agreeing to return your money if you are not perfectly satisfied; however, if you prefer to see and examine this gun before paying for it, you can send us $1.00, and we will send the gun to you by express C. O. D., subject to examination. You can examine it at your express office, and if found perfectly satisfactory and exactly as represented, you can then pay the express agent the balance, $13.87, and express charges; but if not satisfactory you need not pay one cent, the express agent will return the gun to us at our expense, and we will immediately return your one dollar.

FROM THIS ILLUSTRATION, engraved by our artist from a photograph, you can get just some little idea of the appearance, high finish and points of superiority worked out in this genuine American made gun. Do not compare this genuine American made gun with any of the many cheap imported so called foreign machine made guns, for this gun will outshoot and outwear a half dozen of any of the foreign machine made guns that are sold generally at $18.00 to $20.00. This gun can be compared only with the highest grade American made, double barrel, hammer breech loading shotguns.

ILLUSTRATION SHOWING THE DEELEY & EDGE PATENT FORE END, FRAME AND FULL PISTOL GRIP.

OUR PATENT GLOBE SIGHT FURNISHED FREE

with this gun. This sight can be instantly adjusted to or taken off from any shotgun without in any way marring or scratching the gun barrel. When the gun is aimed at a bird on the wing, no matter how swiftly it flies, or how inexperienced the marksman, it describes a large circle around the bird, and once the bird is within the circle and you fire, you are sure of hitting the mark. It makes possible the most effective and accurate wing shooting even in the hands of an inexperienced hunter. Remember, this Globe Sight will be furnished free with every one of these guns, at $14.87.

SPECIAL FEATURES of this, the highest grade, genuine Damascus barrel, elaborately engraved, American made gun, made by the American Gun Company of New England. THIS GUN IS SUPERIOR to all other American guns that can be had within $5.00 to $10.00 of the price in the following particulars: **First.** Barrels are genuine 2-blade Damascus steel. **Second.** This gun has the celebrated patent Deeley & Edge fore end. **Third.** Heavy solid reinforced ball breech. **Fourth.** Solid nitro firing pins. **Fifth.** Latest style bar locks. **Sixth.** Elaborately engraved locks and frame. **Seventh.** Celebrated taper choke bored for hard, long range shooting. **Eighth.** The latest style "L" shaped automatic locking extension rib, preventing the gun from coming loose or shaky. **Ninth.** Interchangeable parts. This gun being made on automatic machines each part is interchangeable. If, perchance, any part should break a new part can be immediately furnished that will fit in the place perfectly. **Tenth.** It has a strong double bolt lock. This gun combines the strong, up to date features of all other high grade American made double barrel breech loading shotguns, with the defects of none, and is the equal of any double barrel breech loading hammer gun you can buy at almost any price, and at our $14.87 price is offered to you at about one-half the price charged by others.

HOW WE CAN MAKE THE PRICE $14.87.

We take the output of the factory of the American Gun Company on this celebrated, high grade, two blade, Damascus steel breech loading shotgun. The automatic gun making machinery use in the making of this high grade gun runs constantly on these guns for us, thus reducing the cost of manufacture to the very minimum. To the actual cost to produce, the cost of material and labor (the labor being reduced to the very minimum by the employment of the most up to date automatic gun making machinery), we add but our one small percentage of profit, and sell you this high grade, genuine two blade Damascus steel barrel, all American made gun at about one-half the price charged by others for any American made gun that will compare with this.

$14.87

No 6C368

No. 6C368

$14.87

ORDER BY NUMBER.

WE RECOMMEND this, our highest grade American Gun Company's gun at $14.87 in preference to all other double barrel, hammer, breech loading shotguns. While we sell cheaper double barrel breech loaders as low as $6.75, we advise by all means when selecting a double barrel breech loading hammer gun, that you select this, the highest grade gun made by the American Gun Company. We recommend it for the reason that it is the greatest value ever offered by us or any other house. We guarantee you will find in this such a gun as was never before seen in your section at anything approaching the price.

DETAILED DESCRIPTION.

BARRELS. The barrels used in this gun are the genuine two-blade Damascus steel, and should not be compared with any of the cheaper barrels, such as imitation Damascus, often sold as genuine Damascus, nor with the plain steel barrels, nor even with the genuine twist or laminated steel barrels, since these are guaranteed the genuine two-blade Damascus steel, and a pair of these barrels cost to produce more than double the cheaper barrels referred to. They are made, bored and finished for shooting either smokeless, nitro or black powder; they are choke bored by the celebrated taper system in such a way as to confine the gas behind the charge of shot, giving the greatest possible penetration for the longest range shooting, especially for wing shooting, where the greatest possible penetration with the best possible target is required, and especially where you wish to use smokeless or nitro powder, we advise you to select a gun made with genuine Damascus barrels like this, our $14.87 gun. The barrels are beautifully finished within and without, they are nicely shaped, have a handsome matted rib. They must be seen, examined and compared with the barrels furnished on the ordinary guns sold generally at $15.00 to $20.00 to appreciate the real value we are offering in this highest grade gun of the American Gun Company. All are fitted with double bolt lugs.

MOUNTINGS. The mountings include the very latest style low circular hammers, which are beautifully engraved and elaborately decorated with fancy case hardening, and adjusted so that they are out of the line of sight. Locks are rebounding and the hammers come back automatically to half cock when being fired. Plungers are the latest nitro style, with heavy firing pins intended for nitro or smokeless powder. Break is the very latest, neat, handsomely shaped top lever, beautifully engraved and mottled. Locks are the latest style of bar lock, beautifully shaped, accurately fitted, elaborately engraved by hand, finished with a beautiful mottled case hardened effect, **and the parts of the lock are extremely simple, very powerful and almost impossible to get out of order.** Each piece being interchangeable can be instantly replaced at next to no cost. The shell extractor works automatically, extracts the shell far enough so it can be easily removed by the fingers. The "L" shaped extension rib fits into the frame in such a secure way as to prevent any possible shaking loose. Action is made with two heavy lugs which securely lock the barrel to the frame, making it one of the strongest actions found on any breech loading shotgun. This double bolt action is found only on the highest grade guns, guns that sell generally at about double our price.

FRAME. This is a strong, extra high grade, genuine steel shaped and finished frame, with heavy ball breech, made with flat water table found only on high grade guns, accurately milled, beautifully shaped and finished and very elaborately engraved and decorated by hand, finished with a beautiful mottled case hardened effect found only on the highest grade American made guns.

STOCK. This gun comes with a handsome straight grained, selected, well seasoned black walnut stock. Stocks are beautifully finished, handsomely shaped, very latest style, insuring a perfect balance of the gun. They are full pistol grip, with handsome pistol grip rosette and heavy fancy butt plate. Full pistol grip is handsomely checkered in the new design. The stocks are made to fit perfectly.

DEELEY & EDGE FORE END. This gun at $14.87 is furnished with the celebrated patent Deeley & Edge fore end. The fore end is made from a carefully selected piece of black walnut, beautifully finished with handsome design of hand checkering, and to this is fitted the celebrated patent Deeley & Edge attachment, as shown in the illustration, by which the fore end is securely locked, thus preventing any possible loss by accident, and securely locking the gun at all times.

ENGRAVING. This handsome $14.87 gun is elaborately engraved by hand. The design is entirely new, covers the entire frame, lower hammer guard and top lever. It is one of the most artistically and elaborately hand engraved guns on the market. There is nothing shown by any maker at anything approaching the price that will begin to compare with this gun in the way of elaborate hand engraving, and with this handsome design worked out covering the entire frame, blending beautifully as it does with the mottled case hardening effect and that with the beautiful Damascus mottled effect of the barrel, together with the handsomely finished stock, with the beautiful hand checkering, gives a finished gun at $14.87 such as was never before offered by any house.

SHOOTING QUALITIES. We guarantee this gun in shooting qualities equal to any gun made, regardless of price. It is so constructed, the barrels are so made and bored, it is so fitted, that no gun will shoot stronger; there is no gun made at any price that will make a better target at a longer range than this, our $14.87 American gun. We are perfectly willing to send it to any one on conditions that if they do not find it as a shooter the equal of any gun made, they can return it to us at our expense, and we will immediately return their money.

12-GAUGE. This gun comes in 12-gauge only. Barrels are either 30 or 32-inch barrels. 32 inches long, as desired, and in ordering be sure and state whether you wish 30 or 32-inch barrels.

No. 6C368 12-gauge, 30 or 32-inch barrels. Weight, 7¾ to 8 pounds. Price..**$14.87**

LOADED SHELLS $1.29 PER 100 See Page 316

$2.98 BUYS THE LONG RANGE WINNER

Our Globe Sight is Free with this Gun.

AT $2.98, reduced from $5.50, our original price, and afterward reduced to $4.45, we now offer the genuine Long Range Winner as one of the highest grade automatic shell ejecting, single barrel breech loading shotguns made for white or black powder.

$2.98 barely covers the cost of material and labor in our own gun factory with but our one small percentage of profit added. It is lower than dealers can buy in any quantity, a gun the equal of guns that retail everywhere at from $7.00 to $10.00.

OUR $1.00 OFFER. While nearly all of our customers send cash in full with their orders, we will, on receipt of $1.00, send this gun to any address by express C. O. D., subject to examination, the balance of $1.98 and express charges to be paid after the gun is received and found perfectly satisfactory and in every way as represented. We recommend that you send the full amount of cash with your order, as we guarantee the gun to reach you in perfect condition. We guarantee every part and piece that enters into the construction of the gun to be absolutely perfect, and if you do not find it equal to any automatic, single barrel, long range gun that retails at $7.00 to $10.00, you may return the gun to us immediately at our expense of express charges both ways and we will return your money.

COMPARE THIS, OUR $2.98 LONG RANGE WINNER, with any of the single barrel, automatic shell ejecting, breech loading guns on the market, those catalogued by other houses at $4.50 to $6.00, those that retail generally at $7.00 to $10.00, and if you do not find our Long Range Winner at $2.98 the equal of any other shell ejecting breech loader, you can return the gun to us at our expense of express charges both ways and we will immediately return your money.

HOW WE MAKE THE PRICE *$2.98.*

WE OWN THE FACTORY in which these guns are made and control the entire output. The cost to us is gotten down to merely the cost of the raw material and labor, and to this we add our one small percentage of profit, naming the heretofore unheard of price of $2.98. This gun is made in our own factory at Hopkinton, Mass., and the factory is in charge of one of the best single gun makers in the world, and we believe under his management, utilizing the modern machinery we do, that we produce a better automatic shell ejecting single barrel shotgun at a lower cost than any other factory.

WE MAKE AND FINISH MORE BARRELS of this kind than any other maker, thus reducing the cost. On the item of barrels alone there is a saving to us in the cost of every gun over other manufacturers of about 50 cents. Where nearly all makers of single guns import the barrels, the barrels being made in Belgium, we make our barrels in our own factory from solid bars of genuine Wilson welded steel. To make the barrels we buy the highest grade of genuine Wilson welded steel in solid bars of about 12 foot lengths. We cut this steel up into lengths of 30 and 32 inches, and in a new improved automatic barrel boring machine we bore two barrels at a time, and by this process we not only reduce the cost of the barrels about 50 cents each, but we furnish a higher grade, truer, stronger, better finish, and hence a better shooting barrel than is furnished on any single gun made.

BY OUR SYSTEM each barrel is choke bored for strong and long range shooting, made and bored to shoot either white, nitro or black powder, is more highly polished, better finished and blued than any similar gun on the market. We have installed special machinery for making every screw, every piece and every part for the milling, cutting, polishing, shaping, making and fitting of stock, the most economical and finest case hardening plant, everything combined to turn out a perfect gun at the very minimum of cost, and to this actual cost we add our one small percentage of profit, and quote the ridiculously low price of $2.98.

WE LOCATED OUR SINGLE GUN FACTORY at Hopkinton as a matter of economy and efficiency of labor. Hopkinton, Mass., is located in the very center of the gun and revolver making industry of America. Within a short radius of our factory, nearly all the American gun and revolver factories are located, hence we have the most skilled labor concentrated and always at our disposal. The supply usually being in excess of the demand of other factories, we are able to build this gun at a lower wage scale at Hopkinton than at any other point in the country.

ALL THIS HELPS TO MAKE POSSIBLE OUR SPECIAL $2.98 PRICE.

ALWAYS STATE LENGTH OF BARREL WANTED

WILSON'S WELDED STEEL.

TAPER CHOKE BORED

$2.98

LOADED SHELLS, $1.29 PER 100.

See Page 316

SPECIAL POINTS OF EXCELLENCE.

We claim for the Long Range Winner superiority over other single barrel guns, especially on the following points: First, genuine Wilson welded steel barrels, choke bored and finished in our own factory, smoother, stronger and better than other makers furnish, and bored for nitro or black powder.

AUTOMATIC SHELL EJECTOR, stronger, more sure, and less liable to get out of order than any other single barrel, shell ejecting device made.

LOCKING BOLT. The heaviest, strongest and best locking bolt used on any single gun.

FRAME AND ACTION. The strongest, handsomest, most simple, neatest and best finished case hardened frame and action used on a single barrel ejector.

SHOOTING QUALITIES. Above all, we claim for our $2.98 Long Range Winner the best shooter of any single barrel gun of this type on the market. Our barrels and frames are made and the gun is hung in a way that insures a better target at longer range than you will get from any single barrel gun you can buy from any other house at $1.00 to $3.00 more money.

UNDERSTAND, we accept your order and money with the agreement to immediately return your money to you and pay the express charges both ways if the gun is not found perfectly satisfactory.

$2.98

Loaded Shells, $1.29 per 100. See page 316.

Illustration shows the action of our Long Range Winner.

T is the Hammer.
U is the Top Lever.
V is the Top Lever Spring.
W is the Locking Bolt.
X is the Mainspring.
Y is the Trigger Spring.
Z is the Trigger.
G is the Stock.
1 is the Extractor Cam Spring.
2 is the Extractor Cam.
3 is the Extractor Hook.
4 is the Fore End.
5 is the Trigger Guard.
5 is the Screw Key.

DETAILED DESCRIPTION.

THE BARREL is bored from a solid bar of the highest grade, extra fine, thoroughly tested genuine Wilson welded steel, choke bored by the celebrated taper system, each barrel is blued, decarbonized finish, fitted with automatic shell ejector, one of the strongest, positive, perfect working automatic shell ejectors made, so constructed that when you open the gun the empty shell is automatically thrown clear from the gun.

The illustration shows the action of the shell as it is being automatically ejected. By this device there is no stopping to remove the shell by hand, it being thrown clear from your way ready to receive the new loaded shell. This makes possible very rapid firing; in fact, you can load and unload very much faster than with the ordinary extractor gun. The device is only appreciated by those who have used automatic shell ejecting guns, and such people would have no other; in fact with this single barrel automatic shell ejecting gun you shoot almost as rapidly and do almost the same execution that you can accomplish with a double barrel hammer breech loading shotgun.

FRAME. The $2.98 Long Range Winner has one of the very strongest solid steel frames, made extra heavy, reinforced at all parts, nicely shaped, perfectly finished. It is given a handsome mottled finish on the outside. It has the latest rebounding hammer, positive springs, the very latest top snap break. The gun is the latest type of take-down or detachable model. By simply removing the thumbscrew the barrel and fore end can be detached from the frame.

STOCK. This gun is fitted with an extra quality, thoroughly seasoned straight grain walnut stock, with pistol grip as illustrated, and the stock is fitted with a fancy butt plate. The fore end is of selected straight grained seasoned black walnut.

GENERAL FINISH. This gun is gotten up to present a more symmetrical, shapely and in every way a better general appearance than the ordinary single barrel gun. With its neat stock, handsome butt plate, beautifully decarbonized frame and trimmings, highly finished blued barrel, nicely proportioned parts and fittings throughout, even at our special $2.98 price it is one of the handsomest single guns on the market.

GAUGE. This gun comes in 12-gauge only, and being made and bored for white or black powder, made extra strong throughout, the gun is suitable for any kind of shooting where any shotgun can be used, suitable for game, geese, ducks, chickens, partridge, quail, snipe, rabbits, squirrels, etc.

LENGTH OF BARREL. The barrel is either 30 or 32 inches in length as desired. When ordering be sure to state the length of barrel wanted.

NOTE THE ILLUSTRATION.

From this large illustration, engraved by our artist from a photograph taken direct from the gun, showing the ejector and action automatically throwing the shell from the gun, you can form a good idea of the general finish and style of this, our $2.98 Long Range Winner, but it is a gun you must see and compare with other guns to appreciate the value we are offering.

ABOUT THE EXPRESS CHARGES

The gun weighs, packed for shipment, about 10 pounds, and you will find the express charges will amount to next to nothing as compared with what we will save you in price. The express charges will average for 300 miles, 40 cents; for 500 miles, 50 to 65 cents; 1,000 miles and upwards 75 cents to $1.00.

OUR $2.98 GUN weighs about 7 pounds, making a light gun to carry, very convenient and at the same time one of the strongest shooting guns made, and in this respect is more convenient than a double barrel gun, for it is in shooting qualities equal to a double barrel gun that would weigh from 8 to 10 pounds. Weight, packed for shipment, about 10 pounds.

No. 6C401 ORDER BY NUMBER

No. 6C401 LONG RANGE WINNER, 12-gauge, 30 or 32-inch barrel. Weight about 7 pounds. Price.... **$2.98**

THE WORLD'S CHALLENGE AUTOMATIC EJECTOR, $4.40

A GENUINE TWIST BARREL, FANCY CHECKERED FULL PISTOL GRIP, AUTOMATIC SHELL EJECTING, SINGLE BARREL BREECH LOADING SHOTGUN FOR ONLY $4.40.

NOTE THE SPECIAL STRONG POINTS OF EXCELLENCE.

No. 1. Genuine twist barrel. See our booklet explaining how twist barrels are made, and do not compare the genuine twist barrel with any of the plain steel barrels usually found in single guns. This is a genuine twist barrel, sometimes known as laminated steel.

No. 2. Case hardened frame. The frame used in the **World's Challenge Ejector** is the very latest style, extra heavy and strong, beautifully mottled, case hardened finish effect, accurately milled and nicely fitted.

No. 3. Full pistol grip. The World's Challenge Ejector has a good straight grained walnut stock and a full pistol grip. The stock is nicely shaped, close and firmly fitted, with the result that the gun hangs beautifully.

No. 4. Checkered grip. The full pistol grip on the **World's Challenge Ejector** is nicely checkered by hand. Note the fancy checking as shown in the illustration, and bear in mind that none of the cheaper single barrel guns are finished in this way.

No. 5. Taper Choke Bored. The World's Challenge Ejector is choke bored by the celebrated taper system. The barrel is so taper choke bored as to confine all the gas behind the charge, insuring the greatest possible penetration, and the barrels being twist or laminated steel, are of the very greatest strength, hence are perfectly safe for the use of either smokeless or black powder.

DON'T COMPARE THIS GENUINE twist or laminated steel single barrel, checkered grip, automatic shell ejecting, breech loading shotgun with any of the many cheaper grades of single barrel shotguns of which there are many on the market. **This single barrel gun is made in our own factory** at Hopkinton, Mass., and the barrels, frame, action, stock, in fact all the parts, all the material and workmanship are calculated to give our customers a higher grade single barrel breech loading shotgun than they could get from any other factory. If you want a cheaper single barrel breech loader, and yet a thoroughly reliable gun, select our **Long Range Winner Automatic Shell Ejector at $2.98,** shown on another page; but if you want one of the highest grade single barrel guns made, a genuine twist or laminated steel barrel, a single barrel automatic shell ejector, combining the good points of all single barrel shotguns made with the defects of none, then pay a little more; add $1.42 more to the price of our $2.98 Long Range Winner and select this, the **World's Challenge Ejector at...... $4.40**

THE WORLD'S CHALLENGE AUTOMATIC EJECTOR...

which we offer at $4.40, is made in our [illegible] gun factory at Hopkinton, Mass., the [illegible] up to date, thoroughly [illegible]ory in America. We started [illegible] a view of turning out a uniformly high grade of guns and revolvers, and by employing the most modern type of automatic gun making machinery, and buying our material in large quantities for cash, reduced the cost of manufacture, so that after adding our one small percentage of profit, we could furnish our customers direct from our own factory the

HIGHEST GRADE GUNS AND REVOLVERS

at but a fraction of the price charged by other makers. In our own factory at Hopkinton, using nothing but the most modern type of automatic gun making machinery, having no traveling salesmen, no high salaried officers, making no losses by bad debts, we can produce and sell direct to our customers the highest grade guns and revolvers at about one-half the price charged by others.

THE ILLUSTRATION **does not do the gun justice,** since by picture we are unable to show the difference between a twist barrel and the plain steel barrel. We are unable to show satisfactorily the difference between this and a cheaper frame. The many points of excellence in this, **OUR WORLD'S CHALLENGE EJECTOR,** can only be appreciated when you have seen and examined the gun and compared it with other single guns, and particularly after you have put it through the test of long range shooting, and more particularly **after it has stood the test of years of service.**

TAPERCHOKE BORED

$4.40

WE FURNISH FREE

with every WORLD'S CHALLENCE EJECTOR at $4.40 our own patent Globe Sight as illustrated.

THIS GLOBE SIGHT IS OWNED BY US **and can be had only from us,** and is furnished free with every World's Challenge Ejector at $4.40. You cannot afford to buy a single barrel shotgun from any other house when you can get our **World's Challenge Ejector at $4.40 and our patent Globe sight attachment FREE.** With this globe sight you can do wing shooting which it would be impossible to do without the sight. By the aid of this sight the most swift winged game can be instantly targeted, and, unless you are an expert wing shot, you will with this attachment, get three birds where you would not get more than one without it.

DON'T FAIL TO CONSIDER OUR FREE GLOBE SIGHT, which we furnish with the World's Challenge Ejector at $4.40.

REMEMBER OUR LIBERAL TERMS by which you can give this gun ten days' free trial, and if not found satisfactory you can return it to us at our expense and have your money returned to you. Remember, this is a twist barrel gun, not a plain steel barrel gun. Note that

IT HAS A CHECKERED FULL PISTOL GRIP...

not a plain half pistol grip. **REMEMBER, WE GUARANTEE it combines the good points of all high grade single barrel automatic ejectors, with the defects of none.** It is, in short, the only single barrel shotgun to buy. **There is no need of paying more money for any single barrel ejector made.**

THE MAIN POINTS to be considered when buying a single barrel breech loading shotgun are these: Are the barrels bored true to gauge, so they will shoot well? Are they so strong, they will withstand black, nitro or smokeless powder? Are the stocks well seasoned so they will not open in the grain after being fitted on the gun? Is the frame case hardened and strong? Is the hammer rebounding, and does it come back to half cock so you do not have to raise it every time you to open the gun? Is the **automatic ejector simple, so that the gun can be taken apart to be cleaned?**

ALL THESE POINTS are covered in the World's Challenge Ejector, and we are satisfied that if you send us your order for one of these guns you will not part with it for three times the cost if you could not get another.

Order our $4.40 World's Challenge Ejector Gun and we will send it to you with the understanding and agreement that you can give it ten days' free trial, during which time you can put it to every test; you can compare it with other guns for long range shooting, for target and for penetration, for quality of barrels, for workmanship and finish, for strength and durability, and if you do not find our **World's Challenge Ejector** better than any single gun you can buy elsewhere at anything like the price, you can at any time within ten days return the gun to us at our expense and we will immediately return your money, together with any express charges you may have paid; further, we guarantee every piece and part of the material that goes into the construction of the gun. Any part proving defective by reason of defective material or workmanship within one year will be replaced or repaired free of charge.

DETAILED DESCRIPTION.

THE BARREL. The barrel of the World's Challenge Ejector is twist, which is sometimes known as laminated steel, and is made by hand by skilled workmen, who have spent years of their lives learning this art, and no machine has ever been invented which could do this work. It is made by a hand welding process of iron and steel, which makes one of the strongest barrels conceivable, free from flaws and defects. All barrels in the World's Challenge Ejector are made with a view of using black or nitro smokeless powder.

STOCK. The stocks are made from carefully selected straight grain, well seasoned walnut, turned out and finished from the solid plank, and the full pistol grip is handsomely checkered.

FORE END. The fore end is made from the same grade of material as the stock.

PARTS. All the parts which go into this gun are made accurate and true to gauge and are interchangeable, so if you accidentally break a hammer top lever or similar part, it may be replaced without the assistance of a gunsmith.

CHOKE BORED. The World's Challenge Ejector Gun is choke bored on the latest scientific principles, choke bored by the taper system, which insures the best possible target at the longest possible range.

BUTT PLATE. Each gun is fitted with a handsome fancy butt plate of neat design.

EJECTING DEVICE. Our ejecting device is made with the fewest possible parts, which renders it less liable to get out of order than any other ejecting device made, and throws out the shell automatically when opening the gun.

HAMMER. The hammer is rebounding and comes back to half cock, so the gun may be opened without cocking the hammer.

GAUGE. The World's Challenge Ejector comes in 12-gauge only, and is bored for either black, nitro or smokeless powder.

LENGTH OF BARREL. These guns come in 30 or 32-inch barrel. **When ordering, state which you prefer.**

Loaded Shells, $1.29 per 100. See page 316.

WEIGHT, PACKED FOR SHIPMENT, ABOUT 10 POUNDS. No. 6C422

No. 6C422 **Our World's Challenge Ejector.** 12-gauge, 30 or 32-inch barrel, as desired; state length wanted; every barrel guaranteed genuine twist. Weight, about 6¼ pounds. Price, including our Globe Sight... **$4.40**

Weight, packed for shipment, about 10 pounds.

OUR $4.48 QUICK SHOT HAMMERLESS AUTOMATIC EJECTOR

FOR THE MOST RAPID FIRING, SAFEST, STRONGEST SHOOTING, SINGLE BARREL BREECH LOADING SHOTGUN MADE, WE RECOMMEND THIS FULL HAMMERLESS AUTOMATIC SHELL EJECTING SINGLE BARREL BREECH LOADING SHOTGUN

In preference to any other breech loading single barrel shotgun, and we put it out under our binding guarantee as positively the highest grade, strongest, safest, most rapid firing single barrel shotgun on the market, and we also guarantee it to kill at as long a range as any single or double barrel shotgun made, regardless of name, make or price.

How this **HAMMERLESS AUTOMATIC SHELL EJECTING BREECH LOADING SHOTGUN** excels all other hammerless single barrel guns made.

THE FRAME is the strongest and most perfectly constructed single barrel frame made. The lock and working parts, as shown in the illustration, are made very strong, accurate, true to gauge, therefore positive; simple, not liable to get out of order, so constructed as to guarantee perfect and positive operation under all conditions.

THE BARRELS are made and bored for smokeless or black powder and are choke bored by the celebrated taper system, bored from a solid bar of the finest Wilson steel.

THE AUTOMATIC SHELL EJECTOR is the strongest, most positive shell ejecting construction built.

RAPID FIRING. We claim for this gun that it is, by reason of its superior hammerless and shell ejecting construction, capable of far more rapid firing than any other single barrel breech loader made. Every time you open the gun it cocks automatically and is ready to shoot; thus saving the time it takes to cock the hammer.

SAFETY OF OPERATION. By the positive hammerless lock construction, our own special safety device, in connection with our new automatic shell ejecting device, accidental discharge of the gun is made almost next to impossible; in short, this gun is so built that practically all the danger of the ordinary hammer gun is removed. With no chance for accidental discharge, with the strong frame, with the unusual strong lock, safety self cocking and extracting mechanism, with the Wilson steel barrels for smokeless or black powder, with the extremely heavy bolt construction, with its locking connections, with the perfect fitting arrangement, all chance of accident, such as the bursting of any piece or part, accidental discharge, or other possible danger, is thoroughly removed.

THIS HAMMERLESS single barrel automatic shell ejecting shotgun not only excels all other single barrel hammerless guns, but is, in many respects, superior to any double barrel hammer breech loading shotgun made, for with its hammerless, and therefore, its invisible automatic self-cocking mechanism, in connection with its automatic shell ejecting mechanism, you can shoot and load almost, if not quite, as rapidly as with the best double barrel hammer breech loading shotgun made, and you have the advantage of having a much safer firearm, at the same time you have quite a material saving in the weight of the gun, a feature every sportsman will appreciate who carries a gun all day, not to speak of the great saving in price our $4.48 price offers.

ILLUSTRATION SHOWING ACTION OF OUR $5.50 QUICK SHOT HAMMERLESS AUTOMATIC EJECTOR.

No. 1 is the Main Spring. No. 2 is the Hammer. No. 3 is the Locking Bolt. No. 4 is the Trigger. No. 5 is the Trigger Guard. No. 6 is the Top Lever. No. 7 is the Screw Key. No. 8 is the Frame. No. 9 is the Barrel. No. 10 is the Fore End. No. 11 is the Stock. No. 12 is the Cocking Lever. No. 13 is the Extractor.

Why We Can Furnish the Best Single Barrel Hammerless Gun Made in the World, and Sell it at About One-half the Price Others Charge for Inferior Hammerless Guns.

THE MAIN REASON is we own our own gun factory, which is operated for us by the best gun maker in America. The cost to us covers only the cost of material and labor in our own factory, with no selling expenses, no traveling salesmen's salaries or expenses to pay, no bad debts, none of the many wastes common to other factories who sell to wholesale dealers, and to this actual cost of material and labor we add only our one small percentage of profit, making the price $4.48. We make the gun better than any other single barrel hammerless gun, for the reason that we have in our factory every new improved, up to date, labor saving gun making machine. We have equipped our factory with every facility for making everything the very best. None of the old style machinery common to other gun factories will be found in our Hopkinton factory. We use only the highest grade gun materials, all materials are carefully inspected. In the modeling of the gun we have employed the most skillful designers, inventors, machinists and other mechanics with a view to getting out a gun absolutely perfect in all its parts, combining the good points of all other high grade guns, eliminating all the objectionable features. All this you will quickly see and greatly appreciate when you have seen the gun and compared this, our $4.48 quick shot automatic shell ejecting hammerless single barrel shotgun with guns of like style made by other makers.

HOW THIS GUN IS MADE.

Made in our own factory at Hopkinton, Mass., by the Hopkinton Fire Arms Co., and offered for only $4.48 in competition with hammerless shotguns of inferior make that sell at wholesale at $6.00 to $8.00. We offer this gun on the basis of the actual cost of material and labor in our own factory, with but our one small percentage of profit added.

FOR $4.48 you have in this, OUR NEW IMPROVED AUTOMATIC SHELL EJECTING HAMMERLESS SINGLE BARREL BREECH LOADING SHOTGUN, in a

$4.48

all and even more than it would be possible to give you in a double gun of similar construction at less than three to five times the price.

TAPER CHOKE BORED

$4.48

OUR TEN DAYS' FREE TRIAL AND GUARANTEE OFFER.

As a guarantee that you will find this gun perfectly satisfactory and in every way a better hammerless automatic shell ejecting gun than you can buy elsewhere, even at $8.00 to $10.00, as a guarantee that you will find that this hammerless shell ejecting gun combines every good point of every other high grade single barrel gun, with the defects of none, and many improvements over other hammerless guns, that you will find it surrounded by more safety devices, and by reason of its positive operation and shell ejecting device a more rapid firing gun, as a guarantee that you will find it will kill at as long a range and make as good a target as any other gun made, single or double, regardless of name, make or price, we make this liberal ten days' free trial offer.

ORDER THIS GUN, enclose our price, we will send the gun to you with the understanding and agreement that if you do not find it perfectly satisfactory and all we claim for it, after giving it ten days' thorough trial and putting it to every test, you can return the gun to us at our expense, and we will cheerfully refund your money, together with any express charges paid by you. Every gun is covered by our binding guarantee, guaranteeing every piece and part that enters into the gun, the barrels, the frame, the lock and all the mechanism, every part is covered by our binding guarantee, and any piece or part that breaks or fails to perform its duty by reason of defective material or workmanship will be replaced or repaired by us, within one year, free of cost to you.

OUR FREE GLOBE SIGHT

With every one of these quick shot hammerless automatic shell ejecting shotguns which we offer at $4.48 we also furnish free of cost, one of our celebrated Globe sights, a sight that can be instantly attached to or taken from the gun at will. By the use of this sight the most swift wing game can be instantly targeted and unless you are an expert wing shot you will, with this attachment, hit three birds where you would not get more than one without this Globe sight. While these sights can be had only from us, as we own the patent, and they are made only by our factory at Hopkinton, Mass., they nevertheless are furnished free with this hammerless gun which we offer at OUR SPECIAL

$4.48 PRICE.

ALIGNMENT AND DESCRIPTION.

BARRELS. The barrels are made from solid bars of the very finest genuine Wilson steel. They are taper choke bored by the celebrated taper system, made with a view to shooting smokeless or black powder. There is no steel barrel made that will stand a greater strain than the barrels we furnish in this $4.48 gun. They are all beautifully finished and polished. By our system of boring on the new type of gun boring machine we get a perfect, true, smooth and absolutely accurate gauge, which insures for you closer, harder and far more accurate shooting results than you will get on any gun at any price that is bored on any other machine. Each barrel is fitted with an extra strong lug and bolt and is made extra heavy at the breech. This construction is intended to make the gun firm in the frame and protect it against any possible strain.

ALIGNMENT. This is a very important feature in a gun and is overlooked by nearly every maker of single barrel guns and by many makers of double barrel guns. We claim for this that we have the only single barrel gun made with perfect alignment. In this respect it is all you will get in the most expensive double barrel gun made. It is so scientifically balanced as to shape, weight, distribution of weight, measurement, size and general lines as to make it the ideal gun for quick wing shooting or for general purpose. This you will instantly appreciate when you take the gun to your shoulder.

FRAME. The frame is made extra strong, beautifully case hardened by the celebrated Fyrberg mottled case hardening process. It is accurately gauged, perfectly shaped, truly fitted and we believe the best frame ever used on a single barrel shotgun.

LOCK. The lock, the great essential in the building of a gun, is the most simple, yet strongest and most accurate, the only thoroughly positive concealed self cocking, self-acting lock used on a single barrel gun. All parts are carefully machine milled, perfectly finished and are interchangeable. For details of lock mechanism see separate illustration and description.

STOCK. These guns are fitted with carefully selected straight grain, thoroughly well seasoned black walnut stocks, made full pistol grip, fancy butt plate and grip cap, full checkered grip and handsome, full finished black walnut fore end.

AUTOMATIC SHELL EJECTOR. This gun is fitted with the celebrated Fyrberg patent automatic shell ejecting device, a positive self acting device, in every way superior to any other single barrel shell ejecting mechanism made. By this shell ejecting device the instant you fire the gun and open the barrel the empty shell is automatically thrown free from the gun, at the same time the gun is automatically cocked by the concealed lock mechanism and the gun is then ready to load. You can insert the shell, close the gun and it is cocked, loaded and ready to shoot. This operation can be repeated every time you shoot and you have, in short, approximately, as rapid a firing gun as you would have in any double barrel breech loading non-ejecting shotgun.

This, our new $4.48 quick shot hammerless gun, comes only in 12-gauge, in 30 or 32 inch barrels as desired. When ordering, be sure to state whether you wish 30 or 32-inch barrels, and remember it can only be had in 12 gauge. We furnish this gun either in Wilson steel barrels, as above described, or in genuine twist barrels at the following special prices:

No. 6C427 Price of gun, with Wilson steel barrel, 12 gauge, 30 or 32-inch barrels as desired. State length wanted. Wt., about 7 lbs. $4.48
No. 6C428 Price of gun, with genuine twist or laminated steel barrels, 12 gauge, 30 or 32-in. State length wanted. Wt., about 6½ lbs. 5.25
Weight, packed for shipment, about 10 pounds.

LOADED SHELLS $1.29 PER 100. See Page 316.

WE FURNISH FREE WITH THIS GUN OUR PATENT GLOBE SIGHT.

$1.29 PER 100 FOR BLACK POWDER, $1.67 FOR SMOKELESS, BUYS BEST GRADE 12-GAUGE LOADED SHELLS. SEE PAGE 316.

Our 36 and 40-Inch SINGLE BARREL SHOTGUNS

OUR NEW 36 AND 40-INCH BARREL, AUTOMATIC EJECTOR, SINGLE BARREL BREECH LOADER, $4.85 AND $5.35

In response to the many inquiries for a 36 and 40-inch 12 and 16-gauge Single Barrel Breech Loading Shotgun, we have had some special barrels made and are now able to furnish a single barrel gun with 36 and 40-inch barrels for our southern and western trade. As all 12 and 16-gauge guns are usually made in 30 and 32-inch barrels, all makers have their machinery arranged and set for the 30 and 32-inch barrels only, and will not go to the expense of changing the machinery for making and handling 36 and 40-inch barrels; **we have gone to this expense and now offer you 36 and 40-inch single barrel, breech loading guns in 12 and 16-gauge** for only

$4.85 AND $5.35

BORED FOR NITRO POWDER

GENUINE ARMORY STEEL.

No. 6C510

These Special 36 and 40-inch Barrel Guns are made of the best material throughout, with automatic shell ejectors, made on the latest improved principle, choke bored by the latest taper system, fine quality of walnut stock, and fore end nicely finished; and bored for nitro or black powder.

ORDER BY NUMBER.

The automatic ejector device is very strong and simple and less liable to get out of order than any other device known.

The frame is made from the best material that money can buy; the barrel from Wilson's best quality Armory steel, and we consider it one of the **best guns that was ever put upon the market.**

The frame and trigger guard are **case hardened and beautifully finished**; all are made with pistol grip walnut stocks. The hammer is hung in the center of the frame so as to strike the shell squarely, the butt plate is of ornamental design and the gun can be taken down by removing the patent fore end.

Catalogue No.	Grade	Style of Barrel	Gauge	Length of Barrel, inches	Weight of Gun, pounds	PRICE
6C510	Ejector	Genuine	12	36	7 to 7¼	$4.85
6C510½	Ejector	Armory	16	36	6¾ to 7	
6C511	Ejector	Steel,	12	40	7¼ to 7½	5.35
6C511½	Ejector	choke bored	16	40	to 7¼	

WEIGHT, PACKED FOR SHIPMENT, ABOUT 12 POUNDS.

OUR $3.39 NEW WHITE POWDER WONDER AUTOMATIC EJECTOR.

12-gauge only. Choke bored.

$3.39

OUR PATENT GLOBE SIGHT is furnished free with this Gun. It is invaluable to shooters.

No. 6C514

DESCRIPTION of Our New White Powder Wonder Ejector. This gun is made in our own factory at Hopkinton, Mass. Each and every gun is fitted with utmost care, and of the thousands of guns which we have sold we have yet to hear that they have not given universal satisfaction. The **White Powder Wonder Ejector** is fitted with top snap break (strongest break made), Wilson's best Armory steel barrel; the hammer is rebounding and hung in the center so it strikes the primer squarely in the center; straight grain walnut stock and fore end, well seasoned; full pistol grip capped with fancy rosette, choke bored by the celebrated taper system, fancy ornamental butt plate, latest improved automatic ejector, which throws out the shell when the gun is opened, frame beautifully mottled and case hardened, finely finished in every way.

Order by catalogue number and state length wanted.

Catalogue No.	Grade	Style of Barrel	Gauge	Length of Barrel, inches	Weight of Gun	Price
6C514	W.P.W.Ej.	Armory Steel	12	30 or 32	7 pounds	$3.39

Weight, packed for shipment, about 10 pounds.

$1.29 PER 100 FOR BLACK POWDER, $1.67 FOR SMOKELESS, BUYS BEST GRADE 12-GAUGE LOADED SHELLS. See Page 316.

OUR 16-GAUGE TWIST AUTOMATIC EJECTOR SINGLE GUN.

LOADED SHELLS $1.29 PER 100.

See page 316.

Our Patent Globe Sight is furnished FREE with this Gun.

Guaranteed Genuine Twist Steel Barrel and **Choke Bored.** 16-gauge only. 30 or 32-inch barrel. Weight, about 6½ pounds.

$4.55

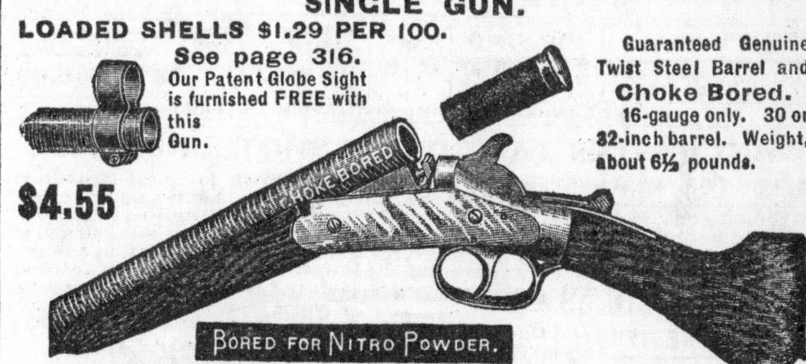

BORED FOR NITRO POWDER.

Our $4.55 16-gauge Ejector Single Gun is fitted with a genuine twist barrel, walnut pistol grip stock, walnut fore end, bored smooth and true to gauge, choke bored for field shooting and has fancy butt plate. The hammer is hung in the center so as to strike the cartridge square. **The automatic ejector device** is very strong and simple and cannot get out of order. The barrel is detachable, making it convenient to carry the gun apart in a Victoria style gun case. It has rebounding lock, top snap break, and the **frame and trigger guard are case hardened and beautifully finished.** Shell is thrown out automatically when you open the gun. State length of barrel wanted. Weight, boxed for shipping, 10 pounds.

No. 6C535 16-gauge, 30 or 32-inch barrel. Price.......................................$4.55

THE GENUINE REMINGTON SEMI-HAMMERLESS, AUTOMATIC EJECTING, SINGLE BARREL BREECH LOADING SHOTGUN.

ALL HAVE AUTOMATIC EJECTORS.

$6.25

BEWARE OF IMITATIONS. All Genuine Remington Guns Bear the Name "REMINGTON ARMS CO., ILION, N.Y."

No. 6C515

HANDSOME AND WELL MADE. CAN YOU MATCH IT?

The manufacturer fixes the prices at which we shall sell these guns and will not allow us or any other house to sell them cheaper.

The Remington Semi-Hammerless Single Barrel Breech Loading Shotgun, top lever break, the best break made, blued armory steel barrel, **choke bored, side cocking lever,** case hardened frame and butt plate, pistol grip stock, rebounding lock. The material, finish and shooting qualities are the same high standard as the **Remington double barrel gun. Every gun is warranted** perfect and a strong shooter. They are all put to a test before leaving the factory and none are allowed to go out until a perfect pattern has been shown. You take no risk in buying the old and reliable **Remington.**

No. 6C515 12-gauge; 30 or 32-inch barrel; weight, 6 to 6½ pounds. State length wanted. Price.......................................$6.25

No. 6C515¼ 16-gauge; 30 or 32-inch barrel; weight, about 6 lbs. Price, 6.25

Weight, packed in box, about 10 pounds.

BEWARE OF IMITATIONS. Many houses are selling guns that are similar, but not genuine. **We guarantee our guns to be as represented or money refunded.**

RUSTED AND DAMAGED GUNS. **Do not return to us a gun, revolver or rifle which is rusted, pitted or** has the finish worn off, for we have no way of selling these guns. If you have a gun, revolver or rifle which needs repairing, first write us fully describing the article and what is broken, as we may be able to send you the part necessary, thus saving the express charges on the gun both ways.

NOTICE—On any goods not described or listed in this catalogue and bought for your convenience, we must ask cash in full with the order, and they cannot be returned under any circumstances. We make no charge for boxing and packing guns for shipment.

THE BELGIAN MUZZLE LOADING DOUBLE BARREL SHOTGUN.

$6.98

No. 6C542

These guns are imported direct from Belgium, and all have the Belgian Government test same as our breech loaders.

Our Bar Lock Gun has genuine patent breech, genuine twist barrels, case hardened bar lock plates, checkered pistol grip stock, wood ramrod, German silver escutcheons, iron butt plate, case hardened and blued mountings. This illustration is made from a photograph of the gun and is an exact copy. It is our best grade muzzle loading double gun. Made in 12 and 14-gauge, 34-inch barrels; weight, 7½ to 8 pounds. Weight, packed for shipping, about 13 pounds.

No. 6C542 Mention length and gauge wanted. Price.............**$6.98**

HOW DAMASCUS GUN BARRELS ARE MADE.

D A B C

The above illustration shows, as near as possible, how the Damascus gun barrels are made. The three strips, A, B and C, each consist of from 40 to 60 layers of iron and steel welded together into one square strip, then they are twisted (D) while hot and rewelded into one strip about ⅝-inch wide, and ⅛-inch thick: the object being that if any one of these numerous layers of iron or steel has a flaw, the welding process entirely eliminates the flaw. After these numerous layers of iron and steel are twisted and rewelded into one strip, the strip is twisted around a mandrel and welded together as shown in the illustration. **These barrels are all hand made** by skilled mechanics who have spent years in learning this art. They cannot be made by machinery. When a barrel is made from three strips it is called three-blade Damascus, when made from two strips it is called two-blade Damascus, and when made from one strip it is called laminated steel. The more strips used in making the barrel, the finer is the figure of the barrel, and the more costly to make.

TO LOAD SHELLS. **If you load your own shells and put one card wad and two black edge and then another cardboard wad over the powder and one card wad over the shot, it takes 1¼ pounds of black powder, 6¼ pounds of shot, 200 black edge wads and 300 cardboard wads to load 100 shells with 3 drams of powder and 1 ounce of shot.**

WINCHESTER REPEATING SHOTGUNS $16.03 TO $18.59.

SMITH'S PATENT SIGHT. SEE THAT SIGHT

The small illustration will give you an idea of the Smith Patent Rear Sight, which may be used on Winchester repeating shotguns. This sight is not adapted to any other shotgun and is easily adjusted by simply unscrewing the band screw on each side of the barrel, inserting the sight, and then setting the screws back to place. This ingenious patented rear sight is very desirable for getting quick aim with a Winchester repeating shotgun.

No. 6C545 The Smith Patent Rear Sight. Price....(Postage extra, 1 cent).......**25c**

MODEL 1897. REPEATING SHOTGUN, $16.03.

THIS GUN IS KNOWN AS THE WINCHESTER PUMP GUN. MODEL 1897.

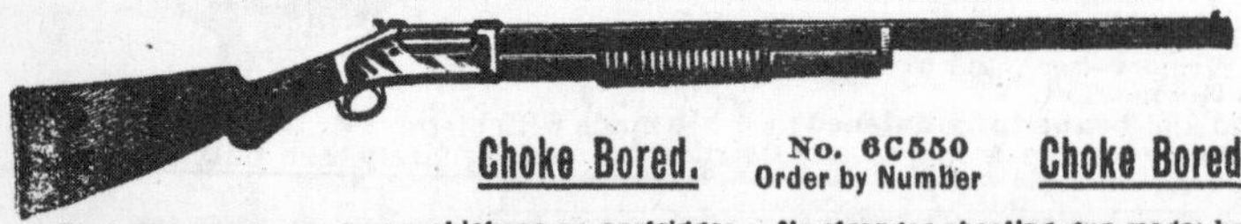

Choke Bored. No. 6C550 Order by Number **Choke Bored.**

Best gun made for ducks, chickens or partridges. No stronger shooting gun made; has wonderful penetration and makes a perfect pattern. Operated by sliding forearm below the barrel. **When the hammer is down the backward and forward motion of this slide unlocks and opens the breech lock, ejects the cartridge or fired shell and replaces it with a fresh cartridge.** The construction of the arm is such that **the hammer cannot fall on the firing pin and strike the cartridge until the breech block is in place and locked fast; while the hammer stands at the full cock notch the gun is locked against opening.** In this position the firing pin must be pushed forward to open the gun. When the hammer stands at half cock, the gun is locked both against opening and pulling the trigger.

Finest quality patent rolled steel barrel, fine selected walnut stock, pistol grip; length of stock, 13¾ inches; drop of stock, 2½ inches; weight, 7¾ pounds; shoots six times without reloading.

Catalogue No.	Grade	Style of Barrel	Gauge	Length of Barrel	Number of Shots	Weight	Price
6C550	Solid frame Model 1897	Rolled Steel Choke Bored	12	30 or 32 in.	6	7¾ lbs.	$16.03

Weight, packed for shipment, about 14 pounds.

WINCHESTER TAKE DOWN SHOTGUNS, $17.31.

$17.31 FOR WINCHESTER Latest Model Take Down, Six-Shot Repeater, 12-gauge Shotgun. Is a shooter equal to any $100.00 gun. We target every gun and they are carefully inspected before leaving our place. Greatest shotgun value ever offered. Order this gun and if you do not find it equal to any gun made, regardless of price, return it at our expense. **Our $17.31 price we guarantee the lowest wholesale price to dealers.**

$17.31 AND $18.59

THE WINCHESTER Take Down Repeating Shotgun is the popular model 1897, with a strong, simple, serviceable and handy take down system applied to it. This gun may be taken apart and put together again as quickly and easily as a double barrel shotgun and carried in a Victoria case, packed in a trunk or rolled up in camp bedding. The system used is similar to that used on Winchester take down rifles, and has been thoroughly tested and found to be faultless.

Catalogue No.	Grade	Style of Barrel	Gauge	Length of Barrel	Number of Shots	Weight	Price
6C560	Model 1897 take down	Rolled Steel Choke Bored	12	30 or 32 in.	6	7¾ lbs.	$17.31
6C565	Brush Gun	Rolled Steel Cylinder Bored	12	26 inches	5	7½ lbs.	18.59

Weight, packed for shipment, about 14 pounds.

The brush gun is simple in construction, very few parts and not liable to get out of order. Most rapid action made, cylinder bored to do the best shooting possible with buckshot.

MARLIN TAKE DOWN SHOTGUNS, $16.25.

The Marlin Take Down Repeating Shotgun, model 1898, can be taken apart and put together very quickly and easily. Made in 12-gauge, 30-inch barrel only. Weight, about 7 pounds. Barrel made of blued steel, choke bored, guaranteed for nitro powder. Pistol grip stock. This gun has been tried and thoroughly tested by the best shooters in the country and found to be perfect in every detail. Magazine holds five shells, and one in the chamber, making six shots.

No. 6C580 A Grade. Factory price, $24.00. 12-gauge, 30-inch barrel only. With Globe sight. Price..........(Weight, packed in box, about 14 pounds)..........**$16.25**

Our Ladies' Little Breech Loading Double Barrel Shotgun.

$10.35 44-Caliber, or 40-65 Caliber Shotgun.

No. 6B276

We have had this gun built for ladies or boys who like to hunt and for whom a 12-gauge gun kicks too hard. It is very effective for squirrels, birds or small game, and is made to take the 44 X. L. shot cartridge No. 6C2717 It can also be furnished to take the 40-65 primed shell which is about 3 inches long, and can be loaded heavier than the 44 X. L. shot cartridges are loaded. We cannot furnish the 40-65 shells loaded. The 40-65 shells are large enough to take about 40 grains of powder and ½-ounce of shot while the 44 X. L. will use only about one-half as much powder and shot. This little breech loader is fitted with 25-inch barrels and weighs about 4 pounds. Our patent Globe Sight is not made small enough for this gun.

No. 6B276 Our 44-Caliber Double Barrel Breech Loading Shotgun, top snap, pistol grip stock, rebounding hammers, laminated steel finished barrels. Price........................**$10.35**

No. 6C2717 Shot Cartridges Caliber 44 X. L. Price, per box of 50..........**.75**

No. 6C277 Caliber 40-65 Loading Tools, consisting of re-capper, cap extractor, wad cutter and charge cup. Price, per set..........................**$1.25**

No. 6B4716 16-ounce Canvas Gun Cover with leather muzzle and lock protector for this gun. Price..........................**75c**

This gun alone when packed for shipment, weighs about 8 pounds.

$1.29 for Best 12-Gauge Loaded Shells, See Page 317.

HOW A SHOTGUN BARREL IS CHOKE BORED.

For the benefit **of our customers who are not familiar with choke boring, we give here** illustration of how a shotgun barrel is choke bored. From the illustration you will imagine that a shotgun barrel has been cut in two the entire length, and you are looking at the inside of the barrel. You will notice that the chamber is large, the rest of the bore (cylinder bore) is smaller and of the same diameter until you come to about one inch from the muzzle, which is smaller than the cylinder bore from the chamber to the choke. **This is known as taper choke;** that is to say, the diameter is the same after it leaves the chamber until it meets the choke about one inch from the muzzle, when it tapers slightly, leaving the muzzle about ten one-thousandth of an inch smaller than the diameter of the cylinder bore from the chamber forward. **It requires fine reamers and skill to taper choke a shotgun barrel.** The difference between the cylinder and choke bore is hardly great enough to notice with the naked eye and the philosophy of choke bore is that the shot travels normally until it meets the choke, when it becomes concentrated while leaving the barrel, and being concentrated, puts a larger number of pellets in a 30-inch circle than if the shotgun was cylinder bored. Cylinder bored shotguns are similar, **except that they are not smaller at the muzzle, the bore being the same from the chamber to the muzzle end of the barrel**

FLOBERT RIFLES.

NOTE. WE DO NOT RECOMMEND NOR GUARANTEE FLOBERT RIFLES. Buy a good rifle. It will pay in the end. We recommend Nos. 6C665 and 6C666. We think No. 6C666 is the best value for the money.

$2.20 REMINGTON SYSTEM FLOBERT RIFLE.

Remington system, for 22-caliber short rim fire cartridges, polished octagon barrel, Remington action, trigger guard, light barrel, rifled, oiled stock, dark mountings, fine checkered pistol grip, 22-inch barrel. Weighs about 4½ pounds. **19 CENTS PER 100 FOR 22-CALIBER SHORT CARTRIDGES. See page 317.**

No. 6C657 Shoots cartridges No. 6C2336. Our cash with order price **$2.20**

Weight, packed for shipment, about 8 pounds.

WARNANT SYSTEM FLOBERT RIFLE.

22-CALIBER $2.50 and $2.75.

See page 317. **19 Cents per 100 for 22-Caliber Short Cartridges.**

Warnant or Springfield action, polished medium heavy octagon barrel, pistol grip, fancy butt, trigger guard, checkered stock, dark mountings, 22-inch barrel. Weight, about 4¾ pounds. Uses 22-caliber short or long rim fire cartridges No. 6C2336 or No. 6C2338.

No. 6C658 Shoots cartridges No. 6C2336 or No. 6C2338. Our cash with order price..............................**$2.50**

No. 6C659 Same as above, but heavier, with 24-inch barrel, well made and well finished. The safest rifle for boys. Shoots cartridges No. 6C2336 or No. 6C2338. Weight about 6 pounds. Our cash with order price..**$2.75**

Weight, packed for shipment, about 8 pounds.

NEW MODEL WARNANT ACTION.

32-CALIBER $2.80.

No. 6C663 New Model Warnant Action, oiled walnut stock, checkered pistol grip, 24-inch octagon barrel, 32-caliber short rim fire, shell extractor, barrel very finely finished. Weight, 6½ pounds. Shoots cartridges No. 6C2352.

No. 6C663 Our cash with order price.**$2.80**

Weight, packed for shipment, about 10 pounds.

NOTICE. 22-caliber short cartridges are good for 35 yards, 22-caliber long cartridges are good for 50 yards, and 22-caliber long rifle cartridges are good for 100 yards.

OUR ATLAS TARGET RIFLE.

22-Caliber, $2.35

The Atlas Target Rifle has a 20-inch round steel barrel, which is beautifully tapered from the breech to the muzzle, plain open sights, straight grained walnut stock, case hardened hammer and trigger, and is intended to shoot caliber 22 short, 22 long and 22 long rifle cartridges, mechanism is very simple, and cannot possibly get out of order. This rifle is made so that it can be taken down, by removing the screw in front of the trigger guard, and the rifling of the barrel is equal to the highest priced rifles made.

No. 6C664 Atlas Rifle, with 20-inch barrel; weight, about 2¾ pounds. Price........(If by mail, postage extra, 48 cents).......... **$2.35**

THE GENUINE NEW PIEPER RIFLE FOR $2.50.

With Remington Action. Good for 35 to 100 yards.

19 CENTS PER 100 FOR 22-CALIBER SHORT CARTRIDGES. See page 317.

THE BEST BOYS' RIFLE MADE FOR SQUIRREL AND SMALL GAME.

The New Pieper Rifle. Patented 1897. This is the best boys' rifle made. It fills a long felt want, and is first class in every respect. This rifle **has the celebrated Remington action, which is the best action used. It is entirely machine made. All parts are interchangeable, which is a great advantage. It shoots accurately, is adapted to and will shoot either 22-caliber No. 6C2336 or No. 6C2338 cartridges, or BB caps, has 20-inch finely rifled octagon barrel.** Weighs about 3¾ pounds. **Just the rifle for squirrels, rabbits and small game. Don't buy a cheap rifle when you can get a genuine Pieper for $2.50.**

No. 6C665 Pieper Rifle, 22-caliber, 20-inch barrel. Price..... **$2.50**

Weight, packed for shipment, about 8 pounds.

THE STEVENS' CRACK SHOT TAKE DOWN RIFLE FOR $3.00.

19 CENTS PER 100 for 22-CALIBER SHORT CARTRIDGES. SEE PAGE 317.

FOR $3.00 we furnish you the STEVENS' CRACK SHOT RIFLE which is well worth $5.00.

This is a strictly American made rifle, smooth, well bored and well rifled, all the working parts are of steel and interchangeable, and if any part breaks we can furnish you another part to replace it. It is an excellent rifle for boys.

The CRACK SHOT RIFLE will shoot accurately and is chambered to take a BB cap No. 6C2331, No. 6C2332, or 22-caliber cartridges Nos. 6C2336, 6C2338 or 6C2340. We recommend using any of the above cartridges in it. It has a blue steel barrel, solid breech block, as shown in illustration, and can easily be taken apart by unscrewing the screw in front of the guard. We guarante the stock to be of the best American walnut. The CRACK SHOT has 20-inch barre and weighs about 4 pounds, and is good for 35 to 100 yards.

No. 6C666 Steven's Rifle, 22-caliber, 20-inch barrel. Price............ **$3.00**

Weight, packed for shipment, about 8 pounds.

QUACKENBUSH SAFETY CARTRIDGE RIFLE. $3.70 AND $3.95.

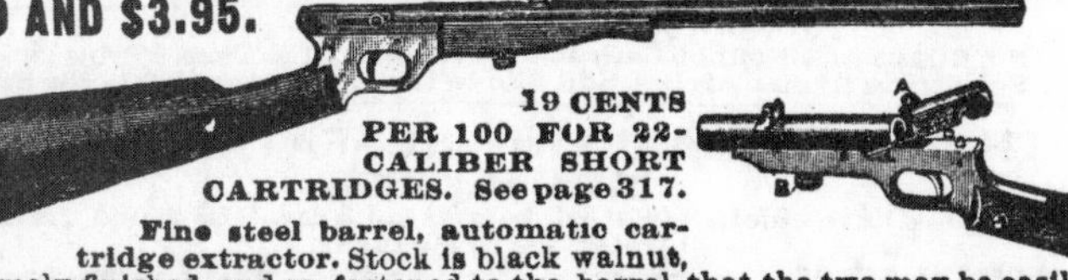

19 CENTS PER 100 FOR 22-CALIBER SHORT CARTRIDGES. See page 317.

Fine steel barrel, automatic cartridge extractor. Stock is black walnut, handsomely finished, and so fastened to the barrel that the two may be easily and quickly separated, making the rifle handy to carry in a trunk, valise or package. The barrel is rifled, and parts are well and durably nickeled, except the breech block, which is case hardened in color. Whole length, 33 inches, 18 or 22-inch barrel, 22-caliber. Shoots cartridges Nos. 6C2336, 6C2338, 6C2340, or 6C2535; good for 35 to 100 yards. Plain open sights, as shown in illustration. Weight, about 4½ pounds. Guaranteed good shooters.

Catalogue No.	Caliber	Barrel, inches	Shoots Cartridge	Good for	Price
6C674	22 Rim Fire	18	No. 6C2336 No. 6C2338 No. 6C2340 No. 6C2535	35 to 100 yards	$3.70
6C676	22 Rim Fire	22			3.95

Weight, packed for shipment, about 8 pounds.

No. 6C4716 18-ounce Canvas Victoria Gun Cover, leather lock and muzzle protector. Price........ 75c

OUR NEW No. 4 REMINGTON TAKE DOWN RIFLE, $4.50.

19 CENTS PER 100 FOR 22-CALIBER SHORT CARTRIDGES. SEE PAGE 317.

These are the Genuine Remington Rifles. Don't buy imitations offered by many houses. They are worthless. All have walnut stock, case hardened frame and mountings, open front and rear sights. As finely rifled as any rifle in the market, and made of the very best rifle material. Perfectly accurate and every one warranted as represented.

22 and 32-calibers. RIM FIRE

No.	Caliber	Barrel	Shoots Cartridge	Good for	Price
6C678	22 Short or Long RimFire	22½ in.	No. 6C2336 No. 6C2340	35 to 100 yards	$4.50
6C680	32 Short Rim Fire	24 inches	No. 6C2352	100 to 200 yards	

Weight, packed for shipment, about 8 pounds.

No. 6C4716 18-ounce Canvas Victoria Gun Cover. Price........75c

19 CENTS PER 100 FOR 22-CALIBER SHORT CARTRIDGES. SEE PAGE 317.

OUR NEW NO. 6 REMINGTON TAKE DOWN RIFLE, $2.85

The New Remington No. 6 Take Down Rifle is placed upon the market with the view of giving the best possible value at a low price. This new No. 6 Remington Rifle is made from the best material that money can buy, and the shooting quality is of a high order, and each rifle is bored and rifled with the same accuracy and precision that follows the entire line of Remington rifles which have become famous for their shooting qualities. It is made in 22-caliber only, shoots the 22-caliber cartridges Nos. 6C2336 or 6C2338, and is good for 35 yds.

No. 6C681 Remington Rifle No. 6, 22-caliber, 20-inch round barrel; weight, 3¾ pounds; walnut stock and fore end; case hardened frame; take down model. Weight, packed for shipment, about 8 pounds. Price........ **$2.85**

THE GENUINE REMINGTON RIFLE No. 2, FOR $6.75.

19 CENTS PER 100 FOR 22-CALIBER SHORT CARTRIDGES. SEE PAGE 317.

5½ to 6 lbs.

22 and 32-Caliber Rim Fire.

New Model.

Single Shot. All fitted with Octagon Barrel.

Case hardened frame, walnut stock, rifle butt plate, steel octagon barrel fitted with sporting front and rear sights. The ejector used in this rifle automatically throws the shell out of the chamber. We handle only the genuine Remington Rifles. We do not handle the imitation Remington Rifles. They are worthless.

Catalogue No.	Caliber	Barrel	Shoots Cartridge	Good for	Price
6C682	22 Rim Fire	24 inches	No. 6C2336	35 to 100 yards	$6.75
6C684	32 Rim Fire	26 inches	No. 6C2352	100 to 200 yards	

Weight, packed for shipment, about 10 pounds.

No. 6C4698 18-ounce Canvas Rifle Cover, for above rifle. Price..... 69c

If any of the above rifles are wanted with Lyman sights, add 25 cents to the cost of the sights for fitting them to rifle.

HOPKINS & ALLEN'S TAKE DOWN RIFLE, $2.65.

For $2.65 we offer you the latest model Hopkins & Allen Take Down Rifle, factory No. 722. We have bought a large quantity of these rifles thus insuring ourselves the very lowest price and by adding our one small percentage of profit we are able to make you this unheard of price of $2.65 for a genuine Hopkins & Allen rifle, which the factory sends out under their No. 722. As the factory price is $3.50 on this rifle you can readily appreciate the bargain you will get by buying this rifle from us. Description—This Hopkins & Allen Take Down Rifle has a finely rifled steel barrel. The frame, breech and trigger guard, as well as all working parts, are case hardened, making them durable. The stock and fore end are of selected straight grain walnut. The rifle is fitted with fancy butt plate and plain open sights. In order to take the barrel from the frame, unscrew the screw in front of the trigger guard.

No. 6C695 Hopkins & Allen Rifle, 22 caliber, suitable for cartridges Nos. 6C2336 and 6C2338, 19-inch barrel, weight, about 3¼ pounds. Weight, packed for shipment, about 8 pounds. The factory price, $3.50, our price........ $2.65

STEVENS' FAVORITE RIFLE WITH DETACHABLE BARREL.

All our Stevens' Favorite Rifles are carefully selected for finish, accuracy and workmanship, and we do not send out any rifle which has not passed a rigid inspection at the factory. The manufacturer fixes the price at which we shall sell these rifles, and will not allow us or any other house to sell them cheaper. The prices are guaranteed to be as low as offered by any reliable house in the United States, and should you be offered these rifles lower by any dealer, you will confer a great favor by advising us, to give us an opportunity of adjusting the prices. All our Favorites are made to our special specifications.

19 CENTS PER 100 FOR 22-CALIBER SHORT CARTRIDGES. SEE PAGE 317.

$5.10

THE FAVORITE

Is guaranteed as well finished and rifled a barrel as found in the most costly rifles. Entirely new model. The barrel is held to stock by a set screw, and is easily separated or put together. Rifling and quality of barrel same as the higher cost rifle. All have case hardened frame, walnut stock, finely finished, warranted accurate; all shoot rim fire cartridges and have open sights, 22-inch barrel and weigh about 4½ pounds.

Catalogue No.	Caliber	Barrel	Shoots Cartridge	Good for	Price
No. 6C708	22 Rim Fire	22 inches	No. 6C2336 No. 6C2338 No. 6C2340	35 to 100 yards	$5.10
No. 6C709	25 Rim Fire	22 inches	No. 6C2346	75 to 150 yards	5.10
No. 6C710	32 Rim Fire	22 inches	No. 6C2352	100 to 200 yards	5.10

Weight, packed for shipment, about 8 pounds.

No. 6C4716 18-ounce Canvas Victoria Gun Cover, for above rifle. Price, 75c

For fitting Lyman Sights, add 25 cents to cost of sights for fitting same.

ANY DEVIATION FROM THIS CATALOGUE MAY CAUSE A DELAY IN YOUR ORDER.

STEVENS' LATEST MODEL IDEAL RIFLE, 7 TO 7¼ POUNDS.

The Ideal Rifle is manufactured by the Stevens' Arms & Tool Co., Chicopee Falls, Mass. These rifles are made from the very best material that money can buy, and made to our specifications for accuracy, superior workmanship and finish, and all parts are interchangeable, so that if you accidentally break a piece or part of a Stevens' Ideal Rifle it may be replaced at a nominal cost without taking it to a gunsmith to have the piece or part fitted. The barrel is made so that it can be instantly detached from the frame, and put into a Victoria Gun Cover. The rifling in the barrel is equal to any rifle made, regardless of price, and the Ideal Rifle, as made for us, will be found extremely accurate. Finish—The barrel is blued and fitted with sporting rear and sporting front sight; the frame is handsomely case hardened, and the lock works are hardened to insure them being good wearing parts; stock and fore arm are made from selected straight grain, well seasoned walnut, and, in fact, the Ideal Rifle is all that its name implies, an Ideal Rifle. The manufacturer fixes the price at which we shall sell these rifles, and will not allow us or any other house to sell them cheaper. These prices are guaranteed to be as low as offered by any reliable dealer in the United States, and should you be offered these rifles lower by any dealer, you will confer a great favor by advising us, in order to give us an opportunity of adjusting prices.

19 CENTS PER 100 FOR 22-CALIBER SHORT CARTRIDGES. SEE PAGE 317.

$8.40

STEVENS IDEAL No44

This rifle meets the demand for a reliable and accurate rifle at a moderate price. It is recommended by us and fully guaranteed by the maker. All have half octagon barrel, oiled walnut stock and forearm, rifle butt, sporting rear and Rocky Mountain front sights, 7 to 7¼ lbs.

Catalogue No.	Caliber	Length of Barrel	Shoots Cartridge No.	Good for	Weight, about	Price
6C718	22 Rim Fire	24 inches	6C2336 6C2338 6C2340	35 to 100 yds.	7¼ pounds	$8.40
6C719	25 Rim Fire	24 inches	6C2346	100 to 150 yds.	7 pounds	8.40
6C720	25-20 C. F. S. S.	26 inches	6C2373	200 to 300 yds.	7 pounds	8.40

Weight, packed for shipment, about 12 pounds.

No. 6C4716 18-ounce Canvas Victoria Gun Cover. Leather lock and muzzle protector, for this rifle. Price........ 75c

If wanted with Lyman Sights, add 25 cents to cost of sights for fitting.

THE LATEST NEW WINCHESTER 22-CALIBER RIFLE, MODEL 1902.

19 CENTS PER 100 FOR 22-CALIBER SHORT CARTRIDGES. SEE PAGE 317.

$3.40

The New Winchester Single Shot, Model 1902, is the latest creation of the Winchester Repeating Arms Company, and enables us to place upon the market a rifle bearing the name of the Winchester Arms Company, at the extremely low price of $3.40. The rifle is guaranteed to shoot as well as any 22-caliber rifle made and is adapted to the 22-short or 22-long rim fire cartridges. 18-inch round barrel. 12¾-inch stock, 2¾-inch drop and fitted with plain front and rear sights. This rifle cannot be furnished any other way. The rifle can be taken apart in an instant, by simply unscrewing the thumbscrew on the fore end, so that it can be carried in a trunk or a grip. Shoots cartridges Nos. 6C2336 or 6C2338. Good for 35 to 100 yards. Weight, packed for shipment, about 6 pounds.

No. 6C723 Price, 18-inch barrel, weight, 3 pounds........ **$3.40**

NOTICE WE HAVE NO SPECIAL PRICES. Our prices as stated in our catalogue are our lowest, regardless of quantity purchased.

NOTICE. Any goods not described or listed in this catalogue and bought for your convenience, or made to special order, cannot be returned under any circumstances if sent as ordered.

MARLIN REPEATING RIFLES.

THE MARLIN SITUATION.

CUSTOMERS PLEASE NOTICE. The Marlin Fire Arms Co. have refused to furnish us any of their rifles or shotguns, and they try to prevent other dealers from supplying us with Marlin goods, because we will not charge our customers as much profit on them as they insist we should.

OUR POLICY is to supply our customers with goods on a small margin of profit, and the Marlin Fire Arms Co. will not permit us to do this with their goods, so they make it as troublesome as possible for us to obtain any of their rifles or shotguns.

WE ARE ABLE to get supplies of their goods from time to time, even though they try to make it impossible for us to buy them from other dealers.

WE PRINT BELOW A COPY OF A LETTER which the Marlin Fire Arms Co. has sent to nearly all the wholesale dealers in the United States. The letter explains itself and our customers will form their own opinions of it.

> August 1, 1902.
>
> NOTICE TO THE JOBBING TRADE:
>
> Messrs. Sears, Roebuck & Co., of Chicago, Ill., print prices on Marlin Arms in their catalogues direct to consumers, that do not leave a fair margin of profit to regular jobbing and retail trade. Our requests to have such cut prices discontinued having been ignored, we have declined to sell them any more goods of our make.
>
> This notice is to advise you of the conditions and of our action to protect the regular trade, and to request you to refrain from supplying Messrs. Sears, Roebuck & Co. with any Marlin Arms. Should you assist them, after receiving this notice, in obtaining our goods, you will be considered as having violated your contract with this company.
>
> Respectfully,
> THE MARLIN FIRE ARMS CO.,
> M. H. Marlin, President.

THE MARLIN CO. pay a rebate of 10 per cent every six months to houses who charge the prices which they designate and any house who sells below those prices is considered as having violated the contract and forfeits the 10 per cent rebate on all the goods that they buy from the Marlin Co. up to the time they cut the prices. They also forfeit the 10 per cent rebate if they furnish us with goods.

MARLIN RIFLE, TAKE DOWN MODEL 1897.

22-CALIBER.

19 CENTS PER 100 BUYS HIGHEST GRADE 22-CALIBER SHORT CARTRIDGES MADE. See page 317. We undersell all makers on ammunition of all kinds.

The New Marlin Model '97, Take Down Rifle, is the latest 22-caliber arm on the market. This rifle is practically the model '92 with the addition of the "take down" feature and many other valuable improvements. It has a finely tapered barrel and a neat rubber butt plate; the receiver is made of special steel, same as is used in the high power smokeless rifles, and is finely case hardened. This rifle is very easily cleaned; by simply removing the side plate (by use of the thumbscrew for the purpose), makes ready access to the inside of this rifle. It comes in 22-caliber only. Magazine holds 25 cartridges 22-caliber short, 20 cartridges 22-caliber long, and 18 cartridges 22-caliber long rifle. Shoots cartridges No. 6C2336, No. 6C2338 or No. 6C2340.

Catalogue Number	Caliber	Length of Barrel	Shoots Cartridge	Good for	Weight	Price
6C734	22 rim fire	24-in. Octagon	6C2336, 6C2338, 6C2340	35 to 100 yds.	5¾ lbs.	$12.75
6C735	22 rim fire	24-in. Round		35 to 100 yds.	5½ lbs.	11.50

Weight, packed for shipment, 14 pounds.

No. 6C4698 18-ounce Canvas Full Length Rifle Cover, leather lock and muzzle protector, for above rifle. Price........................9c

For fitting Lyman Sights, add 25c to the cost of the sights for fitting.

BLACK POWDER CARTRIDGES. RIM FIRE—22-caliber short, are accurate to 35 yards; 22-caliber long, to 50 yards, and 22-caliber long rifle, to 100 yards in good rifles. CENTRAL FIRE—32-20, 38-40, 44-40, etc., are accurate and good for 100 to 300 yards; 38-56, 32-40, 38-55, etc., are good for 100 to 400 yards; 25-35, 30-30 are accurate for 100 to 600 yards, and 45-70 government and 50-70 government are good for 1,000 yards.

THE NEW MARLIN REPEATING RIFLES. MODEL 1892.

The Model 1892 Rifles have BLUED FRAMES.

19 CENTS PER 100 BUYS HIGHEST GRADE 22-CALIBER SHORT CARTRIDGES MADE. See page 317. We undersell all makers on ammunition of all kinds.

$10.25
11.05

Made in 22-caliber rim fire, 32-caliber rim fire and 32-caliber center fire.

In the 22-caliber rifles any or all of the following rim fire cartridges may be used: 22-short, 22-long, and 22-long rifle. This is the only repeater that will do this. Other systems require two or three rifles to do the same work. This model takes entirely to pieces without tools, allowing of perfect cleaning. The magazine holds 25 cartridges 22-short, 20 cartridges 22-long and 18 cartridges 22-long rifle.

All 32-caliber rifles are sent out with two firing pins. This rifle is so made that in the same rifle may be used 32-short rim fire, 32-long rim fire cartridges, and by changing the firing pin, 32-short center fire and 32-long center fire cartridges may be used. The magazine holds 18 cartridges 32-caliber short and 15 cartridges 32-caliber long. This ammunition is cheap, and as compared to repeaters using the 32-20 cartridge will save the entire cost of the rifle on first 2,000 cartridges.

Catalogue Number	Caliber	Length of Barrel	Shoots Cartridges	Good for	Weight	Price
6C740	22 rim fire	24-in. Octagon	6C2336, 6C2338, 6C2340	35 to 100 yds.	5¾ lbs.	$11.05
6C741	22 rim fire	24-in. Round		35 to 100 yds.	5¾ lbs.	10.25
6C742	32 caliber rim or central fire	24-in. Octagon	6C2352, 6C2353	100 to 200 yds.	6 lbs.	11.05
6C743	32 caliber rim or central fire	24-in. Round	6C2380, 6C2381	100 to 200 yds.	6 lbs.	10.25

Weight, packed for shipment, 14 pounds.

No. 6C4698 18-ounce Canvas Full Length Rifle Cover, leather lock and muzzle protector, for above rifle. Price........................69c

For fitting Lyman Sights, add 25c to the cost of the sights for fitting.

THE NEW MARLIN REPEATING RIFLES. MODEL 1894.

ALL HAVE CASE HARDENED FRAMES.

This illustration shows the action of the Model 1894 Marlin Repeating Rifle.

$ 9.85
10.70

This is the latest and most improved repeating rifle to use the popular 25-20, 32-20, and 38-40 caliber center fire cartridges, and is the natural successor to the well known Model 1889. In the Model 1894 rifle every desirable feature of the 1889 which tended to make that arm the sportsman's favorite wherever used, is retained and the improvements suggested by five more years of experience and experiment are added. This rifle is practically the Model 1893 rifle adapted to the shorter cartridges and good for 100 to 300 yards.

Catalogue No.	Caliber	Barrel	Using Cartridge No.	Weight	No. of Shots	Price
6C750	25-20	Octagon, 24-inch	6C2374	6⅞ lbs.	14	$10.70
6C751	25-20	Round, 24-inch	6C2374	7¼ lbs.	14	9.85
6C752	32-20	Octagon, 24-inch	6C2384	6⅞ lbs.	14	10.70
6C753	32-20	Round, 24-inch	6C2384	7¼ lbs.	14	9.85
6C754	38-40	Octagon, 24-inch	6C2396	6⅞ lbs.	14	10.70

Weight, packed for shipment, 14 pounds.

No. 6C4698 18-ounce Canvas Full Length Rifle Case. Price.........69c

For fitting Lyman Sights, add 25c to the cost of the sights for fitting.

THE NEW MARLIN REPEATING RIFLES. MODEL 1893.

These rifles have smokeless steel barrels and case hardened frames and weigh 7¾ to 8 pounds.

$11.60 AND $12.60

Made in 32-40 caliber, using cartridges No 6C2429 or smokeless; 38-55 caliber, using cartridges No. 6C2432 or smokeless; 30-30 caliber, using cartridges No. 6C2605 or No. 6C2607.

This model is similar in principle to the 1894 Model, and is made in response to the many demands for a rifle in 30-30, 32-40 and 38-55 calibers. These rifles have exactly the same barrels as were used in the famous Ballards. The standard length of barrel is 26 inches, and a rifle with octagon barrels of this length weighs about 7¾ pounds. This weight, we believe, will be found about right for hunting purposes. The Model 1893 rifles, 32-40 and 38-55 caliber, are good for 100 to 400 yards; the 30-30 calibers are good up to 600 yards. All rifles of this model have case hardened frames. The barrels of these rifles are made of special smokeless steel. **We can furnish smokeless powder cartridges of all these calibers.**

Catalogue No.	Caliber	Smokeless Steel Barrels	Using Cartridge No.	Weight	No. of Shots	Price
6C762	32-40	Octagon, 26-inch	6C2429	7¾ lbs.	10	$12.60
6C764	38-55	Octagon, 26-inch	6C2432	7¾ lbs.	10	12.60
6C765	38-55	Round, 26-inch	6C2432	8 lbs.	10	11.60
6C766	30-30	Octagon, 26-inch	6C2607	7¾ lbs.	10	12.60

Weight, packed for shipment, 14 pounds.

No. 6C4698 18-ounce Canvas Full Length Rifle Case. Price.........69c

For fitting Lyman Sights, add 25c to the cost of the sights for fitting.

A FEW WORDS ABOUT RIFLES AND RANGES OF CARTRIDGES.

30-30-160 Winchester | 30-30-160 Winchester

This illustration shows bullet before shooting. After shooting.

Our customers frequently ask us: **What is the range of such and such cartridge?** This is a difficult question to answer, because some may mean the range to kill game and others may mean the flight of the bullet. The killing range would depend upon what kind of game you wish to kill and where the bullet hits the game. In former years hunters used large caliber rifles, such as 45-70, 40-82, 50-70, etc., for deer and other large game. At the present time they use small caliber rifles and smokeless cartridges, and get the same results. For instance, the 30-30 Winchester cartridges with soft point bullets, as shown in the illustration, are effective and accurate up to 1,000 yards. The 25-35 and 25-36 smokeless cartridges are effective up to 600 yards, while the 30-caliber Army is accurate up to 2,000 yards. It is difficult to see any game at 500 yards, and a man becomes invisible at 1,000 to 1,500 yards. Most game is killed within 100 yards in the woods, but in open places it may be killed at 100 to 500 yards. **For hunting purposes we recommend soft point bullets in smokeless cartridges, as the point expands on hitting the game.** Full metal patched bullets are liable to go right through the game and they do not produce the shock that soft point bullets do. All governments are beginning to use full metal patched bullets in war, as they do not tear or shatter the bones of a man when hit, but disable him, unless he is struck in a vital place. It must be remembered that when a bullet leaves the rifle, it revolves in its flight, and it really bores a hole through the object.

WINCHESTER MODEL 1892 REPEATING RIFLES, $9.84 AND $10.65.

This illustration shows the action of the Model 1892 Winchester Repeating Rifle. The system is the same as the Model 1886, now so well known, but it is made up in a lighter rifle, and weighs 6¼ to 6¾ pounds. It is manipulated by a finger lever, the firing pin is first withdrawn, the gun unlocked and opened, the shell or cartridge ejected, and a new cartridge presented and forced into the chamber, the firing pin held back until the gun is again locked. The locking bolts are always in sight, and when the gun is closed they support the breech bolt substantially against the force of the explosion. The Model 1892 Rifle uses the same cartridges as the Model 1873, in **32-20 and 38-40-calibers central fire,** and in addition they also take the **25-20 W. C. F.** The gun is light, strong, handsome, and simple in construction, and good for 200 to 400 yards.

6¼ to 6¾ pounds.

Catalogue Number	Caliber	Barrel	Using Cartridge No.	Weight Pounds	Number of Shots	Price
6C792	38-40 W. C. F.	Octagon, 24-inch	6C2396	6¾	15	$10.65
6C793	38-40 W. C. F.	Round, 24-inch	6C2396	6½	15	9.84
6C794	32-20 W. C. F.	Octagon, 24-inch	6C2384	6¾	15	10.65
6C795	32-20 W. C. F.	Round, 24-inch	6C2384	6½	15	9.84
6C796	25-20 W. C. F.	Octagon, 24-inch	6C2374	6¾	15	10.65
6C797	25-20 W. C. F.	Round, 24-inch	6C2374	6½	15	9.84

Weight, packed for shipment, 14 pounds.

No. 6C4698 18-ounce Canvas Full Length Rifle Cover, leather lock and muzzle protector, for above rifle. Price.............................69c

For fitting Lyman Sights, add 25 cents to cost of sights for fitting.

WE RECOMMEND THE FOLLOWING CALIBERS OF RIFLES:

For Squirrels, Muskrats and similar game, - - 22-Caliber Rim Fire
For Rabbits, Birds and similar game, - 32-Caliber Rim or Center Fire
For Mountain Sheep and similar game, 25-20 or 32-20-Caliber Center Fire
For Small Deer and similar game, - - - 38-40-Caliber Center Fire
For Moose, Bear and similar game, - 32-40, 38-55, 30-30 or 30 Army

WINCHESTER REPEATING RIFLE, MODEL 1890, "TAKE DOWN," 22-CALIBER, $8.74.

19 CENTS PER 100 FOR 22-CALIBER SHORT CARTRIDGES. SEE PAGE 317.

This illustration shows the rifle Take Down and Assembled.

Made in 22-Caliber only.

Our Model 1890 Winchester Take Down Rifle is one of the most popular 22-caliber repeating rifles on the market. The rifle is cocked and loaded by a sliding action of the forearm. This rifle is fitted with 24-inch octagon barrel, adjustable, Model 1890, rear sight, weighs about 5¾ pounds, can be easily and quickly taken apart by unscrewing a thumbscrew on the left side of the frame, is made in 22-caliber rim fire only and is the most popular shooting gallery rifle. The 22-caliber short is good for 35 yards, the 22-caliber long is good for 50 yards, and the 22-caliber Winchester special is good up to 200 yards. When ordering, state which cartridge you wish to shoot, as one rifle will only shoot one style of cartridge. These rifles cannot be furnished in any other way.

Catalogue Number	Caliber	Barrel	Weight	Shoots Cartridge Number	Number of Shots	Price
6C804	22 Short Rim	24-Inch Octagon	5¾ Lbs.	6C2336 only	15	$8.74
6C806	22 Long Rim	24-Inch Octagon	5¾ Lbs.	6C2338 only	12	
6C808	22 Winchester Special	24-Inch Octagon	5¾ Lbs.	6C2344 only	10	

Weight, packed for shipment, 14 pounds.

No. 6C4698 18-ounce Canvas Full Length Rifle Cover, leather lock and muzzle protector for above rifles. Price........................69c

For fitting Lyman Sights on any of the above rifles, add 25 cents to cost of sights for fitting. We box and pack guns free of cost to you. Some houses charge extra for this.

DON'T use dense shotgun powder in rifle or revolver shells or you may burst your rifle or revolver barrel.

WHEN ORDERING PARTS for guns, rifles or revolvers always give the name, caliber, gauge of the gun, rifle or revolver. This will save us from writing you for this information. If you can mail us the broken part do so.

THE POINT BLANK RANGE of a rifle means that if you hold the rifle perfectly horizontal the bullet will travel in a true horizontal line up to a certain distance, and after this distance the bullet will necessarily drop toward the earth as it cannot remain in the air. A bullet falls at the rate of 16 feet per second per 1000 yards coming out of a rifle.

The point blank range of rifles using 22-caliber cartridges is 30 to 35 yards and on larger caliber black powder cartridges the point blank range is from 50 to 75 yards, and with smokeless cartridges, such as 303 Savage and 30-30 Winchester, the point blank range is 100 yards, and the rear sight should be kept at the lowest notch for these ranges. For longer ranges elevate the rear sight according to the distance you intend to shoot. All Winchester rifles are point blank at 50 yards.

Savage Hammerless Repeating Rifles, $18.00.

MADE BY THE SAVAGE ARMS CO., UTICA, N. Y.

A Bullet Shot from a Savage has a velocity of 2,000 feet per second.

POWERFUL SHOOTERS.

MODEL 1899.

The Savage is a hammerless rifle made on scientific principles and one of the most powerful shooting rifles yet produced. A steel boiler plate ⅜-inch thick has been perforated by bullet—caliber 303—fired from a Savage rifle at a distance of 30 feet and it will penetrate 35 pine boards ⅞-inch thick. The Savage Hammerless Rifle is good up to 1500 yards with a regular caliber 303 smokeless cartridge, but if wanted for short range shooting, 100 to 200 yards, the caliber 303 miniature cartridge will do the work. In fact the Savage is an all around rifle.

The manufacturer fixes the prices at which we shall sell these rifles and will not allow us to sell them any cheaper.

The Savage Hammerless Repeating Rifle is simple in construction, light in weight. Ejects shells from side. Length of barrel, 26 inches; weight, 8 pounds. Magazine holds five cartridges. Velocity, 2,000 feet per second. Shoots cartridges No 6C2605, No. 6C2607, No. 6C2608, or No. 6C2609.

No.	Caliber	Barrel	Shoots Cartridges	No. of Shots	Wght.	Price
6C819	30-30 Winchester	Octagon, 26-inch	No. 6C2607	6	8 lbs.	$18.00
6C821	303 Savage	Octagon, 26-inch	No. 6C2609	6	8 lbs.	

No. 6C4286 Winchester Loading Tools, caliber 303, without bullet moulds. Price........................$1.50

For fitting Lyman Sights, add 25 cents to cost of Sights for fitting them.

WE BOX AND EXAMINE ALL GUNS CAREFULLY BEFORE SHIPPING and GUARANTEE SATISFACTION. WE CHARGE YOU NOTHING FOR BOXING RIFLES FOR SHIPMENT—SOME HOUSES DO.

Testing Rifles for Accuracy.

When testing rifles for accuracy, sit down while firing, and rest the muzzle, securing a solid rest for the arms and body. In this way extreme accuracy can be obtained suitable for testing the rifle. Do not, in any case, attempt to get accuracy by screwing the rifle in a vise. No reliable results can be obtained in that way, and even an accurate rifle will shoot wild.

Keep both eyes open when shooting. This is the best way to shoot when you acquire the habit.

Always keep the barrel cleaned and oiled when not in use. This prevents pitting in the bore of the rifle.

Always remember that all eyes are not focused alike, so it is necessary to become familiar with your gun. Try to learn to shoot with both eyes open. This is the best way to get quick sight.

WINCHESTER MODEL 1894 REPEATING RIFLES.

26-inch barrels; 32-40, 38-55, also the new 30-30 and 25-35 calibers.

Our Model 1894 Winchester rifles are similar to the Model 1892, but made to take the 32-40, 38-55, 25-35, 30-30 calibers, and are placed upon the market as medium weight, strong shooting rifles for large game and long range work. The 32-40 and 38-55 calibers are good for 500 yards. The 30-30 and 25-35 calibers are good for 750 yards. By using short range ammunition, these rifles can be used at short range of 100 to 200 yards by changing the elevation of the sights. These rifles are adapted to black or smokeless powder cartridges, have the reinforced locking bolt and are fitted with sporting rear and sporting front sights, except the 30-30 and 25-35 which are fitted with express sights.

No.	Caliber	Barrel	Shoots Cartridges	No. of Shots	Wght.	Price
6C830	32-40 C. F.	Octagon, 26-inch.	No. 6C2429	10	7½ lbs.	$10.65
6C831	32-40 C. F.	Round, 26-inch.	No. 6C2429	10	7¼ lbs.	9.84
6C832	38-55 C. F.	Octagon, 26-inch.	No. 6C2432	10	7½ lbs.	10.65
6C833	38-55 C. F.	Round, 26-inch.	No. 6C2432	10	7¼ lbs.	9.84
6C836	30-30 Winch.	Octagon, 26-inch.	No. 6C2607	10	7½ lbs.	$12.58
6C838	25-35 Winch.	Octagon, 26-inch.	No. 6C2601	10	7½ lbs.	

Weight, packed for shipment, 14 pounds.

No. 6C4698 18-ounce Canvas Full Length Rifle Cover, leather lock and muzzle protector, for above rifle. Price........................69c

For fitting Lyman Sights on any of the above rifles allow 25 cents to the cost of the sights for fitting.

RUSTED AND DAMAGED GUNS OR RIFLES. Do not return to us a gun, revolver or rifle which is rusted, pitted or has the finish worn off, for we have no way of selling these goods. If you have a gun, revolver or rifle which needs repairing, first write us, fully describing the article and what is broken and we may be able to send you the part necessary, thus saving the express charges on the gun both ways.

NOTICE—WHEN ORDERING SIGHTS GIVE NAME ALSO THE MODEL AND CALIBER OF RIFLE.

LYMAN AND OTHER SIGHTS.

This illustration shows how game appears to the hunter when using the Lyman Patent Combination Rear Sight. It resembles a ring or hoop and when using one of these sights it is not necessary to get a real fine sight, as is the case with open sights, in order to get the game. When the game is seen in the ring or hoop you generally get it.

NOTICE. Many customers are of the opinion that one Lyman Sight will fit any rifle. This is not a fact, for the sights vary for the different rifles and we carry this line of sights for nearly all model rifles, so when ordering, give the name and caliber of your rifle, also, if possible, give the model of same so we can send you the correct sights.

Combination No. 1 Rear Sights.

No. 6C1005 Our Rifleman's Combination Rear Sight No. 1. Anyone can attach it to the tang of the rifle in a few minutes with the assistance of a screwdriver. If they don't "pitch" right, place a piece of writing paper under them. When ordering, state the name of your rifle, also the caliber and model of same, as these sights are made to fit each particular model and caliber of rifle. In other words, one sight will not do for any rifle, but we furnish them for nearly all styles of rifles on the market. When using this sight the regular rear sight should be removed. Price........$2.00
Extra for fitting sight to rifle, allow.......25
If by mail, postage extra, 6 cents.

Lyman's Receiver Sight.

No. 6C1007 No. 21 Receiver Sight, for use only on the models 1886 and 1895 Winchester and the models 1893 and 1895 Marlin. Intended for rifles having long firing bolts, which prevents the use of No. 6C1005 sight. Price...............$2.60
For fitting this sight to rifle we make an extra charge of 50 cents.

Patent Ivory Front Sight.

No. 6C1008 No. 26, Patent Ivory Front Sight, to be used only with No. 6C1007 and will fit only 30-40 caliber Army model 1895 Winchester Rifles. It will not fit any other rifle. Price.........45c
If by mail, postage extra, 2 cents.

TO REMOVE SIGHTS drive from left to right, facing the muzzle, and use a brass or copper punch so that it will not deface the sight. To put on a sight, drive from right to left.

Ivory Bead Front Sights.

No. 6C1009 Ivory Bead Jack Front Sight, for quick shooting. Good for shooting when the light is poor. Mention name and caliber of rifle. Price....................60c
If by mail, postage extra, 2 cents.

No. 6C1010 Ivory Bead Front Sight. This sight gives the sportsman a clear white bead which can be seen distinctly against any object in the woods or in the bright sunlight. Mention name and caliber of rifle. Price....................60c
If by mail, postage extra, 3 cents.

No. 6C110 Our Combination Ivory Bead and Jack Sight. This sight may be used as an Ivory Bead Sight, and by reversing it you transform it into a Jack Sight. Price..55c
If by mail, postage extra, 3 cents.

No. 6C1012 Improved Ivory Front Hunting Sight. This sight is better than the bead sight for a hunting rifle. The ivory is so well protected by the surrounding metal that there is no danger of its being injured. Mention name and caliber of rifle. Price, 35c
If by mail, postage extra, 3 cents.

Lyman's Patent Ivory Shotgun Sights.

No. 6C1014. Lyman's Patent Ivory Shotgun Sight with reamer. Front and rear, for double barrel guns only. State whether front or rear is wanted.
Price, each........35c
Per pair........70c
If by mail, postage extra, 2 cents.

6C1015 No. 5, Lyman's Patent Combination Ivory Front Sight. One illustration shows the sight on the barrel and the other with the globe turned up and the ivory turned down. Mention name and caliber of rifle. Price....70c
If by mail, postage extra, 3 cents.

No. 6C1030 No. 12, Blank Piece to replace the crotch sight which is usually on the barrel when the rifle is purchased and which should always be removed when peep sights are used. Mention name and caliber of rifle. Price, 17c
If by mail, postage extra, 3 cents.

IN ORDERING RIFLE SIGHTS BE SURE to state the maker's name, also the model and caliber of your rifle.

Sporting Front and Rear Sights

No. 6C1036 Sporting Rear Sight. Graduated from 50 to 300 yards. Mention name and caliber of rifle. Price....................45c
If by mail, postage extra, 2 cents.

No. 6C1046 Knife Blade Front Sight. German silver blade. Mention name and caliber of rifle. Price....................45c
If by mail, postage extra, 2 cents.

No. 6C1048 Rocky Mountain Front Sight. Mention name and caliber of rifle. Price.........44c
If by mail, postage extra, 3 cents.

IN ORDERING SIGHTS BE SURE TO STATE the kind of rifle, also the model and caliber in order to insure a perfect fit.

HAND ENGRAVED, AUTOMATIC, SELF-COCKING REVOLVER, $3.15.

FOR $3.15 we furnish this, the highest grade, automatic, self-cocking revolver, elaborately engraved by hand, as shown in illustration, each revolver heavily nickel plated and highly polished or beautifully blued and highly polished.

THIS HAND ENGRAVED REVOLVER is made in our own factory at Hopkinton, Mass., which alone makes possible our $3.15 price, a price that barely covers the cost of material and labor, less than one-half the price at which revolvers of inferior grades and other makes are sold everywhere.

OUR BINDING GUARANTEE, MONEY REFUND, FREE TRIAL TEST AND COMPARISON OFFER.

As a guarantee that this is one of the handsomest, strongest and best revolvers made, as a guarantee that it is superior to revolvers that are sold generally at double the price, we make this extraordinary offer:

SEND US $3.15 and we will send the revolver to you by express with the understanding and agreement that you can give it ten days' trial, during which time you can put it to every test. You can compare it with revolvers sold by others at double the price, you can compare it piece for piece and part for part, note the difference in our safety device, note our cocking device, the automatic shell action, the safety, note the alignment, shape and finish, note the beautiful hand engraving in comparing with other revolvers, and after you have given the revolver a ten days' test and compared it with revolvers of other makes, if you are not satisfied you have received for your money, $3.15, double the value you would get in any other revolver, you can return the revolver to us at our expense and we will immediately return your money.

COMPARE THIS, our special hand engraved, elaborately finished, automatic, self-cocking hammer revolver which we offer at $3.15 with any of the half dozen or more cheap makes on the market that are retailed at from $3.50 to $5.00. If you want to know how our revolver differs from those cheap makes of revolvers, how in quality of material, workmanship and finish, in the action, in the various devices, in the mechanism, in the shooting qualities and practically in every respect our revolver is superior to revolvers sold generally at $3.50 to $6.00, order one of our revolvers, compare it with any of these and decide for yourself. If you are not perfectly satisfied you have gotten such a revolver as you could not get elsewhere at anything like the price, return it to us at our expense and we will immediately return your money.

DON'T BUY A CHEAP REVOLVER of any kind until you have seen our own high grade, automatic, self-cocking, hand engraved, nickel plated or blued steel revolver which we offer from our own factory at Hopkinton, Mass., at the bare cost of material and labor, with but our one small percentage of profit added.

From the illustration, engraved by our artist from a photograph, you can get some idea of the appearance of this handsome revolver, although it must be seen, examined and compared with the cheaper makes of revolvers to appreciate the value we are giving.

HOW OUR REVOLVER EXCELS, IN STRENGTH, DURABILITY, STYLE, FINISH, SHAPE AND SHOOTING QUALITIES, ANY OTHER REVOLVER MADE AND SOLD AT NOT LESS THAN DOUBLE THE PRICE.

SPECIAL POINTS OF SUPERIORITY.

OUTLINE. Our revolvers have an evenness of balance, shape and outline, a modeling that we do not feel is approached by any other revolver on the market sold at double the price.

PATENT BARREL LATCH. Our revolvers have a patent barrel latch, made under letters patent and owned by us, that far excels any other device made for the secure, rigid fastening of the barrel to the frame. Different from many of these devices, the perfect sight is not interfered with, and we get an evenness of finish not found on other revolvers.

SHELL EXTRACTOR. Our special device for operating the shell extractor is a great improvement over all others, stronger, more simple, less liable to get out of order, positive in its action, always ready for work, no danger of sticking and never missing.

LOCK MECHANISM. We claim for our lock mechanism an advantage over all other revolvers in being more simple, stronger, positive in its action and less liable to get out of order than any other lock mechanism made.

SHOOTING QUALITIES. We claim for our revolver that you can shoot more accurately and farther than with any other revolver made and sold at double the price.

FINISH. Our revolvers are given the highest possible finish. The nickel finished revolvers are all heavily nickel plated and highly polished, the blued steel finished revolvers are always given the highest grade blued finish. The trigger and trigger guards are beautifully mottled and case hardened in the finish, have handsome monogram and checkered rubber handles, one of the latest raised ribbed sights, a revolver that is gotten out with a view of combining the good qualities of all high grade revolvers, with the defects of none.

Catalogue No.	Caliber Center Fire	Length of Barrel	Finish	No. of Shots	Shoots Cartridge No.	Weight, ounces	Handles	Price
6C1121	32 c. f.	3 in.	Nickeled and	5	6C2377	12	Rubber	$3.15
6C1122	38 c. f.	3¼ in.	hand engraved	5	6C2388	15	Rubber	
6C1123	32 c. f.	3 in.	Blued steel and	5	6C2377	12	Rubber	3.55
6C1124	38 c. f.	3¼ in.	hand engraved	5	6C2388	15	Rubber	

Extra for pearl handles on any of the above revolvers.......................$1.00

If by mail, postage extra, 32-caliber, 18 cents; 38-caliber, 22 cents.

$3.90 BUYS OUR NEW HAND ENGRAVED, HAMMERLESS, AUTOMATIC SHELL EJECTING, SELF-COCKING REVOLVER.

FOR $3.90 we offer from our own factory at Hopkinton, Mass., one of the highest grade revolvers made, a price that barely covers the cost of material and labor, with but our one small percentage of profit added, a revolver the equal in every way of revolvers that sell at three to five times the price, a revolver we guarantee superior to any revolver you can buy elsewhere at less than $7.00.

THERE HAS BEEN A DEMAND for an especially fine revolver, a revolver given an extra finish, extra care throughout, a revolver accurately trued, perfectly gauged, a revolver for long, strong, hard shooting, a revolver with special lines and special finish, a revolver elaborately hand engraved, and to supply this demand we have gotten out this one special, extra high grade, extra well finished revolver in our latest hammerless, automatic, self-cocking, shell ejecting style, which we furnish in either 32 or 38 caliber, under our guarantee that the revolver is far superior to revolvers sold by others at $5.00 to $8.00, with the privilege of your returning the revolver and getting your money back if you, too, do not conclude that it is far superior.

YOU WILL FIND IN THIS, our specially finished, extra high grade, full hand engraved revolver that you have every essential point, every high grade, up to date feature of the highest priced revolvers made with a number of new and valuable additions, several very essential improvements.

THE ADVANTAGE OF BUYING A REVOLVER OR SHOTGUN OF OUR OWN MAKE.

In our own firearms factory at Hopkinton, Mass., where this, our finest revolver is made, and where our other styles of revolvers and shotguns are made, we control the material that goes into the construction, we control every detail in the process of manufacture, and since our aim is to get out revolvers and other firearms that combine the good qualities of every other high grade firearm made, with the defects of none, we know we can give you a better revolver or other firearm than you can get from any other house. Where we have practically none of the expense common to other firearms factories, known as overhead expense, traveling salesmen, high salaried officers, collections, losses, etc., the expense, which in many gun factories amounts to more than the actual factory cost of the firearms themselves, we can well afford to make our revolvers and guns as good as the best material that money can buy and the most skilled labor that can be employed can possibly produce. In addition, we have in our Mr. Fyrberg, a gentleman of mechanical genius not excelled, if indeed equaled in any other firearms factory in the country. This accounts for the many little points of superiority in mechanical construction and mechanical devices found in our revolvers and other firearms of our manufacture, accounts for the perfect fitting, perfect adjustment, accurate alignment, the real intrinsic value which you will find in this revolver and other firearms of our make which you will not find in firearms of other makes sold at even double our price.

From this illustration, engraved by our artist from a photograph, you can get some idea of this, our new design, our very latest, our highest grade, elaborately engraved, richly finished, hammerless, automatic, self-cocking, shell ejecting revolver.

REMEMBER this revolver comes in either the nickel plated or blued steel, as desired, either in 32 or 38 caliber. We will be glad to accept your order for one of these revolvers, to be sent to you with the understanding and agreement that if it isn't perfectly satisfactory when received, a better revolver than you could buy elsewhere at less than double the price, you can return it to us at our expense and we will immediately return your money together with any express charges paid by you.

OUR NEW IMPROVEMENTS.

WE CLAIM for our revolver which we are offering in the special finished style with elaborate hand engraving, a hammerless revolver for only $3.90, that it is superior to all other revolvers made in that it has the strongest, most simple, best finished, only absolutely positive self-acting, self-cocking device on the market. It is a self-cocking, self-acting, automatic, rebounding lock, full hammerless action that is next to impossible to get out of order; can never wear out, positive in its action; is rigid, firm, strong as a solid piece of steel, by far the best automatic action made.

BARREL LATCH. Under our own patent we manufacture for this revolver a special barrel latch, which securely locks the barrel to the frame, preventing any side shake, preventing any possibility of wearing loose, giving a square top finish and adding security and strength, an essentially strong feature not found on any other revolver made.

SHELL EXTRACTOR. We have a new automatic shell extracting device that is simple in construction, positive in its action, stronger and better than any other shell extractor on any other revolver made.

OUTLINE. This revolver, as shown in the illustration, has an outline, a shape, an even balance, a style and finish, in our judgment, not approached by any other revolver made, regardless of make, name or price.

SHOOTING QUALITIES. This, our specially finished revolver, is so accurately adjusted, so perfectly fitted, so evenly balanced, so accurately bored, rifled and finished, so sighted, so constructed in the frame as to insure for it accurate and strong shooting, superior to that accomplished on any revolver you can buy elsewhere at less than double the price.

FINISH. Nothing has been left undone to give this, our automatic, hammerless, full hand engraved revolver the highest possible finish. Whether you order the revolver in nickel plated or in blued steel, you will get a revolver elaborately hand engraved and hand carved. If in the nickel, heavily nickel plated and highly polished; if in the blued steel, given the finest colors and brightest blued finish shown on any revolver made, you will get a revolver combining the good qualities of all high grade automatic shell rejecting revolvers, with the defects of none.

Don't buy a revolver of any kind from anyone at home or elsewhere until you have first seen and examined one of our own make, and especially the finest revolver we make, this, our special automatic, shell ejecting, self-cocking, hammerless, full hand engraved revolver.

The 32 caliber takes cartridge No. 6C2377. The 38 caliber takes cartridge No. 6C2388.

Catalogue No.	Caliber Center Fire	Length of Barrel	Finish	No. of Shots	Shoots Cartridge No.	Weight, ounces	Handles	Price
6C1141	32 c. f.	3 in.	Nickeled and	5	6C2377	12	Rubber	$3.90
6C1142	38 c. f.	3¼ in.	hand engraved	5	6C2388	15	Rubber	
6C1143	32 c. f.	3 in.	Blued steel and	5	6C2377	12	Rubber	4.30
6C1144	38 c. f.	3¼ in.	hand engraved	5	6C2388	15	Rubber	

Extra for pearl handles on any of the above revolvers.......................$1.00

If by mail, postage extra, 32-caliber, 20 cents; 38-caliber, 24 cents.

$2.75 BUYS OUR AUTOMATIC --SELF-- COCKING REVOLVER.

MANUFACTURED FOR US BY ANDREW FYRBERG & CO., HOPKINTON, MASS.

AT $2.75 we offer you from our own revolver factory, in Hopkinton, Mass., an automatic shell ejecting, double action, 32 or 38-caliber revolver, under our guarantee that it is superior in every way to automatic revolvers of other makes that sell at much higher prices. We established our own revolver factory at Hopkinton, Mass., for the sole purpose of turning out a uniformly higher grade revolver than those usually furnished by other makers, and yet at a cost to us that would enable us to supply our customers at a lower price than we could possibly supply other makes

MAKERS HAVE, in our judgment, for several years been asking too much money for revolvers. There has been too much profit to the manufacturer and too much profit to the retail dealer, and it was with a view of changing this condition, getting a lower cost and a lower price to our customers, and a better made revolver, that we have established our own revolver factory.

THE CUSTOMER who reads this description can have little idea of the effort and outlay of money necessary to produce such a revolver for $2.75. From the time the manager of this department conceived the idea of building a factory and making our own revolvers, for nearly two years, we have been busy with a large force of men making special machines, getting out designs, making dies, jigs, gauges, tools, etc., before the first revolver could be produced.

IT HAS REQUIRED nearly two years time, a large force of mechanics and a big outlay of money to first build the equipment necessary to produce the finished revolver at the price. We are now fully equipped. Our revolver factory, like one of our gun factories, is also located in Hopkinton, Massachusetts, is in charge of one of the best revolver makers in the country. We have one of the most, if not the most modern, up to date revolver making plants in America. We have every facility for turning out the neatest, handsomest, most up to date design, best finished and best shooting revolver on the market and at the very lowest possible cost, and our special $2.75 price to you represents the net cost to us with but our one small percentage of profit added.

IF YOU WANT A REVOLVER you will find far greater value in one of our own make, one of the revolvers illustrated on this page, than in any other revolver made. This we positively guarantee. We will accept your order with the understanding that if the revolver is not perfectly satisfactory when received, if you are not convinced that it is the greatest revolver value offered by any house and in every way equal, and in many ways superior, to revolvers that sell at double the price, you can return it to us at our expense of express charges both ways and we will immediately return your money.

$2.75

FROM THE ILLUSTRATION, engraved by our artist from a photograph, you can get some idea of the general appearance of the revolver. This illustration shows the exact size of the 32-caliber revolver just as it appears in the photograph, yet you must see, examine and compare the revolver with others to appreciate what we are turning out and how much money you save by sending your order to us.

WE HAVE ENDEAVORED to make this revolver superior to the regular line of automatic revolvers, not only in what we consider a handsomer design, a neater and better shape, and a more beautiful outline, but we believe we have the best shell extracting device, the best cylinder catch and barrel latch, the simplest, strongest and best self-cocking action that is produced on any revolver made, regardless of price, and if you order one of these revolvers we leave it to you to be the judge. All are 5-shot and take center fire cartridges. Same size as Smith & Wesson revolvers. In our nickeling and bluing department we believe we get a finer finish than is furnished on other revolvers. We have endeavored in this respect to turn out a revolver unexcelled, if equaled by any revolver made.

THESE REVOLVERS are made from the very finest decarbonized steel procurable. The cylinders are neatly fluted, the barrels are bored true to gauge and full rifled. They have the latest style high rib, as illustrated, are accurately sighted, made with handsome monogram rubber handle, neatly shaped trigger guard, trigger and hammer, a compact, well made and well finished automatic revolver, built with a view of combining the good qualities of all automatic revolvers with the defects of none, and yet offered at a price lower than offered by any other concern, a price that barely covers the cost of material and labor, with but our one small percentage of profit added, only $2.75.

OUR BINDING GUARANTEE. Each and every one of these revolvers is covered by our binding guarantee, by the terms and conditions of which we will replace or repair any part which may break within one year by reason of defective material or workmanship.

38-CALIBER CARTRIDGES
91 CENTS Per 100
SEE PAGE 317.

The 38-caliber takes this cartridge.

No. 6C2388

The 32-caliber takes this cartridge.

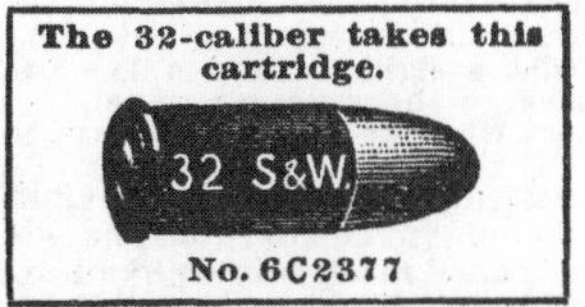

No. 6C2377

32-CALIBER CARTRIDGES
70 CENTS Per 100
SEE PAGE 317.

No. 6C1161 32-caliber, 3 -inch barrel, full nickel plated finish, rubber handles, 5-shot, weight, 12 ounces, shoots cartridge No. 6C2377. Price........$2.75
No. 6C1162 38-caliber, 3¼-inch barrel, full nickel plated finish, rubber handles, 5-shot, weight, 15 ounces, shoots cartridge No. 6C2388. Price........ 2.75
No. 6C1163 32-caliber, 3 -inch barrel, blued steel finish, rubber handles, 5-shot, weight, 12 ounces, shoots cartridge No. 6C2377. Price 3.15
No. 6C1164 38-caliber, 3¼-inch barrel, blued steel finish, rubber handles, 5-shot, weight, 15 ounces, shoots cartridge No. 6C2388. Price 3.15

If by mail, postage extra, 32-caliber, 18 cents; 38-caliber, 22 cents.

OUR 5-INCH BARREL AUTOMATIC REVOLVER.

THE 5-INCH BARREL REVOLVER is made the same as our regular 3 and 3¼-inch revolver, except in length of barrel. A 5-inch barrel revolver is preferable for target shooting while the 3 or 3¼-inch barrel is used mostly for defense.

$3.25

When ordering, write catalogue number in full and mention caliber, length of barrel and finish wanted. All these revolvers are 5-shot.

Catalogue Number	Caliber	Length of Barrel	Finish	Handles	No. of Shots	Weight, ounces	Shoots Cartridge	Price
6C1165	32 C. F.	5 inches	Nickel Plated	Rubber	5-shot	15	6C2377	$3.25
6C1166	38 C. F.	5 inches	Nickel Plated	Rubber	5-shot	18	6C2388	3.25
6C1167	32 C. F.	5 inches	Blued Steel	Rubber	5-shot	15	6C2377	3.65
6C1168	38 C. F.	5 inches	Blued Steel	Rubber	5 shot	18	6C2388	3.65

If by mail, postage extra, 32-caliber, 22 cents; 38-caliber, 26 cents.

ON RECEIPT OF $1.00 we will send any revolver by express, C. O. D., subject to examination, balance to be paid after the revolver is received and found perfectly satisfactory. We recommend, however, that you send cash in full with your order and save the small extra charge which the express companies ask on a C. O. D. shipment. Nearly all our customers send cash in full with their orders.

OUR PEARL HANDLE AUTOMATIC REVOLVER.

THIS IS OUR REGULAR AUTOMATIC REVOLVER, as illustrated and described on this page, but fitted with first quality pearl handles instead of rubber handles.

When ordering, write catalogue number in full and mention caliber, length of barrel and finish wanted.

If by mail, postage extra, 22 to 25 cents.

$3.75

Catalogue Number	Caliber	Length of Barrel	Finish	Handles	No. of Shots	Weight, ounces	Shoots Cartridge	Price
6C1161P	32 C. F.	3 inches	Nickel Plated	Pearl	5-shot	12	6C2377	$3.75
6C1162P	38 C. F.	3¼ inches	Nickel Plated	Pearl	5-shot	15	6C2388	3.75
6C1163P	32 C. F.	3 inches	Blued Steel	Pearl	5-shot	12	6C2377	4.15
6C1164P	38 C. F.	3¼ inches	Blued Steel	Pearl	5-shot	15	6C2388	4.15
6C1165P	32 C. F.	5 inches	Nickel Plated	Pearl	5-shot	15	6C2377	4.25
6C1166P	38 C. F.	5 inches	Nickel Plated	Pearl	5-shot	18	6C2388	4.25
6C1167P	32 C. F.	5 inches	Blued Steel	Pearl	5-shot	15	6C2377	4.65
6C1168P	38 C. F.	5 inches	Blued Steel	Pearl	5-shot	18	6C2388	4.65

$3.50 FOR OUR HAMMERLESS AUTOMATIC SHELL EJECTING SELF COCKING REVOLVER.

The 32-caliber takes this cartridge.

32 S&W

No. 6C2377
Price, per hundred.....70c

AT $3.50 WE OFFER THIS HAMMERLESS AUTOMATIC SHELL EJECTING REVOLVER in 32 or 38-caliber, built in our own factory and GUARANTEED SUPERIOR IN EVERY RESPECT to hammerless revolvers of other makes that sell at much higher prices.

THIS HAMMERLESS REVOLVER AT $3.50 like our special $2.75 Automatic Hammer Revolver, illustrated on preceding page, is built in the same factory—a factory we own and control at Hopkinton, Mass.—and our special $3.50 price barely covers the cost of material and labor with but our one small percentage of profit added. It is made from the same materials, on the same machines, by the same skilled labor as our $2.75 revolver described on preceding page. It differs only in that it is hammerless instead of a hammer revolver.

The 38-caliber takes this cartridge.

.38 S&W.

No. 6C2388
Price, per hundred 91c

IN EVERY DETAIL, in the making of the barrel, frame, cylinder and stock, this is the exact same type of a revolver as our special $2.75, as illustrated and described on the preceding page. It is gotten out with a view of giving our customers the highest type of hammerless revolver it is possible to make yet at the very minimum price, a price much lower than you can buy for elsewhere.

IF YOU ARE IN THE MARKET FOR A REVOLVER of any kind, we especially urge that you select either this $3.50 hammerless or our $2.75 hammer revolver, shown on the preceding page, on the condition that if when received you do not consider it better than other makes at much higher prices return it at our expense, and we will immediately return your money.

OUR BINDING GUARANTEE AND REFUND OFFER.

ORDER ONE OF OUR OWN REVOLVERS at our special price, and we will send it to you with the understanding that if it is not perfectly satisfactory when received, you can return it to us at our expense of express charges both ways, and we will immediately return your money. Further, we guarantee every piece and part that goes into these revolvers, and if any revolver proves defective when received, in any piece or part, it can be returned to us at our expense of express charges both ways, and we will exchange it for another or your money will be refunded at your option.

$3.50

THIS ILLUSTRATION IS THE EXACT LIFE SIZE of our 32-caliber revolver, engraved by our artist direct from a photograph of the revolver, and from it you can get a general idea of the outline and style of the revolver, and we believe you will agree with us that it carries a distinctiveness in beauty of design and general style, and above all, we guarantee it to excel in workmanship and general finish any revolver on the market approaching it in price.

32-CALIBER CARTRIDGES
70 CENTS Per 100
SEE PAGE 317.

WHY WE RECOMMEND THE HAMMERLESS REVOLVER OVER ALL OTHERS. We especially recommend that you select this our hammerless revolver at $3.50 in preference to the hammer revolver at $2.75. We recommend this additional outlay of 75 cents in the interest of safety. There is no hammer revolver that can be carried with absolute safety to the owner, for, the hammer being exposed, a fall, stumble or other accident that may bring the horn of the hammer immediately in contact with a rigid surface is liable to drive the hammer on the cartridge and discharge the revolver. Such accidents are not infrequent with hammer revolvers, whereas it could not happen with a hammerless revolver; the trigger being protected by a guard and the revolver being hammerless, there is no possibility of accidental discharge.

WHILE THE PROFIT IS EXACTLY THE SAME TO US whether you order a hammerless revolver or a hammer revolver, for the above reasons we especially recommend that you order the hammerless in place of the hammer revolver. All are 5-shot and use center fire cartridges.

38-CALIBER CARTRIDGES
91 CENTS Per 100
SEE PAGE 317.

WE FURNISH THIS REVOLVER in either nickel plate or steel blued finish, either in 32-caliber, using cartridge No. 6C2377, or 38-caliber, using cartridge No. 6C2388, with fancy rubber handles at the following prices:

No. 6C1171 32-caliber, 3 -inch barrel, nickel plated finish, rubber handles, 5-shot, weight, 12 ounces, shoots cartridge No. 6C2377. Price............$3.50
No. 6C1172 38-caliber, 3¼-inch barrel, nickel plated finish, rubber handles, 5-shot, weight, 15 ounces, shoots cartridge No. 6C2388. Price............3.50
No. 6C1173 32-caliber, 3 -inch barrel, blued steel finish, rubber handles, 5-shot, weight, 12 ounces, shoots cartridge No. 6C2377. Price............3.90
No. 6C1174 38-caliber, 3¼-inch barrel, blued steel finish, rubber handles, 5-shot, weight, 15 ounces, shoots cartridge No. 6C2388. Price............3.90

If by mail, postage extra, 32-caliber, 18 cents; 38-caliber, 24 cents.

OUR 5-INCH BARREL AUTOMATIC HAMMERLESS REVOLVER.

THE 5-INCH BARREL REVOLVER is made exactly the same as our Automatic Hammerless Revolver except that the barrel is 5 inches long, which makes it preferable for target shooting, while the 3 or 3¼-inch barrel revolver is mostly used as a pocket or home revolver for defense.

When ordering, write catalogue number in full and mention caliber, length of barrel and finish wanted.

$4.00

Catalogue Number	Caliber	Length of Barrel	Finish	Handles	Wgt.	No. of shots	Shoots Cartridge	Price
6C1175	32 C. F.	5 ins.	Nickel Pl't'd	Rubber	12 oz.	5shot	No. 6C2377	$4.00
6C1176	38 C. F.	5 ins.	Nickel Pl't'd	Rubber	15 oz.	5shot	No. 6C2388	4.00
6C1177	32 C. F.	5 ins.	Blued Steel	Rubber	12 oz.	5shot	No. 6C2377	4.40
6C1178	38 C. F.	5 ins.	Blued Steel	Rubber	15 oz.	5shot	No. 6C2388	4.40

If by mail, postage extra, 32-caliber, 22 cents; 38-caliber, 26 cents.

32-CALIBER CARTRIDGES FOR THESE REVOLVERS. PRICE, PER HUNDRED... 70c
38-CALIBER CARTRIDGES FOR THESE REVOLVERS. PRICE, PER HUNDRED... 91c

OUR PEARL HANDLE AUTOMATIC HAMMERLESS REVOLVER.

THIS IS OUR REGULAR AUTOMATIC HAMMERLESS REVOLVER, but fitted with pearl handles instead of rubber handles. The pearl used is strictly first class quality. We use no seconds or inferior pearl.

When ordering, write catalogue number in full and mention caliber, length of barrel and finish wanted.

$4.50

Catalogue Number	Caliber	Length of Barrel	Finish	Handles	Wgt.	No. of shots	Shoots Cartridge	Price
6C1171P	32 C. F.	3 ins.	Nickel Plated	Pearl	12 oz.	5shot	No. 6C2377	$4.50
6C1172P	38 C. F.	3¼ ins.	Nickel Plated	Pearl	15 oz.	5shot	No. 6C2388	4.50
6C1173P	32 C. F.	3 ins.	Blued Steel	Pearl	12 oz.	5shot	No. 6C2377	4.90
6C1174P	38 C. F.	3¼ ins.	Blued Steel	Pearl	15 oz.	5shot	No. 6C2388	4.90
6C1175P	32 C. F.	5 ins.	Nickel Plated	Pearl	15 oz.	5shot	No. 6C2377	5.00
6C1176P	38 C. F.	5 ins.	Nickel Plated	Pearl	18 oz.	5shot	No. 6C2388	5.00
6C1177P	32 C. F.	5 ins.	Blued Steel	Pearl	15 oz.	5shot	No. 6C2377	5.40
6C1178P	38 C. F.	5 ins.	Blued Steel	Pearl	18 oz.	5shot	No. 6C2388	5.40

If by mail, postage extra, 18 to 26 cents.

NOTE—These Revolvers not made for Rim Fire Cartridges.

WHILE WE ESPECIALLY URGE THE PURCHASE OF A REVOLVER MADE IN OUR OWN FACTORY, as illustrated and described on the preceding pages, we show on this and the following pages A LINE OF THE WELL KNOWN DOUBLE ACTION MAKES, AND AT PRICES LOWER THAN YOU CAN BUY ELSEWHERE.

IN ORDERING A SINGLE REVOLVER we advise sending it by mail. This can be done by enclosing enough extra money to cover postage. The postage is 1 cent per ounce, or fraction thereof. If sent by insured mail, allow 5 cents extra for revolvers valued at $5.00 or less, and 10 cents extra for revolvers costing $10.00 or less; and 15 cents extra for revolvers costing $15.00 or less, and if lost in transit you will be entitled to a new revolver.

ON RECEIPT OF $1.00 we will send any revolver by express C. O. D., subject to examination, balance to be paid after the revolver is received and found perfectly satisfactory. We recommend, however, that you send cash in full with your order and save the small extra charge on a C. O. D. shipment. Nearly all our customers send cash in full with their orders.

DON'T FAIL TO COMPARE OUR PRICES WITH OTHER HOUSES.
WE CAN SAVE YOU MONEY.

HOW TO TEST A PISTOL OR REVOLVER.

PLEASE NOTE that expert pistol and revolver shooting can only be accomplished by experience and when once you become an expert shot, it is difficult for you to do poor shooting when you are in good form. **ALL REVOLVERS ARE TESTED** at 12 to 20 yards except the high power strong shooting arms, which are tested at 50 yards, and if you do not make a good target, it is not the fault of the revolver, but is usually the fault of the sighting; for instance, a revolver that is tested at a target at 12 yards, and you can do good shooting at this range, you will find if you shoot the same revolver at 50 yards the bullets will fall under the target, so in order to become an expert shot it is quite necessary for you to become acquainted with the revolver you intend to shoot, and in a short time you will know whether to hold above or below the bull's eye in order to hit it. **WHEN TESTING A REVOLVER** always take a muzzle rest, and shoot 5 or 6 consecutive shots at a bull's eye without stopping, then examine your target and see how the shots group and how near the group is to your bull's eye. This will give you an idea whether you should hold high, low, to the right or to the left of your mark. Always bear in mind that the wind has more or less effect on target shooting, and 5-inch barrel revolvers are better than 3-inch for target shooting. It requires long practice to become skilled with a 3-inch barrel.

OUR NEW MODEL DOUBLE ACTION REVOLVERS, $1.65.

$1.65

All full nickel plated and checkered rubber handle, octagon steel rifled barrel, forged parts, and made from the best material that money can buy. Made in 32-caliber rim fire, 32-caliber central fire and 38-caliber central fire.

Catalogue Number	Caliber	Length of Barrel	Finish	No. of Sh'ts	Shoots Cartridge	Weight	Price
6C1183½	32 r.f.	2 in.	Nickel Plated	5	6C2352	10 oz.	$1.65
6C1185	32 c.f.	2½ in.		6	6C2377	16 oz.	
6C1186	38 c.f.	2½ in.		5	6C2388	16 oz.	

Extra for pearl stock for any of the above revolvers. Price $1.00

If by mail, postage extra, 12 to 20 cents.

CARTRIDGES, 70 AND 91 CENTS PER 100. SEE PAGE 317.

OUR $1.90 AND $2.15 REVOLVERS HAVE 4½ AND 6-INCH BARRELS.

THESE REVOLVERS ARE STRICTLY FIRST CLASS IN EVERY RESPECT, and made especially for us under season contract. The quality of material and workmanship is the best. All have octagon rifled barrels and are good shooters; 5 or 6-shot. These are not toys, but good guns. No one can meet our prices on these goods.

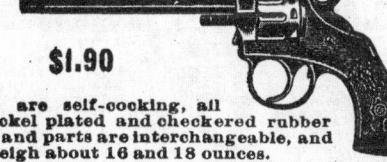

$1.90

They are self-cocking, all full nickel plated and checkered rubber stocks, and parts are interchangeable, and they weigh about 16 and 18 ounces.

Catalogue Number	Caliber	Length of Barrel	Finish	No. of Sh'ts	Shoots Cartridge	Weight	Price
6C1189	32 c.f.	4½ in.	Nickel Plated	6	6C2377	16 oz.	$1.90
6C1190	38 c.f.	4½ in.		5	6C2388	18 oz.	
6C1191	32 c.f.	6 in.		6	6C2377	16 oz.	2.15
6C1192	38 c.f.	6 in.		5	6C2388	18 oz.	

Extra for pearl stock $1.00

If by mail, postage extra, 20 to 27 cents.

CARTRIDGES, 70 AND 91 CENTS PER 100. SEE PAGE 317.

OUR $1.65 DOUBLE ACTION REVOLVER.

Manufactured by the Hopkins & Allen Manufacturing Co., who bought the Forehand & Wadsworth factory.

Forehand & Wadsworth New Double Action, Self Cocking Revolver, full nickel plated, rubber stock, octagon rifled barrel, safe and reliable, accurate, rebounding lock, parts are interchangeable.

Catalogue Number	Caliber	Length of Barrel	Finish	No. of Sh'ts	Shoots Cartridge	Weight	Price
6C1195	32 c.f.	2½ in.	Nickel Plated	6	6C2377	15 oz.	$1.65
6C1196	38 c.f.	2½ in.		5	6C2388	15 oz.	

If by mail, postage extra, 20 cents.

If you wish us to send a revolver by insured mail, see top of this page for rates of insurance.

CARTRIDGES 70 AND 91 CENTS PER 100. SEE PAGE 317.

OUR $1.65 SAFETY HAMMER DOUBLE ACTION REVOLVER.

70c PER 100 FOR 32-CALIBER CARTRIDGES. 91c PER 100 FOR 38-CALIBER CARTRIDGES. SEE PAGE 317.

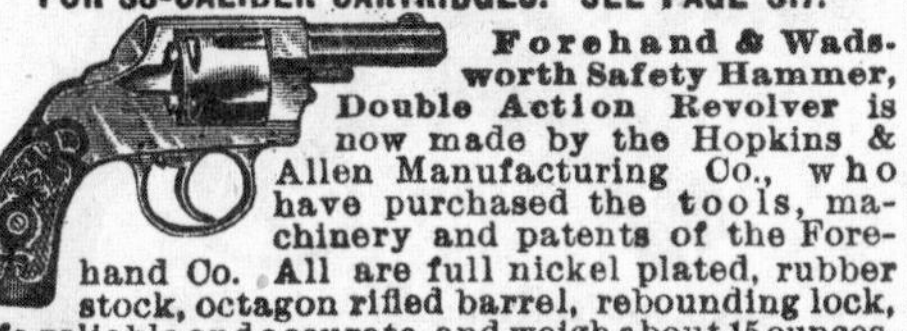

Forehand & Wadsworth Safety Hammer, Double Action Revolver is now made by the Hopkins & Allen Manufacturing Co., who have purchased the tools, machinery and patents of the Forehand Co. All are full nickel plated, rubber stock, octagon rifled barrel, rebounding lock, safe, reliable and accurate, and weigh about 15 ounces.

Catalogue Number	Caliber	Length of Barrel	Finish	No. of Sh'ts	Shoots Cartridge	Weight	Price
6C1197	32 c.f.	2½ in.	Nickel Plated	6	6C2377	15 oz.	$1.65
6C1198	38 c.f.	2½ in.		5	6C2388	15 oz.	

If by mail, postage extra, 20 cents.

These goods are genuine, and new from the factory. Beware of imitations and shop worn goods, which are sold for new goods by some firms. We handle nothing but first class goods.

OUR $2.75 AUTOMATIC — AND — $3.50 HAMMERLESS REVOLVERS

ARE GUARANTEED TO BE EQUAL TO ANY REVOLVER USUALLY SOLD AT DOUBLE THIS PRICE

Send us your order, compare our revolver with any revolver costing more money, keep it ten days, if at that time you are in any way dissatisfied, return the revolver to us and we will refund your money and transportation charges paid by you.

OUR BABY HAMMERLESS REVOLVER.

$1.80

Our Baby Hammerless Revolver is manufactured by Henry M. Kolb, Philadelphia, Pa., who guarantees the revolver against defective parts. It is made to carry in the vest pocket, length of revolver is 4 inches, all parts made interchangeable. All have folding trigger, rifled steel barrel, fancy rubber stock, fluted cylinder, can be loaded from the side, rebounding hammer, full nickel plated; taking 22-caliber rim fire cartridge No. 6C2336.

No. 6C1249 Our Baby Hammerless Revolver, 22-caliber rim fire, taking cartridge No. 6C2336, weight 4½ ounces. 6-shot. Price.. .... $1.80

No. 6C1250 The same revolver fitted with pearl handles $2.70

If by mail, postage extra, 8 cents.

22-CALIBER CARTRIDGES, 19c PER 100. SEE PAGE 317.

THE STEVENS' NEW MODEL TIP UP.

22-CALIBER CARTRIDGES, 19c PER 100. SEE PAGE 317.

22-caliber only. 3½-inch barrel.

Stevens' Single Shot Pistol. Tip up barrel, nickel plated finish, 3½-inch blued steel barrel, 22-caliber only, rim fire. No better material put in rifles. A fine target pistol. Rifled barrel and well made throughout.

No. 6C1343 For 22-caliber short cartridges No. 6C2336. (Postage extra, 15c.) Price $1.95

REMINGTON DERRINGERS.

This is the genuine Remington Double Derringer. Don't buy imitations. The Remington Double Derringer, 41-caliber short, rim fire, takes cartridge No. 6C2360; checkered rubber stock; length of barrels, 3 inches, entire length of pistol is 5 inches; nickel plated.

$4.25

No. 6C1347 Price, nickel plated $4.25
No. 6C1348 Same, blued. Price ....
If fitted with pearl handles, extra 1.25

If by mail, postage extra, 24 cents.

HARRINGTON & RICHARDSON'S YOUNG AMERICA, LADIES' REVOLVER.

Double Action, Reduced Size, 22-Caliber, Rim Fire. 19 CENTS PER 100 FOR THESE CARTRIDGES. SEE PAGE 317.

Young America. $1.65 and $2.55

Full nickel plated, 22-caliber, 7-shot, 2-inch rifled octagon barrel.

The Young America can be carried in the vest pocket as conveniently as a watch, and is designed especially for ladies' use. Takes cartridge No. 6C2336.

22 SHORT

No. 6C1354

No. 6C1352 22-caliber, rubber stocks, 7 ounces. Price $1.65

No. 6C1354 22-caliber, fitted with pearl handles. Price.. (Postage extra, 13 cents).. 2.55

HARRINGTON & RICHARDSON'S YOUNG AMERICA, SELF COCKER.

70 CENTS PER 100 FOR CARTRIDGES. SEE PAGE 317.

Reduced Size, 32-Caliber, Double Action, Rifled Barrel, Central Fire.

32-caliber only. $1.65 and $2.55

Young America.

Full nickeled, rubber stocks, 5-shot, 2-inch rifled octagon barrel, 9 ounces. Takes the 32-caliber S. & W. cartridge No. 6C2377.

No. 6C1355 32-caliber, central fire. Price $1.65

No. 6C1357 32-caliber, with pearl stocks. Price $2.55

If by mail, postage extra, 15 cents.

HARRINGTON & RICHARDSON'S YOUNG AMERICA, SAFETY HAMMER, SELF COCKER.

70 CENTS PER 100 FOR CARTRIDGES. SEE PAGE 317.

Reduced Size, Full Nickeled, Rubber Stocks, 5-Shot Rifled Barrel with Safety Hammer.

32-caliber only. $1.65 and $2.55

The Young America.

Safety hammer, 32-caliber only, central fire, 2-inch barrel. Takes 32-caliber S. & W. cartridge No. 6C2377.

No. 6C1359 32-caliber, central fire, 9 ounces. Price $1.65

No. 6C1361 32-caliber, with pearl handles. Price......(Postage extra, 15 cents.)....... 2.55

HARRINGTON & RICHARDSON'S VEST POCKET, SELF COCKER.

70 CENTS PER 100 FOR CARTRIDGES. SEE PAGE 317.

A neat little Vest Pocket 5-Shot Revolver, full nickel plated, fancy rubber handles. Made to carry in the vest pocket, with 1⅛-inch round barrel. Weight, 8¼ ounces. Takes 32-caliber central fire S. & W. cartridge No. 6C2377. $1.65 and $2.55

No. 6C1363 32-caliber, central fire, with rubber handles. Price $1.65

No. 6C1365 32-caliber, central fire, with pearl handles. Price $2.55

If by mail, postage extra, 14 cents.

STEVENS' DIAMOND MODEL TARGET PISTOL.

22 CALIBER CARTRIDGES 19 CENTS PER 100. SEE PAGE 317.

The Celebrated Stevens' Target Pistol, the best pistol made for fine, close shooting. It has fine, blued barrel, nickel plated frame, rosewood stock, 6-inch tip up barrel; fitted with fine globe and peep target sights, 22-caliber, rim fire. Shoots either 22 long rifle or 22 short cartridges; good for 50 yards. 22-caliber, 6-inch barrel.

No. 6C1344 Diamond model, with globe and peep sights. Price $3.95

No. 6C1345 The same pistol, but with open sights. (Postage extra, 16c.) Price.. 3.97

HARRINGTON & RICHARDSON'S YOUNG AMERICA, TARGET REVOLVER.

22-CALIBER CARTRIDGES, 21c PER 100. SEE PAGE 317.

Double Action, Reduced Size, 22-Caliber, Rim Fire, with 6-inch Rifled Octagon Barrel.

$2.15 and $3.05

The Young America is full nickeled, rubber or pearl stocks, 7-shot, 6-inch rifled octagon barrel; takes cartridge No. 6C2336 and weighs 10 ounces.

Catalogue Number	Caliber	Length of Barrel	Finish	No. of Sh'ts	Shoots Cartridge No.	Handles	Price
6C1368	22 r.f.	6 in.	Nickel	7	6C2336	Rubber	$2.15
6C1369	22 r.f.	6 in.	Plated	7	6C2336	Pearl	3.05

This is the only 22-caliber, 7-shot, target pistol on the market and we were the first to offer it to our customers. **If by mail, postage extra, 14 cents.**

HARRINGTON & RICHARDSON'S NEW MODEL PREMIER, 22-CALIBER, 3-INCH BARREL.

22-CALIBER CARTRIDGES, 19c PER 100. SEE PAGE 317.

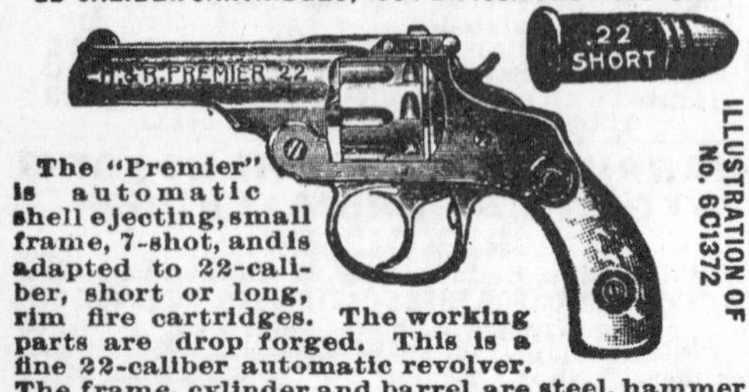

ILLUSTRATION OF No. 6C1372

The "Premier" is automatic shell ejecting, small frame, 7-shot, and is adapted to 22-caliber, short or long, rim fire cartridges. The working parts are drop forged. This is a fine 22-caliber automatic revolver. The frame, cylinder and barrel are steel, hammer is hardened, automatic shell ejector, rubber stocks. Full nickel plated or blued finish, rifled barrel. Weighs 13 ounces. A good pocket size revolver and takes cartridge No. 6C2336.

Catalogue Number	Caliber	Length of Barrel	Finish	No. of Sh'ts	Shoots Cartridge No.	Handles	Price
6C1370	22 r.f.	3 in.	Nickeled	7	6C2336 or 6C2338	Rubber	$3.35
6C1371	22 r.f.	3 in.	Blued	7		Rubber	3.60
6C1372	22 r.f.	3 in.	Nickeled	7		Pearl	4.35
6C1373	22 r.f.	3 in.	Blued	7		Pearl	4.60

If by mail, postage extra, 20 cents.

HARRINGTON & RICHARDSON'S NEW MODEL PREMIER, 22-CALIBER, WITH 5-INCH BARREL.

22-CALIBER CARTRIDGES, 19c PER 100. SEE PAGE 317.

$3.85 AND $4.10

It is automatic shell ejecting, small frame, 7-shot, and is adapted to 22-caliber, short or long, rim fire cartridges. The working parts are drop forged. This is a fine 22-caliber automatic revolver. The frame, cylinder and barrel are steel, hammer is hardened, automatic shell ejector, rubber stocks, rifled barrel. Full nickel plated or blued finish. Weight, about 14 ounces. Shoots cartridges No. 6C2336 or No. 6C2338.

Catalogue Number	Caliber	Length of Barrel	Finish	No. of Sh'ts	Shoots Cartridge No.	Weight, Ounces	Price
6C1374	22 r.f.	5 in.	Nickeled	7	6C2336	14	$3.85
6C1375	22 r.f.	5 in.	Blued	7	6C2338	14	4.10

Extra for pearl handles on these revolvers............$1.00

If by mail, postage extra, 22 cents.

OUR $3.25 FOREHAND AUTOMATIC.

Hopkins & Allen's Celebrated Forehand Automatic Revolver for $3.25; a revolver that retails **at from $5.00 to $6.00.** The very latest improved model, **automatic shell extractor, rebounding locks, double action, self cocking, simple and accurate, inter**changeable parts made from drop steel forgings. The frame is cast steel, no malleable iron about it; **nickel plated throughout;** fancy rubber stock, every revolver is fully warranted; length of barrel, **3¼ inches; weight, 17 ounces; entire length, 7⅜ inches.** The fact that our sales are constantly increasing on these revolvers is evidence of the general satisfaction they give.

32 and 38-Caliber.

Catalogue Number	Caliber	Length of Barrel	Finish	No. of Sh'ts	Shoots Cartridge	Weight	Price
6C1380	32 c.f.	3¼ in.	Nickel	6	6C2377	17 oz.	$3.25
6C1382	38 c.f.	3¼ in.	Nickel	5	6C2388	17 oz.	3.25

If by mail, postage extra, 24 cents.

OUR REVOLVER STOCK, 65c.

Our Revolver Stock is made to be attached to any revolver and is a great assistance to revolver shooters for getting steady aim. With this stock you practically make a rifle out of your revolver. To attach this stock, wrap a piece of cloth around the revolver handle to prevent it from becoming marred, and screw it fast with the thumb nut. This stock will not take the Colt's Automatic Pistol as it interferes with the magazine of same.

No. 6C1398 Our Revolver Stock. Price..............**65c**

If by mail, postage extra, 20 cents.

HARRINGTON & RICHARDSON'S REVOLVERS.

70 AND 91 CENTS PER 100 FOR CARTRIDGES. SEE PAGE 317.

32 and 38-Caliber.

$3.25

Over 3,000,000 Harrington & Richardson's Revolvers now in use.

OUR $3.25 AUTOMATIC REVOLVER.

This revolver would retail in any first class gun store at from $5.00 to $6.00. The celebrated Harrington & Richardson's Improved Automatic, self extracting, double action, self cocking revolver, modeled on the Smith & Wesson pattern, beautifully nickel plated, rubber stock, as accurate and durable as any revolver on the market, and equal to the Smith & Wesson in shooting. Weight, 18½ ounces, 3¼-inch barrel. The 32-caliber is 6-shot, and the 38-caliber is 5-shot.

Catalogue Number	Caliber	Length of Barrel	Finish	No. of Sh'ts	Shoots Cartridge	Weight, Ounces	Price
6C1385	32 c.f.	3¼ in.	Nickel	6	6C2377	18½	$3.25
6C1386	38 c.f.	3¼ in.	Plated	5	6C2388	18½	3.25

Pearl handles on either of the above will cost extra...$1.10

If by mail postage extra, 18 to 24 cents.

OUR NEW LIBERTY 22-CALIBER REVOLVER, $1.15.

Owing to the many calls which we have had for a cheap 22-caliber single action revolver, we have ordered a quantity of the Liberty revolvers with 2½-inch barrel, 7-shot, fancy rubber saw handle, full nickel plated throughout, taking the 22-caliber, rim fire, short cartridge. Weight, about 7 ounces. Full length, 5⅞ inches. These revolvers are not quite as good as the Young America revolver, but are intended to take the place of a cheap single action revolver. They are as well made as any single action revolver yet produced.

No. 6C1399 Our Liberty Single Action Revolver, 22-caliber, 2½-inch barrel, using cartridges No. 6C2336. Price.......**$1.15**

If by mail, postage extra, 10 cents.

22-CALIBER CARTRIDGES FOR THIS REVOLVER 19 CENTS PER 100. SEE PAGE 317.

HARRINGTON & RICHARDSON'S HAMMERLESS REVOLVERS.

70 AND 91 CENTS PER 100 FOR CARTRIDGES. SEE PAGE 317

32 or 38-Caliber, Adapted to S. & W. Cartridges

$3.75

This is Harrington & Richardson's latest production. The revolvers have automatic shell ejectors, forged parts, steel barrels and rubber stocks. The 32-caliber has a small light frame, making them a good convenient pocket size. They are full nickel plated. The 32-caliber uses cartridge No. 6C2377; 38-caliber uses cartridge No. 6C2388

Catalogue Number	Caliber	Length of Barrel	Finish	No. of Sh'ts	Shoots Cartridge	Weight	Price
6C1411	32 c.f.	3 in.	Nickel	5	6C2377	13 oz.	$3.75
6C1412	38 c.f.	3¼ in.	Plated	5	6C2388	18 oz.	3.75

Pearl handles on above revolvers, extra.........$1.10

If by mail, postage extra, 18 to 24 cents.

OUR $3.75 FOREHAND HAMMERLESS.

70c PER 100 FOR 32-CALIBER CARTRIDGES. 91c PER 100 FOR 38-CALIBER CARTRIDGES.

SMALL FRAME.

32 and 38-Caliber.

We offer you at $3.75 our Hopkins & Allen's Forehand hammerless revolver which has never been retailed at less than $6.00. No other house will meet our price. Make a comparison and decide for yourself.

This is the celebrated Forehand new style hammerless revolver, made by the Hopkins & Allen Manufacturing Co., who have bought out the Forehand Arms Co. No better revolver made. **Automatic shell extractor,** double action, self cocking, rebounding lock, absolutely safe catch to lock hammer, made of best material, beautifully finished throughout, accurate and reliable. All center fire, and nicely nickel plated finish. Uses Smith & Wesson center fire cartridges, **32-caliber and 38-caliber, 5-shot.**

Catalogue Number	Caliber	Length of Barrel	Finish	No. of Sh'ts	Shoots Cartridge	Weight	Price
6C1425	32 c.f.	3 in.	Nickel	5	6C2377	14 oz.	$3.75
6C1427	38 c.f.	3¼ in.	Nickel	5	6C2388	16 oz.	$3.75

If by mail, postage extra, 19 to 24 cents.

OUR $3.65 FRONTIER REVOLVER

This Frontier Revolver is offered as the BEST strong shooting arm made at a medium low price. The best revolver for the money for frontier use. This large, strong shooting and well finished revolver retails everywhere at from $6.00 to $8.00.

$3.65

Takes Cartridge 6C2409

It is a 5½-inch barrel 6 shooter, with **fine engraved rubber stock,** 44-caliber, **center fire, full nickel plated or blued finish. This revolver is adapted to 44-caliber Winchester cartridges, so that a person having a rifle need not change** ammunition, but can use the same cartridges in both. Weight, 35 ounces.

No. 6C1434 Price, nickel plated....**$3.65**

No. 6C1436 Same revolver, blue finish. **4.15**

If by mail, postage extra, 40 cents.

THE GENUINE COLT'S MAGAZINE REVOLVERS.

MADE BY THE COLT'S FIRE ARMS CO., HARTFORD, CONN.

NOTICE—The manufacturer fixes the prices at which we shall sell these revolvers, and will not allow us or any house to sell them any cheaper. THESE PRICES ARE GUARANTEED to be as low as offered by any reliable dealer in the United States and should you be offered these goods lower by any dealer you will confer a great favor by advising us, in order to give us an opportunity of adjusting the prices.

COLT'S AUTOMATIC MAGAZINE PISTOL, 32-CALIBER, $15.00

The opposite illustration engraved direct from a photograph will give you some idea of the Colt's Automatic Pistol made in caliber 32 to shoot smokeless cartridges for powerful long range shooting. This is the latest creation of the Colt's Patent Fire Arms Co., of Hartford, Conn. The Colt's Automatic Pistol is designed and proportioned for a pocket size automatic pistol.

QUARTER SIZE

Specifications. The entire pistol is made from the very best grade of crucible steel which can be procured regardless of price, the mechanism is of the same high order which follows the Colt line throughout their entire output; the parts are simple and strong, not liable to get out of order, the barrel is finely rifled for long range shooting; all metal parts are handsomely blued, fancy rubber handles, latest improved safety on the grip which renders the pistol perfectly safe until the owner is ready to shoot, the entire length of the Colt's Automatic Pistol is 7 inches, the weight is 24 ounces, will hold 8 cartridges in the magazine and 1 in the barrel, making it a 9-shot pistol, is accurate up to 300 yards, and will penetrate four one-inch pine boards at a distance of 15 feet. To shoot the pistol, first cock the pistol, fill the magazine and put a cartridge in the chamber. Each shot throws out the shell and puts in a new cartridge. All you have to do is pull the trigger.

No. 6C1500 Colt's Automatic Pistol, 32-caliber, 4-inch barrel, weight, 24 ounces. Price..............**$15.00**

If fitted with pearl handles, extra..............1.75

Extra magazine for the above pistol. Price.......... **.90**

If by registered mail, postage extra, 36 cents.

No. 6C2560 32-caliber Automatic Smokeless Rimless Cartridges with metal patched bullet. Price, per box of 50, **72c**

Cartridges cannot be sent by mail.

COLT'S AUTOMATIC MAGAZINE PISTOL ONLY $19.50

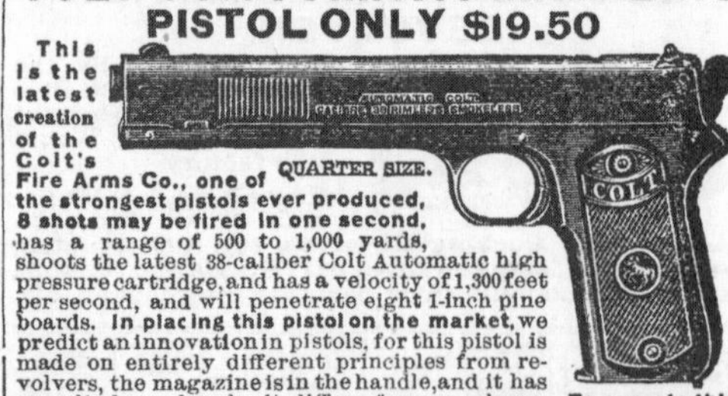

QUARTER SIZE.

This is the latest creation of the Colt's Fire Arms Co., one of the strongest pistols ever produced, 8 shots may be fired in one second, has a range of 500 to 1,000 yards, shoots the latest 38-caliber Colt Automatic high pressure cartridge, and has a velocity of 1,300 feet per second, and will penetrate eight 1-inch pine boards. **In placing this pistol on the market,** we predict an innovation in pistols, for this pistol is made on entirely different principles from revolvers, the magazine is in the handle, and it has no cylinder, whereby it differs from revolvers. **To operate this pistol, place seven cartridges in the magazine, and one in the chamber, raise the hammer, and all you have to do after that is to pull the trigger, for the pistol cocks itself after every shot is fired by its own recoil,** ejects the cartridge which has been fired, places a new cartridge in the chamber, and is ready to shoot again as soon as you are ready to pull the trigger, in other words, the pistol shoots, raises the hammer, ejects the empty shell, replaces another cartridge in the chamber, as fast as you can pull the trigger; the entire eight loads may be fired in eight seconds.

The Colt's Automatic Pocket Pistol has 4½-inch barrel.

Catalogue Number	Caliber	Length of Barrel	Finish	No. of Sh'ts	Shoots Cartridge	Weight	Price
6C1503	38 aut.	4½ in.	Blued	8	6C2580	31 oz.	$19.50
6C1505	38 aut.	6 in.	Steel	8	6C2580	35 oz.	

Extra for pearl stocks, fitted to the above pistol...... **2.00**

Extra magazines for above pistol. Each.............. **1.35**

If by registered mail, postage extra, 48 cents.

No. 6C2580 38-caliber automatic smokeless cartridges with metal patched bullets. Price, per box of 50.......**$1.07**

COLT'S NEW NAVY REVOLVER.

Illustration showing the revolver open. 38 and 41-caliber.

This revolver has been adopted by the U. S. navy, and every one must pass a rigid inspection and test. Colt's New Navy double action, self cocking, automatic shell ejecting revolver, rubber stock, beautifully finished, finest material, length about 12½ inches; six shooter; weight, 2 lbs.; blued steel finish. The 38-caliber takes cartridges No. 6C2391 or No. 6C2392, and the 41-caliber takes cartridges No. 6C2400 or No. 6C2401.

Catalogue Number	Caliber	Length of Barrel	Finish	No. of Sh'ts	Shoots Cartridge No.	Weight Ounces	Price
6C1521	38 c.f.	4½in.	Blued	6	6C2391 or 6C2392	32	$13.90
6C1523	38 c.f.	6 in.	Blued	6		32	
6C1525	41 c.f.	4½in.	Blued	6	6C2400 or 6C2401	32	13.90
6C1527	41 c.f.	6 in.	Blued	6		32	

If fitted with pearl stocks, extra........................$2.75

If by mail, postage extra, 40 cents.

COLT'S DOUBLE ACTION REVOLVER.

38 and 41-Caliber.

Colt's Double Action, sliding ejector. Every one warranted. 38 or 41-caliber, 6-shooter, center fire, rubber handles, blued steel finish, as desired, 4½ or 6-inch barrel. The 38-caliber takes cartridges No. 6C2391 or No. 6C2392, and the 41-caliber takes No. 6C2400 or No. 6C2401.

Catalogue Number	Caliber	Length of Barrel	Finish	No. of Sh'ts	Shoots Cartridge No.	Weight Ounces	Price
6C1531	38 c.f.	4½in.	Blued	6	6C2391 or 6C2392	26	$11.60
6C1533	38 c.f.	6 in.	Blued	6		28	
6C1537	41 c.f.	6 in.	Blued	6	6C2400 or 6C2401	28	12.95

If fitted with pearl stocks, extra........................$2.75

If by mail, postage extra, each, 40 cents.

91 CENTS PER 100 FOR 38-CALIBER CARTRIDGES.

70 CENTS PER 100 FOR 32-CALIBER CARTRIDGES.

SEE PAGE 317.

COLT'S NEW ARMY MODEL 1892.

38 and 41-Caliber.

Colt's New Army Model 1892. Double action, self cocking. Weight, 2 pounds, 6-shooter, 38 or 41-caliber, length of barrel, 4½ or 6 inches. Blued steel finish, rubber handles. The 38-caliber takes cartridges No. 6C2391 or No. 6C2392 and the 41-caliber takes No. 6C2400 or No. 6C2401.

Catalogue Number	Caliber	Length of Barrel	Finish	No. of Sh'ts	Shoots Cartridge No.	Wgt. Oz.	Price
6C1541	38 c.f.	4½in.	Blued	6	6C2391 or 6C2392	32	$13.90
6C1543	38 c.f.	6 in.	Blued	6		32	
6C1545	41 c.f.	4½in.	Blued	6	6C2400 or 6C2401	32	13.90
6C1547	41 c.f.	6 in.	Blued	6		32	

If fitted with pearl stocks, extra........................$2.75

If by mail, postage extra, each, 40 cents.

WE RECOMMEND THE FOLLOWING CALIBERS OF COLT'S REVOLVERS:

For small game, 32 short, 32 long and 41 short.
For medium size game, 32-20, 38 short, 38 long and 41 long.
For deer, bear, etc., 44-40 and 45-caliber.
For quantity of powder and weight of bullet in each above caliber, see central fire cartridges, loaded with black powder, on another page.

COLT'S NEW SERVICE DOUBLE ACTION REVOLVER.

45-CALIBER.

The New Service Double Action Revolvers, jointless solid frame, combined with simultaneous ejector, using 45-caliber Colt's double action cartridges; 7½-inch barrel, rubber handles, blued steel finish only. Weight, about 2 pounds. They are powerful shooters and take cartridges No. 6C2413.

Catalogue Number	Caliber	Length of Barrel	Finish	No. of Sh'ts	Shoots Cartrid No.	Wgt. Oz.	Price
6C1563	45 c.f.	7½in.	Blued Steel	6	6C2413	36	16.20

If fitted with pearl stock, extra........................$5.50

If by mail, postage extra, 44 cents.

Nickel Plated Colt's Revolvers are not carried in stock, but we ship these from factory. Send cash in full with order, as we cannot send C. O. D.

COLT'S SPECIAL PEARL HANDLE REVOLVER.

SINGLE ACTION FRONTIER.

This is our special. Cowboy's Six Shooter with pearl handles. The right handle has an Ox Head carved in raised design and makes a handsome revolver. This illustration is engraved from a photograph of the revolver and will give you some idea of its appearance. Made in blued steel finish only. We handle these regularly in 32-20 and 44-40-calibers but can furnish them on special order in caliber 41 c. f. or 45 Colt's c. f. with 5½ or 7½-inch barrel at $20.00 each. Weight, 41 ounces. **When ordering, say which length barrel you prefer.**

Catalogue Number	Caliber C. F.	Length of Barrel	Finish	No. of Sh'ts	Shoots Cartridge No.	Wgt. Oz.	Price
6C1587	32-20	5½in.	Blued Steel	6	6C2384	41	20.00
6C1589	32-20	7½in.		6	6C2384	41	
6C1591	44-40	5½in.	Blued Steel	6	6C2409	41	20.00
6C1593	44-40	7½in.		6	6C2409	41	

Above may be had in 41 and 45-calibers or in blued steel to special order, cash with order.

If by mail, postage extra, 46 cents.

COLT'S SINGLE ACTION BISLEY MODEL.

The Colt's Bisley Model Revolver is patterned after the Single Action Army Revolver, but has a longer handle, a different shape hammer, and the lock work is somewhat different, and it makes a good smooth working revolver. The frame is case hardened, and the barrel and cylinder are blued. This revolver embodies all the high grade workmanship of the famous Colt's revolvers. We carry this revolver regularly in 32-20 caliber, using cartridges No. 6C2384, but we can furnish it to special order (cash with order), to take the 45 Colt's, 38-40 and 44-40 caliber rifle cartridges.

Catalogue Number	Caliber	Length of Barrel	Finish	No. of Sh'ts	Shoots Cartridge No.	Weight Ounces	Price
6C1610	32-20	5½in.	Blued Steel	6	6C2384	40	13.90
6C1611	32-20	7½in.		6	6C2384	40	

If by mail, postage extra, 45 cents.

COLT'S SINGLE ACTION "COWBOY" FRONTIER ARMY.

32, 41, 44 and 45-Caliber.

This is the old reliable **Cowboys' Gun,** and our price is **$13.90** for all calibers. **Blued steel finish only.** Colt's single action, 6-shooter, rubber stock, solid frame, the best quality and finish; warranted perfect and accurate in every detail. Barrel 5½ or 7½ inches; entire length, 12½ inches; 32, 41, 44 or 45-caliber, as desired. We can furnish these in blued finish only.

Catalogue Number	Caliber C. F.	Length of Barrel	Finish	No. of Sh'ts	Shoots Cartridge No.	Wgt. Oz.	Price
6C1571	32-20	5½in.	Blued Steel	6	6C2384	40	13.90
6C1573	32-20	7½in.		6	6C2384	40	
6C1575	41 c. f.	5½in.	Blued Steel	6	6C2401	40	13.90
6C1577	41 c. f.	7½in.		6	6C2401	40	
6C1579	44-40	5½in.	Blued Steel	6	6C2409	40	13.90
6C1581	44-40	7½in.		6	6C2409	40	
6C1583	45 c.f.	5½in.	Blued Steel	6	6C2413	40	13.90
6C1585	45 c.f.	7½in.		6	6C2413	40	

Pearl stocks on any of the above revolvers, extra....$4.00

If by mail, postage extra, 44 cents.

THE GENUINE SMITH & WESSON REVOLVERS.

OUR 22-CALIBER SMITH & WESSON SIDE EJECTING REVOLVER, $10.50

Solid frame, side ejecting, rebounding look, rubber stock, blued steel or nickel plated; made in 22-caliber, taking rim fire cartridges Nos. 6C2336, 6C2338 or 6C2340; weighs about 10 ounces; 7-shot. This is the latest model Smith & Wesson Revolver, and the highest grade 22-caliber revolver made.

Catalogue No.	Caliber	Length of Barrel	Finish	Handle	No. of Shots	Shoots Cartridge	Weight, ounces	PRICE
6C1700	22 Rim	3½ in.	Nickeled	Rubb'r	7	6C2336 6C2338 6C2340	10	$10.50
6C1701		3½ in.	Blued	Rubb'r	7		10	

IF FITTED WITH PEARL HANDLES, EXTRA........................90c

If by mail, postage extra 14 cents.

SMITH & WESSON MILITARY AND POLICE REVOLVER, $14.00.

Double action, center fire, 6-shot, with solid frame, swing-out cylinder and hand ejecting mechanism; weight, 30 ounces; 5 and 6½-inch barrel; blued steel or nickel plated finish; using 38-caliber long Colt DA cartridge Nos. 6C2391 or 6C2392. **This revolver is Smith & Wesson's latest creation and is a revolver that is built for business.** It will withstand hard usage and has a movable firing pin on the nose of the hammer, which absolutely closes the firing pin hole and prevents any possible gas from going back of the frame. It is highly recommended for target shooting, and made in blued steel or nickel plated finish.

Catalogue No.	Caliber	Length of Bar'el	Finish	Handle	No. of Shots	Shoots Cartr'ge	Weight	PRICE
6C1714	38 c f	5 in.	Nickel	Rubb'r	6-Shot	6C2391 or 6C2392	30 oz.	$14.00
6C1715	38 c f	5 in.	Blued	Rubb'r	6-Shot		30 oz.	
6C1716	38 c f	6½ in.	Nickel	Rubb'r	6-Shot		32 oz.	14.00
6C1717	38 c f	6½ in.	Blued	Rubb'r	6-Shot		32 oz.	

FIRST QUALITY PEARL STOCKS, EXTRA........................$2.00

If by mail, postage extra, 40 cents.

We cannot furnish Smith & Wesson Revolvers for 38-40 cartridges.

COLT'S NEW POLICE REVOLVER.

32-Caliber Colt's New Police Double Action Side Ejecting Revolver, jointless solid frame combined with simultaneous ejector, using the 32 short or 32 long Colt double action, center fire cartridges. This is the revolver adopted by the New York City Police Department. Length of barrel, 4 inches. Weight, 18 ounces.

No. 6C1511 32-caliber, 4-inch barrel, blued steel finish, takes cartridges No. 6C2380 or No. 6C2381. Price........$12.70

If fitted with pearl stocks, extra........................2.00

If by mail, postage extra, 26 cents.

THE GENUINE SMITH & WESSON DOUBLE ACTION REVOLVERS.

These revolvers are warranted genuine Smith & Wesson. Manufactured by Smith & Wesson, Springfield, Mass. **Self cocking, double action,** automatic shell extractor, fine rubber stocks, nickel plated or blued steel finish. Made of the finest material that money can buy and the workmanship is equal in finish to that of any ordinary watch. If you want the best work for your money buy a Smith & Wesson. The 32-caliber takes cartridge No. 6C2377 and the 38-caliber takes cartridge No. 6C2388.

Catalogue No.	Caliber	Length of Barrel	Finish	No. of Shots	Shoots Cartr'ge	Weight	PRICE
6C1724	32 c f	3½ inches	Nickel	5-Shot	6C2377	13 ounces	$11.00
6C1725	32 c f	3½ inches	Blued	5-Shot	6C2377	13 ounces	
6C1726	32 c f	6 inches	Nickel	5-Shot	6C2377	15 ounces	11.00
6C1727	32 c f	6 inches	Blued	5-Shot	6C2377	15 ounces	
6C1730	38 c f	3¼ inches	Nickel	5-Shot	6C2388	18 ounces	12.00
6C1731	38 c f	3¼ inches	Blued	5-Shot	6C2388	18 ounces	
6C1732	38 c f	4 inches	Nickel	5-Shot	6C2388	18 ounces	12.00
6C1733	38 c f	4 inches	Blued	5-Shot	6C2388	18 ounces	
6C1734	38 c f	5 inches	Nickel	5-Shot	6C2388	19 ounces	12.00
6C1735	38 c f	5 inches	Blued	5-Shot	6C2388	19 ounces	
6C1736	38 c f	6 inches	Nickel	5-Shot	6C2388	20 ounces	12.00
6C1737	38 c f	6 inches	Blued	5-Shot	6C2388	20 ounces	

FIRST QUALITY PEARL STOCKS FOR 32 OR 38-CALIBER, EXTRA............$1.00

If by mail or prepaid express, 32-caliber, 18 cents; 38-caliber, 24 cents.

The GENUINE SMITH & WESSON HAMMERLESS.

Made by Smith & Wesson, Springfield, Mass. Latest type, new model hammerless, automatic shell ejector, patent safety catch, self locking rebounding locks, double action, blued steel or nickel plated finish. This is positively the best hammerless revolver made. "A thing of beauty is a joy forever." If you own one of these revolvers you are certain to own one of the best revolvers made and one which always has a market value. The 32-caliber takes cartridge No. 6C2377 and the 38-caliber takes cartridge No. 6C2388.

Catalogue Number	Caliber	Length of Barr'l	Finish	Handle	Number of Shots	Shoots Cart'rge	Weight	Price
6C1756	32 c f	3¼ in.	Nickel	Rubb'r	5-Shot	6C2377	15 oz.	$12.00
6C1757	32 c f	3½ in.	Blued	Rubb'r	5-Shot	6C2377	15 oz.	
6C1760	38 c f	3¼ in.	Nickel	Rubb'r	5-Shot	6C2388	17 oz.	13.00
6C1761	38 c f	3¼ in.	Blued	Rubb'r	5-Shot	6C2388	17 oz.	
6C1762	38 c f	4 in.	Nickel	Rubb'r	5-Shot	6C2388	18 oz.	13.00
6C1763	38 c f	4 in.	Blued	Rubb'r	5-Shot	6C2388	18 oz.	
6C1764	38 c f	5 in.	Nickel	Rubb'r	5-Shot	6C2388	19 oz.	13.00
6C1765	38 c f	5 in.	Blued	Rubb'r	5-Shot	6C2388	19 oz.	
6C1766	38 c f	6 in.	Nickel	Rubb'r	5-Shot	6C2388	19 oz.	13.00
6C1767	38 c f	6 in.	Blued	Rubb'r	5-Shot	6C2388	19 oz.	

FIRST QUALITY PEARL STOCKS ON ANY OF THE ABOVE REVOLVERS, EXTRA $1.00

If by mail, postage extra, 18 to 30 cents. ☞ See our prices on cartridges.

THE IMPORTED AUTOMATIC DOUBLE ACTION REVOLVER.

IMITATION OF SMITH & WESSON.

$4.50 AND $5.00

This illustration, engraved from a photograph by our artist, will give you some idea of the revolver. It is central fire, and has 5½-inch barrel, finished in blued or nickel plated. Made in 44-caliber only.

It has rebounding hammer, rubber stock, weighs 35 ounces and is automatic shell ejecting. This revolver takes the same cartridge as the Winchester Rifle, 44-caliber (No. 6C2409), so that a man who has a 44-caliber rifle can use the same ammunition in both the rifle and this revolver. We have contracted for a large lot of these revolvers in order to get the price so we can sell them with our one small percentage of profit at these figures.

If by registered mail, 45c extra.

Takes No. 6C2409 Cartridges.

No. 6C1780 44-caliber, rubber stock, 5½-inch barrel, nickel plated finish. Price..$4.50

No. 6C1781 44-caliber, rubber stock, 5½-inch barrel, blued finish. 5.00

If by mail, postage extra, 45 cents.

ATTENTION, BOYS! Look at These Prices on AIR RIFLES.

THE NEW MODEL KING AIR RIFLE, SINGLE SHOT.

Our King Rifles we Guarantee the Highest Grade Made.

58 CENTS.

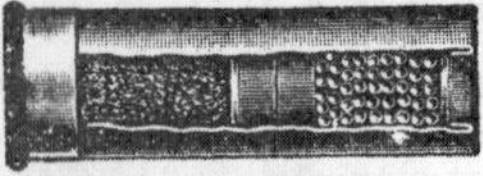

All metal, nickel plated, shoots BB shot. Length of barrel, 19 inches; length over all, 34 inches. Weight, 2 pounds. The New Model King Air Rifle shoots common BB shot accurately and with sufficient force to go through ¼-inch soft pine. The barrel and all working parts are made from the best material possible; no castings to break in case it falls to the ground. Each gun is sighted with movable sights.

No. 6C1832 The New Model King Air Rifle. Price..................58c

If by mail, postage extra, 35 cents.

THE COLUMBIAN 1,000-SHOT AIR RIFLE, $1.10.

The Columbian 1,000-Shot Air Rifle, as now made, with improved lock parts and magazine, is an air rifle which will give universal satisfaction. The loading device is very similar to that of the old model air rifle, that by pushing the sleeve forward you fill the magazine with BB shot, and to operate the rifle, hold the gun in the left hand, turn the muzzle toward the ceiling, throw the lever forward, same as you would with the Winchester rifle, and the gun loads itself. Every time you throw the lever you put a shot in the barrel. It is best to shoot after you load the gun or you will get several pellets in the barrel. Should an imperfect shot get into the barrel, it can easily be removed by cocking the gun and inserting a wire from the muzzle, which pushes the shot into the chamber, from which it can easily be removed. The Columbian Repeating Air Rifle will hold about 1,000 pellets of BB shot in the magazine and can be shot repeatedly until the magazine is empty. The entire length of the Columbian 1,000-Shot Air Rifle is 34¼ inches; the barrel is nickel plated and the frame is japanned; the stock is of good seasoned hard wood. The gun weighs about 4¼ pounds. It looks like a Winchester, works like a Winchester and pleases the boys.

No. 6C1846 The Columbian Air Rifle. Price....................$1.10

Cannot be sent by mail.

LOADED SHOTGUN SHELLS. LOADED SHOTGUN SHELLS AT $1.29 PER HUNDRED AND UP.

WE GUARANTEE our loaded shells to be equal or superior in velocity, penetration, pattern and uniformity to any loaded shells made, regardless of name, make, brand or price. Send us your order for loaded shells and if they are not exactly as we state and satisfactory in every way, you may return them to us immediately at our expense and we will return your money. WHAT MORE CAN WE SAY?

OUR LINE OF BLACK POWDER LOADED SHELLS.

Why not get your friends to join with you and buy shells by the case or 1,000 and ship by freight! It will save you money in freight charges.

A case of 500 12-gauge shells weighs about 65 pounds. A case of 500 10-gauge shells weighs about 75 pounds. Our terms on loaded shells are cash with order. We do not ship them C. O. D.

Order by catalogue number and load number.

Catalogue No. 6C2212 12-Gauge.

LOADED WITH BLACK POWDER.

Load No.	Drams of Black Powdr	Oz. of Shot	Size of Drop Shot	Price per box of 25 Shells	Price per 100 Shells
76, 78, 70	3	1	6, 8, 10	34c	$1.29
84, 86, 88	3	1⅛	4, 6, 8	36c	$1.40
112, 114, 115, 116, 117, 118	3¼	1⅛	2, 4, 5, 6, 7, 8	37c	$1.43
144, 146	3½	1⅛	4, 6	38c	$1.45
17BB	3¾	1⅛	BB	42c	$1.59
5B	3½	1⅛	4 BUCK	43c	$1.60

Catalogue No. 6C2210 10-Gauge.

LOADED WITH BLACK POWDER.

Load No.	Drams of Black Powdr	Oz. of Shot	Size of Drop Shot	Price per box of 25 Shells	Price per 100 Shells
282, 284, 286, 288	4¼	1⅛	2, 4, 6, 8	40c	$1.59
19BB	5	1⅛	BB	45c	$1.80

Catalogue No. 6C2216 16-Gauge.

LOADED WITH BLACK POWDER.

Load No.	Drams of Black Powdr	Oz. of Shot	Size of Drop Shot	Price per box of 25 Shells	Price per 100 Shells
416, 418, 419, 420	2¾	1	6, 8, 9, 10	37c	$1.45

Catalogue No. 6C2220 20-Gauge.

LOADED WITH BLACK POWDER.

Load No.	Drams of Black Powdr	Oz. of Shot	Size of Drop Shot	Price per box of 25 Shells	Price per 100 Shells
4206, 4208	2½	⅞	6, 8	37c	$1.48

We have taken great pains to select loads which are suitable for most purposes and these loads should meet all requirements.

WE DO NOT SEND SHELLS C. O. D.

OUR SMOKELESS POWDER LOADED SHELLS.

We have done considerable experimenting with medium and high priced smokeless loaded shells, and as far as pattern, carrying power, and penetration are concerned, we find that by shooting the medium grade smokeless shells, and the high priced grade smokeless shells, in the same guns, the pattern, penetration and carrying power is almost identical and we therefore abandon all high grade and high priced smokeless powder loaded shells, believing that we should not ask our customers to pay any more for high priced goods than is necessary when the medium priced goods answer the same purpose.

LOADED WITH DROP SHOT.

Catalogue No. 6C2232 12-Gauge.

LOADED WITH SMOKELESS POWDER.

Load No.	Grains of Smokeless Powder Equal to	Wt. of Shot	Size of Drop Shot	Price per box of 25 Shells	Price per 100 Shells
316x 6, 316x 8, 316x 10	3 Drams	1 Ounce	No. 6, No. 8, No. 10	44c	$1.67
317x 2, 317x 4, 317x 6, 317x 7, 317x 8	3 Drams	1⅛ Ounce	No. 2, No. 4, No. 6, No. 7, No. 8	47c	$1.82

Catalogue No. 6C2230 10-Gauge.

LOADED WITH SMOKELESS POWDER.

Load No.	Grains of Smokeless Powder equal to	W'ght of Shot	Size of Drop Shot	Price per box of 25 Shells	Price per 100 Shells
321 x 2, 321 x 4, 321 x 6, 321 x 7, 321 x 8, 321 x 9	3¼ drams	1⅛ ounce	No. 2, No. 4, No. 6, No. 7, No. 8, No. 9	50c	$1.99

Catalogue No. 6C2236 16-Gauge.

LOADED WITH SMOKELESS POWDER.

Load No.	Grains of Smokeless Powder equal to	Ounces of Shot	Size of Drop Shot	Price per box of 25 Shells	Price per 100 Shells
616 x 6, 618 x 8	2½ drams	1	6, 8	48c	$1.90

Catalogue No. 6C2238 8-Gauge.

HAND LOADED WITH SMOKELESS POWDER.

Load No.	Gr'ins of Smokeless Powder equal to	Ounces of Shot	Size of Drop Shot	Price per box of 25 Shells	Price per 100 Shells
8BB	5½ drams	1½	BB	$1.25	$5.00

SMOKELESS POWDER SHELLS, LOADED WITH CHILLED SHOT.

Shells loaded with smokeless powder and chilled shot give better penetration and more even patterns than drop shot. Loaded in 12-gauge only. The No. 7½ shot is our celebrated trap load.

Order by catalogue number and load number.

Catalogue No. 6C2242 12-Gauge.

LOADED WITH SMOKELESS POWDER.

Load No.	Gr'ins of Smokeless Powder equal to	Wt. of Shot	Size of Chilled Shot	Price per box of 25 Shells	Price per 100 Shells
317C4, 317C6, 317C7½, 317C8	3 Drams	1⅛ oz.	No. 4, No. 6, No. 7½, No. 8	50c	$1.95

Empty Pin Fire Paper Shells.

We cannot furnish these loaded. Order your ammunition and reloading tools from us and load your own shells to your own liking. These shells come 100 in a box and we cannot sell less than a box.

Catalogue No.	Gauge	Weight Per 100	Price Per 100
6C2250	20 Pin Fire	1½ pounds	55c
6C2252	16 Pin Fire	1¾ pounds	55c
6C2253	12 Pin Fire	2 pounds	65c

Shells cannot be sent by mail.

Pin Fire Primers for Above Paper Shells.

No. 6C2256 Primers for Pin Fire Paper Shells. Cannot be sent by mail. Price, per box of 100..................19c

FIRST QUALITY EMPTY BRASS SHELLS.

Not loaded. We cannot furnish brass shells loaded.

BEST QUALITY BRASS SHELL

These shells come in two qualities, first quality and second quality; the first quality shell is a trifle heavier than the second quality shell, but they are both good, durable and serviceable shells and may be reloaded many times. These shells come put up 25 shells in a paper box and all use the No. 2 primer and cannot be used in the magazine of repeating shotguns.

Catalogue Number	Gauge of Shell	Length of Shell	Wt. Per Box of 25	Price Per Box of 25
6C2301	8	3 in.	2 lbs.	$2.00
6C2303	10	2⅞ in.	1¾ lbs.	1.15
6C2304	12	2⅝ in.	1⅜ lbs.	1.10
6C2307	16	2½ in.	1⅛ lbs.	1.10
6C2308	20	2½ in.	1¼ lbs.	1.10

Brass shells cannot be sent by mail.

Second Quality Empty Brass Shells.

Catalogue Number	Gauge of Shell	Length of Shell	Wt. Per Box	Price Per Box of 25
6C2316	12	2⅝ in.	1⅛ lbs.	75c
6C2318	10	2⅞ in.	1⅜ lbs.	75c

Brass shells cannot be sent by mail.

NOTICE On any goods not described or listed in this catalogue and made to order, we must ask cash in full with the order, and they cannot be returned under any circumstances.

Any deviation from this catalogue may cause a delay in your order.

RUSTED AND DAMAGED GUNS.

Do not return to us a gun, revolver or rifle which is rusted, pitted or has the finish worn off, for we have no way of selling these guns. If you have a gun, revolver or rifle which needs repairing, first write us, fully describing the article and what is broken, and we may be able to send you the part necessary, thus saving the express charges on the gun both ways.

Pearl and Stag Handle Daggers.

No. 6C4523 Our Finest Quality Ladies' Dagger. This is a little beauty, with the very finest quality of steel in blade. Length of blade, 4 inches, both edges sharp, with beautiful pearl handle and dagger hilt, furnished with fancy leather sheath. This is the finest quality of a dirk knife, and the metal is warranted. Price. (Postage extra, 8c.)..**$1.10**

No. 6C4524 Our Stag Handle Dagger. 4-inch blade of good quality steel, with leather sheath. Price......(Postage extra, 8c).....**65c**

Hunting Knife Sheath.

No. 6C4530 Leather Hunting Knife Sheaths.
For 6-inch Bowie. **20c** | For 8-inch Bowie. **28c**
For 7-inch Bowie. **24c** | For 9-inch Bowie. **32c**
If by mail, postage extra, 4 cents.

No. 6C4771 Leather Belts, for knife sheaths. 1½ inches wide. Price..........**19c**
If by mail, postage extra, 8 cents.

Hunters' Axes.

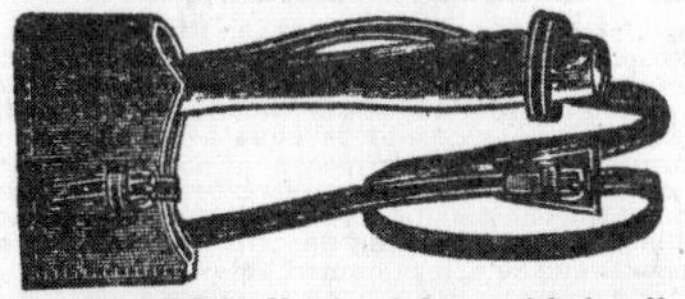

No. 6C4533 Hunters' Axe. with handle, extra cast steel blade, weight, 1¾ pounds; with heavy russet leather sheath, as per illustration. A very convenient tool; makes a light axe or a heavy hatchet for putting up tents, etc., when camping. Weight, with sheath, 2 pounds.
Price, with carrying sheath...............**80c**

Gun Grease, Gun Oil, Etc.

American Gun Grease.

No. 6C4543 The American Gun Grease is the best rust preventer manufactured. For any steel or polished iron surface, and for inside or outside of gun or rifle barrels, it has no equal. Put up in neat metallic tubes. Price, per tube.........**10c**
If by mail, postage extra, per tube, 5 cents.

Gun Oil.

No. 6C4546 S. R. & Co.'s Sperm Gun Oil; put up exclusively for guns, gunlocks and fine machinery, prevents rust and will not gum.
Price, per 2-ounce bottle........**8c**
If by mail, postage extra, 8 cents.

DUCK, TURKEY, SNIPE AND OTHER CALLS.

No. 6C4560 Allen's Latest Improved Wood Duck Caller, the most natural toned and easiest blowing. Used on the Duck Pass by the best duck shooters in America. Price..........**35c**
If by mail, postage extra, 6 cents.

No. 6C4563 Duck Calls, with rosewood mouthpiece, horn tip. Good quality. Price.......................**18c**
If by mail, postage extra, 4 cents.

Our Latest Turkey Caller.

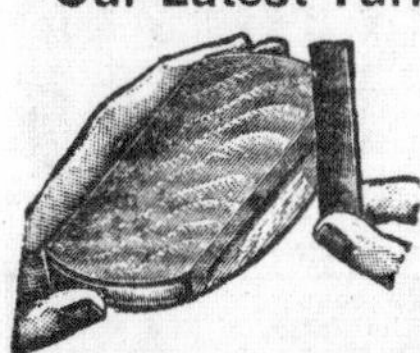

No. 6C4564 Our Turkey Caller is made from well seasoned wood, adapted to make the proper sound for decoying turkeys. Hold the caller in the left hand, as shown in the illustration, and with the right hand rub the slate on the side of the caller, either with the edge or with the flat side, and after a little practice you will be able to decoy turkeys successfully. This caller is 4½ inches long, 2½ inches wide, and may be carried in the pocket. Price.......**45c**
If by mail, postage extra, 3 cents.

No. 6C4565 Turkey Calls, horn tip with rosewood mouthpiece. Calls by sucking into it. Price. (If by mail, postage extra, 4c.)..**20c**

No. 6C4567 Snipe Calls, made of best horn and a perfect snipe call.
Price...(If by mail, postage extra, 2c.)..**15c**

Our Hawk Call, 45 Cents.

No. 6C4568 Our Hawk Call is designed and manufactured by a man who has had much trouble by hawks killing his chickens, and the hawk caller pays for itself many times over every time a hawk is killed. Hold the caller in the left hand, as shown in the illustration and by blowing through it you can soon become expert in decoying hawks toward you.
Price.......................................**45c**
If by mail, postage extra, 2 cents.

Wild Goose Caller.

No. 6C4570 Fuller's Metallic Wild Goose Caller. Very good.
Price..(If by mail, postage extra, 5c.)....**72c**

The Improved Surprise Whistle.

No. 6C4572 The Surprise Whistle, the loudest and best dog call in the market. By squeezing in the bulb at the end you can regulate the sound and produce any effect from purling or muffled notes up to a great swelling, booming, piercing note. A good snipe or plover call also. Price.......................**13c**
If by mail, postage extra, 2 cents.

Horn Whistles.

Horn Whistles, loud and shrill and leaves no bad taste in the mouth.

Catalogue Number	Length	Price	Postage extra
6C4574	2½ inches	15c	2c
6C4575	2¾ inches	20c	2c
6C4576	3 inches	25c	2c

FOR HUNTING BOOTS, WADERS, ETC., SEE OUR SHOE DEPARTMENT.

Cedar Wood Decoy Ducks.

In making these decoys great care has been used to select only sound white cedar for their construction and to secure a perfect balance. They are light, substantial and naturally painted. They will not sink if you shoot them. $2.50 and $3.70 per dozen. Each dozen contains 8 drakes and 4 females. We cannot furnish them any other way except by special order, which causes delay. Decoys below these prices cannot be properly made and painted to look natural. For highest grade wood decoy ducks, these prices are **BELOW ANY COMPETITION.**

They come in mallard, canvasback, redhead, bluebill, teal or sprigtail. Weight, 35 to 40 pounds per dozen. State which style you wish.

REMEMBER—We can only furnish 8 drakes and 4 females in each dozen.

No. 6C4595 No. 1, our best decoy ducks, nicely painted in natural colors, with glass eyes. State which style you wish.
Price, each..............................**$0.40**
Per dozen.......................................**3.70**

No. 6C4596 No. 3, good decoy ducks, nicely painted in natural colors, but with painted eyes. State which style you wish.
Price, each..............................**$0.30**
Per dozen.......................................**2.50**

No. 6C4597 Anchors with cord for decoys. Price, per dozen.....**40c**

Collapsible Ducks.

No. 6C4600 Collapsible Canvas Decoy. A good imitation of the natural duck. Made of the best canvas, beautifully painted in natural colors, waterproofed, inflated with air, and when not in use the air can be let out and ducks folded. Weight, 4 ounces each. Packed one dozen in a neat box. 2⅝x9 inches, and a dozen when packed will weigh 8 pounds. **We sell in any quantity. We handle these decoys in Mallard species only.** To inflate, put cork in mouth, inflate and adjust the cork with the tongue.
Price, per dozen.............................**$5.45**

Canvas Collapsible Geese.

No. 6C4602 Canvas Geese Decoys, made of best sea island domestic canvas, covered with **waterproof dressing, painted exactly like a wild goose.** They are not affected by the heat or cold and will last almost indefinitely. **They are very easily inflated**, and when the air is let out can be packed in a very small space. Weight, per dozen, packed, 12 pounds.
Price, per dozen...........................**$11.75**
If by mail, postage extra, each, 20 cents.

Victor Brand Traps.

The Victor Brand Traps are made by the Oneida Community and are sold to compete with the various imitations of their Newhouse traps. We have sold large quantities of them and have had no complaints.

No. 9C04876 Victor Traps, 3½-inch jaw, with chain. Size, No. 0. Weight, 14 ounces.
Price, each......................................**9c**
Per dozen.......................................**97c**

No. 9C04877 Victor Traps, 4-inch jaw, with chain. Size, No. 1. Weight, 14 ounces.
Price, per dozen, **$1.13**; each.............**10c**

For a full and complete line of game traps for large and small game, see our Hardware Department.

Canvas Shell Bags for Carrying Loaded Shells.

No. 6C4665 10-oz. Brown Canvas Bags, leather bound, with pocket. To hold 50 shells. Price...**30c**
To hold 75 shells.
Price...........**33c**
To hold 100 shells.
Price...........**35c**
If by mail, postage extra, 10 to 14 cents.

OUR GUN AND RIFLE COVERS.

We have selected the following line of gun and rifle covers and placed a large season contract for them, so as to enable us to give you the best possible value for the least amount of money in this line of goods. When you order a gun cover from us you are getting it at a price based on the actual cost of material and labor with only our one small percentage of profit added. You will assist us materially when ordering these goods if you will give us the name of your gun or rifle, also length of barrel, and advise us whether it is a single barrel, double barrel, repeating shotgun or rifle for which you want the cover; this will enable us to furnish you the exact cover you wish without any delay. For special lengths not mentioned in this catalogue allow us one week's time to make them.

NOTICE. 8-oz. canvas means a yard weighs 8 oz.
10-oz. canvas means a yard weighs 10 oz.
12-oz. canvas means a yard weighs 12 oz.
The more ounces to the yard, the heavier the canvas.

Mention length of barrel and name of gun or rifle when ordering a gun cover.

Our 44-Cent Leather Bound Cover.

No. 6C4695 Rifle and Gun Cover, best 8-ounce brown canvas, leather bound, leather sling, cotton flannel lined, best quality. For 24, 26, 28, 30 or 32-inch barrel. Mention length of barrel when ordering and say if you wish it for a rifle or shotgun. Price..............**44c**
If by mail, postage extra, 13 cents.

Special Value for 69 Cents.

No. 6C4698 Heavy Tan 18-ounce Duck Cover, for rifles and shotguns. Full leather bound, with heavy sole leather lock and muzzle protector, with handle and sling. For 24, 26, 28, 30 or 32-inch barrels. Price..............**69c**
If by mail, postage extra, 16 cents.

Our $1.45 Leather Rifle and Shotgun Cover.

No. 6C4701 Soft Leather Cover, made of heavy, soft russet bag leather, with combined sling and handle. Bright trimmings. For 24, 26, 28, 30 or 32-inch barrels; give length of barrel and name of gun or rifle when ordering. Absolutely waterproof. The finest gun cover made. Price..........................**$1.45**
If by mail, postage extra, 25 cents.

Give name of rifle or shotgun and length of barrel when ordering.

Rifle and Carbine Sheath.

No. 6C4703 Rifle Sheath, made of best russet leather, for sporting rifles. These sheaths are not full length covers, but are intended for carrying rifle on saddle, leaving stock of rifle exposed so it may be easily grasped when needed. Be sure to give name of rifle, model and length of barrel when ordering, as different makes require different sheaths. We furnish these for 24, 26 and 28-inch barrel rifles only.
Price...**$1.15**
If by mail, postage extra, 30 cents.

No. 6C4704 The same identical sheath for carbines. State name of carbine and length of barrel when ordering. We furnish these for 20 and 22-inch barrel carbines only.
Price...**$1.10**
If by mail, postage extra, 25 cents.

Give name of rifle or shotgun and length of barrel when ordering.

Our 85-Cent Duck Gun Case.

Victoria Style.

No. 6C4706 Heavy 18-ounce tan duck, waterproof, leather bound, with straps and tool pocket, leather lock and muzzle protector, flannel lined, for 28, 30 or 32-inch barrels. State length wanted. Price........................**85c**
If by mail, postage extra, 30 cents.

Our Victoria Gun Case, $1.00.

No. 6C4707 Victoria Gun Case, heavy 18-ounce waterproof canvas, reinforced with leather lock and muzzle protector, with pocket for cleaning rod; also shell bag to hold 50 shells. The most complete cover offered to sportsmen and trap shooters. For 28, 30 or 32-inch barrel. State length wanted. Price...........**$1.00**
If by mail, postage extra, 35 cents.

REVOLVER AND PISTOL HOLSTERS.

Our Line of Revolver Holsters.

By taking advantage of the leather market and laying in a supply of leather before the advance, we are enabled to make you the following prices. When you order holsters of us you are buying them on our system of one small percentage of profit from the maker to the consumer, and we are sure you will agree with us, that, quality considered, our prices are below any competition. When ordering holsters, always give the name of your revolver, length of barrel and caliber, to enable us to give you the exact size, for these holsters vary in size, according to caliber and length of barrel.

Our Acme Rubber Pocket Holsters.

Made of black rubber and lined with drilling, soft and pliable, with nickel plated clasp to hook to pocket, and made for pocket size revolvers only up to 4-inch barrel. Order by catalogue number in full.

Catalogue Number	Caliber of Revolver	Length of Barrel, Inches	Price, Each	Postage Extra
6C4755B	32	3 to 4	20c	5c
6C4755E	38	3¼ to 4	22c	5c
6C4755G	44	4 to 5	25c	6c

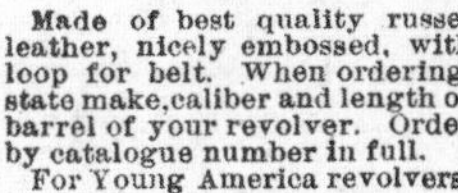

Our Leather Flap Holsters.

Made of best quality russet leather, nicely embossed, with loop for belt. When ordering, state make, caliber and length of barrel of your revolver. Order by catalogue number in full.
For Young America revolvers.

Catalogue Number	Caliber of Revolver	Length of Barrel, Inches	Price, Each	Postage Extra
6C4756A	22	2	21c	4c
6C4756XA	22	6	22c	4c

For Smith & Wesson, Harrington & Richardson, Hopkins & Allen, Forehand, Iver Johnson, Colt's New Pocket, Colt's Police and our own revolvers. Order by catalogue number in full.

Catalogue Number	Caliber of Revolver	Length of Barrel, Inches	Price, Each	Postage Extra
6C4756B	32	3 to 4	23c	6c
6C4756C	32	4½ to 5	24c	6c
6C4756D	32	5½ to 6	25c	6c
6C4756E	38	3½ to 4	26c	7c
6C4756F	38	4½ to 5	27c	7c
6C4756G	38	5½ to 6	28c	7c

For Colt's New Navy, Colt's New Army, Colt's Double Action and Smith & Wesson Military revolvers. Order by catalogue number in full.

Catalogue Number	Caliber of Revolver	Length of Barrel, Inches	Price, Each	Postage Extra
6C4756H	38 or 41	4½ to 5	33c	8c
6C4756J	38 or 41	5½ to 6½	34c	8c

For large frame revolvers, such as Colt's Frontier, Army, Single Action and Double Action, 32-20, 38-40, 44 and 45 caliber. Order by catalogue number in full.

Catalogue Number	Caliber of Revolver	Length of Barrel, Inches	Price, Each	Postage Extra
6C4756K	32-20 to 45	4½ to 5	35c	10c
6C4756L	32-20 to 45	5½ to 6	36c	10c
6C4756M	32-20 to 45	7½	37c	10c

Our Colorado Open Top Holsters.

These Holsters are made of good quality russet leather, nicely embossed, with loop for belt. When ordering, give name of revolver and length of barrel. Write catalogue number in full.

Cat. No.	Caliber of Revolver	Length of Barrel, Inches	Price, Each	Postage Extra
6C4761A	22	2	16c	4c
6C4761XA	22	6	16c	4c

Holsters, continued on next page.

HOLSTERS—Continued.

For Smith & Wesson, Harrington & Richardson, Hopkins & Allen, Forehand, Iver Johnson, Colt's New Pocket, Colt's New Police and our own revolvers.

Catalogue Number	Caliber of Revolver	Length of Barrel, Inches	Price, Each	Postage Extra
6C4761B	32	3 to 4	17c	6c
6C4761C	32	4½ to 5	18c	6c
6C4761D	32	5½ to 6	19c	6c
6C4761E	38	3½ to 4	20c	6c
6C4761F	38	4½ to 5	21c	7c
6C4761G	38	5½ to 6	22c	7c

For Colt's Double Action, Colt's New Navy, Colt's New Army and Smith & Wesson Military revolvers. Order by catalogue number in full.

Catalogue Number	Caliber of Revolver	Length of Barrel, Inches	Price, Each	Postage Extra
6C4761H	38 or 41	4½ to 5	22c	8c
6C4761J	38 or 41	5½ to 6	23c	8c

To fit the large frame Army and Frontier revolvers, 32-20, 38-40, 44 and 45 caliber. Order by catalogue number in full.

Catalogue Number	Caliber of Revolver	Length of Barrel, Inches	Price, Each	Postage Extra
6C4761K	32-20 to 45	4½ to 5	24c	10c
6C4761L	32-20 to 45	5½ to 6	25c	10c
6C4761M	32-20 to 45	7½	26c	10c

Our Hand Carved Mexican Style Cowboy Holsters.

Made of heavy russet saddle leather, to match our fancy cowboys' saddle. These holsters are all hand carved, and are not to be compared with the holsters that other houses sell as the fine cowboy holster, which are embossed under a large press; but these are the most handsome and best holsters in the market. The following holsters are made to fit the Smith & Wesson, Harrington & Richardson, Hopkins & Allen, Forehand, Iver Johnson, Colt's New Pocket and New Police and our own make revolvers in 38 caliber only. They are not made for 32 caliber revolvers. When ordering give the catalogue number in full.

Catalogue Number	Caliber of Revolver	Length of Barrel, Inches	Price, Each	Postage Extra
6C4767E	38	3½ to 4	$0.90	8c
6C4767F	38	4½ to 5	.95	8c
6C4767G	38	5½ to 6	1.00	8c

The following holsters are made to fit the Colt's Double Action, Colt's New Navy and New Army revolvers and Smith & Wesson Military and Police revolvers.

Catalogue Number	Caliber of Revolver	Length of Barrel, Inches	Price, Each	Postage Extra
6C4767H	38 or 41	4½ to 5	$1.10	10c
6C4767J	38 or 41	5½ to 6½	1.15	10c

The following holsters are made to fit the large Frontier and Army frame revolvers, 32-20, 38-40, 44-40 and 45 caliber.

Catalogue Number	Caliber of Revolver	Length of Barrel, Inches	Price, Each	Postage Extra
6C4767K	32-20 to 45	4½ to 5	$1.20	10c
6C4767L	32-20 to 45	5½ to 6	1.25	10c
6C4767M	32-20 to 45	7½	1.35	10c

Texas Shoulder Holster.

Keeps revolver always safe and ready. Made of fine soft russet leather, nicely embossed, with leather strap to pass around the chest to hold holster on shoulder, as shown in the illustration. When ordering, always give catalogue number in full and state the make and style of your revolver, give length of barrel, and we will fit your revolver.

No. 6C4768A For 22-Caliber Young America Revolvers. Mention length of barrel wanted. Price. . . (Postage extra, 5c.).....40c

For Smith & Wesson, Harrington & Richardson, Hopkins & Allen, Forehand, Iver Johnson, Colt's New Pocket and New Police and our own revolvers.

Catalogue Number	Caliber of Revolver	Length of Barrel, Inches	Price, Each	Postage Extra
6C4768B	32	3 to 4	45c	5c
6C4768C	32	4½ to 5	46c	5c
6C4768D	32	5½ to 6	.47c	5c
6C4768E	38	3½ to 4	48c	5c
6C4768F	38	4½ to 5	48c	5c
6C4768G	38	5½ to 6	49c	5c

To fit Colt's Double Action New Navy and New Army, 38 and 41 caliber, and Smith & Wesson Military and Police revolvers.

Catalogue Number	Caliber of Revolver	Length of Barrel, Inches	Price, Each	Postage Extra
6C4768H	38 or 41	4½ to 5	50c	8c
6C4768J	38 or 41	5½ to 6½	51c	8c

To fit large frame 44 or 45 caliber revolvers.

Catalogue Number	Caliber of Revolver	Length of Barrel, Inches	Price, Each	Postage Extra
6C4768K	32-20 to 45	4½ to 5	52c	8c
6C4768L	32-20 to 45	5½ to 6	53c	8c
6C4768M	32-20 to 45	7½	55c	8c

OUR HOLSTER AND CARTRIDGE BELTS.

We would like you to compare our line of belts with any line offered by any other house, and, quality considered, we think you will find that our prices are equal to those paid by the largest dealers. Our leather goods are the best in the market. Always give waist measure and caliber when ordering.

Plain Leather Belts and Cartridge Belts.

No. 6C4771 Belts only, russet leather, 1¼ inches wide, finely embossed, without loops for cartridges. Length, 32 to 40 inches. Give length wanted. Price..........18c

If by mail, postage extra, 5 cents.

No. 6C4772 Belts only, russet leather, nicely embossed edge, with loops for cartridges; 22, 32, 38, 41 or 44 caliber, 1½ inches wide, plain roller buckle, 30 to 40 inches long. Give length and caliber wanted. Price..........29c

If by mail, postage extra, 5 cents.

No. 6C4773 Belts only, fine russet leather, nicely embossed edge, with loops for cartridges, 32, 38, 44 or 45 caliber; 2¼ inches wide, large nickel plated buckle, 32 to 40 inches long. Give length and caliber wanted. Price..........44c

If by mail, postage extra, 10 cents.

Combination Cartridge and Money Belts.

Mexican Combined Cartridge and Money Belt. Made of the very best soft russet leather; belt is 3 inches wide; soft and pliable and will not get hard and crack; neatly embossed. Mention caliber wanted.

No. 6C4774 32-caliber, give waist measure. Price..........90c

No. 6C4774¼ 38-caliber, give waist measure. Price..........90c

No. 6C4774½ 44 or 45 caliber, give waist measure. Price..........90c

No. 6C4774¾ 50-caliber, give waist measure. Price..........90c

Don't forget to state caliber wanted, also waist measure.

If by mail, postage extra, 15 cents.

No. 6C4775 The Cowboy Combined Cartridge and Money Belt. Made of heavy russet tanned leather; strong and durable; nicely embossed; edges double stitched; designed to match our cowboy scabbard and holster; 32, 38, 44 or 45 caliber. Mention caliber wanted and give waist measure. Price..........$1.15

If by mail, postage extra, 18 cents.

Web Cartridge Belts.

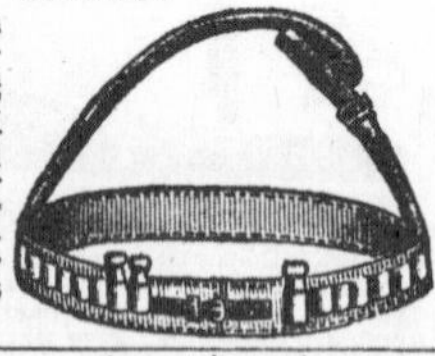

No. 6C4776 Web Belts, for rifle and pistol cartridges; 32, 38, 44 or 45 caliber. Made of heavy web with loops for cartridges. A very strong and durable belt, not impaired by any kind of weather. Mention caliber and waist measure wanted when ordering. Price..........35c

If by mail, postage extra, 17 cents.

Shell Belts for Shotgu Shells.

Shell Belts with loops for carrying shotgun shells. Made of web and russet leather and with shoulder straps to go over the shoulder. Order by number and give waist measure.

Catalogue Number	Made of	Size Gauge	Price	Postage extra
6C4786A	Web	12	32c	8c
6C4786B	Web	10	32c	8c
6C4786C	Web	16	32c	8c
6C4786D	Web	20	32c	8c
6C4787A	Rus. Leather	12	45c	10c
6C4787B	Rus. Leather	10	45c	10c
6C4787C	Rus. Leather	16	45c	10c
6C4787D	Rus. Leather	20	45c	10c
6C4787F	Rus. Leather	8	65c	16c

The New Anson Mills Woven Shell Belts.

No. 6C4791 In these Mills belts the loops are woven into the belts, making them very strong and durable in all kinds of weather; 10 or 12-gauge, with shoulder strap and game hooks. Mention gauge wanted. Price..$1.20

If by mail, postage extra, 22 cents.

No. 6C4794 Anson Mills Hunters' Belt. The loops are woven, closed at the bottom, protecting the crimped end of the shell; no sewing whatever on the belt; 10, 12 or 16-gauge. Mention gauge wanted. Price....82c

If by mail, postage extra, 20 cents.

Grass Suits Reduced to 83c.

83c PER SUIT is our price and thousands are being worn by sportsmen everywhere.

No. 6C5112 For wild goose, duck and all kinds of shore bird shooting; made of long, tough imported marsh grass into a cape coat with hood. They weigh about five pounds and are convenient to wear and shoot from. Make good waterproofs in rainy weather, are easily packed and carried. Hunters appreciate the value of these suits, as no blind or bough house is necessary when shooting on marshes. Weight, about 5 pounds. Cannot be sent by mail. Price, per suit..83c

For Indian Snow Shoes

See Our Shoe Department.

Ski or Norwegian Snow Shoes.

Our Expert Ski, made especially for us in accordance with suggestions made by expert ski men. The Expert Ski are broad in the front and curved a little at the side in the center of the ski, to facilitate turning without lifting the ski. The bottom is grooved. They are hand slaved and oiled, fitted with toe straps and finely finished in every respect, are made of the best white ash, which we consider better adapted for work of this kind than any of the cheaper wood used by various manufacturers in making these goods.

No. 6C5115 Our 8-foot white ash Expert Ski. Price, per pair..........$4.30

No. 6C5116 Our 9½-foot white ash Expert Ski. Price, per pair..........$4.95

No. 6C5118 Professional Ski Pole. Price, each..........70

OUR HUNTING CLOTHING.

We are the largest handlers of hunting clothing direct to the consumer in the United States, and we know that we are able to offer greater value in this line of goods than it is possible for you to obtain elsewhere. Our hunting clothing is guaranteed to be made of the highest grade full weight canvas, full size, made with the same care and finish found in tailor made goods. **Quality, both in material and workmanship, considered, our prices cannot be equaled,** as they are based on our one small profit, manufacturer to consumer plan, and by reason of our enormous trade in this line, our cost of production is far smaller than that experienced by other manufacturers. In ordering, state number of inches around the chest under the arms, and state what size dress coat you wear. **Special sizes not mentioned in the following descriptions, will have to be made specially, and will cost 20 per cent more than the prices named below.**

Our Best 12-Ounce Canvas Coat, $3.65.

6C5135 Our Very Best Quality Hunting Coat, made of the very best quality 12-ounce army duck, dead grass color, double stitched throughout, lined throughout the entire back with best quality 8-ounce army duck, sleeves lined with Walker's sateen, corduroy collar and adjustable cuffs lined with corduroy, reinforced waterproof padded leather shoulder pieces, leather bound throughout, including the pocket flaps; silk crow's foot stitching at the pockets and silk stitched buttonholes. The pockets are made on the cut in principle, with large flaps, which is very neat, and the game pockets are made so as to be accessible from the front and under the armpits, as shown in illustration. This is our best hunting coat, has six outside pockets and three spacious game pockets, with best quality of horn buttons, and no pains have been spared to make this hunting coat the best canvas hunting coat on the market, and is as nearly waterproof as a canvas coat can be. It comes in sizes of 36 to 46 inches. Give measure when ordering. Price..........$3.65

Cannot be sent by mail, as it weighs over 4 pounds. 12-ounce canvas weighs 12 ounces to the yard.

Our 10-Ounce, Leather Bound Hunting Coat, $2.20.

No. 6C5137 Best quality 10-oz. army duck, dead grass color, lined with 8-oz. army duck, full pattern, reinforced shoulders, corduroy collar, corduroy lined adjustable cuffs, six outside pockets with flaps, three game pockets with entrance from front edge and side seam, double stitched throughout; leather bound all around. Sizes, chest measure, from 36 to 46 inches. Give chest measure when ordering. Price........$2.20

If by mail, postage extra, 45 to 55 cents.

Our 10-Ounce Canvas Special Value Coat for $1.85.

No. 6C5139 Hunting Coat, made of 10-oz. duck, dead grass color, three-quarter drill lined, corduroy collar and adjustable cuffs, lined with corduroy, shoulders reinforced, double stitched throughout, five outside shell pockets with flaps, reinforced, three game pockets with entrance from front edge and side seam, fancy stitching around entrance to game pockets. Sizes, chest measure, from 36 to 46 inches. Give chest measure when ordering. Price..........$1.85

If by mail, postage extra, 35 to 45 cents.

Our 8-Ounce Canvas Hunting Coat, $1.35.

No. 6C5143 Hunters' Coat, made of 8-oz. duck (a yard of this canvas weighs 8 ounces), skirt drill lined, dead grass color, corduroy collar, adjustable cuffs, lined with corduroy, five outside pockets with flaps, three game pockets with entrance from front edge and side seams, shoulders reinforced, double stitched, three buttons. Sizes, chest measure, 36 to 46 inches. Give chest measurement when ordering. Price..........$1.35

If by mail, postage extra, 35 to 45 cents.

No. 6C5144 Exactly the same coat as No. 6C5143, but made from heavy, 10-ounce canvas instead of 8-ounce canvas. Sizes, chest measure, from 36 to 46 inches. Give chest measure when ordering. Price.......$1.55

If by mail, postage extra, 35 to 45 cents.

No. 6C5147 Made of heavy drill, dead grass color, five outside pockets, two inside skirt game pockets. A nice, light hunting and fishing coat for mild weather. This coat has no flaps over pockets and is not adjustable sleeve. Sizes, chest measure, 36 to 46 inches. Give chest measure when ordering. Price.56c

If by mail, postage extra, 20 to 35 cents.

Our Boys' Hunting Coat, $1.35.

No. 6C5150 We have had so many calls for Boys' Hunting Coats that we were persuaded to put in a line of these in 30, 32 and 34 inches chest measure. Made of 10-ounce canvas, has five outside pockets with flaps, two game pockets, corduroy collar, adjustable cuffs lined with corduroy, and made up in first class style, same as our regular men's coats. **Give chest measure when ordering.** Price..........$1.35

If by mail, postage extra 28 to 34 cents.

HUNTING COATS make good, serviceable coats to use on the farm, in the woods, etc. They are cheap, strong and have plenty of pockets.

Our $2.85 Corduroy Coat.

No. 6C5152 is made of good quality corduroy, mouse color, well stitched, flaps over pockets, four outside pockets, two inside game pockets of large size, lined with drilling, reinforced shoulders. A dandy for the money, made in 36, 38, 40, 42 and 44 inches chest measure. Give chest measure when ordering. Price...$2.85

If by mail, postage extra, 35 to 42 cents.

Hunting Vests, 73c.

No. 6C5155 Hunting Vest, with loops for cartridges. Made of 8-ounce duck, unlined; holds about 36 shells, 10 or 12-gauge. Sizes, from 34 to 44 inches. **Give gauge and chest measure when ordering.** Price..........73c

If by mail, postage extra, 12 to 18 cents.

Duck Hunting Pants.

No. 6C5158 Hunting Pants. Made of 8-ounce duck; dead grass color, with four patch pockets. Sizes, from 28 to 40 inches waist measure. **Give waist measure and leg measure of inseam when ordering.** Price, per pair.......**73c**

If by mail, postage extra, 25 to 30 cents.

No. 6C5159 Duck Hunting Pants. Made of 10-ounce army duck, dead grass color, business style. Cut in front and back pockets. Sizes, from 30 to 42 inches waist measure. **Give waist measure and leg measure of inseam when ordering.**

Price, per pair...........**$1.20**

If by mail, postage extra, 30 to 36c.

Corduroy Hunting Suit.

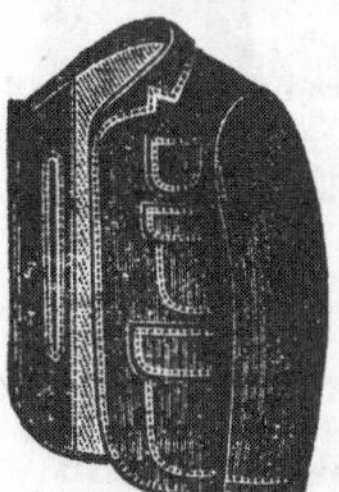

No. 6C5172 Corduroy Coat, made of best imported drab mouse color corduroy, sateen lined, seven outside pockets, three game pockets, adjustable cuffs. This is positively as fine a corduroy coat as can be made and the equal of coats sold at $8.00 to $12.00 by other dealers. We furnish it in sizes 36 to 44 inches chest measure.

Price.........**$4.95**

If by mail, postage extra, 60 to 75 cents.

No. 6C5174 Corduroy Vest. Business style, with pockets, to match above coat. Give chest measure when ordering. Price...............................**$2.25**

If by mail, postage extra, 20 to 25 cents.

No. 6C5175 Corduroy Pants. Business style. To match above coat. Give waist measure and inseam of leg measure when ordering. Price, per pair.............**$3.25**

If by mail, postage extra, 30 to 38 cents.

OIL TANNED HORSEHIDE AND CORDUROY REVERSIBLE COATS.

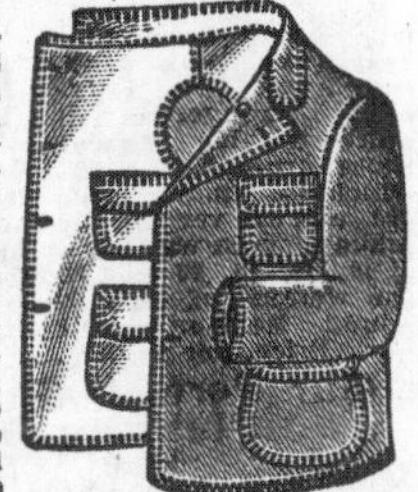

No. 6C5179 Oil Tanned Horsehide Coat, russet color, waterproof, soft and pliable, and will always remain so. A splendid garment for rough, cold and stormy weather, and is made so that it may be reversed, being corduroy on one side and horsehide on the other, and it has three pockets on the leather side and three pockets on the corduroy side, with flaps over pockets. It may be worn either as a horsehide or corduroy coat. Sizes, 36 to 46 inches chest measure. Positively the best reversible coat on the market, regardless of price. Give chest measure when ordering. Weight, 4½ to 4½ pounds.

Price...............................**$11.35**

Our Reversible Leather and Corduroy Hunting Coat, $7.50.

No. 6C5180 Our Reversible leather and Corduroy Hunting Coat. For $7.50 we furnish this hunting coat, made of tan colored, soft tanned, pliable leather on one side and mouse colored corduroy on the reverse side, double stitched at all essential places, three pockets on the leather side and three pockets on the reverse or corduroy side, making six pockets in all, with flaps over pockets. This is one of the best coats ever offered by any house, and for rainy or stormy weather it is by far the best, warmest and most useful coat ever made; it can be worn in stormy weather with the leather side out, and in clear weather it may be worn with the corduroy side out, making a nice, neat, dressy coat, a coat which will please you. Weight, about 4½ pounds. These coats come in 36, 38, 40, 42 and 44 inches chest measure. Give measurement of chest when ordering.

Price...............................**$7.50**

HUNTING HATS AND CAPS.

Canvas Cape Cap, 38 Cents.

No. 6C5189 Canvas Cape Cap, made of 8-o nce duck, dead grass color, single stiff visor, full cape, flannel lined, an excellent rough or cold weather cap. State size wanted.

Price............**38c**

If by mail, postage extra, 7 cents.

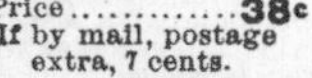

Our $1.32 Klondike Cap.

No. 6C5197 The greatest winter cap made. Just the thing for farmers, teamsters and the Klondike. Made of heavy duck, lined with soft tanned sheepskin with the wool left on, with flap over face and strap and buckles, large visor, green lined, to protect the eyes, with nose protector. The best cap on the market to protect you from extreme cold weather. State size wanted. Price...........................**$1.32**

If by mail, postage extra, 20 cents.

DOG MUZZLES.

NOTICE—When ordering Dog Muzzles, please give measurement around the dog's neck and around snout, 1 inch from the tip of the nose, and the length from tip of the nose to the top of head where the strap goes around his neck, and you will assist us in fitting the muzzle, for muzzles vary considerably in size.

Leather Strap Dog Muzzle.

Leather Strap Dog Muzzle, to buckle around neck and buckles to take up length around head if too large. Give measure when ordering.

No. 6C5347 Small size. Price........**30c**
No. 6C5348 Large size. Price........**40c**

If by mail, postage extra, 4 cents.

OUR LINE OF DOG COLLARS.

Big Bargains.

We engrave names on collars for 3 cents per letter. Cash with order. If you wish a name engraved on the name plate, write the name PLAINLY, so we will not get it wrong.

NOTE—In taking measurements for dog collars the measures below are the length of collar from staple and middle hole, but for convenience of our customers we suggest that you give us the actual measurement around dog's neck by inches, specifying in the order actual measurement, and we will fit him every time. **Prices on dog collars do not include padlocks.**

Our Chain Dog Collars.

These collars have nickel plated flat links, as shown in illustration, lined with leather. When ordering, give catalogue number and length of collar that will fit your dog's neck.

Catalogue Number	Neck Measure	Width of Collar	Price of Collar	Postage Extra
6C6260	11 inches	½ inch	20c	5c
6C6262	13 inches	¾ inch	25c	7c
6C6264	15 inches	1 inch	30c	12c
6C6266	17 inches	1 inch	35c	16c

Engraving extra, 3 cents per letter. Write name plainly and send cash with order.

Our Studded Dog Collars.

Our Studded Collars are made of russet leather, one row of round studs on the small collars and two rows on the large ones, made to lock and all have name plate. When ordering, give measure of dog's neck and give catalogue number of the size collar that is nearest to size wanted.

Catalogue Number	Neck Measure	Width of Collar	Price of Collar	Postage Extra
6C6290	7 inches	½ inch	20c	6c
6C6292	9 inches	½ inch	22c	8c
6C6294	11 inches	¾ inch	25c	10c
6C6296	13 inches	¾ inch	30c	12c
6C6298	15 inches	1 inch	35c	14c
6C6300	17 inches	1 inch	40c	16c
6C6302	19 inches	1 inch	45c	18c
6C6304	21 inches	1¼ inch	50c	20c

Engraving extra, 3 cents per letter. Write name plainly and send cash with order.

Our Heavy Collars for Mastiffs and Large Dogs.

Our Heavy, Russet Color, Double Harness Leather Collar, fine russet finish. Double stitched. Heavily studded, with nickeled studs, solid D ring, nickel plated. Nickeled name plate, staple and trimmings, made to lock; for large dogs. Give catalogue number and length of collar that will fit your dog's neck.

Catalogue Number	Neck Measure	Width of Collar, Inches	Price of Collar	Postage Extra
6C6306	15 inches	1¼	$0.53	18c
6C6308	17 inches	1¼	.60	20c
6C6310	19 inches	1¼	.65	22c
6C6312	21 inches	1½	.85	25c
6C6314	23 inches	1½	.90	27c
6C6316	24 inches	2	1.15	30c

Engraving extra, 3 cents per letter. Write the name plainly so we will not get it wrong, and send cash with order.

Drilled Key Dog Collar Locks.

No. 6C6400 Padlock, 1x¾ inch, all nickel plated, with key. Price.............................**17c**

No. 6C6401 Padlock, 1x¾ inch, brass, with key. Price.......**15c**

If by mail, postage extra, 1 cent.

No. 6C6402 Our Little Secret Dog Collar Lock. A very neat and substantial lock; as strong as any lock and does not require a key. Keyhole has centerpost and is opened by pressing pin to the right. Price.........................**10c**

If by mail, postage extra, 2 cents.

Kennel Chains.

Kennel Dog Chain, polished steel, round wire, new style safety links, three swivels, two snap hooks, so it will not kink; well made and durable; no dog can break it; comes in two lengths and two sizes.

Catalogue No.	Size Links	Length Chain	Price	Postage Extra
6C6420	Medium	4½ feet	22c	10c
6C6421	Medium	6 feet	27c	10c
6C6423	Heavy	4½ feet	30c	12c
6C6425	Heavy	6 feet	35c	16c

Spratt's Dog Cakes.

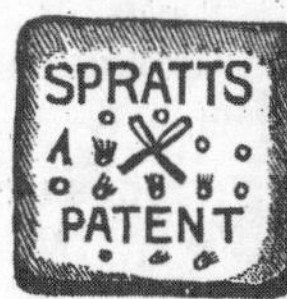

No. 6C6454 Spratt's Patent Fibrine Dog Cakes (with beetroot); these celebrated biscuit are supplied to all the leading kennels and are used at the principal dog shows in America and England, and have been before the public for more than a quarter of a century; 5-pound boxes. Per box...**$0.40**

No. 6C6455 25-pound boxes. Price, per box.......................**1.60**

Each cake weighs 5 to 6 ounces. 2 to 4 cakes per day for pointers and setters, 3 to 5 cakes per day for mastiffs, is considered sufficient food.

LAWN TENNIS GOODS.

Our line of tennis rackets has been selected with great care and we know that we are offering better rackets for far less money than any other house. Even our cheapest racket is a hand polished racket. These rackets are made especially for us; we guarantee them to exceed any rackets on the market in finish, stringing and balance. We recommend our Seroco Racket, in 12-ounce weight, as being an excellent racket for ladies.

No. 6C6650 Our Junior Racket is made from second growth ash, walnut throat, cedar handle, well strung with American gut, well balanced; for boys and girls.

Price...............................**85c**

No. 6C6651 Our Oak Park Racket, full size head; made from second growth ash, with walnut throat, cedar handle; closely strung with best American gut, leather capped, well balanced. An excellent low priced racket for youths and misses. Price...............**$1.25**

No. 6C6652 Our Seroco Racket, full size head; made from selected second growth ash, with walnut throat, cedar handle; strung with good quality selected imported gut, leather capped. Designed for rapid, effective work, well strung and well balanced.

Price...............................**$1.75**

No. 6C6653 Our Volley Racket, full size, highly polished head; is made from selected second growth ash, five-piece walnut and maple throat, polished and scored cedar handle, closely strung with a fine quality imported gut, leather capped and well balanced. A racket suitable for amateur or professional work.

Price...............................**$2.50**

No. 6C6655 Our Expert Racket. This is a racket which is especially built for us, has full size extra highly polished head; the frame is made of the very best selected second growth ash, and head tapers slightly from the rim toward the gut; five-piece walnut and maple throat; polished and scored cedar handle; strung with the very finest imported gut, leather capped, well balanced; designed especially for professional work, 12-ounce, 13-ounce and 14-ounce weights. This racket is as well made as any racket can be regardless of price, name or brand and usually sells at $5.00 to $6.50.

Our price...........................**$3.50**

If by mail, postage extra, 14 to 16 cents.

RACKETS RESTRUNG WITH BEST CLEAR GUT, $1.50.

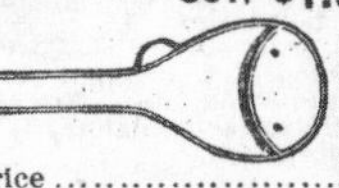

No. 6C6657 Soft Felt Racket Cover. Keeps moisture from racket, saves racket and gut from injury.

Price...............................**35c**

If by mail, postage extra, 6 cents.

Lawn Tennis Balls.

No. 6C6658 Regulation Tennis Balls. Felt covered, an excellent ball.

Price, each...............**$0.25**
Per dozen.................**2.70**

No. 6C6659 Goodrich Championship Tennis Balls, adopted by the United States Lawn Tennis Association. Positively the best ball made. Price, per dozen, **$3.75**; each...........**33c**

If by mail, postage extra, 3 cents.

No. 6C6660 Wright & Ditson Championship Balls. Price, per doz., **$3.95**; each, **35c**

Lawn Tennis Nets.

Note our hand made double center net for $2.50.

No. 6C6661 Tennis Nets, 27x3 feet, 12-thread. Weight, packed, 31 ozs. Price.....**65c**

No. 6C6662 Tennis Nets, 36x3 feet, 15-thread. Weight, packed, 36 ozs. Price.**$1.00**

No. 6C6663 Tennis Nets, 42x3 feet, 15-thread. Weight, packed, 36 ozs. Price.**$1.25**

No. 6C6664 Tennis Nets, 42x3 feet, 15-thread, canvas bound. Price............**$1.65**

No. 6C6665½ Double Center Net, 42x3ft., 21-thread, hand made, canvas bound. Price **$2.50**

No. 6C6666 Back Stop Net to prevent balls from rolling out of grounds, 50x8 feet, 12-thread. Price...........................**$2.25**

Seroco Tennis Net Poles.

No. 6C6667 Solid (one piece) Tennis Poles, nicely finished, complete with guy ropes and pegs. Price, per pair...............**98c**

Dry Tennis Court Marker.

No. 6C6668 Uses marble dust or air slaked lime, no mixing of material required. The wheel revolves on its axle. Comes fitted with handle.

Price...............................**$1.00**

Our Seroco Croquet Sets

No. 6C6678

No. 6C6670 Our Junior Four-ball Croquet Set, four striped mallets, four hardwood varnished and striped balls and striped and varnished stakes, ten wire arches; put up in neat, strong wood box with hinged cover. Weight, about 13 pounds. Price, per set.**55c**

No. 6C6672 Our Amateur Eight-ball Croquet Set, eight striped mallets, eight hardwood varnished and striped balls, two striped and varnished stakes, ten wire arches; put up in a strong wood box with hinged cover. Weight, about 22 pounds. Price, per set.........**75c**

No. 6C6674 Our Favorite Eight-ball Croquet Set, consists of eight nicely painted and varnished mallets with five-inch heads, eight striped and varnished balls, two large fancy striped stakes, heavy wire arches; an excellent set at a low price; put up in a strong, durable wood box with hinged cover. Weight, about 24 pounds. Price, per set................**$1.25**

No. 6C6676 Our Champion Eight-ball Croquet Set, consisting of eight finely finished striped mallets, with eight-inch heads, eight hard maple striped and varnished balls, two striped fancy stakes, heavy pointed wire arches; well made and finished set in every respect, put up in strong wood box with hinged cover. Weight, about 27 pounds.

Price, per set......................**$1.50**

Our Professional Croquet Set.

No. 6C6678 Our Professional Eight-ball Croquet Set, consists of eight finely finished varnished and striped mallets, with eight-inch heads, eight finely finished striped hardwood balls, two handsome beaded striped stakes, heavy wire arches; an excellent set in every respect; put up in a strong wood box, hinged cover. Weight, about 31 pounds.

Price, per set......................**$2.25**

OUR BOXING GLOVE DEPARTMENT.

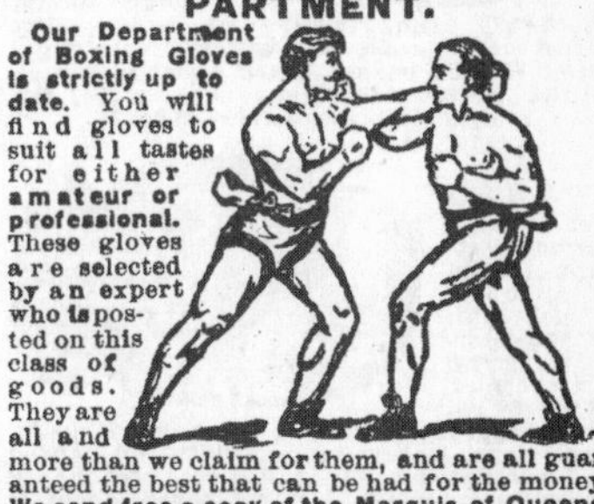

Our Department of Boxing Gloves is strictly up to date. You will find gloves to suit all tastes for either **amateur or professional.** These gloves are selected by an expert who is posted on this class of goods. They are all and more than we claim for them, and are all guaranteed the best that can be had for the money. **We send free a copy of the Marquis of Queensbury Rules with every set. A set consists of four gloves, two pairs, packed in a box.**

No. 6C6800 Boys' size, made of soft tanned kid leather, ecru color, stuffed with good quality short hair, ventilated palm, laced wristband, good shape, a well made and durable glove. Weight, per set, boxed, about 28 ounces. Price, per set of four gloves.**85c**

If by mail, postage extra, 31 cents.

No. 6C6801 Youths' size. Made of wine colored kid leather, soft and pliable, stuffed with good quality curled hair; stitched fingers, laced wristband, ventilated palm. Weight, per set, boxed, about 34 ounces. Price, per set of four gloves..........**$1.10**

If by mail, postage extra, 37 cents.

BOXING GLOVES continued on next page

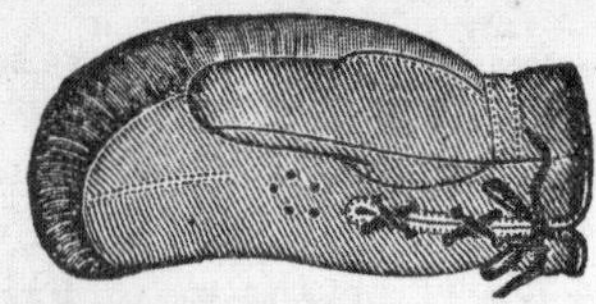

No. 6C6802 Jy. Simon's Men's Size Standard Pattern. Made of ecru kid leather, stuffed with good quality short hair, ventilated palm, laced wristband, drill lined. Weight, per set, boxed, about 46 ounces.
Price, per set of four gloves..........**$1.10**
If by mail, postage extra, 49 cents.

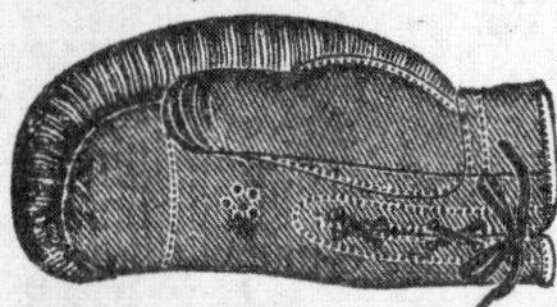

No. 6C6803 Our Frank Snyder Glove, Men's Standard Pattern, Improved. Made of claret colored California napa leather, with padded finger ends, ventilated palm, split and laced wrist, stuffed with good quality curled hair, drill lined. Weight, per set, boxed, about 46 ounces.
Price, per set of four gloves..........**$1.25**
If by mail, postage extra, 49 cents.

No. 6C6804 Our Ben Hoerstal Corbett Pattern. Claret back, palm and wrist; ventilated palm, drill lined, laced wristband, stuffed with good quality curled hair. Weight, per set, boxed, about 46 ounces.
Price, per set of four gloves..........**$1.50**
If by mail, postage extra, 49 cents.

No. 6C6805 Our Wm. Thiel Corbett Pattern. Made of wine colored kid leather, serge lining, stitched fingers, ventilated palm, split wrist with laced wristband and padded cuffs; stuffed with best quality curled hair. Weight, per set, boxed, about 50 ounces.

Price, per set of four gloves..........**$1.65**
If by mail, postage extra, 53 cents.

No. 6C6806 Ed. Campbell's Corbett Pattern. Made of selected green California napa leather, with stitched fingers, serge lining, laced wrist, ventilated palm, stuffed with best quality curled hair. Weight, per set, boxed, about 48 ounces.

Price, per set of four gloves..........**$1.75**
If by mail, postage extra, 51 cents.

No. 6C6808 Ed. Field's Corbett Pattern. Made of selected especially tanned wine color kid, laced wrist, padded cuff, leather bound; best serge lining, ventilated palm, stuffed with extra quality curled hair, double silk stitched, with finger grip. Weight, per set, boxed, about 48 ounces.

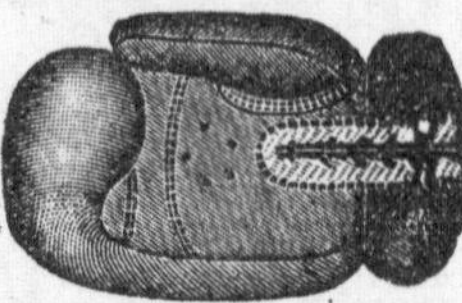

Price, per set of four gloves..........**$3.00**
If by mail, postage extra, 51 cents.

No. 6C6810 Geo. Stoll's Corbett Pattern. Made of selected French kid, of tan color, with grip across center of fingers, lined throughout, double stitched with silk, laced wrist, leather binding, with full padded cuff, ventilated palm; stuffed with best quality curled hair. Weight, per set, boxed, about 48 ounces. Guaranteed equal to gloves that retail generally at $5.00.
Price, per set of four gloves..........**$3.25**
If by mail, postage extra, 51 cents.

The Dudley Club Special, $3.80

No. 6C6811 The Dudley Club Special Boxing Glove. Corbett pattern, full heel pad below the lacing, center palm grip, full padded cuff, laced wristband, double stitched with silk, made from special selected, tan color, California tanned kid, stuffed with finest quality white curled hair, a new departure in boxing gloves, the latest on the market. Weight, per set, boxed, about 50 ounces.
Price, per set of four gloves..........**$3.80**
If by mail, postage extra, 55 cents.

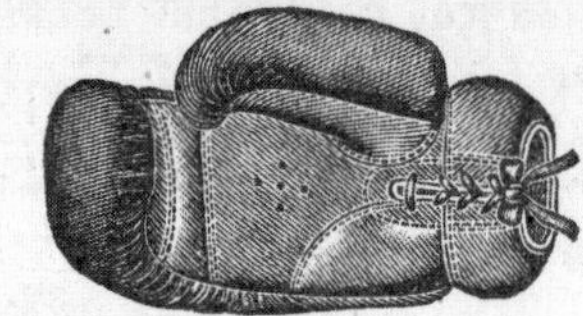

No. 6C6812 Barry Pattern. Made of selected, especially tanned French kid leather, green color with grip in center, thumb well padded on top, affording absolute protection, serge lined and leather binding, laced wrist with tape laces, wrist extra full padded, hand sewed; stuffed with extra quality curled hair, double stitched throughout with silk. Weight per set, boxed, about 48 ounces. Price, per set of four gloves..**$3.50**
If by mail, postage extra, 51 cents.

No. 6C6813 Billy Foster's Amateur Pattern Men's Size Gloves, made of best green color California kid leather, with finger grip and toe padded, ventilated palm, padded wrist, best serge lining, leather binding, laced wrist, stuffed with best quality curled hair, double stitched throughout. A good sparring glove.
Price, per set of four..........**$2.15**
If by mail, postage extra, 48 cents.

Our Highest Grade Gloves at $3.10 per Set.

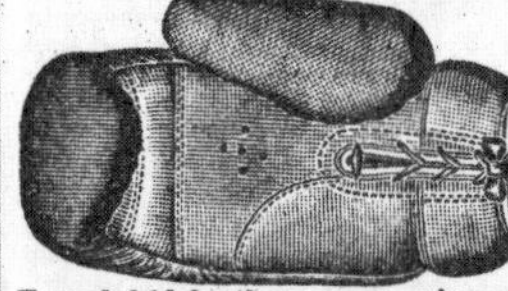

No. 6C6814 Special Fitzsimmons Pattern, with California thumb. Made of selected French kid leather, green color, with grip and side or heel pad, serge lined and leather binding, laced wrist with tape laces, wrist made with extra padded roll, hand sewed; stuffed with extra quality curled hair, double stitched throughout with silk. Weight, per set, boxed, about 52 ounces. Price, per set........**$3.10**
If by mail, postage extra, 53 cents.

Professional Fighting Gloves.

No. 6C6815 Our Geo. Peacock Pattern Professional Fighting Glove. Made of selected green California napa leather, with grip in center and toe pad, ventilated palm, lined throughout, laced and leather bound wrist; stuffed with very best quality curled hair, made extra strong for hard usage, double stitched with linen thread, padded cuff. Weight, per set, boxed, about 45 ounces.
Price, per set of four gloves..........**$2.10**
If by mail, postage extra, 48 cents.

5-Ounce Fighting Gloves.

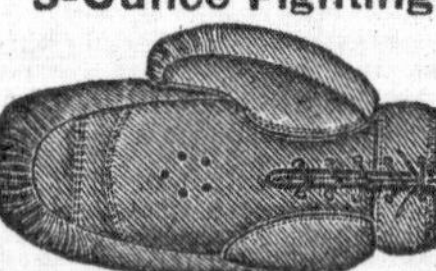

No. 6C6816 The Genuine Root Pattern Fighting Gloves, made of the very finest quality, selected tan color kid leather, and leather lined, made with padded wrist, finger grip, ventilated palm, deep laced wrist, double stitched with silk, stuffed with very best quality white curled hair. Each glove weighs 5 ounces. Regular price, $5.00; our price..........**$3.97**
If by mail, postage extra, 35 cents.

STRIKING BAGS.

Affords much amusement, keeps your health good and is excellent exercise.

Our line of bags is the most complete and finest in the market. All are carefully tested before they are put in stock. Our bags all have the best grade of bladder that money can buy. The buyer of a bag wants a strong, substantial article that can be relied on, and a rubber inside that will not burst the first time it is used. All our bags are lined to keep their original shape. **32 inches is the regulation size. Prices include the bag and bladder complete, with a piece of rope and screw eye.**

Single End Bags.

No. 6C6824 Made of good strong leather, drill lined, strong loop, all well made. This is a good practice bag for a very little money. Weight, about 10 ounces. Price, complete, **90c**

No. 6C6825 Made of gold tan napa leather with strong loop. Drill lined, good, desirable and strong, 30 inches circumference when inflated. Weight, complete, about 10 ounces. Price, with bladder..........**$1.15**

No. 6C6828 Made of olive tan leather, with strong loop and drill lined, very good strong bag, 32 inches circumference when inflated. Weight, complete, about 12 ounces.
Price, with bladder..........**$1.25**

No. 6C6829 Best quality, claret color, soft tanned leather, strong loop, drill lined, triple seams, making an extra strong bag, one of the best sellers, 32 inches circumference when inflated. Weight, complete, about 14 ounces. Price, with bladder..........**$1.50**

No. 6C6830 Best quality California olive tan leather, strong loop, drill lined, welted seams, triple stitches, one-piece top, a fine bag and very fast. 32-inches circumference when inflated. Weight, complete, about 12 ounces.
Price, with bladder..........**$1.75**

No. 6C6835 Soft tan satin calf, drill lined, triple seams, welted, strong loop, one-piece top. A good article, retails for $3.50. 32 inches circumference when inflated. Weight, complete, about 14 ounces. Price with bladder..........**$2.20**

No. 6C6836 Expert Bag, made of special selected oil tan horsehide, very strong and tough. Drill lined, triple seams, welted, strong loop, one-piece top, made up first class in every respect; very fast and the finest bag made. 32 inches circumference when inflated. Weight, complete, about 14 ounces.
Price, with bladder..........**$2.45**
If by mail, postage extra, 20 to 25 cents.

Double End Bags.

Here is a line of double end bags which are lively, good and can be put up anywhere where you can put in two screw eyes. Illustration shows a bag put up in a doorway. Bore a 1-inch hole in your door sill, turn a screw eye into it so it will be below the sill and out of the way; fasten a hook to the elastic cord and hook it to the screw eye, and you can take down the bag or put it up in a few seconds any time. These prices include the bag, bladder, a piece of rope, two screw eyes and a piece of elastic cord.

No. 6C6845 Made of gold tan napa leather, with strong loop, drill lined. Double end, good, desirable and strong, 30 inches circumference when inflated. Weight, complete, about 12 ounces. Price, with bladder, rope and elastic cord..........**$1.35**

No. 6C6846 Best quality, claret color, soft tanned leather, drill lined, strong loop, triple seams, making an extra strong double end bag, and one of the best sellers; 32 inches circumference when inflated. Weight, complete, about 14 ounces. Price, with bladder, rope and elastic cord..........**$1.75**

No. 6C6847 Soft tan satin calf, drill lined, triple seams, welted, the best double end bag on the market. A good article, retails for $4.00. 32 inches circumference when inflated. Weight, complete, about 15 ounces. Price, with bladder, rope and elastic cord..........**$2.45**
If by mail, postage extra, 22 to 27 cents.

Our Pear Shape Bag.

This is the latest thing in punching bags. The pear shape bag is so made that the strain is on all sections of the bag instead of one place. The top and bottom are stitched by hand and the bag is built to withstand constant use —in fact, the bag is built for work.

No. 6C6848 Made of napa leather, plain seams, canvas lined, wine color, 30 inches circumference when inflated. Weight, complete, 11 ounces.
Price, with bladder..........**$1.40**

No. 6C6849 Fine quality goatskin, olive green color, napa tanned, bound lips, eyeleted lace holes, welted triple seams, canvas lined, 32 inches circumference when inflated. Weight, complete, 11 ounces.
Price, with bladder..........**$1.85**

No. 6C6850 Fine quality selected horsehide, tan color, bound lips, eyeleted lace holes, welted seams, canvas lined, 32 inches in circumference when inflated, hand stitched top and bottom, with very best quality of rubber bladder that can be had; just the bag for professional bag punchers. Weight, complete, 11 ounces. Price, with bladder..........**$2.50**
If by mail, postage extra, 22 to 25 cents.

Rugby Rubber Football Bladders.

Our bladders are all the best grade. We do not carry cheap bladders. They are worthless.

No. 6C6851¼ Pure Rubber for regulation Rugby footballs.
Price..........**43c**

No. 6C6851½ Rugby Bladders, for boys' footballs. Price..........**35c**
If by mail, postage extra, 8 to 15 cents.

Rubber Striking Bag and Football Bladders.

No. 6C6852 10-inch Bladders, made of pure Para rubber, for 30-inch striking bags and Association foot balls. Price..........**42c**

No. 6C6853 12-inch Bladders, made of finest quality pure rubber, for bags 33 inches in circumference. Price..........**48c**
If by mail, postage extra, 5 cents.

Striking Bag Swivel.

No. 6C6854 Striking Bag Swivel. The latest out; has all improvements and none of the defects of the old swivel. Rope can be taken out without unscrewing from platform and permits bag to be punched in any direction without twisting rope. Price..........**23c**
If by mail, postage extra, 6 cents.

Striking Bag Knuckle Gloves.

No. 6C6855½ The Celebrated Frazer Striking Bag Knuckle Glove, small, neat, made of the best oil tanned horsehide, heavily padded, thus making a complete protection for the knuckles. For ladies and men. Price, per pair..**35c**
If by mail, postage extra, 5 cents.

Striking Bag Mitts.

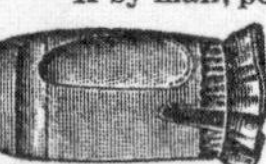

No. 6C6858 Striking Bag Mitts, made of kid, with grip in center, padded back, elastic wristband. This is the only punching bag mitt to use for bag punching.
Price, per pair..........**65c**
If by mail, postage extra, 10c.

Maple Indian Clubs.

No. 6C6856 Sold in pairs only, and made of the best first quality rock maple and finely polished. Weight given is the weight of each club. If you order one pair 1-pound clubs, you get two 1-pound clubs, etc.

Each club weighs	Per pair	Each club weighs	Per pair
½ pound	14c	2 pounds	23c
¾ pound	16c	3 pounds	37c
1 pound	17c	4 pounds	44c
1½ pounds	20c	5 pounds	55c

When ordering, state which weight you want.

Wood Dumb Bells.

No. 6C6857 Wood Dumb Bells, made of polished maple, of best quality and nicely polished. Weight is the same as Indian clubs.

Each bell weighs	Price per pair	Each bell weighs	Price per pair
½ pound	15c	2 pounds	24c
¾ pound	17c	3 pounds	38c
1 pound	18c	4 pounds	45c

Mention the weight you wish when ordering.

Iron Dumb Bells.

No. 6C6859 Our Iron Dumb Bells are cast from pure gray iron, and are very much stronger and more durable than those ordinarily sold, which are usually made from scrap iron, tin, etc., and are very brittle and break easily. We make them in weights as follows: 1, 2, 3, 4, 5, 6, 8, 10, 12, 15, 20 and 25 pounds. These are the weights of each dumb bell. Sold by the pound. Mention weight you wish when ordering. Price, per pound..........**4c**

Our Perfect Chicago Bag Platform, $4.00.

No. 6C6866 From the accompanying illustration, engraved by our artist direct from the platform, you can form some idea of our Perfect Striking Bag Platform. This platform is made of selected wood, 36 inches in diameter, well braced and is so constructed that the platform may be raised or lowered after it is fastened to the wall. This obviates the necessity of lowering or elevating the entire platform to accommodate different sized people. The Chicago punching bag platform should be fastened so that the circle will be about 6¾ feet from the floor. This height will accommodate the average person. Price for the Chicago Punching Bag Platform (this price does not include the punching bag), only..........**$4.00**
Weight, crated for shipment, about 85 pounds.

Elastic Floor Attachments.

No. 6C6867 Elastic Floor Attachments for Double End Bags, made of elastic and covered with braided cotton and used for attaching the bottom of the bag to the floor. Price..........**18c**
If by mail, postage extra, 5 cents.

Exercising or Swinging Rings.

No. 6C6869 Wooden Rings, three pieces, made of walnut and maple, glued together, 6 in. in diameter. Per pair.....**45c**
If by mail, postage extra, 5 cents.

Horizontal Bars.

No. 6C6870 Made of the best quality of second growth, straight grain hickory, square ends.

	Price
4½ feet long.	$1.15
5 feet long.	1.30
5½ feet long.	1.65
6 feet long.	1.85

Weight, 4½ to 6 pounds.

Whiteley Chest Pull.

No. 6C6871 Just the thing to broaden your shoulders and to strengthen the muscles of your back and arms. More beneficial than the heavy chest weights, and far less expensive. Made of three strands of elastic cable, attached to two wood handles with nickel plated trimmings. Comes in three tensions.
A—Light tension, for ladies and children, 27 inches. Price..........**45c**
B—Medium tension, for youths, 30 inches. Price..........**50c**
C—Heavy tension, for men, 33 inches. Price..........**55c**
If by mail, postage extra, 12 cents.

Common Sense Exercisers.

No home is complete without it. Convenient, perfect working, the latest and best on the market and our special price of 34 cents will surely commend it.

No. 6C6872 Our New Common Sense Exerciser, made of heavy elastic cord, the latest and cheapest exerciser yet produced; can be put up in any part of the room. Price...34c
If by mail, postage extra, 11 cents.

Whiteley Exercisers.

No. 6C6873 Made of elastic cord with wood pulleys, plain handles and foot attachment. Price.....$1.55
If by mail, postage extra, 22 cents.

No. 6C6874 Made of elastic cord with metal pulleys running in brass bushings, enameled handles with foot attachment. Price.....$2.35
If by mail, postage extra, 30 cents.

No. 6C6875 Made of elastic cord, with fancy decorated pulleys, nickel plated trimmings, enameled handles with foot attachment. Price...$3.00
If by mail, postage extra, 30 cents.

No. 6C6877 Whiteley Special Exerciser, for adults or children, full size, OO grade, made of elastic cable with plain wood pulleys and wood handles, nickel plated trimmings, complete with hinge attachments, screw eyes, also chart of exercising. Packed in neat paper box. Price...$1.00

BASEBALL GOODS FOR AMERICA'S NATIONAL GAME

Baseball Shoes.

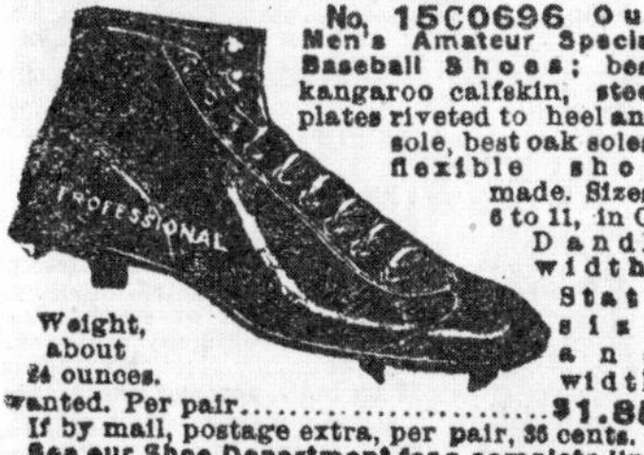

No. 15C0696 Our Men's Amateur Special Baseball Shoes; best kangaroo calfskin, steel plates riveted to heel and sole, best oak soles, flexible shoe made. Sizes, 6 to 11, in C, D and E width. State size and width wanted. Weight, about 24 ounces. Per pair...$1.85
If by mail, postage extra, per pair, 35 cents.
See our Shoe Department for a complete line of baseball, football and running shoes, quoted at lowest wholesale prices.
If by mail, postage extra, 30 cents.

Baseballs.

The Victor League Ball, made entirely by hand, best Para rubber center, the best ball that can be produced; specially prepared, two-piece horse hide cover, stitched with heavy linen thread, makes this the strongest ball on the market, the specifications of the National League are rigidly followed. Guaranteed to hold its shape for nine innings. No better ball made at any price.

No. 6C6885 The Victor League Ball. Price. (If by mail, postage extra, 9 cents.)..90c

No. 6C6886 For those who wish the Spalding League Balls we have them at, each.$1.05
If by mail, postage extra, 9 cents.

No. 6C6887 Our National Association, made of best materials exactly in accordance with approved specifications. A regular dollar ball. Each ball in a separate box and sealed. Price..(If by mail, postage extra, 8 cents)..70c

No. 6C6889 Our High School League. A high grade ball, regulation size, will keep its shape under heavy batting. Price...45c
If by mail, postage extra, 8 cents.

No. 6C6890 Our Pitchers' Pride. A beauty, has horsehide cover, well made; each in a separate box, sealed. A fine ball for boys. Price..(If by mail, postage extra, 8c.)...25c

No. 6C6892 Our Little Victor, the best ball ever offered for the money. Price...10c
If by mail, postage extra, 7 cents.

No. 6C6893 Our Star, an extra well made ball for the money. Not an ordinary ball, but well worth twice our price. Price...5c
If by mail, postage extra, 5 cents.

Baseball Bats.

No. 6C6915 Sereco Professional Model Bat, made of best quality, second growth white grain ash, hand turned, perfectly balanced—special rough grip. 33 and 34 inches. Guaranteed the best bat on the market. Price..60c

No. 6C6916 Men's Champion. Made of fine quality ash. Medium grade bat. Men's size. Price...35c

No. 6C6917 Antique. Good quality ash. Men's size. An extra good bat at a low price. Price...25c

No. 6C6919 Boys' Choice. A good, strong, well finished bat. Price...10c

No. 6C6920 Boys' Comet. 27-inch bat, a daisy for the money. Price...5c

Baseball Mitts.

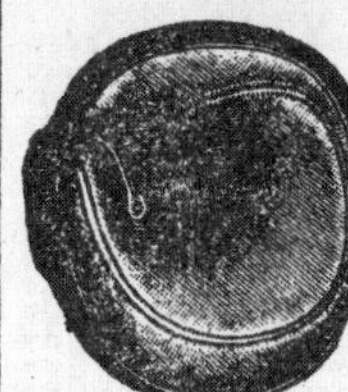

No. 6C6925 The Victor Professional Mitt, made of the highest grade drab horsehide. This mitt is designed especially for professionals and embodies suggestions received from many of the league catchers. Workmanship the best, material the best. Has patent thumb strap and patent lace. The patent thumb strap forms and keeps a deep pocket in the mitt, thus you buy a mitt that is already broken in. Felt lined. No better mitt made at any price. This mitt is 11 inches long and 10 inches wide.
Price....(Postage extra, 38 cents)....$4.75

No. 6C6927 Our Victor Cleveland Mitt. We believe this mitt superior to any $5.00 mitt that was ever put on the market. The front is of best quality horsehide and the back and trimmings are of calf. Has the patent thumb adjusting strap and lace, same as our $4.75 mitt. Made on lines of the professional mitts and felt lined. This mitt is 10½ inches long and 9½ inches wide. Price...$3.75
If by mail, postage extra, 40 cents.

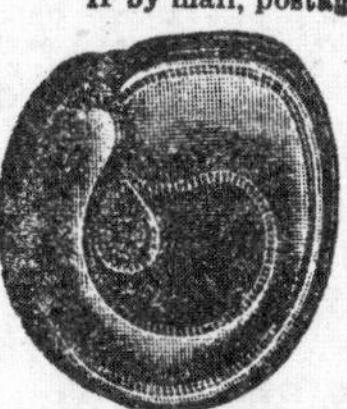

No. 6C6928 Our Amateur League Mitt, 10 inches long, 9 inches wide, made of selected, oil tanned, genuine kip leather, double stitched, leather bound around the edge, padded with good quality heavy felt, same as is used in $5.00 mitts, made with laced heel, the thumb is adjustable with strap and buckle, full crescent heel pad, forming a deep pocket in the palm; thumb reinforced at the base with a quirk. This mitt is regulation size, made after the improved pattern professional league mitt, and of best material and workmanship; warranted to give satisfaction and service. Price. (Postage extra, 33c.)..$2.50

No. 6C6931 Our Commercial League Mitt, made of fine, selected, oil tanned, genuine kip leather throughout, double stitched, leather bound around the edge; has crescent heel pad, the thumb is adjustable with strap and buckle, forming deep pocket in the palm, padded with heavy felt, is 10 inches long and 9½ inches wide, and is first class in every respect; must be seen to be appreciated. Price...(Postage extra, 36c.)....$2.25

No. 6C6933 Our Men's Buck Mitt, made with buckskin palm, goatskin back, calfskin fingers and leather bound around the edge, double stitched, stuffed with good quality felt padding, adjustable strap and buckle on thumb, crescent heel pad; this is a well made mitt, and nicely finished article. Makes an ideal amateur mitt for school or clerical clubs. Price...$1.85
If by mail, postage extra, 30 cents.

No. 6C6934 Our Chelsea Mitt, buckskin palm, back and fingers of selected goatskin, leather bound around the edge, thumb adjustable, crescent heel pad, with deep cup shape palm. An excellent mitt for little money. All are stuffed with felt, and the workmanship is first class. An excellent mitt for school clubs. Price...(Postage extra, 30c.)....$1.65

No. 6C6935 Our Medium Size Amateur Mitt. Palm is made of selected oil tanned calfskin, back is made of selected glove leather, leather bound around the edge, crescent heel pad, well stuffed, and medium deep pocket in the palm. Price.$1.45
Postage extra, 28c.

No. 6C6937 Our Medium Size Amateur Mitt. Palm is made of selected horsehide, back is made of selected glove leather, leather bound around the edge, crescent heel pad, medium deep pocket in the palm, well stuffed; otherwise same mitt as No. 6C6935.
Price....(Postage extra, 28 cents)....$1.25

No. 6C6938 Our Men's Medium Size Amateur Mitt. Palm is made of asbestos buckskin, back is made of light tan color glove leather, leather bound around the edges, well stuffed, with medium size pocket in the palm, an excellent glove for young men for amateur games. Price...(If by mail, postage extra, 28c.)..75c

No. 6C6939 Our Youths' Large Size Mitt, made from yellow or red well tanned leather, crescent heel pad, with medium deep pocket in the palm, machine stitched around the edges, well stuffed; an excellent mitt for youths. Price...40c
Postage extra, 20 cents.

No. 6C6940 S., R. & Co.'s Youths' Mitt, made of selected tan leather, with fingers well padded; a good, strong mitt. Price...30c
Postage extra, 20 cents.

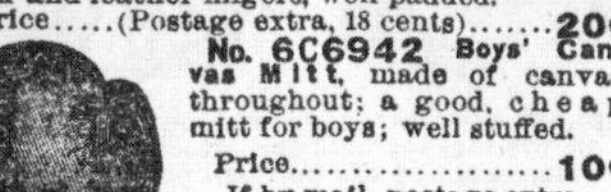

No. 6C6941 Boys' Mitt, made with leather palm, canvas back and leather fingers, well padded. Price.....(Postage extra, 18 cents)......20c

No. 6C6942 Boys' Canvas Mitt, made of canvas throughout; a good, cheap mitt for boys; well stuffed. Price...10c
If by mail, postage extra, 13 cents.

Basemen's Mitts.

No. 6C6943 S., R. & Co.'s Basemen's and Fielders' Mitt, made of the very best and softest tanned buckskin, heavily padded with highest quality felt, with crescent palm and thumb pad, welt seam, leather bound, lace back. It is safe and easy fitting. Very strong and durable. No better mitt made.
Price....(Postage extra, 10 cents.)....$1.25

We always send mitts or gloves for the left hand. If you are left handed, specify "to fit right hand" when ordering.

Basemen's and Fielders' Gloves.

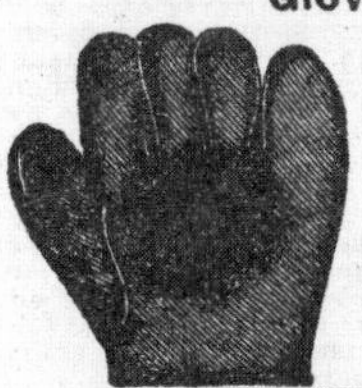

No. 6C6952 The Professional Style Fielder's Glove of latest Improved Pattern, is made of the very best, fine selected oil tanned leather, very soft and pliable, made on very large pattern with large little finger and correctly padded. Has heavy padding at the heel forming a large deep natural pocket in the palm. Leather lined, leather bound, strap and buckle wrist and welted seams. The glove is so constructed that it does not require "Breaking In", and is guaranteed to be equal and to wear as long as any $3.50 glove on the market. No better to be had at any price, and it must be seen to be appreciated. Price...$2.15
If by mail, postage extra, 14 cents.

No. 6C6954 The Victor Professional Fielders' Glove. Made of horsehide, correctly padded, crescent pad extending in a semicircle around palm, with adjustable web between the thumb and first finger, as shown in the illustration, making a deep pocket, correctly padded. The best glove on the market.
Price...$1.95
Postage extra, 11 cents.

No. 6C6956 Basemen's and Infielders' Glove, made of good quality buckskin, crescent heel pad, palm and fingers heavily padded, lined with good quality felt, web between thumb and first finger, a medium priced professional glove and a good one. Price....(Postage extra, 14c.)....$1.27

No. 6C6958 Our Chicago Glove, men's size, made of napa tanned horsehide, well padded, with finger tips; crescent padded palm, full men's size, first class workmanship, a glove that will give you satisfaction. Leather finger tips will be popular this season. Price...$1.00
If by mail, postage extra, 13 cents.

No. 6C6959 Made in men's large size, of buckskin leather, felt lined, crescent heel pad, heavily padded palm, web thumb and first finger, leather bound edges, button wrist; a first class semiprofessional glove. Price...75c
If by mail, post. extra, 10c.

No. 6C6961 Made of Napa tanned glove leather; felt padded palm and fingers, leather bound edges, button wristband. Price...40c
If by mail, postage extra, 8 cents.

Youths' and Boys' Fielders' Gloves.

No. 6C6964 Our Youths' Infielders' Glove, made of finest oil tanned leather heavily padded crescent heel pad, leather bound all around, button fastener. A regular boys' professional glove. Price...35c
If by mail, postage extra, 8c.

Our 18c Boys' Glove.

No. 6C6966 Our Boys' Infielders' Glove, made of fine, colored sheepskin, palm is felt lined and padded, well stitched seams, elastic fastener. Price...18c
If by mail, postage extra, 3 cents.

Baseball Catchers' Masks.

No. 6C6974 Patent Neck Protecting Mask. Has an extension at bottom giving absolute protection to the neck without interfering in the least with the movements of the head. The wire is of the best annealed steel, is extra heavy and covered with black enamel to prevent the reflection of light. The padding is filled with goat hair and faced with finest imported dogskin, which, being impervious to perspiration, always remains soft and pliant to the face. Price...$2.00
If by mail, postage extra, 30 cents.

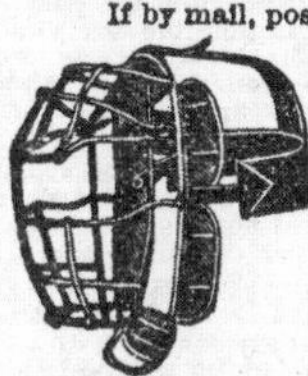

No. 6C6975 Men's Professional League Mask. Black enameled wire of 5-32 and 6-32-inch diameter, which prevents the reflection of the light; temple and cheek pads, with head and chin pieces; weight, 24 ounces; an A1 quality mask; 10½ inches long, 7½ inches wide. A very strong mask. Price...$1.50
If by mail, postage extra, 29 cents.

No. 6C6977 Men's Professional League Mask. Black, enameled wire of 5-32 and 6-32 inch diameter, which prevents the reflection of the light; temple and cheek pads, with head and chin pieces; weight, 22 ounces; an A1 quality mask; 10½ inches long. 7½ inches wide. A strong mask. Price..$1.25
If by mail, postage extra, 27 cents.

No. 6C6978 Men's Professional Mask. Black enameled wire, 5-32 inch in diameter, temple and cheek pads, head and chin pieces; well made; weight, 18 ounces; 10 inches long, 7 inches wide. Price...90c
If by mail, postage extra, 18 cents.

No. 6C6980 Men's Amateur Mask. Bright wire, 4-32 inch in diameter; temple and cheek pads; nicely finished; weight, 11 ounces; 10 inches long, 7 inches wide. Price...50c
If by mail, postage extra, 16 cents.

No. 6C6983 Youths' Mask. Bright wire, 3-32 inch in diameter; temple and cheek pads; nicely finished; weight, 8 ounces; frame, 10 inches long, 6 inches wide. Price...35c
If by mail, postage extra, 9 cents.

No. 6C6984 Boys' Mask. Bright wire, 3-32 inch in diameter; temple and cheek pads; nicely finished; weight, 4 ounces; frame, 9 inches long, 5 inches wide. Price...18c
If by mail, postage extra, 6 cents.

Baseball Catchers' Body Protectors, 60c to $4.00.

No. 6C6990 Our Special Professional League Body Protector, made of the very best rubber, inflated with air; light, pliable, and does not interfere with movements of the wearer. When not in use air may be let out and the protector rolled into a small package. Price...$4.00
Postage extra, 40 cents.

No. 6C6991 Our Special Amateur Body Protector, inflated with air, similar to our league, but has fewer air compartments. It is made with the same care as our professional and all are warranted perfect when they leave our store. Price....$2.75
If by mail, postage extra, 40 cents.

No. 6C6992 Our Boys' Body Protector, made of canvas, well stuffed and quilted, same shape as our league but smaller, for boys. Price...60c
If by mail, postage extra, 20 cents.

No. 6C6993 Our Men's Body Protector, made of canvas, with soft leather front, stuffed and quilted. Price...$1.00
If by mail, postage extra, 30 cents.

League Shoe Plates.

No. 6C6998 League Toe Plates, best quality steel stamping. Price, per pair...18c
If by mail, postage extra, per pair, 3 cents.

No. 6C6999 League Heel Plates, best quality steel stamping. Price, per pair...18c
If by mail, postage extra, per pair, 3 cents.

No. 6C7001 Amateur Shoe Plates, to be used for heel or toe. Steel stamping, for boys' shoes. Price, per pair...9c
If by mail, postage extra, per pair, 3 cents.

Baseball Guides.

No. 6C7028 Annual Baseball Guides, giving official rules of the game. Not issued before April 1st of each year. Price...10c
If by mail, postage extra, 3 cents.

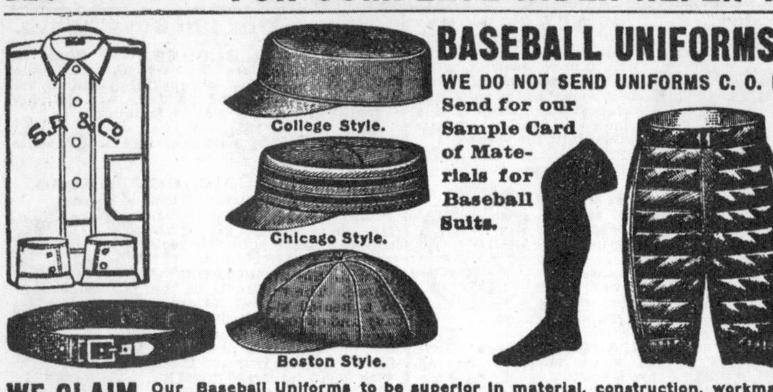

BASEBALL UNIFORMS.

WE DO NOT SEND UNIFORMS C. O. D.

Send for our Sample Card of Materials for Baseball Suits.

WE CLAIM Our Baseball Uniforms to be superior in material, construction, workmanship and finish to any uniforms on the market, and our prices, quality considered, cannot be equaled. We have made the requirements of the baseball player a special study, and by reason of our years of experience gained through the handling of thousands of orders for baseball goods throughout the past seasons, we are enabled to offer greater value in baseball uniforms than it is possible for you to obtain elsewhere, even though you spend far more money for same than the prices we ask. **Send for sample card of baseball uniform samples to satisfy yourself that what we say is true.** (Tape measure, measurement blank and instructions for taking these measurements accompany these samples.)

OUR C. O. D. TERMS do not apply on baseball uniforms, as we do not carry these goods in stock. We find it cannot be done and insure satisfaction to our customers. **We make each and every suit to order in accordance with the specifications furnished, therefore cannot send these goods C. O. D., but we guarantee them to be exactly as ordered and as represented, or money and transportation will be refunded.**

THE TIME REQUIRED TO MAKE. As stated, all our baseball suits are made to order, which involves a delay of four to ten days, except just prior to Decoration Day and 4th of July, when we require orders for suits to be furnished on these two days to be placed **two weeks** in advance. Otherwise we might have to disappoint you on account of the enormous demand for suits at this time of the season.

EXTRAS—3 or 4-inch letters on shirts, per letter....3c
Larger than 4-inch letters on shirt, per letter....10c
Flannel letters on cap, per letter....7c
Detachable sleeves, per shirt....25c

No. 6C7080 OUR AMATEUR UNIFORM is made of very strong, excellent quality twilled material. Suits made of this material present a very neat appearance, and do not catch the dirt like most of the wooly material put in cheap uniforms, and when soiled can be washed, and will look as good as new. We guarantee these suits to be superior to any on the market sold for a similar price. We can furnish these suits only with button front shirt, padded pants with elastic bottom, and college style cap, black cotton ribbed stockings and black belt. We can furnish these suits in the following colors: white, blue mix, green mix, red mix, and a red, green and gray mixture.

No. 6C7080 Shirt, button front only. Mention color wanted. Price, each....$1.25
Pants, elastic bottom. Price, each....1.25
Cap, college style only. Price, each....25
Belt, cotton web. Price, each....20
Stockings, cotton, black only. Price, per pair....25
Uniform Complete. Price....3.00
Do not fail to give size and color when ordering.
For lettering see extras.

No. 6C7081 OUR SERVICE UNIFORM, made from a special grade of strong flannel known as Athletic flannel, and made especially for this purpose. For durability and strength this material cannot be excelled, and is superior to the material used in uniforms sold for twice the price. We furnish these suits with either button or laced front shirts, elastic or tape bottom pants, padded or not padded, any style cap, heavy ribbed black stockings, cotton web belts, and furnish them in the following colors: light gray, pearl gray, dark gray, navy blue and green.

No. 6C7081 Shirt, button front. Mention color wanted. Price, each....$1.50
Pants, elastic bottom. Price, each....1.50
Cap, college or university style, each....50
Belt, cotton web, price, each....20
Stockings, cotton, heavy ribbed, black only. Price, per pair....30
Uniform Complete, Price....3.75
Do not fail to give size and color when ordering.
For lettering see extras.

> Do not fail to send for our sample card, showing flannel used in these uniforms, giving detailed description, before ordering.

> **Uniforms are not sent C. O. D.**

No. 6C7082 OUR SEROCO MEDIUM WEIGHT ALL WOOL UNIFORM, made of all wool flannel, woven especially for us. This material is of a grade very superior to that used in uniforms ordinarily sold for several dollars more. It is well finished and very durable, making this grade of uniform far more serviceable and attractive than any similar priced uniforms sold elsewhere. We can furnish these suits with button front shirts, padded or unpadded pants, with elastic or tape bottom, as desired, any style cap, fine leather belts, black, navy or maroon color stockings, and can furnish these suits in the following colors: pearl gray, dark gray, navy blue, maroon, brown and green.

No. 6C7082 Shirt, button or lace front. Mention color wanted. Price, each....$2.00
Pants, elastic bottom. Price, each....1.80
Cap, Chicago or Boston style. Each....60
Belt, leather, one buckle. Price, each....30
Stockings, wool, medium weight, in black, navy blue or maroon color. Price, per pair....50
Complete Uniform. Price....5.00
For lettering see extras.

Do not fail to give size and color when ordering. Do not fail to send for sample card of flannel used in baseball uniforms, before ordering. We want you to know what we intend to send you.

No. 6C7083 OUR PROFESSIONAL LEAGUE UNIFORMS are the very best made, being made of all wool flannel woven especially for this purpose. For material, style, finish, stitching, workmanship and general appearance they cannot be equaled for less than $10.00 or $12.00 a suit. These are made by the most experienced workmen, and we have taken great care in every detail of construction, endeavoring to make these suits such as any professional player will be proud of. **We could not put better material in these suits if we charged you twice as much for them.** It is the very best and strongest all wool cloth made. These suits come in the following colors: white, pearl gray, Yale gray, navy blue, green and maroon.

No. 6C7083 Shirt, button or lace front. Mention color wanted. Price, each....$2.75
Pants, elastic bottom. Price, each....2.50
Cap, Chicago or Boston style. Each....65
Belt, leather, 1 large buckle. Each....45
Stockings, heavy weight worsted, in black, navy blue or maroon color. Price, per pair....85
Uniform Complete. Price....7.00
For lettering see extras.

NOTE—We strongly advise ordering uniforms for entire teams all in one order as they will then all be identical in style and color, and we can fill an order for nine uniforms quicker than we can nine orders for one uniform each.

Grain Leather Association Round Footballs.

No. 6C7085 The High School Association Football. Made of the best American tanned grain leather, hand sewed, canvas lined, rawhide lace, regulation size. Price, with bladder....$2.10
If by mail, postage extra, 15 cents.

No. 6C7086 Association Football, made of good quality pebbled cowhide, canvas lined, raw hide lace and bladder. A very strong, well made ball, that retails at $2.00. Our price....$1.35
If by mail, postage extra, 15 cents.
For Football Bladders, see No. 6C6852.

The Victor Rugby Football, Oval Pattern.

No. 6C7087 The Victor Intercollegiate Official Rugby Football. Made of best imported grain leather, with all possible stretch removed, stitched with wax thread and has patent double laced opening. The highest grade football on the market, guaranteed; has lacing needle and pump. Price, with bladder....$3.25
If by mail, postage extra, 12 cents.

No. 6C7088 Rugby Football, made of the best quality selected American grain pebbled leather, lined with canvas, stitched on lock stitch machine, with waxed thread, furnished with rawhide lace, lacing needle and pure rubber bladder. An extra strong regulation size ball. Price....$1.50
If by mail, postage extra, 18 cents.

No. 6C7089 Rugby Football, made of good quality pebbled cowhide, canvas lined, full size and well made. Rawhide lace and bladder. A very good strong ball for a little money, that looks like a $2.50 ball. Price....$1.15
If by mail, postage extra, 12 cents.

No. 6C7090 Our Leader Rugby Football, made of good quality pebbled leather, well lined and well made, a genuine bargain for the boys. Will give them satisfaction.
Price, with bladder....75c
If by mail, postage extra, 12 cents.
For Rugby Football Bladders, see No. 6C6851½.

Black Rubber Footballs.

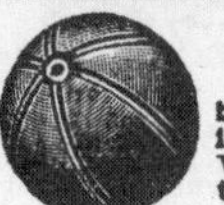

American Round Rubber Footballs. These footballs are inflated through the key. When inflated turn key to right to close the valve.

No. 6C7092 Order by catalogue number and size number.

Size	Diameter	Weight	Price
No. 1	6-inch	6 ounces	34c
No. 2	7-inch	8 ounces	44c
No. 3	8-inch	10 ounces	49c
No. 4	9-inch	13 ounces	54c
No. 5	10-inch	15 ounces	64c
No. 6	11-inch	16 ounces	69c

If by mail, allow 1 cent per ounce.

No. 6C7093 Extra keys for football....5c
If by mail, postage extra, 1 cent.

Football and Striking Bag Inflaters.

No. 6C7094 Pocket Football and Striking Bag Inflaters, nickeled tubes, for pumping up bladders.
Price....(Postage extra, 4 cents)....15c

Basket Balls.

No. 6C7095½ Basket Ball, made of high grade pebbled leather, canvas lined and well made, cheapest basket ball on the market. Will give good service and worth much more than we ask for it.
Price, with bladder....$1.45
If by mail, postage extra, 20 cents.

No. 6C7096 Our College Basket Ball, made of best quality American grain pebbled leather, best lining and stitched with waxed linen thread, furnished with rawhide laces and pure rubber bladder. A ball that will stand lots of hard service. Price....$2.75
If by mail, postage extra, 28 cents.

No. 6C7097 Pure rubber bladders for basket balls. Price....51c
If by mail, postage extra, 5 cents.

Basket Ball Goals.

No. 6C7098 Basket Ball Goals, regulation style, made of iron frame with cotton netting. Price, per pair....$2.75

Superior Football Pants.

The knees and hips of all our pants are heavily padded and quilted in the most approved manner, and all have elastic bottoms.

No. 6C7116 Made of white twilled drilling, laced front, quilted, give waist measure.
Price, per pair....58c

No. 6C7117 Made of white 8-ounce duck, laced front, full quilted, well made; give waist measure.
Price, per pair....95c

No. 6C7119 Made of tan colored army khaki cloth, which is popular this year by reason of its strength, durability and color; made laced front, full padded and quilted at hips and knees, cane reeds at thighs, the latest thing in football pants; well made and well finished; give waist measure. Price, per pair....$1.25
If by mail, postage extra, 28 to 36 cents.

Send for a sample card of football material.

For a complete line of football shoes, see our Shoe Department. For sweaters, see our Furnishing Goods Department.

ATHLETIC ELASTIC BANDAGES.

Elastic Elbow Bandages.

Best made. They are excellent as a support or for sprains. In ordering give circumference above and below elbow and state whether intended for light or strong pressure.

No. 6C7127 Cotton thread and elastic woven. Price, each....$1.15

No. 6C7128 Silk thread and elastic woven. Price, each...(Postage extra 2 cents)...$1.35

Elastic Knee Cap Bandages.

The best thing made for a sprained knee. In ordering give circumference below knee, at knee and just above knee, and state if light or strong pressure is desired.

No. 6C7131 Woven cotton thread and elastic. Price....$1.15

No. 6C7132 Woven silk thread and elastic. Price...(Postage extra, 4 cents)...$1.35

Morton's Supporters.

No. 6C7139 Improved Morton Supporter. Made of canton flannel, lace front. Give waist measure when ordering.
Price....19c

Our Elastic Combination Jockey Strap Suspensory.

No. 6C7142 This Suspensory is made entirely of elastic, except the front piece, which is made of fine balbriggan. It is self adjusting and conforms to the body in any position, is never too loose or too tigh. This is the most practical and by far the most comfortable supporter made. Can be washed in luke warm water. When ordering, give waist measurement. Price....55c
If by mail, postage extra, 6 cents.

Leather Wrist Supporter.

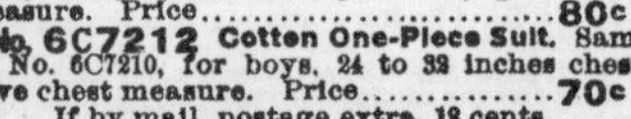

No. 6C7146 A perfect support and protection to the wrist. Invaluable to baseball, tennis and cricket players or in any game where the strain is on the wrist. In domestic grain leather, tan or black. Price, each....17c
If by mail, postage extra, 2 cents.

The Hackey Ankle Supporter.

No. 6C7150 Hackey Supporter relieves pain immediately, cures a sprain in a short time and prevents turning of the ankle. Made of fine, soft calfskin and is worn over stocking, lacing very tight in center, loose at top and bottom. The shoe usually worn can be used. These supporters are not made in children's sizes. Mention size shoe you wear when ordering.
Price, per pair....65c
If by mail, postage extra, 3 cents.

FENCING FOILS.

Weight, 24 to 32 ounces per pair.

No. 6C7175 No. 1 Fencing Foils, with steel blades, iron mounted figure 8 guard, corded handle. Price, per pair....$1.20

No. 6C7176 No. 2 Fencing Foils, with Solingen steel blades, iron mounted figure 8 guard, leather handles. Per pair....$1.75

No. 6C7177 No. 3 Fencing Foils, best Solingen steel blades, 4-inch bell guard or hilt, leather wound handles. Per pair....$2.85
If by mail, postage extra, 32 cents.

Fencing Mask.

No. 6C7178 Our Fencing Mask, Face and Ear Guards, made of finest quality wire, extra small mesh, the best mask made.
Per pair....$2.20
If by mail, postage extra, 40 cents.

Y. M. C. A. Gymnasium Trousers.

No. 6C7180 Our Regulation Y. M. C. A. Gymnasium Trousers are made of good quality gray color athletic flannel, with belt loops and elastic foot straps. The material and style of these pants is the same as is used in nearly all gymnasiums. They are very strong and serviceable. Give measure of waist and inseam when ordering.
Price, per pair....$1.25
If by mail, postage extra, 20 cents.

ATHLETIC THEATRICAL AND SWIMMING SUITS.

Full Sleeve Shirts.

No. 6C7189 Full Sleeve Fine Worsted Shirt, medium quality, black or navy blue color. Give chest measure.
Price....$1.75
If by mail, postage extra, 12c.

No. 6C7190 Full Sleeve Fine Cotton Shirt, black or flesh color. Give chest measure. Price....50c
If by mail, postage extra, 10 cents.

Quarter Sleeve Shirts.

No. 6C7196 Quarter Sleeve Shirt. Medium quality worsted, solid colors, seamless, made in black or navy blue. Give chest measure when ordering.
Price....$1.40
If by mail, postage extra, 12 cents.

No. 6C7197 Cotton Shirt, quarter sleeve, good quality. Made in solid colors of black or navy blue. Give chest measure when ordering. Price....35c
If by mail, postage extra, 10 cents.

Full Length Theatrical Tights.

No. 6C7200 Full Length Tights, made of medium grade worsted, in solid colors of black or navy blue. Give waist and inseam measure when ordering.
Price, per pair....$2.00
If by mail, postage extra, 10 cents.

No. 6C7201 Full Length Cotton Tights, in solid colors of black, navy or flesh color. Give waist and inseam measure when ordering.
Price, per pair....80c
If by mail, postage extra, 8 cents.

Athletic Knee Tights.

No. 6C7203 Made of medium grade worsted in solid colors of black or navy blue. Give waist measure.
Price, per pair....$1.25

No. 6C7204 Cotton Tights. Good quality cotton tights, made in solid colors of black or navy blue. Give waist measure.
Price, per pair....30c
If by mail, postage extra, 6 to 10c.

Velvet Puff Theatrical Trunks.

No. 6C7206 Beautiful Velvet Puff Trunks, made of the finest velvet, full puff, either black, navy, green or maroon color, for theatrical or athletic exhibitions.
Price, per pair....80c
Postage extra, per pair, 7c.

BATHING SUITS.

Our One-Piece Best Cotton Bathing Suit is made like a union suit (buttons over shoulder). It is like an ordinary shirt and knee pants, but all in one piece, made in solid colors and fancy stripes, and ranging in size from 32 to 44 inches chest measure. When ordering give chest measure.

No. 6C7208 Cotton One-Piece Suit, in solid color, black or navy blue; give chest measure. Price....65c

No. 6C7210 Cotton One-Piece Suit, in fancy stripes, assorted patterns; give chest measure. Price....80c

No. 6C7212 Cotton One-Piece Suit. Same as No. 6C7210, for boys, 24 to 32 inches chest. Give chest measure. Price....70c
If by mail, postage extra, 12 cents.

Two-Piece Bathing Suits.

GIVE CHEST AND WAIST MEASURE.

No. 6C7216 Two-Piece Cotton Bathing Suit, consisting of quarter sleeve shirt and knee pants, made in black or navy blue colors. Price, per suit....**55c**

No. 6C7217 Same, in fancy stripes. Price, per suit....**70c**

No. 6C7218½ High grade worsted two-piece Bathing Suit, consisting of sleeveless shirt and trunks. Navy blue or black with fancy stripes around the bottom of the garments. Most up to date and best bargain on the market. If you wear a worsted suit, you will not experience that chill so disagreeable to bathers. Price, per suit....**$2.25**
If by mail, postage extra, 15 cents.

Our Swimming Trunks.

Our Cotton Swimming Trunks, made up in assorted designs of stripes, with draw string; assorted sizes for men or boys. When ordering, give waist measure.

No. 6C7219 Men's Swimming Trunks. Give waist measure. Price, per pair........**20c**

No. 6C7220 Boys' and Girls' Swimming Trunks. Give waist measure or age. Price, per pair..............................**18c**
If by mail, postage extra, 5 cents.

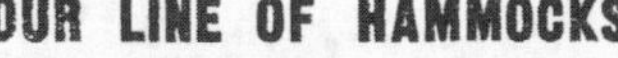

OUR LINE OF HAMMOCKS.

The most select line of hammocks ever placed on the market. We have selected this line of hammocks with a view to giving our customers the best possible value for their money. SEE OUR PRICES.

Our Hand Knitted Seine Twine Hammock, 95c.

This hammock is knitted by hand, of double seine twine, forming a 2-inch square mesh, and each hammock is made in white and one other neat attractive color. The edge on each side is chain braided, and interwoven into the meshes, making a strong, substantial and durable hammock, and with ordinary care will last a number of years. The entire hammock is about 13 feet long and the bed is about 7 feet long, and we furnish it without spreaders.

No. 6C7230 Our hand made double seine twine hammock. Price.......................**95c**
If by mail, postage extra, 32 cents.

Our Hann's Patent Canvas Hammock.

The Hann Patented Hammock is the latest and most comfortable hammock yet produced. It is so constructed that by simply moving the arm rest from one place to another along the ropes, the hammock may be changed from one position to another instantly. By removing the arm rests the hammock may be used as a regular hammock, and by inserting the arm rests, as shown in the above illustration, the hammock has the effect of a reclining chair, and is an excellent thing for invalids as well as being one of the most comfortable hammocks on the market. All are made of striped canvas. Bed is 30 inches wide and 78 inches long, and weighs about 7½ pounds.

No. 6C7233 Made of striped canvas with spreader and pillow. Price.............**$1.10**

No. 6C7234 Made of striped canvas with spreader, pillow and valance. Price...**$1.40**

When hanging a hammock always hang it so that head will be higher than the foot.

Open Weave Cotton Hammock, 55 Cents.

No. 6C7235 Open Weave Cotton Hammocks. Fine cotton weave, quarter color, with fancy colored stripes. Size of bed, 6 feet long, 3 feet wide. Strong and durable; without pillow or spreader. A good hammock for children. Weight, 2 pounds. Price...........................**55c**

Cotton Weave Hammock with Pillow and Spreader, 85 Cents.

No. 6C7237 Cotton Hammock, with close woven body, of the best cotton weave, full fancy colors, with spreader and pillow. Size of bed, 6½ feet long, 3 feet wide. A hammock that sells regularly at $1.25 to $1.50. Weight, 3½ pounds. Price, with fancy pillow and spreader...**85c**

Canvas Weave Hammock with Pillow and Spreader, $1.00.

No. 6C7239 Hammock made of closest fancy canvas weave, in full fancy bright colors. Made with three-ply warps, with fancy colored pillow and spreader. A very strong hammock. Retail from $1.75 to $2.00. Size of bed, 6½ feet long, 3 feet wide. Wt., 3½ lbs. Price....**$1.00**

Special Value with Fringe Valance for $1.25.

No. 6C7241 Cotton Hammock, close excelsior weave, with short fancy fringe valance, full fancy bright colors, with pillow and spreader. Size of bed, 6½ feet long, 3 feet wide. A first class hammock in every respect. Sells regularly at $1.50 to $1.75. Weight, 4 pounds. Price...**$1.25**

Our Leader, $2.25 Value for $1.50.

No. 6C7242 Fine Canvas Weave Hammock, has deep woven valance with fringe, full fancy bright colors, with one spreader and one pillow. Size of bed, 6½ feet long, 3 feet wide. A beauty for the money. Weight, about 5 pounds. Price.................................**$1.50**

Our Damask Weave Hammock, $1.85.

No. 6C7243 Our Big Leader Hammock, made in figured fancy weave, damask pattern, full fancy fluted valance, with fringe and scroll pattern. One strong spreader at head, with fancy pillow, also one short wood spreader at the foot. Size of bed, 40x80 inches. One of the most beautiful hammocks ever placed on the market. Strong and durable, and one which generally sells at retail for $3.00. Weight, 6½ pounds. Price............................**$1.85**

Our Old Gold Pattern Tufted Pillow Hammock, $2.45.

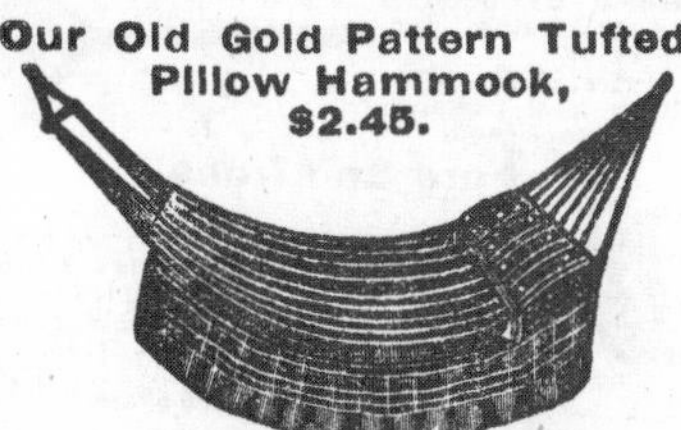

No. 6C7244 Our Large Size, Tufted Pillow Hammock. This hammock is made in full fancy colors, strong spreader and detachable, tufted pillow at one end with extra wood bar at the foot. Full deep valance at the sides. Size of bed, 40x82 inches. Made of heavy three-ply warp, color of old gold effect, and we consider this one of the best bargains which we offer in hammocks. Weight, 10 lbs. Price, for this full size hammock......**$2.45**

Our Jacquard Weave Hammock, $2.75. Tufted Pillow.

No. 6C7245 Hammock, extra heavy fancy close canvas weave, fine fancy bright colors, of jacquard designs, extra deep fluted valance with fancy tufted pillow, heavy strong spreader. One short wood bar at the foot. Size of bed, 40x84 inches. This is a large size hammock, strong, durable and very showy. Weight, 9 pounds. Price.....................**$2.75**

Hammock Hooks.

No. 6C7266 Screw Hammock Hooks, tinned, 7-16 inch diameter, screw in. Price, each........**5c**
Postage extra, 3c.

No. 6C7266

No. 6C7267 Plate Hammock Hooks, tinned, 7-16 inch in diameter to fasten with screws. Price, each.........**6c**

No. 6C7267 If by mail, postage extra, 3 cents.

Lawn Swings, $3.50 and $4.25.

For Children and Adults.

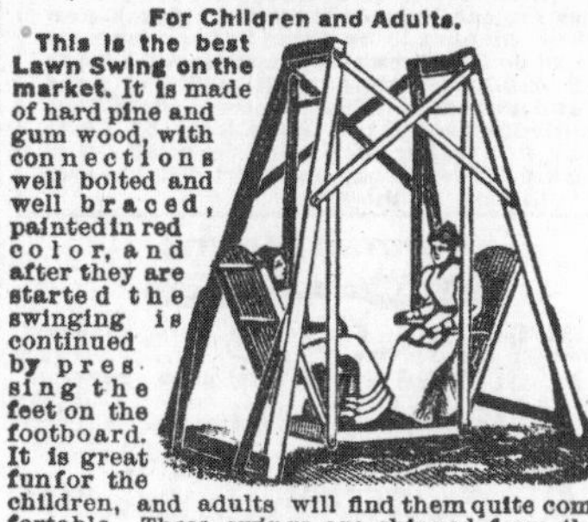

This is the best Lawn Swing on the market. It is made of hard pine and gum wood, with connections well bolted and well braced, painted in red color, and after they are started the swinging is continued by pressing the feet on the footboard. It is great fun for the children, and adults will find them quite comfortable. These swings are shipped from the factory in Illinois and cannot be sent with other goods.

No. 6C7271 Adults' size, about 8½ feet high. The seat is 20 inches wide, which is wider than the ordinary chair, and will hold two grown persons or four children. Weight, about 100 pounds. Shipped from our factory and cannot be sent with other goods. Price.....**$3.50**

No. 6C7272 Large size, 8½ feet high, seat 33 inches wide, large enough to seat four adults or six children. Weight, about 130 pounds. Shipped from our factory and cannot be sent with other goods. Price........**$4.25**

Our Acme Folding Lawn Settee, 86 Cents.

No. 6C7274 For 86 cents we offer you our Acme Lawn Settee, made of selected wood, painted in a bright attractive color and constructed on substantial principles. This lawn settee is made so it may be folded up and set away during the winter or it may be left on a porch, as desired. The Acme lawn settee is a very useful and desirable article and will recommend itself to our customers; in fact, it requires no care or attention and saves many times its value in the wear and tear of regular household furniture. Our Acme lawn settee, 3½ feet long, painted. Weight, 20 pounds. Price..**86c**

The Chicago Folding Porch Chair, 84 Cents.

No. 6C7278 The Chicago Folding Porch Chair. Made of wood frame with denim body. All joints riveted and may be folded when not in use. Weighs about 10½ pounds and the back may be adjusted to various angles for comfort. All have arm rests and high back, are easily carried about and save the household furniture. Price.................................**84c**

Hammock Ropes.

No. 6C7282 Hammock Ropes, 6½ feet long, adjustable anchor fastening that remains where you place it; no knots to tie after attached to hammock, no slipping in hammock. Hammock can be raised and lowered in an instant.
Price, per pair, **16c**; each.....................**8c**
If by mail, postage extra, each, 6 cents.

REPAIR PARTS FOR FLOBERT RIFLES.

NOTICE—These parts are not fitted. They are in a filed state and must be fitted by a gunsmith or mechanic. If possible send us the broken part and we will try to match it as near as we can.

Flobert Breech Blocks.

These parts are not fitted.

No. 6C7300 Remington Action Breech Blocks. Filed, cut nose, not fitted. Price......**25c**
If by mail, postage extra, 2 cents.

No. 6C7301 Remington Action Breech Blocks. Filed, pointed nose, not fitted. Price..............................**25c**
If by mail, postage extra, 2 cents.

Warnant Breech Blocks.

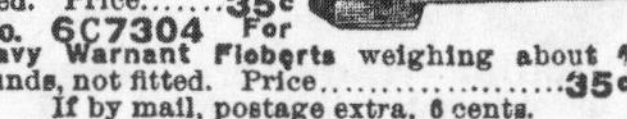

No. 6C7303 For Light Warnant Action Floberts weighing about 4½ pounds, not fitted. Price.......**35c**

No. 6C7304 For Heavy Warnant Floberts weighing about 4 pounds, not fitted. Price.........................**35c**
If by mail, postage extra, 6 cents.

WHEN ORDERING PARTS for guns, rifles or revolvers, always give the name, caliber or gauge of the gun, rifle or revolver. This will save us from writing for this information.

Improved Warnant Breech Blocks.

No. 6C7305 For Light Improved Warnant Action, like our No. 6C658, not finished. Price..........**40c**

No. 6C7306 For Heavy Improved Warnant Action, like our No. 6C659 or 6C663, not finished. Price..............................**45c**
If by mail, postage extra, 5 cents.

Flobert Extractors.

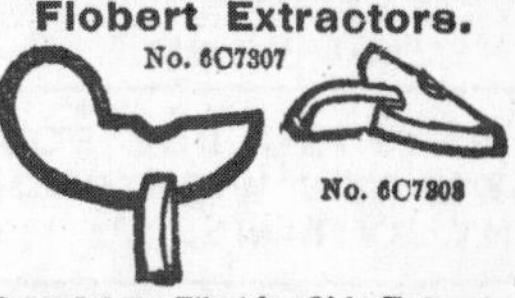

No. 6C7307 Filed for Side Extractor Floberts, not finished. Price..............**15c**

No. 6C7308 Filed for Remington Action Floberts, not finished. Price..............**12c**

No. 6C7309 Filed for Warnant Action Floberts (to go with No. 6C7303), not finished. Price..............................**20c**

No. 6C7310 Filed for Heavy Warnant Action Floberts (to go with No. 6C7304), not finished. Price...(Postage extra, 2 cents)...**25c**

Flobert Hammers, Filed.

No. 6C7311 For Side Extractor Floberts, for our No. 6C655 rifle, not fitted. Price.......**30c**

No. 6C7312 For Light Warnant Action Floberts, old style, not fitted, to go with No. 6C7303. Price..............................**31c**
Remember, these parts must be fitted by a gunsmith or mechanic.
If by mail, postage extra, 7 cents.

No. 6C7313 For Light Remington Action Floberts, for our No. 6C657 rifle, not fitted. Price..............................**30c**

No. 6C7314 For Improved Warnant Action Floberts, for our No. 6C658 rifle, not fitted. Price, **32c**

No. 6C7315 For Heavy Improved Warnant Floberts, for our No. 6C659 or No. 6C663 rifle, not fitted. Price......................**34c**
If by mail, postage extra, 5 cents.

Flobert Hammer Swivels.

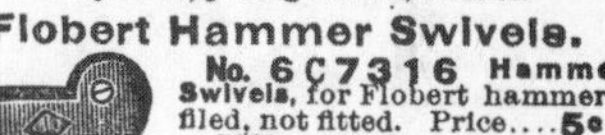

No. 6C7316 Hammer Swivels, for Flobert hammers, filed, not fitted. Price.....**5c**
If by mail, postage extra, 1 cent.

Flobert Main Springs.

No. 6C7317 Flobert Main Springs, suitable for all styles of Floberts, not fitted. Price..............................**18c**
If by mail, postage extra, 2 cents.

Flobert Trigger Springs.

No. 6C7318 Flobert Trigger Springs, suitable for all Floberts, not fitted. Price..............**10c**
If by mail, postage extra, 2 cents.

Flobert Sights.

No. 6C7319 Flobert Front Sights, filed, not fitted. Price...**10c**

No. 6C7320 Flobert Rear Sights, filed, not fitted. Price...**11c**
If by mail, postage extra, 1 cent.

Flobert Triggers.

No. 6C7321 Flobert Triggers, filed, not fitted. Price.........**14c**
Postage extra, 2 cents.

Warnant Buttons.

No. 6C7322 Warnant Buttons, filed and threaded, not fitted. Price..............................**10c**
If by mail, postage extra, 2 cents.

Flobert Screws.

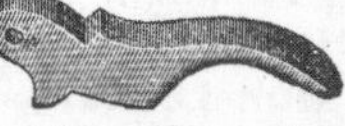

No. 6C7323 Fore End Screws. Price.........**8c**

No. 6C7324 Trigger Spring Screws. Price..............................**9c**

No. 6C7325 Warnant Side Breech Block Screws. Price..............................**10c**
If by mail, postage extra, 1 cent.

GUN TUBES FOR MUZZLE LOADERS.

Number of Threads to the Inch.

The English have 28 threads.
The Belgian have 30 threads.
The Springfield have 24 threads.
The Enfield have 20 threads.
The nipples have the following threads to the inch and of the specified diameter.

	Threads	Diameter
Enfield..............	20 per inch	5-16 inch
Springfield........	24 per inch	5-16 inch
Belgian............	30 per inch	¼ inch
English............	28 per inch	15-64 to 20-64

When ordering English nipples always give diameter or send the old nipple.

Catalogue No.	Style	Polished	Price, Each	Postage Extra
6C7330	English	Shank	5c	1c
6C7331	English	Outside	8c	1c
6C7332	English	Bottom	10c	1c
6C7333	English	Inside	15c	1c
6C7334	Belgian	Medium	10c	1c
		For		
6C7336	Springfield	Musket Caps	10c	1c
6C7337	Springfield	Gun Caps	12c	1c
6C7338	Enfield	Musket Caps	10c	1c
6C7339	Enfield	Gun Caps	12c	1c

Nipple Wrench.

No. 6C7326 Nipple Wrench, polished. Price..............25c
If by mail, postage extra, 5 cents.

Brass Ramrod Heads.

No. 6C7328 Ramrod Heads, brass solid end, sizes assorted, ½, ⅝ and ¾ inch. Price.......................15c
If by mail, postage extra, 1 cent.

ALWAYS INCLUDE POSTAGE IF YOU WISH GOODS SENT BY MAIL. : : : : :

THESE GUN LOCKS are finished, but will have to be fitted to your gun. No two guns are exactly alike and therefore we cannot furnish gun locks to fit exactly. Measure the length of your gun lock and tell us how long it is, or send us a drawing of the lock plate, and we will send you the nearest we have to it. We usually send them a trifle longer because it is easy to cut out the stocks a little more to make them fit. Gun locks usually measure 4½ to 5 inches from end to end.

Back Action Gun Locks for Muzzle Loaders.

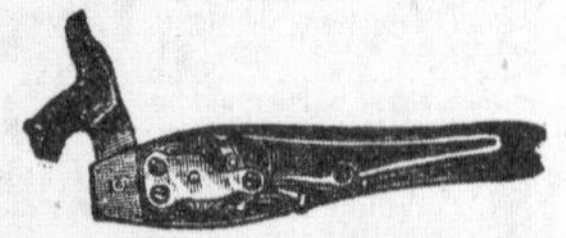

No. 6C7340 American Back Action, polished, for muzzle loaders, right hand, 4½ to 5 inches long; give length wanted. Price..50c
No. 6C7341 American Back Action, polished, for muzzle loaders, left hand, 4½ to 5 inches long; give length wanted. Price..52c
If by mail, postage extra, 6 cents.

Forward Action Gun Locks.

No. 6C7342 American Forward Action, polished, for muzzle loaders, right hand, 4½ to 5 inches long; give length wanted. Price.................................51c
If by mail, postage extra, 6 cents.

No. 6C7343 Forward Action, left hand, 4½ to 5 inches. Price..........................53c

No. 6C7345 C. P. American Forward Action, cut for plug, right hand, for muzzle loading rifles, 4½ to 5 inches long; give length wanted. Price...........................79c
If by mail, postage extra, 6 cents.

Bar Action Gun Locks.

No. 6C7346 American Full Bar, polished, for muzzle loaders, right hand, 4½ to 5 inches long; give length wanted. Don't fail to state length of lock wanted. Price....75c

No. 6C7347 American Full Bar, polished, for muzzle loaders, left hand, 4½ to 5 inches long; give length wanted. Price.................................76c
If by mail, postage extra, 6 cents.

Muzzle Loading Hammers.

No. 6C7353 Muzzle Loading Hammers, 1⅛ to 1⅜ inches from middle of nose to center of hole. Right hand. State size wanted.
Price, each, not fitted.....25c
If by mail, postage extra, 2 cents
No. 6C7354 Muzzle Loading Hammers, 1⅛ to 1⅜ inches from middle of nose to center of hole. Left hand. State size wanted.
Price, each, not fitted..........................25c
If by mail, postage extra, 2 cents.

Walnut Gun Stocks.

No. 6C7361 Rough Turned Gun Stocks, turned to shape, leaving the square end 1⅜ inches wide and 2 inches from top to bottom, length 15¾ inches, butt measure 5¼x1⅝ inches. Made of good American walnut, not fitted, just shaped, for double barrel breech loading guns. Weight, 20 ounces. Price.......................50c
If by mail, postage extra, 27 cents.

NEW STOCKS AND FORE ENDS FITTED TO GUNS.
When stocks of double guns are broken so you can't repair them with glue a new one will have to be fitted by hand and we can do this work all the way from $5.00 to $12.00, according to the quality of wood and amount of labor required. Fore ends fitted to back action guns from $2.75 to $4.00; to bar lock guns from $3.00 to $4.00. You to pay transportation charges both ways on the gun.

German Worms.

No. 6C7365 For double guns, reversed, medium size. Price..........................14c
No. 6C7366 For double guns, reversed, large size. Price..............................15c
If by mail, postage extra, 2 cents.

Tumbler Pins.

No. 6C7369 Tumbler Pins, threaded, for muzzle loading locks.
Price...5c
If by mail, postage extra, 1 cent.

Side Pins.

No. 6C7371 Side Pins, threaded for muzzle loaders. Price...............................5c
If by mail, postage extra, 1 cent.

Cross Pins.

No. 6C7372 Cross Pins for muzzle loading guns. Price..10c
No. 6C7373 Cross Pins, for breech loading guns. Price.......................................15c
If by mail, postage extra, 1 cent.

Inside Lock Screws.

No. 6C7374 Inside Lock Screws, threaded. Price..............8c
If by mail, postage extra, 1 cent.

Tumbler Swivels.

No. 6C7375 Tumbler Swivels, filed, single horn, not fitted. Price...................5c
If by mail, postage extra, 1 cent.

Top Lever Springs.

Order by numbers.
Catalogue No. 6C7376

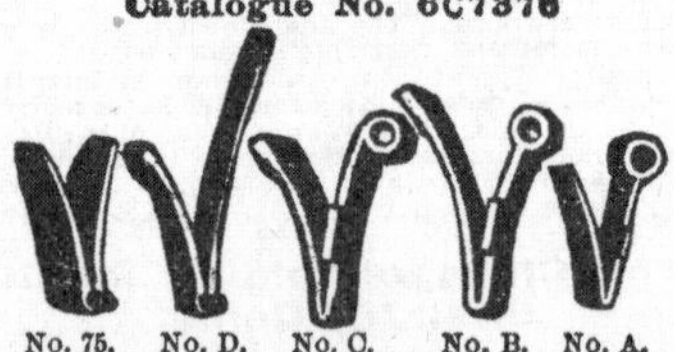

Order by Number.	No. 6C7376	Price
Style No. A	For English guns	22c
Style No. B	For Bonehill guns	23c
Style No. C	For English guns	24c
Style No. D	For Tolley guns	28c
Style No. 75	For Belgian guns	15c

If by mail, postage extra, 2 cents.

Back Action, Double Sear Springs, Filed.

No. 6C7377 Right hand, not fitted. Price...10c
No. 6C7378 Left hand, not fitted. Price...10c
If by mail, postage extra, 1 cent.

Bar Sear Springs, Filed, Not Fitted.

No. 6C7381 Right hand, not fitted. Price..........11c
No. 6C7382 Left hand, not fitted. Price..........11c
If by mail, postage extra, 1 cent.

Brass Front Sights for Double Guns.

No. 6C7383 For Breech Loading Guns. Price (postage extra, 1 cent)...5c

NOTICE—This material is not finished nor ready to put into guns. It has to be fitted by a gunsmith or mechanic. If possible, send us the broken part, so we can better match it.

Breech Loading Gun Hammers.

Flat Hammer for Lefeaucheaux Action Guns. Right or left hand; filed and drilled, 1 to 1¼ inches from middle of nose to center of hole. In ordering, state size wanted.
No. 6C7384 Right hand, not fitted. Price..............20c
No. 6C7385 Left hand, not fitted. Price....................................21c
If by mail, postage extra, 2 cents.

Round Body Hammers.

Round Body Hammer, filed and drilled, right or left hand, 1 to 1¼ inches from middle of nose to center of hole. In ordering, state size wanted.
No. 6C7386 Right hand, not fitted. Price each............25c
No. 6C7387 Left hand, not fitted. Price, each..............26c
If by mail, postage extra, 2 cents.

Circular Hammers.

Circular Hammer, filed and drilled, right or left hand, 1 to 1⅛-inch from middle of nose to center of hole. In ordering, state size wanted.
No. 6C7390 Right hand, not fitted. Price, each....30c
No. 6C7391 Left hand, not fitted. Price, each.......32c
If by mail, postage extra, 2 cents.

Concave Circular Hammers.

Filed and drilled, right or left hand, 1 to 1⅛-inch from middle of nose to center of hole. In ordering, state size wanted.
No. 6C7392 Right hand, not fitted. Price, each..........40c
No. 6C7393 Left hand, not fitted. Price, each..42c
If by mail, postage extra, 2 cents.

Spring Plungers.

No. 6C7395 For Old Style Spring Plunger Guns, not fitted. Price, each..............................10c
No. 6C7396 For Zulu Guns, not fitted.
Price, each..15c
If by mail, postage extra, 1 cent.

Nitro Plungers.

No. 6C7397 For Latest Style Belgian Guns, not fitted.
Price, each..10c
If by mail, postage extra, 1 cent.

Solid Plungers.

No. 6C7398 8-32-inch diameter at head, not fitted.
Price, each..............12c
No. 6C7399 9-32-inch diameter at head, not fitted. State size wanted. Price, each 13c
No. 6C7400 10-32-inch diameter, not fitted. Price, each..................................14c
No. 6C7401 11-32-inch diameter, not fitted Price, each..................................15c
If by mail, postage extra, 1 cent.

Plunger Springs.

No. 6C7402 Taper, for Old Style Double Guns.
Price, each..........10c
No. 6C7403 For Zulu Guns. Price, each.......11c
If by mail, postage extra, 1 cent.

Plunger Seats.

No. 6C7404 For English Guns, 6-cornered shoulder, not fitted. Price, ea..20c
No. 6C7405 For Belgian Guns, round shoulder, not fitted.
Price, each..........................22c
If by mail, postage extra, 1 cent.

No. 6C7405

Milled Extractors.

No. 6C7406 Milled Extractors, in a filed state, not fitted.
Price, each...35c
If by mail, postage extra, 4 cents.

Fore End Irons.

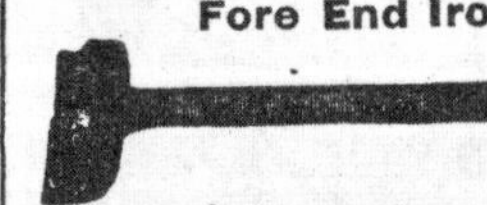

No. 6C7407 Milled Fore End Irons for double guns, not fitted.
Price, each..............................35c
If by mail, postage extra, 5 cents.

Triggers.

No. 6C7408 Right Hand, Filed Trigger, not fitted.
Price, each..........................8c
No. 6C7409 Left Hand, Filed Trigger, not fitted.
Price, each..........................9c
If by mail, postage extra, 1 cent.

Top Levers.

No. 6C7410 Top Levers for Old Style Belgian Guns, filed, not fitted.
Price, each..........................50c
No. 6C7412 Top Levers for New Style Belgian Guns, filed not fitted.
Price, each..........................60c
If by mail, postage extra, 2 cents.

Choke Boring Tools in 10 and 12-Gauge.

No. 6C7413 The Batchelor Choke Boring Tool, made of a brass socket, with two cutting blades as shown in illustration, and a bevel thumbscrew to expand the cutters gradually, as the operation requires. They have a rod 34 inches long, with a shank, so the tool can be used in a brace; made in 10 or 12-gauge. Weight, 3¼ pounds. Price...............$4.25
If by mail, postage extra, 45 cents.

Breech Loading Gun Locks.

We can only furnish the following breech loading gun locks in the sizes which we mention. As gun locks vary so much in size we have put in stock the sizes which are most generally used. These locks are all finished complete and are probably large enough to fit almost any gun where new locks are necessary.
When ordering locks give us the length of your old lock, or if you can do so make a drawing of it on a piece of paper and attach it to your order, and we will send you as near as we can, a lock to match it; but you must not expect a lock that will fit exactly in your gun. It may fit exactly or it may require some little work to make it fit your gun. When ordering do not forget to give us the size or a drawing of your gun lock.

No. 6C7414 Breech Loading, Back Action Gun Lock, complete with hammer. Right hand, 4½ inches long, 1 inch wide at hammer. For breech loaders. Price..........$1.25
No. 6C7415 Back Action Gun Locks, complete with hammer. Left hand, 4½ inches long, 1 inch wide at hammer. For breech loaders. Price..........................$1.30
If by mail, postage extra, 7 cents.

No. 6C7416 Breech Loading, Bar Lock, complete, with hammer. Right hand, 4½ inches long, 1 inch wide at hammer. For breech loaders. Price....$1.50
No. 6C7417 Bar Lock, complete, with hammer. Left hand, 4½ inches long, 1 inch wide at hammer. For breech loaders. Price..............................$1.55
If by mail, postage extra, 7 cents.

Main Springs for Breech Loaders.

If possible send a drawing of the spring, of the old one, so we can match it best. Mark the place where stud goes into the lock plate.
No. 6C7420 Back Action Swivel (main and sear combination) Main Springs, right hand, breech loading, not fitted. Price, each, 25c
No. 6C7421 Back Action Swivel (main and sear combination) Main Springs, left hand, breech loading, not fitted. Price, each 26c
No. 6C7422 Back Action Swivel Rebounding Main Spring, right hand, not fitted. Price, each..................................30c
No. 6C7423 Back Action Swivel Rebounding Main Spring, left hand, not fitted. Price, each..................................32c
No. 6C7424 Bar Action Swivel Rebounding Main Spring, right hand, not fitted.
Price, each.......45c
No. 6C7425 Bar Action Swivel Rebounding Main Spring, left hand, not fitted. Price..................................46c
If by mail, postage extra, 2 cents.

Breech Loading Swivel Tumblers.

No. 6C7430 Back action, rebounding, filed, right hand, not fitted. Price, each. 25c
No. 6C7431 Back action, rebounding, filed, left hand, not fitted. Price, each...........................26c
No. 6C7432 Bar action, rebounding, filed, right hand, not fitted. Price, each. 30c
No. 6C7433 Bar action, rebounding, filed, left hand, not fitted. Price, each. 31c
If by mail, postage extra, 2 cents.

Sears for Gun Locks.

No. 6C7434 Back Action Sears, filed, right hand, not fitted. Price, each.......14c
No. 6C7435 Back Action Sears, filed, left hand, not fitted. Price, each..................................15c
No. 6C7436 Bar Action Sears, filed, right hand, not fitted. Price, each.........16c
No. 6C7437 Bar Action Sears, filed, left hand, not fitted. Price, each.........17c
If by mail, postage extra, 1 cent.

Rubber Butt Plates.

No. 6C7439 Rubber Butt Plates for breech or muzzle loading guns; not fitted. Price, each..........30c
If by mail, postage extra, 3 cents.

Breech Loading Trigger Guards.

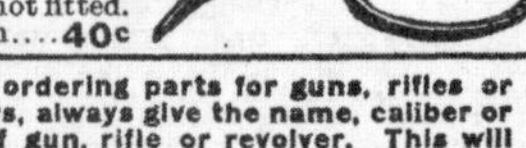

No. 6C7440 Breech Loading Guards, filed and threaded, not fitted. Price, each....40c

When ordering parts for guns, rifles or revolvers, always give the name, caliber or gauge of gun, rifle or revolver. This will save us from writing you for this information.

Breech Loading Trigger Plates

No. 6C7441 Breech Loading Trigger Plates, filed and tapped; not fitted. Price................45c
If by mail, postage extra, 5 cents.

Revolver Trigger Springs.

No. 6C7442 No. 14. Trigger Springs for double action revolvers, 22, 32 or 38-caliber. State for which caliber you wish it and give name of the revolver. Price..................................10c
No. 6C7443 No. 26. Trigger Springs for automatic revolvers made by Harrington & Richardson, 22, 32 or 38-caliber. State caliber wanted and give name of revolver. Price, each..................................10c
If by mail, postage extra, 1 cent.

Revolver Main Springs.

No. 6C7447 Revolver Main Springs for Harrington & Richardson double action and automatic revolvers, 22, 32, 38 and 44-caliber. When ordering state the name of revolver and caliber, or send the broken spring so we can match it. Price, each....20c
If by mail, postage extra, 2 cents.

No. 6C7448 Main Springs for Smith & Wesson revolvers, 32, 38 or 44-caliber. State caliber wanted. Price, each....30c
If by mail, postage extra, 2 cents.

No. 6C7449 Main Springs for Forehand Arms Co. revolvers. Give caliber and name of make, say if wanted for automatic or double action, when ordering. Price, each....20c
If by mail, postage extra, 2 cents.

Air Rifle Main Springs.

No. 6C7451 Main Springs for King, Daisy, Rapid, Cyclold and Rival air rifles. Must be fitted by customer. Price, each....10c
If by mail, postage extra, 2 cents.

Winchester and Marlin Main Springs.

No. 6C7452 Main Springs for Winchester Rifles. Mention caliber and model wanted. Price, each....30c
No. 6C7453 Main Springs for Marlin Rifles. Mention caliber and model wanted. Price, each....30c
If by mail, postage extra, 2 cents.

Main Springs or Gun Springs.

Any main or gun springs not described or listed in this catalogue, will have to be made by hand, and especially to order, and if you will send us the broken spring we will try to have a new one made for you, which will cost on any ordinary spring 40 to 50 cents, and for a main spring which is very difficult to make, the price will be higher, according to how long it takes our spring maker to make the spring. Do not forget to send the broken sample, and if possible tell us the name and caliber or gauge of the gun, revolver or rifle, for which you want the spring.
Price of ordinary springs....40c to 50c
Complicated springs......75c to $1.25

Rubber Revolver Handles.

No. 6C7454 Rubber Stocks for All Double Action and Automatic Revolvers, except Colt, 22, 32, 38 and 44-caliber. When ordering, state name of the revolver and whether right hand or left hand is wanted, also state the caliber. Price, each (not a pair)....25c
No. 6C7454½ Rubber Stocks for Colt's Revolvers, each....35c
If by mail, postage extra, 2 cents

Marlin Stocks and Fore Ends

No. 6C7455 Stocks for "A" grade Marlin Shotguns. Price....$2.50
No. 6C7456 Fore Ends for "A" grade Marlin Shotguns. Price....85c
If by mail, postage extra, 10 to 20 cents.

Stevens' Rifle Parts.

No. 6C7462 Breech Block Screws for Crackshot Rifles. Price....10c
No. 6C7463 Firing Pins for Crackshot. Price....15c
No. 6C7464 Main Springs for Crackshot. Price, each....15c
No. 6C7465 Main Springs for Favorite. Price, each....15c
No. 6C7466 Main Springs for Ideal. Price, each....20c
No. 6C7467 Hammers for Crackshot. Price....45c
No. 6C7468 Breech Block for Crackshot. Price....45c
No. 6C7469 Side Levers for Crackshot. Price....25c
If by mail, postage extra, 2 cents.

Colt's Revolver Repairs.

No. 6C7470 Colt's Revolver Main Springs for New Service Revolver. Price....70c
No. 6C7471 Colt's Revolver Main Springs for other models. Mention name and caliber of revolver when ordering. Price....50c
No. 6C7472 Colt's Double Action Trigger Springs. Price....25c
No. 6C7473 Single Action Sear and Bolt Spring. Price....15c
No. 6C7474 Colt's Bolts for Single Action Revolver. Price....30c
If by mail, postage extra, 2 cents.

Quackenbush Safety Rifle Parts.

No. 6C7475 Main Springs for Air Rifle No. 1. Price....30c
No. 6C7476 Main Springs for Safety Rifles. Price....10c
No. 6C7477 Firing Pins for Safety Rifles. Price....15c
If by mail, postage extra, 2 cents.

Pieper Rifle Parts.

No. 6C7480 Main Springs for Pieper Rifles. Price....15c
No. 6C7483 Firing Pins for Pieper Rifles. Price...(Postage extra, 2 cents)....10c

Remington Gun Springs.

No. 6C7485 Top Lever Springs for Semi-Hammerless Single Guns. Price....25c
No. 6C7486 Main Springs for Semi-Hammerless Single Guns. Price....40c
No. 6C7489 Top Lever Springs for Double Hammer Guns. Price....25c
No. 6C7490 Top Lever Springs for Double Hammerless Guns. Price....50c
No. 6C7495 Main Springs for Remington Rifles Nos. 2, 3, 4 and 6. Mention style wanted. Price..(Postage extra, 2 cents)....40c

Ithaca Gun Springs.

No. 6C7501 Main Springs for Hammer Guns. Price....20c
No. 6C7502 Main Springs for Hammerless Guns. Price....25c
No. 6C7505 Sear Springs for Hammer Guns. Price....15c
No. 6C7507 Sear Springs for Hammerless Guns. Price....25c
If by mail, postage extra, 2 cents.

Davis Gun Springs.

No. 6C7510 Main Springs for Double Hammer Guns. Price....50c
No. 6C7511 Main Springs for Double Hammerless Guns. Price....50c
No. 6C7512 Top Lever Springs for Double Hammer Guns. Price....25c
No. 6C7513 Top Lever Springs for Double Hammerless Guns. Price....25c
If by mail, postage extra, 2 cents.

Forehand Hammerless Single Gun Parts.

No. 6C7525 Main Springs for Forehand Hammerless Single Guns. Price....30c
No. 6C7526 Cocking Levers for Forehand Hammerless Single Guns. Price....50c
If by mail, postage extra, 2 cents.

Revolver Hammers.

Prices vary according to style of revolver and caliber. State caliber and style wanted.
No. 6C7530 Revolver Hammers for Colt's revolvers cost....$1.00 to $1.50
No. 6C7531 Revolver Hammers for Smith & Wesson revolvers cost....50c to 75c
No. 6C7532 Revolver Hammers for Harrington & Richardson revolvers cost,..40c to 50c
No. 6C7533 Revolver Hammers for Forehand revolvers cost....40c to 60c
No. 6C7534 Revolver Hammers for Iver Johnson revolvers cost....35c to 40c
If by mail, postage extra, 2 cents.

Long Range Winner, White Powder Wonder, Gold Medal Wonder and World Challenge Ejector Single Gun Parts.

These Guns Were Made by Three Different Factories.

No. 6C7575 Main Springs. Send broken sample so we can match it. Price....20c
No. 6C7577 Top Lever Springs. Send broken sample so we can match it. Price..8c
No. 6C7580 Barrel Keys. Send broken sample so we can match it. Price....25c
No. 6C7582 Top Levers. Send broken sample so we can match it. Price....35c
No. 6C7585 Firing Pins. Send broken sample so we can match it. Price....15c
If by mail, postage extra, 2 to 3 cents.

Chicago Long Range Wonder Hammerless Double Gun.

Finished, Ready to Put in the Gun.
No. 6C7601 Main Springs. Right or left side, send sample. Price....20c
No. 6C7603 Trigger Springs. Right or left side, send sample. Price....20c
No. 6C7605 Hammer. Right or left side, send sample. Price....35c
No. 6C7607 Sears. Right or left side, send sample. Price, each....30c
No. 6C7609 Top Lever. Send sample. Price....35c
No. 6C7610 Top Lever Spring. Send sample. Price....15c
No. 6C7611 Firing Pins. Send sample. Price....15c

OUR GUN SHOP is equipped with first class, up to date machines, forge, grinders, drill press, tools, etc., and we are prepared to give estimates on almost any kind of repair work. Tell us the make, name, style, model, caliber, gauge of your shotgun, rifle or revolver, say what is broken and the manager of our gun shop will estimate the cost of repairing same and will advise you if it is necessary to send the firearm to us or if he can make or furnish the part or parts necessary so you need not return the firearm to us. We always aim to save you the transportation charges of sending the firearm to us if we can do so.

American Gun Co. Gun Parts.

No. 6C7550 Top Lever Springs. Send broken sample so we can match it. Price 30c
No. 6C7551 Main Springs, right and left. Send broken sample so we can match it. Price 40c
No. 6C7555 Sears, right and left. Send broken sample so we can match it. Price, each 30c
No. 6C7557 Firing Pins. Send broken sample so we can match it. Price....20c
No. 6C7558 Top Lever. Send broken sample so we can match it. Price....60c
If by mail, postage extra, 2 to 4 cents.

FISHING TACKLE DEPARTMENT.

We carry an assortment of the highest grade fishing tackle to supply the wants of anglers of all kinds. We do not handle the cheap grade of tackle which has no practical value, but have selected our line with considerable care and handle only the very best of the hundreds of rods, reels, hooks, lines and baits on the market. There are hundreds of baits and specialties in fishing tackle on the market, but very few of which have practical merit, and you can rest assured that any article you select from this catalogue is exactly as represented, is full value for the money, and fully answers the purpose for which it is intended.

JAPANESE RODS.

We are offering our customers this season a line of Japanese jointed rods which we believe are better value than you can get from any other house in the United States, quality considered.

We have endeavored to get most of this line of Japanese rods all fitted with solid reel seat and zylonite butt, which makes a very attractive and expensive looking rod, and by placing a large contract for these goods, we were able to get the cost of manufacture down to the lowest point, and by adding our one small percentage of profit we are able to give you such value as we believe you cannot get anywhere else in the United States.

Japanese Two-Piece Rod, 7½ to 8½ Feet, 12 Cents.

No. 6C8597 Two-Piece Japanese Bamboo Rod. Natural color, double telescope ferrules, ringed guides for line. Length, about 7½ to 8½ feet. Price....(Postage extra 8 cents)....12c

Japanese Two-Piece Rod with Zylonite Butt, 7 to 8 Feet, 45c.

No. 6C8600 Two-Piece Japanese Rod, about 7½ feet long. Made of genuine Japanese cane, fitted with nickel telescope ferrules, solid reel seat above the grip, black zylonite butt, line guides for line. The best rod on the market for the money. Weight, about 12 ounces. Price....(If by mail, postage extra, 14 cents)....45c

Japanese Three-Piece Rod with Zylonite Butt, 8½ to 9 Ft., 58c.

No. 6C8602 Three-Piece Japanese Rod, about 8½ to 9 feet long, made of genuine Japanese cane, nickel plated telescope ferrules, solid reel seat above the grip, black zylonite butt, line guides for the line. The best 3-piece rod on the market for the money. Weight, about 13 ounces. Price....(If by mail, postage extra, 15 cents)....58c

Japanese Four-Piece Rod, with Zylonite Butt, about 14 Ft., 85c.

No. 6C8604 Four-Piece Japanese Rod, about 14 feet long, made of genuine Japanese cane, fitted with nickel plated telescope ferrules, solid reel seat above the grip, black zylonite butt, line guides for line. The best long rod on the market for the money. Weight, about 24 ounces. A good rod to fish from the shore. Price....(If by mail, postage extra, 26 cents)....85c

Four-Piece Calcutta Trunk Rod, About 8 Feet, 75 Cents.

No. 6C8606 Four-Piece Calcutta Trunk Rod. 7½ to 8 feet long. Made of genuine mottled Calcutta cane, nickel plated telescope ferrules, strong line guides for line, solid reel seat above the grip, zylonite butt, nickel plated trimmings. Each piece is 24 inches long, so it may be carried in a trunk or grip. Weight, 8 ounces. Price....(Postage extra, 12 cents)....75c

Calcutta Four-Piece Splashing Rod, 12 to 16 Feet, 85 Cents.

No. 6C8607 Four-Piece Calcutta Bamboo Rod, double telescope ferrules, ringed for line, with butt cap and reel bands. An excellent rod for splashing or spatting or trolling among the weeds and lily pads. Length, 12 to 16 feet. Weight, about 3 pounds. Price....85c

LANCEWOOD RODS.

There are about thirty to fifty styles of Lancewood rods manufactured by the various makers, and each style necessitates a change in equipment, machinery, etc., and by reducing the number of styles of our lancewood rods, we are able to save the expense of these changes, which expense is necessarily added to the rods when so many styles are handled by one house. We have decided to reduce the number of styles of lancewood rods in order to handle a few styles and manufacture them with the least possible expense. By doing this we were able to reduce the cost of our lancewood rods, and we give you the benefit of this reduction by pricing the following line of rods, based on our reduced cost, adding our one small percentage of profit.

St. Croix River Lancewood Fly Rod, 10 to 10½ Feet, 85 Cents.

No. 6C8616 Our St. Croix River Lancewood Fly Rod, made in three pieces, with an extra tip, genuine lancewood throughout, nickeled mountings and raised telescope ferrules. Silk wound tie guides and silk whippings at each mounting. Solid reel seat below hand. Zylonite corrugated grip. Length, about 10 to 10½ feet. Put up in neat partitioned cloth bag. Weight, about 9 ounces. A fine looking rod. Price....85c
If by mail, postage extra, 12 cents.

GENUINE LANCEWOOD BAIT CASTING ROD FOR 75 CENTS.

No. 6C8621 Owing to a contract we placed early in the season we are able to furnish a genuine lancewood Bait Casting Rod, 8 to 9 feet in length, for 75 cents. This rod is made of genuine lancewood, 3 joints, with extra tip, has double shouldered nickel plated telescope ferrules, select silk wound round wire tie guides, which are guaranteed not to cut the lines, is nicely wrapped with silk, solid nickel plated reel seat above handsome corrugated zylonite grip. Weight, about 9 ounces. This rod is put up in a neat, partitioned cloth bag, is a fine looking rod, very strong and pliable, a regular $1.50 to $2.00 rod. Our price....(If by mail, postage extra, 18 cents)....75c
Agate Tip fitted to this rod, 65 cents extra; Agate Guide fitted to this rod, 65 cents extra; Agate Tip and Guide, $1.20 extra over the stated price of the rod.

Our Delavan Lake 2-Joint, 5½-Foot Lancewood Bass Rod, $2.25.

No. 6C8622 There is a growing demand for a Two-Joint Rod, and to satisfy this demand we have had this rod built especially for us. Our Delavan Lake Rod is made with two joints of lancewood with detachable cork grip, making three pieces in all. This rod is very closely wrapped with red and black silk, fitted with anti-friction trumpet guides, which are wrapped with wire, fitted with double hole frictionless funnel tip, shouldered ferrules and reel seat are heavily nickel plated. This is the most beautiful Lancewood rod ever placed on the market at a price less than $6.00. This rod is very strong, weighs 6 ounces, and has a beautaper from grip to tip, making it well adapted for bait casting; comes put up in a neat partitioned flannel bag. Price....(If by mail, postage extra, 12 cents)....$2.25
Agate Tip fitted to this rod, 65 cents extra; Agate Guide fitted to this rod, 65 cents extra; Agate Tip and Guide, $1.20 extra over the stated price of the rod.

OUR SPLIT BAMBOO RODS.

This illustration will give you as near as it is possible an idea of how a split bamboo rod is made. At first the bamboo cane is split in a sort of triangle shape, as shown in illustration, and glued together, forming a hexagonal shape. This is where the rod derives its name—Split Bamboo—(the bamboo is split and glued together).

Our Western Expert Split Bamboo Bass Rod, 5½ Feet, $2.00.

No. 6C8629 This rod was designed by us to meet the large demand for a high grade short length bait casting rod, and is one that is generally sold for from $4.00 to $5.00. This rod is original with us. It was made in exact accordance with the specifications furnished by us, made by a manufacturer who has been in business for years and whose rods ordinarily sell for very fancy prices. This rod is made of special selected clear straight grain, hand split bamboo, **the joints are beautifully tapered and balanced,** giving this rod **just the right amount of life and elasticity** which has always been so hard to obtain in a cheap rod. It is handsomely and closely wrapped with alternate wrappings of black and red silk, is fitted with **German silver anti-friction trumpet guides, double hole funnel tip,** handsome solid nickel plated reel seat with nickel plated finger hook, corrugated black and white celluloid grip, nickel plated butt cap, heavy welded shouldered ferrules, shouldered dowels, put up three joints and an extra tip in a flannel covered wood form, incased in a flannel bag; a rod that will please the expert at a price fully $2.00 less than it could possibly be duplicated for elsewhere. Weight, 5½ ounces. Length, 5½ feet. Price.... **$2.00**
If by mail, postage extra, 20 cents.

Agate tip fitted to this rod, **65 cents extra**; agate guide fitted to this rod, **65 cents extra**; agate guide and tip fitted to this rod, **$1.20** extra over stated price of the rod.

Our Climax Split Bamboo Bass Rod, 8 to 9 Feet, 78 Cents.

No. 6C8630 Solid reel seat above the hand. This rod is one that we are making a run on at an exceedingly low price and are positive **the rod cannot be duplicated for twice the amount** anywhere in the country. Split and glued bamboo bass rods, **nickel plated telescope ferrules, silk wound line guides,** with alternate wrappings, nickeled mountings, three pieces, with an extra tip. **Put up on a wooden form in a cloth bag.** About 8 to 9 feet long. Weight, about 11 ounces.
Price.....................(If by mail, postage extra, 20 cents.)..................... **78c**

Agate tip fitted to this rod, **65 cents extra**; agate guide fitted to this rod, **65 cents extra**; agate tip and guide fitted to this rod, **$1.20** extra over the stated price of the rod.

Our Acme Split Bamboo Fly Rod, 9½ to 10 Feet, 82 Cents.

No. 6C8634 Solid reel seat below the hand. This rod is the same quality as our Climax, except that the reel seat is below the hand for trout and light fishing. Has silk wound ring guides, with wrappings of fine silk every few inches; solid reel seat and nickel plated telescope ferrules and mountings. Length, about 9½ to 10 feet. Weight, about 11 ounces. **Worth $1.75 anywhere. Comes in three pieces with an extra tip on a wood form and in a cloth bag.** Price.................. **82c**
If by mail, postage extra, 19 cents.

High Grade Split Bamboo Fly Rod, 9 to 10 Feet Long, $2.75.

For $2.75 we offer you our Special Rio Grande High Grade Split Bamboo, Cedar Inlaid Fly Rod, made of six pieces, selected bamboo, split and glued together, with solid reel seat, snake line guides, fancy silk wrappings at short intervals, nickel plated mountings, shouldered ferrules and swelled butt. The bamboo is strengthened at the reel seat by extra inlaying of cedar at the butt, making it very strong and durable. **The rod comes in three pieces with an extra tip,** put up on a covered wood form. Each piece is about 36 inches long, and when the rod is put together the entire length is about 9 to 10 feet, and weighs 8 ounces. This is undoubtedly one of the best fly rods to be had for the money.

No. 6C8669 Our Rio Grande Split Bamboo Fly Rod, about 9 to 10 feet long, with corrugated genuine celluloid butt. Price.......(If by mail, postage extra, 17 cents.)........... **$2.75**

Steel Rod Shortener.

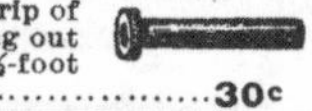

No. 6C8695 Our Steel Rod Shortener. This shortener fits in the grip of jointed steel rods and in doing so takes only the two smallest joints, leaving out the joint which fits in the grip. With this shortener you can make an 8½-foot rod 6 feet long. Price..................(If by mail, postage extra, 2 cents.)................. **30c**

WHITE ASH OARS.

One pair of 6½-foot oars weigh about 6 pounds and one pair of 8½-foot oars weigh about 13 pounds. **All our oars are first quality.**

Plain Ash Oars.

No. 6C8710 Length given is length of each oar.

Length	6 ft.	6½ ft.	7 ft.	7½ ft.	8 ft.	8½ ft.
Price, pr.	89c	94c	$1.00	$1.08	$1.17	$1.24

Copper Tipped Ash Oars.

No. 6C8711 Length given is length of each oar.

Length	6 ft.	6½ ft.	7 ft.	7½ ft.	8 ft.	8½ ft.
Pair	99c	$1.04	$1.12	$1.20	$1.25	$1.34

Copper Tipped Spruce Oars.

No. 6C8713 Genuine Adirondack Spruce Oars, in 7-foot only. Lighter than ash oars and strong, copper tipped.
Price, per pair........................... **$1.25**

Oar Locks.

No. 6C8714 North River Oar Lock, galvanized malleable iron, 2 inches between horns. Weight, per pair, about 2 pounds.
Price, per pair.......................... **20c**

No. 6C8715 Socket Oar Locks, malleable iron. Weight, per pair, 2 pounds. Width, 2 inches between horns.
Price, per pair..... **18c**

No. 6C8717 Safety Side Plate Oar Locks. Impossible to pull horn out of socket accidentally. Made of malleable iron. Weight, per pair, 2½ pounds.
Price, per pair............... **35c**

Universal Bow Facing Oar Locks.

No. 6C8718 Do not row backwards because your grandfather did. Buy a pair of Universal Oar Locks and face the way you are rowing. This oar lock is very simple, made of malleable iron, contains but few parts and can be easily attached to a boat by most anyone. Weight, per pair, 8 pounds.
Price, per pair............................ **$2.15**

Life Preservers.

No. 6C8720 Life Belts, made of square blocks of cork similar to the "Never Sink" and buckles on the same way. **One of the best in the market; safe and durable.** Weight, 8 pounds.
Price....... **$1.15**

Our Capoc Life Belt.

No. 6C8723 Capoc Life Belt is made very similar to the Cork Jacket as illustrated above, except that it is more in the shape of a belt and intended to go around body under the arms. The belt is 8½ inches wide, 52 inches long, and is so arranged with tape that it can be hung over the shoulders and fastened around the body in such a way as to float the average man in the water. Capoc is a short vegetable fibre similar to cotton, and grows in the East Indian Islands. It has a silky appearance, is very buoyant. Our Capoc Life belt weighs but 2 pounds, is tested by the United States Inspector, and makes an ideal light weight life preserver. Price............ **$1.05**
If by mail, postage extra, 34 cents.

Our Special Willowemock Split Bamboo Fly Rod, 9½ to 10 Feet, $1.50.

No. 6C8641 Solid reel seat below the hand. This rod is made of special selected bamboo, hexagonal in shape, with close wrappings of colored silk, full nickel plated telescope ferrules and mountings, cork grasp. Put up in three pieces with an extra tip on a fine covered wood form and in a neat bag. Length, about 9½ to 10 feet. A rod that retails at $3.00 in stores.
Weight, 6 ounces. Price..............(If by mail, postage extra, 18 cents.).............. **$1.50**

THE GENUINE BRISTOL STEEL FISHING RODS. Warranted.

Manufactured by the Horton Manufacturing Co., of Bristol, Conn.

Steel Telescope Fly and Bass Rods 9½ Feet Long.

No. 6C8670 Steel Telescope Bass Rods, 9 feet 6 inches in length, full nickel mounted with solid reel seat above the hand. Line runs through the center of the rod. When telescoped the rod is 32 inches in length, all enclosed within the butt length, as shown in illustration. Weight, 11½ ounces. With genuine celluloid handle. Price..................(If by mail, postage extra, 15 cents.).................. **$2.90**

Steel Telescope Fly Rod, 9½ Feet Long.

No. 6C8672 Same style as above, but with reel seat below the hand for trout fishing. Line runs through the center of the rod. When telescoped, the rod is 32 inches in length. All inclosed within the butt length. Weight, 11½ ounces. With genuine celluloid handle. Price.. **$2.85**
If by mail, postage extra, 15 cents.

Our High Grade 10-Foot Jointed Steel Fly Rod.

No. 6C8674 Steel Fly Rod, 10 feet long, full nickel mounted, **with solid reel seat below the hand.** This rod is jointed and fitted with two-ring German silver tie guide and one-ring German silver fly tip. Is made with three pieces and handle; each joint being 38 inches long. **Does not telescope.** Weight, 9½ ounces. With genuine celluloid wound handle. Price.................(If by mail, postage extra, 13 cents.)................ **$3.60**

$3.25 Genuine Henshall 8½-Foot Steel Bass Rod. $3.25

No. 6C8676 Full nickel mounted with solid reel seat **above the hand.** This rod is jointed and fitted with two-ring German silver tie guides and German silver three-ring tip. Is made with three pieces and handle; each joint being 32 inches long. **Does not telescope. This rod is the best bass or pickerel rod made.** Weight, 10 ounces. With genuine celluloid wound handle. Price............(If by mail, postage extra, 15 cents.)............ **$3.25**

$3.25 The Genuine Expert 6½-Foot Steel Bass Rod. $3.25

No. 6C8680 The Expert Steel Bait Casting Rod, 6½ feet long, full nickel mounted, with **solid reel seat above the hand.** This rod is jointed and fitted with two-ring German silver tie guides and German silver three-ring tip. It is made with three pieces and handle; the joints are 24 inches long. This is a fine rod for long casts and for heavy work. **Does not telescope, but is jointed.** Weight, 8½ ounces. With genuine celluloid wound handle.
Price.........................(If by mail, postage extra, 13 cents.)......................... **$3.25**

No. 6C8688 The New Bristol Steel Bait Casting Rod, 5½ feet long with agate tip and one agate guide, which saves the wear on the line, the other guides are German silver, trumpet style. This rod is intended for those who prefer **a short rod, which is rapidly becoming more and more popular,** being more readily handled and not so severe on the wrist. This rod does not telescope, but is jointed and fitted with genuine celluloid handle. Weight, 8½ ounces. Price........ **$5.25**
If by mail, postage extra, 13 cents.

The Serocol Complete Tackle Outfit.

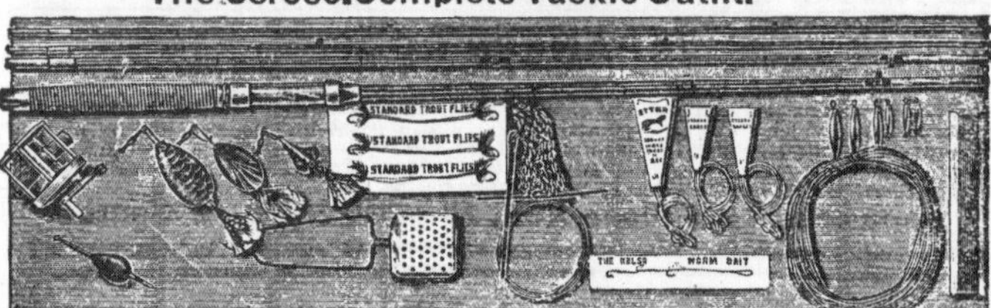

No. 6C8726 This is a first class outfit, one that will please any fisherman, no matter how critical. Same consists of a split bamboo bait casting rod, 8 feet long, three joints and extra tip, zylonite grip, anti-friction tie guides, mounted wood frame in cloth bag, excellent 60-yard wide spool quadruple reel, fitted with click and drag, steel pivot and steel axle, full nickel plated, fancy bone balance handle; 25 yards of hard silk braided casting line, one linen line suitable for trolling or still fishing, one and a half dozen assorted gut hooks, three popular attractive artificial baits, half a dozen trout flies, half a dozen assorted sinkers, one 3-foot double gut leader, one worm gang, one chain fish stringer, one fancy float, one fish scaler; all put up in a durable pasteboard box. This outfit, if the items were purchased separately, would cost about $3.75.
Our price for above outfit as stated........(If by mail, postage extra, 42 cents.)...... **$2.60**

Our Shakespeare Service Quadruple Reel, $3.60.

Has wide spool, click on the left hand side, drag on the top of the right disc, screw off oil caps, balance handle, steel pinion and furnished in 80 yards only. The reel is 2 inches wide and 2 inches in diameter. Weight, about 7 ounces. An excellent casting reel.

No. 6C8730 Price, 80-yard size..... **$3.60**
If by insured mail, postage extra 15 cents.

Our Orleans Reel, single action, raised pillar, riveted brass reel. A very strong and durable reel.

Catalogue Number	Holds No. 4 Line	Click	Price
6C8737	25 yards	With	12c
6C8738	60 yards	With	18c

If by mail, postage extra, 4 to 6 cents.

Double Multiplying Reel.

Raised Pillar, balance handle, screwed connections, polished brass or full nickel plated reel, with patent adjustible slide drag and back sliding click, polished bearings.

Catalogue No.	Finish	Capacity	Price
6C8740	Brass	40 yards	35c
6C8741	Brass	60 yards	40c
6C8743	Nickel Plated	40 yards	43c
6C8744	Nickel Plated	60 yards	50c

If by mail, postage extra, 9 cents.

Rubber Cap Reel.

Double multiplying raised pillar, balance handle, screwed connections, **nickel plated** reels, with patent adjustable **slide drag and back sliding** click.

Catalogue No.	Holds No. 4 Line	Price
6C8746	40 yards	55c
6C8747	60 yards	60c
6C8748	80 yards	70c

If by mail, postage extra, 9 cents.

We offer the genuine Bristol Steel Fishing Rods with the assurance that there are no better rods made at any price. These rods are patented by the makers and no steel rods are genuine except these. All rods are warranted by the makers for one year and if any piece or part gives out by reason of defect in material or workmanship it will be repaired or replaced free of cost to you by The Horton Mfg. Co., Bristol, Conn. Keep a drop of oil on joints to prevent corrosion.

Our Ideal Quadruple Reel.

The best low price Quadruple Reel on the market, has round disc, wide spool, balance handle, screw off oil cap, the oil cap, disc, handle and post are milled, giving a handsome appearance; is fitted with steel axle and steel pinion, also fitted with click and drag, making it a very durable, handsome reel; each reel is carefully examined, guaranteed to run absolutely true.

Catalogue No.	Holds No. 4 Line	Price
6C8750	40 yards	$0.95
6C8751	60 yards	1.10
6C8752	80 yards	1.20

If by mail, postage extra, 14 cents.

Carlton Ideal Reel.

No. 6C8753 The Carlton Ideal Reel is an ideal reel for fly casting. It is doubtless the lightest reel on the market; it is a single action reel but the construction of the spool enables this reel to reel in the line as fast as a multiplying reel, also thoroughly dries the line, as the air can easily get at same. The reel is finely nickel plated, fitted with click and balance handle, the base and side plate are made of one piece of metal, making the reel doubly strong. This reel comes 60 yards only. Price............$1.00

If by mail, postage extra, 10 cents.

Our Genuine Quadruple Pennell Reel.

Each reel is carefully tested for smooth running and carefully adjusted before leaving the factory. We guarantee this to be the genuine Pennell Quadruple Reel, the best reel for bass fishing or trolling. Our Quadruple Pennell Round Disc Reel is fitted with adjustable sliding click and drag, steel pivots, bridge over gear made of the best material possible, handsomely nickeled, fancy bone balance handle.

Catalogue No.	Holds No. 4 Line	Price
6C8755	40 yards	$1.65
6C8756	60 yards	1.90
6C8757	80 yards	2.05

If by mail, postage extra, 15 cents.

Our Celebrated Tournament Agate Cap Quadruple Pennell Reel.

Our Quadruple Agate Cap Reel with balance handle, round disc wide spool fitted with click and drag, all parts made true, to run with the least possible friction. The disc and agate caps are milled, making a very handsome appearance, handsomely nickel plated screw connections, adjustable slide click and drag. These celebrated reels have the genuine agate caps, which makes them smooth and free running.

Catalogue Number	Holds No. 4 Silk Line	Price
6C8762	60 yards	$2.85
6C8763	80 yards	3.15

If by mail, postage extra, 15 cents.

Shakespeare Universal Quadruple Reel.

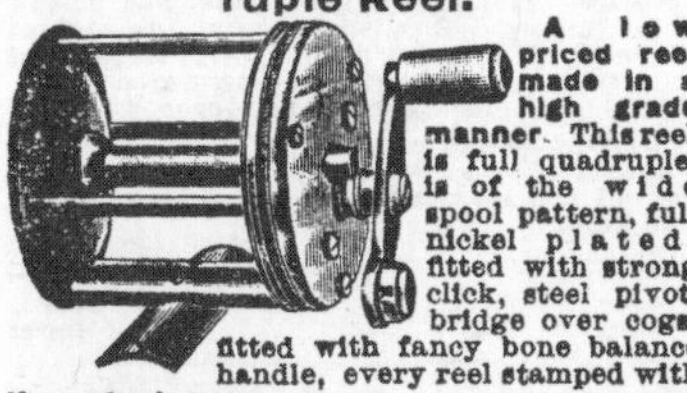

A low priced reel made in a high grade manner. This reel is full quadruple, is of the wide spool pattern, full nickel plated, fitted with strong click, steel pivot, bridge over cogs, fitted with fancy bone balance handle, every reel stamped with the maker's name.

No. 6C8764 40 yards. Price......$0.85
No. 6C8765 60 yards. Price...... 1.00
No. 6C8766 80 yards. Price...... 1.20

If by mail, postage extra, 12 cents.

Shakespeare Standard Reel.

This reel holds the world's record for accuracy and long distance bait casting. It is a beautifully finished reel, accurately made, runs with a freedom and smooth motion that is not experienced in other reels, full quadrupled, heavily silver plated and oxidized on hard drawn and rolled brass, with English silver steel journals and pinons, has the adjustable drag, which prevents the over running and snarling of the line while bait casting; drag and click are placed on top of reel opposite each other, as shown in the illustration. 1⅜-inch wide spool pattern.

No. 6C8768 80 yards. Price..........$5.40

If by mail, postage extra, 15 cents.

The Expert Seroco Agate Rubber Plate Quadruple Reel.

These reels are of the new widespool type, are made especially for us under contract. It is one of the finest reels made, a reel that would ordinarily sell for twice the price we are asking for same. Rubber plates incased with nickel bands, jeweled bearings, the agates being accurately adjusted to the axle, has handsome white bone milled balance handle, is bridged to prevent action from becoming loose, insuring smooth running qualities, gears are carefully cut and adjusted by experts, finely finished, being extra heavily nickel plated, new style cross blade, fitted with click and drag. Made in 60 and 80-yard size.

No. 6C8775 60-yard size. Price...$1.90
No. 6C8776 80-yard size. Price... 2.20

If by mail, postage extra, 15 cents.

Perfection Pennell Take-Apart Reel.

No tools required. This reel may be taken apart in a moment's time by unscrewing the ring at either end. This reel is made by the most skilled mechanics, built on entirely different principles than other reels, and is the strongest, simplest, swiftest reel on the market. Has a scientific friction device by which any degree of friction can be instantly secured on the spool. Principle of the click is entirely new, it is silent when the line is being reeled in, clicks when the line runs out. It is the strongest click ever placed on a reel. Can be thrown off or on as desired. The pinion gear of quadruple style is cut upon a solid steel shaft running through and securely fastened into the non-corrosive German silver spool. The pivots are turned upon this hardened steel shaft and have cone end bearings. The large gear is perfectly cut in bronze, and is securely bridged on the cap of the reel. The fancy bone handle is screwed upon the solid post of this gear and can be placed in four different positions. This reel is of the wide spool pattern, is the best bait casting reel of its kind ever placed upon the market. Absolutely true and accurate.

No. 6C8777 60 yards..............$3.50
No. 6C8778 100 yards.............. 4.00

If by mail, postage extra, 14 cents.

TWISTED COTTON AND LINEN FISH LINES.

NOTE A. This illustration shows as near as possible the size of all twisted fish lines. It is impossible to make an illustration show the sizes exact. This is as near correct as a picture can be made. When ordering, tell us which size you wish. Order by catalogue number.

Excellent Braided Line.

No. 6C8785 Excellent Braided Linen Finished Line. This is a beautifully mottled hard braided line, very strong, put up 50 yards on a nicely finished spool, comes in three sizes. Sizes 4 5 6
Per spool 19c 18c 17c

If by mail, postage extra, 4 cents.

Sea Grass Lines. Twisted in Coils.

No. 6C8790 Sea Grass Line, put up in coils and 6 coils in a bunch. One of the best and strongest lines made; fine as silk. See illustration Note A for sizes. We cannot sell less than a bunch of a size. State size wanted.

No. 1, the smallest, for trout (very strong). Price, per bunch of six coils (about 125 feet)..........38c
No. 2, medium, for bass (very strong). Price, per bunch of six coils (about 70 feet)..........40c
No. 3, largest, for pike (very strong) Price, per bunch of six coils (about 50 feet).. (If by mail, postage extra, 2c.)......44c

Hawser Laid Trolling Lines.

No. 6C8793 Our Hawser Laid Line is a heavy hand laid line of great strength, is finely finished; line No. 3 will hold the largest fish. Put up in coils of 100 feet, 6 coils connected if desired, making 600 feet in one piece.

Size 1, cable laid coils of 100 feet, per coil, 12c
Size 2, cable laid coils of 100 feet, per coil, 14c
Size 3, cable laid coils of 100 feet, per coil, 17c

If by mail, postage extra, 4 cents.

No. 5 4 3 2 1 1-0 2-0 3-0

NOTE B. This illustration shows size of braided lines as near as it is possible to print sizes or to illustrate them. Order by catalogue number and state size you wish.

Braided Cotton Lines.

No. 6C8796 Braided Cotton Lines, put up 24 feet in a coil, strong and durable, made of best Sea Island cotton, guaranteed even strength. Mention size wanted. See Note B for sizes.

Size, Nos......... 5 4 3 2 1 1-0 2-0 3-0
Price, per coil.... 5c 5c 5c 7c 7c 10c 11c 12c

If by mail, postage extra, 3 cents.

The No. 5 is tested to 10 pounds; the No. 3-0 is tested to 40 pounds pull. All others are tested in proportion.

Hard Braided Linen Lines.

No. 6C8798 Hard Braided Linen Lines, put up 25 yards in a coil and may be had four coils connected, making 100 yards. Much stronger than twisted or laid lines. The best bass and trolling line in the market. Made from best Scotch linen fibre, evenly braided and well finished. The No. 5 is tested to 25 pounds; the No. 2-0 to 50 pounds, and all the other sizes are tested in proportion. See illustration Note B for sizes. State size wanted. Order by catalogue number and size number.

Size, Nos... 5 4 3 2 1 1-0 2-0
Per coil.... 13c 14c 15c 16c 17c 17c 18c

If by mail, postage extra, 3 to 10 cents.

NOTE C. This illustration shows as near as possible the size of our silk lines. It is impossible to show the exact size by illustration.

5 4 3 2 1

Our Celebrated Kingfisher Braided Silk Line.

No. 6C8805 This line is made on the latest improved braiding machine, has an even luster finish and tension, and we cannot recommend it too highly. It comes in four sizes, and is the genuine Kingfisher line. Don't buy imitations. It comes put up 25 yards on a block and may be had four blocks connected, making 100 yards, if so wanted. For sizes, see illustration Note C.

State size wanted.
Size, Nos.................. 5 4 3
Price, per 25 yards.......... 24c 30c 35c

If by mail, postage extra, 3 cents.

Our Famous Braided Oil Silk Lines in Coils.

No. 6C8810 Fine Quality Braided Oil Silk Lines, put up 25 yards in a coil and may be had four coils connected, making 100 yards. This is a very strong line, closely braided, of the finest silk, oiled, making it a waterproof line; soft and pliable. A good line for trolling and fly casting. For sizes, see illustration Note C. State size wanted. Order by catalogue number and size number.

Size, Nos........ 5 4 3 2
Price, per 25 yds........ 25c 34c 39c 44c

If by mail, postage extra, 4 cents.

Our Kingfisher Special Silk Bass Lines.

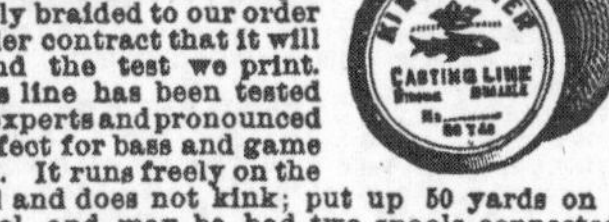

This line is the highest quality dressed silk casting line made. It is specially braided to our order under contract that it will stand the test we print. This line has been tested by experts and pronounced perfect for bass and game fish. It runs freely on the reel and does not kink; put up 50 yards on a spool and may be had two spools connected, making 100 yards, if wanted. This is the genuine Kingfisher line.

Catalogue Number	Size	For Fish Weighing	Price, per Spool
6C8811	No. 5	1 to 3 lbs.	50c
6C8811½	No. 4	3 to 4 lbs.	60c
6C8811¾	No. 3	4 to 10 lbs.	74c

If by mail, postage extra, 7 cents.

Martin's Special Enamel Silk Trout Lines.

No. 6C8814 Our Extra Quality Kingfisher, Enameled Oil Silk Trout Lines are giving excellent satisfaction and the demand for these lines is becoming greater each season, they being of small diameter and possessing great strength. This result is obtained not only by using the highest grade of silk, but by braiding more strands into each line and plaiting very close. Try one of these lines and you will want more. 25 yards on neat card.

Price, per card.. (Postage extra, 3c.)......34c

Kingfisher Special Enamel Finished Potomac Bass Lines.

No. 6C8815 Our Special Potomac Bass Line is the same as No. 6C8814, but bass size. Comes 25 yards in a coil and may be had two or four coils connected, or 50 yards, if so wanted.

Price, per coil of 25 yards...................45c

If by mail, postage extra, 2 cents.

Genuine Italian Braided Silk Bass and Trout Line.

Our Genuine Italian Braided Silk Line is intended for expert fishermen, for the man who wants the best line that money can buy. This line is made from selected stock, perfectly braided over a silk core, is a hard line free from any imperfections. This same line is sold by dealers under various names at $1.50 a spool. It comes put up 50 yards on a spool, 2 spools connected.

Catalogue Number	For	Yards on Spool	Price, per Spool
6C8818B	Bass	50 Yards	90c
6C8818T	Trout	50 Yards	70c

If by mail, postage extra, 2 cents.

Our Genuine Martin Level Enameled Fly Casting Lines.

No. 6C8819 Enameled Silk Waterproof Fly Line, made from the very finest silk that can be obtained, is uniform in size and has enormous strength. Put up 25 yards in a coil and may be had four coils connected, or 100 yards, if desired. A very fine line, guaranteed. State size wanted.

Size, Nos................ 6-H 5-G 4-F 3-E
Price, per 25 yards.... 53c 62c 75c 85c

If by mail, postage extra, 2 cents.

Cuttyhunk Linen Lines.

The Strongest Reel Line Made.

No. 9
No. 12
No. 15
No. 18
No. 21

No. 6C8820 Cuttyhunk Linen Reel Line, the old reliable; the strongest line made for its size. Made of the finest quality of Scotch linen, always runs smooth and even and never kinks. The best linen reel line on the market. Put up 150 feet on a spool, or may be had two spools connected, making 300 feet of line. This line is twisted, and when used with swivel on end will not untwist. Can be used same as a braided line See illustration for sizes. State size wanted. Order by catalogue number and size number.

Size, Nos......... 9 12 15 18 21
Price, per 150 ft.. 24c 28c 33c 40c 45c
Price, per 300 ft.. 45c 50c 65c 78c 90c

If by mail, postage extra, 4 to 9 cents.

Crystal Lake Green Linen Lines.

No. 6C8825 This line is made of the finest quality Scotch flax, is green in color, is especially adapted for game fish. In the manufacture of this line great care is taken to select only the best long fibre Scotch flax, insuring a smooth, perfect line that will not kink, free from all knots, will run free on any reel. Comes in three sizes: No. 9, breaking strength, 18 pounds; No. 12, breaking strength, 24 pounds, and No. 15, breaking strength, 30 pounds. Put up 50 feet on the coil, six coils connected if desired.

Size.................. No. 9 No. 12 No. 15
Price, per coil...... 20c 25c 30c

If by mail, postage extra, 2 cents.

Furnished Lines.

Furnished Lines, rigged complete. Line with hook, float and sinker, all ready to drop in the water. Put up one on a winder, convenient to carry.

No. 6C8826 Medium laid Cotton Line, rigged complete, with fancy adjustable float for still fishing. Price..........5c

If by mail, postage extra, 2 cents.

No. 6C8832 Finest Quality Silk Line, rigged complete, with gut hook, fancy float and sinker, for still fishing. Price..........15c

If by mail, postage extra, 3 cents.

Fish Hooks, Double Refined and Tempered Steel.

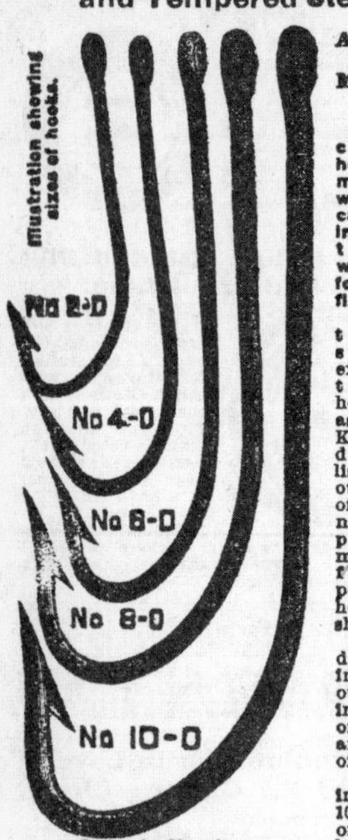

All Best English Manufacture.

There are cheaper hooks in the market, but we do not carry them in stock, as they are worthless for catching fish.

This illustration shows the exact size of the ringed hooks, such as Limerick, Kirby, Aberdeen, Carlisle and all other kinds of hooks, as nearly as possible, measuring from the point of the hook to the shank.

The other difference in the various hooks is in the length of the shank and the style of bend.

Sold only in boxes of 100 and only one size in a box.

Order by Number.

We cannot sell less than 100 hooks of a size.

On above sizes, No. 2-0 is the smallest and No. 10-0 is the largest size. The sizes grow larger gradually from No. 2-0 up, as shown in above illustration.

1 2 3 4 5 6 7 8 9 10 11 12

This illustration shows the Kirby style hooks, about ¾ the actual size. Order by size number and catalogue number. Postage on ringed hooks, sizes 1 to 8, 1 and 2 cents; sizes 1-0 to 10-0, 3 to 22 cents.

Kirby Hooks, Spear Point.

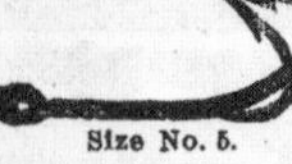

Size No. 5.

No. 6C8848 Kirby Bent Fish Hooks, medium length shank, superfine steel, ringed. Put up in a box of 100 each. We cannot sell less than 100 of a size, but our price is the same whether you buy 100 or 1,000. We give the lowest price always. See illustration of sizes above and state size wanted. Order by catalogue number and size number.

Size, Nos.	12	10	8	7	6
Per 100	4c	4c	5c	5c	5c
Size, Nos.	5	4	3	2	1
Per 100	6c	6c	6c	6c	6c
Size, Nos.	1-0	2-0	3-0	4-0	
Per 100	7c	8c	10c	11c	
Size, Nos.	5-0	6-0	8-0	10-0	
Per 100	13c	14c	20c	35c	

If by mail, postage extra, per box, 2 to 20 cents.

Limerick Hooks, Spear Point.

No. 6C8850 Limerick Fish Hooks, medium length shank, similar to the Kirby; superfine steel, ringed. Put up 100 hooks in a box. We cannot sell less than 100 hooks of a size. See illustration of sizes above and state size wanted. Order by catalogue number and size number.

Size No.	12	10	8	6	5
Per 100	5c	5c	5c	5c	5c
Size No.	4	3	2	1	1-0
Per 100	5c	5c	5c	5c	8c
Size No.	2-0	3-0	4-0	6-0	8-0
Per 100	9c	10c	11c	13c	19c

If by mail, postage extra, per box, 2 to 20 cents.

Carlisle Hooks, Spear Point.

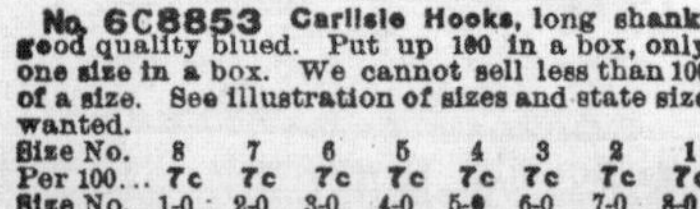

No. 6C8853 Carlisle Hooks, long shank, good quality blued. Put up 100 in a box, only one size in a box. We cannot sell less than 100 of a size. See illustration of sizes and state size wanted.

Size No.	8	7	6	5	4	3	2	1
Per 100	7c	7c	7c	7c	7c	7c	7c	7c
Size No.	1-0	2-0	3-0	4-0	5-0	6-0	7-0	8-0
Per 100	8c	10c	12c	15c	18c	22c	25c	30c

If by mail, postage extra. 1 to 10 cents a box.

The Maloney Weedless Bass Hook.

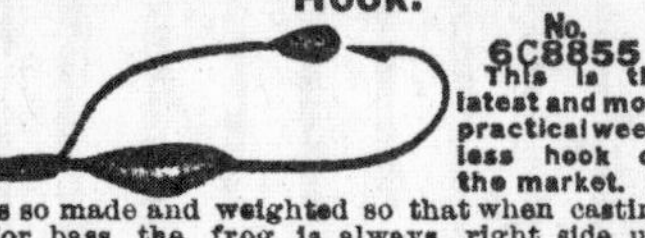

No. 6C8855 This is the latest and most practical weedless hook on the market. It is so made and weighted so that when casting for bass, the frog is always right side up. They are made in sizes 2-0, 3-0, 4-0 and 5-0. See illustration of ringed hooks for sizes and state size wanted. Price, each 8c

If by mail, postage extra, 1 cent.

Greer's New Lever Hooks.

Illustration shows the hook when set and sprung.

Greer's Patent Lever Fish Hooks. No more fish lost and baits to reset no coming home without your largest fish; a dead sure thing on getting your fish if it bites. It is easily adjusted to all kinds of fishing, by sliding the little clamp on the rod. Made of 1-0 and 3-0 Carlisle hooks.

GREER NEW LEVER BASS HOOK — SET — SPRUNG

No. 6C8857 Size, 1-0. Price, each 8c
No. 6C8857½ Size, 3-0. Price, each 9c

If by mail, postage extra, 2 cents.

Spring Fish Hooks.

No. 6C8858 The Snap and Catch 'Em Spring Fish Hook. The hook's spring points outward, and it is easily set. Fish cannot get away when he is once hooked. No. 20, for small fish; No. 19, for medium size fish; No. 18, for large fish. Say which you want. Price, each 8c

If by mail, postage extra, 2 cents.

Kelso Worm Gang.

No. 6C8858½ This is just the thing for still fishing and will catch the nibbler every time. As shown in the illustration, this bait consists of three No. 8 hooks tied to a piece of gut same as an ordinary snell hook, except you have three hooks around which you twine your angle worm. You will not have your bait nibbled off if you use the Kelso Worm Gang when you go still fishing. Price, each 6c

If by mail, postage extra, 1 cent.

AN OUTFIT FOR BASS, PICKEREL, ETC.

Consists of 1 Bait Casting Rod, 5 to 6½ feet. 1 Quadruple Reel, 1 Silk Line, 3 or 4 spoons No. 4 to 4½, a few sinkers, a few pieces of pork rind, 3 inches long, ⅜ inch wide, cut to look like a fish and fastened to one of the treble hooks on the spoon. With this outfit you are ready for business.

If you go on a long trip take an extra cheap rod and a few extra articles in case you break a rod or lose some tackle in the lake.

SNELLED HOOKS.

Our snelled hooks are put up one-half dozen of a size in a package, and we cannot sell less than one-half dozen of a size. All our snelled hooks are specially hand tied and no house can compete with us in quality and prices. All our gut hooks are tied with silk. **Our Carlisle and Cincinnati Bass Hooks** are put in a patent folding metal holder which is in destructible. Will keep your hooks together without tieing or fastening same.

Limerick Spear Point Snelled Hooks.

Tied to best quality single and double gut, full length. We cannot sell less than one-half dozen of a size.

No. 6C8860 Limerick Single Gut.

Size No.	8	7	6	5	4	3
Price, per doz.	10c	10c	10c	10c	10c	10c
Size No.		2	1	1-0	2-0	3-0
Price, per doz.		10c	10c	12c	13c	14c

If by mail, postage extra, per dozen, 2 to 4 cents.

No. 6C8862 Limerick Double Gut.

Size No.		4	3	2	1	
Price, per doz.		12c	12c	12c	12c	
Size No.	1-0	2-0	3-0	4-0	5-0	6-0
Price, per doz.	14c	15c	16c	21c	26c	32c

If by mail, postage extra, per dozen, 2 to 4 cents.

Carlisle Snelled Hooks.

Carlisle Spring Steel Hooks, special quality, silk tied to full length single or double gut. Put up one-half dozen in a **patent metal holder.** We cannot sell less than one-half dozen of a size.

No. 6C8867 Carlisle Single Gut.

Size No.	8	7	6	5	4	3
Price, per doz.	15c	15c	15c	15c	15c	15c
Size No.		2	1	1-0	2-0	3-0
Price, per doz.		15c	15c	19c	21c	24c

No. 6C8869 Carlisle Double Gut.

Size No.	4	3	2	1	1-0
Price, per doz.	18c	18c	18c	18c	21c
Size No.	2-0	3-0	4-0	5-0	6-0
Price, per doz.	23c	26c	30c	34c	40c

If by mail, postage extra, per dozen, 2 to 4 cents.

Plain Treble Hooks.

Don't throw away your spoon bait if you have lost the hook, but buy a hook for it.

No. 6C8884 Plain Treble Hooks; ringed, made of best quality spring steel and well finished. Sizes compare with regular fish hooks.

Size No.				4	3	2	1
Price, each				2c	2c	2c	2c
Size No.	1-0	2-0	3-0	4-0	5-0	6-0	7-0
Price, each	3c	3c	3c	4c	4c	4c	5c

If by mail, postage extra, 1 to 3 cents.

Feathered Treble Hooks.

No. 6C8885 Heavily feathered, well tied, best quality hooks.

Size No.	5	4	3	2	1
Price, each	3c	3c	3c	3c	3c
Size No.	1-0	2-0	3-0	4-0	
Price, each	4c	4c	4c	5c	
Size No.	5-0	7-0	8-0		
Price, each	5c	6c	6c		

If by mail, postage extra, each, 1 cent.

Bucktail Treble Hooks.

No. 6C8886 Our Bucktail Treble Hooks, made from genuine deertail hair, can be attached to almost any spoon bait, makes an excellent hook to interchange with the regular feathered treble hook, an excellent hook for bass, used the same as a frog, either for trolling or casting.

Sizes, 2, 4 and 6. Price, each 10c
Sizes, 1-0 and 2-0. Price, each 12c

If by mail, postage extra, 1 cent.

Egg Shape Adjustable Wood Floats.

No. 6C8888 Egg Shaped Excelsior Wood Floats; painted in two colors and varnished; assorted. This float can be instantly adjusted to any depth water.

Size, inches	2	2¼	2½
Weight, per doz., ounces	8	12	15
Price, each	2c	3c	4c

If by mail, postage extra, per dozen, 6 to 15 cts.

Barrel Shape Cork Floats.

No. 6C8892 Barrel shape, best grade cork, well made. Painted in two colors.

Length, inches	2	3	4
Weight, ounces	3	4	6
Price, each	3c	7c	9c

If by mail, postage extra, 3 to 7 cents.

Brass Box Swivels.

No. 6C8895 Brass Box Swivels. For trolling spoon baits, etc. The length mentioned is the entire length.

No.	8	5	3
Length, inch	⅓	¾	1
Price, per dozen	14c	14c	14c
No.	1-0	2-0	3-0
Length, inches	1¼	1⅓	1¾
Price, per dozen	15c	21c	33c

If by mail, postage extra, per dozen, 2 to 3 cents.

Patent Spring Swivels.

No. 6C8896 Patent Spring Swivel. A broken hook or spoon may be instantly removed without untieing the line.

Nos.	8	4	1-0
Length, inches	⅞	1¼	1¾
Price, per dozen	30c	35c	40c

If by mail, postage extra, 2 to 3 cents per dozen.

Adjustable Sinkers.

No. 6C8898 Patent Adjustable Sinkers. These can be attached or detached by a single turn of the line.

Nos.	1	2	4	5	6
Length, inches	¾	1	1¼	1⅓	1¾
Weight, dozen, oz.	2	3	4	5	6
Price, per dozen	6c	7c	9c	11c	13c

If by mail, postage extra, 1 cent per ounce.

Split Shot Sinkers.

For light sinkers and fly casting when it is windy.

No. 6C8902 Split shot for sinkers, two dozen in wood box. Price, per dozen boxes, 30c; per box 3c

If by mail, postage extra, per box, 1 cent.

Mackinac Adjustable Screw Sinkers.

No. 1 No. 2 No. 3 No. 4

No. 6C8903 is adjustable by screwing the two parts together. Order by catalogue number and mention size wanted.

Nos.	1	2	3	4
Weight, dozen, ounces	1	2	3	5
Price, per dozen	12c	14c	16c	19c

If by mail, postage extra, 1 cent per ounce.

Cincinnati Bass Hooks, Snelled.

No. 6C8875 Cincinnati Bass Hooks. Double Gut, silk tied to best quality double gut, full length, and warranted the best hooks in the market for the money. Put up one-half dozen of a size in a patent metal holder. We cannot sell less than half dozen of a size.

Size No. 24 equal to No. 3, per dozen 18c
Size No. 23 equal to No. 2, per dozen 18c
Size No. 22 equal to No. 1, per dozen 18c
Size No. 21 equal to No. 1-0, per dozen 20c
Size No. 20 equal to No. 2-0, per dozen 22c
Size No. 19 equal to No. 3-0, per dozen 24c
Size No. 18 equal to No. 4-0, per dozen 26c
Size No. 17 equal to No. 5-0, per dozen 30c
Size No. 16 equal to No. 6-0, per dozen 32c

If by mail, postage extra, per dozen, 2 to 5 cents.

Our Aluminum Leader Box.

No. 6C8905 Our Aluminum Leader Box, 4 inches in diameter, with two felt pads for keeping the leaders moist, cannot rust, hinge cover, light and convenient to carry in the pocket. No fisherman should be without one, as leaders should always be kept moist when in use. Price 20c

If by mail, postage extra, 2 cents.

Our Standard Gut Leaders.

We have an entirely new and much superior line of gut leaders for this season. We carry a complete assortment of the highest grades in stock always. These leaders will not peel and weaken, but are made of selected gut and you run no risk of breakage and loss of sport. Imported from Italy or Spain. Leaders should be kept moist when in use.

Catalogue Number	L'g'th of Leader	Kind of Gut	Size for	Color	Price, Each
6C8906	3 feet	Single	Trout	Mist	3c
6C8906½	6 feet	Single	Trout	Mist	6c
6C8908	3 feet	Double	Trout	Mist	6c
6C8908½	6 feet	Double	Trout	Mist	12c
6C8916	3 feet	Double	Salm'n	Mist	20c
6C8916½	6 feet	Double	Salm'n	Mist	40c

If by mail, postage extra, 1 cent.

Our Wire Leaders.

No. 6C8919 A very strong and pliable leader, mounted with connecting link which enables fishermen to instantly attach or detach the bait, also fitted with swivel which prevents kinking of line and leader. Very desirable leader when fishing for pike, pickerel or other large fish having sharp jaws. Comes in one length only, namely, 12 inches; just the right length for bait casting. Price 12c

If by mail, postage extra, 1 cent.

Silkworm Gut Leaders.

Put up 100 in a bunch, for fishermen who make their own snelled hooks, flies and leaders.

No. 6C8920 Size 12, is 11 inches long, medium size. Price, per bunch 30c
No. 6C8920½ Size 8, is 12 inches long, heavy. Price, per bunch 75c

If by mail, postage extra, per bunch, 3 to 5c

TROUT FLIES.

Highest Grade Trout Flies.

Our line of Trout and Bass Flies has been selected with great care. We have carefully selected only such flies as we know from experience to be killers, and know that our flies cannot be excelled for beauty, quality and workmanship. We do not sell anything cheaper than an all silk body fly, knowing that the cheaper grades do not give satisfaction.

B GRADE is a Silk Body Fly, plain wings, finely finished, tied to full length clear gut and good quality hook.
Price, per dozen 30c
If by mail, postage extra, per dozen, 2 cents.

D GRADE is a Full Silk Body, Reversed Wing Fly and as good a fly as can be made, regardless of price. Is hand tied with silk, has hollow point imported English hooks of the highest grade; every fly made by an expert; tied to best quality clear round gut. Price, per dozen **50c**
If by mail, postage extra, per dozen, 2 cents.

NOTICE—When ordering, give size of hooks wanted and state whether B or D grade. **We cannot sell less than one-half dozen flies of one kind.**

	NAME	Size of Hooks
No. 6C8921	Rube Wood	6, 8 or 10
No. 6C8922	Professor	6, 8 or 10
No. 6C8923	Governor	6, 8 or 10
No. 6C8924	Golden Spinner	6, 8 or 10
No. 6C8925	Silver Doctor	6, 8 or 10
No. 6C8926	Seth Green	6, 8 or 10
No. 6C8927	Blue Bottle	6, 8 or 10
No. 6C8928	Cow Dung	6, 8 or 10
No. 6C8929	Queen of Waters	6, 8 or 10
No. 6C8930	King of Waters	6, 8 or 10
No. 6C8931	Grizzly King	6, 8 or 10
No. 6C8934	Brown Hackle	6, 8 or 10
No. 6C8935	Gray Hackle	6, 8 or 10
No. 6C8936	Coachman	6, 8 or 10
No. 6C8937	Royal Coachman	6, 8 or 10
No. 6C8939	Paramachenee Belle	6, 8 or 10
No. 6C8940	Montreal	6, 8 or 10
No. 6C8941	Black Gnat	6, 8 or 10
No. 6C8953	White Miller	6, 8 or 10
No. 6C8959	Yellow May	6, 8 or 10

Midget Trout Flies.

No. 6C8960 Midget, or Small Trout Flies. Superior midget flies, tied on sproat hooks Nos. 12 and 14, of which the following is a list. Silk body—silk tied:

Professor,	Gray Hackle,
Governor,	Coachman,
Golden Spinner,	Royal Coachman,
Cow Dung,	Black Gnat,
Queen of Waters,	White Miller,
Grizzly King,	Yellow May,
Brown Hackle,	March Brown.

The above selections are "killers."
Price, per dozen........................ 35c
If by mail, postage extra, per dozen, 2 cents.

Our Genuine Bucktail Bass Flies.

No. 6C8964 Our Bucktail Bass Flies are guaranteed to be made from genuine bucktail hair, all have hollow point hooks and first quality double gut, well tied, and are so constructed that the hair almost covers the entire hook, making one of the best bucktail bass flies ever produced. Made in sizes 1, 1-0 and 2-0. State which size wanted.
Price, each....... 12c
If by mail, postage extra, 2 cents.

No. 6C8965 Buck Tail Trout Flies. Sizes, 4, 6 and 8. State size wanted. Price......... 9c
If by mail, postage extra, 2 cents.

The trout fisherman often requires a pair of high boots. We quote a fine line of boots in our shoe catalogue.

SPOON AND ARTIFICIAL BAITS.

SIZES OF SPOON BAITS.

NOTE K—The spoons of spoon baits come in various lengths, and the following is a list showing the length of the spoon on baits from Nos. 1 to 8. They may vary a trifle either way, for no two manufacturers make them exactly alike.

Nos.	1	2	3	4	4½
Length, inches	1	1⅛	1¼	1½	1⅞
Nos.	4½	5	6	7	8
Length, inches	1⅞	2⅛	2⅜	2½	3⅛

American Spinner Bait.

No. 6C8967 Best Plated Spoon, one-half hammered, best material and a rapid spinner, for bass, pickerel, etc. Nos. 2, 3, 4 and 5. See Note K for sizes. Price, each.................. 12c
If by mail, postage extra, 2 cents.

Fluted Spoon Bait for Bass.

Fluted Trolling Spoon, full nickel plate, inside painted red, same shape spoon as Skinner's, and same size hook, feathered treble hook, an old, reliable, first class spoon bait. Take a piece of pork rind 3 inches long, ⅜ inch wide, cut it to look like a fish and fasten to one of the treble hooks and you have a good bass or pickerel bait. Order by catalogue number.

No. 6C8968 For small size fish, 1 to 3 pounds. Nos. 2, 3 and 4. Price 8c
No. 6C8968½ For medium size fish, 3 to 6 pounds. Nos. 4½, 4¾ and 5. Price 9c
No. 6C8968¾ For large size fish, 6 pounds and upward. Nos. 6, 7 and 8. Price......... 10c
If by mail, postage extra, 2 cents.

Skinner's Spoon Bait for Bass.

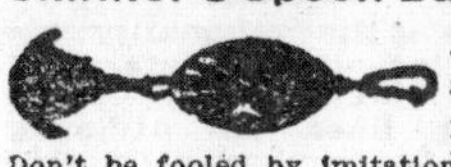

No. 6C8969 The Genuine Skinner Spoon. All have hollow point hooks. Don't be fooled by imitations. Every spoon bears maker's name.

Nos.	1	2	3	4	4½
Length, inches	1	1⅛	1¼	1½	1⅞
Nos.	4½	5	6	7	8
Length, inches	1⅞	2⅛	2⅜	2½	3⅛

Nos. 1, 2, 3, 4, 4½, 4¾, for black bass, trout, etc. Price, each.............. 15c
Nos. 5 and 6, for pickerel, pike, lake trout, etc. Price, each.............. 20c
Nos. 7 and 8, for muskallonge. Price, each.............. 25c
State size wanted. If by mail, postage extra, 3 cents.

The Q. C. Weedless Spoon Bait.

No. 6C8974 This is doubtless the best weedless spoon bait on the market. Fitted with brass box swivel, heavily plated, fluted spoon and single weighted weedless hook. This bait can be used alone or a frog or shiner can be attached to same with excellent results.

Sizes	4-0	5-0	6-0
Price, each	13c	14c	15c

If by mail, postage extra, 3 cents.

The Muskallonge or Tarpon Bait.

The herculean strength of this bait will tell its own story to the fisherman in pursuit of large gamy fish. For the St. Lawrence, the western lakes and rivers and the coast of Florida, they will fill the bill to perfection.

No. 6C8978 Fine Nickel Plated Spoon, treble hook, feathered, very best material.
2¾-inch Spoon, for 10 to 20 lb. fish, Price........................ 18c
3¼-inch Spoon, for 20 to 100 lb. fish. Price 23c
If by mail, postage extra, 3 cents.

The Delevan Spoon Bait.

No. 6C8988 A very popular spoon in Michigan and Wisconsin. Plate is brass, heavily nickel plated, fitted with two first quality removable hooks. Sizes 3, 4 and 5. Price, each........ 10c
If by mail, postage extra, 3 cents.

Our Spinning Coachman.

No. 6C8991 First quality, with 1¼ inch coppered or nickel plated spoon. No. 1 hook tied with double gut, nickel plated box swivel. Each bait comes with a coachman and two other popular bass flies mounted on a handsome enameled card. One of the best bass baits on the market. Price. 20c
If by mail, postage extra, 2 cents.

Our Special Lowe's Star Bait.

No. 6C8993 Oval shape, finished in two colors, the lower half gold and the upper half silver plated. Feathered treble hook, box swivel. An extra fine bait for bass, muskallonge and large, gamy fish. Try this bait. Nearly every customer who tries them buys more. The genuine is stamped Lowe.

Nos.	1-0	1	2	4	6
Length blade, inches	2¾	2¼	2	1¾	1
Price, each	40c	35c	35c	25c	25c

If by mail, postage extra, 3 cents.

Our Aluminum Muskallonge and Pickerel Bait.

This is the latest muskallonge, bass and pickerel bait; made of aluminum, on the principle of a wood auger, which causes it to be an excellent spinner in the water, resembling a fish.
No. 6C8994 For bass and pickerel, 2¼ inches long. Price........................ 25c
No. 6C8995 For muskallonge, 3¼ inches long. Price........................ 35c
If by mail, postage extra, 2 cents.

Our Bucktail Casting Spoon.

No. 6C8998 Our Genuine Bucktail Casting Spoon is made with Nos. 1, 2, 3 and 4 spoons. All have hollow point hooks of best quality, and these are without doubt the best casting spoons ever placed upon the market for pickerel and bass. Price 19c
If by mail, postage extra, 2 cents.

Luminous Tandem Spinner.

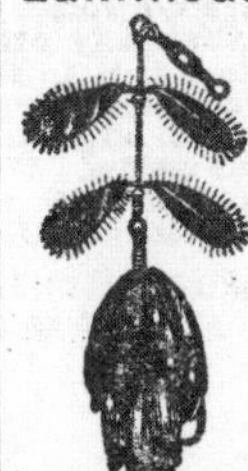

No. 6C9002 This Spinner is considered the most successful spinner used today for bass fishing. Blades revolve in opposite directions, giving a perfect imitation of a struggling minnow. This spinner is luminous, making it doubly attractive on dark days or in deep water. The blades are heavily nickel plated and the treble hook is heavily feathered, making a very handsome bait. When unsuccessful with other baits try a tandem spinner.
No. 1. Price.................. 30c
No. 2. Price.................. 35c
If by mail, postage extra, 2 cts.

Steel Pliers.

No. 6C9004 Steel Pliers, 4 inches long, weight 2 ounces. Every fisherman should have a pair in his tackle box to replace hooks on spoons. If a hook catches in clothes break it off.
Price, per pair.................. 10c
If by mail, postage extra, 3 cents.

Our Wood Casting Minnow.

No. 6C9006 This minnow is made of wood, the belly is painted with aluminum and the top is the color of a minnow, fitted with treble hooks, spinners and box swivel. The body is weighted so the minnow will always swim right side up, and is the latest minnow placed upon the market; an excellent casting bait. We do not advise using a minnow with more than 3 treble hooks, as too many hooks scare away the fish and become tangled.
Price..(If by mail, postage extra, 3 c)..... 35c

Our Phantom Minnow.

No. 6C9008 One of the most successful baits made. The body is made of silk, waterproofed, nicely mounted, assorted in blue, silver and brown colors. We claim our Phantom Minnow equal to any upon the market, regardless of price. Order by catalogue number and mention length of minnow wanted when ordering.

Sizes	1	2	3	4	5	6	8
Length, inches	2	2¼	2¾	3	3½	4	4½
Price, each	25c	25c	25c	28c	29c	32c	38c

If by mail, postage extra, 3 to 7 cents.

Our Porpoise Hide Phantom.

No. 6C9010 Same as the above silk phantom, except made of porpoise hide, which is very tough and strong and always holds its shape. Intended especially for large gamy fish. This minnow is fitted with extra strong hooks with heavy braided, non-corrosive wired mounting. Windings are of non-corrosive wire to guard against the sharp teeth of the fish. Two sizes only.
No. 5, 3½ inches long. Price, each....... 50c
No. 7, 4½ inches long. Price, each....... 60c
If by mail, postage extra, 5 cents.

RUBBER BAITS.

Excellent Substitutes where the Natural Bait Cannot Readily Be Found.

Shrimp Bait.

No. 6C9012 Shrimps, about 3 inches long.
Price.... 20c
If by mail, postage extra, 3 cents.

Helgamites.

No. 6C9014 Helgamite, or Dobson, soft rubber, with swivel. Price.... 17c
Postage extra, 3 cents.

Our Special Fly Minnow.

No. 6C9015 Fly Minnow, 1¾ inches long, a good imitation of a minnow, for still fishing. Price.................. 13c
If by mail, postage extra, 2 cents.

Grasshopper Bait.

No. 6C9019 Grasshopper, soft rubber, 1¾ inches long, quite natural. Price........... 12c
If by mail, postage extra, 1 cent.

Rubber Frogs.

No. 6C9020 Genuine Soft Rubber Frogs, colored as natural as life. An excellent bait for "splashing" or casting. Tied with strong gut loop to treble hook. Colored green and brown. About 1¾ inches long. Price.................. 20c
If by mail, postage extra, 3 cents.

Floating Meadow Frog.

No. 6C9021 Made of satin cork, very artistically painted, has a lifelike appearance. The treble hook is secured to the belly of the frog on a spiral eye, enabling fishermen to change hooks when desired. This treble hook insures hooking your fish when he strikes. Entire length, 3 inches. Price.................. 23c
If by mail, postage extra, 4 cents.

Soft Rubber Angle Worms.

No. 6C9022 Angle Worms; a perfect imitation of red, live worms; about 3 inches long.
Price........ 15c
If by mail, postage extra, 2 cents.

Soft Rubber Froggies.

No. 6C9023 Made of soft, pliable rubber, with string gut loop and treble hook, about 1 inch long. A good lasting bait. Naturally colored.
Price.................. 15c
If by mail, postage extra, 2 cents.

Shakespeare Revolution Bait.

No. 6C9032 This is one of the most popular baits on the market. It is made entirely of aluminum, with two paddles and three treble hooks. The body, head and paddles revolve rapidly when the bait is drawn through the water, resembling a fish, making a very attractive lure. This bait has been on the market but a short time, but its killing qualities has made it one of the most popular baits now on the market. Price.................. 40c
If by mail, postage extra, 2 cents.

Our Sure Catch Minnow Trap.

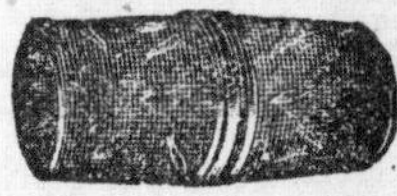

No. 6C9033 Our Sure Catch Minnow Trap is made of galvanized sheet steel and wire screening with cone shaped ends, and so constructed that it may be separated in the center and one end can be telescoped into the other. When baited with stale bread, meat or other bait, the bait is exposed to view through the wire screen and when the minnows, crawfish or other small fish once get into this trap it is difficult for them to find their way out. The Sure Catch Minnow Trap is 18 inches long, 10 inches in diameter and weighs about 3½ pounds. Price 75c

Keystone Fish Stringers.

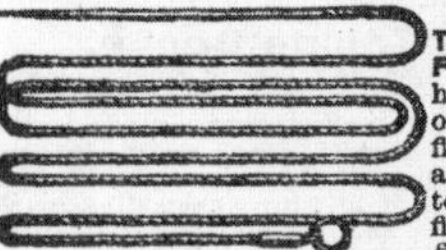

No. 6C9036 The Keystone Fish Stringer has a needle at one end to string fish and a ring at the other end to loop the first fish. After the first fish is looped, you may string as many as the string will hold. The Keystone is 6 feet long. Price........ 15c
If by mail, postage extra, 2 cents.

Chain Fish Stringers.

No. 6C9038 Chain Fish Stringers, brass links, heavy nickel plated, strong and durable; will hold 100 pounds of fish and not break. Price, 15c
If by mail, postage extra, 3 cents.

Fish Spears.

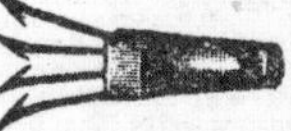

No. 6C9046 Has four tines, 2¾ inches long, with socket for pole.
Price.................. 15c
If by mail, postage extra, 6 cents.

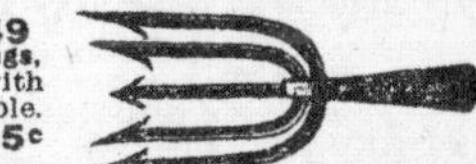

No. 6C9049 Has five prongs, 5 inches long, with socket for pole.
Price...... 45c
If by mail, postage extra, 18 cents.

Our Special Hand Forged Spear.

The best spear on the market.

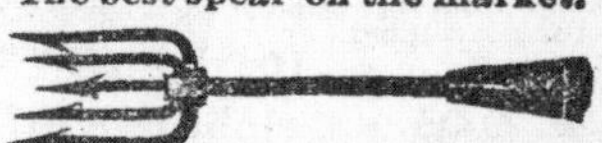

No. 6C9050 Hand Made Fish Spear, all best steel except socket and wedge; beards of each tine made on solid shank, screws into socket and makes its own thread in wood (of handle); the outside tines can be removed if smaller spear is wanted at any time by putting in larger wedge. Width, about 4¾ to 4½ inches; entire length of tines, about 6½ inches; entire length, 22 inches. Weight, about 1¾ pounds. None better. Price. $1.40
If by mail, postage extra, 26 cents.

No. 6C9052 Is same as No. 6C9050 but lighter weight, weighing 8 ounces. Total length, 14½ inches; length of tines, 4½ inches; width across tines, 4 inches. A good hand made spear with threaded shank to screw into the handle and nickeled ferrule. Price........ 65c
If by mail, postage extra, 22 cents.

Our Automatic Gaff Hook.

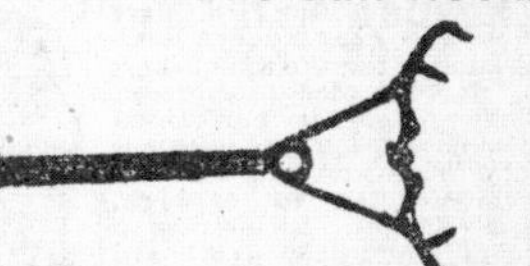

A Gaff Hook is a necessary part of every fisherman's outfit. It possesses numerous advantages over the landing net when handling large game fish. Our automatic gaff hook makes it an easy matter to land your fish in a boat, it only being necessary to reach out and touch the fish, the hook will close automatically and the fish is yours. This gaff hook can be opened by hand or by the foot, is easily operated, positively insures your getting your fish if you can touch him with the hook.

No. 6C9053 No. 1 Gaff Hook, finely nickel plated for fish 15 to 20 pounds, fitted with 30-inch handle, jaws have 7-inch spread.
Price $1.45
If by mail, postage extra, 25 cents.

Tackle Boxes.

This is a very practical and ornamental box, made of heavy tin, double seamed and soldered, japanned and striped, with carrying handle, and will stand hard service.

No. 6C9060 Single Outfit Tackle Box, has three compartments and one tray for tackle. Size, 10½ inches long, 5½ inches wide and 4 inches deep. Price....................55c
If by mail, postage extra, 38 cents.

No. 6C9062 Stock Tackle Box, has two large compartments and two trays, space for large reel, any amount of lines, hooks, etc. They must be seen to be appreciated. All are made finely finished, gilt stripes and ornamentation, with carrying handle. Size, 12 inches long, 5½ inches wide and 5¼ inches deep.
Price........70c
Postage extra, 65

Fly Books

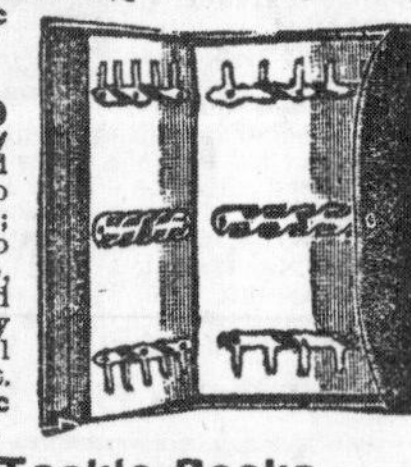

No. 6C9070 Empire City Fly Book; with bar and center clips, two heavy envelopes; imitation morocco durable cover. Size, 6x3½ inches and will hold twenty flies. This size will fit any coat pocket.
Price........25c
Postage extra, 4c.

Seroco Tackle Books.

No. 6C9071 Seroco Tackle Book. Made to hold snelled hooks or flies. This book has durable pebbled leather cover, made with pocketbook fastening. Size, 6x3½ inches. Has four sheets of yellow parchment with bar and center clips to hold four dozen flies, with two flannel leaves for drying, has also deep pocket suitable for gut leaders. This is a neat, durable book, just the right size for the pocket.
Price....................50c
If by mail, postage extra, 6 cents.

Our Bray Style Tackle Book.

No. 6C9072 The cover of this book is heavy calf leather, lined with soft glove leather, has two leather pockets, also two celluloid envelopes. This book has celluloid leaves. Bray style spring in center, holds four dozen flies. In addition it has two flannel leaves for drying flies or keeping leaders moist. Size, 3¾x7 inches, has single strap fastening, all leaves are celluloid, is undoubtedly the best tackle book on the market. Price..........$1.25
If by mail, postage extra, 8 cents.

Bait Boxes.

All our Bait Boxes are of tin, neatly painted and finished.

No. 6C9079 The Padlock Bait Box, 3½ inches wide, 3 inches deep, shaped very much like a fish basket, with a top cover and a safety pin on the back so it can be pinned to the coat—no losing of bait or upsetting of bait box.
Price....................10c
Postage extra, 5 cents.

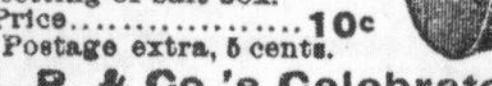

S., R. & Co.'s Celebrated Minnow Buckets.

No. 6C9085 Handiest, lightest, most noiseless and most complete minnow bucket ever put on the market. Free circulation of air and water, attracts the fish to it, thereby making good fishing around the bucket. If desired to keep the minnows fresh while in transit put a little ice in the bottom of your bucket. When you arrive at the lake drop the inside bucket into the water, where it can be kept on the surface by a string tied to the boat. The inside bucket is made of wire screening and so open that it affords full flow of fresh water all the time, bringing to your minnows the insect food upon which they exist, as well as attracting other fish to it. Weight, 3 and 3½ pounds.

Buckets for holding........	8 quarts	10 quarts
Price	70c	90c

Midget Minnow and Frog Bucket.

No. 6C9086 Our Two-Quart Minnow and Frog Bucket is an ideal bucket for the lone fisherman. Same is nicely lacquered in deep blue, has perforated hinged cover, self locking, bail handle. This bucket is 6 inches in diameter, 4½ inches high, weighs 9 ounces. Tie a string to the handle and drop overboard and your bait will remain fresh. Small, strong, neat, efficient.
Price..........................18c
If by mail, postage extra, 12 cents.

Our Universal Live Nets, to Keep Fish Fresh When Caught.

No. 6C9088 These nets are made with wire hoops and tan colored netting, are collapsible and take up very little room. An excellent thing to keep fish alive and fresh when caught.
Price, 10 inches diameter...28c
Price, 12 inches diameter...33c
Price, 14 inches diameter...38c
If by mail, postage extra, 18 cents.

Minnow Dip Nets.

No. 6C9089 Minnow Dip Nets made of No. 20 6-ply Sea Island cotton, superior in strength and durability to linen nets and far less expensive. Prices are for nets only; do not include frames.
Price, 16 inches deep....................17c
Price, 18 inches deep....................20c
Price, 20 inches deep....................25c
Price, 24 inches deep....................30c
Price, 30 inches deep....................40c
Price, 36 inches deep....................55c
If by mail, postage extra, 5 cents.

Linen Landing Nets.

No. 6C9090 Price is for netting only, and does not include the frame. For landing large fish.
Price, 20 inches deep....................15c
Price, 24 inches deep....................20c
Price, 30 inches deep....................30c
If by mail, postage extra, 5 cents.

Our Chicago Landing Net, 85 Cents.

No. 6C9091 Our Complete Landing Net, with solid round ring, fitted with 18-inch net, ⅝-inch mesh and 4-foot jointed handle, finely finished.
Price, complete....................85c
If by mail, postage extra, 27 cents.

Bucket and Aquarium Net.

No. 6C9093 Our Minnow Net is designed to take minnows out of a bucket, which is more convenient than taking them out by hand; this net is made with a round frame, short handle, and can easily be carried in the coat pocket. Price..........18c
If by mail, postage extra, 4 cents.

The Genuine Kelso Folding Net Ring, Complete with Net.

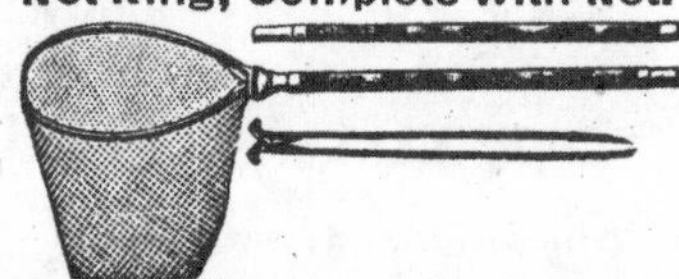

Complete with net and handle. This is undoubtedly the best folding net on the market. Can be taken apart in a moment's time, is very light and strong, being made of the best tempered steel and the ring will positively not turn when in use as it is securely held by a patent lock joint. No parts to get lost, ring can be folded without moving the net. Put up in neat partitioned cloth bag.

No. 6C9095 No. 1 Ring, 14x15 inches, full nickel plated, mounted with a square bottom linen waterproof net, fitted with 4-foot jointed bamboo handle. Price....................$1.80
If by mail, postage extra, 22 cents.

Fishing Hats.

No. 6C9098

No. 6C9099

No. 6C9098 Collapsible Brown Muslin, green lined, rolls up and may be carried flat in the pocket. On a windy day pin it fast to coat collar. The finest thing out, cool and light.
Price....................20c

No. 6C9099 Same as the above, with a mosquito shield, a mosquito proof hat.
Price....................40c
If by mail, postage extra, 4 cents.

Mosquito and Bee Head Nets, 28 Cents.

No. 6C9100 To be worn over the hat or cap. Made of good tarletan. Fitted with four light steel springs, bottom weighted with shot so as to set close to shoulders. Can be folded up and put in an ordinary coat pocket.
Price....................28c
If by mail, postage extra, 7c.
Everybody intending to camp or fish should have a Mosquito Head Net.

Our White Canvas Fishing Hat, 28 Cents.

No. 6C9101 This Hat is made from white canvas, round crown, 4-inch brim, stiffened, and is so constructed that it may be rolled up and carried in the pocket; one of the best fishing hats ever made. Mention size wanted. Price.......28c
If by mail, postage extra, 6 cents.

Trout Baskets with Patent Metal Fastening.

Our baskets are made from select French willow, very strong and light.

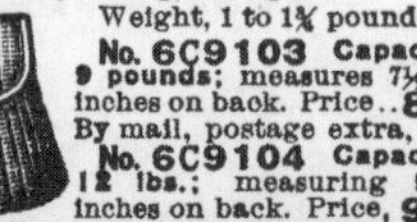

Weight, 1 to 1¾ pounds.

No. 6C9103 Capacity, 9 pounds; measures 7½x12 inches on back. Price..80c
By mail, postage extra, 15c.

No. 6C9104 Capacity, 12 lbs.; measuring 9x13 inches on back. Price, 90c
If by mail, postage extra, 20 cents.

Trout Basket Straps.

No. 6C9109 Seroco Patent Trout Basket Strap, the best trout basket strap made, made of webbing and leather, leaves the arms free. See illustration opposite.
Price....................22c
If by mail, postage extra, 4 cents.

Genuine Agate Rod Tips.

No. 6C9122 Agate Tips do not wear out a line as fast as metal tips and make line run more smoothly. Made for rod tips of the following diameters:

Size No.	¼	½	¾	1
Diameter, inch	3-32	4-32	5-32	6-32

Price, each....................50c
If by mail, postage extra, 2 cents.

Genuine Agate Guides for Rods.

No. 6C9124 Does not wear out the line like metal guides and makes it run smoothly. No. 7 is for tip joint, No. 6 is for middle joint, No. 5 is for grip joint. Price, each....................50c
If by mail, postage extra, 2 cents.

Brower's Reel Seat.

No. 6C9142 Brower's Patent Reel Holder, can be applied to any rod. Just the thing for Calcutta and Japanese rods; no cutting or fitting required. Nickel plated. Price..........25c
If by mail, postage extra, 3 cents.

Foard's Disgorger.

No. 6C9146 No. 2 Foard's Disgorger, single end. Price....................10c
If by mail, postage extra, 3 cents.

Acme Spring Balances.

WEIGH YOUR FISH.

No. 6C9150 Acme Spring Balance, weighs from 1 to 10 lbs. by ¼ lbs. A good scale with tare allowance. Every pair warranted perfect. Price......27c
If by mail, postage extra, 5 cents.

Set Line Snaps.

No. 6C9153 These snaps save tieing on your hooks, permit hooks to be changed instantly, more than save their cost in the price of staging they save. Price, per dozen, set of 12 rings and 12 snaps....................15c
If by mail, postage extra, 2 cents.

The Lightning Fish Scaler.

No. 6C9166 The best and most rapid scaler on the market, neatly made, tinned to prevent rusting, stamped out of one solid piece of sheet steel, it simply rubs the scales off, also excellent for shredding cod fish, preparing Hamburger steak, etc.
Price....................10c
If by mail, postage extra, 6 cents.

Our Rival Camp Stove.

No. 6C9170 Perfect baker, good heater. This stove is made of heavy sheet steel, has heavy half-inch rolls all around bottom line of body, the corners are well mitered, are well braced inside; also has half-inch rolls around the doors to stiffen them, strong steel latches for each door. The cooking top is supported by strong angle braces which connect with the side of the stove, thereby preventing warpage from the weight of cooking vessels. The pipe collar is in the corner, increasing the space for top cooking. The bake oven is corrugated to prevent warpage, and an air space formed by a double wall is made between the fire and the oven; this prevents burning of food in the oven. The stove pipe is nested in six short lengths, so as to pack inside of either the firebox or oven. This stove burns wood; fire is placed on the ground; burns equally well inside or outside of the tent; is an excellent heater; will hold fire all night and keep the tent very comfortable; is undoubtedly the best stove of this kind on the market. The stove is not only for campers, but good for contractors, surveyors, cattlemen, people in all occupations who are compelled to stay in the open air and move from place to place. Length of stove, 29 inches; width, 16 inches; height, 14 inches. Size of oven, height, 9 inches; depth, 16 inches; width, 12 inches. Size of pot holes on top, 7 inches. Weight, crated for shipment, about 40 pounds. Price, $3.15

For a complete line of Blue Flame Oil Stoves, hard and soft coal Cooking and Heating Stoves see our Stove Department.

Metal Telescope Collapsing Cup.

Our Fine Metal Collapsing Cup. It can be folded into a very small space and carried in vest pocket. Neat and substantial, nicely nickel plated and the body fits into the cover. Every sportsman should have one. Small size holds about 4 or 5 tablespoonfuls, large size about size of an ordinary tumbler.

No. 6C9173 Small size. Price.......12c
No. 6C9174 Medium size. Price.....18c
No. 6C9175 Large size. Price.......25c
If by mail, postage extra, 3 to 5 cents.

Hunter's Drinking Cups.

No. 6C9200 Soft, White Rubber Drinking Cup, tumbler shape, will hold about as much as a common table tumbler. Flexible, and can be folded and put in a vest pocket. Price..............13c

No. 6C9203 Same as the above, but made in canoe shape. This cup can also be folded and carried in a vest pocket. Price..........12c
If by mail, postage extra, 3 cents.

SEINES AND NETS.

SEE PRICES ON FOLLOWING PAGE.

Our Seines and Nets are all made under our own supervision, and are guaranteed to be the best in material and workmanship. Our factory is fully equipped, and we are constantly adding improvements, and are able to turn out better nets than any other house. Our seines are all made to order, but we can fill orders two to six days after we receive them, according to the orders we have on hand when we receive your order.

Our terms are cash in full with the order in all cases. You will save delay by complying with our terms. We make these goods specially to your order, and if made as ordered they cannot be returned under any circumstances. We cannot ship seines C. O. D.

WE GUARANTEE QUALITY AND WILL CHEERFULLY REFUND YOUR MONEY IF GOODS ARE NOT AS REPRESENTED.

Lake and River Drag Seines.

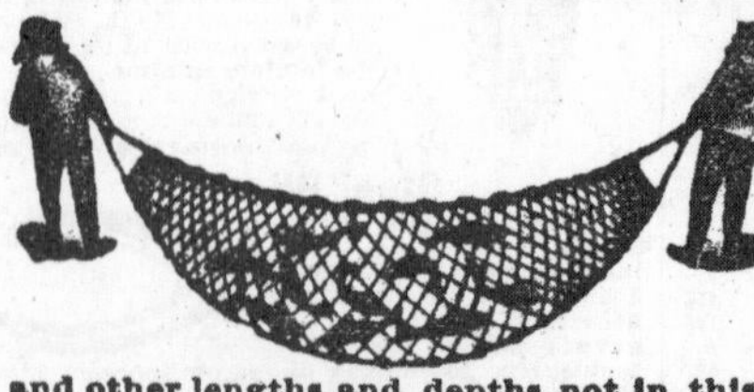

Made of the best quality cotton twine, all complete, with buoys, sinkers, etc., except hauling lines. In ordering seines be particular to give catalogue number, size mesh, length wanted and price. Special prices are given upon request for large lake seines and other lengths and depths not in this list. These seines all have top lines, ¼-inch manila rope, tarred, and bottom lines, ¼-inch manila rope, tarred, doubled, with reversed twist to prevent rolling.

NOTE—A seine mesh is diamond shaped, and a 1-inch square mesh measures 1 inch on each of the four sides. A 1½-inch square mesh measures 1½ inches on each of the four sides, etc. One inch square mesh is 2 inches stretched mesh; 1½-inch square mesh is 3 inches stretched mesh.

1-IN. 1-IN. This illustration shows a 1 INCH SQUARE MESH 1-IN. 1-IN.

The following seines are hung with leads, floats and lines ready for use, except hauling lines. Compare our prices and quality with other houses and you will find that we beat them all.

Weight: A 50-foot seine weighs about 20 pounds; a 100-foot seine weighs about 40 pounds; a 150-foot seine weighs about 80 pounds; a 300-foot seine weighs about 180 pounds.

SEINES AND NETS.

See description on preceding page.

PERFECTION TAPERED DRAG SEINES.

12-Thread Cotton Seine Twine—Square Mesh.

We cannot ship seines C. O. D. **Allow 2 to 6 days for us to make and ship your seine.**

Catalogue No.	Length, feet	Depth, Center, feet	Depth, at ends, feet	1-inch Mesh, Price	1¼-inch Mesh, Price	1½-inch Mesh, Price	2-inch Mesh, Price
6C9685	20	4	3	$0.77	$0.67	$0.64	$0.56
6C9686	30	4	3	1.16	.99	.96	.83
6C9687	40	5	4	1.79	1.51	1.42	1.21
6C9688	50	5	4	2.23	1.88	1.77	1.51
6C9689	60	6	5	2.99	2.50	2.34	1.96
6C9690	72	7	6	4.06	3.33	3.12	2.57
6C9691	90	8	7	5.55	4.52	4.18	3.43
6C9692	100	8	7	6.17	5.02	4.64	3.81
6C9693	120	10	8	8.87	7.20	6.68	5.45
6C9694	150	12	10	12.73	10.20	9.41	7.54

16-Thread Cotton Seine Twine—Square Mesh.

We cannot ship seines C. O. D. **Allow 2 to 6 days for us to make and ship your seine.**

Catalogue No.	Length, feet	Depth, Center, feet	Depth, at ends, feet	1-inch Mesh, Price	1¼-inch Mesh, Price	1½-inch Mesh, Price	2-inch Mesh, Price
6C9699	20	4	3	$0.91	$0.77	$0.68	$0.60
6C9700	30	4	3	1.37	1.16	1.03	.90
6C9701	40	5	4	2.13	1.79	1.54	1.31
6C9702	50	5	4	2.67	2.23	1.94	1.65
6C9703	60	6	5	3.65	3.02	2.58	2.15
6C9704	72	7	6	5.03	4.09	3.46	2.84
6C9706	100	8	7	7.63	6.19	5.21	4.25
6C9707	120	10	8	10.95	8.89	7.48	6.11
6C9709	180	12	10	19.16	15.33	12.79	10.20
6C9710	200	14	10	22.76	18.10	15.06	11.94
6C9712	300	14	10	34.14	27.15	22.60	17.92

Perfection Straight Seines.

The depths given **are straight from end to end** and do not taper. **Hung with leads and floats.** Made of **best soft laid twine. Send cash in full with order. Seines or netting cannot be returned if sent as ordered. Expect a delay of from two to five days.**

NOTE—All our seines are square mesh.

Mesh, inches.	No. 6C9716 Price, per running yard. 12-thread—Soft. Sq. Mesh. 1	1¼	1½	2 & 3	No. 6C9717 Price, running yd. 16-thread-Soft Sq. Mesh. 1	1¼	1½	2 & 3
6 ft. deep	16c	14c	12c	11c	20c	16c	14c	12c
8 ft. deep	20c	16c	15c	12c	24c	20c	16c	14c
10 ft. deep	24c	20c	18c	15c	30c	24c	21c	16c
12 ft. deep	28c	22c	21c	16c	35c	28c	23c	18c
14 ft. deep	30c	25c	22c	18c	39c	30c	26c	20c

Lake or River Drag Seines, made of **Woodbury's best white** cotton, soft laid seine twine. **No better seine made** at any price. Hung with leads, floats and line ready for use. Square mesh. These seines are straight from end to end and do not taper. All complete and ready for use. **We cannot ship seines C. O. D.**

No. 6C9721 9-thread medium laid twine.

Length	Depth	¾-inch Mesh Price	1-inch Mesh Price	1¼-inch Mesh Price	1½-inch Mesh Price
20 feet	4 feet	$1.28	$0.72	$0.62	$0.53
30 feet	5 feet	2.23	1.20	1.07	.91
40 feet	6 feet	3.40	1.76	1.54	1.29
50 feet	7 feet	4.76	2.44	2.13	1.76
60 feet	8 feet	6.40	3.18	2.75	2.26

No. 6C9722 12-thread soft laid twine.

Length	Depth	¾-inch Mesh Price	1-inch Mesh Price	1¼-inch Mesh Price	1½-inch Mesh Price
20 feet	4 feet	$1.56	$0.83	$0.70	$0.67
30 feet	5 feet	2.72	1.42	1.19	1.12
40 feet	6 feet	4.20	2.12	1.74	1.62
50 feet	7 feet	5.92	2.95	2.41	2.23
60 feet	8 feet	8.12	3.87	3.13	2.89
75 feet	8 feet	9.84	4.83	3.90	3.61

No. 6C9723 16-thread soft laid twine.

Length	Depth	¾-inch Mesh Price	1-inch Mesh Price	1¼-inch Mesh Price	1½-inch Mesh Price
20 feet	4 feet	$1.88	$0.98	$0.83	$0.73
30 feet	5 feet	3.44	1.71	1.43	1.23
40 feet	6 feet	5.36	2.58	2.12	1.81
50 feet	7 feet	7.60	3.64	2.95	2.51
60 feet	8 feet	10.28	4.80	3.88	3.26
75 feet	8 feet	12.80	5.98	4.84	4.07

Cotton Seine Netting.

This netting is intended for fishermen who wish to repair or make their own nets. Price quoted is for the netting only and does not include the floats, leads or lines. This netting is made of white seine twine. When ordering, be sure to give the depth, size of mesh and catalogue number of netting desired. We can furnish any depth desired.

No. 6C9727 Cotton Netting No. 12, soft or medium twine, 1-inch square mesh or larger. Price, per pound.............**31c**

No. 6C9728 Cotton Netting No. 16, soft twine, 1-inch square mesh or larger. Price, per pound.....................**29c**

There are approximately 37 square feet of netting, hung measurement, in a pound of netting, 1-inch square mesh, made of No. 12 twine. There are about 31 square feet, hung measurement, in netting made of No. 16 twine with 1-inch square mesh. In netting made of No. 12 twine, 1½-inch square mesh, there are about 64 square feet, hung measurement. In a pound of netting, 16-thread, 1½-inch square mesh, there are about 50 square feet of netting, hung measurement.

Don't fail to state the depth and size of mesh of netting wanted.

Perfection Creek Seines. All fitted with floats and sinkers.

No.	Lengths	1-2 in. center, 1 in. at ends.	4 Ft. Deep	5 Ft. Deep	6 Ft. Deep	7 Ft. Deep
6C9735	10 ft.		$0.46	$0.54	$0.61	$0.69
6C9736	15 ft.		.69	.81	.92	1.04
6C9737	20 ft.		.93	1.08	1.23	1.38
6C9738	25 ft.		1.15	1.35	1.54	1.73
6C9739	30 ft.		1.38	1.65	1.88	2.10

Each end of a creek seine is of 1-inch square mesh, No. 9 twine; **and one-third the length of the seine in center is** ½-inch square mesh, No. 14-6 twine. **When ordering seines give size and price as well as catalogue number. Seines and netting cannot be returned if sent as ordered. We cannot ship seines C. O. D.**

Perfection Minnow Seines.

We cannot ship Seines C. O. D.

These minnow seines are hung complete with leads and floats, made in ⅜-inch, ¼-inch and ½-inch square mesh. Prices on other lengths or depths quoted upon application. When ordering give catalogue number, length, depth and size of mesh. Minnow seine ⅜ and ¼-inch mesh are made of No. 20-6 twine. Minnow seines with ½-inch square mesh are made of 14-6 twine. We do not ship minnow seines C. O. D.

Number	Depth Feet	Size Square Mesh	L'gth 10 feet	L'gth 15 feet	L'gth 20 feet	L'gth 25 feet	L'gth 30 feet
6C9740A	3	⅜-inch	$0.69	$1.04	$1.38	$1.73	$2.10
6C9740B	4	⅜-inch	.87	1.30	1.74	2.18	2.63
6C9740C	5	⅜-inch	1.05	1.58	2.10	2.63	3.14
6C9746D	3	¼-inch	1.13	1.71	2.26	2.83	3.38
6C9746E	4	¼-inch	1.45	2.19	2.91	3.64	4.36
6C9746H	5	¼-inch	1.77	2.67	3.56	4.44	5.33
6C9752I	3	½-inch	.49	.73	.97	1.21	1.46
6C9752J	4	½-inch	.60	.90	1.20	1.50	1.80
6C9752K	5	½-inch	.72	1.07	1.43	1.79	2.13

Minnow Netting.

Minnow Netting, made of cotton twine. **The prices are for the netting only; not rigged with sinkers, floats or lines.** Price is by the running yard, stretched measure. If you wish to make a 50-yard seine it will require 75 yards of netting. **Not sent C. O. D. and cannot be returned if sent as ordered.**

Catalogue Number	Size, Square Mesh	Per Yard 3 Feet Deep	Per Yard 4 Feet Deep	Per Yard 5 Feet Deep	Per Yard 6 Feet Deep
6C9755A	¼-incb	21c	27c	33c	38c
6C9755B	⅜-inch	12c	15c	19c	22c
6C9755C	½-inch	7c	10c	12c	14c
6C9755D	¾-inch	6c	8c	10c	12c

Common Sense Minnow Seines.

Common Sense Minnow Seines, ⅛-inch mesh. Made of woven netting, similar to mosquito netting, but of much heavier material. Just the thing to catch bait minnows. Hung with leads, floats, etc., ready for use. **All these nets are 4 feet deep. We cannot furnish any other depth.**

Catalogue No.	Long feet	Deep feet	Price	Catalogue No.	Long feet	Deep feet	Price
6C9758A	4	4	19c	6C9758E	15	4	$0.69
6C9758B	6	4	28c	6C9758F	20	4	.92
6C9758C	10	4	46c	6C9758G	25	4	1.15
6C9758D	12	4	56c	6C9758H	30	4	1.38

Common Sense Netting.

No. 6C9759 Common Sense Netting only, without floats, leads or lines, made only 4 feet deep, ⅛-inch mesh. **We cannot furnish this any other depth.** Price, per yard..............**11c**

Perfection Brook and Creek Funnel Nets.

Seines and Nets cannot be returned if sent as ordered. We cannot ship Seines C. O. D.

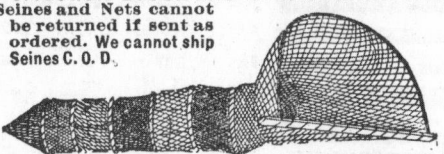

Our New Brook and Creek Funnel Nets, made expressly for fishing in brooks or small streams. The first or large hoop is made D shape to set flat on the bottom of the stream. **These nets are set in the stream and require no wings. Will catch and hold all medium size fish. These nets weigh about 4½ lbs.**

We cannot ship Seines C. O. D. Catalogue No.	Style of Throat	Height of Mouth	Width of Mouth	Length	Number of Hoops	Size of Twine	Size Mesh Front	Size Mesh Middle	Size Mesh Tail	Price
		Ft.	Ft.	Ft		No.	In.	In.	In.	
6C9760	Double	1¼	3	6	8	9	1¼	¾	⅝	$0.58
6C9761	Double	1¾	3½	7	9	9	1¼	¾	⅝	.73
6C9762	Double	1¾	4½	7	9	16-12	1¼	¾	⅝	1.08
6C9763	Double	1⅝	5	8	9	16	1½	¾	⅝	1.14

The Perfection Peerless Fyke or Hoop Net.

Send cash with order. We cannot ship Nets C. O. D.

Lengths which we give on wings are for each wing. **Hoops** are on outside of netting, thus greatly saving the same. **Made of best quality cotton twine.** Hung ready for use. Netting can be furnished without hoops to your order if desired. **Expect a delay of from two to five days.** Cannot be returned if made as ordered.

Wts. 2 ft. 10 lbs.
Wts. 2½ ft. 12 lbs.
Wts. 3 ft. 20 lbs.
Wts. 4 ft. 25 lbs.
Wts. 5 ft. 35 lbs.
Wts. 6 ft. 46 lbs.

No.	Style Throat.	Height, Mouth	Length of Net	Number of Hoops	L'gth Right Wing	Length Left Wing	Size of Twine	Size of Mesh, Inches Square: Front	Middle	Tail	White Twine Price
		ft	ft		ft	ft	No				
6C9765	Single....	2	6	4	6	6	9	¾	¾	¾	$1.27
6C9766	Single....	3	10	6	9	9	24	1¼	1¼	1¼	2.02
6C9768	Double. .	2½	8	6	6	6	16	1	1	1	1.87
6C9769	Double...	3	10	6	9	9	24	1¼	1¼	1¼	2.10
6C9770	Double.:	4	16	7	12	12	24	2	1¾	1½	2.91
6C9771	Double...	4½	18	8	15	15	24	2½	2	1½	3.81
6C9772	Double...	5	18	8	15	15	28	2½	2	1½	3.89
6C9773	Double...	6	18	8	20	20	28	2½	2	1½	5.59

For Fyke Nets made of tarred twine, add one-fourth of the above prices. When hoops are not wanted, deduct one-fifth from above prices.

NOTE. We make all kinds of fish nets to order. If you will fully describe what you want and send diagram of shape, we will quote prices on the style and mesh you wish. They cannot be returned when made as ordered.

PERFECTION FUNNEL NETS, WITHOUT WINGS.

Same style as above, but have no wings. With hoops complete. Made of the best quality cotton twine. When ordering nets give size, price and catalogue number, to avoid error. Expect a delay of from two to five days.

Cannot be returned if sent as ordered and we cannot ship C. O. D. Description: No.	Style Throat	Weight, lbs.	Height Mouth	Length of Net	Number Hoops	Size of Twine	Size of Mesh, Inches Square: Front	Middle	Tail	Price
			ft.	ft		No	in.	in.	in.	
6C9780	Single...	7	2	6	4	9	¾	¾	¾	$0.77
6C9781	Single...	10	3	10	6	24	1¼	1¼	1¼	1.46
6C9783	Double..	9	2½	8	6	16	1	1	1	1.43
6C9784	Double..	15	3	10	6	24	1¼	1¼	1¼	1.54
6C9785	Double..	20	4	16	7	24	2	1¾	1½	2.22
6C9786	Double..	25	4½	18	8	24	2½	2	1½	2.84
6C9787	Double..	30	5	18	8	28	2½	2	1½	2.92
6C9788	Double..	35	6	18	8	28	2½	2	1½	4.07

The Seroco Flat Bottom Steel Boat, $26.00.

The best boat ever made for shooting, fishing or pleasure. Wooden boats are a thing of the past. Uncle Sam does not build wooden warships nowadays, nor are ocean liners built of wood. One good steel boat will outlast six ordinary wood boats, furthermore our steel boat is non-sinkable, non-leakable, it does not expand or contract, it is non-rustable, being made of **Apollo galvanized steel, painted with silver "pegamoid," the preparation with which our steel navy is painted. Our steel boat being properly built, will slide through the water with one-third less friction than a wooden boat of the same dimensions, has 50 per cent more bouyancy than a wood boat and will last forever.**

There are various kinds of steel boats on the market and after experimenting with various makes, we are satisfied that in our Seroco Steel Boat we are giving our customers greater value and better satisfaction than we could possibly do in offering them any other make of boat. This boat has light draft suitable for shallow water, is not as easily capsized as a wooden boat, and if capsized, will float all passengers. Our Seroco Boat has an extra heavy steel bottom and has three oak strips running full length, one in center and one on each side to protect boat from rocks and rough usage. **This boat will not warp, cannot leak, cannot rot, never needs repairs, has air tight chambers at each end. Length, 12 feet.** Width amidship, 41½ inches. Depth amidship, 12 inches. Height of bow, 15 inches. Height of stern, 15 inches. Fitted with three seats. Distance between ribs, 5 inches. Weight, about 100 pounds; crated, about 135 pounds.

No. 6C9808 Price of boat in natural wood finish, including one pair of 6½-foot ash oars fitted with oar locks.............................**$26.00**

These boats are shipped from our factory at Detroit, Mich., and take four times first class freight rate.

PERFECTION LINEN GILL NETTING.

The best linen netting for gill nets or for inside of trammel nets, made of best silver gray, 3-cord linen twine. Any depth required. Mention depth when ordering. This netting is for gill or set nets, and not for drag seines, the twine being too small for such use. **Cannot be returned when made to order.**

No. 6C9810 Size of Twine	1-inch square mesh, per lb.	1¼-inch square mesh, per lb.	1½-inch square mesh, per lb.	1¾-inch square mesh, per lb.	2-inch square mesh, per lb.
18 x 3 cord	$1.52	$1.44	$1.38	$1.34	$1.29
20 x 3 cord	1.61	1.53	1.48	1.43	1.38
25 x 3 cord	1.75	1.67	1.61	1.57	1.52
30 x 3 cord	1.89	1.81	1.75	1.71	1.66
35 x 3 cord	2.19	2.11	2.05	2.00	1.96
40 x 3 cord	2.42	2.34	2.28	2.23	2.19

Size 25x3 cord, 1-inch mesh, contains about 180 square feet to the pound. Size 40x3 cord, 1-inch mesh, contains about 320 square feet to the pound. Larger mesh contains more square feet to the pound in proportion.

See No. 6C9915 for sizes. **We do not send this C. O. D.**

No. 6C9811 Cotton Netting, No. 16 soft twine, intended for outside of trammel nets. Size, 6 to 8-inch square mesh. Price, per pound 29c

IMPROVED PERFECTION TRAMMEL NETS.

OUR PRICES ARE BELOW ANY COMPETITION, QUALITY CONSIDERED.

We handle only the Perfection Nets and Seines, recognized the world over as **THE BEST.** We could furnish **poorer goods at less money,** but the **Perfection Seines** are so far superior to all others, and our prices to you being but our small percentage above actual cost to make, are **so very low,** that we feel sure you will want **the best. Do not buy a cheap net or seine.** You will find it dear at any price. Perfection goods will always satisfy you.

The Perfection Trammel Net has three nets hung upon a single top and a single bottom line. Of the three nets the two outside have large meshes of cotton seine twine. The inside net is made of best linen gilling twine, which is hung slack, forming a bag in which fish coming from either side are caught and unable to escape. **These nets are not "drag seines," but are to be "set" stationary in the water, the same as a gill net. We do not ship C.O.D.**

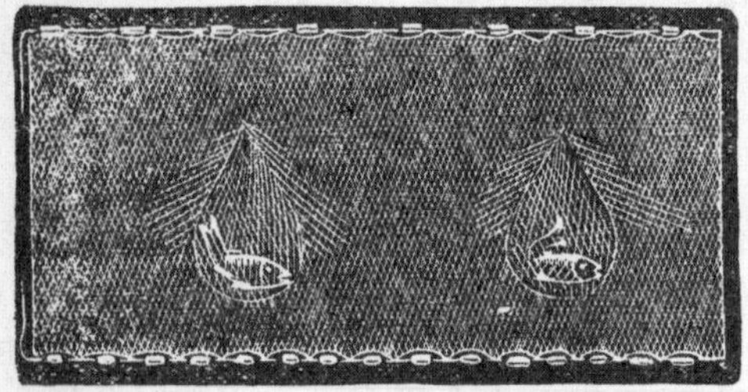

Price is per running yard in length, hung measure, for the net complete. The mesh sizes are square mesh. **Weight, per yard, about ½ pound.**

Nets cannot be returned when made as ordered.

No.	Depth	Outside Mesh	Inside Mesh	Inside Linen Twine	Outside Cotton Twine	Price per Yard
	Feet	Inches	Inches	No.	No.	
6C9820...	3½	6	¾	25	All No. 16-Thread Soft Laid Twine.	16c
6C9821...	3½	6	1	25		14c
6C9822...	3½	6	1¼	25		13c
6C9823...	4	6	1	25		16c
6C9824...	4	6	1¼	25		13c
6C9826...	4½	7	1¼	25		14c
6C9827...	4½	7	1½	18		13c
6C9829...	4½	7	2	18		11c
6C9830...	5	8	1	25		19c
6C9831...	5	8	1½	18		14c
6C9832...	5	8	2½	18		11c
6C9833...	5	8	3	18		11c
6C9834...	6	8	1	25		22c
6C9835...	6	8	1½	18		18c
6C9836...	6	8	2	18		14c
6C9837...	6	8	2½	18		13c
6C9838...	6	8	3	18		13c
6C9838½	7	8	1¼	25		20c
6C9839...	7	8	1½	18		19c
6C9840...	7	8	2	18		16c
6C9842½	8	8	1¼	25		22c
6C9843...	8	8	1½	18		21c
6C9844...	8	8	1¾	18		19c
6C9845...	8	8	2	18		18c
6C9846...	8	8	2½	18		16c
6C9847...	8	8	3	18		15c

Other styles made to order. Meshes as given above are diamond square. Hung complete for use except hauling lines. **When ordering nets give size, price and catalogue number. Allow us two to five days to make.**

NOTE—Trammel Nets are made to order only, and if order is filled correctly we cannot take the goods back, as we seldom have any two orders just alike in every particular. Consequently if the net were returned it would be a dead loss to us.

NOTICE—If you intend to use your net in water where there is a very swift current, same must be rigged accordingly. We can rig nets extra heavy with leads and floats at an additional expense of 10 per cent over catalogue prices.

PERFECTION SQUARE COTTON DIP NETS.

No. 6C9850 Made of cotton seine twine. Roped all around edges, with loops at corners. All are made 1-inch square mesh of No. 12 soft twine. Price is for netting only. No frame comes with these nets. **Cannot be returned if sent as ordered.**

	Price	Postage extra
4x4 feet, square shape	$0.23	10c
5x5 feet, square shape	.36	12c
6x6 feet, square shape	.46	15c
8x 8 feet, square shape	.79	23c
10x10 feet, square shape	1.19	38c
12x12 feet, square shape	1.66	40c

LINEN GILL OR SET NETS.

A gill net is a single net, hung with floats and leads complete, without hauling lines. Made of best imported linen twine. **These nets cannot be used for drag seines,** the twine being too fine. They are set in the water and allowed to remain from 5 to 24 hours.

The fish are caught by the gills, hence the name gill or set nets.

Rigged complete ready for use. Made of linen twine. Price per running yard in length, hung measure. **Weight, per yard, about ¼ pound.**

Nets cannot be returned if sent as ordered. Allow us two to five days to make.

No.	Depth feet	Size Linen Twine	Sq. Mesh, 1 inch Price, pr. yd.	Sq. Mesh, 1¼ in. Price, pr. yd.	Sq. Mesh, 1½ in. Price, pr. yd.	Sq. Mesh, 2 in. Price, pr. yd.	Square Mesh, 2¼ in Price. pr. yd.
6C9860	3½	All 40-3 Cord	......	......	......	6c	....
6C9861	4		12c	11c	8c	7c	....
6C9866	5		13c	12c	10c	7c	7c
6C9873	6		15c	13c	11c	8c	8c
6C9880	7		......	......	12c	10c	....
6C9883	8		......	......	13c	11c	....

Other styles made to order. Our gill nets are made of Knox best Scotch linen twine.

PERFECTION COTTON GILL NETS.

We furnish these nets in the following sizes only, made in 1¼, 1½, and 2-inch square mesh of No. 28 4-ply Sea Island cotton gill netting. **Cannot be returned if sent as ordered. Be sure to specify size of mesh wanted, also depth and number of yards. Following prices are per running yard, hung measure, rigged complete with leads and floats.**

No.	Depth	1¼-inch Mesh, Price, per yard	1½-inch Mesh, Price, per yard	2-inch Mesh, Price, per yard
6C9890A	4 feet	7c	6c	6c
6C9890B	5 feet	8c	7c	6c
6C9890C	6 feet	10c	8c	6c
6C9890D	7 feet	10c	8c	7c
6C9890E	8 feet	11c	10c	7c

PERFECTION COTTON TROT LINES.

Cotton Trot Lines, to use as set lines and top and bottom lines on small nets; in 50-foot coils, six rolls connected or 300 feet. Best quality. Sold in any quantity at dozen rates.

No. 6C9900 No.	Weight, per doz.	Price, per doz. coils or 600 ft.
1	15 oz	$0.17
2	16 oz	.23
3	19 oz	.28
4	20 oz.	.37
5	23 oz	.42
6	24 oz	.57
7	32 oz	.66
8	36 oz	.79
9	44 oz	.93
10	52 oz	1.06
11	56 oz	1.20
No. 12 is $\frac{5}{16}$-inch diameter	96 oz	1.50

PERFECTION COTTON GILL NETTING.

This Gill Netting is made from No. 28x4-ply Sea Island cotton twine, in any depth, and is made to special order, according to your measure, **and cannot be returned if sent as ordered;** when ordering, mention depth desired, also mention size mesh wanted. Understand, this is not a rigged net; it is the netting only and does not have the floats, leads and lines. This cotton netting is very fine and strong, and runs just twice as much to the pound as the heavier, coarser netting, hence the difference in price. **Allow us two to five days to make.**

No. 6C9853 Cotton Gill Netting, 1-inch square mesh, mention depth wanted. Price, per lb.. **$1.61**

No. 6C9854 Cotton Gill Netting, 1¼, 1½, 1¾ or 2-inch square mesh, mention depth and mesh wanted. Price, per pound **$1.38**

PERFECTION LINEN GILLING TWINE.

The Best Quality Imported.

OUR GILL TWINE is made of the **highest grade** linen, and, quality considered, is offered for less money than it has ever been sold before.

Gilling twine is a small, all linen twine used for gill or set nets, and cannot be used to make drag, lake or river nets. For Gill Netting see No. 6C9810.

Prices of Linen Gilling Twine.

Catalogue Number	Size of Twine	No. of yds. per pound.	Comes in balls of	Price, per pound
6C9915 A....	12x3 cord	1,200	½-lb. each	$0.81
6C9915 B....	16x3 cord	1,600	½-lb. each	.89
6C9915 C....	18x3 cord	1,800	½-lb. each	.92
6C9915 D....	20x3 cord	2,000	½-lb. each	.98
6C9915 E....	25x3 cord	2,500	½-lb. each	1.08
6C9915 F....	30x3 cord	3,000	½-lb. each	1.26
6C9915 G....	35x3 cord	3,500	½-lb. each	1.48
6C9915 H....	40x3 cord	4,000	½-lb. each	1.71

PERFECTION WHITE SEINE TWINE.

Comes in skeins or hanks, and we cannot sell less than 2 pounds of one size. State size wanted.

Catalogue Number	Style of laid	No. 6, per pound	No. 9, per pound	No. 12, per pound	No. 16 and larger, per pound
6C9925...	Soft	28c	25c	24c	23c
6C9926...	Medium	28c	25c	24c	23c
6C9927...	Hard	37c	26c	26c	25c

No. 9 Twine will average 600 yards per pound.
No. 12 Twine will average 425 yards per pound.
No. 16 Twine will average 325 yards per pound.

6 12 16 20 24 30 36 40 48 60

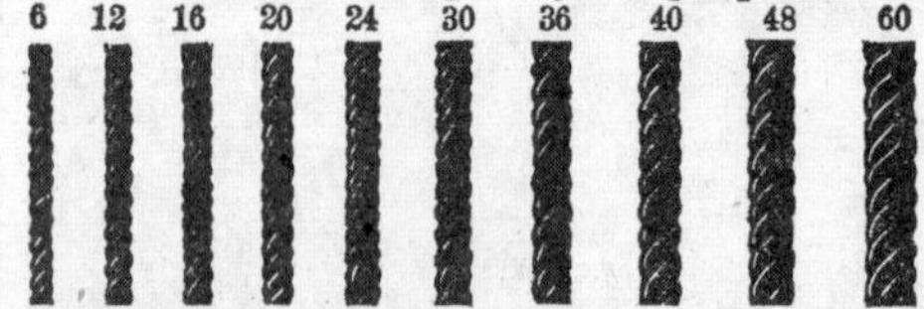

Showing sizes of Seine Twine as near as possible. These illustrations appear larger than the twine.

Our Seine Twine is the best in the market, laid smooth and even and uniform in size. We do not handle the loosely laid, bunchy, cheap goods.

SEINE NEEDLES.

No. 6C9935 Seine Knitting Needles, made of prepared maple wood, finely finished; very tough and strong.

Width, inches..	½	¾	1	1¼	1½
Price, each.....	6c	7c	7c	7c	8c

If by mail, postage extra, 1 cent.

RIGGING MATERIAL.

OUR RIGGING MATERIAL is the best on the market.

No. 6C9950 Cedar Trammel Net Floats.	Size, 1¼ x 5,			per 100, 31c	
No. 6C9951 Cedar Gill Net Floats.	Size, 1¾ x 5,			per 100, 61c	
No. 6C9952 Cedar Seine Floats.	Size, 2 x 3, per 100, 35c	Size, 2½ x 3, per 100, 49c	Size, 2¼ x 4, per 100, 57c	Size, 3 x 4, per 100, 77c	Size, 3 x 5, per 100, 92c

No. 6C9960 Lead Sinkers for trammel nets or seines. 16 to the pound. Price, per pound...... 8c
10 to the pound. Price, per pound............. 8c
4 to the pound. Price, per pound............. 7c

No. 6C9965 Hoops for Fyke and Funnel Nets.
5 in. to 2 ft. in diameter, ¼ in. timber. Price....12c
2¼, 2½, 2¾ and 3 feet in diameter, ⅝x1 in. timber. 13c
3¼, 3½, 3¾ and 4 feet in diameter, ⅝x1 in. timber 18c
4½, 4¾ and 5 feet in diameter, ⅝x1 in. timber....21c
5½ and 6 feet in diameter, ⅝x1 in. timber. Price, 52c

THE OTTER FOLDING CATCH-ALL MINNOW NET.

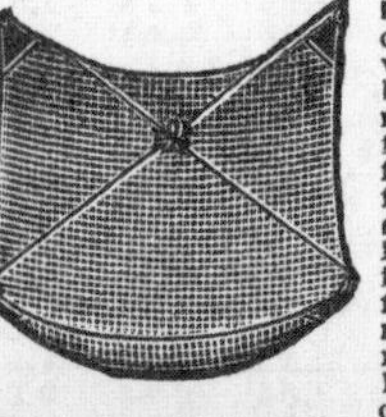

No. 6C9970 This Net supplies a long felt want. A minnow net that can be folded into a small space and when spread out is large enough to be practically used as a minnow dip net. This net has a steel frame, 3½ feet square. This frame can be folded in a moment's time; when folded occupies a space 2 inches square, 2½ feet long. The net itself is heavy common sense netting ¼ inch mesh, reinforced at corners, fitted with a brass ring in each corner to attach to frame. This net is not fitted with handle, frame has a large ring to which a handle or rope can be attached.

Price, complete with bag..$1.25
If by mail, postage extra, 25 cents.

OUR TENT AND COVER DEPARTMENT.

MANUFACTURERS. We manufacture our own tents, stack covers, etc. We are not at the mercy of any manufacturer, but operate and control our own factory, which factory makes tents, covers, etc., exclusively for us. Manufacturing our own tents we can guarantee better service and better tents than any other house on earth.

MATERIAL. We buy every yard of duck used in our factory. We know the grade and quality of every piece of duck used in our tents or covers and we guarantee our duck to be the equal of the best duck ever placed on the market. It is fully 29 inches wide and positively guaranteed to be full weight. We do not buy, handle or permit any 7 or 9-ounce duck to enter our factory. Place one of our 8-ounce tents on a scale and place one of some other make of the same size tent and supposedly made of the same weight canvas as our tent and note which weighs most; and bear in mind we do not use duck that is filled with starch, which will be found to be several ounces per yard under weight after the first rain storm. If you know nothing about canvas, this is the surest test that you are getting full weight canvas for your money.

FINISH AND CONSTRUCTION. Our tents are finished in a first class workmanlike manner. It is impossible for other dealers to sell tents for less money than we do unless they account for the difference in price by the difference in quality. Furthermore, our tents are guaranteed to be full size. Where we specify a tent to have a 7 or 8-foot center pole it is not necessary for the purchaser to cut several inches off of the center pole in order to make the walls reach the ground. Our wagon covers and paulins are constructed in the same high grade manner as our tents.

C. O. D. We do not ship tents, bed sheets, paulins and wagon covers C. O. D., as these goods are all made up especially to customer's order, but we guarantee every article of this kind to be exactly as represented, of full size and full weight of canvas, or money refunded.

DELIVERIES. Allow two to four days after we receive the order to make the goods, and in June and July allow ten to fifteen days, as these two months are the busiest months in the tent business. We aim to ship within the shortest possible time after we receive the order, but our business in June and July, owing to the excellence of our tents, is so very heavy that we desire our customers to anticipate a delay, as stated. If you get the tent in less time we know you will not be disappointed.

RAINS. We have been very careful in buying our canvas to select a grade of canvas that would be most impervious to water. The canvas we have selected is woven especially for our tents, paulins, wagon covers, etc. In states where rains are frequent and heavy, it is advisable to purchase an extra fly, which practically makes two roofs to your tent. A fly usually costs half the price of a tent, for example on a $10.00 tent, an extra fly would cost $5.00.

SPECIAL TENTS. On tents not described or illustrated in this catalogue we invite correspondence. Tell us the style of tent desired and for what purpose the tent is intended, state the size and weight of duck and we will quote you a price and advise you how long it will take to fill your order.

TENTS MADE TO ORDER. As all tents are made to special order, they cannot be returned under any circumstances if sent as ordered.

HOW TO PITCH A TENT. Having unrolled the tent in the exact position you want it to be when up, place the ridge pole, round side up, inside the tent, and on a line with the large eyelet holes, which are in the center of the roof; then insert the uprights in the holes bored in the ridge pole, and let the spikes in the upright pole come through the top of the tent. If a fly is used let the spikes also go through that, in precisely the same way as the tent; then take hold of the uprights and raise tent and fly together; secure the corner guys first and then the others between them. Do not drive the pegs straight, but slanting; they hold very much better in this way. The tent being now up and guys all adjusted so that they bear equal strain, then proceed to dig a V-shaped trench all around the tent, about three inches deep; this will insure you a dry floor at all times. Do not take the tent down when wet or even damp. Heat and dampness are the cause of mildew, which destroys more tents than all other causes combined.

"A" or Wedge Tents.

We do not ship Tents C. O. D.

The weight which we give includes center poles. 10-ounce will weigh one-fourth more, and 12-ounce will weigh one-half more. When poles are not wanted with tents deduct 5 per cent from these prices.

No. 6C10340 The following prices include poles:

Style No.	Length and Breadth	W'ght, 8-oz.	Height	Price, 8-oz. Duck	Price, 10-oz. Duck	Price, 12-oz. Duck
A	7 x 7 ft.	25 lbs.	7 ft.	$3.46	$4.15	$ 5.43
B	7 x 9½ ft.	27 lbs.	7 ft.	4.23	4.95	6.55
C	9½x9½ ft.	32 lbs.	7 ft.	4.65	5.51	7.30
D	9½x12 ft.	38 lbs.	7½ ft.	5.76	6.77	9.00

Miners' Tents.

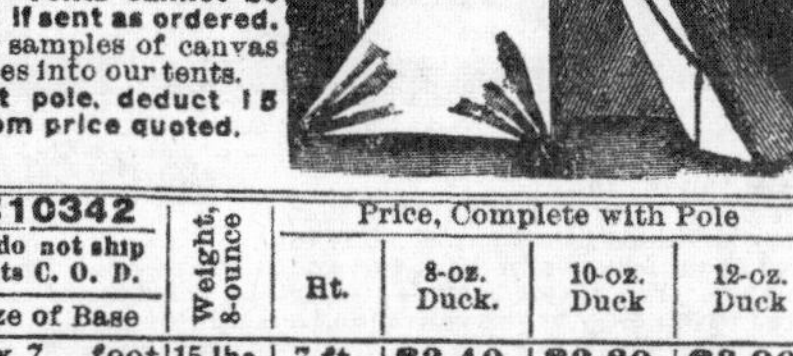

For Miners, Prospectors, or may be used as play tents for children. The weight which we give includes poles. 10-ounce weighs one-fourth more than 8-ounce and 12-ounce one-half more than 8-ounce. Tents cannot be returned if sent as ordered. Send for samples of canvas which goes into our tents.

Without pole, deduct 15 cents from price quoted.

Style No.	No. 6C10342 We do not ship Tents C. O. D. Size of Base	Weight, 8-ounce	Price, Complete with Pole Ht.	8-oz. Duck	10-oz. Duck	12-oz. Duck
A	7 x 7 feet	15 lbs.	7 ft.	$2.40	$2.80	$3.90
C	9½x 9½ feet	22 "	8 ft.	3.69	4.25	5.90
F	12 x12 feet	30 "	9 ft.	5.60	6.45	8.95

REFRESHMENT TENTS.

Oblong or Refreshment Tent, made of plain white duck; not striped, as shown in illustration. Price includes poles, pins, guy ropes, etc., complete, ready to set up. This illustration shows front open and folded at the sides; the front may be closed or stretched out in front for an awning, or taken off altogether, as it is put on with hooks for these changes. **Tents are made to order and cannot be returned if made as ordered.**

NOTICE—Our 12-oz. refreshment tents are made of 12-oz. double filled duck throughout. Some manufacturers make the side walls of lighter duck; we make side walls and top of 12-oz. double filled duck.

No. 6C10344 Cannot be shipped C. O. D.

Size	Weight, 8-ozs.	Hgt., Wall	Height, Center	8-oz. White Duck	10-oz. White Duck	12-oz. D. F. White Duck
9½x14½	50 lbs.	6 ft.	10 ft.	$12.55	$14.25	$17.85
9½x19	80 lbs.	6 ft.	10 ft.	15.60	17.75	21.75
12x19	100 lbs.	6 ft.	11 ft.	17.14	19.60	24.30
14x21½	125 lbs.	6 ft.	11 ft.	21.10	24.10	30.15
14x23½	130 lbs.	6 ft.	11 ft.	26.00	29.75	36.50

Tent Without Poles, 5 per cent Less Than Above Prices.

WALL TENTS.

WALL TENTS. These are the best style tents for all general purposes, such as camping, golfing, to use as an out house, summer kitchen, etc. We can furnish tents in large or small quantities on short notice generally. Our tents are the best quality, they are all full size, and all have a good "pitch" to roof, to turn rain, and all made in a durable and substantial manner. We quote actual measurements, where other dealers quote a 16-foot tent we quote 15½ feet, because we know that a tent cannot be made 16 feet wide without considerable waste of duck which would make the tent very expensive in proportion to other sizes. **Tents cannot be returned,** as they have to be made to order. We warrant them to be exactly as represented. **In ordering, give catalogue number, length, breadth and price. Allow three to five days' time for making tents, and in June and July allow ten to fifteen days, according to the number of orders we have on hand at the time we receive your order. Send for samples of canvas which goes into our tents.**

No. 6C10350 Wall Tent.

We give weight of tents with poles below on 8-ounce tents. 10-ounce will weigh about ¼ more and 12-ounce about ½ more than 8-ounce. **The weights may vary slightly, as poles do not always run alike. Allow three to five days' time to make tent, and in June and July allow ten to fifteen days.** A 9½x12 foot tent makes a good out house or summer kitchen.

Order by Catalogue No. and Style No.

No. 6C10350 We do not ship tents C. O. D.

Style No.	Length and Breadth	Height Wall	Height Pole	Weight, 8-ounce	Our Prices include Poles, Pegs, Guys, Guy Ropes, etc., Complete, ready to set up. 8-oz. Duck	10-oz. Duck	12-oz. Duck
	Feet	Ft.	Ft.	Lbs			
A	7 x 7	3	7	30	$ 4.48	$ 5.24	$ 6.86
B	7 x 9 ½	3	7	35	5.32	6.19	8.18
C	9 ½x 9 ½	3	7½	40	6.13	7.17	9.52
D	9 ½x 12	3	7½	45	7.21	8.43	11.17
E	9 ½x 14	3	7½	50	8.20	9.58	12.68
F	12 x 12	3½	8	55	8.57	10.05	13.30
G	12 x 14	3½	8	60	9.69	11.31	15.01
H	12 x 15½	3½	8	70	10.75	12.57	16.69
J	12 x 18	3½	8	70	11.96	13.96	18.48
K	14½x 14	4	9	70	11.54	13.52	18.01
L	14½x 15½	4	9	80	12.71	14.92	19.88
M	14½x 18	4	9	85	14.20	16.66	22.09
N	14½x 20½	4	9	100	15.79	18.34	24.08
P	14 x 24	4	9	120	17.81	20.66	26.54
Q	15½x 16	5	11	90	15.79	18.59	24.70
R	15½x 18	5	11	110	17.33	20.38	27.02
S	15½x 20½	5	11	120	19.10	22.29	29.20
T	15½x 24	5	11	145	21.76	25.31	33.07
U	15½x 30	5	11	170	26.32	30.66	40.04
W	18 x 20½	5	11	175	21.84	25.41	33.43
X	18 x 24	5	11	180	24.42	28.48	37.24
Y	18 x 30	5	11	240	29.26	34.10	44.79
Z	18 x 35	5	11	290	32.56	37.97	49.87

EXTRAS AND DEDUCTIONS.

Where higher wall is wanted, add 5 per cent of the cost of the tent for each 6 inches extra height of wall.

Poles and pins are included in above prices.

A tent fly makes an extra movable or double roof to a tent, and affords a greater protection from sun and rain, and can be made to serve as an awning, either in front or rear of tent. They are not really necessary, and are not included in prices of tents, but we can furnish them, if ordered, at one-half the price of tents of corresponding size and quality, for instance, **a fly for $10.00 tent will cost $5.00.**

When tent poles are not wanted with tents, deduct 5 per cent from above prices of tents.

Tents cannot be returned if sent as ordered.

Photographers' Tents.

Tents cannot be returned, as they are made to order. It takes three to five days, and in June and July ten to fifteen days to fill tent orders.

We do not ship Tents C. O. D.

No. 6C10360 Weight given below includes poles and may vary on account of poles not always being alike.

NOTICE—We quote 12-oz. double filled duck; most dealers quote 10-oz. double filled duck. The difference between 10-oz. single duck and 10-oz. double duck does not warrant the difference usually asked in the price, whereas 12-oz. double filled duck is much stronger, closer woven and much more impervious to water.

Order by number and size — Size	Weight of 8-oz. Lbs.	Pole	Wall	Price, Complete, Without Dark Room — 8-oz. Single Fill'g Duck	10-oz. Single Filling Duck	12-oz. Double Filling Duck
12x16 ft.	135	11 ft.	6 ft.	$16.52	$18.48	$25.20
12x21 ft.	155	11 ft.	6 ft.	20.16	23.24	31.36
12x24 ft.	175	11 ft.	6 ft.	22.40	25.76	34.70
14x21 ft.	220	12 ft.	6 ft.	22.40	25.76	34.70
14x24 ft.	230	12 ft.	6 ft.	24.36	28.30	38.00
14x28 ft.	240	12 ft.	6 ft.	27.72	32.20	43.65
16x28 ft.	270	13 ft.	6 ft.	30.52	35.56	47.80

Prices on tents include poles, pins, guy ropes, etc. Tents above are complete, fitted with one skylight, **ready to set up. If poles are not wanted deduct 5 per cent from the above prices. Dark rooms, lined with red muslin, extra,** 6x6 feet, **$6.75;** 4¼x4½ ft., **$6.00.** Our dark rooms **are made of same material,** same weight and color as the tent—**all white.** Our dark rooms are hung inside of the tent with snaps and rings, no separate frame or poles being necessary.

Quotations on other sizes on application and at bottom prices. Tents are made to order and cannot be returned if made as ordered.

Prices on stable tents, stable tops, Sibley tents, canopy tops without wall, photographers' tents, square hip-roof tents or any other style, given on application and at bottom prices.

Cowboys' or Stockmen s Bed Sheets.

For herders who are compelled to sleep in a tent or on the ground, or they may be used as sod covers. Fitted with snaps and rings or eyelets as may be ordered. When ordering, say if you wish snaps and rings or eyelets. Made to order of very best heavy white duck, and cannot be returned if sent as ordered. Allow 2 to 6 days for making. We do not ship Bed Sheets C. O. D.

Weight, packed for shipment, 10 to 20 pounds.

No. 6C10362

Style No.	Weight, 13-ounce	Feet	13-oz.	15-oz.	18-oz.
A	4¼ lbs.	6x12	$3.44	$4.17	$4.48
B	4½ lbs.	6x14	3.98	4.82	5.21
C	4¾ lbs.	6x15	4.29	5.17	5.55
D	5 lbs.	6x18	5.09	6.16	6.62
F	4¾ lbs.	7x14	4.59	5.51	6.08
G	4¼ lbs.	7x16	5.27	6.35	7.00
H	5½ lbs.	7x18	5.81	7.00	7.72
L	6 lbs.	8x18	7.35	8.87	9.74

8-ounce duck means a yard will weigh 8 ounces; 10-ounce duck means a yard will weigh 10 ounces; 12-ounce duck means a yard will weigh 12 ounces etc.

Rubber and Paper Blankets.

Our Rubber Blankets are made chiefly for camping purposes, to keep warm while sleeping on cots or on the ground in wet or cold weather, and may also be used for certain kinds of sickness where the mattress is to be preserved. In such cases place the blanket over the mattress and a bed sheet over the blanket. They come in two styles, black rubber, lined with white sheeting, and black rubber lined with black cotton fleece cloth.

No. 6C10364 Black Rubber Blanket, lined with white sheeting, 3¾ feet wide and 6 feet long. Weight, about 3 pounds. Price.................. **$1.10**

No. 6C10366 Black Rubber Blanket, lined with black cotton fleece cloth, 4½ feet wide and 8 feet long. Weight, about 4½ pounds. Price...... **$2.75**

Our Paper Blanket is made from a very fine grade of wood fibre paper, made soft and flexible. The edges are nicely bound, and when placed over or between two sheets makes a nice, warm, light blanket for home use at a moderate price. **Weight, about 2¾ pounds.**

No. 6C10367 Our Paper Blanket, 5½ feet wide and 7 feet long, fits any double bed. Price.... **85c**

If by mail, postage extra, 36 cents.

PAULINS OR STACK AND MACHINE COVERS.

Weight given below is for 8-ounce duck; 10-ounce will weigh one-fourth more than 8-ounce, and 12-ounce will weigh one-half more than 8-ounce. Protect your crops, implements and machinery from snow, rain and inclement weather.

Made to special order. Allow from two to five days, according to the number of orders we have on hand when we receive yours.

We do not ship Paulins or Covers C.O.D.

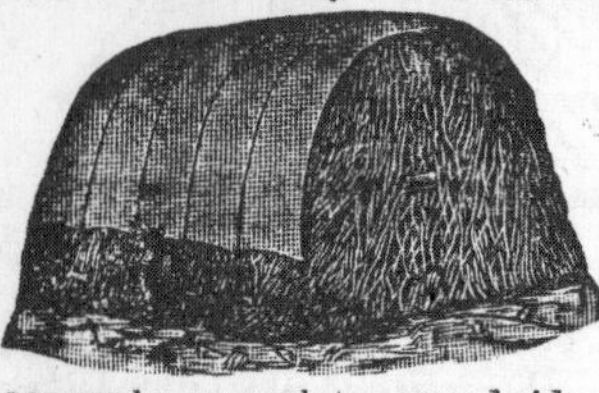

Made of white duck. Always state size wanted when ordering. These goods are not tents, but paulins or stack covers. Stack covers have short ropes, BUT NO POLES; machine and merchandise covers have eyelets around side. Paulins are made to order and cannot be returned if sent as ordered. Write for samples of canvas which goes into our covers. Write for prices for special paulins not quoted in this list.

No. 6C10370

Style No.	Size, Feet	Wgt. of 8-oz.	8-oz. Duck	10-oz. Duck	12-oz. Duck
A	10x16	11 lbs.	$2.68	$3.30	$4.63
B	10x18	12 lbs.	3.03	3.72	5.00
C	12x14	12 lbs.	2.93	3.60	4.69
D	12x16	13 lbs.	3.44	4.13	5.57
E	12x18	16 lbs.	3.78	4.64	6.25
F	12x20	17 lbs.	4.23	5.15	6.88
G	14x16	16 lbs.	4.47	5.46	6.73
H	14x18	18 lbs.	5.02	6.15	7.50
J	14x20	20 lbs.	5.60	6.84	8.38
K	14x24	25 lbs.	6.39	7.84	10.13
L	16x16	18 lbs.	4.88	5.97	7.66
M	16x18	19 lbs.	5.48	6.73	8.63
N	16x20	23 lbs.	6.09	7.44	9.63
P	16x24	26 lbs.	7.30	8.95	11.50
Q	18x20	25 lbs.	6.85	8.40	10.78
R	18x24	30 lbs.	8.24	10.06	12.92
S	18x28	36 lbs.	9.62	11.74	15.07
T	18x30	39 lbs.	10.26	12.59	16.13
U	20x24	34 lbs.	9.15	11.18	14.38
V	20x36	51 lbs.	13.72	16.76	21.50
W	24x30	51 lbs.	13.72	16.76	21.57
X	24x40	68 lbs.	18.26	22.38	28.75
Y	24x50	84 lbs.	22.84	27.95	35.94

CANVAS BINDER COVERS.

No. 6C10371 Weight, 6½ to 7¼ pounds. Fitted to cover the binder and not the whole machine. Will fit any binder. Size 7½x15 feet. Made of white 8 and 10-oz. duck. Price, 8-ounce, $2.21; 10-ounce..$2.47

Allow from two to five days to make.

BLACK OILED OR TARPAULIN WAGON COVERS

These covers, although black and called tarpaulins, have no tar in their composition. Our waterproof dressing is an oil preparation and is entirely free from anything calculated to rot or burn the canvas, but adds to the durability of the cover, being impervious to water and very soft and pliable. It will neither rot nor mildew from damp, or break from being too hard. They are invaluable to persons who are shipping and receiving goods that are liable to be damaged by wet weather. In ordering, give catalogue number, size and price. Weight 9 to 38 lbs.; 6x12, 12 lbs.; 6x9, 9 lbs.; 7x12, 16 lbs.; 7x14, 19 lbs.

Allow from two to five days to make.

No.	Size	Price	Size	Price	Size	Price
6C 10375	6x 8 ft.	$2.32	7x 9 ft.	$3.06	8x10 ft.	$3.87
	6x 9 ft.	2.55	7x10 ft.	3.38	8x12 ft.	4.65
	6x10 ft.	2.94	7x12 ft.	4.02	8x14 ft.	5.42
	6x12 ft.	3.43	7x14 ft.	4.75	8x16 ft.	6.21
	6x14 ft.	4.06	....	....	9x14 ft.	6.12

Prices given on other sizes upon application.

WHITE DUCK EMIGRANT WAGON COVERS.

Always give size when ordering. Weight given below is on 8-ounce covers. 10-ounce weighs one-fourth more and 12-ounce about one-half more than 8-ounce. We do not send wagon covers C.O.D. Write for prices on covers not quoted in this list.

No. 6C10380

Size, Feet	Lbs.	8-oz. Duck	10-oz. Duck	12-oz. Duck
10x10	7	$1.78	$2.26	$3.38
10x12	7½	2.15	2.69	4.08
10x14	7¾	2.50	3.14	4.77
10x15	8	2.69	3.36	5.12
10x16	9	2.87	3.62	5.46
11x13	9	2.62	3.38	4.99
11x15	10	3.02	3.80	5.76
12x15	20	3.37	4.22	6.40
12x16	25	3.68	4.50	6.81
12x20	30	4.52	5.73	8.55

Allow from two to five days to make.

Comstock Malleable Iron Tent Pegs.

They last a lifetime. Cannot be broken.

No. 6C10387 Short Peg, 8¾ inches long. Weight about 4½ ounces each.
Price, per dozen.......................................50c

No. 6C10388 Long Peg, 13½ inches long. Weight, about 7¼ ounces each.
Price, per dozen.......................................70c

Our Palmetto Lawn Tents.

No. 6C10393

These Palmetto Lawn Tents are calculated for temporary use; as playhouses for children and similar purposes. They are made of about 8-ounce awning material and come in stripes of blue and white, are set up with one pole, and a light iron frame sewed into the tent around the eaves; are handsome in appearance upon the lawn and afford great pleasure to children. Order by catalogue number and state size wanted.

Size of Base	Size of Top	Height at Center	Height at Side	Wgt., lbs.	Price, each
7x 7 ft.	2 ft. 4 in.	7 ft. 6 in.	6 ft.	17	$4.21
8x 8 ft.	2 ft. 4 in.	8 ft.	6 ft. 6 in.	19	4.87
9x 9 ft.	3 ft. 6 in.	8 ft. 6 in.	7 ft.	23	5.88
10x10 ft.	3 ft. 6 in.	9 ft.	7 ft. 6 in.	26	6.62

Waterproof Ponchos.

No. 6C10394 Our Luster Ponchos, made of finest quality rubber, lined with fine sheeting and have a hole in center, covered with heavy flap. By using this hole and drawing the poncho over the head, it forms a large rubber cape, protecting the entire body. It is absolutely waterproof and may also be used as a rubber blanket. Size, 45x72 inches. Weight, 3½ pounds.
Price.....................$1.25

Our Combination Tent and Cot.

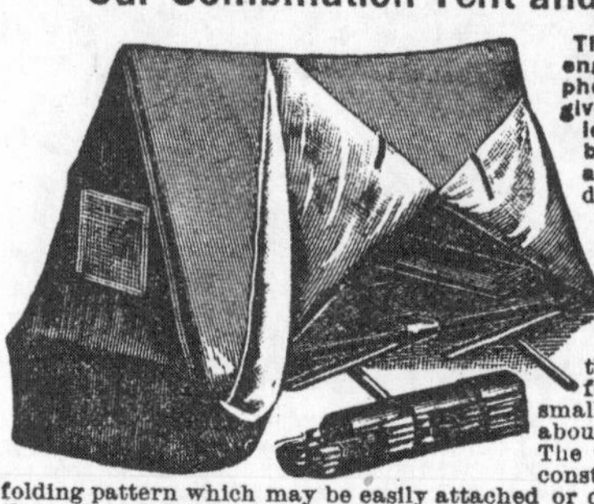

This illustration, engraved from a photograph, will give you some idea of our combination tent and cot, a very desirable article for campers who do not wish to be burdened with a tent. The cot is so constructed that it may be folded into a small package about 3 feet long. The tent frame is constructed on a folding pattern which may be easily attached or detached from the cot and folded in the same manner as the cot, while the canvas tent is made to fit over the cot and tent frame, as shown in the illustration. The cot has a pillow casing attached which may be filled with straw, hay or clothing to act as a pillow, and at each end of the tent there is sewn into it mosquito netting to keep out mosquitoes, as well as to afford ventilation to the occupant. The tent is 6¼ feet long, 2¼ feet wide, 4⅛ feet high, and is made from 10-ounce duck, which makes it practically a waterproof tent, and the entire weight of the cot and tent complete is about 24 pounds. The entire outfit may be folded up, as shown in the above illustration, and carried from place to place at a moment's notice. Weight, packed for shipment, about 30 pounds.

No. 6C10395 Price of the cot and tent complete, as shown in the above illustration.....................$5.50

PORCH CURTAINS.

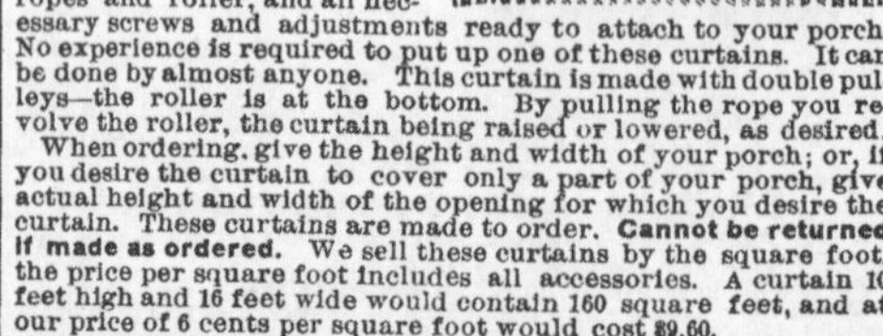

If you have a porch or piazza, a porch curtain will enable you to enjoy the full benefit of same, as it will protect you from the heat of the sun; will also keep out dust and rain, and will help to make your porch very comfortable during the summer months.

Our porch curtains are made of fancy striped duck, furnished complete with pulleys, ropes and roller, and all necessary screws and adjustments ready to attach to your porch. No experience is required to put up one of these curtains. It can be done by almost anyone. This curtain is made with double pulleys—the roller is at the bottom. By pulling the rope you revolve the roller, the curtain being raised or lowered, as desired.

When ordering, give the height and width of your porch; or, if you desire the curtain to cover only a part of your porch, give actual height and width of the opening for which you desire the curtain. These curtains are made to order. Cannot be returned if made as ordered. We sell these curtains by the square foot, the price per square foot includes all accessories. A curtain 10 feet high and 16 feet wide would contain 160 square feet, and at our price of 6 cents per square foot would cost $9.60.

No. 6C10397 Price, per square foot 6c

We are in position to quote prices on special awnings of all kinds. Will be glad to quote prices on store awnings, roller awnings, complete with winding gear, and special awnings for extra wide windows, upon request.

Our Adjustable Window Awning.

Our Adjustable Window Awning is constructed so that anybody can quickly fit same to a window, and can be as quickly removed if desired. It is not necessary to have an experienced awning hanger to hang these awnings. You can do it yourself just as well. They are made of regular awning material, blue and white striped, with scallops at the bottom, as shown in the illustration; are raised and lowered with ropes over pulleys, same as other awnings. These awnings will help to make your home pleasant, keep the sun from fading your carpets and furniture, and will greatly add to the appearance of the house. They come in three sizes to fit windows from 2 feet 4 inches to 4 feet 5 inches wide. When ordering, give width of your window so that we know which of the three sizes to send you.

No. 6C10399 No. 2 Awning will fit any size window from 2 feet 4 inches to 2 feet 10 inches wide..................$1.75

No. 3 Awning to fit any window from 3 feet to 3 feet 7 inches wide.......................... .85

No. 4 Awning to fit any window from 3 feet 10 inches to 4 feet 5 inches wide.......................... 2.00

Weight, packed for shipment, 11 pounds.

Special Awnings for Stores and Residences.

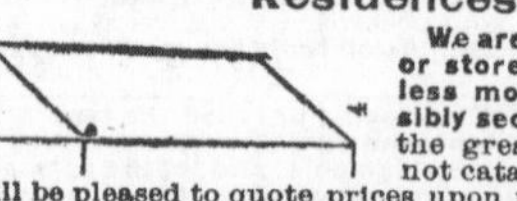

We are able to furnish your home or store with a better awning for less money than you could possibly secure elsewhere. Owing to the great variety of sizes, we do not catalogue special awnings, but will be pleased to quote prices upon receipt of an inquiry, stating size of awning wanted. When writing us regarding a special awning, refer to the above diagram, give us height of awning from 1 to 2, projection from 2 to 3 and width from 3 to 4. Distance from 1 to 2 should be governed by height of store ceiling; allow 7 to 8 feet from bottom of frame (2) to sidewalk. Mention if frame is to be fastened to wood, brick, stone or iron columns. Also if columns to which frame is to be fastened are in line. If not in line, state which ones, and how far back they are set. State whether you desire the awning made of plain white or striped duck and if the awning is to be lettered, and whether lettering is to be placed on roof of awning or on curtain. If you desire new cover only, be sure to so state in your inquiry, also state whether the cover is for a wood or an iron frame.

Camp Chairs and Stools.

No. 6C10431 Canvas Top Camp Stool well made. Weight, 2¾ lbs.
Price.....................22c

No. 6C10432 Canvas Top Camp Chair, same as No. 6C10431, with back. Weight, 3¾ pounds. Price... ....30c

Our Combination Folding Cot and Litter, $1.50.

Our Combination Folding Cot and Litter. Just the thing for camping purposes and may be used as a stretcher; made of 10-ounce duck. This is the lightest, strongest and most compact folding cot made. It has the only practical pillow ever put on a cot. It is made so that you can stuff straw or clothing into the pillow casing. Length, 6 feet 3 inches; width, 29 inches. Dimensions, when folded and ready for shipment, 6 feet 3 inches by 5 inches by 5 inches. Weight, 15 pounds.

No. 6C10435 Price, complete with pillow........$1.50

Our Gold Medal Folding Camp Bed.

This is positively one of the most substantial, well made and well finished folding cots upon the market. It is so constructed that it may be folded into a parcel 3 feet long and about 5 inches in diameter, and is guaranteed to hold 1,000 pounds. The frame is made strong and substantial, and is covered with heavy brown canvas and has a pillow casing which may be stuffed with straw, hay or clothing to act as a pillow. It is about 6½ feet long and 2⅛ feet wide and weighs about 16 pounds.

No. 6C10438 Gold Medal Folding Camp Bed. Price, $2.15

Camping Outfit Complete at $5.40.

No. 6C10455 Pat. March 10, '96.

Illustration of kit unpacked.

No. 6C10455 Wilson's Kamp Kook's Kit. Just the thing for camping out. 53 pieces. Fire jack, two boilers suitable for using as an oven, fry pan, coffee pot and all utensils and tableware for a party of six. Everything first class. Boilers are made of 26-gauge smooth steel. The entire kit nests in small space, and when packed ready for shipment makes a package 14½x10½x8 inches, all nested together and can be firmly locked up by an ordinary padlock. Weight, complete, 20 pounds.
Price, complete............$5.40

PAT. MARCH. 10, 96.

No. 6C10455 Illustration of kit packed for shipment.

This outfit can be packed inside of either the oven or the fire box of our No. 6C9170 Stove. Making the most complete, compact and serviceable combined outfit on the market.

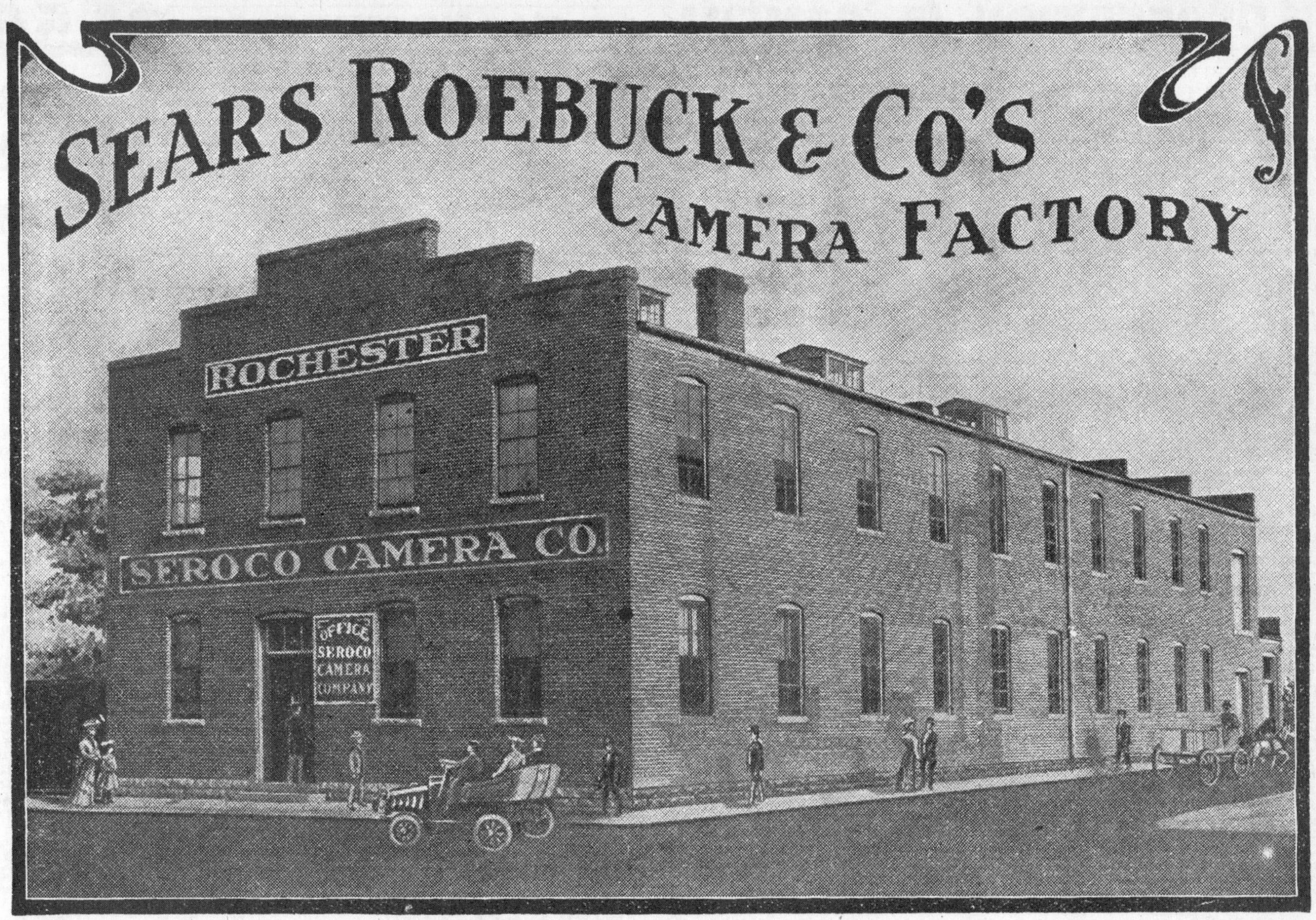

This picture shows our own big new camera factory at Rochester, Minn., where we make the highest grade cameras made in the world, which we sell at about one-half the prices charged by others for cameras that will not compare with those made by us in our factory at Rochester.

OUR NEW CAMERA FACTORY AS SHOWN IN THE ILLUSTRATION, IS THE

MOST MODERN, — MOST UP TO DATE, BEST EQUIPPED CAMERA FACTORY IN AMERICA.

EQUIPPED WITH EVERY MODERN, labor saving and high quality giving machine for camera making, everything made, equipped and managed with a view to giving our customers, as we do, a better camera than goes out of any other camera factory in the world, cameras that combine the good points of all other cameras with the defects of none, and yet, built in our own factory, we can offer the best at about one-half the prices charged by others.

LOW PRICES EXPLAINED.

OUR PRICES, which, quality for quality, are about one-half the prices charged by others, are made possible by reason of our owning, controlling and running our own camera factory, running the factory to its full capacity every day in the year, thus reducing the cost of the highest grade cameras made in the world to the mere cost of material and labor, to which we add only our one small percentage of profit, making our prices (quality considered) about one-half the price others ask.

OUR OFFER.

QUALITY GUARANTEED. PRICE GUARANTEED. TEN DAYS' FREE TRIAL COMPARISON OFFER. OUR CHALLENGE C. O. D. TERMS.

SEND US AN ORDER for any camera. Remember you get the outfit at factory cost. Either enclose our price, as quoted in this catalogue, or $1.00 (balance payable at your express office after you have examined the camera), and we will send the camera you select with the understanding and agreement, first, that it must reach you promptly and in perfect condition; second, that you can give it ten days' free trial, during which time you can put it to any test. You can compare it with cameras sold by others at double our price and if you do not find it

PERFECTLY SATISFACTORY,
LOWER IN PRICE,
BETTER IN QUALITY

and in every way more satisfactory and better than any similar style of camera you can buy elsewhere, you can send the camera back to us at our expense and we will immediately return your money, including any express charges paid by you.

QUALITY GUARANTEED.

EVERY CAMERA we make in our big new camera factory at Rochester is covered by our binding guarantee, by the terms and conditions of which, if any piece or part in any way gives out or fails to perform its duty properly by reason of defective material or poor workmanship, we will replace or repair such camera free of charge and stand the express charges both ways. The cameras of our make are simpler to operate, easier to understand, less liable to get out of order, wear longer and take better pictures than any other cameras made in the world.

DON'T BUY FROM A TRUST.

AS NEARLY ALL the cameras made in the United States are made by one concern, one manufacturer (even though they are sold under several different company names) and this one manufacturer is trying to monopolize the camera business of the United States and thus compel you to pay two or three prices for the camera, if you don't buy from us you will be almost sure to buy a trust camera from anyone else and, quality considered, pay double the price we ask for cameras made in our own factory.

HOW THEY TRIED TO FORCE US TO HIGH PRICES.

THE MANAGER of this big camera monopoly came to us and told us that we must sell their cameras and only theirs under penalty of war. They told us that we must sell at prices fixed by them, at prices unreasonably high. WE REFUSED, AND NOW IT IS WAR TO THE KNIFE. We built our own camera factory in order to make better cameras than the monopoly ever made, cameras to sell at factory cost with only our one small profit added, better cameras than monopoly cameras, and at one-half the prices of monopoly cameras. ARE YOU WITH US IN THIS FIGHT? We need your support. If you buy a camera from us you are not helping to support any trust, any camera monopoly, you are not helping to support high prices, but you will be helping us in waging a low price war, helping us to maintain our factory price plan on the best cameras made in America.

MR. CAMERA DEALER: You know about this war. You know that the Camera Trust has threatened to drive us out of business by refusing to furnish us photographic goods, if we continue to maintain low prices on cameras. You know we are in the right. You know we have got the best cameras. You know the high prices you would have to pay today for cameras if we were not waging this war against the trust. We need your support also. Help us a little by a trial order for a few cameras. Compared side by side our cameras will sell for more money, style for style and size for size, than any other cameras you are now selling. They will cost you less money and please your customer much better.

THE PERFECTION JR. CAMERA AT FACTORY PRICE $1.55

$7.50 OUTFIT FOR $2.56

A HIGH GRADE AND THOROUGHLY PRACTICAL CAMERA.

MADE IN OUR OWN FACTORY and sold to you at manufacturer's price, one-half the prices asked by other concerns for goods of equal merit. There is nothing to get out of order, as they are constructed in the simplest possible form, having no unnecessary springs, catches or adjustments to get out of order and annoy the owner or create a source of expense.

For 3½x3½ PICTURES

$1.55

THE PERFECTION JR. CAMERAS ARE MANUFACTURED IN OUR OWN FACTORY AT ROCHESTER, AND ARE SOLD ONLY BY US.

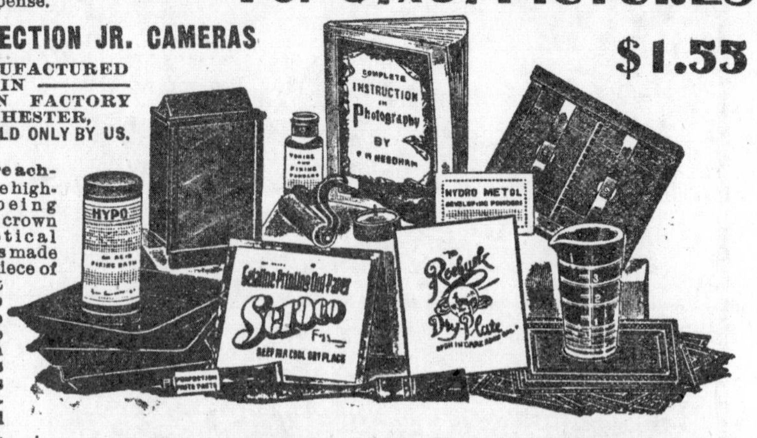

..THE PERFECTION Jr. CAMERA.

The lenses are achromatic of the highest grade, being made of both crown and flint optical glass. (Lenses made of a single piece of glass will not give a sharp focus, as the light rays are reflected in such a way that rays of different colors focus at different distances from lenses.) They are ground and set for a **Universal Focus** and need no adjustment even when pictures are to be taken at different distances. **THE UNIVERSAL FOCUS LENS is a special feature of advantage**, anything in the picture up to within a few feet of the camera, or any distance in the background, being in focus; that is, **sharp and clear. THE SHUTTER** is one of the most simple, but is thoroughly practical and is equally adapted to both **snap shot and time exposures**. It is well made and finished in every respect and has no complications to get out of order. **THE VIEW FINDER** is an important feature of these cameras, for it shows the operator an exact copy of the picture as it will appear when finished, and makes it an easy matter to get the subject to be photographed in the proper position on the plate. **THE COVERING is artistic, neat, has the seal grain finish**, same as used in the highest priced cameras; is creased on all corners; has a handle for carrying, and thoroughly finished in every respect. **THE SIZE, 3½x3½**, is the most popular one for amateur work with the single exception of the 4x5. **GLASS PLATES ONLY** are used in The Perfection Jr. for making negatives, and we recommend them as being much better and easier to handle than films. All of the material used for these cameras is **the same as used by professional photographers**, which places the amateur in a position to do the very best of work. **THE DEVELOPING AND FINISHING OUTFIT** is the most complete and convenient outfit ever offered in this size, and includes everything necessary **for making pictures and finishing them complete, mounted on cards. SIZE AND WEIGHT: The Perfection Jr. Camera** measures 4¾x5¼x7¼ inches, and weighs 18 ounces. The camera has space in the back for three double plate holders, making the carrying capacity six plates. **"Complete Instructions in Photography"** is furnished with this outfit, and even if you have never taken a picture you will be able to make good photographs from the start.

THE PERFECTION JR. OUTFIT CONTAINS:

1 Perfection Jr. Camera. 1 Metal Dark Room Lamp. 1 Tray for Developing Plates. 1 Tray for Fixing Plates. 1 Tray for Toning Prints. 1 Printing Frame. 1 Measuring Glass. 1 Print Roller for smoothing down the prints when mounted. 1 Paste Brush for mounting. ½ doz. Dry Plates for making negatives. 1 doz. Sheets Sensitized Paper. 1 doz. Embossed Border Cards for mounting the pictures. 1 Package Dry Developer (makes 8 oz. of solution). 1 Package Dry Toner (makes 8 oz. of solution), 1 Package Hypo, for fixing negatives and prints. 1 Jar Prepared and Scented Mounting Paste. 1 Copy "Complete Instructions in Photography."

The Camera alone, if purchased from the regular retail dealers, would cost you $4.00, and the complete developing and material outfit as listed above would cost at least $3.50, making the total value of the Perfection Jr. Camera and outfit at retail $7.50. The fact that we make these goods in our own factory enables us to offer you the complete outfit for actually less than the retail dealer can buy it for.

No. 20C2040 The Perfection Jr. Camera and Complete Developing and Material Outfit and one double dry plate holder as described above. Price........ **$2.56**

No. 20C2041 The Perfection Jr. Camera with one double dry plate holder, but without the complete outfit. Price........ **$1.55**

No. 20C2042 Extra Double Plate Holders. Price, each........ **.28**

If by mail, postage extra, 5 cents.

OUR SEROCO JR. FOLDING CAMERA

AT $4.50 FOR THE 4X5 SIZE. AT $7.25 FOR THE 5X7 SIZE.

OUR SPECIAL FACTORY PRICES for the Seroco, Jr., Folding Camera are based on the actual cost of material and labor, with but our one small percentage of profit added, and are the lowest prices ever made for cameras of this grade. The illustrations, engraved by our artist direct from photographs of the camera, will give you some idea of the appearance of our handsome Seroco Jr. Folding Camera; the one illustration showing the camera fully extended and ready for use, another showing the camera closed, and the third illustration showing the appearance of the camera and plate holders when in the carrying case.

Camera Closed.

OUR SEROCO JR. FOLDING CAMERA represents one of the very latest styles for 1905. It embodies all the most up to date features of all high grade folding cameras with the defects of none. With the Seroco Jr. Folding Camera, you can accomplish any results and do any kind of work that can be done with other cameras at from three to five times our prices, **and as we include without extra charge a copy of our new 112-page manual, "Complete Instructions in Photography,"** the making of perfect pictures with this camera is a simple matter, even for those without the slightest previous experience or knowledge of photography. The Seroco Jr. Folding Camera is constructed throughout of selected Honduras mahogany, with highly polished piano finish. It is covered with heavy seal grain black morocco leather of best quality, the bellows are made of an excellent quality of red leather, lined with absolutely light proof black gossamer cloth. The trimmings and all metal parts are finely finished and highly polished, thus making an exceedingly handsome appearance in contrast with the dark, rich finish of the mahogany woodwork.

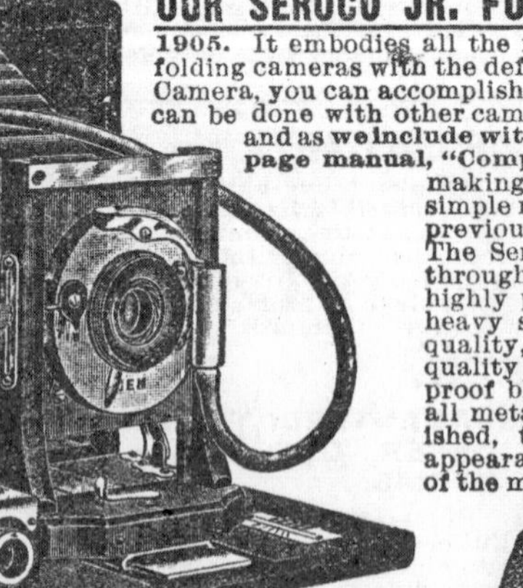

Camera Open.

THE VIEW FINDER IS REVERSIBLE and the camera is fitted with two tripod sockets, thus making it available for either vertical or horizontal pictures, both when used with a tripod or when used as a hand camera, The Seroco Jr. Folding Camera is made with rising and falling front for regulating the relative amount of sky and foreground. It is provided with a ground glass focusing screen for careful and accurate work, and this ground glass is protected from injury, when not in use, by a hinged panel. An accurate focusing scale is carefully adjusted and enables the user to focus the camera instantly when it is not desirable to use the ground glass.

LENSES The lenses used in our Seroco Jr. Folding Camera are made expressly for this camera by the Rochester Lens Company, and are the highest grade of single achromatic lenses which this manufacturer turns out. They possess great depth of focus, covering the plate sharply to the extreme corners, work very rapidly, producing sharp, clear pictures with fine detail.

SHUTTER We use in our Seroco Jr. Folding Camera the Junior Automatic Shutter, one of the latest productions of the celebrated Wollensak Optical Company. It is entirely automatic in its action, requiring only a pressure of the bulb to make any kind of exposure desired. It is so arranged that it may be set for either instantaneous, time or bulb exposures, thus covering the entire range of adjustments, the same as possessed by the very highest priced shutters on the market.

OUR SPECIAL $4.50 AND $7.25 PRICES INCLUDE the Seroco Jr. Folding Camera Complete with lens, Automatic Junior shutter, carrying case and one double plate holder.

GIVE NAME OF CAMERA, CATALOGUE NUMBER AND SIZE WHEN YOU ORDER :: :: :: ::

Carrying Case.

No. 20C2064 The 4x5 Seroco Jr. Folding Camera, complete as above stated. Price........ **$4.50**

No. 20C2066 The 5x7 Seroco Jr. Folding Camera, complete as above stated. Price........ **7.25**

Extra Holders, 4x5, 45 cents each; 5x7, 60 cents each. This camera uses the Seroco Holders, see No. 20C2510 for description.

THE 4x5 DELMAR CAMERA

OUR SPECIAL FACTORY TO USER PRICE, $1.90

MADE IN OUR OWN FACTORY AT ROCHESTER.

THE IMMENSE SALE OF THESE most popular cameras and outfits has made it possible for us to manufacture them in enormous quantities and by purchasing the **chemicals by the barrel**, and the other materials by the thousands of each, and by assembling and boxing the outfits by the thousands, being satisfied with a very small percentage of profit, we are able to **CUT THE PRICE IN TWO**, while other concerns still insist on selling with large profits (which has always been the custom in the photographic line), with the result that they sell small quantities of goods and charge their patrons double what they should.

THE SIZE AND STYLE OF THE DELMAR 4x5 is by far the most popular on the market, and this statement will be better appreciated when we say that we believe at least seven out of ten of all the amateur cameras sold are of this same size and style. While it takes a 4x5 cabinet size picture, its outside dimensions are only 6x7x8¼ inches, and it weighs but 34 ounces. **One Double Plate Holder** for two plates is included with each camera, and there is space in the camera for two extra holders, giving a capacity for six plates.

THE LENS is what is known as the Meniscus Achromatic, and is the finest universal focus lens made; in fact, is the same grade and quality as used in cameras which sell as high as $10.00 to $15.00. It has great depth of focus, which gives full and sharp detail to objects at a distance as well as to those which are near by.

THE SHUTTER is automatic and always set, being operated by a spring in connection with a very ingenious device; is very simple, with no complicated parts to get out of order, but so perfect in its arrangement that it can be instantly changed for either snap shot or time exposures.

THE VIEW FINDERS form a part of the camera, and not only are they of invaluable assistance in locating and centering the objects to be photographed, but they add much to its artistic appearance.

SIMPLICITY. The ease of manipulation is one of the best features of this outfit. **Remember, the shutter is always set**, you don't have to turn any buttons or push any levers before making an exposure, operations which are very apt to be forgotten or wrongly executed in the excitement of the moment; and **you don't have to focus each time a picture is made**, as the lens is of universal focus, **always ready**. With other cameras many a fine picture is lost because of the delay in setting the shutter, focusing, etc. In the meantime the subject is gone or the scene is changed, **but the Delmar Camera is always ready.**

THINK SERIOUSLY of the opportunity to possess a camera and complete outfit for making 4x5 pictures for the small sum of $3.10 and then ask yourself what would afford you more pleasure than to own a photographic outfit with which you could, as the opportunities present themselves, take the pictures of your friends and relatives, brothers and sisters; the pets, such as dogs, cats and horses; the home, both inside and out; pretty landscapes, buildings and places of interest seen while traveling; and especially the picture of the baby in all its cute and amusing positions. It will not be fully realized, until after years, what treasures have been secured in the way of pictures of friends and places or things of interest.

THE COMPLETE OUTFIT CONTAINS:

- 1 4x5 Delmar Camera, with Double Plate Holder.
- 1 Metal Dark Room Lamp.
- 1 Tray for Developing Plates.
- 1 Tray for Fixing Plates.
- 1 Tray for Toning Prints.
- 1 Print Roller for smoothing down the mounted prints.
- ½ Dozen Dry Plates.
- 1 Paste Brush.
- 1 Graduated Glass for Measuring Liquids.
- 1 Dozen Card Mounts with fancy embossed borders.
- 1 Package Concentrated Dry Developer (makes 8 ounces of solution).
- 1 Package Concentrated Dry Toner (makes 8 ounces of solution).
- 1 Dozen Sheets Sensitized Paper.
- 1 Printing Frame.
- 1 Package Hypo for fixing Negatives and Prints.
- 1 Jar of fine Scented Photo Mounting Paste.
- 1 Copy of "Complete Instructions in Photography."

Everything in the outfit is the best that can be secured.

This Picture was taken with the Delmar Camera.

THE PICTURE OF THE FOOTBALL TEAM which we show above, will give you some idea of the style and an exact idea of the size of picture that can be taken with the Delmar Camera. It is, however, impossible for us to show, by means of the above picture the fine detail and delicate shading that appears in the original photograph, as these fine points are lost when we reproduce a photograph by the ordinary process of printing, such as we use in printing this page.

THE DELMAR CAMERA, like the Perfection Junior, is the simplest and by far the most popular and convenient form of amateur camera. It is made of the best seasoned material throughout; is strong, well made in every respect and has absolutely **no complicated parts to get out of order.**

THE DELMAR CAMERA has a beautiful **black seal grain finished covering**, has leather handle for carrying, and two tripod sockets for attaching a tripod when desired, for either perpendicular or horizontal pictures.

DRY PLATES ONLY are used in the Delmar Cameras. The dry plates for negatives are much easier to develop and print from than films, and as dry plates only are used by professional photographers, it is evident that they are the best.

No. 20C2050 The 4x5 Delmar Camera, with one double plate holder and complete developing, finishing and material outfit, as described above............ $3.10

NOTE—If you have no express office near you, we can, by making several packages of this outfit, ship same by mail, the postage required being $1.50.

No. 20C2051 The 4x5 Delmar Camera, with one double plate holder, but without the developing, finishing and material outfits.............. **$1.90**

If by mail, postage extra, 50 cents.

No. 20C2052 Extra Double Plate Holders. Price, each.............. **28c**

If by mail, postage extra, 6 cents.

See following pages for extra supplies, such as dry plates, sensitized paper, developers, toners, etc. Any of the supplies listed in this catalogue are suitable for the Delmar Camera.

SEROCO A CYCLE FOLDING CAMERA, AT $7.40 FOR 4X5 PICTURES; AT $9.90 FOR 5X7 PICTURES.

MADE IN OUR OWN FACTORY AT ROCHESTER AND SOLD TO YOU AT MANUFACTURERS' PRICES.

THE FINEST HONDURAS MAHOGANY, thoroughly seasoned, is used in making this camera, even those portions which are covered being made of mahogany instead of from cheaper wood, as is the case with many cameras now on the market.

ALL METAL PARTS are of lacquered brass, highly polished, carefully and accurately fitted and beautifully finished.

THE COVERING is a fine grade of genuine seal grain leather. We use no imitation leather in any of the Seroco Cameras.

THE BELLOWS IS MADE from an extra quality of red leather, very elegant in appearance, strong and durable and lined with light proof black gossamer cloth.

SEROCO A Cycle Folding Camera Open.

SPECIFICATIONS—Solid Mahogany, Piano Finish, Genuine Leather Covering, Double Rectilinear Lens, Wollensak Regular Double Valve Shutter.

Camera Closed

Carrying Case.

LENS. The lens is a high grade double rapid rectilinear, made especially for the Seroco cameras, by one of the best lens makers; a lens that possesses great depth of focus, covers the plate sharply to the extreme corners and is absolutely guaranteed in every respect.

THE SEROCO A CAMERA is made with rising and falling front for regulating sky and foreground, a spring actuated ground glass focusing screen, an accurately adjusted focus scale and two tripod sockets.

THE FINISH AND WORKMANSHIP on the Seroco A Camera is of the very highest order, these cameras being made in the same factory and by the same workmen who turn out our very highest grade cameras, and they receive the same careful attention, the same rigid inspection and the same strict attention to the smallest detail of construction.

SHUTTER. The Wollensak regular shutter forms a part of the equipment of the Seroco A Camera, and this shutter is universally recognized as one of the best shutters made. It is arranged for making automatic exposures of from $\frac{1}{100}$ of a second to one full second, or time exposures of any desired length.

THE CARRYING CASE is made from the best black sole leather, strongly made, and has room for the camera and four double plate holders.

THESE SPECIAL PRICES include the camera complete with lens, shutter, one double plate holder and carrying case.

No. 20C2085 Seroco A Cycle Folding Camera, 4x5. Price........$7.40
No. 20C2086 Seroco A Cycle Folding Camera, 5x7. Price.......... 9.90
Extra Plate Holders, 4x5, 45c each; 5x7, 60c each; see No. 20C2510. Shoulder Strap, 22 cents extra. For Developing Outfits see Nos. 20C2899 and 20C2900.

SEROCO B CYCLE FOLDING CAMERA, AT $8.75 FOR 4X5 PICTURES; AT $11.25 FOR 5X7 PICTURES.

SEROCO B Cycle Folding Camera Open.

SPECIFICATIONS—Solid Mahogany, Piano Finish, Genuine Leather Covering, Double Rectilinear Lens, Wollensak Shutter, Rack and Pinion Focus Movement, Swing Back.

Camera Closed.

Carrying Case.

LENS. The lens with which the Seroco B Camera is equipped is a special rapid rectilinear double lens of the very best quality—a lens which we can guarantee to do the very highest grade of work and equal in every respect to lenses furnished with many cameras costing from $20.00 to $30.00.

THE SEROCO B CAMERA is made throughout of solid mahogany, no other wood being used in any part of its construction. The covering is a high grade of black seal grain leather, the metal parts are of lacquered brass and the wood work is French polished, regular piano finish.

ADJUSTMENTS. The Seroco B Camera is provided with all necessary adjustments for any ordinary work, including rack and pinion focus movement, swing back, rising and falling front, spring actuated ground glass focusing screen, accurately adjusted focus scale, reversible view finder and two tripod sockets.

THE SEROCO B CAMERA embodies all of the good points of the Seroco A Camera, is constructed throughout in the same careful and substantial manner, with the same rigid attention to the smallest details of construction, and in addition is provided with a finely made rack and pinion focus movement, also an easily operated swing back.

THE RACK AND PINION FOCUS MOVEMENT is a particularly desirable adjustment, as it affords a very convenient means of focusing—the operation being accomplished by turning a milled head screw, instead of sliding the front of the camera out by hand.

THE SWING BACK is also a very desirable adjustment, greatly increasing the efficiency of the camera, especially when photographing buildings, as this adjustment enables one to entirely overcome the distortion which sometimes is unavoidable with cameras which are not provided with a swing.

FOR LANDSCAPE WORK, views of buildings, flash lights, interiors, groups, etc., the Seroco B Camera meets every requirement and it is a camera which we can unhesitatingly recommend and fully guarantee in every respect.

THE CARRYING CASE furnished with the Seroco B Camera is made from the best quality of heavy, black sole leather, strongly and substantially made, and contains room enough for the camera and four double plate holders.

THESE SPECIAL PRICES include the camera complete with lens, shutter, one double plate holder and carrying case.

No. 20C2090 Seroco B Cycle Folding Camera, 4x5. Price........$8.75
No. 20C2091 Seroco B Cycle Folding Camera, 5x7. Price........ 11.25
Extra Plate Holders, 4x5, 45c each; 5x7, 60c each; see No. 20C2510. Shoulder Strap, 22 cents extra. For Developing Outfits see Nos. 20C2899 and 20C2900.

SEROCO C CYCLE FOLDING CAMERA, AT $10.25 FOR 4X5 PICTURES; AT $12.75 FOR 5X7 PICTURES.

WE OFFER THE SEROCO C CAMERA as the equal of any camera in its class on the market, regardless of price. It represents the acme of perfection in this style of a camera, embracing all of the improvements and attachments ever constructed in a camera of this design.

IN CONSTRUCTION AND WORKMANSHIP the Seroco C Camera is strictly high grade in every sense of the word, and the woodwork is made from solid mahogany throughout.

THE COVERING is the very best quality of genuine seal grain morocco leather. The metal work is of lacquered brass, and the entire camera is finished in the most careful and accurate manner.

SEROCO C Cycle Folding Camera Open.

SPECIFICATIONS—Solid Mahogany, Piano Finish, Genuine Morocco Leather Covering, Double Symmetrical Lens, Wollensak Double Valve Shutter, Rack and Pinion Focus Movement, Swing Back, Reversible Back, Piano Hinge, Brilliant Finder.

ANTI-TRUST.

Camera Closed.

Carrying Case.

THE RACK AND PINION FOCUS MOVEMENT makes rapid and accurate focusing very easy, and the piano hinge, by which the bed is connected to the body of the camera, not only adds to the elegant appearance of the instrument, but also increases its strength and rigidity.

LENS. The lens with which the Seroco C Camera is provided is an extra high grade double symmetrical lens, a lens that is the equal in every respect of lenses used on the most expensive cameras, and superior in every way to lenses usually furnished with cameras at moderate prices. We believe that we are the first dealers in cameras to furnish even our moderate priced cameras with strictly high grade lenses.

SHUTTER. The Wollensak double valve shutter is one of the latest and most up to date shutters on the market; and we decided to equip the Seroco C Camera with this shutter only after a most careful and rigid test of its qualities. This shutter makes automatic exposures of any length from $\frac{1}{100}$ of a second to one second, also time or bulb exposures of any desired length. It is provided with a fine iris diaphragm and is without doubt one of the best shutters on the market today.

BRILLIANT FINDERS. The Seroco C Camera is equipped with the latest style of brilliant finder—a finder far superior to the ordinary style—of a special construction which secures a most brilliant and perfect image.

THE REVERSIBLE BACK is a most desirable feature, enabling the operator to take either vertical or horizontal pictures without changing the position of the camera.

IN ADDITION to the reversible back, rack and pinion focus movement, swing back and piano hinge, the Seroco C Camera is also provided with rising and falling front, spring actuated ground glass focusing screen, reversible brilliant finder, accurately adjusted focus scale and tripod socket.

THESE SPECIAL PRICES include the camera complete with lens, shutter, one double plate holder and carrying case.

No. 20C2100 Seroco C Cycle Folding Camera, 4x5. Price........$10.25
No. 20C2101 Seroco C Cycle Folding Camera, 5x7. Price........ 12.75
Extra Plate Holders, 4x5, 45c each; 5x7, 60c each; see No. 20C2510. Shoulder Strap, 22 cents extra. For Developing Outfits see Nos. 20C2899 and 20C2900.

SEROCO LONG FOCUS CAMERA, $12.25

LATEST 1905 . . MODEL . .

$12.25 buys the latest 1905 Model of the Long Focus Reversible Back Seroco Cycle Folding Camera, the highest grade camera in its class, the equal of any other camera made, regardless of price.

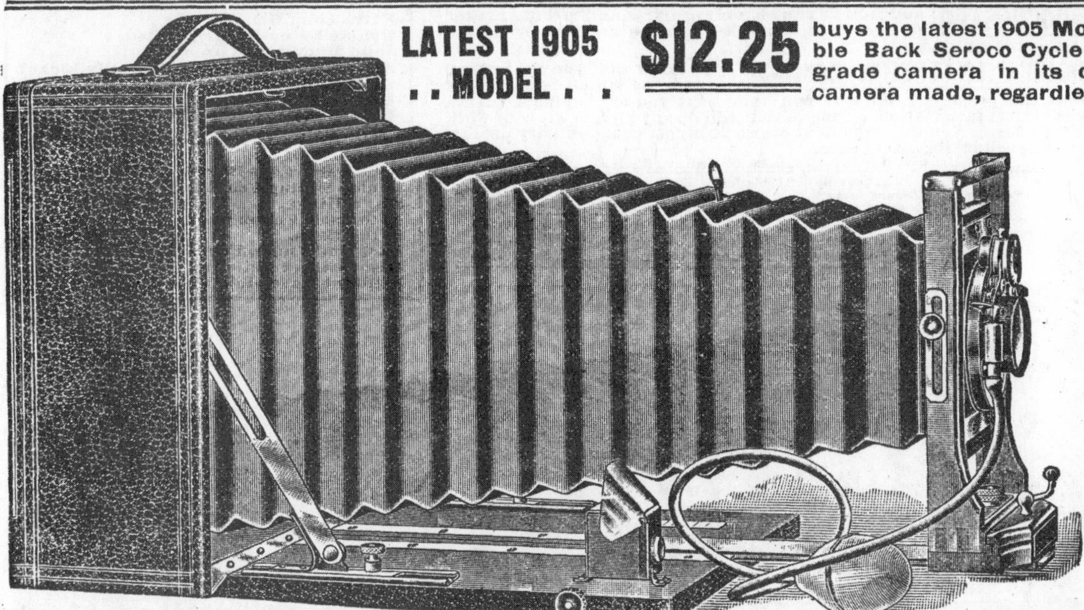
The Seroco Long Focus Camera.

SPECIFICATIONS:

Solid Mahogany throughout,
Lacquered Brass Trimmings,
Morocco Leather Covering,
High Grade Double Symmetrical Lens,
Wollensak Double Valve Shutter,
Swing Back,
Rack and Pinion Focus Movement,
Reversible Back,
Long Bellows,
Removable Lens Board,
Rising and Falling Front
Sliding Front,
Piano Hinge,
Brilliant Finder.

FACTORY PRICES:

4 x 5	$12.25
5 x 7	14.75
6½ x 8½	19.75
8 x 10	25.95

MADE IN OUR OWN FACTORY AT ROCHESTER. The special prices we name on the Seroco Long Focus Cameras are made possible only by the fact that we make these cameras ourselves, in our own factory, and sell them with only one small profit added to the actual factory cost.

Size.	Focal Capacity Ground Glass to Front Board.	Equivalent Focus of Lens.	Focus of Rear Combination of Lens.
4 x 5	12 inches	6¾ inches	10 inches
5 x 7	16½ inches	8¼ inches	14 inches
6½ x 8½	20 inches	11 inches	18 inches
8 x10	23 inches	13 inches	21 inches

OUR ILLUSTRATIONS, engraved by our artist direct from photographs of the camera, give you some idea of the appearance of the Seroco Long Focus Camera, but in order to fully appreciate this instrument, you must see it. The beautifully polished mahogany woodwork and the highly finished, lacquered brass trimmings contrasted with the fine black morocco covering and the rich red leather bellows, gives this instrument a strikingly handsome appearance.

THE LENS. One of the features of this camera is the extra high grade Symmetrical Lens—a double combination lens manufactured expressly for this camera and the very highest grade Symmetrical Lens that we can purchase. Either the front or rear combination of this lens can be used alone when desired, and as the focal length of either combination alone is about double that of the entire combination, the efficiency of the camera is greatly increased, as this is equivalent to having two lenses, one double the focal length of the other.

THE SHUTTER. We equip the Seroco Long Focus Camera with the Wollensak Double Valve Regular Shutter—a shutter that we can absolutely guarantee in every respect, simple and easy to operate, free from liability to get out of order—a shutter that has stood the test of time.

THE BELLOWS. The Seroco Long Focus Camera is equipped with an exceptionally good bellows, made from the best grade of leather, lined with special light proof gossamer cloth, and no glue whatever is employed in its construction, only the best rubber cement being employed. This bellows is made extra long, thus securing results in distant landscape photography, portraiture, copying, etc., which are entirely beyond the capacity of ordinary short bellows cameras. This long bellows also permits the use of the rear combination alone when desired for very long focus work.

THE REVERSIBLE BACK is of the very latest design, a style that is more easily operated and more convenient than any reversible back heretofore made. Changing the plate from one position to another is accomplished simply by pressing a concealed button on either side of the camera. There are no clips or catches of any sort to cause annoyance.

Seroco Long Focus Camera Closed.

THE SWING BACK. The swing with which the Seroco Long Focus Camera is equipped is one of the most perfect devices of the kind ever constructed, being controlled by the two set screws at the base of the side arms on either side of the camera. By simply loosening these screws the back can be swung either forward or backward to any desired angle and securely clamped by tightening the same screws, an adjustment that is quickly and easily made.

IN ADDITION to the special points mentioned above, including the Reversible Back, the Extra Long Bellows and the Swing Back, this camera is also fitted with all the other adjustments with which high grade cameras are usually provided, including a finely made rack and pinion focus movement, detachable lens board, rising and falling front, sliding front, piano hinge, brilliant reversible finder, and accurately adjusted focus scale.

ABOUT THE CARRYING CASES. We furnish with the Seroco Long Focus Camera the very best carrying cases that we can obtain, carefully and strongly made from a fine grade of heavy sole leather. The carrying case furnished with the 4x5 size has room for four plate holders, the 5x7 size has room for five plate holders, the 6½x8½ size has room for six plate holders and the 8x10 size has room for four plate holders.

Shoulder straps are not included unless ordered extra.

PRICES:

No. 20C2140	The Seroco Long Focus Camera, 4 x 5	$12.25
No. 20C2141	The Seroco Long Focus Camera, 5 x 7	14.75
No. 20C2142	The Seroco Long Focus Camera, 6½x 8½	19.75
No. 20C2143	The Soroco Long Focus Camera, 8 x10	25.95

FOR PRICES ON THESE CAMERAS WITH ANASTIGMAT LENSES, SEE PAGE 349.

UNDERSTAND, at the above prices we furnish the Cameras complete with High Grade Symmetrical Lens, Wollensak Shutter, Sole Leather Carrying Case, and one double Plate Holder.

Extra Plate Holders, 4x5, 45c each; 5x7, 60c each; 6½x8½, 79c each; 8x10, $1.10 each. See No. 20C2510. Shoulder strap, 22c extra.

For Complete Developing Outfits suitable for use with the Seroco Long Focus Camera, see No. 20C2900.

TEN DAYS' FREE TRIAL OFFER. Select the size you desire, send us the price as quoted on this page, and we will ship the camera to you, guaranteeing it to arrive in perfect order, and will allow you the privilege of testing it for ten days, during which time you can put it to any test, you can compare it with other cameras at double our price, and if you are not thoroughly convinced that this camera is all and even more than we claim for it, if you do not find it exactly as represented in every way and entirely satisfactory to you, return it to us at our expense and we will return your money in full, including express charges.

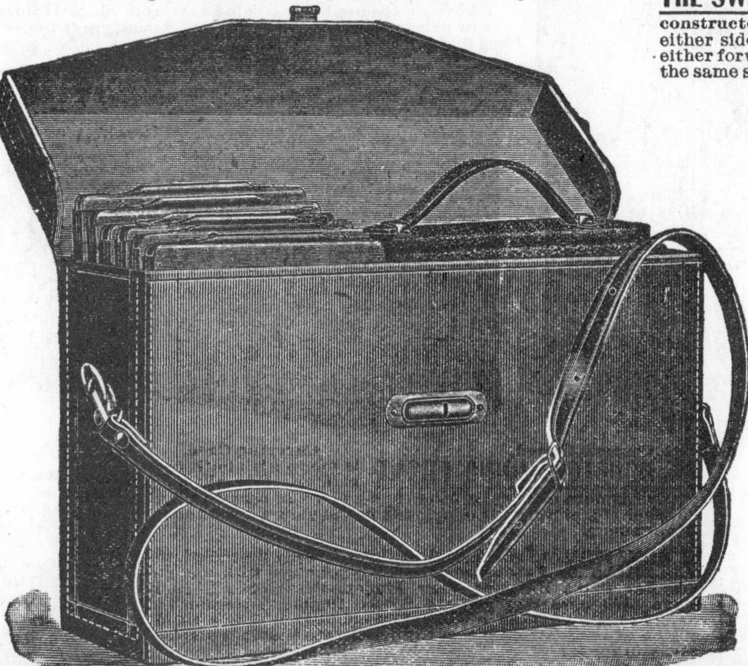
Carrying Case for Seroco Long Focus Camera.

THE SEROCO DOUBLE EXTENSION CYCLE FOLDING CAMERA.

The Very Highest Grade Camera that we Make, the Equal of Any Camera Made, Regardless of Price.

MADE IN OUR OWN FACTORY AT ROCHESTER, and sold to you on our regular small profit, maker to user plan, the only possible method by which cameras of this grade can be sold at the prices we name.

WHEN YOU BUY THE SEROCO DOUBLE EXTENSION CAMERA, you know that you are buying a camera which is as nearly absolutely perfect as the very best makers can possibly produce. You know that you are buying a camera which will be absolutely certain to give you perfect satisfaction, a camera that will do any kind or style of work which you may desire to attempt, and we are offering you this camera at prices no higher than ordinary dealers charge for common, short focus, or, at the best, medium length cameras.

SPECIFICATIONS.

Extra Long Bellows,
Double Extension Triple Bed,
Solid Mahogany Throughout,
All Metal Parts of Brass, Heavily Nickel Plated,
Fine Quality Morocco Leather Covering,
Extra High Grade Rapid Convertible Three-Focus Lens,
Latest Automatic Wollensak Shutter
Reversible Back,
Detachable Lens Board,
Double Sliding Front,
Piano Hinge,
Automatic Pinion Lock,
Swing Back,
Rack and Pinion Focus Movement,
Best Leather Bellows,
Brilliant Reversible View Finder.

Size	Focal Capacity Ground Glass to Front Board	Equivalent Focus of Lens	Focus Rear Combination of Lens	Focus Front Combination of Lens
4 x5	17 inches	6¾ inches	11 inches	14 inches
5 x7	24 inches	8 inches	14 inches	18 inches
6½x8½	32 inches	11 inches	18 inches	22 inches

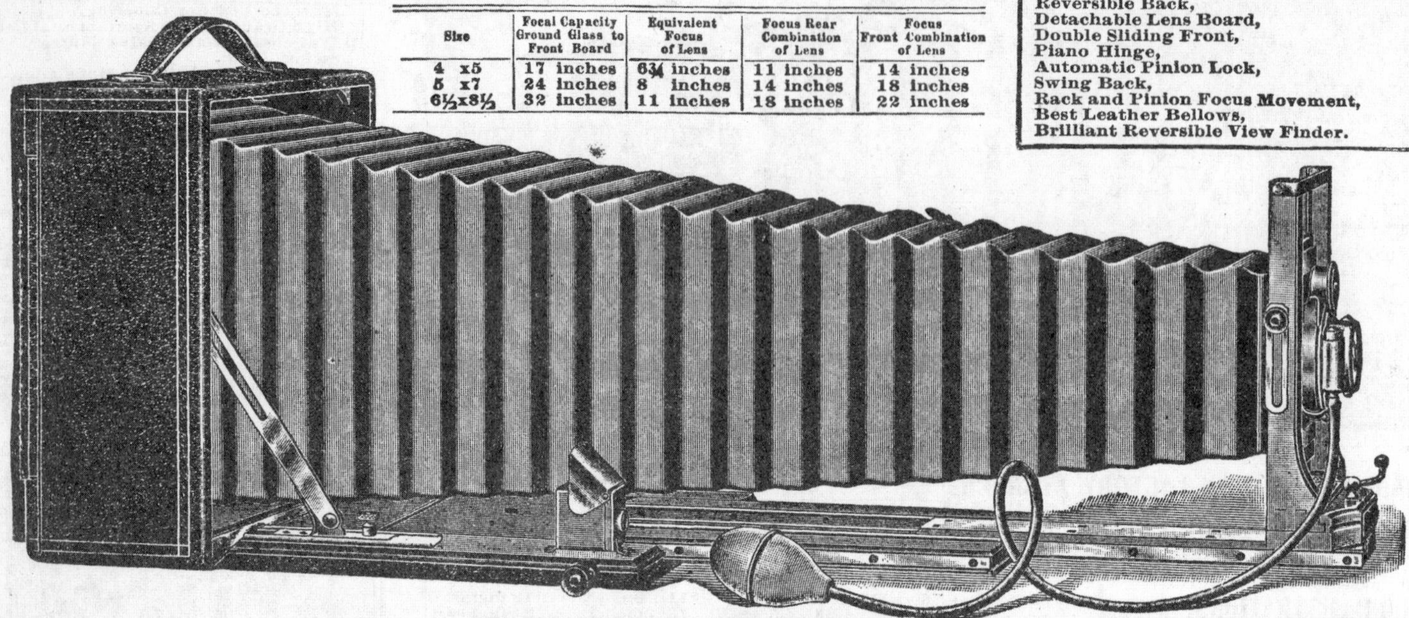

THE SEROCO DOUBLE EXTENSION CAMERA.

THE LENS. We equip the Seroco Double Extension Camera with an extra high grade, convertible, three-focus lens, made expressly for this camera, the very best convertible lens that we can buy. This lens is composed of two perfectly corrected combinations, the front combination having longer focal length than the rear combination. As either the front or rear combination may be used alone, we have three different focal lengths available, thus meeting any possible requirement.

THE SEROCO DOUBLE EXTENSION CAMERA is made throughout from thoroughly seasoned, kiln dried mahogany. No other wood is used in any part of its construction, and this mahogany is carefully selected, with particular attention to fine grain effects. The corners are all rounded and all joints are dovetailed. The bed and front are finished with the highest piano polish.

THE COVERING is the very highest grade of fine, black seal grain morocco leather, the best leather that we can buy.

THE METAL PARTS are made throughout from brass, heavily nickel plated, beautifully polished and accurately fitted.

THE SHUTTER. The Seroco Double Extension Camera is fitted with the new Wollensak Automatic Shutter, a marvel of mechanical ingenuity, of most perfect construction and rigidly tested. This shutter makes automatic exposures of from $\frac{1}{100}$ of a second to one full second, or time exposures of any desired length. The Wollensak Automatic Shutter is always set, one pressure of the bulb making the exposure and at the same time automatically resetting the shutter for the next exposure.

THE TELESCOPIC DOUBLE EXTENSION TRIPLE BED, made in three sections and brass bound, is one of the features of this camera. Its construction is such as to secure the greatest possible strength and rigidity even when the bellows is fully extended. A single pinion moves each section of the bed either forward or back, the first section, carrying the lens and shutter, moving out first, and as soon as it is fully extended automatically locking with the next section, which at once moves forward without the slightest lost motion. By pressing in this pinion the bed is securely locked at any desired point.

No. 20C2150 Seroco Double Extension Camera, 4x5 .... **$16.75**
No. 20C2151 Seroco Double Extension Camera, 5x7 .... **21.75**
No. 20C2152 Seroco Double Extension Camera, 6½x8½ **29.75**

Above prices include carrying case and plate Holder. For prices on these Cameras with Anastigmat Lenses, see page 349.

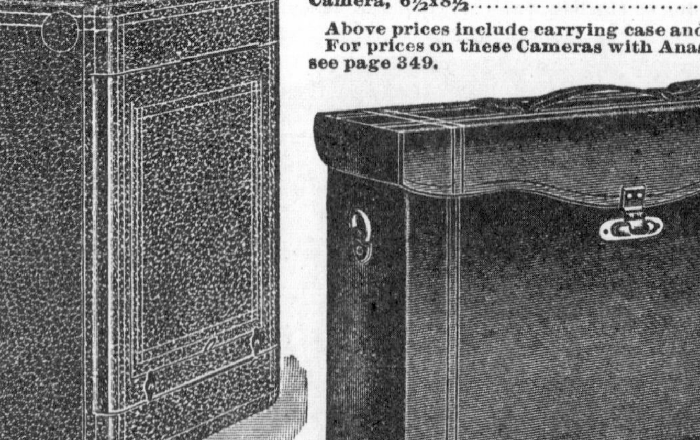

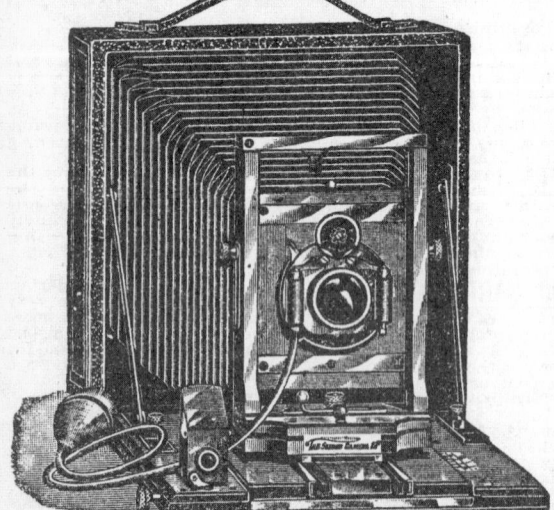

Front View of the Seroco Double Extension Camera. Seroco Double Extension Camera Closed. Carrying Case.

THE BELLOWS is made from the very best grade red leather, lined with a special light proof gossamer cloth, attached with pure rubber cement, which insures the leather remaining soft and pliable.

THE SWING BACK is so constructed that it is easily and quickly adjustable to any desired angle, and firmly held by simply tightening the set screw at the base of either side arm.

THE REVERSIBLE BACK. The Seroco Double Extension Camera is so made that the back can be instantly detached by pressing two concealed buttons, and as readily replaced with the plate in position for either vertical or horizontal pictures; the most easily operated reversible back made, having no clips or catches of any sort to adjust.

THE FINE RACK AND PINION FOCUS MOVEMENT works very smoothly without the slightest lost motion, and when the camera is focused it may be securely locked by simply pressing in the pinion flush with the bed.

THE DOUBLE SLIDING FRONT is made with both vertical motion and side motion, allowing control of the relative amount of sky and foreground, and also permitting more of one side or the other of a picture to be included in the view without changing the position of the camera.

IN ADDITION to the special features already described, the Seroco Double Extension Camera is provided with the latest type of Triple Lens Reversible Brilliant View Finder, Detachable Lens Board and Piano Hinge. When we offer you the Seroco Double Extension Camera as the best camera made, we do so with perfect confidence that a rigid test and examination of the instrument will demonstrate that it is all and even more than we claim for it.

Shoulder strap 22 cents extra. For prices on extra holders see No. 20C2510. For suitable developing outfits see No. 20C2900.

THE SEROCO VIEW CAMERA.

5 x 7 Outfit	$19.00
6½x8½ Outfit	25.00
8 x 10 Outfit	28.00

MADE IN OUR FACTORY AT ROCHESTER.

Our special prices are actual factory cost, with only our one small profit added, less than corresponding trust cameras cost the largest dealers.

SPECIFICATIONS: SOLID MAHOGANY, PIANO FINISH; LACQUERED BRASS METAL WORK; LEATHER BELLOWS; REVERSIBLE BACK; ADJUSTABLE SLIDING FRONT, RACK AND PINION FOCUS MOVEMENT; DOUBLE SWING, CENTRALLY PIVOTED; BOTH FRONT AND BACK FOCUS; EXTRA LONG DRAW; THREE SECTION, DOUBLE GROOVED BED.

THE FOCAL CAPACITY of the Seroco View Camera constitutes a most important feature, the 5x7 size having a bellows length of 22 inches, the 6½x8½ size, 27 inches and the 8x10 size, 30 inches.

The Seroco View Camera and Combination Tripod.

THE SEROCO VIEW CAMERA is the highest grade view camera made, combining convenience, strength, rigidity, compactness and adaptability for the widest possible range of work to a degree never before attained. We honestly believe the Seroco View Camera to be the best view camera made, regardless of price.

THE SEROCO VIEW CAMERA meets all requirements for the very best amateur or professional work. It is a camera that is elegant in appearance, a camera that will give you perfect results and a camera that you will enjoy using.

THE WOODWORK of the Seroco View Camera is solid mahogany throughout, thoroughly seasoned and highly polished.

THE METAL PARTS are all of lacquered brass, highly finished, carefully and accurately adjusted.

FOCUSING may be accomplished by moving either the front or the back, both being operated by fine rack and pinion adjustment.

The Seroco View Camera with rear section of bed detached.

The Seroco View Camera Folded.

THE BACK is reversible and may be instantly changed to either upright or horizontal work.

THE DOUBLE SWING, which is pivoted at the center, is easily and quickly adjusted to any desired angle and securely clamped in place by a large milled head screw.

THE FRONT is adjustable, permitting a wide range of movement either above or below the center, and is securely clamped at any height by simply tightening a milled head screw.

THE BELLOWS is made from the best grade of red keratol, lined with a special light proof gossamer cloth; elegant in appearance, absolutely light tight; strong and durable; the best bellows possible to make.

FOR WIDE ANGLE WORK the back may be racked close up to the front, thus permitting the use of the shortest focus lenses made, leaving no part of the bed in range of the lens.

THE BED is made in three sections, the front section hinged and arranged to fold back against the camera. The rear section is detachable, being necessary only when the extreme length of draw is used.

STRONG, RIGID, SUBSTANTIAL AND AT THE SAME TIME LIGHT AND COMPACT.

THE TRIPOD. We furnish with the Seroco View Camera a high grade Combination Tripod, a combined sliding and folding tripod with detachable head, made from selected ash, strong, substantial, absolutely rigid, the best tripod that can be made. This tripod is easily and quickly set up, readily adjusted to any desired height, and folds up so compactly that it can be put into the carrying case with the camera.

THE LENS AND SHUTTER. We equip the Seroco View Camera with either our Seroco Rapid Rectilinear Lens and Unicum Shutter (for prices see No. 20C2208 below), or with our Seroco Extra Rapid Symmetrical Lens and Automatic Shutter (for prices see No. 20C2209 below.) For illustrations and complete descriptions of these lenses and shutters we refer you to page 348.

THE CARRYING CASE. We put the Seroco View Camera in a fine carrying case, with compartments for containing the camera, the tripod, the lens and shutter and six extra plate holders. Compare the convenience of this outfit in which everything is contained in one easily carried case, with other outfits in which the case contains only the camera and about two holders, making it necessary to carry the lens and shutter, the tripod and the extra plate holders in separate packages.

The Carrying Case, with compartments for Camera, Lens and Shutter, Tripod and six Double Plate Holders.

FOR PRICES On these Cameras with ANASTIGMAT LENSES See Page 349

COMPLETE DEVELOPING, FINISHING AND MATERIAL OUTFITS.

For the convenience of those who desire everything necessary for making, developing and finishing pictures, we put up special outfits suitable for use with the Seroco View Camera. These outfits contain the following complete list of apparatus and materials:

- 1 High Grade Metal Ruby Lamp with Oil Burner.
- 1 Compressed Fibre Tray for developing.
- 1 Compressed Fibre Tray for fixing.
- 1 Compressed Fibre Tray for toning.
- 1 Folding Negative Rack to hold 24 plates.
- 1 8-Ounce Cone Shaped Graduate.
- 1 Print Roller.
- 1 Heavy Printing Frame.
- 1 Paste Brush.
- 1 Fine Gossamer Focus Cloth.
- 1 Dozen Extra Rapid Roebuck Dry Plates.
- 1 Dozen Seroco Sensitized Paper.
- 25 Card Mounts.
- 1 Package Hydro-Metol Developing Powders (makes 24 ounces developer).
- 1 Package Toning and Fixing Powders (makes 24 ounces of Toner).
- 1 Pound Hypo-Sulphite of Soda.
- 1 Jar Photo Paste.
- 1 Copy "Complete Instructions in Photography."

FOR PRICES OF OUTFITS SEE No. 20C2211.

Order by Number.

PRICES:

No. 20C2208 The Seroco View Camera, complete with Seroco Rapid Rectilinear Lens, Unicum Shutter, Combination Tripod, one Double Plate Holder and Carrying Case.

Size	Price
5 x 7	$19.00
6½ x 8½	25.00
8 x 10	28.00

No. 20C2209 The Seroco View Camera, complete with Seroco Extra Rapid Symmetrical Lens, Automatic Shutter, Combination Tripod, one Double Plate Holder and Carrying Case.

Size	Price
5 x 7	$35.00
6½ x 8½	41.00
8 x 10	48.00

No. 20C2210 The Seroco View Camera, with Combination Tripod, one Double Plate Holder and Carrying Case, but **without Lens or Shutter.**

Size	Price
5 x 7	$12.48
6½ x 8½	14.13
8 x 10	15.25

No. 20C2211 Developing, Finishing and Material Outfits, complete, just as described above and shown in the illustration on this page.

Outfit for	Price
5 x 7 Camera	$3.24
6½ x 8½ Camera	3.86
8 x 10 Camera	4.92

Extra Holders, 5x7, 60c each; 6½x8½, 79c each; 8x10, $1.10 each. See No. 20C2510

COMPLETE INSTRUCTIONS IN PHOTOGRAPHY.

OUR NEW 112-PAGE MANUAL.

A SPECIAL FEATURE of our photographic outfits is the book, "Complete Instructions in Photography," which is included free of charge with every camera or complete outfit.

THIS BOOK WAS WRITTEN EXPRESSLY FOR US by one of the most expert photographers in the United States; a man who has spent fifteen years in making photographs, teaching photography, and selling photographic merchandise to both amateur and professional photographers. The experience thus gained, not only in the actual processes of photography, but in contact with other photographers—with amateurs and with beginners—enables him to appreciate and to understand, better than anyone else, the difficulties met with and the errors made by beginners. This experience enables him to understand just what the beginner wants to know, enables him to make it plain and simple, and the success which is attending the efforts of those who are already using "Complete Instructions in Photography" is the best proof we can offer as to its value.

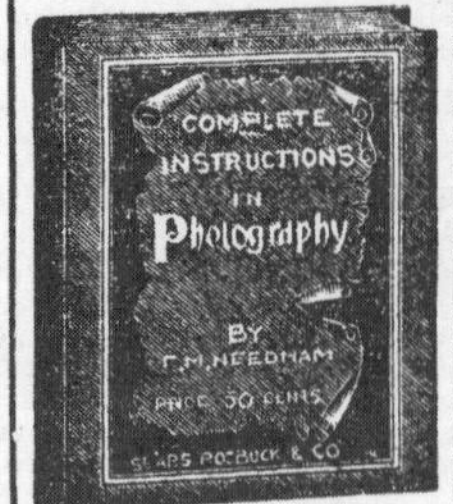

COMPLETE INSTRUCTIONS IN PHOTOGRAPHY answers all your questions, solves all your difficulties, anticipates all your troubles and makes photography easy. Indispensable to the beginner, invaluable to the advanced photographer. Complete Instructions in Photography tells secrets of the trade never before published; gives valuable information heretofore possessed only by a few professional photographers; GIVES DOZENS OF VALUABLE FORMULAS OR RECEIPTS; tells you how to make your own developers, your own solutions of all kinds; tells you how to determine the correct amount of exposure, how to save plates which are wrongly exposed, how to make good portraits, how to make blue paper, how to dry a negative in five minutes, HOW TO MAKE MONEY IN PHOTOGRAPHY, how to avoid all the troubles sometimes met with by beginners, how to select a camera; tells all about a hundred other things which we haven't space to mention here.

REMEMBER, There is no other book like it. It was written expressly for us. It is published only by us, and can be secured only from us.

IT COSTS YOU NOTHING.

WE INCLUDE IT FREE OF CHARGE with every camera which we sell. If you already have an outfit and desire a copy of the book, we will include it free of charge with an order for photographic supplies amounting to $2.50 or more (provided you state in your order that you desire it). We do not sell this book. We had it written and publish it exclusively for the benefit of our customers, but in order to protect ourselves against actual loss, we are obliged to give it only to those who send us an order for at least $2.50 worth of photographic goods, and state in their order that a copy of "Complete Instructions in Photography" is desired.

No. 2 SEROCO FILM CAMERA.

Daylight Loading. For 4x5 Pictures.

FACTORY PRICE, - - - - - - - - - - **$3.75**

No. 20C2252 THE No. 2 SEROCO FILM CAMERA combines simplicity of operation and compactness to the greatest possible degree. It does not require to be focused, the shutter does not need to be set, in short it is ready for instant use at any time without any manipulation or adjustment.

THE LENS is an extra high grade Universal Focus Achromatic Meniscus, the very best 4x5 fixed focus lens that can be made. The shutter is of the rotary style, perfectly balanced and provided with a regulator, permitting either slow, medium or fast instantaneous exposures and time exposures of any length. This camera is provided with a set of three diaphragms, two accurately centered and adjusted view finders and two tripod sockets. The covering is the very finest black morocco leather and all metal parts are finely nickel plated. Workmanship and materials throughout of the same high quality maintained in all our Seroco Film Cameras. Our special factory price.......... $3.75

No. 20C2253 Sole Leather Carrying Case for above camera. Price, 1.10

No. 3 SEROCO FOLDING FILM CAMERA.

Daylight Loading. For $3\frac{1}{4}$x$4\frac{1}{4}$ Pictures.

OUR SPECIAL FACTORY PRICE, **$6.95**

Open.

No. 20C2260 THE No. 3 SEROCO FOLDING FILM CAMERA is an exceedingly compact camera, fitted with high grade Double Rapid Rectilinear Lens of great depth of focus and covering capacity. **THE SHUTTER** is the simplex, designed especially for small compact cameras, entirely automatic in action, always set and provided with Iris diaphgram.

THE BRILLIANT FINDER is reversible.

TWO TRIPOD SOCKETS are provided.

THE COVERING is the highest grade pebbled morocco leather. All metal parts are nickel plated.

THE WOOD WORK is solid mahogany with piano finish. Workmanship and material throughout are the very highest grade. Price.......... $6.95

No. 20C2261 Sole Leather Carrying Case for above camera..... 95c

Closed.

Glass Plate Attachment.

For Use with the Seroco Folding Film Cameras.

No. 20C2289 There are many photographers who prefer on some occasions to use glass plates instead of film, and this glass plate attachment used in connection with our Seroco Folding Film Cameras converts the camera instantly into a regular glass plate camera with spring actuated ground glass focusing screen. These plate holders use a very light and compact single plate holder, with aluminum back and hard rubber slide.

Price complete, including one single plate holder... $1.75
Extra plate holders, $3\frac{1}{4}$x$4\frac{1}{4}$, each.......... .35
Extra plate holders, 4x5, each.......... .45

This plate attachment can be used with the Nos. 3, 4, 5 and 6 Seroco Film Camera only, and the price is the same for each style. In ordering, be sure to state number of camera it is to be used with.

No. 4 SEROCO FOLDING FILM CAMERA.

Daylight Loading. For 4x5 Pictures.

OUR SPECIAL FACTORY PRICE, - - - - **$10.95**

Open.

No. 20C2265 THE No. 4 SEROCO FOLDING FILM CAMERA is similar in general style to the No. 3, but larger, making 4x5 pictures. It is fitted with the very latest improved Bausch & Lomb Automatic Shutter, the highest grade shutter made, provided with Iris Diaphragm and an extra high grade Double Rapid Rectilinear Lens, the very best rapid rectilinear lens made.

THE No. 4 SEROCO FOLDING FILM CAMERA is covered with the best pebbled morocco leather.

ALL METAL PARTS are nickel plated and highly polished.

THE FINDER is of brilliant reversible type.

THE WOOD WORK is solid mahogany with piano finish.

OUR SPECIAL PRICE for the No. 4 Seroco Folding Film Camera is made possible only by the fact that we make these cameras in our own factory and sell them direct to the user at manufacturers' prices. Price.......... $10.95

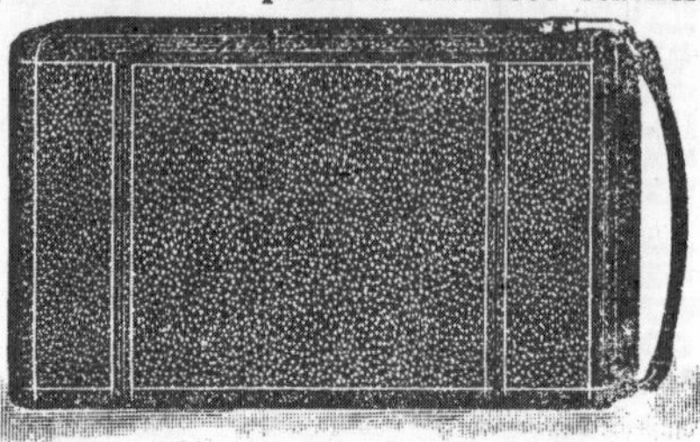

Closed.

No. 20C2266 Sole Leather Carrying Case for above camera..... $1.16

Nos. 5 AND 6 SEROCO FOLDING FILM CAMERAS.

Daylight Loading.

$10.75 for the $3\frac{1}{4}$x$4\frac{1}{4}$ size.

$12.50 for the 4x5 size.

Open.

THE Nos. 5 AND 6 SEROCO FOLDING FILM CAMERAS are made with extra high grade Symmetrical Lens, Extension Bed, Rack and Pinion Focus Movement and Rising and Falling Front. These cameras represent a most decided advance in film cameras, having all the adjustments possessed by the highest grade glass plate cameras. The wood work is solid mahogany with piano finish, the covering is the best morocco leather. All metal parts are nickel plated and highly polished. They are fitted with extra large high grade Symmetrical Lenses, the very b[illegible] symmetrical lenses that ca[illegible] be purchased from the Bausch & Lomb Optical Co., and the latest improved Bausch & Lomb Automatic Shutter.

THE TRUST IS TRYING TO COMPETE WITH US by offering these exact same cameras at $15.00 and $18.00 each, against our special factory prices of $10.75 and $12.50.

Closed.

No. 20C2270 No. 5 Seroco Film Camera, for $3\frac{1}{4}$x$4\frac{1}{4}$ pictures. Price. $10.75
No. 20C2271 No. 6 Seroco Film Camera, for 4x5 pictures. Price.. 12.50
No. 20C2272 Sole Leather Carrying Case for No. 5 Camera...... .95
No. 20C2273 Sole Leather Carrying Case for No. 6 Camera .. 1.10

Nos. 7 and 8 SEROCO FOCUSING FILM CAMERAS.

Daylight Loading.

FACTORY PRICES, according to size,

$12.80 and $13.75

THE Nos. 7 and 8 SEROCO FOCUSING FILM CAMERAS represent a new departure in the line of film cameras, being so constructed that a regulation full size ground glass focusing screen in the rear of the camera may be used the same as in a glass plate camera.

Open.

THESE CAMERAS are made with Rack and Pinion Focusing Movement, Brilliant Reversible Finders, Extension Bed and Extra Long Bellows. They are made throughout of solid mahogany with piano finish. The covering is the best grade of pebbled morocco leather. All metal parts are nickel plated and both material and workmanship throughout are the best that can be obtained.

THE SHUTTER is the latest improved style of Bausch & Lomb's Famous Automatic with retarding device, the highest grade shutter made. The Lens is an Extra Rapid Long Focus Symmetrical, of great depth of focus and covering power.

Closed.

No. 20C2277 No. 7 Seroco Focusing Film Camera for 8¼x4¼ pictures. Our special factory to user price. $12.80

No. 20C2278 No. 8 Seroco Focusing Film Camera for 4x5 pictures. Our special factory to user price.. $13.75

No. 20C2279 Sole Leather Carrying Case for No. 7, $1.60; for No. 8, 1.90

OUR SPECIAL PORTRAIT OUTFIT.

No. 20C2300 This outfit consists of an 8x10 Camera, Camera Stand and Reversible Cabinet Attachment.

CAMERA is made from best hard wood, finely finished. All adjustments are automatic and self locking. Has 30-inch bed, best india rubber bellows.

STAND IS THE WIZARD No. 7, fitted with automatic balancing device, raises and lowers with the lightest touch, can be locked in any position by lever at side. Firm and rigid, made of hardwood, finely finished. Top measures 17x32¼ inches.

THE NELSON AUTOMATIC HOLDER is included, the best studio plate holder made. Plates are put in or removed without turning a button, the back does not require to be opened, no spring to press on back of plate. Takes any size of plate from 8x10 to 2x2.

THE REVERSIBLE CABINET ATTACHMENT has spring actuated ground glass, and uses modern double plate holders.

THE FOLDING RACK is made of hardwood, holds twelve double plate holders, and is attached to side of stand.

KITS FOR 6½X8½, 4¼x6½ AND 3¼x4¼ PLATES are furnished so that the outfit is complete for any size work from 8x10 down.

Price, complete, **$34.75**

No lens or shutter is included. Make selection from pages 348 and 349 to suit your requirements.

Portrait Camera.

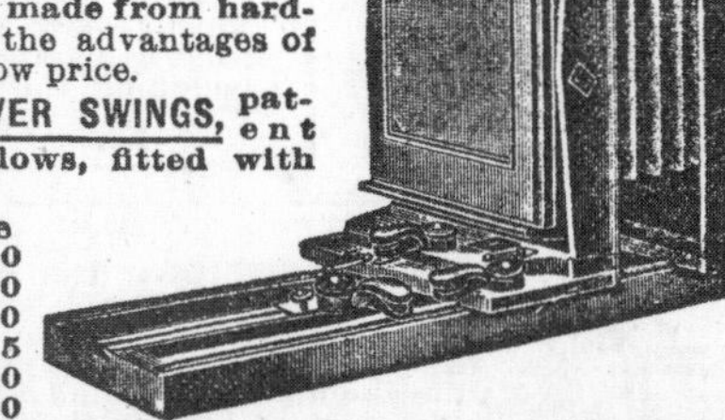

No. 20C2305 This Camera is made from hardwood, finely finished, and has all the advantages of higher priced cameras at a very low price.

AUTOMATIC SELF LOCKING LEVER SWINGS, patent focus lever, india rubber bellows, fitted with regulation curtain slide holder.

Size	Length of Bed	Price
6½x8½	24 inches	$14.60
8 x10	30 inches	17.50
10 x12	34 inches	21.00
11 x14	36 inches	25.75
14 x17	40 inches	30.40
17 x20	43 inches	39.00

IN MAKING UP YOUR ORDER FOR SUPPLIES
REMEMBER THAT
COMPLETE INSTRUCTIONS IN PHOTOGRAPHY IS FURNISHED FREE
IF YOU ASK FOR IT, WITH EVERY $2.50 ORDER.

Studio Camera.

No. 20C2310 This Camera is made from finely finished hardwood, has india rubber bellows, swinging ground glass, double swing and automatic self locking focus lever. Fitted with reversible cabinet attachment, with one 5x7 double plate holder for same, also regular curtain slide holder. Length of bed, 24 inches, made in 8x10 size only. Price, complete with cabinet attachment........ $19.90

Price, without cabinet attachment.................... $13.20

Price of extra holders for cabinet attachment, 98c each.

Improved Victoria Camera for Ferrotype Work.

No. 20C2315 Made from selected hardwood, provided with all the latest adjustments, and finely finished. This camera is made for 5x7 plates, but is also fitted with diaphragms for making 4¼x5½ and 3¼x4¼ pictures with one lens. With four Gem lenses this camera makes either four or eight pictures on a 5x7 plate.

Price, complete with four quarter-size Gem lenses............ $18.90

Price, without lenses..... 9.50

Our Best Penny Picture Camera.

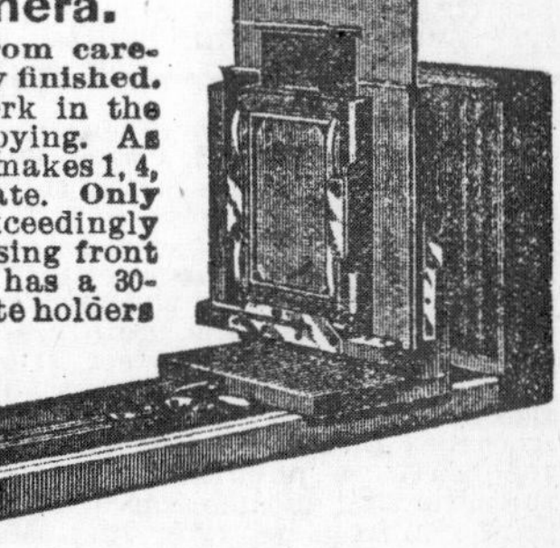

No. 20C2320 This Camera is made from carefully selected hardwood and handsomely finished. It can be used for any regular portrait work in the studio, up to and including 5x7; also for copying. As a multiplying or penny picture camera, it makes 1, 4, 9, 12, 16, 20, 30 or 42 pictures on one 5x7 plate. Only one lens required. The mechanism is exceedingly simple, very easy to operate. Made with rising front and self locking focus lever. This camera has a 30-inch bed, rubber bellows and uses double plate holders of modern style. Price, with one double plate holder................ ..... $16.90

Extra plate holders, each.................. 65c

We especially recommend our Portrait Lens No. 20C2432 for use with this camera.

Special Penny Picture Camera.

No. 20C2325 This Camera is adapted for regular portrait work as well as penny pictures, and makes an excellent all around studio camera. Made from hardwood, well finished, has india rubber bellows, and a sliding back, which makes it unnecessary to remove the holders between exposures. Made in two sizes, 4x5 and 5x7. The 4x5 camera makes 1, 4, 9 or 12 pictures on one 4x5 plate. The 5x7 camera makes 1, 4, 9, 12 or 24 pictures on one 5x7 plate. Uses modern double plate holders. Only one lens is required. Price, 4x5 camera, with one double plate holder.................... $9.85

Price, 5x7 camera, with one double plate holder.................. 13.25

Extra plate holders for 4x5 cameras, each.............................. .60

Extra plate holders for 5x7 cameras, each.............................. .65

See No. 20C2432 for prices on lenses suitable for this camera.

Camera Stands.

No. 20C2350 Camera Stand No. 0. Made of hardwood, with tilting top and automatic lock, by which top is raised or lowered. Top measures 11x19 inches. Can be taken apart or set up without tools. Price.................. $2.80

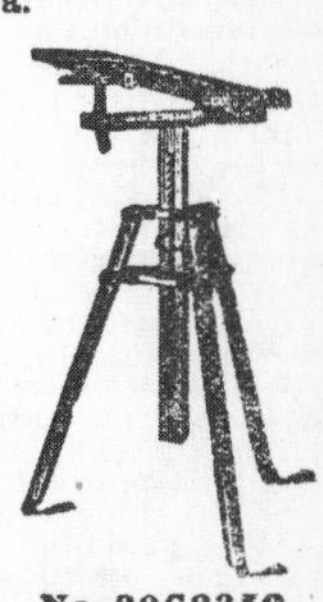

No. 20C2350

No. 20C2354

No. 20C2354 The Wizard Stand No. 7, a very solidly built stand, made of finely finished hardwood. Has automatic balancing device, which can be regulated to balance any camera from 10x12 down. Raises and lowers with the lightest touch, and is firmly locked in any position by lever at side. Very firm and rigid; our best stand. Size of top, 17x32¼ inches; for cameras 10x12 or smaller.

Price................ $13.40

POSING CHAIR, $3.50.

No. 20C2370 Our Special Posing Chair, a neat and well made chair, seat and back of oak, pedestal of steel wire with antique copper finish. Seat can be raised and lowered, or placed in any position and held firmly by tightening knob under seat. Price.................. $3.50

No. 20C2370

The Monarch Wide Angle Lens.

No. 20C2415 The Monarch Wide Angle Lens embraces an angle of 90 degrees, making it especially adapted to photographing the interiors of buildings, out of door views in confined situations; in fact, any work where it is difficult or impossible to get far enough away from the subject in order to get it all on the plate with an ordinary lens. **Our Monarch Wide Angle Lenses** are handsomely mounted in lacquered brass with a set of revolving diaphragms. Made expressly for us by the Bausch & Lomb Optical Company, and represents the latest advances in the making of lenses of this type. **The speed of this lens is F. 16.**

Size of View, Inches	Equivalent Focus, Inches	Back Focus, Inches	Diameter of Lenses, Inches	Diameter Across Hood, Inches	Price
4 x 5	3½	3¼	¾	1 9/32	$5.70
5 x 7	5¼	4⅞	¾	1 9/32	6.80
5 x 8	5½	5⅛	¾	1 9/32	7.10
6½ x 8½	6½	6 1/16	⅞	1 9/32	9.90
8 x 10	8	7½	1⅛	1 9/32	12.80

Seroco Rapid Rectilinear Lens.

The Seroco Rapid Rectilinear Lens.

No. 20C2421 The Seroco Rapid Rectilinear Lens, a double lens of the rapid rectilinear type, very handsomely mounted in lacquered brass with Waterhouse diaphragms. **This lens is perfectly rectilinear,** rendering the straight lines of buildings, or other subjects, absolutely without distortion, possesses a remarkable depth of focus and flatness of field, giving the most brilliant definition and detail. **This lens is unsurpassed for landscape work,** views of buildings, and other architectural subjects, flash lights, groups and instantaneous work. **Represents better value than any other lens on the market, and is superior in every respect to many lenses sold at double the prices.** In sizes 4x5 to 8x10 inches, inclusive, we furnish the Seroco Rapid Rectilinear Lens either with or without the Unicum Shutter. **The speed of this lens is F. 8.**

The Unicum Shutter.

The Unicum Shutter gives automatic exposures of 1 second, ½ second, ⅕ second, 1/25 second or 1/100 second, with one pressure of the bulb. With indicator set to "B" a pressure of the bulb opens the shutter, which remains open until the pressure is released. With indicator set to "T" the first pressure of the bulb opens the shutter, which remains open until the bulb is again pressed. Back of the shutter blades is a perfect **Iris Diaphragm,** the opening being instantly adjustable to any desired size by the index lever at lower margin of shutter. **Accuracy and entire freedom from jarring are secured by a pneumatic retarding device,** and the actuating mechanism of the shutter is fully protected from injury or dust. Made from bronze metal, with nickel plated trimmings, very handsomely finished throughout.

The Seroco Rapid Rectilinear Lens with Unicum Shutter.

Size of View, Inches	Equivalent Focus, Inches	Back Focus Inches	Diameter Image Circle, Inches	Diameter of Lenses, Inches	Diameter Across Hood, Inches	Price of Lens Alone With Waterhouse Stops	Price of Lens Complete With Unicum Shutter
4 x 5	6¾	6	9	1	1½	$ 5.70	$ 8.50
5 x 7	8¾	7½	10½	1⅜	2 1/16	6.80	9.50
5 x 8	9¼	8	11	1⅜	2 1/16	7.10	11.25
6½ x 8½	12	10¼	13¼	1⅝	2 11/32	9.90	14.75
8 x 10	14¾	13	16	2	3	12.80	16.75
10 x 12	17	15	19½	2¼	3 9/16	17.50	Not Made
11 x 14	18½	16½	22½	2 9/16	4 1/16	26.32	Not Made
14 x 17	22½	20	26	2⅞	4 9/16	36.00	Not Made

The Seroco Extra Rapid Symmetrical Lens.

SPEED F. 6. THE QUICKEST RECTILINEAR LENS MADE.

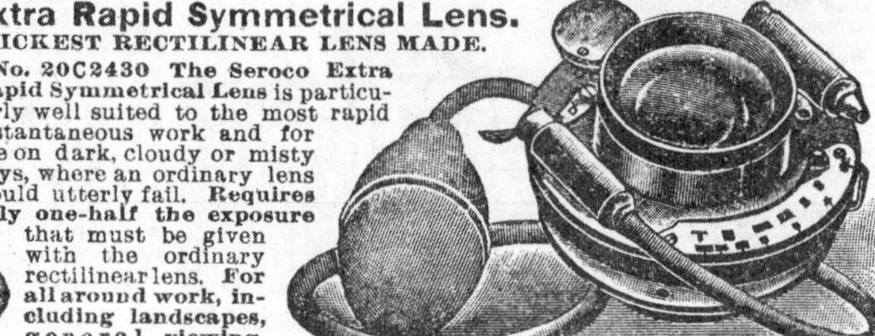

The Seroco Extra Rapid Symmetrical Lens with Iris diaphragm.

No. 20C2430 The Seroco Extra Rapid Symmetrical Lens is particularly well suited to the most rapid instantaneous work and for use on dark, cloudy or misty days, where an ordinary lens would utterly fail. **Requires only one-half the exposure** that must be given with the ordinary rectilinear lens. **For all around work, including landscapes, general viewing, high speed instantaneous work, etc., the Seroco Extra Rapid Symmetrical lens offers advantages over any other existing type of lens on the market today.**

This lens is **perfectly rectilinear,** rendering the straight lines of buildings or other subjects absolutely without distortion, possesses **great depth of focus,** flatness of field and **brilliant definition.**

The great speed of this lens, almost equal to that of an ordinary portrait lens, makes it particularly desirable for **portrait work,** and for those who do not care to invest in both a rectilinear lens and a portrait lens, we can especially recommend the Seroco Extra Rapid Symmetrical Lens, **which will answer both requirements.**

Construction: This lens is composed of two systems, both the front and back systems each being composed of two lenses cemented together. Both front and rear combinations are perfectly corrected and either may be used alone when a greater focal length is desired.

It is provided with a finely adjusted Iris Diaphragm, operated by a small lever, as shown in the illustration, beautifully mounted in lacquered brass. In sizes 4x5 to 8x10 inclusive, we furnish these lenses either with or without the new Bausch & Lomb Automatic Shutter.

Seroco Extra Rapid Symmetrical Lens with Automatic Shutter.

Size of View, Inches	Equivalent Focus, Inches	Back Focus, Inches	Diameter Image Circle, Inches	Diameter of Lenses, Inches	Diameter Across Hood, Inches	Price of Lens Alone with Iris Diaphragm	Price of Lens Complete with Automatic Shutter
4 x 5	6⅜	5 3/16	8¾	1⅛	1 3/16	$15.68	$20.55
5 x 7	8	7	10¾	1⅛	1 13/32	20.10	24.75
6½ x 8½	9 7/16	8¼	12¾	1¼	1 31/32	25.12	29.62
8 x 10	11¼	9 13/16	15⅛	2⅛	2 11/32	32.40	36.60
10 x 12	14¼	12 7/16	19	2⅝	2⅞	41.92	Not Made
11 x 14	17½	15¼	24	3 5/16	3⅝	56.00	Not Made
14 x 17	22¾	19⅜	25¾	3¾	4⅛	72.52	Not Made

The 5x7 lens will cover a 5x8 plate sharply to extreme corners.

The new Bausch & Lomb Automatic Shutter, in general appearance and principles of operation closely resembles the Unicum, which we fully describe under No. 20C2421, but **it requires no setting,** as the mechanism is so constructed that it automatically resets itself after each exposure.

The Seroco Extra Rapid Portrait Lens.

SPEED, F. 4. THE QUICKEST LENS MADE.

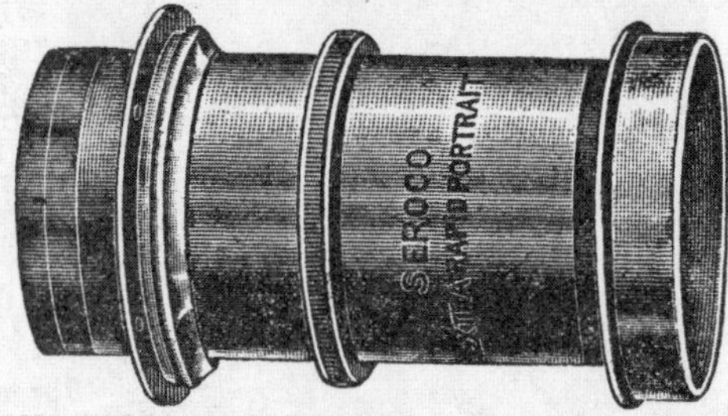

No. 20C2440 At $48.00 we offer the 6½x8½ Seroco Extra Rapid Portrait Lens as the equal in every way of portrait lenses heretofore sold at several times our price. In quality of glass, perfection of finish, careful adjustment and fine workmanship; in softness, delicacy and depth of focus; in speed, flatness of field, and brilliancy of illumination; **the Seroco Extra Rapid Portrait Lens** is not equaled by any other portrait lens on the market, regardless of price or maker. **The Seroco Extra Rapid Portrait Lens** represents the very latest advances in scientific lens grinding, possessing all those peculiar optical qualities and special brilliancy of definition so necessary in high grade portrait work. **The Seroco Extra Rapid Portrait Lens** preserves that softness and roundness so essential in portrait making, even when stopped down, a quality possessed by no other portrait lens made, as all other lenses become distinctly wiry when a small diaphragm is employed. **We particularly invite comparison of the Seroco Extra Rapid Portrait Lens with any other portrait lens on the market regardless of price or maker,** as we know that in all these special points, whereby a portrait lens is judged, the **Seroco Extra Rapid Portrait Lens** is the best that money can buy.

CONSTRUCTION: The Seroco Extra Rapid Portrait Lens is composed of two systems, the elementary lenses of the front system being cemented together, while the elementary lenses of the back system are separated. The back system is mounted in an adjustable mounting, enabling the operator to vary the distance between these lenses, thus varying the depth of focus and quality of definition. Any desired degree of softness, roundness or distribution of focus can be obtained by thus varying the distance between the elementary lenses of the back system. A perfect **Iris Diaphragm** is provided with this lens, thus doing away entirely with loose stops to mislay or lose.

Number	Size of Plate Covered, inches	Diameter of Lenses, inches	Back Focus, inches	Diameter Across Hood, inches	Price
1	5 x 8	3 5/16	8½	4 9/16	$33.75
2	6½ x 8½	4 1/16	11½	5 9/16	48.00
3	8 x 10	4¼	13½	5 9/16	90.00

Distance required between subject and lens to make a standing figure 6 inches high of a person 6 feet tall is as follows: With the 5x8 size, 12 feet; with the 6½x8½ size, 17¼ feet; with the 8x10 size, 19 feet.

OUR TEN DAYS' FREE TRIAL OFFER.

WE SEND OUT

ANY OF OUR LENSES

with the understanding and agreement that you can keep the lens for ten days, during which time you can put it to any test. You can compare it with other lenses of the most celebrated makes, lenses costing two and three times the amount we ask you for our lens, and, if our lens does not prove equal to any lens with which it may be compared in depth of focus, covering power, definition—in short, in all those qualities by which lenses are judged, you may send it back to us and we will refund your money, including the express charges both ways.

THE SEROCO PORTRAIT LENS.

SPEED F. 6.

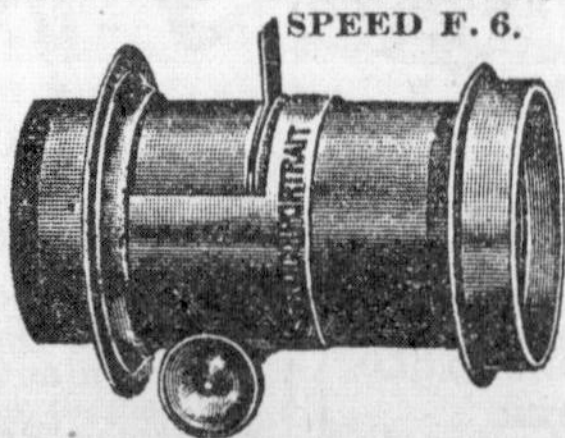

No. 20C2432 This lens possesses those peculiar optical qualities necessary in portrait work, working very rapidly and yielding soft, brilliant negatives. **The ¼-size is particularly suitable for penny picture work** and for small portraits. Many photographers purchase ordinary rectilinear lenses for penny picture work on account of the comparatively low price of such lenses as compared with regular portrait lenses, but in this lens we offer you an opportunity to equip your outfit with a lens designed and made expressly for portrait work, at a price even lower than the cost of a rectilinear lens. **The ½-size and 4-4 size are both designed for regular cabinet work** and of the two the 4-4 size is the most popular, **as it can also be used for small groups and full figures.**

CONSTRUCTION: The Seroco Portrait Lens is a double combination, the front system composed of two lenses cemented together, the rear system of two separated lenses, which is the true portrait method of construction. The lens tube is nickel plated and highly polished, the hood, flange and barrel of lacquered brass, and **a fine rack and pinion movement** is provided for accurate focusing, also a set of Waterhouse diaphragms in morocco case.

Size	Plate covered inches	Diameter lenses, inches	Back Focus, inches	Price
¼	3¼x4¼	1⅝	4½	$ 7.75
½	4¼x6½	2⅜	7	13.70
4-4	6½x8½	3¼	11	24.00

SEROCO SERIES I ANASTIGMAT LENS F. 6.8.

No. 20C2443 The Seroco Series I Anastigmat Lens is a double anastigmat of the most perfect type. It is in every sense of the word a universal lens, being suitable for practically any kind of photographic work, including landscapes, architectural subjects, portraits, groups, studio use and high speed instantaneous work.

The designers of this lens have succeeded in absolutely eliminating all traces of astigmatism and at the same time have produced a lens absolutely free from chromatic or spherical aberration.

In defining power, depth of focus, flatness of field and brilliancy of illumination the Seroco Series I Anastigmat Lens is not surpassed by any anastigmat lens on the market, regardless of price.

The Seroco Anastigmat Lens is of the double symmetrical type, the front and rear combinations being of the same construction. They are ground from the very highest grade Jena optical glass, made expressly for the manufacture of the highest grade anastigmat lenses.

In construction this lens is of the double anastigmat symmetrical type, composed of two systems, each system made up of four elementary lenses. Both the front combination and rear combination are fully corrected and may be used alone, having a focal length about twice that of the complete lens.

We absolutely guarantee the Series I Seroco Anastigmat Lens to be the very highest grade and the very best anastigmat lens on the market, regardless of price.

We furnish this Lens, mounted in either the BAUSCH & LOMB OPTICAL CO.'S AUTOMATIC SHUTTER or the VOLUTE SHUTTER. The Automatic shutter makes automatic exposures of 1 second, ½ second, ⅕ second, 1/25 second, 1/50 second and 1/100 second, and bulb or time exposures of any length, is fitted with Iris diaphragm, entirely automatic in action, with pneumatic release and always set. **The Volute Shutter** is the highest type of Iris diaphragm shutter, extra rapid, very compact, dust proof and durable. It is beautifully finished throughout; made like a watch in point of accuracy and fine workmanship. Recognized everywhere, by experts, as the finest shutter made.

THIS LENS CAN BE FITTED TO ANY FOLDING CAMERA OR VIEW CAMERA. Send us the front board of your camera with your order for the lens, and we will mount it without charge.

Size	Equivalent Focus	Price, with Automatic Shutter	Price, with Volute Shutter
4 x 5	6 inches	$24.75	$36.75
5 x 7	7 inches	30.00	42.00
6½x8½	10½ inches	$42.00	$53.00
8 x10	13 inches	54.00	65.30

These prices are for the lens complete, with shutter, bulb and tube.

Ray Filters.

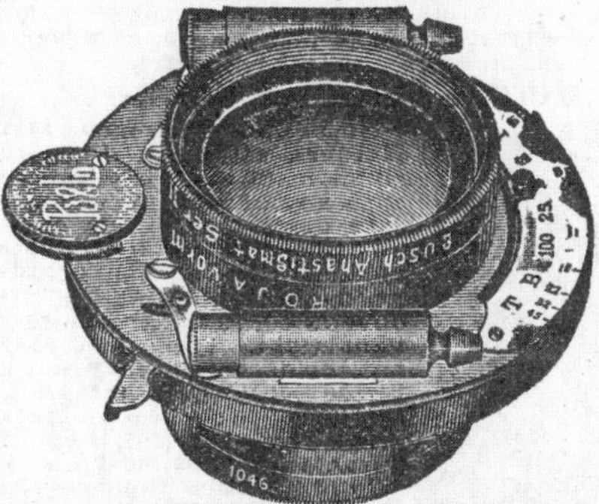

No. 20C2470 A Ray Filter is a small device so constructed that it can be slipped over the hood of the regular camera lens during exposure. **The ray filter** absorbs the violet and ultra-violet rays of light and produces a picture in which the color values are correct, that is, it enables us to produce, in monochrome, photographs with true color values. **Certain colors** or combinations of colors, such as white clouds and blue sky, or reds and yellows, show little or no contrast when photographed without a ray filter. **Clouds in a photograph** improve the artistic value of the picture wonderfully, and except under very unusual conditions they cannot be obtained at all without using a ray filter. **Landscapes** photographed with the ray filter possess a brilliancy and contrast which it is impossible to obtain otherwise; and in the photographing of flowers, paintings or any brightly colored subjects, the ray filter is practically indispensable. **A ray filter, in order to be of any practical value, must be both chemically and optically perfect.** It must be accurately ground from the very best quality of optical glass. **The surfaces must be absolutely true and mathematically parallel.** The color must be chemically pure, transparent and of exactly the right shade according to spectroscopic test. Our ray filters are composed of two pieces of thin optical glass with surfaces ground optically plane, each coated with a spectroscopically accurate yellow tint and firmly cemented together, **the very best ray filter it is possible to produce.**

No. 1 for lenses 1 1/16 inches in diameter	$0.60
No. 2 for fixed focus or box cameras	.60
No. 3 for lenses 1 7/16 inches in diameter	.60
No. 4 for lenses 1½ inches in diameter	.75
No. 5 for lenses 1¾ inches in diameter	.90
No. 6 for lenses 2 inches in diameter	.90
No. 7 for lenses 2¼ inches in diameter	1.05
No. 8 for lenses 2½ inches in diameter	1.20
No. 9 for lenses 2¾ inches in diameter	1.35
No. 10 for lenses 3 inches in diameter	1.50
No. 11 for lenses 3¼ inches in diameter	1.80
No. 12 for lenses 3½ inches in diameter	2.10
No. 13 for lenses 4 inches in diameter	2.50
No. 14 for lenses 4½ inches in diameter	3.00

If by mail, postage extra, on Nos. 1 to 6, 3 cents; Nos. 7 to 10, **5 cents;** on Nos. 11 to 14, **8 cents.**

Any of the above sizes are suitable for lenses ¼ inch less in diameter than size mentioned.

State exact diameter of lens when ordering.

BUSCH ANASTIGMAT LENS.

SERIES III F. 7.7.
Made by Rathenower Optische Industrie-Anstalt, vorm Emil Busch.

No. 20C2445 The Series III Busch Anastigmat Lens, made in Germany by the celebrated **Rathenower Optische Industrie Anstalt, successors to Emil Busch,** is constructed upon entirely new principles, and, although sold at a price representing only a fraction of the amount heretofore asked for anastigmat lenses, is a true anastigmat lens fully and positively corrected for astigmatism.

These Lenses are ground from normal optical glass, absolutely clear, colorless glass, free from bubbles and other imperfections inherent in the abnormal Jena glass ordinarily employed in making anastigmat lenses.

The Series III Busch Anastigmat Lens is composed of two symmetrical combinations, each combination absolutely free from astigmatism, spherical and chromatic aberration. Either combination may be used alone and has about one and three-fourth times the focal length of the complete lens. The use of the single combinations alone will be found particularly advantageous in landscape and portrait work. Each combination of this lens is composed of two elementary lenses, which, contrary to the ordinary custom, are not cemented together, thus eliminating the danger of deterioration of the lens due to the balsam disintegrating, a trouble to which cemented lenses are always more or less subject.

We furnish the Series III Busch Anastigmat Lens, mounted in the latest Wollensak Optical Co.'s Automatic shutter, or the Volute shutter. The Automatic shutter makes automatic exposures from 1/100 of a second to one full second, bulb exposures or time exposures of any desired length. It is made with Iris diaphragms, provided with pneumatic release and is entirely automatic in action, re-setting itself after each exposure.

The Volute Shutter is the highest type of Iris diaphragm shutter, extra rapid, very compact, dust proof and durable. It is beautifully finished throughout; made like a watch in point of accuracy and fine workmanship. Recognized everywhere, by experts, as the finest shutter made.

Size of Plate Covered at Full Aperture	Size of Plate Covered at F. 45	Equivalent Focus	Price, with Automatic Shutter	Price, with Volute Shutter
4x5	5x8	6 inches.	$19.75	$30.00
5x7	7x9	7½ inches.	23.50	33.75
6½x8½	9x12	10 inches.	39.00	48.50
8x10	12x16	13 inches.	49.40	59.75

These prices are for the lens complete, with shutter, bulb and tube.

This lens can be fitted to any folding hand camera or view camera. If you desire us to mount the lens for you, send us the front board of your camera **and we will fit** the lens to it without charge.

Series II Busch Anastigmat Lens, F 5.5.

No. 20C2447 The greatly increasing demand, both by **amateur and professional photographers, for lenses of large aperture and great rapidity has prompted us to make special arrangements with the Rathenower Optische Industrie Anstalt** whereby we are enabled to offer this high grade, extremely fast Busch Double Anastigmat Lens at prices heretofore considered impossible for lenses of this construction.

The Series II Busch Anastigmat Lens works at an aperture of F 5.5, which is about double the speed of the ordinary anastigmat lens.

The Series II Busch anastigmat lens is constructed under the same patents, and has all the advantages possessed by the Series III and works at double the speed.

Absolute flatness of field and complete absence of astigmatism are obtained over the entire angle of 75 degrees, and equal definition is secured over the entire surface of the plate when the lens is used at full aperture. The use of smaller diaphragms greatly increases the covering power and renders the lens very valuable as a **wide angle lens,** when used on a plate larger than the size for which it is listed.

Both the front and rear combinations are perfectly corrected for spherical and chromatic aberration and astigmatism, and the back lens can be used alone for landscape and portrait work, having a focal length one and three-fourth times that of the complete lens.

REMEMBER, that a lens having a large aperture will do any work that a lens of smaller aperture will do, and in addition will do very many things that cannot be done with a lens of smaller aperture. For instantaneous exposures on dark or cloudy days this lens is indispensable. **For portrait work** the length of exposure is greatly shortened, an advantage which will be readily appreciated. **For high speed, instantaneous work** this lens is undoubtedly the very best lens on the market today.

We furnish the Series II Busch Anastigmat Lens in Wollensak Optical Co.'s Automatic Shutter, described in detail under No. 20C2445, or in the celebrated Bausch & Lomb Optical Co.'s Volute Shutter.

The Volute Shutter is the highest type of Iris diaphragm shutter, extra rapid, very compact, dust proof and durable. It is beautifully finished throughout; made like a watch in point of accuracy and fine workmanship. Recognized everywhere, by experts, as the finest shutter made.

This is a large lens and can be fitted only to cameras having large lens boards and plenty of room in front. Send us your front board when you order, and we will mount the lens without charge.

The prices are for the lens complete with automatic shutter, bulb and tube.

Size of plate covered at full aperture	Size of plate covered at F 11	Equivalent Focus, inches	Price, with Automatic Shutter	Price, with Volute Shutter
4x5	5x7	6	$25.00	$34.40
5x7	6½x8½	7½	31.00	40.00
6½x8½	8x10	10	48.00	57.65
8x10	11x14	13	Not furnished.	75.00

Seroco Cameras With Anastigmat Lenses.

ANTI-TRUST CAMERAS, WITH ANTI-TRUST LENSES, AT ANTI-TRUST PRICES.

We are now in position to furnish any of our Seroco Long Focus, Seroco Double Extension or Seroco View Cameras complete with any of our Anastigmat Lenses at the following prices:

Catalogue No.	Camera	Price, with Seroco Series I F 6.8 Anastigmat Lens	Price, with Busch Series III F 7.7 Anastigmat Lens	Price, with Busch Series II F 5.5 Anastigmat Lens
20C2451	4 x 5 Long Focus	$32.95	$28.00	Not furnished
20C2452	5 x 7 Long Focus	40.25	33.75	Not furnished
20C2453	6½x 8½ Long Focus	53.75	50.75	$59.75
20C2454	8 x10 Long Focus	68.00	63.40	*91.70
20C2455	4 x 5 Double Extension	36.00	31.00	Not furnished
20C2456	5 x 7 Double Extension	45.75	39.25	Not furnished
20C3457	6½x 8½ Double Extension	59.00	56.00	$65.00
20C2459	5 x 7 View	42.48	35.98	43.48
20C2460	6½x 8½ View	56.13	53.13	62.13
20C2461	8 x10 View	69.25	64.65	*90.25

The above prices all include Automatic Shutters, except those marked (*) which include Volute Shutters.

IF VOLUTE SHUTTER is wanted add to above price the difference between price of lens with Automatic Shutter and price with Volute Shutter as quoted under Nos. 20C2443, 20C2445 and 20C2447.

With the **Long Focus and Double Extension cameras at above prices, we include sole leather carrying** case and one plate holder.

With the **View cameras, at above prices, we include carrying case, one plate holder and combination** tripod as shown on page 351.

AUXILIARY LENSES.

Sectional view of our auxiliary lens showing perfect optical construction.

The use of Auxiliary Lenses for increasing the efficiency and capacity of ordinary folding hand cameras is becoming almost universal and practically every user of a folding hand camera today finds the use of these auxiliary lenses for enlarging and copying and for portrait work indispensable. The great demand for these auxiliary lenses has induced certain unscrupulous manufacturers to place on the market a line of very cheap goods, which are sold at wonderfully low prices, or given away as premiums. **Our auxiliary lenses** should not for a moment be compared with these trashy goods, which are made from **one piece of common window glass, imperfectly ground and not centered.** Such a lens is not achromatic, it is certain to distort the picture and will counteract all the good properties of the camera lens with which it is used. **Our auxiliary lenses are ground with scientific accuracy from the very best optical glass, the same glass that is used in making the highest grade photographic objectives. Everyone of our auxiliary lenses is accurately centered, the edges are ground and polished and they are mounted in nickel plated brass cells.** Both our enlarging lenses and our portrait lenses are composed of two elementary lenses, one of flint glass and the other of crown glass, cemented together and correctly centered, thus forming an achromatic, optically perfect, scientifically correct lens.

AUXILIARY ENLARGING AND COPYING LENSES.

No. 20C2475 These lenses are used in connection with the regular lens of any folding camera, greatly increasing its power. By the use of these lenses, copying and enlarging may be done with any folding camera, enabling one to copy other pictures or photograph small articles to their full size or even larger. **A 4x5 photograph copied with an ordinary camera will make a picture about the size of a postage stamp, but when copied with the aid of this lens can be made full size or larger.** Many uses for this valuable discovery will readily suggest themselves to the user.

No. 1 for 4x5 camera with lens 1 3/16 in. in diam. . $0.90
No. 2 for 5x7 camera with lens 1 5/16 in. in diam. . . .90
No. 3 for fixed focus or box cameras 90
No. 4 for 4x5 camera with lens 1 3/16 in. in diam. . . .90
No. 5 for 5x7 camera with lens 1 5/16 in. in diam. . . .90
No. 6 for 4x5 camera with lens 1½ in. in diam. . . 1.20
No. 7 for 5x7 camera with lens 1½ in. in diam. . . 1.20
No. 8 any size camera with lens 1¾ in. in diam. . . 1.35
No. 9 any size camera with lens 2 in. in diam. . . 1.50
No. 10 any size camera with lens 2¼ in. in diam. . . 1.65
No. 11 any size camera with lens 2½ in. in diam. . . 1.80
No. 12 any size camera with lens 2¾ in. in diam. . . 1.95
No. 13 any size camera with lens 3 in. in diam. . . 2.10

If by mail, postage extra, on Nos. 1 to 7, **3 cents;** Nos. 8 to 10, **4 cents;** Nos. 11 to 13, **5 cents.**

In measuring your lens, take the outside diameter, remembering that the enlarging lens slips over your regular lens same as a cap.

Any of the above sizes are suitable for lenses ¼ inch less in diameter than size mentioned.

Auxiliary Portrait Lenses.

No. 20C2478 In making portraits with the ordinary folding hand camera, the great difficulty heretofore has been the small size of the faces. This portrait lens, however, entirely overcomes this difficulty and enables anyone with any kind of a folding camera to make portraits in which the faces are large and distinct. Constructed in the same style and used in same manner as the enlarging lens No. 20C2475.

No. 1 for 4x5 camera with lens 1 3/16 in. in diam. $0.90
No. 2 for 5x7 camera with lens 1 5/16 in. in diam. .90
No. 3 for fixed focus or box cameras 90
No. 4 for 4x5 camera with lens 1½ in. in diam. .90
No. 5 for 5x7 camera with lens 1½ in. in diam. .90
No. 6 for 4x5 camera with lens 1½ in. in diam. 1.20
No. 7 for 5x7 camera with lens 1½ in. in diam. 1.20
No. 8 any size camera with lens 1¾ in. in diam. 1.35
No. 9 any size camera with lens 2 in. in diam. 1.50
No. 10 any size camera with lens 2¼ in. in diam. 1.65
No. 11 any size camera with lens 2½ in. in diam. 1.80
No. 12 any size camera with lens 2¾ in. in diam. 1.95
No. 13 any size camera with lens 3 in. in diam. 2.10

If by mail, postage extra, on Nos. 1 to 7, **3 cents;** Nos. 8 to 10, **4 cents;** Nos. 11 to 13, **5 cents.**

In measuring your lens, take the outside diameter, remembering that the portrait lens slips over your regular lens same as a cap.

Any of the above sizes may be used on lenses ¼ inch less in diameter than size given.

REMEMBER, THAT A COPY OF

"COMPLETE INSTRUCTIONS IN PHOTOGRAPHY"

will be included, free of charge (if you ask for it), with every $2.50 order for Photo Goods. **See page 346.**

Duplicators.

No. 20C2480 Duplicator. A device enabling one to photograph a person in two positions on the same plate. Very humorous and interesting pictures can be made in this way. Can be used with any folding camera. Made in same sizes as our auxiliary lenses. **Cannot be used with box cameras. State diameter of lens.**

Price, each, any size 17c

If by mail, postage extra, 3 cents.

Auxiliary Lens Sets.

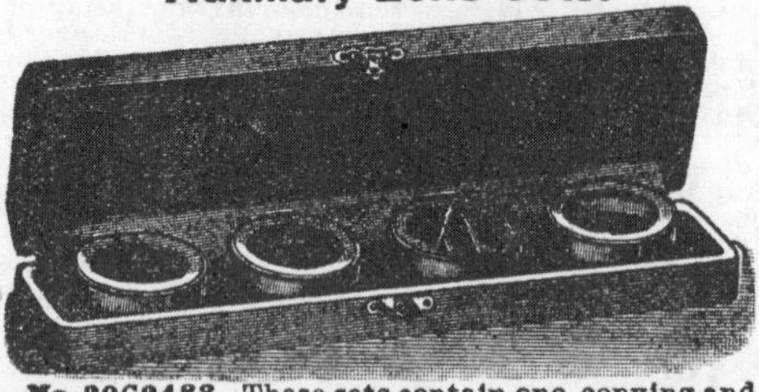

No. 20C2483 These sets contain one copying and enlarging lens, one portrait lens, one ray filter and one duplicator, **all contained in a beautiful plush lined leather case. Put up only in the following sizes:**

Set No. 1 for 4x5 camera with lens 1 3/16 in. diam. . $2.55
Set No. 2 for 5x7 camera with lens 1 5/16 in. diam. . 2.55
Set No. 3 for 4x5 camera with lens 1 3/16 in. diam. . . 2.55
Set No. 4 for 5x7 camera with lens 1 5/16 in. diam. . . 2.55

Postage extra on any size, if sent by mail, 8 cents. Larger sizes are not put up in cases.

PLATE HOLDERS.

We list herewith plate holders to fit the principal and best known makes of cameras on the market. We can also furnish holders to fit other makes of cameras than those mentioned below, but when such holders are ordered the name of the camera which they are to fit, also the manufacturer's name and the size must always be mentioned, as without this information we cannot fill the order.

Seroco Plate Holders.

No. 20C2510 Seroco Plate Holders, with pressed board slides, made expressly for use with any of the Seroco cameras described in this catalogue. Extra high grade holders, made from hardwood throughout, all joints dovetailed, and absolutely light tight. Compact, easy to load, easy to unload. Fitted with the best grade specially coated black pressed board slides, the most durable and the most practical slides made. **Good results are an impossibility with any camera unless the plate holders are perfect.**

Size	4x5	5x7	6½x8½	8x10
Price, each	45c	60c	79c	$1.10

Always state name of camera you want the holders to fit.

No. 20C2510½ Seroco Plate Holders, with hard rubber slides. Although we do not believe that hard rubber slides possess any particular points of superiority over pressed board, and while hard rubber is always liable to breakage, at the same time we appreciate the fact that many of our customers prefer this style of slide on account of the finer appearance, etc., in spite of the greater cost and danger of breakage. We are therefore pleased to furnish them when desired at the following prices:

Size	4x5	5x7	6½x8½	8x10
Price, each	50c	65c	85c	$1.15

What camera do you want the holders for? We must know.

We absolutely guarantee every Seroco Plate Holder to be perfect in every detail.

No. 20C2511 Premo Plate Holders, to fit the Premo Cameras.

Size	4x5	5x7	6½x8½	8x10
Price, each	90c	$1.13	$1.58	$1.80

No. 20C2512 Century Plate Holders, to fit the Century Cameras.

Size	4x5	5x7	6½x8½	8x10
Price, each	72c	90c	$1.35	$1.58

No. 20C2513 Poco Plate Holders, to fit the Poco Cameras and the Rochester View Cameras.

Size	4x5	5x7	6½x8½	8x10
Price, each	90c	$1.13	$1.58	$1.80

No. 20C2514 Wizard Plate Holders, to fit the Wizard Cameras.

Size	4x5	5x7	6½x8½	8x10
Price, each	90c	$1.13	$1.58	$1.80

No. 20C2515 Korona Plate Holders, to fit the Korona Cameras.

Size	4x5	5x7	6½x8½	8x10
Price, each	90c	$1.13	$1.58	$1.80

No. 20C2516 Montauk Plate Holders, to fit the Montauk Cameras.

Size	4x5	5x7
Price, each	68c	88c

No. 20C2517 Seneca Plate Holders, to fit the Seneca Cameras.

Size	4x5	5x7	6½x8½	8x10
Price, each	60c	75c	$1.13	$1.20

No. 20C2518 Ray Plate Holders, fit Ray Cameras.

Size	4x5	5x7
Price, each	48c	60c

No. 20C2519 Perfection Plate Holders, sliding, to fit any of the following view cameras: Empire State, Carlton, Universal, Standard, Monitor and Kenwood.

Size	5x7	6½x8½	8x10
Price, each	86c	$1.20	$1.38

No. 20C2520 Perfection Plate Holders, rabbeted, to fit New Model and New Model Improved Cameras.

Size	5x7	6½x8½	8x10
Price, each	86c	$1.20	$1.38

No. 20C2521 Zephyr Plate Holders, to fit the N. P. A., Novelette, Normandie, Clifton, Champion and other Anthony cameras. **These Holders also fit the Perfection Viewing Camera listed in previous issues of our catalogue.**

Size	5x7	5x8	6½x8½	8x10
Price, each	$1.00	$1.08	$1.28	$1.48

Multiplying Slides.

For Making Six Exposures, All Alike or All Different, on One 4x5 or 5x7 Plate.

One of the latest novelties. A set of three plate holder slides so arranged that six separate exposures can be made on one plate. Can be used with any 4x5 or 5x7 focusing camera. An ordinary plate holder becomes a multiplying plate holder when these slides are used. Very easy to use. Full instructions with each set.

No. 20C2522 Multiplying Slides. For 4x5 plate holder. Price, per set 42c

No. 20C2523 Multiplying Slides. For 5x7 plate holder. Price, per set 63c

Be sure to state name of holder that slides are to be used in. Cannot be used with box cameras.

Photographers' Kits.

KITS are thin wooden frames which fit into a plate holder, the same as an ordinary plate, and the opening in the center holds a plate of smaller size than the holder is designed for. They are to be used when it is desired to take smaller pictures than **the regular size of the camera, and thus save the expense of the larger plates.**

			Price
No. 20C2525	Kit. 4 x5	to hold 3½x3½ plates,	10c
No. 20C2526	Kit. 4 x5	to hold 3¼x4¼ plates,	10c
No. 20C2527	Kit. 4¼x6½	to hold 3¼x4¼ plates,	11c
No. 20C2528	Kit. 5 x7	to hold 3¼x4¼ plates,	13c
No. 20C2529	Kit. 5 x7	to hold 4 x5 plates,	13c
No. 20C2530	Kit. 5 x8	to hold 3¼x4¼ plates,	14c
No. 20C2531	Kit. 5 x8	to hold 4 x5 plates,	14c
No. 20C2532	Kit. 5 x8	to hold 4¼x6½ plates,	14c
No. 20C2533	Kit. 6½x8½	to hold 4 x5 plates,	16c
No. 20C2534	Kit. 6½x8½	to hold 4¼x6½ plates,	16c
No. 20C2535	Kit. 6½x8½	to hold 5 x7 plates,	16c
No. 20C2536	Kit. 6½x8½	to hold 5 x8 plates,	16c
No. 20C2537	Kit. 8 x10	to hold 4 x5 plates,	20c
No. 20C2538	Kit. 8 x10	to hold 4¼x6½ plates,	20c
No. 20C2539	Kit. 8 x10	to hold 5 x7 plates,	20c
No. 20C2540	Kit. 8 x10	to hold 5 x8 plates,	20c
No. 20C2541	Kit. 8 x10	to hold 6½x8½ plates,	20c

We cannot furnish any sizes not quoted in above list.

Camera Tripods.

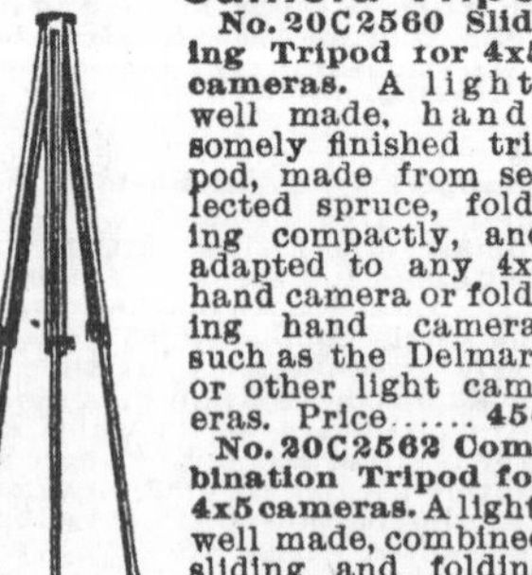
No. 20C2560

No. 20C2560 Sliding Tripod for 4x5 cameras. A light, well made, handsomely finished tripod, made from selected spruce, folding compactly, and adapted to any 4x5 hand camera or folding hand camera, such as the Delmars or other light cameras. Price 45c

No. 20C2562 Combination Tripod for 4x5 cameras. A light, well made, combined sliding and folding tripod, with detachable head; suitable for use with any 4x5 camera, and even for 5x7, provided the camera is not very heavy. Ea, $1.28

No 20C2562

Hardwood Sliding Tripod.

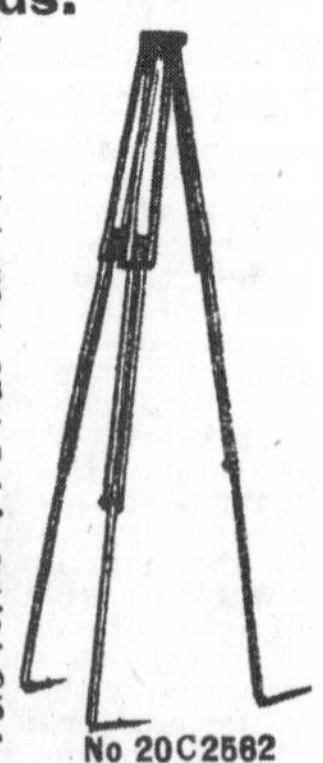

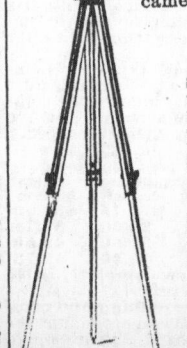

No. 20C2566 Our Best Grade Sliding Tripod is without a doubt the most perfect sliding tripod made. Constructed of best selected spruce, **top of three-piece wood to prevent warping and covered with felt. A special brass binding plate,** operated by set screw, clamps the legs securely at any desired height. **Suitable for hand cameras, folding hand cameras or regular view cameras.**

Size No. 1, for 4x5 or 5x7 cameras. Price 98c
Size No. 2, for 5x8 or 6½x8½ cameras. Price $1.30
Size No. 3, for 8x10 cameras. Price $1.45

Combination Tripod.

No. 20C2569 Combination Tripod, a combined sliding and folding tripod, **one of the most convenient forms yet devised.** Quickly set up for use, readily adjusted to any desired height and perfectly rigid. Made in three sections with detachable head, the lower section slides into the second, while the upper section folds back upon it, thus making a very compact tripod. The best tripod made.

Size No. 1, for 4x5 or 5x7 cameras. Price..................**$1.60**
Size No. 2, for 6½x8½ cameras. Price......................**$1.90**
Size No. 3, for 8x10 cameras. Price........................**$2.25**
Size No. 4, for 10x12 or 11x14 cameras. Price............**$2.48**

The New Silent Shutter.

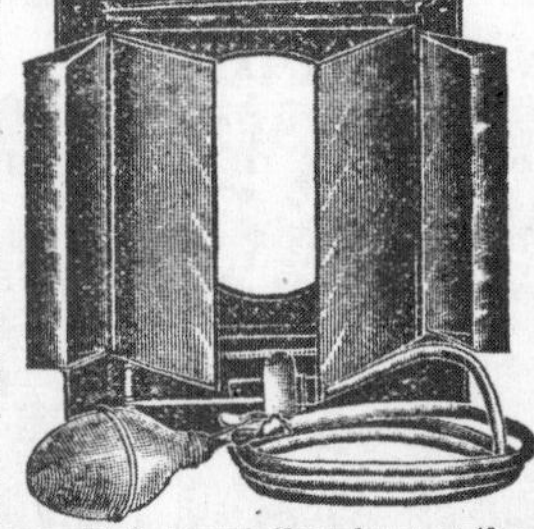

No. 20C2574 The Silent Shutter, a new device absolutely noiseless in opening. The photographer who has experienced repeated failures by reason of a child subject or a member of a group looking toward the lens at the critical moment because he heard the "click" of the shutter will appreciate this new shutter, which opens with **absolute silence.** The cups at the sides form **air cushions** which arrest the wings as they open, thus avoiding all sound. Bulb and 6 foot of rubber hose furnished with each shutter.

This shutter is placed back of lens or inside of front board.

Size of Opening, inches...		2	2½	3	3½
Size of Shutter, inches...		3⅞x4½	4⅜x5	5x5½	5⅜x6
Price...		$4.50	$4.50	$4.50	$4.50
Size of Opening, ins.	4	4½	5	5½	6
Size of Shutter, ins.	6x6½	6½x7	7x7½	7½x8	8x8½
Price...	$4.50	$5.40	$6.30	$7.20	$8.10

Camera Level.

No. 20C2576 This Little Level is intended to be attached to the bed of the camera, enabling the operator to quickly and easily place the camera perfectly level. It is nicely made from brass, finely finished and **accurately adjusted.**
Price..........................**29c**

Camera Bulbs.

No. 20C2577 Bulb and Tube for Camera. Made from the very best quality of red rubber, very elastic; tube is 2 feet long and can be fitted to any shutter. Rubber always becomes hard, brittle or rotten after a certain length of time, and if the bulb and tube you now have has become useless you can easily fit one of these to your shutter.
Price.......**(If by mail, postage extra, 3c)** **18c**

Light Printing Frames.

No. 20C2580 Light Weight Printing Frame. The best light weight frame made and a great improvement over the ordinary style. **A special point of advantage is the piano hinge,** heretofore fitted only to the highest priced frames, giving strength and durability. The finish throughout is good.

Size, inches	2½x2½	3¼x3¼	3¼x4¼	4¼x4¼	4x5	5x7
Price	9c	9c	9c	9c	10c	13c

Not made in larger sizes.

Heavy Weight Printing Frames.

No. 20C2583 Heavy Weight Printing Frames. The finest printing frame manufactured, strongly and substantially constructed throughout, heavy brass springs sliding under brass plates instead of grooves in the wood, thus preventing all wear, mortised corners, back in three pieces to prevent warping, **high grade piano hinge,** finished throughout in the best possible manner. **It pays to get good printing frames, and these frames are the best made.**

Size	Price, per dozen	Price, each	Size	Price, per dozen	Price, each
3¼x 4¼	$2.22	$0.19	6½x 8½	$3.70	$0.32
4 x 5	2.45	.21	8 x10	4.30	.37
4¼x6½	2.68	.23	10 x12	5.59	.48
5 x7	2.78	.24	11 x14	11.06	.95
5 x8	2.90	.25	14 x17	13.97	1.20

Masks.

Every package contains a large assortment of fancy and novel designs.

A NECESSARY ADDITION TO ANY PHOTOGRAPHIC OUTFIT.

No. 20C2587 Made from tough opaque paper, and designed to be placed between negative and sensitized paper while printing, thus producing oval, circular or various fancy shaped prints from any negative. The illustration shows only one of the many sizes of styles. Made for the following negatives: 2¼x3¼, 3¼x3¼, 3¼x4¼, 4¼x4¼, 4x5 and 5x7.
Assortment No. 1 contains one oval, one circle, one rectangle, one round corner rectangle, the balance being a variety of ornamental designs. Assortment No. 2 is composed entirely of ornamental designs, all different from Assortment No. 1.
Price, per package, any size. **18c**
If by mail, postage extra, on small sizes, 2 cents; on size 4x5, 3 cents; size 5x7, 4 cents.
State which assortment you want and size of negative.

Our Special Trays.

No. 20C2588 Our Special Trays. These are the best trays on the market for general purposes, developing negatives, toning, washing prints, etc. **They are manufactured expressly for us from a peculiar composition material known as compressed fibre. These trays are jet black, perfectly smooth, without seam or joint, and perfect in shape. We guarantee them to stand all photographic chemicals without deterioration and to be acid and alkali proof. In shape, finish and durability they are superior to all other composition trays.**

For Plates, inches....	2¼x2½	3¼x3¼	3¼x4¼	4x5	
Price...	5c	7c	7c	9c	
For Plates, inches..	5x7	5x8	6½x8½	8x10	10x12
Price...	16c	17c	25c	38c	83c

Japanned Metal Trays.

No. 20C2590 An entirely new style of japanned metal tray and superior to all others. These trays are stamped from one solid piece of metal without joints or seams, and coated with an enamel which is a special japan and rubber preparation, rendering them entirely chemical proof.

For Plates, inches........	4x5	5x7	5x8	6½x8½
Price...	6c	13c	16c	24c

Deep Hard Rubber Trays.

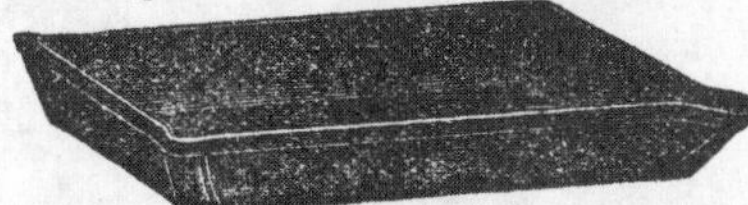

No. 20C2592 Hard Rubber Trays are generally considered the best trays manufactured, and the quality we handle is the best we can buy, **genuine hard rubber** (not composition), made extra deep and with lip at corner for pouring.

For Plates, inches....	4x5	5x7	5x8	6½x8½
Price...	34c	43c	52c	68c
For Plates, inches....	8x10	10x12	12x16	15x19
Price...	$0.85	$1.40	$1.95	$3.90

Porcelain Trays.

No. 20C2593 Porcelain Trays, the best grade of imported white porcelain, extra deep. These trays are very easy to keep clean, are absolutely chemical proof, and are generally considered the finest trays made for toning and other work.

For Plates, inches....5x7	5½x8½	7x9	8x10	
Price...49c	60c	65c	80c	
For Plates, in.... 10x12	11x14	14x17	15x19	19x24
Price... $1.32	$2.11	$4.80	$6.00	$10.00

Measuring Glasses.

No. 20C2600 Tumbler Shaped Measuring Glasses. For liquids; graduated with ounces and drams; not quite as convenient as the regular cone shaped graduate, but preferred by many on account of the extremely low price.
Price, 2 ounce.............................**4c**
Price, 4 ounce.............................**6c**
Price, 8 ounce.............................**9c**
Not mailable.

Pressed Line Graduates.

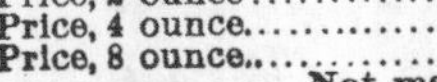

No. 20C2605 Cone Shaped Graduates. For measuring liquids; marked with scale showing ounces and drams. **Perfectly accurate.**
Price, 1 ounce.............................**8c**
Price, 2 ounce.............................**9c**
Price, 4 ounce.............................**12c**
Price, 8 ounce.............................**18c**
Price, 16 ounce............................**27c**

Engraved Graduates.

No. 20C2606 Cone Shaped Graduates, all lines and figures engraved by hand, the most carefully made and accurate graduate on the market.
Price, 1 ounce.............................**12c**
Price, 2 ounce.............................**13c**
Price, 4 ounce.............................**20c**
Price, 8 ounce.............................**32c**
Price, 16 ounce............................**50c**
Price, 32 ounce............................**88c**

Fixing Baths.

No. 20C2610 These Fixing Baths are made of metal, thoroughly coated with a preparation which renders them impervious to the action of hypo.

They are a very great convenience at a very low price. The use of these baths for fixing **avoids the danger of spots and stains,** which is the frequent result of fixing in the ordinary tray. They hold six plates each. **These baths are provided with a rising bottom,** so that the plates are readily raised above the top—a great convenience in removing them from the box and avoiding the danger of scratching.
No. 0, for plates 3¼x3¼. Price.................**38c**
No. 1, for plates 3¼x4¼. Price.................**38c**
No. 2, for plates 4 x5. Price.................**38c**
No. 3, for plates 5x7 or 5x8. Price.................**55c**
If by mail, postage extra, 10, 16 and 22 cents.

Zinc Washing Box.

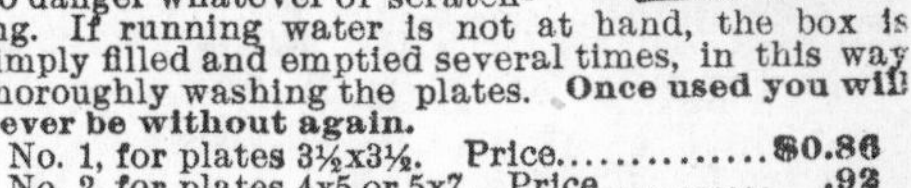

No. 20C2615 Zinc Washing Box, a perfect device for washing plates, and should form a part of every photographic outfit. **Constructed throughout of zinc and cannot rust.** The water enters through the inlet tube, is circulated through the whole area of the box and passes off through the outlet tube. **The patent lifting bottom** is a valuable feature of this box, as the plates can be lifted out with, no danger whatever of scratching. If running water is not at hand, the box is simply filled and emptied several times, in this way thoroughly washing the plates. **Once used you will never be without again.**
No. 1, for plates 3¼x3¼. Price.................**$0.86**
No. 2, for plates 4x5 or 5x7. Price.................**.92**
No. 3, for plates 3¼x4¼, 4¼x4¼ or 4¼x6½. Price.................**.92**
No. 4, for plates 5x7 or 6½x8½. Price......**1.29**
No. 5, for plates 6½x8½ or 8x10. Price......**1.47**
Too heavy to send by mail.

Glass Funnels.

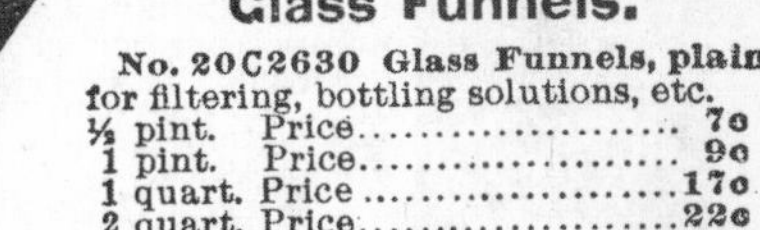

No. 20C2630 Glass Funnels, plain, for filtering, bottling solutions, etc.
½ pint. Price.............................**7c**
1 pint. Price.............................**9c**
1 quart. Price............................**17c**
2 quart. Price............................**22c**

Fluted Glass Funnels.

No. 20C2631 Glass Funnels, fluted, for filtering. More desirable than plain funnels, because filtering is much more rapid.
½ pint. Price.............................**13c**
1 pint. Price.............................**17c**
1 quart. Price............................**23c**
2 quart. Price............................**34c**
Too heavy to send by mail.

New Style Photo Scale for 32 Cents.

No. 20C2656 The best scale yet devised at a low price; answers all the requirements in making up solutions, etc. **Simple, nothing to get out of order, accurate and convenient.** Weighs up to 12 drams. Pan is made of glass and easily cleaned.
Price.............................**32c**
If by mail, postage extra, 10 cents.
Extra Glass Pans for No 20C2656 Scale. Price.10c

An Imported Scale for $1.00.

No. 20C2658 Our Imported Balance Scale, made in Germany, has 2¼-inch brass pans, brass pillar, 6-inch beam, and stands 12 inches high when set up for use. The entire scale packs away in the box on which it is set up, has complete set of weights from ½ grain to 1 ounce and comes complete in oak box.
Price, complete......**$1.00**
If by mail, postage extra, 20 cents.

Print Trimmers.

No. 20C2700 Prints always have to be trimmed before mounting, and while this can of course be done fairly well with scissors or knife, at the same time the advantages of a regular trimmer as here illustrated will be readily apparent. **It trims the prints quickly, easily and squarely.** The blade is made of finest tempered steel, the board of polished hardwood, has graduated measure which also serves as guide for the paper. Our illustration shows way in which this trimmer is used. Trims any size from 4x5 down. Price................45c

No. 20C2701 Trimming Board, same as No. 20C2700, but larger, suitable for prints up to 5x7. Price....................85c

No. 20C2702 Trimming Board, same as No. 20C2700, but with 10½-inch blade, suitable for any size up to and including 8x10. Price.......................... 95c

Our Best Grade Trimmer.

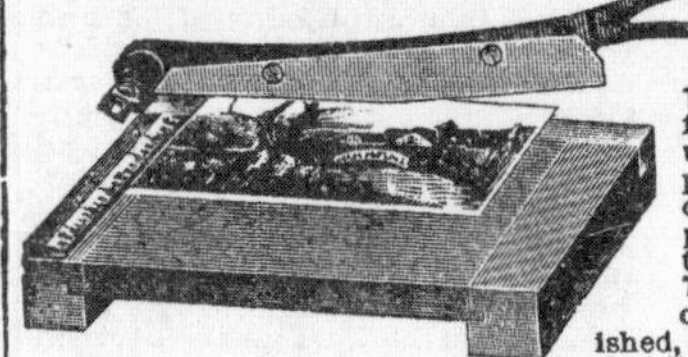

No. 20C2710 The blade is made from the same steel used in the best paper cutting machines, finely tempered and ground to a perfect edge. The board is made of hardwood, polished, and so constructed that it cannot warp. The spring joint, by which the blade is attached, allows a slight lateral motion, so that the two cutting edges are in perfect contact at every point, insuring perfect, clean cut edges to either cards or paper. The illustration shows method of trimming a print.

Length of blade, inches	6½	8½	10½	12½
Price	90c	$1.25	$1.90	$2.30

Our Best Photo Scale.

No. 20C2659 All metal parts are nickel plated; it has large nickel plated pan, 3½ in. in diameter; it is very sensitive, finely finished, accurately adjusted and durable. **Two complete sets of weights** are included, one set of **avoirdupois,** $\frac{1}{16}$ of an ounce to 2 ounces, and one set of **dram, scruple and grain** weights. Price, complete.. ....$1.85

If by mail, postage extra, 40 cents.

Flash Light Cartridges.

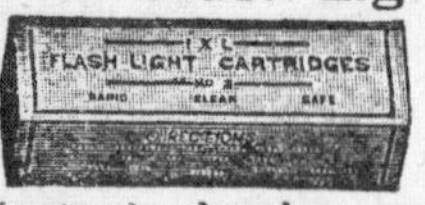

No. 20C2669 For making flash light pictures without a lamp. Each cartridge contains sufficient powder for one exposure, and for use the cartridge is simply placed on a stove shovel or other article which will not be injured and the fuse lighted. A blinding flash of white light follows and the picture is made instantaneously. Made in three sizes and put up in packages of ½ dozen each. Price per pkg.

Size No. 1, ½ dozen 20-grain cartridges..........10c
Size No. 2, ½ dozen 40-grain cartridges..........20c
Size No. 3, ½ dozen 60-grain cartridges..........25c
(Unmailable.)

Folding Negative Racks.

No. 20C2675 The Folding Negative Rack is a very convenient and necessary accessory for the support of negatives **while drying and prevents them from being scratched;** will hold 12 negatives. For plates, 4x5 or smaller. Price..........8c

No. 20C2676 Folding Negative Rack. Same as above, but larger, holds 24 negatives, suitable for any size up to and including 8x10. Price.........9c

Ruby Lamps.

No. 20C2680 Candle Ruby Lamp, constructed of metal, has deep ruby glass, burns candle. A very convenient and satisfactory lamp at a low price. Price..............14c

Extra Candles.

No. 20C2681 Candles to fit this lamp, small flat paraffine candles in pasteboard cups, burn two hours. Made especially for dark room lamps. Price, per dozen ..17c

Oil Ruby Lamp.

No. 20C2683 Oil Ruby Lamp. A strictly first class metal lamp, fitted with both orange and ruby glass, which gives the safest and best light. Has adjustable screen for shielding the eyes, ventilation is perfect, reservoir can be filled from outside and light be turned up or down without opening the lamp. A regular $1.00 lamp. Price..........40c

No. 20C2685 Ruby Oil Lamp, same as No. 20C2683. Regular $1.50 size. Price.........80c

Print Rollers.

Indispensable for smoothing down prints after mounting and for squeegeeing prints on ferrotype plates.

No. 20C2695 4-inch Print Roller, rubber covered, large wood handle, as shown in illustration. Price..........10c

No. 20C2697 6-inch Print Roller, rubber covered, large wood handle, as shown in illustration. Price..........18c

WRITE THE CATALOGUE NUMBER IN FULL ALWAYS.

BACKGROUNDS.

Our backgrounds are all painted in oil on fine muslin, perfectly waterproof, and will not crack, practically indestructible. **Do not compare** our grounds with water color grounds or distemper, which are ruined if touched by water and can hardly be handled without cracking. **A secret process** known only to the painter who makes our backgrounds, enables him to get a perfect dull or dead finished surface in oil, making an ideal background, crack proof, waterproof and photographically correct.

CLOUDED HEADGROUNDS.

No. 20C2721 The following grounds, in clouded designs, No. 40 and No. 41, are especially suitable for bust pictures, although the larger sizes, 5x7 and 6x8 are extensively used for full figure work and small groups. Very artistic, up to date grounds, giving the soft shadowy effects so desirable in portrait work. Painted in oil on the best muslin. No better headgrounds are made at any price.

State whether you want design No. 40 or 41. These grounds are suitable for either right or left light, and several different effects can be obtained by using the ground in different positions.

Price, size, 4x4 feet..................$0.70
Price, size, 5x6 feet.................. .84
Price, size, 5x7 feet.................. 1.05
Price, size, 6x8 feet.................. 1.50

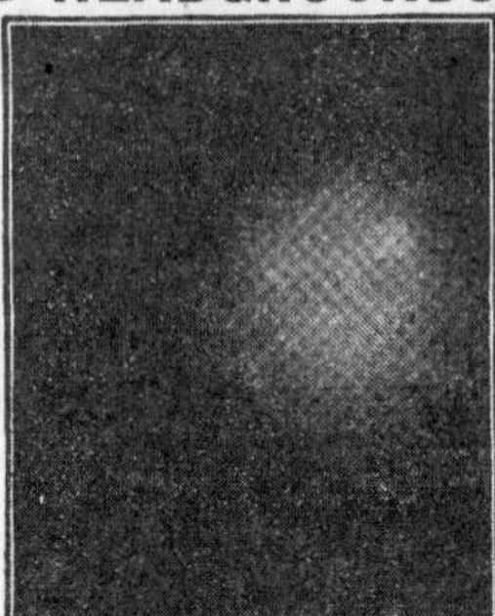

Clouded Design No. 40.

Clouded Design No. 41.

SCENIC BACKGROUNDS.

Scenic Design No. 1.

Scenic Design No. 2.

Scenic Design No. 3.

Scenic Design No. 4.

Scenic Design No. 5.

Scenic Design No. 6.

Scenic Design No. 7.

Scenic Design No. 8.

No. 20C2722 The above illustrations show our line of scenic backgrounds, painted expressly for us, the very latest and most artistic designs, painted in oil, on the best grade of muslin, guaranteed to be waterproof, will not crack, and will stand more rough handling than any other grounds made.

Size, 6x 8 feet. Price..................$3.50
Size, 8x 8 feet. Price.................. 4.30
Size, 8x10 feet. Price.................. 5.40
Size, 8x12 feet. Price.................. 7.39
Size, 6x15 feet. With Floor Extension. Price.................. 5.90
Size, 8x15 feet. With Floor Extension. Price.................. 6.15
Size, 10x15 feet. With Floor Extension. Price.................. 7.48
Size, 12x15 feet. With Floor Extension. Price.................. 8.60

State size, design, and which side light falls on, when ordering. If light falls on right side of sitter, when sitter is in position, it is **"right light."** Right light falls on left side of operator when operator faces sitter. **Do not judge these backgrounds by the prices we ask for them. There are no better grounds painted at any price.**

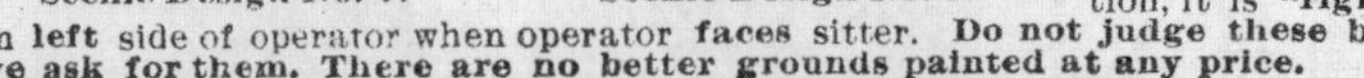

Burnishers.

No. 20C2770 Amateur Burnishers, the only thoroughly practical oil heating, double roller burnishers yet placed on the market at a low price. They are thoroughly well made in every respect, simple, clean, economical and safe. Make your outfit complete by adding one of these excellent machines. **Suitable also for regular professional use.**

Size No. 1.	Price, 6-inch roller	$3.60
Size No. 2.	Price, 8-inch roller	4.40
Size No. 3.	Price, 10-inch roller	5.70
Size No. 4.	Price, 12-inch roller	7.70

Brushes.

No. 20C2790 Bristle Brushes for pasting; an exceptionally well made brush designed especially for photographic use, wood handle, tin bound.

1 inch wide	3c	2½ inches wide	9c
1½ inches wide	4c	3 inches wide	11c
2 inches wide	6c		

No. 20C2795 Camel's Hair Brushes, tin bound, wood handles, very soft and fine, used for dusting plates before placing in holder, dusting negatives, etc.

1 inch wide	11c	2½ inches wide	33c
1½ inches wide	16c	3 inches wide	35c
2 inches wide	21c		

Hard Rubber Bound Brushes.

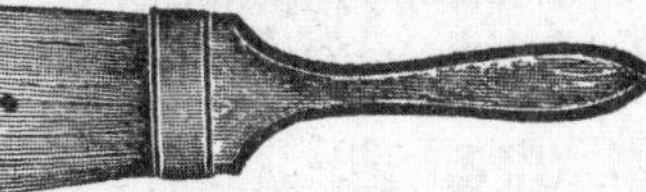

No. 20C2797 These are the best, the highest grade and the most durable brushes made. The bristles never come out, as they are vulcanized in hard rubber, there are no metal parts to rust, and they will last for years. Made with either bristles or camel's hair.

Size, 1 in. wide. Price, bristle, 16c; camel's hair, 32c
Size, 1½ in. wide. Price, bristle, 21c; camel's hair, 48c
Size, 2 in. wide. Price, bristle, 29c; camel's hair, 64c
Size, 2½ in. wide. Price, bristle, 38c; camel's hair, 82c
Size, 3 in. wide. Price, bristle, 42c; camel's hair, $1.15

Blotting Paper.

No. 20C2800 Photographers' Blotting Paper, for mounting prints. Chemically pure and perfectly lintless. Price, 9x12 inches, per dozen 8c
Price, 20x24 inches, per dozen 29c
If by mail, postage extra, per dozen, 8c and 30c.

Filter Paper.

No. 20C2803 Filter Paper; diameter, 8 inches. Price, per package of ten sheets 5c
No. 20C2804 Filter Paper; diameter, 10 inches. Price, per package of ten sheets 6c
No. 20C2805 Filter Paper; diameter, 13 inches. Price, per package of ten sheets 7c
No. 20C2806 Filter Paper; diameter, 18 inches. Price, per package of ten sheets 10c
The 8-inch paper just fits a ½-pint funnel, the 10-inch fits a 1-pint, the 13-inch a 1-quart and the 18-inch fits a 2-quart funnel.

Litmus Paper.

No. 20C2810 For testing solutions to ascertain whether alkaline or acid; very useful in making toning baths. Put up in bottles containing 100 sheets. State whether red or blue is desired.
Price, per bottle 7c
If by mail, postage extra, 3 cents.

Postoffice Paper, 12c Dozen.

No. 20C2815 A yellow paper for dark room use, making ruby light, etc.
Size, 18x22. Price, per dozen sheets 12c
If by mail, postage extra, per sheet, 1 cent.

Ruby Fabric.

No. 20C2820 A good substitute for ruby glass, and not liable to breakage. Size, 15x18.
Price, per sheet 15c
If by mail, postage extra, 1 cent.

Negative Preservers.

No. 20C2825 Envelopes for Preserving Negatives, made of strong manila, the proper size for negatives, open at the end and have notched cut for admitting thumb and finger in removing; **printed on the face with lines for number, description, etc.; put up in packages of 50 each.**

Size	Per pkg.	Size	Per pkg.
½x3½	7c	5 x 8	16c
¼x4¼	8c	6½x 8½	18c
½x5½	11c	8 x10	23c
x7	14c		

Ground Glass.

No. 20C2830 Ground Glass for replacing broken screens in cameras, making transparencies, etc., finest quality, mud ground.

Size	Price	Size	Price
3¼x4¼	8c	8x10	19c
4 x5	8c	10x12	29c
4¼x6½	8c	11x14	38c
5 x7	12c	14x17, double thick	69c
5 x8	12c	18x22, double thick	89c
6½x8½	17c		

Ruby and Orange Glass.

No. 20C2835 Ruby or Orange Glass for dark rooms where it is desired to have the lamp on the outside, replacing broken lantern glass, etc.

Size, 6½x 8½	Price, per light	19c
Size, 8 x10	Price, per light	23c
Size, 10 x12	Price, per light	32c
Size, 11 x14	Price, per light	40c
Size, 16 x20	Price, per light	60c

Be sure and state which color is wanted.

Squeegee Plates.

No. 20C2840 Ferrotype Plates, extra fine quality, for squeegeeing or producing a glossy finish without burnishing.
Size, 5x 7 inches. Price 4c
Size, 7x10 inches. Price 7c
Size, 10x14 inches. Price 9c
If by mail, postage extra, 8 and 10 cents.

Extra Heavy Squeegee Plates.

No. 20C2842 Extra Heavy Squeegee Plates, very fine quality, made in 10x14-inch size only.
Price 19c

Retouching Goods.

No. 20C2851 A. W. Faber's Pencils. The best pencils in the world for retouching; any degree of hardness; 3-H sent unless otherwise ordered.
Price, per dozen, 90c; each 8c
No. 20C2853 A. W. Faber's Artist Style Pencils. With movable lead; any degree of hardness supplied; 3-H sent unless otherwise ordered.
Price of holder and lead complete 18c
No. 20C2855 A. W. Faber's Extra Leads. Any degree of hardness. Price, per box of six 47c
No. 20C2856 Smith's Points. Metallic leads for retouching; used in artist style pencils. Price...11c
No. 20C2857 Sable Brushes. For spotting; polished cedar handles; nickel plated ferrules; Nos. 1 to 6. Price 5c
No. 20C2858 India Ink. Lion Head brand; for spotting. Price, per stick 9c
No. 20C2859 Spotting Colors. Set of three improved spotting colors on celluloid sheets, suitable for any kind of paper; very handy. Price 12c
No. 20C2860 Retouching Glass, 4 inches in diameter; highest grade manufactured; very powerful; nickel plated rim; black wood handle. Price..$1.10
No. 20C2861 Retouching Glass, 4 inches in diameter, ordinary quality, **same as the regular photo supply houses furnish.** Price 78c
No. 20C2862 Calcined Flour. A retouching medium for producing a fine matt surface on negatives so they will take the pencil readily and smoothly. **Guaranteed not to scratch.** Price, per can..17c
No. 20C2863 Retouching Varnish or Dope. A fine retouching medium, suited to either hard or soft pencil. Price, per bottle 15c
No. 20C2864 Retouching Frame. Fitted with adjustable reflector, ground glass and drawer for pencils. **Folds compactly when not in use.** For 8x10 or smaller. Price $2.30
No. 20C2865 "Retouching Negatives and Prints." A complete guide to retouching, describing all the various methods and explaining everything very fully. Price, per copy 25c

Rubber Finger Tips.

No. 20C2870 Made of pure rubber, put up in sets of three; prevents staining the fingers when developing, etc. Price, per set 8c
If by mail, postage extra, 2 cents.

Trimmers.

No. 20C2874 Straight Trimmers, for trimming prints; the cutting knife is a small wheel which revolves and leaves very clean edge. Price..14c
Extra wheels, 8 cents each.

No. 20C2875 Swivel Trimmers, same as above, but cutting wheel is swivel mounted and can follow curved surface. Price 16c
Extra wheels, 8 cents each.
If by mail, postage extra, 4 cents.
NOTE—Prints must be laid on a sheet of metal or piece of glass when using above trimmers.

REMEMBER THAT A COPY OF COMPLETE INSTRUCTIONS IN PHOTOGRAPHY will be included, free of charge (if you ask for it), with every $2.50 order for Photo Goods. SEE PAGE 346.

Rotary Trimmer.

No. 20C2877 Rotary Trimmer, for trimming round, oval or square prints; ball bearing knife, easily and quickly changed; a perfect cutter; very handy; can be carried in vest pocket. Price...19c
No. 20C2878 Extra Knives for 20C2877 regular style. Price 11c
No. 20C2879 Mask Knives, for above rotary trimmer, with shoulder constructed so that a white margin can be left around print. Price 12c

Round and Oval Trimming Forms.

No. 20C2880

No. 20C2880 Perfectly made steel trimming forms, with copper oxidized finish.

	Size		Size
No. 0.	Oval. 1⅜x2	A.	Oval...1½x2½
No. 1.	Oval. 2x2¾, ¼ Cab.	B.	Oval...1⅞x3½ inches
No. 2.	Oval. 3 1/16x4 3/16, ½ Cab.	C.	Oval...2⅝x5 1/16 inches
No. 3.	Oval. 3½x5, Cab	D.	Oval...1 7/16x2 11/16 inches
No. 4.	Oval. 2⅜x3½	E.	Oval...2¼x4 1/16 inches
No. 5.	Oval. 3¾x5¾	F.	Oval...2½x5 1/16 inches
No. 6.	Oval. 4¼x6	G.	Oval...2⅛x5⅝ inches
No. 9.	Circle. 2¾ inches	H.	Oval...1⅞x3¾ inches
No. 10.	Circle. 3 inches	J.	Oval...2¾x5¼ inches
No. 11.	Circle. 3¼ inches	K.	Oval...3⅛x6⅝ inches
		L.	Oval...1⅜x2¾ inches
		M.	Oval...2 9/16x3 9/16 inches

Price, each, any size 13c

Hydrometers.

No. 20C2881 For making up solutions by hydrometer test instead of by using scales and weights; very convenient. Complete, with glass jar, in wooden box. Price 18c
If by mail, postage extra, 10 cents.

Focus Cloth.

No. 20C2890 Fine Quality Black Gossamer Focus Cloth, 36x36 inches.
Price 22c
No. 20C2891 Focus Cloth. Same as above, but double size; 36x72 inches.
Price 44c
If by mail, postage extra, 10 cents.

Complete Developing and Printing Outfits.

No. 20C2899 SERIES A OUTFITS. Complete Developing, Finishing and Material Outfits, Series A, put up in sizes 2¼x2¼ to 4x5 inclusive, containing everything necessary for making and finishing pictures complete. Each outfit contains the following items:

- **1 Candle Ruby Lamp,** metal
- **1 Printing Frame**
- **1 4-inch Print Roller**
- **½ dozen Dry Plates**
- **1 dozen Seroco Sensitized Paper**
- **1 dozen Embossed Border Card Mounts.**
- **1 package Dry Developer** (makes 8 ounces developer)
- **1 Paste Brush**
- **1 package Dry Toner** (makes 8 ounces toning solution)
- **½ lb. Hyposulphite of Soda**
- **3 Trays for Developing, Fixing and Toning**
- **1 Measuring Glass**
- **1 Tube Photographic Paste**
- **1 Copy "Complete Instructions in Photography"**

No camera is included with these outfits.

Outfit for 2¼x2¼ pictures.	Price	$0.98
Outfit for 3¼x3¼ pictures.	Price	1.05
Outfit for 3¼x4¼ pictures.	Price	1.12
Outfit for 4x5 pictures.	Price	1.20

No. 20C2900 SERIES B OUTFITS. Complete Developing, Finishing and Material Outfits, Series B, put up only in sizes 4x5 to 8x10 inclusive. The best and most complete outfits ever sold. Everything strictly high grade, suitable for use with our very best cameras. Each outfit contains the following list of apparatus and materials:

- **1 Fine Oil Ruby Lamp**
- **3 Compressed Fibre Trays for developing, fixing and toning**
- **1 Cone Shaped Graduate**
- **1 Hardwood Negative Rack**
- **1 Heavy Printing Frame**
- **1 Print Roller**
- **1 Fine Gossamer Focus Cloth**
- **1 dozen Roebuck Dry Plates**
- **1 dozen Seroco Sensitized Paper**
- **1 Package Hydro-Metol Developing Powder** (makes 24 ounces developer)
- **1 Package Toning and Fixing Powder** (makes 24 ounces toning solution)
- **1 Pound Hyposulphite of Soda**
- **25 Card Mounts**
- **1 Jar Photographic Paste**
- **1 Paste Brush**
- **1 Copy "Complete Instructions in Photography"**

No camera is included with these outfits.

Outfit for 4 x5 pictures.	Price	$2.25
Outfit for 5 x7 pictures.	Price	3.10
Outfit for 6½x8½ pictures.	Price	3.65
Outfit for 8 x10 pictures.	Price	4.75

SEROCO PAPER

THE HIGHEST GRADE GELATINE PRINTING-OUT PAPER MADE.

OUR SPECIAL PRICE FOR 4x5 SIZE, 10c Per Dozen, 98c Per Gross.

NOT MADE BY THE TRUST.

AT ONLY 10 CENTS PER DOZEN OR 98 CENTS PER GROSS (if ordered in gross lots), for the popular **4x5** size (other sizes at proportionately low prices), **we offer our Seroco Gelatine Printing-Out Paper as the very best photographic paper it is possible to make,** the equal of any gelatine printing-out paper on the market regardless of name or price, that may be offered at much higher prices. Seroco is not to be compared with the many cheap gelatine papers on the market which are offered at various prices.

SEROCO PAPER IS MADE ESPECIALLY FOR US by one of the best **and most perfectly equipped factories in America,** under the personal supervision of an expert and successful maker of sensitized paper. It is a paper that is the result of long experience in the manufacture of sensitized paper, combining the good qualities of all other gelatine printing-out papers and the defects of none, a paper that we feel safe in putting out under our personal guarantee as not only the highest quality paper on the market, but also under our guarantee that the special prices we name **are not to be approached by any** paper of equal quality on the market.

DO NOT COMPARE SEROCO WITH ANY OF THE VARIOUS LOW PRICED PAPERS ON THE MARKET. **Most of these other low priced papers are so called "mill run,"** which is only another name for second quality, and these are the papers that many dealers offer in an attempt to meet the prices on Seroco. We guarantee that every sheet of Seroco is first choice, first quality, carefully sorted, every sheet subjected to the most rigid scrutiny for blemishes or imperfections and every sheet we send out is positively perfect.

OUR CHALLENGE OFFER. **Send us your order for Seroco paper at the special prices as printed opposite, give it a** thorough test, and if you do not find it perfectly satisfactory in every way, exactly as we have described it, by far the best gelatine printing-out paper you have ever used, if you do not find it superior in every respect to any of the low priced papers offered by other dealers, say so, and we will return your money without question or argument.

IMPORTED STOCK. **Seroco is coated on the very best and highest quality genuine imported stock,** only the highest grade and the very best quality gelatine is used, chemically pure gelatine, manufactured expressly for emulsion making, and the paper is coated by the best and most up to date process, under expert handling. **Seroco is rich in silver,** the chemicals used in its preparation are the very best that money can buy, and when we offer Seroco as the best gelatine printing-out paper on the market, we know the result it gives will substantiate our claims. **Seroco is a hardened paper,** the film being absolutely insoluble and it will not soften even in the hottest weather. It can be used in any climate, and its keeping qualities are unexcelled.

SEROCO IS AN EASY PAPER TO WORK. **It can be toned in any ordinary gold toning bath, or if preferred, it may be worked by the combined toning and fixing process.** Seroco prints quickly, and it yields tones of unequaled richness with a wealth of detail in the halftones and a clearness of whites that is unsurpassed.

If you want the very best gelatine printing-out paper it is possible to produce, don't fail to order Seroco. Our special prices, as named below, are based on the manufacturing cost, the cost of material and labor with but our one small percentage of profit added, a price we are able to name only by reason of our immense output of this paper, and while we sell this paper in immense quantities, we pay strictest attention to quality, and can guarantee each and every package.

There are many so called cheap papers on the market. We do not claim that Seroco is the lowest priced paper on the market, unless you take quality into consideration. If we were inclined to sacrifice quality for price, we could offer you cabinet size gelatine printing-out paper as low as 70 cents per gross. **By using domestic stock, lower grade chemicals and less silver,** we could make a paper to sell at this price that would be equal to the best of the so called cheap papers on the market, but our experience has taught us that there is nothing to be gained in using or selling low grade photographic paper. There is no satisfaction for the customer in using a paper of poor quality, for such papers only give dissatisfaction and spoil your work. We therefore urge you to buy the highest grade printing-out paper made, and order Seroco.

Our special prices on Seroco paper are as follows:

No. 20C2910 Seroco Paper.

Size	Dozen	Gross	Size	Dozen	Gross
2½x2½	$0.07	$0.72	6½x 8½	$0,33	$3.07
3½x3½	.08	.92	8 x10	.44	4.75
3¼x4¼	.08	.92	10 x12	.65	7.30
4¼x4¼	.10	.97	11 x14	.87	9.48
4 x5	.10	.98	14 x17	1.31	14.50
3⅞x5½	.13	.98	20 x24	2.55	18.75
4 x6	.15	1.28	4 x 5 Seconds		.70
5 x7	.22	2.12	Cabinet Seconds		.75
5 x8	.24	2.40			

Rolls, 26 inches wide, 10 feet long, each $1.20
Rolls, 26 inches wide, 10 yards long, each 3.16

Less than one gross is sold at dozen rate only. For example: One-half gross of 4x5 (which is 6 dozen) would cost 60 cents; (6 dozen at 10 cents per dozen), and not one-half of 98 cents, or 49 cents. **We cannot violate this rule under any circumstances.**

A DEVELOPING PAPER FOR BLACK AND WHITE PICTURES.

NOT MADE BY THE TRUST.

4x5, PER DOZEN, 10c
5x7, PER DOZEN, 16c

DARKO IS ABSOLUTELY THE BEST DEVELOPING PAPER MADE **easy to work, beautiful in its results and absolutely permanent.** The artistic qualities of Darko are unsurpassed, combining the effects of carbon and platinum.

DARKO IS PRINTED BY LAMP LIGHT. **Sunlight is entirely unnecessary. Printing may be done at night or at any other time, regardless of light or weather.**

ONLY A FEW SECONDS **are required for printing, a few seconds for developing, and then, after fixing and washing, the pictures are complete. For simplicity, speed of manipulation and results, Darko stands without a rival.**

DARKO PAPER IS COATED **on the very best quality of imported stock,** the highest grade and the most expensive raw stock that can be obtained, and it is coated in a factory equipped with all the latest improvements, under the personal supervision of a most experienced and successful maker of developing paper.

ABSOLUTELY PERMANENT. **Prints made on Darko Paper will last as long as the paper itself, and WILL NEVER FADE OR DISCOLOR WITH AGE.**

DARKO PAPER IS MADE IN FOUR STYLES, AS FOLLOWS:

No. 20C2911 CARBON MATT DARKO.
No. 20C2912 ROUGH DARKO.
No. 20C2913 GLOSSY DARKO.
No. 20C2914 SMOOTH PORTRAIT DARKO.

CARBON MATT DARKO AND SMOOTH PORTRAIT DARKO **give results which are practically the same, namely, a fine matt surface or dull finish.** Carbon Matt Darko is best suited to soft negatives, and Smooth Portrait Darko is best adapted to hard negatives, that is, negatives which show considerable contrast.

GLOSSY DARKO, as the name implies, finishes with a glossy or highly polished surface like ordinary gelatine printing-out paper, and should be squeegeed or burnished.

ROUGH DARKO **yields especially artistic effects** and is suitable both for landscape work or portraits. The surface is quite rough, a style of finish which is now very popular.

DARKO WILL KEEP FOR MONTHS **and you can safely order a considerable supply without fear of it spoiling on your hands.**

PRICES ON DARKO. **Order by number, as given above. Prices are the same on any kind of Darko.**

Size	Dozen	½ Gross	Gross	Size	Dozen	½ Gross	Gross
3½x 3½	$0.08	$0.46	$0.87	5 x 7	$0.16	$0.91	$1.73
3¼x 4¼	.09	.52	.98	5 x 8	.19	1.09	2.06
4 x 5	.10	.57	1.08	6½x 8½	.29	1.66	3.14
3⅞x 5½ (Cabinet)	.11	.63	1.19	8 x10	.40	2.28	4.32
4 x 6	.13	.74	1.41				

Order by the gross; it will keep good for months.

DEVELOPER FOR DARKO PAPER

A combination of hydrochinon and metol in dry form put up in tightly sealed pasteboard tubes, six tubes to a package. Each package makes twenty-four ounces of developer for Darko and all other developing papers.

No. 20C2915 Price, per package **19c**

WATER TONE PLATINUM PAPER.

Produces beautiful prints with soft, velvety blacks and clear whites. Develops and tones in plain water.

No. 20C2920

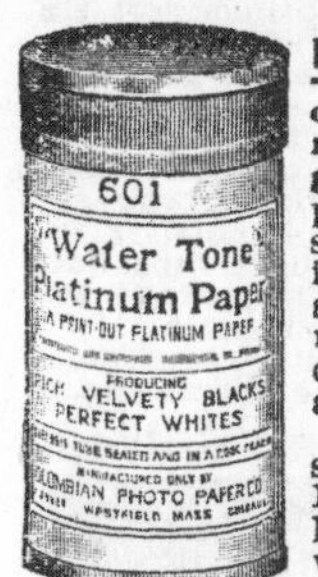

PLATINOTYPE PAPER has always been a favorite with those appreciating the most artistic results in photography, but the high price at which paper of this kind has always been sold has prevented many from using it. We are now able, however, to supply the best platinum paper made at prices no higher than are charged by many dealers for ordinary printing out papers.

Platinum paper produces matt surface pictures in **black and white. No chemicals required** (except a little muriatic acid for fixing) and the **whole process is extremely simple.** The details of the picture show before development; both development and fixing are accomplished very quickly, the entire process of development, fixing and washing not requiring over twenty minutes.

Size	Per dozen	Size	Per dozen
3¼x3¼	18c	3⅞x5½	$0.36
3¼x4¼	23c	5 x7	.54
4 x5	32c	6½x8½	.81
		8 x10	1.17

No. 20C2947 Muriatic Acid, chemically pure to make the fixing bath for platinum paper.
Price, per pound bottle, 44c; 1 ounce bottle.....12c

METALOTYPE PAPER.

No. 20C2922

METALOTYPE PAPER is one of the latest novelties in the line of sensitized papers and is justly becoming very popular. Metalotype is a developing paper, being manipulated just the same as Darko, simply requiring a short exposure to artificial light, after which the picture is developed.

THE DISTINGUISHING FEATURE of this paper is the burnished silvery surface, due to a thin metallic coating, giving a beautiful silvery sheen to the picture and making it at once striking and different from anything else made. Metalotype must be seen to be appreciated; it is impossible to do it justice in a description.

Order enough to give it a fair trial.

Size, 3¼x3¼. Price, per dozen, 12c; per gross, $1.20
Size, 3¼x4¼. Price, per dozen, 12c; per gross, 1.20
Size, 4 x5. Price, per dozen, 20c; per gross, 1.60
Size, 3⅞x5½. Price, per dozen, 20c; per gross, 1.60
Size, 5 x7. Price, per dozen, 28c; per gross, 2.80
Size, 5 x8. Price, per dozen, 32c; per gross, 3.20
Size, 6½x8½. Price, per dozen, 48c; per gross, 4.80
Size, 8 x10. Price, per dozen, 64c; per gross, 7.20

THIS PAPER KEEPS GOOD INDEFINITELY.

You can order by the gross without fear of its spoiling on your hands.

The Best Developer for metalotype paper is the Darko Developer, see No. 20C2915. Price, per package, 19 cents.

FERRO-PRUSSIATE OR BLUE PAPER.

No. 20C2925

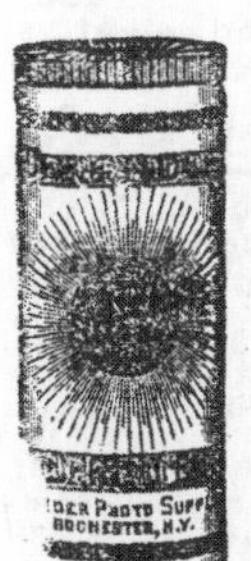

BLUE PAPER is very easy to manipulate, as it requires no toning. Prints can be made from it very rapidly and **no chemicals** are necessary. It is merely printed for about ten minutes in the sunlight and then **washed** thoroughly in clean water. It will retain its sensitiveness longer than any other paper, and full instructions for working accompany each package.

It is a good paper for beginners for printing landscapes, etc.

The prints are of a brilliant blue and white color. Put up in light proof packages of 24 sheets. We guarantee our paper to be the best blue paper made.

Size	Price, per pkg.	Size	Price, per pkg.
3½x3½	12c	5 x 7	25c
3¼x4¼	12c	5 x 8	30c
4 x5	15c	6½x 8½	38c
4¼x6½	23c	8 x10	40c

REMEMBER, THAT A COPY OF

COMPLETE INSTRUCTIONS IN PHOTOGRAPHY"

will be included, free of charge (if you ask for it), with every $2.50 order for Photo Goods. See page 346 . . . . .

AUTOTONE MATT PAPER.

No. 20C2930

AN ENTIRELY NEW PRODUCT in the line of sensitized printing papers, and one which by its simplicity in working, low price and beautiful results, is rapidly making many friends.

This paper tones while printing, and the only treatment necessary after printing is fixing in a plain hypo bath. The tone secured in this way is a beautiful warm sepia, very pleasing, especially for landscapes.

IT HAS THE POPULAR DULL OR MATT SURFACE FINISH, REQUIRING NO BURNISHING.

Size	Price	Price
2½x2½.	Per pkg. 2 doz. sheets, 10c; per ½ gro..	$0.24
3½x3½.	Per pkg. 2 doz. sheets, 13c; per ½ gro..	.32
3¼x4¼.	Per pkg. 2 doz. sheets, 15c; per ½ gro..	.36
4 x5.	Per pkg. 2 doz. sheets, 16c; per ½ gro..	.40
3⅞x5½.	Per pkg. 2 doz. sheets, 20c; per ½ gro..	.48
4 x6.	Per pkg. 1 doz. sheets, 12c; per ½ gro..	.48
5 x7.	Per pkg. 1 doz. sheets, 16c; per ½ gro..	.72
5 x8.	Per pkg. 1 doz. sheets, 20c; per ½ gro..	.88
6½x8½.	Per pkg. 1 doz. sheets, 24c; per ½ gro..	1.04
8 x10.	Per pkg. 1 doz. sheets, 32c; per ½ gro..	1.60

MONOX BROMIDE PAPER.

No. 20C2934

A HIGH GRADE BROMIDE PAPER, coated on the best imported stock, made by the Defender Photo Supply Co. Suitable for either contact work or enlarging. **We guarantee Monox Bromide Paper** to be the best bromide paper which can be produced.

Size, 8x10. Price, per doz. $0.60; per gross, $ 6.75
Size, 10x12. Price, per doz. .90; per gross, 10.13
Size, 11x14. Price, per doz. 1.17; per gross, 13.00
Size, 14x17. Price, per doz. 1.76; per gross, 20.25
Size, 16x20. Price, per doz. 2.40; per gross, 27.00
Size, 20x24. Price, per doz. 3.60; per gross, 41.25

Special prices will be quoted, if desired, on larger sizes up to 40x72, or on rolls.

CARDBOARD ARGO PAPER.

No. 20C2932

A SENSITIZED CARDBOARD, producing results exactly like Darko, and worked in the same way. Instead of being a thin, flexible paper, like all other sensitized papers, Cardboard Argo is a thick, stiff cardboard, and the pictures do not need to be mounted. **The finish is a dull or matt surface, the tone a pure black and white.** Very pleasing results are obtained on Cardboard Argo by printing with a mask, thus leaving a white margin.

Size, 3½x3½. Price, per doz., 8c; per ½ gross, $0.45
Size, 3¼x4¼. Price, per doz., 9c; per ½ gross, .49
Size, 4 x5. Price, per doz., 11c; per ½ gross, .60
Size, 3⅞x5½. Price, per doz., 13c; per ½ gross, .65
Size, 5 x7. Price, per doz., 23c; per ½ gross, 1.20
Size, 5 x8. Price, per doz., 24c; per ½ gross, 1.26
Size, 6½x8½. Price, per doz., 38c; per ½ gross, 2.10
Size, 8 x10. Price, per doz., 45c; per ½ gross, 2.50

Cardboard Argo is developed with the same developer as Darko. See No. 20C2915.

SENSITIZED POSTAL CARDS.

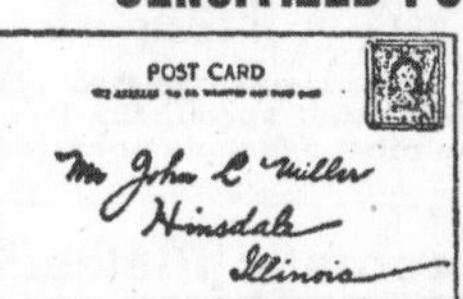

FRONT

No. 20C2950

THIS IS A VERY POPULAR NOVELTY, consisting of regulation size postal cards, printed on one side just like the government postal cards and sensitized on the reverse side. They make delightful souvenirs when printed with your favorite pictures and mailed to your friends. These postal cards are worked just the same as **Darko,** the prints being made by artificial light and developed, yielding beautiful warm black and white tones. Put up only in packages of one dozen or one-half gross.

REVERSE

Price, per half gross, 75c; per dozen..........15c

MONARCH MATTE PAPER.

Beautiful Black and White or Sepia Effects.

A PURE COLLODION MATT PAPER, THE EQUAL OF ANY COLLODION MATT PAPER MADE.

No. 20C2936

MONARCH IS COATED on the highest grade of imported stock, the emulsion is rich in silver and we absolutely guarantee this paper to be equal to any collodion matt paper on the market, regardless of price or maker. **Don't pay a fancy price** just for the privilege of using a paper made by the trust. Monarch is a perfect paper and costs you less money. **Monarch is easy to work,** gives the kind of results that bring trade, and it is **absolutely permanent.**

Size, 3½x 3½. Price, per doz. $0.13; per gross.......$1.31
Size, 4 x 5. Price, per doz. .18; per gross.......1.44
Cabinets.......Price, per doz. .22; per gross.......1.75
Size, 4 x 6. Price, per doz. .26; per gross.......1.97
Size, 5 x 7. Price, per doz. .31; per gross.......2.80
Size, 5 x 8. Price, per doz. .35; per gross.......3.15
Size, 5½x 7¾. Price, per doz. .40; per gross.......3.50
Size, 6½x8 ½. Price, per doz. .48; per gross.......4.46
Size, 8 x10. Price, per doz. .66; per gross.......6.82
Size, 10 x12. Price, per doz. .96; per gross.......10.50
Size, 11 x14. Price, per doz. 1.27; per gross.......13.65
Cabinet Seconds. Price, per gross.......1.40
Rolls, 10 feet long, 24½ inches wide. Price.......1.97
Rolls, 10 yards long, 24½ inches wide. Price.......5.25

No. 20C2938 Gold Solution, absolutely pure; made especially for Monarch paper. Price, size No. 1, 44c; size No. 2.......85c

No. 20C2939 Platinum Solution, to make platinum toning bath for Monarch paper. Absolutely pure; requires only addition of water. Price, size No. 1, 44c; size No. 2.......85c

LUSTRE.

A Developing Paper with Collodion Matt Effect.

No. 20C2940

LUSTRE IS AN ENTIRELY NEW PRODUCT in developing papers, a variety of Argo, the prints having the characteristic surface, finish and general effect of regular collodion matt surface papers. An ideal paper for the professional photographer, as it can be worked by artificial light; prints can be made any time of day or night. Rush work can be gotten out absolutely independent of the weather. **For the professional** or for the amateur this paper takes the place of collodion matt papers, possessing all the good points of collodion matt papers, giving all the peculiarly characteristic effects of tone, surface and detail **as** exhibited in the finest collodion matt prints, but **without** the long complicated and difficult process of double toning in gold and platinum, without being dependent on the weather, and at about one-half the cost. **Simplicity of manipulation** is literally true with Lustre. **Printing is accomplished in a few seconds by artificial light, development is almost instantaneous, and then fixing and washing completes the work. Lustre is coated on the very finest grade of pure imported stock,** the prints are absolutely permanent, and the wealth of detail in the **halftones** was never before produced in a developing paper.

Size	Dozen	Half Gross	Gross	Size	Dozen	Half Gross	Gross
3½x3½	$0.09	$0.50	$0.93	5 x7	$0.18	$0.95	$1.75
3¼x4¼	.10	.57	1.08	6½x8½	.30	1.60	3.15
4 x5	.12	.60	1.15	8 x10	.42	2.30	4.50
3⅞x5½	.12	.65	1.20	10 foot rolls, 26 inches wide, each			1.35
4 x6	.14	.75	1.50	10 yard rolls, 26 inches wide, each			3.25

Lustre keeps indefinitely. Don't hesitate to order in quantity and thus reduce cost of transportation. Lustre Paper is developed with the same developer used for Darko. See No. 20C2915.

THE ROEBUCK DRY PLATES.

NOT MADE BY THE TRUST.

No. 20C2960 We offer the Roebuck Dry Plate as the equal of any dry plate made, a plate that can be depended upon under any conditions, a plate that is suitable for any kind of work.

THE ROEBUCK DRY PLATES are coated on the finest quality of imported Belgium glass, carefully sorted and free from bubbles, scratches or other imperfections.

THE EMULSION IS RICH IN SILVER, yielding strong, vigorous negatives with a wealth of detail and no tendency whatever toward fogging. The factory in which the Roebuck plates are made is one of the most perfectly equipped dry plate factories ever built, furnished with the very latest and most approved styles of coating machines, and a most complete system of ventilation and refrigeration, giving perfect control of both temperature and hygroscopic conditions. It is this perfect equipment, combined with long experience in dry plate making and the most perfect materials, which enables us to produce perfect plates and offer them at prices heretofore considered impossible.

THE ROEBUCK PLATES ARE EXCEEDINGLY RAPID, giving the finest possible results in the studio where short exposures are so desirable. For landscapes, portraiture, interiors, flashlight work, instantaneous exposures; in fact, any work requiring a uniformly rapid and reliable plate, the Roebuck plate is unsurpassed. In brilliancy, detail, uniformity and speed, the Roebuck plate will satisfy the most exacting operator.

Size	Quantity in case, dozen	Price, per case	Price, per dozen	Size	Quantity in case, dozen	Price, per case	Price, per dozen
2 x 2	50	$4.75	$0.10	4¼x 6½	24	$10.95	$0.48
2½x 2½	50	6.18	.13	5 x 7	24	13.22	.58
2½x 4	50	8.55	.18	5 x 8	24	15.28	.67
3¼x 3¼	36	6.50	.19	6½x 8½	12	10.15	.89
3¼x 4¼	36	7.86	.23	8 x10	12	14.25	1.25
4¼x 4¼	30	9.40	.33	10 x12	4	7.41	1.95
4 x 5	30	9.69	.34	11 x14	3	8.41	2.95
4¼x 5½	24	9.35	.41	14 x17	3	11.26	3.95

Cramer's Isochromatic Plates.

MADE BY G. CRAMER DRY PLATE CO.

Not in the Trust.

No. 20C2962 Cramer's Isochromatic Plates are very desirable in photographing landscapes, flowers, paintings, portraits, etc., as they give true color values, that is, they show the true difference between certain shades or colors which cannot be shown if photographed with an ordinary plate. With ordinary plates we have reds that take too black, blues, that take too white, and yellow or orange that takes the same as black, red or green. These plates discriminate in these and other colors and yield surprisingly good results on all subjects where colors are to be contrasted. Landscapes made with this plate possess a brilliancy and beauty not to be obtained with any other plate. Cloud effects are more easily obtained and portraits are greatly improved. Remember, these plates do not actually make colored photographs, they simply produce in light and shade the correct or relative color values.

Made in three speeds: slow, medium and instantaneous.

Size	Quantity in case	Price, per case	Price, per dozen
3¼x 3¼	30 dozen	$ 9.00	$0.32
3¼x 4¼	30 dozen	10.13	.36
4 x 5	30 dozen	14.63	.52
5 x 7	20 dozen	16.50	.88
6½x 8½	12 dozen	14.85	1.32
8 x10	10 dozen	18.00	1.92
10 x12	4 dozen	12.60	3.36
11 x14	4 dozen	18.00	4.80
14 x17	3 dozen	20.25	7.20

State whether you want slow, medium or instantaneous. For general use, we advise the medium.

Cramer's Dry Plates.

MADE BY G. CRAMER DRY PLATE COMPANY.

Not in the Trust.

No. 20C2966 Cramer's Plates are widely known as strictly high grade goods, and are used extensively by the best studios and by the most experienced and successful amateurs. We furnish two speeds, known as the Banner and Crown brands. The Banner plate is the most extensively used for portrait work in the studio, and is rapid enough for ordinary instantaneous work. The Crown brand is extremely rapid and suited to the shortest possible exposures.

Size	Quantity in Case	Crown Price, per Case	Crown Price, per Doz.	Banner Price, per Case	Banner Price, per Doz.
3¼x 3¼	30 doz.	$ 8.40	$0.30	$ 7.80	$0.28
3¼x 4¼	30 doz.	9.45	.34	8.78	.32
4 x 5	30 doz.	13.65	.49	12.68	.46
4¼x 6½	30 doz.	18.90	.68	17.55	.63
5 x 7	20 doz.	15.40	.83	14.30	.77
5 x 8	20 doz.	17.50	.94	16.25	.88
6½x 8½	12 doz.	13.86	1.24	12.87	1.16
8 x10	10 doz.	16.80	1.80	15.60	1.68
10 x12	4 doz.	11.76	3.15	10.92	2.94
11 x14	4 doz.	16.80	4.50	15.60	4.20
14 x17	3 doz.	18.90	6.75	17.55	6.30

Hammer's Dry Plates.

MADE BY HAMMER DRY PLATE CO.

Not in the Trust.

No. 20C2967 Hammer's Dry Plates, another of the well known standard brands, are considered by professional photographers to be one of the best plates made. We furnish this plate in one speed only—the extra fast—suitable for studio work or general all around photography.

Size	Quantity in case, dozen	Price, per case	Price, per dozen
3¼x 3¼	30	$ 7.57	$0.28
3¼x 4¼	30	8.52	.31
4 x 5	30	12.30	.44
4¼x 6½	30	17.03	.62
5 x 7	20	13.90	.75
5 x 8	20	15.77	.85
6½x 8½	12	12.48	1.12
8 x10	12	18.16	1.63
10 x12	4	10.60	2.86
11 x14	4	15.14	4.08
14 x17	3	17.03	6.12

Exposure Tables.

No. 20C2972 A Little Book of Tables which gives you the exact exposure at any hour of the day, and any day of the year with any brand of plates, or any speed of lens. Simple and absolutely correct. No more over exposed or under exposed plates. Price..(If by mail, postage extra, 1c)..15c

Photo Paste in Jars.

No. 20C2975 Perfection Photo Paste. The most perfect paste ever made for mounting photographs. It is always ready for use, of great adhesive power and will not mould, sour or deteriorate in any way. The Perfection Paste is a purely vegetable paste, containing no acids or other ingredients injurious to photographs.

Price, 4-ounce jar..........9c
Price, 8-ounce jar..........15c
Price, 16-ounce jar..........20c
Price, 32-ounce jar..........48c

Unmailable on account of weight.

Photo Paste in Tubes.

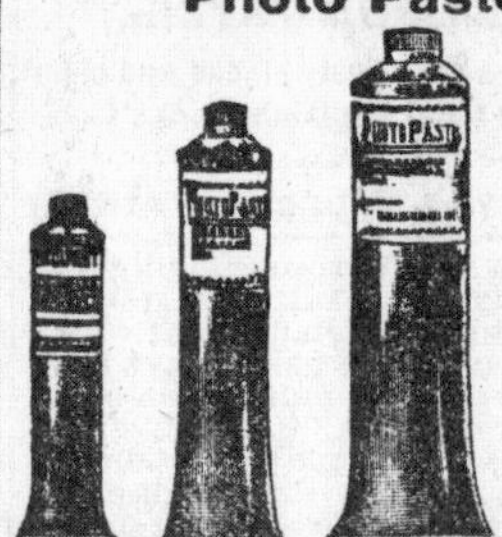

No. 20C2976 This Paste is the same as described under No. 20C2975, but is put up in collapsible soft tin tubes. Paste put up in this way never gets hard or dry and is always ready for use.

Price, 1-ounce tube..4c
If by mail, postage extra, 4 cents.
Price, 2-ounce tube..6c
If by mail, postage extra, 8 cents.
Price, 4-ounce tube..9c
Postage extra, 12c.

Acme Transparent Water Colors.

With these Improved Transparent Water Colors you can color any photograph with the most artistic results quickly and easily. No previous experience or skill required. The coloring of photographs is a beautiful art and a profitable profession. With these colors anyone can do the work and do it well. The Acme Transparent Water Colors are adapted to any and all kinds of photographs, and are also suitable for engravings, halftone pictures, etc.; they are guaranteed to be perfectly pure, brilliant and reliable, the best colors made.

No. 20C2982 Acme Water Colors, large box, as shown in illustration, containing sixteen colors, palette and instructions. Price..........$1.95

No. 20C2983 Acme Water Colors, small box, containing six colors, palette and instructions. Price..........80c

No. 20C2984 "Photographic Coloring," a complete book of instructions for the use of water color paints in coloring photographs. Price..........21c

Opaque.

No. 20C2990 It is frequently desirable to block out or render opaque certain parts of a negative, and this can easily be done with this preparation, which is simply applied to the negative with a small camel's hair brush.

Price, per box..........20c

If by mail, postage extra, 2 cents.

Polish for Ferro Plates.

No. 20C2992 Ferrotype Plate Polish. A small quantity of this solution rubbed over the ferrotype plate before squeegeeing, makes it impossible for the print to stick to the plate. Cannot be sent by mail. Price, per bottle..........10c

Martin's Specialties.

A line of special photographic preparations, radically different from anything on the market and of great merit.

No. 20C2995 Soline, a liquid for sensitizing cloth, paper, postal cards or other materials. Prints made on cloth can be washed without injury; very useful in making sofa pillows, banners, tidies, book marks, etc. Price..........30c

No. 20C2996 Intensine, an intensifier in dry form for glass or film negatives or lantern slides. An extra good intensifier. Price....15c

No. 20C2997 Platyn, a single platinum toner that gives fine platinum tones on any kind of printing-out paper, or on cloth prints made with Soline. Price per ½-ounce bottle, sufficient for 80 ounces toning bath..........30c

LIQUID DEVELOPERS.

Hydro-Metol Developer.

No. 20C3015 We consider this our best developer, being a combination of the well known hydrochinon and metol; works very rapidly, never fogs the plate, brings out all the details and gives a very brilliant negative.

Price, per 8-ounce bottle..........18c

Unmailable on account of weight.

ANSCO FILM. ....DAYLIGHT LOADING....

FOR USE IN ANY KODAK, BUCKEYE, ANSCO, HAWKEYE OR SEROCO FILM CAMERA.

NO. 20C2970 THIS FILM is put up in regular daylight loading cartridges of either six or twelve exposures and is adapted to any modern make of daylight loading film camera, including the Eastman kodaks and the Seroco film cameras.

ANSCO FILM is made by one of the largest and best known film makers in the world, a manufacturer whose name on any article of photographic merchandise is a guarantee of good quality.

EVERY ROLL OF ANSCO FILM which we sell is put out under our binding guarantee to be absolutely perfect, guaranteed to be equal to any film on the market, regardless of price, and we will replace with new film or refund the purchase price on any Ansco film found defective to the slightest extent.

ANSCO FILM IS ANTI-TRUST FILM. It is the only anti-trust film on the market. If you buy another make of film, you are contributing to the support of the trust and to the maintenance of high prices on photographic goods.

Size of picture		Price, 6 exposures	Price, 12 exposures
1½x2	For Pocket Kodak	....	$0.21
2¼x2¼	For No. 1 Brownie	$0.12	....
2¼x3¼	For No. 2 Brownie	.17	....
1⅝x2½	For No. 0 Folding Pocket Kodak	.12	.21
2¼x3¼	For No. 1 Folding Pocket Kodak	.17	.34
2½x4¼	For No. 1A Folding Pocket Kodak	.21	.42
3¼x4¼	For No. 3 Folding Pocket Kodak, No. 3 Weno Hawkeye, Stereo Weno Hawkeye, No.3 Buckeye, No. 4 Ansco and Nos. 3, 5, 7 and Stereoscopic Seroco Film Cameras	.30	.58
3½x3½	For Bullseye, Bullet, Hawkeye and No. 1 Seroco Film Camera	.25	.50
4 x5	For Bullseye, Bullet, Hawkeye and Nos. 2, 4, 6 and 8 Seroco Film Cameras	.38	.75
4¼x3¼	For No. 3 Cartridge Kodak	.30	.55
5 x4	For No. 4 Cartridge Kodak	.38	.75
7 x5	For No. 5 Cartridge Kodak	.67	1.34

DEVELOPING POWDERS.

We especially recommend the purchase of developers in powder form, as they ship better, transportation charges are exceedingly small and the purchaser gets the greatest possible value for the money, as the expense of bottling, compounding, etc., is all saved.

Eikonogen Developing Powders.

No. 20C3020 These powders afford a very convenient means for preparing the liquid Eikonogen developer; avoids the risk of breakage in transportation, and always insures a fresh and stronger developer. Each package contains six sets of powders, which is sufficient to prepare 24 ounces of concentrated developer.

Price, per package...(By mail, extra, 3 cents)...15c

Hydro-Metol Developing Powders.

No. 20C3025 Our Hydro-Metol Developing Powders, a combination of hydrochinon and metol, are made from the purest chemicals, put up in the most careful and exact manner, and will be found a perfect developer in every way. Our Hydro-Metol Developing Powders work very rapidly, do not fog or stain the plate, and produce **brilliant, sparkling negatives,** full of detail and of the most perfect printing quality. **The best Developing Powder made.**

Price, per package containing six powders, sufficient to make 24 ounces of developer 16c

If by mail, postage extra, 3 cents.

Elko-Hydro Developing Powders.

No. 20C3026 A combination of eikonogen and hydrochinon, making a developer equally well suited to time exposures or instantaneous work, and one of our most popular productions. This developer works rapidly, is clean and stainless and produces a bright, snappy negative. Price, per package of six powders, sufficient for 24 ounces of developer..............15c

If by mail, postage extra, 3 cents.

TONERS.

No. 20C3035 Combined Toning and Fixing Solution, a high grade toning and fixing bath in one solution. For toning Seroco paper or any kind of gelatin printing-out paper. Our Combined Toning and Fixing Solution yields a variety of tones, and as it is rich in gold it may be used repeatedly. Price, per 16-ounce bottle, 29c; per 8-ounce bottle..........16c

Unmailable on account of weight.

Gold Toning Solution.

No. 20C3040 Many photographers prefer to work their paper in separate baths, that is the toning and fixing being done in two separate baths; and this is certainly the most correct method, as prints made in a combined toning and fixing bath are very apt to fade or discolor in time. **This gold toning solution** requires only to be diluted with water, and after toning, the prints are fixed in a plain solution of hypo. Concentrated. Price, per 8-oz. bottle..27c

Unmailable on account of weight.

Toning and Fixing Powders.

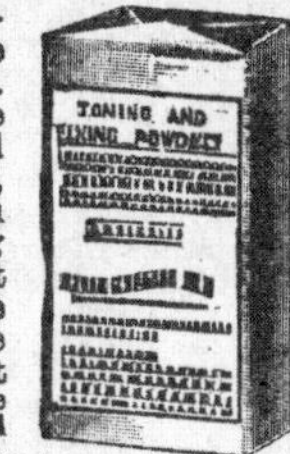

No. 20C3045 Toning and Fixing Powders, for preparing the combined toning and fixing bath. The toning bath made from these powders possesses all the good points of our regular liquid toner, and for use is simply dissolved in water. **These Toning and Fixing Powders** are radically different from any other preparation of the kind on the market, and are the only thoroughly reliable and perfect **toner and fixer in dry form** ever made. Made especially for Seroco paper, but yield splendid results with any gelatin printing-out paper.

Price, per package, sufficient for 24 ounces solution.......15c

If by mail, postage extra, 6 cents.

Platinum Toning Solution.

No. 20C3048 Platinum Toning Solution, for producing black tones on any gelatin printing-out paper, such as Seroco. **The platinum finish** is very popular and this toning bath affords an easy method of obtaining fine black platinum tones at small expense; also produces fine results with Autotone paper.

Price, per 8-ounce bottle, concentrated....................28c

Unmailable on account of weight.

Intensifier.

No. 20C3050 It frequently happens that negatives, from errors in exposure or developing, are too weak, thin, or lacking in detail, to make good prints, and in such cases negatives which might otherwise be thrown away as valueless, **can be so improved by intensifying as to produce good prints.** This intensifier is made from a special formula. It is absolutely the best one made, and there is nothing else on the market like it. Price 38c

Unmailable on account of weight.

Intensifying Powders.

No. 20C3055 Intensifying Powders, for strengthening weak negatives. Require only to be dissolved in water to make ready for use. One package makes 24 ounces of solution.

Price, per package...16c

Unmailable on account of weight.

Reducing Powders.

No. 20C3065 Reducing Powders, for thinning negatives which are too dense. When dissolved in water, this powder forms a reducing solution ready for use. Each package makes 24 ounces of solution. Price, per package..................15c

If by mail, postage extra, 4 cents.

Neg-Dry.

No. 20C3070 Neg-Dry is a hardener for either plates or paper and is a most remarkable preparation. One of the most annoying things in photography is the long time required for a negative to dry after washing. **When treated with this preparation, the negative can be dried in five minutes by artificial heat,** and the film becomes so hard that it can scarcely be scratched or marred in any way. Used with Darko paper, the finished prints can be dried within a few minutes after development. **Can be used over and over again.** Price, per 4-ounce bottle.....17c

Unmailable on account of weight.

Acid Hypo.

No. 20C3075 Acid Hypo is a preparation in dry form for making the acid fixing bath. Requires only the addition of water to make it ready for use. The acid fixing bath is of great advantage, both for plates and films, and for developing papers, having a clearing effect and preventing fog.

Price, per box...(By mail, postage extra, 8c)....8c

Varnishes.

No. 20C3077 Negative Varnish, best quality, for varnishing negatives. Price, per 6-ounce bottle..28c

No. 20C3078 Diamond Varnish, for tintypes or ferrotypes. Price, per 6-ounce bottle. 32c

Unmailable on account of weight.

Photographic Chemicals.

We absolutely guarantee the purity of our photographic chemicals.

No. 20C3090 Pyrogallic Acid, the old reliable developer. **Our Pyro** is a pure, resublimed pyrogallic acid, of the very finest quality, guaranteed equal to any Pyro on the market, regardless of price. Put up in tins.

Price, per pound	$2.30	Price, per ¼-pound	65c
Price, per ½-pound	1.25	Price, per ounce	20c

No. 20C3091 Schering's Pyro, a standard make of pyro, still preferred by many photographers.

Price, per pound	$2.30	Price, per ¼-pound	65c
Price, per ½-pound	1.25	Price, per ounce	20c

No. 20C3092 Hydrochinon, strictly chemically pure, perfectly white, the best hydrochinon we can buy.

Price, per pound	$1.92	Price, per ¼-pound	50c
Price, per ½-pound	.98	Price, per ounce	16c

No. 20C3093 Eikonogen, best grade, imported from Germany. Put up in tins.

Price, per pound	$3.35	Price, per ¼-pound	$1.02
Price, per ½-pound	1.79	Price, per ounce	.30

No. 20C3094 Metol, in original packages.

Price, per pound	$8.00	Price, per ¼-pound	$2.42
Price, per ½-pound	4.46	Price, per ounce	.65

No. 20C3095 Glycin, in original packages.

Price, per pound	$8.00	Price, per ¼-pound	$2.42
Price, per ½-pound	4.46	Price, per ounce	.65

No. 20C3096 Amidol, in original packages.

Price, per pound	$8.00	Price, per ¼-pound	$2.42
Price, per ½-pound	4.46	Price, per ounce	.65

Defendol.

A New Developing Agent for either Plates or Paper.

No. 20C3099 Defendol, the new developing agent, offers advantages over any developer yet produced and is suitable for any paper, such as darko, lustre, etc, or for dry plates. **Defendol is not poisonous,** it does not stain the fingers; plates can be left in it for hours and still remain clear; it is cheaper than other developers; it keeps indefinitely in dry form; it remains clear in solution longer than other developers. **Defendol retains its working qualities** to the last drop, being practically inexhaustible; it can be used over and over again, and it is the best developer known for bromide papers. **No sulphite of soda is necessary in making up Defendol developer, no other chemical except dry carbonate of soda being required.**

	Price
½-oz. package makes about 20 ozs. developer	$0.21
1-oz. package makes about 60 ozs. developer	.40
4-oz. package makes about 7½ qts. developer	1.50
8-oz. package makes about 7½ gals. developer	2.80
16-oz. package makes about 15 gals. developer	5.20

No. 20C3100 Acetic acid, No. 8, 1-oz. bottle, 5c; 1-lb. bottle 20

No. 20C3102 Citric acid, crystals, 1-oz. bottle 10

	Price
No. 20C3104 Muriatic acid (known also as hydrochloric acid), 2-oz. bottle, 18c; 1 lb. bottle	$0.44
No. 20C3106 Nitric acid, 1-oz. bottle, 12c; 1-lb. bottle	.36
No. 20C3108 Oxalic acid, crystals, 2-oz. bottle, 15c; 1-lb. bottle	.30
No. 20C3112 Sulphuric acid, C. P., 1-oz. bottle, 12c; 1-lb. bottle	.33
No. 20C3120 Alcohol, pure, for photographic uses, ½-pint bottle	.25
No. 20C3124 Alum, pulverized, 1-lb. package	.15
No. 20C3126 Alum, chrome, 1-lb. box	.15
No. 20C3128 Ammonia, liquid conc., U. S. P., 1-lb. bottle	.26
No. 20C3130 Ammonium bromide, 1-oz. bottle	.12
No. 20C3132 Ammonium bichromate, 1-oz bottle, 15c; 1-lb. bottle	1.12
No. 20C3134 Ammonium carbonate, 1-lb. bottle	.40
No. 20C3136 Ammonium chloride, 1-oz. bottle, 10c; 1-lb. bottle	.35
No. 20C3138 Ammonium sulphocyanide, 1-oz. bottle,	.15
No. 20C3150 Formalin, put up in 4-oz. bottles. Per bottle	.18
No. 20C3151 Glycerin, very pure, 1-oz. bottle	.08

Gold Chloride at 40 Cents.

Guaranteed Full Weight.

No. 20C3153 Gold chloride, pure, 15-gr. bottle, per dozen, $4.72; each	$0.40
No. 20C3155 Gold and sodium, chloride, 15-gr. bot.	.35
No. 20C3161 Iodine, resublimed, 1-oz. bottle	.33
No. 20C3163 Iron protosulphate, 1-lb. package	.06
No. 20C3165 Iron and ammonia, citrate, 1-oz. bottle,	.12
No. 20C3168 Lead nitrate, 1-oz. bottle	.12
No. 30C3170 Lead acetate (sugar of lead), 1-oz. bot.	.12
No. 20C3175 Mercury bichloride (corrosive sublimate), 1-oz. bottle	.15
No. 20C3177 Magnesium, pure, 1-oz. package	.32
No. 20C3179 Potassium bromide, 1-oz. bottle	.10
No. 20C3184 Potassium carbonate, 1-lb. package	.25
No. 20C3185 Potassium cyanide, 4-oz. can, 20c; 1-lb. can	.60
No. 20C3186 Potassium ferrocyanide (yellow prussiate of potash), 1-oz. package	.12
No. 20C3188 Potassium ferricyanide (red prussiate of potash), 1-oz package	.15
No. 20C3190 Potassium iodide, 1-oz. package	.30
No. 20C3192 Potassium oxalite, neutral, 1-lb. pkg.	.25
No. 20C3200 Platinum chloride, 15-gr. bottle	.45
No. 20C3202 Silver nitrate, 1-oz. bottle	.55
No. 20C3210 Sodium acetate, 1-oz. bottle	.08
No. 20C3212 Sodium bicarbonate, 1-oz. package	.05
No. 20C3213 Sodium bisulphite (acid sulphite), pure, 1-oz. bottle	.12
No. 20C3214 Sodium carbonate (sal soda), crystals, pure, 1-lb. package	.09
No. 20C3216 Sodium citrate, 1-oz. bottle	.14
No. 20C3218 Sodium sulphite, crystals, pure. Per 1-lb. cartons	.10
No. 20C3221 Sulphite of Soda, dry, a very high grade sulphite, guaranteed absolutely chemically pure. Per lb. bottle	.32
No. 20C3224 Carbonate of Soda, dry, a very high grade carbonate (sal soda), guaranteed absolutely chemically pure. Per 1-lb. bottle	.22

100 Pounds of Hypo for $1.90.

No. 20C3225 Hyposulphite of sodium, or Hypo, as the photographers call it, is one of the most important chemicals used in photography, and none but the best grade should ever be used.

OUR HYPO is the best chemically pure pea crystals, free from dirt, small, perfectly formed crystals. Clean and dry. No caking, no waste.

PRICES.

Price, per pound, in 1-pound sealed cartons......................3c

Price, 25 lbs., in wooden pail, as shown in illustration, for....60c

Price, 100 lbs., in original keg, for............................$1.90

Guaranteed best quality hypo or money refunded.

The Little Gem Albums.

You frequently have a few pictures which are especially interesting, and which if mounted on cards are apt to get soiled or misplaced; but this neat little booklet will exactly fill your requirements, bring out the beauty of your photographs and please your friends. **Made in two sizes only, one for 5x7 pictures, the other for pictures 4x5 or smaller.** Has six ash gray flexible leaves, thus holding 12 pictures each, and the covers are handsomely tinted and embellished with halftone engraving.

No. 20C3400 The Little Gem Album for pictures 4x5 or smaller. Price..............................8c

No. 20C3401 The Little Gem Album for pictures 5x7. Price....................................12c

Order several, they are cheaper than card mounts.

Our Flexible Leaf Albums.

These most attractive albums are made with flexible covers and leaves, in either full cloth or full leather, morocco grain binding. The leaves are of the popular ash gray color, and for protection to the prints a sheet of transparent parchment is inserted between each two leaves. These albums are suitable either for the matt surface prints, such as Darko, or for glossy squeegeed prints, and in mounting on the flexible leaves, it is only necessary to put a little paste on each corner of the print.

No. 20C3601	For pictures 4x5	No. of leaves 25.	Price, cloth binding	$0.25
No. 20C3602	For pictures 4x5	No. of leaves 50.	Price, cloth binding	.36
No. 20C3603	For pictures 5x7	No. of leaves 25.	Price, cloth binding	.36
No. 20C3604	For pictures 5x7	No. of leaves 50.	Price, cloth binding	.54
No. 20C3611	For pictures 4x5	No. of leaves 25.	Price, leather binding	.63
No. 20C3612	For pictures 4x5	No. of leaves 50.	Price, leather binding	.75
No. 20C3613	For pictures 5x7	No. of leaves 25.	Price, leather binding	.93
No. 20C3614	For pictures 5x7	No. of leaves 50.	Price, leather binding	1.12

The 4x5 size is also suitable for smaller pictures.

CARD MOUNTS.

Plain White Cards.

No. 20C3300 Good Quality Plain White Cardboard Mounts, square cornered. Enameled on one side. Put up in packages of 50.

Size	Price, per 1000	Per 50
Size, 4¼x5½ inches	$1.54	8c
Size, 5 x7 inches	2.31	12c
Size, 5 x8 inches	2.50	13c
Size, 6½x 8½ inches	3.84	20c
Size, 8 x10 inches	5.38	28c
Size, 10 x12 inches, extra heavy	9.22	48c
Size, 11 x14 inches, extra heavy	11.42	60c

Sizes given are exact outside measurements.

Plain Tinted Cards.

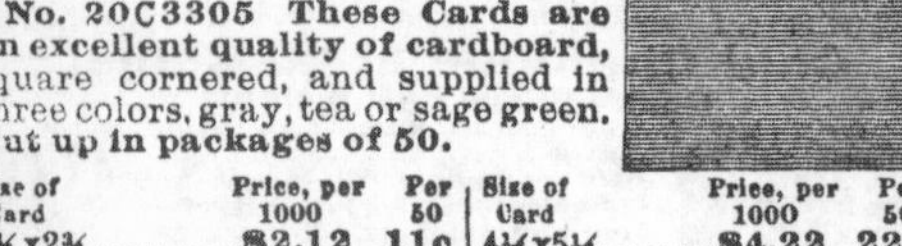

No. 20C3305 These Cards are an excellent quality of cardboard, square cornered, and supplied in three colors, gray, tea or sage green. **Put up in packages of 50.**

Size of Card	Price, per 1000	Per 50	Size of Card	Price, per 1000	Per 50
2¾x2¾	$2.12	11c	4¼x5½	$4.22	22c
3½x4½	3.46	18c	5½x7½	7.30	38c
3¾x3¾	3.27	17c			

Sizes given are exact outside measurements.

Gold Bevel Edge Cards.

No. 20C3310 Fine Quality Card, enameled on one side, gold beveled edge, round corners, supplied in white only. A first class card. **Put up in packages of 25.**

Size of Card	Price, per 1000	Per 25	Size of Card	Price, per 1000	Per 25
2¾x2¾	$3.08	8c	5 x7	$ 8.45	22c
3¾x3¾	3.84	10c	6½x8½	12.68	33c
3½x4½	4.61	12c	8 x10	18.44	48c
4¼x5½	5.37	14c			

Sizes given are exact outside measurements.

Embossed Border Cards.

No. 20C3315 Embossed Border Cards, wide margin cards with fancy embossed border, of very pretty pattern, good quality, furnished in either white enameled, queen's gray or sage green. **Put up in packages of 25.**

For Pictures	Price, per 1000	Per 25	For Pictures	Price, per 1000	Per 25
1½x2	$2.25	7c	3¼x4¼	$ 5.40	14c
2 x2	2.70	8c	4¼x4¼	6.20	16c
2½x2½	3.15	9c	4 x5	6.25	17c
3½x3½	5.40	14c	5 x7	11.75	30c

Sizes given are inside measurements.

Embossed Tinted Border Cards With White Center.

No. 20C3320 Extra Heavy Cards, with white centers and wide embossed sage green borders. When the picture is mounted there is a narrow **margin of the white center left, which forms a pleasing contrast** between the sage green border and the prints. Put up in packages of 25.

For Pictures	Price, per 1000	Per 25	For Pictures	Price, per 1000	Per 25
1½x2	$5.76	15c	3¼x4¼	$8.07	21c
2½x2½	6.52	17c	4 x5	9.98	26c
3½x3½	7.68	20c	5 x7	16.13	42c

Sizes given are inside measurements.

Ash Gray and Ivy Green Mounts.

No. 20C3325 Light, thin matt surface cards, very artistic for prints made on Darko paper, and also extensively used for glossy prints which have been squeegeed. In mounting prints on these cards the paste is applied only to the corners of the print. Made in two colors, ash gray and ivy green, and put up in packages of 25.

Size of Card	For Pictures	Price, per 1000	Per 25
5½x6½	4 x 5 or smaller	$ 6.92	18c
8 x10	5 x 7	14.59	38c
10 x12	6½x 8½	22.28	58c
11 x14	8 x10	23.04	60c

Beveled Edge Melton Cards.

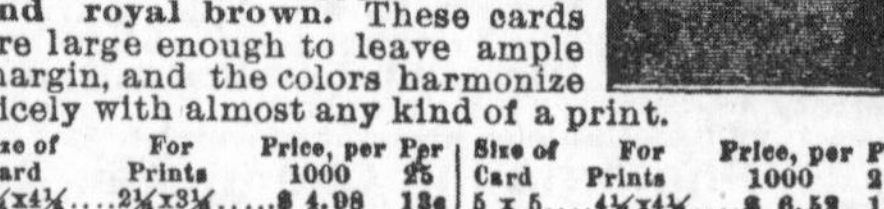

No. 20C3330 Another new card in the stylish Melton stock, perfectly plain, with square corners and beveled edges. Made in two colors, **Egyptian black and royal brown.** These cards are large enough to leave ample margin, and the colors harmonize nicely with almost any kind of a print.

Size of Card	For Prints	Price, per 1000	Per 25	Size of Card	For Prints	Price, per 1000	Per 25
3¼x4¼	2¼x3¼	$ 4.98	13c	5 x 5	4¼x4¼	$ 6.52	17c
4¼x4¼	3¼x3¼	6.16	16c	5 x 6	4 x5	7.68	20c
4¼x5½	3¼x4¼	6.20	16c	6 x 8	5 x7	10.36	27c

Melton Face Embossed Cards.

No. 20C3335 Melton Face Embossed Border Cards, in the new colors, Scotch gray and ivy green. The border is embossed in a very handsome design, and the cards are of the best quality. **State whether you desire the Scotch gray or ivy green.**

For Pictures	Price, per 1000	Per 25	For Pictures	Price, per 1000	Per 25
2¼x3¼	$6.52	17c	4¼x4¼	$9.21	24c
3½x3½	7.20	19c	4 x5	10.75	28c
3¼x4¼	8.44	22c	5 x7	16.13	42c

Special Mounts for 4x5 Pictures.

Owing to the constantly increasing demand for cards and other supplies in the popular 4x5 size, we have made arrangements for furnishing the following new and attractive designs. These cards are all for 4x5 pictures only, and cannot be furnished in any other size.

No. 20C3375 Embossed Border Card, for 4x5 pictures, center white enamel, border very light queen's gray, with handsome embossed design. Outside measurement, 5⅝x6⅝ inches.

Price, per 1,000, **$8.45**; per package of 25.......**22c**

No. 20C3376 White Line Beveled Edge Card, for 4x5 pictures. This card is made from the popular Melton face stock, color very dark gray, with white **beveled edge.** Around the border, about ½ inch from the edge, is a **deeply embossed pure white line,** which forms a very effective contrast with the picture and the dark mount. Outside measurements, 5¼x6¼ inches.

Price, per 1,000, **$11.52**; per package of 25......**30c**

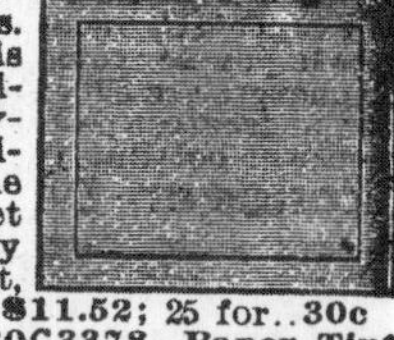

No. 20C3377 Black Line Beveled Edge Card, for 4x5 pictures. This card, like the preceding, is made from the best heavy Melton face stock, with white beveled edges. The color is a beautiful shade of pearl gray, and the deeply embossed line is jet black, making a very pretty card. Outside measurement, 5¼x6¼ inches. Price, per 1,000, **$11.52**; 25 for..**30c**

No. 20C3378 Paper Tint Center Card, for 4x5 pictures, one of the latest ideas. This card is made from Melton face stock, color dark ivy green, with plain straight edges and **plate sunk center.** The center of the card is covered with a plain white paper insert, just large enough so that a narrow white margin is left between the edges of the picture and the dark ivy green border of the card. Outside measurements, 5¼x6¼ inches; plate sunk center, 4⅜x5⅜ inches. Price, per 1,000, **$12.28**; 25 for..**32c**

No. 20C3379 Paper Tint Center Card, for 4x5 pictures, our best card. Made from medium weight Melton face stock of best quality, color a fine Scotch gray, edges perfectly plain and straight. **Plate sunk center with plain white paper insert.** This is an extra large card and one of the most stylish and up to date designs on the market. Outside measurement, 7x8 inches; plate sunk center, 5x6 inches; white center, 4¼x5¼ inches.

Price, per 1,000, **$17.28**; per package of 25....**45c**

Plain Cabinet Cards.

No. 20C3380

No. 20C3380 Round Cornered Cabinet Cards, just what you want for cheap work—supplied in white, gray or sage—4¼x6½.

Price, 1,000 for **$2.72**; 500 for **$1.37**; 250 for..................**70c**

No. 20C3381 White Enameled Cabinet Cards. Excellent quality plain edges, round corners, 4¼x6½.

Price, 1,000 for **$3.49**; 500 for **$1.76**; 250 for..............................**90c**

No. 20C3381

No. 20C3382

No. 20C3382 Gold Bevel Cabinet Cards, of good quality, not enameled, white or primrose. 4¼x6½.

Price, 1,000 for **$4.27**; 500 for **$2.16**; 250 for..............**$1.10**

No. 20C3383 Plain Bevel Cabinet Cards, square corners, good quality of Melton face board, furnished in Scotch gray, ivy green or black. 4¼x6½.

Price, 1,000 for **$4.66**; 500 for **$2.35**; 250 for.................................**$1.20**

No. 20C3383

Cards for Penny Pictures.

No. 20C3386 Embossed cards, white enamel outside, 2¾x2¾, for prints 1¼x1½.

Price, per 1,000, **$1.30**; 500 for **68c**

No. 20C3387 White Enameled Cards, fancy embossed border, outside, 2¾x2¾, for prints 1⅝x1⅝. Very pretty.

Price, per 1,000, **$2.05**; 500 for.....**$1.08**

Fancy Mounts For Portrait Work.

No. 20C3390 Castle Square Panels, fine Melton stock, heavy, fancy border embossed in black around center, wide plain margin, plain beveled edges, square corners. Colors, Scotch gray or Egyptian black.

Size of Card	For Pictures	Price per 100	Price per 1,000
3 x4½	¼ Cabinet	$0.65	$ 6.31
4¼x6	½ Cabinet	.84	8.15
5⅛x7⅛	Cabinet	1.26	12.22

No. 20C3391 Ascot Panel, a very handsome mount, medium weight, hard pebble surface, plate sunk center, tinted paper insert, made in ivory white black or fawn.

Size of Card	For Pictures	Price, per 25	Price, per 100
4¾x7¼	1⅜x3⅜	$0.32	$1.22
8 x10	½ Cabinet	.63	2.44
9 x11	Cabinet	.73	2.83
7¾x11¾	3x7	1.05	4.12

Plankington Oval Opening Cards.

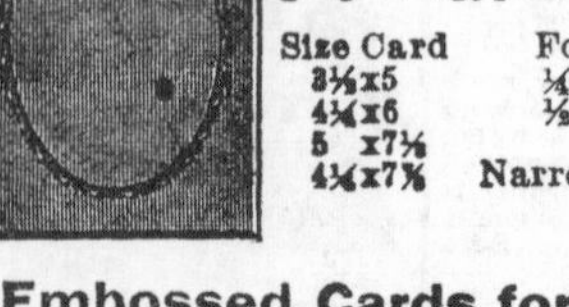

No. 20C3392 Plankington Oval, a thin card, made from very hard stock, with rough surface, with embossed design around oval opening. Colors, white, black or fawn.

Size of Card	Size of Print	Price, per 25	Price, per 100
7 x 9	¼ cabinet	50c	$1.94
8 x10	½ cabinet	70c	2.72
9 x11	cabinet	90c	3.50
5¾x 8⅞	2x5½	70c	2.72

Oval Opening Cards.

No. 20C3393 Alamo Oval, very heavy stock, Melton face, oval opening with tinted paper insert, matched bevel edges. Colors, Egyptian black or Scotch gray.

Size of Card	Size of Print	Price per 25	Price per 100
5 x 7	Narrow oval, 1⅝x2⅝	$0.60	$2.35
5⅝x 8½	Narrow oval, 2⅛x3⅞	.80	3.14
6 x 9½	Narrow oval, 2⅝x5	1.00	3.92
6 x 8	Standard oval, ¼ cabinet	.90	3.53
7 x 9	Standard oval, ½ cabinet	1.10	4.31
8 x10	Standard oval, cabinet	1.30	5.10

No. 20C3394 Mansion Oval, made from heavy stock, plain beveled edges, design around **oval** center embossed in black. Colors, Scotch gray or Egyptian black.

Size Card	For Prints	Price per 25	Price per 100	Price per 1,000
3½x5	¼ cabinet	20c	$0.78	$ 7.76
4¼x6	½ cabinet	25c	.98	9.70
5 x7½	cabinet	32c	1.25	12.42
4¼x7⅞	Narrow oval, 2x5½	40c	1.57	15.52

Embossed Cards for Large Prints.

No. 20C3395 Embossed Border Cards, made from high grade stock, good weight, supplied in white, ivy green or carbon black.

Size Card	For Prints	Price per 25	Price per 100
8x10	5 x 7	$0.38	$1.49
9x12	5 x 8	.47	1.84
10x12	6½x 8½	.57	2.23
11x14	8 x10	.72	2.82
14x17	10 x12	1.24	4.86

SPECTACLES AND EYEGLASSES.

WE PARTICULARLY CAUTION OUR CUSTOMERS against buying the very cheap grades of spectacles or eyeglasses. The lenses of these cheap goods are made of very poor material, are improperly cut, and almost certain to do untold injury to the eyes. An injury to your clothes can be mended or repaired, but an injury to the eyes may never be cured.

THE PROPER READING DISTANCE for ordinary print is from 12 to 14 inches. If it is necessary to hold the reading nearer the eye than this, glasses for near sight are required. If it is necessary to hold the reading more than 12 to 14 inches away from the eye, glasses are required for far sight. Practically everybody should wear glasses after reaching the age of forty years, as the eyes at this time commence to be far sighted, and the longer the wearing of glasses is put off the harder it will be to remedy the trouble. **Near sightedness** is also very common, especially among young people, and should never be neglected, as this trouble is so easily and perfectly relieved by proper eyeglasses or spectacles.

TYPE FOR TESTING THE EYES.

60

The smallest size letters on this card should be read easily at fifteen inches from the eye. If you cannot do so you should wear spectacles. It does not pay to buy cheap spectacles.

52

They distort the rays of light, disturb the angles of vision, cause pain and discomfort and injure the eyesight. When it is necessary to hold work or reading matter farther than fifteen inches from the eyes

44

in order to see distinctly, it is a sure sign of failing vision, and much annoyance, discomfort and pain will be prevented

40

by having a pair of glasses fitted. Pain in the eyes when wearing spectacles is usually caused

36

either by improperly fitted lenses, or from the centres of the lenses not corresponding with

32

the centres of the eyes. To be perfect, a lens must be made with highly polished surfaces

26

of accurate curvatures. Our crystalline lenses are the best in the market.

22

They are made from the clearest and finest material obtainable

20

AND ARE WARRANTED TO BE OF ABSOLUTELY

18

PERFECT CONSTRUCTION.

16

BUY NO OTHER KIND.

13

CRYSTALLINE

11

LENSES

10

ARE THE

8

B E S T.

30F

R E D

40F

O P

50F

N

INSTRUCTIONS FOR ORDERING.

Give the catalogue number of the style of Spectacles or Eyeglasses that you want, and answer very carefully the following test questions.

When ordering spectacles or eyeglasses of any kind to be sent by mail, include 5 cts. extra for postage.

WE WILL REFUND YOUR MONEY IN FULL IF THE SPECTACLES WE SEND YOU DO NOT FIT YOUR EYES PERFECTLY.

TEST QUESTIONS.

No. 1. What is your age?
No. 2. Have you ever worn glasses before, and if so, how long and what number were they?
No. 3. Do your eyes stand out prominently or are they sunken?
No. 4. Do your eyes become tired after slight use?
No. 5. Does the light hurt your eyes?
No. 6. How long is it since your sight began to fail?
No. 7. Do you suffer from headaches or pain over the eyes?
No. 8. Can you see well at a distance without glasses?
No. 9. Do you desire glasses for reading or for seeing at a distance?
No. 10. Can you read test type No. 30F at a distance of 20 feet without glasses? If not, what number can you see at this distance?
No. 11. What is the number of the smallest type that you can easily and distinctly read, when holding this page at a distance of 12 inches from the eyes, without glasses?
No. 12. What is the greatest possible distance at which you can easily and distinctly read paragraph No. 26, without glasses?

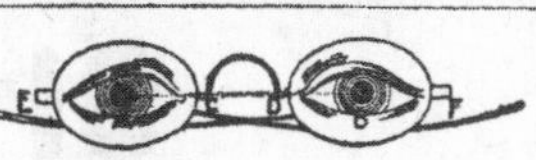

If you desire SPECTACLES answer the following three questions:

No. 13. What is the distance between the pupils (A to B)?
No. 14. What is the width of nose at base (C to D)?
No. 15. What is the distance between the temples (E to F)?

If you desire EYEGLASSES answer the following four questions.

No. 16. What is the width of nose (T to T)?
No. 17. What is the width of nose (P to P)?
No. 18. Is the bridge of your nose prominent or flat?
No. 19. What is the distance from the center or pupil of one eye to the center or pupil of the other eye?

Steel, Alumnico and Solid Gold Riding Bow Spectacles.

The Riding Bow Spectacles, known also as Hook Bow, are to be preferred in all cases where the glasses are to be worn constantly, or nearly so. The shape of the temples prevents the spectacles falling off, and also keeps the lenses more exactly in the proper position all the time.

No. 55C110 Steel Spectacles, riding bow temples, finely tempered, with good quality lenses. Price.................. .35c

No. 55C113 Best Grade Steel Spectacles, the very best riding bow steel spectacle made, nickel plated, finely finished, perfectly tempered, and warranted in every respect. These spectacles are fitted with the **finest quality crystalline lenses,** carefully ground and accurately adjusted. Price................72c

No. 55C115 Alumnico Spectacles, riding bow temples, light and well finished, with fine periscopic lenses. Alumnico is a composition metal in weight and color exactly like aluminum. **Warranted not to tarnish.** Price............................**$1.00**

No. 55C125 Solid Gold Spectacles, riding bow temples, perfection joints, highly polished and fitted with the finest accurately centered crystalline lenses. Price, 14-karat, **$3.30**; 10-karat............**$2.98**

STRAIGHT TEMPLE SPECTACLES.

Straight Temple Spectacles are most suitable for those who wear glasses for near work only, and therefore remove them frequently from the eyes.

No. 55C131 Steel Spectacles; straight temples, finely tempered, with good quality lenses. Price..35c

No. 55C135 Best Grade Steel Spectacles, the best straight temple steel spectacle that can be manufactured, full nickel plated, perfectly tempered, elegantly finished, both frame and lenses guaranteed in every way. These spectacles are fitted with the very best quality of accurately ground crystalline lenses, carefully adjusted. Price........69c

No. 55C136

No. 55C136 Alumnico Straight Temple Spectacles for $1.00. We offer these genuine Alumnico Straight Temple Spectacles as the most satisfactory, most durable and most comfortable straight temple spectacle made, except the solid gold or gold filled styles. They are far superior to steel, as alumnico is a light, silvery metal that **will never rust or tarnish,** but will always keep its fine bright color. These frames are as carefully finished as our best solid gold, and fitted with our highest grade crystalline lenses. Price....**$1.00**

Our Special Gold Filled Straight Temple Spectacles, at $1.65.

No. 55C140 We furnish these extra high grade Straight Temple Spectacles as absolutely the best straight temple gold filled spectacle that can be manufactured. They are genuine gold filled, made with two plates of extra heavy solid gold over an inner plate of hard composition metal, and we will replace without charge any pair that discolors, tarnishes or wears through to the composition metal in **ten years.** Equal in appearance to solid gold, beautifully finished and fitted with the very highest grade crystalline lenses. Price.. ....**$1.65**

No. 55C145 Solid Gold Spectacles; straight temple bows, perfection joint, highly polished, heavy weight; fitted with the finest accurately centered crystalline lenses. Price, 14-K. **$3.45**; 10-K.....**$3.20**

Bifocal Lenses.

The illustration shows appearance of Bifocal Lenses. We recommend Bifocal Lenses in cases where spectacles are required for both near and distant vision. **We furnish these lenses in the style known as cemented bifocal lenses,** which are the latest, best and most satisfactory style made. **Any of the spectacles or eyeglasses** in this catalogue (except the rimless) can be furnished with bifocal lenses for **50 cents extra**; for example, spectacle No. 55C136, the regular price of which is **$1.00**, would be **$1.50** with bifocal lenses.

Flexible Guard Eyeglasses.

The Flexible Guard eyeglasses are generally preferred when glasses are not constantly worn, as they are easily adjusted to the nose.

No. 55C165

No. 55C160 Alumnico Eye-glasses, flexible cork lined guards and oval spring, light and of silvery color, will not tarnish, fitted with finest periscopic lenses. Price..**75c**

No. 55C165 Gold Filled Eyeglasses, flexible cork lined guards and oval spring, warranted for ten years, fitted with finest crystalline lenses. The very highest grade gold filled eyeglass frame that can be produced. Price.......................**$1.25**

Offset Guard Eyeglasses.

The Offset Guard Eyeglasses are used exclusively when glasses are worn constantly, as they are specially adapted to remain in a fixed position.

No. 55C175

No. 55C170 Alumnico Eyeglasses, offset guards cork or shell lined, hoop spring, light and of silvery color, warranted not to tarnish, fitted with finest periscopic lenses. Price...75c

No. 55C175 Gold Filled Eyeglasses, offset guards either cork or shell lined, round hoop spring warranted for ten years, fitted with finest crystalline lenses. The very highest grade gold filled eyeglass frame that can be produced. Price...**$1.25**

Colored Spectacles.

No. 55C212 Colored Lens Spectacles, a high grade steel frame spectacle; with best colored coquille lenses, riding bow temples. Colored spectacles are a great comfort to those whose eyes are weak, protecting them from strong light, and do much toward preserving the sight. Furnished with either smoke or blue lenses. Price..32c

OUR $1.90 GOLD FILLED SPECTACLES.

FOR $1.90 we furnish these fine gold filled riding bow spectacles as the very highest grade spectacles made, the equal of riding bow spectacles furnished by opticians at $5.00 to $10.00.

OUR TEN-YEAR GUARANTEE. As the exceedingly low price at which we offer these spectacles may lead some of our customers to question the quality, we put out every pair under our binding ten years' guarantee, and if they wear through, tarnish, discolor or give out by reason of defect in material or poor workmanship at any time within ten years, we will replace them with a new pair or refund the amount paid for them.

WHY WE CAN SELL SPECTACLES AT PRICES SO MUCH LOWER THAN ARE CHARGED BY OTHERS.

It has always been customary for opticians to make enormous profits and the prices asked are always entirely out of proportion to the actual value of the goods themselves. Opticians attempt to justify their extortionate prices on the plea that their customers are paying them for their skill, their time and their knowledge.

WE ARE ABLE, however, by reason of the enormous number of orders we receive for spectacles, to sell these goods on our regular staple merchandise small profit plan. We buy our spectacles direct from the manufacturer in enormous quantities, thereby securing the very lowest possible price, and, by thus securing the goods at the lowest possible cost and contenting ourselves with an ordinary merchandise profit, we are able to sell the very highest grade spectacles at one-fourth the prices which opticians are compelled to charge for inferior grades.

THIS LARGE ILLUSTRATION, engraved direct from a photograph, will give you an idea of the appearance of our special $1.90, ten-year guaranteed gold filled riding bow spectacles. They are made with a broad nosepiece, they are fitted with the very finest quality crystalline lenses, accurately adjusted and carefully selected by our expert optician in accordance with your answers to our test questions. We send these glasses out with the understanding that if they are not perfectly satisfactory in every way, if they do not fit your eyes perfectly, enable you to see better than any other glasses you have ever worn, they can be returned to us at our expense, and we will refund your money.

No. 55C190 Gold Filled Riding Bow Spectacles. Price........$1.90

No. 55C191 Gold Filled Riding Bow Spectacles, not quite so good quality as No. 55C190, but just the same in general appearance and style of construction; warranted for 10 years. Finest crystalline lenses. Price..$1.40

CABLE BOW GOLD FILLED SPECTACLES $2.10.

CABLE RIDING BOW SPECTACLES are the most comfortable and most satisfactory style of spectacles that can be worn. The secret of their comfort lies in the fact that the bows or temples are of a peculiar twisted construction made from the very highest grade fine gold filled wire twisted together like the strands of a rope, this peculiar construction being plainly shown in our large illustration. This method of making the bows renders them very flexible and somewhat larger than the regulation style, making it impossible for them to cut into the flesh back of the ears, thereby entirely doing away with the discomfort which is often experienced with the ordinary style of bow. CABLE RIDING BOW SPECTACLES are the most comfortable and easiest style of spectacle that can be worn.

OUR CABLE RIDING BOW GOLD FILLED SPECTACLES are made from the very highest grade gold filled stock, two plates of heavy fine solid gold over an inner plate of hard composition metal, beautifully polished and finished and guaranteed the very highest grade, the very best quality gold filled spectacles that can be made.

WE SEND THESE SPECTACLES out with the understanding and agreement that the gold will not wear off, discolor nor tarnish in ten years constant use. If you purchase a pair of these spectacles from us and they give out, through any defect in material or through poor workmanship, or if they tarnish, discolor or wear off at any time within ten years, we will replace them with a new pair absolutely free of charge.

OUR CABLE RIDING BOW GOLD FILLED SPECTACLES are fitted with the highest grade periscopic crystalline lenses, accurately adjusted, carefully selected, in accordance with your answers to our test questions, and, if they do not fit your eyes perfectly, if you do not find them better than any other spectacles you have ever worn, they can be returned to us at our expense, and we will refund your money, including postage both ways.

No. 55C195 Cable Riding Bow Gold Filled Spectacles. Price..$2.10

RIMLESS SPECTACLES AT $2.20.

$2.20

RIMLESS SPECTACLES are the very latest and most stylish spectacles made. They are light and elegant in appearance, comfortable to wear and contribute in no small measure towards giving the wearer a neat and dressy appearance. Our rimless or skeleton spectacles are made expressly for us by one of the largest optical manufacturers in America. The mountings are of the very highest grade 10-karat gold filled stock, guaranteed the very highest grade gold filled stock that can be produced. They are beautifully finished, accurately adjusted and are equal in every respect to gold filled rimless spectacles ordinarily sold by opticians at from $6.00 to $10.00.

OUR RIMLESS SPECTACLES are fitted with the very highest grade crystalline lenses, the very best lenses that can be made, lenses that are accurately adjusted, highly polished and carefully selected in exact accordance with the answers to our test questions, thus insuring a perfect fit. These rimless spectacles are sent out under our binding guarantee to be equal to rimless spectacles sold by opticians at from $6.00 to $10.00.

THEY ARE GUARANTEED to be the very highest grade gold filled rimless spectacles that can be made, regardless of price, and if they do not fit your eyes perfectly, give you better vision than any other spectacle you have ever worn, you may send them back to us and we will refund your money, including the postage both ways. You take absolutely no chance in ordering spectacles from us, as we will return your money immediately if the spectacles are not in every way satisfactory.

IF YOU ALREADY HAVE A PAIR OF SPECTACLES that suit your eyes and would like to own a pair of our high grade, gold filled, rimless spectacles, we suggest that you tell us the number of your lenses, if you know it, or, if not, that you send us your spectacles, and we will select from our stock a pair of these high grade, gold filled spectacles, with lenses of exactly the same strength as your own and of the same dimensions, so that they will fit you just as well as the old pair.

No. 55C198 Gold Filled Rimless Spectacles, as described and illustrated above. Price........$2.20

OUR RIMLESS EYE GLASSES FOR $1.65.

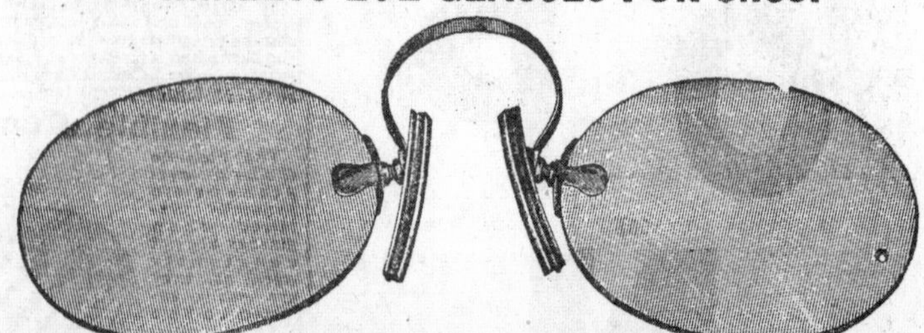

OUR RIMLESS OR SKELETON EYE GLASSES are in every respect equal to the spectacles described under No. 55C198, but, as there is less material used in making an eye glass, and less labor involved, we can sell these rimless eye glasses at only $1.65 and at the same time maintain the same high quality that is represented in our rimless spectacles. Our rimless eye glasses are made with offset guards, lined either with cork or tortoise shell, the mountings are the very highest grade gold filled stock, guaranteed made with two heavy plates of fine solid gold over an inner plate of hard composition metal, beautifully polished and finished, and guaranteed in every respect equal to rimless eye glasses sold by opticians at from $5.00 to $8.00. The lenses are extra high grade periscopic crystalline lenses, made from the very purest optical glass, accurately centered and carefully selected to meet the requirements indicated by your answers to our test questions.

EVERY PAIR OF OUR RIMLESS EYE GLASSES is sent out under our binding ten years' guarantee, under the terms of which we agree to replace any pair that tarnish, wear off, or give out through defective materials or poor workmanship in ten years. A pair of carefully adjusted high grade gold filled rimless eye glasses gives the wearer a distinguished and prosperous appearance which is entirely lacking with the ordinary styles of spectacles.

REMEMBER every order for either spectacles or eye glasses receives the careful personal attention of our expert optician, a graduate of the Northern Illinois College of Ophthalmology, who has for years made a special study of fitting spectacles by mail.

REMEMBER that every pair of spectacles or eye glasses which we sell is sent out with the distinct understanding and agreement that if we fail to fit your eyes perfectly, if you do not find the glasses entirely satisfactory in every way, if they do not enable you to see better than any other glasses you have ever worn, they may be returned to us and your money will be refunded, including postage both ways.

No. 55C200 Rimless Eye Glasses. Price........$1.65

Scenery or Shooting Spectacles.

Nos. 55C230 to 55C234

While these spectacles are commonly known as shooting spectacles, they are largely used by tourists in looking at scenery, especially where the light is bright and dazzling or when the ground is covered with snow, which reflects the light and tires the eyes. **The peculiar amber tint of the lenses, not only improves the view but enables one to see more plainly at a distance,** and is very pleasant and soothing to the eye. **The lenses are known as diaphragm lenses,** being sanded or ground in such a manner as to exclude the view except through the clear circle in the center of each lens.

No. 55C230 Shooting Spectacles, steel frames, straight temples, good quality, nickel plated, amber tinted diaphragm lenses. Price........16c

No. 55C231 Shooting Spectacles, steel frames, straight temples, best quality, finely tempered with bronze finish. Best amber tinted diaphragm lenses. Price........36c

No. 55C232 Shooting Spectacles, steel frames, same as illustration, but with **riding bow temples,** fine quality, extra finish with amber tinted diaphragm lenses. Price........28c

No. 55C234 Shooting Spectacles, steel frames, straight temples, best quality, finely tempered and extra finish, with best grade smoke tinted diaphragm lenses. Price........42c

If by mail, postage extra, each, 5 cents.

Goggles.

The use of Goggles as a protection to the eyes from light, dust, etc., is so common and well known that no comment upon them is necessary.

Nos. 55C240 and 55C241

No. 55C240 Goggles, ordinary quality, wire gauze with common smoke, blue, green or white glasses. Price........7c

No. 55C241 Goggles, good quality, wire gauze, velvet bound edges, with smoke, blue or white glasses. Each pair in cloth bound box. Price........20c

No. 55C243 Goggles, steel frame, velvet bound, finely finished, with stiff nose piece and tempered riding bow temples. Extra fine wire gauze and highest grade light smoke lenses. Each pair in fine case. Price........95c

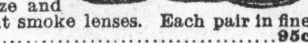

If by mail, postage extra, each, 5 cents.

Eye Protectors.

These eye protectors, being extremely light and also well ventilated, are very comfortable, and as a protection against excessive light, blinding storms of sleet, snow or rain, floating cinders, mud, dust, flying sparks, are unexcelled. They are used by wheelmen, streetcarmen, railroadmen, stonecutters, firemen, millers, harvesters, in fact, by all who are in any way exposed to the danger of injuring the eyes.

No. 55C248 Celluloid Eye Protector, well made from the best transparent celluloid, felt bound, in white, blue or green. Price, including case.....**(If by mail, postage extra, 2 cents)**.....16c

No. 55C249 Mica Eye Protector. Made of selected mica, substantially constructed and bound with corrugated felt. This Eye Protector is hinged at the center, thus folding into small space, and is made with either smoke, blue or white mica. Price, with morocco case....20c

If by mail, postage extra, 2 cents.

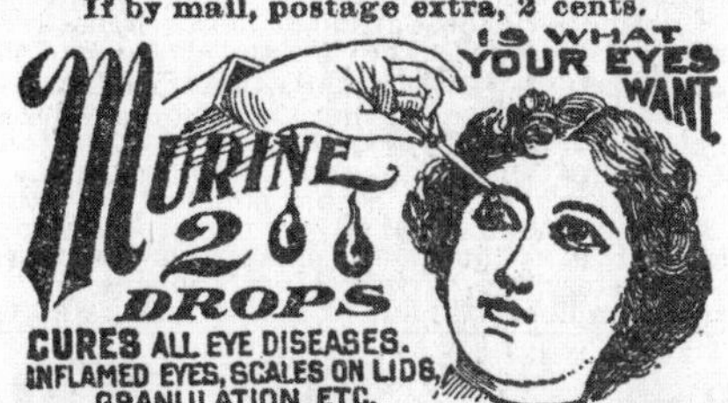

IS WHAT YOUR EYES WANT
Murine
2
DROPS
CURES ALL EYE DISEASES.
INFLAMED EYES, SCALES ON LIDS, GRANULATION ETC.

No. 55C253 Murine is a remedy that cures diseased conditions of the eye, an absolutely harmless, pure distilled product. Murine cures weak eyes, inflamed eyes, sore eyes, relieves tired eyes, cures watering eyes, granulated lids, removes floating spots in eyes, clears vision, brightens dull eyes, relieves pain in injured eyes. **Murine can be used by anybody,** may be used as often as desired, it always benefits the eyes, and never harms them. **School children's eyes are strengthened by Murine,** professional men find relief from eye strain in Murine. Farmers, railroad men and others exposed to wind and weather are greatly benefited by **Murine. Everybody can use Murine** to advantage, and every medicine cabinet should contain a bottle of it. **We know Murine is the best eye medicine in the world.** Price per bottle, complete with dropper........40c

Extra for postage and mailing case, if sent by mail, 10 cents.

Eyeglass Chains and Hooks.

Nos. 55C265 to 55C269

No. 55C265 Eyeglass Chain, gold plated, with snap and hook. Price........38c

No. 55C267 Eyeglass Chain, fine quality, gold filled, fully guaranteed. Price........63c

No. 55C269 Eyeglass Chain, extra fine quality, solid gold. Price........$1.42

If by mail, postage extra, 4 cents.

No. 55C275 Eyeglass Hook, fine quality gold filled. Price........15c

No. 55C277 Eyeglass Hook, solid gold, extra quality. Price........62c

Nos. 55C275 and 55C277.

If by mail, postage extra, 2 cents.

Eye Shades.

No. 55C280 Eye Shade, metal rim, with leather bound edges. Price........9c

No. 55C281 Eye Shade, best grade transparent green celluloid, light and comfortable. Price........12c

If by mail, postage extra, 4 cents.

READING GLASSES

are very desirable for reading fine print, and as they are strong magnifiers and give a large range of vision they are very restful to the eyes and **especially desirable for old people. They are also used for looking at photographs and other pictures,** as they bring out the detail and add greatly to the beauty of the picture, the principle being the same as the graphoscope.

Powerful Burning Glasses.

Any of these reading glasses are powerful sun or burning glasses, readily setting fire to light materials such as paper, shavings, dry leaves, etc. The larger the glass the greater its burning power is.

German Reading Glasses.

These glasses, Nos. 55C335 to 55C339 are fitted with first quality lenses, nickel plated frames and black enameled handles.

Nos. 55C335 to 55C339

No. 55C335 German Reading Glass, 2¼ inches in diameter. Price........24c
If by mail, postage extra 12 cents.

No. 55C336 German Reading Glass, 2¾ inches in diameter. Price........38c
If by mail, postage extra, 14 cents.

No. 55C337 German Reading Glass, 3¼ inches in diameter. Price.**(If by mail, postage extra, 18c)** 65c

No. 55C338 German Reading Glass, 4 inches in diameter. Price........78c
If by mail, postage extra, 20 cents.

No. 55C339 German Reading Glass, 5 inches in diameter. Price..**(Postage extra, 25 cents.)**..$1.47

Best Grade Reading Glasses.

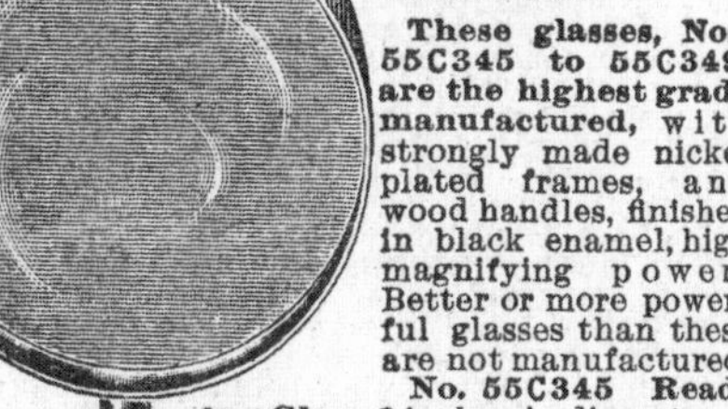

Nos. 55C345 to 55C349

These glasses, Nos. 55C345 to 55C349, are the highest grade manufactured, with strongly made nickel plated frames, and wood handles, finished in black enamel, high magnifying power. Better or more powerful glasses than these are not manufactured.

No. 55C345 Reading Glass, 2 inches in diameter. Price........35c
If by mail, postage extra, 12c.

No. 55C346 Reading Glass, 2½ inches in diameter. Price....48c
If by mail, postage extra, 14c.

No. 55C347 Reading Glass, 3 inches in diameter. Price....63c
If by mail, postage extra, 17c.

No. 55C348 Reading Glass, 4 inches in diameter. Price..$1.10
If by mail, postage extra, 20c.

No. 55C349 Reading Glass, 5 inches in diameter. Price..$1.60
If by mail, postage extra, 25 cents.

Pearl Handle Reading Glass.

No. 55C350 The handle of this beautiful Reading Glass is made of brilliant iridescent oriental pearl, the rim is finely gold plated and the lens is best grade manufactured. Diameter, 3½ inches. The handsome appearance and fine quality make it **especially suitable for a birthday or Christmas gift.** Price..**(If by mail, postage extra, 20c)**...$2.58

Our 70-Cent Dust Protector.

No. 55C400 Against dust it is the greatest protector ever made. For thrashers, grain men, millers, farmers and everyone whose duties call him into dusty places. **It is worth a thousand times its cost as a** protection to the lungs, to the general health and comfort. **Thousands of men are saved from consumption by the use of this protector. It protects the nose and mouth** from the intrusion of dust which is so injurious to the head and lungs. **No miller, grain buyer, thrasher or farmer is safe** without one. They afford perfect protection with perfect ventilation. **Made of fine metal,** handsomely nickel plated, bound with chamois skin, adjustable to anyone by strong elastic band, absolutely indestructible and **worth a thousand times the trifling cost** as a safeguard to health. Each protector comes packed in a neat box with full instructions for use. Price........70c

If by mail, postage extra, 5 cents.

Conversation Tubes.

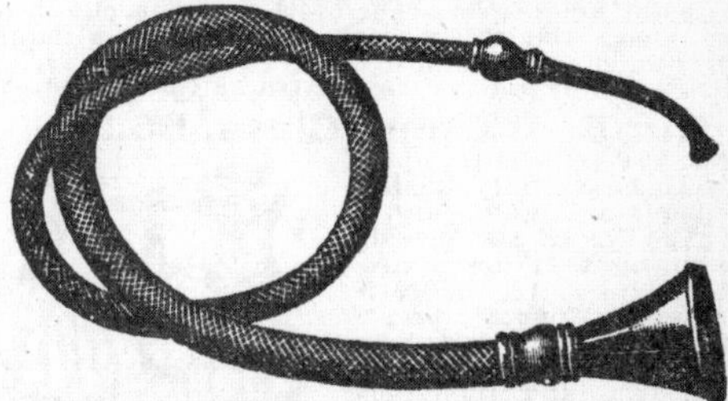

Conversation Tubes are undoubtedly the best device ever made for the relief of deafness, and these are the very highest grade of conversation tubes made; finely constructed throughout, with a peculiar metallic spiral lining, which gives the tube great flexibility and at the same time keeps it fully distended in any position.

No. 55C411 Mohair Conversation Tube, medium size, tapered, covered with flexible mohair, hard rubber ear piece and bell. Price........$1.00

No. 55C412 Mohair Conversation Tube, same as No. 55C411, but larger size, 3 feet in length. Ea. $1.10

No. 55C413 Silk Conversation Tube, very highest grade manufactured, covered with finest quality black silk, tapered tube, medium size. Price. $1.05

No. 55C414 Silk Conversation Tube, same style and quality as No. 55C413, but larger size, 3 feet in length. Price........$1.15

Hearing Horns.

These horns are exactly the same as those advertised by many dealers at prices ranging from $8.00 to $15.00 each. These London Hearing Horns are constructed of light metal upon an entirely new principle. **They** may be carried in the pocket and when in use are easily concealed in the hand. **They are designed for the use of those who are only moderately deaf** and enable one to hear not only an ordinary conversation but **sounds at a distance** as well, making them suitable for use anywhere—at home, in church, or public entertainments.

Made in Two Sizes, with Black Oxidized Finish.

No. 55C420 London Hearing Horn, medium size, 2½ inches in length. Price........$1.00
If by mail, postage extra, 5 cents.

No. 55C421 London Hearing Horn, large size, 4 inches in length. Price........$1.10
If by mail, postage extra, 8 cents.

Your money will be promptly refunded if the horn does not give entire satisfaction.

Miss Greene Hearing Horn.

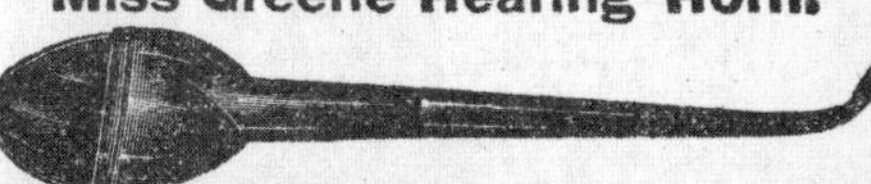

No. 55C425 This is a new device, being an improvement in shape over all other Tin Trumpets, and is more easily carried. The sound receiving end is flat oval shape, 5½ inches in diameter by 1½ inches in depth. Its peculiar formation is especially adapted to gather in sounds and convey them audibly and distinctly to the ear; is one of the best arrangements for conversation or public speaking; can be held to the ear without raising the hand; made of metal, in two pieces, japanned black. Price........90c

Our $1.75 Opera Glass.

No. 55C450 This is a good practical glass, made with a good quality achromatic lenses, 1⅛ inches in diameter; covered with black morocco leather; draw tubes and trimmings are black. It is an excellent instrument for so little money. Price..**$1.75**

If by mail, postage extra, 16 cents.

A Genuine LeMaire Opera Glass, Only $3.75.

No. 55C455 This is a genuine **LeMaire** opera glass. Perfectly plain finish throughout; covering, fine black morocco leather; all metal parts, hard black enamel. Finest achromatic lenses, 1⅛ inches in diameter. The name **LeMaire** is in itself a guarantee of excellence, and if you desire a strictly high grade instrument, where every cent of the cost is put into **fine lenses and substantial construction,** without fancy finish or trimmings, this is the glass to buy.

Price..(**If by mail, postage extra, 18 cents.**) .**$3.75**

Our Best Opera Glass, $6.85.

No. 55C460 This opera glass is beautifully finished in pearl and gold, and is strictly high grade throughout. Finest achromatic lenses, 1⅛ inches in diameter; oriental pearl body, pearl tops and pearl focusing screw. Draw tubes, cross bars and trimmings heavily gold plated.

Price.....(**If by mail, postage extra, 18c**)....**$6.85**

Our $4.29 Pearl Opera Glass.

No. 55C465 We offer this gold and pearl opera glass as the best instrument of the kind ever sold for so low a price. All metal parts are gold plated. Warranted not to tarnish, fine pearl body, good achromatic lenses, 1⅛ inches in diameter.

Price.................**$4.29**

If by mail, postage extra, 18 cents.

Our $7.25 Genuine Jena Aluminum Opera Glass.

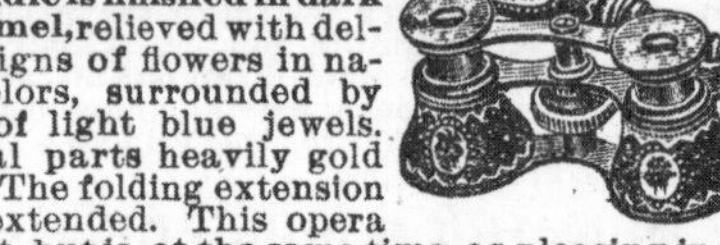

No. 55C470 This is a genuine **Jena Special Opera Glass,** the very highest grade opera glass made. All metal parts of **aluminum,** light, durable and handsome; lenses ground from the famous Jena special optical glass. The draw tubes are highly polished, in the natural silver color of the aluminum; the tops and cross bars are finished with a h rd black enamel, and the covering is the finest morocco leather. This is an extra large opera glass, having lenses 1⅛ inches in diameter, giving very high power and perfect definition. Price...............**$7.25**

If by mail, postage extra, 17 cents.

Our $8.90 Enameled Opera Glass, with Lorgnette Handle.

No. 55C475 This very stylish and beautiful opera glass with handle is finished in dark blue enamel, relieved with delicate designs of flowers in natural colors, surrounded by borders of light blue jewels. All metal parts heavily gold plated, pearl tops, finest achromatic lenses, 1 inch in diameter. The folding extension handle is 4 inches long when closed and 8 inches long when extended. This opera glass is not only a thoroughly practical, serviceable instrument, but is, at the same time, as pleasing in appearance as a fine piece of jewelry. Price............(**If by mail, postage extra, 17 cents.**)............**$8.90**

FIELD GLASSES.

We contract every season with the best known and most famous makers of field glasses in Paris and Germany to furnish us with the largest quantity of high grade field glasses ever purchased by any one house. In this way we induce the manufacturers to figure the cost to us on a basis of the actual cost of material and labor. To this price, figured on actual shop cost, we add simply our one small percentage of profit, and as a result we offer in our cheapest field glass at $3.65, an instrument for which you would pay the ordinary optician from $8.00 to $10.00. In our highest grade field glasses such as the famous LeMaire or our new Jena Special Glass, we offer for only $11.95 and $12.95 instruments which have heretofore been sold at from $20.00 to $35.00. Even our cheapest field glass is fitted with achromatic lenses, and well made. We do not carry in stock at all nor offer for sale the cheap non-achromatic glasses advertised by many dealers; such instruments are worthless and dear at any price. Following the usual custom we indicate the size of our field glasses by giving the diameter of the object glasses, that is the large lenses, in lignes, the French unit of measurement for optical instruments. **All have extension sun shades.**

Our $3.65 Delmar Field Glass.

No. 55C500 For $3.65 we furnish this Delmar Field Glass fitted with genuine achromatic lenses, bars, draw tubes and trimmings finished in black and body covered in black morocco leather. We offer this Delmar Field Glass as the equal of field glasses sold by retail dealers at prices ranging from $8.00 to $10.00. **The Delmar Field Glass** measures 6 inches high when closed and 7¼ inches when extended. The object glasses are 24 lignes in diameter and the weight is 17 ounces. **Magnifying power four times.**

Price, complete with leather case and strap.**$3.65**

If by mail, postage extra, 40 cents.

$6.95 Buys a $15.00 Field Glass.

No. 55C510 This Field Glass is provided with first quality achromatic lenses, carefully fitted, the draw tubes are finished in dead black and the trimmings are in bright black enamel and nickel plate. Although possessing no higher magnifying power than the Delmar Field Glass, the lenses are of better quality, thus giving finer definition and greater clearness. Workmanship and materials throughout are first class. **Our $6.95 Field Glass** measures 5¾ inches high when closed, 7¼ inches when extended. The diameter of the object glasses is 24 lignes, the magnifying power is five times and the weight is 22 ounces.

Price, complete with leather case and strap..**$6.95**

If by mail, postage, extra, 42 cents.

High Grade Tourist's Field Glass for $6.60.

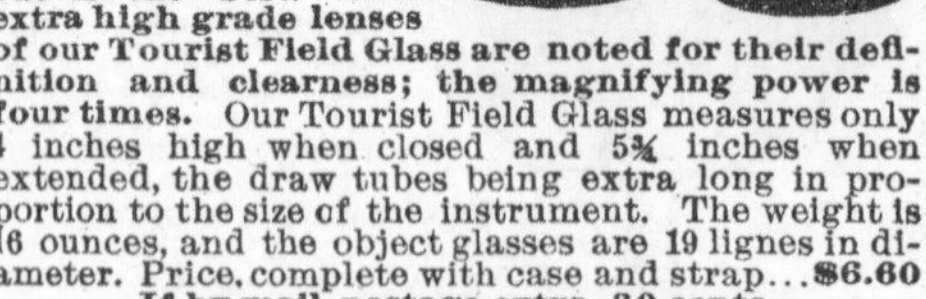

No. 55C525 This is an exceptionally fine field glass, designed especially for tourists or those who expect to carry a field glass to a considerable extent, its small size and light weight making it very desirable. Our high grade tourist's field glass is fitted with the **best achromatic lenses,** very carefully ground, accurately fitted and adjusted. The finish throughout is **extra fine,** the trimmings, cross bars and draw tubes are the best quality black enamel, the covering is the best grade of fine morocco leather, and the workmanship throughout is the best. **The extra high grade lenses of our Tourist Field Glass are noted for their definition and clearness; the magnifying power is four times.** Our Tourist Field Glass measures only 4 inches high when closed and 5¾ inches when extended, the draw tubes being extra long in proportion to the size of the instrument. The weight is 16 ounces, and the object glasses are 19 lignes in diameter. Price, complete with case and strap...**$6.60**

If by mail, postage extra, 30 cents.

Only $12.95 for Our Highest Grade Genuine Jena Special Field Glass.

No. 55C560 This large illustration, engraved by our artist direct from a photograph, will give you an idea of the appearance of our JENA SPECIAL FIELD GLASS. The lenses of this field glass are ground from the famous Jena special optical glass, made in the Jena glass factory in Germany. The sole object of this remarkable factory is the production of new and special kinds of glass for optical purposes. One of their latest productions is a glass especially suited to the requirements of field glass lenses.

It is from **this special new glass,** this latest result of the experiments and investigations of the most skilled and scientific glass makers of Europe, that the lenses for our Jena Special Field Glasses are ground. They are ground by the most skilled lens grinders, they are fitted with the utmost care, and they are accurately adjusted. **These lenses combine, to a degree never before attained, the highest power with the most marvelous definition and clearness.**

We offer the Jena Special Field Glass not merely as the equal of glasses sold by other dealers at several times our price, but we offer it as **absolutely the best field glass that can be obtained at any price.** We sell this glass under a positive guarantee and if you do not find it superior to any field glass to which you may compare it, you may return it at our expense and we will refund your money.

Bear in mind that our special $12.95 price is for the large size Jena Special Field Glass with lenses 26 lignes in diameter. This field glass measures 6 inches high when closed and 7⅜ inches when extended, weighs 33 ounces, and the magnifying power is seven times. The draw tubes, cross bars, tops and trimmings are all finished in fine black enamel and the covering is the best grade of morocco leather.

Price, complete with fine case and strap..**$12.95**

No. 55C561 OUR JENA SPECIAL ALUMINUM FIELD GLASS. Exactly the same as our No. 55C560, except that **all metal parts are made of aluminum,** thus reducing the weight and adding to its handsome appearance. The highly polished draw tubes are finished in the natural silvery color of aluminum, all trimmings are finished in black and the covering is morocco leather. Weight, only 18 ounces.

Price, complete with fine case and strap..**$16.90**

EXCEPTIONAL VALUE AT $9.90.

No. 55C530 We offer our $9.90 Field Glass as the equal of any $25.00 field glass on the market, a strictly high grade, serviceable field glass that we know will give perfect satisfaction. Our **$9.90** field glass is made expressly for us under contract by one of the best field glass makers in Paris; it is made of the very best materials throughout and every one is sold under a binding guarantee. The lenses used in our **$9.90** field glass are the finest quality specially ground achromatic, accurately adjusted, of high magnifying power and fine definition. The finish throughout is perfect, the trimmings, cross bars and tops in black enamel, the draw tubes oxidized in black, and the covering the best grade of morocco leather. Our **$9.90 Field Glass is substantially constructed,** the workmanship is the best, it is a glass that will stand rough handling, a glass that is built for practical purposes and it is a glass that we can absolutely guarantee to give satisfaction. Our **$9.90** field glass measures 5½ inches high when closed, 6¾ inches when extended. The weight is 25 ounces. The magnifying power is five times.

Price, complete with case and strap..............................**$9.90**

If by mail, postage extra, 47 cents.

Maxim Binocular Telescope for $17.60.

An exceedingly small and compact instrument of high magnifying power.

This is a genuine Maxim Double Telescope, made by Maxim, the celebrated Paris telescope maker, and is the handiest and most efficient instrument of this kind ever devised. It is an ideal glass for tourists, farmers, hunters, ranchmen, stockmen or anyone requiring a powerful instrument which at the same time is **small in size, light and compact. Our special Binocular Telescope weighs only 9 ounces and is so compact that it may be carried in the coat pocket as easily as a pocketbook, yet has a magnifying power of nine times or one-half again as high a power as the best field glasses.** Our illustration shows the glass in the fine silk lined morocco leather pocket case, which is included without extra charge. **When closed our Special Binocular Telescope measures only 4¾ inches high, the distance from side to side is only 3½ inches and the barrels are only ¾ of an inch in diameter. The length when extended for use is 6¾ inches.** The lenses with which our Special Binocular Telescope is fitted are the best quality achromatic, accurately fitted and adjusted. The magnifying power is nine times and the definition is exceptionally fine.

No. 55C565 Maxim Double Telescope.

Price complete with morocco pocket case, as shown in illustration....................................**$17 60**

If by mail, postage extra, 20 cents.

TURNER-REICH AND BUSCH BINOCULARS.

THESE INSTRUMENTS REPRESENT THE VERY LATEST ACHIEVEMENTS IN OPTICS AND ARE PRACTICALLY THE CULMINATION OF THREE CENTURIES OF OPTICAL PROGRESS.

FIELD GLASSES **of this type are variously known as Porro Prism Glasses, Binoculars, Binocular Field Glasses and Prism Binoculars.** They are constructed on the formula of Porro, the principle of which is the use of reflecting prisms so placed in the body that they reduce the length of the instrument to about one-third that of ordinary telescopes of corresponding power.

PORRO **was an Italian optician who devised the combination of prisms by means of which the construction of the modern Prism Binocular is made possible.** Porro, however, was unable to place these instruments on the market, owing to the impossibility, at that time, of securing glass of the perfect grade which is essential for the successful production of a prism binocular glass. In 1882 the famous Jena Glass Works were successful in producing a grade of optical glass so perfect that it could be successfully used in instruments of this kind. So incredibly delicate, however, is the workmanship required to produce a serviceable, satisfactory binocular, that even with the perfect materials which became available in 1882, it remained for 20th century skill and ingenuity to render the modern prism binocular glass a commercial possibility.

AS COMPARED WITH FIELD GLASSES **of the ordinary styles, Prism Binoculars offer the following very important points of superiority:**

First—Larger field of view. **Second**—Better defining power. **Third**—Higher magnifying power. **Fourth**—Great reduction in weight and bulk.

OUR GUARANTEE ON PRISM BINOCULARS.

EVERY TURNER-REICH OR BUSCH BINOCULAR **which we sell is sent out under our binding guarantee to be absolutely perfect, both optically and mechanically.** We guarantee the Turner-Reich and Busch Binoculars to be equal to any other prism binocular glasses on the market regardless of price.

OUR TEN DAYS' FREE TRIAL PROPOSITION.

WE SEND THESE INSTRUMENTS **out with the understanding and agreement that they may be kept and used for 10 days, during which time they may be put to any test,** may be compared with any other prism binocular glasses made, and if they do not prove better than any glasses with which they may be compared, you can send them back to us at our expense and we will refund your money, including transportation charges.

ABOUT THE MAGNIFYING POWER.

THE 6-POWER GLASS **is sufficiently powerful for all ordinary purposes and has the advantage of an exceptionally large field of view,** of being very easy to hold steady and is recommended for yachting, races, athletic sports, hunting and similar purposes.

THE 8 AND 9-POWER GLASSES **are recommended as the best all around instruments,** being especially suitable for military, yachting and touring requirements. The magnifying power is ample for the above purposes and the instrument can be held sufficiently steady to involve no inconvenience in this respect.

THE 10-POWER GLASS **is constructed especially for long range observations and is recommended for special purposes where a high magnifying power is desirable,** such as marine and military work, use on ranches and in mountainous countries where a long range is necessary.

Turner-Reich Prism Binoculars.

The bodies of the Turner-Reich Binoculars are made of aluminum and the working parts are of brass. The bodies are covered with the finest quality pebbled morocco leather and all exposed metal parts are finished in lusterless black.

One of the eye piece cells is so made that it may be adjusted to accommodate observers' eyes that are not of the same power, a much commoner defect than is generally supposed and frequently only noticeable when using a high power glass.

Focusing is accomplished very easily by the large mill head in the hinge, which actuates a precision screw.

The Turner-Reich Instruments are adjustable for pupillary distance and provide for any separation of the eyes. An adjustable click may be set at the desired pupillary distance so that the images of both barrels of the instrument may be made coincident by simply turning the barrels until the click springs into position.

No. 55C570 6-power Turner-Reich Prism Binocular. Linear magnifying power, 6 diameters. (Superficial power 36 times.) Real field of view 6 degrees. Diameter field of view at 1000 yards, 315 feet.

Price, with solid sole leather case and shoulder strap..**$34.00**

No. 55C571 8-Power Turner-Reich Prism Binocular. Linear magnifying power, 8 diameters. (Superficial power 64 times.) Real field of view, 4¾ degrees. Diameter field of view at 1000 yards, 246 feet. Price, with solid sole leather case and shoulder strap..**$35.50**

No. 55C572 10-Power Turner-Reich Prism Binocular. Magnifying power, 10 diameters. (Superficial power, 100 times.) Real field of view, 3¾ degrees. Diameter field of view at 1000 yards, 204 feet.

Price, with solid sole leatner case and shoulder strap..**$37.00**

Busch Prism Binoculars.

The Busch Prism Binoculars are made with a view to securing the greatest possible solidity and durability combined with the necessary portability, ease of manipulation and lightness of weight. **The bars and bodies are made from one solid casting of an especially hard alloy of aluminum.** The working parts are of brass. This form of construction makes it possible to use fewer parts, fewer screws, and renders it **almost impossible for the glass to get out of optical adjustment.**

The bodies are covered with the very finest black pebbled morocco leather and all exposed metal parts are finished in fine bright black enamel, highly polished.

The Busch Prism Binocular is adjustable for pupillary distances in a simple way by bending the hinged bars to the necessary width. The focus screw is large and centrally located, as shown in our illustration. The eye piece of the right barrel is made movable to allow for adjustment of differences in the power of the users' eyes.

These Binoculars are made by the RATHENOWER OPTISCHE INDUSTRIE-ANSTALT, one of the largest optical concerns in Europe, noted for the production of extra high grade goods.

No. 55C580 6-Power Busch Prism Binocular. Linear magnifying power, 6 diameters. (Superficial power, 36 times.) Real field of view, 6.9 deg. Diameter field of view at 1,000 yards, 375 feet. Price, with sole leather case and shoulder strap..........**$31.00**

No. 55C581 9-Power Busch Prism Binocular. Linear magnifying power, 9 diameters. (Superficial power, 81 times.) Real field of view, 4.6 deg. Diameter field of view at 1,000 yards, 240 feet. Price, with solid sole leather case and shoulder strap....**$32.00**

GENUINE BARDOU & SON RIFLE RANGE TELESCOPE FOR $16.50

No. 55C675 The Bardou Rifle Range Telescope represents the highest degree of perfection attained in telescope making. The firm of Bardou & Son, Paris, enjoys the reputation of producing the finest telescopes in the world, and this instrument was especially designed by Bardou & Son for the French government, which desired an extra good glass for military purposes. Both ends of the Bardou Rifle Range Telescope are protected by leather caps, which at the same time afford a means of attaching the shoulder strap for convenience in carrying; the barrels are finished in dead black, a great improvement over the usual highly burnished brass draws, which soon tarnish. The body of the Bardou Rifle Range Telescope is covered with the best grade smooth horsehide leather, with black oxidized draw tubes and trimmings, fine quality horsehide leather caps for each end, and shoulder strap. The Bardou Rifle Range Telescope is fitted with absolutely the best achromatic lenses made, giving great clearness and fine definition.

We guarantee the Bardou Rifle Range Telescope to show a bullet mark at a distance of half a mile, in clear atmosphere. The diameter of the object glass is 22 lignes, the length when closed is 11 inches, when extended, 36 inches. **Power is 33 diameters.**

Price, complete..**$16.50**

If by mail, postage extra, 60 cents.

No. 55C676 Astronomical Eyepiece for Bardou Rifle Range Telescope, increasing the power to 50 diameters, thus making it an extra fine instrument for observing the sun, moon and stars.

Price..**$2.70**

If by mail, postage extra, 10 cents.

Our Black Beauty Telescope, $6.67.

No. 55C640 We have had this Telescope especially designed for us by the leading telescope maker of Paris, and offer it this season for the first time. The most distinctive feature in the appearance of this splendid instrument is the **dead black oxidized finish throughout.** All brass parts, draw tubes and trimmings are perfectly black, a finish which is not only pleasing in appearance, but is also permanent and entirely free from liability to tarnish. Our **Black Beauty Telescope** is provided with extra quality achromatic lenses, carefully and accurately fitted, the workmanship and finish throughout is the best that can be produced, and every one is guaranteed to be optically perfect. **The eyepiece of our Black Beauty Telescope is fitted with an adjustable dark glass,** thus making the instrument suitable for observations of the sun. The spots on the sun, the mountains of the moon, the larger satellites of Jupiter, double stars, and many other interesting features of the heavenly bodies are readily seen with this instrument. The diameter of the object glass is 19 lignes, the length when closed is 9¾ inches, when extended, 30 inches. The magnifying power is 25 diameters.

Price, complete..............**$6.67**

If by mail, postage extra, 25 cents.

Delmar Achromatic Spy Glasses, at $1.40 to $2.95.

The Delmar Spy Glass, partly extended.

The Delmar Spy Glasses are fitted with first quality achromatic lenses, accurately fitted. Provided with slide cover for eyepiece and brass cap for front lens. The draw tubes are made from brass tubing, highly burnished. All trimmings are of lacquered brass and the bodies covered with fine black morocco leather. Made in four sections, thus closing to about one-third their total length.

No. 55C600 Delmar Spy Glass, diameter 10 lignes; length closed, 4⅛ inches; extended, 13 inches; magnifying power 10 times. Price........(If by mail, postage extra, 10 cents)........$1.40

No. 55C601 Delmar Spy Glass, diameter 12 lignes; length closed, 5 inches; extended, 14 inches; magnifying power 12 times. Price........1.55
If by mail, postage extra, 12 cents.

No. 55C602 Delmar Spy Glass, diameter 14 lignes; length closed, 6¼ inches; extended, 16¼ inches; magnifying power 16 times. Price........1.98
If by mail, postage extra, 16 cents.

No. 55C603 Delmar Spy Glass, diameter 16 lignes; length closed, 8 inches; extended, 22 inches; magnifying power 20 times. Price........2.95
If by mail, postage extra, 20 cents.

Our Pocket Spy Glass, for $2.80.

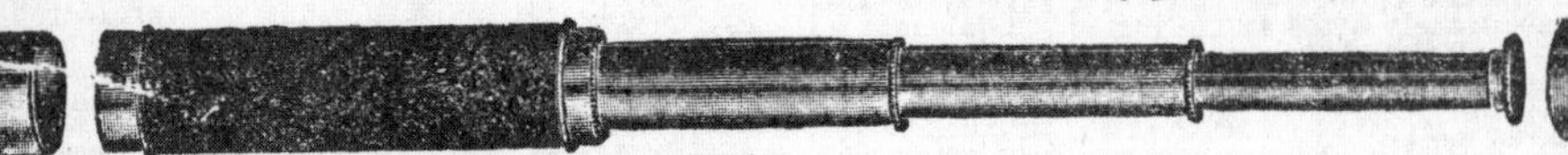

No. 55C615 The special features of this Spy Glass are the extra quality lenses and the rounded, nickel plated caps fitted to each end. These caps not only enhance the appearance of the instrument, but make it **dustproof**, thus protecting the lenses and making it very convenient to carry in the pocket. Our Pocket Spy Glass is fitted with **extra quality** achromatic lenses, the draw tubes are of burnished brass, caps nickel plated, and the body finely covered with the best morocco leather. **Extra fine workmanship and finish throughout.** Length when closed, 6¾ inches; when extended, 16¾ inches; magnifying power, 20 times. Price........(If by mail, postage extra, 16 cents)........$2.80

Telescopes with Sunshade, at $3.95 and $6.75.

Partly Extended.

These Telescopes are made by the same maker who furnishes us with the Delmar Spy Glasses and the workmanship and quality throughout is practically the same as in the Delmar instruments, but they are of larger size and are provided with an additional feature known as a sunshade. This consists of a lacquered brass sleeve, which can be extended forward in such a manner as to shade the object glass from the direct rays of sunlight. These instruments are fitted with first quality achromatic lenses, burnished brass draw tubes, lacquered brass trimmings, morocco leather covering, carefully and accurately made and guaranteed throughout.

No. 55C625 Sunshade Telescope, diameter, 19 lignes; length, closed, 10 inches; extended, 30 inches; magnifying power 25 times. Price........$3.95

No. 55C626 Sunshade Telescope, diameter, 22 lignes; length, closed, 10½ inches; extended, 37 inches; magnifying power 30 times. Price........6.75

If by mail, postage extra, on No. 55C625, 25 cents; on No. 55C626, 45 cents.

22-Ligne Black Lacquered Telescope, $9.85.

GENUINE PARIS MADE TELESCOPE.

POWER 35 TIMES.

No. 55C652 This is an exceptionally fine telescope in every respect, well made throughout, material and workmanship the best, finely finished, the lenses carefully and accurately adjusted, giving high magnifying power and fine definition. This is a splendid instrument for ordinary or terrestrial observations, and also affords excellent views of the sun, moon and other bodies, showing the sun spots, craters on the moon, Jupiter's satellites, etc. The sliding cover in the eyepiece is fitted with a dark glass for observations of the sun. **The magnifying power is 35 diameters.** This telescope measures 36 inches long, when fully extended, and 10¼ inches long when closed. The diameter of the object glass is 22 lignes (2 inches) and the instrument weighs 32 ounces. It is constructed throughout of brass, the very best metal known for scientific instruments, and it is finished with fine black lacquer throughout. **The draw tubes and trimmings are perfectly black, a finish which is permanent and will never tarnish.** This black lacquered finish is much superior to the ordinary highly burnished brass draw tubes furnished with most telescopes. The covering of the body is black pebbled morocco leather.

Price, complete, just as shown in illustration........$9.85

Astronomical Eyepiece, $4.25.

No. 55C653 This Eyepiece is made for use with our No. 55C652 telescope, for astronomical observations only, and increases the power to 55 diameters. Price........$4.25

Extra High Grade 25-Ligne Telescope, $15.90.

Gun Metal Finish. Magnifying Power 55 Diameters.

No. 55C657 This is the most powerful and the very highest grade telescope that we handle, a much higher grade and much finer instrument than is to be found in the best optical stores in the United States. We import this instrument direct from the maker in Paris, a maker whose specialty is extra high grade goods, who does not make any ordinary quality telescopes at all, but directs his entire attention to the making of extra high grade instruments. **While the finish of this instrument** throughout is finer and better than any other telescope with which it may be compared, still it is not the fine finish and workmanship which constitutes its chief points of superiority. **It is the lenses** which make this instrument so much superior to ordinary telescopes, these lenses being especially ground from the finest optical glass, very carefully centered and accurately adjusted. They are made to combine to the greatest possible extent the finest definition and highest magnifying power. **For astronomical work** this telescope forms an ideal instrument, showing clearly and distinctly the interesting changes and mysterious spots on the surface of the sun, the wonderful mountain ranges and apparently extinct craters of the moon, satellites of Jupiter, and the surface markings of this planet, the wonderful rings of Saturn, the canals on the planet Mars, nebulae, double stars, etc. **For observation of the sun a dark glass is mounted in the slide cover of the eyepiece. The magnifying power of this instrument is 55 diameters.** **The draw tubes, trimmings**, and all exposed metal parts are made with fine gun metal finish, the very best and most expensive finish known for optical instruments. This telescope is made throughout from brass, but the fine gun metal finish gives it the appearance of steel, the color being a characteristic glossy steel blue. **This fine steel blue gun metal finish will never tarnish or rust** and the draw tubes always work smoothly and easily. The body of the instrument is covered with a fine grade of pebbled morocco leather. **This telescope is made with sunshade**, a device for protecting the object glass from the direct rays of the sun, adding greatly to the efficiency of the instrument. This sunshade consists of a metal sleeve which can be drawn forward so as to shade the object glass. Instead of a cap it is provided with a hinged metal cover which affords perfect protection to the object glass. The length of this telescope when extended is 41½ inches; when closed, 12¼ inches. Weight, 50 ounces. The diameter of the object glass is 25 lignes (2¼ inches) and the **magnifying power 55 diameters. The high magnifying power**, extra quality lenses, fine workmanship and beautiful finish combine to make this telescope a most desirable instrument. Price, complete........$15.90

Astronomical Eyepiece, $4.65.

No. 55C658 This Eyepiece is made for use with our No. 55C657 telescope, for astronomical observations only, and increases the power to 80 diameters. Price........$4.65

Combination Microscope.

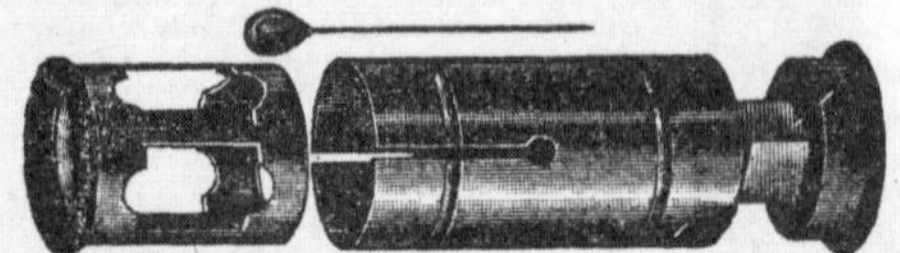

No. 55C719 Combination Microscope with lacquered brass case, 2 inches in length, has two lenses, one of very high power, the other of medium power; is especially adapted for the pocket. Price, including one insect holder..(Postage extra, 5 cents)....19c

Prospectors' Magnifying Glass.

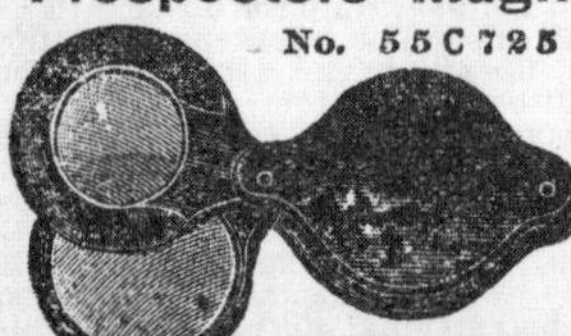

No. 55C725 Prospectors' Magnifying Glass, heavy, well finished hard rubber case, two lenses, 1 inch and 1⅛ inches in diameter, of high magnifying power. Strong and durable. **Especially adapted to the use of mineral prospectors**, being designed by a mining expert of long experience and made expressly for us by one of the best optical manufacturers in the world. Price, $1.95
If by mail, postage extra, 5 cents.

Triple Lens Magnifiers.

These are the most powerful instruments made in this style of construction, having three extra fine quality magnifying glasses, which can be used separately or all together, as desired, thus giving a range of power. The three lenses used together form an extra powerful magnifier. Mounted in finely finished rubber cases.

No. 55C746 Diameter of ½, ⅝ and ¾ inch. Price..43c
By mail, postage extra, 2 cents.

No. 55C747 Diameter of lenses, ⅝, ¾ and ⅞ inch. Price...(Postage extra 2 cents)...57c

No. 55C748 Diameter of lenses, ¾, ⅞ and 1 inch.
Price........(If by mail, postage extra, 4 cents)........72c

FOLDING CODDINGTONS.

These Coddington Magnifiers are made with folding metal cases, nickel plated, making them very convenient for carrying in the pocket. They are fitted with very fine double achromatic lenses of high power.

No. 55C781 Diameter, ¾-inch. Price........$0.75
If by mail, postage extra, 3 cents.

No. 55C782 Diameter, 1 inch. Price........1.00
If by mail, postage extra, 5 cents.

No. 55C783 Diameter, 1¼ inches. Price........1.25
If by mail, postage extra, 5 cents.

No. 55C784 Diameter, 1½ inches. Price........1.40
If by mail, postage extra, 8 cents.

Our $17.85 College Microscope.

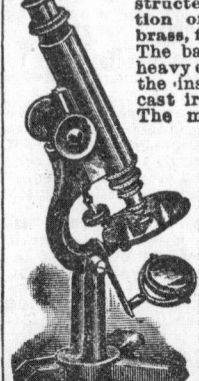

No. 55C820 This microscope is constructed throughout, with the exception of the base and arm, from brass, finely finished and lacquered. The base, which is extra broad and heavy enough to give great stability to the instrument, is constructed from cast iron with black enamel finish. The mirror is concave and can be swung to any angle either above or below the stage. **Our College Microscope** is fitted with a 1-inch Huyghenian eyepiece and a ⅔ and 1-6 divisible objective, giving powers of 96 and 460 diameters. The coarse adjustment is accomplished by a fine diagonal rack and pinion movement, and the fine adjustment by a micrometer screw located at base of arm and working in a hardened steel nut. Everything in connection with this instrument is strictly **high grade**; the materials used throughout are the best and it is just as carefully constructed and just as accurately adjusted as the highest priced instrument. Price, complete with fine polished hardwood case....$17.85
Shipping weight, 12 pounds.

ALL OUR MICROSCOPES are sold with the understanding and agreement that they may be used for ten days, compared with microscopes costing double the price that we ask, and if not found mechanically and optically perfect, better than corresponding instruments regardless of price, they may be returned to us at our expense and your money will be refunded.

Professional Microscope, $29.40.

No. 55C830 Made of brass throughout, highly polished and lacquered, complete in the smallest details of construction. The base, made of cast iron, finished in black enamel, is large and heavy, making the instrument very stable and steady at any angle of inclination. **The coarse adjustment** is operated by a very fine diagonal rack and pinion movement, and **the fine adjustment** is operated by a micrometer screw.

The draw tube is nickel plated, graduated in millimeters, and is adjustable in the cloth lined sleeve of the main tube.

The mirror is so mounted that it may be swung to any obliquity, either above or below the stage; **the stage** is provided with a **fine Iris diaphragm.**

Our Professional Microscope is provided with a DOUBLE NOSEPIECE for instantly changing objectives and is provided with two extra high grade objectives, a ⅔-inch and ⅙-inch, and the best quality 1-inch Huyghenian eyepiece. With the objectives furnished with this instrument, any kind of pathological or histological work and urinary analysis may be accomplished, and will detect tuberculosis germs and some other easily recognizable forms. This microscope is of large size, standing from 13 to 15½ inches high according to tube length. With the objectives which we furnish, a range of magnifying power from 96 to 540 diameters is available. Price, complete in fine, polished hardwood case.. **(Shipping weight, 14 pounds)... $29.40**

No. 55C845 One-twelfth inch Oil Immersion Objective, suitable for use with above or any standard microscope. Price.............. **$25.90**

OUR HIGHEST GRADE PHYSICIANS' MICROSCOPE.

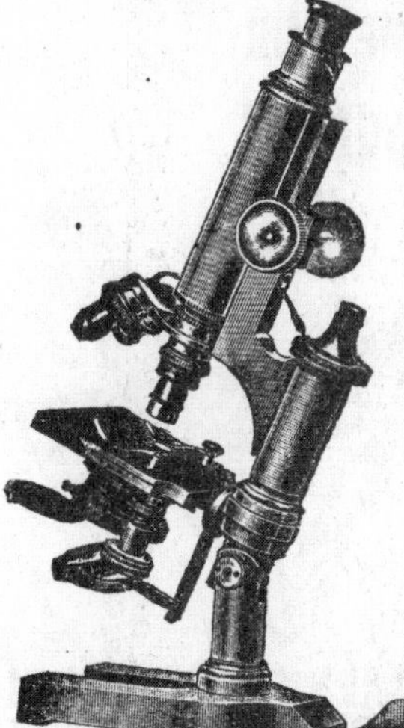

THE STAND of this, our very highest grade physicians' microscope, is made of brass throughout, with extra large and heavy base.

THE COARSE ADJUSTMENT is operated by diagonal rack and pinion with provision to compensate for wear.

THE FINE ADJUSTMENT is by means of a very delicate micrometer screw, operated by an extra large milled head, graduated for accurate adjustment.

THE DRAW TUBE is arranged for either long or short standard, is graduated in millimeters and works with remarkable smoothness. The large, square stage is fitted with removable spring clips and Iris diaphragm of special design, operated from beneath.

THE ABBE CONDENSER is mounted on a quick acting screw substage, by means of which it can be quickly and accurately focused or rapidly removed from the path of light. The objectives included with this instrument are the very highest grade, absolutely guaranteed to be optically perfect in every respect.

THIS MICROSCOPE will fully meet all requirements for the most exact scientific work, both in the physician's office and in the scientist's laboratory. It is suitable for all pathalogical and histological work, urinary analysis and bacteriology.

OUR HIGHEST GRADE PHYSICIANS' MICROSCOPE is sent out with the understanding and agreement that it may be used ten days, during which time it can be put to any test, compared with instruments costing $100.00 or more, and if not found perfect in every respect, absolutely correct both optically and mechanically, and better than any instrument with which it may be compared, it can be returned to us at our expense, and your money will be refunded to you.

No. 55C835 Our Highest Grade Physicians' Microscope, complete with two eye pieces, 1 inch and 2-inch; three objectives, ⅔-inch and ⅙-inch dry and $\frac{1}{12}$-inch oil immersion; triple nose piece; highest grade Abbe Condenser and screw substage attachment, put up in a handsome hardwood polished case. Price........................... **$68.00**

THERMOMETERS.

Tin Case Outdoor Thermometers.

No. 55C905 Japanned Tin Case Thermometer, ordinary grade, black figures on light metal scale; mercury tube. Length, 8 inches. Price................**10c**
If by mail, postage extra, 7 cents.

No. 55C908 Japanned Tin Case Thermometer, good quality, heavier, better made and more accurate than the preceding style; **seasoned tubes of standard size,** mercury only, good reliable thermometers for ordinary use. Length, 8 inches. Price............................**19c**
If by mail, postage extra, 8 cents.

No. 55C911 Japanned Tin Case Thermometer, best grade made, white figures and graduations upon black oxidized scale, thoroughly **seasoned tubes** of **large size,** good material and workmanship throughout, and **guaranteed absolutely accurate;** mercury only. Length, 8 inches. Retails everywhere at $1.00. Price **58c**
If by mail, postage extra, 10 cents.

No. 55C911

No. 55C913 Japanned Tin Case Thermometer, with red spirit tubes, graduated to **50 or 60 degrees below zero.** Carefully tested for accuracy and is perfectly reliable. Length, 12 inches. Price.........**39c**
If by mail, postage extra, 13 cents.

Storm Glass Thermometers.

No. 55C930 Poole's Barometer, a combined storm glass and thermometer, mounted upon varnished wood case, 3 inches wide by 9 inches long. This storm glass foretells the weather with a fair degree of accuracy for 24 hours in advance, and the thermometer shows correct temperature. Price.............................**16c**
If by mail, postage extra, 12 cents.

No. 55C930

No. 55C932 Antique Oak Storm Glass and Thermometer combined, mounted upon carved oak back with fancy beaded edge, black oxidized metal scale to thermometer with brass mountings, extra large storm glass with etched lettering. A reliable and handsome instrument. Price...........................**58c**
If by mail, postage extra, 17c.

No. 55C934 Copper Case Storm Glass and Thermometer, case made of polished copper, silvered metal scale, high grade thermometer with standard size tube, mercury. A very serviceable instrument for outdoor use. Price... **(Postage, 14c)......40c**

Fever Thermometers.

Clinical or fever thermometers are used, as the name implies, for taking the temperature in cases of sickness. **No family should be without a good fever thermometer,** and we handle only the highest grade, as a cheap or inaccurate instrument is worse than useless.

No. 55C940 Fever Thermometer, 4 inches long, magnifying tube, self registering, in hard rubber case, very accurate and guaranteed. A certificate of accuracy given with each one. Price...............**78c**
If by mail, postage extra, 3 cents.

No. 55C942 Fever Thermometer, 4 inches long, self registering, in hard rubber case, magnifying tube, very carefully tested and guaranteed, **registers in one minute.** Each thermometer accompanied by certificate of accuracy. Price................**98c**
If by mail, postage extra, 3 cents.

No. 55C944 Fever Thermometer, 4 inches long, self registering; in black enameled case with gold trimmings, chain and clasp; cannot be lost out of pocket; magnifying tube; very carefully tested and certificate of accuracy with each one. Price.....**89c**
If by mail, postage extra, 3 cents.

Dairy Thermometers.

No. 55C950 Churn Thermometer, with flange scale, tested at 62 degrees, for churning. Price...........**9c**
If by mail, postage extra, 4 cents.

No. 55C958 Dairy or Bath Thermometers, all glass. A very desirable instrument and easy to keep clean. Price......(Postage extra, 5 cents) **12c**

No. 55C960 Dairy Thermometer, all glass. This thermometer floats in the cream in upright position **with entire scale exposed to view.** Scale is **hand graduated and very accurate. Red spirit,** magnifying tube, making it very easy to read. Price..(If by mail, postage extra, 11 cents) ..**39c**

Incubator Thermometers.

Thermometers for use in Incubators should have thoroughly seasoned tubes and be specially tested. No ordinary thermometer will answer the purpose. Our Incubator Thermometers are guaranteed.

No. 55C965 Incubator Thermometer, extra large bulb and tube, very sensitive, white graduations on black oxidized metal plate. Absolutely accurate; 6 inches long. Price..........**42c**
If by mail, postage extra, 6 cents.

No. 55C966 Incubator Thermometer, same style and grade as No. 55C965, but 4½ inches long. Price...............................**37c**
If by mail, postage extra, 6 cents.

No. 55C965 No. 55C966

No. 55C967 Incubator Thermometer, same quality as preceding styles, but triangular in shape, will stand upright among the eggs with scale showing plainly. Price...........**45c**
If by mail, postage extra, 8 cents.

Hydrometers.

No. 55C977 Hydrometers, for testing specific gravity of liquids, eleven kinds as follows: Acids, alkalis, ammonia, coal oil, gasoline, salt, spirits, sirup, vinegar, liquids lighter than water, liquids heavier than water. **State kind wanted.** Price, any style................................**29c**
If by mail, postage extra, 5 cents.

POCKET COMPASSES.

Watch Style, 18 Cents.

No. 55C1010 Pocket Compass, watch style, open face, bevel edge glass, paper dial, brass case. Diameter, 1⅛ inches. Price...............................**18c**
If by mail, postage extra, 3 cents.

Good Compass for 43 Cents.

No. 55C1015 This Watch Style Pocket Compass is made with silvered metal dial, protected by heavy bevel edged glass, substantial brass case, and provided with **sliding stop.** Diameter, 1¾ inches. Price..(Postage extra, 3c)..**43c**

Jeweled Compass, 72 Cents.

No. 55C1020 This fine Pocket Compass has strong brass case with cap cover, heavy bevel edged glass, silvered metal dial, with full circle divisions, sliding stop and **jeweled cap to needle.** Diameter, 1¾ inches. An extra good compass at a very low price. Price.......**72c**
If by mail, postage extra, 4 cents.

Jeweled Compass, 98 Cents.

No. 55C1030 Our Watch Style Jeweled Pocket Compass is made with finely finished strong brass case with hinged cover, heavy beveled edge glass, **silvered metal dial** with full circle divisions and **sliding stop.** The needle is very sensitive and mounted with **jeweled cap.** Diameter, 2 inches. A compass that will last a lifetime and give perfect satisfaction under any conditions. Price...........**98c**
If by mail, postage extra, 5 cents.

Fine Jeweled Compass, $1.78.

No. 55C1033 An extra high grade pocket compass, made throughout in the most careful and accurate way. Strongly made lacquered brass case, 2⅜ inches in diameter, with cap cover, **extra heavy** beveled glass, automatic stop and best grade **jewel mounted English bar needle.** Bottom of compass is oxidized in black, with white lettering, and the full circle divisions **are engraved on a silvered metal dial raised to level of needle.** Price........................**$1.78**
If by mail, postage extra, 10 cents.

High Grade Compass, $1.90.

No. 55C1050 This is a very fine, compact compass, very convenient for carrying in pocket, made like a watch with **nickel plated dust proof case, spring** hinged cover, opened by pressing on stem, best jewel mounted English bar needle, automatic stop and heavy beveled glass. The full circle divisions are engraved on a silvered metal dial raised to level of needle. Diameter, 2 inches. Price.........................**$1.90**
If by mail, postage extra, 5 cents.

EXCEPTIONAL VALUES IN STEREOSCOPES AND STEREOSCOPIC VIEWS.

AT 12 CENTS TO 60 CENTS FOR STEREOSCOPES AND 40 CENTS TO $3.10 FOR STEREO-GRAPHOSCOPES WE OFFER SUCH A SELECTION OF EXCEPTIONAL VALUES IN THE LATEST STYLE STEREOSCOPES AND STEREO-GRAPHOSCOPES AS WAS NEVER BEFORE OFFERED.

OUR VERY LOW PRICES are based on the actual cost to manufacture, the cost of material and labor, with but our one small percentage of profit added. In stereoscopic views we offer a line of specially high grade values at prices ranging from **36 cents** to **81 cents per dozen**, the equal of stereoscopic views that sell generally at several times our special prices.

OUR VERY LOW PRICES ON STEREOSCOPIC VIEWS ARE MADE POSSIBLE BY REASON OF OUR ARRANGING WITH THE MANUFACTURER TO GIVE US A BIG PART OF HIS ENTIRE OUTPUT, GREATLY REDUCING THE COST OF MANUFACTURE.

SPECIAL NOTICE TO AGENTS. **Agents who are selling Stereoscopic Views and Stereoscopes are especially** requested to compare our prices with the prices you are now paying to see the big saving you can make by sending your order to us. Understand, we accept all orders for stereoscopes and stereoscopic views with the understanding that if they are not perfectly satisfactory they can be returned to us at our expense, and your money will be immediately returned to you. Our sales of stereoscopic views and stereoscopes have been so very large that we have been induced to greatly increase the department and increase our manufacturing facilities, thus reducing the cost of manufacture, and we give you the benefit of all this saving in the incomparably low prices we name.

A GOOD STEREOSCOPE FOR 12 CENTS.

No. 55C1305 This Stereoscope is made with hardwood frame, wood screw handle, small but first quality lenses, and the hood is made from pressed strawboard, stained and varnished in imitation of rosewood.

Price, per gross, **$15.90**; per dozen, **$1.38**; each........**12c**

If by mail, postage extra, each, 18 cents.

OUR BIRDSEYE MAPLE STEREOSCOPE FOR 20 CENTS.

No. 55C1311 The hood of this stereoscope is made from a good quality of birdseye maple. The frame is of cherry wood and it is fitted with **a patent folding handle.** The lenses are small but of first quality.

Price, each................ **$0.20**
Per dozen................ **2.32**

If by mail, postage extra, each, 20 cents.

No. 55C1313 This stereoscope is made with birdseye maple hood, cherry frame and folding handle, same as our No. 55C1311, but has first quality medium sized lenses, instead of small lenses.

Price, per dozen, **$2.75**....(**If by mail, postage extra, each, 20 cents.**) ....each..**24c**

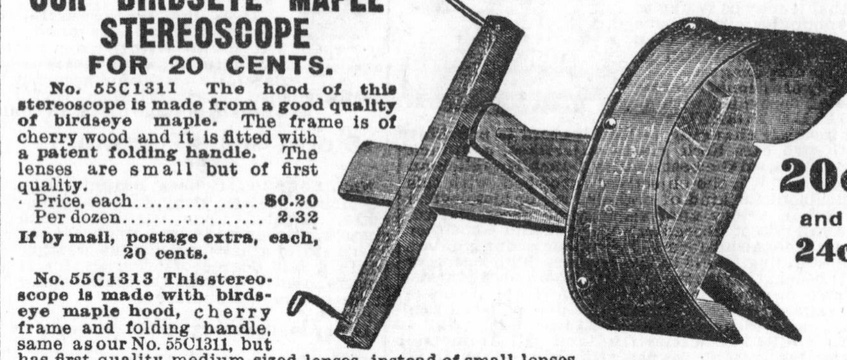

OUR SPECIAL ALUMINUM STEREOSCOPE FOR 49c

No. 55C1319 This Elegant Stereoscope is made with fine aluminum hood, beautifully engraved and bound with dark red velvet. The frame is of cherry wood, carefully finished and varnished, with patent folding handle. The lenses are extra quality, of good size, carefully ground from the highest grade of fine, clear glass and accurately adjusted. **Our Special Aluminum Stereoscope is a universal favorite** with canvassers, who find that the elegant appearance and sterling good qualities which it possesses make it a very ready seller. **The very low price which we quote on this stereoscope** is made possible only by the fact that we have contracted for the largest quantity of high grade stereoscopes ever handled by any one dealer and have thus been enabled to reduce the manufacturing cost to the lowest possible figure. Price, per dozen, **$5.64**; each..............**49c**

If by mail, postage extra, each, 25 cents.

OUR LARGE LENS WALNUT STEREOSCOPE FOR 60c

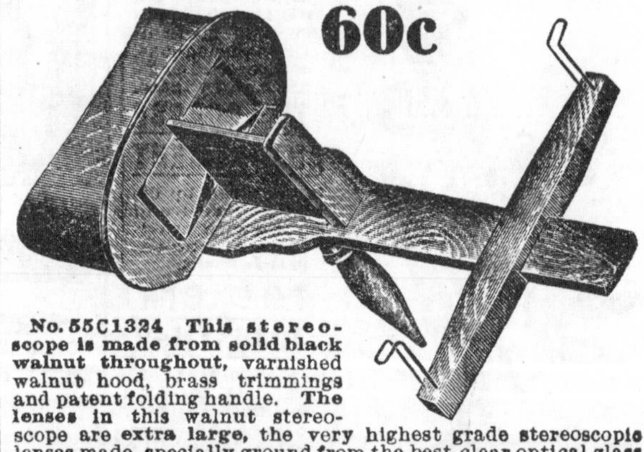

No. 55C1324 This stereoscope is made from solid black walnut throughout, varnished walnut hood, brass trimmings and patent folding handle. **The lenses in this walnut stereoscope are extra large,** the very highest grade stereoscopic lenses made, specially ground from the best clear optical glass and accurately adjusted. Best workmanship and carefully selected materials throughout; an extra good stereoscope.

Price, per dozen, **$6.95**; each........ ....**60c**

If by mail, postage extra, each, 20 cents.

STEREO-GRAPHOSCOPES

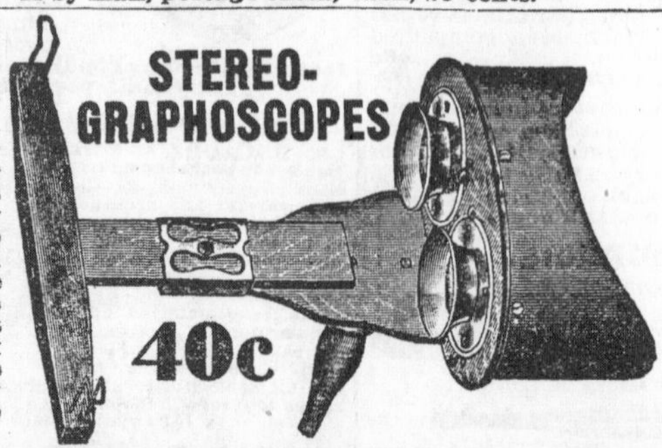

The Stereo-Graphoscope is an instrument made upon a new principle by means of which it can be adjusted for either regular stereoscopic views or single photographs and other pictures by simply reversing the lenses. The manner in which the lenses are mounted and the shape of the hood shuts out all light, making a dark chamber around the eyes and giving a very clear, beautiful effect to the pictures.

No. 55C1335 Stereo-Graphoscope, cherry frame, varnished cherry hood, brass trimmings and wood screw handle. Medium size lenses of best quality.

Price, per dozen, **$4.68**; each..**40c**

If by mail, postage extra, each, 25 cents.

No. 55C1336 Stereo-Graphoscope, cherry frame, varnished mahogany hood, brass trimmings and patent folding handle. Best grade lenses of large size, a first class instrument throughout. Price, per dozen, **$6.48**; each.......**56c**

If by mail, postage extra, each, 25 cents.

No. 55C1337 Our Best Stereo-Graphoscope, made with oiled cherry frame, fine varnished mahogany hood, all trimmings nickel plated and highly polished, patent folding handle, first quality materials and best workmanship throughout. Extra large lenses of very highest quality. Price, per dozen, **$8.15**; each...**70c**

If by mail, postage extra, each, 25 cents.

OUR IMPORTED STEREO-GRAPHOSCOPE FOR $3.10

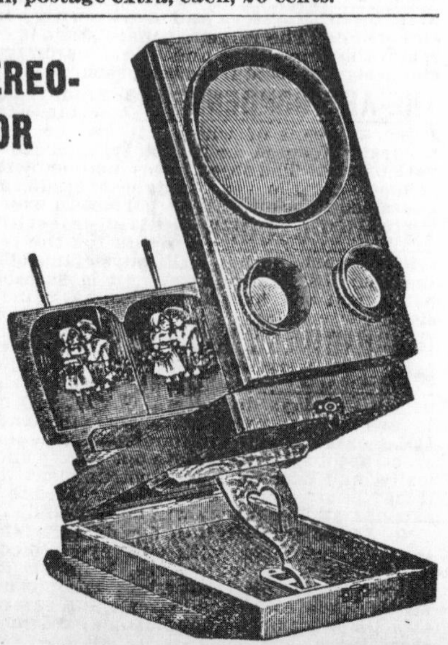

No. 55C1345 This instrument, a combination stereoscope and graphoscope, is designed for both stereoscopic pictures and single photographs, being fitted with a pair of very high grade specially ground stereoscopic lenses for the former and with a large double convex graphoscope lens, 4 inches in diameter, for the single pictures. Made from polished mahogany, very finely finished throughout, folds compactly when not in use, measuring when closed only 8⅝ inches long by 5⅛ inches wide by 2⅜ inches deep. An ornament to any parlor, and the source of great interest and amusement. Price, complete......**$3.10**

If by mail, postage extra, each, 35 cents.

A TOUR OF THE WORLD WITH THE STEREOSCOPE.

THIS OUTFIT consists of one hundred magnificent colored reproductions of original photographic stereoscopic views. The original photographs from which these views are reproduced were especially selected for this set, the greatest care being exercised to obtain only views of particular interest, unusual beauty and the most perfect stereoscopic effect.

THIS SET illustrates some of the most noted places in the world—mountain scenery both in America and Europe—waterfalls and other famous natural phenomena, some of the world's most famous buildings, places of historical interest and places famous for beautiful architecture or beautiful natural scenery. **This set is of the greatest educational value,** presenting, as it does, such realistic likenesses of scenes and places that we all should know about.

THERE ARE ONE HUNDRED VIEWS IN THE SET, all different and every one good. All are finished in natural colors, made by a new and secret process, which enables us to offer these colored, high grade stereoscopic views at a price heretofore impossible. **Understand,** these views are reproductions in natural colors, made from

ORIGINAL RETOUCHED PHOTOGRAPHS

by a recently perfected secret process, combining the principles of halftone photography and lithography.

THE STEREOSCOPE which we furnish with this set of pictures, is made with hardwood frame, wood screw handle, fair quality lenses and varnished pressed board hood. While it is not the best stereoscope made, it is a very serviceable instrument, and, if you prefer

ONE OF OUR HIGHEST GRADE STEREOSCOPES,

you can order this set of views alone at 85 cents and make your own selection of stereoscope from page 366.

No. 55C1360 Complete Outfit, 100 Views of the World and Stereoscope.
Price.. **95c**
If by mail, postage extra, 44 cents.

No. 55C1361 Views of the World, without Stereoscope.
Price.. **85c**
If by mail, postage extra, 24 cents.

FUN, LAUGHTER AND AMUSEMENT WITH THE STEREOSCOPE.

THIS SPLENDID SET OF PICTURES consists of one hundred exquisitely colored stereoscopic pictures, made by our new secret process which, by a combination of well known lithographic and halftone processes, enables us to reproduce with photographic fidelity in all their natural colors these genuine photographic views, and enables us to sell them at one-tenth the actual cost of stereoscopic views made by the old process.

THESE ONE HUNDRED PICTURES ARE ALL PHOTOGRAPHED FROM LIFE. There are no copies of paintings or drawings, but every picture is made with a camera direct from life. The coloring in these comic views is exceptionally good and our new process has enabled us to bring out the details and present the subjects in the most realistically lifelike manner. Great care has been exercised in selecting the subjects for this set so that only unusually good views are included. There is not a vulgar picture in the entire set, not a picture to which the most refined could possibly object, but at the same time every picture in the set is interesting, and they will be looked at over and over again, forming a never failing source of pleasure and relaxation.

EVERYBODY LIKES A GOOD LAUGH, and every picture in this big set is good for one big, hearty laugh. Laughable hugging and kissing scenes, humorous scenes of domestic tribulations, amusing bathing scenes, photographs of children engaged in childish occupations—

FUNNY, ENTERTAINING AND LAUGHABLE PICTURES.

They will amuse you and help to entertain your friends. **Understand,** this big set consists of one hundred comic colored views, every picture a good one, and our special hardwood, pressed board hood, wood screw handle, stereoscope, all complete, scope and pictures, for 95 cents. If you want a better stereoscope, just order the views alone and pick out your scope from page 366.

No. 55C1364 Complete Outfit, 100 Comic Views and Stereoscope.
Price.. **95c**
If by mail, postage extra, 44 cents.

No. 55C1365 Comic Views, without Stereoscope.
Price.. **85c**
If by mail, postage extra, 24 cents.

A TRIP TO THE FAIR WITH THE STEREOSCOPE.

THIS SET OF ONE HUNDRED BEAUTIFUL COLORED STEREOSCOPIC VIEWS **of the St. Louis Exposition** were all made from original photographs taken on the fair grounds by our special photographer, reproduced in natural colors by our new lithographic halftone process. This set of views is particularly interesting, not only to those who have visited St. Louis, but by particularly to those who have not been fortunate enough to see the beautiful buildings magnificent grounds, fountains, cascades, drives and lagoons of this great exposition.

THE LOUISIANA PURCHASE EXPOSITION IN ST. LOUIS is considered one of the most beautiful **Expositions of the World.** The naturally picturesque surroundings have been developed and turned to the best possible account by famous architects and celebrated landscape gardeners, and this realistic set of colored stereoscopic pictures will serve to perpetuate the memory of

THE MOST BEAUTIFUL EXPOSITION BUILDINGS AND GROUNDS EVER DESIGNED.

REMEMBER, these views are all reproduced from genuine original photographs. No copies, no paintings or drawings were used—

NOTHING BUT ORIGINAL PHOTOGRAPHS MADE ON THE GROUNDS BY OUR SPECIAL PHOTOGRAPHER.

OUR PRICE FOR THIS SET of one hundred colored stereoscopic pictures all complete with our hardwood screw handle stereoscope is 95 cents, but, if you prefer a better stereoscope, one of our highest grade stereoscopes as shown on page 366, you can buy the views alone for 85 cents and select any style of scope that you prefer.

No. 55C1372 Complete Outfit, 100 World's Fair Views and Stereoscope.
Price.. **95c**
If by mail, postage extra, 44 cents.

No. 55C1373 World's Fair Views, without Stereoscope.
Price.. **85c**
If by mail, postage extra, 24 cents.

300 BEAUTIFULLY COLORED STEREOSCOPIC VIEWS AND OUR HIGHEST GRADE ALUMINUM SCOPE $2.88

THREE BIG SETS.

100 VIEWS OF THE WORLD. 100 COMIC VIEWS.
100 ST. LOUIS EXPOSITION VIEWS.

THESE THREE BIG SETS of colored stereoscopic views, all complete, each set in a separate box, with our highest grade large lens velvet edge aluminum hood stereoscope, present a most attractive proposition, offering, as they do, the very largest number of pictures, covering a range of subjects unexcelled in their educational value, subjects of current interest, subjects of international importance, with just enough comic and laughable subjects to give spice to the entertainment

REMEMBER under the terms of this special offer you get 300 colored stereoscopic views made by our new combination lithographic and halftone process, exactly as described on preceding page, together with our highest grade aluminum stereoscope, for only $2.88.

No. 55C1380 Three sets, Views of the World, Comic, and St. Louis Exposition, with Aluminum Stereoscope. Price....................$2.88

No. 55C1381 Three sets, as described above, but without stereoscope. Price....................2.40

If sent by mail, postage extra, 70 cents.

FINE VIEWS AT 36 CENTS PER DOZEN

THE FOLLOWING SERIES ARE ALL GENUINE PHOTOGRAPHIC VIEWS, PRINTED FROM NEGATIVES UPON REGULAR PHOTOGRAPHIC PAPER, FINELY FINISHED AND MOUNTED ON GOOD CARDS.
IF BY MAIL, POSTAGE EXTRA, PER DOZEN, 5 CENTS.

Chicago World's Fair.

No. 55C1410 Chicago World's Fair Series. The White City in all its glory, and choice views along the Midway Plaisance. Price, per 100, assorted, $2.85; per dozen, all different....................36c

Norwegian Views.

No. 55C1411 Norwegian Series. A splendid collection of views from Norway, illustrating the famous scenery of the country, its cities, etc. Price, per 100, assorted, $2.85; per dozen, all different, 36c

American Picturesque.

No. 55C1412 American Picturesque Series. A beautiful collection of subjects illustrating the picturesque features of the American continent.
Price, per 100, assorted, $2.85; per dozen, all different....................36c

Views in Sweden.

No. 55C1413 Swedish Series. A very fine assortment of pictures taken in Sweden, showing the magnificent scenery of this picturesque country, glimpses of its cities, etc. Price, per 100, assorted, $2.85; per dozen, all different....................36c

Sportsmen's Views.

No. 55C1414 Sporting Series. Choice views illustrating camp life, hunting and fishing scenes, game, etc. Price, per 100, assorted, $2.85; per dozen, all different....................36c

American Cities.

No. 55C1416 American Cities Series. Glimpses of streets, parks, public buildings, etc., in the principal cities of America. Price, per 100, assorted, $2.85; per dozen, all different....................36c

Yellowstone National Park.

No. 55C1418 Yellowstone Park Series. Beautiful views showing the canyons, geysers, hot springs and wonderful rock formations. Price, per 100, assorted, $2.85; per dozen, all different....................36c

Foreign Picturesque.

No. 55C1420 A splendid series of views illustrating the most beautiful and striking scenery and points of interest throughout Europe. Price, per 100, assorted, $2.85; per dozen, all different......36c

Ruins and Antiquities.

No. 55C1422 Antiquities Series. A very interesting series of pictures showing subjects of historical interest, old castles, wonderful architectural works of ancient times, etc. Price, per 100, assorted, $2.35; per dozen, all different....................36c

Foreign Cities.

No. 55C1424 Foreign Cities Series. Glimpses of interesting points, streets, celebrated buildings, etc., in the great cities of Europe. Price, per 100, assorted, $2.85; per dozen, all different.......36c

Comic Views.

No. 55C1426 A large series of very comical and amusing scenes, all photographed from life. One of the most popular series we handle. Price, per 100, assorted $2.85; per dozen, all different......36c

Colored Views, 54 Cents per Dozen.

Beautifully Hand Colored Photographic Views. If by mail, postage extra, 5 cents per dozen.

Yellowstone National Park.

No. 55C1435 Yellowstone Park Series. Beautifully colored views, spouting geysers, brilliant deposits from hot springs, mountains, cliffs and rivers. Price, per 100, assorted, $4.28; per dozen, all different....................54c

American Scenery.

No. 55C1437 American Picturesque Series. Beautifully colored views showing the most picturesque places throughout our country. Price, per 100, assorted, $4.28; per dozen, all different........54c

Foreign Scenery.

No. 55C1439 Foreign Picturesque Series. Beautifully colored views illustrative of the grandest scenery of Europe. Price, per 100, assorted, $4.28; per dozen, all different....................54c

Comic Views from Life.

No. 55C1441 Comic Series. Beautifully colored views, various comical scenes, child life, amusing situations, etc., all photographed from life.
Price, per 100, assorted, $4.28; per dozen, all different....................54c

Special High Grade Views at 58 Cents per Dozen.

We have only a limited number of subjects in the following series, but they are all extra fine and represent exceptionally good value. These views are all printed from original negatives and finished by the new platinum toning process, giving beautiful results in black and white.
If by mail, postage extra, per dozen, 6 cents.

Comic Series.

No. 55C1445 Comic Views, a very fine series of highly amusing pictures, groups from life, charming pictures of child life, all new and attractive About forty different subjects. Price, per 100, assorted, $4.60; per dozen, all different....................58c

(58-cent Views continued on next page.)

American Scenery.

THE BROOKLYN BRIDGE

No. 55C1446 American Scenery, a most interesting series of views illustrating the many beautiful and picturesque portions of the American continent, including views in the large cities. About forty different subjects. Price, per 100, assorted, **$4.60**; per dozen, all different **58c**

Foreign Scenery.

MORRO CASTLE, SANTIAGO.

No. 55C1447 Foreign Scenery, an elegant collection of choice views from all over the world, every one of exceptional merit, especially selected for this series. About forty different subjects.

Price, per 100, assorted, **$4.60**; per dozen, all different **58c**

American Battleships.

BATTLESHIP WISCONSIN

No. 55C1448 Battleships, a very popular series consisting of a fine collection of views of the battleships of our navy. **Extra good.** About 30 different subjects. Price, per 100, assorted, **$4.60**; per dozen, all different **58c**

100 Views, All Different, for $4.75.

No. 55C1449 We have made up this special collection of 100 views, all different, comprising the very best subjects from the Comic, American Scenery, Foreign Scenery and Battleship series Nos. 55C1445 to 55C1448 as described above. We put up this fine collection of 100, all different, specially selected high grade views in a substantial cloth lined box with a black seal grain covering. Price, complete.... **$4.75**

Shipping weight, 6½ pounds.

Our Highest Grade Views at 81 Cents per Dozen.

We offer the following series of extra high grade views as the very best Stereoscopic Views that can be made, regardless of price.

Every one of our highest grade views is made from an original retouched negative, printed upon the finest quality of photographic paper and mounted on the best grade heavy cards.

If by mail, postage extra, per dozen, 6 cents.

Yellowstone National Park.

No. 55C1455 Yellowstone National Park, a magnificent series of pictures taken in this world famous region; canyons, spouting geysers, castled rocks, terraces and boiling springs, towering mountains, wonderful rock formations and beautiful waterfalls. Nearly 200 different subjects.

Price, per 100, assorted, **$6.42**; per dozen, all different **81c**

Yosemite Valley and Big Trees.

CATHEDRAL SPIRES

No. 55C1457 Yosemite Valley and Big Trees, a series of beautiful views exhibiting in a most striking manner the varied scenes of California's marvelous wonderland. Price, per 100, assorted, **$6.42**; per dozen, all different **81c**

Sporting Series.

QUAIL SHOOTING

No. 55C1459 Sporting Views. This splendid collection of hunting, fishing and camp life scenes, all photographed direct from life, will be especially interesting to those who appreciate the pleasures of rod or gun. They bring back memories of pleasant days in the woods, on the marshes or along some shady stream, revive the memories of dead camp fires, and anticipate the pleasures of days to come. Over 200 different subjects. Price, per 100, assorted, **$6.42**; per dozen, all different **81c**

Comic Views.

THE SANDMAN'S COMING

No. 55C1461 Comic Views. In addition to scores of the most humorous and laughter provoking scenes, all photographed direct from life, this series contains some of the choicest views of child life, showing the little ones engaged in their various and amusing occupations, and pretty bits of scenery caught with the artist's camera. A very popular series, with over 250 different subjects. Price, per 100, assorted, **$6.42**; per dozen, all different **81c**

If by mail, postage extra, per dozen, 6 cents.

Religious Views.

JESUS APPEARS TO MAGDALEN

No. 55C1485 Life of Christ Set. Twelve splendid views portraying in the most vivid manner the story of our Savior's life before and after the crucifixion.

Price, per set, plain, **48c**; colored **60c**

THE CRUCIFIXION

No. 55C1486 The Crucifixion Set. Twelve splendid views representing the Nativity, Early Life, Crucifixion and Resurrection of Christ.

Price, per set, plain, **48c**; colored **60c**

JUVENILE MAGIC LANTERN OUTFITS.

The young people not only derive great pleasure from giving MAGIC LANTERN EXHIBITIONS, but the business training which they gain in all the various details connected with the management of an entertainment, putting up advertising posters, **selling tickets**, etc., gives them ideas of the rudiments of **money making** which starts them on the highway to business success. REMEMBER that each outfit is complete, containing **a fine Magic Lantern, a splendid assortment of Colored Views, a large supply of Advertising Posters, plenty of Tickets.**

INTERESTING INSTRUCTIVE AND PROFITABLE

You will easily make the original cost of the outfit in your first exhibition; after that it's all profit.

The Home Magic Lantern Outfits.

Our illustration gives a very exact idea of the general appearance and construction of the Home Magic Lantern. The body of this lantern is made of metal, japanned in black, **handsomely decorated in gilt** and mounted on wood baseboard. Burns ordinary kerosene or coal oil.

No. 55C1500 The Home Magic Lantern Outfit No. 1, with Home Magic Lantern as described above, using slides 13-16 inches wide and magnifying pictures to about 1 foot in diameter. The complete outfit contains lantern, six colored slides, three to four pictures on each slide, twenty-five advertising posters and twenty-five admission tickets.

Price, complete **59c**

No. 55C1502 Home Magic Lantern Outfit No. 2, same as No. 55C1500, but using slides 1 9-16 inches wide, magnifying pictures to 2 feet and including **twelve colored slides** instead of six. Price, complete **$1.28**

No. 55C1504 Home Magic Lantern Outfit No. 3, same as No. 55C1500, but using slides 2 inches wide, magnifying pictures to about 3 feet in diameter. Price, complete **$1.98**

The Brilliant Magic Lantern Outfits.

The Brilliant Magic Lanterns are very handsome instruments of the upright style, finely finished in brass, bronze and nickel plate, with the body of the lantern enameled in bright red. They are provided with **double convex condensing lens** and finely ground projecting lens. In addition to the regular long glass slides, these lanterns also use a slide in the form of **a round disc with six views.** Each lantern contained in neat wood box with handle.

No. 55C1509 The Brilliant Magic Lantern Outfit No. 1, with Brilliant Magic Lantern as described above, **using slides 1⅜ inches wide** and magnifying pictures to about 2 feet in diameter. The complete outfit consists of lantern, six long glass colored slides, three to four views on each slide, three glass discs with six colored views on each disc, twenty-five advertising posters and twenty-five admission tickets. Price, complete **$1.90**

No. 55C1512 Brilliant Magic Lantern Outfit No. 2, same as No. 55C1509, but **using slides 1¾ inches wide**, magnifying pictures to about 3 feet in diameter. Price, complete **$2.98**

No. 55C1514 Brilliant Magic Lantern Outfit No. 3, same as No. 55C1509, but **using slides 2 inches wide**, magnifying pictures to about 4 feet in diameter. Price, complete **$3.75**

Gloria Magic Lantern Outfits.

The Gloria Magic Lantern, our best grade lantern, is finely finished in Russia sheet iron, lacquered, with brass lens tube and trimming. **The Gloria Lantern is provided with a pair of convex condensing lenses,** and finely ground projection lens, and has blue glass window in door to protect the eyes from the dazzling light. The lamp with which the Gloria lantern is fitted is of the duplex or double burner style, giving a very brilliant illumination. Burns ordinary kerosene or coal oil. **A fine instrument for parlor exhibitions.**

No. 55C1518 Gloria Magic Lantern Outfit No. 1, with Gloria Magic Lantern as described above, using **slides 2 inches wide** and magnifying pictures to about 3 feet in diameter. **The complete outfit consists of the lantern, twelve colored slides, three to four pictures on each slide, one comic slip slide, one movable scenery slide, one brilliantly colored chromotrope or artificial fireworks slide, fifty large advertising posters and fifty admission tickets.** Price, complete.......................$3.95

No. 55C1520 Gloria Magic Lantern Outfit No. 2, same as No. 55C1518, but **using slides 2⅜ inches wide,** magnifying pictures to about 4 feet in diameter. Price, complete.......................$4.95

No. 55C1522 Gloria Magic Lantern Outfit No. 3, same as No. 55C1518, but **using slides 2¾ inches wide,** magnifying pictures to about 5 feet in diameter. Price, complete.......................$5.80

Extra Chimneys and Wicks.

No. 55C1532 Chimney to fit any of the Home or Brilliant Magic Lanterns. Price, each, any size..10c
If by mail, postage extra, 6 cents.

No. 55C1537 Wicks, to fit any of our magic lanterns. Price, six for.......................5c

N. B.—When ordering chimneys or wicks be sure to state which lantern they are to fit.

Colored Slides.

No. 55C1540 These slides are all highly colored and each slide has from three to four views. They are put up in packages of one dozen slides and each package contains an assortment of both comic and scenic views. **We cannot sell less than one package,** and we are unable to furnish any special subjects.

Plain Colored Slides.

Width	Price
1⅛ inches, package of 1 dozen	$0.20
1⅜ inches, package of 1 dozen	.30
1½ inches, package of 1 dozen	.36
1¾ inches, package of 1 dozen	.51
2 inches, package of 1 dozen	.64
2⅜ inches, package of 1 dozen	.85
2¾ inches, package of 1 dozen	1.11

Comic Movable Slides.

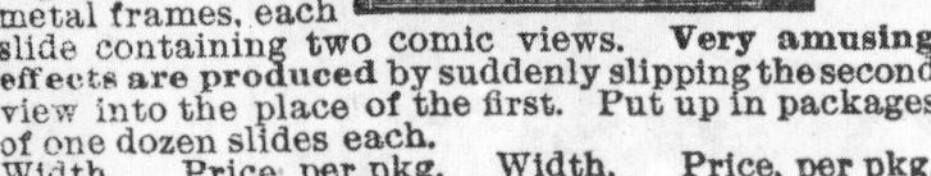

No. 55C1542 These pictures are painted in bright colors on glass slips, which slide in metal frames, each slide containing two comic views. **Very amusing effects are produced** by suddenly slipping the second view into the place of the first. Put up in packages of one dozen slides each.

Width, inches	Price, per pkg. of 1 dozen	Width, inches	Price, per pkg. of 1 dozen
1⅜	60c	2	$1.08
1½	67c	2⅜	1.28
1¾	92c	2¾	1.48

The Brilliant Slides.

No. 55C1544 The most economical slides made, printed on celluloid and affording a class of pictures **never before offered** in anything but high priced slides. Made in one size only, 2 inches wide, but can be used in any lantern using slides 2 inches or wider. If your lantern uses slides 2⅜ or 2¾ inches wide, we will include, **for 8c extra,** a small wooden carrier by means of which you can use these **Brilliant Slides.** Each series of **the Brilliant Slides** contains twelve slides, three pictures on each slide, making a total of **thirty-six views in each series.** Order by series.

Series		Price
A	Noted Places Around the World	36c
B	Miscellaneous Views, mostly very comic	36c
H	Old and New Testament Bible Views	36c
I	Comic, each good for a laugh	36c
M	American and Foreign Scenery	36c

All the Brilliant Slides are 2 inches wide.
If by mail, postage extra, per set, 1 cent.

Chromotropes.

No. 55C1546 These Slides, known also as **artificial fireworks,** consist of two glass discs, painted in bright colors in radiating geometrical patterns, which are revolved in opposite directions by means of the small crank, producing a **very brilliant effect.** Several different patterns of each size can be furnished.

Width, 1⅛ inches; price	25c
Width, 1⅜ inches; price	30c
Width, 2 inches; price	33c
Width, 2⅜ inches; price	36c
Width, 2¾ inches; price	39c

Genuine Photographic Slides.

We are able to offer this season for the first time the following series of actual photographic views, all popular and up to date subjects, in sizes suitable for use with our Juvenile Magic Lanterns. By making up these slides in great quantities, and putting four views on a slide, we are able to furnish them at astonishingly low prices. Heretofore real photographic slides could be obtained only in the regular professional size, suitable only for use with the large professional stereopticons; they were made with only one view on a slide, and cost from 35 cents to 50 cents per view. **Each set of our genuine photographic slides contains twelve slides, and there are four views on each slide, making a total of forty-eight views in every set. With every set we include a printed lecture, giving a complete description of every view.**

The Spanish-American War.

No. 55C1548. A splendid set of forty-eight views, illustrating the most interesting features of the late war between the United States and Spain. Portraits of prominent officers, battleships, camp life, battle scenes, etc. Twelve slides in the set, four views on each slide, making a total of forty-eight views.

Width, 1⅛ inches; price, per set, with lecture,	$1.13
Width, 2 inches; price, per set, with lecture,	1.35
Width, 2⅜ inches; price, per set, with lecture,	2.48
Width, 2¾ inches; price, per set, with lecture,	2.93

Sold only in sets. We cannot sell less than a set.

Russian-Japanese War.

No. 55C1550 This very interesting set of views is descriptive of the most important events in the war between Russia and Japan. It contains portraits of prominent officers, pictures of the Japanese and Russian battle ships, soldiers in camp and on the march, views in Manchuria, Corea and Japan. Twelve slides in each set, 4 pictures on each slide, making a total of 48 pictures.

Width, 1⅛ inches; price, per set, with lecture,	$1.13
Width, 2 inches; price, per set, with lecture,	1.35
Width, 2⅜ inches; price, per set, with lecture,	2.48
Width, 2¾ inches; price, per set, with lecture,	2.93

Sold only in sets. We cannot sell less than a set.

The St. Louis Exposition.

No. 55C1552 This is a beautiful set of slides containing pictures of the most prominent buildings at the Fair, views of the grounds, lagoons, drives, parks and other **interesting views on the** Fair grounds. There are 12 slides in the set, each slide containing 4 pictures, a total of 48 magnificent photographic views of the most beautiful exposition ever held.

Width, 1⅛ inches; price, per set, with lecture,	$1.13
Width, 2 inches; price, per set, with lecture,	1.35
Width, 2⅜ inches; price, per set, with lecture,	2.48
Width, 2¾ inches; price, per set, with lecture,	2.93

Sold only in sets. We cannot sell less than a set.

NOTE—These photographic slides can be used with any of our Juvenile Lanterns, except Nos. 55C1500 and 55C1509. Note in the description of the lanterns the size of slide used, and select the corresponding size in these photographic slides.

DRAWING INSTRUMENTS.

92 Cents Buys This Scholars' Set.

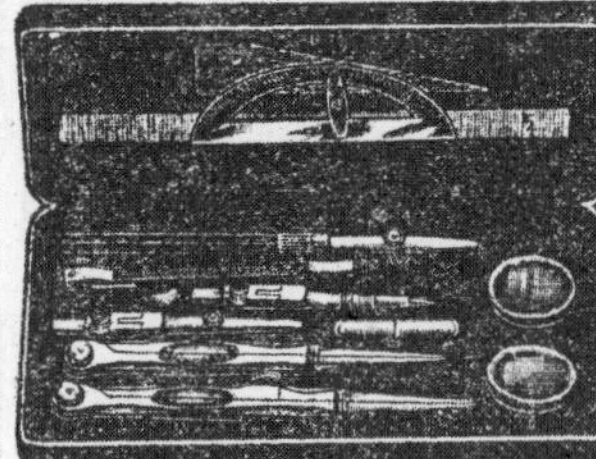

No. 55C1620 Scholars' Drawing Set, consisting of: 4½-inch Plain Dividers, Lengthening Bar for Compasses, Graduated Rule, Case of Leads, Small Wood Triangle, 5-inch Compasses with both pen and pencil points, 4¾-inch Ruling Pen, Metal Protractor and Key. Contained in a handsome velvet lined leatherette case. Per dozen, $10.50; each....92c
If by mail, postage extra, 12 cents.

Exceptional Value at $1.68.

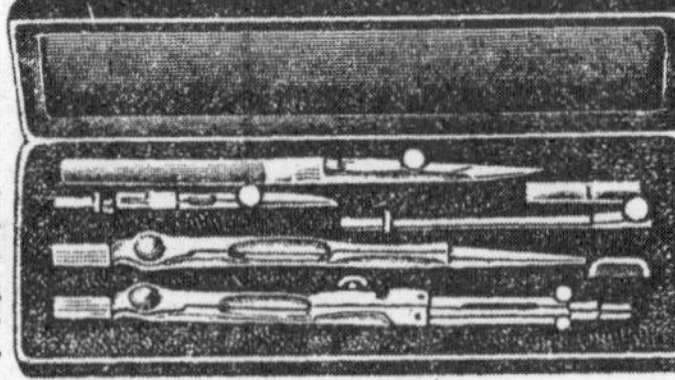

No. 55C1630 Fine German Silver Drawing Set, consisting of: 5-inch Plain Dividers, 5½-inch Compasses with pen and pencil points, 5½-inch Ruling Pen, Lengthening Bar for Compasses, Box of Leads and Key. These well made instruments are contained in genuine leather, velvet lined pocket case. Price, per dozen, $19.25; each.......................$1.68
If by mail, postage extra, 13 cents.

A Good Set for $1.98.

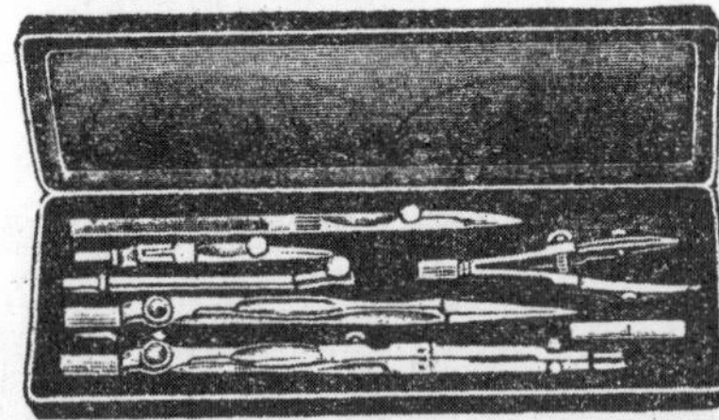

No. 55C1635 Fine German Silver Drawing Set, consisting of: 5½-inch Ruling Pen, 5-inch Plain Dividers, 5½-inch Compasses with pen and pencil points, Lengthening Bar for Compasses, 3½-inch Steel Spring Bow Pen, Box of Leads and Key. Contained in genuine leather, velvet lined pocket case. Fully meets the requirements for use in manual training schools or elementary work in engineering colleges. Price, per dozen, $22.80; each....$1.98
If by mail, postage extra, 14 cents.

Our Pivot Joint Set for $2.90.

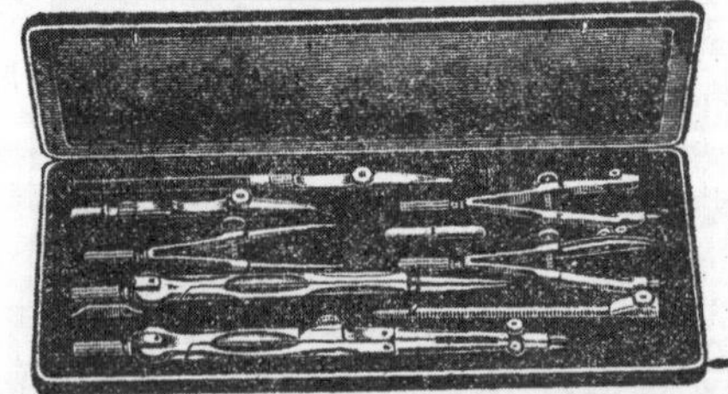

No. 55C1637 Fine Quality German Silver Drawing Set, consisting of 5½-in. Ruling Pen with Spring, 3½-inch Steel Spring Bow Divider, 3½-inch Steel Spring Bow Pencil, 3½-inch Steel Spring Bow Pen, 5¾-inch Pivot Joint Dividers, 5-inch Pivot Joint Compass with pen and pencil point, Lengthening Bar for Compass, Box of Leads. The best set ever sold for less than $5.00.
Price, per dozen, $33.40; each.......................$2.90
If by mail, postage extra, 15 cents.

Our $4.20 Pocketbook Set.

No. 55C1638 Fine German Silver Drawing Set, consisting of 5-inch Ruling Pen, 3½-inch Steel Spring Bow Pencil, 3½-inch Steel Spring Bow Pen, 5½-inch Pivot Joint Dividers, 6-inch Pivot Joint Compass with pen and pencil points, Lengthening Bar for Compass, Case of Leads. Contained in a genuine morocco leather folding pocketbook case, lined with plush. This makes a splendid set for either school or college use or home work. Strictly first class quality throughout.

Price, each.......................$ 4.20
Per dozen.......................48.00

If by mail, postage extra, 14 cents.

$4.35 BUYS THIS BIG DRAWING SET.

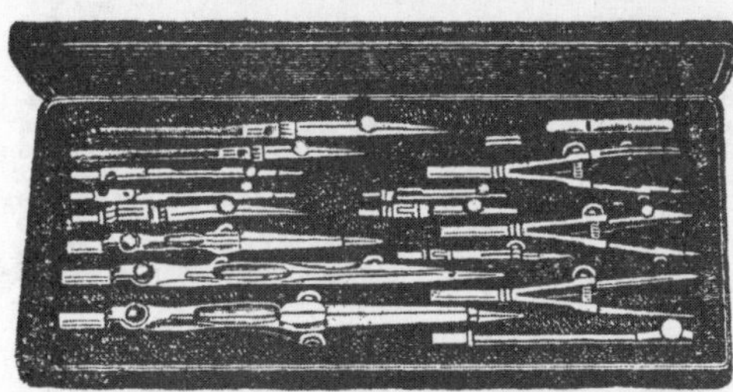

No. 55C1640 Fine German Silver Drawing Set. The instruments contained in this set are the same high grade of German silver and English steel construction as those of set No. 55C1635, but the number of pieces is greater, in fact the set includes everything that would be required for the most advanced work. The set consists of: 5½-inch Plain Dividers, 3¾-inch Compasses with pen and pencil points, Needle Points for 3¾-inch Compasses, 5½-inch Compasses with pen and pencil points, Needle Point for 5½-inch Compasses, 4-inch Ruling Pen with joint, 5½-inch Ruling Pen with joint, 3½-inch Steel Spring Bow Pen, 3½-inch Steel Spring Bow Pencil, 3½-inch Steel Spring Bow Dividers, Lengthening Bar for Compasses, Box of Leads and Key. This very complete set is contained in a fine leather pocket case of the regular style, velvet lined. Price, per dozen, $49.20; each....$4.35

If by mail, postage extra, 22 cents.

WONDERFUL VALUE AT $5.75.

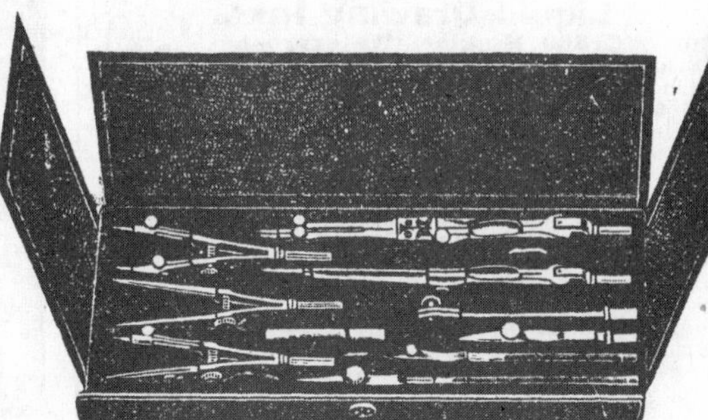

No. 55C1645 Superior German Silver Drawing Set. The instruments of this set are made from the finest grade of hard German silver, carefully tempered and highly finished. The tongues of the joints, needle points and other steel parts are made from the best English steel, finely tempered and hardened. Both the dividers and compasses are made with the **famous pivot joint**, universally accepted by draftsmen as the most desirable joint made. The following instruments are included: 6¼-inch Ruling Pen with spring, 5-inch Ruling Pen with spring, 5-inch Hair Spring Dividers with pivot joint; 5½-inch Compasses, pivot joint, with pen, pencil and needle points; Lengthening Bar for Compasses; 3½-inch Spring Bow Dividers with metal handle; 3½-inch Spring Bow Pencil with metal handle; 3½-inch Spring Bow Pen with metal handle; Box of Leads. **This elegant set is contained** in our new style folding pocketbook case, made of genuine seal grain morocco leather, and lined with silk velvet.

Price, per dozen, $66.25; each....$5.75

If by mail, postage extra, 18 cents.

Extra High Grade Set, $7.85.

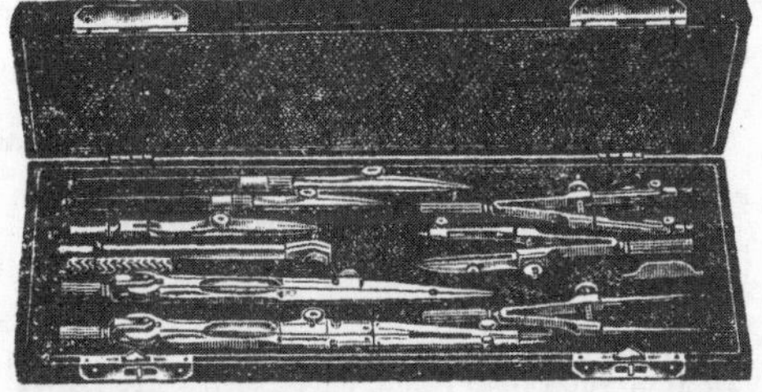

No. 55C1648 This is one of our most popular sets containing the best possible assortment of instruments for mechanical draftsmen. Every instrument in the set is strictly high grade and absolutely guaranteed. The set consists of 5½-inch Ruling Pen, 4½-inch Ruling Pen, 3½-inch Steel Spring Bow Divider, 3½-inch Steel Spring Bow Pen, 3½-inch Steel Spring Bow Pencil, 5¼-inch Pivot Joint Hair Spring Divider with straightening device, 6-inch Pivot Joint Compass set with straightening device and pen and pencil points, Lengthening Bar for Compasses, Case of Leads.

We direct particular attention to the straightening device with which the divider and compasses in this set are equipped. This device is recognized by expert draftsmen as the most marked improvement made in drawing instruments for many years.

This set is contained in a new style hardwood hinged cover pocket case, covered with the best morocco leather and lined with silk velvet.

Price, per dozen, $90.00; each....$7.85

If by mail, postage extra, 18 cents.

High Grade Wrought Metal Set for $8.30.

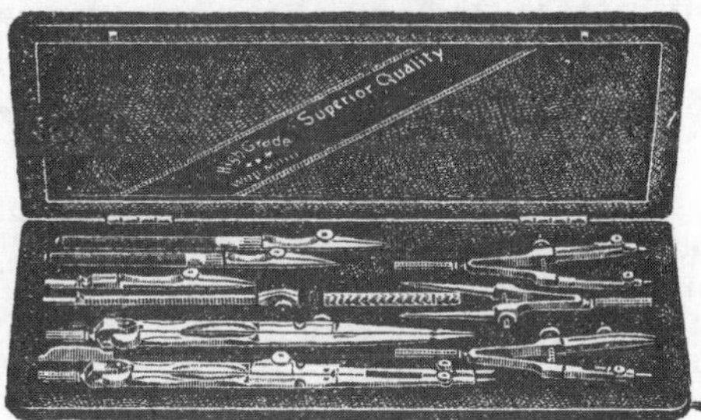

No. 55C1649 Extra High Grade German Silver Wrought Metal Drawing Set, consisting of 5-inch Ruling Pen, 4½-inch Ruling Pen, 3½-inch Steel Spring Bow Divider, 3½-inch Steel Spring Bow Pen, 3½-inch Steel Spring Bow Pencil, 6-inch Pivot Joint Hair Spring Divider with straightening device, 6-inch Pivot Joint Compass with straightening device, pen and pencil points, Lengthening Bar for Compass, Case of Leads.

We guarantee this set to equal in quality any set sold by ordinary dealers at $15.00. It is a set that will meet the requirements in the very best technical schools in this country. This set is put up in the regulation leather covered pocket case, lined with silk velvet.

Price, per dozen, $95.60; each....$8.30

If by mail, postage extra, 20 cents.

Our Special Wrought Metal Set at $9.75.

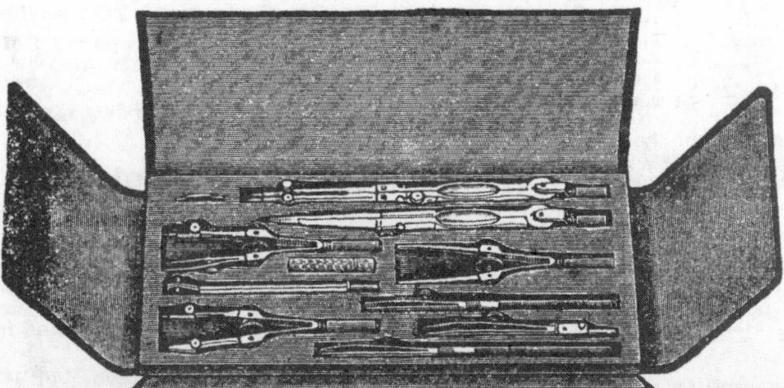

No. 55C1652 Extra High Grade German Silver Drawing Set, consisting of 5-inch Ruling Pen, 4½-inch Ruling Pen, 3½-inch Steel Spring Bow Divider, 3½-inch Steel Spring Bow Pen, 3½-inch Steel Spring Bow Pencil, 6-inch Pivot Joint Hair Spring Divider with straightening device, 6-inch Pivot Joint Compass with straightening device, pen and pencil points, Lengthening Bar for Compass, Case of Leads. We cannot recommend this set too highly. Every instrument is made with the utmost care and guaranteed to be perfect. Workmanship and materials used throughout are the very highest grade, and we know that this set is equal in quality to any set sold regardless of price. This set is put up in the very latest style folding pocketbook case, made with the finest quality morocco leather and lined with brown chamois skin, giving the set an exceptionally rich appearance. It is a case well fitted to contain this exceptionally high grade set of instruments. Price, per dozen, $112.00; each....$9.75

If by mail, postage extra, 20 cents.

$11.25 for This Big Pivot Joint Drawing Set.

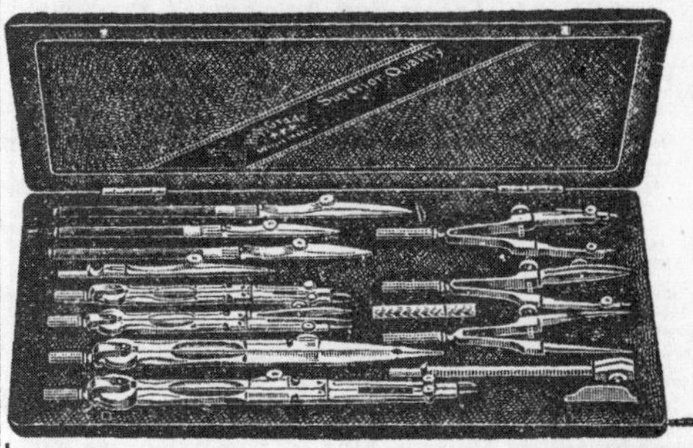

No. 55C1655 This is the largest and most complete set of extra high grade pivot joint German Silver Instruments that we handle and is designed especially to meet the requirements of those who desire not only the very highest grade of instruments, but at the same time the most complete assortment and largest number of pieces. This set consists of 5½-inch Ruling Pen, 5-inch Ruling Pen, 4½-inch Ruling Pen, 3½-inch Steel Spring Bow Divider, 3½-inch Steel Spring Bow Pen, 3½-inch Steel Spring Bow Pencil, 5¾-inch Pivot Joint Hair Spring divider with straightening device, 6-inch Compass set with straightening device and pen and pencil points, 4½-inch Pivot Joint Compass with straightening device, pen point and needle point, 4½-inch Pivot Joint Compass with straightening device, needle point and pencil point, Lengthening Bar for the 6-inch Compass, Case of Leads. The largest set of strictly high grade absolutely guaranteed instruments ever sold for less than $25.00. **This** set is put up in the regulation style morocco covered pocket case, lined with fine quality silk velvet.

Price, per dozen, $129.00; each....$11.25

If by mail, postage extra, 22 cents.

Complete Draughting Outfit at $6.45.

Suitable for correspondence school work and much superior to outfits usually furnished for this work.

No. 55C1666 This complete outfit contains the following items:

1 set of our No. 55C1637 pivot joint instruments, with three bow instruments, compass, divider, pen, etc. See page 370 for description of this set.
1 15x21 Drawing Board.
1 24-inch T Square, mahogany, ebony lined.
1 6-inch German Silver Protractor, engine divided.
1 12-inch Triangular Boxwood Scale.
1 8-inch Transparent Celluloid Triangle, 30x60 degrees.
1 6-inch Transparent Celluloid Triangle, 45 degrees.
1 Hard Rubber Curve.
1 Dozen Brass Thumb Tacks, fine quality.
1 Faber's Pencil, HHHH.
1 Bottle Higgins' Waterproof Ink.
1 Ink and Pencil Eraser.
2 Sheets 16x21 Tracing Cloth.
6 Sheets Whatman's Best Drawing Paper, 15x20.

Price, complete....$6.45

Spring Bow Instruments.

No. 55C1710 Spring Bow Dividers, finely tempered English steel, German silver handle; 3½ inches long. Price....34c

No. 55C1711 Spring Bow Pencil, finely tempered English steel, German silver handle; 3½ inches long. Price....57c

No. 55C1712 Spring Bow Pen, finely tempered English steel, German silver handle; 3½ inches long. Price....57c

No. 55C1713 Spring Bow Set, consisting of instruments Nos. 55C1710, 55C1711 and 55C1712 in fine morocco covered case. Price....$2.18

Protractors.

Used for dividing circles into any number of equal parts and determining angles.

No. 55C1725 Brass Protractor. Diameter 4½-inch half circle, 1 degree graduations, a high grade instrument. Price....22c

If by mail, postage extra, 3 cents.

No. 55C1728 Celluloid Protractor. Transparent, half circle, diameter 6 inches, ½ degree graduations. Price....63c

If by mail, postage extra, 6 cents.

No. 55C1729 German Silver Protractor. Half circle, diameter 5½ inches, ½ degree graduations. Price....45c

Triangular Boxwood Scales.

No. 55C1741 Architects' Triangular Boxwood Scale, divided 1/32, 1/16, 1/8, 1/4, 3/8, 1/2, 3/4, 1, 1 1/2, 3-inch to the foot, 1/16-inch. Best seasoned boxwood, engine divided, U. S. standard; 12 inches long.
Price.......................................38c

No. 55C1742 Architects' Triangular Boxwood Scale, same as No. 55C1741, but with white edges, 12 inches long.
Price.......................................$1.26

No. 55C1746 Engineers' Triangular Boxwood Scale, divided, 10, 20, 30, 40, 50, 60 parts to inch, best seasoned boxwood, engine divided, U. S. standard, 12 inches long.
Price.......................................38c

No. 55C1747 Engineers' Triangular Boxwood Scale, same as No. 55C1746, but with white edges, 12 inches long.
Price.......................................$1.26

Do not judge these scales by the price, we will refund your money if you do not find them equal to the highest priced scales offered by other dealers.

Straight Edges.

No. 55C1755 Straight Edge, made of mahogany, ebony lined, with beveled edge.

Length, inches	24	30	36	42
Price	38c	47c	56c	69c
If by mail, postage extra	4c	6c	10c	12c

Wooden Triangles.

No. 55C1765 Cherry Triangles, 30 by 60 degrees, mortised joints.

Size, inches	7	9	11	14
Price	11c	13c	16c	22c
If by mail, postage extra	3c	4c	5c	6c

No. 55C1768 Cherry Triangles, 45 degrees, mortised joints.

Size, inches	6	8	9	12
Price	11c	13c	17c	22c
If by mail, postage extra	3c	4c	5c	6c

Transparent Celluloid Triangles.

These triangles allow more rapid and accurate work owing to their transparency, do not collect dust, and keep their edges almost like metal tools.

No. 55C1770 Transparent Celluloid Triangles, 30 by 60 degrees, open center.

Size, inches	4	6	8	10	12	14
Price	16c	24c	33c	45c	63c	86c
If by mail, postage extra	2c	3c	4c	5c	6c	8c

No. 55C1772 Transparent Celluloid Triangles, 45 degrees, open center.

Size, inches	4	6	8	10	12	14
Price	24c	33c	48c	63c	$1.14	$1.19
If by mail, postage extra	2c	3c	4c	5c	6c	8c

T Squares.

No. 55C1780 T Square, with cherry blade and fixed head.

Length, inches	15	18	24	30	36	42
Price	12c	15c	17c	21c	25c	29c

Weight of 15, 18, and 24-inch, packed 11, 14 and 26 ounces. Larger sizes not mailable.
For postage rate see page 4.

No. 55C1785 T Square, maple blade and black walnut fixed head.

Length, inches	24	30	36	42	48	54
Price	29c	33c	38c	42c	47c	60c

Weight of 24-inch, packed, 26 ounces. Larger sizes not mailable.
For postage rate see page 4.

No. 55C1790 T Square, cherry blade and movable head, with improved clamping swivel.

Length, inches	24	30	36	42
Price	57c	68c	75c	90c

Weight of 24 inch, packed, 26 ounces. Larger sizes not mailable.
For postage rate see page 4.

No. 55C1792 T Square, mahogany, ebony lined blade and fixed head. A very fine square.

Length, inches	24	30	36	42	48
Price	72c	88c	$1.04	$1.20	$1.40

Weight of 24-inch, packed, 26 ounces. Larger sizes not mailable.
For postage rate see page 4.

Drawing Boards.

No. 55C1800 Drawing Board, made of pine with two drawing surfaces and side ledges.

Size, inches	12x17	15x21	20x24½	23x31
Price	57c	70c	80c	$1.24

No. 55C1805 Drawing Board, made of thoroughly seasoned pine, with hardwood ledges dovetailed into the board to allow contraction and expansion.

Size, inches	20x24½	23x31	31x42
Price	98c	$1.55	$2.55

Thumb Tacks.

No. 55C1820 Steel Thumb Tacks, stamped from one piece of steel. An excellent tack at a very low price. Put up only in boxes of 100.
Diameter, 5/16 inch. Price, per box of 100.......24c
Diameter, 3/8 inch. Price, per box of 100.......30c
Diameter, 1/2 inch. Price, per box of 100.......39c
If by mail, postage extra, per box, 5, 6 and 7 cents.

Brass or German Silver Thumb Tacks.

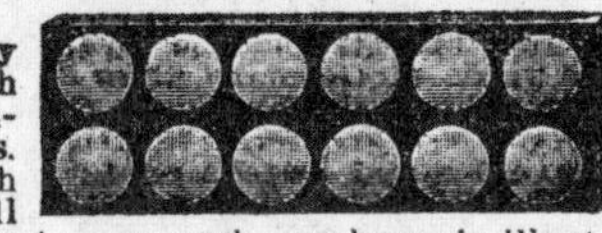

No. 55C1825 First quality Tacks, made with either German silver or brass heads, cannot push through nor pull out. Each dozen put up on cork, as shown in illustration.

Diameter, inch	3/8	1/2	5/8
Brass. Price, per dozen	6c	7c	8c
German silver. Per dozen	9c	10c	11c

If by mail, postage extra, per dozen, 2c.

Irregular Curves.

No. 55C1840 Irregular Curves, accurately made from hard rubber, and invaluable for drawing in irregular curves
Price.......................................27c
If by mail, postage extra, 5 cents.

No. 55C1845 Irregular Curves, same as No. 55C1840 but made of transparent celluloid. Price.......................................39c
If by mail, postage extra, 5 cents.

Liquid Drawing Inks.

No. 55C1860 Higgins' Waterproof Ink, an intensely black liquid India ink, which becomes waterproof when dry, and therefore especially adapted to drawings which have to stand handling, moisture or color washes. Stopper is fitted with quill for filling drawing pen. Weight, packed, 13 ounces.
Price, per dozen, $2.25; per bottle..19c
For postage rate see page 4.

No. 55C1870 Colored Drawing Inks, indelible, put up in same style bottles as No. 55C1860, with quill for filling pen; yellow, orange, scarlet, carmine, blue, green or brown. Weight, packed, 13 ounces.
Price, per bottle.......................................20c
For postage rate see page 4.

India Ink.

No. 55C1875 Lion Head India Ink, first quality black. Small size.......................................9c
Medium size.......................................12c
Large size.......................................21c
If by mail, postage extra, 1 cent.

Hardmuth's Koh-i-Noor Pencils.

No. 55C1890 Hardmuth's Koh-i-Noor Drawing Pencils, six degrees of hardness, designated as 1H, 2H, 3H, 4H, 5H and 6H. 1H is hard, 2H is a degree harder, and so on up to 6H, which is extra hard.
Price, per dozen, 95c; each.......................................9c
If by mail, postage extra, 1 cent.

Crow Quill Pens.

No. 55C1910 Crow Quill Pens, very fine and stiff, put up on cards of one dozen, with hard rubber holder. Genuine Gillott's.
Price, per dozen.......................................48c

No. 55C1911 French Crow Quills.
Price, per dozen.......................................19c
If by mail, postage extra, 5 cents.

Sponge Rubber.

No. 55C1920 Sponge Rubber, extra fine grade, very soft and pure, with solid rubber back. Very useful in cleaning drawings and erasing pencil lines, without disturbing ink lines. Price.........24c
If by mail, postage extra, 3 cents.

Drawing Papers.

No. 55C1950 German Drawing Paper, an excellent white paper, strong, stands pencil erasing well, has slightly grained surface, suitable for work in pencil, ink or color.
Size, 10x13½ inches. Price, per quire (24 sheets) 18c
Size, 13½x20 inches. Price, per quire (24 sheets) 35c

No. 55C1955 Whatman's Drawing Paper, either hot or cold pressed. This paper is hand made from the finest linen stock and is universally conceded by draftsmen to be the finest drawing paper made. The hot pressed has a smooth surface, mostly used for very fine drawing. The cold pressed has a finely grained surface, used for general drawings and water color work.

Size	Price, per quire
13x17 inches	$0.53
15x20 inches	.78
19x24 inches	1.50
22x30 inches	2.60
27x40 inches	4.65

Always specify whether "hot" or "cold" pressed is desired.

No. 55C1960 Cream Drawing Paper, the best paper made for preliminary drawings and sketching. Stands erasing perfectly, and takes pencil, ink, or water color well. The cream tint is agreeable to the eye, and admits of much handling without showing soil. Does not break when folded.
Width, 21 inches. Price, per yard.......9c
Width, 27 inches. Price, per yard.......11c
Width, 36 inches. Price, per yard.......13c
Width, 42 inches. Price, per yard.......18c

Tracing Cloth.

No. 55C1970 Tracing Cloth, fine quality, one side glazed, the other side dull.

Width	Price, per roll of 24 yds.	Per yd.
30 inches	$6.35	28c
36 inches	7.52	33c
42 inches	9.56	42c

Devoe's Prepared Oil Colors.

IN COLLAPSIBLE TUBES.

No. 55C2000 Genuine Devoe Oil Colors for Artists, in collapsible tubes, made by F. W. Devoe & Co. These tube paints are prepared from the most carefully selected pigments, thoroughly incorporated with the purest oil. Although sold at a price much lower than is charged for the imported paints, they are guaranteed to be the very highest grade paints made, equal to any other paints on the market, regardless of price. They are guaranteed to be of that firm consistency and fineness of texture demanded by the most experienced and successful artists. Furnished in the following colors:

Class A Colors.

*American Vermilion, Antwerp Blue, Asphaltum, Bitumen, Blue Black, Bone Brown, Brown Pink, Brown Ochre, Burnt Roman Ochre, Burnt Sienna, Burnt Umber, Caledonian Brown, Cappah Brown, *Carmine Lake, Cremnitz White, Chrome Green, light, Chrome Green, medium, Chrome Green, deep, *Chrome Yellow, lig't, *Chrome Yellow, medium, *Chrome Yellow, deep, Chrome Yellow, Chrome Orange, Cologne Earth, Crimson Lake, Chinese Blue, Emerald Green, Flake White, Gamboge, *Geranium Lake, Ivory Black, Indian Lake, Indian Red, Indigo, Italian Pink, King's Yellow, Light Red, Lamp Black, Magenta, Mauve, Meglip, Mummy, *Naples Yellow, light, *Naples Yellow, medium, *Naples Yellow, deep, Neutral Tint, New Blue, Oxford Ochre, Olive Green, Orpiment, Payne's Gray, Permanent Blue, Purple Lake, Prussian Blue, Raw Sienna, Raw Umber, Roman Ochre, *Rose Lake, *Rose Pink, Sap Green, Scarlet Lake, Silver White, Sugar of Lead, Terre Verte, Transparent G'ld Ochre, Vandyke Brown, Venetian Red, Verdigris, Verona Brown, Yellow Lake, Yellow Ochre, *Zinnober Green, Light, *Zinnober Green, medium, *Zinnober Green deep, Zinc White

The name Devoe on oil colors is an absolute guarantee of quality.
Single Tube size. Price, per dozen, 55c; each.5c
Double Tube size. Price, per dozen, 90c; each.8c

Class B Colors, 13 and 17 Cents.

No. 55C2002 Genuine Devoe Oil Colors, Class B, as follows:
Brown Madder, Chinese Vermilion, French Vermilion, Perfect Yellow, Carnation Lake, Citron Yellow, Green Lake, Ruben's Madder, Cerulean Blue, English Vermilion, Imperial Orange, Sepia

Single Tube size. Price, each.......................13c
Double Tube size. Price, each.......................17c

Class C Colors, 17 and 21 Cents.

No. 55C2003 Genuine Devoe Oil Colors, Class C, as follows:
Carmine, No. 2, Cobalt Blue, Cobalt Green, Emeraude Green, Indian Yellow, Lemon Yellow, Madder Lake, Malachite Green, Oxide of Chromium, Orange Vermilion, Pink Madder, Purple Madder, Rose Dore, Rose Madder, Scarlet Madder, Scarlet Vermilion, Strontian Yellow, Ultramarine, Viridian

Single Tube size. Price, each.......................17c
Double Tube size. Price, each.......................21c

Class D Colors 20 and 26 Cents.

No. 55C2004 Genuine Devoe Oil Colors, Class D, as follows:
Cadmium Lemon, Cadmium Deep, Cadmium Yellow, Cadmium Pale, Cadmium Orange

Single Tube size. Price, each.......................20c
Double Tube size. Price, each.......................26c

Quadruple White Oil Colors at 20 Cents.

No. 55C2012 Devoe's Quadruple Prepared Colors. Flake white, silver white, cremnitz white.
Price, each.......................20c
If by mail, postage and mailing case extra, per tube, 19 cents.

Windsor & Newton Colors.

No. 55C2015 Winsor & Newton Oil Paints. In collapsible tubes. These are the well known imported paints, made in England, and, although more expensive than the American colors, are preferred by many artists. We furnish the Winsor & Newton Paints in all of the colors specified under No. 55C2000, except those marked with a star (*), and in addition the following colors:
Chrome Yellow, Chrome Lemon, Chrome Deep, Cinnabar Green, Light, Cinnabar Green, Medium, Cinnabar Green, Deep, Naples Yellow, French, Naples Yellow

Furnished in single tubes only.
Price, per dozen, 95c; each.......................8c

Devoe's Moist Water Colors.

No. 55C2030 Genuine Devoe's Moist Water Color Paints, in half pans. These water colors are made by F. W. Devoe & Co. Guaranteed in every respect, unexcelled in brilliancy of color, smoothness and permanency. Furnished in the following colors:

Blue, Antwerp	Emerald Green	New Blue
Blue Black	Flake White	Olive Green
Brown Pink	Gamboge	Payne's Gray
Brown Ochre	Hooker's Green No. 1	Prussian Green
Burnt Umber	Hooker's Green No 2.	Prussian Blue
Burnt Sienna	Indian Red	Raw Sienna
Charcoal Gray	Indigo	Raw Umber
Chinese White	Ivory Black	Sap Green
Chrome, Light	Kings' Yellow	Terre Verte
Chrome, Yellow	Lamp Black	Vandyke Brown
Chrome, Deep	Light Red	Venetian Red
Chrome, Orange	Mauve	Vermilion
Cologne Earth	Naples Yellow	Yellow Lake
Dragon's Blood	Neutral Tint	Yellow Ochre

Price, per dozen, **$1.00**; each....................9c
If by mail, postage extra, per dozen pans, 10 cents.

Extra Soft French Pastel Crayons.

Each crayon wrapped in tissue paper.

No. 55C2053 Box containing 44 crayons, assorted colors. Price, per box....................**75c**
No. 55C2055 Box containing 30 crayons, assorted colors. Price, per box....................**40c**
No. 55C2057 Box containing 30 crayons, white or black. Price, per box....................**45c**
No. 55C2061 Box containing 64 crayons, assorted colors. Price, per box....................**$1.65**
No. 55C2063 Box containing 126 crayons, assorted colors. Price, per box....................**$2.85**
Unmailable.

Hard French Pastel Crayons.

No. 55C2067 Box containing 12 sticks, assorted colors. Weight, 4 ounces. Price....................**9c**
No. 55C2072 Box containing 18 sticks, assorted colors. Weight, 5 ounces. Price....................**15c**
No. 55C2074 Box containing 24 sticks, assorted colors. Weight, 6 ounces. Price....................**20c**

Oils, Varnishes, Etc.

Unmailable.
Always include a supply in your express and freight orders.

No. 55C2102 Linseed Oil, purified. Price, 2-ounce bottle....................**11c**
No. 55C2104 Pale Drying Oil. Price, 2-ounce bottle, **14c**
No. 55C2106 Nut Oil. Price, 2-ounce bottle....................**15c**
No. 55C2108 Poppy Oil. Price, 2-ounce bottle....................**14c**
No. 55C2110 Picture Mastic Varnish. Price, 2-ounce bottle....................**23c**
No. 55C2112 Picture Copal Varnish. Price....................**19c**
No. 55C2114 Retouching Varnish. Price, 2-oz. bottle, **19c**
No. 55C2116 French Retouching Varnish. For oil or water color painting. Price....................**20c**
No. 55C2118 Genuine Mastic Varnish. Price....................**33c**
No. 55C2120 White Damar Varnish. Price, 2-oz. bottle, **17c**
No. 55C2122 Siccatif de Harlem. Price, 2-oz. bottle, **25c**
No. 55C2124 Siccatif de Courtry. Price, 2-oz. bottle, **23c**
No. 55C2126 Spirits of Turpentine, rectified. Price, 2-ounce bottle....................**9c**
No. 55C2128 Japan Gold Size. Price, 2-ounce bottle, **18c**
No. 55C2130 Fixatif, for charcoal and crayon drawings. Price, 2-ounce bottles....................**13c**
No. 55C2140 Japanned Tin Atomizer. Price....................**9c**

Japanned Tin Boxes of Oil Colors.

No. 55C2160 Contains 24 single and 1 double tube of oil colors; 6 super bristles, 4 red sable and 2 Bright's bristle artists' brushes; badger blender, No. 4; bottle each pale drying and poppy oils and spirits of turpentine; steel palette knife; palette cup and charcoal. Weight, packed for shipment, 8 pounds. Price....................**$5.50**

The Scholar's Box of Oil Colors, Etc.

No. 55C2165 Polished Wood Box. Size, 11 inches long, 6 inches wide, 2 inches deep. Contains 13 single tubes of prepared artists' oil colors, 1 palette knife, bottles of pale drying oil and spirits of turpentine, sable and bristle artists' brushes, badger blender, palette cup, mahogany palette, tracing and transfer papers, 4 studies and academy board. Weight, packed for shipment, 2¼ pounds. Price....................**$1.15**

Rembrandt Boxes.

No. 55C2180 Our Special Rembrandt Box, contains 12 moist water colors in half pans. Cover arranged as palette. Size, 6½x3 inches. Price....................**20c**
If by mail, postage extra, 8 cents.

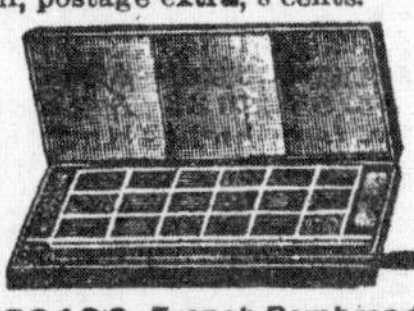

No. 55C2185 Large Size Rembrandt Box, containing 18 moist water colors in half pans, 1 tube Chinese white, 1 tube ochre, 1 brush and directions. Cover arranged as palette. Size, 3¾x7½ inches. Price....................**40c**
If by mail, postage, extra, 12 cents.

No. 55C2190 French Rembrandt Box, containing 12 French moist water colors in half pans and brush. Cover arranged as palette. Size, 8x6¼ inches. Price....................**28c**
If by mail, postage extra, 8 cents.

Murillo Boxes.

No. 55C2195 Murillo Box, containing 12 moist water colors in pans, 1 tube sepia, 1 tube Chinese white and brushes. Cover arranged as palette. Size, 3¼x6½ inches. Price....................**48c**
If by mail, postage extra, 12 cents.

No. 55C2199 Murillo Box, containing 16 moist water colors in pans, 1 tube of sepia, 1 tube Chinese white and brushes. Flap and cover arranged as palette. Size, 3¼x7¾ inches. Price....................**70c**
If by mail, postage extra, 18 cents.

Moist Water Color Outfit.

No. 55C2210 Containing Ten School Moist Water Colors in half pans, together with one No. 7 camel hair brush. Japanned tinned box with removable trays. Size of box, 2x8 inches. Price....................**50c**
If by mail, postage extra, 10 cents.

No. 55C2211 Extra School Moist Water Colors in half pans for use in the above outfit. When ordering, be sure to mention color wanted, whether burnt sienna, charcoal gray, Chinese white, crimson, gamboge, ivory black, light red, new blue, new green, orange, Prussian blue, sepia, violet, vermilion, yellow, ochre and vandyke brown.
Price, each....................**5c**
If by mail, postage extra, 6 cents.

Crayon Outfits.

No. 55C2250 Crayon Outfit. Size, 6¼x9½ inches and 1¾ inches deep; fitted. Containing white, black and red square crayons, sauce crayons, colored crayons, Conte's black crayon pencil, charcoal, paper, leather and rubber stumps, thumb tacks, porte crayon, crayon pointer, bevel rubber, crayon paper and studies. Shipping weight, 2 pounds.
Price....................**$1.75**

No. 55C2255 Palette Crayon Outfit. Size, 5½x6¾ inches, containing square black crayons, velour sauce crayons, leather and paper stumps, tortillon stumps and porte crayon. The box is so arranged that it can be held in the hand and the chamois lined cover used for stumping. Price....................**90c**
If by mail, postage extra, 12 cents.

No. 55C2275 Conte's Square Black Crayon, hard, medium and soft. Weight, 3 ounces. Price..**2c**

French Charcoal.

No. 55C2279 First Quality, 6 inches long, in boxes of 50 sticks. Price, per box....................**15c**
If by mail, postage extra, 5 cents.

No. 55C2281 First Quality, 8 inches long, in boxes of 50 sticks. Price, per box....................**35c**
If by mail, postage extra, 8 cents.

Crayon Holders.

No. 55C2288 Crayon Holders, brass.
Price, 6-inch, 7c; 5-inch, 6c; 4-inch....................**5c**
If by mail, postage extra, 2 cents.

Crayon Sauce.

No. 55C2301 Conte's Crayon Sauce, put up in full packages. Weight, 2 ounces. Price....................**5c**
Per dozen....................**55c**

Stumps.

No. 55C2321 Tortillon Stumps, paper, 12 in a package, white or gray. Price....................**4c**
If by mail, postage extra, 2 cents.

No. 55C2323 Nigrivorine Stumps, rubber.
Small. Price, 2 for....................**5c**
Medium. Price, 2 for....................**9c**
Large. Price, 2 for....................**12c**
If by mail, postage extra, 2 cents.

Prepared Canvas for Oil Painting.

No. 55C2360 First quality, smooth, 30 inches wide. Price, per roll (6 yards), **$3.45**; per yard **$0.62**
36 inches wide. Price, per yard.................... **.68**
Per roll (6 yards).................... **3.95**
Weight, per yard, 2 pounds.

Prepared Smooth Sketching Canvas for Oil Painting.

No. 55C2372 28 inches wide. Price, per yard, **$0.45**
Per roll (6 yards).................... **2.15**
31 inches wide. Price, per yard.................... **.50**
Per roll (6 yards).................... **2.65**
37 inches wide. Price, per yard.................... **.60**
Per roll (6 yards).................... **3.30**
Weight, per yard, 2 pounds.

French Pastel Papers.

No. 55C2390 French Pastel Paper, Royal, 19x25 inches. Price, per dozen sheets, **$1.98**; per sheet **18c**
Super Royal, 22x28 inches. Price, per dozen sheets, **$2.50**; per sheet....................**23c**
Unmailable. Always include a supply in your freight and express orders.

Crayon Papers.

No. 55C2395 French Tinted Crayon Paper, Royal, 19x24 inches,
Price, per quire, 95c; per ½ dozen sheets......**25c**
Super Royal, 22x28 inches.
Price, per quire, $1.30; per ½ dozen sheets......**35c**
Unmailable. Always include a supply in your freight and express orders.

No. 55C2398 French Charcoal Paper. Size 19x25. Price, per quire **50c**; per ½ doz. sheets, **14c**

Academy Board.

No. 55C2400 We furnish this Academy Board in two surfaces, smooth or rough. When surface is not specified, we always send smooth.

Size, 6x 9.	Price, per dozen, $0.28;	each.......3c
Size, 8x12.	Price, per dozen, .52;	each.......5c
Size, 12x18.	Price, per dozen, 1.00;	each.......8c
Size, 18x24.	Price, per dozen, 2.20;	each.......20c
Size, 22x27.	Price, per dozen, 4.25;	each.......35c
Size, 23x30.	Price, per dozen, 5.25;	each.......45c

As it is unprofitable to send academy board by mail, we suggest that you order it in as large quantities as possible when you have a freight or express shipment coming, thus effecting the greatest possible saving.

No. 55C2450 Paper Mache Plaques, round.
Price, 12 inches in diameter, 30c; 8 inches......**17c**

Interchangeable Stretcher Strips.

These strips are double mortised and tenoned, strong and will not warp.

No. 55C2501 Regular width, 1¾ inches. Any length from 6 to 36 inches (in even inches). Price, per dozen....................**56c**
No. 55C2502 Narrow Strips, 1¼ inches wide. Any length, 6 to 12 inches (in even inches).
Price, per dozen....................**36c**
No. 55C2503 Narrow Strips, 1¼ inches wide. Any length, 13 to 18 inches. Price, per dozen..**40c**
No. 55C2504 Narrow Strips, 1¼ inches wide. Any length, 19 to 24 inches. Price, per dozen...**50c**

Miscellaneous.

No. 55C2510 Mahogany Palettes.
Price, 10-inch, oiled, 13c; 9-inch, oiled........**9c**
Price, 10-inch, polished....................**35c**
No. 55C2525 Japanned Palette Cups with cover. Price, double, 15c; single....................**12c**
No. 55C2530 Improved Single Palette Cup, concaved bottom, liquidproof cover. Price........**13c**
No. 55C2535 Wooden Canvas Pins.
Price, per dozen....................**20c**
No. 55C2545 Ebony Handled Palette Knife.
Price, 5-inch, each, 27c; 4-inch, each.......**23c**
Price, 3½-inch, each, 20c; 3-inch, each........**19c**

Artists' Brushes.

These Brushes are made by the leading manufacturer of this class of goods. This guarantees you the best brushes it is possible to produce. At our prices you get the finest at a saving of 50 to 60 per cent.

No. 55C2601 Artists' Red Sable Brushes, for oil painting, photographers, etc., polished handles, round or flat, in the following sizes and prices:

No. 1 Price, 4c	No. 5 Price, 6c	No. 9 Price, 7c
No. 2 Price, 5c	No. 6 Price, 6c	No. 10 Price, 9c
No. 3 Price, 5c	No. 7 Price, 6c	No. 11 Price, 9c
No. 4 Price, 5c	No. 8 Price, 7c	No. 12 Price, 10c

No. 55C2607 Artists' Red Sable Flat "Brights" Brushes, for oil painting, square touching. Polished handles, nickel ferrules, in the following sizes and prices:

No. 1 Price, 6c	No. 4 Price, 12c	No. 7 Price, 17c
No. 2 Price, 8c	No. 5 Price, 14c	No. 8 Price, 18c
No. 3 Price, 10c	No. 6 Price, 16c	No. 9 Price, 22c

No. 55C2609 Artists' Russia Sable Brushes, for oil painting, polished handles, nickel ferrules, round or flat in the following sizes and prices:

No. 1 Price, 4c	No. 3 Price, 5c	No. 5 Price, 6c
No. 2 Price, 4c	No. 4 Price, 5c	No. 6 Price, 6c

No. 55C2612 Red Sable Water Color Brushes, polished handles, nickel ferrules, in the following sizes and prices:

No. 0 Price, 6c	No. 3 Price, 12c	No. 6 Price, 25c
No. 1 Price, 8c	No. 4 Price, 15c	No. 7 Price, 30c
No. 2 Price, 10c	No. 5 Price, 20c	

No. 55C2615 English Bristle Artists' Brushes, super quality, polished handles, in the following sizes and prices:

No. 1 Price, 4c	No. 5 Price, 5c	No. 9 Price, 7c
No. 2 Price, 4c	No. 6 Price, 6c	No. 10 Price, 7c
No. 3 Price, 5c	No. 7 Price, 6c	No. 11 Price, 8c
No. 4 Price, 5c	No. 8 Price, 7c	No. 12 Price, 8c

Any one of the above brushes by mail, postage extra, 3 cents.

Our Favorite Gold Enamel.

No. 55C2703 Decorates anything and everything. It is used on furniture, frames, slippers, shoes, bicycles, baby carriages, baskets, tables, chairs, railing, artificial flowers, albums, statues, bric-a-brac, glasses, bottles, ornamental candles, gas fixtures, ceilings, centerpieces, candlesticks, flower pots, inkstands, clocks, grates, iron bedsteads, sewing machines, earthenware, etc. Can be washed with soap and water.
Small size. Price....................**17c**
Large size. Three times as much as in the small size. Price....................**30c**
If by mail, postage extra, on small size, 12 cents; on large size, 20 cents.

Our Family Gold Enamel.

No. 55C2705 Our Family Gold Enamel, for gilding picture frames, bric-a-brac, earthen and iron ware, and all kinds of ornamental work. Can be washed with soap and water. Absolutely guaranteed.
Small size. Price....................**12c**
Large size. Three times as much as in the small size. Price....................**22c**
If by mail, postage extra on small size, 12c; on large size, 20 cents.

No. 55C2706 Our Family Gold Enamel Outfit, contains six ¼-ounce bottles of powder, five different shades of gold and one of aluminum; also two brushes, two mixing pans and a 2-ounce bottle of mixing liquid. Just the thing for getting different shades on your decorating work.
Price....................**15c**
If by mail, postage extra, 12 cents.

Japanese Gold Paint.

No. 55C2708 For gilding ornamental candles and all kinds of wax work, gilding fancy baskets, frames and every variety of woodwork, gilding metallic ornaments, albums, stationery and all kinds of paper work, etc. Put up in attractive highly polished wooden box with brush. Price....................**15c**
If by mail, postage extra, 5 cents.

Flitters.

No. 55C2725 Bronze Flitters or Leaf Brocades, for sign work. Highest grade flitters made. Used everywhere by professional sign painters and decorators.

Color.	Price, per lb.	Price, per oz.
Pale gold and rich gold	$0.68	6c
Copper and crimson	.72	7c
Blue, orange, fire, green and lemon	.83	8c
Silver and aluminum	1.10	9c

One-half pound lots furnished at pound rates. Less than one-half pound lots at ounce rates only.

No. 55C2730 Best Gold Bronze Powder, for ornamental and decorative purposes. Furnished in three shades, light or rich gold, medium or pale gold and deep gold. Price, per pound, 72c; per ounce, 7c

No. 55C2735 Liquid for Mixing Bronze Powder.

Price, per 4-oz. bottle	Price, per 1-pint can	Price, per 1-quart can	Price, per 1-gallon can	Price, per 5-gallon can
8c	14c	25c	90c	$3.50

No. 55C2736 Banana Liquid for Mixing Bronze Powder; made with wood alcohol. Works better than the common liquid, but owing to disagreeable odor, is generally used only by professional workers. Put up only in one-gallon cans. Price, per gallon..$1.85

Passe-Partout Binding

No. 55C2801 New Pebbled, Gummed Passe-Partout Paper Binding, put up in continuous rolls, 36 feet in length, for binding pictures, embroidered linen frames, mats and prints of all kinds that require protection under glass. Colors, black, white, brown, green, gray, red or blue.

Price, per dozen rolls, 90c; per roll..............8c

If by mail, postage extra, per roll, 3 cents.

No. 55C2802 Passe-Partout Paper Binding, pebbled, gummed, 36 feet to roll. Colors, silver and gold. Price, per dozen, $1.80; per roll..........16c

If by mail, postage extra, per roll, 3 cents.

No. 55C2807 Brass Rings and Metal Fasteners, used for backs of passe-partout frames, put up in envelopes containing 12 rings and 12 fasteners.

Price, for the 12 rings and 12 fasteners...........8c

If by mail, postage extra, 5 cents.

Passe-Partout Hangers.

No. 55C2812 Leaf Shaped Passe-Partout Hangers, with suspension rings.

Packed 25 in box. Price..............................8c
Packed 100 in box. Price...........................25c

If by mail, postage extra, per box of 25, 5 cents; per box of 100, 7 cents.

Passe-Partout Outfits.

No. 55C2817 Passe-Partout Outfit, containing 1 roll of passe-partout binding, 1 tube of paste, 8 cloth hangers, suspension rings, etc., packed in hinged cover boxes. Size, 4x3x1 inches. Weight, packed for shipment, 4 ounces.

Price..........................20c

If by mail, postage extra, 12 cents.

No. 55C2826 Passe-Partout Outfit, containing 6 printed cardboard mats, round and square openings, easel supports, 1 roll of black gummed binding, tube of paste, glass cutter, assortment of hanging devices, and a book of instructions. Put up in telescope covered box. Size, 10¼x7⅛x1 inches. Weight, packed for shipment, 12 ounces.

Price..............45c

If by mail, postage extra, 25 cents.

No. 55C2831 Passe-Partout Outfit, containing 12 tinted cardboard mats, round and oval openings with mounts and easel, 8 rolls of binding, assorted colors, 1 tube of paste, 1 tube of glue, 1 glass cutter, instruction book and an assortment of devices for hanging pictures, etc. Put up in telescope case box. Size, 10x12 inches. Weight, packed for shipment, 2½ pounds. Price.......................................89c

If by mail, postage extra, 55 cents.

Surveyors' Compasses with Levels.

No. 55C3001 Surveyors' Compass with folding hooked sights, fine English bar needle, jewel mounted, with sliding stop, full circle divisions engraved on silvered metal dial, raised to level of needle.

This Compass is fitted with two spirit levels, greatly increasing the accuracy and efficiency. Length of needle, 2¼ inches. Price complete, including Jacob staff mounting with ball and socket joint, as shown in the illustration $8.40

If by mail, postage extra, 28 cents.

No. 55C3003 Surveyors' Compass, same as No. 55C3001, but larger. Length of needle, 3 inches.

Price, complete..............................$9.45

If by mail, postage extra, 35 cents.

Surveyors' Vernier Compasses. $13.95 and $15.95.

No. 55C3011 Surveyors' Vernier Compass. Best English make, finest materials and workmanship throughout, bronze finish. Made with two very sensitive spirit levels for accurate adjustment. **A fine vernier for close readings. Best agate mounted English bar needle and set screw stop.** The full circle divisions are engraved on a silvered metal dial raised to level of needle. **Length of needle, 3½ inches.** Shipping weight, 4 pounds. Price, complete, including ball and socket joint mounting suitable for either Jacob staff or tripod.............$13.95

No. 55C3012 Surveyor's Vernier Compass, same as No. 55C3011, but larger. **Length of needle, 4⅛ inches.** Shipping weight, 5 pounds.

Price, complete...................................$15.95

NOTE—Tripods are not included at above prices. See No. 55C3033 for prices on suitable tripods.

Extra High Grade Vernier Compass at $32.40.

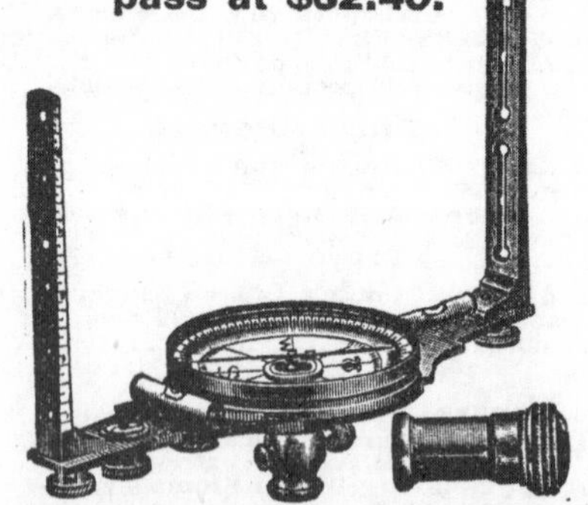

No. 55C3021 This Surveyor's Vernier Compass is an extra high grade instrument, made throughout in the most careful and accurate manner, the very best compass on the market at any price.

The sights, which are detachable, are very firm and rigid, and graduated for taking angles of elevation and depression.

The vernier for adding or subtracting magnetic variations of the needle is placed under the glass. **Two straight levels,** very sensitive, are provided for adjustment, and the entire construction throughout is very heavy and substantial, highly finished and accurately adjusted.

The Needle is 5 inches long, made of special magnetic steel, swung on a jeweled center, and very sensitive.

This Compass is put up in a substantial, finely finished mahogany box with lock and carrying strap. Shipping weight, 25 pounds.

Price, without tripod.............................$32.40

Jacob Staff Mountings with ball and socket joint, extra...$1.50

NOTE—If compass is to be used with tripod the Jacob Staff mountings will not be needed.

See No. 55C3036 for prices on suitable tripod.

Compass Tripods and Jacob Staffs.

No. 55C3030 Jacob Staff, a straight, hardwood stick with metal shoe and tapered top, suitable for any of the compasses previously described. Price.................75c

No. 55C3033 Compass Tripod, light weight, good quality, suitable only for compasses Nos. 55C3011 and 55C3012. Price............$3.90

No. 55C3036 Compass Tripod, extra quality, heavy, made especially for compass No. 55C3021.

Price.........................$4.60

55C3033 55C3036

Architects' Level $44.75.

No. 55C3049 This level exactly meets the requirements of architects, builders, millwrights, engineers, surveyors or others engaged in construction, sanitary work, drainage, road leveling, etc. This level is provided with an extra high grade perfectly achromatic telescope, 12 inches long, magnifying power 20 diameters, fitted with fine crosshairs, and adjustable eyepiece for precise focusing of the crosshairs. With this telescope a leveling rod can be read at a distance of 600 feet. The instrument revolves upon a horizontal circle 3⅝ inches in diameter, graduated from 0 to 90 each way and is read to 5 minutes by vernier fixed to spindle. The level, ground absolutely true, with very sensitive bubble, is graduated and securely mounted under the telescope. We furnish this level complete with metal trivet, substantial tripod, fine hardwood box with lock and strap. Shipping weight, 22 pounds. Price, complete.................$44.75

Vernier Transit Compass, $69.00.

No. 55C3057 This Transit is an ideal instrument for county surveyors or others who want to do good land surveying, but do not care to invest the large amount usually charged for a transit. This instrument is provided with a very substantial leveling arrangement, with two straight levels, a powerful telescope 8 inches long, with fine crosshairs and rack and pinion focus movement. The compass is 6¼ inches in diameter, with variation plate inside the circle. Length of needle, 5¼ inches. Provided with clamp and tangent screw to center. This instrument is no heavier than an ordinary compass, the weight without tripod being only 8 pounds. We include with this instrument a **good tripod,** plumb bob, shade, adjusting pin, screwdriver, magnifying glass and substantial mahogany box with lock and carrying strap. Shipping weight, 28 pounds. Price, complete...............$69.00

No. 55C3058 Vernier Transit Compass, same as No. 55C3057, but with level and clamp to telescope, making instrument available for regular leveling work. Price, complete...............$82.00

Chesterman Chains.

No. 55C3101 Iron Chain, made of best iron wire, with two oval rings between links, brass swivel handles, brass tallies.

Length	Price
Length, 2 poles.	Price....$1.60
Length, 4 poles.	Price.... 2.50
Length, 50 feet.	Price.... 1.80
Length, 100 feet.	Price.... 2.75

No. 55C3103 Steel Chain, made of best cast steel wire, hardened, tempered and polished, two oval rings between links, brass swivel handles and brass tallies.

Length	2 poles	4 poles	50 feet	100 feet
Price	$2.45	$4.50	$2.65	$5.00

No. 55C3105 Brazed Steel Chain, same as No. 55C3103, but with all joints brazed, making a solid chain. **The best chain made.**

Length	2 poles	4 poles	50 feet	100 feet
Price	$4.00	$7.50	$4.25	$7.75

NOTE—The 2-pole and 4-pole chains are divided into links and tallied every 10th link. The 50-foot and 100-foot chains are divided into feet and tallied every 10 feet.

Arrows or Marking Rings.

No. 55C3109 Arrows or Marking Pins, iron, 15 inches long, in sets of eleven. Per set....55c

No. 55C3110 Arrows or Marking Pins, steel, best grade, 15 inches long, in sets of eleven.

Price, per set...85c

Leveling Rods and Poles.

No. 55C3131 Philadelphia Rod, heavy, hardwood, divided into feet and 10ths, vernier reading to 100ths, with target, vernier and clamp. 7 feet long, sliding out to 13 feet. Price...........................$9.90

No. 55C3133 Architects' Rod, hardwood, divided into feet, inches and ⅛ inches; with target, vernier and clamp. 5⅝ feet long, sliding out to 10 feet.

Price...$5.10

No. 55C3145 Ranging Pole, best seasoned wood; octagonal, painted red and white, alternating every foot.

Price, 6 feet..$1.70
Price, 8 feet.. 1.92
Price, 10 feet.. 2.12

Drainage Level, $23.90.

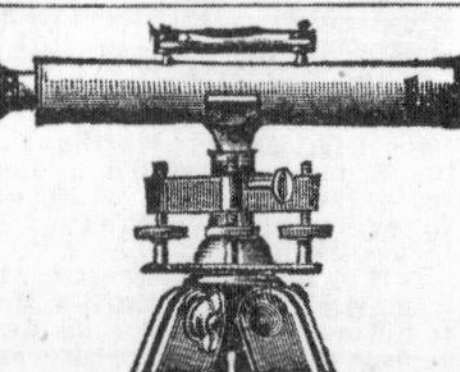

No. 55C3046 This is a thoroughly practical, accurately constructed level, designed especially for the use of farmers and ditchers. As shown in the illustration this level is provided with tripod and leveling head, by means of which the instrument can be perfectly leveled up and kept so when revolved. **The telescope is a powerful, high grade, achromatic instrument,** 8½ inches long and made with fixed crosshairs inside which cannot get out of adjustment. With this telescope a leveling rod can be read at a distance of 500 feet. The telescope carries a carefully ground spirit level, adjustable by two nuts and so sensitive that a difference of ⅛ of an inch in 100 feet can be easily determined. The entire instrument is constructed of bronze metal, finely finished, with the best workmanship throughout.

Price, complete with tripod and box ....$23.90 Shipping weight, 12 pounds.

GRAPHOPHONE DEPARTMENT.

OUR $5.00 GRAPHOPHONE TALKING MACHINE.

THIS IS A GENUINE TYPE A Q COLUMBIA GRAPHOPHONE, made by the Columbia Phonograph Co., of New York and London, and uses the regular Columbia Phonograph Co.'s standard size wax cylinder records.

THIS GRAPHOPHONE, as shown in the illustration, is one of the latest 1905 styles, made with clockwork spring motor enclosed in a dustproof metal barrel. It is provided with a speed regulator and leveling screw and has a high grade governor for maintaining a

UNIFORM SPEED,

just the same as furnished with the highest grade talking machines.

A NEW AND IMPROVED FEED SCREW DEVICE carries the reproducer along over the surface of the record, holding it firmly in place and preventing it from slipping or injuring the record.

THE LARGE SIZE ALUMINUM REPRODUCER, made with mica diaphragm, is securely attached to the 10-inch japanned amplifying horn, and will reproduce standard size wax cylinder records with the most wonderful clearness and fidelity. Uses any standard size wax cylinder records.

No. 21C102 Price, complete, without records.......................$5.00

AQ GRAPHOPHONE AND SIX COLUMBIA RECORDS $5.90

No. 21C103 When sorting out our enormous stock of standard size genuine Columbia records to make up into collections of twelve, twenty-five and fifty, as explained on page 382, we made up a large quantity into collections of six, little assortments of extra nice records, and we now offer the A Q Graphophone, as shown above, together with one of these extra good collections of six records, for only $5.90, thus presenting an exceptional opportunity for you to get a complete outfit for very little money.

Remember, the outfit is complete, the A Q Graphophone and six genuine Columbia records, all different. Price..................................$5.90

THE COLUMBIA TYPE Q GRAPHOPHONE AT $7.50.

THIS IS THE COLUMBIA PHONOGRAPH CO.'S GENUINE TYPE Q MACHINE, one of the most perfectly constructed talking machines ever placed on the market for so low a price.

$7.50

THIS MACHINE will run the regular standard size wax cylinder records just as perfectly as the higher priced machines and it is especially well suited for home entertainment purposes.

THE CAREFULLY CONSTRUCTED SPRING MOTOR which operates this graphophone is encased in a dustproof barrel, and the high grade governor, with latest style speed regulator, insures perfect uniformity of speed.

THE REPRODUCER, made with best mica diaphragm and sapphire reproducing point, is detachable and reproduces the musical and talking records as perfectly as many machines costing two and three times as much. We particularly recommend this graphophone to anyone desiring a strictly high grade instrument for home amusement at a very moderate price. We call your special attention to the possibility of making up a very moderate priced graphophone outfit by purchasing this little machine and an assortment of twelve, twenty-five or fifty of the Columbia Phonograph Co.'s records, which we are now selling in lots of 50 at 15 cents each, as explained on page 382.

No. 21C110 Type Q Graphophone, complete with 10-inch japanned horn and high grade aluminum reproducer, but without records.
Price..$7.50

RECORDS MUST BE PURCHASED EXTRA, and this machine will use either the XP records, illustrated and described on pages 380 and 381, or the Columbia records, which we are now offering, while they last, in lots of 50 at 15 cents each, as explained on page 382.

A LARGE AMPLIFYING HORN makes a wonderful difference in the effect produced with a graphophone. By attaching a large amplifying horn to a graphophone, you increase its efficiency 50 per cent. If you buy either the $7.50, $8.60 or $20.00 graphophone, we would suggest in addition that you order an amplifying horn, of which we give a selection on page 378. You can hardly appreciate what a difference in the volume of sound an amplifying horn produces until you have made the trial. It is the cheapest way of making a high grade graphophone out of a cheap machine.

RECORDS AT 15 CENTS.

At 15 cents each, in lots of 50, we sell

Genuine Columbia Standard Size Wax Cylinder Records

suitable for use with any graphophone described on this page. For full information regarding this

GREAT RECORD SALE SEE PAGE 382.

$8.60 BUYS OUR SPECIAL HOME TALKING MACHINE.

THIS BEAUTIFULLY FINISHED and thoroughly practicable home entertainment graphophone is made expressly for us by the Columbia Phonograph Co., of New York and London, and we offer it to our customers as a talking machine which is more brilliant in its reproduction and in every way better than any other low priced machine on the market today.

$8.60

CAREFULLY MADE THROUGHOUT, with powerful clockwork spring motor, perfectly adjusted governor for maintaining an absolutely uniform speed of reproduction, and high grade aluminum reproducer with French diaphragm glass.

THE HEAVILY NICKEL PLATED and highly ornamental base and the large 14-inch aluminum amplifying horn, finished in the natural silvery color of aluminum, make this machine in every respect a little beauty, a machine that will brighten the home, entertain yourself, your family and your friends and keep you in touch with the best and latest music of the finest bands and orchestras and the most celebrated public singers. Uses standard size wax cylinder records.

No. 21C115 The Home Graphophone, complete with nickel plated ornamental metal base, 14-inch aluminum amplifying horn and reproducer, just as shown in our illustration, but without records. $8.60

As a machine for home amusement or parlor entertainment, where a low priced graphophone is desired, there is no talking machine that will answer the purpose better or give better satisfaction than this, our special $8.60 Home Talking Machine. In the first place, it is a strictly high grade machine, well made, perfectly constructed, with all improvements, and with the 14-inch aluminum amplifying horn which is included, gives a wonderful volume of sound. In the second place, it is a very handsome machine, and will prove an ornament as well as a source of entertainment in any home.

When you consider that you can buy 50 different records and selections, the very best musical and talking records, for only $7.50, 15 cents each in lots of 50, and when you can get a full sized, substantial, perfectly operating graphophone from $5.00 up, there seems to be no reason why everyone should not take advantage of these offerings.

See page 382 for our wonderful offer on the regular Columbia records.

THE TYPE AT COLUMBIA GRAPHOPHONE FOR $20.00

RUNS STANDARD SIZE WAX CYLINDER RECORDS.

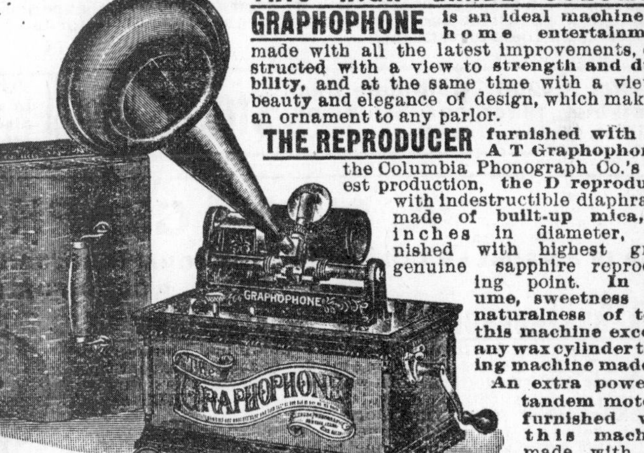

THIS HIGH GRADE COLUMBIA GRAPHOPHONE is an ideal machine for home entertainment, made with all the latest improvements, constructed with a view to strength and durability, and at the same time with a view to beauty and elegance of design, which makes it an ornament to any parlor.

THE REPRODUCER furnished with this A T Graphophone is the Columbia Phonograph Co.'s latest production, the D reproducer, with indestructible diaphragm, made of built-up mica, 1¼ inches in diameter, furnished with highest grade genuine sapphire reproducing point. In volume, sweetness and naturalness of tone, this machine exceeds any wax cylinder talking machine made.

An extra powerful tandem motor is furnished with this machine, made with the most perfect governor and speed regulating device, insuring perfect reproduction, and it runs five records with one winding. The cabinet is constructed from solid quarter sawed oak, of elegant design and beautifully finished.

YOU CAN MAKE YOUR OWN RECORDS with this machine, as we furnish with each one the latest improved recorder, and half the pleasure in owning a graphophone is derived from record making. Successful record making cannot be accomplished without a machine that is as perfect in its operation as a watch, and this graphophone fulfills all requirements.

With this A T Columbia Graphophone you have an additional opportunity for entertainment and instruction, for the reason that you can make your own records. You can put on a blank record and have any one sing or talk into the machine, and then keep this record indefinitely and reproduce it as often as you care to. Just think of preserving the voices of each and every one in the family, and what a pleasure it would be to listen to these voices and reproduce these records in after years.

If you are willing to invest as much as $20.00 in a graphophone, we especially recommend the purchase of this machine. It is a strictly high grade graphophone, beautifully built in a handsome, solid quarter sawed oak cabinet, with a beautiful bent oak cover to protect it from dust and dirt when the machine is not in use. All of the operating parts are thoroughly protected, the machine throughout is built extra strong and durable and runs five records with one winding. With each machine we include a D reproducer, the latest improved recorder for making records, and a 14-inch aluminum horn, exactly as illustrated.

No. 21C120 Columbia A T Graphophone, complete with D reproducer, recorder and 14-inch aluminum horn, but without records.
Price..$20.00

For list of XP records suitable for this machine see pages 380 and 381.
For price of blank records see No. 21C875, page 378.

$8.75 BUYS THE HARVARD DISC TALKING MACHINE.

THIS TALKING MACHINE uses the wonderful disc records, the most marvelously realistic reproductions of sound ever made. This machine is strictly high grade in every respect, made from the very best materials, constructed in the most careful, accurate and substantial manner, exactly the same machine that is being sold today by other dealers for $15.00, and never before sold for less than $15.00. **THIS DISC TALKING MACHINE** is made with extra powerful clockwork spring motor, made with machine cut bevels and gears, and an improved form of governor, insuring an absolutely uniform rate of speed. **THE MECHANISM** is entirely enclosed within the case in such a way that it is perfectly protected from dust or injury and will require practically no attention whatever. **THE CABINET** is strongly and substantially constructed from solid oak made in a very handsome design and finely finished.

THE SOUND BOX, also known as the reproducer, is of an improved type, made with the latest mica diaphragm, producing a volume of sound combined with a fullness and roundness of tone which is a revelation to those accustomed to the ordinary wax cylinder talking machines. This talking machine uses **THE NEW PROCESS DISC RECORDS, THE GREATEST IMPROVEMENT IN RECORD MAKING SINCE THE INVENTION OF TALKING MACHINES.**

THE DISC RECORDS ARE LOUDER AND CLEARER, and the reproduction is more perfect and more absolutely true to the original sound than has ever before been produced by any process. Those who have been accustomed to hearing the ordinary talking machine and the ordinary wax cylinder records will be astounded when listening for the first time to the latest new process disc records as used by this and our other disc machine.

FOR PUBLIC EXHIBITION WORK the disc machine is the only machine that should ever be used, as it is the only talking machine which reproduces the human voice, bands, orchestras and other instrumental music with sufficient volume, musical quality and absolutely perfect fidelity. **THIS TALKING MACHINE WITH THE NEW PROCESS HARVARD OR COLUMBIA DISC RECORDS MUST BE HEARD TO BE APPRECIATED.** It is impossible for anyone not having heard these wonderful machines to appreciate in any way the marvelous results which they give.

No. 21C207 Harvard Disc Talking Machine, complete, as shown in illustration, with 16-inch japanned horn, improved sound box and 100 needles. Price.... .... **$8.75**

THE HARVARD TALKING MACHINE USES THE 7-INCH HARVARD RECORDS, 7-INCH OR 10-INCH COLUMBIA RECORDS, OR ANY OTHER MAKE OF 7-INCH OR 10-INCH DISC RECORDS.

COMPLETE PUBLIC EXHIBITION OUTFIT FOR $18.25.

REALIZING THE SUPERIORITY of the disc machine over all other types of talking machines and realizing also that the disc machine is the only talking machine suitable for public exhibition work, no other machine being sufficiently loud, clear and perfect in its reproduction of musical sounds, we recommend that for public exhibition work a disc machine be used in all cases. At $18.25 we furnish a complete public exhibition outfit, an outfit which we know from practical experience in this line of work will meet all requirements for the public exhibitor and prove a profitable business investment.

THIS COMPLETE PUBLIC EXHIBITION TALKING MACHINE OUTFIT AT $18.25 includes everything necessary for public exhibition work, and consists of the following items: One improved Harvard Disc Talking Machine, the same as shown in the above illustration and described under No. 21C207; Twenty-four Genuine Harvard Improved 7-inch Disc Records, your own selection, see page 379. Five Hundred Posters, large size; One Thousand Admission Tickets; One Fine Rubber Printing Outfit with movable type, for filling in dates, etc.

No. 21C208 Complete Disc Talking Machine Exhibition Outfit. Price....... .... **$18.25**

YOU CAN MAKE BIG MONEY with one of these outfits, giving entertainments in churches, school houses, concert halls, etc. It is so loud and clear that it is also suitable for outdoor use and will prove a profitable venture at picnics and other out of door gatherings.

A $12.00 GRAPHOPHONE FOR $8.40.

THIS IS A REGULAR COLUMBIA PHONOGRAPH CO.'S HIGH GRADE $12.00 GRAPHOPHONE NEVER BEFORE SOLD BY ANY DEALER IN THE WORLD FOR LESS THAN $12.00. OUR PRICE, $8.40

THIS GRAPHOPHONE IS THE REGULAR TYPE B X, exactly the same as furnished by the Columbia Phonograph Co., and by all dealers in talking machines at $12.00, except that instead of the little 10-inch horn which all other dealers furnish with this machine at $12.00 we furnish a **LARGE CONCERT SIZE,** 26-inch Japanned Amplifying Horn with 12-inch bell and folding japanned horn stand, this horn and stand alone being sold by other dealers at from $1.00 to $2.00.

THIS COLUMBIA PHONOGRAPH CO.'S BX GRAPHOPHONE is an exceedingly handsome machine, thoroughly well made in every respect and perfectly finished. The operating power is furnished by a powerful spring motor guaranteed not to get out of order. **THE GEARS AND PINIONS** are all machine cut, thus insuring perfect accuracy of action. **THE GOVERNOR AND TENSION SCREW** effectively maintain the speed at an absolutely uniform rate. **LARGE SIZE REPRODUCER** extra loud, made from aluminum, with sapphire reproducing point and latest improved mica diaphragm.

THIS GRAPHOPHONE is substantially mounted on a handsome oak base with highly finished bent oak cover with handle, thus forming in itself a convenient and effective carrying case for the machine.

$8.40
GRAPHOPHONE
THIS B X
GRAPHOPHONE
AND
50 RECORDS
$14.95

NO BETTER, HANDSOMER OR MORE DURABLE talking machine was ever before offered by any dealer for less than $12.00, and our special price of $8.40 represents the very lowest price at which a strictly high grade first quality reliable talking machine has ever been sold.

No. 21C216 Columbia Phonograph Co.'s B X Graphophone, complete with aluminum reproducer, mammoth 26-inch amplifying horn and folding horn stand. Price...... **$8.40**

No. 21C217 COMPLETE B X GRAPHOPHONE OUTFIT, consisting of Columbia B X Graphophone with 26-inch Amplifying Horn, japanned stand, large aluminum reproducer, just as shown in illustration and 50 genuine Columbia standard size wax cylinder records, as illustrated and described on page 382. Shipping weight, 48 pounds.
Price for the entire outfit, all complete........................ **$14.95**

THE A K DISC GRAPHOPHONE

THIS MACHINE IS ONE OF THE COLUMBIA PHONOGRAPH CO.'S

VERY LATEST PRODUCTIONS

$15.00

EMBODYING ALL OF THE FEATURES OF THE HIGHEST GRADE TALKING MACHINES AND YET SOLD AT A MODERATE PRICE.

IT IS MADE with extra powerful clockwork spring motor and contained in a fine oak cabinet of very handsome design.

THE SOUND BOX OR REPRODUCER is the very latest type concert style with improved knife edge bearings, heavy mica diaphragm, and is absolutely the highest grade sound box furnished with any talking machine, regardless of price.

THE ORNAMENTAL HORN SUPPORTING ARMS, which are detachable, are of very handsome design and made of aluminum, this metal being most perfectly adapted for this purpose.

THE BLACK AND GOLD HORN is the highest grade horn made for Disc Talking Machines, the body of this horn being made from fine sheet steel with black oxidized finish and the bell of polished brass, giving it a very ornamental appearance.

EITHER THE 7-INCH OR 10-INCH RECORDS MAY BE USED WITH THIS MACHINE, AND ON PAGES 383 AND 384 WE GIVE A VERY COMPLETE LIST OF SELECTIONS WHICH WE CAN FURNISH IN THESE MARVELOUS DISC RECORDS.

No. 21C230 The Columbia Phonograph Co.'s Type A K Disc Graphophone, complete with latest improved knife edge reproducer, 16-inch black and gold horn and 100 needles........ **$15.00**

No. 21C231 Type A K Columbia Disc Graphophone, equipped with 22-inch black and gold horn, otherwise same as described above. Price.. **18.50**

THE A J DISC GRAPHOPHONE

AT **$20.00**

THE TYPE **A J DISC GRAPHOPHONE** IS MADE WITH DETACHABLE CABINET TOP, THUS GIVING EASY ACCESS TO THE MOTOR FOR THE PURPOSE OF OILING OR CLEANING. : : :

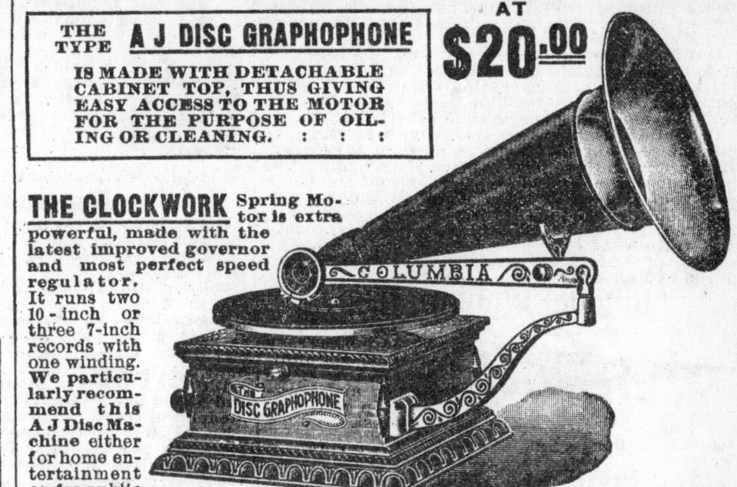

THE CLOCKWORK Spring Motor is extra powerful, made with the latest improved governor and most perfect speed regulator. It runs two 10-inch or three 7-inch records with one winding. We particularly recommend this A J Disc Machine either for home entertainment or for public exhibition work, as it has proven the most popular talking machine we have ever handled.

THIS DISC GRAPHOPHONE similar to the type A K described opposite, is a somewhat larger machine with a larger, heavier and more handsomely designed cabinet made from solid quarter sawed oak.

THE SOUND BOX OR REPRODUCER is the latest knife edge style, extra large size, made with mica diaphragm, and is the very highest grade sound box furnished with any talking machine, regardless of price.

The Wonderful Disc Records, the records which have created a sensation wherever heard, and made it possible to say that the talking machine has at last been perfected, are used with this machine.

SEE PAGES 383 AND 384 FOR SELECTIONS. EITHER 7-INCH OR 10-INCH CAN BE USED.

No. 21C240 The Columbia Phonograph Co.'s Type A J Disc Graphophone, complete with knife edge reproducer, 16-in. black and gold horn with polished brass bell and 100 needles. **$20.00**

No. 21C241 Type A J Columbia Disc Graphophone, same as described above, except that cabinet is more elaborate and more highly finished, making the machine very ornamental. Price.. **$22.50**

No. 21C242 Type A J Columbia Disc Graphophone, same as described under No. 21C241, but equipped with large 22-inch black and gold horn. Price.......................... **25.00**

THE A H DISC GRAPHOPHONE FOR $30.00

THE TYPE A H DISC GRAPHOPHONE IS THE VERY HIGHEST GRADE AUTOMATIC TALKING MACHINE MADE BY THE COLUMBIA PHONOGRAPH CO., and represents the highest degree of perfection yet attained in the making of talking machines.

THE CABINET IS EXTRA LARGE AND HEAVY

OF A VERY HANDSOME AND ORNAMENTAL DESIGN, made from solid quarter sawed oak, and very finely finished throughout.

THE SOUND BOX IS THE VERY LATEST IMPROVED KNIFE EDGE PATTERN, extra large, with heavy mica diaphragm, the most perfect reproducer yet constructed.

THIS GRAPHOPHONE

RUNS EITHER THE 7 OR 10-INCH DISC RECORDS,

A COMPLETE LIST OF WHICH YOU WILL FIND ON PAGES 383 AND 384.

THE POWERFUL DOUBLE SPRING MOTOR

WITH SPECIAL GOVERNOR AND IMPROVED SPEED REGULATOR

IS EASILY ACCESSIBLE FOR CLEANING AND OILING, AND RUNS THREE 10-INCH RECORDS, OR FIVE 7-INCH RECORDS WITH ONE WINDING.

The motor is absolutely noiseless. The only disc machine motor made which operates entirely without sound.

IF YOU WANT A TALKING MACHINE

WHICH WILL CREATE A SENSATION IN YOUR LOCALITY : : : :

A Machine Which People Will Come Miles to Hear, Order This A H Machine and a Selection of 10-inch Records. . . . .

THE FINE BLACK AND GOLD HORN is of extra large size, being 22 inches long, with 11½-inch bell, the body of this horn being constructed from the finest quality sheet steel, oxidized in black, and the bell is made of extra heavy polished brass. This type of horn greatly improves the quality and sweetness of tone.

No. 21C250 The Columbia Phonograph Co.'s Type A H Graphophone, complete with the latest improved knife edge sound box, 22-inch black and gold horn and 100 needles. Price.. **$30.00**

No. 21C251 Type A H Columbia Disc Graphophone, same as described above, but with extra large black and gold horn, 30 inches long, with 16½ inch bell. Price.. **40.00**

No. 21C252 Type A H Columbia Disc Graphophone, same as described above, but with extra large 36-inch aluminum horn. Price.. **45.00**

AMPLIFYING HORNS.

SOLID BRASS OR BLACK AND GOLD.

A large amplifying horn adds wonderfully to the volume of sound, improves the tone quality greatly and in every way increases the efficiency of any style of talking machine.

Our black and gold horns are made with sheet steel bodies, oxidized in black, and burnished brass bells, giving them an exceedingly handsome appearance, and the use of steel for the body enables us to sell them cheaper than the solid brass horns.

Our solid brass horns are made from brass throughout, the very finest horns it is possible to produce. In our opinion there is very little, if any, difference in the quality of reproduction or tone of the black and gold and solid brass horns, although many users consider the tone of the brass horn superior to the black and gold. **The volume of sound, purity and fullness of tone** is very largely influenced by the size of the bell, the very finest effects being produced by horns having the widest bells.

Regular Width Horns.

No. 21C350 These horns have bells of the ordinary width. The quality and workmanship are the very best.

Length, inches	Width of Bell, inches	Price, Solid Brass	Price, Black and Gold
18	7⅜	$0.63	$0.60
30	13¾	1.54	1.26
36	16⅛	2.73	2.38
42	16¾	3.50	3.15
48	20½	5.46	4.90
56	20½	6.44	5.60

Wide Horns.

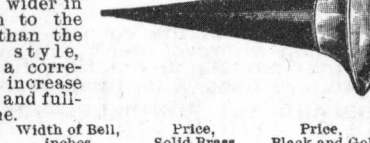

No. 21C365 These wide bell horns have bells which are wider in proportion to the length than the preceding style, and give a corresponding increase in volume and fullness of tone.

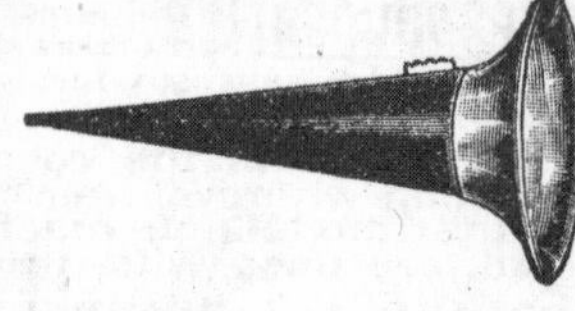

Length, inches	Width of Bell, inches	Price, Solid Brass	Price, Black and Gold
24	13¾	$1.40	$1.23
30	16⅛	2.10	1.75
36	20½	4.41	3.99
42	20¼	4.90	4.55
56	23¾	9.10	8.04

Extra Wide Flaring Horns.

No. 21C380 These extra wide flaring horns are the largest and finest horns made, regardless of price. In volume of sound and fullness of tone they are not equaled by any other horns made.

Length inches	Width of Bell inches	Price, Solid Brass	Price, Black and Gold
30	20⅛	$ 4.20	$ 3.85
42	23¾	8.54	7.35
56	28	13.30	12.25

Any of our horns can be used with either wax cylinder or disc machines of any make. A horn stand, as described below, is necessary with any of the above horns.

Folding Horn Stands.

No. 21C540 Horn Stand, black japanned, folds into small space, suitable for 30-inch and smaller horns. Price....35c

No. 21C542 Imperial Horn Stand, a handsome and efficient folding stand, finely made throughout and nickel plated; adapted to any size horn up to 42-inch. Price....82c

No. 21C544 No. 1 Horn Stand, our best stand, extra strong and heavy; adapted to any size horn, including the largest 48-inch and 56-inch; nickel plated; folds very compactly. Price....$1.40

Cases for Records.

No. 21C560 Record Boxes, for standard size wax cylinder records. Made of strong pasteboard, covered with imitation leather, affording a convenient means of keeping the records safe and easily accessible.

No. 1 size, holds 12 records. Price....23c
No. 2 size, holds 24 records. Price....40c

No. 21C565 Carrying Cases for Standard Size Wax Cylinder Records, black seal grain covering, with improved pegs for records, full nickeled trimmings, two snap locks and lock and key. Best record cases made.

No. 1, holds 24 standard size records. Price..$2.00
No. 2, holds 36 standard size records. Price.. 2.25
No. 3, holds 72 standard size records. Price.. 3.40

Disc Record Cases.

No. 21C570 Disc Record Cases, strongly and substantially made from wood, covered with black seal grain imitation leather, nickel plated trimmings, two snap catches, lock and key and leather handle. Provided with numbered separators and numbered blank on inside of cover for list of selections, so any desired record may be instantly found.

No. 1, holds 50 7-inch disc records. Price....$1.35
No. 2, holds 50 10-inch disc records. Price.... 1.55

Miscellaneous.

No. 21C585 Recorder, for Q, QC, QQ, or our special Home Graphophone. Price....$2.50

No. 21C590 Recorder, for BX, AT, AO, or Gem Graphophone....$5.00

No. 21C595 Reproducer, for Q, QC, QQ, or our special Home Graphophone. Price....$2.50

No. 21C599 Reproducer, Style D, for any wax cylinder graphophone **except** Q, QC, QQ and our special Home, latest improved style, extra large, with built up mica diaphragm. Price....$5.00

SPECIAL OFFER: Send us your old reproducer and $3.00 in cash and we will send you this latest model improved "D" Reproducer.

No. 21C625 Diaphragm Glasses, best French glass. Price, per dozen, 30c; each....4c

No. 21C628 Mica Diaphragms, for "D" reproducers only, best quality, built up. Price, each ..19c

No. 21C632 Mica Diaphragms, for sound boxes of any style Disc Graphophone. Price, each....10c

No. 21C640 Rubber Gaskets, for reproducers or recorders. Price, per set of three, ordinary size...5c
Per set of two, for large "D" reproducer....4c

No. 21C650 Reproducer Ball, made of Brazilian pebble, but sold by many dealers as sapphire. Price, each....20c

No. 21C651 Reproducer Ball, made of genuine sapphire, highest grade. Price, each....75c

MISCELLANEOUS—Continued.

No. 21C660 Recorder Points, made of Brazilian pebble, but often sold as sapphire.
Price, each, in setting, flat edge....52c
Price, each, in setting, cupped edge....60c

No. 21C661 Recorder Points genuine sapphire, highest grade made.
Price, each, in setting, flat edge....$1.10
Price, each, in setting, cupped edge.... 1.80

No. 21C670 Main Spring, single, for Q, QC, QQ, BX, AB and our special Home Graphophones.
Price, each....21c
State kind of Graphophone for which spring is wanted.

No. 21C672 Main Spring, single, for AT, AK, AJ and our $8.75 Disc Graphophones.
Price, each....55c

No. 21C674 Main Spring, single, for AH Graphophones. Price, each....60c

No. 21C800 Speaking Tube, for use in record making, mohair covered, with spiral spring, lining and hard rubber mouthpiece; 22 inches long. Price 75c

No. 21C830 Camel's Hair Brushes, 1½ inches wide, for dusting records. Price, each....15c

No. 21C850 Needle Box, two parts, for used and unused needles. Price, each....15c

No. 21C875 Blank Cylinders, for record making. Standard size, same as P or XP records.
Price, each....15c

Needles at 4 Cents per 100.

No. 21C900 These Needles, for disc talking machines of any make, are made from cold drawn, oil tempered steel wire, and guaranteed to be the finest needles manufactured. Put up in envelopes of 100 each. Price, per 100....4c
If by mail, postage extra, 2 cents
Per 1,000....37c
If by mail, postage extra, 8 cents.

No. 21C920 Rubber Hose, large size, for connecting large horns to any style talking machine.
Price, per foot....16c

No. 21C930 Rubber Hose, small size, for hearing tubes, etc. Price, per foot....3c

NEW RECORDS EXCHANGED FOR OLD ONES

7-INCH COLUMBIA DISC RECORDS AT 25 CENTS (IN EXCHANGE)	10-INCH COLUMBIA DISC RECORDS AT 50 CENTS (IN EXCHANGE)

OUR NEW RECORD EXCHANGE PROPOSITION

ENABLES YOU TO KEEP UP YOUR ASSORTMENT OF RECORDS AT

ONE-HALF REGULAR COST

How to Get Genuine Columbia, Latest Improved, Brand New, 7-Inch Disc Records for 25 Cents Each.

For each new 7-inch Columbia record that you desire, send us one old or worn 7-inch record of either Columbia or Victor make and 25 cents in cash. In exchange for your old record and 25 cents we will send you one new 7-inch Columbia disc record, your own selection.

Remember, one old record and 25 cents cash buys one new record. Twelve old records and $3.00 cash buys twelve new records, and so on in the same way for any desired quantity, large or small.

How to Get Genuine Columbia, Latest Improved, Brand New, 10-Inch Disc Records for 50 Cents Each.

For each new 10-inch Columbia record that you desire, send us one old or worn 10-inch record of either Columbia or Victor make, and 50 cents in cash. In exchange for your old record, and 50 cents, we will send you one new 10-inch Columbia disc record, your own selection.

Remember, one old record and 50 cents cash buy one new record. Two old records and $1.00 in cash buys two new records. Twelve old records and $6.0 cash, buys twelve new records, and so on in the same way for any desired quantity, large or small.

CONDITIONS OF THIS OFFER.

THIS EXCHANGE PROPOSITION makes it possible for you to keep up your supply with the latest, up to date, improved disc records, at just **one-half the regular** cost, but each and every exchange must be subject to the following rules and regulations:

1st. Each exchange must be complete in itself, and the worn records must reach us in good order. (They may be worn, but they must not be broken.)

2nd. The old records must be sent to us, CHARGES PREPAID.

3rd. We cannot receive any old records to be credited against future purchases, but the exchange must be complete and the transaction closed at the time the records are sent.

4th. We cannot make a cash allowance for old records under any circumstances. We accept old records only in accordance with the above proposition as part payment for an equal number of new records.

AS AN EXAMPLE: Suppose you have on hand twenty-four 10-inch disc records, either Columbia or Victor make, which have been used until they are no longer clear and satisfactory, send us these twenty-four old, worn records and $12.00 in cash (50 cents for each record), and we will send you in exchange twenty-four new Columbia 10-inch records, your own selection of subjects.

WHEN SENDING YOUR RECORDS TO US FOR EXCHANGE, be sure to pack them very securely, because we cannot allow credit for any records received broken. Be sure to put your name and address on the outside of the package (don't forget this) and mark the package, "Old records for exchange." If you send the old records to us by express, you can enclose your letter (telling us what records you want in exchange) with the package of records. But if you send your old records to us by mail, do **not** put your letter in the package; send your letter separately; just put your own name and address on the outside of the package. Don't fail to prepay all charges (express or postage) on records returned to us.

Be sure to put your name and address on the package and prepay the charges.

This proposition does not apply to the Harvard disc records. We cannot make any exchange proposition on Harvard disc records, owing to the exceedingly low price at which we sell them.

REMEMBER, we accept only Columbia disc or Victor records in part payment for new records as explained above.

ON XP OR OTHER WAX CYLINDER RECORDS WE DO NOT MAKE ANY EXCHANGE PROPOSITION. We cannot allow any credit whatever for wax cylinder records of any kind.

GENUINE HARVARD DISC RECORDS.

30c EACH
$3.50 Per Dozen.

THE LOUDEST, THE SMOOTHEST, THE CLEAREST, THE SWEETEST, THE MOST NATURAL RECORDS MADE. CAN BE USED ON ANY STYLE OF DISC TALKING MACHINE.

WHILE WE SELL THE HARVARD DISC RECORDS at only 30 cents each, or $3.50 per dozen, the lowest price ever made for high class, up to date disc records, **IT IS THE QUALITY OF THESE RECORDS** rather than the price to which we wish to direct your particular attention.

THE HARVARD DISC RECORDS are, without any exception whatever, the very best disc records on the market today. They are the very latest, most up to date and most perfect talking machine records made.

IN THE PRODUCTION OF THESE RECORDS, we have been able to utilize the very latest discoveries, the very latest improvements and the greatest possible skill and experience in record making. They are made for us in one of the largest and most perfectly equipped talking machine factories in the world.

MANY OF THE STANDARD DISC RECORDS today on the market, are made from "masters" which were produced as much as two and three years ago. During the past two or three years great improvements have been made in record making, and the reason that the Harvard records surpass in quality many of the regular fifty cent and one dollar records on the market today, is largely due to the fact that every one of the "masters" from which the Harvard records are made has been produced since the first of September this year, thus enabling the makers of these records to take advantage of the very latest and most up to date improvements.

N MUSICAL QUALITY, naturalness of tone and volume of sound, the Harvard disc records are not surpassed by any records on the market, regardless of make or price.

AS STRICTLY HIGH GRADE first quality records of this size have never before been sold for less than 50 cents each, we know that many people will question the quality of the Harvard records because we sell them at 30 cents each, and we wish to particularly impress upon the minds of our customers the fact that our Harvard records are the very best records it is possible to make.

THE COST OF MANUFACTURING these records is just as much, and in some instances more, than the cost of manufacturing the 50-cent records, and it is only by reason of the fact that we control the output of these records and handle them upon our regular one small percentage of profit plan that we are able to make this special price of

30 CENTS EACH, OR $3.50 PER DOZEN.

EVERY ORDER WHICH WE RECEIVE for the Harvard Disc Records is accepted and filled with the distinct understanding and agreement that the records may be carefully tested upon any style of disc talking machine, and if not found entirely satisfactory in every respect, equal or superior to records sold at 50 cents and $1.00 each, they may be returned to us, at our expense, and the money paid for them, including all transportation charges, will be refunded.

We can furnish the following selections in the Harvard disc records. Give both name and number of selection wanted and order Harvard disc records No. 21C1080.

No. 21C1080 Harvard 7-inch Disc Records. Price, per dozen, **$3.50**; each........30c

BAND.

3928 "An Arkansas Husking Bee."
3406 "At a Georgia Camp Meeting."
1372 "Cavalleria Rusticana."
3322 "Columbia Phonograph Company March."
3325 "Dancing in the Dark." Song and dance with clogs.
3361 "Dixie."
3372 "Dream on the Ocean." Waltz.
3479 "Forge in the Forest." With bells, cock crow and anvil effects.
3418 "Hands Across the Sea." March. Sousa.
3427 "In the Village Tavern." Song and dance with clogs.
3628 "Jolly Coppersmith, The." With bell effect and anvil chorus.
1587 "Jack Tar March." Sousa
3478 "Liberty Bell March." Sousa
3495 "Love's Dreamland Waltz"
3240 "Mendelsohn's Wedding March."
3639 "McKinley Memorial." Introducing President McKinley's last speech and "Lead Kindly Light," by brass quartette.
3522 "Mr. Thomas Cat." March Comique. Trombone imitations.
3507 "Marching Through Georgia."
379 "Mosquito Parade, The." A Jersey Review
3526 "Nearer, My God, to Thee."
1009 "Paderewski's Famous Minuet."
3553 "Stars and Stripes Forever." March. Sousa.
3555 "Star Spangled Banner."
3972 "Stradella Overture."
3564 "Till We Meet Again." Waltz.

ORCHESTRA.

3592 "Bugler's Dream." Introducing "Just Before the Battle, Mother," bugle calls, etc., and ending with "Nearer, My God, to Thee."
3595 "Circus Galop." Clown tells new jokes; applause, snapping of whip, etc.
3330 "Creole Bells."
31431 "Dixie Land March."
3596 "Dancing in the Kitchen." Song and dance with clogs.
3600 "Darkie Tickle." Plantation medley, with clogs, shouts, etc.
3602 "Down on the Suwanee River." Pulling in the gang plank, steamboat bells, whistle, dance on board, with negro shouts and clogs.
337 "Go 'Way Back and Sit Down."
309 "Husking Bee." Introducing rural characters and scenes, with country dance and calls in dialect.
608 "Happy Days in Dixie." Plantation medley, with clogs, shouts, etc.
29 "He Laid Away a Suit of Gray to Wear the Union Blue."
155 "Hiawatha."
3616 "Kentucky Jubilee Singers." Plantation medley, with clogs, shouts, etc.
1571 "Laughing Water."
3243 "Night Alarm." With all the familiar descriptive effects, representing a fire alarm at night, fire bells, cries, horses' hoofs, winding of hose reel, whistling of engine, ending with firemen's chorus.
3637 "Over the Wave Waltz." String orchestra.
31555 "Peaceful Henry."
31043 "Prince of Pilsen."
31111 "Spring Blossom Gavotte."
1689 "Uncle Sammy March and Two-Step."
1679 "Winona Two-Step." A wigwam wooing.

CLARIONET SOLOS.

398 "Intermezzo." Cavalleria Rusticana.

BANJO SOLOS.
By Vess L. Ossman.

3461 "A Coon Band Contest."
3465 "Creole Belles."
3292 "Medley of Coon Songs."
3463 "Medley." Introducing "When Mr. Shakespeare Comes to Town," and "Go 'Way Back and Sit Down."

VIOLIN SOLOS.

3212 "Schubert's Serenade."
3216 "Then You'll Remember Me."
3217 Waltz from "Faust."

PICCOLO SOLOS.
By George Schwenfest.

3498 "Ragtime Skedaddle.."

CHIMES.

3438 "Nearer, My God, to Thee."
3446 "Lead, Kindly Light."

BUGLE CALLS.

3638 "Bugle Calls of the Rough Riders in Their Charge up San Juan Hill."
3640 "Bugle Calls of the United States Army."

MINSTRELS.
With Orchestra and Quartette Chorus.

3641 "Coon, Coon, Coon."
333 "Dese Bones Shall Rise Again."
3642 "Hear Dem Bells."
3798 "I've a Longing in My Heart for You, Louise."
3805 "My Old Kentucky Home."
3804 "Old Folks at Home."
3644 "The Laughing Song."
3645 "The Old Log Cabin."

VOCAL QUARTETTE.
Male Voices.

3511 "Carry Me Back to Old Virginia."
3456 "Coon Wedding in Southern Georgia, A."
3451 "Dixie Land."
3455 "Farm Yard Medley." With farm yard fowl and animal imitations.
3453 "Hymns and Prayers from the Funeral Service over President McKinley."
3753 "I'se Gwine Back to Dixie."
3512 "My Old Kentucky Home."
3518 "Nearer, My God, to Thee."
3458 "Night Trip to Buffalo." Descriptive of things that might happen in a sleeping car.
3512 "Old Oaken Bucket, The."
3450 "Sleigh Ride Party, The." A descriptive record with good singing, sleigh bell effect and comedy by everybody.
3520 "Soldier's Farewell."
3514 "Tenting Tonight on the Old Camp Ground."
3457 "Trip to the County Fair, A." Imitations of railway, fakirs and Reubens.
3714 Way Down Yonder in the Corn Field."

VOCAL DUETS.

3789 "Coon, Coon, Coon." (Comic duet.) Baritone and tenor.
3257 "Girl I Loved in Sunny Tennessee, The." Baritone and tenor.
3597 "I Got Mine." Baritone and tenor.
3792 "I Never Trouble Trouble until Trouble Troubles Me." Baritone and tenor.
3258 "In the Shadow of the Pines." Baritone and tenor.
3262 "Just as the Sun Went Down." Baritone and tenor.
3259 "Mid the Green Fields of Virginia." Baritone and tenor.
39,0 "Under the Bamboo Tree." (Very popular.) Baritone and tenor.
3261 "While the Leaves Came Drifting Down." Baritone and tenor.
3790 "Whoa! Bill." (Comic Rube duet.) Baritone and tenor.

VOCAL TRIOS.

3649 "Camp Meeting." Opening with chorus by trio, followed by a negro sermon and ending with song by trio.
3652 "In Front of the Old Cabin Door." Old man, negro character, clog dance, whistling chorus by trio.
3653 "The Mocking Bird Medley." Tenor solo; whistling chorus by trio.

WHISTLING SOLOS.
By Joe Belmont.

3215 "The Mocking Bird."
3213 "The Whig-poor-will Song."

YODLE SONG.

3589 "Snyder, Does Your Mother Know You're Out."

VOCAL SOLOS.
With Church Organ Accompaniment.

3397 "Nearer, My God to Thee."

VOCAL SOLOS.
With Piano Accompaniment.

3221 "Absence Makes the Heart Grow Fonder." Tenor.
3378 "Ain't Dat a Shame." (Coon song.) Baritone.
3346 "Any Old Place I Can Hang My Hat is Home, Sweet Home to Me." Baritone.
3405 "Carrie Nation in Kansas." (With axe effect). Baritone
3113 "Good Bye, Dolly Gray." Tenor.
3381 "Good Morning, Carrie." Baritone.
3377 "Go 'Way Back and Sit Down." (Comic.) Baritone
3230 "Hello, Central! Give Me Heaven." Tenor.
31579 "Hiawatha." Baritone.
31406 "Hiawatha." Tenor.
3326 "He Laid Away a Suit of Gray to Wear the Union Blue."
3149 "Holy City, The." Baritone.
344 "Home, Sweet Home." Baritone.
3324 "I Can't Tell Why I Love You, But I Do." Tenor.
3357 "I'll Be With You When the Roses Bloom Again." Tenor.
31014 "In the City of Sighs and Tears." Baritone.
355 "In the House of Too Much Trouble." Tenor.
3940 "In the Good Old Summer Time." Baritone.
31650 "I'm Wearing My Heart Away for You." Baritone.
386 "Just Because She Made Dem Goo Goo Eyes." (Coon song.) Tenor.
3320 "My Old Kentucky Home." Tenor.
3571 "Way Down Yonder in the Corn Field." (Coon song.) Baritone.
353 "When the Harvest Days are Over." Tenor.
3558 "When You Were Sweet Sixteen." Baritone.
3199 "Where is My Wandering Boy Tonight?" Tenor.
3403 "Where the Sweet Magnolias Bloom." Baritone.

LAUGHING SONGS.

3210 "Negro Laughing Song." By George W. Johnson.
322 "I'm Old, but I'm Awfully Tough." Rube song, by Mr. Cal Stewart.
3105 "And Then I Laughed." Rube song, by Mr. Cal Stewart.

SONG WITH WHISTLING CHORUS.
By George W. Johnson.

3211 "The Whistling Coon."

GERMAN SONG.
By Emil Muench.

3108 "Die Wacht Am Rhein."

UNCLE JOSH WEATHERBY'S LAUGHING STORIES.
By Cal Stewart.

370 "Arrival in New York, Uncle Josh's."
31518 "Automobile, Uncle Josh on a."
371 "Base Ball Game, Uncle Josh at a."
372 "Bicycle, Uncle Josh on a."
368 "Department Store, Uncle Josh in a."
374 "Lightning Rod Agent, Uncle Josh and a."
376 "Troubles in a Hotel, Uncle Josh's."
31409 "Street Car, Uncle Josh in a."

TALKING RECORDS.
By H. C. Spencer.

319 "Husking Bee." Giving a correct imitation of a New England dance on the barn floor, with the fiddle playing appropriate music; figures called.
321 "The Arkansas Traveler." Descriptive of a native sitting in front of his hut, scraping a fiddle, and answering the interruptions of a stranger with witty sallies.
323 "Schultz on Kissing." Dutch dialect.
334 "Stump Speech on Love."
335 "A Negro Sermon."
3398 "Backyard Conversation Between Two Irish Washerwomen." Full of real comedy and back talk.
3833 "Address by the Late President McKinley at the Pan-American Exposition."
3662 "Vaudeville Selection." Imitation of the Irish comedian, John Kernell, Frank Mayo in "David Crocket," and Miss May Irwin singing a coon song.
3160 "Lincoln's Speech at Gettysburg."

TALKING.
By Len Spencer.

3664 "The Twenty-third Psalm and the Lord's Prayer."
3884 "Blazing Rag Concert Hall." Introducing a bouncer, a tipsy soubrette, a professor and a fight.
3887 "The Dog Fight."

No. 21C1080 Harvard 7-inch Disc Records. Price, per dozen, **$3.50**; each........30c

Give both numbers and names wanted and specify **Harvard 7-inch Disc Records.** These records can be used on any kind of disc talking machine.

COLUMBIA XP "GOLD-MOULDED" RECORDS

REDUCED TO 25c EACH OR $3.00 PER DOZEN.

THESE ARE THE GENUINE COLUMBIA HIGH SPEED EXTRA LOUD GOLD-MOULDED RECORDS; THE GENUINE GOLD-MOULDED RECORDS AS WIDELY ADVERTISED BY THE COLUMBIA PHONOGRAPH CO.

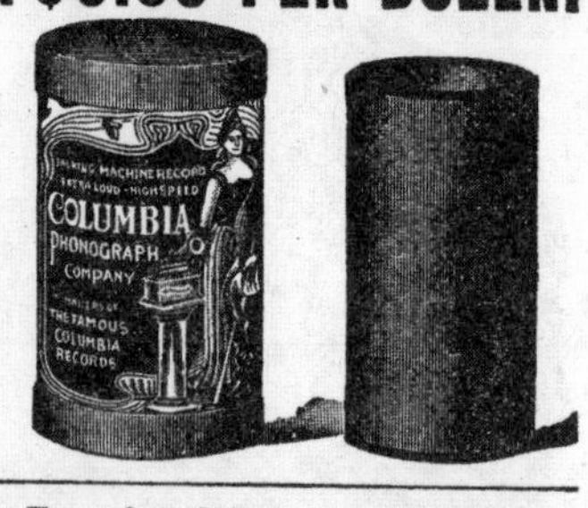

FOR VOLUME OF SOUND, SMOOTHNESS AND SWEETNESS OF TONE, these records are vastly superior to any wax cylinder records ever produced under earlier methods. Made by an entirely new process, whereby the records are moulded from a permanent gold master record, insuring absolute uniformity of product, each record being exactly like every other record from the same mould. As compared with other wax cylinder records, these new moulded XP records show a wonderful improvement in volume, in brilliancy and musical quality, and absolute freedom from harsh, grating sounds. A harder wax is used in making these moulded records than was possible when records were made by the old process of duplication, hence much greater wearing capacity.

CAN BE USED IN ANY GRAPHOPHONE OR PHONOGRAPH USING STANDARD SIZE WAX CYLINDER RECORDS.

Cornet Solos.

32021 Columbia Polka
32491 Marriage Bells (with chimes effect)
31861 Nearer, My God, to Thee
32030 Sweet Sixteen Waltz

Cornet Duets.

3807 Home, Sweet Home
3814 'Mid the Green Fields of Virginia
3813 My Old Kentucky Home
3812 Nearer, My God, to Thee
3815 She Was Bred In Old Kentucky

Records by Sousa's Band.

32311 Anona (intermezzo two-step) by Mabel McKinley
32389 Bedelia, medley march (introducing "He Was a Sailor")
533 Bride Elect March, The
32413 By the Sycamore Tree (medley)
509 Circus Galop (descriptive)
538 Coon Band Contest
529 Dancing in the Dark (song and dance with clogs)
518 Directorate March
32274 Dixie Girl
514 El Capitan March
31781 Hail to the Bride March
31483 Hail to the Spirit of Liberty March
535 Hands Across the Sea March
501 High School Cadets March
526 Honeymoon March
31762 Imperial Edward Coronation March
507 Jolly Coppersmith (descriptive)
506 King Cotton March
500 Liberty Bell March (bell effect)
537 Man Behind the Gun March
519 Manhattan Beach March
32362 Any Rags (schottische)
521 Off to Camp March
32322 Parsifal (prelude to opera)
516 Say Au Revoir, But Not Good-Bye
530 Semper Fidelis March
532 Stars and Stripes Forever March
32275 Sunburst (a novelty)
520 Washington Post March

Records by Gilmore's Band.

1544 Admiral's Favorite March
1514 America
31652 American Eagle March
1541 American Republic March
31529 American Students' Waltz
32155 Amoureuse Waltz (a dreamy favorite)
1582 Anvil Chorus (with anvil effect)
31867 Arkansaw Husking Bee, An
1553 Artists' Life Waltz
1505 "Bohemian Girl," Selections from
1572 Boston Commandery March
31530 Bunch of Blackberries (cake walk)
1593 "Cavalleria Rusticana," Intermezzo
1637 Charge of the Light Brigade March
31486 Colored Major, The (ragtime march)
1550 Columbia Phonograph Co. March
1518 Die Wacht Am Rhein
1516 Dixie
32154 Down South (American sketch with clog dances—a winner)
1508 El Miserere, from "Il Trovatore"
1510 "Faust," Selections from
31644 First Brigade March
31775 In a Cozy Corner
1642 International Cake Walk
1580 In the Village Tavern (song and dance, with clogs)
1579 Irish Airs, Medley of
32297 Jack Tar March (Sousa's latest, introducing sailor's hornpipe, eight bells, boatswain's whistle)
31841 "King Dodo," Selections from
1526 La Marseillaise
31625 Love's Dreamland Waltz
1638 Marching Through Georgia
31888 Mill in the Forest, The
31808 Morning, Noon and Night Overture
31643 Mosquito Parade
1509 My Pretty Peggy (with cornet solo)
1522 Nearer, My God, to Thee (with cornet solo)
31543 Queen's Trumpeters (cornet duet)
1539 Rock of Ages
32187 Rocked in the Cradle of the Deep (with saxhorn solo)
31526 Sousa's Band's Coming (descriptive patrol)
31626 Spring and Love Waltz
1512 Star Spangled Banner
32156 "Sultan of Sulu," Selections from
1523 "Tannhauser," Grand March from
1560 Then You'll Remember Me, from "Bohemian Girl"
1563 Thunderer March
1588 Till We Meet Again Waltz
1564 Under the Double Eagle March
1561 Vacant Chair, The (with trombone solo)
31417 Warm Reception, A
1524 "William Tell," Overture to

Records By the Columbia Orchestra.

Every musician in this great orchestra has been selected with special reference to the creation of an organization representing the highest achievement in the art.

32393 Always in the Way
15132 Angels' Serenade (piccolo and cornet duet)
32380 Babes in Toyland, (selections from the musical extravaganza)
15194 Battle of Manila (descriptive)
15065 Belle of New York March
31648 Birds and the Brook, The
15162 Blue Danube Waltz
15206 Bugler's Dream, The (descriptive—introducing "Just Before the Battle, Mother," Bugle Calls, etc., and ending with "Nearer, My God, to Thee")
15191 Capture of Santiago (descriptive—The Bugle Call, Fall In, March, Opening of the Battle, In the Thick of the Fight, Caring for the Wounded, Cease Firing, The Battle Won, Patriotic Music)
31862 Chinese Honeymoon, (medley march)
15141 Circus Galop (descriptive—clown tells new joke, applause, snapping of whip, etc.)
31668 Creole Belle
32302 Cumming's Indian Congress at Coney Island (a very realistic descriptive selection, introducing Indian yells, sham battle, etc.)
32445 Dance of the Song Birds (with bird imitations)
15010 Dancing in the Kitchen (song and dance with clogs)
15025 Dancing on the Housetops (song and dance with clogs)
15145 Darky's Dream (with clogs)
15159 Darky Tickle (plantation medley, with clogs, shouts, etc.)
15229 Dewey's Return (descriptive, with steamboat whistles, cheers, etc. Music, "See The Conquering Hero Comes")
32191 Dixieland March, introducing "Dixie" and "Old Black Joe"
15064 Down on the Suwanee River (descriptive —pulling in the gang plank, steamboat bells, whistle, dance on board, with negro shouts and clogs)
31525 Echoes of the Forest (descriptive)
15117 "El Capitan," Lanciers from Opera (with figures called)
32337 "Erminie" (selections from)
15114 Flora Waltz (cornet solo, with full orchestra accompaniment)
15030 Forge in the Forest, The (descriptive—with cock crow, anvil, etc.)
15202 Georgia Camp Meeting, At a (march and two-step)
32460 Gondolier (intermezzo two-step, the latest popular success)
15007 Happy Days in Dixie (plantation medley, with clogs, shouts, etc.)
15216 Hello, My Baby
32092 Hiawatha (a summer idyl)
15142 Husking Bee (descriptive, introducing rural characters and scenes, with country dance and call in dialect)
15210 I Guess I'll Have to Telegraph My Baby (cake walk)
31868 I Have Grown So Used to You (with xylophone solo)
15039 Jolly Coppersmith (descriptive—with bell effect and vocal chorus)
15151 Jolly Fellows Waltz
15028 Kentucky Jubilee Singers (plantation medley with clogs, shouts, etc.)
32283 Laughing Water
15121 Let Her Rip (quadrille, with figures called)
32303 Levee Scene (introducing darky songs, plantation melodies, pickaninny band, etc.)
15139 Limited Express, The (descriptive)
32321 Lucky Duck, A (a web foot promenade)
32467 Maple Leaf Forever
31869 "Messenger Boy, The," March (with xylophone solo)
15063 Night Alarm (with all the familiar descriptive effects, representing a fire alarm at night—fire bells, cries, horses' hoofs, winding of hose reel, whistle of engine, ending with firemen's chorus)
15014 Nightingale and the Frog, The (with piccolo solo)
32263 Peaceful Henry (a slow drag)
15171 Popular Airs, Medley of
31876 Queen of the Blue Grass March
15004 Rastus on Parade (plantation medley, with clogs, shouts, etc.)
15205 Return of the Troops (descriptive—drum solo and fife effect, cheers, etc. "When Johnny Comes Marching Home")
15195 Roosevelt's Rough Riders, Charge of
15044 Rose from the South Waltz
15211 "Runaway Girl, A," March from
15097 Sambo at the Cake Walk (plantation medley with clogs, shouts, etc.)
15067 Santiago Waltz (with castanets)
32221 Soko (march and two-step) a Moorish intermezzo
15045 Schubert's Serenade (cornet solo)
15220 Smoky Mokes March
15107 Stars and Stripes Forever March
31594 Tell Me, Pretty Maiden (from "Florodora")
15013 Titl's Serenade (piccolo and cornet duet)
15059 Virginia Skedaddle (plantation medley, with clogs, shouts, etc.)
31794 When Mr. Shakespeare Comes to Town
15203 Whistling Rufus
32387 Winona (intermezzo two-step, a wigwam wooing)
15077 Zenda Waltz

Drum, Fife and Bugle Corps.

12801 Marching Thro' Georgia and Dixie
12800 The Girl I Left Behind Me and Auld Lang Syne

Records by Vienna Orchestra.

The Violin Effects of a String Orchestra Are Here Shown to Their Best Advantage.

31681 Life in Vienna Waltz
31847 Night in Venice Waltz, A
31683 Over the Waves Waltz
31844 Tales from the Vienna Woods Waltz
31766 Vienna Beauties Waltz
31843 Village Swallows Waltz

Bugle Calls.

3769 Rough Riders in Their Charge Up San Juan Hill, Bugle Calls of the
3768 United States Army, Bugle Calls of the

Orchestra Bells.

32527 American Beauty Mazurka
12516 Chiming Bells
32472 Easter Lilies. Gavotte
32423 Little Beauty Mazurka
32422 Marriage Bells
12517 Mill in the Forest, The
12518 Popular Airs, Medley of

Violin Solos.

27002 Ben Bolt (special arrangement)
31495 Carnival de Venice
31492 Holy City
27006 Imitation of Bagpipes and Scotch Airs, special arrangement.
27005 Scenes That Are Brightest, from "Maritana"

Gilmore's Brass Quartette.

2713 Come Where My Love Lies Dreaming
2707 Scotch Medley

Clarionet Solos.

3400 Massa's In the Cold, Cold Ground (with variations)
3409 My Old Kentucky Home (with variations)
3408 Old Black Joe (with variations)
3406 Southern Plantation Echoes

Banjo Solos.

3851 Bunch of Rags
32442 Cocoanut Dance (morceau characteristic)
3850 Coon Band Contest, A
32443 Darkies' Awakening (with clog effects)
3816 Darky's Dream
3825 El Capitan March
3856 Eli Green's Cake Walk
32256 Hiawatha (Moret)
3860 Old Folks at Home (with variations)
3830 Rag Time Medley (introducing "All Coons Look Alike to Me," and "Oh, Mr. Johnson")
3863 "Runaway Girl" Selections
3859 Whistling Rufus
31780 Whoa Bill!
31590 Colored Major, The. Duet
31589 Mosquito Parade. Duet

Xylophone Solos.

12003 Carnival of Venice (with variations)
12020 Dancing in the Sunlight
12009 Mocking Bird, The
12010 Then You'll Remember Me

Piccolo Solos.

23501 Darkies' Jubilee
23505 Hornpipe Polka
23503 Irish Reel
23509 Old Folks At Home (with variations)

Whistling Solos.

12606 Anvil Chorus
12604 Home, Sweet Home
7701 Mocking Bird, The (with bird imitations running throughout the record)

Minstrels.

These records each embrace overture, new jokes, laughter and applause, and end with song given in title, with orchestra and vocal quartette.

31609 Coon, Coon, Coon.
13000 Dese Bones Shall Rise Again
13007 Golden Harp, Play on the
13006 Golden Shore, Upon the
13008 Good-Bye Dolly Gray
13005 Hear Dem Bells
13009 Hello, My Baby
32392 Squash Town Amateur Minstrels. (The local talent attempts to emulate the "reg'lar professionals." Exceptionally funny)
31691 I'd Leave My Happy Home for You
13004 Laughing Song, The
31692 My Creole Sue
13010 Old Folks at Home
31610 Sadie Ray

No. 21C1100 Columbia XP Records. Our special price, each.......$0.25
Per dozen.......3.00

State No. 21C1100, also the name and number of each record when ordering. The price is the same on all XP Records, 25 cents each or $3.00 per dozen. LIST OF XP RECORDS CONTINUED ON NEXT PAGE.

An Evening With the Minstrels

This series of twelve records constitutes a complete minstrel performance. Each record, however, is complete in itself, and is entirely suitable to be purchased separately if desired.

32045A Introductory Overture by the entire company
32045B Our Land of Dreams, Ballad. Baritone solo by J. W. Myers, with chorus by the entire company. Orchestra accompaniment
32045C End Man Stories, by George Graham
32045D End Man Song, "I'm a Nigger That's Living High," by Billy Golden
32045E Jokes between Interlocutor and End Man
32045F I'm Wearing My Heart Away for You. Tenor solo by George J. Gaskin, with chorus by the entire company
32045G Jokes between Interlocutor and End Man
32045H End Man Song, "My Friend from Home" (coon song), by Len Spencer, with chorus by the entire company. Orchestra accompaniment
32045I Finale, "Black Hussars March." Baritone solo by J. W. Myers, with chorus by the entire company
32045J Musical Specialty, by Albert Bode. Trumpet solo
32045K Monologue by George Graham
32045L Banjo Solo, "Yankee Doodle," by Vess L. Ossman, with orchestra accompaniment

Vocal Sextettes—Mixed Voices

31604 Tell Me, Pretty Maiden (from 'Florodora")

Mendelssohn Quartette—Mixed Voices.

32074 Good Night, Good Night, Beloved
32332 Home, Sweet Home, by John Howard Payne
32075 Refuge (sacred)
32073 Sweet and Low
32238 The Lord's Prayer and Gloria Patria

Vocal Quartettes.

MALE VOICES.

These are deservedly among the most popular of Columbia records. The songs are finely rendered, and the effect is so natural that no stretch of the imagination is required to bring the singers so strongly forward in spirit that their actual presence seems to be achieved.

9014 Annie Laurie
31842 Barbecue in Old Kentucky, A
9071 Blue and The Gray, The
9063 Bridge, The
9067 Camp Meeting Jubilee (negro shout)
9068 Carry Me Back to Old Virginia (coon song)
9039 Church Scene from "The Old Homestead" (with church bell effect)
9046 Coon Songs, Medley of
32242 Coon Wedding in Southern Georgia, A
32498 Dear Old Girl. (solo and chorus)
9037 Farmyard Medley (imitation of fowl, cattle, etc.)
9049 Fireman's Duty, The (descriptive—the horses' hoofs, gallant rescue. etc.)
9053 Honey, Youse My Lady Love (coon song)
32237 Hoosier Hollow Quilting Party (Rube gags in song and story)
31654 Hymns and Prayer from the Funeral Service over President McKinley
9070 I'd Leave My Happy Home for You (coon song)
9010 I'se Gwine Back to Dixie (coon song)
31693 Laughing Quartette, The
31668 Lead, Kindly Light
9015 Little Alabama Coon (with baby cry and clog)
32499 Little Cotton Dolly (plantation lullaby)
9022 Louisiana Lou (negro love ditty)
9032 Massa's in the Cold, Cold Ground (coon song, with banjo imitation)
9008 Moonlight on the Lake
9019 My Old Kentucky Home
9045 My Old New Hampshire Home
32192 My Dinah (Perrin)
9012 Nearer, My God, To Thee
9050 Old Black Joe (coon song)
9030 Old Folks at Home, The
9018 Old Oaken Bucket, The
9044 Oregon Before Santiago, On Board the (descriptive)
31583 Owl and the Pussy Cat, The
32241 Plantation Songs, Medley of (introducing "In the Evening by the Moonlight," "Down in the Cornfield," "Carry Me Back to Old Virginia" and "My Old Cabin Home")
9011 Rocked in the Cradle of the Deep
9064 Rock of Ages
9040 Sleigh Ride Party, The (descriptive)
31548 Soldier's Farewell, The
9041 Steamboat Medley (descriptive)

32236 St. Patrick's Day at Clancy's ("Loike Ould Times in Kilkenny, begorra")
9052 Sweetest Story Ever Told, The
9048 Tenting on the Old Camp Ground
9038 Trip to the County Fair (imitation of railway, fakirs and Rubes)
9029 Way Down Yonder in the Cornfield (coon song)
9061 Where is My Wandering Boy Tonight?
9069 Where the Sweet Magnolias Bloom

Vocal Trios.

7708 Alpine Specialty (yodle song, tenor solo, chorus by trio)
7707 Camp Meeting (opening with chorus by trio, followed by a negro sermon and ending with song by trio)
7705 Mocking Bird Medley, The (tenor solo, whistling, chorus by trio)
9352 Farewell, My Own (from "Pinafore")
32273 Praise Ye (from "Attila-Verdi"). Mixed voices

Vocal Duets.

8416 Almost Persuaded. Baritone and tenor
31760 Back, Back to the Woods. Baritone and tenor
8410 Banks of the Wabash, On the. Baritone and tenor
32408 Barney (A song full of blarney). Baritone and tenor
8404 Bye and Bye You Will Forget Me. Baritone and tenor
31686 Coon, Coon, Coon. Baritone and tenor
31865 Cuckoo Song, The (with whistling chorus). Baritone and tenor
32485 Dixie (with fife and drum corps effect). Baritone and tenor
31856 First Rehearsal for the Husking Bee (comic Rube duet). Baritone and tenor
32381 He Was a Sailor. Baritone and tenor
32327 Hiawatha, Parody on. Baritone and tenor
32217 Hurrah for Baffin's Bay (From "The Wizard of Oz"). Baritone and tenor
31343 I Loved You Better than You Knew. Baritone and tenor
32209 It's a Lovely Day for a Walk (seriocomic). Contralto and baritone
31878 Jerry Murphy is a Friend of Mine. Baritone and tenor
32184 Marching Through Georgia (with drum, fife and bugle corps effect). Baritone and tenor
31703 McManus and the Parrot (comic Irish song). Baritone and tenor
32333 Moriarity (A Rousing Irish Song). Baritone and tenor
8411 Mother of the Girl I Love, The. Baritone and tenor
32218 Oh, Didn't He Ramble (comic). Baritone and tenor
32517 Possum Pie, or the Stuttering Coon. Baritone and tenor
31611 Reuben and Cynthia (a duet interspersed with humorous dialogue between male and female characters. One of Hoyt's great successes). Soprano and baritone
32309 Scene in a Country Blacksmith's Shop. Baritone and tenor
8420 Shadow of the Pines, In the. Baritone and tenor
31687 Tell Us, Pretty Ladies, (Weber & Field's burlesque on "Tell Me, Pretty Maiden," from "Florodora"). Baritone and tenor
32150 They Were All Doing the Same. Baritone and tenor
32267 Two Rubes in an Eating House. Baritone and tenor
31877 Two Rubes in a Tavern. Baritone and tenor
32409 Under the Anheuser Bush. Baritone and tenor
31910 Under the Bamboo Tree (as sung by Miss Marie Cahill in the musical comedy "Sally in Our Alley"). Baritone and tenor
32308 Waiting for the Dinner Horn to Blow. Baritone and tenor
32310 When We Were Boys. Baritone and tenor
8421 While the Leaves Came Drifting Down. Baritone and tenor
31684 Whoa, Bill (a trombone extravaganza). Baritone and tenor

Vocal Duets with Orchestra Accompaniment.

32551 Down on the Brandywine (with chime effects). Very tuneful and catchy. Baritone and tenor
32531 Listen to the Mocking Bird (with bird imitations). Contralto and baritone.
32532 Nobody's Lookin' but de Owl and de Moon. Contralto and baritone

Vocal Solos with Church Organ Accompaniment.

31359 All Hail the Power of Jesus' Name. Baritone
32496 I Need Thee Every Hour. Tenor
31364 Jesus, Lover of My Soul. Baritone
31356 Nearer, My God, To Thee. Baritone
31358 Rock of Ages. Baritone
31367 There is a Fountain. Baritone
31357 Where is my Wandering Boy Tonight? Baritone

Vocal Solos with Banjo Accompaniment.

32269 Banjo Evangelist, The (song, interspersed with the philosophy of an old time darky preacher). Baritone
7200-c Hot Time in the Old Town Tonight. Baritone
31403 If You Love Your Baby, Make the Goo Goo Eyes. Baritone
7200-h Little Old Log Cabin in the Lane. Baritone
7200-g Old Black Joe. Baritone
31405 That Minstrel Man of Mine. Baritone

Vocal Solos with Piano Accompaniment.

31549 Absence Makes the Heart Grow Fonder. Tenor
31677 Ain't Dat a Shame (coon song). Baritone
4028 Alabama Coon, Little (coon song). Tenor
7178 Almost Persuaded. Baritone
32202 Alic Busby, Don't Go Away (by the composer of "Bill Bailey, Won't You Please Come Home?"). Baritone
6318 And the Parrot Said (comic). Tenor
31809 As Your Hair Grows Whiter. Tenor
32287 Because You Were an Old Sweetheart of Mine. Baritone
31786 Bill Bailey, Won't You Come Home? (coon song). Baritone
5842 Blue and the Gray, The. Baritone
4586 Break the News to Mother. Baritone
32089 C-h-i-c-k-e-n; That's the Way to Spell Chicken. Baritone
31338 Columbia, the Gem of the Ocean. Baritone
4640 Come Back to Erin. Baritone
31603 Coon, Coon, Coon (coon song). Baritone
31680 Creole Belle. Baritone
4615 Darling Nellie Gray. Baritone
32282 Dear Old Girl. Baritone
32323 Down on the Farm. (ballad). Baritone
4004 Drill, Ye Tarriers, Drill (realistic drill effects, blast fire, etc.) Tenor
31678 Every Darky Had a Raglan On. (coon song). Baritone
32201 Every Morn I Bring Her Chicken (a coon's answer to "Violets"). Baritone
32505 Face to Face (with violin obligato). Sacred. Baritone
31851 Fare Thee Well, Molly Darling. Baritone
5851 Fatal Rose of Red, The. Baritone
32357 Gen. Hardtack on Guard. Baritone
7181 Girl I Loved in Sunny Tennessee, The. Baritone
32243 Glory (marching song, sung with great success in "The Billionaire"). Baritone
32216 Ghost of Benjamin Binns (an international comic hit). Tenor
31311 Good-Bye, Dolly Gray. Baritone
31645 Good Morning, Carrie. Baritone
31649 Go Way Back and Sit Down. Tenor
5097 Handicap Race, The (describing the progress of a horse race, cheers, horses' hoofs, etc.) Tenor
31671 He Laid Away a Suit of Gray to Wear the Union Blue. Tenor
31628 Hello, Central; Give Me Heaven (sentimental). Baritone
5801 Holy City, The. Baritone
32161 Home Ain't Nothing Like This (coon song). Baritone
31646 Honeysuckle and the Bee, The. Baritone
6309 I Couldn't (comic). Tenor
7486 I'd Leave My Happy Home For You (coon song). Baritone
31706 If Time Was Money, I'd Be a Millionaire (coon song). Baritone
31315 If You Love Your Baby, Make the Goo-Goo Eyes (coon song). Tenor
32434 If You're Such a Great Star, Why Don't You Shine? Baritone
32335 "I Like You, Lil, for Fair." (Tough song from Peggy from Paris) Tenor
4672 I'll Come Back When the Hawthorne Blooms Again. Baritone
32162 I'm a Jonah Man (Williams and Walker's big coon hit). Baritone
32194 I'm Thinking of You All of de While (coon love song). Baritone
31698 I'm the Man That Makes the Money in the Mint (comic). Tenor
31725 I Need the Money (comic). Tenor
31753 In Old New York. Baritone
32259 In the Sweet Bye and Bye (Von Tilzer's Popular Waltz Song). Baritone
32355 "It Takes the Irish to Beat the Dutch." Baritone
32261 It Was the Dutch (Lew Dockstader's latest song hit). Tenor
31695 I've a Longing in My Heart For You, Louise. Tenor
32163 I've Got to Go Now, 'Cause I Think It's Going to Rain (comic coon song). Baritone
4592 I Want to Go To-Morrow (intensely funny). Baritone
31790 Jennie Lee. Baritone
5850 Jerusalem. Baritone
7184 Just As The Sun Went Down. Baritone
32136 Last Wish, The (Abt). Bass
31745 Letter Edged in Black, The. Baritone
4282 Little Bit Off The Top, A (comic). Baritone
31701 Little Boy in Blue, A. Tenor
31776 Mansion of Aching Hearts, The. Baritone
31791 Meaning of U. S. A., The. Baritone
31674 Minnie Ha Ha. Baritone
6365 Miss Helen Hunt (comic). Tenor
31779 Mister Dooley (as sung in "The Chinese Honeymoon"). Tenor
31718 My Lady Hottentot (coon song). Baritone
31881 My Starlight Queen (the Rogers Brothers' big coon song hit in their latest farce, "In Harvard"). Tenor
7118 Ninety and Nine. Baritone
6301 Oh, Don't It Tickle You? (Comic). Tenor
32245 On a Moonlight Night (waltz song). Baritone
31755 On A Sunday Afternoon. Baritone
32260 Penny Whistler, The (English comic—introducing the penny whistle. When in doubt whistle it). Tenor
31788 Please Let Me Sleep (coon song). Baritone
31582 Reuben Haskins from Skowhegan (Rube song and dance with clog effect). Baritone
31726 Rip Van Winkle was a Lucky Man (from "The Sleeping Beauty and the Beast"). Tenor
4507 Rocked in the Cradle of the Deep. Baritone
4085 Safe in the Arms of Jesus. Baritone
32144 Same Old Crowd, The (from "The Jewel of Asia"). Tenor
32244 She's My Girl (song hit of "The Runaways", the latest Broadway success). Baritone
4254 Strike Up the Band, Here Comes a Sailor (comic). Tenor
31584 Sweet Annie Moore. Tenor
32257 There's Music in the Air. Tenor
32140 Things Ain't the Same Babe, I'm Coming Home (a great coon movement). Baritone
32176 Three Little Owls and the Naughty Little Mice, The (Yankee nursery rhyme). Baritone
31619 Village Choir, The (illustrating an amusing and characteristic country choir rehearsal. Imitation of four different voices). Baritone
31676 Way Down Yonder in the Corn Field (new ballad). Baritone
4275 Way to Kiss a Girl, The. Tenor
31647 Wedding of the Reuben and the Maid, The. Baritone
5068 What Do You Think of O'Hooligan? (comic.) Tenor
31744 When I Hold Your Hand in Mine. Tenor
32143 When It's All Going Out, and Nothing Coming In (coon song, as sung by Williams and Walker before His Royal Highness, King Edward VII). Tenor
31651 When Mr. Shakespeare Comes to Town. Baritone
31588 When the Blue Sky Turns to Gold. Tenor
31724 When the Roses Bloom Again. Baritone
32262 Whistling Bowery Boy, The. Tenor
32306 Wouldn't It Make You Hungry? (The plaintive wail of a half starved coon) Baritone
32314 "You're as Welcome as the Flowers in May." Baritone
31699 Yarns the Captain Told the Mate (comic). Tenor
6355 You Didn't Tell Me That Before We Married (comic). Tenor
31758 You Give Me Your Love, and I'll Give You Mine. Tenor

Soprano and Contralto Solos.

As faithful reproductions of the female voice in great range and sweetness, these records must be heard to realize their wonderful beauties.

32340 Angel's Serenade (with violin obligato). Contralto
6601 Ben Bolt. Soprano
32520 Cupid Has Found My Heart (from "The Yankee Consul"). Contralto
32339 Happy Days (with violin obligato). Contralto
31761 I'll Be Your Rainbeau. Soprano
32507 I Want to be a Lidy (from "A Chinese Honeymoon"). Soprano
6603 Killarney. Soprano
32199 My Little Pansy (from "The Billionaire"). Soprano
31814 My Mother Was a Northern Girl. Soprano
6608 Old Kentucky Home. Soprano
31715 Stay in Your Own Back Yard. Soprano
32200 Tell Me That Beautiful Story. Soprano
32519 Toyland (with male chorus, as sung in "Babes in Toyland"). Contralto
32341 Whisper and I Shall Hear (with violin obligato). Contralto

Laughing Songs.

With Rube Laughing Chorus.

31756 And Then I Laughed
7601 Negro Laughing Song. (An old standard)
31764 Ticklish Reuben
14032 I'm Old, But I'm Awfully Tough

Negro Shouts.

Songs with laughing and whistling choruses. A characteristic representation of the Alabama negro of the old slave days.

7711 Bye Bye, Ma Honey
7713 Negro Songs, Medley of
7703 Turkey in the Straw

Songs with Whistling Chorus.

31696 Whip-poor-will Song, The (with bird imitations)
12653 Whistling Susanna

Yodle Songs—Tenor.

The Yodling is distinct and agreeable, with good voice effect.

8001 Hush-a-Bye Baby
8000 Katharina
8902 Snyder, Does Your Mother Know You're Out?

Vaudeville Records.

31783 Bird Imitations
30402 "Musical Moke"

Vocal Solos with Orchestra Accompaniment.

32489 Ain't It Funny What a Difference Just a Few Hours Make. (From "The Yankee Consul.") Tenor
32545 All Aboard for Dreamland (The latest New York waltz song). Tenor
32382 Always in the Way. Baritone
32377 Any Rags? (This is a good one). Baritone
32375 Bedelia (The best Irish coon song of the century.) Tenor
32515 Blue Bell (Marching Song and Chorus) A big success. Tenor
32328 By the Sycamore Tree. Baritone
32282 Cordalia Malone. (Bedelia's sister). A new song by the composer of Bedelia. Tenor
32471 For Sale, a Baby (by the composer of "Always in the Way"). Tenor
32500 Gondolier (Vocal arrangement of the $5,000 intermezzo). Tenor
31750 Good-Bye, Dolly Gray. Baritone
32539 Good-bye, Eliza Jane (A popular coon hit). Baritone
32546 Good-Bye, Little Girl, Good-Bye (A popular hit) Tenor
32512 Good-Bye, My Lady Love. (One of the latest hits). Tenor
32508 "Hannah, Won't You Open that Door?" (A big hit). Baritone
32379 Happy Days. Baritone"
32509 "He Done Me Wrong"; or The Death of Bill Bailey. Baritone
32518 If I Were Only You (A new song by the composer of Navajo). Tenor
32503 I Heard the Voice of Jesus Say (with violin obligato). Sacred. Baritone
32397 I'm just Barely Living, Dat's All (A hard luck tale of a speculative coon). Baritone
32352 I'm On The Water Wagon Now (From "The Office Boy"). Baritone
32358 I'm Wearing My Heart Away For You. Baritone
32490 In the Days of Old. (From "The Yankee Consul.") Tenor
31879 In the Good Old Summer Time. Baritone
32446 In the Village By the Sea (popular hit). Baritone
32540 "I've Got A Feelin' for You" (Popular coon song). Baritone
32376 Lazy Bill (A Volunteer of Rest). Baritone
31752 Little Boy in Blue. A. Baritone
32535 Man in the Overalls. Baritone
32368 Mary Ellen. Baritone
32488 Meet Me in St. Louis, Louis. Tenor
32495 McGinty at the Living Pictures. Tenor
32493 My Little Irish Canary. (MaryAnn). Tenor
32514 My San Domingo Maid. Tenor
32363 Navajo (From the musical comedy "Nancy Brown.") Tenor
32536 On a Good Old Trolley Ride. Baritone
32541 Oysters and Clams (A popular coon shout). Baritone
32367 Plain Mamie O'Hooley (From the Office Boy) Tenor
32353 Pretty Little Dinah Jones. Baritone
32373 Sammy (From "The Wizard of Oz,") Tenor
32394 "There's a Little Street in Heaven that They Call Broadway." (Very good) Tenor
32456 "The Man Behind." (Lew Dockstader's big hit). Tenor
31749 Way Down in Old Indiana. Baritone
32534 Wedding of Barney and Bedelia. Tenor
32318 When Mamie, Sweet Mamie,'s a Bride. Tenor
32419 Whistling Riley (with whistling effects). Tenor
32366 Woodchuck Song, The. (Very popular) Baritone
32459 You're Always Behind, Like An Old Cow's Tail (from Dockstader's minstrels) Baritone
32384 Under the Anheuser Bush (This one is good)

Uncle Josh Weathersby's Laughing Stories.

14000 Arrival in New York, Uncle Josh's
14005 Base Ball Game, Uncle Josh at a
14011 Bicycle, Uncle Josh on a
14028 Chinese Laundry, Uncle Josh in a
14004 Department Store, Uncle Josh in a
14008 Fifth Avenue Bus, Uncle Josh on a
14031 Husking Bee Dance, Uncle Josh's (giving a correct imitation of a New England dance on the barn floor, with the fiddler playing appropriate music and Uncle Josh calling the figures)
31574 Jim Lawson's Horse Trade, Uncle Josh on
31765 Last Day of School at Pumpkin Center, The
14029 Lightning Rod Agent, Uncle Josh and the
31573 Meeting of the Ananias Club at Pumpkin Center, Uncle Josh at a
32406 Ohio, Uncle Josh on the (descriptive with bells and steamboat imitations)
32405 Political Meeting at Pumpkin Center. (Introducing speech by Uncle Josh, national airs by county band and the Pumpkin Center Glee Club)
14027 Society, Uncle Josh in
32403 Thrashing Time at Pumpkin Center (with imitations of steam thrasher, song with banjo and chorus by the farm hands)

Talking Records.

31566 Address of the late President McKinley at the Pan-American Exposition
11098 Arkansaw Traveler, The (descriptive of a native sitting in front of his hut scraping his fiddle and answering the interruptions of the stranger with witty sallies. Record is full of jokes and laughter)
31836 Auction Sale of a Bird and Animal Store (with bird and animal effects)
11102 Backyard Conversation Between Two Jealous Irish Washerwomen (full of real comedy and back talk)
1102- "Blazing Rag" Concert Hall, The (introducing the bouncer, the tipsy soubrette, the professor, and the fight—very realistic)
10501 Stump Speech on Love
31839 Daybreak at Calamity Farm (with animal effects)
11021 Dog Fight, The
32354 Ghost Scene from Hamlet
31838 Passing of the Circus Parade, The (with animal and band effects)
10006 Sale of Household Furniture. (The leather lunged auctioneer)
10001 Sale of Pawnbroker's Goods. (The leather lunged auctioneer)
31694 Scene in a Police Court
31837 Trip to the Circus, A (with animal and band effects)

Special Talking Records

By Joseph Jefferson.

Genuine records by Mr. Jefferson, the Dean of the American Stage.

32229 Scene in the Mountain (From second act, "Rip Van Winkle")
32230 Rip Meets Meenie after Twenty Years Absence (From "Rip Van Winkle")

These records, aside from their dramatic merit, are valuable as souvenirs of this great actor.

Vocal Solos in German.

32096 Das Haidenroeslein
31855 Dein Gedenk Ich, Margaretha
32106 Die Heimath
8206 Die Wacht Am Rhein
32104 Der Rattenfaenger
8218 Es Hat Nicht Sollen Sein (Nessler)
32103 Freiheit Die Ich Meine
32105 Gute Nacht, Fahrewohl
32097 Staendchen von Schubert
32101 Ueber den Sternen ist Ruh
32102 Wie Mag es Wohl Gekommen Sein

Descriptive.

32461 Clarence the Copper. (Clarence leaves his beat to call on his best girl. The sergeant appears and Clarence is transferred)
32483 Evening time at Pumpkin Center. (Descriptive, introducing the evening hymn at the fireside of the country homestead)
32494 Flogging Scene from Uncle Tom's Cabin. (With incidental orchestra effects)
32468 Leander and Lulu. (Leander attempts to propose while riding down town on elevated railway. Charlie Onthespot, his hated rival, is on the spot as usual)
32426 The Ebony Emperors of Melody. (A lively vaudeville specialty)

No. 21C1100 Columbia XP Records. Price, per dozen, $3.00; each, 25c

State No. 21C1100, also name and number of each record, when ordering. Price of all records listed on this page, 25 cents each or $3.00 per dozen.

DO NOT ORDER RECORDS for Disc Machines from this list, as these numbers are furnished in XP Wax Records only. XP Records fit any graphophone or phonograph using standard size wax cylinder records.

A LARGE AMPLIFYING HORN will greatly increase the volume of sound and the purity of tone. See No. 21C350.

WE SELL HORNS AT THE LOWEST PRICES EVER KNOWN.

GENUINE COLUMBIA STANDARD SIZE WAX CYLINDER RECORDS AT 15c

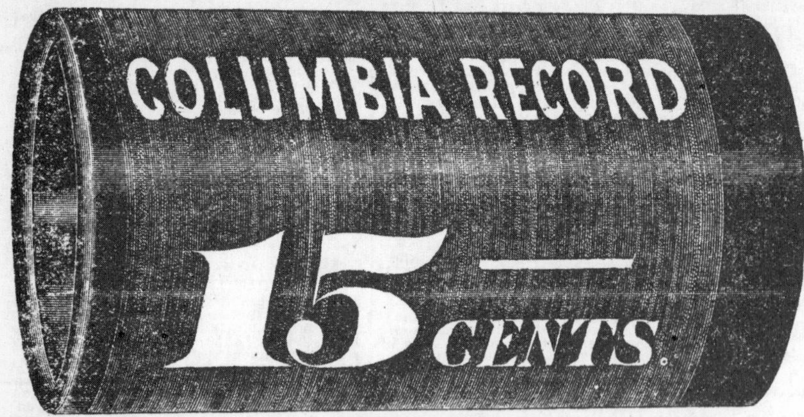

50 Standard Size Wax Cylinder Records, all different, **$7.50**
25 Standard Size Wax Cylinder Records, all different, **3.95**
12 Standard Size Wax Cylinder Records, all different, **1.95**

Can be used on any make of graphophone, phonograph or other talking machine using standard size wax cylinder records.

THIS ILLUSTRATION shows the exact style and quality of these standard size wax cylinder Columbia records, which we are closing out in lots of 50 for $7.50; lots of 25 for $3.95; lots of 12 for $1.95.

UNDERSTAND, these are strictly high grade records, records that we absolutely guarantee, the exact same records which have been sold for years by the Columbia Phonograph Company, and by all dealers in talking machines for 50 cents each. We are now closing them out at less than one-third this price, and when this lot of four hundred thousand is gone there will be no more. We are advised by the Columbia Phonograph Company that never again will they permit their regular standard size wax cylinder records to be sold for less than the full retail price.

BAND RECORDS.	VOCAL TRIO RECORDS.
ORCHESTRA RECORDS.	CORNET AND TROMBONE DUET RECORDS.
VIENNA ORCHESTRA RECORDS.	BUGLE CALL RECORDS.
ORCHESTRA BELLS RECORDS.	BANJO DUET RECORDS.
CORNET SOLO RECORDS.	PICCOLO SOLO RECORDS.
MINSTREL RECORDS.	XYLOPHONE SOLO RECORDS.
VOCAL QUARTETTE RECORDS.	BANJO SOLO RECORDS.
VOCAL DUET RECORDS.	CLARIONET SOLO RECORDS.
LAUGHING SONG RECORDS.	MANDOLIN SOLO RECORDS.
VOCAL SOLO RECORDS.	VIOLIN SOLO RECORDS.
UNCLE JOSH WEATHERSBY'S LAUGHING STORY RECORDS.	WHISTLING SOLO RECORDS.
NEGRO SHOUTS.	SPECIAL TALKING RECORDS.
VOCAL SEXTETTE RECORDS.	COMIC RECORDS.
	VAUDEVILLE RECORDS.

ORDER BY NUMBER.

No. 21C1115	50	Genuine Columbia Records. Price,	$7.50
No. 21C1116	25	Genuine Columbia Records. Price,	3.95
No. 21C1117	12	Genuine Columbia Records. Price,	1.95

WE GUARANTEE EVERY RECORD. We guarantee that you will find these records the genuine Columbia Records, high grade, standard size, wax cylinder records; the exact same records that have been advertised and sold by the Columbia Phonograph Co., by us and by other dealers for years at 50 cents each. If you will place your order immediately, ordering twelve, twenty-five or fifty records, enclosing with your order our special close out price of $1.95, $3.95 or $7.50, according to the quantity wanted, the records will go forward to you by return express. **You can examine these records when you receive them. You can test them on your talking machine.** You can compare them with any wax cylinder records that you have, or that you have ever seen, and if you do not find them just as good as any records you have ever purchased, if you do not find them equal to the very highest priced records on the market, if you do not find them entirely satisfactory in every respect, **you can return them to us at our expense, and we will refund the amount paid for the records, also the transportation charges.**

FIFTY GENUINE COLUMBIA STANDARD SIZE RECORDS AT 15c EACH

THIS ILLUSTRATION, engraved directly from a photograph, shows our assortment of 50 records, just as we put them up, ready to ship. 50 high grade records, at **15 cents each**; every one guaranteed.

WHY WE CAN SELL STANDARD SIZE GENUINE COLUMBIA WAX CYLINDER RECORDS FOR 15c.

LAST SPRING WE PURCHASED from the Columbia Phonograph Co. three hundred thousand wax records, which we offered for sale at 17, 18 and 19 cents each, according to quantity. This was at the time the largest purchase of talking machine records ever made, and our competitors predicted that it would be impossible for us to dispose of this enormous quantity, but the price at which we offered them, the lowest price ever known for talking machine records, enabled us to sell the entire three hundred thousand records. Our success in disposing of this enormous quantity of records prompted us to go again to the Columbia Phonograph Co., this time with **a proposition to take an even larger quantity of high grade, standard size wax cylinder records at a price even lower** than we paid for the first lot, and the quantity which we agreed to take was so large that the manufacturer accepted our proposition (in consideration of a spot cash payment for the entire lot), and we therefore find ourselves again in possession of hundreds of thousands of standard size genuine Columbia wax cylinder records which we can sell at prices lower than ever before. **We bought these new records for less money than we paid for the first lot, and we are giving our customers the benefit of this additional reduction in cost. That is why we can now offer these records in lots of fifty for $7.50; in lots of twenty-five for $3.95 and lots of twelve for $1.95.**

WE HAVE UNDERTAKEN TO CLOSE OUT this enormous lot of four hundred thousand standard size wax cylinder records at less than one-third the price we have for years been compelled to charge for these records. We have undertaken to close them out at a very small margin of profit to ourselves, a margin of profit so small that in order to insure ourselves against actual loss we must reduce the entire cost of handling, the cost of boxing, the cost of filling the orders to the very minimum. In order to do this, we must arrange to ship these records out boxed in lots of even numbers and we have decided on lots of twelve, twenty-five and fifty records and, therefore, all of the records which we sell at these special prices, at $7.50 for fifty, $3.95 for twenty-five and $1.95 for twelve, must be shipped out in lots of twelve, twenty-five and fifty.

IN ORDER TO BOX THESE RECORDS IN ADVANCE and keep the cost of handling down to the very lowest possible figure, we must, of course, make our selection of subjects in advance and in order that every one of our customers may have the very choicest selection of subjects we have arranged the division in such a way that the very best variety of subjects will be found in the twelve, twenty-five and fifty lots.

UNDERSTAND, this entire lot of records, numbering more than four hundred thousand standard size wax cylinder records, is now packed up, boxed, and ready for shipment in lots of twelve, twenty-five and fifty, and we must ask our customers to accept the subjects we have selected, as you will readily see how impossible it would be to open up and go through these boxes in search of any special selection which might be desired.

We have put this entire stock of more than four hundred thousand standard size wax cylinder records up in lots of twelve, twenty-five and fifty records. Therefore, we can accept orders for these records only in lots of twelve, twenty-five and fifty.

NO ORDER WILL BE ACCEPTED FOR LESS THAN TWELVE RECORDS and, if you wish more than twelve, you must order twenty-five; if you wish more than twenty-five you must order fifty.

EVERY COLLECTION OF TWELVE RECORDS which we furnish at $1.95 is as good as it is possible to get together in so small a number of records, while our collections of twenty-five and fifty records, which we furnish at $3.95 and $7.50 respectively, are, by reason of the larger number, better selected, a bigger variety, more entertaining, including band records, orchestra selections, vocal solos, duets, quartettes, with just enough vaudeville, comic, minstrel and special talking and novelty records to make each assortment positively the very best, the most attractive, and most satisfactory assortment that could be got together.

COLUMBIA RECORDS AT 10 CENTS.

While sorting out and packing the enormous stock of records, as described above, we set apart and reserved all those records which were made in other languages than English, and we have put these foreign records, these songs in German, Hungarian, Norwegian, Swedish, French, Hebrew, Polish, Russian, Italian and Spanish, up into special collections of twelve, twenty-five and fifty and we are closing them out at **10 CENTS EACH.**

IN MUSICAL QUALITY THESE RECORDS ARE EXCEPTIONALLY GOOD. Although sung in languages which you may not be able to understand, these records are just as delightful to listen to, just as musical, just as pleasing and just as satisfactory as though they were sung in English. Among these foreign selections are some splendid old German songs, weirdly sweet Hungarian music, Swedish and Norwegian airs that remind one of the far away Northland, vivacious French selections, comical Hebrew songs that make you laugh though you cannot understand the words, patriotic Polish airs, harmonious Russian selections, beautiful Italian songs that carry one's thoughts to the sunny Mediterranean, and Spanish love songs. We have put all of these foreign song records up in collections of twelve, twenty-five and fifty. Every collection contains a complete assortment of all the different languages, beautiful songs, musical selections that are certain to please you.

UNDERSTAND, THESE ARE STRICTLY HIGH GRADE, FIRST QUALITY, GENUINE COLUMBIA RECORDS, just as good as any other records which we sell at higher prices and just as good as any records sold by any other dealer at 50 cents each. These records were all made to sell at 50 cents each. They are the exact same quality of record which has been sold for years by the Columbia Phonograph Co. and by all dealers in talking machine goods at 50 cents each—strictly high grade, first quality, absolutely guaranteed records.

REMEMBER, this special price of 10 cents each is good only while this stock lasts. We have fifty thousand of these foreign selections and when they are gone it will be impossible to supply any more except at full regular prices. **Order now, before the stock is exhausted.** Do not miss this opportunity to get fifty high grade genuine Columbia records at 10 cents each, a price actually less than the cost of the material alone.

No. 21C1125	Fifty Foreign Records, all different. Price........	$5.00
No. 21C1126	Twenty-five Foreign Records, all different. Price.	2.65
No. 21C1127	Twelve Foreign Records, all different. Price......	1.28

NEW PROCESS COLUMBIA DISC RECORDS.

7-INCH 50 CENTS EACH. $5.00 PER DOZEN.
10-INCH $1.00 EACH. 10.00 PER DOZEN.
BE SURE TO STATE SIZE WANTED.

THE LOUDEST, CLEAREST AND MOST PERFECT RECORDS EVER PRODUCED.

THESE NEW PROCESS FLAT DISC COLUMBIA RECORDS represent the greatest advance made in the reproduction of sound since the original invention of the talking machine.

SO PERFECT that they are often mistaken for actual singing and talking, even by those accustomed to them. Until these new process disc records were perfected, all talking machines had a peculiar nasal sound and a scratching noise, this peculiar sound being so characteristic that no one could ever mistake a talking machine record of any kind for actual talking, singing or instrumental music.

IN VOLUME OF SOUND, musical quality and naturalness of tone these disc records are so far superior to all other records that no comparison is possible, and at the same time they possess other points of superiority over all other records, first in importance being

DURABILITY. The material of which these records are made is a very hard wear resisting composition, making them practically indestructible. They can be handled roughly, played hundreds of times and still retain their original brilliancy and perfection.

MADE IN THE FORM OF FLAT DISCS, measuring only 7 or 10 inches in diameter and only ⅛-inch in thickness, a large number may be put into a very small space. They are easy and convenient to handle and the cost of shipping is very slight.

THE ONLY RECORDS ever made that are loud enough for use out of doors. Think of the delightful possibilities for open air concerts that can be given with a disc graphophone on a moonlight summer night, possible only with these marvelous New Process Columbia Disc Records, these records that make it possible to say truthfully,

7-INCH COLUMBIA DISC RECORD.

10-INCH COLUMBIA DISC RECORD.

AT LAST THE TALKING MACHINE IS PERFECTED.

No. 2C1200 Columbia Disc Records, 7-inch size. Price, per dozen, $5.00; each $0.50
No. 2C1201 Columbia Disc Records 10-inch size. Price per dozen 10.00; each 1.00

ALL OF THE SELECTIONS LISTED BELOW (UNLESS OTHERWISE SPECIFIED) ARE MADE IN BOTH 7-INCH AND 10-INCH SIZES.

Band.

234 Admiral's Favorite March
235 America
32 American Eagle March
138 American Republic March (Thiele)
297 American Student's Waltz
1376 Amoureuse Waltz (a dreamy favorite)
1597 Anona (Intermezzo two-step), Vivian Grey
84 Anvil Chorus, from "Il Trovatore" (Verdi)
1654 Any Rags! Schottische
923 Arkansas Husking Bee
298 Artists' Life Waltz
181 Baltimore Centennial March (Herbert)
37 Boston Commandery March (introducing "Onward, Christian Soldiers")
1372 "Cavalleria Rusticana," Selections from
368 Charge of the Light Brigade
1015 Chariot Race March (with whistling solo)
253 Chopin's Funeral March
322 Columbia Phonograph Co. March
957 Convivial March (introducing old German drinking song, "Down Deep Within the Cellar")
251 Coon, Coon, Coon
825 Dancing in the Dark (song and dance with clogs)
354 Die Wacht am Rhein
355 Directorate March (Sousa)
361 Dixie
1567 Dixie Girl (characteristic two-step)
1375 Down South (introducing Big Boot Dancers, and Cake Walk)
872 Dream on the Ocean Waltz
1021 Echoes from the Metropolitan Opera House
838 El Capitan March (Sousa)
250 El Miserere, from "Il Trovatore"
183 "Faust," Waltz from (Gounod)
244 "Florodora," March from (Stuart)
826 "Flying Dutchman, The" Selections from
479 Forge in the Forest, The (descriptive, with bells, cock crow and anvil effects)
406 Georgia Camp Meeting, At a
410 God Save the King
868 Good Morning, Carrie—Medley March
416 Hail to the Spirit of Liberty (Sousa)
252 Hallelujah Chorus, from the "Messiah"
418 Hands Across the Sea (Sousa)
420 High School Cadets March (Sousa)
421 Hurrah Boys March
424 Indian Chase, An (descriptive galop)
425 In Shadow Land Waltz
427 In the Village Tavern (song and dance with clogs)
249 Invincible Eagle March, The (Sousa)
428 Irish Airs, Medley of
1587 Jack Tar March (Sousa's latest, introducing Sailor's Hornpipe, Eight Bells, Boatswain's Whistle)
628 Jolly Coppersmith, The (anvil effect and vocal chorus)
268 Jolly Fellows' Waltz (with bell effect)
437 Killarney (with trombone solo)
470 King Cotton March (Sousa)
1203 King of France, The (Sousa)
473 La Chasse Infernal Galop
474 La Golondrina
475 La Marseillaise
478 Liberty Bell March (with bell effect)
482 Little Chatterbox Gavotte
185 "Lohengrin," Bridal Chorus from
495 Love's Dreamland Waltz
502 Man Behind the Gun, The (March) (Sousa)
503 Manhattan Beach March (Sousa)
507 Marching Through Georgia
509 Marriage Bells (with cornet solo)
639 McKinley Memorial (introducing President McKinley's last speech, and "Lead Kindly Light" by brass quartette)
949 Mill in the Forest
79 Mosquito Parade, The (from "A Jersey Review"—Whitney)
528 Mr. Thomas Cat (march comique; trombone imitations)
526 Nearer, My God, to Thee
1910 New Colonial March
537 O, Promise Me, from "Robin Hood"
1611 "Parsifal," Prelude to Opera
1529 "Peggy from Paris," Selections from (new musical comedy by George Ade)
431 President's March, The
548 Rock of Ages
1426 Rocked in the Cradle of the Deep (with saxhorn solo)
549 Scotch Airs, Medley of
550 Southern Airs, Medley of
551 Spring and Love Waltz
553 Stars and Stripes Forever March (Sousa)
555 Star Spangled Banner
972 Stradella Overture
1377 Sultan of Sulu," Selections from "The (Ade and Wathall's Broadway success)
1568 Sunburst (A novelty)
233 "Tannhauser," Grand March from
82 Tell Me, Pretty Maiden, from "Florodora"
1535 Tenderfoot," Selections from "The
562 Then You'll Remember Me, from "Bohemian Girl" (with trombone solo)
564 Till We Meet Again Waltz
1601 Tone Pictures of the 71st Regiment leaving for Cuba (F. Hager)
568 Vacant Chair, The (with trombone solo)
570 Washington Post March (Sousa)
573 Wedding of the Winds Waltz
240 Wedding March (Mendelssohn)
580 Wine, Women and Song Waltz
35173 Intentions. A romance played by the Private Band of the Czar, Nicholas II, conducted by Mæstro Hugo Warlich, St. Petersburg. The music is marvelously shaded, the tones soft, mellow and pleasing, more nearly approaching the magnificent harmony of a great pipe organ. Made in 10-inch disc only.

Orchestra.

64 Angel's Serenade—piccolo and cornet duet
38 Artists' Life Waltz
1672 "Babes in Toyland" (Selections from the musical extravaganza)
582 Belle of New York March
49 Birds and the Brook, The (with bird imitations)
264 Blue Danube Waltz (Strauss)
1186 "Broadway Hits," Medley March
592 Bugler's Dream, The (descriptive introducing "Just Before the Battle, Mother," Bugle Calls, etc., and ending with "Nearer, My God, To Thee)
594 "Cavalleria Rusticana," intermezzo from
1066 "Country Girl, The," Selections from
595 Circus Galop (descriptive—clown tells new joke, applause, snapping of whip, etc.)
330 Creole Belles (with violin—J. B. Lampe)
1550 Cummings' Indian Congress at Coney Island (descriptive—grand entree of the Indians and Mexicans, preceded by the Carlisle Indian Band, Princess Wininah, the champion rifle shot of the world. Indian sham battle and realistic scene introducing the war song, the attack of the Mexicans who are routed amidst the yells and whoops of the Indians, who celebrate by their battle cry of victory. A record full of thrilling interest)
596 Dancing in the Kitchen (song and dance with clogs)
598 Dancing on the Housetops (song and dance with clogs)
599 Darkey's Dream (with clogs)
600 Darkey Tickle (plantation medley, with clogs, shouts, etc.)
1563 Departure of a Hamburg-American Liner (descriptive—the big whistle sounds. "All ashore going ashore". The band plays popular airs, friends shout farewells, the giant liner back into midstream and the music is drowned in the cheering.
1556 Dixie Girl (characteristic two step)
1431 Dixieland March (introducing "Dixie" and "Old Black Joe")—Haines
602 Down on the Suwanee River (descriptive—pulling in the gang plank, steamboat bells, whistle, dance on board, with negro shouts and clogs)
263 Echoes of the Forest (descriptive, with bird effects)
604 Estudiantina Waltz (with castanets)
605 Flora Waltz (cornet solo, with full orchestra accompaniment)
231 "Florodora," selections from (introducing "The Shade of the Palm"—Stuart)
247 Forge in the Forest, The (descriptive with cock crow, anvil, etc.)
132 Good-bye, Dolly Gray; March
337 Go 'Way Back and Sit Down
907 Harmony Mose (by the composer of "Rastus on Parade," "Happy Days in Dixie" and "At a Georgia Camp Meeting")
608 Happy Days in Dixie (plantation medley, with clogs, shouts, etc.)
129 He Laid Away a Suit of Gray to Wear the Union Blue
1155 Hiawatha (a summer idyl)
338 Honeysuckle and the Bee, The (with violin)
385 Hunky Dory (Abe Holzman)
609 Husking Bee (descriptive, introducing rural characters and scenes, with country dance and call in dialect)
1549 In Old Alabama—Cruger (a Barn Dance in the Land of Cotton.) The catching melody is interspersed with negro shouts, concluding with a quartette melody.
1588 Jack Tar March (Sousa)
616 Kentucky Jubilee Singers (plantation medley, with clogs, shouts, etc)
1571 Laughing Water (F. W. Hager)
1551 Levee Scene (as the darkies load the cotton, the boat's band plays a lively plantation melody, a warning whistle is sounded, and the roustabouts sing "What you gwine do in de winter?" As the steamer is departing the coon chorus serenades with a levee song, accompanied by the pickaninny band.
1610 Lucky Duck, A (a web foot promenade)
620 Merry Sleigh Bells, The (with sleigh bell effect)
621 Midway, On the (descriptive—introducing the fakirs and theatre)
387 My Old Kentucky Home—Fantasia.
395 Nearer, My God, to Thee (with Brass Quartette)
243 Night Alarm (with all the familiar descriptive effects, representing a fire alarm at night—fire bells, cries, horses' hoofs, winding of hose reel, whistle of engine, ending with firemen's chorus)
622 Nightingale and the Frog, The (with piccolo solo)
394 "Onward, Christian Soldiers," and "Old Hundred" (with organ)
1772 Polly Prim (Greatest march and two-step. A new one and a good one)
274 Popular Airs, Medley of
1555 Peaceful Henry (a slow drag)
1043 "Prince of Pilsen, The" Medley March from the Musical Comedy, (introducing "The Tale of the Sea Shell" and "The Stein Song")
937 Queen of the Blue Grass March
671 "Runaway Girl, A" March from
624 Santiago Waltz (with castanets)
625 Sea Flower Polka (cornet solo)
626 Serenade Waltz, from "The Serenade"
627 Smoky Mokes March
1442 Song Without Words "To Her"
1111 Spring Blossoms (caprice gavotte)
1578 Sun Dance, The (characteristic Indian dance)
128 Tell Me, Pretty Maiden, from "Florodora"
630 Titi's Serenade (piccolo and cornet duet)
632 Village Orchestra, The (They do the best they can. From Percy Gaunt's Musical Burlesque, as played between the acts in "A Trip to Chinatown")
634 Virginia Skedaddle (plantation medley, with clogs, shouts, etc.)
121 When Reuben Comes to Town March
283 Whoa! Bill (A country characteristic—Von Tilzer)

Vienna Orchestra.

The Violin Effects of a String Orchestra are Here Shown to their Best Advantage.

635 Armoureuse Waltz
636 Life in Vienna Waltz
637 Over the Waves Waltz
908 Night in Venice Waltz, A
894 Tales from the Vienna Woods Waltz
862 Vienna Beauties Waltz
893 Village Swallows Waltz

Cornet Solos.

Selections by Jules Levy are made in 10-inch discs only.

918 Alice Where Art Thou! By Jules Levy
1081 Columbia Polka. By Bohumir Kryl
1089 Facilita. By Bohumir Kryl
15 Flora Waltz (grand concert solo)
921 Nearer, My God, to Thee. By Jules Levy
919 Robin Adair. By Jules Levy.
1090 Sweet Sixteen Waltz. By Bohumir Kryl
1082 Theresa Polka. By Bohumir Kryl

Bugle Calls.

638 Rough Riders in Their Charge Up San Juan Hill, Bugle Calls of the
640 United States Army. Bugle Calls of the

Violin Solos.

214 "Ballet," Fantasie (De Beriot)
218 El Miserere, from "Il Trovatore"
217 "Faust," Waltz from
62 Intermezzo Sinfinico from "Cavalleria Rusticana")
212 Schubert's Serenade
216 Then You'll Remember Me

Clarionet Solos.

91 Comin' Thro' the Rye (with variations)
96 Old Folks at Home (with variations)
879 Sally in Our Alley

Banjo Solos.

1619 Anona. By Mabel McKinley.
460 Colored Major, The
461 Coon Band Contest, A
292 Coon Songs
465 Creole Belle
464 Hot Corn
462 Invincible Eagle March, The
1613 Jack Tar March. Sousa. (Duet.)
1618 Jack Tar March. Sousa.
254 Mosquito Parade, The
1706 Navajo (two-step). (Duet with orchestra accompaniment.)
1620 Peaceful Henry (a slow drag)
469 Rusty Rags Medley
463 "When Mr. Shakespeare Comes to Town," and "Go 'Way Back and Sit Down"

Piccolo Solos.

497 Comin' Thro' the Rye (Grand Fantasia)
499 Irish Medley Jig
500 Nigger Fever
498 Rag Time Skedaddle, A

Xylophone Solos.

534 Believe Me If All Those Endearing Young Charms
530 Happy Days in Dixie
529 Kiss Me, Honey, Do (dinah song)
531 My Old Kentucky Home
528 Pickaninny Polka
532 Suwanee River Medley

Chimes.

441 Almost Persuaded
446 Lead Kindly Light (with voice and organ)
438 Nearer, My God, to Thee
445 Old Hundred (with voice and organ)
439 Rock of Ages
444 Safe in the Arms of Jesus

Whistling Solos.

229 Independence March
215 Mocking Bird, The

Minstrels.

Each record embraces introduction by orchestra, jokes and witty sayings and ends with song given in title accompanied by orchestra and quartette.

641 Coon, Coon, Coon
33 Dese Bones Shall Rise Again
642 Hear Dem Bells
643 High Old Time, A
798 I've a Longing in My Heart for You, Louise
644 Laughing Song, The
800 Mandy Lee
799 My Heart Loves You Too
805 My Old Kentucky Home
801 My Wild Irish Rose
804 Old Folks at Home
645 Old Log Cabin, The
802 Tell Me
803 When the Autumn Leaves Are Falling

Vocal Sextette—Mixed Voices.

647 Tell Me, Pretty Maiden (from "Florodora")

Vocal Quartettes.

716 Annie Laurie
511 Carry Me Back to Old Virginia
456 Coon Wedding in Southern Georgia, A
451 Dixie Land
455 Farm Yard Medley (with farm yard fowl and animal imitations)
453 Funeral Service Over President McKinley
513 Good Bye, Dolly Gray
1621 Home, Sweet Home, by John Howard Payne (Made in 10-inch only)
820 I Can't Think of Nothin' Else But You
753 Ise Gwine Back to Dixie
510 Lead, Kindly Light
519 Little Darling, Dream of Me
1516 Lord's Prayer and "Gloria Patria"
750 My Creole Sue
452 My Dinah
512 My Old Kentucky Home
518 Nearer, My God, to Thee
458 Night Trip to Buffalo (very funny)
521 Old Oaken Bucket, The
754 Onward Christian Soldiers
751 Owl and the Pussy Cat, The
651 Patriotic Songs, Medley of

List of Disc Records Continued on Next Page.

COLUMBIA DISC RECORDS.—Continued from Preceding Page.

459 Sidewalks of New York, The
450 Sleigh Ride Party, The. (A descriptive record with good singing, sleigh bell effects)
520 Soldier's Farewell
454 Steamboat Medley
818 Suwanee River
514 Tenting Tonight on the Old Camp Ground
457 Trip to the County Fair, A. (All of the familiar scenes at a country fair are here. The peanut man, the elastic skin man, and the fakir in all his glory)
714 Way Down Yonder in the Cornfield

Vocal Trios—Male Voices.

548 Alpine Specialty. (Yodle song, tenor solo, chorus by trio)
549 Camp Meeting. (Opening with chorus by trio, followed by a negro sermon and ending with song by trio)
552 In Front of the Old Cabin Door. (Old man negro character, clog dance, whistling chorus by trio)
553 Mocking Bird Medley, The. (Tenor solo, whistling chorus by trio)

Vocal Duets.

763 Back, Back to the Woods. Baritone and tenor
789 Coon, Coon, Coon. (Comic duet). Baritone and tenor
1201 Deed I Do (coon love song). Contralto and baritone
3616 First Rehearsal for the Husking Bee. (comic Rube duet), Baritone and contralto
257 Girl I Loved in Sunny Tennessee, The. Baritone and tenor
1673 He Was a Sailor. (A good comic song) Baritone and tenor
597 I Got Mine. Baritone and tenor
792 I Never Trouble Until Trouble Troubles Me. Baritone and tenor
258 In the Shadow of the Pines. Baritone and tenor
1461 It's a Lovely Day for a Walk. Contralto and baritone
262 Just as the Sun Went Down. Baritone and tenor
256 Larbord Watch. Baritone and tenor
259 'Mid the Green Fields of Virginia. Baritone and tenor
1522 Moriarity (A regular Irish shout). Baritone and tenor
1492 Oh, Didn't He Ramble. (Comic). Baritone and tenor
1184 Oh that We Two Were Maying. Contralto and baritone
1460 Reuben and Cynthia. (Gaunt). Contralto and baritone
1558 Scene in a Country Store, A. Baritone and tenor
1417 They Were All Doing the Same. Baritone and tenor
1559 Two Rubes in an Eating House. Baritone and tenor
970 Under the Bamboo Tree (as sung in the musical comedy "Sally in Our Alley"). Baritone and tenor
791 Wedding of the Reuben and the Maid, The. (From "Rogers Brothers in Washington"). Baritone and tenor
816 When We Are Married. Contralto and baritone
261 While the Leaves Came Drifting Down. Baritone and tenor
790 Whoa! Bill (Comic Rube duet). Baritone and tenor

Duets with Orchestra Accompaniments.

1777 Dixie (with fife and drum corps effect). Made in 10-inch only. Baritone and tenor
1776 Marching Through Georgia (with drum, fife and bugle corps effect). Made in 10-inch only. Baritone and tenor
1749 Under the Anheuser Busch. (Made in 10-inch only). Baritone and tenor

Vocal Solos with Piano Accompaniment.

221 Absence Makes the Heart Grow Fonder. Tenor
1603 Abide With Me. Sacred. Tenor
1625 At the Seaside (from "A Princess of Kensington"). Tenor
1449 Alic Busby, Don't Go Away (coon song, by the composer of "Bill Bailey Won't You Please Come Home"). Baritone
378 Ain't dat a Shame (coon song). Baritone
172 And the Parrot Said (comic). Tenor
346 Any Old Place I Can Hang My Hat, is Home, Sweet Home, to Me. Baritone
1614 Any Rags. Tenor
401 Armful of Kittens and a Cat, An (comic—with cat imitations). Baritone
208 Ben Bolt. Tenor
563 Birds Sing Sweeter, Lad, at Home, The. Baritone
1248 Boys Will be Boys (from De Wolf Hopper's new comic opera "Mr. Pickwick"). Tenor
146 Calvary. Baritone
405 Carrie Nation in Kansas (with axe effect). Baritone
1371 Congo Love Song, A (from "Nancy Brown"). Baritone
1578 Dear Old Girl. Baritone
170 Doing His Duty-ooty-ooty. Tenor.
383 Every Darky Had a Raglan On (coon song). Baritone
1410 Every Little Dog Must Have His Day. Tenor
1448 Every Morn I Bring Her Chicken (coon song). Baritone
77 Fare Thee Well, Molly Darling. Baritone
1190 Gambling Man, The (coon song). Baritone
113 Good Bye, Dolly Gray. Tenor
381 Good Morning, Carrie. Baritone
1575 Goodnight, Beloved, Goodnight. Baritone
377 Go 'Way Back and Sit Down (comic). Baritone
230 Hello, Central! Give Me Heaven. Tenor
1579 Hiawatha. Baritone
1406 Hiawatha. Tenor
149 Holy City, The. Baritone
1387 Home Ain't Nothin' Like This (coon song). Baritone
44 Home, Sweet Home. Baritone
311 Honeysuckle and the Bee, The. Tenor
167 Honey, You'se My Lady Love (coon song). Tenor
1508 Hosanna. Bass
1404 Hurrah for Baffin's Bay (from "The Wizard of Oz"). Baritone
1624 I Like You, Lil, for Fair (tough song from "Peggy From Paris"). Tenor
1543 In the Sweet Bye and Bye (the popular waltz song). Baritone
380 I Ain't Agoin' to Weep No More (coon song). Baritone
324 I Can't Tell Why I Love You, But I Do. Tenor
423 I Got Married This Morning (comic). Tenor
195 I Heard the Voice of Jesus Say. Baritone
1361 I Wants a Man Like Romeo (coon song). Tenor
357 I'll Be With You When the Roses Bloom Again. Tenor
1388 I'm a Jonah Man (coon song). Baritone
349 I'm Tired (comic.) Baritone
1441 I'm Thinkin' of You All of de While (coon love song). Baritone
55 In the House of Too Much Trouble. Tenor
402 In the Shade of the Palm (from "Florodora"). Baritone
1399 In Sunny Africa (coon song). Baritone
1553 It Was the Dutch (Lew Dockstader's latest song hit). Tenor
1389 I've Got to Go Now, Cause I Think It's Goin' to Rain (coon song). Baritone
226 I've a Longing in My Heart for You, Louise. Tenor
86 Just Because She Made dem Goo Goo Eyes (coon song). Tenor
356 Killarney. Tenor
1457 Like a Star That Falls from Heaven. Tenor
1419 Limerick Girls, The. Tenor
176 Little Bit Off the Top, A (comic). Tenor
1420 Marriage is Sublime (from "Mr. Bluebeard"). Baritone.
1585 Mighty Like a Rose. Baritone
1589 Miner's Home, Sweet Home, A (the great American home song). Baritone.
1531 Must You (Laughable English Dialect Song from "The Wizard of Oz"). Tenor
1572 My Little Coney Isle. Baritone
320 My Old Kentucky Home. Tenor
1592 My Wild Irish Rose. Tenor
1507 Nazareth. Sacred. Bass
303 New Born King, The (sacred). Baritone
1411 Noreen Mavourneen. Tenor
1398 Oh My (comic coon song). Baritone
1523 On a Moonlight Night. Cahill. Baritone
106 On a Sunday Afternoon. Baritone
1580 Over the Pommery Foam. Baritone
1552 Penny Whistler, The (English comic, introducing the penny whistle. When in doubt whistle it). Tenor
1192 Please, Mamma, Buy Me a Baby. Tenor
1522 Rocked in the Cradle of the Deep. Baritone
1359 Same Old Crowd, The (sung by Blanche Ring in "The Jewel of Asia"). Tenor
353 Sing Again that Sweet Refrain. Tenor
1576 Star of My Life. Baritone
52 Sweet Annie Moore. Tenor
1163 Tessie, You Are the Only, Only, Only. Tenor
1360 There's a Lot of Things You Never Learn at School (from "The Wizard of Oz"). Tenor
1403 Things ain't the Same, Babe, I'm Coming Home (a great coon movement). Baritone
1541 There's Music in the Air. Tenor
1118 Thy Beaming Eyes. Baritone
1574 Up in the Cocoanut Tree. Baritone
571 'Way Down Yonder in the Corn Field (coon song). Baritone
488 What Do You Think of O'Hoolihan? (comic two-voice specialty). Tenor
1530 When He's Not Near (from "Peggy from Paris" great Chicago hit). Baritone
1358 When It's All Going Out and Nothing Coming In (as sung by Williams and Walker before His Royal Highness, King Edward VII). Tenor
318 When Reuben Comes to Town. Tenor
53 When the Harvest Days are Over. Tenor
558 When You Were Sweet Sixteen. Baritone
1241 When We are Married (comic English song as sung by Billy West with Rogers Brothers. Tenor
199 Where Is My Wandering Boy Tonight? Tenor
1092 Where the Silv'ry Colorado Wends Its Way. Baritone
403 Where the Sweet Magnolias Bloom. Baritone
200 While the Band is Playing Dixie. Tenor
1554 Whistling Bowery Boy, The. Tenor
111 Who Threw the Overalls in Mistress Murphy's Chowder. Tenor
1600 You're as Welcome as the Flowers in May. Baritone

Yodle Songs—Tenor.

587 Emmet's German Yodle
591 Hi! Le! Hi! Lo!
708 Hush-a-Bye, Baby
585 Hush! Don't Wake the Baby
707 Lauderbach
706 Life in the Alps
589 Snyder, Does Your Mother Know You're Out!

Laughing Songs.
With Laughing Choruses.

105 And Then I Laughed (Rube song)
22 I'm Old, but I'm Awfully Tough
210 Negro Laughing Song (an old standard)
1105 Roll on the Ground.
759 Ticklish Reuben. (Rube song)
1101 Turkey in the Straw. (Negro laughing song)

Songs with Whistling Choruses.

213 Whip-poor-will Song, The (with bird imitations)
211 Whistling Coon, The (the old favorite)

Soprano Solos.

283 Ben Bolt
1628 Home Sweet Home. (Made in 10-inch only)
837 I've a longing in My Heart for You, Louise
1629 My Old Kentucky Home. (Made in 10-inch only)
1717 The Last Rose of Summer, (with violin obligato. One of the finest soprano records ever made. Made in 10-inch only)

Vocal Solos in German.

148 Auch ich war ein Jungling
123 Deutschland, Deutschland
108 Die Wacht am Rhein
143 Es hat nicht sollen sein
144 In dunkler Nacht
147 Schneiders Hollenfahrt
125 Wohlauf, noch getrunken

Vaudeville Records.

662 Imitation of the Irish Comedian, John Kernell, Frank Mayo in "Davy Crockett," and Miss May Irwin singing a coon song
663 "Musical Moke." (Drum and fife corps effect)

Talking Records.
Dutch Dialect Series.

26 Schultz as the Man Behind the Gun
28 Schultz on Christian Science
24 Schultz on George Washington
23 Schultz on Kissing
27 Schultz' Trip to Chicago

Talking Records.

21 Arkansas Traveler, The. (Record is full of jokes and laughter)
398 Back Yard Conversation Between Two Jealous Irish Washerwomen
833 Address by the Late President McKinley at the Pan American Exposition
1606 Con Clancy's Christening. (with violin accompaniment)
160 Lincoln's Speech at Gettysburg
162 Little Red Riding Hood (for the children)
35 Negro Sermon, A
34 Stump Speech on Love
1604 Stuttering Monologuist, The (with violin accompaniment)
664 Twenty-third Psalm, and the Lord's Prayer

Special Talking Records.
By Joseph Jefferson.

Genuine records by Mr. Jefferson, the Dean of the American stage.

1469 Rip Meets Meenie after Twenty Years Absence (from "Rip Van Winkle")
1468 Scene in the mountain (from Second Act, "Rip Van Winkle")

These records aside from their dramatic merit, are valuable as souvenirs of this great actor.

Uncle Josh Laughing Stories.

70 Arrival in New York, Uncle Josh's
1518 Automobile, Uncle Josh in an (a new one by Stewart). Very laughable
71 Base Ball Game, Uncle Josh at a
72 Bicycle, Uncle Josh on a
1490 Chinese Laundry, Uncle Josh in a
1488 Circus, Uncle Josh at a
68 Department Store, Uncle Josh in a
19 Husking Bee Dance (giving a correct imitation of a New England dance on the barn floor, with the fiddler playing appropriate music; figures called)
1510 Invitation to Visit Him on His Farm, Uncle Josh's
1512 Jim Lawson's Hogs
74 Lightning Rod Agent, Uncle Josh and the
1489 Society, Uncle Josh in
1409 Street Car, Uncle Josh on a
1502 Trip to Boston, Uncle Josh's
1486 Trip to Coney Island, Uncle Josh's
76 Troubles in a Hotel, Uncle Josh's

Vocal Solos With Church Organ Accompaniment.

1780 I Need Thee Every Hour. Tenor
396 Lead, Kindly Light. Baritone
397 Nearer, My God, to Thee. Baritone
1774 One Sweetly Solemn Thought. Tenor
1747 Safe in the Arms of Jesus. Sacred. (Made in 10-inch only). Tenor

Vocal Solos With Orchestra Accompaniment.

1667 Bedelia. (the best Irish coon song) Tenor
1715 Coonville Cullud Band. (A descriptive, up to date coon marching song. This is an extra good one.) Baritone
1800 Hannah, Won't You Open That Door? (Made in 10-inch only) Baritone
1671 Happy Days. Baritone
1054 Heidelberg (Stein Song from the musical comedy, "The Prince of Pilsen")
1644 I'm on the Water Wagon Now. (Made in 10-inch only) Baritone
1650 I'm Wearing My Heart Away for You. Baritone
1014 In the City of Sighs and Tears
940 In the Good Old Summer Time. Baritone
1660 Mary Ellen. Baritone
1792 Meet Me in St. Louis, Louis. Tenor
1721 Navajo. (Made in 10-inch only) Baritone
1659 Plain Mamie O'Hooley. (from "The Office Boy). Baritone
1665 Sammy (The big hit in "The Wizard of Oz.") Tenor
1052 Tale of the Sea Shell, The (from the Musical Comedy, "The Prince of Pilsen"). Baritone
1676 Under the Anheuser Bush. (One of the best new ones). Baritone
1658 Woodchuck Song, The (a new one that is good). Made in 10-inch only. Baritone.
1688 Wouldn't It Make You Hungry? (The plaintive wail of a half starved coon). Baritone

Grand Opera Columbia Disc Records. Price, $2.00 Each.

Wonderful records by the world's greatest singers. The Genius, the Art and the Talent of the highest priced Artists on the Operatic Stage brought within the reach of ever one.

The Columbia Phonograph Company have induced the world famed singers, such as Marcella Sembrich, Edouard de Reszke, Ernestine Schumann-Heink, Guieseppe Campanari, Suzanne Adams, etc., to sing into special recording graphophones for permanent records in the shape of these 10-inch flat disc indestructible records, and thousands of dollars were paid for the services of these famous singers in making these records.

NEVER UNTIL THE NEW PROCESS Columbia disc records were perfected, would these famous singers consent to sing into a talking machine for the reason that the records heretofore made would not do justice to their voices. But these new process disc records make it possible to obtain an absolutely true record, reproducing with absolute fidelity the highest soprano notes, the deepest bass tones, the most beautifully rounded contralto phrases, the wonderful trills and entrancing sweetness of such voices as Sembrich, Schumann-Heink, Adams, the marvelous technique of such masters as De Reszke, Scotti, and the other world known operatic singers.

Soprano Solos by Marcella Sembrich. (Piano Accompaniment.)

1364 Scena e Cavatina, from the opera "Ernani"—Ernani, involami—Ernani, rescue me. (Italian.) Verdi.
1365 Waltz Song, Voci di Primavera—Voices of Spring—Fruhlingsstimmen. (Italian.) Johann Strauss.
1366 Aria from "Traviata"—Ah, fors' e lui—'Tis thus perchance. (Italian.) Verdi.

Bass Solos by Edouard de Reszke. (Piano Accompaniment.)

1221 Aria from "Ernani," Infelice—O, Cruel Fortune. (Italian.) Verdi.
1222 Canzone del Porter, from "Martha"—porter song. (Italian.) Von Flotow.
1223 Serenade. Don Juan. (Italian). Tschaikowsky.

Contralto Solos by Ernestine Schumann-Heink.
Piano Accompaniment.

1378 Arioso, from the opera "Le Prophete." (French.) Meyerbeer.
1379 Trinkleid aus Lucretia Borgia—Brindisi—drinking song. (German.) Donizetti.
1380 Dalilah's Grand Aria, from the opera "Samson et Dalila." (German.) Saint-Saens.

Baritone Solos by Guiseppe Campanari. (Piano Accompaniment.)

1224 Cavatina, from "Faust"—Dio Possente—Even Bravest Heart. (Italian.) Gounod.
1225 Serenade. (Italian.) Sepilli.
1227 Toreador Song, from "Carmen." (Italian.) Bizet.

Soprano Solos by Suzanne Adams. (Piano Accompaniment.)

1194 Sunbeams. (English.) Ronald.
1195 Printemps Nouveau—Early Spring. (French.) Leo Stern.
1197 Valse Aria, from "Romeo et Juliette"—waltz song. (French.) Gounod.
1198 Coquette. (French.) Leo Stern.
1243 Jewel Song, from "Faust." (French.) Gounod.

Baritone Solos by Antonio Scotti. (Piano Accompaniment.)

1205 Toreador Song, from "Carmen." (Italian.) Bizet.
1206 Prologue, from "Il Pagliacci." (Italian.) Leoncavallo.
1207 Serenade and Air de Champaign, from "Don Giovanni." (Italian.) Mozart.

Baritone Solos by Charles Gilibert. (Piano Accompaniment.)

1234 La Vierge a la Creche. (French.) Perilliou.
1236 Obstination—A Resolve. (French.) Fontenailles.
1251 Les Rameaux—The Palms. (French.) J. Faure.

Duet by M. and Mme. Charles Gilibert. (Piano Accompaniment.)

1254 Colinette. (French.) G. Alary

No. 21C1300 Columbia Grand Opera Disc Records, made in 10-inch size only. Price, each.... $2.00

State No. 21C1300, also name and number of each record when ordering.

STEREOPTICON DEPARTMENT

MAGIC LANTERNS, MOVING PICTURE MACHINES, SLIDES, FILMS, SUPPLIES AND COMPLETE EXHIBITION OUTFITS

Our Model "A" Single Stereopticon, $17.50.

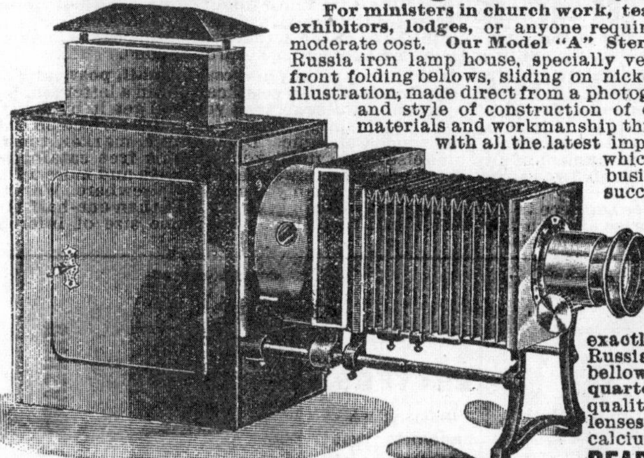

For ministers in church work, teachers in class room work, public exhibitors, lodges, or anyone requiring a strictly high grade lantern at moderate cost. Our Model "A" Stereopticon is made with extra large Russia iron lamp house, specially ventilated, provided with extension front folding bellows, sliding on nickel plated rods. The accompanying illustration, made direct from a photograph, shows the general appearance and style of construction of our Model "A" Stereopticon. The materials and workmanship throughout are the best, it is equipped with all the latest improvements and all the adjustments which long experience in the exhibition business has taught us are requisite for successful projection work. **This lantern may be used with Calcium Light, Electric Light, Sun Rival Vapor Light,** or any system of lighting at present employed by the best public exhibitors.

AT $17.50 We furnish our **Model "A" Single Stereopticon complete,** exactly as shown in the illustration, with **Russia iron lamp house, adjustable bellows, high grade Bausch & Lomb quarter size projecting lens,** extra quality 4½-inch imported condensing lenses, slide carrier and latest improved calcium burner.

BEAR IN MIND that any kind of light can be used with this lantern, but at our special price, $17.50, the light is not included. The additional expense for proper light equipment will depend upon the style selected by the purchaser.

No. 21C2000 Model "A" Stereopticon, complete as described. Price.......................... **$17.50**

If ready made oxygen and hydrogen gases are purchased in steel tanks, no additional apparatus will be required, except six feet of small rubber tubing (at 10 cents per foot) to connect tanks to lantern, and a can of limes (costing 65 cents).

No. 21C2010 Our Special Single Stereopticon and Vapor Light Outfit, consisting of Model "A" Stereopticon, and our new Sun Rival Vapor Light (burns common gasoline). An ideal outfit for ministers, educators, lodges, etc. Price, complete.......................... **$29.50**

No. 21C2020 Our Special Single Stereopticon with Calcium Light Outfit, consisting of Model "A" Stereopticon and our new Oxygen Gas Making Outfit (see Nos. 21C2000 and 21C2300). Price, complete. **$48.00**

For list of slides, lecture sets and supplies suitable for these outfits, send for Our Special Free Magic Lantern Catalogue.

Our Model "AA" Double Stereopticon for Dissolving Views, $39.50.

THIS EQUIPMENT consists of two high grade Model "A" Stereopticons, mounted one above the other, perfectly matched and accurately adjusted, a perfect instrument for producing dissolving views and the most effective scenic results so much desired in public exhibition work. Dissolving effects are produced by having two different views, one in each stereopticon, turning the gas gradually from one jet to the other so that while one view fades away the other grows brighter, until one view has faded away altogether and the other developed to full brilliancy.

Our new Oxygen Gas Making Outfit can be used with this lantern, thus doing away entirely with the heavy steel tanks and the inconvenience of sending away for ready made gases. See No. 21C2300.

AT $39.50 we furnish this high grade Model "AA" Double Stereopticon complete, with finest Russia iron lamp houses, extra large adjustable bellows, two perfectly matched high grade Bausch & Lomb quarter size projecting lenses, two pairs of extra quality imported 4½-inch condensing lenses, two slide carriers, two improved calcium jets and highest grade dissolving key.

THIS LANTERN is designed for calcium light only, but can be equipped for electricity if desired. If the oxygen and hydrogen gases are purchased ready made in tanks, no additional apparatus of any kind is required to make the outfit complete, except a few feet of rubber tubing and a can of limes.

No. 21C2100 Our Model "AA" Double Dissolving View Stereopticon, complete as described above. Price.......................... **$39.50**

No. 21C2119 Our Special Complete Professional Outfit, consisting of Model "AA" Double Dissolving Stereopticon, with our New Oxygen Gas Making Outfit (see Nos. 21C2100 and 21C2300). Price, complete.......................... **$69.00**

OUR FREE MAGIC LANTERN CATALOGUE

SHOWS THE MOST COMPLETE LINE OF

STEREOPTICONS	LECTURE SETS
MOVING PICTURE MACHINES	MOVING PICTURE FILMS
LANTERN SLIDES	PROJECTION LENSES

EXHIBITOR'S SUPPLIES AND ACCESSORIES OF ALL KINDS

ALL SOLD AT THE LOWEST PRICES EVER KNOWN FOR HIGH GRADE APPARATUS

We will be glad to send this catalogue to you.

Our New Oxygen Gas Making Outfit, $37.50.

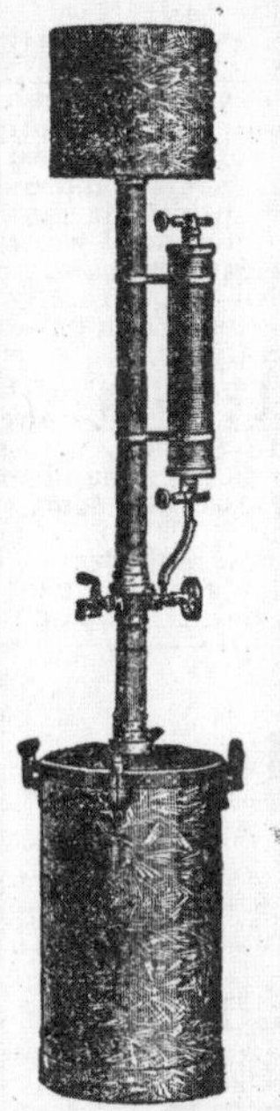

Our New Oxygen Gas Making Apparatus represents the greatest advance made in magic lantern apparatus since the original invention of the lantern. This new apparatus, which enables the operator to instantly and easily produce a supply of absolutely pure oxygen gas at any time, will, we confidently predict, revolutionize the exhibition business. It is a well known fact to exhibitors that outside of the electric light, which is available only in the larger cities, the only practicable light for public exhibition work, either for stationary or moving pictures, is the calcium light, and until the invention of this wonderful new oxygen gas making outfit, which we now place upon the market for the first time, the only means of producing the calcium light was by an expensive, heavy, cumbersome gas making outfit, very difficult to operate, actually dangerous owing to frequent explosions, and successful only in the hands of expert and experienced chemists. **Our New Oxygen Gas Making Outfit does away with all the danger,** with all the trouble and with practically all of the expense attached to the operation of these old style gas making outfits. Our illustration, engraved direct from a photograph of the apparatus, shows how simple, compact and portable it is. It can be packed into a small carrying case, measuring only about 10 inches square by 30 inches long, and weighs complete only about 30 pounds. **The only chemical required in operating this new oxygen gas making outfit is oxylythe,** and a small package of this oxylythe, weighing only a few ounces, is sufficient for an evening's entertainment. The operation of this outfit is simplicity itself. There is no possible chance for mistakes, no possible chance for failure and absolutely no danger. A small quantity of the oxylythe is placed in the tank, which contains a little water, and the generation of oxygen gas commences at once, and is conveyed from the gas making outfit by means of a small rubber tube directly to the burner of the lantern.

As there is no high pressure developed in the process of making oxygen gas with this apparatus, the danger of explosion, which is inherent in all other gas making outfits, is entirely obviated. The apparatus cannot possibly under any conditions, even with the grossest mismanagement, explode or cause damage, even to the slightest extent. **It is as safe in the hands of the inexperienced novice as in the hands of the oldest and most experienced operator.** The light produced by this apparatus is just as powerful and just as effective for exhibition work as the light produced by the most expensive forms of oxyhydrogen apparatus, or by the use of ready made gases supplied in steel tanks by the Calcium Light Companies. The chemical, oxylythe, used in this oxygen making apparatus is known to chemists as binoxide of sodium. This is not a new chemical. It has been known to chemists for years and its properties have been understood, but the great expense of producing it heretofore has made its use prohibitive for practical work. A celebrated French chemist, however, has recently perfected a method of producing this binoxide of sodium at a very low cost, making it possible to utilize this wonderful substance for the production of oxygen gas for the oxyhydrogen or calcium light in magic lantern work.

Oxylythe, or, chemically speaking, binoxide of sodium, possesses the peculiar property of evolving or giving off pure oxygen gas when it comes in contact with water. In this respect its action is very similar to calcium carbide, which, when placed in contact with water, gives off acetylene gas. The production of oxygen gas from binoxide of sodium corresponds exactly to the production of acetylene gas from calcium carbide. In operation the oxygen gas, which is formed in the galvanized iron cylinder forming the base of the apparatus, passes upward into the short brass cylinder called the saturator, shown in the illustration, and this short cylinder is filled with ether, through which the oxygen gas passes, this ether supplying the hydrogen element which is necessary for the production of the oxyhydrogen or calcium light. **Remember that no additional apparatus is required.** The machine as shown in our illustration is complete and ready to attach to the lantern, a small piece of rubber tubing being used for this purpose. The production of oxygen gas, after the oxylythe is placed in the apparatus, is immediate and instantaneous and the exhibitor is ready to proceed with his entertainment as soon as he has placed the oxylythe in the generator. Remember that the apparatus is simple and easy to operate, that the element of danger is absolutely eliminated. Remember that the light which is produced is as brilliant and as steady and as satisfactory in every way as any calcium light that can be produced by any known method. Remember that it can be used for the projection of either stationary or moving pictures with perfect success. Remember that the complete outfit can be packed into a small carrying case, measuring only about 10x10x24 inches, and that it weighs only about 30 pounds.

No. 21C2300 Our New Oxygen Gas Making Apparatus complete. Price.......................... **$37.50**

No. 21C301 Oxylythe, for use with above outfit, put up in 2-pound boxes. Price, per box...... **$1.35**

MEMORIAL DEPARTMENT.

A SMALL SAMPLE PIECE OF THIS MARBLE WILL BE MAILED ON RECEIPT OF 10 CENTS.

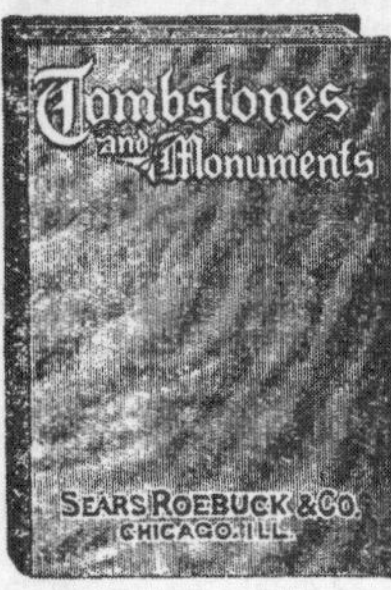

OUR FREE TOMBSTONE CATALOGUE. This handsome special catalogue of tombstones and monuments is the handsomest, most complete and most up to date catalogue of tombstones and monuments furnished to buyers. With large, handsome illustrations and very complete descriptions, it shows a big variety of tombstones and monumental work, which we furnish at the quarries at prices that barely cover the cost of material and labor, with but our one small percentage of profit added—prices less than one-half the prices asked by dealers generally.

A FINE SELECTION of handsome headstones or markers at prices ranging from $4.40 to $40.00, with some very choice designs from $5.00 to $8.00; a handsome line of tombstones at from $6.60 to $50.00, with some specially fine designs ranging from about $10.00 to $15.00; a grand variety of monuments at from $7.70 to $160.14, many new and elegant designs in the way of entirely new shapes and finishings; a big line of shaft monuments ranging in price from $7.70 to $117.30, with a big assortment up to $35.00.

WE USE ONLY THE CHOICEST VERMONT blue and white Rutland Italian marble. Our free catalogue shows handsome illustrations, shows all the different shapes, different carvings, shows how each piece will look when set up, explains our liberal terms, our guarantee and is the most complete, most interesting and by far the lowest priced tombstone and monument catalogue ever published.

THIS FREE CATALOGUE tells all we know about tombstone and monumental work. It gives you the advantage of buying right at the quarry on the basis of the actual cost of quarrying, making and finishing, with only our one small percentage of profit added.

THIS BOOK IS FREE, will be sent to any address, by mail, postpaid, on application. On a postal card or in a letter, simply say: "Send me your free Tombstone Catalogue," and you will get it by return mail, postpaid. Either order one of the pieces illustrated and described on this page or write for our free Tombstone Catalogue. Don't buy a marker, tombstone or monument of any kind elsewhere until you see this free catalogue. We will furnish you something handsomer, newer, more stylish and more up to date, and in every way more satisfactory than you can buy elsewhere. We will guarantee the piece in every way, and you can get it at less than one-half the lowest price at which any dealer will furnish you the same size of inferior workmanship and finish.

OUR $4.40 PRICE includes the Marker and Base complete, but without any lettering, and the price is based on the actual cost of cutting the work out of the quarry with but our one small percentage of profit added. **This stone is handsomely polished, and as shown in the illustration, it is trimmed with tracing and beveling.** Height, with base, 1 foot 6 inches; size of base, 16x8x6 inches; marker, 12x12x4 inches. Weight, 125 lbs.

No. 22C700 Price, Acme Blue, Dark Vein .. $4.40
No. 22C701 Price, White Acme Rutland Italian 5.22

THIS BEAUTIFUL TOMBSTONE with a sleeping lamb on the top is furnished at the heretofore unheard of prices of $10.45 in Acme Blue, Dark Vein Vermont Marble, and at $11.55 in White Acme Rutland Italian Marble.

DIMENSIONS: Nos. 22C792 and 22C793. Total height over all, 2 feet and 2 inches. Size of bottom base, 1 foot 6 inches by 10 inches by 8 inches. Size of upper base, 1 foot 2 inches by 6 inches by 4 inches. Size of tablet, 1 foot 2 inches by 1 foot by 4 inches. Weight, 235 pounds.

No. 22C792 Price, Acme Blue, Dark Vein $10.45
No. 22C793 Price, White Acme Rutland Italian 11.55

LETTERS.

Ordinary Sunk Inscription, name and dates, 6 cents per letter.

Sunk Verse, 2½ cents per letter.

2-inch Letters, raised ⅛-inch in Panel, 15 cents per letter.

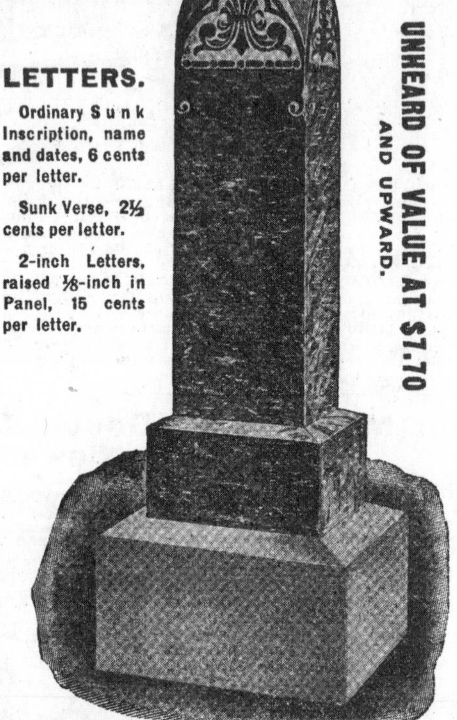

UNHEARD OF VALUE AT $7.70 AND UPWARD.

LIKE EVERY ONE of our higher grade tombstones, this monument is made in the same famous quarry, and by reason of having been made there, you are guaranteed a quality which you might not expect anywhere else.

DIMENSIONS: Nos. 22C844 and 22C845. Total height over all, 3 feet 4 inches. Size of bottom base, 1 foot by 1 foot by 8 inches. Size of upper base, 9 inches by 9 inches by 4 inches. Size of shaft, 2 feet 4 inches by 6 inches by 6 inches. Weight, 235 pounds.

No. 22C844 Price, Acme Blue, Dark Vein, $7.70
No. 22C845 Price, White Acme Rutland Italian $9.62

DIMENSIONS: Nos. 22C846 and 22C847. Total height over all, 3 feet 8 inches. Size of bottom base, 1 foot 4 inches by 1 foot 4 inches by 8 inches. Size of upper base, 1 foot by 1 foot by 6 inches. Size of shaft, 2 feet 6 inches by 8 inches by 8 inches. Weight, 455 pounds.

No. 22C846 Price, Acme Blue, Dark Vein, $12.65
No. 22C847 Price, White Acme Rutland Italian $14.82

DIMENSIONS: Nos. 22C848 and 22C849. Total height over all, 4 feet 6 inches. Size of bottom base, 1 foot 6 inches by 1 foot 6 inches by 10 inches. Size of upper base, 1 foot 2 inches by 1 foot 2 inches by 8 inches. Size of shaft, 3 feet by 10 inches by 10 inches. Weight, 809 pounds.

No. 22C848 Price, Acme Blue, Dark Vein, $20.47
No. 22C849 Price, White Acme Rutland Italian $25.98

DIMENSIONS: Nos. 22C850 and 22C851. Total height over all, 4 feet 10 inches. Size of bottom base, 1 foot 10 inches by 1 foot 10 inches by 1 foot. Size of upper base, 1 foot 4 inches by 1 foot 4 inches by 8 inches. Size of shaft, 3 feet 2 inches by 1 foot by 1 foot. Weight, 1,270 pounds.

No. 22C850 Price, Acme Blue, Dark Vein, $30.45
No. 22C851 Price, White Acme Rutland Italian $37.80

Give us four to six weeks to finish, letter and ship.

OUR SPECIAL $13.12 NEW DESIGN LOW ROLL MONUMENT.

Delivered on the Cars at our Quarry and Marble Works in Vermont.

THIS TOMBSTONE is quarried from the Acme Blue Marble Quarry, cut and polished by expert artisans, traced and carved by artists in their line of work, and the result is the **beautiful and imposing monument** shown in the illustration.

DIMENSIONS: Nos. 22C798 and 22C799. Total height of base and roll, 1 foot 10 inches. Size of base, 2 feet by 1 foot by 1 foot. Size of roll, 1 foot 8 inches by 10 inches diameter. Weight, 524 pounds.

No. 22C798 Price, Acme Blue, Dark Vein $13.12
No. 22C799 Price, White Acme Rutland Italian $15.22

DIMENSIONS: Nos. 22C800 and 22C801. Total height of base and roll, 2 feet 2 inches. Size of base, 2 feet 4 inches by 1 foot 2 inches by 1 foot 2 inches. Size of roll, 1 foot 10 inches by 1 foot diameter. Weight, 828 pounds.

No. 22C800 Price, Acme Blue, Dark Vein $18.37
No. 22C801 Price, White Acme Rutland Italian $22.05

Foot Stones, 6x2 inches, sand rubbed, each, **50 cents.** Corner Posts, 4x4 inches, for cemetery lots, each, **$1.00.** Corner Posts, 6x6 inches, for cemetery lots, each, **$1.65.**

A small sample piece of marble in any of the above colors will be mailed on receipt of 10 cents.

GIVE US FROM FOUR TO SIX WEEKS IN WHICH TO FINISH, LETTER AND SHIP.

Remember two things: The rate of freight is very low on marble. The work is the finest in America.

Ordinary sunk inscription letters, **6 cents each.** Sunk verse, **2½ cents each.** 2-inch letters, raised ⅛ inch in panel, **15 cents each,** and other sizes in proportion.

ALL MARBLE WORK is carefully boxed and delivered on the cars at our quarry in Vermont, and guaranteed to reach you in perfect order or we will replace it free of charge. Where we quote prices delivered on the cars at quarry it is done to save the expense of freight, cartage and handling into and out of our store in Chicago, and all the saving goes to the customer in the low prices we make—prices only made possible by eliminating all the handling expenses.

HOUSE FURNISHING HARDWARE DEPARTMENT.

COMPLETE KITCHEN OUTFITS.

ABOUT THE QUALITY. Different from any department or novelty stores who sell assortments of inferior goods, our assortments are all made up from regular stock merchandise of the highest grade. Every article that goes into every combination we offer is strictly a high standard quality and so guaranteed, and if not found to be such in every instance, you are at liberty to return goods to us and we will cheerfully refund your money. We are able to make this extraordinary offer on combination outfits by reason of buying up immense quantities of the different articles during the dull seasons, when the manufacturers have little to do and are willing to make very close prices; at the same time when it is quiet with us we can assemble the outfits, pack them and get them ready for shipment. As it costs no more to handle the complete outfit once ready for shipment than one single item in the lot, we can afford to figure our profit even lower than on a general line. All this you get the benefit of in our prices.

IRONSTONE ENAMELED WARE OUTFITS.

We guarantee our Ironstone Enameled Steel Ware to be the most durable and toughest enameled ware known. It is absolutely acid proof and will last two or three times as long as the fancy colored wares costing twice our price or more. The body of the vessels is of sheet steel and is covered with two coats of vitrified porcelain enamel. In color, it is a dark brown with fine white mottling, having a rich, glossy and pleasing appearance.

Ironstone Enameled Ware Outfits containing almost everything necessary in the kitchen for only $2.25 to $2.85. Ironstone Enameled Steel Ware is the most durable and toughest enameled ware made. The material used in the enamel is guaranteed to be absolutely pure. It is united with the steel body at an enormous temperature (more than twice as high as required in ordinary enameling) and is not only vitrified but forms a perfect union or clinch with the steel, making it tough and lasting. We furnish three assortments suitable for Nos. 7, 8 and 9 stoves respectively, containing the following articles:

Catalogue No.	No. 23C3001	No. 23C3002	No. 23C3003
Suitable for stove size	No. 7	No. 8	No. 9
Shipping weight	40 lbs.	45 lbs.	55 lbs.
Price	$2.25	$2.50	$2.85
	Size of Vessels	Size of Vessels	Size of Vessels
1 Tea Kettle	7	8	9
1 Tea Pot	1½ quart	2 quart	3 quart
1 Coffee Pot	2 quart	3 quart	4 quart
1 Preserving Kettle	4 quart	5 quart	6 quart
1 Wash Basin	10½ inch	11½ inch	12½ inch
1 Pudding Pan	1½ quart	2 quart	3 quart
2 Pie Plates	9 inch	9 inch	9 inch
1 Soap Dish to Hang	6½x4 inch	6½x4 inch	6½x4 inch
1 Ladle	3⅞ inch	3⅞ inch	4½ inch
1 Dipper	¾ quart	1 quart	2 quart
1 Sauce Pan	3 quart	4 quart	5 quart
1 Basting Spoon	10 inch	12 inch	14 inch
1 Drinking Cup	1 pint	1 pint	1 pint

These great big Ironstone Enameled Steel Ware Outfits containing everything necessary in the kitchen for the largest family at only $4.25 to $5.35. Ironstone Enameled Steel Ware is the most durable and lasting ware made by anyone. It will easily last twice as long as ordinary enameled ware. We have contracted for the entire output of this brand and offer these complete outfits at one half what regular dealers must charge you for ordinary enameled ware, which will not last you half as long.

Catalogue No.	No. 23C3004	No. 23C3005	No. 23C3006
Suitable for stove size	No. 7	No. 8	No. 9
Shipping weight	65 lbs.	75 lbs.	90 lbs.
Price	$4.25	$4.80	$5.35
	Size of Vessels	Size of Vessels	Size of Vessels
1 Tea Kettle	7	8	9
1 Coffee Pot	2 quart	3 quart	4 quart
1 Tea Pot	1½ quart	2 quart	3 quart
1 Double Boiler for Rice or Milk	1 quart	2 quart	3 quart
1 Berlin Kettle	4 quart	6 quart	8 quart
1 Sauce Pan	2 quart	3 quart	4 quart
1 Sauce Pan	4 quart	5 quart	6 quart
1 Preserving Kettle	6 quart	8 quart	10 quart
3 Pie Plates	9 inch	9 inch	9 inch
3 Jelly Plates	9x1 inch	9x1 inch	9x1 inch
1 Dish Pan	14 quart	17 quart	17 quart
1 Pudding Pan	1½ quart	2 quart	3 quart
1 Pudding Pan	3 quart	4 quart	5 quart
1 Milk Pan	2 quart	2 quart	3 quart
1 Basting Spoon	10 inch	12 inch	14 inch
1 Windsor Dipper	1 quart	2 quart	2 quart
1 Ladle	3⅞ inch	3⅞ inch	3⅞ inch
1 Soap Dish to Hang	6½x4 inch	6½x4 inch	6½x4 inch
1 Drinking Cup	1 pint	1 pint	1 pint
1 Wash Basin	11½ inch	11½ inch	12½ inch

No. 23C3007........$3.15
No. 23C3008........ 3.50
No. 23C3009........ 3.98
ORDER BY NUMBER.

Peerless Gray Enameled Steel Ware Outfits.

We have made up a combination of Peerless Gray Enameled Steel Ware in three different sizes, which we are able to offer in the complete assortment as listed below, at **$3.15**, **$3.50** and **$3.98**, in competition with anything you can buy anywhere at double the price. This Peerless Gray Enameled Steel Ware is the highest grade, strictly first, not seconds, made by the best makers in America. These outfits consist of the following articles:

- 1 Peerless Enameled Steel Tea Kettle.
- 1 Peerless Enameled Steel Coffee Pot.
- 1 Peerless Enameled Steel Tea Pot.
- 2 Peerless Enameled Steel Preserving Kettles.
- 1 Peerless Enameled Steel Sauce Pan
- 2 Peerless Enameled Steel Pudding Pans.
- 1 Peerless Enameled Steel Wash Basin.
- 1 Peerless Enameled Steel Windsor Pattern Dipper.
- 4 Peerless Enameled Steel Pie Plates, 9 inches in diameter.
- 1 Peerless Enameled Steel Soap Dish to hang on the wall.
- 1 Peerless Enameled Steel Dish Pan.
- 1 Peerless Enameled Steel Soup Ladle.

No. 23C3007 Our Peerless Enameled Steel Outfit for No. 7 Stove. Weight, 45 pounds. Price, complete....................$3.15

No. 23C3008 Our Peerless Enameled Steel Outfit for No. 8 Stove. Weight, 50 pounds. Price, complete....................$3.50

No. 23C3009 Our Peerless Enameled Steel Outfit for No. 9 Stove. Weight, 60 pounds. Price, complete....................$3.98

TRUE BLUE ENAMELED WARE OUTFITS.

The Highest Grade Made, at $4.88 $5.63 and $6.15.

Our True Blue Enameled Ware is the highest grade it is possible to procure. The purity of the material used in its composition, excellency of workmanship and beauty of design are unequaled. It is strong and durable, yet light and convenient to handle. The body of the ware is sheet steel, triple coated on the inside with absolutely pure white porcelain and on the outside with a bright glossy, mottled blue and white enamel presenting a very handsome effect, every piece matching perfectly. Covers are enameled also and will never rust. It is as easily cleaned as china and the best and most durable ware for family use made. **We furnish three assortments suitable for size No. 7, 8 and 9 stoves respectively, containing the following articles: Note the reduced prices.**

Catalogue No.	No. 23C3012	No. 23C3013	No. 23C3014
Suitable for stove size	No. 7	No. 8	No. 9
Shipping weight	50 lbs.	55 lbs.	65 lbs.
Price	$4.88	$5.63	$6.15
	Size of Vessels	Size of Vessels	Size of Vessels
1 Tea Kettle	7	8	9
1 Coffee Pot	2 quart	3 quart	4 quart
1 Tea Pot	1½ quart	2 quart	3 quart
1 Berlin Kettle with enameled cover	3½ quart	5 quart	7 quart
1 Handled Sauce Pan	2½ quart	4 quart	5 quart
1 Pudding Pan	3 quart	3 quart	4 quart
1 Wash Basin	11½ inch	11½ inch	11½ inch
1 Double Boiler for Rice, Milk, etc.	2 pint	4 pint	4 pint
1 Dish Pan	10 quart	14 quart	14 quart
1 Soap Dish to Hang	6½x4 inch	6½x4 inch	6½x4 inch
1 Basting Spoon	12 inch	14 inch	14 inch
2 Pie Plates	9 inch	9 inch	9 inch
1 Dipper Windsor Pattern	1 quart	1 quart	1 quart
1 Soup Ladle	3½ inch	3½ inch	3½ inch

Porcelain Enameled Dinner Set.

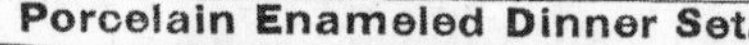

No. 23C3016 Dinner Set, contains 6 dinner plates, 6 coffee cups, 6 saucers, 1 platter, 1 vegetable dish and 1 bowl. The articles in this set are made of sheet steel coated inside and out with absolutely pure white porcelain, and ornamented with a bright blue border. Cannot be broken, are not easily chipped, and are less than one half the weight of crockery. Will not discolor and as easily cleaned as china. For miners, camping parties or children's use, it is just what is wanted. Also desirable for ordinary household use. Weight, boxed for shipment, 25 pounds
Price, set complete, as shown....................$2.48

OUR NEW LINE OF WALL PAPER PATTERNS IS THE VERY BEST WE HAVE EVER BEEN ABLE TO OFFER.
We make our own wall paper in our own factory and sell at about one-half the prices usually asked. If you will write and ask for it we will gladly send you a complete book of samples showing the entire line of new designs from the very cheapest to the best. Don't buy a roll of wall paper from anyone until you first get our free sample book.

STOVE FURNISHING SETS.

Made up from full size, first quality goods.

The first figure in stove size designates the size furniture that fits the stove.

THUS... No. 8-18 stove takes No. 8 furniture.
No. 9-18 stove takes No. 9 furniture.

Queen Assortment.

1 Copper Bottom Tin Wash Boiler
1 Copper Bottom Tin Tea Kettle
1 Cast Iron Stove Kettle
1 Cast Iron Spider
1 Wrought Iron Fry Pan, polished, 10 inches
1 4-pint Tin Tea Pot
1 5-quart Tin Coffee Pot
1 10-quart Retinned Dish Pan
1 Revolving Flour Sifter
2 Black Dripping Pans, 10x12 and 10x14 inches
1 Tin Bread Pan, 5¾x10¾x3 inches
2 Com'n Square Bread Tins, 7¾x11¾x1½ inches
1 Box Grater
1 Biscuit Cutter
1 Dover Egg Beater
1 Dozen 3-inch Plain Patty Pans
½ Dozen 9-inch Tin Pie Plates
1 14-inch Basting Spoon
1 Cake Turner
1 1-quart Tin Cup
1 Vegetable Fork
1 Tin Dipper
1 Flat Handled Skimmer
1 Fire Shovel
1 Tin Wash Basin
1 Tubed Cake Pan, 10-inch

No. 23C3017 Queen Assortment for No. 7 Stove. Weight, 65 pounds. Price......$2.95
No. 23C3018 Queen Assortment for No. 8 Stove. Weight, 70 pounds. Price...... 3.15
No. 23C3019 Queen Assortment for No. 9 Stove. Weight, 75 pounds. Price...... 3.35

Acme Assortment.

1 Heavy IX Tin Copper Bottom Wash Boiler
1 Iron Stove Kettle
1 Tin Cover to fit
1 Nickel Plated Copper Tea Kettle
1 Iron Spider
1 Fry Pan, 10 inches
1 Stove Shovel, heavy steel
1 Nickel Plated Copper 5-pint Coffee Pot
1 Nickel Plated Copper 4-pint Tea Pot
1 Retinned Preserving Kettle
1 Cover to fit
1 Retinned Sauce Pan
1 Cover to fit
1 Basting Spoon
1 Tin Muffin Frame, 12 cups
½ Dozen Tin Pie Plates, 9-inch
1 Extra Heavy Retinned Dishpan, 14-qts.
1 Pieced Tin Cup, 1 pint
1 Heavy Copper Bottom Water Dipper, 2 quarts
1 Flathandled Skimmer
1 Vegetable Fork
3 Tin Bread Pans
2 Tin Cake Pans
2 Drip Pans, 10x12 and 10x14 inches
1 Dozen Assorted Patty Pans
1 Rolling Pin
1 Cake Turner
1 Retinned Colander
1 Cake Cutter
1 Biscuit Cutter
1 Doughnut Cutter
1 Nutmeg Grater
1 Large Grater
1 Revolving Flour Sifter
1 Dover Egg Beater
1 Covered Japanned Dust Pan
1 Butcher Knife
1 Paring Knife
1 Mincing Knife
1 Bread Board
1 Wood Potato Masher
1 Oval Hardwood Chopping Tray
1 Steamer
1 Set Mrs. Potts' Sad Irons, consisting of Three Irons, Handle and Stand.

No. 23C3027 Acme Assortment for No. 7 stove. Weight, 110 pounds. Price......$6.55
No. 23C3028 Acme Assortment for No. 8 stove. Weight, 115 pounds. Price...... 6.75
No. 23C3029 Acme Assortment for No. 9 stove. Weight, 120 pounds. Price...... 7.10

Our Special $1.10 Housekeepers' Outfit of Tinware.

Every piece we show in this lot is strictly high grade, standard goods. There is not a piece in the whole outfit but what is in every day use. If there happens to be one or more articles in this outfit you have no use for, do not hesitate to take advantage of the offer; you are getting a good portion of the outfit for nothing, and when you get the $1.10 price you can afford to pay $1.10 for this outfit if you give away one-third of the articles. The remainder will be very cheap at $1.10.

Our $1.10 Set of Tinware consists of the following articles:

1 Heavily Retinned Dishpan, 10-quart size
3 Retinned Pudding Pans, 1 each 1, 2 and 3 quart size
1 Retinned Milk Pan, 4-quart size
1 Spout Strainer, to attach to spout of Teapot
1 Wire Handle Bowl Strainer, diameter 5 inches, to strain soups, etc.
1 Retinned Wire Soap Bracket, to hang on the wall
1 Doughnut Cutter, diameter 3 inches
1 Biscuit Cutter, diameter 3 inches
1 Soap Saver. Uses up all the small pieces of soap
1 Wire Pot Chain. 1 Nutmeg Grater
1 Pieced Tin Cup, 1-pint size
1 Wood Handle Slotted Mixing Spoon
1 Tinned Steel Kitchen Fork, 12½ inches long, 3 prongs
1 Apple Corer, size, 3½x6 inches
1 Wire Potato Masher, heavy retinned wire and hardwood handle
1 Dover Egg Beater, regular family size
1 Rubber Scraper, used for cleaning windows and also for cleaning sinks
1 Dredge Box, japanned, size, 3x3½ inches
2 Tin Graters, with enameled wood handles, 1 each size, 5½x13 and 3x6½ inches
1 Retinned Wire Broiler, size, 9x6 inches
1 Heavy Asbestos Stove Mat, 9 inches in diameter, with metal rim
1 Wood Handle Preserving Spoon
1 Glass Cutter

No. 23C3033 Price for the entire outfit as listed above, weight 15 pounds.....$1.10

Our $4.05, $4.40 and $4.95 Stove and Kitchen Tinware Outfit.

Everything needed in the kitchen or in the home. More tinware than you would be able to buy in any retail store at more than double the price. The goods we offer in this outfit are all strictly high standard grades. Full sizes and quality guaranteed. Outfit includes the following:

1 IX Tin Wash Boiler, with flat copper bottom
1 IX Tin Tea Kettle, with flat copper bottom
1 IX Tin Coffee Pot, with copper bowl bottom and enameled wood handle
1 IX Tin Teapot, with copper bowl bottom and enameled wood handle
1 Retinned Wash Basin
1 IX Tin Dipper, with heavy copper bottom
3 Heavily Retinned Preserving Kettles
1 Heavily Retinned Sauce Pan.
2 Retinned Pudding Pans. 1 IC Tin Colander
1 Heavily Retinned Dishpan
1 IC Tin Steamer, with rimmed cover
4 Tin Pie Plates, 9 inches in diameter
3 Tin Bread Pans. 1 Tin Oblong Pan
1 Deep Oblong Pan
1 Tin Measure, 1-quart size, graduated by one half pints. 1 Tin Funnel
1 Tin Grater, with enameled wood handle
1 Retinned Soup Ladle, with enameled wood handle.
1 Tin Gravy Strainer
10 Assorted Cake, Cookey, Biscuit and Doughnut Cutters. 1 Nutmeg Grater
1 Retinned Flat Handle Skimmer
1 Cake Turner, with enameled wood handle
12 Assorted Tin Patty Pans
1 Patent Rotary Flour Sifter
1 Covered Japanned Dustpan
2 Retinned Threaded Basting Spoons
1 Tinned Kitchen Fork, 3 prongs, length, 12¼ inches.
1 Dover Egg Beater
3 Assorted Tin Pot Covers, to fit kettles and saucepan. 1 Square Japanned Match Box
1 Polished Lipped Frying Pan, with always cool handle
2 Sheet Iron Dripping or Roasting Pans

No. 23C3037 Our Stove and Kitchen Tinware Set for No. 7 Stove. Weight, 55 lbs., complete. Price......$4.05
No. 23C3038 Our Stove and Kitchen Tinware Set for No. 8 Stove. Weight, 60 lbs., complete. Price......$4.40
No. 23C3039 Our Stove and Kitchen Tinware Set for No. 9 Stove. Weight, 70 lbs., complete. Price......$4.95

GREATEST VALUES EVER KNOWN IN WASHING MACHINES.

We Ask Your Orders for These Well Known and Highest Grade Machines Made, Because We Offer the Best and Can Save You Money.

WASHING MACHINES, formerly considered a mechanical luxury, are now a household necessity. At the prices we name, which are the lowest ever known for highest grade washing machines, no family can afford to be without one. By their use anyone can do washing, blue Monday becomes a thing of the past, and sighs and groans are turned into smiles. Clothes are washed perfectly clean by gentle friction and agitation and without rubbing them to pieces on a washboard. They will save your health, patience and time. You can wash as much in one hour with a good washing machine as you can in three by hand and do better work. No matter which style you may select you can rest assured you will receive the most perfect washing machine of its kind and one which will give splendid satisfaction. To attain perfect results, to wash cleaner and easier and in less than one-third the time required to do the same work by hand, to wash the clothes to snowy whiteness, follow closely the simple directions which we furnish with each machine and we will guarantee splendid satisfaction.

ALWAYS GIVE CATALOGUE NUMBER WHEN ORDERING.

The Home Queen Rotary Washer, $4.55.

EQUAL TO WASHING MACHINES WIDELY ADVERTISED AT DOUBLE OUR PRICE.

No. 23C101 Saves three-fourths of the time and labor and will do an average washing in an hour. The simple high speed, light running gearing is the best and most durable made, the wearing parts being made of steel and malleable iron. The rotary motion is by far the easiest for the operator. It will run forward or backward and washes the clothes by gentle friction and agitation; rubs off no buttons and tears no clothes. The tub is made of the best Louisiana cypress with the inside corrugated like a washboard. It will wash a few pieces or a tub full; blankets or handkerchiefs and napkins with equal ease. We fully guarantee the Home Queen to be the best rotary washer ever offered at the price and to please you in every way. Inside dimensions, 24x14 inches. Weight, 75 pounds. Price......$4.55

The Chicago American Washer, No. 22.

$2.48

Interior View of No. 23C102

No. 23C102

No. 23C102 **The old reliable Chicago American, made better than ever before.** Tub is now made of the best Louisiana cypress, corrugated on the inside like a wash board. Has our improved gearing and adjustable pin wheel agitator. Handsomely finished and varnished and is warranted to do perfect work and to be worth double the price of the washers of this pattern commonly sold. Inside dimensions, 24x14 inches. Weight 50 pounds. Price......$2.48

No. 23C104

$2.45

READ THIS.

You can WASH AS MUCH IN ONE HOUR with a good washing machine as you can in three by hand. Clothes are washed to snowy whiteness with little labor. They save your health and patience and make blue Monday a thing of the past.

The Desplaines American Washer No. 5.

No. 23C104 This machine was gotten up at special request of some of our customers. It is the same make and finish as our No. 22 Chicago American. Staves and bottom are corrugated; in fact, it is the No. 22 Chicago American reversed. Inside dimensions, 22½x11 inches. Weight, 44 pounds. Price......$2.45

The Curtis Washer.

No. 23C110 This machine is made on the rubber principle, the same as used in the Quick and Easy, but has two cylinders working in opposite directions at the same motion of the crank shaft, thus cleaning the clothes quicker and more thoroughly than the former machine.

It will not tear the clothes, and on account of the balance wheel the machine will work so easily that a child can work it without being fatigued. Made of selected Louisiana cypress, finished with two coats of paint and one coat each of graining color and coach varnish. Has heavy non-rusting galvanized bottom and all the iron parts coming in contact with the water are heavily tinned or galvanized to prevent spotting the clothes. Inside dimensions, 18x24x13 inches. Weight, 103 pounds.

Price, wringer not included **$5.10**

$5.10

Columbia Rotary Washer.

$4.98

No. 23C144 Columbia Rotary Washer. Easiest and lightest running washer made. Has improved roller bearings, metal parts aluminum coated; no clutches, cams or springs to wear or get out of order. The mechanism is never in the way. Has extra large tub made of perfectly seasoned selected Virginia white cedar, fully corrugated like a washboard. Top hoop is flat, middle and bottom hoops are of electric welded galvanized wire, can never come off. It washes the most delicate laces or the heaviest bedding easily, quickly, perfectly. Balance wheel turns in either direction and washes equally well when turned slowly or rapidly. The tub is steamtight as well as watertight giving out no odor of foul steam, and making no sloppy floors. No other machine combines so many labor saving devices with good workmanship and perfect material. Fully guaranteed, and if not the easiest running machine made, can be returned at our expense and money will be refunded. Weight, 65 pounds.

Price....................**$4.98**

Our Cascade Rocker Washer.

No. 23C121 Rocks like a cradle and almost as easily. You can do your washing while sitting on a chair. Cannot possibly tear the clothes, has large capacity and washes quickly and easily. The galvanized cover is water and steam tight. No sloppy floors or foul steam to endanger your health if you use our Cascade Rocker. Has space for attaching a wringer, and can be instantly locked in a level position. It is extra well made and strongly braced, has no parts to wear or break and is the most durable machine manufactured. Inside dimensions, 16x25 inches. Weight, 60 pounds. Price....................**$3.98**

The Golden Crown Rotary Washer.

A $10.00 WASHER AT ONLY $5.45

No. 23C137 This is the genuine Golden Crown Washer, a machine that has always sold for $10.00. Exactly the same as the $10.00 machine in every way—has every improvement, including the high speed heavy draft gearing, by which you can wash a heavy load in one-half the time required to wash a light load in any other machine. We fully guarantee the Golden Crown Washer to wash more clothes at a time and to do it in one-half to two-thirds the time of any other washer. This illustration, which is reproduced from a photograph, gives a little idea of the strength and durability of this machine. It is built of selected red Louisiana cypress, which will resist the action of water and acid better than any other known wood, the extra heavy stave legs are strongly bolted to the chime of the tub, cross braced and reinforced with steel rods. We guarantee the gearing for five years and should any part give out within that time we will replace it entirely free of charge. The inside is fully corrugated. The heavy well balanced fly wheel can be run either way with little effort and the machine washes anything from a lace curtain to a horse blanket perfectly. Finished with three coats of cream colored pure lead paint, with red hoops and gold bronzed gearing and fly wheel. Remember, we guarantee the Golden Crown washer to wash one-third easier and quicker than any other. Every one is shipped out on 30 days' trial and if after using it 30 days you are not more than satisfied with your purchase, return it to us at our expense and we will refund your money and all transportation charges you have paid. Shipped set up and ready for use by attaching fly wheel which can be done in a few moments. Shipping weight, 80 pounds. Price....................**$5.45**

The Revolving Wheel All Metal Steam Washer.

No. 23C149 Having all the latest improvements. Boiler is made of heavy galvanized iron, 21¾x12x10¼ in., inside measurement. The cylinder is made from heavy tin plate, is 18¾ inches in diameter and 9¾ inches wide. The clothes are placed in this cylinder and washed by the action of the steam. Prints and ginghams can be washed in from five to eight minutes, white flannel in five minutes; red flannel in about one minute; lace curtains in from ten to fifteen minutes. No washboard rubbing is necessary, and clothes will last twice as long. In washing it is not necessary to turn all the while. You turn the cylinder one or two minutes, then go about your other work for a while, then turn the cylinder a minute or two again. You can wash much cleaner in this washer than you can by hand, and the clothes will always keep white and never turn yellow. Does not wear the clothes or pull off the buttons. This machine is made of the best material and should last from five to ten years. Remember, the clothes are not boiled, but cleansed by steam. This is a process which is used by the celebrated French steam cleaning establishments. A heavy tin cover fits closely on the top of this machine, and closely confines the steam. Shipping weight, 30 pounds. Price....................**$3.75**

The Genuine Improved Scott's Western Washer.

The standard family machine. The make up and finish of our Scott's Western will be the same as heretofore, and will not be excelled by any other make. All of the bolts, washers, nuts, nails, in fact all iron parts that come in contact with the clothing are heavily tinned, absolutely no danger of rust spots on the clothes. Fitted up with our patent post and pinwheel, the greatest invention of the age in washing machines. Made in two sizes, No. 2 and No 3. The former is the family size.

No. 23C124 Scott's Western Washing Machine, Size No. 2. Inside dimensions, 17¾x23½x10½ inches. Weight, 62 pounds. Price.......**$2.47**

$2.47

No. 23C126 Scott's Western Washing Machine, Size No. 3. Inside dimensions, 19½x25½x11¼ inches. Weight, 63 pounds. Price....................**$2.67**

Quick and Easy Washer.

No. 23C135 This machine is called the Quick and Easy Washer and we are satisfied that by buying it every householder will find that it is true to its name and will relieve his wife of a great burden. Sides are each made of one piece of selected lumber, has heavy, rustless galvanized iron bottom, removable corrugated double rubbers, nicely finished in red with iron parts japanned. Inside dimensions, 19x28x13 inches. Weight, 43 lbs.

$1.98

Price....................**$1.98**

Electric Washer.

$3.33

No. 23C140 Constructed of the best Virginia white cedar, and is stronger, more nicely finished, and larger than any round machine on the market. Supplied with our improved gearing fully galvanized. Inside of machine is fully corrugated, similar to a washboard, there being no nails or blocks of any kind on the inside. The machine is made with large end of tub down, allowing plenty of room for water and clothes. The hoops are made of extra heavy galvanized wire, are electric welded, and are warranted not to break or fall off. Instead of using a square wooden post to work the dolly, we use a square galvanized iron rod, making it impossible to tear the most delicate fabric, as the dolly and standard are automatically adjusted to the quantity of clothes contained in the machine. The Electric closes tight and retains the heat in the washer for a long time, and prevents the odor of foul steam from clothes. The washer can be used on a carpet without soiling same. Large, convenient place for holding the wringer, which need not be moved while using the machine. Shipping weight, 50 pounds. Price....................**$3.33**

Our Ideal Washer.

No. 23C154 Our Ideal Washer. It does washing equal to any large washing machine, but with greater ease and more rapidity. It washes a tub, pail or boiler full of clothes all at one time, without the usual wear and tear received by all old methods. It forces compressed air, steam and water through the fabric, quickly removing all dirt. It has no equal for dainty fabrics, lace curtains, blankets, woolens, disagreeable cloths, etc. If it does not do all we claim for it, it may be returned and money will be refunded. Made of best tin. Weight, 1½ pounds. Price....................**42c**

WRINGERS.

Rolls in our warranted wringers are made of solid white rubber, and vulcanized immovably to shaft. When we state that a wringer is guaranteed for a certain period, we mean, that should the rolls turn on the shaft, become loose, bulge, or give out because of defects within the time specified, we will replace them free of charge. When we guarantee a wringer for one year, it does not mean that we do not think, and that you cannot expect that the wringer will last longer than that time. If a wringer is defective it will certainly show within one year, and if it does not show within that time, we take it for granted that the wringer is perfect in material and workmanship, and will last according to the care and usage it receives, from five to twenty years. **When ordered with a washing machine a wringer adds little or nothing to the freight charges.**

The Curtis Star Wringer.

With large 11-inch rolls.

No. 23C206 The Genuine Curtis Star 5-Year Guaranteed Wringer with relief screws is similar to the Acme Star in design but has the highest grade solid white rubber rolls made, size, 11x1¾ inches. Sets down close to tub and is easy to operate. The best wringer made for galvanized tubs. Weight, boxed, 22 pounds.

Price....................**$2.87**

The Keene Wringer.

No. 23C210 The Keene Wringer is a strictly high grade, up to date wringer. It has all the improvements known to wringer manufacturers. It has wheel top screws, but screws that will fasten to galvanized iron, fibre or wooden tubs, steel pressure springs, double cog wheels. It is guaranteed for two years. Size of rolls, 10x1¾ inches. Weight, boxed, 21 pounds.

Price....................**$1.98**

The Wonder Wringer.

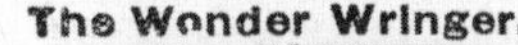

No. 23C200 The Wonder is an ordinary grade wringer, not guaranteed. It has iron frame, and apron, iron tub clamps, steel springs; rolls are 10x1¾ inches. This wringer is not warranted, and we do not advise its purchase. Weight, boxed, 14½ lbs. Price. **$1.25**

The Acme Star Wringer.

No. 23C205 The Acme Star Wringer with cog wheels. Special features of merit in the Acme Star iron frame wringers are that they have steel spiral pressure springs and thumb nuts, by which the pressure can be adjusted the same as any wood frame wringer. They are furnished with high grade rolls, size, 10x1¾ inches, guaranteed for three years. Weight, boxed, 21 pounds. Price....................**$2.08**

The Dandy Wringer.

No. 23C202 The Dandy Wringer has a frame and apron of the same general appearance as the Wonder wringer, but the rolls are high grade and are warranted for one year. It is furnished with tub clamps that will fasten to galvanized iron, fibre or wooden tubs. Size of rolls, 10x1¾ inches. Weight, boxed, 15 pounds.

Price....................**$1.65**

The Fowler Wringer.

No. 23C209 The Fowler Wringer has wood frame with two adjusting screws, iron tub clamps, as shown in illustration. The rolls are ordinary grade, not warranted, and while we recommend our 5-year guaranteed Curtis wringer, we offer this as a wringer for less money. Rolls, 10x1¾ inches. Weight, boxed, 20 pounds. Price....................**$1.42**

The Scott Wringer.

No. 23C214 This Wringer has wheel top screws, tub clamps that will fasten to galvanized iron, fibre or wooden tubs, double gear cog wheels, spiral steel pressure springs, high grade rolls fully warranted for two years. Rolls, 10x1¾ inches. Weight, boxed, 22 pounds. Price........$2.05

The Seroco Ball Bearing Wringer.

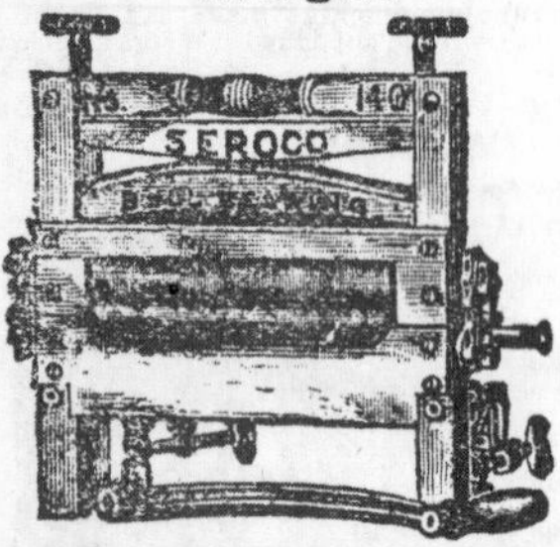

No. 23C218 This Wringer has wheel top screws, steel adjustment spring, double gear cog wheels, tub clamps that will fasten to galvanized iron, fibre or wooden tubs. The tub clamp is fastened to the wringer by a bolt, which passes entirely through the wringer, making the strongest fastening known. The ball bearings reduce the friction to a minimum and materially lighten the hardest part of the wash day. The ball bearings in this wringer are so constructed that it is absolutely impossible for them to break or get out of order in any way. We wish to caution users against putting too much pressure against the rolls. This wringer turns so easily that if you have been accustomed to using a wringer with ordinary bearings, you will think that this one is not wringing dry because it turns so easily. You should not put much pressure on the top screws or you will destroy the rolls. If you will simply put enough pressure on the rolls to wring the clothes dry you will find that this wringer will work better than any you can find in the market. The rolls are high grade, guaranteed for two years. Size, 10x1¾ inches. Weight, boxed, 23½ pounds. Price.....$2.28

The Genuine Curtis Five-Year Wringer.

Guaranteed for 5 Years.

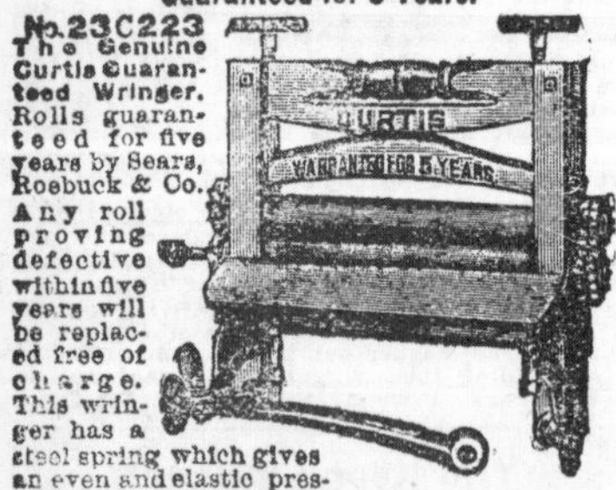

No. 23C223 The Genuine Curtis Guaranteed Wringer. Rolls guaranteed for five years by Sears, Roebuck & Co. Any roll proving defective within five years will be replaced free of charge. This wringer has a steel spring which gives an even and elastic pressure, and an improved guide board, which spreads the clothes as they pass between the rolls, causing the rolls to wear more evenly and lessening the wear on the clothing. You cannot buy a better wringer than this, because better rolls are not made. We have contracted for the entire output of this wringer and must sell them. Our price, combined with our guarantee, should enable us to dispose of them quickly. Size of rolls, 11x1¾ inches. Weight, boxed, 23 lbs. Guaranteed for five years. Price.....$3.15

MRS. POTTS' SAD IRONS.

Set consists of one iron with rounded end, for polishing, weight, 4 pounds; two with regular ends, one weighing 5½ pounds and one 5¾ pounds; one detachable wood handle, always cool, and one iron stand.

No. 23C345 Mrs. Potts' Sad Irons, in sets of three, with detachable wood handle and iron stand, as described above; finely polished. Price, per set........64c

No. 23C346 Set of three Mrs. Potts' Sad Irons, as above, finely polished and heavily nickel plated. Price, per set........67c

Mangles.

Comparatively few people appreciate the value of a mangle; in fact, many have never heard of a mangle, but in Europe they are very extensively used and considered as indispensable as a wringer. It is an established fact that clothes which have been mangled are more healthful than when finished by the hot iron, for the reason that the meshes of the material are left open, whereas the hot iron closes them. Articles mangled, retain original whiteness and never spoil by scorching. N. B.—They are not suitable for shirts and clothes with buttons.

No. 23C250 Household Mangle with Ball Bearings, which reduce the friction to a minimum and make it easy to operate. Can be attached to any table. Size of wood rolls, 24x3½ inches. Shipping weight, 58 lbs. Price....$4.48

Universal Mangle.

No. 23C256 Universal Mangle. For heavy work in laundries, hotels and institutions where a great deal of laundry work is done. Also suitable for large families; it is not suitable for shirts and clothes with buttons. Size of wood rolls, 24x4½ inches. Shipping weight, 94 pounds. Price........$12.85

Mop Handles.

No. 23C300 Mop Handle and Brush Holder Combined. A reliable article, made from latest improved patterns, with free working and effective screw, hardwood handle. Weight, 1¼ pounds. Price....8c

No. 23C315 Cotton Mops. 9 pounds to the dozen. Price........11c

No. 23C316 Cotton Mops. 12 pounds to the dozen. Price........14c

Self Wringing Mop.

No. 23C324 The Erie Self Wringing Mop. The mops made of cotton coils, large and full size. The hands do not come in contact with the water, the mop being wrung at arm's length. The use of scalding water is another important advantage. The floor washes easier, cleaner and quicker and dries more readily. Weight, 2 pounds. Price.......25c

Sad Iron Handle.

No. 23C352 Sad Iron Handle. Fits any Mrs. Potts' pattern sad irons; is all steel and cannot be broken. Asbestos insulated and the coolest handle made. Fits the hand and does not tire the wrist. Nice japanned finish. Price........9c

Sensible Sad Irons.

No. 23C356 Sensible Sad Irons. A handsome outfit, containing three highly nickel plated and polished solid sad irons, ground by perfect machinery which makes every iron true; and face shaped to make ironing easier than with the old style irons. These solid irons hold the heat longer than the ordinary Mrs. Potts' irons. The handle is the strongest and best made, will not shake, fits the hand perfectly and can not become accidentally detached. Irons are double pointed and weigh 5, 6 and 7 pounds respectively. Price, per set of three irons, detachable handle and stand. 83c

No. 23C359 Sensible Sleeve Iron. For laundering shirt waists and children's clothes. Will iron a plait or tuck to the seam. Is nickel plated and polished, with detachable handle. Weight, 4 pounds. Length, 8 in. Price....29c

No. 23C375 Old Style Sad Irons, with face finely polished. The 2½-pound is handsomely nickel plated and splendid for laundering shirt waists and other light articles.

Weight, lbs....	2½	5	6	7	8	9
Price........	23c	14c	17c	20c	23c	26c

Charcoal Irons.

No. 23C407 Family Charcoal Irons, with removable top and hardwood handle with shield. Handsomely nickel plated and elegantly finished, with top finished in gold bronze. Is self heating and requires little attention. Uses ordinary charcoal as fuel, is easily regulated to any desired heat and does away with the hot fire on ironing day. Agents charge $2.00 to $2.50 for this iron. Weight, 7 pounds. Price........98c

No. 23C408 Family Charcoal Iron. Same pattern as above. Plain polished finish. Weight, 6½ pounds. Price........70c

Tailor's Goose.

No. 23C412 Tailor's Goose, with extra polished face.

Weight, lbs.....	12	14	16	18	20	22
Price........	51c	60c	68c	77c	85c	94c

Crown Hand Fluter.

No. 23C442 Crown Hand Fluter. Plate, 5¼ inches long and 3 inches wide; roll, 1¾ inches diameter. Japanned cast base. To heat the plate, it is simply lifted off the base and placed on the stove. Plate and roll are finely polished. The handle and yoke to hold roll are of malleable iron. Weight, 2¾ pounds. Price........58c

CARPET SWEEPERS.

A Carpet Sweeper saves time and money. costs no more than four or five good brooms and will outwear several dozen. Will follow a broom on any carpet and remove more dirt and dust than the broom did with very much less labor. Does not wear out a carpet as a broom does, and in this way alone will quickly save its cost. Sold under our universal guarantee, If not satisfactory, return it and your money will be refunded.

No. 23C470 The Acme Carpet Sweeper is the best low priced carpet sweeper ever offered. It has broom action, reversible bail, improved dumping device, the new improved braid band, which never comes off, strictly pure bristle brush, handsomely finished case. The metal parts are japanned finish. Weight, boxed 9¼ pounds. Price........$1.55

Imperial Carpet Sweeper.

No. 23C473 Our Imperial Carpet Sweeper contains the famous broom action, and every other feature necessary in a first class sweeper. Made from the best selected cabinet woods in an assortment of attractive finishes. Full nickel plated trimming. Nickel plated on copper, which is the best method known, permits the highest possible finish and will not rust or tarnish. Has the new improved braid band furniture protector encircling the case, patent reversible bail. Wheels outside the case, our everlasting pure bristle brush; pans operate independently by an easy pressure of the finger. Weight, boxed, 9¼ pounds. Price.....$1.98

Bissell's Sanitary Sweeper.

No. 23C479 Bissell's Sanitary Sweeper is made by the Bissell Carpet Sweeper Co. of Grand Rapids, Mich., the largest manufacturers of carpet sweepers in the world. It has the renowned Bissell broom action, reversible bail, new improved braid band furniture protector which never comes off. Bissell's reliable new improved spring dumping device, pure bristle sweeping brush, handsomely finished case. All metal parts are nicely japanned. Weight, boxed, 9½ pounds. Price........$1.80

Bissell's Grand Rapids, Cyco Bearings.

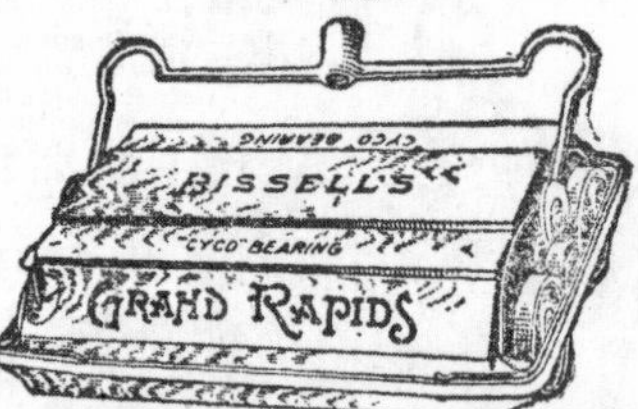

No. 23C480 Bissell's Grand Rapids, Cyco Bearings, Carpet Sweeper. The best known and most widely sold carpet sweeper in the world. Contains the famous Bissell broom action, the anti-raveling collector brush ends, the dustproof axle tubes, the new improved Bissell's ball socket, and every other desirable feature necessary in a first class sweeper. Made from the best selected cabinet woods in an assortment of attractive finishes. Has improved braid band furniture protector encircling the case, Bissell's patent reversible bail spring, wheels outside the case, our everlasting pure bristle brush; both pans open at once by an easy pressure of the finger. Fully guaranteed. Weight, boxed, 9½ pounds. Price, Cyco bearings, japanned metal trimmings........$2.50

Bissell's Prize, Cyco Bearings, Carpet Sweeper.

No. 23C483 Bissell's Prize Carpet Sweeper, the latest of the Bissell patterns. A sweeper of the highest grade, with one of the handsomest patent case designs. The case is hand polished. The bail, trimmings and iron end pieces are plated with nickel, brass or antique copper, according to the finish of the case. It contains the Bissell broom action, has patent reversible bail, patent bail sockets, the improved braid band furniture protector and our pure bristle wire staple brush, adapted to be easily removed from the sweeper. Its spring dumping device is convenient, opening one pan at a time. Length of case, 14 inches. Its construction throughout is as perfect as care and skill can make it. This is in our opinion the handsomest design and the best finished carpet sweeper made by the Bissell Carpet Sweeper Co. Weight, boxed, 10¼ pounds.

Price, with Cyco bearings........$3.00

Pot Chain and Scraper.

No. 23C510 The Sensible Pot Chain and Scraper is a new and useful article, each ring is double, which makes it very durable. The handle is malleable iron; the blade is steel; the handle and scraper are tinned. Weight, 4 ounces.

Price, per dozen, 85c; each........8c

MAKE UP A FREIGHT ORDER OF 100 LBS. OR MORE BY INCLUDING GOODS FROM OTHER DEPARTMENTS THAT YOU WILL SOON NEED.

Bench Wringers. $2.75

No. 23C234 The Alpine Bench Wringer. We have often heard said, "It's more work to hold the tubs than to turn the wringer." Use a bench wringer and you don't have to hold the tub. The bench is strong and durable, large enough to accommodate two large tubs. When not in use bench folds up, taking but little more room than an ordinary wringer and much less than the old fashioned washbench. The apron is reversible so clothes can be put in from either side. The wringer is well made. Rolls are guaranteed for one year. Size of rolls, 10x1¾ inches. Weight, crated, 41 pounds. Price........$2.75

The Genuine Curtis 5-Year Guaranteed Bench Wringer.

No. 23C236 The King of Wringers. Nothing better has ever been produced; has pure elastic Para rubber rolls, size, 11x1¾ inches, which will wring drier and last longer than any other. We warrant these rolls for five years, and with ordinary care they should last 15 years in family use. The folding bench, holding two tubs, has an oscillating drainboard which conducts the water into either tub. Has best lignum vitæ bearings; improved guideboard, steel pressure spring, is constructed in the most substantial manner, and when folded will occupy but little more floor space than an ordinary wringer. Shipping weight, 43 pounds. Price........$3.85

Can Openers.

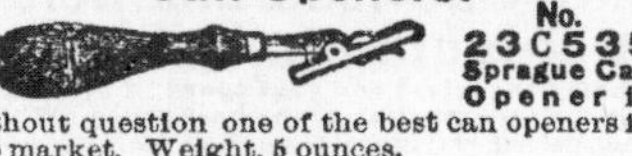

No. 23C535 Sprague Can Opener is without question one of the best can openers in the market. Weight, 5 ounces.
Price, per dozen, 39c; each..............4c

No. 23C537 Surecut Can Opener. Opens any can, round or square or any size quicker and easier than others. Has tool steel blade and varnished wood handle.
Price..............9c

Mincing Knife.

No. 23C557 Double Mincing Knife. Polished steel blades; enameled handle. Weight, 8 ounces. Price, per dozen, 48c; each..5c

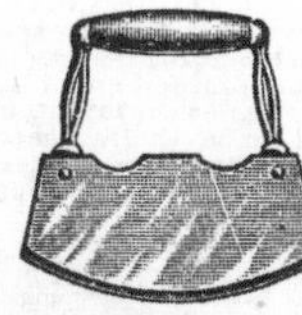

No. 23C560 Mincing Knife. Cast steel blade, ground sharp; solid malleable iron handle, black enameled which can't split or get loose. Weight, 9 ounces.
Price..............7c

Fruit Jar Wrench.

No. 23C595 Fruit Jar Cover Wrench, will not break the cover or can, will not slip or become worthless from long or careless use. It is stamped out of sheet steel and riveted together. It saves jars, rubbers and covers and insures the fruit being properly sealed during the canning season. Weight, 6 oz. Price, per doz., 75c; each..7c

Henis Fruit Press.

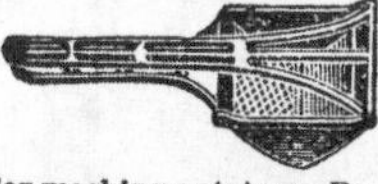

No. 23C610 Henis Fruit and Vegetable Press and Strainer; can be used for a variety of purposes; is especially recommended for mashing potatoes. Potatoes, after being forced through the strainer have a delicious creamy taste that no other method of mashing will impart. It is not necessary to peel the potatoes, as it mashes and removes the skin of boiled potatoes in one operation. Weight, 20 ounces. Price......18c

Steak Pounder.

No. 23C647 The Star Steak Pounder, Ice Pick and Shave. Malleable iron, full nickel plated.
Weight, 10 ounces. Price..............9c

Revolving Grater.

No. 23C680 Revolving Grater, for grating horseradish, cocoanut, pumpkins, squash, lemons, crackers, cheese, etc. The cylinder is 3 inches in diameter and 3 inches long. No family should be without one. Weight, 1 lb. 10 oz. Price...47c

Bread and Bacon Slicer.

No. 23C695 Bread and Bacon Slicer enables any one to produce slices of any desired thickness all exactly alike and all perfectly straight and even; a great time saver for hotels and restaurants; for making sandwiches alone this slicer is worth many times its cost. Strongly made and very simple in operation. Can be used with any bread knife, but the serrated edge knife, as shown in illustration, is best.
Price, Slicer without knife..............15c
Slicer and Knife complete..............22c

Perfect Cherry Stoner.

No. 23C714. This Perfect Cherry Stoner does not crush the cherry or cause any loss of juice; a perfect machine for large, small or California cherries. The seed extracting knife drives the seeds into one dish and actually throws the cherries into another. The mark of the knife can scarcely be seen on the seeded fruit. It seeds from 20 to 30 quarts per hour. No grinding; mashing; no loss of juice. Heavy tinned to prevent rust. Weight, 1½ pounds. Price..............70c

Raisin and Grape Seeder.

No. 23C720 Enterprise Raisin and Grape Seeder is simple in construction, easily adjusted, does the work rapidly and effectually, seeding the raisins wet or dry, better work being obtained if wet. The ordinary washing given by every good housekeeper makes the raisins sufficiently wet. Will seed grapes for preserving and cooking purposes. The raisins should be sprinkled in the hopper as fast as the roller will grasp them. The best results will be obtained by feeding them one at a time. Will seed a pound in five minutes. Weight, 2½ pounds.
Price..............80c

Potato Parer.

No. 23C732 White Mountain Potato Parer. Can be used every day in the year in every household. Pares any shape or kind of potato better and easier than can be done by hand. Enters into and cleans out the eyes and by taking a thinner paring saves at least 50 per cent of the outside of the potato that is ordinarily wasted. Very simple and durable. Also suitable for quinces and pears. Weight, 1½ pounds. Price..............49c

Apple Parers.

No. 23C736 White Mountain Apple Parer. Pares, cores and slices the fruit and pushes off apple and core separately, or can be used to pare without coring and slicing if desired. Simple and easy to operate, cannot get out of order. Weight, 1½ pounds. Price..............37c

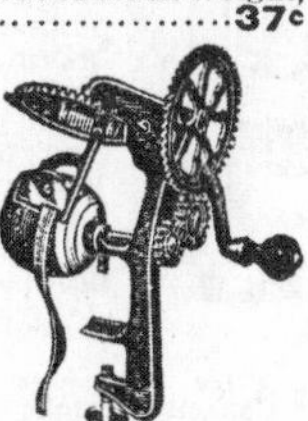

No. 23C739 Turn Table 98 Apple Parer. Pares very close to both ends of the apple, but does not core or slice. All parings fall clear of the machine. Has automatic push off, and after paring, knife recedes so as to leave room to place another apple on the forks. Very rapid and strong, and the best to use where paring only is desired. Weight, 2¾ pounds. Price..............46c

No. 23C740 New Lightning Apple Parer. The most rapid hand paring machine in the world. One forward movement of the hand pares an apple from stem to blossom. A return of the handle pushes the apple off of the fork. Very simple, yet strongly built; does not core or slice. Weight, 2¾ pounds.
Price..............59c

Pepper and Spice Mill.

No. 23C852 Pepper and Spice Mill. Buy the pure, unground pepper and spice, and grind it as you use it, thus preventing adulteration and retaining its full strength. This mill is made of walnut, highly polished, with nickeled top. Height, 4½ inches; diameter, 2 inches. Weight, 4 ounces.
Price..............20c

COFFEE MILLS.

Tin Canister Coffee Mill.

No. 23C875 Tin Canister Coffee Mill. Made with japanned tin canister holding one pound of coffee and cup for catching and measuring the ground coffee. The canister is practically air tight and by buying the coffee in the bean and grinding it just as you need it, you secure the full strength of the bean, as it is well known that coffee rapidly loses its strength if allowed to stand after grinding. Weight, 3 pounds. Price..............26c

The X-Ray Mill.

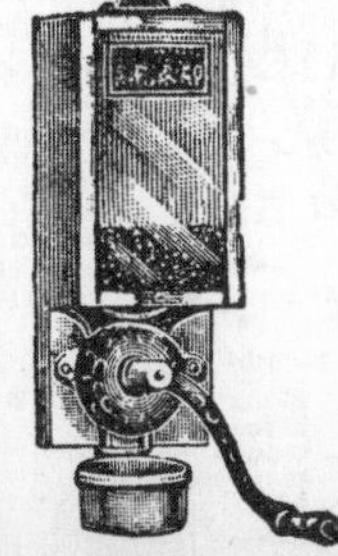

No. 23C879 The X-Ray Mill, has wood frame and wood hopper with glass front, so coffee is always in sight. A 1-pound capacity wall mill of entirely new design. Easily regulated to grind fine or coarse, as desired. Turns easy. Grinds fast. The mill is well made, strong and durable, and is warranted to give satisfaction. Weight, 5 pounds.
Price..............43c

Jewel Coffee Mill.

No. 23C882 Jewel Coffee Mill. With heavy ornamental glass canister. Capacity, one pound. Graduated on one side to show exact amount of coffee on hand. It is provided with our latest improved grinding burrs. Will grind fine or coarse or pulverize coffee if desired. The iron parts and receiving cup are finished in red enamel, and the Jewel is without exception the best and most attractive mill in the market. Each one is packed in a wood box. Weight, 6½ pounds. Price..............65c

New Home Coffee Mill.

No. 23C892 New Home Coffee Mill. Wood top, iron cover and side handle. This mill has a large hopper capacity, holding over a pound of coffee. It is constructed of the best materials. The box is made of hardwood, highly polished and varnished, and supplied with our improved grinding burrs, which are warranted to pulverize coffee, if desired. Size, 6¾x6¾x8 inches. Weight, 4¾ pounds.
Price..............44c

No. 23C904 Raised Hopper Mill with hinged cover, hardwood box and dovetailed corners, highly polished and covered with best copal varnish, bronzed finish, patent regulator and improved grinding burrs that will thoroughly pulverize coffee when desired. This mill has an ornamental iron top to the box, which makes it strong and durable. Size, 6x6x5 inches. Weight, 4½ lbs. Price..40c

No. 23C912 A Raised Hopper Open Top Mill, hardwood box, dovetailed corners, highly polished and covered with best copal varnish, japanned iron patent regulator and improved grinding burr. Size of box, 6x6x3¾ in. Weight, 2¼ lbs.
Price..............24c

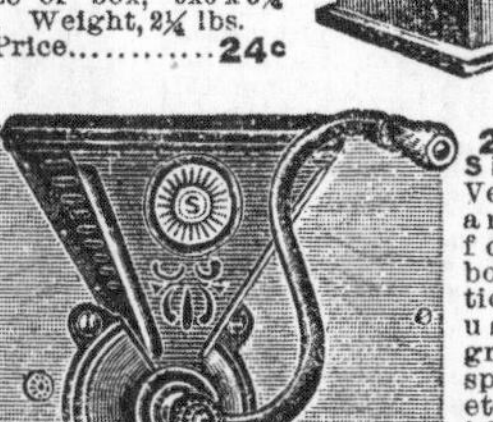

No. 23C925 Side Mill. Very large and strong, for steamboat, plantation or store use. Will grind grain, spices, drugs, etc. Varnished hardwood back, steel grinders. Capacity of hopper, 1½ pounds of roasted coffee. Weight, 9 pounds. Price..............80c

National Coffee Mills.

National Coffee Mills are beautiful in design and most handsomely finished. They are fast grinders and easy runners. We guarantee material and workmanship and in grinding capacity they are equal to other makes of mills of corresponding sizes regardless of price.

Counter Mill.

No. 23C947 National Counter Mill, handsomely finished in red and gold. Fly wheels, 11¾ inches in diameter. Iron hopper holding 1 pound. Height, 18 inches. Shipping weight, 37 pounds. Will grind ½ pound per minute. Price..............$3.75

No. 23C954 National Coffee Mill. Handsomely finished in red and gold with decorated iron hopper holding 2 pounds of coffee. Is 24½ inches high; fly wheels are 16¾ inches in diameter. Will grind 1 pound of coffee per minute. Shipping weight, 72 pounds. Fully warranted.
Price..............$6.60

Bird Cages.

Our various styles of japanned cages are superior to any other japanned cages manufactured. The rails or cross bands of these cages are made of the best charcoal tin plate, double punched, making a stronger and lighter cage than can be made of any other material. Feed cups, perches and swings sent with cages, no extra charge. Our bird cages are all very carefully packed and we guarantee they will reach our customers in good order.

No. 23C1455 Japanned Bird Cage. Size, 11x7½ inches; height, 16 inches. Shipping weight, 10 pounds.
Price..............87c

Our $1.44 Japanned Bird Cage.

With Revolving Perch.

No. 23C1458 Japanned Bird Cage with revolving perch. Body, 9x13¼ inches; height, 19 inches. Shipping weight, 13½ lbs. Price..$1.44

Breeding Cages.

With Partition, Metal Drawer and Flat Back.

No. 23C1467 20 inches long, 10 inches wide, 14 inches high. Shipping weight, 17 pounds.
Price...... $1.58

Mocking Bird Cages.

With Metal Drawers (Opening in Front.)

These cages are suitable for mocking birds, red birds and robins.

No. 23C1479 24 inches long, 16 inches wide, 22 inches high. Shipping weight, 27 pounds.
Price...$2.26

Brass Cages.

The best spring brass wire is used in the construction of our brass cages. Every wire is firmly riveted to the rails by machinery, no solder being used. This gives these cages a strength and firmness combined with lightness and durability unequaled by any other in the market.

No. 23C1500 Brass Bird Cage. Body, 9⅝x6¼ inches; base, 12¾x9⅞ inches; height, 12¾ inches. Shipping weight, 10 lbs.
Price..............89c

No. 23C1505 Brass Bird Cage with brass guard to prevent seed from scattering. Body 10½x7½ inches; base, 13¼x10¾ inches; height, 13½ inches. Shipping weight, 10 pounds.
Price..............$1.58

Parrot Cages.

No. 23C1554 Parrot Cage. Constructed with tinned steel rails and No. 12 tinned wire, plain zinc bases, with new door fastenings, the rails and upright wires being riveted the same as our brass cages. Upright wires are 1⅛-inch space; 17½ inches diameter. Shipping weight, 28¾ pounds.
Price..............$2.90

Bright Tin Squirrel Cages.

Wheel Outside.

No. 23C1572 Red Squirrel or Chipmunk Cage. Body, 9¼x8¼ inches; wheel, 8¼x7¼ inches; height, 11 inches. Shipping weight, 15 lbs.
Price..............$1.80

No. 23C1576 Gray Squirrel Cage. Body, 14¾x12¾ inches; wheel, 12x10¼ in.; height, 16¼ inches. Shipping weight, 16¾ pounds.
Price..............$2.40

Bird Cage Hook.

No. 23C1600 Bronzed Iron Bird Cage Hook, to swing; length 10 inches. Price..............7c

Bird Cage Spring.

No. 23C1604 Bird Cage Springs. Price..............2c

REFRIGERATORS

OUR MICHIGAN REFRIGERATORS are built to las…nd to be economical in the consumption of ice, as a refrigerator that wastes ice is dear at any price. The inside case is made of thoroughly seasoned lumber, upon which is placed our special insulation, mineral felt, which is securely held in place by hardwood cleats, to which is fastened the outside case or cabinet, leaving a space for dead air between the outer wall and filling, the whole forming the most perfect insulation known to science. Outside cases are made of thoroughly seasoned selected ash lumber, finished in antique and handsomely carved and ornamented.

ALL OUR REFRIGERATORS have full metal lining, highest grade solid brass or bronze trimmings, galvanized iron provision shelves, swinging baseboard, which permits the use of a large pan to catch the drippings from waste pipe. Lids are constructed of 1¼-inch lumber, making them very heavy, which prevents warping. Backs are hardwood, paneled. Waste pipe is removable for cleaning. Have perfect dry air circulation. All are thoroughly well built, and have every modern improvement. We give extreme outside measurements, including casters.

THE ICE CAPACITY IS OBTAINED FROM THE NUMBER OF CUBIC INCHES IN THE ICE CHAMBER. REFRIGERATORS THAT HAVE ICE CHAMBER DOOR IN FRONT ARE NOT MADE WITH WATER COOLER.

CATALOGUE OF REFRIGERATORS FREE.

WE ESPECIALLY RECOMMEND that you select a refrigerator from the ones illustrated and described in this big catalogue,

rather than to delay to first write for our free Special Refrigerator Catalogue, since we guarantee that any refrigerator you may order as selected from these pages will reach you in perfect condition, will prove in every way satisfactory to you and that you will find it a very much better refrigerator than you could buy elsewhere at anything like the price we offer, guarantee you will make a big saving in cost; otherwise you can return the refrigerator to us at any time within 10 days at our expense and we will immediately refund your money, together with any freight charges paid by you. If, however, you are unable to make a selection from the illustrations and descriptions shown in this catalogue, and you feel that you would like to have a larger variety to select from, larger illustrations and more complete descriptions, then don't think of buying a refrigerator of any kind from anyone until you first get our free Special Refrigerator Catalogue.

OUR FREE SPECIAL REFRIGERATOR CATALOGUE shows by very large, handsome illustrations, bringing out every little detail, our complete line of refrigerators, all that are shown in this catalogue and many more. Tells how it is possible for us to sell the highest grade refrigerators made at about one-half the prices charged by others. This free catalogue tells all we know about refrigerators, and unless you order at once from these pages, don't think of buying a refrigerator elsewhere until you first write for our free Special Refrigerator Catalogue. In a letter or on a postal card simply say "Send me your free Refrigerator Catalogue" and it will go to you by return mail, postpaid, free with our compliments.

OUR BINDING GUARANTEE. We guarantee every Michigan Refrigerator to be made of the very best materials throughout, to be constructed on the latest improved and most scientific principles, to be found exactly as represented in every respect, and to give universal satisfaction, and if found otherwise than stated we will refund any money sent us and pay freight charges both ways.

REFRIGERATORS are shipped from our factory in Southern Michigan. Refrigerators are accepted as second class freight rate by all railroad companies, which is usually from 40 to 60 cents per 100 pounds for 500 miles. By referring to pages 7 to 11 in front of the book you will get the second class freight rate per 100 pounds to a point nearest you, which is almost exactly the same as to your town, and you will see the freight will amount to next to nothing as compared to what you will save in price.

MICHIGAN SINGLE DOOR REFRIGERATORS

have handsomely finished solid ash cases, solid bronze trimmings, full metal linings, galvanized provision shelves.

A HIGH GRADE LINE AT A LOW PRICE

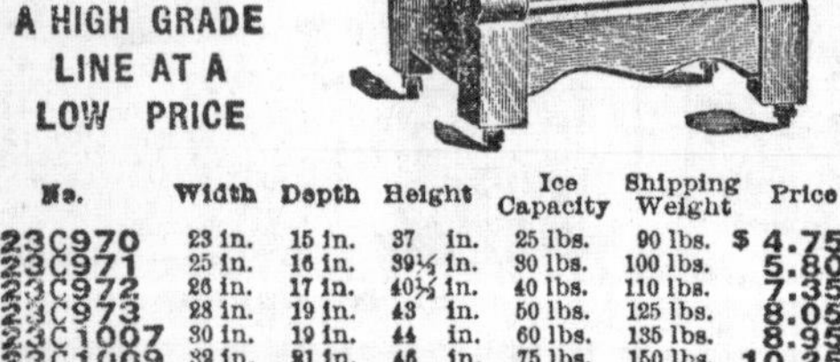

No.	Width	Depth	Height	Ice Capacity	Shipping Weight	Price
23C970	23 in.	15 in.	37 in.	25 lbs.	90 lbs.	$ 4.75
23C971	25 in.	16 in.	39½ in.	30 lbs.	100 lbs.	5.80
23C972	26 in.	17 in.	40½ in.	40 lbs.	110 lbs.	7.35
23C973	28 in.	19 in.	43 in.	50 lbs.	125 lbs.	8.05
23C1007	30 in.	19 in.	44 in.	60 lbs.	135 lbs.	8.95
23C1009	32 in.	21 in.	46 in.	75 lbs.	150 lbs.	10.25

The following refrigerators are exactly the same as Nos. 23C970 to 23C1009, except that they are furnished with a porcelain lined water cooler, and faucet to match trimmings, which reduces the capacity of the ice chamber.

No.	Width	Depth	Height	Ice Capacity	Shipping Weight	Price
23C976	25 in.	16 in.	39½ in.	25 lbs.	110 lbs.	$ 7.60
23C977	26 in.	17 in.	40½ in.	35 lbs.	120 lbs.	8.95
23C978	28 in.	19 in.	43 in.	40 lbs.	135 lbs.	9.75
23C1015	30 in.	19 in.	44 in.	45 lbs.	145 lbs.	10.85
23C1016	32 in.	21 in.	46 in.	65 lbs.	165 lbs.	12.40

Michigan Refrigerators. These refrigerators combine large capacity with small floor space and are very convenient where space is limited. All have handsomely carved solid ash cases and are constructed as described in the heading.

No.	Width	Depth	Height	Ice Capacity	Shipping Weight	Price
23C1017	24 in.	18 in.	50 in.	50 lbs.	120 lbs.	$ 8.55
23C1018	28 in.	19 in.	55 in.	75 lbs.	160 lbs.	10.55
23C1020	31 in.	23 in.	57 in.	100 lbs.	195 lbs.	12.50

Michigan Large Double Door Family Refrigerator, has beautifully carved solid ash case, dark antique finish, solid bronze trimmings, most perfect insulation, full metal lining, and all improvements. Very economical for natural or artificial ice.

No.	Width	Depth	Height	Ice Capacity	Shipping Weight	Price
23C1022	36 in.	21 in.	46 in.	100 lbs.	165 lbs.	$11.85

No. 23C1024 Same as No. 23C1022, but with porcelain lined water cooler and faucet, which reduces ice capacity to 80 pounds. Shipping weight, 185 pounds. Price......**$14.10**

This elegant line of large double door refrigerators for hotels, boarding houses and private families, are stylish in appearance, of the most durable construction and very economical; have hand carved cases, beautifully finished, and solid brass trimmings. See heading for description of construction and insulation. Fully guaranteed in every way. All have provision chamber divided into two compartments, except smallest size.

No.	Width	Depth	Height	Ice Capacity	Shipping Weight	Price
23C1026	37 in.	20 in.	51 in.	125 lbs.	195 lbs.	$14.95
23C1027	40 in.	24 in.	52 in.	170 lbs.	290 lbs.	19.60
23C1028	42 in.	27 in.	54 in.	190 lbs.	340 lbs.	22.25
23C1029	45 in.	28 in.	56 in.	220 lbs.	370 lbs.	24.50

MICHIGAN ICE CHESTS.

Michigan Ice Chests are made of solid ash, nicely finished and insulated in the same manner and with the same care as our refrigerators. They are very economical in the use of ice, and while they lack the cold dry air circulation which is a feature of our refrigerators, they will give good satisfaction. Very strongly constructed, full zinc lined, with ice and provision racks and mounted on patent casters.

No.	Length	Depth	Height	Shipping Weight	Price
23C1031	25 in.	17 in.	25 in.	70 lbs.	$ 4.10
23C1032	29 in.	20 in.	25 in.	85 lbs.	4.99
23C1034	32 in.	21 in.	26 in.	105 lbs.	5.67
23C1035	35 in.	23 in.	29 in.	125 lbs.	6.88
23C1036	37 in.	25 in.	31 in.	145 lbs.	7.88
23C1037	41 in.	27 in.	33 in.	185 lbs.	9.28

Puritan White Odorless Enameled Refrigerators.

In this line is embodied the latest and best ideas of scientific and sanitary refrigerator construction of the best grade. While there are many higher priced refrigerators on the market, there is no other line in which all the essentials, namely: durability, economy in the use of ice, and ease of cleaning are combined to such an extent as in our Puritan line.

Construction—Made of selected thoroughly seasoned ash lumber. Paneled on side, top and back to prevent warping; front ornamented with raised beveled panels, finished in antique, handsomely polished. Hinges and automatic air tight locks used are solid brass, Roman gold finish. Lids are extra heavy and will not warp. Ice racks and ice chambers are heavy galvanized steel, fitted with self closing drip cup, removable waste pipe, swinging baseboard and patent casters. The metal lining to provision chamber, shelves and drain pipe are enameled with a pure white sanitary odorless enamel, which is a mineral substance, containing no white lead, oil or turpentine. It is applied in three coats and baked on in ovens under a high temperature; after cooling, a coating of white shellac is applied, which gives it a high glossy finish, easily cleaned with warm water and a damp cloth. Others use an enamel the same as used on iron beds, which is poisonous, bad smelling and not sanitary.

Our system of insulation is acknowledged to be the best known, and consists of six distinct walls as follows: Outside ash casing, sheet of mineral felt, dead air space, sheet of mineral felt, inner casing and metal lining. The doors are insulated in the same manner, with mineral felt and dead air space. The money you will save in the smaller consumption of ice through this perfect insulation will in a single season more than pay the difference in cost between a Puritan refrigerator and the ordinary grades which waste a large quantity of ice.

Puritan White Enameled Solid Ash Refrigerator, constructed as described above with single door to provision chamber and ice receptacle opening on top. Has perfect dry cold air circulation and it is impossible for provisions to become mouldy or tainted as long as ice supply is kept up. It is economy to keep ice chamber well filled with ice as the ice will melt slower and maintain a lower temperature.

No.	Width	Depth	Height	Ice Capacity	Shipping Weight	Price
23C1038	30 in.	20 in.	46 in.	75 lbs.	150 lbs.	$11.75
23C1039	33 in.	22 in.	48 in.	90 lbs.	180 lbs.	13.70

Puritan White Odorless Enameled Refrigerator. This style is very convenient where space is limited, as they combine large capacity with small floor space. Ice chamber door is in front, making it easy of access. If properly supplied with ice the Puritan line will maintain the lowest temperature and use less ice than any other made.

No.	Width	Depth	Height	Ice Capacity	Shipping Weight	Price
23C1045	29 in.	20 in.	54 in.	65 lbs.	175 lbs.	$13.10
23C1046	31 in.	22 in.	56 in.	100 lbs.	210 lbs.	14.85

Puritan White Odorless Enameled Refrigerator. Double door style with two compartments in provision chamber. This is an advantage, as less warm air is admitted when only one side is opened at a time. Has perfectly dry cold air circulation. The white enamel lining makes the interior of provision chambers look fresh, clean and inviting at all times and adds much to the beauty of the box.

No.	Width	Depth	Height	Ice Capacity	Shipping Weight	Price
23C1047	40 in.	24 in.	49 in.	150 lbs.	275 lbs.	$18.55

Puritan White Odorless Enameled Refrigerator, $24.45.

Puritan White Odorless Enameled Refrigerator, large size for hotels, boarding houses, restaurants and private families; has double doors to both ice and provision chambers, two compartments in provision chamber, very roomy and economical in the use of ice. This size and grade is not carried in stock by any except a few high class stores in the large cities, and their price is about double what we ask.

No. 23C1048 Width, 42 inches; depth, 27 inches; height, 54 inches; ice capacity, 190 pounds; shipping weight, 340 pounds. Price **$24.45**

If you want more information about our REFRIGERATORS, why they are BETTER THAN THOSE OFFERED BY OTHERS, write for our free Refrigerator Catalogue.

FLOWER STANDS.

Flower Stands for potted plants. Extra strong and heavy, with patent casters, very handsome designs, painted green and tastefully decorated in gold bronze.

Semi-Circular Flower Stands.

No. 23C1660 With Trellis, 4 feet 6 inches wide, 28 inches deep, 5 feet 8 inches high, will hold from 18 to 24 pots, weight, 81 pounds. Price...... **$3.32**

No. 23C1661 Small Semi-circular Flower Stand same as above, except that it has no trellis, 36 inches high. Weight, 15 pounds. Price, **$2.60**

No. 23C1664 With Trellis, 6 feet 8 inches high, 4 feet long, 32 inches deep. Weight, 30 pounds. Price..... **$4.75**

No. 23C1665 Stand same as above without trellis, 3 feet 8 inches high. Weight, 24 pounds. Price..... **$3.95**

Arched Flower Stands.

No. 23C1668 With Arch, three shelves 3 feet 3 inches long, 6 feet 6 inches high, 30 inches deep. Will hold from 24 to 30 pots. Weight, 25 pounds. Price includes arch and basket. Price.... **$3.80**

No. 23C1669 Stand, the same as above, without arch or basket. 42 inches high, shelves 3 feet 2 inches long. Weight, 20 pounds. Price **$3.00**

Pyramid Flower Stands.

No. 23C1672 Pyramid Flower Stand with gothic arch and basket, 6 feet 6 inches high, 4 feet wide and 22 inches deep. Will hold from 35 to 40 pots. Weight, 35 pounds. Price.. **$4.70**

No. 23C1673 Stand, same as above without arch, 42 inches high. Weight, 29 pounds. Price.. **$3.95**

Window Flower Pot Shelves.

Note the greatly reduced prices.

Window Flower Pot Shelves are intended to be put on the outside of window frame sill or they may be used inside to set flower pots on. They are 7 inches wide with border 4½ inches high, finished in green and gold.

No. 23C1692 33 inches long. Weight, 2¾ pounds. Price **32c**

No. 23C1694 36 inches long. Weight, 3 pounds. Price **35c**

No. 23C1696 39 inches long. Weight, 3¼ pounds. Price **38c**

Flower Pot Brackets.

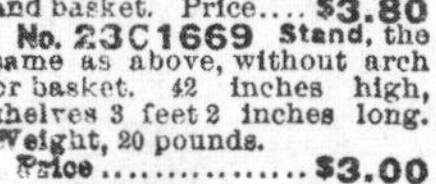

No. 23C1730 Bronzed Iron. 5-inch arm, shelf 4 inches in diameter. Weight, 12 ounces. Price........ **7c**

No. 23C1733 Dark antique bronzed iron, two shelves, 12-inch arm, one 5½-inch shelf and one 4-inch shelf. Weight, 25 ounces. Price..**39c**

No. 23C1735 Flower Pot Brackets. Enameled; length of arm, 12 inches; diameter of dishes, one 5-inch and one 6-inch. Weight 3½ lbs. Price **24c**

No. 23C1738 Flower Pot Bracket. Enameled; length of arms, 12 inches; diameter of dishes, two 5-inch and two 6-inch, complete as shown. Weight, 6¾ lbs. Price. **50c**

Tack Hammers.

No. 23C1762 The head of this hammer is magnetic, and it will pick up and hold tack for driving; hickory handle with steel claw. Weight, 5 ounces. Price......... **8c**

Tack Claws and Pullers.

No. 23C1770 Forged Steel Tack Claws. Polished blade, riveted tang. The best we can buy. Weight, 3 oz. Price... **6c**

No. 23C1773 Tack Puller. sure and quick; does not bend the tacks; ebonized handle; steel jaws. Weight, 3 oz. Price, each........ **4c**
Per dozen **35c**

Carpet Stretchers.

No. 23C1793 Carpet Stretcher, is light and durable, simple in construction and powerful, as it has a short fulcrum and good length of lever, which makes it easy to operate and is warranted not to injure the finest carpet. It holds the carpet in position after it is drawn to its proper place, giving the operator the free use of both hands with which to do the nailing. Weight, 12 ounces. Price **30c**

No. 23C1795 Carpet Stretcher, with tack hammer and claw. The drawbar is long enough to get enough bearing on carpet, so there is no danger of tearing. The takeup is automatic. Weight, 1 pound, 11 ounces. Price... **49c**

Nut Crackers.

No. 23C2000 Nut Cracker, nickel plated. Length, 5 inches. Price, per dozen **40c**; each........ **4c**

No. 23C2007 Lever Nut Cracker. The kind that confectioners, bakers and dealers in nuts use. Cracks any kind of a nut. Mounted on wood base. Price **15c**

Broom Holders.

No. 23C2012 The Acme Broom Holder is much superior to any that we have ever seen. It is handsomely nickel plated and has hooks to hang the dust pan and brush on. Projects 4 inches from the wall. Weight, 5 ounces. Fastens to wall with two screws. Price **7c**

Picture Knobs.

No. 23C2143 White Porcelain Picture Knobs with screw. Medium size. Price, per dozen, **17c**; each, **2c**

No. 23C2144 White Porcelain Picture Knobs with screw. Large size. Price, per dozen, **18c**; each.... **2c**

Picture Nails.

No. 23C2150 Picture Nails; porcelain heads; gilt rims. Price, per dozen, **10c**; each........ **1c**

Wall Hooks.

No. 23C2155 Brass Wall Hooks for hanging pictures, etc. Put up with an ordinary wire nail. The round plate is removed while nail is being driven and when replaced covers the head of nail. Very ornamental.

	Size	Price, per doz.	Each
Small...	⅝x1¼	16c	2c
Large...	⅞x1¾	32c	4c

Picture Wire.

No. 23C2174

No. 23C2176

Braided Wire Picture Cord, silver finish. Moths can't eat it off; comes in coils of 25 yards. We do not cut coils.

No. 23C2174 Braided Wire Picture Cord, as above, No. 2, suitable for medium weight pictures. Price, per coil of 25 yards......... **5c**

No. 23C2176 Braided Wire Picture Cord, as above, No. 4, suitable for heavy pictures. Price, per coil of 25 yards........ **10c**

Hat Racks.

No. 23C2310 Six-Hook Hat Rack. Size 4x32 inches. Weight, 1 pound. Price........ **9c**

No. 23C2312 Four-Hook Hat Rack. Size, 4x21 inches. Weight, ¾ pound. Price........ **6c**

No. 23C2315 Improved Hat Rack. Will safely hold a stiff hat. Five hooks. Weight, 1¾ pounds. Price **15c**

No. 23C2316 Seven hooks. Weight, 1¾ pounds. Price **18c**

No. 23C2325 Thirteen-Pin Folding Rack. The regulation folding pattern hat rack. Made of hardwood; walnut stained. Weight, 1¼ pounds. Price, **12c**

Wall Paper Cleaner.

No. 23C2359 Elastic Wall Paper Cleaner for cleaning wall paper, fresco, water colors and window shades. Prepared ready for instant use; requires no mixing; you do not have to raise your carpet or move your furniture, as it makes no dirt. It takes off all the dust and dirt and makes the walls as clean as new. Does not crumb, stick or leave streaks. Price, per pound can **10c**

Jewel Carpet Renovator.

No. 23C2364 Dirty carpets are unhealthy and dangerous, but Jewel Carpet Renovator will take all the dust, dirt, grease spots, fruit stains and coal soot out of carpets and rugs, and disinfect them. Will destroy moths and raise the nap and restore the colors, making old carpets as clean and bright as new, all without injury to the fabric, and without removing the carpet from the floor. The work is as simple and easy as scrubbing the floor. Carpets can be renovated in the morning, and company received on them in the afternoon, they being thoroughly dry and clean, and bright as new. One cake cleans from 15 to 20 yards of carpet. Price, per cake......... **15c**

Scraper.

No. 23C2365 Scraper to be used in connection with the Jewel Carpet Renovator. Made of heavy galvanized iron with wood handle. Used for removing the material from the floor, and necessary for perfect results. Price......... **9c**

Scrubbing Brushes.

Palmetto Scrubbing Brushes, double pointed with one piece solid hard maple backs. Palmetto fibre is very stiff and tough and not affected by acids or lye.

No. 23C2450 Small size. Size of face, 8½x2 inches. Weight, 6 ounces. Price...... **6c**

No. 23C2451 Medium size. Size of face, 10x2 inches. Weight, 8 ounces. Price..... **9c**

No. 23C2452 Large size. Size of face, 12x3 inches. Weight, 10 ounces. Price..... **9c**

No. 23C2460 Hub Ox Fibre Brush. Cleans quickly and thoroughly and will outwear three ordinary brushes. Will resist scalding water. Edges are beveled and will clean the corners. Solid hard maple block shaped to fit the hand and varnished. Best scrub brush made. Size of face, 10x2¾ inches. Weight, 7 ounces. Price......... **18c**

White Tampico Scrub Brushes. Finest selected Mexican tampico used in these brushes. Will wear down to the block without any tufts coming out. Double pointed solid hardwood blocks.

No. 23C2465 Small size. Size of face, 9x2½ inches. Weight, 8 ounces. Price...... **9c**

No. 23C2466 Medium size. Size of face, 10½x2½ inches. Weight, 9 ounces. Price. **11c**

No. 23C2467 Large size. Size of face, 11¼x2¾ inches. Weight, 11 ounces. Price **13c**

Rice Root Scrub Brushes.

No. 23C2474 Rice Root Scrub Brushes. Very stiff for rough work. Hard wood backs. Tufts securely stapled in solid block, square end. Size, 9x2¾ inches. Weight, 10 ounces. Price......... **7c**

Combination Brush and Scraper.

No. 23C2483 Combination Floor Scrub Brush and Drier. Block size, 11x3 inches, filled with best Mexican tampico stock with rubber scraper inserted in side for drying floor. Handle not furnished. Weight, 2 pounds. Price **20c**

Hand or Nail Scrub Brush.

No. 23C2490 White Tampico Hand or Nail Scrub Brush, hardwood block, size, 4½x1¼ inches, used for washing hands, etc. Weight, 3 ounces. Price **3c**

Handy House Brush.

No. 23C2492 White Tampico Handy House Brush with handle for scrubbing vegetables, cleaning wash basins, etc. Size of block, 4½x1¼ inches. Weight, 4 ounces. Price **4c**

Stove Brushes.

No. 23C2596 Tampico Straight Back Single End Stove Brush. Five rows; length of block, 10 inches. Weight, 8 ounces. Price......... **9c**

No. 23C2602 Tampico Curved Back Stove Brush. Five rows well filled with good stock. Varnished hardwood back. Length, 10½ inches. Weight, 11 ounces. Price......... **14c**

No. 23C2606 Curved Back Stove Brush. Five rows well filled with pure bristles and horsehair. Varnished hardwood back. Length, 10 inches. A handsome, durable brush. Weight, 9 ounces. Price......... **20c**

Window or Cobweb Brush.

No. 23C2672 Pure Bristle Window or Cobweb Brush. Stock, 2 inches long. To go on long handle for washing windows or brushing cobwebs from the ceiling. Handle not furnished by us. Weight, 6 ounces. Price.... **35c**

Oblong Window Brush.

No. 23C2675 Oblong Window Brush. Length of block 8¼ inches; 7 rows of strictly pure stock, 2 inches long. Handle not furnished by us. Weight, 11 ounces. Price **45c**

Floor Brushes.

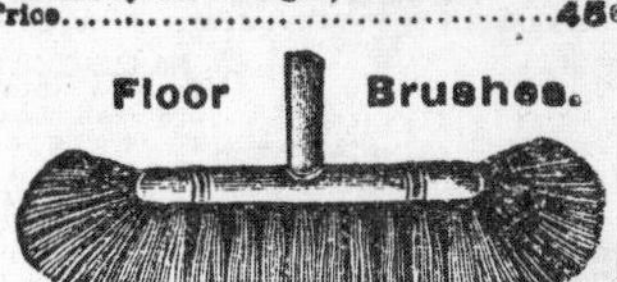

No. 23C2690 Floor Brush. Pure bristle, black center, white outside row, polished back, with handles, best for hardwood or painted floors.

Length, inches....	12	14	18
Weight, pounds...	2½	2¾	3 5-16
Price	72c	88c	$1.12

Counter Dust Brushes.

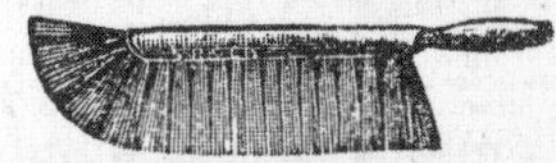

No. 23C2707 Standard, All Gray Bristle Dust Brush, enameled handle, 14 inches long. Weight, 6 ounces. Price......... **20c**

No. 23C2709 Dust Brush, gray and white bristles, varnished handle; an extra fine brush. Weight, 7 ounces. Price......... **30c**

Turkey Feather Dusters.

Containing 100 good quality turkey feathers. Size given is length of feathers.

	Size	Weight	Price
23C2721	10-inch	7 ounces	13c
23C2722	12-inch	8 ounces	18c
23C2723	14-inch	9 ounces	23c
23C2724	16-inch	12 ounces	28c
23C2725	18-inch	13 ounces	32c

Wool Dusters.

The best duster for furniture, pianos, etc. Made of softest duster fleece; charming colors, never scratches, easily washed when soiled.

No. 23C2748 Length of handle, 8 inches, wool 5 inches. Weight, 3 ounces. Price....8c

No. 23C2749 Length of handle, 12 inches, wool 7 inches. Weight, 4 ounces. Price..14c

No. 23C2750 Length of handle, 12 inches, wool 8 inches. Weight, 5 ounces. Price..27c

No. 23C2752 Length of handle, 12 inches. Wool 10 inches, extra fine. Weight, 10 ounces. Price....45c

Carpet or Rug Beater.

No. 23C2776 Carpet or Rug Beater. Made of coppered spring steel wire, doubled so as to give four points of contact with the carpet, thus avoiding danger of injury as the force of the blow delivered is distributed over a greater surface. Has black enameled handle, length 30 inches. Price....9c

Mail Boxes.

No. 23C2800 Storm Proof Mail Box with spring wire attachment to hold newspapers, etc. Size, 12x5¼ inches. Made to lock with padlock. Price is without padlock. Weight, 4½ pounds.
Price, each....$0.35
Per dozen....3.65

Mail Boxes for Rural Mail Delivery.

THE RURAL MAIL BOXES listed below are all officially accepted by the Postmaster General, and are so stenciled, and are also marked "U. S. Mail," and a space is left on which patron's name can be painted if desired. We stencil the user's name on any box when so ordered, and give you a heavy fibre paper stencil, which is very useful for stenciling implements, grain bags, etc., free of charge. Name should be printed or written very plainly to avoid mistakes.

OUR BIG 50-CENT LEADER.

Approved by the Postmaster General.

No. 23C2803 The Johnson Rural Mail Box. Officially approved by the postoffice department and every box so stenciled. Size, 18x6 inches. Constructed of heavy galvanized steel throughout. Equipped with hasp and signal and overlapping cover; is strongly riveted at joints; storm and dustproof. Will last just as long and give just as good service as any rural mail box, no matter how high priced. Lettered with your name free of charge when so ordered and heavy fiber paper stencil included free. Our 50-cent bargain price barely covers the cost of material and labor and is the lowest ever known for an officially accepted box. Weight, 6½ pounds.
Price, per dozen, $5.95; each....50c

Smith's Standard Rural Mail Box.

Approved by the Postmaster General.

No. 23C2804 Smith's Standard Mail Boxes, strongly constructed of galvanized iron, riveted at joints; has overlapping cover which protects hinges and contents from rain, snow and ice. Cover closes automatically and cannot be left open, has red painted signal to notify carrier of outgoing mail, etc., which raises automatically when cover is lifted. While not as carefully made as our more expensive boxes, it is remarkable value at the price and will give good satisfaction. Size, 7x18 inches. Weight, 7 pounds.
With brass spring hasp. Price, each..$0.65
Per dozen....7.25

Smith's Eureka Rural Mail Box.

Approved by the Postmaster General.

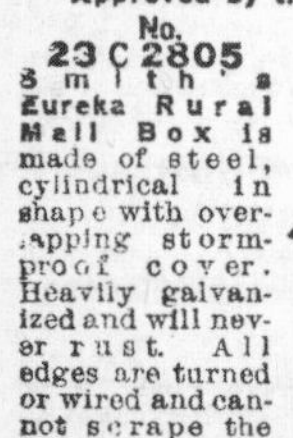

No. 23C2805 Smith's Eureka Rural Mail Box is made of steel, cylindrical in shape with overlapping storm-proof cover. Heavily galvanized and will never rust. All edges are turned or wired and cannot scrape the hand. Has red painted signal flag which raises automatically when cover is lifted. Has automatic spring brass hasp and can be used with padlock if desired. (Padlock not furnished at price of box). Size, 6x18 inches. A popular low priced box. Weight, 6¼ pounds.
Price, per dozen $8.90; each....80c

Smith's National Rural Mail Box.

Approved by the Postmaster General.

No. 23C2806 Smith's National Rural Mail Box is made of 22-gauge galvanized steel. Full size, 7 inches in diameter by 18 inches long. It is absolutely rain and dustproof, and cover cannot be blown open by a strong wind. It is handsomely finished with weatherproof aluminum bronze, has spring hasp and can be locked with a padlock if desired. (Padlock not furnished with box unless ordered separately.) Has handsomely decorated signal flag which raises automatically when cover is lifted. Is fastened to post by a substantial bracket shaped brace, which holds it very rigid. We recommend it for its simplicity and durability. Weight, 6¼ pounds.
Price, each....$0.95
Per dozen....9.95

The Roesch Rural Mail Box.

Approved by the Postmaster General.

No. 23C2809 The Roesch Rural Mail Box is most simple in operation, having no hinges or springs to get out of order. The inside of the box is in the shape of a half cylinder mounted on steel pivots and is easily revolved for the insertion or withdrawal of mail. Closes automatically and surely. Opening box causes signal to drop into place where it remains in plain view until pushed back by the one who removes the mail. A very strongly braced box of large capacity. Size, 19 inches long, 8 inches wide and 10 inches high. Made of 22-gauge galvanized iron and is storm and dustproof. Weight, 11¼ pounds. Price, each....$1.25
Per dozen....14.50

Padlocks for Rural Mail Boxes.

Self-locking Padlocks for Rural Mail Boxes, with heavy cast brass case, galvanized steel shackle heavy corrugated key cylinder; inside parts solidly built. Each lock is furnished with two corrugated keys for owner, and can furnish any quantity up to eighteen locks, all different. One master key which will unlock all the locks furnished with each dozen, for use by the mail carrier. Height, including shackle, 2 inches.

No. 23C2815 Padlock without chain, with two keys. Price, each....$0.17
Per dozen, with one master key....2.00

No. 23C2816 Padlock with chain, as shown in illustration, with two keys.
Price, each....$0.19
Per dozen, with one master key....2.25

No. 23C2817 Extra Master Keys, to fit any number of locks up to one dozen. Price...10c

Adjustable Firebacks.

No. 23C3200 Readily adjusted to fit all sizes of cook stoves. The only fireback that will adjust itself in both length and width. Length, 14½ to 21 inches, width, 5 to 6 inches. Weight, 7 pounds. Price....32c

Patent Stove Pipe.

No. 23C3210 Patent Stove Pipe. Made of smooth steel. This pipe is not made up, but the seam is made and edges turned over, and any one with a mallet or hammer can put it together in a few minutes' time. Has patent self-locking seams and cannot slip or collapse. It is left this way to facilitate shipping, as a dozen joints do not occupy any more space than one joint put together. 24 inches long. Made from 28-gauge steel.

Diameter, inches	5	6	7
Weight, per joint, pounds	1⅝	2⅛	2⅝
Price, per length	$0.08	$0.08	$0.10
Per crate of 50 joints	3.75	3.95	4.90

No. 23C3212 Polished Blue Steel Pipe, made the same as No. 23C3210 above. Length, 28 inches. Only an expert can tell this from genuine Russia iron pipe. The best pipe to use.

Diameter, inches	5	6	7
Weight, per joint, lbs.	2¾	2⅝	2⅞
Price, per length	16c	17c	20c

No. 23C3230 Taper Joints. 7 inches at one end and 6 inches at the other. Seamed but not put together. Length, 24 inches. Weight, 2¼ pounds. Smooth steel. Price....12c

No. 23C3232 Taper Joints. Polished blue steel, same as above. Length, 28 inches. Weight, 2⅜ pounds. Price....23c

Adjustable Safe Thimbles.

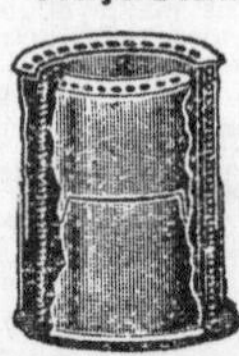

Adjustable Thimbles are perfect safe guards against fire from overheated stove or furnace pipes passing through floors or partitions. They can be used with ceiling and register plates for conducting heat to room above and for closing opening when not in use.

No.	Size, in.	Exte'd from	Wt. lbs.	Price, Thimbles only	Thimble complete with Ceiling and Register Plate
23C3283	6	4 to 8 in.	2¼	25c	61c
23C3284	6	6 to 12 in.	3¼	28c	64c
23C3285	7	4 to 8 in.	2 15-16	30c	69c
23C3286	7	6 to 12 in.	3¾	33c	72c

Hot Air Registers.

No. 23C3310 Black Japanned; can be used in floor or side wall. We do not furnish borders with register unless at an additional cost. These registers fit boxes of the size indicated.

Size, inches	6x8	8x10	9x12	10x12	12x15	14x18
Wt., lbs.	4½	6⅜	8	10½	18½	23½
Price	35c	37c	48c	55c	$1.02	$2.05

Register Borders.

No. 23C3312 Black Japanned Register Borders to match No. 23C3310 registers.

Size in.	Weight, lbs.	Price
6x8	3¼	$0.24
8x10	3⅞	.25
9x12	4	.33
10x12	4⅜	.33
12x15	6⅞	.65
14x18	9⅛	1.02

Register Face.

No. 23C3314 We furnish a Register Face which is used for ceilings; finished in white.

Size, inches	6x8	8x10	9x12	10x12	12x15	14x18
Weight, lbs	1⅜	3¼	4	4½	8¾	11¾
Price	29c	32c	47c	48c	66c	$1.44

Stovepipe Elbows.

No. 23C3330 Smooth Steel Elbows, four-piece.

Diameter, inches	5	6	7
Weight, pounds	⅝	¾	1¼
Price	5c	6c	9c

No. 23C3335 Smooth Steel Corrugated Elbows, made from one piece smooth steel.

Diameter, inches	5	6	7
Weight, pounds	1	1½	1¾
Price	8c	9c	12c

No. 23C3336 Polished Blue Steel Elbows, corrugated, made from one piece of polished blue steel.

Diameter, inches	5	6	7
Weight, pounds	1¼	1⅜	1⅞
Price	15c	18c	23c

Adjustable Elbows.

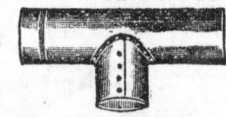

No. 23C3337 Adjustable Elbows, smooth steel. Can be quickly adjusted to any angle.

Diameter, inches	5	6	7
Weight, pounds	1	1⅛	1¼
Price	9c	9c	12c

No. 23C3338 Adjustable Elbows. Polished Blue Steel.

Diameter, inches	5	6	7
Weight, pounds	1	1⅛	1¼
Price	12c	14c	18c

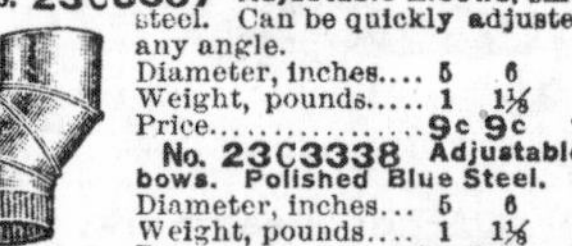

T Joints.

No. 23C3345 T Joints, smooth steel. 6 inches. Weight, 2⅜ pounds. Price...30c

Stove Polishing Mitten.

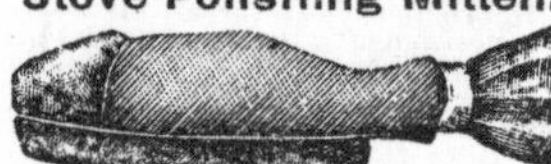

No. 23C3359 Stove Polishing Mitten. Was originally intended for blacking and polishing stoves, but is now also used for polishing household furniture, cleaning bicycles, polishing tan shoes, etc. It cannot scratch the most delicate material or varnish, while the finest possible polish can be produced, and the hands are kept clean. Has a waterproof back and is made with thumb; the whole front is made of the most durable and soft selected sheepskin, tanned with long fleecy wool on. Extra wool dauber with heavy wire handle packed with each one. Weight, 3 ounces. Price....12c

No. 23C3360 Stove Polishing Mitten, made without thumb and with dauber on back, otherwise same as above but with shorter fleece. Price, per dozen, 85c; each....8c

Stove Pipe Dampers.

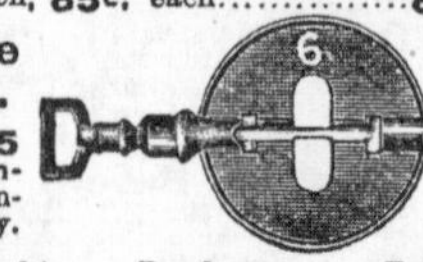

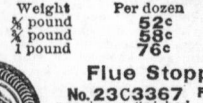

No. 23C3365 Stove Pipe Dampers. Cold handle. Put in easily.

Size	Weight	Per dozen	Each
5-inch	⅝ pound	52c	5c
6-inch	¾ pound	58c	6c
7-inch	1 pound	76c	7c

Flue Stopper.

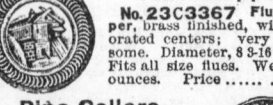

No. 23C3367 Flue Stopper, brass finished, with decorated centers; very handsome. Diameter, 8 3-16 inches. Fits all size flues. Weight, 4 ounces. Price....5c

Pipe Collars.

No. 23C3370 Decorated, gold lacquered.

Size, inches	Weight ounces	Price, dozen	Price, each
5	2	26c	3c
6	2	29c	3c
7	3	38c	4c

Stove Shovels.

The Double Handle Steel Stove Shovel. Made extra strong, unlike the cheap article ordinarily sold. The handle cannot be broken; it is hollow and of an oval shape, and fits the hand nicely; it will outwear any other shovel.

No. 23C3380 The Double Handle Steel Shovel, No. 7. Size of scoop, 5x7¾ inches; full length, 16 inches. Weight, ⅜ lb. Price....7c

No. 23C3381 The Double Handle Steel Shovel, No. 9. Size of scoop, 5x8¾ inches; full length, 22 inches. Weight, 1¼ pounds. Price....10c

No. 23C3382 The Double Handle Steel Shovel, No. 11. Size of scoop, 5½x9 inches; full length 25 inches. Weight, 1⅜ pounds. Price....12c

Stove Lid Lifters.

No. 23C3391 Nickel Plated Cover Lifter. The handle is formed of a spiral coil of plated wire which permits the air to circulate fully and makes it the coolest lifter in the market. Weight, 5 ounces. Price..5c

Stove Pokers.

Extra Heavy Pokers; the kind that don't bend up when you want to use them; always cool wire handles; full nickel plated. Length, 26 inches; diameter, 7-16 inch. Weight, 1 pound.

No. 23C3397 Straight. Price....9c

No. 23C3398 Bent. Price....9c

Kitchen Sets.

No. 23C3410 Kitchen Sets, enameled, with shovel, tongs and poker to match. Height, 18 inches. Weight, 10 pounds. Price, per set complete, as shown....$1.00

Iron Fire Dogs.

No. 23C3430 Iron Fire Dogs, ring top, japanned.

Height, inches	Weight, pounds	Price, per pair
11	5½	34c
13	8	47c
16	12	63c

Open Coal Hods.

No. 23C3450 Open Coal Hods, japanned.

Size, inches	Weight, lbs.	Price
16	2⅜	21c
17	2½	23c
18	2¾	26c

No. 23C3451 Open Coal Hods, galvanized.

Size, inches	16	17	18
Weight, pounds	2¾	3	3½
Price	27c	30c	32c

Funnel Coal Hods.

No. 23C3454 Funnel Coal Hods, japanned, 17-inch; weight, 2¾ pounds. Price....29c

No. 23C3455 Funnel Coal Hods, galvanized, 17-inch; weight, 3½ pounds. Price....36c

Mosaic Stove Boards.

Made of sheet steel enameled under a temperature of 240 degrees of heat. Will not rust or fade. Not affected by heat from any stove. Can be scrubbed like oilcloth and will retain their colors. Made to represent mosaic tiling, which is a new feature in a stove board. The metal is 20 per cent heavier than any other board and as much better as enameled ware is better than tinware. They are lined with wood.

No.	Size, inches	Weight	Price
23C3471	26x26	7¾ lbs.	$0.57
23C3472	26x28	9¾ lbs.	.64
23C3473	28x28	8¼ lbs.	.65
23C3474	28x34	10 lbs.	.71
23C3475	30x30	9¾ lbs.	.72
23C3476	33x33	11¾ lbs.	.87
23C3477	30x38	12¾ lbs.	.98
23C3478	36x36	13¾ lbs.	1.01
23C3479	32x42	15¾ lbs.	1.07

Stove Pipe Shelves.

No. 23C3374 Cast Iron, Japanned; is 18 inches square, made for 6-inch pipe. This shelf is very complete in itself and is easily applied or raised and lowered. A heavy weight upon it only strengthens its grasp and assists in holding it in place, making the grip on the pipe tighter. Weight, 6¾ pounds.
Price....55c

Stove Lining.

No. 23C3490 Asbestos Plastic Stove Lining, composed of asbestos and other fireproof materials; is easily applied with a trowel and makes a durable and economical lining for cook stoves; useful for repairing broken brick or iron lining. Price, 5-lb. pails, **24c**; 10-lb. pails, **43c**

No. 23C3492 The Acme Stove Lining Cement for lining stoves, ranges, etc., and repairing old brick lining. It never sets until it is burned. If directions are closely followed it will not crack or crumble. The 12-pound package is enough to brick a stove. The 6-pound package will make a back. Full directions with each package so that no one can make a mistake.

Price per box, containing 6 pounds.... **22c**
Price per box, containing 12 pounds.... **40c**

Brass Preserving Kettles.

No. 23C3510 Full size, made in one piece with extra heavy bottoms.

Size	Dimensions	Price
1½ gallons	9x6 inches	91c
2 gallons	10x7 inches	$1.10
3 gallons	12x9 inches	$1.48
4 gallons	12x9½ inches	$1.85
6 gallons	16x11 inches	$2.75
8 gallons	17x11½ inches	$3.17
10 gallons	18x1[illegible] inches	$3.98
14 gallons	20x14 inches	6.48
18 gallons	22x15½ inches	7.80
25 gallons	24x17 inches	.3 75

Porcelain Lined Cast Preserving Kettles.

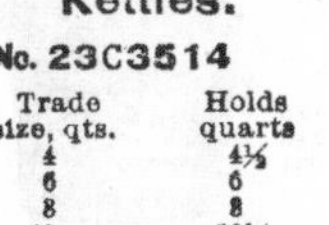

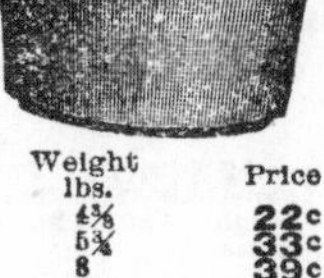

No. 23C3514

Trade size, qts.	Holds quarts	Weight lbs.	Price
4	4½	4¾	22c
6	6	5¾	33c
8	8	8	39c
10	10½	10½	42c
12	11½	11	47c
14	13½	12	53c

CAST IRON STOVE WARE.

The number denotes the size stove the vessel is most suited for, although they can be used on stoves of other sizes if desired.

Iron Tea Kettles.

No. 23C3521 Iron Tea Kettles, wood handle.
No. 7, weight, 8 pounds. Price **31c**
No. 8, weight, 9 pounds. Price **35c**
No. 9, weight, 11 pounds. Price **38c**

Stove Pots.

No. 23C3522 Iron Stove Pots. Inside ground.

No.	7	8	9
Size, inches	9½	10½	11½
Weight, lbs.	7¼	8¾	10¾
Price	35c	39c	46c

Stove Kettles.

No. 23C3523 Iron Stove Kettle. Inside ground.

No.	7	8	9
Size, ins.	9½	10½	11½
Wt., lbs.	6¼	7¼	11
Price	30c	33c	39c

Scotch Bowls.

No. 23C3524 Iron Scotch Bowl. Inside ground.

Diameter at top, inches	10	11	12
Weight, lbs.	4¾	5¾	6
Price	21c	23c	28c

NOTE—Sometimes water in certain localities causes iron kettles to rust or discolor articles cooked in them. This can easily be prevented by using the kettle the first time for boiling salted meat; or Mrs. Rorer recommends boiling suet and salt before using iron kettles.

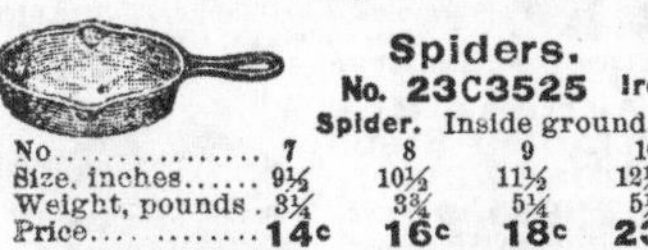

Spiders.

No. 23C3525 Iron Spider. Inside ground.

No.	7	8	9	10
Size, inches	9½	10½	11½	12½
Weight, pounds	3½	3¾	5¼	5½
Price	14c	16c	18c	23c

Griddles.

No. 23C3526 Iron Side Handle Griddles.

No.	Size	Weight	Price
8	10½ inches	2½ pounds	13c
9	11½ inches	3¾ pounds	14c

Bailed Griddles.

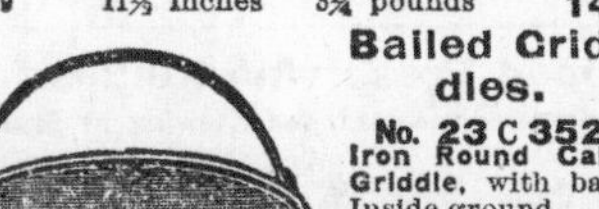

No. 23C3528 Iron Round Cake Griddle, with bail. Inside ground.

Size, in.	12	14
Wt., lbs.	6	7½
Price	24c	29c

Long Griddles.

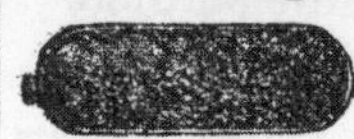

No. 23C3530 Long Griddles.

For stove No.	8	9
Wt., lbs.	5½	6½
Price	24c	29c

Pancake Griddles.

No. 23C3536 The Sun Pancake Griddle is made of wrought steel; is strong and durable, heats quickly and is lighter than any other griddle made. The batter is first poured into the little round hinged pans. When done on the first side the round pans are turned over with a fork into the long pan, and while the cakes are finishing the round pans are refilled, and so on, thus baking at the actual rate of six cakes a minute. Weight, 1¾ pounds. Price **26c**

Flat Iron Heaters.

No. 23C3538 Iron Flat Iron Heaters. Will save one-half the time in heating irons. Deep pattern.

For stove size	7	8	9
Weight, pounds	5¼	6	7
Price	21c	25c	31c

Flat Iron Heater.

No. 23C3540 Sad Iron Heater, for gas, gasoline or oil stoves, heats three irons at one time and will keep two rapid ironers supplied with hot irons. The heat coming in direct contact with the irons heats them much faster than can be done on heaters with closed sides. Weight, 2¼ lbs. Price **19c**

Gem Pans.

No. 23C3542 Iron Gem Pan, deep; 11 cups. Weight, 5 lbs. Price **20c**

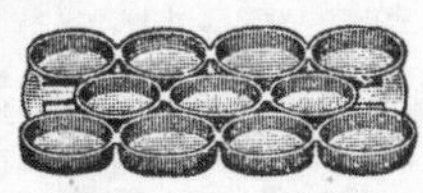

No. 23C3543 Iron Gem Pan, round pattern. Weight, 3¾ pounds, 11 cups; shallow. Price **15c**

IMPERIAL STOVE HOLLOW WARE.

Imperial Stove Hollow Ware is made of smooth cast gray iron, heavily coated on the inside with pure white porcelain and on the outside with mottled blue and white enamel, all of which is united with the cast iron at an intense heat, thereby forming a perfect union of the two, which no subsequent heating can destroy. It is easy to clean, of pleasing appearance, and we warrant every piece to give satisfaction. The numbers given designate the size of stove the article is intended for.

Imperial Spiders.

No. 23C3565 Imperial Enameled Cast Spider. Enameled inside and out.

Number	7	8	9
Dimensions at bottom, inches	8½	9¼	10½
Weight, pounds	3	4	5
Price	33c	36c	39c

Imperial Kettles.

No. 23C3567 Imperial All Enameled Cast Kettle.

Number	7	8	9
Diameter at top, inches	9½	10¾	11½
Depth, inches	6½	7¾	8
Weight, pounds	5¾	7¼	9
Price	60c	62c	63c

Imperial Stove Pots.

No. 23C3570 Imperial All Enameled Cast Stove Pots.

Number	7	8	9
Diameter at top, inches	9¼	10¾	11½
Depth, inches	6¾	7¾	8½
Weight, pounds	6¾	8	11½
Price	66c	67c	69c

Imperial Tea Kettles.

No. 23C3574 Imperial All Enameled Cast Stove Tea Kettles.

Number	7	8	9
Capacity, quarts	5½	6½	9
Weight, pounds	7¾	8½	11
Price	90c	96c	$1.05

New Idea Kettles.

No. 23C3577 New Idea Cast Iron Kettles. White porcelain lined, enameled on outside with mottled blue porcelain. Smooth as glass and as easy to clean as a china dish. An ideal kettle for preserving fruits, etc., as it is not affected by acids, does not stain and will not discolor anything cooked in it.

Capacity, quarts	4	6	8	10
Weight, pounds	4¾	6½	7½	8¾
Price	44c	54c	64c	69c
Capacity, quarts	12	16	20	24
Weight, pounds	11¼	15	17¼	19¼
Price	74c	$1.00	$1.24	$1.49

Ham Boilers.

No. 23C3585 Ham Boiler. Made of cast iron and lined with white porcelain; also used by many as a wash boiler; will not rust or discolor the clothes and with ordinary care should last a lifetime. Size indicates the size stove it will fit.

Size	7	8	9
Length, inches	19	21½	24
Width, inches	9⅝	11	13
Weight, pounds	20	22½	31
Price	$1.03	$1.23	$1.35

Asbestos Stove Mat.

No. 23C3700 A household necessity. This mat is made of asbestos of superior quality, and is scorchproof as well as fireproof. Any cooking utensil used upon it becomes absolutely scorchproof. Diameter, 9 inches, with metal ring. Weight, 2 ounces.
Price, per dozen, **24c**; each **3c**

Lightning Bread Toasters.

No. 23C3705 Toasts four slices of bread in two minutes and boils tea or coffee at the same time on any gas, gasoline or oil stove, and for a quick meal beats a red hot coal fire. All heavy steel, braced and dovetailed at corners. Weight, 1½ pounds. Price **20c**

Waffle Irons.

No. 23C3712 Simple in construction, convenient to handle, easy to clean, no better made.

Size	8	9
Weight, lbs.	8¼	10
Price	66c	79c

Soapstone Griddles.

Soapstone Griddles make delicious griddle cakes and require no greasing. Heat gradually and rub with a little dry salt before using.

No. 23C3732 Round Soapstone Griddle, hooped, with handles. Never use grease.

Diam.	Weight	Price
10 inches	5½ lbs.	42c
12 inches	6⅞ lbs.	59c
14 inches	9½ lbs.	77c
16 inches	13⅞ lbs.	90c

Oval Soapstone Griddles.

No. 23C3733 Oval Soapstone Griddles, hooped, with handles.

Size, inches	8x16	9x18	10x20	11x22
Weight, lbs.	7¼	9¼	11¼	13½
Price	60c	70c	86c	$1.05

Soapstone Foot Warmers.

No. 23C3741 Soapstone Foot Warmer. Can be heated in oven or on top of an ordinary stove and will hold the heat a long time. Will keep the feet warm when sleighing. Much used for bed warming.

Size, inches	6x8	8x10	10x12	12x15
Weight, lbs.	5¾	9½	15¾	22½
Price	15c	18c	23c	28c

Sugar Kettles.

No. 23C3775 Sugar or Wash Kettles, with bails, milled and painted. No. 8, 40-gallon kettle, is the largest cast iron kettle, with bail, made. Average weight of kettles is given below.

No.	Actual Measure	Weight	Price
No. 1	8 gallons	25 pounds	$0.97
No. 2	10 gallons	30 pounds	1.23
No. 3	15 gallons	42 pounds	1.55
No. 4	18 gallons	48 pounds	1.95
No. 5	21½ gallons	52 pounds	2.20
No. 6	25 gallons	65 pounds	2.67
No. 7	30 gallons	85 pounds	3.10
No. 8	40 gallons	120 pounds	4.20

Copper Kettles.

Hand made from one piece of pure copper, without seams. Will never rust; lighter than iron kettles and with proper use will last a lifetime.

No.	Size, gal.	Weight, about	Diam. on top inside	Deep, in.	Price
23C3780	12	20 lbs.	19 in.	13	$5.20
23C3781	14	22 lbs.	19½ in.	13¼	5.72
23C3782	16	23 lbs.	20 in.	13¾	5.98
23C3785	18	25 lbs.	21¾ in.	13¾	6.50
23C3786	20	27 lbs.	22 in.	14½	6.98
23C3787	25	30 lbs.	23½ in.	15	7.80
23C3788	30	38 lbs.	24½ in.	17½	9.68
23C3789	36	44 lbs.	26 in.	19	11.45
23C3790	40	46 lbs.	27 in.	19¼	11.98

Dripping Pans.

No. 23C3815 Refined Smooth Steel Dripping Pan.

Size, inches	7x10	7x14	8x12	10x12
Weight, pounds	¾	1⅛	1	1¼
Price	7c	9c	9c	10c
Size, inches	10x14	11x16	12x17	14x17
Weight, pounds	1½	1¾	2	2⅜
Price	12c	14c	15c	16c

Self Basting Roasting Pans.

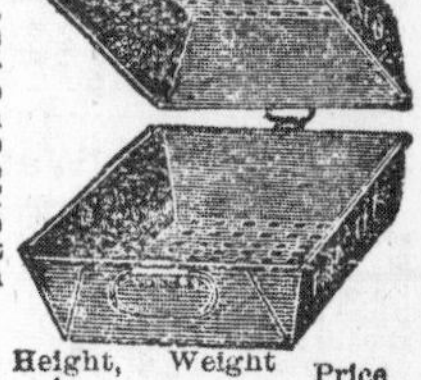

No. 23C3817 Self Basting Roasting Pan. This is an entirely new pan. The projections shown in the illustration collect the condensation from the steam and cause it to fall on the meat instead of running down the sides of the pan. It is made of smooth iron.

Length, in.	Width, in.	Height, in.	Weight	Price
15½	10½	8	2⅜ lbs.	23c
17½	12½	9	4 lbs.	32c

The Acme Roasting Pans.

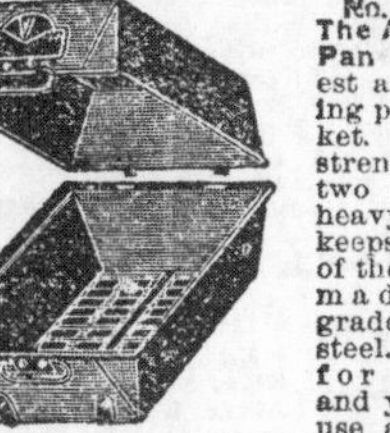

No. 23C3820 The Acme Roasting Pan is the strongest and best roasting pan in the market. The bottom is strengthened by two ribs. Has a heavy rack which keeps the meat out of the gravy. It is made of a fine grade of smooth steel. Try the pan for baking bread and you will never use anything else.

Notice the very low prices. They are sold by agents at more than twice our price.

Number	1	2	3	4
Width, inches	9	10	11	13
Length, inches	13	15	16	18
Height, inches	7½	7½	8½	9½
Weight, pounds	3½	4	4½	6⅜
Price	39c	47c	55c	67c

Acme Frying Pans.

No. 23C3830 Stamped Seamless Lipped Frying Pans. Polished, with patent handle, always cool.

Number	3	4	5	6
Diameter at top, in.	9⅞	10⅜	10⅞	11¾
Weight, pounds	1	1⅛	1½	1¾
Price	11c	13c	16c	18c

No. 23C3833 Brooklyn Steel Skillet. Made of one piece of highly polished cold rolled steel, with always cool handle. Will never break.

For stove No.	7	8	9
Diameter at bottom, in.	8	9	10
Price	18c	19c	22c

Steam Cookers.

No. 23C3837 You can cook sauerkraut, onions, cabbage and pudding at the same time, without any one of them partaking of the odor or flavor of the other. It cooks well but never burns. It saves fuel, stove space, fits any stove, and saves one-quarter of the food which is lost when cooked the old way. Specially adapted for oil, gas and gasoline stoves where space is limited. Well made from good heavy tin, with copper bottom on bottom vessels.

Vessels	4	4	4	5	5
Qts. each	2	3	5	3	5
Diam., in.	7⅝	9	10¼	9	10¼
Wt., lbs.	3½	4⅞	5½	6¼	7
Price	95c	$1.12	$1.28	$1.[illegible]	$1.56

Crown Steel Broiler.

No. 23C3808 Crown Self Basting Steel Broiler; broils and bastes perfectly. The juices of the meat are retained by the corrugated bars, and the meat is being thoroughly basted on one side while the other is broiling. Turn the broiler frequently and you will get the best results. Can be used over coal, gas or gasoline fire and is strong and light. Diameter, 10½ inches. Weight, 1¾ pounds. Price **20c**

Arnold Steam Cooker.

Arnold Steam Cooker will cook perfectly anything that can be boiled, baked or roasted. Retains all the nutriment, richness and flavor of the food. It makes burning or scorching impossible and saves watching. No steam or odor can escape into the room. A good cook can cook better with one than without, and a poor cook cannot spoil a meal if she tries. Everything cooked is healthier and more easily digested than when cooked in any other way and it saves nearly one-third of the food which is lost by the old way. You simply put your entire dinner in the cooker at once, set it on any kind of a stove and let it alone until ready to serve. Price includes meat kettle, vegetable steamer and pudding pan. Also complete directions and valuable recipes.

No. 23C3839 Capacity, 3 gallons; 3 compartments; adapted for family of 3 to 6. Price........**$2.59**

No. 23C3840 Capacity, 4 gallons; 3 compartments; adapted for family of 7 to 10. Price........**$3.03**

No. 23C3841 Capacity, 5 gallons; 3 compartments; adapted for family of 11 to 15. Price........**$3.42**

Sanitary Water Still.

No. 23C3855 Set the still on any kind of a stove, filled with any kind of water and no matter how foul, it is quickly converted into water of crystal purity, revitalized and sterilized, delicious and palatable to the taste. Handsomely and durably made of best hard rolled sheet copper. The interior surfaces are lined with pure block tin, as it is insoluble in distilled water, so as to prevent corrosion. The outside of the still is beautifully planished. Every part is accessible and can be easily cleaned when necessary. Weight, about 6 pounds. Price........**$3.70**

Solid Steel Ware.

No. 23C3891 Solid Steel Seamless Taper Stove Kettles are made from one piece of wrought steel. The bottom is much thicker than the sides. Tinned to prevent rusting. Flat bottom.

Number	7	8	9	10
Diameter, inches	8½	10	11	12
Depth, inches	6	7	7¼	7
Weight, pounds	2⅞	4	4¾	5
Price	64c	74c	91c	99c

Seamless Spiders.

No. 23C3893 Solid steel, solid handle. Pressed hot from No. 14 Stubbs' gaugo steel and guaranteed not to warp; polished.

Number	7	8	9	10	12
Dia. at top, inches	9¼	10⅜	11½	12⅝	13½
Dia. at bottom, inches	8	9	10	11	12
Weight, pounds	2	3	4	4¼	5½
Price	23c	26c	32c	39c	45c

SOLID STEEL LAVA ENAMELED WARE.

Our Solid Steel Lava Enameled Ware is made of heavy steel, rolled especially for this purpose, and is covered with three coats of very hard and elastic enamel, the surface of which is as smooth as the most delicate of china. The inside or lining is a pure white porcelain and the outside is white mottled with a delicate shade of brown. For purity of materials, durability and excellence of workmanship, this ware is without an equal. We guarantee every piece, and while it costs a trifle more than ordinary enameled ware, it will be found to be the cheapest in the end.

Spiders.

No. 23C3896 Solid Steel Lava Enameled Spiders, made from one piece of 14-gauge steel, triple coated with enamel.

Number	7	8	9	10	12
Diameter at bottom, in.	8	9	10	11	12
Weight, pounds	3	4	5¼	5½	6½
Price	36c	42c	50c	62c	73c

Solid Steel Lava Enameled Kettle.

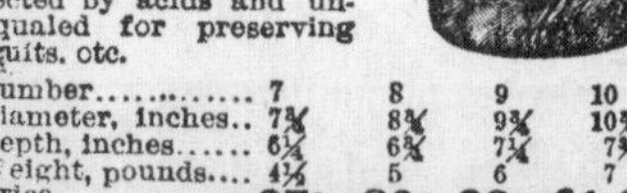

No. 23C3897 Solid Steel Lava Enameled Taper Stove Kettle. Flat bottom. Made of 16-gauge stoel, The heaviest enameled kettlo made. Not affected by acids and unequaled for preserving fruits, otc.

Number	7	8	9	10
Diameter, inches	7¾	8¾	9¾	10¾
Depth, inches	6¼	6¾	7¼	7⅝
Weight, pounds	4½	5	6	7
Price	67c	80c	93c	$1.07

Solid Steel Enameled Lava Tea Kettle.

No. 23C3898 Solid Steel Lava Enameled Tea Kettle. Latest pattern seamless body, flat bottom. With ordinary care a tea kettle of this ware should outlast a dozen tin tea kettles.

Number	7	8	9
Capacity, quarts	5	7	8
Weight, pounds	3½	3¾	4
Price	93c	$1.12	$1.30

Solid Steel Lava Enameled Wash Basin.

No. 23C3899 Solid Steel Lava Enameled Wash Basin. Durable and easy to clean.

Number	28	30	32
Diameter, inches	11¼	12¼	13
Weight, pounds	1½	1¾	2
Price	22c	29c	32c

Lava Enameled Filters.

No. 23C3912 They are as easily kept clean as a china dish, and unlike the common crock filters cannot be broken. Filtration in this filter is obtained by percolation through a porous natural stone by force of gravity. No filth or putrid matter can possibly get below the surface. The first few buckets of water filtered have a slight taste of the rock, but it is in no way injurious to health. Two or three times a week scrub off the top of the stone with a small broom or brush, and the filter is then ready for use again. Each vessel holds 3 gallons. Capacity, 8 gallons per day; Weight, 13½ pounds. Price........**$3.05**

PEERLESS ENAMELED STEEL WARE.

Our Peerless Enameled Steel Ware is formed from sheet steel, and after being put together is enameled inside and outside a gray color, handsomely mottled. For cleanliness, purity, durability and beauty, this ware is unexcelled by any other gray enameled steel goods on the market. It is entirely free from lead, arsenic and antimony, metals so often used in enamels of this appearance. We buy enameled ware from the makers and are satisfied with our usual small profit. No seconds or imperfect goods sold.

About Sizes—All Tinware and Enemeled Ware is usually listed by all manufacturers and dealers at what is known as trade measure. Some articles actually hold more than trade measure, most articles hold about the same, and a few articles do not hold the quantity indicated by trade measure. For the guidance of those who are not familiar with trade size, we also give actual capacity on each utensil. When comparing our price with those of other dealers, remember that our goods are standard size, and same size as listed by all manufacturers and dealers as the same trade size.

Peerless Enameled Steel Coffee Boiler.

No. 23C4000 Peerless Enameled Steel Flat Bottom Coffee Boiler, with retinned cover.

Size 6. Holds 6 qts., wgt., 2¼ lbs. Price, **61c**
Size 8½. Holds 8 qts., wgt., 2½ lbs. Price, **67c**
Size 11½. Holds 11 qts., wgt., 3¼ lbs. Price, **80c**

Peerless Enameled Steel Teapots.

No. 23C4002 Peerless Enameled Steel Teapots, with retinned cover.

			Price
Size, 1 qt.,	holds 1 qt.	Weight, ⅝ lb.	22c
Size, 2 qts.,	holds 2 qts.	Weight, 1 lb.	29c
Size, 3 qts.,	holds 2¾ qts.	Weight, 1¼ lb.	33c
Size, 4 qts.,	holds 3½ qts.	Weight, 1⅜ lb.	36c
Size, 5 qts.,	holds 4 qts.	Weight, 1½ lb.	45c

Peerless Enameled Steel Coffee Pots.

No. 23C4004 Peerless Enameled Steel Lipped Coffee Pots. Retinned covers. Actual capacity and weights same as teapot of same size.

Size, 1½ quarts. Price.. **27c**
Size, 2 quarts. Price.. **29c**
Size, 3 quarts. Price.. **33c**
Size, 4 quarts. Price.. **36c**
Size, 5 quarts. Price.. **45c**

Enameled Steel Flat Bottom Tea Kettles with Enameled Covers.

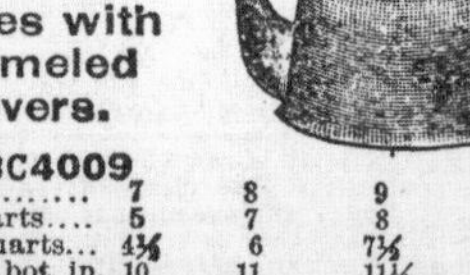

No. 23C4009

No.	7	8	9	10
Size, quarts	5	7	8	11
Holds, quarts	4⅜	6	7½	9½
Diam. of bot. in.	10	11	11¼	12
Weight, lbs	2¼	2½	3	3⅛
Price	55c	66c	85c	$1.05

Peerless Enameled Steel Colanders.

No. 23C4011 Peerless Enameled Steel Family Colanders.

Inches	10 x 4	12 x 5½
Weight, pounds	⅝	1⅛
Price	26c	38c

Peerless Enameled Steel Wash Basins.

No. 23C4012 Peerless Enameled Steel Wash Basins, with patent rings.

No.	26	28	30	32
Inches	10⅝x2⅝	11⅝x2⅞	12¼x3⅛	13x3⅜
Weight, lbs	½	⅝	⅝	¾
Price	13c	14c	16c	23c

Peerless Enameled Steel Deep Dishpans.

No. 23C4015 Peerless Enameled Steel Seamless Deep Dishpans.

Size, quarts	10	14	17	21
Holds, quarts	9	12	15	18
Inches	14¼x5	15⅝x5¼	17⅜x5⅝	19¼x6
Weight, pounds	1⅞	2¼	3	4½
Price	40c	48c	57c	65c

Peerless Enameled Steel Seamless Climax Cook Pots.

Arranged with patent Climax bottom which prevents burning or scorching and affords protection to that portion of the vessel that in ordinary usage receives the most wear.

No. 23C4018 Peerless Enameled Steel Seamless Climax Cook Pot, with retinned cover. Sizes are actual capacity.

Quarts	3	5	7
Inches	8x4½	9x5	9⅝x6
Weight, pounds	1¾	2½	2¾
Price	48c	55c	61c

Peerless Enameled Steel Climax Saucepans.

With patent Climax bottom same as above. Milk and cereals can be cooked in these vessels without danger of scorching or burning.

No. 23C4020 Peerless Enameled Steel Covered Seamless Climax Saucepans, with retinned cover.

Sizes are actual capacity.

Quarts	2	3	5	7
Inches	6¾x4	8x4½	9x5	9⅝x6
Weight, pounds	1¼	1¾	2½	2¾
Price	41c	48c	55c	61c

Peerless Enameled Strong Steel Lipped Saucepan.

No. 23C4021

Quarts		2	3
Holds, quarts		1½	2¾
Inches		7x3½	8½x3¾
Weight, pounds		⅝	⅞
Price		13c	18c
Quarts	4	5	6
Holds, quarts	3¼	4¼	6
Inches	9x4	9¾x4¼	11x5
Weight, pounds	1	1¼	1¾
Price	21c	25c	28c

Peerless Enameled Steel Berlin Saucepans.

No. 23C4022 Peerless Enameled Steel Seamless Covered Berlin Saucepans, with retinned covers. Size are actual capacity.

Quarts	2	3	5	7
Inches	7x4	8x4½	9x5½	10x6¼
Weight, pounds	1	1¼	1½	2¼
Price	26c	32c	40c	47c

Peerless Enameled Steel Covered Seamless Berlin Kettles With Retinned Covers.

No. 23C4025 Sizes are actual capacity.

Quarts	2	3	5	7
Inches	7x4	8x4½	9x5½	10x6¼
Weight, pounds	1	1¼	1½	2¼
Price	26c	32c	40c	47c

Peerless Enameled Steel Covered Seamless Stove Pots.

No. 23C4032 Peerless Enameled Steel Covered Seamless Stove Pots, retinned covers, flat bottom. Sizes are actual capacity.

No. 7, 9 quarts, 9¼x9, inches. Weight, 3 pounds. Price........**72c**

No. 8, 13 quarts, 10½x9¼ inches. Weight, 4¼ pounds. Price........**96c**

No. 9, 17 quarts, 12x10½ inches. Weight, 5¼ pounds. Price........**$1.20**

Peerless Enameled Steel Deep Pudding Pans.

No. 23C4045 Peerless Enameled Steel Deep Pudding Pans.

Quarts	Size, inches	Holds, quarts	Weight, pounds	Price
1	7⅛x2½	1	⅜	9c
2	8⅝x3	1¾	½	13c
3	9⅜x3¼	2½	⅝	14c
4	10¼x3⅜	3¼	¾	16c
5	11 x3½	4	⅞	17c
6	11⅞x3⅜	5	1	20c

Peerless Enameled Steel Straight Milk Pans.

No. 23C4046

Quarts	Holds, quarts	Inches	Weight, ounces	Price
1	¾	7 x5⅛	6	8c
2	1½	8½x2	8½	10c
3	2	9¼x2¼	9	12c
4	2⅜	10⅝x2½	10	14c
6	4¼	12⅝x2¾	16	18c
8	5½	13¼x2⅞	18	24c
10	6	14¼x3	22	29c
12	6½	15 x3⅛	29	34c

Peerless Enameled Steel Water Pails.

No. 23C4051 Peerless Enameled Steel Seamless Straight Water Pails, flat bottom.

Qts.	Holds, qts.	Inches	Weight, lbs.	Price
10	8½	10½x7¾	2⅜	48c
12	11½	11½x8¾	3	60c
16	14	12 x 9¾	3½	72c

No. 23C4058 Peerless Enameled Steel Pie Plates. Full size.

Inches	7	8	9
Wt., ozs.	2	4	6
Price, ea.	6c	8c	$0.09
Per doz.	72c	93c	1 05

Inches	10
Weight, ounces	8
Price, each	$0.11
Per dozen	1.25

No. 23C4059 Peerless Enameled Steel Extra Deep Pie Plates. Full size.

Inches	9	10
Weight, ounces	6	8
Price, each	$0.10	$0.13
Per dozen	1.15	1.46

No. 23C4062 Peerless Enameled Steel Flat Bottom Dinner Plates.

Full size, 9x1 inches.
Weight, ounces........ 8
Price, each........ **$0.11**
Per dozen........ **1.25**

No. 23C4065 Peerless Enameled Steel Deep Jelly Cake Pans. Full size.

Inches	9x⅜	9x1¼
Weight, ozs.	8	8
Price, each,	$0.11	$0.13
Per dozen	1.30	1.50

No. 23C4072 Peerless Enameled Steel Muffin Pans. Medium sized cups.

Number of cups on frame	6	8	12
Weight, pounds	½	⅝	1¼
Price	21c	25c	34c

No. 23C4077 Peerless Enameled Steel Flaring Coffee Cups. Holds 1 pint. Weight, 6 ounces. Size, 4½x3 inches.
Price, per dozen, **$1.18**; each........**10c**

Peerless Enameled Steel Saucers.

No. 23C4078 Peerless Enameled Steel Saucers. Size, 6⅝x1 inch. Weight, 4 ounces.
Price, per dozen, **82c**; each........**7c**

Peerless Enameled Steel Bread Raiser.

No. 23C4080 Peerless Enameled Steel Bread Raiser, with retinned ventilated cover. Sizes are actual capacity.

Size, quarts	10	14	17	21
Weight, lbs	2⅜	4	4¾	6¼
Price	87c	$1.01	$1.21	$1.38

Peerless Enameled Steel Lipped Preserving Kettles.

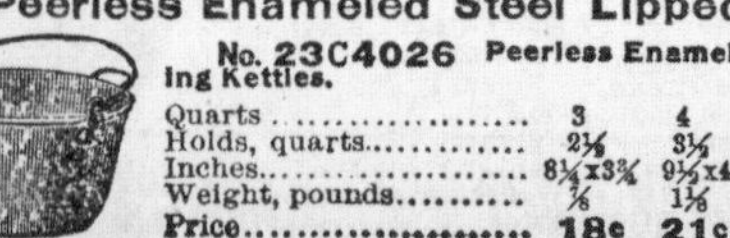

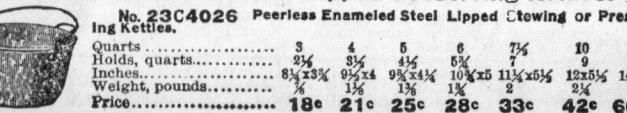

No. 23C4026 Peerless Enameled Steel Lipped Stewing or Preserving Kettles.

Quarts	3	4	5	6	7½	10	14
Holds, quarts	2½	3½	4½	5¾	7	9	13⅜
Inches	8¼x3¾	9½x4	9¾x4¼	10⅜x5	11¼x5½	12x5½	14x6⅜
Weight, pounds	⅞	1⅛	1⅜	1¾	2	2¼	3
Price	18c	21c	25c	28c	33c	42c	60c

Peerless Enameled Steel Seamless Water Pitcher.

No. 23C4089

Size, quarts	1½	2	3	4
Holds, quarts	1	2	2½	3
Weight, pounds	¾	1	1⅛	1⅜
Price	30c	36c	42c	54c

Peerless Enameled Steel Seamless Oblong Pans.

No. 23C4094

Inches	13x9x2½	15x10½x2½	16x11x2½	17x11¾x2½
Weight, lbs.	1⅞	2½	2¾	3
Price	32c	40c	46c	52c

Granite Steel Bread Pans.

No. 23C4098 Granite Steel Bread Pans.

Sizes, inches	Price
9¾x4½x3	16c
10½x5½x3	20c
11½x6 x3	24c

Peerless Enameled Steel Seamless Milk or Rice Boiler.

No. 23C4110 Peerless Enameled Steel Seamless Milk or Rice Boiler, with retinned cover that fits both vessels.

Quarts, inside boiler	1	2	3	4
Holds, quarts	1½	1⅞	3	4½
Weight, pounds	1⅜	2	2½	3⅝
Price	44c	56c	72c	90c

Peerless Enameled Steel Windsor Dippers.

No. 23C4115 Peerless Enameled Steel Windsor Dippers.

Quarts	1	2
Holds, quarts	¾	1¼
Inches	5½x3	6½x3¼
Weight, ounces	8	9
Price	15c	20c

Peerless Enameled Steel Soup Ladles.

No. 23C4118 Peerless Enameled Steel Soup Ladles. Size, 3¼x1⅜ inches. Weight, 4 ounces. Price... 9c

Peerless Enameled Steel Wall Soap Dish with Drainer.

No. 23C4134 Weight, 4 ounces.
Inches... 6½x4x1½
Price... 11c

Peerless Enameled Steel Chambers.

No. 23C4140

No.	Inches	Pounds	Price
1	7 x4⅛	⅝	21c
1½	8¼x4¼	1	26c
2	9¾x5⅛	1¼	32c

Peerless Enameled Steel Chamber Covers.

No. 23C4141

To fit chamber No.	1	1½	2
Weight, lbs.	½	⅝	¾
Price	11c	13c	15c

Unbreakable Enameled Steel Bed Pans at Less Than the Price of Ordinary Crockery.

No. 23C4146 Weight, 2¾ pounds. Price... $1.45

Unbreakable Enameled Steel Bed or Douche Pans.

No. 23C4147
Inches... 15¾x11¾x3
Weight... 3 pounds.
Price... 93c

White Porcelain Enameled Ware.

Porcelain Enameled Ware is made from sheet steel, heavily coated inside and outside with absolutely pure white porcelain, and ornamented with a bright blue border. It cannot be broken, is not easily chipped and is less than one-half the weight of crockery. It will not discolor and is as easily cleaned as china. For miners, camping parties or children's use it is just what is needed. Also desirable for ordinary household use.

No. 23C4200 White Porcelain Enameled Dinner Plates.

Diameter, inches	7¾	8¾	9½
Price, each	$0.10	$0.12	$0.14
Per dozen	1.15	1.30	1.45

No. 23C4202 White Porcelain Enameled Cups.

Diameter, inches	3	3½	4
Price, each	$0.10	$0.11	$0.12
Per dozen	1.10	1.20	1.28

No. 23C4204 White Porcelain Enameled Saucers.

Diameter, inches	5	5½	6
Price, each	7c	8c	9c
Per dozen	80c	88c	95c

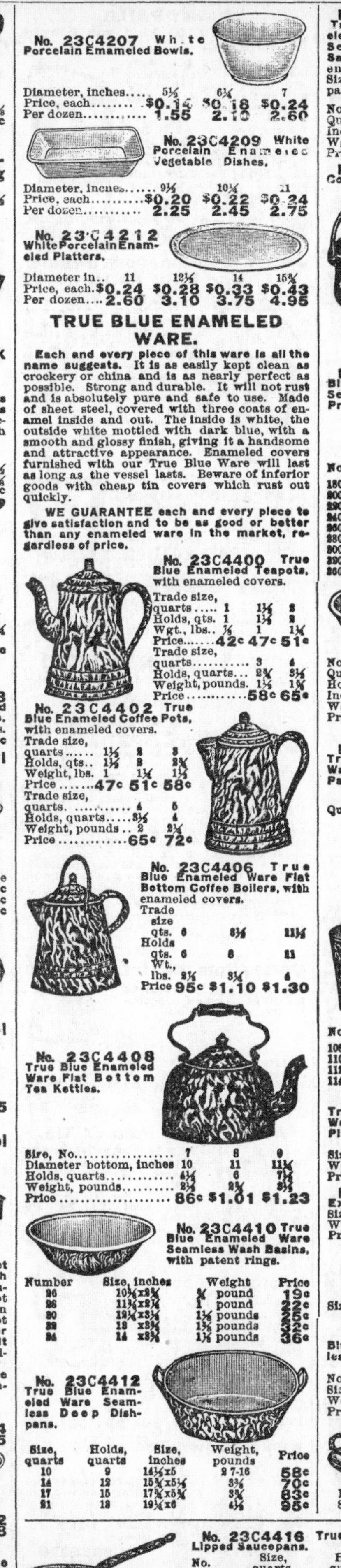

No. 23C4207 White Porcelain Enameled Bowls.

Diameter, inches	5½	6½	7
Price, each	$0.14	$0.18	$0.24
Per dozen	1.55	2.10	2.60

No. 23C4209 White Porcelain Enameled Vegetable Dishes.

Diameter, inches	9½	10½	11
Price, each	$0.20	$0.22	$0.24
Per dozen	2.25	2.45	2.75

No. 23C4212 White Porcelain Enameled Platters.

Diameter in.	11	12½	14	15¾
Price, each	$0.24	$0.28	$0.33	$0.43
Per dozen	2.60	3.10	3.75	4.95

TRUE BLUE ENAMELED WARE.

Each and every piece of this ware is all the name suggests. It is as easily kept clean as crockery or china and is as nearly perfect as possible. Strong and durable. It will not rust and is absolutely pure and safe to use. Made of sheet steel, covered with three coats of enamel inside and out. The inside is white, the outside white mottled with dark blue, with a smooth and glossy finish, giving it a handsome and attractive appearance. Enameled covers furnished with our True Blue Ware will last as long as the vessel lasts. Beware of inferior goods with cheap tin covers which rust out quickly.

WE GUARANTEE each and every piece to give satisfaction and to be as good or better than any enameled ware in the market, regardless of price.

No. 23C4400 True Blue Enameled Teapots, with enameled covers.

Trade size, quarts	1	1½	2
Holds, qts.	1	1½	2
Wgt., lbs.	⅞	1	1¼
Price	42c	47c	51c

Trade size, quarts	3	4
Holds, quarts	2¾	3½
Weight, pounds	1¼	1½
Price	58c	65c

No. 23C4402 True Blue Enameled Coffee Pots, with enameled covers.

Trade size, quarts	1½	2	3
Holds, qts.	1½	2	2¾
Weight, lbs.	1	1¼	1½
Price	47c	51c	58c

Trade size, quarts	4	5
Holds, quarts	3½	4
Weight, pounds	2	2¼
Price	65c	72c

No. 23C4406 True Blue Enameled Ware Flat Bottom Coffee Boilers, with enameled covers.

Trade size qts.	6	8½	11½
Holds qts.	6	8	11
Wt., lbs.	2⅞	3¼	4
Price	95c	$1.10	$1.30

No. 23C4408 True Blue Enameled Ware Flat Bottom Tea Kettles.

Size, No.	7	8	9
Diameter bottom, inches	10	11	11¾
Holds, quarts	4½	6	7½
Weight, pounds	2⅛	2⅜	2⅝
Price	86c	$1.01	$1.23

No. 23C4410 True Blue Enameled Ware Seamless Wash Basins, with patent rings.

Number	Size, inches	Weight	Price
26	10⅝x2¾	¾ pound	19c
28	11⅜x2⅞	1 pound	22c
30	12¼x3⅛	1⅛ pounds	25c
32	13 x3⅜	1⅜ pounds	32c
34	14 x3⅜	1½ pounds	36c

No. 23C4412 True Blue Enameled Ware Seamless Deep Dishpans.

Size, quarts	Holds, quarts	Size, inches	Weight, pounds	Price
10	9	14½x5	2 7-16	58c
14	12	15¾x5¼	3⅜	70c
17	15	17¾x5¾	3¾	83c
21	18	19¼x6	4½	95c

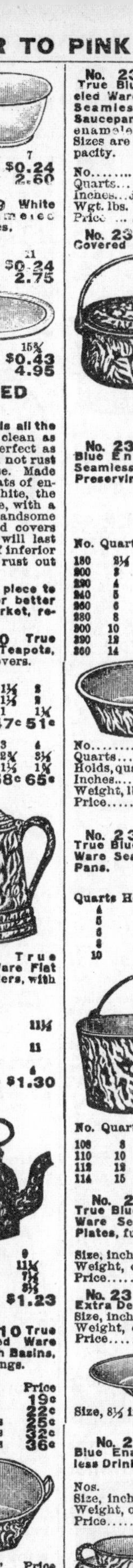

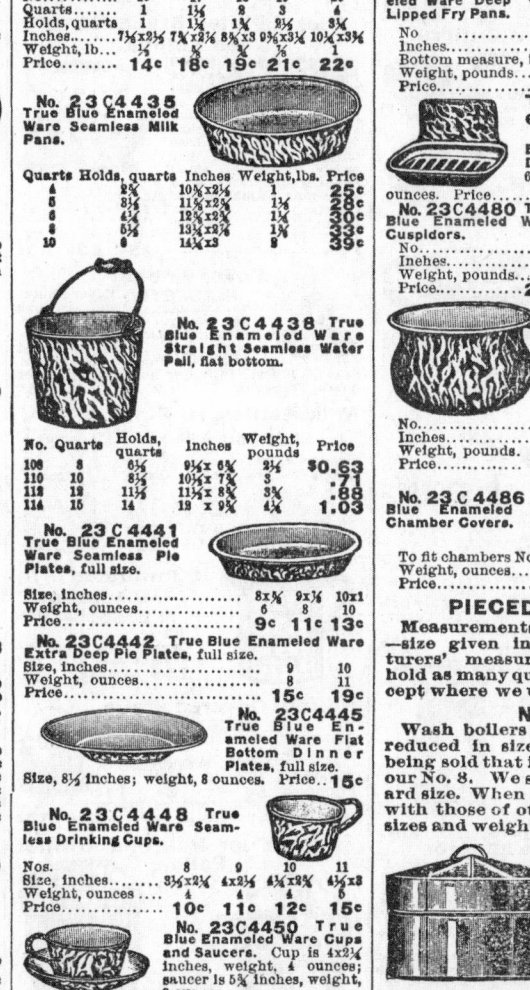

No. 23C4419 True Blue Enameled Ware Covered Seamless Berlin Saucepans, with enameled covers. Sizes are actual capacity.

No.	02	03	04	06	08
Quarts	1½	2½	3½	6	8
Inches	5⅞x3¼	6⅜x4¼	8x4⅞	8⅞x5⅝	9⅞x6⅜
Wgt. lbs.	1	1½	1⅝	2½	3⅛
Price	40c	47c	56c	66c	82c

No. 23C4423 True Blue Enameled Ware Covered Seamless Berlin Kettles. Sizes are actual capacity.

No.	03	04
Quarts	2½	3½
Inches	7⅛x4¼	8⅜x4⅞
Wgt. lbs.	1¼	1⅜
Price	48c	56c
No.	06	08
Quarts	6	8
Inches	9¼x5¾	10⅛x6¾
Wgt. lbs.	2⅝	3
Price	66c	82c

No. 23C4426 True Blue Enameled Ware Seamless Strong Lipped Preserving Kettles.

No.	Quarts	Holds, quarts	Inches	Weight, pounds	Price
180	2½	2	7¾ x 3½	1	25c
200	3	2½	8⅝ x 3⅝	1⅛	30c
220	4	3½	9½ x 4	1¼	32c
240	5	4½	9⅝ x 4¼	1½	40c
260	6	5⅝	10⅜ x 5	2	43c
280	8	7	11¼ x 5½	2½	51c
300	10	9	12 x 5½	2⅝	60c
320	12	11	13 x 5⅝	3¼	68c
360	14	13½	14 x 6⅝	3½	88c

No. 23C4432 True Blue Enameled Ware Seamless Extra Deep Pudding Pans.

No.	16	17	18	19	20
Quarts	1	1½	2	3	4
Holds, quarts	1	1¼	1¾	2½	3¼
Inches	7⅛x2½	7¾x2⅝	8⅝x3	9⅝x3¼	10¼x3⅜
Weight, lb.	½	⅝	¾	⅞	1
Price	14c	18c	19c	21c	22c

No. 23C4435 True Blue Enameled Ware Seamless Milk Pans.

Quarts	Holds, quarts	Inches	Weight, lbs.	Price
4	2⅝	10⅝x2½	1	25c
5	3½	11⅝x2⅝	1⅛	28c
6	4¼	12⅝x2¾	1¼	30c
8	5½	13¼x2⅞	1⅜	33c
10	6	14¼x3	2	39c

No. 23C4438 True Blue Enameled Ware Straight Seamless Water Pail, flat bottom.

No.	Quarts	Holds, quarts	Inches	Weight, pounds	Price
108	8	6½	9½x 6⅝	2¼	$0.63
110	10	8½	10½x 7¾	3	.71
112	12	11½	11½x 8¾	3⅝	.88
114	15	14	12 x 9¾	4¼	1.03

No. 23C4441 True Blue Enameled Ware Seamless Pie Plates, full size.

Size, inches	8x⅝	9x⅞	10x1
Weight, ounces	6	8	10
Price	9c	11c	13c

No. 23C4442 True Blue Enameled Ware Extra Deep Pie Plates, full size.

Size, inches	9	10
Weight, ounces	8	11
Price	15c	19c

No. 23C4445 True Blue Enameled Ware Flat Bottom Dinner Plates, full size.

Size, 8½ inches; weight, 8 ounces. Price.. 15c

No. 23C4448 True Blue Enameled Ware Seamless Drinking Cups.

Nos.	8	9	10	11
Size, inches	3½x2¼	4x2½	4¼x2¾	4½x3
Weight, ounces	4	4	4	5
Price	10c	11c	12c	15c

No. 23C4450 True Blue Enameled Ware Cups and Saucers. Cup is 4x2¼ inches, weight, 4 ounces; saucer is 5¾ inches, weight, 3 ounces.

Price, cups, per dozen, $1.49; each... 13c
Saucers, per dozen, 98c; each... 9c

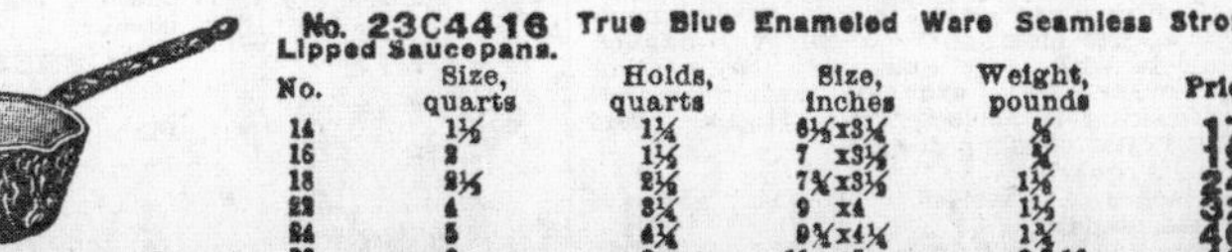

No. 23C4416 True Blue Enameled Ware Seamless Strong Lipped Saucepans.

No.	Size, quarts	Holds, quarts	Size, inches	Weight, pounds	Price
14	1½	1¼	6½x3¼	⅝	17c
16	2	1½	7 x3½	¾	19c
18	2½	2½	7¾x3½	1⅛	24c
22	4	3¼	9 x4	1½	32c
24	5	4¼	9¾x4¼	1¾	40c
26	6	6	11 x5	2 7-16	43c

No. 23C4452 True Blue Enameled Ware Soup Bowls.
Size, inches... 5⅜x2⅜.
Weight... 8 ounces.
Price, each... 14c

No. 23C4455 True Blue Enameled Ware Seamless Water Pitchers.

No.	Qts.	Holds, qts.	Wgt., lbs.	Price
1	1½	1	⅞	50c
2	2	2	1⅛	58c
3	3	2½	1⅜	67c
4	4	3	1⅝	87c

No. 23C4458 True Blue Enameled Ware Patent Seamless Milk or Rice Boilers, enameled cover to fit both vessels.

No.	Quarts, inside boiler	Holds quarts	Weight, pounds	Price
52	1	1½	1⅞	$0.69
53	2	1⅞	2⅜	.92
54	3	3	3½	1.19
56	4	4½	3⅞	1.40

No. 23C4463 True Blue Enameled Ware Windsor Dippers, with round handles.

No.	410	412	414
Inches	5x2½	5¼x3	6½x3¼
Weight, oz.	8	9	11
Price	20c	25c	29c

No. 23C4468 True Blue Enameled Ware Soup Ladles, threaded handles. No. 38, 3¼x1⅞ inches. Weight, 7 oz. Price... 12c

No. 23C4471 True Blue Enameled Ware Threaded Basting Spoons.

Inches	12	14	16
Weight, ounces	2	3	5
Price	10c	11c	13c

No. 23C4474 True Blue Enameled Ware Deep Lipped Fry Pans.

No	3	4	5
Inches	9¾x1¾	10x2	11¼x2
Bottom measure, in.	7½	8	9
Weight, pounds	1¼	1½	1⅞
Price	28c	33c	38c

True Blue Enameled Soap Dishes.

No. 23C4477 True Blue Enameled Ware Wall Soap Dishes, with grates. No. 60, 6½x4x1½ inches. Weight, 8 ounces. Price... 17c

No. 23C4480 True Blue Enameled Ware Cuspidors.
No... 1
Inches... 7x4
Weight, pounds... ¾
Price... 24c

No. 23C4485 True Blue Enameled Ware Seamless Chambers.

No.	1	1½	2
Inches	7x4⅛	8½x4⅛	9¾x5⅛
Weight, pounds	1	1½	2
Price	33c	43c	51c

No. 23C4486 True Blue Enameled Ware Chamber Covers.

To fit chambers No.	1	1½	2
Weight, ounces	7	11	13
Price	14c	17c	21c

PIECED TINWARE.

Measurements in inches are correct—size given in quarts is manufacturers' measure. Vessels will not hold as many quarts as size given, except where we use the word HOLDS.

Notice.

Wash boilers are being constantly reduced in size. A No. 9 boiler is being sold that is not any larger than our No. 8. We shall maintain standard size. When comparing our prices with those of others, please compare sizes and weights also.

Tin Wash Boilers, IX.

No. 23C5000 Flat copper bottoms, full sizes. Drop handles.

No.	Inches	Weight lbs.	Price
7	9½x18½	5	70c
8	10⅜x20¼	6	72c
9	11⅝x22½	6½	78c

Copper Rim Wash Boilers, IX.

No. 23C5002 Copper rim, flat copper bottoms, full sizes. Drop handles.

Nos.	8	9
Inches	10⅜x20¼	11¾x22⅜
Weight, pounds	6¼	6¾
Price	90c	98c

Copper Wash Boilers.

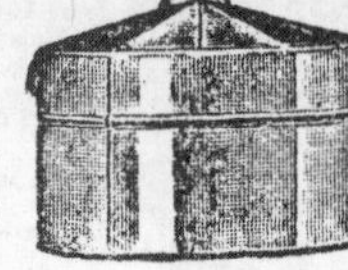

No.23C5007 Polished Copper, 14-ounce flat copper bottoms, tin covers, full sizes.

Nos.	7	8	9
Inches	9½x18½	11x21	12x22½
Weight, pounds	6¾	7½	8
Price	$1.85	$1.90	$2.08

Acme Copper Wash Boilers.

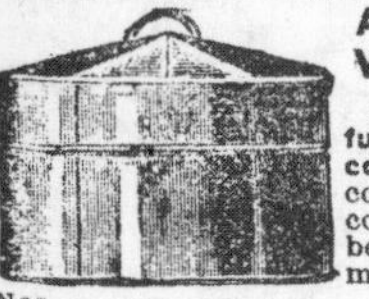

No.23C5008 Oval, full size, 16-ounce copper, polished flat copper bottoms, tin covers. Heaviest and best all copper boiler made. Full sizes.

Nos.	8	9
Inches	11½x21	12x22½
Weight, pounds	8¾	9½
Price	$2.35	$2.48

Tin Colanders, IC Tin.

No.23C5032 Eastern Pattern.

Inches	10	12
Weight, pounds	⅝	¾
Price	9c	13c

Cake Cutters, IC Tin.

No. 23C5038 Animal. Assorted styles. Weight, 2 ounces.
Price, each.....3c
Per dozen.....27c

Biscuit Cutters, IC Tin.

No. 23C5044 Size, 3 inches. Weight, 2 ounces.
Price, each.....2c
Per dozen.....18c

Doughnut Cutters, IC Tin.

No. 23C5046 Size, 3 inches. Weight, 2 ounces.
Price, each.....3c
Per dozen.....25c

Cooky Cutters, IC Tin.

No. 23C5047 Size, 3½ inches. Weight 2 ounces.
Price, each.....3c
Per dozen.....28c

Card Party Cake Cutters.

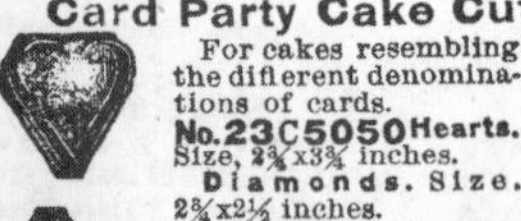

For cakes resembling the different denominations of cards.
No.23C5050 Hearts. Size, 2⅜x3⅜ inches. Diamonds. Size, 2⅜x2½ inches. Clubs. Size, 2¾x3 in. Spades. Size, 2¾x3 in. Sold in sets of four cutters only. Weight, per set, 8 ounces.
Price, per set.....9c

Drinking Cups.

No. 23C5062 Straight Drinking Cups, IC tin.

Pints	½	1
Holds, pts.	⅜	⅞
Inches	3¼x2	3⅝x2⅜
Wght., oz.	3	4
Price	2c	2c
Per doz.	17c	22c

Quarts	1	2
Holds, Quarts	¾	1¾
Inches	4⅜x4½	5⅜x4⅞
Weight, ounces	6	8
Price, each	5c	6c
Per dozen	48c	63c

Water Dippers.

No. 23C5090 Tin Bottom, IC.

Quarts	1	2
Holds, quarts	⅝	1⅛
Inches	5½x3	6½x3⅜
Weight, ounces	5	6
Price	6c	7c

No. 23C5092 Water Dipper, Copper Bottom, IX Tin. Two quarts; holds 1⅛ quarts; weight, 8 ounces; size, 6½x3⅜ inches.
Price.....11c

Climax Fruit Jar Filler.

No. 23C5098 Made with standard thread to fit any ordinary screw top jar. Mason'sincluded. By using this the cook can take the jar right to the kettle, filling the fruit in HOT, so that it will KEEP perfectly. Weight, 4 ounces. Price.....8c

Funnels, IC Tin.

No. 23C5106

Pints	½	1
Inches	3¾	4⅜
Weight, ounces	2	3
Price	3c	3c

Quarts	1	2	4
Inches	5⅞	6½	7½
Weight, ounces	4	5	6
Price	4c	6c	8c

ABOUT SIZES. All dealers sell tinware and enameled ware by what is known as manufacturers' measure. It does not hold the number of quarts represented. We give both manufacturers' size and actual capacity.

Graters.

No. 23C5119 Nutmeg Grater. It will not clog, tear the fingers, nor drop the nutmeg. It grates the nutmeg very fine, distributes it evenly, and grates it all up, leaving no pieces. It is simple and durable. Weight, 4 ounces.
Price, each.....6c
Per dozen.....63c

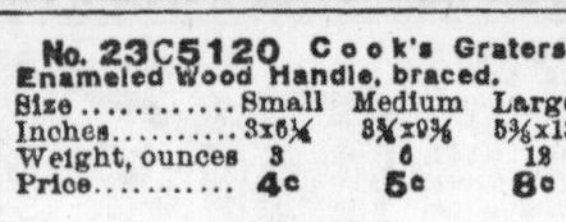

No. 23C5120 Cook's Graters. Enameled Wood Handle, braced.

Size	Small	Medium	Large
Inches	3x6½	3⅝x9⅝	5⅜x13
Weight, ounces	3	6	12
Price	4c	5c	8c

Combined Grater and Slaw Cutter.

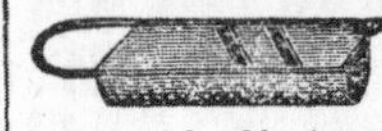

No. 23C5126 Grater and Slaw Cutter Combined. The slicer sheet is detachable. Two knives made of best quality of steel and can be sharpened. Length, not including handle, 4⅝x10 inches. Weight, 1 pound. Price.....17c

Tin Tea Kettles, IX Tin.

No. 23C5133 Flat Copper Bottoms.

No.	7	8	9
Diameter of bottom, inches	8½	9½	10½
Weight, pounds	1½	1¾	2½
Price	38c	44c	49c

Nickel Plated Copper Tea Kettles.

No. 23C5142 Nickel Plated Copper Tea Kettles. 14-ounce copper, heavily coated with pure block tin on the inside, highly polished and nickel plated on the outside. Body made from one piece of metal. Spout double seamed to body, patented. Strongest ear with handle rest patented.

No.	7	8	9
Diameter of bottom, inches	8½	9½	10½
Weight, pounds	1½	2	2½
Price	69c	73c	78c

Nickel Plated Brass Range Tea Kettles.

No. 23C5145 Nickel Plated Brass Range Tea Kettles. Made of solid brass heavily tinned on inside and nickel plated and polished on outside. Will fit on back of a base burning stove, and very handy to heat a small quantity of water in a short time for making tea, etc.

Quarts	1½	2	3½
Diameter at bottom, inches	6⅝	7⅛	8⅛
Weight, pounds	1	⅞	1⅛
Price	45c	53c	63c

Cover Knobs.

No.23C5150 Cover Knobs, with washers and nut. Any one can apply. When ordering, state if wanted for tea kettle or coffee pot. Enameled wood knob, tin flanges. Weight, per dozen, 5 ounces. Price, per hundred, 55c; per dozen, 7c; each.....1c

Milk Kettles, IC Tin.

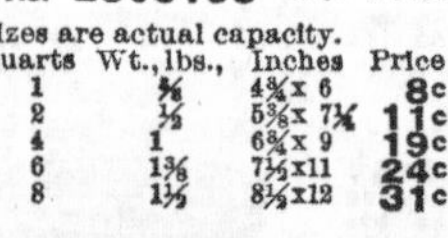

No. 23C5158 With bails.

Sizes are actual capacity.

Quarts	Wt., lbs.	Inches	Price
1	⅜	4⅜x 6	8c
2	½	5⅜x 7¼	11c
4	1	6⅜x 9	19c
6	1⅜	7½x11	24c
8	1½	8⅜x12	31c

Graduated Tin Measures.

No.23C5164 With lips.

Capacity, qts.	1	2
Weight, ozs.	6	8
Price, each	5c	9c

Round Covered Pails.

No. 23C5167

Quarts	1	2	3	4
Holds, qts.	1	2	2¾	3⅝
Inches	3⅝x4⅝	4¼x6	4⅞x6⅝	5⅝x7⅞
Weight, lb.	⅜	⅜	⅝	⅞
Price, each	5c	6c	8c	11c

Quarts, 6, holds, quarts, 5½; inches, 6x8⅛; weight, pounds, 1. Price, each.....14c

Miners' or Railroad Dinner Pails.

No. 23C5182 Miners' or Railroad Dinner Pail. Extra strong and heavy, made from IXX polished tin plate. Is oval-shaped, making it easy to clean and convenient to handle. Complete with large and small tray nesting together, and cup. Cover fits down over outside making it perfectly water tight. Best and handiest dinner pail made.

Capacity, quarts	4	5	6
Size, inches	9x5½x6	9x5½x7	9x5½x8
Weight, pounds	2	2¼	2½
Price	44c	49c	54c

DAIRY PAILS.

Better than the kind you bought 50 years ago.

No. 23C5191 Dairy Pails made of IX tin. Well soldered with best solder. Patent bottom; will never leak. Sizes are actual capacity.

Quarts	10	12	14
Weight, lbs.	1½	2	2½
Price	18c	21c	25c

No. 23C5194 Steel Clad Dairy Pails. Made of heavy IXXXX tin. Best dairy pails made. Sizes are actual capacity. Note the weights.

Quarts	10	12	14
Inches	11x 9½	11½x10	11½x10¾
Weight, pounds	3¼	3½	3¾
Price	32c	34c	36c

Jersey Combination Strainer and Dairy Pails.

No. 23C5199 Jersey Combination Strainer and Dairy Pail, made of IX tin plate. Strainer can be detached in a moment, making it easy to clean, smoothly finished and well soldered, with no corners or rough places where milk can collect and sour.

Capacity	Size, in.	Price
10 qts.	10¾x9	38c
12 qts.	11½x9½	39c
14 qts.	12x9½	43c

Sap Pails.

No.23C5210 Tin Sap Pails, well made from IC tin plate.

Quarts	10	12
Holds, quarts	9	11
Size, inches	10x8⅜	12x8¾
Price, per doz.	$1.23	$1.55
Crate, 6 doz.	7.10	8.75

No. 23C5214 Galvanized Sap Pails. Heavy galvanized. Will never rust or leak.

Quarts	10	12
Holds, quarts	9	11
Size, inches	11½x9¼	11½x10¼
Price, per dozen	$1.75	$2.02
Price, per crate of 6 dozen	10.45	12.10

A crate of 10-quart tin sap pails weighs about 78 pounds; 12-quart, about 95 pounds. We carry a large stock of sap pails and can ship promptly.

Sap Spouts.

No. 23C5220 Malleable Sap Spout, open top, tinned heavily. Will not break, are not liable to clog. Will take a long time to stop by freezing. Will thaw out quicker and obtain more sap from a tree than any other spout known. All the sap must run through the spout and drop in the bucket. Will not injure the tree. Will not drop out or loosen by frost, and as they are the only spout with a hook for pail provided in one piece, no parts can be lost, and they are always ready for use. Made to fit a hole bored with a ½-inch bit. Weight, per 100, 7 pounds.
Price, per dozen.....$0.21
Per 100.....1.40

Coffee Pots, IX Tin.

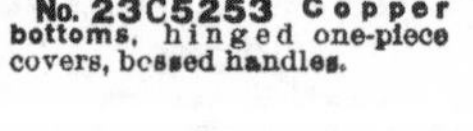

No. 23C5253 Copper bottoms, hinged one-piece covers, bossed handles.

Quarts	3	4	5	6
Holds quarts	2½	3½	4	5¼
Inches	6x8½	7x9	7½x9⅛	8⅛x9⅜
Weight, pounds	⅞	1	1⅛	1⅜
Price	22c	25c	29c	36c

Acme Coffee Pots, IX Tin.

No.23C5262 Copper bowl bottoms, enameled wood handles, hinged one-piece covers.

Quarts	2	3	4	5
Holds qts.	1½	2½	3½	4½
Inches	6⅝	6	6½	7
Wgt., lbs.	¾	⅞	1	1⅛
Price	26c	29c	31c	34c

Acme Teapots, IX Tin.

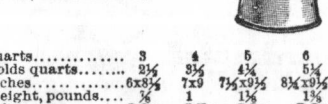

No.23C5270 Copper bowl bottoms, enameled wood handles, hinged one-piece covers.

Quarts	1½	2	3	4	5
Holds, quarts	1	1⅜	2½	3½	4⅜
Inches	6½	5⅝	6	6½	7
Weight, pounds	⅝	⅝	⅞	1	1⅛
Price	23c	26c	29c	32c	35c

Nickel Plated Tea and Coffee Pots.

Have copper bottoms, enameled handles, metal knobs; all satin finished inside, outside highly polished.

No. 23C5276 Teapot.

Pints	Holds, pints	Price
3	2½	33c
4	3⅜	35c
5	4	37c
6	5½	40c

No. 23C5278 Coffee Pot.

Pints	Holds, pints	Price
3	2¾	33c
4	3⅜	35c
5	4	37c
6	5½	40c

All Copper, Nickel Plated Tea and Coffee Pots.

Made of full weight 14-ounce copper, heavily coated with pure block tin on the inside, and highly polished and heavily nickel plated on the outside.

Nickel Plated Copper Teapots.

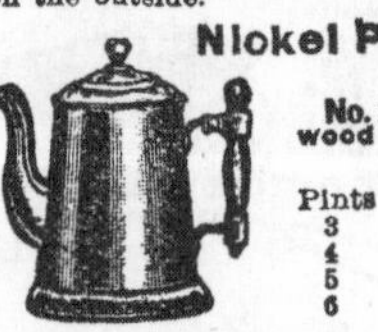

No. 23C5280 Patent wood handle, always cool.

Pints	Holds pints	Weight lbs.	Price
3	2⅜	¾	44c
4	3⅜	⅞	48c
5	4	1	52c
6	5½	1¼	59c

Nickel Plated Coffee Pots.

No. 23C5282 Patent wood handle, always cool.

Pints	Holds, pints	Weight, lbs.	Price
4	3⅜	⅞	47c
5	4	1	52c
6	5½	1⅛	57c
8	6½	1¼	66c

Pan-American Tea and Coffee Pots.

Pan-American Tea and Coffee Pots are of the latest low pattern, superior in finish and design. Made of 14-ounce copper, heavily nickel plated and polished outside, with heavy satin finished silver lining. Have improved hinged covers and rubberoid always cool handles.

Pan American Teapots.

No. 23C5292 Pan-American Nickel Plated Teapots, silver lined.

Capacity, pints	2	3	4	5	6
Price	68c	72c	78c	85c	92c

Pan-American Coffee Pots.

No. 23C5294 Pan-American Nickel Plated Coffee Pots, silver lined.

Capacity, Pints	3	4	5
Price	72c	78c	85c

Cap., pints	6	8
Price	92c	$1.03

Royal Nickel Plated Tea and Coffee Pots.

An elegant design in the highest grade of nickel plated ware. Equal to silver in appearance and durability. Have solid 18-ounce copper bodies, quadruple nickel plated with silver lining. Genuine ebony handles with beautifully embossed covers and metal knobs. An ornament to any table and guaranteed to please you.

No. 23C5297 Royal Nickel Plated Tea Pots. Silver lined.

Capacity, pints	Price, each
2	$1.03
3	1.08
4	1.15
5	1.22
6	1.29

No. 23C5298 Royal Nickel Plated Coffee Pots. Silver lined.

Capacity, pints	Price, each
2	$1.02
3	1.07
4	1.14
5	1.21
6	1.28

Steamers, IC Tin.

No. 23C5312 Rimmed Covers.

No.	Inches	Weight lbs.	Price
7	9½x5	1¼	20c
8	10⅜x5	1⅜	22c
9	11⅜x5½	1½	25c

Bread Pans.

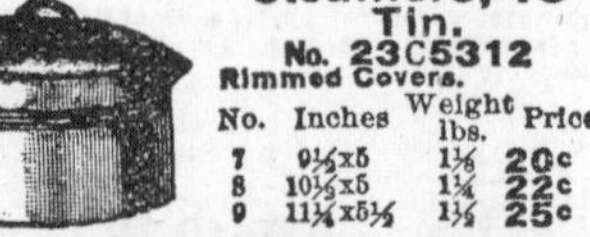

No. 23C5314 Sanitary Bread Pans. Extra well made with all rounded corners and edges. No grease, dirt or dough can embed itself in the edges as in ordinary pans. Full wired. Guaranteed not to leak.

No.	6	7
Size, inches	8¾x4½x2¾	9½x4½x3½
Price, each	6c	7c
Per dozen	65c	78c

No.	8	9
Size, inches	10¼x5½x2¾	11¼x7¾x2¾
Price, each	7c	8c
Per dozen	79c	90c

Deep Bread Pans, IC Tin.

No. 23C5316

No.	1	2	3
Inches	9½x5x3	10¼x6¼x3¼	12x6¾x3⅜
Weight, ozs.	6	8	10
Price, each	6c	7c	8c
Per dozen	60c	69c	85c

Handled Bread Pan, IC Tin.

No. 23C5318 Size, 14x9x2½ inches. Weight, 15 ounces. Price, per doz. $1.45; each....13c

Square Pans, IC Tin.

No. 23C5319 Common. Size, 7⅞ x 11⅜ x 1⅜ inches. Weight, 6 ounces. Price, each............5c
Per dozen............52c

No. 23C5320 Deep. Size, 6⅛x10⅛x2⅛ inches. Weight, 7 ounces. Price, each......5c
Per dozen. 57c

Ideal Bread Pans.

The Ideal Bread Pan makes a crisp, moist and wholesome loaf a certainty. It bakes evenly through and through. There is no danger of burning, and no special care is required. The crust is smooth and even, and the loaf of beautiful shape, the bread is more nutritious, more tasty and more digestible. There is no heavy crust.

No. 23C5324 Double Pan. Size, 13⅝x10 inches. Weight, 10 ounces. Price..........20c

No. 23C5326 Single Pan. Size, 13⅝x5 inches. Weight, 8 ounces. Price. 9c

Tin Brass Bottom Milk Strainer.

No. 23C5333 Tin, Brass Bottom Milk Strainer, with hoop. Size, 10 inches. Weight, 10 ounces.
Price........11c

Retinned Wash Bowls, IC Tin.

No. 23C5345 With eyelets.

Inches	10⅛	11⅛	13
Weight, ounces	8	9	10
Price	7c	8c	11c

Family Colanders.

No. 23C5348 Retinned. 11⅝ inches. Weight, 10 ounces.
Price......16c

Retinned Water Dippers.

No. 23C5352 Size, 1 quart, holds ⅝ quart. Weight, 5 ounces.
Price..........6c
Size, 2 quarts, holds 1 quart. Weight, 6 ounces.
Price, each..........7c

Retinned Preserve Kettles.

No. 23C5359

Size, qts.	Holds, quarts	Inches	Wt. lbs.	Price
4	3½	9½x4	¾	12c
5	4	9⅞x4½	⅞	13c
6	5	10½x4⅛	⅞	17c
8	6½	11½x4⅞	1	19c

Retinned Soup Ladles.

No. 23C5362 Wood handles.

Inches	3⅜	4⅛
Weight, ounces	3	4
Price	5c	6c

Scalloped, Tubed Cake Pans.

No. 23C5377 With tubes.

Inches	8	10
Weight, ozs.	4	6
Price	5c	6c

Retinned Round Cake Pans.

No. 23C5382 Deep, with tubes.

Quarts	3	6
Holds qts.	2½	4½
Inches	9¼x3⅜	11¼x3⅞
Weight, ozs	6	12
Price	10c	15c

Retinned Angel Cake Pan, IC Tin.

No. 23C5387 With tube. Size, 9⅝x4 inches. Weight, 12 ounces,
Price............18c

Plain Muffin Pans.

No. 23C5396 Plain Muffin Pans.

Inches	7⅛x14⅛	10⅝x14⅛
Cups	8	12
Size of cups	3⅛x1	3⅛x1
Weight, pound	½	¾
Price	11c	16c

Corn Cake Pans.

No. 23C5398 Corn Cake Pans, plain. Same as No. 23C5396 Muffin pans, but with deeper cups.

Inches	7⅛x14⅛	10⅝x14⅛
Cups	8	12
Size of cups	3x1½	3⅛x1½
Weight, pound	⅝	⅞
Price	12c	17c

Retinned Sauce-Pans.

No. 23C5402 Lipped.

Quarts	1	2
Holds, qts.	¾	1½
Inches	5⅞x2⅝	7x3⅛
Weight, ounces	4	8
Price	6c	9c

Quarts	3	4	5
Holds, quarts	2	3	4
Inches	8⅛x3⅞	9⅛x4	9⅝x4⅛
Weight, ounces	12	13	14
Price	12c	13c	14c

Retinned Milk Pans, IC Tin.

No. 23C5405

Quarts	Inches	Holds qts.	Weight, ozs.	Price, each	Per dozen
4	10⅞x2⅛	2⅞	8	8c	$0.92
5	11⅞x2⅝	3⅞	10	9c	1.03
6	12⅞x2⅝	4⅛	11	10c	1.17
8	13⅞x2⅝	5⅞	12	12c	1.33
10	14⅞x3	6	13	14c	1.57
12	15⅞x3⅛	7	14	16c	1.87

Retinned Pudding Pans, IC Tin.

No. 23C5409

Quarts	1	2	3
Inches	7x2⅞	8⅛x3	9⅛x3⅛
Holds, qts.	1	1⅞	2½
Weight, oz.	4	5	6
Price, each	6c	8c	9c
Per dozen	61c	84c	92c

Quarts	4	5	6
Inches	10x3⅛	10⅝x3⅝	11⅛x3⅛
Holds, quarts	3⅛	4	5
Weight, ounces	7	8	10
Price, each	$0.09	$0.11	$0.11
Per dozen	1.03	1.16	1.20

Retinned Dish Pans, IX.

No. 23C5415

Quarts	10	14	17	21
Inches	14⅛x5⅛	16⅛x5⅛	17⅞x5⅝	19⅛x6
Holds, qts.	9	12	15	18
Weight, lbs.	1¼	1⅞	2	2⅛
Price	23c	28c	33c	39c

Retinned Dish Pans, IXXX.

No. 23C5417 Extra heavy.

Quarts	10	14	17	21
Holds, qts.	9	12	15	18
Inches	14⅛x5⅛	16⅛x5⅛	17⅞x5⅝	19⅛x6
Weight, lbs.	1⅞	2⅛	3	3⅞
Price	37c	44c	47c	53c

Retinned Bread Raisers.

No. 23C5420 Sizes are actual capacity. Extra heavy.

Quarts	10	14	17	21
Inches	14⅛	16⅛	17⅞	19⅛
Weight, pounds	2⅛	2⅝	3	4⅛
Price	50c	58c	70c	80c

Easy Bread Maker.

No. 23C5423 Easy Bread Maker will do in 3 minutes by turning the crank what it takes 30 minutes hard work to do by the old method. It is a combined mixer, kneader and raiser, does all these perfectly and your hands do not touch the dough. Thoroughly mixes all the ingredients in three minutes. Then cover with a cloth and set in a warm place to raise. After raising cut around edges with a knife, loosening dough from pail, turn crank, when it will form into a round mass and the kneading is accomplished. Remove mixer from pail, push off dough, cut up and put in pans for baking same as you have been accustomed to do. Has heavy non-rusting tin pail with cover, not shown in illustration, is readily cleaned, nothing to get out of order. The easy way to make bread.

Size No. 1. Capacity, 4 loaves. Price..$1.35
Size No. 2. Capacity, 10 loaves. Price.. 1.75

Retinned Flat Skimmers.

No. 23C5438 Flat handles.
4⅛ inches. Weight, 4 ounces. Price..........5c
5⅛ inches. Weight, 6 ounces. Price..........7c

Cake Turner.

No. 23C5445 Enameled wood handles. 3⅛x3⅞ inch blade. Weight, 2 ounces. Price...3c

Retinned Covered Scoops.

No. 23C5450

Size, inches	6⅞x4⅞	9⅞x6⅞
Weight, ounces	5	8
Price	15c	23c

Pie Plates.

No. 23C5465 Shallow Pie Plates, full size. All ⅞ inches deep.

Inches	Weight, doz., lbs.	Price, each	Per dozen
6	1⅛	2c	17c
7	1⅜	3c	21c
8	1⅞	3c	26c
9	2⅜	3c	30c
10	3⅜	4c	37c
11	3⅞	5c	50c

No. 23C5467 Deep Pie Plates, 1⅛ inches deep.

Diameter, inches	9	10
Weight, per dozen, pounds	2⅛	3⅛
Price, each	4c	4c
Per dozen	37c	40c

Jelly Cake Pans.

No. 23C5471 Deep Jelly Cake Pans, 1 inch deep.

Diameter, inches	9	10
Weight, per dozen, pounds	2⅞	3⅜
Price, each	4c	4c
Per dozen	38c	44c

Tin Tart or Patty Pans.

No. 23C5494 Set of Six Assorted Tin Tart or Patty Pans. One of each pattern shown in illustration; also used as individual jelly moulds. We do not break sets. Weight, per set, 3 ounces. Price, per set of 6 pans.......10c

Loose Bottom Pie or Layer Cake Pans.

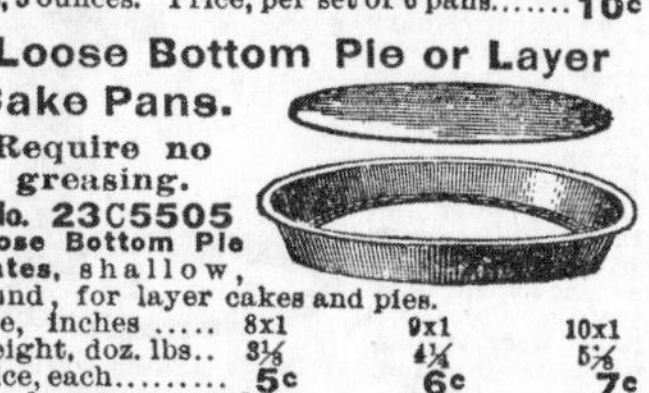

Require no greasing.

No. 23C5505 Loose Bottom Pie Plates, shallow, round, for layer cakes and pies.

Size, inches	8x1	9x1	10x1
Weight, doz. lbs.	3⅛	4⅛	5⅛
Price, each	5c	6c	7c
Per dozen	49c	60c	67c

Loose Bottom Square Cake Pans.

No. 23C5510 Loose Bottom Square Cake Pan.

Size, inches	8⅝x8⅝x1⅛	9x9x2⅝
Weight, ounces	10	12
Price	12c	16c

Divided Saucepans.

No. 23C5525 Divided Saucepans enable you to cook three articles at one time on one burner of gasoline or oil stove; three pans. Capacity each pan, 2⅛ quarts. Good quality tin. Weight, per set, 3 pounds. Price, per set..........55c

Flour Sifters.

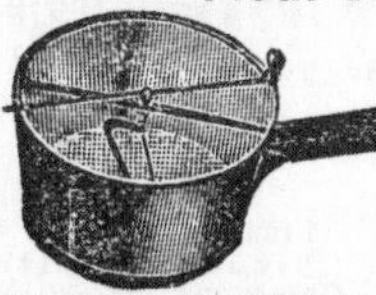

No. 23C5528 Flour Sifter. One of the quickest sifters made. For mixing baking powder with the flour it cannot be surpassed. Has a detachable and adjustable agitator. As a fruit strainer and washer there is nothing better on the market. Size of body, 3x6 inches. Weight, 8 ounces. Price 9c

No. 23C5529 The Genuine Hunter's Flour Sifter. The old reliable, made of heavy tin plate, also used as a scoop, measure or strainer. Weight, 10 oz. Price..12c

No. 23C5530 Imitation Hunter Sifter. Same pattern as above, but made of lighter tin. Weight, 8 ounces. Price..........9c

No. 23C5533 Favorite Flour Sifter. The finest sifter made, heavily nickel plated and polished, fancy enameled wood handle, extra strong and durable. Weight, 11 oz. Price...23c

Flour Sieves.

No. 23C5536 Tin Rim Sieve, plated wire bottom, 18 meshes to the inch, 12⅛ inches diameter, well put together; made of heavy tin. Weight, 6 oz. Price, 11c

Ringed Pot Covers, IC Tin.

No. 23C5545 Hemmed edges.

Inches	8⅛	9	9⅛
Price	3c	3c	4c
Inches	10	10⅛	11
Price	4c	5c	5c
Inches	11⅛	12	12⅛
Price	6c	6c	7c

JAPANNED WARE.

Flour Boxes.

No. 23C6000 Hinged covers, decorated.

Holds, pounds	25	50
Weight, pounds	2⅛	4
Size, inches	9⅝x16⅜	12⅛x20⅛
Price	53c	75c

Holds, pounds	100
Weight, pounds	7
Size, inches	15⅛x26⅛
Price	$1.05

Perfect Flour Bin and Sifter.

No. 23C6002 Japanned and nicely ornamented. The sifter is protected from pressure by the flour in the bin by our new shield, which enables the reels to work easily and smoothly, and obviates all grinding through of foreign substances. A tin skirt below the sifter prevents the flour from scattering all over the bottom of the bin, but instead directs it into the proper receptacle. The sifter is easily removed for cleaning.

Holds, pounds	25	50	100
Weight, crated, lbs.	10⅛	16	21
Size, inches	10⅛x23	12⅛x27¼	15⅛x34
Price	$1.34	$1.55	$2.20

Square Bread Boxes.

No. 23C6005 Nicely japanned and decorated.

Inches	9⅛x9⅛x13⅛	10⅛x11⅛x15	10⅝x12⅛x17
Wgt., lbs.	2⅛	3	3⅞
Price	47c	52c	61c

Fog or Dinner Horns.

No. 23C6037 Fog or Dinner Horns, 18 inches long with improved mouthpiece; nicely japanned. Price 12c

Comb Cases.

No. 23C6043 Comb Cases, Assorted colors, 2⅜x5⅛x7 inches. Weight, 4 ounces. Price, each, 5c
Per dozen........54c

Match Box Holder and Safe.

No. 23C6055 Match Box Holder and Safe. Holds full box of 200 matches. Nicely finished. Weight, 4 ounces.
Price..........8c

Light Cash Boxes.

No. 23C6080 Flat top, sunk handle, nicely japanned, with lock.

Length, in.	8⅜	9⅛	10⅞	11⅛	12⅜	13⅛	15
Width, in.	5⅜	6⅜	7⅜	8⅜	8⅜	10	11
Height, in.	3⅛	3⅜	4⅛	5	5⅛	6⅛	7
Price	35c	38c	44c	49c	50c	62c	79c

Combination Lock Cash or Treasure Boxes.

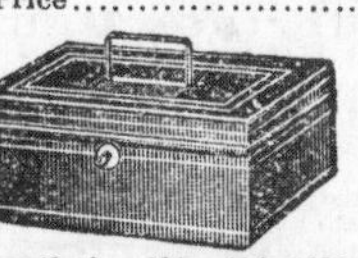

No. 23C6090 These boxes are made from very heavy stock, finished in black enamel striped with rich gold bronze. The dial is large and legible. The owner can set a new combination as often as may be required without taking the lock to pieces. Trays are not furnished with boxes. For trays see following number. Knobs project ⅜ inch beyond the ribs.

Length, outside	Width	Depth	Price
9⅛ in.	6⅜ in.	3⅜ in.	$1.95
10⅞ in.	7⅜ in.	4⅛ in.	2.08
12⅜ in.	8⅜ in.	5⅛ in.	2.19
14⅛ in.	10⅛ in.	6⅛ in.	2.35
16⅛ in.	12 in.	7 in.	2.70
18⅛ in.	13⅛ in.	8⅛ in.	2.98

No. 23C6092 Inside Partitioned Trays, to fit inside our No. 23C6090 cash box. The middle compartment with slide is omitted from the 9⅛ inch tray.

Size, in.	9⅛	10⅞	12⅜	14⅛	16⅛	18⅛
Price	16c	23c	25c	48c	65c	80c

Fireproof Cash Box.

No. 23C6094 Fireproof Cash Box. The fireproof walls of this box are sufficiently thick to make it absolutely fireproof in any residence. It is a perfectly safe receptacle for deeds, bonds, contracts, mortgages, notes, insurance policies, tax receipts, jewelry, etc. To test this box we had one subjected to an intense heat in a furnace. Not only was the iron heated red hot, but it reached a white heat, which is the point just before iron melts. The contents of box were not even marred. No fire could ever occur out in the open air to equal the intense heat to which this box was subjected. Furnished with a first class padlock with two keys. Dimensions: Outside, 13 inches long, 9 inches wide, 7 inches deep; inside, 10 inches long, 6¼ inches wide, 3 inches deep. Approximate weight, 50 pounds. Price......**$4.65**

Cuspidors.

No. 23C6112 Cuspidors, japanned tin, with gold band. Weight, 5 ounces. Size, 4x7 inches.
Price, each.......**8c**
Per dozen.......**88c**

No. 23C6116 Nickel Plated Cuspidors. Weight, 8 ounces. Size, 5x7½ inches.
Price......**22c**

No. 23C6119 Cast Iron Cuspidors. White enameled inside, outside painted, assorted colors, banded. Weight, 5½ pounds. Size, 6x8 inches. Price....**39c**

Fancy Water Coolers.

No. 23C6130 Water Coolers. Double wall, filled with non-conducting material, galvanized iron reservoir, handsomely decorated in various colors, side handles, nickel plated faucets.

Gallons	2	3		
Weight, crated, lbs.	18	20		
Price	**$1.20**	**$1.55**		
Gallons	4	6	8	10
Weight, crated, lbs.	25	30	45	55
Price	**$1.80**	**$2.15**	**$2.58**	**$3.35**

Chamber Pails.

No. 23C6158 Chamber Pails. Assorted colors; nicely japanned inside and outside.

Quarts	10	12
Holds, qts.	9	11
Size	10½x10½	11x11½
Wgt. lbs.	2	2½
Price	**30c**	**31c**

Quarts	14
Holds, qts.	13
Size	11¼x12¾
Wgt. lbs.	2¾
Price	**39c**

Challenge Odorless Commode and Slop Bucket Combined.

No. 23C6162 It is impossible for the foul air to escape, even when the lid is removed, as there is inside the lid a receptacle that holds a deodorizer, and which neutralizes all gases inside the commode. The disinfectant (2 tablespoonfuls of chloride of lime), needs only to be renewed once in two weeks at a small cost. It is indispensable in the sick room, especially in cases of contagious diseases and fevers. Does not have to be emptied until filled, no matter how long it stands. Illustration shows construction. Made of heavy galvanized iron, and has no paint to hold stench or disease germs. Has removable seat, etc. It needs only to be seen to convince you of its wonderful merit. Holds 9 quarts. Weight, 6¾ lbs. Price **$1.35**

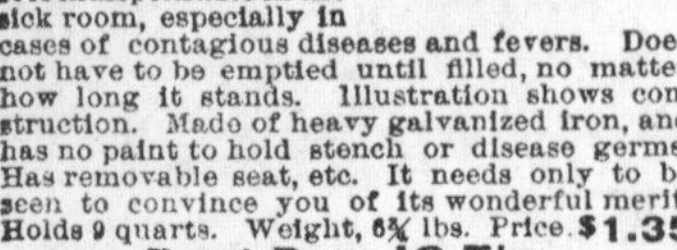

Dust Pan, IC Tin.

No. 23C6175 Japanned, round tin handles. Weight, 6 ounces. Size, 9 x 13 inches.
Price, each......**6c**
Per dozen......**64c**

Covered Dust Pan, IC Tin.

No. 23C6177 Japanned, round tin handles. Weight, 8 ounces. Size, 9 x 13 inches.
Price, each......**9c**
Per dozen......**95c**

Quaker Dust Pan.

No. 23C6179 Quaker Dust Pan, made of XXX tin plate, extra heavy, with stiff, sharp edge. Built for wear, and will stand rough usage. Japanned finished. Size, 12¾x8½ inches.
Price.........**17c**

Crumb Pans and Brushes.

No. 23C6186 Assorted colors. Black Tampico brushes. Pan, 6x9¼ inches. Weight, 6 ounces. Price..............**19c**

No. 23C6189 Large shell pattern. Extra fancy. Assorted colors. Black and white bristle brushes, 8¾x10½ inches. Weight, 8 ounces.
Price......**33c**

Crumb Tray and Brush.

No. 23C6194 Crumb Tray and Brush, finely polished and nickel plated. Weight, 8 ounces.
Price, for tray and brush..**52c**

No. 23C6195 Crumb Tray and Scraper, same design as shown above, with scraper instead of brush. Weight, 8 ounces.
Price for tray and scraper..............**25c**

Japanned Oval Tea Trays.

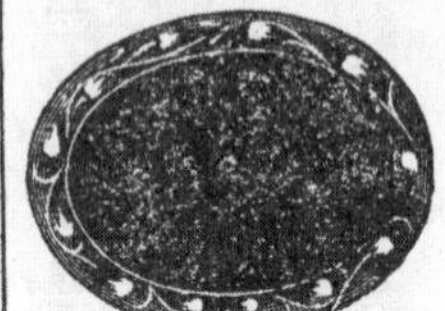

No. 23C6212

Inches, diameter	14	18	22	26
Weight, pounds	¾	1	1¾	2½
Price	**10c**	**15c**	**22c**	**33c**

Toilet Stand.

No. 23C6260 Toilet Stand. Will hold any ordinary sized wash basin. Easily attached to wall, post or the side of a wooden pump, and can be folded up out of the way when not in use. Complete with soap holder, as shown in illustration, and towel hook. Made of steel, nicely japanned and is unbreakable. Weight, 2 pounds. Price..........**18c**

Towel Rack.

No. 23C6475 Towel Rack. All steel, nicely nickel plated, with three swinging arms. 12½ inches long. Weight, 6 ounces. Price......**9c**

Wire Broilers.

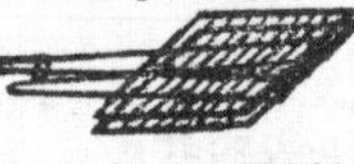

No. 23C6500 Heavy Retinned Wire Broilers.

Size	Weight	Price
9x 6 inches	4 ounces	**6c**
9x 8 inches	6 ounces	**7c**
9x12 inches	12 ounces	**10c**
9x14 inches	14 ounces	**12c**

Vegetable Boilers.

No. 23C6508 Made of wire. Can also be used for boiling eggs.

Size, inches	7	8	9
Weight, ounces	4	5	6
Price	**5c**	**6c**	**7c**

Wire Dish Covers.

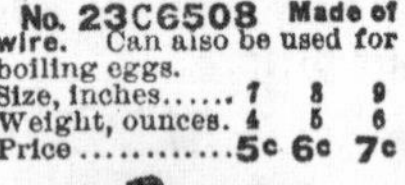

No. 23C6512 Blued Wire Dish Covers.

Size, inches	6	7	8	9	10
Price	**5c**	**6c**	**7c**	**8c**	**10c**

Per set, one each, 6 to 10 inches. Weight, per set, 12 ounces. Price..........**33c**

Soap Holders.

No. 23C6519 Soap Holder. We furnish one different from illustration with tooth brush rack. Weight, 2 ounces. Price..**7c**

No. 23C6521 Soap Holder. Has black and gold enameled iron frame with glazed crockery soap dish. Can be used as a stand or hung on wall. Weight, 6 ounces.
Price..........**10c**

Wire Dish Drainer.

No. 23C6537 Extra Heavy Wire Dish Drainers, 12x16 inches, strong and well made, heavily coated with tin to prevent rust. Weight, 1½ pounds.
Price..............**18c**

Basting Spoons.

No. 23C6544 Forged Steel Basting Spoons, strong, heavy and durable. Heavily tinned.

Length	Weight	Price
10-inch	3½ ounces	**4c**
12-inch	4 ounces	**6c**
14-inch	6 ounces	**7c**
16-inch	7 ounces	**8c**
18-inch	7½ ounces	**10c**

Aluminum Soup Ladle.

No. 23C6546 Soup Ladle. Made in one piece of solid cast aluminum and highly polished. Will not tarnish, rust or corrode, no plating to wear off. Equal to solid silver in appearance and durability at about one-tenth the price. Length, 12 inches. Weight, 3 ounces.
Price..............**48c**

Wood Handle Mixing Spoon.

No. 23C6547 Wood Handle Mixing Spoon. Retinned. Length, 10 inches. Weight, 2 ounces. Price..............**5c**

Slotted Mixing Spoon.

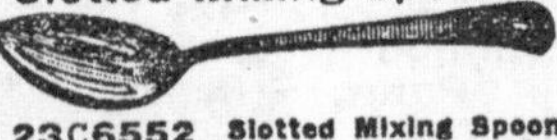

No. 23C6552 Slotted Mixing Spoon or Cake Beater. Forged from one piece of steel and heavily retinned. Smooth and easily cleaned. Length, 11½ inches. Weight, 4 ounces.
Price..............**7c**

Kitchen Fork.

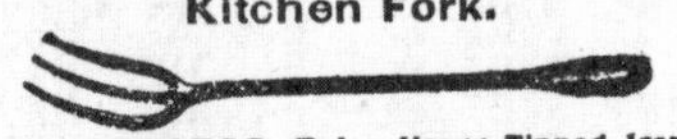

No. 23C6563 Extra Heavy Tinned Iron Kitchen Fork. Three prongs. Length, 15 inches. Weight, 5 ounces. Per doz., **75c**; each.....**7c**

Handy Kitchen Set.

No. 23C6567 Handy Kitchen Set, consisting of one forged steel flesh fork, 11½ inches long; one forged steel basting spoon, 11½ inches, and one 9-inch cooking spoon, all heavily retinned and mounted on card. Weight, 12 ounces. Price, for set of three pieces......**18c**

Wire Coat or Garment Hanger.

No. 23C6568 Wire Coat or Garment Hanger, 17 inches. Garments when hung on this device do not lose their shape as when hung on hook or nail. Weight, 4 ounces.
Price, per dozen, **34c**; each..........**4c**

Potato Masher.

No. 23C6577 Potato Masher, the best kitchen utensil ever used; heavy retinned wire, twisted shank and hardwood handle. Weight, 6 ozs. Price, per doz., **42c**; each..**5c**

Corn Poppers.

No. 23C6582 Heavy wire. One quart. Weight, 6 ounces.
Price..............**8c**

No. 23C6583 Heavy wire. Two quarts. Weight, 8 ounces. Price..........**12c**

Soap Saver.

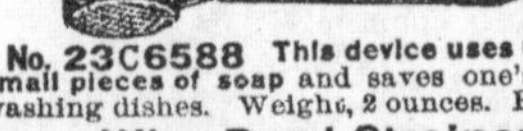

No. 23C6588 This device uses up all the small pieces of soap and saves one's hands in washing dishes. Weight, 2 ounces. Price...**5c**

Wire Bowl Strainer.

No. 23C6595 Wire Bowl Strainer, twisted wire handle, tinned wire gauze body with tin rim, 5 inches. Weight, 1½ ounces.
Price, per dozen, **48c**; each..........**5c**

Strainers.

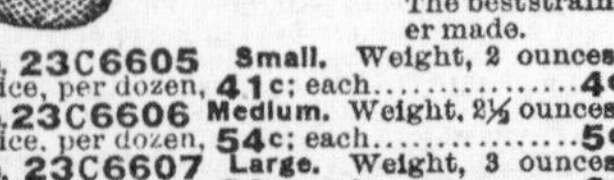

Enameled Handle Strainer, with extra fine wire gauze. The best strainer made.

No. 23C6605 Small. Weight, 2 ounces. Price, per dozen, **41c**; each..........**4c**

No. 23C6606 Medium. Weight, 2½ ounces. Price, per dozen, **54c**; each..........**5c**

No. 23C6607 Large. Weight, 3 ounces. Price, per dozen, **66c**; each..........**6c**

Tea or Coffee Balls.

Tea or Coffee Balls. Tinned wire with hinge and catch. Put the tea or coffee in the ball and drop it into the pot and boil in the usual way. You will get the full strength of the tea or coffee without grounds or tea leaves, and a strainer is not necessary.

No. 23C6612 Small Size, 1½x2½ inches. Weight, 1 ounce. Price..........**5c**

No. 23C6614 Large Size, 2¼x3¼ inches. Weight, 1 ounce. Price..........**7c**

Holt's Patent Egg Beater.

No. 23C6628 Holt's Patent Egg Beater will whip a pint of cream fine in two or three minutes; beats eggs in twenty seconds. We guarantee it to beat eggs or whip cream in one-third the time of the best Dover beater. Is larger and stronger than the regular Dover beater, and has improved flaring dashers.
Price..............**15c**

Surprise Egg Beater.

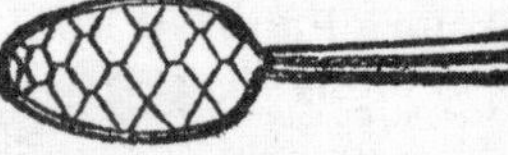

No. 23C6632 Considered the best cream whip. Weight, 1 ounce.
Price, per dozen, **14c**; each..........**2c**

Dover Egg Beaters.

No. 23C6633 Dover Egg Beater. Length, 9 inches. Weight, 5 ounces. Wheels and handle are Tuscan bronzed; beater and frame heavily tinned and retinned. The size and kind commonly sold for 10 to 15 cents. Price..........**5c**

No. 23C6634 Dover Egg Beater. Length, 10½ inches. Weight, 7 ounces. All parts tinned and retinned to prevent rust. Easy to clean.
Price..............**8c**

No. 23C6636 Dover Egg Beater. Length, 12½ inches. Weight, 15 ounces. The hotel size; strong and durable; wheels and handle are Tuscan bronzed; beater and frame heavily tinned.
Price..............**12c**

Champion Fly Trap.

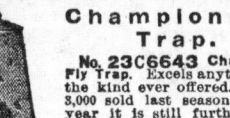

No. 23C6643 Champion Fly Trap. Excels anything of the kind ever offered. Over 3,000 sold last season. This year it is still further perfected, better than ever. Weight, 7 ounces.
Price, each........**$0.10**
Price, per dozen...**1.18**

Wire Fly Killer.

No. 23C6647 Wire Fly Killer. Kills a fly on the wall without crushing it and picks it up without staining the wall or paper. The wire cuts the air, so the fly does not feel any fanning of the air and will not get away. Weight, 2 ounces. Price..........**7c**

Card Racks and Holders.

No. 23C6655 Folding Card Racks. These are very useful articles for holding cards, photos, etc. It admits of very handsome decoration with ribbons. Just the thing for amateur photographers. Made of twisted steel wire, brightly tinned. It folds up into a small package and cannot be injured in shipping.

Size, inches	11x17	14½x21	17x26	20½x28
Holds pictures	28	45	66	91
Weight, ounces	2	3	4	5
Price	**7c**	**8c**	**11c**	**12c**

Galvanized Chamber Pails.

No. 23C6817 Worth a dozen cheap tin or wooden pails. 12 quarts. Holds 11½ quarts. Weight, 2½ pounds.
Price..........**35c**

Galvanized Water Pails.

No. 23C6820 Will never rust, no hoops to fall off. Sizes are actual capacity.

Quarts	10	12	14
Weight, lbs.	2	3	3½
Price	**16c**	**18c**	**20c**

Galvanized Washtubs.

No. 23C6836 Heavy Galvanized Washtubs; no leaking, no hoops to fall off, strong and durable.

No.	1	2	3
Size	20x17½x10½	22x17½x10½	24½x21½x10½
Weight	8 lbs.	8 lbs.	9 lbs.
Price	**50c**	**56c**	**64c**

Wringer Attachments.

No. 23C6837 For clamping wringer on galvanized tub. A set consists of two devices like illustration. Weight, 6 ounces. Price, per set...**6c**

Galvanized Steel Baskets.

Galvanized Steel Bushel Baskets are provided with extra heavy corrugated bottoms, thus insuring great strength.

No. 23C6845 1 bushel. Weight, 5½ pounds. Price..52c

No. 23C6846 1½ bushel. Weight, 7 pounds. Price, 68c

OIL CANS.

Spout Oil Cans.

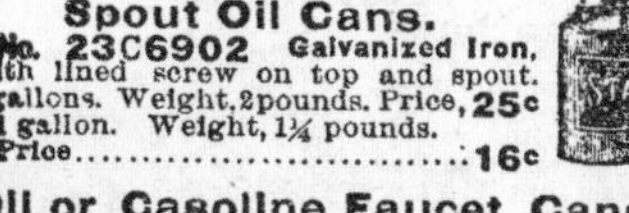

No. 23C6902 Galvanized Iron, with lined screw on top and spout. 3 gallons. Weight, 2 pounds. Price, 25c
1 gallon. Weight, 1¼ pounds.
Price........................16c

Oil or Gasoline Faucet Cans.

No. 23C6907 The Faucet Can. The most desirable faucet can made. Corrugated galvanized iron; brass faucet, nickel plated.
3 gallons. Weight, 2½ lbs.
Price......................38c
5 gallons. Weight, 3¾ lbs.
Price......................47c

Copperized Steel Oilers.

No. 23C6950 Seamless Copperized Steel Oilers are cheap, durable and elegant. They are heavily electro copper plated on the inside to prevent rust and to prevent the oil from becoming gritty. On the outside they perfectly resemble solid burnished copper. The 9-inch nozzles are bent; all others are straight. Have block steel spring bottoms.

Diam. of bottom	2¾	3⅜	3⅜	3⅜	3¾	4⅛	4⅛
Length of nozzle, inches	2½	3	3	5	3	3	9
Weight, ounces	2	3	4	5	6	7	8
Price	13c	15c	16c	18c	22c	26c	30c

Mowing Machine Oilers.

Mowing Machine Oilers. Tin; bent or straight spout; hold about ⅓ pint. Weight, 5 ounces.
No. 23C6975 Bent spout. Price..5c
No. 23C6976 Straight spout.
Price..........................5c

Copper Plated Mowing Machine Oiler.

No. 23C6983 Copper plated inside and outside. Made of one piece of steel, holds about ½ pint. Weight, 6 ounces. Price...14c

TUBULAR LANTERNS.

Dietz Victor Side Lift Tubular Lantern.

For Kerosene.

No. 23C7002 Can be filled, lighted, regulated and extinguished without removing the globe. A side crank raises globe for lighting, and also securely locks it down to burner. Has No. 1 burner with ⅝-inch wick and No. 0 globe. Fount holds enough oil to burn 17 hours. Weight, 1⅞ pounds.
Price........................45c

Dietz Crystal Tubular Lantern.

No. 23C7005 This is a strongly guarded tubular lantern with a glass fount instead of tin. This enables the user to see how much oil is in the fount, and the fount will never leak. Fitted with our improved side lift. While the fount on this lantern is strongly guarded and is not liable to breakage, still in case of accidentally breaking it can easily be renewed and a new one put in. No. 1 burner; ⅝-inch wick; No. 0 globe. Weight, about 2½ pounds. Price.......62c

Dietz Royal Tubular Lantern.

For Kerosene.

No. 23C7012 This lantern has the No. 2 burner, 1-inch wick and No. 0 Globe, and should fill a want where a large amount of light is needed in a hand lantern. The oil pot holds 1¼ pints of oil, and the lantern will burn nineteen hours without refilling. Weight, about 2 pounds.
Price......................62c

Ham's Cold Blast Tubular Lantern.

No. 23C7015 Cold Blast No. 2 Round Tube, Bottom Lift, Tin Tubular Lantern. No. 2 burner, 1-inch wick, No. 0 globe. Globe removable without taking off the guard, and is easily raised to light. This lantern is made on the same principle as a street lamp, with wind break, making it a superior lantern in its burning qualities. Very desirable for use in places where there are strong drafts of wind. In mills and other places where there is considerable dust, the burner will not clog up. Weight, 2¼ pounds.
Price......................80c

Dietz Junior Cold Blast Lanterns.

No. 23C7016 Only 12 inches high and gives a light equal to many lanterns double its size. It can be filled, lighted, regulated and extinguished without removing the globe. It burns on the cold blast principle, taking most of its air supply from above the globe and will not blow out in the strongest wind. Our Junior Cold Blast possesses all the advantages of our regular No. 2 cold blast lantern, but in more compact form, and is unequaled where a light handy lantern is required. Price..........60c

No. 23C7018 Dietz Junior Cold Blast Lantern, same as No. 23C7016, except it is made of brass, highly polished. Price............90c

No. 23C7019 Dietz Junior Cold Blast Lantern, same as No. 23C7016, except it is made of brass and is highly polished and nickel plated. Price.......................$1.10

Dietz Safety Tubular Mill Lantern.

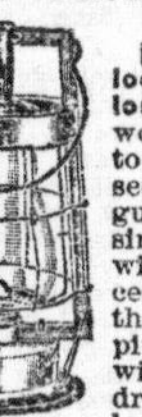

No. 23C7017 The burner is locked in place by two positive locks on globe frame, which work automatically. In addition to this a padlock may be used to secure the globe frame and the guard frame permanently, if desired. The guard has our patent wind break, which prevents access to the flame over the top of the globe. The oil fount holds 1½ pints of oil, will burn 19 hours without refilling, has a solid drawn, retinned oil fount. This lantern has been endorsed by insurance men wherever shown as the safest kerosene burning lantern made. Improved burner, ⅝-inch wick. No. 0 globe. Weight, 2½ pounds.
Price........................90c

Dietz Buckeye Dash Lantern.

No. 23C7025 This is really a very handy combination; it serves as a hand lantern and a side or dash lamp. The lamp can be fastened under the body of the vehicle by means of a holder. (See No. 23C7052.) We furnish this lamp with our new bull's eye lens—a bull's eye attached to the perforated plate. It is superior in every way to the bull's eye globe. No. 1 burner, ⅝-inch wick. No. 0 globe. Wt., about 2¼ lbs. Price, 63c

Dietz No. 0 Reflector Tubular Lantern.

For Kerosene.

No. 23C7027 The globe can be raised for lighting. The hood is 6 inches deep, fitted with a 5-inch silvered glass reflector and a spring fastening for dash. Can also be used as a hand lantern or wall lamp. It is a desirable lantern for night driving, and will throw a strong light over 100 feet. We have never heard of one of them blowing or jarring out. The lamp can be fastened under the body of the vehicle, by means of our Warner holders. (See No. 23C7052.) No. 1 long cone burner, ⅝-inch wick. No. 0 globe. Wt., about 2⅜ lbs. Price, $1.10

Cold Blast Dash Lamp.

No. 23C7030 Cold Blast Dash Lamp. No. 2 burner, 1-inch wick, No. 0 globe. This lamp is intended for use when a very powerful light is required. It will not blow out in the strongest wind, and does not flicker as much as a lantern without windbreak. We furnish this lantern japanned blue. Weight, 2¾ pounds.
Price $1.00

Dietz Tubular Driving Lamp.

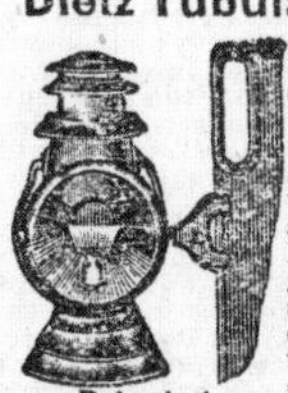

Patented.

No. 23C7040 It is a practicable and perfect driving lamp. It will not blow out; it gives a clear, white light; it looks like a locomotive headlight; it throws all the light straight ahead; it burns kerosene. Handsomely finished; japanned. By means of a spring on the back, the lamp can be instantly placed on the front of dash; by means of the holder it can be attached to either side of the dash. It can also be placed on the bracket of a carriage. Fount holds oil to burn 21 hours. 11 inches high; 6 inches in diameter. Weight, 2½ pounds. Price, japanned..............$2.10

Dietz Tubular Hunting Lamp.

No. 23C7045 Looks like a locomotive headlight. It will not blow nor jar out. The hood over the front works perfectly and without noise; when the hood is down no light escapes. It will throw a powerful light. It burns kerosene oil and will burn ten hours without refilling. It is compact and handsome. Has bail and can be used as a hand and wall lantern in camp. Gives a brilliant light, and is absolutely safe. 11 inches high; 6 inches in diameter. Weight, 2½ lbs. Price...$3.00

Lantern Holder.

No. 23C7052 Warner Tubular Lantern Holder. For holding a tubular lantern under the body of a wagon for night driving. Weight, 6 ounces.
Price..........................20c

Wire Bottom R. R. Lantern.

Burns Lard Oil.

No. 23C7069 The strongest railroad lantern made. The bail is made so that when the lantern is put down the bail stands up. Hinge top, removable globe, wire bottom, casts no shadow, bail fastened to guard. Bayonet catch on oil pot. Weight, 2½ pounds.
Price..........................70c

Police or Dark Lanterns.

No. 23C7125
No. 23C7126

No. 23C7125 Police or Dark Lanterns, 2¼-inch bull's eye. Weight, 12 ounces. **Burns lard or sperm oil.** Price....33c

No. 23C7126 Police Lanterns, 3-inch bull's eye. Weight, 16 ounces. Price.............36c

No. 23C7130 Special quality dark lanterns, made of heavy tin, nickel plated, finest finish and strongest in the market; furnished with the best quality fire polished lens. Weight, each, 14 ounces, with 2½-inch lens. **Burns lard or sperm oil.**
Price......................98c

No. 23C7130
No. 23C7131

No. 23C7131 With 3-inch lens. Weight, 18 ounces. Price...................$1.18

Dietz Search Light.

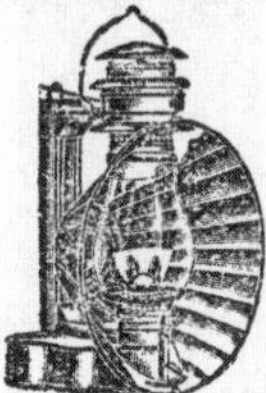

No. 23C7148 For outdoor or indoor use. Will not blow out. Gives a powerful and brilliant light. Simple and effective device for raising globe, for lighting and trimming. No. 2 burner, 1-inch wick. No. 0 globe. Weight, 3¾ pounds.
Price.....................$1.50

10-inch Square Traction Engine Headlight.

No. 23C7150 This headlight is especially adapted for traction engines, as it gives a very strong light, and the draft is so arranged that the flame will not smoke or blow out in high winds, nor jar out in passing over rough roads. Size, 21¾x12x9¼ inches. Has silver plated copper reflector, 10 inches in diameter, and improved locomotive headlight burner. Packed complete with attachments to fit to engine. Weight, crated, 32 pounds. Price..................$6.20

Dietz Tubular Hanging Street Lamp.

No. 23C7181 Will not blow out in the strongest wind. No chimney, new globe lifter, improved burner, outside wick regulator, automatic extinguisher, does not smoke. Light equal to gas, at a less cost. Is useful wherever a strong light is desired. Has No. 3 burner, 1½-inch wick, No. 3 globe. Weight, packed for shipment, 31 pounds.
Price.......................$3.38

Dietz Corporation Street Lamp.

No. 23C7191 This Lamp is fitted with a glass oil fount, kerosene burner and chimney, and has a removable cast iron socket that will fit a post or bracket. The upper part of lamp is removable and they nest close for shipment. Packed one in each case. Average weight, with case, 40 pounds. Net, with socket, 15 pounds. Height, 32½ inches. No. 2 burner. 1-inch wick. No. 2 Sun chimney. Price.............$3.20

Dietz No. 3 Globe Tubular Street Lamp.

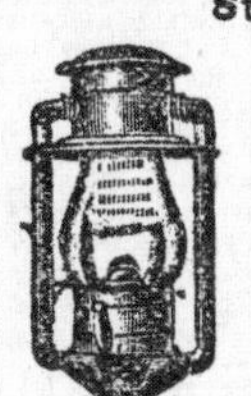

No. 23C7196 Warranted to give perfect satisfaction. More sold than all other makes combined. No chimney. Light equal to gas at a less cost. New globe lifter. Outside wick regulator. Does not smoke. Casts no shadow. Will not blow out in the strongest wind. Can be regulated to burn a certain number of hours. This lamp never fails to give perfect satisfaction. It can be filled, lighted and regulated without removing the globe. The reflector is painted white and the lamp painted green. Packed one each in a case. Weight boxed, 30 pounds; 27 inches high; No. 3 burner; 1½-inch wick; No. 3 globe.
Price......................$3.38

Gasoline and Oil Torches.

No. 23C7300 The Acme Gasoline Torches, for indoor or outdoor lighting; are not affected by wind, rain, cold or heat. They produce a large, brilliant, white flame, equal in volume to ten gas jet flames. The reservoir holds nearly six quarts, and when filled will burn full flame for nine hours. Weight, 3¼ pounds. Price..........84c

No. 23C7302 Acme Gasoline Torch, with two burners, controlled by separate valves, so only one may be used if desired. The burners are 24 inches apart. Weight, 5¼ pounds. Price....$1.50

Torch Burner.

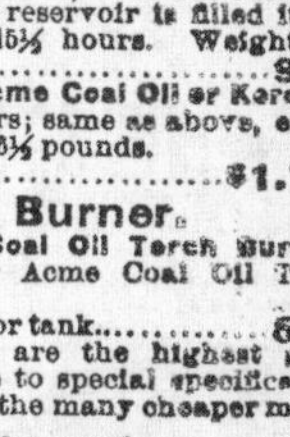

No. 23C7305 Gasoline Torch Burners, same as used on our Acme Gasoline Torch. Weight, 1¼ pounds.
Price, without pipe or tank..........45c

Kerosene Torches.

No. 23C7308 The Acme Coal Oil or Kerosene Torch, is similar in general appearance to the gasoline torch, with the exception of burner. When the reservoir is filled it will burn full flame for 15½ hours. Weight, 3¾ pounds. Price.........................94c

No. 23C7310 Acme Coal Oil or Kerosene Torch with two burners; same as above, except the burner. Weight, 6½ pounds.
Price.......................$1.75

Torch Burner.

No. 23C7312 Coal Oil Torch Burners, same as used on our Acme Coal Oil Torch. Weight, 1¼ pounds.
Price, without pipe or tank..............63c

Our Acme Torches are the highest grade made. They are made to special specifications and are worth double the many cheaper makes.

Washboards.

No. 23C8085 Brass Washboard. The finest family size washboard manufactured. The rubbing surface is made of a sheet of hard spring brass; it will not corrode, crack or get out of shape; has the latest improved corrugated cable crimp and will do the washing with one half the labor required on ordinary boards. It is not necessary to rub hard, the board will do the work. Has protector top and open back braced by bent truss rods so that rubbing surface can never sag. We guarantee every one of these washboards for five years and will replace any that give out within that time. Weight, 2½ pounds. Price..................32c

No. 23C8088 Glass Washboard. Rubbing surface consists of a thick heavy corrugated plate of best flint glass. Can never tarnish, corrode or get out of shape. Gives a perfect and easy washing surface. Price.........30c

No. 23C8090 The Old Reliable Banner Globe Double Washboard. Standard family size; double zinc surface; globe crimp on one side and plain crimp on the other; hardwood frame and stationary protector top; strong and well made. One of the most popular washboards made. Weight, 2⅜ pounds. Price........24c

No. 23C8096 Leader Washboard. Single zinc rubbing surface with globe crimp. Protector top. A strong and durable board at small price. Weight, 2 pounds. Price..........17c

Clothes Pins.

No. 23C8115 Hoyt's Spring Clothes Pins are made of white basswood and the spring is one continuous piece of galvanized spring wire. Simple and convenient and the cheapest when durability is considered. Weight, per gross, 3 pounds.
Price, per gross, 35c; per dozen.........3c

No. 23C8117 Hold Fast Clothes Pins. Will not tear the most delicate fabric. Easily removed when frozen to line. Has galvanized steel spring warranted never to rust. Weight, per gross, 4¼ pounds.
Price, per gross, 58c; per dozen..........5c

No. 23C8120 Clothes Pins, standard goods, full count. Weight, per gross, 3¼ pounds. We do not sell less than one gross. Price, per gross........12c
Price, per box, containing 5 gross..........55c

Clothes Lines.

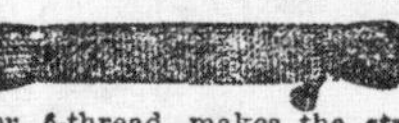

No. 23C1930 Manila Rope, ⅜ inch diameter, 6-thread, makes the strongest and most durable clothes line you can get. 100 feet is the ordinary clothes line length, but we will sell any quantity desired.
Price, per foot...........................½c
Price, per 100 feet.......................45c

Empire Braided Cotton Clothes Lines.

Warranted Full Length. Each Line All One Piece Solid Braid—no Filler.

No. 23C1946 Length, 50 feet. Price..........................13c
No. 23C1947 Length, 75 feet. Price..........................20c
No. 23C1948 Length, 100 feet. Price.........................27c

SIZE OF NO. 20.

SIZE OF NO. 18.

Galvanized Wire Clothes Lines.

No. 23C1960 Wire Clothes Line, 100 feet long, made of six strands of No. 18 wire. Flexible, and will not rust.
Price.....................................22c

No. 23C1962 Wire Clothes Line, 100 feet long, made of six strands of No. 20 wire. Price...........................16c

Clothes Line Hooks.

No. 23C1980 Clothes Line Hooks, japanned, heavy. Weight, 6 ounces.
Price, each 2c
Per dozen 20c

Clothes Line Reel.

No. 23C1992 Line Reel or Clothes Drier Casting. Has a socket which fastens over the top of a post. The reel revolves on this socket and is made for four bars. From 100 to 200 feet of line can be strung on bars according to length of bars, and this can be hung full of clothes without moving basket or wading through deep snow in the winter. Weight, 12¼ pounds. Price 48c

Rat Traps.

No. 23C981 The Genuine French Marty Rat Trap is a wonderfully effective rat catcher. Is used in the leading hotels, market houses, and public institutions. Many testimonials prove that they will catch rats up to their full capacity night after night, as long as the rats hold out. Family size, 17 inches long; capacity, 20 rats. Weight, 1¾ lbs. Price 52c

No. 23C982 American Rat Trap, same size and pattern as the genuine Marty, but wires are not as close together nor as strongly secured, although it is an excellent rat catcher. Price 32c

Mouse Traps.

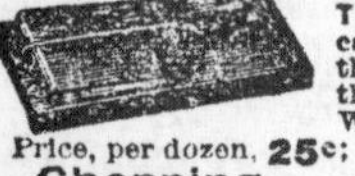

No. 23C991 Mouse Trap. This is the most successful mouse catcher ever invented. One mouse sets the trap for the next one that comes along; will hold several. Weight, 6 ounces. Price 9c

No. 23C994 Mouse Trap. As a sure mouse catcher it is a certain thing. Mice can't touch the bait and live. Weight, 2 ounces.
Price, per dozen, 25c; each 3c

Chopping Bowls.

No. 23C8140 Chopping Bowls. Polished maple. Extra quality, with heavy rims, prevents checking.

Inches	13	15	17	19
Weight, lbs.	1¾	2¾	3¼	4
Price	9c	15c	26c	42c

Oblong Chopping Trays.

No. 23C8142 Oblong Chopping Trays. Cut from a solid piece of hard maple.

Size	12x22	11x21	10½x19½
Weight, lbs.	3½	2½	2¼
Price	38c	29c	24c

Potato Masher.

No. 23C8161 Potato Masher, made complete with handle, all from one piece of hard maple. Weight, 10 ounces. Price 4c

Kitchen Spoon.

No. 23C8165 Wood Kitchen Spoon, polished maple, 14 inches long. Weight, 3 ounces. Price 4c

Rolling Pin.

No. 23C8172 Rolling Pin, best solid maple, revolving handles. Weight, 1¾ pounds. Price 8c

Egg Timer.

No. 23C8177 Egg Timer. Hour glass pattern with fancy wood frame. Height, 3 inches. Weight 1 ounce. Price 10c

Toothpicks.

No. 23C8190 Orangewood Toothpicks, imported from Portugal. Whittled out by hand to fine point on each end. The best toothpick made. Put up in bunches of 400 picks. Weight, per bunch, 3 ounces. Price 8c

No. 23C8192 Hardwood Toothpicks, double points. Standard size box holding about 1,800 picks. 100 boxes in case. Weight, per box, 8 ounces.
Price, per box $0.02
Per case 1.95

Fruit and Vegetable Slicer.

No. 23C8220 Fruit and Vegetable Slicer. For slicing apples, pears, bananas, potatoes, beets, carrots, cucumbers, turnips, radishes, etc. Makes dainty and attractive perforated flutings and Saratoga chips, also shoestrings, etc. No waste; anybody can use it. Illustration shows perforated slices made with this slicer. Weight 10 ounces. Price, each, $0.15
Per dozen 1.65

Slaw Cutter.

No. 23C8223 Slaw Cutter. For slicing cabbage, potatoes and all vegetables. Size 17x6¼ inches, hardwood. Weight, 2 pounds. One knife, adjustable. Price 12c
Two-knife, adjustable. Price 20c

Vegetable Slicer.

No. 23C8224 Potato or Vegetable Slicer. A household convenience for making Saratoga chips, cutting slaw or slicing fruits or vegetables for pies, soups, etc. Made of hardwood with steel knife. Size, 10¾x3¼ inches. Weight, 4 ounces. Price 10c

Adjustable Knife Kraut Cutters.

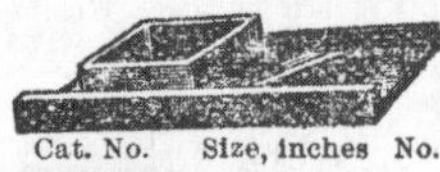

With slide box and tool steel knives easily adjusted to cut fine or coarse.

Cat. No.	Size, inches	No. of Knives	Price
23C8235	8x24	2	$0.72
23C8236	8x24	3	.83
23C8237	8x24	4	.95
23C8226	9x30	3	1.49
23C8239	12x36	4	2.98

Spice Cabinet.

No. 23C8250 Spice Cabinet. Neatly constructed, an ornamental cabinet for holding and preserving spices. Eight drawers marked for contents. Very handsome for any use to which a cabinet can be put. Made of ash, oil finish. Size, 12x18 inches. Weight, 5¼ pounds. Price 39c

Salt Box.

No. 23C8261 Salt Box, made of nice clear wood, is 4½x5 inches square, and will hold two small bags of salt. Weight, 14 ounces. Price 8c

Hardwood Salt Box.

No. 23C8263 Hardwood Salt Box. The front is made of alternating strips of dark and light wood, varnished and highly polished to bring out the beautiful grain of the wood. Has fancy metal plate, engraved with the word Salt. An artistic kitchen necessity. Will hold a small sack of salt. Is 10 inches high and 5¼ inches wide. Weight, 1 pound. Price 18c

Towel Rollers.

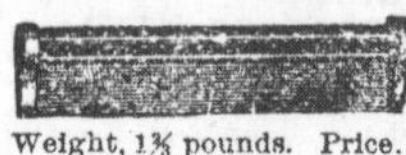

No. 23C8355 Towel Roller, white wood, plain. Size of roller, 18 x 1¾ inches. Weight, 1¾ pounds. Price 7c

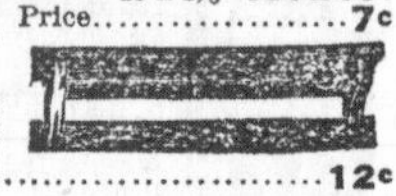

No. 23C8357 Towel Roller, hard wood, varnished. Size of roller, 1¾x18 inches. Weight, 1¾ pound. Price 12c

Clothes Bar or Towel Rack.

No. 23C8392 Clothes Bar or Towel Racks with bronzed bracket and birch arms. Any desired number of the arms can be used and the others drop down out of the way. Necessary in every kitchen.
Price, 5 arms, 18 inches long 7c
Price, 7 arms, 24 inches long 12c

Eureka Adjustable Clothes Bars.

No. 23C8395 Eureka Clothes Bar, intended to fasten to the wall. When not in use takes the space of an ordinary broom. The bars are 3 feet in length. A very convenient household article. Weight, 4 pounds. Price 39c

No. 23C8396 Same as No. 23C8395, with six bars, 2 feet long. Weight, 1½ lbs. Price 19c

Folding Ironing Board.

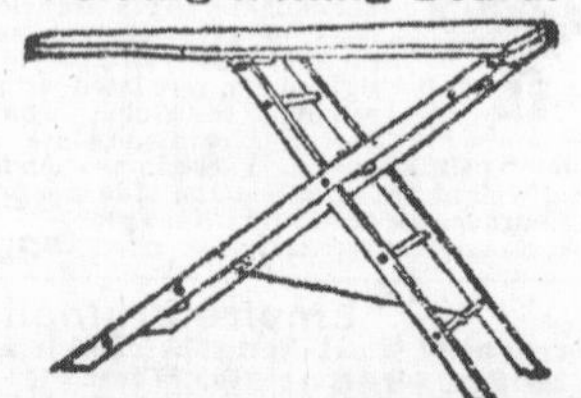

No. 23C8414 This convenient household article is in great favor wherever shown. It has basswood top. The legs are of hardwood, and the table may be easily and quickly adjusted to three different heights. When not in use occupies but little more space than the common ironing board. Weight, 14 lbs. Price, 55c

Curtain Stretchers.

No. 23C8461 Folding Curtain Stretchers for drying Lace Curtains. Extends to 6x12 feet and will hold any ordinary sized curtain; made from 1¼-inch stock with center brace; very light and strong. Rods stamped with measuring rule. Has all brass triple nickel plated stationary pins, one inch apart, which is close enough to fit the scallops of any curtain made. For center connections of frames we use a stamped steel plate hinge, fastened to side rails by bolts which permits the stretcher to be folded into the smallest possible space when not in use. Weight, 8½ pounds. Price 75c

No. 23C8464 Folding Curtain Stretcher. Can be adjusted to fit any size curtain. Triple nickel plated pins, guaranteed not to rust. At the cost of laundering two pair of lace curtains the housekeeper can secure one of these stretchers, and also obviate the customary laundry damage to curtains. Size, 6x12 feet. Weight, 8½ pounds. Price 67c

Extension Ladders.

Extension Ladders are always shipped direct from our Chicago factory. Weight about 3 pounds per foot.

No. 23C8542 Made from selected and seasoned Norway pine and hickory rungs. Our new double roller, single piece top iron is much stronger than the angle rollers, and strengthens the ladder in its weakest place. Our hooks are also the best. This is the best extension ladder manufactured. We do not allow for lap. Made in two sections. Length, 20 to 60 feet.
Price, per foot 11c
If made in three sections, per foot 12c

23C8542

Rope Extension Ladder.

No. 23C8544 Top section raised and lowered by rope and pulley attachment, easily handled. Has new roller, iron automatic locking hooks, and made same as our regular extension. We put our crank attachment for raising and lowering section on all these ladders and crank and rope are furnished. Made only in two sections. Length, 20 to 60 feet. Price, per foot 18c

Chair Seats.

Illustration shows shape of ball top seat. These chair seats are made from three pieces of birch veneer with grains crossing. Glued together under great pressure. They cannot split. Sizes given are measurements across the widest place.

No. 23C8570 Ball Top Chair Seats.
No. 23C8571 Square Chair Seats.

Size, inches	10	11	12	13	14	15
Weight, ounces	6	7	8	9	10	11
Price	3c	4c	4c	5c	5c	5c

Size, inches	16	17	18	20
Weight, ounces	12	14	18	20
Price	7c	7c	9c	10c

Splasher Mats.

No. 23C8640 Splasher Mats, for protecting wall above wash stand. Made of waterproof sewed wood splints with assorted hand decorated centers. Size, 17¼x29¼ inches. Weight, 8 ounces. Price, per dozen, 75c; each 7c

Table Mats.

No. 23C8646 Table Mats, made of Japanese matting, assorted colors, with fancy plaited straw edges. These are light, neat and durable. Set consists of three mats, one each, 6, 8 and 11 inches long. Weight, per set, 2 ounces. Price, per set 18c

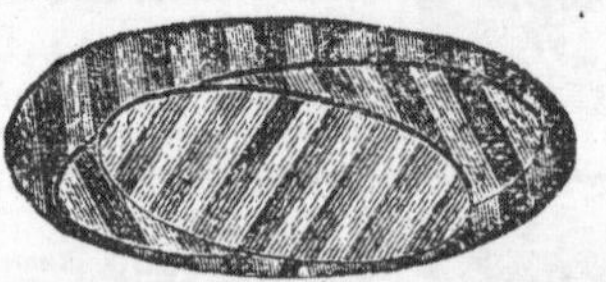

No. 23C8648 Table Mats. Made of alternating strips of light and dark hardwood, highly polished and securely glued to the cotton flannel back; can be rolled up into a small space. Set consists of three mats, lengths, 6¾, 8¾ and 10 inches. Weight, per set, 6 ounces. Price, per set 20c

No. 23C8650 Fine Palm Leaf Table Mats. Strong and neatly woven, for use under hot platters, etc. Prevents burning of table cloth and marring finish of table. Set consists of four oblong mats; length, 8, 9¾, 11, 12¾ inches, respectively. Sold in sets only. Weight, per set 10 ounces. Price, per set of four, one of each size. 45c

Chair Cane in Hanks.

No. 23C8579 Chair Cane. Extra No. 1, all long, in hanks of 1,000 feet. This is a high grade chair cane. We carry in stock fine, common and medium width.
Fine. Price, per hank 56c
Medium. Price, per hank 67c
Common. Price, per hank 73c

No. 23C8581 Binding Cane. Extra No. 1 grade, in hanks of 500 feet. Price 63c

DEPARTMENT OF DAIRY SUPPLIES.

Clean Easy Milk Cans.

We make all of our milk cans at our own factory and after the most approved modern designs. Our patterns were submitted to dairymen and milk shippers of long experience before the dies were made and embody every improvement that experience could suggest. Special attention has been given to the clean easy feature; there are no sharp angles, grooves or rough seams in which milk can collect and sour. The breasts are full and rounding, all seams are heavily loaded with solder and all rivet heads smoothly soldered over. Every can is as smooth and easily cleaned inside as a glass dish. Nothing but the best grade of steel plate is used in making; tinned and retinned by the palm oil process, which makes the most durable plate known. The Elgin, New York, Cleveland and St. Louis cans have our improved bottom hoop with offset, which supports the entire weight of the can and contents, so that no amount of jarring can strain the seams or rivets. Half round top hoops where used, are heated and shrunk immovably onto the breast, the same as the tire is shrunk onto a wagon wheel; breast and hoop are then forced onto the cylinder by heavy machinery and would never loosen even if no solder were used. Breast handles are our improved, full round pattern, which cannot cut the hands or collect dirt. Soldering is done by expert workmen and every seam is loaded with as much pure solder as it will carry.

The weight of a milk can governs the price and when comparing prices always compare weights. We guarantee actual and full capacity. Remember that we will not only guarantee to furnish you with the best can of the weight that money can buy, but also guarantee to save you from 25 to 65 cents on every can you buy, or refund your money and pay transportation charges both ways. No other maker dare do this.

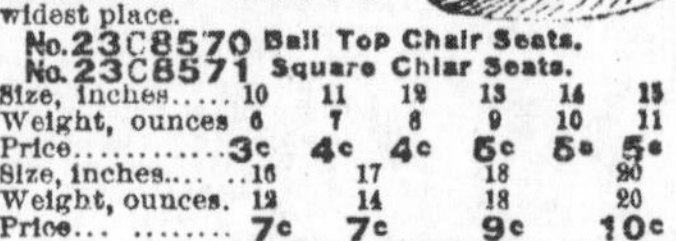

No. 23C9003 The Iowa Pattern Railroad Stiff Steel Milk Shipping Can. Is constructed to give great service; has seamless neck and cover with non-pull-off handle, improved round breast handles to prevent cut hands, stamped seamless breast with ⅜-inch half round steel bumping band to protect can from getting jammed in. Heavy stiff steel body, will not dent; riveted and soldered, drawn steel bottom, heavy tinned steel bottom hoop which supports the entire weight of the can and contents; bottom is flanged and riveted through hoop and body. Extra well soldered making them leak proof and durable.

Capacity, gallons	5	8	10
Average weight, lbs.	13½	18¼	20
Price	$1.48	$1.64	$1.63

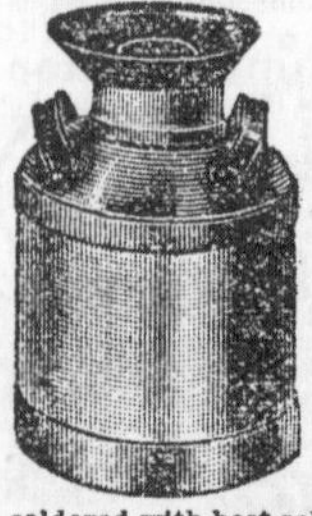

No. 23C9000 The Wisconsin Pattern Milk Can, seamless neck and cover, improved round handle, stamped seamless breast, heavy steel body, drawn steel bottom, strong heavy bottom hoop 2½ inches wide, half round breast, hoop shrunk immovably onto breast, then forced over body and heavily soldered. Body is double seamed. Bottom is flanged and riveted to body and bottom hoop, all parts tinned and retinned before being put together. All inside seams soldered with best solder and perfectly smooth. This style can is in use all over the United States for a wagon can for hauling milk or cream to creameries, but is not as durable for shipping purposes as our heavier cans. We guarantee them to be actual capacity.

Capacity, gallons	8	10
Average weight, pounds	15	16½
Price	$1.42	$1.47

No. 23C9006 The Elgin Pattern Railroad Stiff Steel Milk Shipping Can. Has seamless neck and cover with non-pull-off handle, improved round breast handles to prevent cut hands, stamped heavy steel breast with ⅜-inch half round steel bumping band. Heavy stiff steel body (will not dent), riveted and soldered, drawn steel bottom, extra heavy reversed bottom hoop, 1¼ inches wide with offset which takes all strain off seams and rivets; riveted through flange of bottom and body and projecting just far enough below body and bottom to protect both. Material in the body, breast and bottom is of extra heavy steel carefully retinned. While this can is stronger than those having outside hoops, the hoops are shorter and lighter owing to the improved construction.

Capacity, gallons	5	8	10
Average weight, lbs.	13½	17	19
Price	$1.45	$1.69	$1.80

Milk Shipping Cans.

No. 23C9014 Western Pattern Railroad Extra Stiff Steel Milk Shipping Can. Has seamless neck and cover, with non-pull-off handle. Extra heavy stiff steel seamless breast. Improved round breast handles. Extra stiff heavy steel body; riveted and soldered, heavy stiff drawn steel bottom; bottom rivets pass through flange of bottom, body of can and bottom hoop, making the strongest construction known. Breast and bottom hoops are 2½ inches wide, and are offset and riveted on ends, and soldered top and bottom. This can is intended to stand the roughest kind of usage. All seams are loaded by floating into them the best pure solder. The entire inside of can is smooth and easy to clean.

Capacity, gallons	8	10
Average weight, pounds	22	24¼
Price	$1.81	$1.93

No. 23C9017 New York Pattern Railroad Extra Stiff Steel Milk Shipping Can, one of our best patterns, has 7-inch seamless neck, extra heavy cover, will support a cake of ice without injury, and the cover is shaped so the cans can be piled two or three high. Has stamped steel breast with malleable drop handles, extra stiff heavy steel body riveted and soldered, heavy drawn steel bottom; bottom hoop is 1¾ inches wide, with offset which body and bottom rest on and which supports the weight of the can and contents; breast hoop, ⅜-inch half round welded steel shrunk onto breast to act as a bumper and prevent can from jamming in. Smoothly soldered and a very easy can to clean on account of the large neck and rounding corners. We guarantee full capacity.

Capacity, gallons	5	8	10
Average weight, lbs.	15⅝	19½	22¼
Price	$1.52	$1.86	$1.90

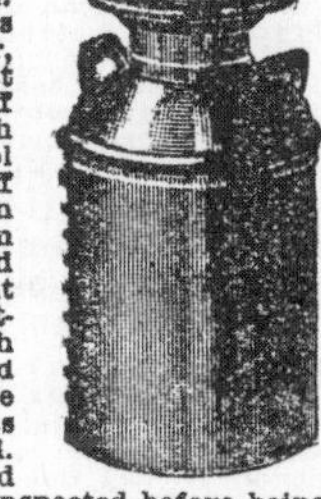

No. 23C9026 The Cleveland Pattern Stiff Steel Railroad Milk Can. Deep, 7-inch seamless neck, extra heavy cover, improved, round breast handles, stamped stiff steel breast with ⅜-inch half round welded steel bumping band, heavy stiff steel body, heavy drawn steel bottom, bottom hoop is extra heavy and supports the entire weight of can and contents. Bottom rivets pass through flange of bottom, body and bottom hoop, making the construction almost as strong as a solid weld. All parts are tinned and retinned and carefully inspected before being put together. We guarantee actual capacity.

Capacity, gallons	8	10
Average weight, pounds	19¾	22¼
Price	$1.80	$1.89

No. 23C9029 St. Louis Pattern Railroad Milk Shipping Cans. 7-inch seamless neck, extra heavy cover malleable drop handles; seamless stamped steel breast with ⅜-inch half round welded steel bumping band to protect can from being jammed in, heavy stiff steel body, riveted and soldered; drawn steel bottom; outside bottom hoop 1¾ inches wide, having offset on the inside on which the bottom and body rests, taking all strain off the seams and rivets. Unusual care is taken in soldering this can, all seams are loaded by floating into them the best pure solder until seams are smooth as glass, leaving no shoulders or rough places where milk can collect and sour. We guarantee actual capacity.

Capacity, gallons	5	8	10
Average weight, lbs.	12¾	19½	22¼
Price	$1.51	$1.80	$1.90

Our Sturges Pattern Steel Can.

No. 23C9035 The Old Reliable Well Known Sturges Pattern Railroad Milk Shipping Can. Has seamless neck and cover with non-pull-off handle. Seamless stamped steel breast; round steel breast handles. Drawn steel bottom. Breast hoop 2½ inches wide, soldered top, bottom and ends. Bottom hoop 2½ inches wide. Bottom rivets pass through flange of bottom body and bottom hoop. All parts are tinned and retinned and carefully inspected before being put together. This pattern can has been on the market for thirty-five years and is better this year than ever before. We guarantee actual capacity.

Capacity, gallons	5	8	10
Average weight, lbs.	10	19¾	22
Price	$1.39	$1.57	$1.65

READ OUR
GREAT CREAM SEPARATOR OFFER
ON PAGE 408.

Milk Can Links and Washers.

No. 23C9047 Milk Can Links and Washers. We always use this washer to strengthen can and prevent its wearing. We can fit any of our milk cans with link and washer, at an additional charge of, per can.....5c

Milk Can Letters and Figures.

No. 23C9048 Copper Milk Can Letters or Figures. Size, 1⅜ inches, soldered onto can at, per letter or figure.....1½c

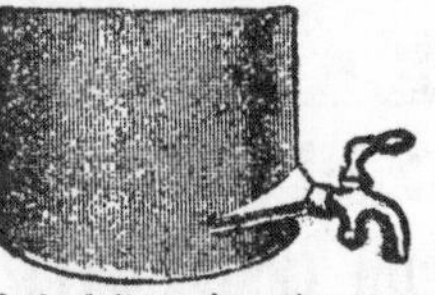

Brass Faucet.

No. 23C9050 The illustration shows ⅜-inch brass faucet fitted to milk can for delivery purposes. When desired, it can be put on any of our cans at an additional cost, including price of faucet and labor of.....$1.45

No. 23C9056 Jersey Milk Can Brush. Best ox fibre stock, wide flaring ends. Will clean corners perfectly and never mat down. Cleaned with scalding water. Size of face, 9 by 5 inches. Weight, 7 ounces. Price.....29c

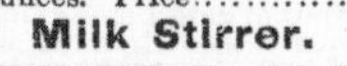

Milk Stirrer.

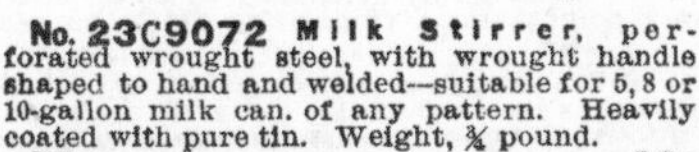

No. 23C9072 Milk Stirrer, perforated wrought steel, with wrought handle shaped to hand and welded—suitable for 5, 8 or 10-gallon milk can, of any pattern. Heavily coated with pure tin. Weight, ¾ pound. Price.....22c

Stamped Milk Can Strainer.

No. 23C9080 Retinned, with 4½-inch brass wire strainer cloth bottom. Just the thing to use in connection with railroad milk cans. Heavy large bowl and straining surface. It measures 10½ in. across the top and the brass cloth measures 4½ inches which will accommodate the milk as fast as poured in. It is retinned, easily cleaned and always bright. Weight, ¾ pound, Size, 10½ in. Price...27c

Milk Can Strainer.

No. 23C9082 Milk Can Strainer, is made of the best quality IXX charcoal tin plate; well soldered, with brass strainer. Has detachable hoop for holding straining cloth. The bowl or hopper is large enough to prevent milk overflowing. Strong, heavy and durable. Weight, 1½ pounds. Price.....55c

Milk Coolers and Aerators.

No. 23C9085 Makes the milk keep longer, takes out all animal heat and odors and thoroughly cools and aerates it. Pour the milk into the hopper, and by the time you are through milking, it is cooled and aerated. It can be used either with running water or filled from a well, spring or with ice. The milk will be cooled to within a few degrees of the temperature of the water used in cooling. One filling with ice will cool 500 to 600 quarts of milk down to a temperature of 60 degrees. Attach rubber hose to water inlet and fill water compartment with cold water, or lift off top and fill from bucket, being careful to place the cooler and aerator where there is plenty of pure fresh air. Use the agitator freely to draw the warm water from the sides. The water overflow will permit of your keeping a running stream of water constantly passing through, and is desirable where such can be resorted to. Built of heavy tin plate with galvanized steel bottom and painted inside with two coats of best anti-rust paint. With little care, should last for years. Securely crated for shipment.

Number	Capacity of Milk Receiver	Number of Cows	Takes Care of	Weight, Crated	Price
2	18 quarts	5 to 25	3 Milkers	21 lbs.	$4.20
3	34 quarts	25 to 50	5 Milkers	29 lbs.	4.75
4	52 quarts	50 to 100	8 Milkers	40 lbs.	5.75

Prices include double cheese cloth strainer and spring pins. Special descriptive circular sent free on request.

Milkeep.

No. 23C9090 Simply stir one tablespoonful into a 10-gallon can of milk to keep the milk perfectly sweet without ice for 36 to 48 hours in the warmest weather. For cream use double this quantity. If it is desired to keep the milk sweet a longer time, add the same quantity of Milkeep at the end of 30 hours. It contains no acid, leaves no odor, cannot be detected by analysis; guaranteed to be absolutely harmless, a child can drink a glassful of Milkeep and it will have no more effect on the system than pure water.

Price, 1 quart bottle.....$0.75
½ gallon.....1.30
1 gallon.....2.25

Deep Cover Cream Setting Cans.

Without Gauge. With Gauge.

Have Air Tight Covers, with Self Locking Bails. It requires no locking device to hold the cover down, and is the only cream can that can be completely submerged in water without leaking. The graduated glass gauge enables you to watch and measure the rising cream. **Note special price in lots of six cans.**

No. 23C9100 Made of IX tin plate, without gauge.

Quarts	14	18	20
Weight, pounds	2½	3	3½
Price, each	$0.30	$0.33	$0.36
Per crate of six cans	1.56	1.71	1.87

No. 23C9103 Made of IXX tin plate, with gauge.

Quarts	14	18	20
Weight, pounds	3½	4	4½
Price, each	$0.42	$0.45	$0.48
Per crate of six cans	2.18	2.34	2.49

Dairyman's Quick and Easy Cleaner.

No. 23C9119 A pure white flake, containing neither grease, caustic, alkali, animal or vegetable matter. A wonderful cleaner, and will sweeten and purify milk cans, churns, milk bottles, separators, test tubes, strainer cloths, and all dairy woodwork. Invaluable for milk cans and separator parts, as it will instantly remove all grease and cream, and will not rust or corrode the tin. It makes no lather, is easily rinsed off and is tasteless, quickly removes all grease and stain from milk bottles, leaving them sweet, clean and highly polished. Where you have been using 5 to 7 pounds of sal soda or similar washing compound, 1 pound of Dairyman's Quick and Easy Cleaner will do the work. Put up in wooden boxes with complete directions for use.

Price, per box, containing 6 pounds.....25c
Price, per box, containing 12 pounds.....48c

Glass Milk Jars.

Strictly first quality flint glass; smooth, clear and heavy, with deep rim at top to hold stopper.

No. 23C9126 Capacity, two quarts. Price, per doz.....$1.22
Per gross.....13.75
No. 23C9128 Quarts. Price, per gross, $6.88; per dozen.....60c
No. 23C9129 Pints. Price, per gross, $4.98; per dozen.....44c
No. 23C9127 Half Pints. Price, per gross, $4.80; per dozen.....43c

Milk Jar Stoppers.

No. 23C9130 Waterproof Fibre Stoppers for either size glass milk jars. Weight, per 1,000, 4 pounds. Price, per 1,000.....20c
Price, per bushel basket containing 6,000 stoppers.....$1.20
Price, per barrel containing 50,000 stoppers.....$9.00

Milk Bottle Filler.

No. 23C9131 Built of IXXXX Cookley K imported tin plate. Capacity 60 quarts. Has two faucets on bottom and operates fully as fast as any automatic device. Faucets are straight bore and easily cleaned and are equipped with filters which remove all particles that may be in the milk and cause it to flow in smooth, even columns. Made so strong and heavy that it will last a lifetime. The sensible way to fill bottles. Price.....$3.30

Milk Jar Delivery Baskets.

No. 23C9132 Milk Jar Delivery Basket. Extra heavy wire, double tinned after being made, which solders every joint and makes it strong and durable. No. 1, holds 6 1-quart bottles. Price.....42c
No. 2, holds 4 1-quart and 2 1-pint bottles. Price.....45c

Milk Bottle Brushes.

No. 23C9134 Milk Bottle Brush. Best Russian bristles, securely fastened, with stiff tampico tufts for cleaning corners and bottom; length, 16 inches. Price.....12c

Cheese Factory Milk Cans at Greatly Reduced Prices.

No. 23C9140 Factory Cans. Made of heavy steel, heavily coated with pure block tin. Has the improved handle and seamless floating cover, strictly first quality in every way.

Holds, gal.	15	20
Weight, lbs.	22	25
Price	$2.40	$2.70
Holds, gal.	30	40
Weight, lbs.	32	40
Price	$3.18	$3.90

Factory Milk Can.

No. 23C9145 Has ventilated floating cover which slides down on to the milk and prevents churning and agitation. Body made from one piece Cookley K IXXXX best charcoal tin plate, double seamed and soldered. Bottom is extra heavy. Bottom hoop is 1¾ inches wide welded steel, having a bead on which bottom rests. Bottom rivets pass through flange on bottom body and bottom hoop. Top and center hoops, 2½ inches wide welded steel. Improved recessed malleable iron handle, fits snugly over the middle hoop and is riveted on both sides, so when these cans are riding together in a wagon the handles cannot punch holes in the body of can. All hoops are soldered top and bottom. Great care is taken in soldering these cans, to assure strength and no leaks. The weight of this can indicates plainly its actual value; although the price may seem high, when durability is considered, it's the cheapest can we or anyone else can offer. We guarantee actual capacity.

Cap., gals.	15	20	30	40
Av. wt., lbs.	30	32	38½	47¾
Price	$3.68	$3.93	$4.52	$5.60

Dairy Pails.

No. 23C9170 Heavy Dairy Pail, with drawn steel bottom, heavy steel bail. Stock is tinned and retinned before being put together. Well soldered, smooth seams, strong and durable.

Actual capacity, quarts	12	14
Weight, lbs.	3½	3¾
Price	34c	36c

For other Dairy Pails, Strainer Pails, etc., see Index. For Dairy and Butter Salting Scales, see page 413.

Improved Dilution Cream Separator.

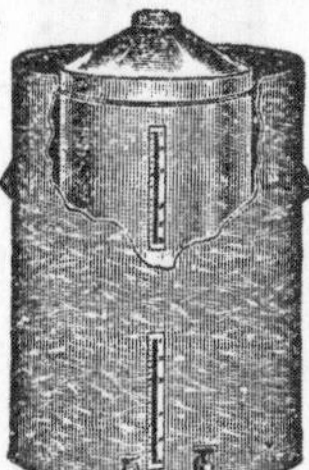

No. 23C9189 Improved Dilution Cream Separator separates the cream from the milk in thirty to fifty minutes, and gives you the sweet diluted milk which is far superior to the sour milk from the pan system for stock food, and with a little oil meal added, makes a most nourishing ration. To use: Reverse the cover which also contains a brass strainer and attach conducting tube; pour in any quantity of milk up to half the capacity of the separator. Now slowly pour in an equal quantity of pure cold water, then reverse cover, unscrew tube and attach aerating plate. The water entering at the extreme bottom diffuses evenly upwards through the milk, separating the cream globules, which being lighter than either, rise quickly to the top. The rising of the cream can be watched through the glass gauges in the side, and when all has risen, draw off the skim milk through faucet at apex of the cone shaped bottom until cream line passes below lowest gauge. Then remove milk can and draw off the pure cream in another vessel. Made of heavy XXX charcoal tin plate, enameled and decorated on the outside and furnished complete with legs.

Capacity Gallons	Outside Measure	Shipping Weight	Price, Complete
10	12x30 in.	10 pounds	$3.75
14	14x30 in.	15 pounds	4.20
18	15x30 in.	20 pounds	4.65
21	16x30 in.	25 pounds	5.10
24	18x36 in.	30 pounds	5.60
32	19x38 in.	35 pounds	5.95

Economical Creamers.

No. 23C9190 Economical Creamer, will separate the cream from the milk in 4 to 6 hours and produce perfect separation in warm or cold weather. Has removable inner can, permitting thorough cleaning of both inner and outer cans. No loose parts to wear or get lost. No labor wasted in toilsome skimming, lifting or handling of crocks. The milk is aerated and ventilated and is not churned as in a centrifugal separator. Milk compartment can be removed and cleaned as easily as one crock. Gives you pure, sweet, undiluted milk for family use. Glass gauges at top and bottom enable you to watch the progress of the cream rising and to draw off the milk and cream separately through valve in bottom. Inner can is made of heavy tinned steel, painted on outside to prevent rust. Outer can made from galvanized iron with double seamed bottom. All carefully soldered. Cover is cone shaped and by reversing forms a strainer, as it is provided with removable cone shaped brass wire strainer and also perforated plate for ventilating and aerating the milk. Special descriptive circular mailed on request.

Capacity of inner can	Size, crated	Shipping weight	Price
4 gals.	18x18x22	20 pounds	$3.20
6 gals.	19x19x24	22 pounds	3.60
8 gals.	24x24x24	25 pounds	3.95
10 gals.	24x24x26	28 pounds	4.30
12 gals.	28x28x26	32 pounds	4.65

For other creamers see page 410.

THE IMPROVED ECONOMY CREAM SEPARATOR, $38.75

AT $38.75 TO $53.50, according to capacity, we offer this genuine Improved Economy Cream Separator, as the very best and highest grade, and most improved cream separator on the market. Guaranteed the closest skimmer, the easiest running, strongest, most convenient, easiest cleaned, and most satisfactory hand cream separator manufactured today, the superior of any separator on the market, regardless of name, make or price.

$38.75 BUYS THIS IMPROVED ECONOMY CREAM SEPARATOR

$10.00 TO $15.00 A YEAR ON EACH COW CAN EASILY BE SAVED by using the improved Economy Separator. The farmer who has only three cows is simply throwing away money (in the percentage of cream he loses) if he is without a good separator. The Improved Economy is guaranteed to save you time, labor and money, and to be the easiest running, closest skimming and most durable separator made.

IT IS NOT SAFE To buy any separator, no matter who it is made by, unless you get a long term written guarantee against defects of all kinds with it.

WE GUARANTEE SAFE DELIVERY ALSO. Every separator is set up and carefully tested before packing and leaves us in perfect condition, and we guarantee it to reach you in the same perfect condition and if by chance any part should be damaged or lost by rough or careless handling in transit, we agree to replace or repair it or furnish another separator free of all expense to you.

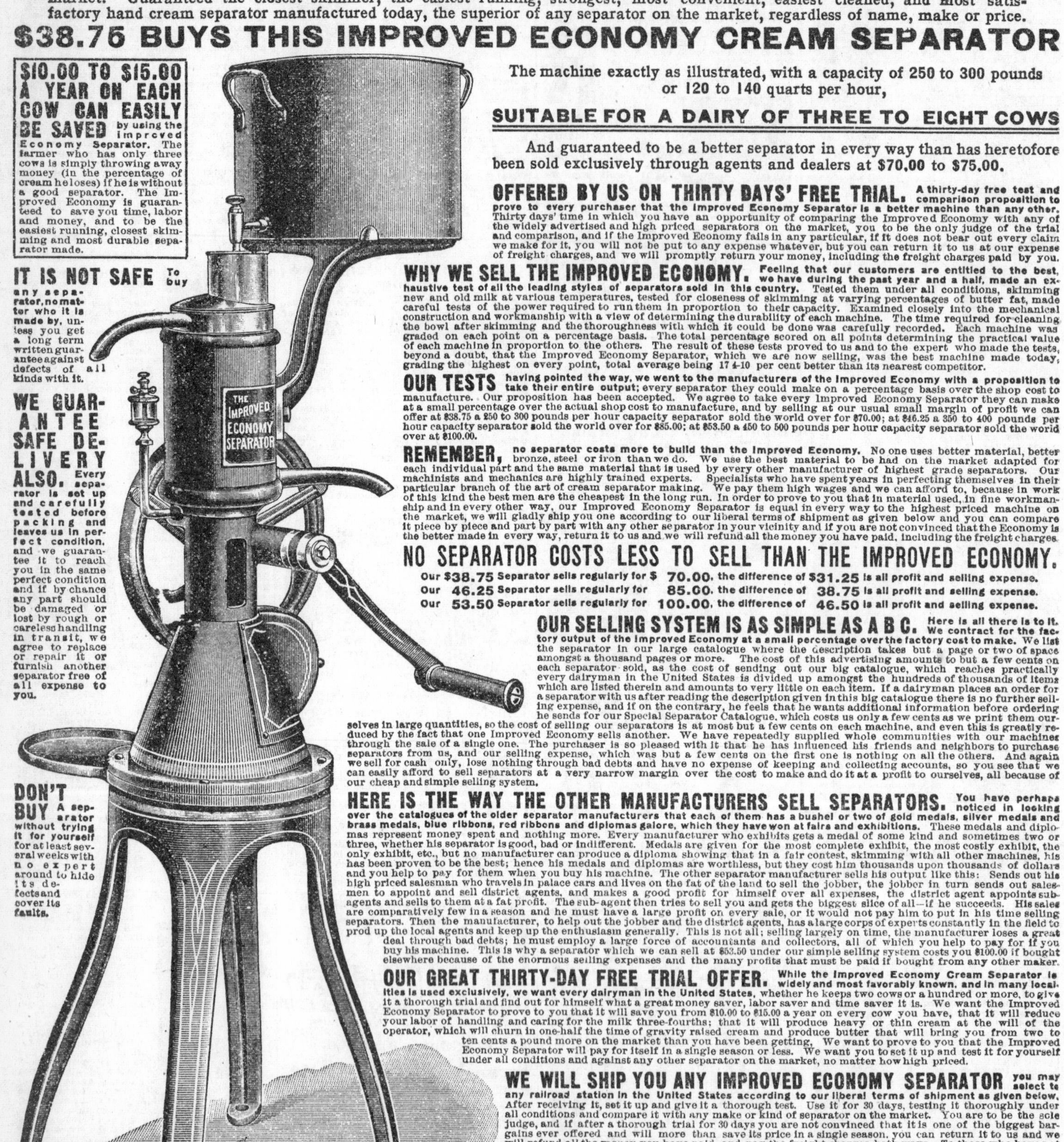

DON'T BUY A separator without trying it for yourself for at least several weeks with no expert around to hide its defects and cover its faults.

DON'T PAY More than our price for any other separator of the same capacity. No separator costs more to build than the Improved Economy and the extra price is all profit for the man who is trying to sell you.

The machine exactly as illustrated, with a capacity of 250 to 300 pounds or 120 to 140 quarts per hour,

SUITABLE FOR A DAIRY OF THREE TO EIGHT COWS

And guaranteed to be a better separator in every way than has heretofore been sold exclusively through agents and dealers at $70.00 to $75.00.

OFFERED BY US ON THIRTY DAYS' FREE TRIAL. A thirty-day free test and comparison proposition to prove to every purchaser that the Improved Economy Separator is a better machine than any other. Thirty days' time in which you have an opportunity of comparing the Improved Economy with any of the widely advertised and high priced separators on the market, you to be the only judge of the trial and comparison, and if the Improved Economy fails in any particular, if it does not bear out every claim we make for it, you will not be put to any expense whatever, but you can return it to us at our expense of freight charges, and we will promptly return your money, including the freight charges paid by you.

WHY WE SELL THE IMPROVED ECONOMY. Feeling that our customers are entitled to the best, we have during the past year and a half, made an exhaustive test of all the leading styles of separators sold in this country. Tested them under all conditions, skimming new and old milk at various temperatures, tested for closeness of skimming at varying percentages of butter fat, made careful tests of the power required to run them in proportion to their capacity. Examined closely into the mechanical construction and workmanship with a view of determining the durability of each machine. The time required for cleaning the bowl after skimming and the thoroughness with which it could be done was carefully recorded. Each machine was graded on each point on a percentage basis. The total percentage scored on all points determining the practical value of each machine in proportion to the others. The result of these tests proved to us and to the expert who made the tests, beyond a doubt, that the Improved Economy Separator, which we are now selling, was the best machine made today, grading the highest on every point, total average being 17 4-10 per cent better than its nearest competitor.

OUR TESTS having pointed the way, we went to the manufacturers of the Improved Economy with a proposition to take their entire output; every separator they could make on a percentage basis over the shop cost to manufacture. Our proposition has been accepted. We agree to take every Improved Economy Separator they can make at a small percentage over the actual shop cost to manufacture, and by selling at our usual small margin of profit we can offer at $38.75 a 250 to 300 pounds per hour capacity separator sold the world over for $70.00; at $46.25 a 350 to 400 pounds per hour capacity separator sold the world over for $85.00; at $53.50 a 450 to 500 pounds per hour capacity separator sold the world over at $100.00.

REMEMBER, no separator costs more to build than the Improved Economy. No one uses better material, better bronze, steel or iron than we do. We use the best material to be had on the market adapted for each individual part and the same material that is used by every other manufacturer of highest grade separators. Our machinists and mechanics are highly trained experts. Specialists who have spent years in perfecting themselves in their particular branch of the art of cream separator making. We pay them high wages and we can afford to, because in work of this kind the best men are the cheapest in the long run. In order to prove to you that in material used, in fine workmanship and in every other way, our Improved Economy Separator is equal in every way to the highest priced machine on the market, we will gladly ship you one according to our liberal terms of shipment as given below and you can compare it piece by piece and part by part with any other separator in your vicinity and if you are not convinced that the Economy is the better made in every way, return it to us and we will refund all the money you have paid, including the freight charges.

NO SEPARATOR COSTS LESS TO SELL THAN THE IMPROVED ECONOMY.

Our $38.75 Separator sells regularly for $ 70.00, the difference of $31.25 is all profit and selling expense.
Our 46.25 Separator sells regularly for 85.00, the difference of 38.75 is all profit and selling expense.
Our 53.50 Separator sells regularly for 100.00, the difference of 46.50 is all profit and selling expense.

OUR SELLING SYSTEM IS AS SIMPLE AS A B C. Here is all there is to it. We contract for the factory output of the Improved Economy at a small percentage over the factory cost to make. We list the separator in our large catalogue where the description takes but a page or two of space amongst a thousand pages or more. The cost of this advertising amounts to but a few cents on each separator sold, as the cost of sending out our big catalogue, which reaches practically every dairyman in the United States is divided up amongst the hundreds of thousands of items which are listed therein and amounts to very little on each item. If a dairyman places an order for a separator with us after reading the description given in this big catalogue there is no further selling expense, and if on the contrary, he feels that he wants additional information before ordering he sends for our Special Separator Catalogue, which costs us only a few cents as we print them ourselves in large quantities, so the cost of selling our separators is at most but a few cents on each machine, and even this is greatly reduced by the fact that one Improved Economy sells another. We have repeatedly supplied whole communities with our machines through the sale of a single one. The purchaser is so pleased with it that he has influenced his friends and neighbors to purchase separators from us, and our selling expense, which was but a few cents on the first one is nothing on all the others. And again we sell for cash only, lose nothing through bad debts and have no expense of keeping and collecting accounts, so you see that we can easily afford to sell separators at a very narrow margin over the cost to make and do it at a profit to ourselves, all because of our cheap and simple selling system.

HERE IS THE WAY THE OTHER MANUFACTURERS SELL SEPARATORS. You have perhaps noticed in looking over the catalogues of the older separator manufacturers that each of them has a bushel or two of gold medals, silver medals and brass medals, blue ribbons, red ribbons and diplomas galore, which they have won at fairs and exhibitions. These medals and diplomas represent money spent and nothing more. Every manufacturer who exhibits gets a medal of some kind and sometimes two or three, whether his separator is good, bad or indifferent. Medals are given for the most complete exhibit, the most costly exhibit, the only exhibit, etc., but no manufacturer can produce a diploma showing that in a fair contest, skimming with all other machines, his has been proven to be the best; hence his medals and diplomas are worthless, but they cost him thousands upon thousands of dollars and you help to pay for them when you buy his machine. The other separator manufacturer sells his output like this: Sends out his high priced salesman who travels in palace cars and lives on the fat of the land to sell the jobber, the jobber in turn sends out salesmen to appoint and sell district agents, and makes a good profit for himself over all expenses, the district agent appoints subagents and sells to them at a fat profit. The sub-agent then tries to sell you and gets the biggest slice of all—if he succeeds. His sales are comparatively few in a season and he must have a large profit on every sale, or it would not pay him to put in his time selling separators. Then the manufacturer, to help out the jobber and the district agents, has a large corps of experts constantly in the field to prod up the local agents and keep up the enthusiasm generally. This is not all; selling largely on time, the manufacturer loses a great deal through bad debts; he must employ a large force of accountants and collectors, all of which you help to pay for if you buy his machine. This is why a separator which we can sell at $53.50 under our simple selling system costs you $100.00 if bought elsewhere because of the enormous selling expenses and the many profits that must be paid if bought from any other maker.

OUR GREAT THIRTY-DAY FREE TRIAL OFFER. While the Improved Economy Cream Separator is widely and most favorably known, and in many localities is used exclusively, we want every dairyman in the United States, whether he keeps two cows or a hundred or more, to give it a thorough trial and find out for himself what a great money saver, labor saver and time saver it is. We want the Improved Economy Separator to prove to you that it will save you from $10.00 to $15.00 a year on every cow you have, that it will reduce your labor of handling and caring for the milk three-fourths; that it will produce heavy or thin cream at the will of the operator, which will churn in one-half the time of gravity raised cream and produce butter that will bring you from two to ten cents a pound more on the market than you have been getting. We want to prove to you that the Improved Economy Separator will pay for itself in a single season or less. We want you to set it up and test it for yourself under all conditions and against any other separator on the market, no matter how high priced.

WE WILL SHIP YOU ANY IMPROVED ECONOMY SEPARATOR you may select to any railroad station in the United States according to our liberal terms of shipment as given below. After receiving it, set it up and give it a thorough test. Use it for 30 days, testing it thoroughly under all conditions and compare it with any make or kind of separator on the market. You are to be the sole judge, and if after a thorough trial for 30 days you are not convinced that it is one of the biggest bargains ever offered and will more than save its price in a single season, you can return it to us and we will refund all the money you have paid and pay the freight charges both ways. To those who have not been accustomed to using a centrifugal cream separator, and may perhaps hesitate to order one on that account, we may say that by following the plain, simple directions which we send out with every separator, any 14-year old boy can set up and learn to operate the Improved Economy Separator perfectly in less than an hour.

OUR LIBERAL TERMS OF SHIPMENT. While nearly all of our customers, especially those who have had dealings with us and hence know that we are reliable, send cash in full with their order, saving the extra charge of usually 25 to 50 cents which all express companies make for the collection of C. O. D. and the return of the money to us, to those who prefer to see and examine the separator before paying for it, we will, upon receipt of $1.00 ship any of our separators to any part of the United States, you can examine the separator at your nearest railroad station, and if found to be perfectly satisfactory pay the agent our price and the freight and collection charges, less the $1.00 sent with the order, and take up the shipment subject, of course, to our 30-day free trial offer as explained above.

OUR WRITTEN 20-YEAR BINDING GUARANTEE goes with every Improved Economy Separator, by the terms and conditions of which, if any piece or part gives out within 20 years by reason of defect in material or workmanship, we will replace or repair it free of charge. This is the longest, strongest and most binding guarantee furnished by any separator manufacturer and backed, as it is by our house with a capital of over two million dollars, you are made absolutely secure against any possible defect of any kind.

THE IMPROVED ECONOMY IS THE CLOSEST SKIMMER IN THE WORLD

UNDER ALL CONDITIONS AND WE CAN PROVE IT. THERE IS NO OTHER JUST AS GOOD.

WE WILL GIVE $1,000.00 IN GOLD to the separator manufacturer who can produce a machine that will outskim the Improved Economy at temperatures of 50, 60, 70, 80 and 90 degrees. This offer is made to the makers of the De Laval, Sharples, Empire, United States and every other machine sold in the United States. WE HAVE TESTED THEM ALL AND WE KNOW WHAT WE ARE TALKING ABOUT. The Improved Economy ranks first, the best of the others is a poor second.

DETAILS OF CONSTRUCTION. In the Improved Economy Separator the whole milk is fed from the supply tank at the top of the machine into a cup shaped vessel, where the flow is regulated and from there passes down into the bowl, which is revolved at a high rate of speed by a series of three gear wheels operated by turning the crank. In passing through the bowl, the cream is separated by the centrifugal force, assisted by our wonderful skimming device, the skim milk, from which all the cream has been removed, passing out through the bottom of the bowl while the cream flows out through the upper cover where it can be regulated to any desired thickness.

THE BOWL OF THE IMPROVED ECONOMY IS WONDERFULLY EFFECTIVE, and is the result of many years of thought and careful experimenting by a mechanical genius, the Edison of the separator world, and as it now stands perfected is miles in advance of any other.

In the Improved Economy the currents are controlled perfectly from the time the whole milk enters the bowl until the skim milk and cream leave it by their respective exits, the conflict of the moving particles of skim milk and cream each striving to reach their respective levels impelled by centrifugal force, is reduced to a minimum, the currents being directed in such a way that practically all the cream is separated instantaneously the moment the whole milk enters the bowl. The very minute particles of butter fat, which are affected but little by the force of gravity, are acted upon over and over by our skimming device and are practically all separated and carried to the center or cream wall long before the skim milk reaches the bottom of the bowl. So perfect is the control of the currents and so complete is the separation, that we have frequently run 1,000 to 1,100 pounds of milk per hour through our 450 to 500-pound capacity bowl at 65 turns of the crank per minute, which is but 5 turns more than the regular speed and skimmed to 1-100th of one per cent, that is to say we left but 1½ ounces of butter fat in 1,000 pounds of skim milk. No other separator can approach this record, but few can reach it even at their rated capacity.

THE PARTS OF THE BOWL.

THE BOWL.

MILK AT A TEMPERATURE OF 85 DEGREES IS COMPARATIVELY EASY TO SKIM, AT 70 DEGREES IT IS MUCH HARDER, AT 60 DEGREES BUT FEW MACHINES WILL SKIM SUCCESSFULLY, AT 50 DEGREES IT IS FRIGHTFULLY HARD and but one other separator will approach the Economy in closeness of skimming; and it will leave from two to three times as much butter fat in the skim milk. If you want to skim but once a day in winter when the cows are giving but little milk, you can do it with the Improved Economy. With other machines you must heat the milk up before skimming, which necessitates building a fire, a lot of heavy lifting and considerable time wasted.

AN EASY RUNNING SEPARATOR MUST HAVE A SMALL BOWL; A LARGE HEAVY BOWL IS HARD TO GET IN MOTION AND IS RETARDED BY FRICTION OF THE AIR AND THE FRICTION UPON ITS BEARINGS. The bowl of the Improved Economy is but 3 5-16 inches in diameter, making it a remarkably easy running machine. A boy or girl can run it with little effort. After having operated one of the old fashioned heavy bowl machines, which are sold by so many of the separator manufacturers, it seems to almost run itself, the effort required to run it is so little in comparison.

EASE OF CLEANING IS MOST IMPORTANT. SOME WIDELY SOLD SEPARATORS HAVE A GREAT MANY SMALL PARTS INSIDE OF THE BOWL and actually require more time to clean after skimming than they do to skim. The Economy bowl is most simple, only five parts to the bowl, viz.: the bowl proper or shell, two cores, feed rod and cover, just as shown in the illustration. By running two or three quarts of hot water through the machine after skimming and following the simple directions which we furnish with each machine, it flushes out perfectly and can be cleaned in 3 or 4 minutes easily.

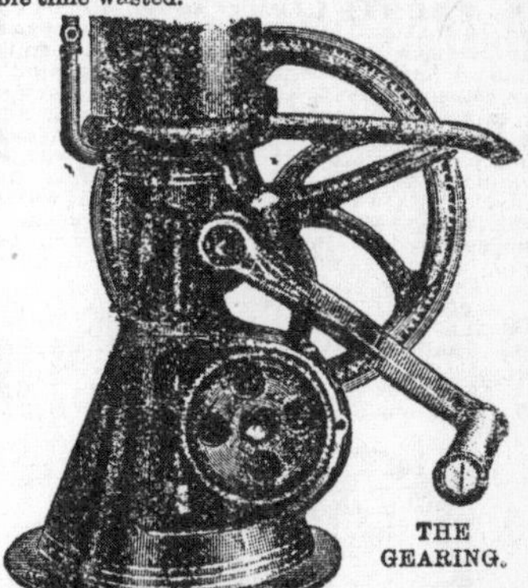
THE GEARING.

THE IMPROVED ECONOMY CREAM SEPARATOR IS BUILT TO LAST

AND IS A MACHINE WHICH ANY MAN, WOMAN, BOY OR GIRL CAN UNDERSTAND AND RUN.

IT REQUIRES NO EXPERT to nurse it and tinker with it as some others do. Simply keep it oiled and cleaned properly and give it the same care you would any other piece of farm machinery, and it is always ready for business, will harvest your crop twice every day in the year and pay for itself quicker than any piece of machinery you ever saw.

THE IMPROVED ECONOMY SEPARATOR is the simplest of any; there is nothing complicated or hard to understand about it. By removing three small screws and taking off the plate at the base of the frame, the entire gearing is exposed and the relation of the different moving parts to each other can be plainly seen. They consist only of the large gear wheel, which is revolved by the crank and meshes with a small steel gear wheel that is mounted on a shaft, on the other end of which is the bronze gear that in turn operates the worm spindle that revolves the bowl. It is all so simple that it can be understood at a glance. The bowl is equally simple, consisting of only the shell or bowl proper, two inside cores, cover and feed rod. Five parts in all, and cleaning the bowl is the work of a few minutes only, in fact it is almost self cleaning. The frame is strong and substantial and as can be seen from the illustration is well proportioned and of the latest design. It is handsomely finished in dark blue enamel, decorated with gold stripings. The supply tanks are of large capacity and are extra heavy, being made of DXXXX Cookley K charcoal tin plate with concaved bottoms and will drain clean to the last drop. The supply tank faucet is solid brass, heavy, nickel plated, with removable key. The cream pan and spout are of heavy steel, carefully tinned and soldered so that there are no rough edges or crevices where milk can collect and sour. The oil cup is nickel plated brass and is of the latest automatic sight feed design, and once regulated, require no attention except to start and stop the flow of oil. The bowl spindle is made in two parts, the lower or worm spindle being permanently seated in an anti-friction metal bushing and revolving on a steel ball, and is not disturbed when the bowl is removed from the machine. It is not affected by any slight vibration of the bowl, will always run true and smooth and never cut the worm wheel, as the one-piece bowl spindles frequently do. The bowl and spindle are solid steel forgings of enormous tensile strength, the feed rod and bowl head are turned from solid steel, and the cores are also of steel. All are heavily retinned to prevent corrosion or rust. The gear wheels are cut by expensive automatic machinery and are mathematically correct, reducing the wear to a minimum. All moving parts run on anti-friction bronze bushings, provided with apertures for oiling. The bowl spindle runs in bushings of a special anti-friction metal alloy used only in the finest high speed machinery and are constantly supplied with oil by our automatic oil cups. Every part, seen or unseen, is made as carefully as skilled mechanics of long experience, assisted by the finest automatic machinery, can make it. The measurements are taken in thousandths of an inch and the various parts are fitted as carefully as in a watch. The Improved Economy Separator is built on honor and will last a lifetime and save its cost several times over every year it is in use.

IF YOU KEEP COWS, NO MATTER HOW MANY, you are losing money every day you are without the Improved Economy Separator. The Improved Economy will save you money because it takes practically all the butter fat out of the milk, it skims to a small fraction of one per cent, to a trace so small that it frequently cannot be measured in a test tube. No other separator can skim as close. The best gravity raising systems lose 10 to 25 per cent of the butter fat that never raises to the top. If raised in crocks and pans 30, 40 and often 50 per cent of the butter fat is wasted. With the Improved Economy you can easily make as much butter from the milk of three or four cows as from the milk of five cows by the old way. The separator cream will churn in one-half the time and the butter will bring from 2 to 10 cents per pound more on the market. The tiresome hand skimming, the everlasting handling and cleaning of crocks and pans and pumping of water is done away with. Half an hour after the milking is done all the cream is separated from the milk and cared for, the separator has been washed and the warm sweet skim milk fed to the calves, pigs or chickens. The value of the fresh warm skim milk as a food for young animals cannot be overestimated. It contains all the nourishment of the whole milk and the addition of a small quantity of cotton seed or flax seed meal at a trifling cost makes a perfect food. Calves and pigs raised on this diet will bring twice the price on the market of the slop fed animal. If you are hauling your whole milk to the creamery, or having it hauled, the cost of hauling in time and labor will pay for an Improved Economy in less than a year. Then there is the wait for the skim milk at the creamery, which is usually the longest in the busy season. You bring it home icy cold in winter and it has to be heated before it can be used. In summer it is usually thick, sour and disgusting, causing sickness and death among the animals to which it is fed.

ABOUT REPAIRS. There is almost no call for repairs for the Improved Economy Separator, as it is built to run for years without repairs. But, if through accident any part should be broken, we can always furnish repairs promptly and at about one-half what is usually charged by other makers.

BUYING SEPARATORS ON TIME OR EASY PAYMENTS. Agents will offer to sell you almost any of the high priced separators on time or easy payments, but you must pay them an outrageous price for the accommodation. For example, should you borrow the money to purchase our No. 23C9175, 500 pounds per hour capacity Improved Economy Separator, for one year at 10 per cent (it will pay for itself twice over in that time) the interest on the borrowed money would be $5.35, making the total cost of your separator $58.85, including interest. Now the agent will ask you at least $100.00 (in some cases $125.00) for a separator of the same capacity that does not cost one cent more to build than the Improved Economy, and which we will guarantee will not do as good work, so that when you pay $100.00 for any other make of this capacity, you are paying about 80 per cent interest on the real value of the separator for the privilege of paying for it on time, when it should not cost you more than 10 per cent at the very outside.

AFTER A FAIR TRIAL in which the Improved Economy has outclassed any of the high priced, big profit separators in closeness of skimming, easy running, easy cleaning, and in every other way, the agent may tell you, as a last resort, "It will not last." To this we may say that the Improved Economy is, piece for piece and part for part, the strongest and most durable separator manufactured. You are fully protected by our 20-year written, binding guarantee which goes with every Improved Economy Separator. Remember, no other make of separator is guaranteed at all.

THIS IS OUR GUARANTEE. We guarantee the Genuine Improved Economy Cream Separator to positively skim closer at a wider range of temperature, to be easier to run and easier to clean, to be more durable, to be better in construction finish and in every other way than any hand separator manufactured, regardless of name, make or price. We will gladly accept your order for an Improved Economy Separator with the understanding and agreement on our part that if after thirty days' trial you do not find by comparison that it is better than any separator made you can return it at our expense and we will immediately refund your money and any transportation charges you have paid.

PRICE LIST

OF THE GENUINE IMPROVED ECONOMY CREAM SEPARATORS.

PLEASE NOTE.—It is always advisable to buy a separator with a capacity in excess of present requirements. You will not only save time in separating and provide for fluctuations in the milk supply, but are in a position to increase the size of your herd and hence your profits in the future. Our 450 to 500-pound capacity separator is practically no harder to run or to care for than our 250 to 300-pound capacity machine, but will separate any quantity of milk in about one-half the time of the smaller machine.

No. 23C9173 The Improved Economy Cream Separator. Capacity, 250 to 300 pounds per hour. As a quart of milk weighs a little over two pounds, this size has a capacity of 120 to 140 quarts per hour. A perfect little machine and a wonder in its way; runs as smoothly and as evenly as a watch and does its work quickly and thoroughly. Easy to operate and manage and no trouble to clean and keep in order. This machine is suitable for a dairy of three to seven cows. It will easily save its cost the first year, and if properly oiled and taken care of will last a lifetime. Shipping weight, 135 pounds. Price.................. **$38.75**

No. 23C9174 Improved Economy Cream Separator. Capacity, 350 to 400 pounds, or about 170 to 190 quarts of milk per hour. Constructed exactly the same as our No. 23C9173 separator, but is larger and heavier, has a greater capacity and speed, and hence will do a given amount of work much quicker. It is always advisable to buy a machine with a capacity in excess of present requirements. You not only save time in separating and provide for fluctuations in the milk supply, but are in a position to increase the size of your herd, and hence your profits, in the future. This size is practically no harder to run or to care for than our No. 23C9173, 250 to 300-pound size, and will handle the product of a dozen or more cows nicely. Weight, securely boxed for shipment, 180 pounds. Price.................. **$46.25**

No. 23C9175 Improved Economy Cream Separator. Capacity, 450 to 500 pounds, or 220 to 240 quarts of milk per hour. This is our largest hand power separator and is guaranteed to be the lightest running machine of its capacity made, and requires but little more power to operate than our smaller sizes. It is exactly suited for large home dairies, whether butter making or cream selling is the object in view. A separator that is always ready for use and will skim at any temperature. Will skim a heavier cream than any other make. Will do this every day, under all sorts of conditions, and with proper care will last a lifetime. We especially recommend this size on account of its large capacity, almost double that of our No. 23C9173, 250 to 300-pound size, and yet requiring no more care, and is almost as easy to run. Weight, boxed for shipment, 200 pounds. Price.................. **$53.50**

WITH EACH MACHINE we send our great 20-year written, binding guarantee. Our 30-day free trial offer, as explained in full on the previous page, absolutely protects you and makes you the sole judge of the machine, and if after giving it a thorough trial for 30 days, you are not satisfied with it, you are at liberty to return it at our expense and we will refund all your money and all transportation charges you have paid.

OUR FREE SPECIAL CREAM SEPARATOR CATALOGUE.

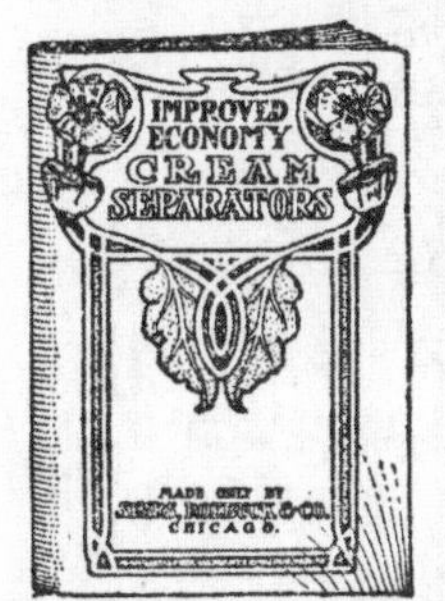

If you can use a cream separator; if you keep only a few cows and would like to save $10.00 to $15.00 a year on every cow you have, we ask that you send us your order for one of our guaranteed Improved Economy Cream Separators, direct from this page, always with the understanding and agreement that if it is not perfectly satisfactory after thirty days' trial, you can return it to us and we will return all your money, including all transportation charges paid by you. You are thoroughly protected by our twenty years' binding guarantee, our liberal thirty-day trial proposition, and you need not hesitate to send us your order direct from this catalogue, without waiting to get any further information. At the same time, if there is any point you are at all doubtful about, any question you wish answered, any information in regard to cream separators that you desire, whether it is about the Improved Economy or any other cream separator, do not fail to first write and get our new Free Special Cream Separator Catalogue. Our new Special Free Cream Separator Catalogue is the most complete, most comprehensive, and finest catalogue of separators ever published. It covers every detail of information regarding the manufacture and sale of separators; tells just how the Improved Economy Separator is built; shows illustrations of all the different parts that enter into the construction of the Improved Economy Separator; explains the good points of all other cream separators and why the improvements of the Improved Economy excel all others. It gives the complete history of cream separators from their first invention down to the present day, and especially the Improved Economy Separator. Therefore, if you do not send us your order for a cream separator direct from this catalogue and you are interested in this subject, do not under any circumstances buy a separator from anyone or place your order elsewhere before you first write and get our Free Cream Separator Catalogue and become thoroughly posted on the subject. It will give you a world of valuable separator information, and whether you buy from us or not will give you such valuable information that you will be enabled to buy to the best advantage. It states the facts about the different makes of separators and the relative efficiency of each as proven by expert tests. It will prove to you that to pay more than our price for any separator of the same capacity, no matter what name plate it bears, is simply throwing your money away. This Free Separator Catalogue contains many letters from well known dairy experts who have given it a series of careful tests and they tell what they think of it. It also contains valuable instructions on the care and operation of cream separators, and instructions for butter making that will be worth many dollars to you. This Cream Separator Catalogue is Free. It enables us to go into the subject in a much more exhaustive manner than the space in this catalogue permits, and while, as stated before, we would like your order sent immediately from this catalogue, and you are taking no chances whatever in doing so, and you have every privilege and inducement that we are able to offer, nevertheless if you are not thoroughly convinced, please write and get our Free Cream Separator Catalogue. Simply send us a letter or a postal card saying "Send me your Free Cream Separator Catalogue," and the book with all the information, all the instructions, all the tests, all the letters from experts, in fact, everything regarding the subject, will be sent to you immediately by return mail, postpaid.

No. 23C9191 Similar to No. 23C9190 except that outside water tank is oblong and is provided with two separate oval inner milk cans so that the morning and evening's milk can be kept separate and new milk need never be mixed with the old, which is a great advantage. Inner cans are made from heavy charcoal tin plate and each provided with a combined strainer and cover and painted on outside with anti-rust paint. Outside water tank is heavy galvanized iron, double seamed and soldered at joints. Inner cans can be easily detached and taken out for cleaning.

No.	Capacity of each inner can	Outside measure of tank	Shipping weight	Price
10..	5 gallons	25x16½x20 in.	30 pounds	$5.95
14..	7 gallons	27x18 x22 in.	35 pounds	6.75
18..	9 gallons	29x20 x24 in.	40 pounds	7.40
23..	11 gallons	31x22 x26 in.	45 pounds	8.25

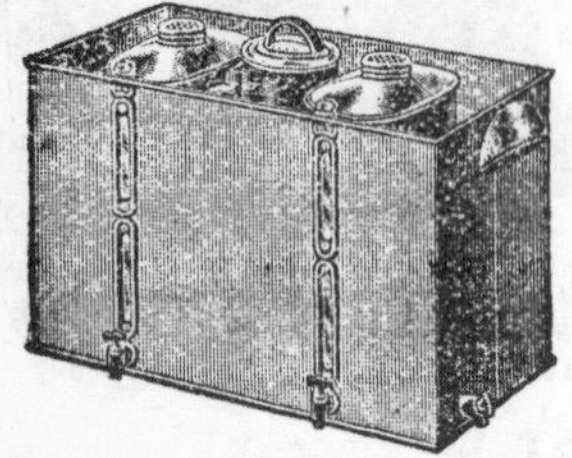

No. 23C9193 Our Best Economical Creamer has two oval inside cans for milk and a smaller can in which to keep the cream from the different skimmings in good condition until ready to ripen for churning. Always stir the cream when you add more to it. Outside tank is made of heavy galvanized iron, strongly braced. Inner cans are best charcoal tin and are removable for cleaning. Milk cans and tank are provided with glass gauges to watch the rising of the cream. Made in the same careful manner as our other Economical creamers, but larger and more convenient.

No.	Capacity of each Inner Milk Can, Gallons.	Capacity of Cream Can, Gallons.	Outside Measure of Tank, Inches.	Shipping Weight, Pounds.	Price.
22	5	3	31x16½x20	35	$7.45
26	7	4	35x18x 22	40	8.25
30	9	4	35x20x 24	45	8.95
34	11	4	35x20x 26	50	9.75

The Peerless Home Creamery.

No. 23C9192 The Peerless Home Creamery is a cabinet made in refrigerator style, with galvanized iron lining and having double walls with felt lining and a dead air space between, which greatly assists in maintaining a low temperature within. The milk cooling cans are oblong, 14 inches long, 5 inches wide and 14 inches deep, capacity 18 quarts, and are immersed in cold water with or without ice. By using ice and water and holding temperature at 45 degrees all cream can be raised in 12 hours, or by using running water at a temperature of 55 degrees cream can be obtained in 24 hours. Each can is provided with glass gauge for observing cream and faucet for drawing off both milk and cream. Tank is strongly made and well painted and with fair usage will last a lifetime.

No.	No. of cans	No. of cows	H'gt, in.	L'th, in.	W'th, in.	W't, lbs.	Price
2	2	4 to 6	35	25	23	100	$19.35
3	3	7 to 9	35	34	23	125	23.60
4	4	10 to 12	35	41	23	160	28.65
5	6	13 to 18	35	61	23	220	37.30
6	8	19 to 24	35	77	23	230	43.90
7	10	25 to 30	35	80	23	320	50.15
8	12	31 to 36	35	96	23	440	57.70

Rectangular Churns.

No. 23C9216 The Rectangular Churn works the easiest and quickest of any churn on the market. At the Dairy Fair, held in Chicago, it received the highest award, a cash premium and diploma, in competition with the world. Wisconsin butter won five medals at the Centennial Exhibition at Philadelphia, and four of these were awarded to butter made in the Rectangular Churn.

Churn. Nos.	Holds Gals.	Churns Gals.	Weight	Price
0	7	1 to 3	30 pounds	$3.38
1	10	2 to 4	33 pounds	3.63
2	12	2 to 6	35 pounds	3.80
3	20	3 to 9	55 pounds	4.37
3½	26	4 to 12	65 pounds	5.35
4	40	6 to 18	130 pounds	6.95
5	60	8 to 30	200 pounds	10.35

Union Churns.

You can make, gather, work and salt your butter without removing from the Union Churn or without touching the butter with your hands. It churns with ease by the extra power and motion gained by gear wheels.

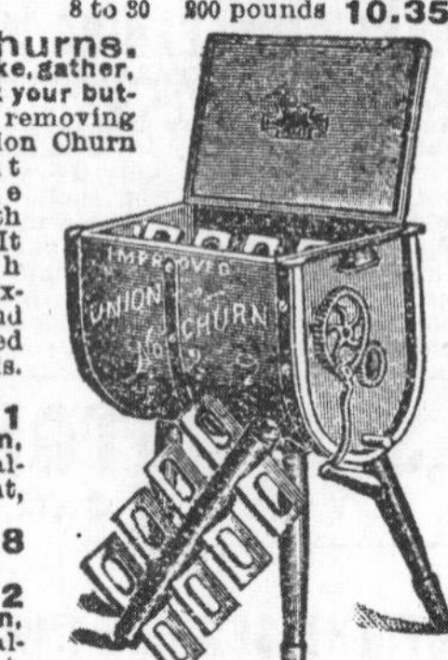

No. 23C9221 Union Churn, holding 5 gallons. Weight, 38 pounds. Price...**$3.18**

No. 23C9222 Union Churn, holding 7 gallons. Weight, 40 pounds. Price...........**$3.67**

No. 23C9223 Union Churn, holding 10 gallons. Weight, 45 pounds. Price **$4.22**

No. 23C9225 Union Churn, holding 15 gallons. Weight, 60 pounds. Price....**$6.20**

NOTE—To attain best results, churns should not be filled more than half full.

Improved Cedar Cylinder Churns.

No. 23C9226 White Cedar Cylinder Churn. We use a double dasher, and the crank is locked to the churn with a clamp and thumbscrew, which prevents leakage. Look cannot break.

The top is large and dasher easily removed. The hoops are galvanized iron and will not rust. The best churn in use. Weights vary from 15 to 25 lbs.

Nos.	1	2	3	4
Will hold, gal.	3	4	7	10
Will churn, gal.	2	3	4	5
Price	$1.63	1.93	2.30	2.58

No. 23C9234 White Cedar Dash Churn. The old way is considered by many the best, and we can safely recommend our Cedar churns as the best dash churn made. Cedar is peculiarly adapted for milk and butter purposes.

Gallons	4	5	6
Sizes, inches	18	20	22
Weight, lbs.	6¾	9½	10¾
Price	70c	80c	98c

Reid Butter Workers.

No. 23C9246 Size, 14x23 inches, to work 10 pounds of butter. Shipping weight, 20 pounds. Price...............**$3.58**

No. 23C9247 Size, 17x27 inches, to work 20 pounds of butter. Shipping weight, 25 pounds. Price...............**$4.40**

No. 23C9248 Size, 20x36 inches, to work 30 pounds of butter. Price...............**$4.75**

No. 23C9249 Size, 23x36 inches, to work 50 pounds of butter. Price...............**$5.70**

When it is to our customers' advantage to do so we ship from our factory in Pennsylvania.

The Star Barrel Churns.

This style of churn is old, tried and reliable, easy to operate and keep clean; it is absolutely impossible for this churn to leak, as the wear can be taken up as simply as one can turn a thumbnut. The fasteners are attached to the outside of the churn, and it will be seen from the illustration that the bail and cover fastening is a compound leverage which increases the pressure ten times more than any other make of churn.

No. 23C9200 Six-gallon Barrel Churn, for 1 to 3 gallons of cream. Weight, 32 pounds. Price...............**$2.39**

No. 23C9201 Ten-gallon Barrel Churn, for 1 to 5 gal. of cream. Weight, 45 pounds. Price...............**$2.57**

No. 23C9202 Fifteen-gallon Barrel Churn, for 1 to 7 gallons of cream. Weight, 50 pounds. Price...............**$2.70**

No. 23C9203 Twenty-gallon Barrel Churn, for 2 to 9 gallons of cream. Weight, 67 pounds. Price...............**$2.97**

No. 23C9204 Twenty-five-gallon Barrel Churn, for 2 to 12 gallons of cream. Weight, 77 pounds. Price...............**$3.62**

No. 23C9205 Thirty-five-gallon Barrel Churn, for 3 to 16 gallons of cream. Weight, 95 pounds. Price...............**$4.75**

Lever Butter Workers.

No. 23C9250 Its simplicity, saving of time, ease of operation and very low price commends it to every dairy. No. 0 size, 20 inches wide; weight, 22½ pounds; works 15 pounds. Price..**$3.33**

No. 23C9251 No. 1 size, 30 inches wide; weight, 39½ lbs.; works 25 lbs. Price...**$4.33**

No. 23C9252 No. 2 size, 40 inches wide; weight, 50 lbs.; works 35 lbs. Price....**$4.95**

Family Cheese Making Apparatus.

No. 23C9256. This is a very simple apparatus, adapted to the wants of all farmers or dairy men who keep from 2 to 10 cows, or more. It will make from 2 to 10 pounds of cheese each operation, according to the quantity of milk. It makes a perfect cheese each time, whether 2 pounds or 10 pounds. The milk is heated by a coal oil lamp, which is easily kept under control. The heating vat is so constructed that the lamp gives all the heat that is necessary. The management of the heat is the secret of success in making good cheese. The entire apparatus is so light in weight that a lady can move it from one place to another with ease. A lady can make cheese in the kitchen or pantry, and carry on her household work at the same time. With each machine we send simple and full instructions how to make cheese successfully. Every apparatus is complete with heating vat and iron stand, upright automatic spring cheese press; galvanized iron outer press hoop, inner cylinder for press; thermometer; oil lamp heater; curd stirrer, curd knife, test iron, bandages, rennet tablets, cheese color; in fact, everything necessary to make cheese.

Number	Capacity, gallons	Weight, pounds	Price
1	10	100	$11.70
2	20	155	14.20
3	30	160	16.25

The National Babcock Milk Tester.

The latest and best. Runs as smoothly and quietly as a high grade cream separator and gives perfect results. Heretofore moderate priced testers have been made with cast iron gearing and working parts, making them noisy, easily broken and hard to run. The National Babcock Tester has cut bronze spiral gear wheel and steel spindle with worm thread enclosed in heavy case, is fitted with swinging pockets and malleable heads; it turns easily without vibration or jar and can be attached to any table or bench; it will tell you the exact quality of each cow's milk. Remember the cost of feeding a good cow is no greater than a poor one. To make dairying pay and to know the profit derived from each individual cow a milk tester is a necessity. Price includes bottle of acid, test bottle brush, acid measure, pipette, test bottles and full directions for making test. Weight, boxed, about 11 pounds.

No. 23C9270 2-Bottle complete, for testing milk. Price...............**$3.90**

No. 23C9271 4-Bottle complete, for testing milk. Price...............**$4.90**

No. 23C9272 2-Bottle complete, for testing milk and cream. Price...............**$4.40**

No. 23C9273 4-Bottle complete, for testing milk and cream. Price...............**$5.40**

Fancy Square and Round Butter Moulds

Made from selected maple wood, and every one guaranteed perfect.

No. 23C9302 Size of mould, 1 lb. Fancy carving, round. Weight of mould, 1 lb. Price...............**12c**

No. 23C9303 Size of mould, 1 lb. Jersey cow, round. Weight of mould, 1 lb. **21c**

No. 23C9306 Size of mould, 1 lb. Fancy carving, square. Weight of mould, 1¼ lbs. Price...............**18c**

No. 23C9312 One-Pound Brick Butter Mould. Hard maple with dovetailed corners. Hand carved in fancy designs. Weight, 1 pound. Price...............**23c**

Butter Mould, Philadelphia Pattern.

No. 23C9331 One-pound size. Very firm bricks made quickly by pressing down with a rocking motion and removed from mould by reversing and pushing out with plunger. Weight, 1¾ pounds. Price...............**97c**

Butter Ladles and Spades.

No. 23C9362 The Acme Ladle. Solid hard maple. Weight, 4 ounces. Price...............**4c**

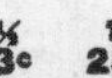

No. 23C9363 Hard Maple Butter Spade. Weight, 4 ounces. Price...............**4c**

Chr. Hansen's Rennet Extract.

No. 23C8700 1-gallon bottles, per bottle...............**$1.48**

Chr. Hansen's Rennet Tablets.

No. 23C8702 Can of 100 No. 1 tablets...............**$4.25**

No. 23C8705 Can of 200 No. 2 tablets...............**2.15**

No. 23C8707 Sample boxes, 50 No. 2 tablets...............**.80**

No. 23C8709 Sample boxes, 24 No. 2 tablets...............**.44**

No. 23C8711 Bavarian Rennets, dry. Price, per dozen, **$1.20**; each..... **.12**

Cheese Color.

No. 23C8713 Chr. Hansen's Cheese Color. 1-gallon bottles...............**$1.48**
4-ounce bottles, each...............**.18**

No. 23C8715 Chr. Hansen's Cheese Color Tablets. Per vial of 12 tablets.....**23c**

Butter Color.

No. 23C8717 Chr. Hansen's Danish Butter Color. 4-ounce bottle...............**$0.18**
9-ounce bottle...............**.37**
20-ounce bottle...............**.70**
Gallon cans...............**2.35**

Butter Paper.

No. 23C8730 White Waxed Butter Paper, grease proof.
12x18 inches. Per package, 480 sheets, **33c**
8x11 inches. Per package, 480 sheets, **12c**

Parchment Dairy Paper.

Cut in the sizes as quoted and put up in packages of 1,000 sheets.

No. 23C8732

Size	Price 1,000 sheets	Size	Price 1,000 sheets
6x 6........	29c	8x11......	$0.81
8x 8........	58c	9x12......	.88
9x 9........	78c	10x10......	.90
		12x12......	1.18

BUTCHERS' TOOLS AND SUPPLIES.

Genuine Hand Forged (GENUINE A WARRANTED) Butcher Knives.

For more than fifty years the Genuine Diamond A brand of butcher knives has been made especially for the meat cutting industries and are universally and favorably known. They are just the right shape and weight to satisfy the expert butcher who takes pride in doing good work, and for toughness of steel and edge holding qualities are unequaled. Every knife is absolutely hand forged from the bar, hardened and tempered by a secret process used only at this factory, ground and finished by hand and honed to an edge by skilled workmen. They are finished in the best possible manner and subjected to a rigid inspection before leaving the factory. Every knife branded thus (Genuine Diamond A Warranted), is fully guaranteed by the factory and ourselves to be the best that can be produced at any price, and if you are not perfectly satisfied with it after giving it a thorough trial, return at our expense and we will refund your money or exchange, as you wish.

No. 23C9400 Genuine Diamond A Butcher Knives, beechwood handles. Hand forged blades. Fully warranted.

Length of blade, inches	6	6½	7	8	9	10	12	14
Price	18c	23c	25c	30c	36c	59c	76c	$1.10

No. 23C9402 Genuine Diamond A Skinning Knives, beechwood handles. Every knife of this brand fully guaranteed.

Length of blade, in.	5½	6	6½	7
Price	21c	24c	25c	30c

No. 23C9401 Genuine Diamond A Sticking Knives, best beechwood handles. Guaranteed hand forged from best steel.

Length of blade, inches	6	6½	7
Price	19c	23c	25c

Genuine Diamond A Butcher Knives.—Continued.

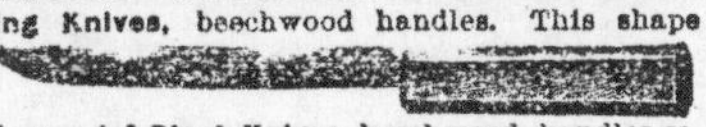

No. 23C9403 Genuine Diamond A Boning Knives, beechwood handles. This shape is a favorite with the butchers everywhere.
Length of blade, inches........... 6 6½
Price........................ 24c 26c

No. 23C9404 Genuine Diamond A Steak Knives, beechwood handles securely riveted through blade, best hand forged steel blades. Right shape and right temper guaranteed.
Length of blade, inches... 10 12 14
Price... 65c 79c $1.14

Genuine Wilson Butcher Knives.

STAMPED I. WILSON.

Imitations of this knife are frequently sold. If not stamped on blade I. WILSON they are counterfeits.

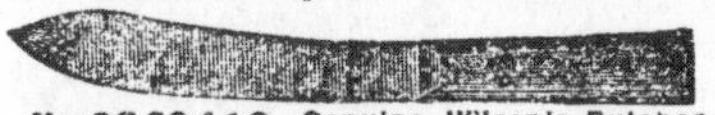

No. 23C9410 Genuine Wilson's Butcher Knives, beechwood handles.
Length of blade, inches: 5 5½ 6 7 8 10
Price........17c 20c 23c 33c 43c 64c

No. 23C9411 Genuine Wilson's Sticking Knives, beechwood handles.
Length of blade, inches. 5½ 6 6½
Price......................... 22c 24c 29c

No. 23C9412 Genuine Wilson's Skinning Knives, beechwood handle. 
Length of blade, inches .. 6 6½ 7
Price.................... 26c 28c 34c

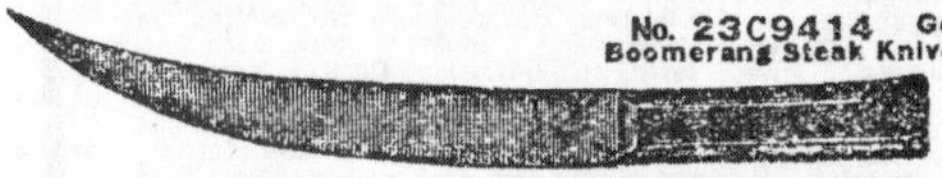

No. 23C9414 Genuine Wilson's latest pattern Boomerang Steak Knives, beechwood handle.
Length of blade, inches: 10 11 12
Price.. 67c 85c $1.00

Butchers' Steels.

No. 23C9418 The Genuine Wilson's Butchers' Steel, cocoa handle, very best material and finish; the favorite with butchers in all parts of the world.
Length, inches. 10 12 14
Price........ 75c 90c $1.10

No. 23C9419 The Genuine Wilson's Butchers' Steel, stag handle, finest quality, best finish.
Length, inches 10 12 14
Price.........84c 95c $1.15

Butchers' Saws.

No. 23C9424 The Fulton Butcher Saw. Flat polished steel frame. Blue clock spring blade. Fully warranted.
Size, inches........ 20 22 24 26
Weight, pounds.. 1⅝ 1¾ 2 2⅛
Price.............. 70c 75c 80c 86c

No. 23C9425 Star Butcher Saws are furnished with blades that are tempered so that they will cut about six times as long as the old kind, which have to be left soft enough to file. The Star Blades can take a file temper, as they are to be thrown away when dull, for we sell a new blade at the usual cost of sharpening the old style blades. After cutting bone for six weeks, one of these blades will cut through a half-inch rod of iron twenty times.

Price List of Frames with one Blade.
For length of blade,
inches......... 18 20 22 24 26
Weight, lbs.... 2½ 2⅝ 2¾ 3 3¼
Price..........90c 97c $1.08 $1.13 $1.18

Butcher Saw Blades.

No. 23C9427 Star Butcher Saw Blades. While wearing out one of these blades it would be necessary to file an old style blade five or six times, hence we claim that though the Star blades must be thrown away when worn out, they are cheaper in the end. Will fit any frame. Weight, 1 to 3 ounces.
Length, ins. 18 20 22 24 26
Price, each. $0.09 $0.09 $0.10 $0.10 $0.11
Per dozen. 1.00 1.00 1.12 1.12 1.22

No. 23C9428 The Fulton Butcher Saw Blades, 1⅛ inches wide. Made from finest spring tempered steel and all ready for use. Every blade warranted. Weight, 1 to 3 ounces.
Length, inches 20 22 24 26
Price, each........ 19c 21c 23c 25c

Beef Splitting Saw.

No. 23C9431 Beef Splitting Saw. Extra heavy steel frame, hardwood handles on both ends. Weight, 5 to 6 pounds. 32-inch blade, 2 inches wide. Price.............................$2.80

No. 23C9432 Extra Blades for Beef Splitting Saws, 32x2 inches. Price.............45c

Kitchen Saws.

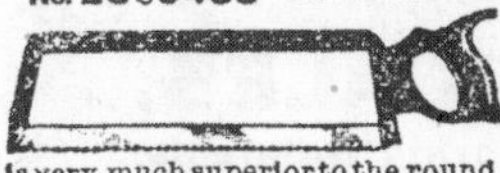

No. 23C9435 Kitchen Saws. Flat polished steel frame. Good steel blade. Beech handle with two screws. This frame is very much superior to the round or oval frame commonly sold. Size, inches.. 12 14 16
Weight, ounces................ 10 11 12
Price.............................. 18c 19c 20c

No. 23C9436 Star Kitchen Saw. Polished steel frame with beech handle. They have what most other kitchen saws do not have—an arrangement for straining the saw, which adds much to their value. Length of blade, 14 inches. Weight, 14 ounces.
Price, frame with one blade...................29c

No. 23C9437 Extra Blades for Star Kitchen Saws. Price...............................9c

Butchers' Cleavers.

Our Butchers' Market Cleavers are of the most desirable pattern, forged from a special high grade steel and carefully tempered. Blades are extra strong and heavy and have best varnished hickory handles that never get loose. Every one fully warranted.

No. 23C9440 7-inch cut. Weight, 1½ lbs. Price.............................57c
No. 23C9441 8-inch cut. Weight, 1¾ lbs. Price.............................67c
No. 23C9442 9-inch cut. Weight, 3¼ lbs. Price.............................74c
No. 23C9443 10-inch cut. Weight, 4 lbs. Price.............................$1.10
No. 23C9444 12-inch cut. Weight, 5 lbs. Price.............................$1.24

The Family Cleaver.

No. 23C9456 Family Cleaver, cast steel blade forged and hardened. Is a very handy household article and should be in everyone's kitchen. Weight, 14 ounces. Price.....................23c

Hog Hook.

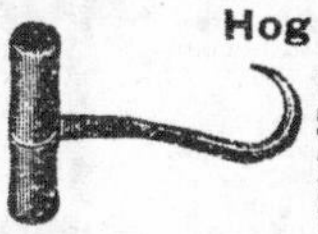

No. 23C9478 Hog Hooks, forged from best steel, diameter of steel, 7-16-inch. Length of hook, 7¾ inches; length of handle, 9 inches. Weight, ¾ pounds. Price.....20c

Sargent's Gem Food Choppers

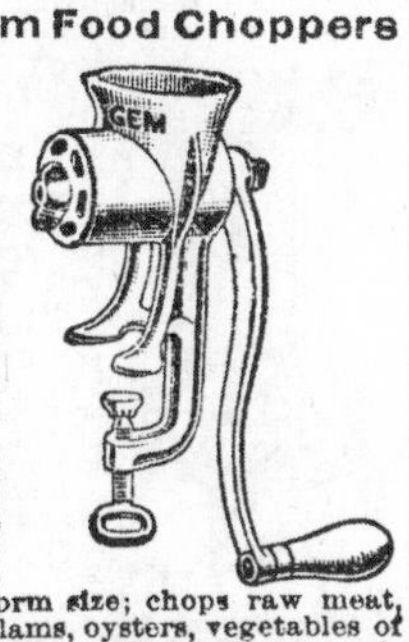

Sargent's Gem Food Chopper is easy to take apart; easy to put together; easy to adjust; easy to use; can be cleaned in a jiffy and with less trouble than a chopping bowl. With each machine there are four steel cutters, one each for fine, medium and coarse chopping, and one for pulverizing. They will not break; they are self sharpening: each cutter chops in pieces of its uniform size; chops raw meat, cooked meat, fish, clams, oysters, vegetables of all kinds, fruit, bread, crackers, cheese, nuts and many other articles used in making substantial dishes and dainty desserts. A copy of The Gem Cook Book free with each one. The Sargent Gem Food Chopper is carefully made, nicely tinned, self cleaning and self sharpening. No. 23C9493, size 20, is generally purchased for family use; No. 23C9494, size 22, stands higher from the table and has a larger hopper; No. 23C9495, size 24, is extra large and heavy.

Catalogue No.	Size	Capac. per Minute, lbs.	Diam. of Hopper. Inside, inches	Outside inches	Height from Table to Bottom of Barrel	Weight, pounds	Price
23C9493	20	2	3	3¼	2¼ in.	5¼	$0.78
23C9494	22	2½	3¾	4	2¾ in.	5¾	1.02
23C9495	24	3	4⅝	4⅞	3½ in.	9⅛	1.35

Stuffing Attachments.

No. 23C9497 Stuffing Attachment for Gem Food Choppers. Can be screwed on to size 22 chopper and used to stuff sausage. Weight, 1 pound. Price.............................16c

No. 23C9498 Stuffing Attachment for Gem Food Chopper. Size 24. Weight, 1¼ pounds. Price.............................17c

Enterprise Food Choppers.

No. 23C9502 The Enterprise Food and Meat Chopper. It will chop raw meat, cooked meat, vegetables of all kinds, bread and crackers, and will make peanut butter. It will chop any kind of food any size you wish for any kind of dish. Can be cleaned in a minute, is always ready and never gets out of order. Four knives, one each, fine, medium and coarse, and nut butter cutter furnished with each machine. The bearing is of phosphor bronze, which reduces the friction, makes the machine easier to turn and will last much longer. Will chop two pounds of meat per minute. Weight, 4½ pounds. Price..92c

Classic Food Choppers.

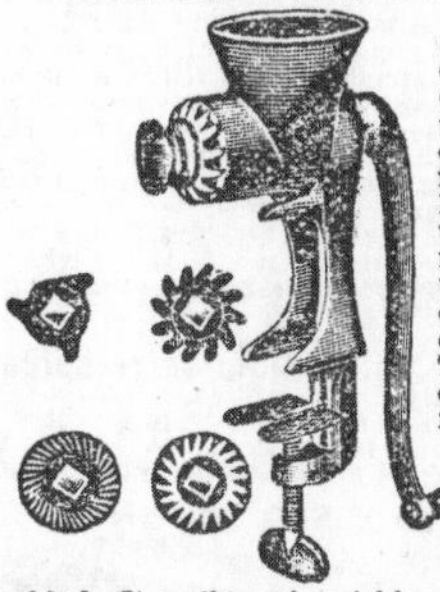

The best that money can buy. Classic Food Choppers can be used in the kitchen every day in the year. In household use they will last for many years and will save their cost several times over every year. This perfect food chopper embodies the best features found in other makes with several valuable improvements added. It easily and quickly chops all kinds of meats, fruits or vegetables, fine or coarse, and does not mash or choke up. In cutting juicy fruits with other choppers there is always some leak at the back end onto the floor; our perfect drip spout catches and saves this juice and prevents spots on the floor or carpet. The face of the chopper is concaved and knives are carefully machined to an exact fit, giving a fine, clean cut. Has improved table clamp, which holds fast easy; can be taken apart in a jiffy and is very easy to clean. All handsomely tinned and an ornament to any kitchen. Each chopper is furnished with four cutters, coarse, medium, fine and nut butter cutters, except No. 23C9505, which has no nut butter cutter.

No. 23C9503 Size 1, chops 2 pounds of meat per minute; size of hopper, 2½x3 inches. Weight, 4½ pounds. Price.....................95c

No. 23C9504 Size 2, chops 2½ pounds of meat per minute; size of hopper, 3x4 inches. Weight, 5 pounds. Price.....................$1.15

No. 23C9505 Size 3, chops 3½ pounds of meat per minute; size of hopper, 4x5 inches. Weight, 9 pounds. Price.....................$1.58

The Enterprise Meat Choppers.

The Enterprise Choppers cut the meat as with a pair of scissors, and do not grind or tear it. It is impossible for any strings, sinews or gristle to pass through without being chopped. The small quantity of uncut meat remaining in the machine can be cut by running through some of the already cut meat a second time. All parts are interchangeable and can be replaced at small cost. The cutting parts being steel, they are vastly superior to the cast iron ones of other makes of choppers.

By means of the stuffing attachment, which we furnish at a small additional cost, they make excellent sausage stuffers.

No. 23C9506 Genuine Enterprise Meat Choppers, small family size, with clamp (No. 5), chops 1½ pounds per minute. Weight, 4½ pounds. Price.......$1.60

Our $2.40 Meat Chopper.

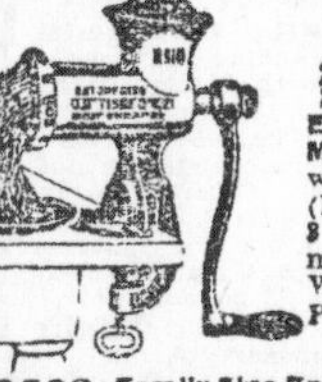

No. 23C9507 Family Size Enterprise Meat Chopper, with clamp (No. 10) chops 3 pounds per minute. Weight, 8 lbs. Price, $2.40

No. 23C9508 Family Size Enterprise Meat Chopper, with legs to screw on bench or table (No. 12), chops 3 pounds per minute. Weight, 9 pounds. Price.............................$2.20

No. 23C9509 Hotel Size Enterprise Meat Chopper, with legs to screw to table or bench (No. 22), chops 4 pounds per minute. Weight, pounds. Price...$3.60

No. 23C9510 Butchers' Size Enterprise Meat Chopper with legs to screw on table or bench (No. 32), chops 5 pounds per minute. Weight, 18 pounds. Price.............................$4.80

No. 23C9512 Butchers' Size Enterprise Meat Chopper, with fly wheel (No. 232), chops 5 lbs. per minute. Weight, complete, 38 pounds. Price. $7.60

Improved Stuffing Attachments for Enterprise Meat Choppers.

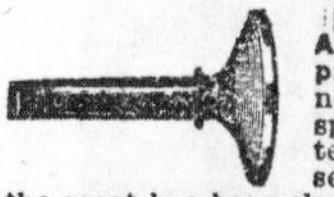

No. 23C9516 Stuffing Attachments for Enterprise Meat Chopper, with new patented corrugated spout, prevents air entering casing thus preserving the sausage. After the meat has been chopped, remove the knife and plate, place the attachment against the cylinder, screw the ring up moderately tight and the machine is ready for work. They are made of spun brass, nickel plated, and are very strong and durable. Made in two sizes of tubs, namely: ⅝-inch and 1⅛-inch. When ordering be sure to give number of chopper for which attachment is wanted. Weights vary from 2 to 5 ounces.

Price, with ⅝-inch tube. To fit chopper—
No. 5 No. 10 No. 12 No. 22 No. 32 No. 232
37c 40c 40c 50c 58c 58c

Price, with 1⅛-inch tube. To fit chopper—
No. 5 No. 10 No. 12 No. 22 No. 32 No. 232
57c 60c 60c 70c 90c 90c

Knives for Enterprise Meat Choppers.

No. 23C9517 Knives for Enterprise Meat Choppers. Weights vary from 1 to 3 oz.

To fit chopper—	Price	To fit chopper—	Price
No. 5	20c	No. 22	40c
No. 10	24c	No. 32	60c
No. 12	24c	No. 232	60c

Plates for Enterprise Meat Choppers.

No. 23C9518 Extra Plates for Enterprise Meat Choppers. When ordering be sure to give number of chopper for which the plate is wanted. The plate having 3-16-inch holes is most commonly used, and is what is furnished with choppers. Weight, 2 to 16 ounces, according to size. With 3-16, ¼, 5-16 or ⅜-inch holes.
Price, to fit chopper—
No. 5 No. 10 No. 12 No. 22 No. 32 No. 232
24c 40c 40c 60c 80c 80c

Enterprise Sausage Stuffer, Fruit and Lard Press.

Unexcelled for butchers' or farmers use for stuffing sausages and pressing lard. For kitchen use there is nothing like it for pressing fruit for making jellies, wine, etc. Full directions for use are sent with each press.

No. 23C9523 2 quart size, japanned rack movement. Weight, 21 pounds. Price.............................$2.90

No. 23C9524 4-quart size, japanned, screw movement. Weight, 30 pounds. Price.....$4.15

No. 23C9525 8-quart size, japanned, screw movement. Weight, 44 pounds. Price.....$5.25

Sausage Stuffers.

Lever Sausage Stuffer. Iron japanned. No. 0 for butcher's use No. 1, for family use.

Weight, 11¾ pounds.
Weight, 8¾ pounds.
No. 23C9530 Size 0. Price........88c
No. 23C9531 Size 1. Price........63c

Family Size Sausage Stuffer.

No. 23C9533 Railroad Sausage Stuffer. The castings are heavy and nicely japanned. Barrel is made of heavy tin plate. Suitable for family and hotel use. Capacity, 3½ pounds. Weight, 9 pounds. Price......79c

Fruit and Lard Presses.

A well made and handsome press for making jellies, wines, syrups, lard, etc. Made with special reference to strength, and guaranteed against breakage under any fair usage. Cylinders are heavy tin and all parts tinned all over. Can be taken apart in a moment for cleaning. All parts are interchangeable and can be replaced at a slight expense in case of breakage.

No. 23C9538 2-quart size. Weight, 9½ pounds. Price......$1.33
No. 23C9539 4-quart size. Weight, 21 pounds. Price......$2.65
No. 23C9540 10-quart size. Weight, 54 pounds. Price......$3.95

Lard Presses.

No. 23C9543 Lard Press. The frame is made of heavy hardwood and nicely finished. Castings are heavy and properly machined; screw is very strong with heavy thread. It has cast iron swivel follower on the lower end, also supplied with substantial wood follower that goes on top of the cracklings to squeeze the lard out. Colander is made of heavy tinned steel, perforated ⅔ of the way up and provided with hinge to open for removing cake. Splasher is high enough to keep the grease inside of the pan. Hand wheel on top is made to admit the use of a lever to assist in screwing down. All parts very heavy and substantial and well put together.

No.	Diameter of cylinder	Weight	Price
1	12 inches	90 pounds	$ 4.50
2	14 inches	150 pounds	7.90
3	17 inches	290 pounds	12.60
4	20 inches	350 pounds	17.00

Fruit, Wine and Jelly Press.

No. 23C9552 Combination Fruit, Wine and Jelly Press. Can be used for many purposes, such as making wines, jellies and fruit butter from fruits, the entire substance being extracted in one operation. Weight, 12½ pounds. Price......$2.65

Wrought Steel Meat Hooks.

No. 23C9562 Wrought Steel Tinned Mutton Hooks, for 2-inch bar, made of 5-16-inch square steel. Weight, per dozen, 2½ pounds. Price, per dozen......37c

No. 23C9563 Wrought Steel Tinned Beam Hooks. Very heavy, for 2-inch bar, made of 7-16-inch square steel. Weight, per dozen, 4½ pounds. Price, per dozen......55c

No. 23C9564 Wrought Steel Tinned Beam Hooks, with large round bend, very heavy, for 3-inch bar; made of ½-inch steel. Weight, per dozen, 10½ pounds. Price, per dozen......67c

Hog Scrapers.

No. 23C9568 Hog Scraper. Will pay for itself the first time used. Wood handle with bolt extending through scraper. Made of No. 18 sheet steel. Weight, 8 ounces. Price......18c

No. 23C9569 Hog Scraper. Made of No. 20 sheet iron. Weight, 7 ounces. Price......8c

Twine.

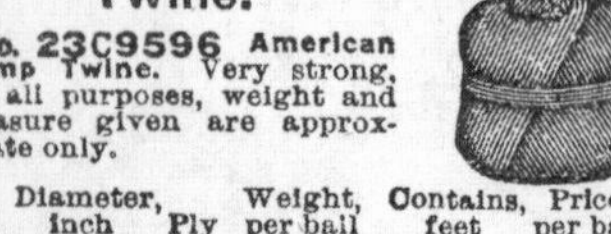

No. 23C9596 American Hemp Twine. Very strong, for all purposes, weight and measure given are approximate only.

No.	Diameter, inch	Ply	Weight, per ball	Contains, feet	Price, per ball
18	1-16	3	½ lb.	575	9c
35	3-32	3	½ lb.	300	8c
4½	⅛	2	½ lb.	150	6c
3	5-32	3	1 lb.	200	11c
3	3-16	3	1½ lbs.	196	16c

No. 23C9598 Cotton Wrapping Twine. Good quality for grocers' or household use. 6 balls to the pound. Price, per ball......$0.05
Per sack containing 5 pounds......1.10

Saltpetre.

No. 23C9606 Saltpetre for butcher' use. Granulated, very pure. Price, per pound..8½c

Ice Saws.

No. 23C9592 Hand Ice Saw, with iron handle. Fully warranted,

Length, inches......	24	26	28	30
Price......	81c	87c	95c	99c

Ice Tongs.

Drop forged of solid steel. This ice tong is far better and stronger than others commonly sold.

No. 23C9636 Ice Tongs, No. 1, opens 13 in., family size. Wgt., 4½ lbs. 39c
No. 23C9637 Ice Tongs, No. 2, opens 17 inches. Weight, 5 lbs. Price, 47c
No. 23C9638 Ice Tongs, No. 3, opens 24 inches, wagon size. Weight, about 6 pounds. Price......57c
No. 23C9639 Ice Tongs, No. 6, opens 14 inches, with bail top, family size. Weight, about 2½ pounds. Price......37c

ICE CREAM FREEZERS AND SUMMER SUPPLIES.

The Alaska Ice Cream Freezers.

No. 23C9627 Alaska Ice Cream Freezers. Miles in advance of any other make. The only freezer with perpetual motion, aerating spoon dasher, with spoon shaped floats open in center, mounted on the arms which carry the wood scrapers; as these rapidly revolve the freezing mixture is removed from the sides of the can and thrown to the center, where it is rapidly beaten and aerated until frozen into the smoothest and most deliciously mellow cream you ever tasted. The Alaska Freezers have clear kiln dried northern pine tubs, which are treated to a special waterproofing preparation, and are guaranteed to outlast any cedar tub; have heavy galvanized steel hoops, which can never come off; can has steel body and heavy malleable bottom and cover, all heavily retinned with pure block tin. Gearing is heavily galvanized. Guaranteed to make better cream and freeze quicker with less ice and salt than any other freezer made or money refunded.

Size, quarts	1	2	3	4	6
Weight, lbs.	10	11	12	17	21
Price......	$1.26	$1.46	$1.72	$2.10	$2.68

Size, quarts......	8	10	12	15
Weight, lbs......	27	31½	35	50
Price......	$3.40	$4.40	$5.76	$6.72

Size quarts with Fly Wheel......	8	10	12	15
Weight, pounds...	41	45	50	68
Price......	$4.84	$5.92	$8.10	$9.24

Ice Cream Brick Moulds.

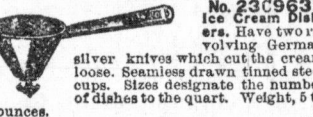

No. 23C9629 Ice Cream Brick Moulds for packing ice cream into a convenient shape for selling or serving. Made of heavy IX tin plate with single or double cover. Illustration shows double cover which is the best to use, making the removal of the cream rapid and in perfect shape.

Capacity, Pints,	Single Cover, each	Single Cover, per dozen	Double Cover, each	Double Cover, per dozen
2	18c	$1.98	26c	$2.90
3	21c	2.29	29c	3.25
4	26c	2.90	34c	3.90
6	31c	3.50	41c	4.65
8	33c	3.70	47c	5.30

Ice Cream Dishers.

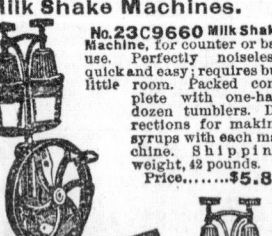

No. 23C9632 Ice Cream Dishers. Have two revolving German silver knives which cut the cream loose. Seamless drawn tinned steel cups. Sizes designate the number of dishes to the quart. Weight, 5 to 7 ounces.

Sizes......	4s	5s	6s	8s	10s
Price......	19c	18c	17c	16c	15c

Milk Shake Machines.

No. 23C9660 Milk Shake Machine, for counter or bar use. Perfectly noiseless, quick and easy; requires but little room. Packed complete with one-half dozen tumblers. Directions for making syrups with each machine. Shipping weight, 42 pounds. Price......$5.88

Our Best Milk Shake Machine for $8.50.

No. 23C9661 The Imperial Milk Shake Machine, handsomely painted, with nickel plated trimmings. Glass caps for tumblers. It can be securely fastened to the floor, and does not shake counter. One-half dozen tumblers packed with each shaker, and directions for making syrups included. Weight, packed for shipment, 73 pounds. Price......$8.50

Many purchasers of our Milk Shake Machines write us that they have paid for the machine in one day at their county fair.

Extra Parts for Milk Shake Machines.

These parts will fit either of our machines.

No. 23C9662 Glass tops. Price......14c
No. 23C9663 Glass tumblers. Price, per dozen......95c
No. 23C9664 Rubbers that go between glass top and tumbler. Price......12c
No. 23C9665 Extra friction rubbers for No. 23C9660 fly wheel. Price......23c

Ice Shave.

No. 23C9672 Imperial Ice Shave, nickel legs, galvanized top. Finely finished hardwood base. Occupies but little space; can be conveniently used on soda counters. Weight, 8½ pounds. Price......$1.53

Ice Cutting Machines.

A small, compact, simple, strong and cheap machine, which cuts the ice into small diamond shaped pieces with the utmost ease and rapidity. Can be attached by screws to any table, counter or shelf, and occupies a space only 8 inches square and about 12 inches high. For iced tea or coffee or ice cream it has no equal.

No. 23C9674 For bar tops and soda counters. Occupies a space 6 inches square, 12½ inches high. Weight, 7½ pounds. Price......$2.80

No. 23C9675 For family and universal use. Occupies a space 7 inches square, 14 inches high. Weight, 14 pounds. Price......$4.00

Lemon Squeezers.

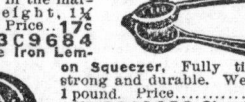

No. 23C9682 Lemon Squeezer. Japanned, with heavy cast aluminum bowl to hold juice when squeezing. Weight, 1½ pounds. Price......25c

No. 23C9683 Lemon Squeezer. Bowls are made of white porcelain; plunger from hardwood and is detachable. The frame is of gray iron, japanned finish; the handsomest and most complete lemon squeezer in the market. Weight, 1½ pounds. Price......17c

No. 23C9684 Malleable Iron Lemon Squeezer. Fully tinned strong and durable. Weight, 1 pound. Price......8c

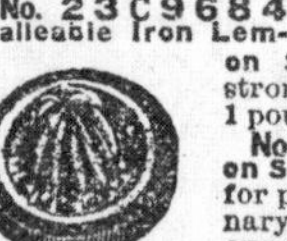

No. 23C9686 Glass Lemon Squeezer. The best made for private use; fits any ordinary size tumbler. Weight, 6 ounces. Price......5c

No. 23C9689 Acme Lemon Squeezer. No soda fountain complete without it. Cuts the lemon and squeezes the juice out with one movement of the lever. Strongly made of malleable iron. Finely nickeled. Cups tinned and easily removed for cleaning. It is small enough to be used on street stands. Weight, 3 pounds. Price......$1.48

Corkscrews.

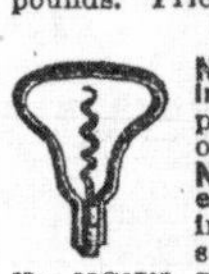

No. 23C9705 Folding Corkscrew, nicely polished. Weight, 2 ounces. Price......5c

No. 23C9706 Pocket Corkscrew. Each in nickel case, case serving as handle, which is passed through ring in screw. Weight, 2 ounces. Price......10c

No. 23C9705 No. 23C9706

Hot Water Urns.

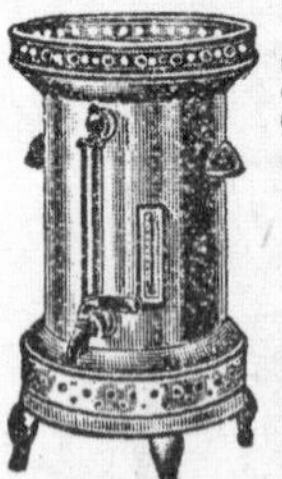

This very handsome urn is entirely new in design and construction and makes an elegant bar ornament as well as being very useful. It is constructed throughout of the best 20-ounce cold rolled copper stock and is extra heavily nickel plated and polished. It is equipped with thermometer, gauge and the latest pattern nickel plated faucet. The design is simple and rich and the absence of elaborate ornamentation makes it easy to keep clean and bright. It can be used equally well as coffee urn if desired and is the most popular pattern for restaurants and bars. Price.

No. 23C9732 Capacity, 2 gal. $4.90
No. 23C9733 Capacity, 3 gal. 5.70
No. 23C9734 Capacity, 4 gal. 6.50

Gasoline Burner.

No. 23C9737 Lightning Gasoline Burner, especially adapted for the above urns, to which it can be easily attached by anyone. Heavily nickel plated, with improved burner, and a rapid heater. Price......$1.33

Hot Water Urn.

No. 23C9738 Hot Water Urn. Made of best 14-ounce cold rolled copper, highly polished, with the latest improved pattern faucet. Extra well made, all joints double seamed and soldered. For barber shops, bars, restaurants or private families where hot water is required it is indispensable. Price

2-gallon capacity, polished copper......$1.72
3-gallon capacity, polished copper......2.08
4-gallon capacity, polished copper......2.38

Gasoline Vapor Stove.

No. 23C9740 Gasoline Vapor Stove. For heating hot water and coffee urns, all nicely nickel plated, with six jets. Capacity about 1 quart. Price......45c

Keyless Fly Fan.

No. 23C9798 Keyless Fly Fan. Will positively keep the flies from the lunch counter or table. Runs one hour and a quarter at each winding and is rewound by simply turning crosspiece at top of base. Invaluable in the dining room, sick room or office. It insures cleanliness at meals, comfort and rest to the weary, and is a blessing in the sick chamber, as while running there is entire freedom from the annoyance of flies. It is run by clockwork and wings are easily set at any angle. Height, 30 inches; spread of wings, 50 inches. Weight 3½ pounds. Price......$1.92

Electric Cigar Lighters.

No. 23C9799 Electric Cigar Lighter. Hangs from the ceiling on incandescent electric wire, with batteries on shelf. Each lighter is packed complete with 15 feet of the best double lamp cord and three of the best batteries to be procured. Complete instructions sent with each lighter. The metal parts are solid brass, nickel plated. Shipping weight, 10 pounds.

Price for lighter, complete with batteries and spark coil as described......$3.65

Cash Register.

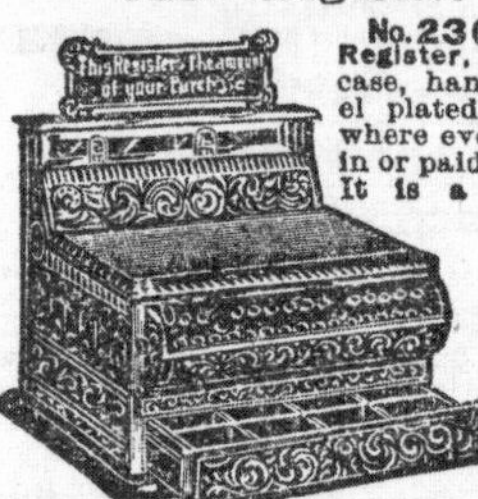

No. 23C9804 Cash Register, with metal case, handsomely nickel plated. Shows you where every cent taken in or paid out has gone. It is a detail adder, strong and simple in construction. Works on the principle of leverage and gravity and has the smallest number of springs of any cash register made. Mechanism is metal throughout, securely mounted in metal frame. Pushing the thumb lever cancels former registration uncovers the keys, opens the drawer and sounds the alarm. The next sale must be registered before drawer can be closed. Adds in detail. Capacity over $2,400. Standard arrangement of keys is as follows, reading from left to right: Top row, 3c, 4c, 5c, 10c, 20c, 30c, 40c, 50c, 65c, 75c, 90c, $2.00, $4.00, $10.00 ticket; lower row, 1c, 3c, 5c, 10c, 15c, 25c, 35c, 45c, 60c, 70c, 80c, $1.00, $3.00, $5.00, $20.00. Any special tabulation desired can be supplied at an additional cost of 75 cents. Cash drawer contains six coin hoppers and three bill compartments. Dimensions: Height, 21 inches; width, 19½ inches; depth, 13 inches. Shipping weight, 80 pounds. Price......$30.00

Note. For show cases and other store fixtures send for our Free Barber Supply Catalogue.

Money Drawer.

No. 23C9806 Money Drawer. It is a safeguard against sneak-thieves. Gong sounds every time drawer is opened, or whenever an attempt is made to open it. It is opened by a combination which may be changed as often as desired. Can be opened by one knowing the combination on which it is set as quickly as any drawer. Has sliding coin tray, with partitions underneath for paper money. Weight, 15 pounds. Price......97c

Tobacco Cutter.

No. 23C9808 Tobacco Cutter with image. Cast iron, with steel blade. Japanned finish. Weight, 6 pounds. Price......42c

SCALES.

Spring Balances.

No. 23C9875 Spring Balance, to weigh 24 pounds by ½ pounds. Shipping weight, 9 ounces. Price, 5c

No. 23C9876 Spring Balance, to weigh 48 pounds by pounds. Shipping weight, 12 ounces. Price......12c

No. 23C9877 Spring Balance, with round tin dish; weighs 24 pounds by ½ pounds. Shipping weight, 1½ pounds. Price......15c

No. 23C9878 Spring Balance, with round tin dish; weighs 50 pounds by pounds. Shipping weight, 2½ pounds. Price......22c

23C9875 23C9877

Ironclad Ice Scales.

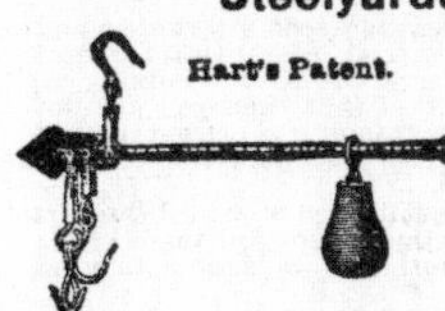

No. 23C9880 The Famous Ironclad Ice Balance, made entirely of steel and malleable iron and cannot break. Compact and durable and not liable to get out of order. Fully guaranteed. Marked to 5-pound graduations.

Will weigh	200 lbs.	300 lbs.
Weight, pounds	4½	5
Price	$2.40	$2.85

Steelyards.

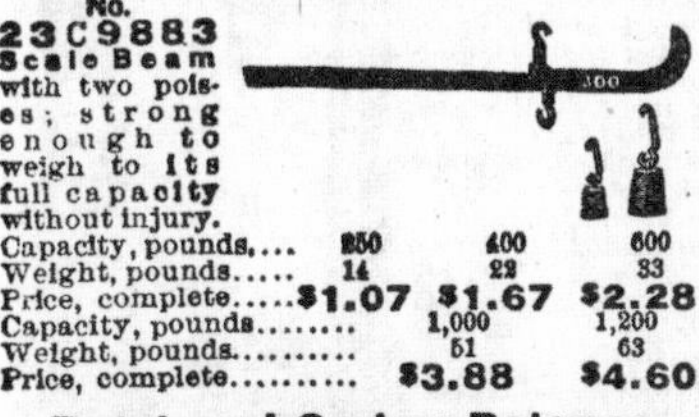

No. 23C9882 Hart's Patent Steelyards, with steel bars guaranteed to weigh absolutely correct. We could sell you cheaper steelyards that could not be depended on, for a very little less money, but we don't care to handle such goods. The 50-pound size weighs by ¼ pounds, larger sizes by ½ pounds.

Cap'ty lbs.	50	100	150	200	250	300
Weight, lbs.	3½	4	5	6¾	8⅜	8½
Price	60c	67c	79c	98c	$1.19	$1.40

Scale Beams.

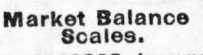

No. 23C9883 Scale Beam with two poises; strong enough to weigh to its full capacity without injury.

Capacity, pounds	250	400	600
Weight, pounds	14	22	33
Price, complete	$1.07	$1.67	$2.28
Capacity, pounds		1,000	1,200
Weight, pounds		51	63
Price, complete		$3.88	$4.60

Butchers' Spring Balance Scales.

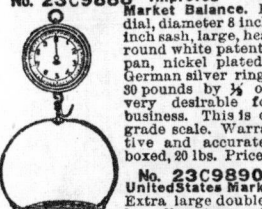

No. 23C9885 Circular Spring Balance. This scale is for butchers' use exclusively. It weighs 30 pounds by ounces, has 7-inch dial with nickel plated glass sash, large figures, white enameled front, tinned iron bows, hooks and swivel, and has a fine porcelain pan. Sensitive and accurate; fully warranted. Weight, boxed for shipment, 19 pounds.
Price..............$4.80

No. 23C9886 Butchers' and Grocers' Hanging Circular Spring Balances, aluminum dial, 6 inches in diameter, will not corrode or tarnish, black figures, white patent enameled pan, 11 inches in diameter, tinned iron bows and hooks. Weighs 24 pounds by ounces. Warranted sensitive and accurate. This is our leader. Weight, 4 pounds.
Price..............$2.14

Market Balance Scales.

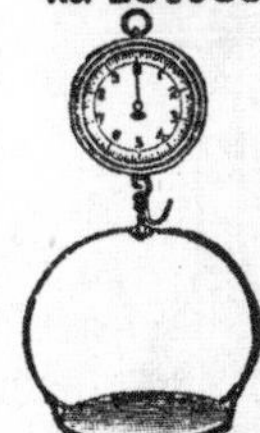

No. 23C9888 Improved Market Balance. Extra large dial, diameter 8 inches, and 10-inch sash, large, heavy figures, round white patent enameled pan, nickel plated bows and German silver rings. Weighs 30 pounds by ½ ounces, and very desirable for butcher business. This is our highest grade scale. Warranted sensitive and accurate. Weight, boxed, 20 lbs. Price...$7.20

No. 23C9890 Improved UnitedStates Market Balance Extra large double dial, 8 in. in diameter with 10-inch sash. Dial can be seen from both sides. Large, heavy figures, nickel plated sash and bows and German silver ring, round white patent enameled pan, warranted not to break. Weighs 30 pounds by ounces and used in all large markets. Sensitive and accurate. Weight, boxed, 22 pounds. Price...$10.80

Agate Bearing Butcher Counter Scales.

No. 23C9893 Agate Bearing Butcher Counter Scales. Even balance, 10-inch double dial. Dial can be seen from both sides. Finely nickel plated sash, agate bearings, handsome black enameled base and marble slab; weighs 30 pounds by ounces. This is the only spring balance on the market that has agate bearings, and is consequently very sensitive and accurate and thoroughly reliable. Weight, boxed, 59 pounds. Price..............$11.98

Butchers' Scales.

No. 23C9895 Butchers' Scale, marble slab; tested to weigh 32 pounds by ounces. Weight, carefully packed in box for shipment, 40 pounds. Price..............$7.38

No. 23C9896 Same as No. 23C9895, to weigh 64 pounds by 2 ounces. Weight, carefully packed in box for shipment, 40 pounds.
Price..............$7.65

American Family Scale.

No. 23C9900 Made of steel, with steel top, white enameled dial. Beautifully enameled and ornamented. It weighs 24 pounds by ounces. Occupies but little space, is light and easily moved. It can be regulated by turning brass screw on top. Is always ready and is easily understood. It is a convenient scale to use and has no weights that can be lost. You can look this one in the face to prove its accuracy without looking for weights. Every scale examined before leaving the factory and warranted correct. Weight, boxed, 6 pounds. Price..............88c

Our Household Scale for 98c.

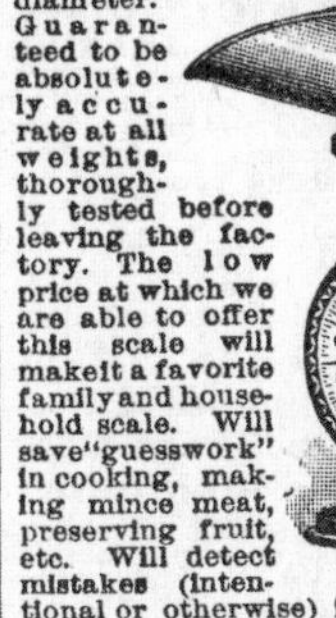

No. 23C9901 The Acme Household Scale. A handsome and reliable scale; weighs to 24 pounds by ounces; has tin scoop, handsome enameled dial 5 inches in diameter. Guaranteed to be absolutely accurate at all weights, thoroughly tested before leaving the factory. The low price at which we are able to offer this scale will make it a favorite family and household scale. Will save "guesswork" in cooking, making mince meat, preserving fruit, etc. Will detect mistakes (intentional or otherwise) in weighing articles you buy. Every farmer and every family should by all means have one or more scales. Our prices place scales within the reach of everyone. Weight of scale, boxed for shipment, 7 pounds.
Price..............98c

The U. S. Family Scale.

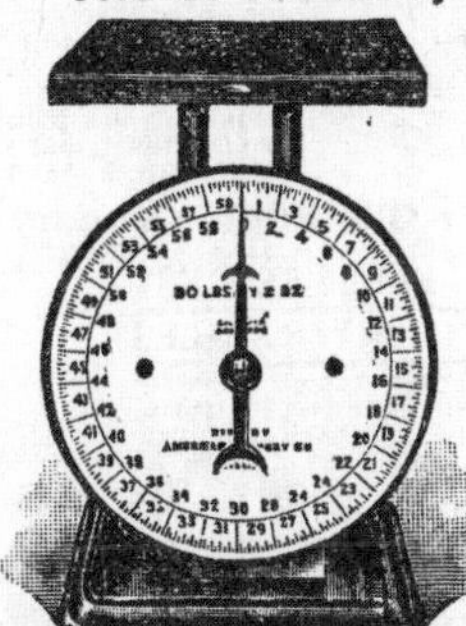

$1.75

No. 23C9902 The U. S. Family Scale. The most practical all purpose scale made. Capacity, 60 pounds by 2 ounces. Body is made of 18-gauge drawn steel, finished in black enamel, and dial is of extra large size, finely enameled, which will never tarnish or become dull. We guarantee it to be absolutely correct at all weights. The springs used in these scales are tempered one at a time in oil and afterwards flashed in tallow, which retains the carbon in the steel, making a tough, pliable spring which will never weaken, but will retain its strength exactly the same for years. Has extra heavy post and top and will hold anything that can be weighed on a scale of this capacity. Height, 10 inches. Shipping weight, 12 pounds. Price, with steel platform as shown in illustration.......$1.75
Price, with forks and heavy tin scoop 16½ inches long..............$2.05

Our 68-Cent Family Scale.

No. 23C9904 Our 68-cent price should induce every family in the land to own a pair of these 4-pound scales. You may save the cost in one day's use. Even balance scales. Plain japanned. To weigh 4 pounds, with good tin scoop. Weight, boxed, 8¼ pounds. Price 68c

Our $1.62 Family Scales.

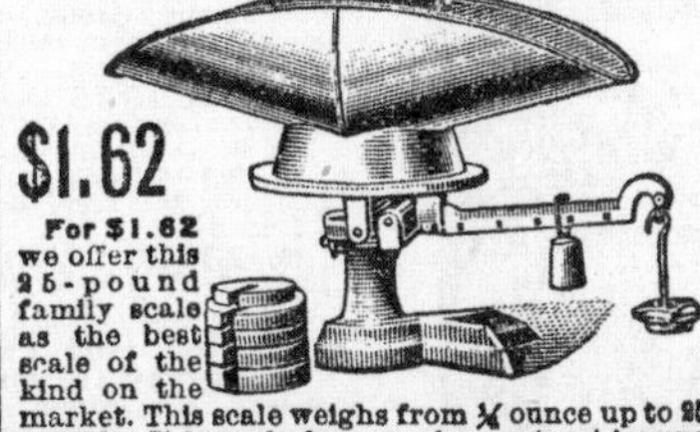

$1.62

For $1.62 we offer this 25-pound family scale as the best scale of the kind on the market. This scale weighs from ¼ ounce up to 25 pounds. It is made for us under contract by one of the best makers. Every scale is guaranteed and if it is not found perfect in every respect it can be returned to us at our expense and your money will be refunded. It will pay you to buy this scale and weigh your grocery and meat purchases; weigh the butter. Boxed for shipment, they weigh about 20 pounds. Beam marked 1½ pounds by ¼ ounces.
No. 23C9905 Price..............$1.62

Our Dairy Scale with Butter Salter Attachment.

No. 23C9910 Capacity, ¼ ounce to 240 pounds. Same grade scale, same material and workmanship as described under our No. 23C9915. By using this scale the butter can be weighed and salted without figuring, avoids all guesswork, and makes every lot of butter the same. Beam marked 44 pounds by ¼ ounces. Will weigh 240 pounds with all weights on. Size of platform, 10x13¼ inches. They are sealed carefully with the United States standard and are absolutely correct. Shipping weight, 46 pounds. Price, complete......$3.75

No. 23C9911 Extra High Grade Dairy Scale with Butter Salter Attachment. Capacity ¼ ounce to 250 pounds. Size of platform, 9⅞x13 inches. All steel bearings sensitive, accurate and durable. The mechanism is perfect. The castings are correct; pivots are the finest tool steel, case hardened. Beam marked 44 pounds by ¼ ounces. Shipping weight, 52 pounds.
Price..............$5.25

Our $1.95 Platform Counter Scales.

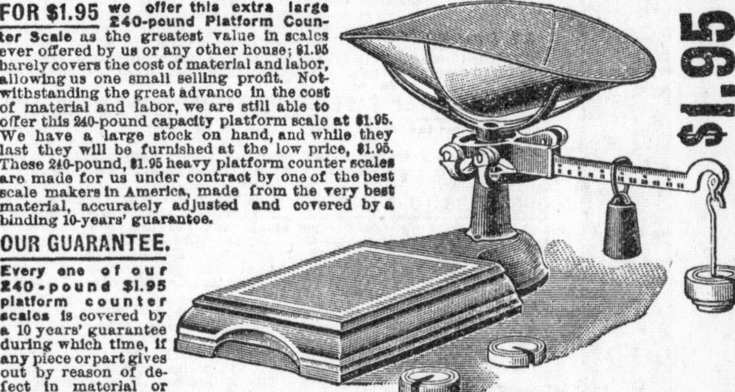

FOR $1.95 we offer this extra large 240-pound Platform Counter Scale as the greatest value in scales ever offered by us or any other house; $1.95 barely covers the cost of material and labor, allowing us one small selling profit. Notwithstanding the great advance in the cost of material and labor, we are still able to offer this 240-pound capacity platform scale at $1.95. We have a large stock on hand, and while they last they will be furnished at the low price, $1.95. These 240-pound, $1.95 heavy platform counter scales are made for us under contract by one of the best scale makers in America, made from the very best material, accurately adjusted and covered by a binding 10-years' guarantee.

OUR GUARANTEE.

Every one of our 240-pound $1.95 platform counter scales is covered by a 10 years' guarantee during which time, if any piece or part gives out by reason of defect in material or workmanship, we will replace or repair it free of charge.

THIS OUR SPECIAL $1.95 SCALE is an all purpose scale, and unless you have a larger scale or a full standard platform scale, do not fail to take advantage of our special $1.95 price, for you will be repaid many times over during the year. These scales weigh from ¼ ounce to 240 pounds. They take the place in many ways of the regular platform scale. They have fine steel bearings, tin scoop, heavy accurately graduated beam. Weight, boxed for shipment, about 40 pounds. You will find the freight will amount to next to nothing, as compared with what you will save in price. There are a number of scales of from 200 to 250 pounds capacity being advertised at prices ranging very nearly the same as we offer this scale. We wish to say with reference to scales so advertised that this scale could be cheapened and offered for considerably less money, but if you want the best single beam platform scale we handle, our 10-year guaranteed scale, you will get no such platform scale elsewhere at anything like the price. Beam marked 44 pounds by ¼ ounces.
No. 23C9914 Price..............$1.95

Our $2.38 Double Beam Platform Counter Scales.

FOR $2.38 we offer this high grade, 10-year guaranteed, double beam counter scale as the equal of any counter scale made. $2.38 is a price based on the actual cost of material and labor, with but our one small percentage of profit added. A 240-pound platform counter scale for only $2.38. These heavy double beam platform counter scales are made for us under contract by one of the best scale makers in this country. They are made from the best material that can be secured, and only the most skilled mechanics are employed. They are carefully tested, accurately adjusted, and are covered by a binding guarantee.

OUR 10-YEAR GUARANTEE.

Every special $2.38, 240-pound Platform Counter Scale is covered by a binding 10-year guarantee, during which time if any piece or part gives out by reason of defect in material or workmanship, we will replace or repair it free of charge. From the illustration, engraved from a photograph, you can form some idea of the appearance of our special $2.38, 240-pound Platform Counter Scale. If you do not wish to invest in a regular platform scale at $6.33 to $13.54, do not fail to order one of our counter scales. You will be repaid many times over for the $2.38 purchase price, in detecting errors, if not dishonesty, in the goods you buy and the produce you sell. These scales have a capacity of 240 pounds, they are extra large, extra strong and will serve almost any purpose. Boxed for shipment, they weigh about 45 pounds.

THESE SCALES are made with extra heavy accurately graduated beam, extra heavy tare beam. This is a great convenience and makes the scale one of the handiest in use. Every scale is tested before leaving the factory, and we guarantee them to be mechanically perfect. Beam marked 44 pounds by ¼ ounces.

AT $2.38 the scales come complete with double beam, scoop and extra weights, securely boxed, and we guarantee safe delivery.
No. 23C9915 Price..............$2.38

Our Extra Best Union Platform Grocers' Counter Scales.

WITH BRASS SCOOP AND SLIDING POISE.

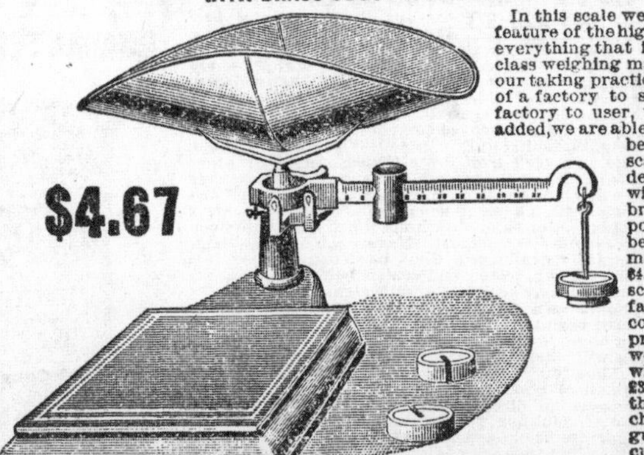

$4.67

In this scale we have every essential feature of the highest priced scale sold; everything that is necessary to a first class weighing machine. By means of our taking practically the entire output of a factory to sell them direct from factory to user, with one small profit added, we are able to offer you this extra best high grade grocers' scales, handsomely decorated and finished, with heavy polished brass scoop, sliding poise, heavy solid brass beam, we are able to make a price of only $4.67 on this scale. This scale is suitable for fancy groceries, teas, coffees, etc., and our price is no more than you would pay for the scale which we sell under No. 23C9914 if you bought it through the ordinary channels of trade. It is guaranteed to weigh accurately on either corner of the platform or in the scoop. Capacity ¼ ounce to 240 pounds. Finished in red enamel and gilt, handsomely decorated. Platform is 9⅞x12⅞ inches. Carefully packed in a wooden box for shipment. Beam marked 40 pounds by ¼ ounces.
No. 23C9916 Price..............$4.67

OUR $6.33 PLATFORM SCALES

GUARANTEED TEN YEARS.

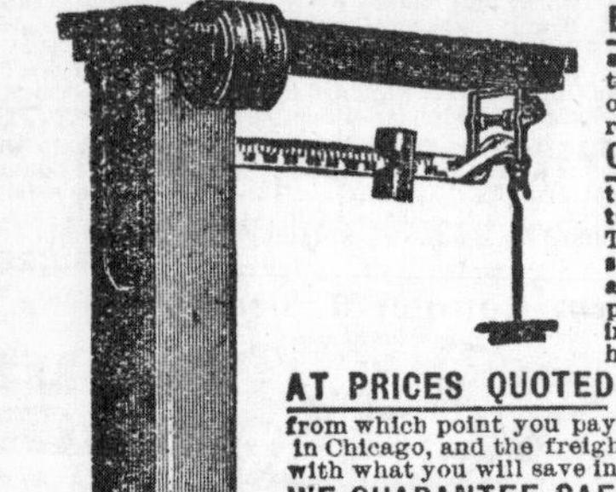

EVERY PLATFORM SCALE sold by us is covered by a binding ten years' guarantee, during which time, if any piece or part gives out by reason of defect in material or workmanship, we will replace or repair it **free of charge.**

OUR PLATFORM SCALES are made for us under contract by one of the best makers in the country, made from the very best of material. They are accurately adjusted, they are very strong and substantial; they are sensitively accurate in weight and any farmer will be repaid a dozen times over in a very short time in the saving effected by weighing everything he sells and everything he buys.

AT PRICES QUOTED we furnish these scales carefully boxed, delivered on board the cars at the factory, from which point you pay the freight; no expense for extra handling in Chicago, and the freight will amount to next to nothing compared with what you will save in price.

WE GUARANTEE SAFE DELIVERY. These scales are very carefully packed in a strong box and we guarantee them to reach you in the same perfect condition they leave us.

From the illustration shown, engraved from a photograph, you can form an idea of the appearance of our highest grade, ten-year guaranteed $6.33 platform scales.

OUR $6.33 TO $9.40 PRICE is based on the actual cost of material and labor, with but our one small percentage of profit added, and is the lowest price ever named for the highest grade platform scales. We furnish these scales in capacity from 600 to 1,500 pounds at from $6.33 to $9.40 as quoted below. With our platform scales you can weigh every load of grain you sell before going to market, everything on the farm can be weighed, and it is not safe to do otherwise.

THESE SCALES are provided with the best steel pivots, carefully hardened and finished; have no check rods to bind or get out of place. The platform rests on adjustable chill bearings, which take the wear directly off the steel pivots, and the pivots remaining sharp, the scales act quick and sensitive. The scales are fitted with heavy, smoothly finished wheels, heavy wood center platform, sliding poise beam, sealed and tested.

EACH AND EVERY SIZE OF PLATFORM SCALE which we sell is made at the same factory and by the same skilled workmen, and it is just as much of an impossibility for a high class man to turn out crude, unfinished work as it is for the ordinary common factory hand to **turn out the high class of goods** that are made by our expert mechanics.

NOTE SIZE OF PLATFORM. Some dealers add extra weights to increase the capacity of the scales they sell. A 400-lb. scale, with weights to weigh 600 pounds, is not a 600-lb. scale.

Catalogue Number	Capacity	Beams Marked	Size of Platform	Shipping Weight	Price
23C9920	600 lbs.	50 lbs. by ¼ lb.	16½x24 inches	150 lbs.	$ 6.33
23C9921	800 lbs.	50 lbs. by ¼ lb.	17 x24½ inches	160 lbs.	6.95
23C9922	1,000 lbs.	50 lbs. by ¼ lb.	17½x25 inches	170 lbs.	7.30
23C9923	1,250 lbs.	100 lbs. by ½ lb.	18 x26 inches	235 lbs.	8.45
23C9924	1,500 lbs.	100 lbs. by ½ lb.	20 x28 inches	245 lbs.	9.40

We furnish the above grade of scales with bag rack as follows:

Catalogue No.	Capacity	Beams Marked	Size of Platform	Price
23C9925	600 lbs.	50 lbs. by ¼ lb.	16½x24 inches	$ 7.98
23C9926	800 lbs.	50 lbs. by ¼ lb.	17 x24½ inches	8.20
23C9927	1,000 lbs.	50 lbs. by ¼ lb.	17½x25 inches	8.55
23C9928	1,200 lbs.	100 lbs. by ½ lb.	18 x26 inches	10.65

OUR SCALES ARE GUARANTEED TO BE ABSOLUTELY ACCURATE AND TRUE.

WE ACCEPT YOUR ORDER with the understanding that the scale you get from us will be the greatest value you ever saw, otherwise it can be returned to us, and we will return your money, and stand transportation charges both ways.

Our Extra Best Heavy Portable Platform Scales.

NOTHING BETTER CAN BE MADE—AT $7.50 TO $14.35 THE GREATEST SCALE VALUE EVER OFFERED.

BUILT TO WITHSTAND HEAVY STRAINS and to weigh accurately under all conditions. For continuous use, day in and day out, this is the best scale that can be made. The levers, the pivots, loops, platforms, frame and, in fact, every part that is subjected to strain is built extra heavy and of the best material that can be procured. We especially recommend these scales for those who use a scale constantly and require a scale to be absolutely accurate under all conditions. Has solid brass beam, accurately graduated with sliding poise, best English tool steel pivots, hardened and tempered, heavy wood center platform. In design it is similar to the illustration of No. 23C9920, but is built stronger and heavier in every part. It is guaranteed to be equal in strength and accuracy to any scale made, regardless of name and price, and far superior to the so called standard scales usually sold at 50 to 75 per cent more than the prices we ask.

Our extra heavy portable platform scales are sold under our great ten-year guarantee, and to make you absolutely secure, we make you this great 30-day free trial offer. Order one of these scales according to our liberal terms of shipment as given on page 2. After receiving it, use it for thirty days and subject it to every test and if at the end of that time you are not more than satisfied with it and convinced that it is a wonderful bargain at our price, return it at our expense and we will refund the money you have paid and pay transportation charges both ways. You run no risk, you can not lose a single penny.

AT PRICES QUOTED we furnish these scales carefully boxed, delivered on board the cars at the factory, from which point you pay the freight; no expense for extra handling in Chicago, and the freight will amount to next to nothing compared with what you will save in price.

Catalogue No.	Capacity	Beams Marked	Size of Platform	Price
23C9930	600 pounds	50 pounds by ¼ pound	16½x24 inches	$ 7.50
23C9931	800 pounds	50 pounds by ¼ pound	17 x24½ inches	7.80
23C9932	1,000 pounds	50 pounds by ¼ pound	17½x25 inches	8.45
23C9933	1,200 pounds	100 pounds by ½ pound	18 x26 inches	9.10
23C9934	1,600 pounds	100 pounds by ½ pound	20 x28 inches	11.25
23C9935	2,000 pounds	100 pounds by ½ pound	25 x33 inches	13.75
23C9936	2,500 pounds	100 pounds by ½ pound	25 x34 inches	14.35

Our Special High Grade Portable Platform Two-Beam Creamery Scale.

$8.75

Made especially for the severe usage which a scale of this character must be subjected to. These scales are used for weighing milk. Empty can may first be weighed with one of the poises, and the other poise left free for weighing the milk itself. All scales have graduations to 50 pounds on each bar. They have heavy double brass beam and sliding poises, and are as good as we know how to make them.

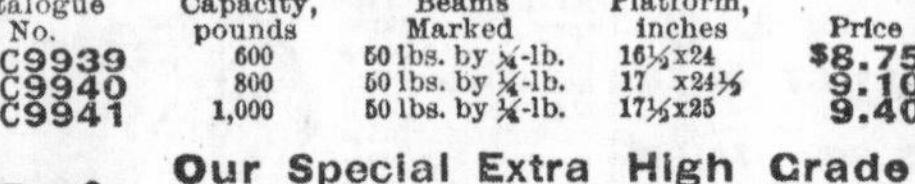

Catalogue No.	Capacity, pounds	Beams Marked	Size of Platform, inches	Price
23C9939	600	50 lbs. by ¼-lb.	16½x24	$8.75
23C9940	800	50 lbs. by ¼-lb.	17 x24½	9.10
23C9941	1,000	50 lbs. by ¼-lb.	17½x25	9.40

Our Special Extra High Grade Five-Beam Creamery Milk Weighing Scale.

No. 23C9942 These scales are very convenient for the creamery, as they have different beams for taking the tare and enable the buyer to weigh several customers' milk without emptying the can until full, each beam representing a customer. There are no loose weights to be lost or stolen. Scales mounted on wheels. Size of platform, 16½x24 inches. Capacity, 600 pounds. Beams marked by ½ pounds. Made only in one size. Price..................$10.95

No. 3C05228 The United States Standard Scale Books. Size, 8½x11 inches. Durably bound in boards; marble sides; cloth back. Contains 500 weigh forms. Printed on a good quality of paper, with stubs attached. Weight, packed for shipment, 24 ounces. Price..................25c

We guarantee safe delivery of the goods and entire satisfaction on everything you order or refund your money. **About the Freight.** Scales are accepted by most railroad companies as second class freight, usually at from 40 to 50 cents per 100 pounds for 500 miles. By referring to pages 7 to 11 in the front of the book you can get the second class freight rate per 100 pounds to a point nearest you which is almost exactly the same as to your town, and you will see it amounts to next to nothing as compared with the saving you will make in price.

Our Gilt Edge Grocery Platform Counter Scales.

OUR GILT EDGE GROCERY PLATFORM COUNTER SCALES with heavy brass scoop, capacity 1 ounce to 250 pounds. Platform, 12x15 inches. Scales of the same pattern as this are sold by dealers at more than double our price. This style of scale is very desirable for use in stores. It combines extreme sensitiveness with accuracy and large capacity. The beam is on a level with the eye; the platform is large enough to hold a barrel of flour, and the scale is quick enough to weigh teas and spices. Instead of using a weight to balance the scoop, we use a poise which cannot get lost. It has a heavy brass beam graduated on both sides. The scale is handsomely decorated and securely packed for shipment. Capacity, 1 ounce to 250 pounds. Size of platform, 12x15 inches. Beam marked 55 pounds by ounces.

No. 23C9918 Price ...$8.95

WAGON SCALES

A farmer who is without a wagon scale is blind to his own interests. He is taking risks no business man would dare take and is placed entirely at the mercy of others for the results of his brain and labor. Our high grade wagon scales will last you a lifetime and put money in your pocket every time they are used. You will more than pay for them in weighing a single season's crops, and the increase in your yearly profits will surprise you.

OUR STEEL KING WAGON SCALES, $24.95.

GUARANTEED FOR 10 YEARS.

AT $24.95, $26.90 AND $27.50 for our three, four and five-ton wagon scales we offer a high grade steel trussed lever wagon scale.

ABOUT THE QUALITY We claim for these scales that they are stronger than other makes that weigh as much or even more because of the improved shape of the levers and the manner in which they are trussed. While these scales are not as heavy and do not have the improved compound beam, which does away with the use of weights, as in our No. 23C9958 New Century Scale, they are superior to the best cast iron lever scales offered by other makers, as owing to the nature of the material used, no cast iron lever scale can be made that will stand the same amount of rough usage and abuse that a wagon scale with all steel levers will. Cast iron levers often contain hidden imperfections and blow holes which will cause them to break just when they are needed the most. Have double brass beams with sliding poises accurately graduated. Best hardened English tool steel pivots. Every scale set up, tested and sealed before leaving our factory and guaranteed absolutely accurate at all weights.

EVERY FARMER should own either a set of wagon scales or platform scales. A farmer should not sell a load of grain, a bale of cotton, a hog or a steer, that has not been weighed on his own scales. Your scales will check mistakes and detect dishonesty, and will pay the cost ten-fold in a few years. In order to sell these high grade wagon scales at the smallest possible advance over the actual cost to manufacture, we ship them all direct from our factory in Western Ohio, saving the expense of handling, freight, storage, transfer charges, etc., which we would otherwise be obliged to add to the cost. On the next page we give the rate per hundred pounds on wagon scales to various points. Note that the rate to eastern and southern points is even cheaper than it would be from Chicago, and to western points is only slightly more. In any case the freight charges amount to very little compared to the saving in price you will effect by buying this 10-year guaranteed high grade scale from us.

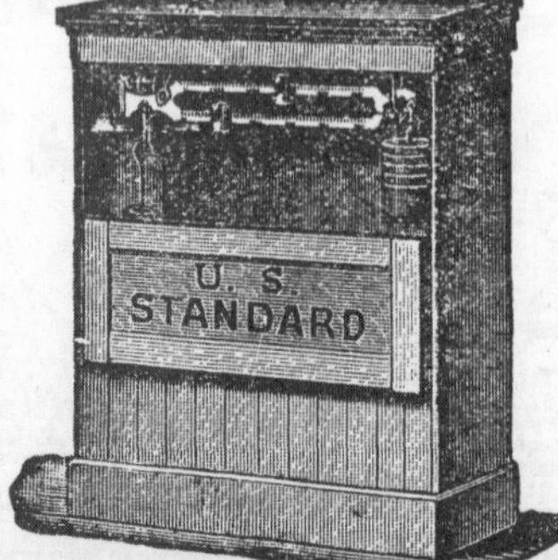

WITH EVERY SET OF WAGON SCALES we send building plan and full directions so that you can set the scales up without any trouble whatsoever. The scales come complete with beam box, brass beam, sliding poises and steel pivots.

OUR BINDING GUARANTEE. With every Steel King wagon scale we issue a written binding ten years' guarantee, by the terms and conditions of which if any piece or part gives out by reason of defect in material or workmanship within ten years, we will replace or repair it **free of charge.** With care, our wagon scales will last a lifetime.

No. 23C9945 Capacity, 3 tons. Shipping weight, 450 pounds. Size of platform, 8x14 feet; double beam marked to 1,500 pounds. Price..................$24.95

No. 23C9946 Capacity, 4 tons. Shipping weight, 475 pounds. Size of platform, 8x14 feet; double beam marked to 1,500 pounds. Price..................$26.90

No. 23C9947 Capacity, 5 tons. Shipping weight, 500 pounds. Size of platform, 8x14 feet; double beam marked to 1,500 pounds. Price..................$27.50

Sealed Test Weight.

No. 23C9948 Fifty-pound sealed test weight, guaranteed correct, U. S. standard, which can be used to test any scale. Every owner of a wagon or platform scale should have one. Price..................$1.90

SOME AGENTS OR DEALERS may tell you that at prices 25, 50 or 100 per cent higher than ours they will furnish a better scale. Get a building plan of their scale, send for a building plan of our scale, **free** for the asking, compare the two and decide for yourself **which is the better scale.**

ATLAS GUARANTEED WAGON SCALES, $31.50 TO $53.50.

WITH TRIPLE BRASS BEAMS. NO LOOSE WEIGHTS.

AT $31.50 TO $53.50 we offer the Atlas 25-year guaranteed wagon scales as the strongest and most accurate wagon scales made, regardless of name or price. Scales of a similar grade to this are made only by two or three of the best manufacturers in this country and have heretofore been sold through agents only and at prices ranging from $65.00 to $125.00. Our prices on these Atlas steel trussed scales are but a small margin over the actual cost of the material and the skilled labor that goes into them, and is only made possible by manufacturing them in large quantities, loading directly onto the cars at our factory door, so that we have no cartage or handling expense, and by selling only through our catalogue, thus cutting out all expense for agents and salesmen. You pay for material and labor and just one small profit, nothing more, and are thus enabled to get these Atlas highest grade scales at one-half the regular price.

OUR 25-YEAR BINDING GUARANTEE. With every Atlas steel trussed lever wagon scale we send our written binding 25-year guarantee, by the terms and conditions of which, if any piece or part gives out by reason of defect in material or workmanship within twenty-five years, we will replace or repair it free of charge. With ordinary care and attention our Atlas scales will last more than a lifetime. We guarantee our Atlas scales to be remarkably quick and sensitive, the slightest weight on the platform causing the beam to act. We guarantee them to weigh exactly the same on every corner of the platform as on the center. We guarantee them to be tested and sealed and to be absolutely accurate at all weights.

THE TRIPLE BEAM is made of solid brass of the highest grade and the graduations are mathematically exact. It has three weighing bars or beams. The lower bar is graduated by 2½-pound graduations to 500 pounds, and has sliding poise. The upper bar is graduated by 10-pound graduations to 2,000 pounds and can be used as a tare beam to weigh empty wagons, etc. It is equipped with sliding poise with leather tipped set screw to hold it at any desired place without marring the polished finish of the beam. The center bar is notched in 500-pound graduations to the balance of the capacity of the scale. A small steel spur on the poise sets down into the notches and insures absolute accuracy in weighing as these Atlas scales are sealed on every notch and there can be no deviation. The beam pivots are of the finest tempered tool steel and each one is provided with a spring steel friction pin, which prevents the loops from chafing or wearing the beam. Beam is also provided with screw balance ball for balancing the platform. Carefully hardened loops and a 7-16 inch steelyard rod connects the beam with the wrought steel shelf lever, also provided with tempered steel pivots, in the beam box, which in turn is connected with the platform levers by a ¼-inch steel steelyard rod, at the lower end of which is an all steel built up shackle or stirrup in which the long levers are each hung separately and centerally, each lever having a cone shaped tempered steel point resting in a tempered steel cup welded into the shackle.

ALL LEVERS ARE OF WROUGHT T SHAPED STEEL with heavy steel truss rods from end to end and are perfectly rigid and unbreakable. Tension of the trusses is adjustable by means of a right and left hand nut. Heavy cast head are riveted to each end of the levers, and the pivots, which are of ¾-inch tool steel, ground to a diamond edge and tempered, pass through heads and mortise into lever, making head absolutely immovable. Long and short levers connect by a square steel shackle and cannot bind; both are equipped with cone shaped hardened steel pivots and bearing cups. All levers are hung from ⅜-inch wrought steel corner irons, which are set into holes drilled in the sills and serve also to bind them together. Beam box is furnished with each scale and is built of 1-inch matched lumber, with heavy moulded top, painted two coats of white paint and fitted with flat key lock. Plain simple building directions and timber specifications are furnished with each scale. The parts are few and their relation to each other is plainly shown so that any one can set them up without previous experience. Depth of pit required is but 18 inches to bottom of sills or 24 inches including sills.

PRICE IS FOR SCALE COMPLETE WITH BEAM BOX. The timber and masonry for pit to be furnished by the purchaser. Scales are delivered free on board cars at our Western Ohio factory and purchaser must pay freight, which amounts to little or nothing compared to your saving in price.

Catalogue No.	Capacity, Tons	Size of Platform	Shipping Weight	Price
23C9949	3	14 x 8 feet	500 pounds	$31.50
23C9950	4	14 x 8 feet	500 pounds	32.50
23C9951	5	14 x 8 feet	505 pounds	33.50
23C9952	6	16 x 8 feet	520 pounds	42.00
23C9953	8	16 x 8 feet	920 pounds	46.00
23C9954	10	16 x 8 feet	925 pounds	53.50

NEW CENTURY STEEL LEVER WAGON SCALES, $29.75.

BY MAKING THOUSANDS OF THESE SCALES EVERY YEAR ALL EXACTLY ALIKE, by devoting our entire energy to making a single size and capacity (namely 5 tons), in our New Century Scale our workmen employed day after day in a single pattern and size have become expert and rapid, the work on this scale has been so systematized and our output is so large that we are now making this particular style at a lower cost than it can be produced at any other scale factory in the country. Our price of $29.75 for a 25-year guaranteed steel lever wagon scale with solid brass compound beam and beam box has been heretofore unheard of. It is actually lower than the factory cost to make in other scale plants and is just a single small margin of profit over the shop cost to build. **THIS SCALE IS PRACTICALLY UNBREAKABLE FROM OVERWEIGHT OR MISUSE AND WITH EACH ONE WE FURNISH OUR WRITTEN TWENTY-FIVE YEAR GUARANTEE AGAINST ALL DEFECTS IN MATERIAL OR WORKMANSHIP.**

We ship direct from our Western Ohio factory and the freight charges, which you must pay, amount to really nothing compared to your saving in price. To Eastern and Southern points they are less than from Chicago, and to Western points but a trifle more.

OUR NEW CENTURY WAGON SCALE is provided with a solid brass compound beam, which registers the full capacity of the scale, and no loose weights are required.

The upper bar or beam is graduated by 5-pound marks to 1,000 pounds and the lower beam to 9,000 pounds by 500-pound graduations. Both beams have heavy brass front sliding poises and lower poise is equipped with a leather tipped set screw which holds the poise in any desired position and does not mar the polished surface of the beam. Beam is provided with an adjustable screw ball for balancing the weight of the platform and the tempered tool steel pivots are equipped with spring steel friction pins preventing all wear on the beam. In construction, our New Century Wagon Scales are exactly the same as our Atlas Scales described above, except that the short levers do not have truss rods, as they are not required in this scale. All levers are of heavy T shaped steel, all pivots are of the finest tool steel ground to a knife edge and carefully tempered. Pivot loops and bearing irons are hardened to a file temper and will never wear or cut.

EVERY SCALE is set up and tested at our factory and sealed to all weights and in every corner of the platform. The knife edge steel pivots and fine workmanship throughout make this scale remarkably quick and sensitive and **WE GUARANTEE IT TO BE ABSOLUTELY ACCURATE AT ALL WEIGHTS.**

It comes complete with compound solid brass beam and substantial, well painted and finished beam box, steel levers and in fact everything except the timber to build the platform and frame and the masonry.

Simple complete directions go with each scale, which enables any one to set them up in a short time.

No. 23C9958 **New Century Steel Lever Wagon Scale,** capacity, 5 tons, size of platform, 14 feet long, 8 feet wide. Shipping weight, 500 pounds. Furnished with beam box. Price........ **$29.75**

ABOUT THE FREIGHT. Scales are accepted by most railroad companies as second class freight, usually at from 40 to 50 cents per 100 pounds for 500 miles. Thus the freight rate from our factory in Western Ohio on wagon scales, per 100 pounds, to Chicago, is 30 cents; Cleveland, 23 cents; Detroit, 23 cents; Louisville, Ky., 30 cents; Dubuque, Ia., 40 cents; Kansas City, Omaha or Sioux City, 80 cents; St. Paul, 68 cents; St. Louis, 40 cents and Denver, $1.80. The shipping weight of each wagon scale is given in the description, and by computing the freight to the town mentioned above, which is nearest to you, you can closely estimate what the freight will cost you.

FOLDING STOCK RACK.

No. 23C9960 **Folding Stock Rack for Wagon Scales.** Fits any farm scale made and can be changed from weighing stock to a position suitable for weighing wagons loaded with hay, grain, etc., in fifteen seconds, without taking off of the scale platform or re-balancing the scale. Rack is simply folded back in a self-supporting position, allowing ample room to drive through with any kind of a load, and as rack is balanced on platform it does not affect the accuracy of the weight should hay crowd against it. End gates open in or out, as desired, and sides can be folded together and weatherboarded to protect the scale in winter. We furnish the hardware only, including the hinges, gate fastenings, etc., also plain directions for erecting and specifications for lumber required. About 200 feet of lumber is needed, which purchaser must furnish. Weight of irons boxed for shipment, 40 pounds. Price........ **$4.35**

Descriptive circular sent on application.

GUARANTEED FIREPROOF SAFES AT ONE-HALF THE REGULAR PRICES.

FIREPROOF SAFES—FOR FREE CATALOGUE SEE NEXT PAGE.

THE VULCAN SAFE AND LOCK CO. ARE MANUFACTURERS OF ABSOLUTELY FIREPROOF, GUARANTEED SAFES OF THE HIGHEST GRADE. Not only guaranteed to be absolutely fireproof, but also to be equal in the quality of material used, in the workmanship, in finish and in every detail of construction to any safe manufactured, regardless of name, make or price. We have contracted for the entire output of this well known manufacturer of highest grade safes and by making shipments direct from the factory in Central Ohio and avoiding all expense of handling, cartage, etc., by selling direct to the user, by employing no salesmen or agents who, making but few sales, must have a large profit on every one, by selling for cash only, losing nothing through bad debts, we are enabled to offer the genuine Vulcan Fireproof Safes, which cost just as much to manufacture as other safes of the highest grade, at prices which are but a small margin over the actual cost to produce in largest quantities. At a profit which would be but a mere incident in the heavy selling expense of a manufacturer who sells safes through agents in the old way.

READ CAREFULLY THE DETAILS OF THE HIGH GRADE CONSTRUCTION. Body is constructed of one continuous plate of heavy wrought steel forming top, bottom and sides which is securely riveted with heavy boiler rivets to the heavy wrought steel front and back frames which are each made from one continuous angle of bar steel heavily reinforced at each corner and passing entirely around the body of the safe. The bottom being made double to insure greater rigidity. The back is of one piece of selected plate steel. The front of the door is a solid plate of heavy hammered wrought steel. The inner walls are also of wrought steel. The body of the safe is riveted and braced in a manner that insures enormous strength and avoids all danger of breaking open by falling from great heights or being crushed by falling walls or heavy timbers.

OUR FIREPROOF FILLING is an absolutely fireproof, non-conducting preparation which is introduced between the inner and outer walls of our safes in a semi-liquid state, filling every crevice and adhering firmly to the steel body. In a short time it becomes perfectly dry and as hard as granite adding greatly to the strength of the safe. Our fireproof filling is the best and most costly that can be procured. There is nothing better to be had. It insures perfect safety to the contents of the safe in the hottest and fiercest fires. The chemical change which it undergoes when subjected to great heat evolves a vast quantity of vapor which filling every pore of the filling forms a cool moist wall entirely surrounding and protecting the contents of the safe. **REMEMBER OUR SAFES ARE GUARANTEED TO BE ABSOLUTELY FIREPROOF.**

DOORS are secured by heavy round bolts projecting from both sides into the jambs of the safe and have from three to seven flanges, which serve to prevent the entrance of heat. The locks are fitted to the inner edge of the doors, making them easy of access for oiling or changing combination and are protected on the inside by a removable steel plate. A heavy wall of our fireproof filling makes the door as fireproof as the body of the safe and serves to protect the locks and contents.

HINGES. We use outside hinges, securely riveted to the steel angle frame and to the door plate without cutting, and insuring great strength. They are fitted with finely nickel plated tips, easily unscrewed for oiling.

LOCKS. We use two patterns of the highest grade Yale unpickable combination locks, which are more fully described below.

BOLT WORK is of the special Vulcan design, very strong and simple in design, is easily operated and never gets out of order. All bolts are turned, polished and nickel plated. No part of the bolt work is in any way connected with the lock plate but is operated independently by a cold rolled steel handle to the left of the lock dial.

CABINET WORK is handsomely finished, filled and varnished, nicely carpeted, equipped with iron sub-treasury with high grade lock, and two flat keys, also drawers, pigeonholes and book spaces, as described.

FINISH AND TRIMMINGS. Vulcan safes are finished in black, beautifully ornamented with gold stripings and decorated with artistic and original designs and finished with the best varnish. We use only the highest grade filler and the best oil colors. Our decorators are the best in the business and take pride in turning out beautiful work. Bolt handles, dial knobs and hinge tips are finely nickel plated.

WE LETTER NAME OF PURCHASER IN GOLD OVER DOOR, free of charge when so ordered, but not otherwise. The name of the makers, The Vulcan Safe & Lock Co., is lettered on inside of outside door unless otherwise desired. **OUR NAME DOES NOT APPEAR ON THE SAFE.**

PLEASE NOTE that in stating dimensions we give first, the height, second, the width and third, the depth, in inches.

ABOUT THE FREIGHT. All safes are shipped from the factory in Central Ohio. Safes take third class rate of freight, and the freight charges amount to next to nothing compared to your saving in price. For example, third class freight will be, for 200 miles, 15 to 20 cents per 100 pounds; 400 miles, 30 to 40 cents per 100 pounds; 700 miles, 40 to 50 cents per 100 pounds; 1,000 miles, 60 to 75 cents per 100 pounds, from which you can calculate very closely what the freight will amount to.

WEIGHTS given are approximate only, as safes of the same size will vary considerably in weight owing to the nature of the filling.

Our Free Special Catalogue of Safes.

While we especially recommend that you order your safe direct from this big catalogue, even though the illustrations are small, and we accept your order with the understanding that if the safe is not perfectly satisfactory in every way, you can return it at our own expense and your money will be refunded, nevertheless, if you want to first see larger illustrations and more complete descriptions of these guaranteed fireproof safes, write and ask for our free Safe Catalogue. We issue a special catalogue of safes in which we are able to show large, handsome pictures of every one of these safes, as well as more elaborate and detailed descriptions than we have space to display in this big book, and if you cannot decide just what safe to order, **don't fail to write for this free Safe Catalogue.**

High grade reliable fireproof safes built and finished just as described; equipped with the genuine Yale triplex three-tumbler combination lock, a lock which defies the most expert, is absolutely unpickable, and yet so simple that the combination can be easily changed by the owner in a few minutes at any time by simply removing the inner steel door plate and following the simple directions which accompany every safe. Absolute protection against fire at small cost. A necessity in every home and to every merchant. In the following safes the cabinet work is arranged just as shown in the accompanying illustration.

No. 23C8802 **Dimensions:** Outside measure, 24x14⅛x16⅝ inches; inside measure, 12x8⅛x9 inches; arrangement of cabinet work, one 5x4-inch iron cash box with high grade lock with two flat keys; one 3x4-inch drawer with knob; one 3½x4-inch pigeonhole; one 12x3½-inch book space. Shipping weight, about 300 pounds. Price....................**$11.95**

This size is not made with inner door.

No. 23C8804 **Dimensions:** Outside measure, 25⅛x17x17⅛ inches; inside measure, 13⅜x10⅛x10 inches; arrangement of cabinet work, one 6x4⅜-inch iron cash box with high grade lock with two flat keys; one 3x4⅜-inch drawer with knob; one 5⅜x4⅜-inch pigeonhole; one 13x4⅛-inch book space. Shipping weight, about 400 pounds. Price....**$14.25**

No. 23C8805 Same as No. 23C8804, but with extra inner steel door, with high grade lock, with two flat keys. Price....................**$15.50**

Absolutely fireproof safes made by skilled workmen, of the best material that can be procured, perfect in every detail, finished in the finest possible manner, guaranteed to please you and to be equal in fireproof qualities and in every other way to any safe on the market regardless of name or price, direct from the factory to the user, at one-half the price agents must ask for even inferior grades. In the following safes the cabinet work is arranged just as shown in the accompanying illustration. All are equipped with the genuine Yale triplex combination locks, absolutely unpickable, cannot get out of order and combination can be changed by owner at any time.

No. 23C8808 **Dimensions:** Outside measure, 28⅛x17x18⅝ inches; inside measure, 15⅛x10 3-16x11 inches. Arrangement of cabinet work: One 6x4⅜-inch iron cash box, with high grade lock, with two flat keys; one 3x4⅜-inch drawer with knob; one 3x4⅜-inch pigeonhole; one 2⅝x4⅜-inch pigeonhole; one 15x4⅜-inch book space. Shipping weight, about 450 pounds. Price....................**$16.95**

No. 23C8809 Same as No. 23C8808, but with extra inner steel door, with high grade lock, with two flat keys. Price....................**$18.20**

No. 23C8812 **Dimensions:** Outside measure, 31⅛x20⅛x20⅝ inches; inside measure, 17⅛x12x12 inches. Arrangement of cabinet work: One 6x4⅜-inch iron cash box, with high grade lock, with two flat keys; one 3x4⅜-inch drawer with knob; one 3x4⅜-inch pigeon hole; one 4⅛x4⅜-inch pigeonhole; one 17⅛x6⅜-inch book space. Shipping weight, about 600 pounds. Price....................**$18.90**

No. 23C8813 Same as No. 23C8812, but with extra inner steel door, with high grade lock, with two flat keys. Price....................**$20.40**

No. 23C8816 **Dimensions:** Outside measure, 34x22⅛x21⅝ inches; inside measure, 19x14x12½ inches. Arrangement of cabinet work: One 6x4⅜-inch iron cash box, with high grade lock, with two flat keys; one 3x4⅜-inch drawer with knob; one 3x4⅜-inch pigeonhole; one 6x4⅜-inch book space; one 19x8⅜-inch book space. Shipping weight, about 750 pounds. Price....................**$20.90**

No. 23C8817 Same as No. 23C8816, but with extra inner door, with high grade lock and two flat keys. Price....**$22.15**

Our Line of Heavy Wall Safes.

While our regular line of safes are absolutely fireproof and in strength and durability are superior to almost all of the so-called high grade safes sold through agents at about double our prices, we have, to meet the demands of those who require an even greater factor of safety, constructed a line of safes with extra heavy walls. Heavier steel is used in the bodies and in the angles, the hinges and bolt work is heavier and the doors are thicker. They are heavier in every way. A line of the highest grade heavy wall safes insuring absolute safety from loss by fire or from being broken open by falling from great heights or being crushed by masonry.

All our heavy wall safes are equipped with the genuine Yale O. B. 3-tumbler combination locks, which are recognized by safe makers everywhere as the best manufactured, absolutely unpickable and susceptible to one million different combinations. Changes in combination can be easily and quickly made by following the simple directions which accompany every safe. All inside doors and cash boxes have Yale pattern flat key locks with duplicate keys. In the following safes the cabinet work is arranged as shown in the accompanying illustration, except that the Nos. 23C8840 to 23C8845, inclusive, have but one pigeonhole.

No. 23C8840 **Dimensions:** Outside measure, 26⅛ x 18 x 17⅛ inches; inside measure, 13⅜x10⅛x10 inches. Arrangement of cabinet work: one 6x4⅜-inch iron cash box, with high grade lock with two flat keys; one 3x4⅜-inch drawer with knob; one 4x4⅜ inch pigeonhole; one 13⅜x5⅛-inch book space, shipping weight, about 400 pounds. Price.......**$15.60**

This size is not made with inner door.

No. 23C8844 **Dimensions:** Outside measure, 29⅛x18x18⅝ inches; inside measure, 15⅜x10⅛x11 inches. Arrangement of cabinet work: one 6x4⅜-inch iron cash box with high grade lock with two flat keys; one 3x4⅜-inch drawer; one 5⅜x4⅜-inch pigeonhole; one 15⅜x5⅛-inch book space. Shipping weight, about 475 pounds. Price....................**$18.60**

No. 23C8845 Same as No. 23C8844, but with extra inner steel door with high grade lock, with two flat keys. Price....................**$20.10**

No. 23C8848 **Dimensions:** Outside measure, 35⅛x23⅜x24⅛ inches; inside measure, 19x14x14 inches. Arrangement of cabinet work: One 6x4⅜-inch iron cash box with high grade lock with two flat keys; one 3x4⅜-inch drawer with knob; two 4⅛x4⅜ inch pigeonholes; one 19x9-inch book space. Shipping weight, about 1,075 pounds. Price....................**$25.80**

No. 23C8849 Same as No. 23C8848, but with extra inner steel door with high grade lock, with two flat keys. Price....................**$27.60**

No. 23C8852 **Dimensions:** Outside measure, 38⅛x26⅛x24⅛ inches; inside measure, 20⅝x15x14 inches. Arrangement of cabinet work: One 6x4⅜-inch cash box with high grade lock, with two flat keys; one 3x4⅜-inch drawer with duplicate flat key lock; one 3x4⅜-inch pigeonhole; one 7⅜x4⅜-inch book space; one large book space, 20⅝x10 inches. Shipping weight, about 1,200 pounds. Price....................**$30.60**

No. 23C8853 Same as No. 23C8852, but with extra inner steel door with high grade lock, with two flat keys. Price....................**$32.40**

Massive, Heavy Wall Vulcan, Absolutely Fireproof Safes at $36.00 and $38.40.

For merchants, bankers, insurance and real estate men and others, who insist on having a thick wall safe. This safe has a 5-inch wall, is heavy and massive in construction, and as an absolute protection against loss from fire will meet any requirement. It is equipped with the genuine Yale O. B. combination lock, susceptible to one million different combinations. Is handsomely finished and decorated. Cabinet work is arranged as shown in the accompanying illustration.

No. 23C8856 **Dimensions:** Outside measure, 42x29x26⅝ inches; inside measure 24x18x15⅝ inches. Arrangement of cabinet work: One 6½x5½-inch iron cash box with high grade lock, with two flat keys; two 3x5⅝-inch drawers with duplicate flat key locks; two 3x5½-inch pigeonholes; one 10 9/16x5½-inch book space; one large book space, 20 1/16 x 12 1/16 inches. Shipping weight, about 1,550 pounds. Price....................**$36.00**

No. 23C8857 Same as No. 23C8856, but with extra inner steel door with high grade lock, and two flat keys. Price....................**$38.40**

Extra Large Vulcan Heavy Wall Single Door Fireproof Safes at $45.60 to $60.00.

Extra large single door Vulcan fireproof safes, massive in construction with solid 5-inch walls. Heavy reinforced wrought steel angles, our highest grade bolt work built by experts of long experience insuring absolute security. This line is suitable for large stores, country banks, public institutions, societies, town boards and other places where a roomy safe is required. Equipped with the genuine Yale O. B. combination lock, susceptible to one million changes and absolutely unpickable. The Yale O. B. lock is conceded by all safe makers to be the best in use. In this line the cabinet work is arranged as shown in the accompanying illustration.

No. 23C8860 **Dimensions:** Outside measure, 46x29⅛x30⅛ inches; inside measure, 27⅛x18⅛x17 inches. Arrangement of cabinet work, one 6½x5½-inch iron cash box with high grade lock with two flat keys; two 3⅛x6⅜-inch drawers with duplicate flat key locks; four 3x4⅛-inch pigeonholes; four 3⅛x6⅜-inch pigeonholes; two 14x6⅜-inch book spaces; one large book space 17⅛x5⅛ inches. Shipping weight, about 2,000 pounds. Price.**$45.60**

No. 23C8861 Same as No. 23C8860, but with extra inner steel door with high grade lock with two flat keys. Price....................**$48.00**

No. 23C8864 **Dimensions:** Outside measure, 51x31⅜x32⅛ inches; inside measure, 29⅛x18⅜x18 inches. Arrangement of cabinet work, one 6½x5½-inch iron cash box with high grade lock with two flat keys; two 3⅛x6⅜-inch drawers with duplicate flat key locks; four 3x4⅛-inch pigeonholes; four 3⅛x6⅜-inch pigeonholes; two 15⅜x6⅜-inch book spaces; one large book space 19⅜x5½ inches. Shipping weight, about 2,500 pounds. Price....................**$57.60**

No. 23C8865 Same as No. 23C8864, but with extra inner steel door with high grade lock and two flat keys. Price....................**$60.00**

Vulcan double door fireproof safes with massive double outside doors equipped with the genuine Yale O. B. combination lock which is absolutely unpickable and susceptible to one million changes. Has the high grade Vulcan bolt work made doubly secure with heavy top and bottom bolts. Double folding steel inside doors with high grade key lock affords additional security. Heavy 6-in. walls with wrought steel angles make this line absolutely fireproof in the hottest and most prolonged fires. Arrangement of cabinet work is shown in above illustration.

No. 23C8868 **Dimensions:** Outside measure, 47⅛x37⅛x29⅛ inches; inside measure, 26⅛x24⅜x17 inches. Arrangement of cabinet work: one 6½x5½-inch iron cash box with high grade lock with two flat keys, cash box is provided with a 3x5⅛-inch drawer; twelve pigeonholes 3x4½ inches; one pigeonhole 3x5⅛ inches; two 3x6-inch drawers with duplicate flat key locks; two 13⅛x6-inch book spaces; two large book spaces, 16⅛x6 inches. Has massive double folding outside doors and double steel inside doors. Shipping weight, about 2,300 lbs. Price.**$72.00**

Extra large size Vulcan fireproof safes with double folding outside doors equipped with the genuine Yale O. B. unpickable combination locks, a lock which defies the most expert and is susceptible to one million combinations. Extra heavy bolt work of the highest grade made doubly secure with heavy top and bottom bolts, double folding steel inside doors with high grade key lock. The massive 6 inch solid walls, the wrought steel angles, highest grade lock and bolt work, make this line unequaled for security from loss. The finish is the finest and our decorations are most artistic, making these safes a pleasing ornament, which will give tone and finish to any office or store. Arrangement of cabinet work is as shown in above illustration.

No. 23C8872 **Dimensions:** Outside measure, 55⅛x38⅛x29⅛ inches; inside measure, 34⅛x26⅛x17 inches. Arrangement of cabinet work: One 8x7-inch cash box with high grade duplicate flat key lock; cash box is provided with a 3x7-inch drawer; eight pigeonholes, 3⅛x5 inches; two pigeonholes, 2⅞x6 inches; two 3x7-inch drawers, with duplicate flat key locks; two 15⅛x4-inch book spaces; two 15⅛x6⅜-inch book spaces; two large book spaces, 18⅛x6⅛ inches. Has massive double folding outside doors and double steel inside doors. Shipping weight, about 2,800 pounds. Price....................**$90.00**

No. 23C8874 **Dimensions:** Outside measure, 61⅛x37⅛x30⅛ inches; inside measure, 40⅛x24⅜x18 inches. Arrangement of cabinet work: one 8x7-inch cash box, with high grade duplicate flat key lock; cash box is provided with a 3x7-inch drawer; eight pigeonholes, 3⅜x4⅜ inches; two pigeonholes, 2⅞x6 inches; two 3x7-inch drawers with duplicate flat key locks; two 14⅛x6 inch book spaces, two 22⅛x6-inch book spaces, two large book spaces, 25⅛x6 ins.; double folding outside doors and double steel inside doors. Shipping weight, about 3,300 lbs. Price **$102.00**

CHANGES IN CABINET WORK. We can arrange the cabinet work in any of our safes in any way desired, charging only the exact cost to us of making the change. Complete change of cabinet work usually necessitates a delay of two or three weeks in making shipment. Send us a diagram of what is wanted and we will promptly advise you what the additional cost will be, if any.

Vulcan safes cost more to build than others, more for material and more for labor. They are built to resist great strains and shocks, to be absolutely fireproof in the hottest and most prolonged fires. Our expense of selling is practically nothing. Our output is so large that our factory runs continuously. Were we to sell our safes through agents and on time, as others do, our selling expenses would be enormously increased and we would be obliged to ask double the prices we quote. In the following line the cabinet work is arranged just as shown in this illustration. All are equipped with the genuine Yale unpickable triplex combination lock.

No. 23C8820 **Dimensions:** Outside measure, 37⅜x24x22⅜ inches. Inside measure, 20⅜x15x13 inches. Arrangement of cabinet work: one 6x4⅜-inch iron cash box with high grade lock, with two flat keys; one 3x4⅜-inch drawer with knob; two 2⅜x4⅜-inch pigeonholes; one 3x4⅜-inch pigeonhole; one large book space, 14⅜x9⅜ inches; one small book space, 14⅜x4⅜ inches. Shipping weight, about 875 pounds. Price....................**$23.95**

No. 23C8821 Same as No. 23C8820, but with extra inner steel door with high grade lock and two flat keys. Price....................**$25.80**

No. 23C8824 **Dimensions:** Outside measure, 39x25x23⅜ inches. Inside measure, 22x16⅛x14 inches. Arrangement of cabinet work: one 6x4⅜-inch iron cash box with high grade lock with two flat keys; one 3x5⅜-inch drawer with knob; two 2⅜x5⅜-inch pigeonholes; one 3x5⅜-inch pigeonhole; one large book space, 15⅜x11⅛ inches; one small book space, 15⅜x4⅜ inches. Shipping weight, about 1,000 pounds. Price....................**$26.40**

No. 23C8825 Same as No. 23C8824 but with extra inner steel door with high grade lock and two flat keys. Price..... **28.20**

No. 23C8828 **Dimensions:** Outside measure, 40½x26⅜x23⅜ inches. Inside measure, 24x18x14 inches. Arrangement of cabinet work: one 6½x5½-inch iron cash box with high grade lock with two flat keys; one 3x5⅜-inch drawer with knob; two 2⅜x5⅜-inch pigeonholes; one 3x5⅜-inch pigeonhole; one large book space, 17⅜x12⅛ inches; one small book space, 17⅛ x 5⅛ inches. Shipping weight, about 1,250 pounds. Price....................**$29.40**

No. 23C8829 Same as No. 23C8828, but with extra inner steel door with high grade lock with two flat keys. Price.... **31.80**

CUTLERY DEPARTMENT.

The goods in our Cutlery Department are in finish and workmanship equal to any in the market, but our greatest effort is made to furnish goods made from good steel and tempered to cut and hold an edge. We exercise the utmost care to see that even the very lowest priced goods are the very best that can be had for the money. We sell no pot-metal trash and do not handle imperfect goods known as seconds. Our rapidly increasing sales in this department show that this is the policy that pays. All orders will be filled at prices printed in the latest edition of our catalogue.

SILVER PLATED TABLE WARE.

Silver Plated Knives and Forks.

No. 5C0166 Sears, Roebuck & Co.'s Seroco Brand Plain Medium Knives, 6-dwt. plate. Price, per dozen....................**$1.80**

No. 5C0168 Sears, Roebuck & Co.'s Seroco Brand Plain Medium Forks, 6-dwt. plate. Price, per dozen....................**$1.80**

No. 5C0170 Sears, Roebuck & Co.'s Seroco Brand Plain Medim Knives, 8-dwt. plate. Price, per dozen....................**$2.00**

No. 5C0172 Sears, Roebuck & Co.'s Seroco Brand Plain Medium Forks, 8-dwt. plate. Price, per dozen....................**$2.00**

No. 5C08104 Sears, Roebuck & Co.'s Paragon Brand Medium Knives. Price, per dozen.....**$2.60**

No. 5C08106 Sears, Roebuck & Co.'s Paragon Brand Medium Forks. Price, per dozen......**$2.60**

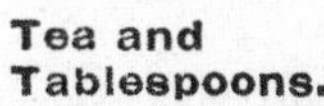

Tea and Tablespoons.

No. 5C08550 Sears, Roebuck & Co.'s Paragon Brand Plain Teaspoons. Price, per dozen....**$1.58**

No. 5C08553 Sears, Roebuck & Co.'s Paragon Brand Plain Tablespoons. Price, per dozen..**$3.16**

FOR A FULL LINE OF SILVERWARE in all makes and grades, including flat ware as well as castors, cake dishes and all hollow ware, at prices unheard of before, see our Silverware Department, pages 265 to 270.

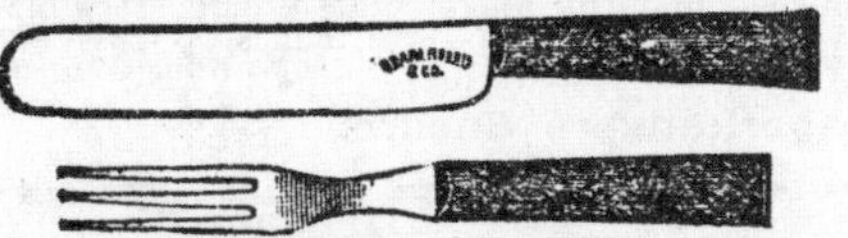

No. 28C112 Cocobolo Handle Knives and Forks, no bolster. Per set, 6 knives and 6 forks.........**37c**

No. 28C113 Knives only. Price, per dozen...**48c**

No. 28C114 White Bone Handle Knives and Forks, no bolster. Per set, 6 knives and 6 forks..**67c**

No. 28C115 Knives only. Price, per dozen...**78c**

No. 28C125 Cocobolo Handle Knives and Forks, single bolster. Per set, 6 knives and 6 forks......**55c**

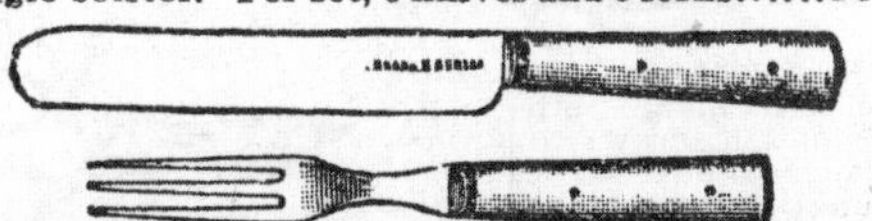

No. 28C127 White Bone Handle Knives and Forks, single bolster. Per set, 6 knives and 6 forks......**84c**

No. 28C134 Fancy Ring Pattern, Cocobolo Handle Knives and Forks, swaged scimiter blades. Price, per set, 6 knives and 6 forks............**82c**

No. 28C136 Same as No. 28C134, with white bone handles. Price, per set, 6 knives and 6 forks...**$1.15**

No. 28C143 Fancy Shape Cocobolo Handle Knives and Forks, with one cross pattern bolster. Swaged scimiter blades. Taper point handle. Price, per set, 6 knives and 6 forks..........**$1.02**

No. 28C152 Double Bolstered Cocobolo Handle Knives and Forks. Per set, 6 knives and 6 forks. **68c**

WE FURNISH KNIVES ONLY in any of the styles sold by us (unless otherwise noted in description) at 20 cents per dozen more than price of set of same knives and forks.

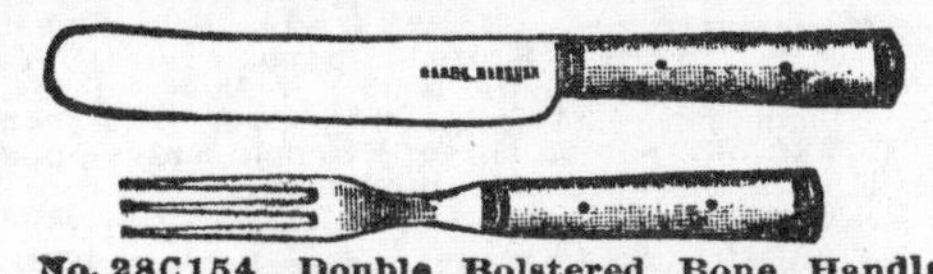

No. 28C154 Double Bolstered Bone Handle Knives and Forks. Per set, 6 knives and 6 forks. **93c**

No. 28C170 Double Ring Pattern Knives and Forks, cocobolo handles. Price, per set, 6 knives and 6 forks.............**83c**

No. 28C171 Same as No. 28C170, with ebony handles. Price, per set, 6 knives and 6 forks....**96c**

No. 28C172 Same as No. 28C170, with swaged scimiter blades, with bone handles. Price, per set, 6 knives and 6 forks.. ....**$1.25**

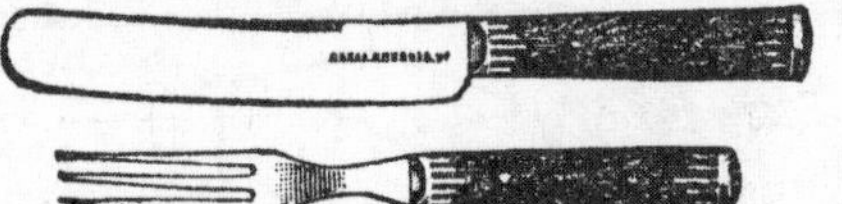

No. 28C179 German Style, Cocobolo Handle Knives and Forks, swaged scimiter blades. Price, per set, 6 knives and 6 forks..........**$1.00**

IF SENT BY MAIL, Postage on Knives and Forks is from 35 cents to 40 cents extra, per set.

No. 28C188 Cross pattern, double bolstered cocobolo handles, swaged scimiter blades, Knives and Forks. Price, per set, 6 knives and 6 forks. **$1.00**

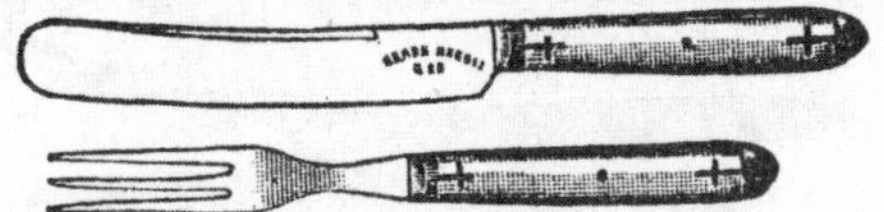

No. 28C226 Our latest style cross pattern, white bone handles, swaged scimiter blades. Price, per set, 6 knives and 6 forks..........**$1.65**

No. 28C225 Same as No. 28C226, with ebony handles. Price, per set, 6 knives and 6 forks...**$1.30**

No. 28C224 Same as No. 28C226, with cocobolo handles. Price, per set, 6 knives and 6 forks...**$1.20**

No. 28C265 Imitation Stag Handle, Double Bolster Knives and Forks, swaged scimiter blades. Price, per set, 6 knives and 6 forks..........**$1.25**

No. 28C274 White Celluloid Handle Medium Knives and Forks. Price, per set, 6 knives and 6 forks...........**$2.50**

No. 28C275 White Celluloid Handle Medium Knives only. More durable than ivory. Will not crack or change color. Ordinarily used with silver forks. Preferred to a plated knife because they can be sharpened. Price, per dozen................**$2.67**

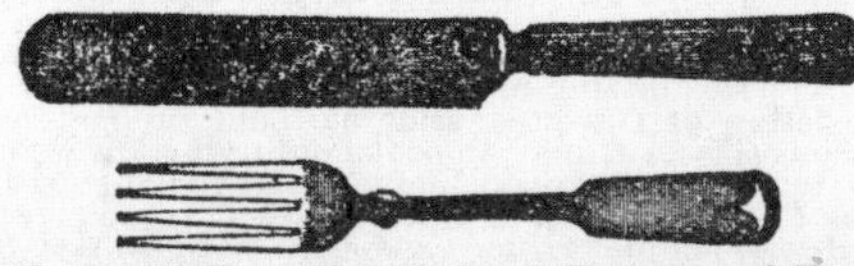

No. 28C283 Tinned Steel Knives and Forks. Forged from steel, and are heavily coated with pure block tin to prevent rust. **We do not break sets.** Price, per set, 6 knives and 6 forks.............**45c**

No. 28C284 Tinned Steel Knives only. Price, per dozen.. ....**68c**

No. 28C287 Tinned Steel Table Knives and Forks. Put up in cardboard case as illustrated. Handles of forks are same as knives. We do not break sets. Price, per set, 6 knives and 6 forks........**72c**

If by mail, postage extra, 44 cents.

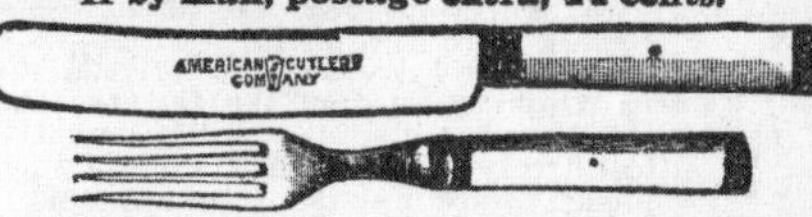

No. 28C299 White Bone Handle Knives and Four-Tined Forks. Double bolster; swaged scimiter blade. A handsome and durable article. Price, per set, 6 knives and 6 forks..........**$1.35**

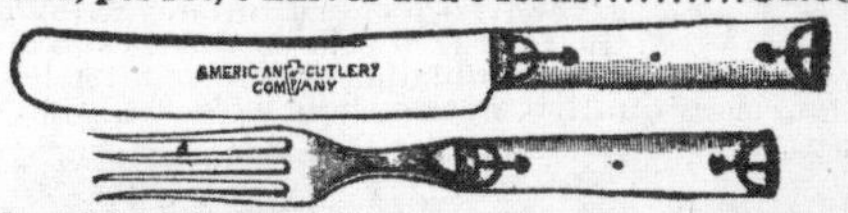

No. 28C307 White Bone Handle Knives and Four-Tined Forks. Double fancy bolsters; swaged scimiter blades. Price, per set, 6 knives and 6 forks.........**$1.58**

No. 28C304 Cocobolo Handle Knives and Four-Tined Forks. Double fancy bolster; swaged scimiter blades. Price, per set, 6 knives and 6 forks..**$1.12**

No. 28C310 Cocobolo Handle Knives and Four-Tined Forks. Double fancy bolsters; swaged scimiter blades. A very neat and attractive pattern. Price, per set, 6 knives and 6 forks..........**$1.30**

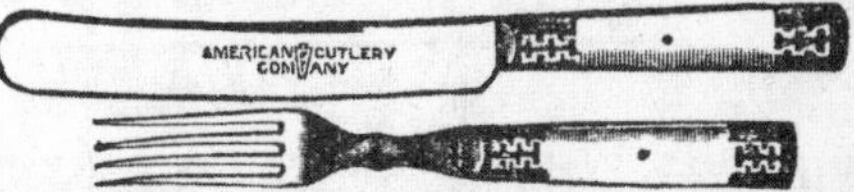

No. 28C314 White Bone Handle Knives and Four-Tined Forks. Double fancy bolster; swaged scimiter blades. Price, per set, 6 knives and 6 forks..........**$1.77**

Tea and Tablespoons.

No. 28C383 Heavy Retinned Steel Teaspoons, tipped pattern. Weight, per dozen, 9½ ounces. Price, per dozen...............**11c**

No. 28C384 Heavy Retinned Steel Tablespoons, tipped pattern. Weight, per doz., 17¾ ounces. Price, per dozen, **22c**

No. 28C386 Heavy Retinned Steel Teaspoons, fancy pattern. Wgt., per doz., 8 ounces. Price, per doz. **17c**

No. 28C387 Heavy Retinned Steel Tablespoons, fancy pattern. Weight, per doz., 20 ounces. Price, per dozen....................................**34c**

Aluminum Spoons.

These spoons are highly polished and in appearance are equal to the best solid silver goods, and as they are made of the same material throughout (having no plating to wear off) they will not tarnish nor corrode, but will have the appearance of new goods even after years of use.

No. 28C392 Cast Aluminum Tipped Teaspoons. Full size. Very finely finished. Pure as solid silver. Never wear out or tarnish. Price, per set of six..........................**28c**

If by mail, postage extra, 3 cents.

No. 28C393 Cast Aluminum Tipped Tablespoons. Full size in every way. Length, 8¼ inches. Price, per set of six......... ....**47c**

If by mail, postage extra, 7 cents.

Carving Knives and Forks.

No. 28C408 Carvers, have stag handles with solid steel bolster. The blades are 8 inches long, made from the best of steel and tempered to cut. The finish is first class and every pair is fully warranted. Price, per pair...........................**$1.25**

If by mail, postage extra, 20 cents.

Bread Knives.

No. 28C576 T. T. C. solid handle fancy bolster, best crucible steel blade slicer or bread knife. Blade is 9 inches long, made of the best crucible steel, swaged and finely polished. A better blade could not be made. Price....(Postage extra, 10c.)...**30c**

No. 28C577 T. T. C. Crackerjack Slicer, or general household knife, cocoa handle, three large head brass rivets, single bolster, clip point, swaged blade. Length of blade, 9¼ inches. The blade of this knife is made of the best crucible steel. A better blade could not be made, and it is fully guaranteed. Price....(If by mail, postage extra, 10c.)....**35c**

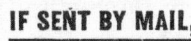

Christy Pattern Knife Sets.

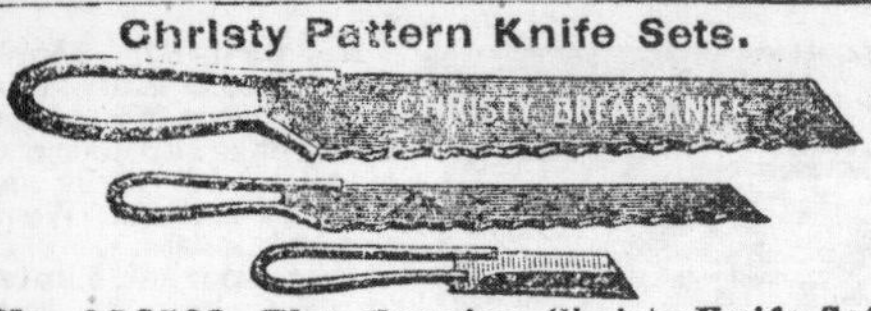

No. 28C583 The Genuine Christy Knife Sets. Every blade warranted to be made of the best cutlery steel. Bread, cake and paring knife.
Price, per set of three knives........................48c

No. 28C586 Christy Pattern Knife Sets, made of the best cold rolled nickel steel. Will give satisfaction. Handles firmly swaged to the blade and will never come loose. Set consists of bread, cake and paring knife. Price, per set of three knives......16c

Butcher Knives.

Butcher Knives are guaranteed to give satisfaction or money refunded. Nearly the total cost of these knives is in the blade. They are intended to sell on their quality, not on their looks.

No. 28C603 T. T. C. Butcher Knife. Beech handle. Fully warranted in every way.

L'gt. of blade, in.	5	5½	6	7	8	10	12
Price	10c	11c	12c	13c	16c	25c	40c

No. 28C605 T. T. C. Butcher Knife. Solid cocoa handle, fancy bolster butcher knife with best crucible steel blade, tempered to cut, swaged and highly finished. It is impossible for this blade to get loose in the handle, and as there are no joints or places for grease and dirt to collect it is the most sanitary knife ever made. It is fully warranted in every way.

Length of blade, inches	6	6½	7	8
Price	21c	23c	27c	33c

No. 28C623 Our Prussia Pattern Butcher Knife. Forged from the bar, ground and finished by hand, and fully guaranteed. It has cocobolo handle, large head brass rivets. Warranted.

Length of blade, inches	6	7	8
Price	25c	27c	30c

Kitchen Knives.

No. 28C590 Kitchen Knife, sharp point, steel ferrule, natural wood handle, steel blade. Length of blade, 3 inches. Price, per dozen, 35c; each......4c

No. 28C591 Kitchen Knife; with diagonal point, steel ferrule, natural wood handle. Length of blade, 3 inches. Price, per dozen, 35c; each...............4c

No. 28 C 592 Kitchen Knife, clip point, steel ferrule, natural wood handle. Length of blade, 3 inches. Steel blade. Price, per dozen, 35c; each..............4c

No. 28C593 Set of three Kitchen Knives, one each of the three preceding numbers.
Price, per set of three..................................10c

No. 28C594 Kitchen Knife, diagonal point, fancy curved handle, crucible steel blade. Length of blade, 3 inches. Price, per dozen, 45c; each..................5c

No. 28C595 Kitchen Knife, sharp point, walnut handle, three brass rivets, swaged blade. This knife is made of the very best crucible steel, and it's far better than any knife we have ever seen.
Price, per dozen, 68c; each..................................7c

No. 28C596 Kitchen Knife, walnut handle, three brass rivets, clip point, swaged blade. This knife is made of the best crucible steel, and will cut and hold its edge. We have never seen a better kitchen knife. Price, per dozen, 68c; each..............7c

No. 28 C589 Vegetable Parer. Takes off an even peel. Is easily sharpened and cleaned. Just the thing for Saratoga chips.
Price, per dozen, 50c; each..................................5c

No. 28C974 Emery Knife Sharpener; has nickel plated shield, whole length (including handle) 12 inches. Weight, 6 ounces. Price, per dozen, 54c; each..........................5c

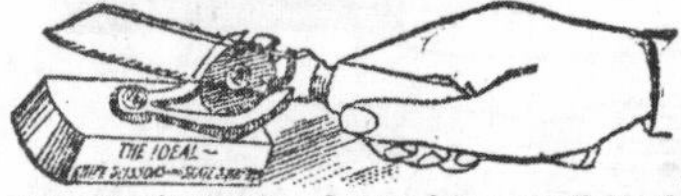

No. 28C599 Knife, Scissors and Skate Sharpener. A few seconds only is required to sharpen the kitchen knives or a pair of scissors. Screwed to a small block of wood of a suitable size for the hand, it makes a neat skate sharpener that will concave the skate runner.
Price, per gross, $4.80; per dozen, 55c; each....5c
If by mail, postage extra, each, 3 cents.

Pocket Scissors

No. 28C756 T.T.C. Pocket Scissors. They are full nickel plated and warranted.

Full lgth inches	Lgth of cut, ins.	Price
4	1¾	27c
4½	2	28c
5	2¼	29c

Barbers' Shears.

T.T.C. Barbers' Shears fit the hand perfectly and work easily and smoothly. The blades are laid with a special steel and tempered by a patent process. Every shear is highly finished and must pass a rigid inspection before leaving factory, and we fully guarantee every pair we send out to give perfect satisfaction.

No. 28C758 T. T. C. Barbers' Shears. Full nickel plated and polished; warranted.

Whole length, inches	7	7½	8	8½	9
Length of cut, inches	3	3¼	3½	3⅞	4⅛
Price, per pair	35c	38c	40c	43c	48c

No. 28C759 T. T. C. Barbers' Shears, with enameled handles and full nickel plated blades; warranted.

Whole length, inches	7	7½	8	8½	9
Length of cut, inches	3	3¼	3½	3⅞	4⅛
Price, per pair	32c	35c	36c	40c	44c

No. 28C740 T. T. C. Solid Steel Barbers' Shears. Light pattern, full nickel plated, forged from a bar of special shear steel, tempered by a patented method, and are fully warranted.

Size, inches	7	7½	8	8½	9
Length of cut, inches	3¼	3½	3¾	4	4¼
Price	45c	48c	50c	53c	56c

No. 28C741 T. T. C. Solid Steel Left Hand Barbers' Shears. Full nickel plated, light pattern. Size, 8 inches. Length of cut, 3¾ inches. Fully warranted. Price..58c

Heinisch Barbers' Shears.

No. 28C775 Heinisch Barbers' Shears. Japanned handles. Laid steel blades; warranted.

Size, inches	8	8½	9
Price	42c	45c	48c

No. 28C776 Heinisch Barbers' Shears. Finely polished and full nickel plated; laid steel blades. Every pair warranted.

Size, inches	8	8½	9
Price	59c	62c	65c

Paperhangers' Shears.

No. 28C742 T. T. C. Paperhangers' or Bankers' Shears. Nickel plated steel laid blades and enameled handles. Fully warranted.

Size, inches	10	12	14	16
Length of cut, inches	5¾	7	8⅜	10
Price	57c	72c	95c	$1.20

T.T.C. BRAND SHEARS AND SCISSORS.

OUR GUARANTEE. If they are not in every way satisfactory **they may be returned within thirty days,** and money will be refunded or another pair sent to replace them. The shape of the blades makes them very stiff. **They have steel laid blades** and are finished in a superior manner. **The fitting of the joints is as near perfect** as the highest mechanical skill and careful inspection can make it. A drop of oil should be put on the joints of shears and scissors occasionally, and the blades should be kept free from dust and grit, which quickly causes the blades to become dull. **Don't use the shears to pull carpet tacks, draw corks, lift stove lids, etc., and then expect them to cut.** While we claim our shears are the **best on earth,** they cannot be used for such purposes and give good satisfaction. **Size of shears is the entire length.**

T.T.C. Shears, Straight Trimmers.

No. 28C751 T. T. C. Shears (Straight Trimmers). Japanned handles, nickel plated steel laid blade. Will cut clear to the points and keep sharp longer than any other we know of. **Fully warranted, as explained in heading above.**

Whole length, inches	6	7	8	9	10
Length of cut	2¾	3¼	3⅞	4¼	5
Price	27c	32c	36c	43c	57c

No. 28C752 T. T. C. Shears (Straight Trimmers). Full nickel plated, otherwise like those previously quoted. While the cutting qualities are the same in all shears of our brand, the nickel plated shear is most popular because it costs but very little more and looks much nicer.

Whole length, inches	6	7	8	9	10
Length of cut	2¾	3¼	3⅞	4¼	5
Price	30c	35c	40c	48c	63c

No. 28C750 T. T. C. Left Hand Shears. Full nickel plated; fully warranted.

Size, inches	7½	8½
Length of cut, inches	3¼	3⅞
Price	43c	48c

T.T.C. Shears, Bent Trimmers.

No. 28C753 T.T.C. Shears (Bent Trimmers). Japanned handles, nickel plated steel laid blade. For use on a table or board or for following a line the bent handle shear is most convenient. **Fully warranted.**

Whole length, inches	8	9	10
Length of cut, inches	3⅞	4¼	5
Price	39c	50c	61c

No. 28C754 T. T. C. Shears (Bent Trimmers). Full nickel plated, otherwise same as described under preceding number. Will cut clear to the points. Will cut more thicknesses of cloth, will keep sharp longer than other brands. **They are fully warranted.**

Whole length, inches	8	9	10
Length of cut, inches	3⅞	4¼	5
Price	43c	55c	67c

Heinisch Straight Trimmers.

No. 28C762 Heinisch Straight Trimmers, laid steel blades, full nickel plated, fully warranted.

Size, inches	6	6½	7	7½	8	8½	9
Price	43c	48c	53c	56c	57c	63c	68c

No. 28C755 T. T. C. Ladies' Scissors are made of special steel of superior quality. Tempered, fitted and inspected with the greatest care. They are fully guaranteed both in quality and finish. Finely polished and full nickel plated. Every piece warranted.

Full length	3	3½	4	4½	5	6	7
Length of cut	1	1¼	1¾	2	2¼	2⅞	3½
Price	23c	25c	26c	27c	28c	30c	33c

Imported Scissors.

The following line of scissors, Nos. 28C782 to 28C791, are made in Europe and generally give satisfaction to the user, but they are not warranted.

No. 28C782 Buttonhole Scissors, with adjustable thumbscrew, highly polished.
Price..................................25c

No. 28C783 Buttonhole Scissors, nickel plated, with inside set screws to adjust blades for cutting, best steel. Length, 4½ inches..........35c

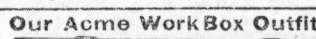

No. 28C788 Folding Pocket Scissors, in case; nickel plated; length when open, 4 inches; length folded, 2¼ inches, fair grade......20c

No. 28C791 Good Grade Folding Pocket Scissors. Same as No. 28C788, except that it is better finished and made of better material. Price...42c
If by mail, postage on scissors is from 6c to 10c.

Our Acme Work Box Outfit.

No. 28C800 Our Acme Work Box Outfit consists of a well made nicely finished hardwood box, 12⅜ inches long, 8¼ inches wide and 4⅝ inches deep with brass hinges and hasps. It contains 1 pair 10-inch bent shears, 1 pair 8-inch straight shears, 1 pair 5-inch scissors and 1 pair 3½-inch lace scissors, all of **T. T. C.** brand, nicely finished and heavily nickel plated; 1 pair good grade German buttonhole scissors, 1 tracing wheel with hollow metal handle, 1 needle case containing 4 packages gold eye needles of assorted sizes (Sharps), a tape needle, steel bodkin, crewel needles, tape needles (27 pieces;) an assortment of black head black drapery pins (14 pieces), a steel crochet needle and a package of needle pointed pins of various sizes, part of them being black; 1 set knitting needles (5 pieces), a crochet hook set consisting of two steel and one bone crochet needles of various sizes, 1 Globe pin book containing 8 rows of needle pointed pins (one row being black) of various sizes, 1 package of 24 safety pins of assorted sizes, 1 package of finest quality mending tissue, 1 spool (100 yards) black linen finished thread, 1 spool (500 yards) white basting cotton, 1 spool (200 yards (best six-cord white cotton thread, 1 spool (50 yards) Corticelli sewing silk, 2 German silver gilt thimbles with fancy tricolor band, medium and large sizes. Price for complete outfit in handsome and durable box as described..$3.00

No. 28C801 Our Acme Work Box, empty..50

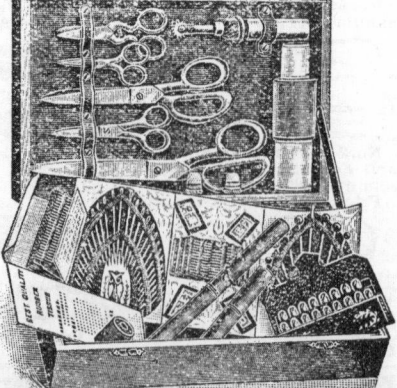

NEW POCKET KNIVES DIRECT FROM OUR OWN FACTORY.

WE CALL YOUR ATTENTION ESPECIALLY to this line of highest grade American made pocket and penknives, our  brand.

THE BLADES ARE FORGED from S. C. Wardlow's best English special blade steel, the finest and the best that can be procured for knife blades. We also use Wardlow's steel for the springs, which costs nearly double the price at which ordinary spring steel can be bought, but which greatly improves the wearing qualities of the knife and adds greatly to its durability. **Every blade, from the cheapest to the best, which bears our brand, is hammered out by hand.** Instead of using iron for the lining of our cheaper knives, we pay more for steel because it makes a much stronger and better knife. All work is done by skilled mechanics, particular attention being paid to making a keen cutting knife that will carry a lasting edge.

OUR POCKET KNIVES are fully guaranteed in every way. This means we guarantee the blades to be free from flaws, and guarantee them to be neither too hard nor too soft. This does not mean that we guarantee the knives not to break. If we were to do this, we would be obliged to temper them so soft they would be of no practical use for cutting. They are not intended to be used as mortising chisels, tack pullers, can openers, screwdrivers, crowbars, nor for any of the purposes by which pocket knives are frequently misused.

ALL POCKET KNIVES should occasionally be oiled at the joint so the blade will not wear into the spring. Vaseline makes a very good lubricant for this purpose.

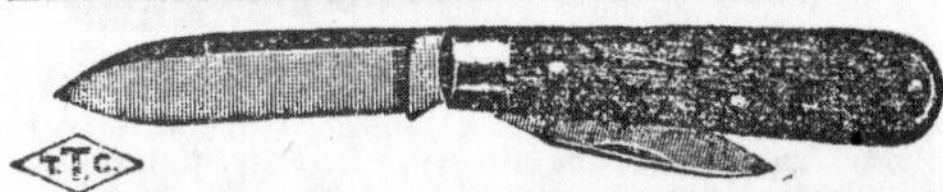

No. 28C830 T. T. C. Pocket Knife. Has rosewood handle, steel lining, iron bolster. Length of handle, 3⅜ inches. Length with large blade open, 6 inches. Price....................18c
If by mail, postage extra, 4 cents.

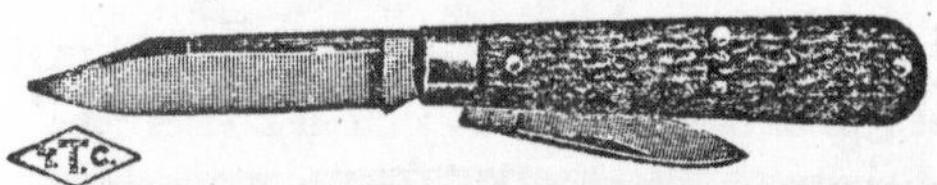

No. 28C833 T. T. C. Pocket Knife, clip point, stag handle, two blades, steel lining, iron bolster. This is a standard size full weight knife; is durable, and will give splendid satisfaction. Length of handle, 3⅜ inches. Length with large blade open, 6⅛ inches. Price....................20c
If by mail, postage extra, 5 cents.

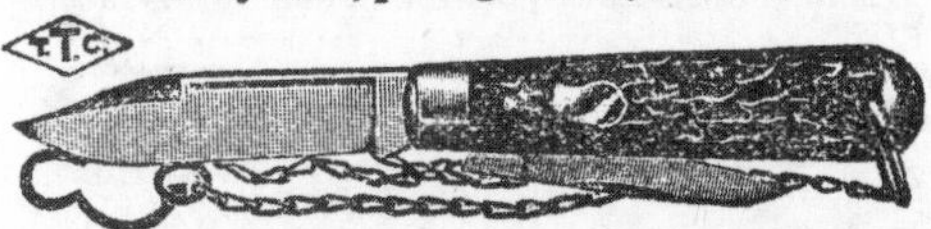

No. 28C838 T. T. C. Stag Handle Chain Knife, clip point, two blades, steel lining, iron bolster and caps, German silver shield, with chain of suitable length to fasten over button. Length of handle, 3⅝ inches. Length with large blade open, 6¼ inches.
Price...(If by mail, postage extra, 6 cents)....35c

No. 28C840 A medium weight, finely finished **T. T. C. Knife, with white bone handle,** brass lining, finished inside and out, German silver bolster, caps and shield. Length of handle, 3⅝ inches. Length with large blade open, 6⅛ inches.
Price...(If by mail, postage extra, 5 cents)....39c

No. 28C842 T. T. C. Jack Knife, stag handle, swell butt, steel lining, iron bolsters, German silver shield. Length of handle, 3⅝ inches. Length with large blade open, 6⅛ inches. Price............35c
If by mail, postage extra, 5 cents.

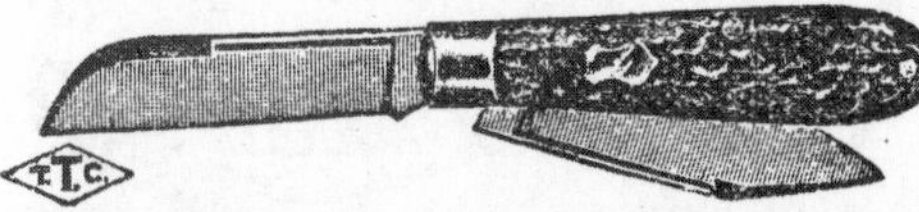

No. 28C847 T. T. C. Carpenters' Sensible Knife, having two large blades, one with clip point and one sheep's foot or carpenter's marking blade. The blades of this knife are made of 11-gauge steel; has stag handle, steel lining, iron bolsters, German silver shields, finished inside and out. Length of handle, 3¾ inches. Length with large blade open, 6¼ inches.
Price...(If by mail, postage extra, 6 cents)....43c

No. 28C850 T. T. C. Easy Opener Pocket Knife, with stag handle, German silver bolster, caps and shield, brass lining. Finished inside and out. Length of handle, 3½ inches. Length with large blade open, 6⅛ inches. Price....................47c
If by mail, postage extra, 6 cents.

No. 28C861 T. T. C. Gentlemen's Jack Knife, stag handle, German silver bolster, caps and shield, brass lining, thoroughly finished in every particular inside and out. Length of handle, 3¼ inches. Length with large blade open, 5¾ inches. Price..........42c
If by mail, postage extra, 5 cents.

No. 28C864 T. T. C. Equal End Pocket Knife, has cocoa handle, German silver bolster, caps and shield, brass lined, finished inside and out. Length of handle, 3¼ inches. Length with large blade open, 5¾ inches. Price....................40c
If by mail, postage extra, 5 cents.

No. 28C895 T. T. C. Texas Toothpick, has stag handle, German silver bolsters and shield, brass lining, finely finished inside and out. Clip point saber blade. While the blade is long and slim, the peculiar shape makes it very strong and durable as well as an excellent whittler. Length of handle, 3⅞ inches; length with large blade open, 6⅞ inches.
Price....................45c
If by mail, postage extra, 6 cents.

No. 28C875 T. T. C. Balloon Shaped Knife, stag handle, fancy German silver bolster, caps and shield, brass lining, finished inside and out. Length of handle, 3⅝ inches. Length with large blade open, 6⅛ inches. Price....................53c
If by mail, postage extra, 6 cents.

Pearl Handle Knife.

No. 28C869 T. T. C. Gentlemen's Pearl Handle Jack Knife. Has pearl handle, German silver bolster, caps and shield, German silver lining, satin finish. The blades are full crocus polished. The knife is in every way finished as finely as the best penknife you ever saw. Length of handle, 3¼ inches; length with large blade open, 5¾ inches. Price.........90c
If by mail, postage extra, 5 cents.

No. 28C856 T. T. C. Equal End Jack Knife. Has cocoa handle, brass lining, finished inside and out, German silver bolster, caps and shield. Length of handle, 3½ inches; length with large blade open, 6⅛ inches. Price....................42c
If by mail, postage extra, 6 cents.

No. 28C857 T. T. C. Equal End Knife, has stag handle, brass lining, German silver bolster, cap and shield. Length of handle, 3½ inches; length with large blade open, 6⅛ inches. Price....................45c
If by mail, postage extra, 6 cents.

No. 28C866 T. T. C. Little Giant Equal End Pocket Knife, with saber clip blade, stag handle, German silver bolster, caps and shield, brass lined, finished inside and out. The amount of work which this knife will do is something never before attained in a knife of its size. Length of handle, 3¼ inches; length with large blade open, 5⅝ inches. Price...43c
If by mail, postage extra, 5 cents.

No. 28C908 T. T. C. Missouri Favorite, has clip point saber blade made of full 12-gauge steel. Has ebony handle, long German silver bolsters, caps and shield, brass lined, finished inside and out. Length of handle, 3⅝ inches; length with large blade open, 6 inches. Price....................50c
If by mail, postage extra, 6 cents.

No. 28C845 T. T. C. Solid Worth Jack Knife, Stag handle, brass lining, finished inside and out, iron bolsters and caps, German silver shield. Length of handle, 3⅝ inches; length with large blade open, 6¼ inches. Price....................40c
If by mail, postage extra, 6 cents.

No. 28C886 T. T. C. Jumbo Pocket Knife, with ebony handle 4 inches long; German silver bolster and shield, brass lined, finished inside and out. The blades are made of full size 10-gauge steel. This is a big, strong, heavy, durable knife. Length of handle, 4 inches; length with large blade open, 6⅞ inches. Price....................43c
If by mail, postage extra, 6 cents.

No. 28C896 T. T. C. Austrian Hunter. It has a clip point blade, stag handle, fancy iron bolster and caps, German silver shield, steel lining, finely finished inside and out. Length of handle, 3¾ inches; length with large blade open, 7 inches. Price..75c
If by mail, postage extra, 6 cents.

No. 28C920 T. T. C. Hunter's Pride Knife. It has stag handle, long, heavy German silver bolsters, caps and shield, brass lining, highly finished inside and out. Length of handle, 4½ inches; length with large blade open, 8 inches.
Price..(If by mail, postage extra, 6 cents)..60c

No. 28C945 T. T. C. Arkansas Hunter. A knife in which nearly every cent of the cost is spent in quality, and not looks. It has clip point saber blade, flush lock back so blade cannot shut on the fingers, curved stag handle which just fits the hand nicely, fancy iron bolsters, steel lining. Length of handle, 4½ inches; length with blade open, 8⅛ inches.
Price....................65c
If by mail, postage extra, 7 cents.

No. 28C946 T. T. C. Hudson Bay Hunting Knife A very nicely finished hunting knife. Clip point saber blade, flush lock back, curved stag handle, fancy German silver bolster, caps and lining. Length of handle, 5¼ inches; length with blade open, 9⅝ inches. Price....................$1.00
If by mail, postage extra, 8 cents.

For other Hunting Knives and a full line of Hunters' Goods, see Sporting Goods Department.

No. 28C884 T. T. C. Sampson Pruning Knife. Blade made of 10-gauge steel. The shape of blade, method of grinding, etc., being according to the ideas of one of the best fruit growers in the country, made just exactly the way he wanted it regardless of expense. Length of handle, 4 inches; length with blade open, 7 inches.
Price..(If by mail, postage extra, 6 cents)...35c

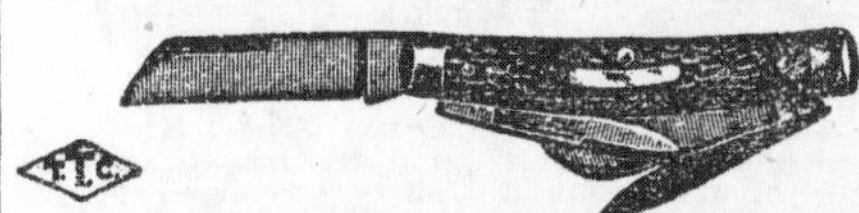

No. 28C980 T. T. C. Large Congress Knife, has two large blades and two pen blades, stag handle, German silver bolsters and shield, brass lined, nicely finished throughout. Length of handle, 3⅝ inches; length with large blade open, 6 inches.
Price...(If by mail, postage extra, 5 cents)..74c

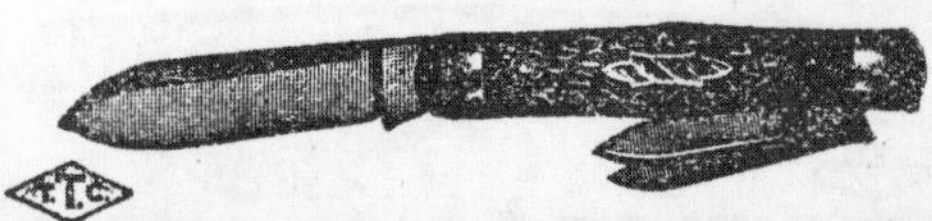

No. 28C969 T. T. C. Compact Three-Blade Pocket Knife. The large blade is wide and strong; has two pen blades, stag handle, German silver bolsters and shield, brass lining, finely finished inside and out. Length of handle, 3⅝ inches; length with large blade open, 5⅝ inches. Price....................65c
If by mail, postage extra, 5 cents.

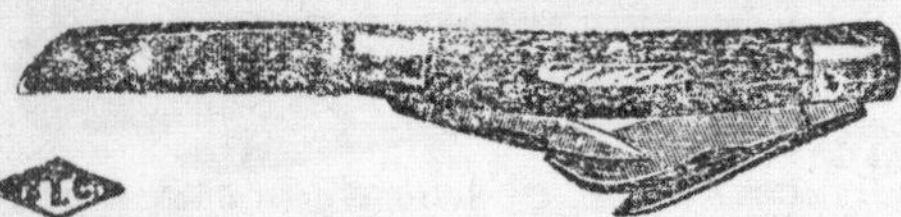

No. 28C983 T. T. C. Jumbo Congress Knife, with two large blades and two pen blades. Stag handle, iron bolsters, German silver shield, steel lined. Finely finished. Those who prefer a congress pattern knife and want something strong and heavy will find this a most desirable pattern. Length of handle, 4⅛ inches; length with large blade open, 6⅞ inches. Price 75c
If by mail, postage extra, 5 cents.

No. 28C925 T. T. C. New England Workmen's Knife. A great favorite with carpenters, cabinetmakers and other woodworkers. It has stag handle, German silver bolster and shield, brass lining, finely finished, and polished inside and out. Length of handle, 3⅝ inches; length with large blade open, 6 inches. Price ..(If by mail, postage extra, 4 cents).....50c

No. 28C890 T. T. C. Favorite Double Ender, with spear and clip point blades. Stag handle. German silver fancy bolsters and shield, brass lined and finished inside and out. Length of handle, 3⅝ inches; length with clip point blade open, 5⅞ inches. Price....(Postage extra, 5 cents).....55c

IF A RAZOR EDGE is put on any of the **T. T. C.** blades we will guarantee any of them to shave, but a razor edge should never be put on a pocket knife. To get a proper edge on a pocket knife blade, the blade should be held at an angle of about 20 or 25 degrees, and drawn from shoulder to point on each side until a true edge is obtained. This makes a stiff, keen cutting edge, and enables us to furnish a much higher tempered knife blade than we would were the blade to be laid flat and brought down to a razor edge.

No. 28C892 T. T. C. Western Chief. Has clip point saber blade, very heavy, made of full 10-gauge steel; has stag handle, German silver bolsters and shield, brass lining, finished inside and out. The large blade has a flush lock back, which prevents the blade from closing on the hand. Length of handle, 4 inches; length with large blade open, 8⅝ inches. Price..(Postage extra, 6 cents)......95c

No. 28C911 T. T. C. Junior Cattle Knife. Has spear, pen and sheep's foot blades. It has stag handle, German silver bolster and shield, brass lining, finished inside and out. Length of handle, 3⅛ inches; length with large blade open, 5⅜ inches. Price ...(If by mail, postage extra, 5 cents)....60c

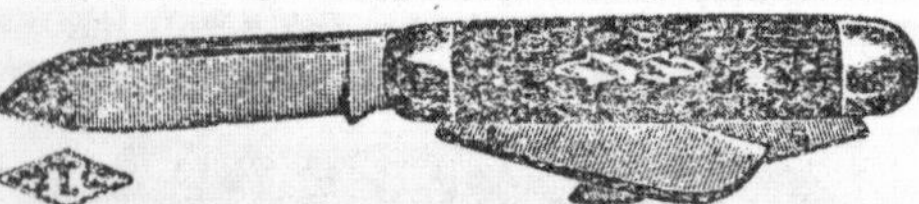

No. 28C913 T. T. C. Wild West Cowboys' Knife Has spear, sheep's foot and pen blades, stag handle, iron bolsters, German silver shield, brass lined; finished inside and out. This is a strong, heavy knife, and is a great favorite with stockmen, hunters, trappers and others who wish a strong, heavy knife in as compact form as possible. Length of handle, 3⅝ inches; length with large blade open, 6¼ inches. Price.......................65c
If by mail, postage extra, 6 cents.

No. 28C881 T. T. C. Texas Stock Knife. A pattern of knife which is popular with stock raisers all over the world, has clip, sheep's foot and spaying blades, stag handle, German silver bolsters and shield, brass lined, highly finished inside and out. This is our most popular cattle knife, and is made just as good as we know how to make them. Length of handle, 4 inches; length with clip point blade open, 6⅞ inches. Price..........................75c
If by mail, postage extra, 5 cents.

No. 28C899 T. T. C. Ranchero Cattle Knife. Has pearl handle, German silver bolsters and shield, German silver lining, satin finish. The blades are full crocus polished. It cannot fail to give satisfaction to those who want a knife of superior cutting qualities, workmanship and beauty. Length of handle, 3⅝ inches; length with large blade open, 6⅜ inches. Price..(Postage extra, 5 cents)....$1.35

No. 28C901 T. T. C. Montana Beauty Stockmen's Knife. Has clip, sheep's foot and spaying blades, pearl handle, German silver lining, satin finish; the blades are beautifully crocus polished. In our ordinary grades of knives, knives which must sell at popular prices, we pay very much more attention to quality and workmanship than we do to beauty and finish, but in this particular knife we excel all others in finish as well as in quality. Length of handle, 3⅞ inches; length with large blade open, 6⅜ inches. Price...(If by mail, postage extra, 5c)......$1.50

No. 28C954 T. T. C. Popular School or Ladies' Knife. Pearl handle, German silver bolsters and lining, finished inside. Length of handle, 2⅞ inches; length with large blade open, 4⅝ inches. Price..........................50c
If by mail, postage extra, 3 cents.

No. 28C961 T. T. C. Four-Blade Stag Handle Senator Pattern Penknife, with large blade, two pen blades and nail blade, stag handle, German silver tips and shield, brass lining, finely finished inside and out, all blades full crocus polished. Length of handle, 3¼ inches; length with large blade open, 5¼ inches. Price..........................65c
If by mail, postage extra, 4 cents.

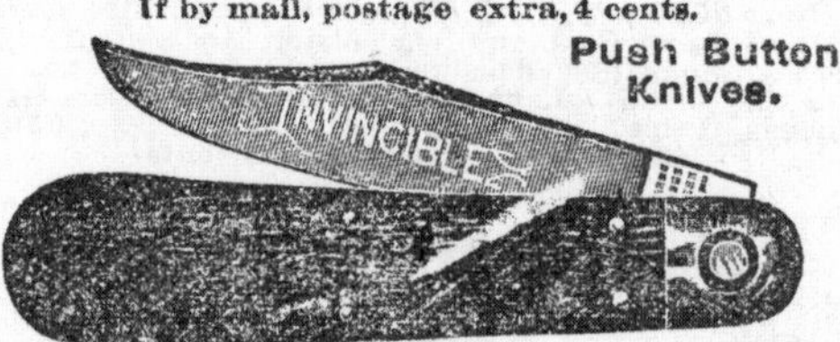

No. 28C962 T. T. C. Small Congress Knife, has one large blade, two pen blades and one nail blade, stag handle, German silver bolsters and shield, brass lined, finely finished throughout. Length of handle, 3⅛ inches; length with large blade open, 5⅝ inches. Price..................70c
If by mail, postage extra, 4 cents.

Push Button Knives.

No. 28C1324 Push Button Knife. One blade, clip point, stag handle, single bolster, iron lined. Length of handle, 4⅝ inches; length with blade open, 8⅝ inches. Price..........................66c
If by mail, postage extra, 5 cents.

No. 28C1320 Push Button Knife. One blade, clip point, stag handle, single bolster, iron lined. Length of handle, 3⅞ inches; length with blade open, 6⅞ inches. Price..........................57c
If by mail, postage extra, 5 cents.

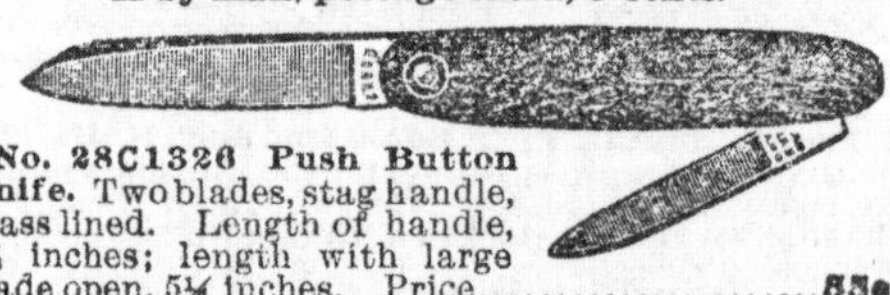

No. 28C1326 Push Button Knife. Two blades, stag handle, brass lined. Length of handle, 3⅝ inches; length with large blade open, 5¼ inches. Price..........................53c
If by mail, postage extra, 4 cents.

No. 28C1136 Combination Knife. Has stag handle, German silver bolsters, steel lining, spear blade, reaming awl, hoof cleaver, screwdriver, wire cutter, pliers and wrench. All tools are practical and serviceable. Warranted. Length of handle, 4½ inches. Price..........................98c
If by mail, postage extra, 6 cents.

Genuine Imported Swedish Hunting Knives.

Blade can be removed, folded into its frame, and replaced in the handle. This knife is a popular woodworkers' tool, as well as a hunting knife. Has solid boxwood handle. **The blade is best of steel, and cutting qualities and temper are fully guaranteed.**

No. 28C1301 Genuine Imported Swedish Hunting Knife, as described above. Length of handle, 2⅞ inches. Price..........................38c
No. 28C1302 Genuine Imported Swedish Hunting Knife, as described above. Length of handle, 3¼ inches. Price..........................45c
No. 28C1303 Genuine Imported Swedish Hunting Knife, as described above. Length of handle, 4⅝ inches. Price..........................50c
If by mail, postage extra, 6 cents.

Geo. Wostenholm & Sons' I X L Pocket Knives.

We show some of the most desirable patterns of George Wostenholm & Sons' Celebrated IXL Pocket Knives, which are favorably known all over the world.
If by mail, postage extra, 6 cents.

No. 28C1138 George Wostenholm & Sons' Genuine IXL Pocket Knife; ebony handle, German silver bolster, brass lined. Length of handle, 3⅝ inches. Price..........................52c

No. 28C1140 George Wostenholm & Sons' IXL Pocket Knife; genuine stag handle, German silver bolster and shield, brass lined. Length of handle, 3⅝ inches. Price..........................57c

No. 28C1142 George Wostenholm & Sons' IXL Pocket Knife; genuine stag handle, iron bolster, iron lined. Length of handle, 3⅞ inches. Price..66c

No. 28C1144 George Wostenholm & Sons' IXL Pocket Knife; stag handle, German silver bolsters and shield, brass lined. Length of handle, 3⅝ inches. Price..........................75c

No. 28C1146 George Wostenholm & Sons' IXL Pocket Knife; cocobolo handle, German silver bolster and shield, brass lined, finely etched. Length of handle, 3⅞ inches. Price..........................70c

No. 28C1148 George Wostenholm & Sons' IXL Cattle Knife; genuine stag handle, German silver bolsters and shield, brass lined. Length of handle, 3⅝ inches. This knife has spear, sheep's foot and pen blades. Price..........................$1.34

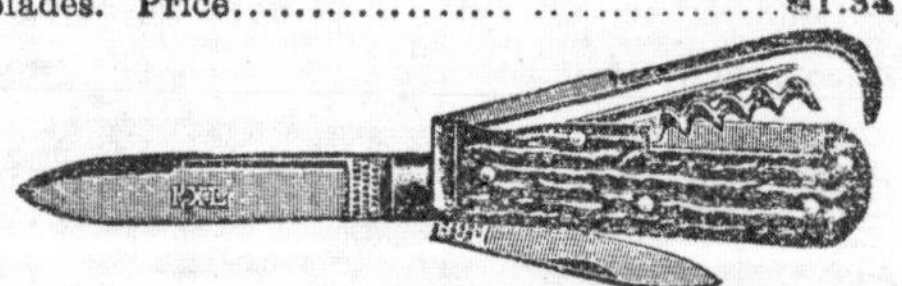

No. 28C1150 George Wostenholm & Sons' IXL Sportsmen's Knife; genuine stag handle, iron bolster, iron lined. Length of handle, 3⅞ inches. This knife has spear and pen blades, hoof cleaner, nut crack, champagne opener, corkscrew and reamer. Price..........................$1.47

No. 28C1152 George Wostenholm & Sons' IXL Congress Knife; stag handle. This knife has sheep's foot blade, two pen blades and nail blade, iron bolsters, brass lining. Length of handle, 4⅛ inches. Price..........................$1.24

No. 28C1154 George Wostenholm & Sons' IXL Lock Back Hunting Knife; stag handle, iron bolster, iron lining, saber clip point blade. Length of handle, 4⅝ inches. Price..........................70c

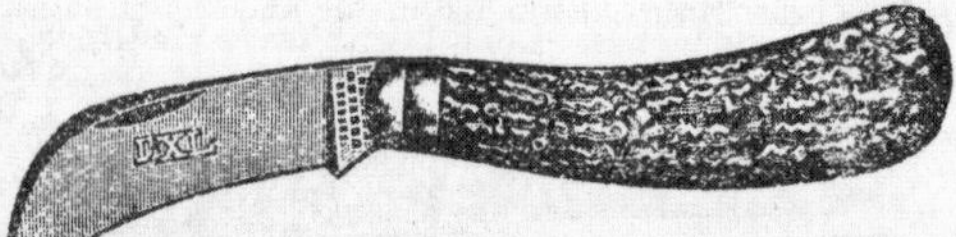

No. 28C1156 George Wostenholm & Sons' IXL Pruning Knife; genuine stag handle, iron bolster, iron lining. Length of handle, 4⅝ inches. Price, 97c
No. 28C1158 George Wostenholm & Sons' IXL Pruning Knife; same as above, except has cocobolo handle. Price..........................80c

No. 28C1160 George Wostenholm & Sons' I X L Pen Knife; stag handle, German silver tips and bolster, brass lined. Length of handle, 3 inches. This knife has spear and pen blades. Price......76c

No. 28C1162 George Wostenholm & Sons' I X L Pen Knife; stag handle, German silver tips and shield, pen blade and fancy nail blade. Length of handle, 2⅞ inches. Price......80c

No. 28C1164 George Wostenholm & Sons Medium Size Congress Knife; stag handle, iron bolster, brass lining. Length of handle, 3½ inches. This knife has sheep's foot, two pen and one nail blade. Price......$1.07

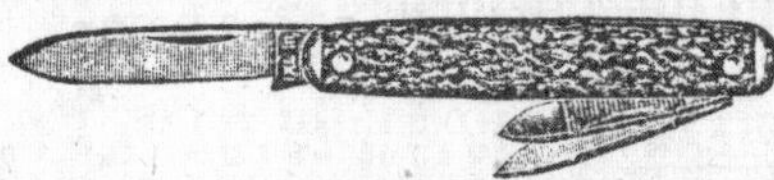

No. 28C1166 George Wostenholm & Sons' Pen Knife; stag handle, German silver tips, brass lined. Length of handle, 3 inches. This knife has spear, pen and nail blades. Price......$1.08

No. 28C1168 George Wostenholm & Sons' Pen Knife; pearl handle, German silver tips, brass lined. Length of handle, 3 inches. This knife has spear and pen blades. Price......$1.25

No. 28C1170 George Wostenholm & Sons' IXL Pen Knife; pearl handle, German silver tips and shield, brass lined. Length of handle, 3 inches. This knife has spear, pen and nail blades. Price....$1.60

No. 28C1172 George Wostenholm & Sons' IXL Physicians' Knife; buffalo horn handle, German silver bolster and butt, brass lined. Length of handle, 3¾ inches. This knife has spear and pen blades. Price......$1.04

IMPORTED KNIVES.

The following pocket knives are imported from Europe and are not guaranteed. In order that our customers may not be misled, we have described them as good, fair and cheap. The cheap grade is good for the price, but the price is not enough for a good knife. Fair will usually give satisfaction. The good grades are commonly sold as warranted, but we do not warrant them. Any of these goods will be better value than you can secure elsewhere for the same money.

No. 28C1004 Ebony Handle Knife, one blade, iron lined; blade, 2⅝ inches. Cheap grade. Price......5c
If by mail, postage extra, 4 cents.

No. 28C1021 A well finished, fair grade, single blade, Boys' Jack Knife. Length of handle, 3⅛ inches; length with large blade open, 5⅝ inches. Rosewood handle, iron lined. Price......9c

No. 28C1012 White Bone Handle Jack Knife, two blades, iron lined. Cheap grade knife, 2¾ inches. Price......8c
If by mail, postage extra, 5 cents.

No. 28C1020 Boys' White Bone Handle Knife, with bolster. Two blades, iron lined, 3½ inches. Cheap grade. Price......15c
If by mail, postage extra, 6 cents.

No. 28C1026 A well finished, fair grade, German Jack Knife; length of handle, 3½ inches, dogwood handle, two blades. Price......18c

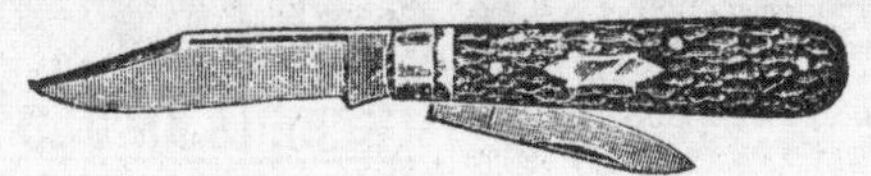

No. 28C1030 Stag Clip. A fair grade German knife. Stag handle, clip blade. Entire length open, 6¼ inches; length of handle, 3⅝ inches. Price . 18c

20-Cent Easy Opening Knife.

No. 28C1024 This Knife has the easy opening feature, which saves the finger nails, and an 18-inch security chain, which prevents loss. Has two blades, stag handle and is iron lined. Length of handle, 3¼ inches; length with large blade open, 6 inches. A fair grade German knife. Price......20c
If by mail, postage extra, 6 cents.

No. 28C1025 Another Easy Opening Security Knife, the same as No. 28C1024, but with cocoa handle, which, being smooth, is preferred by many. Length of handle, 3¼ inches; length with large blade open, 6 inches. Price......20c
If by mail, postage extra, 6 cents.

No. 28C1032 Stockmen's Knife. Three blades, stag handle, brass lined. Length of handle, 4 inches; length with large blade open, 7 inches. This is a good grade German knife, though we do not warrant it. Price......40c

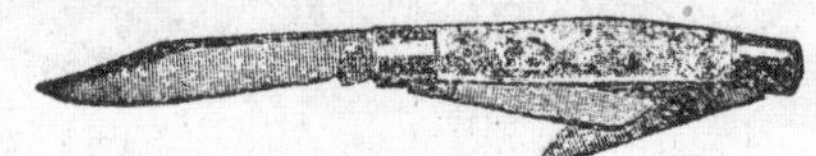

No. 28C1034 Pearl Handle, Three-Blade Small Cattle Knife. Length of handle, 3¼ inches; length with large blade open, 5⅞ inches. Finely finished and a good grade knife, but not warranted. Price......75c

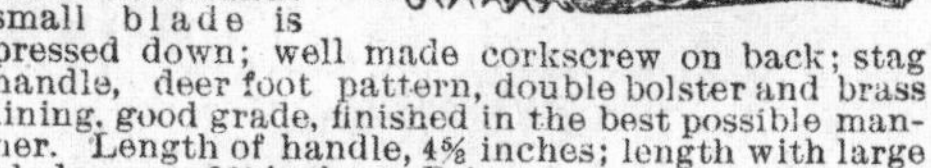

No. 28C1028 Has one small blade and one large clip point blade which cannot be closed until small blade is pressed down; well made corkscrew on back; stag handle, deer foot pattern, double bolster and brass lining, good grade, finished in the best possible manner. Length of handle, 4⅝ inches; length with large blade open, 8⅜ inches. Price......70c

No. 28C1500 Ladies' Two-Blade Pearl Handle Penknife, brass lined. Length of handle, 2⅝ inches; a pretty knife. Price......15c

No. 28C1505 Ladies' Two-Blade Corrugated Pearl Handle Penknife, polished steel blades, and a beauty. Length, 2¾ inches. Price......30c

No. 28C1510 Ladies' Two-Blade Penknife. Good grade; pearl handle, brass lined, finely finished. Length of handle, 2¾ inches. Price......28c

No. 28C1512 Two-Blade Pearl Handle Penknife. Good grade; German make. Length of handle, 3⅛ inches; length with large blade open, 5 inches. Good value for the money. Price......40c

No. 28C1515 Three-Blade Pearl Handle Penknife with nail blade. Length of handle, 3¼ inches; length with large blade open, 5¼ inches. Fair grade; not warranted. Price......50c

No. 28C1519 A Good Grade German Penknife. Pearl handle, three blades with fancy long nail blade. Length of handle, 3 inches; length with large blade open, 4⅞ inches. Price......65c

No. 28C1520 A three-blade with one nail blade, pearl handle, high grade German penknife. Finely finished. Length of handle, 3 inches; length with large blade open, 5⅛ inches. This is an extra good grade German knife, but we do not warrant it. Price......75c

No. 28C1507 A Medium Grade German Penknife, three blades, one nail blade, stag handle, iron lined. Length of handle, 3⅜ inches; length with large blade open, 5⅛ inches. Not warranted. Price......25c

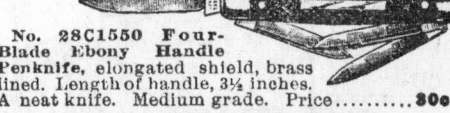

No. 28C1508 A Medium Grade German Penknife, four blades, stag handle, Congress pattern. Length of handle, 3¼ inches; length with large blade open, 5⅝ inches. Not warranted. Price.25c

No. 28C1550 Four-Blade Ebony Handle Penknife, elongated shield, brass lined. Length of handle, 3¼ inches. A neat knife. Medium grade. Price......30c

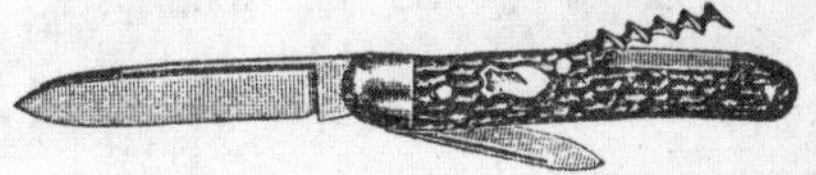

No. 28C1509 A Medium Grade German Penknife, four blades, stag handle. Length of handle, 3¼ inches; length with large blade open, 5⅝ inches. Not warranted. Price......28c

No. 28C1513 Stag Handle Corkscrew Knife. Length of handle, 3½ inches; length with large blade open, 6 inches. A good grade knife, but not warranted. Price......45c

No. 28C1517 A Good Grade German Penknife; not warranted. Length of handle, 3⅜ inches; length with large blade open, 5⅞ inches. Three blades. One pen blade. Brass lined. Price......38c

Cheap Assorted Knives, $1.25 per Dozen.

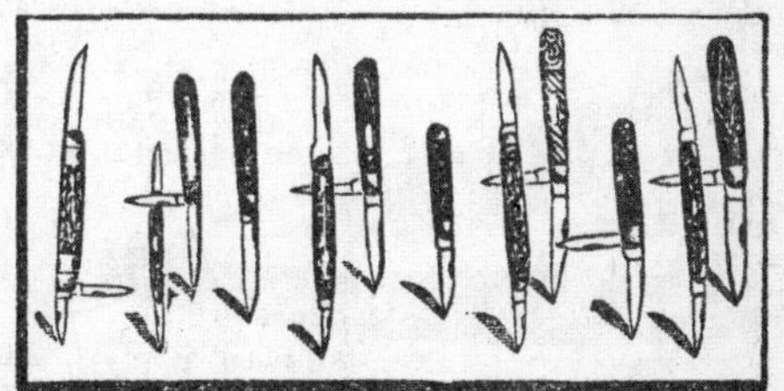

No.28C1332 Assorted Knives. We have had many calls for cheap knives for knife racks, and we furnish an assortment of twelve styles of knives suitable for this purpose. **We do not sell less than a dozen and do not break dozens.** They are as good or better than the class of goods usually sold for this purpose, but they are not good enough for our customers to use.
Price, per dozen assorted......$1.25

We can furnish rack knives at $1.50, $2.00 $2.50, $3.00, $3.50 or $4.00 per dozen, if a better assortment is desired.

No. 28C1334 Wood Rings for Knife Racks. Price, per dozen......10c

Pocket Emery Hone.

No. 28C1676 Pocket Emery Hone. A fine emery knife hone in case. Price......9c

Knife Purses.

No. 28C1678 Leather Knife Purse. For knives having handles not longer than 4¼ inches. Give length of handle of knife you intend to carry in purse. When ordered with knife, we send purse to fit. Price..6c

SOME FACTS ABOUT A RAZOR.

A GREAT MANY PEOPLE spoil a good razor by the use of a poor strop. The majority of people strop a razor too much and bear too hard on the strop.

WHEN YOU FIRST GET A RAZOR FROM US, it is in perfect condition and ready to use at once. If it shaves you well the first time you use it, if you keep it in the same condition, it will always shave you satisfactorily. If at first you are unable to do this, you should at once learn how to keep your razor in good condition. The first thing is to get a good strop. Hold the blade lightly and evenly on the strop, being careful not to drop the hand toward the end of the stroke. Dropping the hand pulls the edge of the razor across the rough edge of the strop, which usually holds more or less dust or grit, and will quickly ruin the edge of any razor.

DO NOT STROP THE RAZOR TOO MUCH.

IF ANY OF OUR RAZORS are properly cared for, they should never require honing for private use. When one of our razors shows the need of honing, it also shows that the razor has been stropped too much, or stropped on a poor strop. Dust on a good strop will spoil a razor. It is quite a common practice to use a swing strop, having it hung up in some convenient place where dust will settle on it. Then if you take a cloth and wipe off this dust, still there is enough grit that cannot be removed, to affect the edge of the razor. The strop should be kept as free as possible from dust.

THERE IS AN OLD ADAGE, that the man who is well lathered is half shaved. Any man's beard will collect dust and grit that will spoil the edge of a razor. It is a good plan to thoroughly wash the face before commencing to apply the lather. Use good soap and rub the lather well on the skin. Five minutes spent in rubbing in the lather will make a big difference in the comfort of your shave. The razor blade should be laid as nearly flat as possible when shaving and given a slightly drawing motion from point to heel. This requires considerable practice to enable one to do it nicely without danger of cutting oneself. The proper use of a razor is to cut and not scrape. You never will shave with the extreme of comfort until you learn to hold the razor blade in the proper position, and give it a drawing motion.

Now as before stated, every razor that we send out is stropped and ready for use, and should shave satisfactorily the first time you use it. If it does not, it never will and you should return it to us at once, giving us the following information:

- How many years have you shaved?
- How often do you shave?
- What is the color of your beard?
- Is your beard fine or coarse?
- Is your beard hard or soft?
- Is your skin tender?
- Do you have a "GOOD" strop?

Answers to these questions will help us in making a selection of a razor to suit you. As a rule, it is not necessary to select some other style of razor. The same style razor with the edge either a little stiffer or not quite so stiff as your answers indicate would be likely to give you entire satisfaction.

T.T.C. RAZORS.

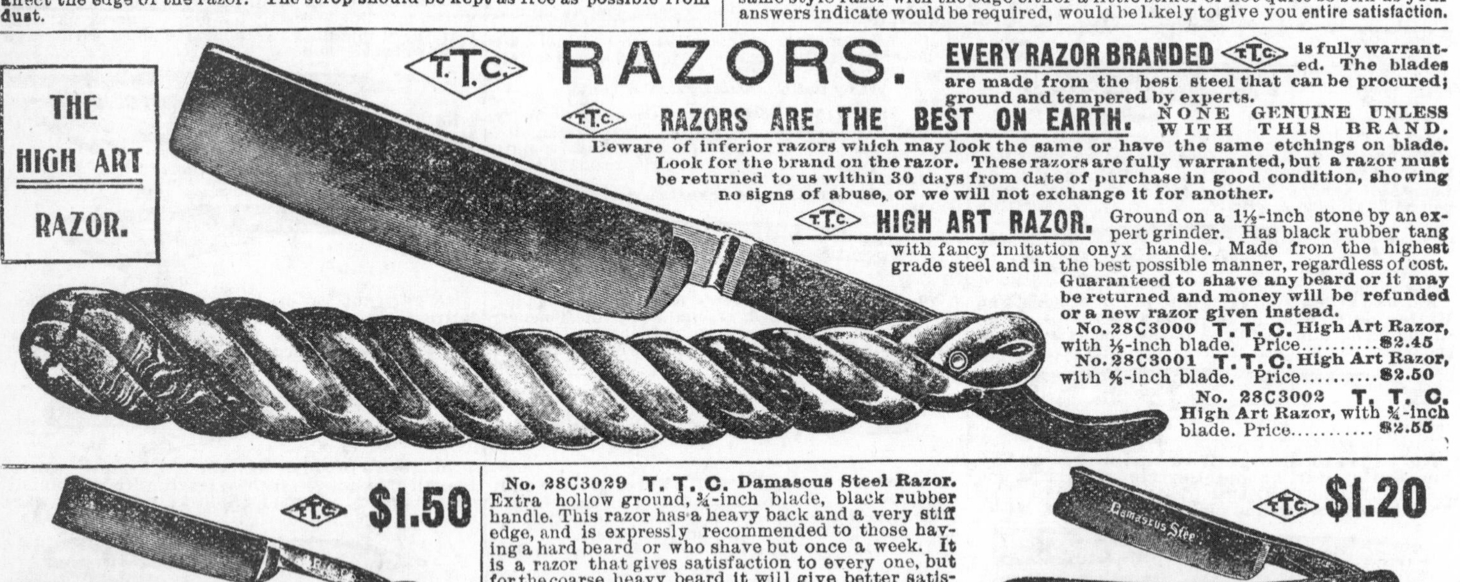

EVERY RAZOR BRANDED T.T.C. is fully warranted. The blades are made from the best steel that can be procured; ground and tempered by experts.

T.T.C. RAZORS ARE THE BEST ON EARTH. NONE GENUINE UNLESS WITH THIS BRAND.

Beware of inferior razors which may look the same or have the same etchings on blade. Look for the brand on the razor. These razors are fully warranted, but a razor must be returned to us within 30 days from date of purchase in good condition, showing no signs of abuse, or we will not exchange it for another.

T.T.C. HIGH ART RAZOR. Ground on a 1⅛-inch stone by an expert grinder. Has black rubber tang with fancy imitation onyx handle. Made from the highest grade steel and in the best possible manner, regardless of cost. Guaranteed to shave any beard or it may be returned and money will be refunded or a new razor given instead.

No. 28C3000 T. T. C. High Art Razor, with ⅝-inch blade. Price..........$2.45

No. 28C3001 T. T. C. High Art Razor, with ⅝-inch blade. Price..........$2.50

No. 28C3002 T. T. C. High Art Razor, with ¾-inch blade. Price..........$2.55

No. 28C3006 T. T. C. Barbers' Razor. Extra hollow ground, ½-inch blade. Fully warranted. Price....$1.50

No. 28C3009 T. T. C. Barbers' Razor. Extra hollow ground, ⅝-inch blade. Fully warranted. Price....$1.50

No. 28C3015 T.T.C. Barbers' Razor. Extra hollow ground, ¾-in. blade. Fully warranted. Price, $1.50

T.T.C. 50c

HOLLOW GROUND

No. 28C3019 T.T.C. Medium Hollow Ground Razor. Hollow point, ⅝-in. blade. Price....50c

T.T.C. 75c

Reliable

No. 28C3020 Our T.T.C. Reliable Razor, ⅝-inch blade, hollow ground, hollow point, fancy thumb hold. Imitation tortoise shell handle. Guaranteed to give satisfaction. Price, 75c

If razors are sent by mail, postage extra is 6 cents for each razor.

No. 28C3024 T. T. C. Original "Naval" Razor is a favorite pattern; medium hollow ground, ⅝-inch blade. Price..........75c

No. 28C3029 T. T. C. Damascus Steel Razor. Extra hollow ground, ¾-inch blade, black rubber handle. This razor has a heavy back and a very stiff edge, and is expressly recommended to those having a hard beard or who shave but once a week. It is a razor that gives satisfaction to every one, but for the coarse heavy beard it will give better satisfaction than a lighter razor. It is finely finished and fully guaranteed. Price..........$1.20

T.T.C. $1.20

Damascus Stee

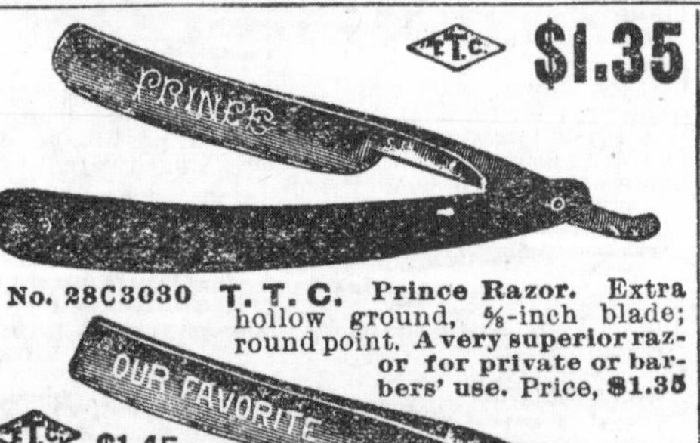

No. 28C3030 T. T. C. Prince Razor. Extra hollow ground, ⅝-inch blade; round point. A very superior razor for private or barbers' use. Price, $1.35

OUR FAVORITE

T.T.C. $1.45

No. 28C3033 T. T. C. Our Favorite Razor is a very thin, extra hollow ground razor for barbers' use. This razor requires careful handling to be kept in proper condition, but if properly used will give excellent satisfaction in private use, ⅝-in. blade, $1.45

No. 28C3034 T. T. C. Our Premier Razor. ⅝-inch blade. Fancy celluloid handle, extra hollow ground; for barbers' or private use. Fancy cut back. Gimped tang. Full crocus polished. A beautiful razor for a present, one that cannot fail to give satisfaction in use, and fully warranted. Price..$1.50

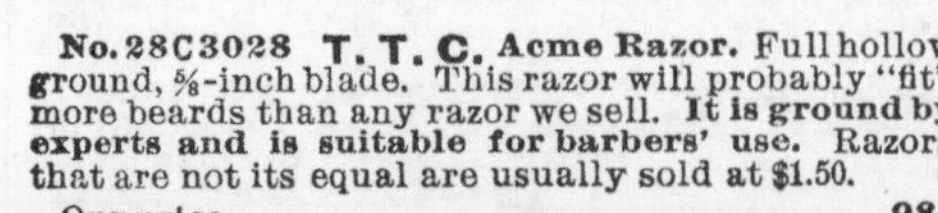

No. 28C3028 T. T. C. Acme Razor. Full hollow ground, ⅝-inch blade. This razor will probably "fit" more beards than any razor we sell. It is ground by experts and is suitable for barbers' use. Razors that are not its equal are usually sold at $1.50.

Our price..........98c

If razors are sent by mail, postage extra is 6 cents for each razor.

No. 28C3035 T. T. C. Extra Hollow Ground Razor, with fancy grained celluloid handle, for barbers' or private use; ⅝-in. blade. A very handsome razor, $1.60

CLEAN SHAVE

T.T.C. $1.65

No. 28C3044 T.T.C. Clean Shave Razor is another finely ground fancy razor suitable for either barbers' or private use. Has ⅝-in. blade. Fancy celluloid handle..$1.65

No. 28C3050 T. T. C. Ivory Tang Razor is a very finely ground razor with ivory tang and fancy grained celluloid handle. Only an expert would know this was not a real ivory handle. It makes an elegant present and is a first class shaver. Has ⅝-inch blade. Price..$2.00

No. 28C3052 T. T. C. Fancy Celluloid Handle Razor. One of the best razors made for private or barbers' use. Full hollow ground; warranted best material: ⅝-inch blade. Price..........$2.00

GERMAN RAZORS.

MADE IN TWO SIZES

$1.25

THE "BISMARCK" RAZOR FOR BARBERS' USE.

The "Bismarck" Razor is ground in Germany by the most expert grinders and is recommended for barbers or private use. A razor ground as finely as this will not give satisfaction unless it is carefully taken care of, but the expert barber, the man who knows how to care for a razor, will appreciate the "Bismarck." The ridge running lengthwise of the blade which supports the edge can be plainly seen with the naked eye. The man who shaves himself will get good results from this razor provided he knows how to keep it in order. The illustration is the exact size of the "Bismarck" Razor with ¾-inch blade. It has a black rubber handle.

No. 28C3090 "Bismarck" Razor for Barbers' Use. Width of blade, ¾ inch. Price, each....... $1.25
Three for....... 3.50
Six for....... 6.00

No. 28C3091 "Bismarck" Razor for Barbers' Use. Width of blade, ⅝ inch. Price, each....... $1.25
Three for....... 3.50
Six for....... 6.00

A barber will find no trouble in selling these razors to his customers at $2.00 each.

Herman Boker & Co.'s Tree Brand Razors.

65c

No. 28C3126 H. Boker & Co.'s Tree Brand Razor, medium hollow ground, black rubber handle. Width of blade, ⅝ inch. Hollow point. Price... 65c

$1.25

No. 28C3128 H. Boker & Co.'s Tree Brand Razor, extra hollow ground, fully warranted, black rubber handle. Width of blade, ⅝ inch. Price.... $1.25

$1.50

No. 28C3135 H. Boker & Co.'s Tree Brand Razor, extra full hollow ground, black rubber handle. Width of blade, ⅝ inch. Price....... $1.50

$2.40

No. 28C3136 H. Boker & Co.'s Tree Brand Razor, ⅝-inch blade, extra full hollow ground, black rubber handle, pearl tang; a beautiful razor for private or barbers' use. Price....... $2.40

30c

No. 28C3165 A Fair Grade German Razor, ⅝-inch blade, Extra hollow ground, etched "fully warranted," but not warranted by us. It is a razor that is usually sold at from 50 cents to $1.00. Price....... 30c

Our 65-Cent German Razor.

65c

No. 28C3166 A Good Quality German Razor, ⅝-inch blade. Extra hollow ground, made of best steel, magnetized, warranted. Price....... 65c

ENGLISH RAZORS.

Jos. Allen & Sons' Celebrated NON-XLL Razors.

$1.25

No. 28C3100 NON-XLL Razor, grained celluloid handle, imitation ivory; full hollow ground, square point, ⅝-in. blade, finely polished and etched; is made by Jos. Allen & Sons, one of the leading cutlery manufacturers of Sheffield, England, and is fully warranted. Price.. $1.25

$1.25

No. 28C3102 NON-XLL Razor, fancy carved celluloid handle, ⅝-inch blade with round point, full hollow ground, polished and etched. A razor which is warranted and which cannot fail to give satisfaction. Price $1.25

Wostenholm Razors.

We offer a line of razors made by George Wostenholm & Sons, of Sheffield, England, manufacturers of the genuine IXL cutlery and the Pipe Brand razors, which are so widely known all over the world. Every Wostenholm razor which we sell is guaranteed to give satisfaction and the assortment includes the very best razor Wostenholm makes, down to the medium price razor that is not so finely ground.

75c

No. 28C3055 George Wostenholm & Sons' Genuine, Original and True Pipe Razor, medium hollow ground, black rubber handle. Width of blade, ⅝ inch. This razor is known all over the world and has established a most enviable reputation. Price....... 75c

90c

No. 28C3057 George Wostenholm & Sons' Original Pipe Razor, hollow ground. Width of blade, ⅝ inch. A first class razor for general use. Price....... 90c

$1.00

No. 28C3058 George Wostenholm & Sons' Original and True Pipe Razor, medium hollow ground. Width of blade, ⅝ inch. A fine razor for the beginner; also used for shaving a second time over; has black rubber handle, file cut tang. Price....... $1.00

$1.25

No. 28C3061 George Wostenholm & Sons' Celebrated IXL Razor, full hollow ground, black rubber handle. Width of blade, ⅝ inch. Price....... $1.25

$1.40

No. 28C3063 George Wostenholm & Sons' Original and True Pipe Razor, black rubber handle, full hollow ground. Width of blade, ⅝ inch. Price....... $1.40

$1.50

No. 28C3065 George Wostenholm & Sons' Celebrated IXL Razor, ⅝-inch blade, hollow ground, round point, imitation ivory handle; an excellent razor for private use. Price....... $1.50

$2.00

No. 28C3066 George Wostenholm & Sons' Original and True Pipe Razor; ⅝-inch blade, the best razor Wostenholm makes. Black rubber handle, file cut gimped back tang. A razor that if properly cared for will give the very best satisfaction. Price....... $2.00

Wade & Butcher's Razors.

75c

No. 28C3115 Wade & Butcher's Hollow Point. Medium Hollow Ground Razor, rubber handle. Fully warranted and a superior cutter, ⅝-inch blade. Price....... 75c

$1.50

No. 28C3121 Wade & Butcher's Special Razor. Full hollow ground. A superfine barbers' razor. Black rubber handle. Width of blade, ⅝ inch. Price....... $1.50

No. 28C3122 Wade & Butcher's Special Razor. Same as above, except blade is ¾ inch wide. Price....... $1.50

Joseph Rodgers & Sons' Razors.

70c

No. 28C3160 Joseph Rodgers & Sons' Medium Hollow Ground Razor, with ⅝-inch blade. Black rubber handle. Price....... 70c

$1.40

No. 28C3162 Joseph Rodgers & Sons' Extra Hollow Ground Special Barbers' Razor, with square point. Black handle.

Width of blade	½ inch	⅝ inch	¾ inch
Price	$1.40	$1.50	$1.60

Swedish Razors.

98c

No. 28C3145 Genuine Joh. Engstrom Swedish Razor. A popular pattern, finely ground, warranted best ⅝-in. steel blade. Price....... 98c

OUR SHAVING OUTFITS.

No. 28C3176 Our High Art Shaving Set consists of a High Art razor with ⅝-inch blade, our best double leather swing strop, a seamless aluminum shaving mug, hand engraved, a fancy celluloid shaving brush and a cake of Yankee shaving soap.
Price, for complete set........................**$3.75**

No. 28C3177 Our High Art Shaving Set. Same as above, except razor has ¾-inch blade.
Price, for complete set........................**$3.80**

No. 28C3178 Our Bon Ton Shaving Set consists of your choice of any razor quoted by us, at $2.00 or less, a good leather and prepared web double swing strop, a fancy celluloid handle shaving brush, a seamless hand engraved aluminum shaving mug and a cake of Yankee shaving soap. **Make your order for the above shaving set thus: "No. 28C3178, 1 shaving set with No. .....razor,"** filling in the blank with the catalogue number of the razor you select. Price, for entire outfit..............**$2.75**

No. 28C3179 Our Premier Shaving Set consists of a Premier razor, a double leather swing strop, a seamless hand engraved aluminum mug, a good fancy celluloid handle shaving brush and a cake of Yankee shaving soap. Price, for complete set.....**$2.40**

No. 28C3180 Our Damascus Shaving Outfit consists of our Damascus steel razor, a good double leather swing strop, a seamless hand engraved aluminum cup, a good barbers' shaving brush and a cake of Yankee shaving soap.
Price, for complete set........................**$2.00**

No. 28C3181 Our Competition Shaving Set consists of a fair grade medium hollow ground razor, not warranted, a fair double swing leather and prepared web razor strop, a seamless aluminum shaving mug, a good brush and a cake of shaving soap. Price, for the complete outfit........................**95c**

No. 28C3182 Our Acme Shaving Set consists of our Acme razor, a good double swing horsehide and prepared web razor strop, a good shaving brush, a seamless hand engraved aluminum shaving mug, and a cake of Yankee shaving soap. **Remember the razor is fully warranted.**
Price, complete set, **$1.75**

No. 28C3087 Our Shaving Set in Case, is made up of No. 28C3034 razor, a seamless aluminum cup, No. 28C3372 shaving brush, a fine double swing horsehide strop, and a cake of the genuine Williams' Yankee soap, all packed in an imitation leather covered case, nicely lined. Price, per set, complete..................**$3.25**

No. 28C3401 Oak Shaving Cabinet. Golden oak finish. Height, 13 inches; width, 9¾ inches; depth, 7¾ inches. Partitioned inside as illustrated. The door has strong brass butts and has a mirror 7x10 inches on inside of door. This is a nicely finished cabinet and very convenient. Weight, about 5 pounds.
Price........................**$1.30**

Aluminum Shaving Mugs.

No. 28C3167 Aluminum Shaving Mug. Seamless, ebony finish body, engraved, with polished band and beading on top. Size, 3⅛ inches high and 3⅛ inches across the top.
Price..................................**30c**

No. 28C3168 Aluminum Shaving Mug. Same as above, with satin finish body, engraved.
Price..................................**25c**

No. 28C3169 Aluminum Shaving Mug. Same as above, with satin finish body, plain. Price..................**18c**

China Shaving Mugs.

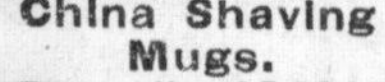

No. 28C3170 Carlsbad China Shaving Mug. Floral decorations. Gold line. Price....**15c**

No. 28C3172 Genuine Austrian China Shaving Mug. Floral decorations. Heavily gold stippled.
Price......**25c**

No. 28C3173 German China Shaving Mug, with partition for soap. Floral decorations. Gold line.
Price.......**20c**

No. 28C3175 Genuine Hapsburg China Shaving Mug, with partition for soap. Neat floral decorations, heavily gold stippled on edges and handle.
Price..................**50c**

The Sensible Safety Razor.

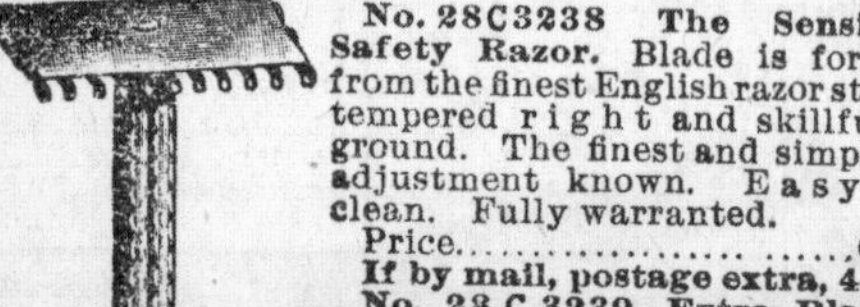

No. 28C3238 The Sensible Safety Razor. Blade is forged from the finest English razor steel, tempered right and skillfully ground. The finest and simplest adjustment known. Easy to clean. Fully warranted.
Price........................**62c**
If by mail, postage extra, 4c.

No. 28C3239 Extra Blades for Sensible Safety Razors.
Price........................**50c**

The Winner Safety Razor.

No. 28C3245 The Winner Safety Razor. Impossible to cut yourself. Blades full hollow ground. Any Winner Safety Razor that is not satisfactory may be returned any time within sixty days and a new razor given in exchange or money paid will be returned. Price.....**75c**
If by mail, postage extra, 5 cents.

No. 28C3246 Extra Blades for the Winner Safety Razor.
Price..............................**50c**

Adjustable Razor Guard.

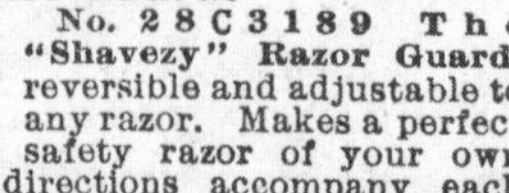

No. 28C3189 The "Shavezy" Razor Guard, reversible and adjustable to any razor. Makes a perfect safety razor of your own favorite blade. Full directions accompany each guard. It is finely finished and heavily nickel plated.
Price, per dozen, $2.00; each.............**18c**
If by mail, postage extra, each 2 cents.

The Genuine Star Safety Razor.

No. 28C3190 Star Safety Razor with the latest improved frame. Blades of best steel and full concave, which can be easily removed and placed in handle for stropping. Full nickel plated, packed in latest improved box.
Price..............................**$1.45**
If by mail, postage extra, 6 cents.

No. 28C3191 Extra Blades for Star Safety Razor.
Price..............................**83c**

No. 28C3195 Stropping Machine for Star Safety Razor, without strop. **A swing strop should be used with this machine.** Price............**$1.50**
If by mail, postage extra, 12 cents.

No. 28C3199 The Improved Diagonal Finish Leather Strop for the Star Safety razor. Price.**75c**
If by mail, postage extra, 10 cents.

Star Safety Razor Sets.

No. 28C3220 Star Safety Razor Combination Set consists of a Star Safety razor, stropping machine and diagonal finish leather strop, all packed complete in imitation leather case. Just the thing for tourists' use. Price of complete set..**$3.67**
If by mail, postage extra, 18 cents.

No. 28C3227 Star Safety Razor Set. Elegantly finished in morocco. Contains one safety frame with two blades, and is a gem in the full sense of the word.
Price, per set............**$3.00**
If by mail, postage extra, 8 cents.

No. 28C3229 Star Safety Razor Set. Put up in elegant satin lined morocco case, and contains one safety frame with two perfectly adjusted blades of fine silver steel; box of finely perfumed shaving soap; holder for stropping and honing blades; shaving brush, comb and cosmetique; in fact, everything requisite for an easy, quick and luxurious shave. Price...........**$4.67**
If by mail, postage extra, 14 cents.

No. 28C3232 Star Safety Razor Set. Contains one safety frame and seven blades—one blade for each day in the week. This case is especially adapted to the wants of those who find a razor works easier by frequent changing. It is a very elaborate and handsome affair, put up in box covered with morocco and lined with satin. Price.....**$8.50**
If by mail, postage extra, 12 cents.

Our $12.00 Complete Outfit.

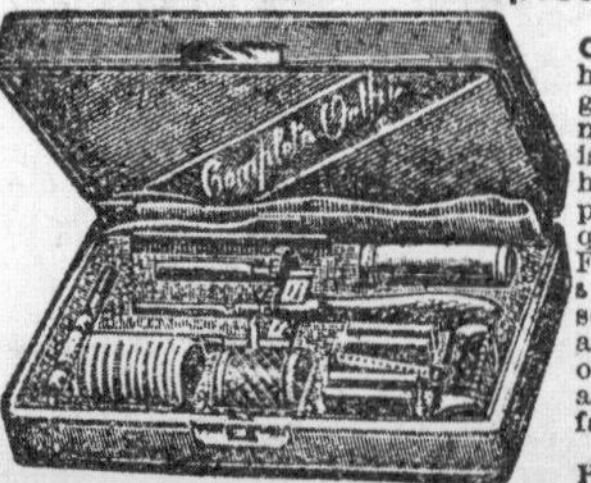

No. 28C3237 Complete Outfit. This handsome case with its galaxy of everything necessary for shaving, is a perfect beauty. It holds four highly tempered blades of the first quality, one frame, one Famous strop machine, strop, razor handle, soap, cosmetique comb, and brush. The interior of the case is of doeskin and the covering of fancy leather.
Price.......**$12.00**
Postage extra, 40 cents.

RAZOR STROPS.

The best razor is no good without a first class strop

No. 28C3250 Combination Four-Side Extension Razor Strop. A fair strop for little money.
Price......(If by mail, postage extra, 10c)....**20c**

No. 28C3253 Belt Two-Side Extension Razor Strop. A fair grade strop. Price...............**25c**
If by mail, postage extra, 10 cents.

No. 28C3256 Combination Four-Side Extension Razor Strop with cushion buff. A fine strop.
Price......(If by mail, postage extra, 12c)...**35c**

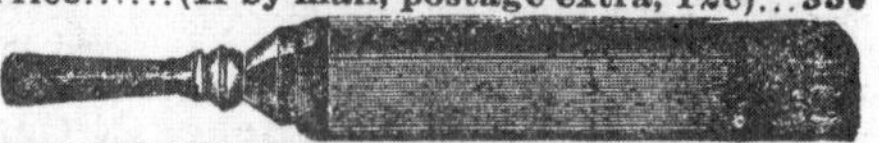

No. 28C3257 Cushion Strop, Four-Side. This is a very superior strop of this old favorite style.
Price......(If by mail, postage extra, 14c)..**50c**

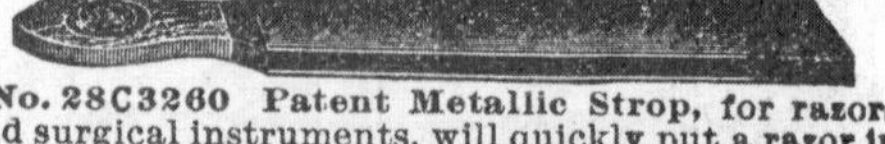

No. 28C3260 Patent Metallic Strop, for razors and surgical instruments, will quickly put a razor in condition to split a hair and shave easy. Sharp as the best hone without its harshness. You cannot spoil your razor with this strop. Price **65c**

No. 28C3263 Swing Cushion Strop. This strop combines all the advantages of the swing strop and the stiff cushioned strop. It is better for the inexperienced user, as one is not so likely to round the edge of the razor. It is finished on one side for use when razor is dull; the other side for finishing. **Made with heavy nickel plated swivel in handle, fashioned** filled leather handle. Price.......**$1.25**
If by mail, postage extra, 10 cents.

No. 28C3264 Double Swing Razor Strop, black leather on one side, tubular cotton hose on the other; has swivel and black enameled wood handle. **Width, 2** inches; entire length, 22½ inches. Price. . .**25c**
If by mail, postage extra, 6 cents.

No. 28C3265 Double Swing Razor Strop. Porpoise hide oil finished leather on one side and prepared tubular cotton hose on the other; has a **swivel** and fashioned handle. Width, 2 inches; **entire** length, 23 inches. Price.......................**35c**
If by mail, postage extra, 6 cents.

No. 28C3267 Our 50-cent Leader. This strop is better value than we have ever before been able to offer at this price. This is a double swing strop. Special porpoise hide oil finished leather on one side and extra prepared webbing on the other. **Has swivel** and padded leather handle. Width, 2¼ inches; entire length, 24 inches. Price...............**50c**
If by mail, postage extra, 8 cents.

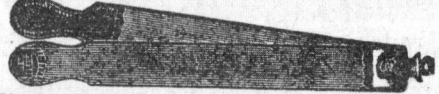

No. 28C3272 Double Swing Strop, porpoise hide oil finished leather on one side and pure Irish linen hose, prepared and polished, on the other. **Nickel plated removable swivel, fashioned handle. A fine** strop for professional barbers. Width, 2¼ inches; entire length, 25 inches. Price..................**75c**
If by mail, postage extra, 8 cents.

No. 28C3276 Double Swing Strop, very extra quality, satin finished genuine horsehide leather on one side and pure Irish linen hose, prepared and polished, on the other. **Removable nickel plated swivel, fashioned handle.** A superior strop, good and durable, for any use. Width, 2¼ inches; entire length, 25 inches. Price.....................**$1.00**
If by mail, postage extra, 8 cents.

No. 28C3280 Single Swing Barbers' Strop, porpoise hide oil finished prepared leather. The strop that barbers buy. **Fashioned handle and eyelet.** Width, 2¼ inches; entire length 24 inches. Price.....(If by mail, postage extra, 4 cents.)..**25c**

No. 28C3287 Extra Fine Selected Shell Horsehide Razor Strop. Single swing. Width, 2¼ inches; entire length, 24 inches. Used by first class barbers. Price..........................**75c**
If by mail, postage extra, 4 cents.

Razor Strops.

No. 28C3284 Single Swing Barbers' Strop. Pure Irish linen, prepared and polished especially for professional barbers' use. **Fashioned leather handle and eyelet.** Width, 2¼ inches; entire length, 24 inches. Price.(Postage extra, 4c)...35c

No. 28C3290 Double Leather Swing Razor Strop. Width, 2 inches. Length of stropping surface, 12½ inches; length over all, 19½ inches. Both strops are leather—one for sharpening, the other for finishing. Nickel plated swivel; sewed on handle.
Price..(If by mail, postage extra, 8 cents).....45c

No. 28C3291 Double Leather Swing Razor Strop. Army and Navy style. Width, 2 inches. Length of stropping surface, 14 inches; length over all, 20 inches. Both strops are leather—one for sharpening, the other for finishing. Heavy nickel plated swivel. Heavy nickel plated loop for handle.
Price..(If by mail, postage extra, 8 cents).....65c

No. 28C3292 Double Leather Swing Razor Strop. Width, 2¼ inches. Length of stropping surface, 17½ inches; length over all, 24 inches. Both strops are leather—one for sharpening, the other for finishing. Nickel plated bolt swivel; sewed on handle on one strop; fashioned handle on the other.
Price....(If by mail, postage extra, 10c)......75c

Razor Strop Paste.

No. 28C3296 Stropine. Guaranteed absolutely harmless to either razor or strop. It contains no acid or mineral substance. A jar will last for years, always retaining its moisture. Puts the strop in shape to put the proper kind of an edge on a razor. Price..............9c
Stropine cannot be sent by mail.

Razor Hones.

No. 28C3300 A Very Good Belgian Razor Hone, that will give satisfaction in private use. We sell them for the same amount of money you must pay to have your razor honed once. Price....................25c

No. 28C3302 A Superfine Belgian Razor Hone, special selection for our trade. Each hone packed in neat cardboard case; every one perfect; suitable for private or barbers' use. Price 50c

No. 28C3305 Extra Superfine Belgian Razor Hones for professional use. Price............75c

No. 28C3306 Barbers' Special Belgian Hone, selected especially for the best barbers' trade. In quality it is the very best and in shape the most convenient for barbers' use. Each hone packed in strong paper box. Size, 5x2¼ inches. Price.........$1.75

No. 28C3307 Barbers' Special Belgian Hone, same as above, only smaller. Size, 4x2 inches.
Price..................................83c

RAZOR HONES ARE LIABLE TO BE BROKEN IF SENT BY MAIL.

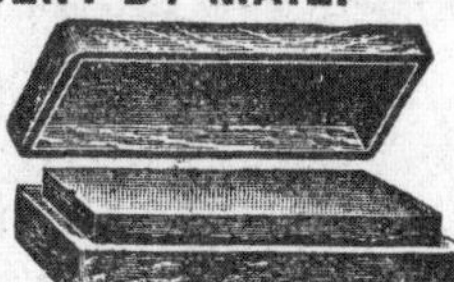

No. 28C3309 Special No. 1 Fine Belgian Razor Hone. Size, 5x1⅝ inches, mounted in polished hardwood box. A hone that gives general satisfaction. Price..65c

Genuine Swaty Hones.

Each one branded Franz Swaty, Marburg, Austria.

No. 28C3308 The Genuine Swaty Hones. Length, 5½ inches; width, 2 inches. For private use.
Price..45c

No. 28C3312 The Genuine Swaty Hones. For barbers' use. Length, 8 inches; width, 2 inches. Considered by many barbers the best. Price...72c

Emery Razor Hones.

No. 28C3315 Emery Razor Hone, is far superior to natural stone and at the same time much lower in price. Size, 5½x2x½ inches. Price..........................40c
If by mail, postage extra, 15 cents.

German Water Hones.

No. 28C3318 Dark Blue German Water Hones with "rubbers." Length, 7 inches. Price.........20c

No. 28C3319 Barbers' Gem German Water Hones, especially selected for barbers' use. Size, 5x2½ inches. Put up in a strong paper box.
Price......(If by mail, postage extra, 25c).......50c

Shaving Brushes.

Aluminum Ferrule Shaving Brushes, No. 28C3244 to 28C3249 are put together with waterproof cement under heavy pressure and will wear to the handle without shedding bristles. They have no twine to foul, no metal that will corrode, no horn to crack. Made from sterilized, odorless, fine French bristles, with non-corrosive aluminum ferrule, ebonoid handle. They are the best line of shaving brushes we have seen.

No. 28C3244 Aluminum Ferrule Shaving Brush for private use. Length of bristles, 1⅞ inches. Inside diameter of ferrule, ⅞ inch. Has flat end handle permitting brush to be stood on end. Price..............15c
If by mail, postage extra, 4 cents.

No. 28C3247 Aluminum Ferrule Shaving Brush for private use. Length of bristles, 2⅛ inches. Inside diameter of ferrule, ⅞ inch. Has flat end handle permitting brush to be stood on end. Price.....20c
If by mail, postage extra, 4 cents.

No. 28C3248 Aluminum Ferrule Shaving Brush, for barbers' or private use. Length of bristles, 2⅛ inches. Inside diameter of ferrule, ⅞ inch. Price, ...(Postage extra, 5 cents) 25c

No. 28C3249 Aluminum Ferrule Shaving Brush, for barbers' use. Length of bristles, 2¼ inches. Inside diameter of ferrule, 1⅛ inch. Price..........3

No. 28C3354 Cherry Enameled Handle Shaving Brush. White bristles; nickel plated metal ferrule. Length of bristles, 1⅞ inches. Diameter of brush at ferrule, ¾ inch. **A well set, durable brush.**
Price.. ....(If by mail, postage extra, 3c).......10c

No. 28C3372 Fancy Carved White Celluloid Shaving Brush. White bristles. Length of bristles, 1¾ inches. Diameter of brush at ferrule, ¾ inch. Bristles well set. Price.......................................25c

No. 28C3378 Fancy Celluloid Handle Shaving Brush. Genuine badger hair. Fancy carved horn ferrule. Length of hair, 2⅛ inches. Diameter of brush, ¾ inch. Every hair in this brush is guaranteed genuine badger hair. **It is well set and a brush that cannot fail to please.**
Price...75c

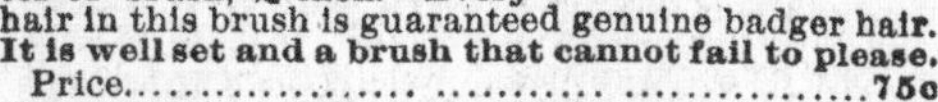

No. 28C3380 Barbers' Shaving Brush, No. 1 or Standard Size. This is a popular professional barbers' brush, with boxwood handle. Rubber ferrule. Guaranteed never to shed bristles. The bristles are 2 inches long. Diameter of brush at ferrule is ¾ inch. Price...20c

No. 28C3381 Barbers' Shaving Brush. Size No. 3, boxwood handle, rubber ferrule. Length of bristles, 2⅝ inches. Diameter of brush at ferrule, 1 inch. Same style and quality as No. 28C3380 only larger. **Guaranteed never to shed bristles.** Price.................29c

Patent Folding Handle Tourists' Shaving Brush.

No. 28C3362 White bristles, nickel ferrule. Length of bristles, 1⅝ inches. Diameter of brush at ferrule, ⅝ inch. **Illustration shows brush ready for shaving.** When not in use the ferrule can be unscrewed and placed in the hollow handle, making the package only 2¾ inches long and 1 inch in diameter. All metal parts are made from brass and are heavily nickel plated. Price 18c

Shaving Soaps.

No. 7C1842 Yankee Shaving Soap, very choice, 1 dozen in box.
Price, per cake..................$0.09
Per box.................................1.00

Williams' Shaving Soap.

No. 7C1843 Williams' Shaving Soap, finest made, 6 cakes to pound.
Price, per cake........$0.05
Per pound..................28
Per 10-pound box.....2.70

Barbers' Shaving Soap, 4 Cents.

No. 7C1844 At 4 cents per single cake or 20 cents per roll of 6 cakes, we offer our barbers' shaving soap as a strictly high grade article. Price, per single cake........... 4c
Per roll of 6 cakes.........................20c

Genuine Cuticura Shaving Soap.

No. 7C1845 Genuine Cuticura Shaving Soap, medicated; square cup cakes; makes an excellent lather.
Price, per dozen cakes, $1.45; per cake..................14c

Colgate & Co.'s Shaving Sticks.

Colgate & Co.'s Dulcemont Shaving Stick. Convenient to carry around when traveling. Each in metal box. Perfumed with roses.

No. 7C1846 Large size. Price, per stick....$0.14
Per dozen sticks...1.40

No. 7C1846½ Small size. Price, per stick..........$0.09
Per dozen sticks...1.00

Williams' Shaving Sticks.

No. 7C1847 Genuine Williams' Shaving Sticks. In leatherette box; handy when traveling; also for home use. No waste; always clean and ready for use. Price, per box..........$0.16
Per dozen boxes......................1.75

Colgate's Shaving Soap.

No. 7C1852 Colgate's Shaving Soap, 8 cakes to pound. Price, per cake.....$0.05
Per pound 27
Per 10-pound box.....................2.50

Barbers' Hair Clippers.

For Human Hair Only. For Horse and Dog Clippers, see Harness Department.

SPECIAL NOTICE—**When ordering repairs for clippers be sure to give us the NAME of the clipper and all marks that appear on it. We do not furnish springs or repairs for any clipper except those that have been purchased from us.**

No. 28C3452 The Fulton Hair Clipper is full size, well made of good steel, properly tempered, finely finished and nickel plated. It has concealed three-coil music wire spring, which lasts about five times as long as ordinary springs and can be easily replaced if broken. Cuts hair ⅛ inch long. Price.... ....50c
If by mail, postage extra, 12 cents.

No. 28C3453 Springs for the Fulton Hair Clipper. Price 5c

No. 28C3460 The Washington Hair Clipper is exactly like the Fulton, except it has a three-coil music wire spring between the handles. Will do fine work. Price... ......55c
If by mail, postage extra, 12 cents.

No. 28C3461 Springs for the Washington Hair Clipper. Price.......10c

No. 28C3468 The Scott Hair Clipper is the old French pattern clipper with flat steel springs, which has been so popular for years. It is very carefully made, tempered to cut, and we guarantee it is better than any other clipper of this pattern in the market. Finely finished and heavily nickel plated. Cuts hair ⅛ inch long. Price..80c
If by mail, postage extra, 12 cents.

No. 28C3469 Springs for the Scott Hair Clipper, with notch in end. Price..........................10c

No. 28C3470 Springs for the Scott Hair Clipper, with projection on end. Price.....................10c

No. 28C3480 The Acme Hair Clipper is very carefully made from the very best material, finely finished and heavily nickel plated. It has a fluted and hollowed bottom plate, fitting the head, and making it easy cutting. This clipper is recommended to professional barbers as one which will please.
Price.. (If by mail, postage extra, 12c.)......75c

No. 28C3481 Springs for the Acme Hair Clipper. Price...................5c

This illustration shows the fluted and curved bottom plate which is furnished on our Keene, Acme and Waldorf Clippers.

No. 28C3500 The Keene Barbers' Hair Clipper. We claim the equal of this clipper has not yet been made. It was designed by a barber who knew what a barber required in a clipper. It is made from the very best material. The main tension bolt is set forward almost directly over the teeth, and it is a double tension clipper, having an extra tension bolt, insuring ease and perfection of working. The bottom plate is grooved and hollowed so only the points of teeth touch the scalp. The clipper is finely finished and heavily nickel plated, and is guaranteed to be better than some that are sold at double our price. Cuts hair ⅛-inch long. Price...........98c

No. 28C3501 The Keene Barbers' Hair Clipper, same as above, only to cut very close—almost equal to shaving.
Price.......(If by mail, postage extra 15 cents)........$1.12

No. 28C3503 Springs for Keene Hair Clipper. Price.5c

No. 28C3508 The Waldorf Anti-Friction Dustproof Roller Bearing Barbers' Hair Clippers, with fluted and curved bottom plate. Very easy working and very comfortable to your customers. Has three-coil music wire spring which is guaranteed to last five times as long as springs made from ordinary spring wire. Used by barbers who cater to the best trade. Extra carefully finished and heavily nickel plated. Better clippers than the Waldorf are not made. Why pay more! Price... ....$1.25
If by mail, postage extra, 12 cents.

No. 28C3509 Springs for Waldorf Hair Clipper. Price.5c

Adjustable Comb.

No. 28C3515 Adjustable Comb to fit either the Fulton, Washington, Acme, Keene, Scott or Waldorf Clippers. Will not fit other makes. Can be adjusted instantly to increase the cut from ⅛ to ⅝ inch. It does not fall off in use, and is the only practical adjustable comb we have ever seen. It is finely finished and full nickel plated.
Price........(If by mail, postage extra, 4 cents)...........37c

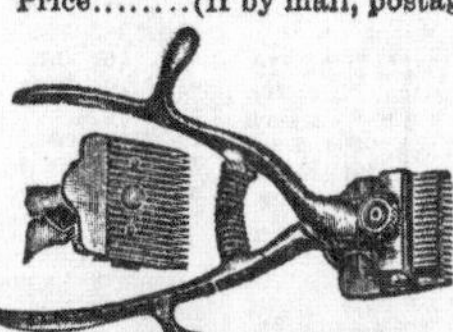

No. 28C3530 French Pattern Toilet Clipper. Modeled on the lines of the original French Toilet Clipper. Has excellent cutting qualities. Workmanship and finish first class. Spring has adjustable tension. Cuts ⅛ inch.
Price......................$2.00
If by mail, postage extra, 15c.

No. 28C3533 Springs for French Pattern Toilet Clipper. Price.........10c

No. 28C3538 "Neck Shave" Toilet Clipper, for trimming the beard and neck. Has corrugated bottom plate. Very carefully made; light and a favorite with barbers.

Cuts very close, almost equal to shaving. **Heavily nickel plated.**
Price........(If by mail, postage extra, 15 cents).....$1.95

No. 28C3539 Spring for Neck Shave Clipper. Price 10

Brown & Sharpe's Barbers' Clippers, Bressant Pattern.

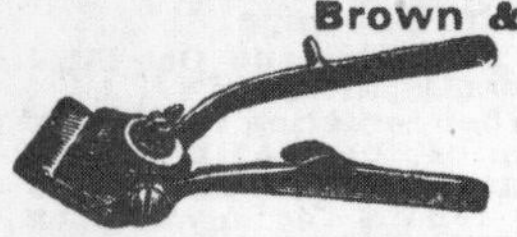

No. 28C3540	No. 0. B.&S., cuts 1/32 in. Price	$2.25
No. 28C3541	No. 1. B.&S., cuts ⅛ inch. Price	2.25
No. 28C3542	No. 2. B.&S., cuts ¼ inch. Price	2.55
No. 28C3543	No. 3. B.&S., cuts 5/16 inch. Price	3.00
No. 28C3544	Springs for above clipper, each	.05

If by mail, postage extra, 15 cents.

A FREE CATALOGUE OF BARBER CHAIRS AND SUPPLIES.

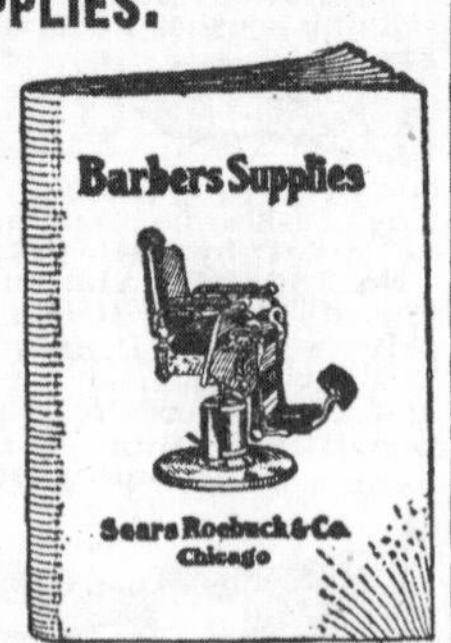

We issue a handsome special Barbers' Supply Catalogue, showing our entire line of new up to date styles of barbers' chairs, large, handsome illustrations, showing the details in every particular, showing the many ways in which our barbers' chairs are superior to any chairs you can buy elsewhere at anything like the price we offer. This free catalogue also shows our entire line of new up to date barbers' furniture and fixtures, everything in the very latest style, all valued at the actual factory cost, with but our one small percentage of profit added, priced at only a little more than one-half the price you have been in the habit of paying.

All these goods are shown in large, handsome illustrations, showing every little detail, full descriptions and priced at astonishingly low prices.

In this free Barbers' Special Catalogue we show some very attractive values in special razors, hones, strops, shaving soap and every sort of barbers' accessories and supplies. Want of space in this catalogue prevents our showing the complete line.

If you don't order from this catalogue, don't buy anything in barbers' supplies until you get our special free Barbers' Supply Catalogue, for such values, such offers, such liberal terms, such inducements, such up to date things in the entire line are offered by no other house at anything approaching our price. **If you are running a barber shop** or you are thinking of establishing a barber shop and you wish to buy a new outfit, or add to your present outfit, you will see from our free Barbers' Supply Catalogue that your money will go about twice as far in this line by dealing with us as it would in dealing with any exclusive barbers' supply house in America. While we always urge our customers to order direct from this catalogue if they can make a suitable selection, nevertheless, if you are running a barber shop or contemplate opening a barber shop and, therefore, will be in need of supplies from time to time, you cannot afford to be without our free Barbers' Supply Catalogue. **On a postal card, or in a letter, simply say: "Send me your free Barbers' Supply Catalogue," and it will go to you by return mail, postpaid, free with our compliments.**

Our Revolving and Reclining Barber's Chair, $19.20.

Woodwork is Oak, Legs are Protected with Brass Mountings. All Metallic Parts are Strong and Well Finished.

No. 28C4225 Our Revolving and Reclining Barbers' Chair, upholstered in mohair plush; colors, crimson, maroon, green or old gold. If color desired is not stated in order, we make the selection. Complete as shown in illustration, except it has no scroll on the sides, being perfectly plain with metal parts japanned. Weight, packed, about 210 pounds. Price...$19.20

No. 28C4218 Same chair, exactly as illustrated, upholstered in plush, with metal parts nickel plated. Price...$21.60

No. 28C4226 Same chair, without scroll on sides, upholstered in leather, any color, japanned trimmings. Price...$21.65

No. 28C4219 Same chair, exactly as illustrated, upholstered in leather, with metal parts nickel plated. Price...$24.00

BUILDERS' HARDWARE.

THE GOODS WE LIST in this department are guaranteed for quality. They are made in proper proportions and are not only beautiful in design, but a. e correct from a mechanical standpoint. Dealers make a big profit in the sale of locks, door knobs, hinges, latches, sash fixtures, etc., and we sell all of these goods so close that no matter how little you wish to buy, we will save you enough to pay you for sending to Chicago for the goods.

THE FREIGHT RATES on hardware and building material are low and will amount to almost nothing compared to the saving in price.

IF YOU ARE GOING TO BUILD, make out a list, or have your carpenter or architect make it out for you, of all the goods you will require in this line. Refer to these goods in this catalogue for prices, or if you wish, send the list to us and we will quote you the price for each and every article, and for the entire bill delivered at your nearest railroad station. **You will find that our prices will surprise you in the money you can save,** and if you do not order your goods from us, it will prevent your paying too much elsewhere, and in any case **we will save you money.**

DON'T BE PERSUADED to use a poor quality of hardware. Hardware in a building is a small item in the total cost, even if the very best is used. For example, the difference in cost between good locks and poor locks is so little that the owner would not consider it a saving to use poor locks if he were posted on the matter. Because the work is so easily concealed, poor locks are used to save a few cents. **We furnish complete lines in the desirable finishes.**

WE HAVE MADE THE DESCRIPTIONS SO EXPLICIT, and so arranged the goods that anyone can select that which pleases him, or which suits his particular work, with the assurance of getting just what is desired. **Every article is guaranteed to be exactly as we represent it, and if not found so it may be returned and the money will be refunded.**

WE SHOW SIX LINES. We show two lines of plain goods in all the popular finishes and four lines of ornamental goods. We can save you so much money on these goods that you cannot afford to buy them from your local dealer, whose cost, in many cases, is more than our price to you.

All builders' hardware commonly used will be found in this catalogue, but if there are certain goods needed not found here, you should send for our free Special Catalogue of Builders' Hardware, which contains a very complete line.

ORNAMENTAL GENUINE BRONZE LOCK SETS.

Antique Copper Sand Finish Front Door Cylinder Locks.

ACME DESIGN.

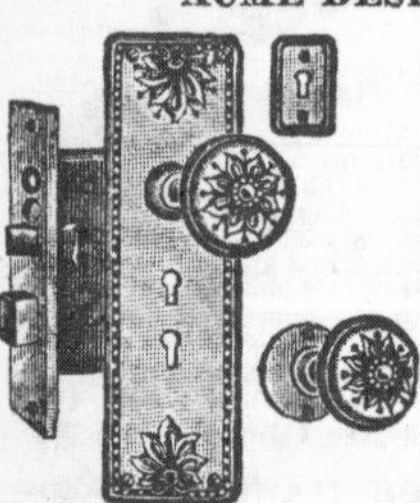

No. 9C325 Genuine Bronze Acme Front Door Lock Set. Size of lock, 4¾x3½ inches, one nickel plated steel key for lock bolt and two for night latch; cast bronze front and bolts; easy spring; wrought bronze knobs, 2¼ inches in diameter. 5-16 inch swivel spindle One wrought bronze escutcheon for outside of door, size, 7½x2¼ inches. Packed complete with screws. The front, strike and all the trimmings are finished antique copper, sand finish.

Price, per set...$1.83

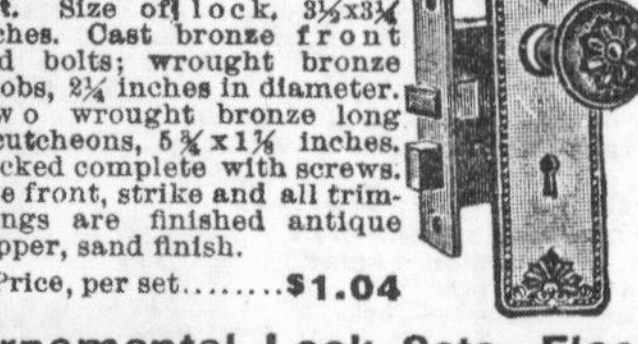

No. 9C332 Genuine Bronze Acme Inside Lock Set. Size of lock, 3½x3¼ inches. Cast bronze front and bolts; wrought bronze knobs, 2¼ inches in diameter. Two wrought bronze long escutcheons, 5¾x1⅛ inches. Packed complete with screws. The front, strike and all trimmings are finished antique copper, sand finish.

Price, per set...$1.04

Ornamental Lock Sets, Electro Copper Plated, Antique Copper, Sand Finish.

FULTON DESIGN.

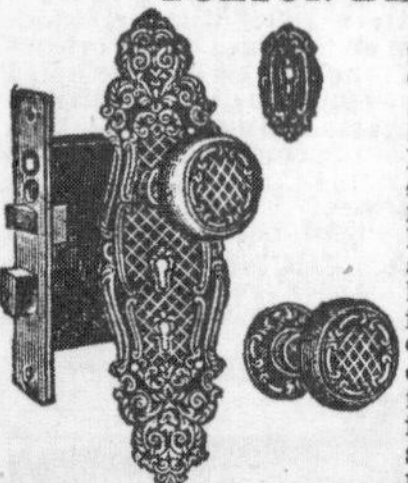

No. 9C373 Ornamental Electro Copper Plated Fulton Front Door Lock Set. Easy spring lock, 4¾x3½ inches. One nickel plated steel key for lock bolt and two for night latch. Knobs, 2¼ inches in diameter. One long escutcheons for outside of front door, 11x2¾ inches. The front, strike and all trimmings are electro copper plated, antique copper, sand finish. Packed complete with screws.

Price, per set...94c

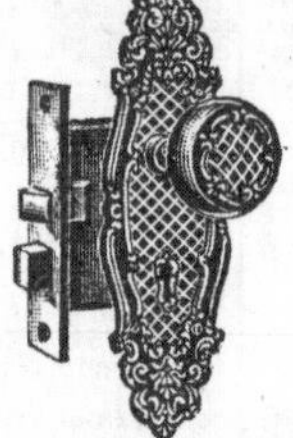

No. 9C378 Ornamental Electro Copper Plated Fulton Inside Lock Set. Lock 3½x3¼ inches, with nickel plated steel key, wrought front; knobs 2¼ inches in diameter; two long escutcheons, 9x2⅜ inches. The front, strike and all trimmings are heavily electro copper plated, antique copper, sand finish. Packed complete with screws.

Price, per set...$0.58
Per dozen sets...6.88

No. 9C391 Ornamental Electro Copper Plated Fulton Hook Sash Lift. Finished antique copper, sand finish. Size, 2x1⅛ inches. Price, per dozen, 37c; each...4c

Butts.

No. 9C392 Ornamental Electro Copper Plated Fulton Door Butts. Finished antique copper, sand finish. Packed complete with screws.

Size	3x3	3½x3½	4x4	4½x4½
Per pr	25c	28c	33c	38c

Bokay Design Lock Sets, Etc.

Genuine Bronze and Electro Bronze Plated. The parts of illustrations which show dark are finished in black enamel. The parts which show light are plain polished, bronze finish.

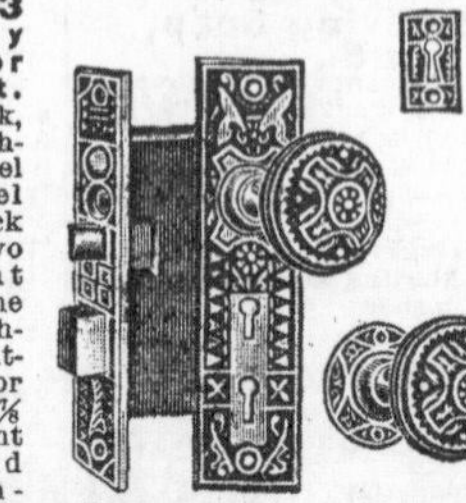

No. 9C453 Bokay Front Door Lock Set. Size of lock, 4¼x3½ inches, one nickel plated steel key for lock bolt and two for night latch. One long escutcheon for outside of door is 7¼x1⅞ inches. Front of lock and all trimmings are electro bronze plated.

Price of lock set complete...$1.06

No. 9C423 Bokay Front Door Lock Set. Same as No. 9C453, except has genuine bronze bolts, front and strike. All trimmings genuine bronze. Price of lock set complete...$1.34

No. 9C473 Bokay Hook Sash Lifts. Electro bronze plated. Size of plate, 1⅝x⅞ inch.

Price, each...2c
Per dozen...23c

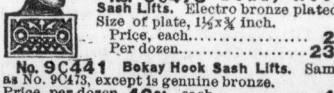

No. 9C441 Bokay Hook Sash Lifts. Same as No. 9C473, except is genuine bronze. Price, per dozen, 40c; each...4c

No. 9C456 Bokay Inside Lock Set. Nickel plated steel key. Has wrought steel front, wrought steel knobs, 2¼ inches in diameter. Two wrought steel escutcheons 5½x1⅝ inches. Front of lock and all trimmings are electro bronze plated. Packed complete with screws. Price, per dozen sets, $4.45; per set...38c

No. 9C424 Bokay Inside Lock Set. Same as No. 9C456, except has genuine bronze bolts, front and strike. All trimmings genuine bronze.

Price, per doz. sets; $7.60; per set...64c

No. 9C457 Bokay Inside Lock Set. Nickeled key. Has jet knobs. Two escutcheons, 5¼x1½ inches. Front of lock and all trimmings are electro bronze plated. Packed complete with screws.

Price, per set. $0.27
Per dozen sets 3.20

No. 9C425 Bokay Inside Lock Set. Same as No. 9C457, except has genuine bronze bolts, front and strike. All trimmings genuine bronze. Per dozen sets...$6.25 Per set...53c

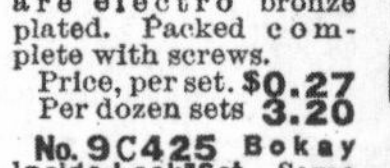

No. 9C1300 Bokay Electro Bronze Plated Door Butts. Packed complete with screws.

Size, inches	3x3	3½ x 3½	
Per pair	22c	24c	
Size, in.	4x4	4½x4½	5x5
Per pair	29c	34c	39c

No. 9C1343 Bokay Cupboard Catch. Electro Bronze Plated. Size, 1¼x1⅞ inches with screws. Price, per dozen, 67c; each...6c

No. 9C1350 Bokay Cupboard Turns. Electro Bronze Plated. With patent diamond no-friction latch. Size, 1¾x2⅛ inches. Packed with screws. Price, per doz. $1.30; each 11c

No. 9C1353 Bokay Electro Bronze Plated Cupboard Turns. Size, 1¾x2⅛ inches. Packed with screws.

Price, each. $0.11
Per dozen... 1.29

No. 9C1365 Bokay Electro Bronze Plated Drawer Pulls. Size, 3½ inches. Packed with screws.

Price, per dozen, 45c; each...4c

Plain Lock Sets Etc. Genuine Bronze and Electro Copper Plated, Antique Copper Finish.

CHICAGO DESIGN.

No. 9C555 Chicago Design Front Door Lock Set. Easy spring lock. One nickel plated steel key for lock bolt; two for night latch; wrought steel knobs, One long escutcheon for outside of door is 7x1⅛ inches. Front of lock and all trimmings electro copper plated, antique copper finish. Packed complete with screws. Price, per set..$1.10

No. 9C515 Chicago Design Front Door Lock Set, same as No. 9C555, except has genuine bronze bolts, front and strike and all trimmings are genuine bronze, antique copper finish.

Price, per set complete...$1.20

No. 9C559 Chicago Design Inside Lock Set. Wrought steel front; wrought steel knobs. Two long escutcheons, 5⅛ x 1⅛ inches. Front of lock and all trimmings electro copper plated, antique copper finish. Packed complete with screws.

Price, per set, $0.42
Per dozen...5.00

No. 9C522 Chicago Design Inside Lock Set same as No. 9C559, except has genuine bronze bolts, front and strike and all trimmings are genuine bronze, antique copper finish.

Price, per set...$0.69
Per dozen sets...8.17

No. 9C562 Chicago Design Inside Lock Set. Front of lock and all trimmings are electro copper plated, antique copper finish. Same description as No. 9C559, except it has jet knobs instead of metal.

Price, per set. $0.32
Per dozen sets 3.75

No. 9C525 Chicago Design Inside Lock Set. Bolts, front, strike and all trimmings are genuine bronze, antique copper finish. Same description as No. 9C522 except has jet knobs instead of bronze.

Price per dozen sets, $6.75; per set..57c

No. 9C543 **Chicago Design. Genuine Bronze Hook Sash Lift,** antique copper finish, beveled edges. Size, 1½x1½ inches. Packed with screws.
Price, per dozen, **38c**; each........................**4c**

No. 9C575 **Chicago Design Hook Sash Lift.** Wrought steel, electro copper plated, antique copper finish. Size, 1⅞ inches. Packed with screws. Price, each.......................**2c**
Per dozen.......................................**20c**

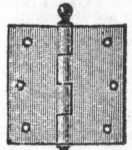

No. 9C943 **Plain Electro Copper Plated Steel Butts,** antique copper sand finish. Packed complete with screws.

Size, inches	3x3	3½x3½	4x4
Price, pair	27c	29c	32c
Size, inches	4½x4½	5x5	
Price, per pair	35c	42c	

The above butts match lock sets in sand finish.

No. 9C946 **Plain Electro Copper Plated Steel Butts,** polished antique copper finish. Packed complete with screws.

Size, inches	3x3	3½x3½	4x4	4½x4½	5x5
Price, per pair	20c	23c	25c	28c	34c

The above butts match lock sets, either solid bronze or bronze plated, in antique copper finish.

No. 9C947 **Plain Electro Copper Plated Steel Butts,** antique copper finish (not polished). Packed complete with screws.

Size, inches	3x3	3½x3½	4x4
Price	13c	15c	19c

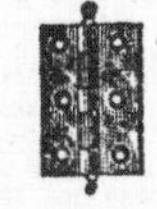

No. 9C983 **Genuine Wrought Bronze Ball Tip Butts,** antique copper finish, highly polished. Packed with screws.

Size, inches, open	2½x1⅞	3x3
Price, per pair	24c	39c

Burglar Proof Sash Fasts.

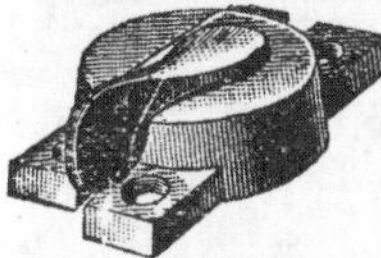

No. 9C1129 **Electro Copper Plated Antique Copper Sash Fasts.** Matches any antique copper finish goods.
Price, each..........**8c**
Per dozen...........**88c**

Cupboard Catches.

No. 9C1160 **Electro Copper Plated, Antique Copper Finish Cupboard Catch,** wrought steel patent triangular bolt. Packed complete with screws. Matches any antique copper finish goods.
Price, per dozen, **69c**; each........................**6c**

Cupboard Turns.

No. 9C1183 **Electro Copper Plated, Antique Copper Finish Cupboard Turn.** A new and beautiful design. Will match any antique copper finish goods.
Price, each.........**$0.13**
Per dozen..........**1.45**

No. 9C1194 **Electro Copper Plated, Antique Copper Sand Finish Cupboard Turn,** with patent diamond no-friction bolt, T handle. Will go on stile inch wide. Packed complete with screws. Matches any antique copper sand finish goods.
Price, each..........................**$0.21**
Per dozen...............................**2.44**

Drawer Pulls.

No. 9C1231 **Electro Copper Plated, Antique Copper Finish Drawer Pull.** Large, 3⅞ inches long. Will match any antique copper finish goods.
Price, per dozen, **26c**; each........................**3c**

Sliding Door Lock Sets.

Small illustration to the left shows astragal front.

Sliding Door Lock Sets are furnished with trimmings of same material and design as are used on inside sets of the design they are to match.

Catalogue Number	To Match Inside Set	Design	For Single or Double Doors	Style of Front	Price, per Set
336	9C332	Acme	Single	Flat	$1.43
337	9C332	Acme	Double	Flat	1.47
338	9C332	Acme	Double	Astragal	2.14
383	9C378	Fulton	Single	Flat	1.18
384	9C378	Fulton	Double	Flat	1.50
385	9C378	Fulton	Double	Astragal	1.80
C430	9C424	Bokay	Single	Flat	.94
C431	9C424	Bokay	Double	Flat	1.35
C432	9C424	Bokay	Double	Astragal	1.63
463	9C456	Bokay	Single	Flat	.83
464	9C456	Bokay	Double	Flat	1.25
465	9C456	Bokay	Double	Astragal	1.50
530	9C522	Chicago	Single	Flat	1.07
531	9C522	Chicago	Double	Flat	1.38
532	9C522	Chicago	Double	Astragal	1.88
566	9C559	Chicago	Single	Flat	1.00
567	9C559	Chicago	Double	Flat	1.50
568	9C559	Chicago	Double	Astragal	1.82

Parlor Door Hangers.

Steel Ball Bearing Parlor Door Hanger with overhead center stop floor guides and screws complete—wheel has noiseless fibre tread.

The hanger has a vertical adjustment of about three-quarters of an inch, and the set screw which regulates the adjustment is easily accessible with a screwdriver at either edge of the door. These hangers are furnished complete with 14 feet of steel track for double doors and with 8 feet of steel track for single doors.

If more track is wanted than is furnished with set we will furnish it at 5 cents per foot.

No. 9C900 **For Double Doors,** complete with 14 feet of steel track.
Price, per set.......................................**$2.50**

No. 9C901 **For Single Doors,** complete with 8 feet of steel track. Price, per set......**$1.25**

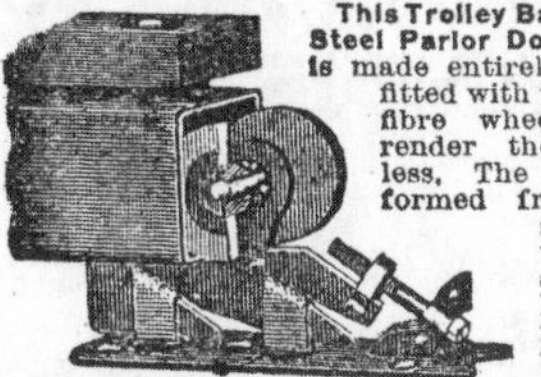

This Trolley Ball Bearing Steel Parlor Door Hanger is made entirely of steel, fitted with vulcanized fibre wheels, which render them noiseless. The track is formed from sheet steel, is very rigid and firm. Each piece is fastened to a wood header by three adjusting screws and can be furnished in any length to 10 feet without joint. While the first cost of this hanger may seem high when compared with others, the saving in material and labor for putting them up will nearly if not quite offset the extra cost. Complete directions packed with each set.

No. 9C908 **For Double Doors.** Price, per set
Size of opening, 5 feet..........................**$2.77**
Size of opening, 5 feet 6 inches...............**2.78**
Size of opening, 6 feet..........................**2.79**
Size of opening, 6 feet 6 inches...............**2.89**

No. 9C909 **For Single Doors.** Price, per set
Size of opening, 4 feet..........................**$1.62**
Size of opening, 4 feet 6 inches...............**1.74**
Size of opening, 5 feet..........................**1.86**
Size of opening, 5 feet 6 inches...............**1.98**
Size of opening, 6 feet..........................**2.09**

STORE DOOR HANDLES AND LOCKS.

Elegant Bronze Store Door Handle.

No. 9C1500 **Genuine Bronze Metal, Antique Copper Finish Door Handle,** with cylinder lock. Size of lock, 5⅛x3½ inches. Reversible. Easy spring. Three German silver keys. Size of plates, 12⅞x2½ inches, with fancy bar grip with ball tips. A very strong, secure and handsome lock, packed with screws.
Price, complete...**$6.93**

No. 9C1510 **Genuine Bronze Metal Store Door Handle and Lock.** Plain polished easy spring lock, reversible, for right or left hand doors. Size of lock, 4¼x3 inches. Lock has three tumblers. Two nickel plated steel keys. Size of plate is 12⅞x2½ inches. Packed complete with screws.
Price, complete...**$3.50**

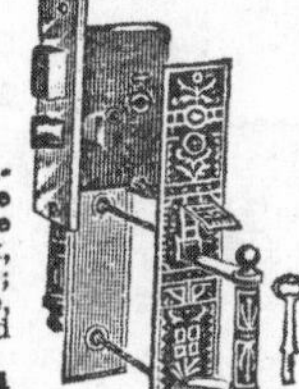

No. 9C1513 **Ornamental Electro Bronze Plated Store Door Handle and Lock.** Size of lock, 4¼x3 inches. Reversible; easy spring. Size of plate, 12⅞x2½ inches. Packed complete with screws.
Price..............**$1.54**

Rim Knob Locks.

NOTICE—Door knobs are not furnished with latches and locks quoted below. If knobs are wanted, order them separately.

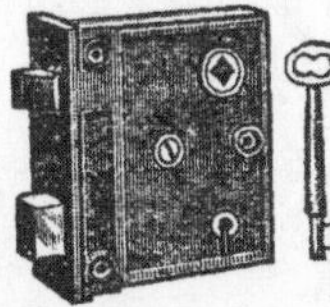

No. 9C1633 **Upright Rim Knob Lock,** for either right or left hand door. Japanned, with stop, iron bolts, iron key, one tumbler, packed complete with screws and japanned keyhole escutcheons, without door knobs. If knobs are wanted, order them separately. Size, 4x3¼ inches. Weight, 2⅛ pounds.
Price, per dozen, **$1.13**; each.............**10c**

SEND TO US FOR ALL THE GOODS YOU NEED. WE SAVE YOU MONEY ON EVERYTHING.

No. 9C1636 **Horizontal Rim Knob Lock,** for either right or left hand door. Size, 3¼x4½ inches, japanned, with stop, iron bolts, iron key, japanned keyhole escutcheons, one tumbler. Packed with screws, without door knobs. If knobs are wanted, order them separately. Weight, 2¼ pounds.
Price, per dozen, **$1.00**; each.............**9c**

No. 9C1639 **Upright Rim Knob Lock,** for either right or left hand door. Size, 4x3¼ inches. Japanned, with three brass bolts, nickel plated steel key, japanned keyhole escutcheons. Packed complete with screws. One tumbler, without door knobs. If knobs are wanted, order them separately. Weight, 2¼ pounds. Price, per dozen, **$2.20**; each..**19c**

No. 9C1645 **Horizontal Rim Knob Lock,** for either right or left hand door. Japanned, with three brass bolts, nickel plated steel key, one tumbler, japanned keyhole escutcheons. Packed complete with screws. Without door knobs. If knobs are wanted, order them separately. Size, 4x3¼ inches. Weight, 2¼ pounds.
Price, per dozen, **$3.38**; each.............**29c**

Wrought Steel Rim Locks.

The cases of these locks are made of wrought steel, finished in ivory black. The locks are lighter than cast iron goods and they cannot be broken.

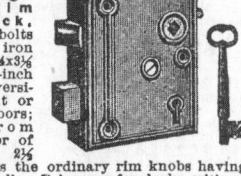

No. 9C1660 **Upright Wrought Steel Rim Knob Lock,** with iron bolts and tinned iron key. Size, 4x3½ inches, ⅝-inch thick. Reversible, for right or left hand doors; distance from face to center of keyhole, 2½ inches; takes the ordinary rim knobs having 5-16-inch spindle. Prices are for locks without knobs. If knobs are wanted, order them separately. See Nos. 9C1941, 9C1942 or 9C1943 for knobs to go with this lock. Packed complete with keyhole escutcheons and screws to match.
Price, per dozen, **$1.93**; each.............**17c**

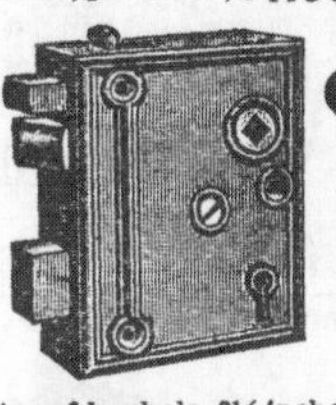

No. 9C1664 **Upright Wrought Steel Rim Knob Lock,** with thumb bolt. Three iron bolts, nickel plated steel key. Size, 4x3½ inches, ⅝-inch thick, reversible, for right or left hand doors; distance from face to center of keyhole, 2½ inches; takes knobs same as above. Prices are for locks without knobs. Packed complete with keyhole escutcheons and screws to match.
Price, per dozen, **$2.85**; each.............**24c**

No. 9C1668 **Upright Wrought Steel Rim Knob Lock,** same as preceding, except it has brass bolts.
Price, per dozen, **$3.07**; each.............**26c**

Rim Knob Locks and Latches.

No. 9C1675 **Horizontal Wrought Steel Rim Knob Lock,** with iron bolts and tinned iron key. Size, 4½x3¼ inches, ⅝ inch thick. Reversible for right or left hand doors. Distance from face to center of keyhole, 2½ inches; to center of knob hub, 3⅝ inches. Takes the ordinary rim knobs. See Nos. 9C1941, 9C1942 or 9C1943. Prices are for locks without knobs. Packed complete with keyhole escutcheons and screws to match.
Price, per dozen, **$2.07**; each.............**18c**

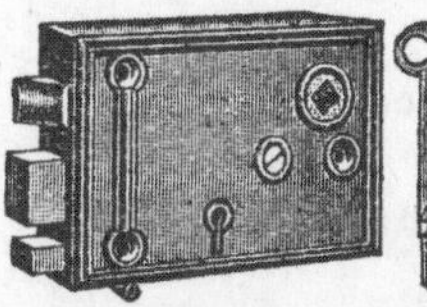

No. 9C1679 **Horizontal Wrought Steel Rim Knob Lock,** with thumb bolt. Three brass bolts. Nickel plated steel key. In other ways same as preceding lock. Price, per doz. **$4.00**; each, **34c**

No. 9C1726 **Horizontal Rim Knob Latch.** Size, 3½x2½ inches. Reversible for right or left hand door. Iron bolt; iron thumb bolt; japanned case. Packed with screws; without knobs; if knobs are wanted order them separately. Price, per doz., **$1.28**; each, **11c**

Rim Night Latches.

Rim Night Latches cannot be used with door knobs. They are operated from the outside by key only and on the inside by the knob; the bolt may be fastened back at will by the spring catch inside of case.

No. 9C1758 **Horizontal Cylinder Rim Night Latch,** plain japanned case. Size, 2½x2⅞ inches, bronze bolt, bronze escutcheon, three German silver keys for either right or left hand doors, from ⅞ to 3 inches thick. Packed complete with screws. Safe and durable.
Price..**$1.05**

No. 9B1763 **Horizontal Tubular Rim Night Latch.** Right or left hand. Size, 3½x2⅜ inches. Two flat steel keys. For doors, 1 to 1⅞ inches thick. Packed complete with screws.
Price..**30c**

Store Door Locks.

No. 9C1765 **Upright Rim Store Door Lock.** Size, 5x3½ inches; japanned case, iron bolt, two nickel plated folding steel keys. Packed complete with screws.
Price.....**48c**

No. 9C1780 **Mortise Knob Latch.** Size, 1⅞x3½ inches; japanned iron case, iron front, bolt and strike, without knobs. Weight, 12 ounces.
Price, each.........**6c**
Per dozen..........**68c**

No. 9C1785 **Mortise Knob Latch,** same as above, with brass front, bolt and strike, without knob. Price, per dozen, **$1.85**; each..**16c**

Reversible Mortise Knob Locks.

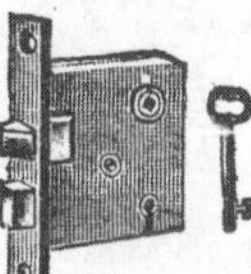

No. 9C1800 **Reversible Mortise Knob Lock.** Size, 3½x3½ inches; japanned iron case; lacquered iron front, strike and bolts; malleable iron keys; japanned escutcheons; one tumbler. Weight, 1⅛ pounds; without knobs.
Price, each....**$0.11**
Per dozen.....**1.22**

No. 9C1804 **Reversible Mortise Knob Lock.** Size, 3½x3½ inches; japanned iron case, cast brass front and bolts. Strike is wrought iron, brass plated; nickel plated steel key; japanned escutcheons; one tumbler; without knobs.
Price, per dozen, **$2.19**; each..........**19c**

Door Knobs.

These door knobs will fit any standard make of lock and doors from ⅞ to 2¼ inches thick. The knob is 2¼ inches in diameter. Spindle, 5-16 inch.

No. 9C1941 **Mineral Rim Knobs,** with japanned shanks and rose; fits rim knob locks. Color, mottled brown. Weight, 1 lb. Per doz, **66c**; each, **6c**

No. 9C1942 **Porcelain Rim Knobs,** with japanned shanks and rose; fits rim knob locks. Color, white. Weight, 1 pound.
Price, per dozen., **73c**; each..............**7c**

No. 9C1943 **Jet Rim Knobs,** with japanned shanks and rose; fits rim knob locks. Color, black. Weight, 1 lb. Per dozen, **73c**; each, **7c**

Door Knobs for Mortise Locks.

No. 9C1951 **Mineral Mortise Knobs,** with japanned shanks and roses; fits mortise knob locks. Color, mottled brown. Weight, 1 pound. Price, per dozen, **66c**; each.........**6c**

No. 9C1952 **Porcelain Mortise Knobs,** with japanned shanks and roses; fits mortise knob locks. Color, white. Weight, 1 pound.
Price, per dozen, **73c**; each...........**7c**

No. 9C1953 **Jet Mortise Knobs,** with japanned shanks and roses; fits mortise knob locks. Color, black. Per doz., **73c**; each, **7c**

Door Butts.

No. 9C2000 **Loose Pin Cast Iron Butts,** plain finish. The sizes given are measurements when butt is open, and length is always given first.
Screws not included at prices quoted.

Size, inches	2x2	2½x2½	3x3	3½x3½	4x4
Wt., per pair, ozs.	9	12	15	18	28
Price, per pair	3c	4c	5c	6c	8c
Per dozen pairs	27c	37c	48c	64c	79c

Loose Pin Steel Butts.

No. 9C2004 **Wrought Steel Loose Pin Butts,** for either right or left hand doors. Plain finish.
Prices are for butts without screws.

Sizes	2½x2½	3x3	3½x3½	4x4	4½x4½
Price, per pair	4c	5c	6c	8c	$0.10
Doz. pairs	34c	49c	71c	87c	1.1'

Japanned Steel Door Butts.

No. 9C2006 Wrought Steel Loose Pin Butts, with ball tips, for right hand doors; japanned. Prices are without screws.

Size, inches	Size Screw required	Per dozen pairs	Per pair
2½x2½	8	$0.68	6c
3 x3	9	.79	7c
3½x3½	10	.90	8c
4 x4	10	1.12	10c
4½x4½	11	1.35	12c
5 x5	12	1.68	14c

Flat Head Japanned Screws.

No. 9C4124 With black japanned heads, suitable for No. 9C2006 butts.

Length	Size No.	Per Grs.	Per Doz.
⅞-inch	8	17c	2c
1 -inch	8	18c	2c
1 -inch	9	19c	3c
1¼-inch	9	21c	3c
1 -inch	10	20c	3c
1¼-inch	10	22c	3c
1 -inch	11	22c	3c
1¼-inch	11	23c	3c
1½-inch	11	25c	4c
1 -inch	12	24c	3c
1¼-inch	12	25c	4c
1½-inch	12	27c	4c

Narrow Wrought Butts.

Prices are for butts without screws.

No. 9C2012 Narrow Wrought Steel Butts. Fast joints.

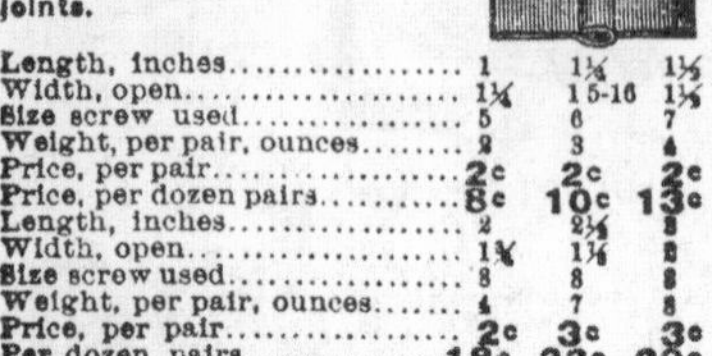

Length, inches	1	1⅛	1½
Width, open	1¼	1 5-16	1½
Size screw used	5	6	7
Weight, per pair, ounces	2	3	4
Price, per pair	2c	2c	2c
Price, per dozen pairs	8c	10c	13c
Length, inches	2	2½	3
Width, open	1⅞	1⅞	2
Size screw used	8	8	8
Weight, per pair, ounces	4	7	8
Price, per pair	2c	3c	3c
Per dozen pairs	18c	22c	29c

Screws are not furnished with butts.

Brass Butts and Hinges.

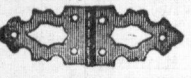

No. 9C2022 Light Wrought Brass Butts. Prices are without screws.

Size	¾x⅝	1x⅞	1¼x1	1½x1
Weight, per pair	2 ozs.	3 ozs.	4 ozs.	4 ozs.
Price, per pair	2c	2c	2c	3c
Per dozen pairs	12c	15c	20c	24c
Size	1½x1¼	2x1¼	2½x1¾	3x1½
Price, per pair	4c	4c	6c	$0.10
Per dozen pairs	34c	37c	68c	1.00

No. 9C2023 Fancy Light Brass Box Hinge, for work boxes and small cases. Intended to be put on with brass escutcheon pins. Entire length, open 1½ inches. Width, ½-inch. Made of brass buffed and lacquered. Price, per pair 3c
Per dozen pairs 25c

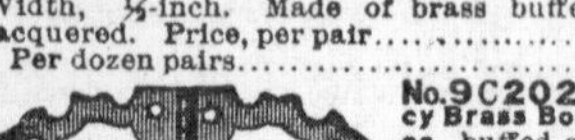

No. 9C2024 Fancy Brass Box Hinges, buffed and lacquered. Entire length, open, 3 inches. Width, 1 inch. Intended to be put on with round head brass screws or escutcheon pins. Weight, per pair, ½ ounce. Price, per pair 5c
Per dozen pairs 50c

Wrought Brass Hinges.

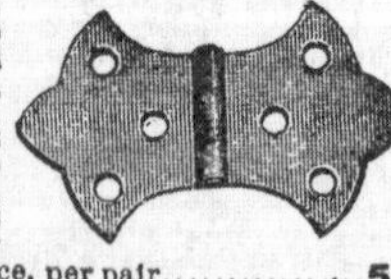

No. 9C2025 Wrought Brass Flap Hinges, buffed and lacquered. Size, when open, length, 3 inches; width at joint, 1 inch. Made to be put on with flat head brass screws. Weight, per pair, 2 ounces. Price, per pair 5c
Per dozen pairs 50c

Floor Hinge.

No. 9C2032 Floor Hinge, can be applied with less trouble than any other double acting floor spring hinge on the market. The door works on a ball bearing pivot and the spring has an adjustable tension. Doors cannot sag. No jamb strip required. We carry the following in stock, but will quote other sizes and finishes in solid bronze metal on request. Packed complete with pivot for top of door and all screws.

Thickness of Door, Inches	Price, Iron, Dull Japanned	Price, Iron, Polished Antique, Copper Plated
⅞ to 1⅜	$1.26	$1.73
1¾ to 2	1.62	2.16

Niles' Spring Hinge

No. 9C2037 Niles Double Acting Spring Hinge, (to swing both ways) requires no jamb strip. They are easily put on, doors can not sag, they have adjustable tension. For a set we furnish our spring and pivot for top of door. We carry in stock the sizes and finishes listed below but can furnish other styles. Price quoted on request:

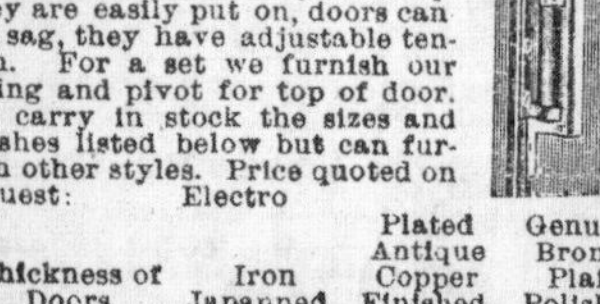

Thickness of Doors	Iron Japanned	Electro Plated Antique Copper Finished	Genuine Bronze Plain Polished
⅞ in. to 1 1-16 in.	$0.58	$1.08	$2.88
1⅛ in. to 1¼ in.	.80	1.29	3.60
1⅜ in. to 1½ in.	1.00	1.52	3.96
1¾ in. to 1⅞ in.	1.30	1.73	5.40
2 in. to 2⅛ in.	1.88	2.15	6.34
2¼ in. to 2⅜ in.	2.16	2.52	7.20

Double Acting Spring Butts.

No. 9C2031 Spring Butts, reversible for right or left hand doors; japanned iron. The largest hinge that the thickness of the door will permit works best.

Size	For doors	Per pair
3-inch	⅝ to 1 inches thick	$0.80
4-inch	⅞ to 1¼ inches thick	1.00
5-inch	1 to 1½ inches thick	1.25
6-inch	1¼ to 1¾ inches thick	1.70

Thumb Latches.

No. 9C2100 Enameled Thumb Latch; very handsome. Weight about 1 pound. Packed complete with screws. Suitable for doors ¾ to 1¾ inches thick.
Price, each 5c
Per dozen 58c

Barn Door Latches.

No. 9C2110 Barn Door Latches, Japanned, extra heavy; with wrought latch.
Price, each $0.10
Per dozen 1.00

ALUMINUM LETTERS AND FIGURES.

Our letters and figures are provided with prongs on back for the purpose of securing them to wood. By the use of these letters and figures you can make durable and elegant signs at a less price than you could have an inferior sign made by a sign painter.

Aluminum Letters.

No. 9C2112 Cast Aluminum Letters, 3 inches high.
Price, any letter, each, 7c
Per 100 $6.25

No. 9C2113 Cast Aluminum Periods or Commas, for use with above.
Price, per 100, $1.25; each 2c

Aluminum Figures.

No. 9C2114 Cast Aluminum Figures. 2 inches high. Flat.
Price, any figure, each $0.04
Per 100 3.75

No. 9C2115 Cast Aluminum Figures. 3 inches high. Oval.
Price, any figure, each $0.06
Per 100 5.10

Postage on 2-inch, per dozen, 5 cents; 3-inch, per dozen, 7 cents.

Foot Scrapers.

No. 9C2125 Made from Bessemer steel, 6 inches wide, 3¾ inches high. Will not bend, and being made of steel, cannot be broken by a sharp blow.
Price, each 7c
Per dozen 68c

No. 9C2131 Foot Scraper, fancy pattern, japanned iron.
Price, each 4c
Per dozen 42c

No. 9C2133 Extra Heavy Unbreakable Foot Scraper. The best and strongest foot scraper we have ever seen. Weight, 14 ounces. Price, each, 5c
Per dozen 47c

Wrought Iron Door Bolts.

No. 9C2140 Wrought Iron Door Bolts. Japanned plate; brass knob; polished bolt.

Length of bolt, in.	2½	3	4	5	6
Price, each	3c	4c	4c	5c	5c
Per dozen	28c	35c	39c	45c	53c

Cupboard Catches.

No. 9C2155 Cupboard Catch, japanned iron, porcelain knob. Wt., 4 ounces.
Price, each 3c
Per dozen 30c

Elbow Catches.

No. 9C2160 Elbow Catches, japanned; used on double cupboard doors to hold one door closed, the other being fastened with outside catch.
Price, each 2c
Per dozen 22c

Door Stops.

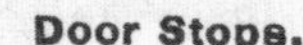

No. 9C2170 Base Knob, to screw into baseboard to prevent door knob striking against the wall; bronzed iron, brass rim, rubber tip, wrought iron screw.
Price, per dozen, 21c; each 2c

No. 9C2173 Birchwood Base Knob, with rubber tips.
Price, each 2c
Per dozen 12c

Hat and Coat Hooks.

No. 9C2180 Wire Coat and Hat Hook; gimlet screw points. Will not break. No tools required to put them up. Lighter than cast iron hooks. Copper finished.
Length, 3 inches. Price, per dozen 5c
Per gross 55c

No. 9C2181 Wire Coat and Hat Hook, same as above, japanned finish.
Length, 3 inches. Price, per dozen 6c
Per gross 58c

No. 9C2186 Iron Japanned Hat and Coat Hook, 2½ inches. Weight, per dozen, 1¼ pounds.
Price, per dozen 6c
Per gross 69c

No. 9C2188 Iron Japanned Hat and Coat Hook, 3½ inches. Weight, per dozen, 1 lb. 5 ozs.
Price, per dozen 8c
Per gross 85c

No. 9C2193 Iron Japanned Triple Hat and Coat Hook, 4 inches. Weight, per dozen, 1 pound 13 ounces. Price, per gross, $1.12; per dozen 10c

No. 9C2200 The Safety Coat and Hat Hook will easily hold a stiff, straw or soft hat; projects from the wall about 4 inches; whole length 10 inches. Rough nickel plated.
Price, each 5c
Per dozen 47c

No. 9C2201 Polished and nickel plated. Price, each 9c
Per dozen 98c

Schoolhouse Hooks.

No. 9C2208 Iron Japanned Schoolhouse Hooks are heavier and stronger than the ordinary hat or coat hooks and are sometimes preferred for wardrobe use for that reason. Double hook, 2½ inches, no screws. Weight, per dozen, 3 pounds 13 ounces.

Price, per dozen $0.16
Per gross 1.87

Extra Heavy Harness Hooks.

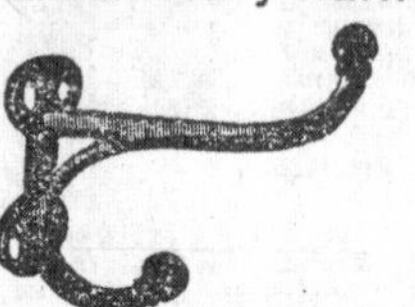

No. 9C2220 Harness Hooks, japanned, extra heavy.
Length 6 inches
Price, each 4c
Per dozen 42c
Length 8 inches
Price, each 5c
Per dozen 53c
Length, 10½ inches.
Price, per dozen, $1.58; each 14c

Wardrobe Hooks.

No. 9C2225 Coppered Wire Wardrobe Hook. Length, 2 inches.
Price, per dozen 6c
Per gross 68c

No. 9C2226 Japanned Wire Wardrobe Hook. Length, 2½ inches.
Price, per doz. 8c
Per gross 85c

Shelf Brackets.

No. 9C2262 Shelf Brackets. German bronzed, fancy design, same as illustration.

Size, inches	Price, per doz. pairs	Per pair
4x5	$0.75	7c
5x7	1.05	10c
6x8	1.24	11c
8x10	1.88	17c
9x12	2.52	23c

No. 9C2263 Wrought Steel Shelf Brackets; japanned; will never break. They are rapidly taking the place of the common cast iron shelf brackets, which are brittle and unreliable. Price does not include screws.

Size, inches	Price, per doz. pairs	Per pair
3x4	$0.19	3c
4x5	.26	3c
5x7	.46	5c
6x8	.58	6c
7x9	.69	7c
8x10	.81	8c
10x12	1.14	11c
12x14	1.72	16c

Ives' Sash Locks.

Ives' Burglar Proof Sash Lock is pronounced by architects and builders to be the best in use. When locked they draw the two sashes tightly together, which prevents their rattling. They cannot be opened from the outside by putting a thin knife blade between sash and pushing the hook open, as is the case with common sash locks. They are ornamental and easily put on. Packed with screws.

No. 9C2324 Ives' Burglar Proof Sash Locks, small size, ornamental iron bronzed.
Price, per dozen, 32c; each 3c

No. 9C2325 Ives' Burglar Proof Sash Locks, medium size, ornamental iron; bronzed.
Price, per dozen, 41c; each 4c

No. 9C2328 Ives' Burglar Proof Sash Locks, medium size, ornamental iron, bronzed, with genuine bronze metal knob.
Price, per dozen, 72c; each 6c

No. 9C2329 Ives' Burglar Proof Sash Locks, medium size, ornamental iron, electro copper plated, to match Bokay design lock sets.
Price, per dozen, $1.25; each 11c

No. 9C2331 Ives' Burglar Proof Sash Locks, large size, ornamental iron, bronzed.
Price, per dozen, 50c; each 5c

No. 9C2334 Ives' Burglar Proof Sash Locks. Large size, ornamental iron, with bronze metal knob.
Price, per dozen, 89c; each 8c

No. 9C2336 Ives' Burglar Proof Sash Lock, medium size, electro copper plated, antique copper finish. Price, each 8c
Per dozen 89c

No. 9C2337 Ives' Bell Tip Plain Sash Fasts Medium size, highly polished electro copper plated. Plain polished bronze finish. Price, each $0.12
Per dozen 1.42

No. 9C2340 Ives' Bell Tip Plain Sash Fasts, Medium size, genuine bronze metal. Plain polished bronze finish, highly polished.
Price, per dozen, $2.50; each 21c

No. 9C2355 Burglar Proof Sash Fasts, ornamental iron.
Price, each 4c
Per dozen 35c

No. 9C2356 Burglar Proof Sash Fasts, electro copper plated, antique copper finish.
Price, per dozen, 53c; each 5c

No. 9C2357 Burglar Proof Sash Fasts, electro bronze plated, to match lock sets Nos. 9C423 to 9C491.
Price, per dozen, $1.03; each 9c

No. 9C2360 Burglar Proof Sash Locks. Plain iron, bronzed.
Price, each 4c
Per dozen 35c

No. 9C2361 Burglar Proof Sash Locks. Electro copper plated, antique copper finish.
Price, per dozen 53c; each 5c

No. 9C2362 Burglar Proof Sash Locks. Electro copper plated, highly polished antique copper sand finish.
Price, per dozen 97c; each 9c

No. 9C2363 Burglar Proof Sash Locks. Electro copper plated, plain polished bronze finish. Price, each 9c
Per dozen 98c

No. 9C2350 Sash Lock holds the window securely closed or open to any position desired. Finished in nickel plate. Packed complete with screws.
Price, each 6c
Per dozen 63c

No. 9C2352 Sash Lock same as preceding, electro copper plated, antique finish.
Price, each 6c
Per dozen 62c

Window Springs.

No. 9C2390 Window Springs, screw socket, self fastening iron case. Malleable iron bolt. Fits ¾-inch hole.
Price, per gross, $2.57; per dozen 22c

Window Spring Bolts.

No. 9C2397 Window Spring Bolts, japanned silvered tip, tin case.
Price, per gross, $1.13; per dozen 10c

No. 9C2402 Tinned Norway Iron Window Spring Bolts, with zinc case.
Price, per gross, $1.57; per dozen 14c

No. 9C2395 Window Spring Bolt, for screen frames, japanned tin case. Length of case ¾-inch; entire length, 3 inches.
Price, per gross, $1.22; per dozen 11c

Stop Bead Screws with Beveled Washers.

No. 9C2406 Antique Copper Plated (on Iron) Stop Bead Screws and Washers complete.
Price, per gross, 68c; per dozen 7c

No. 9C2408 Genuine Bronze Stop Bead Screws and Washers, plain bronze finish, complete. Price, per dozen $0.15
Per gross 1.44

Sash Pulleys.

No. 9C2424 Steel Sash Pulleys are provided with a durable bushing in the wheels to take the wear. Every part is steel. They save screws, breakage, freight and time putting them in. Diameter of wheel, 2 inch.
Price, per dozen 21c

No. 9C2430 The Common Sense Pattern Pulley. Mortise made with a 1-inch bit. It can be applied by hand at the rate of 80 per hour. It is firmly held by screws through its face plate, and easily removable when occasion requires. Plain face, polished 2-inch wheel.
Price, per dozen 18c

Vanderbilt Sash Balances.

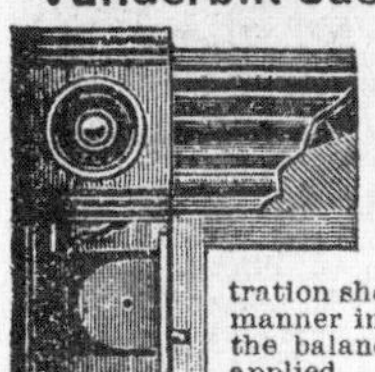

All Vanderbilt Balances are all coppered inside as well as outside, therefore are not liable to rust.

All balances are tested with great care and we fully warrant every one. The illustration shows the manner in which the balances are applied. Directions are sent with each set.

No. 9C2440 Vanderbilt Side Balances. Per set of four balances, enough for two sashes.

Size No.	Weight of each sash, pounds	Height of sash, inches	Price, per set
[illegible]	4 to 6	34	$0.79
[illegible]	6 to 8	34	.86
[illegible]	8 to 10	34	.88
[illegible]	10 to 12	44	1.02
[illegible]	12 to 14	44	1.17
[illegible]	14 to 16	44	1.23
[illegible]	16 to 18	48	1.33
[illegible]	18 to 20	48	1.44
[illegible]	20 to 22	48	1.50
[illegible]	22 to 24	48	1.60
[illegible]	24 to 26	50	1.70
[illegible]	26 to 28	50	1.82
[illegible]	28 to 30	50	1.86
[illegible]	30 to 32	50	1.92
[illegible]	32 to 34	50	1.99
[illegible]	34 to 36	50	2.06

We furnish any size balance up to 58 pounds. Prices quoted on application.

Sash Cord.

No. 9C2445 Silver Lake Braided Sash Cord, size 8-32. Put up in bundles of 100 feet. Weight, about 2½ pounds to the bundle.

Price, per bundle............................76c

No. 9C2446 Standard Braided Cotton Sash Cord. We have sold this cord for several years and it has always given the best of satisfaction. Size 8-32. Put up in bundles of 100 feet.

Price, per bundle............................65c

Transom Lifters.

With this device transoms may be lowered or raised at will with great ease and locked in any position; no other fastenings required; when ordering, give length of lifter. They are made from round iron rods, bronzed and nicely finished.

No. 9C2452 For transom hinged at top or hung in the middle.

Length		Diameter, ¼-inch	Diameter, 5-16-inch	Diameter, ⅜-inch
[illegible] feet.	Price..	11½c	.....	.....
[illegible] feet.	Price..	11½c	.....	.....
[illegible] feet.	Price........		19c	.....
[illegible] feet.	Price........		21c	27c
[illegible] feet.	Price........		24c	31c
[illegible] feet.	Price........		.....	35c

Iron Storm Threshold.

No. 9C2120 No rain will beat under your door if you use this iron storm threshold. Size given is width between jambs.

Size, inches.	28	30	32	34	36
Weight, lbs.	9	9½	10	10½	11
Price........	38c	42c	46c	50c	60c

See Nos. 9C2475 to 9C2484 for weather strips.

Ashpit or Fuel Door.

No. 9C2496 Ashpit or Fuel Door. Heavy cast iron, well made. Size indicates size of opening in inches.

Size of opening	Price, each	Per doz.
8x 8	35c	$4.05
8x10	38c	4.45
10x12	52c	6.08
10x14	58c	6.76

Shutter Knobs.

No. 9C2498 Porcelain Shutter Knobs. Loose, round head, tinned screw; used for drawer pulls, cupboard door knobs, etc.

Size, inches	Price, each	Per dozen	Per gross
⅞	1c	7c	$0.78
1	1c	8c	.84
1¼	2c	11c	1.21
1½	2c	13c	1.52

Fancy Handles and Pulls.

No. 9C2507 Tuscan Bronzed Drawer Pulls. 3½-inch. Packed complete with screws. Each weighs 4 ounces.

Price, Per dozen..19c, each..............2c

No. 9C2510 Fancy Stamped Furniture Handles. Gilt finish. Size of plate, 4x1⅜ inches.

Price, each...2c
Per dozen...22c

No. 9C2512 Fancy Stamped Furniture Handles. Gilt finished. Size of plate, 4⅜ x 1⅝ inches.

Price, each....3c
Per dozen....25c

No. 9C2515 Fancy Stamped Furniture Handles. Gilt finish. Size of plate, 5 x 2½ inches. Price, each......5c
Per doz. 49c

No. 9C2521 Fancy Cast Furniture Handles. Gilt finish. A new and handsome design. Size of plate, 4¼x2 inches.

Price, each .. 7c
Per dozen ..81c

No. 9C2527 Drop Ring Pulls. Gilt finish, plate 1⅞-inch in diameter. The ring of this pull is iron, brass plated, making a strong, durable pull.

Price, each..........2c
Per dozen...........19c

No. 9C2530 Drop Ebony Pulls. Gilt finish plate. Size of plate is 1⅜ inches in diameter; diameter of knob is 1¼ inches. Can be used on wood not thicker than 1¼ inches. Price per dozen, 34c; each 4c

No. 9C2536 Fancy Cast Brass Knob Pulls. Diameter, 1⅛ inches.

Price, each 5c
Per dozen........54c

No. 9C2546 Fancy Stamped Escutcheon. Gilt finish. Used with any of our stamped handles. Size of plate, 1⅞x1⅛ inches; length of opening for key, ⅝ inch. Per dozen, 13c; each.......2c

No. 9C2548 Fancy Cast Escutcheon. Size, 2⅛x1⅛inches; length of opening for key, ⅝ inch. Used with any of our cast pulls or handles. Price, each.3c; per dozen....25c

Strap and T Hinges.

NOTICE—Screws are not furnished with hinges at prices quoted. For screws see Index.

No. 9C2600 Light Wrought Steel T Hinges. Size given is measure from joint to end of hinge.

Size, in...	3	4	6	8
Weight, per pair...	4 ozs.	5 ozs.	8 ozs.	12 ozs.
Price, per pair...	3c	3c	4c	5c
Per dozen pairs....	23c	24c	36c	45c

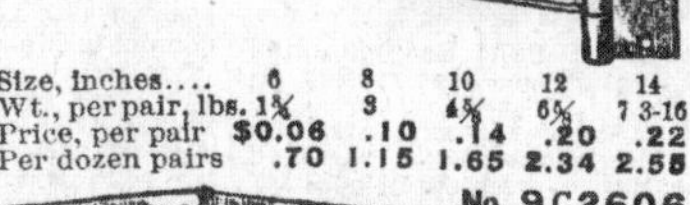

No. 9C2603 Extra Heavy Wrought Steel T Hinges, without screws.

Size, inches....	6	8	10	12	14
Wt., per pair, lbs.	1⅛	3	4⅜	5⅝	7 3-16
Price, per pair	$0.06	.10	.14	.20	.22
Per dozen pairs	.70	1.15	1.65	2.34	2.55

No. 9C2606 Light Wrought Steel Strap Hinges, without screws. Size given is measurement from joint to end of hinge.

Size, inches..........	3	4	5	6
Price, per pair	3c	3c	4c	5c
Per dozen pairs......	23c	30c	36c	47c

No. 9C2609 Heavy Wrought Steel Strap Hinges, without screws.

Size, inches.....	6	8	10	12	14
Wt., per pair, lbs...	1⅛	3	4½	6⅛	7⅜
Price, per pair.	$0.06	.08	.12	.17	.19
Per dozen pairs..	.60	.88	1.34	1.91	2.20

Screw Strap Hinges.

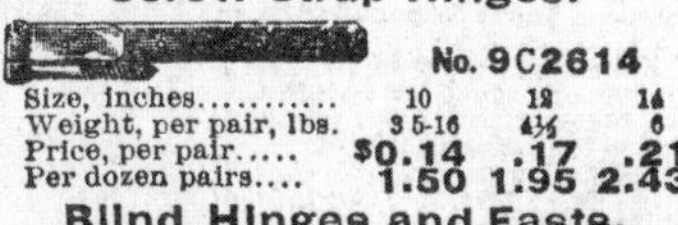

No. 9C2614

Size, inches........	10	12	14
Weight, per pair, lbs.	3 5-16	4⅛	6
Price, per pair....	$0.14	.17	.21
Per dozen pairs....	1.50	1.95	2.43

Blind Hinges and Fasts.

No. 9C2620 Clark's or Shepard's Gravity Locking Blind Hinges and Fasts, for wood houses; throws the blind 1½ inches from the casing. Price, per set......7c
Per dozen sets.........75c

Gate Hinges.

No. 9C2635 Self Closing Gate Hinges, to swing both ways; no springs to get out of order. Weight, 2½ pounds.
Price, per set 14c
Per dozen..$1.57

No. 9C2638 Self Closing Gate Hinges, to swing both ways, with wrought upper hinge.
Price, per set...32c

Gate Latches.

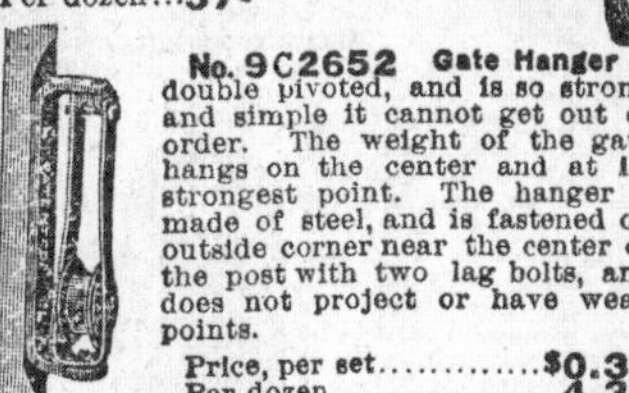

No. 9C2642 Gate Latches, for either right or left hand gates, to swing both ways. No springs to break or get out of order. Weight, 1 pound.
Price, each.....5c
Per dozen...57c

No. 9C2652 Gate Hanger is double pivoted, and is so strong and simple it cannot get out of order. The weight of the gate hangs on the center and at its strongest point. The hanger is made of steel, and is fastened on outside corner near the center of the post with two lag bolts, and does not project or have weak points.

Price, per set.............$0.37
Per dozen 4.30

Hooks and Staples.

No. 9C2655 Wrought Iron Hooks and Staples.

Length, inches	3	4	5	6
Weight, ounces.	3	4	4	5
Price, each...........	1c	1c	2c	2c
Per dozen............	8c	9c	11c	13c

No. 9C2658 Bright Iron Wire Hooks and Screw Eyes.

Length, inches.........	2	3	4
Weight, ounces............	2	2	3
Price, each..................	1c	1c	2c
Per dozen....................	5c	6c	8c

No. 9C2662 Safety Gate Hooks. Malleable hook with steel staples, all heavily tinned to prevent rusting.

Length, inches..............	4	6
Price, each..................	4c	5c
Per dozen.....................	44c	56c

Hasps and Staples.

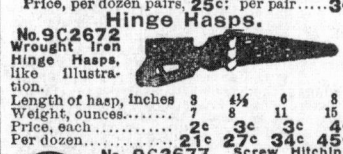

No. 9C2668 Wrought Iron Hasps and Staples, complete with double hook.

Length, inches.......	5	6	8	10
Weight, ounces......	4	5	9	13
Price, each...........	2c	2c	2c	3c
Per dozen	12c	14c	18c	25c

No. 9C2669 Security Combined Hook, Hasp and Staple. The most popular hasp on the market today. Length, 8 inches. complete with staples. Price, per doz. 31c
Each..............................3c

Padlock Eyes.

No. 9C2670 Padlock Eyes of Malleable Iron. Length, 2¼ inches; weight, per pair, 4 ounces. These padlock eyes take the place of the old time hasps and staples. They are more secure, as the screws which fasten them to the door or jamb are covered up so they cannot be gotten at.

Price, per dozen pairs, 25c; per pair.....3c

Hinge Hasps.

No. 9C2672 Wrought Iron Hinge Hasps, like illustration.

Length of hasp, inches	3	4½	6	8
Weight, ounces.......	7	8	11	15
Price, each	2c	3c	3c	4c
Per dozen..............	21c	27c	34c	45c

No. 9C2677 Screw Hitching Rings. These rings have heavy wrought steel screw and malleable ring. Heavily galvanized to prevent rust. Diameter of ring, 2¼ inches.

Price, per dozen, 47c; each.................5c

Roller Bearing Anti-Friction Steel Barn Door Hanger.

Is fully covered, has cold rolled steel axle and anti-friction rollers. With the exception of the wheel, it is made entirely of wrought steel, is built to stand the roughest usage and can be used on any standard track. We do not furnish bolts at prices quoted. **For bolts see Index.**

No. 9C2687 Roller Bearing Anti-Friction Steel Barn Door Hanger. For small doors. Frame, 4⅜x11½ inches, made of 3-16x1 inch wrought steel; 3-inch wheel. Weight, per pair, 6¼ pounds; per dozen pairs crated, 81 pounds. Use 5-16 bolts. For bolts see Index.

Price, per pair..........................$0.31
Per case containing 12 pairs........... 3.63

No. 9C2688 Roller Bearing Anti-Friction Steel Barn Door Hangers. For ordinary doors. Frame, 6¼x12¼ inches, made of ¼x1 inch wrought steel; 4-inch wheel. Weight, per pair, 8¼ pounds; per dozen pairs crated, 106 pounds. Use 5-16 bolts. For bolts see Index.

Price, per pair..........................$0.38
Per case containing 12 pairs........... 4.45

No. 9C2689 Roller Bearing Anti-Friction Steel Barn Door Hangers. Strong enough to hang the heaviest door. Frame, 7x14 inches, made of ¼x1¼ wrought steel; 5-inch wheel. Weight, per pair, 11½ pounds; per dozen pairs crated, 144 pounds. Use 5-16 bolts. For bolts see Index. Price, per pair.............$0.46
Per case containing 12 pairs............ 5.42

Anti-Friction Steel Barn Door Hanger With Loose Axle.

This hanger is made entirely of heavy steel, with the exception of the wheel, and is fully covered to protect it from snow and ice. Runs smoothly, and is built to stand continuous hard service. The wheel has a deep groove to prevent jumping the track. Bolts are not furnished with hangers. For bolts see Index.

No. 9C2703 Anti-Friction Steel Barn Door Hangers, with loose axle. For ordinary doors. Frame, 9x10¼ inches, made of ¼x1-inch wrought steel. 3-inch wheel, 8-foot run. Weight, per pair, 8 pounds; per half dozen pairs, crated, 58 pounds. Use 5-16 bolts to fasten to door.

Price, per pair.........................$0.45
Per crate of six pairs... .... 2.63

No. 9C2704 Anti-Friction Steel Barn Door Hangers, with loose axle. For wide doors. Frame, 11x11¾ inches, made of ¼x1-inch wrought steel. 4-inch wheel, 10-foot run. Weight, per pair, 9¾ pounds; per half dozen pairs, crated, 65 pounds. Use 5-16 bolts to fasten to door. Price, per pair...............$0.54
Per crate of six pairs................. 3.15

No. 9C2705 Anti-Friction Steel Barn Door Hangers, with loose axle. For wide and heavy doors. Frame, 12x12¼ inches, made of ¼x1¼-inch wrought steel. 5-inch wheel, 11-foot run. Weight, per pair, 13¼ pounds; per half dozen pairs, crated, 86 pounds. Use 5-16 bolts to fasten to door. Price, per pair...............$0.66
Per crate of six pairs................. 3.85

Braced Barn Door Rail.

No. 9C2720 Braced Barn Door Rail. Standard size, 3-16x1, made solid and strong. Will carry the largest doors. Comes in 4, 6, 8 or 10-foot lengths. Requires No. 12 screws to fasten to building. Prices quoted do not include screws.

Length, feet.......	4	6	8	10
Price, per length...	10c	15c	20c	25c

Trolley Roller Bearing Steel Barn Door Hanger.

No. 9C2700 Hangers have lateral adjustment and are suitable for doors from 1½ to 2½ inches thick, weighing 400 pounds or less. A pair of hangers consists of two hangers and carriers, one right end bracket, one left end bracket, one center bracket, complete with wood screws for hangers and lag screws for brackets. Weight, per pair, 10 pounds. The number of extra track brackets required depends upon the weight and width of door. In any case they should not be more than 3½ feet apart and on very heavy doors it is best to have them about 2 feet apart.

Price of hangers, complete as described, per pair.....................................$1.25

No. 9C2701 Trolley Track for our trolley barn door hanger, made of 16-gauge steel. Weight, per foot, 1¾ pounds. Prices given below are for track only, without brackets.

Length, feet.......	4	5	6	8	10
Price, per length,	40c	50c	60c	80c	$1.00

No. 9C2702 Center Track Brackets, for above track. Remember that end brackets and one center bracket are furnished with hangers.

Price, each.................................10c

The Rockwell Barn Door Hanger.

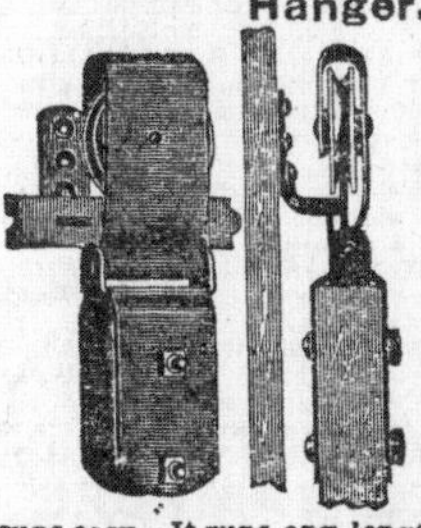

No. 9C2730 The Rockwell Flexible or Hinge Joint, Roller Bearing, Steel Barn Door Hanger. It is made with a hinge joint so it cannot bind when door is swung in or out. It has a guard that runs under and inside the track, making it impossible to throw the wheels off the track. It runs easy. It runs any length of track. It is warranted to carry any door. Made only one size, for doors 1⅜-inch thick. (Will not run on the common track. For track for this hanger see next number.) Weight, per pair, 5½ pounds.

Price, per doz. pairs. $6.14; per pair. 52c

No. 9C2731 Track for the Rockwell Flexible Barn Door Hanger. Made of round edge steel, 1¼x3-16 inches. Strong enough to carry the heaviest door. To put this track up it requires three screws to each foot. The diameter of each screw should be No. 12, the length either one inch or longer, as required. Screws are not furnished at price named. If wanted, please order them separately. See No. 9C4112.

Length, feet.......	4	6	8	10
Price, per length.	17c	26c	34c	43c

No. 9C2733 Barn Door Steel Rollers, to screw; wrought iron shank. Weight, 14 ounces.

Price, per dozen, 50c; each 5c

No. 9C2738 Barn Door Stay Rollers, adjustable to any thickness of door. Will always stay in the right position. The strongest adjustable stay in the market.
Price, each......7c
Per dozen......75c

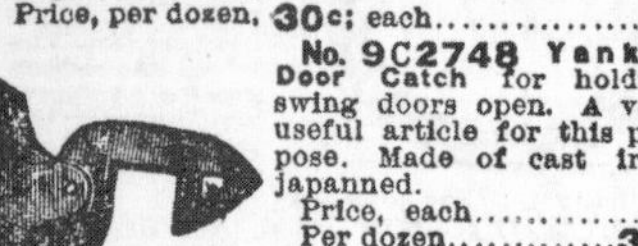

No. 9C2746 Barn Door Pulls, extra heavy, japanned. Weight, 10 ounces.
Price, per dozen, 30c; each......3c

No. 9C2748 Yankee Door Catch for holding swing doors open. A very useful article for this purpose. Made of cast iron, japanned.
Price, each............4c
Per dozen............38c

PADLOCKS.

No. 9C2762 Solid Steel Padlock, heavily brass plated to prevent rust. Brass bushing. Two flat steel keys. Self locking. Width, 1½ inches. Length over all, including shackle, 2¼ inches. Price, per dozen, 57c; each.........5c

No. 9C2765 Solid Wrought Steel, heavily brass plated to prevent rusting. Self locking. Two flat steel keys to each lock. In each dozen locks there are five key changes. Width, 2¼ inches. Length, including shackle, 3¼ inches.
Price, each.......8c
Price, per doz....94c

No. 9C2766 Our Heavy Wrought Steel Padlock, brass plated to prevent rusting, self locking. It has extra heavy spring shackle; six secure levers; two double bitted keys to each lock, all different in a dozen. Width, 2 inches. Length, including shackle, 3 inches. Price, each..................$0.14
Per dozen..................1.63

No. 9C2770 A Cracker Jack Padlock, wrought steel case, black rustless finish, with brass rivets and brass bushing. Two nickel plated corrugated steel keys to each lock. In each dozen there are six key changes. Self locking strong steel swivel shackle. Width of lock, 2 inches. Length, including shackle, 2¾ inches. Price, each..................$0.16
Per dozen..................1.88

No. 9C2780 The finest padlock made. Ball bearing, pin tumbler cylinder. Heavy flat bronze case. Heavy case hardened spring shackle. Two German silver keys to each lock and no two locks alike. Shackle cannot be cut with a hack saw or filed. Width of case, 2 inches; length including shackle, 3 inches. Price..........$1.05

Solid Brass Padlocks.

No. 9C2771 Solid Brass Padlock. Self locking spring shackle. Four secure levers. Two flat steel keys to each lock. All different in a dozen. Width, 2 inches. Length, including shackle, 2⅞ in.
Price, each.......$0.19
Per dozen.......2.25

No. 9C2772 Our Samson Eight-Lever Padlock is solid wrought steel, self locking, extra heavy spring shackle, eight secure levers, two flat bow fancy double bitted steel keys. The lock is heavily brass plated inside and out to prevent rusting. Width, 2¾ inches. Length, including shackle, 3⅞ inches. A strong, safe lock; a lock that cannot be picked; a lock that cannot be opened by any key in your town, and a better lock than you have ever seen sold at the price.
Price, per dozen, $2.38; each.........20c

No. 9C2776 Our Gun Metal Six-Lever Lock with Chain. Two nickel plated flat steel keys to each lock, all different in a dozen. Width, 2¼ inches. Length, including shackle, 3 inches.
Price, each, $0.38
Per dozen.. 4.50

No. 9C2777 Our Pin Tumbler Spring Shackle Lock. Steel body, rustless gun metal finish. Brass cylinder, two German silver keys with each lock. No two locks alike. This makes an excellent lock for stores and warehouses, as it cannot be picked and is very strong. Width, 1⅞ inches. Length, including shackle, 3 inches.
Price, each..................$0.59
Per dozen..................6.89

No. 9C2818 Double Link Self Locking Chest Lock, made of iron. Width, 2⅜ inches. Depth, 1⅞ inches. Distance from top of lock to center of key pin, ⅞ inch. This lock has secret wards double bitted keys, all different in a dozen. It is furnished with brass escutcheon.
Price..................30c

No. 9C2820 The Old Favorite Spring Chest Lock, with double bitted key and brass keyhole escutcheon. This lock is 4 inches wide and 2¼ inches deep. Distance from top of lock to center of key pin, 1⅛ inches, it has secret wards and the keys are all different in a dozen.
Price..................38c

No. 9C2829 All Brass Chest Lock, double link, secure ward self locking. Two nickel plated flat steel keys to each lock. All different in a dozen. Size of lock, 3½ inches wide, 2¼ inches deep. Distance from top of lock to center of cylinder, 1⅛ inches. Diameter of cylinder, ⅝-inch. Made for wood 1 inch thick. Price........56c

No. 9C2842 Drawer Lock, made of steel with brass cylinder. Size of lock, 1⅞ inches wide, 1⅞ inches deep. Diameter of cylinder, ⅝ inch. Distance from selvage to center of cylinder, ⅝ inch. Made for wood ⅞ inch thick. Has broad, heavy bolt, two secure levers, two nickel plated flat steel keys to each lock. All different in a dozen. Weight, 1½ ounces. Price......17c

No. 9C2844 Drawer Lock, made entirely of brass. Made to put on without cutting the wood. Size of lock, 1⅞ inches wide by 1⅞ inches deep. Diameter of cylinder, ⅝ inch. Has broad bolt, two secure levers, two nickel plated flat steel keys to each lock, all different in a dozen. For wood ⅞ inch thick. Weight, 3 ounces.
Price..................20c

Combination Drawer Locks.

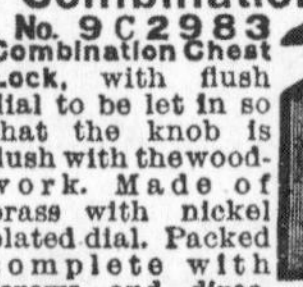

No. 9C2977 Combination Drawer Lock. Size of lock case, 2x2¼ inches; drop 1¼ inches; projects ⅝ inch. Made of bronze and brass with the knob and dial handsomely nickel plated.

Thickness of wood, inch,	½	¾	⅞
Price..............	$1.08	$1.10	$1.12

Combination Chest Locks.

No. 9C2983 Combination Chest Lock, with flush dial to be let in so that the knob is flush with the woodwork. Made of brass with nickel plated dial. Packed complete with screws and directions. Size of lock case, 4x2¼ inches; drop 1⅞ inches.

Thickness of wood, inches.	½	1	1¼	1½
Price......	$1.90	$1.91	$1.92	$1.93

BUILDING PAPER.

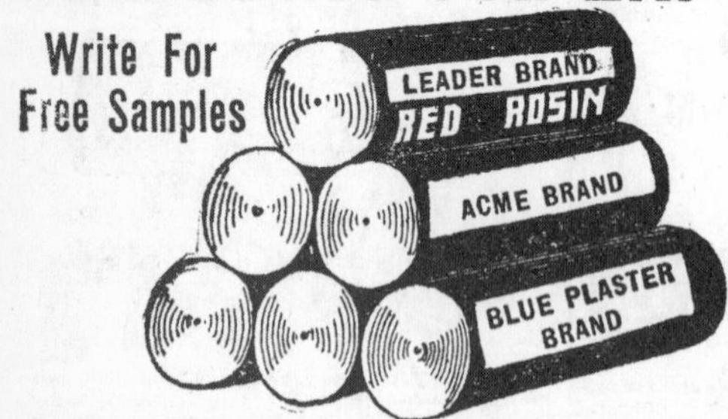

We buy our building paper from the largest and most reliable makers in large quantities for spot cash, and sell it at our usual small profit. Building paper is not intended to be exposed to the weather, but is intended to be used under shingles, clapboards, floors, etc. **The cost is very little**, and can be saved in one season in your fuel bills, to say nothing of the comfort secured by its use.

No. 9C3000 Leader Brand Red Rosin Sized Sheathing is a strong, smooth finish, durable, waterproof paper, put up in rolls of 500 square feet, 36 inches wide, weighing about 40 pounds. Clean to handle. Price, per roll..................69c

No. 9C3001 Fulton Brand Red Rosin Sized Sheathing Paper, same as Leader brand, except it is heavier. Weight, about 50 pounds to the roll. Price, per roll..................87c

No. 9C3003 Acme Brand Red Rosin Sized Sheathing is the same grade as Leader Sheathing but is not quite as heavy. Put up in rolls of 500 square feet, 36 inches wide, weighing about 35 pounds. Price, per roll..................61c

No. 9C3007 The Competition Brand Red Rosin Sized Sheathing Paper. A strong, clean paper, nearly waterproof and lays smooth; better and cheaper than common strawboard. Put up in rolls of 500 square feet, 36 inches wide and weighing about 20 pounds. Price, per roll..................35c

No. 9C3009 Tarred Strawboard Sheathing Paper is put up in rolls weighing from 50 to 75 pounds, 32 inches wide.
Price, per pound..................1¼c

No. 9C3012 Blue Plaster Board. A strong, tough sheathing paper also used on walls and ceilings in place of plaster. For cheap or temporary partitions it is used extensively. It is put on with tacks and covered with wall paper. Price, per roll containing 250 square feet, weight, 30 pounds..................77c

No. 9C3013 Blue Plaster Board. Price, per roll containing 500 square feet, weight, 60 pounds..................$1.50

We do not cut rolls of building paper.

No. 9C3004 Wool Deadening Felt, 36 inches wide, put up in rolls weighing from 60 to 80 pounds. Weight, 1 pound to the square yard. Price, per pound..................2½c

No. 9C3006 Wool Deadening Felt, 36 inches wide, put up in rolls weighing from 70 to 85 pounds. Weight, 1½ pounds to the square yard. Price, per pound..................2½c

If you don't find the sheathing paper you want in this catalogue send for our FELT ROOFING CATALOGUE.

FREE SAMPLES OF BUILDING PAPER AND ROOFING PAPER

WE WILL GLADLY SEND FREE ON REQUEST

by mail postpaid, samples of our entire line of building and roofing paper. It is not really necessary to ask for samples as you can order direct from this catalogue without waiting to see samples and still be assured of receiving perfectly satisfactory goods. In fact, we recommend that you send your order direct from this catalogue without getting samples, under our binding guarantee that the goods we send you will prove perfectly satisfactory in every way, otherwise we will immediately return your money and pay freight charges both ways, but for the benefit of those who want samples, we will be very glad, indeed, to send them free on request.

IF YOU ARE INTERESTED **simply write us a letter or postal card and say: "Send me your samples of building and roofing paper,"** and the complete line of samples with plain descriptions and full information will be sent to you immediately by mail, postpaid, free of any cost to you.

FELT ROOFING.

Flint Surfaced "Asphalt-Felt" Ready Roofing.

We consider our Flint Surfaced "Asphalt-Felt" Ready Roofing and "Bestovall" Rubberized Felt Roofing the best roofing on the market today.

Made from heavy, fibrous wool felt, thoroughly saturated and heavily coated with pure, imported asphalt and surfaced with fine flint. Positively no coal tar or products of coal tar used in this roofing. Will not require coating or painting for several years. Saves cost of coating, gravel and labor to apply same. Will not "run" from the heat of the sun. Packed in rolls 32 inches wide and 40 feet long, which will cover roof 10x10 feet (or 100 square feet), allowing for laps. In the center of roll is packed cement for laps, roofing caps and roofing nails sufficient for same. We do not cut rolls.

No. 9C3011 Flint Surfaced "Asphalt-Felt" Ready Roofing, as described above. Weight, per square, about 80 pounds, complete with trimmings. Price, per roll..................$1.90

No. 9C3015 Flint Surfaced "Asphalt-Felt" Ready Roofing, described above. Weight, per square, about 70 pounds, complete with trimmings. Price, per roll containing 1 square......$1.70

No. 9C3016 Flint Surfaced "Asphalt-Felt" Ready Roofing, as described above. Weight, per square, about 60 pounds, complete with trimming.
Price, per roll containing 1 square..................$1.45

No. 9C3018 Flint Surfaced "Asphalt-Felt" Ready Roofing, as described above. Weight, per square, about 50 pounds complete with trimmings. Price, per roll..................$1.30

No. 9C3017 Pure Imported Especially Prepared Asphalt Paint for "Asphalt-Felt" roofing. Equally good for any felt, iron, steel, tin or shingle roof. Jet black. An excellent paint for any iron surface. Furnished in the following packages:

Packed in flat top wood jacket tin cans:

Gallons..........	1	2	3	5	10
Price..........	53c	$1.00	$1.43	$2.19	$3.75

Put up in barrels:

Gallons..........	25	50
Price..........	$9.32	$15.75

"Bestovall" Rubberized Felt Roofing.

The "Bestovall" Rubberized Felt Roofing has the appearance of rubber, although no rubber is used in its manufacture. It is elastic and pliable, strong and tough, practically fireproof, no odor, not affected by changes of the climate, acid and alkali proof, not affected by gases or vapors, can be used on steep or nearly flat roofs, any workman can put it on, will not shrink or crack, does not taint water, requires no coating or painting for about three years. Our No. 9C3017 Roof Paint should be applied **before it seems to be needed**, say once every three or four years. We make this roofing in three weights. The quality is all alike.

WEIGHTS OF "BESTOVALL" RUBBERIZED FELT ROOFING.

Standard..........	30 to 32 pounds, per 108 square feet.
Heavy..........	40 to 42 pounds, per 108 square feet.
Extra Heavy..........	50 to 52 pounds, per 108 square feet.

The above weights do not include the trimmings. This roofing is packed in rolls containing 108 square feet, which will lay 100 square feet on roof (allowing for laps). With lap cement, tin caps and nails sufficient to put it on, packed in the center.

No. 9C3031 "Bestovall" Rubberized Felt Roofing, Standard, complete with trimmings. Weight, about 35 pounds.
Price, per roll..................$1.56

No. 9C3032 "Bestovall" Rubberized Felt Roofing, Heavy, complete with trimmings. Weight, about 45 pounds.
Price, per roll..................$2.00

No. 9C3033 "Bestovall" Rubberized Felt Roofing, Extra Heavy, complete with trimmings. Weight, about 55 pounds.
Price, per roll..................$2.38

Samples sent free on request.

Duck Brand Prepared Felt Roofing.

We do not recommend Duck Brand Roofing for painted buildings, because there is a possibility that if not properly applied the coating may run from the heat of the sun and spoil the paint on the walls of the building. **This is true of all roofings using** coatings produced from coal tar under names such as "asphaltum," etc. Once in a while any of them give this trouble.

For painted buildings we advise the use of our **"Asphalt-Felt" or "Bestovall" Roofing.** Understand, however, that Duck Brand Roofing will last just as long as any roofing on the market, and for roof for a barn or other outbuilding it has no equal at the price.

This roofing has been used in all climates and has given universal satisfaction. It is easily and cheaply applied, no tools being required except a jack knife, hammer and brush. Complete directions with each roll. The two-ply roofing consists of two layers of felt roofing with a layer of waterproof cement between. The three-ply roofing consists of three layers of felt roofing with two layers of waterproof cement between, the whole being united under great pressure. This roofing is 32 inches wide, and is put up in rolls containing 108 square feet. Allowing for laps, each roll will cover 100 square feet. The two-ply roofing weighs about 45 pounds per roll and the three-ply roofing weighs about 65 pounds per roll without cement, nails, etc. If this roofing is kept well coated with our roofing cement it is practically indestructible. Write for free samples.

No. 9C3022 Two-ply Duck Brand Roofing, only, per roll containing 108 square feet. Wt., about 45 lbs per roll. Price. 61c

No. 9C3023 Three-ply Duck Brand Roofing, per roll containing 108 square feet. Wt., about 65 lbs. per roll. Price.. 83c

No. 9C3028 Barbed Roofing Nails, ⅞-inch long (1 pound required for each roll of roofing). Price, per pound.........4c

No. 9C3029 Tin Roofing Caps (1½ pounds required for each roll of roofing). Price, per pound.........5c

Roof Coating.

No. 9C3035 Roof Coating, for Duck Brand Roofing (2 gallons required for two coats each roll of roofing).
Contents of package,

Gallons..............	2	5	10
Price, per package..............	56c	95c	$1.75

25 to 35-gallon barrels. Price, per gallon..........13¾
50-gallon barrels. Price, per gallon..........11

OUR FELT ROOFING CATALOGUE contains full directions for applying roofing, testimonials from our customers who have used it and several items that are not listed in our general catalogue. It is sent free on request.

Roofing Brushes.

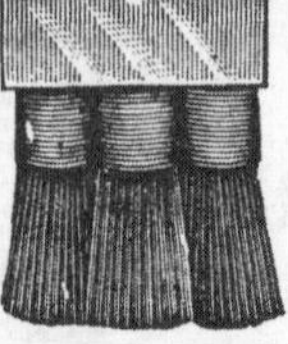

No. 9C3038 Roof Paint Brushes.

Knots..............	2	3
Price..............	33c	50c

No. 9C3039 Roof Paint Brushes, mixed center, gray bristles, outside round ferrules.

Knots..............	2	3	4
Price..............	56c	83c	$1.05

Tarred Roofing Felts.

We sell three grades of Roofing Felts. They are made of carefully selected material, and the greatest possible care is exercised in manufacturing them.

No. 9C3050 Tarred Roofing Felt. Is generally used in specifications for gravel roofing where a No. 1 thickness and grade is required, and we can recommend same for strictly first class work. Also used extensively for roofing lumber camps and temporary buildings. Put up in rolls of about 230 square feet, 32 inches wide, weighing about 60 pounds to the roll.
Price, per pound..................1½c

No. 9C3054 Tarred Roofing Felt. Is the regular felt used in gravel roofing, where four or more plys are specified. Put up in rolls of about 340 square feet, 32 inches wide, weighing about 60 pounds to the roll. Price, per pound..........1½c

No. 9C3055 Tarred Roofing Felt. This is used for gravel roofing where cheap work is required. Is specially recommended as a No. 1 lining under slate, shingles or metal roofing, and for general sheathing purposes. Put up in rolls of about 480 square feet, 32 inches wide, weighing about 60 pounds to the roll. Price, per pound..........1⅛c

STEEL ROOFING.

THE CHIEF MERITS OF STEEL ROOFING are its cheapness, durability, ease of application and protection against fire. Our painted roofing is coated on both sides with iron oxide, re-ground in pure boiled linseed oil, applied with brushes. **A layer of roofing felt should invariably be laid under all metal roofing,** where gas or steam is used in the building, or where there is heat next to the roof. It will prevent dripping or sweating from condensation in cold weather, protect the paint on the under side of roof and serves as a non-conductor of heat and cold.

WHILE OUR ROOFING IS OF THE FINEST QUALITY it will rust if not protected with paint. As soon as applied on a building, we recommend that the roofing be well coated with the best iron oxide or graphite paint. After a period of a year another coat should be applied, and then at intervals of three or four years, as may be found necessary.

TERMS: Our terms on steel roofing, eaves troughs, conductor, sheet steel and tin plates are cash in full with the order.

WE ISSUE A SPECIAL STEEL ROOFING CATALOGUE containing a full line of metal roofings, ornamental steel sidings, sidings, etc., and all accessories. It will be sent free on request. If you don't find the goods you want in this book, send for our free Steel Roofing Catalogue. Painted roofing weighs about 70 pounds per 100 square feet. Galvanized roofing weighs about 90 pounds per 100 square feet.

V-Crimped Roofing.

This is the cheapest of all roofing offered and costs less to put it on the roof. Any person can apply it who can drive a nail. It is put down with an end lap only, or with end locks shown; the latter being the better method. When end locks are turned, a cleat should be used in the middle of the end lock, which prevents the sheet from rattling. It is made in two ways, namely, with side crimps only, or 2-V crimp as illustrated, and with side and center crimps or 3-V crimp, having a crimp in center of sheet. 1 pound, 1¾-inch No. 10 barbed wire nails, 1 pound dry mineral paint, 50 feet V sticks are required to lay a square of this roofing. 100 feet V sticks required for 3-V crimp roofing.

V-Crimped Roofing, 2-V crimp, 28-gauge steel, painted both sides. Sheets will lay 24 inches from center to center of crimps. The ends of sheets should be lapped not less than 3 inches. May be laid over sheathing, shingles, lath or direct to rafters placed 24 inches from center, on any roof having a pitch of more than 2 inches to the foot. The ends of sheets can either be lapped 3 inches or more, or put together with lock joint.

To lay direct to rafters, without sheathing: Set rafters 24 inches from center to center, and nail V wood strips on top surface of rafters. Place crosspiece between rafters, level with the top of rafters, to support and nail the end of sheet. Begin at left hand corner of eaves, and end of building, and lay sheets from eaves to ridge, allowing 3 inches for end lap and one crimp for side lap. Nail through the crimp about every 8 inches. At end lap use four nails to the lap. When laid without end locks, no special tools are required. When end locks are made, a joiner, snips and mallet will be required.

No. 9C3077 2-V Crimp Roofing, painted both sides.

Length of sheet, feet	5	6	7	8	9	10
Price, per sheet	21c	25 2/10c	29 4/10c	33 6/10c	37 8/10c	42c

No. 9C3078 2-V Crimp Galvanized Roofing.

Length of sheet, feet	5	6	7	8	9	10
Price, per sheet	35c	42c	49c	56c	63c	70c

The above price is for roofing only and does not include sticks, nails or paint.

No. 9C3081 V Sticks for V Crimp Roofing. Sold in any quantity (50 feet required for each square of 2-V roofing and 100 feet for 3-V roofing). Price, per 100 feet....20c

No. 9C3085 3-V Crimp Roofing, painted both sides. Lays 23½ inches from center to center of outside crimps.

Length of sheet, feet	5	6	7	8	9	10
Price, per sheet	22 2/10c	26 6/10c	31c	35 5/10c	40c	44 4/10c

No. 9C3086 3-V Crimp Roofing, galvanized.

Length of sheet, feet	5	6	7	8	9	10
Price, per sheet	36 6/10c	43 9/10c	51¼c	58 6/10c	65 9/10c	73 2/10c

No. 9C3087 Dry Red Mineral Paint. (One pound required for each square of roofing.) Price, per pound....2c

No. 9C3088 Barbed Wire Roofing Nails, 1¾ inches long. (One pound required for each square of roofing.) Price, per lb....4c

Plain Roll and Cap Roofing.

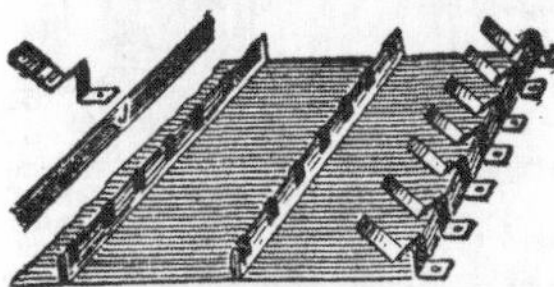

This roofing is used on all classes and kinds of roofs with entire satisfaction.

For a square of this roofing we furnish as follows: 1 roll 50 feet long by 26¼ inches wide, 50 side cleats, 51 lineal feet of caps.

Plain Roll and Cap Roofing, made of 28-gauge steel, painted both sides. Weight, per square about 70 pounds.

No. 9C3070 Price, per square, as described above, painted....$2.52

No. 9C3071 Price, per square, galvanized (weight, 90 pounds)....4.14

The tools needed to apply this roofing are as follows: **1 pair edging tongs, 1 pair squeezing tongs, 1 pair tinners' snips and mallet.**

We sell full rolls only of this roofing. A square is 10 feet each way, or 100 square feet.

We issue a special catalogue of
METAL ROOFING, STEEL CEILINGS, ETC.
which will be sent free on request.

Pressed Standing Seam Roofing.

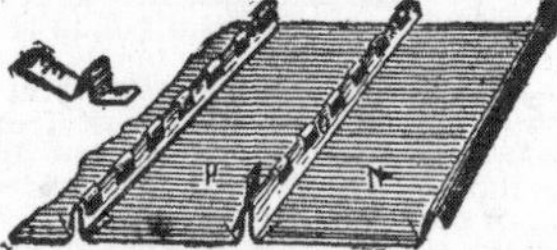

This is also known as Double Cap Roofing. It is a universal roofing and used for all kinds of buildings. Its distinctive feature is the outside cleat. This feature is no objection to its use, and only slightly objectionable regarding its appearance. **It has many points to recommend it, not the least among which is the rapidity with which it can be laid.** This roofing lays 24 inches center to center. We furnish sufficient cleats to lay the roofing. For paint and nails see No. 9C3087 and No. 9C3088. One-half pound nails and one pound paint required for each square.

No. 9C3075 Pressed Standing Seam Roofing, made of 28-gauge sheet steel, painted both sides. Weight, per square, about 71 pounds.

Length of sheet, ft.,	5	6	7	8	9	10
Per sheet	22 2/10c	26 5/10c	31c	35 5/10c	40c	44 4/10c

No. 9C3076 Pressed Standing Seam Roofing, made of 28-gauge steel, galvanized.

Length of sheet, ft.,	5	6	7	8	9	10
Per sheet	36 6/10c	43 9/10c	51¼c	58 6/10c	65 9/10c	73 2/10c

The following tools are required to lay this roofing: **1 pair squeezing tongs, 1 jointer, 1 pair snips and 1 mallet.** A square is 10 feet each way, or 100 square feet.

Edging Tongs.

No. 9C3090 Edging Tongs; used in turning up the standing seam in roll cap roofing. Price....35c

Squeezing Tongs.

No. 9C3093 Squeezing Tongs; used in squeezing the seams on roll cap and pressed standing seam, or double cap roofing. Price....35c

Jointer.

No. 9C3095 Jointer or End Locker; used in making the end locks on V-crimp and pressed standing seam, and other roofings....30c

Pressed Corrugated Sheets For Siding, Ceiling, Fireproof Partitions, Etc.

The strongest sheet metal known to the trade, and the most widely used is corrugated. For structures of moderate cost or light, inexpensive framings that are intended to be fireproof, no better material can be had. The rigidity imparted to comparatively light sheets by corrugating makes them self supporting. For siding, 1-inch end laps will do. If used for roofing, the roof should have a pitch of not less than 3 inches to the foot. Sheets should have 3 to 6 inches end lap and one and one-half or two corrugations side lap. Nails should always be driven through the crown of corrugation. While the corrugated sheets are used extensively in some sections for roofing, we believe our V-crimped roofing is better and cheaper.

Corrugated Sheets, 28-gauge, with 2½-inch corrugations. Sheets are 26¼ inches wide. Allowing one corrugation for lap on each side, it leaves a covering surface 24 inches wide, which lays to advantage on rafters or studding 24 inches center to center. The end lap should be from 1 to 6 inches. Sheets are 5, 6, 7, 8, 9 and 10 feet long.

No. 9C3105 Corrugated Sheets. 28-gauge, 2½-inch corrugations. Painted both sides.

Length of sheet, feet	5	6	7	8	9	10
Price, per sheet	22¾c	27 3/10c	31 9/10c	36 4/10c	41c	45½c

No. 9C3106 Corrugated Sheets. 28-gauge, 2½-inch corrugations. Galvanized.

Length of sheet, feet	5	6	7	8	9	10
Price, per sheet	37c	44½c	51 9/10c	59 3/10c	66 7/10c	74 1/10c

Above prices do not include paint or nails.

No. 9C3107 Corrugated Sheets, with 1¼-inch corrugations. Allowing one corrugation for side lap, it lays 24 inches wide, 28 gauge, painted both sides.

Length of sheet, feet	5	6	7	8	9	10
Per sheet	23 6/10c	28 3/10c	33c	37 7/10c	42 5/10c	47 2/10c

No. 9C3108 Corrugated Sheets with 1¼-inch corrugations, 28-gauge, galvanized.

Length of sheet, feet	5	6	7	8	9	10
Price, per sheet	37 6/10c	45 1/10c	52 7/10c	60 2/10c	67 7/10c	75 2/10c

For paint and nails, see Nos. 9C3087 and 9C3088.

Beaded Siding and Ceiling.

Made from the best quality box annealed steel, painted on both sides with the best iron oxide paint, ground in pure linseed oil. Sheets, when beaded, cover 24 inches from center to center of outside beads, and can be furnished any length up to 8 feet. The beads are small corrugations, ⅜ inch wide by ⅜ inch deep and 3 inches from center to center. In applying, no special tools are required. The sheets should be lapped 1 or 2 inches at ends, and over one crimp at side. They can be applied perpendicularly or horizontally (as desired) to boards, studding or joists placed the proper distance apart, or put on over old plaster.

No. 9C3115 Beaded Siding or Ceiling. Painted.

Length, feet	4	5	6	7	8	9	10
Per sheet	20c	25c	30c	35c	40c	45c	50c

For Ornamental Steel Ceilings and Side Walls send for our Steel Roofing Catalogue. It gives plain instructions for ordering and illustrates how metal roofing and sidings should be applied. Sent free on request.

Round Ridge Caps.

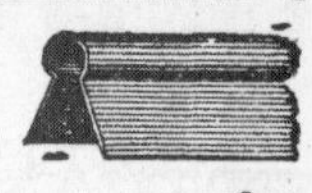

No. 9C3145 Round Ridge Roll. Makes a neat waterproof cap for the ridge of roofs. It is made in 8-foot lengths. We do not furnish cut lengths.

Diameter of roll, inches....2
Width of apron, inches....2½
Girth, inches....10
Price, per length, painted....27c

No. 9C3144 Round Ridge Roll, galvanized.

Diameter of roll, inches....2
Width of apron, inches....2½
Girth, inches....10
Price, per length, painted....30c

FOR FINIALS, CRESTINGS, WEATHER VANES, SKYLIGHTS, CORNICES, ETC., WRITE FOR SPECIAL STEEL ROOFING CATALOGUE.

Lap Joint Eaves Trough.

No. 9C3150 Galvanized Lap Joint Eaves Trough. Made of 28-gauge steel, in 10-foot lengths. We do not furnish cut lengths.

Size, inches	3½	4	4½	5	6
Weight, per length, pounds	5	5½	6	7	8
Price, per length	24c	28c	31c	33c	40c

Patent Slip Joint Eaves Trough.

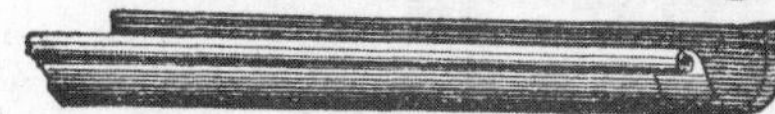

When ordering slip joint trough, state whether right or left is wanted. Right hand means that the water is to discharge at right hand end of trough. Left hand that the water is to discharge at the left hand end. The above picture shows a right hand. The same rule also applies to corners, etc.

No. 9C3148 Slip Joint Eaves Trough. Right hand.
No. 9C3149 Slip Joint Eaves Trough. Left hand.
Galvanized Slip Joint Eaves Trough. Made of 28-gauge steel. Made in 10-foot lengths. We do not furnish cut lengths. Size is taken inside of bed. Price includes one slip joint with each length of trough. Weighs about ½ pound per length more than lap joint.

Size, inches	3½	4	4½	5	6
Price, per length	26c	29c	33c	35c	41c

FOR PLAIN ROOF GUTTER, WRITE FOR STEEL ROOFING CATALOGUE.

Outside and Inside Corner Mitre.

These mitres are made complete, ready for use, for both inside and outside bead, either slip or lap joint. If slip joints are ordered be sure to state if wanted right or left.

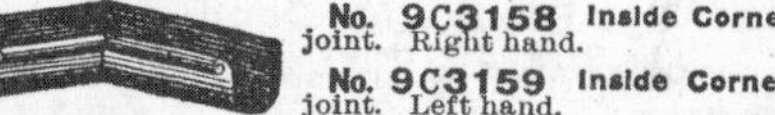

No. 9C3158 Inside Corner, slip joint. Right hand.
No. 9C3159 Inside Corner, slip joint. Left hand.
No. 9C3154 Inside Corner, lap joint.

Size, inches	3½	4	4½	5	6
Price, slip joint	14c	15c	16c	17c	19c
Price, lap joint	12c	13c	14c	15c	17c

No. 9C3162 Outside Corner, slip joint. Right hand.
No. 9C3163 Outside Corner, slip joint. Left hand.
No. 9C3156 Outside Corner, lap joint.

Size, inches	3½	4	4½	5	6
Price, slip joint	14c	15c	16c	17c	19c
Price, lap joint	12c	13c	14c	15c	17c

OUR PRICES ON
Metal Roofing, Conductors, Eaves Trough, Etc.
Are Subject to Market Changes.

PRICES are correct at the time we go to press, but the market on this class of goods is in an unsettled condition and prices are liable to advance any day. We will not advance our prices so long as our present stock lasts. We ship Metal Roofing, Conductor and Eaves Trough from factory if ordered in large quantities, when it will save freight charges for our customers.

Adjustable Outlets and End Cap.

The central illustration represents outlet in position, with end of trough closed with slip joint end cap. Outlet shown in small illustration to the left is complete, and can be slipped on the trough at any point; the lip turned over the back edge of trough makes it perfectly secure and tight. Anyone can put this on. No soldering needed.

No. 9C3160 Adjustable Outlet, shown in small illustration on the left. To fit eaves trough, sizes

Sizes	3½	4	4½	5	6
Fitted for conductor, size	2 in.	2 in.	3 in.	3 in.	4 in.
Price	11c	12c	13c	16c	19c

No. 9C3161 End Cap Slip Joint, shown in small illustration on the right. To fit eaves trough, size

Size	3½	4	4½	5	6
Price	5c	6c	6c	6c	8c

Wire Eaves Trough Hangers.

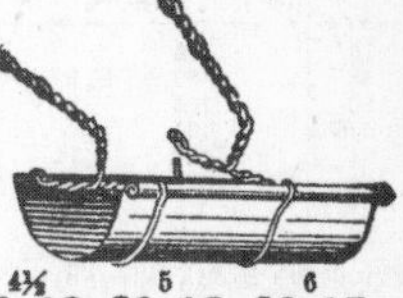

No. 9C3170 Wire Eaves Trough Hanger.

Size, inches	3½	4	4½	5	6
Price, per doz	$0.10	$0.11	$0.12	$0.13	$0.15
Per gross	1.07	1.19	1.32	1.43	1.67

Steel Brick Siding.

Steel Brick Siding, painted both sides. It can be applied by any mechanic, lays perfectly smooth, and, after painting, cannot be distinguished from the finest Philadelphia pressed brick. It costs no more than the best wood siding and about one-fifth that of brick. In beauty of appearance, durability, cheapness and as a protection against fire, we claim this siding has no equal. Insurance underwriters as a rule, give it the same rating as brick or stone. This siding is manufactured of the best soft steel, and shipped in lengths of 60x28 inches.

No. 9C3116 Price, per sheet, painted....27 3/10c
No. 9C3117 Galvanized Brick Siding. Price, per sheet....41 1/10c

It requires about ¾ pound of ⅞-inch barb wire roofing nails to lay a square of this roofing. See No. 9C3028.

A square of pressed brick siding consists of 8½ sheets.

FOR STONE SIDING WRITE FOR SPECIAL STEEL ROOFING CATALOGUE.

Acme Eaves Trough Hangers.

No. 9C3172 Acme Eaves Trough Hangers, complete with rods and nuts.

Size, inches	3½	4	4½	5	6
Price, per dozen	$0.24	$0.25	$0.26	$0.27	$0.29
Price, per gross	2.70	2.87	2.94	3.04	3.38

No. 9C3173 Hanger Tongs and Wrench Combined. Price....20c

Corrugated Expanding Conductor.

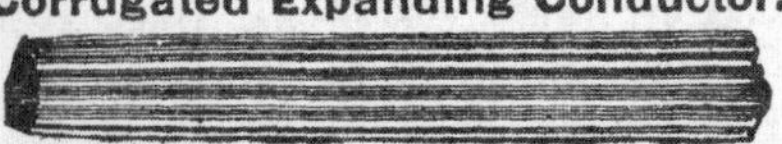

Galvanized Corrugated Conductor is made in 10-foot lengths, without a cross seam. Will not burst when full of ice. No cut lengths furnished. Size of conductor suitable for eaves trough:

Size of eaves trough	3½	4	4½	5	6	7	8
Size of conductor	2	2	3	3	4	5	6

No. 9C3180 Round Corrugated Galvanized Conductor.

Sizes, inches	2	3	4	5	6
Price, per length	28c	32c	43c	54c	64c

Elbows and Shoes.

Galvanized, Flat Crimped, Expanding. When ordering, always specify by number the angle desired, as shown here.

No. 1. No. 2. No. 3. No. 3 Shoe.

No. 9C3181 Conductor Elbow, Angle No. 1.
No. 9C3182 Conductor Elbow, Angle No. 2.
No. 9C3183 Conductor Elbow, Angle No. 3.

Size, inches	2	3	4	5	6
Price, each	6c	7c	9c	$0.11	$0.13
Per dozen	61c	73c	97c	1.21	1.45

No. 9C3184 Round Galvanized Corrugated Shoes.

Size, inches	2	3	4	5	6
Price	7c	8c	11c	13c	18c

Conductor Fastenings.

No. 9C3185 Tinned Conductor Hooks for round corrugated conductor.

Size, inches	2	3	4	5	6
For wood, per doz.	39c	52c	65c	78c	$1.00

No. 9C3186 For brick, per dozen

For brick, per dozen	46c	59c	72c	85c	$1.12

Hooks for Conductors.

No. 9C3189 Tinned Conductor Hooks for corrugated round conductor.

Size, inches	2	3	4	5	6
For wood, dozen	12c	16c	24c	32c	40c
For brick, dozen	16c	22c	34c	48c	60c

Conductor Strainers.

No. 9C3194 Galvanized Wire Conductor Strainers, placed in the outlet of eaves trough, prevents leaves, etc., from entering or stopping up the conductor. The size given designates the size outlet strainer will fit.

Size, inches	2	3	4	5	6
Price	3c	4c	5c	7c	$0.12
Per dozen	29c	37c	53c	78c	1.25

Rain Water Cut Off.

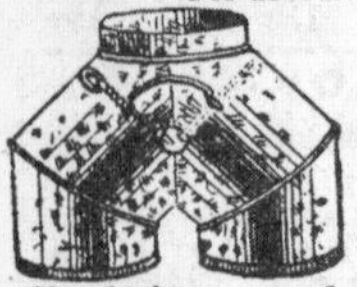

No. 9C3193 For Corrugated Conductor.

No. 9C3195 For Plain Conductor. Galvanized Rain Water Cut-off; simple, durable and cheap.

Size, inches	2	3	4	5	6
Price each	$0.14	$0.16	$0.22	$0.40	$0.46
Per dozen	1.50	1.71	2.35	4.28	5.13

Valley Tin.

No. 9C3198 Made of a good grade of tin plate in a continuous strip, locked and soldered. Full lengths are 50 feet, but we can furnish any quantity.

Width, inches	14	20	28
Price, per lineal foot	$0.05	$0.06½	0.09½
Per 50-foot lengths	1.78	2.35	3.32

Tin Shingles or Flashings.

No. 9C3199 Made of a good grade of roofing tin and cut to exact sizes. Useful for repairing old roofs and making a tight joint around chimney, etc.

Size, 5x7 inches. Price, each...$0.01¼
Per 100....81
Size, 7x10 inches. Price, each....02¼
Per 100....1.62

Black Sheet Steel.

No. 9C3220 Size of sheet, 30x96 inches.

Gauge	Average Weight per Bundle, Lbs.	Number of Sheets in a Bundle	Price, per Sheet	Price, per Bundle
16	150	3	$1.22	$3.56
18	160	4	1.03	4.00
20	150	5	.68	3.25
22	125	5	.64	3.08
24	140	7	.54	3.59
26	120	8	.45	3.35
27	124	9	.42	3.50
28	125	10	.38	3.53

Prices on Black Sheet Steel are subject to changes of the market.

Galvanized Sheet Steel.

Absolutely flat and free from buckles. Every sheet warranted of finest working quality.

No. 9C3228 Galvanized Sheets. Size of sheet, 30x96 inches.

Gauge	Average Weight per Bundle, Lbs.	Number of Sheets in a Bundle	Price per Sheet	Price, per Bundle
16	159	3	$1.54	$4.52
18	172	4	1.36	5.30
20	166	5	1.06	5.10
22	141	5	.96	4.64
24	162	7	.79	5.33
26	145	8	.67	5.10
27	152	9	.66	5.67
28	156	10	.65	6.17

Prices on Galvanized Sheet Steel are subject to changes of the market.

Roofing Tin.

Roofing Tin, guaranteed to be full size and free from defects. Prices subject to change without notice, but always furnished at lowest market prices.

No. 9C3238 IC Light Roofing Tin, lead finish. Cut to exact sizes.

Size, inches	14x20	20x28
Number of sheets in box	112	112
Weight, per box, pounds	100	200
Price, per sheet	$0.06	$0.11
Price, per box	4.20	8.40

No. 9C3239 No. IC Roofing Tin, high grade, lead finish, for porches, etc., smooth, even finish; cut to exact sizes, used mostly for flashings and covering roofs.

Size, inches	14x20	20x28
Number of sheets in box	112	112
Weight, per box, pounds	110	220
Price, per sheet	$0.06	$0.11
Price, per box	4.38	8.75

No. 9C3240 No. IX Roofing Tin, same quality as our IC, but much heavier; has more coating than any roofing tin on the market.

Size, inches	14x20	20x28
Number of sheets in box	112	112
Weight, per box, pounds	136	272
Price, per sheet	$0.07	$0.12
Price, per box	5.40	10.80

FOR BRIGHT CHARCOAL TIN PLATE
WRITE FOR METAL ROOFING CATALOGUE.

Soldering Coppers.

No. 9C3250 Soldering Coppers, with square points, for common use. When ordering give number wanted, but don't state weight.

Number	1½	2	3	4	5	6	8
Weight, lbs	¾	1	1½	2	2½	3	4
Price	19c	24c	36c	47c	61c	71c	95c

Soldering Copper Handles.

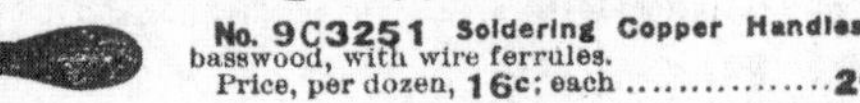

No. 9C3251 Soldering Copper Handles, basswood, with wire ferrules. Price, per dozen, 16c; each....2c

Tinners' Solder.

No. 9C3254 Tinners' Solder, strictly half and half; bars weigh from 1¼ to 1½ pounds. Please notice a bar costs from 24 to 29 cents. Price, per pound....20c
Price on solder is subject to market fluctuations.

Tinners' Snips.

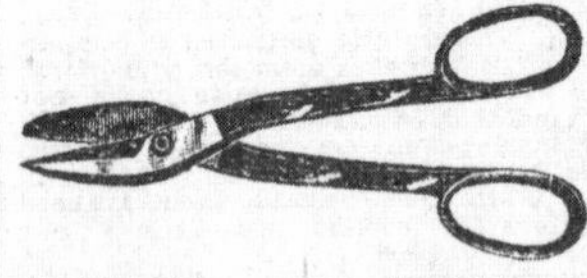

No. 9C3259 The Fulton Tool Co. Tinners' Snips, forged from one solid piece of steel and laid full length of cutting surface with finest cutlery steel, carefully tempered. Warranted.

Full Length	Length of Cut	Weight	Price
8 inches	2 inches	¾ pound	$0.47
9 inches	2¼ inches	1 pound	.56
10 inches	2½ inches	1¼ pounds	.65
11½ inches	3 inches	1¾ pounds	.70
13 inches	3½ inches	2¼ pounds	.93
14½ inches	4 inches	2¾ pounds	1.16

Tinners' Snips.

No. 9C3260 The Fulton Tool Co. Tinners' Snips, for cutting scrolls and circles as well as straight lines. These shears are especially adapted to cornice and tin work. The blades are rounding front and back and very sharp pointed, and can be used for the most delicate work. They are made of the best material, have forged handles and steel blades, and are fully warranted.

Cut 3 inches. Weight, 1¾ pounds. Price....$0.87
Cut 3½ inches. Weight, 2¼ pounds. Price....1.18
Cut 4 inches. Weight, 2¾ pounds. Price....1.48

No. 9C3265 Handy Snips, laid with a special steel of superior quality. Have nickel plated blades and enameled handles. This snip is just the thing for cutting flashing, putting up stove pipe, or cutting any material not heavier than 28-gauge.

Full Length	Length of Cut	Weight	Price
6¾ inches	1¾ inches	4 ounces	38c
7¾ inches	2 inches	5 ounces	42c

The Handy Pipe Crimper.

No. 9C3268 This is a convenient and very practical crimper, and fills a long felt want for a low priced hand crimper, to be sent out on jobs and for shop use. Weight, 13 ounces. Price....25c

Tinners' Fire Pots.

No. 9C3275 Tinners' Fire Pot, with shaking grate; hinged hearth door, double damper, reversible flue. When the fire is well started shut the front damper and open the back damper. This gives a downward draft directly on the coppers, concentrating the heat where it is required. Weight, packed for shipment, 14 pounds. Price....$1.45

For Plumbers' Furnaces See Department of Plumbing Goods and Plumbers' Tools.

No. 9C3285 The Turner Gasoline Brazing Torch No. 2-S. with double jet burner. Gives twice the heat. Saves half the time of the workman. Reservoir 6 inches high, 4 inches in diameter; capacity, 1 quart. About 3,500 degrees of heat can be obtained with this torch, which is nearly double the capacity of all single valve burners. Burner is hooded, and for outdoor work in windy weather it is unsurpassed. Weight packed for shipment, 5 lbs. Price....$4.15

No. 9C3290 A complete tool for soldering, brazing, burning paint, melting metals, for heating soldering coppers, frozen pipes, heavy soldered joints, etc. A convenient, durable, reliable tool, adapted for a hundred purposes. This is the best torch made with a single jet burner. Weight, packed for shipment, 4¼ pounds. Price....$2.05

ORNAMENTAL STEEL CEILINGS

ARE BEING USED VERY EXTENSIVELY.

WE SHOW A COMPLETE LINE IN OUR STEEL ROOFING CATALOGUE and any carpenter or workman can put them up by following the plain and simple directions we furnish. Our prices are right. If interested, write for our Steel Roofing Catalogue. Sent free on request.

CARPENTERS, CONTRACTORS AND BUILDERS should not fail to study our catalogue carefully, and especially this section of our catalogue, for we can save them an immense amount of money on all the goods they use. If you have a big contract job, or want to estimate on a job, before turning in your estimate, don't fail to check over the material required, figure out our prices on the goods, and you will see wherein you can buy the greater majority of material and supplies from us to better advantage than you could get from any other source. If mill work is included, don't under any circumstances fail to send for our free Special Catalogue of Mill Work, showing the very lowest market prices, lower than you could possibly get from any other source. If the work includes anything in the line of metal roofing or ornamental steel ceiling, don't forget that we carry a most complete line at the lowest prices, but for lack of space are unable to show this line in this catalogue. We, therefore, issue a special catalogue of steel ceilings and roofing, and this catalogue will be sent free on application.

WHETHER YOU WANT TOOLS, MILL WORK OR BUILDERS' HARDWARE, YOU CANNOT AFFORD IN JUSTICE TO YOUR OWN INTEREST TO OVERLOOK OUR GOODS AND PRICES.

MILL WORK.

Sash, Doors, Blinds, Mouldings, Porch Material, Stair Material, Grilles, Etc.

SEND FOR FREE SPECIAL CATALOGUE ON MILL WORK.

IN THIS LINE we are prepared to save money for our patrons, and give them strictly reliable goods. Don't buy lumber and mill work together. Have separate itemized estimate made of your mill work, and compare piece for piece with our prices.

OUR PRICES are always right at the bottom. You cannot afford to build a house without first consulting our catalogue, even if only to see that you are buying at right prices. Remember, our goods are guaranteed to be strictly up to official grades adopted by the Sash, Door and Blind Manufacturers' Association of the Northwest.

FREIGHT RATES are very low on mill work. Do not let the matter of freight rates prevent you from sending your orders to us. We guarantee the rate will be exactly the same to you as to your dealer. We pack all shipments so they should reach destination in the same condition they leave the mill—clean and bright.

WE GUARANTEE SAFE DELIVERY, and will replace broken glass on condition that consignee sends in paid expense bill, indorsed by freight agent, as to condition of doors or windows on arrival at destination.

SEND FOR OUR BIG MILL WORK CATALOGUE. IT'S FREE FOR THE ASKING, and may save considerable money.

WOOD SCREWS

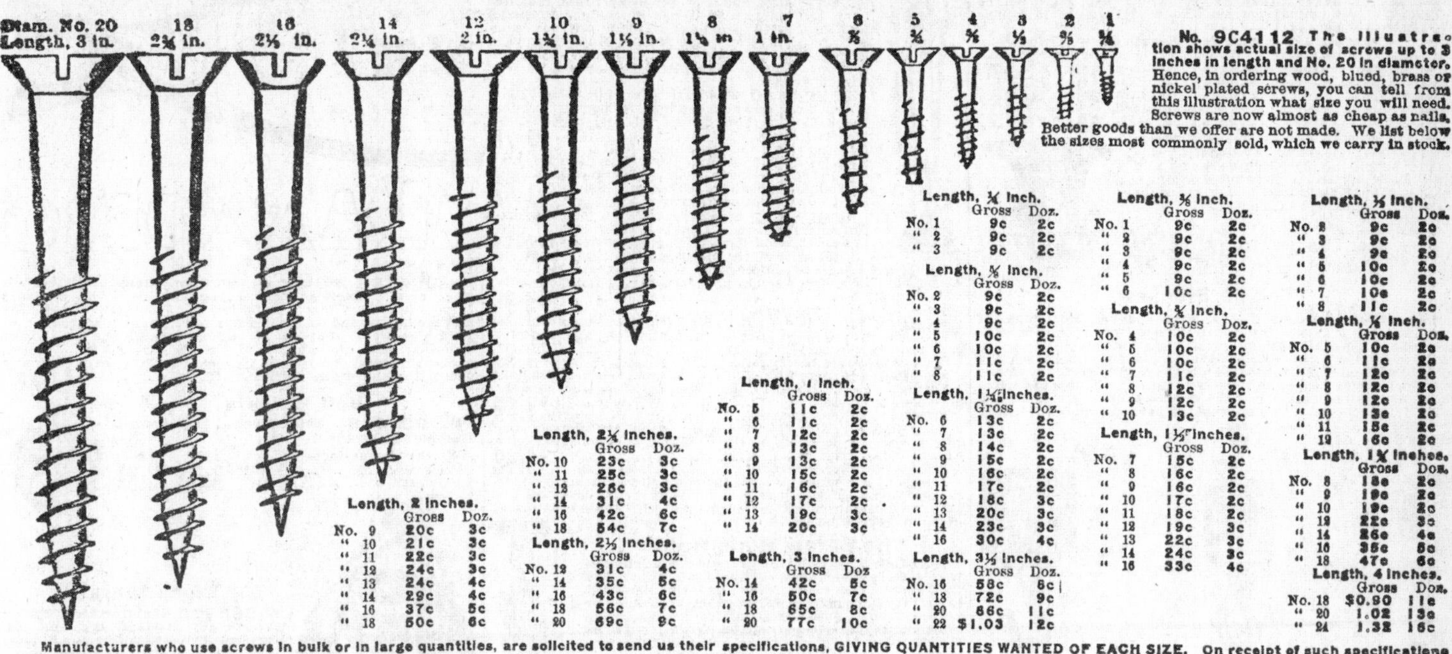

No. 9C4112 The illustration shows actual size of screws up to 3 inches in length and No. 20 in diameter. Hence, in ordering wood, blued, brass or nickel plated screws, you can tell from this illustration what size you will need. Screws are now almost as cheap as nails. Better goods than we offer are not made. We list below the sizes most commonly sold, which we carry in stock.

Length, 2 inches.

No.	Gross	Doz.
No. 9	20c	3c
" 10	21c	3c
" 11	22c	3c
" 12	24c	3c
" 13	24c	4c
" 14	29c	4c
" 16	37c	5c
" 18	50c	6c

Length, 2¼ inches.

No.	Gross	Doz.
No. 10	23c	3c
" 11	25c	3c
" 12	26c	3c
" 14	31c	4c
" 16	42c	6c
" 18	54c	7c

Length, 2½ inches.

No.	Gross	Doz.
No. 12	31c	4c
" 14	35c	5c
" 16	43c	6c
" 18	56c	7c
" 20	69c	9c

Length, 1 inch.

No.	Gross	Doz.
No. 5	11c	2c
" 6	11c	2c
" 7	12c	2c
" 8	13c	2c
" 9	13c	2c
" 10	15c	2c
" 11	16c	2c
" 12	17c	2c
" 13	19c	3c
" 14	20c	3c

Length, 3 inches.

No.	Gross	Doz.
No. 14	42c	5c
" 16	50c	7c
" 18	65c	8c
" 20	77c	10c

Length, ¼ inch.

No.	Gross	Doz.
No. 1	9c	2c
" 2	9c	2c
" 3	9c	2c

Length, ⅜ inch.

No.	Gross	Doz.
No. 2	9c	2c
" 3	9c	2c
" 4	9c	2c
" 5	10c	2c
" 6	10c	2c
" 7	11c	2c
" 8	11c	2c

Length, 1¼ inches.

No.	Gross	Doz.
No. 6	13c	2c
" 7	13c	2c
" 8	14c	2c
" 9	15c	2c
" 10	16c	2c
" 11	17c	2c
" 12	18c	3c
" 13	20c	3c
" 14	23c	3c
" 16	30c	4c

Length, 3½ inches.

No.	Gross	Doz.
No. 16	58c	8c
" 18	72c	9c
" 20	86c	11c
" 22	$1.03	12c

Length, ⅜ inch.

No.	Gross	Doz.
No. 1	9c	2c
" 2	9c	2c
" 3	9c	2c
" 4	9c	2c
" 5	9c	2c
" 6	10c	2c

Length, ¾ inch.

No.	Gross	Doz.
No. 4	10c	2c
" 5	10c	2c
" 6	10c	2c
" 7	11c	2c
" 8	12c	2c
" 9	12c	2c
" 10	13c	2c

Length, 1½ inches.

No.	Gross	Doz.
No. 7	15c	2c
" 8	16c	2c
" 9	16c	2c
" 10	17c	2c
" 11	18c	2c
" 12	19c	3c
" 13	22c	3c
" 14	24c	3c
" 16	33c	4c

Length, ½ inch.

No.	Gross	Doz.
No. 2	9c	2c
" 3	9c	2c
" 4	9c	2c
" 5	10c	2c
" 6	10c	2c
" 7	10c	2c
" 8	11c	2c

Length, ⅞ inch.

No.	Gross	Doz.
No. 5	10c	2c
" 6	11c	2c
" 7	12c	2c
" 8	12c	2c
" 9	12c	2c
" 10	13c	2c
" 11	15c	2c
" 12	16c	2c

Length, 1¾ inches.

No.	Gross	Doz.
No. 8	18c	2c
" 9	19c	2c
" 10	19c	3c
" 12	22c	3c
" 14	26c	4c
" 16	35c	5c
" 18	47c	6c

Length, 4 inches.

No.	Gross	Doz.
No. 18	$0.90	11c
" 20	1.02	13c
" 24	1.32	16c

Manufacturers who use screws in bulk or in large quantities, are solicited to send us their specifications, GIVING QUANTITIES WANTED OF EACH SIZE. On receipt of such specifications we will quote a delivered price.

Round Head Blued Screws.

No. 9C4115

Length, ½ inch.

No.	Gross	Dozen
No. 3	11c	2c
" 4	11c	2c
" 5	12c	2c

Length, ⅝ inch.

No.	Gross	Dozen
No. 5	13c	2c
" 6	13c	2c
" 7	14c	2c
" 8	15c	2c

Length, 1¼ inches.

No.	Gross	Dozen
No. 6	15c	2c
" 7	16c	2c
" 8	17c	2c
" 9	16c	2c
" 10	19c	3c

Length, ¾ inch.

No.	Gross	Dozen
No. 4	12c	2c
" 5	12c	2c
" 6	13c	2c

Length, 1 inch.

No.	Gross	Dozen
No. 6	14c	2c
" 7	14c	2c
" 8	15c	2c
" 10	18c	2c

Length, 1½ inches.

No.	Gross	Dozen
No. 10	20c	3c
" 12	24c	3c
" 14	29c	4c

Length, 1¾ inches.

No.	Gross	Dozen
No. 12	26c	4c
" 14	32c	4c
" 16	42c	5c

Steel Brads.

No. 9C4007 Wire Brads in quarter-pound and pound papers.

1-IN.

Length, inches	½	⅝	¾	⅞	1	1¼	1½
Size wire	19	18	18	17	16	15	15
Per ¼ lb. paper	3c	3c	3c	2c	2c	2c	2c
Per lb. paper	10c	8c	7c	6c	5c	5c	5c

Brass Head Nails.

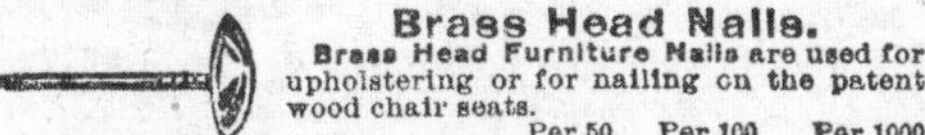

Brass Head Furniture Nails are used for upholstering or for nailing on the patent wood chair seats.

		Per 50	Per 100	Per 1000
No. 9C4012	Small size... Price	3c	4c	25c
No. 9C4013	Large size. Price..	4c	6c	50c

Handy Nail Assortment.

No. 9C4014 Handy Assortment of Wire Nails. A big lot of nails for $1.00. Not the so called "Farmers' Nails," which are "culls" from the factory, but all perfect nails, well assorted in sizes from 3 to 40 penny.

Price, per box, containing 30 pounds of nails............**$1.00**

NAILS IN KEGS.

Send for our free special price list of NAILS. Prices are always "right at the bottom."

Tacks.

All tacks quoted by us by the paper are guaranteed strictly genuine half weight papers. For ingrain carpet use 8-oz. tacks; for Brussels carpet use 10-oz. tacks; for extra thick Brussels carpet use 12-oz. tacks. To tack curtains on spring shade rollers use 1-oz. tacks. There are 370 tacks in a half weight paper of 8-oz. cut tacks or nearly four times as many as in count tacks of 100 in a paper.

No. 9C4016 American Iron Cut Tacks.

Size, ounces	1	2	3	4	6	8	10	12	16
Price, per paper	2c	2c	2c	2c	2c	2c	2c	3c	3c
Per doz. papers	8c	9c	10c	12c	14c	17c	20c	23c	29c

No. 9C4020 Tinned Carpet Tacks. In half weight papers.

Size, ounces	6	8	10	12
Price, per paper	2c	2c	3c	3c
Per dozen papers	17c	20c	25c	29c

No. 9C4022 Double Pointed Tacks, Blued. Sometimes called Staple Tacks. The only thing for straw matting. In packages containing 120 tacks.

Size, ounces	10	11	12
Price, per paper	1c	1c	1c
Per dozen papers	8c	9c	10c

Bill Posters' Tacks.

No. 9C4026 Put up in 1-pound papers and in boxes containing 25 pounds.

Size, ounces	2	3	4	6	8
Price, per lb.	$0.10	$0.08	$0.07	$0.06	$0.05
Per box	2.14	1.68	1.50	1.33	1.16

No. 9C4029 Swede's Iron Upholsterers' Tacks. In bulk; sold in any quantity by the pound.

Ounces	2	2½	3	4	6
Price, per pound	$0.10	$0.09	$0.08	$0.07	$0.07
Per box of 25 lbs	2.14	1.85	1.68	1.50	1.33

Ounces	8	10	12	16
Price, per pound	$0.06	$0.06	$0.05	5c
Per box of 25 lbs	1.16	1.10	1.04	93c

No. 9C4059 Flush Chest Handles, enameled, extra heavy, riveted.

Width of plate, inches	4	5
Price, per pair	15c	24c

Chest Handles

No. 9C4060 Chest Handles, 3½ inches, japanned, heavy. Weight, per pair, 1 pound 5 ounces. Without screws. Price, per pair, 5c
Per dozen pairs............50c

No. 9C4061 Chest Handles, 4 inches, japanned, heavy. Weight, per pair, 1¾ pounds. Without screws. Price, per pair, 7c
Per dozen pairs............69c

No. 9C4062 Chest Handles, 4½ inches, japanned, heavy. Weight, per pair, 2 pounds 6 ounces. Without screws. Price, per pair.........8c
Per dozen pairs............82c

Wrought Brass Box Corners.

Packed with screws to match, suitable for trimming tool chests, etc.

No. 9C4065 Wrought Brass Box Corners. Size, 2½x⅞ inches. Highly polished.
Per dozen, 88c; each........8c

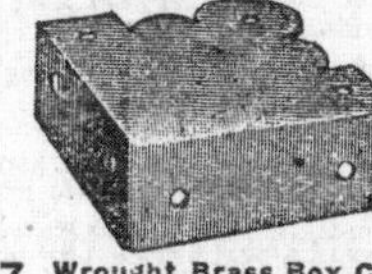

No. 9C4067 Wrought Brass Box Corners. Size, 1⅞x½ inch. Highly polished.
Price, each............4c
Per dozen............40c

No. 9C4069 Wrought Brass Box Corners. Size, 1⅞x1⅝ inch. Highly polished.
Price, each...5c
Per dozen ...46

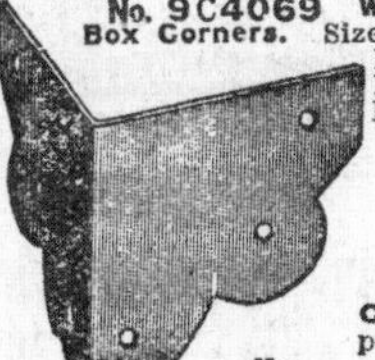

No. 9C4071

No. 9C4071 Wrought Brass Box Corners. Size, 2½x2½ inches, highly polished.
Price, per dozen, 88c; each.......8c

Wrought Brass Box Corners.

No. 9C4073 Wrought Brass Box Corners. Size, 2½x2½ inches, highly polished.
Price, per dozen, 88c; each.....8c

No. 9C4073

Ladder Sockets.

No. 9C4135 Iron Ladder Sockets. The use of these sockets avoids boring holes in the side pieces. With them a ladder can be made much lighter and stronger. A broken round can be replaced without taking the ladder apart. Diameter of hole, 1 inch. Weight, per 100, about 14 pounds.
Price, per 100, 92c; each............1c

Brass Cup Hooks.

No. 9C4155 Brass Screw Hooks for bangle boards.

Size, inch	½	⅝	¾
Price, per doz	5c	5c	5c
Per gross	47c	49c	50c

No. 9C4157 Brass Cup Hooks.

Size, inch	⅝	¾	⅞	1
Price, per doz	5c	5c	6c	6c
Per gross	49c	50c	57c	66c

No. 9C4155 No. 9C4157

Screw Eyes.

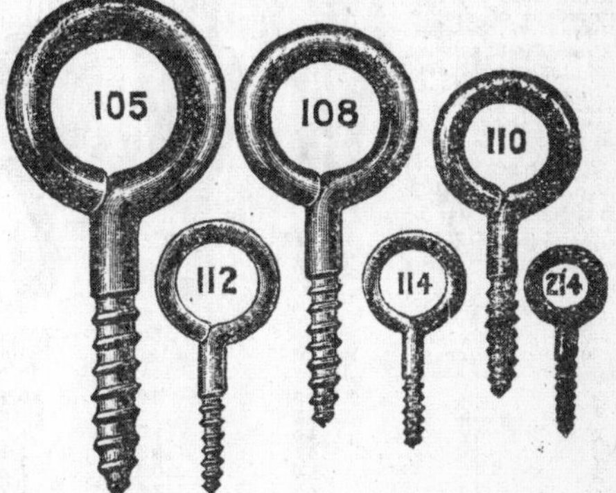

No. 9C4160 Screw Eyes. Bright iron. Illustrations show size.

Nos.	105	108	110	112	114	214
Price, per dozen	3c	2c	2c	2c	2c	2c
Per gross	27c	16c	13c	10c	9c	8c

Casters.

No. 9C4250 Plate Casters, ⅞-inch bronzed iron wheel. Philadelphia pattern.
Price, per set of four............4c

No. 9C4262 Bed Casters, 1⅝-inch bronzed iron wheel.
Price, per set complete............7c

Anti-Friction Casters.

The plate revolves upon steel rollers, which gives an even bearing and relieves the pivot of all friction, They are without doubt the best casters made.

No. 9C4275 Anti-Friction Caster with Common Stem. With 1⅜-inch iron wheel.
Price, per set, 18c; per dozen sets...$2.05

No. 9C4276 With 1⅜-inch lignum vitae wheel. Price, per set, 19c; per doz. sets, $2.17

No. 9C4280 Anti-Friction Caster with Bedstead Stem, with 1⅝-inch iron wheel.
Price, per set............$0.23
Per dozen sets............2.56

No. 9C4283 With 1⅝-inch lignum vitae wheel.
Price, per set............$0.24
Per dozen sets............2.70

No. 9C4284 With 2-inch lignum vitae wheel.
Price, per set............$0.32
Per dozen sets............3.65

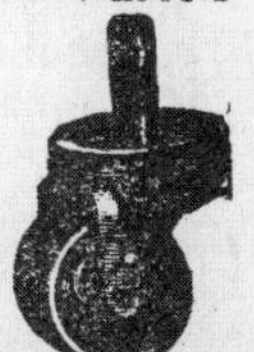

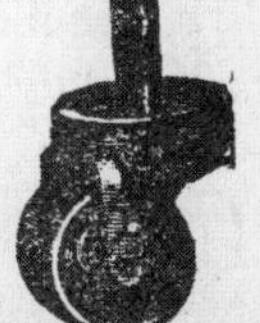

Box or Truck Casters.

Set consists of four casters. No. 9C4297 and No. 9C4298 are suitable for trucks or heavy boxes. They are very strong. No. 9C4297 weighs 8 pounds per set. No. 9C4298 weighs 15 pounds per set.

No.	Kind of Wheel	Diameter of Wheel	Length of Plate	Price, per set	Price, doz. sets
9C4290	Iron	1¼-inch	1¾-inch	15c	$1.62
9C4291	Lig. Vitae	1½-inch	1¾-inch	16c	1.76
9C4296	Iron	2 -inch	2½-inch	30c	3.38
9C4297	Iron	2½-inch	4½-inch	65c	7.43
9C4298	Iron	3½-inch	5 -inch	89c	10.13

No. 9C4311 Box or Truck Casters, cast iron, japanned, stationary. One caster should be placed on each end and two in the middle. A piece of ⅞ or 1-inch board should be placed under **middle** casters so truck will turn corners.

Diameter of wheel, inches..	3	4	4½
Price, each.....	$0.11	$0.15	$0.17
Per dozen......	1.17	1.65	1.87

Tackle Blocks.

Iron Strapped Tackle Blocks. Iron sheaves, steel pins. If two single blocks are ordered for a set, one should be with becket and the other without. If a single and double block are ordered for a set, the single block should be with becket, the double without. If two double blocks are ordered for a set, one should be with becket and one without. If a double and triple block are ordered for a set, the double should be with becket, the triple without. The more sheaves used the more the lifting capacity is increased.

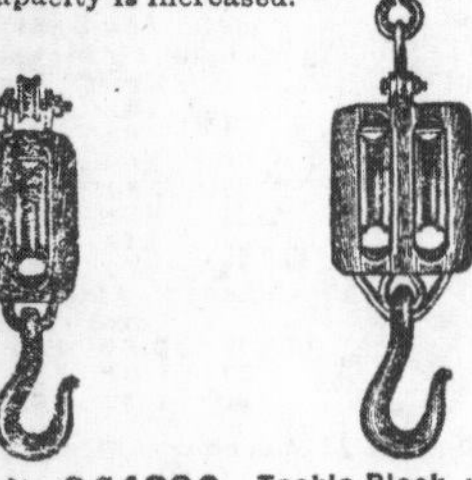

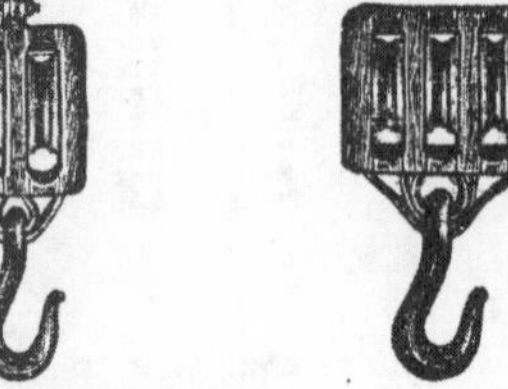

No. 9C4390 Tackle Block, with becket.
No. 9C4391 Tackle Block, without becket.

Size of shell	For Rope	Single Pulley, Price	Double Pulley, Price	Triple Pulley, Price
3	5-16-inch	$0.18	$0.33	$0.44
3½	⅜-inch	.19	.37	.50
4	½-inch	.22	.40	.54
5	⅝-inch	.23	.44	.57
6	¾-inch	.28	.50	.73
7	⅞-inch	.33	.60	.88
8	1 -inch	.42	.72	1.07
10	1⅛-inch	.69	1.13	1.63
12	1¼-inch	1.12	1.88	2.67
15	1½-inch	2.00	3.25	4.50

All Metal Tackle Blocks.

With loose hooks and edges of plates rounded to protect the rope, steel straps, steel pins, steel rivets, gray iron sheaves, turned out true and interchangeable. The best block made.

No. 9C4395 Tackle Block. Without becket.

No. 9C4396 Tackle Block. With becket.

Length of Shell, inches	For Diameter Rope, inches	Single Pulley, Price	Double Pulley, Price	Triple Pulley, Price
4	½	$0.29	$0.55	$0.79
5	⅝	.32	.60	.86
6	¾	.40	.70	1.02
7	⅞	.47	.85	1.25
8	1	.58	1.00	1.49
9	1 1-16	.75	1.24	1.72
10	1⅛	.97	1.60	2.19
12	1¼	1.57	2.58	3.68
14	1⅜	2.35	3.67	5.16
12 Heavy	1½	2.82	4.62	6.75

Steel Tackle Blocks.

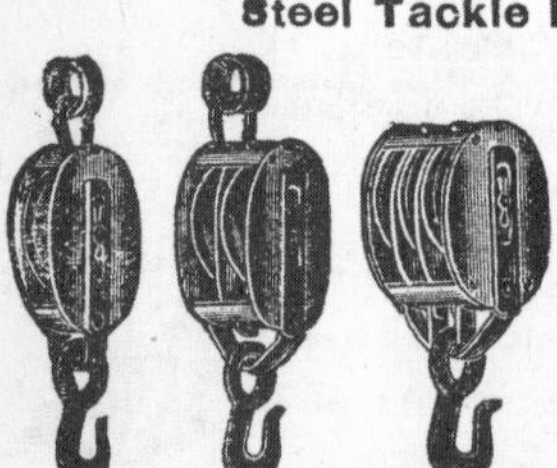

No. 9C4397 Steel Tackle Block, without Becket.

No. 9C4398 Steel Tackle Block with Becket. These blocks are intended for lighter work than the preceding metal block. The shells are pressed from sheet steel, edges well turned to prevent wearing the rope. Hooks and straps of open hearth steel. The straps extend below the pins making the strongest block of this class.

Size of shell	For Rope, Inches	Single Pulley, Price	Double Pulley, Price	Triple Pulley, Price
3	⅜	$0.17	$0.32	$0.42
4	½	.20	.38	.50
5	⅝	.21	.41	.53
6	¾	.26	.47	.68
7	⅞	.31	.56	.82
8	1	.39	.67	.99

Metal Snatch Blocks.

No. 9C4402 Our Metal Snatch Blocks recommend themselves for their neatness, strength and durability. They are almost as light as wood blocks, and yet 30 per cent stronger and stiffer.

Length of Shell, inches	For Diameter Rope, inches	Size of Sheave, inches	Price
7	⅞	3½x1¼	$1.72
8	1⅛	4 x1½	2.33
10	1⅜	5½x1⅞	3.45
12	1½	[illegible]	[illegible]

Burr Steel Safety Lift.

The Burr Safety Lifts are made of the best selected steel. No part of the lift can be worn out by ordinary usage, and it is far cheaper than the ordinary lock blocks, as it has no wedge, eccentric, springs or teeth to get out of order and need constant repairs. The brake against which the rope is locked being perfectly smooth, can in no way injure the rope. Special descriptive circular will be sent free on request.

No. 9C4410 The Burr Safety Lift. Size 3. For ⅜-inch rope; one man can hoist 300 pounds. Double lower block. Weight, 4½ pounds; capacity, 800 pounds. Price............$0.90
Price, with roller bearings............1.95

No. 9C4411 Size 4. For ½-inch rope; one man can hoist 350 pounds. Double lower block. Weight, 6½ pounds; capacity, 1,500 pounds. Price....$1.67
Price, with roller bearings............2.75

No. 9C4412 Size 5. For ⅝-inch rope; one man can hoist 400 pounds. Double lower block. Weight, 11 pounds; capacity, 2,000 pounds. Price....$2.12
Price, with roller bearings............3.50

No. 9C4413 Size 6. For ¾-inch rope; one man can hoist 450 pounds. Double lower block. Weight, 17 pounds; capacity, 2,500 pounds. Price............$2.60
Price, with roller bearings............4.25

No. 9C4414 Size 4½. For ½-inch rope; one man can hoist 600 pounds. Triple lower block. Weight, 10 pounds; capacity, 3,000 pounds. Price............$3.05
Price, with roller bearings............4.85

No. 9C4415 Size 5½. For ⅝-inch rope; one man can hoist 700 pounds. Triple lower block. Weight, 20 pounds; capacity, 3,500 pounds. Price............$3.65
Price, with roller bearings............5.85

No. 9C4416 Size 6½. For ¾-inch rope; one man can hoist 850 pounds. Triple lower block. Weight, 28 pounds; capacity, 5,000 pounds. Price............$4.25
Price, with roller bearings............6.75

The above prices and weights include upper and lower block. No rope furnished at above prices. With roller bearings one man can hoist considerable more than with plain bearings as given in description above.

The Safety Rope Hoist.

The Safety Rope Hoist illustrated herewith hoists, lowers, locks and unlocks, without the bother of a trip rope. The heavier the load the tighter it locks. It can be used in any position, horizontal or perpendicular. Just the thing for erecting windmills and taking out and putting down pumps. It is made of the best malleable iron and fully warranted. All sizes have double lower block.

No. 9C4422 Made to take ⅜-inch rope. One man can lift 600 pounds. Capacity, 1,000 pounds.
Price, without rope............87c

No. 9C4423 Made for ½-inch rope. One man can lift 600 pounds. Capacity, 1,500 pounds.
Price, without rope............$1.67

No. 9C4424 Made for ¾-inch rope. One man can lift 600 pounds. Capacity, 2,500 pounds.
Price, without rope............$2.80

Manila Rope.

Prices on cordage change considerably from time to time, and we cannot guarantee these prices for the season, but will always furnish at lowest market prices. We guarantee our cordage to be strictly first quality.

No. 9C4490 Manila Rope once cut from the coil cannot be returned if sent as ordered. We sell any quantity at 100-foot rate.

Diam., inch,	¼	5-16	⅜	½	⅝	¾
100 ft.....	28c	44c	63c	98c	$1.88	$2.25

Diameter, inches...	⅞	1	1¼	1½
Price, per 100 feet....	$3.50	$4.05	$6.28	$9.10

State size wanted when ordering.

Lariat Rope.

No. 9C4495 Four Strand Hard Laid Pure Manila Lariat Rope. Diameter, 7-16 inch. Price, per foot............1¾c

Hog Ringers.

No. 9C4550 Hill's Pattern Hog Ringer. Black japanned.
Price....6c
Perdoz..60c

No. 9C4549 Hill's Hog Ringers made of malleable iron. Much stronger than above. Head painted red.
Price, per dozen, 85c; each............8c

No. 9C4551 Hill's Pattern Hog Rings for above ringer; 100 rings in a box. Price, per dozen, 43c; per box............4c

No. 9C4552 Hill's Pattern Shoat Rings for above ringer; 100 rings in a box. Price, per dozen, 43c; per box............4c

No. 9C4553 Hill's Pattern Pig Rings for above ringer; 100 rings in a box. Price, per dozen, 43c; per box............4c

Perfection Hog Ringer.

No. 9C4554 Perfection Hog Ringer. Made of malleable iron.
Price, each............8c
Per dozen............90c

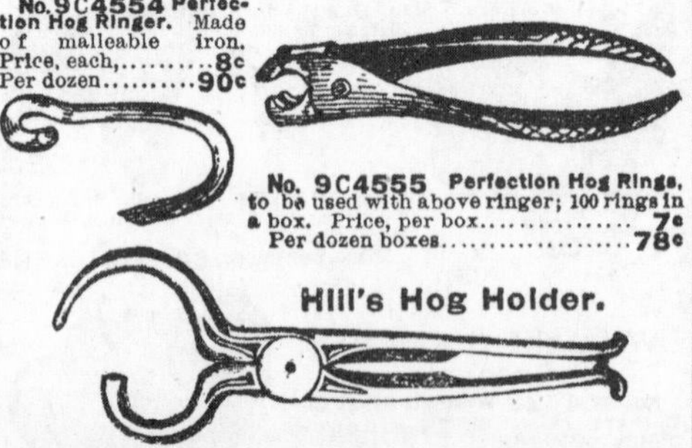

No. 9C4555 Perfection Hog Rings, to be used with above ringer; 100 rings in a box. Price, per box............7c
Per dozen boxes............78c

Hill's Hog Holder.

No. 9C4560 Hill's Malleable Iron Hog Holder, for holding hogs when placing rings in nose.
Price, per dozen, $1.88; each,............18c

Stock Marking Punch

$1.75

Nos. 1 2 3 4 5 6 7 8 9 10 11

No. 9C4586 Strong malleable iron handles, best steel cutting dies. Practical, strong and durable. The dies are from ¾ to ⅞ inch long; entire length of tool, 11½ inches. The dies are hollow and cut, which is more humane than the use of solid dies, which simply punch a hole through the ear. When ordering, state the number of the die you prefer. Weight, packed for mail or express, 1½ pounds. Your choice of any one of the above dies. Price............$1.75

Well Wheels.

No. 9C4482 Well Wheels, japanned. Weight, 3 to 6 pounds.

Width of frame, inches	8	10	12
Price, each............	$0.18	$0.21	$0.25
Per dozen............	2.00	2.35	2.85

Stock Marks.

No. 9C4600 Cast Iron Stock Marks with raised letter—never wear out. Used with Perfection Ring and Ringer. Made only with any one single letter. Price, per 100, 35c; per dozen..5c

Ear Labels.

Metal Ear Labels for sheep, cattle and hogs; name on one side and numbered from 1 upward, or any numbers desired on the reverse side; they are very light and will not tear out. If there are more than seven letters in your name the initials only can be put on labels.

No. 9C4561 Sheep and Hog Size No. 9C4562 Cattle Size No. 9C4563 Extra Cattle Size	Sheep and Hog Size	Cattle Size	Extra Cattle Size
100 with name and numbers..........	$1.50	$2.00	$2.50
50 with name and numbers..........	1.00	1.25	1.50
25 with name and numbers..........	.65	.75	1.00
100 name only or number only........	1.00	1.50	1.75
50 name only or number only........	.75	1.00	1.25
25 name only or number only........	.50	.60	.60

If by mail, postage extra, 20 cents per 100 on Cattle labels an 10 cents extra per 100 on Sheep labels.

Oval Ear Punches.

No. 9C4566 Oval Ear Punches.
Extra Cattle Size Ear Punch. Price............$1.20
Cattle, Sheep and Hog Size Ear Punch. Price.......75
If by mail, postage extra, 10 cents.

Tattoo Stock Markers.

No. 9C4572 The Tattoo Ear Marker for horses, cattle, sheep, swine and dogs. It is well known that a mark tattooed into the skin of a man or an animal will remain visible as long as the wearer lives. It cannot be changed or removed as ear labels or buttons frequently are, and will therefore, prevent fraud and stop all controversies as to the indentification of registered animals. It is the only brand or mark which may be applied to a horse without disfiguring. The letters are interchangeable, and can be quickly removed and others attached in their place. The letters are ½ inch square, and cut out of solid metal. If the letters are kept oiled they should last a lifetime. Directions for using. First smear the letters with the tattoo oil, punch the ear, and then rub the oil well into the punctures with the thumb or fingers. It takes three to five days for the ear to heal and the brand to show out clear and distinct. On a white, pink or yellow skin the brand is a jet black, but on a brown or black skin it makes a clear blue brand.

Marker fitted with three letters or figures. Price...$2.00
Extra letters or figures. Price each............30
Set of ten figures, 0 to 9. Price............2.75
Complete alphabet, A to Z. Price............6.25
Tattoo Oil, per bottle (marks 500 ears). Price.......50
Tattoo Oil, per bottle (Red, for extra dark skins). Price.......60

If by mail, postage on marker, 25 cents; postage on oil, 8 cents.

Ear Buttons.

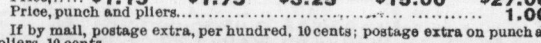

No. 9C4573 Ear Buttons. Suits all animals. Clinches tight. Cannot come out. Name and address on top as shown and number on bottom. Best and cheapest on the market. All pure aluminum.

	25	50	100	500	1000
Price,.....	$1.15	$1.75	$3.25	$15.00	$27.00

Price, punch and pliers............1.00

If by mail, postage extra, per hundred, 10 cents; postage extra on punch and pliers, 10 cents.

Hog Tamer and Stock Marker.

No. 9C4615 Never Root Hog Tamer. Cuts across tip of nose with curve at each side and severing same in the middle, making two projections, their weight causing them to drop apart and heal quickly in that position. The cutter is of fine quality of steel, is T shaped and reversible, one edge for pigs and shoats, the other for large hogs. This cutter is self adjusting to the gauges on back of cutting plate, gauging the proper depth of cutting on various sizes of hogs. We also furnish an extra knife for stock marking. Weight, 15 ounces. Price, with two knives......58c

Dehorning Saw.

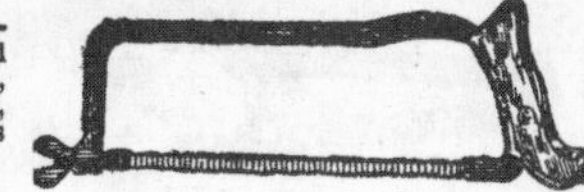

No. 9C4625 Dehorning Saw, with japanned malleable iron frame, beech handle, complete, with blade, 9½ inches long, ⅜ inch wide.
Price...45c

No. 9C4626 Extra Blades for this saw.
Price, per dozen, 87c; each.......................................8c

SEE PAGES 95 to 98 for the GREATEST Values in STOCK SADDLES Ever Heard of.

Newton & McGee's Draw Cut Patent Dehorner.

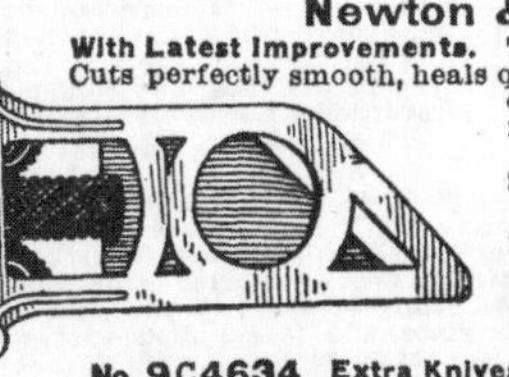

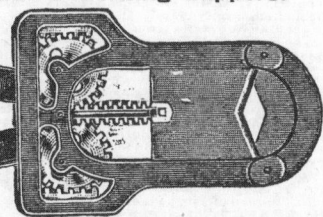

With Latest Improvements. The frames are made of best malleable iron and the blades of the best steel. Cuts perfectly smooth, heals quickly and causes the animal very little pain. They are fully guaranteed in every respect, and if any part should break from a flaw or defect, we will replace same without expense to the purchaser. They are made in three sizes.

No. 9C4631 No. 1 Draw Cut Dehorner, is for calves only. Has a 2-inch opening. Length, 2 feet 3 inches. Weight, 4½ pounds. Price...$2.90

No. 9C4632 No. 2 Draw Cut Dehorner, as described above, for young and medium aged cattle. Has a 3½-inch opening. Length, 3 feet 4 inches. Weight, 12 pounds. Price.......................$5.20

No. 9C4633 No. 3 Draw Cut Dehorner as described above, is for either young or old cattle. Has 4½-inch opening. Length, 3 feet 8 inches. Weight, 17 pounds. Price.......................$5.25

No. 9C4634 Extra Knives for No. 9C4631 Dehorner, Price.......... .95
No. 9C4635 Extra Knives for No. 9C4632 Dehorner, Price.......... 1.00
No. 9C4636 Extra Knives for No. 9C4633 Dehorner, Price.......... 1.00

Leavitt's "V" Shape Blade Dehorning Clippers.

LARGE SIZE, $5.00
SPECIAL SIZE, $4.00

Leavitt's V-shape Blade Dehorning Clipper, cuts all around horn as handles are closed. Knives cannot interlock, or cut into each other. This style dehorner in the large size will clip any size horn from cattle of any age smooth and clean. The special size will clip any ordinary size horn. In opening the blades, the handles do not go far enough apart to prevent the operator having ample purchase, and twice the power of any other dehorner made. This is a very desirable feature, as it has power enough to clip any large horn, with perfect ease to the operator. The material used in manufacturing this clipper is the best quality. The handles and U head frame are malleable, while the knives are of the best crescent steel; can be easily cleaned and do not tarnish, thus preventing all possibility of blood poisoning, often occurring from the use of inferior machines. Every clipper is thoroughly tested before being sent out. Twisting or prying will cause the blades to break. We will not replace blades broken from this cause. Shipping weight, 14 pounds.

No. 9C4640 Leavitt's V Blade Dehorner. Large size. Knives open 3½ inches. Price, each..................$5.00

No. 9C4641 Extra Sliding Knife for V Blade Dehorner.
Price...40

No. 9C4642 Extra Stationary Knife for V Blade Dehorner. Price.......................................40

No. 9C4637 Leavitt's V Blade Dehorner. Special size. Knives open 3 inches. Large enough for any ordinary stock.
Price, each...$4.00

No. 9C4638 Extra Sliding Knife for V Blade Dehorner.
Price...40

No. 9C4639 Extra Stationary Knife for V Blade Dehorner. Price.......................................40

SHEEP SHEARS.

Our Sheep Shears are made of a high grade of cutlery steel, which is produced specially to meet the peculiar requirements of our goods. They are made with the best modern appliances and machinery, and our system of inspection is so thorough as to prevent any but perfect goods being sent out. In finish and appearance, as well as in quality and durability, our shears are superior to any other line on the market, either imported or domestic. We guarantee every pair of shears to be perfect. Each pair of sheep shears is examined and tested in wool before packing. The blade of each shear is etched as follows: "If this shear does not prove as good or better than any shear you ever had return it and money will be refunded." Our prices are based on cost to manufacture with only our one small profit added. We do make the best shear it is possible to produce, and sell it at a price that cannot be named on shears which must bear a large advertising expense and the middlemen's profits.

No. 9C4652 Great Western Sheep Shears. Double bow. Straight back and edge. Full polished blades. The shape and style used by professional shearers of the West. Don't let our low price cause you to doubt the quality of these shears. They are etched on blade as follows: "If this shear does not prove as good or better than any shear you ever had return it and money will be refunded."

Length of blade, inches	5	6½	7
Price	70c	74c	78c

No. 9C4654 Great Eastern Sheep Shears, single bow. Bent handles. Full polished and swaged. The shape and style used in the Central and Eastern States. Same quality, workmanship and finish as described under preceding number.

Length of blade, inches	5½	6	6½
Price	69c	73c	77c

No. 9C4656 Sheep Shears are made of the same high grade steel used in above shears, but they are not so nicely finished nor so carefully inspected. They do not carry the same guarantee as those described above, but they will do good work and are good enough for anyone who has only a small flock and does his own shearing. Bent handles. Half polished blades.

Length of blade, inches	5½	6
Price	52c	55c

For Sheep Shearing Machines, see Index.

No. 9C4659 The Celebrated Burgon & Ball's "B. B. A." Sheep Shears, double bow, straight swage blades, polished; the kind that is used by professional sheep shearers.

Size, inches	6½	7
Price	95c	$1.00

Cattle Leaders.

No. 9C4677 Malleable Iron Cattle Leaders, with brass spring; full size; regular goods, same as you pay double the price for or more.
Price, per dozen, 50c; each..........5c

Bull Rings.

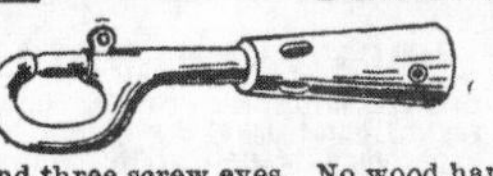

No. 9C4679 Copper Bull Rings, 2½ inches in diameter; polished, with screwdriver to fit.
Price, per dozen, $1.00; each...........9c

No. 9C4683 Same as No. 9C4679, 3 inches in diameter.
Price, per dozen, $1.25; each..........11c

Bull Snaps.

No. 9C4687 Patent Bull Snap. Every one who handles a bull should have and always use this snap. We furnish with snap three feet of chain, with ring on end and three screw eyes. No wood handle furnished.
Price, per dozen, $2.34; each..........20c

Brass Ox Balls.

No. 9C4690 Brass Ox Balls, to put on the tips of the horns of vicious cattle. Octagon pattern. Medium size, ⅝-inch. Price, per dozen, 27c; each..........3c
Large size, ⅞-inch. Price, per dozen, 44c; each...4c

Cattle Tie Irons.

No. 9C4695 Cattle Tie Irons, tinned, with patent covered spring bolt snap. Complete with thimble for rope ⅝-inch or smaller. Weight, complete, 6 ounces.
Price, per dozen.......49c; Complete, each..........5c

German Pattern Cow Ties.

No. 9C4698 Welded Links. Ohio pattern cow ties, with two toggles. No. 2-0, length, 4½ feet.
Price, each..........$0.12
Per dozen..........1.33

Niagara Cow Ties.

The Niagara Wire Link is formed on the principle of a square knot. The greater the strain the tighter holds the knot, so that no force will pull its fastenings apart. Being made entirely by automatic machinery this chain can be turned out at a less cost than other patterns of chain and is therefore sold cheaper.

No. 9C4699 Niagara Wire Link Ohio Pattern Cow Ties, with toggle. Size, 2-0, suitable for ordinary size cows. This is the size and weight commonly sold.
Price, each..........$0.12
Per dozen..........1.35

No. 9C4700 Niagara Wire Link Ohio Pattern Cow Ties, with toggle. Size, 4-0, large and strong enough for the largest cow.
Price, per dozen, $1.98; each..........17c

American Cow Ties.

The links of the American Cow Ties are stamped from a piece of steel, and chain is constructed entirely without welds, making the strongest and safest chain that can be produced. The flat chain is easier on stock.

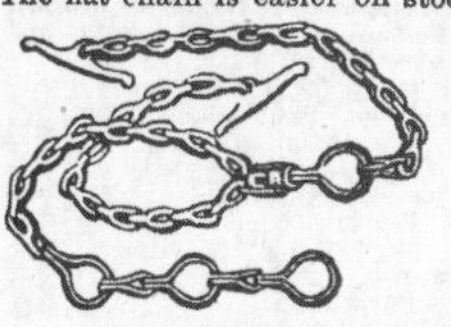

No. 9C4707 The American Flat Link Ohio Pattern Cow Tie with two toggles. Size, 3-0. Larger and stronger than the size commonly sold.
Price, each..........$0.16
Per dozen..........1.81

No. 9C4708 The American Flat Link Ohio Pattern Cow Tie with two toggles. Size, 5-0. The largest and strongest cow tie made. Will hold the biggest bull. Price, per dozen, $2.75; each..........23c

Combination Ohio Pattern Cow Ties.

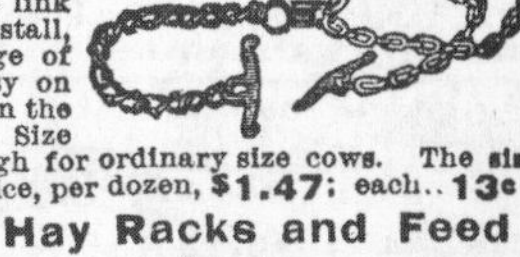

No. 9C4713 Combination Ohio Pattern Cow Ties, with two toggles. This tie has the American link to go around the neck and the Niagara wire link to fasten to stanchion or stall, thus giving the advantage of the flat link, which is easy on the neck, at little more than the price of the regular chains. Size 2-0, large and strong enough for ordinary size cows. The size that is commonly sold. Price, per dozen, $1.47; each..13c

Hay Racks and Feed Boxes.

No. 9C4720

No. 9C4720 Cast Iron Corner Hay Rack. Projects from corner 22 inches; height, 27 inches. Weight, 29 pounds.
Price..........88c

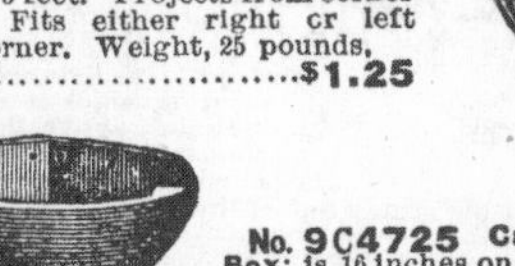
No. 9C4721

No. 9C4721 Wrought Steel Corner Hay Rack; made from round steel rods, ½ inch in diameter. Frame, flat steel 1¼x3-16 inches. Height, 3 feet. Projects from corner 2 feet. Fits either right or left hand corner. Weight, 25 pounds.
Price..........$1.25

No. 9C4725 Cast Iron Corner Feed Box; is 16 inches on each side; 10 inches deep. Weight, 28 pounds. Price.87c

No. 9C4726 Cast Iron Corner Feed Box, with roll rim. Size, 16x16x10 inches.
Price..........98c

No. 9C4728 Cast Iron Corner Salt Box, Size, 6x6x5 inches.
Price..........25c

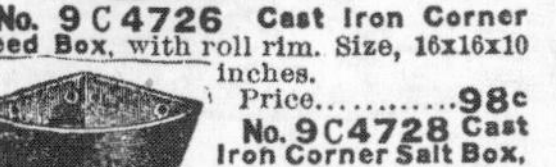
No. 9C4728

No. 9C4726

Picket Pins and Chains.

No. 9C4735 Straight Fluted Malleable Iron Picket Pins, 15 inches long, with swivel. Weight, 1½ pounds.
Price, per dozen, 75c; each..........7c

Eureka Wire Link Picket or Tie-out Chains are stronger, better and more durable than a rope. These chains have a stake ring 3½ inches in diameter on one end, a steel swivel snap on the other and a swivel in the center.

No. 9C4743 Eureka Wire Link Picket Chain. Size 1. Light, but strong enough for a docile animal.

Length, feet	20	30	50
Price	39c	56c	90c

No. 9C4744 Eureka Wire Link Picket Chain. Size 2-0. Heavy and strong enough for unruly animals.

Length, feet	20	30	50
Price	52c	78c	$1.20

Lariat Swivels.

No. 9C4747 Malleable Iron Lariat Swivels, 3 inches long. One eye ⅝ inch inside, the other ⅜ inch inside.
Price, per dozen, 22c; each..........2c

Calf Weaners.

Not mailable.

No. 9C4754 No sharp points in front to prick or gouge the cow. Perfectly safe and harmless. Is the only weaner having any side protection to prevent sucking sidewise, and is warranted to wean the most obstinate case without cruelty or injury. Does not go through the nose or swing loose to wear the nose or make it sore. Patented October 2, 1886.

No. 1, for small calves. Price, per dozen $1.69; each..15c
No. 2, for large calves. Price, per dozen 1.70; each..15c
No. 3, for yearlings. Price, per dozen 1.97; each..17c
No. 4, for two-year olds and cows.
Price, per dozen, $2.25; each..........19c

Not Mailable.

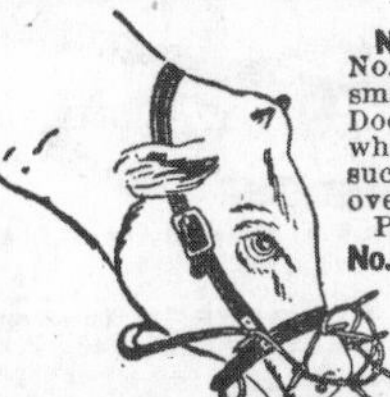

No. 9C4763 Hoosier Calf Weaner. No. 1 will adjust to fit smallest calves or small yearlings. Weight, about 1½ lbs. Does not interfere with feeding, but when the head is raised in position to suck, the weight forces the muzzle over his mouth. Price, each..$0.24
Per dozen..........2.82

No. 9C4764 Hoosier Range Weaner, same as above only larger. Suitable for large calves, yearlings or colts. Weight, about 2 pounds.
Price, each..........$0.32
Per dozen..........3.75

No. 9C4765 Hoosier Cow Weaner will adjust to fit large yearlings or large cows. The halter is made of heavy, oil filled waterproof leather. The frame is made of ⅝x3-16 wrought steel. The points of No. 5 steel wire; all metal parts are tinned to prevent rust. Weight about 3 pounds. Price, each..$0.40
Per dozen..........4.69

Basket Weaners.

Basket Weaners have been thoroughly tested and have given the best of satisfaction in every way. The straps are well filled with oil; substantial and durable; when the head is raised in position to suck, the wire basket drops over the mouth.

No. 9C4771 Size 1. For calves. Price, each...$0.20
Per dozen.........2.35
No. 9C4772 Size 2. For yearlings. Price, each $0.22
Per dozen.........2.58
No. 9C4773 Size 3. For cows. Price, each.....$0.26
Per dozen.........3.05

Genuine Newhouse Traps.

The Genuine Newhouse Game Traps are branded on the pan "S. Newhouse" and are manufactured by The Oneida Community (Limited) at Kenwood, N. Y. They are the standard for excellence the world over and are fully warranted.

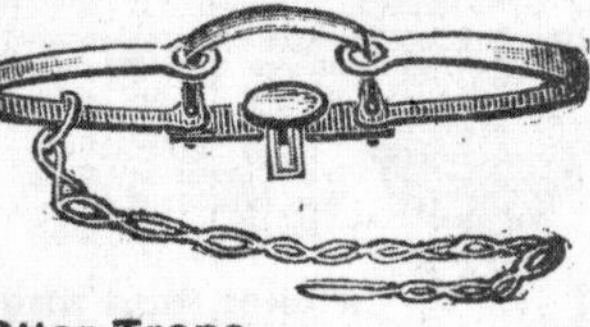

No. 9C4836 Genuine Newhouse Traps. Spread of jaws, 3½ inches; with chain. Size No. 0; weight, 13 ounces.
Price, each.......$0.18
Per dozen.........2.13

No. 9C4837 Genuine Newhouse Traps. Spread jaws, 4 inches; with chain. Size No. 1. This is the size most used. Weight, 17 ounces. Price, per dozen, $2.50; each..........21c

No. 9C4838 Genuine Newhouse Traps. Spread of jaw, 4½ inches; with chain. Size No. 1½. This is called the mink trap. Often used for catching foxes. Weight, 1 pound 6 ounces.
Price, per dozen, $3.75; each..........32c

No. 9C4835 Newhouse Trap with Webbed Jaws. Occasionally animals free themselves from traps by gnawing their legs off just below the trap jaws where the flesh is numb from pressure. Noting the jaws, as illustrated, it is plain the animal can only gnaw off its leg at a point quite a distance below the meeting edges of the jaws. The flesh left above the point of amputation and below the jaws will swell, and make it impossible to draw the leg stump out of the trap. Made in Newhouse quality only and in only one size. Spread of jaws, 4 inches. Price, per dozen, $2.75; each..........24c

Fox Traps.

No. 9C4839 The Genuine Newhouse Trap, with double spring and chain. Size No. 2, the fox trap; spread of jaws, 4⅞ inches. Weight, 1 pound 10 ounces.
Price, each $0.44
Per dozen, 5.25

Otter Traps.

No. 9C4840 The Genuine Newhouse Trap, with double spring and chain. Size No. 3, the otter trap; spread of jaws, 5½ inches. Weight, 2½ pounds.
Price, per dozen, $7.00; each..........59c

Beaver Traps.

No. 9C4841 The Genuine Newhouse Trap, with double spring and chain. Size No. 4, the beaver trap; spread of jaw, 6½ inches. Weight, 3 pounds 2 ounces.
Price, per dozen, $8.25; each..........69c

Single Spring Otter Traps.

No. 9C4844 Newhouse (Size 2½) Single Spring Otter Trap was designed in response to requests from old and experienced trappers. It is used more especially for catching otter on their "slides." For this purpose a thin, raised plate of steel is adjusted to the pan so that when the trap is set the plate will be a trifle higher than the teeth on the jaws. The points of the teeth are made very sharp, to pierce the animal's breast, and the raised plate can be readily detached if desired, making the trap one of general utility. Spread of jaws, 5 inches.
Price, per dozen, $8.25; each (with chain)..........69c

No. 9C4845 Newhouse (Size 3½) Otter Trap, single spring, with chain. In some localities the otter grows to an unusual size, with great proportionate strength, so that we sell an especially large and strong pattern for those who prefer a single spring trap. The No. 3½ Newhouse was designed to meet these requirements. All the parts are heavier than the No. 2½, the spread of jaws is greater, and the spring stiffer. Spread of jaws, 6½ inches. Price, per dozen, $9.25; each..........78c

Newhouse Deer Trap.

No. 9C4852 Newhouse Deer Trap No. 14, with chain. This trap is the same in size as the No. 9C4841, but has heavier and stiffer springs, and offset jaws, which allow the springs to rise higher when the animal's leg is in the trap, and is furnished with teeth sufficiently close to prevent the animal from drawing its foot out. Spread of jaws, 6½ inches.
Price, per dozen, $8.75; each..........73c

Wolf Traps.

No. 9C4853 The Genuine Newhouse Trap. Size No. 4½, especially adapted to catching wolves. This trap has 8-inch spread of jaws, with the other parts in proportion, and is provided with a pronged drag, a heavy snap and an extra heavy steel swivel and chain, 5 feet long, warranted to hold 2,000 pounds. The trap, complete with chain and drag, will weigh about 9 pounds.
Price, per dozen, $20.00; each..........$1.67

Bear Traps.

No. 9C4857 The Genuine Newhouse Trap No. 5 size, with teeth on jaws. This trap weighs 17 pounds, and has a spread of jaws of 11¾ inches. It is used for taking the common black bear, and is furnished with a chain and swivel sufficiently strong; double spring. Price..........$8.00

No. 9C4858 The Genuine Newhouse Trap, No. 6, for grizzly bear. This is the strongest trap made; it will hold a lion, cougar, tiger or moose, as well as the great grizzly bear. Spread of jaws, 16 inches. Weight, 42 pounds. Price..........$10.00

No. 9C4861 Newhouse Bear Trap No. 15, with chain. To meet the views of certain hunters whose judgment we respect, we designed a style of jaw for this trap, making an offset of ¾ of an inch, so as to allow the springs to come up higher when the bear's leg is in the trap. This gives the spring a better grip. Spread of jaws, 11¾ inches. Price..........$5.00

WE BUY YOUR RAW FURS AND SKINS. WRITE FOR PRICES AND INSTRUCTIONS.

Game Traps.

The Hawley & Norton Game Traps are manufactured by The Oneida Community (Limited) at Kenwood N. Y., the makers of the genuine Newhouse traps.

The Hawley & Norton, while almost identical in form, is made somewhat lighter than the Newhouse throughout, and therefore cheaper; but it is a good, reliable trap, with a great reputation of its own. The springs are all tested before leaving the factory, and all the other parts are carefully inspected, the traps being set and sprung to insure their working correctly. We do not illustrate the Hawley & Norton traps, as the illustrations of same sizes in the genuine Newhouse traps—which is the previous line listed—will show what they look like.

No. 9C4865 The Hawley & Norton Game Trap, size 0, with chain. Spread of jaws, 3½ inches. Per doz., $1.44; each....12c
No. 9C4866 The Hawley & Norton Game Trap, size 1, with chain. Spread of jaws, 4 inches. Per doz., $1.69; each....15c
No. 9C4867 The Hawley & Norton Game Trap, size 1½, with chain. Spread of jaws, 4½ inches. Per doz., $2.54; each....22c
No. 9C4868 The Hawley & Norton Game Trap, size 2, with chain. Double spring. Spread of jaws, 4⅞ inches.
Price, per dozen, $3.55; each..........30c
No. 9C4870 The Hawley & Norton Game Trap, size 3, with chain. Double spring. Spread of jaws, 5½ inches.
Price, per dozen, $4.73; each..........40c
No. 9C4872 The Hawley & Norton Game Trap, size 4, with chain. Double spring. Spread of jaws, 6½ inches.
Price, per dozen, $5.57; each..........47c

Victor Brand Traps.

The Victor Brand Traps are made by The Oneida Community and are sold to compete with the various imitations of their Newhouse traps. We have sold large quantities of them and have had no complaints.

No. 9C4876 Victor Traps. 3½-inch jaws, with chain. Size No. 0. Weight, 14 ounces. Price, per dozen, $1.07; each....9c
No. 9C4877 Victor Traps. 4-inch jaws, with chain. Size No. 1. Weight, 14 ounces. Price, per dozen, $1.25; each....11c
No. 9C4878 Victor Traps. Size No. 1½, mink trap; 4½-inch jaws; single spring, with chain. Per doz., $1.88; each....16c
No. 9C4879 Victor Traps. Size No. 2, fox trap; 4⅞-inch jaws; double spring, with chain. Per doz., $2.63; each....22c
No. 9C4880 Victor Traps. Size No. 3, the otter trap; 5½-inch jaws; double spring, with chain. Per doz., $3.50; each....30c
No. 9C4881 Victor Traps. Size No. 4, the beaver trap; 6½-inch jaws; double spring, with chain. Per doz., $4.13; each....35c

Setting Clamps.

No. 9C4889 For setting game traps.
No. 4, for setting No. 4 trap. Price..........11c
No. 5, for setting No. 5 trap. Price..........25c
No. 6, for setting No. 6 trap. Price..........42c

No. 9C4891 Sears, Roebuck & Co.'s Lightning Tanner. Will tan furs and skins perfectly and satisfactorily in from 24 to 36 hours. No experience is needed to do first class work. No special tools are required. Simple directions are sent with each box. This size box will tan two raccoon skins in 36 hours. Price, per box..........10c
If by mail, postage extra, per box, 5 cents.

No. 9C4892 Sears, Roebuck & Co.'s Lightning Tanner in box containing about three times as much as above. One box will tan a large deer skin. 3 boxes are required for a horse or cow hide. Price, per box..........25c
If by mail, postage extra, per box, 15 cents.

Stop Thief Traps.

No. 9C4898 Stop Thief Trap, No. 1. Small size, for rats, ground squirrels and all small burrowing animals. A light and effective trap made of spring steel. Give this trap a test and its effectiveness will astonish you.
Price, per dozen, 97c; each.....9c

No. 9C4899 Stop Thief Trap, No. 2. Large size for rabbits, mink, muskrats, weasels, etc. If properly set this trap is sure to catch. To successfully catch mink, select a place on the bank of a stream where mink tracks are seen and where there is but little room between the bank and the water. Make a hole in the bank 6 or 7 inches deep and a little smaller than the bow of the trap. Cut bait in small pieces and put in back end of the hole. Set trap over the hole so the trigger will be down. When set this way the animal will throw the trap with its body when it makes an effort to remove the bait. This insures catching around the neck or body, which kills at once and saves the skin and fur in good condition. Price, each..........$0.12
Per dozen..........1.39

No. 9C4901 Stop Thief Trap, No. 3. Extra large size, for catching skunks, Southern raccoons, etc.; same as above only larger. Price, per dozen, $1.57; each..........14c

No. 9C4902 Stop Thief Trap No. 3½. Special size for Northern raccoons. Can be used for skunks, minks, opossums, etc. Price, per dozen, $2.67; each..........23c

Gopher Traps.

No. 9C4897 Out o' Sight Gopher Traps. This is a perfect trap and better suited for the purpose intended than all other makes. We guarantee it to catch nineteen out of twenty gophers if set according to directions which accompany each trap.
Price, each.....$0.12
Price, per dozen..........1.33

No. 9C4904 Improved Gopher Trap, with wood sides. Can be set easier than above. Price, each..........$0.14
Price, per dozen..........1.67

Mole Traps.

No. 9C4900 The Bulldog Mole Trap is the simplest, most durable and effective on the market. Directions:—Find the main trail, which usually starts from a wood pile, a fence or any place where ground is not often disturbed. Remove dirt from top of trail. Set the trap, pressing handles together and inserting the tongue. Place the trap in the trail, the tongue touching bottom. Cover loosely with dirt, leaving handles exposed.
Price, per dozen, $2.25; each..........23c

No. 9C4903 Mole Trap. Has 30 pounds pressure when set. The spears are 5 inches long, made of hard steel, and are firmly set in a malleable plate. The plunger is made of hard steel, is firmly fastened in the center of the spear plate, and is supplied with a finger or hand hold at its upper end. It has a notch filed in for the trigger to catch in when set. It can be altered very easily so the trap will throw to suit the ground, as it should throw with less pressure in sand than clay or sod. The trigger and trip are simple and durable; they are automatic, set by gravity. Price, per doz., $5.00; each, 45c

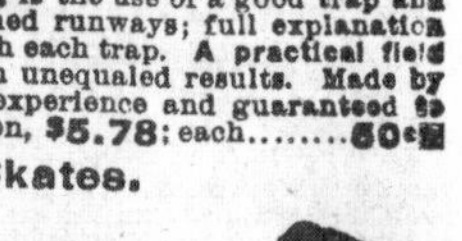

No. 9C4906 Out o' Sight Mole Trap. The latest improved mole trap. A new departure, having many advantages over all others, on account of its simplicity. Not complicated or easy to get out of order, easily set without danger to yourself, and can be used in hotbeds without interfering with the glass cover. This trap can be set without disturbing the runway, the pedal being so sensitive that it is impossible for the mole to pass under without throwing the trap. The secret of mole catching is the use of a good trap and to know their habits and established runways; full explanation of the habits, etc., furnished with each trap. A practical field trial has been given this trap with unequaled results. Made by practical trap makers of long experience and guaranteed to give satisfaction. Price, per dozen, $5.78; each..........50c

Roller Skates.

No. 9C4920 Improved Extension Sidewalk Skate, full strapped. Has high grade homogeneous steel tops, is strong and durable; trucks are stamped and corrugated and made from Swedish steel, are very light and strong. Trimmed with black pebbled leather straps, tongue buckles and nickel plated heel bands. Maple wheels. This skate is an extension—"one skate for all sizes"—is easily adjusted, and will stay where it is put and gives no trouble. Weight, per pair, 28 ozs. Price, per pair......33c

No. 9C4922 Plain Bearing, all Clamp Rink Roller Skate, for men. An extension roller skate, combines all the latest improvements in materials, designs and ideas. The tops, trucks, clamps and stampings being made of the best cold rolled Swedish steel insures fine appearance and strength. Trucks are oscillating, with best rubber cushions, and turn in three-foot circle. No straps. Clamps are neat, easily removed for repairs, cleaning or side adjustment and will hold to shoe like a vise. Furnished with hemacite rolls. Skate will extend and fit all sizes from 8½ to 11½ inches. Adjustment is easily made and will hold. Weight, per pair, 54 oz.
Price, per pair..........$0.73
Per 100 pairs f. o. b. factory..........66.00

No. 9C4923 Plain Bearing, Full Heel Rink Roller Skate, for women. An extension skate, combining all of the latest and best ideas, mentioned in description No. 9C4922. Furnished with hemacite rolls. Skate extends to fit all sizes from 7½ to 10½ inches.
Weight, per pair, 52 oz.
Price, per pair..........$0.73
Per 100 pairs f. o. b. factory..........66.00

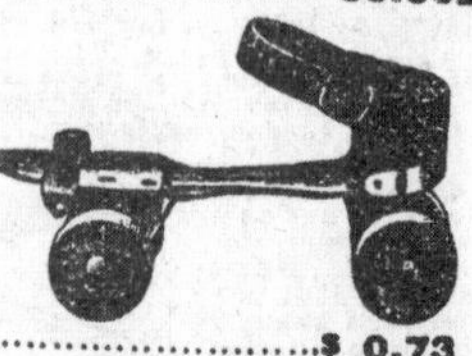

No. 9C4925 Ball Bearing, Half Clamp Rink Roller Skate, for either men or women. This is an extension roller skate, and combines all the latest improvements in materials, designs and ideas, as mentioned in description of No. 9C4922. Straps are best russet grain leather, with nickel buckles and trimmings. Furnished with hemacite rolls. Skate will extend to fit all sizes from 8½ to 11½ inches.
Weight, per pair, 63 ozs. Price, per pair..........$1.98
Per 100 pairs f. o. b. factory..........172.50

No. 9C4926 Ball Bearing, all Clamp Rink Roller Skate, for men. An extension roller skate. It combines all the latest improvements in design and manufacture mentioned in description of No. 9C4922. Furnished with hemacite rolls. Skate extends to fit all sizes from 8½ to 11½ inches. Weight, per pair, 63 ozs
Price, per pair..........$1.98
Per 100 pairs f. o. b. factory..........172.50

ORDERS for 100 pairs roller skates, made up from Nos. 9C4922, 9C4923, 9C4925 and 9C4926 will be sold at 100 pairs price. NOTE—100 pairs price is f. o. b. factory; pair price f. o. b. Chicago.

WE ARE HEADQUARTERS FOR POULTRY NETTING, WOVEN WIRE FENCING,

WIRE GATES, BARBED WIRE, SMOOTH WIRE.

Everything in Wire at Manufacturers' Lowest Prices.

OUR NETTING, FENCING AND WIRE GOODS

will be found superior to those carried by the average retail dealer or offered by other mail order houses. **We offer you these goods in all the various size meshes and size wire suitable for the different uses for the ranch, farm, lawn and garden.** We guarantee all our fencing and netting to be made of size wire as stated in our description. **When comparing our prices with others, please remember this and be sure competing price is for the same size wire. WE GUARANTEE EACH BALE** to contain the quantity specified.

ABOUT THE FREIGHT. Freight amounts to next to nothing compared with what you will save in the price. For 500 miles it will, as a rule, add not more than five per cent to our price.

Poultry Netting.

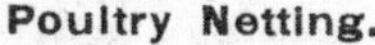

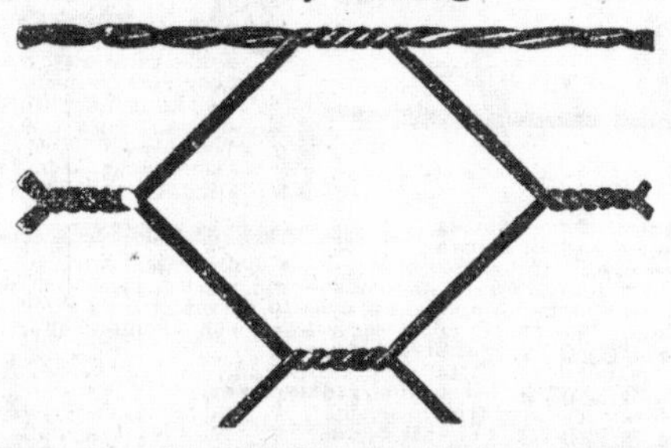

Genuine Acme Galvanized Bessemer Hard Steel Wire Netting, made for poultry fences, vine supports, trellises, etc. Superior in quality to what you will be likely to get elsewhere, and by reason of our very favorable contract, we can quote it at even less than light and inferior goods are offered. The Acme netting will last much longer than netting made from soft steel wire, is stronger and makes the best and cheapest poultry fences; cannot blow down; very easily put up, also excellent for pea vine supports and training ornamental vines.

Where it is to the advantage of our customer, we will ship our Acme Galvanized Poultry Netting Nos. 9C5450, 9C5456, 9C5462 and 9C5468 from the factory in Massachusetts. Small lots of this netting will be shipped from Chicago.

2-Inch Mesh.

No. 9C5450 Galvanized Poultry Netting, with 2-inch mesh, made from No. 19 hard steel wire with double and twisted selvage. Put up in rolls 150 feet long. This is the standard size mesh most generally used for poultry yards and light farm purposes. Some of our competitors sell 2-inch mesh poultry netting made from **No. 20 wire.** We do not consider No. 20 wire heavy enough to be serviceable in a 2-inch mesh netting, hence do not handle it.

We positively will not sell part of a roll.

Width, inches	Weight, per bale	Per bale of 150 ft.	Width, inches	Weight, per bale	Per bale of 150 ft.
12	12 pounds	$0.63	42	37 pounds	$2.20
18	16 pounds	.94	48	43 pounds	2.52
24	22 pounds	1.26	54	48 pounds	2.82
30	27 pounds	1.57	60	52 pounds	3.15
36	32 pounds	1.89	72	63 pounds	3.78

1½-Inch Mesh.

No. 9C5456 Galvanized Poultry Netting, with 1½-inch mesh, made from No. 19 wire with double and twisted selvage. Rolls are 150 feet long. Used for poultry yards, pigeon cotes, etc.

We positively will not sell part of a roll.

Width, inches	Weight, per bale	Per bale of 150 ft.	Width, inches	Weight, per bale	Per bale of 150 ft.
12	18 pounds	$0.88	42	50 pounds	$3.08
18	24 pounds	1.32	48	58 pounds	3.52
24	30 pounds	1.76	54	64 pounds	3.96
30	36 pounds	2.20	60	69 pounds	4.40
36	44 pounds	2.64	72	82 pounds	5.28

1-Inch Mesh.

No. 9C5462 Galvanized Poultry Netting, with 1-inch mesh, made from No. 20 wire, with double and twisted selvage. Rolls are 150 feet long. This netting is used at the bottom of fences to keep the small chickens inside and prevent vermin intruding.

We positively will not sell part of a roll.

Width, inches	Weight, per bale	Per bale of 150 ft.	Width, inches	Weight, per bale	Per bale of 150 ft.
12	19 pounds	$1.39	36	47 pounds	$4.15
18	25 pounds	2.08	42	53 pounds	4.85
24	34 pounds	2.77	48	60 pounds	5.54
30	38 pounds	3.46			

2½-Inch Mesh Lawn Fence.

No. 9C5468 Galvanized Lawn Fencing, with 2½ inch mesh, made from No. 15 wire, with double and twisted selvage. Put up in rolls 150 feet long. This makes a close, heavy, strong and durable fence for lawns, gardens, cemeteries, etc. Poultry raisers use this for poultry yards—putting a narrow width of No. 9C5462 around the bottom inside—thus making a good fence that will stop everything and last for many years.

We positively will not sell part of a roll.

Width, inches	Weight, per bale	Per bale of 150 ft.	Width, inches	Weight, per bale	Per bale of 150 ft.
12	29 pounds	$1.57	42	92 pounds	$5.47
18	41 pounds	2.35	48	103 pounds	6.25
24	53 pounds	3.13	54	113 pounds	7.03
30	66 pounds	3.91	60	123 pounds	7.81
36	79 pounds	4.69	72	144 pounds	9.37

"No Sag" Woven Wire Fencing.

Made of the best galvanized wire. Will not sag. The line wires, running as they do through the mesh wires, form a truss which prevents sagging. For ordinary farm fences this extra fencing, 48 inches high, 3⅜x12-inch mesh, will make a good substantial fence. For hog pastures, where it is used in connection with barbed wire, the 18, 23 or 30-inch fence, 3⅜x12-inch mesh will answer. For garden fences use the 2x4 or 3⅜x6-inch mesh whatever height is needed. This fencing is made of No. 14 galvanized wire for the line and mesh wires, with a rope selvage of two strands of No. 12 wire. This wire is carried in stock at factory, put up in rolls of 20 rods (330 feet) each, but we can furnish any number of even rods direct from the factory in Joliet, Illinois, but do not cut less than six rods.

No. 9C5509 "No Sag" Woven Wire Fencing. Size of mesh, 3⅜x12 inches.

Width	Weight, per rod	Price, per rod	Width	Weight, per rod	Price, per rod
18 inches....	4½ lbs.	17½c	42 inches....	8 lbs.	33c
23 inches....	5 lbs.	22c	48 inches....	9½ lbs.	35c
30 inches....	6½ lbs.	26¼c	54 inches....	10½ lbs.	37¼c
37 inches....	7½ lbs.	30¾c	60 inches....	12 lbs.	39½c

No. 9C5511 "No Sag" Woven Wire Fencing. Size of mesh, 3⅜x6 inches.

Width	Weight, per rod	Price, per rod	Width	Weight, per rod	Price, per rod
18 inches....	5½ lbs.	26¼c	42 inches....	9½ lbs.	41¾c
23 inches....	6 lbs.	30¾c	48 inches....	11 lbs.	43¾c
30 inches....	7½ lbs.	35c	54 inches....	12 lbs.	46c
37 inches....	8½ lbs.	39½c	60 inches....	13 lbs.	48¼c

Extra Heavy "No Sag" Woven Wire Fencing.

This fencing is made like the fence described above, excepting that it is heavier and will consequently last longer. The selvage is made of two No. 12 wires twisted together, the line wires No. 12, and the mesh wires No. 14, all galvanized. **This is without doubt the best woven wire fencing to be had.** Put up in rolls of 20 rods (330 feet), but we can furnish any number of even rods above six. It is shipped direct from factory in Joliet, Illinois.

No. 9C5514 "No Sag" Extra Heavy Woven Wire Fencing. Size of mesh, 3⅜x12 inches.

Width	Weight, per rod	Price, per rod	Width	Weight, per rod	Price, per rod
18 inches....	5 lbs.	22c	42 inches....	10½ lbs.	39½c
23 inches....	6 lbs.	26¼c	48 inches....	12 lbs.	43¾c
30 inches....	7½ lbs.	30¾c	54 inches....	13½ lbs.	48¼c
37 inches....	9 lbs.	35c	60 inches....	15 lbs.	52½c

No. 9C5516 "No Sag" Extra Heavy Woven Wire Fencing. Size of mesh, 3⅜x6 inches.

Width	Weight, per rod	Price, per rod	Width	Weight, per rod	Price, per rod
18 inches....	7 lbs.	30¾c	42 inches....	12½ lbs.	48¼c
23 inches....	8 lbs.	35c	48 inches....	14 lbs.	52½c
30 inches....	9½ lbs.	39½c	54 inches....	15½ lbs.	57c
37 inches....	11 lbs.	43¾c	60 inches....	17 lbs.	61¼c

Write for Special Wire Fence Circular, for our complete line of Wire Fencing.

Our Sheep and Hog Fence With 3x3-Inch Mesh. Less Than 23 Cents per Rod.

No. 9C5545 For those who wish a low priced hog fence we offer in competition with what is commonly sold, a fencing made of No. 16 wire, with 3x3-inch mesh. We have this put up in bales 150 feet long, and do not cut bales. While the price is lower it is no cheaper, quality considered, than is our "No Sag" fencing. (23 inches wide). Remember, our prices are governed by the quality of the goods we furnish.

Sheep and Hog Fencing. Mesh, 3x3 inches; made of No. 16 wire, with double and twisted wire selvage. Weight, per bale, 35 pounds. Price, per bale, 150 feet long, 24 inches wide..**$2.07**

STEEL GATES.

All our steel gates have extra heavy T steel frames, to which are securely riveted strong malleable iron latch and hinges. All frames are thoroughly painted with a special metallic paint, which prevents corrosion. Distance between posts should be 4 inches greater than width of the gate.

WHEN ORDERING GATES ALWAYS GIVE WIDTH FIRST. This will prevent misunderstanding, errors and delays.

Single Walk Gates, with Ornamental Tops.

No. 9C5562 Single Gates, covered with woven wire fence (mesh 2x4). Complete with hinges and latch.

Height	36 inches	42 inches	48 inches	54 inches
36 inches wide........	$2.66	$2.67	$2.68	$2.73
42 inches wide.......	2.76	2.77	2.78	2.82
48 inches wide.......	2.83	2.84	2.85	2.87

Double Drive Gates.

With ornamental tops. Distance between posts should be 5 inches greater than width of both gates.

No. 9C5566 Covered with woven wire fence (mesh 2x4), complete with hinges and latch.

Height	36 inches	42 inches	48 inches	54 inches
5 feet wide. Per pair....	$7.74	$7.75	$7.76	$7.87
6 feet wide. Per pair...	7.88	7.89	7.90	8.05

Width given is for each gate.

Fence Ornaments.

No. 9C5572 Malleable Iron Fence Picket, japanned. Length, 18 inches; height, 6 inches. They are especially adapted for the top rail of any fence, board partitions, veranda roofs, etc. They may be used inverted for ornaments under veranda roofs.

Price, per 100, **$4.38**; each........................**5c**

Galvanized Staples.

Our staples are sharp pointed, will drive well and are perfectly bent and cut.

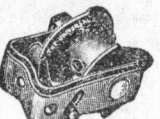

No. 9C5595 Galvanized ⅞-inch staples, for poultry netting, 550 to the pound. Price, per pound **5c**

No. 9C5596 Galvanized 1-inch staples, for poultry netting, 230 to the pound. Price, per pound..........**5c**

No. 9C5597 Galvanized 1¼-inch staples, for woven wire fencing, smooth or barbed wire, 100 to the pound. Price, per pound..........**3¾c**

No. 9C5598 Galvanized 1½-inch staples, for woven wire fencing, smooth or barbed wire, 80 to the pound. Price, per pound..........**3¾c**

Wire Fence Ratchet.

No. 9C5611 The Universal Wire Fence Ratchet and Tightener is reversible and cannot get out of order. The frame is of steel. The lock is positive and automatic. Can be used at the posts or midway between the posts.

Price, each.......................**$0.03**
Per box containing 100........**2.80**

No. 9C5614 Fence Ratchet, for stretching plain, barbed, or woven wire fencing. The catch works automatically. It will adjust itself to a round or flat surface, and will neither tip or turn sidewise. Can also be used as a center stretcher. Weight, each, 12 ounces.

Price, per 100, **$3.75**; each.......**4c**

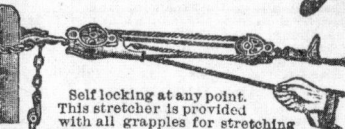

No. 9C5618 Tackle Block Wire Stretcher.

Self locking at any point. This stretcher is provided with all grapples for stretching barbed wire, strand and woven wire fencing. It is also a complete safety rope hoist for ordinary use, with which one man can raise 500 pounds. Weight, 4½ pounds.

Price, complete with 16 feet of ⅜-inch rope..........**73c**

No. 9C5619 The Bulldog Wire Grip. The more you pull, the tighter it grips the wire and never slips. When attached to a handspike it makes a splendid stretcher for either barbed or smooth wire. The grip can be attached to any wire stretcher.

Price..........................**22c**

Wire Stretchers.

No. 9C5621 The Well Known Elwood Wire Stretcher. Full weight, regular size.

Price..........**42c**

The Handy Andy.

No. 9C5625 The Handy Andy Combination Tool serves as a hammer, hatchet, pincers, staple puller, wire cutter, nail claws, screwdriver and leather punch. Forged from tool steel, propealy tempered. An excellent tool for fence building or repairing. Length, 12 inches. Weight, 2¼ pounds. Price..........**75c**

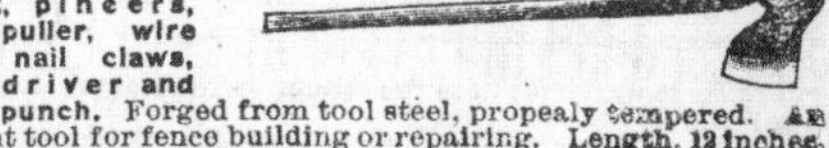

Staple Pulling Pliers.

No. 9C5623 The Improved Genuine Russell Staple Pulling Buttons' Pliers. Made by the Utica Drop Forged & Tool Co. Drives, pulls and saves the staples; cuts and splices wire. Weight, 1½ pounds. Length, 10 inches. Price..........**80c**

No. 9C5624 Latest Improved 1905 Fencing Plier. Drives, pulls and saves the staples; cuts and holds wire for splicing. The cutter will take in and easily cut the double and twisted barbed wire or No. 9 smooth wire. The jaws are shaped to grasp the staple on its bend when the staple is farthest out of the wood. It draws the staples straight so they can be used again. One side of the plier is provided with a cutting edge to use in chipping away the wood when a staple is embedded in the post or when a wire has been attached to a tree and the tree grown over it. It is an all-round farm plier, wire cutter and hammer. Every tool warranted against defects in material or workmanship. Length, 10 inches. Weight, 23 ounces. Price..........**70c**

If by mail, postage extra, 30 cents.

Buttons' Pliers and Cutters.

No. 35C3744 Buttons' Pliers and Cutters. Forged steel; not as well made or as finely finished as our special Buttons' Pliers, but one that will give satisfaction in general use.

Price, 4½-in. **17c**; 6-inch, **19c**; 8-inch, **25c**; 10-in. **31c**.

No. 35C3746 Our Special High Grade Buttons' Pliers and Cutters. Made from the best tool steel that can be procured; made by skilled workmen and finely finished; will cut heavier wire than corresponding sizes made by other manufacturers. The cutters are tempered just right. The best plier for fence builders that can be produced.

Price. 4½-inch. **22c**; 6-inch. **24c**; 8-inch. **31c**; 10-inch. **42c**

The above illustration shows our two-point Glidden Pattern Barbed Wire. Notice that the barbs have two turns around the main wire—will not come loose.

Our Barbed Wire, both galvanized and painted, is made of the best grade of soft Bessemer steel, perfectly drawn and thoroughly annealed. The wire is thoroughly and uniformly galvanized, and the wire is nicely prepared on good, stout reels, which average in weight from 95 to 110 pounds each.

No. 9C5400 Two-Point Painted Hog Wire, barbs 3 inches apart............
No. 9C5401 Two-Point Painted Cattle Wire, barbs 5 inches apart............
No. 9C5402 Four-Point Painted Hog Wire, barbs 3 inches apart............
No. 9C5403 Four-Point Painted Cattle Wire, barbs 5 inches apart............
No. 9C5404 Two-Point Galvanized Hog Wire, barbs 3 inches apart............
No. 9C5405 Two-Point Galvanized Cattle Wire, barbs 5 inches apart............
No. 9C5406 Four-Point Galvanized Hog Wire, barbs 3 inches apart............
No. 9C5407 Four-Point Galvanized Cattle Wire, barbs 5 inches apart............

Price is liable to advance or decline any day, so we quote prices on application. Write us for Wire Price List. We will save you money.

Wire Cable Fencing.

No. 9C5412 Wire Cable Fencing. Galvanized. Made of two strands of No. 12 soft Bessemer steel wire, thoroughly annealed and heavily and uniformly galvanized. It is same as barbed wire, except it has no barbs. Send for Wire Price List.

Smooth Fence Wire.

Price per 100 pounds.

Size No. 9 10 11 12 13 14 15 16 18

No. 9C5416 Galvanized............
No. 9C5417 Not galvanized............

Send for Wire Price List.

Coiled Spring Fence Wire.

No. 9C5419 Coiled Spring Fence Wire. Galvanized. The coil allows for expansion and contraction caused by changes in the temperature. It is made from a special hard steel wire, and is very carefully galvanized. Put up in bundles running from 95 to 110 pounds.

Size No. 9 10 11 12

Send for Wire Price List.

Fencing Staples.

No. 9C5429 Plain, 1¼ inches long............
No. 9C5430 Plain, 1½ inches long............
No. 9C5431 Galvanized, 1¼ inches long............
No. 9C5432 Galvanized, 1½ inches long............

Send for Wire Price List.

Grave Guard with Arch.

No. 9C5751 To protect and ornament a grave. Prevents small children from picking the flowers; keeps dogs, cats, etc., off the grave. It is strongly made and nicely painted. Has angle steel frame fastened together with bolts. Is taken apart and securely crated for shipment, but can be easily and quickly put together by anyone. This makes freight charges less and insures the guard reaching destination in good condition.

Length, feet	Width, inches	Height, inches	Price
4	21	24	$4.88
5	24	24	6.10
6	30	27	7.32
7	30	27	8.54

Painted Wire Cloth.

The illustration shows you the exact size of mesh. You can make your own screen doors and windows. Order just what you require, but note the reduction in price when ordering in full rolls.

Best Acme Bessemer Steel Wire, painted black or green, double selvage, 12-mesh (the standard).

No. 9C5640 Green Painted Wire Cloth.
No. 9C5641 Black Painted Wire Cloth.

Width	Per roll of 100 running feet	Per lineal foot	Width	Per roll of 100 running feet	Per lineal foot
24 in.	$2.52	3¼c	38 in.	$3.99	5c
26 in.	2.73	3½c	40 in.	4.20	5¼c
28 in.	2.94	3¾c	42 in.	4.41	5½c
30 in.	3.15	4c	44 in.	4.62	5¾c
32 in.	3.36	4¼c	46 in.	4.83	6c
34 in.	3.57	4½c	48 in.	5.04	6¼c
36 in.	3.78	4¾c			

No. 9C5642 Galvanized Wire Cloth. Made from galvanized steel wire, 14 mesh (fine). Rolls contain 100 lineal feet.

Width	Per roll	Per lineal foot	Width	Per roll	Per lineal foot
24 in.	$4.32	5c	32 in.	$5.76	6¼c
26 in.	4.68	5¼c	34 in.	6.12	6¾c
28 in.	5.04	5½c	36 in.	6.48	7c
30 in.	5.40	6c			

Wire Cloth Staples.

No. 9C5646 Blued Steel Wire Cloth Staples are much superior to common tacks. Two points enter the wood. They lap over three wires, hence hold the wire better, and not so many tacks required.

Price, per pound, 8c; per paper of 120 staples.... 1c

Window Screens.

No. 9C5858 Extension Window Screen. Has a perfect adjustment; frames are made of selected hardwood finished in oil, beaded both sides. Wire cloth is painted black and is the best to be obtained in the market. We claim for this screen a perfect adjustment, stronger construction, better material and smoother finish than can be found in any other. Made in the following sizes and no other sizes furnished:

Height	Width adjustable	Price, per crate containing 12 screens	Price, each
18 inches	From 20 to 33½ inches	$1.96	18c
24 inches	From 22 to 37½ inches	2.49	23c
30 inches	From 22 to 37½ inches	3.03	27c
36 inches	From 22 to 37½ inches	3.92	35c

SCREEN DOORS.

The line we offer is the result of years of experience. The styles are artistic and we are positive will meet the requirements of all users. All doors are made one inch longer than size listed, to allow for the trimming and fitting. All our lumber is thoroughly seasoned, and steam kiln dried, insuring a first class door which will not become loose at joints and will last for years. Weights vary from 13 to 22 pounds.

Douglas Pattern Screen Door.

No. 9C5667 Douglas Pattern Screen Door. Three-panel. Made of kiln dried yellow pine, stained walnut, ⅞ inch thick, 3-inch stiles, flush moulding, best black wire cloth. Furnished only in sizes listed below.

Width	Height	Price
2 feet 6 inches	6 feet 6 inches	59c
2 feet 8 inches	6 feet 8 inches	60c

Greveland Screen Door.

No. 9C5668 Greveland Screen Door, fancy pattern, 3-panel. Yellow pine, finished in the natural, with one coat of varnish, 1⅛ inches thick; 3-inch stiles. Joints secured with heavy corrugated hardwood dowels, well glued, making strongest possible construction. Has flush beaded mouldings, best thick painted wire cloth.

Width	Height	Price
2 feet 6 inches	6 feet 6 inches	75c
2 feet 8 inches	6 feet 8 inches	76c
2 feet 8 inches	7 feet	77c
2 feet 10 inches	6 feet 10 inches	78c
2 feet 10 inches	7 feet	79c
3 feet	7 feet	80c

Kenwood Pattern Screen Door.

No. 9C5669 Kenwood Screen Door. This popular pattern is made from choice selected kiln dried yellow pine lumber with ⅞-inch turned spindles, finished with two coats of varnish, 1⅛-inch stock with 3-inch stiles. Strongest glued hardwood dowel joint construction, best black wire cloth beaded flush mouldings, easily removed to replace wire cloth when necessary.

Width	Height	Price
2 feet 6 inches	6 feet 6 inches	$0.95
2 feet 8 inches	6 feet 8 inches	.96
2 feet 8 inches	7 feet	.97
2 feet 10 inches	6 feet 10 inches	.98
2 feet 10 inches	7 feet	.99
3 feet	7 feet	1.00

No. 9C5669

Hyde Park Pattern Screen Door

No. 9C5670 Hyde Park Pattern Screen Door. A beautiful design suitable for front doors. A carpenter would be obliged to ask $5.00 to $7.00 for a door of this style and quality. Made of the best selected 1⅛-inch yellow pine, finely finished with two coats of best varnish; 3-inch stiles with ⅝x8 turned spindles in lock rail; has flush beaded moulding with highest grade black double selvage 12-mesh steel wire cloth, stretched tight and tacked before moulding is nailed on. Extra strong glued hardwood double joints—will never become loose at joints and will last for years.

Width	Height	Price
2 feet 6 inches	6 feet 6 inches	$1.09
2 feet 8 inches	6 feet 8 inches	1.10
2 feet 8 inches	7 feet	1.11
2 feet 10 inches	6 feet 10 inches	1.12
2 feet 10 inches	7 feet	1.13
3 feet	7 feet	1.14

No. 9C5670

Screen Corner Brackets.

No. 9C2051 Japanned Iron Corner Brackets for Window Screen Frames, packed with screws, four brackets to a set.

Price, per set.... 5c
Per dozen sets.... 50c

No. 9C2054 Japanned Iron Corner Brackets for screen door frames, with screws. Four large corner brackets and two center pieces to a set.

Price, per set, $0.16
Per dozen sets, 1.75

Screen Door Brace.

No. 9C2053 Can be used on any screen door, and will cure and prevent sagging, so that the door will swing freely and close tight.

Price, each.... 5c
Per dozen.... 55c

Spring Hinges

No. 9C2036 Hold Back Spring Hinges. Holds the door securely shut, and when opened past the center holds it open. These are full size, heavy goods. Weight, per pair, 1 pound.

Price, per pair, without screws.... 7c
Per dozen pairs.... 81c

No. 9C2035 Spring Hinges. The action of this hinge is strong and free. Being extra heavy there are no parts liable to break or get out of order. May be used on either right or left hand doors.

Price, per pair.... 7c
Per dozen pairs.... 73c

No. 9C2039 Double Action Spring Hinges, for screen doors, to swing both ways; japanned iron; for doors not more than 1⅜ inches thick.

Price, per pair $0.17
Per dozen pairs 1.88

Door Springs.

No. 9C2061 The Old Favorite Warner Door Spring. Latest improved designs.

Price, each.... 6c
Per dozen.... 63c

No. 9C2065 Coiled Wire Door Spring, made of heavy steel spring wire, japanned, adjustable tension. Weight, 11 ounces. Price, per dozen, 83c; each.... 8c

No. 9C2066 Torrey Door Spring, is without doubt the best cheap door spring made. So well known, description is not necessary. Weight, 12 ounces.

Price, each.... $0.10
Per dozen.... 1.15

Spiral Door Spring attached to door by two screw eyes. It consists of a closely coiled steel wire spring, made in four different sizes, of the best crucible steel wire, with hooks at each end and screw eyes to be inserted in door and casing. If properly adjusted, nothing can be more effective.

No. 9C2071 For screen doors. Price, per dozen, 33c; each.... 3c
No. 9C2072 For ordinary inside door. Price, per dozen, 38c; each.... 4c
No. 9C2073 For outside door. Price, per dozen, 42c; each.... 4c
No. 9C2074 For heavy outside door. Price, per dozen, 46c; each.... 4c

Screen Door Catches.

No. 9C2080 Screen Door Catch, German bronzed iron with stop for doors from ⅞ to 1⅜ inches thick. This is the style commonly used, and is for inside of doors opening out. Packed complete with knobs and screws.

Price.... 11c

No. 9C2081 Screen Door Catch. Same as shown above, electro bronze plated.

Price.... 19c

No. 9C2082 Screen Door Catch. Electro bronze plated, for doors from ⅞ to 1⅜ inches thick for inside of doors opening in. This is not much used. Be sure to order the right catch. Packed complete with knobs and screws.

Price.... 20c

No. 9C2083 Screen Door Catch, same as above, German bronzed. Price.... 12c

ALWAYS WRITE THE CATALOGUE NUMBER PLAINLY AND IN FULL.

Acme Ball Bearing High Grass Mower.

Our Acme Ball Bearing High Grass Lawn Mower is made on the same general lines as our regular Acme Lawn Mowers, except it is made heavier to withstand the severe strain caused by mowing tall grass. This mower is furnished with four cutting blades. It is a general rule that any "high grass" mower requires more power to push than the regular kind, but the Acme requires only a very little more power than our regular style and runs easier than most ordinary mowers. It will cut grass 10 inches high and can be adjusted to leave the grass as tall as 2 inches. It will also cut short grass very close and leave the lawn nice and smooth, which is something most "high grass" lawn mowers will not do. It is guaranteed to give satisfaction.

Nos.	9C6001	9C6003	9C6005	9C6007
Width of cut, inches	15	17	19	21
Weight, lbs.	52	59	65	70
Price	$8.00	$8.67	$9.33	$10.66

Our Acme Lawn Mowers, $3.40 to $4.50.

HAVING FOUR CUTTING BLADES.

The Acme Mowers have the latest patent micrometer adjustment. This is our standard high grade Acme machine and strengthened and improved for this season. The drive wheels are open for 1 inch below the tread, though the working parts are completely enclosed. It is the easiest running lawn mower made, because the handle is so attached to the drive wheel that the power is applied to the center of motion. This mower has our patent micrometer adjustment, continuous cut, spring bedknife, noiseless ratchet, long heavy bearings of phosphor bronze. Diameter of traction wheels, 9½ inches; diameter of reel, 6 inches, with four cutting blades. The 16-inch size is most popular.

No. 9C6014 14-inch mower. Weight, 47 lbs. Price.... $3.40
No. 9C6016 16-inch mower. Weight, 49 lbs. Price.... 3.70
No. 9C6018 18-inch mower. Weight, 51 lbs. Price.... 4.15
No. 9C6020 20-inch mower. Weight, 57 lbs. Price.... 4.50

Acme Ball Bearing Lawn Mowers.

Our Acme Ball Bearing Mower is of the same design as our Acme, illustrated above. It is constructed on first class principles, adjustable throughout. Silent in operation. Cones and cups made of solid cone steel, no pressed cups used. Ground perfect. Best quality steel balls. The cups, cones and balls are dustproof, and made with as great a degree of perfection as the best bicycle. Wheels, 9½ inches high. Four bladed revolving cutter. Cutter, 6 inches diameter. Front bar 6½ inches from the ground. Cuts close and does fine work. High wheels, easy running. Four cutting blades. Spring bed knife, continuous cut. The ball bearings will never need adjustment. Guaranteed to give satisfaction or money refunded. We offer our Ball Bearing Mower at the following prices:

No. 9C6035 14-inch mower. Weight, 46 lbs. Price, $5.75
No. 9C6036 14-inch mower. Weight, 50 lbs. Price, 6.00
No. 9C6037 18-inch mower. Weight, 57 lbs. Price, $6.25
No. 9C6038 20-inch mower. Weight, [illegible] lbs. Price, 6.75

Our Sunrise Lawn Mowers, $2.25 to $2.60.

In our New Sunrise Lawn Mower we claim to have the easiest running, best made and most complete medium priced lawn mower made. It is made from the best material and all parts are interchangeable. The reel knife shaft is made of solid steel, and runs in split phosphor bronze bushings. It is fitted with large driving wheels, incased gearing, continuous spiral steel reel knives, accurately ground, adjustable handle, self acting and positive pawls, steel handle braces, and a bed knife made from the best lawn mower knife steel, which is finely ground and self sharpening. **Wheels are 8¼ inches high. Wheel revolves when turning corners either way, as there is a ratchet in each wheel. Makes very little noise.**

Nos.	9C6022	9C6024	9C6026	9C6028
Size	12-inch	14-inch	16-inch	18-inch
Shipping weight	38 pounds	40 pounds	42 pounds	45 pounds
Price	$2.25	$2.30	$2.35	$2.60

Ball Bearing Horse Lawn Mower.

No. 9C6033 High Grass Ball Bearing Mower, with Horse Attachment. Height of drive wheels, 10 inches. Diameter of cutter, 7 inches—four-bladed, 31-inch cut. This mower is the same (except size) as our Acme High Grass Mower excepting the extra bracing of handle, and draft attachment, together with extra heavy shaft and heavy ball bearings. The lower straight blade on this mower is of the laid steel pattern, very heavy. The singletree, or pull, is so arranged that it will draw from either end of the mower, so horse can walk on cut grass. The mower can be used by one man in ordinary grass; the draft attachment can be removed without trouble. This machine fills the bill exactly for a light running and durable, low priced horse mower; cutting a wide swath; very suitable for large lawns with much shrubbery. Width, 31 inches. Weight, 80 pounds. Price, **$16.25**

Grass Catchers.

Attach a grass catcher to your lawn mower and when you have mowed your lawn you have finished the job. The grass is gathered cleaner than can be done with a rake without time or labor and without injury to the lawn which cannot be avoided when using a rake.

No. 9C6046 The Carroll Adjustable Grass Catcher, made of striped canvas on a galvanized steel frame. The spring in the front hem holds the catcher securely to the mower. Adjustable to fit mowers from 12 to 18-inch cut. Price **40c**

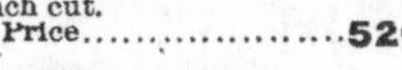

No. 9C6047 The Carroll Adjustable Grass Catcher, to fit mowers from 18 to 24-inch cut. Price **52c**

No. 9C6048 The Ironclad Adjustable Grass Catcher is made of bright striped canvas, with galvanized steel bottom. This combines lightness with durability and is especially designed for those who want the best. Adjustable to fit all mowers not wider than 18-inch cut. Price **80c**

No. 9C6049 The Ironclad Adjustable Grass Catcher, adjustable to fit all mowers from 18 to 24-inch cut. Price **93c**

Sharpening Paste for Lawn Mowers.

No. 9C6040 McClelland's Sharpening Paste for Lawn Mowers will quickly put a good edge upon the knives of a lawn mower if directions are followed. One package is sufficient to keep a lawn mower in good condition for a season. Put up in tin boxes with full directions for use. Weight, per box, 12 ounces. Price, per box........................**25c**

SCHOOLHOUSE AND FACTORY BELLS AT $4.83 TO $15.90. CHURCH BELLS AT $17.47 TO $79.24.

Bells for farm, schoolhouse, church and elsewhere, we will sell at prices based on the actual cost to manufacture, the cost of material and labor, with but one small percentage of profit added. If you are in the market for a high grade, perfect toned, guaranteed bell for schoolhouse, church, farm or home, we are prepared to furnish you such a bell under our guarantee for quality and at a saving of from 25 to 50 per cent in price as against any price you can get from any dealer anywhere.

QUALITY. Our bells are made for us under contract by one of the best makers in this country. They are made from a very fine crystalline metal, making them loud, clear, round and sweet in tone, and cannot be compared with the cheap cast iron bells that are advertised by many.

OUR GUARANTEE: We put out every bell under our binding guarantee against breakage for five years, and if it is not perfectly satisfactory as to quality of tone, volume, finish, weight and durability; if it is not satisfactory in every way, and if you do not find it lower in price than any bell you can buy elsewhere, you are at liberty to return it to us **AT OUR EXPENSE AND WE WILL REFUND YOUR MONEY.**

Beware of Imitations of the Crystalline Metal Bell.

The Bell Trust and those dealers who co-operate with them are advertising a bell under a name somewhat similar to Crystalline Metal, admitting that their bell is not first class. Our bells are pronounced by purchasers and users the best made and they should not be compared with anything except the very best quality made by anyone. If you have any doubt about the quality of our bells send for our Special Bell Catalogue, containing testimonials from users (some of whom you may know), who say our bells are louder and better toned than other bells in their vicinity.

Church, Schoolhouse and Factory Bells.

No. 9C6050 These bells are CRYSTALLINE METAL and can be relied on under all circumstances and in all seasons. Nos. 20 to 28 are school or factory bells, and are not recommended for churches. Nos. 30 to 48, inclusive, are recommended for churches. Bells are numbered by the diameter in inches.

Nos.	Complete, lbs.	Price, without Tolling Hammer	Price, with Tolling Hammer	Nos.	Complete, lbs.	Price, without Tolling Hammer	Price, with Tolling Hammer
20	165	$4.83	$6.13	34	765	$22.24	$23.97
22	205	5.93	7.22	36	950	28.45	30.46
24	250	7.50	8.80	38	1,010	35.05	37.07
26	350	10.50	11.79	40	1,300	39.90	41.92
28	450	14.60	15.90	44	1,790	61.45	63.45
30	570	17.47	19.24	48	2,280	77.23	79.24
32	640	18.57	20.30				

We do not advise tolling hammer to be used with bells smaller than No. 30.

The weights and prices named are for complete bells, and include wood sills and wheel for rope. The above prices are for bells delivered free on board cars at our factory in Central Ohio. **For further information regarding Bells, for testimonials from users in every state, send for our Bell Catalogue, sent free on request.**

For Fire Alarm Bells send for Bell Catalogue.

OUR BIG 87-CENT FARM BELL.

Illustration of sizes No. 1, 2, 3 and 8

At 87 cents for 37½ pounds, $1.23 for 53 pounds, $1.64 for 71 pounds, and $2.24 for 96 pounds, we offer this large, handsome crystalline metal farm bell as the greatest value ever offered in a bell of this kind. This bell is hung on a heavy, strong and substantially built frame which bolts to a pole. The bell is full bronzed and at our special 87-cent to $2.24 price, according to weight.

THE BELL COMES COMPLETE WITH ALL MOUNTINGS.

No. 9C6051 Size No. 1. Diameter at mouth, 14¼ inches. Weight of bowl, 23½ pounds. Weight, with hangings, 37½ pounds. Price.....**87c**

No. 9C6052 Size No. 2. Diameter at mouth, 16¼ inches. Weight of bowl, 33 pounds. Weight, with hangings, 53 pounds. Price..........**$1.23**

No. 9C6053 Size No. 3. Diameter of mouth, 18 inches. Weight of bowl 48 pounds. Weight, complete with mountings, 71 pounds. Price..**$1.64**

No. 9C6058 Size No. 8. Diameter of mouth, 19½ inches; weight, complete with mountings, 96 pounds. Price........................**$2.24**

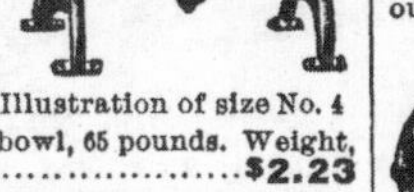

Illustration of size No. 4

No. 9C6054 Size No. 4. Diameter at mouth, 19½ inches. Weight of bowl, 65 pounds. Weight, with mountings, 96 pounds. Price........................**$2.23**

We do not include bolts to fasten frame to post. If wanted, please order them separately. The holes in frame are made to take bolts ⅜ inch in diameter.

When to our customers' advantage we ship farm bells from factory in Central Ohio.

New Departure Door Bell.

It gives the electric ring. Made with either push button or turn plate, as described. No springs to get out of order. It is simple and durable.

No. 9C6060 New Departure Cast Iron Rotary Turn Plate Door Bell. Electro copper plated, antique copper finish. Diameter of bell, 3 inches. Size of turn plate, 3⅝x1¼ inches. Very handsome design and wonderfully cheap. Price..............**48c**

No. 9C6063 New Departure Rotary Door Bell. Nickel plated bell, 3½ inches in diameter. Wrought bronze metal turn plate, finished antique copper. Size of turn plate, 2x4½ inches. Price, complete.........**76c**

No. 9C6066 New Departure Push Button Door Bell. Nickel plated bell. 3½ inches in diameter. Wrought bronze metal push button case. Antique copper finish. Size of case, 2x4½ inches. (Illustration shows push plate only). Bell is same as No. 9C6063. Price..............**89c**

For electric bells and burglar

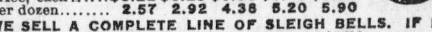

Sargent & Co.'s Patent Rotary Electric Ring Door Bells.

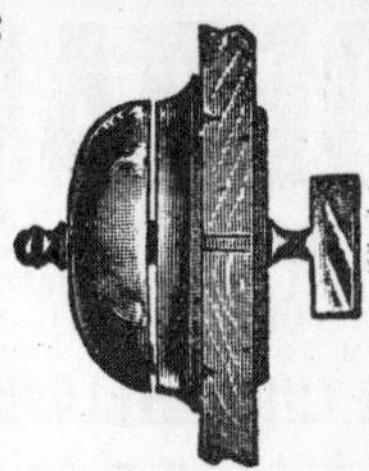

No. 9C6074 To turn. Requires no winding. Has the effect of the electric bell without any electric appliance. There are no springs to get out of order, there is no battery to replace, no winding required. Nickel plated bell metal, 3½ inches in diameter, with plain genuine bronze turn plate, polished bronze finish. Packed complete with screws. Price, complete....**63c**

No. 9C6077 Door Bell, same as No. 9C6074, except the turn is antique copper finish. Price complete....**64c**

Open Polished Bells.

No. 9C6100 Open Polished Bell. Metal bells may be used for a variety of purposes; make good sheep bells, a harness bell for milk wagons, drays, etc. Genuine bell metal. Full weight goods. Best shape for sound. Not made with extra flare to increase diameter of mouth.

Nos....	1	2	3	4	5	6
Diameter of mouth, in.	2⅛	2⅜	2½	2⅞	3¼	3½
Weight, per dozen, lbs.	2⅜	3½	4¼	6	7	9
Price, each	7c	9c	$0.11	$0.16	$0.18	$0.23
Per dozen...........	64c	94c	1.20	1.62	1.87	2.60

Hand Bells.

No. 9C6112 Genuine Bell Metal. Full weight goods. Finely polished, enameled wood handle.

Nos.	Actual weight, ounces	Diameter, inches	Price
1	4	2⅜	$0.08
3	7	3	.13
5	13	3¾	.24
7	20	4⅝	.38
9	30	5⅜	.66
13	50	7⅜	1.16
14	54	7⅞	1.32

Trip Gong Bells.

No. 9C6125 Trip Gong Bells. Genuine bell metal.

3-inch, weight, 1 lb. 5 ozs........**$0.39**
4-inch, weight, 1½ lbs...............**.49**
6-inch, weight, 2 lbs. 13 ozs.........**.90**
8-inch, weight, 6 lbs...............**1.68**
10-inch, weight, 9¾ lbs..............**3.08**

Swiss Cow Bells.

These Swiss Cow Bells are made from Swiss bell metal. They are celebrated for their pure musical tone, which can be heard a long distance and sounds entirely different from common bells.

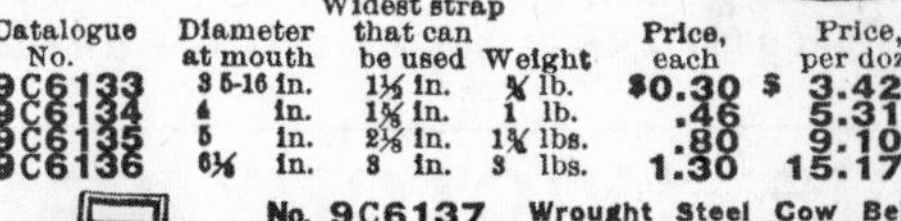

Catalogue No.	Diameter at mouth	Widest strap that can be used	Weight	Price, each	Price, per doz.
9C6133	3 5-16 in.	1½ in.	¾ lb.	$0.30	$ 3.42
9C6134	4 in.	1⅝ in.	1 lb.	.46	5.31
9C6135	5 in.	2⅛ in.	1¾ lbs.	.80	9.10
9C6136	6¾ in.	3 in.	3 lbs.	1.30	15.17

No. 9C6137 Wrought Steel Cow Bell. Made of one piece of solid steel with malleable iron loop; warranted not to crack. The tone is entirely different from the ordinary cow bell, and can be heard much farther. It is heavily electro copper plated, giving it the appearance of a copper bell.

Diameter of mouth, inches	3⅜	5
Price, each....................	$0.11	$0.24
Per dozen......................	1.24	2.79

Cow Bells.

No. 9C6140 The Old Standard Cow Bell. Very loud tone and extra well made.

Nos...........	0	2	3	5
Size of mouth	6x4½	5½x3⅞	4½x3	3¼x2⅜
Height........	6½	5	4¾	3¾
Price, each....	$0.25	$0.17	$0.12	8c
Price, per doz.	2.85	1.90	1.43	95c

Cow Bell Straps.

No. 10C02601 Fine Black Leather Cow Bell Straps. Made with roller buckle and loop.

Width, 1½ inches. Price..............................**29c**
Width, 2 inches. Price..............................**45c**
Width, 3 inches. Price..............................**65c**

Sheep Bells.

Sheep Bells, cast from bell metal. Complete with straps of suitable size.

No. 9C6141 Sheep Bell, like illustration; height, 1⅝ inches; size of mouth, 1⅜x1⅞ inches, with strap. Price, per dozen, **$1.73**; each. **15c**

No. 9C6142 Sheep Bell, like illustration; height, 1¾ inches; size of mouth, 1½x2 inches, with strap. Price, per dozen, **$2.05**; each.....................**18c**

No. 9C6143 Round Sheep Bells. Made of wrought steel malleable iron loop, copper plated, very durable; will not crack; furnished with straps of suitable size.

Diameter, inches................	2 7-16	2⅞	3⅜
Price, each....................	$0.13	$0.14	$0.18
Per dozen.......................	1.45	1.59	2.06

Turkey Bells.

No. 9C6146 Polished Bell Metal Turkey Bell. Diameter, 1⅛ inches; enables the flock to be easily located, makes the foxes shy. Furnished complete with strap as shown. Weight, each, 3 ounces. Price, per dozen, **99c**; each **9c**

Loose Sleigh Bells.

No. 9C6260 Polished Loose Sleigh Bells, for the convenience of those who wish to make their straps of bells. Made of genuine bell metal, natural finish.

We will furnish any quantity at dozen prices.

Numbers......	0	1	2	3	4	5	6	7
Diameter, in..	1	1⅛	1¼	1⅜	1½	1⅝	1¾	1⅞
Price, per doz.	18c	20c	28c	36c	44c	52c	58c	72c
Numbers.....	8	9	10	12	14	16	18	
Diameter, in.	2⅛	2¼	2⅜	2⅝	3	3¼	3¾	
Price, per doz.	82c	$1.00	$1.19	$1.63	$2.38	$3.60	$4.27	

Loose Swedish Sleigh Bells.

No. 9C6265 Loose Swedish Sleigh Bells; made of genuine high grade cast bell metal, polished. These bells have a distinct tone, entirely different from the common sleigh bells, which makes them a great favorite in some localities.

Numbers..........	7	9	11	13	15
Diameter, inches.	2	2¼	2½	2¾	3¼
Price, each	$0.22	$0.25	$0.38	$0.45	$0.51
Per dozen........	2.57	2.92	4.38	5.20	5.90

WE SELL A COMPLETE LINE OF SLEIGH BELLS. IF IN-

DEPARTMENT OF MECHANICS' TOOLS.

IT IS CONCEDED that we sell more tools to the consumer than any other three concerns in the United States, which is conclusive evidence that our goods are satisfactory. Those who purchase tools from us are protected by our guarantee as well as the manufacturer's on warranted goods. Repairs can always be furnished at reasonable prices for all goods sold by us. A boy can buy tools from us just as well as an experienced mechanic, for our illustrations and descriptions are accurate and everything is exactly as represented. For harness makers' tools, watchmakers' tools, shoemakers' tools, blacksmiths' tools or other lines of tools refer to index.

IN THIS CATALOGUE we list all tools most commonly used; we show a more complete line of tools in our Special Mechanical Tool Catalogue, sent free on application. If there is any kind of a tool you want, not shown in this catalogue, don't fail to write for our FREE MECHANICAL TOOL CATALOGUE.

OUR $9.00 "CHAMPION" TOOL SET

FOR $9.00 WE FURNISH THE TOOLS AS LISTED BELOW COMPLETE WITH TOOL CHEST AS ILLUSTRATED.

THE TOOLS ARE SELECTED from our regular stock, and quality of everything is guaranteed. There is ample space in the chest to keep more tools, as you may add to the set from time to time.

DO NOT COMPARE THE QUALITY OF THESE TOOLS WITH THOSE COMMONLY SOLD IN CHESTS AT ABOUT THIS PRICE.

SO FAR AS WE KNOW we are the only firm putting up a tool set at this price and using high grade tools, tools that will satisfy any carpenter or mechanic; goods that will make friends and customers for us.

No. 35C6007 Our "Champion" Tool Set consists of the following tools:

- 1 **Springfield Hand Saw**, 24-inch.
- 1 **Springfield Rip Saw**, 26-inch.
- 1 **Standard Compass Saw**, 12-inch.
- 1 **Adjustable Jack Plane**, with wood bottom. Length, 15 inches, with 2-inch cutter.
- 1 **Iron Block Plane.** Length, 7½ inches, with 1¾-inch cutter.
- 1 **Adze Eye Bell Face Nail Hammer.** Weight, 1 pound. Warranted.
- 3 **Socket Firmer Chisels**, with leather top handles. Sizes, ¼, ½ and 1 inch. Warranted.
- 1 **Ratchet Bit Brace**, 10-inch sweep.
- 5 **German Gimlet Bits.** Sizes, 1/16, ⅛, 3/16, ¼ and 5/16 inch.
- 5 **Best Tool Steel Double Spur and Lip Auger Bits.** Sizes, ⅜, ½, ⅝, ¾ and 1 inch.
- 1 **Countersink** for wood.
- 1 **Countersink** for metal.
- 1 **Reamer.**
- 1 **Boxwood Rule**, 2-ft., four-fold, square joints with drafting scale.
- 1 **Try Square**, 6-inch blade.
- 1 **Screwdriver**, 5-inch blade.
- 1 **Nail Set**, 3/32-point.
- 1 **Steel Shingling Hatchet**, 4-inch cut. Warranted.
- 1 **Drawing Knife**, 8-inch cut. Warranted.
- 1 **Mounted Oil Stone**, 6-inch.
- 1 **Steel Square**, No. 7, extra quality.
- 1 **Pair 6-inch Button's Pliers.**
- 1 **Monkey Wrench**, 10-inch.
- 1 **Slim Taper File**, 6-inch.
- 1 **Universal Tool Handle.**

No. 35C6007 Price of the above tools packed in chest as illustrated and described. **$9.00**

WEIGHT, PACKED FOR SHIPMENT, 75 POUNDS.

OUR "VICTOR" CARPENTER CHEST OF TOOLS FOR $14.95.

EACH AND EVERY ARTICLE GUARANTEED TO BE EXACTLY AS DESCRIBED.
EVERY TOOL GOOD ENOUGH FOR ANY CARPENTER OR MECHANIC.

$14.95 BUYS A $25.00 OUTFIT.

QUALITY. We cannot too strongly emphasize the fact that all these tools are strictly FIRST CLASS, HIGH GRADE GOODS. To build up the enormous tool trade which we have established, it was necessary for us to furnish the best goods we could procure; and to hold and still further increase our tool trade, it is necessary that we continue to deal with our patrons as in the past.

READ CAREFULLY THE DESCRIPTION OF GOODS AND REMEMBER THAT EVERY ARTICLE IS GUARANTEED EXACTLY AS REPRESENTED.

No. 35C6010 ORDER BY NUMBER.

LIST AND DESCRIPTION OF TOOLS IN OUR "VICTOR" CHEST OF TOOLS:

- 1 **"Odd Jobs" Rip Saw**, 28 inches long.
- 1 **Fulton Hand Saw**, 26 inches long, fully warranted.
- 1 **Fulton Panel Saw**, 18 inches long, fully warranted.
- 1 **Compass Saw**, length, 14 inches.
- 1 **Adjustable Wood Smooth Plane.** Length, 8 in., with 1¾-in. cutter.
- 1 **Adjustable Wood Jack Plane.** Length, 15 in., with 2⅛-in. cutter.
- 1 **Adjustable Wood Fore Plane.** Length, 20 in., with 2⅜-in. cutter.
- 1 **Adjustable Iron Block Plane.** Length, 5½ in., with 1¼-in. cutter.
- 1 **S., R. & Co.'s Improved Morrill's Pattern Saw Set.**
- 1 **Saw Clamp.** To hold saws for filing. Jaws are 9½ inches long, adjustment is by a lever.
- 2 **Slim Taper Saw Files.** One 4½ inches long, and one 6 inches long.
- 1 **No. 7 Steel Square.**
- 1 **Carpenters' Pincers.** Length, 8 inches.
- 1 **Combination Wire Cutter and Pliers.** Length, 5½ inches.
- 1 **Knurled Cup Point Nail Set.**
- 1 **Spring Tube Punch**, for cutting holes in leather, etc.
- 100 **Slotted Rivets**, assorted lengths, in nice tin box.
- 1 **Iron Bench Screw.** Length, 13 inches; diameter, 1 inch.
- 4 **Iron Clamps.** Open, 2¼ inches.
- 1 **Beechwood Improved Marking Gauge. Made by The Stanley Rule & Level Co.**
- 1 **Pair of Wing Dividers.** Length, 8 inches, polished forged steel, with adjusting screw.
- 1 **Reel and Awl, for Chalk Line**, as shown in illustration.
- 1 **Braided Cotton Chalk Line.** Medium size.
- 12 **Cakes of Carpenters' Chalk.** Assorted colors, red, white and blue, and 1 **Carpenters' Lead Pencil** of good quality.
- 1 **Plumb and Level, adjustable.** Made by **The Stanley Rule & Level Co.**, polished mahogany, arched top plates; two side views. Length, 28 inches.
- 1 **Try Square.** Brass lined with rosewood handle, square inside or outside. Length of blade from inside the handle, 6 inches. It is made by **The Stanley Rule & Level Co.**
- 1 **Sliding T Bevel**, with rosewood handle, brass tipped, 8-inch blade, flush adjusting screw, so bevel can be used right or left hand, either side up. It is made by **The Stanley Rule & Level Co.**
- 1 **Boxwood Rule.** Made by **The Stanley Rule & Level Co.**, two-foot, four-fold, square joints, edge plates, spaced 8ths, 10ths, 12ths and 16ths, with drafting scale, 1 inch wide.
- 1 **Shingling Hatchet.** Weight, 1 pound 7 ounces, **warranted.**
- 1 **Nail Hammer.** Weight, 1 pound, **warranted.**
- 1 **Monkey Wrench.** Length, 10 inches.
- 1 **Draw Knife.** Length of cut, 8 inches.
- 1 **Spoke Shave**, with double cutter, one straight and one concave.
- 1 **Socket Framing Chisel.** Width, 1-inch, with ring on handle to prevent splitting.
- 3 **Socket Firmer Chisels.** 1 each, ¼, ½ and 1-inch chisels. **Fully warranted.**
- 1 **Cold Chisel**, made of ½-inch octagon steel.
- 1 **Screwdriver**, with beech handle and 6-inch blade.
- 1 **Ratchet Bit Brace**, made of 7/16-inch cold drawn steel rod. Head and handle of hardwood, 10-in. sweep.
- 7 **Auger Bits.** 1 each size, ¼, 5/16, ⅜, ½, ⅝, ¾ and 1 in.
- 3 **German Pattern Gimlet Bits.** 1 each size, 1/16, ⅛ and 3/16 inch.

We pack the "VICTOR" set of Carpenters' Tools in a hardwood chest, with one tray, well made, finished and varnished, with hinges, handles and lock. Weight, packed for shipment, 90 pounds. SEE FREIGHT RATES IN FRONT OF BOOK.

No. 35C6010 OUR PRICE FOR ALL THE ABOVE TOOLS PACKED IN THIS CHEST IS ONLY $14.95.

OUR "INVINCIBLE" TOOL CHEST.

FOR $24.10 WE FURNISH A STRICTLY HIGH GRADE SET OF MECHANICS' TOOLS, THE EQUAL OF ANYTHING YOU CAN BUY ANYWHERE AT $35.00 TO $40.00.

WE PACK THIS SET OF TOOLS in a tool chest with sliding tray; well and strongly made, with hinges and lock. Inside measurements of chest, 31½ inches long, 16¾ inches wide, 9½ inches deep. Read carefully the list and description of tools in this set. Remember, we fully guarantee each and every tool to be perfect in material and workmanship. Consider the reputation of the brands; consider our reputation as dealers in fine high grade mechanics' tools, and we are sure you will agree that the price we name for the complete outfit of tool chest is indeed wonderfully low.

BELOW IS A COMPLETE LIST OF THE DIFFERENT TOOLS FURNISHED IN THIS OUR SPECIAL $24.10 "INVINCIBLE" MECHANICS' TOOL SET.

1 Fulton Tool Co.'s Warranted Shingling Hatchet, all steel, full polished and etched, 3⅞-inch cut.
1 Fulton Tool Co.'s Warranted Hammer, highly nickel plated. Has octagon poll and polished hickory handle. Size, 1½. Weight, 1 pound.
1 Adjustable Saw Clamp. Can be instantly adjusted to any angle.
1 Sears, Roebuck & Co.'s Original Morrill's Pattern Saw Set, with improved anvil, will set hand, panel, rip, meat, buck or band saws.
1 Stanley's Combined Try and Mitre Square, 7½-inch blade, brass lined rosewood handle and graduated steel blade.
1 Stanley's Sliding "T" Bevel, 10-inch blade, rosewood handle, brass tipped with flush adjusting screw and steel blade.
1 2-foot Rule, full brass bound, double arch joints, four-fold with drawing scale, 1⅜-inch wide.
1 Stanley Improved Marking Gauge, made of beechwood with boxwood thumbscrew. Marked in inches.
1 Sears, Roebuck & Co.'s Quick Cut Oil Stone. Size, 7x2 inches. Mounted in finished chestnut case.
1 Awl and Tool Set, with 10 forged steel awls and tools and hollow cocobolo handle which holds tools when not in use.
4 Warranted High Grade Socket Firmer Chisels, have bevel edge blades, 6 inches long and polished handles. One each of the following sizes: ¼, ½, 1 and 1½-inch.
1 Combined Pliers and Wire Cutter, 6-inch.
1 Pair Carpenters' Pincers. 8-inch. With claw on handle. Forged from superior steel.
1 Wrought Iron Bench Screw. 1 inch in diameter, with patent collar, double thread and wood handle.
1 Warranted Forged Steel Draw Knife. 10-inch razor blade.
1 Polished Forged Steel Wing Divider. 8-inch.
1 Warranted Tool Steel Machinists' Screwdriver. 6-inch blade. Round, corrugated, imitation rosewood handle.
1 Warranted High Grade Fulton Rip Saw. 28-inch.
1 Warranted High Grade Fulton Hand Saw. 26-inch.
1 Warranted High Grade Fulton Panel Saw. 20-inch.
1 Nest of Saws, consisting of 1 Handle, 1 Keyhole Blade, 1 Compass Blade, 1 Pruning Blade. All interchangeable in the handle.
1 No. 3 Extra Quality Steel Square. Size of body, 24x2 inches; size of tongue, 16x1½ inches. Marked in sixteenths, twelfths and fourths, and also with Brace and Essex Board Measure.
1 Stanley Adjustable Plumb and Level, mahogany polished, Proved Glasses, Arched Top Plates, brass tipped, with two side views.
1 Genuine Bailey Adjustable Wood Smooth Plane, with handle. Length, 9 inches. 2-inch cutter.
1 Genuine Bailey Adjustable Wood Jack Plane. Length, 15 inches. 2⅛-inch cutter.
1 Genuine Bailey Adjustable Wood Jointer Plane. Length, 26 inches. 2⅝-inch cutter.
1 Genuine Bailey Adjustable Knuckle Joint Block Plane, with nickel plated trimmings. Length, 6 inches. 1¾-inch cutter.
1 10-inch Sweep Fray's Ratchet Brace. Lignum vitae head. Well finished and heavily nickel plated.
10 Fulton Extension Lip, Double Spur, Tool Steel Auger Bits. All fully warranted. 1 each of the following sizes: ¼, 5/16, ⅜, 7/16, ½, 9/16, ⅝, ¾, ⅞ and 1 inch.

No. 35C6014 Price, $24.10.

8 Forged Steel, German Pattern, Gimlet Bits. 1 each of the following sizes: 1/16, 3/32, ⅛, 5/32, 3/16, 7/32, ¼ and 5/16-inch.
1 Fulton Tool Co.'s Warranted Full Polished and Etched, All Steel Broad Hatchet. 4½-inch cut.
2 Countersink Bits, forged from steel and polished. 1 each; flat head for metal and snail head for wood.
1 Screwdriver Bit, for use in bit brace, 5½ inches long, forged from steel.
1 Square Reamer Bit, for use in bit brace, forged from steel.
3 Knurled Cup Point Nail Sets. Assorted sizes.
1 Iron Handle Spoke Shave, with 2⅛-inch steel cutter.
3 Fulton brand Slim Taper Saw Files. 1 of each size; 4, 5 and 6-inch.
1 Monkey Wrench. 10-inch.
1 Nickel Plated Coping Saw, with 1 dozen extra blades.
1 Bench Stop, screw adjusting, with reversible cast steel head.
2 Sets 10-inch Hand Screw Clamps, made of seasoned hardwood.
1 Square Hickory Mallet, mortised handle. Head is 6½x2¾x3¾ inches.
6 Cakes Assorted Colors Carpenters' Chalk.
1 Beechwood Chalk Line Reel and Awl.
3 Hanks Braided Chalk Line.

Shipping weight, 100 pounds.

ALL THE ABOVE HIGH GRADE TOOLS ARE FIRST CLASS IN EVERY WAY. PACKED IN TOOL CHEST, AS DESCRIBED. No. 35C6014 FOR $24.10.

Our $2.25 Every Day Tool Set.

A splendid set of tools for home use. Every farmer should have one. Will save its cost in three months' use.

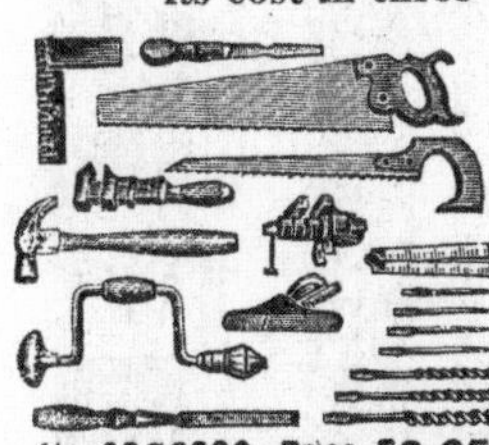

No. 35C6000 Price, $2.25

$2.25 for a set of tools you could not buy in any market for less than $3.50. Tools that would retail in any hardware store at from $3.50 to $4.50. This special set at $2.25 consists of the following strictly standard grade tools: 1 Panel Saw, blade 18 inches long; 1 Warranted Nail Hammer; 1 Bit Brace; 4 Double Cut Gimlet Bits, assorted sizes; 3 Warranted Cast Steel Double Spur Auger Bits, 1 each ⅜, ½ and ⅝ inch; 1 Compass Saw, 14-inch, which can also be used as a Rip Saw; 1 Carpenters' Two-Foot 4-Fold Boxwood Rule; 1 Screwdriver with forged steel blade 5 inches long; 1 Monkey Wrench, length 8 inches; 1 Iron Block Plane, length 5½ inches; 1 Warranted Socket Firmer Chisel, ½-inch; 1 Combined Anvil and Vise, 1½-inch jaws, opens 1¾-inch, weight 1¼ pounds; 1 Rosewood Handle Try Square with 6-inch blade.

No. 35C6000 18 Tools. Price..............**$2.25**
Weight, packed for shipment, 15 pounds.

Carpenters' Empty Tool Chests, at $2.50 to $5.75.

Take care of your tools by providing a good chest. These are the best made and sell in regular hardware stores at $7.00 and $8.00.

Made of selected hardwood, hardwood mouldings, sliding tray, fitted with lock and key, and nicely varnished.

No. 35C3609 Empty Tool Chest, 28x15x14 inches (inside measurements), with two sliding trays, saw rack, etc. Price......**$4.38**

No. 35C3613 Empty Tool Chest, 32x18x16 inches (inside measurements), with two sliding trays, having saw racks to take in full length saws. Price....**$5.75**

No. 35C3615 Carpenters' Special Hardwood Tool Chest. Same as illustrated with Invincible Tool Chest. Furnished with hinges, lock, handles and one sliding tray as illustrated. Inside measurements: Length, 31½ inches; width, 16 inches; depth, 9½ inches. Made with moulding around the bottom and extension top with edges finished round. Well made, well finished and varnished. Weight, securely crated for shipment 87 pounds. Price..............................**$2.50**

Our $5.55 Wood Butchers' Set.

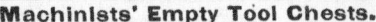

No. 35C6003 Price, $5.55.

The tools included in this set are selected from our regular stock and are all strictly high grade tools. We pack them in a neat wooden box with tray, furnished with hinges and lock. The box is large enough to hold other articles you might wish to keep in your tool box. All the tools are not shown in the illustration. Read the list. The set consists of the following tools: 1 Springfield Panel Saw, 22 inches long, fully warranted; 1 Two-foot Rule, 4-fold, 1-inch wide, made by The Stanley Rule & Level Co.; 1 Try Square, with rosewood handle, brass lined; length of blade, 6 inches, made by The Stanley Rule & Level Co.; 1 Combination Pliers and Wire Cutter, 5½ inches long; 1 Bit Brace, 10-inch sweep, like illustration; 4 Auger Bits, 1 each size, ⅜, ½, ¾ and 1 inch; 5 Gimlet Bits, German pattern, 1 each size, 1-16, ⅛, 3-16, ¼, 5-16; 1 Solid Steel Nail Hammer, warranted, weight, 1 pound; 1 Draw Knife, 8-inch cut; 1 Spoke Shave, with two cutters, one straight and the other convex; 2 Socket Firmer Chisels, 1 each, ½ and 1 inch; 1 Screwdriver, 5-inch blade; 1 Beech Jack Plane, 16 inches long, 2¼-inch double iron; 1 Iron Block Plane, 5½ inches long, 1¼-inch cutter; 1 good Carpenters' Pencil.

No. 35C6003 We furnish our Wood Butchers' Set with this neat box, as described, for..............................**$5.55**

Weight packed for shipment, 40 pounds. See freight rates in the front of book.

Machinists' Empty Tool Chests.

These chests are made of selected hardwood and are furnished with Yale pattern locks, nickel plated draw pulls and cup handles. Each chest is provided with a brass elbow to hold up lid, and a device to lock all the drawers at once, automatically.

No. 35C3602 With two drawers. Outside dimensions, 20⅝ inches long by 13 inches wide by 9⅞ inches high. Inside dimensions are as follows: Receptacle under lid, 18x10¼x3⅛ inches; first drawer, 16⅞x9x1⅜ inches; second drawer, 16⅞x9x2⅝ inches; space under second drawer, 1 inch deep. With two drawers, made of chestnut, with black walnut panels.
Price..............................**$4.65**

No. 35C3604 With three drawers. Outside dimensions, 23½ inches long by 14½ inches wide by 12 inches high. Inside dimensions are as follows: Receptacle under lid, 21x11¾x3⅛ inches; first drawer, 20x10½x1 inches; second drawer, 20x10½x1½ inches; third drawer, 20x10½x2½ inches; space under bottom drawer, 1⅜ inches. With three drawers, made of chestnut, with black walnut panels.
Price..............................**$5.85**

CIRCULAR SAWS.

PATENT GROUND AND TEMPERED SOLID TEETH OF EXTRA QUALITY, SUPERIOR WORKMANSHIP. WARRANTED.

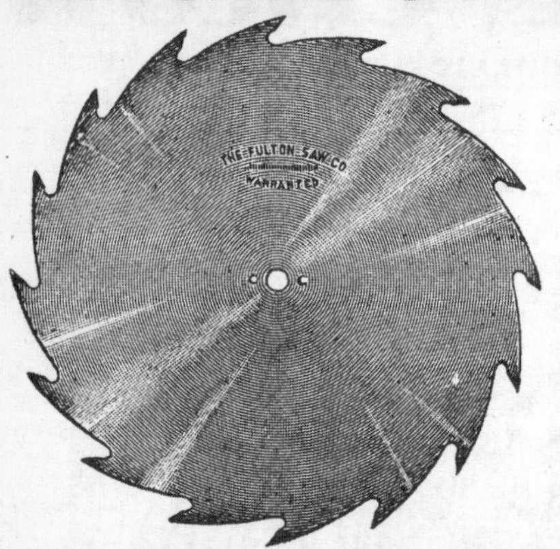

THE FULTON SAW CO.'S CIRCULAR SAWS are not excelled by any in the market in any particular. As we sell many saws for cordwood and pole sawing machines, which are handled by men who are not skilled in filing or caring for saws, we believe a few words in regard to the proper handling of a saw will not be out of place, and if these suggestions are followed no purchaser of one of our circular saws will have cause to make complaint. On most of the complaints we receive we find that the fault lies not with the saw, but the way it is fitted. The only part of the saw which should come in contact with the lumber is the point of the teeth. These points must be kept sharp to do good work. The teeth should have enough set to clear the blade of the saw, but no more than is necessary. If too much set is used it requires more power to run the saw and puts unnecessary strain upon the saw, which may cause it to crack, especially if it is run when dull. A saw should always be tried before and after the collars are tightened, for if it does not hang true, an attempt to run it is liable to spoil it entirely.

A CIRCULAR SAW must be perfectly round or it will not do good work. If some tooth is long, it brings more strain on that portion of the blade, which will make the saw work poorly and may cause a crack at the gullet. During cold weather, be sure to take the frost out of the saw before attempting to set the teeth or use the saw, as the better the steel used in the saw the more easily it is broken when frosted. The mandrel must be heavy enough so it will not spring and the collars must be true. **ANY SAW IS LIABLE TO CRACK IF SQUARE CORNERS ARE FILED IN THE GULLET. We positively will not replace a cracked saw if filed with square corners in the gullet.**

FOR CROSS CUT SAWS the points of the teeth and the points only should be beveled. The body of tooth and the gullets should be filed straight across. The heavier the cutting the less bevel should be filed on front edge of point. If too much bevel is filed on the front edge of teeth they will be forced out of line into the sides of cut. This will cause a lateral strain and chattering and a probability of breakage, particularly if the teeth are dull.

NEARLY EVERY BROKEN CIRCULAR SAW that has ever been returned to us has not been properly filed or set. This is no fault of ours, nor of the quality of the saw, and we therefore now sell all saws filed and set.

WE AIM TO CARRY IN STOCK at all times, ready for prompt shipment, saws 36 inches in diameter and smaller, with holes as listed and number of teeth ordinarily used, but can ship saws with odd size holes or made to order with as little delay as any saw maker. If a saw is wanted with pin holes, send a paper pattern giving exact location. Order blanks for ordering saws will be furnished on request.

WE CANNOT ATTEMPT to fill orders for saws larger than 36 inches without the following specifications: Size of mandrel hole, number of teeth wanted in saw, size of pin holes, distance of pin holes from center to center, gauge at center, gauge at rim, spring or swage set, temper, speed, feed, to cut hard or soft wood, right or left hand.

Blank for ordering circular saws sent free on request. We require from 5 to 30 days to fill orders for circular saws which are not regular or which are not carried in stock. We cannot accept cancelation of order after saw is in work in our factory.

We carry the following saws at factory so we can finish and ship within five days after order reaches us, and usually same day order reaches us. All have 2-inch mandrel hole with ⅝-inch pin holes, spaced 3-inch center to center.

Diameter, inches	Gauge at Hole	Gauge at Rim	Teeth	Diameter, inches	Gauge at Hole	Gauge at Rim	Teeth	Diameter, inches	Gauge at Hole	Gauge at Rim	Teeth
42	9	10	32	52	8	9	36	60	8	9	38
44	9	10	32	54	8	9	36	62	8	9	40
46	9	10	34	56	8	9	38	64	8	9	40
48	9	10	34	58	8	9	38	66	7	8	40
50	9	10	36								

No. 35C101 Cut Off Saw. Fulton Saw Co.'s warranted.
No. 35C102 Rip Saw. Fulton Saw Co.'s warranted. Read remarks above before making out your order.
Circular saws 42 inches in diameter and larger beveled, two gauges (if so ordered) without extra charge.

Diameter, inches	Thickness, Gauge	Size of Hole, inch	Price, Each, Cut off Saw	Price, Each, Rip Saw	Diameter, inches	Thickness, Gauge	Size of Hole, inch	Price, Each, Cut off Saw	Price, Each, Rip Saw	Diameter, inches	Thickness, Gauge	Size of Hole, inch	Price, Each, Cut off Saw	Price, Each, Rip Saw
4	19	¾	$0.52	$0.46	20	13	1 5-16	$3.67	$3.53	44	8	2	$18.34	$17.20
5	19	¾	.61	.56	22	12	1 5-16	4.30	4.14	46	8	2	21.88	20.66
6	18	¾	.71	.68	24	11	1½	5.07	4.94	48	8	2	25.35	24.06
7	18	¾	.84	.77	26	11	1½	5.93	5.74	50	7	2	28.85	27.46
8	18	⅞	.97	.89	28	10	1½	6.75	6.54	52	7	2	32.42	30.92
9	17	⅞	1.18	1.10	30	10	1½	7.59	7.33	54	7	2	35.92	34.32
10	16	1	1.38	1.31	32	10	1⅝	8.38	8.13	56	7	2	41.12	39.42
11	16	1	1.60	1.51	34	9	1⅝	9.44	9.16	58	7	2	46.43	44.63
12	16	1	1.71	1.62	36	9	1⅝	10.66	10.34	60	6	2	51.63	49.73
14	15	1⅛	2.03	1.94	38	9	1⅝	11.34	11.03	62	8	2	......	57.60
16	15	1⅛	2.45	2.34	40	9	2	13.11	12.78	64	8	2	......	64.80
18	15	1¼	3.06	2.93	42	8	2	15.56	14.48	66	7	2	......	72.00

Please note that above prices are for saws **set and filed**; also note that prices for saws larger than 36 inches are for saws delivered on board cars at factory, from which point customer pays freight.

We are prepared to furnish circular saws up to 76 inches in diameter. Prices quoted on application.

Inserted Tooth Circular Saws.

Prices on inserted tooth circular saws will be quoted on application. When asking for prices state diameter of saw, right or left hand gauge at eye, gauge at rim, speed, number of teeth wanted, diameter of mandrel hole, diameter of pin holes, distance from center to center of pin holes. State if Rip or Cut-off saw is wanted, the kind of lumber to be sawed and the speed and feed of mill.

Circular Saw Mandrels.

No. 35C125 Circular Saw Mandrels, with pulley on right hand side when saw is running toward you with left hand thread.

Diam. of Pulley, inches	Face of Pulley, inches	Diam. of Flange, inches	W'g't. lbs.	Length of Shaft, inches	Diam. of Shaft, inches	Size of hole in Saw, inches	Price of Mandrel Complete
2½	3½	2½	18½	16½	1 1/16	1	$4.00
3	4	3	22½	19	1 3/16	1⅛	4.33
3½	4½	3½	32	21½	1 5/16	1¼	4.68
4	5	4	38	24	1 7/16	1 5/16	5.32
4½	5½	4½	44½	26	1 7/16	1 5/16	6.00
5	6	5	46	28	1 7/16	1⅜	6.34
5½	6½	5½	49	30½	1 7/16	1⅜	7.20
6	7	6	59	32½	1 9/16	1½	9.33
7	8	6	75	37	1 11/16	1⅝	10.67
8	8	6	80	41	1 13/16	1⅝	12.00

Mandrel will not safely run larger saws than those having same size hole in price list of circular saws above. To illustrate: The first mandrel will not safely carry a saw larger than 12 inches in diameter, and the last mandrel will not run a saw larger than 36 inches in diameter.

No. 35C126 Circular Saw Mandrel with pulley in center. Sizes and prices same as No. 35C125.

Mixter's Swages.

Genuine Mixter's Saw Swage, with improved patent guides, is the most satisfactory and reliable swage ever made. The spreading recess acts upon the teeth of a saw back from the cutting edge and spreads them to the required width without materially reducing their lengths. It makes strong and substantial shoulders to the teeth when necessary, which will stand hard work and frozen timber, and it spreads them more on the underside, which causes the saw to cut easily, clear well and steadies it in the cut. Full directions sent with each swage.

No. 35C263 Genuine Mixter's Patent Duplex Swage, with patent guides (size No. 3), for saws from 5 to 10 gauge. Weight, 1½ pounds. Price........ $4.67

No. 35C264 Genuine Mixter's Patent Duplex Swage, with patent guides (size No. 2), for saws from 8 to 12 gauge. Weight, 1 pound. Price........ $3.98

No. 35C265 Genuine Mixter's Patent Duplex Swage, with patent guides (size No. 1), for saws 10 gauge and thinner. Weight, 10 ounces. Price........ $3.34

No. 35C266 Genuine Mixter's Patent Duplex Swage (size No. 0), for small thin saws. Weight, 5 ounces. Price...... $2.67

Mixter's Celebrated Champion Gummer.

With Patent Automatic Self Feed.

It is self acting, throwing itself out of gear when the teeth are cut to the required depth, making them of uniform length. The line of the teeth can be cut at any angle desired from horizontal to perpendicular. It cuts very rapidly and with no risk of bending, breaking or case hardening the saw. Full directions sent with each machine.

No. 35C277 The Mixter Patent Automatic Self Feeding Champion Gummer, including three cutters, size, ⅜, ½ and 1 inch, grinder and wrench. Price........ $18.00

No. 35C279 Small Size Patent Automatic Self Feeding Champion Gummer, especially adapted for cross cut saws and small and medium circular saws, including three cutters, ⅜, ½ and ⅝ inch grinder and wrench. Price........ $15.00

Genuine Mixter's XX Gummer Cutters.

No. 35C281 In ordering cutters, be sure and give size of hole, as well as size of cutter required, or you can send us an impression of one end of cutter on paper. Be particular to state what size gummer they are to be used in. We furnish cutters for Mixter's gummers only.

One Mixter's XX Cutter will do as much work as six ordinary ones. No cutter genuine unless stamped "Mixter's XX". Cutters ⅜, ½ and ⅝ inch have 3-16-inch holes. Cutters, ½, ⅝ and ¾ inch have 5-16 inch holes. Cutters ¾, ⅞, 1, 1⅛, 1¼ and 1½ inch have ½-inch holes, the standard size for regular arbor in the Champion gummer.

Size, inches	⅜	½	⅝	¾	⅞c
Price	46c	47c	48c	56c	66
Size, inches		1	1⅛	1¼	1½
Price		75c	85c	94c	$1.18

No. 35C278 Extra Arbors for cutters with 5-16-inch holes. Price, each........ $1.98

No. 35C280 Extra Arbors for cutters with 3-16-inch holes. Price, each........ $1.95

Side File.

No. 35C285 Large size. For dressing the sides of the points of teeth of circular saws to make them true. Price........ 83c

No. 35C288 Extra Files for Side File. Price........ 30c

Band Saws, Filed and Set.

Warranted.

No. 35C290 Band Saws. Not joined.
No. 35C291 Band Saws. Joined.

Width	Gauge	Price, per foot, not joined.	Extra for joining
¼ in.	21	5¼c	20c
⅜ in.	21	6 c	20c
½ in.	21	6½c	20c
⅝ in.	21	7¼c	25c
¾ in.	20	8¼c	25c
⅞ in.	20	8¾c	25c
1 in.	20	9½c	30c
1⅛ in.	20	10¼c	30c
1¼ in.	19	11¼c	30c
1⅜ in.	19	12¾c	40c
1½ in.	19	13¾c	40c

No. 35C292 Silver Solder for Brazing Band Saws. We do not sell less than one ounce. Price, per ounce........ 88c

CROSS CUT SAWS.

The Fulton Saw Co.'s Cross Cut Saws Are Fully Warranted.

We do not sell second quality brands in cross cut saws.

No. 35C201 The Fulton Saw Co.'s Champion Tooth Two-Man Narrow Cross Cut Saws. Warranted. Without handles.
Length, 5½ feet, weight, 3¾ pounds. Price........ 83c
Length, 6 feet, weight, 4 pounds. Price........ 90c

No. 35C204 The Fulton Saw Co.'s Champion Tooth Two-Man Cross Cut Saw. Two gauges thinner on back than on teeth. Price quoted is without handles.

Length, feet	5	5½	6	6½	7
Weight, pounds	6	7	8	8¾	9
Price	$1.29	$1.42	$1.55	$1.68	$1.80

No. 35C206 The Fulton Saw Co.'s Champion Tooth Two-Man Cross Cut Saw, without handles. This saw is ground four gauges thinner throughout the entire back, and will retain its gauge as the saw wears narrow. The very best tough sabre steel is used in this saw, and each saw is set and sharpened ready for use.

Length, feet	5	5½	6	6½	7
Price	$1.50	$1.65	$1.80	$1.95	$2.10

No. 35C210 The Fulton Saw Co.'s Plain Tooth Two-Man Cross Cut Saws. Two gauges thinner on back than on teeth. Price quoted is without handles.

Length, feet	5½	6	7
Price	$1.53	$1.67	$1.94

No. 35C215 The Fulton Saw Co.'s Great American Tooth Two-Man Cross Cut Saw. Four gauges thinner on back than on teeth and is well adapted for all kinds of timber, 14-gauge on tooth edge, 18-gauge on the back. Price quoted is without handles.

Length, feet	4½	5	5½	6
Price	$1.53	$1.70	$1.87	$2.04

No. 35C217 The Fulton Saw Co.'s Diamond Tooth Two-Man Cross Cut Saw. Two gauges thinner on back than on teeth. Price quoted is without handles.

Length, feet	4½	5	5½	6	7
Price	$1.35	$1.50	$1.65	$1.80	$2.10

No. 35C219 The Fulton Saw Co.'s Perforated Lance Tooth Two-Man Cross Cut Saw. This saw is made from the best tough sabre steel and with much care. It is ground four gauges thinner on the back. Price quoted is without handles.

Length, feet	5	5½	6	6½
Price	$1.70	$1.87	$2.04	$2.21

Cross Cut Saw Handles.

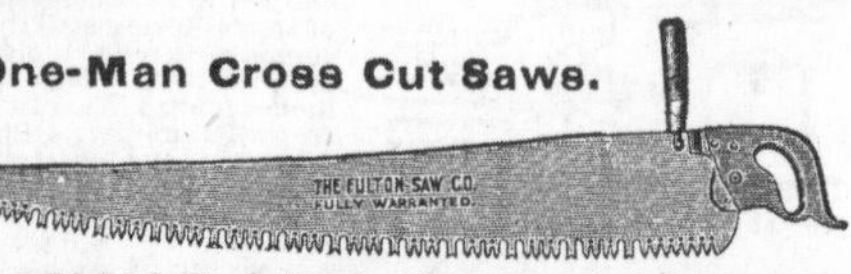

No. 35C254 Patent Loop Cross Cut Saw Handles.
Price, per pair........ 9c
Per dozen pairs........ 97c

No. 35C255 Reversible Cross Cut Saw Handles.
Price, per pair........ $0.10
Per dozen pairs........ 1.05

One-Man Cross Cut Saws.

No. 35C226 The Fulton Saw Co.'s Skew Back One-Man Cross Cut Saw. Ground four gauges thin on back. Perforated lance tooth. Supplementary handle. The fastest cutting and easiest working one-man cross cut saw in the market. Hangs just right in work. Your money refunded if not perfectly satisfactory.

Length, feet	3	3½	4	4½	5
Weight, pounds	3½	4	5	6	6½
Price	$1.55	$1.80	$2.05	$2.28	$2.53

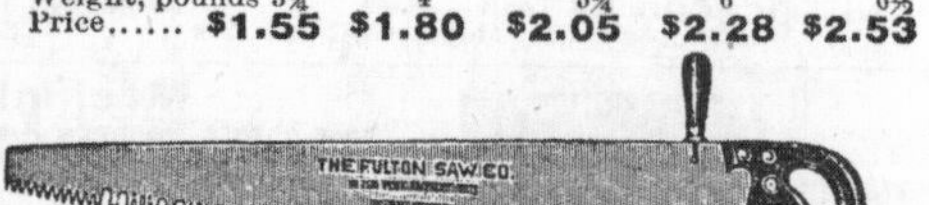

No. 35C229 The Fulton Saw Co.'s One-Man Cross Cut Saw. Ground four gauges thin on back. Perforated lance tooth. Supplementary handle. The easiest and fastest cutting saw ever produced. No expert required to keep in good working order. Warranted "if not satisfactory in every way return it within 30 days and your money will be refunded, together with cost of transportation both ways."

Length, feet	3	3½	4	4½	5
Weight, pounds	3¾	4	5¼	6	6½
Price	$1.45	$1.70	$1.95	$2.18	$2.43

One Man Cross-Cut Saws.

No. 35C221 The Fulton Saw Co.'s One-Man Cross Cut Saws. Two gauges thinner on back than on teeth. Champion tooth; supplementary handle. **Warranted.**

Length, feet	Weight, lbs.	Price	Length, feet	Weight, lbs.	Price
3	3¾	$0.88	4	5½	$1.18
3½	4¼	1.05	4½	6¼	1.33

Saw Handles.

No. 35C250 Handle for One-Man Cross Cut Saw. Price.......12c

No. 35C251 Supplementary Handle for One-Man Cross Cut Saw. Price.......8c

Cross Cut Saw Tools.

No. 35C276 Saw Tool, comprises a side file, jointer, tooth gauge, setting device, and a setting gauge, by the aid of which cross cut saws may be kept in perfect order. Full directions for using accompany each set of tools. It is one of the most popular set of saw tools on the market, and an expert is not needed to use them. Weight, 20 ounces. Price.......36c

Cross Cut Saw Sets.

No. 35C275 The Whiting Pattern Saw Set for Cross Cut Saws only. Simple and effective and a favorite with lumbermen. Fully warranted. Price.......33c

No. 35C686 Sears, Roebuck & Co.'s Improved Anvil, Morrell's Pattern Saw Set No. 3, for common tooth circular and cross cut saws from 20 to 14 gauge. Weight, 1 pound 6 ounces. Price.......55c

No. 35C687 Sears, Roebuck & Co.'s Improved Anvil, Morrell's Pattern Saw Set No. 4, for Champion or M-tooth cross cut saws from 22 to 14 gauge. Weight, 1½ pounds. Price.......54c

The Fulton Saw.

The Fulton Saw is a hand made saw. It is made upon honor and sold on its merits; it is made from the best steel that can be produced; it has extra thin back, the blade is ground four gauges thinner on back, allowing the saw to run freely with little set. It is smithed and blocked equal to "trust" saws that sell for 40 or 50 per cent more. Good smithing and blocking make a good saw, but because this work is expensive and doesn't show until saw has been used it is too often slighted; when it is honestly done, the saw works right, not only while it is new, but as long as it lasts, if properly used. Every Fulton saw is carefully examined to see that the smithing and blocking is not slighted. Every Fulton saw is highly tempered, hence care must be used when setting or teeth may be broken out. The set should not extend down more than one-third the length of the tooth. When a tooth is broken out through improper setting we do not consider the saw defective or that it has failed to give satisfaction. If everybody used the Taintor saw set (see No. 35C690) there would be little complaint from this cause. The Fulton Saw is hand set, full bevel hand filed, ready for use, hollow back, handsome handle, perfectly plain, with four improved screws, the neatest looking handle ever put on a saw. **It is guaranteed as follows:** "If this saw is not perfectly satisfactory in every way return it to your dealer and he will refund the amount you paid for it." If you have been accustomed to pay $1.85 or more for a 26-inch saw we will be pleased to have you order a Fulton saw at $1.25 with the understanding that if you do not consider it equal in every way to saws that sell in a regular way at $1.85 and upward you may return it to us within 30 days and we will refund the price paid and pay transportation charges both ways.

No. 35C304 The Fulton Panel or Hand Saws.

Length	Points to the inch	Price
18-inch Panel	9, 10, 11 or 12	$0.90
20-inch Panel	9, 10, 11 or 12	1.02
22-inch Panel	9, 10, 11 or 12	1.15
24-inch Hand	7, 8, 9, 10, 11 or 12	1.20
26-inch Hand	6, 7, 8, 9, 10, 11 or 12	1.25
28-inch Hand	6, 7 or 8	1.43
30-inch Hand	6, 7 or 8	1.64

No. 35C305 The Fulton Rip Saws.

Length	Points to the inch	Price
24-inch Rip	5, 5½, 6 or 6½	$1.22
26-inch Rip	5, 5½ or 6	1.27
28-inch Rip	4, 4½, 5, 5½ or 6	1.45
30-inch Rip	4½ or 5	1.66

We cannot furnish these saws in points other than listed above.

The Springfield Saw.

The Springfield Saw is ground nearly three gauges thinner on back, carefully smithed and blocked, carved handle, four improved screws, hollow back. Hand made full bevel, hand filed, hand set and warranted as follows: "If this saw does not prove satisfactory and equal to saws made by other manufacturers that sell at 40 per cent more money, return it to your dealer, within thirty days, and he will refund the price paid for it." If you have been accustomed to pay $1.40 to $1.65 for a 26-inch hand saw, we will be pleased to have you order a Springfield saw at $1.00, with the understanding that if you do not consider it in every way equal to saws that usually sell at $1.40 and upwards, you may return it to us within thirty days and we will refund your money.

PRICE LIST OF THE SPRINGFIELD SAW.

No. 35C306 The Springfield Panel or Hand Saws.

Length	Points to the inch	Price
18-inch Panel,	9, 10, 11 and 12	$0.79
20-inch Panel,	9, 10, 11 and 12	.84
22-inch Panel,	9, 10, 11 and 12	.90
24-inch Hand,	7, 8, 9, 10, 11 and 12	.95
26-inch Hand,	6, 7, 8, 9, 10, 11 and 12	1.00

No. 35C307 The Springfield Rip Saws.

Length	Points to the inch	Price
26-inch Rip,	5, 5½ and 6	$1.02
28-inch Rip,	5, 5½ and 6	1.12

The Odd Jobs Saw.

The Odd Jobs Saw is warranted but it is not ground thin on the back and it is not smithed or blocked or filed as carefully as our Fulton or Springfield saws. It is set and sharpened and will give satisfaction to anyone who wants a saw only for odd jobs. **We do not advise a first class carpenter to buy it.** It is as good as saws commonly retailed at $1.25 (for 26-inch size) and better than any saw we ever saw retailed for $1.00. You need not hesitate to buy this saw for doing odd jobs.

No. 35C308 The Odd Jobs Panel or Hand Saws.

Length	Points to the inch	Price
20 inches, Panel,	9, 10 or 12	62c
24 inches, Hand,	7, 8, 9 or 10	67c
26 inches, Hand,	7, 8, 9 or 10	70c

No. 35C309 The Odd Jobs Rip Saws.

Length	Points to the inch	Price
26 inches, Rip,	5, 5½ or 6	72c
28 inches, Rip,	5, 5½ or 6	82c

No. 35C350 While this saw is not warranted, it is a fair grade saw, and has given excellent satisfaction. Blade is cast steel, patent ground and tempered, walnut handle with steel plate on handle, three brass screws; filed and set.

Length, inches	18	22	26	28 Rip
Price	45c	50c	53c	65c

Henry Disston & Sons' Saws.

Below we show the leading number of this well known brand. We guarantee them to be the genuine Disston's Saws.

No. 35C363 Disston D-8, Hand and Rip Saws. Skew back, apple handle, polished edge, five improved screws. Rip saws have thumb hold in handle. **Warranted.**

26-inch, hand, 6, 7, 8, 9, 10, 11 and 12 points. Price.......$1.35
28-inch, rip, 4½, 5, 5½ and 6 points. Price.......1.53

THE FULTON SAW IS NOT MADE BY A TRUST.

If you are opposed to trusts and combinations (which usually keep prices higher than they should naturally be), you can fire one shot at the enemy by buying the FULTON SAW, and provided you find it exactly as we say, recommending it to your fellow workmen.

C. E. Jennings & Co.'s Saws.

All C. E. Jennings & Co.'s Saws are patent ground and tempered. Hand hammered. Hand filed and set ready for use. They are fully warranted in every particular.

No. 35C353 Jennings' A 7½ Hand Panel and Rip Saw. This saw is 6 inches wide at butt and 1½ inches at point. It can be used for many purposes where a full width saw is unwieldly. They are made of the best refined spring steel, ground four gauges thin on back, full beveled, filed and set, carved and full polished handle, four improved brass screws. The 18, 20, 22 and 24-inch sizes come in 9, 10, 11 and 12 points. The 26-inch size comes 6, 7, 8, 9, 10, 11 and 12 points. The 28-inch size comes 4½, 5, 5½ and 6 points to the inch. Every saw is warranted.

Length in.	18	20	22	24	26	28 Rip
Price	$1.05	$1.19	$1.33	$1.47	$1.54	$1.75

C. E. Jennings & Co.'s No. 12½ Straight Back Saw. Extra London refined spring steel highly polished blade; apple handle, carved and polished. Four improved brass screws, patent ground and tempered. Hand hammered and hand filed and set ready for use. This saw is, in our opinion, better made, better filed, and better in every way than saws made by other manufacturers that we could sell at about the same price. Cabinet makers, car builders, inside finishers, millwrights, bridge builders and other high class woodworkers call this "the finest hand saw made." We take back or exchange any that are defective in any particular.

No. 35C354 C. E. Jennings & Co.'s No. 12½ Panel or Hand Saw.

Length, 20-inch Panel, 9, 10, 11 or 12 points. Price.......$1.45
Length, 22-inch Panel, 9, 10, 11 or 12 points. Price.......1.58
Length, 24-inch Hand, 8, 9, 10, 11 or 12 points. Price.......1.72
Length, 26-inch Hand, 6, 7, 8, 9, 10, 11 or 12 points. Price.......1.84

No. 35C355 C. E. Jennings & Co.'s No. 12½ Rip Saws.

Length, 26-inch Rip, 5, 5½ or 6 points.......$1.86
Length, 28-inch Rip, 5, 5½ or 6 points.......2.10

C. E. Jennings & Co.'s No. 212 Skew Back Hand Saw is the same as No. 12½ described above, except it has skew back, which is preferred by most workmen.

No. 35C356 C. E. Jennings & Co.'s No. 212 Panel or Hand Saw.

20-inch Panel, 9, 10, 11 or 12 points. Price.......$1.52
22-inch Panel, 9, 10, 11 or 12 points. Price.......1.65
24-inch Hand, 8, 9, 10, 11 or 12 points. Price.......1.78
26-inch Hand, 6, 7, 8, 9, 10, 11 or 12 points. Price.......1.90

No. 35C357 C. E. Jennings & Co.'s No. 212 Rip Saw.

26-inch Rip, 5, 5½ or 6 points. Price.......$1.92
28-inch Rip, 5, 5½ or 6 points. Price.......2.17

Back Saws.

No. 35C384 The Fulton Back Saw with extra heavy blued steel back giving weight to the saw and insuring a steady cut. Made from extra spring steel. Hand hammered. Hand filed and ready for use. Has apple handle. Fully warranted.

Size, inches	10	12	14	16
Price	85c	$1.02	$1.14	$1.25

No. 35C387 The Springfield Back Saw with blued steel back, Beech handle. It is not so finely finished as our Fulton back saw and the handle is not so expensive. It is, however, a first class saw and is warranted to give satisfaction.

Size, inches	10	12	14	16
Price	62c	74c	87c	93c

Mitre Box Saws.

No. 35C388 The Fulton Mitre Box Back Saw, measuring 4 inches under the back. Length of saw is entire length of blade, the toothed edge being about 2 inches shorter.

Length, inches	22	24	28
Price	$1.60	$1.80	$2.05

No. 35C389 The Fulton Mitre Box Back Saw, measuring 5 inches under the back.

Length, inches	24	28
Price	$1.98	$2.31

Compass Saws.

No. 35C392 Standard Compass Saws. Spring steel, beech handle with 2 screws.

Length, inches	10	12	14
Price	11c	12c	13c

No. 35C396 The Fulton Compass Saw. Thin back, evenly tempered from butt to point, hand hammered, full bevel hand filed and set ready for use. Extra finished handle, two improved screws.

Length, inches	10	12	14	16
Price	28c	30c	32c	36c

Nests of Saws.

No. 35C401 Superior Nest of Saws, consisting of 1 handle, 1 keyhole blade, 1 compass blade, 1 panel or pruning blade; **all interchangeable in the handle.** Price.......68c

Saw Handles.

No. 35C405 Hand Saw Handles, common beechwood, with varnished edges. Weight, 10 ounces. Price.......7c

No. 35C406 Panel Saw Handles, common varnished edges. Price.......7c

No. 21. No. 23. No. 31.

No. 35C425 Brass Saw Handle Screws.

No.	Price, per dozen	each
No. 21	14c	2c
No. 23	25c	3c
No. 31	20c	2c

Coping Saws.

No. 35C440 Coping Saws, nickel plated, adjustable frames. All wire, 6-inch bent end blades. Depth of cut, 4 inches. Complete, with 1 dozen extra blades. Price.......15c

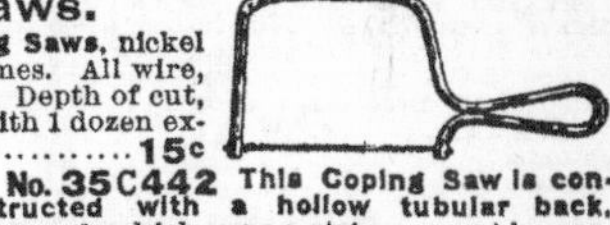

No. 35C442 This Coping Saw is constructed with a hollow tubular back, through which runs a string or cable connecting both ends of saw frame, which causes the blade to run to any angle by turning the handle only, without removing it from the work. Nickel plated and furnished complete with one-half dozen blades packed in pasteboard box. Price.......90c

No. 35C443 Extra Blades for Coping Saws. Six inches long with bent ends. Price, per dozen.......9c

Braced Frame Buck Saw.

No. 35C636 Braced Frame Wood Saw, maple frame, with rod and 30-inch Fulton Saw Co.'s round breasted blade. Warranted. Price.......35c

No. 35C637 Braced Frame Wood Saw, maple frame, painted red, best tinned rod, 30-inch, Fulton Saw Co.'s brand blued blade. Warranted. Price.......43c

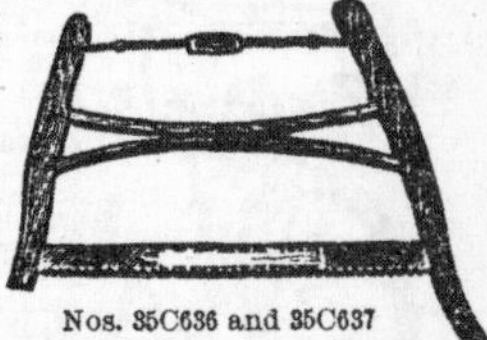

Nos. 35C636 and 35C637

No. 35C638 The "Fulton Special" Buck Saw. Made especially for wood sawyers. Frame is selected natural hard wood, varnish finish, heavy tinned rod with japanned turn. Threads will not strip. The blade is the main feature of this saw. It is made of the best clock spring tempered steel with round breast. It is taper ground extra thin on the back, hand filed and set ready for use. The peculiar shape of the tooth, the extra thin back, the expert hand filing, the high grade steel used and the extreme care exercised in its manufacture, make the "Fulton Special" the fastest and easiest cutting buck saw in the world. If you cannot saw a cord of wood faster and easier with the "Fulton Special' buck saw than with any buck saw you have ever used you may return it to us within thirty days and we will refund the price paid and stand the cost of the transportation charges both ways. Price.......70c

Buck Saw Rods.

No. 35C650 Loop Buck Saw Rods, will span from 19 to 22 inches. Weight, 7 ounces. Price.......5c

No. 35C651 Best Tinned Loop Saw Rods, span from 19 to 22 inches. Heaviest saw rod made—threads will not strip. Weight, 12 ounces. Price.......7c

Buck Saw Blades.

No. 35C655 Buck Saw Blades, Fulton Saw Co.'s brand. Same as used in No. 35C636 buck saw. Price.......23c

No. 35C656 Buck Saw Blades, Fulton Saw Co.'s brand blued. Same as used in No. 35C637 buck saw. Warranted. Price.......24c

Buck Saw Blades.

No. 35C658 Buck Saw Blades, C. E. Jennings & Co.'s brand, round breast, extra spring steel, patent ground and tempered, full bevel filed, set ready for use; length, 30 inches.
Price..**35c**

No. 35C659 The "FULTON SPECIAL" buck saw blade as described under No. 35C658 (length 30 inches). Price.......**40c**

Buck Saw Frames.

No. 35C664 Buck Saw Frames, same style as used in No. 35C636, made of hardwood, finished in the white.
Price, each..**$0.12**
Per dozen...**1.33**

No. 35C665 Buck Saw Frames, same as No. 35C664, painted red. Price, each..**$0.15**
Per dozen...**1.69**

No. 35C666 Buck Saw Frames, same as No. 35C664, made of selected hardwood, natural finish, varnished.
Price, each..**$0.18**
Per dozen...**2.05**

Hack Saw Frames.

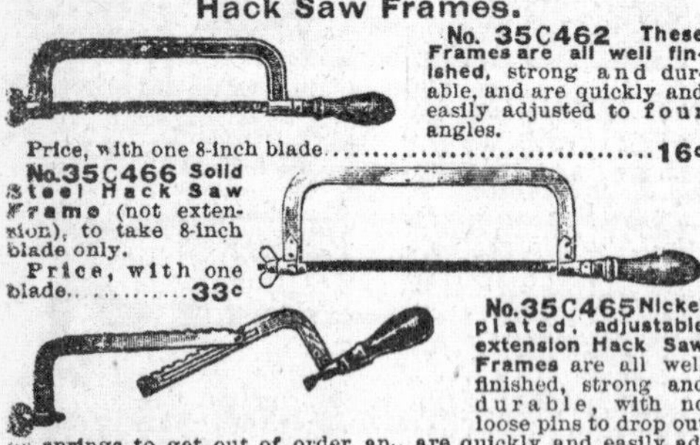

No. 35C462 These Frames are all well finished, strong and durable, and are quickly and easily adjusted to four angles.
Price, with one 8-inch blade..............................**16c**

No. 35C466 Solid Steel Hack Saw Frame (not extension), to take 8-inch blade only.
Price, with one blade............**33c**

No. 35C465 Nickel plated, adjustable extension Hack Saw Frames are all well finished, strong and durable, with no loose pins to drop out or springs to get out of order, and are quickly and easily adjusted to four angles, or to any lengths, from 8 to 12 inches.
Price, with one 8-inch blade...............................**48c**

No. 35C470 This is the stiffest Hack Saw Frame made. It is made of steel, highly polished, heavily nickel plated, and will face the blades in four directions. The handle is ebonized. This will hold all blades from 6 to 12 inches.
Price, with one 10-inch blade, as shown in illustration.....**80c**

Hack Saw Blades.

No. 35C480 Hack Saw Blade is made from the best clock steel, soft on the back with highly tempered teeth. It is unbreakable, and is preferred by many. Has 14 points to the inch.

Length, inches	8	9	10	12
Price, each	3c	3c	4c	4c
Per dozen	31c	33c	39c	45c

No. 35C481 Hack Saw Blades, 24 points to the inch, for cutting brass, drill rods, black pipe tubing and similar work. Soft on the back with highly tempered teeth.

Length inches	8	9	10	12
Per dozen	32c	34c	40c	46c

No. 35C483 Genuine Star Hack Saw Blades are never to be filed and are tempered so high that one will last four times as long as an ordinary saw with one filing. We fully warrant all saws marked with a star sold by us. These saw blades are made with 14 teeth to the inch and have a good set.

Length, inches	8	9	10	12
Price, each	5c	6c	7c	8c
Price, per dozen	58c	63c	74c	95c

Hand Bracket Saws.

No. 35C498 Bracket Saw, nickel plated, rosewood handle; frame, 5x12; with 50 designs, 6 saw blades, 1 awl, 1 sheet impression paper, and directions packed in pasteboard box. Weight, 1¼ pounds.
Price, for outfit.....................**83c**

Bracket Saw Blades.

No. 35C500 Bracket Saw Blades, 5 inches long. We do not sell less than a dozen of any one size.

Size	00	0	1	2	3	4	5	6	7	8	9	10
Per doz.	5c	5c	5c	5c	5c	5c	5c	5c	6c	6c	7c	7c
Per gro.	50c	50c	50c	50c	50c	50c	50c	50c	55c	60c	65c	70c

The above blades also fit Nos. 35C512, 35C514 and 35C521 saws.

Foot Power Bracket Saws.

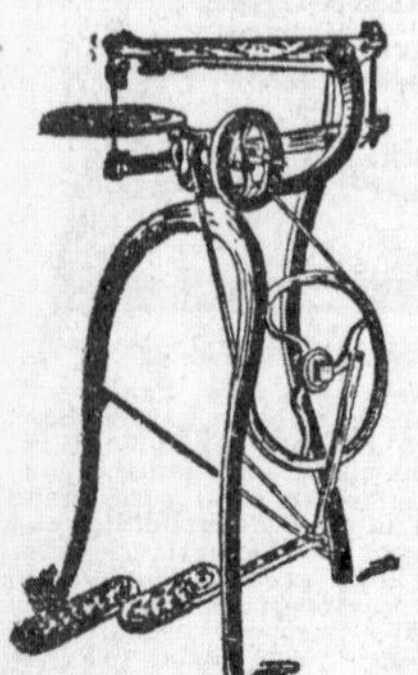

No. 35C512 Bracket Saw. Has a rubber dust blower, improved clamps for holding the saw blade and a roller inserted in the table back of the saw, which makes it run perfectly true. The arbors are made of steel, carefully gauged and fitted to their bearings. The balance wheel is 4½ inches in diameter, with iron spoke center and rim of solid emery. The attachment for drilling is on the right hand side of machine, which is an advantage. With each machine we give 12 saw blades, wrench, sheet of designs and 3 drill points. The saw alone weighs 25 lbs.; when boxed for shipment, about 42 lbs.
Price..........................**$3.25**

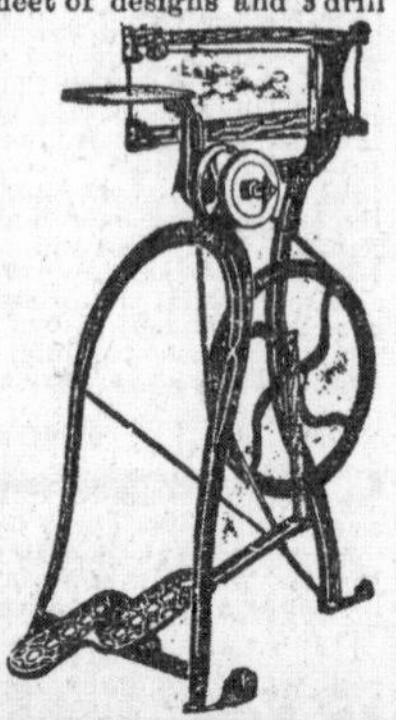

No. 35C514 The Star Scroll Saw is a better machine than No. 35C512. It has a heavier drive wheel. The emery wheel is fastened by adjustable clamps, which can also be used for holding various other sizes of emery wheels, grindstones, buffing wheels, etc. It has a chuck for holding drill points. It weighs, net, 37 pounds, and boxed, 55 pounds. With each machine we give 12 saw blades, wrench, sheet of designs and 3 drill points. Price, complete.....**$4.40**

THE FOOT POWER BRACKET SAWS Nos. 35C512 and 35C514 are not practical tools for carpenters, etc. They are intended only for amateurs or light work.

Foot Power Lathe.

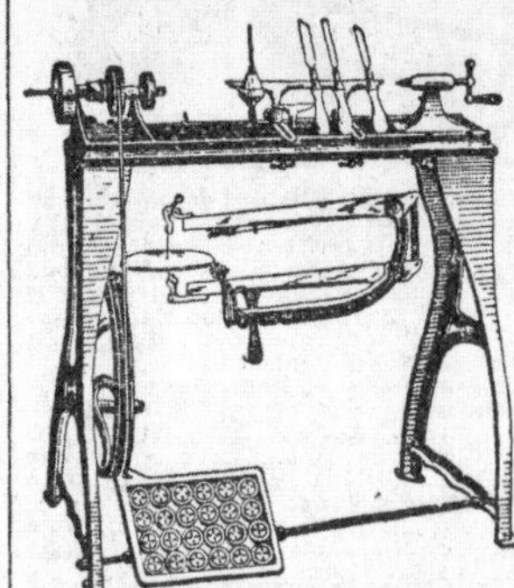

No. 35C520 This Lathe is provided with a long and short tool rest, five turning tools, wrench and drill points. Swing of lathe, 5 inches; length of bed, 24 inches; distance between center, 15½ inches. The large drive wheel has two grooves of varying depths on its face to give it a change of speed; the higher speed is 11 to 1; the lower, 7 to 1; the lathe head has a 2-inch face plate, a spur center, a screw center for turning cups and also a drill chuck to hold from 1-32 to ¼-inch round twist drills for drilling wood or iron. The lathe is thoroughly built and highly finished, the plain and polished parts being nickel plated. Weight, 56 pounds; weight, boxed, ready to ship, 70 pounds. Price..........**$8.15**

No. 35C521 The same Lathe, with scroll saw attachment. Weight, boxed, ready to ship, 70 pounds. Price..........**$9.80**

No. 35C522 Circular Saw Attachment for this lathe, complete with 3-inch saw. Price...........................**$1.00**

No. 35C523 Extra Clamps to hold saw blades in saws. Nos. 35C510-35C512 and Scroll Attachment to Goodell Lathe. Sold in pairs only. Price, per pair...........................**29c**

No. 35C520 LATHES ARE NOT SUITABLE FOR MECHANICS. They are only intended for the use of boys and amateurs. Not a tool for the carpenter shop, as they are too light for heavy work.

Screw Cutting Lathes.

No. 35C558 Nine inch Screw Cutting Lathe with foot power. Weight, 350 pounds.
Price........**$46.00**

For Speed Lathes, Screw Cutting Lathes and Engine Lathes write for special catalogue. Sent free on request.

Lathe Sets.

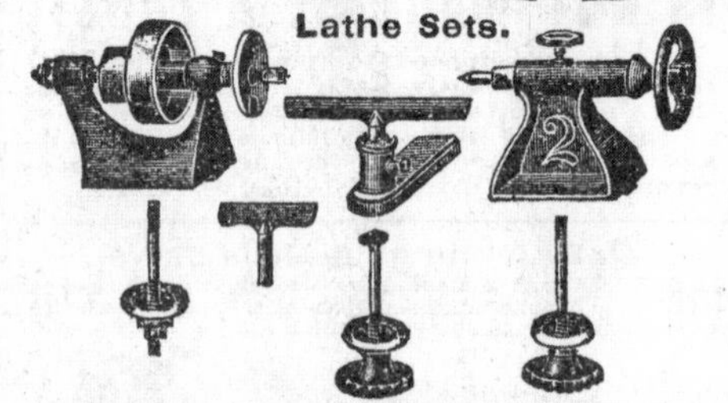

No. 35C574 Lathe Sets are well made and the bottoms are planed to bring the centers in line. The No. 1 and No. 2 have steel head spindles running in cast iron bearings. The Nos. 3 and 4 have babbitt bearings, and the centers are the No. 2 Morse taper. The cones are carefully balanced, being turned on the inside, and no better made lathes have ever been placed upon the market. Each set of heads consists of 1 head stock, 1 rest socket, 1 face plate, 1 common center, 3 bolts, 1 tail stock, 2 T rests, 1 spur center, 2 hand wheel nuts, and 3 flanges.

No.	1	2	3	4
Swing	6 in.	8 in.	11 in.	13 in.
No. of speeds on Cone	2	2	3	4
Width of Belt	1 in.	1¼ in.	1½ in.	1½ in.
Price	$6.33	$9.33	$16.00	$26.50

No. 35C576 Countershaft, to fit No. 35C574 Lathe Set, with step pulleys to match each size.

No.	1	2	3	4
Price	$4.00	$5.00	$7.33	$8.67

Ball Bearing Saw Machines.

For Foot and Hand Power and Light Belt Power.

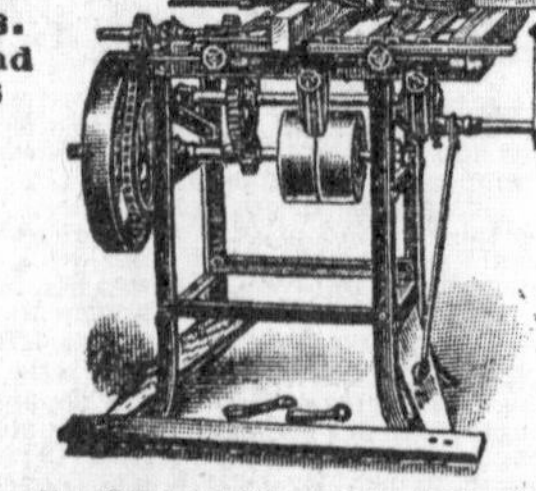

No. 35C4200 Price, $29.40

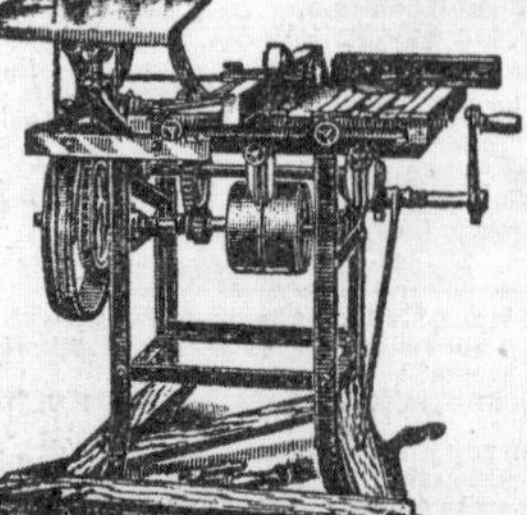

Every wagon maker, cabinet maker, boat builder, carpenter and contractor can make one of these machines pay for itself in a very short time. They are good, practical machines, guaranteed to give satisfaction, and are sold at prices that are lower than have ever been made on such machines. If interested ask for our Special Saw Machine catalogue. It will be sent free on request.

No. 35C4211 Price, $50.40

Other combinations from $8.40 to $78.50.

Saw Sets.

No. 35C682 Saw Set is made with a revolving eccentric anvil having the required bevel of all saw teeth ranging from 4 to 16 to the inch. The figures on the dial indicate the number of teeth to the inch. The indicator and dial being on the outside at the end of the tool makes it easier to set than others. Hardened anvil and plunger. Finely tempered steel spring. Highly polished finish. Length, 6¾ inches; weight, 10 ounces. Price.......**59c**

No. 35C684 Saw Set. The lever is placed on the lower side, where it is operated by moving the fingers only, thus doing away with the motion of the entire hand, which is necessary in operating the older types of saw sets in which the lever is above the body of the tool. The anvil and plunger are hardened; the spring is of tempered steel. The surface is polished, then heavily nickel plated and buffed to a high finish. Length, 6¾ inches. Weight, 10 ounces.
Price...**36c**

No. 35C685 Sears, Roebuck & Co.'s Improved Anvil, Original Morrell's Pattern Saw Set No. 1, for setting hand, band, panel, buck and meat saws. If this saw set is used intelligently it will be impossible to break a tooth out of a saw while setting it. No prying required. Simply shutting the handles sets the tooth. The point of tooth when in position on anvil can be seen by the operator. Weight, 9 ounces.
Price...**27c**

The Taintor Positive Saw Set is made entirely of steel, is light, strong and durable, and every part guaranteed. The anvil is a block of steel, having ten sides and faces, which are numbered. The faces are of three lengths, placed in lettered divisions—F for fine, M for medium and C for coarse teeth. These faces will produce any setting ordinarily required, but for fine adjustment a washer is provided, which, when placed between the anvil and frame, causes each face to bend the tooth nearer its point, producing less set. Never use a face that reaches below the root of the tooth. In use the anvil should be screwed tightly down, with its side accurately in line with the clamping jaw. Bring the handles together with sufficient force to press the tooth hard against the face of the anvil, but not hard enough to crush it or draw it out of shape. To return to any setting, note the number of anvil face on which it was done.

No. 35C690 The Taintor Positive Saw Set.
Price...**56c**

Aiken's Hammer Saw Set.

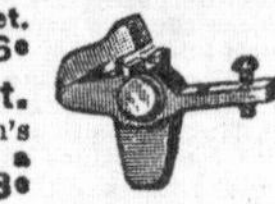

No. 35C693 Hammer Saw Set. Aiken's genuine forged steel. So well known a description is not necessary. Price..........**48c**

Saw Jointer and Skate Sharpener.

No. 35C700 The Perfect Saw Jointer and Skate Sharpener. Adjustable to any thickness of blade. Uses any common file. So simple that directions are not necessary.
Price, with file..........**35c**

Saw Clamps.

No. 35C719 Saw Clamp, may be firmly attached to any bench almost instantly. It will hold the saw firmly and is instantly adjustable. Length of jaws, 12½ inches. Occupies a space 13x3¼x3 inches. Weight, 2¾ pounds.
Price...**36c**

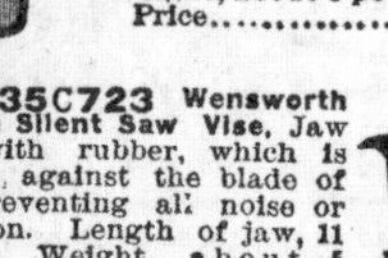

No. 35C720 Saw Clamps; jaws are 9½ inches. To open clamp, throw the lever down; place saw between the jaws and bring the lever back, and saw is securely held for filing; nicely japanned. Weight, about 3 pounds.
Price...**24c**

No. 35C723 Wensworth Pattern Silent Saw Vise, Jaw faced with rubber, which is pressed against the blade of saw, preventing all noise or vibration. Length of jaw, 11 inches. Weight, about 5 pounds. Price..........**45c**

No. 35C726

No. 35C726 Ball and Socket Adjustment Saw Clamp is adjustable in every direction; length of jaw, 9½ inches; saw is secured by tightening thumbscrew; nicely japanned. Weight, about 9 pounds. Price, **54c**

No. 35C730 Adjustable Saw Clamp, with clamp to secure it to bench or table. This clamp holds saw securely at any angle. Jaws are 9½ inches. **The adjustable feature**, which can be readily understood by looking at illustration, makes this the **most popular and best selling saw clamp in the market.** Weight, about 5 pounds.
Price...**25c**

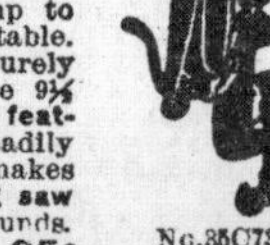

No. 35C730

No. 35C737 The Fulton Improved Noiseless Saw Clamp with filing guide attachment. The vise is adjustable to the clamp which fastens it to the bench by a ball and socket joint, enabling the operator to adjust the vise to any angle. The jaws are 10½ inches long and are fitted with rubber, making it noiseless. The saw is clamped in the vise by a cam lever. The filing guide is adjustable in every direction by the ball and socket joint. The file is adjusted to any angle, and by means of this clamp and filing guide anyone can file a saw with perfect accuracy. Weight, 7¾ pounds. Price....................**$1.38**

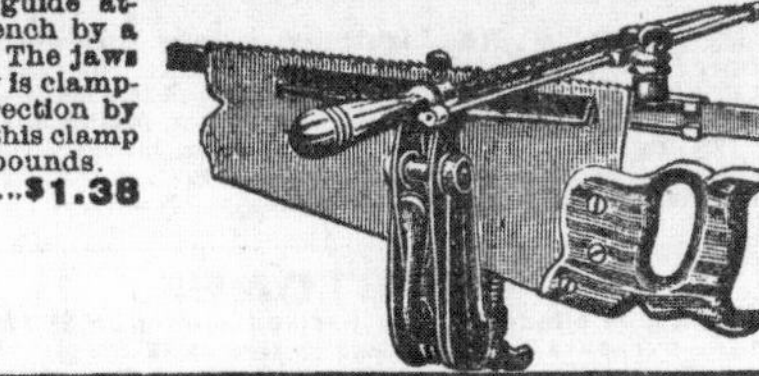

No. 35C738 This Saw Vise has the same adjustments as our No. 35C730, and it has the same filing guide attachment as No. 35C737. Its use enables anyone to file a saw accurately. Length of jaws, 9½ inches. Weight, 6 pounds. Price.....**$1.00**

No. 35C739 Saw Filing Guide, with adjustments to file any angle, any bevel and exact depth. Anyone can file a saw accurately with this guide. Can be used with any vise. Weight, 2¼ pounds. Price..........**78c**

Mitre Boxes.

No. 35C748 The Stanley Improved Mitre Box No. 50, for use with either back or panel saw. Adjustable. Will cut 4½ inches wide at mitre to 7 inches wide at square. Will take stuff 3 inches thick with saw 5 inches under back. Length, 20 inches. Price, without saw, **$4.22**

No. 35C749 The Perfection Mitre Box. The saw guide can be instantly set and rigidly held by the setscrew at any angle wanted. Any saw may be used, back saw, panel or hand. For cutting to exact depths, use a back saw, the back rib resting on the shoulders within the swinging guide, this guide adjusted to the proper height, will determine the depth, at the same time that it keeps to the angle to be cut. May be detached in a minute from the wood box and folded to carry in tool chest. Price....................**$2.67**

No. 35C750 The Genuine Langdon New Improved Mitre Box, made by The Millers Falls Company, with saw 22x4, gives 6 inches width at right angles and 4 inches at mitre. This box, by using the circular arms or guides, cuts from right angles to 75 degrees on 2¼-inch stuff, varying more or less with width of stuff. Ajustable for mitreing circular work in patterns and segments of various kinds. Weight, 10½ pounds. Price, with saw..........**$8.20**

No. 35C753 The Langdon New Improved Mitre Box, with saw 24x4, gives 9½ inches at right angles and 6½ inches at mitre. Weight, 11½ pounds. Price, with saw..........**$9.45**

No. 35C756 The Langdon New Improved Mitre Box, with saw 28x5, gives 9½ inches width at right angles and 6½ inches at mitre. Weight, 12½ pounds. Price, with saw..........**$11.48**

No. 35C767 Latest Improved Mitre Box and Saw Guide. Stronger, simpler and more accurate than any tool of this class. Instantaneous adjustment to cut square and at angles of 25, 30 and 45 degrees, and can be rigidly held at any adjustment by clamping the saw guide to the post by a few turns of the thumbscrew. Any panel or hand saw may be used. Just the thing for clapboarding and general house finishing. Will cut mouldings of any width or depth. Can be fastened to the bench or placed on top of the work. Weight, 3¼ pounds. Price, each..**$1.25**

No. 35C766 Picture Frame Makers' Combined Mitre Sawing Machine and Vise. Adjustable for mouldings from ¼ inch to 5 inches wide. The most delicate mouldings of any shape are held firmly while being sawed, and drawn tightly together in exact position while being nailed. Price, complete, without saw..**$5.50**

This machine requires our No. 35C388 Mitre Box Saw, length, 22 inches.

No. 35C775 Lyon Universal Trimmer, size No. 4. For cutting joints square, bevel, or at any angle, leaving a smooth and accurate finish. It cuts up to 4 inches high and 7 inches wide. For cutting off the ends of siding, flooring, casings, mouldings, etc., it will pay for itself on one job. Every machine is sold with the distinct understanding that if it does not work entirely to your satisfaction, if you want to return it for any reason whatever, or without any reason, we will immediately refund the amount you have paid us and stand the cost of transportation charges both ways. It is safely packed for transportation. Shipping weight is about 34 pounds. Price....**$11.33**

No. 35C776 Extra Knives for above machine. Price, per pair..........**$2.75**

THE FULTON BRAND OF FILES. THE BEST MADE.

The tang or part of file which goes into handle is not included when giving sizes of files.

We sell any quantity at dozen price. For the convenience of our customers we print the price of one, figured within the fraction of a cent.

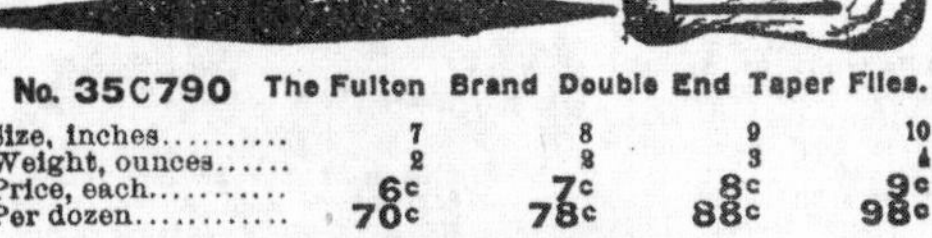

No. 35C790 The Fulton Brand Double End Taper Files.

Size, inches	7	8	9	10
Weight, ounces	2	2	3	4
Price, each	6c	7c	8c	9c
Per dozen	70c	78c	88c	98c

No. 35C793 The Fulton Brand Regular Taper Files.

Size, in.	Weight, oz.	Price, each	Price, per doz.	Size, in.	Weight, oz.	Price, each	Price, per doz.
3	2	4c	42c	5½	4	5c	$0.60
3½	2	4c	42c	6	4	6c	.68
4	3	4c	44c	7	4	8c	.86
4½	3	4c	48c	8	6	9c	1.08
5	4	5c	52c				

No. 35C795 The Fulton Brand Slim Taper Files.

Size, in.	Weight, oz.	Price, each	Price, per doz.	Size, in.	Weight, oz.	Price, each	Price, per doz.
3	2	4c	42c	5½	4	5c	58c
3½	2	4c	42c	6	4	6c	62c
4	3	4c	44c	7	4	7c	76c
4½	3	4c	46c	8	6	8c	90c
5	4	5c	50c				

No. 35C798 The Fulton Brand Mill Files.

Size, in.	Weight, oz.	Price, each	Price, per doz.	Size, in.	Weight, oz.	Price, each	Price, per doz.
6	6	6c	$0.70	12	16	13c	$1.50
8	7	8c	.86	14	21	18c	2.14
10	10	10c	1.12				

No. 35C800 The Fulton Brand Mill Files, with one round edge.

Size, inches	Weight, oz.	Price, each	Per doz.
8	7	8c	$0.96
10	10	11c	1.26
12	16	14c	1.68

No. 35C805 The Fulton Brand Flat Bastard Files.

Size, in.	Weight, oz.	Price, each	Price, per doz.	Size, in.	Weight, oz.	Price, each	Price, per doz.
4	2	7c	$0.74	10	12	12c	$1.40
5	4	7c	.78	12	20	17c	1.94
6	4	8c	.86	14	29	23c	2.66
8	7	9c	1.06				

No. 35C808 The Fulton Brand Half Round Bastard Files.

Size, in.	Weight, oz.	Price, each	Price, per doz.	Size, in.	Weight, oz.	Price, each	Price, per doz.
6	4	11c	$1.22	12	18	20c	$2.36
8	8	13c	1.50	14	28	26c	3.10
10	11	16c	1.82				

No. 35C810 The Fulton Brand Round Bastard Files. Sometimes called Rat Tail Files.

Size, in.	Weight, oz.	Price, each	Price, per doz.	Size, in.	Weight, oz.	Price, each	Price, per doz.
4	2	5c	60c	8	6	8c	$0.86
5	4	6c	64c	10	8	10c	1.12
6	5	6c	70c	12	12	13c	1.50

No. 35C813 The Fulton Brand Square Bastard Files.

Size, inches	4	5	6	8	10	12
Weight, ounces	2	4	4	7	12	20
Price, each	7c	7c	8c	$0.10	$0.13	$0.17
Per dozen	76c	82c	92c	1.10	1.48	2.04

No. 35C819 The Fulton Brand Flat Smooth Files.

Size, inches	4	5	6	8	10	12
Weight, ounces	2	2	4	7	10	20
Price, each	8c	8c	$0.09	$0.11	$0.15	$0.21
Per dozen	94c	95c	1.06	1.32	1.74	2.42

No. 35C824 The Fulton Brand Half Round Wood Rasps.

Size, inches	8	10	12	14
Weight, ounces	6	11	18	24
Price, each	$0.17	$0.23	$0.32	$0.42
Per dozen	2.02	2.74	3.74	4.96

No. 35C826 The Fulton Brand Half Round Cabinet Rasp, same shape as wood rasps, but not so coarse cut.

Size, inches	6	8	10	12	14
Price, each	$0.17	$0.22	$0.30	$0.38	$0.50
Per dozen	2.02	2.56	3.50	4.56	5.92

For Horse Rasps, see Blacksmith Tool Department.
For Horse Tooth Rasps, consult the index.

No. 35C828 The Fulton Brand Half Round Cabinet Files.

Size, inches	8	10	12
Price, each	$0.17	$0.23	$0.32
Per dozen	2.02	2.74	3.74

No. 35C832 The Fulton Brand Cant Saw Files

Size, inches	5	6	8	10
Price, each	$0.09	$0.09	$0.11	$0.15
Per dozen	.98	1.08	1.28	1.74

No. 35C837 Fulton Brand Band Saw Files.

Size, inches	4	5	6	8
Price, each	$0.05	$0.06	$0.08	$0.12
Per dozen	.58	.70	.94	1.34

No. 35C840 Fulton Safe Back Cant Saw Files, especially adapted for Disston's No. 120 Saw. Size, 6 inches. Price, per dozen, **$1.10**; each..........**10c**

No. 35C841 Fulton Great American File. Especially adapted for great American tooth saw.

Size, inches	8	10
Price, each	$0.13	$0.16
Per dozen	1.50	1.82

Needle Files.

No. 35C850 Needle Files, with Wire Handles; assorted, two each—flat, square, round, half round and oval; one each—three square and knife; sold only in above assortment. We positively will not break packages. Price, per doz., assorted as above, **67c**

File Brushes.

No. 35C858 File Brush or Cleaner. Steel wire set in leather. The most durable file brush in the market. Price..........**9c**

File Handles.

No. 35C860 File Handles. Large, medium or small. Weight, 2 ounces. Price, per dozen, **9c**; each.......**1c**

No. 35C869 File Handle and Tool Holder, malleable iron, 5 inches long, japanned finish. It will hold equally well all sizes files, twist drills, gimlets, screwdrivers and all tools with shanks less than ⅜ of an inch square, round or flat. Weight, 6 ounces. Price..........**8c**

EMERY WHEELS.

The Emerundum Wheel is made especially for us and they give satisfaction as a general purpose wheel. Remember, no one has yet succeeded in making one wheel that will do all kinds of work satisfactorily. The wheel that is best for grinding tools will be unsatisfactory on rough castings. When ordering state what kind of work wheel is wanted for and give size of mandrel hole.

Price List of Emerundum Emery Wheels.

No. 35C870 Flat Face. **No. 35C871** Bevel Face. **No. 35C872** Round Face.

Diam. Wheel	Thickness ¼	⅜	½	⅝	¾	1	1¼	1½	2	2½	3
2	$0.09	$0.11	$0.12	$0.13	$0.14	$0.15	$0.16	$ 0.17	$ 0.20	......	......
2½	.10	.14	.16	.17	.18	.21	.23	.26	.30	......	......
3	.12	.16	.20	.22	.23	.27	.30	.34	.41	......	......
3½	.15	.20	.23	.26	.27	.33	.38	.42	.52	......	......
4	.18	.23	.27	.30	.33	.39	.45	.51	.63	$ 0.75	$ 0.87
5	.24	.29	.34	.39	.44	.53	.63	.72	.92	1.10	1.30
6	.34	.39	.42	.51	.58	.72	.89	1.05	1.35	1.65	1.94
8	.50	.56	.62	.74	.86	1.10	1.35	1.58	2.05	2.42	2.90
10	.72	.76	.80	1.00	1.15	1.42	1.80	2.10	2.67	3.46	4.10
12	.....	.80	.84	1.15	1.26	1.55	1.89	2.25	2.94	3.65	4.35
14	.....	.....	1.31	1.54	1.77	2.24	2.70	3.15	4.05	5.00	5.90
16	.....	.....	.....	.....	2.28	2.88	3.48	4.08	5.25	6.45	7.65
18	.....	.....	.....	.....	2.48	3.17	3.87	4.57	6.15	7.37	8.75
20	.....	.....	.....	.....	.....	3.55	4.34	5.14	6.70	8.28	9.85
22	.....	.....	.....	.....	.....	4.38	5.43	6.48	8.58	10.68	12.72
24	.....	.....	.....	.....	.....	5.08	6.30	7.53	9.98	12.43	14.93
26	.....	.....	.....	.....	.....	.....	7.53	8.93	11.73	14.53	17.30
30	.....	.....	.....	.....	.....	.....	.....	10.68	14.53	18.38	22.20
36	.....	.....	.....	.....	.....	.....	.....	.....	22.05	27.50	32.90

DIRECTIONS FOR ORDERING. In ordering always give the details of the work to be ground, whether iron or steel and whether surface or edge work and if for wet or dry grinding. ALSO GIVE THE DIAMETER, THICKNESS, SIZE OF HOLE AND SHAPE OF FACE AND SPEED OF WHEEL. Manufacturers may send us orders giving full details as above with the understanding that they are to test THE STAR wheel with any other and if THE STAR does not turn out as much or more work in the same time they may return it to us and we will refund the price paid and stand transportation charges both ways. Many manufacturers have done this to THEIR ADVANTAGE.

The Star Wheel is a time saver and "time is money." Piece workers can earn more money with the Star Wheel than with any other. The Star is made in various grades to suit any kind of work. Our grades are so carefully selected there is absolutely no kind of work that we cannot suit. Every Star Wheel is guaranteed to be satisfactory on the work it is ordered for, but if you do not state fully the work the wheel is for we do not guarantee it.

We carry in stobk flat and round face, in all sizes that are commonly sold. Other sizes and grades will be shipped direct from factory, from which point purchaser pays the freight.

Price List of The Star Wheels.

No. 35C873 Flat Face. **No. 35C874** Bevel Face **No. 35C875** Round Face.

Before writing order read note at bottom of preceding page.

Diam.	Thickness.										
	¼	⅜	½	⅝	¾	1	1¼	1½	2	2½	3
2	$0.11	$0.14	$0.15	$0.17	$0.18	$0.19					
2½	.12	.17	.20	.21	.22	.26					
3	.15	.20	.24	.27	.29	.33	$0.38	$0.42			
3½	.18	.24	.29	.32	.33	.41	.47	.53			
4	.23	.29	.33	.38	.41	.48	.56	.63	$0.78		
5	.30	.36	.42	.48	.54	.66	.78	.90	1.14		
6	.42	.48	.53	.63	.72	.92	1.11	1.31	1.70	$2.09	
8	.63	.71	.78	.93	1.08	1.38	1.68	1.98	2.58	3.18	$3.78
10	.90	1.01	1.10	1.31	1.50	1.91	2.31	2.72	3.35	4.34	5.15
12	1.08	1.14	1.20	1.65	1.80	2.22	2.70	3.21	4.20	5.22	6.23
14		1.55	1.88	2.21	2.54	3.20	3.86	4.52	5.84	7.16	8.48
16					3.26	4.11	4.97	5.82	7.50	9.24	10.95
18					3.98	5.10	6.23	7.35	9.60	11.85	14.10
20						6.08	7.43	8.78	11.48	14.18	16.88
22								11.10	14.70	18.30	21.90
24								12.90	17.10	21.30	25.50

Do not forget to state fully what the wheel is to be used for.

Emery Wheel Dresser.

No. 35C947 Emery Wheel Dresser. It removes glaze and leaves the wheel clean and sharp and in the best possible condition for cutting. Price, with two sets cutters.......**37c**

No. 35C948 The Genuine Huntington Extra Cutters. Made by the Chicago Screw Co. Will fit any Huntington Dresser; quality the best.
Price, per 100 sets, **$6.00**; per dozen sets, **78c**; per set....**7c**

Emery Wheel Stands.

No. 35C891 Emery Wheel Stand for power. Will run two 6-inch emery wheels, 1-inch thick; has ⅜-inch steel spindle, ½ inch between flanges. Pulley, 2 inches in diameter, 1⅜-inch face. Weight, 8 pounds. Price......**$2.15**
Price does not include wheels.

No. 35C892 Will run two wheels 10 inches in diameter and 1½ inches thick, has steel spindle ⅞ inch in diameter in bearings, ¾ inch between flanges. The bearings are 2 inches long and adjustable; mounted with brass oil cups. Pulleys, 2¼ inches diameter, 1¾-inch face. Two adjustable knuckle joint rests, as shown in illustration. Weight, 18 pounds. Price.......**$4.65**

No. 35C893 Emery Wheel Stand. Will run two wheels 12 inches in diameter and 2 inches thick; has steel spindles 18 inches long and 1 1-16 inches diameter in bearings, 1 inch between flanges. The bearings are 2¼ inches long and same style as engine lathe bearings, mounted with brass oil cups. Pulleys, 3½ inches diameter, 2¼-inch face. Weight, 38 lbs. Price.......**$7.20**

No. 35C894 Emery Wheel Stand. Will run two wheels 16 inches in diameter and 2½ inches thick, has steel spindles 1⅜ inches diameter in bearings, 1¼ inches between flanges. The bearings are 4 inches long and same style as engine lathe bearings, mounted with brass oil cups. Pulley, 5 inches diameter, 4¼-inch face. These stands are provided with two rests which are knuckle jointed and can be set at any desired angle. Weight, 76 pounds. Price.......**$9.50**

Counter Shafting.

No. 35C911 Counter Shaft. The shaft is ⅞ inch in diameter; fast and loose pulleys, 3¾ inch in diameter, 1¾-inch face; driving pulley, 8 inches in diameter, 1¾-inch face; suitable for No. 35C891 grinder. Weight, 21 pounds. Price.....**$2.75**

No. 35C912 Counter Shaft. The shaft is 1⅛ inch in diameter; fast and loose pulleys, 5 inches in diameter, 2¼-inch face; driving pulley, 10 inches diameter, 2¼-inch face, suitable for No. 35C892 grinder. Weight, 34 pounds. Price.......**$4.10**

No. 35C913 Counter Shaft. The shaft is 1¼ inches in diameter; fast and loose pulleys, 6 inches in diameter, 3-inch face; driving pulley, 12 inches in diameter, 2¾-inch face; suitable for No. 35C893. Weight, 49 pounds. Price.......**$5.45**

No. 35C914 Counter Shaft. Shaft is 1½ inches in diameter; fast and loose pulleys, 6 inches in diameter, 4½-inch face; driving pulley, 16 inches in diameter, 4-inch face. Suitable for No. 35C894 grinder. Weight, 75 pounds. Price.......**$7.50**

Polishing Heads.

No. 35C925 Polishing Head. Height, 6 inches; length of spindle, 9 inches; taper left hand screw, 2½ inches long. Drill chuck and collars on other end. Pulley, 2 inches in diameter, for cord or belt. Weight, 3 pounds. Price.......**73c**

Emery Oil Stones.

No. 35C961 The Lightning rapidity with which they sharpen a tool, without taking the temper from the steel, is marvelous. A keen edge may be obtained in half the time required by the use of the quarried stone. They are made with a coarse and fine side, thus combining two stones in one, the coarse side to be used for taking out nicks and for rapid cutting; the fine side for putting on a fine, keen edge.

Length, inches	8	6
Width, inches	2	2
Thickness, inches	1	¾
Price	**20c**	**17c**

OIL STONES.

QUICK CUT oil stones—the best oil stones on the market for general purposes. Guaranteed to give satisfaction. Fine grit, fast cutters. Use lard oil; if necessary, reduce with alcohol. If used with water only they surpass the ordinary oil stone.

No. 35C980 Quick Cut Oil Stones, mounted in a finely finished chestnut case.

Size of stone	Price
3½x1½	**11c**
6 x2	**20c**
7 x2	**24c**
8 x2	**26c**

No. 35C981 Quick Cut Oil Stones, without case.

Size	Price
5x1½x ⅝	**8c**
8x2 x ⅝	**16c**
8x2 x1½	**24c**

No. 35C982 Lily White Oil Stone, is perfectly white, of uniform texture, free from foreign substances. It is the most satisfactory oil stone for carpenters' and general woodworkers' tools. It is a soft, free grit, quick cutting stone. Weight, about 1 pound. Price.......**45c**

No. 35C983 Lily White Oil Stone, soft, free grit. Weight, about 1½ pounds. Price.......**68c**

No. 35C984 Lily White Oil Stone, medium hard, fine grit. Will stand under a tool of hard temper and give a very smooth edge. Weight, about 1 pound. Price.......**45c**

No. 35C985 Lily White Oil Stone, medium hard, fine grit. Weight, about 1½ pounds. Price.......**68c**

No. 35C988 Soft Arkansas Oil Stone, weight about 1 pound. Price.......**$1.08**

No. 35C989 Soft Arkansas Oil Stone, weight about 1½ pounds. Price.......**$1.83**

No. 35C998 Washita Oil Stone, extra select quality stones, weighing about 1 pound. Price.......**27c**

No. 35C999 Washita Oil Stone, extra select quality, weighing about 1½ pounds. Price.......**41c**

No. 35C1012 Round Edge Washita Slips, same quality as our Washita Oil Stones. From 5 to 5½ inches long. Price.......**16c**

Grindstones and Fixtures.

No. 35C1025 Kitchen Grindstone with water trough and frame, as illustrated; solid first quality stone. Malleable iron mountings. Will put a keen edge on all kinds of tools.

Diam. of Stone..	6-in.	8-in.	10-in.
Price	**63c**	**83c**	**$1.05**

Mounted Grindstones, complete; frame, foot power, crank and fixtures. It is taken apart for shipment, but it is quickly and easily set up. The usual thickness of stones is from 1¾ to 2½ inches. Nothing but a select grade of first quality stone used. We do not sell second quality stones. **Furnished with malleable iron fixtures.**

No. 35C1031 No. 1 stone, Weighs 100 to 110 pounds. Price.......**$3.20**

No. 35C1032 No. 2 stone. Weighs 70 to 80 lbs. Price, **$3.00**

No. 35C1033 No. 3 stone. Weighs 40 to 60 lbs. Price, **$2.85**

No. 35C1038 Unmounted Grindstones of the best quality Huron grit, without frame or fixtures of any kind. Weight, from 40 to 200 pounds. Price, per pound.......**1¼c**

No. 35C1039 Lathe Grindstones, fine, even grit, free from gravel or hard spots. Every one turned true; far better than an emery wheel for putting a cutting edge on tools.

Diameter, inches	6	8	10	12
Thickness, inches	1 to 1½	1 to 1¾	1¼ to 1¾	1¼ to 2
Price	**50c**	**54c**	**62c**	**75c**

No. 35C1040 Grindstone Fixtures. No danger of splitting stone as is the case when a common shaft is used and held with wood wedges.

Inches long	15	17	19	21
Weight, lbs.	5½	6½	7	8
For stone, lbs.	40	60	80	100
Price	**27c**	**29c**	**32c**	**36c**

No. 35C1041 Extra Heavy Grindstone Fixtures, with extra heavy broad faced turned anti-friction rollers; much stronger and better than fixtures quoted above.

Length of shaft, inches	19	21	24	28
Weight, pounds	11¼	12	12½	13½
Suitable for stone, pounds	150	175	200	225
Price, per set	**66c**	**72c**	**81c**	**90c**

No. 35C1048 Double Treadle Grindstone, with wrought steel frame and seat. Weight of stone, 50 to 60 pounds. Price, complete, **$3.60**

No. 35C1049 Double Treadle Grindstone, with wrought steel frame, (as illustrated) and ball bearings. Price.......**$3.85**

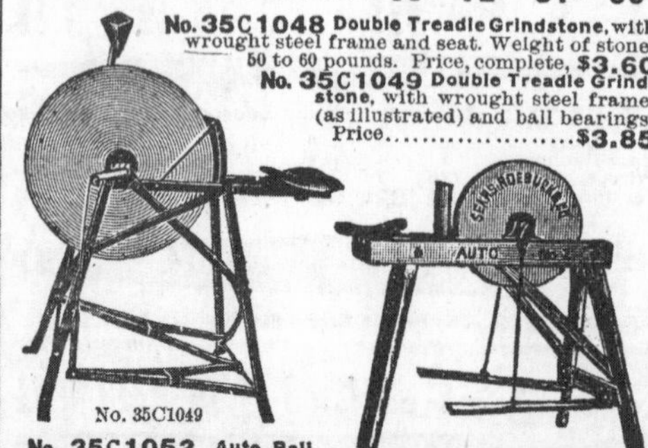

No. 35C1049

No. 35C1052 Auto Ball Bearing Grindstone. The frame is extra heavy, made of seasoned hardwood, fitted with detachable fixtures, with ball bearings on the pitman rods as well as on the shaft. It has a comfortable saddle. The usual thickness of stones is from 1¾ to 2½ inches. They are shipped "knocked down," but can be easily and quickly set up by anyone.

Size stone, pounds	100 to 110	70 to 80	40 to 50
Price	**$3.60**	**$3.45**	**$3.35**

No. 35C1053 The Gem Mounted Grindstone with unbreakable malleable iron fixtures. Adapted to all kinds of light grinding, sickles, scythes, axes, tools, knives, etc. One person supplies the power and does the grinding. No assistant necessary, runs the stone at much greater speed and performs faster and better work than with the ordinary grindstone. Weight, securely crated for shipment, about 75 pounds.
Price, complete.......**$2.85**

No. 35C1054 The Gem Mounted Grindstone with ball bearings.
Price, complete.......**$3.10**

Leveling Instrument.

This instrument consists of a tripod, to the head of which is connected an upper plate carrying a graduated arc and an iron level with a plain sight tube. The tripod is of iron, and has improved extension legs. The upper parts are hollow to receive within them the lower parts, which may be held at any desired length by clamp screws. The upper plate is connected to the tripod head by a ball and socket joint, and can be leveled by the leveling screws. This plate is recessed to contain a graduated arc below its upper surface, and has a center stud on which the arc and level turn. The graduated arc is of steel, and has on it one-half of a circumference divided to degrees and properly numbered. This arc turns on the center stud of the upper plate, independent of the level or sight tube. The sight tube is a brass tube 12 inches long, and in one end is a small eye aperture, while the other end has the usual cross wires. With long extension legs, the height can be adjusted from 2 feet 8 inches to 4 feet 8 inches. The sight tube, level case and graduated arcs are nickel plated, the other parts are japanned. Put up in a nicely finished box. Weight, boxed, about 15 pounds.

No. 35C1058 Price for instrument complete...$10.00

Cook's Patent Levels.

The bulb tube is set in a frame, which is faced on either side with glass and can be seen from any position, and shows the bulb in a clear light. It can be used in many positions which would not be possible with the ordinary level. Two bulb tubes are used, one for leveling and one for plumbing. The inside ring being made of solid drawn brass, and so made as to fit in the grooves of the outside ring, it must necessarily turn on its own center to adjust, which can be done by turning the adjusting screws, one of which reaches to either edge of the stock.

No. 35C1060 Cook's Patent Level, cherry with brass trimmings. Lengths, 24, 26, 28 or 30 inches. Price.......**$1.60**

No. 35C1066 Cook's Patent Level, mahogany strips glued together to prevent warping. Lengths, 24, 26, 28 or 30 inches. Price.......**$2.33**

STANLEY'S PLUMBS AND LEVELS.

All wood levels made by The Stanley Rule and Level Co. have the "Handy" feature. In climbing ladders, walking on stagings or on the frame of a building, the peculiar form of the level is appreciated by the workman who carries it. We have these levels made with proved level glasses on account of their increased strength and accuracy.

No. 35C1072 Stanley's Level. Cherry stained, without plumb. **Has groove for hand hold; not shown in illustration.** Proved glass; not adjustable. Weight, about 1 pound. Length, 12 inches. Price.......**19c**

No. 35C1075 Stanley's Plumb and Level. Mahogany polished. **Proved glasses;** not adjustable; arch top plate; two side views. Weighs about 2½ lbs. Lengths, 24, 26, 28 or 30 in. Price, **37c**

No. 35C1077 Stanley's Adjustable Plumb and Level. Polished, proved glasses, adjustable **arch top plate,** two brass lipped side views. Weighs about 3¼ lbs. Lengths, 24, 26, 28 and 30 in. Price **53c**

No. 35C1080 Stanley's Adjustable Plumb and Level. Mahogany polished, **proved glasses, arch top plates,** two side views, tipped. Weighs about 3¼ lbs. Lengths, 26, 28 or 30 in. Price, **61c**

No. 35C1082 Stanley's Adjustable Plumb and Level. Made of three pieces glued together so it cannot warp or spring; arch top plate; two ornamental brass lipped side views; proved glasses; polished and tipped. Weight, about 3¼ pounds. Lengths, 26, 28 or 30 inches. Price.......**91c**

Stanley's Duplex Plumbs and Levels.

These levels have the ordinary form of leveling glass set in the top surface of the stock. For any uses where an observation of the glass, sidewise, may be found convenient, an additional leveling glass is set in the side, at the opposite end from the plumb. Both glasses are protected by brass discs; can be seen from either side, and are inserted in the level with the least possible removal of wood from the stock.

No. 35C1088 Stanley's Duplex Patent Adjustable Plumb and Level, cherry, arch top plate, improved duplex side views, polished and tipped. Lengths, 24, 26, 28 or 30 inches. Price....**91c**

No. 35C1089 Stanley's Duplex Patent Adjustable Plumb and Level, cherry, and made of three pieces glued together. Arch top plate, improved duplex side views, polished and tipped. Lengths, 24, 26, 28 or 30 inches. Price.......**$1.21**

Plumbs and Levels with Ground Glasses.

The inside surfaces of these glasses are ground perfectly smooth, making the bubble extremely sensitive.

No. 35C1093 Stanley's Mahogany Plumb and Level, arch top plate, two brass lipped side views, tipped with ground glasses. Lengths, 24, 26, 28 or 30 inches. Price $1.84

No. 35C1095 Stanley's Brass Bound Mahogany Plumb and Level, two brass lipped side views, with ground glasses. Lengths, 24, 26, 28 or 30 inches. Price $3.40

No. 35C1097 Stanley's Masons' Plumb and Level, with arch top plate, two side views and adapted to be used with a plumb bob and line. Plumbs and level glasses are adjustable and can be trued up when necessary in a few moments with an ordinary screwdriver. 42 inches long. **Plumb bob and line shown in illustration not furnished at price of level.** Price 88c

No. 35C1104 Stanley's Improved Level Sights, when adjusted to an ordinary carpenters' level, afford a convenient and accurate means for leveling from one given point to another at a distance away. The price given below is for sights only. Level is not included. Price per pair, for wood levels, 46c

No. 35C1105 Stanley's Improved Level Sights for iron levels. Price, per pair 46c

No. 35C1106 Stanley's Iron Level. Japanned, nickel plated trimmings, with proved glasses, two plumbs.

Size, inches	6	9	12	18	24
Price	61c	76c	91c	$1.06	$1.21

No. 35C1107 Stanley's Iron Level; nickel plated, with ground glasses and Eclipse cases; two plumbs. The outer shell of the level case can be turned so as to completely protect the glass from damage when not in use.

Length, in.	12	18	24
Price	$1.82	$2.12	$2.42

No. 35C1113 Davis' Machinists' Adjustable Iron Plumb and Level and Inclinometer.

Length, inches	6	12	18	24
Price	$1.80	$2.25	$2.70	$3.15

No. 35C1117 Stanley's Eclipse Levels. The outer shell of the level case can be turned so as to completely protect the glass from damage when not in use. Nickel plated, with ground glasses and V bottoms (for leveling shafing, etc.)

Size, inches	4	6	8	10
Price	61c	76c	$1.06	$1.37

No. 35C1123 Stanley's Pocket Level, which can be quickly attached to the edge of a steel square or a straight edge. Body is iron, brass top plate. Weight, 3 ounces. Price 7c

No. 35C1150 Japanned Iron Plumb Bob. Adjusted top.

Weight	9 oz.	1 lb.	2 lbs.
Price	5c	9c	13c
Weight, lbs.	3	4	
Price	20c	27c	

No. 35C1151 Iron Plumb Bobs, accurately made from fine quality soft gray iron, highly finished in full nickel plate.

Weight, oz.	5	13½
Each	8c	11c

No. 35C1152 Cast Brass Plumb Bob, with hardened steel point, screw top.

No. 35C1150 No. 35C1152 No. 35C1160

Weight, ounces	6	11½	16
Price	26c	39c	43c

No. 35C1160 Machinists' Plumb Bobs; brass, highly polished, with steel points.

Weight, ounces	2	3	4	6	8
Price	32c	35c	38c	47c	64c
Weight, ounces	10	12	16	20	24
Price	79c	90c	$1.10	$1.32	$1.53

Carpenters' Boxwood Rules.

Our Carpenters' Boxwood Rules are manufactured by The Stanley Rule & Level Co., and cost more and are worth more than other makes. Remember this when comparing our prices with those of other houses.

Drafting Scales are used for laying out work where a scale of ⅛-inch, ¼-inch, ⅜-inch or 1-inch to the foot is found convenient.

Octagonal Scales are used to lay out eight-square work, from 1-inch to 24 or 34-inch diameter.

No. 35C1176 Stanley's Two-Foot Rule. No. 68. Round joint, middle plates, spaced 8ths and 16ths, four-fold, 1 inch wide. Weight, 3 ounces. Price, per dozen, 88c; each 8c

No. 35C1182 Stanley's Two-Foot Rule. No. 63. Square joints, edge plates at joints, spaced 8ths, 10ths, 12ths and 16ths, with drafting scale, four-fold, 1-inch wide. Weight, 4 ounces. Price, per dozen, $1.42; each 12c

No. 35C1184 Stanley's Two-Foot Rule. No. 72. Square joints, edge plates at joints, spaced 8ths, 10ths and 16ths, and drafting scale, four-fold, 1⅜ inches wide. Weight, 4 ounces. Price per dozen, $1.77; each 15c

No. 35C1186 Stanley's Two-Foot Rule. No. 62. Square joints, full brass bound, spaced 8ths, 10ths, 12ths and 16ths, and drafting scale, four-fold, 1-inch wide. Price, per dozen, $2.83; each 24c

No. 35C1193 Stanley's Two-Foot Rule. No. 52. Arch joints, outside edges brass bound, spaced 8ths, 10ths, 12ths and 16ths and drafting scale, four-fold, 1-inch wide. Price, per dozen, $2.48; each 21c

No. 35C1196 Stanley's Two-Foot Rule. No. 54. Arch full brass bound, spaced 8ths, 10ths, 12ths and 16ths, and joints, drafting scale, four-fold, 1-inch wide. Price, per dozen, $3.02; each 26c

No. 35C1199 Stanley's Two-Foot Rule. No. 76. Arch joint, full brass bound, spaced 8ths, 10ths, 16ths, and drafting scales, four-fold, 1⅜ inches wide. Price, per dozen, $3.54; each 30c

No. 35C1200 Stanley's Two-Foot Rule. No. 78½. Double arch joints, full brass bound, spaced 8ths, 10ths and 16ths, drafting scale, four-fold, 1⅜ inches wide. **The best boxwood rule made.** Price, per dozen, $4.25; each 36c

No. 35C1198 Stanley Two-Foot Rule. No. 60. Double arch joints, full brass bound; spaced, 8ths, 10ths, 12ths and 16ths, and drafting scale. Four-fold, 1 inch wide. Price, per dozen, $3.73; each 32c

No. 35C1201 Stanley's Blindman's Rule. No. 7. Two foot, four (4) fold; square joints, spaced 8ths and 16ths inches, 1⅜ inches wide; rule is very light yellow and figures are black. Price, per dozen, $3.90; each 33c

No. 35C1202 Rule is a combination of a carpenter's rule, spirit level, square, plumb, bevel, inclinometer, brace scale, drafting scale, T-square, protractor, right angled triangle. Full directions for use furnished with each rule. One foot, two-fold. Width, 1⅜ inches. Thickness, ⅜-inch. Weight, 7ozs. Price, each.. $1.60

No. 35C1204 Stanley's Three-Foot, Four-Fold Rule. No. 66½. Arch joint middle plates, four-folds, spaced 8ths and 16ths. 1 inch wide. Price, per dozen, $1.77; each 15c

No. 35C1207 Stanley's Carriage Makers' Four-Foot, Four-Fold Rule. No. 94. Arch joint, bound, spaced 8ths and 16ths 1⅜ inches wide. Price, per dozen. $8.50; each 72c

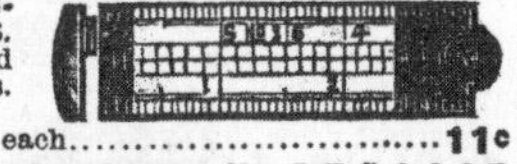

No. 35C1214 Stanley's One-Foot Caliper Rule. No. 32½. Arch joints, full brass bound, spaced 8ths, 10ths, 12ths and 16ths, four-fold; width, 1 inch. Price, per dozen, $3.54; each 30c

No. 35C1216 Stanley's One-Foot Caliper Rule. No. 32. Four-fold, arch joints, edge plates at joints, spaced in 8ths, 10ths, 12ths and 16ths. One inch wide. Price, per dozen, $2.13; each 18c

No. 35C1218 Stanley's 6-inch Caliper Rule. No. 36. Two-fold, square joints, spaced 8ths, 10ths, 12ths and 16ths. Width, ⅝ inch. Price, per dozen, $1.24; each 11c

No. 35C1225 Stanley's Two-Foot Architects' Rule. No. 53½. Arch joint, edge plates, spaced 8ths, 10ths, 12ths and 16ths, with inside beveled edges and architects' drafting scale, four-fold, 1 inch wide. Price, per dozen, $2.66; each 23c

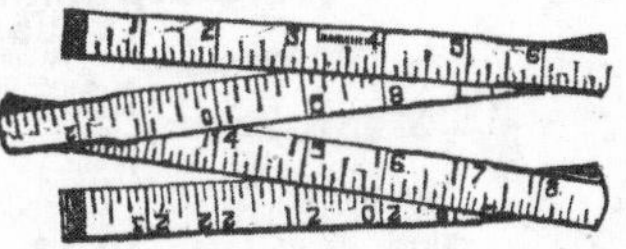

No. 35C1233 Stanley's Zigzag Rules. Much superior to the cheap imported rule of this style which is commonly sold.

Length, feet	2	3	4	5	6	8
Price, each	$0.10	$0.15	$0.19	$0.24	$0.29	$0.38
Per dozen	1.13	1.70	2.27	2.84	3.40	4.53

Measuring Tapes.

No. 35C1340 Pocket Tape. Nickel plated case; patent spring with stop. ⅝-inch linen tape. To measure 5 feet. Price 35c

No. 35C1344 Pocket Steel Tape. German silver cases, spring wind with stop. Marked one side only. Length, 50 inches with ¼-inch steel tape, marked inches and sixteenths. Price 75c

Brass bound case, folding handle, with ⅝-inch oiled cotton tape. **This is a good low priced tape for family use.** Millwrights, surveyors, and others who use line much should buy a higher priced one.

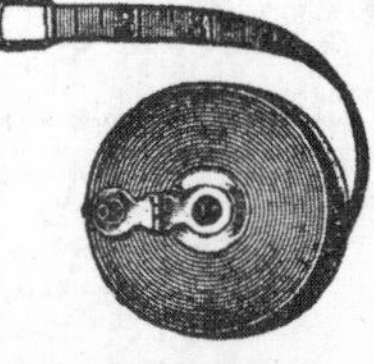

No. 35C1350 To measure 25 feet. Price 18c

No. 35C1351 To measure 50 feet. Price 24c

No. 35C1353 To measure 66 feet. Price 29c

No. 35C1354 To measure 100 feet. Price 43c

This Tape Line is a durable, reliable, accurate and strong tape line. A metallic warp is woven in with the linen, which prevents stretching. Has a heavy red leather case, folding handle; spaced in feet and 12ths of feet.

No. 35C1360 Metallic Warp Tape Line. To measure 50 feet. Price $1.90

No. 35C1362 To measure 66 feet. Price $2.28

No. 35C1363 To measure 100 feet. Price $3.04

Steel Tape Lines.

No. 35C1368 Steel Tape Lines with Leather Case. The measurements are guaranteed accurate. The case is compact, very durable and will not break. The winding drum is large, has a long crank, winds easily and the handle folds nearly flush with the case. We can safely recommend this tape to the purchaser as an article which is first class, durable and perfectly accurate. Marked feet and twelfths (inches) and eighths.

To measure feet	25	50	75	100
Price	$2.33	$2.85	$3.75	$4.82

Carpenters' Squares.

No. 35C1400 Iron Square. Body is 24 inches long, 1½ inches wide. Tongue is 12 inches long, 1 inch wide, spaced in 8ths on both sides. Not warranted. Price 22c

No. 35C1402 Iron Square. Body is 24 inches long, 2 inches wide. Tongue, 12 inches long, 1½ inches wide, spaced in eighths on both sides. Not warranted. Price 25c

Steel Squares.

Both body and tongue are tapered, the ends being thinner. This gives strength where it is needed, and makes square lighter than it would otherwise be. We guarantee these squares to be equal to any made, and exactly as represented.

No. 35C1409 Steel Square No. 7, extra quality, 2 inches wide, marked on both sides, spaced ⅛, ¼ and 1 inch, Essex new board measure, giving feet and inches in full. Size of body, 24x2 inches; size of tongue, 16x1½ inches. The face is marked ⅛-¼; back is marked, ¼-1-¼-⅛. Price 47c

No. 35C1412 Steel Square No. 3, extra quality; size of body, 24x2 inches; size of tongue, 16x1½. Marked on face, 1-16 ⅛ 1-16, marked on back, 1-12 ¼ 1-12 ¼; with brace measure and Essex new board measure, giving feet and inches in full. Price 55c

No. 35C1416 Nickel Plated Steel Square No. 103. Marked same as No. 35C1412. .... 70c

No. 35C1419 Nickel Plated Steel Square No. 103. Marked same as No. 35C1412, with 18-inch tongue. Price 71c

No. 35C1423 Blued Rustless Finish Steel Square No. 3. Marked same as No. 35C1412. Price 79c

No. 35C1426 Blued Rustless Finish Steel Square No. 3. Marked same as No. 35C1412, with 18-inch tongue. Price 80c

No. 35C1429 Blued Rustless Finish Steel Square No. 2. Body, 24x2; tongue, 16x1½; marked same as No. 35C1412, with rafter scale, giving length, pitch and bevel of rafters; easily understood by any carpenter and the most practical and desirable scale yet put on a steel square. Price 87c

No. 35C1431 Steel Square No. 100. Extra quality. Body, 24x2 inches; tongue, 16x1½; brace measure, 8 square and Essex board measure giving feet and inches in full; marked on face, 1-16 ⅛ 1-16 ⅛; marked on back, 1-12 1-32 1-12 1-10. Price 80c

No. 35C1433 Same Square as No. 35C1431, except it has an 18-inch tongue. Price 81c

No. 35C1436 Nickel Plated Steel Square No. 200. Marked same as No. 35C1431. Price $1.00

No. 35C1439 Nickel Plated Steel Square No. 200. Marked same as No. 35C1431, except it has an 18-inch tongue. Price $1.01

No. 35C1442 Blued Rustless Finish Steel Square No. 100. Marked same as No. 35C1431. Price $1.04

No. 35C1446 Blued Rustless Finish Steel Square No. 100. Marked same as No. 35C1431, except it has an 18-inch tongue. Price $1.05

No. 35C1450 Steel Square No. 112. Nickel plated. Size of body, 12x1½ inches; size of tongue, 8x1 inch. Marked on face, 1-16 ⅛ 1-16 ⅛; marked on back, 1-12 ⅛ 1-12 ⅛. This square will be found very convenient, as it may be put in an ordinary tool chest. Price 58c

Practical Use of the Steel Square.

In Two Volumes.

By Fred T. Hodgson. Complete modern treatise. It is thorough, accurate, clear, and easily understood. It is an exhaustive work, including a brief history of the squares that are now and have been in use, including some very ingenious devices for laying out bevels or rafters, braces and other inclined work; also chapters on the square as a calculating machine, showing how to measure solids, surfaces and distances—very useful to builders and estimators. Instructions on roofing and how to form them by the aid of the square. Octagon, hexagon, hip and other roofs are shown and explained, and the manner of getting the rafters and jacks given; on heavy timber framing, showing how the square is used for laying out mortises, tenons, shoulders, inclined work, angle corners and similar work, and thousands of other subjects too numerous to mention. Size, 5½x7 inches.

No. 3C09369 Volume 1, cloth. Retail price, $1.00. Our price 58c

No. 3C09370 Volume 2, cloth. Retail price, $1.00. Our price 58c

If by mail, postage extra, each, 12 cents.

Try Squares.

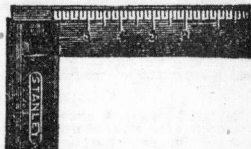

No. 35C1460 Stanley's Try Square. Brass lined rosewood handle, graduated steel blade. Square inside or out. Blade is measured from inside of handle.

Size blade, in.	4½	6	7½	9	12
Price, each	$0.11	$0.15	$0.16	$0.19	$0.25
Per dozen	1.28	1.70	1.86	2.21	2.89

No. 35C1462 Stanley's Try Square. Nickel plated, iron handle, graduated steel blade. Square inside and out. Blade is measured from inside of handle.

Size blade, inches	4	6	8
Price	13c	16c	20c

No. 35C1465 Stanley's Combined Try and Mitre Square, brass lined rosewood handle, graduated steel blade. Square inside and out. Blade is measured from outside of handle.

Size blade, inches	6	7½	9	12
Price, each	$0.19	$0.23	$0.27	$0.34
Per dozen	2.27	2.72	3.18	4.08

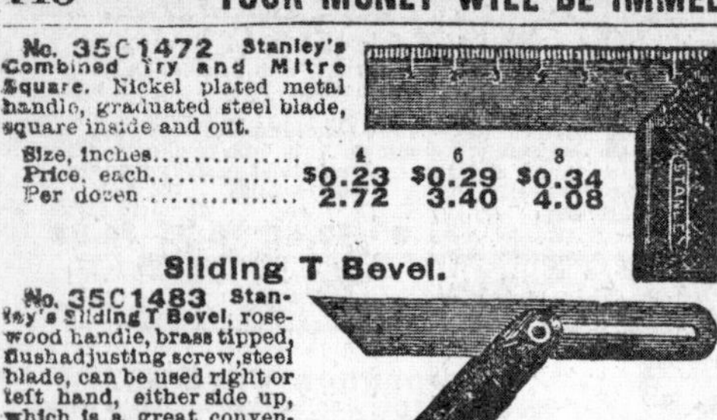

No. 35C1472 Stanley's Combined Try and Mitre Square. Nickel plated metal handle, graduated steel blade, square inside and out.

Size, inches	4	6	8
Price, each	$0.23	$0.29	$0.34
Per dozen	2.72	3.40	4.08

Sliding T Bevel.

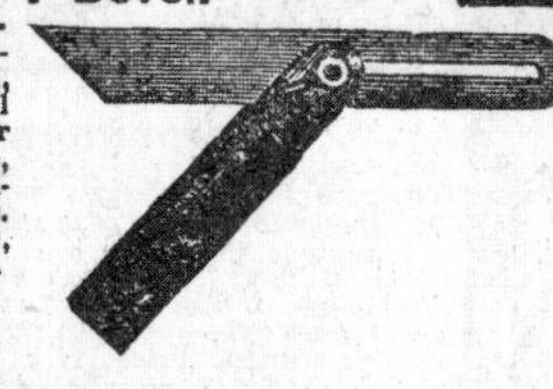

No. 35C1483 Stanley's Sliding T Bevel, rosewood handle, brass tipped, flush adjusting screw, steel blade, can be used right or left hand, either side up, which is a great convenience. Weight, 7 to 10 ozs.

Length, inches	Price, per dozen	Price, each
6	$1.67	14c
8	1.82	16c
10	1.97	17c
12	2.12	18c

Eureka Sliding T Bevel.

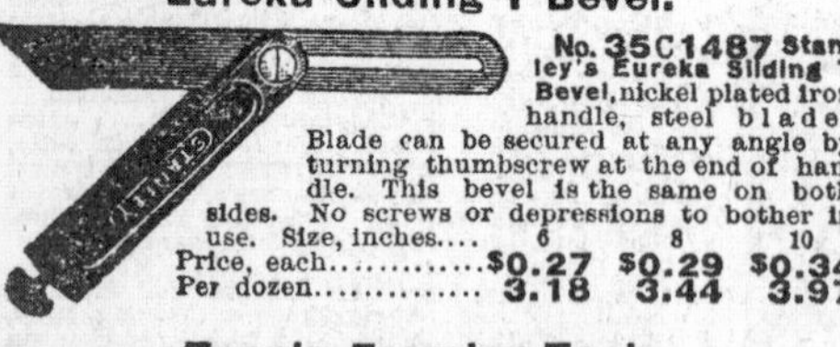

No. 35C1487 Stanley's Eureka Sliding T Bevel, nickel plated iron handle, steel blade. Blade can be secured at any angle by turning thumbscrew at the end of handle. This bevel is the same on both sides. No screws or depressions to bother in use.

Size, inches	6	8	10
Price, each	$0.27	$0.29	$0.34
Per dozen	3.18	3.44	3.97

Topp's Framing Tool.

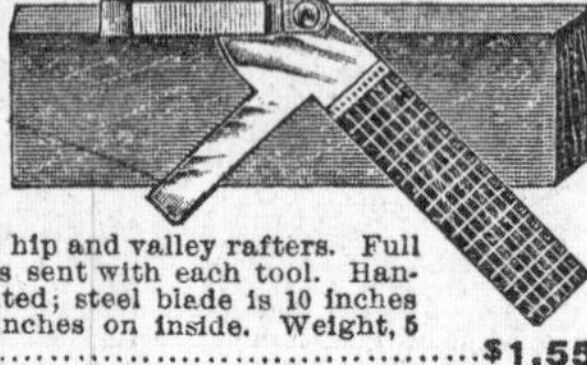

No. 35C1481 Topp's Framing Tool is a T Square, Try Square and Adjustable Bevel. It is graduated on one side of blade with pitches and scales used in cutting principal rafters; on the other side with pitches and scales used in cutting both jack and hip and valley rafters. Full and complete directions sent with each tool. Handle is wood, brass mounted; steel blade is 10 inches long on outside and 8 inches on inside. Weight, 5 ounces. Price $1.55

Marking Gauges.

No. 35C1488 Marking Gauge, beechwood bar and head, boxwood thumbscrew, marked bar. Steel point. Weight, 7 ounces.

Price, per dozen, 38c; each 4c

No. 35C1489 Stanley's Improved Marking Gauge, will run a gauge line with accuracy, either straight or around curves of any degree, either concave or convex; beechwood, boxwood thumbscrew, oval bar, marked in inches.

Price, per dozen, 76c; each 7c

No. 35C1492 Improved Marking Gauge, boxwood, brass thumbscrew and shoe, plated head, adjustable steel point.

Price, per dozen, $2.65; each 23c

Marking and Mortise Gauge.

No. 35C1496 Stanley's Patent Mortise and Marking Gauge. Rosewood, plated head, improved screw slide, brass thumbscrew and shoe, oval bar, marked, steel points.

Price, per dozen, $3.78; each 32c

No. 35C1500 Stanley's Double Gauge. A marking and mortise gauge combined, beechwood, polished, boxwood thumbscrew, marked in inches.

Price, per dozen, $1.51; each 13c

Butt and Rabbet Gauges.

No. 35C1503 Stanley's Improved Butt and Rabbet Gauge. The most convenient gauge for hanging doors, mortising, marking, etc. Weight, 15 ounces.

Price, per dozen, $9.05; each 76c

No. 35C1505 Stanley's Improved Butt Gauge nickel plated. Has one bar with two steel cutters fixed upon it. When the cutter at the outer end of this bar is set for gauging on the edge of the door, the cutter at the inner end of the bar is already set for gauging from back of the jamb. The other bar has a steel cutter to accurately gauge for the thickness of the butt. It is so constructed that the bars cannot fall out of the stock.

Price, per dozen, $5.43; each 46c

Marking Gauges.

No. 35C1512 Barrett's Combination Marking and Mortise Roller Gauge. Made entirely of metal. The marker is a revolving steel wheel, which will not follow the grain of the wood. Wgt., 15 oz. Price, 64c

Clapboard Tools.

No. 35C1526 Clapboard or Siding Gauge or Holder, is used as shown in illustration. When in this position, press the handle over sidewise and it will be held securely. Two of them are as good as an extra man. Adjustable to lay clapboards to the weather any width desired. Price, each $0.31
Per dozen 3.62

No. 35C1530 Clapboard Marker. By moving this tool half an inch (when placed in position as shown) it will make a full line across the clapboard exactly over the edge of the corner board. Saw to the mark and you have a perfectly close joint.

Price, per dozen, $3.62; each 31c

Shingling Brackets.

No. 35C1536 Stanley's Shingling Brackets. The parts are of spring steel, firmly riveted together. Light, strong, safe. Quickly put up and taken down, leaving no nail holes in the roof. Will pay for themselves in laying twenty thousand shingles and last a lifetime. Price, per dozen, $1.81; each 16c

Awls and Blades.

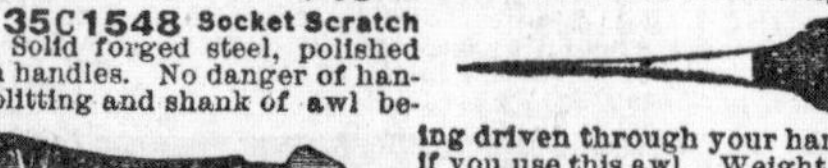

No. 35C1540 Handled Brad Awls, steel shouldered awl, polished handle with ferrule. Sizes, small, medium and large. Weight, 6 ounces. Price, per dozen, 45c; each 4c

No. 35C1548 Socket Scratch Awl. Solid forged steel, polished beech handles. No danger of handle splitting and shank of awl being driven through your hand if you use this awl. Weight, 8 ounces. Price, each 9c

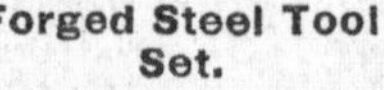

Awl and Tool Set.

No. 35C1560 Awl and Tool Sets, with forged steel awls and tools. Hollow cocobolo handle, which holds tools when not in use. Very convenient and serviceable. Weight, 9 ounces. Price 32c

Forged Steel Tool Set.

No. 35C1562 Forged Steel Tools. Handle is hollow to hold tools. Tools are 4½ inches long, forged from regular tool steel, hardened in oil and carefully finished.

Price, complete 70c

Chalk Line Reel and Awl.

No. 35C1572 Beechwood Chalk Line Reel and Awl. Weight, 6 ounces.
Price for both 5c

No. 35C1549 Steel Scratch Awl, with beech handle and brass ferrule.
Price 3c

Braided Cotton Chalk Lines.

No. 35C1575 Braided Cotton Chalk Lines, in hanks of 18 feet each. One dozen hanks connected. Braided lines do not kink or snarl.

	Small	Medium	Large
Price, per hank	2c	3c	4c
Per dozen hanks	24c	30c	38c

Carpenters' Chalk.

Six dozen in a box.

		Per doz.	Per box
No. 35C1577	White	2c	12c
No. 35C1578	Red	2c	16c
No. 35C1579	Blue	3c	19c

Carpenters' Pencils.

No. 3C05880 Carpenters' Pencils, oval, polished cedar; 7 inches long. Weight, per dozen, 8 ounces.
Price, per gross, $2.25; per dozen, 20c; half dozen 12c

No. 3C05882 Carpenters' Pencils, oval, polished cedar, 9 inches long, best quality lead. Weight, per dozen, 7 ounces.
Price, per gross, $2.45; per dozen, 25c; six for 15c

No. 3C05884 Carpenters' Pencils, polished cedar, 12 inches long, good quality lead. Weight, per dozen, 8 ounces.
Price, per gross, $3.25; per dozen, 30c; half dozen 18c
If by mail, postage extra for two, 2 cents.

Wing Dividers.

No. 35C1637 Wing Dividers, polished forged steel. Held at any desired point by a set screw. Thumbscrew for slight and accurate adjustment.

Size, inches	6	8	10
Weight, ounces	7	8	16
Price, each	$0.12	$0.16	$0.22
Per dozen	1.38	1.88	2.50

Wood Bench Planes.

Our Wood Bench Planes are correctly proportioned, nicely finished and furnished with warranted plane irons.

No. 35C1700 Beechwood Smooth Plane; length, 8¼ inches, 2-inch double iron; weight, 2½ lbs.
Price 44c

No. 35C1703 Beechwood Jack Plane; length, 16 inches, 2⅛-inch double iron; weight, 4½ pounds. Price 49c

No. 35C1706 Beechwood Fore Plane; length, 22 inches, 2⅜-inch double iron; weight, 6½ pounds. Price 68c

No. 35C1708 Beechwood Jointer Plane; length, 26 inches, 2⅜-inch double iron; weight, 9 pounds. Price 73c

No. 35C1709 Beechwood Jointer Plane; length, 28 inches, 2⅜-inch double iron; weight, 10 pounds. Price 77c

Plane Handles.

No. 35C1720 Jack Plane Handles; beechwood. Price 2c

No. 35C1721 Fore or Jointer Plane Handles; beechwood.
Price 4c

No. 35C1720 No. 35C1721

YOU BUY

FULTON BRAND TOOLS

from us with the understanding and agreement that if they are not entirely satisfactory to you, if you want to return them for any reason, or, without stating any reason, we will refund the price paid and also stand cost of transportation both ways. It is perfectly safe to buy Fulton tools.

The Fulton Planes.

The Fulton Planes are brought out to meet the demand for a reliable, good working plane at a moderate price. The irons are made of the best shear steel, carefully made and tempered by experts, and the planes are guaranteed to give satisfaction in general use.

. The Fulton Wood Bottom Planes. The bottoms are made of carefully selected, air seasoned beech. The castings are smooth and strong. The working parts are made by automatic machinery, and all parts are interchangeable. Repairs may be had from us at any time in the future, at reasonable prices.

Catalogue Number	Length, Inches		Width of Cutter, inches	Weight, pounds	Price, each
No. 35C1710	8	Smooth	1¾	2¾	63c
No. 35C1711	8	Smooth	2	3¼	64c
No. 35C1712	9	Handled Smooth	2	3¼	79c
No. 35C1713	10	Handled Smooth	2⅜	3½	86c

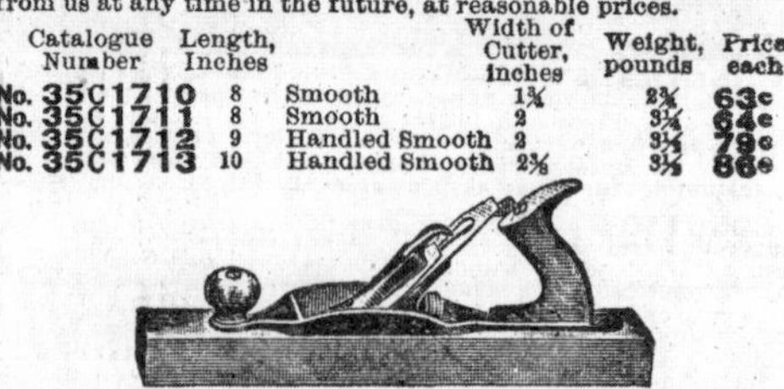

Catalogue Number	Length, inches		Width of Cutter, inches	Weight, pounds	Price, each
No. 35C1714	15	Jack	2	3¾	$0.71
No. 35C1715	15	Jack	2⅛	4	.79
No. 35C1716	15	Jack	2¼	4	.80
No. 35C1717	18	Fore	2⅜	4½	.86
No. 35C1718	20	Fore	2⅜	5¾	.87
No. 35C1719	22	Jointer	2⅜	6	.94
No. 35C1722	24	Jointer	2⅜	6½	.94
No. 35C1723	26	Jointer	2⅝	7¼	1.02
No. 35C1724	28	Jointer	2⅝	7¾	1.03
No. 35C1725	30	Jointer	2⅝	8¼	1.10

The Fulton Line of Iron Bench Planes.

The Fulton Iron Bench Planes are made of strong, smooth, heavy castings. The face is ground perfectly. The working parts are all made by automatic machinery, and all are interchangeable. While repairs will seldom, if ever, be needed, we can always furnish them at any time in the future at reasonable prices. The cutters are made from the best shear steel, carefully made, and tempered to cut and hold an edge. Every plane is guaranteed to give satisfaction in use. They are made with both smooth and corrugated bottoms, as described below.

The Fulton Iron Planes with Smooth Bottoms.

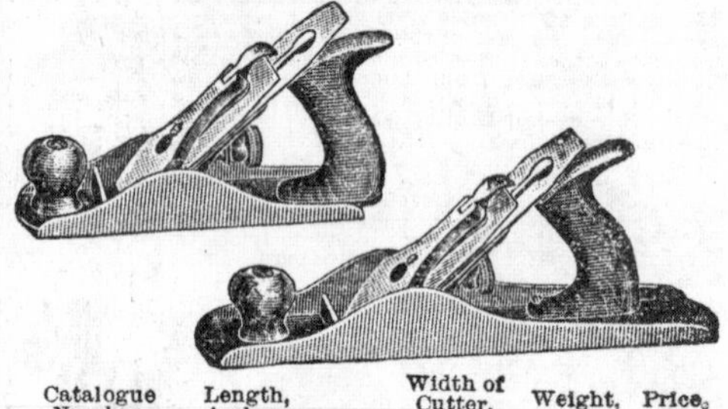

Catalogue Number	Length, inches		Width of Cutter, inches	Weight, pounds	Price, each
No. 35C1726	8	Smooth	1¾	3	$0.94
No. 35C1727	9	Smooth	2	3½	1.02
No. 35C1728	10	Smooth	2⅜	5	1.18
No. 35C1729	14	Jack	2	4¾	1.19
No. 35C1731	15	Jack	2¼	4¾	1.33
No. 35C1733	18	Fore	2⅜	7	1.49
No. 35C1735	22	Jointer	2⅜	8½	1.72
No. 35C1736	24	Jointer	2⅝	9¾	2.04

The Fulton Iron Planes with Corrugated Bottoms.

Catalogue Number	Length, inches		Width of Cutter, inches	Weight, pounds	Price, each
No. 35C1738	8	Smooth	1¾	3	$0.94
No. 35C1740	9	Smooth	2	3½	1.02
No. 35C1741	10	Smooth	2⅜	5	1.18
No. 35C1742	14	Jack	2	4¾	1.19
No. 35C1743	15	Jack	2¼	4¾	1.33
No. 35C1744	18	Fore	2⅜	7	1.49
No. 35C1745	22	Jointer	2⅜	8½	1.72
No. 35C1746	24	Jointer	2⅝	9¾	2.04

Bailey's Bench Planes.

The Genuine Bailey Planes, made by the Stanley Rule & Level Company, are so well and favorably known to mechanics the world over that they need no recommendation from us. The cutter is stamped from a solid piece of the best quality of English cast steel, of equal thickness throughout, finely tempered and ground sharp, ready for use. By means of a lever, located under the plane iron and working sidewise, the cutting edge can easily be brought into a position exactly square with the bottom of the plane. The patents having expired, planes of same style are made by various manufacturers and offered as Bailey pattern, or even for the genuine goods. We sell the genuine only.

Genuine Bailey Adjustable Smooth Planes. Order by catalogue number.

Catalogue Number	Stanley's Number	Length, inches	Width of Cutter	Weight, pounds	Price
35C1751	22 Smooth	8	1¾-inch	2¾	$0.76
35C1755	24 Smooth	8	2 -inch	3¼	.77
35C1760	35 Handle Smooth	9	2 -inch	3½	.97
35C1763	36 Handle Smooth	10	2⅜-inch	3½	1.0[illegible]

Genuine Bailey Adjustable Jack Fore and Jointer Planes, made by the Stanley Rule & Level Co. Order by catalogue number.

Catalogue Number	Stanley's Number		Length, inches	Width of Cutter	Weight, pounds	Price
35C1769	26	Jack	15	2 -inch	3¾	$0.85
35C1772	27	Jack	15	2⅛-inch	4	.96
35C1775	27½	Jack	15	2¼-inch	4	.97
35C1778	28	Fore	18	2⅜-inch	4½	1.05
35C1780	29	Fore	20	2⅜-inch	5¾	1.06
35C1782	30	Jointer	22	2⅜-inch	6	1.13
35C1784	31	Jointer	24	2⅜-inch	6½	1.14
35C1787	32	Jointer	26	2⅝-inch	7¼	1.25
35C1789	33	Jointer	28	2⅝-inch	7¾	1.26
35C1791	34	Jointer	30	2⅝-inch	8¼	1.33

The Genuine Bailey Adjustable Iron Bench Planes, made by the Stanley Rule & Level Co. Instructions for adjustment sent with each plane.

Catalogue Number	Stanley's Number		Length, inches	Width of Cutter	Weight, pounds	Price
35C1850	1	Smooth	5½	1¼-inch	1½	$0.85
35C1851	2	Smooth	7	1⅝-inch	2¼	1.05
35C1854	3	Smooth	8	1¾-inch	3	1.14
35C1856	4	Smooth	9	2- inch	3½	1.25
35C1859	4½	Smooth	10	2⅜-inch	5	1.41
35C1862	5	Jack	14	2- inch	4¾	1.42
35C1864	5½	Jack	15	2¼-inch	4¾	1.62
35C1867	6	Fore	18	2⅜-inch	7	1.81
35C1870	7	Jointer	22	2⅜-inch	8½	2.07
35C1873	8	Jointer	24	2⅝-inch	9¾	2.47
Bailey Iron Planes with Corrugated Bottom.						
35C1879	2c	Smooth	7	1⅝-inch	2¼	$1.05
35C1880	3c	Smooth	8	1¾-inch	3	1.14
35C1882	4c	Smooth	9	2- inch	3½	1.25
35C1885	4½c	Smooth	10	2⅜-inch	5	1.41
35C1889	5 c	Jack	14	2- inch	4¾	1.42
35C1892	5½c	Jack	15	2¼-inch	4¾	1.62
35C1895	6c	Fore	18	2⅜-inch	7	1.81
35C1898	7c	Jointer	22	2⅜-inch	8½	2.07
35C1899	8c	Jointer	24	2⅝-inch	9¾	2.47

Stanley's "Bed Rock" Planes.

The "Bed Rock" Planes are as solid as one-piece planes, but have more adjustments than any planes ever produced. The entire bottom surface of the frog and the seat of frog in plane body are machined and fitted accurately. The tongues and grooves on frog and in seat are also machined. There can be no shifting of the frog and it is always at a true right angle to the mouth. The cutting iron has the same solid bed as if resting on the plane body itself. With the "Bed Rock" Plane one can change from working hardwood to pine with but a moment's delay. The "Bed Rock" Plane is made by the Stanley Rule & Level Co., who have an established reputation for making the highest grade tools on the market; and in our opinion it is a practical and decided improvement over any plane that has yet been produced.

Catalogue Number	Stanley's Number		L'gth, ins.	Width of Cutter	Weight,	Price, each
35C1802	602	Smooth	7	1⅝	2 lbs. 2 oz.	$1.30
35C1803	603	Smooth	8	1¾	2 lbs. 13 oz.	1.39
35C1804	604	Smooth	9	2	3 lbs. 8 oz.	1.51
35C1806	604½	Smooth	10	2⅜	4 lbs. 6 oz.	1.75
35C1809	605	Jack	14	2	4 lbs.	1.76
35C1812	605½	Jack	15	2¼	5 lbs. 7 oz.	1.97
35C1814	606	Fore	18	2⅜	6 lbs. 2 oz.	2.12
35C1816	607	Jointer	22	2⅜	6 lbs. 13 oz.	2.54
35C1817	608	Jointer	24	2⅝	8 lbs. 4 oz.	3.02
Stanley's Bed Rock Planes with Corrugated Bottoms.						
35C1822	602C	Smooth	7	1⅝	2 lbs. 2 oz.	$1.30
35C1823	603C	Smooth	8	1¾	2 lbs. 13 oz.	1.39
35C1824	604C	Smooth	9	2	3 lbs. 3 oz.	1.51
35C1826	604½C	Smooth	10	2⅜	4 lbs. 6 oz.	1.75
35C1829	605C	Jack	14	2	4 lbs.	1.76
35C1832	605½C	Jack	15	2¼	5 lbs. 7 oz.	1.97
35C1834	606C	Fore	18	2⅜	6 lbs. 2 oz.	2.12
35C1836	607C	Jointer	22	2⅜	6 lbs. 13 oz.	2.54
35C1837	608C	Jointer	24	2⅝	8 lbs. 4 oz.	3.02

Weights given are for plane only without packing of any kind.

Chaplin's Improved Patent Iron Planes.

WITH CORRUGATED BOTTOMS AND CHECKERED RUBBER HANDLES.

The improvements made in these Planes have reduced the number of working parts, and consequent liability to get out of order, and gain the simplest and most arbitrary adjustment for regulating the depth of the cut.

This adjustment, working as an eccentric, will carry the cutting bit to any variation of depth desired with absolute accuracy, and hold it securely against any displacement.

There is also a **lateral adjustment** for bringing the edge of the cutting bit to an exact and even bearing on the work.

The Checkered Rubber Handle gives added strength, a firm grip and largely increased durability, while at the same time it adds to the beauty and finish of the tool.

The corrugations forming the bottoms of these planes, and designed to relieve the suction and clinging tendency of the smooth face, are divided by ribs **through the bottom**, giving increased strength and rigidity without adding to the weight. The air spaces so formed **reduce the traction and friction to the minimum.**

The peculiar shape and finish of these planes gives an easy feeling in the hand, always appreciated, while for beauty of appearance they are unrivaled.

No. 35C1840 Smooth Plane, 8 inches long, 1¾-inch cutter. Price........ **$1.30**

No. 35C1841 Smooth Plane, 9 inches long, 2-inch cutter. Price........ **$1.40**

No. 35C1842 Jack Plane, 15 inches long, 2⅛-inch cutter. Price........ **$1.70**

No. 35C1843 Fore Plane, 18 inches long, 2¼-inch cutter. Price........ **$2.00**

No. 35C1844 Jointer Plane, 22 inches long, 2½-inch cutter. Price........ **$2.30**

No. 35C1845 Jointer Plane, 24 inches long. 2⅝-inch cutter. Price........ **$2.70**

The Fulton Line of Block Planes.

Will be found far superior to any similar line offered at about the same price. The cutters are as good as can be made in every way. The castings are smooth and strong. The workmanship is good in every particular, and they are fully guaranteed.

No. 35C2000 The Fulton Iron Block Plane, length, 5½ inches; width of cutter, 1¼ inches; weight, 13 ounces. Price, **13c**

No. 35C2001 The Fulton Iron Block Plane, length, 7¼ inches; width of cutter, 1⅜ inches; weight, 1¼ pounds. Price...... **19c**

No. 35C2002 The Fulton Iron Block Plane. This plane has two slots, and two cutter seats. It can be used as a block plane, or, by reversing the position of the cutter and the clamping wedge, it can be used to plane close up into corners, or other difficult places. Length, 8 inches; width of cutter, 1⅜ inches; weight, 1½ pounds. Price.... **25c**

No. 35C2003 The Fulton Adjustable Iron Block Plane. Length, 5½ inches; width of cutter, 1¼ inches. Weight, 12 ounces. Price........ **19c**

No. 35C2004 The Fulton Adjustable Iron Block Plane. Length, 7½ inches; width of cutter, 1⅜ inches. Weight, 1¼ pounds. Price........ **27c**

No. 35C2008 The Fulton Iron Block Plane, with screw adjustment to regulate the thickness of the shaving. It also has adjustment for opening or closing the throat as may be required for coarse or fine work. Length, 6 inches, Width of cutter, 1⅜ inches; weight, 22 ounces. Price........ **47c**

No. 35C2009 The Fulton Iron Block Plane, same as preceding number, except the length is 7 inches; weight 24 ounces. Price. **50c**

Stanley's Iron Block Planes.

No. 35C2100 Stanley's Iron Block Plane, No. 101; length, 3½ inches, 1-inch cutter. Not a toy, but a practical tool for light work. Weight, 9 ounces. Price........ **9c**

No. 35C2107 Stanley's Iron Block Plane, No. 102; length, 5½ inches, 1¼-inch cutter. Weight, 14 ounces. Price........ **17c**

No. 35C2112 Stanley's Iron Block Plane, No. 110; length, 7½ inches, 1⅜-inch cutter. Weight, 1 pound 14 ounces. Price........ **26c**

No. 35C2109 Stanley's Iron Block Plane, No. 103; adjustable, 5½ inches in length, 1¼-inch cutter. Price.. **26c**

No. 35C2113 Stanley's Iron Block Plane, No. 120; adjustable, 7½ inches in length, 1⅜-inch cutter. Price........ **34c**

No. 35C2116 Stanley's Iron Block Plane, No. 130; double ender; length, 8 inches, 1⅜-inch cutter. By reversing the cutter and clamping wedge, as shown by dotted lines in illustration, this plane can be made to plane close up into corners. Weight, 1 pound 14 ounces. Price........ **34c**

No. 35C2120 Stanley's Iron Block Plane, adjustable, No. 220; 7½ inches in length, 1⅜-inch cutter. Price........ **34c**

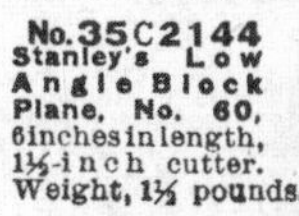

No. 35C2144 Stanley's Low Angle Block Plane, No. 60, 6 inches in length, 1⅜-inch cutter. Weight, 1½ pounds. Price........ **65c**

No. 35C2124 Bailey's Patent Iron Block Plane, No. 9½, length, 6 inches; 1⅝-inch cutter. Adjustable cutter, adjustable throat. Weight, 1 lb. 10 oz. Price.... **57c**

No. 35C2127 Same shape and adjustments as above, No. 15, 7 inches long, 1⅝-inch cutter. Weight, 1 pound 14 ounces. Price........ **63c**

No. 35C2138 Bailey's Knuckle Joint Plane, No. 18, as above. Length, 6 inches, 1⅝-inch cutter. Weight, 1 pound 10 ounces. Price, **68c**

No. 35C2161 Stanley's Rabbet and Block Plane, No. 140, detachable side, 7 inches long, 1⅜-inch cutter. A detachable side will easily change this tool from a block plane to a rabbet plane, or vice versa. The cutter is set on askew. Price........ **76c**

No. 35C2182 The Fulton Circular Plane. This plane has a flexible steel face, which can be easily shaped to any required arc, either concave or convex, by turning the knob on the front of the plane. Length of face, 10½ inches; width of cutter, 1¾ inches. Weight, 3½ pounds. Price........ **$1.58**

Circular Plane.

No. 35C2184 Stanley's Adjustable Circular Plane No. 113, with flexible steel face, which, by turning the knob on the front of the plane, can be easily shaped to any required arc either concave or convex. Weight, 3⅜ pounds. Price.... **$1.66**

Tonguing and Grooving (Match) Plane.

No. 35C2218 Stanley's Tonguing and Grooving Plane No. 48. (Commonly called match plane), which will match boards of any thickness from ¾ to 1¼ inches thick. Weight, 2⅜ pounds. Price........ **$1.51**

No. 35C2219 Stanley's Tonguing and Grooving Plane, No. 49, which will match board any thickness from ⅜ to ¾ inch. Weight, 2⅜ pounds. Price........ **$1.50**

Stanley's Bull Nose Plow and Matching Plane.

Two interchangeable front parts go with this tool. The form shown in illustration is that of a bull nose plow, and the cutter will easily work up to and into a ⅛-inch hole or any larger size—as in sash fitting, stair work, etc. With the other front on, it takes the ordinary form of a plow, and is adapted to all regular uses. With each tool eight plow bits (⅛, 3-16, ¼, 5-16, ⅜, 7-16, ½, ⅝-inch) and a slitting blade are furnished; also a tonguing tool ¼-inch.

No. 35C2223 Nickel plated, with ten tools, bits, etc. No. 143. Price........ **$3.02**

Stanley's Universal Plane $9.66.

No. 35C2228 Stanley's Patent Universal Plane, No. 55, nickel plated, including moulding plane, match, sash, chamfer, beading, reeding, fluting, hollow, round, plow, dado, rabbet, filletster and slitting plane, with 52 cutters, packed in four separate cases, and the whole outfit packed in a neat wooden box. This tool, in the hands of an ordinary carpenter, can be used for all lines of work covered by a full assortment of so called fancy planes. Price, complete........ **$9.66**

Illustration shows the plane adjusted for making moulding.

Traut's Adjustable Dado, Plow, etc., No. 46.

No. 35C2230 Made by the Stanley Rule & Level Co. This tool is accompanied by eight plow and dado bits (3-16, ¼, 5-16, ⅜, ½, ⅝, ⅞ and 1¼-inch), a filletster cutter, a slitting tool and a tonguing tool. All except the slitting blade are secured in the main stock on askew. Price, nickel plated, including eleven tools, plow bits, slitting and tonguing tools, etc........ **$4.23**

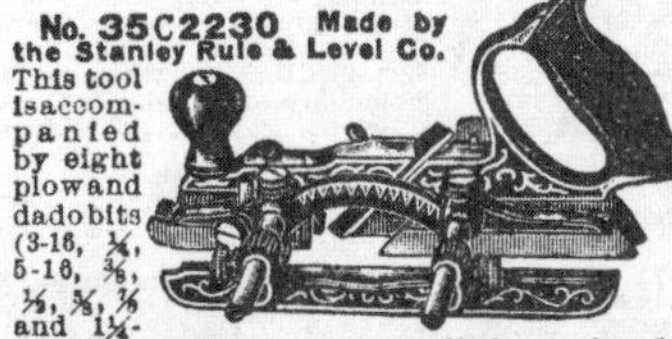

Stanley's Adjustable Beading and Matching Plane.

No. 35C2255 Stanley's Patent Adjustable Beading and Matching Plane No. 50, will do all the work for which fourteen common wood bead planes would be required. Has spur cutter for use when beading across the grain. By adjustment of the fence center, beading can be done any distance up to 5 inches from the edge of a board. Price, complete, including seven beading tools, sizes ⅛, 3-16, ¼, 5-16, ⅜, 7-16 and ½ inch and a pair of ⅜-inch matching tools. Price........ **$2.42**

Modern Carpentry.

A Book Every Carpenter, Machinist, Mechanic and Apprentice Needs.

By Fred T. Hodgson. A New Complete Carpenters' Guide. Contains 100 quick methods of performing general carpenter work, such as laying roofs, rafters, stairs, joints and joining, timber splicing, mouldings, bevels, hand railing, circular and splayed work, etc. Written in a very simple style, easily understood. The illustrations of which there are many, are explanatory, making it possible for amateurs and carpenters generally to understand. This is the most complete, authentic and latest book on the subject published. It is thoroughly practical and reliable. Size, 5¼x7¾ inches. Retail price, $1.00.

No. 3C09308 Cloth. Our price.... **58c**

If by mail, postage extra, 11 cents.

Stanley's Beading, Rabbet and Slitting Plane.

No. 35C2237 Stanley's Patent Adjustable Beading, Rabbet and Slitting Plane No. 45. This in each of its several forms will do first class work, even in the hands of an ordinary mechanic. Directions for forming the different tools which can be made from this plane accompany each plane, and are easily understood by any one of ordinary intelligence. This plane embraces (1) beading and center beading plane; (2) rabbet and filletster; (3) dado; (4) plow; (5) matching plane; (6) sash plane; (7) a superior slitting plane. Each plane has seven beading tools (⅛, 3-16, ¼, 5-16 ⅜, 7-16 and ½-inch) ten plow and dado bits (⅛, 3-16, ¼, 5-16, ⅜, 7-16, ½, ⅝, ¾ and ⅞-inch), a slitting blade, a tonguing tool, and a sash tool. Weight, 6¼ pounds.

Price, complete with tools as above........ **$4.83**

Extras for No. 35C2237 Plane.

The following tools can be used with above plane, but are not included in above combination.

No. 35C2239 Hollows and Rounds for above plane. Nos...	6	8	10	12
Cutter, width, inch........	½	⅝	¾	1
Works, circle, inches........	¾	1	1¼	1½
Price, per pair........	85c	85c	85c	85c

Nosing Tools.

No. 35C2241 Nosing Tool, 1⅛-inch. (Attach same as above.) Price........ **61c**

Cabinet Scrapers.

No. 35C2287 Stanley's Cabinet Scraper. Raised handles, 11-inch, 2⅛-inch blade. Price.........61c

No. 35C2553 Cabinet Scraper, a sheet of finely tempered saw steel about 3x5 inches. Price.........5c

No. 35C2554 C. E. Jennings & Co.'s Extra Quality Cabinet Scraper, No. A1. Made from best saw steel, smithed and blocked by hand, edges finished ready for use. Size, 3x6 inches. Price.........16c

Jointer Gauge.

No. 35C2549 Jointer Gauge. This tool can be readily attached to any iron or wood plane, and will enable the operator to accurately plane either square or bevels of any desired angle, and will do away with the continued use of a bevel or try square. It is made entirely of iron and steel. Illustration shows gauge attached to plane. We do not furnish plane. Price, without plane, $1.20

Sand Paper.

No. 35C2557 Sand Paper. Nos. 1 and 1½ are commonly used. No. 00 is the finest and No. 3 the coarsest. State numbers wanted when ordering. 24 sheets to the quire. If a quire is made up of assorted numbers we charge the sheet price. Quire price is not good for less than a quire of any number.

No.	00	0	½	1	1½	2	3
Per sheet	1c	1c	1c	1c	1c	1c	1c
Per quire	13c	13c	13c	14c	15c	16c	19c

Emery Cloth.

No. 35C2563 24 sheets to the quire.

No.	00	0	½	1	1½	2
Price, per sheet	3c	3c	3c	3c	3c	3c
Price, per quire	53c	53c	53c	57c	60c	62c

C. Hammond's Hatchets.

The C. Hammond Brand denotes the very highest quality in tools. C. Hammond has been established at his present location since 1843, and for many years prior to that time was located in Boston, Mass.

The C. Hammond Bronzed Hatchets Nos. 35C2570, 35C2571, 35C2572 and 35C2573 are forged from Swedish iron with best tool steel on poll and inserted for cutting edge. They have bronzed body and polished bit. All hatchets are furnished with selected second growth, extra white, hickory handles of special patterns and shapes. **They are fully warranted.**

No. 35C2570 C. Hammond's Shingling Hatchet. Weights given do not include handles.
Width of cut, 3¼ inches, weight, 1 lb. Price.....41c
Width of cut, 3½ inches, weight, 1¼ lbs. Price...44c
Width of cut, 3¾ inches, weight, 1½ lbs. Price...47c
Width of cut, 4 inches, weight, 1¾ lbs. Price...50c

No. 35C2571 C. Hammond's Half Hatchet. Weights given do not include handles.
Width of cut, 3¼ inches, weight, 1¼ lbs. Price......47c
Width of cut, 3½ inches, weight, 1½ lbs. Price......50c
Width of cut, 3¾ inches, weight, 1¾ lbs. Price......53c
Width of cut, 4 inches, weight, 2 pounds. Price......59c

No. 35C2572 C. Hammond's Claw Hatchet. Weights given do not include handles. Width of cut, 3¼ in., weight, 1¼ lbs. Price.....50c
Width of cut, 3¾ inches, weight, 1½ lbs. Price.....53c
Width of cut, 4 inches, weight, 1¾ lbs. Price.....59c

No. 35C2573 C. Hammond's Broad Hatchet. Weights given do not include handles.
Width of cut, 4 inches, weight, 1 pound 6 ounces. Price......65c
Width of cut, 4½ inches, weight, 1 pound 10 ounces. Price.......70c
Width of cut, 5 inches, weight, 2¼ lbs. Price, 76c
Width of cut, 5½ inches, wt., 2 lbs. 10 ozs. Price, 82c
Width of cut, 6 inches, weight, 3 pounds. Price.........91c

Nos. 35C2580, 35C2581, 35C2582 and 35C2583 are forged from the best refined crucible steel. They cannot be excelled for light work. For rough heavy work those made with Swedish iron body are stronger. They are furnished with selected second growth white hickory handles of special shapes. Fully warranted.

No. 35C2580 C. Hammond's Adze Eye Bell Poll Shingling Hatchet. Weights given do not include handles.

Width of cut, in.	3¼	3½
Weight, pounds	1	1¼
Price	70c	74c

No. 35C2581 C. Hammond's Adze Eye Bell Poll Half Hatchet. Weights given do not include handles.

Width of cut, inches	3	3¼
Weight, pounds	1	1¼
Price	70c	74c

No. 35C2582 C. Hammond's Adze Eye Bell Poll Lath Hatchet. Width of cut, 2⅛ inches; weight (not including handle), 1 pound. Price.........70c

No. 35C2583 C. Hammond's Chicago Pattern Milled Head Lath Hatchet. Width of cut, 2⅛ inches. Weight (not including handle) 1 pound. Price.........85c

FULTON TOOL CO.'S HATCHETS.

The Fulton Tool Co.'s Hatchets are the best that can be produced from the best materials by the very best mechanical skill. Before we decide to handle any article it is subjected to the most critical examination, practically compared and tested with other goods, and must be able to bear out our guarantee—"As good or better than any you ever had. If not found so, return to us and money will be refunded." Every hatchet branded Fulton Tool Co. is sold subject to this guarantee.

All hatchets sold by us have handles, but the weight of handle is not included when we state weight of hatchet.

No. 35C2600 Fulton Tool Co.'s Shingling Hatchets, phantom bevel, soft steel body; tool steel bit and poll. Full polished and etched.

Size	Weight, without handle	Width of bit in.	Price
1	1 lb.	3⅛	68c
2	1 lb. 6 ozs.	3⅞	70c
3	1 lb. 12 ozs.	4⅛	72c

No. 35C2606 Fulton Tool Co.'s Brand Half Hatchets, phantom bevel. Soft steel body. Tool steel bit and poll. Full polished and etched. Warranted.

Size	Weight, without handle	Width of bit	Price
1	14 oz.	3⅛ in.	71c
2	1 lb. 4 ozs.	3⅞ in.	73c
3	1 lb. 10 ozs.	4 in.	75c

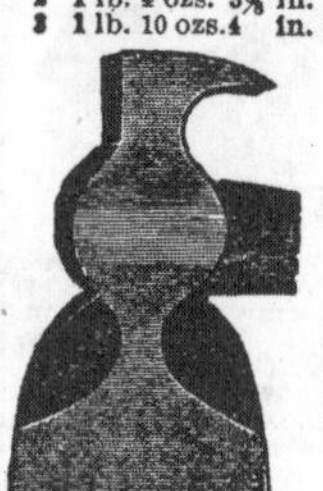

No. 35C2612 The Fulton Tool Co.'s Brand Claw Hatchets. Phantom bevel. Soft steel body. Tool steel bit and poll. Full polished and etched. Warranted.

Size	Weight, without handle	Width of bit, inches	Price
1	1 pound 2 ounces	3⅛	63c
2	1 pound 8 ounces	3⅞	65c
3	1 pound 14 ounces	4⅛	68c

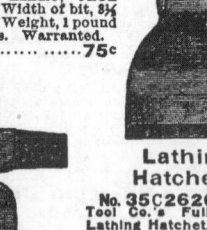

No. 35C2616 The Fulton Tool Co.'s Shingling Hatchet. Adze eye, bell poll, solid cast steel, full polished, hickory handle; thin blade. Width of bit, 3⅛ inches. Weight, 1 pound 4 ounces. Warranted. Price.........75c

Lathing Hatchets.

No. 35C2620 Fulton Tool Co.'s Full Polished Lathing Hatchet. Solid cast steel, thin blade, adze eye, hickory handle. Width of bit, 2⅛ inches. Weight, 1 pound. Warranted. Price.........68c

No. 35C2624 The Fulton Tool Co.'s Underhill Pattern Lathing Hatchet. Full polished, solid cast steel, extra thin blade, 2⅛ inches wide. Weight, 15 ounces. Large size head and full grip handle; warranted. Price.........83c

No. 35C2626 The Fulton Tool Co.'s Boston Pattern Lath Hatchet. Solid tool steel, full polished, polished hickory handle. Width of bit, 2⅛ inches. Weight (not including handle), 14 ounces. Price..80c

Broad Hatchets.

No. 35C2629 The Fulton Tool Co.'s Brand Broad Hatchets. Soft steel body, tool steel bit and poll. Full polished and etched. Warranted.

Size	Weight, without handle	Width of bit	Price
2	1 pound 12 ounces	4½ inches	68c
3	2 pounds 2 ounces	5 inches	80c
4	2 pounds 8 ounces	5½ inches	87c
5	2 pounds 14 ounces	6 inches	96c

No. 35C2633 The Fulton Tool Co.'s Shingling Hatchet, extra cast steel, bronzed; polished bit, hickory handle, finely finished and tempered. Fully warranted.
No. 1. Weight, without handle, 1 lb. 1 oz; width of bit, 3¼ inches. Price.........40c
No. 2. Weight, without handle, 1 lb. 7 ozs.; width of bit, 4 inches. Price.........43c
No. 3. Weight, without handle, 1 lb, 13 ozs.; width of bit 4½ inches. Price.........45c

No. 35C2636 The Fulton Tool Co.'s Lathing Hatchet. Extra forged steel, bronzed; polished bit, hickory handle. Fully warranted.

No.	0	1	2
Width, in.	2	2⅛	2⅜
Weight	10 oz.	14 oz.	1 lb. 1 oz.
Price	38c	40c	43c

No. 35C2637 The Fulton Tool Co.'s Claw Hatchet. Extra forged steel, bronzed. Polished bit, hickory handle. Carefully tempered and finely finished. Warranted.
No. 1. Width, 3½ inches; weight, 1 lb. 5 ozs. Price.........45c
No. 2. Width, 4 inches; weight, 1 lb. 9 ozs. Price.........48c
No. 3. Width, 4½ inches; weight, 1 lb. 15 ozs. Price.........50c

No. 35C2640 The Fulton Tool Co.'s Broad Hatchets or Carpenters' Bench Axes. Extra forged steel, bronzed; polished bit, hickory handle. Warranted.
Width, 4½ inches; weight, 1 lb. 12 ozs. Price.........58c
Width, 5 inches; weight, 2 lbs. 2 ozs. Price.........65c
Width, 5½ inches; weight, 2 lbs. 8 ozs. Price.........73c
Width, 6 inches; weight, 2 lbs. 14 ozs. Price.........83c

Hatchet Handles.

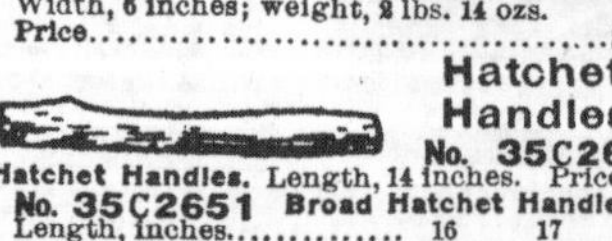

No. 35C2650 Hatchet Handles. Length, 14 inches. Price. 4c

No. 35C2651 Broad Hatchet Handles.

Length, inches	16	17	18
Price	5c	6c	7c

Broad Axes and Adzes.

The Fulton Tool Co.'s Adzes and Broad Axes are warranted as follows: If they prove too soft so the edge bends or if they break from a flaw and are returned to us within 30 days, a new one will be given in exchange. If a tool shows a clean break it will be considered done accidentally and will not be exchanged.

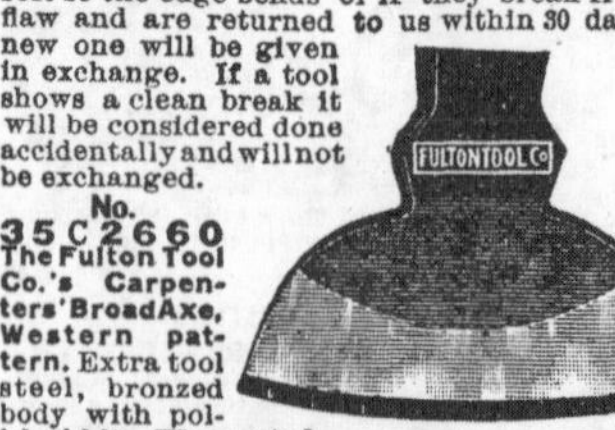

No. 35C2660 The Fulton Tool Co.'s Carpenters' Broad Axe, Western pattern. Extra tool steel, bronzed body with polished bit. Warranted.

Weight, pounds	6	6½	7	7½
Width of cut, inches	11	11½	12	12½
Price	$1.60	$1.65	$1.70	$1.75
Weight, pounds	8		8½	9
Width of cut, ins.	13		13½	14
Price	$1.80		$1.85	$1.90

No. 35C2661 The Fulton Tool Co.'s Carpenters' Broad Axe, Canada pattern. Extra tool steel bronzed body with polished bit. Warranted.

Weight, pounds	6	6½	7	7½
Width of cut, inches	10½	11	11½	12
Price	$1.89	$1.94	$1.96	$2.07
Weight, pounds	8		8½	9
Width of cut, ins.	12½		13	13½
Price	$2.10		$2.14	$2.18

Broad Axe Handles.

No. 35C2667 Extra Selected Quality Broad Axe Handles. Reversible for either right or left hand. Price.........20c

No. 35C2668 The Fulton Tool Co.'s Carpenters' Adze. Extra cast steel, bronzed; polished bit.

Width of cut, in.	3½	4	4½
Weight, pounds	3⅛	3½	3⅞
Price	$1.07	$1.08	$1.09

No. 35C2668

No. 35C2670 The Fulton Tool Co.'s Ship Carpenters' Adze, with spur head. Warranted.

Width of cut, inches	4½	4½
Price	$1.31	$1.32

No. 35C2670

Adze Handle.

No. 35C2674 Selected Quality Carpenters Adze Handle, 34 inches long. Price.......17c

OUR LINE OF AXES is selected from the most popular patterns of the oldest and best known axe makers in the world. All have taper eye, which is largest on the outside. This binds the handle and prevents its getting loose. The cheapest axe we sell is made from just as good material as is used in our best axe, and it is made and tempered with the same care. The difference in our price represents the difference in cost of labor in making. While our Red Ridge will give satisfaction, our Hubbard's Hollow Ground Lippincott Brand will chop easier and is well worth every cent of the additional cost. **We also give you the exact weights you want.** You can have a dozen of weights as desired at dozen prices; you don't have to take them as packed assorted by the manufacturers. **EVERY AXE, like everything else sold by us, IS GUARANTEED TO GIVE SATISFACTION.**

Red Ridge Michigan Pattern Axe.

No. 35C2677 Red Ridge Michigan Pattern Axe. This axe is handsomely finished in red with polished bit. In its manufacture a full portion of the best quality crucible steel is used. Each axe is carefully tempered by hand, is hand hammered and carefully inspected in every process of manufacture. The special bevel in this axe enables it to enter and leave the timber with the least possible resistance. Aside from this valuable feature, it is larger than the ordinary axe of the same weight, which makes it well balanced.

Weight, lbs.	3	3½	3¾	4	4½	5
Price, ea.	$0.59	0.60	0.61	0.62	0.64	0.66
Per doz.	6.50	6.55	6.75	6.80	7.00	7.25

Red Ridge Michigan Pattern Double Bit Axe.

No. 35C2678 Red Ridge Michigan Pattern Double Bit Axe. Is made in like manner and finish as above.

Weight, lbs.	3½	3¾	4	4½	5	5½
Price, ea.	$0.76	0.78	0.79	0.81	0.83	0.85
Per doz.	8.50	8.75	8.80	9.00	9.25	9.50

Red Ridge, Single Bit, Handled, Michigan Pattern Axe.

No. 35C2679 Red Ridge, Single Bit, Handled, Michigan Pattern Axe. Same as described under No. 35C2677, with a good hickory handle, correctly put in. Weight does not include handle.

Weight, lbs.	3[illegible]	4	4½
Price, each	$0.72	$0.74	$0.76
Per dozen	[illegible].00	8.25	8.50

Hunt's Superior Axes. Yankee Pattern.

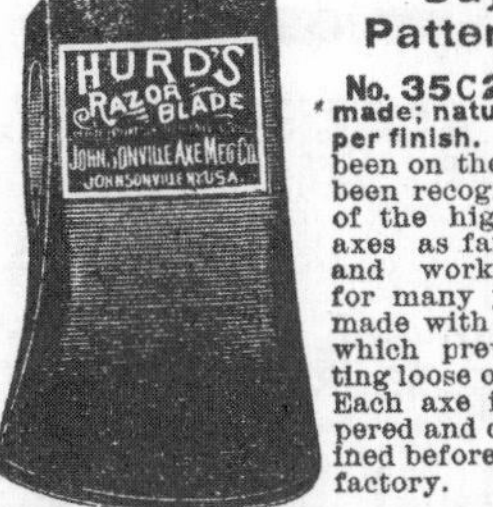

No. 35C2680 These are finished in black with polished bit. The first axe of this brand was manufactured from best refined tool steel in 1826 and the company has been most careful to maintain the high reputation it has always enjoyed. Each one is hand tempered and carefully inspected before leaving the factory.

Weight, lbs.	3	3½	3¾	4	4½	5
Price, ea.	$0.61	0.62	0.64	0.65	0.67	0.68
Per doz.	6.75	6.80	7.00	7.05	7.25	7.50

Hurd's Razor Blade Single Bit Dayton Pattern Axe.

No. 35C2682 Hand made; natural gas temper finish. This axe has been on the market and been recognized as one of the highest quality axes as far as quality and workmanship go for many years. It is made with a taper eye, which prevents it getting loose on the handle. Each axe is hand tempered and closely examined before leaving the factory.

Weight, lbs.	3	3½	3¾	4	4½	5
Price, each.	$0.61	0.62	0.63	0.64	0.66	0.68
Per dozen	6.75	6.80	7.00	7.05	7.25	7.50

No. 35C2683 Hurd's Razor Blade Double Bit Wisconsin Pattern Axe. Same hand made, natural gas temper finish as single bit described previously.

Weight, lbs	3½	3¾	4	4½	5	5½
Price, each,	$0.78	0.80	0.81	0.83	0.85	0.87
Per dozen	8.75	9.00	9.05	9.25	9.50	9.75

The Jamestown Axe, Western Crown Pattern.

No. 35C2686 Full polished and etched with blue phantom bevel. It has been in the market a number of years and the verdict of the choppers is that it is correctly made. Each axe is hand hammered and tempered by hand. It is so made that it enters and leaves the wood freely and will not become stubbed after grinding.

Weight, lbs.	3	3½	3¾	4	4½	5
Price, each.	$0.66	0.67	0.68	0.69	0.71	0.73
Per dozen	7.25	7.30	7.50	7.55	7.75	8.00

No. 35C2687 Jamestown Axe, double bit, Michigan pattern, quality and finish same as above.

Wt., lbs.	3½	3¾	4	4½	5	5½
Price, ea.	$0.82	0.84	0.85	0.86	0.88	0.90
Per doz.	9.25	9.50	9.55	9.75	10.00	10.25

C. W. Hubbard's Patented Easy Chopping Hollow Ground Axe.

No. 35C2688 C. W. Hubbard's Patented Easy Chopping Hollow Ground Axe (Lippincott Brand, Dayton Pattern). Altogether a new innovation and promises to be the axe of the future, for the reason that from the peculiar construction of the bit it is the easiest chopping axe in the world. Look at the illustration and notice that the axe is hollow ground. This feature enables it to enter and leave the wood with the least possible amount of resistance, and considerably less grinding is necessary to keep it in good condition than with the ordinary axe. The axe is finely finished and deeply etched and is not only the best and easiest chopping, but the handsomest axe on the market today. All of our axes are made with a taper eye, which prevents them from becoming loose on the handle.

Weight, lbs.	3	3½	3¾	4	4½	5
Price, each.	$0.68	0.69	0.70	0.71	0.72	0.74
Per dozen	7.50	7.55	7.75	7.80	8.00	8.25

No. 35C2689 C. W. Hubbard's Patented Easy Chopping Hollow Ground Double Bit Axe. Lippincott brand, Wisconsin pattern. Natural gas temper.

Weight, pounds	3½	3¾	4
Price, each	$0.84	$0.86	$0.87
Per dozen	9.50	9.75	9.80
Weight, pounds	4½	5	5½
Price, each	$0.88	$0.90	$0.92
Per dozen	10.00	10.25	10.50

No. 35C2690 Boys' Niagara Handled Axe, made from best cast steel, handsomely finished in red with blue bevels. They are made with the same care and go through the same inspection as our men's axes. Weight, including handle, which is about 28 inches in length, is about 3¼ pounds.

Price, per dozen, $6.00; each........54c

Hurd's Hunters' Hatchet.

No. 35C2693 Ideal black finish, made by the same skilled workmen who make our regular Hurd's axes. The handle is about 14 inches long. It is a convenient tool for household use as it takes the place of either axe, hatchet or hammer. It weighs only about 1½ pounds with handle. Price, each.......$0.44
Per dozen............5.15

Axe Handles.

No. 35C2735 Common Quality Turned Axe Handle, 36 inches long. Price..........9c

No. 35C2738 Standard Quality Turned Axe Handle, 36 inches long. Price........14c

No. 35C2740 Boys' Standard Quality Turned Axe Handle, 28 inches. Price....15c

No. 35C2745 Selected Quality Hand Shaved Axe Handle, 36 inches long. Price..18c

No. 35C2747 Extra Selected Quality Hand Shaved Axe Handle, 36 inches long. The best handle we can find. Price..............23c

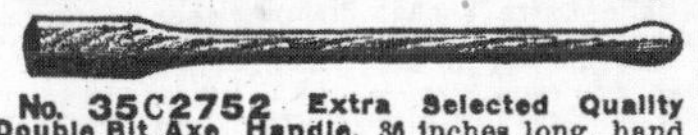

No. 35C2752 Extra Selected Quality Double Bit Axe Handle, 36 inches long, hand shaved. Excellent value. Price..........20c

Axe Wedges.

No. 35C2755 So well known, description is not necessary. Weight, 2 ounces.
Price, each.........2c
Per dozen.........18c

No. 35C2759 Wood Choppers' Solid Steel Wedges. Weight, 4 pounds.
Price, each.........12c
Weight, 5 pounds. Price..........15c

No. 35C2762 Truckee Pattern Wood Choppers' Wedge, tool steel, oil finished.

Weight, pounds	4	6	8
Price, each	13c	16½c	26c

No. 35C2766 Oregon Pattern Wood Choppers' Wedge, tool steel, oil finished.
Price, each
4-pound......24c
6-pound......36c
8-pound......48c

No. 35C2767 The Fulton Special Oregon Pattern Wood Choppers' Wedge. Made from the best materials and tempered right.

Weight, pounds	4	6	8
Price, each	32c	48c	64c

No. 35C2769 Falling Wedge, tool steel, oil finished.

Weight, pounds	4	6	8
Price, each	36c	54c	72c

Saw Log Wedge.

No. 35C2772 Saw Log Wedge, improved pattern, extra tool steel, oil finished.

Weight, pounds	1½	2	2½	3
Price, each	12c	14c	18c	21c

Wood Choppers' Mauls.

No. 35C2775 Wood Choppers' Maul, straight cut pattern, extra tool steel. Polished bit and poll, body painted blue.

Weight, lbs.	5	6	7	8	10
Price, each	40c	48c	56c	64c	80c

No. 35C2778 Wood Choppers' Maul, Oregon pattern, extra tool steel, oil finished, polished face.

Weight, lbs.	5	6	7	8	10
Price, each	40c	48c	56c	64c	80c

The Fulton Tool Co.'s Nail Hammers.

With Ebonized Hickory Handles.

Guaranteed. If not satisfactory return to us and money will be refunded.

The handsomest hammer you ever saw and it's just as good as it looks.

No. 35C2800 The Fulton Tool Co.'s Brand Nail Hammer. Octagonal neck and poll. Made of the very best tool steel; finely polished and nickel plated. They are proportioned right; they hang right; claws are right shape to draw a nail without breaking the claw; temper is right. Ebonized hickory handle.

Size	1	1½	2
Weight, without handle,	1¼ lbs.	1 lb.	13 ozs.
Price	65c	63c	61c

THE FULTON SPECIAL NAIL HAMMERS

are just as good as the most skillful workmen can make them. We don't know where better material could be bought. Great care is used in tempering. The face is tempered right. The claws are tempered to pull nails and not break. The eye is left soft so it will not crack. The "Never Rust" finish is dark in color and gives the hammer a handsome appearance.

No. 35C2801 The Fulton Special Nail Hammer. Adze eye, Plain face. "Never Rust" finish. Hickory handle. Every hammer warranted to give satisfaction.

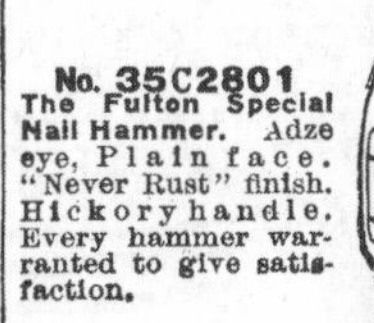

Weight	1 lb. 4 oz.	1 lb.	13 ozs.	7 oz
Price	43c	41c	38c	36c

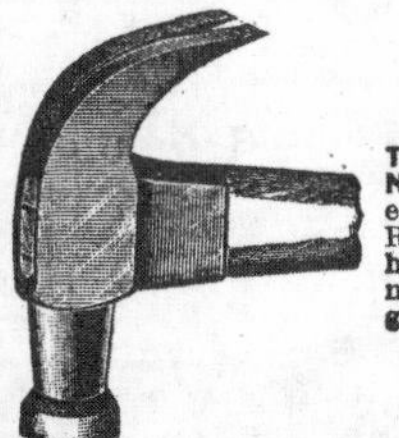

No. 35C2802 The Fulton Special Nail Hammer. Adze eye. Bell face. "Never Rust" finish. Hickory handle. Every hammer warranted to give satisfaction.

Weight	1 lb. 4 oz.	1 lb.	13 oz.	7 oz.
Price	44c	42c	39c	37c

Nail Holding Hammer.

No. 35C2803 Nail Holding Hammer, made from the best quality crucible steel. By the improved form of the groove this hammer will hold any size or shape of cut or wire nail. With it one can drive nails beyond ordinary reach. Only one size and shape made. Weight, 1 pound 3 ounces, without handle.
Price, with handle..........72c

Wedge Plate Hammer.

No. 35C2806 Wedge Plate Hammers are forged from the best tool steel; handles of the best second growth hickory. The malleable wedge plate strengthens the handle and at the same time keeps the head from getting loose or coming off. We guarantee every hammer to be first class. Weight of head, 1 pound; bell face.
Price..........51c

No. 35C2807 Same Hammer, plain face.
Price..........50c

David Maydole's Nail Hammers.

No. 35C2810 The Genuine David Maydole's Nail Hammers. Adze eye, plain face, polished hickory handles. Weights do not include handles.

Nos.	1	1½
Weight	1¼ lbs.	1 lb.
Price	54c	49c

No. 35C2811 The Genuine David Maydole's Nail Hammers. Adze eye, bell face, polished hickory handles. Weights do not include handles.

Nos.	11	11½	12	13
Wgt.	1 lb. 3 ozs.	1 lb.	12 oz.	7 oz.
Price	54c	49c	46c	41c

Forged Steel Nail Hammers.

Hammers No. 35C2815 and No. 35C2816 are forged from steel, and are warranted against flaws and not to be soft. For common use they give excellent satisfaction.

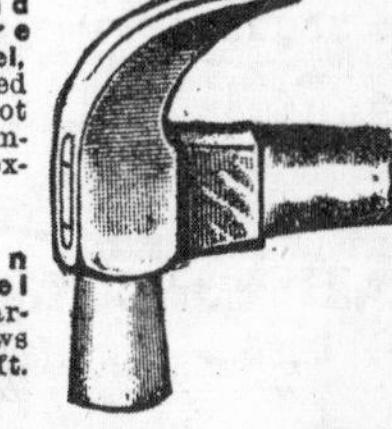

No. 35C2815 Adze Eye, Plain Face, Forged Steel Nail Hammer, warranted against flaws and not to be too soft.

Size	Weight	Price
1	1¼ lbs.	30c
1½	1 lb.	28c
2	13 ozs.	26c

Weight of handle not included in stating weight.

No. 35C2816 Adze Eye, Bell Face Forged Steel Nail Hammers. Warranted against flaws and not to be too soft.

Size	Weight	Price
11	1¼ lbs.	30c
11½	1 lb.	28c
12	13 ozs.	26c

Cast Iron Nail Hammers.

No. 35C2820 Cast Iron Hammers are positively no good. We have a few of these hammers in stock, which we would rather keep than sell to our customers. If you must have them, we will sell you a light one for 7 cents or a full size for 8 cents. You will be sorry if you buy one. Can't you afford to pay 28 cents for a hammer that will give you satisfaction. See No. 35C2816.

Hammer Handles.

No. 35C2825 Selected Quality Adze Eye Nail Hammer Handles. Length, 14 inches.
Price..........5c

Nail Puller.

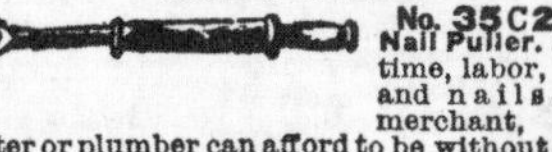

No. 35C2845 Nail Puller. Saves time, labor, cases and nails. No merchant, carpenter or plumber can afford to be without a nail puller. It pays for itself.
No. 1. Weight, 5 pounds. Price..........42c

Mallets.

No. 35C2850 Square Hickory Mallets. Head is 6½x2¾x3¾ inches; mortised handle. Weight, about 1¾ pounds. Price, 12c

No. 35C2853 Square Lignum Vitae Mallets. Head is 6½x2¾x3¾ inches. Weight, 2¼ pounds.
Price..........23c

No. 35C2856 Round Malleable Iron Mallet, with inserted hickory faces. Head is 5¼x3 inches. Weight, 3½ pounds.
Price..........36c

No. 35C2860 Rawhide Bound Mallets. Positively will not split. The spring, of the hide facing cushions the blow and prevents jarring, greatly relieving the arm of the user.
2-inch face. Price..........29c
2½-inch face. Price..........37c
3-inch face. Price..........46c

FULTON TOOL CO.'S HIGH GRADE WARRANTED CHISELS.

We warrant all chisels sold by us to be perfect when they leave the store, so far as the material and workmanship are concerned. If a tool proves too soft and bends on the edge or breaks in consequence of a flaw in the steel, and is returned to us within 30 days from date of purchase, a new tool will be given in exchange. If it shows abuse or is broken where the steel is sound, it will not be exchanged.

No. 35C2880 Fulton Tool Co.'s Socket Firmer Chisels, with leather tipped handles. Blades are 6 inches long. For quality of material, finish and cutting qualities these chisels cannot be equaled at the price. They are high grade, first class tools. Warranted.

Size, inch	¼	⅜	½	⅝	¾	
Price	16c	17c	18c	20c	22c	
Size, inches	⅞	1	1¼	1½	1¾	2
Price	23c	24c	26c	28c	30c	32c

No. 35C2881 Fulton Tool Co.'s Socket Firmer Chisels, beveled edge, leather tipped handles. These are high grade tools, made in the best manner of the best materials. Bevel blade, 6 inches long. Warranted.

Size, inch	⅛	¼	⅜	½	⅝	¾	⅞
Price	21c	22c	23c	24c	26c	28c	29c
Size, inches	1	1¼	1½	1¾	2		
Price	30c	32c	34c	36c	38c		

No. 35C2887 Fulton Tool Co.'s Socket Framing Chisels, blade, 8 inches long; high grade, fine finish, with handles. Handles have iron rings on end to prevent splitting. Warranted.

Size, in	⅜	½	¾	1	1¼	1½	1¾	2
Price	23c	24c	28c	32c	36c	40c	44c	48c

No. 35C2889 Fulton Tool Co.'s Socket Corner Chisel; extra tool steel, polished outside, with handle. Handle has iron ring on end to prevent splitting. Size given is width of each face.

Size, inches	¾	1	1¼
Price	56c	64c	72c

No. 35C2893 Fulton Tool Co.'s Socket Slick Chisel; extra tool steel, polished, with handle as shown in illustration. Warranted.

Size, inches	2½	3	3½	4
Price	80c	88c	$1.04	$1.19

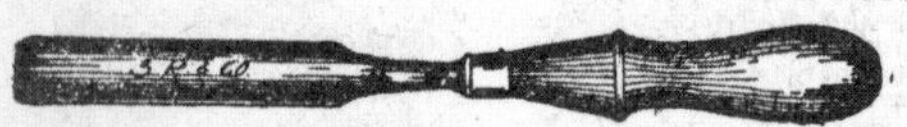

No. 35C2894 The Fulton Tanged Firmer Gouges, beveled outside, ground sharp, with selected hickory handles. The 1-inch blade is 5½ inches long from the bolster. **Other sizes in proportion. Warranted.**

Size, inches	⅛	3-16	¼	5-16	⅜	½	⅝
Price, each	26c	27c	28c	29c	30c	32c	34c
Size, inches	¾	⅞	1	1¼	1½	1¾	2
Price, each	37c	41c	43c	56c	67c	79c	93c

No. 35C2895 The Fulton Turning Chisel, without handles. The 1-inch size is 10¼ inches over all. Sharpened and honed. Warranted.

Size, inches	⅛	3-16	¼	5-16	⅜	½	⅝
Price, each	18c	19c	19c	20c	21c	23c	25c
Size, inches	¾	⅞	1	1¼	1½	1¾	2
Price, each	29c	31c	36c	45c	58c	70c	83c

No. 35C2896 The Fulton Turning Gouges, without handles; beveled on the outside. The 1-inch size is 10¼ inches over all. Sharpened and honed. Warranted.

Size, inches	⅛	3-16	¼	5-16	⅜	½	⅝
Price, each	23c	24c	25c	27c	28c	31c	33c
Size, inches	¾	⅞	1	1¼	1½	1¾	2
Price, each	38c	44c	49c	64c	83c	98c	$1.21

Chisel Sets.

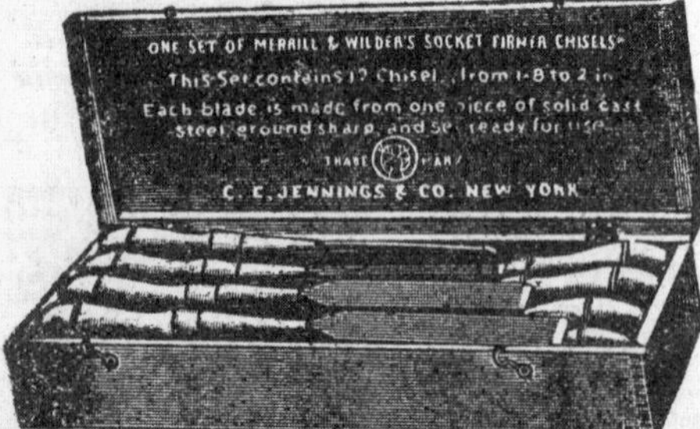

No. 35C2915 Set of 12 Merrill & Wilder's Extra Socket Firmer Chisels, made by C. E. Jennings & Co., with selected handles. Solid tool steel, sharpened ready for use. Blades are 6 inches to shoulder; sizes ⅛ to 2 inches. **Fully warranted.** Put up in fancy wood box as illustrated. Wt., 8½ lbs. Per set, **$3.80**

No. 35C2916 Set of 12 Merrill & Wilder's Beveled Edge Extra Selected Socket Firmer Chisels, made by C. E. Jennings & Co., with selected handles. Solid extra refined tool steel, sharpened ready for use. Blades are 6 inches to shoulder; sizes ⅛ to 2 inches. **Fully warranted.** Put up in fancy wood box, as illustrated. Weight, 8½ pounds. Price, per set **$4.40**

Chisel Handles.

All Chisel Handles sold by us are made from selected hickory timber, and are cheap at our price, when quality is considered.

No. 35C2950 Selected Hickory Handles for tanged chisels or gouges, with brass ferrules. Price, per dozen, **22c**; each... **2c**

No. 35C2951 Selected Hickory Handles for socket firmer or paring chisels or gouges. Price, per dozen, **15c**; each.... **2c**

No. 35C2952 Selected Hickory Handles for socket framing or corner chisels, with malleable iron ferrule on end to prevent splitting. Price, per dozen, **25c**; each.... **3c**

No. 35C2963 Leather Capped Hickory Chisel Handles, with three layers of solid sole leather in cap; for socket firmer chisels from ⅛ to 2 inches. Price, per dozen, **50c**; each.... **5c**

No. 35C2964 Leather Capped Chisel Handles, with three layers of solid sole leather in cap; for socket framing chisels. Price, per dozen, **56c**; each.... **5c**

No. 35C2965 Leather Capped Chisel Handles, with three layers of solid leather in cap and seamless brass tube ferrule; for tanged firmer chisels. Price, per dozen, **64c**; each.... **6c**

When ordering chisel handles, give size of chisel for which they are wanted.

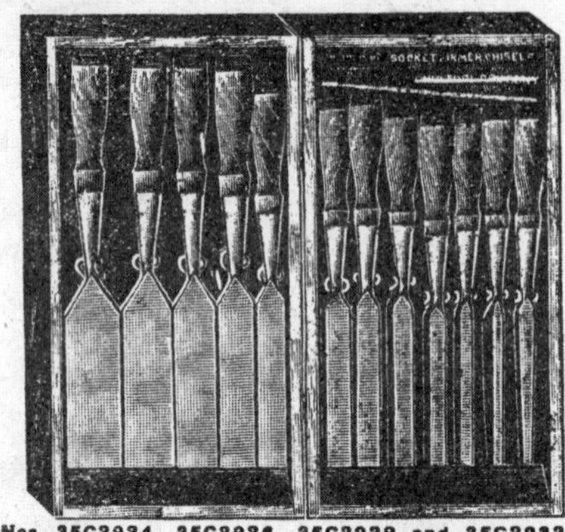

Nos. 35C2924, 35C2926, 35C2929 and 35C2932 are sets that no other dealers sell—not even anything which they claim is "just the same" or "just as good."

No. 35C2924 Fulton Tool Co.'s Extra Socket Firmer Chisels. Forged steel, with ebonized hickory leather tipped handles. Blades highly polished and heavily nickel plated. Twelve chisels, sizes, ⅛ to 2 inches, put up in wood box like illustration. Fully warranted. Price, per set.... **$4.20**

No. 35C2925 Fulton Tool Co.'s Extra Socket Firmer Chisels. Forged steel, with leather tipped hickory handles. Guaranteed to give satisfaction; twelve chisels, sizes, ⅛ to 2 inches, put up in a wood box like illustration. Fully warranted. Price, per set.... **$3.25**

No. 35C2926 Fulton Tool Co.'s Extra Socket Firmer Chisels. Forged steel, with ebonized hickory leather tipped handles. Blades highly polished and heavily nickel plated. Six chisels in a set; one each size, ¼, ½, ¾, 1, 1½ and 2 inches. Put up in wood box like illustration. Price, per set.... **$2.55**

No. 35C2928 Fulton Tool Co.'s Extra Socket Firmer Chisels. Forged steel, with leather tipped hickory handles. Six chisels in a set; one each size, ¼, ½, ¾, 1, 1½ and 2 inches. Put up in a wood box like illustration. Price, per set.... **$1.93**

No. 35C2929 Fulton Tool Co.'s Extra Socket Firmer Chisels, with bevel edge. Ebonized hickory leather tipped handles. Blades highly polished and heavily nickel plated. Guaranteed to give satisfaction; twelve chisels, ⅛ to 2 inches, put up in wood box like illustration. Fully warranted. Price, per set.... **$4.82**

No. 35C2931 Fulton Tool Co.'s Extra Socket Firmer Chisels, with bevel edge. Leather tipped handles. Guaranteed to give satisfaction; twelve chisels, ⅛ to 2 inches, put up in a wood box like illustration. Fully warranted. Per set... **$3.87**

No. 35C2932 Fulton Tool Co.'s Extra Socket Firmer Chisels, with bevel edges. Ebonized hickory leather tipped handles. Blades highly polished and heavily nickel plated. Fully warranted. Six chisels in set, one each size, ¼, ½, ¾, 1, 1½ and 2 inches. Put up in wood box like illustration above. Price, per set.... **$2.85**

No. 35C2933 Fulton Tool Co.'s Extra Socket Firmer Chisels, with bevel edges. Leather tipped handles. Fully warranted. Six chisels in set, one each size, ¼, ½, ¾, 1, 1½ and 2 inches. Put up in a wood box like illustration above. Price, per set.... **$2.24**

Drawing Knives.

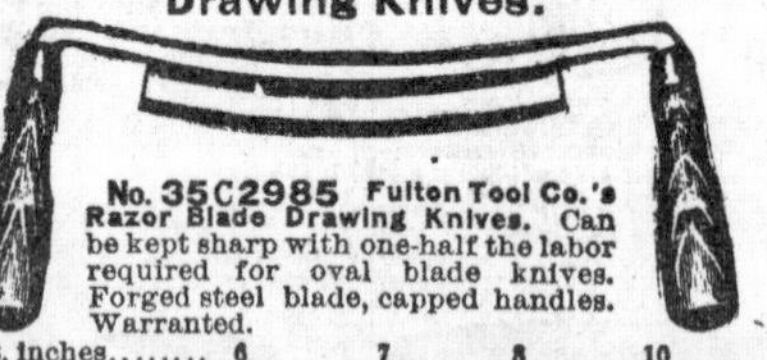

No. 35C2985 Fulton Tool Co.'s Razor Blade Drawing Knives. Can be kept sharp with one-half the labor required for oval blade knives. Forged steel blade, capped handles. Warranted.

Size cut, inches	6	7	8	10	12
Weight, pounds	1	1¼	1¼	1½	1¾
Price	34c	36c	38c	42c	46c

Folding Handle Drawing Knives.

No. 35C2987 Folding Handle Razor Blade Drawing Knife. Handles fold to protect cutting edge and save space in tool chest. Forged from best steel. Fully warranted.

Size cut, inches	6	8	10	12
Price, each	61c	65c	69c	73c

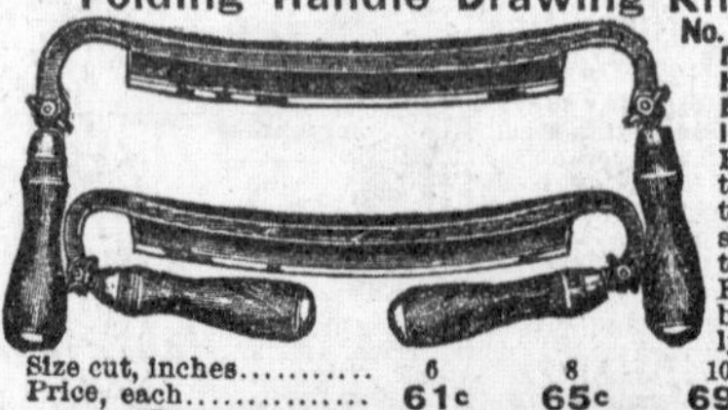

No. 35C2990 The Genuine Wilkinson's Folding and Adjustable Handle Drawing Knife, made of best cast steel; cutting edge protected. Handy, compact. Warranted.

Length of blade	6-inch	7-inch	8-inch	9-inch
Price	$1.06	$1.13	$1.21	$1.32

For carriage makers' drawing knife see department of blacksmiths' tools.

Shingle Knife.

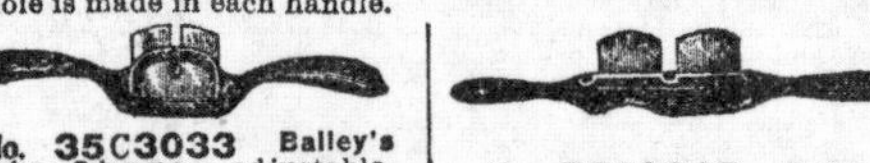

No. 35C3012 Fulton Tool Co.'s Shingle Knife. Blade is 1¾ inches wide, best steel blade, beechwood handles. Warranted. Length of cutting edge, 14 inches. Price.... **63c**

Bailey's Spoke Shaves.

Made by the Stanley Rule & Level Co., are in perfect working order when sent from the factory. They can be hung up, as a hole is made in each handle.

No. 35C3033 Bailey's Spoke Shave, adjustable, raised handle, 10-inch, 2⅛-inch cutter. Price.... **20c**

No. 35C3038 Bailey's Model Spoke Shave, double iron hollow face, 10-inch, 2⅛-inch, cutter. Price.... **14c**

No. 35C3041 Bailey's Model Spoke Shave, double iron, 10-inch, 2⅛-inch cutter. Price.... **14c**

No. 35C3045 Bailey's Spoke Shave, double cutter, hollow and straight, 10-inch, 1¾-inch cutter. Price.... **20c**

No. 35C3060 Goodell's Spoke Shave, rosewood handles, 2-inch cast steel cutter; either handle may be removed to work in close places; will work in smaller circles than any other shave made. Price.... **63c**

Screwdrivers.

No. 35C3073 Screwdrivers, forged steel blades. Beech wood handle, brass cap ferrule.

Size of blade, inches	2	3	4	5	6	8
Whole length, inches	5½	7½	9	10½	12½	15
Price	4c	5c	6c	7c	8c	12c

No. 35C3077 The Genuine Champion. Made by Tower & Lyon. We guarantee every blade not to turn, pull out or develop any imperfections in temper, quality or finish. Handle is dyed rosewood and has a high gloss finish. Ferrule and blade polished.

Size of blade, inches	3	4	5	6	8	10
Whole length, inches	7½	9	11½	12½	15	17
Price	15c	20c	24c	26c	35c	44c

No. 35C3082 Screwdriver, forged from a very tough grade of crucible steel. Rosewood finished handle, steel ferrule. This screwdriver will stand the most severe usage and is warranted.

Size of blade, inches	3	4	5	6	8	10
Whole length, inches	7½	9	11½	12½	15	17
Price	11c	12c	13c	14c	16c	18c

No. 35C3083 Yankee Ratchet Screwdriver. Right and left hand and rigid. The materials and workmanship are of superior quality in every detail.

Inches	4	5	6	8	10	12
Price	31c	33c	39c	44c	53c	58c

Goodell's Automatic Screwdriver.

Goodell's Automatic Screwdriver can be used as a spiral ratchet or a plain screwdriver.

No. 35C3096 Goodell's Spiral Screwdriver No. 1, stained cherry handle. Length closed, 7½ inches; open, 11½ inches, with three forged steel bits. Price.... **69c**

No. 35C3097 Goodell's Spiral Screwdriver No. 2, stained cherry handle. Length, closed, 9 inches; length, open, 13 inches; with three forged steel bits. Price.... **79c**

Reversible Automatic Screwdriver.

No. 35C3100 Goodell's Reversible Automatic Interchangeable Screwdriver No. 22. Strong and in every way a practical tool for both driving and drawing screws automatically. It has two separate and distinct spirals, each working entirely independent of the other: each furnished with three blades. Weight, 14 ounces. Price.... **$1.08**

Drill Attachment for Goodell's Automatic Screwdrivers consists of a chuck and 8 drill points. This attachment converts the automatic screwdriver into an automatic drill.

No. 35C3101 Drill Attachment, Size 1, fits Goodell's automatic screwdriver size 1, No. 35C3096. Price for attachment with 8 drill points.... **46c**

No. 35C3102 Drill Attachment, Size 2, fits Goodell's automatic screwdriver Nos. 2 and 22, catalogue Nos. 35C3097 and 35C3100. Price for attachment with 8 drill points.... **46c**

No. 35C3106 Yankee Spiral Ratchet Screwdriver No. 30. Standard size, right and left hand, and rigid; can be used to push or ratchet screws in or out; convenient in size and of light weight, yet stronger in these vital points than any similar tool now made. The chuck for holding the bits is simple in construction and positive in its hold on bits. Three bits are included with each tool. The extreme length of tool with bit in chuck is 13¾ inches when closed, and 19¾ in. when extended. Price... **$1.09**

No. 35C3108 Yankee Spiral Ratchet Screwdriver No. 31. Extra large size; with bit in chuck it measures when extended, 26¾ inches. Price.... **$1.47**

Yankee Chuck.

No. 35C3107 Yankee Chuck with drill points, for use in No. 35C3106 Yankee Spiral Ratchet Screwdriver. Eight drill points, 1-16 inch to 11-64 inch, inclusive, are furnished with each chuck. The chuck and eight drill points are put up in a small round wooden box. Price, per set of 1 chuck and 8 drills.... **38c**

No. 35C3109 Yankee Chuck with drill points to fit No. 35C3108 Yankee Screwdriver. Price, per set of 1 chuck and 8 drills.... **38c**

No. 35C3138 Yankee Automatic Drill. Bores holes in hard or soft woods without splitting. Pushing handle down revolves the drill, and a spring pushes handle back to its place. During the return movement the drill point revolves backward to clear chips, etc. The tool is nickel plated and finely finished. Eight drill points are furnished with each tool one each, 1-16, 5-64, 3-32, 7-64, ⅛, 9-64, 5-32, 11-64 inch. The entire length of tool inclusive of drill, as in illustration, is 11¾ inches. Price............**$1.12**

No. 35C3141 Extra Drill Points, to fit drill No. 35C3138 and chucks Nos. 35C3107 and 35C3109 in sets of 8, sizes, 1-16, 5-64, 3-32, 7-64, ⅛, 9-64, 5-32 and 11-64. Price, each, (any size)....**4c**
Per set of eight drills..............................**32c**

Yankee Reciprocating Drill.

No. 35C3145 Yankee Reciprocating Drill, is so constructed that the drill runs continuously to the right, during both the forward and backward movement of the driver. The head of the tool is provided with ball bearing to reduce the friction. The chuck has three jaws, is accurate and strong and will not get out of order. No drill points are furnished with this tool. The chuck will hold any drill with shanks 3-16-inch diameter or less. (See No. 35C3572.) The materials and workmanship throughout are of the best, and each tool is guaranteed. Price......**$1.65**

The Marvel Drill.

Puts holes into iron and brass easier than the common brace and bit does into hardwood. A 3-foot chain is fastened at one end of the feed and loops into the other end between any two links, thus holding the drill to articles of variable size. This drill works on ball bearings. Almost all of the pressure is thus directed to the cutting spot. This is the reason that it cuts so easy.

No. 35C3165 Style A. Takes standard or half-inch round shank drill. See No. 24C860. Price..............**59c**

No. 35C3166 Style B. Takes standard square shank, bit stock drill. See No. 35C3450. Price..............**60c**

No. 35C3167 Style C. Fitted with universal chuck. Will hold 1-16 to ½ inch round shank drills. See No. 35C3572. Price..............**$1.05**

No. 35C3168 Style D. With extra long chuck, a combination of styles A and B. The first opening will fit round drills. Above this is a square taper that will hold a square shank drill. Price..............**68c**

Bit Braces.

No. 35C3180 Bit Brace, with 7-16-inch cold drawn steel sweep and revolving stained head and handle. The best low priced brace made.
8-in. sweep Price.......**19c**
10-in. sweep. Price.......**22c**

No. 35C3179 Bit Brace, with black walnut head and handle, well made and nicely finished. Strong and serviceable.

Sweep, inches	8	10	12
Price, each	32c	35c	38c

No. 35C3181 Fray's Bit Brace. A strictly high grade brace. Steel sweep, forged steel jaws, lignum vitae head and handle. Jaws are blued, all other metal parts finely polished and nickel plated. The spring (of best music wire) attached to jaws, make them open automatically.

Sweep, inches	8	10	12	14
Price	47c	50c	55c	60c

No. 35C3185 Ratchet Bit Brace. Sweep is made of 7-16-inch cold drawn steel rod. The head and handle are stained hardwood. 10-inch sweep. Price.......**44c**

No. 35C3188 Nickel Plated Ratchet Bit Brace. Same as above only a little better finished. The brace is not polished before being plated. This brace will give good service. 10-inch sweep. Price.........**54c**

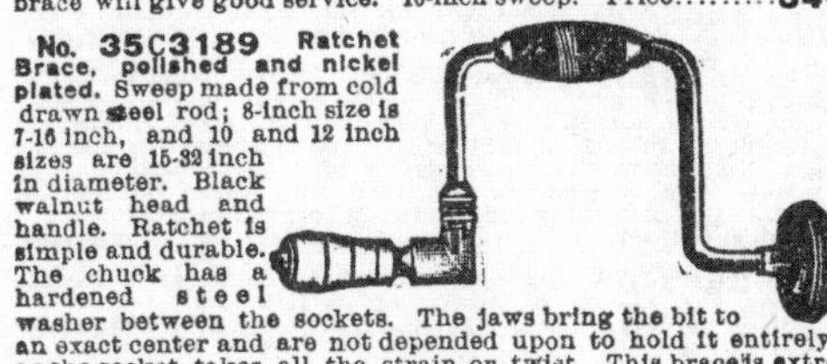

No. 35C3189 Ratchet Brace, polished and nickel plated. Sweep made from cold drawn steel rod; 8-inch size is 7-16 inch, and 10 and 12 inch sizes are 15-32 inch in diameter. Black walnut head and handle. Ratchet is simple and durable. The chuck has a hardened steel washer between the sockets. The jaws bring the bit to an exact center and are not depended upon to hold it entirely, as the socket takes all the strain or twist. This brace is extra strong, and in workmanship and finish is first class.

Sweep, inches	8	10	12
Price	67c	68c	69c

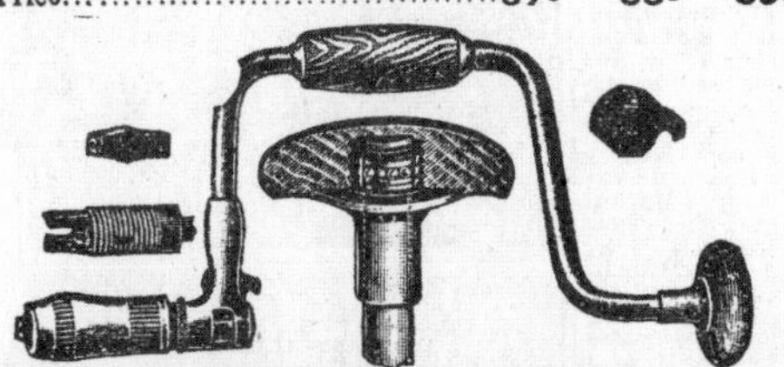

No. 35C3193 Ball Bearing Ratchet Brace, finely polished and heavily nickel plated. The balls run between two hardened steel washers, making a dustproof bearing which cannot get out of order. The sweep is made of cold drawn steel rod—strong and stiff. The 8-inch size is 7-16 inch and the 10 and 12-inch sizes are 15-32 inch in diameter. The chuck has a hardened steel washer between the sockets. The ratchet is simple, durable and handy, and when locked there is scarcely any lost motion. The bit is held by the socket and jaws serve only to center the bit and hold it in the brace when withdrawing from wood. Has lignum vitae head, cocobolo handle. One of the most practical ratchet braces in the market.

Sweep, inches	8	10	12
Price	82c	85c	87c

No. 35C3194 Fray's Ratchet Brace. Steel sweep, forged blued steel jaws and socket milled to fit, lignum vitae head and handle. All parts are made with as much care, but not polished so finely nor finished as expensively as on Fray's highest price braces. For use, they are just as strong. Fully guaranteed.

Sweep, inches	8	10	12	14
Price	80c	93c	$1.04	$1.15

No. 35C3195 Ball Bearing Ratchet Brace. Nickel plated, cocobola head and handles. Steel clad head. The sweep is made from finished cold drawn steel; the sweep on the 8-inch brace is made of 7-16-inch round steel, on the 10 and 12-inch of 15-32-inch, and on the 14-inch is ½-inch in diameter; the chuck has a hardened steel washer between the sockets; the jaws bring the bit to an exact center and are not depended upon to hold the tool entirely, as the interior of the socket is so constructed as to securely hold all sizes of bits, thus giving a perfect center and extra strength. The quality of material, workmanship and beauty of finish are unsurpassed.

Sweep, inches	8	10	12	14
Price, each	$1.00	$1.05	$1.10	$1.15

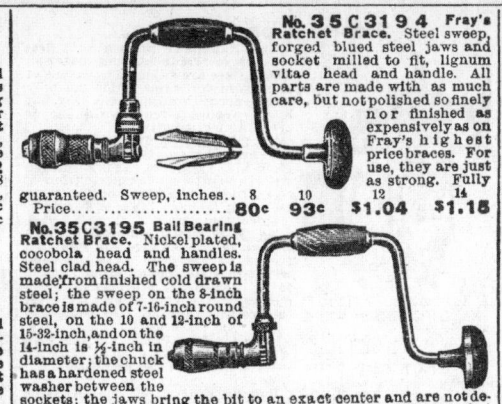

No. 35C3197 Fray's Ball Bearing Ratchet Brace. In these braces the square shank of the bit fits into a socket and is driven thereby the jaws, holding firmly by the round part of bit shank beyond the square, prevent its coming out. Crank, sleeve, jaws, ratchet and pawls are steel. Ball bearing head. Head and handle of cocobolo wood. Metal parts nickel plated. The hardened jaws open automatically as the sleeve is unscrewed until fully open, when a stop screw arrests the further motion of both sleeve and jaw. Fully guaranteed.

Sweep, inches	8	10	12	14
Price	$1.19	$1.30	$1.41	$1.52

Barber Improved Ratchet Braces.

No. 35C3199 The latest improved old reliable genuine Barber Ratchet Braces with alligator jaws and ball bearing head. Made by the Millers Fall Co. Jaws hold round or square shank drills or auger bits of all sizes. The sweep is made from steel. The jaws are forged from steel. The wood handle has brass rings inserted in each end so it cannot split off. The chuck has a hardened steel anti-friction washer between the two sockets, thus reducing the wear. The head has a bearing of steel balls, running on hardened steel plates, so no wear can take place, as the friction is reduced to the minimum. The brace is heavily nickel plated and warranted in every particular. They are made as nearly perfect as is possible in durability, quality of material and workmanship and beauty of finish. The 10-inch sweep is best for general work. The 6-inch size is a favorite with electricians.

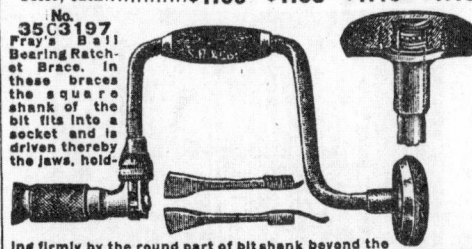

Sweep, inches	6	8	10	12	14
Price	$1.08	$1.19	$1.30	$1.41	$1.52

Ratchet Brace. With Ball Bearing Head and Samson Ball Bearing Chuck.

No. 35C3208 These Braces are finely finished and accurately fitted in every part. Lignum vitae head, rosewood center, positive ratchet, full nickel plated. The sleeve of the chuck is drilled through solid tool steel. The forged steel alligator jaws open parallel or at a slight angle; are interlocking and grip firmly either round, tapering or square shanks the entire length of the jaw, so that square shanks will not slip and round or tapering shanks will not turn or twist. The ball bearings in the chuck enforce a stronger grip than has ever been obtained by any chuck. It will hold equally well large expansive bits or the smallest twist drill. This brace is especially recommended for car, ship and bridge builders, and for all heavy work.

Sweep, inches	8	10	12	14
Price, each	$1.55	$1.65	$1.75	$1.90

Spofford Bit Braces.

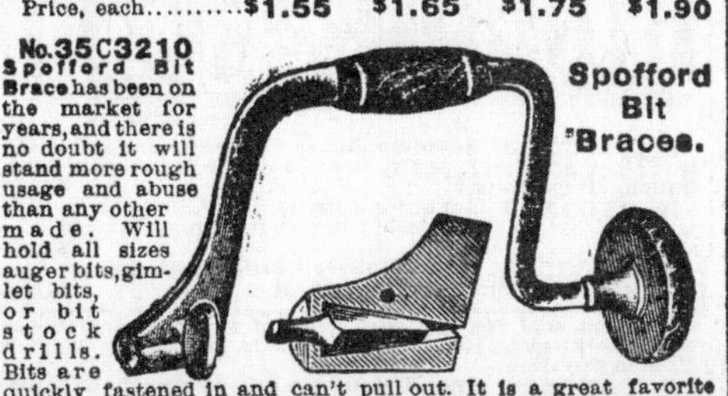

No. 35C3210 Spofford Bit Brace has been on the market for years, and there is no doubt it will stand more rough usage and abuse than any other made. Will hold all sizes auger bits, gimlet bits, or bit stock drills. Bits are quickly fastened in and can't pull out. It is a great favorite with blacksmiths and carriage builders. Solid steel, nickel plated, cocobolo head and handle, adjustable bit holder.

Sweep, inches	8	10	12	14	17
Price	75c	85c	94c	$1.03	$1.13

No. 35C3207 Spofford Bit Brace with metal head. Will hold bits of any size and is made to stand wear and tear.

Sweep, inches	8	10	12	14
Price	60c	69c	78c	88c

Drill and Ratchet Braces.

No. 35C3219 Drill and Rachet Brace. Barber 10-inch nickel plated steel sweep, ball bearing head, alligator jaws, forged from steel; the wood handle has brass rings inserted in each end so it cannot split off. The chuck has a hardened steel anti-friction washer between the two sockets, thus reducing the wear. The head has a bearing of steel balls, running on hardened steel plates. The braces are heavily nickel plated and warranted in every particular. The drill gear is detachable and is easily and quickly adjusted. Jaws hold all kinds of bits and drills. Price..............**$2.46**

Boring Machine.

No. 35C3225

$2.58

No. 35C3225 Angular Boring Machines. Adjustable to bore at any angle. Holds any standard boring machine auger. Strong and well finished. Without augers.
Price....**$2.58**

Two Speed Boring Machine.

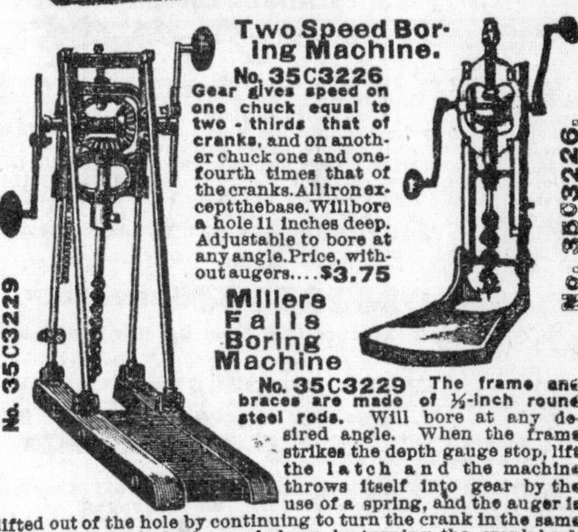

No. 35C3226 Gear gives speed on one chuck equal to two-thirds that of cranks, and on another chuck one and one-fourth times that of the cranks. All iron except the base. Will bore a hole 11 inches deep. Adjustable to bore at any angle. Price, without augers....**$3.75**

Millers Falls Boring Machine

No. 35C3229 The frame and braces are made of ½-inch round steel rods. Will bore at any desired angle. When the frame strikes the depth gauge stop, lifts the latch and the machine throws itself into gear by the use of a spring, and the auger is lifted out of the hole by continuing to turn the crank in the same direction, then it is dropped down by turning the crank back until the auger strikes the wood, when it is thrown out of gear, and proceeds to bore the next hole.
Price, without augers..........................**$6.67**

Boring Machine Augers.

No. 35C3230 Extra Quality Augers for above or any other boring machine of standard make, fully warranted.

Size, inches	1	1¼	1½	1¾	2
Price	25c	30c	36c	42c	50c

No. 35C3231 This auger will bore with less friction, will bore smoother, will bore deeper without withdrawing than any other auger we have ever seen. They are made of a high grade crucible steel, well finished and carefully inspected.

Size, inches	¾	⅞	1	1¼	1½	1¾	2
Price	43c	46c	49c	55c	61c	67c	73c

Carpenters' Augers.

No. 35C3235 Extra Quality Carpenters' Auger. Handle not included at price given. Extra tool steel, full polished; nut on end of shank.

Size, inches	¾	⅞	1	1¼	1½	1¾
Price	16c	18c	20c	24c	30c	36c
Size, inches	2	2¼	2½	2¾	3	
Price	44c	80c	$1.00	$1.19	$1.39	

Auger Handles.

No. 35C3239 Will fit any size auger, and is quickly removed, so augers can be easily packed in tool chest. Only one handle required for a full set of augers. Weight, 1 pound. Price..........**15c**

No. 35C3240 Common Auger Handles. When ordering state for what size auger handle is wanted.
Price..**3c**

Auger Bits.

No. 35C3250 Best Grade Common Pattern Auger Bits. Every bit is made from extra tool steel, with double spur and lip nicely finished. They are fully warranted. For common use or in the hands of one who is not a mechanic, they will give better satisfaction than our higher priced goods.

Size, inch	3-16	¼	5-16	⅜	7-16	½	9-16
Price, each	9c	8c	8c	9c	9c	9c	10c
Per dozen	93c	81c	82c	87c	88c	94c	98c
Size, inch	⅝	11-16	¾	13-16	⅞	15-16	1
Price, each	10c	11c	12c	14c	15c	16c	18c
Per dozen	$1.05	1.17	1.28	1.40	1.51	1.70	1.86

Be sure to state size wanted when ordering.

Extension Lip Auger Bits.

Commonly called Jennings Pattern.

The difference in the price of our auger bits represents the difference in cost of labor in making them. The most expensive operation is fitting the head of the bit and **has everything to do with making a bit work satisfactorily.** The next most expensive operation is polishing the hollow of the twist and adds to appearance only. It does not make a bit work any better. Wishing to offer a bit that for work would be equal to the best, we have brought out the Fulton bit—having the head fitted as good as the best bit-maker in the world can do it, and having the hollow of the twist left unpolished just as it comes from the hammer. We guarantee our Fulton auger bit will bore as smooth and be as satisfactory in every way as the most expensive bit on the market. If not as satisfactory in every way (appearance as well as everything else) they may be returned to us within 30 days and money will be refunded, together with transportation charges.

No. 35C3253 The Fulton Extension Lip Auger Bit with head fitted by hand as good as can possibly be done, unpolished hollow in twist, guaranteed to please the most expert woodworker; coarse thread on screw.

Size, inch	¼	5-16	⅜	7-16	½	9-16	⅝	11-16	¾
Price, each	14c	16c	18c	20c	22c	24c	26c	28c	30c
Size, inches	13-16	⅞	15-16	1	1⅛	1¼	1⅜	1½	
Price, each	33c	35c	38c	41c	46c	52c	57c	63c	

No. 35C3255 Extension Lip Auger Bit, commonly called Jennings Pattern. These bits are made from the finest tool steel and are designed for mechanics' use. Warranted.

Size, inch	¼	5-16	⅜	7-16	½	9-16	⅝
Price	11c	11c	12c	12c	12c	13c	14c
Size, inch	11-16	¾	13-16	⅞	15-16	1	
Price	15c	17c	18c	20c	22c	24c	

Russell Jennings' Bits.

No. 35C3263 The Genuine Russell Jennings' Extension Lip Auger Bits. Every bit fully warranted.

Size, inch	¼	5-16	⅜	7-16	½	9-16	⅝
Price	18c	21c	23c	27c	29c	32c	34c
Size, inch	11-16	¾	13-16	⅞	15-16	1	
Price	37c	40c	44c	47c	51c	55c	

Bailey Auger Bits.

No. 35C3275 The Bailey Auger Bit has one-half of the twist left out, making them single spiral, allowing the chips to pass up and out entirely free, which obviates the necessity of frequently withdrawing the bit to clear the hole. **A high grade of crucible steel is used in them. They are carefully made,** well finished, each bit being closely inspected before leaving the factory.

Size, inch	3-16	¼	5-16	⅜	7-16	½	9-16	⅝	11-16
Price	12c	11c	12c	14c	16c	17c	19c	20c	22c
Size, inches	¾	13-16	⅞	15-16	1	1⅛	1¼	1⅜	1½
Price	24c	26c	28c	30c	32c	36c	40c	45c	49c

Car Bits.

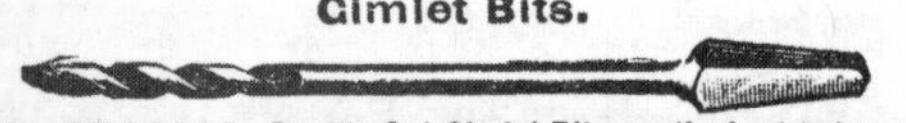

No. 35C3286 Superior Cast Steel Car Bits, with 12-inch twist. Warranted.

Size, inches	4-16	5-16	6-16	7-16	8-16	9-16	10-16	11-16
Price	23c	24c	27c	32c	37c	40c	46c	48c
Size, inches	12-16	13-16	14-16	15-16	16-16	17-16	18-16	
Price	55c	59c	63c	67c	73c	86c	96c	

No. 35C3290 Ship Auger Car Bits, with screws. Length of twist, 12 inches. Used by car builders, millwrights, etc.

Size, inch	5-16	⅜	7-16	½	9-16	⅝	11-16	¾
Price	34c	36c	38c	40c	42c	44c	46c	48c
Size, inches	13-16	⅞	15-16	1	17-16	1⅛	19-16	1¼
Price	50c	52c	56c	58c	62c	64c	68c	70c

Auger Bit File.

No. 35C3295 Auger Bit File. This is the only file ever invented to file all sizes of auger bits without filing the screw and lip away and spoiling your tool.
Price, per dozen, $1.02; each........9c

Gimlet Bits.

No. 35C3299 Double Cut Gimlet Bits are the best to buy if you are not a skilled mechanic. Extra quality tool steel, polished. No. 0 is about 1-16. The other numbers increase gradually up to No. 6, which is about ¼ inch. Be sure to state what number is wanted.

Number	0	1	2	3	4	5	6
Price, each	3c	3c	3c	3c	3c	3c	3c
Per dozen	29c	29c	29c	29c	29c	29c	29c

No. 35C3300 A Set of Gimlet Bits, one of each size. Weight, 10 ounces. Price, per set of seven........16c

No. 35C3305 German Pattern Gimlet Bits. Extra quality tool steel. Will bore with small risk of splitting. The small sizes are easily broken if not handled right, and should be used carefully. Draw the bit when you have bored to depth of pod, and you will have no trouble then to bore as deep as bit will go.

Size, inch	1-16	3-32	⅛	5-32	3-16	7-32	¼	5-16
Price	4c	4c	4c	4c	4c	4c	4c	4c
Per dozen	42c	42c	42c	42c	42c	42c	42c	42c

No. 35C3306 A set of the above bits, one of each size. Weight, 10 ounces. Price, per set of eight........26c

Countersink Gimlet Bits.

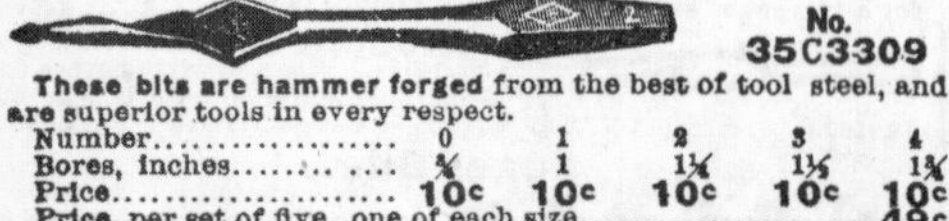

No. 35C3309

These bits are hammer forged from the best of tool steel, and are superior tools in every respect.

Number	0	1	2	3	4
Bores, inches	¾	1	1¼	1½	1¾
Price	10c	10c	10c	10c	10c

Price, per set of five, one of each size........49c

Clark's Expansive Bits.

With this tool you can bore holes of any diameter between sizes mentioned. It is elegantly made and highly polished. Made in two sizes.

No. 35C3320 The Fulton, Clark's Improved Expansive Bit. Small size, with two cutters, one boring from ½ to ⅞ inch, the other from ⅞ to 1½ inches. Price, complete........51c

No. 35C3321 The Fulton, Clark's Improved Expansive Bit. Large size, with two cutters, one boring from ⅞ to 1¾ inches, the other boring from 1¾ to 3 inches. Price, complete........74c

No. 35C3322 Extra Cutters only for small size Clark's Expansive Bits.
No. 1. Cuts from ½ to ⅞ inch. Price........9c | No. 2. Cuts from ⅞ to 1½ inches. Price........11c

No. 35C3323 Extra Cutters only for large size Clark's Expansive Bits. No. 3. Cuts from ⅞ to 1¾ inches. Price........15c
No. 4. Cuts from 1¾ to 3 inches. Price........17c | No. 5. Cuts from 3 to 4 inches. Price........26c

Steers' Expansive Bits.

This Expansive Bit is strictly first class in workmanship and material. The cutters are adjusted by means of a micrometer screw which not only makes accurate adjustment easy, but also prevents the cutters slipping or creeping while boring.

No. 35C3331 Steers' Expansive Bit (small size), to bore any size hole from ⅝ to 1¾ inches. It is furnished with two cutters, one boring from ⅝ to 1⅛ inches, the other boring from 1⅛ to 1¾ inches. Weight, 8 ounces.
Price, complete........$1.15

No. 35C3332 Steers' Expansive Bit (large size) to bore any size hole from ⅞ to 3 inches. It is furnished with two cutters, one boring from ⅞ to 1¾ inches, the other boring from 1¾ to 3 inches. Weight, 14 ounces. Price, complete........$1.35

No. 35C3333 Extra Cutters only for small size Steers' Expansive Bit.
No. 1, to bore from ⅝ to 1⅛ inches. Price........18c
No. 2, to bore from 1⅛ to 1¾ inches. Price........23c

No. 35C3334 Extra Cutters only for large size Steers' Expansive Bit.
No. 3, to bore from ⅞ to 1¾ inches. Price........31c
No. 4, to bore from 1¾ to 3 inches. Price........35c
No. 5, to bore from 3 to 4 inches. Price........73c

Bit Sets in Boxes.

87c to $3.69 for sets of 6, 8 or 13 fine cast steel auger bits in neat polished wood boxes.

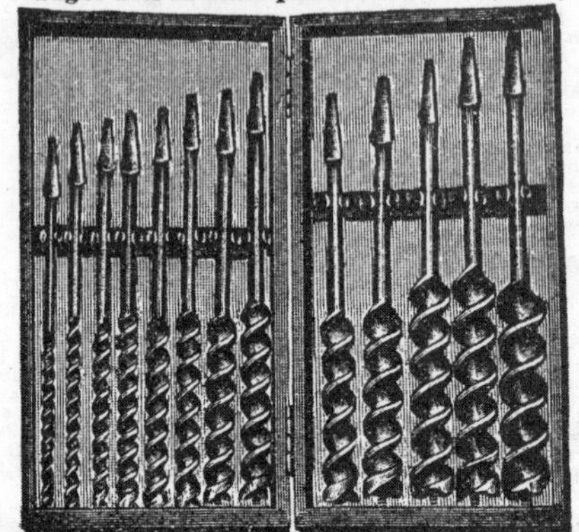

No. 35C3365 Set of Six Selected Extra Tool Steel, Common Pattern Auger Bits, with double spur and lip, nicely finished. Size, ¼, ⅜, ½, ⅝, ¾ and 1 inch. Put up in a finely finished, fancy hardwood box, every bit is fully warranted. Weight, per set, 2 pounds. Price, per set........87c

No. 35C3368 Our Favorite Set of Eight Selected Extra Tool Steel Common Pattern Auger Bits with double spur and lip, nicely finished. Warranted. Size, ¼, 5-16, ⅜, ½, ⅝, ¾, ⅞ and 1 inch. Put up in a nicely finished fancy hardwood box. Weight, per set, 2¾ lbs. Price, per set........$1.12

No. 35C3371 Our Acme Set of Eight Selected Extension Lip Auger Bits, warranted. Sizes, ¼, 5-16, ⅜, ½, ⅝, ¾, ⅞ and 1 inch. Put up in a finely finished hardwood box. Weight, 2¾ pounds. Price, per set........$1.44

No. 35C3372 Our Fulton Bit Set, consisting of eight selected Fulton auger bits as described under No. 35C3253. Fully warranted. One each of the following sizes: ¼, 5-16, ⅜, ½, ⅝, ¾, ⅞ and 1 inch, packed in nicely finished hardwood box, as per illustration. Price, per set........$2.25

No. 35C3374 Set of Thirteen Selected Extra Tool Steel Common Pattern Auger Bits, with double spur and lip, one each size from ¼ to 1 inch, put up in a nicely polished fancy hardwood box. Weight, per set, 5 pounds. Price, per set........$1.73

No. 35C3377 Set of Thirteen Selected Extension Lip Auger Bits, one each size from ¼ to 1 inch, put up in a nicely finished fancy hardwood box. Weight, per set, 5 pounds.
Price, per set........$2.25

No. 35C3378 Our Winner Bit Set consisting of thirteen selected Fulton auger bits as described under No. 35C3253. Fully warranted. One each size from ¼ to 1 inch packed in nicely finished hardwood box, as illustrated. Price, per set........$3.69

Bailey Bits in Sets.

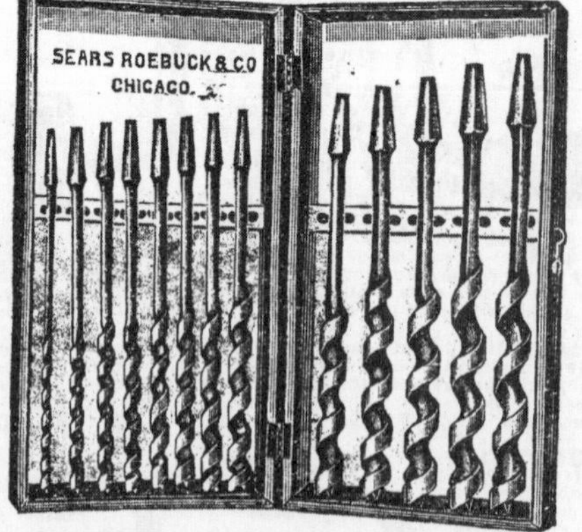

In Fancy Boxes, Nicely Varnished. (For description of bit see No. 35C3275.)

No. 35C3384 Set of Six Bailey Auger Bits, one each size, ¼, ⅜, ½, ⅝, ¾ and 1 inch, put up in same style box as shown in illustration. Price, per set........$1.39

No. 35C3387 Set of Nine Bailey Auger Bits, one each size, ¼, 5-16, ⅜, 7-16, ½, ⅝, ¾, ⅞ and 1 inch, put up in same style box as shown. Price, per set........$2.00

No. 35C3390 Set of Thirteen Bailey Auger Bits, one each size, ¼ to 1 inch in box. Price, per set........$3.00

Jennings' Auger Bits.

No. 35C3399 C. E. Jennings & Co.'s Single Twist Extension Lip Auger Bits. Put up in a quartered oak bit box. One each size, From 4-16 to 16-16 inch. Thirteen bits.
Price, per set..$5.50

No. 35C3266 Set of Thirteen Genuine Russell Jennings' Auger Bits. One each size from 4-16 to 16-16. Put up in a patent three-compartment wooden box. Every bit fully warranted. Price, per set........$4.55

Brace and Bit Sets.

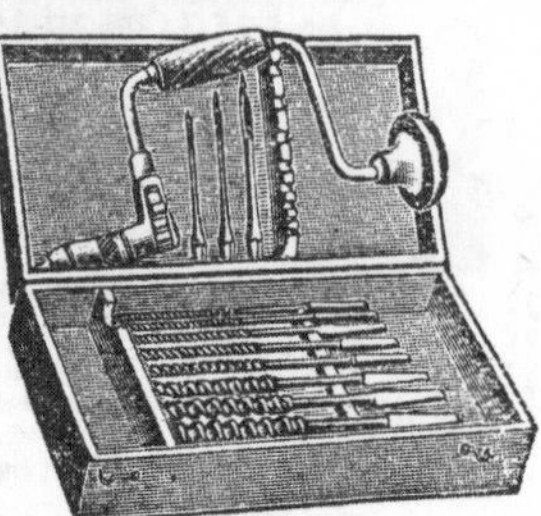

No. 35C3400 Brace and Bit Set. Ball bearing ratchet brace, nickel plated, 10-inch sweep, rosewood head and handle, hardened steel jaws; strictly first class, high grade goods; eight extra selected cast steel auger bits; common pattern, with double spur and lip. Sizes, ¼, 5-16, ⅜, ½, ⅝, ¾, ⅞ and 1 inch. Every bit warranted. Three German gimlet bits, sizes, 1-16, ⅛ and 3-16. All in a finely finished hardwood box.
Price, per set....$2.14

No. 35C3403 Brace and Bit Set. We furnish our No. 35C3197 brace, with 10-inch sweep. Has ball bearing steel capped heads. Rosewood head and handle; will hold round shank twist drill, and all styles square shank bits. The finest finish possible. Heavily nickel plated. Eight extension lip auger bits. Sizes, ¼, 5-16, ⅜, ½, ⅝, ¾, ⅞ and 1 inch. Three German gimlet bits, sizes 1-16, ⅛ and 3-16 inch. One Clark's expansion bit, cutting any size hole from ⅞ to 3 inches. In a hardwood box. Price, per set........$3.60

No. 35C3404 Brace and Bit Set. Same as above except expansion bit is left out. Price, per set........$2.86

No. 35C3405 Brace and Bit Set. Consists of one No. 35C3197. brace, 10-inch sweep. Eight Fulton auger bits No. 35C3253, each size, ¼, 5-16, ⅜, ½, ⅝, ¾, ⅞ and 1 inch. One Steers' expansive bit No. 35C3332. Eight German pattern gimlet bits, one each size, No. 35C3305. One screwdriver bit. One countersink for metal. One countersink for wood. One auger bit file. All packed in a nicely finished hardwood box, as illustrated.
Price, per set........$5.44

No. 35C3406 Brace and Bit Set. Same as preceding, except the Steers' expansive bit is left out.
Price, per set........$4.05

No. 35C3407 Our "Best of All" Brace and Bit Set, consists of a No. 35C3208 ball bearing chuck brace, 10-inch sweep. Eight "Fulton" extension lip auger bits, sizes, ¼, 5-16, ⅜, ½, ⅝, ¾, ⅞ and 1 inch. One Steers' expansive bit, boring any size from ⅞ to 3 inches. Eight German pattern gimlet bits. One screwdriver bit. One countersink for metal. One countersink for wood; one auger bit file. All packed in nicely finished hardwood box. Price, per set........$5.75

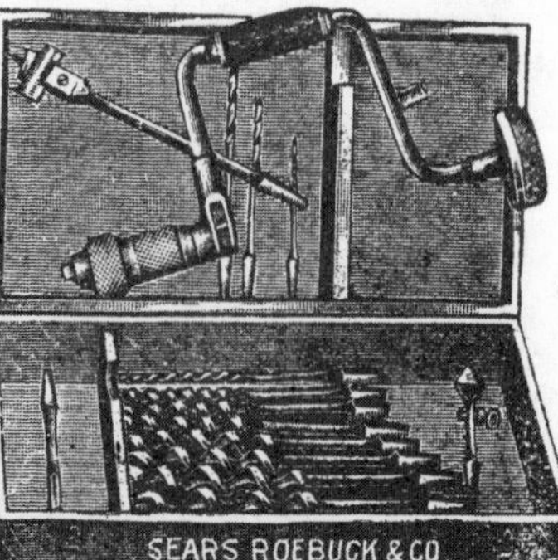

No. 35C3408 Same set as above with expansive bit left out.
Price, per set........$4.50

Screwdriver, Reamer and Countersink Bits.

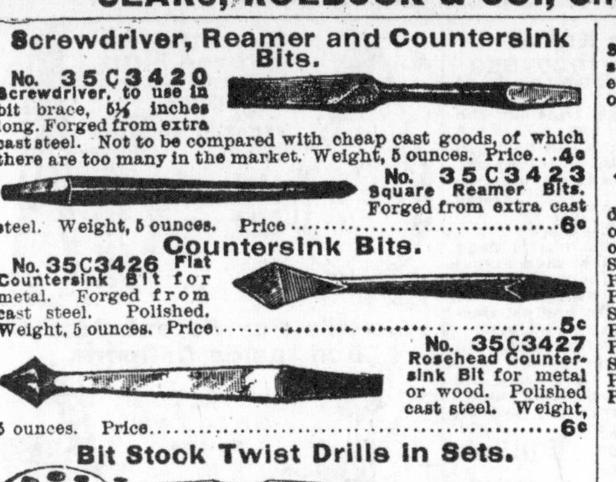

No. 35C3420 Screwdriver, to use in bit brace, 5½ inches long. Forged from extra cast steel. Not to be compared with cheap cast goods, of which there are too many in the market. Weight, 5 ounces. Price....4c

No. 35C3423 Square Reamer Bits. Forged from extra cast steel. Weight, 5 ounces. Price....6c

Countersink Bits.

No. 35C3426 Flat Countersink Bit for metal. Forged from cast steel. Polished. Weight, 5 ounces. Price....5c

No. 35C3427 Rosehead Countersink Bit for metal or wood. Polished cast steel. Weight, 5 ounces. Price....6c

Bit Stock Twist Drills in Sets.

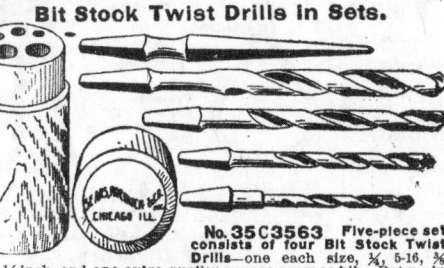

No. 35C3563 Five-piece set consists of four Bit Stock Twist Drills—one each size, ¼, 5-16, ⅜ and ½ inch, and one extra quality square reamer bit. Put up in a round wood case, which serves as a permanent receptacle for the tools. Drills will bore either wood or iron.
Price, for complete set with box....89c

No. 35C3431 Snail Head Countersink for wood. Polished cast steel. Weight, 5 ounces. Price....6c

Twist Drills.

No. 35C3450 Twist Drills for bit brace. Will drill metal or bore wood. The price is now so low that everyone owning a bit brace should have a set of these drills. Keep point of drill well oiled when drilling metal.

Size, inch	1-16	3-32	⅛	5-32	3-16	7-32	¼	9-32
Price, each	4c	5c	6c	7c	$0.09	0.10	0.11	0.13
Per dozen	48c	53c	68c	84c	1.00	1.16	1.32	1.51

Size, inch	5-16	11-32	⅜	13-32	7-16	15-32
Price, each	$0.15	0.17	0.20	0.22	0.24	0.26
Per dozen	1.73	2.02	2.31	2.57	2.82	3.08

Size, inch	½	⅝	¾	⅞	1
Price, each	$0.28	0.44	0.53	0.63	0.76
Per dozen	3.30	5.18	6.33	7.49	9.02

Bit Stock Drill Set.

No. 35C3566 Set of 9 Bit Stock Drills, put up in a wood box similar to No. 35C3563 (without reamer). Sizes are as follows: 1-16, 3-32, ⅛, 5-32, 3-16, 7-32, ¼, 5-16 and ⅜ inch.
Price, per set, complete....85c

Countersink with Gauge.

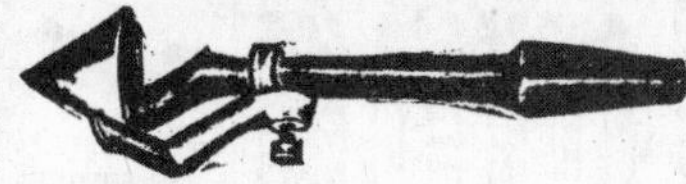

No. 35C3437 Countersink for wood, with gauge. Weight, 5 ounces. Price....14c

Straight Shank Drills.

No. 35C3572 Straight Shank Twist Drills; 64ths of an inch sizes. These drills cannot be used in the ordinary bit brace. They must be used in a chuck made for round shank drills. The shank and twist are the same size. We guarantee the quality equal to any made.

Diameter	Length	Price, per dozen	Price, each	Diameter	Length	Price, per dozen	Price, each
1/16	2½	$0.32	$0.03	19/64	4⅜	$1.23	$0.11
5/64	2⅝	.35	.04	5/16	4½	1.33	.12
3/32	2¾	.38	.04	21/64	4⅝	1.42	.13
7/64	2⅞	.41	.04	11/32	4¾	1.52	.14
⅛	3	.46	.05	23/64	4⅞	1.61	.15
9/64	3⅛	.51	.05	⅜	5	1.70	.16
5/32	3¼	.57	.06	25/64	5⅛	1.80	.17
11/64	3⅜	.63	.06	13/32	5¼	1.89	.17
3/16	3½	.70	.07	27/64	5⅜	2.02	.18
13/64	3⅝	.76	.07	7/16	5½	2.15	.20
7/32	3¾	.84	.08	29/64	5⅝	2.27	.21
15/64	3⅞	.92	.09	15/32	5¾	2.37	.22
¼	4	1.00	.09	31/64	5⅞	2.46	.22
17/64	4⅛	1.07	.10	½	6	2.52	.23
9/32	4¼	1.15	.11				

Pincers and Pliers.

No. 35C3700 Carpenters' Pincers, with claw on handle, forged from superior steel, adapted for the work.
Size, inches.... 6, 8, 10, 12
Price.... 15c, 18c, 21c, 27c

No. 35C3701 Sears, Roebuck & Co.'s Extra High Grade Special Carpenters' Pincers. Pincers have a cutting edge and will cut small wire, brads, etc. They are made from strong, tough steel, carefully finished and tempered. Full polished all over. We have made this just as good as possible, regardless of cost. To this cost we have added only our one small profit. Length, 8 inches. Price....40c

No. 35C3702 The Peck, Stow & Wilcox Co.'s Flat Nose Pliers, with box joint. The best made, best fitted and strongest plier on the market.
Size, inches.... 4, 4½, 5, 6
Price.... 21c, 22c, 24c, 29c

No. 35C3703 The Peck, Stow & Wilcox Co.'s Flat Nose Pliers, with lap joint. Strong and serviceable.
Size, inches.... 4, 5, 6
Price.... 13c, 14c, 17c

No. 35C3704 The Peck, Stow & Wilcox Co.'s Round Nose Pliers, with box joint. The best and strongest made.
Size, inches.... 5, 6, 7
Price.... 25c, 30c, 41c

No. 35C3706 Peck, Stow & Wilcox Co.'s Round Nose Pliers, with lap joint. Strong and serviceable.
Size, inches.... 4, 5, 6
Price.... 14c, 15c, 18c

No. 35C3707 Peck, Stow & Wilcox Co.'s Side Cutting Pliers. Box joint, raised cutters. The strongest and most popular plier on the market today.
Size, inches.... 5, 6, 7, 8
Price.... 60c, 65c, 80c, 95c

No. 35C3709 Peck, Stow & Wilcox Co.'s Side Cutting Pliers. Same as preceding number, nickel plated.
Size, inches.... 5, 6, 7, 8
Price.... 77c, 83c, $1.03, $1.20

No. 35C3710 Peck, Stow & Wilcox Co.'s Side Cutting Pliers, with lap joint, raised cutters. Forged from crucible steel and equal in every respect to any plier in the world, except the Peck, Stow & Wilcox Co.'s box joint pliers. Size, inches.... 5, 6, 7, 8
Price.... 42c, 45c, 57c, 67c

No. 35C3711 Peck, Stow & Wilcox Co.'s Side Cutting Pliers, with splicing attachment. Box joint, raised cutters. This plier is used by linemen and wireworkers for splicing wires.
Size, inches.... 6, 7, 8
Price.... 86c, $1.05, $1.19

No. 35C3714 Peck, Stow & Wilcox Co.'s Side Cutting Pliers, with splicing attachment, lap joint, raised cutters, forged from crucible steel strong and durable.
Size, inches.... 6, 7, 8
Price.... 70c, 84c, 95c

No. 35C3715 Peck, Stow & Wilcox Co.'s Diagonal Cutting Plier. Swedish pattern, box joint, forged from the best crucible steel. The strongest and best plier of this pattern. Size, inches.... 4½, 5, 6
Price.... 60c, 62c, 65c

No. 35C3716 Peck, Stow & Wilcox Co.'s Long Chain Nose Side Cutting Plier. Lap joint. Used by telephone manufacturers, machinists, jewelers, engineers, opticians, electricians, etc. Length, 5½ inches. Price....50c

No. 35C3717 Peck, Stow & Wilcox Co.'s Long Chain Nose Plier, without side cutter. Lap joint. Length, 5 inches. Price....28c

No. 35C3718 Peck, Stow & Wilcox Co.'s End Cutting Nipper. Lap joint, forged from crucible steel. The best end cutting nipper made.
Size, inches.... 4, 5, 6, 8
Price.... 43c, 48c, 57c, 72c

For Other Pliers See Page 437.

No. 35C3758 The Keyes Solid Steel Plier is a good general purpose plier, but not suitable for wireworkers.
Size, inches.... 4, 5, 6, 7
Price, each.... 4c, 5c, 6c, 7c
Per dozen.... 38c, 49c, 57c, 68c

No. 35C3760 End Cutting Nipper, solid steel. Tempered to cut ordinary wire. Will not cut piano wire. The best nipper to be had at anything like the price. Length, 5 inches.
Price....18c

No. 35C3761 Compound Lever Solid Steel Cutting Nippers. Carefully tempered and tested. Will cut all kinds of soft wire, but not intended for piano wire. Length, 5½ inches. Price....35c

No. 35C3739 Family Plier and Cutter and Gas Burner Plier. It's a good one for the money. Length, 6 inches. Weight, 7 ounces. Price....15c

Cold Chisels.

No. 35C3800 Cold Chisels, made from octagon tool steel, ⅝ inch in diameter, with the cutting end drawn out wider, as shown above. Weight, 5 ounces. Price....6c

No. 35C3801 Cold Chisel. Same as above, made from ¾-inch octagon steel. Weight, 1 pound 2 ounces. Price....12c

No. 35C3802 Our Fulton Cold Chisel is hammered from a special grade of tough crucible tool steel, carefully tempered. We could not produce a better chisel. It is full polished all over. Size indicates diameter of octagon stock from which chisel is made.
Size, inches.... ½, ⅝, ¾
Price.... 13c, 20c, 32c

No. 35C3803 Our Fulton Cold Chisel, same as above except it is not polished.
Size, inches.... ½, ⅝, ¾
Price.... 9c, 15c, 23c

The brand "Fulton" means the best that can be produced.

Knurled Punches.

No. 35C3807 Knurled Prick Punch. Diameter, ⅜ inch. Price....7c

No. 35C3808 Knurled Center Punch. Diameter, ⅜-inch. Price....7c

Nail Sets.

No. 35C3825 Knurled Nail Set, with cup or hollow point. Just the thing for starting screws which are rusty or have broken heads. Tempered at both ends. Weight, 4 ounces.

Size of points	2-32	3-32	4-32	5-32
Price, each	5c	5c	5c	5c
Per dozen	50c	50c	50c	50c

No. 35C3826 Set of Four Knurled Nail Sets. Assorted sizes, Price, per set....19c

Bench Screws.

No. 35C3836 Wrought Iron Bench Screws, with well cut double thread, wood handle and movable collars.

Our bench screws are full size, longer and better made than some that are in the market.

Diam., in.	Length, in.	Wt., lbs.	Price
1	16½	4½	24c
1⅛	16½	5¼	28c
1¼	17½	6½	34c
1½	19½	10	62c

Bench Stops.

No. 35C3847 Bench Stops, reversible cast steel, head, screw adjusting. Weight, 1 pound.
Price....23c

Clamps.

No. 35C3860 Quilt Frame Clamp, with improved ball and socket head on screw. Can be used as a cabinet clamp. Nicely japanned. 2½-inch opening.
Price, per doz. 33c; each....3c
3-inch opening. Price, per doz.. 40c; each 4c

No. 35C3863 Quilt Frame Clamps, japanned iron, intended especially to hold quilt frames, but are convenient for many purposes; opens 2¼ inches. Price, per set of four, 9c; each....3c
Price, per dozen....25c

No. 35C3866 Malleable Iron Screw Clamps; swivel head, wrought steel screw.

Opens, inches	Weight, lbs.	Price, per doz.	Price, each
3	1¼	$1.13	10c
4	1½	1.50	14c
5	1¾	1.85	16c
6	2	2.40	21c
7	3	2.85	25c
8	3¼	3.30	29c
10	5¼	4.00	35c

Wood Hand Screw Clamps.

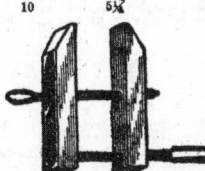

No. 35C3872 Wood Hand Screw Clamps. Picture shows complete set.

Length of jaw, in.	Length of screw, in.	Size of jaw, in.	Price, per doz. sets	Price, per set
8	10	1⅜	$1.75	15c
10	12	1⅝	2.10	18c
12	14	1⅞	2.50	22c
16	18	2⅛	3.50	30c
20	24	2⅜	4.75	40c

Eccentric Clamp.

No. 35C3876 Cabinet Makers' and Builders' Heavy Steel Bar Eccentric Clamp.

In.	Price, per doz.	Price, each	In.	Price, per doz.	Price, each
12	$5.48	47c	30	$8.33	72c
18	6.34	55c	36	9.13	79c
24	7.31	63c	48	10.96	94c

FOR BLACKSMITHS' DRILLS
See Department of Blacksmiths' Tools.

FOR ELECTRICIANS' DRILLS
See Department of Electrical Supplies.
REFER TO INDEX FOR ANY ARTICLE YOU WANT.

Carpenters' Steel Bar Clamps.

No. 35C3877 Carpenters' Steel Bar Clamps. The bar is rolled from a special quality stiff steel; the "T" shape has much more strength for a given weight than is possessed by flat stock. The notches are cut on the lower edge of the bar, affording greater holding power to the sliding jaw than if cut on the upper edge. The wrought iron screw is provided with a deep thread; the head, crank, sliding jaws and pawl are malleable iron, and the handle of wood, ebonized. The sizes given below represent a maximum width of work which each size will take.

Size, feet	2½	3	4	5
Wt., each, lbs.	7½	8½	9½	10½
Price, each	$1.33	$1.44	$1.63	$1.80
Per dozen	15.20	16.22	18.23	20.28

Clamp Attachment.

No. 35C3878 Clamp Attachments for Wood Bar Clamp. Malleable iron clamps. Wrought iron screw. Made for wood bars, 1⅛x2⅛ inches. Run of screw, 4 inches, diameter of screw, ⅝-inch Weight each, 3 pounds. Price, for attachment only, without wood bar....$0.45
Per dozen....5.00

Clamp Heads.

No. 35C3890 Clamp Head, wrought iron screw, revolving head, double thread, iron handle.

Diameter of screw	Price
1 -inch	$0.68
1⅛-inch	.92
1¼-inch	1.02

Patent Flooring Clamp.

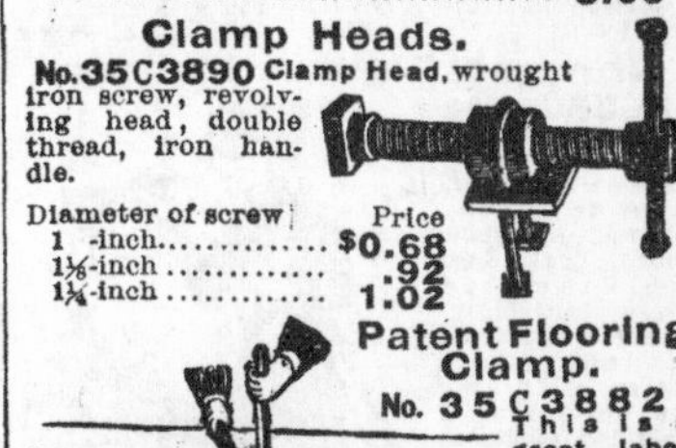

No. 35C3882 This is a great labor saver for a carpenter in laying crooked and warped flooring or in putting on of crooked siding. It can be worked with one hand while using the hammer in the other. Carpenters who have used this tool say: "It pays for itself each day it is used." Price....44c

Clamp Anvil Vises.

The following Clamp Anvil Vises will be found very convenient for light work.

Catalogue Number	Width of Jaw, inches	Weight each, lbs.	Price, each
35C3906	1⅛	1¼	20c
35C3907	1½	1½	28c
35C3908	2	2	36c
35C3909	2¼	2¾	48c
35C3910	2¾	5	95c

Steel Stamps.

No. 35C3963 Steel Letters and Figures for stamping tools, etc. Mark your tools so you can always identify them. An alphabet consists of 26 letters, 1 period and 1 &. Sizes given indicate the length of letter which the stamp makes. Use on untempered part of steel tools. They are not intended to stamp on hardened steel.

Size letter, in.	1-16	⅛	3-16	¼	⅜
Wt. ozs. Per set	16	20	22	28	48
Price, each..	3c	3c	$0.04	$0.05	$0.08
Per alphabet	75c	75c	1.05	1.30	2.00

No. 35C3964 Steel Figures.

Size, inch	1-16	⅛	3-16	¼	⅜
Wt. ozs. Per set	4	6	8	12	30
Price, each	3c	3c	4c	5c	8c
Per set of 9	25c	25c	34c	41c	66c

No. 35C3965 We can furnish a number of letters in one stamp. These stamps are made to order, which requires three or four days' time in busy seasons. Be very careful in ordering these stamps, as they will not be taken back if sent as ordered.

1-16, 3-32 or ⅛-in. letters, each letter costs 10c
3-16-inch letters, each letter costs 15c
¼-inch letters, each letter costs 18c
If by mail, postage extra, per letter, 1 cent.

Key Check Outfit.

No. 35C3966 Key Check Outfit, consists of complete alphabet of 1-16 inch steel letters, a complete set of 1-16 inch figures, a key check anvil with gauge for guiding dies when stamping all kinds of key checks, a steel hammer, 100 assorted German silver key checks, 24 assorted key rings, 144 small key check rings.
Price for complete outfit $6.00

No. 35C3967 Assorted German Silver Key Checks, with lodge emblems and other fancy designs, with scroll for name.
Price, per 100 $2.00

No. 35C3968 Assorted German Silver Key Checks, fancy shapes, plain.
Price, per 100 $1.50

No. 35C3969 Assorted German Silver Umbrella Plates, oblong and oval. Per doz. 12c

No. 35C3970 Assorted Key Rings, of different sizes and shapes. Price, per dozen, 40c

Stencil Sets.

Interchangeable Stencils put up in fonts of letters assorted by printers' rules. We cannot break fonts nor change the assortment. As put up they will make any ordinary name. They are made of spring brass and will not curl up.

No. 35C3975 Font No. 2, 70 pieces, consisting of letters, periods, figures, etc.

Size, inches	⅜	½	1	1¼
Price, per font	65c	71c	76c	81c

No. 35C3983 A large box of Stencil Ink for above stencil sets. Price, per box 22c

No. 35C3984 A small box of Stencil Ink for above stencil sets. Price, per box 9c

Stencil Brushes.

No. 35C3989 Stencil Brush, white stiff bristles. Seamless zinc ferrule.

Size	1	2	3	4
Price	5c	8c	10c	13c

Universal Tinware Mender.

No. 35C4040 Does not require the use of any soldering copper, acid or rosin. Tinware, copperware, brass kettles, enameled ware and hundreds of different household articles can be soldered and mended at home by any woman or child. Three pieces of mender with full directions in each package, enough to mend 75 small holes. Price, per package 8c

Soldering Caskets.

No. 35C4043 Soldering Casket. Consists of a small soldering copper, a scraper, a bar of solder and a box of rosin, all in a neat wood box with a sliding cover. Weight, 1 pound.
Price 25c

Riveting Machine.

No. 35C4122 Monarch Riveting Machine for hollow tubular rivets. The quickest and best riveting machine on the market. Light but strong enough so it will never break.
Price, each $0.35
Per doz. 4.00

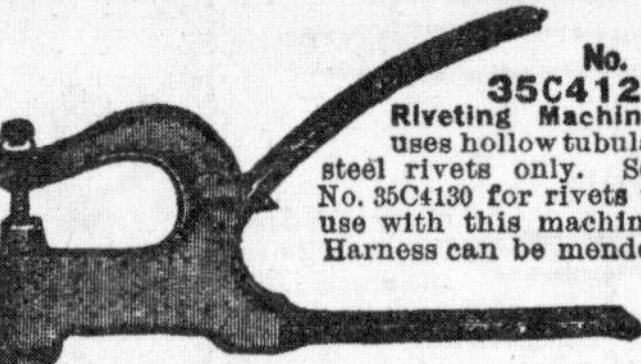

No. 35C4126 Riveting Machine, uses hollow tubular steel rivets only. See No. 35C4130 for rivets to use with this machine. Harness can be mended on a nervous horse, as there is no pounding to disturb it. Simply pulling down the lever punches the hole and completes the job. Weight, 3½ pounds. Price, each $0.23
Price, per dozen 2.65

Hollow Tubular Steel Rivets.

No. 35C4130 Hollow Tubular Steel Rivets, japanned, for use with above or similar riveting machines, put up in boxes containing 50 rivets, assorted lengths, from 3-16 to ½ inch long, for general repair work on harness, etc.
Price, per box 4c
Per dozen boxes 37c

Hollow Tubular Rivets.

No. 35C4131 Hollow Tubular Rivets, japanned, put up in boxes containing 100 rivets all the same length.

Length, inch	3-16	4-16	5-16	6-16	7-16
Price, per box	9c	9c	9c	10c	10c
Length, inch	8-16	9-16	10-16	11-16	12-16
Price, per box	11c	12c	14c	15c	16c

Rivet Set.

No. 35C4133 Rivet Set for Hollow Tubular Rivets. Made of steel ⅜ inch in diameter, tempered on ends. Will set the rivets as nicely as any riveting machine.
Price 9c

Slotted Rivets.

Slotted Clinch Rivets are very popular, as no set or other tool is required except a common hammer. Put up in packages containing 100 rivets. We do not break packages. Made of coppered annealed steel.

No. 35C4136 Slotted Rivets. Size No. 9. Assorted lengths.
Price, per package of 100 rivets 3c
Per dozen packages 32c

Harness or Belt Rivets.

Size numbers refer to diameter, No. 8 being the largest. There are enough burrs for the rivets in each package. We do not break packages.

No. 35C4138 Coppered Iron Rivets and Burrs. Made of soft iron heavily coppered. Put up in ½-pound packages containing about 60 rivets and burrs. Size No. 8, assorted lengths.
Price, per dozen packages, 67c; pkg 6c

Copper Rivets and Burrs.

No. 35C4140 Copper Rivets and Burrs. Size No. 8, either ⅜, ½, ⅝ or ¾-inch long. One length in package.
Price, per lb. package, 21c; ½-lb. pkg., 11c

No. 35C4141 Copper Rivets and Burrs. Size No. 8. Lengths assorted from ⅜ to ¾-inch in each package.
Price, per lb. package, 22c; ½-lb. pkg., 12c

No. 35C4142 Copper Rivets and Burrs. Size No. 9, either ⅜, ½, ⅝ or ¾-inch long. Only one length in a package.
Price, per lb. package, 22c; ½-lb. pkg., 12c

No. 35C4143 Copper Rivets and Burrs. Size No. 9. Lengths assorted from ⅜ to ¾-inch in each package. Price, per ½-lb. pkg 12c
Per 1-pound package 23c

No. 35C4144 Copper Rivets and Burrs. Size No. 10. Either ⅜, ½, ⅝ or ¾-inch long. Only one length in a pkg. Price, per ½-lb. pkg. 12c
Per 1-pound package 22c

No. 35C4145 Copper Rivets and Burrs. Size No. 10. Lengths assorted from ⅜ to ¾-inch in each package. Price, per ½-lb. pkg 13c
Per 1-pound package 24c

No. 35C4147 Copper Rivets and Burrs. Size No. 12. Assorted from ⅜ to ¾-inch in each package. Price, per ½-lb. package 13c
Per 1-pound package 25c

Rivet Sets.

No. 35C4158 Rivet Sets for setting the burrs on harness or belt rivets. No. 7 can be used for smaller rivets, but the No. 10 won't work on larger rivets. The sets are just right for the rivets of same number. Sizes either 7, 8, 9 or 10. Price 8c

Hollow Drive Punches.

Illustration showing size of holes cut by Hollow Punches.

10 8 6 4 2

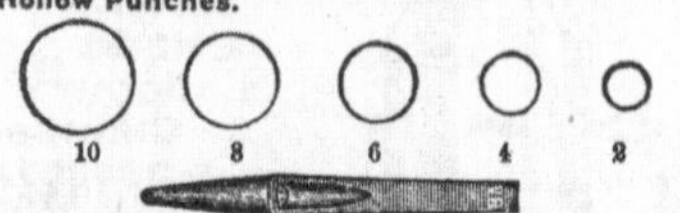

No. 35C4160 Hollow Drive Punches. Made of best tool steel. Weight, 4 ounces. Size 10, 7c; any size, 7 to 9, 6c; any size, 1 to 6 5c

Hollow Spring Punches.

No. 35C4165 Spring Punch, for cutting holes in belts, harness, etc. Full size. Length, 7½ inches; polished. Tube sizes are 4, 6, 8 and 10. State size wanted. Weight, 10 ounces.
Price, per dozen, $1.57; each 14c

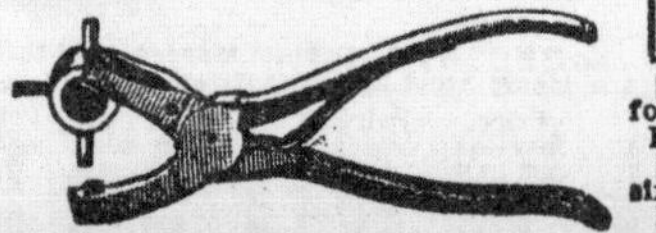

No. 35C4169 Revolving Spring Punch, with four tubes of different sizes. Weight, 14 ounces.
Price, per dozen, $3.45; each 30c

No. 35C4170 Revolving Spring Punch, with six tubes of different sizes. Weight, 14 ounces.
Price, per dozen, $4.85; each 41c

Leather Gauge Knife.

No. 10C07550 This is the best hollow iron handle gauge knife in the market. Will cut from ⅛ to 4 inches in width. It is the same knife used by all practical harness makers. Price 95c

MACHINISTS' TOOLS.

EVERY TOOL listed under this head is made by a manufacturer who has established a most enviable reputation for producing accurate and reliable tools. Every tool listed under this heading is warranted accurate and satisfactory. We can furnish any of Starrett's tools.

SOME PEOPLE STAMP THEIR NAMES on our tools, causing them to spring, and then write us they are defective. Stamping the name on them is the cause of their being "out." We cannot replace or exchange any tool on which a name has been stamped.

Starrett's Steel Rules. English Measure.

Graduations: Our rules are divided into parts of inches as follows:

No. 1 Graduation.	No. 4 Graduation.
1st corner, 10, 20, 50, 100	1st corner 64
2d corner 12, 24, 48	2d corner 32
3d corner 16, 32, 64	3d corner 16
4th corner 14, 28	4th corner 8

Starrett's Spring Tempered Rules.

Thickness, 3-64 inch or No. 18 Gauge.

No. 35C4500 Spring tempered, No. 4 graduation.

No. 35C4506 Spring tempered, No. 1 graduation.

Lengths, ins.	2	3	4	6	12
Price	18c	25c	32c	46c	89c

Starrett's Patent Combination Square.

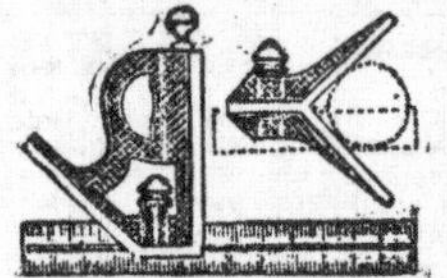

No. 35C4566 Starrett's Patent Combination Square with Mitre Head and Hardened Blade. Every tool warranted accurate.

6-inch, with center head, $0.89; without, $0.60
9-inch, with center head, 1.04; without, .75
12-inch, with center head, 1.19; without, .89
18-inch, with center head, 1.63; without, 1.34

No. 35C4569 Starrett's Protractor Head and Level, only added to No. 35C4566 Square makes a combination set as illustrated under No. 35C4573. When ordering, state what size square it is to fit. Price $1.19

Starrett's Combination Sets.

No. 35C4573 Combination Square, with center head and 7-inch bevel protractor head, with hardened blade, all on the No. 35C4566 square scale. Each head may be instantly removed or replaced and used interchangeably with the scale, thus forming the most useful combination set of tools ever devised for mechanics' use. A small level to be attached in place of the rule removed, forming an adjustable level to show any degree, thus greatly increasing the usefulness of the instrument is now furnished with the set although it is not illustrated. Price, 9-inch set, complete, $2.23
Price, 12-inch set, complete 2.38
Price, 18-inch set, complete 2.82
Price, 24-inch set, complete 3.12

Starrett's Improved Speed Indicator, with New Rubber Tips.

No. 35C4662 Speed Indicator No. 106 is nickel plated, and has a rosewood handle, so that it will not heat the fingers when run at high speed. New rubber tips for both pointed and hollow centers.
Price, in pasteboard box $1.19
Price, in leatherette case 1.59

No. 35C4665 Speed Indicator No. 104 may be run at highest speed without heating, on account of our frictionless bearing, against which the inner end of the spindle revolves (for which patent is pending). The inner plate is frictionally clamped to the revolving gear by a checked waferhead screw. By a pressure and twist with the thumb the plate is loosened, when the O mark may be instantly moved to agree with the starting point, thus saving time revolving the spindle to bring it there.
Price, in pasteboard box $0.79
Price, in leatherette case 1.19

No. 35C4668 Starrett's Registering Speed Indicator No. 107 was devised to automatically register hundreds as well as units and tens, and thus relieve the mind from keeping tally. The instrument will register 5,000 revolutions. Has a hard rubber handle, making a safe insulator when used on electrical machinery. It has our new rubber tips for both pointed and hollow centers.
Price, in pasteboard box $2.37
Price, in leatherette case 2.77

Starrett's Improved Firm Joint Calipers.

No. 35C4700 Outside	No. 35C4702 Inside	Price
3-inch		27c
4-inch		34c
5-inch		38c
6-inch		44c
8-inch		55c
10-inch		61c
12-inch		68c

No. 35C4700 No. 35C4702

Starrett's Fay Patent Outside and Inside Calipers.

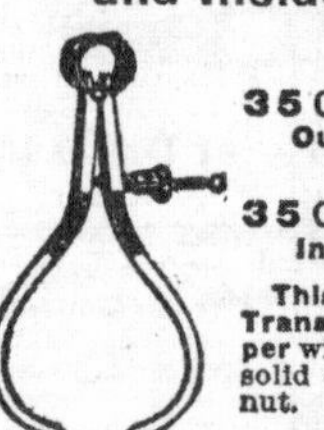

No. 35C4748 Outside.

No. 35C4750 Inside.

This is a new Transfer Caliper with either solid or spring nut.

No. 35C4748 No. 35C4750

Size, inches	2½	3	4	5	6
Price, Solid Nut	67c	68c	74c	75c	$0.92
Spring Nut	78c	79c	85c	86c	1.02

Starrett's Yankee Calipers and Dividers.

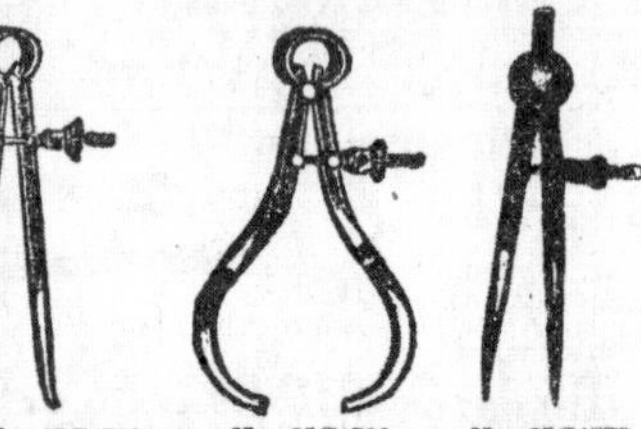

No. 35C4766 No. 35C4768 No. 35C4773

No. 35C4766 Starrett's Yankee Inside Transfer Caliper.
No. 35C4768 Starrett's Outside Caliper.
No. 35C4772 Starrett's Yankee Spring Dividers.

Size	Solid Nut, Price	Spring Nut, Price	Size	Solid Nut, Price	Spring Nut, Price
2½ inches	44c	54c	5 inches	55c	65c
3 inches	48c	58c	6 inches	58c	68c
4 inches	51c	61c	8 inches	68c	78c

WE CAN FURNISH ANY TOOL

MADE BY THE L. S. STARRETT CO. AT MONEY SAVING PRICES. Send us your orders at prices printed in Starrett's catalogue and we will return the difference between the amount you send and our prices.

Starrett's Improved Extension Divider.

No. 35C4790 The head and arms of this tool are made of the best malleable iron, the rest of steel. The points are hardened and warranted first class. The smallest size is 7 inches long; by adjustment of points becomes 9 inches and will scribe a 22-inch circle; will caliper 11 inches outside and 13 inches inside. The second size is 9 inches, by adjustment of points becomes 12 inches, and will scribe a 30-inch circle, and caliper 14 inches outside and 16 inches inside.
Price, 7-inch, with divider legs only $0.86
Price, 9-inch, with divider legs only 1.02
Price, 7-inch, complete 1.34
Price, 9-inch, complete 1.68

Extension Dividers.

No. 35C4797 The Standard Tool Co. Forged Best Tool Steel Extension Dividers with tempered points.
6-inch will scribe a 32-inch circle.
8-inch will scribe a 41-inch circle.
10-inch will scribe a 50-inch circle.
6-inch calipers, outside, 14 inches; inside 16 inches.
8-inch calipers, outside, 18 inches; inside 20 inches.
10-inch calipers, outside, 24 inches; inside 26 inches.
Price, 6-inch with divider legs only $0.69
Price, 8-inch with divider legs only .83
Price, 10-inch with divider legs only .98
Price, 6-inch, complete 1.24
Price, 8 inch, complete 1.38
Price, 10-inch, complete 1.52

Bell Centering Tool.

No. 35C4865 Bell Centering Tool. A very useful little tool; a big saver of time; knurled and nicely polished. Diameter, 1¾ inches.
Price 40c

IF YOU CAN'T FIND THE TOOL YOU WANT

REFER TO THE INDEX ON THE PINK PAGES OR WRITE FOR OUR SPECIAL TOOL CATALOGUE.

DON'T BUY ANY KIND OF A TOOL BEFORE YOU FIRST GET OUR PRICE. WE CAN ALWAYS SAVE YOU MONEY.

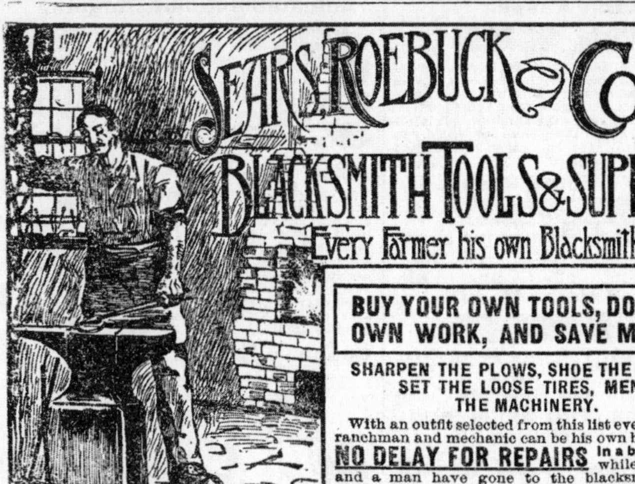

Sears, Roebuck & Co.
Blacksmith Tools & Supplies.
Every Farmer his own Blacksmith.

BUY YOUR OWN TOOLS, DO YOUR OWN WORK, AND SAVE MONEY.

SHARPEN THE PLOWS, SHOE THE HORSE, SET THE LOOSE TIRES, MEND THE MACHINERY.

With an outfit selected from this list every farmer, ranchman and mechanic can be his own blacksmith. **NO DELAY FOR REPAIRS** in a busy season while the team and a man have gone to the blacksmith shop. Again, if you have an outfit you will improve rainy days to fix up things that are showing wear, and avoid costly, vexatious and dangerous breakages in a busy time.

OUR PRICES quality considered, you will find by comparison are far below any competition. Freight is very low on this class of goods, and will add but very little to cost.

Riveting Hammers.

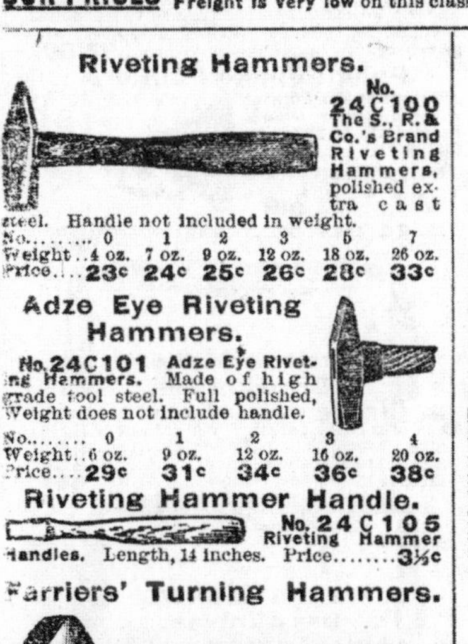

No. 24C100 The S., R. & Co.'s Brand Riveting Hammers, polished extra cast steel. Handle not included in weight.

No.	0	1	2	3	5	7
Weight	4 oz.	7 oz.	9 oz.	12 oz.	18 oz.	26 oz.
Price	23c	24c	25c	26c	28c	33c

Adze Eye Riveting Hammers.

No. 24C101 Adze Eye Riveting Hammers. Made of high grade tool steel. Full polished, Weight does not include handle.

No.	0	1	2	3	4
Weight	6 oz.	9 oz.	12 oz.	16 oz.	20 oz.
Price	29c	31c	34c	36c	38c

Riveting Hammer Handle.

No. 24C105 Riveting Hammer Handles. Length, 14 inches. Price........3½c

Farriers' Turning Hammers.

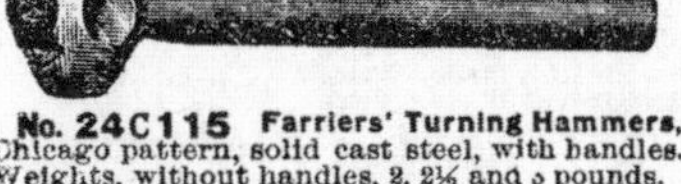

No. 24C115 Farriers' Turning Hammers, Chicago pattern, solid cast steel, with handles. Weights, without handles, 2, 2½ and 3 pounds. Price, any weight........97c

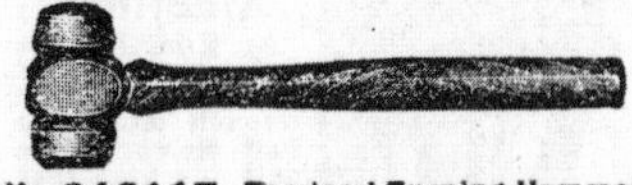

No. 24C117 Farriers' Turning Hammers. New York pattern. Weight, 2, 2½ and 3 pounds; weights do not include handles. Price, $1.00

Plow or Engineers' Hammers.

No. 24C120 Solid Cast Steel, finely polished: complete with handle.
Weight, 1 lb. 2 oz. No. 0. Price........34c
Weight, 2 lbs. No. 2. Price........44c

Blacksmiths' Hand Hammers.

No. 24C122 Blacksmiths' Hand Hammers, extra fine steel; fully warranted; handle not included in weight.

No.	1	2	3	4
Weight	2 lbs.	2 lbs. 10 ozs.	3 lbs.	3½ lbs.
Price	42c	45c	47c	49c

Blacksmiths' Hand Hammer Handles.

No. 24C130 Blacksmiths' Hand Hammer Handles. Length, 16 inches. Price........4½c
Length, 18 inches. Price........5½c

Machinists' Ball Pein Hammers.

No. 24C132 The S., R. & Co.'s Brand Machinists' Ball Pein Hammers, half polished, solid cast steel, hickory handles. Handle not included in weight.

No.	00	0	1	2	3	4
Weight	12 oz.	1 lb.	1¼ lbs.	1½ lbs.	1¾ lbs.	2 lbs.
Price	37c	39c	42c	45c	49c	50c

Machinists' Hammer Handles.

No. 24C135 Machinists' Hammer Handles.
Length, 16 inches. Price........6c
Length, 18 inches. Price........7c

Engineers' Ball Pein Hammers.

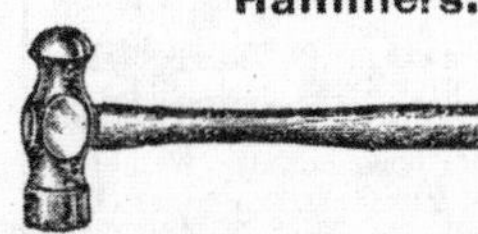

No. 24C139 The S., R. & Co.'s Brand Engineers' Hammer. Made with an extra heavy eye. The great fault with all engineers' or machinists' hammers is the breaking or splitting at the eye. We have here a hammer that we can warrant not to split and to be the finest balanced hammer made—just the thing where heavy work is to be done. Made of the finest English steel—comes full polished. Weight does not include handle.

No.	0	1	2	3	4
Weight	1 lb.	1¼ lbs.	1½ lbs.	1¾ lbs.	2 lbs.
Price	50c	52c	55c	60c	65c

Farriers' Hammer.

No. 24C148 Farriers' Hammer; weight (not including handle), 10 ounces, adze eye, cast steel, round pole, polished. Price, 33c

Adze Eye Farriers' Hammers.

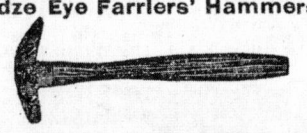

No. 24C150 Solid Cast Steel Farriers' Hammer, full polished; guaranteed to be the best hammer sold by anyone at the price. Weight, 10 ounces. Handle not included in weight. Price........37c

Horseshoers' Driving Hammers.

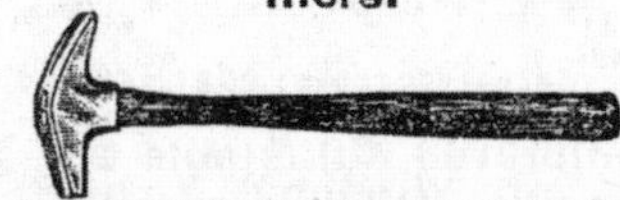

No. 24C153 The Genuine Heller Bros.' Farriers' Hammers. Made of finest quality tool steel. Every hammer warranted. Weight, 11 to 20 ounces. Price........55c

Farriers' Driving Hammers.

No. 24C156 The Genuine Heller Bros.' Heller Pattern Farriers' Hammers. Made of the best quality tool steel. Every hammer warranted. Weight, 13 to 20 ounces. Handle not included in weight. Price........67c

Scotch Farriers' Hammers.

No. 24C158 Round Face Farriers' Hammer. Made of solid steel. This hammer is acknowledged by all to be the best tool of its kind on the market. The rounding claw will draw a nail very easily and will do so without bending the same. Something you cannot do with any other make. Weight, 12 to 20 ounces. Price........54c

Blacksmiths' Ball Pein Hammers.

No. 24C160 The Genuine Heller Bros.' Ball Pein Hammers. Nothing better made. Every hammer fully warranted. Handle not included in weight.

Weight	¾ lb.	1 lb.	1¼ lbs.	1½ lbs.
Price	50c	52c	53c	56c

Horseshoers' Turning Hammers.

No. 24C165 Genuine Heller Brothers' Horseshoers' Turning or Cat's Head Hammer. Made of the best quality tool steel. Weight does not include handle. Weight, 2 to 3 pounds. Price........$1.30

Electric Sharpening Hammer.

No. 24C168 Our Electric Horseshoers' Hammer has no equal for sharpening shoe. Pein is corrugated for drawing out the calks. Made of the best quality English steel; fully warranted. Price..$1.07

Heller Bros.' Rounding Hammers.

No. 24C171 Genuine Heller Bros.' Rounding Hammer. Made of the finest quality tool steel. Every hammer warranted. Weight does not include handle. Weight, 2 to 3 pounds. Price........$1.31

Cast Steel Blacksmiths' Sledges.

No. 24C174 Solid Cast Steel Blacksmiths' Sledges, without handles.

Size, lbs.	8	9	10	11	12
Price	39c	44c	49c	54c	59c
Size, lbs.	13	14	15	16	17
Price	64c	68c	71c	76c	81c

No. 24C176 Handles for above, 36 inches long, shaved hickory. Price........11½c

Horseshoers' Turning Sledges.

No. 24C177 Horseshoers' Turning Sledges. Made of the best cast steel, one solid piece, oil finished with polished faces. Weight, from 6 to 12 pounds. Price, per lb....7½c

Farriers' Pincers.

No. 24C178 Blacksmiths' Pincers, solid hammered cast steel, polished jaws. Length, 14 inches. Weight, 2 pounds 10 ounces. Not for cutting nails. Price........44c

High Grade Farriers' Pincers.

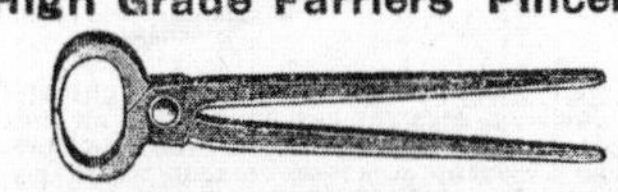

No. 24C180 High Grade Farriers' Pincers, made of the best tool steel, full polished. Something better than generally carried by the hardware trade.
Size, 14 inches. Weight, 2 pounds, 10 ounces, Price........$1.00
Size, 16 inches. Weight, 3 pounds. Price........1.30

Heller Bros.' Farriers' Pincers.

No. 24C181 Genuine Heller Bros.' Farriers' Pincers. Finest tools on the market; nothing better made.
Size, 14 inches. Weight, 2½ pounds. Price........$1.15
Size, 16 inches. Weight, 3 pounds. Price........1.45

Cutting Nippers.

No. 24C183 Solid Cast Steel Cutting Nippers. For cutting horse nails, etc. Also used for cutting horses' hoofs. Do not pry with this nipper, for it is hardened to cut, and prying will almost surely break it. Length, 14 inches. Weight, 1⅜ pounds. Price........62c

High Grade Nail Cutting Nippers.

No. 24C185 High Grade Nail Cutting Nippers, made of imported tool steel. Something better than generally sold by the hardware trade. Every pair fully warranted.
Length, 12 inches. Weight, 1½ pounds. Price........$0.86
Length, 14 inches. Weight, 2 pounds. Price........1.05

Heller Bros.' Cutting Nippers.

No. 24C186 Genuine Heller Bros.' Cutting Nippers. Used by all first class horseshoers; finest goods made; every tool warranted. Size, 10 ins. Weight. 1 lb. Price...$0.87
Size, 12 ins. Weight, 1¾ lbs. Price... 1.10
Size, 14 ins. Weight, 2½ lbs. Price... 1.30

Anvil Tools.

No. 24C192 Hot Cutter (no handle is furnished), 1⅜-inch cut; weight, 2 pounds 4 ounces. Price........28c

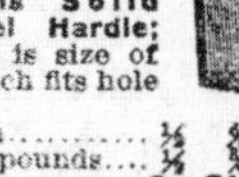

No. 24C195 Cold Cutter (handle is not furnished), 1⅜-inch cut; weight, 2 pounds 4 ounces. Price........29c

Blacksmiths' Hardle.

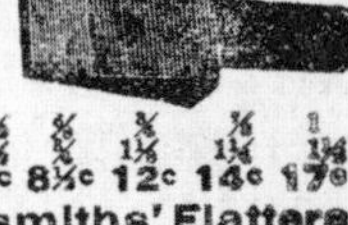

No. 24C198 Blacksmiths' Solid Cast Steel Hardle; size given is size of shank, which fits hole in anvil.

Size, inch	½	⅝	¾	⅞	1
Weight, pounds	½	⅞	1⅛	1¼	1¾
Price	6c	8½c	12c	14c	17c

Blacksmiths' Flatters.

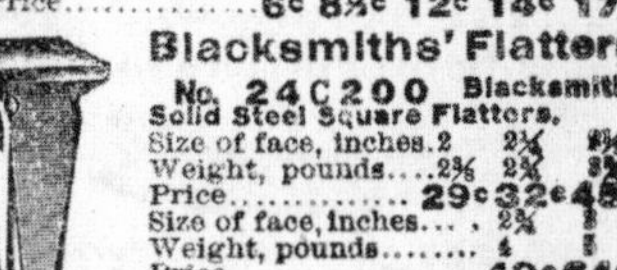

No. 24C200 Blacksmiths' Solid Steel Square Flatters.

Size of face, inches	2	2¼	2½
Weight, pounds	2⅜	2¾	3¾
Price	29c	32c	45c
Size of face, inches	2¾	3	
Weight, pounds	4	5	
Price	49c	64c	

Blacksmiths' Swages.

No. 24C202 Solid Crucible Steel Top Swages.

Size, inch		¼	5-16	⅜	7-16
Weight, lbs		1½	1½	2	2
Price		18c	19c	25c	28c
Size, inch		½	⅝	¾	⅞
Weight, lbs		2	2	2½	2¾
Price		29c	30c	35c	36c
Size, in.	1	1⅛	1¼	1½	2
Wgt. lbs.	2¾	3	3	4	4¼
Price	38c	39c	40c	51c	52c

Swages.

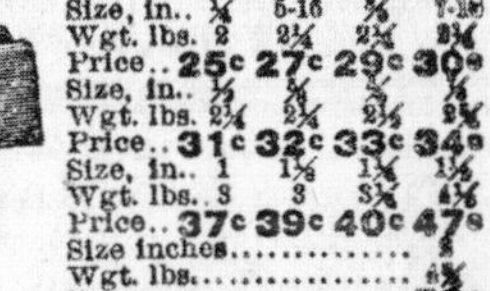

No. 24C204 Solid Crucible Steel Bottom Swages; shanks are iron, ⅞ to 1¼ inches.

Size, in.	¼	5-16	⅜	7-16
Wgt. lbs.	2	2¼	2¼	2¾
Price	25c	27c	29c	30c
Size, in.	½	⅝	¾	⅞
Wgt. lbs.	2¼	2¼	2½	2¾
Price	31c	32c	33c	34c
Size, in.	1	1⅛	1¼	1½
Wgt. lbs.	3	3	3¾	4½
Price	37c	39c	40c	47c
Size inches				2
Wgt. lbs.				4¾
Price				50c

Round Hand Punches.

Blacksmiths' Cast Steel Round Hand Punches, made of ⅝-inch octagon steel, 10 inches long. Be sure and state size wanted.

No. 24C212 Sizes, 3-16-inch, ¼-inch, 5-16-inch, ⅜-inch, either size, Price........12c
No. 24C213 Sizes, 7-16 or ½-inch. Price........15c
No. 24C214 Size, ⅝-inch. Price...22c
No. 24C215 Size, ¾-inch. Price...28c

Heading Tools.

Cast Steel Blacksmiths' Heading Tool. Be sure to state size wanted.

No. 24C220 Sizes, ¼, 5-16, ⅜, 7-16 or ½-inch. Weight, 3¼ pounds. Price........36c
No. 24C221 Sizes, 9-16, ⅝, or ¾-inch. Weight, 4¼ pounds. Price........48c
No. 24C222 Sizes, ⅞ or 1-inch. Weight, 5 pounds. Price........57c

Square or Round Punches.

Blacksmiths' Square or Round Punches. Be sure to give size and kind wanted.

No. 24C226 Sizes, ¼, 5-16, ⅜ or ½-inch. Price........27c
No. 24C227 Sizes, ⅝ or ¾-inch. Price........35c
No. 24C228 Size, ⅞-inch. Price...45c
No. 24C229 Size, 1-inch. Price....57c

Set Hammers.

No. 24C234 Solid Cast Steel Blacksmiths' Set Hammer.

Sizes of square face in inches	1	1¼	1½	1¾	2
Weight, pounds	1⅛	2	2¾	4	5
Price	13c	23c	29c	45c	57c

Horseshoers' Buffer.

No. 24C237 Solid Cast Steel Horseshoers' Buffer. Price........25c

If you are unable to find just the tool you want in this book, write for our Free SPECIAL MECHANICAL TOOL CATALOGUE.

Nielsen's Patent Farriers' Knife.

No. 24C248 The blacksmith, veterinarian, trainer and stock farm manager will use no other. The knife has adjustable blades, and is made in three different shapes. The blades are strictly first class, made of the best imported English steel. A set consists of one handle and three blades as shown in illustration. Price, per set.......................... **75c**

Keystone Farriers' Knife.

The handiest and best knife ever produced for the horseshoer, veterinarian and all horsemen. Blades can be changed in an instant and are held as secure in the handle as in the old style knife.

No. 24C252 Price, complete........ **33c**
No. 24C253 Price, handles only...... **13c**
No. 24C254 Price, blades only....... **10c**

Wostenholm Farriers' Knife.

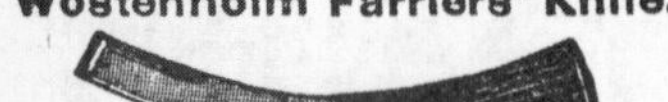

No. 24C256 Wostenholm Farriers' Knife, celebrated IXL brand. Weight, 7 ounces. Price.................................. **24c**

Heller Bros.' Farriers' Knife.

No. 24C258 Heller Bros.' High Grade Farriers' Knife, made of refined steel, finely finished. Price.............................. **24c**

Stone.

No. 24C262 This article is made solid, through and through, of pure ground corundum, but with a steel bar extending its entire length. Length, 10 inches. Price.......... **5c**

Blacksmiths' Straight Lip Tongs.

Blacksmiths' Straight Lip Tongs, drop forged, no welds.

No. 24C263 Length, 20 inches. Weight, 2½ pounds. Price...................... **21c**
No. 24C265 Length, 22 inches. Weight, 3 pounds. Price..................... **24c**

Gad Tongs.

Blacksmiths' Gad Tongs, drop forged from one solid piece of steel.

No. 24C268 Length, 18 inches. Weight, 1½ pounds. Price...................... **23c**
No. 24C270 Length, 22 inches. Weight, 3½ pounds. Price..................... **36c**

Round Bolt Tongs.

Blacksmiths' Round Bolt Tongs. Length, 20 inches. State what size bolts tongs are wanted for.

No. 24C272 For Bolts, 5-16, ⅜ or ½ inch. Weight from 1½ to 2½ pounds. Price, any one size........................ **30c**
No. 24C273 For Bolts, ⅝ to ¾ inch. Weight, 3½ pounds. Price.................. **40c**
No. 24C274 For Bolts, ⅞ to 1 inch. Weight, 3⅝ pounds. Price.................. **45c**

Horseshoers' Tongs.

No. 24C279 Solid Steel Horseshoers' Tongs. Weight, 12-inch, 1 lb. 5 oz.; 14-inch, 1½ lbs. Price, 12-inch.... **19c**
14-inch.......................... **21c**

Heller Bros.' Farriers' Tongs.

No. 24C280 Genuine Heller Bros.' Farriers' Tongs, solid steel, nothing better made. Size, 14 inches. Weight, 1½ pounds. Price.................................. **27c**

Clinch Tongs.

No. 24C282 Clinch Tongs or Nail Clinchers are used in turning the clinch instead of using the hammer. In many cases the horse's foot becomes sore and is very sensitive to the hammer. They are made of the best quality crucible cast steel and are tempered with great care, making them uniform in quality and temper. Weight, 1½ pounds. Price.................................. **90c**

Heller Bros.' Clinch Tongs.

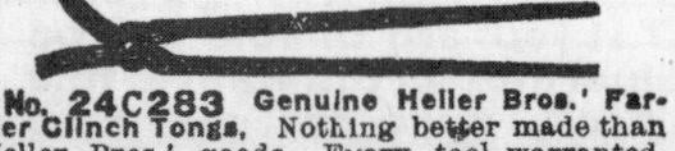

No. 24C283 Genuine Heller Bros.' Farrier Clinch Tongs. Nothing better made than Heller Bros.' goods. Every tool warranted. Size, 14 inches. Weight, 2 lbs Price.. **$1.20**

Round Nose Clinch Tongs.

No. 24C285 Round Nose Clinch Tongs, made of the same material as No. 24C282, but of a different style. Weight, 1½ pounds. Price.................................. **95c**

Samson Hoof Parer.

No. 24C289 The main feature of this parer is that it leaves the shell of the hoof, making a concave cut with a sweep of the knife, and does not interfere with the frog of the foot while being pared. The blade is dovetailed into the head of the parer and also fastened by set screws, and should it need sharpening, all that is necessary to remove it is to loosen the set screw, drive blade out, sharpen on a stone and replace same. Weight, 2⅝ pounds. Price.................. **$1.00**

Hoof Parers.

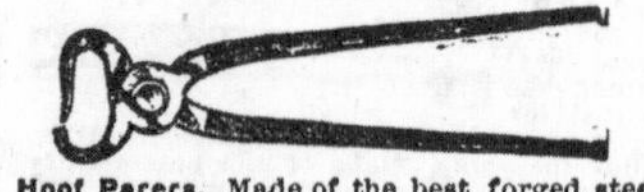

Hoof Parers. Made of the best forged steel, carefully tempered. The most practical tool ever made for paring a horse's foot. Full polished.

	Length	Weight	Price
No. 24C290	12 inches	1½ pounds	$0.85
No. 24C291	14 inches	2 pounds	1.03

Heller Bros.' Hoof Parers.

No. 24C292 Genuine Heller Bros.' Hoof Parers, solid steel, finely finished. Nothing better made.

	Weight	Price
Length, 12 inches	1½ pounds	$1.12
Length, 14 inches	2 pounds	1.30

Our New Hoof Shear.

No. 24C293 Our New Hoof Shear. This is the most practical tool yet produced for paring the foot. The cutting blade being at an angle gives it a drawing cut, which is much easier than any other pattern. The spring brings the tool wide open as soon as the cut is made, and is a great convenience. Weight, 2 pounds. Price.................. **$1.13**

The Giant Hoof Parer.

No. 24C295 The Giant is the lightest, most powerful straight cut hoof parer on the market. In this tool we have a principle that produces a maximum jaw movement, while the handles can be reached with one hand at any time. This tool has the largest amount of leverage, with the least complication of any tool made. Weight, 2 pounds. Price....... **$1.60**

Easy Bolt Clippers.

No. 24C300 Our New Easy Bolt Clippers have all the latest improvements, such as patent adjustment, locking device, rubber buffers, etc. They are made of the best material throughout. Jaws are high grade steel. Every clipper fully warranted. Don't use small clippers on large work, you may break them; or large ones on small work, they are heavy and cost more.

No. 0 For cutting bolts 5-16-inch or less; weight, 3 pounds. Price.................. **$1.75**
No. 1 For cutting bolts ⅜ inch or less; weight, 4½ pounds. Price.................. **$1.95**
No. 2 For cutting bolts ½-inch or less; weight, 7½ pounds. Price.................. **$2.75**
No. 3 For cutting bolts ⅝-inch or less; weight, 12½ pounds. Price.................. **$4.25**

Randall's Improved Bolt and Rivet Clippers with Double Eccentric Adjustment.

No. 24C310 The mechanical construction is greatly improved, workmanship and material the very best. Has double adjustment, a first class clipper in every respect.

No. 0 For bolts 5-16-in. or less. Price.. **$1.80**
No. 3 For bolts ⅜-in. or less. Price.. **2.40**
No. 4 For bolts ½-in. or less. Price.. **3.35**
No. 5 For bolts ⅝ or ¾-inch or less. Price.................................. **4.50**

Average weight, 5 pounds.

Horse Rasps.

No. 24C312 S., R. & Co.'s Horse Rasps. We have sold a great many horse rasps of this brand. Our trade is increasing and we are getting orders again and again from same parties. Order a sample, give it a trial and see if it is not just as good or better than those for which you must pay more.

	12-inch	14-inch	16-inch
Price	20c	27c	36c

Heller's Horse Rasps.

No. 24C314 Heller's Horse Rasps. Flat, not tanged.

Size, inches	12	14	16
Price	27c	38c	53c

Tanged Horse Rasps.

No. 24C316 Genuine Heller Bros., Tanged Horse Rasps.

Size, inches	10	12	14	16
Price	28c	34c	48c	68c

Lightning Tire Setter and Spoke Holder.

Lightning Tire Setter and Repair Outfit. It is not necessary to remove the wheel to repair it, as this outfit contains all the tools necessary to do the job and will do it better than any blacksmith who cuts and welds the tire. A set consists of the complete setter, as shown in illustration, with one dozen assorted holders and two coils of leather washers.

No. 24C320 Price, complete set.. **$1.55**
No. 24C321 Extra spoke holders. Price, per dozen.................. **.80**

Wrenches.

No. 24C322 Solid Cast Steel Alligator Wrench. Length, 5⅝ inches. Capacity, ¼ to ⅝ inch; for holding or turning round or square bolts or nuts. Weight, 7 ounces. Price.................. **10c**

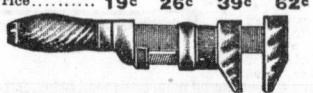

No. 24C323 Always Ready Wrench, forged from steel of superior quality, oil tempered, nickel plated.

Numbers	1	2	2½	3
Holds nuts or pipe, inches	⅛ to ⅝	⅛ to 1¼	⅛ to 1⅜	⅛ to 1⅞
Weight, pounds	½	1	2	2⅝
Price	19c	26c	39c	62c

No. 24C324 Screw Wrench, wrought iron bar, head and screw. The 10-inch size is the best for general purposes.

Size, inches	6	8	10	12	15
Weight	1 lb.	1 lb. 6 oz.	2 lbs.	2½ lbs.	3½ lbs.
Price	17c	18c	22c	25c	43c

No. 24C325 Genuine L. Coes' Improved Knife Handle Wrench. Made of the very best materials, thoroughly case hardened, and every wrench warranted.

Size, inches	6	8	10	12	15	18	21
Will open	⅞	1¼	1½	2	2⅜	3	4½
Weight, pounds	⅝	1½	2	3½	4⅝	6⅞	9
Price	37c	42c	50c	60c	$1.00	$1.26	$1.80

For other wrenches see index.

Improved Adjustable S Wrench.

No. 24C326 Improved Adjustable S Wrench. Handle and frame are malleable iron. Jaws high grade tool steel. Can be used in a thousand and one places where an ordinary wrench will not go.

Size, inches	6	8	10	12	14
Opens, inches	¾	1	1⅜	1½	2
Weight, lbs.	⅜	⅞	1⅜	2½	4½
Price	35c	46c	64c	75c	$1.05

Hollow Auger

No. 24C335 Bonney Pattern Adjustable Hollow Auger is a tool that is first class in material and finish. Cuts eight sizes of tenons from ⅜ to 1 inch. Has adjustable stop to regulate length of tenon. Nickel plated. Weight, 1 pound. Price.................. **48c**

Adjustable Hollow Augers.

No. 24C337 Patent Adjustable Hollow Auger, made of malleable iron and nicely finished. The knife is made of the best tool steel, has adjustable stop, with scale for regulating length of tenon. It cuts 8 sizes, as follows: ⅜, 7-16, ½, 9-16, ⅝, ¾ and 1 inch. Weight, 1 pound 9 ounces.

No. 1 complete. Price, **$2.90**

No. 24C339 Patent Adjustable Hollow Auger No. 3. Cuts any size tenon from ¼ to 1¼ inches; the pivoted jaws are provided with a graduated scale by which the size of the tenon is regulated. To secure required length of tenon a movable stop is operated upon a graduated scale, with rulings to sixteenths. Weight, 1¾ pounds. Price.................. **$2.25**

Goodell's Adjustable Hollow Auger.

No. 24C341 Goodell's Patent Adjustable Hollow Auger. Has fitted to it a nickel plated bit brace sweep with rosewood handle and lignum vitæhead; sweep, 14 inches. As the brace sweep is fitted to it, it will always work true. The auger is adjustable to cut from ¼ to 1¼ inches. Weight, 3½ pounds. Price, complete with sweep.................. **$2.80**

Patent Spoke Pointers.

Patent Spoke Pointer with adjustable shank. Points, 1⅝ inches in diameter.

No. 24C346 No. 1. weight, 12 ounces. Price.......... **33c**
No. 24C347 No. 2, weight, 18 ounces (large). Price.................. **57c**

Carriage Makers' Drawknives.

No. 24C348 Carriage Makers' Drawknives. Made of solid cast steel. Weight about 1½ lbs.

Size, 8-inch blade. Price.......... **49c**
Size, 10-inch blade. Price.......... **55c**
Size, 12-inch blade. Price.......... **66c**

Wagon Makers' Drawknives.

No. 24C349 Wagon Makers' Drawknives. Made of high grade cast steel. Weight about 1¾ pounds.

Size, 8-inch blade. Price.......... **50c**
Size, 10-inch blade. Price.......... **56c**
Size, 12-inch blade. Price.......... **67c**

Reynold's Tire Bolting Machine.

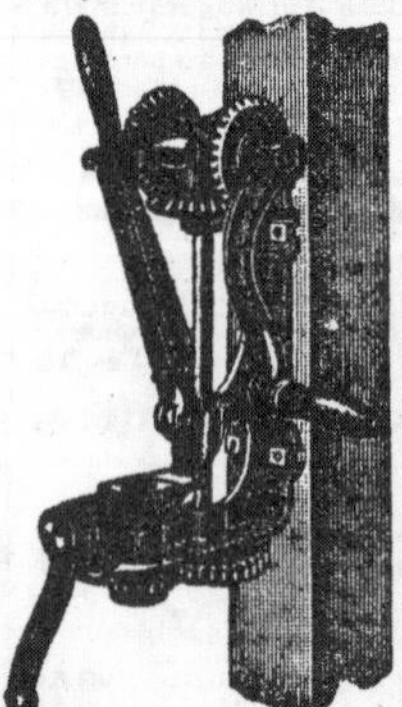

No. 24C351 A Combination Bolt Clipper, Bolt Wrench and Tire Bolt Holder. The only machine that will successfully remove burrs, run them on, or clip off the ends of tire bolts; will fit any sized tap. Either operation can be performed on any ordinary buggy wheel in less than two minutes with perfect ease to the operator. This machine is patented, and the only machine of its kind on the market. Weight, 24¼ pounds. Price.......... **$5.35**

Drop Forged Tire Measuring Wheel.

No. 24C355 This wheel is a drop forging, lathe turned, a perfect running wheel, first class. Weight, 1 pound. Price, **95c**

Graduated Tire Measuring Wheel.

No. 24C356 This wheel is a drop forging made so that the figures and lines are raised above the surface of the wheel, and cannot be filled or defaced with rust or dirt. It is exactly 24 inches in circumference, with index hand. Weight, 1½ pounds.................. **$1.1**

Acme Junior Double Speed Post Drill.

No. 24C807 In our Acme Junior Post Drill we have the neatest, lightest and at the same time most durable drill for the price on the market. The frame is bored, then reamed and polished to a finish. No babbit used. Could not be better at any price. A second or slow speed is obtained by use of handle on fly wheel. This feature will be found very convenient in boring large holes. **Only the best of material is used in its construction.** Has steel mandrel, shafts and feed screw. Light buggy wheel tires can be drilled by removing table and using the forked support as a wheel holder. Has self feed, two speeds, swing table; bores up to ¾-inch hole and drills to center of 12-inch circle. Spindle runs 3 inches. Takes bits or drills with ½-inch round shank. Weight, 85 pounds. Price......**$4.98**

Acme No. 12 Post Drill for Hand Power

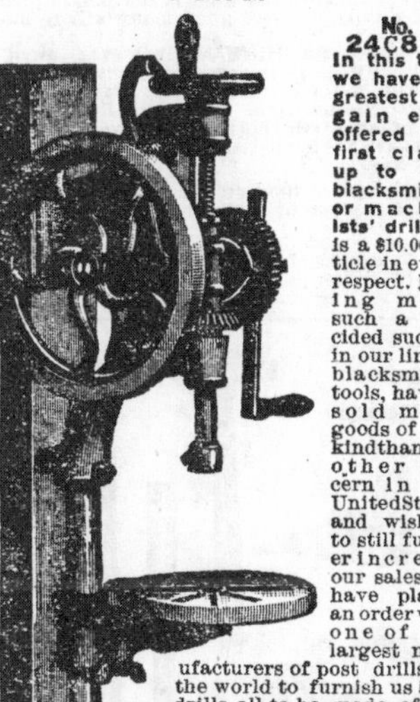

No. 24C816 **In this tool we have the greatest bargain ever offered in a first class, up to date blacksmiths' or machinists' drill.** It is a $10.00 article in every respect. Having made such a decided success in our line of blacksmiths' tools, having sold more goods of this kind than any other concern in the United States and wishing to still further increase our sales, we have placed an order with one of the largest manufacturers of post drills in the world to furnish us 5,000 drills, all to be made of the same material as our high priced goods. We have advanced its weight and quality over all others listed at this price. We believe, with our long experience in handling this line of goods, we know just how to meet the wants of the consumer with a good serviceable drill at the lowest possible cost. This drill has very long, heavy bearings, which are well babbitted, and cannot spring or get out of line as is the case with so many drills put on the market and designated as world beaters; **our automatic feeding device is of the very latest improved mechanical construction**, and is entirely out of the way of the operator, being located behind the spindle, and worked by a cam on inside of main gear wheel. This cam is so constructed as to give nearly a continuous feed, and does not jam the drill into its work all at once, as is so frequently the case in other makes, thus avoiding breakage of bits. It also has two speeds, which can be obtained instantly by changing handle from one shaft to the other, thus giving the operator additional power when drilling very large holes. Drill spindle has run of 3 inches, and is bored to take ½-inch straight shank drills. The upright column, drill spindle and feed screw, are of best steel. Drills to the center of 15-inch circle, and from 0 up to 1¼-inch holes. Weight, 125 lbs.
Price............................**$5.90**

No. 12 Power Drill.

No. 24C820 Same as our No. 24C816, with exception that it is provided with tight or loose pulleys for belt, as shown in illustration; well suited for all kinds of light power.
Price, No. 12, with tight and loose pulleys, no fly wheel...............**$8.00**
No. 24C821 Price, No. 12 with tight and loose pulleys and fly wheel...**$8.75**

No. 24C820

Acme No. 150 Cut Geared Drills.

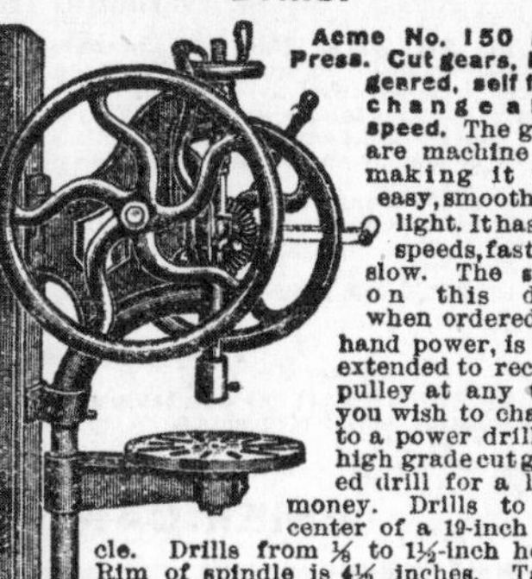

Acme No. 150 Drill Press. Cut gears, back geared, self feed, changeable speed. The gears are machine cut, making it run easy, smooth and light. It has two speeds, fast and slow. The shaft on this drill when ordered for hand power, is left extended to receive pulley at any time you wish to change to a power drill. A high grade cut geared drill for a little money. Drills to the center of a 19-inch circle. Drills from ⅛ to 1½-inch holes. Rim of spindle is 4½ inches. Takes drill bits with ¾-inch round shank. No drill bits furnished at prices given below.

Weight, 175 pounds.

No. 24C830 Price, for hand power, as per illustration............**$13.75**

No. 24C831 Price, for hand and pulley power...................**$15.65**

Acme No. 120 Cut Geared Drill.

In our Acme No. 120 Cut Geared Drill we have one of the best drills on the market. It is a strictly high grade tool. We use cut gears only in this drill; only the best material and the workmanship is perfect. You can not buy a better drill at any price. Drills to the center of a 15-inch circle. Will drill holes ⅛ to 1½ inches in diameter. Takes drill bits with ½-inch round shank. We furnish the drill for both hand and pulley power. Illustration shows pulley power.
Weight, 200 lbs.
No. 24C833 Price, for hand power drill **$19.25**
Price, for pulley power drill **$21.75**

Drill Chucks.

A moderate price chuck that is capable of good work. It is smaller than the ordinary drill chuck, and is well suited to use in connection with the various sizes of hand and light power drills. They are furnished with straight or taper shanks, the former to fit the chuck to hand drills, the latter to fit it to larger drills.

		Holding Drills	For straight shank chuck
No. 24C850	No. 1	...0 to ⅜-inch	**$1.50**
No. 24C851	No. 2	...0 to ½-inch	**2.00**

We send ½-inch straight shank when not otherwise ordered.

Round Shank Countersinks.

No. 24C857 **Steel Countersinks**, with ½-inch round shank. Will fit any of our post drills.
Size, ⅝-inch with ½-inch shank. Price..**29c**
Size, ⅞-inch with ½-inch shank. Price..**42c**

Countersinks for Bit Brace.

Steel Countersinks for Bit Brace, nothing better made.
No. 24C859 Size, ⅝-inch. Price.....**29c**

Round Shank Drills.

No. 24C860 **Twist Drill**, with round shank to be used with any of our post drills. Also our No. 24C809 Horizontal Bench Drill. Will drill metal or bore wood. The shank of all sizes is ½-inch in diameter. They are made of the highest grade Drill Steel and the diameters are absolutely correct. Every drill is inspected carefully after each operation by skillful workmen. We guarantee all drills and will replace, free of charge, any tool found defective in material or workmanship.

Size......	⅛	5-32	3-16	7-32	¼	9-32
Price....	15c	16c	16c	18c	20c	21c
Size......	5-16	11-32	⅜	13-32	7-61	15-32
Price....	23c	24c	25c	26c	26c	27c
Size......	½	17-32	9-16	12-32	⅝	21-32
Price....	28c	29c	30c	31c	35c	36c
Size......	11-16	23-32	¾	25-32	13-16	27-32
Price....	38c	40c	41c	43c	45c	47c
Size..............		⅞	29-32	15-16	31-32	1 inch
Price..............		48c	50c	53c	57c	60c

MAKE YOUR ORDER AS LARGE AS POSSIBLE.

Very likely there are other goods in this catalogue that you need, and if so, our prices will probably interest you. Look them up.

Tiger Steel Blowers with 20th Century Ideas.

No. 24C926 **Handsomest**—Because its constructive design is symmetrical, attractive and beautiful. **Best**—Because made of the best material, by skilled workmen and best mechanical experience that can be obtained. **Superior Points**—No belts, no clutches, no ratchets.

The blower case oscillates on its bearing, permitting nose of case to point down or out or up, as may be desired, meeting any angle of blow pipe, thereby saving one elbow and 10 per cent of blast force, besides valuable room occupied by other blowers. The crank turns forward or backward, as suits operator. **The gears** are cut on the most scientific principle; they are flat and straight cut (insuring double the life of spiral or worm gears), which combined with steel shafts and composition bearings made and assembled perfectly, run noiseless, and make this the best blower in the world. **The gear case** is oil tight and dust proof, permitting gears to run in a bath of oil. **The blast** is very powerful, and as positive and steady as a power blower, and takes less labor to operate than others. The after blast is strong and lasting. The four legs and base give a solid, non-trembling foundation. The room it takes is less than any other blower. Weight, 90 pounds. Fan, 10½ inches outside; fan case, 13 inches. Height, over all, 45 inches. Price......................................**$9.65**

Root's Acme Hand Blowers.

$14.95

No. 24C925 **guaranteed to give blast equal to a 60-inch bellows.** The revolvers are enclosed in an iron case, bored out perfectly true, and are dressed so that they keep up continuous contact with each other during the entire revolution, forcing forward and utilizing all the air taken into the case. The blower occupies a space less than a foot square of floor surface. It is equally well adapted to light or heavy work, as the blast can be varied instantly, at the will of the operator, and will heat 1-inch iron in one minute. Price...............**$14.95**

Vises.

No. 24C880 **Wrought Iron Blacksmiths' Vises**, solid boxes, cast steel jaws.

Weight	Price
35 lbs...........	$3.20
40 lbs...........	3.39
45 lbs...........	3.52
50 lbs...........	3.70
55 lbs...........	3.89
60 lbs...........	4.20
65 lbs...........	4.50
70 lbs...........	4.85
75 lbs...........	5.25
80 lbs...........	5.65
85 lbs...........	6.00
90 lbs...........	6.60
95 lbs...........	7.25
100 lbs...........	7.75
110 lbs...........	7.90

Weight....	120 lbs.	130 lbs.	140 lbs.
Price......	$8.25	$8.95	$9.91
Weight....	150 lbs.	160 lbs.	170 lbs.
Price......	$10.75	$12.25	$13.10
Weight....	180 lbs.	190 lbs.	200 lbs.
Price......	$13.75	$15.50	$16.25

Vise Box and Screws.

Extra Vise Box and Screws for the No. 24C880 Vises.
No. 24C885 1-inch, for vises 35 to 40 pounds. Price...........**$2.90**
No. 24C886 1⅛-inch, for vises 45 to 55 pounds. Price.....**$3.00**
No. 24C887 1¼-inch, for vises 60 to 70 pounds. Price..............**$3.10**
No. 24C888 1⅜-inch, for vises 75 to 90 pounds. Price...........**$3.75**
No. 24C889 1½-inch, for vises 90 to 130 pounds. Price.....................**$5.45**

Farriers' Vises.

$6.75 to $8.90.

No. 24C895 **Our Farriers' Vise** is made with extra heavy steel jaws, which are flattened or beveled on top to form the heels or calks on horse shoes, etc.

Weight	Price
70 lbs................	$6.75
75 lbs................	7.90
80 lbs................	8.25
85 lbs................	8.90

Acme Improved No. 401 Blowers, with Ball Bearings.

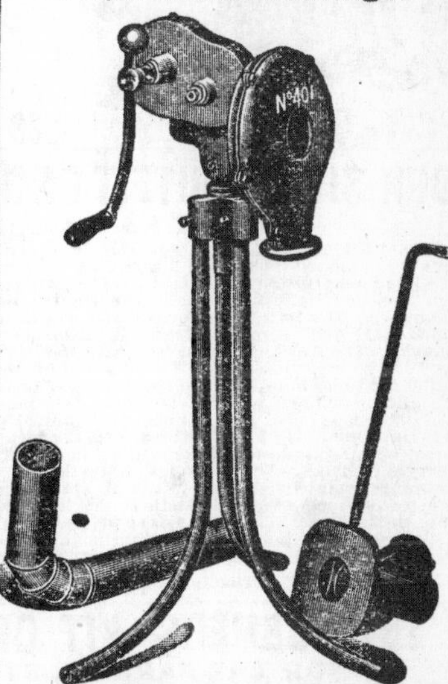

No. 24C935 **In our Acme Improved No. 401 Blower we have, without doubt, the most perfect blacksmith's blower ever put on the market**, when material, workmanship, easy running, high speed and powerful blast are considered. A crank blower of any style or make is a dead failure if it does not run easy and smooth, as the constant jar of a cheaply constructed machine will paralyze the arm of any blacksmith in two hours' time. In our Acme No. 401 we use spiral wheels or gears which run upon a spiral shaft with ball bearings that gives a smoothness and speed to the fan which is perfection in itself.

The Gear Case is air tight, which permits the lower shaft to run in a bath of oil which, in turn, throws the oil over the upper wheel or gear. No hot journals or worn cut boxes. Will last a lifetime if case is kept filled with oil.

The Fan or Case sets upon a swivel base which can be raised or lowered to suit the height of forge. All shafts and gears are made of high grade tool steel. Crank can be turned either to the right or left hand. Height over all, 46 inches. Size of fan, 12 inches. Weight, with Tuyere iron, pipe and elbow, 100 pounds.
Price, complete, as shown in illustration...................................**$13.00**

Western Acme Blowers.

No. 24C905 **For forges, furnaces, ventilating, drying** and cooling. A well made, up to date blower. Sizes 3 and 5 have grease cups in addition to oil cups, so that should oil cups run dry the grease cups will continue to lubricate and prevent heating.

Number of Blower	Height in Inches	Diameter of Inlet	Diameter of Outlet	Diameter of Pulley	Face of Pulley	Revolutions per Minute, 2-ounce Blast for Boiler Fires	Revolutions per Minute, 2-ounce Blast for Forge Fires	Number of Forge Fires	Square feet of Boiler Grate Surface Supplied by Boiler	Weight, Pounds	Price
P 1	10	3¼	2¾	1⅞	1¼	3,675	4,040	1	2	15	$6.00
P 2	15	4½	4¼	3	2½	3,000	4,000	2	5	35	9.00
P 3	18	5¼	4¾	3	2	2,000	3,600	4	6	50	10.00
P 4	20	6½	5¾	4½	2	2,500	3,200	5	8	65	14.00
P 5	24	7	7½	4⅝	3¼	1,928	2,680	7	10	100	16.50

Western Acme Blowers.

The illustrations of the following blowers represent our new and improved Steel Frame Blowers—the BEST, the STRONGEST, the NEATEST in the world and in this we challenge the entire field. By having a frame constructed to support the fan from every side, and to brace each way from the bearings, it stands without trembling when operated, keeping all the bearings in line, working far easier than with a straight upright frame, either of wood or iron. In No. 4 of these blowers we offer to our patrons **the only** practical combined crank and lever blower made. By an ingenious device we **combine both motions in one machine,** and at the same time **each works independent of the other.** When the crank works, thereby doubling the speed, the lever is idle. As soon as the crank is released it drops to the lower side and gear wheels stop. This is the only gear motion that will stop (all gears) while the shaft still revolves. **All gears are cut.**

IMPORTANT FEATURES—Cut gears, solid angle T steel frame, compressed steel shafts, the W. A. Tuyere iron and fire pot, clutch, positive and noiseless and also adjustable; no leathers or ratchets in its construction; reversible nose to fan case for turning the blast to right or left, as desired.

Western Acme Blower, Size 1.

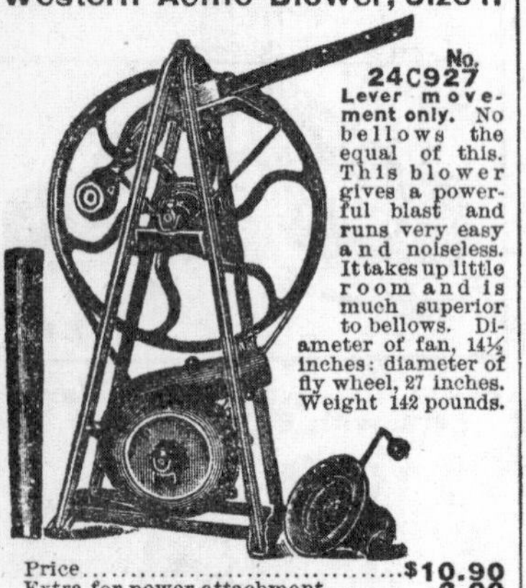

No. 24C927 Lever movement only. No bellows the equal of this. This blower gives a powerful blast and runs very easy and noiseless. It takes up little room and is much superior to bellows. Diameter of fan, 14½ inches: diameter of fly wheel, 27 inches. Weight 142 pounds.

Price......**$10.90**
Extra for power attachment......**2.00**

Western Acme Blower, Size 2.

No. 24C938 Lever movement only. Takes up little room, and is far superior to bellows. Can be furnished to operate with right arm for left handed smiths when desired. Diameter of fan, 16¼ inches; diameter of fly wheel, 27 inches. Weight, 165 lbs.

Price......**$12.50**
Extra for power attachment......**2.00**

ANVILS.

No. 24C975 Cast Iron Anvils, with steel face. The face of this anvil is one solid piece of English tool steel, thoroughly welded to the body of the anvil by a patent process. The horn is covered with and its extremity made entirely of cast steel. The face and horn are then accurately ground and tempered. We do not guarantee this anvil, but it will give satisfaction for light work.

No.	2	3	4	5
Wgt., lbs.	20	30	40	50
Price	**$2.18**	**$2.35**	**$2.87**	**$3.25**
No.	6	7	8	9
Wgt., lbs.	60	70	80	90
Price	**$3.55**	**$3.80**	**$4.10**	**$4.60**

PETER WRIGHT'S ANVILS.

Wrought Iron with Steel Face.

No. 24C981 This well known anvil has stood the test for years, and is today the most popular anvil in the world. It is cheap enough for anybody and good enough for anyone. Don't buy an anvil too light for your work. A light anvil when struck a hard blow with a heavy hammer is sure to jump. We carry a large stock, but occasionally are not able to send the exact weight ordered, but can always come within 5 pounds of the weight ordered. This anvil is sold by the pound, and price per pound varies with the size.

85 to 500 pounds. Price, per pound......**9¾c**
71 to 84 pounds. Price, per pound......**10¾c**
61 to 70 pounds. Price, per pound......**11½c**
51 to 60 pounds. Price, per pound......**11¾c**
50 pounds and lighter. Price, per pound......**12c**

Peter Wright's Farriers' Anvil.

No. 24C982 It has a suitable side horn for drawing toe clips, etc., and a thin steel heel for working small size shoes. Weight, 140 to 150 pounds. Price, per pound,......**10¾c**

AMERICAN WROUGHT ANVILS.

HAVING SECURED THE EXCLUSIVE SALE of one of the best wrought anvils in the world, we have agreed to take the entire output, and in order to do so we have reduced the price to where it will enable us to sell more anvils than any firm in the United States.

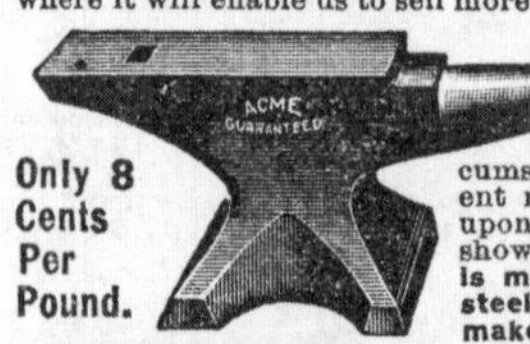

Only 8 Cents Per Pound.

THE TIME HAS PASSED when we must go to England for our best anvils. Having sold both the American and English anvils for a number of years, shipping them to every part of the United States, having been used by all kinds of mechanics, under all circumstances, we are in a position to know the merits of the different makes. In our American Wrought Anvil we have improved upon all foreign makes in shape, style and finish, until we now show the **finest high grade anvil** produced by any one. **The body is made of the best quality wrought iron, with an extra heavy steel face welded to the body by an electric process, which makes it practically a solid steel anvil.**

THE FACE is tempered by a special process, known only to the makers of this anvil, which warrants it against flaws, chipping, or being too soft. This, by the way, is the most difficult obstacle to overcome in anvil making. Hundreds of anvils, made of good material, are made useless by poor tempering, being either too hard or too soft.

THE FACE IS TRUED AND SHAPED BY A SPECIAL MACHINE, so that every anvil is **mechanically perfect; no hollow or uneven places.** The horn is extra long, with the Peter Wright shape, pattern and curve, nicely rounded. The hole for the **hardie is made true and** straight, so you experience no trouble by hardie or flatter sticking or not setting level. While these points seem small, the defects of nine-tenths of all anvils, both foreign and American make, now being sold, rest in the fact that these points are not looked after. **We cannot always furnish even weights; please allow five pounds either way.**

NOTICE—Never leave a hot piece of iron for any length of time on the face of an anvil, as this will surely draw the temper and thus make it soft. A great many anvils are ruined in this way.

No. 24C988 Weight, 80 pounds and up. Price, per pound......**8½c**
Weight 70 pounds to 79 pounds. Price, per pound......**9c**
Weight, 60 pounds to 69 pounds. Price, per pound......**9½c**
Weight, 50 pounds to 59 pounds. Price, per pound......**10½c**

OUR $12.65 OUTFIT OF BLACKSMITHS' TOOLS.

OUTFIT No. 24C995. Order by Number.

This Kit of Tools is far superior to those usually sold, all tools being strictly first quality standard tools, such as are used by mechanics.

Read description of the tools. The Forge is a lever forge, built especially for farmers' use and light repairing. **The Hearth** is 18 inches in diameter. **Fan,** 8 inches in diameter. **The Ratchet** is perfect and cannot get out of order. **The Drill** is a standard horizontal drill, screw feed, and is furnished with chuck to take drills having ½ round shanks. **The Anvil** has a cast base with steel face and horn, same as our No. 24C975 anvils, and can be used the same as a solid wrought iron anvil. We guarantee the face of this anvil not to become detached from body of anvil. Weight, 30 pounds. **The Vise** is our Parallel Bench or Farmers' Vise; has steel face and screw finely finished. A good, serviceable vise. Size, jaws, 3 inches; weight, 11¾ pounds. **The Stock and Dies** cut ⅜ to 3-16 right hand, 14, 18 and 22 threads to the inch, with 6 taps and 3 sets of dies. **The Tongs** are drop forged (no welds), length, 20 inches. **The Pincers** are solid hammered cast steel; length, 14 inches. **The Farriers' Knife** is the celebrated Wostenholm make. **The Hand Hammer** weighs 2 pounds (without handle), solid cast steel. **The Farriers' Hammer** weighs 10 ounces (without handle). All tools are strictly first class in material and workmanship. You will save $12.65, the price of this outfit, in your own time and blacksmiths' bills. Shoe your horses, mend your machinery, your wagons. You can do any ordinary work. Worth five times the price every year for keeping all your tools in perfect order.

No. 24C995 Price for complete outfit as illustrated and described......**$12.65**

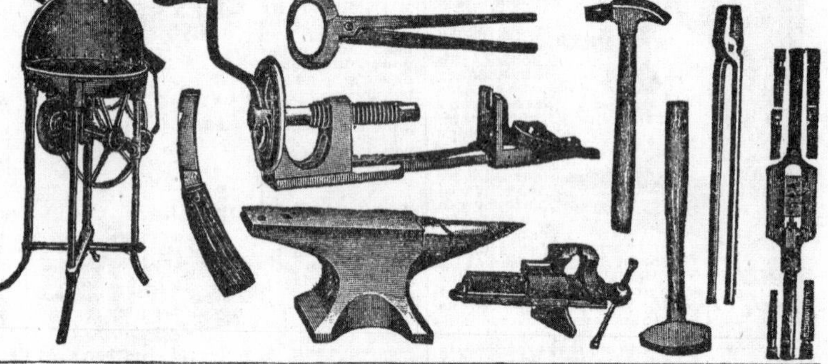

THE FARMERS' KIT OF BLACKSMITHS' TOOLS, $22.50.

FOR THE FARMER, STOCKMAN, PLANTER AND MECHANIC.

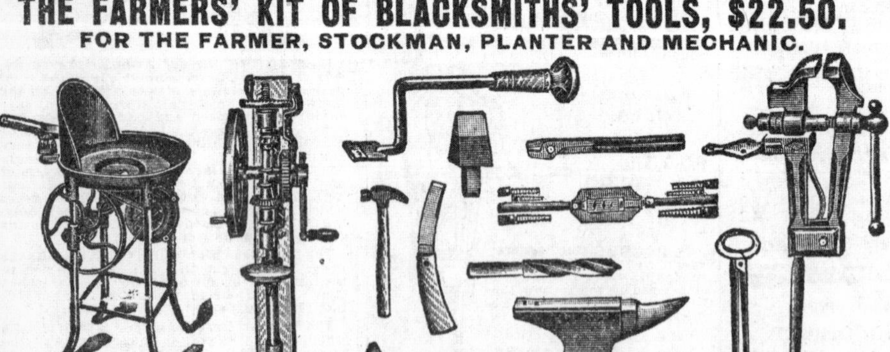

THE ANVIL. We furnish an anvil with steel face, accurately ground and tempered. Weight, 60 pounds. The face of this anvil is one solid piece of English tool steel, thoroughly welded to body of anvil by a patented process. The horn is covered with and its extremity made entirely of cast steel.

ALL TOOLS furnished with this outfit are strictly first class, and are suitable for any small blacksmith's or farmer's use. You can compare this set with anything else in the market, for there's nothing offered like it.

THE VISE. We furnish a wrought iron solid box and screw blacksmith vise, with steel jaws, weighing 35 pounds.

There have been many cheap kits of blacksmith's tools sold, but never before has anyone offered a kit of standard, reliable tools. Read the description of each article.

THE FORGE. We furnish a lever forge having hearth 18 inches in diameter. It is furnished with a 6-inch fan. The gear is the simplest, strongest and best ever put on a forge. Only a slight movement of the lever produces the strongest blast.

THE DRILL. We furnish our Acme Double Speed Drill. The best drill for the money on the market. Drills to the center of a 12-inch circle. Takes drills with ½-inch round shank. Weight, 85 pounds. For a full description of this drill see No. 24C867.

THE SET OF STOCKS AND DIES cuts ⅝ to 3-16-inch right hand, 14, 18 and 22 threads to the inch, with six taps and three sets of dies. **The hot cutter and cold cutter are 1⅜-inch cut. The hardie fits anvil. The tongs are 20 inches long. The pincers 14 inches long. The farriers' knife is the celebrated Wostenholm make. The farriers' hammer weighs** 10 ounces without the handle. **The buttress is 2-inch cut. The drills—We** furnish seven drills to fit drill; one each size, ⅛, 3-16, ¼, 5-16, ⅜, ½ and ⅝-inch.

No. 24C997 Price for complete outfit, as illustrated and described......**$22.50**

THE ACME KIT OF BLACKSMITHS' TOOLS, $26.35.

No. 24C999 Order by Number.

No one will meet our prices on same quality of goods. We will not sacrifice quality for price, but on our high standard of quality, we defy competition.

The Forge. We furnish a lever forge having hearth 21 inches in diameter. It is furnished with 8-inch fan. The gear is the simplest, strongest and best ever put on a forge. Only a slight movement of the lever produces the strongest blast.

The Anvil. We furnish an American wrought anvil, accurately ground and tempered. Weight, 85 pounds. The face of this anvil is one solid piece of English tool steel, thoroughly welded to body of anvil by a patented process. The horn is covered with and its extremity made entirely of cast steel.

The Drill. We furnish our Acme Double Speed Drill. The best drill for its weight on the market. Drills to the center of a 12-inch circle. Takes drills with ½-inch round shank. Weight, 85 pounds. For full description of this drill see No. 24C807.

The Vise. We furnish a wrought iron solid box and screw blacksmith vise, with steel jaws, weighing 35 pounds.

The Set of Stocks and Dies cut ⅝ to 3-16-inch right hand, 14, 18 and 22 threads to the inch, with six taps and one set of three dies. The hot cutter and cold cutter are 1⅜-inch cut. The hardie fits anvil. The tongs are 20 inches long. The pincers 14 inches long. The farriers' knife is the celebrated Wostenholm make. The hand hammer weighs 2 pounds without the handle. The farriers' hammer weighs 10 ounces without the handle. The buttress is 2-inch cut. The drills—We furnish eight drills to fit drill, one each size, ⅛, 3-16, ¼, 5-16, ⅜, ½, ⅝ and ¾-inch.

All tools furnished with this outfit are strictly first class, and are suitable for any small blacksmith or carriage maker's shop. You can compare this set with anything else in the market, for there is nothing offered like it.

No. 24C999 Price for complete outfit as illustrated and described......**$26.35**

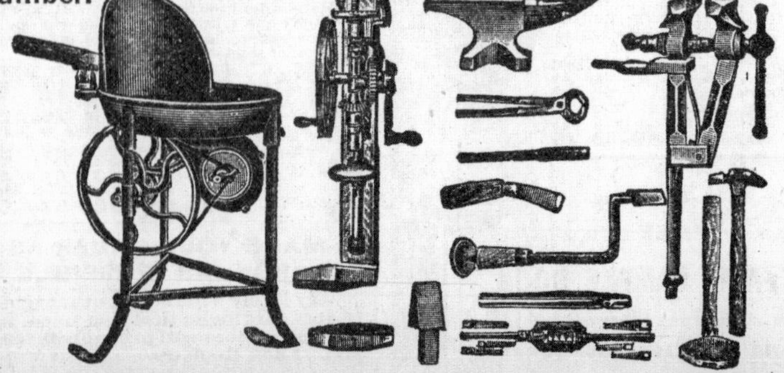

OUR $41.20 SET OF BLACKSMITHS' TOOLS.

ALL TOOLS ARE A1, the best we carry, and are guaranteed to be made of high grade material of perfect workmanship. We replace any tool found defective, free of charge. A set suitable for any blacksmith shop.

THE FORGE. We furnish a lever forge with a half hood; size of fan, 12 inches; height of forge, 30 inches; size of hearth, 35x23 inches. Weight, 145 pounds. It is the best finished and most perfect motion lever forge made. Will produce a welding heat on 3-inch iron in seven minutes.

THE DRILL. We furnish our No. 10 ball bearing post drill, one of the best drills we carry. The shaft and spindle are made of best grade tool steel. Has our improved third gear. The spindle is supplied with steel balls which add greatly to the running of the drill. Takes drills with ½-inch round shank. Weight, 110 pounds. For full description of this drill see No. 24C812.

THE VISE. We furnish a solid wrought iron vise with steel face and jaws; has machine cut screw; an A1 vise in every respect. Weight, 50 pounds.

THE SCREW PLATE. We furnish our Invincible screw plate known to all mechanics as being the most perfect thread cutting tool ever invented. Guaranteed to cut a perfect thread with a single cut. The sizes are ¼, ⅜, ½, ⅝ and ¾-inch; five taps and five pairs of dies. Comes complete in a heavy oak case, as shown in illustration.

THE BLACKSMITHS' APRON. Our regular $1.03 split leather apron, extra large size complete with straps.

Farriers' Knife is the imported IXL Wostenholm. **Hardie** is 1¼-inch and fits the anvil. **Hand Hammer** weighs 3 pounds, is made of best grade tool steel. **Farriers' Hammer** is our S., R. & Co.'s brand, and weighs 1 pound, handle included.

THE DRILLS, of which we furnish eight in number, size ⅛, 3-16, ¼, 5-16, ⅜, ⅜, ⅝ and ¾ have ½-inch round shank and are made to fit the drill. They are what is called the Morse pattern twist drill and are guaranteed against flaws or defects in workmanship.

THE ANVIL. We furnish our 100-pound American solid wrought anvil with steel face, one of the best anvils made in this or any other country. The body and base are wrought iron; face and horn are steel welded together by an electric process which makes practically one solid piece. We warrant this anvil against defects or being too hard or soft.

CUTTING NIPPERS are the V. & B. Brand; are made of a solid piece of steel, no welds, length, 14 inches. **Farriers' Pincers** are the V. & B. brand, made from one solid piece of steel; length, 14 inches. **Flat Lip Tongs** are 22 inches long and are drop forged from one piece of steel; no welds to break. **Bolt Tongs** will hold bolts of iron 5-16 to ½-inch in diameter, are drop forged thus doing away with all welds. **Horse Rasp** is our S., R. & Co.'s make, is double faced hand cut and is 14 inches long. **Hot Cutter** has a 1⅜-inch cut and weighs 2 pounds 2 ounces. **Cold Cutter** has a 1⅜-inch cut, and weighs 2 pounds 14 ounces.

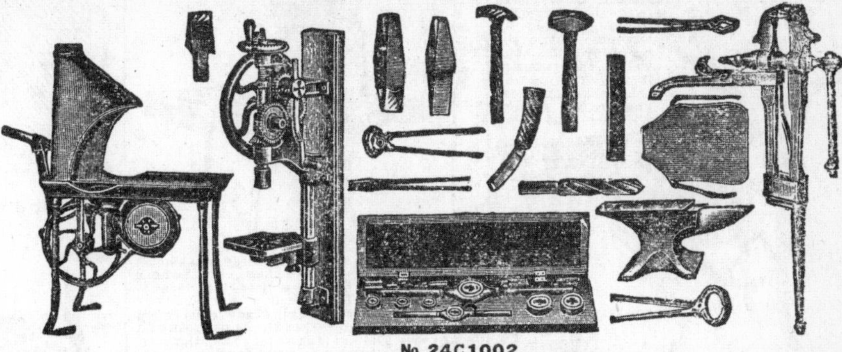
No. 24C1002

To accommodate our customers we will allow them to omit any article in this outfit and substitute any article (pertaining to blacksmiths' supplies only) in exchange at our regular catalogue prices for article omitted, also for new article selected.

No. 24C1002 Price for complete outfit as illustrated and described......**$41.20**

OUR $53.85 SPECIAL SET OF BLACKSMITHS' TOOLS.

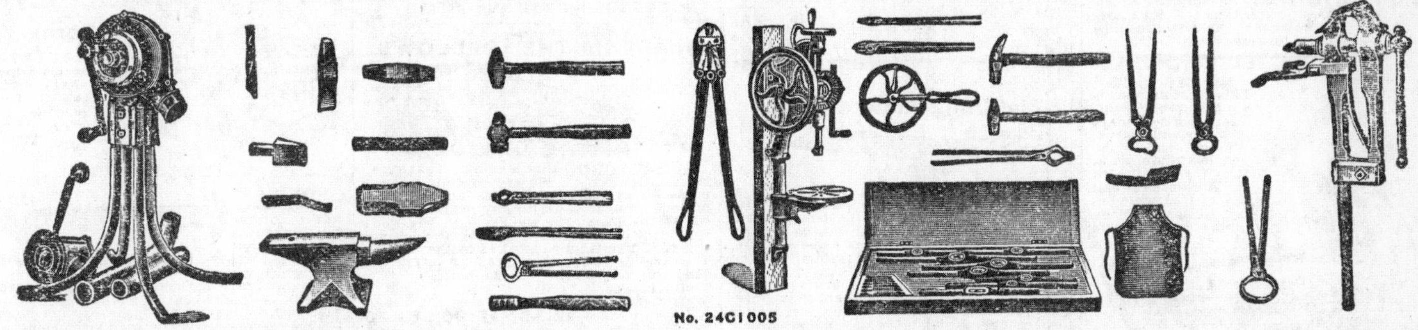
No. 24C1005

IN OUR SPECIAL SET OF BLACKSMITHS' TOOLS we show the most complete up to date outfit sold by anyone. A set that is complete and large enough for any shop. All tools are high grade and the most improved patterns on the market.

THE BLOWER is our Tiger 20th Century, complete with Tuyere iron. A blower that will give a blast equal to a 48-inch bellows.

THE DRILL is our large 125-pound drill, one of the best drills we carry. It has a self feed attachment, is double geared, drills to the center of a 15-inch circle, holds round shank drills and will bore up to 1¼-inch hole.

THE VISE is our solid box wrought vise. Weight, 60 pounds.

THE SCREW PLATE is our Invincible full mounted plate, each die having a separate holder. Cuts seven sizes, ¼ to ¾-inch. Complete in hardwood case.

THE ANVIL is our American wrought. Weight, 125 pounds.

DRILLS. We furnish ten high grade round shank bits that fit the above drill. Sizes, 3-16, ¼, 5-16, ⅜, 7-16, ½, ⅝, ¾, ⅞ and 1-inch. One hot cutter, size 1⅜ inches; one cold cutter, size 1⅜ inches; one hardie that fits anvil; one pair farriers' tongs, 14-inch; one pair flat tongs, 20-inch; one pair flat tongs 22-inch; one pair bolt tongs, 5-16 to ½-inch; one pair bolt tongs, ½ to ¾ inch; one steel blacksmiths' sledge with handle; one pair Maud S farriers' pincers, 14 inch, solid steel; one pair nail cutting nippers, 12-inch, solid steel; one electric sharpening hammer, weight, 2 or 2½ pounds; one blacksmiths' hand hammer, weight 3 pounds; one farriers' hammer, Cincinnati pattern weight 14 to 18 ounces; one Keystone adjustable farriers' knife; one Sears, Roebuck & Co. horse rasp, 14 inches long; one large size blacksmiths' apron; one pair high grade hoof parers, 14 inches long; one pair Randall bolt clippers, cuts up to ½-inch bolt, nothing better made; one riveting hammer, all steel, weight, 9 ounces; one all steel toe knife; one tire measuring wheel, steel, drop forged.

No. 24C1005 Price for complete outfit as illustrated and described......**$53.85**

THE ACME FORGES.—PORTABLE LEVER TYPE.

$4.50

The line of Acme Forges, illustrated on this and the following pages, will be found to contain those of suitable capacity for all classes of blacksmith work. A close examination of the several designs will clearly show that each individual machine is particularly adapted to the requirements for which it is recommended. A careful study of all the desirable features of a forge for a given service has been made and the greatest possible number embodied. In the construction of the Acme forges only the best material and workmanship enter. The greatest accuracy is constantly insisted upon in the erection and assembling of the machines, which results in all parts being brought into the closest relation to each other. The most approved methods of securing them are employed. In consequence there is no gradual rattling loose or becoming wabbly after the machines are used for a time. All these deficiencies, common to cheap forges, will be found to be entirely avoided. **NOTICE: To prevent fire pan from cracking always put in a layer of clay before starting fire. This applies to all forges.**

Our $4.50 Portable Forge Leader.

We believe we are headquarters for everything desirable in portable forges. We have made our contracts with several of the very largest and most reliable manufacturers in the country, concerns who are strictly headquarters for the manufacture of the highest grade portable forges on the market. There are many cheap, inferior forges offered, and some of our competitors may even attempt to meet or cut our prices; but when a forge is offered at within 10 or 20 per cent of the price we are able to name, you can depend upon it you are not getting the same grade of work. There is perhaps no more necessary or economic machine on a farm than one of our strictly high grade portable forges. In one year it will save its cost ten times over in time, to say nothing of the saving in blacksmiths' bills.

WE WANT to sell another 4,000 of these $4.50 forges during the coming year, and with the expectation that we will sell this number, have reduced our price to $4.50. By making our contract on this basis, we were able to get the price down to about the actual cost of material and labor. This forge is accepted by the railroad companies at second class freight rate.

At $4.50 we offer you a strictly high grade, fully guaranteed forge, which you could not duplicate elsewhere, in a wholesale way, at anywhere near what we ask for it. We are able to get the price so low ($4.50) that every farmer in selecting a forge should order this in preference to a cheaper one. The motion is a very simple device. It has a self acting ratchet; no springs or anything to get out of order. It is made from the very best material. The lever is connected with a segment of gears which speeds the driving wheel up to a very high speed. It requires a very slight movement of the lever to get the strongest blast. Having but three legs, it stands very firmly on an uneven foundation, and is purposely made for the work we claim. Height of forge, 30 inches; hearth, 21 inches in diameter; fan, 8 inches. Weight, 80 pounds. This is the largest forge we ever saw offered at anything like the price, and we would ask you to compare the size of **hearth and fan** with other forges at about the same price, and draw your own conclusions.

No. 24C1008 Price.......................................**$4.50**

Our $4.00 Leader Forge.

Remember when you buy a forge from us, all sizes, weights, etc., will correspond with catalogue description. We guarantee weights and sizes to be just as represented or money refunded.

$4.00

No. 24C1009 Sears, Roebuck & Co.'s Portable Forge is especially built for farmers' and planters' use or for light repairing. Blacksmiths should buy a larger forge. This lever motion forge has pipe legs. Has 6-inch fan. Stands 30 inches high. Hearth is 18 inches in diameter. Will produce a welding heat on fine iron in five minutes. Compare weight, size of fan, etc., with any other make and you will see this is the cheapest forge for the size sold by anyone. Weight, 65 pounds. Price....**$4.00**

Our Acme No. 352 Forge.

Only $6.90 for this Splendid Forge

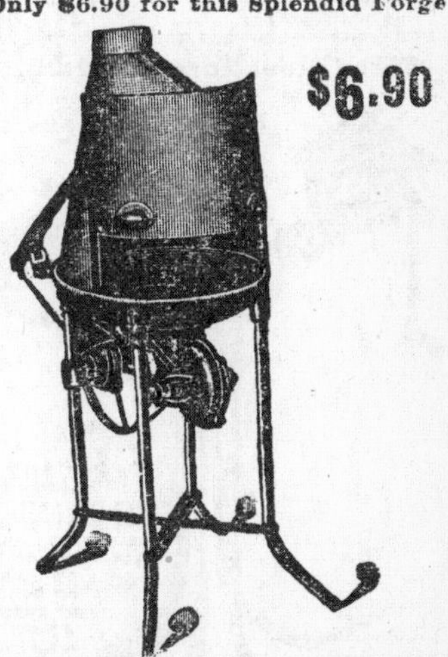
$6.90

No. 24C1012 This forge is of the same high grade as our No. 24C1009, but with hood entirely closed. The large sliding door in front and smaller door in rear affords convenience in handling long bars. The escape of sparks, fumes and smoke is effectually prevented and this type of forge is particularly adapted to places where combustible material is lying about or where bright metal work is attacked by fumes from the fire. Hearth, 18 inches diameter; fan, 8 inches, height, 30 inches. Weight, 75 pounds. Price............................**$6.90**

Acme No. 200 Forge.

We would call your special attention to our No. 200 Acme Forge, inasmuch as we have here the best forge for the money sold by anyone. Notice the make up, size and weight, then compare it with any forge on the market and see if you are not getting 33⅓ per cent more forge for your money than you can get elsewhere. This is a forge of our own design, is made up in quantities of 1,000 forges at a time, which has reduced the cost of manufacture to a minimum. It is large enough for general blacksmithing, and as a forge for the farm or ranch it has no equal. Has a perfect tuyere iron and blast and the size and shape of hearth permits ample room for coal and to lay tools upon. The fan is 12½ inches in diameter; hearth is 36x25 inches, stands 30 inches high, and weighs 165 pounds without crating. Will produce welding heat on 3-inch iron in five minutes.

No. 24C1014 Price, with shield...**$9.95**
No. 24C1015 Price, with half hood, as per illustration, without water tank......**$11.05**

If wanted with water tank, as shown in illustration, add 90 cents to above price.

Acme No. 165 Forge.

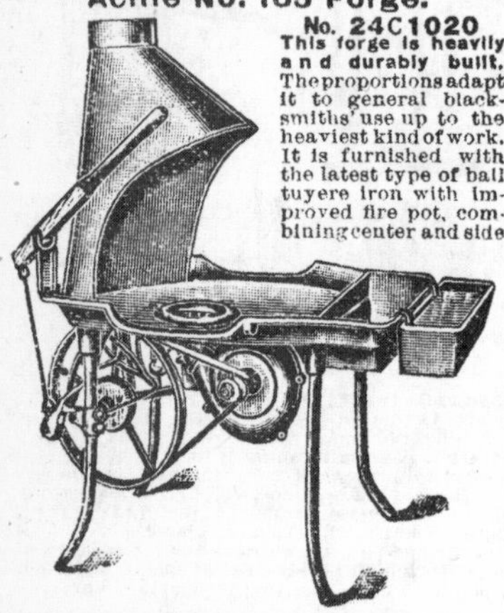

No. 24C1020 This forge is heavily and durably built. The proportions adapt it to general blacksmiths' use up to the heaviest kind of work. It is furnished with the latest type of ball tuyere iron with improved fire pot, combining center and side blast, which is able to stand continuous heavy work without burning out; an improved steel friction clutch is used. This is a high class forge in every detail. Size of hearth, 46x33½ inches; fan, 14½ inches. Height, 30 inches; length over all, 54 inches. Weight, 300 pounds.

Price, with coal box.......... **$16.00**
Price, with coal box and water tank **16.75**

Tiger Steel Forge, $12.25.

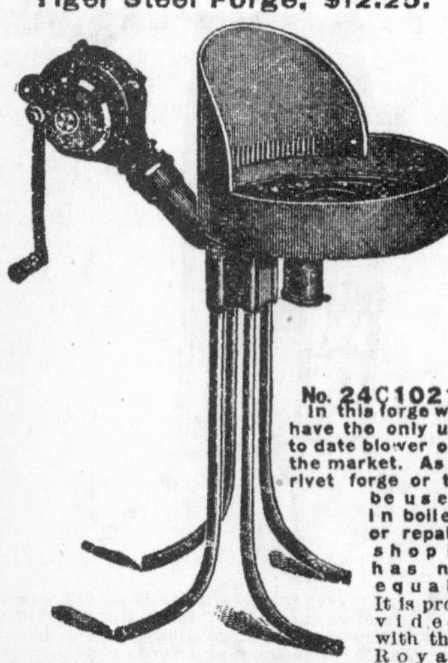

No. 24C1021 In this forge we have the only up to date blower on the market. As a rivet forge or to be used in boiler or repair shop it has no equal. It is provided with the Royal style of blower, which has the flat, straight cut gears, insuring double the life of bevel or worm gears, which combined with steel shafts makes it by far the best forge made by anyone. The gear case is oil tight and dust proof, permitting the gears to run in a bath of oil. We use no belts, clutches or ratchets. The hearth is of sheet steel, making the forge light and neat in appearance. Can be quickly and easily taken apart for transportation, and its extreme lightness and simplicity make it a most desirable move-about forge. The crank turns to right or left as suits operator. Will give a welding heat on 3½-inch iron in about ten minutes. Has 18-inch hearth, 9-inch fan. Height, 30 inches over all. Weight, 70 pounds. Price..**$12.25**

Acme Forge No. 300.

This forge is to be used in large blacksmith shops, plow and railroad shops, etc., where heavy work is done and a first class forge is wanted. In this forge we have combined our Tiger blower, with a high grade cast forge, which combination makes the best outfit sold by anyone. The fan is extra large and the blast is direct from blower to fire. Easy to operate and equal in volume to any demand required. Size of hearth, 33½x46 inches; diameter of fan, 12 inches; height, 30 inches; length over all, 54 inches. Weight, 275 pounds.

No. 24C1024 Price with either coal or water box...................................**$17.10**
No. 24C1025 Price, with both coal and water box...................................**$18.10**

Steel Harrow Teeth.

No. 24C1032 Give length when ordering.

Size, inches	Wt. per doz., lbs.	Per doz.	Size, inches	Wt. per doz., lbs.	Per doz.
½x8	6½	....22c	⅝x9	11¼	....37c
½x8½	7	....25c	⅝x9½	11½	....40c
½x9	7¼	....26c	⅝x10	12	....40c
9-16x8½	9	....30c	¾x10	17	....58c
9 16x9	9½	....37c	¾x11	21	....65c
⅝x8½	11	....39c			

Lightning Plow Shares.

Lightning Plow Share, fully welded and point finished. Perfected to meet the demand for a fully welded plow share, that can be quickly and easily fitted to the different make of plows, thus saving the hard work of welding on the landside and finishing the point. The Lightning share can be fitted to the angle of more plows than any other welded share in the market. The landside extends at the heel and is long enough to cut to fit any plow. Either right or left hand. Be sure and state kind wanted. Average weight, 13 pounds.

No. 24C1033 Made of crucible cast steel.
Price, 12-inch..............................**$1.05**
14-inch..**1.15**
16-inch..**1.25**
No. 24C1034 Made of soft center steel.
Price, 12-inch..............................**$1.70**
14-inch..**1.85**
16-inch..**2.00**

Plow Shares.

They are made of the best soft center and solid crucible cast steel. Perfect shape with an upset edge, and can be easily fitted to any plow. Be sure and state right or left hand. Average weight, 9 pounds.

No. 24C1035 No. 1 Shares. For old ground plows, made from soft center steel.
12-inch. Weight, 7¼ pounds. Price....**$0.78**
14-inch. Weight, 8¾ pounds. Price.... **.95**
16-inch. Weight, 9½ pounds. Price.... **1.00**
No. 24C1036 No. 2 Shares. For old ground plows, made from crucible steel.
12-inch. Weight, 7 pounds. Price.........**60c**
14-inch. Weight, 8¾ pounds. Price.......**74c**
16-inch. Weight, 9¾ pounds. Price.......**78c**

Landside Plates.

No. 24C1037 No. 1 Landside Plates, ready for use, made of soft center steel.
14-inch. Weight, 5¾ pounds. Price.......**56c**
16-inch. Weight, 5¾ pounds. Price.......**61c**
No. 24C1038 No. 2 Landside Plates, ready for use, made of crucible cast steel.
14-inch. Weight, 5½ pounds. Price.......**42c**
16-inch. Weight, 5¾ pounds. Price.......**45c**

New Green River Shoeing Vise and Bolt Header.

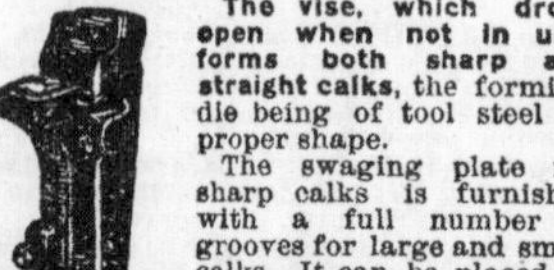

The vise, which drops open when not in use, forms both sharp and straight calks, the forming die being of tool steel of proper shape.

The swaging plate for sharp calks is furnished with a full number of grooves for large and small calks. It can be placed so that the grooves run either way as may be preferred.

Size, ¼, 5-16, ⅜, 7-16, ½, ⅝, ¾ inch. Any length up to 24 inches.

No. 24C1045 Price, complete for shoeing and bolt heading........................**$10.25**
No. 24C1046 Price, for shoeing only (without bolt heading attachment)......**$9.50**

Blacksmiths' Aprons.

No. 24C1050 Split Leather Aprons. Size, 26x34 inches. Price..**90c**

Horseshoers' Aprons.

No. 24C1052 Standard Split Leather Aprons. Our own special brand. Size, 28x38 inches.
Price.....**$1.03**
No. 24C1054 Pigskin Aprons. Size, 28x38 inches.
Price..**$1.73**

Peace's Spoke Tenoning Machine.

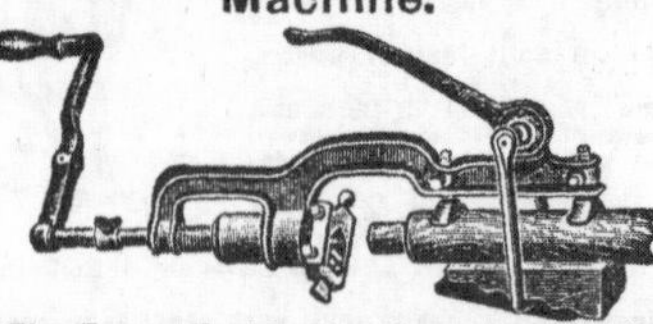

The Peace Machine has been used for the last ten years with general satisfaction. It is made in the most workmanlike manner, all castings being malleable iron and the auger head made extra heavy. The knife starts on the blank of spokes and centers perfectly. The auger is kept cutting by force of the spring. Can be used on any size spoke or disc of wheel and is readily applied without removing from where spokes are driven. Cuts any size from ¾ to 1¾. Weight, 8 pounds.

No. 24C1060 Price, without felloe attachment..**$7.50**
No. 24C1061 Price, with felloe attachment..**8.75**

BLACKSMITHS' BELLOWS.

No. 24C1080 Blacksmiths' Bellows, standard patterns. We use cowhide leather, prepared especially for our use, and we guarantee it to wear equal to any made. We use whitewood, basswood and pine in the wood work, which is kiln dried, making it perfectly dry, that it may not be affected by the climate. The weight of our bellows is about as follows. They may vary a little, but not much:

Width, inches.....	24	26	28
Weight, pounds...	30	35	40
Price...............	$2.55	$2.90	$3.20
Width, inches.....	30	32	34
Weight, pounds...	45	50	60
Price...............	$3.30	$3.60	$4.15
Width, inches.....	36	38	40
Weight, pounds...	68	78	100
Price...............	$4.65	$5.15	$5.90

No. 24C1084 Extra Long Pattern Bellows.

Width, inches	34	36	38	40
Weight, pounds	73	87	105	125
Price.......	$5.40	$5.50	$6.80	$7.40
Width, inches.	44		46	48
Weight, pounds	147		220	225
Price.........	$10.50		$12.50	$14.50

Tuyere Iron.

No. 24C1089 Single Duck's Nest Tuyere Iron. Weight, 12 pounds. Price. **32c**

Clark's Tuyere Irons.

Clark's Extra Heavy Tuyere Irons with patent dump and shaker.

No. 24C1092 No. 2. Weight, 22½ pounds.
Price..**79c**
No. 24C1093 No. 3. Weight, 27½ pounds.
Price..**88c**
No. 24C1094 No. 4. Weight, 45 pounds.
Price..**$1.30**

Sutton's Tuyere Irons.

No. 24C1095 Sutton's Improved Tuyere Irons. Made large enough to answer the purpose of firepot and tuyere iron combined, just the thing where heavy, constant work is required. Weight, 44 pounds.
Price.......................**$2.10**

Norton's Patent Tuyere Iron.

No. 24C1104 This is one of the best tuyeres on the market. The cinders and ashes may be removed by drawing out the small rod which opens the slide. The levers and spring are readily changed to either side for right or left hand use. To regulate the blast, turn the large rod. Weight, about 27 pounds.
Price..**98c**

Warren's Patent Tuyere Iron.

No. 24C1106 Easily adjusted. Open the bottom valve, and all cinders and ashes drop out. The blast is regulated by simply revolving the ball, which has three unequal sides. Weight, about 31 pounds. Price........**$1.10**

Turn Buckles.

No. 24C1113 Pressed Wrought Iron Turn Buckles, made of the best material. Well finished. Average weight, 2½ pounds.

Size	Price	Size	Price
⅜ inch............	21c	¾ inch..........	36c
7-16 inch	24c	⅞ inch	43c
½ inch............	25c	1 inch..........	50c
⅝ inch............	30c		

Larger sizes furnished. Prices quoted upon application.

Cherry Heat Welding Compound.

No. 24C1115 Every weld with compound will be stronger than it would be possible to make at any heat with borax. It is a perfect protection to steel from any degree of heat obtainable in a smith's forge. It will perfectly restore burnt steel. Broken castings can be reunited at a low heat with the compound, and cast iron firmly united to either wrought iron or steel.

1-pound tin can. Price, per can........**13c**
5-pound boxes. Price, per box........**50c**

E-Z Welding Compound.

No. 24C1116 In the E-Z Welding Compound we are presenting a compound entirely without borax. You will find it will make a clean, firm weld. Can be used with a very low heat which, of course, makes a better weld. There is no sluffing or boiling off and there is absolutely no scale. Put up in 5-pound wood boxes. Price per 5-pound box..................**35c**

Borax.

No. 24C1172 Best Quality Strictly Pure Borax. Sold in any quantity.
Price, per pound.....**10c**

Carriage Bolts.

Oval Head Carriage Bolts, forged nuts, full size square shoulder, well cut thread in nut and on bolt, made from soft iron, which will not break easily.

Weight of carriage bolts per 100. ¼-inch carriage bolts weigh about 2½ pounds per 100 for each inch in length; 5-16-inch carriage bolts about 4¼ pounds per 100 for each inch in length; ⅜-inch carriage bolts weigh about 6 pounds per 100 for each inch in length; ½-inch carriage bolts weigh about 13 pounds per 100 for each inch in length.

No. 24C1175 Carriage Bolts, ¼-inch in diameter.

Length inches	Per doz.	Per 100	Length inches	Per doz.	Per 100
1	$0.04	$0.22	3¾	$0.06	$0.31
1¼	.04	.23	4	.06	.32
1½	.04	.24	4¼	.06	.32
1¾	.05	.25	4½	.06	.33
2	.05	.26	5	.06	.35
2¼	.05	.27	5½	.07	.37
2½	.05	.28	6	.07	.39
2¾	.05	.29	6½	.07	.41
3	.05	.30	7	.07	.42
3¼	.05	.30	8	.07	.46
3½	.06	.31			

No. 24C1177 Carriage Bolts, 5-16 inch in diameter.

Length inches	Per doz.	Per 50	Per 100	Length inches	Per doz.	Per 50	Per 100
1¼	$0.05	.13	.26	4¼	$0.08	.20	.40
1½	.05	.14	.27	4½	.08	.21	.42
1¾	.06	.14	.27	5	.09	22	.43
2	.06	.14	.28	5½	.09	.23	.46
2¼	.07	.15	.29	6	.09	.25	.50
2½	.07	.15	.30	6½	.09	.28	.56
2¾	.07	.16	.31	7	.09	.33	65
3	.07	.17	.34	7½	.10	.35	.69
3¼	.08	.18	.35	8	.12	.35	.70
3½	.08	.18	.36	9	.14	.37	.73
3¾	.08	.19	.37	10	.15	.38	.75
4	.08	.19	.38				

No. 24C1179 Carriage Bolts, ⅜-inch in diameter.

Length inches	Per doz.	Per 50	Per 100	Length inches	Per doz.	Per 50	Per 100
1¼	$0.07	.19	.37	4¾	$0.11	.42	.60
1½	.07	.19	.38	5	.11	.45	.63
1¾	.07	.20	.39	5½	.12	.46	.66
2	.08	.22	.43	6	.12	.48	.69
2¼	.08	.22	.44	6½	.13	.50	.80
2½	.08	.23	.45	7	.14	.53	.87
2¾	.09	.23	.46	7½	.14	.55	.92
3	.09	.24	.47	8	.15	.58	.94
3¼	.09	.25	.49	8½	.16	.62	.99
3½	.09	.26	52	9	.17	.63	1.00
3¾	.10	.27	.54	10	.17	.68	1.10
4	.10	.28	.55	11	.19	.73	1.15
4¼	.10	.28	.56	12	.20	.75	1.25
4½	.11	.29	.58				

No. 24C1180 Carriage Bolts, ½-inch in diameter

Len'h in.	Per doz.	Per 50	Per 100	Len'h in.	Per doz.	Per 50	Per 100
1½	$0.10	.38	.76	7½	$0.20	.68	1.36
2	.10	.39	.77	8	.20	.72	1.41
2¼	.10	.39	.78	8½	.22	.74	1.47
2½	.10	.40	.79	9	.22	.77	1.53
3	.11	.42	.84	9½	.23	.79	1.58
3½	.12	.45	.90	10	.24	.82	1.64
4	.12	.47	.94	10½	.25	.85	1.70
4½	.12	.52	1.01	11	.26	.88	1.76
5	.14	.54	1.07	11½	.27	.92	1.81
5½	.14	.57	1.13	12	.28	.94	1.87
6	.14	.60	1.19	13	.29	1.00	1.99
6½	.15	.62	1.24	14	.30	1.05	2.10
7	.15	.65	1.30	15	.30	1.11	2.21

Machine Bolts.

Machine Bolts have square heads and nuts, and are round all the way up to the head. Weights about the same as carriage bolts.

No. 24C1189 Diameter, ¼-inch.

Length inches	Per doz.	Per 100	Length inches	Per doz.	Per 100
1½	$0.07	$0.38	4½	$0.09	$0.50
2	.07	.39	5	.09	.52
2¼	.08	.40	5½	.09	.54
2½	.08	.41	6	.10	.55
3	.08	.44	6½	.10	.57
3½	.08	.46	7	.11	.59
4	.09	.48			

No. 24C1190 Diameter, 5-16 inch.

Length inches	Per doz.	Per 100	Length inches	Per doz.	Per 100
1½	$0.09	$0.45	4½	$0.12	$0.67
2	.09	.47	5	.13	.70
2¼	.09	.50	5½	.14	.72
2½	.10	.52	6	.16	.75
3	.10	.54	6½	.17	.77
3½	.11	.57	7	.18	.80
4	.11	.59			

No. 24C1191 Diameter, ⅜-inch.

Length inches	Per doz.	Per 100	Length inches	Per doz.	Per 100
1½	$0.10	$0.54	5	$0.20	$0.88
2	.11	.58	5½	.21	.92
2½	.12	.61	6	.22	.95
3	.13	.65	6½	.22	.99
3½	.14	.70	7	.23	1.04
4	.17	.72	7½	.23	1.09
4½	.18	.75	8	.24	1.12

No. 24C1192 Diameter, ½-inch.

Length inches	Per doz.	Per 100	Length inches	Per doz.	Per 100
1½	$0.41	$0.81	7	$0.73	$1.46
2	.44	.87	8	.89	1.57
2½	.46	.91	9	.88	1.75
3	.47	.95	10	.89	1.78
3½	.50	1.00	11	1.00	2.00
4	.56	1.11	12	1.08	2.15
4½	.58	1.16	14	1.13	2.25
5	.62	1.21	16	1.20	2.40
5½	.64	1.27	18	1.28	2.55
6	.68	1.35	20	1.40	2.80
6½	.70	1.40			

Round Head Stove Bolts.

Stove bolts are useful for many purposes. For fastening hinges they are cheap and good. For many uses they take the place of carriage bolts at much less cost.

No. 24C1195 Diameter, 3-16-inch, round head.

Length, inches	½	⅝	¾	⅞	1	1¼
Per dozen	$0.03	.03	.03	.03	.03	.03½
Per 100	.17	.17	.17	.18	.18	.19
Length, ins.	1½	1¾	2	2½	3	
Per dozen	$0.03½	.03½	.03½	.04	.04	
Per 100	.20	.22	.23	.24	.26	

No. 24C1196 Diameter, 1-4-inch, round head.

Length, ins.	½	⅝	¾	⅞	1	
Per dozen	$0.03½	.03½	.03½	.04	.04	
Per 100	.20	.20	.20	.21	.21	
Length, in.	1¼	1½	1¾	2	2½	3
Per dozen	$0.04	.04	.04	.04½	.04½	.04½
Per 100	.22	.23	.23	.25	.27	.29

No. 24C1197 Diameter, 5-16-inch, round head.

Length, inches	¾	⅞	1	1¼
Per dozen	$0.05	.05	.05	.06
Per 100	.32	.33	.34	.35
Length, inches	1½	2	2½	3
Per dozen	$0.06	.06	.07	.07
Per 100	.37	.40	.41	.44

Flat Head Stove Bolts. No. 24C1200

Diameter, 3-16-inch, flat head.

Length	½	⅝	¾	⅞	1
Per dozen	$0.03	.03	.03	.03	.03
Per 100	.15	.15	.15	.16	.16
Length	1¼	1½	2	2½	3
Per dozen	$0.03	.03	.03½	.03½	.03½
Per 100	.17	.18	.20	.22	.23

No. 24C1201 Diameter, ¼-inch, flat head.

Length		¾	⅞	1
Per dozen	$0.03½	.03½	.03½	.03½
Per 100	.18	.18	.19	.19

Length	1¼	1½	2	2½	3
Per dozen	$0.03½	.04	.04	.04	.04
Per 100	.20	.21	.23	.25	.27

No. 24C1202 Diameter, 5-16-inch flat head.

Length	½	⅝	¾	⅞	1	1¼
Per dozen		$0.04½	.04½	.05	.05	.05½
Per 100		.26	.26	.27	.28	.30
Length		1½	2	2½	3	
Per dozen		$0.05½	.06	.06	.07	
Per 100		.34	.38	.42	.46	

Bolt Ends.

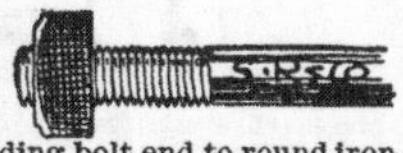

No. 24C1210 Bolt Ends with square nuts, made of a superior grade of soft iron which is very tough. By welding bolt end to round iron of same size, bolts of any required length may be made.

Diameter of iron	½	⅝	¾
Length of ends	8	9	10
Average weight, per dozen	5	11	17
Price, per dozen	$0.24	.36	.47
Diameter of iron		⅞	1
Length of ends		11	12
Average weight, per dozen		25	37
Price, per dozen		$0.72	1.05

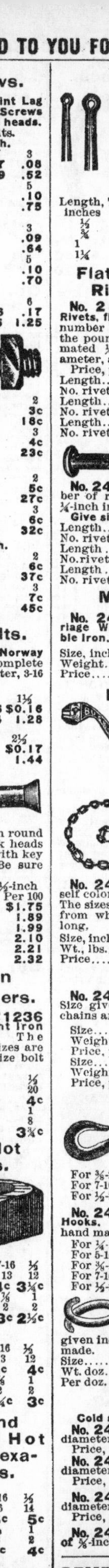

S., R. & Co.'s Lag Screws.

Gimlet Point Lag or Coach Screws with square heads. Weights about the same as carriage bolts.

No. 24C1214 Diameter, 5-16-inch.

Length	1½	2	2½	3
Per dozen	$0.05	.07	.07	.08
Per 100	.39	.45	.49	.52
Length	3½	4½		5
Per dozen	.08	.09		.10
Per 100	.55	.70		.75

No. 24C1215 Diameter, ⅜-inch.

Length	2	2½	3
Per dozen	$0.08	.09	.09
Per 100	.54	.60	.64
Length	3½	4	5
Per dozen	.10	.08	.10
Per 100	.69	.58	.70

No. 24C1216 Diameter ½-inch.

Length	3	4	5	6
Per dozen	$0.13	.15	.16	.17
Per 100	.95	1.05	1.15	1.25

Tire and Iron Work Bolts.

No. 24C1218 Diameter, 3-16 inch.

Length	1¼	1½	1¾	2
Per dozen	3c	3c	3c	3c
Per 100	15c	16c	17c	18c
Length	2¼	2½	2¾	3
Per dozen	4c	4c	4c	4c
Per 100	19c	20c	22c	23c

No. 24C1219 Diameter, ¼-inch.

Length	1¼	1½	1¾	2
Per dozen	4c	4c	4c	5c
Per 100	22c	23c	25c	27c
Length	2¼	2½	2¾	3
Per dozen	5c	5c	5c	6c
Per 100	28c	30c	31c	32c

No. 24C1220 Diameter, 5-16-inch.

Length	1¼	1½	1¾	2
Per dozen	6c	6c	6c	6c
Per 100	34c	35c	36c	37c
Length	2¼	2½	2¾	3
Per dozen	7c	7c	7c	7c
Per 100	39c	40c	43c	45c

T-Head Bolts.

No. 24C1226 Norway Iron T-Head Bolts, complete with burrs. Diameter, 3-16 or ¼-inch.

Length		1	1¼	1½
Per doz.		$0.16	$0.16	$0.16
Per 100		1.20	1.24	1.28
Length	1¾	2	2¼	2½
Per dozen	$0.17	$0.17	$0.17	$0.17
Per 100	1.32	1.36	1.40	1.44

Plow Bolts.

No. 24C1234 Norway Iron Plow Bolts, finished complete, as shown in illustration. The following styles furnished at same price: Plain round countersunk heads; round countersunk heads with square neck; round countersunk with key head, and square countersunk head. Be sure to state which style is wanted.

Length	Size, ⅜-inch Per doz.	Size, ⅜-inch Per 100	Size, ½-inch Per doz.	Size, ½-inch Per 100
1 -inch	14c	$1.00	24c	$1.75
1¼-inch	14c	1.08	25c	1.89
1½-inch	15c	1.13	26c	1.99
1¾-inch	16c	1.19	28c	2.10
2 -inch	17c	1.24	30c	2.21
2¼-inch	17c	1.29	32c	2.32

Iron Washers.

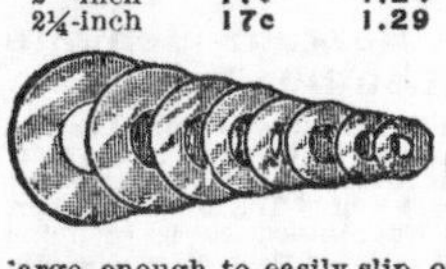

No. 24C1236 Wrought Iron Washers. The various sizes are large enough to easily slip over the size bolt given.

For bolt, in	¼	5-16	⅜	½
No. in lb	139	113	55	20
Per pound	7c	6c	5¼c	4c
For bolt, in	⅝	¾	⅞	1
No. in lb	13	10	9	8
Per pound	4c	4c	3¾c	3¾c

Blank and Threaded Hot Pressed Square Nuts.

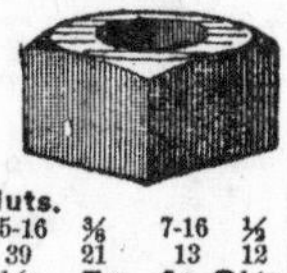

Whether your order is large or small, we welcome it.

No. 24C1250 Blank Nuts.

For bolts, inches	¼	5-16	⅜	7-16	½
No. in pound	74	39	21	13	12
Blank, price, per lb.	9c	6½c	5c	4c	3¼c
For bolts, inches	9-16	⅝	¾	⅞	1
No. in pound	7	6	3	2	2
Blank, price, per lb.	3¼c	3¼c	3c	3c	2½c

No. 24C1252 Threaded Nuts.

For bolts, inches	¼	5-16	⅜	7-16	½
No. in pound	74	39	21	13	12
Threaded, per lb.	11½c	9c	6½c	5c	4c
For bolts, inches	9-16	⅝	¾	⅞	1
No. in pound	7	6	3	2	2
Threaded, per lb.	4c	3½c	3¼c	3¼c	3c

Blank and Threaded Hot Pressed Hexagon Nuts.

No. 24C1256 Blank Nuts.

For bolts, inches	¼	5-16	⅜	7-16	½
No. in pound	88	47	26	16	14
Blank, per lb.	18c	12c	8¼c	6c	5c
For bolts, inches	9-16	⅝	¾	⅞	1
No. in pound	8	5	4	3	2
Blank, per lb.	5¾c	4½c	4¼c	4c	4c

No. 24C1258 Threaded Nuts.

For bolts, inches	¼	5-16	⅜	7-16	½
No. in pound	88	47	26	16	14
Threaded, per lb.	20c	14½c	10½c	8c	6¼c
For bolts, inches	9-16	⅝	¾	⅞	1
No. in pound	8	5	4	3	2
Threaded, per lb.	6c	5¼c	5c	5c	4¾c

Spring Cotters.

No. 24C1262 Made of the best grade English spring steel. Full polished.

Length, inches	Thickness, inches	Per 100	Length, inches	Thickness, inches	Per 100
½	⅛	5c	1½	3-16	16c
¾	⅛	7c	1¾	3-16	18c
1	5-32	10c	2	¼	35c
1¼	3-16	14c			

Flat Head Rivets.

No. 24C1270 Rivets, flat head. The number of rivets to the pound is approximated ¼-inch in diameter, any length. **Give size when ordering.**

Price, per pound ... 4¼c

Length	1	1⅛	1¼	1⅜	1½	1⅝
No. rivets to pound	58	56	54	53	50	48
Length	1¾	1⅞	2	2⅛	2¼	2⅜
No. rivets to pound	46	44	42	40	38	36
Length		2½	2⅝	2¾	2⅞	3
No. rivets to pound		34	32	30	28	26

Oval Head Rivets.

No. 24C1272 Rivets, oval head. The number of rivets to the pound is approximated. ¼-inch in diameter, any length.

Give size when ordering. Price, per lb. 4¼c

Length	1	1⅛	1¼	1⅜	1½	1⅝
No. rivets to lb.	56	54	52	50	48	46
Length	1¾	1⅞	2	2⅛	2¼	2⅜
No. rivets to pound	44	40	37	35	33	30
Length		2½	2⅝	2¾	2⅞	3
No. rivets to pound		28	25	23	22	20

Malleable Wrenches.

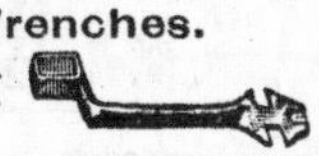

No. 24C1290 Carriage Wrenches, Malleable Iron.

Size, inches	⅞	1	1⅛	1¼	1½
Weight	9 oz.	12 oz.	14 oz.	15 oz.	16oz.
Price	4½c	6c	6½c	7½c	7½c

Buckeye S Wrench.

No. 24C1299 The Handy Buckeye Wrench is made of malleable iron. Small end opens 1 inch, large end, 1½ inches. Size, 10 inches.

Price ... 13c

Log Chains.

No. 24C1310 Cable Log Chains, made of self colored coil chain, with hook on each end. The sizes given below indicate the size of iron from which the link is made. Made 14 feet long.

Size, inch	¼	5/16	⅜	½	⅝
Wt., lbs.	10	16	22	39	56
Price	67c	86c	96c	$1.55	$2.05

Cable Coil Chains.

No. 24C1314 Straight link, hand made. Size given indicates size of iron from which chains are made.

Size	3-16	¼	5-16	⅜
Weight, per foot	8 oz.	12 oz.	1 lb.	1½ lbs.
Price, per pound	8¾c	6¼c	4¾c	4c
Size	7-16	½	⅝	¾
Weight, per foot	2 lbs.	2 lbs.	4¼ lbs.	6 lbs.
Price, per pound	4c	3¾c	3¾c	3½c

Chain Hooks.

No. 24C1318 Common Round Chain Hooks. Made by hand, best grade chain iron used.

For ¼-inch chain. Price ... 7c
For 5-16-inch chain. Price ... 8c
For ⅜-inch chain. Price ... 10c
For 7-16-inch chain. Price ... 17c
For ½-inch chain. Price ... 22c

No. 24C1320 Grab Chain Hooks. Best grade chain iron, hand made.

For ¼-inch chain. Price ... 7c
For 5-16-inch chain. Price ... 8c
For ⅜-inch chain. Price ... 11c
For 7-16-inch chain. Price ... 11½c
For ½-inch chain. Price ... 15c

Repair Links.

No. 24C1325 Repair Links for connecting or repairing chains. Size given indicates size of iron from which link is made.

Size	3-16	¼	5-16	⅜	7-16	½
Wt. doz.	12 oz.	14 oz.	1 lb. 7 oz.	2½ lbs.	2¾ lbs.	3 lbs.
Per doz.	5c	5c	8c	11c	18c	21c

Lap Rings.

Cold shut Lap Rings, made of soft steel.

No. 24C1335 Size, 1½-inch diameter, made of 5-16-inch rod. Price, per dozen ... 10c

No. 24C1337 Size, 1¾-inch diameter, made of ⅜-inch rod. Price, per dozen ... 13½c

No. 24C1339 Size, 2-inch diameter, made of ½-inch rod. Price, per dozen ... 24c

No. 24C1341 Size, 2-inch diameter, made of ⅝-inch rod. Price, per dozen ... 41c

REMEMBER, WE GUARANTEE

TO PLEASE YOU IN EVERY PURCHASE OR WE STAND READY TO IMMEDIATELY RETURN YOUR MONEY AND PAY ALL EXPENSES OF THE TRANSACTION.

Ausable Horse Nails.

No. 24C1530 Ausable Horse Nails are put up in wood boxes of 25 pounds and paper boxes of 5 pounds. We sell any quantity. Nos. 6 and 7 are most used. This is one of the best known nails in the market.

Nos	5	6	7
Length, inches	1⅞	2	2⅛
Price, per pound	15c	14c	13c
Nos	8	9	10
Length, inches	2⅜	2½	2¾
Price, per pound	12½c	12½c	11c

Capewell Horse Nails.

No. 24C1533 The well known Capewell Horse Nails.

Nos	5	6	7
Price, per pound	20c	17½c	16½c
Nos	8	9	10
Price, per pound	16c	15c	15c

Invincible Horse Nails.

No. 24C1534 Our Invincible Brand Horse Nails are made of No. 1 material. Workmanship is perfect, every nail being uniform in size, etc. It is a nail that will hold its own in any company. Made in six sizes: Nos. 5, 6, 7, 8, 9 and 10. City head.

Price, per pound, any size ... $0.12
Price, per box of 25 pounds ... 2.80

Hercules Horse Nails.

No. 24C1535 In our Hercules Horse Nail we have the BEST NAIL made—BAR NONE. We will guarantee this nail to be the equal of the Putnam, Capewell, New Northwest or any other high grade nail. They are made of the highest grade steel, perfectly formed and highly finished. Don't let our low price lead you to believe they are not of a high grade. Money or experience can't make a better nail than the Hercules. Made in six sizes: Nos. 5, 6, 7, 8, 9 and 10. City head.

Price, per pound, any size ... $0.14
Price, per box of 25 pounds ... 3.15

Steel Levers for Jack Screws.

No. 24C1357 For use with 1½-inch jack. Size, 9-16x18 inches long. Price ... 8c

No. 24C1359 For use with 1¾-inch jack. Size, ⅝x20 inches long. Price ... 10c

No. 24C1361 For use with 2-inch jack. Size, ¾x22 inches long. Price ... 14c

Jack Screws.

No. 24C1355 Jack Screws, wrought iron screws, cast iron stands. We do not furnish levers with these screws.

Capacity—1¼-inch screws, 10 tons; 1½-inch screws, 12 tons; 1¾-inch screws, 16 tons; 2-inch screws, 20 tons; 2¼-inch screws, 24 tons; 2½-inch screws, 28 tons; 3-inch screws, 36 tons.

Diam. of Screw, In.	Height of Stand, In.	Height over all, In.	Price	Diam. of Screw, In.	Height of Stand, In.	Height over all, In.	Price
1¼	8	10¼	$0.62	2	12	15¼	$1.40
1¼	10	12¼	.72	2	14	17¼	1.65
1¼	12	14¼	.81	2	16	19¼	1.72
1½	6	8½	.72	2	18	21¼	2.03
1½	8	10½	.78	2¼	8	11¾	1.50
1½	10	12½	.88	2¼	10	13¾	1.62
1½	12	14½	.97	2¼	12	15¾	1.79
1¾	8	10¾	.96	2½	10	14	1.93
1¾	10	12¾	1.06	2½	12	16	2.13
1¾	12	14¾	1.15	2½	14	18	2.38
1¾	14	16¾	1.22	2½	16	20	2.59
2	6	9¼	1.02	2½	18	22	2.88
2	8	11¼	1.13	3	18	22½	4.36
2	10	13¼	1.26				

Cast Iron Jack Screws.

No. 24C1365 Cast Iron Jack or House Mover's Screws, made with cast seamless threads, which make them very smooth and uniform.

Diam. of Screw	Height Over All	Price
3 inches	20 inches	$1.20
3 inches	24 inches	1.32
3 inches	30 inches	1.62
3 inches	34 inches	2.23
3 inches	36 inches	2.26

Bell Base Ratchet Jack Screws.

No. 24C1374 This Jack has wrought iron screw, cast iron stand and cap, and steel ratchet, paw and handle.

Diam. of Screw	Height Over All	Price
2 in.	12 in.	$4.35
2 in.	14 in.	4.45
2 in.	16 in.	4.75
2 in.	20 in.	5.15
2 in.	22 in.	5.25
2¼ in.	18 in.	5.70
2¼ in.	20 in.	5.95
2¼ in.	22 in.	6.25
2½ in.	18 in.	6.10
2½ in.	20 in.	6.35

Capacity.

2 -inch Screws ... 24 tons
2¼-inch Screws ... 28 tons
2½-inch Screws ... 35 tons

Oil Troughs.

Everyone who owns a wagon should have one of these.

No. 24C1376 Oil Trough, for oiling wagon on wheels, for 2-inch tires, made of cast iron. Weight, 12 pounds
Price............**33c**

No. 24C1378 Oil Trough, larger size than No. 24C1376, for wheels with tires as large as 4 inches. Weight, 15 lbs.
Price............**50c**

Self Heating Oil Troughs.

Directions: Place the oil trough as shown in the illustration, after having poured into the chamber two quarts of linseed oil. **Saturate the mineral wool torch** with coal oil or gasoline, and apply match, and place the same under trough, and heat the oil to boiling point. Revolve the wheel slowly in the trough, as shown in illustration, until the wood is thoroughly saturated with the oil, taking care that the boiling oil covers the felloe.

No. 24C1381 For tire up to 4 inches. Weight, 14 pounds. Price..............**95c**

Horseshoes.

No. 24C1541 Horseshoes, not ready to put on, as they must be fitted. A set consists of two front and two hind shoes. Sizes are outside of front shoes.

Nos..........	1	2	3
Width, inches	4½	4¾	5⅛
Length, inches	5½	6	6½
Price, per set	**18c**	**22c**	**25c**
Nos..........	4	5	6
Length, inches	6⅞	7¼	7⅜
Width, inches	5⅜	6	6¾
Price, per set	**28c**	**33c**	**40c**

Price, per keg of 100 pounds, No. 1......**$4.35**
Price, per keg No. 2 and larger........**4.10**

Trotting or Snow Shoes.

No. 24C1542 A light, concave shoe for light shoeing; trotting, or driving. Perkins pattern. A set consists of four shoes.

Weight, per set in oz.	44	52	62	74	84
Price, per set........	**17c**	**21c**	**25c**	**32c**	**40c**

Price, per keg of 100 pounds, No. 1......**$4.40**
Price, per keg No. 2 and larger.........**4.20**

Toe Calks.

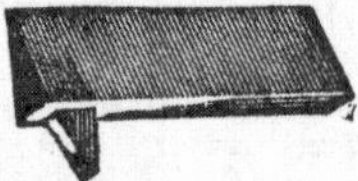

No. 24C1546 Perkins-Dewick or Schoenberger Toe Calks. Made of the best Bessemer steel.

Nos..........	1	2	3	4	5	6
Number calks in pound......	20	12	8	6	5	4

Price, per pound, any size..........**4c**

No. 24C1547 Toe Calks, same as above, sharpened ready for use.
Price, per pound..........**5c**

Tool Steel.

No. 24C1548 American Tool Steel, furnished in round, square or octagon bars cut to any length. A good grade of steel to be used for drills, chisels, punches, etc.

¼-inch, per lb..	**15c**	⅝-inch, per lb.	**11c**
5/16-inch, per lb..	**15c**	¾-inch, per lb.	**11c**
⅜-inch, per lb..	**12c**	1-inch, per lb.	**11c**
½-inch, per lb..	**12c**	1¼-inch, per lb.	**11c**
9/16-inch, per lb..	**12c**	1½-inch, per lb.	**11c**

CARRIAGE HARDWARE AND SUPPLIES.

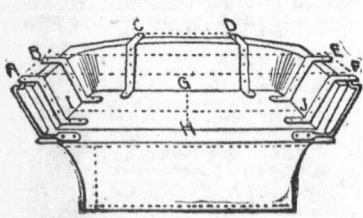

IN CALLING YOUR ATTENTION to this complete department, we are confident that we can supply the great need of thousands of our customers who find it constantly necessary to replace various parts of their vehicles, but who have been paying exorbitant retail prices. We offer a line that has no equal in general excellence of material and finish. At the same time our contracts with manufacturers are so advantageous that we are in a position to make unusually low prices.

IN ORDERING BUGGY TOPS give measurements from center to center of holes in irons, as shown in illustration; width from A to F, from B to E, from A to B, from C to D. State whether you want three or four bows, and give choice of color of lining.

IN ORDERING CUSHIONS give measurements from I to J on bottom of seat; from G to H, width of seat at bottom, and state if square or round corners are wanted.

IN ORDERING CUSHIONS WITH FALL give measurements of cushion as above, and also width of fall at the bottom and distance from bottom of seat to floor of buggy. Our buggy tops are shipped in light but strong crates, and are not liable to injury in transportation.

OUR TERMS are cash with the order. But if anything is not entirely satisfactory when received, return it to us and we will immediately refund your money, including what you paid for transportation charges.

YOU WILL SAVE MONEY by buying your own needed repairs direct from us at manufacturers' lowest prices. Freight amounts to nothing compared with what you save in price. Nearly all these goods are taken at second class rate or lower.

OUR $5.90 COMPLETE BUGGY TOP.

No. 24C2500 For $5.90 we furnish this Buggy Top complete with full length side and back curtains with patent shifting rail, which adjusts itself to any buggy. The latest style top in every way. $5.90 is a special price, based on the actual cost of material and labor, with but one small profit added. **Made in our own factory.**

We build these tops in our own factory here in Chicago; we build them in immense quantities. The bows, bow sockets, shifting rails, joints, prop nuts and finishings are contracted for direct from the largest manufacturers for cash. Our rubber drill, cloth linings and trimmings are contracted for in very large quantities, and it is by reason of the low price at which we have been able to buy the material and by reason of our manufacturing them in our own factory that we are able to name this extremely low price of **$5.90.**

From the two illustrations you can form an idea of the appearance of this, our special **$5.90** buggy top. The one illustration shows the top; the other illustration shows one of the side curtains. We furnish a pair of side curtains and a full length back curtain.

In ordering buggy tops follow our rules for measurement as given above, and we can guarantee the top we furnish you will fit your buggy exactly.

This, our $5.90 Top, is made of thoroughly reliable material. The roof and the quarters are made of good quality extra heavy rubber drill, well padded; roof and back straps lined with No. 14 X cloth, and backstays stiffened with two thicknesses of buckram. Side and back curtains are made of good weight colored back drill. We use nothing but the highest grade tubular steel bow sockets of the latest pattern, full black enameled metal buckle loops. Thomas top props, patent concealed joints, japanned prop nuts, patent curtain fasteners, wrought iron rail with patent buttons, which make it adjustable to any buggy. Side and back curtains are full length, large glass fitted in back curtain, patent button holes used throughout.

No. 24C2500 Price..................**$5.90**
Can furnish this top with gray lining for 50 cents extra.

Our $5.45 Drill Top.

At $5.45 we furnish a Drill Top complete with side and back curtains. It is made of light black enameled drill, light material throughout, made to compete with the many cheap tops now being advertised, and while we do not guarantee it, for a very cheap top it will give good satisfaction.

No. 24C2502 Price..............**$5.45**

The top weighs, crated for shipment, about 50 pounds, and you will find the freight will amount to next to nothing as compared with what you will save in price. Can furnish this top with gray lining for 50 cents extra.

In ordering be sure to give measure as per diagram below. Also state whether three or four-bow is wanted.

Our Special Silver King Top, $8.25.

For $8.25 we furnish this fine Buggy Top as described, a very showy top for a livery line and equal to tops usually sold at a much higher price.

No. 24C2504 This Top is made of the same material and with the same care as our No. 24C2505, but with silver trimmings throughout. Silver prop nuts, silver joints and fastenings on the back stays. The back stays and head linings are hand stitched, nicely corded with pinked edges. It makes a top that can be used on any buggy, especially where a stylish, up to date rig is wanted. **Just the top for a livery or hack line**, the silver trimmings showing off to fine advantage against the black panels of a buggy. Crated singly, weight, 50 pounds. Price..................**$8.25**

22-Ounce Rubber Buggy Top.

No. 24C2505 Our No. 1 Buggy Top has either **three or four bows** as desired. This is a full 22-ounce rubber top with steel bow sockets, **second growth top bows**, wrought iron joints, japanned nuts, iron rivets. Thomas top props, **concealed joints** between two back bows. Top lined with **heavy cloth**, back stays lined, back curtain lined, rubber side curtains, indigo dyed back, glass in back curtains. Price, for **No. 1** Top, as above described, with quarter rail attached..................**$6.75**

28-Ounce Rubber Buggy Top.

No. 24C2506 Our No. 2, 28-ounce, Buggy Top is in appearance just like **No. 1** described in No. 24C2505. However, our No. 2 has **leather quarters** and stay top, **steel bow sockets**, second growth top bows, wrought iron joints, japanned nuts, iron rivets, **Thomas top props**, top lined with all wool cloth, back stays lined, back curtain lined, rubber side curtains, front valance sewed on, indigo dyed No. 12 back, glass in back curtain. **Three or four bows**, as desired. Price, as described, with quarter rail attached..................**$7.50**

Full Moroccoline Leather Top for $10.00.

No. 24C2508 Our No. 5 Top is exactly the same as our No. 4, except that it is covered with moroccoline leather. This is a perfect substitute for leather, it will not show scratches, is guaranteed not to crack or become soft. Moroccoline leather is embossed by the same process as real leather and will last fully as long as the genuine leather. Price...**$10.00**

Our Great Bargain Genuine Split Leather Top.

For $12.25 we furnish this Genuine Leather Top as the equal of any leather top on the market. Made in our own factory. Great value for $12.25. Our No. 4 Buggy Top is full leather, machine buffed, guaranteed to be genuine leather. This top is lined with all wool cloth, nicely corded, back stays lined and stiffened with two thicknesses of buckram, rubber side curtains with colored back; glass in back curtain. Steel bow sockets, second growth top bows, wrought iron joints, japanned nuts, iron rivets. Thomas top props, concealed joints between two back bows. Three or four bows, as desired.

No. 24C2510 Price for our No. 4 full leather top, with quarter rail attached**$12.25**

EXTRAS.

No. 24C2513 Extra for rubber side curtains. Price, per pair..................**$1.90**

No. 24C2514 Extra for moroccoline side curtains. Price, per pair..................**$3.56**

Handy Top.

No. 24C2515 Our Handy Top is light, strong and durable, dispensing with half of the objectionable front bows; permits you to get in and out easily without any exertion whatever.

If this style top is wanted add **25 cents extra** to price of any top shown in our catalogue.

Only $11.75 for Top, Cushions and Seat Complete.

No. 24C2516 The accompanying illustration shows our No. 4 Buggy Top, complete with seat, full back and cushion, with fall. **This top** is made of 24-ounce rubber, has wrought rail and joints. Top and back stays lined with all wool fast color cloth, either blue or green, side and back curtains indigo dyed rubber, cushion and full back made of 12-ounce blue or green cloth, either biscuit or diamond tufted, and filled with selected moss. Front and back valance nailed on. Black prop nuts and rivets. Three or four steel socket bows, as desired.

Price for No. 4 top, complete, as described..................**$11.75**

No. 24C2518 Our No. 5 Buggy Top, complete, with full back and cushion, is a duplicate of our No. 4, with 28-ounce rubber drill and leather quarters and stay, and is complete with seat, wrought rail and joints, three or four steel bows; the top roof, back stays and back curtain lined with all wool fast color cloth. Rubber side curtains and 14-ounce blue or green cloth in full back and cushions. Weight, about 50 pounds. Front valance sewed on. Furnished complete as shown in illustration of No. 24C2516.
Price..................**$15.00**

No. 24C2522 This is a very neat and durable top and seat for liverymen. The roof and quarter back curtain and stays are made of 28-ounce rubber, all lined with covert cloth head lining, colored curtains are lined, corduroy laces in top, seat is white, solid high panel full back with corduroy roll at top and sides, also corduroy facing on front of cushion, covert cloth trimmed. Furnished complete as shown in illustration of No. 24C2516.
Price, complete..................**$15.50**

Machine Buff Leather Top.

No. 24C2523 This is a Machine Buff Leather Quarters and Stays. Roof and back curtain are made of 28-ounce rubber, wool whip cord head lining, nicely corded, back and side curtains lined. Seat is white with solid high back, panel back, trimmed with heavy wool whip cord, springs in back. Thomas malleable top props, japanned joints and prop nuts. Wrought iron rail. Furnished complete as shown in illustration of No. 24C2516.
Price..................**$23.00**

EXTRAS.

No. 24C2530 Extra rubber back curtains.
Price..................**$1.15**

No. 24C2532 Extra rubber back stays.
Price..................**$1.25**

Canopy Top Sun Shades.

Canopy Top Sun Shades to use in connection with any canopy top, furnished complete ready for use. Length, 60 inches.

No. 24C2540 No. 6, Extra Heavy Silesia; color, dark blue. Price..................**69c**

No. 24C2541 No. 3, Sateen; color, fast black. Price..................**85c**

No. 24C2542 No. 1, Austra; color, fast black. Price..................**$1.05**

No. 24C2543 No. 9, Glorioso Silk; color, dark blue or drab; nickel plated trimmings.
Price..................**$1.45**

No. 24C2544 No. 11, English Cloth; nickel plated trimmings, with silk fringe; color, dark blue. Price..................**$2.00**

Canopy Tops.

In measuring for canopy top give exact distance from back of back seat to front end of body. Give exact width of seats from outside to outside on top. These canopy tops have drill roof X-cloth, head lining and fringe all around 7 inches deep. Weight, crated, about 70 pounds.

NOTICE—Please notice we do not furnish curtains or standards at prices given below, and cannot take back tops that have been made up as ordered. Be very careful in taking measurements.

No. 24C2550 Our $6.95 Canopy Top is covered with black drill, lined with all wool X-cloth, and **ornamented with all wool fringe.** Price, for **5-foot length or less top**..**$6.95**

This price is without standards or curtains. See rule for giving measures in ordering **canopy tops above.**

For larger sizes over 5-foot, add extra for each additional foot..................**$1.00**

No. 24C2555 Complete set side and back curtains, indigo dyed rubber, for above tops. Price..................**$4.00**

Extension Tops.

For measuring for extension tops for seats that are ironed: No. 1—Begin at back corner of back seat and measure to goose neck. No. 2—Then from goose neck to eye on front seat. No. 3—Then across the seat from eye to eye. No. 4—Then from eye down to cushion bottom. No. 5—Then give difference in height of seats E to F.

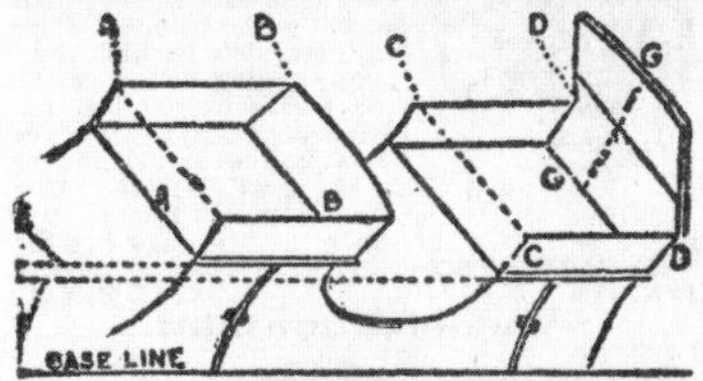

NOTICE—For extension top for seats not ironed: No. 1—Beginning at back corner of back seat on bottom, give width of seat at bottom. No. 2—Then from front of back seat give distance to back corner of front seat at bottom. No. 3—Then give exact width across seat on top, outside to outside. No. 4—Then give difference in height of seats E to F. No. 5—Then measure from top of seat at front down to cushion bottom.

Make a rough sketch of all ironed bodies and where the irons are situated, mark figures on same, plain. We cannot fill these orders without a definite knowledge of what is required.

All tops over 42 inches wide cost from **65c** to **$2.00** extra, in accordance with the extra width.

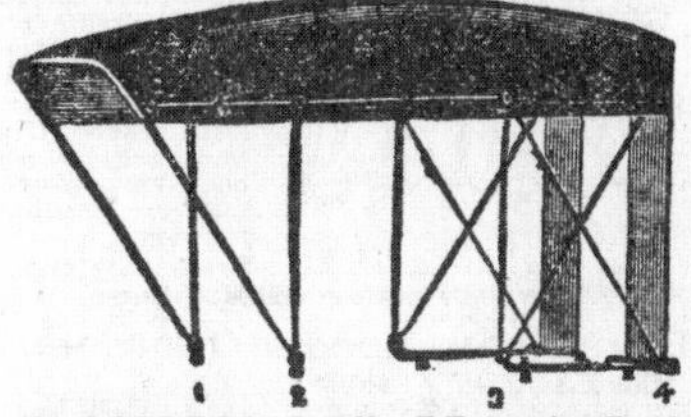

No. 24C2560 Our No. 7 Extension Top is a 4 bow, 22-ounce rubber top, lined throughout with all wool cloth, except side curtains, which are indigo dyed rubber. Wrought iron joints, japanned nuts and iron rivets. Front valance sewed on. No rail. Weight, crated, about 65 pounds. Price.......... **$11.25**

No. 24C2562 Our No. 8 Extension Top, just the same as our No. 7, described above, but has leather quarter and stay. Price... **$15.50**

No. 24C2564 Our No. 9 is a Full Leather Extension Top, otherwise just the same as No. 7, described above. Price........ **$21.00**

Phaeton Tops.

We can furnish Phaeton Tops of same material as Nos. 24C2504, 24C2505, 24C2506, 24C2508 and 24C2510 at same prices.

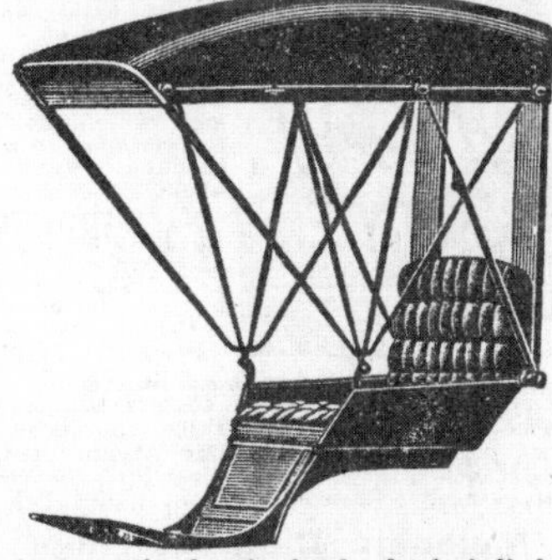

In measuring for phaeton top for body that is ironed: No. 1—Give distance across top of seat at front. No. 2—Give distance across back panel. No. 3—Give distance from front corner of seat down to cushion bottom. No. 4—State whether back is straight or rounding.

Wagon Sunshade Top.

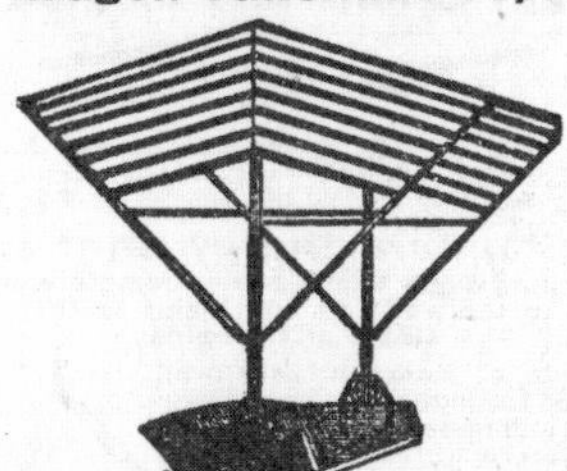

Especially adapted for express and farm wagons. This top is furnished complete with irons and bolts, ready to attach to seat. The irons will fit any kind of a seat. The sizes we keep in stock are for seats measuring from 32 to 44 inches. For extra wide tops the additional cost of making will be added. When ordering, give width of seat outside to outside on top of seat at back corner.

No. 24C2580 Covered with brown duck. Price.......... **$2.30**

No. 24C2582 Covered with awning stripe. Price.......... **$2.40**

While you must pay freight or express charges on the goods you buy of us, you will find that these charges are only a small part of the money we save you.

$1.35 for Best Wagon Umbrella Made.

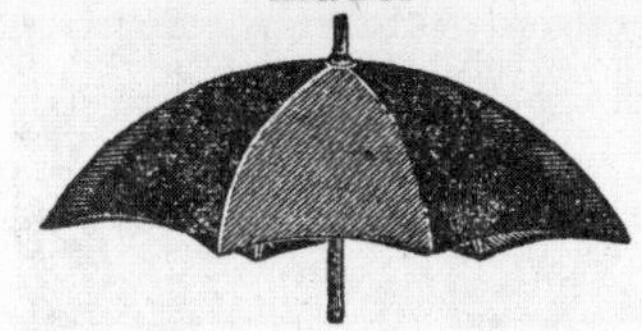

This is the most popular umbrella on the market. Has heavy duck covering, in blue, brown or white. Guaranteed strongest umbrella made. 6 steel ribs, 1½-inch white ash handle, 5 feet 8-inch spread, cover removable. Price includes all fixtures complete.

No. 24C2586 Price.......... **$1.35**

Wagon Umbrellas with Fixture Sockets.

Compare our prices on these goods with those of other houses and see if we cannot save you 25 to 50 per cent on price. These umbrellas come with best quality heavy steel ribs and fixtures. Handles, 1¼-inch seasoned white ash, oiled and varnished. Colors, blue, green or buff. Heavy umbrella cloth muslin. Be sure to state color wanted. The most complete fixtures yet produced. Made of the best malleable iron, light and strong, quickly applied, and holds the umbrella secure. Weight, about 7½ pounds.

No. 24C2587 36-inch, 8 ribs, with fixtures. Price.......... **$1.24**

No. 24C2588 38-inch, 8 ribs, with fixtures. Price.......... **$1.29**

No. 24C2589 40-inch, 10 ribs, with fixtures. Price.......... **$1.37**

No. 24C2590 40-inch, 10 ribs, double face duck, green inside, duck outside, with fixtures. Price.......... **$1.65**

Buggy Cushions and Falls and Full Backs.

These goods are first class in all respects. We make strictly inside prices on these goods and can save you a large percentage on each purchase. The price of full back is just the same as that of the cushion with fall. If you want both the full back and cushion with fall, the price will be just twice that of the cushion and fall alone. All cushions are based on 34-inch length. Larger sizes we charge 7 cents per inch extra. Weight, about 6 pounds.

NOTICE—In ordering cushions give size of seat. Measure length and width on inside bottom of seat and do not include the flare. **We cannot take back cushions or full backs that have been made up as ordered. Be very careful in taking measurements.**

No. 24C2600 Black drill cushion with fall. Price.......... **70c**

No. 24C2602 Black drill cushion without fall. Price.......... **65c**

No. 24C2604 Rubber drill cushion with fall. Price.......... **94c**

No. 24C2606 Rubber drill cushion without fall. Price.......... **80c**

EXTRAS—We can furnish any of these cushions with springs, extra.......... **75c**

Full backs with springs, extra.......... **35c**

Full Backs.

This illustration shows the Full Back furnished with any of our cushions when wanted. If you wish a full back allow price of the cushion you order for same. For example, if No. 24C2600 cushion and full back to match is wanted, allow **70 cents** each or **$1.40** for both.

No. 24C2607 Blue or green cloth cushion, plain top, with fall. Price.......... **$1.55**

No. 24C2608 Blue or green cloth cushion, with fall, biscuit or diamond tufted, filled with moss. Price.......... **$1.75**

No. 24C2610 Fancy leather cushion with fall, plain top. Price.......... **$2.50**

No. 24C2613 Black leather cushion, with fall, plain top. Price.......... **$2.75**

No. 24C2615 Black split leather cushion, with fall, plain top. Price.......... **$2.30**

No. 24C2616 Black split leather cushion, without fall, plain top. Price.......... **$1.75**

No. 24C2617 Green or black artificial leather cushion, with fall. Price.......... **$1.66**

No. 24C2619 Brown corduroy cushion with fall, plain top. Price.......... **$1.60**

No. 24C2620 Brown corduroy cushion, without fall, plain top. Price.......... **$1.60**

No. 24C2622 Light, colored, all wool, whipcord cushion with fall, tufted or plain top. Price.......... **$1.65**

No. 24C2624 Light colored all wool, whipcord without fall, tufted or plain top. Price.......... **$1.60**

Full backs to match, same price as cushions.

NOTICE—We cannot take back cushions or full backs that have been made up as ordered. Be very careful in taking measurements.

Full Backs and Cushions. All Styles Same Price.

In ordering be sure to state style 1, 2 or 3, as wanted.

No. 1. No. 2. No. 3.

Full Backs and Cushions. In sets, or cushion or full back only. We show three patterns of seats which we furnish at the same price. In ordering be sure and give style wanted, No. 1, 2 or 3. If you wish seat and outfit complete give width of seat across the bottom. Order cushions and full backs the regular way, width across bottom, etc.

No. 24C2626 Made of 12-ounce blue or green cloth or whipcord.

Cushion with fall only. Price.......... **$2.15**

Full back only. Price.......... **2.15**

Seat with arm rail, cushion with fall, and full back, complete, as illustrated. Price, **6.50**

No. 24C2627 Made of deep buff leather. Cushion and fall only. Price.......... **3.20**

Full back only. Price.......... **3.20**

Seat with arm rails, cushion with fall and full back, complete, as illustrated. Price **8.25**

No. 24C2628 Made of No. 1 machine buff leather.

Cushion and fall only. Price.......... **3.45**

Full back only. Price.......... **3.45**

Seat with arm rails, cushion with fall and full back, complete, as illustrated. Price, **9.15**

Drivers' Cushions.

No. 24C2630 Drivers' Cushion, made of 12-ounce body cloth or whipcord. Price.. **$2.00**

No. 24C2631 Drivers' Cushion, leather. Black or fancy. Price.......... **$3.00**

High Stick Seats for Driving Wagons.

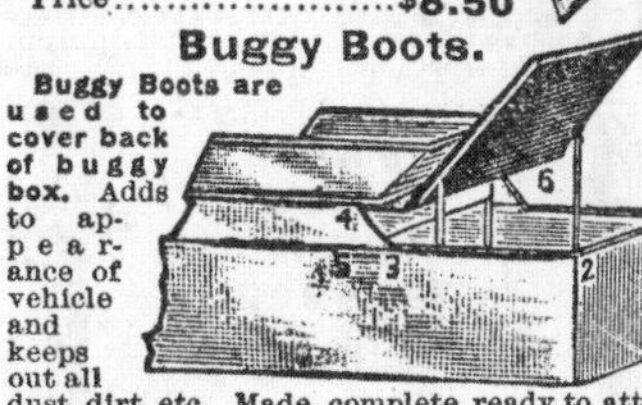

High Stick Seats for driving wagons furnished complete as shown in illustration.

No. 24C2633 Trimmed with light colored covert. Price **$7.00**

No. 24C2634 Trimmed with blue or green cloth, or whipcord. Price.......... **$8.50**

Buggy Boots.

Buggy Boots are used to cover back of buggy box. Adds to appearance of vehicle and keeps out all dust, dirt, etc. Made complete ready to attach to buggy.

No. 24C2644 No. 1 made of enameled drill. Price.......... **70c**

No. 24C2648 No. 2, made of enameled rubber. Price.......... **80c**

No. 24C2650 No. 3, made of leather. Price.......... **$1.75**

In giving measurements give width No. 1 to No. 2, No. 2 to No. 3, No. 3 to No. 4, No. 4 to No. 5, No. 5 to No. 6.

Rubber Boot Straps.

This device is used for fastening buggy boots to buggy bodies. Fastenings are made of tinned wire; straps of pure gum (double thick).

No. 24C2653 Price, per pair.......... **5c**

Plain Full Lazy Backs.

Complete with irons; ready to attach to seat.

No. 24C2672 Covered with drill. Price.......... **$1.20**

No. 24C2673 Covered with brown corduroy. Price.......... **$2.10**

No. 24C2674 Covered with black leather. Price.......... **$2.75**

No. 24C2674½ Covered with 12-ounce body cloth. Price.......... **$2.15**

Top Props.

No. 24C2693 Thomas' Malleable Top Props, complete. Price, per set.......... **9c**

Concealed Joints.

Concealed Buggy Top Joints, furnished complete.

No. 24C2700 Per pair, for 12-inch..... **6c**

No. 24C2701 Per pair, for 14-inch..... **7c**

Single Bow Sockets.

No. 24C2706 Back Socket. Price... **11c**

No. 24C2708 Front, Main or Off Set. Price, each.......... **11c**

Steel Shaft End.

Double Tube, for repairing broken shafts. Used also on new work to prevent breaking. Easy to put on, perfect in strength and finish. Reversible; can be used either right or left. This device consists of two thick steel tubes, the inner tube having a hickory filler and being pressed into the outer tube in such a way that the shafts will break in any other place than where repaired. Anyone can repair a broken shaft with this device in a few minutes. Try it and be convinced.

No. 24C2709 Buggy size, japanned, with nickel shaft tip. Price, each.......... **24c**

No. 24C2710 Surrey or Wagon size, japanned, with nickel shaft tip. Price, each... **34c**

Whip Sockets.

No. 24C2714 Iron Whip Socket and Rein Holder. Can be used on wood or leather dash with line spring. Price **12c**

No. 24C2720 Metal Bell Top Whip Socket, with security band fasteners, nickel shell cap and bands. One of the neatest and best made sockets on the market. Price... **15c**

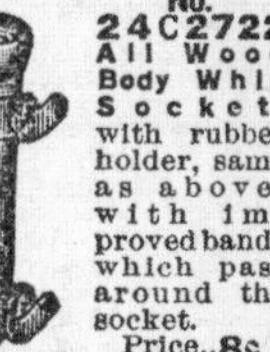

No. 24C2718 Wood Top Whip Socket, with rubber holder; holds whip securely and prevents rattling. Price.. **8c**

No. 24C2722 All Wood Body Whip Socket, with rubber holder, same as above, with improved bands which pass around the socket. Price.. **8c**

We can save you money on almost everything you buy.

Black Enameled Carriage Cloth.

Used for Covering Buggy Tops, Making Cushions, Curtains, etc.

No. 24C2750 Leather Grain Muslin, 45 inches wide, white back. Price, per yard....... **16c**

No. 24C2752 Leather Grain Drill, 50 inches wide, white back. Price, per yard....... **21c**

No. 24C2754 Glazed Drill (patent leather finish), 50 inches wide, white back. Price, per yard....... **21c**

No. 24C2756 Enameled Duck, 50 inches wide, white back. Price, per yard.......... **27c**

No. 24C2758 Tan Back Drill (patent leather finish), 45 inches wide, tan back. Price, per yard.......... **28c**

If Nos. 24C2752, 24C2756 or 24C2758 are wanted with green or blue back, add **8** cents per yard to above prices. We cannot furnish colored back in Nos. 24C2750 and 24C2754.

Moroccoline Leather.

Moroccoline Leather is a perfect substitute for leather. It will not show scratches. It will not crack, does not become soft or sticky, and grease does not affect it. Moroccoline leather is embossed by the same process as genuine leather, will last fully as long, and costs only one-third as much as the genuine leather.

No. 24C2760 Black, 50 inches wide. Price, per yard.......... **59c**

No. 24C2762 Green, 50 inches wide. Price, per yard.......... **59c**

No. 24C2764 Dark Maroon, 50 inches wide. Price, per yard.......... **59c**

No. 24C2766 Tan, 50 inches wide. Price, per yard.......... **59c**

Rubber Carriage Drill.

High Grade Embossed Rubber Carriage Drill for Cushions, buggy tops, etc., **leather grain finish.** We sell only the highest grade Rubber Drill. Nothing better made.

No. 24C2780 18 ounces, white back, 50 inches wide. Price, per yard.......... **27c**

No. 24C2781 22 ounces, white back, 50 inches wide. Price, per yard.......... **30c**

No. 24C2782 28 ounces, white back, 50 inches wide. Price, per yard.......... **35c**

No. 24C2783 22 ounces, blue or green back, 50 inches wide. Price, per yard ... **40c**

No. 24C2784 22 ounces, blue or green back, 36 inches wide. Price, per yard ... **39c**

No. 24C2785 28 ounces, blue or green back, 50 inches wide. Price, per yard ... **45c**

Carriage Broadcloth.

For buggy cushions and backs; all wool, guaranteed first quality. Can furnish in either blue or green. Always state which color you want. Width, 54 inches.

No. 24C2790 10-ounce Indigo Cloth. Price, per yard.......... **$1.10**

No. 24C2792 12-ounce Indigo Cloth. Price, per yard.......... **$1.25**

No. 24C2794 14-ounce Indigo Cloth. Price, per yard.......... **$1.35**

Head Lining for Buggy Tops, etc., Wool.

No. 24C2798 XX Special Head Lining. Width, 38 inches. Price, per yard..........32c

No. 24C2799 7¼-ounce Head Lining. Width, 38 inches. Price, per yard..........55c

Corduroy.

No. 24C2816 Corduroy for buggy cushions, full backs, etc. A good quality suitable for carriage work. Comes in assorted colors, drab, brown or green. Width, 27 inches. Price, per yard..........50c

Carriage Carpets.

Best Grade Tapestry Figured Carriage Carpeting; sold in any quantity.

No. 24C2830 24 inches wide. Per yard...45c

No. 24C2832 27 inches wide. Per yard...55c

Carriage Mats.

No. 24C2850 Velour Center with Wool Fringe. Has an extra heavy lamb's wool fringe. Comes in assorted colors. Size, 12x24 inches. Price..........69c

Carriage Fringe.

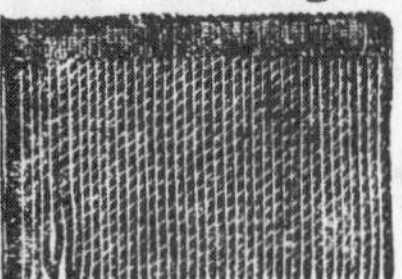

Worsted Bullion Carriage Fringe. Evenly woven; well finished. A good fringe for the money. Either green or blue.

No. 24C2854 4 inches wide. Price, per yd...14c

No. 24C2855 5 inches wide. Price, per yard..........15c

Plain Head Genappe.

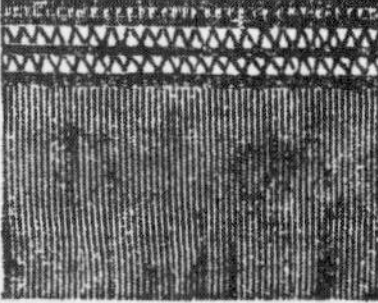

No. 24C2858 Plain Carriage Fringe. Medium quality, closely woven, well made. Comes in blue or green. 7 inches wide. Price, per yard..........19c

Fancy Head Genappe.

No. 24C2860 Best Made Fancy Carriage Fringe. Good enough for any job. Fancy head, all luster genappe, blue or green. 7 inches wide. Price, per yard..........17c

Fancy Cord and Tassel Head Genappe.

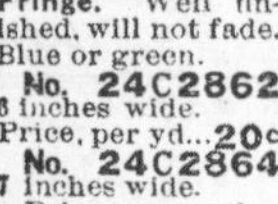

Extra Quality Fancy Cord and Tassel Head Genappe Carriage Fringe. Well finished, will not fade. Blue or green.

No. 24C2862 6 inches wide. Price, per yd...20c

No. 24C2864 7 inches wide. Price, per yard..........21c

Stay Webbing.

No. 24C2870 English Stay Webbing. 1⅛ inches wide, 12 yards in a piece. Price, per piece..........35c

No. 24C2871 English Stay Webbing. 3 inches wide, 72 yards in a piece. Price, per piece..........$1.00

Moss.

No. 24C2885 XXX Moss, in bales of about 150 pounds. Price, per pound..........6½c

Excelsior.

No. 24C2890 Excelsior, put up in bales of about 75 pounds.
Price, less than full bales, per lb..........1½c
Full bales, per pound..........1c

Oval Curtain Lights.

No. 24C2894 New Side Lights for Buggies and Phaetons. Nicely finished. Size, 3½x5⅝ inches inside. French glass. Price..........13½c

Curtain Lights.

Keystone Japanned Curtain Lights, nicely finished, double strength glass.

No. 24C2897 Size opening, 3x4x7 inches; plain glass. Price..........33c

No. 24C2898 Size opening, 3x4x7 inches; beveled glass. Price..........78c

Buttonholes.

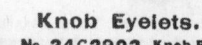

No. 24C2900 Talcott's Elastic Buttonholes for carriage or wagon curtains, round hole, japanned frame, rubber center. Price, per dozen..........19c

Knob Eyelets.

No. 24C2902 Knob Eyelets, japanned frame, goat leather center. Price, per dozen..........2½c

Metallic Loops and Buckles.

No. 24C2908 Single Buckle and Loop. Price..........1½c

Metallic Strap Loop.

No. 24C2910 Price..........1½c

Complete Curtain Fasteners.

No. 24C2911 Complete Curtain Fasteners with metal loops and buckles japanned. Price, as shown in illustration..........2½c

Curtain Straps and Fasteners.

No. 24C2912 Price..........1c

Adjustable Leather Axle Washers.

No. 24C2932 Made from the best oak tanned stock, durable and satisfactory, can be cut out to fit any nut or collar, have been thoroughly tested, and are superior to all others. Put up 100 washers in a box.

Size	½ in.	1 in.	1⅛ in.	1¼ in.	1½ in.
Price, per 100,	10c	12c	13c	16c	22c

Washer Cutter for Bit Brace.

No. 24C2931 Washer Cutter for Bit Brace. Extra fine steel knives, polished. Cuts any size washer with any size hole up to 5½ inches in diameter. Price..........40c

Drive or Rivet Split Shank Carriage Knobs.

No. 24C2934 Japanned Carriage Knobs, to drive or rivet. With split shank. Price, per dozen..........4c

Japanned Carriage Knobs.

No. 24C2936 To drive. Price, per dozen..........2c

No. 24C2937 To screw. For single or double curtains. Price, per dozen..........4c

No. 24C2937 No. 24C2936

Wagon Curtain Patches.

No. 24C2939 Wagon Curtain Patches, with screw eyes. This is the most complete and durable fastening on the market. Complete with screw eyes. Price, per dozen..........19c

Lining Nails.

No. 24C2956 Lining Nails, japanned heads. Size, 4, 6, 8 or 12-ounce.
Price, per paper..........5c
Size, 14 or 16-ounce.
Price, per paper..........6c

No. 24C2958 Cloth Covered Tacks for Carriage Trimming, etc.
Price, per gross, 6-ounce..........15c
Price, per gross, 8-ounce..........15c
Price, per gross, 10-ounce..........15c

Prop Block Rubber.

No. 24C2962 Made of rubber. Sold in pieces 2½ inches long. Price, per pair or two pieces..........4½c

Buggy Dashes.

No. 24C3000 Made of best leather moulding, completely ironed and ready to put on your buggy. All have patent extensions to fit bodies not exact measurement of the dash. **Feet and bolts included in price.** Order by number and be sure to give exact height, width and price of dash wanted.

Irons for square end bodies sent unless ordered for flaring end bodies.

Width	11-in. high Price	13-in. high Price	15-in. high Price
21 inches	$0.78	$0.88	$0.98
22 inches	.82	.92	1.00
23 inches	.85	.93	1.04
24 inches	.88	.95	1.06
25 inches	.90	1.00	1.10
26 inches	.93	1.02	1.11
27 inches	.95	1.05	1 24
28 inches	.98	1.10	1.27
29 inches	1.00	1.12	1 33
30 inches	1.02	1.14	1.35
31 inches	1.15	1.23	1.38
32 inches	1.17	1.27	1 42
33 inches	1.19	1.30	1.45
34 inches	1.25	1.33	1.48
35 inches	1.27	1.35	1.52
36 inches	1.30	1.40	1.54

Buggy Dashes with Iron Hand Holes.

No. 24C3001 High Grade Piano Body Dashes. Every dash guaranteed as first quality. We do not carry seconds. Prices are for dashes, complete, with feet.

Width	11 inches high	13 inches high
21 inches	Price, $1.00	Price, $1.16
22 inches	Price, 1.04	Price, 1.20
23 inches	Price, 1.06	Price, 1.24
24 inches	Price, 1.10	Price, 1.26
25 inches	Price, 1.14	Price, 1.28
26 inches	Price, 1.20	Price, 1.30
27 inches	Price, 1.22	Price, 1.33
28 inches	Price, 1.26	Price, 1.36
29 inches	Price, 1.28	Price, 1.39
30 inches	Price, 1.30	Price, 1.43

Surrey Dashes.

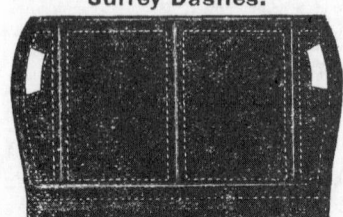

No. 24C3002 High Grade Surrey Dashes. Made of first quality dash leather. We do not carry seconds. Prices are for dashes, complete, with feet.

Width inches	17 inches high.	Width inches	17 inches high.
24	Price....$1 60	29	Price....$1.85
25	Price.... 1.65	30	Price.... 1.88
26	Price.... 1.70	31	Price.... 1.90
27	Price.... 1 75	32	Price.... 1.95
28	Price.... 1.80		

Carriage Dash Rails.

No. 24C3006 Nickel Plated Dash Rails, made adjustable so as to fit any ordinary dash 20 to 36 inches wide; easily attached to dash; no special tools required. Illustration shows rail as it appears on dash. No dash furnished at the price. Price..........24c

Hand Hold Dash Rails.

No. 24C3008 Nickel Plated Dash Rail with rope pattern hand holds. Made of ¼-inch steel; heavily nickel plated; made adjustable, to fit any dash 20 inches to 36 inches wide. Price given below is for rail only. Price..........43c

Double Bar Dash Rails.

No. 24C3010 Fancy Pattern Double Bar Dash Rails, with hand holds. Made of ¼-inch steel; nickel plated; adjustable to fit any dash 20 inches to 36 inches wide. Price given below is for rail only; no dash furnished. Price..........39c

Surrey Fenders.

Leather Surrey Fenders with patent covering. Bolt heads inserted from rear through opening in the frame. Hind fender 6x7x57 inches long by 48¾ inches to center of attaching bars.

Front fender 6x9x31 inches long; 20¾ inches to center of attaching bar.

No. 24C3024 Price, per pair hind fenders..........$2.75

No. 24C3025 Price, per pair front fenders..........$2.25

Rim Bands for Buggy Hubs.

No. 24C3035 Turned Malleable Iron Hub Bands. Do not fail to state size and price of hub bands wanted.

Diameter, inches	1¾ in. Deep, per set	2 in. Deep, per set	Diameter, inches	1¾ in. Deep, per set	2 in. Deep, per set
2	$0.15	$0.20	3⅛	$0.17	$0.25
2⅛	.15	.20	3¼	.18	.26
2¼	.15	.20	3⅜	.19	.27
2⅜	.15	.20	3½	.20	.28
2½	.15	.20	3⅝	.22	.29
2⅝	.15	.20	3¾	.25	.33
2¾	.16	.22	3⅞	.27	.45
2⅞	.16	.22	4	.35	.50
3	.16	.22			

LOOK over the catalogue carefully and send your order for all goods you need. There is hardly any line of merchandise in which we cannot save you money.

Carriage Lamps.

Latest Style Carriage Lamps. Made of the best material by one of the most reliable manufacturers in the United States. Every lamp carefully inspected before being sent out. Black japanned with nickel trimmings. We furnish these lamps with either candle or kerosene burners. Size body, 4¼x3½ inches oval flange, 5½x4½ inches.

No. 24C3050 Price, candle burner, per pair..........$1.70

No. 24C3051 Price, kerosene burner, per pair..........$2.10

Veeder Odometer.

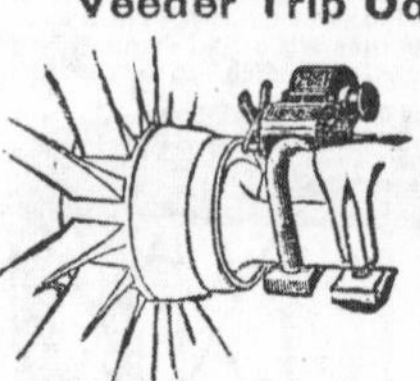

No. 24C3075 The Veeder Odometer registers the distance traveled by a horse. Made for all sized wheels; sizes most used, 38, 40 and 42 inches. In ordering give height of front wheel. Price..........$2.10
If by mail, postage extra, 5 cents.

Veeder Trip Odometer.

No. 24C3076 Veeder Trip Odometer, with band attachment. The small dial registers the number of miles traveled each trip and can be set back when starting on another journey. Price..........$3.00
If by mail, postage extra, 9 cents.

Extra Heavy Veeder Odometer.

No. 24C3077 While our No. 24C3075 Odometer for all ordinary purposes has been a winner, there has been a demand for an odometer of larger size, one that could be attached to heavy vehicles. In the above machine we have the most perfect, as well as substantial article on the market, comes complete with fixtures, same as our No. 24C3075, but can be furnished with a band to attach to automobiles, if so desired. Price..........$5.85
If by mail, postage extra, 12 cents.

Buggy Aprons.

Patent Buggy Aprons. Made of the best grade rubber drill, is adjustable to any dash. A round elastic cord extends across dash with a hook at each end which holds the apron securely to the dash. Weight, about 2½ pounds.

No. 24C3080 Buggy Apron. Made of 22-ounce rubber drill. Size, 50x54 inches. Fits dashes 21 to 30 inches wide. Price......78c

No. 24C3082 Buggy Apron. Made of 22-ounce rubber drill. Size, 50x60 inches. Fits dashes 21 to 30 inches wide. Price..........95c

No. 24C3086 Large Size Apron. Made of 28-ounce rubber drill. Size, 50x72 inches. Fits dashes 22 to 40 inches. Price..........$1.30

Melodain Cloth Carriage Aprons.

No. 24C3087 This is a 28-ounce Melodain Cloth (a smooth gray finish rubber cloth) Apron. Made the same as No. 24C3086. One of the finest aprons made. Size, 50x60 inches. Fits dashes 16 to 30 inches wide. Price..........$1.20

Buggy Evener and Singletree.

No. 24C3092 Buggy Evener and Singletree, finished, painted black and ironed complete ready for use. Price, per set..........$1.20

Standard Buggy Shafts.

Standard Buggy Shafts, ironed complete, either in the white or with paint, leather straps or trimmings.

Made of select hickory well ironed throughout, cross bar mortised and fastened with T-plates, double reinforced shaft irons with extra heavy eye made of one solid piece of steel. No welds to break or become loose. The painted shafts have 17-inch leathers on ends, also on singletree and holdbacks. Have 1-inch eye with 7-16-inch hole; width outside to outside, 44 inches, which is the standard width of all buggies. Weight, about 35 pounds.

No. 24C3096 Finished and ironed in the white, ready to paint, 1⅜x2 inches, which is buggy size. Price, per pair..........$1.50

No. 24C3098 Surrey size, 1½x2¼ inches. Price, per pair..........$1.95

No. 24C3100 Painted black or red, ironed and trimmed complete, as shown in illustration. Buggy size, 1⅜x2 inches. Price, per pr..$2.00

No. 24C3102 Surrey size, 1½x2¼ inches. Price, per pair..........$2.48

Standard Buggy Shafts with Circle Bar.

Standard Buggy Shafts. Same as No. 24C3096 with extra circle, as shown in illustration, which gives greater strength and rigidness. Weight, about 35 pounds.

No. 24C3104 Size, 1⅜x2 inches, finished and ironed in the white, ready to paint. Price........ **$1.85**

No. 24C3105 Size, 1⅜x2 inches, painted black or red, ironed and trimmed complete. Price........ **$2.50**

Standard Carriage Poles.

Standard Carriage Poles, ironed and trimmed complete, either in white or painted black. High grade work at a price the ordinary manufacturer pays for the raw material. We use nothing but select hickory in all our poles; also wrought iron stays and tee plates well finished and ironed throughout. We furnish them complete with doubletree, singletree, neckyoke and stay straps.

No. 1, Buggy Pole, 1¾x2¼ inches, with 1-inch eye, 7-16-inch hole, width of eyes outside to outside, 44 inches.

No. 24C3106 Price, complete in the white........ **$2.85**

No. 24C3107 Price, complete, painted black or red........ **$3.00**

No. 2, Surrey Pole, 2x2½ inches, with 1-inch eye, 7-16-inch hole, width of eyes outside to outside, 44 inches.

No. 24C3110 Price, complete, in the white........ **$2.90**

No. 24C3112 Price, complete, painted black or red........ **$3.10**

Anti-Rattlers and Bolt Holders.

No. 24C3124 Anti-Rattlers and Bolt Holders, made of Crescent patent cold rolled steel. It insures against the rattling of the shafts of any spring vehicle, is perfectly noiseless, will last as long as the buggy, and shafts can be taken off without trouble and replaced by a pole in a minute. Price, per pair........ **7c**

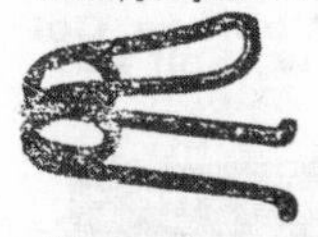

Wire Anti-Rattlers.

No. 24C3128 Wire Anti-Rattlers; made of steel wire; prevents rattling of the shafts. Price, per pair........ **1½c**

The Safety Quick Coupler and Anti-Rattler.

No. 24C3142 In our Safety Coupler we have the best quick shaft shifter sold by anyone. It is a first class anti-rattler as well as a quick shifter. It is impossible to dislocate the bolts even if spring should become broken by accident. We use the best steel springs and hand forged bolts. We furnish these couplers in three sizes as follows: To fit ⅞, 15-16 or 1⅛-inch axles, with ⅜ or 7-16 inch bolt. **Be sure and state size wanted.** Price, per set........ **28c**

Model Buggy Neckyokes.

No. 24C3150 Model Buggy Neckyokes, with steel band around yoke. Made of the best selected hickory with extra heavy leather center. Size, 1⅜ inch diameter; 42 inches long. Price........ **27c**

Acme Buggy Neckyokes.

No. 24C3152 Acme Buggy Neckyokes, with steel band covered with leather. Very neat in construction, well finished and suited to any style pole. Size, 1⅜-inch diameter; 42 inches long. Price........ **30c**

Star Buggy Neckyokes.

No. 24C3154 Star Buggy Neckyokes with Solid Leather Center. This yoke is well finished, has solid malleable tips. Is made of the best grade forest hickory. Guaranteed second to none on the market, price considered. Size, 1¾ inches diameter; length, 44 in. Price........ **55c**

Security Neckyoke Center, Adjustable.

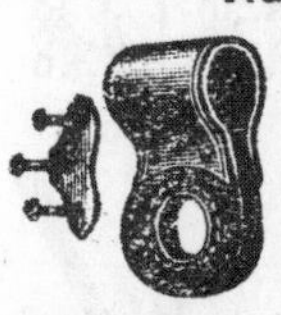

No. 24C3162 The center is made of good, solid harness leather, well stitched and finished, attached to yoke with heavy steel band with leather cover; fastened together with screws and screw plates, as shown in illustration. The best adjustable center on the market, and will not break unexpectedly, as steel centers will do. Sizes, 1⅝, 1¾ or 2 inches. Be sure and state size wanted. Price........ **20c**

Perfection Third Folding Buggy Seat.

No. 24C3165 Perfection Third Folding Buggy Seat. Folds up when not in use and can be placed under cushion. Strong and durable. Price........ **45c**

The New Idea Seats.

No. 24C3166 The New Idea Folding Third Seat. Needs no fastening and fits any buggy or sleigh, so that it can be changed from one vehicle to another instantly. You will readily see the advantage of this if used in a livery, or where two or more rigs are kept. It also makes a good camp stool or can be used in a boat by hunters and sportsmen. Steel enameled frame, upholstered in tapestry Brussels. Price........ **75c**

No. 24C3167 New Idea Seat, with top and bottom covered with velvet. Price........ **85c**

Felloe Plates.

No. 24C3180 Wrought Iron Felloe Plates. Philadelphia pattern.

Size, inches	⅝	⅞	1	1⅛	1⅜
Weight, per doz.	9	7	11	15	21 oz.
Price, per doz.	2½c	3c	4½c	6c	7½c
Size, inches	1½	1⅝	1¾	2	
Weight, per doz.	21	23	35	36 oz.	
Price, per doz.	9c	10c	11c	12c	

Pole Tips.

No. 24C3187 Pole Tips. Plain malleable iron.

Length	6¼	6½	6¾	7	7½
Size of hole, inches	1	1⅛	1¼	1⅜	1½
Weight, ounces	14	14	17	18	23
Price, each	7c	9c	11c	13c	16c

Whiffletree Hooks.

No. 24C3200 Hawleys' Patent Whiffletree Hook.

Diameter, inches	⅞	1	1⅛	1¼	1⅜
Weight, per pair, ozs.	11	12	13	16	18
Price, per pair	17c	17c	20c	22c	25c

Malleable Whiffletree Tongues.

No. 24C3206 With shoulder to screw. Length, 3 inches. Price........ **1½c**

2½ inches long, ⅜-inch shank. Price, **1¾c**

Excelsior Trace Attachments.

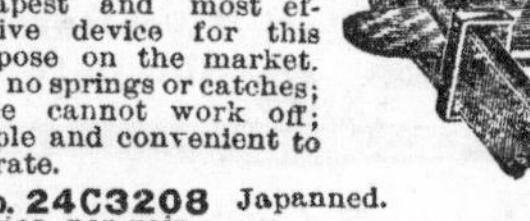

The Excelsior Trace Attachment is the simplest, cheapest and most effective device for this purpose on the market. Has no springs or catches; trace cannot work off; simple and convenient to operate.

No. 24C3208 Japanned. Price, per pair........ **4c**

No. 24C3209 Nickel plated. Price, per pair........ **11c**

Whiffletree Ferrules.

No. 24C3220 Malleable Whiffletree Ferrules.

Size inside large end, Inches	¾	⅞	1	1⅛	1¼
Depth, inches	1	1	1⅛	1⅜	1½
Price, each	1½c	1½c	1½c	2c	2½c

Steel Wagon Seat Corners.

No. 24C3234 Size, ¾-inch wide by 3¼ inches long. Price........ **2c**

Steel Seat Corners.

No. 24C3236 Size, 1 inch wide and 3½ inches long. Price........ **1½c**

Rolled Steel Buggy Rub Irons.

No. 24C3268 Made of one solid piece of steel. Finished complete. Size, 5 inches long; flange, ⅜ inch inside. 1¼ inch wide over all. Price, per pair........ **5c**

Whiffletree Couplings.

No. 24C3287 Whiffletree Couplings, low pattern.

W'th	L'gth	Size hole	Wt., ozs.	Price
1½	4	⅜	4	2c
1¾	4¾	⅜	8	3½c
2	4¾	⅜	9	4c
2½	5¼	7-16	10	4½c
3	6½	7 16	15	7c

Axle Clips.

No. 24C3292 Axle Clips, 5-16-in. shank.

Flat part, 2¼-in., 2¾-in. or 3¼-in. Price........ **1½c**
Flat part, 3¾-in. Price........ **1½c**
Flat part, 4¼-in. Price........ **2c**
Flat part, 4¾-in. Price........ **2c**
Flat part, 5¼-in. Price........ **2½c**
Flat part, 5¾-in. Price........ **2½c**

No. 24C3293 Heavy Axle Clips, ⅜-in. shank.

Flat part, 1¾x4-in. Price........ **2c**
Flat part, 1¾x4½-in. Price........ **2¼c**
Flat part, 1¾x5-in. Price........ **2½c**
Flat part, 1¾x5½-in. Price........ **2¾c**
Flat part, 1¾x6-in. Price........ **3c**
Flat part, 1¾x6½-in. Price........ **3¼c**
Flat part, 1¾x7-in. Price........ **4c**
Flat part, 1¾x7½-in. Price........ **4c**

In ordering, you will avoid errors by stating catalogue number, sizes and prices.

Clip King Bolts, Flanged, with Finished Ends.

No. 24C3300 No. 1, ½-inch at collar; light. Weight, 11 ounces. Price........ **14c**

No. 24C3301 No. 2, 9-16-inch at collar; medium. Weight, 12 ounces. Price........ **15c**

No. 24C3302 No. 3, ⅝-inch at collar; heavy. Weight, 15 ounces. Price........ **19c**

No. 24C3303 No. 4, ¾-inch at collar; extra heavy. Weight, 1 pound 4 ounces. Price........ **25c**

Saddle Clips.

Saddle Clips, half round pattern. A set consists of two clips and one top plate. The flat part of clips are 2, 2¼, 2¾, 3, 3¼ and 3½ inches long for 1¼-inch springs, and run from 2¼ up to 4 inches for 1⅜-inch springs, and from 2½ to 4½ for 1½-inch springs. Give the length of flat part wanted when ordering.

No. 24C3309 For 1¼-inch spring........ **6c**
No. 24C3310 For 1⅜-inch spring........ **6c**
No. 24C3311 For 1½-inch spring........ **6c**

Whiffletree Brace for Buggies.

No. 24C3315 Made of the best grade malleable iron. Length inside, 3 inches or 3½ inches, with 5-16-inch bolt hole. Be sure and give size wanted. Price........ **3c**

Shaft Couplings.

Made of best grade Norway iron, finished beveled ears.

No. 24C3320 ⅞-inch eye, 5-16-inch bolt, 2¾-inch clip, 5-16-inch shank. Weight, 1 pound. Price, per pair **18½c**

No. 24C3321 1-inch eye, ⅜-inch bolt, 3-inch clip, 5-16-inch shank. Weight, 2 pounds 9 ounces. Price, per pair........ **19c**

No. 24C3322 1⅛-inch eye, 7-16-inch bolt, 3¾-inch clip, ⅜-inch shank. Weight, 3½ pounds. Price, per pair........ **23c**

No. 24C3323 1¼-inch eye, 7-16-inch bolt, 4¼-inch clip, ⅜-inch shank. Weight, 3½ pounds. Price, per pair........ **31c**

Pole Couplings.

Finished Pole Couplings. Finished ready for welding to pole irons; made of best Norway iron.

No. 24C3324 ⅞-inch eye, 5-16-inch bolt, 2¾-inch clip. Price, per pair........ **18½c**

No. 24C3325 1-inch eye, ⅜-inch bolt, 3¼-inch clip. Price, per pair........ **19c**

No. 24C3326 1⅛-inch eye, 7-16-inch bolt, 3¾-inch clip. Price, per pair........ **23c**

No. 24C3327 1¼-inch eye, 7-16-inch bolt, 4⅜-inch clip. Price, per pair........ **31c**

Derby Fifth Wheels.

Derby Fifth Wheels. Material and workmanship A1. In ordering, give diameter of wheel wanted; also size of axle wheel is to be used on.

No.	Diam.	Size Iron	To Fit Axle	Price
24C3330	10 in.	⅝ in.	⅞ in.	43c
24C3331	12 in.	⅝ in.	1 or 1⅛ in.	48c
24C3332	14 in.	¾ in.	1⅛ or 1¼ in.	48c
24C3333	16 in.	⅞ in.	1¼ or 1⅜ in.	72c

Solid Steel Toe Rails.

Solid Steel Toe Rails, with braced ends. Made of one piece of steel. Length given is from outside to outside.

No. 24C3363 Size, 20 inches. Price........ **8c**
No. 24C3364 Size, 22 inches. Price........ **8c**

Genuine Bailey Body Hangers.

Rolled Steel Bailey Body Hangers. This is one of the most popular hangers now on the market. Made to clip on springs.

No. 24C3400 Size, 20 inches wide outside to outside, 4-inch drop. Price, per pair........ **85c**

No. 24C3402 Size, 21 inches wide outside to outside, 4-inch drop. Price, per pair........ **85c**

No. 24C3406 Size, 22 inches wide outside to outside, 4-inch drop. Price, per pair........ **85c**

No. 24C3408 Size, 23 inches wide outside to outside, 4-inch drop. Price, per pair........ **85c**

Steel Buggy Steps.

No. 24C3500 Rolled Steel Buggy Steps, made of one solid piece of steel. Size of pad, 3¾x3¼ inches; length of drop, 6¾ inches; projection, 5 inches. Price, per pair........ **18c**

No. 24C3510 Rolled Steel Buggy Steps. Size of pad, 4½x5 inches; length of drop, 9 inches; projection, 8 inches. Price, per pair........ **45c**

Malleable Wagon Clevises.

No. 24C3535 Malleable Clevis, with screw pin, 2 inches, inside measure, 4½ inches in length. Weight, 1 pound 10 ounces. Price........ **6c**

Patent Self Fastening Pin Clevises.

No. 24C3538 Malleable Patent Self Fastening Pin Clevis; inside measure, 2½ inches; whole length, 5½ inches. Weight, 1 pound 13 ounces. Price........ **7c**

Steel Wagon Clevises.

No. 24C3542 Steel Wagon Clevises, with round pin. Size of opening, 2⅛ inches; depth, 4½ inches. Price........ **5c**

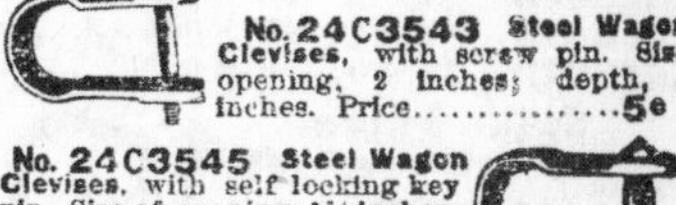

No. 24C3543 Steel Wagon Clevises, with screw pin. Size opening, 2 inches; depth, 4 inches. Price........ **5c**

No. 24C3545 Steel Wagon Clevises, with self locking key pin. Size of opening, 1⅞ inches; depth, 4½ inches. Price........ **5½c**

Patent Steel Wagon Clevis.

No. 24C3548 Patent Steel Wagon Clevis, with clip for square back doubletree. Size, opening, 1¾ inches. Price........ **7c**

Patent Lock Pin Clevis.

No. 24C3550 Patent Lock Pin Clevis, with steel clip and chain stay ring. No chain furnished. Size of opening, 1¾ inches. Price........ **7½c**

The Acme Clevis.

No. 24C3555 Swivel Clevis

No. 24C3556 Swivel Hook

These devices can be attached to any implement where hook or clevis is needed, without a link, adapting themselves to any position desired. The whiffletrees retain their proper position while you handle the plow any way you wish. In passing stumps or trees, the doubletree will accommodate itself to any angle without disturbing the plow.

A harrow, with this device, can be raised to any angle, or turned over if necessary, without affecting the position of the doubletree.

No. 24C3555 Swivel Clevis. Price........ **20c**
No. 24C3556 Swivel Hook. Price........ **18c**

Swivel Hook Clevis.

No. 24C3557 Evener Clevis with Swivel Hook, 2½ inches inside measurement, 9 inches extreme length. Weight, 3 pounds 9 ounces. Price........ **13½c**

End Clevis.

No. 24C3559 Malleable End Clevis. Inside measure, 2⅜ inches, whole length, 5 inches. Weight, 12 ounces. Price........ **2½c**

Whiffletree Hooks and Ferrules.

Whiffletree Hook and Ferrule. Wrought iron hook, malleable ferrule. Weight, 11 ounces.

No. 24C3565 Size, small end, 1⅛ inches. Price........ **4c**

No. 24C3567 Size, small end, 1¼ inches. Price........ **5c**

Steel Singletree Hooks.

No. 24C3578 Steel Singletree Hooks with welded clips and hooks. To be used in center of singletree. Size, round part, ⅝-inch, hook, ½-inch. Price........ **7½c**

End Clip to be Used on End Singletree.

No. 24C3579 Size round part, ¾-inch; size hook, 7-16 inch. Price........ **5c**

No. 24C3580 Size round part, 7-16 inch; size hook, ⅜-inch. Price........ **4c**

Steel Singletree Clips.

Catalogue No.	Size round part	Price
24C3585	7-16 inch	3c
24C3586	½ inch	3½c
24C3587	9-16 inch	3½c
24C3588	⅝ inch	4½c

Steel Singletree Clips with Rings.

No. 24C3595 Size round part of clip, ½-inch. Price........ **4½c**

No. 24C3596 Size round part of clip, 9-16 inch. Price........ **4½c**

No. 24C3597 Size round part of clip, ⅝-inch. Price........ **5½c**

Singletree Strap and Hook.

Strap Singletree Hook, made of the best quality wrought iron nicely finished. Intended to rivet on to singletree wood.

No. 24C3608 Hook and Strap, ⅝-inch. Price........ **6c**

No. 24C3609 Strap only. Price........ **4c**

Neckyoke Attachment.

No. 24C3612 Wrought Iron Neckyoke Attachment, with plate, complete 9-16-inch ring, 7-16-inch eyes, ⅜-inch links.
Price 10c

Steel Neckyoke Ferrules.

In ordering do not fail to give size and price of ferrules wanted.

Catalogue Number	Size Ferrule, inside large end	Size Ring	Price
24C3618	1⅛-inch	3½x⅜-inch	4c
24C3619	1¼-inch	3½x⅜-inch	4c
24C3620	1⅜-inch	3½x⅜-inch	5c

Stake Rings.

Malleable Iron Stake Rings for Wagons.
No. 24C3630 Size for ¾-inch stake. Price, per set of eight...6c
No. 24C3631 Size for ⅞-inch stake. Price, per set of eight........6c
No. 24C3632 Size for 1-inch stake. Price, per set of eight........6c

Steel Bolster Plates.

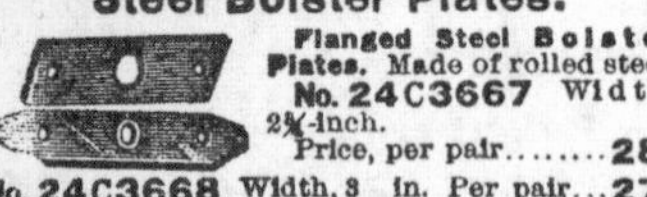

Flanged Steel Bolster Plates. Made of rolled steel. **No. 24C3667** Width, 2¾-inch.
Price, per pair........28c
No. 24C3668 Width, 3 in. Per pair...27c
No. 24C3669 Width, 3¼ in. Per pair...31c
No. 24C3670 Width, 3½ in. Per pair...33c

Wagon Rub Irons.

No. 24C3675 Rolled Steel Wagon Rub Irons, made of one solid piece of steel. Size, 2⅜x5¼ inches.
Price, per pair........8c

Steel Wagon Wrenches.

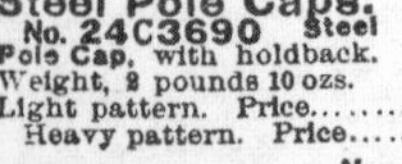

Rolled Steel Wagon Wrenches.
No. 24C3685 Size opening, 2⅛ inches; shank, ⅜x9 inches. Price........7½c
No. 24C3686 Size opening, 2⅜ inches; shank, ⅜x9 inches. Price........7½c
No. 24C3687 Size opening, 2¾ inches; shank, ⅜x9 inches. Price........7½c

Steel Pole Caps.

No. 24C3690 Steel Pole Cap, with holdback. Weight, 2 pounds 10 ozs.
Light pattern. Price........9c
Heavy pattern. Price........9½c
No. 24C3692 Steel Pole Cap, with holdback and wear irons complete. Price........16c

Reach Plates.

No. 24C3715 Cast Reach Plates with flange. Width of reach, 3½ or 4 inches.
Price 20c

Wagon Box Straps.

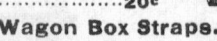

No. 24C3725
A set consists of eight pieces.

Length	Weight, per set	Diam. of screw	Price, per set
10 in.	4 lbs.	⅜ x10 in.	22c
12 in.	5 lbs.	⅜ x12 in.	24c
14 in.	6½ lbs.	9-16x14 in.	30c
16 in.	8½ lbs.	9-16x16 in.	31c
18 in.	9 lbs.	⅝ x18 in.	37c

Hooked Box Straps.

No. 24C3727 A set consists of eight pieces.

Length	Diam. of screw	Price, per set
10 in.	⅜	31c
12 in.	½	35c
14 in.	9-16	40c
16 in.	9-16	45c
18 in.	⅝	52c

The Barten Adjustable Malleable Iron Bolster Stake for Wagons.

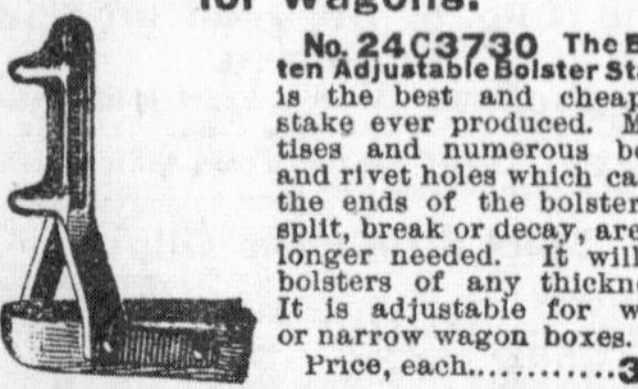

No. 24C3730 The Barten Adjustable Bolster Stake is the best and cheapest stake ever produced. Mortises and numerous bolts and rivet holes which cause the ends of the bolster to split, break or decay, are no longer needed. It will fit bolsters of any thickness. It is adjustable for wide or narrow wagon boxes.
Price, each..........33c

Steel Wagon Box Side Braces.

Steel Wagon Box Side Braces, finished complete, as shown in illustration.

	Size Round Part	Length	Price
No. 24C3735	7-16-inch	15½ inches	3½c
No. 24C3736	½-inch	15½ inches	4½c
No. 24C3737	9-16-inch	15½ inches	5c

Tailboard Fasteners.

No. 24C3745 Rolled Steel Tailboard Fasteners. Just the thing for use in close quarters where common long box rod cannot be taken out. Three pieces as shown in illustration, go on each side of box.
Price, per set, 6 pieces..........7½c

Wagon Box Rods.

Wagon Box Rods, with patent collar; both wide and narrow track; state which you want; wide track is 3 feet 7 inches between collars, and narrow track 3 feet 3 inches. Weight, about 1¾ pounds.
No. 24C3747 Price, for narrow track, each........6c
No. 24C3748 Price, for wide track, each........7c

Stake Irons.

No. 24C3750 Malleable Iron Stake Irons for express wagons. Size for 1⅛ and 2½ stake, 2½ inches deep, with ⅜-inch holes. Length over all, 7 inches.
Price 15c

Bow Staples.

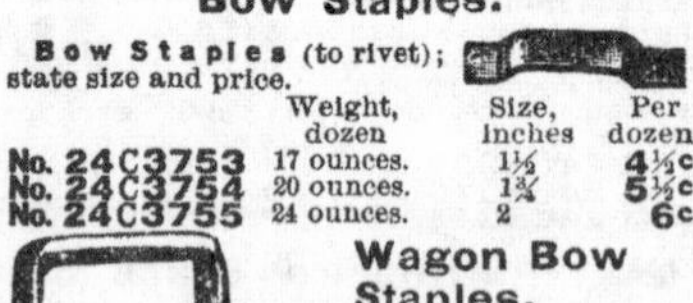

Bow Staples (to rivet); state size and price.

	Weight, dozen	Size, inches	Per dozen
No. 24C3753	17 ounces.	1½	4½c
No. 24C3754	20 ounces.	1¾	5½c
No. 24C3755	24 ounces.	2	6c

Wagon Bow Staples.

No. 24C3759 Wagon Bow Staples (to drive). 1½, 1¾ and 2-inch. Weight, per dozen, 15 ounces. State size wanted.
Price, per dozen........7½c

Steel Stay Chains.

No. 24C3765 Steel Wagon Stay Chains, with twisted links. Size, 5-16-inch; length, 26 inches. Weight, 4 pounds per pair.
Price, per pair........18c

Steel Tongue or Pole Chains

No. 24C3767 Steel Tongue or Pole Chains with twisted links. Size, 5-16-inch; length, 33 inches. Weight, 6 pounds per pair.
Price, per pair........26c

Spiral Tongue Support.

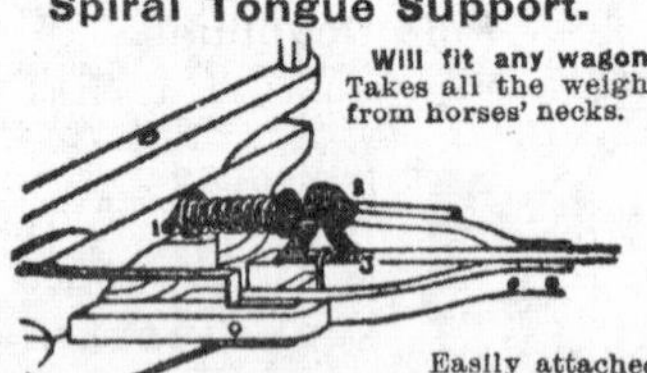

Will fit any wagon. Takes all the weight from horses' necks.

Easily attached to wagon tongue. One of the most simple and durable supports on the market. We have sold thousands of them in the last two years and they have given universal satisfaction.
No. 24C3774 For light spring wagons. Price........88c
No. 24C3775 For ordinary wagons. Price........98c
No. 24C3776 For heavy wagons. Price........$1.08

Lindquist's Wagon Tongue Support.

This Tongue Support will hold any wagon tongue in its proper position, preventing it from falling down. It relieves the necks of the horses from the weight of the tongue, thereby giving them greater ease and comfort. Can be applied in one minute. Will keep the tongue straight under any and all circumstances.
No. 24C3779 ¾-inch, for ordinary farm wagons. Price........$1.25
No. 24C3780 ⅞-inch, for heavy wagons. Price........$1.40

Ironed Neckyokes.

Neckyokes, hickory, ironed complete. Weight, 7¼ pounds.
No. 24C3785 38-inch. Price........39c
No. 24C3788 42-inch. Price........48c
No. 24C3789 48x3-inch. Price........65c

Ironed Evener.

No. 24C3792 Ironed Eveners, 2x4x48 inches, wrought iron plates and malleable clevises, complete, as shown in illustration; oiled. Price........40c

Plow Doubletree.

No. 24C3798 Selected hickory, 36 inches long, 2¾ inches thick, with hook in center. Weight, about 8 pounds. Price........27c

Plow Doubletree Sets.

No. 24C3800 Made of selected hickory, well ironed; a smooth, nice job; 36-inch evener, with singletree clevises, complete. Weight, about 15 pounds. Price, per set........67c

Plow Singletrees.

These are very fine Singletrees, made of selected wood, equipped with center clip hook and ferrule. These singletrees are not painted, but finished smooth and carefully oiled.
No. 24C3810 Plow Singletree, 26-inch, hickory, ironed. Weight, 3¼ pounds. Price, 12c
No. 24C3812 Plow Singletree, 30-inch, hickory, ironed. Weight, 3¾ pounds. Price........14c

Wagon Singletrees.

Wagon Singletree, hickory, ironed, with ferrules and hooks. Weight, 6 pounds.
No. 24C3817 2½x30 inches. Price..22c
No. 24C3818 2½x36 inches. Price..30c
No. 24C3819 3 x38 inches. Price..50c

Strap End Singletrees.

No. 24C3822 Selected Hickory, Strap End Wagon Singletree, hook has ½-inch strap, well riveted on, and ⅜-inch hook. Size, 2½x36 inches. Weight, 6½ pounds. Price........35c

The Celebrated Tubular Steel Doubletrees, Singletrees and Neckyokes.

These goods are past the experimental stage, having stood for the past seven years the most severe and practical tests, and are at present used by hundreds of our customers with the best results. A trial will convince any practical person of their superiority over all similar articles made from wood. They weigh no more than wood of a good quality and will outwear a dozen of the latter. In short, they are practically indestructible and will last a lifetime.

Tubular Steel Two-Horse Wagon Singletrees.

Tubular Steel Two-Horse Wagon Singletrees with ring in center, just the thing for heavy hauling. Will haul the load of three wood singletrees. Coated with a special iron paint baked on, which remains permanent. Will not rust.

No.	Size	Capacity	Weight	Price
24C3860	33-inch.	2,000 lbs.	9lbs.	70c
24C3862	34-inch.	2,500 lbs.	10lbs.	80c
24C3864	36-inch.	4,000 lbs.	12lbs.	89c

Acme Three-Horse Evener.

No. 24C3894 Acme Three-Horse Evener is light, strong, neat and durable. A perfect three-horse equalizer; can be changed for two horses in one minute; is made of selected hickory; the ends of all the eveners are riveted. Single trees have twisted clip and full hooks. Size of woods used: Main evener, 1¾x3½x40 inches; small eveners, 1⅜ x 2¾ x 28 inches; singletrees, 26 inches. Price, per set........$1.60

Tubular Steel Plow Doubletrees.

Tubular Steel Plow Doubletree Sets complete, as shown in illustration. Stronger and as light weight as wood; will last a lifetime. Furnished with hook in center and cockeye hooks pulling from back of singletree. Painted with a patent rustproof iron paint, baked on, which we guarantee to remain permanently.
No. 24C3875 No. 0. Capacity, 2,000 pounds, doubletree 33 inches long, singletree 28 inches long. Price, per set........$1.65
No. 24C3876 No. 1. Capacity, 3,000 pounds, doubletree 36 inches long, singletree 30 inches long. Price, per set........$1.70

Tubular Steel Wagon Doubletree Sets.

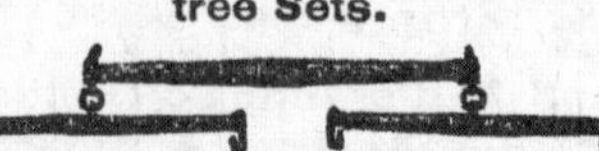

Tubular Steel Wagon Doubletree Sets. Made of the same high grade of steel as No. 24C3875. Just the thing for hauling grain, wood, etc., to market. You can't break them.
No. 24C3880 No. 1. Capacity, 2,500 pounds; evener is 46 inches long, singletree 33 inches long. Weight, 35 pounds. Price, per set, $2.75
No. 24C3882 No. 2. Capacity, 4,000 pounds; evener is 48 inches long, singletree 34 inches long. Weight, 38 pounds. Price, per set, $2.95

Western Brand Collinge Collar, Oil Retaining, Self Lubricating Axle.

Our Western Brand Self Oiling Axle is made with an oil groove which contains an oil retaining, lubricating pad, which holds the oil much longer than any other self oiling axle. Also the Collinge collar, acknowledged to be the nearest dirtproof of any axle made. Only the best grade steel used in their construction. Every axle carefully inspected before sent out.
No. 24C3910 Short bed.
No. 24C3912 Long bed.
Prices are per set of four axles.

Size	Price, short bed	Price, long bed	Size	Price, short bed	Price long bed
⅞x6½	$1.55	$1.75	1¼x6½	$2.75	$2.98
1 x6½	1.75	1.95	1¼x7	2.77	3.00
1⅛x6½	2.10	2.35	1¼x7½	2.79	3.05
1⅛x7	2.11	2.36	1⅜x7	3.95	4.25
1⅛x7½	2.12	2.37	1⅜x7½	4.05	4.35

Tubular Steel Wagon Neckyoke.

No. 24C3868 Tubular Steel Wagon Neckyoke; made of best grade Bessemer steel, coated with patent iron paint which prevents rusting. As light as wood and will outwear three common neckyokes. Give this a trial and see if it is not the best neckyoke you ever used. Weight, 12 pounds. Price for 40-inch........93c

Steel Buggy Axles.

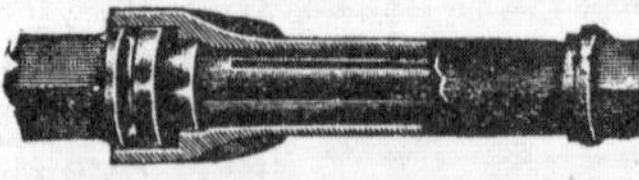

S., R. & Co.'s half patent solid collar welded shoulder steel axles, complete with boxing. We cannot furnish boxes only, nor axles without boxes. A set of short bed axles (commonly called axle stubs), consists of four axles with short bed, which are intended to be welded to old axles. A set of long bed axles consists of four axles with bed long enough to make axle complete by welding in the center. We sell one-half set at one-half price of a full set, and one-quarter set at one-quarter the price of full set. We cannot weld axles or set boxes.
In ordering parts of sets be sure and state whether right or left hand is wanted.
No. 24C3900 Short bed. **No. 24C3902** Long bed.

SIZE	No. 1 Price, short bed	No. 2 Price, long bed	SIZE	No. 1 Price, short bed	No. 2 Price, long bed	SIZE	No. 1 Price, short bed	No 2. Price, ong bed
⅞x6½	$1.18	$1.45	1¼x6½	$1.85	$2.20	1⅜x7½	$2.56	$3.15
1 x6½	1.33	1.60	1¼x7	1.86	2.21	1½x8	3.30	3.90
1⅛x6½	1.56	1.84	1¼x7½	1.87	2.22	1⅝x8	4.50	5.00
1⅛x7	1.57	1.85	1⅜x7	2.55	3.10	1¾x9½	5.60	6.50
1⅛x7½	1.58	1.86						

New Sampson Wagon Jacks.

No. 24C4435

New Sampson Malleable Iron Jack. Raises and lowers automatically. No springs to get out of order. Works by gravity.
No. 24C4433 No. 5, will raise six tons. Weight, about 25 pounds. Price........$2.75
No. 24C4434 No. 6, will raise eight tons. Weight, about 31 pounds. Price........$3.75

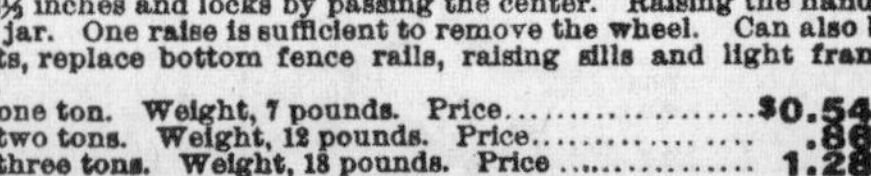

Oliver Improved Standard Wagon Jacks.

The merits of the Oliver Jacks have been established by their general adoption and long continued use. Can be handled with either hand. Is easily adjustable to any height by grasping the handle and sliding the bracket up or down, catching the rivet in any notch. Pulling down the handle will raise 2½ inches and locks by passing the center. Raising the handle will lower the load easily without a jar. One raise is sufficient to remove the wheel. Can also be used to set up machinery, pull posts, replace bottom fence rails, raising sills and light frame buildings. Lifting range, 24 inches.
No. 24C4435 No. 1 will raise one ton. Weight, 7 pounds. Price........$0.54
No. 24C4436 No. 2 will raise two tons. Weight, 12 pounds. Price.........88
No. 24C4437 No. 3 will raise three tons. Weight, 18 pounds. Price........1.28

WIDE TIRE METAL WAGON WHEELS

The demand for Wide Tire Low Metal Truck Wheels is growing every year. It has come to stay. Economy and strength are served when you have a set for use in the hundred and one emergencies arising where they may be used to great advantage. At the same time a day's use of these low metal wheels will convince you that you will save the cost of them in a year. You can do alone with them what would require an extra hand with the old style wheels. You can load your wagon twice as easily, and you can haul twice as much more with the same team.

We warrant all these wheels against defective workmanship or material, and if found defective, under our guarantee we will repair or replace them free of charge if delivered to our factory.

In making out your order, be sure to state size of skein wheel is intended for. The spokes are steel, oval shape. Staggered spokes always sent unless otherwise ordered.

Weights, each, of wheels with ⅜x4-in. tires as follows:

24-inch	28-inch	30-inch	32-inch	34-inch
64 lbs.	73 lbs.	77 lbs.	81 lbs.	88 lbs.
36-inch	38-inch	40-inch	42-inch	
92 lbs.	96 lbs.	114 lbs.	123 lbs.	

Other sizes weigh in proportion.

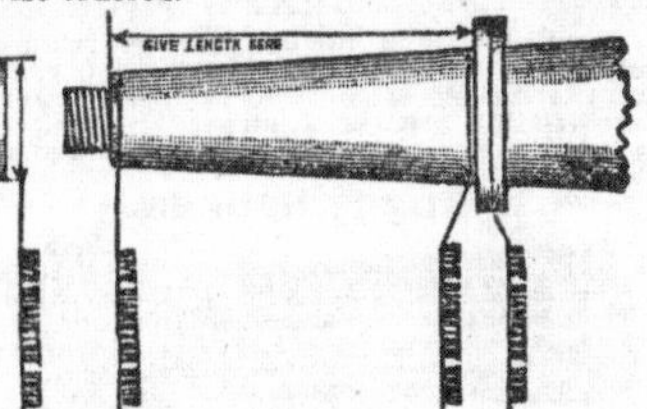

How to Take Measurements.

In ordering be sure to follow instructions on accompanying diagram; also give height of wheels wanted, and size of tire. Prices below are for single wheels. Prices f. o. b. at factory in Central Illinois.

No. 24C3922

Height		Tire ⅜x3	Tire ⅜x4	Tire ⅜x5	Tire ½x3	Tire ½x4
24-inch	Price	$2.38	$2.65	$2.92	$2.73	$3.00
28-inch	Price	2.64	2.95	3.17	2.99	3.30
30-inch	Price	2.92	3.05	3.45	3.27	3.40
32-inch	Price	3.11	3.40	3.62	3.46	3.75
34-inch	Price	3.35	3.50	3.78	3.70	3.85
36-inch	Price	3.61	3.69	4.10	3.96	4.04
38-inch	Price	3.70	3.99	4.39	4.05	4.34
40-inch	Price	3.84	4.17	4.49	4.59	4.52
44-inch	Price	4.49	4.70	4.98	4.84	5.05

Thimble Skeins.

No. 24C3935 Steel Skein.

Cast Skeins.

No. 24C3937 Iron Skeins. These Thimble Skeins are seamless and have cut threads. Set consists of four skeins, but we will sell one only at one-quarter the price of full set, or two only at one-half the price of full set.

When ordering one skein only, state whether right or left is wanted. Always give catalogue number and do not fail to give size and price of skeins.

Size Inches	Weight, pounds Iron	Price, per Set Iron	Price, per Set Steel	Weight, pounds Steel
2¼x 6½	26	$0.80	....	....
2¼x 7	28	.66	$3.35	44
2¼x 7½	30	.91	3.36	46
2½x 7	30	.92	....	....
2½x 7½	34	1.03	3.42	48
2½x 8	36	1.08	3.46	50
2¾x 8	40	1.20	3.66	51
2¾x 8½	48	1.24	3.72	53
3 x 9	56	1.38	3.90	66
3¼x 9	65	1.61	4.44	70
3¼x10	70	1.72	4.50	76
3¼x11	74	1.78	4.56	80
3½x10	74	1.84	4.98	80
3½x11	84	1.90	5.10	94
3½x12	92	2.02	5.40	100
3¾x11	92	2.07	6.00	100
3¾x12	96	2.16	6.05	108
4 x12	116	2.44	7.20	112

Cast Cup and Truss Bar Skeins.

No. 24C3940 Extra Heavy Truss Bar Cast Skeins. This is a first class skein and is rapidly replacing the common old style skein to a large extent. They are considerably heavier than the ordinary skein and on that account seldom break. Underneath the bell which envelops the axle, provision is made for attaching a flat truss, held in place by a so-called cup bar. There is also a little knob on top of the bell to keep the cup tie, which is a piece of ⅜ or 7-16 inch iron, from slipping out of place. It makes a very convenient way of trussing a wagon and attaching a hook for stay chains.

Size, 2½x 8 inches; weight, per set of four, 46 pounds. Price, per set of four.......... **$1.60**

Size, 3 x 9 inches; weight, per set of four, 67 pounds. Price, per set of four.......... **2.12**

Size, 3¼x10 inches; weight, per set of four, 86 pounds. Price, per set of four.......... **2.44**

Size, 3½x11 inches; weight, per set of four, 113 pounds. Price, per set of four.......... **2.88**

Iron Tires.

No. 24C3948 Front tires, 12 feet long; hind, 15 feet. For half set (front tires), one-half the price of full set. For half set (hind tires), add 35 cents to the half set price. Price subject to change of market.

Size	Weight, lbs.	Price, per set	Size,	Weight, lbs.	Price, per set
1¼x⅜	85	$2.13	2½x½	227	$5.67
1⅜x⅜	94	2.35	3 x½	273	6.90
1½x½	137	3.42	3½x½	319	7.65
1⅝x½	148	3.70	4 x½	364	9.10
1¾x½	160	4.00	4 x⅝	455	11.35
2 x½	180	4.50			

FARM WAGON WHEELS

The material used in the construction of these wheels is carefully graded by expert workmen, and the wheels are made by skilled mechanics who make a special feature of fine workmanship.

We cannot set boxes in the hubs and guarantee them to fit your old skeins, hence we price you the wheels complete, except boxes in the hubs, and also complete with boxes in the hubs and skeins to fit your axles. If you want new boxes you must order new skeins as well, which we furnish to you at the actual cost of manufacturing.

Order by number and give full description, size and grade of wheels wanted.

The following prices are per set of four wheels, f. o. b. our factory in Southern Wisconsin.

Height of front wheels, 3 feet 8 inches; height of rear wheels, 4 feet 2 inches and 4 feet 6 inches.

For broken sets add 35 cents per wheel extra. For irregular sizes we require cash in full, as on all other goods.

As these wheels are made to your order there will be a delay of from six to ten days.

WE CAN NOT TAKE BACK WHEELS THAT HAVE BEEN MADE UP AS ORDERED. BE VERY CAREFUL IN TAKING MEASUREMENTS.

Catalogue Number	Size of Skein Wheels are to Fit	Size of Tire	In White, Not Ironed or Painted	In White, Tire Set, Not Painted, without Boxes in the Hubs	Painted, Tire Set, but without Boxes in the Hubs	Painted, Tire Set, Boxes in Hubs and Cast Skeins to Fit	Extra for each ½-inch Width of Tire	Extra for Steel Skeins in place of Cast Skeins
24C4445	2¼x7	1¼x¼	$ 8.85	$12.75	$14.00	$16.15	....	$2.15
24C4447	2½x8	1⅜x⅜	8.90	14.00	15.75	18.25	$1.20	2.19
24C4449	2¾x8½	1⅜x⅜	8.95	15.25	16.75	19.35	1.20	2.22
24C4451	3 x9	1½x½	9.70	16.50	18.50	20.50	1.40	2.25
24C4453	3¼x10	1½x½	9.90	16.75	19.00	22.50	1.50	2.30
24C4455	3½x11	1⅝x⅝	10.25	16.50	22.50	24.00	1.60	3.25
24C4457	3¾x12	1¾x⅝	12.30	20.50	23.00	27.50	1.90	4.20
24C4459	4 x12	2 x¾	14.00	24.50	26.00	30.75	2.30	5.00

SARVEN PATENT WHEELS

WITH TIRES.

Read our Prices for Genuine Sarven Patent Wheels, and you will readily see we are the Leaders in the Wheel Business.

WE DO NOT HESITATE TO SAY OUR STANDARD GRADE WHEELS are the best Wheels for the money, quality and workmanship considered, sold by anyone. The hubs are second growth elm, spokes and rims of second growth Ohio hickory. We receive a great number of letters from our customers asking how we can sell **standard grade** Sarven Patent Wheels, made of honest stock and of good workmanship, at the low price quoted in our catalogue. This is easily answered when you stop to consider that we are the largest buyers of tired buggy wheels in the United States, having bought and sold twice as many wheels the past year as any other firm; that we buy for **spot cash,** and by placing such large orders with one firm they are able to manufacture wheels the year around.

A wheel factory generally runs about six months in the year, so you can readily see they are willing to make a great concession by reducing prices for this reason. It is much more profitable to keep running, if at a small loss, as the machinery becomes rusted, belting rots out and a general decay takes place the minute you shut down. As we stated above, all our wheels are made by a firm whose reputation for honest wheels is second to none in this country. Every wheel is carefully inspected before leaving the factory and if found imperfect in any way is rejected; the same care is taken when the wheels are received by us. They are made with the object of giving value received to the purchaser and are sold on their merits.

RUBBER TIRED BUGGY WHEELS. Sarven Patent Buggy Wheels with Highest Grade Guaranteed Goodyear Rubber Tires. The tires are put on by machinery after first setting a steel channel tire on wheels, bolting same between every spoke, thus avoiding any chance of becoming loose from the rim. The rubber used is the **highest grade Para rubber,** carefully vulcanized, and is strictly first class. Prices given below are for a high grade Sarven wheel in the white or oiled, with tires put on ready for use.

WHEELS IN THE WHITE WITH TIRES.

Catalogue Number	Size of Spoke at Hub	Length of Hub where box goes in	Width of Rim	Size of Tire	Weight, per Set of 4 Wheels	Price per Set of 4 Wheels Standard Grade	Price per Set of 4 Wheels with Rubber Tires
	Inches	Inches	Inches	Inch	Pounds		
24C4416	1 1-16	6½	⅞	5-16	90	$ 5.98	$19.00
24C4418	1⅛	6½	1	¼	100	6.25	22.00
24C4420	1¼	7	1⅛	5-16	125	7.70	29.00
24C4422	1⅜	7½	1¼	⅜	160	9.90	34.00
24C4424	1½	8	1½	½	240	16.50	....
24C4426	1¾	9	1¾	⅝	375	27.00	....

Diameter of above wheels, 3 feet 2 inches, 3 feet 4 inches, 3 feet 6 inches, 3 feet 8 inches, 3 feet 10 inches and 4 feet.

There should be 4 inches difference between front and hind wheels.

For example, 3 feet 4 inches and 3 feet 8 inches correspond; 3 feet 6 inches and 3 feet 10 inches; 3 feet 8 inches and 4 feet.

GIVE HEIGHT OF WHEELS WANTED. If no height is mentioned we use our judgment in filling orders. These prices are for a set of four wheels, any height listed above. Half sets furnished at one-half the price of a set. The hub length is length of box which goes in the hub, rim band and hub or sand band not being measured.

NOTICE—We cannot paint wheels, furnish or set boxes. Please do not ask it as it will only delay order. Sarven patent wheels with tires.

WE CARRY A LARGE STOCK OF WHEELS and can make prompt shipment. If no height is mentioned we send 3 feet 8 inches and 4 feet wheels. In ordering wheels for repair work give length of box in your old wheel, which will be the length of hub required. Two wheels sold at half the price of a set, one wheel at one-quarter the price of a set. **In ordering parts of sets be sure to give height.**

NOTICE—As there seems to be more or less confusion existing as to the right size axles to use in different size wheels, we give below the standard table of sizes. We have a great many orders for light wheels and say 1¼-inch axles, and the consequence is, the hub is cut entirely out putting the box in, leaving only ⅜ or ½-inch of spoke tenon and the result is the wheel soon goes to pieces, is condemned as no good. By following the table below, you will avoid all this.

For No. 24C4416 Wheels use ⅞x6½ or 1 x6½ Axles.
For No. 24C4418 Wheels use ⅞x6½ or 1 x6½ Axles.
For No. 24C4420 Wheels use 1x7 or 1⅛x7 Axles.
For No. 24C4422 Wheels use 1⅛x7½ or 1¼x7½ Axles.
For No. 24C4424 Wheels use 1⅜x8 or 1½x8 Axles.
For No. 24C4426 Wheels use 1½x9 or 1⅝x9 Axles.

We carry in stock wheels 3 feet 2 inches, 3 feet 4 inches, 3 feet 6 inches, 3 feet 8 inches, 3 feet 10 inches and 4 feet, and can make prompt shipment. Prices on other sizes quoted on application.

WRITE US FOR PRICES ON HEAVIER SARVEN WHEELS, being careful to give size of spoke, length of hub, tread, depth of rim and height of wheel wanted. Thimble skeins cannot be used in Sarven wheels. Steel axles must be used.

Buggy and Carriage Springs.

Oil tempered, half bright.

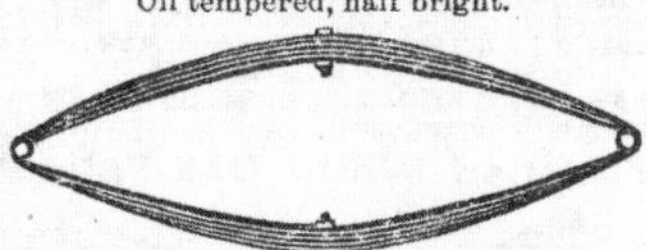

No. 24C3980 Carriage Springs, regular elliptic shape, double sweep same price as single. Avoid mistakes by giving catalogue number and do not fail to state size and price of spring wanted.

Width, inches	No. of Leaves	Length, inches	Av. Weight per single spring, pounds	Price, each
1¼	3	34	16½	$0.88
1¼	3	36	17½	.97
1¼	4	34	18½	1.00
1¼	4	36	20	1.10
1⅜	4	34	20	1.15
1⅜	4	36	22½	1.25
1½	4	36	23½	1.35
1½	5	36	27½	1.50
1¾	5	36	32½	1.85
1¾	6	36	37	2.20

Platform Springs.

No. 24C3984 Side Springs.

No. 24C3985 Cross Springs. Best grade oil tempered side and cross springs. Guaranteed against imperfections. Prices given below are for either side or cross spring.

Width inches	No. of Leaves	Length Inches Side	Length Inches Cross	Av. Weight each	Price, each
1¼	3	38 or 40	40 or 42	10 lbs.	$0.60
1¼	4	38 or 40	40 or 42	16 lbs.	.96
1⅜	3	38 or 40	40 or 42	11½ lbs.	.70
1⅜	4	38 or 40	40 or 42	15 lbs.	.90
1⅜	5	38 or 40	40 or 42	20 lbs.	1.20
1½	4	38 or 40	40 or 42	18 lbs.	1.08
1½	5	38 or 40	40 or 42	21 lbs.	1.26
1½	6	40	42	26 lbs.	1.56

Give length, width and number of leaves.

Sweet's Seat Springs.

No. 24C3990 Seat Springs, two-leaf, 1¼x26 inches. Weight, per pair, 18 pounds. Price, per pair.......... **52c**

No. 24C3992 Seat Springs, three-leaf, 1¼ x 28 inches. Weight, per pair, 20 pounds. Price, per pair.......... **88c**

Glover's Patent Seat Springs.

No. 24C3996 These springs are longer, require no seat hooks or spring bars, and can be attached to seat by anyone, requiring no blacksmith. They are not so easily broken as the old style, and it is nearly impossible to break them within two inches from each end, where the old style usually gives way. Price, per pair, 1¼-inch, two-leaf springs.......... **43c**

Our Fruit and Dairy Bolster Springs.

Our Fruit and Dairy Bolster Springs are especially adapted for fruit or dairy hauling, but are used extensively on all kinds of wagons. We put them up to fit 36, 38, 42 or 44-inch bolster, and they have extension end shoes to fit odd sized bolsters. Always give exact size between bolster stakes.

Prices are per set of two springs.

No.		Price
24C4130	To carry 1,000 pounds...	$1.75
24C4131	To carry 1,500 pounds...	2.00
24C4132	To carry 2,000 pounds...	2.20
24C4133	To carry 2,500 pounds...	2.20
24C4134	To carry 3,000 pounds...	2.60

The Acme Bolster Springs.

The Acme Bolster Springs are so constructed that they will not strike the bolster. They are made on the same principle as an elliptic carriage spring. Every set warranted to carry the number of pounds represented or money refunded. A set consists of two complete springs ready for use. We carry in stock and can ship at once 38-inch size, which is the regular standard size. Any other size furnished on short notice at a slight advance in price. 38-inch always sent unless otherwise ordered. In ordering give distance between bolster stakes.

NOTICE—Springs over 38 inches wide, 75 cents per set extra.

No.	Width of Steel, inches	No. of Leaves	Springs to carry pounds	Weight, per set, pounds	Price, per set
24C4150	1¼	3	1,000	66	$3.50
24C4151	1¼	4	1,500	75	3.75
24C4152	1½	4	2,000	90	4.50
24C4153	1¾	5	2,500	105	5.00
24C4154	2	5	3,000	120	5.20
24C4155	2	6	4,000	135	6.00
24C4156	2	7	5,000	150	6.35
24C4157	2½	6	6,000	170	7.70

Miller's Patent Wagon Jack.

No. 24C4440
For buggy..........50c
For wagon..........60c
For truck..........80c

Bent Heel Buggy or Cutter Shafts.

Finished Bars included. Give size when ordering. Not ironed.

	Size, inches	Weight, per pair, lbs.	Price, per pair XXX	Black Hickory
No. 24C4470	1⅜x1⅛	11¼	$0.66	$1.00
No. 24C4471	1½x2	12½	.72	1.03
No. 24C4472	1½x2¼	14½	.85	1.05
No. 24C4473	1⅝x2¼	15	1.00	1.30

Buggy Poles.

No. 24C4492 Single Bend Poles.
No. 24C4493 Double Bend Poles.

Buggy Poles, finished, including finished circles. The prices below are for one single or double bend pole and circle, which are called a set. Give size when ordering.

Size	Weight	Price XXX	Black Hickory
1⅞x2¼ inches.	14 pounds.	$0.95	$1.26
2 x2½ inches.	15 pounds.	.96	1.29
2 x2¾ inches.	17 pounds.	1.10	1.47
2 x3 inches.	19 pounds.	1.20	1.53

Be sure and state which style is wanted, single or double bend.

Buggy Singletree Woods.

No. 24C4540 **Buggy Singletree Woods,** forest hickory, 1½, 1⅝, 1¾, 1⅞-inch center. Give size when ordering. Price..........9½c
No. 24C4542 Extra select hickory. Price..........13c

Buggy and Express Doubletree Woods.

Select Hickory Buggy and Express **Doubletree Woods.** Not ironed.

		Price
No. 24C4550	Size, 1⅜x2¼x48 in. long	15c
No. 24C4552	Size, 1½x2½x48 in. long	16c
No. 24C4554	Size, 1¾x3x48 in. long	18c

Buggy Neckyoke Woods.

Select Hickory Buggy Neckyoke Woods, not ironed; weight, 2½ pounds; acorn tips.
No. 24C4560 Size, 1⅝x42 in. long....14c
No. 24C4562 Size, 1¾x42 in. long....14c
No. 24C4564 Size, 2 x42 in. long....15c

Hickory Wagon Singletree Woods.

Select Hickory Wagon Singletree Woods, not **ironed.** Weight, 3½ pounds.
No. 24C4626 Oval, 2½-inch center, 36 inches long. Price..........8½c
No. 24C4628 Oval, 2⅝-inch center, 36 inches long. Price..........9c
No. 24C4630 Oval, 2¾-inch center, 36 inches long. Price..........10c

Neckyoke Woods.

Select Hickory Neckyoke Woods, not ironed Weight, 3 to 5 pounds.
No. 24C4636 2½-inch center, 38 inches long. Price..........13c
No. 24C4638 2⅝-inch center, 40 inches long. Price..........13½c
No. 24C4640 2¾-inch center, 42 inches long. Price..........14c

Wagon Evener Woods.

Hickory Wagon Evener Woods in the white. Not ironed. Weight, 8 pounds.
No. 24C4650 Size, 2 x4 x48 in. long, 16c
No. 24C4652 Size, 2¼x4¼x52 in. long, 29c
No. 24C4654 Size, 2½x5 x52 in. long, 30c

Plow Doubletree Woods.

No. 24C4659 **Select Hickory Plow Doubletree Woods, not ironed.** Size, 1⅞x3½x42 inches long. Price..........11c

White Ash Finished Wagon Tongues.

Select Ash Wagon Tongues, finished ready for use. Square butts.
No. 24C4670 Size, where doubletree goes, 3 inches. Price..........95c
No. 24C4672 Size, where doubletree goes, 3½ inches. Price..........$1.00
No. 24C4674 Size, where doubletree goes, 4 inches. Price..........$1.05

Wagon Bows.

Wagon Bows, round or square top, five pieces to a set (be sure to say whether for narrow or wide track). Weight, per set, 30 pounds.
No. 24C4700 Round top, size, 1⅛x⅜ inches. Price, per set..........50c
No. 24C4702 Square top, size, 1⅛x⅜ inches. Price, per set..........55c

Finished Wagon Bolsters.

Select White Oak Wagon Bolsters, rounded and finished.
No. 24C4720 Size, 3¼x4¼ inches, regular size. Front. Price..........38c
No. 24C4722 Size, 3⅜x4¾ inches, full size. Front. Price..........40c
No. 24C4724 Size, 2⅝x3¾ inches, full size. Hind. Price..........27c

Finished Wagon Hawns.

No. 24C4745 **Select White Oak Finished Hind Wagon Hawns,** turned ready for use. Price, per pair of two pieces.....35c

Surfaced Front Hawns.

No. 24C4747 **Made of Select White Oak.** Price, per pair of two pieces..........32c

Finished Tongue Hawns.

No. 24C4758 **Select White Oak Wagon Tongue Hawns,** ready for use. Price, per pair of two pieces..........29c

Surfaced Sway Bars.

No. 24C4762 **Select White Oak, Surfaced or Planed Wagon Sway Bars.** Price..........13c

Finished Sand Bars.

No. 24C4766 **Select White Oak Finished Sand Bars,** ready for use. Price..........29c

Turned and Finished Wagon Axles.

Select Hickory Finished Wagon Axles, ready to put in wagon. A saving of labor as well as transportation charges. No kiln dried lumber used. Every axle warranted to be free from knots, etc.
No. 24C4780 2¼-inch skein, wide or narrow track. Price, each..........65c
No. 24C4781 2½-inch skein, wide or narrow track. Price, each..........72c
No. 24C4782 3-inch skein, wide or narrow track. Price, each..........82c
No. 24C4783 3¼-inch skein, wide or narrow track. Price, each..........88c
No. 24C4784 3½-inch skein, wide or narrow track. Price, each..........92c

Finished White Oak Felloes.

No. 24C4845 **Select White Oak Finished Sawed Wagon Felloes,** made of well seasoned stock, free from knots, etc. We cannot sell less than one-half full set. A set consists of twelve front, fourteen hind felloes. Furnished 3 feet 8 inches and 4 feet 6 inches only; except 1⅜x2⅜, which we can furnish from 3 feet to 4 feet 6 inches.

	Weight	Per set
1⅜-inch tread, 2¼-inch depth..	71 lbs.	$1.55
1⅜-inch tread, 2½-inch depth..	75 lbs.	1.60
1⅜-inch tread, 2⅝-inch depth..	77 lbs.	1.65

We cannot furnish sizes different from above.

Wagon Spokes.

No. 24C4856 **Wagon Spokes, forest oak,** 52 to a set. Always state what size and grade is wanted.

Size, inches	Weight, pounds	Price, per set C grade	B grade	A grade
2	55	$1.15	$1.50	$2.25
2⅛	60	1.20	1.60	2.40
2¼	65	1.27	1.65	2.55
2⅜	73	1.35	1.75	2.65
2½	80	1.40	1.80	2.80
2⅝	90	1.50	2.00	3.05
2¾	95	1.60	2.20	3.70
3	110	1.75	2.50	3.80

A set consists of two bundles, one front and one hind, the two bundles containing enough spokes for one set of wheels. **Front bundles are half the price of a full set. Hind bundles are half the price of a full set plus 25 cents.**

Buggy Spokes.

No. 24C4858 **Buggy Spokes,** hickory, 1 to 1⅜, 60 to a set. 1½, 52 to a set. We do not break sets. Can be used **only in wood hub wheels.**

Inches		C grade	B select	A select
Size 1	Price, per set,	$1.00	$1.75	$2.55
Size 1⅛	Price, per set,	1.02	1.77	2.60
Size 1¼	Price, per set,	1.05	1.80	2.65
Size 1⅜	Price, per set,	1.10	2.05	2.80
Size 1½	Price, per set,	1.25	2.35	3.10

Be sure to state size and grade wanted.

Buggy Seats.

When ordering, give length of Buggy Seat from outside to outside on the bottom.

No. 24C4902 **Buggy Seat,** square corners, ironed, ready for lazy back, as shown in illustration. Size, 30 to 42 inches wide, 15 inches deep. Weight, 15 pounds. Price..........$1.45

High Back Stick Seats.

No. 24C4906 **High Back Stick Seat,** finished complete in the white. No irons. 27 inches and 29 inches long on bottom. Weight, about 18 pounds.
Price..........$3.50

Cutter Stuff.

This illustration shows the Swell Body Cutter stuff.

Square Box Cutter Stuff.

Square Box Cutter Stuff, complete.
No. 24C4920 Size, 1¼ inches; for one seat. Weight, about 36 pounds. Price, per set..90c
No. 24C4922 Size, 1¼ inches; for two seats. Weight, about 41 pounds. Price, per set..........$1.00

Bent Cutter Stuff.

Bent Cutter Stuff for Portland cutters, consisting of runners, raves and fenders; put up in the bundle.
No. 24C4924 Size, 1¼ inches; for one seat. Weight, 35 pounds. Price, per set......$1.05
No. 24C4926 Size, 1¼ inches; for two seats. Weight, 40 pounds. Price, per set......$1.10

Cutter Stuff for Swell Body Cutters.

No. 24C4930 Size, 1¼ inches; for one seat. Weight, 35 pounds. Price, per set......$1.65
No. 24C4933 Size, 1¼ inches; for two seats. Weight, 40 pounds. Price, per set..........$2.30

Bob Runners.

Bent Bob Runners. Made of select rock elm. Entire length, 6 feet. Set consists of four single runners.

	Size	Weight, lbs.	Per set
No. 24C4940	2x3	45	$1.25
No. 24C4942	2x3½	60	1.35
No. 24C4944	2x4	65	1.75

Cutter Shoes.

No. 24C4975 **Steel Cutter Shoes,** tapered and bent.

Size	Weight	Per pair	Size	Weight	Per pair
⅝x⅞	17 lbs.	55c	½x⅞	19 lbs.	60c
⅝x1	18 lbs.	60c	½x1	21 lbs.	70c
⅝x1¼	25 lbs.	75c	½x1¼	26 lbs.	80c

Cast Iron Bob Shoes.

No. 24C4978 **Cast Iron Bob Sleigh Shoes,** interchangeable for right or left hand; 1½-inch tread, 2-inch on top and 1¾-inch thick.

Length	Weight, per set of four	Price, per set of four
36 inches	74 pounds	$1.25
38 inches	79 pounds	1.40
40 inches	84 pounds	1.70
42 inches	89 pounds	1.80
44 inches	94 pounds	1.85
46 inches	99 pounds	2.00
48 inches	104 pounds	2.25

Sleigh Shoe Bolts.

No. 24C4980 Made of the best Norway iron.

Length, inches	Diameter	Price, per set of 16	Length, inches	Diameter	Price, per set of 16
4½	7-16 inch	19c	6½	7-16 in.	30c
5	7-16 inch	20c	7	7-16 in.	35c
5½	7-16 inch	23c	7½	7-16 in.	37c
6	7-16 inch	26c	8	7-16 in.	38c

Piano Buggy Body.

No. 24C5065 **Piano Buggy Bodies** in the white, not ironed or painted; 24 and 25 inches wide, and 48 or 50 and 52 inches long; panels, 8 inches deep. Weight, about 50 pounds. Made of the best seasoned material. The panels are well glued, clamped and screwed to frame, which make them stand the hard usage to which they are put. Dimensions given above are on bottom, outside to outside. Finished and crated ready for shipment. We can furnish these bodies in sizes quoted in catalogue only. Price..........$3.45

Corning Buggy Body.

No. 24C5068 **Corning Buggy Body** is one of the standard styles. Next to the piano body it is the best selling body on the market. We use only thoroughly dry material. Panels are clamped and screwed to posts or frame and put up by first class mechanics. Sizes, 24 inches wide and 49 inches long. No paint or irons furnished. Finished in white, and crated ready for shipment. Weight, about 65 pounds. Price..........$3.60

F. & A. Business Gears.

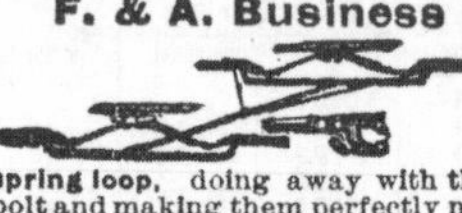

This gear is made with our new improved cone hanger and spring loop, doing away with the wear on the bolt and making them perfectly noiseless; made in two tracks only, 4 feet 8 inches and 5 feet. When ordering, give track, length and width of body.

		Axle, in.	Lbs.	Cap. lbs.	Price
24C5100	No. ½	⅞x6½	75	450 to 600	$8.90
24C5102	No. 1	1x6½	100	600 to 800	10.10
24C5104	No. 2	1⅛x7	125	1,000	11.25

Prices f. o. b. Factory.

Fitch's Combination Singer Duplex and Elliptic Gears.

We furnish this gear complete, as shown in illustration, ready to bolt body to gear. It hangs as low as our regular duplex gear and is adapted for delivery, express or pleasure wagons. When ordering, give track, width and length of body to be used on same.

		Axle, in.	Lbs.	Cap. lbs.	Price
24C5112	No. 1	1x6½	125	800	$11.90
24C5114	No. 2	1⅛x7	125	1,000	12.85
24C5116	No. 3	1¼x7	135	1,500	15.80
24C5118	No. 4	1⅜x7½	150	1,800	19.60
24C5119	No. 5	1½x8	175	2,200 to 2,500	25.00

Prices f. o. b. Factory.

Double Elliptic End Spring Drop Axle Gear.

This gear is adapted for milk, bakery and grocery wagons; hangs very low and rides easy. We make this gear in two sizes and furnish spring bars on both.
No. 24C5138 No. 1 gear has 1x6½-inch axles; capacity, 800 pounds. Weight, 150 pounds. Price..........$17.10
No. 24C5140 No. 2 gear has 1⅛x7-inch axles; capacity, 1,000 pounds. Weight, 150 lbs. Price..........$18.80
Prices f. o. b. Factory.

Combination End Springs and Platform Gear.

Notice—When ordering gears of this style, please state whether the body is to be hung on loops in front or to set on top of front spring bar. Also state width of track and width and length of body to be used.

No.	No. Gear	Axles	Front Spring	Hind Spring, side	Cross Springs	Capacity	Price
24C5142	1	1 x6½	1⅛x4x36 light	1⅛x4x36 light	1⅛x5x43 light	800	$15.95
24C5143	2	1⅛x7	1¼x4x36 heavy	1¼x4x36 heavy	1¼x5x43 heavy	1,000	17.10
24C5144	3	1¼x7	1¼x5x36 heavy	1¼x4x36 heavy	1¼x6x43 heavy	1,500	19.10
24C5145	4	1⅜x7½	1¼x6x36 heavy	1¼x5x36 heavy	1¼x7x43 heavy	1,800	23.95

PUMP DEPARTMENT.

PROBABLY THERE IS NO OTHER LINE OF GOODS that we sell on which we can save our customers more money than we can on pumps. We fit all our pumps so that anyone can set them in the well without any trouble. The only special tool required is a pipe tong. We sell a 1¼-inch pipe tong for 66 cents, and everyone should have one.

IF IN DOUBT WRITE US, giving us this information: How deep is well? Is force pump or lift pump wanted? How much water is wanted per day? When water is to be drawn from a distance or forced to a distance, send a rough drawing showing position of pump, position of well, giving all angles and measurements. We will name our price on the best outfit.

Pitcher Spout Pumps.

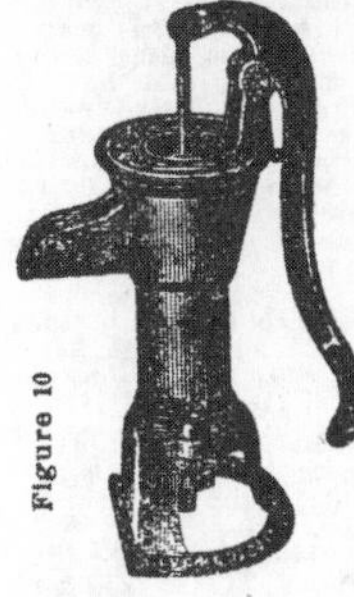

Figure 10

This illustration represents our close top Pitcher Spout Pump. These pumps are made in the very best manner and have the revolving bearer which by loosening the set screw allows handle to be placed on either side or back, in any position desired. The cylinders of these pumps are bored true and polished. They have trip valves, by which the water may be let out of the pump in the winter by raising the handle until it trips the lower valve. They are fitted with connection for either lead or iron pipe. Pipe is not included in price. (See No. 24C5710 for pipe.) We also make this pump with brass lined cylinder. It is a well known fact that leather plungers operating in brass cylinders are almost indestructible. **We can fully recommend them where the best is wanted.**

	Iron	Brass lined
No. 24C5200 No. 1. 2½-inch cylinder for 1¼-inch pipe. Price	$0.92	$2.15
No. 24C5202 No. 2. 3-inch cylinder for 1¼-inch pipe. Price	.98	2.40
No. 24C5204 No. 3. 3½-inch cylinder for 1¼-inch pipe. Price	1.12	2.85
No. 24C5205 No. 4. 4-inch cylinder for 1¼-inch pipe. Price	1.37	3.10

Acme Cistern Pumps.

In the Acme Cistern Pump we have the most up to date pump made. Extra finish, high grade, gray iron and brass, machine fitted. We have this pump in two styles, iron body and brass lined body. All are fitted for 1¼-inch lead or iron pipe and back outlet for 1-inch pipe as per illustration.

Figure 20

No. 24C5214 3-inch iron body. Price.........**$4.00**

No. 24C5215 3-inch brass lined body. Price.........**$4.95**

Same pump without cock spout, but with common round spout and hose attachment.

No. 24C5221 3-inch iron body. Price.........**$3.05**

No. 24C5222 3-inch brass lined body. Price.........**$4.20**

Iron and Brass Lined Force Pumps.

With Air Chamber, Revolving Bearer and Brass Piston Rod.

This is a staple pump for house use. It is usually placed on a kitchen sink or elevated platform, and used to force water up into a tank or reservoir to supply bathrooms and wash basins. The air chamber is fitted with an outlet into which a draw cock may be screwed if desired. Hose may also be attached to the cock for sprinkling or fire purposes, in which case it is best to put a stop cock on the upward discharge. These pumps have brass valve seats, and are fitted for iron or lead pipe. Will not work satisfactorily in well or cistern over 25 feet deep. Complete as shown in illustration.

Figure 25

	Iron	Brass Lined
No. 24C5226 No. 2. 2½ inch cylinder for 1¼-inch pipe. To fit ¾-inch hose coupling. Price	$5.40	$6.80
No. 24C5228 No. 4, 3-inch cyliner for 1¼-inch pipe. To fit 1-inch hose coupling. Price	6.00	7.65

Iron and Brass Lined Force Pumps.

This pump is similar to our No. 24C5226 and the same description is applicable. It is only different in that it bolts to a plank and is designed to be fastened to the wall. No. 2. 2½-inch cylinder for 1¼-inch pipe. No. 4, 3-inch cylinder for 1¼-inch pipe. Complete as shown in illustration.

Figure 30

No. 24C5233
No. 2, Iron.........**$5.40**
No. 2, Brass lined, **6.98**

No. 24C5235
No. 4, Iron.........**$5.50**
No. 4, Brass lined, **7.65**

We can fully recommend our brass lined pumps to be equal to an all brass one, and much cheaper. The cylinder is lined with a seamless drawn brass tube. The plunger, piston rod, stuffing nut, and all working parts are brass, and have leather plungers operating in brass cylinders which are known to be almost indestructible.

House Force Pumps.

With Revolving Bearer and Brass Piston Rod.

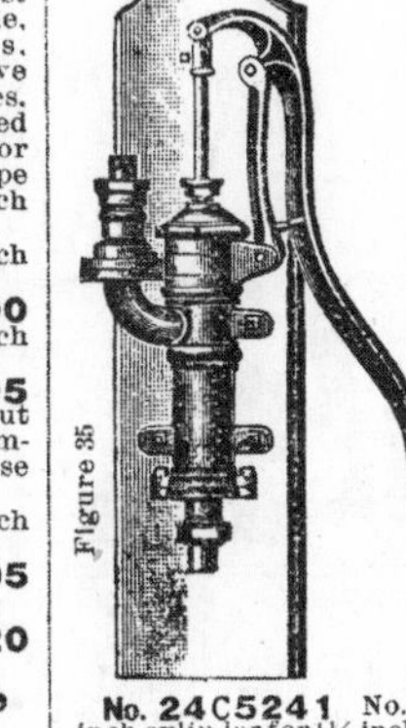

Figure 35

This House Pump is used to force water up into a tank or reservoir. It has a brass seat valve and is arranged for attaching either iron or lead pipe. It comes fastened to plank as shown in illustration, which can be placed against the wall, thus being out of the way of sink. It is a high class article and is guaranteed to do good work.

	Iron	Brass Lined
No. 24C5241 No. 2, 2½-inch cylinder for 1¼-inch pipe. Price	$4.10	$5.98
No. 24C5242 No. 4, 3-in. cylinder for 1¼-in. pipe. Price	4.60	5.50

HOW TO ORDER A PUMP.

When a pump is ordered for a well more than 25 or 30 feet deep, the cylinder should be placed within 10 feet of the bottom of the well. It might be well to add here that the nearer the cylinder is placed to the water the better it will work, and when possible it is always advisable to place the cylinder directly in the water. **When so ordered**, it takes more pump rod and pump rod couplings, and requires extra labor, for which we make an extra charge of 5 cents per foot for each foot the cylinder is put down. This charge is to be added to cost of pump and pipe complete.

NOTICE—The cost of pipe is not included in above extra charge. We give below a sample order for pump and pipe complete to reach 70 feet from platform with cylinder put down 65 feet.

No. 24C5278 One pump, No. 6...**$3.75**
No. 24C5710 70 feet black iron pipe. 1¼-inch, at 6½ cents.........**4.55**
To put cylinder down 65 feet at 5 cents **3.25**
Total.........**$11.55**

Anti-Freezing Closed Top Lift Pumps.

Adapted for wells not more than 30 feet deep. Has revolving top, so handle may be placed on either side or at back of spout in **any position desired.** It measures four feet from platform to bottom of cylinder. The pipe connecting cylinder and pump screws into the pump at the spout, thus **leaving an air space around the pipe** above the platform, which is a preventive against freezing. The cylinder is of the best quality and is fitted for 1¼-inch pipe, unless otherwise ordered. If well is more than 20 feet deep, we recommend placing a foot valve on end of pipe at bottom of the well. Pipe to reach from bottom of cylinder to bottom of well is not furnished at prices named below.

Figure 60

No. 24C5256 No. 4, 3-in. cylinder. Price....**$2.60**

No. 24C5257 No. 6, 3½-inch cylinder. Price.........**$3.05**

No. 24C5258 No. 8, 4-inch cylinder. Price.........**$3.50**

10-inch iron cylinders furnished with above pumps.

New Pattern Close Top Lift Pumps.

The bolts on cap and pitman are large, and will many times outwear the small ones in ordinary use. The pipe is screwed into pump just below the spout, which prevents freezing in winter. Has revolving top, so handle may be placed in any desired position. Has swinging fulcrum. The cylinder is of the best quality, and fitted for 1¼-inch pipe. It measures 4 feet from flange at platform to bottom of cylinder. For wells not more than 25 or 30 feet deep, order the pump as shown in illustration, and enough pipe to reach from bottom of cylinder (4 feet from platform) to the bottom of well. Extra pipe is not included with pump. For price of pipe, see No. 24C5710.

Figure 65

No. 24C5264 No. 2, 2½-inch cylinder.........**$2.65**

No. 24C5266 No. 4, 3-inch cylinder.**$2.70**

No. 24C5268 No. 6, 3½-inch cylinder.........**$3.35**

Above pump furnished with 10-inch iron cylinders. Brass cylinders furnished at an extra cost; see No. 24C5545 for difference in prices.

Lift Pump with Windmill Head.

Adapted for wells not more than 60 feet deep. May also be used for hand use. Pipe screws into standard at the spout. Has revolving top and swinging fulcrum. All parts are strong and durable. We can fully recommend it as a first class pump. Measures 4 feet from platform to bottom of cylinder. For wells not more than 25 or 30 feet deep, order pump as shown in illustration and enough 1¼-inch iron pipe to reach from bottom of cylinder (4 feet below platform) to bottom of well. Price of pipe is not included in price of pump. Average weight, 80 pounds. For price of pipe, see No. 24C5710.

Figure 70

No. 24C5274 No. 2, 2½-inch cylinder. Price.........**$3.40**

No. 24C5276 No. 4, 3-inch cylinder. Price.........**$3.55**

No. 24C5277 No. 5, extra heavy, 3¼-inch cylinder. Price.........**$3.60**

No. 24C5278 No. 6, extra heavy, 3½-inch cylinder. Price.........**$3.75**

Above pump furnished with 10-inch iron cylinders; brass body cylinders furnished at an extra cost of difference in price of cylinders. See No. 24C5545 for prices on brass body cylinders. When this pump is ordered for wells more than 25 or 30 feet deep, cylinder should be placed within 10 feet of the bottom of the well, for which we make an extra charge in addition to cost of pump and pipe, same as explained under No. 24C5242.

Extra Heavy Lift Pumps.

For Stockyards and Heavy Work.

This illustration represents our Heavy Set Length Lift Pump, adapted for stock yards and wells where large quantities of water are required. It measures 4 feet from flange at platform to bottom of cylinder. The set lengths are screwed in the pumps at the spout to prevent freezing in winter. The stocks are made very heavy and strong, and the cylinders are large and capable of throwing large quantities of water. We fully recommend it where a large amount of water is desired. Average weight, 88 lbs.

Figure 75

No. 24C5285 3½-inch cylinder, fitted for 1¼-inch pipe. Price....**$3.72**

No. 24C5286 4-inch cylinder, fitted for 1¼-inch pipe. Price.........**$3.98**

The above pumps are fitted with 10-inch iron cylinders; for brass body cylinders, see No. 24C5545. Can furnish brass body cylinders for difference in prices.

Price of pipe is not included in above prices. For pipe, see No. 24C5710.

Force Pumps.

Adapted for wells not more than 60 feet deep. The pipe which connects cylinder to pump is screwed into pump at spout, preventing freezing in winter. It has an outlet in rear of spout where a 1-inch pipe may be attached if desired, as shown in illustration No. 24C5310. Hose may be attached to the spout by means of the clevis which we furnish, as shown in illustration. We can also furnish with cock at spout if so ordered, at extra price. See No. 24C5310. It measures 4 feet from flange at platform to bottom of cylinder. The large pump will give best results in deep water.

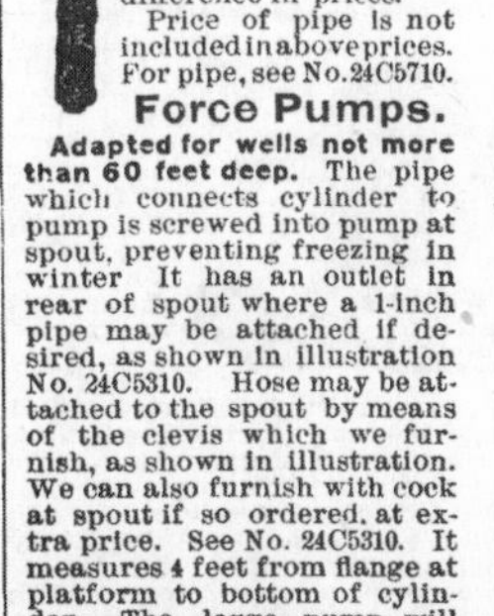

Figure 85

No.	Size	Cylinder	Price
24C5301	3	2½x10	$4.60
24C5302	4	3 x10	4.70
24C5303	5	3¼x10	5.10
24C5304	6	3½x10	5.15

The above pumps are fitted with iron cylinders. If wanted with brass cylinders add difference in price. See No. 24C5545.

Windmill Force Pumps.

This pump is exactly like No. 24C5301, except that it has a windmill head. We can fully recommend both of them as powerful force pumps. Size 8 is fitted for 1½-inch pipe; other sizes fitted for 1¼-inch pipe.

Figure 90

No.	Size	Cylinder	Price
24C5310	2	2½x10	$4.90
24C5312	4	3 x10	5.15
24C5313	5	3¼x10	5.20
24C5314	6	3½x10	5.30
24C5315	8	4 x10	5.70

EXTRAS—The above prices are for pump with Common Round Iron Spout with plug in back of standard for back attachment. Price of pipe to reach from bottom of cylinder to bottom of well is not included. For pipe see No. 24C5710. If this pump is ordered for well more than 25 or 30 feet deep, the cylinder should be placed within 10 feet of the bottom of the well. When so ordered we make an extra charge of 5 cents per foot for each foot the cylinder is put down. For full information read description given under No. 24C5242. These pumps can also be fitted with cock at spout (see illustration of pump No. 24C5310), for which we make an extra charge of 75 cents. These pumps can also be fitted with back attachment (see illustration of pump No. 24C5310), for which we make an extra charge of 90 cents. **Above pumps furnished with iron cylinder.** If wanted with brass cylinders, add difference to price. See No. 24C5545.

Acme Double Acting Force Pumps.

Acme Double Acting Force Pump, with windmill head and revolving spouts, for shallow or deep wells. The upper cylinder is heavy seamless drawn brass tubing. The lower cylinder is furnished with our new style brass poppet valves and brass valve seats. Each pump is furnished with our improved malleable hose attachment and suction strainer. When used in deep wells the lower cylinder should be lowered to within 10 to 15 feet of bottom of well, or, better still, placed in the water. We furnish this pump with windmill head which can be used by hand if so desired. For a deep well pump, say 125 to 150 feet, this pump has no equal.

Figure 95

No. 24C5317 Size cylinder, brass lined, 2½ inches, for 1¼-inch pipe. Price.........**$7.90**

No. 24C5318 Size cylinder, brass lined, 3 inches, for 1¼-inch pipe. Price.........**$8.15**

No. 24C5319 Size cylinder, brass lined, 3½ inches, for 1¼-inch pipe. Price.........**$8.27**

Double Acting Force Pump With Three-Way Cock.

This pump is the same as No. 24C5317 with the exception that it has a vertical three-way cock. With the aid of this three-way cock water can be forced underground into tanks or cisterns. Upper cylinder is brass, lower cylinder brass lined.

Figure 100

No. 24C5323 Size cylinder, 2½ inches, for 1¼-inch pipe. Price.........**$8.90**

No. 24C5324 Size cylinder, 3 inches, for 1¼-inch pipe. Price.........**$9.00**

No. 24C5325 Size cylinder, 3½ inches, for 1½ inch pipe. Price.........**$9.10**

Acme Double Acting Drilled Well Force Pump.

Our Acme Double Acting Drilled Well Force Pump is adapted for drilled wells of small bore, and is so constructed that the cylinder and all of its parts below the platform will enter and pass into the casing or drilled hole, thus avoiding the cutting off of the casing, so that the casing can be run up close to the platform, keeping out the surface water and all other impurities. Although this pump is especially adapted for drilled wells, it has no superior for dug or open wells. Lower cylinder is furnished with brass seat valves and poppet valves; also strainer and hose attachments furnished free of charge. Has brass lined upper cylinder and brass lower cylinder. A first class pump in every respect.

Figure 105

No. 24C5327 Size 2, has 2½-inch cylinder for 1¼-inch pipe. Will go into 3-inch cased well. Price.........**$8.75**

No. 24C5328 Size 4, has 3-inch cylinder for 1¼-inch pipe. Will go into 3½-inch cased well. Price.........**$8.90**

No. 24C5329 Size 6, has 3½-inch cylinder for 1¼-inch pipe. Will go into 4-inch cased well. Price.........**$9.35**

Windmill Head, Double Acting, Drilled Well Force Pump.

This pump is the same as No. 24C5327 except that it has a windmill head, which is an attachment to connect same to windmill. Material and workmanship guaranteed to be A 1. Nothing better made.

No. 24C5332 Size 2, has 2½-inch brass cylinder for 1¼-inch pipe. Will go into a 3-inch cased well. Price............**$8.80**

No. 24C5333 Size 4, has a 3-inch brass cylinder for 1¼-inch pipe. Will go into a 3½-inch cased well. Price............**$8.82**

No. 24C5334 Size 6, has a 3½-inch brass cylinder for 1½-inch pipe. Will go into a 4-inch cased well. Price............**$9.35**

If wanted with brass lined lower cylinder in place of all brass, deduct 50 cents from above prices.

New Acme Drilled Well Force Pumps.

Our New Acme Drilled Well Force Pump discharges a smooth, steady stream, and operates unusually easy, and is adapted for any kind of a well, but especially for cased wells of small diameter. A large air chamber is placed inside the stock. It is so constructed as to avoid any of the parts getting out of order beyond ordinary wear. The cylinders are fitted with our new style, all brass poppet valves. Strainer and hose attachment furnished free of charge.

No. 24C5336 Size 2, has 2½x12-inch brass flush capped cylinder for 1¼-inch pipe. Will go into a 3-inch cased well. Price............**$6.92**

No. 24C5337 Size 4, has a 3x12-inch brass flush capped cylinder for 1¼-inch pipe. Will go into a 3½-inch cased well. Price............**$6.98**

No. 24C5338 Size 6, has a 3½x12-inch brass flush capped cylinder for 1½-inch pipe. Will go into a 4-inch cased well. Price............**$8.75**

New Acme Drilled Well Force Pump, with Windmill Head.

Our New Acme Drilled Well Force Pump, with Windmill Head, is the same as No. 24C5336, except that it has a windmill head, so that it can be attached to a windmill. The best single acting pump sold by anyone.

No. 24C5340 Size 2, has a 2½x12 brass flush capped cylinder for 1¼-inch pipe, will go into a 3-inch cased well. Price............**$7.60**

No. 24C5341 Size 4, has a 3x12 brass flush capped cylinder for 1¼-inch pipe, will go into a 3½-inch cased well. Price............**$7.70**

No. 24C5342 Size 6, has a 3½x12 brass flush capped cylinder for 1½-inch pipe, will go into a 4-inch cased well. Price............**$8.57**

Acme Improved Windmill Force Pump Standards.

Our Improved Acme Windmill Force Pump Head or Standard, has brass stuffing box; hose connection on spout; is furnished at top with a special bushing which prevents the rod from wearing on the bearer. This pump is arranged with outlet back of spout or pump so that pipe can be attached for forcing water to tank or cistern. It is much heavier than the regular size standard, and is intended for deep wells.

NOTICE—If wanted with Cock Spout, add 75 cents to the following prices:

No. 24C5345 Size 1, 6-inch stroke, for 1¼-inch pipe. Price............**$3.35**

No. 24C5346 Size 2, 10-inch stroke, for 2-inch pipe. Price............**$3.70**

Hand and Windmill Force Pump Standard with Long Fulcrum.

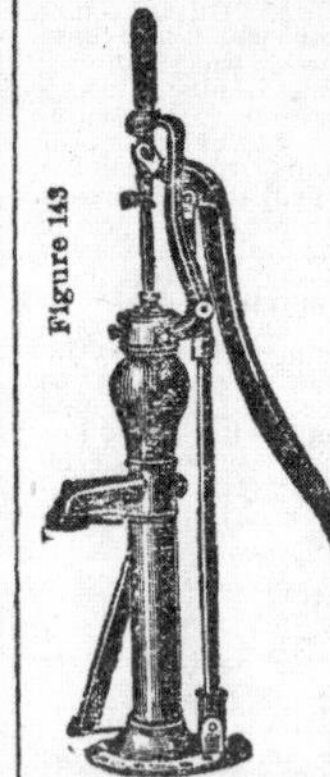

Figure 143

The special features of this pump are the long fulcrum and extra heavy cap and large wrought iron turned pins, making a better standard in every way than the common standard. The long fulcrum takes all strain off the top of pump and gives a greater leverage, therefore works much easier. It is tapped at back so that a pipe may be attached for elevating water into a tank or to the house or barn. Please notice that we furnish a brace with all long fulcrum standards. Prices given below are for standard only, **as shown in illustration.** Cylinder and pipe cost extra. See page 473. Tapped for 1¼-inch pipe. Hose attachment and cut off clevis furnished free of charge.

No. 24C5348 Price, 6-inch stroke. **$4.00**

Extra Heavy Windmill Standards.

This illustration represents our extra heavy Windmill Pump Standard. It is much heavier than our common windmill pump, and the spout is higher from the base. Furnished complete with guides and rods. Tapped for 1¼-inch pipe.

No. 24C5349 6-inch stroke. Price............**$3.00**

No. 24C5350 10-inch stroke. Price............**$3.35**

Underground Valve Force Pumps.

This pump is especially adapted for 2-inch tubular wells, also 1¼-inch pipe for open or drilled wells. By operating the wheel in the top of the gooseneck, the water may be discharged either through the spout or through the underground pipe at the bridgepiece below. It differs from other three-way valve pumps in that the operating screw, which is of brass, is below, near the valve, and not at the gooseneck, consequently there is no liability to chill and freeze. The pipe on the right forms the air chamber. When this pump is used for tubular wells, it is made with a cap at the stuffing box, which, when unscrewed, leaves an opening large enough to pull the plunger up through without disconnecting the pipe or disturbing the pump in any way. This pump is always sent for 2-inch pipe, but may be bushed for smaller sizes, 1¼-inch discharge pipe. Gooseneck to fit 1-inch hose coupling.

No. 24C5352 6-inch stroke. Price............**$7.40**

No. 24C5353 10-inch stroke. Price............**$7.75**

Suction pipe and rod coupling connect at B; discharge pipe connects at A.

NOTICE—The above prices are for the pump stock only; cylinder and pipe are extra. See No. 24C5528 for cylinder, and No. 24C5710 for pipe.

EXTRAS—To make complete outfit, select cylinder desired and quantity of pipe wanted for suction, also number of feet of pipe wanted for discharge. State number of feet cylinder shall be put down, and in addition to cost of standard, cylinder and pipe, add 5 cents per foot for each foot the cylinder is put down.

Acme Rotary Power Force Pumps.

This illustration shows our Acme Rotary Power Pumps, without outside gearing, arranged with tight and loose pulleys. It is well adapted for a small fire pump, and will throw water from 125 to 150 feet horizontally. The driving shaft is made of ample length to permit a balance wheel with handle to be placed on the outside of the bearing, readily enabling it to be worked by hand in an emergency. The spout is screwed for hose on the outer end, and for wrought iron pipe where it connects to the pump. These pumps can be run up to 200 revolutions per minute without injury, although we recommend a lower rate of speed. Should not be placed over 15 to 20 feet distance from water. The second column of figures gives the capacity per minute of 100 revolutions.

Cat. No.	Gal.	Size, Suction Pipe	Size, Discharge Pipe	Size, Pulleys	Price
24C5370	13	1¼ ins.	1 in.	8x2½	$ 6.75
24C5371	14	1¼ ins.	1 in.	8x2½	9.30
24C5372	17	1½ ins.	1¼ ins.	8x2½	12.00
24C5373	27	2 ins.	1½ ins.	12x3½	16.00
24C5374	36	2 ins.	2 ins.	12x3½	18.25

Acme Tank Pump.

No. 24C5386 **Our Acme Low Down Tank Pump** is by far the most powerful pump made. It is made on new principles. The cylinder being in a horizontal position, we gain great strength and simplicity. It is strictly a double acting pump, sucking water at each stroke of the pump. The cylinder is 5 inches in diameter, with a 5-inch stroke. Openings are 2 inches for suction and discharge. Spout is attached to top of pump, is reversible and is so arranged that the largest pail can be placed under it, thus avoiding lead hose when a pail of water is wanted. It has a capacity of 2 barrels per minute and will throw a stream of water 60 feet. Guaranteed to be the best pump of its kind made or money refunded.

Price............**$4.95**

Figure 200

NOTICE—We furnish a large size strainer with each pump free of charge.

Big 6 Double Acting Force Pump.

With Air Chamber and Adjustable Handle.

Our Big 6 Double Acting Force Pump is especially adapted for elevating water from cisterns to tanks in upper stories of residences. It is also used largely for cleaning and filling boilers and for fire protection, or can be used as a deck pump and many other purposes. All sizes are fitted with all brass valves. Brass plugs are provided for draining cylinder to prevent freezing, and also for priming when necessary. The air chamber can be reversed so that discharge may be used on either side. The suction and discharge are always fitted for iron pipe unless otherwise ordered, but can be fitted for hose or lead pipe if specified.

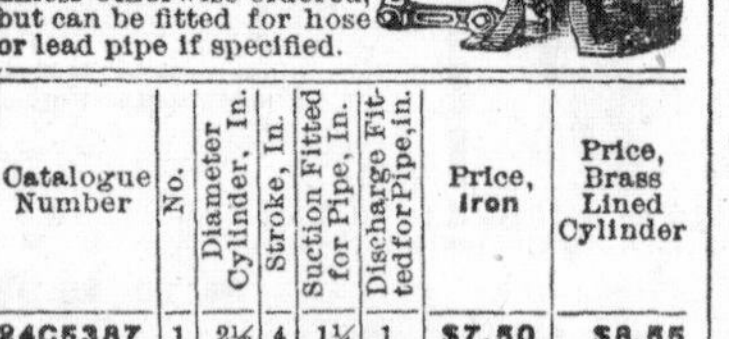

Catalogue Number	No.	Diameter Cylinder, In.	Stroke, In.	Suction Fitted for Pipe, In.	Discharge Fitted for Pipe, in.	Price, Iron	Price, Brass Lined Cylinder
24C5387	1	2½	4	1¼	1	$7.50	$8.55
24C5388	2	3	4	1¼	1¼	8.50	9.90

Tank Hose, Clamp, Etc.

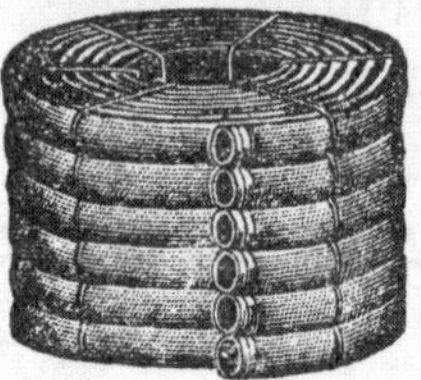

Standard grade, wire lined, smooth bore Tank Hose, sold in 15, 20 and 25-foot pieces only. The 2-inch size is used in connection with our 24C5386 Tank Pumps.

	No. 24C5391		
Size, inches	1¼	1½	2
Price, per foot	19c	22c	23c

High Grade Tank Hose.

Below we list a high grade of 2-inch Suction Hose, wire lined, such as is used on our tank pumps. While our No. 24C5391 is the best hose for the money sold by anyone and is the grade generally sold, we have had calls for something better.

No. 24C5392 Size, 2-inch, Acme brand, per foot......**33c**

Size, 2-inch Sampson brand. Price, per foot............**43c**

No. 24C5393 2-inch Hose Clamps for above hose. Price, **8c**

Hard Rubber Suction Hose.

In smaller sizes than 2-inch, we list a suction hose without any wire insertion, called hard rubber suction. This is made with hard, thick walls to prevent collapsing when in use. We carry two grades of the above hose. Sold in multiples of five feet only, as 5, 10, 15 or 20-foot pieces, etc., and up to and including 50 feet.

No. 24C5394 No. 1 size..1 in. 1¼ in. 1½ in. 2 in. Price, per foot............**29c 36c 43c 65c**

No. 24C5395 No. 2 size...¾ in. 1 in. 1¼ in. Price, per foot............**16c 19c 23c**

Frictionless Non-Chokable Pumps.

This pump is fitted to connect with 2½-inch or 3-inch suction hose and is the best and most efficient hand power pump ever placed upon the market, and also the most desirable pump ever used by sewer contractors, foundation or bridge builders, or in water works. The pump being frictionless, and having large, open valve ways, is especially adapted for sewer departments, or for pumping drainage or sewerage matter, sanitary deposits, mud, gravel, quicksands, etc.

No.	Size of Suction Hose	Capacity per Hour
1....	2½ inches	1,500 gallons
2....	3 inches	3,500 gallons

No. 24C5406 Price, with side or bottom suction, No. 1............**$9.60**

No. 24C5408 Price, with side or bottom suction, No. 2............**$13.00**

Wood Pumps.

Our Wood Pumps are made from selected stock, thoroughly painted, striped and varnished. They are furnished with iron handle brackets and iron spouts. The plunger, which is the vital part of a suction pump, is of the latest improved pattern. Adapted for wells not more than 30 feet deep.

To Select a Pump: For wells 20 feet or less deep, use 6-foot pump. For wells 20 to 25 feet deep, use 7-foot pump. For wells 25 to 30 feet deep, use 8-foot pump. Besides the pump, order enough tubing of size to match pump to reach from bottom of pump to bottom of well. Tubing comes in lengths of 12 feet and less. When more than 12 feet of tubing will be required order a coupling to connect the tubing.

Wood Farm Pumps.

General Purpose Pump is 6 inches square, 3½-inch bore, 9-inch stroke. Capacity, 60 gallons per minute. While this pump throws an ample supply of water, ladies and children can work the pump with ease. Average weight about 47 pounds.

No.	Length	Price, plain pump	Price, with porcelain lined cylinder
24C5412	6 feet	$2.35	$3.20
24C5413	7 feet	2.60	3.25
24C5414	8 feet	2.85	3.60

No. 24C5415 Tubing to fit above pump, 4 inches square, with 1⅝-inch bore. Price, per foot............**8½c**

No. 24C5416 Couplings for tubing. Price............**23c**

Wood Stock Pumps.

Stock Pump is 7 inches square, 4-inch bore, 10-inch stroke. Capacity, 80 gallons per minute. These pumps are particularly adapted to the wants of farmers and stockmen using large quantities of water. They should not be used in wells where the water is more than 15 or 20 feet from the platform, as the quantity of water which the pump lifts at each stroke would cause it to work hard in deep wells. Average weight about 50 pounds.

No.	Length	Price, plain pump	Price, porcelain lined cylinder
24C5418	6 feet.	$3.25	$4.00
24C5419	7 feet.	3.65	4.45
24C5420	8 feet.	4.00	4.70

No. 24C5424 **Tubing for above Pump,** 4 inches square, 2-inch bore. Price, per foot. **10c**

No. 24C5425 **Couplings for Tubing.** Price............**23c**

Acme Improved Purifying Pumps.

Our Acme Purifying Pump is the simplest structure for raising water and at the same time purifying it, in the world. It is adjustable to any well or cistern, and is very durable, being an endless chain composed of links all made from the best of galvanized wire, manufactured and tempered expressly for these pumps. The cups are made of the best grade of galvanized iron.

It always furnishes the water from the bottom of the well, as no water enters the cups until they begin to rise at the bottom of the well, when the air immediately escapes and they are filled with the best and coldest water, and has none of the objections common to other pumps. There are no suckers or valves, no wooden tubing to rot out or rusty iron to come in contact with the water, but everything is kept pure and wholesome.

Average weight about 75 pounds.

No. 24C5442 Complete for 10-foot well. Price...**$4.35**
No. 24C5443 Complete for 15-foot well. Price...**5.35**
No. 24C5444 Complete for 20-foot well. Price...**6.15**
No. 24C5445 Extra Galvanized Buckets and Chain. Price, per foot............**.08¾**

Acme Hydraulic Rams.

Our Hydraulic Ram is one of the oldest makes on the market. Thousands of them in use at the present time. It is made of the best materials; has brass fittings, etc. Sent with a guarantee to be the best ram on the market for anything like what we ask for them.

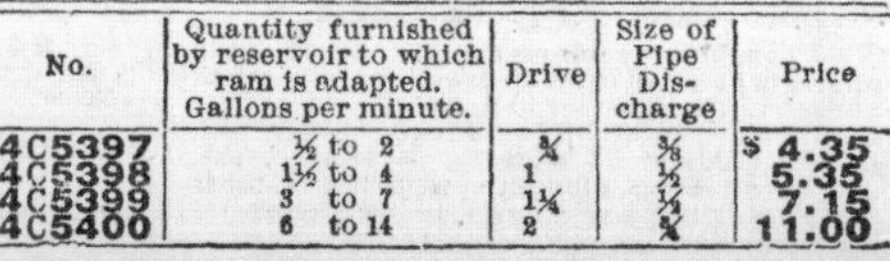

No.	Quantity furnished by reservoir to which ram is adapted. Gallons per minute.	Drive	Size of Pipe Discharge	Price
24C5397	½ to 2	¾	⅜	$ 4.35
24C5398	1½ to 4	1	½	5.35
24C5399	3 to 7	1¼	½	7.15
24C5400	6 to 14	2	¾	11.00

Star Water Elevator and Purifying Pumps.

Our Star Water Elevator is of the same construction as No. 24C5442, purifying the water; a galvanized steel curb in place of wood. This makes a much better pump in every way, will last longer, will not rust or decay; all castings and fittings are extra heavy. Furnished complete with galvanized buckets and chain.

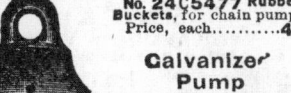

No. 24C5446 Complete with buckets for 10-foot well. Price......**$6.30**
No. 24C5447 Complete with buckets for 15-foot well. Price......**$7.20**
No. 24C5448 Complete with buckets for 20-foot well. Price......**$8.00**
No. 24C5449 Complete with buckets for 25-foot well. Price......**$8.95**
No. 24C5450 Complete with buckets for 30-foot well. Price......**$9.75**
No. 24C5453 **Extra Galvanized Buckets.** Price, per foot......**8¾c**

Star All Galvanized Steel Chain Pump Curb, with Galvanized Steel Tubing.

The Star Patent Galvanized Steel Curbs are made entirely of No. 24 gauge galvanized steel, have many and great advantages over any and all others. They are fitted with a heavy cast iron base at the bottom to support the curb, which allows the body of the curb to project down and into the opening in the well or cistern cover. This, with the special feature of the fixtures being set below the top line of the curb, prevents any water leaking out on the top of the well or cistern cover, and when top of curb is off the fixtures are fully protected by the sides of the curb. These curbs are fitted with our latest improved noiseless roller bearing fixtures that, with their construction, material and workmanship, makes them the most complete chain pump curb on the market. The tubing is made of the best grade No. 24 galvanized steel, is formed perfectly round, with seam air and water tight. We would not advise using this pump in wells over thirty feet deep.

Prices given below include reservoir and all, complete.

No. 24C5455 Price, for 10-foot well, complete......**$3.90**
No. 24C5456 Price, for 12-foot well, complete......**4.20**
No. 24C5457 Price, for 15-foot well, complete......**4.35**
No. 24C5458 Price, for 18-foot well, complete......**4.90**
No. 24C5459 Price, for 20-foot well, complete......**5.00**

Rubber Bucket Chain Pumps.

No. 24C5472 **Rubber Bucket Chain Pump**, complete for well 10 feet deep. Price......**$2.50**
No. 24C5473 **Rubber Bucket Chain Pump**, complete for well 12 feet deep. Price......**$2.70**
No. 24C5474 **Rubber Bucket Chain Pump**, complete for well 15 feet deep. Price......**$3.00**
No. 24C5475 **Rubber Bucket Chain Pump**, complete for well 18 feet deep. Price......**$3.35**
No. 24C5476 **Rubber Bucket Chain Pump**, complete for well 20 feet deep. Price...**$3.50**

We do not advise the use of chain pumps for wells deeper than 20 feet.

Chain Pump Buckets.

No. 24C5477 **Rubber Buckets**, for chain pump. Price, each......**4c**

Galvanized Pump Chain.

No. 24C5478 **Extra Chain** for above pumps. Price, per foot.....**2¾c**

Chain Pump Tubing.

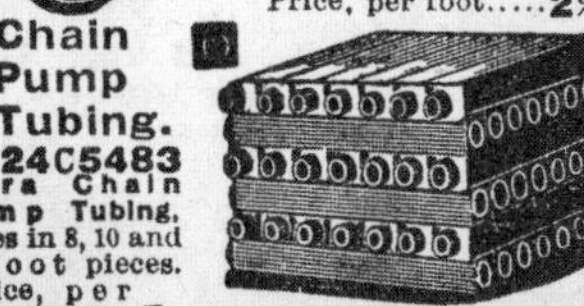

No. 24C5483 **Extra Chain Pump Tubing**, comes in 8, 10 and 12-foot pieces. Price, per foot......**5c**

Galvanized Steel Tubing.

Reservoir Tubing.

Funnel Tubing.

Plain Tubing.

No. 24C5486 **Galvanized Steel Tubing**, to be used in connection with our No. 24C5472 to No. 24C5476 chain pumps. Furnished in 5-foot, 6-foot, 7-foot, 8-foot, 9-foot and 10-foot lengths. Reservoir tubing is used in connection with the pump curb. Funnel tubing goes at bottom of pump, and plain tubing is used for connecting the reservoir and funnel tubing where the two above pieces are not sufficient for the depth of the well. Either style same price. Be sure and state style wanted. Price, per foot......**6c**

Acme Sprayer or Lightning Bug Exterminator.

We have improved our Acme Sprayer for this season, and have now the best low priced sprayer sold by anyone. It is made of heavy IX tin: piston rod is made of a heavy steel rod, with a hardwood stuffing box. Cylinder is 1¾x15 inches. Weight, about 2 pounds.

No. 24C5490 Price, IX tin......**23c**
No. 24C5492 Price, brass tank with brass tube......**50c**

Glass Reservoir Sprayer.

No. 24C5493 **Our Glass Reservoir Sprayer** has detachable glass reservoir, provided with our patent spring leather plunger expander, which at all times keeps the leather washer expanded and will not allow it to wrinkle or dry up, which was the case with former sprayers. It is the only sprayer having a glass reservoir, detachable, encased, so that the operator at all times can see the ingredients mixing, and just how they are working. Weight, about 2½ pounds. Price......**44c**

Acme Sprayer.

A Self-Operating or Automatic Sprayer.

The Climax of all Sprayers; combines every conceivable point of excellence, including economy, durability, low price and ease in carrying and operating. Nothing but galvanized iron and solid brass or copper used in making the Acme Sprayer with four-ply rubber hose—nothing to rust or corrode; eight to ten strokes of plunger in air chamber will compress enough air to discharge the entire contents and make a continuous spray for nine minutes. This means that the Acme Sprayer can be charged in fifteen seconds, when it will work uninterruptedly long enough to spray a quarter acre of potatoes. Weight, about 7½ pounds.

No. 24C5501 Price, sprayer complete, galvanized iron tank......**$3.25**
No. 24C5502 Price, sprayer complete, brass tank......**4.55**
Price, 2-foot extension pipe, galvanized......**.20**
Price, 2-foot extension pipe, brass......**.28**

The Acme Knapsack Sprayer.

Concaved to fit the back. All Brass Pump.

No. 24C5505 **This machine consists of a tank holding four gallons and a pump made entirely of brass, which cannot corrode or rust.** There is a large air chamber placed inside the tank for convenience, which has sufficient capacity to keep up the pressure and continue to discharge the spray for one minute after the operator stops pumping. The lower valve is screwed to bottom of cylinder, hence no trouble or expense to reach the valves. There is a large opening on top for the reception of liquid, with a fine strainer set inside. Four feet of best rubber hose and a brass pipe 15 inches long with a stop cock are furnished with each machine. The nozzle is our combination Vermorel, so highly recommended, and gives universal satisfaction. For vineyards, nurseries, potato, tobacco and cotton fields. Price, with galvanized tank...**$ 6.25**
Price, copper tank, with agitator......**10.00**

Acme High Grade Barrel Spraying Pumps.

Acme New Improved Barrel Spray Pump with brass upper and brass lined lower cylinders, brass plunger, brass check valve and brass valve seats. All working parts coming in contact with the liquid are brass. The body of the pump is a large air chamber and after the pump is under pressure it will discharge a steady spray lasting two minutes or more with one stroke of the handle, thus making it easy to operate. It is double acting, discharging half the water on the up stroke and half on the down stroke of the handle. Each pump is fitted with a jet agitator or can be furnished with a paddle agitator, if preferred, at an extra charge. It can be used for many other purposes besides spraying, such as washing windows, buggies, extinguishing fires, sprinkling lawns, flowers, etc. Prices do not include the barrel.

No. 24C5513 Includes pump, jet agitator, suction pipe and brass strainer (no hose). Price......**$5.40**
No. 24C5514 Includes pump and trimmings, complete, with one lead ½-inch, three-ply discharge hose, 5 feet long and Vermorel nozzle. Price......**$7.00**
No. 24C5515 Includes pump and trimmings, complete, with two leads ½-inch, three-ply discharge hose, each 5 feet long and Vermorel nozzle. Price......**$8.00**

Bordeaux nozzles will be furnished in place of Vermorel, if preferred, at same price.

No. 24C5516 Galvanized extension tubes, 8 feet long. Price......**45c**

Improved Spray and Force Pump.

No. 24C5518 **Improved Spray and Force Pump.** It is beyond question the most perfect and effective hand apparatus ever invented for throwing water. It supplies a universal want, for every family needs some kind of a force sprinkler and pump. In variety of service, simplicity of construction and ease of operation, it has no equal. Is always ready for use, not liable to get out of order, and so light and convenient that it can be used easily and effectively by anyone. Made of heavy, bright tin coated with Egyptian lacquer. Weight, 2¾ pounds. Price......**65c**

Spraying Pump.

No. 24C5520 **The construction of the pump requires the pressure on the handle to be all done on the down stroke**, the pressure on the cylinder acting as a cushion, and partly forcing the handle up again, thus making it very easy of operation, requiring no foot rest or other device to steady it. The hose can be detached at top of pump and a nozzle attached in its place, either for spraying, sprinkling, or throwing a solid stream. It is also arranged so that a small stream is discharged with great force from the bottom of the pump into the bucket or barrel, serving to thoroughly agitate the mixture at all times when the pump is in use. For washing buggies, windows, etc., it is very useful. Weight, about 5 pounds. Price.....**$2.12**

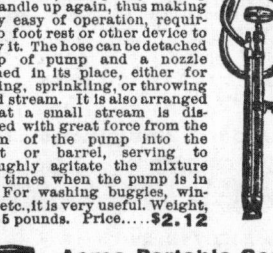

Acme Portable Cast Force Pump.

No. 24C5523 **Our Acme Portable Cast Force Pump is one of the most effective hand pumps on the market.** Is made extra strong; nicely finished. Is adapted for spraying trees, washing windows and wagons, sprinkling lawns, etc. Furnished complete with hose and connections, brass nozzle and sprinkler. Weight, 11¾ pounds. Price......**$4.10**

Acme Fire Extinguisher.

No. 24C5525 **A device that every store, factory and residence should be equipped with.** Absolute protection against loss by fire can now be assured to property owners at a small cost. The Acme Chemical Fire Extinguisher is the simplest and most powerful machine made. It is made of heavy copper securely riveted and soldered and highly polished. Holds three gallons and throws a stream 40 feet when in action. The solution used contains no acids to destroy fabrics, etc., although it is the most powerful fire extinguisher solution known. Solution for re-charging can be obtained from any druggist for 15 cents. Full directions sent with each machine. Weight when ready for use 12 pounds.
Price......**$4.95**

Pump Cylinders.

By means of the cylinder water is raised, and unless the cylinder is well made no good results can be obtained. A good cylinder must be bored true and plunger must fit accurately. Valves must be simple and durable. The cost of repairing a cylinder is usually more than its first cost, so it pays to get the best. Our cylinders are the best that skilled workmen can produce and our prices as low as equally well made goods can be sold for. Cylinders 10 inches long have 6-inch stroke and can be used in wells up to 35 feet deep. Cylinders 12 inches long have 6-inch stroke and can be used in wells up to 75 feet deep. Cylinders 14 inches long have 8-inch stroke and can be used in wells up to 150 feet deep. Cylinders 16 inches long have 10-inch stroke and can be used in wells up to 200 feet deep. Cylinders 2 inches in diameter are fitted for 1-inch pipe. Cylinders 3½ inches in diameter are fitted for 1½-inch pipe. Cylinders 4 inches in diameter are fitted for 2-inch pipe. All others fitted for 1¼-inch pipe.

No.	Diam. inch.	10 in. long	12 in. long	14 in. long	16 in. long	18 in. long
24C5528	2	$0.66	.94	1.03	1.05	1.28
24C5529	2¼	.68	.98	1.10	1.12	1.37
24C5530	2½	.74	1.00	1.17	1.18	1.42
24C5531	2¾	.79	1.10	1.27	1.28	1.52
24C5532	3	.85	1.17	1.40	1.42	1.68
24C5533	3¼	.98	1.34	1.63	1.65	1.98
24C5534	3½	1.18	1.50	1.93	1.95	2.42
24C5535	4	1.50	1.95	2.45	2.50	3.08

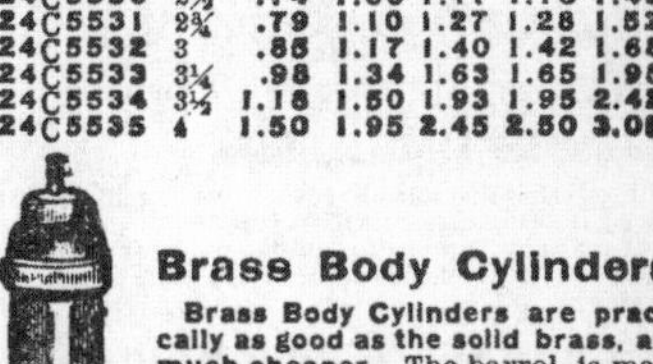

Brass Body Cylinders.

Brass Body Cylinders are practically as good as the solid brass, and much cheaper. The barrel is made of a seamless brass tube, and workmanship, stroke and capacity are all same as iron cylinders. 10 and 12-inch cylinders have 6-inch stroke, 14-inch cylinder has 8-inch stroke and 16-inch cylinder has 10-inch stroke.

No.	Diam. inch.	10 in. long	12 in. long	14 in. long	16-in. long	18 in. long
24C5545	2	$1.80	1.86	2.24	2.26	2.70
24C5546	2¼	1.82	1.88	2.26	2.28	3.00
24C5547	2½	1.83	1.98	2.36	2.38	3.20
24C5548	2¾	1.88	2.02	2.46	2.48	3.36
24C5549	3	2.12	2.18	2.61	2.63	3.50
24C5550	3¼	2.45	2.58	3.12	3.15	3.70
24C5551	3½	2.48	2.60	3.18	3.20	4.20
24C5552	4	3.00	3.25	3.90	3.95	5.50

Artesian Well Brass Cylinders.

This illustration represents our all brass cylinder to be used in artesian wells, the shell being made of heavy seamless brass tubing, fitted with hard brass or bronze ball valves and which are supplied with best cupped oak tanned leathers. This cylinder may be placed in open wells and in drilled wells where the pipe or casing is long enough to take the cylinder attachments. They are adapted to work in the deepest well.

NOTE—The plunger and lower valves may be removed through the connecting pipe, which is larger in diameter than the bore of the cylinder, thus making it convenient when repairs are necessary.

No.	Length of Cylinder, Inches	Stroke, Inches	Inside Diameter, inches	Fitted for Pipe	Price
24C5560	36	16	1⅜	1½-inch	$ 7.50
24C5561	33	16	1¾	2 -inch	9.50
24C5562	43	24	2¼	2½-inch	15.00
24C5563	45	24	2¾	3 -inch	18.00
24C5564	49	24	3¼	3½-inch	25.00
24C5565	51	24	3¾	4 -inch	36.00
24C5566	59	30	4¼	4½-inch	46.00

Ball Valve Pump Cylinders.

In our Ball Valve Cylinder we have the best deep valve cylinder made. In putting down a 75 to 300-foot well, it is very essential that you have a cylinder that will work well at all times, and last a lifetime. Pulling up a pump of this kind costs money. This cylinder is fitted with a four leather plunger and brass bronze ball valve, which will raise a greater amount of water and last longer than any cylinder on the market.

NOTE—Iron cylinders are furnished with outside cap only. Can furnish brass body cylinders with inside cap if so wanted. Be sure to state whether inside or outside cap is wanted. Be sure to state style wanted.

No.	Size, Inches	Fitted Pipe, Inches	Stroke, Inches	Price, Iron	Price, Brass Body
24C5570	2 x16	1¼	8	$2.70	$3.50
24C5571	2¼x16	1¼	8	3.00	4.00
24C5572	2½x16	1¼	8	3.35	4.30
24C5573	2 x18	1¼	10	2.90	4.00
24C5574	2¼x18	1¼	10	3.15	4.35
24C5575	2½x18	1¼	10	3.50	4.70
24C5576	2¾x18	1¼	8	4.45	5.40
24C5577	3 x18	1¼	8	5.70	7.00
24C5578	2 x20	1¼	12	3.05	4.35
24C5579	2¼x20	1¼	12	3.35	4.75
24C5580	2½x20	1¼	12	3.70	4.85
24C5581	2¾x20	1¼	10	4.45	5.95
24C5582	3 x20	1¼	10	5.60	8.00

Tubular Well Cylinders.

Used in deep tubular wells, or in wells where water has given out and you wish to drive pipe further down. It slips inside the pipe and can be set at any desired distance; can be removed for repairing by simply disconnecting handle of pump and drawing cylinder out. No pump tools required. The body is made of seamless drawn brass tubing, with brass valves. Stroke, 12 inches. Not made smaller than 2 inches.

No. 24C5592 Size, 2-inch. Price.................. **$2.10**

No. 24C5593 Size, 2½-inch. Price.................. **$3.25**

No. 24C5594 Size, 3-inch. Price.................. **$4.50**

Little Patent Automatic Pipe Holder.

No. 24C5611 Little Patent Automatic Pipe Holder, simple, strong and quick acting. Has adjustable set screws for different size pipe. Dog and catch are made of best grade steel. Every machine made of best quality material. No. 1 holds 1, 1¼ or 1½-inch pipe. Price........ **$2.60**

Little Giant Pipe Holder.

No. 24C5612 Something new in pipe holders. Will hold either 1, 1¼ or 1½-inch pipe. Dog has corrugated chilled surface; pipe cannot slip. Well made, nicely finished. A practical tool. Price........ **$2.65**

Acme Pipe Pullers.

This puller is made in different sizes to fit pipe from 1 inch to 4 inches in diameter. Dies have threads that will not crush pipe or allow same to slip. Is large enough for the coupling of pipe to pass through. This puller is used in connection with jack screws, which are placed under each lug or ear. For prices on jack screws see No. 24C1355, page 465. For pulling pipe this tool has no equal. Prices given below are for puller and one set of dies only. Be sure and state size wanted. Four or five different sizes can be used in the same holder, however.

No. 24C5613 No. 2 Puller, with one Set of Dies, either 1, 1¼, 1½ or 2-inch. Price, per set........ **$1.35**

No. 3 Puller, with one Set of Dies, either 2, 2½ or 3-inch. Price, per set........ **$2.55**

No. 4 Puller, with one Set of Dies, either 3½ or 4-inch. Price, per set........ **$4.35**

No. 6 Puller, with one Set of Dies, either 4, 4½, 5 or 6-inch. Price, per set........ **$6.20**

Price of Extra Dies.

Extra Dies for No. 2 Holder,	1-in.	1¼-in.	1½-in.	2-in.
Price, each	45c	43c	28c	27c
Extra Dies for No. 3 Holder,	2-in.	2½-in.	3-in.	
Price, each	44c	41c	40c	
Extra Dies for No. 4 Holder,	3½-in.	4-in.		
Price, each	$1.05	95c		
Extra Dies for No. 6 Stock,	4-in.	4½-in.	5-in.	6-in.
Price	$1.50	$1.45	$1.35	$1.20

Babcock Pipe Lifter.

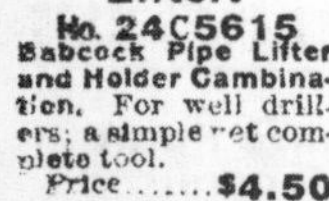

No. 24C5615 Babcock Pipe Lifter and Holder Combination. For well drillers; a simple yet complete tool. Price........ **$4.50**

Pipe Lifting Clevis.

No. 24C5617 Pipe Lifting Clevis. A handy device to prevent pipe from slipping when being taken from well. Price, for 1 or 1¼-inch pipe........ **62c**

Pump Leathers.

No. 24C5655 Plunger Leathers, made of the best grade oak tanned stock. Plain.

Diam. cyl. inches	2	2¼	2½	2¾	3	3½	4
Price	2½c	3c	4c	4c	4½c	5c	6c

Plunger Leathers, Crimped.

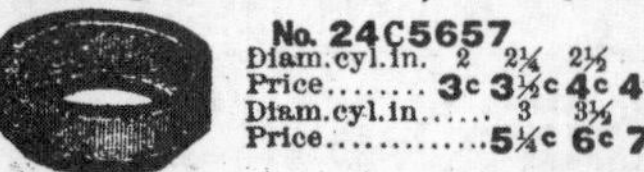

No. 24C5657

Diam. cyl. in.	2	2¼	2½	2¾
Price	3c	3½c	4c	4½c
Diam. cyl. in.	3	3½	4	
Price	5½c	6c	7c	

Lower Valve Leathers.

No. 24C5659 Our special price, 2½c to 6c.

Diam. cyl. inches	2	2¼
Price	2½c	3c
Diam. cyl. inches	2½	2¾
Price	4c	4c
Diam. cyl. inches	3	3½	4
Price	4½c	5c	6c

Well Caps.

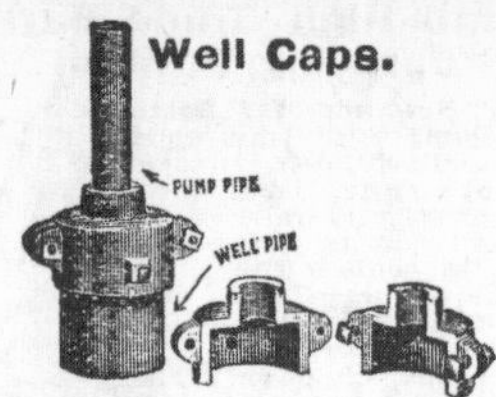

No. 24C5664 Well Caps to be used on drilled wells where well casing is used. Cap fits over end of casing and then clamps on to well pipe which holds same in place; also keeps out all dirt, rats, or any refuse that may drop in from platform of well. Sizes, 3½, 4½ and 5 inches. Give size of your casing. Price, each........ **$1.00**

Water Conductor.

No. 24C5665 This Cast Iron Conductor hangs over and directly under the spout of the pump. The pipe is screwed in at lower outlet on side to conduct water to a tank or trough that may be some distance from the pump. Price, 1¼ or 1½-inch pipe... **23c**

Foot Valves.

We recommend that Foot Valve and Strainer should be placed on lower end of pipe in wells more than 15 or 18 feet deep. It makes pump work much easier and the strainer prevents anything from entering the pipe which might clog the valves in cylinder. Made in two sizes.

No. 24C5670 For 1¼-inch pipe. Price. **24c**

No. 24C5671 For 1½-inch pipe. Price. **35c**

No. 24C5672 For 2-inch pipe. Price. **48c**

Drive Well Points.

Drive Well Points are made of wrought iron pipe, galvanized inside and out after the holes are punched. It is covered with a brass gauze, and gauze is covered and protected by a perforated brass jacket. No. 60 gauze is most commonly used. No. 100 gauze is for quicksand. Either flush point for tubular wells or with cast head for driving. Be sure and state which is wanted.

No. 24C5680 Flush Point.
No. 24C5681 Cast Point.

Diam. inches	Length, inches	60 Gauze, Price	100 Gauze, Price
1¼	24	$0.47	$1.08
1¼	30	.62	1.34
1¼	36	.76	1.61
1¼	42	.88	1.90
1½	30	.80	1.61
1½	36	.96	1.91
2	36	1.40	2.57
2	48	1.70	3.33

24C5680 24C5681

Acme Well Force Pump Packing Heads.

No. 24C5686 Straight Rod Packing Head or Stuffing Box for Windmill and Force Pumps, made of the best grade malleable iron, with brass glands and brass rods. It has ½-inch rod coupling at top and 7-16-inch rod coupling at bottom. Size for pipe, inch, 1 1¼

Price........ **$1.15** **$1.20**

Size for pipe, inch 1½ 2

Price........ **$1.21** **1.22**

Standard Wrought Iron Pipe.

No. 24C5710 Black Iron Pipe.
No. 24C5711 Galvanized Iron Pipe.

Black and Galvanized. For steam, gas and water. When pipe is ordered in full lengths, one coupling is furnished free with each piece. Prices given below are for pipe in random lengths (16 to 20 ft.) Where you specify exact lengths we charge for threads on both ends as per list below. No coupling with pipe cut to exact length. Prices of pipe subject to fluctuations of the market.

Inside Diameter	Pounds per foot	Black, per foot	Galvanized, per foot	Extra threads, per cut
⅛-inch	¼	2c	3c	2c
¼-inch	⅜	2c	3c	2c
⅜-inch	½	2c	3c	2c
½-inch	⅝	3c	4c	2c
¾-inch	1 1/10	3½c	5c	2c
1-inch	1⅝	4¾c	7c	3c
1¼-inch	2⅜	6½c	9½c	3c
1½-inch	3⅛	7¾c	11½c	4c
2 -inch	3¾	10½c	15½c	4c
2½-inch	5¾	16½c	24c	8c
3 -inch	7½	22c	32c	10c
3½-inch	9	27½c	38c½	12c
4 -inch	10⅝	31c	46c	16c
4½-inch	12½	37½c	55c	22c
5 -inch	14½	42c	61c	24c
6 -inch	18¾	54c	81c	32c

Be sure to allow for cost of cutting threads when pipe is ordered cut to exact lengths.

Iron Pipe Fittings.

We illustrate the fittings that are commonly used, but can furnish any fitting that is made. If you want any fitting not quoted here, you can safely order it from us, allowing sufficient money to pay for it, and we will fill your order promptly; or, if you prefer, write us and we will promptly and cheerfully quote price.

About sizes—Remember that the size of iron pipe is inside measure and that fittings are for pipe of corresponding size. We show below the comparative sizes of iron pipe.

Pipe size, inch	⅛	¼	⅜	½	¾
Outside measure, in.	40/100	54/100	67/100	84/100	1 5/100
Pipe size, inches	1	1¼	1½	2	
Outside measure, inches	1 31/100	1 66/100	1 9/10	2 37/100	

Wrought Iron Couplings.

No. 24C5720 Black.

Pipe inches	¼	⅜	½	¾	1	1¼	1½	2
Black, each	2c	2½c	2½c	3½c	4½c	5½c	6½c	9½c

No. 24C5721 Galvanized.

Pipe inches	¼	⅜	½	¾	1	1¼	1½	2
Galv'd, each	2½c	2½c	3½c	4½c	6c	8½c	10½c	14c

Malleable Elbows.

No. 24C5724 Black.

Pipe, inch	¼	⅜	½	¾	1
Black	2c	2½c	3½c	5½c	7c
Pipe, inches	1¼	1½	2		
Black	8½c	11½c	16½c		

No. 24C5725 Galvanized.

Pipe, inches	¼	⅜	½	¾	1	1¼
Galv'd, each	2½c	3c	5½c	7½c	11c	13c
Pipe, inches	1½	2				
Galv'd, each	20c	29c				

45 Degrees Malleable Elbows.

No. 24C5728 Black.

Pipe, inches	¼	⅜	½	¾
Black, each	3½c	3½c	4½c	6½c
Pipe, inches	1	1¼	1½	2
Black, each	9½c	12½c	18½c	27c

No. 24C5729 Galvanized.

Pipe, inches	¼	⅜	½	¾	1	1¼	1½	2
Galv'd, each	5c	5½c	7c	8½c	14c	15½c	26c	38c

Malleable Tees.

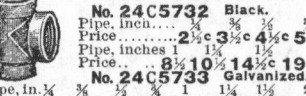

No. 24C5732 Black.

Pipe, inch	¼	⅜	½	¾
Price	2½c	3½c	4½c	5½c
Pipe, inches	1	1¼	1½	2
Price	8½	10½	14½c	19½c

No. 24C5733 Galvanized.

Pipe, in.	¼	⅜	½	¾	1	1¼	1½	2
Price	3½c	3½c	5½c	7c	13c	17c	23c	34c

Malleable Crosses.

All our fittings are Proctor goods, the highest grade made.

No. 24C5736 Black.

Pipe, inch	¼	⅜	½	¾
Price	3½c	4½c	4½c	7½c
Pipe, in.	1	1¼	1½	2
Price	10½c	13½c	19½c	33c

No. 24C5737 Galvanized.

Pipe, inches	½	¾	1	1¼	1½	2
Price	7c	10c	16c	23c	33c	50c

Malleable Unions.

No. 24C5740 Black.

Pipe inches	¼	⅜	½	¾
Price	6½c	7½c	8½c	9½c
Pipe inch	1	1¼	1½	2
Price	10½c	14½c	17½c	23c

No. 24C5741 Galvanized.

Pipe inches	¼	⅜	½	¾
Price	8½c	10½c	11½c	12½c
Pipe inches	1	1¼	1½	2
Price	15½c	20½c	26½c	33c

Malleable Reducers.

To reduce one size—size given is big end.

No. 24C5744 Black.

Pipe inch	⅜	½	¾	1
Price	2c	2c	2c	3½c
Pipe inches	1	1¼	1½	2
Price	5½c	7½c	9½c	15½c

No. 24C5745 Galvanized.

Pipe inches	⅜	¾	1	1¼	1½	2
Price	3½c	5½c	8½c	10½c	14½c	24c

Cast Iron Plugs.

No. 24C5748 Black.

Pipe in.	¼	⅜	½	¾
Price	1½c	1½c	1½c	1½c
Pipe in.	1	1¼	1½	2
Price	2c	2½c	3½c	3½c

No. 24C5749 Galvanized.

Pipe in.	¼	⅜	½	¾	1	1¼	1½	2
Price	2c	2c	2c	2½c	3½c	4½c	5½c	6½c

Bushings.

Reducing one size outside size is given.

No. 24C5752 Black.

Pipe, in.	⅜	¼	¾	1	1¼	1½	2
Price	2c	2c	2½c	2½c	2½c	3½c	4½c

No. 24C5753 Galvanized.

Pipe, in.	⅜	½	¾	1	1¼	1½	2
Price	3½c	3½c	4½c	4½c	5½c	7½c	9½c

Lock Nuts.

No. 24C5755

Pipe, in.	¼	⅜	½	¾
Price	2c	2c	2c	2c
Pipe, in.	1	1¼	1½	2
Price	3c	4c	5c	6c

Pipe Caps.

No. 24C5758 Black.

Pipe, inch	¼	⅜	½	¾
Price	2c	2½c	2½c	3½c
Pipe, inches	1	1¼	1½	2
Price	4c	5c	9½c	13c

No. 24C5759 Galvanized.

Pipe, in.	¼	⅜	½	¾	1	1¼	1½	2
Price	2c	2c	3c	3c	4c	7c	11c	16c

Standard Well Casing.

In random lengths, with threads and couplings, unless otherwise ordered.

No. 24C5712 Black Casing.

Inside Diameter, Inches	Outside Diameter, Inches	Pounds, per foot	Price Black, per foot	Inside Diameter, Inches	Outside Diameter, Inches	Pounds, per foot	Price Black, per foot
2	2¼	2¼	15c	4½	4¾	7	34c
3	3¼	4	25c	5	5¼	8	42c
3¼	3½	4⅛	26c	5⅝	6	10¼	52c
3½	3¾	4¾	27c	6⅝	7	12¼	63c
4	4¼	6	32c	6¾	8⅝	15	76c

Nipples.

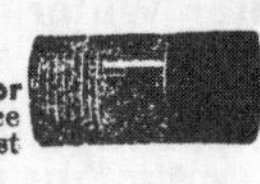

State length wanted.

All nipples 6 inches long or over will be charged at price per foot of iron pipe with cost of cutting threads added.

Size ins.	No. 24C5763 Black short, Price	No. 24C5764 Galvanized short, Price	No. 24C5765 Black long, Price	No. 24C5766 Galvanized long, Price
⅛	1½c	2c	2c	3c
¼	1½c	2c	2½c	3c
⅜	2c	2c	2½c	3½c
½	2c	2½c	3c	4c
¾	2½c	3½c	3½c	5½c
1	3½c	5c	5½c	8c
1¼	4c	7c	6½c	9c
1½	6c	9c	8½c	10c

Malleable Return Bends, Open Pattern.

No. 24C5769 Black.

Pipe, in.	¾	1	1¼
Price	5½c	11½c	16c
Pipe, in.	1½	2	
Price	20c	27c	35c

Brass Straightway Double Gate Valves.

No. 24C5788 These Standard Double Disc Gate Valves have brass seats and rising stem, tested to 100 pounds steam pressure. In the construction of these valves the bearing of the wedge being central it acts uniformly on all parts of the disc, consequently it will force the disc to the seats and have an equal bearing on all parts. These valves are used either for steam or water where a full opening (same size of pipe), is required and will allow the water to be drained from pipes in cold weather.

Sizes	½	¾	1	1¼
Price	40c	52c	70c	$1.05
Sizes	1½	2	2½	3
Price	$1.45	$2.20	$4.00	$5.65

Brass Globe Valves.

No. 24C5826

For pipe, inch	¼	⅜
Price	$0.21	$0.23
For pipe, inch	½	¾
Price	.30	.38
For pipe, inch	1	1¼
Price	54	.75
For pipe, inch	1½	2
Price	1.05	1.45

Brass Angle Valves.

No. 24C5828

For pipe, inch	¼	⅜
Price	$0.21	$0.23
For pipe, inch	½	¾
Price	.30	.38
For pipe, inch	1	1¼
Price	.54	.75
For pipe, inch	1½	2
Price	1.05	1.45

Brass Cross Valves.

No. 24C5830

For pipe, inch	¼	⅜
Price	$0.37	$0.38
For pipe, inch	½	¾
Price	.45	.60
For pipe, inch	1	1¼
Price	.75	1.00
For pipe, inch	1½	2
Price	1.40	2.30

Horizontal Check Valves.

No. 24C5832

For pipe, in.	¼	⅜
Price	20c	21c
For pipe, in.	½	¾
Price	27c	34c
For pipe, in.	1	1¼
Price	48c	67c
For pipe, in.	1½	2
Price	$0.95	$1.35

Brass Three-Way Cocks.

No. 24C5834

For pipe, in.	½	¾
Price	$0.60	$0.70
For pipe, in.	1	1¼
Price	.89	1.40
For pipe, in.	1½	2
Price	1.70	2.45
For pipe, in.	2½	3
Price	4.40	5.25

Steam Cocks.

No. 24C5836 Brass Flat Head Steam Cocks, best quality.

For pipe, in.	¼	⅜
Price	$0.19	$0.25
For pipe, in.	½	¾
Price	.31	.43
For pipe, in.	1	1¼
Price	.57	.90
For pipe, in.	1½	2
Price	1.18	1.80
For pipe, in.	2½	3
Price	3.55	5.15

Vertical Check Valves.

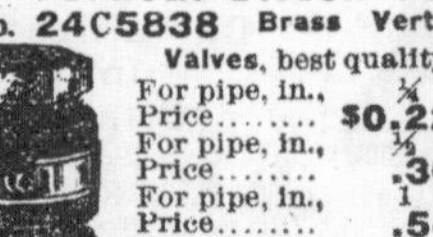

No. 24C5838 Brass Vertical Check Valves, best quality.

For pipe, in.	¼	⅜
Price	$0.22	$0.23
For pipe, in.	½	¾
Price	.30	.38
For pipe, in.	1	1¼
Price	.54	.75
For pipe, in.	1½	2
Price	1.05	1.60

Swing Check Valves.

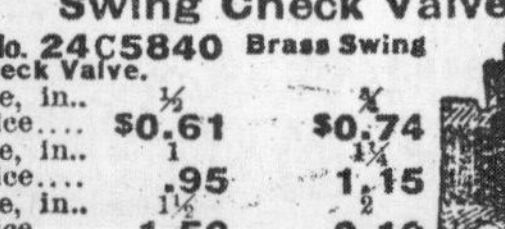

No. 24C5840 Brass Swing Check Valve.

Size, in.	½	¾
Price	$0.61	$0.74
Size, in.	1	1¼
Price	.95	1.15
Size, in.	1½	2
Price	1.50	2.10

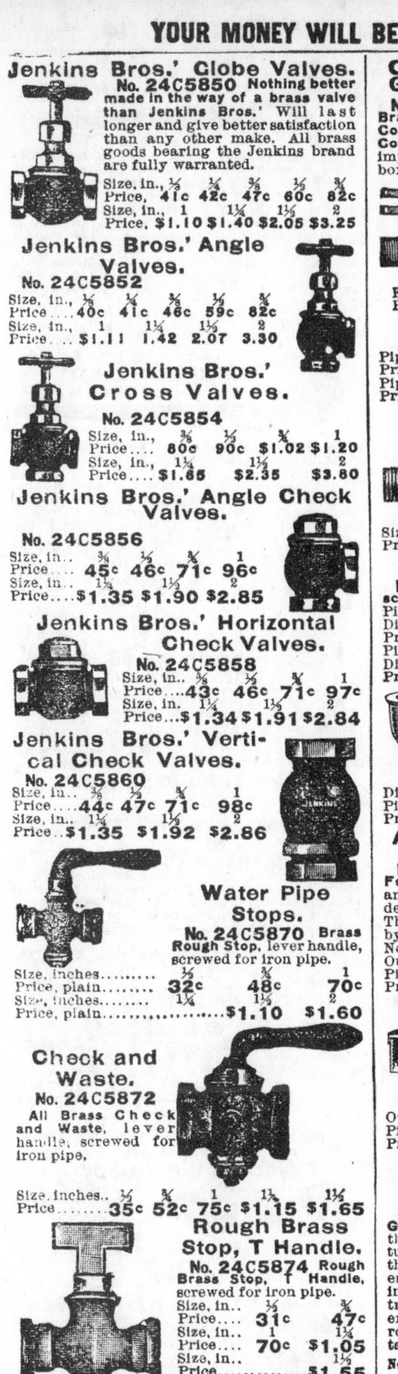

Jenkins Bros.' Globe Valves.

No. 24C5850 Nothing better made in the way of a brass valve than Jenkins Bros.' Will last longer and give better satisfaction than any other make. All brass goods bearing the Jenkins brand are fully warranted.

Size, in.	⅛	¼	⅜	½	¾
Price	41c	42c	47c	60c	82c
Size, in.	1	1¼	1½	2	
Price	$1.10	$1.40	$2.05	$3.25	

Jenkins Bros.' Angle Valves.

No. 24C5852

Size, in.	⅛	¼	⅜	½	¾
Price	40c	41c	46c	59c	82c
Size, in.	1	1¼	1½	2	
Price	$1.11	1.42	2.07	3.30	

Jenkins Bros.' Cross Valves.

No. 24C5854

Size, in.	⅜	½	¾	1
Price	80c	90c	$1.02	$1.20
Size, in.	1	1½	2	
Price	$1.65	$2.35	$3.80	

Jenkins Bros.' Angle Check Valves.

No. 24C5856

Size, in.	⅜	½	¾	1
Price	45c	46c	71c	96c
Size, in.	1¼	1½	2	
Price	$1.35	$1.90	$2.85	

Jenkins Bros.' Horizontal Check Valves.

No. 24C5858

Size, in.	⅜	½	¾	1
Price	43c	46c	71c	97c
Size, in.	1¼	1½	2	
Price	$1.34	$1.91	$2.84	

Jenkins Bros.' Vertical Check Valves.

No. 24C5860

Size, in.	⅜	½	¾	1
Price	44c	47c	71c	98c
Size, in.	1¼	1½	2	
Price	$1.35	$1.92	$2.86	

Water Pipe Stops.

No. 24C5870 Brass Rough Stop, lever handle, screwed for iron pipe.

Size, inches	½	¾	1
Price, plain	32c	48c	70c
Size, inches	1¼	1½	2
Price, plain		$1.10	$1.60

Check and Waste.

No. 24C5872 All Brass Check and Waste, lever handle, screwed for iron pipe.

Size, inches	½	¾	1	1¼	1½
Price	35c	52c	75c	$1.15	$1.65

Rough Brass Stop, T Handle.

No. 24C5874 Rough Brass Stop, T Handle, screwed for iron pipe.

Size, in.	½	¾
Price	31c	47c
Size, in.	1	1¼
Price	70c	$1.05
Size, in.		1½
Price		$1.55

Hydrant Clamp.

No. 24C5880

Malleable Iron Hydrant Clamp, with square hole; always give size hydrant cock clamp is to fit.
Price 5c

Gate Valves.

No. 24C5881 Improved Gate Valves. Double wedge disks, stationary stem. All parts are made of the best steam bronze, except hand wheels, which are iron; japanned. finished trimmings.

Size, in	½	¾	1	1¼	1½	2	2½
Price	37c	48c	67c	95c	$1.30	$2.00	$3.75

Hydrant Cocks.

No. 24C5890 Brass Hydrant Cocks, for iron pipe connections. T handle.

Size, in.	¾	1	1¼
Price	75c	$1.18	$1.80

Ball Gauge Cocks.

No. 24C5915 Ball Gauge Cock, brass body.

Size, inch	½	¾
Price	25c	26c

Compression Gauge Cocks.

No. 24C5918 Solid Brass, Wood Wheel, Compression Gauge Cocks. Complete, with improved stuffing box, finished.

Size, inch	⅜	½	¾
Price	28c	30c	35c

Cylinder Cocks.

No. 24C5921 Traction Engine Cylinder Cocks. Made of brass, finished ready for use.

For pipe, inch	⅛	¼	⅜	½
Price	34c	37c	40c	53c

Air Cocks.

No. 24C5922

Pipe size, in.	⅛	¼
Price	9c	9c
Pipe size, in.	⅜	½
Price	11c	13c

Bibb Nose Air Cocks.

No. 24C5924 All Brass Bibb Nose Air Cocks.

Size pipe, inch	⅛	¼	⅜	½
Price	15c	17c	19c	22c

Brass Oil Cups.

No. 24C5926 All brass with screw top.

Pipe size, inch	⅛	¼	¼
Diam. of body, in.	¾	1	1¼
Price	6½c	9c	14c
Pipe size, inch	⅜	⅜	
Diam. of body, in.	1½	2	
Price	22c	46c	

Elbow Shank Oiler.

No. 24C5929 Brass Elbow Shank Oilers, to attach to an out of the way place where a straight oiler cannot be used. Saves the expense of a nipple elbow and coupling and makes a much better job.

Diam. of body	⅞	1	1¼	1½	1¾	2
Pipe thread	⅛	¼	¼	⅜	⅜	½
Price	15c	21c	29c	40c	50c	65c

Acme Screw Feed Grease Cups.

No. 24C5932 Acme Screw Feed Grease Cup. Very simple and not easily gotten out of order. Made of brass throughout. The best cup for the money sold by anyone.

No.	6	7	8	9
Outside diam., inches	1½	2	2⅜	2¾
Pipe thread, inch	⅛	¼	⅜	⅜
Price	17c	22c	33c	45c

Solid Brass Grease Cups.

No. 24C5936 Solid Brass Grease Cups. Just the cup for traction engines or any machinery where there is more or less vibration, finely finished and fine polished.

Size	00	0	1	2	3	4
Outside diam., in.	1	1¼	1½	2	2½	3¼
Pipe thread, in.	⅛	¼	¼	⅜	½	½
Price	14½c	17½c	24c	31c	49c	60c

Acme Glass Oil Cups.

No. 24C5940 The Acme Glass Body Oil Cups are by far the most perfect cups manufactured. Made of cast brass throughout. Can be used on all engines and machinery bearings. Especially adapted to traction engines and steam rollers, where a cup is subject to rough usage, etc. Easily attached and regulated.

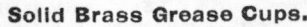

No.	Size of Shank (Pipe Thread)	Height	Capacity	Price
11	⅛ inch	1⅛ inches	½ oz.	$0.25
12	¼ inch	1⅜ inches	1 oz.	.26
13	¼ inch	1⅝ inches	1½ oz.	.32
14	⅜ inch	1⅞ inches	2 oz.	.34
15	⅜ inch	2⅛ inches	3 oz.	.40
16	⅜ inch	2⅜ inches	4 oz.	.56
17	½ inch	3 inches	8 oz.	.78
18	½ inch	4 inches	1 pt.	1.16

Sight Feed Oil Cups.

No. 24C5942 Glass Body Sight Feed Oil Cup. Double glass top and bottom, which enables you to see when oil is not feeding properly; frame is made of solid polished brass, an A1 cup in every respect.

No.	30	31	32
Capacity, oz.	⅛	½	1
Price	36c	39c	45c
Nos.	33	34	36
Capacity, oz.	1½	2	4
Price	49c	53c	73c

The Detroit Spring Compression Grease Cup.

No. 24C5945 Is automatic in its operation. The rate of feed can be regulated by the screw T. The base slopes to the center on the inside, insuring that all the grease will be fed, and it can be screwed into place on the bearing either by using a wrench on the hexagon, or by using a flat piece of iron with the lugs. To fill, turn the thumb nut down until the plunger is drawn up to the cover; then unscrew the cover and fill with grease; then put on cover and turn the thumb nut up to the point you desire the plunger to go down while feeding.

Number	60	61	62	64	66	67
Extreme height over all (Plunger raised)	3⅞	4⅝	5½	6¾	7⅞	9
Shank pipe thread	⅛	¼	¼	⅜	½	½
Capacity, ozs.	⅛	1	1½	3	6	10
Price, brass	36c	48c	59c	76c	99c	$1.35

Brass Lubricators.

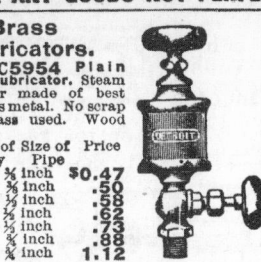

No. 24C5954 Plain Cylinder Lubricator. Steam chest oiler made of best grade brass metal. No scrap or old brass used. Wood wheels.

No.	Diam. of Body	Size of Pipe	Price
80	1 in.	⅜ inch	$0.47
81	1¼ in.	⅜ inch	.50
82	1½ in.	½ inch	.58
83	1¾ in.	½ inch	.62
84	2 in.	½ inch	.73
86	2½ in.	¾ inch	.88
87	3 in.	¾ inch	1.12

Asbestos Moulding Sectional Covering.

No. 24C5966 This form of covering is offered as the most durable and effective moulded and non-conducting covering yet produced. It is supplied in sections 3 feet long, which are provided with metal bands to hold them firmly in place, and can be easily applied by unskilled workmen.

Inside Diam. of Pipe	Covering per Foot	Elbows, Price	Tees, Price
½ and ¾ inches	5½c	6¼c	8¼c
1 inches	5¾c	6¼c	8¼c
1¼ inches	6 c	6¼c	8¼c
1½ inches	6¼c	6¼c	8¼c
2 inches	6¾c	6¾c	9 c
2½ inches	7¾c	7¾c	10¼c
3 inches	9 c	9 c	12 c
3½ inches	10 c	10 c	13¼c
4 inches	11 c	11 c	14¾c

PIPEFITTERS' TOOLS.

Malleable Iron Pipe Vise.

No. 24C5968 Steamfitters, plumbers and gasfitters will find this the handiest vise on the market. The jaws are made of the best tool steel. Weighs only 7 pounds. Can be carried in tool chest. Takes pipe from ⅛ to 2 inches.
Price $1.10

Open Hinge Malleable Iron Pipe Vises.

No. 24C5970 Has interchangeable cut steel jaws, and is constructed to do the heaviest work. Great care has been taken in manufacturing the various parts, putting the strength where most desired. Jaws are warranted.

	No. 1	No. 2
Holds pipe from	¼ to 2 in.	¼ to 3 in.
Weight	20 lbs.	26 lbs.
Price	$1.42	$2.00
No. 24C5971 Extra Jaws	.75	1.15

Prentiss' 20th Century Pipe Vises.

No. 24C5972 The 20th Century Pipe Vise is one of the new up to date tools put upon the market the last year. It is more convenient and more durable than the old style malleable vise. Can be used on bench or post in any position. Finest finish and best material.

Holds ⅛ to 2-inch pipe. Weight, 8 pounds. Price $2.35
Holds ⅛ to 3-inch pipe. Weight, 18 pounds. Price $3.40
Holds ⅛ to 4-inch pipe. Weight, 40 pounds. Price $6.25

Removable Jaw Pipe Vises.

No. 24C5974 This vise can be fastened to bench or post with three lag screws or bolts. The screws are cut from steel bars and of ample size to insure long wear, and with a coarse machine cut thread for rapid and smooth movement. The jaws of these vises are composed of several sections of tool steel. These sections are milled to length and are interchangeable in any size of vise of our manufacture. When the edges of these sections become dull, it is only necessary to loosen the clamp bolts, reverse the sections and tighten the bolts. The sides of the sections are milled to accommodate small projections cast on the clamps to prevent sections being knocked or jarred out.

No. 1 Holds ⅛-inch to 2-inch pipe. Price, $1.85
No. 2 Holds ¼-inch to 3-inch pipe. Price, 2.55
No. 3 Holds ½-inch to 4-inch pipe. Price, 3.60

Improved Swivel Pipe Grip.

An efficient vise attachment for mechanics and others having occasional use for a pipe grip. The swivel adjusts the pipe from a vertical position to a horizontal one, which can be changed to any position on the vise by means of the horizontal slot.

No. 24C5975 Steel Jaws. Made with two-sized holders. Price
No. 67 fits from 2½-inch to 4-inch vise. 75c
No. 68 fits from 4½ inch to 5¾-inch vise. 85c

Genuine Smith Combination Pipe Vises.

No. 24C5976 Extra heavy, has steel removable jaws. Material and workmanship A1. Best vise for the money sold by anyone.

Special prices. No. 1, weight, 45 pounds; takes pipe, ⅛ to 2 inches. Price $3.95
No. 2, weight, 72 pounds; takes pipe, ¼ to 3 inches. Price $4.95

One-Wheel Pipe Cutters.

No. 24C5985 Made of malleable iron with steel rod and tool steel cutter; lighter and stronger than any other one-wheel cutter made.

	No. 1	No. 2	No. 3
Cuts pipe from	⅛ to 1 in.	¾ to 2 in.	1¼ to 3 in.
Price	72c	$1.13	$3.20
Extra wheels	6c	.09	.13

Three-Wheel Pipe Cutters.

No. 24C5987 Made of malleable and wrought iron, with steel pins and wheels of Jessop's best tool steel. Simple and strong in construction and cuts rapidly and easily.

	No. 1	No. 2	No. 3
Cuts pipe from	⅛ to 1 in.	1 to 2 in.	2 to 3 in.
Price	90c	$1.15	$1.95
Extra wheels	5c	.07	.09

Saunder's Pattern Pipe Cutters

No. 24C5996 Saunders' Pattern Pipe Cutters. By referring to illustration it will be seen that the front that rubs on pipe is provided with rollers which reduce the friction, making it a very easy cutting tool. Weight, 3¾ to 6¾ pounds.

	No. 1	No. 2	No. 3
Cuts pipe from	⅛ to 1 in.	1 to 2 in.	2 to 3 in.
Price, complete	75c	$1.10	$2.70
Extra wheels	6c	.07	.14

Pipe Stock and Dies.

Malleable Iron Pipe Stock, with solid steel dies. No taps. See No. 24C6060 for taps. Weights range from 15 to 35 pounds.

No.	24C6000	24C6001	24C6002
	No. 0	No. 1	No. 1½
Pipe size of dies	⅛,¼,⅜,½	¼,⅜,½,¾,1	¾,1,1¼
Dimension of dies	2x½	2½x¾	3x¾
Complete with dies	$2.30	$2.90	$2.65
Extra dies	.41	.54	.68
Extra guides	.07	.11	.15

No.	24C6003	24C6004	24C6005
	No. 1¾	No. 2	No. 3
Pipe size of dies	1, 1¼, 1½	1¼, 1½, 2	2½, 3
Dimension of dies	3x¾	4x⅞	5x1¼
Complete with dies	$2.75	$3.85	$13.00
Extra dies	.68	.95	2.40
Extra guides	.15	.18	.33

Economy Pipe Stock and Dies.

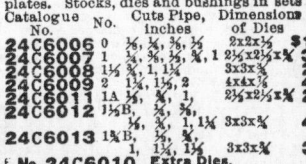

The Economy Stock and Dies are made for strength as well as economy in price. The center part is made of the best malleable iron, handles are made of steel pipe screwed into stock. The knurled handles prevent the hands from slipping; handle finely polished, center part dark finish.

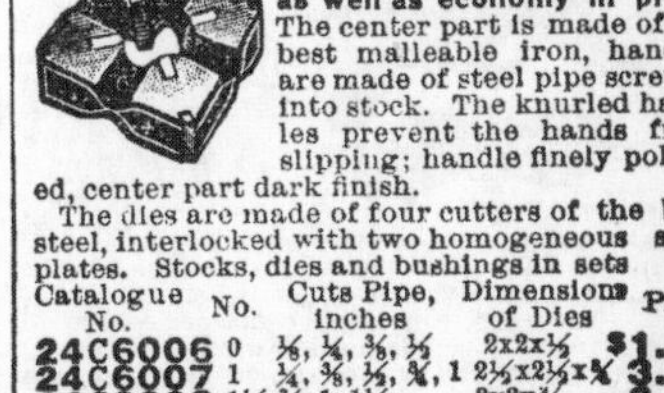

The dies are made of four cutters of the best steel, interlocked with two homogeneous steel plates. Stocks, dies and bushings in sets

Catalogue No.	No.	Cuts Pipe, inches	Dimensions of Dies	Price
24C6006	0	⅛, ¼, ⅜, ½	2x2x½	$1.87
24C6007	1	¼, ⅜, ½, ¾, 1	2½x2½x¾	3.00
24C6008	1½	¾, 1, 1¼	3x3x¾	2.65
24C6009	2	1¼, 1½, 2	4x4x⅞	4.00
24C6011	1A	½, ¾, 1,	2½x2½x¾	2.20
24C6012	1½B	¼, ⅜, ½, ¾, 1, 1¼	3x3x¾	4.20
24C6013	1¾B	½, ¾, 1, 1¼, 1½	3x3x¾	3.70

No. 24C6010 Extra Dies.

Cuts Pipe, inches	Dimension of Dies	Fit Stock No.	Price
⅛, ¼, ⅜, ½	2x2x½	0	31c
⅛, ¼, ⅜, ½, ¾, 1	2½x2½x¾	1	41c
¾, 1, 1¼	3x3x¾	1½ & 1¾	52c
1¼, 1½, 2	4x4x⅞	2	73c

Armstrong's Adjustable Stock and Dies for Threading Pipes.

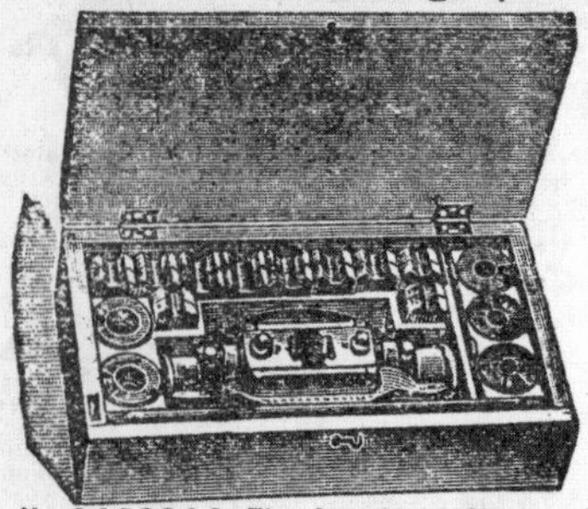

No. 24C6014 **The Armstrong Stock and Dies** are among the best known pipe cutting tools on the market. More of them have been sold in the past 15 years than any other make. The dies can be adjusted to the variations in the size of fittings, and by reason of their peculiar cutting edge can be worked with much less labor and accomplish the desired results in less time than with other dies. The dies have a double taper, that is, the taper at the entrance for the first few threads is greater in degree than the standard taper, which forms a lead to the dies, causing them to start on the pipe without filing, even when there is a swell or burr, and requiring no pressure to start dies on the pipe. No. 2 stock and dies cut five sizes, ¼ inch to 1 inch, right hand.

Price, set complete $3.85
Extra pipe dies, each size, 2 pieces .... .55

Armstrong's No. 2½ Pipe Stock and Dies.

No. 24C6015 **Armstrong's No. 2½ Pipe Stock and Dies** complete, with four dies cutting ½, ¾, 1 and 1¼ inches, right hand. Illustration shows head only. Furnished complete, with handles, dies and guides. Price .. $3.90
Extra pipe dies, each size, 2 pieces. 1.25

Armstrong's No. 3 Pipe Stock and Dies.

No. 24C6016 **Armstrong's Adjustable Stock and Dies**, complete with sizes of dies cutting three sizes, 1¼ to 2 inches; furnished with handles, dies and guides.

Price, complete set $6.40
Extra pipe dies, each size, 2 pieces 1.50

Armstrong's No. 6 Pipe Stock and Dies.

No. 24C6018 **Armstrong's Adjustable Pipe Stock and Dies**, with two dies cutting 2½ and 3-inch pipe, furnished complete with handles, dies and guides.

Price $14.90
Extra pipe dies, each size, 2 pieces. 5.60

Armstrong's No. 7 Pipe Stock and Dies.

No. 24C6020 **Armstrong's Adjustable Pipe Stock and Dies**, cutting 2½, 3, 3½ and 4 inches, right hand, furnished complete with handles, dies and guides.

Price... $21.25

Extra pipe dies, each size, 2 pieces. Price $5.60

Duplex Adjustable Pipe Stock and Dies.

These tools have adjustable dies that are quickly opened and self-centering. It is not necessary to turn back over finished threads with them; dies are thrown open and stock lifted off. The danger of stripping threads, a common occurrence when reversing is thus also avoided. Threads can be made over or under standard sizes, just as desired for fitting. There are four dies or chasers which do the cutting; these when set to size are clamped so securely in every way as to be rigid as a solid die. Furnished complete with pipe cutoff unless ordered without.

No. 24C6025 **For threading pipe:**

No. 1	Price, per set, ⅛, ¼, ⅜, ½, ¾	$ 7.90
No. 2	Price, per set, ¼, ⅜, ½, ¾, 1, 1¼ .	9.90
No. 3	Price, per set, 1, 1¼, 1½, 2	12.90
No. 3½	Price, per set, ½, ¾, 1, 1¼, 1½, 2	14.40

Extra Pipe Dies for No. 24C6025, Duplex Stock. When ordering give size pipe dies are to cut.

No. 1	Price, per set of four pieces	$1.35
No. 2	Price, per set of four pieces	1.60
No. 3	Price, per set of four pieces	1.80
No. 3½	Price, per set of four pieces	1.85

Pipe Taps.

No. 24C6060

Size, inch	⅛	¼	⅜	½	¾
Price	16c	19c	24c	29c	39c
Size, inches	1	1¼	1½	2	
Price	49c	56c	70c	93c	

Pipe Reamers.

No. 24C6062

Size, inch	⅛	¼	⅜	½	¾
Price	17c	22c	28c	34c	48c
Size, inches	1	1¼	1½	2	
Price	52c	62c	74c	95c	

Burring Reamer.

No. 24C6063 **Lightning Burring Reamer.** Made of high grade tool steel. Used for reaming pipe, etc., also countersinking. Size, at point 7-16 by 1¼ inches at base. Price 68c

Monarch Ratchet Drills.

Single Action.

No. 24C6073 **The Monarch Ratchet Single Action Drill** is by far the most perfect tool for the price on the market. The body is drop forged steel, sockets, bars and all parts English steel. Sockets are for square shank drills.

Length of handle	10-inch	12-inch	15-inch
Price	$3.65	$4.10	$4.40

Keystone Double Acting Ratchets.

No. 24C6074 **Keystone Reversible Double Acting Ratchets.** Combination square sleeve ratchet and short boiler socket—interchangeable. The ratchet being entirely enclosed, prevents obstacles from interfering with its working. The body is dropped forged steel. Simple in construction and strong. Nothing to break or get out of order.

Combination complete with 10-inch handle. Price $4.90
Combination complete with 14-inch handle. Price 5.85
Combination complete with 16-inch handle. Price 6.60

Twist Drills for Ratchet Drill Stock.

No. 24C6088 **Best Grade Twist Drills** for our No. 24C6073 and No. 24C6074 ratchet drill stocks. Made extra heavy.

Diam. Inches	Length, Inches	Price	Diam. Inches	Length, Inches	Price
¼	5	$0.60	⅝	6½	$0.84
5-16	5	.62	¾	6½	.93
⅜	6	.72	⅞	7½	1.23
7-16	6¼	.75	1	8½	1.53
½	6¼	.78	1⅛	9	1.86
9-16	6½	.81	1¼	9½	2.19

Care must be used not to force the drill too hard at any time, and especially when the point comes through. Be sure point of set screw in ratchet has a good countersink to work in.

Lightning Dies and Stocks.

No. 24C6095 **Pump Repairers' Dies and Stocks.** Two dies in one stock; always ready for use without changing dies. A first class tool, made of the very best materials and fully warranted. Will do perfect work and cut a full thread at one cut. Size dies, ⅜ and 7-16-inch.

Price $2.25

Brown's Adjustable Pipe Tongs.

No. 24C6122

Number	1	1½	2	3	4
Takes pipe from	⅛ to ⅜	⅜ to 1	½ to 1¼	1 to 2	1¼ to 3
Price	57c	70c	80c	$1.10	$2.50

Drop Forged Steel Gas Pliers.

No. 24C6130 **Full Polished.**

Length, inches	7	8	10
Price	19c	20c	26c

Combination Gas Pliers.

S. R. & Co.'s Combination Wire Cutter, Wrench, Screwdriver and Gas Pliers. Drop forged from best tool steel. This is one of the handiest pliers made, very strong and durable, nicely finished.

Six-inch pliers take up to ⅜-inch pipe; 8-inch and 10-inch take up to 1-inch pipe.

No. 24C6136 **Black Finish.**

Size, inches	6	8	10
Price	40c	48c	54c

No. 24C6137 **Nickel Plated.**

Size, inches	6	8	10
Price	46c	53c	63c

Pipe Wrench Jaws.

No. 24C6140 **Yankee Jaws makes a monkey wrench, a pipe wrench.** Will fit any size monkey wrench. Everybody knows a pipe wrench is a necessary tool to have, but is expensive, but now every one can have one. It can be adjusted to fit pipe or bolts from ⅛ to 3 inches. Made of high grade steel. Will last a lifetime.

Prices are for jaws only.

No. 1, fits wrench 6 inches to 10 inches in size. Price 18c
No. 2, fits wrench 10 inches to 24 inches in size. Price 21c

Victor Wrench.

No. 24C6143 **The Victor is a Drop Forged Wrench.** Has steel jaws, knurled oval handles; will hold square and hexagon nuts, pipe bolts and rods. Few parts, strong, and easily worked. Furnished nickel plated.

Size, 7 inches. Price 66c
Size, 8 inches. Price 80c
Size, 10 inches. Price 98c

Alligator Pipe Wrench.

No. 24C6145

Length, in.	5¾	9	16	22	27
Takes pipe	⅛ to ⅜	⅜ to ¾	½ to 1¼	1¼ to 2	2 to 3
Weight, lbs.	¼	¾	2¾	6¼	13
Price	11c	27c	53c	78c	$1.20

Trimo Special Narrow Jaw Wrench.

No. 24C6146 **This wrench is designed for close quarter work, the jaws narrow materially and it can be used in places where no other wrench would operate.** Light in weight and particularly designed for gasfitters' use; handy around an automobile or bicycle.

Size, inches	6	8	10
Price	85c	86c	95c

Trimo Pipe Wrench.

No. 24C6147 **This wrench is drop forged from bar steel,** is interchangeable in all its parts, does not lock upon the pipe, but releases its hold readily; grips the pipe firmly without lost motion; does not crush the pipe or slip. The movable jaw and the nut are made with a round top and bottom thread, guaranteed not to strip or burr. An inserted jaw is placed in the handle, which can be renewed for little expense when dull or worn.

Length, open, in.	10	14	18	24
Takes pipe	⅛ to 1	¼ to 1½	¼ to 2	¼ to 2½
Price	90c	$1.20	$1.65	$2.40

Stillson Pipe Wrench.

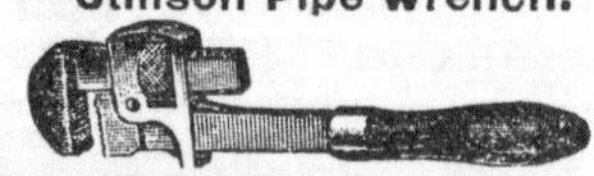

No. 24C6149 **The Stillson Pipe Wrench is too well known** to require a lengthy description of same. They are made of the best imported steel, finely finished and fully warranted.

Length open, inches	6	8	10
Takes pipe from	⅛ to ¼	⅛ to ¾	⅛ to 1
Price	68c	69c	70c
Length open, inches	14	18	24
Takes pipe from	¼ to 1½	¼ to 2	¼ to 2½
Price	$1.10	$1.45	$2.20

American Pipe Wrench.

The American Wrenches are made of the best material throughout, and are very strong and durable. They grip the pipe firmly and release the hold more readily than any other pipe wrench. We furnish this wrench with teeth in back jaw same as Trimo or Stillson wrench. The parts are interchangeable and can be replaced at small expense when necessary. The trade will find **American Wrenches** very efficient and satisfactory in every respect.

No. 24C6160

Length, open inches	Takes pipe from, inches	Price, complete, each
8	⅛ to ¾	$0.72
10	⅛ to 1	.82
14	¼ to 1½	1.05
18	¼ to 2	1.45
24	¼ to 2½	2.15

The V. & B. Automatic Pipe Wrench.

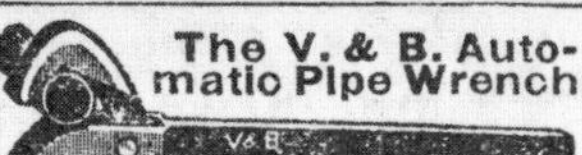

No. 24C6166 **The V. & B. Automatic Pipe Wrench,** as illustrated, shows the jaw open. This is the strongest, lightest, simplest and most perfect working pipe wrench we have ever seen. Carefully made from selected tool steel of superior quality. Material and workmanship are fully guaranteed. The harder you pull on this wrench the tighter the grip. But the grip relaxes instantly when pressure is removed. The grip being distributed over a large surface it is not so liable to crush the pipe by a severe strain.

Length, inches	10	14	24
Takes pipe	⅛ to 1	¼ to 1¼	½ to 2½
Weight	20 oz.	2½ lbs.	7 lbs.
Price	61c	90c	$1.80

Trimo Bulldog Chain Pipe Wrench.

No. 24C6168 **This wrench has a solid head,** to the head is attached a forged steel jaw, enabling it to grip firmly without slipping, and to release its hold readily from the pipe. The chain can be easily placed, and quickly removed at the will of the operator. Points of superiority: Impossible to lock upon the pipe. The strain evenly distributed, each part bearing its proportion. Works equally well whether pulling up or down. Does not crush the pipe nor slip. Will handle close fittings and work in closer quarters than any other chain wrench made.

No.	11	12	13
Length, inches	20	27	37
Takes pipe	¼ to 2	¼ to 3	⅜ to 6
Price	$1.88	$2.58	$3.60

Cotton Waste.

No. 24C6180 **Extra Quality Cotton Waste,** sold in any quantity. No. XX white.

Price, per pound ... 8½c

Roller Tube Expanders.

No. 24C6185 **Has solid steel body,** is finely finished and guaranteed to do good work. In ordering, give outside diameter **(not the inside)** of tube or flue the expander is to be used in. If your tube measures 2¼ inches outside, order a 2¼-inch expander.

Size	1	1¼	1½	1¾
Price	$1.64	$1.65	$1.66	$1.67
Size	2	2¼	2½	3
Price	1.68	1.76	1.77	2.25

Wire Flue Brushes.

No. 24C6190 **Flat Wire Flue Brushes** made of spring steel, with wrought iron stem; when ordering, give outside diameter of tube the brush is to be used in.

Outside diameter of tube, inches	1¾	2	2¼	2½	3
Price	13½c	15c	18c	21c	25c

Favorite Flue Scraper.

No. 24C6192 **Engineers' Favorite Flue Scraper,** one of the most popular tools on the market, has adjustable screw which fits pipe snugly. Sizes are for outside diameter of pipe or flue.

Size	2	2¼	2½	3	3½	4
Price	28c	34c	41c	47c	49c	69c

Combination Flue Brushes and Scraper.

No. 24C6196 **We have here the best flue and brush cleaner made.** By simply turning a rod or handle, the ends contract until it will readily pass into the flue. Then by turning the handle in an opposite direction the cleaner is gradually expanded until it fits the tube perfectly; the brush following, leaves the tube absolutely clean. Sizes are for outside diameter of tube, from 2 inches up.

Size, in.	2	2¼	2½
Price	$1.10	$1.25	$1.40
Size, in.	3	3½	4
Price	1.70	1.98	2.25

Expansion Flue Brushes.

Open.

Closed

No. 24C6198 **The illustration shows our Improved Expansion Tube Brush.** The improvement consists in so arranging the sections that the open space between the sections does not extend the entire length of the brush and thus cleans the whole of the flue each time it is pushed through. **This brush is made entirely of steel and malleable iron, and is the most substantial and effective flue cleaner made. In ordering tube brushes be particular to give the outside measurement of tube.**

Size, in.	1¾	2	2¼	2½	3
Price	56c	65c	73c	83c	97c
Size, in.	3½	4	5	6	
Price	$1.15	$1.30	$1.65	$1.90	

Bemis & Call's Pipe Wrench.

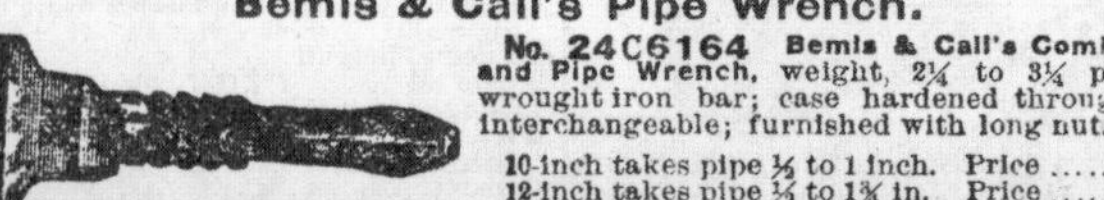

No. 24C6164 **Bemis & Call's Combination Nut and Pipe Wrench,** weight, 2¼ to 3½ pounds; with wrought iron bar; case hardened throughout; parts interchangeable; furnished with long nut.

10-inch takes pipe ⅛ to 1 inch. Price $1.20
12-inch takes pipe ⅛ to 1¼ in. Price 1.30
15-inch takes pipe ⅛ to 2 inches. Price 1.95

Acme Respirator.

No. 24C6205 The Acme Respirator is the most complete article ever offered for protecting the throat and lungs from dust and poisonous gases and all other impurities in places where persons are exposed and many times life endangered. Made of high grade pure white rubber. Nothing better made. Price **$1.00**

Spiral Earth Augers.

No. 24C6210 Spiral Earth Augers for boring wells, prospecting, etc. Made extra heavy, of the best grade of tool steel; will stand hard usage. We furnish them in three styles, No. 1, 2 or 3; be sure and state style wanted.

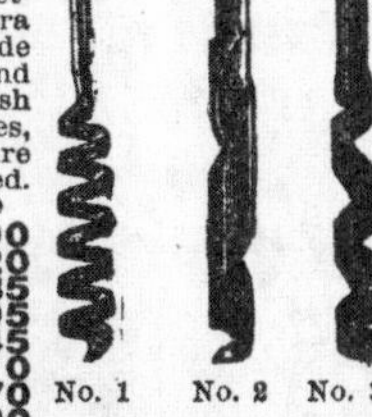

No. 1 No. 2 No. 3

Size, ins.	Price
2	$1.90
2½	2.20
3	2.35
3½	2.95
4	3.45
4½	4.10
5	5.70
6	7.20

The Detroit Lubricators.

No. 24C6250 This lubricator is designed for use on traction and other small engines and steam pumps where it is desirable to discharge the oil either into the steam pipe below the throttle, or into the steam chest direct. On account of its construction, the oil cannot be siphoned out, **and a steady and regular feed is assured at all times. It is well made,** all connections, etc., being one solid piece of brass, finely finished. Size glass in sight full ¾x2½ inches. **Brass finish.**

	⅛-pint	¼-pint	½-pint
Price	$3.00	$3.55	$3.75

Detroit Sight Feed Lubricators.

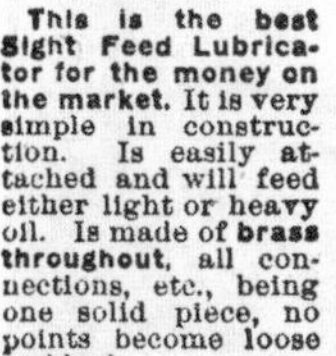

This is the best Sight Feed Lubricator for the money on the market. It is very simple in construction. Is easily attached and will feed either light or heavy oil. Is made of **brass throughout,** all connections, etc., being one solid piece, no points become loose and leak.

Our Guaranty—That this Lubricator has no superior.

No.	Size	Diameter of Engine Cylinder	Price
24C6260	⅛-pint	Up to 8 inches	$3.22
24C6261	¼-pint	8 to 10 inches	3.60
24C6262	1-pint	10 to 18 inches	4.90
24C6263	1-quart	18 to 30 inches	6.60
24C6264	2-quarts	30 and over.	9.60

Zero Cold Weather Lubricators.

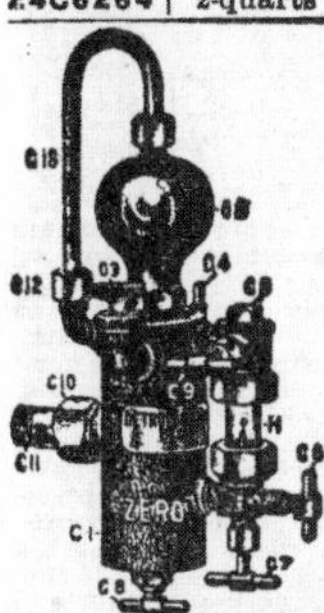

Single Connection.

No. 24C6267 Our Zero Single Connection Lubricator possesses every feature necessary or desirable for traction engine service or for engines working in exposed places, subject to sudden changes of temperature. It will feed the regular number of drops of oil in coldest as well as warm weather. The oil is kept warm by steam, no attention being required. It may be attached to the steam pipe on either side of the throttle or to steam chest direct. This lubricator can be used on traction, stationary, hoisting, portable engines and steam pumps.

Size	¼-pint	½-pint	¾-pint	1-pint
Price	$2.58	$2.80	$3.20	$4.55

Double Connection Zero Lubricators.

No. 24C6271 The Double Connection Zero Lubricators are widely used on such traction and portable engines as have steam pipes suitable for a double connection lubricator. They are also extensively used on steam pumps and on stationary engines, which are exposed more or less to the cold. They possess the same heating features as the single connection style, together with most of that cup's other good qualities. Bronze body, finished trimmings.

Size	¼-pint	½-pint	¾-pint	1-pint
Price	$2.50	$2.62	$3.05	$4.60

The Detroit Kid Sight Feed Lubricators.

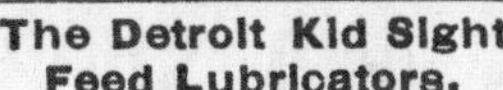

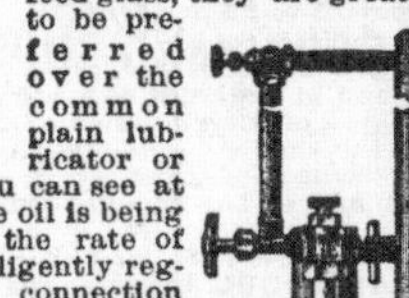

No. 24C6272 The Kid Lubricators are intended for use on small steam engines and small steam pumps. Having the sight feed glass, they are greatly to be preferred over the common plain lubricator or chest oiler, as you can see at once whether the oil is being fed or not and the rate of feed can be intelligently regulated. Single connection size ⅛-pint. Price..........**$1.33**

No. 24C6274 Double Connection Kid Self Feed Lubricators. Size, ⅛-pint. Price..............**$1.30**

Roberts' Single Connection Sight Feed Lubricators.

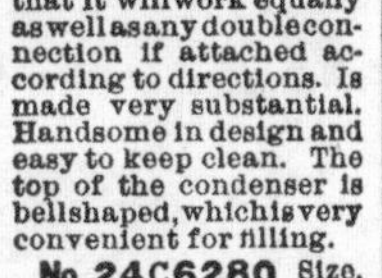

Roberts' Never Fail Single Connection Sight Feed Lubricator. This is one of the best low priced lubricators we have ever sold. It is so constructed that it will work equally as well as any double connection if attached according to directions. Is made very substantial. Handsome in design and easy to keep clean. The top of the condenser is bellshaped, which is very convenient for filling.

No. 24C6280 Size, ⅛-pint. Price.**$1.75**
No. 24C6281 Size, ¼-pint. Price..**$1.85**
No. 24C6282 Size, ⅜-pint. Price.. **2.15**
No. 24C6283 Size, ½-pint. Price.. **2.30**
No. 24C6284 Size, 1-pint. Price.. **3.60**
No. 24C6285 Size, 1-quart. Price.. **4.70**

Penberthy Automatic Injectors

Every Penberthy Injector is carefully tested before leaving the factory, and no machine is allowed to go out that will not work on the following points (while nearly all of them will do much better). Start low, 18 to 22 pounds steam on 4 foot lift; work high, 152 to 160 pounds steam on 4 foot lift; lift water 20 to 22 feet on 60 to 80 pounds steam; handle hot water, 120 to 125 degrees at 60 to 80 pounds steam; handle hot water, 112 to 115 degrees at 100 pounds steam; handle hot water, 85 to 100 degrees at 125 pounds steam. **The Penberthy Injector is one of the oldest as well as most reliable injectors on the market.**

No. 24C6295

Size	Horse Power	Pipe Connections	Capacity per hour, 1 to 3 ft. lift, 50 to 75 lbs. steam pres're		Price
		Inches	Max. gals.	Min. gals.	
100	4 to 8	⅜	80	55	$4.60
A	8 to 16	⅜	135	70	5.25
AA	12 to 22	½	180	100	5.85
B	17 to 32	½	260	140	7.30
BB	20 to 45	¾	355	170	8.85
C	40 to 65	1	475	300	11.75
CC	45 to 80	1	600	350	13.00
D	50 to 100	1¼	800	425	16.00

The above capacities are based on actual tests and are guaranteed. As will be seen from above, any size "Penberthy" will deliver more water than the corresponding size of any other make, while the capacity can be cut down about one-half by simply throttling water supply valve.

The Hancock Inspirators. Stationary Type.

No. 24C6300 The Hancock Inspirator, Stationary Type, for Feeding Stationary, Marine and Portable Boilers. It works with low or high steam, on all lifts up to 25 feet, and when taking water under a head with hot feed water as well as cold feed water. It requires no adjustment for varying steam pressures. Owing to the peculiar construction of this form of the Hancock Inspirators, it can be used for other purposes when not feeding the boiler. When desired, the lifter side or lifting apparatus can be used as an ejector for delivering water to a tank, or for other purposes. Water can be elevated above the Hancock Inspirator about 2½ feet for each pound of steam pressure. With 45 pounds steam pressure, water can be lifted 25 feet and elevated 112½ feet above the inspirator, a total elevation of 137½ feet.

No. 24C6300

Size	Prices, Stationary type	Pipe connections: Steam	Suction and Delivery	Overflow	Capacity per hour with 60 lbs. steam pressure, gallons	Horse Power: For the ordinary type of Boiler and Engine	On a basis of 30 lbs. Evaporation per H. P. per hour
7½	$ 4.60	⅜	⅜	¼	60	4 to 6	5 to 8
8¾	5.40	⅜	½	⅜	90	6 to 8	8 to 15
10	6.00	⅜	½	⅜	120	8 to 15	15 to 25
12½	7.50	½	¾	½	220	15 to 30	25 to 35
15	9.00	½	¾	½	300	30 to 40	35 to 60
17½	12.00	¾	1	¾	420	40 to 60	60 to 75
20	13.50	¾	1	¾	540	60 to 75	75 to 100
22½	16.50	1	1¼	1	710	78 to 90	100 to 130

Prices on larger sizes quoted upon application.

Metropolitan Automatic Injector.

Every Injector is guaranteed, and if it does not prove perfectly satisfactory, you can return it at our expense and we will refund your money.

The Metropolitan Automatic Injector is the result of combining in an automatic injector the correct principle, good mechanical design and perfect construction necessary to make a perfect automatic injector, and in eliminating the weak features common in injectors of this type. Special circular sent on application which gives a full description of the Metropolitan Injector, how constructed, which size to order, etc.

No. 24C6304

Size	Size of pipe connection	Capacity with Steam Pressure 80 lbs., 2-ft. Lift	Horse power	Price
2	⅜	60 gals.	4 to 6	$ 4.50
3	⅜	80 gals.	6 to 8	4.80
3½	½	120 gals.	8 to 15	5.40
4	½	165 gals.	15 to 20	6.00
5	¾	250 gals.	20 to 30	7.50
6	¾	350 gals.	30 to 45	9.00
7	1	500 gals.	45 to 65	12.00
8	1	600 gals.	65 to 80	13.50
9	1¼	800 gals.	80 to 100	16.50

The H-D Ejector or Jet Pump. Made with Independent Couplings and Tubes.

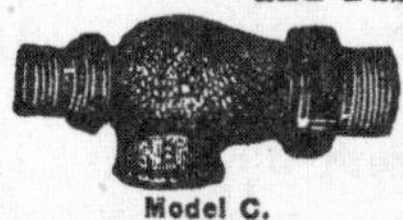

Model C.

No. 24C6312 They are used for lifting and conveying water and other liquids from one level to another in mines, pits, wells, tanneries, paper mills, chemical works—in fact in every place where it is desired to transport liquids of any kind. The H-D Ejector will lift 24 feet. When it is desired to raise the liquid to a greater distance, place the Ejector near the liquid and elevate it. With a steam pressure of 65 pounds it will elevate 50 to 60 feet, and with 100 pounds steam up 70 to 80 feet.

Size, No.	Pipe Connections: Steam	Suction and Delivery	Capacity per Hour	Price
1 Brass	⅜	⅜	250 gals.	$1.80
2 Brass	⅜	¾	500 gals.	2.25
3 Brass	¾	1	960 gals.	3.35
4 Brass	1	1¼	1300 gals.	4.50
5 Brass	1¼	1½	2000 gals.	5.63
6 Iron	1¼	2	4000 gals.	7.68
7 Iron	1½	2½	8000 gals.	10.13
8 Iron	2	3	11000 gals.	12.38

Farm Engine and Yacht Pop Valve.

No. 24C6330 Made of brass, finely finished, full relieving capacity and very sensitive. Connect valve as close to boiler as possible. When pipe connections are used, have them full diameter of valve or larger, and as short and free from bends as possible. In ordering, state horse power, size of boiler, highest working pressure.

Size	Size Steam connection	Horse power	Price
¾-inch	¾-inch	8	$1.48
1 -inch	1 -inch	12	1.65
1¼-inch	1¼-inch	18	2.05
1½-inch	1½-inch	20	2.95
2 -inch	2 -inch	30	3.95

Steam Whistles with Valve.

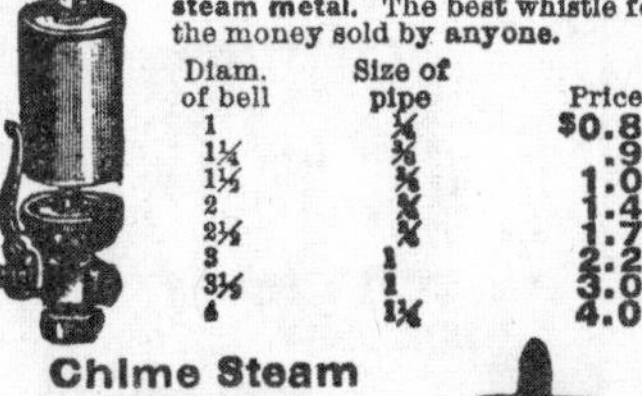

No. 24C6350 The bell is made of brass; valve, etc., of steam metal. The best whistle for the money sold by anyone.

Diam. of bell	Size of pipe	Price
1	⅜	$0.80
1¼	⅜	.98
1½	½	1.05
2	½	1.40
2½	¾	1.70
3	1	2.25
3½	1	3.05
4	1¼	4.00

Chime Steam Whistles.

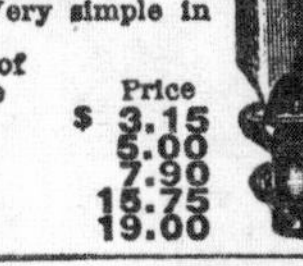

No. 24C6354 Single Bell Chime Whistle, made of highly polished brass. Gives three distinct tones. Very simple in construction.

Diameter of bell	Size of pipe	Price
2	½	$ 3.15
3	¾	5.00
4	1	7.90
5	1¼	15.75
6	1½	19.00

Steam Gauges.

Our Steam Gauges are the best made and worth two of the many cheaper ones. Our price of 98 cents and upwards will mean a great saving for you.

No. 24C6362 Steam Gauge, Iron Case, japanned, to register 200 pounds or less, single spring.

Size, inches	3½	4½	5
Price	98c	$1.00	$1.05

No. 24C6364 Steam Gauges, Iron Case, double spring for steamboats, portable and traction engines. Size, 4½ inches. Graduated 200 pounds. Price..............**$1.95**

Safety Valves.

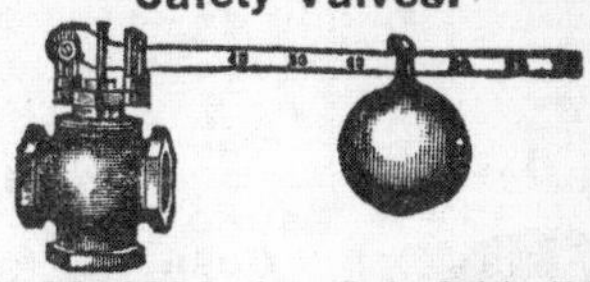

No. 24C6390 Iron Body Safety Valves with brass mounting. Screwed.

Size	1	1¼	1½
Price	$1.50	$1.55	$1.80
Size	2	2½	3
Price	2.45	4.20	5.30

Eclipse Governors.

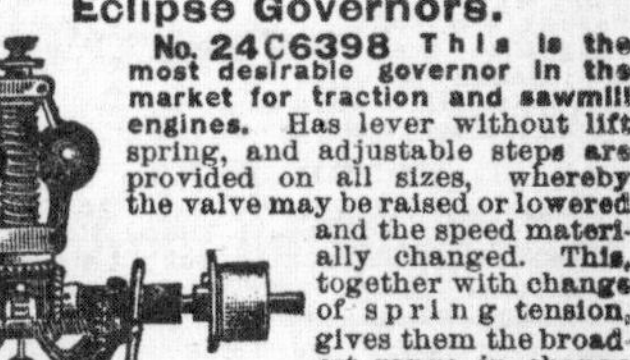

No. 24C6398 This is the most desirable governor in the market for traction and sawmill engines. Has lever without lift spring, and adjustable steps are provided on all sizes, whereby the valve may be raised or lowered and the speed materially changed. This, together with change of spring tension, gives them the broadest range in change of speed of any governor in the market. This governor is especially designed for traction engine service, and where it is necessary to change the speed of engine while it is running. By this device the speed can be increased or diminished from 25 to 30 per cent without changing the tension of spring. Also with this improvement the engineer can give the engine sufficient speed for any kind of road service, and immediately change it to the proper speed of threshing, or other purposes, without stopping. This governor is otherwise constructed so the jolting of the engine over rough and uneven ground or roads has but slight effect on the regulation. In ordering it is always best to give the make of engine; how fast you intend to run it; diameter of pulley on engine; shaft to drive the governor; diameter of base flange and if wanted for threaded pipe.

Size, In.	Height, In.	Pulley Diam. Face	Speed	Engine Cylinder Diam.	Price
½	10	1½x1¼	700	1¼ to 2½	$6.90
¾	13	2¼x1½	600	2 to 3	7.90
¾	13½	2¼x1½	600	3 to 4	8.90
1	15	2¼x1½	600	4 to 5	9.85
1¼	16	2¾x1½	600	5 to 6	10.80
1½	20	3 x1¾	450	6 to 7	12.30
2	22	3 x1¾	450	7 to 8	14.75
2½	26	3½x2¼	400	8 to 10	19.80
3	27	3½x2½	350	10 to 12	23.50

The Pickering Governor.

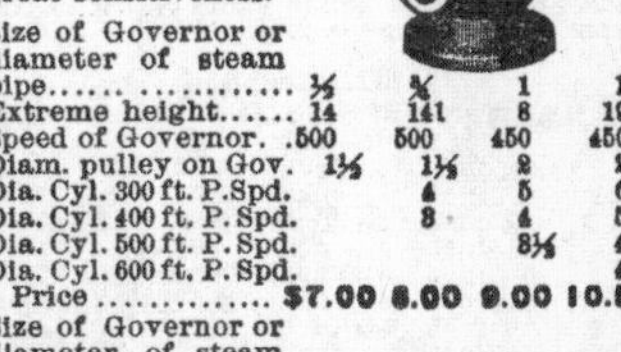

No. 24C6400 This Governor, by its accurate regulation and good workmanship, will commend itself wherever used. We guarantee to regulate accurately any size or style of engine and under all circumstances. For durability in all its parts, simplicity of construction, and economy in fuel, it cannot be excelled. Having no joints, its action is direct, thereby insuring great sensitiveness.

Size of Governor or diameter of steam pipe	½	¾	1	1¼
Extreme height	14	141	18	19
Speed of Governor	500	500	450	450
Diam. pulley on Gov.	1½	1½	2	2
Dia. Cyl. 300 ft. P.Spd.		4	5	6
Dia. Cyl. 400 ft. P.Spd.		3	4	5
Dia. Cyl. 500 ft. P.Spd.			3½	4½
Dia. Cyl. 600 ft. P.Spd.				4
Price	$7.00	8.00	9.00	10.50

Size of Governor or diameter of steam pipe	1½	2	2½	3
Extreme height	25	26	31½	35
Speed of Governor	420	420	380	320
Diam. pulley on Gov.	2½	2½	3	4
Dia. Cyl. 300 ft. P. Spd.	7	9	12	14
Dia. Cyl. 400 ft. P. Spd.	6	8	10	12
Dia. Cyl. 500 ft. P. Spd.	5	7	9	10
Dia. Cyl. 600 ft. P. Spd.	4½	6	8	9
Price	$12.50	15.00	19.85	30.00

Mocking Bird Whistles.

No. 24C6356 This is a simple and practical variable sound Steam Whistle, especially adapted for traction engines, locomotives, steamboats, factory and mill use. It makes an excellent fire alarm, and is attached like any ordinary whistle. The bell is provided with a piston, which is pulled downward by a chain running between pulleys, and when not in use is always at the top, being drawn upwards by means of a spring. To change the sound pull the chain. The bell must be raised or lowered to suit the steam pressure by screwing same up or down.

Diameter of Bell, inches	Size of Pipe Connection, inches	All Brass with Valve. Price
2½	¾	$ 4.55
3	¾	6.00
3½	1	8.65
4	1¼	12.00
5	1¼	17.00
6	1½	22.00

Water Gauges.

No. 24C6402 With brass body, iron wheels and two guards to protect the glass tube. Prices are for gauges complete, as shown in illustration.

Size	Rough	Finished
Pipe ⅜, Glass ⅝x10. Price,	67c	$0.94
Pipe ½, Glass ⅝x12. Price,	69c	1.08

Genuine Scotch Glass Tubes.

For Water Gauges.

No. 24C6406 These gauge glasses are imported by us direct, size labeled on end of each, and we warrant them equal to any. Lengths not regular, charged price of next longer tubes of same diameter.

Length		½	⅝	¾
10 inches	Price,	5c	5c	6c
11 inches	Price,	6c	6c	6c
12 inches	Price,	7c	7c	7c
13 inches	Price,	7c	7c	8c
14 inches	Price,	7c	7c	8c
15 inches	Price,	8c	8c	9c
16 inches	Price,	8c	8c	10c

Gauge Glass Gaskets.

No. 24C6407 Rubber Glass Gaskets or Washers.
Size, ½-inch. Per dozen....7c
Size, ⅝-inch. Per dozen....7c
Size, ¾-inch. Per dozen....7c

Water Gauge Glass Cutter.

No. 24C6410 Patent Water Gauge Glass Cutter. Made of the best material. Cutters made of the finest imported Jessops steel. Price 32c

Babbitt Metal.

No. 24C6450 The best low priced Babbitt Metal sold by anyone. Used largely on mowers, farm machinery, pulleys, etc. No. 4, per lb.....6½c

No. 24C6452 No. 3 Babbitt Metal. This grade is suitable for separators, horse powers. Price, per pound............7½c

No. 24C6454 No. 1 Babbitt Metal. This grade metal is used for same purposes as above metal, No. 24C6452, but a better grade. Price, per pound............10½c

No. 24C6456 No. 1 Lubricant Grade Babbitt Metal. This is a special grade of copper mixed metal used on high speed engines or on any piece of machinery where speed and durability are required. Price, per lb....15½c

Old Hickory Babbitt Metal.

No. 24C6461 Old Hickory Babbitt Metal is the highest grade babbitt on the market. Can be used on any journal, but is especially recommended for high speed machinery. It is made in round bars of 2½ pounds each, one side cone shaped, which fits the bottom of the melting ladle evenly thus all parts of metal melt at once. We cannot sell less than 2½ pounds.
Price, per pound............25c

Plumbers' Solder.

No. 24C6462 High Grade Plumbers' Solder, half and half. Comes in bars of about 1½ pounds each. We do not sell less than a bar
Price, per pound............17c

Pig Lead.

No. 24C6464 Genuine Pig Lead. Comes in pigs of about 80 pounds each.
Price, per pound............5½c

Block Tin.

No. 24C6466 Pure Block Tin. Comes in pigs of about 100 pounds; can also furnish bar tin in 1½-pound bars.
Price, bar tin, per pound............35c
Price, block tin, per pound............34c

Crucibles.

No. 24C6470 Plumbago or Graphite Crucibles.

	Height	Diameter	Price
No. 2...	3⅛-inch.	2⅝-inch.	27c
No. 3...	4 -inch.	2⅞-inch.	31c
No. 3...	4½-inch.	3½-inch.	36c
No. 4...	5 -inch.	4 -inch.	40c
No. 5...	5½-inch.	4½-inch.	47c
No. 6...	5¾-inch.	4¾-inch.	56c
No. 8...	6½-inch.	5¼-inch.	60c
No. 10...	7⅝-inch.	6 -inch.	80c

Valve or Float.

No. 24C6475 This Valve and Float is used to regulate the supply of water in a watering trough. The float is attached to the end of the lever, and as the water rises in the trough it shuts the valve. It has brass valve seat. By changing position of lever it will either open or close when used either on bottom or side of tank, or when two levers are used it can be used to open or close.

Size in...	¾	1	1¼	1½	2	2½
Price...	75c	80c	90c	$1.75	$2.65	$4.50

PLUMBERS' GOODS AND SUPPLIES

EVERYTHING IN THE LINE OF PLUMBERS' TOOLS, MATERIALS AND SUPPLIES.

Please compare our prices on this line of goods with prices quoted for goods of equal quality by specialty houses and exclusive dealers in Plumbers' Supplies. We feel sure a comparison of our prices will show where we can save you from 15 to 35 per cent.

THIS DEPARTMENT OF PLUMBING GOODS AND SUPPLIES is only one of the many merchandise departments in our house, and our margin of profit on these goods is exactly the same as our profit on the most staple lines of merchandise. Our prices in every instance are based on the manufacturing cost with the smallest possible percentage of profit added. We have the most economical method of marketing goods, namely, through the medium of our catalogue, without any traveling salesmen or any of the expense common to the usual methods of selling this line of goods.

NOTICE: IF INTERESTED IN PLUMBING, STEAM OR HOT WATER HEATING, WRITE US FOR OUR SPECIAL PLUMBING CATALOGUE, which shows a most complete line of Plumbing, Sectional and Magazine Heaters, Radiators, etc. Space will not permit showing our complete line. We can save you 50 per cent on these goods.

A Complete Special Catalogue sent free for the asking. Write us at once.

Enameled Iron Hopper Closets.

No. 24C7500 Enameled Iron Straight Hopper, self raising seat, complete as shown in illustration. No waste or supply pipes or tank furnished at the price.
Price $4.15

Frost Proof Closets.

No. 24C7503 Our Frost Proof Closets have frost proof brass valves for outside and exposed places. The valve is below frost line, and is connected with hopper by a heavy chain, fastened to seat; when seat is depressed the valve is opened and hopper is flushed; when seat is relieved the supply is shut off and waste pipe opened, allowing the water which is in pipe to drain direct into trap; therefore valve and pipe are at all times free from water.

We furnish above, complete with cast iron hopper, enameled inside, self raising seat, frost proof valve, 5-foot length of pipe, cast iron P trap complete with chain and lever. For cold or exposed places this outfit is the best on the market, water is always below frost line, it is easily connected, is substantially constructed and avoids rotting away of wooden supports, as all water wastes direct into sewer.

Price, complete............$8.00

Low Tank, Wash Down, Siphon Combination Closet, Special Price, $11.90.

No. 24C7504 Our Low Tank, Wash Down Siphon Combination is by far the most up to date closet sold by anyone, and at the price we ask for it, is 50 per cent lower than a closet of this kind was ever sold at before. Don't let the price lead you to believe it is a cheaply constructed affair, made only to sell. We guarantee it to be the equal of any wash out closet ever put on the market. The tank, seat and cover are made of solid oak, golden oak finish, tank is copper lined; has copper floats, solid brass valve, improved flushing valve. All trimmings, hinges, etc., made of cast brass, heavily nickel plated. Supply pipe is ⅜-inch in diameter, made of brass, also nickel plated. A slight pressure of the valve button gives a flush that empties the tank complete. Furnished complete as shown in the illustration.

Price, complete with plain bowl....$11.90

If wanted with embossed bowl, add 60 cents to the above price.

Low Tank, Siphon Jet Combination Closet.

No. 24C7505 Low Tank, Siphon Jet Combination Closets. The low tank closet is by far the most popular closet now on the market. It does away with the long supply pipes and high tank. Has a 2-inch opening in bowl, which insures a positive flush every time; is noiseless and neat in appearance. Can be placed in out of the way place or under stairs where high tank will not go. The tank is made of solid oak, golden oak finish, is lined with heavy sheet copper, has copper float, brass valve, etc. The valve is our improved positive flush valve, cannot get out of order. A slight pressure of the valve lever or button empties the tank complete. The seat and cover are made of oak, all trimmings, hinges, etc., of brass, heavy nickel plated; supply pipe is ⅜-inch in diameter, nickel plated; furnished complete ready to set up. The bowl is high grade vitreous English earthenware—siphon jet style, by far the best pottery made.

Price, complete with plain earthenware bowl............$17.50

If wanted with embossed bowl, add $1.00 to above price.

Acme Water Closets.

At $12.75 we offer this water closet as the equal of closets that plumbers sell at $16.00 to $20.00.

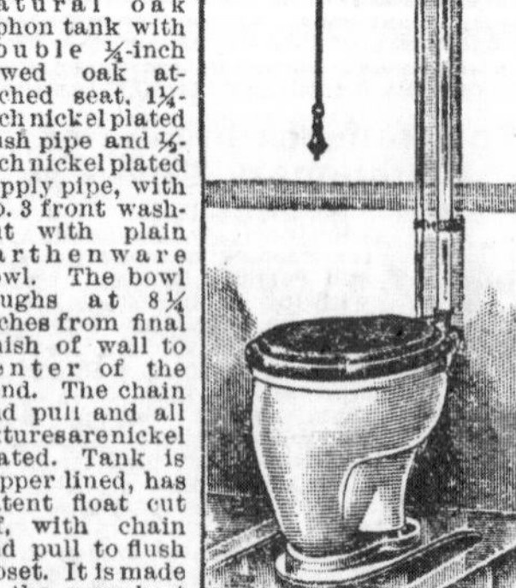

No. 24C7510 Our Acme Water Closet is by far the best finished and most up to date closet on the market. It has a round cornered natural oak siphon tank with double ⅜-inch sawed oak attached seat, 1¼-inch nickel plated flush pipe and ⅜-inch nickel plated supply pipe, with No. 3 front washout with plain earthenware bowl. The bowl roughs at 8¼ inches from final finish of wall to center of the bend. The chain and pull and all fixtures are nickel plated. Tank is copper lined, has patent float cut off, with chain and pull to flush closet. It is made of the very best materials throughout and the workmanship and finish are perfect. Furnished complete, ready for use, no fitting or extras required.
Price............$12.75

No. 24C7512 Closet, same as No. 24C7510, only without supply and waste pipes. Price............11.25

If wanted with embossed bowl, add 60 cents to above prices.

Acme Combination Hopper and Trap Closet.

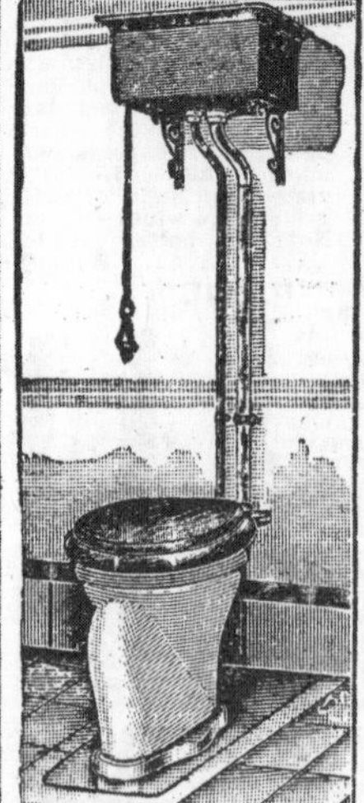

No. 24C7513 Combination Hopper and Trap or Wash Down Siphon Closet. This makes one of the best low priced outfits we carry. The tank, pipe and fittings are the same as described in our No. 24C7510 below. Everything is first class. Could not work better nor last longer at any price. A great many prefer this combination hopper to the regular No. 3 front washout as shown in No. 24C7510, as it gives a more positive flush, has greater force, etc.
Price, complete, ready to set up, $13.00

If wanted with embossed bowl, add 60 cents to above price.

Siphon Jet Water Closets.

No. 24C7514 Water Closets, complete as shown in illustration. Tank is copper lined. Outside made of quarter sawed oak; has siphon jet; 1¼-inch nickel plated flush pipe; ⅜-inch nickel plated supply pipe. Has double oak seat attached to bowl; chain and pull nickel plated. Furnished complete, with chain, pull, striker and floor bolts. A very neat and substantial closet at a moderate price.
Price $17.95

No. 24C7516 Closet, same as No. 24C7514, but without supply and waste pipes.
Price $16.35

If wanted with embossed bowl, add 75 cents to the above prices.

Something New in Steel Bath Tubs.

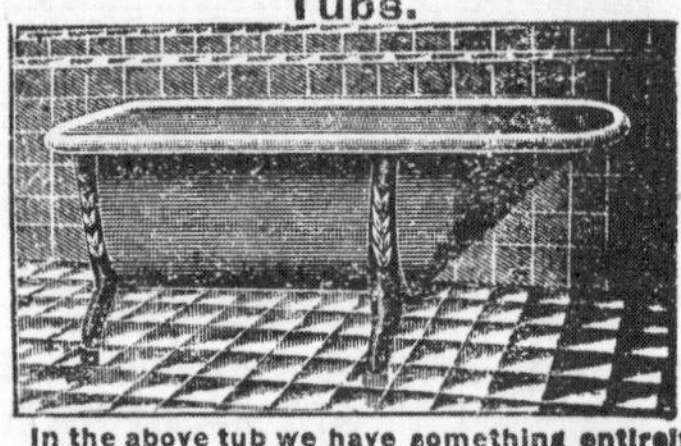

In the above tub we have something entirely different from the regular steel clad tub we have sold for several years. It is made of the finest rolled galvanized steel, carefully finished inside with our special white Japan enamel, baked on to a fine porcelain finish. The most serviceable and durable enamel yet produced. The outside is enameled in a nile green color, which gives the tub a very artistic appearance. The cap, or rim, instead of being wood, as heretofore, is made of cast metal, cast in one piece, with lugs to fasten to legs, and is finished with our special white enamel, baked on, giving the tub the appearance of a cast iron porcelain tub. Has patent overflow and waste connection and plug and chain, making it by far the most up to date tub now on the market.

NOTICE—We would call your special attention to the cast metal rim feature of this tub. There is no wood used whatever, all steel and iron, enameled in pure porcelain white. We experienced considerable trouble with the wood rim tubs, inasmuch as the joints soon become loose, varnish comes off, etc. With the cast rim, we have overcome all this. This is the only tub now on the market with a metal rim. Furnished complete in hardwood crate, with patent overflow and waste, also plug and chain. All tubs fitted for No. 4½ Fuller cocks. Shipping weight, 90 pounds.

NOTICE—For No. 4½ Fuller Hot and Cold Combination Cock, add $1.75 to prices given.

No. 24C7520 Size, 4 ft., 6 in. Price $5.65
No. 24C7521 Size, 5 feet, Price....6.15
No. 24C7522 Size, 5 feet 6 in. Price 6.48
No. 24C7523 Size, 6 feet. Price.......7.68

Nickeloid Bath Tubs.

These tubs are constructed with an outer casting of heavy sheet steel and inner lining of heavy sheet zinc, both sides deposited with copper, and outside heavily nickel plated, planished and polished to a mirror finish. The interior of our shells are coated with our non-corrosive sheet steel mixture. The nickel plated zinc sheets are finely fitted into a heavy steel shell, and capped with our patent cast metal rim; legs are of same style and similarly secured; fitted with a patent connected waste and overflow, and outside connections for 1½ L. P. gauge. Finished on the outside in a beautifully tinted nile green, and all rims are pure white enameled, baked on to a hard fine porcelain finish. Legs bronzed in pure gold. Rims are patent cast metal, with lugs cast therein to secure legs, and cross ribs with notches to retain body of tubs. No screws or tacks used, which always get loose, and no joints to come apart as on the old style wood rim. There is no wood used whatever on these tubs, nothing but iron, steel and copperized nickel plated zinc. Furnished complete with overflow and waste, also plug and chain. Fitted for No. 4½ Fuller cocks. Shipping weight, 90 pounds.

NOTICE—For No. 4½ Fuller Hot and Cold Combination Cock, add $1.75 to prices given below.

No. 24C7525 Size 4 ft. 6 in. Price $8.50
No. 24C7526 Size 5 ft. Price..... 8.95
No. 24C7527 Size 5 ft. 6 in. Price $9.95
No. 24C7528 Size 6 ft. Price.... 10.60

Copper Lined Bath Tubs.

These tubs are constructed with an outer casing of heavy sheet steel, and inner lining of tinned copper, planished and polished. The interiors of the shells are coated with our special non-corrosive sheet steel mixture. They are designed to meet the demand for a well made, carefully finished, copper lined steel tub. They are constructed on the shape and model of our patent enameled tub; the rim and legs are of the same style and similarly secured. Patent overflows and outside connections of threads are for 1½ L. P. gauge. Finished on outside in a beautiful tinted nile green. All rims are pure white enameled, baked on to a hard fine porcelain finish, legs bronzed in a beautiful gold or silver aluminum. Rims are patent cast metal, cast in one piece, with lugs cast therein to secure legs, and cross ribs with notches to retain the body of tub. No screws or tacks used, which become loose, and no joints to come apart as on the old style wood rim. There is no wood used whatever on these tubs, nothing but steel, iron and copper, and all parts heavy, making it strong and substantial, and the artistic design of same gives it a neat and tasty appearance. Copper lining is as smooth, well tinned and polished as it is possible to make it, and finely fitted to steel shell; copper guaranteed up to weight. Fitted for No. 4½ Fuller cocks. Weight averages 90 lbs.

NOTICE—For No. 4½ Fuller Hot and Cold Combination Cock, add $1.75 to prices given below.

No. 24C7529 Size, 4 feet 6 inches. Price....$10.75
No. 24C7530 Size, 5 feet. Price. 11.00
No. 24C7531 Size, 5 feet 6 inches. Price.... 12.00
No. 24C7532 Size, 6 feet. Price. 14.00

Roll Rim Porcelain Enameled Iron Baths.

No. 24C7535 Best Grade Porcelain Enameled Bath Tub, made of high grade cast iron, extra heavy weight enameling, put on by a patent process, which we guarantee not to flake or peel off. We furnish the tub with 2½-inch wide enameled rolled rim; nickel plated overflow and waste plug with strainer. Height on legs, 27 inches; width over all, 29 inches; depth inside, 20 inches. Enameled inside, painted one coat outside. Average weight, 300 pounds.

NOTICE—For No. 4½ Fuller Hot and Cold Combination Cock, add $1.75 to prices given below.

Size of tub, 4½ feet; length over rim, 4 feet 9 inches; length over all, 4 feet 10 inches. Price....$14.95
Size of tub, 5 feet; length over rim, 5 feet 3 inches; length over all, 5 feet 4 inches. Price.... 16.95
Size of tub, 5½ feet; length over rim, 5 feet 9 inches; length over all, 5 feet 10 inches. Price.... 18.95
Size of tub, 6 feet; length over rim, 5 feet 10 inches; length over all, 6 feet ½ inch. Price.... 21.95

Porcelain Enameled Bath Tub, Complete.

No. 24C7536 Roll Rim Porcelain Enameled Bath Tub, made of high grade cast iron, complete with No. 4½ Fuller Combination Cock. Has patent overflow, nickel plated plug and chain, ½-inch nickel plated supply pipe and outside nickel plated waste pipe. Stands 27 inches high, 29 inches wide over all, 20 inches deep and 2½-inch roll rim. This is one of the best tubs on the market. Everything about it is new and up to date. We guarantee the enameling not to crack or peel off. A first class tub in every respect. Good enough for any residence. Manufactured by one of the largest makers of plumbing goods in the United States and guaranteed to be perfect in every respect. Enameled inside, painted one coat outside. Price includes everything complete, ready for use. Average weight, 300 pounds.

Size	4½ feet	5 feet	5½ feet	6 feet
Price	$19.00	$21.00	$23.00	$26.00

WHILE OUR PRICES on everything in the line of plumbing are extremely low, please bear in mind that the goods are strictly high class in every way. We guarantee the quality of everything we sell and any goods that do not prove perfectly satisfactory can be returned to us at our expense of transportation charges both ways and we will promptly return your money.

Improved Bath Heater.

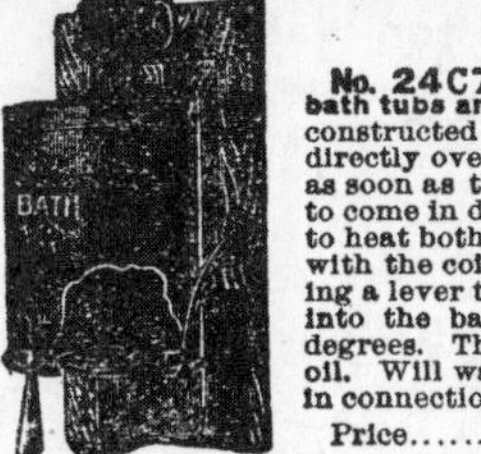

No. 24C7543 This heater is the same as used in connection with our bath tubs and is made of the best galvanized iron. Consists of a round coil constructed of ⅜-inch copper tubing, attached to the bottom of heater and directly over the burners in such a way as to cause the water to circulate as soon as the burners are lighted, and at the same time allowing the flame to come in direct contact with the bottom of heater, thus causing the water to heat both by circulation and radiation at the same time. In connection with the coil, we employ a three-way cock, which is so arranged that by raising a lever the circulation through heater is shut off, and the water drawn into the bath tub. By so doing the temperature of the water is raised 20 degrees. The heater is arranged to burn either gasoline, gas, natural gas or oil. Will warm 20 gallons of water in from 25 to 30 minutes, and can be used in connection with water service.

Price....$10.00

Oval Foot Tubs.

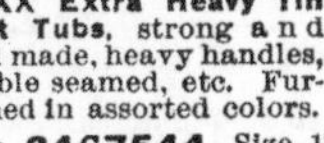

XXX Extra Heavy Tin Foot Tubs, strong and well made, heavy handles, double seamed, etc. Furnished in assorted colors.

		Price
No. 24C7544	Size, 17x13¼ inches	28c
No. 24C7545	Size, 18x14⅜ inches	33c
No. 24C7546	Size, 20x16½ inches	45c

Infants' Bath Tubs.

Infants' Heavy XXXX Tin Bath Tubs, well made, double seamed, strong rim and handles. Nicely japanned.

No. 24C7547	Size, 27 in. Price..	$0.78
No. 24C7548	Size, 30 in. Price..	.88
No. 24C7549	Size, 33 in. Price..	1.00
No. 24C7550	Size, 36 in. Price..	1.32
No. 24C7551	Size 42 in. Price..	1.55

Plunge Bath Tubs.

No. 24C7552 Extra Heavy Tin Plunge Bath Tubs, double seamed, heavy roll at top, extra wood bottom, waste pipe at end of tub. Nothing better made in a tin tub.

Size, 4 feet. Price....$4.30
Size, 5 feet. Price.... 5.95
Size, 6 feet. Price.... 5.55

Open Plumbing Marble Lavatories.

Italian marble slab, 20x24 inches, 1¼ inches thick, 8-inch back, 14-inch round patent overflow basin, nickel plated metal plug with rubber stopper, nickel plated S trap; No. 1 Fuller basin cocks, chain and stays, and nickel plated brackets.

No. 24C7563 Tennessee Marble.
Price, with 14-inch round bowl....$ 9.00
Price, with 14x17-inch oval bowl.... 10.00

No. 24C7564 Italian Marble.
Price, with 14-inch round bowl.... 9.85
Price, with 14x17-inch oval bowl.... 10.75

Open Plumbing Marble Lavatory, furnished complete, as shown in illustration. Back and bottom slabs are made of Italian and Tennessee pink marble, highly polished. Back slab is 8 inches high; bottom slab 20x24 inches, with 14-inch earthenware patent overflow bowl; nickel plated No. 1 basin cocks; nickel plated brackets, with nickel plated supply pipe and air chamber; plug and chain nickel plated. We guarantee all parts to be made of the best materials and workmanship to be perfect. Being all nickel plated, it does not require much care to keep it clean. Will not rust or corrode. We furnish everything complete, ready for use.

No. 24C7566 Tennessee Marble.
Price, with 14-inch round bowl....$11.40
Price, with 14x17-inch oval bowl.... 12.35

No. 24C7567 Italian Marble.
Price, with 14-inch round bowl.... 12.15
Price, with 14x17-inch oval bowl.... 13.15

Open Plumbing Corner Lavatories.

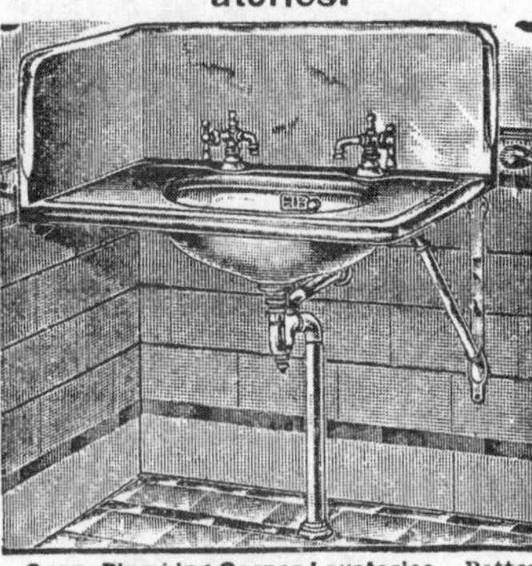

Open Plumbing Corner Lavatories. Bottom slab is 20x24 inches; backs 8 inches high, in either Italian or Tennessee marble. We use nothing but the **best grade of marble.** Furnished complete, ready for use, with brass nickel plated S-trap, No. 1 Fuller nickel plated cocks, chain, stay and brackets, nickel plated. **Everything first class. For either right or left hand corner. Be sure and state which is wanted. Illustration shows left hand corner.**

No. 24C7569 Tennessee Marble.
Price, with 14-inch round bowl....$10.45
Price, with 14x17-inch oval bowl.... 11.20

No. 24C7570 Italian Marble.
Price, with 14-inch round bowl.... 11.45
Price, with 14x17-inch oval bowl.... 12.20

Open Plumbing Marble Lavatories.

Marble Lavatories, A1 material and finish. Furnished with nickel plated brass legs, nickel plated brass trap, with improved nickel plated brass bibbs, chain and plug. Slab is 20x24 inches, 1¼ inches thick. Has 8-inch back with oval or round bowl. Comes complete ready to set up.

No. 24C7571 Tennessee Marble.
Price, with 14-inch round bowl....$ 9.70
Price, with 14x17-inch oval bowl.... 10.60

No. 24C7572 Italian Marble.
Price, with 14-inch round bowl.... 10.50
Price, with 14x17-inch oval bowl.... 11.35

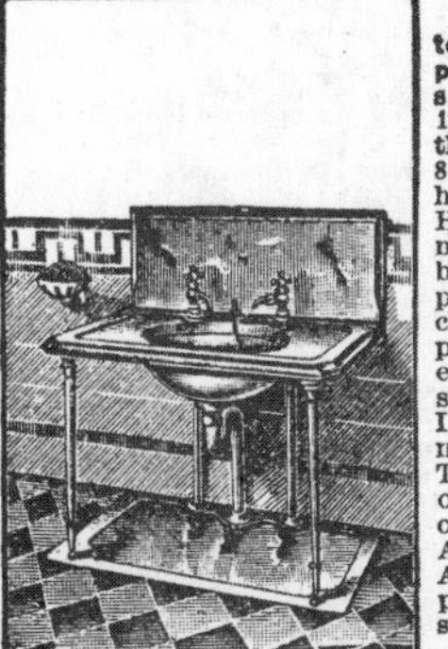

Marble Lavatories with Supply Pipes. The slab is 20x24 in., 1¼ inches thick, with an 8-inch back, highly finished. Has improved nickel plated bibbs, nickel plated stay, chain, rubber plug, etc., nickel plated brass supply pipes. Legs are brass, nickel plated. This makes one of the neatest outfits we sell. All material is A1. Comes complete, ready to set up.

No. 24C7574 Tennessee Marble.
Price, with 14-inch round bowl....$12.00
Price, with 14x17-inch oval bowl.... 12.95

No. 24C7575 Italian Marble.
Price, with 14-inch round bowl.... 12.75
Price, with 14x17-inch oval bowl.... 13.70

ENAMELED IRON WARE.

In buying enameled sinks, lavatories, tubs, etc., from us, remember you get **first quality goods**—no seconds, and any piece found imperfect in any way can be returned to us at our expense. Our low prices may lead you to believe there is something wrong in the quality. All we ask is a trial order. There is no better ware made—quality, style and finish considered, than the following line of enameled ware.

It is made in one of the most modern and complete foundry and enameling plants. Only skilled workmen employed who have had years of experience in enameling. We have made our prices low, as we intend to sell more goods of this kind than any jobber in the United States.

All the following Enameled Cast Lavatories, taking brackets, are furnished with our improved Acme Bracket, unless otherwise ordered. This bracket always insures a rigid, firm lavatory, as a thin board can be nailed to studding, when the bracket can be screwed on to the board. It is not always possible to strike a studding when bracket is screwed to the wall.

Enameled Iron One-piece Lavatories.

Enameled Iron One-piece Lavatories. Includes waste plug and coupling, rubber stopper, chain stay and nickel plated overflow strainer. Also two high grade compression cocks, brass nickel plated. Length of back, 14 inches; height of back, 6 inches. Patent overflow basin, 12 inches in diameter.

No. 24C7501 Price, enameled inside, bronzed exterior....$3.75
No. 24C7502 Price, enameled all over.... 5.40

Enameled Iron One-piece Corner Lavatories.

Enameled Iron One-piece Corner Lavatories. Includes waste plug and coupling, rubber stopper, chain stay and nickel plated overflow strainer. Length of sides, 15 inches; height of back, 6 inches. With patent overflow 12-inch round basin. Also two high grade brass nickel plated compression cocks.

No. 24C7507 Price, enameled inside, with bronzed exterior....$3.76
No. 24C7508 Price, enameled all over.... 5.50

Enameled Iron One-piece Lavatories.

Enameled Iron, One-piece, Half Circle Lavatories, with sanitary nickel plated brass soap tray. Waste plug and coupling, rubber stopper, chain stay, nickel plated overflow strainer and brackets. Also two high grade compression cocks. To make this lavatory complete add one of our Nos. 24C7701, 24C7702, 24C7703 or 24C7706 traps. Slab is 17x19 inches; height of back, 6 inches; patent overflow D bowl, 10x14 inches.

No. 24C7515 Price, enameled inside, bronzed exterior....$4.60
No. 24C7517 Price, enameled all over.... 5.75

IF YOU EXPECT TO DO ANYTHING IN THE LINE OF PAINTING, Don't fail to write for our **FREE PAINT SAMPLE BOOK.**

Enameled Iron One-piece Lavatories.

Enameled Iron, One-piece, Half Circle Lavatories, with waste plug and coupling, rubber stopper, chain stay, nickel plated overflow strainer and brackets, also two high grade nickel plated compression cocks. Slab is 18x2 inches; height of back, 8 inches, with patent overflow bowl, 11x14 inches.

No. 24C7578 Price, enameled inside, bronzed exterior........**$4.95**

No. 24C7579 Price, enameled all over........**6.75**

These lavatories can be used in connection with our traps Nos. 24C7701, 24C7702, 24C7703 and 24C7706.

Enameled Iron One-piece Lavatories.

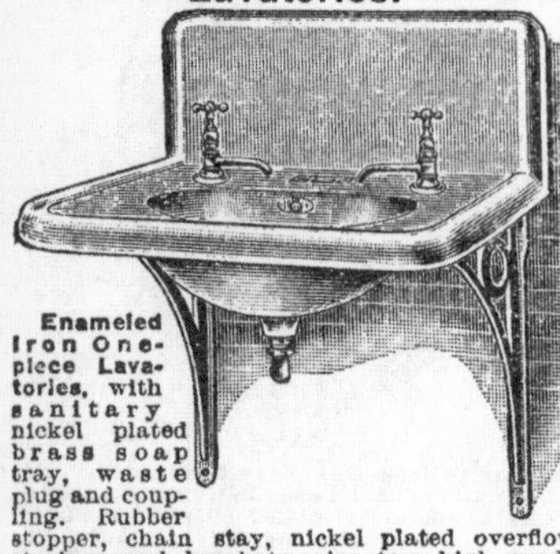

Enameled Iron One-piece Lavatories, with sanitary nickel plated brass soap tray, waste plug and coupling. Rubber stopper, chain stay, nickel plated overflow strainer and brackets, also two high grade nickel plated compresssion cocks. Backs are 10 inches high.

No. 24C7540 Size, 18x24-inch slab with patent overflow basin 11x15 in. Price..**$6.00**

No. 24C7541 Size, 20x24-inch slab with patent overflow basin 12x16 in. Price...**$7.65**

These lavatories can be used in connection with our nickel plated traps. Nos. 24C7701, 24C7702, 24C7703 or 24C7706.

Enameled Iron One-piece Lavatories.

Enameled Iron One-piece Half Circle Apron Lavatories with sanitary, nickel plated brass soap tray, waste plug with coupling, rubber stopper, chain stay, nickel plated overflow strainer and brackets; also two high grade nickel plated compression cocks. Slab is 18x21 inches, with 8-inch high back patent overflow D bowl 10x14 inches.

No. 24C7542 Enameled inside, bronzed exterior. Price........**$5.90**

No. 24C7543 Enameled all over. Price........**7.75**

Can be used in connection with our traps Nos. 24C7701, 24C7702, 24C7703 and 24C7706.

Enameled Iron One-piece Lavatories.

Enameled Iron, One-piece Half Circle Apron Lavatories with nickel plated model waste and brackets, also two high grade nickel plated compression cocks. Slab, 18x21 inches; height of back, 8 inches; patent overflow D bowl 10x14 inches.

No. 24C7556 Price, enameled inside, bronzed exterior........**$7.35**

No. 24C7557 Price, enameled all over........**8.62**

Can be used in connection with our traps Nos. 24C7701, 24C7702, 24C7703 and 24C7706.

Enameled Iron One-piece Lavatories.

Enameled One-piece Apron Lavatories, with sanitary nickel plated brass soap tray; with waste plug and coupling, rubber stopper, chain stay, nickel plated overflow strainer and enameled iron brackets, also two high grade nickel plated compression cocks. Made in two sizes, as follows:

No. 24C7565 Size, 18x24 inches, with 10-inch high back, patent overflow D bowl 11x15 inches. Price........**$7.90**

No. 24C7568 Size, 20x24 inches with 12-inch high back, patent overflow D bowl 11x15 inches. Price........**$8.40**

This lavatory can be used in connection with our traps Nos. 24C7701, 24C7702, 24C7703 and 24C7706

Enameled Iron One-piece Corner Lavatories.

No. 24C7573 Enameled Iron One-piece Corner Apron Lavatory, with sanitary nickel plated brass soap tray, waste plug and coupling; rubber stopper, chain stay, nickel plated overflow strainer and wall brackets; also two high grade nickel plated compression cocks. Length on sides, 20 inches; height of back, 6 or 8 inches; patent overflow D bowl 10x14 inches.

Size, 6-inch high back, enameled inside, bronzed outside. Price........**$6.20**

Size, 6-inch high back, enameled all over. Price........**$7.80**

Size, 8-inch high back, enameled inside, bronzed outside. Price........**$7.05**

Size, 8-inch high back, enameled all over. Price........**$8.75**

This lavatory can be used in connection with our traps Nos. 24C7701, 24C7702, 24C7703 and 24C7706.

Enameled Iron One-piece Lavatories.

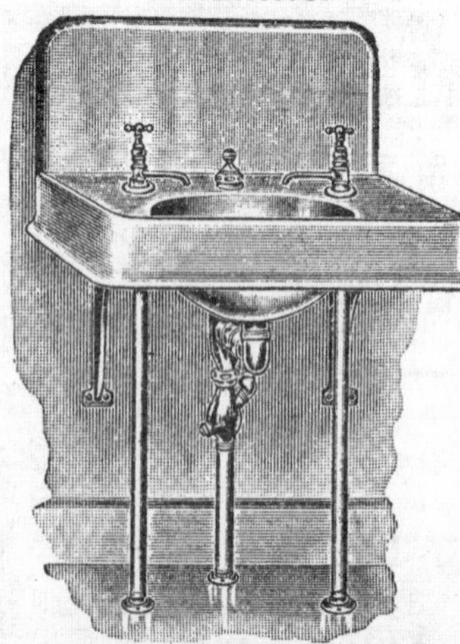

No. 24C7574 Enameled Iron One-piece Apron Lavatory, with nickel plated model waste and enameled iron brackets, complete with brass, nickel plated, compression cocks, brass, nickel plated, supply pipes and brass, nickel plated Acme patent traps. One of the most up to date lavatories on the market. Slab is 20x24 inches; height of back, 12 inches. Has oval bowl, 11x15 inches.

Enameled outside. Price........**$14.00**

Roll Rim Iron Wash Stands.

No. 24C7581 Roll Rim White Enameled Iron Lavatories to place in corner of room. In ordering, be sure and state which corner of the room stand is to be placed, right or left hand.

NOTICE—Can furnish with S trap and floor plate at same price if so desired.

Price........**$12.40**

If wanted with nickel plated supply pipe, add $1.25 to the above price.

If you are interested in Plumbing Goods, Steam or Hot Water Heating, write us for our Special Plumbing Catalogue. Sent free of charge for the asking.

Enameled Iron Sectional Lavatories.

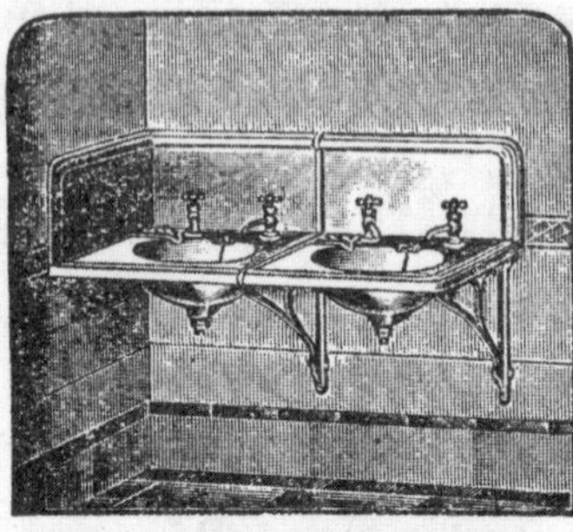

No. 24C7582 Enameled Iron Sectional Lavatories are especially adapted for hotel, restaurant and schoolhouse use. Size of each section, 18x24 inches. Height of back, 10½ inches. Length over all, 48 inches. Size of bowl, 12x15 inches. Furnished complete with four nickel plated compression basin cocks and two brackets, overflow, plug and chain.

Price........**$20.00**

In ordering, state whether right or left hand end is wanted.

Flat Rim Roll Back Sinks.

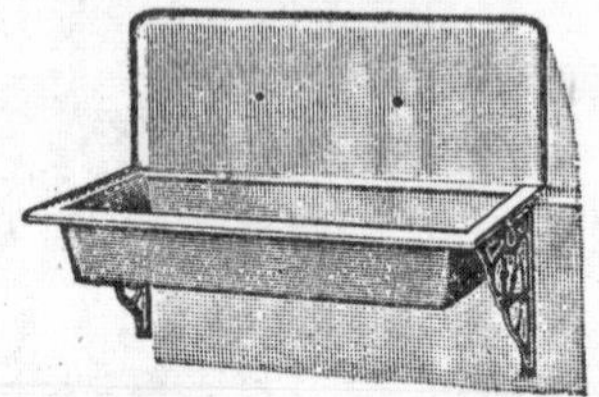

No. 24C7583 Porcelain Enameled Cast Iron Flat Rim Roll Back Sinks. White enameled inside with enameled back, complete with cast iron painted brackets. This makes a very neat sanitary sink at a small cost. Backs are 12 inches high; made extra deep so that faucets and pipe connections can be placed back of same. Makes a neat job, as nothing shows from the outside except the faucets. Made with holes for two faucets. Complete with all connections and strainer. Faucets not furnished at prices given below. For faucets, see No. 24C7880 to No. 24C7888.

Size, 18x30 inches. Price........**$3.95**
Size, 18x36 inches. Price........**4.85**
Size, 20x30 inches. Price........**4.25**
Size, 20x36 inches. Price........**4.75**
Size, 20x40 inches. Price........**4.90**

Enameled Iron Roll Rim Kitchen Sinks.

No. 24C7589 High Grade Cast Iron Enameled Roll Rim Kitchen Sinks, with 12-inch high, 2¼-inch deep roll rim back, nickel plated brass strainer and bronzed iron brackets. Also two high grade brass Fuller cocks.

Size, 18x30 inches. Price........**$5.40**
Size, 18x36 inches. Price........**7.90**
Size, 20x30 inches. Price........**7.30**
Size, 20x36 inches. Price........**8.10**
Size, 20x40 inches. Price........**9.40**

PLUMBERS WILL DO WELL to compare our prices on these goods with prices asked by others, whether wholesalers or jobbers. We are not in the plumbing goods trust, and you will find that our prices on many items are lower than you can secure from any other source. You can save money by buying from this catalogue.

Enameled Iron Roll Rim Corner Kitchen Sinks.

No. 24C7594 Enameled Iron Roll Rim Corner Kitchen Sinks, with 15-inch high, 2½ inch deep roll rim back and nickel plated brass strainer. Also two high grade Fuller cocks and bronzed bracket.

Size, 18x30 inches. Price........**$ 9.00**
Size, 18x36 inches. Price........**10.75**
Size, 20x30 inches. Price........**10.15**
Size, 20x36 inches. Price........**11.00**
Size, 20x40 inches, Price........**12.00**

If wanted with air chambers, add 60c extra.

Enameled Iron Roll Rim Kitchen Sinks.

No. 24C7597 Enameled Iron Roll Rim Kitchen Sinks, on bronzed iron legs, with 15-inch high roll rim back, extending over drain board, nickel plated strainer, 24-inch enameled iron drain board on bronzed bracket, also two high grade Fuller cocks. Furnished with either right or left hand drain board; illustration shows right hand. **Be sure and state which is wanted.**

Size, 18x30 inches. Price........**$13.35**
Size, 18x36 inches. Price........**14.65**
Size, 20x30 inches. Price........**13.65**
Size, 20x36 inches. Price........**15.15**
Size, 20x40 inches. Price........**16.15**

If wanted with air chambers, add 60c extra.

Enameled Iron Roll Rim Corner Kitchen Sinks.

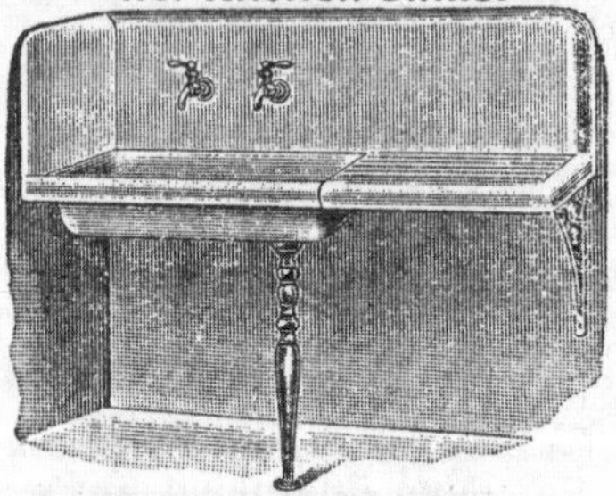

No. 24C7598 Enameled Iron Roll Rim Sinks on bronzed legs, with 15-inch high roll rim back, extending over drain board; nickel plated strainer, 24-inch enameled iron drain board on bronzed bracket, also two high grade Fuller cocks. Furnished either right or left hand; illustration shows left hand end with right hand drain board. **Be sure and state which is wanted.**

Size, 18x30 inches. Price........**$14.75**
Size, 18x36 inches. Price........**16.00**
Size, 20x30 inches. Price........**15.70**
Size, 20x36 inches. Price........**16.90**
Size, 20x40 inches. Price........**18.00**

If wanted with air chambers, add 60c extra.

Enameled Iron Roll Rim Kitchen Sinks.

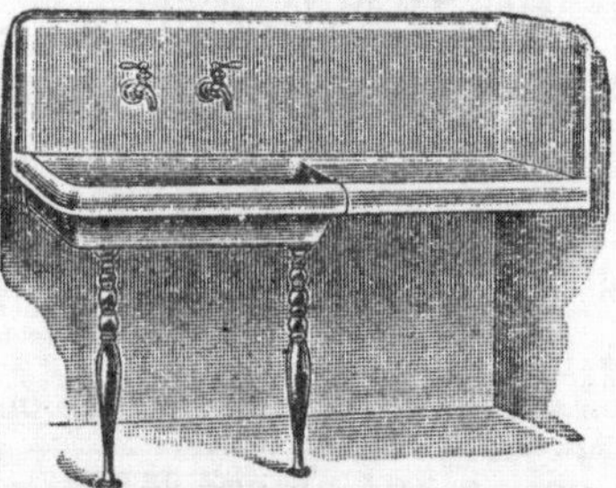

No. 24C7599 Enameled Iron Roll Rim Sinks, on bronzed legs, with 15-inch high roll rim back, extending over drain board. Nickel plated brass strainer and 24-inch enameled iron drain board with end piece. Also two high grade Fuller cocks. Furnished either right or left hand, illustration shows right hand end piece. **Be sure and state which is wanted.**

Size, 18x30 inches. Price........**$14.00**
Size, 18x36 inches. Price........**14.65**
Size, 20x30 inches. Price........**15.50**
Size, 20x36 inches. Price........**16.85**
Size, 20x40 inches. Price........**17.90**

If wanted with air chambers add 60c extra.

Enameled Iron Roll Rim Kitchen Sinks.

No. 24C7601 Enameled Iron Roll Rim Sinks, on bronzed legs, with 12-inch high and 2¼-inch deep roll-rim back. Nickel plated brass strainer; two enameled drain boards on bronzed brackets, also two high grade Fuller cocks.

Size, 18x30 inches. Price.........$13.40
Size, 18x36 inches. Price.........14.50
Size, 20x30 inches. Price.........14.60
Size, 20x36 inches. Price.........15.40
Size, 20x40 inches. Price.........16.50

If wanted with air chambers, add 60c extra.

Enameled Iron Roll Rim Kitchen Sinks.

Enameled Iron Roll Rim Sinks, on bronzed iron legs, 15-inch high roll rim back, extending over drain boards; with drain boards on bronzed iron brackets. We furnish this sink with either ash or enameled iron drain boards.

No. 24C7602 Prices for sinks with 18-inch double ash drain boards.

Size, 18x30 inches. Price.........$14.50
Size, 18x36 inches. Price.........14.86
Size, 20x30 inches. Price.........14.90
Size, 20x36 inches. Price.........15.10
Size, 20x40 inches. Price.........17.15

No. 24C7603 Prices for sinks with 18-inch double enameled iron drain boards.

Size, 18x30 inches. Price.........$16.60
Size, 18x36 inches. Price.........17.00
Size, 20x30 inches. Price.........17.45
Size, 20x36 inches. Price.........17.65
Size, 20x40 inches. Price.........19.75

If wanted with air chambers, add 60c extra.

Acme Stoneware Kitchen Sinks.

No. 24C7587 Our Acme Stoneware Sinks with 14-inch high back, patent metallic rim, brass strainer and waste connection; mosaic drain board, two Fuller faucets, two 18 to 24-in. extension legs (painted), and galvanized hanging soap cup. Guaranteed against leakage for ten years.

Size of Sink	Size of Drain Board	Total length	Price
18x30x8 in.	18x20	50 in.	$13.50
20x36x8 in.	20x20	56 in.	14.85
20x40x8 in.	20x24	64 in.	16.25

Can furnish above sinks with brass rims in place of metallic rims for $2.50 in addition to price of any of above sizes.

Acme Enameled Stoneware Kitchen Sinks.

No. 24C7588 Double Drain Board, polished mosaic, with detachable 15-inch stoneware high back, including patent metallic rim, brass strainer and waste connection. Sink is made of steel, enameled, set in granitine; will last a lifetime. Furnished complete with Fuller cocks and extension legs.

No.	Size of Enam. Sink Inches	Size of Enam. Drain Board	Total Length	Zinc Rim, Price
100	16x24x7	16x18 in.	60 in.	$17.00
101	18x30x7	18x18 in.	66 in.	19.00
102	20x30x7	20x18 in.	66 in.	19.75
03	18x36x7	18x18 in.	72 in.	21.00
4	20x36x7	20x18 in.	72 in.	22.00

Granitine Combination Kitchen Sink and Laundry Tubs.

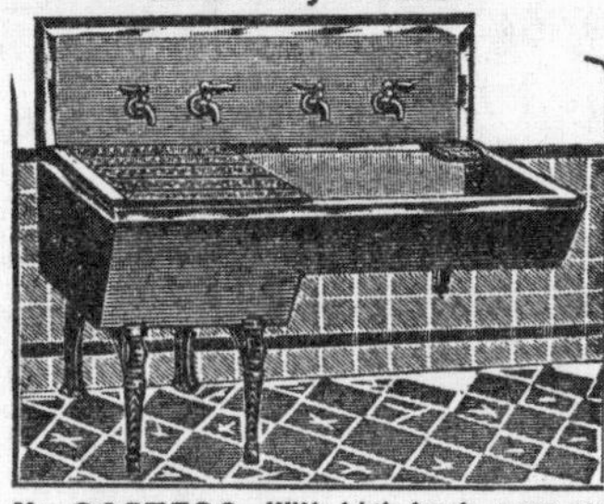

No. 24C7590 With high back, soap cup, strainer and painted iron legs. Backs higher than 14 inches will be charged extra. We do not furnish faucets unless specially ordered, but 14-inch back, and faucet holes in the back, will be sent unless otherwise ordered. All measurements are outside. If wanted with hardwood drain board as shown in illustration, add 75 cents to the prices given below.

Total length, inches...	48	54	60
Width, feet...	2	2	2
Depth, tub part, inches	16	16	16
Depth, sink part, ins...	8	8	8
Price, 14-inch back.....	$13.90	$15.25	$17.40

Two-Compartment Granitine Laundry Tubs.

Without High Backs.

No. 24C7591 Two-Compartment Granitine Laundry Tubs. With patent metallic rim, brass plugs, strainers, overflows and waste connection. This tub is the same as our No. 24C7592 without the high back. Furnished with zinc rim, no faucets furnished at prices given below. See No. 24C7595 for faucets.

No	Length	Width	Depth	Zinc Rims, Price
6	48 in.	24 in.	16 in.	$7.60
7	54 in.	24 in.	16 in.	8.60
8	60 in.	24 in.	16 in.	8.95

Two-Compartment Granitine Laundry Tubs.

No. 24C7592 We do not furnish faucets unless specially ordered. Tubs have zinc rim and 6-inch back and faucet holes in the high back will be sent unless otherwise ordered. All measurements are outside.

Length, feet.....	4	4½	5
Width, feet.....	2	2	2
Depth, inches...	16	16	16
Price, 6-in. back.	$10.30	$11.95	$12.95

Laundry Tub Faucets.

No. 24C7595 Finished Brass Laundry Tub Faucets. Used in connection with our Laundry Tubs, Nos. 24C7590 and 24C7592. Complete with flange screwed for iron pipe connection.
Price, each......$1.00

Cast Iron Sinks.

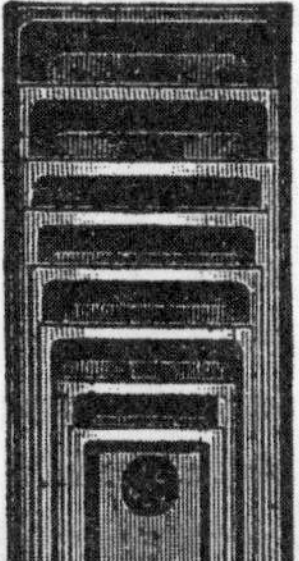

No. 24C7600 Cast Iron Sinks. Made of high grade gray iron, painted or white enameled inside; flat rim, fitted for 1¼-inch lead pipe.

Size	Painted	White Enameled Inside, Painted Outside
16x24 in.	$0.87	$2.15
18x30 in.	1.20	2.25
18x36 in.	1.45	3.20
20x30 in.	1.40	3.00
20x36 in.	1.79	3.50
20x40 in.	1.93	4.00

Cast Iron Slop Sinks.

No. 24C7604 Extra Heavy Cast Iron Slop Sinks.

Size	Price
16x16x10 inches....	$1.30
14x20x12 inches....	1.65

Cast Iron Corner Sinks.

No. 24C7606 Cast Iron Corner Sinks.
No. 1. Size, 20-inch sides, 28-inch front by 6 inches deep. Price.........84c
No. 2. Size, 22-inch sides, 31-inch front by 6½ inches deep. Price.........$1.00

Steel Kitchen Sinks.

Wrought Steel Kitchen Sinks. These sinks are made from one plate of steel and superior to cast iron sinks in every particular, being lighter, stronger and more durable; are fitted for 1¼-inch lead or 1½-inch iron pipe, and come painted or galvanized in the following sizes:

No. 24C7608 Painted.

Size	Wt., lbs.	Price	Size	Wt., lbs.	Price
16x24x6	6	$1.35	20x30x6	12½	$1.83
18x30x6	12½	1.60	20x36x6	15½	2.15
18x36x6	14	1.95	20x40x6	19	2.50

No. 24C7609 Galvanized.

Size	Wt. lbs.	Price	Size	Wt. lbs.	Price
16x24x6	9	$1.60	20x30x6	15	$2.15
18x30x6	14½	1.95	20x36x6	18	2.50
18x36x6	15½	2.30	20x40x6	19½	2.90

Seamless Wrought Steel Sinks with turned edges. This sink is adapted for exposed or open plumbing and has improved brass strainer couplings. They are made of one piece of steel, and are finely finished and one of the strongest sinks made. Cannot crack or rust out. Fitted for 1¼-inch lead pipe or 1½-inch iron pipe. Furnished in three finishes and sizes as follows:

No. 24C7613 Painted.

Size	Wt. lbs.	Price	Size	Wt. lbs.	Price
16x24x6	8	$1.34	20x30x6	13	$1.83
18x30x6	13	1.58	20x36x6	15½	2.13
18x36x6	14	1.93	20x40x6	19	2.48

No. 24C7614 Galvanized.

Size	Wt. lbs.	Price	Size	Wt. lbs.	Price
16x24x6	9	$1.56	20x30x6	15	$2.14
18x30x6	14	1.92	20x36x6	17½	2.48
18x36x6	16	2.28	20x40x6	20	2.82

No. 24C7616 White Enameled Sinks, nicely finished; outside color blue.

Size	Wt. lbs.	Price	Size	Wt. lbs.	Price
16x24x6	9	$3.00	20x30x6	15	$3.90
18x30x6	15	3.60	20x36x6	18	4.40
18x36x6	17	4.00	20x40x6	21	4.85

Adjustable Sink Brackets.

Malleable Iron Adjustable Sink Brackets. Will fit all sizes of sinks that we carry. Made to be fastened to wall. Very neat in appearance.

No. 24C7620 Painted. Price, per pair.........24c
No. 24C7621 Galvanized. Price, per pair.........43c

Enameled Iron Round Basins.

No. 24C7605 Enameled Iron Round Basins. With waste plug, rubber stopper and nickel plated overflow strainer. Size, 13½ inches.

Patent overflow, enameled inside. Price.........$1.86
Patent overflow, enameled all over. Price.........3.10

Enameled Iron Oval Basins.

No. 24C7607 Enameled Iron Oval Basins, with waste plug, rubber stopper and nickel plated overflow strainer.

Patent overflow, 14x17 inches, enameled inside. Price.........$2.00
Patent overflow, 14x17 inches, enameled all over. Price.........$3.25
Patent overflow, 15x19 inches, enameled inside. Price.........$2.05
Patent overflow, 15x19 inches, enameled all over. Price.........$3.30

ALL OF OUR PLUMBING GOODS ARE STRICTLY HIGH GRADE, AND OUR PRICES ARE BELOW COMPETITION.

Steel Wash Basins.

No. 24C7635 Seamless Steel Wash Basins, crystal enameled; common overflow; diameter, 14 inches; complete with stopper, fitted for either lead or iron pipe. Price.........$1.62

Earthenware Basins.

Patent Overflow White Earthenware Basins for metal or rubber plugs, smooth standard goods. Size, 14 inches in diameter.

No. 24C7640 Price for metal plug.........70c
No. 24C7641 Price, for rubber plug.........80c

Oval Earthenware Basins.

White Earthenware Oval Basins with Patent Overflow. Oval in shape. Size, 14x17 inches, for rubber or metal plugs.

No. 24C7643 Price, for rubber plug, $1.80
No. 24C7644 Price, for metal plug. 1.55

Above prices on basins do not include plugs. For price on plugs see No. 24C7674.

Marble Slabs with Right or Left Hand Ends.

No. 24C7645 Right or Left Hand End Marble Slabs. Best grade white Italian, finished for 14-inch round bowls. Size, 20x24 inches.

Illustration shows right hand end.

Notice—In ordering, be sure and state whether right or left hand end is wanted.

Price, with 8-inch back.........$6.41
With 10-inch back.........6.97
With 12-inch back.........7.60

No. 24C7646 Same as above; made of high grade Tennessee marble. State whether right or left hand end is wanted. Illustration shows right hand end.

Price, with 8-inch back.........$5.42
With 10-inch back.........5.87
With 12-inch back.........6.47

Marble Slabs With Straight Back.

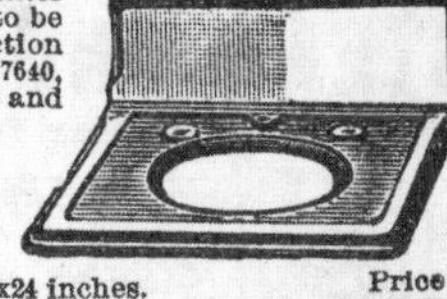

Best Grade White Marble Slabs, to be used in connection with Nos. 24C7640, 24C7641, 24C7643 and 24C7644 basins, finely finished, 14-inch round or oval bowl; complete ready for use. Size, bottom slab, 20x24 inches.

No.		Price
No. 24C7648	With 8-inch back...	$5.37
No. 24C7649	With 10-inch back..	5.75
No. 24C7650	With 12-inch back..	6.00

Same size and style as above. Made of Tennessee marble.

No.		Price
No. 24C7655	With 8-inch back...	$4.57
No. 24C7656	With 10-inch back..	4.84
No. 24C7657	With 12-inch back..	5.12

Marble Slabs for Corner.

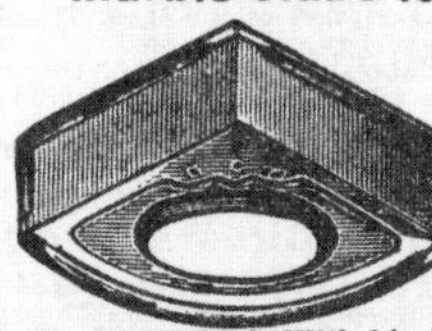

White Marble Slabs for Corner Basin, finished and polished complete, ready for use. Price includes two backs for corner. Size, square part, 20 inches.

No.		Price
No. 24C7659	With 8-inch back...	$5.62
No. 24C7660	With 10-inch back..	6.17
No. 24C7661	With 12-inch back..	6.73

Same size and style as above. Made of Tennessee marble.

No.		Price
No. 24C7665	With 8-inch back...	$4.77
No. 24C7666	With 10-inch back..	5.22
No. 24C7667	With 12-inch back..	5.77

Brackets for Basin Slabs.

No. 24C7671 Steel Brackets, nickel plated, suitable for Nos. 24C7648 to 24C7667 basin slabs. Size, 16x18 inches. Price, per pair.........47c

Metal Plugs With Rubber Stoppers.

No. 24C7672 Patent Overflow Basin Plugs with rubber stoppers; made of solid brass, nickel plated, to fit Nos. 24C7640 or 24C7644 basins...30c

Rubber Stoppers.

No. 24C7674 Rubber Plugs, to fit our No. 24C7641 and No. 24C7643 basins. Price.........6c

Urinals.

No. 24C7682 Iron Half Circle Urinal, enameled. Size, 12 inches; fitted for lead pipe.
Price 79c

Philadelphia Pattern Hopper Closets.

No. 24C7690 Enameled Iron Philadelphia Hoppers are enameled inside and painted outside. Must be connected with lead pipe directly to water pressure. This makes a very cheap and neat outfit for use in basement or outside places.
Price, for hopper only........$1.00

Acme Gas Water Heaters.

Circulating Water Heaters to attach to side of range boiler. A reliable, inexpensive heater that will do the work of a hard coal range at a much less cost. It is not necessary to start the range to have hot water. Will heat the contents of the range boiler in a few moments. In the summer time, when your range is not used over once a week, you are obliged to start a fire every time you wish a little hot water. With this heater, which can be easily attached to your boiler, you can have hot water any time of day or night in five minutes' time. The illustration shows the heater attached to boiler. We furnish the heater only, at prices given below. These heaters are made with plain black pipe and cast iron water chamber with black pipe covering and burn common illuminating gas.

No. 24C7730 Cold water supply pipes, ½ inch. Hot water outlet, ¾ inch. Capacity, thirty to forty-gallon boiler. Price, each $4.75

No. 24C7731 Cold water supply pipes, 1 inch. Hot water outlet, 1 inch. Capacity, fifty to sixty-gallon boiler. Price, each......$6.45

FREE CATALOGUE ON STEAM AND HOT WATER HEATERS. (Illustrated below.)

For $122.00 we furnish a complete outfit for heating a house, consisting of boiler, radiators, pipes, valves, fittings, etc. If you are interested, write for our Free Catalogue on Steam and Hot Water Heating.

Lavatory Traps.

No. 24C7701 Heavy Brass Nickel Plated P Traps, to be used in connection with lavatories. Comes complete, as shown in illustration.
Price, 1¼-inch..................$1.25

Lavatory Traps.

No. 24C7702 Extra Heavy Lavatory S Traps, 1¼-inch, vented. Complete with pipe to floor and vent to wall, and flanges. Made of brass, nickel plated.
Price........$1.80

Lavatory Traps.

No. 24C7703 Extra Heavy S Lavatory Traps, plain, not vented. Made of brass, heavily nickel plated. Complete, as shown in illustration. Size, 1¼ inches.
Price..........................$1.20

Lavatory Traps.

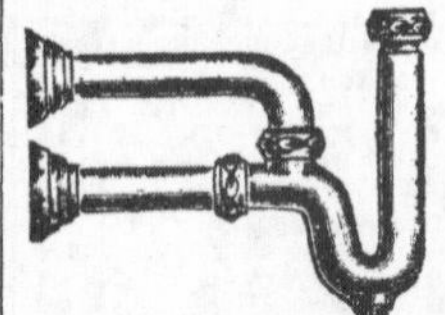

No. 24C7706 Extra heavy 1¼-inch P Lavatory Trap, vented, with waste and vent to wall, complete with flanges.
Price...$1.70

Range Boilers.

Range Boilers are used only where there is a water supply furnished with constant pressure through pipes—which can only be obtained in towns and cities having water works.

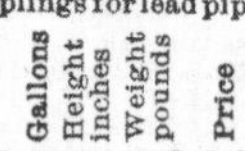

Galvanized Steel Range Boilers, tested to 200 pounds pressure. We furnish our boilers complete with stands, inside tubes and brass couplings for lead pipe.

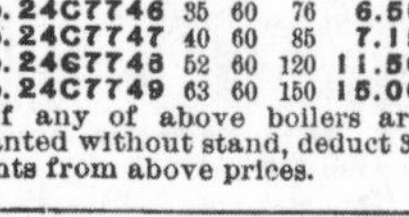

	Gallons	Height inches	Weight pounds	Price
No. 24C7745	30	60	72	$ 6.00
No. 24C7746	35	60	76	6.50
No. 24C7747	40	60	85	7.15
No. 24C7748	52	60	120	11.50
No. 24C7749	63	60	150	15.00

If any of above boilers are wanted without stand, deduct 35 cents from above prices.

STEAM AND HOT WATER HEATERS.

OWING TO THE GROWING DEMAND FOR STEAM AND HOT WATER HEATERS (an article which has heretofore been sold by agents at an enormous profit), we have made arrangements with the manufacturers whereby we are able to offer our customers the best line of water heaters on the market and at prices which you will find tobe 50 percentless than you were ever offered a heater at before. Our Hercules line of heaters has been on the market for years, over 50,000 being in constant use. If you are building or contemplating changing your heating plant write us for our Special Catalogue on Steam and Hot Water Heating. This catalogue gives a complete description of the Hercules Boilers, their construction, capacity, size to buy, weight, etc. You can then send us your plans and we will make you a net price on the complete outfit comprising heaters, radiators, valves, pipe, etc. There is no more difficult stronghold of conservatism in the world than the question of right heating. Our special catalogue explains clearly why steam or hot water heating, as applied by the Hercules Heater, is better than any other system of heating.

WE HAVE ADDED new features to the construction and working that makes the 1905 TYPE A WORLD BEATER.

Acme Direct Steam or Water Radiators.

No. 24C7760 Our Acme Radiators are the latest thing in radiator design and construction; occupy less floor space for amount of heating surface than any other. Guaranteed to contain full area of heating surface claimed. The openings are large and unobstructed, no angles to check free and perfect circulation. If a connection at top of a hot water radiator is desired, it can readily be made by simply removing the ornamental plug. This is an important feature, as it is often called for in certain systems of piping. The castings are made of the best gray iron and are of uniform thickness. They are adapted to high or low pressure.

Number of sections	Length, Inches	Heating Surface—Square Feet: 45 Inches High, 5¼ square feet per section	37 Inches High, 4¼ square feet per section	31 Inches High, 3½ square feet per section	25 Inches High, 2¾ square feet per section	20 Inches High, 2¼ square feet per section
5	11 9-16	26¼	21¼	17½	13¾	11¼
6	13⅞	31½	25½	21	16½	13½
7	16 3-16	36¾	29¾	24½	19¼	15¾
8	18½	42	34	28	22	18
9	20 13-16	47¼	38¼	31½	24¾	20¼
10	23⅛	52½	42½	35	27½	22½
11	25 7-16	57¾	46¾	38½	30¼	24¾
12	27¾	63	51	42	33	27
13	30 1-6	68¼	55¼	45½	35¾	29¼
14	32⅜	73½	59½	49	38½	31½
15	34 11-16	78¾	63¾	52½	41¼	33¾
Height, inches		45	37	31	25	20
Price, per square foot		19c	20c	21c	24c	27c

Width of section, 7½ inches. To ascertain the cost of a radiator, multiply the number of square feet in the radiator you wish by the cost per square foot. For example, a 10-section radiator 37 inches high contains 42½ square feet, at 20 cents, will cost $8.50.

Boiler Couplings.

No. 24C7756 Boiler Couplings for iron boilers, for lead pipe, straight. Size, ¾-inch. Price..................37c

Brass Soap Cups.

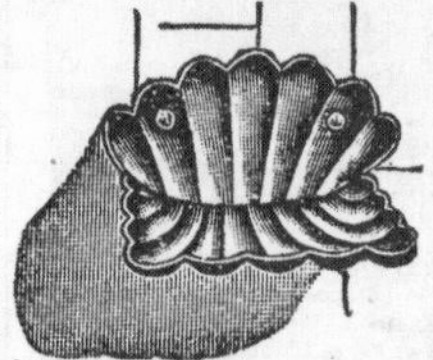

No. 24C7822 Shell Pattern Brass, Nickel Plated Soap Cups, to be fastened to the wall. Finest finish, extra fine goods. Size, 4x3 inches. Price..................29c

No. 24C7828 Soap Cups for the rim of the bath, solid brass, nickel plated, finely finished. Hanging rods can be adjusted so as to fit any tub. Size, 6x3½ inches.
Price..........63c

No. 24C7832 Sponge Holders. To be used on rim of bath tub. Made of brass, nickel plated. Heavy, high grade goods. Nothing better made. Price....$1.40

Towel Racks.

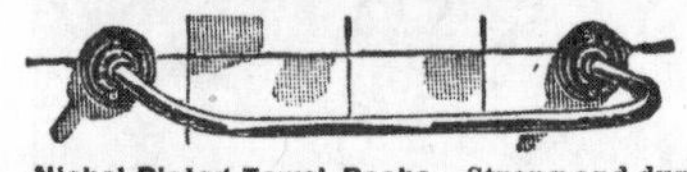

Nickel Plated Towel Racks. Strong and durable; finely finished bar is ½-inch in diameter; projects 2½ inches from wall.

No. 24C7836 Length 15 inches. Price, 32c
No. 24C7837 Length 18 inches. Price, 35c
No. 24C7838 Length 24 inches. Price, 43c

Extra Heavy Towel Rack.

No. 24C7840 Extra Heavy Towel Rack. Made of brass, nickel plated. Diameter of bar, ⅝ inch; width from wall, 3 inches.
Size, 15 inches. Price..................60c
Size, 18 inches. Price..................70c
Size, 24 inches. Price..................85c

Two-Arm Towel Rack.

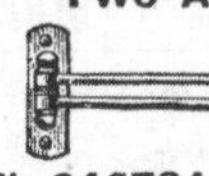

No. 24C7841 Nickel Plated Towel Rack. Two-arm; diameter of bars, ⅜ inch.
Price..................41c

Toilet Paper Holder.

No. 24C7848 Solid Brass Toilet Paper Holder. Nickel plated, takes standard size paper.
Price..............68c

Bath Spray.

No. 24C7855 Nickel Plated Bath Spray, 5 feet of rubber tubing to attach to faucet; rose is made of brass, nickel plated. Price..................70c

Bath Tub Seats.

No. 24C7856 Bath Tub Seat. Fits any style bath tub. Seat is natural oak. Hangers made of brass, nickel plated. Size, 18¾x5¾ inches. Price..................80c

Excelsior Shower Bath.

No. 24C7858 The Best Shower Bath Made. Made of best rubber tubing, with celluloid eyelets and nickel hook. A hip bath can be taken without wetting the shoulders, or either limb may be showered separately. It leaves the arms entirely free and it can be as readily adjusted to a child as to an adult. Only a small quantity of water being necessary for the shower bath, it enables several persons to take a bath from a single tank of hot water. Can be attached to any faucet. Comes complete with 7 ft. of hose—all trimmings are made of brass, nickel plated.
Price..........70c

Compression Basin Cocks.

No. 24C7870 Compression Basin Cocks, T handle. Made of brass, finely finished and polished.
Price..................45c

Fuller Basin Cocks.

No. 24C7872 High Grade Fuller Basin Cocks, furnished complete, nickel plated. In ordering single faucets be sure and state whether left or right hand is wanted.
Price, each..............55c

Combination Bath Cocks.

No. 24C7874 No. 4½ Fuller Cast Brass, Combination Hot and Cold Bath Cocks. Nickel plated, complete, ready for use. Nothing better made.
Price..................$1.75

Compression Plain Bibbs, with Flange.

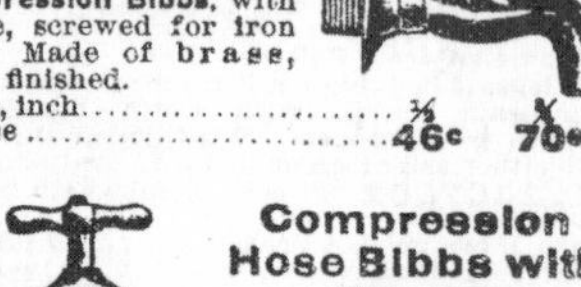

No. 24C7880 Plain Compression Bibbs, with flange, screwed for iron pipe. Made of brass, finely finished.

Size, inch	½	¾
Price	46c	70c

Compression Hose Bibbs with Flange.

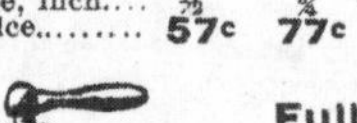

No. 24C7882 Compression Hose Bibbs, with flange, screwed for iron pipe. Made of brass, finely finished.

Size, inch	½	¾
Price	50c	70c

Compression Hose Bibbs, with Flange.

No. 24C7886 Compression Hose Bibbs, with flange, for lead pipe connection. Made of brass, highly finished.

Size, inch	½	¾
Price	57c	77c

Fuller Bibbs, Plain, with Flange.

No. 24C7888 Fuller Bibbs, plain, with flange, screwed for iron pipe. Made of brass, highly finished.

Size, inch	½	¾	1
Price	57c	75c	$1.50

Fuller Bibbs, Plain.

No. 24C7896 Plain Fuller Bibbs for lead pipe connection, made of brass, highly polished.

Size, inch	½	¾	1
Price	46c	62c	$1.23

Fuller Hose Bibbs.

No. 24C7898 Fuller Hose Bibbs for lead pipe connections. Made of brass, highly polished.

Size, in.	½	¾	1
Price	52c	65c	$1.40

Bibbs.

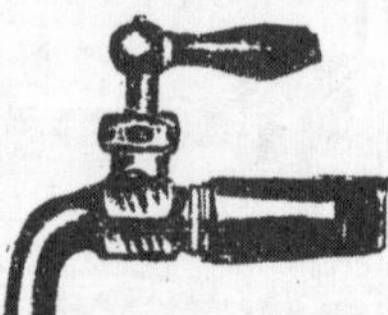

No. 24C7900 Fuller Pattern Plain Bibbs, for iron pipe, finished brass.

Size, inch	Price
½	$0.43
¾	.58
1	1.20

Rubber Balls for Fuller Bibbs.

No. 24C7901 Size for bibbs, ½-inch, 5c; ¾-inch, 5c; 1-inch......6c

Fuller Pattern Hose Bibbs.

No. 24C7902 Fuller Pattern Hose Bibbs, for iron pipe, finished brass.

Size, inch	½	¾
Price	52c	68c

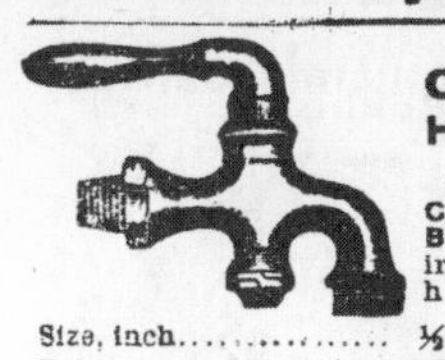

C. C. Brand Hose Bibbs.

No. 24C7904 C. C. Brand Hose Bibbs, screwed for iron pipe. Lever handle, finished.

Size, inch	½	¾	1
Price	53c	95c	$1.50

Compression Hose Bibbs.

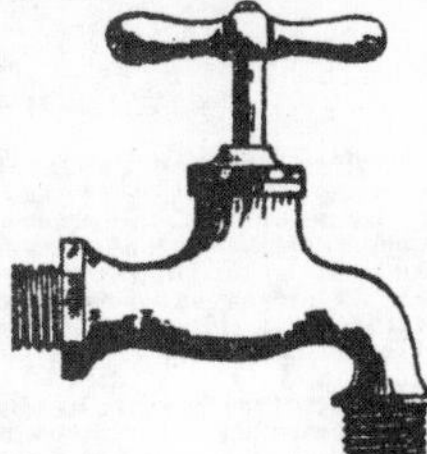

No. 24C7906 C. C Brand. Screwed for iron pipe with shoulder; finished.

Size, in.	Price
½	$0.40
¾	.55
1	1.13

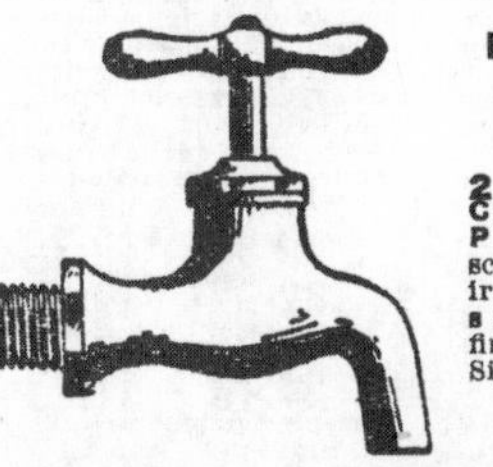

Compression Plain Bibbs.

No. 24C7908 Compression Plain Bibbs, screwed for iron pipe, with shoulder, finished.

Size, in.	Price
½	$0.32
¾	.53
1	1.05

Compression Sill Cocks.

No. 24C7917 Compression Sill Cocks, finished ready for use. Size, ¾-inch. Price..........85c

Lever Handle Stop and Waste for Iron Pipe.

No. 24C7922 Lever Handle Stop and Waste, for iron pipe, finished and polished.

Size, inch	½	¾
Price	70c	$1.00

T Handle Rough Stop and Waste.

No. 24C7926 T Handle Rough Stop and Waste, for lead pipe. Complete as shown in illustration.

Size, in.	½	¾	1
Price	46c	55c	85c

T Handle Rough Stop and Waste.

No. 24C7927 T Handle Rough Stop and Waste, screwed for iron pipe.

Size, inch	½	¾	1
Price	40c	65c	82c

Drawn Lead Traps.

Full S Standard Heavy Drawn Lead Traps for Sinks, Basins, etc.

No. 24C8015 Size, 1¼ inches. Price..........31c

No. 24C8016 Size, 1½ inches. Price..........48c

No. 24C8017 Size, 4 inches. Price..........$1.75

Extra Long S Lead Traps.

Extra Long Standard S Lead Traps for Sinks, Basins, etc.

No. 24C8019 Size, 1¼ inches. Price..........49c

No. 24C8020 Size, 1½ inches. Price..........72c

Combination Lead Bends and Ferrules.

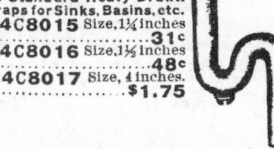

No. 24C8029 Combination lead bends and ferrules, to be used in connecting soil pipe with closet bowl.

Size, inches	4x12	4x14	4x18
Price	$1.17	$1.29	$1.49

Short Bends.

Lead Short Bends, standard grade and sizes.

No. 24C8030 Size, 1¼ in. Price 13c

No. 24C8031 Size, 1½ in. Price 19c

No. 24C8032 Size, 2 in. Price 30c

No. 24C8033 Size, 3 in. Price..........45c

No. 24C8034 Size, 4 in. Price..........80c

Lead Drum Traps.

No. 24C8046 Lead Drum Traps. Diameter, 4 inches; length 9 inches, with brass screw. Price..........96c

Cast Iron Soil Pipe.

Single Hub Cast Iron Soil Pipe, best grade; come in 5 feet pieces only.

No. 24C8050 Price, per foot, standard, 2-inch size..........11c

No. 24C8051 Price, per foot, standard, 4-inch size..........16c

No. 24C8054 Price, per foot, extra heavy, 2-inch size..........12½c

No. 24C8055 Price, per foot, extra heavy, 4-inch size..........24c

Double Hub Soil Pipe.

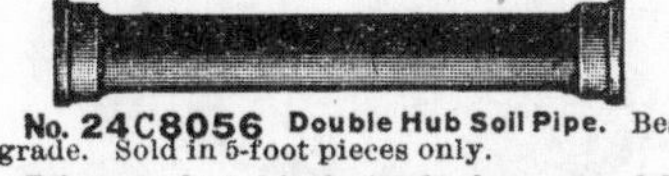

No. 24C8056 Double Hub Soil Pipe. Best grade. Sold in 5-foot pieces only.

Price, per foot, 2-inch standard..........14c
Price, per foot, 2-inch, extra heavy..........16c
Price, per foot, 4-inch standard..........17½c
Price, per foot, 4-inch, extra heavy..........25c

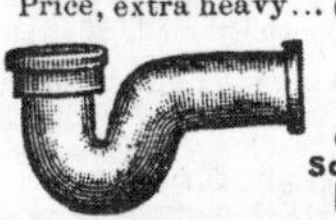

Cast Reducers.

No. 24C8078 Cast Reducers for Soil Pipe.
Size, 4x2 inches, standard. Price..........19c
Size, 4x2 inches, extra heavy. Price..........23c

Cast S Traps.

Cast S Traps for Soil Pipe. Plain. Size, 4 inches.

No. 24C8085 Price, standard..........39c

No. 24C8086 Price, extra heavy..........65c

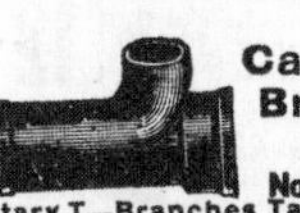

Cast Half S Traps.

Cast Half S Traps, for Soil Pipe. Size, 4 inches.

No. 24C8087 Price, standard..........39c

No. 24C8088 Price, extra heavy..........65c

Lead Trap.

No. 24C8091 Lead Trap for closet connection. Half S style. Price..........$1.25

Cast Sanitary T—Branches Tapped for Iron Pipe.

No. 24C8099 Cast Sanitary T—Branches Tapped for Iron Pipe.

Size, 4x1½-inch. Standard. Price..........50c
Size, 4x2 inch. Standard. Price..........57c
Size, 4x1½-inch. Extra heavy. Price..........60c
Size, 4x2 -inch. Extra heavy. Price..........63c

Cast Iron Cesspools.

Cast Iron Cesspools, with bell trap, to be used in connection with soil pipe.

No. 24C8110 Size, 6x6 inches. Price..........36c

No. 24C8111 Size, 9x9 inches. Price..........48c

No. 24C8112 Size, 13x13 inches. Price..........72c

Street Washers.

No. 24C8115 All parts with which water comes in contact are at the bottom, hence free from frost. Valves can be pulled out at top, thus avoiding digging up for repairs.

Size, inch	¾	¾
To set in ground	3 ft.	4 ft.
Price	$2.65	$3.10
Size, inch	1	1
To set in ground	3 ft.	4 ft.
Price	$5.00	$5.50

Pipe Hydrants.

No. 24C8117 When a cheap but serviceable hydrant is desired, we recommend our pipe hydrant. It attaches to the underground pipe below freezing point and is furnished with a brass shut off valve, the drip from which drains the hydrant as soon as it is turned off, and prevents injury from frost.

	¾-inch	1-inch	1¼-inch
4 feet long	$1.55	$1.85	$2.85
5 feet long	1.60	1.92	3.00
6 feet long	1.65	2.00	3.20

No. 24C8117

No. 24C8130

Gasoline Fire Pots.

No. 24C8130 Acme, fixed pump, two detachable shields for holding melting pot, complete with cast iron melting pot. Price..........$3.20

Bulb Blast Furnace.

No. 24C8131 Same style as No. 24C8130 with rubber bulb instead of pump. Price..........$2.75

No. 24C8131

Plumbers' or Melting Ladles.

No. 24C8140 Steel bowl with wrought iron handle.

Size across bowl, 3 inches. Price..........9c
Size across bowl, 4 inches. Price..........11c
Size across bowl, 5 inches. Price..........13c

Lead Pipe.

No. 24C8264 Lead Pipe. Prices subject to change without notice.

	Price, per foot
Lead Pipe, ½ in. in diam., 10 oz. to foot	5c
Lead Pipe, ¾ in. in diam., 1 lb. to ft.	7c
Lead Pipe, 1 in. in diam., 1½ lbs. to ft.	10½c
Lead Pipe, 1¼ in. in diam., 2 lbs. to ft.	14c
Lead Pipe, 1½ in. in diam., 3 lbs. to ft.	21c
Lead Pipe, 2 in. in diam., 3 lbs. to ft.	22c

Strong Lead Pipe.

No. 24C8266

	Price, per foot
Lead Pipe, ½-in. diam., 1¾ lbs. to foot	10c
Lead Pipe, ¾-in. diam., 2 lbs. to foot	14c
Lead Pipe, ¾-in. diam., 2¼ lbs. to foot	16c
Lead Pipe, 1-in. diam., 3¼ lbs. to foot	23c

Handy Force Pump.

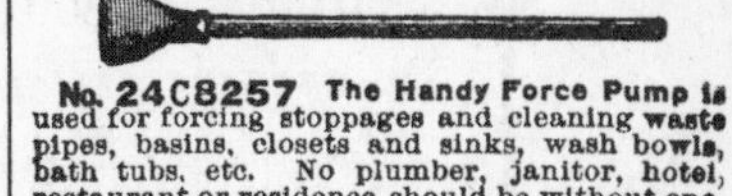

No. 24C8257 The Handy Force Pump is used for forcing stoppages and cleaning waste pipes, basins, closets and sinks, wash bowls, bath tubs, etc. No plumber, janitor, hotel, restaurant or residence should be without one. One stoppage of your pipes will pay for it. Thousands of them sold with the best results. It is made with a heavy rubber cup on the end of a 3-foot wooden handle. Price, each..45c

Sheet Lead, Zinc and Copper.

No. 24C8268 Sheet Lead. In ordering give thickness wanted. Price, per lb.....7½c

No. 24C8270 Best Grade Sheet Zinc. Cannot sell less than half sheet. 26-gauge, No. 9, 36 inches wide by 84 inches long. Weight, about 14 pounds.

Price, per sheet..........$1.20
Price, per half sheet..........68

No. 24C8272 Soft Sheet Copper. Not polished. Tinned on one side.

Size of Sheet	Weight of Sheet	Price per Sheet
14x48 in.	4 lbs. 5 oz.	$1.00

We do not sell less than half sheet. Prices on other sizes and kinds of copper quoted upon application.

GAS FIXTURES AND SUPPLIES.

SPACE WILL NOT PERMIT OUR SHOWING our complete line of these goods, although you will find the goods listed on these pages very comprehensive. If, however, there is anything you want in the way of gas fixtures or supplies and you do not find it listed herein, write us and describe what you want, for we know we can furnish it and we know that we can save you about 50 per cent on the price.

THE GOODS WE QUOTE are manufactured by one of the very best makers in the country. They are made of the very best material by skilled workmen and each and every article is carefully inspected before it leaves the factory. We put out every article under our binding guarantee for quality, and if anything is not entirely satisfactory when received, simply return it to us and we will promptly refund your money.

NOTICE—We can furnish gas fixtures for natural gas at an extra cost of 12 cents for each tip or burner.

Gas Brackets.

No. 24C8400 Polished Brass Gas Brackets, finished complete. Price....19c

No. 24C8402 Single swing tube. Price, 27c

Gilt Finish Gas Brackets, finished complete.

No. 24C8405 Two-swing. Price..........40c

Double Burner Gas Fixtures.

No. 24C8412 Plain Gilt Finish, Double Burner Gas Fixtures, finely finished, complete. Length, 36 inches. Spread, 16 inches. Two-light.

Price..........87c

NOTICE—Gas fixtures for natural gas take a special tip or burner. When so fitted there will be an extra charge of 12 cents for each tip.

Polished Gas Fixtures.

No. 24C8416 Polished Gas Fixtures, complete with shade as shown in illustration.

Length, 30 inches. Price..........53c
Length, 36 inches. Price..........58c

Polished Gas Fixtures.

No. 24C8418 Polished Gas Fixtures, complete with shade as shown in illustration.

Length, 30 inches. Price..........$1.12
Length, 36 inches. Price..........$1.18

Hall Gas Fixtures, No. 170.

No. 24C8418 No. 24C8420

No. 24C8420 No. 170 Hall Gas Fixtures, polished. A very neat fixture for a little money. Comes complete as shown in illustration. Length, 36 inches. Price..........$1.35

Hall Gas Fixtures, No. 171.

No. 24C8424

No. 24C8424 No. 171 Hall Gas Fixtures, polished, complete as shown in illustration. Length, 36 inches. Price..........$2.10

Gilt Gas Fixtures, Style 200.

No. 24C8428 Gilt Gas Fixtures, a strong, well made fixture, comes complete as shown in illustration, Length, 36 inches, spread, 16 inches.

Price, two-light..........$1.70
Price, three-light..........$2.10
Price, four-light..........$2.65

Gilt Gas Fixtures, Style 199.

No. 24C8430 High Grade Gilt Finish Gas Fixtures, one of the best fixtures we sell for the money. Length, 36 inches, spread 19 inches.

Price, two-light $1.70
Price, three-light, 2.25
Price, four-light, 2.95

Gilt Finish Gas Fixtures, Style 199.

No. 24C8432 Gilt Finish Gas Fixtures, well made, strong and durable. Length, 36 inches. Spread, 21 inches. Comes complete as shown in illustration.

Price, two-light...$2.25
Price, three-light. 2.85
Price, four-light.. 3.25

IN OUR
Free Electrical Goods Catalogue
sent on application, we show a complete line of
ELECTRICAL FIXTURES

Gilt Finish Gas Fixtures, Style 201.

No. 24C8434 Style 201 Gas Fixtures, well made, finely finished. Comes complete with glass ware as shown in illustration. Length, 36 inches, spread, 22 inches.
Price, two-light...**$2.50**
Price, three-light. **3.10**
Price, four-light.. **3.30**

Polished Gas Fixtures, Style 186.

No. 24C8438 Style 186 Gas Fixtures, a well made, up to date fixture. Comes complete with shades, tips, etc. Length, 36 inches, spread, 21 inches.
Price, two-light.....**$3.25**
Price, three-light... **3.75**
Price, four-light.... **4.35**

Polished Gas Fixtures, Style 185.

No. 24C8440 Style 185 Gas Fixtures, a very neat, well made fixture. One of the best fixtures we show. Comes complete with shades, tips, etc. Length, 36 inches, spread, 19 inches.
Two-light....**$3.45**
Three-light... **4.15**
Four-light.... **4.80**

Crystal Gas Shades.

No. 24C8450 Crystal Gas Shades, a clear cut crystal glass. Made to fit a 4-inch shade holder.
Price..............**11c**

No. 24C8454 Crystal Glass Gas Shades, clear cut glass. Made to fit a 4-inch shade holder. Price....**11c**

Opalescent Gas Shades.

No. 24C8458 Opalescent Gas Shades. Made to fit 4-inch shade holder.
Price..............**24c**

Gas Lighters.

No. 24C8706 Gas Lighter. Hardwood handle, silver finish, metal parts.
Price..............................**10c**
No. 24C8708 Wax Tapers for above, 50 tapers in a box. Price, per box....**5c**

Gas Light Tubing.

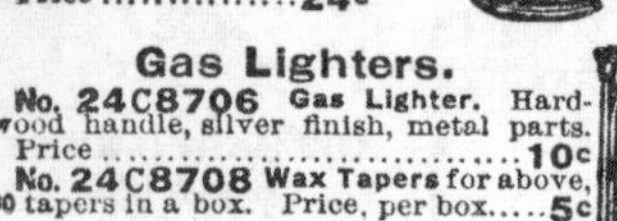

No. 24C8717 Portable or Drop Light Tubing. Pure India rubber inner tube with braided mohair covering. Comes complete with metal ends to connect to gas jet and lamp. Furnished in 6, 8 and 10-foot pieces only.
Price, per foot.........................**4½c**

Complete Safety Gas Lights.

No. 24C8780 This light consists of brass burner, mantle, patent safety chimney, either plain or corrugated, opal shade and improved glass draft attachment. Will cut your gas bill one-half. Fits any gas fixture.
Price......................................**46c**

Acme No. 10 Incandescent Gas Light.

No. 24C8782 There is no other gas light in existence as popular as our Acme No. 10. They are used by the thousands all over the United States. As a light producer and saver it has no equal. It is impossible to force more gas throught than is burned. Fits any fixture. We use only the best grade mantle. We furnish these burners for artificial or natural gas. In ordering be sure and state which is wanted. Price..........................**45c**

Big 6 Gas Light.

No. 24C8785 The Big 6 Gas Light is the simplest, most economical and best light on the market. It develops 390-candle power on a consumption of four feet of gas per hour. Furnished complete with mantle, burner and globe, ready to fasten on the gas fixtures. The globe is made of imported glass with patent air holes.
Price.....................**65c**

Gas and Gasoline Mantles.

We handle only the best grades of mantles and warrant them to give a bright, clear light. They come securely packed one in a box with full directions on each box how to place and adjust on lamp.

No. 24C8790 No. 1. Standard Grade Mantles, 60-candle power.
Price.....................**8c**

No. 24C8792 No. 3. XXX Grade Mantles, 80-candle power.
Price.....................**12c**

No. 24C8794 No. 5. Extra Grade Mantles, 100-candle power.
Price.....................**14c**

No. 24C8795 No. 6. Heavy weave, especially for high pressure gasoline lamps; 5 inches long; nothing better made.
Price.....................**19c**

Double Weave Mantle with Wire and Cap.

No. 24C8796 Extra Quality Double Weave Mantle with wire and cap, ready to put on burner. No adjusting or fitting.
Price.....................**15c**

Triple Weave Mantle.

No. 24C8797 Our Triple Weave Double Wire Mantle attached to cap is by far the longest lived mantle we sell. Cannot break by handling. Wire will not kink or drop over sideways. Will last longer than any mantle on the market.
Price.....................**18c**

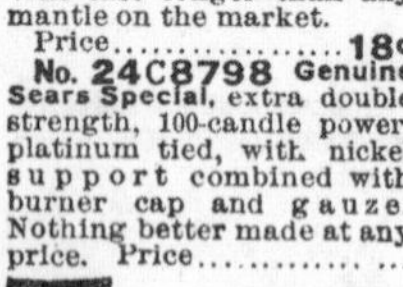

No. 24C8798 Genuine Sears Special, extra double strength, 100-candle power, platinum tied, with nickel support combined with burner cap and gauze. Nothing better made at any price. Price..................................**21c**

Mica Chimney.

No. 24C8882 Mica Chimney—cannot break, will last forever. Length, 7 inches. Fits our Nos. 24C8782 or 24C8780 burners.
Price...............................**6½c**

Opal Smoke Shades.

Opal Smoke Shades to hang over gas fixtures. Complete, ready for use.

No. 24C8887 Size, 6-inch. Price.... **8c**
No. 24C8888 Size, 7-inch. Price.... **10c**
No. 24C8889 Size, 8-inch. Price.... **13c**

Pure Lead Glass Chimney.

No. 24C8905 Pure Lead Chimneys, high grade. Size, 1½x7 inches, will fit our No. 24C8780 burner.
Price.....................**6c**

Combination Cylinder Chimney.

No. 24C8907 Pure Lead Glass Combination Cylinder Chimney. Price includes asbestos washers. Fits our No. 24C8780 Burner.
Price.....................**7c**

Opal Shades.

No. 24C8911 Best Quality Opal Shades, fluted pattern, 8 inches in diameter. Price.........**8c**

LEATHER BELTING.

We sell only the best grades in medium and full weight stock, made from carefully selected hides of oak tannage. If a cheaper belt is wanted we advise the use of a rubber belt. Quality considered, you will find we will save you fully 33⅓ per cent on anything in belting.

Double Thick or 2-Ply Belts Twice the Price of Single Ply. **Extra Heavy Belts, Extra Prices.**

Prices quoted are per foot.

Width In.	No. 24C8920 Acme	No. 24C8921 Standard B	No. 24C8922 Standard A
1	3½c	4c	4¼c
1¼	4½c	5c	5¾c
1½	5¾c	6½c	7¼c
1¾	7c	7½c	8¾c
2	8¼c	9c	10¼c
2¼	9½c	10½c	12c
2½	10½c	11½c	13c
2¾	11½c	13c	14½c
3	12¾c	14c	16c
3½	15c	16¼c	19c
4	17½c	19c	22c

Width In.	No. 24C8922 Standard A
4½	24c
5	27c
5½	30c
6	33c
7	39c
8	58c
9	65c
10	70c
11	82c
12	86c

In ordering, state where belts are to run. We do not guarantee belts to run on the quarter turn, unless they are especially made for that purpose.

Endless belts made to order at short notice. For cost of making endless belts add the price of 3 feet of belt for lapping.

Round Leather Belting.

Solid and Twisted Leather Belting, made of the best oak tanned leather; warranted to be of uniform size and twist. **In ordering, be sure and state the size and kind wanted.**

No. 24C8924 Solid.

Size	Price	Size	Price
3-16-inch. Per foot,	2c	5-16-inch. Per ft.,	3½c
¼-inch. Per foot,	2c	⅜-inch. Per ft.,	6½c

No. 24C8925 Twisted.

Size	Price	Size	Price
¼-inch. Perfoot,	7c	⅝-inch. Per foot,	21c
5-16-inch. Per ft.	9c	¾-inch. Per foot,	25c
⅜-inch. Perfoot,	11c	⅞-inch. Per foot,	34c
½-inch. Perfoot,	18c	1-inch. Per foot,	42c

Improved Steel Belt Couplings.

No. 24C8928 Coupling for Round Belts, or Bands, easily attached, strong and durable. The best coupling of the kind on the market.

Size.	3-16	¼	5-16	⅜	½	⅝	¾	⅞	1
Price	9c	10c	10c	12c	15c	24c	36c	60c	72c

RUBBER BELTING.

Our Rubber Belting is composed of the best quality of cotton duck and India rubber, made in the best manner possible. These belts will stretch less than any other belts made. On this account the friction always remains firm. Not only is stretching an exceedingly troublesome defect, but it also loosens the friction and destroys the strength of the belt. They are not suitable for threshers or sawmill belts. We do not guarantee the Standard belt, but it is all right for nearly any place where a light, narrow belt is used. We make endless belts only in extra quality. For making endless we charge as much as three feet of belt would cost. **Be careful in making orders for belt, for if it is sent as ordered, it will not be taken back or exchanged.**

2-Ply Rubber Belting.

No. 24C8932 Standard quality, not guaranteed. Extra quality, guaranteed.

Size, Inch	Standard, per ft.	Extra, per ft.	Size, Inch	Standard, per ft.	Extra, per ft.
1	1¾c	2½c	2½	4½c	6c
1¼	2¼c	3¼c	3	5½c	7¾c
1½	2¾c	4c	3½	6½c	9c
2	3¾c	5¼c	4	7½c	10c

3-Ply Rubber Belting.

No. 24C8933 Standard quality, not guaranteed. Extra quality, guaranteed.

Size, Inch	Standard, per ft.	Extra, per ft.	Size, Inch	Standard, per ft.	Extra, per ft.
1½	3½c	4½c	7	15c	21½c
2	4½c	6c	8	17½c	24¼c
2½	5½c	8c	9	20c	29c
3	6½c	9¼c	10	22½c	32½c
3½	8c	10¾c	11	25c	36c
4	9c	12¼c	12	27c	39c
5	11c	15½c	13	29½c	42½c
6	13c	18¾c	14	32c	46c

4-Ply Rubber Belting.

No. 24C8934 Standard quality not guaranteed. Extra quality guaranteed.

Size, Inch	Standard, per ft.	Extra, per ft.	Size, Inch	Standard, per ft.	Extra, per ft.
3	9¼c	11c	10	32c	38½c
3½	11c	13c	11	35c	42½c
4	12½c	15c	12	39c	47c
4½	14c	17c	13	42c	50c
5	15½c	18½c	14	46c	55c
6	18½c	22½c	15	50c	60c
7	22c	26c	16	53c	63c
8	25c	30c	18	60c	72c
9	28c	34c			

Stitched Canvas Belting.

We have the strongest Stitched Canvas Belting that is manufactured. The rows of stitches are sewed so close together that the piles cannot separate. It is painted with a composition of a red color, which gives it a good friction and makes it thoroughly waterproof. Oil (no matter in what quantity) will not injure the belting in the least. Stitched cotton belting is cheaper, more durable and much stronger than leather belting, as has been shown by various tests. All belting is thoroughly stretched before leaving the factory. Use an awl in making holes for lacing canvas belting. Never use a belt punch as it cuts the threads.

No. 24C8938 4-ply Stitched Canvas Belt.

Width, inches....	1½	2	2½	3	3½	4	4½	5	6	7	8	9	10	12
Price, per foot..	4½c	6c	7½c	9c	10½c	12c	13½c	15c	18c	21c	24c	27c	30c	36c

No. 24C8939 6-ply Stitched Canvas Belt.

Width, inches...	3	4	5	6	7	8	9	10	12	14	16	18
Price, per foot..	13c	17½c	22c	26c	30c	35c	39c	43½c	52c	64c	73c	82c

Endless Stitched Canvas Belting.

Endless Stitched Canvas Thrasher Belt is far superior to all other canvas thrasher belting on account of the process of its manufacture. The splice is made in such a manner that the belt is no thicker at this point, and is **just as strong and flexible as any other part of the belt.** It is painted with a composition of a reddish color and is thoroughly waterproof, and is not affected by any change of temperature, neither by oil. It is sewed with rows of stitches throughout its entire length, which makes it practically **impossible for the piles to separate.** We carry the following lengths of these 4 and 5-ply belts in stock and can ship promptly. The actual length of these belts is three feet less than stated, as it requires the price of three feet for labor in making belt endless. Other lengths made to order, which require from two to three weeks to make.

No. 24C894[illegible] Four-ply Endless Belt.

Length, ft.	6-in. 4-ply	7-in. 4-ply	8-in. 4 ply
80	$11.65	$13.55	$15.50
100	14.50	16.95	19.40
120	17.45	20.35	23.35
130	18.90	22.00	25.20
140	20.35	23.75	27.15
150	21.85	25.45	29.10
160	23.25	27.15	31.15

No. 24C8943 Five-ply Endless Belt.

Length, ft.	6-in. 5-ply	7-in. 5-ply	8-in. 5-ply
130	$24.35	$27.60	$30.95
140	26.30	29.75	33.25
150	28.10	31.85	35.60
160	30.00	34.00	38.00

Warren's Liquid Pulley Cover.

APPLIED WITH A BRUSH

No. 24C8949 Best on the market for over five years. It is applied (like paint) with a brush, to any kind of pulley, dries hard and is ready for use in from four to six hours. Prevents slipping, allows belts to run slack, reduces wear on belts, bearings and machinery, saves fuel, increases output and is very durable. Put up in tin can, each can in separate box, with brushes, material for cleaning pulleys and full directions for use. Price............**$12.00**
Special case, sufficient for 40 square feet pulley surface. Price.........................**$5.00**
No. 3 case, sufficient for 15 square feet pulley surface. Price.........................**$2.50**

Rawhide Lace Leather.

No. 24C8954 We sell the best grade of Rawhide Lace Leather in sides of from 5 to 15 square feet. (We do not cut sides.)
Price, per square foot.....................**19c**

Cut Lacing.

No. 24C8955 Cut Lacing comes in bunches of 100 feet. Will sell half a bunch at one-half the price of full bunch.

Width	Price, per 100 feet	Width	Price, per 100 feet
¼ inch..........	38c	½ inch......	$0.78
5-16 inch..........	48c	⅝ inch......	.98
⅜ inch..........	58c	¾ inch......	1.18

Our 25-Cent Lace Leather Cutter.

No. 24C8957 Lace Leather Cutters, adjusted to cut various widths. Price.............**25c**

The Acme Belt Hooks.

No. 24C8960 The Acme Belt Hook is the simplest and most durable made. They will stand more strain than any lacing; can be used on any diameter pulley; will not cut out of the belt or become loose. As good for rubber and canvas as for leather belting. Made from the very best annealed coppered steel wire, so that the points will not break in clinching. **Put up in boxes of 200 hooks,** assorted No. 0 to No. 3 or all one size, as desired.
No. 0—⅜ inch wide. | No. 2—⅝ inch wide.
No. 1—½ inch wide. | No. 3—1 inch wide.
Price, per box, any size...................**19c**

Composition Wire Belt Lacing.

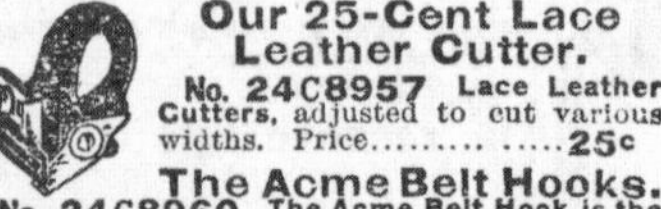

No. 24C8962 There is no friction or wear on the lace while in contact with the pulley, as the strands lie flush with the face of the belt. For all work where the belts are speeded or run with idlers, or at a severe strain, a single trial will establish its claim as a perfect means of sewing the ends of machine belting. **50 feet on each spool, and each spool in a box.** No. 1—For all single belts 6 inches wide and under. No. 2—For all belts 6 to 20 inches wide.
Price per spool...........................**28c**

Belt Studs.

No. 24C8964 Blake's Pattern Belt Studs. Recognized as the best belt fastener made.

No.	00	0	1	2	3	4
Length bet. Shoulders	15-16	11-16	¾	9-16	½	7-16
Per dozen	11c	9c	7c	6c	4c	4c
Per 100	74c	59c	50c	38c	26c	26c

Rubber Garden Hose.

Our entire line of hose is made entirely by machinery from start to finish, so there is no possibility of poor goods caused by careless operatives. All our hose is made with seamless tube. It is sold in lengths of 25 and 50 feet only. Couplings are not furnished. If you want couplings, order them separately, giving catalogue number and price, and we will put them on for you. When not in use hose should be kept in a cool place.

No. 24C8975 Our Competition Hose is what is commonly sold. It is not guaranteed as a high pressure hose, although it will give excellent service for all ordinary purposes. We have this season secured the best hose of this grade that we have ever seen. We sell it in 50-foot lengths only, without couplings. Size, ¾-inch, 3-ply.

Price, per length of 50 feet............**$3.00**

No. 24C8977 Our Leader Hose is good enough for ordinary use. Prices, without couplings. Sold in 25 or 50 feet pieces only.

	3-ply		4-ply	
Diameter, inch......	¾	1	¾	1
Price, per foot......	8c	12½c	9c	15½c

No. 24C8978 Our Acme Grade Hose is constructed of the best possible material. Will stand more pressure and wear longer than the Leader grade. Sold in 25-foot or 50-foot pieces only.

	3-ply			4-ply		
Diameter, inch	½	¾	1	½	¾	1
Price, per foot,	7½c	8½c	13½c	9c	10¾c	16¾c

Cotton Garden Hose.

The increased demand for light, durable, strong and absolutely reliable hose, suitable for sprinkling gardens, lawns and other places, has induced us to place on the market our New Process Rubber Lined Cotton Hose. The fabric is made from specially selected long fibre cotton and is perfect in construction. The rubber lining is of the very best quality. Put up in lengths of 50 feet with brass couplings. **We cannot sell less than full lengths of 50 feet. No extra charge for couplings.**

No. 24C8980 ¾-inch standard quality. Price, per foot..........8½c

No. 24C8981 ¾-inch extra standard quality. Price, per foot..........10c

Steam Hose.

No. 24C8982 Strictly Standard Made Steam Hose. This brand of hose needs no special introduction, having been on the market for years and giving universal satisfaction. For ordinary steam pressure it may be depended on to answer every requirement.

Inside Diam.	Ply	Pressure, pounds	Price, per foot	Inside Diam.	Ply	Pressure, pounds	Price, per foot
½-in.	3	40	18c	1¼-in.	4	26.7	$0.50
¾-in.	4	53.3	28c	1½-in.	6	53.3	.80
1 -in.	4	40	34c	2 -in.	6	40.	1.00
1¼-in.	4	32	45c				

Cotton Mill Hose.

No. 24C8984 Our Seamless Rubber Lined Cotton Mill Hose is adapted for hand engines, factories, warehouses, hotels, steamboats, public institutions, and wherever a light, durable and reliable hose for fire protection is required. It is full weight, made in the most careful manner, every section being mildew-proofed and guaranteed to stand water pressure of 250 pounds. Sold only in 25 or 50-foot pieces. We cannot sell less. Seamless, rubber lined. Diameter, inches.......... 1½ 2

Price, per foot.......... 19½c 24½c

Mill Hose Couplings.

No. 24C8986 For use on rubber and cotton fire hose. Same style as No. 24C8998.

Size, inches.......... 1½ 2

Price, per pair.......... 55c 80c

Hose Pipes or Nozzles.

No. 24C8988 Hose Nozzles, made of brass, finely finished, to be used in connection with our No. 24C8984 fire hose.

Size, inches..........	1½	2
Length, inches..........	12	12
With screw tips. Price....	$0.82	$1.10
With cock or cut off. Price..	1.75	2.30

Hose Splicers.

No. 24C8993 Metal Hose Menders. Where hose is broken or worn, the defective place may be cut out and the two ends joined together with the splicers.

Size, inch.......... ½ ¾ 1

Price.......... 2c 2½c 4c

Double Hose Clamps.

No. 24C8994 For use with Hose Splicers. One clamp does the work of two.

Size, inch.......... ½ ¾

Price.......... 3c 3c

Hose Nipples.

No. 24C8996 Brass Hose Nipples, to be used in connecting hose to iron pipe.

Size, inch.......... ½ ¾ 1

Price.......... 10c 11c 15c

All Brass Hose Couplings.

No. 24C8997 All Brass Hose Couplings. The lightest and easiest working coupling made. Size, ¾-inch.

Price, per pair..........7c

Hose Couplings.

No. 24C8998 Metal Hose Couplings. Will fit any kind of hose of inside measure as given.

¾ inch, per pair.... 6c | 1¼ in., per pair... 30c

1 inch, per pair.... 12c | 1½ in., per pair... 42c

2 inch, per pair.......... 68c

Sure Grip Hose Clamps.

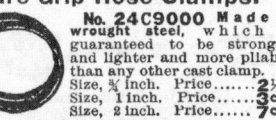

No. 24C9000 Made of wrought steel, which is guaranteed to be stronger and lighter and more pliable than any other cast clamp.

Size, ¾ inch. Price........ 2½c

Size, 1 inch. Price........ 3c

Size, 2 inch. Price........ 7c

Rubber Tubing.

No. 24C9005 Pure Rubber Tubing is used for siphoning liquors out of vats or barrels, for nursing bottles, syringes and numerous other purposes. It will not stand much pressure. Made in two grades. Thin wall is 1/16 inch thick. Thick wall is 3/32 inch thick.

Diam. inch.	Thin wall, per foot	Thick wall, per foot	Diam. inch.	Thin wall, per foot	Thick wall, per foot
⅛	3c	3½c	⅜	8c	9c
3/16	3c	4½c	½	8½c	10c
¼	5c	6c	⅝	9c	11c
5/16	6c	7c	¾	10c	13c

Gem Hose Nozzles.

No. 24C9007 The Improved Gem Hose Nozzle, by far the best combination nozzle made, throws a spray or solid stream. For ¾-inch hose.

Price..........23c

Hose Nozzles.

This Nozzle can be regulated to throw either a solid stream or a spray by simply turning the cock.

No. 24C9009 ¾-inch. Price..........33c

No. 24C9010 1-inch. Price..........58c

Reversible Lawn Sprinkler.

No. 24C9022 This sprinkler is suitable for either high or low pressure. The cap is reversible and a high or low spray, covering a wide area of ground, may be secured by simply reversing the cap. The standard is threaded to fit ¾-inch hose connection, and is provided with an internal rubber packing. It will not clog, there being no small holes to fill up and thus retard the spray. Price..........40c

Crescent Lawn Sprinkler.

No. 24C9025 This illustration shows our Crescent Lawn Sprinkler. It has four arms, which revolve when the water is turned on. Can be moved from place to place without detaching. Price..........$1.05

Turbine Lawn Sprinkler.

No. 24C9026 At last we have a lawn sprinkler that will do the work that a lawn sprinkler is intended to do; do it right and will last a lifetime without repairs. Lawn sprinklers, as a rule, are mere toys, get out of order, easily broken, etc. The arms in our Turbine sprinkler are made of ¼-inch 18 gauge brass tubing with five ⅛-inch holes in each end. The spread is 22 inches. Standard is made of ½-inch steel pipe with coupling to attach to ¾-inch hose. The swivel is made of cast brass and is constructed in such a manner that the bearings simply ride upon the stream of water when sprinkler is in operation. Five pounds pressure will operate it. It stands 2½ feet high and weighs 4½ pounds. With 15 pounds pressure it will cover 30 feet of ground. With 30 to 40 pounds pressure it will cover 50 feet of ground. Sold with a guarantee of being the best lawn sprinkler made or money refunded. Price..........$2.20

Hose Reels.

No. 24C9028 Hose Reel, strong and well made of hardwood, iron wheels. No hose included. Weight, 11 pounds. Price..........50c

Packing.

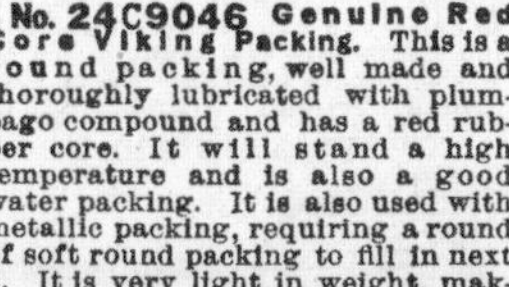

No. 24C9046 Genuine Red Core Viking Packing. This is a round packing, well made and thoroughly lubricated with plumbago compound and has a red rubber core. It will stand a high temperature and is also a good water packing. It is also used with metallic packing, requiring a round of soft round packing to fill in next to the gland. It is very light in weight, making the cost very low. We have sold the Viking for over six years, and experience has proved it superior to all cut spiral packing. **Strictly Engine Packing.** Size, inches, ¼, 5-16, ⅜, 7-16, ½, 9-16, ⅝, ¾, 1. Price, per pound, any size..........67c

Sheet Packing.

No. 24C9052 Cloth Insertion Sheet Packing. Cloth on one or both sides, made of the best stock and guaranteed to be the best sheet packing for the price ever sold. Comes in sheets one yard wide. Can furnish any quantity, but must be a cut the whole width of sheet (or 1 yard wide).

Thickness..........	1-32 in.	1-16 in.	⅛ in.
Weight, per square yd.	3 lbs.	6 lbs.	12 lbs.
Price, per pound.......	11c	11c	11c

Cardinal Brand Sheet Packing.

Our Cardinal Packing is far superior to all Red Sheet Packings for gas, air and ammonia compressors, and is not easily dissolved by contact with oil. Will make a tighter cold joint than other packings; has a smooth surface, is firm and substantial, and does not show a porous condition under microscopic examination. It is also good for steam and differs from other packings in the fact that it does not cling to the flanges and can be easily removed at any time.

No. 24C9054 Comes in sheets one yard wide, and sold in any quantity, but not less than whole width of sheet. For example we can't furnish a piece 2 inches wide, but it must be one yard long.

Thickness..........	1-32 in.	1-16 in.	⅛ in.
Weight, per square yd.	3 lbs.	6 lbs.	12 lbs.
Price, per pound.......	42c	42c	42c

Standard Wire Hoisting Rope.

This rope is almost universally employed for hoisting purposes on account of its flexibility. It is made of six strands, each of which is formed by twisting nineteen wires together, and a hemp core or center.

The Standard Hoisting Rope is very pliable, and will wind on moderate sized drums and pass over reasonably small sheaves without injury.

In ordering steel rope, it is well to use the same size as the iron, thereby taking full advantage of the increased wearing capacity of steel over iron. The best steel is the only one to use, as inferior grades are not as serviceable as good iron, because the constant vibrations to which ropes are subjected cause the poor steel to become brittle and unsafe.

We now list two grades of wire rope, one made of Swedish iron, the other cast steel. The Swedish iron is the kind generally sold and will give good service, but where great strength is required or where lives are at stake, as in mines, etc., we would recommend the cast steel as being best suitable for the purpose.

Parties ordering wire rope for the first time should give full particulars of the work, the size of drums, pulleys, curves, etc., and if rope ordered is not suitable, advice will be given. We cannot take back wire rope that has been cut to order.

No. 24C9060 Swedish Rope.

Diam.		Per foot	Diam.		Per foot
⅜ in.	Price....	3½c	¾ in.	Price....	8c
½ in.	Price....	4c	⅞ in.	Price....	10c
⅝ in.	Price....	6c	1 in.	Price....	13c

No. 24C9061 Cast Steel Rope. This rope is made the same as No. 24C9060 only steel is used in its construction instead of Swedish iron.

Diam.		Per foot	Diam.		Per foot
⅜ in.	Price....	4¼c	¾ in.	Price....	8c
½ in.	Price....	5c	⅞ in.	Price....	10½c
⅝ in.	Price....	6½c	1 in.	Price....	13½c

Galvanized Iron Rope.

No. 24C9062 This rope is composed of six strands (seven wires to a strand) with a hemp center. All the wires of each strand are coated with zinc so that the rope is proof against the action of the atmosphere. **This rope is not suitable to be run over drums or pulleys, but is to be used for guys, etc.**

Diam. in inch.....	5-16	⅜	½	⅝	¾
Price, per foot....	2c	2½c	3½c	4¾c	5¾c

Galvanized Wire Strand.

No. 24C9063 This cable is similar to the above guy rope, but is much stiffer, and cannot be used in connection with a pulley or drum. It is used for smoke stack guys, signal strand, trolley line span wire and other purposes. **It is composed of seven wires twisted together.**

Diameter in inches.........	¼	⅜	½
Weight, per 100 feet, lbs...	13	30	52
Price, per foot.........	1c	1½c	2½c

Wire Rope Clips and Clamps.

No. 24C9064 Clips and Clamps for Wire Rope are used to make an eye in the end of wire rope without splitting. Anyone can put them on.

Diam., inch.......	¼	5-16	⅜	½
Price.........	15c	15c	15c	18c
Diam., inch.......	⅝	¾	⅞	1
Price.........	22c	24c	28c	31c

Galvanized Steel Wire Rope Thimbles.

No. 24C9065 Galvanized Steel Wire Rope Thimbles, to be used in connection with our wire rope and strand.

Size	Price	Size	Price
5-16 inch..........	5c	¾ inch..........	10c
⅜ inch..........	6c	⅞ inch..........	11c
½ inch..........	7c	1 inch..........	15c
⅝ inch..........	9c		

Attachment Links for Chain Belting.

No. 24C9068 These Attachment Links are made to fit the sizes of chain listed under No. 24C9074, and should not be ordered except to match the sizes we state they will fit.

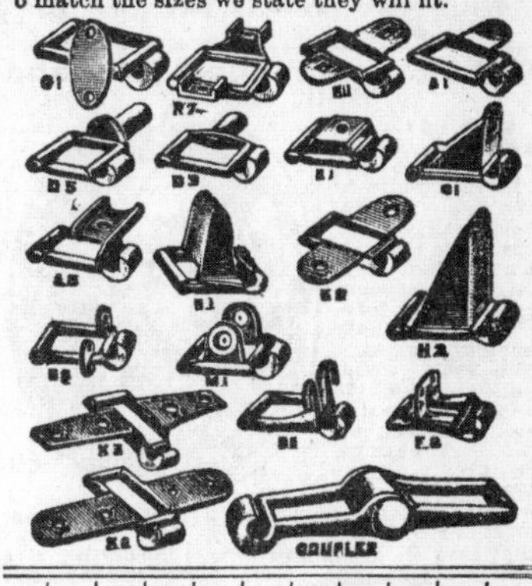

No. 25	No. 33	No. 35	No. 42	No. 45	No. 51	No. 52	No. 55	No. 57	No. 62	No. 67
A3	A1	A1	A1	A1	A1	A1	A1	A1	A1	A1
D3	A6	C1	K1	C1	K1	C1	C1	D5	C1	D5
E1	A13	K1	K3		K7	D4	D3	E1	D5	E1
G1	A14	cplr	S1	D5	S1	D5	F2	F2	K1	F3
H2	D3		cplr	E1		F2	K1	H2	K5	H1
K5	cplr			F2		G1	K5	K1	cplr	S2
K6				G1		K1	M1	S2		cplr
M1				H2		K5	S1	cplr		
S1				K5		cplr	cplr			
cplr				S1						
				S5						
				cplr						

Price on attachment links, 25 and 33......3c

Price on attachment links, 35, 42, 45, 51...4c

Price on attachment links, 52, 55, 57, 62...5c

Price on attachment links, No. 67...........6c

Improved Rigid Pillow Block.

No. 24C9072 Improved Rigid Pillow Block. This pillow block is provided with relief screws, independent of the screws that fasten the cap, thus permitting the cap to be set on the shaft at any desired pressure.

Size, in.	15-16	1 3-16	1 7-16	1 11-16	1 15-16	2 3-16
Price	75c	94c	$1.00	$1.50	$1.60	$1.80

Link Chain Beltings.

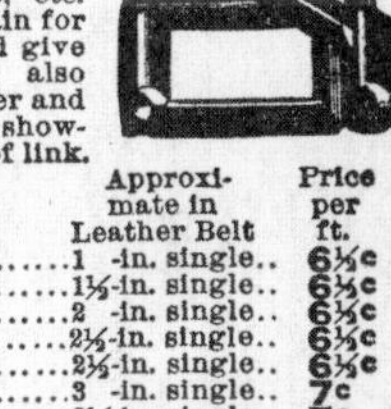

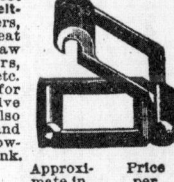

No. 24C9074 Best Quality Link Chain Belting, for use on mowers, reapers, corn and wheat drills, corn shellers, straw stackers, feed cutters, traction engines, etc. When ordering chain for repairs be sure and give number of chain; also lay one link on paper and mark around same, showing size and shape of link.

No.	Links, per ft.	Working Strain	Approximate in Leather Belt	Price per ft.
25	13.3..	75 lbs......	1 -in. single..	6½c
32	10.4..	150 lbs......	1½-in. single..	6½c
33	8.6..	200 lbs......	2 -in. single..	6½c
34	8.6..	225 lbs......	2½-in. single..	6½c
35	7.4..	250 lbs......	2½-in. single..	6½c
42	8.8..	300 lbs......	3 -in. single..	7c
45	7.4..	350 lbs......	3½-in. single..	7c
51	10.4..	375 lbs......	3½-in. single..	8½c
52	8..	500 lbs......	4 -in. single..	9½c
55	7.4..	450 lbs......	4 -in. single..	9½c
57	5.2..	600 lbs......	6 -in. single..	9½c
62	7.3..	650 lbs......	6½-in. single..	13c
67	5.2..	700 lbs......	7 -in. single..	14c

Ribbed Compression Couplings.

No. 24C9080 All Compression Couplings furnished complete with key.

For	Price	For	Price
1 3-16-in. shaft.	$2.15	1 11-16-in. shaft.	$2.70
1 5-16-in. shaft.	2.25	1 15-16-in. shaft.	3.10
1 7-16-in. shaft.	2.35	2 3-16-in. shaft.	3.35

Shafting.

No. 24C9093 Cold Drawn Steel Shafting.

Diam. in.	W'ght. per ft. lbs.	Price per ft.	Diam. in.	W'ght. per ft. lbs.	Price per ft.
¾	1.50	6c	1 5-16	4.61	18½c
⅞	2.03	8c	1⅜	5.08	20c
1	2.64	10½c	1½	6.00	22c
1 1-16	3.00	12c	1⅝	7.04	26c
1⅛	3.33	13¼c	1¾	8.16	27½c
1 3-16	3.74	15c	1⅞	9.39	34c
1¼	4.16	16½c	2	10.65	39c

Prices quoted are for shafts 1 to 24 feet, inclusive.

For full bars of 12, 14, 16, 18, 20 or 24 feet, deduct 1 cent per foot from above prices.

Adjustable Ball and Socket Hangers.

No. 24C9084 Adjustable Ball and Socket Hangers. Single Brace with plain standard bearings.

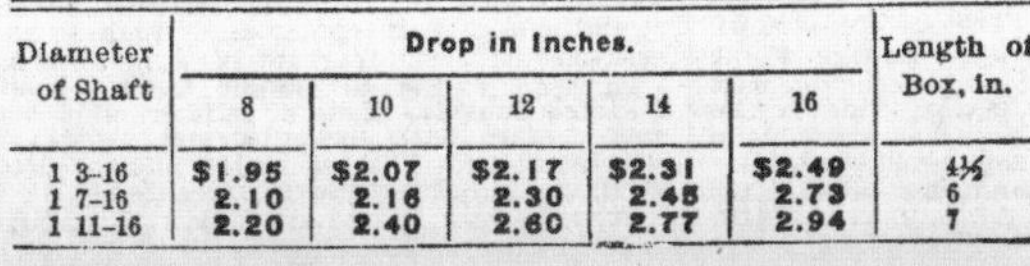

Diameter of Shaft	Drop in Inches.					Length of Box, in.
	8	10	12	14	16	
1 3-16	$1.95	$2.07	$2.17	$2.31	$2.49	4½
1 7-16	2.10	2.16	2.30	2.45	2.73	6
1 11-16	2.20	2.40	2.60	2.77	2.94	7

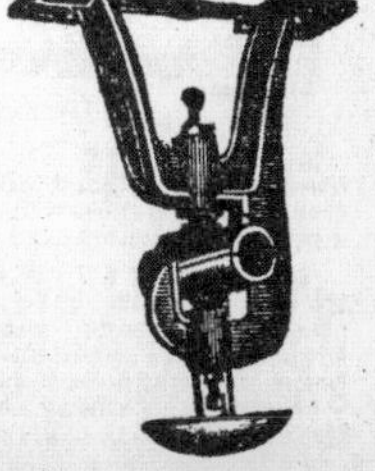

Shafting Collars.

No. 24C9083 Cast Collars for shafting, with set screw. Finished ready for use.

Size, in.	15/16	1	1⅛	1 3/16	1¼	1 5/16	1 7/16	1½	1 11/16	1 15/16	2 3/16
Price	14c	14c	14c	15c	15c	15c	16c	17c	20c	23c	26c

PULLEYS—Finished Iron and Split Wood.

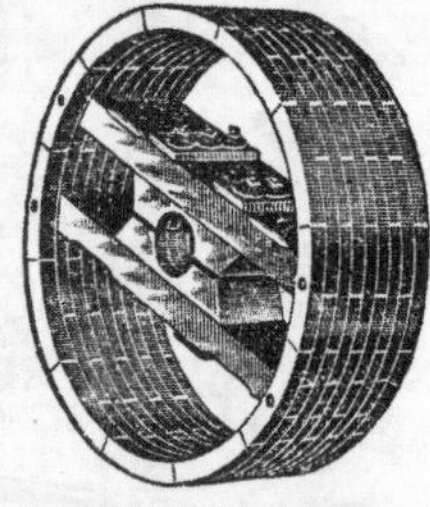

Best grade pulleys, cast iron or wood. The cast pulleys are made of the best quality gray cast iron, turned and fitted by lathe so that each one is absolutely perfect as to balance, hang, etc. The split wood pulleys, which are always made split, are one of the best pulleys on the market. They are made with interchangeable bushing so that they fit any size shaft.

No. 24C9090 Split Wood.

In ordering, give diameter, width of face, size of shaft pulley is to be used on, also kind wanted, if crowning or straight face is wanted. You cannot be too explicit in ordering. We furnish set screws with all pulleys unless ordered key seat. As most pulleys must be made to order, that is, bored to fit your shafting, there may be a delay of three or four days for doing this work.

No. 24C9089 Solid Cast.

PRICE LIST OF PULLEYS.

Write us for prices on any size pulley not listed below. Space will not permit our listing our full line.

No. 24C9089 Solid Cast Pulleys.
No. 24C9090 Split Wood Pulleys.

Diam., in.	Face, in.	Solid Cast	Split Wood	Diam., in.	Face, in.	Solid Cast	Split Wood
3	3	....	$0.68	18	8	$3.55	$2.42
3	4	....	.72	18	10	4.07	2.81
3	5	....	.75	18	12	4.78	3.24
3	6	....	.81	20	6	3.25	2.30
4	3	....	.72	20	8	3.93	2.74
4	4	....	.76	20	10	4.65	3.24
4	5	....	.80	20	12	5.46	3.75
4	6	....	.86	22	8	4.40	3.05
5	3	....	.75	22	10	5.25	3.60
5	4	....	.80	24	6	4.02	2.81
5	5	....	.87	24	8	4.88	3.40
5	6	....	.93	24	10	5.80	4.00
6	3	$1.02	.80	24	12	6.81	4.68
6	4	1.10	.85	26	6	4.52	3.10
6	5	1.20	.92	26	8	5.55	3.78
6	6	1.34	.99	28	6	4.99	3.42
7	3	1.10	.83	28	8	6.15	4.18
7	4	1.19	.86	28	10	6.83	5.04
7	5	1.31	.94	30	6	5.54	3.82
7	6	1.45	1.00	30	8	7.15	4.68
8	4	1.29	.93	30	10	8.66	5.62
8	5	1.41	.99	30	12	10.23	6.65
8	6	1.55	1.08	30	14	11.85	7.70
9	5	1.50	1.09	32	6	6.46	4.15
9	6	1.65	1.17	32	8	7.92	5.00
10	4	1.47	1.09	32	10	9.57	6.00
10	5	1.59	1.18	34	6	7.10	4.67
10	6	1.78	1.26	34	12	12.25	8.00
12	4	1.65	1.23	34	14	14.25	9.30
12	5	1.83	1.34	36	6	7.80	5.20
12	6	2.02	1.40	36	8	9.35	6.30
12	8	2.39	1.64	36	10	11.45	7.50
12	9	2.60	1.77	36	12	13.45	8.55
14	4	1.97	1.34	36	14	15.45	10.00
14	6	2.30	1.57	38	6	8.50	5.70
14	8	2.73	1.84	38	8	10.45	6.95
14	9	2.94	2.00	38	10	12.55	8.20
16	6	2.57	1.80	38	12	14.65	9.30
16	8	3.08	2.16	38	14	16.75	10.70
16	9	3.30	2.34	40	6	9.45	6.25
18	6	2.88	2.06	40	8	11.45	7.55

Sprocket Wheels.

No. 24C9078 Sprocket Wheels, bored and set, screwed or key seat. Made of high grade gray iron.

No. 52

Pitch. Diam. In.	No. of Teeth	Price
3½	7	$0.71
4	8	.76
4½	9	.84
5	10	.91
5½	12	1.00
6	13	1.08
6½	14	1.14
7	15	1.20
7½	16	1.27
8	17	1.35
9	19	1.49
10	21	1.62
12½	26	1.95
18	38	2.92
20	42	3.25
30½	64	5.20

Nos. 35, 45, 55

Pitch. Diam. In.	No. of Teeth	Price
2½	5	$0.58
3	6	.65
3¾	7	.71
4¼	8	.81
4¾	9	.87
5¼	10	.95
5¾	11	.99
6	12	1.07
6½	13	1.12
7¼	14	1.20
8½	16	1.33
9	17	1.39
9½	18	1.46
10	19	1.50
10½	20	1.52
11½	22	1.70
12	23	1.75
12¾	24	1.82
13	25	1.88
14¼	27	2.14
16	31	2.40

No. 32

Pitch. Diam. In.	No. of Teeth	Price
2	5	$0.52
2½	6	.53
3	8	.61
3½	9	.69
4¼	11	.74
4¾	13	.82
6	16	.95
8½	23	1.26
9	24	1.35
12	33	1.69

No. 42

Pitch. Diam. In.	No. of Teeth	Price
3	7	$0.71
3¾	9	.78
4½	11	.86
5¾	13	.94
6¾	14	1.04
8	18	1.24
9½	19	1.46
10½	22	1.56
14	32	2.08
18	41	2.60

No. 62

Pitch. Diam. In.	No. of Teeth	Price
3¾	7	$0.87
4¼	8	.91
7¼	14	1.30
8	15	1.35
9¾	18	1.60
10½	20	1.78
11½	22	2.04
12	22	2.08
14¾	28	2.59
16	30	2.75
18	34	3.16
20	38	3.60
24	45	3.90

Nos. 57, 67, 77

Pitch. Diam. In.	No. of Teeth	Price
4½	5	$0.87
5	6	.95
5½	7	1.00
6	8	1.10
7¼	10	1.30
8	11	1.39
8¾	12	1.48
9½	13	1.61
10¼	14	1.77
12½	17	2.10
14	19	2.38
15½	21	2.63
17	23	2.90
20	28	3.68
22	30	4.05
26	36	5.00
30	41	5.85

No. 25

Pitch. Diam. In.	No. of Teeth	Price
1½	5	$0.48
2	7	.52
2¼	8	.55
2¾	9	.58
3¼	11	.65
3½	12	.69
3¾	13	.71
4	14	.73
4½	15	.74
4¾	16	.78
5	17	.82
6	21	.95
6¼	22	.97
7½	26	1.10
8	28	1.17
10	35	1.21
10¼	36	1.39
12	42	1.56
13¾	48	1.75
15	52	1.88
16	56	2.00
17¼	60	2.15
18½	64	2.34
24	84	3.25

Nos. 33 and 34

Pitch. Diam. In.	No. of Teeth	Price
4	9	$0.74
5½	12	.94
6½	15	1.10
7	16	1.17
8½	19	1.30
9¾	22	1.47
12	27	1.69
16	36	2.20

No. 51

Pitch. Diam. In.	No. of Teeth	Price
2½	7	$0.65
4	11	.81
4½	12	.84
5	14	.91
6¼	17	1.04
8	22	1.30
10	27	1.52
12	33	1.82
14	39	2.08
16	45	2.40

Order by Catalogue Number.

GARDEN TOOLS.

In this line we offer only strictly high grade goods, made by concerns of well known and established reputation, and on this class of goods we are prepared to save you money. We can supply you at as little or less money than your dealer can buy in quantities. It will pay you to include all these goods in your order. Let us ship by freight and get you the correct freight rate. One trial order will demonstrate. Our economic one small profit plan works a great saving to the buyer.

D Handle Square Point Spades.

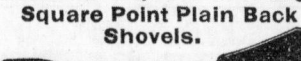

No. 24C9115 D Handle Square Point Steel Spades. Back and front strap, riveted. Size, 7½x12 inches, which is full regular size. Every spade warranted. Price............44c

No. 24C9117 D Handle, Square Point Polished Spade, made of solid crucible cast steel. Plain back, wide straps. This is the highest grade spade on the market, every blade being made of selected crucible cast steel, fully warranted. Nothing better made. Size, 7½x12 inches. Price............50c

Long Handle Square Point Spades.

No. 24C9122 Long Handle Square Point Steel Spades. Back and front strap. Size, 7½x12 inches, full regular size. Warranted selected hickory handles. Price............44c

No. 24C9124 Long Handle Square Point Polished Spade. Made of solid crucible cast steel. Plain back socket straps. Same grade as our No. 24C9117. Fully warranted. Price...50c

Square Point Plain Back Shovels.

No. 24C9126 D Handle Square Point Shovels. Back and front straps riveted. Size, 9¾x12 inches. Full regular size. Made of the best selected steel. Warranted. Price....44c

No. 24C9128 D Handle Square Point Polished Shovels. Made of solid crucible cast steel. Plain back socket straps. Made of selected stock. Nothing better made. Size, 9¾x12 inches. Every shovel warranted. Price............50c

Long Handle Square Point Shovels.

No. 24C9134 Long Handle Square Point Steel Shovels. Back and front strap. Size, 9¾x12 inches. Made of selected steel. Price.....44c

No. 24C9136 Long Handle Square Point Shovels. Made of solid crucible cast steel. Plain smooth back and socket straps, same grade as our No. 24C9128. Every shovel warranted. Best selected hickory handles. Price.........50c

Round Point Solid Steel Shovels.

No. 24C9138 D Handle Round Point Steel Shovels. Back and front straps riveted. Made of steel, not iron. Size, 9¾x12 inches. Price...44c

No. 24C9140 D Handle, Round Point Polished Solid Crucible Cast Steel Shovels. Made of the highest grade cast steel. Nothing better made. Plain back socket straps. Every shovel warranted. Price............50c

Long Handle, Round Point Shovels.

No. 24C9143 Long Handle, Round Point Shovels. Steel. Front and back straps. Size, 9¾x12 inches, full regular size. Price............44c

No. 24C9145 Long Handle, Round Point Polished Solid Crucible Cast Steel Shovels. Plain, smooth back socket straps. Made of the finest cast steel. Nothing better made. Full warranted. Price............50c

Coal Shovels.

No. 24C9147 D Handle Cleveland Pattern Coal Shovels. Made of extra fine cast steel. Makes an excellent shovel for snow, grain or sawdust. Made in three sizes as follows:

	Size of blades.	Price
No. 1.	13 inches wide, 14 inches long...	42c
No. 2.	14 inches wide, 14¾ inches long...	47c
No. 3.	14¾ inches wide, 15½ inches long...	49c

Manure Fork Handle.

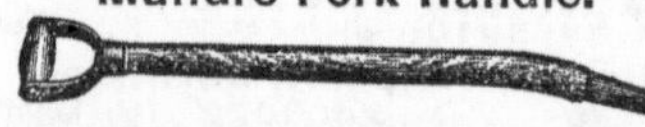

No. 24C9149 Selected Quality Manure Fork Handle, with malleable D. Price....17c

Shovel and Spade Handles.

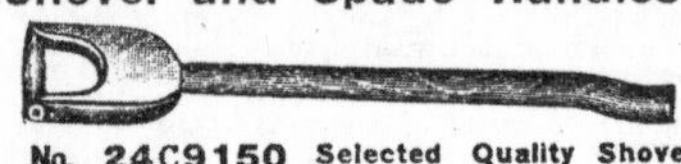

No. 24C9150 Selected Quality Shovel Handle, with wood D. Price............19c

No. 24C9151 Selected Quality Spade Handle, with wood D. Price............20c

No. 24C9152 Selected Quality Long Shovel Handle. Price............16c

No. 24C9153 Selected Quality Long Spade Handle. Price............14c

Scoop Shovels.

No. 24C9156 Steel Scoop. Chisholm's pattern, half polished. Wide mouth. A first-class farmer's scoop.

	No. 6	No. 7	No. 8	No. 9	No. 10
Width....	13½ in.	13¾ in.	14¼ in.	14½ in.	14½ in.
Price.....	54c	58c	61c	65c	68c

Furnace Scoops.

No. 24C9161 All Steel Furnace Scoops, D. handle, narrow mouth. Length of blade, 13 inches; width at point, 9¼ inches. Made in one size only. Price............40c

Scoop Shovel Handles.

No. 24C9162 A1—Best quality Scoop Shovel Handles. Price............20c

Vaterland Spades.

No. 24C9163 Vaterland Spades. Made of the highest grade steel, full polished. The cutting edges being angular, no steps are required, which allow the blade to scour from end to end. You can do more work with this spade than with any tool made. We use extra all white hickory handles. Every spade fully warranted. Try one. Price............84c

Wire Potato Scoop.

No. 24C9170 Wire Potato Scoop. Size, 13½x16 inches. Price............$1.10

Drain Spades.

Drain Spade, solid steel plain back, D handle, round point, blade tapers from 5½ inches at the step to 4½ inches at the point.

No. 24C9175 Length, 18 inches. Price............88c

No. 24C9176 Length, 20 inches. Price............90c

Post Spades.

No. 24C9179 Post Spade, solid steel square point, D handle, plain back. Size, 6½x12 inches. Price............90c

No. 24C9180 Same as No. 24C9179, 6½x20 inches. Price............91c

Drain Cleaners.

This Drain Tool is an improvement over any drain tool on the market. It is very strong and intended to last a long time. The parts are made of the best malleable iron, and the blade of shovel steel. The handle can be placed at any angle by raising the spring. When the spring is in position the blade is locked tightly and will not move or have a side motion.

No. 24C9190 Size, 4x16 inches. Price............59c

No. 24C9191 Size, 5x16 inches. Price............60c

No. 24C9192 Size, 6x16 inches. Price............63c

Spading Forks.

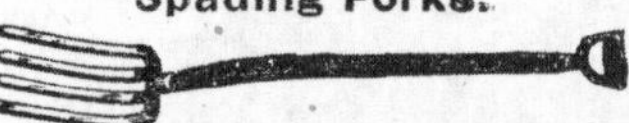

No. 24C9198 D Handle, Capped Ferrule, Spading Fork, four flat steel tines. Price 42c

No. 24C9199 D Handle, Strap Ferrule, Spading Fork, four steel tines. The strongest and best spading fork made. Price.....52c

Coke Forks.

Coke Forks. Made of best cast steel, strapped ferrule, D handle.

No. 24C9205 Price, 10-tooth....$1.20
No. 24C9206 Price, 12-tooth.... 1.40
No. 24C9207 Price, 14-tooth.... 1.70

Manure Hook.

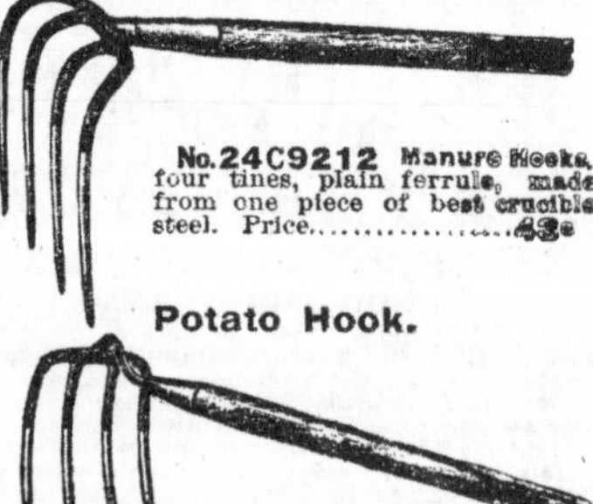

No. 24C9212 Manure Hooks, four tines, plain ferrule, made from one piece of best crucible steel. Price............43c

Potato Hook.

No. 24C9214 Potato Digger, 4 round tines. Price............31c

No. 24C9215 Potato Digger, 4 flat tines. Price............40c

D Heads for Fork or Shovel Handles.

No. 24C9217 Malleable D for fork or shovel handles. Price............6c

Hay Forks.

This illustration shows the plain Ferrule.

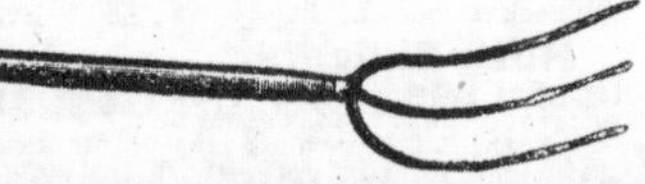

Straight Handle, Plain Capped Ferrule Hay Forks, three oval tines, standard size and length; selected handles.

No.	Length of handle	Price
24C9220	4 feet	31c
24C9221	4½ feet	32c
24C9222	5 feet	33c
24C9223	5½ feet	35c
24C9224	6 feet	36c

Straight Handle, Capped and Strapped Ferrule Hay Forks, three oval tines, standard size and length, selected handles.

No.	Length of handle	Price
24C9226	4 feet	36c
24C9227	4½ feet	37c
24C9228	5 feet	38c
24C9229	5½ feet	39c
24C9230	6 feet	41c

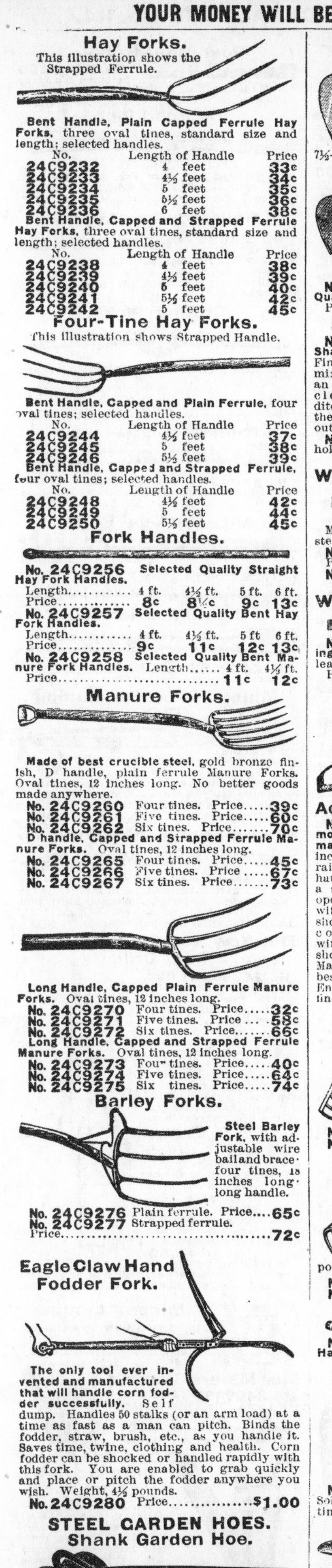

Hay Forks.

This illustration shows the Strapped Ferrule.

Bent Handle, Plain Capped Ferrule Hay Forks, three oval tines, standard size and length; selected handles.

No.	Length of Handle	Price
24C9232	4 feet	33c
24C9233	4½ feet	34c
24C9234	5 feet	35c
24C9235	5½ feet	36c
24C9236	6 feet	38c

Bent Handle, Capped and Strapped Ferrule Hay Forks, three oval tines, standard size and length; selected handles.

No.	Length of Handle	Price
24C9238	4 feet	38c
24C9239	4½ feet	39c
24C9240	5 feet	40c
24C9241	5½ feet	42c
24C9242	6 feet	45c

Four-Tine Hay Forks.

This illustration shows Strapped Handle.

Bent Handle, Capped and Plain Ferrule, four oval tines; selected handles.

No.	Length of Handle	Price
24C9244	4½ feet	37c
24C9245	5 feet	38c
24C9246	5½ feet	39c

Bent Handle, Capped and Strapped Ferrule, four oval tines; selected handles.

No.	Length of Handle	Price
24C9248	4½ feet	42c
24C9249	5 feet	44c
24C9250	5½ feet	45c

Fork Handles.

No. 24C9256 Selected Quality Straight Hay Fork Handles.

Length	4 ft.	4½ ft.	5 ft.	6 ft.
Price	8c	8½c	9c	13c

No. 24C9257 Selected Quality Bent Hay Fork Handles.

Length	4 ft.	4½ ft.	5 ft	6 ft.
Price	9c	11c	12c	13c

No. 24C9258 Selected Quality Bent Manure Fork Handles.

Length	4 ft.	4½ ft.
Price	11c	12c

Manure Forks.

Made of best crucible steel, gold bronze finish, D handle, plain ferrule Manure Forks. Oval tines, 12 inches long. No better goods made anywhere.

No. 24C9260 Four tines. Price.....39c
No. 24C9261 Five tines. Price.....60c
No. 24C9262 Six tines. Price.....70c

D handle, Capped and Strapped Ferrule Manure Forks. Oval tines, 12 inches long.

No. 24C9265 Four tines. Price.....45c
No. 24C9266 Five tines. Price.....67c
No. 24C9267 Six tines. Price.....73c

Long Handle, Capped Plain Ferrule Manure Forks. Oval tines, 12 inches long.

No. 24C9270 Four tines. Price.....32c
No. 24C9271 Five tines. Price.....58c
No. 24C9272 Six tines. Price.....66c

Long Handle, Capped and Strapped Ferrule Manure Forks. Oval tines, 12 inches long.

No. 24C9273 Four tines. Price.....40c
No. 24C9274 Five tines. Price.....64c
No. 24C9275 Six tines. Price.....74c

Barley Forks.

Steel Barley Fork, with adjustable wire bail and brace four tines, 18 inches long long handle.

No. 24C9276 Plain ferrule. Price....65c
No. 24C9277 Strapped ferrule. Price.....72c

Eagle Claw Hand Fodder Fork.

The only tool ever invented and manufactured that will handle corn fodder successfully. Self dump. Handles 50 stalks (or an arm load) at a time as fast as a man can pitch. Binds the fodder, straw, brush, etc., as you handle it. Saves time, twine, clothing and health. Corn fodder can be shocked or handled rapidly with this fork. You are enabled to grab quickly and place or pitch the fodder anywhere you wish. Weight, 4½ pounds.

No. 24C9280 Price.....$1.00

STEEL GARDEN HOES.
Shank Garden Hoe.

No. 24C9290 Common Shaped Shank Garden Hoes, with cast steel blade welded to shank. Selected handle, full regular size, 7½-inch blade. Price.....27c

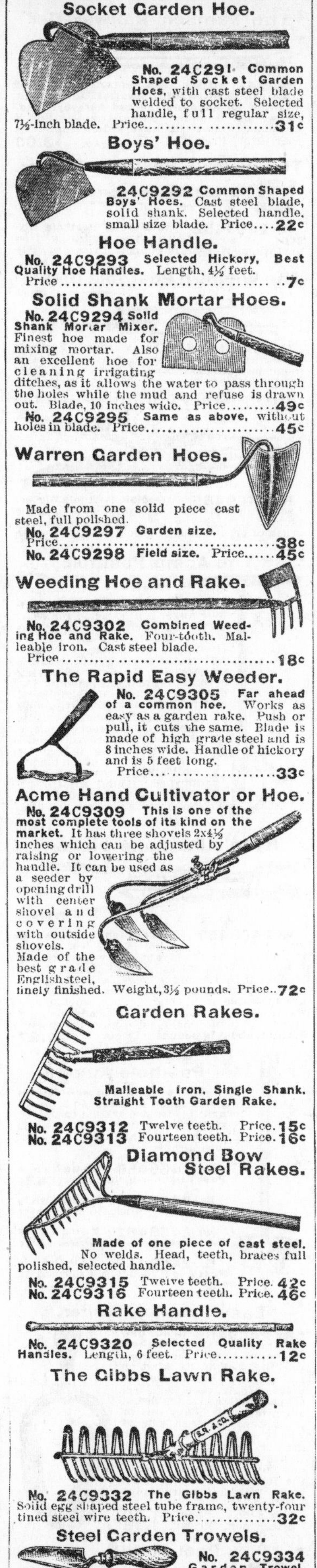

Socket Garden Hoe.

No. 24C9291 Common Shaped Socket Garden Hoes, with cast steel blade welded to socket. Selected handle, full regular size, 7½-inch blade. Price.....31c

Boys' Hoe.

24C9292 Common Shaped Boys' Hoes. Cast steel blade, solid shank. Selected handle, small size blade. Price....22c

Hoe Handle.

No. 24C9293 Selected Hickory, Best Quality Hoe Handles. Length, 4½ feet. Price.....7c

Solid Shank Mortar Hoes.

No. 24C9294 Solid Shank Mortar Mixer. Finest hoe made for mixing mortar. Also an excellent hoe for cleaning irrigating ditches, as it allows the water to pass through the holes while the mud and refuse is drawn out. Blade, 10 inches wide. Price.....49c

No. 24C9295 Same as above, without holes in blade. Price.....45c

Warren Garden Hoes.

Made from one solid piece cast steel, full polished.

No. 24C9297 Garden size. Price.....38c
No. 24C9298 Field size. Price.....45c

Weeding Hoe and Rake.

No. 24C9302 Combined Weeding Hoe and Rake. Four-tooth. Malleable iron. Cast steel blade. Price.....18c

The Rapid Easy Weeder.

No. 24C9305 Far ahead of a common hoe. Works as easy as a garden rake. Push or pull, it cuts the same. Blade is made of high grade steel and is 8 inches wide. Handle of hickory and is 5 feet long. Price.....33c

Acme Hand Cultivator or Hoe.

No. 24C9309 This is one of the most complete tools of its kind on the market. It has three shovels 2x4½ inches which can be adjusted by raising or lowering the handle. It can be used as a seeder by opening drill with center shovel and covering with outside shovels. Made of the best grade English steel, finely finished. Weight, 3½ pounds. Price..72c

Garden Rakes.

Malleable Iron, Single Shank, Straight Tooth Garden Rake.

No. 24C9312 Twelve teeth. Price..15c
No. 24C9313 Fourteen teeth. Price..16c

Diamond Bow Steel Rakes.

Made of one piece of cast steel. No welds. Head, teeth, braces full polished, selected handle.

No. 24C9315 Twelve teeth. Price..42c
No. 24C9316 Fourteen teeth. Price..46c

Rake Handle.

No. 24C9320 Selected Quality Rake Handles. Length, 6 feet. Price.....12c

The Gibbs Lawn Rake.

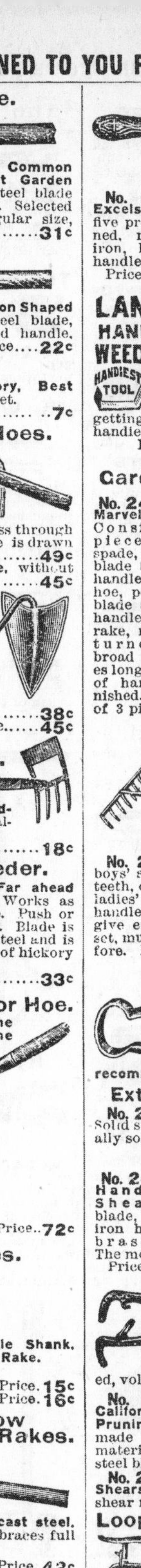

No. 24C9332 The Gibbs Lawn Rake. Solid egg shaped steel tube frame, twenty-four tined steel wire teeth. Price.....32c

Steel Garden Trowels.

No. 24C9334 Garden Trowel. Steel blade, 6 inches long, steel shank. Hardwood handle, cherry finish. Price.....3½c

No. 24C9335 All Steel Garden Trowels. Made from one piece of metal, a better trowel than generally carried by the retail trade. Size, 6 inches. Price.....19c

Garden Fork.

No. 24C9337 Garden Fork. Malleable, hardwood handle. Price..7c

Weeders.

No. 24C9339 Excelsior Weeder, five prongs, japanned, malleable iron, hardwood handle. Price.....4c

No. 24C9342 The Lang Hand Weeder, is a tool that should be owned by all who do gardening or raise flowers. It has an elegant steel blade, sharpened to cut both ways. For getting around plants and flowers, it is the handiest tool made. Price.....15c

If by mail, postage extra, 4 cents.

Garden Sets.

No. 24C9345 The Marvel Garden Set. Consists of three pieces as follows: spade, polished steel blade 5½x3¾ inches, handle 18 inches long; hoe, polished steel blade 5½x3½ inches, handle 30 inches long; rake, malleable iron turned. 5¾ inches, broad handle 30 inches long. All handles of hardwood, varnished. Price, per set of 3 pieces.....20c

Acme Garden Set.

No. 24C9347 Acme. Comprises a steel boys' spade with D handle, a rake with eight teeth, of a new and improved pattern, and a ladies' hoe, with solid steel shank and spring handle. This set is made for service and will give entire satisfaction. A large, well made set, much better quality than ever offered before. Price, per set.....67c

Grass Shears.

No. 24C9354 Grass Shears, like illustration; bent handles; length of blade, 5½ inches. Not recommended for shearing sheep. Price, 16c

Extra Grade Grass Shears.

No. 24C9355 Extra Grade Grass Shears. Solid steel blades. A better article than generally sold by the retail trade. Price.....25c

Pruning Shears.

No. 24C9357 Hand Pruning Shears, steel blade, malleable iron handles, brass springs. The most popular hand pruning shear made. Price.....16c

No. 24C9358 Henry Pattern Pruning Shears, well made and finished, high grade steel blades, warranted, volute springs. Price.....24c

No. 24C9359 California Pattern Pruning Shears, made of the best material, polished steel blades, volute springs. Price.....30c

No. 24C9360 Extra High Grade Pruning Shears. 9-inch full nickel plated. Finest shear made. Price.....48c

Loop Handle Pruning Shears

No. 24C9361 Loop Handle Pruning Shears. Blades are made of high grade English steel. A neat, well made shear. Price.....27c

Buckeye Pattern Pruning Shears.

No. 24C9363 Buckeye Pattern Pruning Shears, ash handle, 22 inches long, 2-inch cast steel cutter. Price.....48c

Patent Fruit Gatherer.

No. 24C9367 The Acme Patent Fruit Gatherer, is a device for gathering fruit. It will pick apples, pears, plums and similar fruit from otherwise inaccessible places without bruise or injury of any kind. Price.....70c

No. 24C9367

Acme Telegraph Tree Pruner.

No. 24C9368 This improvement was originally designed for the use of telephone and telegraph men in keeping the wires free from overhanging branches of trees. The blade can be taken out to be sharpened; there is a steel coil spring for throwing out the blade; the socket has a thread on the inside and can thus be easily screwed on to a pole of any length. Price.....75c

Extra blades.....8c
Extra springs.....9c

The Waters' Tree Pruner.

The Waters' Tree Pruner, with latest improvements, is considered by fruit growers and gardeners the best on the market. Although the cutting blade is very thin, it being supported on both sides by the hook, makes it strong and durable. It will cut off the largest bough the hook will admit, and also clip the smallest twig. No ladders are required, as pruning can be done while standing on the ground.

No. 24C9370

Length, feet	4	6	8	10	12
Weight, lbs.	2¼	3	3½	4	4½
Price	38c	43c	47c	46c	52c

No. 24C9369 Extra knives for above pruners.....9c

Hedge Shears.

No. 24C9373 Hedge Shears, high grade steel blades, ... hardwood handles. Nothing better made.

Size	8	9	10	12
Price	93c	$1.18	$1.28	$1.95

Hedge Knives.

No. 24C9375 Hedge Knives, made of the best English steel. Has strong ferrule, with rivet through ferrule and shank. Length of blade, 18 inches; finely finished. Price..49c

Foundry Riddles.

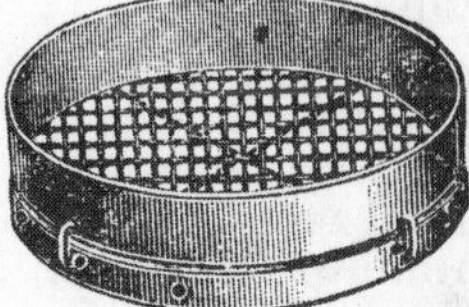

No. 24C9394 Foundry Riddles. Wood rims with brass or steel wire. Sieves made of heavy wire with extra strong rims.

Steel wire, Nos. 4, 6 or 8. Price.....40c
Brass wire, Nos. 4, 6 or 8. Price.....75c

Mill Pick.

No. 24C9401 Mill Picks, made of special tool steel. Tempered by a secret process which insures an even temper; well finished ready for use. Weight, 1½ to 3 pounds each. Price, per pound.....32c

Sandstone Crandles.

No. 24C9402 Sandstone Crandles, used for surfacing stone. Teeth are adjustable, and can be taken out and sharpened; furnished complete with handle.

Price, 12-tooth crandle.....$2.35

Brick Trowels.

Our Brick Trowels are made with great care by experienced workmen from the best steel—tempered to stand the most severe usage. They are forged from the bar, shank and blade all one piece. We do not handle the cheap trowel with stamped blade riveted to shank.

No. 24C9380 The Fulton Mason's Brick Trowel, London pattern. Finely finished and correctly tempered. Warranted.

Size, inches	10	10½	11
Price	32c	34c	36c

No. 24C9381 The Fulton Mason's Brick Trowel, Philadelphia pattern, has square heel which brings weight of mortar nearer the hand. Warranted.

Size, inches	10	10½	11
Price	35c	37c	39c

Pointing Trowels.

No. 24C9383 The Fulton Pointing Trowel, same shape as No. 24C9380 trowel, only smaller, forged steel blade, polished, welded to shank. Warranted.

Size, inches	4	5	6
Price	14c	15c	16c

WE ACCEPT ALL ORDERS with the understanding and agreement that goods may be returned at our expense and transportation charges and your money promptly refunded, if anything we send you is not satisfactory.

Plastering Trowels.

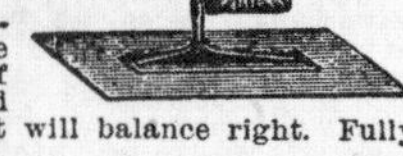

No. 24C9384 The Fulton Plastering Trowel is made of the very best of steel finely finished and handled so it will balance right. Fully warranted

Size, inches	10	10½	11	12
Price	29c	32c	33c	41c

No. 24C9385 The Cincinnati Pattern Plastering Trowel, is made of the very best steel, extra fine finish, carefully mounted. The easy fit to the hand has made this trowel very popular with the best plasterers in all sections of the country. Fully warranted.

Size, inches	11	11½	12
Price	78c	81c	84c

Corner Trowel.

No. 24C9386 Corner Trowels, cast steel. Length, 6 inches. Price........35c

Plasterers' Cork Floats.

No. 24C9387 Plasterers' Cork Floats, made from one thickness of cork, carefully smoothed on both sides.

Size, 12x4x1 inches thick. Price........28c
Size, 12x5x1¼ inches thick. Price........42c
Size, 12x6x1½ inches thick. Price........51c

Stone Sledges.

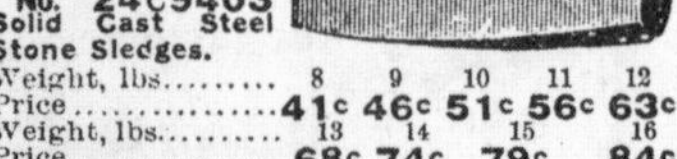

No. 24C9403 Solid Cast Steel Stone Sledges.

Weight, lbs.	8	9	10	11	12
Price	41c	46c	51c	56c	63c
Weight, lbs.	13	14	15	16	
Price	68c	74c	79c	84c	

Drilling Hammers.

No. 24C9405 Solid Cast Steel Drilling or Striking Hammers, without handles.

Weight, lbs.	2½	3	3½	4	4½
Price	23c	23c	26c	30c	30c
Weight, lbs.	5	6	7	8	9
Price	30c	30c	35c	45c	55c

Stonemasons' Hammers.

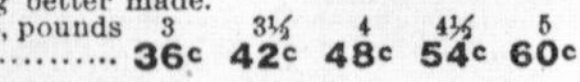

No. 24C9406 High Grade Steel Stonemasons' Hammers. Bronzed axe finish. Nothing better made.

Weight, pounds	3	3½	4	4½	5
Price	36c	42c	48c	54c	60c

Stonemasons' Hammers. With Teeth.

No. 24C9407 High Grade Stonemason's Hammers. Bronzed axe finish. With teeth. Nothing better made.

Weight, pounds	3	3½	4	4½	5
Price	38c	44c	46c	65c	75c

Drilling Hammer Handles.

No. 24C9408 Drilling Hammer Handles. Length, 16-in., price 5c. Length, 18-in. price 5c

Single Face Spalling Hammers.

No. 24C9409 Single Face Spalling or Stone Hammers. Solid cast steel, polished face, oil finish. Nothing better made.

Weight, lbs.	2½	3	3½	4	4½	5
Price	25c	28c	32c	38c	40c	41c
Weight, lbs.	6	7	8	9	10	
Price	45c	53c	60c	68c	75c	

Stone Bush Hammers.

No. 24C9410 Stone Bush Hammer, with milled teeth. Made of extra quality tool steel, oil finished.

Weight, lbs.	3	3½	4
Price	$1.50	$1.75	$2.00
Weight, lbs.	4	5	6
Price	$2.25	$2.50	$3.00

Double Face Spalling Hammers.

No. 24C9411 Double Face Spalling or Stone Hammers. Solid cast steel, polished face, oil finish.

Weight, lbs.	2½	3	3½	4	4½	5
Price	25c	28c	32c	38c	40c	41c
Weight, lbs.	6	7	8	9	10	
Price	45c	53c	60c	68c	75c	

Stonemasons' Hammer Handle.

No. 24C9412 Stonemasons' Hammer Handle, Length, 18 inches. Price........5c

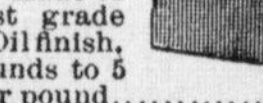

Stone Axe.

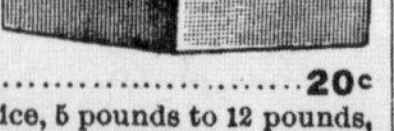

No. 24C9414 Stone Axe. Made of the highest grade tool steel. Oil finish. Price, 3 pounds to 5 pounds, per pound........20c

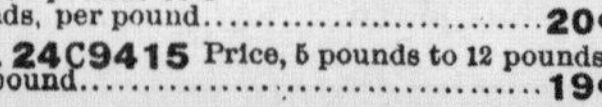

No. 24C9415 Price, 5 pounds to 12 pounds, per pound........19c

Brick Hammers, Chicago Pattern.

No. 24C9417 Solid Cast Steel Brick Hammers, oil finished. Nothing better made.

Size 1, weight 1 lb. 8 oz. Price .60c
Size 2, weight 2 lbs. Price.....65c
Size 3, weight 2 lbs. 8 oz. Price........70c

Brick Chisels.

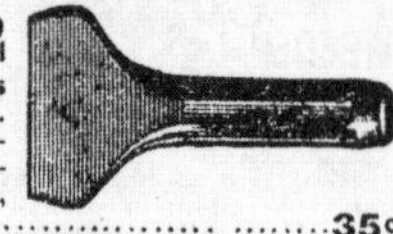

No. 24C9419 Highest Grade Tool Steel Brick Chisels nicely finished. Made of ⅝-inch octagon steel, 4½ inches wide. Weight, 1¾ pounds. Price........35c

Mallet Head Stonecutters' Points.

No. 24C9420 Mallet Head Stonecutters' Points, made of 9-16-inch highest grade tool steel. Weight, 11 ounces. Price........16c

Pitching Tools.

No. 24C9421 Pitching Tools, made of the highest grade tool steel. Size, 2 inches. Weight, 1 pound 12 ounces. Price........35c

Stonecutters' Chisels.

No. 24C9422 Mallet Head Plain Stonecutters' Chisels, made of the highest grade 9-16-inch octagon tool steel.

Width of blade, inches	¾	1	1¼
Weight, ounces	10	10	11
Price	15c	15c	16c

No. 24C9423 Stonecutters' Mallet Head Chisels, with teeth, made of the highest grade 9-16-inch octagon tool steel.

Width of blade, inches	¾	1	1¼
Weight, ounces	10	10	11
Price, each	16c	16c	17c

Hand Chipping Chisels.

No. 24C9424 Hand Chipping Chisels, made of the highest grade tool steel.

Size, inch	½	⅝	¾
Weight, pound	½	½	1
Price	10c	14c	20c

Cement Sidewalk Edgers.

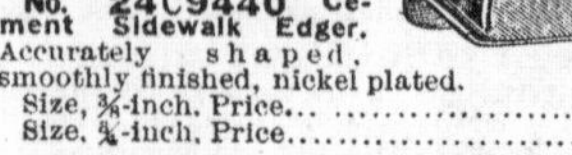

No. 24C9440 Cement Sidewalk Edger. Accurately shaped, smoothly finished, nickel plated.

Size, ⅜-inch. Price........43c
Size, ⅝-inch. Price........54c

Cement Sidewalk Groovers.

Cement Sidewalk Groovers. Accurately shaped, smoothly finished, nickel plated. We can furnish these groovers with or without steel centers. Curved on both ends like illustration, or square at one end. Also with curves adapted for sidewalks or those suitable for driveways. All cast for sidewalks.

No. 24C9441
Price........42c
No. 24C9442 Steel centers for sidewalks.
Price........68c
No. 24C9442½ Driveway Groovers.
Price........52c

Sand Rammers.

No. 24C9443 Cast Iron Sand Rammers; wood handle.

No. 2, size, 5x6 inches. Price........$0.65
No. 2, size, 6x7 inches. Price........ .75
No. 2, size, 7x8 inches. Price........ 1.00

No. 24C9444 Cast Iron Sand Rammers. Wood handles.

No. 1, size, 8x8 inches. Price........$ .85
No. 1, size, 10x10 inches. Price........ 1.15

Our Little Steel Handy Pinch Bars.

No. 24C9445 Is the real thing for use about store, warehouse, factory, barn, on truck (teaming) or about house or farm. You can move almost anything with one of them. Handy everywhere, and a single use when you need it will save many times the trifling cost. It is hammered steel, ¾-inch in the square, 3 feet long, with tempered points as shown in illustration. Weight, 3¾ pounds.

Price, black........28c
Price, full polished........40c

Crowbars.

No. 24C9447 Solid Steel Crowbar. Either Wedge or Pinch Point. The top illustration shows wedge point; bottom, pinch point. We have them weighing from 12 to 20 pounds.

Weight	12 lbs.	14 lbs.	16 lbs.	18 lbs.	20 lbs.
Price	36c	42c	48c	54c	60c

The Samson Railway Car Mover.

No. 24C9450 The Samson is the most practical, positive and powerful device ever invented for handling railroad cars by hand, and we sell it under that guarantee. Buy a Samson and have a little switch engine of your own. Price........$3.00

The Eureka Posthole Digger.

No. 24C9452 The Eureka Posthole Digger, cast steel blades with malleable iron mounting. Weight, 10 pounds. Price......59c

The Western Posthole Digger.

No. 24C9454 The Western Posthole Digger, cast steel blades, heavy malleable mounting, selected handles. Price........72c

Invincible Posthole Digger.

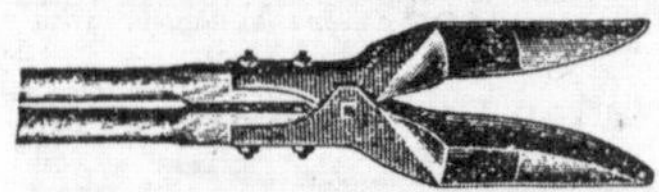

No. 24C9455 Invincible Posthole Digger. Each blade and shank dropped out of a single piece of steel. No welds or malleable parts to break or become loose. Price........69c

The Acme Posthole Auger.

No. 24C9456 The Acme Posthole Auger is unexcelled for easy, quick and efficient work. It has readily adjustable blades to bore from 6½ to 8-inch holes, by simply setting out two of the blades; this obviates the necessity of having several different sized augers. The dumping mechanism is simple and effective. The superior advantages of the Acme in general utility, speed, wide difference of operation with improved results make it the king of posthole augers. Spring steel blades, malleable iron castings nicely finished. Radial adjustment, automatic downward feed, earth packs hard against disc.

Price........$1.25

Ryan's Posthole Digger.

No. 24C9457 Ryan's Patent Posthole Digger. Will dig a 7-inch hole three feet deep in one minute. It is warranted to work perfectly in any soil, from sticky mud to dry sand. The load is cut free from the blades and forced out by simply spreading the handles. All castings are maleable iron; blades of crucible cast steel; cleaner rods, spring steel, and handles second to none. Sold strictly on its merits. Weight, about 10 pounds. Price........$1.37

Posthole Augers.

These are the well known goods made by Vaughan & Bushnell; blades are of solid cast steel, spring tempered. The tube is hollow. They are made in the following sizes:

No. 24C9460 Vaughan's Post Auger, 6-inch. Price...49c
No. 24C9461 Vaughan's Post Auger, 7-inch. Price...49c
No. 24C9462 Vaughan's Post Auger, 8-inch. Price...49c
No. 24C9463 Vaughan's Post Auger, 9-inch. Price...49c

Easy Posthole Auger.

No. 24C9466 In our new Improved Easy Posthole Auger we have the easiest working tool of its kind on the market. The blades are made of high grade tool steel shaped similar to a double cut auger bit with heavy lips or projections, on each side of which, while giving a much greater cutting power, also insures a straight hole without any special attention of the operator. Comes complete with 3-foot iron pipe handle.

Size, 8-inch. Price..$1.10
Size, 9-inch. Price.. 1.15

Post Mauls.

No. 24C9468 Post Mauls, solid cast iron with hickory handles.

Weight, lbs.	10	13	16	18	20
Price	24c	30c	35c	39c	45c

Post Maul Handle.

No. 24C9469 Selected quality Post Maul Handles. 36 inches long.
Price........10½c

Railroad Pick.

No. 24C9474 Adze Eye, cast steel, axe finish railroad picks. Weight, 5 to 6 pounds.
Price........28c

Railroad Pick Handle.

No. 24C9476 Selected Quality Railroad Pick Handles, 36 inches long.
Price........11c
Railroad pick handles are also used for mattocks.

Drifting Picks.

No. 24C9480 Drifting Picks, adze eye, oil finish.

Nos.	1	2	3	4
Weight, pounds	3	4	4½	5
Price	35c	37c	38c	43c

Drifting Pick Handle.

No. 24C9481 Selected Quality Drifting Pick Handle, 34 inches long, for above picks.
Price........13c

Adze Eye Coal Picks.

No. 24C9485 Adze Eye Coal Picks, made of refined iron with steel points, ground and oil finished.

Wgt, lbs.	2	2½	3	3½	4	4½	5
Price,	36c	39c	42c	44c	46c	50c	52c

Coal Pick Handle.

No. 24C9486 Select Hickory Coal Pick Handles, 34 inches long. Price........11c

Miners' Short Ear Cutting Pick.

No. 24C9489 High Grade Short Ear Miners' Cutting Picks. The best shaped miners' pick sold by anyone. Made by one of the largest concerns devoted to mining tools only, in the United States. Every tool guaranteed. Weight, 2, 2¼ and 2½ pounds.
Price, any weight........30c

Miners' Short Ear Mining Pick.

No. 24C9490 Miners' Short Ear Mining Picks. Made by one of the largest makers of mining tools in the United States. Material, shape and finish first class. Every tool guaranteed. Weight, 2, 2¼ and 2½ pounds. Price, any weight......33c

The New Acme Coal Miners' Post Drill.

No. 24C9493 Our New Improved Acme Coal Miners' Post Drill is by far the best, simplest and lightest running machine on the market. It is the result of years of experience by practical miners. We warrant the machine in every particular. The thread box is made of highest grade alloy, which will outlast a dozen of the usual thread boxings made of malleable iron. Furnished with three augers. Weight, about 100 pounds.

Price, shipped direct from factory in Southern Illinois, complete with side and end gear and three augers......$9.75

Complete with end gear only and three augers, $8.60

In ordering, be sure to give height of vein of coal drill is to be used in. Also state whether side or end gear is wanted.

Miners' Lamp.

No. 24C9497 One Hook. Weight, 2 ounces.
Price........8c

Star Miners' Lamp.

No. 24C9498 Star Miners' Lamp. Made of XXX tin; well made, nicely finished.
Miners' Lamp. Price, each 10c
Drivers' Lamp, each.....12c

Genuine Frostburg Drivers' Lamps.

No. 24C9499 Star Drivers' Lamp. Well made and nicely finished. The best drivers' lamp on the market. Price, for single spout, each........18c
For double spout, each........20c

Coal Miners' Cap.

No. 24C9500 Miners' Caps. Well made. Best lamp attachment used by anyone. No. 1 brown duck, as shown in illustration. Sizes, 6⅜ to 7¼. Price...18c

Stone Picks.

No. 24C9503 Solid Cast Steel Stone Picks. High grade steel, with polished points. Weights, 5 lbs., 5½ lbs., 6 lbs., 6½ lbs., 7 lbs., 8 lbs.
Price, per pound........................11c

Pick Mattock.

No. 24C9507 Pick Mattock is a pick on one side and a mattock on the other, as shown in illustration. Adze eye, extra tool steel, axe finish. Price 35c
No. 24C9508 Handles for above.
Price............................11c

Mattocks.

No. 24C9510 Mattock. Long cutter, cast steel, adze eye, axe finish. Weight 5 to 6 pounds. Price 35c
No. 24C9511 Mattock. Short cutter, same as above. Weight, 4½ lbs. Price....34c
No. 24C9512 Handles for above. Hickory, 36 inches long. Price..................11c

Grub Hoes.

No. 24C9514 Grub Hoes, adze eye, cast steel, axe finish, blade is about 4 inches wide. Price, 2½ pounds....26c
Price, 3 pounds........................27c

Grub Hoe Handle.

No. 24C9515 Selected Quality Grub Hoe Handles, 36 inches long. Price 11c

Hazel Hoes.

No. 24C9517 Hazel Hoes. Size about 6-inch cut. 10 inches long, and weighs about 3 pounds. Adze eye, cast steel, axe finish. Price....33c
No. 24C9518 Handles for above. Price 13c

Planter's Eye Hoes.

Solid Forged Steel Planters' Hoes, without handles. Made of refined cast steel. Half polished blade. Prices are for blade only, without handles.

No.	24C9520	24C9521	24C9522
Size	7 inches	7½ inches	8 inches
Price	19c	20c	22c

Bush Hooks.

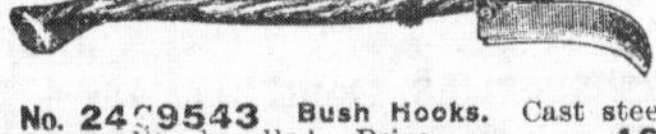

No. 24C9543 Bush Hooks. Cast steel, extra quality, handled. Price..............46c

Grass Hooks.

No. 24C9545 Grass Hooks. Made of high grade steel, tempered in oil.
Price. 15c

Extra Quality Grass Hooks.

No. 24C9547 Extra Quality Grass Hooks. A heavier and better finished hook than our No. 24C9545. Made of English tool steel, full polished. Price 25c

Scythe Grass Hook.

No. 24C9548 Barden's Grass Hook and Lawn Trimmer. The cutting edge is made of crucible steel, overlaid with soft steel, which protects the thin edge steel in center of blade. The handle is so arranged as to protect the hand from coming in contact with the ground. Price..............25c

Common Cant Hook.

No. 24C9550 Common Cant Hook, made of high grade steel with hardwood hand turned handle. A first class hook in every way.

Size of Stock	Style of Hook	Price
2⅝ inches.	No. 1 chisel point.	92c

Grain Cradle.

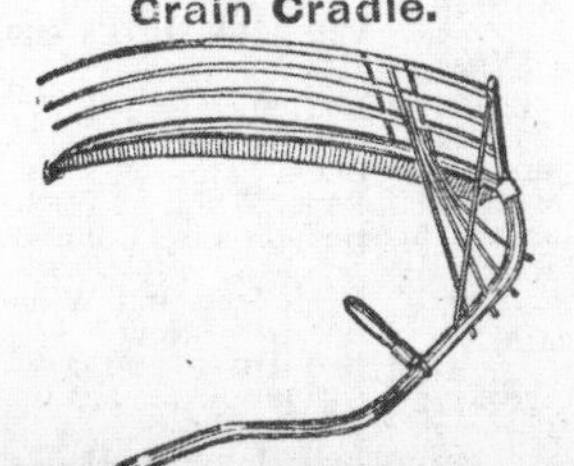

No. 24C9560 Morgan Pattern Grain Cradle, four fingers, iron brace, ring fastening, complete with silver steel scythe.
Price...........................$2.25

Standard Clipper Scythe.

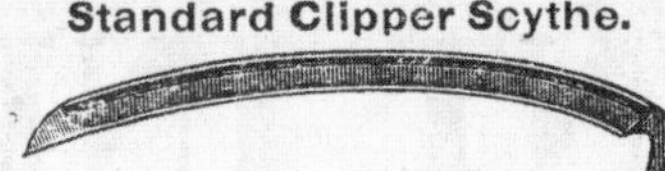

No. 24C9561 Standard Clipper Pattern Steel Grass Scythes. Edge of back is polished, with bronze web. The best scythe for the money sold by anyone. Length, 28 to 32 inches.
Price.................................45c

Standard Western Dutchman Scythes.

No. 24C9562 Standard Western Dutchman All Steel Grass Scythes, extra wide heel. Edge of back is polished, with bronzed web. Nothing better made, price and quality considered. Comes in lengths of 28 to 32 inches.
Price..................................47c

Extra Grade Grass Scythes.

Extra Grade All Steel Grass Scythes. Both back and web full polished. Has the double rib, which gives greater strength and rigidness. We furnish this scythe in both the Clipper and Western Dutchman patterns. (The above illustration shows the Clipper pattern.) The Western Dutchman pattern has the extra wide heel. Comes in lengths 28 to 32 inches.
No. 24C9563 Clipper Pattern. Price..56c
No. 24C9564 Western Dutchman Pattern.
Price 55c

English Steel Grass Scythe.

No. 24C9565 English Steel Grass Scythes, extra quality and finish. This scythe is made to meet the demand for an extra fine tool. While it will not cut any better than our extra grade scythes, it has the finish and imported steel that no other scythe on the market has. In short, you cannot buy a better scythe no matter how much you pay for it. Every scythe warranted. Comes in lengths 28 to 32 inches.
Price...................................60c

Weed Scythe.

No. 24C9567 Weed Scythes. High grade, extra cast steel. Sizes, 26 to 30 inches. Price..............46c

Bush Scythe.

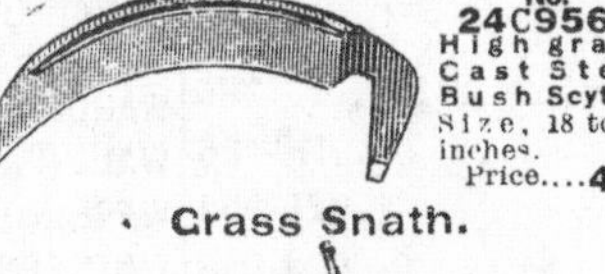

No. 24C9568 High grade Cast Steel Bush Scythe. Size, 18 to 22 inches.
Price....47c

Grass Snath.

No. 24C9570 Patent Loop Scythe Snath for grass scythes (not heavy enough for brush scythes), complete with wrench. Price....52c

Bush Snath.

No. 24C9572 Bush Snath for Bush Scythes. Price 55c

Scythe Stones.

No. 24C9584 The Black Diamond Stone. Finest stone on the market. Nothing better. Price 7c

No. 24C9585 Emery Scythe Stones; will put the right kind of an edge on a scythe and do it quickly. Size, 10x1¼x⅜ inches. Price 3c

Hay or Straw Puller.

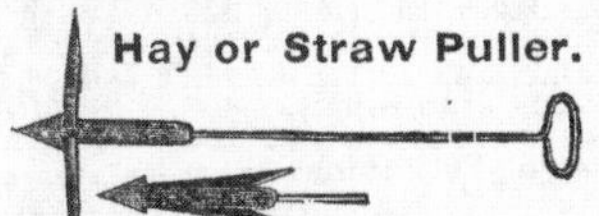

No. 24C9588 In using this Puller, push it into the stack a short distance with the hooks in a horizontal position. Turn it slightly and draw it out and the hay or straw will come out with it. Should you get more than you can draw out, push the puller further into the stack, turn it again to a horizontal position, then draw it out. It is made of steel, japanned. Length, 4 feet, 4 inches. Width, open, 12 inches. Weight, 3½ pounds. Price..................40c

Sickle Edge Hay Knife.

No. 24C9589 This is without doubt, the best hay knife sold by anyone. The blade is made in three pieces or sections, riveted to strong metal back. Sections can be replaced at any time at a very small cost. Have a mower tooth edge; it always remains sharp. Price.................74c

Sears' New Improved Saw-Cut Hay Knife.

No. 24C9592 Extra Quality Sears' Hay Knives. Made of the best grade tool steel. Well finished, finely tempered. Price.....44c

Spear Point Hay Knife.

No. 24C9594 Genuine Spear Point Hay Knives. Made of the best steel, finely tempered. One of the oldest makes of hay knives on the market.
Price..65c

Hay Knife.

No. 24C9596 The Heath Upright Hay Knife. Made of the best material. Cast steel sections, same as used on a mowing machine.
Price.......................................64c

Clipper Corn Knife.

No. 24C9600 The Clipper Corn Knife. Made from high grade steel, tempered in oil.
Price.......................................13c

Acme Clipper Corn Knife.

No. 24C9601 Hand forged, hardened and tempered in oil, hardwood, beaded handle, which prevents turning in the hand. Made from a fine quality of cutlery steel. We will replace any knife found defective in temper or workmanship. Price.........................19c

The Acorn Corn Knife.

No. 24C9603 The Acorn Corn Knife. Cast steel blade. This knife has always been a big seller in the Western States. Price.......17c

Lightning Corn Knife.

No. 24C9606 Made of the finest oil tempered steel, full polished. Price. 19c

Steel Grain Scoops.

Acme Steel Grain Scoop is the best and strongest scoop in the market. It is made of fine planished sheet steel and will outwear a dozen common scoops. One man can do double the work that can be done with an ordinary long handle scoop. Anyone who handles much grain cannot afford to be without it.
No. 24C9615 Half bushel size. Price.......................$1.20
No. 24C9616 Bushel size. Price 1.40

Steel Elevator Buckets.

Made of sheet steel formed up from one piece, with round corners and round bottom. They are constructed in such a manner that the lap comes on the end, making a double thickness and brace, which adds largely to the strength and stiffness of the cup. The back of the cup is perfectly smooth and flat, which is a great advantage in saving wear on the belt.

No.	Width on Belt	Projection	Price, each
24C9630	3 -inch	3 -inch	5¼c
24C9632	3½-inch	3 -inch	6c
24C9634	4 -inch	3½-inch	7c
24C9636	4½-inch	3½-inch	8c
24C9638	5 -inch	4 -inch	10c
24C9640	6 -inch	4 -inch	12c

Elevator Bucket Bolts.

No. 1 Elevator Bucket Bolts, with corrugated slot heads.

	Size	Per doz.
No. 24C9650	¾x¼-inch....	10c
No. 24C9652	⅞x¼-inch....	10c
No. 24C9654	1 x¼-inch....	11c

Warehouse Trucks.

Warehouse Truck (like illustration). Hardwood, well ironed, **neatly finished. Axles turned and wheels bored. Steel nose, side straps, axles and legs. We guarantee this the best truck on the market, and, quality considered, 20 per cent cheaper in price than any other.**

No.	Length, handles	Width	Weight	Price
24C9682	3 ft. 11 in.	19 in.	44 lbs.	$2.45
24C9683	4 ft. 4 in.	20 in.	56 lbs.	3.20
24C9684	4 ft. 8 in.	22 in.	77 lbs.	4.30

Daisy Truck.

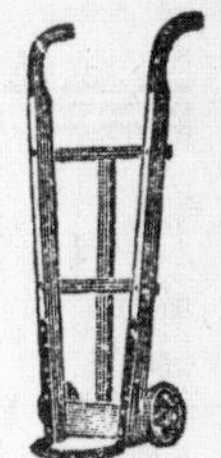

No. 24C9690 Daisy Truck, with steam bent handles. Length of handle, 46 inches; width at nose, 12 inches; at upper crossbar, 17½ inches. Weight, 30 pounds. Price..........$1.35

Wheelbarrows.

This Wheelbarrow is well made. Has full sized tray; wheel, 16 inches in diameter. When packed for shipment wheel is bolted on inside of tray and legs are folded on side of handle. Can be easily set up by anyone.
No. 24C9701 Half Bolted Railroad Wheelbarrow, with steel wheel. Price......$1.32

Acme Steel Tray Wheelbarrow.

No. 24C9704 The handles and frame of these barrows are made of the very best selected hardwood. Trays are of heavy sheet steel with edges turned over. Just the thing for canal, firemen, etc. Tray is made of No. 16 sheet steel with No. 1 steel wheels.
Price..................................$2.30

Garden Wheelbarrow.

Well Painted, Striped and Varnished.

No. 24C9708 With finely shaped handles, black tipped. Braced with steel. Size of bed, 27 inches; depth, 12½ inches; length over all, 62 inches. This barrow is fitted with steel wheels, 20 inches in diameter and are a light but very strong bread tired wheel. Weight, about 50 pounds. Price..................$2.25

Heavy Steel Tray Barrow.

No. 24C9723 The tray is made of one piece of No. 16 steel of the same thickness throughout. The edges of the trays are flanged and turned over a 5-16 inch steel rod. This rod prevents the tray from breaking at the edge and makes it **very much stronger.** As the steel of the tray is of **uniform thickness, there are no thin corners to give out after using a short time.** These barrows are made to dump forward and are so constructed that at the dumping point they will not run back on the operator. They are well bolted and braced and made of the **best material and painted.** The wheel revolves on a heavy bolt which also passes through the handles and so materially strengthens the barrow.
Price...................................$4.35

Solid Pressed Steel Tray Barrow.

Coal and Coke Barrow, with one piece tubular steel frame extending around in front of the wheel. Frame strongly braced and well ironed. The tray is made of best quality of steel, with wire edge. They will carry from 400 to 450 pounds of coal or five bushels of coke. Fitted with our extra heavy No. 4 wheel, 17 inches in diameter, tire 2¼x7-16 inch, nine 9-16-inch spokes, ⅜-inch axle.
No. 24C9726 Gauge of steel in tray, 15; length of tray on top, 41½ inches; width of tray on top, 33 inches; depth of wheel, 12 inches; capacity, 6 cubic feet. Weight, 95 pounds.
Price...................................$8.00
No. 24C9727 Gauge of steel in tray, 13; length of tray on top, 41½ inches; width of tray on top, 33 inches; depth of wheel, 12 inches; capacity, 6 cubic feet. Weight, 110 pounds.
Price...................................$8.50

DEPARTMENT INDEX.

TO THOSE WHO WISH TO REFER TO ANY ONE DEPARTMENT and not to any special item, we direct you to the following abridged department index; but if you are looking for any special item you will find it in the itemized index arranged alphabetically on these colored pages.

IF YOU FAIL TO FIND THE ITEM YOU ARE LOOKING FOR UNDER THE ITEMIZED INDEX, refer to the department and search carefully for the article you are looking for; otherwise you might overlook it, as we may have the exact same article indexed under a different number. In other words, if you should fail to find the item you are looking for in the itemized index, by referring to the department you are almost sure to find it, for there is scarcely an article imaginable that will not be found in our great stock of merchandise.

WHEN YOU REFER TO A CERTAIN PAGE and the item you are looking for is not shown on such page, but a special catalogue is described, don't fail to write for the special catalogue mentioned. In the special catalogue described you will find a large and complete line of the goods you are looking for.

INDEX.

ELECTRICAL GOODS.

Our Big, Free, Special Catalogue of Electrical Goods shows our complete line of push buttons, wet and dry batteries, annunciators, electric fans and fan motors, searchlights and other dry battery novelties, linemen's supplies of all kinds, electric light supplies, lamps, sockets, switches, cut-outs, telegraph instruments, etc. This catalogue shows our big line of electric and combination fixtures, shades, lamps, etc., gas engine spark coils and igniters, dynamos, motors and power house supplies of all kinds.

OUR COMPLETE LINE OF TELEPHONES is shown in this special catalogue with large illustrations, complete descriptions of each and every part used in these telephones, together with a complete line of telephone materials, including wire, insulators, brackets, linemen's tools, etc., all quoted at the lowest prices ever known for high class, absolutely guaranteed, thoroughly dependable goods.

This catalogue is mailed free of charge to any address. Send for it; ask for the Free Electrical Goods Catalogue.

Iron Box Bells.

No. 48C101 3-inch Iron Box Bell, for door and call bell use. Neat and very well made. Pure German silver contacts. No complicated parts to get out of adjustment. Will ring 50 feet on one cell of battery. Price....20c

If by mail, postage extra, 10 cents.

No. 48C103 4-inch Iron Box Bell. Same as above except larger. For use where a louder call is necessary. Price....35c

If by mail, postage extra, 14 cents.

Skeleton Bells.

No. 48C120 Skeleton Bell, for fire alarms, burglar alarms, and use on long circuits; with pivoted armature and 4-inch gong. Price....$1.20

No. 48C122 Same as above, with 6-inch gong. Price....$1.90

No. 48C124 Same as above, with 8-inch gong. Price....$3.25

Electric Bell Outfits.

For Door and Call Bell Service.

No. 48C170 Electric Bell Outfit, consisting of one dry battery, one wood push button, one 3-inch iron box bell, 75 feet No. 18 annunciator wire and necessary staples. Weight, 3¼ pounds when packed. Price....58c

No. 48C171 Electric Bell Outfit, consisting of one dry battery, one bronze push button, one 3-inch iron box bell, 75 feet No. 18 annunciator wire and necessary staples. Weight, 3¼ pounds when packed. Price....63c

No. 48C172 Electric Bell Outfit, consisting of one round carbon wet battery, one bronze push button, one 3-inch iron box bell, 75 feet No. 18 annunciator wire and necessary staples. Weight, 4¾ pounds when packed. Price....75c

No. 48C173 Electric Bell Outfit, consisting of two cells of dry battery, one bronze push button, one 3-inch iron box bell, 150 feet of annunciator wire and necessary staples. Weight, 5¼ pounds when packed. Price....$1.10

Our Special Economy Wet Battery.

No. 48C230 Our Special Economy Wet Battery, a strictly first class open circuit battery for door bells, telephones, etc., easily recharged when exhausted, consists of round carbon, square zinc and **jar and one** charge of sal ammoniac.

Price, complete....26c

No. 48C231 Carbon only. Price....15c

No. 48C232 Square Zinc. Price....3c

No. 48C233 Sal Ammoniac. Price, per charge, 4c

Price, per pound....10c

Weight, 4½ pounds when packed. Cannot be sent by mail.

Gravity Battery.

The Gravity Battery is a closed circuit battery and is used almost entirely for telegraph work, and can also be used for operating electric bells, small motors. Battery requires from one to three pounds of blue vitriol or blue stone to charge it. Full directions for charging this battery are contained in the Manual of Telegraphy **sent with each telegraph instrument.**

No. 48C240 Gravity Battery. Size 5x7; consisting of jar, copper and zinc. Weight, 5 pounds. Price, complete....39c

No. 48C241 Gravity Battery. Size, 6x8; consisting of jar, copper and zinc. Weight, 6 pounds. Price, complete....48c

NOTE—Blue Vitriol is not furnished with these batteries, it is always sold extra. They cannot be sent by mail.

No. 48C242	Battery Jar, glass, 5x7. Price....	15c
No. 48C243	Battery Jar, glass, 6x8. Price....	17c
No. 48C244	Zinc, for 5x7 battery. Price....	18c
No. 48C245	Zinc, for 6x8 battery. Price....	25c
No. 48C246	Copper, for 5x7 battery. Price..	6c
No. 48C248	Copper, for 6x8 battery. Price..	6c
No. 48C247	Blue Vitriol. Price, per pound.	7c

Stand By Batteries.

The 1½x4-inch size can be shipped by mail, but the larger sizes are too heavy for mail shipment and must be sent by express or freight.

The Stand By Dry Batteries are extra high grade batteries and tests will show them to be superior to all others. They will produce more current and last longer than any other dry cell batteries of their size on the market. The Stand By Batteries live up to their name. They are made in five sizes suitable for different kinds of experimental work and the larger sizes are adapted especially to gas engine work where heavy discharges are necessary for short periods only.

	Size, inches	Weight	Price
No. 48C310	1½x4	9 ozs.	16c
No. 48C311	2 x5	1 lb. 2 ozs.	18c
No. 48C312	2½x6	2 lbs.	23c
No. 48C313	3 x7	3 lbs. 7 ozs.	49c
No. 48C314	3½x8	5 lbs.	57c

If by mail, postage extra, on 1½x4-inch size, 12 cents.

Seroco Dry Battery.

No. 48C300 The Seroco Dry Battery shown here is made especially for us by one of the largest dry battery manufacturers in the country. It is the best low priced battery on the market today. It is 2½x6 inches in size and weighs about 2 pounds. Is especially adapted for door bell and call bell use and for dry cell medical batteries. It is also one of the best telephone batteries made.

Price, each....14c

In barrel lots of 125, each....13c

If by mail, postage extra, 36 cents.

Push Buttons.

No. 48C500 Wood Push Buttons, in oak, ash or walnut.

Price, each....6c

In lots of 100, each....5c

If by mail, postage extra, 4 cents.

No. 48C500

No. 48C512 Solid Cap Stamped Brass Buttons.

Price, each....12c

If by mail, postage extra, 4 cents.

No. 48C512

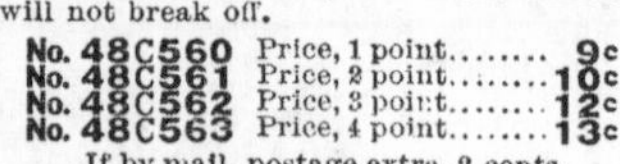

Wood Base Switches.

For use on telephones, closed circuit bell systems, burglar alarms, etc.

Wood base switches, with metal handles, will not break off.

No. 48C560	Price, 1 point....	9c
No. 48C561	Price, 2 point....	10c
No. 48C562	Price, 3 point....	12c
No. 48C563	Price, 4 point....	13c

If by mail, postage extra, 2 cents.

TELEGRAPH INSTRUMENTS.

Our Complete Learner's Telegraph Outfit.

PRICE $1.50

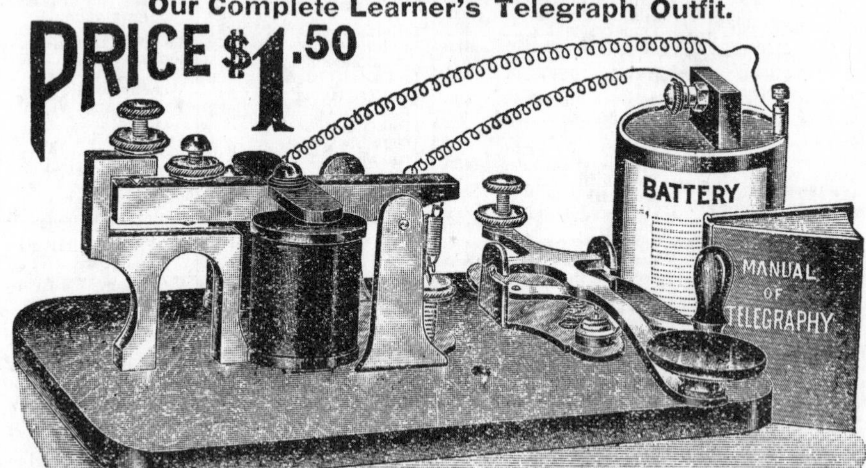

FOR $1.50 we furnish a learner's complete telegraph outfit, consisting of key and sounder, working battery, wire and Manual of Telegraphy (a complete instruction book), a regular $5.00 outfit. Use this outfit, follow the instructions and you will soon become a telegraph operator. Positions are open for operators on railroads everywhere at $40.00 to $60.00 per month.

THIS OUTFIT as illustrated, consists of a full size key and sounder, mounted on a polished cherry base. It comes complete with one cell of dry battery, instruction book and wire, ready to set up. The key has a nickel bar, latest thumb nut adjustment and hard rubber key knob and cut out, platinum points and stamped base. The sounder has covered magnets wound to 4 ohms resistance, polished brass sounding bar and frame, thumb nut adjustment. The latest stamped sounder frame and key base assures an easy working and very sensitive instrument, the very best on the market for the money; a thoroughly serviceable and practical instrument for short lines, with copper wire not to exceed 100 feet.

INSTRUCTION BOOK. The instruction book, or Manual of Telegraphy, furnished with this outfit gives full instructions how to read and write the alphabet, figures, punctuation, etc., by the Morse system; teaches you how to send and receive messages, teaches you everything pertaining to telegraphy, enables you, by carefully following the instructions and using the outfit in practice, by your own efforts to become an expert telegraph operator.

No. 48C1200 Learner's Telegraph Outfit, complete as described above. Price....$1.50

This outfit weighs 4½ pounds; it cannot be sent by mail.

4-Ohm Learner's Instrument.

No. 48C1201 4-Ohm Learner's Instrument, exactly the same as the instrument included with outfit No. 48C1200, but without battery or connecting wire. Price....$1.38

If by mail, postage extra, 24 cents.

20-Ohm Learner's Instrument.

No. 48C1202 20-Ohm Learner's Instrument consists of full size sounder and key, mounted on polished cherry base, with magnets wound to 20 ohms; otherwise the same as No. 48C1200, except no batteries are sent with the instrument. The instrument is intended for long distance work and can be used on lines ½ mile or more in length. It requires two batteries to operate the instrument.

Price, as described.... (If by mail, postage extra, 24 cents)....$1.70

The Omnigraph. A Learner's Automatic Telegraph Instrument.

$3.25

No. 48C1210 The Omnigraph Automatic Telegraph Instrument will tick off any character in the Morse alphabet absolutely correct and at any speed. The dots, dashes and spaces can be both seen and heard, thus making it very easy to learn. By listening to the instrument you can quickly memorize the letters and be able to read messages as well as an experienced operator. By means of the key you are able to duplicate these sounds as fast as you learn them, thus becoming an efficient operator. The Omnigraph consists of regular key and sounder, mounted on a polished mahogany base, the sounder having a polished brass bar and frame with thumb nut adjustment and magnets wound to 5 ohms. The key lever is of nickel, with hard rubber handle and cut out. The Omnigraph transmitter is a mechanical device operated by a small crank between the key and sounder. The three instruments are mounted upon a polished cherry base. It requires two cells of battery to operate this successfully. The Omnigraph can be operated as an ordinary instrument without the transmitter and will work perfectly satisfactorily on short lines not to exceed 100 feet. **We furnish this Omnigraph complete, with two cells of dry battery, connecting wire, and an instruction book for setting up the Omnigraph, for....$3.25**

Weight, 6½ pounds. Cannot be sent by mail.

The Omnigraph No. 3.

No. 48C1212 This is a new style of the Omnigraph and consists of the transmitter mounted upon a polished cherry base, with binding posts. Measures 5¼x9½ inches. With book, "How to Become an Experienced Operator." Guaranteed to work perfectly with any instrument or on any line. Weight, 1 pound.

Price, as described, with one disc.......... **$1.75**

If by mail, postage extra, 16 cents.

No. 48C1215 Extra dials with sentences, numbers and punctuation marks; twelve different styles. Price, each.......... **4c**

Price, for the complete set of twelve dials, all different.......... **45c**

If by mail, postage extra, per dial, 2 cents.

Aluminum Lever Giant Sounders.

Our New Aluminum Lever Giant Sounders excel all other sounders in tone, loudness and quick action, being in every respect the finest and best sounders made. The sounding bar is made from **aluminum**, the balance of the instrument is of brass, and the magnets are covered with polished hard rubber. The base is of highly polished mahogany, and the entire instrument is finished with the most careful attention to details and appearance. Special attention is directed to the way in which the wooden base is connected to the instrument, an open space being left between the wood and the metal, which greatly increases the sound and improves the tone. **The Western Union Telegraph Co. has thousands of these sounders in use on their main lines,** a fact which in itself speaks for their quality.

No. 48C1225 Aluminum Lever Giant Sounder, as described and illustrated above, with magnets wound to 4 ohms resistance, for lines one-quarter mile or less in length. Price.......... **$1.60**

If by mail, postage extra, 24 cents.

No. 48C1226 Aluminum Lever Giant Sounder, as described and illustrated above, with magnets wound to 20 ohms resistance, for lines one-half mile or more in length. Will work on lines up to fifty miles in length. Price.......... **$1.80**

If by mail, postage extra, 24 cents.

Extra High Grade Private Line Instruments.

$2.60

No. 48C1235 4-Ohm Private Line Instrument, for practice on short lines. This instrument consists of an extra high grade sounder and fine steel lever key, mounted on highly polished mahogany base. Materials and workmanship are the best. **The sounder magnets are wound to 4 ohms resistance** and covered with polished hard rubber, the sounding bar is made from aluminum, and for tone, loudness and quick action is unsurpassed. The fine steel lever key, has hardened platina points and thumbscrew trunnion adjustments. Price.......... **$2.60**

If by mail, postage extra, 48 cents.

No. 48C1236 20-Ohm Private Line Instrument, exactly the same as No. 48C1235, except that the sounder magnets are wound to 20 ohms resistance, **making** the instrument suitable for long distance **work.** Can be used on lines one-half mile or more in **length.** Price.......... **$3.00**

If by mail, postage extra, 48 cents.

Steel Lever Keys.

No. 48C1245 Steel Lever Key, legless. This is the standard Western Union Key, of the **latest and most improved type,** the lever and trunnions being made of solid steel, nickel plated, instead of brass, as in the old type of instrument. The same strength is secured with much lighter weight and the liability of loose trunnions completely avoided. This is without doubt **one of the handsomest and best working keys on the market.** Its adoption by the **Western Union Company** is certainly a sufficient recommendation for it. Price.......... **$1.30**

If by mail, postage extra, 10 cents.

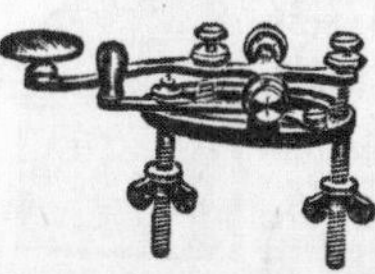

No. 48C1246 Steel Lever Key, with legs. A standard Western Union key, just the same in general construction, material, workmanship and efficiency as No. 48C1245, but made with two legs which go through the table, connection thus being made from below.

Price.......... **$1.20**

If by mail, postage extra, 10 cents.

Kenco Battery Fan Motor.

COSTS ONE CENT PER HOUR TO RUN. GIVES A FINE BREEZE.

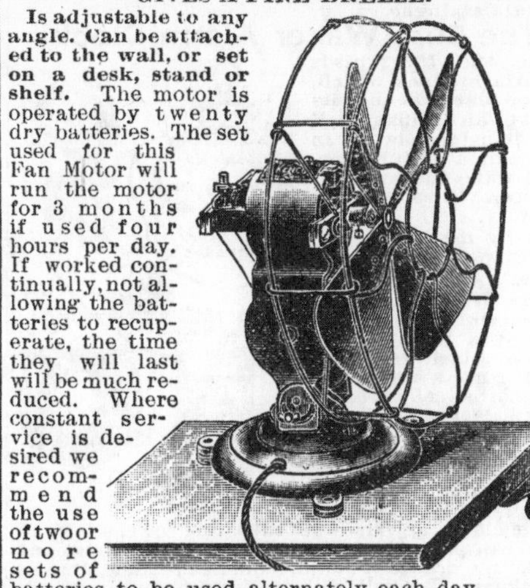

Is adjustable to any angle. Can be attached to the wall, or set on a desk, stand or shelf. The motor is operated by twenty dry batteries. The set used for this Fan Motor will run the motor for 3 months if used four hours per day. If worked continually, not allowing the batteries to recuperate, the time they will last will be much reduced. Where constant service is desired we recommend the use of two or more sets of batteries to be used alternately each day.

No. 48C705 The Motor complete, with fan, guard, 20 feet of cord and twenty dry cells, wired and packed in a neat case ready to connect to the motor when received. Weight complete, 52 lbs. Price, **$8.90**

No. 48C709 Motor, with fan and guard, without batteries and cord. Weight, 7 pounds. Price.. **$4.95**

No. 48C701 Battery for this motor, consisting of twenty high grade cells, packed in a neat wooden case, wired, ready to connect to motor. Weight, 45 pounds. Price.......... **$4.00**

Permanent Horseshoe Magnets.

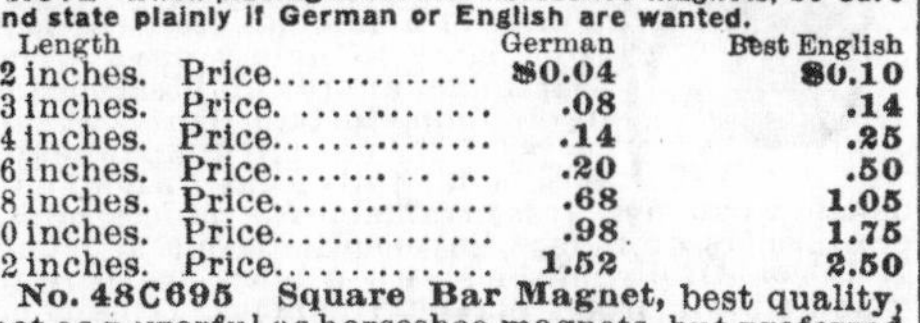

No. 48C675 We furnish Horseshoe Magnets in two qualities, the ordinary quality, made in Germany, and the best quality, made in England.

NOTE—When placing orders for horseshoe magnets, be sure and state plainly if German or English are wanted.

Length		German	Best English
2 inches.	Price..........	$0.04	$0.10
3 inches.	Price..........	.08	.14
4 inches.	Price..........	.14	.25
6 inches.	Price..........	.20	.50
8 inches.	Price..........	.68	1.05
10 inches.	Price..........	.98	1.75
12 inches.	Price..........	1.52	2.50

No. 48C695 Square Bar Magnet, best quality, not as powerful as horseshoe magnets, but preferred in many cases on account of the shape.

Price, 6 inches long, 18c; 4 inches long.......... **12c**

No. 48C696 Lodestone or Natural Magnet. A naturally magnetic iron ore, very interesting as a curiosity and useful in certain peculiar arts and sciences. Ours is the genuine article.

Price, per pound, 50c; per ounce.......... 10c

The Electrohit.

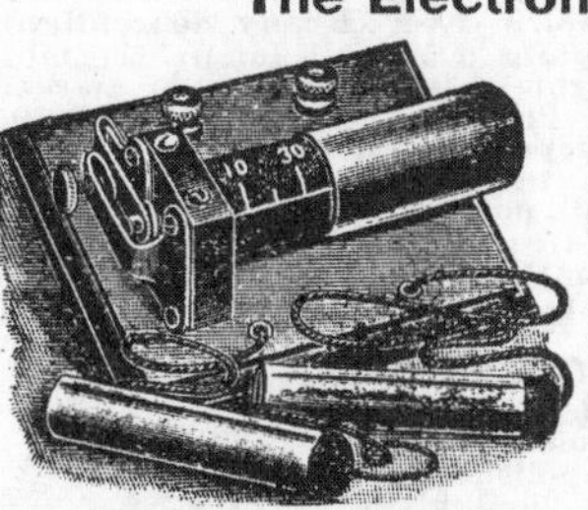

No. 48C1330 The Electrohit is a coil mounted on a wood base, with binding posts and full instructions. It is the best coil on the market for the money. Many interesting and amusing tricks can be played with this instrument. For instance, partly fill a metallic basin with water, drop in a coin, hold one handle against the basin, ask a person to take the other handle and reach for the coin. The results will be interesting. This coil is especially made for those who are interested in the construction of induction coils and in performing small experiments, and we are sure it will please you.

Price, without battery..(**Postage extra, 10c**)..**66c**

NOTE—One Seroco Dry Battery, price 14 cents, will operate this coil perfectly.

No. 48C1320 Magneto Electric Thriller, is mounted on a neat wooden base, finished in red enamel, with full nickel plated trimmings, fitted with flexible cords and nickel plated handles. It shows the principles of the magneto electric machine, and affords great amusement as well as instruction. The current can be so regulated that it will make a strong man tremble, or so mild as not to injure a child. Price.......... **65c**

65c

If by mail, postage extra, 25 cents.

Little Hustler Motor.

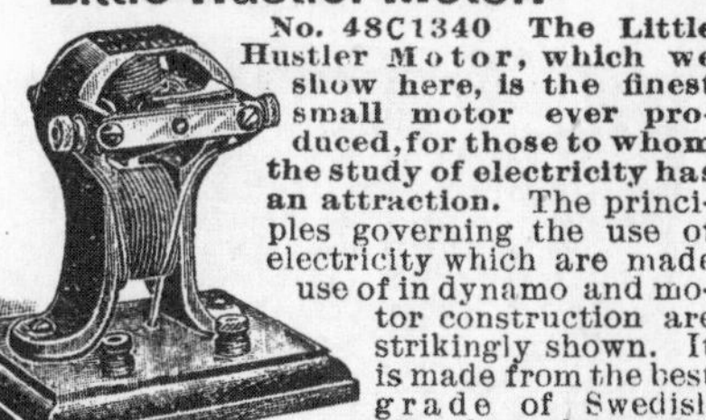

No. 48C1340 The Little Hustler Motor, which we show here, is the finest small motor ever produced, for those to whom the study of electricity has an attraction. The principles governing the use of electricity which are made use of in dynamo and motor construction are strikingly shown. It is made from the best grade of Swedish iron, has three-part armature, extra long bearings, binding posts, is mounted on a neat wood base, is finished in black enamel, with **nickel plated trimmings.** This motor will run on a single cell of dry or wet battery, and is also fitted with a groove pulley. Price.......... **90c**

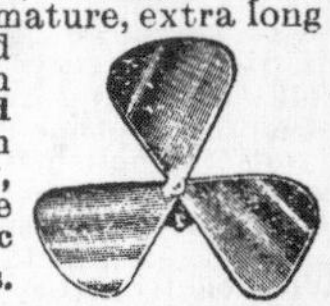

If by mail, postage extra, 15 cents.

No. 48C1341 Little Hustler Motor. With one cell wet battery. Price.......... **$1.20**

Cannot be sent by mail.

No. 48C1345 Nickel Plated 5-inch Fan, for Little Hustler Motor only.

Price.......... **20c**

If by mail, postage extra, 2 cents.

Little Hustler Motor Parts.

No. 48C1350 Little Hustler Motor Parts. For boys and others interested in experimental electrical work no better method of learning the principles of electric motor construction exists than by being able to build one. We furnish a set of motor parts, which are complete with the necessary wire for winding armature and field as well as all the screws, etc., necessary to put the machine together. With the instructions which accompany each set, anyone can construct a motor.

Price, complete.......... **68c**

If by mail, postage extra, 15 cents.

Medical Battery.

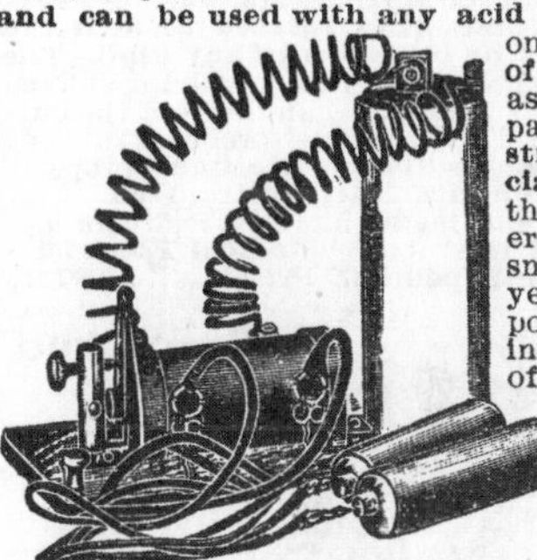

No. 48C1600 This instrument is very strong and can be used with any acid battery or with one or two cells of dry battery, such as are listed on page 500. **This instrument is especially desirable** for the use of travelers, as it is very small and portable, yet it has all the power of the larger instruments. Size of base, 5¾x2¾ inches. Comes complete, including pair of hand electrodes, cords, one cell of dry battery and our complete instructions. **"Medical Electricity at Home."** Weight, 2¾ pounds.

Price.......... **$1.50**

Price, without battery.......... **1.36**

Anti-Doc Battery.

No. 48C1605 This Dry Cell Medical Battery is the most compact, reliable, durable and neatest medical battery ever placed before the public, and combines with these qualities the most important one of cheapness. It is furnished in a polished hardwood case with carrying handles and nickel plated trimmings, and is furnished with two nickel plated hand electrodes, one sponge electrode, one electrode handle, one nickel plated foot plate, one pair silk conducting cords with tips, the whole making the most desirable outfit ever manufactured. It will furnish three different currents, namely: primary, secondary and combined primary and secondary. Outside measurement of case, 7⅜x5¼x3½ inches. Complete, including instruction book **"Medical Electricity at Home."** Weight, 4½ pounds.

Price.......... **$2.25**

Gem Battery, $2.65.

No. 48C1610 The Gem Battery is the best medical battery on the market. It uses a dry cell, thus doing away entirely with the annoyance of acids or other liquids, and is contained in a very handsome polished wood case. **The compact form, ease of operation,** handsome appearance and strong, even current of this battery, make it a universal favorite. All metal parts are finely **nickel plated.** With each battery is furnished: **One pair silk battery cords, wood handle, one pair metal handles, one nickel plated foot plate, one pair sponge electrodes, one copy "Medical Electricity at Home,"** a complete guide to the use of electricity in the treatment of diseases. Weight, 6½ pounds.
Price.................................$2.65

Davis & Kidder Magneto Battery.

$7.25

No. 48C1625 This is the genuine Davis & Kidder Battery and not the cheap imitation which is so extensively sold at present. **Operated without the use of chemicals or batteries of any kind.** The electric current is produced by the revolving of fixed electro magnets by turning a handle from the outside of the case. This machine produces a very powerful current and **will last a lifetime** if properly cared for. **Every one absolutely guaranteed.** Complete, with cords and metal handles, ready for use, and our complete instructor **"Medical Electricity at Home."** Weight, 7 pounds. Price..........$7.25

Improved Double Cell Battery.

$6.95

No. 48C1630 This Medical Battery is an extra large and powerful instrument, made in accordance with our own plans. It is furnished with two high grade dry cells in a case of highly polished hardwood, strongly made and handsomely finished. In addition to adjustments for regulating strength of current from either mild to very strong, it has an improved pole changer, by means of which the current may be changed from positive to negative, or vice versa. It is also furnished with a special rheotome or adjustable vibrator, for treatment of various muscular diseases, such as rheumatism, paralysis, etc. By means of this adjustable vibrator, the current, either the primary or secondary, or a combination of them, can be applied with slow or rapid vibrations. The vibrator on this instrument is of the latest improved type and has very fine adjustments. The coil is very high grade. All metal parts are nickel plated. The battery is provided with an electric hair brush, metallic foot plate, one pair of metallic hand electrodes, one pair of silk covered cords, one pair wood handles, one pair sponge electrodes, one metallic scourge and our book, **"Medical Electricity at Home,"** explaining the proper method of using electricity for any kind of disease. Weight, 10 pounds. Price, complete....................$6.95

Medical Battery Supplies.

We can furnish special electrodes, extra cords and other supplies. Send for our Special Electrical Catalogue.

The Sure Waker Alarm Clock.

No. 48C1750 This is an Alarm Clock which, when placed in the circuit of an ordinary bell outfit, using a switch in place of a push button, will wake the soundest sleeper. Price, of clock only...................98c
If by mail, postage extra, 24 cents.

No. 48C1752 The Sure Waker Alarm Clock Outfit consists of our Sure Waker alarm clock, 3-inch iron box bell, one wood base switch, one cell of Seroco dry battery and 75 feet of annunciator wire with necessary staples. The diagram shows the method of connection, which is very simple and can be made by anyone. **Just the thing** for the farmer, who can place the bell anywhere in the house and wake the occupant of the room at the same time he awakens. The bell will continue to ring until the switch is shut off. Weight, 5 pounds.
Price, all complete...........................$1.56

Famous Ever Ready Searchlight.

The Ever Ready Searchlight was the pioneer on the market; it has always been the very best and still maintains its reputation. It has been greatly improved and today has no equal. It consists of a special electric lamp contained in a silver plated reflector placed in the end of a cylinder which contains the batteries. The lamp is lighted by pressing the small ring on the side, and the light can be directed in whatever direction is necessary. We guarantee an absolutely fresh and perfect battery with each light. It is not designed for steady use, however, as used in this way it would last only about two hours, while by using it for intervals of a few minutes will last from sixty to ninety days. The searchlight affords an ideal means of obtaining instant light. It can be placed in a keg of gunpowder or in a cellar full of gas without any danger whatever. It is invaluable for miners, hunters, farmers, or, in fact, anyone who is out at night. It is beautifully finished with a black leatherette case and full nickel plated trimmings. This is no imitation but is the Ever Ready lamp.

No. 48C1800 No. 1 Ever Ready Searchlight, 8½ inches long, 1⅛ inches in diameter, good for from 4,000 to 5,000 flashes. Weight, 1 pound.
Price..(**If by mail, postage extra, 24 cents.**).$1.80
No. 48C1801 Extra battery for No. 1 Ever Ready.
Price...(**If by mail, postage extra, 14 cents**)...24c
No. 48C1802 Extra lamp for No. 1 Ever Ready.
Price....(**If by mail, postage extra, 2 cents**)...34c
No. 48C1806 No. 3 Ever Ready Searchlight. 1½x13 inches, contains a 5½-volt lamp; the most powerful searchlight of its kind on the market. Weight, 2 pounds. Price.......................$2.95
If by mail, postage extra, 32 cents.
No. 48C1807 Extra battery for No. 3 Ever Ready.
Price..(**If by mail, postage extra, 20 cents.**) .42c
No. 48C1808 Extra lamp for No. 3 Ever Ready.
Price....(**If by mail, postage extra, 2 cents.**)..36c

The Ever Ready Electric Vest Pocket Light.

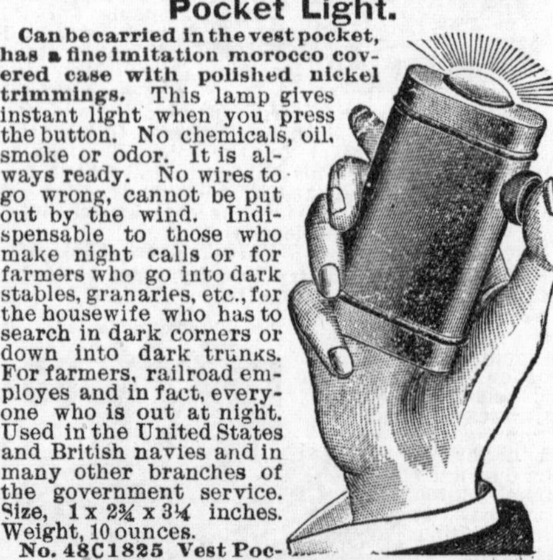

Can be carried in the vest pocket, has a fine imitation morocco covered case with polished nickel trimmings. This lamp gives instant light when you press the button. No chemicals, oil, smoke or odor. It is always ready. No wires to go wrong, cannot be put out by the wind. Indispensable to those who make night calls or for farmers who go into dark stables, granaries, etc., for the housewife who has to search in dark corners or down into dark trunks. For farmers, railroad employes and in fact, everyone who is out at night. Used in the United States and British navies and in many other branches of the government service. Size, 1 x 2¾ x 3¼ inches. Weight, 10 ounces.

No. 48C1825 Vest Pocket Searchlight, strong metallic case, with black seal grain covering. Price, complete.............95c
If by mail, postage extra, 15 cents.
No. 48C1826 Extra battery. Price...........24c
If by mail, postage extra, 10 cents.
No. 48C1827 Extra bulb. Price...............32c
If by mail, postage extra, 2 cents.

Electric Scarf Pins.

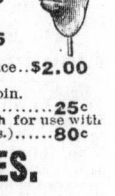

We handle three different styles of electric scarf pins, the Jeweled Horseshoe Pin, the Scull Pin and the Elk's Head Pin. To use these, the pin is attached to the scarf or to the lapel of the coat, the battery placed in an inner pocket, with the little switch where you can reach it easily. By closing the switch a bright, strong light issues from the bulb located in the pin. Using these pins a second or two at a time, from 1,500 to 2,000 flashes can be obtained before renewing the battery. To renew the battery simply unscrew the small binding nuts and insert the wires on the new battery, screwing down the nuts tightly. There is no danger of fire or of any inconvenience. The dry battery is very small and compact and can easily be carried in the pocket.

No. 48C1835 Electric Jeweled Horseshoe Pin, complete with battery. Price...............$1.20
If by mail, postage extra, 16 cents.
No. 48C1836 Electric Scull Pin.
Price.......................................$1.65
If by mail, postage extra, 16 cents.
No. 48C1837 Electric Elk's Head Pin. Price..$2.00
If by mail, postage extra, 16 cents.
No. 48C1840 Battery for any style of scarf pin.
Price.........(If by mail, postage extra, 12 cents).........25c
No. 48C1844 Extra Lamp, Cord and Switch for use with any style of pin. Price.... .(Postage extra, 2 cents.)......80c

SEROCO TELEPHONES.

Series Telephones.

Our Series Telephones are made with 80-ohm ringers and powerful four-magnet series generators guaranteed to ring through 25,000 ohms resistance. This generator is made with extra long heavy laminated armature wound with silk insulated wire, wide noiseless gear and automatic shunt, highest grade bi-polar receiver, long distance back transmitter, self contained long lever switch hook and Maltese lightning arrester. The best series telephone that can be made regardless of price.

Series Telephone with Compact Cabinet.

No. 48C2101 Series Telephone, as described above, with latest style compact cabinet. Price, each....$ 7.70
Per dozen.............. ...... 88.70

Series Telephone with Double Battery Cabinet.

No. 48C2106 Series Telephone, as described above, with large double battery cabinet.
Price, each...................$ 8.20
Per dozen.... .... 94.25

Two dry batteries are included with each series telephone at above prices. If wet batteries are wanted instead of dry batteries add 26 cents to the price of each phone. Wet batteries can be used only with the double battery cabinet. Weight of one telephone when packed, about 50 pounds.

Bridging Telephones.

These telephones are used on party lines where a number of instruments are installed, and no switchboard or central office is used. Our bridging telephones are equipped with a special high grade ringer, designed especially for bridging work, and extra powerful four-magnet or five-magnet generators. The generators, transmitters, receivers, ringers, switch hooks, lightning arresters and cabinets are all of the highest grade, exactly as illustrated and described below and on next page. We guarantee our bridging telephones to be the best that skilled labor, money and expert electrical knowledge can produce.

Four-Magnet Bridging Telephones.

These telephones, equipped with four-magnet generators, are adapted to party lines having twenty or less instruments.

With Compact Cabinets.

No. 48C2151 Four-Magnet Bridging Telephone, with compact cabinet; 1000-ohm ringer. Price, each, $ 9.25
Per dozen.....................106.15
No. 48C2152 Four-Magnet Bridging Telephone, with compact cabinet; 1600-ohm ringer. Price, each, $ 9.50
Per dozen.....................109.30
No. 48C2153 Four-Magnet Bridging Telephone, with compact cabinet; 2000-ohm ringer. Price, each. $ 9.80
Per dozen.....................112.50

Two dry batteries are included with each of our four-magnet bridging telephones at above prices. Weight of one telephone when packed, about 50 pounds.

With Double Battery Cabinets.

No. 48C2156 Four-Magnet Bridging Telephone, with double battery cabinet; 1000-ohm ringer. Each $10.00
Per dozen..... ....$116.85
No. 48C2157 Four-Magnet Bridging Telephone, with double battery cabinet; 1600-ohm ringer. Each $10.25
Per dozen...................$118.70
No. 48C2158 Four-Magnet Bridging Telephone, with double battery cabinet; 2000-ohm ringer. Each $10.50
Per dozen...................$121.70

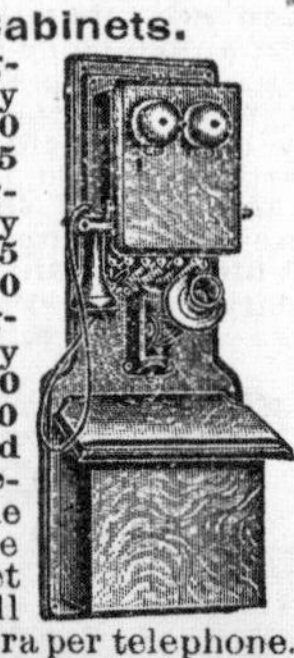

Two dry batteries are included with each of these bridging telephones at above prices. The double battery cabinet, however, is large enough to accommodate two wet batteries, and if preferred we will include wet batteries for 26 cents extra per telephone.
Weight of one telephone when packed, about 50 pounds.

Five-Magnet Bridging Telephones.

These telephones, equipped with extra powerful five-magnet generators, are adapted to lines on which from twenty to forty instruments are installed.

With Compact Cabinets.

No. 48C2171 Five-Magnet Bridging Telephone, with compact cabinet; 1000-ohm ringer. Price, each, $ 10.00
Per dozen 115.50

No. 48C2172 Five-Magnet Bridging Telephone, with compact cabinet; 1600-ohm ringer. Price, each, $ 10.30
Per dozen 118.70

No. 48C2173 Five-Magnet Bridging Telephone, with compact cabinet; 2000-ohm ringer. Price, each, $ 10.60
Per dozen 121.70

Two dry batteries are included with each of our five-magnet bridging telephones at above prices.

Weight of one telephone when packed, about 50 pounds.

With Double Battery Cabinets.

No. 48C2176 Five-Magnet Bridging Telephone, with double battery cabinet; 1000-ohm ringer. Price, each $ 10.60
Per dozen 121.70

No. 48C2177 Five-Magnet Bridging Telephone, with double battery cabinet; 1600-ohm ringer. Ea. $ 10.85
Per dozen 124.90

No. 48C2178 Five-Magnet Bridging Telephone, with double battery cabinet; 2000-ohm ringer Ea. $ 11.15
Per dozen 128.00

Two dry batteries are included with each of these bridging telephones at above prices. The double battery cabinet, however, is large enough to accommodate two wet batteries, and if preferred we will include wet batteries for 26 cents extra per telephone.

Send for our Big Free Catalogue of telephones, showing large illustrations and detailed descriptions of our complete line. Weight of one telephone when packed, 50 pounds.

Portable Desk Telephone.

No. 48C2200 Our Portable Desk Telephone is of the very latest pattern. It is equipped with **our high grade standard receiver, our own solid back transmitter,** designed especially for long distance work, induction coil mounted in the base, self contained switch hook and conducting cords. The base is of cast brass, the standard is of the best steel tubing, the springs have platinum contacts, and the entire instrument is heavily nickel plated. The ringer and generator used with a desk telephone must be the same size as used with the telephones on the line to which it is connected. Our desk telephone can be used on any line and we can furnish the generator and ringer to attach to any line. **The price of the desk set complete with ringer and generator is $1.25 more than the price of the Double Battery Telephone of the same size.**

Our Best Magneto Call Telephone, $11.90 per Pair.

FOR PRIVATE LINES, GOOD UP TO FIVE MILES.

No. 48C2270 Our Magneto Call Telephones are designed to be used with only two instruments on the line (and cannot be used with any other phone), on distances not to exceed five miles. The case is made of golden oak, highly polished. It is equipped with a powerful three-bar generator, an 80-ohm ringer, high grade transmitter and receiver and standard induction coil, self contained switch hook and carbon lightning arrester. All metal parts are heavily nickel plated. **We furnish two dry batteries with each instrument.** The greatest value ever given for those who desire a short line. Weight of complete outfit, 32 pounds.

Price, per set of two telephones, complete with four dry batteries $11.90

Our Special Battery Call Telephone, $7.85 per Pair.

FOR SHORT PRIVATE LINES.

No. 48C2275 Our Special Battery Call Telephone is designed for short distances, not to exceed 1,000 feet, and for two instruments only on the line. In battery call telephones the ringing as well as the talking is accomplished by batteries. The instruments are furnished with a double gong vibrating bell, with our standard bi-polar receiver, our high grade transmitter and self contained switch hook. **It is furnished in golden oak,** highly polished, and all metal parts are heavily nickel plated. **We furnish two dry batteries with each telephone,** which are all that is necessary for talking and ringing a distance of 700 feet on copper line wire. For longer distances, from four to six additional cells will be required at each end of the line. Weight of complete outfit, 17 pounds.

Price, per set of two telephones, complete with **four** dry batteries $7.85

Telephone Parts.

		Price.
No. 48C2400	80-ohm Extension Bell	$1.15
No. 48C2401	160-ohm Extension Bell	1.50
No. 48C2405	1000-ohm Extension Bell	2.00
No. 48C2410	1600-ohm Extension Bell	2.25
No. 48C2415	2000-ohm Extension Bell	2.50

No. 48C2375 Our Solid Back Transmitter, the very best and of the latest design. Our transmitter talks. Price, complete $1.05

No. 48C2385 Our Bi-Polar Receiver is the result of twenty years' experience. They are in use on over 150,000 telephones today. Price $0.85
Extra caps. Price, each .20

If by mail, postage extra, 2 cents.

Ringers.

No. 48C2430 80-ohm Series Ringer. Price $0.75
No. 48C2432 160-ohm Ringer. Price .90
No. 48C2434 500-ohm Ringer. Price 1.05

No. 48C2435 Adjustable 1000-ohm Bridging Ringer. Price $1.45

No. 48C2440 Adjustable 1600-ohm Bridging Ringer. Price $1.55

No. 48C2445 Adjustable 2000-ohm Bridging Ringer. Price $1.70

No. 48C2450 Gong Stands, complete, with nickel plated gongs for style of ringer.
Price, each 20c

No. 48C2400 5-Magnet Bridging Generator. Price $3.35

No. 48C2403 4-Magnet Bridging Generator. Price $2.60

No. 48C2405 3-Magnet Bridging Generator. Price $2.00

No. 48C2489 Long Lever Switch Hook, very heavily made, with extra heavy contact springs and platinum contacts; heavily nickel plated. Price 35c

Silk Wound Induction Coils, with square fiber ends.

No. 48C2490 250-ohm Induction Coil. Price 35c

No. 48C2492 500-ohm Induction Coil. Price 50c

No. 48C2534 Worsted Receiver Cords, with metallic tips. Length, 36 inches. Price, per pair 12c

No. 48C2546 Hard Rubber Mouthpieces, for either male or female thread, to fit any transmitter. Price 9c

If by mail, postage extra, 3 cents.

No. 48C2240 Single Pole Western Union Style Fuse Block with Carbon Lightning Arrester. Porcelain base and brass mountings, upright carbons, with either silk or mica insulation. Western Union or Postal style. Price, each $0.11

No. 48C2242 Price, per 100 9.00

No. 48C2244 Double Pole Fuse Blocks with Carbon Lightning Arrester, either Western Union or Postal style. Price, each 18c

No. 48C2275 Veribest Glass Inclosed Fuses, for Western Union fuse blocks. Price, each $0.01½
Price, per 100 1.40

Galvanized Steel Line Wire.

Our Double Galvanized Steel Line Wire is especially made for telegraph and telephone use. IT IS NOT FENCE WIRE. We guarantee this wire to be genuine BB and steel and to stand any standard test, which has double the breaking strain of iron wire. **For long spans, steel wire is always preferable.** The No. 10 wire will weigh about 275 pounds to the mile, the No. 12, 165 pounds, and the No. 14 about 96 pounds.

This wire is sold in half-mile coils only. Prices subject to change without notice.

	B.W.G. Gauge	Price, per 100 pounds on B. B. Iron Wire	Price, per 100 pounds on Steel Line Wire
No. 48C2600	No. 10	$3.00	$2.62
No. 48C2601	No. 12	3.12	2.75
No. 48C2602	No. 14	3.37	3.00

Write for special prices on large quantities.

Office and Annunciator Wire.

No. 48C2625 Annunciator Wire, No. 18, in ½ and 1-pound coils.
Price, per pound 28c

No. 48C2630 Office Wire, No. 18, in 1-pound coils. Price, per pound 30c

Magnet Wire, B. & S. Gauge.

No. 48C2705 Our line of Double Cotton Covered Magnet Wire is most complete and we can furnish any size listed below in quantities as specified. In sizes from 0000 to and including 6, will be sold only in lots of 10 pounds and over; from 7 to 14 in lots of 5 pounds and over; 15 to 18, 1-pound lots; 19 to 24 in lots of ½ pound; and from 24 to 40, in lots of 1 ounce and upward. In sizes from 24 to 40, an extra charge of 5 cents will be made for the spool when ordered in lots of less than ½ pound.

Double Cotton Covered.

Size	Price, per lb.	Size	Price, per lb.	Size	Price, per lb.
0000 to 6	$0.24	22	$0.55	32	$1.50
7 and 8	.25	23	.60	33	1.87
9 and 10	.28	24	.70	34	2.15
11 and 12	.30	25	.80	35	2.55
13 and 14	.32	26	.90	36	3.25
15 and 16	.34	27	1.00	37	4.85
17 and 18	.36	28	1.10	38	6.35
19	.40	29	1.20	39	8.00
20	.45	30	1.30	40	10.00
21	.50	31	1.40		

Insulators.

No. 48C2755 Pony Glass Insulator for telephone, telegraph and fire alarm work. Packed 400 in barrel. Weight, per 1,000 packed, 725 pounds.
Price, each $ 0.01½
By the barrel, per 1,000 11.90

No. 48C2760 Double Groove Pony Glass Insulator for telephone, telegraph, fire alarm work, etc. Packed 400 in barrel. Weight, per 1,000 packed, 700 pounds.
Price, each $ 0.01½
Price, by the barrel, per 1,000 11.90

No. 48C2765 Porcelain Insulator No. 4½, new code; requiring 1 inch space between botom and groove. Height, 1⅜ inches; diameter, 1¼ inches; hole, 3/16 inch; groove, 3/16 inch.
Price, per 100 75c
Price, in standard packages of 2,000, per 1,000 $7.25

No. 48C2770 Porcelain Insulator No. 5½, new code; requiring 1 inch space between bottom and groove. Height, 1 3/16 inches; diameter, 1 inch; hole, ¼ inch; groove, 3/16 inch. Price, per 100 $0.55
In standard packages of 5,000, per 1,000 5.00

No. 48C2830 Oak Pony Telephone Wood Bracket, painted and dipped one coat.
Price, each $ 0.01½
Price, per 1,000 10.00

No. 48C2835 1¼-inch Oak Pony Pin for telephone work, sawed and split timber, painted one coat. Price, each $0.01
Price, in sacks, per 1,000 6.70

No. 48C2840 Small Wiring Staples, for office and annunciator work. Price, per pound 15c

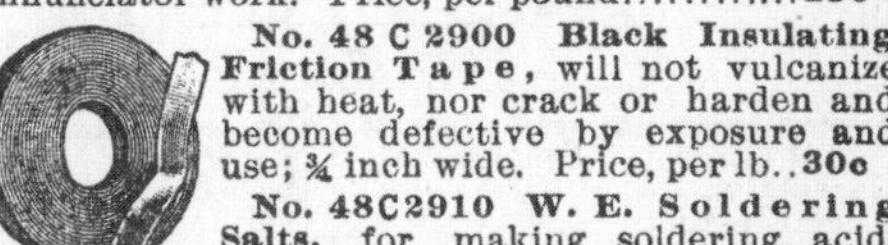

No. 48C2900 Black Insulating Friction Tape, will not vulcanize with heat, nor crack or harden and become defective by exposure and use; ¾ inch wide. Price, per lb. 30c

No. 48C2910 W. E. Soldering Salts, for making soldering acid. Mixed with water only. Will not corrode the finest metal. Directions on bottle. In ½-pound bottles. Price, per pound 28c

No. 48C2915 Soldering Stick, a soldering flux in solid form, superior to any style of acid, very portable, used by applying on heated joint.
Price, per stick 15c

No. 48C2920 Soldering Paste, 2-ounce box.
Price, per box 9c

No. 48C2925 Wire Solder, for ordinary electric work. Price, per pound 27c

No. 48C2930 Special Rosin Solder. This solder requiring no other flux, will not corrode the wires.
Price, per pound 45c

No. 48C3000 The Elgin Adjustable Linemen's Wrench is particularly useful to the lineman as well as other electrical workers, owing to its wide range of work. It will hold pipe, nipples, collars, round or square rods and square, hexagon or round nuts. Length, 7 inches. Weight, 10 ounces.
Price 75c

No. 48C3010 Extra jaws for above. Price 25c

No. 48C3060 Utica Drop Forge & Tool Co.'s Knot Tieing, Splicing and Side Cutting Plier. A handy tool for linemen or electrical workmen. Made from a special brand of Brescian steel. Toughness and hardness of cutting edge unequaled.

Length, inches	7	8
Price	$1.03	$1.26

No. 48C3015 Linemen's Clamps or Connectors. Made from electro boracic Swedish steel. Spring tempered handles with round edges; will not wear out clothes. The best that mechanical skill can produce. Fully warranted. Length, 11 inches; full polished; for No. 3 wire and smaller, B. & S. gauge. Two oval and two round holes.
Price $1.50

No. 48C3020 Linemen's Clamps; same grade as above. Length, 11 inches; full polished; for No. 8 wire and smaller, B. & S. gauge. Four round holes. Price $1.50

Hargraves' Climbers.

We guarantee these climbers to be made of the very best steel, perfectly tempered, finely finished, the very best, strongest and safest climbers made. We carry these climbers in standard lengths, namely, 15, 15½, 16, 16½, 17 and 17¼ inches, in stock.

No straps are furnished with our climbers at prices as listed below.

No. 48C3500 Hargraves' Climbers, Eastern Pattern.
Price, per pair, with spurs $1.70

No. 48C3501 Extra Spurs, for Eastern Pattern Climbers.
Price, per pair, with rivets 55c

Climber Straps.

No. 48C3510 These straps are furnished with a large leather pad, which prevents the climber from digging into the knee. Can be used with any make of climber, either Eastern or Western.

Price, per set of four $1.00

AGRICULTURAL IMPLEMENTS

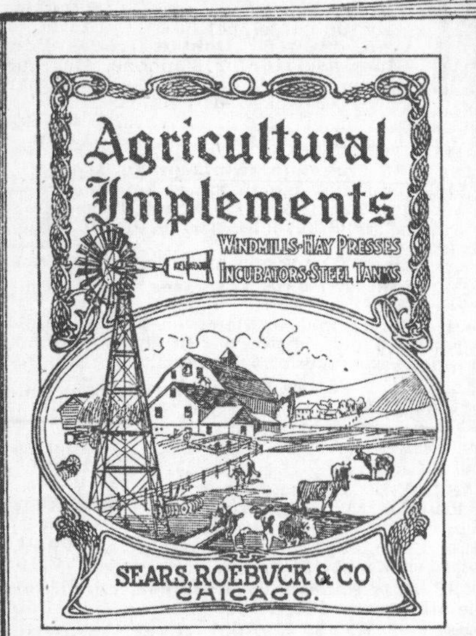

LOWER PRICES, GREATER VALUES, GREATER VARIETY, AND A MORE COMPLETE LINE THAN EVER BEFORE OFFERED BY US OR BY ANY OTHER CATALOGUE HOUSE OR DEALER. EVERY ARTICLE GUARANTEED TO BE PERFECTLY SATISFACTORY TO THE PURCHASER OR THE PURCHASE PRICE AND FREIGHT CHARGES REFUNDED.

SEND FOR OUR FREE

AGRICULTURAL IMPLEMENT CATALOGUE

TO PROPERLY ILLUSTRATE AND DESCRIBE **our complete line of AGRICULTURAL IMPLEMENTS and kindred goods,** and to give our customers anything like a correct idea of the great variety which we sell, of the **extremely low prices** which we place on the goods, of their universal **high quality**, and of the **great values** which we offer in this line, we have found it necessary to devote the **entire space of a very large catalogue to this one line of goods.** If you are interested in agricultural implements and wish to see large and correct illustrations and accurate descriptions of a very much larger line of agricultural implements, farm supplies and labor saving machinery than is carried by any other mail order house in the world, **of a better quality,** and at prices very much lower than were ever before offered, **don't fail to write for our free Agricultural Implement Catalogue,** and on receipt of your application, the catalogue **will be sent to you by return mail, postage prepaid, free.**

IN THIS GENERAL CATALOGUE, **"THE GREAT PRICE MAKER," we show only a few seasonable articles, with small illustrations and short descriptions.** We do this not only to show you a very few of **our great values** but to enable you to order at once such implements as you are likely to wish to obtain without waiting for another catalogue, **but our complete line of implements and kindred goods is described only in our large SPECIAL AGRICULTURAL IMPLEMENT CATALOGUE,** which we will be glad to send to you **FREE** if you will ask for it.

SO THAT YOU **may gather some idea of the extensiveness of our line of implements, we print below a condensed list of the contents of our SPECIAL AGRICULTURAL IMPLEMENT CATALOGUE.**

NAME OF ARTICLES

Agricultural Boilers
Bag Holders and Trucks
Barrel Carts
Barrel Headers
Bean Planters
Bean Separators
Bee Hives
Bee Keepers' Supplies
Bee Smokers
Bee Veils
Beet Weeders
Boilers, Steam
Bone Cutters and Mills
Brooders and Incubators
Bushel Crates
Cane Mills
Canvas Tighteners, Harvester
Cart and Cultivator Wheels
Carts, Hand and Barrel
Cider Mills
Clod Crushers
Contractors' Supplies
Corn and Cob Mills
Corn Cribs, Portable
Corn Planters and Drills
Corn Shellers
Corn Shock Compressers
Corn Slicers
Cotton Planters
Coulters, Rolling
Cultivator Teeth and Sweeps
Cultivators
Derrick Winches
Dipping Tanks
Disc Plows
Disc Grinders and Sharpeners
Dog Powers
Drag Sawing Machines
Egg Cabinets
Egg Carriers and Crates
Egg Cartons
Egg Testers
Engines and Boilers
Ensilage Cutters and Shredders
Evaporator Pans and Furnaces
Fanning Mills
Feed Cutters and Shredders
Feed Grinders
Feed Troughs, Poultry
Fence Machines
Fodder Ties
Food Cookers and Steamers, Stock
Fountains, Poultry
French Buhr Mills
Fruit Evaporators
Furnace Fronts and Grates
Garden Tools
Gasoline Engines
Gauge Wheels
Georgia Stocks
Grading Plows
Grinding Mills
Grist Mills
Grubbers
Hand and Delivery Carts
Harrow Teeth
Harrows
Hay Carrier Outfits
Hay Carriers, Forks, Pulleys, etc.
Hay Loaders
Hay Presses
Hay Rack Brackets
Hay Rakes, Horse
Hay Tedders
Hen House Warmers
Hens' Nests, Wire
Hog Troughs, Steel and Cast Iron
Holsters, Handy
Hoisting Crabs
Honey Extractors
Honey Sections
Honey Shipping Cases
Horse Hoe Attachments
Horse Power Couplings
Horse Power Jacks
Horse Powers
House Tanks
Incubators and Brooders
Jointers, for Plows
Kettles and Jackets
Kraut Cutters
Land Rollers
Leg Bands, Poultry
Lifting Jacks
Marine Engines, Gasoline
Mower and Binders, Section Guards, Knives, Heads, etc.
Nest Eggs, Sanitary
Oat Cleaners, for Stables
Pea Hullers
Pig Troughs, Cast Iron
Plant Setters
Plows and Attachments
Potato Hillers and Diggers
Potato Planters
Poultry Catchers
Poultry Punches
Poultry Supplies
Propeller Wheels
Pumping Jacks
Racks, Stock, Hay and Grain
Root and Vegetable Cutters
Saw Blades
Saw Frame Irons
Sawing Machines
Scrapers, Drag, Ditching and Wheeled
Seat Springs, Anti-Jolt
Seed Carriers
Seed Strippers, Grass
Seeders and Grain or Seed Drills
Shoveling Boards
Shovel Plows
Sickle and Tool Grinders
Stalk Cutters
Stanchions, Cattle
Steam Engines and Boilers
Steel Tank Structures
Steel Tanks and Covers, Galvanized
Stock Tanks
Stock Waterers
Stone Boats
Storage Tanks
Stump Pullers and Attachment
Sugar Evaporators
Swarm Catchers
Sweep Feed Mills
Tank Heaters
Tank Lugs and Band Fasteners
Tanks, Galvanized Steel and Wood
Thresher Tanks
Tool Grinders
Umbrella Holders, Harvester
Vegetable and Root Cutters
Wagon Tanks
Wax Comb Foundation
Weeders
Wheel Hoes
Windlass
Windmill Pump Springs and Couplers
Windmill Regulators
Windmills, Towers and Attachments
Wine Presses
Wire Reel Attachments, for Carts
Wooden Tanks
Wood and Pole Sawing Machines

AND MANY OTHER USEFUL ARTICLES, TOO NUMEROUS TO MENTION OR WHICH CANNOT BE PROPERLY DESIGNATED IN A GENERAL INDEX.

WE CAN SAVE YOU A GREAT DEAL OF MONEY **on agricultural implements.** **Although the illustrations of the implements** which are shown in this general catalogue are small and the descriptions are limited, you can order any **article** shown herein with every assurance that you will be perfectly satisfied with your purchase, otherwise you can return the goods and your money will be returned to you together with the freight charges. We advise you to make your selection from this catalogue when you can, rather than to delay to first write for our free special implement catalogue, but if you are unable to make a satisfactory selection, or if you wish to learn all about our implements, **about obtaining repairs for same, about our special trial offers and our broad guarantee,** or if you wish to purchase any kind or size of agricultural implement, farm tool, or machine not shown on these pages, **then don't think of buying from anyone until you get our big Free Special Agricultural Implement Catalogue.** It will be sent to you **FREE,** postage prepaid, if you will write and ask us to send it.

Kenwood Steel Walking Plows.

$8.60 to $10.60

WOOD OR STEEL BEAM. RIGHT OR LEFT HAND.

The strongest, best constructed, most perfect and easiest running plows made. Stubble plows have mouldboard with short, quick turn, for old land. Turf or sod plows have mouldboard with long, easy turn; they are for sod and general purpose work and known as "Scotch Clipper Plows." **Mouldboards,** landsides and shares are soft center plow steel, all carefully hardened, ground and polished and will scour perfectly. **Landsides** are medium weight. Mouldboards and shares are double shinned. These plows have an adjustable slip heel. **Shipped** knocked down from factory near Chicago.

Catalogue No.		Wood Beam Wt. Lbs.	Wood Beam Price	Steel Beam Price
32C101	12-in. Stubble Plow	95	$8.60	$ 9.30
32C102	14-in. Stubble Plow	100	9.10	9.80
32C103	16-in. Stubble Plow	105	9.60	10.50
32C105	12-in. Turf or Sod Plow	100	8.65	9.35
32C106	14-in. Turf or Sod Plow	105	9.45	10.35
32C107	16-in. Turf or Sod Plow	110	9.75	10.60
32C109	Steel Fin Cutter	4		.55
32C110	Rolling Coulter	21		2.15
32C111	Gauge Wheel	13		.70

Kenwood Riding Attachment.

$10.25

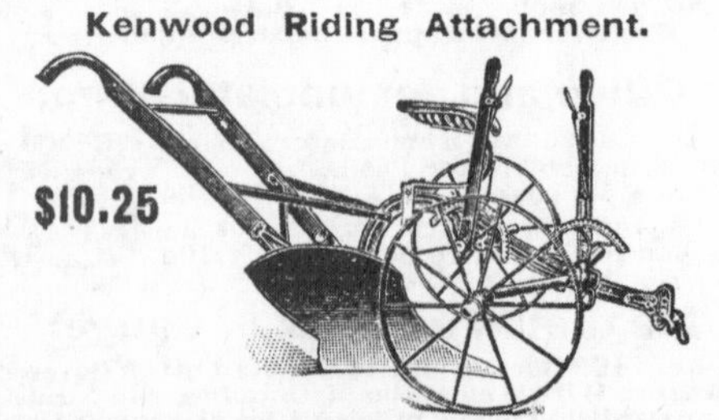

With this riding attachment you can make a first class, up to date sulky plow of any wood beam or steel beam single plow you may have, no matter whether it is right or left hand. It can also be used on middle breakers, and by making a pole extension you can use it on any kind of harrows. It will convert an ordinary walking plow into a perfect working sulky with no perceptible increase of draft. It turns square corners, either right or left, while in the ground. It has absolutely no side draft. It will plow to any depth from one to twelve inches. It is made of malleable iron and steel and will last a lifetime. Weight, 110 pounds.

No. 32C115 Riding Attachment. Price..**$10.25**

Kenwood Steel Pony Plows.

$1.85 to $4.65

RIGHT HAND ONLY.

Especially adapted for cotton and corn land and for garden purposes, the large sizes being suitable for stubble and light sod plowing. Commonly known as black land plows. Mouldboards, landsides and shares are wrought steel, nicely ground. Frogs are solid steel, also the standards and standard caps of the wood beam plows. Each plow is fitted with an **adjustable slip heel** and one extra steel share. Shipped knocked down.

Catalogue No.	Size	Wood Beam Weight	Wood Beam Price	Steel Beam Weight	Steel Beam Price
32C121	7-in. Plow	38 lbs.	$1.85	60 lbs.	$2.75
32C122	8-in. Plow	43 lbs.	2.15	65 lbs.	3.10
32C123	9-in. Plow	47 lbs.	2.40	70 lbs.	3.40
32C124	10-in. Plow	63 lbs.	3.45	87 lbs.	4.20
32C125	11-in. Plow	69 lbs.	3.85	92 lbs.	4.65

32C126 Gauge Wheel. Weight, 11 lbs. Price, **.50**

IF YOU CANNOT MAKE A SATISFACTORY SELECTION FROM THESE PAGES, DON'T THINK OF BUYING FROM ANYONE UNTIL YOU HAVE SENT FOR AND RECEIVED OUR BIG FREE SPECIAL AGRICULTURAL IMPLEMENT CATALOGUE.

KENWOOD DISC PLOWS.

One-Furrow, **$24.75** Two-Furrow, **$33.50** Three-Furrow, **$42.25**

Guaranteed to be as good disc plows as you can buy from anyone at any price and to be better plows than plows for which others ask from $32.00 to $60.00. If you want a disc plow don't doubt the quality because our prices are low; the plows are perfect tools, and should you send us your order you have the privilege of returning the plow at our expense if it does not prove perfectly satisfactory. All we ask is that you make an honest comparison, give our plow a fair trial, and we know you would not part with it for double its price, or trade it for any other plow made. These plows are not intended for turf or sod plowing, but they are the best plows made for stubble or old land plowing, no matter how hard the ground may be. They are very strong, of light draft and easy to operate. They will do the most satisfactory work and are convenient to handle. They can be made rigid for rolling ground or flexible for level ground. The discs revolve on chilled bearings. The hitch can be quickly adjusted or changed as desired. The furrow wheel is flexible, controlled by a lever which permits set of plow in or out of land at will. Depth of furrow is adjusted by a lever within easy reach. The rear castor wheel permits of a square turn to right or left. When throwing furrow it can be locked for deep or hard plowing or left flexible, but it is under full control of team at all times. All sizes have 24-inch wheels and **24-inch polished discs**, and can be adjusted to cut a furrow any depth from 6 to 8 inches. The one-furrow plow will turn a furrow from 10 to 14 inches wide and has a two-horse hitch. The two-furrow plow will turn furrows up to 28 inches wide and has a three-horse hitch. The three-furrow plow will turn furrows up to 36 inches wide and has a four-horse hitch. Will furnish three-horse hitch on the one-furrow plow, or four-horse hitch on the two-furrow plow, without extra charge if so ordered. Shipped knocked down from factory in Ohio.

No. 32C157 **One-Furrow Disc Plow.** Weight, 595 pounds. Price........$24.75
No. 32C158 **Two-Furrow Disc Plow.** Weight, 745 pounds. Price........33.50
No. 32C159 **Three-Furrow Disc Plow.** Weight, 895 pounds. Price........42.25

Kenwood Steel Frame Sulky Plows.

$29.25 to $29.80

These plows are a perfect combination of strength and simplicity, built to stand hard service. Frame is steel and very rigid. Nearly all cast parts are malleable iron or cast steel. Plow handles with ease and levers are within easy reach of driver. Weight is equally distributed on each wheel. Rear wheel is locked in line and released by foot lever and castors at turn. Loose lever principle makes plow ride and handle easily, and insures even depth of furrow, both on smooth and rough land. They have soft center steel mouldboard, landside and share, and mouldboards and shares are double shinned. Can furnish either tongueless, as shown in this illustration, or with pole, and either right or left hand. Be careful to state whether you want right or left hand, tongueless or with pole. Weight, from 475 to 525 pounds. Shipped knocked down from factory near Chicago.

Catalogue No.		Price, 12-inch	Price, 14-inch	Price, 16-inch
32C132	Stubble Sulky Plow	$29.25	$29.50	$29.75
32C133	Turf or Sod Sulky Plow	29.30	29.55	29.80

Kenwood Orchard Gang Plows.

$15.65 TO $22.80

STEEL FRAME. RIGHT HAND ONLY.

Adapted to all kinds of shallow plowing. Furnished regularly with outside rear wheel, but can furnish with rear wheel inside the frame so that plow can be used close to vines or trees. Bottoms are each 9 inches wide, entire cut being 27 inches. Steel mouldboards, shares and landsides are all made of soft center plow steel. Will plow sod from 2 to 4 inches deep and stubble from 3 to 6 inches deep. Gangs having chilled shares are furnished with one extra set of shares. Weight, 300 pounds. Shipped knocked down from factory in Southeastern Wisconsin.

No. 32C150 **Orchard Gang Plow,** with cast mouldboards, chilled landsides and chilled shares. Price........$15.65
No. 32C151 **Orchard Gang Plow,** with steel mouldboards, chilled landsides and chilled shares. Price........$17.30
No. 32C153 **Orchard Gang Plow,** with steel mouldboards, steel landsides and steel shares. Price........$22.80

Kenwood Wood Beam Brush Plows.

$8.60 and $9.30

RIGHT HAND ONLY.

A splendid general purpose plow. Beam is made extra heavy directly over and forward of the standard, and has heavy iron strap on under side. Mouldboard is soft center plow steel turf and stubble shape, carefully hardened, ground and polished. Landside and share are wrought steel. Has steel standard and standard cap, and entire plow is strongly braced. Price is for plow complete, with gauge shoe, reversible coulter and adjustable clevis. Shipped knocked down from factory in Southeastern Wisconsin.

No. 32C165 **12-inch Brush Plow.** Weight, 95 pounds. Price........$8.60
No. 32C166 **14-inch Brush Plow.** Weight, 100 pounds. Price........9.30
No. 32C167 Gauge Wheel. Weight, 12 pounds. Price........68

Kenwood Steel Beam Brush Plow.

$7.80

RIGHT HAND ONLY.

An excellent plow for road work and for breaking up rough and rooty land. Beam is made of two steel bars placed side by side and bolted together. Mouldboard is soft center plow steel, hardened, ground and polished. Share and landside are chilled iron. Handles and entire plow are strongly braced to stand heavy work. Plow measures about 11 inches across the bottom, but will turn a 13-inch furrow. Price includes one extra share, but does not include coulter or gauge wheel. Shipped knocked down from factory in Southeastern Wisconsin.

		Weight	Price
No. 32C172	Steel Beam Brush Plow	128 lbs.	$7.80
No. 32C173	Gauge Wheel	11 lbs.	.70
No. 32C174	Foot Coulter	11 lbs.	1.40
No. 32C175	Knife Coulter	8 lbs.	.92

Kenwood Sod Breaker Plows.

$6.55 TO $7.05

STEEL BEAM RIGHT HAND ONLY.

This plow is intended for turning heavy sod and for use in prairie plowing, but is not suitable for light or sandy soil. Adjustable steel rods take the place of a mouldboard. Share is wrought steel. Price includes gauge shoe, fin cutter and one extra share. Weight, about 67 pounds. Shipped knocked down from factory near Chicago.

		Price
No. 32C186	12-inch Sod Breaking Plow...	$6.55
No. 32C187	14-inch Sod Breaking Plow...	6.80
No. 32C188	16-inch Sod Breaking Plow...	7.05

Kenwood Vineyard Plows.

$6.50 and $7.80

WOOD BEAM. RIGHT HAND ONLY.

Especially adapted for nurseries, orchards, vineyards and all one-horse work. Beam is adjustable so horse can walk in furrow or on the land. Mouldboard is shaped to make light draft and to clean out the furrow in loose soil. Landslide and share are chilled iron. Will turn furrow from 8 inches to 12 inches wide and from 3 inches to 8 inches deep. Price is for plow complete, with gauge wheel, knife coulter, clevis and one extra share. Shipped knocked down from factory in Southeastern Wisconsin.

No. 32C190 **Vineyard Plow,** with cast mouldboard. Weight, 103 pounds. Price........$6.50
No. 32C191 **Vineyard Plow, with steel mouldboard.** Weight, 103 pounds. Price........$7.80

Kenwood Full Chilled Plows.

$1.95 to $5.95. WOOD BEAM. RIGHT HAND.

These are genuine modern, full chilled plows with a general purpose shape. Can be used for any work which a chilled plow will do. Beams are heavy and of good proportions, and entire plow is strongly braced. Mouldboards, landsides and shares are perfectly chilled, ground and polished. One extra share furnished with each plow. Jointers and coulters can only be used on No. 32C207 and larger. Six-inch to 9-inch plows are suitable for one horse; 9-inch to 12-inch plows for two horses. **Can furnish Nos. 32C207 and 32C211 in left hand, if so ordered.** Shipped knocked down from factory near Chicago.

No. 32C203 **6-inch Chilled Plow.** Width of furrow, 7 inches. Weight, 43 pounds. Price...$1.95
No. 32C205 **7-inch Chilled Plow.** Width of furrow, 8 inches. Weight, 48 pounds. Price...$2.75
No. 32C206 **8-inch Chilled Plow.** Width of furrow, 9 inches. Weight, 54 pounds. Price...$3.05
No. 32C207 **9-inch Chilled Plow.** Width of furrow, 10 inches. Weight, 68 pounds. Price...$4.40
No. 32C209 **10-inch Chilled Plow.** Width of furrow, 12 inches. Weight, 92 pounds. Price..$5.50
No. 32C210 **11-inch Chilled Plow.** Width of furrow, 13 inches. Weight, 112 pounds. Price.$5.70
No. 32C211 **12-inch Chilled Plow.** Width of furrow, 14 inches. Weight, 120 pounds. Price.$5.95
No. 32C212 **Cast Jointer.** Wt., 12 lbs. Pr..$1.40
No. 32C213 **Gauge Wheel.** Wt., 13 lbs. Pr. .70

Kenwood Prairie Breaking Plows.

$7.95 TO $8.55

WOOD BEAM. RIGHT HAND ONLY.

These plows are intended for use in breaking either old or new sod in any kind of soil, but can be used for other classes of work. The mouldboard is so shaped that it will turn the sod upside down and lay it perfectly flat. Standard and standard cap are steel. Mouldboard is soft center steel, landside and share are wrought steel, all hardened, ground and polished, but share is left soft enough to file. Entire plow is strongly braced. One extra share is furnished with each plow. Wheel and coulter are not included in price of plow, and, unless you have them, they should be ordered with the plow. Shipped knocked down from factory near Chicago.

			Price
No. 32C220	12-inch Plow.	Wt., 132 lbs..	$7.95
No. 32C221	14-inch Plow.	Wt., 135 lbs..	8.25
No. 32C222	16-inch Plow.	Wt., 138 lbs..	8.55
No. 32C223	Gauge Wheel.	Wt., 11 lbs..	.65
No. 32C225	Rolling Coulter.	Wt., 21 lbs..	1.85

Kenwood Hillside Swivel Plows.

$3.60 TO $6.50

WOOD BEAM

Especially adapted for hillside plowing, but will also do perfect work on level land.

Swivel is arranged to swing very easy. Mould board, landside and share are chilled iron, ground and polished. One extra share furnished with each plow. The 6 and 8-inch plows are for one horse, the 10-inch for two, and the 12-inch for three horses. Jointer can be used only on 10 and 12-inch plows. Shipped knocked down from factory near Chicago.

		Width of Furrow	Weight	Price
No. 32C226	6-in. Plow.	8 in.	70 lbs.	$3.60
No. 32C227	8-in. Plow.	10 in.	78 lbs.	4.40
No. 32C228	10-in. Plow.	12 in.	105 lbs.	5.70
No. 32C229	12-in. Plow.	14 in.	112 lbs.	6.50
No. 32C230	Gauge Wheel.	Wt., 12 lbs....		.70
No. 32C231	Reversible Jointer.	Wt., 14 lbs.		1.58

IF YOU CANNOT MAKE A SATISFACTORY SELECTION FROM THESE PAGES, DON'T THINK OF BUYING FROM ANYONE UNTIL YOU HAVE SENT FOR AND RECEIVED OUR BIG FREE SPECIAL AGRICULTURAL IMPLEMENT CATALOGUE.

Star Gauge Wheel.

90c

The strongest, lightest and best gauge wheel made. Will fit any make of plow, either wood or steel beam. All parts are malleable iron; can be set to always run straight with plow. The post has a loose spindle which, when worn out, can be replaced at a very small cost.

No. 32C300 Star Gauge Wheel. Weight, 9 pounds. Price........ ......90c

Star Jointer.

Will fit any make of wood or steel beam plow. Perfect adjustable features allow this jointer to be set as desired. Mouldboard and point are solid steel. Point is reversible and has three distinct wearing points. Weight, 14 pounds.

$1.55

No. 32C305 Left Hand Star Jointer. Price........$1.55

No. 32C306 Right Hand Star Jointer. Price.... ....$1.55

King Rolling Coulters.

$1.60 and $1.90

Adjustable in every way. Strong and light. Will fit any make of wood or steel beam plows. The adjustment only requires the loosening of one bolt. Hub has device for taking up wear and will outwear the blade.

No. 32C315 12-inch King Coulter. Wt., 15 lbs. Pr., $1.60

No. 32C317 14-inch King Coulter. Weight, 17 lbs. Price..................$1.90

Star Rolling Coulters.

$1.70 to $2.00

Can be attached to any make of wood or steel beam plows. Adjustable to run deep or shallow or to right or left, without releasing clamp. Has conical chilled hubs and is very durable. This is the best and most convenient rolling coulter made and is recommended by us as a most desirable selection. The beam clamps, sockets and disc arms are malleable iron, and the entire coulter is strong and durable.

No. 32C325 12-inch Star Coulter. Weight, 17 pounds. Price...................................$1.70

No. 32C326 13-inch Star Coulter. Weight, 18 pounds. Price...................................$1.85

No. 32C327 14-inch Star Coulter. Weight, 19 pounds. Price...................................$2.00

Farmer's Delight Disc Sharpener.

$1.25

Made entirely of steel and can be sharpened on any grindstone. It is fitted with an emery block to polish and finish the cutting edge of the disc. Disc harrows and cultivators may be sharpened without taking discs apart.

No. 32C400 Farmer's Delight Disc Sharpener. Wt., 6½ lbs. Price..$1.25

Kenwood Disc Sharpener.

$2.70

Powerfully back-geared. Suitable for farm or shop use. For sharpening disc harrows and cultivators. Will sharpen discs from 12 to 20 inches diameter. Centers perfectly and does not chatter. Disc is supported by a roller carrier. Knife is best quality tool steel.

No. 32C405 Kenwood Disc Sharpener. Weight, 40 pounds. Price...................................$2.70

Handy Disc and Tool Grinder.

$1.35 and $2.05

More desirable than the ordinary disc sharpener because it grinds instead of cutting the edge of the disc. Easy to operate and does rapid and perfect work. Will grind harrow discs or coulter blades of any diameter up to 24 inches, at any desired bevel. Can be used as a tool grinder without removing the disc attachment. Price is for the machine complete with disc attachment, tool rest and a 4x1¼-inch tool stone, made of fine emery. As a tool grinder only it does not have the disc attachment. Shipped knocked down and boxed.

No. 32C410 Handy Disc and Tool Grinder. Weight, 18 pounds. Price......................$2.05

No. 32C411 Handy Tool Grinder only. Weight, 15 pounds. Price.............................$1.35

Kenwood Combined Disc Harrow and Cultivator.

$13.25 and $14.50

This machine is designed to meet the requirements of gardeners and small farmers, but owing to its many desirable features it is adapted to a great range of work. The discs can be set at any desired angle and can be reversed to throw the dirt in or out. They can be set close together for harrowing or can be separated to 14¼ inches apart for cultivating. When discs are close together the six-disc machine cuts about 2¾ feet and the eight-disc machine about 3¾ feet wide. Bearings are chilled and as nearly dustproof as they can be made. Discs are 16 inches in diameter, and scrapers are attached to springs so that they keep the discs clean and bright. Shipped knocked down from factory in Southwestern Ohio.

No. 32C420 Disc Harrow and Cultivator with six discs. Weight, 260 pounds. Price.........$13.25

No. 32C421 Disc Harrow and Cultivator with eight discs. Weight, 275 pounds. Price.........$14.50

Kenwood Steel Frame Disc Harrows.

$14.40 to $24.15

Perfect in construction and operation, substantially built and up to date in every respect. Bearings are as near dustproof as can be made. Draft is entirely from the axles, four draft rods being attached directly in front of the bearings. Discs are oil tempered and carefully ground. Weight of driver balances pole. On single lever harrows, both gangs are operated and set at equal angles by the one lever. With double lever harrows each gang is operated by its own lever and the two gangs may be set at different angles. Illustration shows double lever harrow. Unless otherwise ordered, we will ship harrows with the size of hitch shown in the price list, these sizes being recognized as standard in all sections of the country. Always state size of hitch wanted. Shipped knocked down from factory in Southwestern Ohio.

Catalogue No.	Discs No.	Discs Size	Hitch	Width of Cut	Weight	Price with Single Lever	Price with Double Lever
32C425	8	16-in.	2-horse	4½ ft.	315 lbs.	$14.40	$15.35
32C426	10	16-in.	2-horse	5½ ft.	340 lbs.	15.60	16.55
32C427	12	16-in.	3-horse	6½ ft.	370 lbs.	17.10	18.05
32C428	14	16-in.	4-horse	7½ ft.	395 lbs.	18.10	19.05
32C429	16	16-in.	4-horse	8½ ft.	445 lbs.	19.70	20.65
32C430	10	18-in.	3-horse	5½ ft.	375 lbs.	17.40	18.35
32C431	12	18-in.	3-horse	6½ ft.	405 lbs.	18.50	19.45
32C432	14	18-in.	4-horse	7½ ft.	440 lbs.	20.30	21.25
32C433	16	18-in.	4-horse	8½ ft.	495 lbs.	22.10	23.05
32C434	10	20-in.	3-horse	5½ ft.	400 lbs.	19.20	20.15
32C435	12	20-in.	4-horse	6½ ft.	435 lbs.	20.00	20.95
32C436	14	20-in.	4-horse	7½ ft.	475 lbs.	21.40	22.35
32C437	16	20-in.	4-horse	8½ ft.	530 lbs.	23.20	24.15

Kenwood Disc Harrow Broadcast Seeders.

$31.10 to $35.05

These are our regular Kenwood disc harrows with seeder attachments. The seeder attachment will sow broadcast, wheat, oats, barley or other similar seeds, but will not sow grass seed. It has a force feed and can be adjusted to sow any desired quantity per acre. Harrow can be set at an angle so as to cover either deep or shallow, and has a center drag tooth. These seeders can only be furnished with twelve discs. Illustration shows single lever machine. Shipped knocked down from factory in Southwestern Ohio.

Catalogue No.	Discs No.	Discs Size	Seeder Attachment	Weight	Price with Single Lever	Price with Double Lever
32C442	12	16-in.	Full Seeder	550 lbs.	$31.10	$32.05
32C445	12	18-in.	Full Seeder	585 lbs.	32.60	33.55
32C448	12	20-in.	Full Seeder	615 lbs.	34.10	35.05

Kenwood Steel Frame Lever Harrows.

$4.30 to $18.15

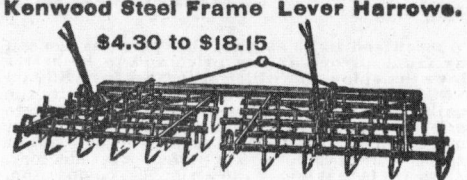

Frames are made of best quality steel "U" bars, connected by steel cross bars and braced with diagonal cross braces. Teeth are square, all with upset heads, except at corners, which are supplied with runner teeth, The teeth can be set at any angle by adjusting the ratchet levers or harrow can be tilted to ride on the runner teeth. Made in sections. Each section has thirty teeth and cuts about 5 feet wide. Price includes drawbar. 90-tooth and 120-tooth harrows have accommodation eveners. Shipped knocked down from factory in Southwestern Ohio.

Catalogue No.	Harrow	½-in. Teeth Wt. lbs.	½-in. Teeth Price	⅝-in. Teeth Wt. lbs.	⅝-in. Teeth Price
32C455	30-Tooth	115	$ 4.30	130	$ 4.65
32C456	60-Tooth	225	8.50	250	9.15
32C457	90-Tooth	355	12.60	395	13.65
32C458	120-Tooth	485	16.70	535	18.15

Kenwood Wood Frame Lever Harrows.

$4.40 to $16.80

Very strong and durable, lighter than steel. Bars are made of seasoned oak, strongly riveted at each tooth and connected by iron and steel pivot plates and cross pieces. Made in sections. Each section has thirty-five ½-inch square teeth with dagger points and cuts about 5 feet wide, and the rachet levers permit of several adjustments in the pitch of the teeth or allow the harrow to ride on the runner teeth. Price includes drawbar. 105-tooth and 140-tooth harrows have accommodation eveners. Shipped knocked down from factory in Southeastern Wisconsin.

Number		Weight, lbs.	Price
32C463	35-Tooth Harrow.	100	$4.40
32C464	70-Tooth Harrow.	195	8.60
32C465	105-Tooth Harrow.	290	12.60
32C466	140-Tooth Harrow.	385	16.80

Kenwood Boss Harrows. $4.65 to $11.25.

Made in sections, so that harrow can be used wide or narrow, as desired. Frames are made of seasoned oak, strongly riveted at each tooth and firmly braced. Teeth are ½-inch square with dagger points. Sections are independently connected to drawbar with drop link clevices. The 60-tooth harrow cuts 10½ feet and consists of one center and one side section. The 78-tooth harrow cuts 13 feet and consists of one center and two narrow side sections. The 102-tooth harrow cuts 16½ feet and consists of one center and two wide side sections. The 150-tooth harrow cuts 26 feet and consists of one center, two wide and two narrow side sections. Price includes drawbar. The 150-tooth harrow has chain equalizers, and 102-tooth and 150-tooth harrows have accommodation eveners. Shipped knocked down from factory in Southeastern Wisconsin.

		Weight	Price
No. 32C471	60-Tooth Harrow.	155 lbs.	$ 4.65
No. 32C472	78-Tooth Harrow.	190 lbs.	5.90
No. 32C473	102-Tooth Harrow.	240 lbs.	7.60
No. 32C474	150-Tooth Harrow.	390 lbs.	11.25

Kenwood Flexible Frame Harrows.

$4.45 to $16.85

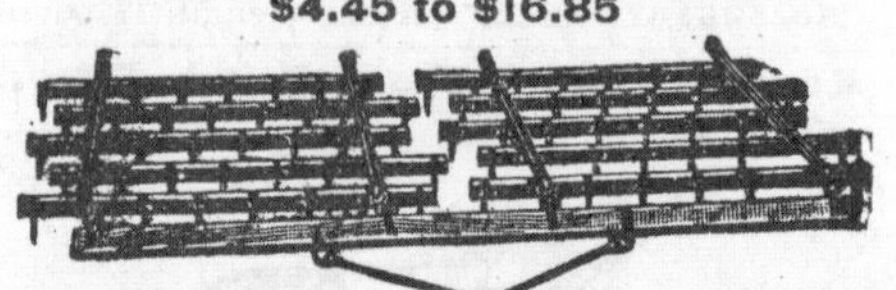

Frames are made of well seasoned oak, strongly riveted at each tooth, and are connected by specially designed iron link bars, which make the harrows flexible, allowing the harrow to adjust itself to uneven surfaces. Made in sections. Has forty ½-inch square dagger point teeth to each section, and each section cuts about 5¾ feet wide. Price includes drawbar, which can be attached to either side of harrow. Drawing the harrow one way, the teeth are slanting, drawing the other way, they are perpendicular. 120-tooth and 160-tooth harrows have accommodation eveners. Shipped knocked down from factory in Southeastern Wisconsin.

No. 32C481 40-Tooth Harrow. Weight, 110 pounds. Price..................................$4.45

No. 32C482 80-Tooth Harrow. Weight, 215 pounds. Price $8.65

No. 32C483 120-Tooth Harrow. Weight, 320 pounds. Price..................................$12.65

No. 32C484 160-Tooth Harrow. Weight, 425 pounds. Price..................................$16.85

Kenwood Scotch Harrows.

$3.70 to $7.80

Frames are made of seasoned oak, riveted at each tooth and strongly braced. Made in two weights and with two styles of teeth. The square teeth are ½ inch square with dagger points. The diamond teeth are ⅝x⅝ inch with diamond shear points. Cuts about 2 feet wide for each twelve teeth. 48 and 60-tooth harrows have two sections, 72 and 90-tooth harrows have three sections. Price includes drawbar. Shipped knocked down from factory in Southeastern Wisconsin.

Catalogue No.	Harrow	Square Teeth Weight	Square Teeth Price	Diamond Teeth Weight	Diamond Teeth Price
32C490	48-Tooth.	115 lbs.	$3.70	125 lbs.	$4.25
32C491	60-Tooth.	135 lbs.	4.70	150 lbs.	5.35
32C493	72-Tooth.	175 lbs.	5.60	190 lbs.	6.40
32C494	90-Tooth.	195 lbs.	6.95	225 lbs.	7.80

Kenwood Angle Bar Harrows.

$3.77 to $7.78

Will harrow lengthwise of sod and not track. Harrows square up on the ends and requires no lap to complete the work. Frame is seasoned oak, strongly riveted at each tooth and firmly braced. Made in two weights and with two styles of teeth. The square teeth are ½ inch square with dagger points. The diamond teeth are ⅝x⅝ inch with diamond shear points. Cuts about 2 feet wide for every twelve teeth. 48 and 60-tooth harrows have two sections, 72 and 90-tooth harrows have three sections. Price includes drawbar. Shipped knocked down from factory in Southeastern Wisconsin.

Catalogue No.	Harrow	Square Teeth Weight	Square Teeth Price	Diamond Teeth Weight	Diamond Teeth Price
32C495	48-Tooth.	125 lbs.	$3.77	140 lbs.	$4.27
32C496	60-Tooth.	150 lbs.	4.85	175 lbs.	5.34
32C498	72-Tooth.	190 lbs.	5.80	200 lbs.	6.34
32C499	90-Tooth.	210 lbs.	7.20	260 lbs.	7.78

Kenwood Steel Frame Spring Tooth Lever Harrow.

$13.70 and $14.70

The most desirable spring tooth harrow made. It is constructed of steel throughout and furnished with standard weight, length and size teeth. The levers pitch the teeth at any desired angle. Can be furnished either on wheels, as shown in the illustration, or on shoes. Shoes are steel, broad and of good length. This harrow has seventeen teeth, cuts about 6 feet wide and weighs about 300 pounds. Price includes drawbar.

No. 32C520 Harrow on Wheels. Price..**$14.70**
No. 32C521 Harrow on Shoes. Price.... **13.70**

Kenwood Wood Frame Spring Tooth Harrows.

$5.85 to $7.70

Frames are made of seasoned oak. Teeth are of standard weight, length and size, made of best quality of spring steel, finely tempered in oil and firmly secured to the bars. Fitted with stump guard around the sides and front. Made either without or with steel bottom lining and called "unlined" and "lined" harrows. The 16-tooth harrow cuts 5 feet, the 18-tooth cuts 6 feet and the 20-tooth cuts 7 feet wide. Price includes drawbar. Shipped knocked down from factory in Southeastern Wisconsin.

Catalogue No.	Harrow	Unlined Weight	Unlined Price	Lined Weight	Lined Price
32C524	16-Tooth.	160 lbs.	$5.85	170 lbs.	$6.50
32C525	18-Tooth.	170 lbs.	6.35	182 lbs.	7.10
32C526	20-Tooth.	180 lbs.	6.85	194 lbs.	7.70
32C530	Extra Teeth. Wt., 5 lbs. Price, each..				.20

Acme Cotton and Corn Planter.

$8.50

Especially adapted for southern trade. Frame and hopper are steel. All other parts except handles are steel and iron. Gearing is strong, is protected from dirt and cannot break or slip. Center shovel has breakpin, side shovels friction slip. The cotton picker wheel and the force wheel prevent bunching, and make the feed perfect, even and certain. Furnished complete with five regular plates and one blank plate. Weight, 96 pounds. Shipped from factory near Chicago.

No. 32C643 Acme Cotton and Corn Planter. Price..........................**$8.50**

Kenwood Two-Horse Corn and Cotton Planter.

$18.25 to $25.80

This is the most perfect corn planter ever put on the market. Wheels are concave, 30 inches high with 6-inch tires and staggered spokes, and can be set to run either over or off the seed row. Made in three sizes, namely: **narrow**, for rows 3 feet 4 inches or 3 feet 6 inches apart; **standard**, for rows 3 feet 6 inches or 3 feet 8 inches apart; **wide**, for rows 3 feet 8 inches or 3 feet 10 inches apart. **Standard** will always be sent unless narrow or wide is ordered, and when check rower is ordered, unless otherwise specified, wire will have buttons 3 feet 8 inches apart. **It is a full combination rotary feed planter**, with double cut-off, which insures perfect work. When fitted for check rowing or for hand dropping three sets of hill plates are furnished. When fitted for drilling, three sets of drill plates and one set of blank plates are furnished. These drill plates will drop one kernel of corn either 12, 16, 18, 19, 20, 21, 23, 24, 30, 31 or 37 inches apart. This machine can be furnished as a two-row cotton planter only or it can be furnished as a corn planter with a cotton planting attachment. Automatic reel will be furnished with check rower planters for **75 cents extra**, and it adds 40 pounds to weight. Shipped knocked down from factory in Southwestern Ohio.

No. 32C610 Corn Planter. Fitted for drilling and for hand hill dropping, but without check rower and wire. Weight, 400 pounds. Price.............**$18.25**
No. 32C611 Corn Planter. Fitted with check rower and 80 rods of wire, but without drill and hand hill dropper. Weight, 460 pounds. Price.....**$24.70**
No. 32C612 Corn Planter. Fitted for drilling and for hand hill dropping and with check rower and 80 rods of wire. Weight, 490 pounds. Price.....**$25.80**
No. 32C613 Fertilizer Attachment. Weight, 50 pounds. Price.............................**$9.25**
No. 32C616 Extra Check Rower Wire. Per rod. Weight, ¼ pound. Price.............................3½c
No. 32C619 Cotton Planting Attachment. Weight, 45 pounds. Price.............................**$6.00**
No. 32C620 Cotton Planter. For cotton planting only. Weight, 400 pounds. Price.............**$21.25**

Kenwood One-Horse Corn Drill, Fertilizer and Cotton Planter.

$7.80 as drill only

Adapted for drilling corn, peas, beans or other small seeds. Furnished with three plates for different sizes of corn, three plates for planting different distances apart and one blank plate. Can be used to plant small seeds in almost any desired quantity. As regularly furnished will drop one grain of corn either 12, 15, 16, 18, 20, 22, 24, 28, 41, 44 or 47 inches apart. Can be furnished with fertilizer attachment, as shown in the illustration. Price does not include whiffletree or either of the attachments which are listed separately. Shipped from factory in Southwestern Ohio.

No. 32C633 Kenwood Corn Drill only. Weight, 100 pounds. Price.............................**$7.80**
No. 32C634 Fertilizer Attachment. Weight, 25 pounds. Price.............................**$2.45**
No. 32C635 Cotton Planting Attachment. Weight, 20 pounds. Price.............................**$2.50**

Kenwood Potato Planter.

$17.60

The most desirable, the most durable, the simplest and the cheapest high class potato planter made. Marks, drops and covers all at the same time. Is furnished with three sizes of sprocket wheels to plant 13, 16 or 19 inches apart, and will plant at any desired depth from 3 to 6 inches. The wheels are adjustable, they determine the distance between the rows and when returning, one horse follows the last wheel track. Weight, 170 pounds. Shipped knocked down from factory in Northern Illinois.

Price
No. 32C660 Kenwood Potato Planter...**$17.60**

Kenwood Wood Frame Two-Row Cotton Planter.

$14.25

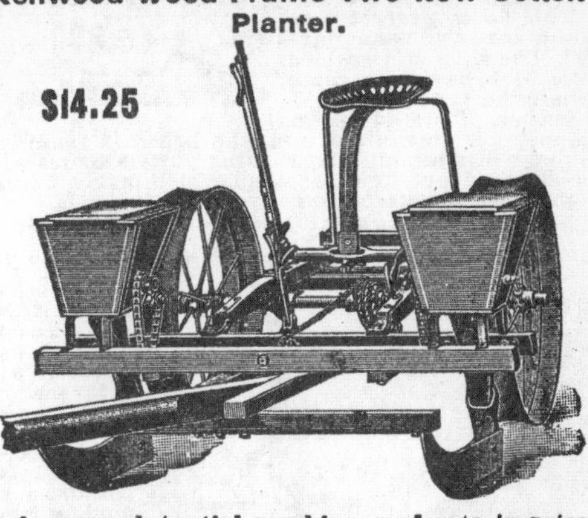

A very substantial machine, moderate in price but reliable in operation and first class in every respect. Has 30-inch steel wheels with 6-inch concave tires. Runners are steel and will scour nicely. Has pick feed dropping device. Drills two rows at a time at any desired quantity per acre, either thickly or sparse, the quantity being regulated by slides in the hoppers and by a combination sprocket wheel on the axle. Never misses planting. Runners can be set at any depth by the lever. Will plant rows 3 feet 8 inches apart, but can furnish for rows 3 feet 6 inches apart, if so ordered. Shipped knocked down from factory in Southwestern Ohio.

No. 32C650 Wood Frame Cotton Planter. Weight, 280 pounds. Price.............................**$14.25**

Fulton Potato Planter and Digger. $24.95 Combined.

$20.75

A splendid machine which can be used as an automatic potato planter or as a riding potato digger. As a planter it drops and covers at the same time. The automatic dropper is fed by hand, insuring more perfect work than can be done with a self drop planter. The driver walks, the feeder rides and feeds with both hands. The wheels are adjustable for width and mark the rows. One horse follows the last wheel track. Will plant hills either 13, 16 or 19 inches apart and any depth from 3 to 6 inches. As a digger the driver rides. It can be set to run any desired depth to raise the potatoes and will not run too deep or too shallow. The separator bars are diamond steel, set edgewise. They raise the potatoes to the surface and separate them from the dirt so they may be picked up easily. This machine can be furnished as a combined potato planter and digger, or as a potato planter only, or as a potato digger only. Shipped knocked down from factory in Northern Illinois.

$18.50

No. 32C666 Fulton Potato Planter and Digger. Weight, 240 pounds. Price.............................**$24.95**
No. 32C667 Fulton Potato Planter only. Weight, 190 pounds. Price.............................**$20.75**
No. 32C668 Fulton Potato Digger only. Weight, 180 pounds. Price.............................**$18.50**

Triumph Corn Planters.

50c and 75c

Adapted to all sorts of soil. Never clog. Operator can see the corn deposited in the ground. All working parts made of malleable iron and blades made of steel. Can be used on sod or plowed ground. The No. 1 is for planting corn only. The No. 2 is for planting corn and has pumpkin seed attachment. Weight, 4½ pounds.

Price
No. 32C700 No. 1 Triumph Corn Planter..**50c**
No. 32C701 No. 2 Triumph Corn Planter..**75c**

Eclipse Corn Planter.

72c

The handiest corn planter made. Has a positive force feed, and is furnished with four different seed plates. Is extremely simple, nothing to get out of order, works very easily and is made of the best of materials. Weight, 7¼ pounds.

No. 32C703 Eclipse Corn Planter. Price..**72c**

☞ YOU CANNOT MAKE A SATISFACTORY SELECTION FROM THESE PAGES, DON'T THINK OF BUYING FROM ANYONE UNTIL YOU HAVE SENT FOR AND RECEIVED OUR BIG FREE SPECIAL AGRICULTURAL IMPLEMENT CATALOGUE.

Segment Corn and Bean Planter.

80c

This is a perfect one-hand corn and bean planter. The slide is a segment of a circle having its center where the jaws are pivoted together. The seed box and hopper are galvanized iron, the brush is genuine Chinese bristles, and the working parts are pressed or stamped out of sheet steel, which makes them light, strong and accurate. Weight, 4¼ pounds.

No. 32C705 Segment Corn Planter. Price..80c

Kenwood Potato Planters.

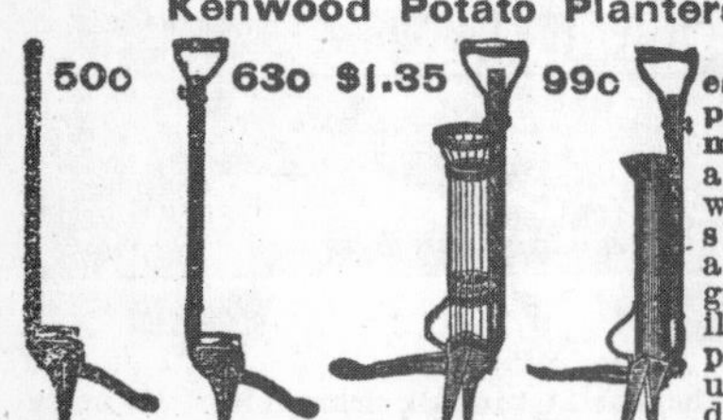

The highest grade planters made. Jaws are steel with sharp, slim beak and enter ground easily. Plants potatoes at a uniform depth and releases them automatically. Jaws are closed and held, when out of ground, by side springs. Spade handle can be adjusted 3 inches. The tube planters are 3 inches in diameter. The wire tube planter is the most desirable planter made. The solid tube is made of galvanized steel.

Catalogue No.		Weight, pounds	Price
32C707	Straight Handle Potato Planter.	3¼	$0.50
32C708	Spade Handle Potato Planter..	3½	.63
32C709	Wire Tube Potato Planter......	4½	1.35
32C710	Solid Tube Potato Planter......	4½	.99

Masters' Rapid Plant Setter.

A perfect mechanical plant setter. All kinds of plants, such as cabbage, tobacco, tomatoes, seed potatoes, etc., can be set, watered and covered at one operation, with the roots below the surface where the ground is cool and damp. It makes no difference how hot the weather or how dry the season may be, this setter does sure work because it sets each plant with either water or liquid fertilizer. No waiting for rain, no loss of plants, no wasted labor. The conical jaws are heavy sheet steel, the main body or water reservoir and plant tube are heavy tinned plate; valves and other fittings are brass and steel. Weight, crated for shipment, 7 lbs.

No. 32C715 Plant Setter. Price..........$3.25

Kenwood Single Row Stalk Cutter.

$19.25

For cutting corn stalks, cotton, etc., in the field, to prepare field for plowing. Frame and wheels are steel. Knives are best tool steel, carefully tempered and ground. Has a chop stroke which cuts successfully. Has a draft equalizing spring to offset motion of the cylinder. Stalk hooks or gatherers are steel and raise automatically with the cylinder. All bearings protected from dirt and dust. Price does not include whiffletrees or neckyoke. Shipped knocked down from factory near Chicago.

No. 32C750 Stalk Cutter. Wt., 490 lbs. Price, $19.25

Kenwood Clod Crushers.

$18.50 TO $27.70

Made like a land roller, but with heavy cast iron cutting wheels, each 24 inches in diameter, in place of drums. These wheels revolve independent of each other, on a 1½-inch, smooth steel axle, and the cutting edges of the wheels are so formed that they crush and pulverize the soil thoroughly and leave the field in a perfect condition. The axle revolves independent of the wheels, and all but the 8-wheel crushers have a bearing in the center as well as at each end. Platform frame is heavy angle steel. Shipped knocked down from factory in Southwestern Ohio.

No. 32C760 8-Wheel Clod Crusher. Length, 5 feet. Weight, 800 pounds. Price..........**$18.50**

No. 32C761 10-Wheel Clod Crusher. Length, 6½ feet. Weight, 1,000 pounds. Price..........**$22.90**

No. 32C763 12-Wheel Clod Crusher. Length, 7¾ feet. Weight, 1,200 pounds. Price..........**$27.70**

Kenwood Steel Drum Land Rollers.

$14.90 to $19.95

The drums of these rollers are 24 inches diameter, made of heavy high carbon steel plates, well rivited to heavy cast iron heads. The shaft is steel, 1¾ inches diameter, and runs in reversible chilled iron bearings, with sand guards over ends of shaft. Each drum turns independently of the other. Seat is mounted on a steel standard. The side bars of the platform frame are heavy angle steel, firmly bolted to the end brackets. Absolutely the best and highest grade steel land rollers made. Shipped knocked down from factory in Southwestern Ohio.

No. 32C755 6-Foot, 2-Section Steel Land Roller. Weight, 575 pounds. Price..........**$14.90**

No. 32C754 6-Foot, 3-Section Steel Land Roller. Weight, 625 pounds. Price..........**$15.75**

No. 32C756 7-Foot, 3-Section Steel Land Roller. Weight, 675 pounds. Price..........**$17.65**

No. 32C757 8-Foot, 3-Section Steel Land Roller. Weight, 725 pounds. Price..........**$18.80**

No. 32C758 8-Foot, 4-Section Steel Land Roller. Weight, 775 pounds. Price..........**$19.95**

Kenwood Steel Frame Tongueless Cultivators.

$10.80 TO $14.70

This cultivator has all modern improvements. Both wheels and gangs are pivoted, always in line. Draft bars have adjustable hitch, gauging depth perfectly. Gangs can be raised or lowered, or set at any distance, in or out. They are independent, so that each horse pulls its own plow. Frame is provided with gang rests, handles are adjustable. Breakpin shovels are adjustable for angle, depth, or suction, and spring trip shovels are adjustable for angle and depth. Wheels are 30 inches high. Price includes whiffletrees and fenders. Two bull tongue blades are also furnished with four shovel gangs. The illustration shows the cultivator with four break pin shovels. For style of spring trip shovels, see illustration of Kenwood tongue cultivator. Weight, 170 pounds. Shipped knocked down from factory in Southwestern Ohio.

No. 32C810 Tongueless Cultivator, with four 5-inch breakpin shovels. Price..........**$10.80**

No. 32C811 Tongueless Cultivator, with six 3½-inch breakpin shovels. Price..........**$11.35**

No. 32C812 Tongueless Cultivator, with eight 2-inch breakpin shovels. Price..........**$11.90**

No. 32C813 Tongueless Cultivator, with four 5-inch spring trip shovels. Price..........**$13.20**

No. 32C809 Tongueless Cultivator, with six 3½-inch spring trip shovels. Price..........**$14.70**

Kenwood Steel Frame Tongue Cultivators.

$11.70 to $15.60

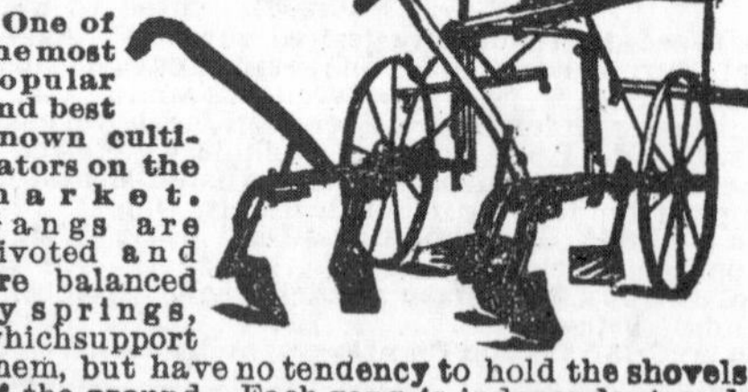

One of the most popular and best known cultivators on the market. Gangs are pivoted and are balanced by springs, which support them, but have no tendency to hold the shovels out of the ground. Each gang is independent and can be adjusted for width, or raised and lowered. Cultivator is provided with gang rests and handles are adjustable. Breakpin shovels are adjustable for angle, depth or suction, and spring trip shovels are adjustable for angle and depth. Wheels are 30 inches high. **Price is for cultivator with single tongue and includes whiffletrees, neckyoke and fenders. Will furnish with double tongue for 65 cents extra.** Two bull tongue blades are also furnished with four shovel gangs. The illustration shows the cultivator with four spring trip shovels. For style of breakpin shovels, see illustration of Kenwood tongueless cultivator. Weight, 215 pounds. Shipped knocked down from factory in Southwestern Ohio.

No. 32C814 Tongue Cultivator, with four 5-inch breakpin shovels. Price..........**$11.70**

No. 32C815 Tongue Cultivator, with six 3½-inch breakpin shovels. Price..........**$12.25**

No. 32C816 Tongue Cultivator, with eight 2-inch breakpin shovels. Price..........**$12.80**

No. 32C817 Tongue Cultivator, with four 5-inch spring trip shovels. Price..........**$14.10**

No. 32C818 Tongue Cultivator, with six 3½-inch spring trip shovels. Price..........**$15.60**

Kenwood Wood Frame One-Horse Weeder.

$5.25

An excellent tool for surface cultivation. Has 35 round spring steel teeth. Width, 7 feet. End sections, which are 2 feet long, can be detached, making weeder 3 feet wide for use in narrow places or between rows. Weight, 75 pounds. Shipped knocked down from factory in S. E. Wisconsin.

No. 32C775 Wood Frame Weeder. Price, $5.25

Kenwood Steel Frame One-Horse Weeder.

$5.50

Frame is made of heavy angle steel and is strongly braced. Weeder is 7½ feet wide, has 38 teeth, which are made of square spring steel and pointed, and is adapted for use in any soil. Price, includes trace hooks. Weight, 85 lbs. Shipped knocked down from factory in Southern Pennsylvania.

No. 32C777 Steel Frame Weeder. Price, $5.50

Kenwood Steel Frame Riding or Walking Cultivators.

$18.20 TO $22.30

A perfect combination riding or walking cultivator. Adjustable for wide or narrow rows. Suitable for any soil and for any class of work. Has more desirable features than any other cultivator on the market. Has springs which can be adjusted to carry the shovels to any desired lift or to be non-acting when at work. Wheels are 42 inches high and have wide tires. Gangs are spring balanced and easily guided by the feet. Seat is suspended and adjusted so as to balance perfectly and ride easily. Draft bars have adjustable hitch. Balance springs are adjustable. Breakpin shovels are adjustable for angle, depth or suction, and spring trip shovels are adjustable for angle and depth. Price includes whiffletrees, neckyoke and fenders. Two bull tongue blades are also furnished with four shovel gangs. The illustration shows the cultivator with six breakpin shovels. For style of spring trip shovels, and manner of attaching handles, see illustration of Kenwood tongue cultivator. Weight, 350 pounds. Shipped knocked down from factory in Southwestern Ohio.

No. 32C822 Riding Cultivator, with four 5-inch breakpin shovels. Price..........**$18.20**

No. 32C823 Riding Cultivator, with six 3½-inch breakpin shovels. Price..........**$18.80**

No. 32C824 Riding Cultivator, with eight 2-inch breakpin shovels. Price..........**$19.40**

No. 32C825 Riding Cultivator, with four 5-inch spring trip shovels. Price..........**$20.60**

No. 32C821 Riding Cultivator, with six 3½-inch spring trip shovels. Price..........**$22.30**

Kenwood Steel Frame Spring Tooth Cultivator.

$19.15

An up to date and very desirable spring tooth riding cultivator. Wheels are 44 inches high, with 1¾-inch tires, and have removable boxes. Draft is direct from gang arch. Gangs are adjustable for width and depth. Wheels can be set either 4 or 5 feet apart. Each gang has five springteeth with 2¼-inch reversible points. Seat arm can be adjusted up or down and seat forward or back. Center gang can be used when wheels are set 5 feet apart. Price is for cultivator complete with pair of fenders, pair of hilling shovels, neckyoke and whiffletrees, but does not include center gang. **Handles, 75 cents extra.** Can furnish shovel gangs for this cultivator at special low prices. Shipped knocked down from factory in Southern Michigan.

No. 32C826 Spring Tooth Cultivator. Weight, 360 pounds. Price..........**$19.15**

No. 32C832 Center Gang only, with three spring teeth and shovels. Wt., 30 lbs. Price, **$1.90**

IF YOU CANNOT MAKE A SATISFACTORY SELECTION FROM THESE PAGES, DON'T THINK OF BUYING FROM ANYONE UNTIL YOU HAVE SENT FOR AND RECEIVED OUR BIG FREE SPECIAL AGRICULTURAL IMPLEMENT CATALOGUE.

Kenwood Steel Riding Disc Cultivator.

$22.25

A strong, substantial and perfect working disc cultivator. Wheels are 54 inches high and have broad tires. Has six discs, each 16 inches in diameter. Discs can be set to plow at any depth, and as the depth is gauged by the wheels the gangs will not plow deeper in soft places than in hard soil. Gangs can be set at any desired angle and to throw the dirt in or out. The gangs are guided by feet of operator. Depth is fixed and regulated by levers and strong depth springs. Drafts bars have adjustable hitch, draft being from both discs and tongue. The scrapers are arranged so that by the pressure of the foot the discs are cleaned from center to the cutting edge. The gangs can be set at any distance apart from 1½ inches to 1 foot. Price includes whiffletrees and neckyoke, but does not include shovel gangs. Weight, 500 pounds. Shipped knocked down from factory in Southwestern Ohio.

No. 32C836 Riding Disc Cultivator, with disc gang only. Price....$22.25

No. 32C837 Pair of Shovel Gangs, with six 3½-inch breakpin shovels. Wt., 80 lbs. Price.....$5.75

Kenwood Endgate Broadcast Seeder.

$5.25

Suitable for sowing broadcast all kinds of seeds and dry fertilizers. Has large hopper, strong gearing, spring clutch on end of shaft, perfectly shaped distributor and pinion. Either or both sides of feed may be cut off at will and seeder may be thrown out of gear. End board and main shaft are made long enough for either wide or narrow track wagon or box. Weight, 95 pounds. Shipped from factory in Southeastern Wisconsin.

No. 32C850 Endgate Seeder. Price.......$5.25

Kenwood Agitator Feed Broadcast Seeder.

$12.75

Sows all kinds of grain broadcast and can be furnished with grass seed attachment. Hopper is deep and has three cast iron partitions, with oil tube at each partition. Steel wheels are 36 inches high with broad tires. Discharge is low. Axle extends full length of seeder. Adjustment of feed is convenient and accurate. If grass seed attachment is wanted it must be ordered with the seeder; it cannot be furnished separately. Shipped knocked down from factory in Eastern Indiana.

No. 32C855 11-Foot Agitator Seeder. Weight, 375 pounds. Price....$12.75

No. 32C856 Grass Seed Attachment. Weight, 40 pounds. Price....$2.40

Kenwood Wheelbarrow Grass Seeders.

$4.90 to $6.80.

Wheelbarrow grass seeders are the most accurate and economical machines for sowing clover, timothy, alfalfa and other small seeds broadcast. The single hopper seeder sows all kinds of smooth grass seeds, either mixed or separate, **but will not sow light, chaffy seeds.** The double hopper seeder will sow smooth seeds and also light, chaffy seeds. Weight, about 50 pounds. Shipped knocked down from factory in Southern Michigan.

No. 32C865 12-Foot Single Hopper Seeder. Price....$4.90

No. 32C866 12-Foot Double Hopper Seeder. Price....$6.20

No. 32C867 14-Foot Single Hopper Seeder. Price....$5.20

No. 32C868 14-Foot Double Hopper Seeder. Price....$6.50

No. 32C869 16-Foot Single Hopper Seeder. Price....$5.50

No. 32C870 16-Foot Double Hopper Seeder. Price....$6.80

Kenwood Five-Hoe Grain Drill.

Especially adapted for drilling small grain between corn rows or for drilling grain with 1 horse. Can be adjusted while in operation from 31 to 40 inches wide. Has wood frame, force feed, rear lift, and can be thrown in or out of gear while in motion. Shipped knocked down from factory in Eastern Indiana.

$9.60

No. 32C863 Grain Drill. Wt., 145 lbs. Price, $9.60

Fulton Jr. Geared Broadcast Seeder.

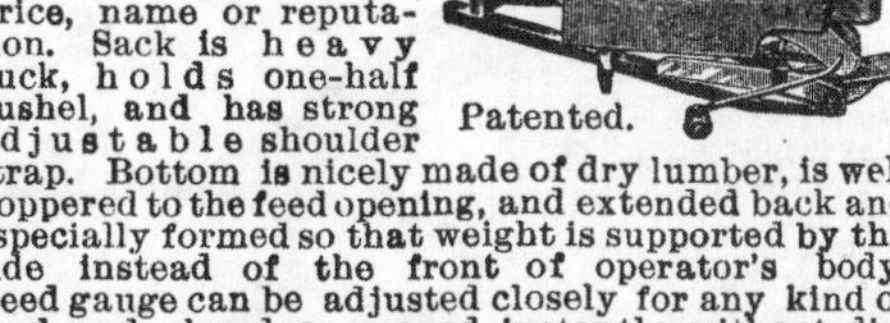

This seeder is very similar to our regular line of Fulton seeders. It rests against the front of the body like seeders of other makes instead of resting against the side like our regular Fulton seeders do. The sack is made of heavy cotton duck, and holds about half a bushel. It is provided with an adjustable neck strap. The crank is above the distributor. Feed gauge can be adjusted closely for any kind of seed, and closed or opened instantly without disturbing the adjustment. Has a force feed, which insures a uniform flow, and an even distribution of the seed. The distributor is a 11-inch disc with four double flanges, has no joints and will distribute the seed at practically the same widths as stated in connection with our regular Fulton seeders. The gearing is strong and very simple. Stationary handle can be changed and crank can be used on either side. It is shipped in a paper box and weighs 2¾ pounds.

No. 32C882 Fulton Geared Seeder. Price...76c

Fulton Hand Broadcast Seeders. 95 Cents and $1.15.

The best and most desirable hand seeders made, regardless of price, name or reputation. Sack is heavy duck, holds one-half bushel, and has strong adjustable shoulder strap. Bottom is nicely made of dry lumber, is well hoppered to the feed opening, and extended back and especially formed so that weight is supported by the side instead of the front of operator's body. Feed gauge can be adjusted closely for any kind of seed and closed or opened instantly without disturbing adjustment. Shake feed insures perfect seeding. Distributor has four arms, is made of tin, double flanged and has no soldered joints; it will distribute perfectly. The fiddle bow seeder has free arm movement, and is operated by a leather cord attached to a steel bow. The geared seeder has good strong gearing which fits perfectly, and is operated by a crank. Weight, 3¼ pounds; crated, 5 pounds.

Patented.

No. 32C884 Fulton Geared Seeder. Price, $1.15

No. 32C885 Fulton Bow Seeder. Price.... .95

Genuine Man-Weight Garden Seeder, Cultivator, Plow, Hoe and Rake.

This is not a cheap imitation or infringement of the celebrated patent man-weight garden tool, but is the genuine article. It cannot be sold for less than our price and is worth more than double the price of imitations. As a seeder it will drop seeds in hills from 3 to 48 inches apart or will sow continuously in drills. Has an agitator force feed to insure even sowing. Will sow the desired quantity accurately at any depth from ¼ inch to 4 inches. Sows and covers the seed, presses or firms the ground and marks the next row all at one operation. As a cultivator, plow, hoe, rake and harrow, it has no superior and as such, it is fitted with one pair of 2-inch cultivator teeth, one pair of small plows, one pair of 8-inch single end hoes, one pair of 4-inch double end hoes and one pair of 7-inch rakes. These tools are always furnished whether the machine is ordered complete or as a cultivator only, but price of cultivator only, does not include the seeder attachment. Wheels are 18 inches high and are 13 inches apart. Machine can be used either as a double or a single wheel hoe or cultivator. Arch is high enough to pass over crops 25 to 30 inches high. Machine is propelled by the operator leaning the weight of his body against the push bar, leaving his hands free to guide the tools around the plants.

Patented.

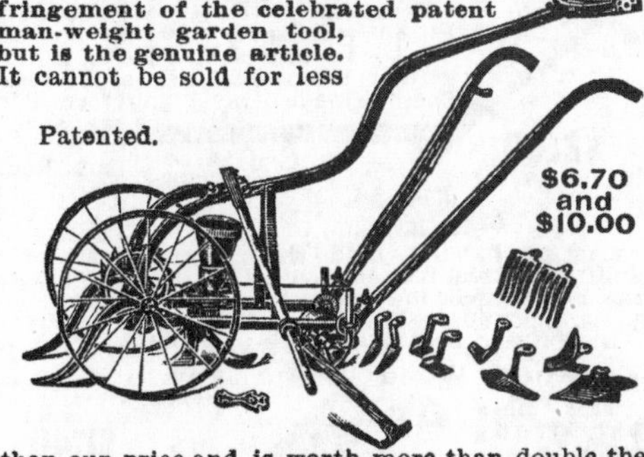

$6.70 and $10.00

No. 32C895 Man-Weight Seeder and Cultivator Complete. Weight, 80 pounds. Price.......$10.00

No. 32C896 Man-Weight Cultivator only. Weight, 60 pounds. Price.......$6.70

New Universal Model Hill and Drill Seeder.

$7.25

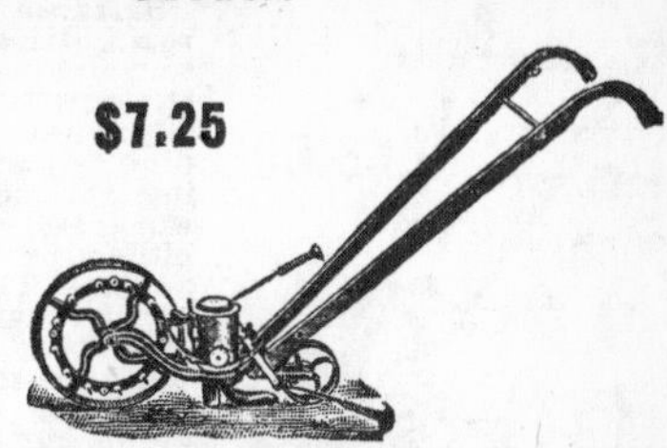

This is a combination hill and drill seeder. It will drop in hills at either 4, 6, 8, 12, 16, 24 or 48 inches apart, or can be used for sowing continuously in drills. For hill dropping, the distance apart is varied by the number of pins placed in the driving wheel, against which the agitator strikes, the agitator opening and closing the holes in the bottom of the seed box. The change from hill to drill top is made by one thumbscrew in detaching the cut-off from the agitator and fastening it back on the frame. This machine has a large hopper, an agitator force feed, a steel furrow opener, drags to throw the soil over the seed, a concaved roller or rear wheel to press and compact the soil which covers the seed, improved markers on each side of the machine, and a patent indicator, conveniently located, bearing the names of the different kinds of seeds. It will drop in hills or drill any kind of small seed in any desired quantity, at any desired uniform depth and covers perfectly. Weight, 57 pounds. Shipped knocked down and boxed.

No. 32C901 Hill and Drill Seeder. Price, $7.25

New Universal Constellation Drill Seeder, Hoe, Rake, Cultivator, Plow and Marker.

$6.50 AND $8.50

The most convenient and desirable full combination garden tool outfit on the market. Can be used either as a one or two-wheel tool. Six tools in one. The outfit consists of the drill complete, one cultivator frame, one pair of hoes, one pair plows, one pair of rakes, one pair of narrow cultivator teeth, one pair of wide cultivator teeth, one center cultivator tooth and one pair of improved markers, exactly as shown in the illustration. The drill has a large hopper, an agitator force feed, a steel furrow opener, drags to cover the seed, a concaved roller or rear wheel to press and compact the soil which covers the seed, and a patent indicator conveniently located, bearing the names of the different kinds of seeds. Will drill any kind of small seeds, in any desired quantity, at any desired uniform depth, and covers perfectly. Weight, 73 pounds. We can also furnish this machine as a single wheel drill seeder only, without any of the cultivating tools. Weight, 56 pounds. Shipped knocked down and boxed.

	Price
No. 32C903 Constellation Drill Outfit...	$8.50
No. 32C900 Drill Seeder only..........	6.50

New Universal Model Gem Drill Seeder, Hoe, Cultivator, Plow and Marker.

$5.00 AND $7.75

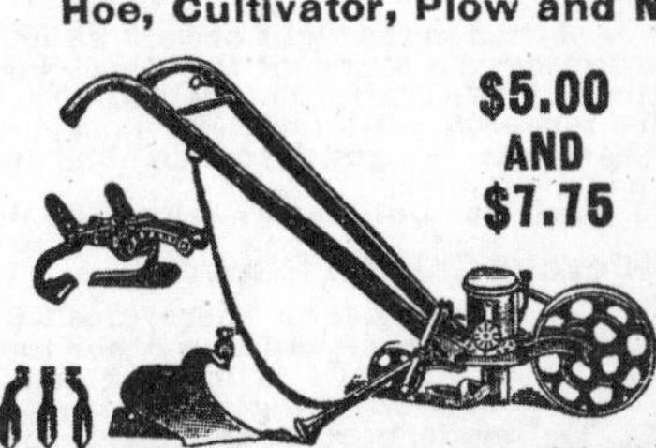

This is a splendid combination of gardening tools, large enough and complete enough for the average small gardener. The complete outfit consists of the drill complete, one cultivator frame, one pair of hoes, three cultivator teeth, one large right hand plow and one reversible marker, exactly as shown in the illustration. The drill has a good sized hopper, a reliable feed, a furrow opener, drags to cover the seed, a concave roller or rear wheel to press and compact the soil over the seed, and a patent indicator bearing the names of the different kinds of seeds. Will drill any kind of small seed in any desired quantity, at a uniform depth and covers perfectly. Weight of complete outfit, 52 pounds. We can also furnish the Gem drill without the hoe, cultivator teeth and plow, but with marker. Weight, 39 pounds. Shipped knocked down and boxed.

No. 32C905 Gem Drill Outfit. Price....$7.75

No. 32C906 Gem Drill only. Price...... 5.00

Our Special Implement Catalogue (sent free), shows larger pictures of these goods.

IF YOU CANNOT MAKE A SATISFACTORY SELECTION FROM THESE PAGES, DON'T THINK OF BUYING FROM ANYONE UNTIL YOU HAVE SENT FOR AND RECEIVED OUR BIG FREE SPECIAL AGRICULTURAL IMPLEMENT CATALOGUE.

New Universal Double Wheel Hoe, Cultivator, Plow and Rake.

$5.50

Suitable for straddle row cultivation, that is to work both sides of the row at once. Has adjustable arch with nine adjustments gauging the depth of the work, and teeth can be pitched to any desired angle. The complete outfit consists of frame complete, one pair of vine guards, one pair of hoes, one pair of plows, one pair of rakes, one pair of narrow cultivator teeth and one pair of wide cultivator teeth, and weighs 42 pounds. Shipped knocked down and boxed. Price,

No. 32C911 Double Wheel Hoe Outfit. $5.50

New Universal Single Wheel Hoe Outfits.

$4.25 and $4.75

Can be used on either side of the row, or by setting the wheel to one side it can be used for straddle row cultivation. Can be furnished in two different ways, namely: No. 1, single wheel hoe outfit, consisting of frame and handles complete, one vine guard, one pair of hoes, one pair of small plows, one pair of rakes, one pair of narrow cultivator teeth, one pair of wide cultivator teeth, and one center cultivator tooth, weight 35 pounds. No. 2, single wheel hoe outfit, consisting of frame and handles complete, one pair of hoes, three cultivator teeth and one large right hand plow, weight 30 pounds. Neither outfit includes all the tools shown in the illustration. Shipped knocked down and boxed. Price,

No. 32C915 No. 1 Single Wheel Hoe. $4.75
No. 32C916 No. 2 Single Wheel Hoe. 4.25

Easy Hand Cultivator, Plow and Rake.

$2.25 and $2.40

Light, strong and easy to operate. Just the tool for gardens and small shrubs. Wheel is 18 inches high. Is furnished with one plow, one cultivator tooth and one cultivator sweep and either with or without rakes. Weight, 22 pounds. Shipped knocked down and bundled.

No. 32C921 Cultivator, without rake. Price, $2.25
No. 32C922 Cultivator, with rake. Price, 2.40

Push Bar Cultivator, Hoe and Plow.

$2.60

This cultivator is easy to operate. It is provided with a push bar which the operator places against his body, thus leaving the hands free to shift the cultivator. The cultivator is flexible, the wheel bars being hinged at the axle of the wheel, and where they join the cultivator frame. This allows the frame of the cultivator to be shifted to the right or left without in any way affecting the course of the wheel, and without making any side draft. The tools furnished are five cultivator teeth, one large right hand plow and one right hand hoe. Weight, 23 pounds. Shipped knocked down and bundled.

No. 32C929 Push Bar Cultivator. Price....$2.60

Bicycle Garden Plow.

$3.25 Patented.

Possesses more excellent features than any other tool of its kind. Will push easier than any single wheel plow made, because the wheels govern the depth. For this reason the weeder or sweep can be used most successfully and the various tools can be set to retain the depth and angle best suited for the work. Can be adjusted to enter the ground from a fraction of an inch to 5 inches deep. Both front and rear wheels are adjustable for depth handles for height. Wheels are 18 inches high. Can be used as a single wheel plow by removing the rear wheel. It is fitted with one plow, one double end cultivator tooth, one sweep and one wide rake. Weight, 25 pounds. Shipped knocked down and crated.

No. 32C931 Bicycle Garden Plow. Price..$3.25

Kenwood Steel Beam Single Shovel Plows.

$1.35 and $1.40

Beams are made of 1¾-inch by ¾-inch steel. The handles are nicely formed and securely braced. The No. 1 size is fitted with 10x12-inch shovel blade. The No. 2 size is fitted with 12x12-inch shovel blade. Weight, 32 pounds. Shipped knocked down.

No. 32C940 No. 1 Steel Beam Single Shovel Plow. Price........$1.35
No. 32C941 No. 2 Steel Beam Single Shovel Plow. Price........$1.40

Kenwood Steel Beam Double Shovel Plows.

$1.50 and $1.85

Width of cut, 20 inches. Beams of No. 1 plows are made of 1¼-inch by ⅝-inch steel. Beams of No. 2 plows are made of 1¾-inch by ¾-inch steel. No. 2 plows have a tie rod between the handles and shovels are extra heavy. Handles are perfectly formed and strongly braced. Shovels are 6 inches wide and 11 inches long. Shipped knocked down.

No. 32C948 No. 1 Steel Beam Double Shovel Plow. Weight, 34 pounds. Price........$1.50
No. 32C950 No. 2 Steel Beam Double Shovel Plow. Weight, 46 pounds. Price........$1.85

Kenwood Steel Beam Breakpin Double Shovel Plow.

$2.15

This plow is practically the same as our No. 2 double shovel plow, except that it is fitted with breakpin shovels. The breakpin foot is attached to the standard by a bolt and a wooden pin, or you can attach it with two bolts when you do not wish to use the breakpin feature. The foot is adjustable so that the blade can be set at any desired angle or slant, and it is slotted so that any style blade can be attached by means of a heel bolt. Beams are made of 1¾-inch by ¾-inch steel. Shovels are extra heavy, 6 inches wide by 11 inches long. Weight, 48 pounds. Shipped knocked down.

No. 32C952 Steel Beam Breakpin Double Shovel Plow. Price........$2.15

Kenwood Steel Beam Wing Shovel Plow.

$2.00

Very light, strong and durable. Fitted with same blade as on our wood beam wing shovel plow. Adapted for hilling and digging potatoes. Beam is made of steel plate formed in the shape of a "U" bar. Rear part of frame forms a socket for handles, holds them firm and prevents splitting. Steel foot can be set at different angles and blade can be lowered as it wears. Weight, complete, 43 pounds. Shipped knocked down. Price,

No. 32C955 Steel Beam Wing Shovel Plow. $2.00

Kenwood Wood Beam Single Shovel Plow.

$1.40

This plow has strong wood beam, standard and handles, well set and braced. Fitted with a heavy blade, 12 inches wide by 14 inches long. Shipped knocked down.

No. 32C960 Wood Beam Single Shovel Plow. Weight, 27 pounds. Price........$1.40

Kenwood Wood Beam Double Shovel Plow.

$1.45

One of the most substantial plows made. Has strong oak beam, standard and handles, is well braced and fitted with heavy steel shovels 7 inches wide by 9 inches long. Shipped knocked down.

No. 32C946 Wood Beam Double Shovel Plow. Weight, 30 pounds. Price........$1.45

Kenwood Wood Beam Wing Shovel Plow.

$1.75

Has strong wood beam, standard and handles, well set and braced. Fitted with single shovel blade, having adjustable steel wings which can be set at any angle and held in position by means of the spread rods. Especially adapted for hilling and digging potatoes. Weight, 33 pounds. Shipped knocked down.

No. 32C958 Wood Beam Wing Shovel Plow. Price........$1.75

Kenwood Potato Hiller and Digger.

$5.75

A practical hiller and digger combined. Has heavy oak beam standard and handles, is well braced and is fitted with adjustable gauge wheel and rear depth shoe. The wing shovel blade leaves the soil loose and destroys the weeds. The digger works perfectly, leaving the potatoes in excellent condition on top of the soil, and runs as steady as a plow. Weight, 68 pounds. Shipped knocked down from factory in Southeastern Wisconsin. Price

No. 32C965 Potato Hiller and Digger....$5.75

Kenwood-One Horse Cultivator and Wing Shovel Plow.

$3.75

Especially adapted for cultivating corn and other heavy work. As it appears in the illustration, it is adapted for cultivation and the rear teeth are adjusted to act as hoes. By taking out two bolts, you can remove the cultivator parts and put on the adjustable wing shovel blade in place of the rear center tooth. Frame is made of best quality hardwood and all steel and iron parts are strictly first class in every way. Cultivator is adjustable from 8 inches to 40 inches in width. A splendid tool for heavy work. Shipped knocked down.

No. 32C968 Wood Frame Cultivator. Weight, 80 pounds. Price........$3.75

Kenwood 14-Tooth Steel Frame Lever Harrow.

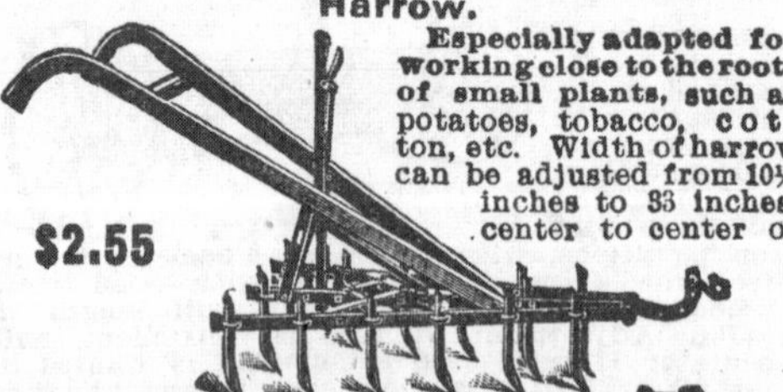

$2.55

Especially adapted for working close to the roots of small plants, such as potatoes, tobacco, cotton, etc. Width of harrow can be adjusted from 10½ inches to 33 inches, center to center of teeth. Teeth can be reversed or turned as desired, presenting four different points. This harrow is fitted with patent compound lever expander. Outside handle braces No. 32C985, and front wheels No. 32C983, are very desirable attachments which can be used on this harrow. Weight, 59 pounds. Shipped knocked down. Price

No. 32C972 Steel Frame Lever Harrow. $2.55

Kenwood Spring Tooth Steel Frame Cultivator.

$2.80

The frame is same as the frame of our 5-tooth cultivators, the only difference being in the teeth. Width can be adjusted from 12 inches to 28 inches, center to center of teeth. Has patent compound lever expander for adjusting width. Outside handle braces No. 32C985 and front wheels No. 32C983 are desirable attachments which can be used on this cultivator. Weight, 55 pounds. Shipped knocked down.

No. 32C981 Spring Tooth Cultivator. Price........$2.80

IF YOU CANNOT MAKE A SATISFACTORY SELECTION FROM THESE PAGES, DON'T THINK OF BUYING FROM ANYONE UNTIL YOU HAVE SENT FOR AND RECEIVED OUR BIG FREE SPECIAL AGRICULTURAL IMPLEMENT CATALOGUE.

Kenwood 5-Tooth Steel Frame Cultivators.

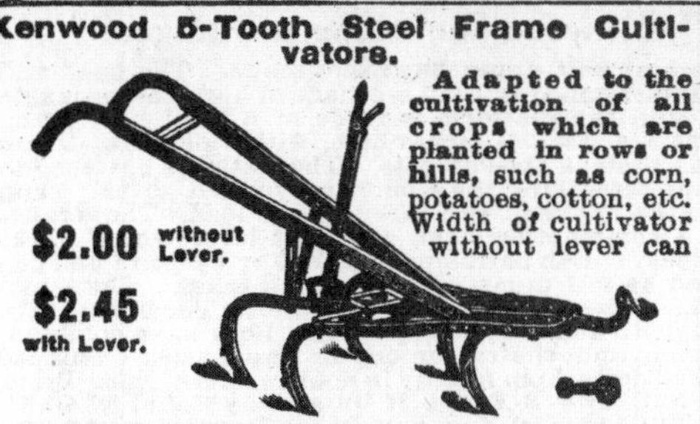

Adapted to the cultivation of all crops which are planted in rows or hills, such as corn, potatoes, cotton, etc. Width of cultivator without lever can be adjusted from 9 inches to 25 inches; width of cultivator with lever can be adjusted from 10 inches to 26 inches, center to center of teeth. Has five 3-inch reversible teeth which can be adjusted to suit all kinds of soil. The No. 1 cultivator has no adjusting lever. The No. 2 and No. 3 cultivators are made with patent compound lever expander, as shown in the first illustration. Outside handle braces No. 32C985, front wheel No. 32C983, cultivator teeth No. 32C993, cultivator sweeps No. 32C995 and horse hoe attachments No. 32C997 can be used on these cultivators, making them **universal tools**, and all are very desirable attachments.

The lever cultivator is also made in a special combination, as shown in the second illustration.

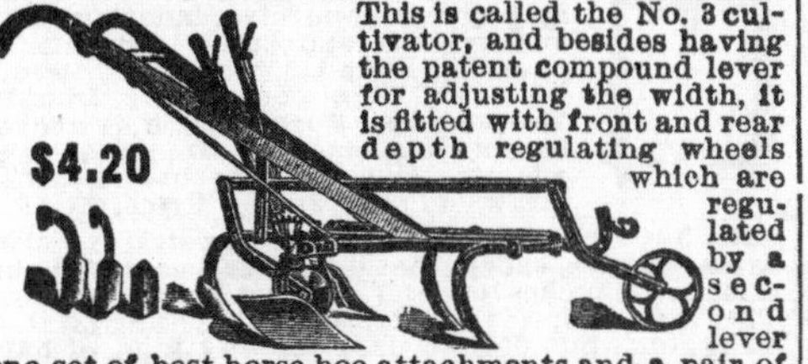

This is called the No. 3 cultivator, and besides having the patent compound lever for adjusting the width, it is fitted with front and rear depth regulating wheels which are regulated by a second lever one set of best horse hoe attachments and a pair of outside handle braces. We especially recommend this combination because it fits the tool for the cultivation of almost any crop. Shipped knocked down.

			Price
No. 32C975	No. 1 Cultivator.	Wt., 47 lbs.	$2.00
No. 32C976	No. 2 Cultivator.	Wt., 55 lbs.	2.45
No. 32C977	No. 3 Cultivator.	Wt., 94 lbs.	4.20

Front Wheel.

30c

This illustration shows our Plain Front Wheel, for use with our No. 32C972 harrow and our Nos. 32C975, 32C976 and 32C981 cultivators. It is a very substantial wheel and is adjustable for depth.

No. 32C983 Plain Front Wheel. Weight 5 pounds. Price........30c

Outside Handle Braces.

Pair of Outside Handle Braces, for use with our No. 32C972 harrow and our Nos. 32C975, 32C976 and 32C981 cultivators, to make handles perfectly rigid. Weight, 2½ pounds.

No. 32C985 Handle Braces. Price, per pair..15c

Reversible Cultivator Teeth.

No. 32C993 Reversible Cultivator Teeth complete with bolts. Made of high grade steel, nicely ground. Will fit our 5-tooth shovel cultivators and most any style of garden cultivator or plow stock.

Width, 1¼ inches. Weight, 10 ounces. Price....5c
Width, 2 inches. Weight, 13 ounces. Price....6c
Width, 3 inches. Weight, 14 ounces. Price....7c
Width, 4 inches. Weight, 16 ounces. Price....8c

Cultivator Sweeps.

No. 32C995 Steel Cultivator Sweeps, complete with bolts; made of high grade steel, nicely ground. Will fit our 5-tooth shovel cultivators and most any style of garden cultivator or plow stock.

Width, 10 inches. Weight, 1¼ pounds. Price....13c
Width, 12 inches. Weight, 1½ pounds. Price....15c
Width, 14 inches. Weight, 1¾ pounds. Price....17c

Horse Hoe Attachments.

47c and 77c

Our Best Horse Hoe Attachments are for use on our 5-tooth shovel cultivators. They consist of a center, right and left hand hoe, and are made to swivel without detaching them from the standard, so that the dirt is thrown to or from the crop, an entirely new feature in attachments. Our common horse hoes are of the standard pattern.

No. 32C997 Best Horse Hoe Attachments. Weight, 15 pounds. Price, per set..........77c
No. 32C998 Common Horse Hoe Attachments. Weight, 8 pounds, Price..........47c

Handy Sickle and Tool Grinder.

The best in construction, the best in use, the most complete outfit and the greatest value for the money. The base has four holes so that grinder can be fastened to a bench or plank and is fitted with a wheel clamp so that the grinder can be clamped to the wheel of a mower. The knife holder is pivoted at both front and back and can be adjusted, while the machine is in motion, so as to grind either more or less on either the front or back. Any desired tension can be put upon the knife holder. The sickle stone arm is oscillated by an eccentric movement which makes the stone travel back and forth over the sections and, as the knife lies in front of the operator, the whole grinding surface is in plain sight. For grinding sections close to the knife head, the machine can be adjusted by changing the position of the oscillating device so as to prevent the wheel from striking the knife head. When used as a tool grinder, the arm which carries the arbor is raised to a horizontal position where it is held in place firmly. The stones make 24 revolutions to each turn of the crank, or about 1,400 revolutions per minute. We can furnish at the extra price shown, a disc grinding attachment with which you can grind perfectly, any harrow disc or coulter blade up to 24 inches diameter, and can also furnish a saw gumming stone for cross cut saws. Shipped knocked down and boxed.

No. 32C1130 Handy Grinder, with sickle stone, tool stone, tool rest and wheel clamp. Weight, 25 pounds. Price..........$2.20
No. 32C1123 Disc Grinding Attachment. Weight, 3 pounds. Price..........70c
No. 32C1133 Saw Gumming Stone. Weight, 1¼ pounds. Price..........38c

Kenwood Combination Grinding Machine.

$6.85

This is an ideal tool for general farm use. It combines six tools in one, and each tool is perfect. It can be operated either by foot power or by hand. The grinder can be removed and bolted to a bench or it can be secured to the drive wheel of a mower. When run by hand the stones make about 1,400 revolutions per minute, but when run by foot power they can be run up to 4,000 revolutions per minute. The sickle grinder is entirely automatic in its grinding movements. It can be adjusted to grind exactly as desired. The knife clamp is arranged so that you grind four sections at one setting. A spring tension holds the knife against the stone and an adjusting screw stops it at the proper point. When used for tool grinding, the frame, which carries the stones, is held rigidly in place on a level line, and the adjustable tool rest can be used or not as desired. We furnish the machine complete with one beveled sickle stone, one tool stone, one saw gummer stone, one polishing wheel, one tool rest, one wheel clamp and one wrench. As useful to a blacksmith, a carpenter, or anyone who uses a grinder as it is to the farmer. The disc grinding attachment, No. 32C1123, shown in connection with our Handy Sickle and Tool Grinder, will fit and can be used on this machine. Weight, boxed, 70 pounds. Shipped knocked down.

No. 32C1135 Combination Grinding Machine. Price..........$6.85

MOWER AND BINDER SUNDRIES.

Our sections are put up in boxes of twenty sections complete with six head rivets and thirty-four bar rivets. We do not break packages, because our prices are so extremely low that we could not afford the labor or the broken stock which would result. We can furnish sections to fit almost any make of mower or binder in use at the present time.

Directions for ordering sections—When ordering sections you should give our catalogue number, the size of the section wanted and the name and kind of machine for which the sections are wanted, stating how many boxes of sections you want. You should also take one of the old sections from the knife, lay it on a piece of paper, and with a sharp pencil mark around the outside of the section, and mark the exact size and position of the rivet holes; then send the paper pattern to us with your order. **Be sure that your pencil is very sharp, and that the lines you draw and the holes you mark show the exact size of the section and the exact size and position of the holes,** because even the width of a pencil mark may make it so that your order could not be filled correctly. If you will be careful in ordering and in making pattern, we will guarantee to furnish the correct size of sections.

Mower and Flax Sections.

Before writing your order, read the directions for ordering sections. These sections are put up in boxes of twenty sections complete with rivets. They are smooth on the cutting edges and are guaranteed to fit the machines for which they are made. The average weight is 3 pounds per box.

No. 32C1072 Box of Smooth Sections. Price, 62c

Reaper and Harvester Sections.

Before writing your order read the directions for ordering sections. These sections are put up in boxes of twenty sections, complete with rivets. They are rough or serrated on the cutting edges and are guaranteed to fit the machines for which they are made. The average weight is 2 pounds per box.

No. 32C1097 Box of Rough Sections. Price..........64c

Section Rivets.

No. 6 or 3-16-inch Section Rivets in 1-pound boxes. We do not break or mix packages. Can furnish ½-inch or 1-inch long with bung heads or with countersunk heads. State which length and which style of head you want.

No. 32C1102 Box of Section Rivets. Price..........8c

Mower and Binder Guard Plates.

These plates are put up in boxes of twenty plates complete with rivets. We do not break packages. Can furnish guard plates to fit almost any mower or reaper in use at the present time. **When ordering guard plates be sure to tell us the name of the machine, whether it is a mower or reaper and tell us what numbers or letters are on the guards the plates are to fit, and send us a paper pattern with the shape of the plate and the size and position of the rivet holes carefully drawn with the sharp point of a pencil.** Mower plates have rough edges, binder plates have smooth edges. Weight, about 1¾ pounds per box.

No. 32C1103 Box of Guard Plates. Price..........50c

Mower and Binder Guards.

18c

We can furnish guards to fit almost any make of mower or binder in use at the present time. Our guards are complete with guard plates riveted in. When ordering guards, always tell us the name of the machine, whether it is a mower or binder and be sure to tell us what numbers or letters are on the old guards. Weight, about 1 pound each.

No. 32C1104 Guard. Price, each..........18c

Mower and Binder Knives or Sickles.

$1.80 to $2.10.

Our mower knives with smooth sections, and our binder or reaper sickles with rough or serrated sections, are furnished complete, with sections and head riveted to the bar, and are guaranteed to fit the machines for which they are made. We can furnish knives or sickles to fit almost any mower or binder in use at the present time. When ordering be sure to tell us whether you want a mower knife with smooth sections or a binder sickle with serrated sections, also tell us the name of the machine and what figures or letters are on the old knife or sickle head, also be sure to tell us how many cutting sections are on the old knife or sickle. If there are no numbers on the old head, send us paper pattern of the head, showing the exact position of the rivet holes and also send us a paper pattern of the section as you would if you were ordering sections only. Weights are for knives or sickles packed for shipment.

No. 32C1105 Knife or Sickle, with 18 cutting sections or less. Weight, 9 pounds. Price..........$1.80
No. 32C1106 Knife or Sickle, with 19 or 20 cutting sections. Weight, 10 pounds. Price..........$1.90
No. 32C1107 Knife or Sickle, with 21, 22, 23 or 24 cutting sections. Weight, 12 pounds. Price..........$2.00
No. 32C1108 Knife or Sickle, with 25, 26, 27 or 28 cutting sections. Weight, 14 pounds. Price..........$2.10

Mower Knife Heads or Binder Sickle Heads.

20c and 25c

Some knife or sickle heads are made of malleable iron, others are made of steel. A steel head cannot be furnished in place of a malleable head, neither can a malleable head be furnished in place of a steel head. We can furnish knife or sickle heads to fit almost any make of mower or binder in use at the present time. When ordering, be sure to tell us the name of the machine and the figures or letters which are on the old head. If there are no figures or letters on the old head, then send us a paper pattern of the old head, showing the exact position of the rivet holes and give us such other information as you may think we will need to fill your order correctly. Average weight, 1¾ pounds each.

No. 32C1109 Malleable Knife Head. Price..........20c
No. 32C1110 Steel Knife Head. Price..........25c

Fulton Sickle and Tool Grinder.

FITTED WITH CARBORUNDUM WHEELS.

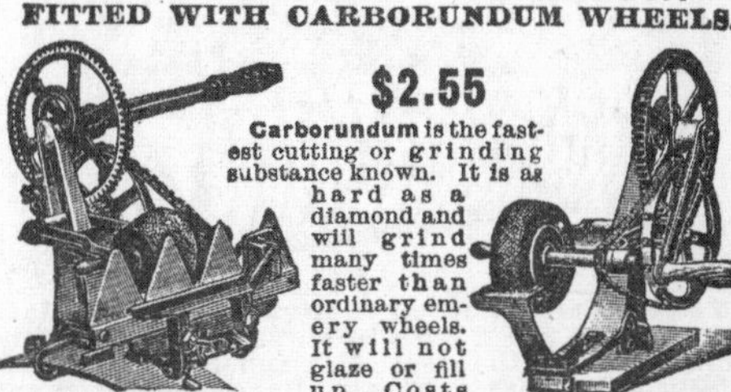

Carborundum is the fastest cutting or grinding substance known. It is as hard as a diamond and will grind many times faster than ordinary emery wheels. It will not glaze or fill up. Costs more, but is worth more than it costs. This machine as a sickle grinder can be fastened to a bench or clamped on to the wheel of a mower. The movement of a stone up and down can be adjusted so as to stop the downward movement at any desired point. The sickle clamp will hold any knife made, can be adjusted to or from the stone and also has a tension adjustment and an angle adjustment. As a tool grinder the wheel carrier arm is set and held firmly in a level position and the tool rest is attached in place of the sickle clamp. Price is for the machine complete with a base board, a wheel clamp, a tool rest, a carborundum sickle stone and a carborundum tool stone. Carborundum wheels cannot be furnished for other grinders. Shipped knocked down and boxed.

No. 32C1115 Fulton Sickle and Tool Grinder. Weight, 22 pounds. Price..........$2.55

KENWOOD HARVESTER CANVAS TIGHTENERS.

13c

The prongs of the hook engage with the buckle, the end of the lever is placed in one of the strap holes and the movement of the lever draws the canvas together. Weight, 5 ounces.

No. 32C1120 Canvas Tightener. Price..........13c

IF YOU CANNOT MAKE A SATISFACTORY SELECTION FROM THESE PAGES, DON'T THINK OF BUYING FROM ANYONE UNTIL YOU HAVE SENT FOR AND RECEIVED OUR BIG FREE SPECIAL AGRICULTURAL IMPLEMENT CATALOGUE.

Kenwood Grass Seed Stripper.

$1.47

For gathering grass seed. The steel fingers strip the heads off the grass, retaining the heads in the stripper. Twenty bushels of grass or clover heads may be gathered in a day. The blades are tempered steel. The stripper is nicely painted and varnished and will last a lifetime. Weight, 4 pounds.

No. 32C1125 Grass Seed Stripper. Price........................$1.47

Acme Hay Rack Brackets and Clamps.

$1.35 and $1.40

A very convenient set of eight brackets and fittings with which anyone can build their own hay rack. No holes to bore through the upper cross pieces or sills. No. 1 is for 2x4-inch cross pieces. No. 2 is for 2x6-inch cross pieces. Weight, 20 pounds per set.

No.32C1140 No. 1 Acme Rack Brackets. Price, per set..................$1.35
No. 32C1141 No. 2 Acme Rack Brackets. Price, per set..................$1.40

Hemm's Patent Hay Rack Brackets.

$2.10 and $2.15

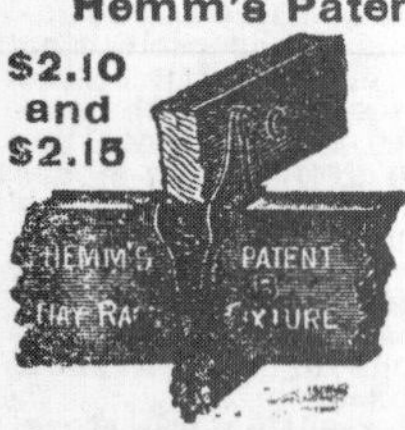

With these brackets any size or style of rack can be made. They are the only brackets with which you can make either a straight or a narrow front rack or box. They can be used with any width of sill or any width of cross bars. A set consists of 8 brackets and 24 bolts. No. 1 has bolts for 2x6-inch sills, No. 2 has bolts for 2x8-inch sills. No vertical holes to bore through the frame. Weight, 25 pounds per set. Per set

No. 32C1144 No. 1 Hemm's Rack Brackets.$2.10
No. 32C1145 No. 2 Hemm's Rack Brackets. 2.15

Kenwood Revolving Hay Rakes.

$2.95 and $3.10

Made from best quality of hardwood. Teeth are square and 45 inches long. Heads are 9 feet long. Dumps only when handles are raised. Weight, 90 pounds. Shipped knocked down from factory in Eastern Indiana. Price

No.32C1158 Revolving Rake, with 14 teeth.$2.95
No.32C1159 Revolving Rake, with 16 teeth. 3.10

Acme Hand Dump Hay Rake.

$10.80

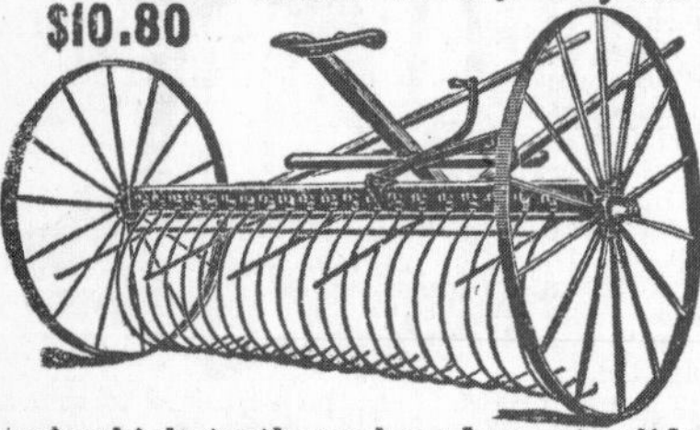

Made in one size only, 8 ft. wide with 20 teeth. Frame, thills and seat post are wood; wheels are steel and 54 inches high; teeth are shaped so as to glide under and collect the hay without scratching the ground. Dumps very easy and raises high, dropping all the hay gathered. Thills are hinged so that draft of horse assists in releasing lock lever and discharging hay. Price includes singletree. Weight, 250 pounds. Shipped knocked down from factory in Southwestern Ohio. Price,

No.32C1160 8-Foot Hand Dump Hay Rake.$10.80

Kenwood Hand and Foot Dump Hay Rakes.

$13.60 AND $14.75

The highest grade hay rake on the market. Made in two sizes: 8-foot with 20 teeth and thills for one horse, 10-foot with 25 teeth and combination pole and shafts, for one or two horses. Rake head, shafts and seat posts are made of best quality of timber. Wheels are steel, 54 inches high. Teeth are the best tempered spring steel, coiled at base and firmly held in place. Can be dumped by hand and foot, or by hand alone, or by foot alone. Operates easily on the heaviest of work. Shafts are attached and hinged so that draft assists in dumping and discharging hay. Prices include singletrees. Weights, 8-foot, 280 pounds; 10-foot, 315 pounds. Shipped knocked down from factory in Southwestern Ohio. Price,

No.32C1161 8-Ft. Foot Dump Hay Rake. $13.60
No.32C1162 10-Ft. Foot Dump Hay Rake. 14.75

$14.25 AND $16.00

Kenwood Self Dump Hay Rakes.

The best self dump hay rakes made. The head and axle and the cleaner head are made of high carbon angle steel, and the platform is made of a steel "I" beam. Wheels are steel, 54 inches high, with wide tires. Dump shields protect the ratchets. The teeth are flattened to prevent scratching the ground, are formed so as to run under the hay, and will carry a large load. These rakes have a combination hand and foot lever which works very easy. Can be dumped by foot or by hand and can be used as self dump or hand dump rakes. The 8-foot rake has 20 teeth and weighs 280 pounds. The 10-foot rake has 25 teeth and weighs 315 pounds. Both have combination pole and shafts for one or two horses. Shipped knocked down from factory in Southwestern Ohio. Price,

No. 32C1168 8-Foot Self Dump Hay Rake. $14.25
No. 32C1169 10-Foot Self Dump Hay Rake. 16.00

Kenwood Hay Carriers and Haying Tools.

Our line of hay carriers, forks, pulleys, etc., is complete in every respect and each and every article in this line is strictly high grade; in fact, the very best that can be produced.

Our hay carriers and sling carriers are made to be used with either ¾-inch or ⅞-inch manila carrier rope. They cannot be used with larger than ⅞-inch rope. They cannot be used with wire rope.

Kenwood Double Swivel Hay Carriers.

$2.90 $2.95

Absolutely the most perfect and most satisfactory hay carriers made. They reverse by swiveling and will work either way from the stop and at either end of the barn without changing the rope or any part of the carrier, and the swivel is so perfectly constructed that it holds in line with the track as firmly as a plain reversible carrier, but is easily swiveled when desired. The wood track carrier will work on ordinary dressed 4x4-inch track, and weighs 33 pounds. The steel track carrier is to run on our double angle steel track only, and weighs 30 pounds. Price includes stop and fork pulley. Carrier will work with any style fork. If carrier is to be used with wagon slings, a sling pulley will be required. The sling pulley is extra, and is not included in the price of carrier. Price

No. 32C1200 Wood Track Hay Carrier.....$2.90
No. 32C1201 Steel Track Hay Carrier..... 2.95

Kenwood Reversible Cable Hay Carrier.

$3.00

This carrier is made to run on a ½-inch wire cable or rod, adapting it especially for use with hay stacking outfits or with barn outfits where it is not desirable to place a permanent track. Price includes stop and fork pulley. Carrier will work either way and with any style of fork. If carrier is to be used with wagon slings, a sling pulley will be required. The sling pulley is extra and is not included in price of carrier. This carrier is made in the reversible pattern, as it is generally used as a carrier for a stacking outfit where a swivel carrier is not so desirable. Weight, 26 pounds. Price

No. 32C1208 Cable Hay Carrier..........$3.00

Kenwood Double Swivel Sling Carriers.

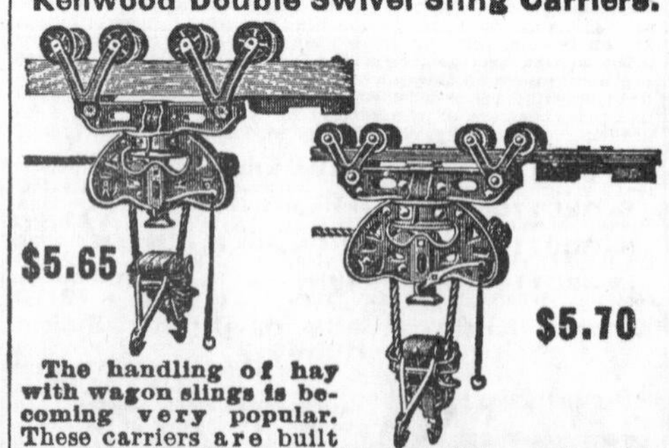

$5.65 $5.70

The handling of hay with wagon slings is becoming very popular. These carriers are built especially for this work. No special sling pulleys are required, as the carriers have sling pulleys of their own. They reverse by swiveling and will work either way from the stop and at either end of the barn without changing the rope or any part of the carrier, and the swivel is so perfectly constructed that it holds in line with the track as firmly as a plain reversible carrier, but is easily swiveled when desired. The wood track carriers will run on ordinary dressed 4x4-inch track. The steel track carrier is to run on our double angle steel track only. Slings can be locked and dumped at any height desired. Can also be used with any kind of hay forks and two forks can be used at once. Weight, 68 pounds. Price,

No. 32C1210 Wood Track Sling Carrier...$5.65
No. 32C1211 Steel Track Sling Carrier... 5.70

Kenwood Single Harpoon Hay Fork.

No. 32C1215 Single Harpoon Hay Fork. Full regular size and perfect in operation. Weight, 15 pounds. Price..............................$1.35

Kenwood Double Harpoon Hay Forks.

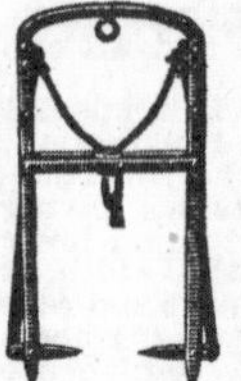

No. 32C1217 Short Tine, Double Harpoon Hay Fork, with 24-inch tines and 16 inches between points. The size and style of fork which is in general use and which we furnish in our regular hay carrier outfits. Made from best quality iron and steel. Weight, 18 pounds. Price.......................90c

No. 32C1218 Long Tine, Double Harpoon Hay Fork. Same as above, except that tines are 30 inches long, adapting this fork for use in loose straw, etc. Wt., 21 lbs. Price, $1.05

No. 32C1219 Alfalfa Double Harpoon Hay Fork. Same as above, except that it is extra heavy and the tines are 34 inches long and 24 inches between points. This fork is especially adapted for handling alfalfa, straw, etc., but can be used for any kind of hay. Weight, 30 pounds. Price...................$1.85

Kenwood Grapple Forks.

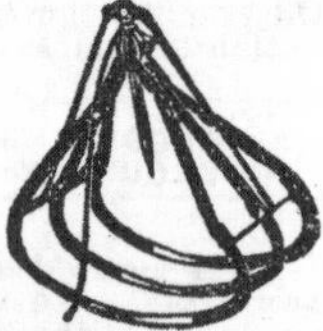

No. 32C1221 Four-Tine Grapple Fork. For ordinary use. Weight, 35 pounds. Price..$3.25

No. 32C1222 Six-Tine Grapple Fork. Same as shown in illustration. For short hay, loose straw, etc. Weight, 55 pounds. Price.......................$3.90

Kenwood Derrick Forks.

For handling straw, marsh hay, corn fodder, etc.

No. 32C1225 4-Foot Derrick Fork, with 4 tines. Weight, 50 pounds. Price......$6.45

No. 32C1226 5½-Foot Derrick Fork, with 6 tines. Weight, 70 pounds. Price..............$8.25

Kenwood Wagon Slings.

The most rapid manner of handling hay, straw, corn stalks, etc., is with wagon slings. Three slings are generally used for the load. Prices are for single slings, not for sets. Our slings are adjustable to suit any length of rack and have reliable trip locks. 4-foot slings have two ropes between the cross bars; 5-foot and 6-foot slings have four ropes. The trip rope is long enough to allow you to trip the sling easily, and there is a small rope attached to each end ring so that you can pull the ends of the sling together without difficulty. Sling pulleys or sling carriers must be used with wagon slings.

No. 32C1227 Four-Foot Wagon Sling. Weight, 18 pounds. Price, each..................$1.45
No. 32C1229 Five-Foot Wagon Sling. Weight, 22 pounds. Price, each....................$1.75
No. 32C1228 Six-Foot Wagon Sling. Weight, 25 pounds. Price, each....................$1.95

Trip Locks and Sling Irons.

To accommodate those who want to make their own wagon slings, we can furnish the trip lock only, which weighs 1 pound, or a complete set of irons for our wagon sling, consisting of 1 trip lock, 2 end rings, 1 small pulley block, 1 staple hook, 1 harness ring and 8 bolts for ends of spreader bars. Weight, 3 pounds.

No. 32C1231 Trip Lock. Price.............40c
No. 32C1232 Sling Irons. Price, per set..70c

Kenwood Sling Pulleys.

For use with our hay carriers only. Not required with sling carriers. Will lock at any place, no matter whether the sliding load be great or small. Cannot be used with sling carriers or with hay carriers of other makes. Weight, 10 pounds.

No. 32C1235 Sling Pulley. Price....................................$1.50

Kenwood Pulley Conveyor.

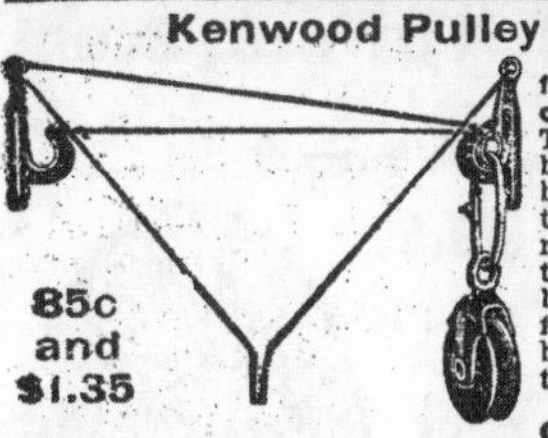

For changing hay pulley from one end of barn to the other without climbing. The conveyor consists of a bracket for each end of the barn, a loop link to carry the pulley, a wire to connect the brackets and carry the link from one end of the barn to the other, and sufficient rope for a 60-foot barn, but does not include the pulley.

85c and $1.35

No. 32C1233 Pulley Conveyor Complete. Weight, 9 pounds. Price........................$1.35

No. 32C1234 Pulley Conveyor, without rope or wire. Weight, 5 pounds. Price........................85c

Kenwood Hay Pulleys.

Our hay pulleys can be used with any manila rope up to 1 inch, but cannot be used with wire rope.

No. 32C1237 Snatch Pulley Block. To shorten travel of horse without reducing power. Horse travels only half the distance hay is carried. Rope can be thrown off and returned to load in half the time. Has iron sheave. Weight, 5 pounds. Price........................42c

No. 32C1241 Iron Yoke, Common Frame Pulley, with large, loose hollow pin and 5½-inch maple sheave. A very popular pulley. Weight, 3½ pounds. Price........................15c

No. 32C1245 Wood Yoke, Common Frame Pulley, with steel inner yoke and axle box, malleable eye and swivel, large loose hollow pin and 5-inch maple sheave. Weight, 3½ pounds. Price........................19c

No. 32C1247 Steel Yoke Knot Passing Frame Pulley, with 5½-inch maple sheave. The most popular pulley made and recommended by us as the best selection. The style of pulley we furnish with hay carrier outfits. Weight, 3½ lbs. Price........................18c

No. 32C1249 Malleable Yoke Knot Passing Frame Pulley, with large, loose, hollow pin and 5½-inch maple sheave. A very desirable pulley and the best knot passing pulley made. Weight, 4 lbs. Price, 20c

No. 32C1251 Swivel Rope Hitch. Made of malleable iron. Can be used on any manila rope up to 1 inch. Fastens anywhere. No cutting or tieing of rope necessary and no twisting. Weight, 2 pounds. Price........................12c

Kenwood Double Angle Steel Track.

No. 32C1253 For our line of hay carriers and sling carriers only. Furnished only in multiples of five feet; that is 10-foot main pieces with two 5-foot pieces to break joints. Price includes couplings and bolts, and with 30 feet or more, two end bumpers are furnished. Price does not include rafter brackets or hanging hooks. Weight, 2½ pounds per foot. Price, per foot........................8c

No. 32C1255 Rafter Bracket. For hanging hay carrier track. Can be attached with nails or screws. Weight, ½ pound. Price........................2c

No. 32C1257 Wood Track Hanging Hook, 14 inches long, under bend, for hanging wood track. Wt., 1 lb. Price, 5c

No. 32C1259 Steel Track Hanging Hook. For hanging our double angle steel track. Weight, 1½ pounds. Price........................6c

No. 32C1263 Floor Hook, ¾-inch diameter. To screw into floor or barn timbers to hold rope pulleys. Weight, 1¼ pounds. Price........................6c

Hay Carrier Sundries.

No. 32C1269 Eye Bolt. For fastening hay carrier cable to end of barn. Has long thread to take up slack. Weight, 3 pounds. Price........................20c

No. 32C1271 Long Bolt. To go through the cross of stacking outfit posts. Weight, 1 pound. Price........................4c

No. 32C1273 Clamp for ⅜-inch hay carrier cable. Weight, ¼ pound. Price........................8c

No. 32C1274 Clamp for ½-inch hay carrier cable. Weight, ⅜ pound. Price........................10c

No. 32C1276 Square Collar for ½-inch hay carrier cable. Weight, 1¼ pounds. Price........................14c

Steel Hay Carrier Cable.

Our Hay Carrier Cable is made up of seven strands of galvanized steel wire, tightly twisted together as shown in the illustration.

No. 32C1277 ⅜-inch Hay Carrier Cable, for stacking outfit end guys. Not suitable for carrier track. Weight, ⅙ pound per foot. Price, per foot........................1¼c

No. 32C1278 ½-inch Hay Carrier Cable, for cable carrier track. Weight, ½ pound per foot. Price, per foot........................2c

Manila Hay Carrier Rope.

For Hay Carrier Rope we furnish only the very best quality of long fibre white manila rope, in fact the highest grade of manila rope that is made. Second quality rope is not fit to use for hay carriers, because it will neither wear well or stand the strain.

No. 32C1281 ⅜-inch Hay Carrier Check Rope. Weight, 1-24th pound per foot. Price, per foot........................⅝c

No. 32C1282 ¾-inch Hay Carrrier Rope. Weight, 1-6th pound per foot. Price, per foot........................2¼c

No. 32C1283 ⅞-inch Hay Carrier Rope. Weight, ¼ pound per foot. Price, per foot........................3½c

Kenwood Hand Hay Press.

$24.75 **One of the greatest money making and money saving machines ever invented.** No matter how much or how little baling is done with a power press, there is always a certain amount of hay, straw, corn husks, flax-tow, hops, cotton, etc., which will go to waste unless there be some means of saving it. **Our Kenwood Hand Hay Press provides this means. It is cheap, compact, powerful, and above all, it is practical.** With it two men, or one man and a boy, can bale from one to two tons per day, turning out perfect bales of uniform size, weighing from 75 to 90 pounds per bale, depending upon the condition of the hay. Press can be operated freely in a space of about 6x14 feet. Height from floor to bottom of charging chamber is 3 feet 9 inches, charging chamber is 17x21 inches. **Makes a bale 17x21 inches by 3 feet 6 inches long.** This machine will readily pay for itself in from 6 to 8 days' time, but you must not expect it to take the place of a power press. Weight, 425 pounds. Shipped from factory in Southwestern Michigan.

No. 32C1181 Hand Hay Press. Price..$24.75

Kenwood Quarter Circle Hay Press.

$82.50 and $99.50

This press is designed to meet the requirements of the individual farmer, who may desire to bale his own hay, straw, etc., yet does not wish to purchase a more expensive power press. It is a quarter circle press; makes a plunge both going and coming; horse travels 27 feet; sweep is 12 feet long; has an adjustable feed table. Feed opening is 16 inches by 24 inches in the clear; bale chamber is 16 inches by 20 inches; plunger travels 30 inches to each stroke; length of bale can be governed to suit. This press is very easy to operate with one horse and will make bales of hay weighing from 85 to 125 pounds, depending on length of bales and condition of hay. Will bale any material such as hay, straw, clover, shredded fodder, etc. Furnished either with or without trucks. Can be used either on or off trucks. Capacity, from five to seven tons per 10 hours. Shipped knocked down from factory in Central Indiana.

No. 32C1171 Quarter Circle Hay Press, without trucks. Weight, 1,550 pounds. Price...$82.50

No. 32C1172 Quarter Circle Hay Press, with trucks, whiffletrees and neckyoke. Weight, 1,900 pounds. Price........................99.50

Kenwood Full Circle Hay Press.

$125.00 and $140.00

This hay press is made largely of steel. Such parts as are cast iron are made very heavy so that breakage is almost impossible. The plunger is 16 feet long, works forward on a 36-inch stroke, and makes two strokes to one round of the horses. When in use the trucks are removed and the press is set on the ground. The draught on the horses is very light as they are crossing the plunger and connecting rod, the hard pulling being done when the horses have a clear track. The rebound of the hay throws the plunger back and it goes back without jar.

The baling chamber is 14x18 inches and long enough so that three bales of hay may be in process at one time. The chamber is made of heavy angle steel at each corner, the balance being of heavy steel plate. The opening for feeding the hay is 30 inches long and 14 inches wide. The wheels are cast, have steel spokes and are fitted to heavy steel axles. The feed table on top of the baling chamber is large and the press is furnished with a feed fork, and is supplied with a spring folder. The power is connected to the baling chamber by an 8-inch heavy steel channel and also by a heavy steel rod. Bales can be made from 36 to 40 inches long and full weight, capacity from seven to ten tons per day. **Furnished either with or without trucks. Price includes a lifting jack.** Shipped knocked down from factory in Southeastern Minnesota.

No. 32C1178 Full Circle Hay Press, without trucks. Weight, 2,250 pounds. Price......$125.00

No. 32C1179 Full Circle Hay Press, with trucks, whiffletrees and neckyoke. Weight, 2,760 pounds. Price........................$140.00

For other hay presses, see next page.

Standard Hay Carrier Outfits. $7.65 to $15.10.

Our Complete Standard Hay Carrier Outfits are carefully made up of such articles as our extensive experience teaches us make the most desirable and satisfactory outfits. In case you wish a longer outfit or an outfit in any way different from the outfits which we list, please make up your order from the different articles previously described, giving catalogue numbers, quantity required and price of each separate item. The total price would be the same in either case. Do not attempt to add to or subtract from or change the outfits, because this might cause confusion and possible errors, either on your part or ours. However, if you want an outfit complete as listed and want additional items, then order the outfit under its catalogue number and price, and the additional items under their respective catalogue numbers and prices.

The number of brackets and hanging hooks which we furnish in the outfits places the hooks about 2½ feet apart. You can order additional brackets and hanging hooks under their catalogue numbers and prices, if you wish to place them closer together.

The amount of hay carrier rope and check rope which we furnish in the barn outfits is ample for unloading at the center of the barn, or for unloading at one end with the horse hitched at the other end, but if you wish to unload at the end of the barn and hitch the horse at the same end, you will need additional carrier rope equal in feet to the length of the barn, and additional check rope equal in feet to one-half the length of the barn. We furnish ¾-inch manila carrier rope in our standard outfits because it is abundantly strong and is more pliable than ⅞-inch rope, but ⅞-inch rope can be used.

Our Standard, Wood Track, Hay Carrier Outfit for a 30-foot barn consists of 1 double swivel wood track hay carrier, 1 short tine double harpoon hay fork, 12 rafter brackets, 12 wood track hanging hooks, 4 floor hooks, 3 steel yoke knot passing pulleys, 90 feet of ¾-inch manila hay carrier rope and 35 feet of ⅜-inch manila check rope. For each 5 feet additional length of barn we add 2 rafter brackets, 2 wood track hanging hooks, 10 feet of ¾-inch manila hay carrier rope and 5 feet ⅜-inch manila check rope.

No.	Outfit	Weight	Price
No. 32C1300	30-foot Wood Track Outfit.	Weight, 100 pounds.	$ 7.65
No. 32C1301	35-foot Wood Track Outfit.	Weight, 105 pounds.	8.05
No. 32C1302	40-foot Wood Track Outfit.	Weight, 110 pounds.	8.45
No. 32C1303	45-foot Wood Track Outfit.	Weight, 115 pounds.	8.80
No. 32C1304	50-foot Wood Track Outfit.	Weight, 120 pounds.	9.20
No. 32C1305	55-foot Wood Track Outfit.	Weight, 125 pounds.	9.60
No. 32C1306	60-foot Wood Track Outfit.	Weight, 130 pounds.	10.00

Our Standard, Steel Track, Hay Carrier Outfit for a 30-foot barn consists of 1 double swivel steel track hay carrier, 1 short tine double harpoon hay fork, 30 feet of double angle steel track complete, 12 rafter brackets, 12 steel track hanging hooks, 4 floor hooks, 3 steel yoke knot passing pulleys, 90 feet of ¾-inch manila hay carrier rope and 35 feet of ⅜-inch manila check rope. For each 5 feet additional length of barn, we add 5 feet of double angle steel track complete, 2 rafter brackets, 2 steel track hanging hooks, 10 feet of ¾-inch manila hay carrier rope and 5 feet of ⅜-inch manila check rope.

No.	Outfit	Weight	Price
No. 32C1320	30-foot Steel Track Outfit.	Weight, 175 pounds.	$10.25
No. 32C1321	35-foot Steel Track Outfit.	Weight, 193 pounds.	11.05
No. 32C1322	40-foot Steel Track Outfit.	Weight, 211 pounds.	11.85
No. 32C1323	45-foot Steel Track Outfit.	Weight, 229 pounds.	12.65
No. 32C1324	50-foot Steel Track Outfit.	Weight, 247 pounds.	13.45
No. 32C1325	55-foot Steel Track Outfit.	Weight, 265 pounds.	14.30
No. 32C1326	60-foot Steel Track Outfit.	Weight, 283 pounds.	15.10

Our Standard, Cable Track, Hay Carrier Outfit for a 30-foot barn consists of 1 reversible cable hay carrier, 1 short tine double harpoon hay fork, 30 feet of ½-inch steel hay carrier cable, 2 eye bolts, 2 ½-inch cable clamps, 4 floor hooks, 3 steel yoke knot passing pulleys, 90 feet of ¾-inch manila hay carrier rope and 35 feet of ⅜-inch manila check rope. For each 5 feet additional length of barn, we add 5 feet of ½-inch steel hay carrier cable, 10 feet of ¾-inch manila hay carrier rope and 5 feet of ⅜-inch manila check rope.

No.	Outfit	Weight	Price
No. 32C1340	30-foot Cable Track Outfit.	Weight, 100 pounds.	$8.10
No. 32C1341	35-foot Cable Track Outfit.	Weight, 105 pounds.	8.45
No. 32C1342	40-foot Cable Track Outfit.	Weight, 110 pounds.	8.80
No. 32C1343	45-foot Cable Track Outfit.	Weight, 115 pounds.	9.15
No. 32C1344	50-foot Cable Track Outfit.	Weight, 120 pounds.	9.50
No. 32C1345	55-foot Cable Track Outfit.	Weight, 125 pounds.	9.90
No. 32C1346	60-foot Cable Track Outfit.	Weight, 130 pounds.	10.25

Our Standard 40-foot Hay Stacking Outfit consists of 1 reversible cable hay carrier, 1 short tine double harpoon hay fork, 40 feet of ½-inch steel hay carrier cable, 2 ½-inch cable clamps, 2 square collars for ½-inch cable, 100 feet of ⅜-inch steel hay carrier cable (in two 50-foot pieces) for end guys, 4 ⅜-inch cable clamps, 2 long bolts for top of posts, 2 steel yoke knot passing pulleys, 80 feet of ¾-inch manila hay carrier rope and 50 feet of ⅜-inch manila check rope. For each 10 feet additional length of outfit we add 10 feet of ½-inch steel hay carrier cable, 10 feet of ¾-inch manila hay carrier rope and 10 feet of ⅜-inch manila check rope.

No.	Outfit	Weight	Price
No. 32C1355	40-foot Stacking Outfit.	Weight, 130 pounds.	$ 9.30
No. 32C1357	50-foot Stacking Outfit.	Weight, 137 pounds.	9.75
No. 32C1359	60-foot Stacking Outfit.	Weight, 144 pounds.	10.25

NOTE—Outfits more than 60 feet long are not practicable. To build longer stacks, move your end posts.

IF YOU CANNOT MAKE A SATISFACTORY SELECTION FROM THESE PAGES, DON'T THINK OF BUYING FROM ANYONE UNTIL YOU HAVE SENT FOR AND RECEIVED OUR BIG FREE SPECIAL AGRICULTURAL IMPLEMENT CATALOGUE.

Windmills, Windmill Towers, Windmill Attachments, Suburban Outfit Towers, Steel Structures for Tanks, Tanks of Every Description, etc.

A SPECIAL WINDMILL CATALOGUE MAILED FREE ON REQUEST.

Our line of this class of goods is so extensive and so complete that we have found it necessary to issue a very large special catalogue, devoted exclusively to windmills and kindred goods. This handsome and complete windmill catalogue will be sent to you free if you will write and ask us for it. We show some of the most popular sizes of back geared steel pumping windmills and angle steel windmill towers in this general catalogue, and you can make your selection from the windmills and towers we list herein, with every assurance that they will give you perfect satisfaction, or your money and the freight charges will be refunded; but if you want a larger pumping windmill, or a higher tower, or a direct stroke steel windmill, or a direct stroke wood windmill, or a steel power windmill, or a suburban outfit tower, or a steel tank structure, or in fact anything in the windmill line not shown in this general catalogue, or wish to learn more about the goods, how and of what materials they are made, **and why our windmills are better than any other windmill made, don't think of buying from anyone until you have sent for and received our big free Special Windmill Catalogue. We will save you money and furnish you with better goods than you can obtain from any other source.**

Kenwood Back Geared Galvanized Steel Pumping Windmills.

$11.50 TO $21.75

These windmills are the heaviest, strongest, best made and most handsomely finished mills on the market at the present time. The engine head is simple, strong and durable. The wind sails are very heavy, are securely attached to the wheel frame and are perfectly proportioned. The vane or tail has the strongest backbone made and it cannot blow into the wheel. **On 8-foot, 10-foot and 12-foot windmills the turntable is ball bearing and the wheel is provided with a ball bearing end thrust.** Every bolt in our windmills has two nuts, others have only one. A perfect self governing windmill, safe and reliable. **The ends of the sails and the vane are tipped with red** and the entire windmill is handsome and strong in every detail. Price includes pump pole, pull-out wire and a perfect pull-out reefing gear. When a pumping windmill is ordered without a steel tower, it is regularly furnished with fittings for a wood tower, but, instead of the wood tower fittings, if so ordered, we will furnish a set of mast fittings. With proper pump cylinder the 4-foot windmill is suitable for a 35-foot well, the 6-foot windmill for a 75-foot well, the 8-foot windmill for a 125-foot well and the 10-foot windmill for a 200-foot well, but either size will pump as much or more water than any other windmill of same size with the same cylinder and depth of well. Shipped knocked down from factory in Northeastern Indiana.

No. 32C4000 4-Foot Back Geared Steel Pumping Windmill. Weight, 280 pounds. Price........**$11.50**

No. 32C4001 6-Foot Back Geared Steel Pumping Windmill. Weight, 350 pounds. Price........**$12.95**

No. 32C4002 8-Foot Back Geared Steel Pumping Windmill. Weight, 450 pounds. Price........**$16.75**

No. 32C4003 10-Foot Back Geared Steel Pumping Windmill. Weight, 575 pounds. Price........**$21.75**

Kenwood Direct Stroke Wood Windmill.

$15.50 AND $19.50

This is a very strong and powerful windmill. The engine head is exactly like that of our direct stroke steel pumping windmills. The wheel and vane are made of wood and the ends of the sails and the vane are tipped with red, making it a very handsome windmill. Price includes pump pole, pull-out wire, and our improved reefing gear. Can be used on our steel windmill towers. When a steel tower is not ordered with this windmill we regularly furnish it with fittings for wood tower, but will furnish with mast fittings if so ordered. Shipped knocked down from Northeastern Indiana.

No. 32C4023 8-Ft. Direct Stroke Wood Pumping Windmill. Weight, 380 pounds. Price........**$15.50**

No. 32C4024 10-Ft. Direct Stroke Wood Pumping Windmill. Weight, 450 pounds. Price........**19.50**

Kenwood Galvanized Angle Steel Windmill Towers.

$10.50 to $27.00.

Our steel windmill towers are built very strong, are banded and braced in a most thorough manner, and are the easiest towers made to put together and erect, and the most staunch after they are up. We make both 3-post and 4-post towers in 20, 30, 40, 50 and 60-foot heights but show in this catalogue only the most popular sizes. Price is for tower complete with platform, anchor posts and anchor plates. Height is above the anchor posts. The corner posts are made in 10-foot lengths, making them easy to handle and strengthening the tower at each joint. Shipped knocked down from factory in Northeastern Indiana.

No. 1 Three-Post Windmill Towers, for 4-ft., 6-ft. and 8-ft. Windmills.

No.	Description	Weight	Price
No. 32C4131	20-Ft. No. 1 Three-Post Windmill Tower	280 lbs.	$10.50
No. 32C4132	30-Ft. No. 1 Three-Post Windmill Tower	400 lbs.	15.75
No. 32C4133	40-Ft. No. 1 Three-Post Windmill Tower	535 lbs.	21.00

No. 2 Three-Post Windmill Towers, for 8-ft. and 10-ft. Windmills.

No.	Description	Weight	Price
No. 32C4143	20-Ft. No. 2 Three-Post Windmill Tower	295 lbs.	$11.90
No. 32C4144	30-Ft. No. 2 Three-Post Windmill Tower	430 lbs.	17.85
No. 32C4145	40-Ft. No. 2 Three-Post Windmill Tower	595 lbs.	23.80

No. 1 Four-Post Windmill Towers, for 4-ft., 6-ft. and 8-ft. Windmills.

No.	Description	Weight	Price
No. 32C4168	20-Ft. No. 1 Four-Post Windmill Tower	335 lbs.	$12.30
No. 32C4170	30-Ft. No. 1 Four-Post Windmill Tower	470 lbs.	18.45
No. 32C4172	40-Ft. No. 1 Four-Post Windmill Tower	630 lbs.	24.60

No. 2 Four-Post Windmill Towers, for 8-ft. and 10-ft. Windmills.

No.	Description	Weight	Price
No. 32C4194	20-Ft. No. 2 Four-Post Windmill Tower	375 lbs.	$13.50
No. 32C4196	30-Ft. No. 2 Four-Post Windmill Tower	545 lbs.	20.25
No. 32C4198	40-Ft. No. 2 Four-Post Windmill Tower	700 lbs.	27.00

Peerless Windmill Regulator.

$2.45

The best regulator made. Can be attached to any make of wood or steel windmill. Takes full charge of the windmill. Weight crated, 44 lbs.

No. 32C1500 Windmill Regulator. Price, $2.45

Kenwood Geared Power Hay Press.

$180.00 and $195.00

Absolutely the best power hay press made. The illustration shows the No. 4 press fitted to be run by the tumbling rod of a sweep horse power. The No. 3 press is fitted to be run by belt or engine power and does not have the jack shaft. This press is driven by two pinions and two large gears in connection with four sprocket wheels with heavy link belting. The crank pin in making a complete revolution of the sprocket wheels never gets further than 4½ inches from the center, thus developing tremendous power. It takes about 15 to 20 strokes of the plunger to make one bale of hay weighing from 100 to 110 pounds. The truck wheels are steel. The chamber is lined with steel. The baling chamber is 14x18 inches and the press will make a bale from 36 to 40 inches long. The No. 3 press is fitted with a 16x8-inch pulley. The main shaft of the No. 4 press makes two revolutions to each revolution of the jack shaft, and the jack shaft is fitted with a slip coupling. The capacity is from 2 to 3 tons per hour with 8 to 10-horse power. Weight, 4,500 pounds. Shipped set up on flat car from factory in Southeastern Minnesota.

No. 32C1175 No. 3 Engine Power Hay Press. Price........**$180.00**

No. 32C1176 No. 4 Horse Power Hay Press. Price........**195.00**

For other hay presses, see preceding page.

KENWOOD GALVANIZED STEEL TANKS.

GENERAL DESCRIPTION—All of our Galvanized Steel Tanks are guaranteed to be made of the best quality of standard No. 20-gauge galvanized sheet steel or heavier. The tops are bound with angle steel. Bottoms of all tanks over 1 foot in height, except house tanks, are secured between two pieces of flat steel, or between a piece of angle steel and a piece of flat steel, this depending upon the size of the tank. Sides are firmly braced, when size and shape require it, with angle steel bars. Round end, square end and oval tanks over 5 feet long and the larger sizes of round storage tanks have angle steel bars across the top, the number of these bars being governed by the length or size of the tank. This construction and the fact that **we do not use light weight or under gauge steel,** makes our steel tanks the strongest, best made and most durable tanks on the market, and they are warranted not to leak or break down.

A tank made of No. 18-gauge steel will cost one-fifth more, or a tank made of No. 16-gauge steel will cost two-fifths more than the prices on tanks made of No. 20-gauge steel, or a tank made of No. 16-gauge steel will cost one-sixth more than the prices on tanks made of No. 18-gauge steel, and weights will increase in about one-half of this proportion.

We will not cut pipe connection holes in steel tanks. These holes you can easily cut for yourself exactly where you want them by using a cold chisel and cutting against the end of a block of hardwood. We cannot, under any circumstances, accept the return of steel tanks in which holes have been cut. Pipe connections, consisting of 1 close nipple, 2 leather washers, 2 lock nuts and 1 pipe cap will be furnished at the following prices: ¾-inch 20c; 1-inch, 25c; 1¼-inch, 30c; 1½-inch, 50c; 2-inch, 70c.

When tanks are shipped knocked down, all holes are punched, every part is fitted together at the factory and sufficient solder and rivets are sent with which to put the tank together. Capacities shown in barrels are based on 31½ gallons to the barrel.

☞ **Certain tanks which are regularly shipped set up, can and will be shipped knocked down if so ordered,** and when such tanks weigh much over 200 pounds and are to be shipped over 500 miles or when any size of such tanks which weigh 125 pounds or more are to be shipped over 1,000 miles, we advise you to order them knocked down, because you will then save in freight charges more than it should cost you to put the tank together.

Kenwood Galvanized Steel Round Tanks.

$4.65 to $12.25

Made of No. 20-gauge steel. Always shipped set up unless otherwise ordered. As stated in general description (see ☞), these tanks can and will be shipped knocked down when so ordered. Shipped from factory in Southwestern Michigan.

Catalogue No.	Size No.	Diam. feet	Height, feet	Capacity, bbls.	Weight, lbs.	Price
32C1523	1	4	2	6	90	$4.65
32C1524	2	4	2½	7	100	5.25
32C1525	3	4	3	9	110	5.70
32C1526	4	4	4	12	135	6.50
32C1527	5	5	2	9½	115	5.80
32C1528	6	5	2½	12	125	7.00
32C1529	7	5	3	14	140	7.75
32C1530	8	5	4	19	170	9.50
32C1533	9	6	2	14	160	8.25
32C1534	10	6	2½	17	170	9.55
32C1535	11	6	3	20	190	10.00
32C1536	12	6	4	27	230	12.25

Kenwood Galvanized Steel Round End Tanks.

$2.65 to $12.05

Made of No. 20-gauge steel. Always shipped set up unless otherwise ordered. As stated in general description, (see ☞), these tanks can and will be shipped knocked down when so ordered. In figuring the capacities no allowance has been made for the round corners, therefore these tanks will not hold quite as much as the table shows. Shipped from factory in Southwestern Michigan.

Catalogue No.	Size No.	Lgth., feet	Width, feet	Hght., feet	Capacity, bbls.	Wt., lbs.	Price
32C1547	C17	4	2	1	1½	50	$2.65
32C1548	C18	6	2	1	2½	60	3.90
32C1549	C19	8	2	1	3½	85	4.95
32C1551	C12	4	2	2	3¾	80	3.65
32C1553	B13	6	2	2	5¾	110	5.20
32C1554	13	8	2	2	7½	125	5.85
32C1555	14	8	2	2½	9½	135	6.00
32C1556	15	8	2¼	2	9½	135	6.05
32C1557	16	8	2½	2½	12	150	6.55
32C1558	17	8	3	2	12	145	6.60
32C1559	18	8	3	2½	14	165	7.80
32C1560	19	8	4	2	15	155	8.30
32C1561	20	8	4	2½	17	175	9.60
32C1564	22	10	3	2	14	165	7.85
32C1565	23	10	3	2½	18	190	9.75
32C1567	25	10	4	2	19	215	10.05
32C1568	26	10	4	2½	24	235	12.05

IF YOU CANNOT MAKE A SATISFACTORY SELECTION FROM THESE PAGES, DON'T THINK OF BUYING FROM ANYONE UNTIL YOU HAVE SENT FOR AND RECEIVED OUR BIG FREE SPECIAL AGRICULTURAL IMPLEMENT CATALOGUE.

Kenwood Galvanized Steel Square End Tanks.

$2.60 to $6.10

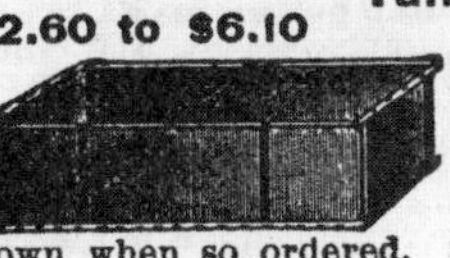

Made of No. 20-gauge steel. Always shipped set up unless otherwise ordered. As stated in general description (see 49), these tanks can and will be shipped knocked down when so ordered. Shipped from factory in Southwestern Michigan.

Catalogue No.	Size No.	Lgth., feet	Width, feet	Hgt., feet	Capy., bbls.	Wt., lbs.	Price
32C1600	45	4	2	1	2	50	$2.60
32C1597	04	6	2	1	2¾	60	3.75
32C1598	05	8	2	1	3¾	85	4.45
32C1601	46	4	2	2	4	80	3.90
32C1602	47	6	2	2	6	95	5.15
32C1603	28	8	2	2	7½	110	6.10

Kenwood Galvanized Steel Round Storage Tanks.

$12.10 to $38.15

All made of No. 20-gauge steel, except sizes A8 and A12 which are made of No. 18-gauge steel. These tanks are always shipped knocked down. They cannot be shipped set up because they are too large to go into the door of a freight car. Shipped from factory in Southwestern Michigan.

Catalogue No.	Size No.	Diam., feet	Height, feet	Capacity, Barrels	Weight, pounds	Price
32C1636	A23	6	6	39⅓	330	$17.20
32C1637	A 8	6	8	53⅓	360	25.30
32C1638	A27	8	2	24	240	12.10
32C1639	A28	8	2½	30	260	14.20
32C1640	A24	8	5	60	390	22.00
32C1641	A25	8	6	71⅓	450	26.00
32C1642	A12	8	8	95	520	38.15

Kenwood Galvanized Steel Oval Tanks.

$3.25 to $10.95

Made of No. 20-gauge steel. Always shipped set up. Cannot be shipped knocked down. Largest sizes have supporting truss in the center as well as at each end. Shipped from factory in Southwestern Michigan.

Catalogue No.	Size No.	Length, feet	Width, feet	Depth, inches	Capac'y Barrels	Weight, pounds	Price
32C1660	68	8	1⅓	14	4	90	$4.15
32C1661	67	8	2	12	4	90	4.20
32C1662	63	8	2	20	6	130	5.90
32C1663	62	8	2⅛	18	6	130	5.95
32C1667	64	10	1⅓	8	2	60	3.25
32C1668	66	10	1⅓	14	5	100	4.70
32C1669	65	10	2	12	5	100	4.75
32C1671	60	10	2⅛	18	8	150	7.10
32C1672	70	10	3	24	13	175	8.45
32C1674	73	10	4	24	20	200	10.95

Kenwood Galvanized Steel Dipping Tanks.

Made of No. 20-gauge steel. **Always shipped set up,** because shape of tank makes it difficult to put together. The incline of our dipping tanks allows sheep to walk out easily. All sizes are 2 feet wide at top and 1 foot wide at bottom, and are furnished with end ladder. Shipped from factory in Southwestern Michigan.

$6.40 to $12.30

Catalogue No.	Size No.	Length, Top	Length, Bottom	Height, feet	Weight, pounds	Price
32C1690	B1	6 feet	3 feet	3	120	$6.40
32C1691	B2	8 feet	5 feet	3	155	8.45
32C1692	B3	8 feet	4 feet	4	190	9.95
32C1694	B6	10 feet	6 feet	4	230	12.30

Kenwood Galvanized Steel Wagon Tanks.

$6.75 to $12.75

Made of No. 20-gauge steel. Always shipped set up. Cannot be shipped knocked down. Made with water tight top, having 14-inch round manhole. Has 1-inch pipe connection near bottom in rear end. Can be used on any wagon by laying boards on the wagon gear. Capacity is not quite as much as shown in table, as no allowance has been made for round corners. Shipped from factory in Southwestern Michigan.

Catalogue No.	Size No.	Length, feet	Width, feet	Height, feet	Capacity, Barrels	Wgt. lbs.	Price
32C1700	E1	6	2	2	5⅓	120	$6.75
32C1701	E2	8	2	2	7⅓	155	8.10
32C1702	E3	8	2½	2	9⅓	170	9.70
32C1703	E4	8	3	2	12	190	11.35
32C1704	E5	10	3	2	14	235	12.75

Kenwood Galvanized Steel Hog Troughs.

$1.45 to $2.75

Made of No. 20-gauge steel. **Always shipped set up.** Cannot be shipped knocked down. Ends are cast iron having flat bottoms with a hole at each corner so that trough can be bolted down. Cross bars are about 12 inches apart. Shipped from factory in Southwestern Michigan.

Catalogue No.	Size No.	Length, feet	Width, in.	Depth, in.	Weight, lbs.	Price
32C1720	H1	4	14	8	34	$1.45
32C1721	H2	6	14	8	43	1.85
32C1722	H3	8	14	8	52	2.25
32C1723	H4	10	14	8	61	2.75

Kenwood Galvanized Steel Thresher Tanks.

$18.00 to $22.00

Made of No. 20-gauge steel. The construction of these tanks makes them exceedingly strong and durable. Fuel box is large and its bottom is lined with 1-inch plank. Rear end of top has a 14-inch round manhole which has a tight fitting cover. These tanks have 1-inch feed pipe connection in the bottom between the trusses. They will fit a 38-inch bolster or we will bolt a piece of 2x4-inch lumber to each side of each truss to make tank fit a 42-inch bolster. **Price of tank does not include truck.** Shipped set up from factory in Northern Indiana.

Catalogue No.	Size No.	Length, feet	Width, in.	Height, feet	Capacity, Barrels	Wgt. lbs.	Price
32C1705	8	8	38	2	9⅓	350	$18.00
32C1706	10	10	38	2	12	375	20.00
32C1707	12	10	38	2⅓	15	400	22.00

Cast Iron Feed Troughs.

Very strong and durable. Will stand firmly on the ground. All sizes are 12 inches wide inside and 4¾ inches deep. The 3-foot trough has one, the 4-foot trough has two and the 5-foot trough has three wrought iron cross bars cast into them across the top, to strengthen them and separate the animals.

$1.10 to $2.60

No. 32C1726 **2-Foot Cast Iron Feed Trough.** Weight, 44 pounds. Price........ $1.10
No. 32C1727 **3-Foot Cast Iron Feed Trough.** Weight, 55 pounds. Price........ $1.65
No. 32C1728 **4-Foot Cast Iron Feed Trough.** Weight, 79 pounds........ $2.10
No. 32C1729 **5-Foot Cast Iron Feed Trough.** Weight, 88 pounds........ $2.60

No. 1 Kenwood Stock Waterer.

$1.10

Operated by a simple automatic float, connected to a rustproof valve, which is protected by the partition. Pan and nipple are cast solid and cannot leak. Partitions and lid are cast in one piece, so that waterer can be cleaned without taking apart. Nipple has outside thread to screw into barrel, and is also tapped for a ¾-inch iron pipe. Each end of trough holds about one gallon. Weight, 16 pounds.

No. 32C1775 **No. 1 Stock Waterer. Price. $1.10**

No. 2 Kenwood Stock Waterer.

$1.15

The best and most satisfactory automatic stock waterer on the market. It is operated by a metal ball float, connected to a rust proof valve which closes on a rubber valve seat. As soon as pan fills up to near the top, the float shuts the water off. Float chamber is inside the barrel or tank, out of all mud and dirt. Requires a 2-inch hole for stem of float chamber to pass through and is easily attached. Inlet is tapped so that it can be connected to ¾-inch iron pipe. Weight, 11 pounds.

No. 32C1777 **No. 2 Stock Waterer. Price, $1.15**

Peerless Tank Heaters.

$2.40 to $3.05

The best tank heaters made. The heater is 24 inches high, made with No. 20 gauge galvanized steel sides and bottom and with a swinging cast iron top in which there is an air damper. **The sides are double riveted in fireproof cement and the bottom is soldered. Every heater is warranted not to leak.** The heater is 16 inches in diameter and can be furnished with hinged grate or basket grate. It is also made with an improved heat deflector which directs the heat against the sides of the heater, doubling its efficiency and making it far more economical. **Prices are for the heaters complete with shovel, poker, holding down rods and one joint of 5-inch galvanized pipe with damper, spark arrester and hood.** Shipped from factory in Southwestern Michigan.

Plain Tank Heaters.		Wt. lbs.	Price
No. 32C1810	No. 1 with hinged grate.	47	$2.40
No. 32C1812	No. 1 with basket grate.	51	2.60
Tank Heaters with Deflectors.		**Wt. lbs.**	**Price**
No. 32C1814	No. 1 with hinged grate.	57	$2.85
No. 32C1816	No. 1 with basket grate.	61	3.05

Kenwood Agricultural Boilers.

$9.00 to $12.75

These Boilers or Furnaces and Kettles are exceedingly popular among both farmers and butchers. They are made of cast iron throughout, have very smooth kettles and can be used for rendering lard, cooking food for stock, or other similar purposes. Price is for furnace and kettle complete with elbow, but does not include pipe. **Boilers for coal have fire brick lining in furnace.** Shipped from factory in Central Ohio.

No. 32C1820 30-Gallon Boiler, for wood. Weight, 275 pounds. Price........ $9.00
No. 32C1821 30-Gallon Boiler, for coal and wood. Weight, 310 pounds. Price........ $10.50
No. 32C1822 45-Gallon Boiler, for wood. Weight, 355 pounds. Price........ $11.25
No. 32C1823 45-Gallon Boiler, for coal and wood. Weight, 410 pounds. Price........ $12.75

Kenwood Food Cookers.

Can be used to cook food for stock or to heat water. The boilers are made of heavy galvanized sheet steel. Illustration shows 100-gallon size with double hinged cover. The 35 and 50-gallon sizes have single hinged cover, and the 20-gallon size has single cover to lift off. The body of the fire box is heavy sheet steel, the ends, door, hearth, etc., are cast iron. All sizes have elbow for 6-inch stove pipe, but price does not include pipe. Nos. 1, 2, 6 and 7 burn wood only, Nos. 3, 4 and 5 burn either wood or coal. Shipped crated from factory in Western Illinois.

$4.35 to $11.60

Catalogue No.	Size No.	Cap. gals.	Total Ht., in.	L'gth in.	Size of Boiler Width in.	Size of Boiler Depth in.	Wt. lbs.	Price
32C1825	1	20	29	24	17	13	60	$4.35
32C1826	2	35	31	30	20	15	70	5.95
32C1827	3	35	31	30	24	15	120	7.00
32C1828	4	50	39	30	24	18	130	9.15
32C1829	5	100	41	48	26	20	170	11.60
32C1830	6	50	39	30	24	18	95	7.60
32C1831	7	100	41	48	26	20	135	9.95

Handy Food Cookers.

$9.00 TO $12.35

The most convenient and desirable steel boiler food cooker made. The boiler is made entirely of heavy galvanized sheet steel, strongly bound at top and bottom and has a close fitting hinged cover. The fire box, fire flue and grate are cast iron. These cookers will burn wood, coal or cobs. Can be used for cooking feed, boiling water and for many other purposes. Price is for cooker complete with elbow and one joint of 6-inch stove pipe. Shipped from factory in Southwestern Michigan.

Catalogue No.	Size No.	Cap. gal.	Total Ht. in.	L'gth in.	Size of Boiler Width in.	Size of Boiler Depth in.	Wt. lbs.	Price
32C1841	3	60	27	48	24	12	200	$9.00
32C1842	2	90	33	48	24	18	215	9.60
32C1843	1	115	33	60	24	18	250	10.75
32C1844	0	160	33	72	28	18	300	12.35

Acme Food Cooker and Steamer.

$22.25

Made of heavy plate steel with heavy cast iron heads. The fire box extends the entire length of boiler, which is 40 inches long. The boiler, which is directly over the fire box, extends downward on each side to the bottom of the fire box, giving great heating surface. Will burn wood, cobs or coal. Price is for the steamer complete, with hand pump, safety weight, water cocks, three pieces of iron pipe with fittings, two valves, 2 feet of hose and elbow for 6-inch smoke pipe, but does not include smoke pipe. Weight, 435 pounds. Shipped from factory in Eastern Iowa.

No. 32C1868 **Cooker and Steamer.** Price........ $22.25

OUR SPECIAL FREE IMPLEMENT CATALOGUE

shows this entire line of goods by means of larger illustrations and more complete descriptions.

IF YOU CANNOT MAKE A SATISFACTORY SELECTION FROM THESE PAGES, DON'T THINK OF BUYING FROM ANYONE UNTIL YOU HAVE SENT FOR AND RECEIVED OUR BIG FREE SPECIAL AGRICULTURAL IMPLEMENT CATALOGUE.

Farmers' Friend Food Cookers.

$5.40 to $11.40

These cookers are constructed so as to give the best possible results from the very smallest amount of fuel. The jacket or casing is heavy cold rolled steel plate supported at the bottom by a heavy wrought iron band. The kettle is made of fine grained charcoal cast iron and is very smooth inside. The rim of the kettle rests on top of the jacket and the kettle can be easily removed. There are no legs and no bottom to this cooker. It is intended to set on the ground wherever it is most convenient to use it. For indoor use, it should be set on a base made of brick and sand. Can be used for cooking food, rendering lard or for any other purpose where an ordinary kettle can be used. The kettle, however, is not ground and polished, Prices are for the cooker for burning wood, complete with elbow, damper and one joint of 6-inch pipe. Coal grates and wood hinged covers are extra. Shipped from factory in Southern Michigan.

Catalogue No.	Size No.	Cap., gal.	H'ght in.	Inside Kettle Diam. in.	Depth in.	Wt. lbs.	Price
32C1851	2	22	26	23	15	125	$ 5.40
32C1852	3	30	28	27	16	200	6.70
32C1853	4	40	28	29	18½	235	7.90
32C1854	5	55	30	32	21	275	9.00
32C1855	6	65	28	34	21	300	10.20
32C1856	7	75	32	36	22	375	11.40
32C1857	Coal grate. Weight, 50 lbs.						1.85
32C1858	Wood Hinged Cover. Weight, 15 lbs.						.35

Hercules Boiler and Steam Food Cooker.

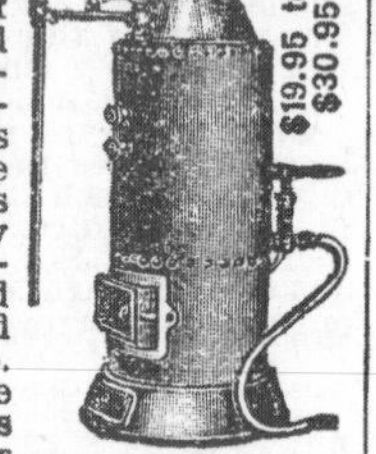

$19.95 to $30.95

Made of boiler plate steel which has a tensile strength of 60,000 pounds, hand riveted and tested to 100 pounds water pressure. Has regular 2-inch lap-welded boiler flues which pass through the water and give large heating surface. The fire door is large and the grate will burn any kind of fuel. Can be used for cooking or steaming any kind of food for stock in a barrel or vat, and for many other purposes. The No. 3 size has a water leg around the fire box and is tested at 150 pounds water pressure. Price is for boiler complete with hand pump, safety valve, two gauge cocks, two valves, 2 feet of hose and with regular amount of iron pipe and fittings. Is fitted for 8-inch smoke stack, but stack is not furnished with boiler. Shipped from factory in Western Michigan.

Catalogue No.	Size No.	Total Height	Size of Shell, Diam.	Height	No. of Flues	Weight lbs.	Price
32C1870	1	54 in.	19 in.	40 in.	9	360	$19.95
32C1871	2	58 in.	19 in.	44 in.	13	430	21.25
32C1872	3	58 in.	19 in.	44 in.	13	450	30.95

Model Stone Boat.

$2.75

This Stone Boat is made of a good quality of 2-inch oak and hard maple. Bottom planks and side pieces are sawed to shape from the log. The side pieces and wide end pieces are firmly bolted to the bottom. Length, 7 feet. Width, about 28 inches. Weight, 150 pounds. Shipped from factory in Southwestern Wisconsin.

No. 32C1910 Stone Boat. Price..........$2.75

Kenwood Pressed Bowl Steel Road Scrapers.

$3.45 to $4.95

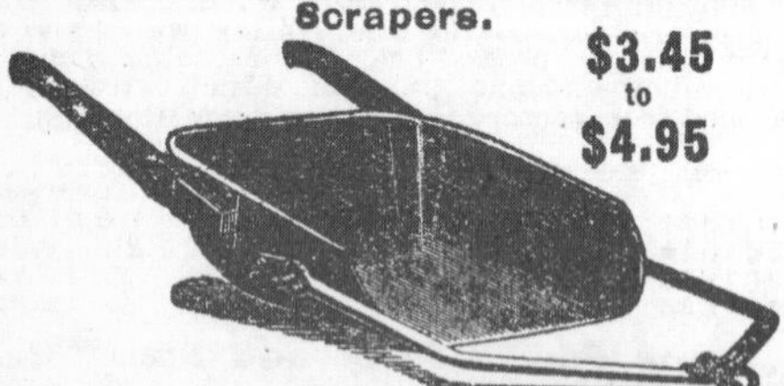

The bowl of these scrapers is pressed from a single sheet of heavy specially hardened steel plate, making a round cornered and perfectly formed bowl, which scours and cleans easily. **Absolutely the best and most substantial scraper on the market. Made of the highest grade of high carbon scraper steel and worth double the price of the low grade tank steel scrapers which are made to meet our prices.** Made in three sizes. No. 3 holds 3½ cubic feet and weighs 80 pounds. No. 2 holds 5 cubic feet and weighs 90 pounds. No. 1 holds 7 cubic feet and weighs 100 pounds. Smooth bottom scrapers do not have runners on the bottom. Double runner scrapers have two steel runners each about 1½ inches wide and ⅜ inch thick. Broad runner scrapers have a broad single runner made of a single heavy steel plate. Shipped from factory in Western Ohio.

		Price
No. 32C1950	No. 3 Scraper. Smooth bottom.	$3.45
No. 32C1951	No. 2 Scraper. Smooth bottom.	3.65
No. 32C1952	No. 1 Scraper. Smooth bottom.	3.95
No. 32C1953	No. 3 Scraper. Double runner.	3.70
No. 32C1954	No. 2 Scraper. Double runner.	3.90
No. 32C1955	No. 1 Scraper. Double runner.	4.20
No. 32C1956	No. 3 Scraper. Single runner..	4.30
No. 32C1957	No. 2 Scraper. Single runner..	4.60
No. 32C1958	No. 1 Scraper. Single runner..	4.95

Genuine Smith's Tree and Stump Pullers.

$14.25 to $55.40

The Smith Stump Pullers are the strongest, simplest and most durable stump pullers made. They embody every conceivable improvement, and when used according to the directions furnished, will do all and more than we claim for them. The illustration shows the No. 2 size, anchored with a 6-foot anchor loop. The larger sizes are supplied with a 25-foot anchor rope for anchoring to a tree or close to a stump. No sweeps or lead poles are furnished, as purchaser can cut these in the timber and thus save freight and cost of same. Pull ropes have hook and coupling attached. **The stump puller rope which we use is made from the best quality of selected steel wire.** It is especially adapted to this class of work, owing to its great strength and flexibility, and when used according to the instructions which we furnish, will outwear two ropes such as are ordinarily furnished with stump pullers. When this rope is used in accordance with our instructions, we guarantee it in every particular, but there is no steel rope made and none can be made, which will not break if it is allowed to kink or if it is bent around a very short turn, because this throws all the strain upon a very few strands of the rope. The rope furnished is abundantly heavy for all ordinary work, but it is always desirable to use either a snatch pulley or a pulley block of some kind, because it makes the work easier and increases the power and life of the rope and the machine. Size of stump which machines will pull depends upon the kind of timber and the condition of the soil, and upon the operator following the instructions which are sent with each machine. Shipped knocked down from the factory in Southeastern Minnesota.

No. 32C1915 No. 1 Smith's Stump Puller. Suitable for use by hand or for one horse on an 8-foot sweep. Furnished with a 5-foot anchor loop and 45 feet of ⅝-inch best steel pull rope. Weight, 150 lbs. Price, $14.25

No. 32C1916 No. 2 Smith's Stump Puller. Suitable for either one or two horses on a 12-foot sweep. Furnished with a 6-foot anchor loop and 50 feet of ¾-inch best steel pull rope. Will pull 12-inch stumps. Weight, 275 pounds. Price..........$24.00

No. 32C1917 No. 3 Smith's Stump Puller. Suitable for one or two horses on a 14-foot sweep. Furnished with a 25-foot anchor rope and 50 feet of ¾-inch best steel pull rope. Will pull 15-inch stumps. Weight, 400 pounds. Price..........$33.60

No. 32C1918 No. 4 Smith's Stump Puller. Suitable for one or two horses on a 16-foot sweep. Furnished with a 25-foot anchor rope and 75 feet of ¾-inch best steel pull rope. Will pull 30-inch stumps. Weight, 500 pounds. Price..........$38.70

No. 32C1919 No. 11 Smith's Stump Puller. Suitable for one or two horses on a 20-foot sweep. The strongest machine made. Furnished with a 25-foot anchor rope and 75 feet of ¾-inch best steel pull rope. Will pull 48-inch stumps. Weight, 800 pounds. Price..........$55.40

No. 32C1928 Combination Snatch Blocks. Increases the power four times. The hitch rope is 12 feet long. This attachment is a valuable aid in pulling large stumps and trees. Weight, 80 pounds. Price..........$10.80

No. 32C1929 Single Pulley Block, with 10-foot hitch rope. Weight, 50 pounds. Price..........$7.20

No. 32C1930 Patent Stump Puller Snatch Block. A great assistance in the pulling of large trees and stumps. Complete with 15-foot hitch rope. Weight, 73 pounds. Price..$13.55

No. 32C1932 Patent Low Stump and Root Hook. Length, 3 feet; depth of beam, 4 inches. Weight, 70 pounds. Price..........$9.60

No. 32C1933 Patent Rope Shortener, complete with hitch rope. Should always be used to shorten pull rope. Weight, 46 pounds. Price $4.95

No. 32C1934 Double Pointed Wrought Steel Root Hook. Weight, 40 pounds. Price..........$6.65

Kenwood Tongue Scraper and Ditcher.

$4.70

Adapted for cutting and cleaning out ditches and moving large quantities of earth rapidly. The draw bars and bit are made of best quality steel. Body, tongue, cross bar and handles are made of well seasoned hardwood lumber, well ironed and bolted. Width, 48 inches. Weight, 135 pounds. Shipped from factory in Western Ohio.

No. 32C1964 Tongue Scraper. Price......$4.70

Kenwood Wheeled Scrapers.

$25.50 to $35.25

The bowl or box is made from a single sheet of the highest grade of high carbon scraper steel, 3/16-inch thick and is shaped so as to give the greatest amount of strength and carrying capacity. Cannot sag under the most severe strain. Hound hooks are stationary, very heavy, well braced and strongly riveted, they carry the bowl high up from the ground. Axle is high, and of best quality square steel. Spindles are turned and polished and fully protected by close fitting sand bands. Made in three sizes: **No. 1** has 3x¼-inch wheel tires and 1⅛-inch axle. The other sizes have 3x5/16-inch wheel tires and 1¼-inch axles. Price is for scrapers with heavy wood hub wheels, and does not include doubletrees and neckyoke. Shipped knocked down from factory in Western Ohio.

Catalogue No.	Size No.	Capacity	Wheels	Weight	Price
32C1966	1	9 cu. ft.	36 in.	450 lbs.	$25.50
32C1967	2	13 cu. ft.	40 in.	600 lbs.	30.50
32C1968	3	17 cu. ft.	44 in.	750 lbs.	35.25

Fulton One-Horse Sweep Power.

$17.75

A good, strong external geared one-horse sweep power, speeded at 25 revolutions to one round of the horse. Furnished complete with two tumbling rods, one slip coupling, two safety couplings, two rod rests, one sweep and one lead pole. Shaft is squared for 1-inch couplings. Shipped knocked down from factory in Southeastern Wisconsin.

No. 32C2014 Fulton One-Horse Power. Weight, 500 pounds. Price..........$17.75

Acme Sweep Horse Powers.

$21.20 TO $43.50

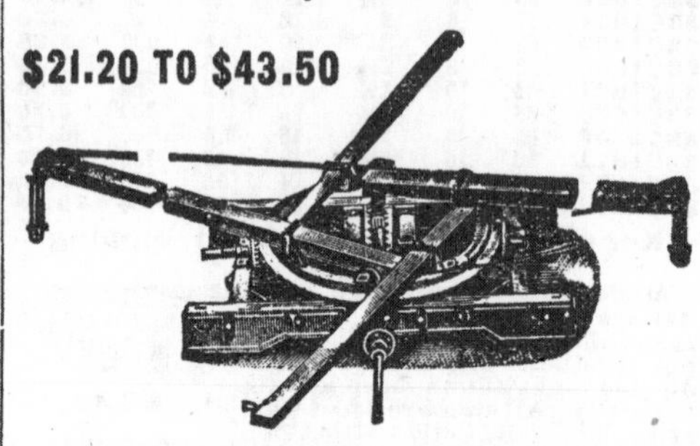

There are no Horse Powers Made at Any Price which are Better Than These Powers.

Made from the original patterns for this style of powers from which all others are copied. These powers are both high and low speed powers and are adapted for all classes of work. A high speed shaft extends from each side of the power, one shaft running with and the other against the horses. The low speed shaft is at one end of the power. The illustration shows the 4-horse power and the general construction of the 6-horse and 8-horse powers. The 2-horse power is of slightly different construction, but is built on the same general principles. Each power is furnished complete with sweeps, two tumbling rods, three couplings, one rod block, one platform and a coil spring draft hitch for each sweep.

The 2-horse power has two sweeps and two lead poles. The tumbling rod is squared for 1-inch couplings. The high speed shafts make 32 and the low speed shaft makes 10 revolutions to one round of the horses and the power weighs 750 pounds.

The 4-horse power has two sweeps and two lead poles. The high speed shafts make 56 and the low speed shaft makes 10¾ revolutions to one round of the horses. The tumbling rod is squared for 1⅛-inch couplings and the power weighs 1,050 pounds.

The 6-horse power is the same as the 4-horse power, except that it has four sweeps and no lead poles and it weighs 1,150 pounds.

The 8-horse power has four sweeps and no lead poles. The high speed shafts make 65 and the low speed shaft makes 12¼ revolutions to one round of the horses. The tumbling rod is squared for 1⅛-inch couplings and the power weighs 1,400 pounds.

A horse power jack and pulley is required when you wish to transmit power by belt. Shipped knocked down from factory in Southeastern Wisconsin.

		Price
No. 32C2001	**Two-Horse Power.**	$21.20
No. 32C2002	**Four-Horse Power.**	29.20
No. 32C2003	**Six-Horse Power.**	31.00
No. 32C2004	**Eight-Horse Power.**	43.50

IF YOU CANNOT MAKE A SATISFACTORY SELECTION FROM THESE PAGES, DON'T THINK OF BUYING FROM ANYONE UNTIL YOU HAVE SENT FOR AND RECEIVED OUR BIG FREE SPECIAL AGRICULTURAL IMPLEMENT CATALOGUE.

Acme Horse Power Jacks.

$5.20 to $6.25

Our Horse Power Jacks are made in two styles and sizes. The light spur and light bevel gear jacks are suitable for use with 1-horse and 2-horse powers. The shafts are squared for 1-inch couplings. The heavy spur and heavy bevel gear jacks are suitable for use with 4-horse, 6-horse and 8-horse powers, but can be used with 1-horse and 2-horse powers. The shafts are squared for 1⅛-inch couplings. Shipped from factory in Southeastern Wisconsin.

No. 32C2010 Light Spur Gear Jack. Increases speed 2¼ to 1. Weight, 90 pounds.
Price, with 12x6-inch pulley.......................**$5.20**

No. 32C2011 Light Bevel Gear Jack. Increases speed 2½ to 1. Weight, 80 pounds.
Price, with 12x6-inch pulley.......................**$5.35**

No. 32C2012 Heavy Spur Gear Jack. Increases speed 4 to 1. Weight, 160 pounds.
Price, with 16x6-inch pulley.......................**$6.20**

No. 32C2013 Heavy Bevel Gear Jack. Increases speed 3⅓ to 1. Weight, 160 pounds.
Price, with 16x6-inch pulley.......................**$6.25**

Kenwood Overhead One-Horse Power.

$18.25

This style of horse power is especially adapted for use in a barn. The power can be bolted to the timbers above the driveway and machines can be set on the floor either above or below the power. When not in use the center post can be lifted from its socket and set out of the way, leaving the floor clear for other purposes. The center post is made of 6-inch by 6-inch timber and is 12 feet long. The driving pulley is 18 inches in diameter with 3-inch face and makes 37½ revolutions to one round of the horse, or about 135 revolutions per minute. Length of sweep from center of post to eyebolt is 7 feet 6 inches. Shipped knocked down from factory in Southeastern Wisconsin.

No. 32C2015 Kenwood Overhead Horse Power. Weight, 400 pounds. Price.......................**$18.25**

Kenwood One-Horse Sweep Power.

$14.75

Especially adapted for well drilling, running feed cutters, corn shellers and other light work. Tumbling rod is 10 feet long, squared for 1-inch couplings and makes nine revolutions to one round of the horse. Furnished complete with tumbling rod, lead pole, sweep, hitch and two couplings. Weight, 350 pounds. Shipped knocked down from factory in Southeastern Wisconsin.

No. 32C2018 Kenwood One-Horse Power.
Price.......................**$14.75**

Acme Horse Power Couplings.

No. 32C2020 Safety Horse Power Couplings. Made in three sizes to fit tumbling rods; squared 1-inch, 1⅛-inch and 1¼-inch. Always state in your order which size you want. Weight, 14 pounds.
Price.......................65c

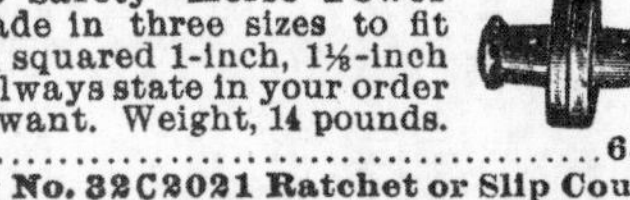

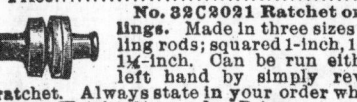

No. 32C2021 Ratchet or Slip Couplings. Made in three sizes to fit tumbling rods; squared 1-inch, 1⅛-inch and 1¼-inch. Can be run either right or left hand by simply reversing the ratchet. Always state in your order which size you want. Weight, 24 pounds. Price.......................**$1.26**

Kenwood Light Animal or Dog Powers.

Made in three styles. For one **$10.25 to $11.75** animal only. The No. 0 is fitted with balance wheel from which power can be transmitted by a belt and is also fitted with a crank attachment for operating machines which are run with a crank. No. 1 machine is the same except that in place of the crank attachment it is fitted with an adjustable stroke walking beam for running dash churns, pumps, etc. No. 2 is a combination of the Nos. 0 and 1 and has balance wheel, adjustable stroke walking beam and crank attachment. The incline of the treads can be changed instantly by means of a ratchet lever so as to set the treads at any desired angle. The balance wheel is 25 inches in diameter with a 2-inch face and makes about 42 revolutions per minute. Average weight of power is 150 pounds. Shipped knocked down from factory in Eastern New York.

No. 32C2025 No. 0 Dog Power. Price...**$10.25**
No. 32C2026 No. 1 Dog Power. Price... **11.00**
No. 32C2027 No. 2 Dog Power. Price... **11.75**

Hustler Hand Grist Mill.

$1.90

These are perfect grist mills, having removable hard iron burrs, which can be adjusted so as to grind to any degree of fineness. They will grind corn, wheat, rye, peas, salt, or in fact, almost anything else which it is desirable to grind, and will make splendid table meal. Will grind from ¾ to 1¼ bushels per hour. Weight, 30 pounds.

No. 32C2100 Hustler Grist Mill. Price.....**$1.90**

Yankee Hand Grist Mills.

$1.50 to $2.95

These mills will grind all kinds of small grain, including corn, and are splendid grinders for coffee, spices, etc. The burrs can be adjusted to grind fine or coarse and are easily removed. Made in two sizes. The No. 1, or small size, is made to bolt to a table. No. 2½ is made to bolt to a post. The No. 1, with balance wheel, will grind from ½ to 1 bushel per hour, No. 2½ from 1 to 2 bushels per hour, depending upon the fineness of the grinding.

No. 32C2104 No. 1 Yankee Grist Mill, with Crank. Weight, 14 pounds. Price.......................**$1.50**

No. 32C2105 No. 1 Yankee Grist Mill, with Balance Wheel. Weight 24 pounds. Price...**$1.95**

No. 32C2106 No. 2½ Yankee Grist Mill, with Balance Wheel. Weight, 45 pounds. Price....**$2.95**

Acme Hand Grist Mills.

$1.55 to $4.25

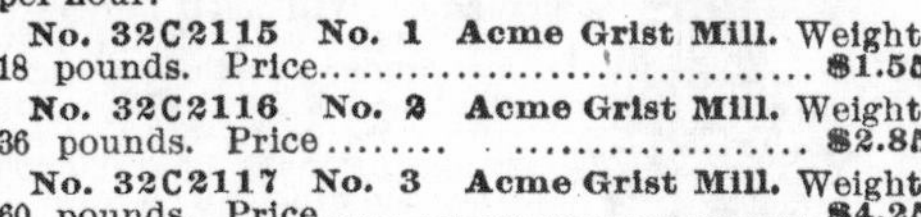

These are the handsomest, most durable, most rapid and most easily regulated grinders made. The burrs are steel alloy. Suitable for grinding small grains, shells, roots, barks, salt and feed for chickens, also for making table meal. The burrs can be adjusted to grind coarse or fine. Made in three sizes. **No. 1,** with a capacity of ½ to 1 bushel per hour; **No. 2,** with a capacity of ¾ to 1½ bushels per hour; **No. 3,** with a capacity of 1¼ to 2½ bushels per hour.

No. 32C2115 No. 1 Acme Grist Mill. Weight, 18 pounds. Price.......................**$1.55**

No. 32C2116 No. 2 Acme Grist Mill. Weight, 36 pounds. Price.......................**$2.85**

No. 32C2117 No. 3 Acme Grist Mill. Weight, 60 pounds. Price.......................**$4.25**

Little Wonder Grinding Mill.

$10.20

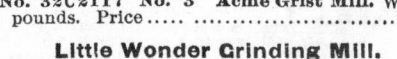

Especially adapted for use with power windmills and other light motive powers. Burrs are 5½ inches diameter and can be adjusted for grinding coarse or fine. Will grind all kinds of small grains, coffee, etc. Driving pulley is 7 inches diameter with 4-inch face, and should make from 700 to 1,300 revolutions per minute. Capacity is from 5 to 15 bushels of mixed feed per hour, depending upon the speed of grinder and fineness of grinding. Requires from one to three horse power to run it. Is furnished with one set of coarse burrs in the mill and one extra set of fine burrs. Shipped set up and crated from factory in Northern Illinois.

No. 32C2130 Little Wonder Grinding Mill. Weight, 90 pounds. Price.......................**$10.20**

Big Giant Double Feed Grinders.

$28.75 and $37.40

These Grinders are the same as the regular Big Giant Feed Grinders, but are double; consequently they have double the capacity of the single grinders, and require double the power. Made in two sizes. **No. 6** with three pair of 6-inch right hand, and three pair of 6-inch left hand burrs. **No. 5** with three pair of 8-inch right hand and three pair of 8-inch left hand burrs. In each case two pairs of the burrs are coarse, two pairs are medium and two pairs are fine. The pulley on these grinders is 8 inches in diameter with 8-inch face. Shipped from factory in Southeastern Minnesota.

No. 32C2146 No. 6 Big Giant Double Grinder. Weight, 350 pounds. Price.......................**$28.75**

No. 32C2147 No. 5 Big Giant Double Grinder. Weight, 445 pounds. Price.......................**$37.40**

Big Giant Feed Grinders.

$16.10 to $23.00

The genuine and original Diamond Grinders, made especially for us and with our special brand. For grinding small grains and shelled corn only. Burrs are adjustable and flexible while running. Made in two sizes, each being furnished with one set of coarse, one set of medium and one set of fine burrs. **No. 9** has 6-inch right hand burrs and is fitted with a pulley 6½ inches in diameter with 6-inch face. **No. 7** has 8-inch right hand burrs and is fitted with a pulley 9 inches in diameter with 6-inch face. The No. 9 should be run from 400 to 1,000 revolutions per minute. It requires from 2 to 8 horse power, and will grind from 8 to 30 bushels per hour. The No. 7 should be run from 600 to 1,000 revolutions per minute. It requires 4 to 12 horse power and will grind from 12 to 40 bushels per hour. Capacity depends upon the speed, horse power and fineness of grinding. **No. 10** is the same as No. 9, and **No. 8** is same as No. 7 except that they have no driving pulley, are fitted with left hand burrs, and have a geared countershaft, squared 1-inch to connect with a horse power tumbling rod, on which there is a 12x3¼ inch pulley, which can be used to drive corn shellers, etc. Shipped from factory in Southeastern Minnesota.

No. 32C2140 No. 9 Big Giant Feed Grinder. Weight, 195 pounds. Price.......................**$16.10**

No. 32C2141 No. 7 Big Giant Feed Grinder. Weight, 265 pounds. Price.......................**$20.70**

No. 32C2142 No. 10 Big Giant Geared Feed Grinder. Weight, 235 pounds. Price.......................**$18.40**

No. 32C2143 No. 8 Big Giant Geared Feed Grinder. Weight, 300 pounds. Price.......................**$23.00**

Acme Power Feed Grinder.

$12.65

This mill is for grinding small grains and shelled corn for feed only. Can be adjusted for either coarse or fine grinding and has large capacity. Pulley is 5 inches in diameter, with 5-inch face and should run from 1,200 to 1,800 revolutions per minute. Burrs are 9 inches in diameter and an extra set is furnished with each grinder. Grinder requires from 4 to 8 horse power to run it, and its capacity is from 15 to 30 bushels of mixed feed per hour, depending upon the speed of the grinder and the fineness of the grinding. State whether you want coarse or fine burrs. Coarse burrs will be shipped unless fine are ordered. Shipped from factory in Eastern Ohio.

No. 32C2156 Acme Power Feed Grinder. Weight, 200 pounds. Price.......................**$12.65**

Kenwood Corn and Cob Mill.

$18.80 and $20.50

This mill is scientifically built, simple, strong and durable, and perfect in operation. The burrs are made from a mixture of steel and iron. The shaft has a **ball bearing end thrust.** Made in two sizes to be run by belt power, and can be furnished with tumbling rod attachment to be run from either end by a sweep horse power. No. 1 has 9½-inch burrs, 12 by 5-inch driving pulley, requires from 4 to 6-horse power, and has a capacity of from 6 to 10 bushels of coarse meal or 15 to 20 bushels of feed per hour. No. 2 has 12-inch burrs, 12 by 6-inch driving pulley, requires 6 to 8-horse power, and has a capacity of from 10 to 15 bushels of coarse meal or 20 to 30 bushels of feed per hour. Capacity and power required, is based on the burrs running 600 revolutions per minute. Can be run at more or less speed with proportionate increase or decrease in capacity and power. Will not grind table meal. Will grind corn and cobs or corn or small grain only. Does not have or require a fly wheel but one can be furnished at extra price. Furnished with one set of coarse and one set of fine burrs. Shipped from factory in Southwestern Ohio.

No. 32C2150 No. 1 Kenwood Corn and Cob Mill. Weight, 275 pounds. Price.......................**$18.80**

No. 32C2151 No. 2 Kenwood Corn and Cob Mill. Weight, 325 pounds. Price.......................**$20.50**

No. 32C2154 Fly Wheel. Weight, 59 pounds.
Price.......................**$2.45**

No. 32C2155 Tumbling Rod Attachment. Weight, 60 pounds. Price.......................**$3.70**

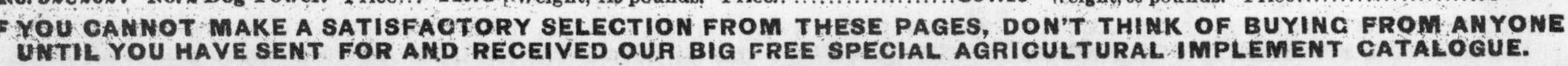

IF YOU CANNOT MAKE A SATISFACTORY SELECTION FROM THESE PAGES, DON'T THINK OF BUYING FROM ANYONE UNTIL YOU HAVE SENT FOR AND RECEIVED OUR BIG FREE SPECIAL AGRICULTURAL IMPLEMENT CATALOGUE.

Acme Power Cob Crusher and Feed Grinder.

$23.65 and $25.80 We consider this one of the best cob crushers and feed grinders made. The hopper is divided by a partition and has a suitable feeding device so that ear corn and small grain can be successfully fed and ground at the same time, or either can be ground separately. The fly wheel is inclosed within the mill. Burrs are made of chilled iron and steel mixed. These grinders should run from 800 to 1,200 revolutions per minute and are fitted with driving pulley, 10 inches diameter by 8-inch face. **The No. 1** has 12-inch burrs, requires from 6 to 10 horse power and has a capacity of from 20 to 40 bushels per hour. **The No. 2** has 14-inch burrs, requires from 10 to 16 horse power and has a capacity of from 30 to 50 bushels per hour. Capacity depends entirely upon speed, power applied and fineness of grinding. Furnished complete with one extra pair of burrs. Shipped from factory in Eastern Ohio.

No. 32C2166 No. 1 Acme Cob Crusher and Feed Grinder. Weight, 390 pounds. Price.........$23.65
No. 32C2167 No. 2 Acme Cob Crusher and Feed Grinder. Weight, 440 pounds. Price.........$25.80

Acme Sweep Feed Mills.

$13.50 to $17.20

These are the highest grade single geared sweep mills on the market. They are made in two sizes and two styles. The No. 10B and No. 20B mills are without legs, but are mounted on a feed box made of good heavy lumber. The No. 10L and No. 20L mills have iron legs and a heavy wooden platform, as shown in the illustration. The grinding rings are made of our standard mixture of hard iron and steel. They are adjustable and can be gauged to grind the crushed cobs and corn to any desired fineness suitable for ordinary feeding purposes. The average capacity of the **No. 10 Mill**, based on coarse grinding of dry corn and cobs, is from 8 to 12 bushels per hour; that of the **No. 20 Mill**, is from 10 to 16 bushels per hour. The regular grinding rings furnished with these mills are coarse and are intended for coarse grinding of corn and cobs or shelled corn for feeding purposes. For finer grinding of shelled corn or for grinding other small grain, fine grinding rings are required. Grinding medium or fine or grinding with fine rings reduces the capacity from one-third to one-half. Price is for the feed mill complete with one pair of grinding rings, sweep and hitch hook. When ordering always state whether you want coarse or fine grinding rings. **Coarse rings will be shipped unless otherwise specified.** Shipped knocked down from factory in Southwestern Ohio.

	Price
No. 32C2179 No. 10B Feed Mill. Wt., 390 lbs.	**$13.50**
No. 32C2180 No. 20B Feed Mill. Wt., 470 lbs.	15.90
No. 32C2181 No. 10L Feed Mill. Wt., 450 lbs.	14.70
No. 32C2182 No. 20L Feed Mill. Wt., 530 lbs.	17.20

Kenwood Triple Geared Ball Bearing, Sweep Feed Mill.

$19.75 AND $20.75

Absolutely the best and most efficient sweep feed mill which money and skilled labor can produce. Made in one size only, but in two styles. The **No. 1** is without legs, but is mounted on a feed box made of good heavy lumber. The **No. 2** is mounted on iron legs, as shown in the illustration, and has a heavy wooden platform. This feed mill being geared three to one, has nearly double the capacity of the ordinary single geared mill. The grinding rings are made of our standard mixture of hard iron and steel. The discharge is through a spout directly under the mill. The grinding rings can be gauged to grind the crushed corn and cobs to any desired fineness suitable for feeding purposes. The regular grinding rings furnished with this mill are coarse and are intended for coarse grinding of corn and cobs, or shelled corn for feeding purposes. For finer grinding of shelled corn or for grinding other small grains, fine grinding rings are required. The average capacity of this mill, based on coarse grinding of dry ear corn is from 15 to 25 bushels per hour. Grinding medium or fine or grinding with fine rings reduces the capacity from one-third to one-half. When ordering always state whether you want coarse or fine grinding rings. **Coarse rings will be shipped unless otherwise specified.** Price is for the mill complete with one pair of grinding rings, sweep and hitch hook. Shipped knocked down from factory in Southwestern Ohio.

	Price
No. 32C2193 No. 1 Feed Mill. Wt., 525 lbs.	**$19.75**
No. 32C2194 No. 2 Feed Mill. Wt., 550 lbs.	20.75

Hustler Corn Sheller.

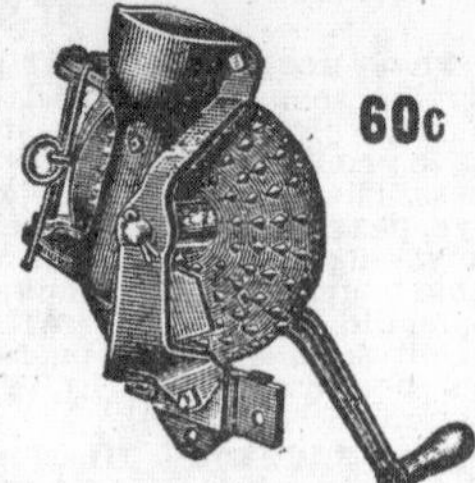

60c

The best cast iron corn sheller made. Will shell any size of field corn and is fitted with a popcorn attachment. Popcorn attachment must be removed when shelling field corn. Has adjustable spring tension. Can be attached to any box or board. Weight, 15 pounds.

No. 32C2227 Hustler Corn Sheller. Price, 60c

Blackbird Corn Sheller.

$1.38

Made largely of malleable iron, all bearings chilled. The sheller will last a lifetime. Any broken or defective part furnished free. Will shell all sizes of field corn easily and rapidly. Adjustable spring tension. Sheller can be instantly clamped to any box or plank (no holes to bore). Weight, 15 pounds.

No. 32C2229 Blackbird Corn Sheller. Price.............$1.38

Universal Duplex Corn Sheller.

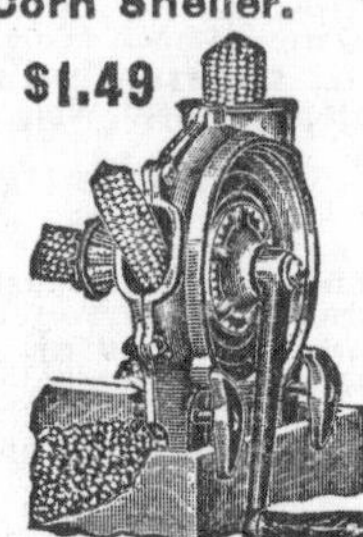

$1.49

This sheller has a compound disc driven by triple gearing, making it very easy to operate and causing it to do perfect work. It is also supplied with a butting and tipping attachment. Will shell any kind of field, seed or pop corn, and can be adjusted to any desired tension. Furnished complete with clamps.

No. 32C2228 Universal Corn Sheller. Weight, 19 pounds. Price........$1.49

Star Ball Bearing Corn Sheller.

$1.35

The easiest running sheller made. Will shell large or small ears of ordinary field corn under the same adjustment, and is fitted with a pop corn attachment, but this attachment must be removed when shelling field corn. A heavy spiral spring produces an even and uniform pressure, holding the ears of corn firmly against the shelling disc. Furnished complete with bolt and clamp. No holes to bore.

No. 32C2231 Star Ball Bearing Corn Sheller. Weight, 20 pounds. Price.............$1.35

Kenwood Two-Hole Corn Sheller.

$10.50

This is a medium grade sheller adapted for general farm, warehouse or custom mill use. The balance wheel is heavy and large. The feed spout is directly over the shelling wheels and the rag irons and springs which control them are adjustable, so that any size of field corn can be shelled. The cob rake separates the shelled corn from the cobs, delivers the cobs at a distance from the foot of the sheller and allows the sheller to be run at a good speed and with good capacity without throwing corn out with the cobs. This sheller is always furnished complete with fan, feed table, crank and an 8-inch diameter by 4-inch face pulley. When run by power, this pulley should make from 300 to 400 revolutions per minute. Capacity is from 25 to 35 bushels of shelled corn per hour. Weight, 250 pounds. Shipped from factory in Southeastern Wisconsin.

No. 32C2239 Kenwood Two-Hole Corn Sheller. Price.............................$10.50

Kenwood One-Hole Corn Sheller.

$4.95

An excellent corn sheller. Not to be compared with the ordinary corn shellers which are cheaply constructed, with price the only object in view. The sheller is tastefully ornamented and handsomely finished. The balance wheel is large and very heavy. The feed spout is placed directly over the shelling wheels, and the shelling wheels grip the ears of corn firmly. The rag iron and the springs which control it are adjustable and can be set so that any size of field corn can be shelled. The capacity is from 10 to 15 bushels of shelled corn per hour. Always furnished complete with crank, fan and feed table. Shipped from factory in Southeastern Wisconsin.

No. 32C2235 Kenwood One-Hole Corn Sheller. Weight, 135 pounds. Price.....................$4.95

Fulton Two-Hole Corn Sheller.

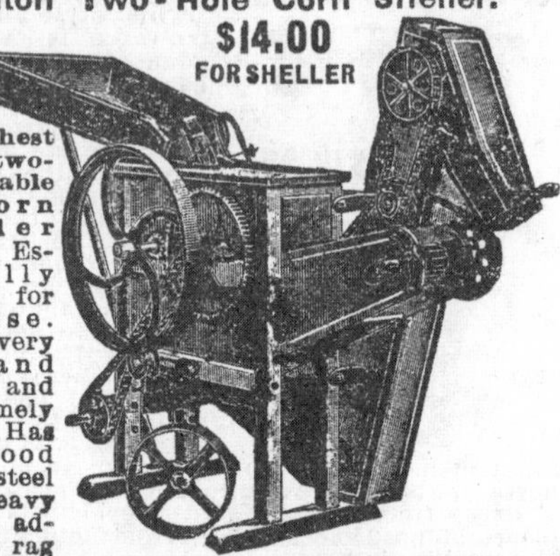

$14.00 FOR SHELLER

The highest grade two-hole table feed corn sheller made. Especially adapted for power use. Made very strong and durable and handsomely finished. Has hardwood frame, steel shafts, heavy gearing, adjustable rag irons and springs, an excellent blast fan and a perfect wire cob rake. Capacity 350 to 400 bushels per day at 350 revolutions per minute. Furnished with 12 by 3½-inch pulley, feed table, fan and crank. Either cob stacker, sacking elevator, wagon elevator or tumbling rod attachment can be used but are furnished only at extra price. Shipped from factory in Central Ohio.

No. 32C2240 Fulton Two-Hole Corn Sheller. Weight, 290 pounds. Price.............$14.00
No. 32C2246 6-Foot Cob Stacker. Weight, 60 pounds. Price.............$4.90
No. 32C2247 5-Foot Sacking Elevator. Weight, 75 pounds. Price.............$6.00
No. 32C2248 8-Foot Wagon Elevator. Weight, 100 pounds. Price.............$9.25
No. 32C2250 Tumbling Rod Attachment. Weight, 50 pounds. Price.............$4.95

Nos. 8 and 10 Kenwood Hand Feed Cutters.

$9.35 and $12.50

The best hand Feed Cutters made. Have feed gearing to change length of cut, and lever to govern the feed. Knives are tempered tool steel and make a downward shearing cut against a hardened cutting bar. Each machine has two knives and will cut either ¼ inch, ⅝ inch or 1 inch long, and length of cut may be doubled by removing one knife. The shaft is 1⅛ inches diameter and extended so pulley can be attached outside of the fly wheel. Pulley is extra. By power, machine should run 400 to 500 revolutions per minute.

The No. 8 Cutter has a heavy safety wheel. Its knives are 8¼ inches long. Capacity, by hand, 150 to 200 pounds of hay or dry fodder, or 300 to 400 pounds of green fodder per hour. Capacity, by power, 400 to 500 pounds of hay or dry fodder, or 600 to 800 pounds of green fodder per hour.

The No. 10 Cutter has a heavy safety fly wheel. Its knives are 10½ inches long. Capacity, by hand, 300 to 450 pounds of hay or dry fodder, or 600 to 900 pounds of green fodder per hour. Capacity, by power, 800 to 1,200 pounds of hay or dry fodder, or 1,200 to 1,800 pounds of green fodder per hour. Shipped knocked down from factory in Central Ohio.

No. 32C2315 No. 8 Feed Cutter. Weight, 160 pounds. Price.............$9.35
No. 32C2316 No. 10 Feed Cutter. Weight, 255 pounds. Price.............$12.50
No. 32C2319 10x3-inch Pulley. Weight, 10 pounds. Price.............$1.00

IF YOU CANNOT MAKE A SATISFACTORY SELECTION FROM THESE PAGES, DON'T THINK OF BUYING FROM ANYONE UNTIL YOU HAVE SENT FOR AND RECEIVED OUR BIG FREE SPECIAL AGRICULTURAL IMPLEMENT CATALOGUE.

Success Feed Cutters and Shredders.

The Success Cutters and Shredders cut the fodder into short lengths and at the same time shred each piece into small parts. This is accomplished by a series of small steel knives set spirally on the cylinder shaft and as the cutting is continuous these machines require much less power than the ordinary cylinder feed cutter. The safety fly wheel is controlled by a positive and reliable friction grip. **This is the only style of shredder which will do satisfactory work when run by hand or at varying speed.**

$22.25 and $24.75

The No. 11 and 13 machines may be run either by hand or with power, and they can be driven at any desired speed, but to obtain the full capacity, the driving pulley should make 1,000 revolutions per minute. The driving pulley of Nos. 11 and 13 is 6x6 inches and is attached to the balance wheel. Each size makes cuts ½ inch, ¾ inch, 1 inch and 1¼ inches long. The No. 11 has an 11-inch cylinder head with 88 knives. It will cut 1½ to 2 tons of dry fodder, or 3 to 4 tons of green ensilage per hour and requires 1 to 2-horse power to run it. The No. 13 has a 13-inch cylinder head with 42 knives. It will cut 2 to 3 tons of dry fodder, or 4 to 6 tons of green ensilage per hour and requires 2 to 3 horse power to run it. Shipped knocked down from factory in Eastern Ohio.

No. 32C2331 No. 11 Success Feed Cutter and Shredder. Weight, 325 pounds. Price.......**$22.25**

No. 32C2332 No. 13 Success Feed Cutter and Shredder. Weight, 375 pounds. Price.......**$24.75**

No. 5 Acme Feed Cutter.

This cutter is made especially to meet the demands for a good, well made, yet cheap and durable machine. The steel cutting knife is 11¼ inches long, and makes a downward shearing cut. Knife makes three cuts to one turn of crank, and length of cut is adjustable from ⅝ inch to 1½ inches. Capacity per hour, 150 to 200 pounds of dry fodder; 300 to 400 pounds of green fodder. Weight, 165 pounds. Shipped knocked down from factory in Central Ohio.

$6.20

No. 32C2361 No. 5 Feed Cutter. Price.....**$6.20**

Star Lever Feed Cutter.

$2.45

The highest grade lever feed cutter on the market. Frame is heavy hardwood and varnished in natural wood. Knife is best quality solid steel, curved so as to give a shearing cut. Adjustment of knife is positive. Gauge plate is adjustable for different lengths of cut. Weight, 65 pounds. Shipped knocked down.

No. 32C2304 Star Lever Feed Cutter. Price..**$2.45**

Kenwood Pea and Bean Huller and Cleaner.

A thoroughly modern and up to date machine, designed to meet the requirements of the small bean and pea raisers. Will hull and clean perfectly any kind of peas or beans after they have been stripped from the vines, and can be used for chaffing and rough cleaning any kind of small grain. A strongly built and handsomely finished machine. Has large gearing, a strong blast and runs very easily. The cylinder and concave are 14 inches long and are built on the same principle as a thresher. The hulls are discharged through the inclined spout and drop at a distance from the machine. The peas or beans drop onto the sieving, where they are thoroughly cleaned. Price is for the machine with one pea and one bean sieve. Shipped set up from factory in Southeastern Minnesota.

$15.60

No. 32C2408 No. 1 Pea and Bean Huller. Weight, 170 pounds. Price.....................**$15.60**

Fulton Farm Fanning Mill.

$8.95

The best all around general purpose fanning mill made. A vast improvement over the ordinary mill. Has very large screening surface, does very rapid and perfect work. Thoroughly well made, of good material and handsomely finished. Will clean, separate and grade any kind of grain raised, and when fitted with proper sieving it will be found the best seed cleaner, separator and grader ever used. Has end shake movement to shoe, a large hopper with adjustable feed, a strong wind blast which can be controlled perfectly so that the most difficult separations can be made, and runs very easily. Price is for the mill complete with grain outfit only, which consists of one three-sieve hurdle with zinc top for wheat and rye, one sieve for oats and corn, one sieve for barley, one long mesh screen for cheat, one coarse screen and one fine screen. **FOR SUCCOTASH, that is, the separating of wild oats from other kinds of grain, this mill cannot be excelled, but the succotash hurdle, which has three zinc sieves, is not furnished except at extra price. Seed sieving is also extra.** Sieves are 23 inches wide. Capacity is from 40 to 60 bushels per hour, depending upon kind and quality of grain. Shipped knocked down from factory in Southeastern Minnesota.

No. 32C2437 No. 1 Fulton Fanning Mill. Weight, 140 pounds. Price.........................**$8.95**

No. 32C2438 No. 1 Succotash Hurdle. Weight, 10 pounds. Price.........................**$1.25**

No. 32C2439 No. 1 Clover Attachment. Weight, 12 pounds. Price.........................**90c**

No. 32C2440 No. 1 Timothy Attachment. Weight, 12 pounds. Price.........................**95c**

No. 32C2441 No. 1 Alfalfa Attachment. Weight, 12 pounds. Price.........................**$1.00**

No. 32C2442 No. 1 Red Top Attachment. Weight, 12 pounds. Price.........................**$1.75**

No. 32C2443 No. 1 Flax Attachment. Weight, 12 pounds. Price.........................**$1.10**

No. 32C2444 No. 1 Bean Attachment. Weight, 12 pounds. Price.........................**$1.15**

No. 32C2445 No. 1 Pea Attachment. Weight, 12 pounds. Price.........................**$1.20**

Kenwood Hand Feed Drag Sawing Machine.

$36.45

This is a light, strong and perfect drag saw to be driven by a two or a four-horse sweep power. Suitable for logs up to 24 inches in diameter. The log is moved by a lever in either direction as required. The stroke of the saw can be shortened or lengthened to suit the power used. The log is rigidly held by dogs, and a guide prevents the saw from whipping. The log carriage is 14 feet long, and the car is strong, with heavy flanged wheels. The saw blade is 5½ feet long, filed and set ready for use, and made to cut one way only. These machines are regularly fitted with gearing suitable for our Nos. 32C2001 and 32C2002 horse powers, but we can usually arrange gearing suitable for any motion of horse power. The upper shaft is 1$\frac{7}{16}$ inches and is extended so that a single pulley can be put on at any time. Saw may be driven at from 75 to 175 strokes per minute, but the best speed is at from 125 to 150 strokes per minute. Capacity is from 15 to 30 cords per day. **When ordering for use with a sweep horse power,** which you have, always state whether the top of the tumbling rod turns to the right or to the left when you stand at the center of the power and face the rod, also how many horses you will use, how many revolutions the tumbling rod makes to one round of the horses, and the size of the square on the tumbling rod. When ordering with a pulley to be driven by a belt, be sure to tell us the diameter and the face of the engine pulley or other pulley which will drive the saw, and how many revolutions said pulley makes a minute. Price includes the saw blade, but does not include horse power, coupling or pulley. We can furnish either 12, 16, 20 or 24-inch iron pulleys with 6-inch face. **For single pulleys add $3.00; for tight and loose pulleys add $6.75 to price of machine.** Shipped knocked down from factory in Southeastern Wisconsin.

No. 32C2480 Hand Feed Drag Sawing Machine. Weight, 750 pounds. Price.....................**$36.45**

Star Model Pea Huller.

$25.00 and $27.00

For hulling, cleaning and separating all kinds of field peas and navy beans, after they have been stripped from the vines. When run by hand this machine will hull and clean 10 to 15 bushels per hour, or if run by power, 20 to 30 bushels per hour. Has two 18-inch cranks, and when ordered for power it also has a 14-inch pulley. This machine is not high grade in finish but it does excellent work. Weight, 375 pounds. Shipped set up from factory in Southern Tennessee.

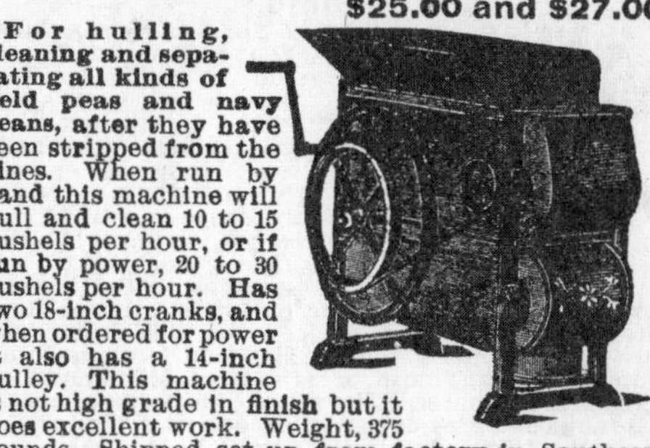

No. 32C2410 Star Hand Pea Huller. Price.........................**$25.00**

No. 32C2411 Star Hand and Power Pea Huller. Price.........................**$27.00**

Kenwood Self Feed Drag Sawing Machine.

$47.15

For use with not less than a four-horse sweep power. Adapted to cutting logs, rails or poles into any desired lengths. The self feed for moving the log forward is very simple and perfect. With the hand feed lever the operator can move the log either forward or back. The log is rigidly held by dogs, and a guide prevents the saw from whipping. The log carriage is 20 feet long and the car is very strong, with heavy flanged wheels. The saw blade is 5½ feet long, filed and set ready for use. When machine is for a four-horse power we furnish a saw to cut one way only, when for six-horse power or more we furnish a saw to cut both ways. With saw cutting both ways machine is suitable for logs up to 30 inches in diameter. These machines are regularly built without gearing and are suitable for our Nos. 32W2003 or 32W2004 horse powers, but **for $2.80 extra we can usually arrange gearing suitable for any motion of horse power.** The shaft is 1⅝ inches and is extended so that a single pulley can be put on at any time. Saw may be driven at from 75 to 175 strokes per minute, but the best speed is at from 125 to 150 strokes per minute. Capacity is from 40 to 80 cords per day, depending upon kind of timber and amount of power applied. When ordering, give same information as for hand feed machine. Price includes the saw blade but does not include horse power, coupling or pulley. For sizes and prices of pulleys, see hand feed machine. Shipped knocked down from factory in Southeastern Wisconsin.

No. 32C2484 Self Feed Drag Sawing Machine. Weight, 1,500 pounds. Price.....................**$47.15**

Kenwood One-Man Sawing Machine.

$4.95

An easy running and very efficient sawing machine, adapted for sawing logs, poles or wood, but not for cutting down trees. Its construction enables the operator to stand erect and to exert his full force and weight on the lever which operates the saw. Has a 5-foot alligator tooth saw blade, filed and set ready for use. Shipped knocked down.

No. 32C2507 Sawing Machine. Weight, 44 pounds. Price.........................**$4.95**

Kenwood Tilting Table Wood Saw Frame.

$11.25

For sawing regular 4-foot cord wood. The shaft is 4 feet 5 inches long, with 5-inch arbor flanges. It has grooves in the boxes to prevent end play. The boxes are connected together by an iron frame which keeps them in perfect alignment. Driving pulley is 5 inches diameter with 6-inch face. Price is for saw frame with 100-pound balance wheel. The cast iron saw guard is adjustable to fit saws from 20 inches to 30 inches in diameter. The arbor hole in saw must be 1⅝ inches. **Price does not include saw blade.** Can furnish either right or left hand frame, but **we always ship right hand frame, unless left hand frame is ordered.** Shipped knocked down from factory in Southeastern Minnesota.

No. 32C2517 Tilting Table Wood Saw Frame. Weight, 335 pounds. Price.........................**$11.25**

No. 32C2518 Pole Extension Parts. Weight, 30 pounds. Price.........................**65c**

For other saw frames, see next page.

IF YOU CANNOT MAKE A SATISFACTORY SELECTION FROM THESE PAGES, DON'T THINK OF BUYING FROM ANYONE UNTIL YOU HAVE SENT FOR AND RECEIVED OUR BIG FREE SPECIAL AGRICULTURAL IMPLEMENT CATALOGUE.

Kenwood Sliding Table Wood Saw Frame.

$12.95

For sawing regular 4-foot cord wood. The table is run on two iron ways which form a part of the frame, and slides on rollers, thus being very easy to operate. The shaft is 4 feet 5 inches long, with 1⅜ inch arbor, and 5-inch arbor flanges. It has grooves in the boxes to prevent end play. Driving pulley is 5 inches diameter, with 6-inch face. Price is for saw frame with 100-pound balance wheel. The hood is made to accommodate any size of saw from 20 inches to 30 inches in diameter. The arbor hole in saw must be 1⅜ inches. **Price does not include saw blade.** Can furnish either right or left hand frame, but we always ship right hand frame unless left hand frame is ordered. Shipped knocked down from factory in Southeastern Minnesota.

No. 32C2521 Sliding Table Wood Saw Frame. Weight, 370 pounds. Price....................**$12.95**

Kenwood Combined Saw Frame and Jack.

For Sawing Either Cordwood or Long Poles.

$17.95 and $19.65

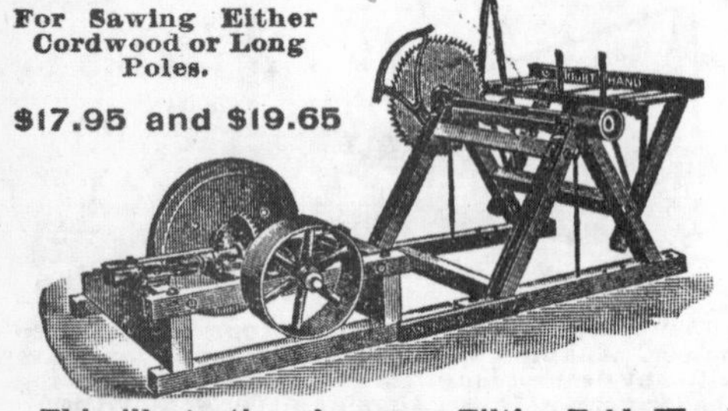

This illustration shows our Tilting Table Wood Saw Frame with Jack Attachment. Our sliding table wood saw frame is also made up in the same manner with jack attachment. In each case the saw frames are exactly the same as described under Nos. 32C2517 and 32C2521, except that the mandril shaft is 4 feet 1 inch long, there is no balance wheel on the frame itself and the frame work of the sliding table saw frame is changed slightly so as to provide foundation timbers at the bottom of the frame. This combination of a saw frame and jack is especially adapted for use with a sweep horse power, so that the power may be attached direct to the jack. The jack is geared three to one, and the large gear shaft is squared 1⅛ inches to connect direct with the tumbling rod of a horse power. Pulley shaft is 1¼ inches diameter. The driving pulley on the jack is 15 inches diameter, with 6-inch face. When ordering these frames, unless you also order the horse power and the saw blade from us at the same time, you should tell us how many revolutions the tumbling rod of your horse power makes to one round of the horses, how many horses you will use and what diameter of saw you will use. With 15-inch pulley it requires 12 feet of 6-inch three or four ply rubber belting. **Price does not include either saw blade or driving belt.** Price is for frame and jack with 100-pound balance wheel on the jack. Can furnish either right or left hand frame, but **we always ship right hand frame unless left hand is ordered.** Shipped knocked down from factory in Southeastern Minnesota.

No. 32C2523 Tilting Table Saw Frame and Jack. Weight, 555 pounds. Price............**$17.95**

No. 32C2524 Sliding Table Saw Frame and Jack. Weight, 590 pounds. Price............**$19.65**

Kenwood Pole Saw Frame.

$13.95

The strongest, best constructed and most popular Saw Frame made in the United States. Suitable for sawing cord wood and long poles of every description. The mandrel shaft is 4 feet 1 inch long, with 1⅜-inch saw arbor and 5-inch arbor flanges. It has grooves in the boxes to prevent end play. The mandrel shaft boxes are connected together by an iron frame which keeps them in perfect alignment. The center tightening pulley is hung on a heavy cast iron bracket with heavy steel shaft, and is so strongly made that it cannot get out of line. All pulleys are 5 inches diameter with 6-inch face. Price is for saw frame with 100-pound balance wheel. The cast iron saw guard is adjustable to fit saws from 20 inches to 30 inches in diameter. The arbor hole in saws must be 1⅜ inches. **Price does not include saw blade.** Can furnish either right or left hand frame, but **we always ship right hand frame unless left hand frame is ordered.** Shipped knocked down from factory in Southeastern Minnesota.

No. 32C2542 Pole Saw Frame. Weight, 415 pounds. Price....................**$13.95**

For other saw frames, see preceding page.

Kenwood Saw Frame Irons.

$7.20

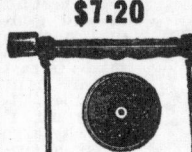

We can furnish Saw Frame Irons such as are used on our tilting table wood saw frames, either in separate items or in complete sets, as listed below. Can furnish either right or left hand mandrel shaft, but **we always ship right hand unless left hand is ordered.** These Saw Frame Irons and their measurements are the same as described with our saw frame, and the arbor hole in saws to be used with them must be 1⅜ inches. Shipped from factory in Southeastern Minnesota.

No. 32C2545 Mandrel Shaft, with arbor collars. Weight, 36 pounds. Price....................**$3.50**

No. 32C2546 5x6-inch Driving Pulley. Weight, 11 pounds. Price....................**80c**

No. 32C2547 100-pound Balance Wheel. Weight, 100 pounds. Price....................**$2.60**

No. 32C2548 Connected Boxes, with rods. Weight, 35 pounds. Price....................**$1.30**

No. 32C2549 Plain Set of Saw Frame Irons, complete. Weight, 182 pounds. Price.........**$7.20**

Fulton Circular Cut-off Saw Blades.

$3.67 to $7.59

These saw blades are especially made for use on our wood and pole saw frames, and all sizes have 1⅜-inch arbor hole to fit the mandrels of our saw frames. When ordering a saw frame and a saw blade, or when ordering a saw blade to fit one of our saw frames, always order one of these saws and be **sure to give the correct catalogue number.** These saws are all filed and set ready for use. They are fully guaranteed, and if kept properly filed and set, and run at the proper speed they will do perfect work and give perfect satisfaction. To operate cut-off saws at full capacity with sweep horse powers it requires about 2-horse power for 20 and 22-inch saws, about 4-horse power for 24 and 26-inch saws, and about 6-horse power for .. and 30-inch saws, but with engines not less than 4-horse power should be used.

Catalogue No.	Diam., inches	Gauge No.	Revolutions per Minute From	To	Weight crated	Price
32C2530	20	13	1,000	1,500	11 lbs.	$3.67
32C2531	22	12	925	1,400	14 lbs.	4.30
32C2532	24	11	850	1,300	17 lbs.	5.07
32C2533	26	11	800	1,200	20 lbs.	5.93
32C2534	28	10	750	1,100	26 lbs.	6.75
32C2535	30	10	700	1,000	29 lbs.	7.59

Buckeye Evaporator Pans and Rocker Furnaces.

FOR MAPLE SYRUP.

Pans, $5.40 to $23.80
Furnaces, $7.70 to $10.95

The construction of the Buckeye pans makes them especially adapted for maple syrup, but they are equally as good for sorghum or sugar cane. The illustration shows a Buckeye evaporator pan combined with a rocker furnace, making a complete portable evaporator. **We list the pans and furnaces separately, so that you may order a pan only, to be set stationary on a brick arch with furnace front and grate.** These pans are substantially constructed of either galvanized steel or planished sheet copper, heavily bound, riveted and soldered. The sides and ends are turned up square and surplus metal at corners is lapped around against the ends and held in position by the wood sides. Wood sides do not come in contact with the juice or syrup. Scum cannot pass from one section to another and flow of juice can be regulated or stopped at will. No seams exposed to the fire. Price of pan includes two wide skimmers. Capacity is based on sugar cane or sorghum, where it takes 10 to 15 gallons of juice to make 1 gallon of syrup. On maple syrup the capacity will be much less, because it requires about 40 gallons of sap to make 1 gallon of syrup. Furnaces are mounted on angle steel rockers and price is for the furnace complete with fire door, grates and chimney, but does not include fire brick and it does not include the pan. **If furnace is wanted with pan, order a pan and a rocker furnace, and allow price of each.** Pans are all 42 inches wide. Shipped from factory in Southwestern Ohio.

Cat'ge No	Size No.	Lgth. of Pan	Gals. Syrup in 12 Hrs.	Galv. Pan, Wt. lbs.	Price	Copper Pan, Wt. lbs.	Price	Rocker Wt. lbs.	Furnace. Price
32C2642	2	64 in.	30 to 40	85	$5.40	100	$13.50	180	$7.70
32C2643	3	80 in.	40 to 60	95	6.80	110	17.40	190	8.65
32C2644	4	96 in.	60 to 80	105	8.10	125	20.70	200	9.70
32C2645	5	112 in.	80 to 100	125	9.15	140	23.80	210	10.95

Furnace Fronts With Grates.

$3.15 and $6.25

For use in brick arches for evaporator pans. These fronts with grates consist of the door frame, door, anchor rods and grate complete. The No. 1 is suitable for use with Nos. 2 and 3 pans. It has a single door, 12x12 inches, and a single grate 18x36 inches. The No. 2 is suitable for use with Nos. 3, 4 and 5 pans. It has a single door, 13x16 inches and a single grate 20x42 inches. Shipped from factory in Southwestern Ohio. Weight Price

No. 32C2651 No. 1 Furnace Front. 85 lbs. **$3.15**

No. 32C2652 No. 2 Furnace Front. 140 lbs. **6.25**

Hustler Hand Bone Mill.

$1.95

This mill is intended for crushing and grinding bones after they have been burned or dried so that they can be ground easily. It will also grind oyster shells in the same condition. It will not cut green bones. Weight, 30 pounds.

No. 32C2700 Hustler Bone Mill. Price....................**$1.95**

No. 0 Acme Green Bone Cutters.

$4.90 AND $6.85.

This cutter is geared, is for hand use only and is suitable for a flock of 75 fowls. Has bone box 3¼x4⅝x6 inches inside, has split nut, and is fed by hand, the operator turning the feed screw. Can be furnished with crank or with balance wheel, and is for use on a bench or table.

No. 32C2703 No. OC Bone Cutter, with crank. Weight, 50 pounds. Price....................**$4.90**

No. 32C2704 No. OB Bone Cutter, with balance wheel. Weight, 75 pounds. Price.....**$6.85**

No. 1 Acme Green Bone Cutter.

$7.80

This cutter is not back geared. It has a larger bone box and will do more work than geared machines at corresponding prices, but requires more power to operate it, the object being to obtain the greatest capacity at the lowest price. It is a hand machine with handle attached to rim of disc, and is suitable for a flock of 150 to 200 fowls, has bone box 4x3x13 inches inside solid nut, and adjustable automatic feed. Shipped from factory in Western Pennsylvania.

No. 32C2710 No. 1LL Bone Cutter. Weight, 108 pounds. Price....................**$7.80**

Nos. 9 to 12 Acme Green Bone Cutters.

$8.40 TO $14.00.

These cutters are the popular sizes for general use. They are all geared and can be furnished on high legs, as shown in this illustration, or on low legs, as shown in illustration of No. 1. In the price lines LL indicates low legs and HL indicates high legs. No. 9 is suitable for a flock of 150 fowls, has bone box 3¼x3x11 inches inside, has solid nut and adjustable automatic feed. No. 10 is same as No. 9 except that it has a split nut. No. 11 is suitable for a flock of 250 fowls, has a bone box 4x3x13 inches inside, has solid nut and adjustable automatic feed. No. 12 is same as No. 11 except that it has a split nut. Price is for cutter with handle on rim of balance wheel to be run by hand. Pulley, 12 inches in diameter with 4-inch face, to adapt machine for belt power, will be furnished for **$1.30 extra.** Shipped from factory in Western Pennsylvania.

Catalogue No.			Weight, pounds	Price
32C2714	No. 9LL	Bone Cutter.	107	$8.40
32C2715	No. 9HL	Bone Cutter.	125	10.10
32C2716	No. 11LL	Bone Cutter.	120	10.95
32C2717	No. 11HL	Bone Cutter.	138	12.40
32C2718	No. 10LL	Bone Cutter.	108	10.15
32C2719	No. 10HL	Bone Cutter.	126	11.75
32C2720	No. 12LL	Bone Cutter.	121	12.45
32C2721	No. 12HL	Bone Cutter.	139	14.00

Kenwood Poultry Vegetable and Root Cutter, $3.80.

Exclusively for poultry, not for stock. Cuts all kinds of roots and vegetables into fine ribbon like shavings, which are easily eaten by all kinds of poultry. Has adjustable steel knives and is fitted with an iron grating which allows all dirt and gravel to escape before reaching the knives. Suitable for a flock of any number of fowls, up to 1,000. Price does not include the measure.

No. 32C2735 Poultry Root Cutter. Weight, 40 pounds. Price....................**$3.80**

Humpty-Dumpty Folding Egg Crate.

24c

Will hold twelve dozen eggs and is complete with standard fillers. When empty, can be folded for shipping, as shown in the illustration, and can be put away in small space. Strongly made with hardwood slats. Ships best in lots of six.

No. 32C2753 Folding Egg Crate. Weight, 5¾ pounds. Price, each......**24c**

IF YOU CANNOT MAKE A SATISFACTORY SELECTION FROM THESE PAGES, DON'T THINK OF BUYING FROM ANYONE UNTIL YOU HAVE SENT FOR AND RECEIVED OUR BIG FREE SPECIAL AGRICULTURAL IMPLEMENT CATALOGUE.

Kenwood Poultry Fountain and Hen House Warmer, $3.95.

Made of heavy sheet metal and nicely painted. Holds 10 gallons of water and is so constructed as to supply the poultry with water just as fast, and no faster, than they drink it. The heat from the lamp warms the water and the radiation from the lamp and water keeps the hen house comfortable. The cups from which the poultry drink, fill automatically. Water is always clean and fresh. Weight, 30 pounds.

No. 32C2754 Poultry Fountain and Warmer. Price **$3.95**

Kenwood Folding Egg Tester.

This is a very simple and inexpensive egg tester, but perfect in every respect. It is made of pasteboard with holes to receive the eggs and with a mirror in the bottom to reflect the light. Weight, ¼ pound.

No. 32C2757 Folding Egg Tester. Price.... 10c

Kenwood Spring Lever Poultry Punch.

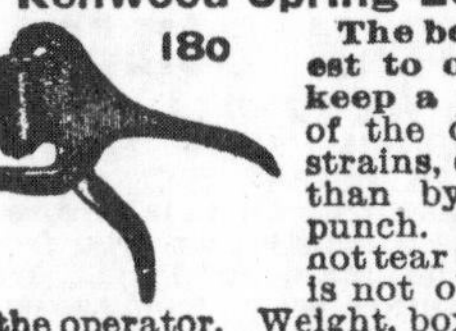

The best, the simplest and easiest to operate. If you wish to keep a record of your chickens, of the different breeds, hatches, strains, etc., there is no better way than by using our spring lever punch. It makes a clean cut, will not tear the web, and its operation is not obstructed by the hands of the operator. Weight, boxed, 2 ounces.

No. 32C2759 Poultry Punch. Price.......... **18c**

Sanitary Nest Eggs, 4 Cents.

These eggs are not intended to take the place of regular nest eggs, but are a sanitary article, the proper use of which will kill lice and mites, without damage to the fowls. They will also kill the germs which so often cause roup, and being a disinfectant, they destroy offensive odors. Put up in boxes of four eggs with instructions on each box. Should be ordered in lots of four or in even dozens.

No. 32C2760 Sanitary Nest Eggs. Weight, 1 ounce. Price, per egg.............................. **4c**

Kenwood Woven Wire Hen's Nests.

These nests are made of japanned steel wire. They are clean and afford no place for vermin. Can be fastened to the wall with two nails or screws. They are made with 1¼-inch mesh solid woven wire cloth, which prevents eggs from dropping out. Should be lined with hay or straw, so as to make a clean, natural nest. The No. 1 nest is 12½ inches in diameter and weighs 5 ounces. The No. 2 nest is 14½ inches in diameter and weighs 8 ounces.

No. 32C2761 No. 1 Wire Hen's Nest. Price... **5c**
No. 2 Wire Hen's Nest. Price.. **8c**

Kenwood Round Poultry Fountains, 23 to 38 Cents.

These fountains are made of galvanized steel, and will not burst open should the water be allowed to freeze in them, unless they are entirely full and freeze solid. As the parts are easily separated, they can be scalded and kept clean at all times. No. 1, holds ½ gallon; weighs, 1 pound. No. 2 holds 1 gallon; weighs 1½ pounds. No. 3 holds 2 gallons; weighs 2 pounds.

No. 32C2767 No. 1 Fountain. Price **23c**
No. 32C2768 No. 2 Fountain. Price......... **30c**
No. 32C2769 No. 3 Fountain. Price.......... **38c**

Kenwood Outdoor Brooders.

$4.65 to $14.15

In this illustration we show our 300-Chick Outdoor Brooder. The 100-chick and 200-chick brooders are practically the same, except that they do not have the hinged door and wire netting in the end. The 50-chick brooder is built on exactly the same principles, but with its top slanting all one way and the door for the chicks to pass in and out is on the side instead of on the end. All of these brooders are supplied with overhead heat, by a double heating system which provides heat on the mother hen plan, and in the quantity required for outdoor use. One lamp produces all the heat necessary, and it is surrounded by a metal jacket, which protects it from storm and wind, and makes a safeguard against accidents. The top is wood, but it is covered with iron sheathing, and this iron is protected by two coats of paint. The heat, whether by hot air or hot water, is distributed by pipes, which are so arranged that the heat is uniform and is easily kept at the required temperature. These brooders can be used indoors as well as outdoors. Furnished complete with runway and thermometer. Shipped set up from factory in Western Illinois.

No. 32C6226 50-Chick Outdoor Hot Air Brooder. Weight, 60 pounds. Price......... **$4.65**

No. 32C6227 50-Chick Outdoor Hot Water Brooder. Weight, 62 pounds. Price......... **$5.40**

No. 32C6228 100-Chick Outdoor Hot Air Brooder. Weight, 65 pounds. Price......... **$6.00**

No. 32C6229 100-Chick Outdoor Hot Water Brooder. Weight, 70 pounds. Price......... **$7.80**

No. 32C6230 200-Chick Outdoor Hot Air Brooder. Weight, 84 pounds. Price......... **$9.30**

No. 32C6231 200-Chick Outdoor Hot Water Brooder. Weight, 86 pounds. Price......... **$10.90**

No. 32C6232 300-Chick Outdoor Hot Air Brooder. Weight, 125 pounds. Price....... **$11.75**

No. 32C6233 300-Chick Outdoor Hot Water Brooder. Weight, 161 pounds. Price....... **$14.15**

INCUBATORS, BROODERS AND POULTRY SUPPLIES.

A Special Catalogue of Incubators and Brooders mailed free on request.

Our line of these goods is so extensive that we issue a big special catalogue devoted entirely to Incubators, Brooders, Combined Incubators and Brooders, Bone Cutters and general supplies for the poultry raiser, and containing a great deal of very interesting information pertaining to successful poultry raising. This handsome and complete **Incubator and Brooder Catalogue** will be sent to you free if you will write and ask us to send it. We show a few of the most popular incubators, brooders and poultry supplies in this catalogue and you can make your selection with every assurance that the goods will give you perfect satisfaction or your money and freight charges will be refunded, but if you want a different incubator or brooder or other poultry supplies, or want to learn more about these goods, how and of what materials they are made and why they are better than you can buy elsewhere at much higher prices than ours, then write for our free **Incubator and Brooder Catalogue.**

Kenwood Improved Incubators.

An exceedingly popular line of medium priced incubators. We recommend them to all classes of poultry raisers and guarantee that they will do as good work as any incubator made, regardless of price. The walls of these incubators are double, the space between them being carefully insulated with the best non-conductors of heat known. The tops and bottoms are also double, both being carefully and thoroughly insulated, so as to overcome any possibility of the outside temperature affecting the egg chamber. All sizes have single doors with double glass, leaving a dead air space between the glass. The doors close tightly against jambs, thus excluding all air from the egg chamber, except that which reaches the chamber through the ventilating system. The glass door enables the operator to observe the thermometer, which can be easily seen and read at all times. The eggs in these incubators are turned by hand in the ordinary manner. The 60-egg, 100-egg and 210-egg incubators each have single trays; the 290-egg incubators have two trays. All trays are strongly made with crossbars on the under side. Furnished complete with egg tester, thermometer, directions and everything complete to make the machine ready for operation. Shipped from factory in Western Illinois.

No. 32C6024 60-Egg Improved Hot Air Incubator. Weight, 44 pounds. Price............... **$7.20**

No. 32C6025 60-Egg Improved Hot Water Incubator. Weight, 46 pounds. Price......... **$8.40**

No. 32C6026 100-Egg Improved Hot Air Incubator. Weight, 115 pounds. Price............ **$9.60**

No. 32C6027 100-Egg Improved Hot Water Incubator. Weight, 118 pounds. Price...... **$11.45**

No. 32C6028 210-Egg Improved Hot Air Incubator. Weight, 165 pounds. Price........... **$12.95**

No. 32C6029 210-Egg Improved Hot Water Incubator. Weight, 170 pounds. Price...... **$14.10**

No. 32C6030 290-Egg Improved Hot Air Incubator. Weight, 195 pounds. Price........... **$17.70**

No. 22C6031 290-Egg Improved Hot Water Incubator. Weight, 205 pounds. Price...... **$21.25**

OUR INCUBATORS AND BROODERS

are made by the best and foremost manufacturer of this line in the country.

They are the highest grade, most improved, easiest operated, and most successful machines on the market.

Kenwood Special Incubators.

$3.95 to $10.85

These incubators are intended only for use within a room or building where the temperature is practically even at all times, and when so used they will produce as good results as any incubator made. The walls are single, without dead air space or packing. The bottom is double, with a single layer of insulation between. The top is double, and is carefully and thoroughly insulated. This construction serves to prevent the outside temperature of the room from affecting the egg chamber. The doors are single, with double glass, leaving a dead air space between the glass. They close tightly against a jamb, thus excluding all air from the egg chamber, except that which reaches the chamber through the ventilating system. The glass door enables the operator to observe the thermometer, which can be easily seen and read at all times. The eggs in these incubators are turned by hand in the ordinary manner. The 60-egg and 100-egg incubators each have single trays. The 220-egg incubator has two trays. Furnished complete with egg tester, thermometer, directions and everything complete to make the machine ready for operation. Shipped from factory in Western Illinois.

No. 32C6048 60-Egg Special Hot Air Incubator. Weight, 44 pounds. Price........................ **$3.95**

No. 32C6050 100-Egg Special Hot Air Incubator. Weight, 58 pounds. Price.................. **$6.30**

No. 32C6052 220-Egg Special Hot Air Incubator. Weight, 105 pounds Price......... ..... **$10.85**

Kenwood Indoor Brooders.

$2.75 to $11.50

The illustration is of the 300-Chick Brooder. The 50-chick, 100-chick and 200-chick brooders are exactly the same, except that they have a round door and the draft pipe projects at the end opposite from the lamp. The heating system of these brooders is overhead, providing heat the same as from a mother hen. The bottom of the brooder is raised above the ground to give ventilation and keep the brooder from gathering dampness. The heat, whether it be hot air or hot water, is distributed by pipes which are so arranged that the heat is uniform and is easily kept at the required temperature. Furnished complete with runway and thermometer. Shipped set up from factory in Western Illinois.

No.	Description	Price
No. 32C6200	50-Chick Indoor Hot Air Brooder. Weight, 35 pounds. Price	$ 2.75
No. 32C6201	50-Chick Indoor Hot Water Brooder. Weight, 37 pounds. Price	4.30
No. 32C6202	100-Chick Indoor Hot Air Brooder. Weight, 50 pounds. Price	5.15
No. 32C6203	100-Chick Indoor Hot Water Brooder. Weight, 53 pounds. Price	6.60
No. 32C6204	200-Chick Indoor Hot Air Brooder. Weight, 57 pounds. Price	7.25
No. 32C6205	200-Chick Indoor Hot Water Brooder. Weight, 60 pounds. Price	9.65
No. 32C6206	300-Chick Indoor Hot Air Brooder. Weight, 79 pounds. Price	9.70
No. 32C6207	300-Chick Indoor Hot Water Brooder. Weight, 83 pounds. Price	11.50

Kenwood Bee Hives.

$7.50 for Five.

These are known as 1½-Story Bee Hives; that is, they consist of a complete brood hive, and one complete hive super. They are regular standard size, all parts being interchangeable with standard dovetailed hives. They are 18¼ inches long, 12¼ inches wide, the brood hive 9½ inches deep and the hive super 4¾ inches deep, all being inside measurements. A complete brood hive consists of one body, eight self spacing brood frames, one division board or follower, one bottom board and one lock cap cover. A complete hive super consists of one body, six scalloped section holders, five separators scalloped on the lower edge, one adjustable follow board, twenty-four 4¼x4¼x1⅞ inch scalloped sections, and two steel pressure springs. **Wax comb foundation for brood frames and sections is not included in price. It must be ordered, if wanted, and is sold only by the pound.** These hives are not painted. They are shipped partly knocked down and crated. They are generally sold in lots of five or multiples of five, therefore, they are put up in crates of five complete brood hives and five complete hive supers. On orders for less than five we are compelled to make a little higher price to cover cost of special packing. Our scalloped sections are No. 1 grade, 4¼x4¼x1⅞ inches, and are sold only in the quantities we name; price does not include foundation starters.

No. 32C2825 Crate of five 1½-Story Bee Hives, in knock down, complete. Wt. 130 lbs. Price.. **$7.50**

No. 32C2827 Crate of five Hive Supers, in knock down, complete. Weight, 38 pounds. Price. **$2.60**

No. 32C2828 Single 1½-Story Bee Hive, in knock down, complete. Weight, 26 pounds. Price.. **$1.80**

No. 32C2831 Single Hive Super, in knock down, complete. Weight, 8 pounds. Price............ **65c**

No. 32C2832 Crate of 500 sections, in knock down. Weight, 36 pounds. Price............ **$2.45**

No. 32C2833 Crate of 250 sections, in knock down. Weight, 18 pounds. Price............ **$1.45**

IF YOU CANNOT MAKE A SATISFACTORY SELECTION FROM THESE PAGES, DON'T THINK OF BUYING FROM ANYONE UNTIL YOU HAVE SENT FOR AND RECEIVED OUR BIG FREE SPECIAL AGRICULTURAL IMPLEMENT CATALOGUE.

Wax Comb Foundation.

Made of strictly pure, bright yellow wax, very tough and perfectly free from grit and dirt. Bright and easily worked by bees. Sold only in even pounds.

No. 32C2835 Medium Brood Foundation. Sheets, 8x16¼ inches. Seven sheets are called one pound. Price, per pound........51c

No. 32C2836 Thin Super Foundation. For section boxes only. Sheets, 3¾x16¼ inches. Twenty-seven sheets are called 1 pound. Price, per lb....58c

Kenwood Bee Smoker.

75c

A convenient, well made and very serviceable smoker. Has 3¼-inch fire chamber made of heavy tin, beaded. The metal parts which attach the fire chamber to the bellows are riveted to the fire chamber and screwed to the bellows. Nozzle is hinged to the top of bellows. Weight, 1¼ pounds.

No. 32C2843 Kenwood Bee Smoker. Price, 75c

Kenwood Delivery Carts.

$4.60 and $5.65

These carts are absolutely the best, strongest, lightest and most durable carts which can be made. The axles are solid steel; wheels have heavy steel rod spokes set closely together, firmly riveted into broad half oval steel tires and into both ends of the long wheel hubs. Boxes are made of ⅝-inch lumber with iron bound tops. Side boards are held in place by iron stakes and sockets. End boards set between cleats on the side boards and are securely held by end rods. Both ends and sides can be removed, leaving bottom flat. Boxes are supported by strong steel leaf springs. Handles are strong iron tubing and are firmly braced with steel rods. When standing still, the end of the two-wheel cart is supported by a hinged steel drop leg. The three-wheel cart has a 14-inch third wheel under rear end of cart, but does not have a drop leg. These carts may be pushed or pulled and will carry 200 to 400 pounds. They have ⅝-inch square axle with ⅝-inch spindles, 28-inch wheels with 1-inch tires; box is 34 inches long by 18¾ inches wide and 7 inches deep inside. Shipped knocked down and crated.

No. 32C2901 Two-Wheel Delivery Cart. Weight, 70 pounds. Price........$4.60

No. 32C2903 Three-Wheel Delivery Cart. Weight, 85 pounds. Price........5.65

Kenwood Hand Cart.

$4.35

This cart is strongly constructed and for ordinary use it will be found just as useful and as desirable as our higher priced carts. The box is made of ⅝-inch lumber and measures 36 inches long, 21 inches wide and 9¼ inches deep inside. The handles are strong bent wood with a convenient crossbar. The axle is 1-inch round steel. The wheels are 36 inches high, with 1¼-inch half oval tires. End boards are held in place by steel rods. Entire box can be removed or both end boards can be taken out, leaving the bottom clear. Weight, 90 pounds. Shipped knocked down.

No. 32C2907 Kenwood Hand Cart. Price. $4.35

Kenwood Steel Frame Barrel Cart.

$2.85

Will outlast several wood frame carts. Made entirely of steel and iron. The steel wheels are 36 inches high, with 1¼ x ¼-inch steel tires. The steel frame is bolted solidly to the axle castings, and these castings are made to fit the side of a barrel to which they are to be bolted. A kerosene, molasses or vinegar barrel can be used. Price includes bolts to attach to barrel and one iron bracket or rest for bottom of barrel. Weight, 55 pounds. Shipped knocked down.

No. 32C2909 Barrel Cart. Price........$2.85

Kenwood Adjustable Swinging Cattle Stanchion.

95c

This stanchion is much superior to any other stanchion now on the market. It is self locking, easily unlocked, allows the animal to lie down or turn its head with perfect freedom, and is held square and firm when open. The stanchion is 4 feet high, with 6¼-inch space between the upright bars. The bars are made of the best quality of hardwood and are strongly braced by iron brackets at top and bottom. Both top and bottom are made of steel and iron, and the pivots are iron. Sold in any quantity, but the freight on six or eight is only about the same as on one.

No. 32C2939 Kenwood Cattle Stanchion. Weight, 15 pounds. Price........95c

Kenwood General Utility Cart.

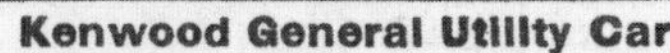

Cart - $3.55
Box - 1.45

Almost indispensable on any farm. Can be used as a barrel cart in connection with any number of barrels only requiring an extra pair of barrel irons for each extra barrel. Can also be used with the box, and the box can be dumped easily or removed instantly. Wheels are steel and 36 inches high with 1¼ x ¼-inch steel tires. Frame is hardwood and is strongly braced. Can be used with a kerosene, molasses or vinegar barrel. Price of the cart includes one set of barrel irons and bolts for attaching. Box is about 40 inches long by 26 inches wide and 6 inches deep inside. Wire reel attachment can be used for paying out or winding up barbed wire. Shipped knocked down.

No. 32C2911 Utility Cart, without box. Weight, 80 pounds. Price........$3.55

No. 32C2912 Cart Box. Weight, 47 pounds. Price........$1.45

No. 32C2913 Pair of Barrel Irons. Weight, 8 pounds. Price........44c

No. 32C2914 Wire Reel Attachment. For barbed wire reels. Weight, 18 pounds. Price, $1.40

Kenwood Stock, Grain and Hay Rack.

$15.00 TO $16.50

There is no better rack made at any price. Worth two of the ordinary cheaply constructed racks. Box bottom is 1-inch matched southern hard pine, with 2x4-inch oak cleats. Box sides are 1⅛-inch Norway pine, 9¼ inches deep, with wrought iron braces, 7/16-inch end rods and 19-inch front end. Rack sides are 1¾x2-inch white oak posts, with 1-inch hard pine side strips, all firmly put together with iron hinges, bolts and rivets. Sides and ends of rack can be lifted out of sockets and removed from box. Front ladder is 6 feet high. When closed, the rack is 38 inches high from bottom of box. When opened, it is 7 feet 3 inches wide. Weight, 500 pounds. Shipped knocked down from factory in Northeastern Indiana.

No. 32C2950 14-Foot Combination Rack for 38-inch bolster. Price........$15.00

No. 32C2951 14-Foot Combination Rack for 42-inch bolster. Price........$15.50

No. 32C2952 16-Foot Combination Rack for 38-inch bolster. Price........$16.00

No. 32C2953 16-Foot Combination Rack for 42-inch bolster. Price........$16.50

GASOLINE ENGINES, STEAM ENGINES AND STEAM BOILERS.

A SPECIAL ENGINE CATALOGUE MAILED FREE ON REQUEST.

OUR LINE OF STATIONARY GASOLINE ENGINES, MARINE GASOLINE ENGINES, VERTICAL STEAM ENGINES, HORIZONTAL STEAM ENGINES, VERTICAL STEAM BOILERS, HORIZONTAL STEAM BOILERS, ETC. is so complete and so extensive, that we find it necessary to issue a special catalogue which is devoted exclusively to this line of goods. This handsome and complete Engine Catalogue will be sent to you free if you are desirous of purchasing an engine and will write and ask us to send the catalogue to you. We show some of our most popular engines in this catalogue, and you can make your selection from the engines we list herein, with every assurance that the engine will give you perfect satisfaction, or your money and transportation charges will be refunded, but if you want a different engine, or wish to learn more about the engines before placing your order, how they are made, what materials they are made of, why they are better engines than you can purchase elsewhere at much higher prices, then write for our free Engine Catalogue.

Kenwood New Model Vertical Stationary Gasoline Engines.

$71.00 TO $135.00

These engines are complete within themselves and are adapted for generating power for such purposes as pumping water, operating farm machinery of all kinds that can be run by belt power, running machinery in blacksmith, carpenter and jobbing shops of all kinds, and for operating small manufacturing plants, grain elevators, printing offices, etc. They are mounted on skids and the water tank and gasoline tank are on the skids and connected to the engine, and the jump spark electric igniters have the batteries wired up and connected, so that when you receive the engine it is ready for work. They are furnished complete with muffler, tools and instruction book. The 1-horse power engine has 6 by 3-inch pulley, makes 400 revolutions per minute and weighs 580 pounds. The 2½-Horse power engine has 6 by 4-inch pulley, makes 400 revolutions per minute and weighs 660 pounds. The 4-horse power engine has 8 by 5-inch pulley, makes 350 revolutions per minute and weighs 900 pounds. Shipped from factory in Southwestern Ohio.

No. 32C4801 One-Horse Power Vertical Gasoline Engine. Price........$71.00

No. 32C4804 Two and One-Half-Horse Power Vertical Gasoline Engine. Price........$98.00

No. 32C4807 Four-Horse Power Vertical Gasoline Engine. Price........$135.00

Kenwood Vertical Steam Engines and Boilers.

$39.00 to $82.00

$35.00 to $98.00

These engines are of the center crank type, strong and well built, nicely finished and handsomely painted. They are furnished complete with governor, oil cups, throttle valve, lubricator, pulley and fly wheel. The boilers are made of 60,000-pound tensile strength flange steel, have lap welded tubes, a water leg, four hand holes and are tested at 150 pounds hydrostatic pressure. They are furnished complete with base, hood, grates, injector, steam gauge, water gauge, gauge cocks, pop safety valve and blow off, check and stop valves. When engines and boilers are ordered together, they will be shipped on separate bases unless ordered on combined base. Price includes steam and exhaust pipe only when engine and boiler are both ordered. Shipped from factory in Southwestern Michigan.

Engines.

Catalogue No.	Size of Engine	Size of Pulley	Rev. per Minute	Wt. lbs.	Price
No. 32C5100	1½-H. P.,	6x3½-in.	400	250..	$39.00
No. 32C5101	2 -H. P.,	10x4½-in.	350	325..	50.00
No. 32C5102	3 -H. P.,	10x4½-in.	350	350..	54.00
No. 32C5103	4 -H. P.,	12x4½-in.	325	500..	62.00
No. 32C5104	5 -H. P.,	12x4½-in.	325	550..	71.00
No. 32C5105	6 -H. P.,	14x6½-in.	250	750..	82.00

Boilers.

Catalogue No.	Description	Weight	Price
No. 32C5121	2-H. P. Boiler.	Wt., 560 lbs..	$53.00
No. 32C5122	3-H. P. Boiler.	Wt., 620 lbs..	57.00
No. 32C5123	4-H. P. Boiler.	Wt., 890 lbs..	70.00
No. 32C5124	5-H. P. Boiler.	Wt., 1060 lbs..	76.00
No. 32C5125	6-H. P. Boiler.	Wt., 1300 lbs..	87.00
No. 32C5126	8-H. P. Boiler.	Wt., 1550 lbs..	98.00
No. 32C5263	2-inch Whistle fitted to boiler,		2.60

Kenwood New Model Horizontal Stationary Gasoline Engines.

$152.00 TO $265.00

Our horizontal gasoline engines are adapted for generating power for all purposes where power is transmitted by belt, and are adapted for private electric light plants, they being steady running and close governing engines. They are furnished complete with water tank and fittings, gasoline tank and fittings, jump spark electric igniter, muffler, tools and instruction book. The 4-horse power engine has 12 by 6-inch pulley, makes 325 revolutions per minute and weighs 1,100 pounds. The 6-horse power engine has 12 by 7-inch pulley, makes 280 revolutions per minute and weighs 1,500 pounds. The 8-horse power engine has 16 by 8-inch pulley, makes 260 revolutions per minute and weighs 2,200 pounds. Shipped from factory in Southwestern Ohio.

No. 32C4821 Four-Horse Power Horizontal Gasoline Engine. Price........$152.00

No. 32C4824 Six-Horse Power Horizontal Gasoline Engine. Price........$209.00

No. 32C4827 Eight-Horse Power Horizontal Gasoline Engine. Price........$265.00

IF YOU CANNOT MAKE A SATISFACTORY SELECTION FROM THESE PAGES, DON'T THINK OF BUYING FROM ANYONE UNTIL YOU HAVE SENT FOR AND RECEIVED OUR BIG FREE SPECIAL AGRICULTURAL IMPLEMENT CATALOGUE.

BOOK DEPARTMENT.

IN THE FOLLOWING PAGES will be found an interesting and comprehensive list of books on subjects that appeal to everyone, no matter what his hobby, inclination or occupation. These titles have been selected with great care from our large Special Book and Stationery Catalogue, a copy of which you should have.

PLEASE INCLUDE YOUR ORDER FOR BOOKS WITH YOUR ORDER FOR OTHER MERCHANDISE. We do not accept orders for less than 50 cents, as explained on page 2. You can save nearly all the express or mail charges on books by including them with your order for other goods to go by freight. The extra freight charges by reason of including the books with your shipment, will amount to practically nothing.

ABOUT MAIL SHIPMENTS. WHEN BOOKS ARE TO BE SENT BY MAIL BE SURE TO ENCLOSE ENOUGH EXTRA TO PAY POSTAGE. If you send too much we will immediately return the balance, but if you do not send enough we will be compelled to hold your order and write for the balance. DO NOT OVERLOOK THE NECESSARY POSTAGE IN ORDERING BOOKS BY MAIL.

OUR CLUB ORDER SYSTEM COMMENDS ITSELF TO BOOK BUYERS, for you will observe in looking over this catalogue that we have been able to figure our prices so low on many of the books that we can quote them to you at but little more than the cost of postage. For example, our Standard Books, beautiful cloth bound books at 12 cents each, postage, 10 cents per volume.

It is therefore much cheaper to have books shipped by express or freight, freight being preferable. The transportation cost per volume is then reduced to next to nothing. To take advantage of the lowest transportation rate, it is desirable to make up a freight order. This you can do by getting your friends and neighbors to join with you and make up a club order.

We always advise our readers to make their book orders large enough that we may ship by freight, but if one or more books are wanted by mail, the EXTRA POSTAGE must be included.

OUR FREE SPECIAL BOOK CATALOGUE.

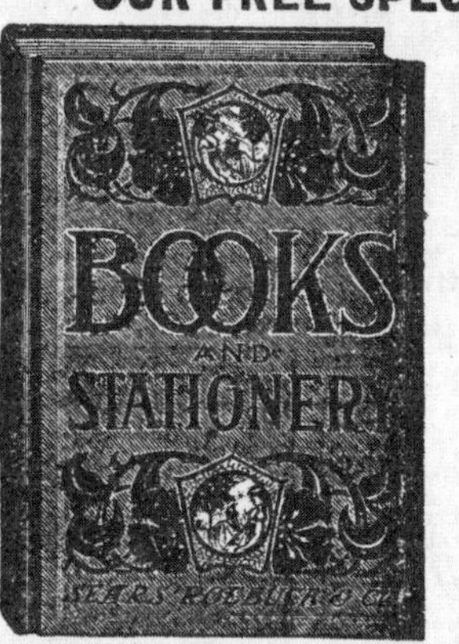

IF YOU ARE UNABLE TO FIND JUST THE BOOK YOU WANT ON THESE PAGES, write and ask for our free Book Catalogue. Our line of books is so very large, embracing all the best books on all subjects, that we find it impossible to illustrate and describe our complete line of books in this, our general catalogue, and we therefore issue a special 238-page catalogue covering books and stationery exclusively, and if you do not find the book you want in this large catalogue, don't fail to write for our free special Book Catalogue. On the following pages you will find our greatest values in books, the best bargains we have to offer, almost a complete line on every subject and it is really unnecessary to first write for our free Book Catalogue if you can make a selection from the ones in this catalogue. At the same time, if you don't find the book you want, or if you are buying books constantly and want the most complete book and stationery catalogue ever issued, write and ask for our free Book Catalogue to be sent to you immediately by mail, postpaid.

AGRICULTURE.

Gardener's Assistant, American.

By Thomas Bridgeman. A new and enlarged edition. Contains practical directions for the cultivation of vegetables, flowers, fruit trees, etc. Illustrated. Cloth. Size, 5¾x7¾ inches. Retail price, $1.00.
No. 3C9159 Our price............75c
If by mail, postage extra, 12 cents.

Small Fruit Culturist.

By Andrew S. Fuller. This book covers the whole ground of propagating small fruits, their culture, varieties, packing for market, etc. Finely and thoroughly illustrated. 298 pages. Cloth. Size, 5x7 inches. Retail price, $1.00.
No. 3C9205 Our price 70c
If by mail, postage extra, 10 cents.

SEND FOR OUR FREE BOOK CATALOGUE.

It contains the best books on Agriculture, Farming, Gardening, Fruit Culture and Flowers.

ARCHITECTURE.

Embracing modern building, house and barn plans, carpentry, estimating, stone masonry, carpenters' tools and their uses, etc.

American Architecture Palliser's.

American Architecture; or, Every Man a Complete Builder. Contains 104 pages; giving detailed plans and instructions how to build cottages, double houses, brick block houses, costing from $300.00 to $6,500.00 each, etc. Size, 10¾ x 13¾ inches.
No. 3C9260 Paper. Price.........58c
If by mail, postage extra, 11 cents.

American Ideal Homes.

Radford's Celebrated Book.

Latest and best book published. Illustrating new houses, summer cottages, churches, barns and lumber sheds, etc., ranging in price from $550.00 to $6,500.00 each, giving all the comforts and conveniences, and suited to every taste, location, want, etc. Cloth. Size, 7½x10½ inches.
No. 3C9268 Price.....................63c

IMPORTANT.—We can furnish any blue print or plan in any book we list at 10 per cent less than the prices listed. Do not fail to give number of blue print wanted.

American Sanitary Plumbing.

By James J. Lawler. Revised edition. A practical work on the best methods of modern plumbing, illustrating with original sketches, the fundamental principles of everything the plumber should know. Illustrated. Cloth. Size, 5½ x 8¾ inches. Retail price, $2.25.
No. 3C9280 Our price...............$1.29
If by mail, postage extra, 12 cents.

Barn Plans and Outbuildings.

A new work, full of ideas, hints, suggestions, plans, etc., for the construction of barns and outbuildings. Many chapters are devoted to the economic erection and use of grain houses, cattle and sheep barns, corn, smoke and ice houses, etc. Cloth. Size, 7½x5¼ inches. 235 pages. Retail price, $1.00.
No. 3C9282 Our price.................75c
If by mail, postage extra, 10 cents.

Builders' Architectural Drawing Self Taught.

By Fred T. Hodgson. This work is especially designed for carpenters and architects and other wood workers who desire to learn drawing at home, and who have not the means, time or opportunity for taking a regular course in school or college, or availing themselves of the offers made by one or other of the "Correspondence Schools." Over 300 fine line engravings made especially for the work, each drawn to scale, 18 large double folding plates with full explanation for each. Also contains perspective views and floor plans of 50 low and medium priced houses. Cloth. Size 5¾x7¾ inches. 300 pages.
No. 3C9298 Price..................$1.25
If by mail, postage extra, 14 cents.

Modern Carpentry.

By Fred T. Hodgson. A practical manual for carpenters and wood workers. A new, complete guide, containing hundreds of quick methods for performing work in carpentry, joining and general woodwork. Like all of Mr. Hodgson's books, it is written in a simple, everyday style, and does not bewilder the workingman with long mathematical formulas or abstract theories. The illustrations, of which there are many, are explanatory, so that anyone who can read, will be able to understand them easily and to follow the work in hand without difficulty. Cloth, 320 pages, 230 illustrations. Size, 5¼x7¾ inches.
No. 3C9308 Price.....................58c
If by mail, postage extra, 11 cents.

Cottage Homes and Details.

By George Palliser. Contains 160 new and original designs for cottages and villas, costing from $75.00 to $7,500, giving all the comforts and conveniences, and suited to every taste, location, want, etc. Fifty new designs for city brick block houses. Twelve new designs for stable and carriage houses. 1,500 detail drawings, covering the whole range of interior finishing and exterior construction and ornamentation of the plans of this work, and all to a uniform scale. Printed on heavy cream plate paper, handsomely bound, with leather back. Boards. Size, 11x14 inches.
No. 3C9312 Price.................$1.98
If by mail, postage extra, 30 cents.

Foundations and Foundation Walls.

By George T. Powell. New and enlarged edition. A valuable book for architects, engineers, masons, builders and others. Explains all about pile driving, building stones and brick. Contains illustrations of foundations, piers, wall construction. Cloth. Retail price, $2.00. Size, 6¼x9 inches.
No. 3C9332 Price.................$1.48
If by mail, postage extra, 15 cents.

Practical Housebuilder.

Contains 50 plans and specifications of dwellings, summer cottages, barns, churches, etc. Ranging in cost from $450.00 to $6,200.00 each. Adapted to all conditions of town and country, with accurate estimates of material and cost. Size, 4½x6¾ inches.
No. 3C9338 Paper. Price.................14c
No. 3C9341 Cloth. Price.................27c
If by mail, postage extra, paper, 8c; cloth, 5c.

Hodgson's Estimator and Contractors' Guide.

By Fred T. Hodgson. Describing reliable methods of pricing builders' quantities for competitive work. Contains a concise explanation of the various methods of estimating builders' work by the square, by the cubic foot, in rough quantities, accurate quantities and other methods. The mason, plasterer, carpenter, bricklayer, contractor, painter and plumber will find rules and methods given in this volume for estimating the cost of work, how much material the work on hand will require, to which is added rules and memoranda tables showing quick methods for obtaining results in estimating. 300 pages, fully illustrated. Cloth. Size, 5½x7¾ inches.
No. 3C9345 Our price...............$1.05
If by mail, postage extra, 12 cents.

Hot Water Heating, Steam and Gas Fitting.

By James J. Lawler. New Revised Edition. A book for plumbers, steam fitters, architects, builders, apprentices and householders. Showing the latest and most approved devices and appliances used; also, the quickest method of doing hot water heating, steam and gas fitting up to the present date. Illustrated. Size, 6x8¾ inches. Cloth. Retail price, $2.00.
No. 3C9346 Our price...............$1.30
If by mail, postage extra, 12 cents.

Hodgson's Low Cost American Homes.

By Fred T. Hodgson, M. O. A. A. This book contains perspective views and floor plans of one hundred houses, churches, schoolhouses and barns, and is, without a doubt, the most practical work ever issued. The plans shown have been built from, and many of them duplicated many times over. All are practical, the creation of the well known author, and many other architects throughout the United States and Canada. Cloth, 200 pages, 200 illustrations. Size, 5¼x7¾ inches.
No. 3C9356 Price......................60c
If by mail, postage extra, 10 cents.

Common Sense Stair Building.

By Fred T. Hodgson. The systems outlined in this book are new, simple, plain, and may be learned in an hour, and are such as are employed by the most successful carpenters. It contains not only the simplest system of stairbuilding, outlining newel and platform stairs chiefly, and gives instructions for their building, planning, and decorations, but also outlines the best methods known in the art of hand railing, with complete instructions for laying out and working handrails suitable for any kind of stairs. Cloth. Size, 5¼x7¾ inches. Retail price, $1.00.
No. 3C9365 Our price.................60c
If by mail, postage extra, 11 cents.

COMPLETE BUILDER'S LIBRARY
BY FRED T. HODGSON.
Consisting of No. 3C9298, No. 3C9308, No. 3C9345, No. 3C9356, No. 3C9365, No. 3C9371 and No. 3C80466, all listed on this page for only $5.75.
Send for Free Book Catalogue, or write for full information.

The Steel Square and Its Uses.

Complete Modern Treatise. By Fred T. Hodgson. This is the only work on the steel square and its uses published. It is an exhaustive work, written in simple language and including some very ingenious devices for laying out bevels for rafters, braces and other inclined work; also chapters on the square as a calculating machine, showing how to measure solids, surfaces, and distances—very useful to builders and estimators. Chapters on roofing and how to form them by the aid of the square. Chapters on heavy timber framing, showing how the square is used for laying out mortises, tenons, shoulders, etc. The work also contains a large number of diagrams, showing how the square may be used in finding bevels, angles, etc. 350 pages in each volume. Cloth. Illustrated. Size, 5¼x7 inches.
No. 3C9369 Volume I. Price..$0.58
No. 3C9370 Volume 2. Price.. .58
No. 3C9371 Two Vols. Price... 1.10
If by mail, postage extra, either volume 12 cents.

Useful Details.

By George Palliser. A new and practical work on every description of modern architectural detail. Contains 40 plates, size, 20x26 inches. Given on a very large scale, and embraces a variety of constructional drawings for all kinds of work, exterior and interior, pertaining to the erection of buildings of every description. Size, 14x22 inches. Retail price, $2.00.
No. 3C9384 Portfolio style. Our price..............................98c
If by mail, postage extra, 16 cents.

NOTE—Our Book Catalogue contains a complete list of the best books published on Architecture, Carpentry, Building, Stone and Stone Working. It's free, send for a copy.

ASTROLOGY, PALMISTRY, HYPNOTISM, PHRENOLOGY, MAGIC AND OCCULT SCIENCES.

Astrology, Practical.

By Comte C. de Saint Germain. The language of the stars easily comprehended. Unfolding the wonderful wisdom of the Chaldean, Egyptian, Greek and Arabian astrologers. Simple, amusing, instructive and elevating. Learn from the stars what you are, what possibilities you have, and what dangers beset your path. Illustrated. Size, 5¼x7½ inches. Retail price, 50c.
No. 3C9400 Cloth. Our price......................30c
No. 3C9402 Paper cover. Retail price, 25 cents. Our price..........................18c
If by mail, postage extra, paper, 7c; cloth, 12c.

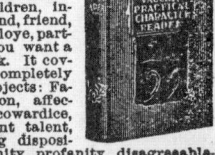

Character Reading, Practical.

By Prof. L. A. Vaught. How to read men, women and children at sight. If you wish to read the character of your children, intended wife, husband, friend, enemy, lover, employe, partner or relative, you want a copy of this book. It covers fully and completely the following subjects: Fanaticism, flirtation, affection, revenge, cowardice, superstition, latent talent, the domineering disposition, bigamy, vanity, profanity, disagreeableness, awkwardness, longevity, bashfulness, reliability, curiosity, goodness, memory, credulity, beauty, impulsiveness, sensuality, executive talent, ambition, borrowing trouble, etc. Cloth. Illustrated. Size, 5¼x7¾ inches. Retail price, $1.00.
No. 3C9407 Our price 59c
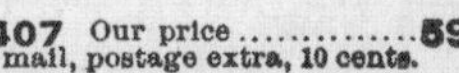
If by mail, postage extra, 10 cents.

Cheirosophy, Practical, or Science of the Hand.

By E. Herron-Allen. A synoptical study of the science of the hand. Contains chapters on the hand, superstitions and customs, etc. Fully illustrated. Cloth. Size, 5x6½ inches. Retail price, 75 cents.

No. 3C9418 Our price........45c

If by mail, postage extra, 6 cents.

Descriptive Mentality.

By Prof. Holmes W. Merton. A new book on physiognomy, phrenology and palmistry, with over 600 original drawings. The most accurate, comprehensive and clearest book on the subject ever published. Persons, by comparing their own hands with the drawings, can read their own nature and destiny as portrayed by those signs, lines and meanings that are present in their hands. Cloth. Size, 6¼ x 9¼ inches. Retail price, $1.50.

No. 3C9422 Our price..........98c

If by mail, postage extra, 15 cents.

Egyptian Secrets; or the White and Black Art for Man and Beast.

A book of nature and hidden secrets and the mystery of life unveiled. Contains the forbidden knowledge of ancient philosophers. This book is held by thousands to be the only sure means to avoid sickness in their families; to make them fortunate in their crops and stock raising, etc. Paper cover. Size, 4⅝x6⅜ inches. Retail price, $1.00.

No. 3C9426 Our price..........32c

If by mail, postage extra, 4 cents.

Faciology.

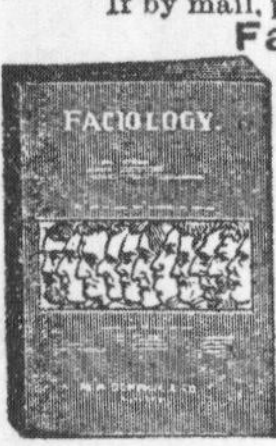

By La Vergne Belden Stevens. New, practical, scientific. All about human nature, brains, forms and character, covering all parts of the face, forehead, hair, wrinkles, etc.; also character and method of salutation and hand shaking. Illustrated. Paper cover. Size, 5 x 7¼ inches. Retail price, 30 cents.

No. 3C9429 Our price..........16c

If by mail, postage extra, 5 cents.

Hypnotism and Magnetism, Practical Lessons in.

By Prof. L. W. De Laurence, instructor of hypnotism, personal magnetism, mesmerism, magnetic healing, suggestive therapeutics, etc. This book gives the only course which starts the student out upon a plain and common sense basis of hypnotizing people; prepared for self instruction of beginners as well as for the use of advanced students and practitioners. Every subject is fully and systematically explained. It contains from ten to thirty practical lessons; many illustrations taken from life; fully illustrated. Size, 5¼x7¾ inches. Retail price, 50c.

No. 3C9433 Paper cover. Our price.....26c

No. 3C9437 Bound in cloth. Illustrated cover. Retail price, $1.00. Our price......58c

If by mail, postage extra, paper, 7c; cloth, 12c.

Magic, Herrmann's Book of.

Or, How to Perform Modern Tricks, by Professor Herrmann. The professor has included in this book only such tricks as have never before appeared in print. Contains a great variety of material for conjurors and sleight-of-hand performers. Coins, cards, silk hat, handkerchiefs and balls are introduced in the many programs offered, thus affording one an endless variety from which to select for parlor and stage amusements. Size, 4⅛x6⅜ inches.

No. 3C9452 Paper cover. Price.......14c

No. 3C9453 Cloth. Price............27c

If by mail, postage extra, paper, 3c; cloth, 6c.

Palmistry Simplified.

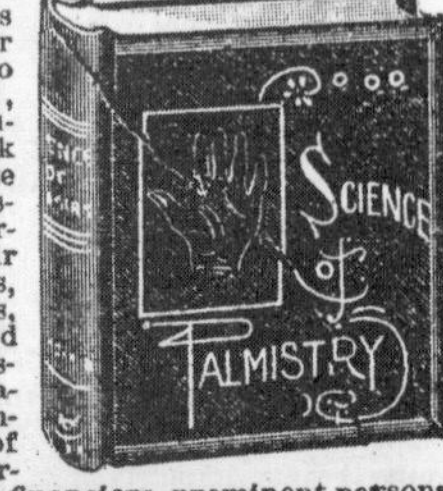

By S. Fuillevert. Everyone is more or less eager to know how to read the past, present and future. This book covers all these subjects. It illustrates the different hands, their shape, lines, mounts, fingers, thumbs and nails, also illustrates many famous hands, including those of well known murderers, lunatics, financiers, prominent persons, many society women and others. Cloth. Size, 6⅛x8⅛ inches. Retail price, $1.75.

No. 3C9480 Our price..........40c

If by mail, postage extra, 18 cents.

Zancig's Complete Palmistry.

By Zancig. There is no trait, no characteristic, no inherited tendency that is not marked on the palm of the hand and can be traced with unerring accuracy. In this volume we have all the discoveries, investigations and researches of centuries; all are summed up in this practical treatise. Size, 5½x7 inches.

No. 3C9483 Paper, price.....14c

No. 3C9484 Cloth, gilt top, price,....27c

If by mail, postage extra, paper 4c, cloth 8c.

Sixth and Seventh Book of Moses, The.

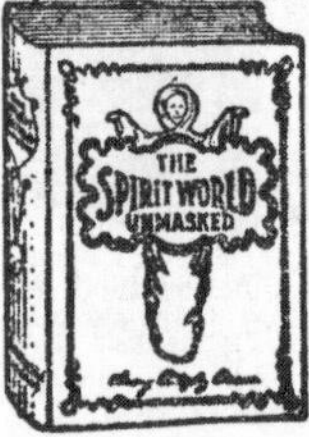

This wonderful translation is of the greatest importance to the Christian, Jew or Gentile, Episcopalian or Roman Catholic, and dissenters of every denomination. It contains 125 seals, signs, emblems, etc., used by Moses, Aaron, the Israelites and Egyptians. Contains the White and Black Art, together with the ministering spirits which were hidden from David; the seal of treasures, respect, affection, admiration, etc. Paper cover. Size, 5⅜x7 inches. Retail price, $1.00.

No. 3C9492 Our price..........33c

If by mail, postage extra, 4 cents.

Spirit World Unmasked, The.

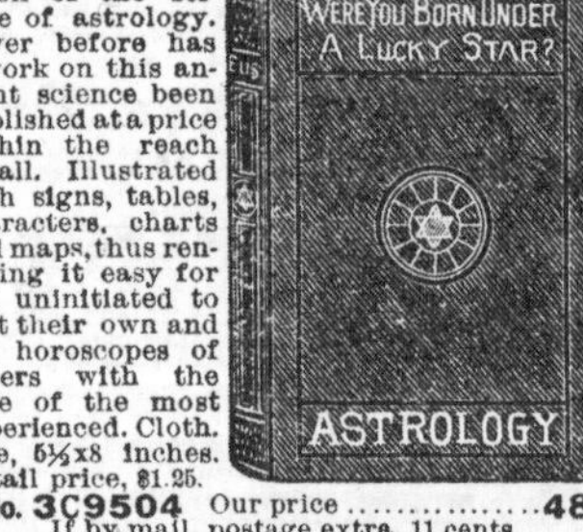

By Henry R. Evans. Illustrated investigations into the phenomena of spiritualism and theosophy. The author has endeavored to give an accurate account of the lives and adventures of celebrated mediums and occultists, which will prove of interest to every reader. Cloth. Size, 5¼ x 7½ inches. Retail price, 75 cents.

No. 3C9497 Our price..........42c

If by mail, postage extra, 12 cents.

Were You Born Under a Lucky Star?

By A. Alpheus. A complete exposition of the science of astrology. Never before has a work on this ancient science been published at a price within the reach of all. Illustrated with signs, tables, characters, charts and maps, thus rendering it easy for the uninitiated to cast their own and the horoscopes of others with the ease of the most experienced. Cloth. Size, 5½x8 inches. Retail price, $1.25.

No. 3C9504 Our price..........48c

If by mail, postage extra, 11 cents.

ATHLETICS AND PHYSICAL CULTURE.

Science of Boxing.

By Professor M. Donovan, ex-middle weight champion of America. It contains fifty-eight beautifully executed halftone illustrations, photographed from life, showing every movement in the hit and get-away science. Demonstrates the famous solar plexus blow, McCoy's corkscrew twist and Jeffries' crouch. Paper covers. Size, 5x7¼ inches. Retail price, 50 cents.

No. 3C9563 Our price..........30c

If by mail, postage extra, 3 cents.

Physical Culture and Self Defense.

By Robert Fitzsimmons. New edition, containing about forty illustrations from poses in his different fighting attitudes. It is an acknowledged fact among famous athletes, trainers and doctors who have known Robert Fitzsimmons, that he has upset more of their theories and done more to revise and better the rules for training and for the care of the health than any other man. His thorough, scientific knowledge of anatomy, and of medicine is uniquely accurate. Cloth. Size, 5½x8¼ inches. Retail price, $1.50.

No. 3C9584 Our price..........68c

If by mail, postage extra, 10 cents.

Wrestling, Art of.

A handbook of instruction in wrestling, giving the methods of Muldoon, Tom Sharkey, Rooney, the giant gripman, showing the half-Nelson, the hammer-lock, etc., with the accepted rules to be observed in the different methods of wrestling generally adopted at the present time. Illustrated. Paper covers. Size, 4x6¼ ins.

No. 3C9606 Our price..........18c

If by mail, postage extra, 3 cents.

BIBLES

Including Combination, Reference and Teachers' Bibles, Young People's Bibles, Hymnals, Testaments, Catholic and Episcopal Prayer Books, Key of Heaven and a complete line of Family Bibles.

Combination Bible.

A Bible for Ministers, Teachers, and Students.

PRINTED IN BOURGEOIS TYPE.

THIS BIBLE IS PERFECTLY PLAIN. The reading matter on the illustration does not appear on the Bible.

New Self Pronouncing, with the old and revised versions on same page. Containing 64 full page illustrations. The wonderful progress of archaeology has made necessary a reinvestigation and consequent modification of many former theories as to the history of the Jews and of the various races by which they were surrounded. In addition to the combination and self pronouncing features, it contains all standard helps to the study of the Bible. It is the most complete and best Bible for general use published. Size, 6x9 inches.

No. 3C10000 Extra French seal, divinity circuit, overlapping edges, round corners, red under gold edges, silk lined. Retail price, $5.50. Our price..........$1.39

No. 3C10002 Same as No. 3C10000, but with new improved index. Retail price, $6.00. Our price..........$1.58

No. 3C10004 Imperial seal, divinity circuit, round corners, red under gold edges. Leather lined. Retail price, $7.00. Our price..........$1.69

No. 3C10006 Same as No. 3C10004, but with new improved index. Retail price, $7.50. Our price..........$1.88

If by mail, postage extra, any style, 26 cents.

Red Letter Self Pronouncing Bibles.

PRINTED IN BOURGEOIS TYPE.

The Red Letter Art Bible with the words of Jesus printed in red, is an entirely new addition to Bible literature and is unquestionably a great help in studying the Holy Scriptures. It includes nearly 100 beautiful engravings of great events and scenes of the Bible, and has complete helps for Bible students. Has beautiful maps, accurate references, large, clear print, fine bindings and is of convenient size. Every word uttered by our Savior while on earth will be found printed in red, all the other matter in the Bible being in black ink.

No. 3C10007 Bound in French Seal, limp, round corners, carmine under gold edges. Size, 6x9 inches. Price..........$1.45

No. 3C10009 Bound in French Seal, divinity circuit, round corners, carmine under gold edges, extra grained lining. Price.$1.67

No. 3C10011 Same as No. 3C10009, with leather linings. Price..........$1.82

If by mail, postage extra, either style, 28 cents.

We can furnish any of the above styles of Bibles, with patent thumb index by which all the letters can be read at one time, enabling the reader to at once find any book, at an additional charge of 20 cents.

Sunday School Teachers' Reference Bible.

PRINTED IN MINION TYPE.

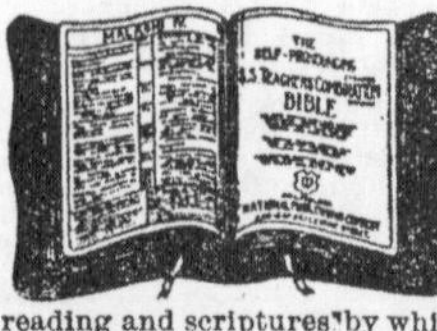

Beautifully bound and illustrated. Size, 4⅝ x 6⅞ inches. Contains illustrated aids and helps to the study of the Bible, thousands of references. Calendar for daily reading and scriptures by which the Bible may be finished in one year; the chronology and history of the Bible and its related periods; Old Testament chronology; combined concordance alphabetically arranged, also hundreds of other special features not usually found in regular teachers' Bibles.

No. 3C10014 French morocco, improved divinity circuit, round corners, red and gold edges, extra grained lining. Retail price, $1.75. Our price..........$1.05

No. 3C10018 Assyrian levant, improved divinity circuit, round corners, red and gold edges, silk head bands and marker, silk sewed, extra grained kid lining. Retail price, $2.25. Our price..........$1.29

If by mail postage extra, either style, 17 cents.

Large Minion Type Self Pronouncing Bibles.

A full and complete Sunday School Teachers' Bible with the self pronouncing feature, references, helps and maps. Printed from clear minion type, on a specially prepared Bible paper, adorned with 17 maps, printed in colors. Size, 5¼x7⅞ inches. Contains complete Bible helps prepared by eminent authorities, embracing the latest researches in the Holy Land.

No. 3C10030 French morocco, divinity circuit, self pronouncing, round corners, red and gold edges, extra grained lining. Retail price, $2.25. Our price..........$1.12

No. 3C10031 Same as No. 3C10030, with patent index cut on edge. Price.....$1.27

No. 3C10032 Roumanian seal, improved divinity circuit, self pronouncing, silk head bands and marker, round corners, red and gold edges, silk sewed. Retail price, $2.75. Our price..........$1.35

No. 3C10033 Same as No. 3C10032, with gold index cut on edge. Price.........$1.50

If by mail, postage extra, either style, 20 cents.

An Ideal Bible for Young People.

Printed in Minion Type.

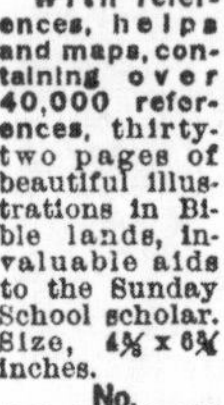

With references, helps and maps, containing over 40,000 references, thirty-two pages of beautiful illustrations in Bible lands, invaluable aids to the Sunday School scholar. Size, 4⅜ x 6⅞ inches.

No. 3C10042 Genuine morocco, divinity circuit; red and gold edges. Retail price, $3.00. Our price..........89c

No. 3C10044 Same as No. 3C10042, but with Dennison's Patent Index cut out on edge. Price..........$1.05

No. 3C10050 Roumanian seal, divinity circuit, lined with English kid, red and gold edges, silk head bands and marker. Retail price, $4.25. Our price..........$1.12

No. 3C10052 Same as No. 3C10050, but with Dennison's Patent Index on edge. Price..........$1.27

If by mail, postage extra, either style, 17 cents.

Reference Bibles.

Minion, 8vo. Size, 5x7¾x1½ inches.

With references, helps and maps. Containing also a beautiful frontispiece, and 32 pages comprising all the valuable illustrations and descriptions of recent Biblical researches and discoveries in Assyria, Babylonia, Egypt and Palestine. The Oxford Helps comprise nearly 400 pages. Don't forget to enclose 24 cents extra for postage when bibles are to go by mail.

No. 3C10090 Florentine seal, divinity circuit, gold edges. Retail price, $3.00. Our price..........75c

No. 3C10092 American seal, divinity circuit, gold edges, imitation silk, cloth lined. Retail price, $3.50. Our price..........90c

If by mail, postage extra, each, 24 cents.

NOTE—We can furnish either of these Bibles with patent index cut on edge for 20 cents extra.

Hand and Pocket Reference Bibles.

Containing the text only, without references, teachers' helps, concordance or other additional matter. For Sunday schools, Christian endeavor societies, home reading, etc., The exclusion of all matter other than the text makes them very desirable for general use. Size 3½x5⅛ inches.

No. 3C10140 Imitation roan, padded, round corners, red edges, 6 maps, pearl type. Price..........28c

If by mail, postage, extra 5c.

No. 3C10144 French morocco, limp, red under gold edges, round corners, 6 maps, pearl type, boxed. Price..........43c

If by mail, postage extra, 7 cents.

No. 3C10146 Assyrian levant, divinity circuit (overlapping edges), round corners, red under gold edges, 6 maps, pearl type, boxed. Price..........59c

If by mail, postage extra, 7 cents.

No. 3C10148 French levant, limp, divinity circuit, overlapping edges, red under gold edges, round corners, 6 maps, kid lined to the edge and silk sewed. Pearl type. Price, 85c

If by mail, postage extra, 8 cents.

Hand Bibles With Self Pronouncing Text.

No. 3C10150 Self pronouncing, imitation roan, red edges, round corners, 6 maps. Minion, 24mo. Price....39c
If by mail, postage extra, 8 cents.

No. 3C10152 Self pronouncing, Assyrian levant, divinity circuit, overlapping edges, round corners, red under gold, 6 maps. Minion, 24mo. Price....69c
If by mail, postage extra, 8 cents.

No. 3C10156 Self pronouncing, Persian morocco, divinity circuit, overlapping edges, red under gold, 6 maps, silk head bands and marker. Minion, 24mo. Price....95c
If by mail, postage extra, 8 cents.

No. 3C10160 Gift Bible, imitation ivory, gold, silver and illuminated floral sprays, round corners, full gilt, leather backs, gilt edge, rims and clasp. Minion. Retail price, $1.15. Our price....(If by mail, postage extra, 8c)....59c

No. 3C10164 Large type, self pronouncing text Bibles for old folks, containing six maps without references or teachers' helps. Imitation roan, limp, red edges, round corners, embossed bands, large clear long primer type. Size, 4⅝x7⅛ inches. Price....69c
If by mail, postage extra, 14 cents.

No. 3C10168 French morocco, limp, gold edges, round corners, six maps. Size, 4⅝x7⅛ inches. Long primer. Price....98c
If by mail, postage extra, 14 cents.

Large Type Bible for Old Folks.

Small Pica.

New Self Pronouncing Edition. Very clearly printed. Size, 5½x8¼ inches, contains 17 maps, with diacritical markings, according to the latest revision of Webster's International Dictionary. To make the system of pronouncing as thorough as possible, every syllable of the proper name is indicated and every vowel is diacritically marked. Printed from large bold type on especially prepared Bible paper. Size, 6x9 inches.

No. 3C10176 Imitation roan, red edges, round corners, embossed bands. Contains family record, etc. Price....79c

No. 3C10180 Morocco, limp, gilt edges, round corners, silk head band and marker. Contains family record, etc. Price....$1.15

No. 3C10184 Persian levant, divinity circuit, overlapping edges, round corners, red under gold edges, silk head band and marker, extra grained lining. Price...$1.55
If by mail, postage extra, each, 24 cents.

Testaments.

No. 3C10198 Bound in linen cloth. Limp, cut flush, sprinkled edges. Size, 3½x5¼ inches. Retail price, 15 cents. Our price....5c
If by mail, postage extra, 3c.

No. 3C10199 Bound in leatherette. Cut flush, round corners, red edges. Size, 2⅞x3⅞ inches. Retail price, 25 cents.
Our price....10c
If by mail, postage extra, 4c.

No. 3C11000 French seal. Limp, round corners, red under gold edges. Ruby, 48mo. Size, 2⅜x4 inches. Retail price, 40 cents.
Our price....18c
If by mail, postage extra, 3 cents.

No. 3C11004 Same style Testament as No. 3C11000, but with Book of Psalms. Size, 2⅜x4 inches. Price....30c
If by mail, postage extra, 3 cents.

No. 3C11008 French morocco. Improved divinity circuit, round corners, red under gold edges. Size, 2⅜x4¼ inches. Retail price, 60 cents. Our price....32c
If by mail, postage extra, 3 cents.

No. 3C11010 Same style Testament as No. 3C11008, but with Book of Psalms. Size, 2⅜x4¼ inches. Price....40c
If by mail, postage extra, 3 cents.

Largest Type Self Pronouncing Old Folks' New Testament Published.

No. 3C11036 Imitation roan, limp, red edges, round corners, embossed bands. Size, 5⅛x7⅛ inches.
Price....39c
Postage extra, 10 cents.

No. 3C11038 Same style as No. 3C11036, but with the Book of Psalms. Size, 5⅛x7⅛ inches.
Price....55c
Postage extra, 11 cents.

No. 3C11040 Morocco, limp, gold edges, round corners. Size, 5⅛x7⅛ inches. Price....69c
Postage extra, 10 cents.

Red Letter Testaments.

This beautiful edition of the New Testament is printed in red and black inks. The portions in red being the words uttered by our Saviour while on earth. Beautifully printed on extra quality of thin Bible paper. Handsomely bound. Illustrated with five multi-colored plates. Size, 3⅛x4⅞ inches.

No. 3C11060 Imitation roan, round corners, gold edges and gold lettering on the side. Price....47c

No. 3C11064 Leather, limp, red and gold edges, round corners, gold lettering on side, silk marker. A soft and pliable binding. Price. 64c

No. 3C11068 Genuine morocco, soft and flexible, divinity circuit, over lapping edges, round corners, red and gold edges. Price..78c
If by mail, postage extra, any style, 3 cents.

Christian Workers' Testaments.

This testament is marked in red on every subject connected with the theme of Salvation. No Testament has ever been prepared to compare with it in usefulness. Size, 3⅛x5 inches.

No. 3C11072 Red Russia cloth, round corners, gilt edges. Retail price, 70 cents.
Our price....47c

No. 3C11076 Morocco limp, round corners, red under gold edges. Retail price, $1.00.
Our price....64c

No. 3C11079 Morocco, divinity circuit, overlapping edges, round corners. Retail price, $1.25. Our price....78c
If by mail, postage extra, any style, 4 cents.

Dictionary of the Bible.

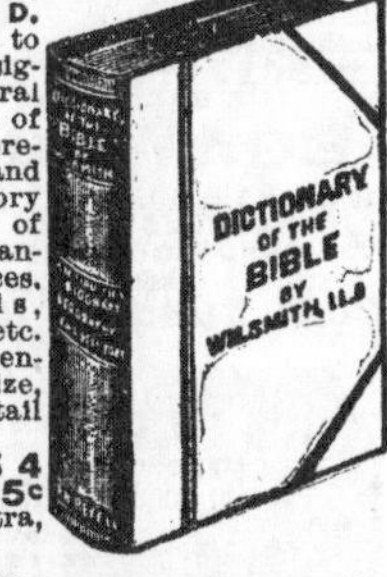

DICTIONARY OF THE BIBLE BY WM. SMITH, LL.D.

New Workers' Edition, by Wm. Smith, LL. D. A complete guide to pronunciation and significations of scriptural names; the solution of difficulties of interpretation, authority and harmony. Also a history of and description of Biblical customs, manners, events, places, persons, animals, plants, minerals, etc. Contains over 500 engravings. Cloth. Size, 6½x9 inches. Retail price, $1.00.

No. 3C32154
Our price....65c
By mail, postage extra, 25 cents.

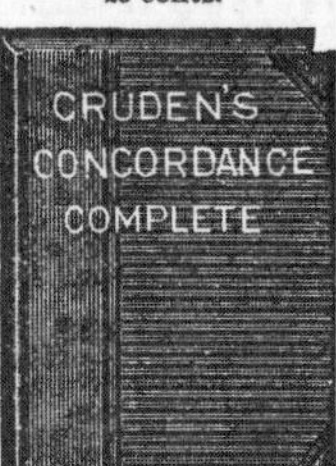

Complete Concordance to the Holy Scriptures.

By Alexander Cruden. A dictionary and alphabetical index to the Bible. New edition. Cloth. Size, 6⅞x9⅞ inches. Retail price $1.00.

No. 3C92237
Our price....65c
If by mail, postage extra, 14 cents.

Episcopal Prayer Books and Hymnals in Sets.

Prayer Books according to the standard. The Hymnals revised and enlarged. Prayers with hymnal. Printed on superior thin white paper. Minion, 48mo. Size, 2⅞x4 inches.

No. 3C11140 Morocco grain cloth, enameled cross or I. H. S., square corners, red edges. Retail price, $1.00.
Our price....65c

No. 3C11144 French morocco, limp, blind frame, blind cross, round corners, gilt edges. Retail price $1.50. Our price....98c

No. 3C11146 Venetian morocco, limp, round, corners red under gold edges. Retail price, $1.75. Our price....$1.35

No. 3C11150 Seal grain, limp, gilt cross, round corners, red under gilt edges, gold roll. Retail price, $1.75. Our price....$1.35

No. 3C11152 French morocco, limp, gilt I. H. S., blind blocked and gilt continuous border, round corners, red under gold edges. Retail price, $2.00. Our price....$1.60

No. 3C11160 Persian calf, limp, round corners, red under gold edges. Illustrated with 12 gravures. Retail price, $2.25.
Our price....$1.80
If by mail, postage extra, any style, 10 cents.

Child's Catholic Prayer Book.

New and complete large type edition, with 36 illustrations of the Mass. Contains 288 pages. Size, 2½x3⅞ inches.

No. 3C11210 Fine black cloth, gilt side stamp. Price, each, or in any quantity....9c

No. 3C11214 American seal, limp, gold title and monogram, red under gold edges. Retail price, 75 cents. Our price....28c

No. 3C11220 Genuine, white celluloid with beautiful floral design on cover, gilt rims and clasp, full gilt edges. Retail price, $1.00. Our price....49c
If by mail, postage extra, any style, 4 cents.

Key of Heaven.

With Epistles and Gospels. 48mo. Size, 2⅛x3⅞ inches. 576 Pages.

No. 3C11242 Persian calf, leather padded, gold cross bands, with beautiful parchment picture of St. Anthony and prayer to this great saint, printed in gold inside of both front and back covers, red under gold edges. Retail price, $1.75.
Our price....79c

No. 3C11246 Pure, white celluloid cover, beautifully decorated in pearl and gold, celluloid clasp, full gold edges. Retail price, $1.50. Our price....69c

No. 3C11250 Persian calf, leather padded, gold crown of thorns on side, beautiful pearl cross and indulgence prayer inside of front cover, red under gold edges. Retail price, $1.75.
Our price....86c
If by mail, postage extra, any style, 6 cents.

FAMILY BIBLES.

SUCH VALUES IN BIBLES WERE NEVER OFFERED BEFORE.

These are really beautiful works, the kind that are usually sold only through agents, and then at double our prices.

Our Leader in Family Bibles.

Size, 10x12¼x3 inches. Contains Old and New Testaments, King James' Text, origin and history of the books of the bible, pronouncing dictionary of proper names, department of references, with maps and illustrations, marriage certificate and record, temperance pledge and triumphal entry, new Lord's Prayer, etc. Weight, packed for shipment, 7 pounds. Retail price, $3.50.

No. 3C12360 Imitation leather, back and side titles stamped in gold, marbled edges.
Price....80c

No. 3C12362 Same style and contents as No. 3C12360, but with full gold edges.
Price....98c

No. 3C12364 Same style and contents as No. 3C12360, but bound in genuine leather, with full gold edges. Retail price, $5.00.
Our price....$1.65

Large Type Illustrated Family Bible, only $2.49.

Holy Family Bible, self pronouncing edition, containing 48 magnificent full page illustrations, illuminated title page, marriage certificate, record of marriages, births, deaths and temperance pledge, numerous full page Dore illustrations, chronological index to the Holy Bible; giving years when remarkable events occurred and passages wherein they are recorded, a summary of its contents and many valuable aids and helps to Bible students, etc. Size, closed, 10⅞x12¼x2⅞ inches. Genuine American morocco, raised panels, gold side and back titles. mottled edges.

No. 3C12375 Price....$2.49
Weight, packed for shipment, 13 pounds.

New Combination Padded Family Bible, only $2.79.

Self pronouncing edition, contains illuminated title page, family record of births, marriages and deaths, thousands of halftone and other illustrations. The text is conformable to that of the Universities of Oxford and Cambridge, with a complete concordance of the Psalms of David in meter. This Bible shows also in simple form all changes, additions and omissions made by the revisers of the Old and New Testaments, arranged in parallel columns, etc., enabling the reader to see at a glance wherein the two versions differ. Size, 10x12⅝x2⅛ inches. Genuine padded leather, gold sides and back title, full gold edges.

No. 3C12378 Price....$2.79
Weight, packed for shipment, 13 pounds.

Self Pronouncing Combination Family Bible, $3.69.

New illustrated edition, containing two colored and 24 full page Dore engravings, history of the books of the Bible illustrated with 48 full page engravings, complete concordance of the Holy Scripture, Psalms of David in meter, Chronological index to the Holy Bible, complete history of the Bible with a summary of its contents and many valuable aids and helps to Bible students, illuminated marriage certificate, family record, etc. Size, 9x12x2½ inches. American calf padded sides, round corners, gold title on side and back, full gold edges.

No. 3C12382 Price....$3.69

Family Bible, only $3.89.

An entirely new Bible, containing all changes, additions and omissions made by the revisers of the Old and New Testaments, and enables readers to see at a glance wherein the two versions differ. This Bible contains in addition to the combination text the following features: Marginal references, many multi-colored plates, including presentation plates, ten colored parable plates, ten commandments and Lord's prayer, family record, family temperance pledge, etc., scenes and incidents in the life of Christ, Proverbs of Solomon, St. Paul's Journeys. Hoffman gallery of original New Testament illustrations, printed in colors with descriptions. Cruden's Complete Concordance, 4,000 questions and answers on the Old and New Testaments, etc. American morocco, calf finish, raised panel sides, embossed in gold with gold edges. Size, 10½x12⅛x4 inches.

No. 3C12387 Price....$3.89

A Superb Self Pronouncing Family Bible, only $4.87.

This Family Bible contains the authorized and revised versions of both the Old and New Testaments; arranged in parallel columns, line for line marginal references; marriage certificate and family record; history of the books of the Bible; the ten commandments and our Lord's Prayer, illuminated; a gallery of seventy-two scriptural illustrations and descriptions of the Israelites' Tabernacle; Life of our Lord and Saviour; cities and towns of the Bible; colored maps of Palestine; Ancient and Modern Jerusalem. French morocco, padded sides, round corners, fancy side stamped, full gold edges. Size, 9½x12½x3½ inches.

No. 3C12392 Price....$4.87

$12.00 Family Bible only $4.89

This Bible shows in simple form, all changes, additions and omissions made by the revisers of the Old and New Testaments, and contains in addition to the Combination Text, the Proverbs of Solomon and the Parables of our Lord, illustrated; contains 10 multi-colored plates, 4 superb halftone engravings, in gold and colors; Jewish Worships, Tabernacles and Vestments, Holy Apostles with descriptions; Sacred Biography of the Holy Apostles and the Evangelists; 9 pages of maps of the Bible land; 6 beautiful steel and 32 full page Dore engravings. Illuminated family record of births, marriages and deaths, temperance pledge, etc. Persian morocco, padded round corners, full gold edges. Size, 10x12¼x3 inches.

No. 3C12395 Price....$4.89

Combination Self Pronouncing Family Bible, Only $6.59.

Magnificent Family Bible, containing illustrated presentation page; parable and ten commandments in colors; marriage certificate; family record of births and deaths; colored temperance pledge; scenes and incidents in the life of Christ; Proverbs of Solomon; path of Jesus; Grecian, Persian and Roman empires; Hoffman's gallery of original New Testament illustrations; Cruden's Complete Concordance and his life. Beautifully bound in genuine Turkey morocco; title stamped on back and side in gold; full gold edges. Size, 10x12⅛x8 inches.

No. 3C12403 Price....$6.59

Holy Catholic Family Bibles.

Holy Catholic Bible, approved by His Eminence, Cardinal Gibbons. Contains the entire canonical scriptures according to the decree of the Council of Trent, translated from the Latin Vulgate, diligently compared with the Hebrew, Greek and other editions of divers languages. Contains also a complete history of the books of the Bible, an illustrated and comprehensive Bible Dictionary; the parables of our Lord and Saviour Jesus Christ, illuminated; life of the blessed Virgin Mary; the stations of the Holy Way of the Cross; portraits of supreme pontiffs, archbishops and bishops; new illustrated plates of the tabernacle, etc. Gallery of full page illustrations by Dore. Weight, packed for shipment, 8 pounds. Retail price. $6.00. Size, 10½x12½ inches.

No. 3C12412 American morocco, crushed paneled sides, combed (mottled) edges.
Our price....$3.65

No. 3C12414 American morocco, raised paneled sides, marbled edges. Size, 10½x12½ inches. Weight, packed for shipment, 11 pounds. Retail price, $9.00. Our price. $4.48

No. 3C12416 Extra fine imported morocco, raised paneled sides, full gold edges. Size, 10½x12½ inches. Weight, packed for shipment 14 pounds. Retail price, $15.00.
Our price....$5.98

BIOGRAPHY.

Biographical Library.

Series No. 3C12168 Durably bound in library cloth, with an individual cover design in colors on each book, printed on extra quality, high grade book paper. Size, 5¼x7½ inches. Retail price, 60 cents.
Our price, per volume....................**27c**
If by mail, postage extra, 12 cents.

Life of John Quincy Adams. William Henry Seward.
Life of Daniel Boone. Edward S. Ellis.
Life and Services of Henry Clay. Mr. Epes Sargent and Horace Greeley.
Life of Colonel David Crockett. Edward S. Ellis.
Life of Oliver Cromwell. Henry William Herbert.
Life of William Henry Harrison. H. Montgomery.
Life of Patrick Henry. Wm. Wirt.
Life of Andrew Jackson. John S. Jenkins.
Life of Napoleon. M. A. Arnault.
Life of Zackary Taylor. H. Montgomery.
Life of George Washington. Geo. Bancroft.
Life of Daniel Webster. B. F. Tefft, D.D., LL.D.

Famous Frontiersmen, Pioneers and Scouts.

By E. G. Cattermole. A thrilling narrative of the lives and marvelous exploits of the most renowned heroes, trappers, explorers, adventurers, scouts and Indian fighters, including Boone, Crawford, Girty, Molly Finney, the McCulloughs, Wetzel, Kenton, Clark, Brady, Crockett, Houston, Carson, California Joe, Wild Bill, Texas Jack, Captain Jack, Buffalo Bill, etc., also Custer's Last Fight. 540 pages. Cloth. Size, 6x9 inches. Retail price, $1.25.

No. 3C12354 Our price..............**36c**
If by mail, postage extra, 19 cents.

Grant, General U. S., Life of

By Hon. Ben. Perley Moore and the Rev. O. H. Tiffany, D.D. An account of the hardships and struggles of his youth, its poverty and following his glorious and victorious career from West Point to the head of the army; comprising his many victories that crowned his later years, as President of the United States. 594 pages. Cloth. Size, 6½x9 inches. Retail price, $1.00.

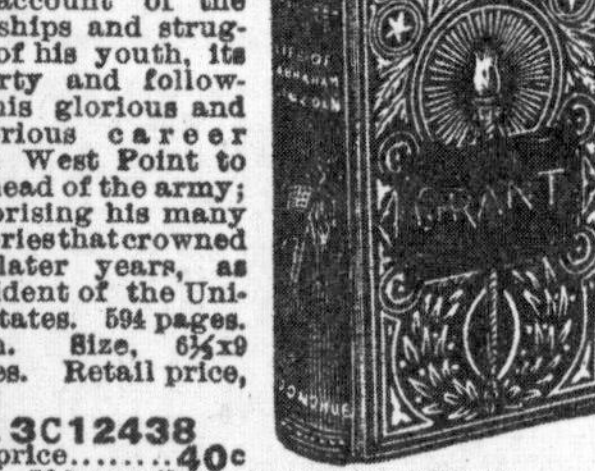

No. 3C12438
Our price..........**40c**
If by mail, postage extra, 18 cents.

Lincoln, Abraham, Life, Stories and Speeches of.

Edited by Paul E. Selby (a personal friend of Lincoln's). A most interesting and entertaining life of Lincoln. The stories, anecdotes and yarns have been compiled from the most reliable sources. The great speeches of Lincoln are arranged in chronological order. Gilt top. Cloth. Size, 5½x7½ inches. 469 pages. Retail price, $1.25.
No. 3C12662 Our price..................**69c**

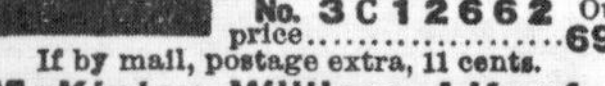

If by mail, postage extra, 11 cents.

McKinley, William, Life of.

By Rt. Rev. Bishop Samuel Fallows, D. D., LL.D. The changing scenes and vicissitudes, lights and shadows, hopes and fears, ambitious struggles, defeats and victories, his invincible courage and the tragic story of his death are pictured in faithfulness to truth in their true colors. Contains also a history and biography of our two other martyred presidents, Lincoln and Garfield. Illustrated with halftone engravings. Cloth. Size, 7x9½ inches. Weight, 3 pounds. Retail price, $1.50.

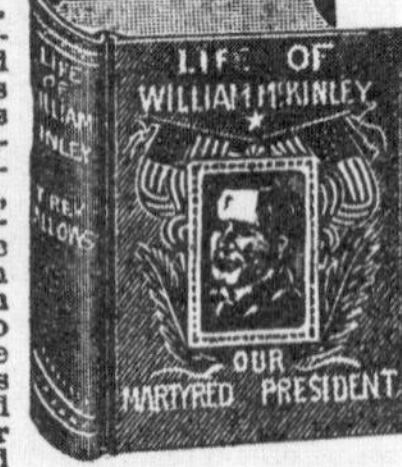

No. 3C12736 Our price.......**64c**
If by mail, postage extra, 25 cents.

Plutarch's Lives.

Translated by John Dryden and others. An authenticated unabridged edition, with complete life of Plutarch. This is unquestionably the best edition published. Durably bound, gilt top, averaging 600 pages to the volume. Cloth. Size, 5½x7½ inches. Retail price, $2.50.

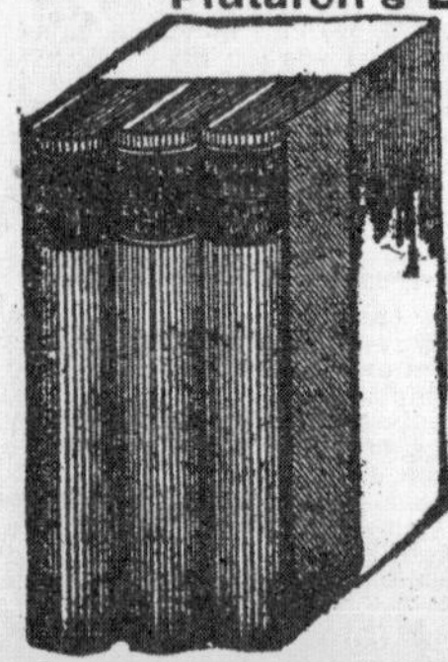

No. 3C12879 Our price, per set of three volumes........**69c**
If by mail, postage extra, per set, 40 cents.

Washington, George, and His Generals of the American Revolution.

By John T. Headley. The only edition published containing biographies of the leading generals of the Revolutionary war. Illustrated with numerous portraits. Complete in two volumes. Bound in cloth. Size, 5½x7½ inches. Retail price, $1.50.
No. 3C13354 Our price, per set of two volumes........................**59c**
If by mail, postage extra, per set, 24 cents.

BIRTHDAY GIFT BOOKS.

Forget-Me-Not.

Selections from F. R. Havergal. Contains a quotation from the Bible and appropriate verses for each month in the year. Artistically printed on calendered paper. Beautifully bound in genuine leather, stamped in gold. Cloth. Size, 4x5 inches. Retail price, $1.00.

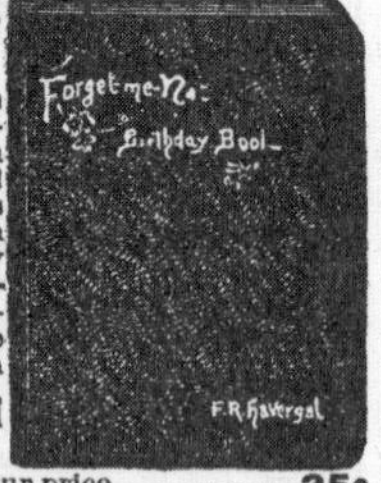

No. 3C14378 Our price..............**35c**
If by mail, postage extra, 5 cents.

Sands of Time, The.

Compiled by Thomas W. Hanford. A book of birthday gems, containing a sentiment and a proverb for each day in the year. Selected from the works of 150 different authors. With blank spaces for autographs. Superbly illustrated with thirteen full page engravings. Printed on calendered paper. Cloth, stamped in colors. Size, 4x5½ inches. Retail price, $1.00.

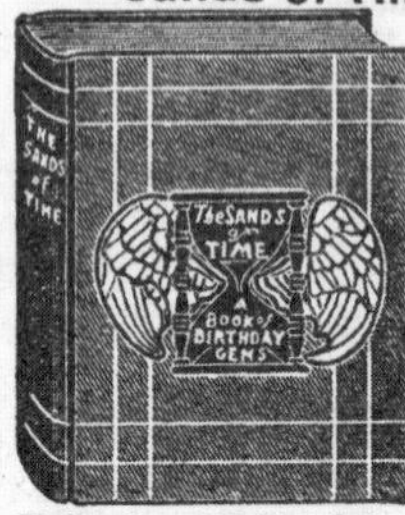

No. 3C15106 Our price..............**55c**
If by mail, postage extra, 11 cents.

Shakespeare's Birthday Book.

Containing twelve delightful drawings in colors of correct scenes described by the greatest dramatist; a special quotation for each month and one for each day in the year, with ruled lines for autographs. Bound in cloth, padded. Gilt edges. Boxed. Cloth. Size, 3¾x4¾ inches. Retail price, $1.50.

No. 3C15112
Our price..............**99c**
If by mail, postage extra, 7 cents.

BLACKSMITHING, BOOKS ON.

Manual of Blacksmithing.

By an Expert Blacksmith. A new guide to blacksmithing, written by a man of thirty years' experience. This book covers the minor details, as well as the most difficult problems in blacksmithing. It is filled with rules and recipes of great value to farmers, horseshoers, wagon makers, machinists, liverymen, etc. The following subjects are fully treated: Forges and appliances, hand tools, drawing down and upsetting, bending and ring making, miscellaneous examples of forged work, cranks, model work and die forging, home made forges, etc. Cloth, illustrated. Size, 5¼x7½ inches.

No. 3C16160 Price..................**49c**
If by mail, postage extra, 7 cents.

Blacksmithing, Modern.

By J. G. Holstrom. An entirely new work on rational horseshoeing and wagon making. Written by a man of thirty years' experience. Contains nothing but elementary rules, thus avoiding technical terms and enabling the young man to master the principles without unnecessary delay and study. The book is filled with rules and recipes of great value to farmers, horseshoers, wagonmakers, machinists, liverymen, well drillers, manufacturers, as well as amateurs and young men on the farm. Illustrated. Cloth. Size, 5¼x7½ inches. Retail price, $1.00.

No. 3C16166 Our price..............**70c**
If by mail, postage extra, 12 cents.

Practical Horseshoeing.

By G. Fleming. An invaluable treatise on the subject of the humane treatment of the horse, and the scientific treatment of the hoofs, by which the utility and endurance of this invaluable animal are increased two-fold. Concisely written, containing only the best methods known. No horseman can afford to be without a copy of this valuable book. Cloth. Illustrated. Size, 5¼x8 inches. Retail price, 75 cents.

No. 3C16178 Our price..............**35c**
If by mail, postage extra, 8 cents.

Correct Horse, Mule and Ox Shoeing.

By J. G. Holstrom. A standard treatise adapted to the demands of veterinarians, amateurs and professional horseshoers. Concisely written, containing only the best methods. It contains no long articles, and the principles laid down in this book are followed by the most experienced and best horseshoers in this country and England. Illustrated. Cloth. Size, 5¼x7½ in. Retail price, $1.00.
No. 3C17114 Our price..............**35c**
If by mail, postage extra, 10 cents.

BOAT BUILDING.

SEND FOR OUR FREE BOOK CATALOGUE, IT INCLUDES BOOKS ON ROWING AND CANOE CONSTRUCTION, YACHTING, SAILING, ETC.

Boat Building for Amateurs, Practical.

By Adrian Nelson, C. E. Contains full and complete instructions for designing and building all manner of sailing boats, such as punts, skiffs, canoes, rowing and sailing boats. Embraces all that anyone will require, save the simplest tools and necessary materials; to build any desired boat. There are nearly one hundred pictorial drawings and illustrations. Cloth. Size, 5½x7¾ inches. Retail price, $1.00.

No. 3C18182
Our price..............**58c**
If by mail, postage extra, 8 cents.

BUSINESS GUIDES, FORMS AND LETTER WRITERS.

Brown's Business Letter Writer.

By C. W. Brown, A.M. One of the most complete practical compendiums of correspondence and business forms ever published. Gives full instructions for writing, and specimens of business letters, legal forms, leases, deeds, wills, contracts; how to address the president and government officials. Also leading synonyms. It will tell you everything you really need in the way of a letter. 208 pages.

No. 3C22182 Paper Cover. Price...**14c**
No. 3C22183 Cloth. Price.............**27c**
If by mail, postage extra, paper 3c, cloth 6c.

Business Pointers.

A Complete Commercial Instructor and Counsellor, embracing everything known in the commercial world; beginning with elementary principles of business and covering in a general manner, information for every occupation. On the desk of an accountant, in the hands of a merchant, contractor, and business man of every class, including the farmer, stock raiser, etc., it will prove a ready guide. Much unpleasant litigation is the result of ignorance concerning proper forms of legal business and points of commercial law. Cloth, illustrated. Size, 5¾x8¾ inches.

No. 3C22190 Price..................**69c**
If by mail, postage extra, 14 cents.

Commercial Calculator.

By G. W. Conklin, for merchants, farmers, contractors, mechanics, iron and steel dealers, hardware men, engineers, accountants, architects and others. New and greatly improved volume, containing calculations covering every possible business requirement, including decimal reckoning table, improved interest, grain and wage tables. A complete short rule arithmetic and original system of lightning methods of calculation, with full directions for estimating all kinds of work, and a useful table showing the value of various foods for feeding chickens, cattle, hogs, etc. Size, 2¾x5½ inches.
No. 3C22238 Cloth. Retail price, 25 cents.
Our price..............**18c**
No. 3C22240 Full leather. Retail price, 50 cents. Our price.....**35c**
If by mail, postage extra, either style, 4 cents.

Practical Business Instructor.

By Prof. H. T. Tanner. A practical book of daily reference. The rules and explanations for opening, conducting and closing all kinds of account books are so simple, plain and practical, that this book will commend itself to business men, managers, buyers, accountants, cashiers, students, etc. Contains chapters on buying and selling goods, loss and gain, method of computing the maturity of notes and bills, and thousands of other subjects. Cloth.

No. 3C94184 Price..................**96c**
If by mail, postage extra, 12 cents.

Safe Methods of Stock Speculation.

How to make money on the stock market. By W. Y. Stafford. An invaluable guide to the stock speculator or others who desire to know something regarding stock speculation. It describes the modes of manipulation which have hitherto remained a secret. The character of different markets, how to recognize and profit by them. Many valuable hints on how to steer clear of the pitfalls and take advantage of the opportunities for making money. Cloth. Size, 4½x7 inches.
No. 3C23106 Price..............**58c**
If by mail, postage extra, 10 cents.

CATTLE, SHEEP, HORSES, POULTRY AND MISCELLANEOUS VETERINARY BOOKS.

Castration, Animal.

By Dr. Liautard. The only work on the subject in the English language. A concise and practical treatise on the castration of domestic animals. Cloth. Size, 5¼x7½ inches. Retail price, $2.25.
No. 3C26208 Our price.........**$1.55**
If by mail, postage extra, 14 cents.

Dogs, Their Diseases, Symptoms and Treatment.

By Hugh Dalziel. New edition. In this popular book the author makes clear the symptoms of all diseases to which the most favored of animals is subject, including antidotes for poisoning, administering medicines, etc. Unlike the human being, life in the different climates requires different applications and, not infrequently, different remedies. Alphabetically arranged. Illustrated. Size, 5x7½ inches.

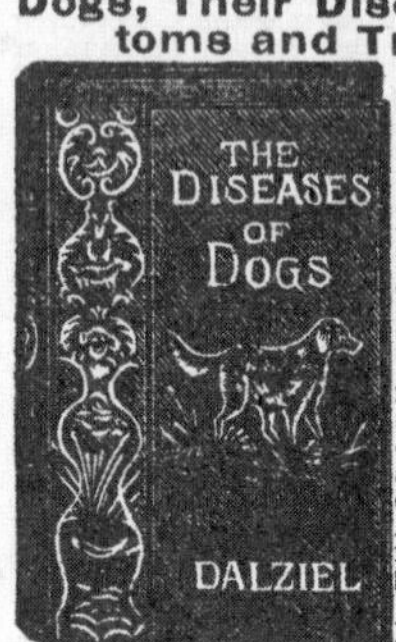

No. 3C26274 Paper. Retail price, 25 cents. Our price..........................**14c**
If by mail, postage extra, 5 cents.
No. 3C26275 Stiff cloth and edges stamped in gold. Retail price, 50 cents.
Our price..........................**27c**
If by mail, postage extra, 7 cents.

Farm and Stock Book, Standard.

By D. Magner. The most complete and authentic work of its kind published. No farmer, stock raiser, dairyman, breeder, trainer, drover, driver, gardener, grafter, blacksmith, etc. can afford to be without it. It comprehensively treats of the principles and details of their professions in a plain, easily understood manner by an author whose name stands preeminent among those of his profession. This book embodies the most essential subjects from all the earlier writings of the author and without doubt is the most complete book of its kind published. Size, 8x10½ inches.
No. 3C26366 Cloth. Price.....**$0.98**
No. 3C26367 Half Russia. Price, **1.52**
If by mail, postage extra, either style, 44 cents.

Farmers' Encyclopedia, The.

By D. Magner. Worth hundreds of dollars to every farmer and stock raiser. Contains principles and treatment in training horses, cure of viciousness; how to encourage, control, and manage them; many chapters are devoted to horseshoeing, also diseases of horses, their cure, etc. How to raise sheep, swine, poultry, bees; their care, diseases, prevention and cure. Contains thousands of other subjects pertaining to the farm and its management too numerous to mention. Cloth. Size, 6x9 inches. Retail price, $1.50.
No. 3C26368 Our price..............**65c**
If by mail, postage extra, 28 cents.

Gleason's Veterinary Handbook.

Contains a new and complete system of horse training and exhaustive treatise on veterinary science, including diseases of horses, cattle, swine, sheep, poultry, dogs, birds, etc. The language is plain, simple and direct, adapted to the understanding of the ordinary farmer and stock raiser. Buckram cloth. Size, 5¼x7½ inches.

No. 3C26432 Price..............**58c**
If by mail, postage extra, 14 cents.

Horse, Diseases of The. How to Treat Them.

By Robert Chawner. A brief, popular and reliable handbook of veterinary science, which treats of the horse and his diseases. A valuable book for horsemen, farmers, students, etc., free from technicalities, and in language plain and simple. Cloth. Size, 5¼ x 7½ inches. Retail price, $1.25.

No. 3C26462 Our price..............**98c**
If by mail, postage extra, 10 cents.

Horse Taming.

By William Mullen. The art of breaking, educating and handling all kinds of horses. It contains instructions for breaking and educating colts; teaching horses to drive and for use under the saddle. This is the most complete book on the art of how to tame and train horses published, and will be found an invaluable assistant to farmers, stockmen and all who handle horses. Cloth. Size, 5¼x8 inches. Retail price, $1.00.
No. 3C26465 Our price..........60c
If by mail, postage extra, 11 cents.

Live Stock, Diseases of, and Their Most Efficient Remedies.

By W. B. Miller. A popular guide for the medical and surgical treatment of all domestic animals, including horses, cattle, cows, sheep, swine, fowl, dogs, etc., giving in brief and plain language the description of all the usual diseases to which these animals are liable, and the most successful treatment of American and English veterinarians. Cloth. Size, 9x6x2½ inches.
No. 3C26690 Price..........$1.12
If by mail, postage extra, 28 cents.

Standard Perfection Poultry Book.

By C. C. Shoemaker. The recognized standard work on poultry in this country; adopted by the Poultry Breeders' Association. It contains a complete description of all the varieties of fowls, including turkeys, ducks and geese; how and what to feed them, how to market them; also full directions for operating incubators and brooders. Fully illustrated. Size, 4½x6½ in.
No. 3C26860 Paper. Price..........14c
No. 3C26862 Cloth. Price..........27c
If by mail, postage extra, paper, 3c; cloth, 5c.

COOK BOOKS, ETIQUETTE, ETC.

Candy Making, Modern.

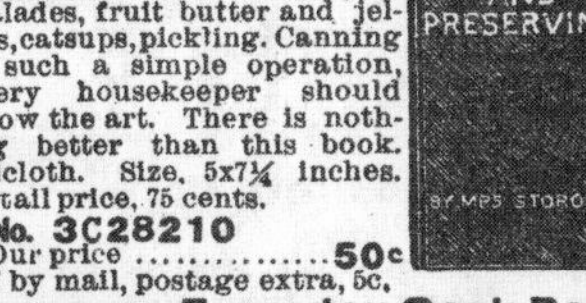

By James S. Wilson. An up to date guide and working manual, with full instructions for making plain and fancy candies, bonbons, caramels, taffy, molasses candy, etc., for the home or market. This book is very simple in its explanations, and is by far the best working manual on the subject of candies published. Size, 4½x6¾ inches.
No. 3C28206 Paper. Price..........20c
No. 3C28208 Cloth. Price..........35c
If by mail, postage extra, paper, 2c; cloth, 4c.

Canning and Preserving.

By Mrs. S. T. Rorer. How to can and preserve fruits and vegetables. Contains also the best method of making marmalades, fruit butter and jellies, catsups, pickling. Canning is such a simple operation, every housekeeper should know the art. There is nothing better than this book. Oilcloth. Size, 5x7¼ inches. Retail price, 75 cents.
No. 3C28210
Our price..........50c
If by mail, postage extra, 5c.

Everyday Cook Book.

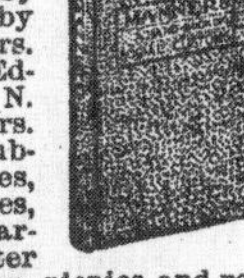

By Miss E. Neill. We have just secured another large edition which we will close out at 18 cents each. Cyclopedia of practical recipes. Economical, reliable, excellent. 315 pages. Bound in oilcloth. Size, 5¼x7¼.
No. 3C28340 Price..........18c
If by mail, postage extra, 12c.

Manners; A Book of Etiquette and Social Customs.

The rules laid down in this volume are those followed by the best society, endorsed by Mrs. Theodore Roosevelt, Mrs. Chauncey M. Depew, Mrs. Edward J. Woolsey, Mrs. Burton N. Harrison, and many others. Embraces the following subjects: Balls and evening parties, cards, calls and visits, carriages, clubs, chaperons, weddings, garden and lawn parties, letter writing, letters of introduction, picnics and receptions, etc. Size, 4½x6 inches.
No. 3C42736 Cloth. Price..........32c
No. 3C42737 Paper. Price..........17c
If by mail, postage extra, cloth, 5c; paper, 3c.

Tasty Dishes.

Every wise and prudent housewife should have a copy of "Tasty Dishes." Prepared with care and intelligence. It deserves a place in every housekeeper's library; has all the requirements of a complete, thoroughly up to date cook book.
No. 3C29159
Price..........29c
If by mail, postage extra, 8 cents.

Household Cook Book.

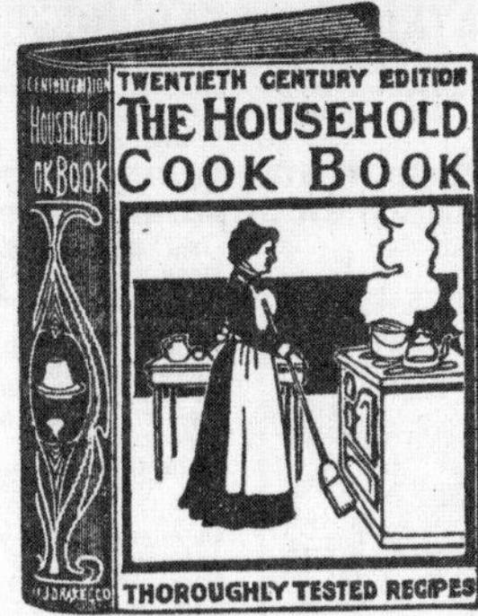

A brand new edition. A new and complete guide for housekeepers; thoroughly reliable, practical and economical. Contains a complete and comprehensive collection of new, choice and thoroughly tested recipes, including every department of domestic cookery, especially adapted for household use. Also containing medical and toilet hints, invalid cookery, plans for setting the table, carving and a great variety of information valuable for every housewife. Years have been spent in gathering the material for this book and no labor or expense have been spared in its preparation. Contains 654 pages. Printed from entirely new plates on extra quality of book paper. White oilcloth, marble edges. Size, 7x10 inches. Retail price, $1.50.
No. 3C28468 Our price..........45c
If by mail postage extra, 28 cents.

The Original White House Cook Book Only 60 Cents.

Authentic and unabridged edition by Hugo Ziemann, President Roosevelt's chef, and Mrs. F. L. Gillette. The art of cooking in its latest perfection. By special arrangements with the publishers we are able to offer this household compendium at less than actual cost to produce; contains over 600 household recipes; nothing relating to practical housekeeping is omitted. Embraces cooking, toilet and household recipes, menus, dinner giving, table etiquette, care of the sick, health suggestions, facts worth knowing, and thousands of other subjects too numerous to mention. Enameled cloth. Illustrated. Size, 7¾x9¾ inches.
No. 3C29328 Price..........60c
If by mail, postage extra, 28 cents.

Practical Etiquette.

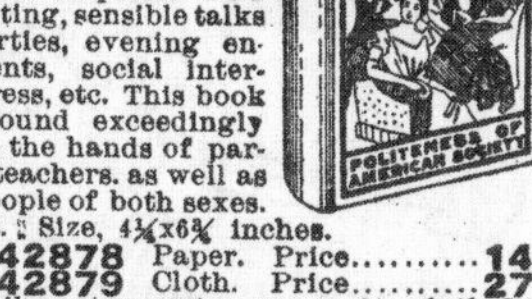

A strictly modern book on politeness. Just what one needs to keep in touch with what is correct at the present time. Hints on politeness and good breeding, sensible talks about etiquette for home, visiting, sensible talks about parties, evening entertainments, social intercourse, dress, etc. This book will be found exceedingly helpful in the hands of parents and teachers, as well as young people of both sexes. 160 pages. Size, 4½x6¾ inches.
No. 3C42878 Paper. Price..........14c
No. 3C42879 Cloth. Price..........27c
If by mail, postage extra, paper, 3c; cloth, 5c.

DICTIONARIES

We quote but a few dictionaries in this catalogue. In our book catalogue (sent free on application), is listed a full and complete line of dictionaries, covering all languages.

Electrical Dictionary.

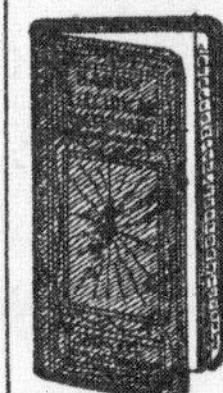

Edited by Wm. L. Webster, M. E. Revised and corrected to date. Complete, concise and convenient. All electrical words, terms and phrases are intelligently defined, containing 4,000 distinct words, terms and phrases, with their definitions. It is absolutely indispensable to all interested in electricity. Size, 2¾x5¾ inches.
No. 3C32328 Cloth. Indexed. Price..........14c
No. 3C32329 Full leather. Indexed. Price..........28c
If by mail, postage extra, either style, 3 cents.

Cassell's French-English and English-French Dictionary.

Compiled from the best authors of both languages, by Professors De Lome, and Wallace, and Henry Bridgeman. Revised, corrected and enlarged by Prof. E. Roubaud, B. A. Contains 1,122 pages. Cloth, two colors. Size, 5x8 inches. Retail price, $1.50.
No. 3C32350 Our price..........$1.05
If by mail, postage extra, 15 cents.

Cassell's German-English and English-German Dictionary.

Compiled from the best authors in both languages. Edited by Elizabeth Wier. Revised, corrected and enlarged. Contains 1,112 pages. Cloth, in two colors. Size, 5x8 inches. Retail price, $1.50.
No. 3C32410 Our price..........$1.05
If by mail, postage extra, 15 cents.

Cassell's English-Latin and Latin-English Dictionary.

An entirely new edition recently revised by J. R. V. Marchant, M. A., assisted by Jos. S. Charles, B. A. In preparing this new edition the reviser's principal aim has been to so adapt the work that it would be suitable for students as well as teachers. This is pre-eminently the best and most complete Latin dictionary published, 927 pages. Bound in cloth, two colors. Size, 5¼x8 inches. Retail price, $1.50.
No. 3C32660 Our price..........$1.05
If by mail, postage extra, 16 cents.

Modern Webster.

Modern Webster Pronouncing and Defining Dictionary of the English Language. An excellent school and office dictionary, being concise, handy and entirely up to the times. Containing all words sanctioned by good authority, together with a collection of words, phrases, maxims and mottoes from classical and modern foreign languages; abbreviations in common use, and instructions in proofreading, etc. Illustrated and indexed. Size, 4½x5¾ inches.
No. 3C32732 Cloth. Price..........29c
No. 3C32733 Morocco, full gilt. Price..........58c
If by mail, postage extra, either style, 7 cents.

Vest Pocket Webster's Pronouncing Dictionary.

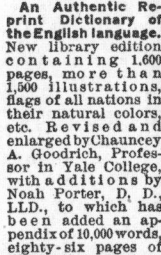

Every doubtful, disputable or difficult word in current speech or popular literature, correctly spelled, properly pronounced and defined. Contains rules of parliamentary procedure; legal holidays in all the states; rates of postage; rules for spelling, punctuation and the use of capitals; abbreviations in common use; foreign words and phrases, etc. Vest pocket (time-saving) size.
No. 3C33286 Full leather, gilt edges, indexed. Price..........18c
If by mail, postage extra, 3 cents.

Webster's Dictionary.
$1.12 buys this $5.00 book.

An Authentic Reprint Dictionary of the English language. New library edition containing 1,600 pages, more than 1,500 illustrations, flags of all nations in their natural colors, etc. Revised and enlarged by Chauncey A. Goodrich, Professor in Yale College, with additions by Noah Porter, D. D., LLD., to which has been added an appendix of 10,000 words, eighty-six pages of illustrations portraying over 3,000 subjects. Biographical Dictionary, also Losette's system of memory culture, electricity up to date, and Roman, Greek, English, Hebrew, Ethiopic, Arabic, Chaldaic, deaf and dumb alphabets. Sheepskin, marble edges, leather label, indexed. Library style. Size, 8¾x10½x4 inches. Retail price, $5.00.
No. 3C33322 Our price, indexed..$1.12
Weight, packed for shipment, 8 pounds.

Webster's Unabridged Dictionary, $1.98.
New 1903 Copyrighted Edition.

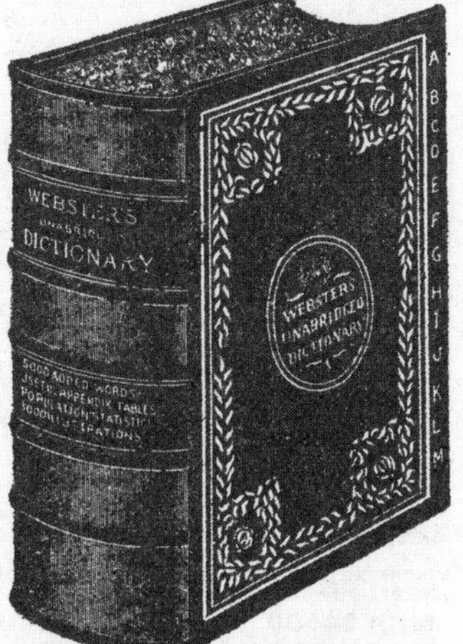

The authorized Webster's Dictionary is universally recognized as an authority in the English Language. The well known G. & C. Merriam & Co.'s edition of the Unabridged Dictionary has now been thoroughly modernized and enriched by a new supplement to meet the wants of those who require a good dictionary at a low price. This dictionary contains 1,764 pages. The dictionary proper with supplement, has over 118,000 words and meanings. An explanatory and pronouncing vocabulary of the names of noted fictitious persons, places, etc. The population of the principal countries and cities of the world, United States Census for 1900. Pronouncing vocabulary of common English christian names. Over 2,500 quotations, words, phrases, proverbs, etc. 68 full page illustrations. Memoirs of Noah Webster, a brief history of the English language, principles of pronunciation and orthography, rules for spelling, etc. Size, 11x9¾x4 inches. Retail price, $5.00.
No. 3C33342 Our price for full law sheep, with patent index cut on edge....$1.98
Weight, packed for shipment, 9 pounds.

Webster's System of Memorizing Difficult Words.

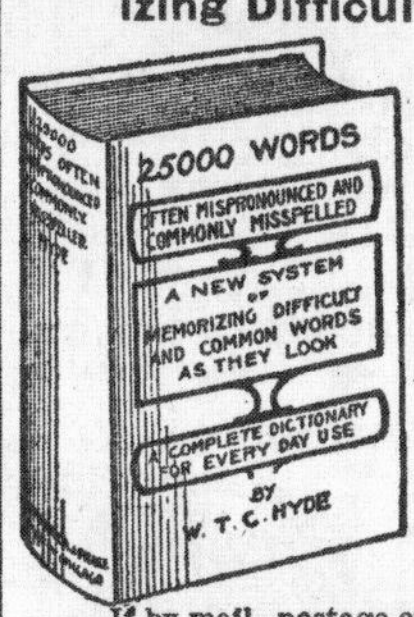

By Wm. T. C. Hyde. A new system of memorizing difficult and common words. A book for business men, teachers, students and educators generally. This work also contains an appendix, in which are defined many commercial and business terms and abbreviations in every day use. Cloth. Size, 5x7 inches. Retail price, 50 cents.
No. 3C33460
Our price...25c
If by mail, postage extra, 6 cents.

Webster's Imperial Dictionary, $3.95.

If you would own the best dictionary in existence—a dictionary that is as reliable as the law of gravitation—the IMPERIAL is the dictionary you want.

Only, **$3.95**—less than one-third the original price, we offer Webster's Imperial Dictionary, the latest, most complete and best edition of Webster ever published.

For years Webster's Unabridged Dictionary has been the standard authority of the English speaking world—today Webster's Imperial is the accepted authority. There is no more reason for buying an inaccurate, poorly printed, reprint dictionary than there is for buying a shoddy suit of clothes. In clearness, convenience of arrangement, accuracy and in all that goes to constitute an ideal dictionary, the Imperial embodies every qualification. It defines more words than Webster's International. It is truly a dictionary that all can use profitably to mind and pocket. A dictionary for the home, for the school, for the student, for the author, editor, for professional use, in fact, for all who have any use for a dictionary. Ideally complete. A triumph of practical and scientific methods. Wonderfully compact, a marvel of learning and of cheapness. Useful, reliable, attractive, lasting. We have purchased the entire first edition of this magnificent work and offer, for only $3.95, the best edition of Webster, the most complete and accurate dictionary of the English language extant. Bound in full law sheep with patent index cut on edge. Size, 9x11¼x4½ inches. Weight, packed for shipment, 16 pounds.
No. 3C33330 Price..........$3.95

ELECTRICITY.

Including Dynamo Tending, Testing, Repairing, Automobiles, Telephones, Telegraphy, etc.

Bell Hangers' Handbook.

By F. B. Badt. This is just the book for people engaged in selling, installing or handling electric batteries, electric bells, elevators, house or hotel annunciators, burglar or fire alarms, gas lighting apparatus, electric heating apparatus, etc. Cloth. Illustrated. Size, 4x6 inches.
No. 3C34160 Price, 65c
If by mail, postage extra, 5c.

Books That Will Help You.

EACH BOOK COMPLETE AND UP TO DATE.

When ordering, be sure and mention Series No. 3C34178 and give title of books wanted.

- **How to Make a Dynamo.**
- **How to Make a Telephone.**
- **How to Make an Electric Motor.**
- **How to Make a Storage Battery.**
- **How to Make a Wimshurst Static Electric Machine.**
- **How to Make a Magnetic Machine.**
- **How to Make a Medical Induction Coil.**
- **How to Make a Pocket Accumulator.**
- **How to Make a Plunge Battery.**
- **How to Make a Voltmeter.**
- **How to Make a Galvanometer.**
- **How to Make a Hand Dynamo.**
- **How to Make a ⅛ H. P. Dynamo Motor.**
- **How to Make a Toy Motor.**
- **How to Make an Electric Bell.**
- **How to Make a Telegraph Instrument.**

Series No. 3C34178 Illustrated.
Price, each..........8c
If by mail, postage extra, each, 2 cents.

Dynamo Tenders' Handbook.

By F. B. Badt. Containing instructions and rules required by practical men, as dynamo tenders, linemen, stationary engineers and operators of all kinds of electric plants. This is the best book of the kind in print. Cloth. Illustrated. Size, 3½x6 inches.

No. 3C34292 Price, **65c**
If by mail, postage extra, 4c.

Electricity, Arithmetic of.

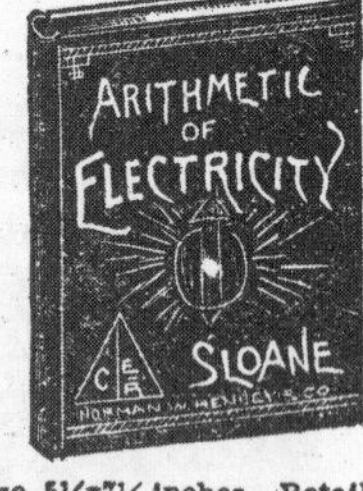

By T. O'Connor Sloane. The latest edition. A practical treatise on electrical calculations of all kinds reduced to a series of rules, all of the simplest forms and involving only ordinary arithmetic. The principal object of this work is to give a practical review of the mathematics of electricity within the scope of those who are not acquainted with algebra and higher mathematics. Illustrated. Cloth. Size, 5¼x7½ inches. Retail price, $1.00.

No. 3C34306 Our price **63c**
If by mail, postage extra, 6 cents.

Electrical Experiments, Easy, and How to Make Them.

By L. P. Dickinson. Elementary handbook of lessons, experiments and inventions. Explains in simple and easily understood language everything about galvanometers, batteries, magnets, induction coils, motors, voltometers, dynamos, storage batteries, simple and practical telephones telegraph instruments, rheostat, condensers, electrophorous, resistance, electro plating, electric toy making, etc. Cloth. Illustrated. Size, 4½x6 inches.

No. 3C34326 Price **68c**
If by mail, postage extra, 12 cents.

Electricity and Magnetism.

By Sylvanus P. Thompson. A book full of practical information. A book for the beginner; for the advanced student. These lessons in electricity and magnetism are intended to afford to beginners a clear and correct knowledge of the experiments upon which the science of electricity and magnetism are based. Cloth. Illustrated. Size, 5¼x7¼ inches.

No. 3C34330 Price **56c**
If by mail, postage extra, 12 cents.

Electrician, How to Become a Successful.

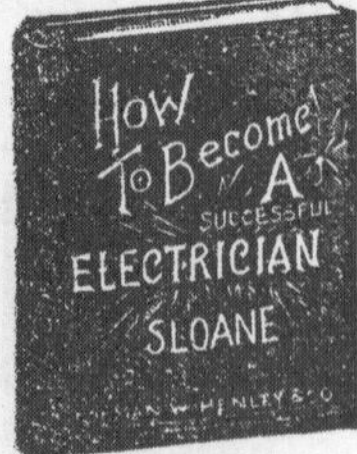

By Professor T. O'Connor Sloane. It is the ambition of thousands of young and old to become electrical engineers. Not every one is prepared to spend several thousand dollars upon a college course, but the book is designed to tell how to become a successful electrician without the outlay usually made in acquiring the profession. Illustrated. Cloth. Size, 5¼x7¼ inches. Retail price, $1.00.

No. 3C34334 Our price **60c**
If by mail, postage extra, 8 cents.

Electric Toy Making.

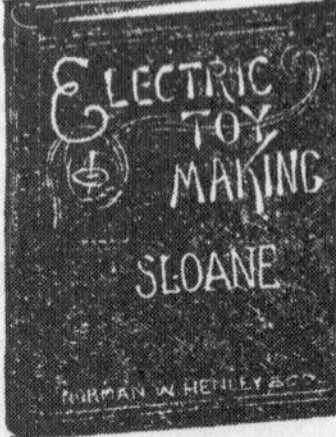

By T. O'Connor Sloane. A work especially designed for amateurs and young folks. This work treats of the making at home of electrical toys, electrical apparatus, motors, dynamos and instruments in general, and is designed to bring within the reach of young and old the manufacture of genuine and useful electrical appliances. Cloth. Size, 5¼x7¼ inches. Retail price, $1.00.

No. 3C34382 Our price **60c**
If by mail, postage extra, 8 cents.

Electrical Transmission Handbook.

By F. B. Badt. In simple language the author has avoided as much as possible the use of scientific terms. This is a book easily understood, and one that should be in the hands of students, amateurs and professional electricians. Illustrated. Size, 3½x6 inches. Cloth.

No. 3C34384 Price **65c**
If by mail, postage extra, 5 cents.

Horseless Vehicles, Automobiles and Motor Cycles.

By Gardner D. Hiscox, M. E. A practical treatise for automobilists, and everyone interested in the development, care and use of the automobile. This book is written on a broad basis, and comprises in its scope a full description with illustrations and details of the progress and manufacturing of one of the most important innovations of the times. This book is up to date and fully illustrated with various types of horseless carriages, automobiles, and motor cycles. Cloth. 316 illustrations. 460 pages. Size, 6x9¼ inches. Retail price, $3.00.

No. 3C34283 Our price **$1.98**
If by mail, postage extra, 24 cents.

How to Make, Test and Repair Dynamos and Motors.

By T. Edwin Lowell. Handbook for electrical amateurs and students, with instructions, working drawings for making small dynamos and motors of various sizes. Chapters on armatures and how to wind them, tables of windings for smal dynamos and motors, valuable hints on testing and repairing, chapter on field magnets, commutator and other details, etc. Cloth. Illustrated. Size, 5x7 inches.

No. 3C34294 Price **45c**
If by mail, postage extra, 5 cents.

Incandescent Wiring Handbook.

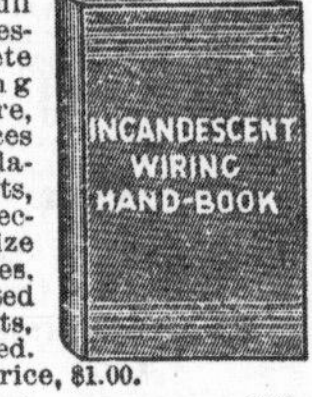

By Lieut. F. B. Badt. Full instructions for incandescent wiring and complete information concerning methods of running wire, location of safety devices and switches, splices, insulation and testing for faults, wire gauges, general electrical data, calculating size of wires, wiring of fixtures, elevators, buildings, isolated and central station plants. Cloth, profusely illustrated. Size, 4x6 inches. Retail price, $1.00.

No. 3C34524 Our price **65c**
If by mail, postage extra, 5 cents.

Induction Coils.

How to Make, Repair and Use Them.

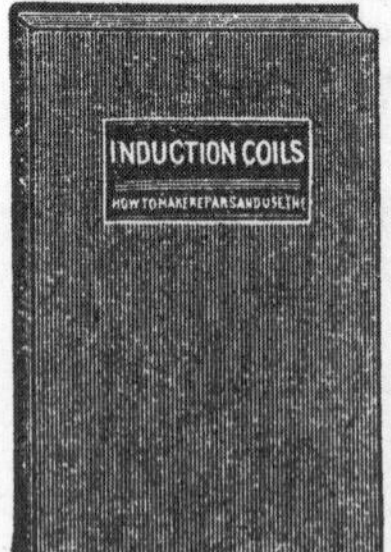

By T. E. Lowell. The induction coil has always been a popular piece of apparatus with amateurs and students interested in electrical science, so numerous and fascinating are the experiments that can be performed with it. This is a practical book on the construction and use of induction coils, containing full instructions for making a powerful shocking coil, ½-inch spark coil, and 4-inch spark coil, and other hints on experiments with induction coils. Fully illustrated. Size, 5x7½ inches. Retail price, $1.00.

No. 3C34530 Our price **45c**
If by mail, postage extra, 5 cents.

Telegraphy Self Taught.

Telegraph operators are always in demand by railroads, corporations, telegraph companies newspaper offices, etc. Explains all about batteries, operating keys, Morse code, block signals, commercial messages, earth as a conductor; how to count the words in a message, order of transmission; railroad rules for telegraph operators and movements of trains by telegraphic orders, train order form. Cloth. Illustrated. Size, 5¼x7¾ inches.

No. 3C35162 Price **58c**
If by mail, postage extra, 11 cents.

ENTERTAINMENTS, AMATEUR THEATRICALS, READINGS, ETC.

Embracing Stump Speeches, Comic Lectures, Conundrums and Riddles, Monologues, Vaudeville Jokes, Tricks (Card and Coin), Etc.

American Star Speaker and Modern Elocutionist, The.

By Charles Walter Brown. A book for schools, churches, libraries, societies, lodges, etc. This is unquestionably one of the best books of its kind published in recent years. Contains a treatise on acting, Delsartism, elocution, oratory, and physical and vocal culture, by the late Isaac Hinton Brown, professor of those subjects in the Missouri State University, halftone illustrations. Size, 7x9¾ inches. Cloth. Retail price, $1.50.

No. 3C38125 Our price **59c**
If by mail, postage extra, 14 cents.

Brudder Gardner's Stump Speeches and Comic Lectures.

Containing some of the best hits of the leading negro delineators of the present day, comprising the most amusing and side splitting contributions of oratorical effusion which have ever been produced. Paper cover. Size, 4½x6½ inches.

No. 3C38158 Price **14c**
If by mail, postage extra, 3 cents.

Card Tricks and How to Do Them.

Principles of Sleight of Hand, by Professor A. Roterberg. Illustrated. This book explains all card tricks, among which are the animated card, dealing five from the bottom, causing a chosen card to appear at any given number in the pack; method of dealing one's self all the trumps in whist; how to palm a card, etc. Size, 4½x6¾ inches.

No. 3C38206 Paper. Price **14c**
No. 3C38207 Cloth, gold titles. Price **27c**
If by mail, postage extra, paper, 3c; cloth, 5c.

Choice Dialect and Vaudeville Stage Jokes.

A new collection of readings, recitations, jokes, gags, monologues in Irish, Dutch, Scotch, Yankee, French, Italian, Spanish, Chinese, Negro and other dialects, representing every phase of sentiment, from the keenest humor or the tenderest pathos to that which is strongly dramatic. Size, 4¼x6¾ inches.

No. 3C38218 Paper. Price **14c**
No. 3C38219 Cloth. Price **27c**
If by mail, postage extra, paper 3c; cloth, 5c.

Comic Recitations and Readings.

Contains some of the best efforts of such world renowned humorists as Mark Twain, Josh Billings, Artemus Ward, Ezra Kendall, Brete Harte, Bill Nye, Ben King, George Thatcher, Lew Dockstader, William S. Gilbert, Jame Whitcomb Riley and others. Suitable for recitations in drawing room entertainment and amateur theatricals. Size, 4¾x6½ inches.

No. 3C38238 Paper cover. Price **14c**
No. 3C38239 Cloth. Price **27c**
If by mail, postage extra, paper, 3c; cloth, 5c.

Conundrums and Riddles.

Collected and arranged by John Ray. Containing upward of 4,000 choice, new intellectual conundrums and riddles which will sharpen your wit and lead you to think quickly. They are always a source of great amusement and pleasure, whiling away tedious hours and putting every one in a good humor. Any person with this book may take the lead in entertaining a company and keep them in roars of laughter for hours. 160 pages. Size, 4¾x6½ inches.

No. 3C38242 Paper. Price **14c**
No. 3C38243 Cloth. Price **27c**
If by mail, postage extra, paper, 3c; cloth, 5c.

Dick's Diverting Dialogues.

Consisting of twenty comedies and farces, by some of the best known authors. Adapted for parlor performance by young ladies and youths, and also includes elaborate decorations for exhibiting living pictures, etc. Size, 4¼x6½ inches.

No. 3C38268 Board cover. Price. **30c**
No. 3C38269 Paper cover. Price. **18c**
If by mail, postage extra, board, 5c; paper, 3c

Dutch Dialect.

Jokes and Recitations, as told by our foremost vaudeville stars, Weber and Fields, Rogers Brothers, Marshall P. Wilder, Ezra Kendall, George Fuller Golden, Gus Williams and others. Every lover of German dialect, wit and humor ought to procure a copy of this new and up to date book, as it contains the choicest emanations of the most celebrated and renowned Dutchcomedians and humorists of the present day. Size, 4½x6½ inches.

No. 3C38290 Paper cover. Price ... **14c**
No. 3C38291 Cloth. Price **27c**
If by mail, postage extra, paper 3c; cloth 5c.

Debaters' Manual.

By Charles Walter Brown, A. M. This book fills a place occupied by no other. It is not only a manual of parliamentary usages, but a complete guide pertaining to matters of organization. Debating clubs will find this book unequaled. It tells us all about how to start the machinery, how to outline and prepare a debate. It gives full debates, so that the inexperienced speaker may know about what he is expected to say. 160 pages. Size, 4¾x6¾ inches.

No. 3C38258 Paper cover. Price ... **14c**
No. 3C38259 Cloth. Price **27c**
If by mail, postage extra, paper, 3c; cloth, 5c.

Little Folks' Dialogues and Dramas.

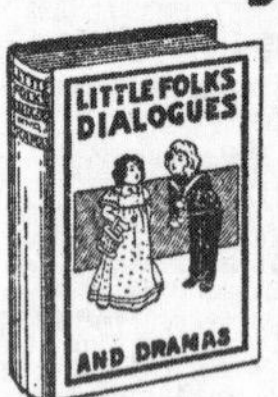

A collection of original dialogues and dramas by various authors. Sprightly and sensible, particularly adapted for little people from 3 to 12 years old, on subjects and ideas fitted to their age, and developing the germs of mimicry and appropriate action, so often observed in even children of tender age. Size, 4¾x7

No. 3C38660 Price ....
No. 3C38661 Price ....
If by mail, postage extra, paper, 3c; cl

Little Folks' Speaker.

Containing cute and catchy pieces for small children ten years and much younger, including speeches of welcome and short dialogues for opening and closing children's entertainments. The subjects are such as delight the infantile mind, and the language, while childlike, is not childish. Size, 4¾x6¾ inches.

No. 3C38664 Paper. Price **14c**
No. 3C38665 Cloth, gold title. Price **27c**
If by mail, postage extra, paper, 3c; cloth, 5c.

Negro Minstrels.

By Jack Haverly. A complete handbook written to encourage, help and guide amateurs in their efforts to form troupes and give a successful evening's performance. An entire program is arranged with full details, consisting of a first part with the brightest dialogue between Tambo, Bones and the Middleman; the introduction of ballads, songs, gags, conundrums, side splitting stump speeches, etc. 150 pages. Size, 4¼x6¾ inches.

No. 3C38762 Paper cover. Price **14c**
No. 3C38763 Cloth. Price **27c**
If by mail, postage extra, paper, 3c; cloth, 5c.

Patriotic Recitations and Readings.

For children. This is the choicest, newest and most complete collection of patriotic recitations published, and includes all the best known selections, together with the best utterances of many eminent statesmen. Selections for Decoration Day, Fourth of July, Washington's and Lincoln's Birthday, Arbor Day, Labor Day and all other patriotic occasions. Size, 4¾x6½ ins.

No. 3C38858 Paper cover. Price. 14c
No. 3C38859 Cloth. Price **27c**
If by mail, postage extra, paper 3c; cloth 5c.

Toasts and After Dinner Speeches.

Edited by William Young Stafford. How many times have you been called upon to respond to some toast or speech? What would you not give for the ability to be rid of this embarrassment? This book contains presentation speeches, at and after dinner speeches, political speeches, welcomes, congratulations, school commencements, valedictories, etc., also toasts and welcomes on various subjects. Size, 4¼x6¾ inches.

No. 3C39174 Paper. Price..........14c
No. 3C39175 Cloth. Price..........27c
If by mail, postage extra, paper, 3c; cloth, 5c.

Tricks with Coins.

By T. Nelson Downs, "King of Koins." Embracing every sleight and subtlety invented and known. Full and complete expose of the author's world famous coin creation, "The Miser's Dream," including the correct method of executing the continuous back and front hand palm. A series of new passes with coins, including eleven distinct and different methods of causing the disappearance of a single coin. Size, 4¼x6¾ inches.

No. 3C39180 Paper. Price..........14c
No. 3C39181 Cloth. Price..........27c
If by mail, postage extra, paper, 3c., cloth, 5c.

Young Folks' Dialogues.

By Charles C. Shoemaker. Everything especially written for this volume. One of the best dialogue books in print. For children of 15 years. Size, 4¾x7 inches.

No. 3C39440 Paper cover. Price......15c
No. 3C39441 Board cover. Price......25c
If by mail, postage extra, paper, 3c; board edition, 5c.

Young People's Speaker.

By E. C. and L. J. Rook. An entirely new book composed of bright, cheery, wholesome recitations, especially adapted for children of from 10 to 14 years.

No. 3C39444 Paper. Price..........9c
No. 3C39445 Boards. Price..........18c
If by mail, postage extra, paper, 3 cents; boards, 6 cents.

"Deestrick Skule."

Of Fifty Years Ago. The most popular entertainment ever published. Always a success wherever given, and we most highly recommend it. Fifteen to fifty people are required. Old fashioned costumes of fifty years ago are worn, grown men and women dressing as the boys and girls of that time in America. No scenery required. Paper cover.

No. 3C39915 Price, each..........35c
If by mail, postage extra, 2 cents.

Hageman's Make-Up Book.

By Maurice Hageman. A useful and up to date handbook on practical make-up, especially prepared for amateurs and professionals. This book contains chapters on how to make up for old, middle aged and adults, juvenile parts, comedy and character parts. Contains chapters on the use of wigs, beards, and other accessories for the face. Also contains chapters on grease paints, their origin, use, application and removal. Size, 4¾x7⅛ inches. Over 60 pages. Retail price, 25c.

No. 3C39920 Our price 15c
If by mail, postage extra, 3 cents.

FICTION.

Latest Copyrighted Fiction only 96c.

The best fiction of the day at prices that have no competition. Books that are listed everywhere at $1.50, and for which book sellers are asking $1.08 to $1.35, at the astonishingly low price of 96 cents. The list given below does not pretend to be a complete record of all the new fiction published, but includes only the more popular and best selling books of the last six months.

Beverly of Graustark. By George Barr McCutcheon
Bruver Jim's Baby. By G. V. Mighels
Call of the Wild. By Jack London
Clansman, The. By Thomas Dixon
Cost, The. By David Graham Philips
Crossing, The. By Winston Churchill
God's Good Man. By Marie Corelli
Gordon Keith. By Thomas Nelson Page
In the Bishop's Carriage By Frances Lynde
Christmas Eve on Lonesome. By John Fox, Jr.
Little Union Scout, A. By Joel Chandler Harris
Lady Rose's Daughter. By Mrs. Humphrey Ward
Memoirs of a Baby. By Josephine Daskam
Old Gordon Graham. By the author of Letters of a Self Made Merchant to His Son
Prodigal Son, The. By Hall Caine
Rebecca of Sunny Brook Farm. By Kate D. Wiggins
Rulers of Kings. By Gertrude Atherton
Sir Mortimer. By Mary Johnston
Virginian, The. By Owen Wister

No. 3C44000 Our price..........96c
If by mail, postage extra, each, 12 cents.

Recent Novels at Popular Prices.

Biennerhassett. By Charles Felton Pidgin
David Harum. By E. Noyes Westcott
Eternal City. By Hall Caine
Girl at the Halfway House. By Emerson Hough
Janice Meredith. By Paul Leicester Ford
Manxman, The. By Hall Caine
Quincy Adams Sawyer. By Charles F. Pidgin
Tommy and Grizel. By J. M. Barrie
Mississippi Bubble. By Emerson Hough
Captain Ravenshaw. By R. N. Stephens
Cecilia. By F. M. Crawford
Children of Destiny. By Molly Elliott Seawell
Hearts Courageous. By Hallie Erminie Rives
Janet Ward. By Margaret Sangster
Lazarre. By Mary H. Catherwood
Long Straight Road. By George Horton
Loom of Life. By C. F. Goss
Richard Rosny. By Maxwell Gray
Seats of the Mighty. By Gilbert Parker
Those Black Diamond Men. By W. F. Gibbons
Two Vanrevels. By Booth Tarkington
Under the Rose. By Frederick S. Isham
When Knighthood Was in Flower. By Charles Major
Wings of the Morning. By Louis Tracy

No. 3C44950 Cloth. Price..........45c
If by mail, postage extra, each, 11 cents.

Eggleston, Edward S., Works of.

New edition of this famous author's works. Uniformly bound in cloth. Illustrated. Size, 5x7 inches. Retail price, $1.00. Do not fail to give title of book wanted.

The Hoosier Schoolmaster. A thrilling, intensely interesting and humorous story of backwoods life in Southern Indiana. Illustrated by F. Opper.

The Mystery of Metropolisville. Wonderfully graphic, intensely vivid and thoroughly human. Finely illustrated.

The End of the World. A love story. Thirty-two fine illustrations.

No. 3C44314 Our price..........60c
If by mail, postage extra, 12 cents.

Evans, Augusta J., Works of.

The author's genius and fascinating style are as fresh today in her later books as they were in her earlier, which after thirty-six years of constant use still hold their popularity. Size, 5¼x7¾ in. Retail price, $1.50.

Speckled Bird (new)
Beulah
Macaria
Inez
St. Elmo
Vashti
Infelice
At the Mercy of Tiberius

No. 3C44345 Our price, per volume..96c
If by mail, postage extra, 12 cents.

Holmes, Mary J., Works of.

New edition, library style, uniform. Cloth. Size, 5¼x7¾ inches. Retail price, per volume, $1.50.

Rena's Experiment (new)
The Cromptons (new)
Tracy Diamonds (new)
Merivale Banks (new)
Daisy Thornton
Chateau d'Or
Hugh Worthington
Ethelyn's Mistake
Edna Browning
Cameron Pride
Dr. Hethern's Daughters
Darkness and Daylight
Bessie's Fortune
Mildred
Gretchen
West Lawn
Queenie Hetherton
Madeline
Paul Ralston
Marguerite
Rose Mather
Meadow Brook
Forest House
Millbank
Marion Gray
Lena Rivers
Edith Lyle

No. 3C44481 Our price..........70c
If by mail, postage extra, 12 cents.

Read, Opie, Works of.

New popular edition. Cloth. Size, 4¾x7½ inches. Retail price, per volume, 75 cents.

An Arkansas Planter
A Kentucky Colonel
A Tennessee Judge
A Yankee from the West
Emmett Bonlore
Len Gansett
My Young Master
Odd Folks
Old Ebenezer
On the Suwanee River
The Captain's Romance
The Carpetbagger
The Jucklin's
The Waters of Caney Fork
The Wives of the Prophet
Up Terrapin River

No. 3C44962 Our price, per volume 33c
If by mail, postage extra, per volume, 10 cents.

Roe, E. P., Works of.

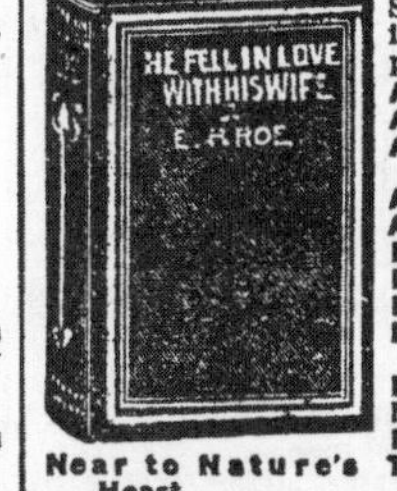

New uniform edition. Bound in silk cloth. Size of volume, 5¼x7½ inches. Retail price, per volume, $1.25.

A Day of Fate
A Face Illumined
A Knight of the XIX Century
A Young Girl's Wooing
An Original Belle
Barriers Burned Away
Driven Back to Eden
From Jest to Earnest
He Fell in Love with His Wife
His Sombre Rivals
Miss Lou
Nature's Serial Story
Taken Alive, and Other Stories
The Earth Trembled
The Home Acre
What Can She Do?
Without a Home
Near to Nature's Heart
Opening a Chestnut Burr
Success with Small Fruits

No. 3C44125 Our price, per volume or in quantity..........63c
If by mail, postage extra, per volume, 12 cents.

Wallace, General Lew, Works of.

Ben Hur. Retail price, $1.50. Cloth. Size, 5¼x7¾ inches. Our price..........96c
Fair God, The. Price..........$1.05
Boyhood of Christ. Price..........$2.48
Prince of India. Price..........$1.78

Order by No. 3C45305 and do not fail to state name of book wanted.
If by mail, postage extra per volume, 14 cents.

FORTUNE TELLING AND DREAM BOOKS.

Dream Book, Gypsy Witch.

This is one of the most complete books of dreams published. Contains an alphabetical list of dreams on every subject, including the lucky numbers, given names of both males and females and their lucky numbers. Birthdays and their significance, lucky days, rules to learn the number of saddle gigs and horses in any given row of numbers and what amount they will bring, combination tables, etc. 208 pages. Size, 4¼x6¾ inches.

No. 3C46278 Paper cover. Price.....14c
No. 3C46279 Cloth. Price..........27c
If by mail, postage extra, paper, 3c; cloth, 5c.

How to Tell Fortunes by Cards.

By Madame Zancig. It describes the methods that are commonly used by gypsies and others when they "read your fortune." Many have witnessed a great number of most wonderful and useful conclusions which have been produced by this science, and many future events have been foretold. Anyone can tell the present, past and future by following these simple instructions. 150 pages. 50 illustrations. Size, 4¼x6¾ inches.

No. 3C46370 Paper cover. Price.....14c
No. 3C46371 Cloth. Price..........27c
If by mail, postage extra, paper, 3c; cloth, 5c.

Gypsy Witch Fortune Telling Cards.

By Mme. Le Normand.

The author has left behind her such a reputation, the memory of so unusual a talent, that we believe we shall do a favor to the admirers of her system, by publishing the cards, which were found after her death. They are the same cards with which she prophesied to Napoleon I. his future greatness, and the downfall of many princes and great men of France. Each pack contains fifty-two illustrated cards, lithographed in colors, with inscriptions. Full directions accompany each pack.

No. 3C46445 Per pack of 52 cards. Price..........20c
If by mail, postage extra, 5 cents.

GIFT BOOKS.

Embracing Birthday, Souvenir and Friendship Books. These are particularly fine examples of the bookmakers' art, and are worthy of a place in any home.

America Photographed.

A portfolio of photographs covering points of scenic and historic interest in North America, Mexico, Alaska and Canada. A collection of 160 halftone reproductions of photographs forming a complete panorama of the continent of America. The pictures include mountain and river scenery, picturesque landscapes, buildings, parks, fountains, etc. Cloth. Cover stamped in silver and aluminum. Size, 12¾x10¾ inches. Retail price, $2.00.

No. 3C48138 Our price..........79c
If by mail, postage extra, 25 cents.

Baby's Book.

By Ida Scott Taylor. Illustrated by Frances Brundage. An album in which may be recorded the mother's story of the chief events of the baby's life. A record regarding the baby and the most interesting events of babyhood, with place for entry of date of birth; full names; photographs. Contains full page colored illustrations and numerous black and white drawings, with appropriate poetical selections. Size, 7½x10 inches.

No. 3C14158 Imitation leather, watered silk pattern, pink or baby blue. Retail price, 50 cents. Our price..........30c
If by mail, postage extra, 11 cents.
No. 3C14159 Same as above, but bound in padded silk. Retail price, 75 cents. Our price..........50c
If by mail, postage extra, 14 cents.

Because I Love You.

A beautiful gift book for a sweetheart, friend, birthday, Christmas or wedding gift. A choice collection of love poems, edited by Anna E. Mack. Miss Mack has selected with discriminating taste some of the sweetest, tenderest lines in our language, dealing with the one imperishable subject, love. Beautifully bound. Deckle edge, uncut. Boxed. Cloth. Size, 5x7 inches.

No. 3C48162 Price..........99c
If by mail, postage extra, 12 cents.

World, Glimpses of The.

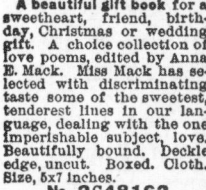

By John L. Stoddard. Contains hundreds of full page views portraying scenes all over the world, reproduced by the perfected halftone process from photographs collected by the celebrated traveler and lecturer, John L. Stoddard, by whom the pictures are described in graphic language. Size, 11x14 inches. Weight, packed for shipment, 7½ lbs. Retail price, $3.50.

No. 3C49342 Cloth. Our price..........$1.69
No. 3C49343 Full leather, gold stamped, gilt edges. Retail price, $7.50. Our price, $3.39
If by mail, postage extra, 64 cents.

Wedding Bells, The.

Illustrated by Frances Brundage. Arranged for exhaustive record of all events connected with the marriage ceremony; Photos of the bride and bridegroom, names of the guests, list of the presents, description of the gown, etc. Has full page color illustrations and numerous black and white drawings, with appropriate poetical selections. Illustrated. Cloth, blue and silver. Size, 8x10 inches. Retail price, 50 cents.

No. 3C49318 Imitation leather, watered silk pattern. Our price..........30c
If by mail, postage extra, 12 cents.
No. 3C49319 Same as No. 3C49318, but beautifully bound in padded silk. Retail price, 75 cents. Our price..........50c
If by mail, postage extra, 17 cents.

REWARD OF MERIT CARDS.

Reward of Merit Cards. For day, Sunday school and graduating exercises. (Sold only in packages.) 10 assorted cards, lithographed in 12 colors and gold, showing landscapes and children's designs. Size, 3⅛x5⅜ inches.

No. 3C49473 Price, per package of 10 cards..........6c
Per box of 100 cards..........50c

Reward of Merit Cards. (Sold only in packages.) Assorted designs of beautiful cards, lithographed in 12 colors and gold and silver, showing winter landscapes and children's designs. An exceptionally pretty card. Size, 4x6 inches.

No. 3C49475 Price, per package of 10 cards..........10c
Per box of 100 cards..........90c

Reward of Merit Cards. (Sold only in packages.) Assorted designs, showing landscapes, flowers, etc. Size, 4⅜x6⅛ inches.

No. 3C49477 Price, per package of 10 cards..........$0.14
Per box of 100 cards..........1.10

Reward of Merit Cards. (Sold only in packages.) Assorted designs of beautiful cards, showing flowers, landscapes, children's designs, etc. Beautifully embossed, fancy cut out border, lithographed in 12 colors and gold. Size, 4⅜x7⅞ inches.

No. 3C49479 Price, per package of 10 cards..........$0.17
Per box of 100 cards..........1.50

Reward of Merit Cards. (Sold only in packages.) Assorted designs of beautiful cards lithographed in designs. A very attractive card. Size, 4¾x6¾ inches.

No. 3C49481 Price, per package of 10 cards..........$0.22
Per box of 100 cards..........1.85
If by mail, postage extra, on any of above numbers, per 10 cards, 5 cents.

Sunday School Text Reward Cards.

Sunday School Text Cards. Assorted designs, beautifully lithographed in 12 colors, floral designs, with embossed fancy border. Size, 3⅜x5⅛ inches.

No. 3C49483 Price, per package of 10 cards.....10c
Per box of 100 cards.....85c

Sunday School Reward Cards. Assorted designs, lithographed in 14 colors and gold; beautiful floral and ribbon effects. Size, 4⅝x5⅞ inches.

No. 3C49485 Price, per package of 10 cards.....$0.15
Per box of 100 cards.....1.35

Sunday School Reward Cards. Assorted designs, lithographed in 12 colors and silver; embossed floral designs with rustic border. Size, 4⅛x5⅞ inches.

No. 3C49487 Price, per package of 10 cards.....$0.20
Per box of 100 cards.....1.85
If by mail, postage extra, per ten cards, 5 cents.

Relief Scrap Pictures.

An assortment of scrap pictures, 10 sheets, each sheet containing from four to thirty pictures, representing fruit, flowers, figures, animals, birds, etc. New designs. No two alike.

No. 3C49489 Box of 10 sheets. Price, 10c
If by mail, postage extra, per box, 5 cents.

Ten superb assorted sheets of scrap pictures, highly embossed, from four to twenty pictures on a sheet. No two sheets alike. Average size of sheet, 7x8 inches.

No. 3C49491 Box of 10 sheets. Price, 15c
If by mail, postage extra, per box, 8 cents.

Twenty entirely different style sheet scrap pictures. With from four to twenty pictures on a sheet. No two sheets alike. Size, 9x13 inches.

No. 3C49493 Box of 20 sheets. Price, 25c
If by mail, postage extra, per box, 24 cents.

Marriage Certificates.

Marriage Certificates. Attractive design, printed on heavy paper, lithographed at the top, with blank spaces for name, location and date. Size, 16x20 inches. Put up in a heavy pasteboard tube, ready for mailing.

No. 3C49495 Price, gilt.....18c

Marriage Certificates. Handsome design, printed on extra heavy, white paper with monogram and description, and spaces for names and dates. Size, 16x20 inches. Put up in a heavy pasteboard tube, ready for mailing.

No. 3C49497 Price, colors.....14c
If by mail, postage extra, either style, 5 cents

HISTORICAL

Including Travels, World's Wonders, Civil War Experiences, History of Western Life. Etc.

Blue and the Gray, The;

Or, the Civil War as Seen by a Boy. Tells of the great war as seen from the camp and saddle. A true story of camp life, daring adventure, footsore marching, heartrending battles. It tells of battle scenes, of farewell requests, hairbreadth escapes, the picket charges, rough riders, etc. Illustrated by Frank Beard. Contains 150 war photographs, two magnificent water color plates. Bound in cloth, lithographed in colors. Size, 7⅛x9⅛ inches.

No. 3C60173 Price.....65c
If by mail, postage extra, 18 cents.

Camp Fire Stories.

By Edward Anderson. A series of sketches of the Union army in the Southwest. Profusely illustrated with over 100 original drawings made especially for the work. This is a collection of short stories, telling in an interesting and vivid manner the various scenes in army life. It portrays in glowing words fun and pathos, the drama and the tragedy, as well as every day scenes of soldier life in camp and on the battlefield, on the march, etc. Cloth. Gilt top. Size, 5⅛x7⅛ inches.

No. 3C60216 Price.....45c
If by mail, postage extra, 13 cents.

Cowboy Life in Texas.

A realistic and true recital of wild life on the boundless plains of Texas. The extraordinary experience of twenty-seven years of exciting life of a genuine cowboy among the roughs and toughs of Texas. Fully illustrated. Contains 290 pages. Cloth. Size, 5⅛x7⅞ inches.

No. 3C60238
Price.....39c
By mail, postage extra, 12c.

Greatest Things in the World, The

Science, invention, commerce, manufacture, etc. Contains history's most remarkable events, men's mightiest achievements, nature's marvels, famous explorations and discoveries, wonderful architectural creations, loftiest mountains largest lakes, rivers, canals, bridges, etc. Over 600 large double column pages, hundreds of superb phototype engravings. Cloth. Size, 7⅞x9⅞ inches. Retail price, $2.50.

No. 3C52439 Polychromatic stamping. Our price.....(Postage extra, 39c).....95c

History of Our Wild West.

A record of exciting events on the western borders, massacres, desperate battles, extraordinary bravery, grand hunts, adventures by flood and field, curious escapes, etc., and the melange of incidents that make up the melodramas of civilization in the march over mountains and prairies to the Pacific. A history of Boone, Crockett, Carson, Buffalo Bill and others. 766 pages. 250 illustrations. Cloth. Size, 7x9 inches. Retail price, $1.25.

No. 3C52468 Our price.....45c
If by mail, postage extra, 20 cents.

Indian Horrors; or, Massacres by the Redmen.

By H. D. Northrop. Startling descriptions of fantastic ghost dances; mysterious medicine men; desperate Indian braves; scalping of helpless settlers; burning their houses, etc. Illustrated with fine engravings printed in colors—battles, massacres, and other thrilling scenes among the Indians. Bound in cloth, marbled edges. Size, 6⅛x8⅛ inches.

No. 3C52525 Price.....49c
If by mail, postage extra, 13 cents.

Indian Wars of the United States.

By Edward S. Ellis. A fascinating history of the Indians, their methods of warfare, customs and manners; thrilling scenes and bloody battles with merciless savages, massacres, etc. The history of the Indian wars is a record of one continuous scene of blunders, frauds, oppression, injustice and crime that is a reproach to our nation. Illustrated with a colored frontispiece, many full page and other illustrations. 484 pages. Cloth. Size, 6⅞x7⅛ inches. Retail price, $3.50.

No. 3C52527 Our price.....60c
If by mail, postage extra, 34 cents.

The Marvelous Story of Man.

By G. Dallas Line. Embracing his origin and antiquity; primitive condition; races, languages, religions, superstitions, customs and peculiarities, life of prehistoric man, stone, bronze and iron ages, the mound builders, the dawning of history; in fact, everything from the beginning of man down to and including the present generation, etc. Cloth. Illustrated. Size, 6⅞x8⅛ inches.

No. 3C52718 Price.....52c
If by mail, postage extra, 21 cents.

Museum of Wonders, or, Curiosities of the World.

By Henry Davenport Northrop. Containing marvels of natural history, with graphic descriptions of monsters of the ancient world, wild animals of forest and plain, beautiful birds and insects, wonderful trees, flowers and plants, sublime natural scenery, etc., including thrilling stories in the polar and tropical regions, remarkable traits of strange people, etc., 500 large double column pages, 200 fine engravings. Cloth, polychromatic stamping. Size, 8x10 inches. Retail price, $2.50.

No. 3C52796 Our price.....79c
If by mail, postage extra, 32 cents.

Story of Stanley and His Travels Through the Wilds of Africa.

A thrilling narrative of this remarkable adventurer's terrible experiences, wonderful discoveries and amazing achievements in the Dark Continent. His explorations to the Congo, the relief of Emin Bey, with its terrible experiences of slavery, misery and death are told in a graphic manner. Profusely illustrated. Cloth. Size, 7x9 inches. Retail price, $2.50.

No. 3C53176 Our price.....48c
If by mail, postage extra, 25 cents.

United States Secret Service of the Late Civil War.

By Gen. Lafayette C. Baker. Exciting experiences in the North and South, fearless adventures, hairbreadth escapes and valuable services of the detectives of the late civil war. Fully illustrated. Contains 480 pages. Cloth. Size, 6x8½ inches. Retail price, $2.50.

No. 3C53226 Our price.....59c
If by mail, postage extra, 16 cents.

HISTORY.

Bancroft's History of the United States.

By Geo. Bancroft. An entirely new edition, partly rewritten and thoroughly revised. From the discovery of the continent to the establishment of the Constitution in 1789. Complete in six volumes. Blue cloth, gilt top. Size, 6x9 inches. Retail price, $15.00. Weight, packed for shipment, 15 pounds.

No. 3C54158 Our price.....$12.95

Gibbon's Complete History of the Decline and Fall of the Roman Empire.

New five-volume edition for only $1.85. Large type edition, printed from new type set plates, on extra quality paper, substantially bound in cloth. A new gilt top edition, library style, complete in five volumes. Size, 5½x7½ inches. Published to retail at $3.50.

No. 3C54416 Our price, per set of five volumes.....$1.85
Weight, packed for shipment, 12 pounds.

Green's History of the English People.

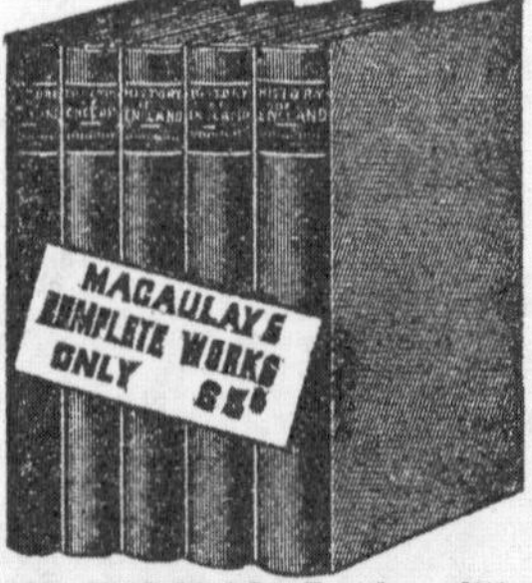

Complete in four volumes. This is really a wonderful production. There is a freshness and originality breathing from one end to the other, a charm of style and power, both narrative and descriptive, which lifts it altogether out of the class of books to which at first sight it seems to belong. Cloth. Size of volumes, 5x7⅞ inches.

No. 3C54438 Price, per set of four volumes.....98c
If by mail, postage extra, per set, 38 cents.

History of Greece.

By Geo. Grote. New edition. Mr. Grote has illustrated and invested with an entirely new significance a portion of the past history of humanity. He has made great Greeks live again before us and has enabled us to realize Greek mode of thinking. Illustrated. Cloth, gilt top. Size, 5½x7½ inches. Complete 4 volumes. Retail price, $5.00. Weight, packed for shipment, 6½ pounds.

No. 3C54440 Our price.....$2.89
If by mail, postage extra, 56 cents.

Josephus Flavius, Works of

Translated by William Whiston, A. M., with an introductory essay by Rev. H. Stebbing, D. D. Standard edition. Comprising the histories and the antiquities of the Jews, with the Destruction of Jerusalem by the Romans, to which are added the seven dissertations concerning Jesus Christ, John the Baptist, John the Just, God's Command to Abraham, Sacrifice of Isaac, together with a discourse on Hell, etc. Size, 6x9 inches. Retail price, $2.50.

No. 3C54578 Cloth. Our price.....70c
No. 3C54579 Bound in full sheep, marbled edges. Retail price, $3.50. Our price.....$1.18
If by mail, postage extra, 30 cents.

Macaulay, Thomas B., Works of.

History of England. New and large type edition, printed from new type set plates on extra quality of paper. Substantially bound. Each volume size, 5⅛x7½ inches.

No. 3C54708 Popular edition, printed from same plates as the above. Price, per set of five volumes.....65c
If by mail, postage extra, per set, 48 cents.

Conquest of Peru.

By Wm. H. Prescott.

With portraits and notes. It is a noble work, judiciously planned and admirably executed; rich with the spoils of learning, easily and gracefully woven. Two volumes complete. Cloth. Size, 5⅛x7⅞ inches.

No. 3C54238 Price, per set of two volumes.....65c
If by mail, postage extra, per set, 25 cents.

Ridpath's History of the United States.

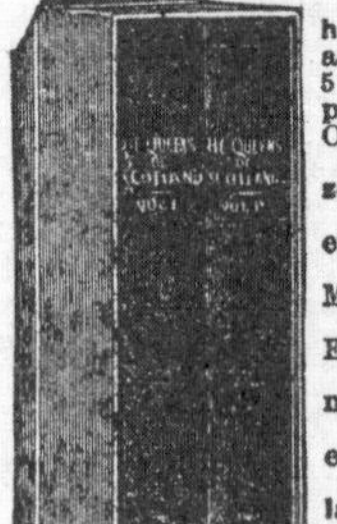

The most complete history of the United States of America published. Never before has there been published a book so rich in historical incident, so instructive in its method of presentation and so brilliant and fascinating in its narrative. Profusely illustrated with sketches, portraits and diagrams. A magnificent volume with over 800 pages, 300 illustrations. Size, 10¼x7¾x2⅛ inches.

No. 3C54966 Price.....89c
Weight, packed, 80 ounces.
If by mail, postage extra, 40 cents.

Standard Histories.

A new series of popular histories, richly bound and well illustrated. Size, 5⅛x7⅛ inches. Retail price, per volume, 75 cents. Order by number and title.

History of America. Hezekiah Butterworth.
History of China. Robert K. Douglas.
History of the Civil War. Mrs. C. Emma Cheney.
History of Egypt. Clara Erskine Clement.
History of India. Fannie Roper Feudge.
History of Mexico, Frederick A. Ober.
History of the Netherlands. Alexander Young.
History of Our Own Times (2 volumes). Justin McCarthy.
History of Russia. Nathan Haskell Dole.
History of Spain. Jas. A. Harrison.
History of Switzerland. Harriet D. S. Mackenzie.

No. 3C55142 Silk cloth, gold and blu stamped. Our price, per volume.....45c
If by mail, postage extra, per volume, 12 cents.

New Standard History of the World.

Revised and Corrected to Date. An entirely new work on general history, both ancient and modern, of all the nations of the globe. An opportunity to purchase at less than the actual cost to produce a history of the world, a history of all nations, a record of every important event since the beginning of time. Magnificently illustrated with portraits and halftone engravings. Size of volumes, 1⅞x7⅛x10⅛ inches.

No. 3C54764 Half Russia library edition, two volumes. Price, for two volumes.$2.80
Weight, packed for shipment, 7 pounds.

No. 3C54765 Complete in two volumes. Cloth. Price, for two volumes.....$2.10
Weight, packed for shipment, 7 pounds.

No. 3C54766 Complete in one volume. Cloth. Price.....$1.69
Weight, packed for shipment, 5 pounds.

HUMOROUS.

Consisting of the works of Bill Nye, M. Quad, Mark Twain, Riley, Burdette, Eli Perkins and many others.

Bill Nye's Remarks.

By Edgar W. Nye. This is the author's greatest and best book. "It is one that will live for weeks after other books have passed away." Contains a selection of the best works of this gifted humorist. 594 pages. Cloth. Size, 6⅞x9 inches. Retail price, $1.50.

No. 3C56162 Our price.....35c
If by mail, postage extra, 18 cents.

Hot Stuff.

A Collection of Witty Writings by Mark Twain, Robert J. Burdette, Eli Perkins, Josh Billings, Alexander Sweet, Bill Nye, Henry Ward Beecher, Geo. W. Peck, Bret Harte, T. De Witt Talmage and nearly fifty others. Humor, wit, pathos, satire and ridicule, repartee, bulls and blunders, clerical wit and humor, lawyers' wit and humor, anecdotes of great men, puns and conundrums, doctors' wit and humor, riddles, puzzles, etc. Contains over 800 pages. Illustrated. Cloth, Size, 6⅛x9 inches.

No. 3C56480 Price.....63c
If by mail, postage extra, 21 cents.

Irish Wit and Humor.

For playfulness, for sarcastic keenness, for gracefulness and for red hot scornfulness, nothing is more effective than some of the examples of wit and humor of the Irishman, as told in this timely volume. 160 pages. Size, 4⅞x6⅞.

No. 3C56535 Paper cover. Price.....14c
No. 3C56536 Cloth. Price.....27c
If by mail, postage extra, paper edition 3 cents; cloth, 5 cents

Jack Henderson. "Down East."

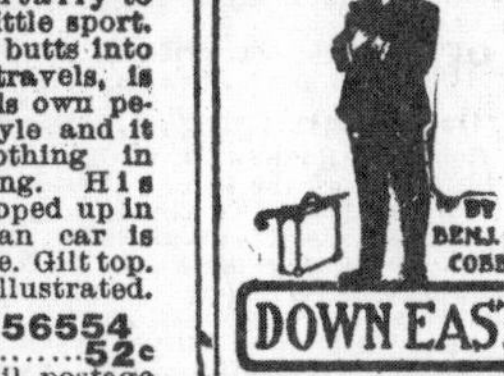

By Benj. F. Cobb. A story told in a series of letters of a Chicago rounder, who takes a trip down East to burn some money, and incidentally to have a little sport. What he butts into in his travels, is told in his own peculiar style and it loses nothing in the telling. His being cooped up in a Pullman car is laughable. Gilt top. Cloth. Illustrated.

No. 3C56554 Price..........52c
If by mail, postage extra, 6 cents.

Samantha at Saratoga.

By Josiah Allen's Wife. The funniest book of all. Written amid the whirl of fashion at Saratoga. Take-off on fashion, flirtations, low neck dresses, dudes, pug dogs, the water craze, toboggans, etc., in the author's inimitable, mirth provoking style. The 100 illustrations by Opper are "just killing." Cloth. Size, 6½x9 inches.

No. 3C57116 Price..................59c
If by mail, postage extra, 15 cents.

Samantha at the St. Louis Exposition.

By Josiah Allen's Wife (Marietta Holley).

The warm welcome given to all of Miss Holley's books the world over will surely be accorded to her latest. All who have read her former "Samantha Books" will find in this the same mixture of wit and pathos, eloquence and practical common sense, besides excellent descriptions of the various buildings and scenes at the St. Louis Exposition. Fully illustrated. Bound in cloth. Size, 5x7 inches. Retail price $1.50.

No. 3C57500 Our price.............95c
If by mail, postage extra, 15 cents.

[illegible]hams, or, Uncle Ben's Ex[illegible]erience With Hypocrites.

By Jno. S. Draper. A delightfully humorous and entertaining book, giving a clear picture of everyday life in rural districts. All who have crossed a farm or halted in front of a country school house, will enjoy its reading. Uncle Ben's trip to the city of Chicago and to California, and his amusing experiences with the shams and sharpers of the metropoli[illegible]trated by True Williams. Cloth. [illegible]hes. Retail price, $1.00.

[illegible]26 Our price...............33c
[illegible]mail, postage extra, 18 cents.

[illegible]bles of Mr. Bowser, The.

[illegible]uthentic account of some of Mr. Bowser's doings at home and abroad. The most excruciatingly funny book of modern times. In Mr. Bowser the author has succeeded in creating a laughable and readable adventure at least one day or evening out of the seven, and would perhaps do a little better if Mrs. were not at hand to sit down on him just at the right moment, or dampen his enthusiasm. Cloth. Fully illustrated. Size, 5¼x7¾ inches.

No. 3C57180 Price..................49c
If by mail, postage extra, 10 cents.

Twenty Years of Hus'ling.

By John P. Johnson. A book bubbling with merriment, overflowing with fun, full of ridiculous incidents, replete with comic situations. A story of twenty years of a man's life, more interesting than fiction, portraying the peculiar and amusing incidents, laughable situations, failures and successes of a man who tried almost every kind of business. Illustrated. Size, 5x8 inches. Retail price, $2.50.

No. 3C57194 Cloth. Our price.....47c
No. 3C57195 Paper. Our price.....21c
If by mail, postage extra, cloth, 16c; paper, 10c.

Wit and Humor.

By Edgar Wilson Nye and James Whitcomb Riley. Amusing prose sketches and quaint dialect poems by these two favorite humorists. A happy combination of wit and humor, melody and pathos. A remarkable book, 544 pages. Illustrated. Cloth. Size, 6½x8¾ inches. Retail price, $1.50.

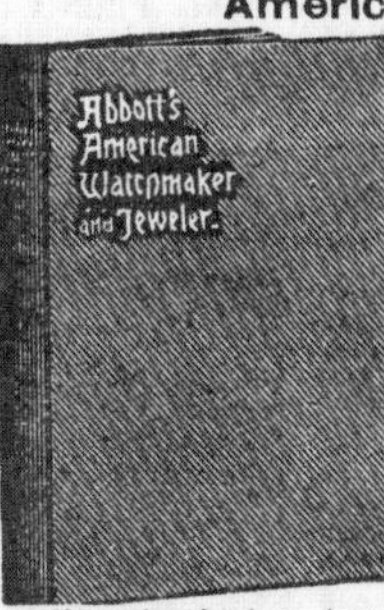

No. 3C57318
Our price....49c
If by mail, postage extra, 19 cents.

HOROLOGY.

Watchmaker and Jeweler, American.

By Henry G. Abbott. Compiled from the best and most reliable sources. Contains complete directions for using all the latest tools, attachments and devices for watchmakers and jewelers; electroplating, bronzing and staining all metals, soldering and directions for making all kinds of hard and soft solder and fluxes; steel, its treatment in annealing, hardening, tempering, etc.; watchcleaning, repairing, etc., a treatise on wheels and pinions, and hundreds of miscellaneous recipes, formulas, and hints on all kinds of work, of great value to every workman. 367 pages. Illustrated with 288 engravings. Cloth. Size, 5¼x7½ inches. Retail price, $1.25.

No. 3C59312 Our price...............98c
If by mail, postage extra, 10 cents.

Watch Repairing.

By N. B. Sherwood. A practical book, written in a practical manner, by a practical man. Informs about the bench and its accessories, the vise and the oilstone, lathe appliances, the jacot lathe, depthing tool, expanding the web of a wheel, the spreading tool and its use, the rounding-up tool, stud remover, opening the regulator, roller remover, replacing broken teeth, graining, polishing blocks, polishing steel work, pivots, hardening, stamping, etc. Illustrated. Size, 5¼x7¾ inches.

No. 3C59330 Price..................28c
If by mail, postage extra, 5 cents.

JUVENILE BOOKS.

WE LIST ONLY THE BEST made, best illustrated, best bound and lowest priced illustrated books for the little folks.

Always include these books—in fact, all books—in your express and freight shipments. If you order them by mail do not forget to include extra money for postage.

Alcott's, Louisa M., Works.

Only 95c Cents per Volume. Probably the most popular books for children ever written. Miss Alcott's books are enduring, true to nature and beautifully written. Cloth. Size of volume, 5½x7½ inches.

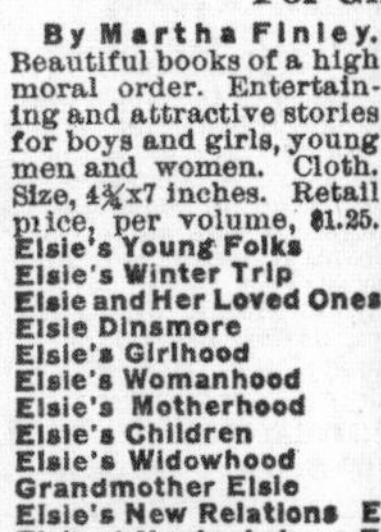

An Old Fashioned Girl
Eight Cousins
Jack and Jill
Jo's Boys
Little Men
Little Women
Rose in Bloom
Under the Lilacs

No. 3C12113 Price, per volume.............95c
If by mail, postage extra, per volume, 12 cents.

Famous Elsie Books.

For Girls.

By Martha Finley. Beautiful books of a high moral order. Entertaining and attractive stories for boys and girls, young men and women. Cloth. Size, 4¾x7 inches. Retail price, per volume, $1.25.

Elsie's Young Folks
Elsie's Winter Trip
Elsie and Her Loved Ones
Elsie Dinsmore
Elsie's Girlhood
Elsie's Womanhood
Elsie's Motherhood
Elsie's Children
Elsie's Widowhood
Grandmother Elsie
Elsie's New Relations
Elsie at Nantucket
Elsie at Home
The Two Elsies
Elsie's Kith and Kin
Elsie and the Raymonds
Elsie's Holiday at Roseland
Elsie's Friend at Woodburn
Christmas with Grandmother Elsie
Elsie Yachting with the Raymonds
Elsie's Journeys on Inland Waters
Elsie's Vacation
Elsie at Viamede
Elsie at Ion
Elsie at the World's Fair
Elsie on the Hudson
Elsie in the South

No. 3C60365 Our price, per volume..69c
If by mail, postage extra, per volume, 12 cents.

Fun for the Little Folks.

Delightfully interesting book. Full of just the kind of jolly reading to gladden the hearts of children and help them entertain themselves. Contains charming stories and amusements, including tales of animals and pets, youthful sports and adventure, and choice reading for the little ones, together with picture alphabet, illustrated numbers, etc. Lithographed cover. Size, 6½x9¾ inches.

No. 3C60392 Price..................18c
If by mail, postage extra, 9 cents.

Gem Library.

For Children. Six beautiful little books, bound in cloth, containing charming stories in prose and verse by well known writers. Profusely illustrated with colored and black and white pictures by Frances Brundage and other well known juvenile artists. Complete set of 6 books, comprising

Effie's Little Mother
Tic-tac-too
Betsey Brian's Needle
Seven Plaits of Nettles
Rainbow Queen
Mildred and Her Mills

In fancy case. Sold only in sets. Cloth. Size, 4¼x6 inches.

No. 3C60415 Price, per set.........95c
If by mail, postage extra, 16 cents.

Illustrated Natural History.

By Rev. J. G. Woods, M. A., F. L. S. This is the greatest book on natural history ever written for the young. It contains pictures of almost every known animal both on land and sea. Written in simple, easily understood language. Beautifully lithographed cover, cloth back. Size, 7¾x10 inches. Retail price, 75 cents.

No. 3C60575
Our price.....22c
If by mail, postage extra, 15 cents.

Mother Goose Complete Melodies.

Containing nursery rhymes and a collection of alphabet tales and jingles, with illustrations; 288 pages. Printed in two colors. The only complete edition of this famous book published. Lithographed cover, cloth back. Size, 7x9 inches.

No. 3C60736 Price..................34c
If by mail, postage extra, 20 cents.

Mother Goose Nursery Tales and Jingles.

New complete edition. A splendid collection of melodies, alphabets, tales, jingles, and rhymes by the dear old lady, so beloved by children. This edition contains many illustrations, some colored, others outlined drawings. Cloth. Size, 5½x8 inches. Retail price, $1.00.

No. 3C60738
Our price, 45c
If by mail, postage extra, 16 cts.

New Child's Life of Christ.

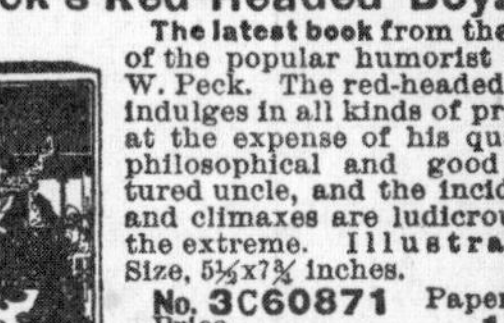

By Hesba Stretton. New edition of this beautiful story profusely illustrated showing the pathways trodden, the scenes visited, the burdens borne, the help rendered, the blessings bestowed, and the lessons taught by Jesus, the Christ, when on His earthly Pilgrimage from the Manger to the Throne. Cloth. Size, 9⅜x7½ ins. Retail price, $1.00.

No. 3C60768
Our price, 38c
If by mail, postage extra, 18 cents.

PECK'S, GEO. W., WORKS.

Peck's Bad Boy and His Pa.

Together with Peck's Compendium of Fun. In this new edition the most celebrated writings of the famous Peck can be found. Every page is filled with wit and humor, and every line is certain to produce a hearty laugh. Profusely illustrated in appropriate and original designs, showing the funny positions occupied by the bad boy. This book is respectfully dedicated to the boys, to the men who have been boys, and the girls who like boys. Cloth. Size, 6⅜x8½ inches.

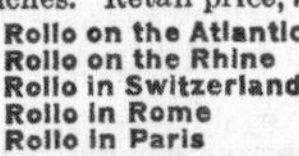

No. 3C60865 Price...............34c
If by mail, postage extra, 21 cents.

Peck's Uncle Ike.

The name of Geo. W. Peck has been immortalized by its being the name of the author of Peck's Bad Boy and His Pa. Uncle Ike is made to share all the troubles of his brother, and from none of them does he escape with less embarassment. Illustrated. Size, 5¼x7¾ inches.

No. 3C60867 Paper. Price.............15c
No. 3C60868 Cloth. Price.............28c
If by mail, postage extra, paper, 4c; cloth, 15c.

Peck's Sunbeams.

Some of the best and most laughable of Geo. W. Peck's humorous writings. Everyday facts, fancies and fads are taken up, and in the well known light vein of humor of the author are made to appear in an altogether different light. Illustrated. Size, 5½x7¾ inches.

No. 3C60869 Paper. Price.............15c
No. 3C60870 Cloth. Price.............28c
If by mail, postage extra, paper, 4c; cloth, 12c.

Peck's Red-Headed Boy.

The latest book from the pen of the popular humorist Geo. W. Peck. The red-headed boy indulges in all kinds of pranks at the expense of his quaint, philosophical and good natured uncle, and the incidents and climaxes are ludicrous in the extreme. Illustrated. Size, 5½x7¾ inches.

No. 3C60871 Paper. Price.............15c
No. 3C60872 Cloth. Price.............28c
If by mail, postage extra, paper, 4c; cloth, 12c.

Five Little Peppers and How They Grew.

By Margaret Sidney. This is a new edition of the most popular book by the celebrated author of the Pepper books. Excellent print on a good quality of paper. Illustrated. Board covers. Size, 5½x7½ inches.

No. 3C60881 Price..................18c
If by mail, postage extra, 12 cents.

Rollo Books of Travel.

By Jacob Abbott. The Rollo books are probably the best known books of travel for young people, and are found in nearly every Sunday school library, an evidence of their popularity. These books are uniformly bound in binders silk cloth, gilt top. Printed from clear type, on a good quality of book paper. Size, 5x7 inches. Retail price, 75 cents.

Rollo on the Atlantic
Rollo on the Rhine
Rollo in Switzerland
Rollo in Rome
Rollo in Paris
Rollo in Naples
Rollo in Scotland
Rollo in Holland
Rollo in London
Rollo in Geneva

No. 3C99912 Price, per volume...19c
If by mail, postage extra, 11 cents.

Uncle Tom's Cabin, or Life Among the Lowly.

By Harriett Beecher Stowe. For years this book has held a leading place in the literary world. It is just as popular now as it was a generation ago. Beautifully illustrated with colored photographs, reproduced from life. Cloth. Size 5¼x8 inches. Retail price, $1.00.

No. 3C61229
Our price....45c
If by mail, postage extra, 16 cents.

What Tommy Did Series.

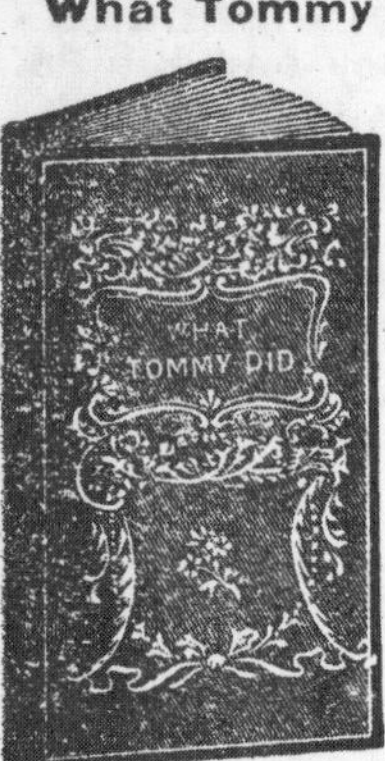

A Series of books for boys. Each complete in one volume. Each written by an author of recognized ability. Bound in cloth. Size, 5⅛x7¾ inches. Retail price, 50 cents.

Black Beauty
Captain George; or the Drummer Boy
Dog of Flanders
J. Cole
Laddie
Miss Toosey's Mission
The Golden Gate
What Tommy Did
Wonder Book for Boys and Girls

No. 3C61318 Our price, per volume..........**28c**
If by mail, postage extra, each, 5 cents.

Young People's Natural History.

By Isaac Thorne Johnson, A. M., forming a popular history of animals, birds, reptiles, fishes and insects, and describing in easy, simple language how wild creatures great and small look, live and act, comprising also many thrilling stories of adventure with them, and amusing anecdotes about them. Illustrated with 200 photos, engravings true to life, showing animals, birds and reptiles. 450 pages. Cloth, lithographed cover. Size, 7¾x9¾ inches. Retail price, $1.00.

No. 3C61443 Our price..............**54c**
If by mail, postage extra, 24 cents.

Linen Toy Books.

Cosy Corner Series. Printed on genuine linen, untearable. A very interesting collection of rhymes about A B C, in which the domestic animals are introduced for the instruction of very young folks. Each book illustrated and printed on linen cloth. Size, 5⅜x7⅞ inches. Embracing a series of six books, different kinds:

Friends in the Meadow
Little Chicks **On Guard** **Pet Lambs**
Neddy Bray **The Pet Goat**

No. 3C60665 Linen cover, handsomely printed in colors. Price, each..........**6c**
Per dozen..........**68c**
If by mail, postage extra, each, 1 cent; per dozen, 9 cents.

SEND FOR OUR
FREE BOOK CATALOGUE
It contains complete lists of Juvenile and Toy Books.

LAW.

Civil and Business Law.

By Prof. Geo. W. Conklin. Most legal difficulties arise from ignorance of the minor points of law. This book furnishes a busy man or woman information on just such points as are likely to arise in every day affairs and forestall them against mental worry and financial loss. How to keep out of trouble, and how to get out if you happen to get in, etc. Don't consult a lawyer. Buy this book.

No. 3C91706 Cloth, colored edges. Retail price, 25 cents. Our price..........**14c**
No. 3C91708 Full leather, gilt edges. Retail price, 50 cents. Our price..........**28c**
If by mail, postage extra, either style, 3 cents.

Law, and How to Keep Out of It.

By Paschal H. Coggins, Esq. Most legal difficulties arise from ignorance of the minor points of law. This book furnishes to the busy man and woman information on just such points as are most likely to arise in every day affairs, and thus forstall them against mental worry and financial loss. Cloth. Size, 4½x6 inches. Retail price, 50 cents.

No. 3C62658 Our price..........**30c**
If by mail, postage extra, 5 cents.

Law at a Glance.

A complete work, embracing every known subject, among which are the following: Affidavits, agents, agreements, arbitration, assignments, power of attorney, bankruptcy, bills of lading, exchange and sale, chattel mortgages, co-partnership, corporations, damages, debts, deeds, frauds, forms of guarantee, injunction, injury, insolvency, insurance, judgment, sales; husband and wife—their relations, divorce, losses, etc. Cloth. Size, 5⅛x7⅛ inches.

No. 3C94606 Price..........**58c**
If by mail, postage extra, 12 cents.

LIQUORS.

Including Books on the Art of Compounding Liquors, Wines, Mixing Cocktails, Fancy Drinks, Etc.

Drinks, as They are Mixed.

By a leading buffet manager. A new, up to date guide to the art of mixing fancy beverages, in vest pocket (time saving) size. This is the only complete and practical book on the subject published. It is especially adapted to the home, buffet or club. The recipes are simple, making it possible for the butler or the lady of the house to properly prepare them. Paper cover. Size, 2¾x5½ inches.

No. 3C64275 Cloth. Price..........**18c**
No. 3C64276 Leather. Price..........**30c**
If by mail, postage extra, either style, 3 cents.

Independent Liquorist.

By L. Monzert. The art of manufacturing all kinds of syrups, bitters, cordials, champagnes, wines, lager beer, ale, porter, beer, punches, tinctures, extracts, brandies, gin, essences, flavorings, colorings, sauces, catsups, pickles, preserves, etc. Cloth. Size, 5⅛x7⅛ inches. Retail price, $3.00.

No. 3C64527 Our price..........**$1.98**
If by mail, postage extra, 12 cents.

LOVE AND COURTSHIP.

Comprising Lovers' Guides, Letter Writing, Art of Making Love, How to Write Love Letters, Etc.

Because I Love You.

The Book of Love, Courtship and Marriage. It fully explains how maidens become happy wives, and bachelors become happy husbands in a brief space of time and by easy methods. Also complete directions for declaring intentions, accepting vows and retaining affections. Tells plainly how to begin courting, the way to get over bashfulness, and is just the treatise to be in the hands of every young bachelor or maiden. 200 pages. Size, 4¼x6¾ inches.

No. 3C66163 Paper cover. Price..........**14c**
No. 3C66164 Cloth. Price..........**27c**
If by mail, postage extra, paper edition, 3 cents; cloth edition, 5 cents.

Lovers' Guide and Manual.

Contains full directions for conducting a courtship with ladies of every age and position in society. Explains all about love, young men and marriage, young women and matrimony, courtship, bachelors, influence of matrimony, marriage, etiquette of courtship, essence of good breeding, proposals, love thoughts of famous writers, love letters. Contains also poems of love, funny love stories, language of flowers, code of flirtations, fortune telling, and character reading, including rules for good society, handkerchief, parasol, fan, hat, postage stamp, cigar, glove, eye, whip, pencil flirtation, and lovemaking. Paper cover. Size, 4½x6¾ ins.

No. 3C66676 Price..........**15c**
If by mail, postage extra, 2 cents.

Modern Art of Making Love, The.

A complete manual of etiquette, love, courtship and matrimony. Something every boy and girl, man and woman ought to know. Tells how to begin a courtship, when and whom to marry, the advisability of long and short courtships, points to be observed in the selection of a husband or wife, the secret of pleasing a sweetheart, how to address and win the favor of ladies, etc. Also contains a complete system of love telegraphy, handkerchief flirtation, the language of flowers, precious stones and their signification, etc. Size, 4½x6¾ inches.

No. 3C66140 Paper cover. Price..........**18c**
No. 3C66141 Cloth. Price..........**30c**
If by mail, postage extra, paper, 3c; cloth, 6c.

North's Book of Love Letters.

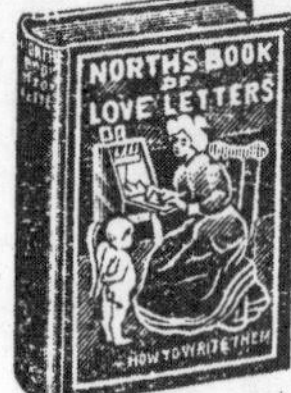

With directions how to write and when to use them. This is a branch of correspondence which fully demands a volume alone to provide for the various phases incident to love, courtship and marriage. Few persons, however otherwise fluent with the pen, are able to express in words the promptings of the first dawn of love. It tells how to follow up a correspondence with the dearest one in the whole world, and how to smooth the way with those who need to be consulted in the matter. It also contains the art of secret writing, the language of love portrayed, and rules in grammar, etc. 160 pages. Size, 4¼x6¾ inches.

No. 3C66778 Paper cover. Price..**14c**
No. 3C66779 Cloth. Price..........**27c**
If by mail, postage extra, paper, 3c; cloth, 6c.

MECHANICS.

TO MACHINISTS, ENGINEERS, FIREMEN AND MECHANICS, our Book Catalogue will be invaluable, as it describes only the best books, embracing every branch of mechanics, including gun making, die cutting, glass working, mechanical drawing, etc. Best works on mineralogy, metallurgy, mines and mining.

Modern Air Brake Practice. Its Use and Abuse.

By Frank H. Dukesmith. The new airbrake book. Invaluable to trainmen, engineers, firemen, conductors, electric motormen and mechanics. The latest and best 1904 edition. With questions and answers for locomotive engineers and electric motormen. While there have been many air brake books written, we feel safe in saying that never before has the subject been treated in the same lucid, understandable manner. The book is fully indexed and cross-indexed, so that any subject can be turned to immediately, as desired. Cloth. 303 pages; hundreds of illustrations. Size, 5x7 inches. Retail price, $1.50.

No. 3C68118 Our price..........**98c**
If by mail, postage extra, 12 cents.

Catechism, Locomotive.

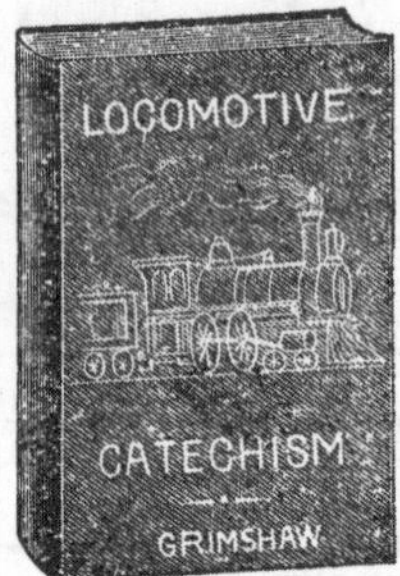

By Robert Grimshaw. A new revised edition. How to run a locomotive. Contains 1,600 questions and gives 1,600 simple, plain and practical answers about the locomotive. Also official form of examination of firemen for promotion and of engineers for employment. 450 pages. 200 illustrations. 12 large folding plates. Cloth. Size, 5¼x7½ inches. Retail price, $2.00.

No. 3C68218 Our price...**$1.29**
If by mail, postage extra, 12 cents.

Catechism, Steam Engine.

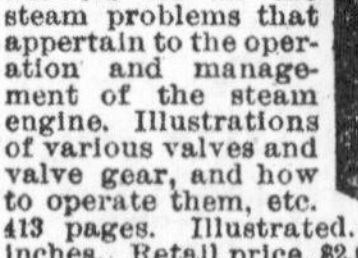

By Robert Grimshaw, M. E. A series of direct practical answers to direct practical questions, not only intended for young engineers and for examination questions, but a handy volume for everyone interested in steam. Also contains formulas and worked out answers for all the steam problems that appertain to the operation and management of the steam engine. Illustrations of various valves and valve gear, and how to operate them, etc. 413 pages. Illustrated. Cloth. Size, 4¼x5¾ inches. Retail price, $2.00.

No. 3C68220 Our price..........**$1.29**
If by mail, postage extra, 8 cents.

Combustion of Coal.

By William M. Barr. New edition. Prepared with special reference to the generation of heat by the combustion of the common fuels found in the United States, and particularly with the conditions necessary to the economic, and smokeless combustion of bituminous coal in stationary and locomotive steam boilers. How to make steam. Contains 800 practical questions and answers on the science of steam making. 85 illustrations. 349 pages. Cloth. Size, 5x7 inches. Retail price, $1.50.

No. 3C68237 Our price..........**$1.10**
If by mail, postage extra, 12 cents.

Dies, Their Construction and Use for the Modern Working of Sheet Metals.

By Joseph V. Woodworth. A treatise upon the designing, constructing and use of tools, fixtures and devices, together with the manner in which they should be used in the power press. A book written by a practical man for practical men and one that diemakers, machinists, toolmakers or metal working mechanics cannot afford to be without. Illustrated. Cloth. Size, 7x8¾ inches. Retail price, $3.00.

No. 3C68265 Our price..........**$1.98**
If by mail, postage extra, 25 cents.

Engines, Gas, Gasoline and Oil.

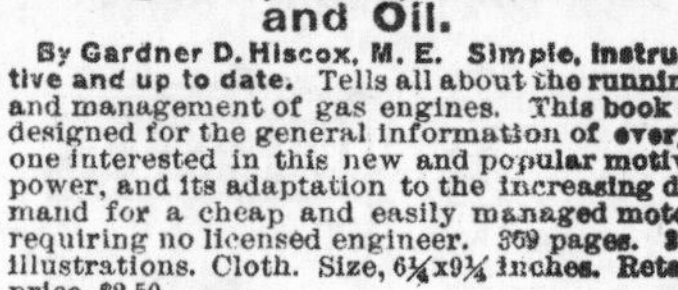

By Gardner D. Hiscox, M. E. Simple, instructive and up to date. Tells all about the running and management of gas engines. This book is designed for the general information of everyone interested in this new and popular motive power, and its adaptation to the increasing demand for a cheap and easily managed motor requiring no licensed engineer. 369 pages. 312 illustrations. Cloth. Size, 6¼x9¼ inches. Retail price, $2.50.

No. 3C68325 Our price..........**$1.69**
If by mail, postage extra, 21 cents.

Engine Runners' Catechism.

By Robert Grimshaw, M. E. Latest edition. Tells how to erect the principal steam engines in the United States. To young engineers this catechism will be of great value, especially those who may be preparing to go forward to be examined for certificates of competency, and to engineers generally it will be of no little service, as they will find in this volume more really practical and useful information than is to be found anywhere else within a like compass. 336 pages. Illustrated. Cloth. Size, 4½x5¾ inches. Retail price $2.00.

No. 3C68330 Our price..........**$1.29**
If by mail, postage extra, 8 cents.

Farm Engines and How to Run Them.

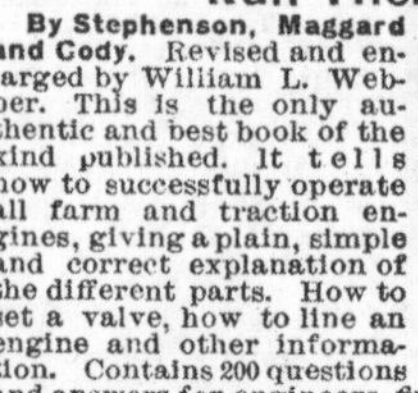

By Stephenson, Maggard and Cody. Revised and enlarged by William L. Webber. This is the only authentic and best book of the kind published. It tells how to successfully operate all farm and traction engines, giving a plain, simple and correct explanation of the different parts. How to set a valve, how to line an engine and other information. Contains 200 questions and answers for engineers, firemen, etc. Cloth. Illustrated. Size, 5¼x8 inches.

No. 3C68362 Price..........**58c**
If by mail, postage extra, 10 cents.

Practical Gas Engineer.

By E. W. Longanecker. A Manual of Practical Gas and Gasoline Engine Knowledge. Being a complete, plainly written treatise, telling what a gas and gasoline engine is; how to purchase it; how to operate it; how to care for it and what to do with it when it gets stubborn, in short how to handle it successfully. Containing 144 pages. Cloth. Size, 4¼x6¾ inches.

No. 3C68410 Price..........**60c**
If by mail, postage extra, 6 cents.

Locomotive Engineers, Ready Help for.

By Norman Gardenier. Contains matters of the utmost value for locomotive firemen seeking promotion; for the scholar and student, for the help of the examiner. It compri[illegible] remedy for every conceivable breakdow[illegible] may occur to the locomotive. Cloth. Si[illegible] inches. Retail price, $1.00.

No. 3C68670 Our price..........
If by mail, postage extra, 6 cents.

Locomotive Up to Date,

By Chas. McShane. An absolute authority on all subjects relating to the locomotive. The greatest accumulation of new and practical matter ever published, treating upon the construction and management of modern locomotives, both simple and compound. More than 100 prominent railway officials and inventors of special railway appliances have furnished practical information about air brakes, break downs, blows and combustions, link and valve motions, setting, steam indicator, injectors and lubricators; examination questions and answers for locomotive firemen and hundreds of other subjects of interest. Contains 736 pages. Cloth. 3[illegible] illustrations. Size, 6¼x9 inches.

No. 3C68672 Price..........**$1.89**
If by mail, postage extra, 22 cents.

Motorman's Guide, The.

By G. H. Gayetty. A new, up to date edition. A practical treatise on street railway motors, containing everything a motorman should know about the care and running of electric cars. Cloth. Illustrated. Size, 4¾x6¾ inches.

No. 3C68772 Price..........**33c**
If by mail, postage extra, 8 cents.

Railroad Men, Standard Handbook For.

By A. Kilburn. A complete, practical and instructive treatise on the modern railroad locomotive and all its attachments. Contains questions and answers on all points referring to engineering, automatic air brakes, link motion, injector breaks, break downs, signaling, etc. Illustrated with full set of double trip daily time sheets and other illustrations. Cloth. Size, 6¾x4 inches. Retail price, $1.00.

No. 3C68908 Our price..........**59c**
If by mail, postage extra, 8 cents.

Rubber Hand Stamps, and the Manipulation of India Rubber.

By T. O'Connor Sloane. A practical treatise on the manufacture of all kinds of rubber hand stamps, small articles of india rubber, United States Government composition dating hand stamps, the manipulation of sheet rubber, toy balloons, india rubber solutions, cements, blackings, renovating varnish, and treatment for india rubber shoes, etc.; the hectograph, stamp inks, and miscellaneous notes; with a short account of the discovery, etc. Illustrated. Cloth. Size 5½x7½ inches. Retail price $1.00.

No. 3C68987 Our price..............**68c**
If by mail, postage extra, 8 cents.

Saws, Saw Filing and Management.

By Robert Grimshaw, M. E. A practical book on filing, gumming, swaging, hammering, and the brazing of band saws, the speed, work and power to run circular saws, etc. A handy book for those who have charge of saws or for those mechanics who do their own filing, as it deals with the proper shape and pitches of saw teeth of all kinds and gives many useful hints and rules for gumming, setting and filing, and is a practical aid to those who use saws for any purpose. Illustrated. Cloth. Size, 4¼x6¼ inches. Retail price $1.00.

No. 3C69110 Our price..............**68c**
If by mail, postage extra, 10 cents.

Shop Kinks.

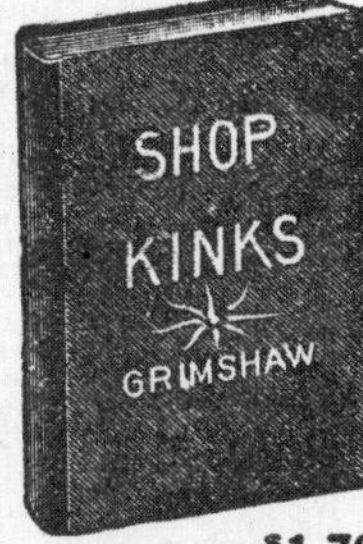

By Robert Grimshaw. A book for machinists. It is indispensable to every machinist or practical man. It is different from any other book published on the subject, showing a special way of doing work better, quicker and cheaper. Full of pointers as to how work is done in the best American and European shops. Full of helpful suggestions. Illustrated. Cloth. Size, 5¼x8 in. Retail price, $2.50.

No. 3C69116
Our price..............................**$1.70**
If by mail, postage extra, 13 cents.

Soldering, The Art of Hard.

By Henry G. Abbott. Contains information pertaining to lamps and blowpipes, character and use of the flame, soldering appliances, the uses and nature of fluxes, soldering and alloys, etc. Cloth. Size, 4¾x6¼ inches.

No. 3C69125 Our price..............**40c**
If by mail, postage extra, 5 cents.

Switchwork, Practical.

By D. H. Levelt. New revised edition. An instructor and guide for roadmasters, section foremen and construction foremen. Contains new, exact and concise methods for laying out railroad curves, switches, forge angles and crossings. A large number of tables, giving all necessary figures for the quick and correct construction of any switch. Curves have been treated in a plain and thorough manner. This book covers everything in switch or yard work. Cloth. Size, 4x6½ inches. Retail price, $1.00.

No. 3C69164 Our price..............**65c**
If by mail, postage extra, 4 cents.

Twentieth Century Hand Book for Steam Engineers and Electricians.

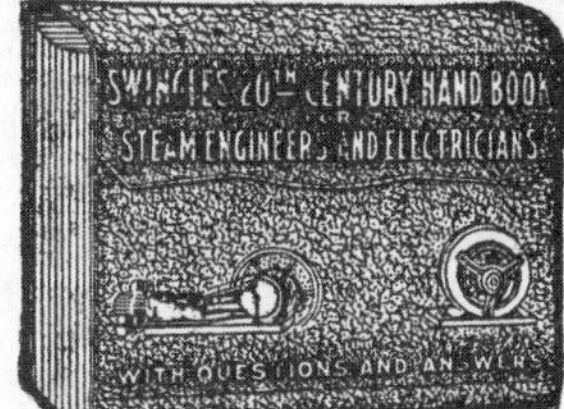

By C. E. Swingle, M. E. A compendium of useful knowledge appertaining to the care and management of steam engines, boilers and dynamos. Thoroughly practical, with full instructions in regard to making evaporation tests on boilers. The adjustment of the slide valve, corliss valves, etc., fully described and illustrated together with the application of the indicator and diagram analysis. The electrical division is written by engineers for engineers and is a clear and comprehensive treatise on the principles, construction and operations of dynamos, motors, lamps, etc. We guarantee this work to be the latest and best work on engineering and electricity for steam engineers published, containing 512 pages, 275 illustrations. Handsomely bound in full leather, gold edge, pocketbook style. Size, 5x6¾x1 inches thick.

No. 3C69192 Price..............**$1.68**
If by mail, postage extra, 12 cents.

Tools Modern Machine Shop.

By W. H. Vandervoort, M. E. The work is logically arranged; the various hand and machine tools being grouped into classes, and description of each is given in proportion to their relative importance. The illustrations represent the very latest tools and methods, all of which are clearly described. This book is strictly up to date in all respects, and is the most complete, concise, and useful work ever published on the subject. Illustrated. Cloth. Size, 7x8½ inches. Retail price $4.00.

No. 3C69181 Our price..............**$2.48**
If by mail, postage extra, 14 cents.

Trackman's Helper, The.

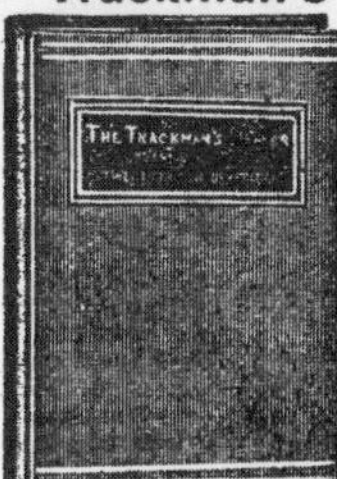

By J. Kindelan. New revised edition. A practical guide for American trackmen. It should be in the hands of every section foreman, track foreman, roadmaster and laborer in the line for promotion; it is just the kind of a book they require. It contains a great deal of valuable information which it would be impossible for the men to get in any other way. Profusely illustrated. Cloth. Size, 5¼x7½ inches. Retail price, $1.50.

No. 3C69187 Our price..............**98c**
If by mail, postage extra, 10 cents.

Universal Assistant and Complete Mechanic.

Contains industrial facts, calculations, recipes, processes and trade secrets for every known business. Also 200,000 items for gas, steam, civil and mining engineers, machinists, iron founders, plumbers, miners, assayers, woodworkers, manufacturers, etc.; information for engineers, firemen, boilermakers, engine and car builders, watchmakers, jewelers, gilders, platers, silversmiths, opticians, diamond cutters, enamelers, cabinetmakers, piano, organ and picture manufacturers, etc. Cloth. Illustrated. Size, 5¼x7½ inches.

No. 3C69240 Price..............**65c**
If by mail, postage extra, 21 cents.

MEDICAL.

Embracing Medical Guides, Home Family Physicians, Advice to Young Girls, Marriage Guides, Motherhood, Advice to Young Men, etc.

American Family Physician, New.

A popular guide for the household management of diseases, giving the history, cause, means of prevention, and symptoms of all diseases and the most approved methods of treating, with plain instructions for the care of the sick, full and accurate directions for treating wounds, injuries, poisoning, etc. Illustrated with lithographic manikins of the body and of the head, etc. Cloth. Size, 7x9½ inches. Retail price, $3.00. Weight, packed for shipment, 5 pounds.

No. 3C70124 Our price..............**$1.29**
If by mail, postage extra, 47 cents.

Creative Life.

By Alice B. Stockham. A special message to young girls. Gives high ideals, the knowledge of which leads to a purity of thought and life. It will be a blessing to many in guiding aright the first conscious recognition of the sexual instinct. The author wisely teaches that this impulse should be trained, and directed as a sacred trust, to conserve personal health and morals, and for effective service in the world. Paper covers. Size, 4¾x7¼ inches. Retail price, 50 cents.

No. 3C70230 Our price..............**18c**
If by mail, postage extra, 3 cents.

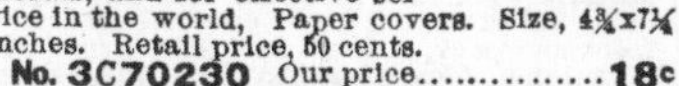

Dr. Foote's Plain Home Talk.

This work embraces plain, clearly written treatises on all diseases, and indicates the proper treatment in each case. Contains 1,000 pages, 200 illustrations, 10 colored charts, 36 chromos, showing signs of life, etc. A complete list of medicines. Cloth. Size, 5½x7½ inches.

No. 3C70280
Price..............**58c**
If by mail, postage extra, 17 cents.

Science of Life.

By Prof. Fowler. This work treats of "Sexual Science," which is simply that great code of natural laws by which the Almighty requires the sexes to be governed in their mutual relations. A knowledge of these laws is of the highest importance. It is pure, elevating in tone, eloquent in its denunciation of vice. Cloth. Size, 6½x9¼ inches. Retail price $2.50.

No. 3C70381 Our price..............**98c**
If by mail, postage extra, 24 cents.

Karezza.

By Alice B. Stockham. Ethics of Marriage. Written expressly for married men and women. It gives a high ideal to parental functions, and pleads for justice to the unborn child. Karezza controverts the prevailing idea of baseness and degradation associated with the sexual nature. It is presented to the world with a deep abiding faith that its teachings will lead individuals to purer lives, to right understanding and appreciation of the sex functions. etc. Cloth. Size, 5x7¼ inches. Retail price, $1.00.

No. 3C70612 Our price..............**59c**
If by mail, postage extra, 9 cents.

The Ladies' New Medical Guide

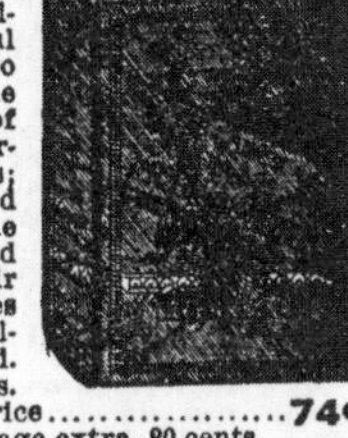

By Dr. S. Pancoast. An instructor, counselor and friend in all delicate and wonderful matters peculiar to women, explaining the nature and mystery of the reproductive organs in both sexes; pregnancy, labor and childbirth, with the causes, treatment and symptoms of all their own special diseases and diseases of children. Illustrated. Cloth. Size, 5¾x8 inches.

No. 3C70658 Price..............**74c**
If by mail, postage extra, 20 cents.

STORY OF A LIVING TEMPLE, THE

By Frederick M. Rossiter and Mary Henry Rossiter.

The first time in the history of medicine that a book embracing the subjects contained in "The Story of a Living Temple," a book that anyone can understand without first making a study of medicine, has been published. **HERE IS A BOOK** that will save you hundreds of dollars in doctors' bills. A book that tells in the most simple and beautiful language how the body is constructed, how to take care of it and keep it strong and well. A book that cannot fail to lead young people and children to take a greater interest in health and hygiene. A book that tells how to avoid the evils of dyspepsia, nervousness, sleeplessness, premature old age and ill health in general. Cloth. Stamped in gold. Size, 5x7½ inches. Retail price, $1.00.

No. 3C71140 Our price, any quantity..............**45c**
If by mail, postage extra, 12 cents.

"The Young Mothers' Tokology" and Preparation for Motherhood.

By Anna C. Hoffman, M. D. If every mother and child were cared for according to the principles taught in this book, the illness following childbirth and the enormous fatality among infants and young children would be averted. Size, 5¼x8¼ inches.

No. 3C71165 Cloth.
Price..............**72c**
If by mail, postage extra, 9 cents.

Text Book of Nursing.

By Clara S. Weeks. A book for the use of nurses, training schools, families and private students. This is undoubtedly the best book on the subject published, thoroughly practical and up to date, with illustrations, vocabulary and index. Cloth. Size, 5¼x7¾ inches. Retail price, $1.75.

No. 3C71168 Our price..............**$1.25**
If by mail, postage extra, 14 cents.

True Manhood.

By E. R. Shepherd. The Secret of Power. A manual of science and guide to health, strength, and purity. Reveals physiological facts and uncovers truth with a chaste and gentle hand. This work is devoted to the presentation of facts, which are eagerly sought by all boys verging upon manhood. Cloth. Size, 5½x7¾ inches.

No. 3C71175
Price..............**59c**
If by mail, postage extra, 11 cents.

True Marriage Guide, or, Talks on Nature.

A book for adults, married or single, and parents. This book takes the ground that children have a right to be well born. It is a standard treatise on sexual physiology and is just such a book as is needed for self instruction. Written in language that can readily be understood. The following are a few of the many subjects treated: Marriage, maternity, procreation, limitation of offspring, painless midwifery, vital subjects, general debility, unwise habits, syphilis, varicocele, etc. Fully illustrated. Size, 5½x7¼ inches.

No. 3C71178 Paper. Price..............**20c**
No. 3C71179 Cloth. Price..............**39c**
If by mail, postage extra, paper, 5c; cloth, 12c.

What all Married and Those Contemplating Marriage Ought to Know.

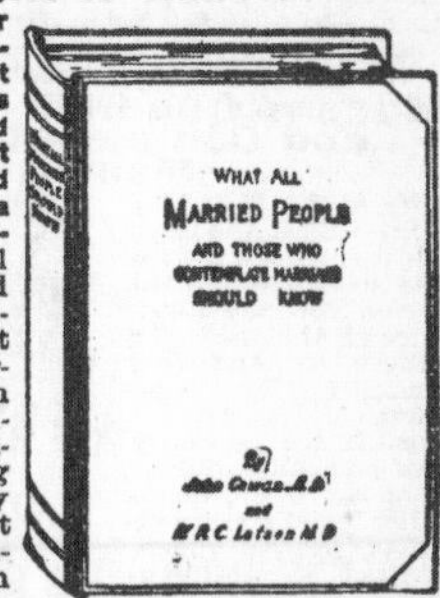

No man or woman who anticipates a bright future and wishes to enjoy married life in its fullest sense can afford to be without a copy of this valuable book. To all who are married or are contemplating marriage, it will give information worth hundreds of dollars, besides conferring a lasting benefit not only upon them but upon their children. It tells in a matter of fact, easily understood way, the thousand and one questions that occur to the minds of both young and old, but about which they feel a delicacy in consulting their physician. It divulges all secrets known to medical science, embracing confidential talks applied to cause, prevention and cure of chronic diseases, etc. Durably bound in cloth. Size, 6¾x7½ inches.

No. 3C71315 Price..............**95c**
If by mail, postage extra, 10 cents.

Mineralogy, Mines and Mining.

Mining, A B C of.

By Charles A. Bramble. A handbook for prospectors, treating fully of exploratory and preparatory work, of the physical properties of ores, field geology, the occurrence and association of minerals, methods of chemical analysis and assay, blow pipe tests promising indications and simple methods of working valuable deposits, etc., and information on placer mining, with chapters on camp life and medical hints. 182 pages. Cloth; cut flush. Size, 4¼x6¾ inches. Retail price, $1.00.

No. 3C72718 Our price..............**60c**
If by mail, postage extra, 6 cents.

Minerals and How to Study Them.

By Prof. Edward S. Dana. A book for beginners in mineralogy. 380 pages, 319 illustrations. Cloth. Retail price, $1.50.

No. 3C72770 Our price..............**$1.25**
If by mail, postage extra, 20 cents.

Moulder's and Founder's Pocket Guide, The.

By Fred Overman, M. E. A treatise on moulding and founding in green sand, dry sand, loam and cement; the moulding of machine frames, mill gear, hollow ware, ornaments, trinkets, bells and statues; description of moulds for iron, bronze, brass and other metals; plaster paris, sulphur, wax, etc., construction of melting furnaces, the melting and founding of metals, the composition of alloys, and their nature, etc. Contains articles on statuary and ornamental mouldings, ordnance, malleable iron castings, etc. 44 engravings. 342 pages. Cloth. Size, 5¼x7¼ inches. Retail price, $2.00.

No. 3C72738 Our price..............**$1.75**
If by mail, postage extra, 11 cents.

Prospectors' Field Book and Guide, The.

By Prof. H. S. Osborn, LL.D. Revised edition. A complete and thoroughly reliable guide and companion to the intelligent and enterprising searcher after ores and other useful minerals, including gems and gem stones. The following subjects are fully treated: The blowpipe and its uses, crystallography, surveying, analysis of ores, special mineralogy —gold, tellurium, platinum, silver, copper, lead and tin, zinc, iron, mercury, bismuth, nickel, cobalt and cadmium, aluminum, antimony, manganese, various other useful minerals; petroleum, ozocerite, asphalt, peat, gems and precious stones. 339 pages. Illustrated. Cloth. Size, 5¼x7¼ inches. Retail price, $1.50.

No. 3C72877 Our price..............**$1.20**
If by mail, postage extra, 10 cents.

Hood's Plain Home Talk Health Book and Common Sense Medical Adviser.

Relating to All the Delicate and Wonderful Matters Pertaining to the Nature and Relation of the Sexes.

It explains everything. No man or woman who anticipates a bright future and wishes to enjoy married life in its fullest sense can afford to be without a copy of this valuable book. Here are answered in plain language a thousand questions that occur in the minds of both young and old, but about which they feel a delicacy in consulting their physician. It tells in a matter of fact, easily understood way, the thousand and one questions that occur to the mind of both young and old, divulges all secrets known to medical science. It treats of the natural relations of men and women to each other; society, courtship, love and marriage, parentage, children, nursing and care of the sick, prescriptions, indications of diseases, domestic surgery, hygiene, skin diseases, etc. It covers thousands of other subjects, among which are valuable suggestions to those contemplating marrying, factors to be considered in entering the marriage relation. Size, 7¼x9¼ ins. Subscription price, $5.00.

No. 3C70480 Our price..............**$1.12**
If by mail, postage extra, 46 cents.

MUSIC AND DANCING.

Complete Songster.

By Charles K. Harris. New, complete edition, containing 150 latest popular songs, among which are the following: For Old Times' Sake, There'll Come a Time, Cast Aside, I Love You in Spite of All, Just One Kiss, I Used to Know Her Years Ago, She's the Only Lady Friend I Know, etc. 200 pages. Size, 4¼x6⅝ inches.
No. 3C75138 Paper cover. Price......14c
No. 3C75139 Cloth. Price......27c
If by mail, postage extra, paper, 3c; cloth, 5c.

Dancing.

By Marguerite Wilson. A complete instructor, beginning with the first positions and steps, and leading up to the square and round dances. It contains also a full list of calls for all of the square dances, and the appropriate music for each figure, the etiquette of the dances and 100 figures for the German. It is unusually well illustrated by a large number of original drawings. Cloth. Retail price, 50 cents. Size, 4½x6.
No. 3C74407 Our price......30c
If by mail, postage extra, 5 cents.

Modern Quadrille Call Book and Complete Dancing Master.

By A. C. Wirth. Contains all the new, modern square dances and tabulated forms for the guidance of the leader or others in calling them, full and complete directions for performing every known square dance, such as plain quadrilles, polka quadrilles, prairie queen, United States quadrille, presidential quadrille, varieties quadrille, Francaise, cake walk quadrille, Dixie figure, Girl I Left Behind Me, Old Dan Tucker, money musk, waltz lanciers, Oakland minuet, waltz quadrille, the German, etc. In the round dances a special feature consists of the Wirth and other new methods of teaching the steps of the waltz, etc. 160 pages. Size, 4½x6⅝ inches.
No. 3C74900 Paper cover. Price......14c
No. 3C74901 Cloth. Price......27c
If by mail, postage extra, paper, 3c; cloth, 5c.

NATURE BOOKS.

Bird Life.

By Frank M. Chapman. Mr. Chapman has earned his place as the leading popular scientific writer upon birds. His descriptions are accurate, his style interesting. This book is filled with beautifully colored illustrations showing birds as they are. It gives the portraits and names of the familiar birds of Eastern and North America. Cloth. Handsome cover design. Size, 5⅛x8 inches. Retail price, $1.50.
No. 3C75167 Our price......$1.29
If by mail, postage extra, 18 cents.

Bird Neighbors.

By Neltje Blanchan. Contains 50 superb full page pictures in colors, many of them life size. Cloth. Size, 7½x10½ inches. Retail price, $2.00.
No. 3C75169 Our price......$1.35
If by mail, postage extra, 18 cents.

Butterfly Book, The

By W. J. Holland, LL. D. Beautifully illustrated, containing photographs of the butterflies in colors. Printed from new plates. Cloth. Size, 7½x10½ inches. Retail price, $3.00.
No. 3C75187 Our price......$2.35
If by mail, postage extra, 29 cents.

PAINTS AND PAINTING.

Including Oil, Water Color, House Painting, Carriage Painting, Graining, Varnishing, Gilding, Etc.

Alphabets, Book of.

Designed for the use of painters, draughtsmen, sign writers, etc. Contains all the standard styles and many new and popular ones. French, German, Old English, etc. Paper bound. Size, 6x9½ inches. Retail price, 50 cents.
No. 3C80122 Our price......27c
If by mail, postage extra, 5 cents.

Amateur Art, or Painting Without a Teacher.

Teaches landscape and flower painting in oil and water colors, cameo, oil, china painting, transferring photographs and prints to glass, coloring photographs in oil and water colors, painting on velvet, Kensington painting, painting on silk, satin, wood and glass, crayon portraiture, charcoal drawing, modeling in clay, etc. Contains a prepared table for mixing colors. Boards. Size, 6⅝x8½ inches.
No. 3C80128 Price......68c
If by mail, postage extra, 7 cents.

Carriage and Wagon Painting.

Full instructions and detailed directions in plain language for painting carriages, wagons and sleighs, including lettering, scrolling, ornamenting, striping, varnishing and coloring, with numerous recipes for mixing colors. 200 illustrations. Cloth. Size, 5½x7½ inches. Retail price, $1.00.
No. 3C80210 Our price......65c
If by mail, postage extra, 10 cents.

Draw and Paint, How to.

Contains instructions in outline, light and shade, perspective, sketching from nature, figure drawing, artistic anatomy, landscape, marine and portrait painting, the principles of coloring applied to painting, etc., 100 engravings. Cloth. Size, 4½x7¼ inches.
No. 3C80232 Price......33c
If by mail, postage extra, 7 cents.

Everybody's Paint Book.

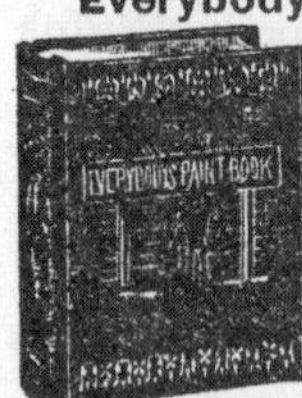

This book is especially designed to teach people how they may do their own house painting and save the expense of a professional painter. Contains full directions for mixing and applying paints, varnishes, polishing, staining and calcimining, etc. Cloth. Size, 5½x7½ inches.
No. 3C80396 Price......59c
Postage extra, 11 cents.

Hardwood Finishing.

By Fred T. Hodgson. Gives rules and directions for finishing in natural colors, and in antique, mahogany, cherry, birch, walnut, oak, ash, redwood, sycamore, pine and all other domestic woods; also staining, polishing, dyeing, gilding and bronzing. This book must not be confounded with the old book published 10 years ago. Cloth. Size, 5x7½ inches.
No. 3C80466 Price......59c
If by mail, postage extra, 8 cents.

Painters' Manual, The.

Including sign and carriage painting. Contains practical lessons in plain painting, varnishing, polishing, staining, paper hanging, kalsomining, etc., together with a full description of the tools and material used. Precise directions are given for mixing paints for all purposes, etc. Boards. Retail price, 50 cents.
No. 3C80257 Our price......27c
If by mail, postage extra, 4 cents.

Painters' Encyclopedia, The.

By F. B. Gardner. Contains definitions of all important words in the art. Plain and artistic painting with details of practice in coach, carriage, railway car, house, sign and ornamental painting, including graining, marbling, staining, varnishing, lettering, stenciling, gilding, bronzing, together with valuable hints and helps in scene painting, porcelain painting, plain and distemper painting. This is an invaluable book for every painter, no matter with what branch of the art he may be connected. Cloth. Size, 5½x7½ inches. Retail price, $1.50.
No. 3C10715 Our price......98c
If by mail, postage extra, 12 cents.

Painters, Decorators and Paper Hangers, Hints for.

A selection of useful rules and suggestions for house, ship and furniture painting, gilding, color mixing, etc. Paper cover. Size, 4⅞x7 inches. Retail price, 25 cents.
3C80859 Our price......15c
If by mail, postage extra, 2 cents.

Painters' Gilders' and Varnishers' Companion.

By William T. Brannt. New revised edition. Comprising the manufacture and test of pigments, the art of painting, graining, marbling, staining, sign writing, varnishing, glass staining and gilding on glass; together with coach painting and varnishing, and the principles of the harmony and contrast of colors. Cloth. Size, 5¼x7½ inches. Retail price, $1.50.
No. 3C80862 Our price......$1.15
If by mail, postage extra, 12 cents.

Sign Writing and Glass Embossing. Practical.

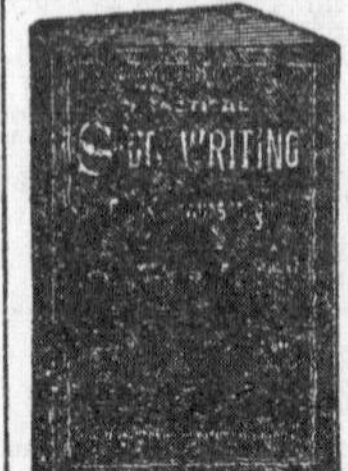

By James Callingham. A complete, practical, illustrated manual on the art of sign writing and glass embossing, with newly engraved illustrations. Paper cover. Size, 4½x7 inches. Retail price, 75 cents.
No. 3C81118 Our price......48c
If by mail, postage extra, 5 cents.

PHOTOGRAPHY.

First Steps in Photography.

By F. D. Todd. A practical guide for amateurs and professionals. Paper cover. Size, 4½x6 inches. Retail price, 25 cents.
No. 3C84367 Our price......15c
If by mail, postage extra, 2 cents.

Second Steps in Photography.

By F. D. Todd. A companion volume to "First Steps in Photography," but more advanced. Size, 4½x6 inches. Retail price, 50 cents.
No. 3C85110 Paper cover. Our price, 30c
If by mail, postage extra, 5 cents.

Photographic Instruction.

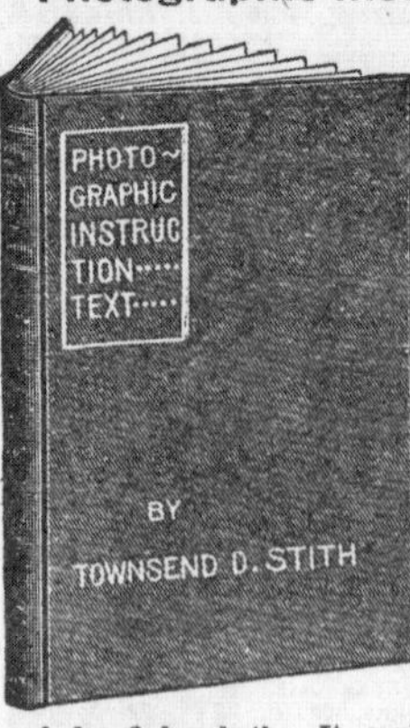

There is a best in everything and this is the best book on photography published. It contains more practical and better information than all other books on photography combined. This book is designed to give systematic, practical instruction and useful information to beginners, advanced amateurs and professional photographers. It gives rules for developing correct exposures, formula for developer and for fixing bath. It explains all about the different methods of toning, trimming, mounting, platinum toning and printing, platinotypes, blue prints and carbon, finishing plates and sensitized papers; all about flashlights, groups and retouching; complete instructions for copying, making lantern slides and enlargements; formula for and methods of using intensifier and reducer; chapters on the choice of a camera, directions for loading films and plates; requirements of dark rooms and fittings, etc. This is a work we can recommend. Cloth. Size, 5x7 inches.
No. 3C86863 Price......35c
If by mail, postage extra, 10 cents.

Photography, Modern, Its Theory and Practice.

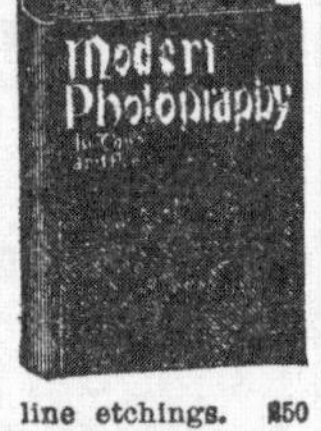

By Henry C. Abbott. A complete guide to photography for the amateur. Thoroughly up to date, describes all the various types of cameras, action of light, plates, loading the holders, keeping records, the exposure, development, fixing, washing, the dark room, its location and general plan, developers and fixing baths and their uses, intensification, reduction, retouching, etc. Illustrated with full page halftones and line etchings. 250 pages. Size, 5½x8 inches.
No. 3C84867 Paper cover. Retail price, $1.00. Our price......55c
If by mail, postage extra, 8 cents.
No. 3C84868 Cloth, stamped in gold. Retail price, $1.25. Our price......88c
If by mail, postage extra, 13 cents.

POETRY.

Ben King's Verse.

A new edition with additional poems, including "If I Should Die Tonight." Containing sketch of Mr. King's life by Opie Read. This new edition will be welcomed not only by his many friends and admirers, but by elocutionists and readers generally. Cloth, gilt top. Size, 5½x7½ inches. Retail price, $1.25.
No. 3C88165 Our price......85c
If by mail, postage extra, 10 cents.

Library Edition of the Poets.

An entirely new edition. Printed from new plates on a superior quality of book paper and uniformly bound in gilt cloth with gilt top, ornamental stamping from original design on front and back. Illuminated title page. Size of volume, 5¼x7½ inches. Gilt top. Retail price, per volume, $1.00.

Browning, Robert	Longfellow
Browning, Elizabeth	Lowell
Bryant	Milton
Byron	Moore
Burns	Poe
Campbell	Pope
Chaucer	Proctor
Coleridge	Scott
Cowper	Schiller
Dante:	Shelley
Goethe	Shakespeare
Goldsmith	Tennyson
Hood	Thackeray
Hemans, Mrs.	Whittier
Holmes	Wordsworth
Kipling	

No. 3C88418 Our price......45c
If by mail, postage extra, per volume, 12 cents.

Poems that Never Die.

Compiled and edited by Margaret M. Browning. Golden thoughts from the world's best authors, comprising poems on mother, home, heaven, the fireside, friendship, love, matrimony, sentiment, reflection, parting, absence, sorrow, religion, death, nature, patriotism, freedom, peace, war, labor, temperance, fancy, etc. An ideal gift book. Illustrated. Cloth, stamped in gold and colored inks. Size, 7x9½ inches. Retail price, $2.50.
No. 3BC8870 Our price......89c
If by mail, postage extra, 24 cents.

James Whitcomb Riley's Works.

(The Hoosier Poet.)

Tastefully bound in English silk cloth, uniform. Size of volumes, 5x7 inches.
Series No. 3C88912
Price, per volume......88c
If by mail, postage extra, per volume, 10 cents.
Neighborly Poems.
Sketches in Prose.
Afterwhiles.
Pipes o' Pan.
Rhymes of Childhood.
The Flying Islands of the Night.
Green Fields and Running Brooks.

Songs That Never Die.

A collection of famous words and melodies. This magnificent book contains songs of the sea, of home and country, of the great Civil War, national airs, Scotch and Irish melodies, lyrics of love and sentiment, songs of the church, a charming collection of instrumental music, etc. Enriched with valuable historical and biographical sketches of renowned authors and composers. Size, 8x10½ inches.
No. 3C89130 Cloth. Price......87c
No. 3C89132 Extra fine, full morocco leather, gilt edges. Retail price, $4.00. Our price......$1.25
If by mail, postage extra, either style, 32 cents.

REFERENCE BOOKS.

Including Atlases, Encyclopedias, Business Calculators, Parliamentary Law, Formulas, Civil Service Manuals, etc.

Imperial Atlas of the World.

Authorized Census Edition. Contains the 1900 census, maps of every country, and special county maps of each state in the United States, maps of large cities, etc. Also a brief historical, descriptive, statistical and political review of the United States and the territories of the United States. Cloth. Size, 11½x14½ inches.
No. 3C90135 Price......$1.12
If by mail, postage extra, 24 cents.

New Twentieth Century Atlas.

Combination Atlas, Gazetteer, Encyclopedia and Pictorial History of the World. Contains new maps, new texts, new illustrations and new features. In fact, new from cover to cover. The latest census, description of the different people of the world, their civilization, religion, etc. Also climate, productions, manufactures, rivers, valleys, lakes, mountains, minerals, and every subject of interest is given. Cloth. Size, 12x17 inches.
No. 3C90139 Price......$1.98
If by mail, postage extra, 76 cents.

Business Calculator.

For Farmers, Merchants and Machinists. Vest pocket edition. This is one of the best, most complete and authentic works on the science of arithmetic published. This book shows at a glance the correct value of grain, stock, cotton, hay, coal, lumber, cattle, in fact, everything. Gives also the square and cubic measurements of lumber, logs, land, stone, hay, grain, cisterns, wagon bins, corn cribs, etc. Vest pocket size.
No. 3C90146 Cloth. Price......12c
No. 3C90147 Leather. Price......22c
If by mail, postage extra, either style, 3 cents.

Chamber's Encyclopedia.

Complete in 15 Volumes, Worth $15.00. Our Special Cut Price Only $5.68.

New popular edition, rewritten and revised to date. A complete work of reference on art, science, history, literature, music, biography, geography, etc. A valuable set of books for students, teachers, business men and literary people generally. Size of each volume, 5½x7½ inches.
No. 3C90216 Complete, 15 volumes. Retail price, $15.00. Our price......$5.68
Weight, packed for shipment, 35 pounds.

Civil Service Manual.

A detailed history, aims, opportunities, rules, regulations and requirements of the Civil Service Law. Tells how to prepare for examinations, how to obtain positions, giving questions for examinations, so that every man, woman and child desiring better positions in the national, state, county or city governments can, with the aid of this book, pass every examination. Vest pocket size.
No. 3C90218 Cloth. Price......16c
No. 3C90219 Leather. Price......32c
If by mail, postage extra, either style, 4 cents.

Commission in the United States Army, Three Roads to a.

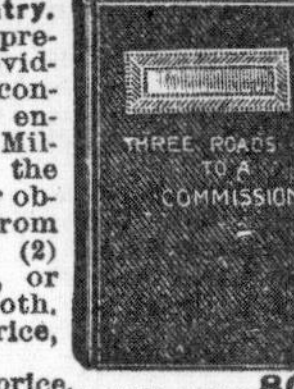

By Lieutenant W. P. Burham, 6th U. S. Infantry. This handbook has been prepared with a view to providing popular information concerning the manner of entering the United States Military Academy, and the courses to be pursued for obtaining a commission from either (1) The Academy, (2) The ranks of the army, or (3) Civil life. 259 pages. Cloth. Size, 5x6 inches. Retail price, $1.00.
No. 3C90236 Our price..........80c
If by mail, postage extra, 6 cents.

Cyclopedia Britannica.

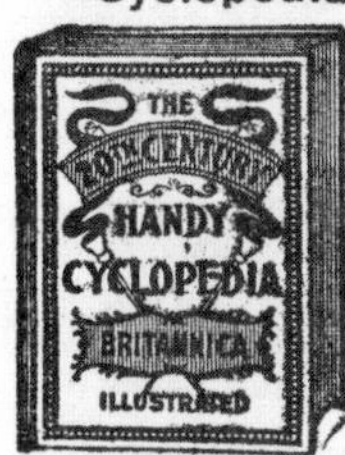

By Alfred B. Chambers. Twentieth Century Handy Edition. Contains over 15,000 articles of intense interest, alphabetically arranged, and covering almost every known subject; law, business, history, geography, biography medicine, chemistry, etc. Size, 4½ x 5½ inches.
No. 3C90246 Flexible cloth, cut flush. Retail price, 25 cents. Our price..........17c
If by mail, postage extra, 3 cents.
No. 3C90247 Stiff cloth, red edges. Retail price, 50 cents. Our price..........30c
If by mail, postage extra, 9 cents.

Dr. Chase's Recipes; or, Information for Everybody.

Contains an invaluable collection of about 800 practical recipes for merchants, grocers, saloon keepers, physicians, druggists, tanners, shoe and harness makers, painters, jewelers, blacksmiths, tinners, gunsmiths, barbers, dyers, farmers and families generally. Also contains rules for the preservation of health, advice to mothers, etc. Cloth. Size, 6x8¼ inches.
No. 3C90268 Price..........68c
If by mail, postage extra, each, 16 cents.

Dr. Lester's Book of Secret Information.

A practical book for all purposes. Tells how to cure and gives the remedies for all ills. Secret information for farmers and stock raisers. Diseases of the domestic animals, with methods of treatment. Something on cooking and valuable information for housewives, recipes and information on the preparation of every known useful article, and thousands of other subjects too numerous to mention. Cloth. Size, 5¾x8 inches.
No. 3C90270 Price..........95c
If by mail, postage extra, 18 cents.

Housekeepers' Handy Book.

The most complete, authentic, reliable and best recipe book published. The only complete ready reference book which is especially adapted to the home. It embraces every known subject of value pertaining to housekeeping, such as cooking, what to eat and how to prepare it, care of the health, teeth and complexion, how to remove freckles, sunburn, etc. Size, 5x7 inches.
No. 3C90478 Paper. Price..........20c
No. 3C90480 Cloth. Price..........35c
If by mail, postage extra, paper, 4c; cloth, 15c.

Lee's Home and Business Manual.

Absolutely new; thoroughly reliable. The teaching of the renowned specialist on all that constitutes a solid American business education, penmanship, letter writing, bookkeeping, banking, every day law, social forms, mercantile and technical terms, speeches for all occasions, and hundreds of other subjects fully and practically discussed. Size, 4¾x5½ inches.
No. 3C90660 Flexible cloth, cut flush. Price..........14c
No. 3C90661 Stiff silk cloth, red edges. Price..........28c
If by mail, postage extra, either style, 6 cents.

Lee's Priceless Recipes.

A unique collection of tried formulas and simple methods for druggists, chemists, etc.; three thousand secrets for the home, work shop, farm, dairy, in fact all the trades and professions, embracing every department of human endeavor. Size, 4¼x5¾ inches.
No. 3C90662 Flexible cloth, cut flush. Retail price, 25 cents. Our price..........14c
No. 3C90663 Stiff silk cloth, red edges. Retail price, 50 cents. Our price..........27c
If by mail, postage extra, either style, 6 cents.

Cushing's Manual of Parliamentary Practice.

Revised edition. Containing rules of procedure and debate in deliberative assemblies, with additional rules, including the Constitution of the United States and the Declaration of Independence. Size, 4¾x6 inches.
No. 3C90856 Paper cover. Retail price, 25 cents. Our price..........12c
No. 3C90857 Cloth. Retail price, 50 cents. Our price..........20c
If by mail, postage extra, paper, 3c; cloth, 5c.

Robert's Rules of Order.

By Lieut. Col. H. M. Roberts, Corps of Engineers, U. S. A. Revised edition. The standard of parliamentary authority. Experienced legislators, leading newspapers and prominent critics pronounce Robert's Rules of Order the best parliamentary guide in the English language, and its wonderful success everywhere entitles it to the claim of being the recognized authority in parliamentary law. Cloth. Size, 4x6 inches. Retail price, 75 cents.
No. 3C90863 Our price..........45c
If by mail, postage extra, 5 cents.

Ropp's Commercial Calculator.

A book that should be in the hands of every student, farmer, commercial and business man. Ropp's Commercial Calculator saves labor, time and money; simple, rapid, reliable; adapted to all kinds of business, trades and professions. Size, 4¼x6¾ inches.
No. 3C90980 Waterproof leatherette. Price (If by mail, postage extra, 3 cents.) 10c
No. 3C90981 Fine colored cloth with pocket..........24c
No. 3C90982 Elegant leather with pocket, silicate slate and account book. Price....63c
No. 3C90983 Fine seal grain, gilt edges with pocket silicate slate and account book. Price..........79c
If by mail, postage extra, either style, 5 cents.

Werner's Universal Encyclopedia.

An Encyclopedia which brings all history, all art, all science, and all literature up to date.

A superb reference library covering authoritatively every subject of interest. The growth of the nations, discoveries in science and great inventions are treated exhaustively, as well as the thousands of questions on historical, scientific and philosophical subjects, etc. No home, library, or school is complete without a set of these books. Complete in 12 large volumes, containing over 25,000 columns of reading matter, thousands of illustrations, etc. Size of volumes, 7¾x9½ inches.
No. 3C91314 Silk cloth. 12 volumes. Price..........$7.95
No. 3C91315 Sheepskin leather, 12 volumes. Price..........$12.95
Weight, packed for shipment, 46 pounds.

RELIGIOUS.

Under this heading will be found only the best books by the best authors on the best and oldest story in the world. Including the works of Canon Farrar, Bishop Fallows, T. DeWitt Talmage, Matthew Henry, Prof. Swing and many others.

Commentary on the Old and New Testaments.

Jamieson, Fauset and Brown's edition. Critical, practical and explanatory. Tried, tested and proven during one of the most active periods ever known in biblical research. That it has not been found wanting is evident in the still unabated demand. At considerable outlay the publishers have issued a new edition of this valuable work at a low price. Four volumes. Cloth. Weight, per set, 8¾ pounds. Size of volume, 1¾x5½x8 inches.
No. 3C92242 Price, per set of four volumes..........$3.89
If by mail, postage extra, 68 cents.

The Life of Christ.

By Canon Farrar. The author's exact scholarship is specially shown in his valuable notes at the foot of nearly every page, and a large number of fine, truthful engravings make this the best Life of Christ ever written. It comprises the birth, infancy and early life of Jesus, His baptism and public ministry, beautiful parables and discourses, etc. Cloth. Illustrated. Size, 6½x9½ inches.
No. 3C92670 Price..........79c
If by mail, postage extra, 43 cents.

From Eden to Calvary.
Or, Through the Bible in a Year.

By Grandpa Reuben Prescott. Especially arranged to take the reader through the Bible in a year, there being fifty-two appropriate chapters, one for each Sunday, in which the Bible stories from Genesis to Revelations are represented in a fascinating manner, and furnish entertainment and instruction for the young people during the long Sabbath afternoons. 254 pages. Cloth. Size, 7¾x9¾ inches. Retail price, $1.50.
No. 3C92382 Our price..........48c
If by mail, postage extra, 13 cents.

Matthew Henry's Works.

A commentary on the Bible. Complete in six volumes. Biblical students, who are most familiar with the very best commentaries of this generation are most able to appreciate the unfading freshness, the clear analysis, the spiritual force, the quaint humor and the evangelical richness of Matthew Henry's Exposition of the Old and New Testaments. There is nothing to be compared with Matthew Henry's Commentary for pungent and practical applications of the teachings of the text. Cloth. Size, 9x11½ inches. Retail price, $15.00. Weight, packed for shipment, 40 pounds.
No. 3C92730 Our price, per set of six volumes..........$7.75

The Home Beyond; or, Views of Heaven.

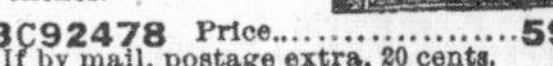

By Rt. Rev. Samuel Fallows, D. D. Taken from the works of over 400 prominent thinkers and writers. Complete treatise on the following: Man, Life, Death, the Dying, the Death of Children, Immortality, the Resurrection, Heaven, Recognition, Angelic Ministry, Saintly Sympathy. Cloth. Size, 5½x7½ inches.
No. 3C92478 Price..........59c
If by mail, postage extra, 20 cents.

MOODY, D. L., WORKS OF.

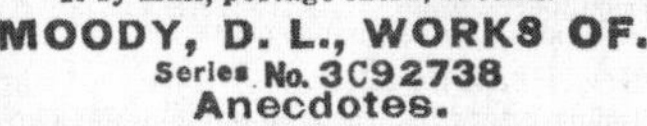

Series **No. 3C92738**

Anecdotes.

Containing several hundred interesting stories told by the great evangelist in his wonderful work in Europe and America. Cloth. Size, 5¼x8 inches. Retail price, $1.00. Our price..........57c

Life Work and Latest Sermons.

As delivered by the great evangelist in his great revival work in Great Britain and America. Together with a biography of the author, and his co-laborer, Ira D. Sankey, 335 pages. Cloth. Size, 5¼x8 inches. Retail price, $1.00. Our price..........57c

Child Stories.

A book adapted to children, but interesting to adults. Illustrated with 16 full page Dore illustrations and 106 other illustrations. 237 pages. Cloth. Size, 5¼x8 inches. Retail price, $1.00. Our price..........35c

Hold the Fort.

A book worth while. Cloth. Gilt tops. Size, 5½x8 inches. Retail price, 75c. Our price, 37c
If by mail, postage extra on the above, each, 12 cents.

Royal Path of Life.

Our Aims and Aids to Success and Happiness. All subjects are treated in a common sense way. It contains something of interest for the young and old, rich and poor, married and single, boys and girls, men and women, grandmothers and grandfathers. Contains full page steel engraved frontispiece and 32 full page engravings. Cloth, marble edges. Gold back stamp. Size, 6½ x 9 inches.
No. 3C92992 Price..........88c
If by mail, postage extra, 23 cents.

SELF TEACHING BOOKS.

Containing complete lessons in Algebra, French, German, Latin, Chemistry, English Composition, Bookkeeping, Law, Mechanical Drawing and hundreds of other subjects.

Algebra Self Taught.

By W. Paget Higgs, M. A. D. Sc. For home study. For the use of mechanics, young engineers and home students. As a guide and helper in the perplexities of algebraic problems, this book can be recommended with confidence to the large number of private students who have found the study always discouraging and sometimes fruitless. Cloth. Size, 5½x7½ inches.
No. 3C94122 Price..........58c
If by mail, postage extra, 12 cents.

Bookkeeping, Self Taught.

By Philip C. Goodwin. A complete self instructor of infallible bookkeeping for teachers, pupils and business men and women. With accounts in illustration, exercises for practice and a glossary of commercial terms. Mr. Goodwin's treatise on bookkeeping is an entirely new departure from all former methods of self-instruction and one which can be studied systematically and alone by the student with quick and permanent results, or taken up in leisure moments with an absolute certainty of acquiring the science in a very short time and with little effort. Cloth. Size, 5x7 inches.
No. 3C94180 Price..........65c
If by mail, postage extra, 12 cents.

Bookkeeping Without a Master.

For Home Study, by John W. Whinyates. A complete self instructor in bookkeeping for students, clerks, tradesmen, and merchants. It is an entirely new, easily understood system, a departure from all former methods, and one that can be studied systematically alone by the student with quick and permanent results. Cloth. Size, 6x9½ inches.
No. 3C94182 Price..........56c
If by mail, postage extra, 7 cents.

Boyd's Syllabic Shorthand.

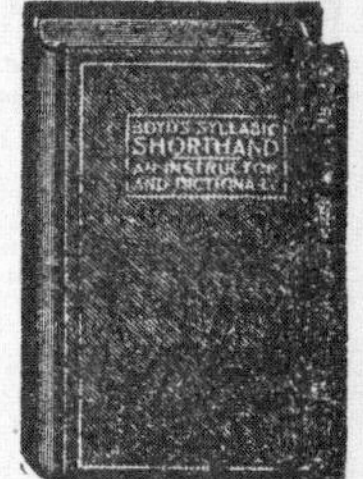

Easily learned in one month. A new system of shorthand in which the characters represent syllables, and are so arranged that when the student learns sixteen syllables, he knows how to write eighty syllables. The English language may be expressed in one hundred and twelve syllables, over one-half of which are rarely used. Each word is a complete line, no dots, no shading and no positions are used. This new system is capable of much greater speed than the older systems, is simpler, briefer and more easily learned, and can be mastered in one month. Cloth. Size, 5x7 inches. Retail price, $1.25.
No. 3C94183 Our price..........85c
If by mail, postage extra, 10 cents.

French Without a Master in Six Easy Lessons.

By A. H. Monteith. A complete course of lessons in the French language are the "Robertsonian Methods," intended for the use of all persons studying the French language without a teacher. Bound in paper. Size, 5¼x8 inches. Retail price, 25 cents.
No. 3C94378 Our price..........12c
If by mail, postage extra, 2 cents.

German Without a Master in Six Easy Lessons.

By A. H. Monteith. Best method of learning German without the aid of a teacher. Paper. Size, 5½x7½ inches. Retail price, 25 cents.
No. 3C94412 Our price..........12c
If by mail, postage extra, 2 cents.

Latin Without a Master in Six Easy Lessons.

By A. H. Monteith. By the aid of this valuable book anyone can read, write, and speak the Latin language without the aid of a teacher. Paper cover. Size, 5¼x7¾ inches. Retail price, 25 cents.
No. 3C94660 Our price..........12c
If by mail, postage extra, 2 cents.

Grammar Without a Master.

English Grammar of William Cobbett. Carefully revised and annotated by Alfred Ayres. The most readable grammar ever written. For the purpose of self education it is unrivalled. Persons who studied grammar when at school and failed to comprehend its principles (and there are many such) as well as those who have never studied grammar at all, will find the book specially suited to their needs. Cloth, with index. Size, 4¾x6¾ inches. Retail price, $1.00.
No. 3C94441 Our price..........68c
If by mail, postage extra, 10 cents.

The Simple Life.
By Chas. Wagner.

President Roosevelt says; "I am preaching your book to my countrymen." To aspire to the simple life is to rightly aspire to the fulfillment of human destiny. Cloth. Size, 5x7 ins.
No. 3C93120 Price..........30c

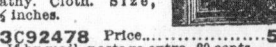

Guide to Successful Auctioneering, A.

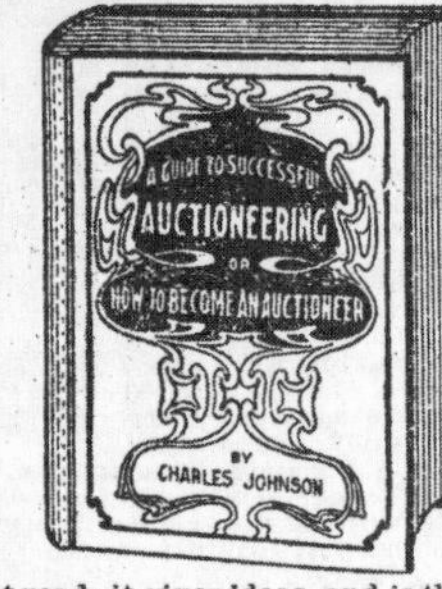

Or, How to Become an Auctioneer, by Chas. Johnson. There is no money making occupation which admits of greater advantages than auctioneering. Auctioneers are in constant demand, and are needed in every line of merchandise. The field is large and the opportunities great. This book starts you on the right road; it gives ideas, and is the only thoroughly practical work of the kind extant. Size, 5x7 inches.

No. 3C94485 Heavy paper cover. Price.....35c
No. 3C94486 Cloth. Library edition. Price.....48c
If by mail, postage extra, paper, 5c; cloth, 11c.

Hawkins' Mechanical Drawing.

For home study. The education of the mechanic is incomplete without a thorough knowledge of mechanical drawing and other branches inseparably connected with it. The drawing board and scientific book must go hand in hand with practical experience. One should not only be able to work practically, but he should be able to express his designs, his improvements and inventions on paper. The practical instructions given in this volume are in plain terms, such as a teacher would use. Cloth. Size, 7x10 inches.

No. 3C94406 Price.....$1.49
If by mail, postage extra, 10 cents.

Modern Penmanship.

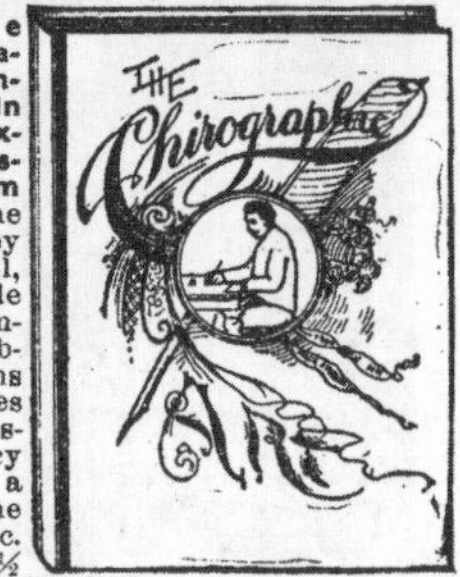

For home study, Chirographic Art. A complete course in penmanship, explaining the muscular or free arm movement. The only system by which a graceful, rapid and legible style of penmanship can be obtained. Contains 28 specimen plates of up to date business and fancy writing; also a skeleton outline of letters, etc. Cloth. Size, 8x10½ inches. Retail price, $1.00.

No. 3C94739 Our price.....65c
If by mail, postage extra, 11 cents.

One Hundred Lessons in Business.

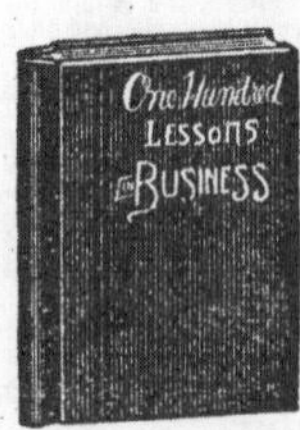

By Seymour Eaton. Containing sound business advice and safe business rules, hints and helps for corresponding purposes, for accountants, for advertisers; something about business figures and how to handle them; decimal numbers and what they are for; making out accounts, percentage, receipts, orders, due bills, trade discounts, invoices, etc. Cloth. Size, 6x9¼ inches.

No. 3C94838 Our price.....29c
If by mail, postage extra, 8 cents.

Cooper's Sea Tales.

By J. Fenimore Cooper, author of Leather Stocking Tales. Complete in five volumes. Uniform in size with Leather Stocking Tales. Comprising the following:

Red Rover
The Pilot
The Two Admirals
The Water Witch
Wing and Wing

A handsome library edition. Cloth. Size of volumes, 5½x7¼ inches.

No. 3C98240 Price, per set.....68c
Weight, packed for shipment, 8 pounds.

Corelli in Five Volumes.

New five-volume edition of Marie Corelli's works. Uniformly bound in cloth, printed from large, clear type. Size of volumes, 5½x7¼ inches. Weight, packed for shipment, 8 pounds. Retail price, $2.00. Comprising the following: **Ardath, Wormwood, Vendetta, Thelma, Romance of Two Worlds**

No. 3C98242 Our price, per set.....58c

Dumas' Romances.

In six volumes. Alexandre Dumas' D'Artagnan romances complete in six volumes. Size, 5½x7½ inches. Uniform cloth. Weight, packed for shipment, 8 pounds. Embraces the following:

Louise de la Valliere
Three Guardsmen
Man in the Iron Mask
Twenty Years After
Son of Porthos
Vicomte de Bragelonne

No. 3C98286 Price, per set.....68c

Dumas', Alexandre, Works, $1.63.

This popular set comprises eight of his renowned romances, each one intensely interesting; in fact, the reader who commences any one can scarcely be persuaded to lay down the volume until completed. Uniformly bound in cloth. Comprising the following: **Son of Porthos,** Louise de la Valliere, Count of Monte Cristo, Vicomte de Bragelonne, **The Three** Guardsmen, The Man in the Iron Mask, **Twenty** Years After, and Edmund Dantes. **Retail price,** $6.00. Cloth. Size of volumes, 5¼x7¼ inches.

No. 3C98288 Our price, per set of eight volumes.....$1.63
Weight, packed for shipment, 8 pounds.

The Self Educator Series.

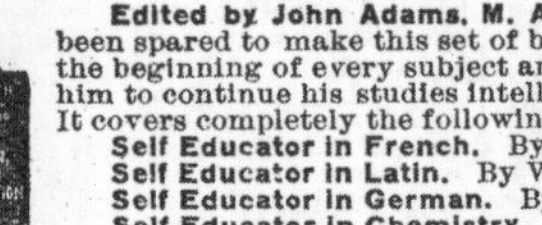

Edited by John Adams, M. A., B. Sc. For home study. No effort has been spared to make this set of books self contained. Each book begins with the beginning of every subject and carries the student far enough to enable him to continue his studies intelligently and successfully on his own account. It covers completely the following subjects:

Self Educator in French. By John Adams.
Self Educator in Latin. By W. A Edward.
Self Educator in German. By John Adams.
Self Educator in Chemistry. By James Knight.
Self Educator in English Composition. By G. H. Thornton.

No. 3C95118 Cloth. Price, per volume.....58c
If by mail, postage extra, per volume, 10 cents.

Surveyors' Guide, Practical.

By Andrew Duncan. New edition. Contains the necessary information to make any person of common capacity a finished land surveyor without the aid of a teacher. Cloth. Size, 5½x7½ inches. Retail price, $1.50.

No. 3C99792 Our price.....$1.15
If by mail, postage extra, 10 cents.

SPORTSMEN'S BOOKS, HUNTING, ETC.

OUR NEW BOOK CATALOGUE contains the best books published on Trapping, Trap Making, Taxidermy, etc. **SEND FOR ONE. IT'S FREE.**

Camp Life in the Woods and the Tricks of Trapping and Trap Making.

By W. Hamilton Gibson. Comprehensive hints on camp shelter of all kinds, boat and canoe building, valuable suggestions on the trappers' food, etc., with extended chapters on the trappers' art, containing all the "tricks" and valuable bait recipes of the profession. Full directions for the use of the steel trap, and for the construction of traps of all kinds; detailed instructions for the capture of all fur bearing animals; valuable recipes for the curing and tanning of fur skins, etc. Cloth. Illustrated. Size, 5x7 inches.

No. 3C96222 Price.....(If by mail, postage extra, 10 cents.).....68c

Taxidermists' Manual.

By Graham Allen. Complete instructions in the art of taxidermy with directions how to prepare, mount and preserve all kinds of birds, animals and insects. Paper cover. Profusely illustrated. Size, 4½x7 inches. Retail price, 25 cents.

No. 3C97110 Our price.....(If by mail, postage extra, 3 cents.).....18c

Amateur Trapper and Trap Makers' Guide.

By Stanley Harding. A new work based upon the experience of the most successful trappers, trap makers and hunters, containing plain directions for constructing the most approved traps, snares, nets and dead falls; the most successful baits for attracting all kinds of animals, birds, etc. Chapters for preparing skins and furs for the market, and for tanning them for future use; with concise and comprehensive instructions for preserving and stuffing specimens of birds and animals, etc. Illustrated. Size, 5x7½ inches.

No. 3C96124 Paper covers. Price.....18c
No. 3C96125 Cloth. Price.....27c
If by mail, postage extra, paper, 3c; cloth, 5c.

STANDARD LIBRARY SETS.

WE CAN POSITIVELY SAVE YOU from 50 to 100 per cent on all standard works. Never before in the history of book making have such wonderful values been offered to the public. We have taken special pains to include all the standard authors, whose works are prime favorites with every reader.

THESE SETS ORDINARILY ought not to be ordered sent by mail, as they usually weigh over the four-pound limit, which would make it necessary to take the books out of the box and wrap each one separately. We do not break sets and cannot sell separately any particular volume in these editions.

THE BOOKS ARE PUT UP IN COMPLETE SETS, including all or nearly all of the writings of each author and bound uniform. Printed on excellent paper from large, clear type, and when the exceedingly low price is considered, you can fully appreciate the wonderful bargains you will secure upon receipt of such books as you may order.

Mrs. Alexander's Five Best Books.

Uniform Edition Bound in binders' silk cloth. Size, 5½x7½ inches. Weight, packed for shipment, 7 pounds. Comprising the following:

Blind Fate
Broken Links
Crooked Path
Mona's Choice
Snare of the Fowler

No. 3C98195 Price, per set 58c

Cooper's Leather Stocking Tales.

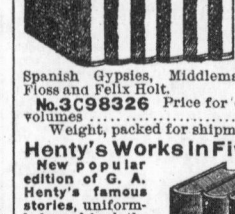

An entirely new edition. Printed from large, clear type on extra quality paper and handsomely bound in cloth, consisting of the following:

The Deerslayer
The Pathfinder
The Prairie
The Pioneers
The Last of the Mohicans

Size of volumes, 5½x7¼ inches.

No. 3C98238 Price, per set.....68c
Weight, packed for shipment, 8 pounds.

Dickens' Works Complete, 15 Volumes, Only $2.69.

This, the most popular priced 15-volume set of Dickens' complete works, is printed from new, clear type on a good quality of book paper. Bound in cloth, with gold titles and **an attractively** embossed cover design. Comprising same titles as No. 3C98260.

These books were made to retail at $7.50 per set, and are being sold by other houses wholesale at $2.95 per set.

No. 3C98258 Our price, per set, 15 volumes, $2.69

Dickens' Complete Works, Library Edition, Only $4.29.

We have purchased for spot cash an entire edition, printed from the best plates **on the market,** and while they last you can procure the 15 volumes at only $4.29. The set consists **of the following** stories:

Bleak House	**Old Curiosity Shop**	**Great Expectations**
Martin Chuzzlewit	**Oliver Twist**	**Little Dorritt**
Pickwick Papers	**Christmas Stories**	**Nicholas Nickleby**
Barnaby Rudge	**Child's History of England**	**David Copperfield**
Tale of Two Cities	**Our Mutual Friend**	**Dombey and Son**

He who has never read the works of Charles Dickens has missed one of the **greatest treats in** the literary world. No home or library is complete without a set of these books. Volumes are uniform. Bound in silk cloth. Retail price, $9.00. Size, 5½x7½ inches. Weight, packed for shipment, 30 lbs. (Handsome gift edition.)

No. 3C98260 Our price, per set of 15 volumes.....$4.29
No. 3C98261 Illustrated, gilt top. Price.....5.95

Eliot's, George, Complete Works, $1.48.

Six volumes, only $1.48. This is a remarkably low price for this author's complete works. Each volume bound in cloth. Size, 5½x7½ inches, comprising the following: Adam Bede, Romola, Silas Marner, Daniel Deronda, Scenes of Clerical Life, Spanish Gypsies, Middlemarch, Mill on the Floss and Felix Holt.

No. 3C98326 Price for complete set, six volumes.....$1.48
Weight, packed for shipment, 10 pounds.

Henty's Works in Five Volumes

New popular edition of G. A. Henty's famous stories, uniformly bound in cloth. Size, 5½x7½ inches. Weight, packed for shipment, 8 pounds. Retail price, $2.00. Consisting of

By Right of Conquest
True to the Old Flag
With Lee in Virginia
With Wolfe in Canada
Under Drake's Flag

No. 3C98465 Our price, per set.....58c

Holmes' Works in Five Volumes.

Five of Mary J. Holmes' popular and well known works. Uniformly bound in binders' silk cloth. Size, 5½x7½ inches. There is a steady and constantly increasing demand for these books. Retail price, $2.00. Weight, packed for shipment, 8 pounds. Embracing the following:

Lena Rivers | **Meadowbrook Farm**
English Orphans | **Tempest and Sunshine**
Homestead on the Hillside

No. 3C98482 Our price, per set.....58c

Marlitt's Works.

In five volumes. New uniform edition. Cloth. Size, 5½x7½ inches. Embracing the following:

Gold Elsie
Owl's Nest
Old Mam'selles Secret
Princess of the Moor
Second Wife

No. 3C99114 Price, per set.....58c

Hugo's, Victor, Complete Works, Only $1.58.

As illustrated. We have just published a new, popular edition of this favorite author's works, complete in seven volumes, which we can sell at the unheard of price of $1.58 for the complete set. The set consists of the following:

Les Miserables, Vol. 1	**History of a Crime**
Les Miserables, Vol. 2	**Toilers of the Sea**
By Order of the King	**Ninety-Three**
Hunchback of Notre Dame	

The volumes are uniformly bound in English cloth. Size of volume, 5⅛x7⅛ inches. Retail price, $6.00.

No. 3C98492 Our price for seven volumes.........**$1.58**
Weight, packed for shipment, 10 pounds.

Interlinear Translations.

The Hamilton Locke and Clark series have long been the standard and are now the best translated and most complete series of interlinears published. Titles:

Virgil. By Hart and Osborn.
Horace. By Sterling, Nuttal and Clarke.
Sallust. By Hamilton and Clarke.
Juvenal. By Hamilton and Clarke.
Homer's Iliad. By Thomas Clarke.
Caesar. By Hamilton and Clarke.
Cicero. By Hamilton and Clarke.
Ovid. By George W. Hellig.
Livy. By Hamilton and Clarke.
Xenophon's Anabasis.

Cloth. Size of volumes, 5x7½ inches. Retail price, $1.50.

No. 3C98527 Our price..............**98c**
If by mail, postage extra, per volume, 12 cents.

$1.48 Buys a $5.50 Set of Washington Irving's Works.

Taking into consideration the quality of paper, high class printing, binding and general appearance of this set, it cannot be duplicated for less than double our price.

The set consists of the following:

Vol. 1—Astoria, Salmagundi, Capt. Bonneville. Vol. 2—Tales of a Traveler, Abbottsford, Newstead Abbey, Bracebridge Hall, Wolfert's Roost. Vol. 3—Sketch Book, Knickerbocker's New York, Crayon Papers. Vol. 4—Tales of the Alhambra, Conquest of Granada, Conquest of Spain, Spanish Voyages. Vol. 5—Life and Voyages of Columbus, Tour of the Prairies. Vol. 6—Life of Mahomet, Oliver Goldsmith, Moorish Chronicles. Cloth. Size of each volume, 5⅛x7⅛ inches. Retail price, $5.50.

No. 3C98538 Our price, per set of six volumes..........**$1.48**
Weight, packed for shipment, 12 pounds.

Rudyard Kipling's Works.

Consisting of In Black and White, Phantom Rickshaw, Plain Tales from the Hills, Soldiers Three and The Light that Failed. Uniformly bound in cloth. Size of volumes, 5⅛x7⅛ inches. Published to retail at $3.50. Weight, packed for shipment, 8 pounds.

No. 3C98615
Our price for complete set..............**58c**

Longfellow's Works Complete in Five Volumes.

New five-volume edition, bound in ribbed cloth, printed from clear, new, large type. Size, 5⅛x7⅛ inches. Weight, packed for shipment, 8 pounds. Cloth. Retail price, $2.00. Embracing the following:

Evangeline	**Book of Poems**
Golden Legend	**Courtship of Miles Standish**
Hiawatha	

No. 3C98682 Our price, per set......**58c**

Lyall's Works Complete in Five Volumes.

New, uniform edition, bound in binders' silk cloth, printed from large, clear type on superior quality of book paper. Size, 5⅛x7⅛ inches. Weight, packed for shipment, 8 pounds. Cloth. Retail price, $2.00. Comprising the following:

Donovan	**In the Golden Days**
Knight Errant	**We Two**
	Won by Waiting

No. 3C98696 Our price, per set......**58c**

Optic's, Oliver, Works.

New edition, uniformly bound in cloth, embracing All Aboard, The Boat Club, Now or Never, Poor but Proud, Try Again. Size of volumes, 5⅛x7⅛ inches.

No. 3C98840 Price, per set........**58c**
Weight, packed for shipment, 8 pounds.

Ruskin's, John, Works.

New 5-Volume Edition, embracing **Crown of Wild Olives, Mornings in Florence, Queen of the Air, Sesame and Lilies, and True and Beautiful.** Attractively bound in cloth. Size of volumes, 5⅛x7⅛ inches.

No. 3C98988 Price, per set..........**58c**
Weight, packed for shipment, 8 pounds.

Shakespeare's Complete Works only $1.45.

A saving of from 50 to 60 per cent. Authentic and unabridged edition. The illustration will give you some idea of the appearance of these books. You can only form an idea of the wonderful value which we are giving by personal examination. Cloth. Size of each volume, 6x7⅛ inches. Retail price, $5.75.

No. 3C99118 Our price, per set of seven volumes..........**$1.45**
Weight, packed for shipment, 10 pounds.

Shakespeare's Complete Works, $2.05.

William Shakespeare, complete in eight volumes. Containing all the tragedies, all the comedies, all the poems and sonnets, and embracing a history of the early drama, an exhaustive biography, Shakespeare's will, an introduction to each play, names of actors and actresses of Shakespeare's day, index of characters, glossary of obsolete words, notes on each play, etc. From the works of Collier, Knight, Dyce, Douce, Hunter, Richardson, Verplanck and Hudson. Edited by George Long Duyckinck, suitable for teachers, students, clubs and homes. Uniform in size and style of binding, 32 full page illustrations. Cloth, stamped in gold. Size of volume, 4⅞x7⅛ inches.

No. 3C99122 Price, per set.......**$2.05**
Weight, packed for shipment, 10 pounds.

Shakespeare, Readers' Library Edition of.

$7.00

Complete in eight volumes. With explanatory notes by Malone, Stevens, Reed, Johnson and others, together with a biography, index to characters, glossary of obsolete terms and a concordance covering over 3,200 familiar passages. Illustrated with 23 fine line steel engravings and ten photo gravures, eight of these being portraits of the best modern actors, from special photographs. Uniform volumes. Size, 5⅛x8 inches. Retail price, $14.00. Weight, packed for shipment, 16 pounds.

No. 3C99128 Cloth. Gilt top. Gold lettering. Our price.... .. ..**$7.00**

Robert Louis Stevenson's Works.

This excellent set is uniformly bound in cloth, library style, embracing **Dr. Jekyll and Mr. Hyde, Master of Ballantrae, Misadventures of John Nicholson, New Arabian Nights, Treasure Island.** Size of volumes 5⅛x7⅛ inches. Weight packed for shipment, 8 pounds.

No. 3C99135 Price, for five volumes.**58c**

Scott's Famous Waverly Novels, $3.60.

Complete in 12 volumes. New popular edition at $3.60. At less than 35 cents per volume, we are offering Scott's complete work, which only recently cost the publishers from 75 cents to $1.00 per volume to produce. Bound in cloth. Uniform. Size, 5⅛x7⅛ inches. Weight, packed for shipment, 30 pounds. Retailed at from $8.00 to $14.00 per set.

Monastery	**Abbot**		
Rob Roy	**Midlothian**		
Waverly	**Woodstock**	**Red Gauntlet**	**Pirate**
Guy Mannering	**Anne of Geierstein**	**Peveril**	**Betrothed**
Lammermoor	**Montrose**	**Fair Maid**	**Antiquary**
Black Dwarf	**Quentin Durward**	**Nigel**	**Count Robert**
Ivanhoe	**Talisman**	**Kenilworth**	**St. Ronan's Well**

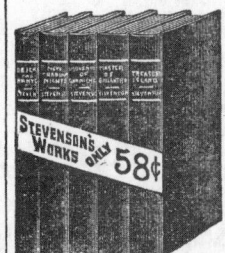

No. 3C99116 Our price, per set, 12 volumes..........................**$3.60**

Thackeray's Works, Complete in 10 Volumes $2.15.

Wm. Makepeace Thackeray. New library edition at $2.15 is beyond competition in price. Only by placing immense contract orders for these sets are we able to offer them at this absurdly low price. This set is durably bound, uniform. Size, 5⅛x7⅛ inches. Weight, packed for shipment, 12 pounds. Published to retail at $6.00. It consists of the following stories:

Vanity Fair	**Virginians**
Christmas Book	**Pendennis**
Newcomes	**Roundabout Papers**
Paris Sketches	**Barry Lyndon**
Phillip	**Henry Esmond**

No. 3C99120 Cloth. Our price for the complete set, 10 volumes..................**$2.15**

CLOTH BOUND STANDARD BOOKS AT 12 CENTS.

This series represents the writings of world renowned authors and is by far the cheapest series of cloth bound library books published. Contains 350 titles, durably bound in cloth, ornamented side, worked in colored inks, head bands, etc. Size of each volume, 5⅛x7⅛ inches.

From this series you can select complete works of well known authors, such as: C. M. Braeme, Washington Irving, Haggard, Bertha M. Clay, Bulwer-Lytton, Alexander Dumas, A. Conan Doyle, Charles Dickens, Samuel Lover, Marie Corelli, J. F. Cooper, Rosa N. Carey, Mrs. E. D. E. N. Southworth, Oliver Optic, The Duchess, Edna Lyall, Jules Verne, Harriett Beecher Stowe, Captain Mayne Reid, Beatrice Harraden, Mary J. Holmes, and other prominent writers.

No. 3C99175 Price, each......**12c**

If by mail, postage extra, per volume, 10 cents.

Adam Bede. By Eliot
Adventures of a Brownie. By Mulock
Aesop's Fables
Age of Fable. By Bulfinch
Alexander the Great. By Jacob Abbott
Alice in Wonderland. By Carroll
Allan Quatermain. By Haggard
All Aboard (Sequel to Boat Club.) By O. Optic
All Sorts and Conditions of Men. By Besant and Rice
Alone. By Marion Harland
Among Malay Pirates. By G. A. Henty
American Wit and Humor. By Peck, Nye and Quad
Andersen's Fairy Tales
Arabian Nights
Ardath. By Marie Corelli
As in a Looking Glass. By F. C. Phillips
At the World's Mercy. By Florence Warden
Aunt Diana. By Rosa N. Carey
Autocrat of the Breakfast Table. By Oliver Wendell Holmes
Averil. By Rosa N. Carey
Bacon's Essays
Barbara Heathcote's Trial. By Rosa N. Carey
Bay Path. By J. G. Holland
Belle of Lynne, The. By Braeme
Beside the Bonnie Brier Bush. By Ian Maclaren
Between Two Loves. By Charlotte M. Braeme
Beulah. By Augusta J. Evans
Beyond Pardon. By C. M. Braeme
Black Beauty. By Anna Sewell
Black Rock. By Ralph Connor
Blind Fate. By Mrs. Alexander
Boat Club. By Oliver Optic
Bondman, The. By Hall Caine
Bonnie Prince Charlie. By Henty
Boy Knight. By G. A. Henty
Boy Slaves. By Capt. Mayne Reid
Boy Tar. By Capt. Mayne Reid
Bracebridge Hall. By Irving
Bravest of the Brave. By G. A. Henty
Bride's Fate, The. (A Sequel to the Changed Brides.) By Mrs. Southworth
Broken Wedding Ring, A. By B. M. Clay
Browning, Robt., Poems
Browning's, Mrs., Poems
Bryant's Poems
Burdette's Book of Parodies and Dialect Reciter
By England's Aid. By G. A. Henty
By Order of the King. By Hugo
By Pike and Dyke. By G. A. Henty
By Right of Conquest. By G. A. Henty
By Sheer Pluck. By G. A. Henty
California and Oregon Trail. Francis Parkman
Camille. By Alex. Dumas, Jr.
Capitola, The Madcap. (Sequel to the Hidden Hand.) By Mrs. Southworth
Capt. Bailey's Heir. By G. A. Henty
Changed Brides, The. By Mrs. Southworth
Children of the Abbey. By Roche
Child's History of England. By Dickens
Child Wife. By Capt. Mayne Reid
Chimes, The. By Chas. Dickens
Christmas Carol. By Chas. Dickens
Christmas Stories. By Dickens
Claribel's Love Story. By Charlotte M. Braeme
Cleopatra. By H. Rider Haggard
Confessions of an Opium Eater. By De Quincey
Count of Monte Cristo. By Dumas
Courting of Dinah Shadd. By Rudyard Kipling
Courtship of Miles Standish. By Longfellow
Cousin Maude. By Mary Jane Holmes
Cranford. By Mrs. Gaskell
Crown of Wild Olives. By Ruskin
Crucifixion of Philip Strong. By Sheldon
Cruel as the Grave. By Southworth.
Daniel Deronda. By Eliot
Dark Marriage Morn. By Bertha M. Clay
Dark Secret. By Mrs. May A. Fleming
David Copperfield. By Dickens
Death Shot. By Capt. Mayne Reid
Deemster. By Hall Caine
Deerslayer. By Cooper
Deserted Wife. By Southworth
Dombey & Son. By Dickens
Donovan. By Edna Lyall
Don Quixote. By Cervantes
Dora Deane. By Mary J. Holmes
Dora Thorne. By Charlotte Braeme
Dragon and the Raven. G. A. Henty
Dream Life. Ik Marvel
Drummond's Addresses
Duke's Secret. By Charlotte M. Braeme
East Lynne. By Wood
Education. By Spencer
Edmund Dantes. (Part I of Count of Monte Cristo.) By Alexandre Dumas
Egyptian Princess. By Ebers
Elizabeth and Her German Garden
Emerson's Essays
Emerson's Poems
English Orphans. By Mary J. Holmes
Erie Train Boy, The. By Alger
Ernest Maltravers. By Bulwer-Lytton
Esther. By Rosa N. Carey
Ethics of the Dust. By Ruskin
Evangeline. By Longfellow
Facing Death. By G. A. Henty
Facing the Flag. By Jules Verne
Farmer Holt's Daughter. By Charles Garvice

(Continued on next page).

CLOTH BOUND STANDARD BOOKS.—Continued.

No. 3C99175 Price, each **12c**
If by mail, postage extra, per volume, 10 cents.

Favorite Poems
Felix Holt. By George Eliot
Fifteen Decisive Battles. By Edward Creasy
File No. 113. By Emile Gaboriau
Firm of Girdlestone. By A. Conan Doyle
First Violin. By Jessie Fothergill
Flower Fables. By Louisa M. Alcott
Footprints of the Creator. By Miller
For Another's Sin. By Braeme
For Name and Fame. By G. A. Henty
Forging the Fetters. By Mrs. Alexander
Four Destinies. By Theophile Gautier
Fox's Book of Martyrs
Franklin, Benjamin, Life of
French Revolution, The. By Thos. Carlyle
Friends, Though Divided. By G. A. Henty
From Dawn to Daylight. By H. B. Stowe
From the Earth to the Moon. By Jules Verne
Giraffe Hunters. By Capt. Mayne Reid
Grandfather's Chair. By Hawthorne
Great Expectations. By Dickens
Great Rebellion, History of the. By Moore
Grimm's Fairy Tales.
Gulliver's Travels. By Swift
Guy Mannering. By Scott
Handy Andy. By Lover
Hard Times. Dickens
Hardy Norseman. By Edna Lyall
Harry Lorrequer. By Chas. Lever
Hawthorne's Book of Ready Made Speeches and Album Selections
Hawthorne's Champion Book of Recitations and Dialogues
Her Martyrdom. By Bertha M. Clay
Her Only Sin. By Charlotte M. Braeme
Heroes, Hero Worship and Heroic in History. By Carlyle
Hiawatha. By Longfellow
Hidden Hand, The. Part 1. See Capitola. By Mrs. Southworth
History of a Crime. By Victor Hugo
History of the World. By Lardner
Homestead on the Hillside. By Mary J. Holmes
Household Angel in Disguise. By Mrs. Madeline Leslie
House of the Seven Gables. By Nathaniel Hawthorne
House of the Wolf, The. By Stanley J. Weyman
Hunchback of Notre Dame. By Hugo
I Have Lived and Loved. By Mrs. Forrester
Idle Thoughts of an Idle Fellow, The. By Jerome K. Jerome
In Freedom's Cause. By G. A. Henty
In His Steps. By Chas. M. Sheldon
In the Reign of Terror. By G. A. Henty
In the Golden Days. By Edna Lyall
In Times of Peril. By G. A. Henty
Inez. By Augusta J. Evans
Ishmael. Southworth
Ivanhoe. By Scott
Jack Archer, Tale of Crimea. By G. A. Henty
Jane Eyre. By Bronte
John Halifax, Gentleman. By Mulock
Kenilworth. By Sir Walter Scott
Kidnapped. By R. L. Stevenson
Knight Errant. By Edna Lyall
Lamplighter. By Cummins
Last Days of Pompeii. By Bulwer
Last of the Mohicans. By Cooper
Legacy of Cain. By Collins
Lena Rivers. By Mary J. Holmes
Light That Failed, The. By Rudyard Kipling
Lion of St. Mark. By G. A. Henty
Lion of the North. By G. A. Henty
Little by Little. By Oliver Optic
Little Minister. By Barrie
Lone Ranch, The. By Capt. Mayne Reid
Longfellow's Poems
Lord Lynn's Choice. By B. M. Clay
Lorna Doone. By Blackmore
Lost Heir. By G. A. Henty
Lover or Friend. By Rosa N. Carey
Lucile. By Meredith
Macaria. By Augusta J. Evans
Maggie Miller. By M. J. Holmes
Man in the Iron Mask, The. By A. Dumas
Marble Faun. By Hawthorne
Marvel. By The Duchess
Master of Ballantrae. By Stevenson
Meadowbrook Farm. By M. J. Holmes
Merle's Crusade. By Rosa N. Carey
Micah Clarke. By A. Conan Doyle
Michael Strogoff. Jules Verne
Middlemarch. By George Eliot
Mill on the Floss. By George Eliot
Mine Own People. By R. Kipling
Minister's Wooing. By H. B. Stowe
Molly Bawn. By The Duchess
Monte Cristo's Daughter. By Dumas
Mosses from an Old Manse. By Nathaniel Hawthorne
Moss-Side. By Marion Harland
Mysterious Island. By Jules Verne
Natural Law in the Spiritual World. By Drummond
Ninety-Three. By Victor Hugo
No Quarter. By Capt. Mayne Reid
Not Like Other Girls. By Carey
Now or Never. By Oliver Optic
Old Curiosity Shop. By Dickens
Old Mam'selle's Secret. By E. Marlitt
Oliver Twist. By Dickens
One of the 28th. By G. A. Henty
Only the Governess. By R. N. Carey
Our Bessie. By Rose N. Carey
Out of the Pampas. By G. A. Henty
Palmer Cox's Brownie Book
Pathfinder. By J. Fenimore Cooper
Patrick Henry, Life of
Phantom Rickshaw and Wee Willie Winkie. By Rudyard Kipling
Pilgrim's Progress. By Bunyan
Pilot, The. By J. Fenimore Cooper
Pioneers. By J. Fenimore Cooper
Plain Tales From the Hills. By Rudyard Kipling
Pleasures of Life. By Lubbock
Poor and Proud. By Oliver Optic
Prairie. By J. Fenimore Cooper
Prince of the House of David. By Ingraham
Prisoners and Captives. By Merriman
Professor at the Breakfast Table. By O. W. Holmes
Prue and I. By Geo. W. Curtis
Queechy. By Wetherell
Queen of the Air. By Ruskin
Quo Vadis. By Sienkiewicz
Ralph Raymond's Heir. By Alger
Rasselas. By Johnson
Red Rover. By J. Fenimore Cooper
Representative Men. By Emerson
Reveries of a Bachelor. By Marvel
Rienzi. By Bulwer-Lytton
Rifle Rangers. By Capt. Mayne Reid
Robert Elsmere. By Mrs. Humphrey Ward
Robert Hardy's Seven Days. By Sheldon
Robinson Crusoe. By D. DeFoe
Rocky Mountain Adventures. By Edwin Bryant
Romance of Two Worlds. By Corelli
Romola. By George Eliot.
Rosamond. By M. J. Holmes
Salathiel, The Wandering Jew. By George Croly
Samantha at Saratoga. By Holley
Sapho. By Daudet
Scalp Hunters. By Capt. Mayne Reid
Scarlet Letter. By Hawthorne
Schools and Schoolmasters. By Hugh Miller
Scottish Chiefs. By Jane Porter
Self-Help. By Samuel Smiles
Self-Raised. By Southworth
Sesame and Lilies. By Ruskin
Shadow of a Crime. By Hall Caine
Shadow of a Sin. By C. M. Braeme
She. By H. Rider Haggard
She Fell in Love with Her Husband. By E. Werner
Ships that Pass in the Night. By Beatrice Harraden
Sign of the Four. By A. Conan Doyle
Silence of Dean Maitland, The. By M. Gray
Sketch Book. By Irving
Snow Image. By Hawthorne
Soldiers Three. By Rudyard Kipling
Son of Porthos. By Alexandre Dumas
Spy, The. By J. Fenimore Cooper
Squire's Darling. By Bertha M. Clay
St. George for England. By G. A. Henty
Stepping Heavenward. By Mrs. E. Prentiss
Sticket Minister. By Crockett
Story of an African Farm. By Schreiner
Study in Scarlet. By A. C. Doyle
Sturdy and Strong. By G. A. Henty
Swiss Family Robinson. J. R. Wyss
Switzerland, History of. Heinrich Zschokke
Taking Manila. By Williams
Tale of Two Cities. By Dickens
Tales from Shakespeare. By Lamb
Tanglewood Tales. By Hawthorne
Tempest and Sunshine. By M. J. Holmes
Tennyson's Poems
Ten Nights in a Bar Room. By Arthur
Terrible Temptation. By Reade
Thaddeus of Warsaw. By Porter
Thelma. By Marie Corelli
This Wicked World. By Cameron
Thorns and Orange Blossoms. By Braeme
Three Guardsmen. By Alexandre Dumas
Three Men in a Boat. By J. K. Jerome
Through the Fray. By G. A. Henty
Through the Looking Glass. Carroll
Toilers of the Sea. By Hugo
Tom Brown's School Days. By Hughes
Tom Brown at Oxford. By Hughes
Tour of the World in Eighty Days. By Verne
Treasure Island. By Stevenson
Tried for Her Life (A sequel to "Cruel as the Grave.") By Mrs. Southworth
True to the Old Flag. By G. A. Henty
Try Again. By Oliver Optic
Trooper's Adventures in the War for the Union
Twenty Thousand Leagues Under the Sea. By Jules Verne
Twice-Told Tales. By Nathaniel Hawthorne
Two Admirals. By J. F. Cooper
Two Years Before the Mast. By Dana
Uncle Tom's Cabin. By Harriett Beecher Stowe
Under Drake's Flag. By G. A. Henty
Under Two Flags. By Ouida
United States, History of. By Frost
Vanity Fair. By Thackeray
Vendetta. By Marie Corelli
Vicar of Wakefield. By Goldsmith
Vicomte de Bragelonne. By Alexandre Dumas
Vivian, the Beauty. By Edwards
Washington, Life of. By Townsend
Water Witch. By J. F. Cooper
Webster, Daniel, Life of
Wedded and Parted. By Bertha M. Clay
We Two. By Edna Lyall
What Gold Cannot Buy. By Mrs. Alexander
White Company, The. By Doyle
Whittier's Poems
Wide, Wide World. By Wetherell
Wife in Name Only. By Braeme
Wife of Monte Cristo. By Alexandre Dumas
Willy Reilly. By Carleton
Wing and Wing. By J. F. Cooper
With Clive in India. By G. A. Henty
With Lee in Virginia. By G. A. Henty
With Wolfe in Canada. By Henty
Woman Against Woman. By Mrs. Holmes
Woman's War. By Bertha M. Clay
Won by Waiting. By Edna Lyall
Wonder Book for Boys and Girls. By Hawthorne
Wormwood. By Marie Corelli
Yellow Aster. By Iota
Young Acrobats. By Horatio Alger
Young Buglers. By G. A. Henty
Young Carthaginians. By G. A. Henty
Young Colonists. By G. A. Henty
Young Midshipman. By G. A. Henty
Young Voyagers. By Mayne Reid

GILT TOP LIBRARY BOOKS AT 19 CENTS.

Comprising best works of the world's most celebrated authors. A selected list of classics and modern literature.

These are unquestionably the best made, best bound, and altogether the best library books in the market. Assorted cover designs, stamped in gold, gilt tops, making a very attractive, durable and substantial book for public and all library purposes. **Size of volume,** $5\frac{1}{2}$x$7\frac{1}{2}$ inches. Retail price, per volume, 50 cents.

No. 3C99912 Cloth. Our price, each, or in any quantity **19c**
If by mail, postage extra, each, 11 cents.

Abbe Constantin. Halevy
Adam Bede. George Eliot
Aesop's Fables
Adventures of a Brownie. Mulock
Alexander The Great. Jacob Abbott
Alhambra, The. Irving
Alice. Bulwer
Alice's Adventures in Wonderland. L. Carroll
All Aboard. Oliver Optic
Alone. Marion Harland
Andersen's Fairy Tales
Arabian Nights Entertainment
Ardath. Marie Corelli
Artist's Love, The. Southworth
Attic Philosopher in Paris, An. Souvestre
Aunt Diana. Rosa N. Carey
Autocrat of the Breakfast Table. O. W. Holmes
Bacon's Essays
Bay Path. J. G. Holland
Beside the Bonnie Brier Bush. Ian Maclaren
Beulah. Augusta J. Evans
Beyond Pardon. Clay
Biglow Papers. Lowell
Bill Nye's Sparks
Black Rock. R. Connor
Black Beauty. A. Sewell
Bleak House. Dickens
Blithedale Romance. Hawthorne
Boat Club, The. Oliver Optic
Bondman, The. Hall Caine
Bonnie Prince Charlie. Henty
Book of Golden Deeds. C. M. Yonge
Boy Hunters, The. Mayne Reid
Boy Knight, The. A Tale of the Crusades. Henty
Boy Slaves. Capt. Mayne Reid
Boy Tar. Capt. Mayne Reid
Bracebridge Hall. Irving
Bravest of the Brave; or, with Peterborough in Spain. Henty
Bride of Llewellyn. Southworth
Brooks' Addresses
Browning's, Mrs., Poems
Browning's, Robt., Poems
Bryant's Poetical Works
Buffalo Bill
Burns' Poems
By Order of the King. Hugo
By Right of Conquest; or, with Cortes in Mexico. Henty
Byron's Poems
California and Oregon Trail. F. Parkman
Character. Samuel Smiles
Charles O'Malley. Charles Lever
Children of the Abbey. Roche
Child's History of England. Chas. Dickens
Christmas Carol. Dickens
Christmas Stories. Chas. Dickens
Cloister and the Hearth. Reade
Columbus. Wilkie
Conquest of Peru. Prescott
Count of Monte Cristo. Dumas
Courting of Dinah Shadd. Kipling
Courtship of Miles Standish. Longfellow
Cousin Maude. Mary J. Holmes
Cranford. Mrs. Gaskell
Crucifixion of Philip Strong. Sheldon
Curse of Clifton. Southworth
Daily Food for Christians.
Daniel Deronda. Eliot
Data of Ethics. Spencer
David Copperfield. Dickens
Deemster, The. Hall Caine
Deerslayer. Cooper
Descent of Man. Darwin
Discarded Daughter. Southworth
Dombey and Son. Charles Dickens
Donovan. Edna Lyall
Don Quixote. Cervantes
Dora Deane. Mary J. Holmes
Drummond's Addresses
Duty. Samuel Smiles
East Lynne. Mrs. Henry Wood
Education. Spencer
Elizabeth and Her German Garden
Emerson's Essays
Emerson's Poems
English Orphans, The. Mary J. Holmes
English Woman's Love Letters, An
Esther. Rosa M. Carey
Evangeline. H. W. Longfellow
Fairy Land of Science. Buckley
Familiar Quotations
Fatal Secret. Southworth
Faust. Goethe
Favorite Poems
Felix Holt. George Eliot
Fifteen Decisive Battles. Creasy
Firm of Girdlestone. A. Conan Doyle
First Violin. Fothergill
Flower Fables. Louisa M. Alcott
Footprints of the Creator. Hugh Miller
Forbidden Fruit. Boucicault
For the Term of His Natural Life. Clarke
Foul Play. Chas. Reade
Franklin, Benjamin. Autobiography of
French Revolution. Carlyle
Goethe's Poems
Gold Dust. C. M. Yonge
Gold Elsie. Marlitt
Goldsmith's Poems
Grandfather's Chair. Hawthorne
Gray's Elegy
Great Expectations. Charles Dickens
Grimm's Fairy Tales
Gulliver's Travels. Jonathan Swift
Guy Mannering. Sir Walter Scott
Handy Andy. Samuel Lover
Hardy Norseman. Edna Lyall
Haunted Homestead. Southworth
Heart of Midlothian. Scott
Hemans' Poems
Her Girlhood's Lover. Bertha M. Clay
Her Shadowed Life
Hiawatha. H. W. Longfellow
Hidden Hand. Southworth
History of a Crime. Victor Hugo
Holmes' Poems. O. W. Holmes
Holy Roman Empire. Bryce
Homestead on the Hillside. Mary J. Holmes
House of Seven Gables
How Women Love. Max Nordeau
Humphrey Clinker. Smollet
Hunchback of Notre Dame. Victor Hugo
Hypatia. Charles Kingsley
Idle Thoughts of an Idle Fellow. Jerome
Iliad, Homer's
Imitation of Christ. Thos. A'Kempis
India, or the Pearl of Pearl River. Southworth
Inez, a Tale of the Alamo. Augusta J. Evans
In His Steps. Charles Sheldon
In Memoriam. Tennyson
Intellectual Life. Hamerton
In the Golden Days. Edna Lyall
Ishmael. Southworth
Ivanhoe. Sir Walter Scott
Jane Eyre. Charlotte Brontë

GILT TOP LIBRARY BOOKS.—Continued.

John Halifax, Gentleman. Miss Mulock
Joseph Balsamo. Dumas
Josephine. Jacob Abbott
Julius Caesar. Jacob Abbott
Kept for the Master's Use. Havergal
Kenilworth. Sir Walter Scott
Kidnapped. Robert Louis Stevenson
King of the Golden River. Ruskin
Kipling's Ballads. Rudyard Kipling
Knight Errant. Edna Lyall
Koran of Mohammed, The
Laddie
Lady of the Isle. Southworth
Lady of the Lake. Sir Walter Scott
Lalla Rookh
Lamplighter. Cummins
Last Days of Pompeii. Bulwer-Lytton
Last of the Mohicans. J. Fenimore Cooper
Lena Rivers. Mary J. Holmes
Les Miserables. Victor Hugo
Life of Christ. Farrar
Light of Asia. Sir Edwin Arnold
Light that Failed
Lincoln, Life of. Raymond
Little by Little. Oliver Optic
Little Lame Prince
Little Minister. Barrie
Locksley Hall
Longfellow's Poems
Lorna Doone. Blackmore
Lost Heir of Linlithgow. Southworth
Love's Labor Won. Southworth
Lover or Friend. Rosa N. Carey
Lowell's Poems.
Lucile. Owen Meredith
Macaria. Augusta Evans
Maggie Miller. Mary J. Holmes
Marble Faun. Hawthorne
Marmion. Sir Walter Scott
Mary, Queen of Scotts. Jacob Abott
Master and Man. Count Leo Tolstoi
Meditations of Marcus Aurelius. Translated by Geo. Long
Memoirs of A Physician. Dumas
Micah Clarke. A. Conan Doyle
Middlemarch. George Eliot
Midnight Queen. Mrs. May A. Fleming
Mill on the Floss, The. George Eliot
Mine Own People. Kipling
Minister's Wooing. Harriet Beecher Stowe
Missing Bride, The. Southworth
Miss Toosey's Mission. Whitaker
Moore's Poems
Mosses from an Old Manse. Hawthorne
Moss-Side. Marion Harland
My Friend, the Murderer. A. Conan Doyle
Mysteries of Paris. Eugene Sue
Mysterious Island. Jules Verne
Napoleon and His Marshals. Headley
Natural Law in the Spiritual World. Drummond
Ninety-Three. Hugo
Noble Lord. Southworth
Not Like Other Girls. Rosa N. Carey
Now or Never. Oliver Optic
Odyssey, Homer's
Old Curiosity Shop. Charles Dickens
Old Homestead, The. Ann S. Stephens
Old Mam'selle's Secret. E. Marlitt
Oliver Twist. Charles Dickens
Only the Governess. Rosa Nouchette Carey
Orange and Green. G. A. Henty
Origin of Species. Darwin
Other Worlds Than Ours. Proctor
Our Bessie. Rosa N. Carey
Out on the Pampas. G. A. Henty
Palmer Cox's Brownie Book. Palmer Cox
Paradise Lost. John Milton
Past and Present. Carlyle
Pathfinder. James Fenimore Cooper
Paul and Virginia. By St. Pierre
Pendennis. William M. Thackeray
Pickwick Papers. Charles Dickens
Pilgrim's Progress. John Bunyan
Pilot, The. James Fenimore Cooper
Pioneers. James Fenimore Cooper
Plain Tales from the Hills. By Rudyard Kipling
Plutarch's Lives. By John Dryden
Poe's Poems
Poor and Proud. Oliver Optic.
Prairie, The. James Fenimore Cooper
Pride and Prejudice. Jane Austen
Prince of Darkness. Southworth
Prince of the House of David. Rev. J. H. Ingraham
Princess. Tennyson
Professor at the Breakfast Table. Holmes
Prue and I. Geo. W. Curtis
Put Yourself in His Place. Charles Reade
Queechy. Elizabeth Wetherell
Queen's Necklace. Alexandre Dumas
Quo Vadis. Sienkiewicz
Rab and His Friends. Brown
Red Rover. James F. Cooper
Representative Men. Emerson
Retribution. Southworth
Robert Hardy's Seven Days. Chas. M. Sheldon
Robinson Crusoe. DeFoe
Rosamond. Mary J. Holmes
Rollo in Geneva. Jacob Abbott
Rollo in Holland. Jacob Abbott
Rollo in London. Jacob Abbott
Rollo in Naples. Jacob Abbott
Rollo in Paris. Jacob Abbott
Rollo in Rome. Jacob Abbott
Rollo in Scotland. Jacob Abbott
Rollo on the Atlantic. Jacob Abbott
Rollo on the Rhine. Jacob Abbott
Rollo in Switzerland. Jacob Abbott
Romance of Two Worlds. Marie Corelli
Romola. George Eliot
Rubaiyat of Omar Khayyam. Fitzgerald
Salathiel, the Wandering Jew. Geo. Croly
Samantha at Saratoga. Holley
Sam Jones' Sermons
Sapho. Daudet
Sartor Resartus. Carlyle
Scarlet Letter. Nathaniel Hawthorne
Scott's Poems
Scottish Chiefs. Porter
Second Wife. Marlitt
Self Help. Samuel Smiles
Self Raised. Southworth
Sesame and Lilies
Shadow of a Crime, The. Hall Caine
Shakespeare's Complete Works.
Shakespeare's Quotations
She Fell in Love with Her Husband. E. Werner
She's All the World to Me. Hall Caine
Ships that Pass in the Night. Harraden
Silence of Dean Maitland, The. Maxwell Grey
Single Heart and Double Face. Chas. Reade
Sketch Book, The. Irving
So Runs the World. Sienkiewicz

Continued on Next Page.

Gilt Top Library Books.—Continued.

No. 3C99912 Price, each..........(If by mail, postage extra, each, 11 cents)............19c

Song of Miriam. Marie Corelli
Spectre Lover. Southworth
Spy, The. James F. Cooper
Stepping Heavenward. Mrs. E. Printiss
Story of an African Farm. Olive Schreiner
Sunshine and Roses. Bertha M. Clay
Swiss Family Robinson. J. R. Wyss
Tain's English Literature
Taking Manila; or, In the Philippines with Dewey
Tale of Two Cities. Charles Dickens
Tales from Shakespeare. Charles and Mary Lamb
Tanglewood Tales. Nathaniel Hawthorne
Tempest and Sunshine. Holmes
Ten Nights in a Bar Room. T. S. Arthur
Tennyson's Poems
Testimony of the Rocks. Hugh Miller
Thaddeus of Warsaw. Porter
Thelma. Marie Corelli
Thorns and Orange Blossoms. C. M. Braeme
Three Guardsmen. Alexandre Dumas
Three Men in a Boat. Jerome K. Jerome
Thrift. Samuel Smiles
Through the Looking Glass. Carroll
Toilers of the Sea. Victor Hugo
Tom Brown at Oxford. Thomas Hughes
Tom Brown's School Days. Thomas Hughes
Treasure Island. Stevenson
True and Beautiful. John Ruskin
True to the Old Flag. Henty
Try Again. Oliver Optic
Twenty Years After. Dumas
Twice Told Tales. Hawthorne
Uncle Tom's Cabin. Harriett Beecher Stowe
Under Drake's Flag. Henty
Under Two Flags. Ouida
Unwilling Bride, An. Mary J. Holm
Vanity Fair. Thackeray
Vendetta, The. Marie Corelli
Vicar of Wakefield. Goldsmith
Wandering Jew. Eugene Sue
Water Babies. Chas. Kingsley
Waverley. Sir Walter Scott
Wedding Trip, A. Bazan
Week on Concord and Merrimac Rivers. Thoreau
Westward Ho. Chas. Kingsley.
We Two. Edna Lyall
White Company, The. A. Conan Doyle
Whittier's Poems
Wide, Wide World. E. Wetherell
Widow Bedott Papers. Whitcher
Willy Reilly. Will Carleton
With Fire and Sword. Sienkiewicz
With Lee in Virginia. Henty
With Wolfe in Canada. Henty
Won by Waiting. Lyall
Wonder Book. Nathaniel Hawthorne
Wordsworth's Poems
Workingman's Wife, The. Frederick
Wormwood. Marie Corelli
Young Voyagers, The; or, The Boy Hunters in the North. Capt. Mayne Reid

STATIONERY DEPARTMENT.

On this and the following pages, we list only the best Blank Books, Letter Copying Books and Tablets, Stationery, Typewriter Paper and Supplies, Inkstands, Paper Weights, Fountain Pens, Pens, Pencils and Holders, Inks, Glues, Paste and General Office Supplies. We are well prepared to take care of Grammar and High School Supplies as well as Academies, Colleges, etc. We are quoting School Ink, Blackboards, Blackboard Erasers and School Supplies generally at from 35 to 45 per cent lower than the manufacturers. It will pay you to investigate before placing your order elsewhere.

GLOBES.

Every office, home, library and school room should be supplied with a globe. We are aware that heretofore many school boards, while recognizing the necessity of a globe, have been prevented from procuring one by its **high cost.** We have here listed a series of globes, which are the best made, and at the prices quoted are within the reach of all. The spheres are made with great care and are warranted not to check or crack; every improvement, in engraving, printing, coloring and mounting the maps has received critical attention.

No. 3C4844 Wire Mounted Globe, 6 inches in diameter, strongly made. The details on the globe are the same as on the more expensive ones. Retail price, 50 cents. Our price.......**25c**
If by mail, postage extra, 16 cents.

Mounted Globes.

No. 3C4828 Mounted on oxidized copper stand. The printing and coloring in this globe is clear, accurate and stands out distinctly, making it equally desirable for home or school use. Height of globe, 16½ inches. Diameter of ball, 8 inches. Has movable meridian. Retail price, $8.00. Our price..............**$3.70**
Weight, packed for shipment, 17 pounds.

No. 3C4810 Mounted same as No. 3C4828 but without meridian. Retail price, $5.00. Our price..............**$1.50**
Weight, packed for shipment, 9¾ pounds.

WE QUOTE in our new book catalogue, a complete line of Globes, up to date Wall Maps, Book Holders, at prices beyond competition. The catalogue is free. **SEND FOR ONE.**

The New Noyes Dictionary and Book Holder.

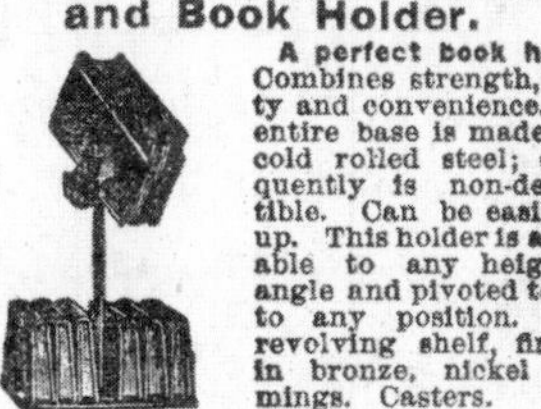

A perfect book holder. Combines strength, beauty and convenience. **The entire base is made from cold rolled steel; consequently is non-destructible. Can be easily set up. This holder is adjustable to any height or angle and pivoted to turn to any position. With revolving shelf, finished in bronze, nickel trimmings. Casters.**

No. 3C4744 Single Adjustable Book Holder. Price.........**$1.89**

No. 3C4746 Double Adjustable Book Holder. Otherwise same as No. 3C4744. Price......**$2.98**
Weight, packed 18 lbs.

PAPETERIES.

It is unprofitable to ship boxed papeteries by mail. Include a supply to go in your freight and express order with other goods.

Our Leader at 4 Cents.

No. 3C4850 Our Leader contains high grade cream wove ruled writing paper, 24 sheets, with baronial envelopes to match. Size of paper, 5x7½ inches. Price, per box.........**4c**
Per dozen......**40c**
If by mail, postage extra, each 4 cents.

Decorated Stationery.

No. 3C4857 Illuminated Stationery, with beautiful floral decoration in upper left hand corner, contains 24 sheets of fine ruled writing paper with envelopes to match. Size of paper, 4½x7 inches.
Price, per box........**8c**
Per dozen boxes....**90c**
If by mail, postage extra, 8 cents.

Full Value. 1-2 Pound for 8c.

No. 3C4860 Contains ½-pound cream wove ruled octavo note paper, with envelopes to match. Size of paper, 4¾x7½ inches.
Price, per box.........**8c**
Per doz.......**88c**
If by mail, postage extra, each, 10 cents.

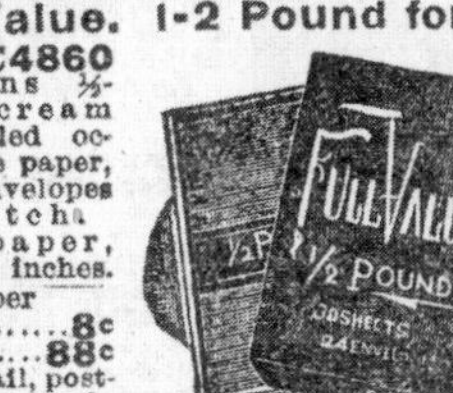

Unwritten History.

No. 3C4864 Unwritten History, a book shaped box containing 24 sheets of ruled paper, with baronial envelopes to match. Put up in a book shaped box, imitation morocco binding, gold edged. Size of paper, 4½x7 inches.
Price, per box..**$0.10**
Per dozen boxes, **1.05**
If by mail, postage extra, each, 12 cents.

Decorated Stationery.

No. 3C4870 Plate Paper, Fancy decorated ruled stationery. Each sheet illuminated with an attractive and animated design, envelopes to match. Size of paper, 4½x7 inches.
Price, per box..........**$0.11**
Per dozen boxes..........**1.08**
If by mail, postage extra, 7 cents.

13 Cents Per Pound; Worth 25 Cents.

No. 3C4872 One pound box of writing paper, containing 50 sheets cream wove, smooth finish, fine quality ruled octavo note paper, baronial envelopes to match; put up in tinted box. Size of paper, 5x7 inches.
Per box........**13c**
If by mail, postage extra, 21 cents.

Perfumed Society Stationery.

No. 3C4877 New Society Correspondence. Perfumed. Contains very best grade of pure white ruled paper; envelopes to match; banded and tied with silk ribbon. Size of paper, 5x7 inches.
Price, per box........**14c**
If by mail, postage extra, 11 cents.

Edinburg Linen.

No. 3C4880 Imported linen, ruled, best quality note paper with envelopes to match, banded and tied with silk ribbon, suitable for general correspondence. Size of paper, 4½x7 inches. Price, per box....................**9c**
If by mail, postage extra, 10 cents.

Overland Mail.

No. 3C4882 For Foreign Correspondence; very thin pure white bond writing paper. Commercial size, with water lines instead of ordinary ruling. Envelopes to match. Size of paper, 4½x7 inches.
Price, per box, **18c**
If by mail, postage extra, 5 cents.

Travelers' Companion.

No. 3C4894 Desk Box and Traveling Companion. An artistically shaped box, easily conformed into a lap desk, contains two sizes of popular style note paper, ruled, with desk pad and blotter on inside of cover, handsomely lithographed top. Size of box, 7x9⅞ inches.
Price........**18c**
If by mail, postage extra, 11 cents.

Imperial China Silk.

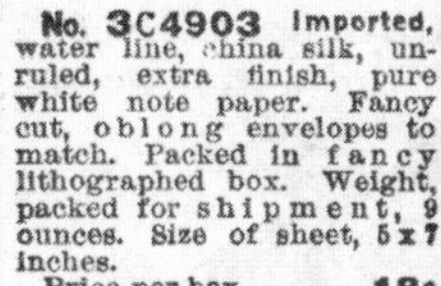

No. 3C4903 Imported, water line, china silk, unruled, extra finish, pure white note paper. Fancy cut, oblong envelopes to match. Packed in fancy lithographed box. Weight, packed for shipment, 9 ounces. Size of sheet, 5x7 inches.
Price, per box.........**18c**
If by mail, postage extra, 9 cents.

Landsdowne Linen.

No. 3C4906 Landsdowne Linen; pure linen, silk finish note paper, unruled, with fancy cut envelopes to match. Size of paper, 5x6⅛ inches.
Price, per box, **22c**
If by mail, postage extra, 12 cents.

Society Stationery.

No. 3C4915 Feather Weight Society Stationery, unruled. Contains one quire of pure white, rice finish, octavo note paper and envelopes for foreign correspondence. Size of paper, 5¼x6¼ inches.
Price, per box...**22c**
If by mail, postage extra, 6 cents.

Heliotrope Perfumed Paper.

No. 3C4927 For fine correspondence, superfine tinted wove octavo note paper, ruled, with baronial envelopes to match. Size of paper, 5x6¼ inches.
Price, per box **25c**
If by mail, postage extra, 12 cents.

Royal Coach.

No. 3C4936 New, up to date novelty paper for polite correspondence. Contains one quire of pure linen, white and tinted, hemstitched paper, unruled, making a perfect handkerchief design. New style envelopes to match. Size of paper, 5x6½ inches.
Price, per box.....**$0.38**
Per dozen boxes.. **3.98**
If by mail, postage extra, each, 12 cents.

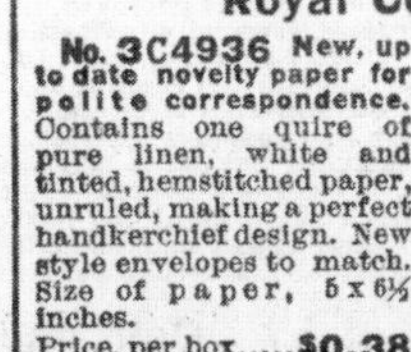

Berkley Colonial Stationery.

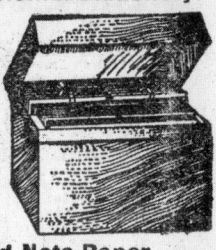

No. 3C4942 An artistically shaped box, containing 2 sizes of pure white, cream wove, unruled writing paper, with envelopes to match, in separate compartments, tied with a silk ribbon. A very desirable gift box. Price, per box....**33c**
If by mail, postage extra, 28 cents.

Unruled Note Paper.

No. 3C4944 Combination Work Basket, made of straw braid, contains one quire of pure white wedding stock, unruled note paper with baronial envelopes to match. Banded and tied with silk ribbon. Size of paper, 5x8 inches. Price, per box......**48c**
If by mail, postage extra, 18c.

Ruled Square Note Paper.

No. 3C4950 Plush Box. Cover lined with sateen, hinges and clasp. Contains crochet hook, bodkin, stiletto and one quire of cream wove square note paper, ruled, with envelopes to match. Box fitted with ball feet. Size of box, 8x2¾x6¼ inches.
Price, per box....Postage extra, 20c..**49c**

White Octavo Note Paper.

No. 3C4956 Contains 24 sheets and 24 envelopes of white octavo note paper, ruled. Put up in a beautiful celluloid box lined with satin, illustrated top, with hinges and clasp. Size of box, 8x5¼x3 inches. Price per box. **79c**
If by mail, postage extra, 20 cents.

Juvenile Paper.

No. 3C4960 Fancy Juvenile Baronial Box of Stationery, containing one quire of smooth, white ruled paper, with envelopes to match, put up in fancy lithographed covered boxes. Size of paper, 5¼x3¾ inches.
Price, per box..........**8c**
Per dozen boxes..........**90c**
If by mail, postage extra, each, 5 cents.

Juvenile Note Paper.

No. 3C4962 Fancy Book Shaped Juvenile Box, with "A Frog Would A-Wooing Go" printed on the back, containing one quire of juvenile ruled white note paper with envelopes to match. Size of paper, 4½x3¾ inches.
Price, per box.. **9c**
Per dozen boxes **90c**
If by mail, postage extra, each, 6 cents.

Juvenile Paper.

No. 3C4964 Gilt Juvenile Drawered Box, with assorted lithographed pictures, printed in colors, containing 24 sheets and 24 envelopes, tied with tinsel twine, extra fine cream wove, juvenile writing paper, ruled, with envelopes to match. Size of paper, 4½x3¾ inches.
Price, per box..**10c**
Per dozen boxes. **99c**
If by mail, postage extra, each, 5 cents.

Juvenile Cream Wove Paper.

No. 3C4970 Fancy Plush Work Box, for children, containing extra white cream wove paper, tied with silk cord, with envelopes to match, crochet hook, bodkin and stiletto. Size of box, 5x8¼ inches.
Price, per box.........**79c**
If by mail, postage extra, 8 cents.

BLANK BOOKS.

No. 3C4975 Half Bound Blank Books, cap folio, full duck, with imitation leather corners, green edges, containing good quality of medium weight paper, a book for general purposes, ruled in journals, day books, single entry and double entry ledgers, cash, record and journal books. Size, 7½x11 inches. Price,

No. pages	per book
100	14c
150	18c
200	25c
250	29c
300	32c

No. of pages	400	500	600
Price, per book	38c	45c	50c

Average weight, per 100 pages, 1 pound.

No. 3C4976 Crown Folio, bound in full sheep, red leather ends and bands, spring back, opens flat, well stayed, contains extra quality of heavy white writing paper. Made in day books, record, cash day books, journals, single entry and double entry ledgers with two and three accounts to the page, unit ruled dollars and cents. Size, 9x14¾ inches.

No. of pages	200	300	400	500
Price, per book	85c	$1.10	$1.25	$1.40
No. of pages	600	800	1,000	
Price, per book	$1.55	$1.70	$1.98	

Average weight, per 100 pages, 1½ pounds.

No. 3C4977 Cap Folio, bound in slate duck, imitation Russia corners, spring back, hubs, green edges, paged, ruled in journals, single entry and double entry ledgers, day, cash and records. Size, 9x13 inches. Average weight, per 100 pages, 1½ pounds.

No. pages	Price
300	59c
400	69c
500	89c

No. 3C4978 Crown Folio, containing extra heavy white wove paper, black cloth sides, Russia back and corners, green edges, sewed strongly on bands, paged, ruled in day book, single entry and double entry ledger, record, cash and journal. Size, 9¾x14 inches.

No. pages	150	200	250	300	400
Price, per book	55c	59c	69c	79c	87c

Average weight, per 100 pages, 1½ pounds.

IMPORTANT—In ordering Blank Books do not fail to state distinctly catalogue number, ruling and number of pages wanted.

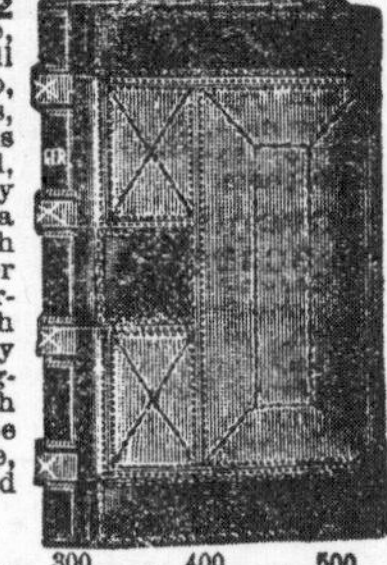

No. 3C4982 Demy Folio. Size, 10¾x16 inches, full bound in buffed sheep, red ends and bands, spring back, opens flat, well stayed, strongly and neatly made. Contains extra quality of fine, smooth finish, white ledger paper. Ruled in journals, day books, cash books, single entry and double entry ledgers and records with one, two and three accounts to the page, unit ruled dollars and cents, indexed.

No. of pages	300	400	500
Price, per book	$1.75	$2.00	$2.35
No. of pages		600	800
Price, per book		$2.50	$3.75

Average weight, per 100 pages, 1½ pounds.

Bookkeeping Blanks.

No. 3C4984 For practice in schools and colleges, excellent quality of white paper, blank book finish, ruled as follows: Day book, record, journal, cash and sales book, double entry ledger, and trial balance, colored press board covers, 34 pages to book. Size, 8½x14 inches. Always mention kind of ruling wanted.
Price, per ¼ dozen..$0.10
Per dozen.......... .36
Per gross.......... 4.25
If by mail, postage extra, for three, 19 cents.

Pocket Receipt Books.

No. 3C4989 Pocket Receipt Book, Best grade pressed board cover, cloth back with stub, perforated. Size, 6½x2 inches. Contains 50 leaves.

POCKET RECEIPTS

Price, per dozen, **55c**; each..........5c
If by mail, postage extra, each, 3 cents.

Draft Books.

No. 3C4991 Draft Books. Best pressed board cover, cloth back, perforated. Contains 50 drafts. Size, 12x3¾ inches.
Price, per dozen, **55c**; each..........5c
If by mail, postage extra, each, 7 cents.

Check Books.

No. 3C4992 Check Books, pressed board cover, cloth back, perforated, contains 50 checks. Size, 12x3¾ inches.
Price, per dozen, **65c**; each..........6c
If by mail, postage extra, each, 7 cents.

Note Books.

No. 3C4993 Note Books. Pressed board cover, cloth back, perforated. Size, 12x3¾ inches. Contains 50 notes.
Price, per dozen, **55c**; each..........5c
If by mail, postage extra, each, 7 cents.

Standard Scale Books.

No. 3C4994 Contains 500 weight forms. Printed on an extra quality of good paper, with stubs attached; marbled paper sides and cloth back. Very durable. Size, 8¼x11 inches.
Price..........22c
If by mail, postage extra, 12 cents.

Complete Account Book and Weather Record.

No. 3C4997 It embraces separate account departments, itemized and consolidated, for all general products and stocks, orchard, dairy, garden, hay, seed, cotton, etc., exemption laws in all states, legal forms, how to rent farms, also information as to how many bushels of seed to the acre, and just how deep to plant various crops, such as wheat, corn, etc. Size, 8¾x14 inches. Cloth. Price..$1.29
If by mail, postage extra, 32 cents.

No. 3C5023 Memorandum Book, bound in leatherette, turned in, gilt edges, aluminum stamp on front cover, extra quality of white paper, ruled in dollars and cents, side opening. Size, 3¼x6 inches. 160 pages.
Price, each..........$0.12
Per dozen..........1.10
If by mail, postage extra, each, 4 cents.

Handy Note Books.

No. 3C5025 Handy Note and Memorandum Books, end opening, contains extra quality of white paper, ruled. Size, 4¼x6¾ inches. 94 pages.
Price, each..........4c
Per dozen..........40c
If by mail, postage extra, each, 4 cents.

Butcher's Pass Book.

No. 3C5041 Butchers' Pass Book. Cap, 8vo., canvas, pressboard cover; contains 40 leaves, extra white paper. Size, 6x3½ inches.
Price, six for..........$0.13
Per dozen.......... .23
Per gross.......... 2.55
If by mail, postage extra, per dozen, 21 cents.

Malleable Iron Letter Press.

Malleable Iron Letter Press, highly enameled in black. Warranted against imperfections in material and workmanship.

No. 3C5079 Size of follower, 10x12½ inches. Weight, packed for shipment, 67 lbs.
Price..........$3.69
No. 3C5081 Size of follower, 10x15 inches. Weight, packed for shipment, 78 pounds.
Price..........$4.38
No. 3C5083 Size of follower, 11x16 inches. Weight, packed for shipment, 90 pounds.
Price..........$6.69

STANDARD LETTER COPYING BOOKS.

No. 3C5075 Half bound, sheep back and corners, black cloth sides, containing best quality of white paper; patent index. Size, 10¼x12¼ inches.
Price, 500 pages, weight, 6 pounds.....$0.80
Price, 700 pages, weight, 7 pounds..... .95
Price, 1,000 pages, weight, 8 pounds.....1.35

TABLETS.

No. 3C5239 Golf Girl Combination Pencil and Ink Tablet. Artistic cover design, printed in colors. Contains the very best quality of pencil paper, permanently bound, cloth back, ruled, 160 leaves (320 pages).
Price, per half dozen.....25c
Per dozen..........47c
If by mail, postage extra, per tablet, 10 cents.

No. 3C5241 Big Bear Pencil Tablet. Containing very best grade of ruled pencil paper, made expressly for home and school use, permanently bound. Contains 170 leaves (340 pages). Size, 5¾x8¾ in. Price, per half dozen..$0.27
Per dozen.......... .51
Per gross.......... 5.90
If by mail, postage extra, per tablet, 12 cents.

No. 3C5244 American Indian Pencil Tablet. An artistic cover design in colors. Permanently bound, perforated. Extra quality of finest pencil paper, ruled. Contains 140 leaves (280 pages). Size, 6x9 inches.
Price, per half dozen..........$0.23
Per dozen.......... .43
Per gross.......... 4.90
If by mail, postage extra, per tablet, 10 cents.

No. 3C5246 Hummer Pencil Paper. Ruled, attractive cover design, permanently bound. Contains 110 leaves (220 pages) white paper. Size, 7¾x10 inches. Price, per half dozen..........$0.27
Per dozen.......... .51
Per gross.......... 5.90
If by mail, postage extra, per tablet, 13 cents.

No. 3C5250 Companion Tablet. Combination pen and pencil tablet. Perforated leaves, made expressly for school work, compositions, essays, etc. Unique cover design, permanently bound. Ruled. Contains 120 leaves (240 pages). Size, 6x9 inches.
Price, per half dozen, $0.25
Per dozen.......... .47
Per gross.......... 5.45
If by mail, postage extra, per tablet, 10 cents.

No. 3C5257 Practice Tablets and Spelling Blanks for school use. New, improved spelling tablet, permanently bound and perforated. Containing 76 leaves (152 pages) of heavy white paper of marginal line and practice ruling. Size, 4x8¾ inches.
Price, each..........$0.04
Per dozen.......... .40
Per gross.......... 4.50
If by mail, postage extra, per tablet, 7 cents.

Desk or Scratch Pads.

No. 3C5258 Perforated Scratch Pads, permanently bound, each sheet perforated near the top; contains extra white, unruled paper for pencil use.
Size, 2¾x4½ inches. Price, per dozen..10c
If by mail, postage extra, per dozen, 16 cents.
Size, 4x6 inches. Price, per dozen.....16c
If by mail, postage extra, per dozen, 27 cents.
Size, 5x8 inches. Price, per dozen.....20c
If by mail, postage extra, per dozen, 38 cents.
Include these pads in your freight and express orders, as owing to their weight they make unprofitable mail shipments.

Old Glory Ink Tablet.

No. 3C5259 U. S. Standard Old Glory Ink Tablet, containing 65 leaves (130 pages) of old U.S. standard, ruled, pure white note paper with blotter attached, suitable for school and commercial use. Size, 5x7¾ inches.
Price, per half dozen..........23c
Per dozen..........44c
If by mail, postage extra, per tablet, 7 cents.

No. 3C5262 Up to Date Ink Tablet. Contains extra quality pure white paper, ruled, with blotter; beautiful cover design, printed in colors; cloth back.
Commercial Note. Size, 5x8 inches. Contains 60 leaves (120 pages).
Price, per half dozen, 21c
Per dozen..........40c
Letter. Size, 8x10 inches. 25 leaves (50 pages).
Price, per half dozen. 18c
Per dozen..........32c
If by mail, postage extra, per tablet, 7 cents.

Blue Ribbon Ink Tablet.

No. 3C5282 Contains extra quality of highly finished, cream wove, ruled writing paper, blotter attached. Fancy cover design.
Commercial Note. Size, 5x8 inches. 200 pages (100 leaves). Price, each.....8c
Per dozen..........80c
Letter. Size, 8x10 inches. 80 pages (40 leaves).
Price, each..........8c
Per dozen..........80c
If by mail, postage extra, per tablet, 11 cents.

University Ink Tablet.

No. 3C5283 Contains extra quality cream laid ruled writing paper, blotter attached, with assorted covers of different colleges, namely, Columbia, Yale, Princeton, Harvard, Cornell and University of Pennsylvania. Size, 5x8 inches.
Price, per half dozen, 27c
Per dozen..........48c
If by mail, postage extra, per tablet 9 cents.

Imperial Wove Bond Tablets.

No. 3C5288 Imperial Wove Bond. Extra quality, medium weight bond writing paper, ruled. Blotter attached.
Commercial Note. Size, 5x8 inches, 200 pages (100 sheets).
Price, each..........$0.15
Per dozen..........1.70
Packet Note. Size, 5½x9 inches, 150 pages (75 sheets).
Price, each..........$0.15
Per dozen..........1.70
Letter. Size, 5½x10 inches. 96 pages (48 sheets). Price, per dozen, **$1.80**; each 18c
If by mail, postage extra, each, 9 cents.

ENVELOPES AT LESS THAN WHOLESALE PRICES.

	PRICE, PER BOX OF 100	250	500	1,000
No. 3C5084 Manila (buff color) Envelopes, No. 5, XXX stock; size, 3 1-16x5½ inches; high cut; made from best jute stock. Weight, per box (500 in box), 3 pounds		$0.15	$0.27	$0.50
No. 3C5085 Manila (buff color) Envelopes, No. 6, XXX stock; high cut; made from best jute stock; size, 3⅝x6 inches. Weight, per box (500 in box), 60 ounces		.16	.28	.54
No. 3C5086 White Envelopes, special grade, manufactured expressly for us; No. 5; size, 3x5½ inches; XXX stock. Weight, per box (250 in box), 32 ounces		.19	.36	.68
No. 3C5087 White Envelopes, same quality as No. 3C5086, but No. 6; size, 3½x6 inches; XXX stock. Weight, per box (250 in box), 35 ounces		.22	.41	.78
No. 3C5089 Duplex Envelopes, white outside, blue inside; writing cannot show through; No. 5, XX stock, extra quality, high cut; size, 3 1-16x5½ inches. Weight, per box (250 in box), 32 ounces		.25	.48	.92
No. 3C5091 Duplex Envelopes, white outside, blue inside; writing cannot show through; No. 6, XX stock, high cut, superior quality; size, 3⅝x6 inches. Weight, per box (250 in box), 37 ounces		.28	.54	1.03
No. 3C5093 White Wove Envelopes, extra quality, high cut, No. 5, XX stock; size, 3 1-16x5½ inches. Weight, per box (250 in box), 33 ounces		.17	.32	.61
No. 3C5095 White Wove Envelopes, No. 6, XX stock, high cut, good quality; size, 3⅝x6 inches. Weight, per box (500 in box), 66 ounces		.27	.51	.97
No. 3C5097 Cream Wove Envelopes, No. 5, XXX stock, superior quality, commercial high cut; size, 3 1-16x5½ inches. Weight, per box (500 in box), 5 pounds		.26	.49	.93
No. 3C5099 Cream Wove Envelopes, No. 6½, XXX stock, superior quality, commercial high cut; size, 3⅝x6½ inches. Weight, per box (500 in box), 5½ pounds	$0.15	.35	.66	1.28
No. 3C5101 Cream Wove Envelopes, baronial high cut, No. 5; size, 4¼x5⅛ inches; XXXX stock. Weight, packed, per box (250 in box), 30 ounces	.16	.36	.69	1.32
No. 3C5103 Cream Wove Envelopes, baronial, high cut, No. 4; size, 3⅞x4¾ inches; XXXX superior stock. This envelope is suitable for general purposes, especially for ladies' correspondence. Weight, packed, per box (250 in box), 34 ounces	.17	.40	.77	1.47
No. 3C5105 White Bond Envelopes, high cut, No. 6; size, 3⅝x6 inches; XXX extra stock. A good envelope for all purposes, especially invitations, etc. Weight, packed, per box (250 in box), 44 ounces	.12	.27	.52	1.00
No. 3C5107 Linen Envelopes, high cut, No. 5; size, 4⅛x5⅛ inches; XXX stock, genuine linen envelopes, suitable for commercial and general use. Weight, packed, per box (250 in box), 33 ounces	.15	.35	.67	1.27
No. 3C5109 Marlborough style, safety seal, wedding flap, high class envelopes for general correspondence, especially for weddings, invitations, parties, etc. No. 6½; size, 3⅝x6 inches; XXX superior stock. Weight, packed, per box (250 in box), 33 ounces	.18	.42	.81	1.55
No. 3C5111 White Wove Official Envelopes, No. 10, best grade paper; size, 4⅛x9½ inches; XX stock, commercial, high cut. Weight, per box (500 in box), 3 pounds	.26	.60	1.16	2.21
No. 3C5113 Manila (buff color) Official Envelopes, No. 10; size, 4⅛x9½ inches; XX extra heavy stock, suitable for general commercial purposes. Weight, packed, per box (500 in box), 7½ pounds	.13	.29	.55	1.06

Coin and Drug Envelopes.

	100	250	500	1,000
No. 3C5117 Coin Envelopes, first quality, No. 1, Manila (buff color) paper; size, 2¼x4¼ inches. Weight, per box (500 in box), 24 ounces		.16	.30	.58
No. 3C5119 Manila (buff color) Envelopes, drug use, No. 3; size, 2 5-16x3⅝ inches. Weight, packed, per box (1,000 in box), 46 ounces		.14	.26	.49

Composition Books.

No. 3C5357 Elk Composition Book. Size, 6½x8¼ inches. Containing an extra grade of heavy, white ruled writing paper, durably bound in cardboard cover, cloth back, handsome cover design, 70 leaves (140 pages).
Price, each, $0.05
Per dozen.. .55
Per gross.. 5.95
If by mail, postage extra, each, 5 cents.

No. 3C5365 Composition Book. Size, 7⅝x9⅜ inches. Contains an extra grade of heavy white writing paper, half bound Linette sides, red imitation leather back and corners, 200 pages (100 leaves).
Price $0.18
Per dozen.............. 1.80
If by mail, postage extra, each, 17 cents.

REAM PAPER—RULED AND FOLDED.

Excellent Quality Fine Paper for Personal and Commercial Correspondence.

No. 3C5384 Jack Rose Commercial Note, superfine white wove. Size, 5x8 inches. 4 pounds to ream.
Per one-half ream......23c
Per ream..................40c

No. 3C5386 Jack Rose Commercial Note, superfine white wove. Size, 5x8 inches. 5 pounds to ream.
Per one-fourth ream....15c
Per ream..................52c

No. 3C5388 Jack Rose Commercial Note, superfine white wove. Size, 5x8 inches. 6 pounds to ream. Per ream, 60c; per one-fourth ream....17c

No. 3C5390 Carrier Dove Letter, white wove. Size, 8x10 inches. 10 pounds to ream.
One-fourth ream..30c
Per ream..........98c

No. 3C5392 Carrier Dove Foolscap, white wove. Size, 8x12½ inches. 14 pounds to ream. One-fourth ream $0.45
Per ream.......... 1.45

No. 3C5394 Carrier Dove Legal Cap, superfine white wove. Size, 8x12½ inches. 14 pounds to ream.
Per ream, $1.45; per one-fourth ream, 45c

Crepe Paper.

No. 3C5482 For covering photograph frames, fancy boxes, making lamp and candle shades, screens, fans, tablecloths, napkins, hats, flower pot covers and other decorations. Assorted colors. When ordering, be sure and mention color wanted.

American Beauty	Gold
Black	Grass Green
Blue, dark	Heliotrope
Blush Pink, dark	Moss Green
Blush Pink, light	Nile Green
Canary	Peacock Green
Celestial Blue	Purple
Cerise	Ruby Red
Coral, dark	Terra Cotta, dark
Coral, pale	Virgin White
Emerald Green	

Put up in 10-foot rolls, 20 inches wide.
Price, per dozen rolls, 75c; per roll.......7c
If by mail, postage extra, per roll, 5 cents.

Shelf Paper.

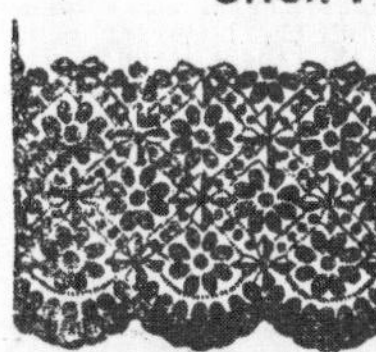

No. 3C5490 Fancy Shelf Paper, extra heavy grade of smooth finish shelf paper, fancy cut out border, embossed and perforated, 12 inches wide and 10 yards long. When ordering be sure and give the color wanted, whether white, blue, pink, yellow or green.
Price, per piece (10 yards)..................4c
Per dozen pieces (120 yards), ...40c
If by mail, postage extra, per 10 yards, 7 cents.

Paper Napkins.

No. 3C5492 Paper Napkins, printed in two colors (new patterns). The finest white silk tissue paper, guaranteed fast colors, assorted, ten patterns to a thousand. We do not sell less than 100 of a pattern. Size, 14x14 inches.
Price, per 1,000 50c; per 100 ....6c
If by mail, postage extra, 10c per hundred.

No. 3C5494.

No. 3C5494 Japanese Crepe Paper Napkins, a good quality soft napkin. Size, 14x14 inches. Price, per 100...........$0.15
Per 1,000....... 1.40

No. 3C5496 Japanese Crepe Paper Napkins, Fancy assorted bright color designs, very fine quality. Size, 14x14.
Price, per 1,000, $1.70; per 100...........18c

Lamp Shade Frames.

No. 3C5498 Wire Frames for Making Lamp Shades, 14 to 18 inches across. Shipping weight, 28 ounces.
Price, each............ 9c
Per dozen..............98c

INKS.

Blue Black Writing Fluid.

Carter's Blue Black Writing Fluid, smooth in flow, absolutely permanent. Best made. Writes blue, turns black.

No. 3C5549 4-ounce round bottle.
Price, per dozen, 79c; each..................7c
Unmailable on account of weight.

New Carmine (Red) Writing Fluid.

This ink has a great brilliancy; does not affect and is not affected by steel pens.

No. 3C5558 Fast Red Fluid. Very brilliant, 1¼-ounce bottle, wide mouth cylinder, black milled top. Price.........................4c

No. 3C5560 2-ounce bottle, wide mouth cylinder. Price..................................7c

No. 3C5562 ½-pint bottle, light glass with hard rubber stopper. Price 45c
Unmailable on account of weight.

Best Black Ink.

Writes black, dries blacker, stays blackest.

No. 3C5564 2-ounce glass bottles. Price, per dozen, 40c; per bottle...4c

No. 3C5568 Pint bottles. Per bottle.........30c

No. 3C5570 Quart bottles. Per bottle.........50c
Unmailable on account of weight.

Premium Raven Black Ink.

No. 3C5578 Carter's Raven Black Ink, 4-ounce wide mouth cylinders.
Price, 4-ounce stand 8c

Copying Ink.

Blue Black Ink, easy flowing and makes perfect copies.

No. 3C5590 4-ounce bottles, wide mouth cylinders.
Price...7c

No. 3C5592 ½-pint bottles with hard rubber tops. Price 30c

No. 3C5594 Pint bottles, with patent pourouts. Price,....................................40c

No. 3C5596 Quart bottles, with patent pourouts. Price..................................75c
Unmailable on account of weight.

Green Ink.

No. 3C5599 Carter's Green Ink, 2-ounce, wide mouth bottle, enameled tops.
Price, per bottle...........4c
Per dozen....................40c
Unmailable on account of weight.

Fountain Pen and Stylographic Ink.

No. 3C5601 Fountain Pen Ink. Writes a brilliant blue, quickly turning black; 4-ounce bottle. French panel, with patent stopper and filler.
Price, per bottle.......$0.20
Per dozen bottles........ 1.89
Unmailable on account of weight.

White, Gold, Invisible Ink, Etc.

No. 3C5606 White Ink. Best grade pure white ink for ornamental writing and flourishing. Used with ordinary steel or automatic pens. Put up in 1-ounce flint glass bottles.
Price, per dozen, 90c; per 1-oz. bottle....9c
If by mail, postage extra, per bottle, 11 cents.

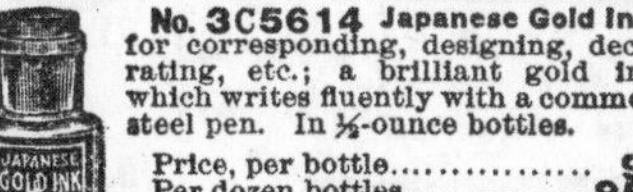

No. 3C5614 Japanese Gold Ink, for corresponding, designing, decorating, etc.; a brilliant gold ink which writes fluently with a common steel pen. In ½-ounce bottles.
Price, per bottle...............9c
Per dozen bottles..............95c
If by mail, postage extra, each, 11c.

No. 3C5617 Invisible Ink. An invisible ink, or secret ink, made readable by application of heat to the paper after the ink is dry, disappearing again when it is cold.
Price, per dozen, 95c; per bottle..........9c
If by mail, postage extra, per bottle 11 cents.

Ink Powders.

No. 3C5619 Ink Powders. Put up in wooden boxes. Each box contains enough powder to make one pint of good ink; blue, green, purple, red or black. In ordering, be sure to give the color wanted.
Price, per dozen, 90c; per box..............9c
If by mail, postage extra, per box, 2 cents.

Carters' Indelible Ink Outfit.

No. 3C5625 Carter's Indelible Ink for marking linen. Labor saving, permanent indelible ink. Requires no preparation and no heat after use. Complete with stretcher, pen and penholder and ink.

Price for complete outfit.................18c
If by mail, postage extra, 5 cents.

Le Page's Prepared Glue.

Strongest glue made, has no offensive odor, is not weakened by age, ready for use, will mend anything: glass, china, wood, leather, marble, crockery, paper, etc.

No. 3C5630 1-ounce bottle.. 6c
No. 3C5634 2-ounce bottle.. 9c
No. 3C5636 4-ounce tin can, 12c
No. 3C5638 ½-pint tin can..22c
No. 3C5640 1-pint tin can...33c
No. 3C5642 1-quart tin can, 55c

Best Mucilage.

No. 3C5648 Best mucilage, flat cylinder stand, flint glass 2-ounce bottle. Price...........5c

No. 3C5650 Best mucilage, 4-ounce bottle. Price..........8c

No. 3C5654 Best mucilage, ½-pint flint glass bottles, with hard rubber tops. Price....15c

No. 3C5660 Best mucilage, 1-pint glass bottles, with hard rubber tops. Price.........25c

No. 3C5662 Best mucilage, 1-quart flint glass bottles. Price......................45c
Unmailable on account of weight.

INKSTANDS.

Smith's Automatic Inkwell.

No. 3C5694 Always ready for use, automatically inks the pen, leaving all surplus ink, and does not soil the fingers. Moulding and evaporation are impossible. Fitted with dip cup stem, admitting the ink at the side instead of the bottom. Completely air tight; 3 inches square.
Price 19c
If by mail, postage extra, 28 cents.

Library Inkstand.

No. 3C5707 Enameled Inkstand, containing two heavy flint glass bottles, mounted on an all iron rack. Size, 4¾x4 inches.
Price......35c
If by mail, postage extra, 24 cents.

Handy Inkstand.

No. 3C5709 Handy Inkstand, finished in bronze, iron cover and case; heavy flint glass bottle, 3 inches high; base, 3½x3½ inches.
Price.........19c
If by mail, postage extra, 18 cents.

No. 3C5726 Common Sense Inkwell, for commercial and general use. No evaporation, no spilling of ink. The most practical and useful inkwell made; 2 inches high.
Price 7c
Postage extra, 12 cents.

Pocket Inkwell, only 28c.

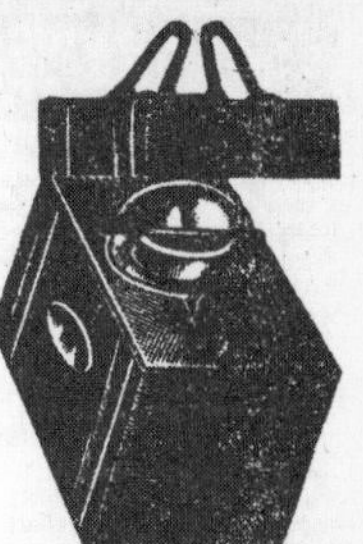

No. 3C5755 New Fancy Pocket and Traveler's Safety Ink Stand. Leather suit case pattern, 2¾ inches long, 1⅝ inches wide. A very desirable gift.
Price...........28c
If by mail, postage extra, 5 cents.

PAPER WEIGHTS.

No. 3C5764 Clear Glass Paper Weight, oblong flat top. Size, 4x2½ inches, with beaded border recess, in which may be mounted photographs, pictures, etc. Price..........6c
If by mail, postage extra, 14 cents.

No. 3C5765 Crystal Glass Paper Weight, same as No. 3C5764, but without beaded border. Size, 4x3½ inches, with picture mounted in recess; assorted subjects. Price 9c
If by mail, postage extra, 14 cents.

No. 3C5766 Crystal Glass Paper Weight, same as No. 3C5765, but without pictures.
Price..3c
If by mail, postage extra, 14 cents.

LEATHER WRITING COMPANIONS.

No. 3C5776 Leatherette, imitation seal, strap with button lock, gusseted pocket inside of flap, pen, and large box compartment for stationery, screw cap inkwell. Size, 6½x10¾ inches. Price..................................52c
If by mail, postage extra, 20 cents.

No. 3C5780 Leather, imitation seal, strap, gusseted pocket with two envelope pockets, otherwise same as No. 3C5776. Size, 8x12 inches. Price..................................98c
If by mail, postage extra, 30 cents.

No. 3C5784 Seal leather, leather strap with large nickel lock and key. Size, 8x12 inches. Price..................................$1.48
If by mail, postage extra, 30 cents.

Peerless Pencil Sharpener.

The Only Practical Machine Made for Sharpening Pencils. Operated without soiling the hands. A child can operate it. Constructed on scientific principles; will sharpen any pencil, short or long, thick or thin, round or angular, to a needle's point, if desired, and never break the lead. It collects its own shavings and graphite chips. It will last a lifetime. Made of best material; cannot get out of order. Used by all colleges, seminaries, and many large business houses, etc.

No. 3C5806 Black enamel. Price..25c
No. 3C5807 Nickel finish, Price..30c
If by mail, postage extra, 48 cents.

LEAD PENCILS.

The following lead pencils are manufactured by one of the largest pencil houses in America. Careful attention has been given to the selection of same with a view of getting not only the very best, but pencils which are especially adapted for school and general purposes at the lowest prices.

No. 3C5810 Graphite Pencils. Round, plain cedar, 7 inches long, extra quality. Weight, per dozen, 6 ounces.
Price, per dozen..............5c
Per gross.......................55c
If by mail, postage extra, per dozen, 6 cents.

No. 3C5813 Self Sharpening Blaisdell Paper Pencil, polished, rubber tip, finest grade lead. Each pencil may be sharpened 30 times, by detaching end of paper with pen knife or any sharp pointed instrument and unrolling, as shown in illustration.
Price, per gross, $1.25; per dozen..................................12c
If by mail, postage extra, per dozen 7 cents.

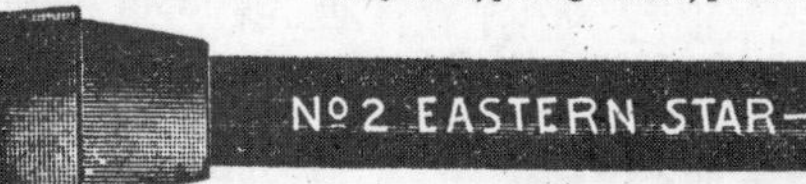

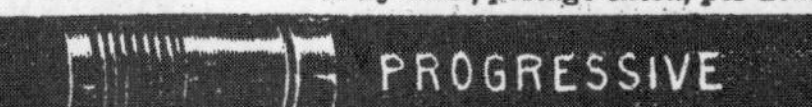

No. 3C5816 Eastern Star Pencil. Round cedar, polished, gilt stamping, fitted with rubber cap, as shown in illustration, 7 inches long; packed one gross in a box.
Price, per dozen........$0.12
Per gross................. 1.38
If by mail, postage extra, per dozen, 5 cents.

No. 3C5820 Express Pencil. Maroon finish, gilt stamp, nickel tip and rubber eraser. This is an A No. 1 pencil, for school and commercial purposes; No. 2 lead. Packed one gross in a box. Price, per gross, $1.30; per dozen..............14c
If by mail, postage extra, per dozen, 5 cents.

No. 3C5823 Progressive. Round, maroon finish, with nickel tip and rubber eraser; extra quality; best pencil for school use; Nos. 2 and 3 lead. Price, per gross, $2.25; per dozen 20c
If by mail, postage extra, per dozen, 6 cents.

No. 3C5827 Fresco Lead Pencil. For school and general purposes. Round, black, polished, with new and special design impressed on the wood. With gilt tip and rubber eraser. Price, per gross, $2.50; per dozen, 23c; per half dozen..........13c
If by mail, postage extra, per dozen, 6 cents.

No. 3C5835 Marvel Lead Pencil. White, polished in spiral and fluted designs. Gilt tip with inserted rubber eraser, stamped in gold; containing extra quality of No. 2 black lead. Packed one dozen in a box.
Price, per gross, **$2.95**; per dozen, **27c**; per half dozen **15c**
If by mail, postage extra, per dozen, 6 cents.

Business Pencils.

MERCANTILE

No. 3C5839 Mercantile, round finished, in black, satin and rosewood, an excellent pencil for general business and commercial purposes; fitted with superior grade Nos. 2 and 3 lead. Weight, per dozen, 6 ounces.
Price, per gross, **$2.80**; per dozen, **25c**; per half dozen **15c**
If by mail, postage extra, per dozen, 6 cents.

817 EAGLE DIAGRAPH No

No. 3C5855 Eagle Diagraph Pencil, with eraser, incased in nickel plated tip; natural polish, stamped in silver. We especially recommend it for accountants, bookkeepers and correspondents. No. 2 and No. 3 lead.
Price, per gross, **$2.80**; per dozen, **24c**; per half dozen **13c**
If by mail, postage extra, per dozen, 5 cents.

No. 3C5859 The Studio Lead Pencil. Highly polished, olive finish, gilt stamp, fitted with nickel tip and rubber eraser. Contains first quality of Nos. 2 and 3 black lead.
Price, per gross, **$4.20**; per dozen, **37c**; per half dozen **20c**
If by mail, postage extra, per dozen, 5 cents.

CARPENTER

Carpenters' Pencils. Containing best grade of Medium No. 2 black lead, oval, polished cedar. Packed one gross in a box.
No. 3C5880 7 inches long. Price, per gross, **$2.25**; per dozen, **20c**; per half dozen **12c**
No. 3C5882 9 inches long. Price, per gross, **$2.45**; per dozen, **25c**; per half dozen **15c**
No. 3C5884 12 inches long. Price, per gross, **$3.25**; per dozen, **30c**; per half dozen **18c**
If by mail, postage extra, per dozen, any length, 8 cents.

MEPHISTO COPYING INK PENCILS.

No 73B "MEPHISTO" COPYING HARDTMUTH

No. 3C5887 Hardtmuth's Copying Ink Pencil, for duplicating, manifolding and all general purposes; violet polished, silver stamped; violet ink lead. The most perfect copying ink pencil made.
Price, per gross, **$4.50**; per dozen **44c**; per half dozen. **24c**
If by mail, postage extra, per dozen, 3 cents.
No. 3C5889 Hardtmuth's Copying Pencil, with enameled mouth piece, made expressly for trainmen, conductors' and travelers' use; otherwise same as No. 3C5887.
Price, per gross, **$4.50**; per dozen, **44c**; per half dozen, **24c**
If by mail, postage extra, per dozen, 4 cents.
No. 3C5891 Hardtmuth's Famous Koh-i-Noor, compressed lead ink copying pencil, yellow polished, gold stamp.
Price, per gross, **$8.25**; per dozen, **90c**; each **8c**
If by mail, postage extra, per dozen, 4 cents.

INDELIBLE COPYING INK PENCIL.

No 79C "Madura" COPYING

No. 3C6180 Madura 79C. It is undoubtedly the best and most durable pencil made in this or the old country. For duplicating, manifolding and all general purposes it is conceded by pencil manufacturers to have no equal. Violet polished, silver stamped, violet ink lead, with enameled mouthpiece. Length, 7 inches.
Price, per gross, **$3.98**; per dozen, **35c**; per half dozen **20c**
If by mail, postage extra, per dozen, 6 cents.

No. 3C5919 Program Pencil. Round, thin, assorted colors, gilt tip and tassels. Suitable for balls, card parties, etc.
Price, per gross, **$1.75**; per dozen **15c**
If by mail, postage extra, per dozen, 3 cents.
No. 3C5927 Perfection Pencil, with Sharpener, round natural finish, with inserted rubber eraser, silver stamp, Nos. 2 and 3 lead. The sharpener is simple in mechanism, clean, neat and useful. Weight, per dozen, 9 ounces.
Price, per dozen, **45c**; each **4c**
If by mail, postage extra, each, 3 cents.

EAGLE PENCIL CO.

No. 3C5941 Magic Automatic Combination Knife and Pencil Sharpener. The easiest knife in the world to open; no stiff joints, consequently no broken thumb nails. The blade moves out or in when pressure is applied on the end opposite the blade. Highly polished black handle; gilt stamped.
Price, per dozen, **$2.00**; each **20c**
If by mail, postage extra, each, 3 cents.

SCHOOL CRAYONS.

We list the celebrated Crayola School Crayons. The crayons that received the award at the St. Louis exposition. They are permanent, waterproof colors, that are not injurious to the hands, and will not soil the clothes. These crayons can be used on almost any surface, and will make bright, clear, permanent colors.
No. 3C5960 Crayola No. 47. For coloring maps or pictures, sketching, etc. Contains twenty-four assorted waterproof crayons, 4 inches long, in cardboard box.
Price, per box **7c**
Per dozen boxes **80c**
If by mail, postage extra, per box, 5 cents.
No. 3C5961 Made expressly for school use, seven bright assorted crayons, 4 inches long, black, blue, green, orange, red, violet and yellow, in cardboard box.
Price, per box **5c**
Per dozen boxes **55c**
If by mail, postage extra, per box, 5c.

No. 3C5962 Crayola No. 41. Fourteen assorted waterproof colors in wooden box, for coloring maps, pictures and general school work. Price, per box **5c**
Per dozen boxes **55c**
If by mail, postage extra, per box, 5 cents.
No. 3C5964 Crayola No. 57. Twelve assorted waterproof colors, 4 inches long, in cardboard box, together with a series of outline pictures for drawing and coloring.
Price, per dozen boxes, **45c**; per box **4c**
If by mail, postage extra, per box, 5 cents.
No. 3C5967 Crayola No. 49. Made especially for studio and educational school work. Fourteen assorted waterproof crayons, 4 inches long, together with a 16-page outline picture book in cardboard box. Price, per box **7c**
Per dozen boxes **80c**
If by mail, postage extra, per box, 5 cents.
No. 3C5969 Colored Crayons for general use. Assorted, round polished wood, gold stamp, full length. Brown, blue, yellow, black, violet, red and green.
Price, per dozen boxes, **$1.95**; per box **18c**
If by mail, postage extra, each, 4 cents.

Staonal Marking Crayons.

STAONAL No. 3.

Staonal No. 3. Waterproof. For marking on leather, lumber, tin, barrels, cases, delivery parcels, checking way bills, newspaper and bulletin work, glass, canvas, etc. Length 5 inches.
No. 3C5984 Black. Price, per dozen, **25c**; two for **5c**
No. 3C5985 Blue. Price, per dozen, **25c**; two for **5c**
No. 3C5986 Red. Price, per dozen, **25c**; two for **5c**
If by mail, postage extra, for two, any color, 3 cents.

No. 3C5988 Star Indelible Marking Crayon. Waterproof. For marking lumber, paper, tinware, etc. 4½ inches long, made in blue, red and black.
Price, per gross, **$1.60**; per dozen **15c**
If by mail, postage extra, per dozen, 7 cents.

Compass and Divider.

No. 3C5992 Eagle Compass and Divider, reliable in its work and useful for school children, mechanics, artists, draftsmen and architects; nickel plated, regulated by spring and screw adjustment, each in neat box, with nickel box containing six extra leads.
Price, per dozen, **$1.80**; each **16c**
If by mail, postage extra, 4 cents.

Pantagraph for Enlarging Purposes.
Full Instructions Accompany Each Outfit.

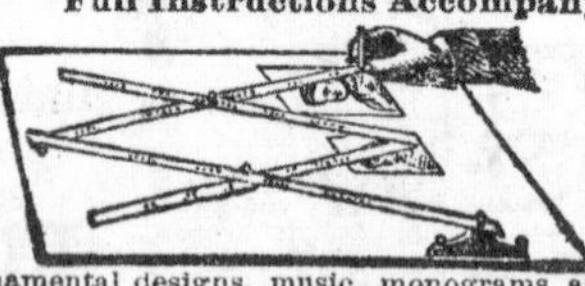

No. 3C5993 Style A. A simple mechanical apparatus, which, without any instruction, enables one to enlarge portraits, using ordinary cabinet sized pictures. Maps, ornamental designs, music, monograms and patterns can be enlarged or reduced to any size by the use of this instrument.
Price, each **10c**
If by mail, postage extra, 12 cents.
No. 3C5994 Style B. Has very neat and substantial trimmings, clean cut figures. Price, in box, each **35c**
No. 3C5995 Style C. Brass Mounted, with brass elbow joint wheel, pencil holder and movable point.
Price, in box, each **$1.25**
No. 3C5996 Style D. Heavily mounted, with nickel plated elbow joint wheel, pencil holder and exchangeable point.
Price, in box, each **$1.90**
If by mail, postage extra, 12 cents.

Penholders.

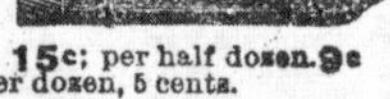

No. 3C6007 Latest Improved Penholder, polished cedar handle, japanned tip. 6¾ inches long. Packed one dozen in a box. Price, per dozen, **15c**; per half dozen **9c**
If by mail, postage extra, per dozen, 5 cents.
No. 3C6013 Swell, Japanned Handle, Double Tip Penholder nickel, highly polished, assorted finishes in natural red and black. 7 inches long. Packed one dozen in a box. Price, per dozen, **25c**; per half dozen **15c**
If by mail, postage extra, per dozen, 6 cents.
No. 3C6029 Cork Tip, Tapering Penholder, cedar, black, highly polished, silver stamp. A very handy and convenient holder. 7 inches long. Packed one dozen in a box.
Price, per dozen, **38c**; per half dozen **25c**
If by mail, postage extra, per dozen, 6 cents.
No. 3C6045 Glass Writing Pen. Twisted glass for point in nickeled barrel. Polished handle. 6¼ inches long.
Price, per dozen, **45c**; each **4c**
If by mail, postage extra, each, 2 cents.

AUTOMATIC SHADING PEN

No. 3C6053 Automatic Shading Pens, for engrossing, fancy lettering, card writing, etc. 7½ inches long.

Nos.	0	1	2	3	4	5
Width	1/16-inch	⅛-inch	3/16-inch	¼-inch	⅜-inch	½-inch

Price, each **9c**
No. 3C6055 No. 6. ¾ inch wide. Price **11c**
No. 3C6057 No. 8. ⅞ inch wide. Price **11c**
If by mail, postage extra, each, 2 cents.

Ink for Automatic Shading Pens.

No. 3C6059 Shading Pen Ink. Prepared especially for use with automatic shading pens, in wide mouth, round flint glass 1½-ounce bottles. Colors, red, violet, blue, green, black or gold. Price, per dozen bottles, **95c**; per bottle **9c**
If by mail, postage extra, per bottle, 13 cents.

Colored Erasive Rubbers.

No. 3C6060 A New Departure in Rubber Erasers. Red erasive rubber, beveled. Specially adapted for school and commercial use.
Price, per dozen, **10c**; per half dozen **7c**
Per pound (120 pieces) **75c**
If by mail, postage extra, per dozen, 3 cents.
No. 3C6062 Same as No. 3C6060, but green erasive rubber.
Price, per dozen, **10c**; per half dozen **7c**
Per pound (120 pieces) **75c**
If by mail, postage extra, per dozen, 3 cents.

Ink and Pencil Eraser.

No. 3C6063 Combined Ink and Pencil Eraser, wood center, best quality erasive rubber.
Price, per dozen **78c**; each **7c**
If by mail, postage extra, each, 3 cents.

Rubber Erasers.

No. 3C6065 Cabinet Bevel Point Oblong Rubber Eraser. Silk finish, superior quality, small size.
Price, per dozen, **8c**; six for **5c**
If by mail, postage extra, for six, 3 cents.

No. 3C6069 New Style Eraser, beveled ends. Contains a superior quality of best erasive rubber. Packed one dozen in a box.
Price, per dozen, **20c**; per half dozen **12c**
If by mail, postage extra, per dozen, 7 cents.

No. 3C6075 Circular Eraser, for typewriter, ink or pencil. The circular eraser is very convenient, giving a sharp, continuous edge for use until worn out.
Price, each **3c**
Per gross, **$3.95**; per dozen **35c**
If by mail, postage extra, each, 2 cents.

Rubber Bands.

No. 3C6079 Assortment of superior quality Rubber Bands, for office and home use, packed in a box 1⅞ x 3½ x 6½ inches. Weight, 6 ounces.
Price, per box **$0.20**
Per dozen boxes **2.25**
If by mail, postage extra, per box, 7 cents.
No. 3C6081 Gray Thread Bands of superior quality, made from best elastic rubber stock. We do not sell less than one ounce packed in a box. When ordering be sure to state whether No. 10, No. 12 or No. 14 is wanted. No. 10, 1½ inches long, 290 bands, one ounce; No. 12, 1⅞ inches long, 225 bands, one ounce; No. 14, 2 inches long, 165 bands, one ounce. Price, per ounce **$0.18**
Per ½ pound **1.30**
Per pound **2.48**
No. 3C6083 Gray Rubber Bands, ⅛-inch wide. No. 000⅛, 3 inches long, 24 bands, one ounce; No. 0000⅛, 3½ inches long, 20 bands, one ounce. Price, per ounce, either size **$0.18**
Per ½ pound **1.30**
Per pound **2.48**
We do not sell less than one ounce.
No. 3C6085 Gray Rubber Bands, ¼ inch wide. No. 00¼, 2½ inches long, 18 bands, one ounce; No. 000¼, 3 inches long, 16 bands, one ounce; No. 0000¼, 3½ inches long, 12 bands, one ounce. Price, per ounce (either style) **$0.18**
Per ½ pound **1.30**
Per pound **2.48**
No. 3C6086 Gray Rubber Bands, ⅜-inch wide. No. 000⅜, 3 inches long, 12 bands, one ounce; No. 0000⅜, 3½ inches long, 10 bands, one ounce. Price, 3 bands for **$0.05**
Per ounce **.16**
Per ½ pound **1.30**
Per pound **2.48**
Postage extra on all rubber bands, 2 cents per ounce.

The Handy Pencil Holder.

No. 3C6091 Handy Pencil Holder, leatherette, plush lined, with metal spring, will hold four pencils.
Price, each **7c**
Per dozen **75c**
If by mail, postage extra, each, 2 cents.

The "Au Fait" Pencil Holder.

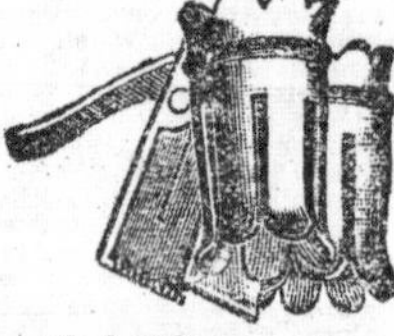

No. 3C6093 Latest Improved Pencil Holder. Can be attached to pocket, suspenders or trousers band; nickel plated. Has double barrel, which may be adjusted to hold any size lead pencil, penholder or fountain pen. Clamp securely attaches holder to garment. Price, each **5c**
Per dozen **55c**
If by mail, postage extra, each, 2 cents.

New Acme Pencil Sharpener.

No. 3C6099 With double edge blade. When one edge becomes dull the blade can be reversed, thus there is an equivalent of two blades with each sharpener. Combines simplicity with perfection.
Price **16c**
If by mail, postage extra, 3 cents.

Envelope Opener.

No. 3C6110 Envelope Opener, made of best quality steel, for opening envelopes and documents, for cutting magazine pages, etc. Length of blade, 4½ inches. Price **10c**
If by mail, postage extra, 5 cents.

Initial Seal Letters.

No. 3C6113 Initial Seal, for use with sealing wax; length, 3 inches; black enamel handle, nickeled metal die with Old English initial letter. In ordering be sure and mention initial letter desired.
Price **9c**
If by mail, postage extra, 3 cents.

Sealing Wax.

No. 3C6117 Sanford's Red Express Sealing Wax; four 4-ounce sticks to pound or eight 2-ounce sticks to pound. Price, per 2-ounce stick **4c**
Per 4-ounce stick, **8c**; per pound (either size) **30c**

No. 3C6119 Perfumed Sealing Wax, for use in fine correspondence; five sticks assorted colors in box. Weight per box, 5 ounces.
Price, per box **$0.15**
Per dozen **1.75**
If by mail, postage extra, per box, 5 cents.

POSTAL SCALES.

No. 3C6123 Scale No. 1. Weighs up to 3 pounds and is 4 inches high, 4 inches wide, 6½ inches long. Price.......96c
If by mail, postage extra, 22 cents.

No. 3C6125 Scale No. 2. Weighs up to 4 pounds and is 4 inches high, 4 inches wide, 6½ inches long. Price...$1.46
If by mail, postage extra, 26 cents.

FOUNTAIN PENS.

STANDARD SELF-FILLING FOUNTAIN PEN.

Not a Novelty—A 20th Century Necessity.

SQUEEZE IT.

No. 3C6130 The Standard fills and cleans itself. The self-filling pen does away entirely with the old fashioned fountain pen dropper, which is always easily broken, easily lost. Any child can fill it, as there is no intricate mechanism, no dropper, no smearing fingers and desk, no overflowing, and no taking apart to clean. The workmanship and material in the Standard are the best. It has perfect under feed, best polished hard rubber barrel, extra heavy 14 K No. 3 solid gold pen, iridium point. Regular length.
Retail price, $2.50; our price..........$1.50
If by mail, postage extra, 5 cents.

No. 3C6133 Challenge Guaranteed 14K Gold Fountain Pen. Absolutely perfect, guaranteed non-leakable, cap feed. This is positively the best low priced fountain pen in the market. Packed complete in cardboard case, with filler and directions.
Price..........50c
If by mail, postage extra, 5 cents.

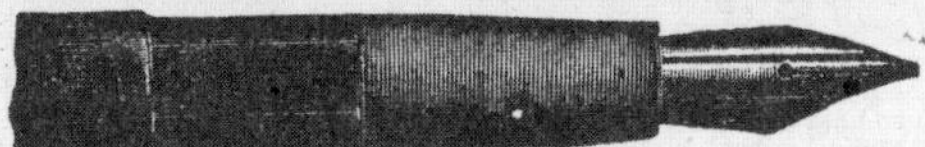

No. 3C6137 High Grade Fountain Pen, fitted with 14K solid gold No. 5 pen. The construction and interior mechanism is of the highest order; under feed, absolutely perfect, hard rubber barrel of best quality and finish. Equal to any $5.00 pen. Packed one pen complete in cardboard case, with filler and directions.
Price..........$1.10

No. 3C6138 Same as No. 3C6137, but fitted with a No. 2 solid gold pen. Price..........75c
If by mail, postage extra, 5 cents.

No. 3C6139 Same as No. 3C6138, but fitted with two solid gold 14K bands around barrel. Packed one pen complete in cardboard box, with filler and directions. Price..........$1.30
If by mail, postage extra, 4 cents.

No. 3C6143 Never Leak Fountain Pen. A new fountain pen, made expressly for ladies. It can be carried with safety in pocket book, shopping bag or pocket. Guaranteed non-leakable. Fitted with No. 2, 14K solid gold, medium point pen. Packed complete in cardboard case, with filler and directions.
Price..........(If by mail, postage extra, 3 cents)..........79c

No. 3C6147 College Fountain Pen. Guaranteed 14-karat solid gold pen. The new feeding device is the simplest and most perfect yet produced. No complicated parts to get out of order. Price..........85c
If by mail, postage extra, 5 cents.

No. 3C6149 Correspondent Fountain Pen, fitted with a 14-karat gold pen and chased hard rubber barrel; absolutely perfect, guaranteed non-leakable. The construction and internal mechanism are of the most improved and highest order, both as to quality and workmanship. Made with latest patented detachable reservoir which unscrews from the bottom and not from the top like the old style pens.
Retail price, $2.50; our price..........$1.10
If by mail, postage extra, 3 cents.

No. 3C6151 Same as No. 3C6149, but handsomely ornamented with heavy 18-karat gold bands. Price..........$1.50
If by mail, postage extra, 5 cents.

No. 3C6155 Fountain Pen, fitted with a No. 2 14-karat gold pen. Made of best quality rubber, with under feed. Packed, one complete, in wooden box, with filler and directions.
Price,..........95c
If by mail, postage extra, 5 cents.

Stylographic Pen.

No. 3C6157 Made of hard vulcanite. The flow of ink is produced and regulated by a steel needle. This is the best and most practical stylographic pen made. Each pen packed in a separate box with glass filler and directions.
Price..........(If by mail, postage extra, 4 cents)..........35c

Fountain Pens for School Use and General Purposes.

No. 3C6171 Eagle Fountain Pen, black enamel finish, hexagon shape, with imitation gilt band, containing glass vial filled with ink, to which is attached the feeder holding a non-corrosive pen; the most complete, useful and finest fountain pen made. Price, per dozen, 70c; each..........6c
If by mail, postage extra, each, 3 cents.

No. 3C6173 Fountain Pen, black enamel finish, round or hexagon, with imitation gilt band. Containing glass vial filled with ink ready for use. The most complete, useful and cheapest fountain pen made. Price..........(If by mail, postage extra, 3 cents)..........9c

STEEL PENS.

The illustrations show exact size of pens. We quote a varied line and warrant every one to be the best made.
If by mail, postage on all pens extra, per ¼ gross, 3 cents; per dozen, 2 cents.

Spencerian Steel Pens.

No. 3C6264 Vertical, No. 37M, particularly adapted for schools and correspondents.
Price, per dozen..........7c
Per ¼ gross (36 pens)..........20c
Per gross..........75c

No. 3C6266 Congressional, No. 28, silverine, point blunt and circular, easy quill action, extra long wearing. Price, per dozen..........7c
Per ¼ gross (36 pens)..........20c
Per gross..........75c

No. 3C6268 Senate, No 26, point medium fine; best pen made for constant use.
Price, per dozen..........7c
Per ¼ gross (36 pens)..........20c
Per gross..........75c

No. 3C6270 Bank, No. 9, point long and flexible; for accountants, tellers and clerks generally. Price, per dozen..........7c
Per ¼ gross (36 pens)..........20c
Per gross..........75c

No. 3C6272 School, No. 5, point fine, medium in flexibility; much used in schools.
Price, per dozen..........7c
Per ¼ gross (36 pens)..........20c
Per gross..........75c

No. 3C6278 College, No. 1. The best pen made; point fine, elastic, action perfect, largely used by the best penmen of this country, Canada and England. Price, per dozen..........7c
Per ¼ gross (36 pens)..........20c
Per gross..........75c

Esterbrook Steel Pens.

No. 3C6280 Bank, No. 14, bronze finish, medium point, an excellent and popular pen for business use.
Price, per dozen..........5c
Per ¼ gross (36 pens)..........14c
Per gross..........42c

No. 3C6281 Falcon 048. Medium point, gray finish. An excellent pen for general business purposes. Price, per dozen..........6c
Per ¼ gross (36 pens)..........17c
Per gross..........52c

No. 3C6283 Ball Pointed Scribe, No. 516 F, gray finish, extra fine point.
Price, per dozen..........8c
Per ¼ gross (36 pens)..........22c
Per gross..........80c

No. 3C6284 Judge's Quill, No. 312, gray finish, fine point stub, a large engrossing pen, very popular.
Price, per dozen..........6c
Per ¼ gross (36 pens)..........17c
Per gross..........52c

No. 3C6286 School, No. 444, bronze finish, medium fine; largely used in the public schools.
Price, per gross, 34c; per ¼ gross (36 pens) 10c

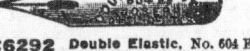

No. 3C6288 Ladies' Falcon 182. Fine and easy action. Especially adapted for ladies. Gray finish. Price, per dozen..........5c
Per ¼ gross (36 pens)..........14c
Per gross..........46c

Gillott's Steel Pens.

No. 3C6290 Magnum Quill, No. 601 E. F., extra fine point, for fine and ordinary writing, very popular for general use. Price, per doz. 6c
Per gross, 53c; per ¼ gross (36 pens)...16c

No. 3C6291 Gillott's Famous Principality Pen, No. 1, bronze finish, extra fine points, an excellent pen for flourishing and ornamental work. Price, per dozen..........7c
Per gross, 78c; per ¼ gross (36 pens)...20c

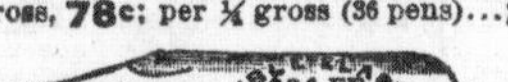

No. 3C6292 Double Elastic, No. 604 E. F., extra fine point. The original double elastic pen, a favorite with professors of penmanship and teachers in business colleges.
Price, per gross, 53c; per ¼ gross (36 pens) 17c

No. 3C6293 Gillott's Famous Extra Fine No. 303 Pen, bronze finish. Price, per doz. 7c
Per ¼ gross (36 pens)..........20c
Per gross..........77c

No. 3C6297 Diamond Stub, No. 1008 a very desirable pen for commercial use. Used by bankers and business men.
Price, per ¼ gross (36 pens)..........17c
Per gross..........55c

No. 3C6301 Gillott's Court House Pen, No. 1064, bronze color. A pen for unshaded and smooth writing, round point.
Per ¼ gross (36 pens)..........25c
Per gross..........85c

Paper Files.

No. 3C6370 Hanging Paper File, tinned wire back and hook with protected point. Weight, packed, 9 ounces. Price, per doz., 32c; each....3c
If by mail, postage extra, each, 2 cents.

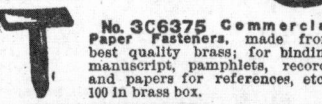

No. 3C6374 Jumbo Standing Paper File, 4-inch lacquered iron base, wire 8 inches long. Weight, packed, 9 ounces.
Price..........5c
If by mail, postage extra, 4 cents.

Paper Fasteners.

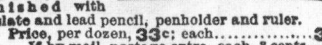

No. 3C6375 Commercial Paper Fasteners, made from best quality brass; for binding manuscript, pamphlets, records and papers for references, etc.; 100 in brass box.

No. 1. Length, ½ inch. Price, per 100......6c
No. 2. Length, ⅝ inch. Price, per 100......8c
No. 3. Length, ¾ inch. Price, per 100......9c
No. 4. Length, 1 inch. Price, per 100......10c
If by mail, postage extra, 3 cents.

SCHOOL SUPPLIES

Scholars' Companion.

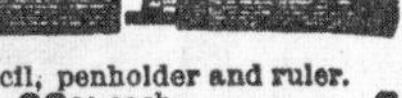

No. 3C6400 Turned Wood Case, furnished with slate and lead pencil, penholder and ruler.
Price, per dozen, 33c; each..........3c
If by mail, postage extra, each, 3 cents.

Swivel Pencil Box.

No. 3C6408 Swivel Pencil Box. Size, 8¼x2x1¼ inches, polished hardwood with chromo top, made in three sections, having eight compartments, fitted with pencil, penholder, pen and rubber eraser.
Price, per dozen, $1.35; each..........12c
If by mail, postage extra, each, 7 cents.

Rosewood Pencil Box.

No. 3C6412 Rosewood Pencil Box. Lithographed top, assorted designs, three compartments, fitted with a glass inkwell, lock and key. Size, 8½x2¾x1¾ inches.
Price, per dozen, 90c; each..........8c
If by mail, postage extra, each, 5 cents.

School Bags.

No. 3C6422 Waterproof School Bag. Made of black oilcloth, bound and stitched, with stitched shoulder strap. Size, 10x13¾ inches. Weight, packed for shipment, 6 ounces.
Price, each..........8c
Per dozen..........90c
If by mail, postage extra, each, 6 cents.

No. 3C6432 Heavy Brown Canvas School Bag, with gusset, bound with tape, fitted with two fancy straps and buckles, extra heavy leather shoulder straps with buckle. Size, 9x11½ inches. Weight, packed for shipment, 11 ounces.
Price..........21c
If by mail, postage extra, 12 cents.

School Straps.

No. 3C6440 Book Straps, flexible leather handle, 36-inch strap.
Price, each, 8c
Per dozen. 90c
If by mail, postage extra, each, 5c.

No. 3C6441 Book or Skate Strap, flexible leather, grained finish. 40 inches long.
Price.....6c
If by mail, postage extra, 5c.

Portable Blackboards.

No. 3C6474 Portable Blackboard of cloth with best black liquid slating surface, mounted on rollers with hook and complete for hanging.

Size	Price	Size	Price
2x2 feet	$0.25	4x4 feet	$0.98
3x3 feet	.60	4x5 feet	1.18
3x4 feet	.70	4x6 feet	1.42
3x5 feet	.98	4x7 feet	1.58
3x6 feet	1.25		

With music lines, $1.25 additional.

Chalk Crayons for School Use.

No. 3C6479 A special prepared white chalk crayon for school purposes. Round. Packed 1 gross in a box, 100 boxes to the case.
Price per dozen boxes, 55c; each..$0.05
For 50 boxes..........2.50
Per case, 100 boxes..........4.85

No. 3C6484 Colored Chalk Crayons; round; one gross, assorted colors in box. Weight, 2¼ lbs. Price, per box (1 gross)..21c

Waverly Arch File.

A double arch file in which the arches swing outward, opening and closing together, either arch operating both; strong, durable and well finished.

No. 3C6520 Note size, 7x12 inches, weight, 20 ounces, file and board only.
Price..........24c

No. 3C6522 Letter size, 9x14½ inches, weight, 18 ounces, file and board only. Price..........24c

No. 3C6524 Cap size, 9x17 inches, weight 20 ounces, file and board only. Price....24c

No. 3C6526 Perforator for Waverly File. Price, (If by mail, postage extra 5c.) 22c

No. 3C6528 Alphabetical Index for Waverly File. Price..........3c
If by mail, postage extra, 2 cents.

Striped Wood Board Clips.

Nickeled Clip, with brass wire spring, improved metal shoulder for papers to square against, and metal eye to hang up by.

No. 3C6534 Note Size. Weight, 14 ounces. Price....27c

No. 3C6536 Letter Size. Weight, 20 ounces. Price....30c

No. 3C6538 Cap Size. Weight, 24 ounces. Price....33c

Unmailable.

Favorite Letter File.

Alphabetically indexed, will hold 3,000 letters, adjusting itself in thickness proportionately to the number of papers it contains. Papers may be returned without tearing or defacing. Indispensable for every office, home and school.

No. 3C6542 Note Size, 6x11¼ in. Price..23c
No. 3C6544 Letter Size, 9x11¼ in. Price..23c
No. 3C6546 Invoice Size, 9¼x15 in. Price 45c
If by mail, postage extra, each, 19 cents.

Falcon Letter File.

No. 3C6552 The only complete file made. It opens automatically. Will stand alone, allowing the free use of both hands for filing letters. Indexed both right and left. Size, 10x12 inches. Price....40c
If by mail, postage extra, 34 cents.

Bankers' Cases.

Made of the very best duck cloth. Arranged so as to hold notes, receipts, bills and all valuable papers in a compact form. Alphabetically indexed.

No. 3C6560 Size, 5x9¾ inches, 21 pockets. Price....70c
If by mail, postage extra, 20 cents.

No. 3C6562 Size, 5x9¾ inches. Monthly; 12 pockets. Price....60c
If by mail, postage extra, 14 cents.

No. 3C6564 Size, 5x9¾ inches. Daily, 31 pockets. Price....75c
If by mail, postage extra, 31 cents.

Improved Paper Fastener.

No. 3C6590 A new, improved Automatic Paper Fastener and Staple Driver, for binding leaflets, papers, pamphlets, etc. Simple in construction, substantially made, cannot get out of order, works perfectly, always ready for use. Price....90c
If by mail, postage extra, 30 cents.

No. 3C6594 Staples for the Improved Automatic Paper Fastener. Price, per 1,000, 40c; per box of 500....23c
If by mail, postage extra, per box, 3 cents.

Blotting Pads.

No. 3C6602 Desk Blotting Pad, 19¼x24¼ inches, for holding No. 3C6608 blotters. Weight, packed for shipment, 32 ounces. Price, without blotters...30c

No. 3C6608 Climax, 19x24 inches, for use in No. 3C6602 desk pad. Price, per sheet....5c
Unmailable.

Hektograph Duplicator.

Hektograph Duplicator for making copies of pen or type written originals in one or more colors. Copies resemble the original, and the manner of using it is so simple that a boy can work it. Invaluable for making circulars, examination papers, postal cards and other notices and all similar work.

No. 3C6644 Postal Size, 4¼x6¼ inches. Price....(Shipping weight, 2 lbs.)....75c
No. 3C6646 Note Size, 6¼x10 inches. Price....(Shipping weight, 3 lbs.)....$1.50
No. 3C6648 Letter Size, 10x12¼ inches. Price....(Shipping weight, 5 lbs.)....$2.60
No. 3C6650 Cap Size, 10x15 inches. Price....(Shipping weight, 6 lbs.)....$3.75
No. 3C6652 Folio Size, 12x18 inches. Price....(Shipping weight, 8 lbs.)....$5.75

Hektograph Supplies.

No. 3C6654 Hektograph Composition for refilling, put up in 2½ and 5-pound tins. Price, per pound....60c

No. 3C6656 Hektograph Duplicating Ink, violet, green, blue or red. Per bottle....20c

No. 3C6658 Black. Price, per bottle....40c
Weight, packed for shipment, 10 ounces.

Duplicator Paper.

No. 3C6660 Note Size, medium. Weight, each, 26 ounces. Per pad of 250 sheets....24c
No. 3C6662 Note Size, heavy. Weight, each, 30 ounces. Price, per pad of 250 sheets....28c
No. 3C6664 Letter Size, medium. Weight, each, 43 ounces. Per pad of 250 sheets....44c
No. 3C6666 Letter Size, heavy. Weight, each, 52 ounces. Per pad of 250 sheets....54c
No. 3C6668 Cap Size, heavy. Weight, each, 4½ pounds. Price, per pad of 250 sheets....72c

The Adder.

No. 3C7488 The Arithmetic Machine of the Century. A thoroughly practical, simple and durable instrument, beautifully finished in nickel. It is mechanically perfect, made of metal throughout; indestructible, will last a lifetime. It will add any number of columns of figures, one, two and three columns at a time, with positive accuracy; for simplicity, durability and beauty of finish, for adding, tallying, verifying mental work, etc., it has no equal. Invaluable to mining engineers, merchants, manufacturers, warehousemen, cotton compressors, coal dealers. Price....$2.75
If by mail, postage extra, 18 cents.

Perfection Adding Machine.

No. 3C7489 A practical article, beautifully and substantially made of nickel, for adding figures. The greatest invention of the age in the mathematical line. It will add figures, proving your trial balance, while you can carry on a conversation at the same time. It will enable experts to add more rapidly and with the certainty of getting the correct result at the first computation. It makes experts of those who could never have mastered ordinary addition. Made entirely of nickel, highly polished. Price, each....39c
If by mail, postage extra, 5 cents.

20th Century Improved Adder.

No. 3C7490 Originated and devised by Prof. Alonzo B. Cole. Improved Adder. The only device made that will add fractions, numerals and whole numbers. Price....8c
If by mail, postage extra, 2 cents.

TYPEWRITERS AND SUPPLIES.

An Up to Date Typewriter for only $35.00.

Chicago Typewriter. This is the most improved typewriter made. It will equal in durability, quality and workmanship, any one of the $100.00 machines, and for all around excellence it is the best that can be found. This is one of the most practical machines in the market. It is easily managed, quickly repaired, and can be taken care of and operated very economically. It has 32 keys, which print 90 different characters, the maximum reached by any typewriter; is fitted with the universal key board and a steel type wheel. These type wheels are interchangeable, and in less than a minute's time can be changed, not only as to style of letter, but also from one language to another, and to the medical and mathematical wheels. The advantage of this will be evident to all. Weight, packed for shipment, 40 pounds.

No. 3C7500 Our special price....$35.00

The Little Gem Typewriter.

No. 3C7491 A practical machine for the household, and a kindergarten instructor or of merit. Simple of operation, adjustable to single or double spacing, easily inked, and may be used to write on a book, package or any other object as well as ordinary typewriter paper. Price....69c
If by mail, postage extra, 15 cents.

The Practical Typewriter.

No. 3C7492 A Strong, Handsome Steel Nickel Plated Typewriter, suitable for business and private use. Made on entirely new principles, easily understood and operated. Has roller feed with spring adjustment, full line of characters, bell, large and small letters, writing always in sight; positive and perfect alignment; will take any width of paper up to 8½ inches. Price....$3.55
Weight, packed for shipment, 5 pounds.

TYPEWRITER SUPPLIES.

Perfection Note Book and Copy Holder.

No. 3C7522 Combination Note Book and Copy Holder. The latest and most practical Stenographers' Note Book and Copy Holder in existence. By opening wire support at the back it is converted into a stand. It will increase the speed of the operator. It may be held in the hand or upon the knee. It is convenient for carrying from place to place and saves much of the labor of writing and copying by keeping the notes in systematic order. Japanned finish. Weight, packed for shipment, 3 pounds. Retail price, $1.50. Our price....98c

No. 3C7524 Typewriter Ink. Colors, black, blue, green, purple or red. Put up in ¼-ounce bottles. Price, per bottle...10c
If by mail, postage extra, including wooden case, 8 cents.

No. 3C7528 Typewriter Ribbons for the Chicago, Smith Premier, Oliver, Caligraph, Hammond, Remington and other standard machines. When ordering, be sure to state whether blue, green, black or copying ribbon is wanted; also give name of machine. Weight, packed for shipment, 4 ounces. Price, per dozen, $4.75; each....45c
If by mail, postage extra, each, 4 cents.

No. 3C7532 Typewriter Oil. Best quality. Weight, packed for shipment, 10 ounces. Price, per bottle....15c
If by mail, postage extra, each, 10 cents.

No. 3C7534 Typewriter Cleaning Brush. Weight, packed for shipment, 3 ounces. Price....18c
If by mail, postage extra, each, 3 cents.

Typewriter Paper. Matchless Brand, for all standard typewriters. 500 sheets to the ream. We do not break reams.

No. 3C7536 Size, 8½x11 inches, plain white paper. Price, per ream....58c
No. 3C7540 Size, 8½x13 inches, plain white paper. Price, per ream....65c
No. 3C7544 Size, 8½x10 inches, linen laid, extra quality paper. Price, per ream....75c
No. 3C7546 Size, 8½x13 inches, linen laid, extra quality paper. Price, per ream....85c
Typewriter paper unmailable on account of weight.

No. 3C7550 Typewriter Carbon Paper, blue, black or purple, for manifold work and copying purposes.
Size, 8 x13 inches. Price, per dozen, 40c; per sheet....4c
Size, 8½x10 inches. Price, per dozen, 30c; per sheet....3c
If by mail, postage extra, per dozen, 2 cents.

SEND FOR OUR FREE STATIONERY CATALOGUE.

RUBBER TYPE OUTFITS.

This picture illustrates the style in which all our type is packed. Represents our 5A6a font of Solid Rubber Type, containing 235 separate pieces, including letters, figures, quads, spaces and tweezers. Our number 2A3a font contains 150 letters, figures, nickel plated tweezers, also pad.

AAaaaBBbbbCCcccDDddd12

No. 3C7578 2A3a font of Type, solid rubber, containing 150 pieces. Same style as above illustration, including a two-line holder 3 inches long and pad. Price....46c
If by mail, postage extra, 10 cents.

No. 3C7580 5A6a font of Rubber Type. Same style type as No. 3C7578, but contains 235 pieces, a four-line holder and pad. Price....(If by mail, postage extra, 15 cents)....95c

AAAAAaaaaaaBB

No. 3C7582 5A6a font of Solid Rubber Type, containing 235 pieces, including a four-line holder 3 inches long. Is especially convenient for the business man, for stamping cards, envelopes, letter heads and miscellaneous printing. Price....89c
If by mail, postage extra, 15 cents.

AAAAAaaaaaaBBBB

No. 3C7586 Rubber Type Outfit. 5A6a font, containing eleven printers' alphabets (5A6a) of type, four sets of figures, two large and two small, punctuation marks, dollar and percentage signs, stars and brackets for fancy work, tweezers, improved self inking pad and type holder for setting up four lines of matter. In addition to the eleven alphabets or letters, contains the following sign words and sentences: "&," "and," "For Sale," "From," "Return in 10 days to," pad and holder. Price...98c
If by mail, postage extra, 20 cents.

AAaaaBBbbbCCcccDD12

No. 3C7588 Success Rubber Type Outfit. 2A3a, contains five printers' alphabets (2A3a) of type, two sets of figures, bottle of indelible ink, one-line holder and ink pad, tweezers, quads, etc. Price....(If by mail, postage extra, 5 cents)....45c

AAaaaBBbbbCCcccDDddd12

No. 3C7590 Special Printing Card Outfit, 2A3a font, containing 150 pieces, two-line holder and pad, is especially convenient for printing calling cards, stationery, etc. Price....59c
If by mail, postage extra, 10 cents.

Extra Holders for Rubber Type Outfits.

Rubber Type Holders, metal base, polished wood handles.

No. 3C7597 Single Line Holders. Price....12c
If by mail, postage extra, 3 cents.
No. 3C7598 Two-Line Holders. Price....17c
No. 3C7599 Four-Line Holders. Price....25c
If by mail, postage extra, 5 cents.

When ordering, always give style and number of type for which holder is desired.

The Home Printing Outfit.

No. 3C7600 Contains alphabet, figures, ink pad, ink holder, tweezers, ornaments, etc. This font of type is especially convenient for marking linen, books, papers, printing cards, etc. Can be changed quickly to any letter or wording. Price....12c
If by mail, postage extra, 3c.

Senior Printer.

No. 3C7604 For marking books, linen, printing name cards, etc., consisting of three sets of alphabets, two sets of figures, ornaments, two-line holder, ink pad and tweezers. Price....23c
If by mail, postage extra, 5 cents.

Boys' Printing Outfit.

No. 3C7606 Contains 120 rubber letters, figures, etc., ink pad, bottle of ink, one-line holder and tweezers. This is one of the most complete boys' printing outfits made. Can be used in printing invitations, cards, etc. Price....24c
If by mail, postage extra, 10 cents.

Mark Your Own Linen.

No. 3C7608 Excelsior Indelible Stamping Outfit; complete with one-line hand stamp (your own name), felt pad, brush and ¼-ounce tube of indelible ink; can be applied to linens, etc. Price, for the complete outfit....22c
If by mail, postage extra, 5 cents.

20th Century Pocket Typewriter.

No. 3C7513 Coffman's Pocket Typewriter. An ingenious writing machine, 7½ inches long, ½ inch wide and ¾ inch thick. Thoroughly practical, writes 78 characters, including capitals, small letters, numbers, punctuation marks, etc. It will write on any plain, smooth surface, in books, on writing tablets, boxes, glass, etc. Can be folded up and carried in the pocket. It is endorsed and used by traveling men, doctors, lawyers, ministers, merchants, teachers, etc. Used in hotels and restaurants in printing bills of fare, etc. Teachers, students and ministers will find this machine very helpful in preparing examination papers, making weekly announcements, etc. All parts are made of first class material and combine best workmanship. Heavily nickeled. Weight, packed for shipment, 18 ounces. Price....$3.90
If by mail, postage extra 18 cents.

SIGN MARKING OUTFITS.

Complete Sign Marking Outfit Only 55 Cents.

No. 3C7634 For making display signs of all kinds. Complete set of rubber stamps, one inch high, consisting of the alphabet, figures, including ¼, ½, ¾, $ and c marks, punctuation points, a bottle of indelible ink, index hand, self-inking pad and gauge. Weight, packed for shipment, 2½ pounds.
Price, for complete outfit......55c

Rapid Sign Marking Outfit.

No. 3C7644 For making display signs of all kinds. Contains two complete sets of the alphabet, capital letters ⅜ inch high, small letters ⅜ inch high, figures from 1 to 0, including ¼, ½ and ¾, $ and c marks. Also the words For, Per, Reduced to, Each, Only; four ornaments, two fists, tube of indelible ink, one ink pad; also one patented gauge and one 14-inch ruler. Put up in a solid wooden case.
Retail price, $3.00; our price......$1.45
Weight, packed for shipment, 5 pounds.

Acme Sign Marking Outfit.

No. 3C7646 The Most Complete Sign and Price Marker Made. Contains two complete sets of alphabets, capitals ¾ inch high, small letters ½ inch high, including set of figures 1½ inches high and set ¾ inch high; also ¼, ½ and ¾, $ and c marks, all punctuation points, stars, fists and other ornaments; also the words Per, Reduced to, Each, For, Only, Per doz., Per yd., a pair, Sale price and Per tin. A tube of ink, pad, 18-inch ruler, etc., in wooden case. Price......$2.27
Weight, packed for shipment, 5¾ pounds.

Display Figures.

No. 3C7648 Large Display Figures for price markers. Complete set of figures from 1 to 0, $ and c. marks, on wood mount with polished base, 2½ inches high. Price, per set...85c
If by mail, postage extra, per set, 10 cents.

No. 3C7650 Same as above, but 1¾ inches high.
Price, per set......60c
If by mail, postage extra, per set, 7 cents.

Fancy Initial Letters.

No. 3C7652 Fancy Initial; rubber, mounted on wood. Any letter, for marking linen, stationery, books, etc. Complete, with indelible ink, and a tube of bronze ready for use.
Price......15c
If by mail, postage extra, 5 cents.

Initial Seals.

No. 3C7654 New Initial Seals, rubber, for marking linen, notepaper, envelopes, letter heads, etc. Mounted. When ordering be sure and mention just what letter is wanted.
Price, per dozen, 60c; each......5c
If by mail, postage extra, each, 2 cents.

Two-Letter Monograms.

No. 3C7656 Any combination of two letters made into a monogram like illustration, to be used for stamping note paper, envelopes, books, linen, music, etc. Mounted. Complete, with inked pad ready for use. When ordering, be sure and mention letters wanted. Price...20c
If by mail, postage extra, 5 cents.

Three-Letter Monograms.

No. 3C7657 Three-Letter Monogram, like illustration. Can be used for marking linen, stamping stationery, books, music, etc. The complete outfit, including ink pad, with ink (any color)......30c
When ordering, be sure and give initials.
If by mail, postage extra, 3 cents.

Convenient Dater, only 9c.

No. 3C7670 A metal holder, provided with revolving rubber type and figures, so arranged that by its use it is an easy matter to stamp the date on all bills and letters. In addition to the names of the months and the figures corresponding to the days of the month, and the years from 1903 to 1909, the dater contains the following words: Rec'd, Ans'd, Paid.
Price, per dozen, $1.00; each......9c
If by mail, postage extra, each, 3 cents.

Notary Public Seals.

New Patented Seal; for notaries, corporations, lodges, courts, etc., with name, county and state. Nickel plated.
No. 3C7732 Star Seal. Weight, 2¼ pounds, 1⅝-inch seal. Price......$1.45
No. 3C7735 Star Seal. Weight, 3½ pounds, 1⅞-inch seal. Price......$1.60
We can furnish seals, using any stock design desired, at $2.45 for the 2¼-pound seal and $2.60 for the 3½-pound seal.
Unmailable on account of weight.

Improved Pocket Seal.

No. 3C7739 For notaries, lodges, corporations, courts, etc., guaranteed to give satisfaction; 1⅝-inch die with plain lettering, nickel plated. Shipping weight, 14 ounces.
Price......$2.25
If by mail, postage extra, 15 cents.

Hand Stamps.

No. 3C7750 Hand Stamp, with your name, business or home address, town and state; for stamping envelopes, letter and bill heads, advertising matter, etc.; on wood mount, polished base and handle. Lines not to exceed three inches in length. Price, one line......10c
Price for each additional line, extra......10c
(Making two-line stamp cost 20c; a three-line stamp, 30c, etc.)
If by mail, postage extra, per stamp, 3 cents.

No. 3C7751 Same style as No. 3C7750, but on cushion mount.
Price, one line......12c
Price for each additional line, extra......12c
If by mail, postage extra, per stamp, 3 cents.

Automatic Self Inking Rubber Stamps.

Always ready for immediate use. With your name and address, town or state, wording not to be in excess of two lines on Nos. 3C7752, 3C7754, 3C7755; and three to six lines on Nos. 3C7756, 3C7759 and 3C7760. Be sure to give your name and address clearly and distinctly to avoid error in spelling.

No. 3C7752 Will print 1⅜x½ inches. Price......45c
No. 3C7754 Will print 1⅞x½ inches. Price......55c
No. 3C7755 Will print 2x11-16 inches. Price......65c
No. 3C7756 Will print 2 7-16x13-16 inches. Price......80c
If by mail, postage on above extra, each, 5c.
No. 3C7759 Will print 2¼x1 inches. Price......90c
If by mail, postage extra, 7 cents.
No. 3C7760 Will print 2¼x1 7-16 inches. Price......$1.20
If by mail, postage extra, 10 cents.

Automatic Pen and Pencil Pocket Stamp.

With Your Name and Address for 18 cents.

No. 3C7761 Self Inking Pocket Stamp. Made of polished metal. Length, 4½ inches. Is neat and strong. Each stamp contains lead pencil and pen on one end, and your name and address on the other (two lines only).
Price......(If by mail, postage extra, 4 cents.)......18c

Handy Pocket Self Inking Name Stamp.

No. 3C7763 New Vest Pocket Stamp; made expressly for stamping letter heads, postal cards, envelopes, linen, etc. The name is mounted on cushion rubber, encased in metal case, highly polished. Price......18c
If by mail, postage extra, 5 cents.
When ordering No. 3C7761 or No. 3C7763, be sure to write your name and address clearly and distinctly to avoid error in spelling.

Excelsior Self Inking Pads.

No. 3C7880 Little Gem. Size, 1½x2⅞ inches; red, blue, green, violet or black. Price......7c
No. 3C7881 Jumbo. Size, 2x3⅝ inches. Any color, red, blue, green, violet or black. Price......10c
No. 3C7882 No. 1. Size, 2⅞x4⅜ inches. Any color, red, blue, green, violet or black. Price......15c
No. 3C7884 No. 2. Size, 3¼x6⅞ inches. Any color, red, blue, green, violet or black. Price......19c
If by mail, postage extra, each 5 cents.

Ink for Rubber Stamps and Pads.

Permanent colors, red, blue, green, violet and black.
No. 3C7888 Half-ounce bottle. Price......8c
No. 3C7890 One-ounce bottle. Price......12c
When ordering, be sure to specify color wanted.
If by mail, postage extra, each, 7 cents, including mailing tube.

Our $2.65 Self Inking Press and Outfit.

No. 3C7909 (No. 5) This press will print a form 2½x3¾ inches. Weight of press and outfit, boxed for shipment, 12 pounds. The self inking feature consists of operating by means of an automatic revolving inking table, over which passes the roller, in turn passing over the face of the type, all of the movements being automatic with one stroke of the hand lever. Consists of the following big assortment: One new improved self inking press, complete with roller and automatic inking table; one font of standard long type; one hundred blank cards; furniture, tweezers, gold and silver bronze, bronzing cotton and a supply of ink. Stands 8 inches high and 12 inches wide with lever extended. Price, complete outfit......$2.65

Our $14.98 Professional Printing Press and Outfit.

No. 3C7920 (No. 12) Prints a form 4½x6¾ inches. Consists of our new improved self inking press, with two inking rollers and inking table; four fonts of type, one 6-inch steel composing stick for setting type, one set of gauge pins, one pair of tweezers, big assortment of furniture, complete set of quoins, one shooting stick for locking up the form, one planer for planing down the form and getting the face of the type even, one oil can, supply of ink, etc. Stands 15 inches high, 23 inches wide. The complete outfit weighs 80 pounds and is without question one of the best built and easiest working printing presses made. Mounted on a handsome cherry base.
Price for the press and complete outfit......$14.98

Our $21.70 Printing Press and Outfit.

No. 3C7924 (No. 13) Prints a form 5½x8 inches. Weight of the press and outfit, boxed, 125 pounds. Complete with five fonts of type, composing stick, planer, furniture, leads and ink, chase, oil can, set of iron quoins, shooting stick and wrench. Our $21.70 press is made in the exact same manner as our $14.98 press described above, with the exception that it is one size larger and will do a greater variety of work, printing a form up to 5½x8 inches in size. This is a size press that will get out circulars and will even print a small newspaper. Full directions are sent with every press and outfit.
Price for the press and complete outfit......$21.70

Our $28.98 New, Large, Self Inking Printing Press and Outfit.

No. 3C7928 (No. 14) Prints a form 6x9 inches. Complete, with two ink rollers, walnut delivery table, hand roller, oil can, set of iron quoins, furniture, leads, shooting stick, gauge pins, ink and seven complete fonts of type. The principle of the operation of our $28.98 press is the same as our smaller and cheaper self inking presses, with the exception of the location of the hand lever. The platen has gripper pins, and with the gauge pins no difficulty will be experienced in securing a perfect make-ready, and neat, clean and perfect work will be turned out. The inking table is especially full size, carries a good supply of ink, revolves at every impression and insures a thorough inking of the form. We furnish seven complete fonts of type, all standard sizes and varieties, two rollers, etc. Weight of the complete outfit packed for shipment, 180 pounds.
Price for the press and complete outfit......$28.98

Autograph Stamps.

Jno. Wymond

No. 3C7908 A cushion mounted Hand Stamp reproducing your signature exactly as you write it. When ordering write your name, just the size you wish it reproduced, with black ink on a clean white card. The wood cut from which the die is made will be sent you with the stamp. This cut can be used for printing if desired. Price......85c
If by mail, postage extra, 5 cents.

Autograph Albums.

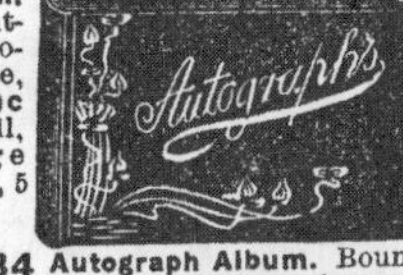

No. 3C6782 Autograph Album. Contains 68 pages, lithographed frontispiece, bound in plush, word Autographs inscribed on front cover. Size, 7x4½ inches. Price......29c
If by mail, postage extra, 5 cents.

No. 3C6784 Autograph Album. Bound in imitation leather, embossed cover, assorted designs, contains 60 pages, full gilt edges. Size, 6½x4½ inches. Price......18c
If by mail, postage extra, 5 cents.

Scrap Books.

No. 3C6786 Scrap Album. New handsome scrap album with embossed cover, assorted designs stamped in colored ink and gold, containing 44 leaves, assorted colors. Size, 10x12¾ inches.
Price......25c
Weight, packed for shipment, 35 ounces.

Twentieth Century Scrap Book.

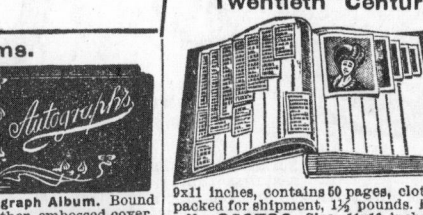

The newest, latest and best way of preserving clippings. Holds three times the capacity of the old style scrap book. It embodies a new idea simple and valuable. (See illustration). Used by editors, architects, actors, platform speakers, musicians, lawyers and business men.

No. 3C6788 Size, 9x11 inches, contains 50 pages, cloth bound, with index. Weight, packed for shipment, 1½ pounds. Price......69c
No. 3C6790 Size, 11x16 inches, contains 50 pages, cloth bound, with index. Weight, packed for shipment, 3 pounds.
Price......98c

Scrap Books.

No. 3C6792 Scrap Book, containing finest grade of manila paper, roan back and corners, gold lines, comb marbled paper sides. Size, 7½x9½ inches; 156 pages. Weight, packed for shipment, 1½ lbs.
Price......48c
No. 3C6794 Scrap Book, crown folio, size, 10x14½ inches; 182 pages; otherwise same as No. 3C6792. Weight, packed for shipment, 3 pounds. Price......72c

EXCEPTIONAL VALUES IN LATEST 1905 MODEL BICYCLES

WE ARE AMONG THE LARGEST DEALERS IN BICYCLES, PROBABLY SELLING MORE BICYCLES DIRECT TO THE CONSUMER THAN ALL OTHER HOUSES COMBINED; CONSUMING, AS WE DO, A LARGE PERCENTAGE OF THE BICYCLE PRODUCTION OF THIS COUNTRY, PRACTICALLY CONTROLLING THE OUTPUT OF THE FACTORY IN WHICH OUR BICYCLES ARE MADE, BASING OUR SELLING PRICES ON THE ACTUAL COST OF MATERIAL AND LABOR, WITH BUT OUR ONE SMALL PERCENTAGE OF PROFIT ADDED.

WE ARE ENABLED TO MAKE EXTREMELY LOW PRICES ON BICYCLES by having them made up in enormous quantities, arranging with the factory in such a way that they may order their tubing and other raw material in very large quantities, contracting for thousands of bicycles to be made up during the dull months of winter when most bicycle factories are closed down, and the highest grade of skilled labor can be had at moderate wages. The exceptional values which we are offering in bicycles should be the most convincing argument in favor of sending us your bicycle order.

AT $10.75 WE OFFER THE HIGH GRADE KENWOOD BICYCLE, a wheel which has given good satisfaction. Our $11.95 Elgin King Bicycle—the Celebrated Red Head Beauty—has been brought strictly up to date, and represents great value for the money. To those desiring to procure a bicycle of the very highest quality, we recommend the celebrated **Three-Crown Nickel Joint Napoleon Bicycle at $13.85.** It represents the acme of perfection in modern bicycle building, having all of the latest improvements. The Napoleon is considered to be the handsomest and best proportioned bicycle on the market.

WE KNOW THAT WE ARE FURNISHING BETTER BICYCLES AT LOWER PRICES than any other concern, and that there are no bicycles made that will compare with ours at the prices for which we offer them.

OUR WONDERFUL TEN DAYS' FREE TRIAL OFFER. All of our bicycles are shipped with the understanding that they can be given a ten days' trial (any ordinary usage), and if for any reason the bicycle is not satisfactory at any time within ten days, it may be returned to us at our expense of transportation charges both ways, and we will cheerfully return the money sent us, with any express or transportation charges which may have been paid by the customer. We would advise our customers to send cash in full with their orders, as it saves the extra charge of from 25 to 50 cents which the express companies always make for collecting and returning the money to us. Also C. O. D. shipments often cause a little inconvenience to the purchaser, as the C. O. D. amount must be paid to the express agent before the goods can be delivered. If the full amount of cash is sent with the order, there is no charge for collecting and returning the money; the bicycle will be shipped direct to you, and you will only have to pay the express or freight charges, which is a very small amount as compared to the great saving in price.

EXCEPTIONAL PAY AFTER EXAMINATION OFFER. If you do not wish to send cash in full with your order, we will gladly, on receipt of $1.00, ship any bicycle to any address, C. O. D., subject to examination. You can examine it at your nearest express office, and if found to be exactly as represented and satisfactory in every way, then pay the express agent our price and express and collection charges, less the $1.00 sent with the order. However, you take no risk in sending cash with the order, for in case you should become dissatisfied with the bicycle at any time within ten days, you have only to avail yourself of our ten days' free trial offer, and we will immediately return your money.

EVERY BICYCLE IS SHIPPED UNDER OUR BINDING GUARANTEE, covering each and every part entering into the construction of the bicycle, including the strongest association guarantee covering the **Celebrated Seroco Single Tube Tires,** with which all of our bicycles are equipped. We have used these tires on our bicycles during the past few years with highly satisfactory results, and do not hesitate to recommend them as one of the highest grade tires made.

REPAIR PARTS ARE SELDOM REQUIRED FOR OUR BICYCLES. However, we carry a complete stock of all parts, so that in the event of accidents or any unusual usage we are enabled to supply parts without delay.

WE WILL EQUIP ANY OF OUR BICYCLES WITH THE CELEBRATED FORSYTH COASTER HUB AND BRAKE FOR $3.00 ADDITIONAL.

$10.75 BUYS THE LATEST 1905 GENTS' KENWOOD BICYCLE.

Equipped with Forsyth Coaster Hub and Brake, **$13.75.**

No. 19C403
Order by Number.

THE KENWOOD BICYCLE IS REALLY TOO WELL KNOWN TO REQUIRE A VERY LENGTHY DESCRIPTION. IT HAS ALWAYS BEEN KNOWN AND SOLD AS A STRICTLY HIGH GRADE WHEEL.

REDUCED from last year's price of $11.75, a reduction of $1.00, and improved in every respect, brought strictly up to date, embodying all the latest features for this season, and the equal of bicycles that sell generally for about double the price.

UNDERSTAND, all Kenwood bicycles are covered by the strongest kind of a **WRITTEN BINDING GUARANTEE,** covering each and every part entering into the construction of this famous wheel. Every possible influence has been brought to bear upon the manufacturers of this high grade bicycle in the way of quantity to be taken and deliveries, in order to procure them at the lowest possible cost. We are pleased to state that in this respect we have been very successful, and offer them to our customers with our one very small percentage of profit added.

THE KENWOOD RECEIVED MEDALS and high awards at the World's Fair, and no expense has been considered in maintaining the high quality which has always marked the Kenwood bicycle as being among the high grade wheels.

FRAME IS THE LATEST STYLE 20, 22 or 24 inches, as desired, made of seamless tubing, flush at every joint, arch crown, good finish, enameled by the latest method in either black or maroon, all bright parts heavily nickel plated. Wheels are 28-inch, with piano wire spokes, high grade hubs, full ball bearing, fitted with ball retainers, latest one-piece hanger, 1905 model sprocket, 7-inch cranks. The Kenwood bicycle is furnished completely equipped with the celebrated Seroco single tube tires, fine saddle, high grade adjustable handle bar with leather grips, rat trap pedals, finely finished tool bag, containing wrench, pump and tube of quick tire repair cement.

THE CELEBRATED FORSYTH COASTER HUB AND BRAKE is the greatest improvement ever made for bicycling purposes. It permits the rider to rest at intervals while riding, as the bicycle will continue in motion while the pedals remain stationary, the coaster hub permitting the wheels to run free without pedalling. The coaster hub is also indispensable in coasting. The bicycle is always under perfect control. As the feet remain on the pedals, the bicycle can be stopped instantly, thereby frequently avoiding accidents. A complete mechanical description will be found under catalogue No. 19C20, on page 553.

No. 19C403 Gents' Kenwood Bicycle. Price.................. $10.75

LADIES' KENWOOD BICYCLE, $11.25

THE LADIES' KENWOOD BICYCLE, made with 20 or 22-inch handsome drop frame, mud and chain guards, nicely laced, and combination rubber pedals. Quality is equal in every way to that of the gents' model.

No. 19C454 Ladies' Kenwood Bicycle. Price.................. $11.25
Above bicycle fitted with the celebrated Forsyth Coaster Hub and Brake.................. 14.25

OUR NEW $13.85 1905 MODEL NAPOLEON BICYCLE

$13.85 buys the Napoleon, our Highest Grade Bicycle, the Highest of High Grade, the Full Three-Crown, Flush Nickel Joint, Full Nickel Head Napoleon. . . .

BROUGHT RIGHT UP TO DATE FOR 1905.

EQUIPPED WITH FORSYTH COASTER HUB AND BRAKE . . $16.85

No. 19C457
Order by Number.

EVERY NAPOLEON BICYCLE is fitted with the Celebrated Seroco Single Tube Tires, one of the highest grade tires it is possible to make, fully guaranteed, finely finished ball bearing pedals, high grade nickel plated adjustable expander handle bar, with fine quality leather grips, extra high grade full grain leather hair padded saddle. Special finished leather tool bag, complete with wrench, pump and tube of quick tire repair cement. In fact, the best of everything throughout, in the highest grade bicycle shown by any maker for the season 1905, and all for **$13.85.**

SPECIAL FEATURES found in our **$13.85 Napoleon Bicycle: Flush jointed frame, made of high carbon seamless steel tubing, handsomely enameled in either black or maroon,** hand rubbed and varnished, with beautiful double hair line gold striping, making a bicycle frame that can only be compared with those used on the highest grade bicycles. A frame which has proven by experience to give the most perfect satisfaction.

THREE CROWNS. **The handsomest, smoothest and best finished frame connections,** rear stay crown, rear fork crown and front fork crown, all highly nickel plated on copper, beautifully polished. In addition to this the head and front fork tips are also nicely nickeled and highly polished, which makes it without exception the handsomest, strongest and altogether best bicycle frame used on any bicycle, regardless of name, make or price.

LATEST 1905 ONE-PIECE HANGER, including one of the handsomest and most highly finished sprockets ever made. The improved 1905 expander in seat post and handle bar, for adjusting bar or post to any position. In fact every up to date feature for 1905 bicycles has been embodied in our latest **$13.85** Napoleon, combining the good points of all high grade wheels, with the defects of none.

OUR BINDING GUARANTEE. With every Napoleon bicycle at $13.85 we issue the strongest kind of a written binding guarantee, covering every piece and part that goes into the bicycle, including the strongest **association guarantee** for the celebrated Seroco Single Tube Tires.

NOTE Owing to the tremendous increase in the sales of this famous bicycle, we have been enabled to place a contract for an enormous quantity, enabling the factory to run continuously during the dull season, thus making the cost of production lower than ever before. We offer them, with only our one small percentage of profit added, at **$13.85,** a price barely covering the cost of material and labor.

WE RECOMMEND THE NAPOLEON BICYCLE above all others. While our $10.75 **Kenwood Bicycle is a perfectly reliable wheel** and the equal of bicycles generally sold at more than double the price, and our Elgin King, the new 1905 **Red Head Beauty,** at $11.95, is strictly high grade, guaranteed in every way and the equal of bicycles that sell for a great deal more money, we especially recommend our highest of high grade bicycles, our **$13.85** Napoleon, which we put out on the strongest written binding guarantee as being more up to date and higher grade than any other bicycle on the market.

THE CLEBRATED FORSYTH Coaster Hub and Brake is the greatest improvement ever made for bicycling purposes. It permits the rider to rest at intervals while riding, as the bicycle will continue in motion while the pedals remain stationary, the coaster hub permitting the wheels to run free without pedalling. The coaster hub is also indispensable in coasting. The bicycle is always under perfect control, as the feet remain on the pedals the bicycle can be stopped instantly, thereby frequently avoiding accidents. A complete description will be found under catalogue No. 19C20, on page 553.

THE JOSEPHINE is the Ladies' Model of our highest grade wheel, the Napoleon. Made in the same high grade manner, equipped with the very highest quality 1905 combination rubber pedals, mud and chain guard, handsomely striped, varnished and laced to match color of frame. Size, 22 inches.

No. 19C458 Ladies' Josephine Bicycle.
Price $14.35
The above bicycle fitted with the Forsyth Coaster Hub and Brake 17.35

DETAILED DESCRIPTION

FRAME—The frame is 22 or 24 inches, as desired, made of the highest grade 1⅛-inch seamless tubing, the very finest 1905 connections. Three-crown frame, flush at every joint, the highest grade, handsomest, smoothest, and strongest full flush joint frame made.

WHEELS—Maple rims, beautifully striped to match frame, piano wire spokes, elegantly nickel plated.

GEAR—72 to 96 as desired.

TOOLS AND TOOL BAG—Napoleon is furnished with a heavy leather tool bag, complete with the best set of bicycle tools, including wrench, pump and tube of quick tire repair cement.

HUBS—We use the celebrated **high grade** Harris hubs, beautifully nickel plated, have hardened cups and cones with ball retainers. They are among the most satisfactory hubs on the market.

HANGER—Latest 1905 one-piece hanger, beautifully finished; ball bearing throughout, latest patent ball retainers, 7-inch cranks.

SPROCKETS—Sprockets are the latest 1905 design, heavily nickel plated and beautifully polished.

TIRES—Every Napoleon is fitted with the celebrated **Seroco single tube tires**—tires that have always given the best of satisfaction, fully covered by the association guarantee. With care these tires will last several years.

PEDALS—On the **$13.85** Napoleon we use a special high grade rat trap pedal, heavily nickel plated, accurately adjusted and full ball bearing.

SADDLE—Strictly high grade full padded grain leather saddle, extra well finished.

NICKEL HEAD—The head is shortened to the latest 1905 design, heavily nickel plated on copper, highly polished and beautifully finished.

HANDLE BAR—We equip the $13.85 Napoleon with a special high grade, full adjustable handle bar, a bar that can be instantly adjusted, up or down turned, as desired, complete with special high grade leather grips.

FINISH—All connections heavily nickel plated on copper, nickel plated at every joint, as illustrated. The **three crowns** nickel plated, **fork ends, head** and **front fork arch crown,** the whole made perfectly flush at every part, including flush **seat post cluster.** The frame is enameled in the best known process, either **black or maroon,** as desired, beautifully striped and without doubt the handsomest bicycle on the market, regardless of price.

No. 19C457 Gents' Napoleon Bicycle. Price **$13.85**

OUR NEW $11.95 ELGIN KING BICYCLE.

EQUIPPED WITH FORSYTH COASTER HUB AND BRAKE, $14.95

No. 19C405

OUR ELGIN KING BICYCLE embodies every new, up to date feature. A bicycle that has a world wide reputation for graceful lines, stability and easy running qualities. This bicycle was formerly sold at $50.00, and in the early bicycle days as high as $100.00. Since coming into our control we have continued to increase the sales, maintaining the high standard of quality, until today we have in the Elgin King—**the celebrated RED HEAD BEAUTY**—a bicycle which is second to none (with the exception of our Napoleon) at a price within the reach of all.

WE ARE SOLE AGENTS for the ELGIN KING bicycle. They can be had only from us, and there is no bicycle on the market which you can buy within $10.00 of the price that will approach the quality of material, workmanship, finish or style.

$12.45

OUR LADIES' ELGIN QUEEN BICYCLE,

exactly same quality as our Elgin King. Equipped with high grade combination rubber pedals; finely varnished dress and chain guard, with latest style lacing. Frame, 20 or 22 inches.

No. 19C456 Ladies' Elgin Queen Bicycle.
Price..$12.45
Above bicycle fitted with Forsyth Coaster Hub and Brake..$15.45

THE ELGIN KING BICYCLE is one of the handsomest bicycles ever made in any factory. The frame is flush at every joint throughout, made of 1⅛-inch seamless tubing, sizes 20 inches, 22 inches or 24 inches, as desired. Enameled by the latest process, consisting of three coats best quality American enamel, hand rubbed and baked at a high temperature, which gives it exceptional wearing qualities, the most beautiful effect in the enameling for which this bicycle is noted, being due to the combination of colors. The main frame and front fork are jet black, the head being handsomely decorated in red or vermilion, this decoration artistically extending on the upper and lower bar. Front fork crown, tips and all other bright parts are highly nickel plated on copper, polished and handsomely buffed. Wheels are 28 inches, with selected maple rims, swaged piano wire spokes and high grade hubs having ball retainers; sprocket of latest 1905 design, one-piece hanger, 7-inch cranks, highest quality $\frac{3}{16}$-inch chain, with latest style expander seat post and handle bar.

OUR BINDING GUARANTEE. With every Elgin King bicycle we furnish a written, binding guarantee, the strongest guarantee issued with any bicycle. This guarantee covers every piece and part including the high grade Seroco single tube tires.

THE ELGIN KING BICYCLE has the highest grade equipment, being equipped with the celebrated Seroco Single Tube Tires; extra fine quality grain leather padded saddle, high grade adjustable expander handle bar, heavily nickel plated, with leather grips, 1905 improved rat trap pedals, fine special grain leather tool bag, containing wrench, pump and tube of quick tire repair cement.

THE CELEBRATED FORSYTH COASTER HUB AND BRAKE is the greatest improvement ever made for bicycling purposes. It permits the rider to rest at intervals while riding, as the bicycle will continue in motion while the pedals remain stationary, the coaster hub permitting the wheels to run free without pedalling. The coaster hub is also indispensable in coasting. The bicycle is always under perfect control. As the feet remain on the pedals, the bicycle can be stopped instantly, thereby frequently avoiding accidents. A complete description will be found under catalogue No. 19C20, on page 553.

No. 19C405 Gents' Elgin King Bicycle. Price..$11.95

BOYS' ELGIN RED HEAD JUVENILE BICYCLES.

$11.95

One of the finest juvenile bicycles that has ever been offered, made of the very best material, of same quality and finish as our celebrated Elgin King and Queen bicycles. The frame, fork and hanger, also every other feature of finish and equipment are of an exceptionally high standard. The frame is enameled in jet black, with head decorated in red or vermilion, this decoration extending on the upper and lower bar, giving a most beautiful effect. The frame and fork are specially reinforced, with a view to making as stanch a bicycle as possible. The hanger is of special one-piece construction, with the latest design sprocket. In fact, this bicycle is made to fill the want of a thoroughly first class juvenile bicycle.

Note—We list three different sizes, suitable for boys of average size ranging from 7 to 16 years. Be very careful in ordering.

DETAILED DESCRIPTION: Tires—The high grade guaranteed Seroco Single Tube. **Pedals**—Full ball bearing, rat trap. **Chain**—3-16-inch, of great tensile strength. **Handle Bar**—Adjustable steel bar, handsomely nickel plated, with leather grips. **Saddle**—Special hair padded, grain leather. **Hubs**—Renowned Harris 1905 tubular. **Hanger**—Special Juvenile, drop forged, one piece, 6-inch crank. **Enamel**—Black with red head, hand rubbed and baked. **Nickel Plating**—All bright parts plated on copper, handsomely buffed. **Tool Bag**—High grade, containing wrench, pump and tube of quick tire repair cement.

No. 19C410 Boys' Bicycle. 16-inch frame, with 24-inch wheels, for boys 7 to 9 years of age. Price...$11.95

No. 19C411 Boys' Bicycle. 18-inch frame, with 26-inch wheels, for boys 9 to 12 years of age. Price... 11.95

No. 19C412 Boys' Bicycle. 20-inch frame, with 28-inch wheels, for boys 12 to 16 years of age.
Price.. 11.95

FREE. With all Elgin Red Head Bicycles we include free of charge a beautiful bell, having 2-inch metal gong made of pure bell metal with the American flag handsomely enameled on top in national colors like illustration.

GIRLS' ELGIN RED HEAD BICYCLES.

Exactly same high grade quality and finish as the boys' Red Head Bicycles described above; having a handsomely drop curved frame, and Rubber Combination Pedals.

No. 19C413 Girls' Bicycle. 16-inch frame, 24-inch wheels, for girls 7 to 9 years of age.
Price..................$11.95

No. 19C414 Girls' Bicycle. 18-inch frame, 26-inch wheels, for girls 9 to 12 years of age.
Price..................$11.95

No. 19C415 Girls' Bicycle. 20-inch frame, 28-inch wheels, fitted with dress and chain guard, for girls 12 to 16 years of age.
Price..................$12.45

$11.95

Any of the above bicycles fitted with the celebrated Forsyth Coaster Hub and Brake at $3.00 additional.

BOYS' ACME WONDER JUVENILES.

$10.75

OUR $10.75 BOYS' BICYCLE.

We have these bicycles made in three sizes, suitable for boys of average size from 7 to 16 years. Be very careful in ordering. This line of bicycles represents exceptional value for the money.

DESCRIPTION: Tires—Seroco, single tube. **Pedals**—Rat trap. **Chain**—Special 3-16-inch. **Handle Bar**—Adjustable nickel plated, with leather grips. **Saddle**—Special Juvenile. **Hub**—High grade, barrel type. **Hanger**—Ball bearing one piece, with new design sprocket. **Finish**—Frames, nicely enameled in black or maroon, all bright parts fully nickel plated.

No. 19C401 Boys' Bicycle, 16-inch frame with 24-inch wheel, for boys 7 to 9 years of age.
Price..$10.75
No. 19C402 Boys' Bicycle, 18-inch frame with 26-inch wheels, for boys 9 to 12 years of age.
Price..$10.75
No. 19C403 Boys' Bicycle, 20-inch frame with 28-inch wheels, for boys 12 to 16 years of age.
Price..$10.75

GIRLS' ACME WONDER JUVENILES.

Made in the same quality as the boys' model, with drop frame and combination rubber pedals.

No. 19C406 Girls' Bicycle, 16-inch frame with 24-inch wheels, for girls from 7 to 9 years.
Price..$10.75
No. 19C407 Girls' Bicycle, 18-inch frame with 26-inch wheels, for girls 9 to 12 years.
Price..$10.75
No. 19C408 Girls' Bicycle, 20-inch frame with 28-inch wheels, fitted with dress and chain guard, for girls 12 to 16 years. Price..$11.25

Any of the above bicycles fitted with the celebrated Forsyth Coaster Hub and Brake at $3.00 additional.

Boys' Velocipedes.

We sell the very best all steel velocipedes; with adjustable seat. Furnished also with rubber tires. Make your selection according to inseam, measured from crotch to heel.

Seats can be raised two or three inches.

Catalogue No.	Front wheel	Inseam Meas.	Ship'g weight	Steel tires	Rubber tires
19C621	16 in.	14 in.	13 lbs.	$1.25	....
19C625	16 in.	14 in.	14 lbs.	.....	$2.50
19C622	20 in.	17 in.	14 lbs.	1.50	....
19C626	20 in.	17 in.	15 lbs.	.....	2.90
19C623	24 in.	19 in.	17 lbs.	1.85	....
19C627	24 in.	19 in.	18 lbs.	.....	3.50
19C624	26 in.	21 in.	18 lbs.	2.50	....
19C628	26 in.	21 in.	19 lbs.	.....	3.95

Instructions for Ordering Tires.

Usually the size can be obtained from the old tires, as nearly all tires have size branded on the side, but when this information cannot be so obtained, it becomes necessary to measure the rim, as illustrated in accompanying diagram. It is not always understood by the rider that the size of tires is governed by the outside diameter when inflated, which explains why a rim measuring 25 inches in diameter from edge to edge requires a 28-inch tire, and other sizes as per our explanatory table given below:

Measuring diameter of rim, edge to edge.
A 17-inch rim requires a 20-inch tire.
A 21-inch rim requires a 24-inch tire.
A 23-inch rim requires a 26-inch tire.
A 25-inch rim requires a 28-inch tire.
A 27-inch rim requires a 30-inch tire.
Then give catalogue number and size desired.

Napoleon Guaranteed Single Tube Tires at $3.10 Per Pair.

The enormous sale of these most popular tires during the past season, has caused us to place a contract for a much greater quantity than we have heretofore, the chief consideration of the contract being that we would accept delivery as fast as they could be made, thus enabling the factory to run continuously during the dull season, and therefore on a most economical basis. Notwithstanding the fact that the cost of material has advanced, by exercising our tremendous purchasing power we have secured these tires at less than ever before, and we offer them to our customers at the actual cost of production, with our one very small percentage of profit added, at the heretofore unheard of price for such high grade tires of $3.10.

The Napoleon single tube tires can be procured only from us. We guarantee them to be one of the highest grade tires it is possible to make, and people in your neighborhood will tell you that they have never received better satisfaction from any other tires.

DESCRIPTION: The inner wall, or air chamber, is made of the finest quality of washed Upper River Para Rubber. Next to the air chamber is placed a protection of the finest Sea Island cotton fabric. Upon this is placed layer after layer of the finest friction fabric to give the tire great wear resisting qualities. This fabric is alternately vulcanized with a fine quality of especially compounded rubber. Over this is placed the outer wall, this being composed of a quality of rubber especially selected for its durability and resiliency. The tire is then vulcanized in the latest designed moulds by the slow process, which is four or five times longer than given to most other tires, which accounts to some extent for the great wear resisting qualities of the Napoleon Tires. It would be impossible in this small amount of space to thoroughly explain the numberless operations and tests to which these tires are subjected before even leaving the factory. After leaving the factory the tires are again tested before shipment to our customers, being inflated under high air pressure to determine as to whether there are any possible defects.

WE GUARANTEE each and every Napoleon Tire to be high grade and absolutely free from any imperfections, either in material or workmanship, and we will gladly replace or repair any tire which is claimed defective, providing the same is sent us, prepaid, for examination within sixty days from date of sale.

NOTICE. Ladies' and Gents' bicycles always require 28-inch tires. Do not order tires of smaller size unless wanted for a Juvenile bicycle. See instructions for ordering tires on page 552.

No. 19C81 Napoleon Single Tube Tires. Size, 28x1⅝ inches. Price, per pair....$3.10
No pump or kit with the above tires. For prices of pumps see pages 554 and 555.

NAPOLEON JUVENILE TIRES. In quality they are identical with the larger size, but to avoid any mistake do not order any of these juvenile tires unless you want them for use on a boys' or girls' bicycle, and then follow the table of instructions for ordering tires given on page 552 of this catalogue.

No. 19C83 Napoleon Juvenile, 26-inch tires. Price, per pair....$3.10
No. 19C85 Napoleon Juvenile, 24-inch tires. Price, per pair....3.10
No pump or kit with the above tires. For prices of pumps see pages 554 and 555.

GENUINE KENWOOD SINGLE TUBE TIRES AT $2.85 PER PAIR.

These are the genuine Kenwood Tires which we have sold for the past number of years with highly satisfactory results. We offer them to our customers with the assurance that they are exceptional value for the money. They are made of the best quality of rubber and friction fabric, and we fully guarantee them to be perfect in every respect. These tires are the equal of any on the market, with the exception of the Napoleon Tires, which are among the highest grade tires possible to make. Every tire is rigidly inspected before shipping.

No. 19C70 Kenwood Tires. Size, 28x1⅝ inches. Price, per pair....$2.85

CUSHION PNEUMATIC TIRES AT $7.95 PER PAIR.

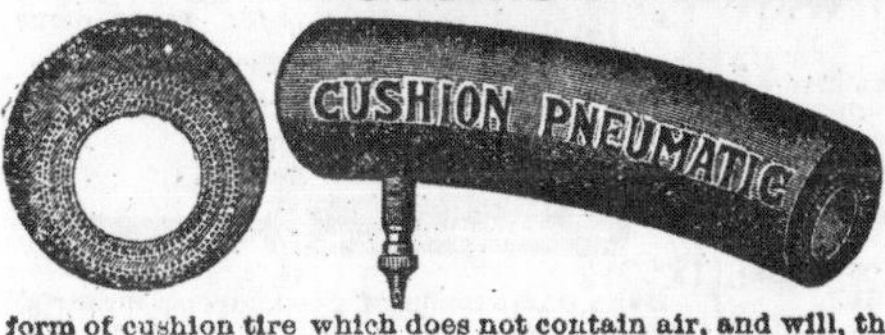

Our sales on these renowned tires have increased so very materially during the past season that we have placed a contract for nearly double the quantity which we have heretofore. This has enabled us to procure the tires from the manufacturers at about the cost of material and labor, owing to the tremendous quantities which we have purchased. We, therefore, offer them to our customers this season for considerably less money than these celebrated tires have ever been sold before.

These tires are unlike any others, and should not be confounded with any other form of cushion tire which does not contain air, and will, therefore, stretch, causing no end of trouble, or with the so called puncture proof tires with which at the present time the market is flooded. Many of them are being offered the unsuspecting rider, not with the idea of building a reputation, but merely to sell. These tires are a late invention, and possess great merit and wear resisting qualities, solely because they are ingeniously made of the highest grade of rubber, in which is amalgamated, by the latest process, many layers of the finest improved friction fabric. This we have tried to illustrate in the small sectional illustration showing the proportionate thickness of the wall in comparison to the diameter of tire. These tires will last for years, as they are heavy, rarely need inflation; are especially desirable and really necessary in those sections of the country where hedge thorns, cacti or sharp stones are encountered. Made in either 28x1½ or 28x1⅝ inches. State size desired.

No. 19C118 Cushion Pneumatic Tires. Price, per pair....$7.95
We will attach these tires to any of our bicycles (in place of regular tires) at $5.00 additional.

Imperial Double Tube Tires.

Recognizing the demand for a thoroughly high grade double tube tire we have contracted with one of the largest and most prominent rubber concerns in this country to make for us a strictly high grade double tube tire. In the Imperial Tire special attention has been given to the outer casing and inner tube, and we offer them to our customers as one of the best double tube tires which can be procured, and exceptional value for the money.

No. 19C86 Imperial Double Tube Tires, 28x1⅝ inches. Price, per pair....$3.45
No. 19C87 Imperial Casings, 28x1⅝ inches. Price, each....$1.25
If by mail, postage extra, each, 25 cents.
No. 19C88 Imperial Inner Tubes, 28x1⅝ inches. Price, each....73c
If by mail, postage extra, each, 12 cents.

Morgan & Wright's Plain Double Tube Tires.

Prices quoted do not include pump or repair kit.

No. 19C30 Size, 28x1½ inches. Price, per pair....$4.50
No. 19C31 Size, 28x1⅝ inches. Price, per pair....4.50
No. 19C33 Size, 26x1½ inches. Price, per pair....$4.50
No. 19C34 Size, 24x1½ inches. Price, per pair....4.15
No. 19C39 Cataplaro Tires. Size, 28x1⅝ inches. Price, per pair....5.25

INNER TUBES.
Monarch Inner Tubes.

Highest quality, every tube guaranteed. If not found to be satisfactory in every way they may be returned and we will replace free of charge.

No. 19C35 Monarch Inner Tubes, 28 inches. Price, each....65c
If by mail, postage extra, 13 cents.
No. 19C36 Morgan & Wright No. 1 Tube, 28-inch. Price, each....73c
If by mail, postage extra, 13 cents.
No. 19C37 Morgan & Wright No. 1 Tube, 26-inch. Price, each....73c
If by mail, postage extra, 12 cents.
No. 19C38 Morgan & Wright No. 1 Tube, 24-inch. Price, each....73c
If by mail, postage extra, 12 cents.
No. 19C45 Morgan & Wright No. 2 Tube, 28-inch. Price, each....58c
If by mail, postage extra, 13 cents.
No. 19C46 Acme Red Tubes. Price, each....90c
If by mail, postage extra, 13 cents.

M. & W. Outer Casings.

Always State Size Desired.

No. 19C43 Cataplaro Casings, 28x1⅝ inches. Price, each....$1.80
If by mail, postage extra, 40 cents.
No. 19C44 Road Casings, 28x1⅝ or 28x1½ inches. Price, each....$1.60
If by mail, postage extra, 32 cents.

IF POSTAGE IS NOT QUOTED, GOODS CANNOT BE SENT BY MAIL.

Dunlop Detachable Tires.

Note that we quote separate prices for tires and rims, as the latter are not included in price of tires. Rims are drilled 32 and 36 holes only. No pump or kit included.

No. 19C60 Dunlop Tires. 28x1⅝ inches. Price, per pair....$7.00
No. 19C61 Inner Tube, 28x1⅝ inches, with valve. Price, each....$1.10
If by mail, postage extra, 15 cents.
No. 19C62 Casings, 28x1⅝ inches. Price, each....$2.64
If by mail, postage extra, 35 cents.
No. 19C63 Dunlop Wood Rims, 28x1⅝ inches. Price, per pair....95c
If by mail, postage extra, per pair, 45 cents.

G. & J. Detachable Tires.

Note that prices are quoted separately for tires and rims. Rims are drilled with 32 and 36 holes. No pump or kit included with these tires.

No. 19C75 G. & J. Tires, 28x1⅝ inches. Price, per pair....$7.00
No. 19C76 Inner Tubes, 28x1⅝ inches with valve. Price, each....$1.10
If by mail, postage extra, 15 cents.
No. 19C77 Casings, 28x1⅝ in. Price, $2.85
If by mail, postage extra, 34 cents.
No. 19C78 G. & J. Rims, 28x1⅝ inches. Price....94c
If by mail, postage extra, 45 cents.

Goodrich Single Tube Tires.

Too well known to require detailed description. No pump or kit included.

No. 19C105 Goodrich 19 Tires, 28x1⅝ inches. Price, per pair....$5.00

Tread Bands for Tires.

These treads are continuous corrugated heavy rubber bands, to be cemented over the worn tread of any 28-inch tire by the aid of ordinary rubber cement, thus often saving the cost of new tires or casings. Sold singly or in pairs.

No. 19C110 Tread Band. Price, each....48c
If by mail, postage extra, 8 cents.

The Forsyth Coaster Hub and Brake.

We guarantee this to be one of the most satisfactory coaster hubs ever placed on the market.

In offering the Forsyth Coaster Hub and Brake we know that it is one of the most valuable devices which has ever been applied to a bicycle, and is considered as great an invention and improvement as the pneumatic tire, as it combines all the elements of ease and comfort in coasting, as well as safety as a brake. It embodies all of the good features of other coaster hubs with none of their defects, together with many new and important improvements which are found only in this hub. **It has absolutely no friction other than its bearings in either driving or coasting.** Wheel is always free and cannot lock. Brake is self releasing. A special composition metal is used for the braking shoe, which works perfectly and silently. It has no ratchets, cams or clutches, therefore cannot slip in changing from one operation to another. It has fewer parts than any other coaster brake made. All parts are accurately turned from the highest quality of tool steel, finely finished, and can be readily adjusted without removing wheel from the frame. This is the only hub having this feature.

In operation the Forsyth Coaster Hub and Brake is entirely automatic. When pedaling forward it acts exactly the same as any ordinary bicycle hub. To coast it is only necessary to stop pedaling, allowing the feet to remain in a stationary position, when the bicycle will continue to glide along. A slight back pressure on the pedals will either decrease the speed or bring the bicycle to a stop at the will of the rider. The Forsyth Coaster Hub and Brake has been pronounced to be the most powerful brake ever placed on the market, which is due to the special construction of the braking surfaces. The braking shoe offers resistance in opposite directions, which gives the maximum of braking power with the minimum of exertion.

There are no hills too steep to coast with perfect safety if your bicycle is equipped with the Forsyth Coaster Hub and Brake. We offer the Forsyth Coaster Hub and Brake to our customers with the absolute guarantee that it will give satisfaction in every respect. We can furnish these hubs complete, with clip for fastening brake arm to lower fork of bicycle, drilled for 32 or 36 spokes, with 7, 8, 9, 10 or 11-tooth sprockets, for either 3-16 or ¼ inch chains. In ordering specify number of spokes and size of sprocket. Unless otherwise specified we will send hub for 36 spokes with 9-tooth sprocket.

This hub can be attached to bicycle by any repair man, or equipped to any of our bicycles at an additional charge of $3.00.

No. 19C20 Forsyth Coaster Hub and Brake. Price....$3.00

Automatic Rear Wheel Brake.

This form of brake is far superior to the old style hand lever brake and much safer. It can be attached to any bicycle, no drilling required. It acts as a positive brake as soon as the rider back pedals. Brake is well made and nicely finished.

No. 19C900 Automatic Brake. Price....60c
If by mail, postage extra, 18 cents.

Our Railroad Attachment.

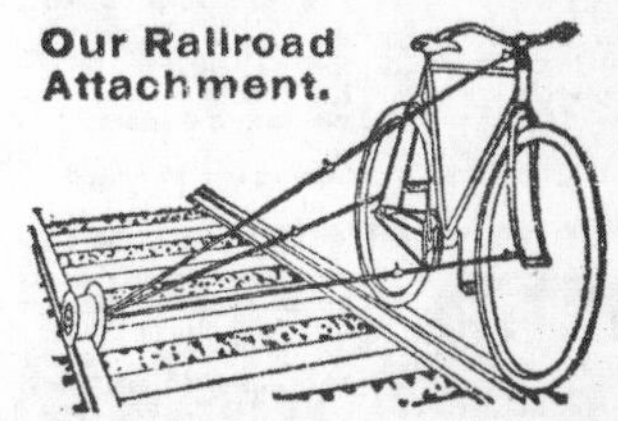

This is the most practical and durable device of its kind on the market, and consists of three braces made of steel tubing, that telescope for convenience in carrying, together with a steel wheel with flanges, the running surface of which is covered with rubber; also the necessary clamps for attaching the braces to the bicycle. Our illustration plainly indicates the manner of attachment which is so simple that anyone can attach or detach the device within the space of a very few minutes, and when not needed for use on the railroad track the parts can be taken down and placed in the cloth carrying case which we furnish with every attachment, and these can then be securely fastened to the bicycle when the latter is used on the road. The parts are substantially made and intended for honest wear, nicely enameled in black and weigh 9 pounds. We have found this device to be very popular with railroad and telegraph employes, male and female.

No. 19C99 Railroad Attachment. Price....$5.50

Padded Saddles.

Thoroughly up to date, well padded, made of grain leather, with nickeled spring and clamp.

No. 19C115 Gents' Saddle. Price.......40c

No. 19C116 Ladies' Saddle. Price.......40c

If by mail, postage extra, 30 cents.

Naber Saddle.

Its perfection is due to the action of the double torsional spring, which, by twisting, not springing, exhausts all the jars and roughness found on country roads. It is made of first class material and makes an ideal saddle.

No. 19C130 Gents' Saddle. Price, $1.05

If by mail, postage extra, 38 cents.

The Rubberneck Saddle.

Its special feature is a patented rubber cushion, honeycombed with air cells, which is placed between the steel base and the leather covering which serves as the top. The material and workmanship is of the best.

No. 19C142 Gents' Road Saddle. Price.......$1.45

If by mail, postage extra, 32 cents.

Gents' Wheeler Saddle.

Made of the finest oaktanned leather, on a wood base, having the new "high back" feature: a very popular saddle.

No. 19C160 Gents' Wheeler Saddle. Price.......75c

If by mail, postage extra, 30 cents.

Saddle Clamp.

Strongly made, will fit any two-spring saddle.

No. 19C926 Saddle Clamp. Price.......5c

If by mail, postage extra, 3 cents.

Our Leader Pedals.

Elegant in design, first class finish and fully guaranteed. Made in standard size, with ½-inch, 20-thread pedal pins. Mated right and left.

No. 19C180 Men's Rat Trap Pedals. Price, per pair.......45c

If by mail, postage extra, 24 cents.

No. 19C181 Combination Pedals. Price, per pair.......60c

If by mail, postage extra, 25 cents.

Our Ideal Pedals.

Made extra heavy, handsomely nickel plated, of a very new and neat design. Made in rat trap or combination. Pedal pins are ½-inch, 20-thread, right and left.

No. 19C193 Gents' Rat Trap Pedals. Price, per pair.......73c

If by mail, postage extra, 22 cents.

No. 19C194 Combination Pedals. Price, per pair.......88c

If by mail, postage extra, 25 cents.

Star Pedals.

These well known pedals are strictly high grade. Threaded ½ by 20, mated right and left.

No. 19C210 Gents' RatTrap Pedals. Price, pair...85c

If by mail, postage extra, 29 cents.

No. 19C211 Combination Pedals. Price, per pair.......95c

If by mail, postage extra, 25 cents.

Universal Pedal Rubbers.

Snap on to any make of pedal without the use of screws, bolts or plates, and do not rattle. Four rubbers constitute the set.

No. 19C219 Pedal Rubbers. Price, per set.......15c

If by mail, postage extra, 5 cents.

Fine Leather Tool Bag.

Excellent quality, large and roomy, thoroughly well made of oak tanned leather, nicely embossed, fastened with patent clasps. This is a fine bag.

No. 19C268 Tool Bag. Price.......17c

If by mail, postage extra, 8 cents.

Tourists' Bicycle Case.

No. 19C276 Tourists' Case. This case is made of heavy pressboard, covered with canvas and lined. The cover is fastened with patent clasps, and straps are provided for attaching to frame. Weight, 1½ lbs. Price.......59c

BICYCLE LAMPS.

In making your selection kindly bear in mind that our oil lamps are made to burn common kerosene or coal oil, obtainable everywhere. The gas lamps require calcium carbide (Catalogue No. 19C364), which can be ordered from us.

NOTE—We cannot accept for credit or exchange lamps that have been used.

The Searchlight Gas Lamp.

Beautifully made of brass, every wearing part reinforced. A handsome design, every part so accurately made as to insure absolute perfection. The only lamp made that can be instantly taken apart for cleaning; has removable dome, top body, tip holder, lens and reflector, all of the very finest construction. The lamp burns loose carbide, has needle valve for regulating flow of water, and gives such a powerful light as to rightly deserve its name, "Searchlight." The bracket supplied with lamp is adjustable to fit any bicycle.

No. 19C343 Searchlight Gas Lamp. Price.......$1.70

If by mail, postage extra, 35 cents.

The 20th Century Gas Headlight.

Burns any loose carbide six to eight hours with one charge. Aluminum parabola reflector, which spreads a wonderful light. A brass carbide holder accompanies every lamp, together with full directions for handling same. New, adjustable lamp bracket, to fit either head or fork.

No. 19C359 20th Century Gas Headlight. Price.......$1.97

If by mail, postage extra, 33 cents.

Duplex Gas Lamp.

Novel construction, made entirely of brass, elegantly nickel plated. Twin cylinders, one for water, the other holding carbide; perfect adjustment, permitting relighting of lamp until carbide is entirely exhausted. Has powerful lens, large reflector, colored sidelights, adjustable bracket. Lamp is also suitable for vehicles or autos.

No. 19C362 Duplex Lamps. Price, $2.25

If by mail, postage extra, 35 cents.

Calcium Carbide.

For use in Acetylene Gas Bicycle Lamps. ¼-inch size, packed in airtight tin cans containing 2 pounds.

No. 19C364 Carbide, 2-pound can. Price.......18c

Not mailable.

OIL LAMPS.

Our Dandy Lamp.

The best low price oil lamp made. Entirely of brass, handsomely nickel plated, no solder to melt, no parts to fall apart while riding. Burns kerosene oil, is 5 inches high and easily kept clean.

No. 19C368 Our Dandy Lamp. Price.......70c

If by mail, postage extra, 18 cents.

The Searchlight Oil Lamp.

Burns kerosene oil; positively the finest lamp of this kind ever constructed. Made of brass with beautiful embossing. Elegantly nickel plated. The oil fount, or bottom, is reversible, so that lamp can be attached to either side of fork or to steering head. It has a double front lens, reflector is detachable and covered with glass, so it will not tarnish.

No. 19C380 Searchlight Oil Lamp. Price.......$1.75

If by mail, postage extra, 30 cents.

HANDLE BARS.

Adjustable Handle Bars.

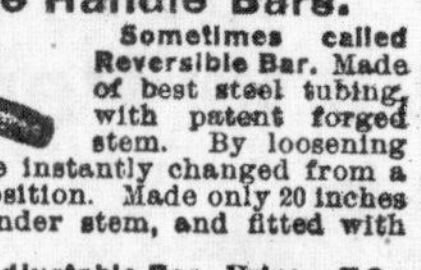

Sometimes called Reversible Bar. Made of best steel tubing, with patent forged stem. By loosening bolt, the bar can be instantly changed from a drop to a raised position. Made only 20 inches wide, ⅞-inch expander stem, and fitted with good grips.

No. 19C427 Adjustable Bar. Price.......50c

If by mail, postage extra, 31 cents.

No. 19C428 Extra Stems. Price.......32c

If by mail, postage extra, 15 cents.

Extension Stem Adjustable Bar.

With 2½-inch forward extension stem, ⅞ inch in diameter, with expander. The upper bar is 20 inches wide, fitted with grips.

No. 19C430 Extension Bar. Price.......95c

If by mail, postage extra, 40 cents.

Kelly Handle Bar.

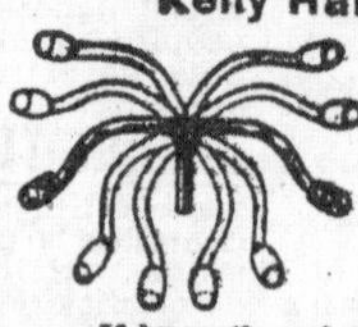

This wellknown bar permits an endless variety of adjustments, the arms being separate. Each bar fitted with grips. Stem is ⅞-inch only, with expander.

No. 19C433 Kelly Bar. Price.......$1.45

If by mail, postage extra, 45 cents.

The Hussey Bar.

Many and varied adjustments are possible with this bar, including forward extension. Each bar is fitted with grips. Stem, ⅞-inch only, with expander.

No. 19C438 Hussey Bar. Price.......$1.55

If by mail, postage extra, 45 cents.

Our 14-Cent Bell.

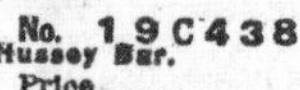

Handsomely nickel plated, 1¾-inch gong, of pure bell metal. Has rotary electric movement.

No. 19C490 Price.......14c

If by mail, postage extra, 8 cents.

Anchor and Shield Bell.

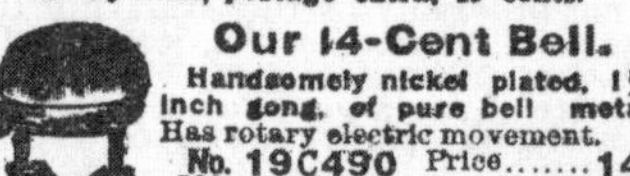

A very pretty design, 1¾-inch gong, with the shield handsomely enameled in colors, and other parts being finely nickel plated. This bell has rotary electric movement.

No. 19C499 Anchor and Shield Bell. Price.......24c

If by mail, postage extra, 8 cents.

Continuous Ringing Bell, With Flag Top.

This is a very handsome bell, having 2⅜-inch gong, the top being enameled, showing the national emblem in natural colors. The mechanism is ratchet electric, continuous ringing.

No. 19C506 Continuous Ringing Flag Bell. Price.......33c

If by mail, postage extra, 12 cents.

Tire Chimes.

A loud, musical, double alarm, continuing as long as rider wishes—simply pull a string, bell does the rest. Easily attached to any front fork, as per directions packed with each bell.

No. 19C517 Tire Chimes. Price.......57c

If by mail, postage extra, 10 cents.

Our Winner Electric Chimes.

The two fine, large, bell metal gongs combined with rotary electric movement produce the most musical alarm ever heard. Strictly high grade.

No. 19C520 Our Winner Electric Chimes. Price.......30c

If by mail, postage extra, 12 cents.

Our Sterling Chimes Bell.

By a slight pressure of the finger a continuous ringing chime can be had, very loud. No clock work or rewinding, the two large, non-revolving, bell metal gongs blending together so harmoniously as to make the sound most musical. Made in the very best possible manner, and is worth several times our price. Just the bell where a loud alarm is needed, such as on bicycles, tandems or automobiles.

No. 19C522 Sterling Chimes Bell. Price.......48c

If by mail, postage extra, 15 cents.

Our Sterling Beauty Chimes.

This is certainly the most beautiful and handsome chimes bell ever produced. The mechanism is perfect, no rewinding, continuous rotary movement, double gong, non-revolving, making a very loud and harmonious alarm. The gongs are of genuine bell metal, 2¼-inch, handsomely decorated. Suitable for use on bicycles, motors, tandems and automobiles.

No. 19C524 Beauty Chimes. Price, 67c

If by mail, postage extra, 15 cents.

Sprocket Lock.

A very handsome appearing lock.

No. 19C563 Sprocket Lock. Price.......8c

Postage extra, 3 cents.

Combination Lock.

No keys to lose, as each lock has a three-tumbler combination which can only be opened by the owner having the combination. Size, 2½x2 inches.

No. 19C578 Combination Lock. Price.......33c

If by mail, postage extra, 4 cents.

Cycle Horn.

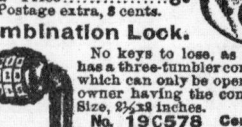

The latest novelty in bicycle alarms, consisting of a handsome brass horn, elegantly nickel plated, combined with high grade rubber bulb. Horn is 6¼ inches long.

No. 19C530 Cycle Horn. Price.......38c

If by mail, postage extra, 6 cents.

The Gem Whistle.

Gives a loud alarm.

No. 19C608 The Gem Whistle. Price, with chain, 11c

If by mail, postage extra, 5 cents.

The Security Cyclometer.

The Security Cyclometer for 28-inch wheels. Positively the most durable cyclometer ever presented to the rider. It fits around the barrel of front hub between the flanges and cannot be knocked or broken off in falls. The interference pin is placed on inside of fork, out of danger. Its mechanism is perfect, with a total register of 10,000 miles. It is finely nickel plated and thoroughly first class in every way.

No. 19C614 The Security Cyclometer. Price.......(Postage extra, 3 cents).......69c

The Veeder Cyclometer.

The Veeder Cyclometer registers 10,000 miles and repeats. So well known to the riding public as to require no special introduction. Weighs but one ounce. It is both dust and water proof, finely nickel plated.

No. 19C617 The Veeder Cyclometer. Price....(Postage extra, 3c)....57c

Hand Pumps.

Hand Pump made of good, strong material, and will last two or three seasons. The favorite style and size, including hose connection which will fit all valves.

No. 19C648 Pump. Price.......7c

If by mail, postage extra, 5 cents.

No. 19C649 Extra Hose and connection. Price.......(Postage extra, 2 cents).......3c

Our 25-Cent Giant Foot Pump.

The Giant Foot Pump is made of the very finest quality of seamless tubing and positively will not corrode. It has a 1¼x12-inch barrel, detachable hose, with a powerful plunger, having at its lower end a patented device whereby the leather washer is continually expanded against the sides of the barrel, thereby making it impossible for the barrel to leak air, thus making it much easier to inflate a tire than with other pumps; will fit all valves, such as the G. & J., Schrader, M. & W., and Dunlop.

No. 19C652 Giant Foot Pump. Price.......25c

If by mail, postage extra, 27 cents.

Our Marvel Foot Pump.

This is an extra heavy pump, having a malleable base wide enough to stand alone, with 12-inch barrel, intended for those requiring a heavy pump; fitted with regular hose and universal connections. Pump is highly finished.

No. 19C654 Marvel Pump. Price.......33c

If by mail, postage extra, 34 cents.

The Giant Pocket Pump.

A very powerful pump. Illustration shows pump extended for use as a foot pump, also when telescoped, ready to carry in pocket. Made of seamless brass, finely nickel plated. Size, when closed, 6½ inches; extended, 15½ inches. Has universal valve connection to fit any tire.

No. 19C660 Giant Pocket Foot Pump. Price.......35c

If by mail, postage extra, 19 cents.

REFER TO OUR BIG CLOTHING DEPARTMENT FOR ANYTHING IN THE LINE OF CLOTHING. We can SAVE YOU MONEY and furnish BETTER MADE and BETTER FITTING CLOTHING than you can buy elsewhere.

The Telescope Bicycle Pump.

This pump is 10½ inches long when closed, and 22½ inches long when ready for use. It will inflate a tire as quickly as an ordinary foot pump. Can be attached to frame by means of clamp accompanying every pump. Made entirely of brass, handsomely nickel plated.

No. 19C661 Telescope Pump. Price, 39c
If by mail, postage extra, 12 cents.

Austin Pump.

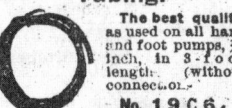

This pump can be carried in the pocket, or attached to frame by means of clamp accompanying pump. Is very powerful, developing a pressure of 100 pounds. No hose connections required. Size, 10x¾-inch. Made of brass, handsomely plated.

No. 19C662 Austin Pump. Price....38c
If by mail, postage extra, 7 cents.

Monarch Foot Pump.

This pump is adapted for heavy work, has 18-inch barrel, hose with universal thread connection. It is strong enough to inflate carriage or vehicle tires.

No. 19C664 Monarch Pump. Price....56c
If by mail, postage extra, 39 cents.

Rubber Pump Tubing.

The best quality, as used on all hand and foot pumps, ⅜-inch, in 3-foot lengths (without connection).

No. 19C6,0 Tubing. Price for 3 feet....11c
If by mail, postage extra, per foot, 2 cents.

Our Child's Seat.

Adapted for use on either ladies' or gents' bicycles; extremely light and does not interfere with the adult rider. Perfectly safe.

No. 19C718 Child's Seat. Price....49c

Our Triumph Oiler.

In this oiler we present one of the neatest patterns, well made, nicely nickel plated.

No. 19C742 Triumph Oiler. Price....5c
If by mail, postage extra, 2 cents.

Adjustable Coasters.

Adjustable Foot Rests or Coasters, very light but strong and neat in design.

No. 19C760 Adjustable Coasters. Price, per pair.......9c
If by mail, postage extra, 6 cents.

Leather Grips.

These grips are made from genuine sole leather and are certainly the most durable made.

No. 19C798 Leather Grips. Price, per pair....5c
If by mail, postage extra, 5 cents.

Fancy End Cork Grips.

With enameled ends inlaid. Maroon or black tips.

No. 19C800 Fancy Cork Grips, Price, per pair....14c
If by mail, postage extra, 7 cents.

Liquid Pistol.

This is a well made nickel plated pistol, with a rubber bulb in handle intended to be filled with ammonia, and by pressing the trigger a fine stream of liquid may be thrown from ten to twenty feet, making a very practical means of defense against dogs, tramps or hoodlums.

No. 19C905 Liquid Pistol. Price....45c
If by mail, postage extra, 5 cents.

Handle Bar Buffer.

Goes on frame and prevents handle bar from knocking off the enamel.

No. 19C910 Handle Bar Buffer. Price....4c
Postage extra, 3 cents.

Patent Trousers Guard.

A neat and handy device for saving the trousers from dirt and grease.

No. 19C916 Patent Trousers Guard. Price, per pair....1c
If by mail, postage extra, 3 cents.

Combination Tool.

Made of steel, nicely nickel plated. Is useful as a nipple grip, screwdriver and wrench for axle nuts.

No. 19C937 Combination Tool. Price, 8c
If by mail, postage extra, 3 cents.

S. R. & Co.'s Bicycle Wrench.

Every rider needs a good wrench for his tool bag. This wrench is made of best quality steel, hardened jaws, handsomely nickel plated.

No. 19C940 Bicycle Wrench. Price....9c
If by mail, postage extra, 6 cents.

Spanner Wrench

A very handy tool, being adjustable, will fit almost any cone or nut. Made of sheet metal, securely riveted.

No. 19C953 Spanner Wrench. Price, 10c
If by mail, postage extra, 4 cents.

Chain Brush.

For cleaning chain, sprocket and other parts. Fine quality.

No. 19C960 Chain Brush. Price.....9c
If by mail, postage extra, 8 cents.

Victor Nipple Grip.

A handy pocket nipple grip, fits any nipple. Nicely nickel plated.

No. 19C982 Victor Grip. Price....12c
If by mail, postage extra, 3 cents.

The Standard Toe Clips.

These Toe Clips are made of tempered steel and are a very popular clip.

No. 19C996 Standard Toe Clips. Price, per pair, 7c
If by mail, postage extra, 10 cents.

Built up Wheels.

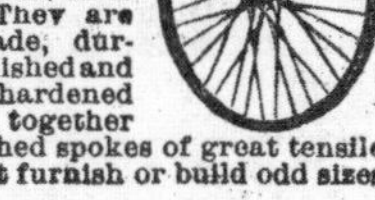

These wheels are especially well constructed, being built in our own factory. The rims are all standard crescent shape to take 28-inch tires, such as Kenwood, M. & W., Seroco, etc. They are built with high grade, durable hubs, highly finished and nickel plated, with hardened cups and cones, together with extra well finished spokes of great tensile strength. We cannot furnish or build odd sizes of wheels.

No. 19C1041 Rear Wheel only. Price....$1.40
No. 19C1042 Front Wheel only. Price....1.10

Wood Rim Wheels for 28-inch G & J. tires as follows:

No. 19C1053 Rear Wheel only. Price....$1.60
No. 19C1054 Front Wheel only. Price....1.30

For price on G. & J. tires, see page 553.

Wood Rim Wheels for 28-inch Dunlop tires, as follows:

No. 19C1056 Rear Wheel only. Price....$1.60
No. 19C1057 Front Wheel only. Price....1.30

For price on Dunlop tires see page 553.

Coaster Brake Wheels.

To accommodate riders who may wish to fit bicycles with a coaster brake rear wheel, we carry a stock of 28-inch built up rear wheels, containing the celebrated Forsyth Coaster Hub and Brake, the best brake on the market, to take 28-inch tires of the cemented type. Sprockets either 7, 8, 9 or 10-tooth. We will send 9-tooth unless otherwise specified.

No. 19C65 Rear Wheel with Forsyth Coaster Brake. Price....$3.75

If G. & J. or Dunlop rims are desired in place of the crescent shaped rim, there will be an extra charge of 25 cents.

Bicycle Hubs.

The bearings are extra heavy, carefully hardened and fitted with ball retainers and oilers. Sprockets 7, 8, 9 or 10-tooth. Hubs drilled with 32 holes in the front and 36 in the rear.

If by mail, postage extra, 15 cents.

No. 19C1049 Rear Hub only. Price....65c
No. 19C1050 Front Hub only. Price, 37c
If by mail, postage extra, 10 cents.

Wood Rims.

Our rims are made of selected stock, thoroughly seasoned. The rim manufacturers have adopted a standard width, viz.: So that a rim to fit a 28x1⅝-inch tire will also fit a 28x1½-inch tire. We cannot supply rims of special color, or drilled other than 32 and 36.

No. 19C1060 Front Rim, 32 holes. Price....35c
If by mail, postage extra, 21 cents.

No. 19C1061 Rear Rim, 36 holes. Price....35c
If by mail, postage extra, 21 cents.

Spokes, Nipples and Washers.

Our spokes are made of piano wire, finely plated, standard gauge, 12⅛ inches long for 28-inch wheels.

No. 19C1100 Spokes and Nipples. Price, per dozen....8c
If by mail, postage extra, 8 cents.

No. 19C1101 Sawtooth Washers, sold only by the 100. Price, per 100....4c
If by mail, postage extra, 5 cents.

Seat Posts.

Front L posts made of best seamless steel tubing, fitted with expander, elegantly nickel plated, 5 inches long, either ⅞, 15-16, 1, 1 1-16, or 1⅛ inches in diameter. State diameter desired plainly.

No. 19C1111 Expander Seat Post. Price........24c
If by mail, postage extra, 12 cents.

No. 19C1112 Expander Seat Post, 19 inches long. Price....35c
If by mail, postage extra, 20 cents.

Spring Seat Post.

In using this post you eliminate all the unpleasant effects of rough roads. This is the best post made, is handsomely finished and plated. Made to fit 15-16 and ⅞-inch (inside measure) seat post mast. It has internal expander to fit flush joint wheels.

No. 19C1115 Spring Seat Post. Price....$1.20
If by mail, postage extra, 28 cents.

Detachable Chain.

Never before could such a chain be bought for so low a price. We furnish these chains in 60-link lengths, suitable for any combination of sprockets, and as every link is detachable they can be readily adjusted if necessary.

No. 19C1150 Detachable Chain, 60 links, 3-16-inch. Price....69c
If by mail, postage extra, 23 cents.

No. 19C1151 Extra Links for same. Price....2c
If by mail, postage extra, 2 cents.

No. 19C1152 Detachable Chain, 60 links, ¼-inch. Price....69c
If by mail, postage extra, 28 cents.

No. 19C1153 Extra Links for same. ¼-inch. Price....2c
If by mail, postage extra, 2 cents.

Roller Chain.

This form of construction removes all friction, and therefore does away with nearly all wear, as the rollers revolve on the rivets. It will outwear several ordinary chains, as rollers and rivets are extra hard and side plates are reinforced. Made 60 links long, for 3-16 inch sprockets only.

No. 19C1155 Roller Chain. Price $1.25
If by mail, postage extra, 30 cents.

No. 19C1156 Extra Links for above. Price....5c
If by mail, postage extra, 2 cents.

Chain Adjuster.

Our adjusters are made from select material, extra strong. Heavily nickeled.

No. 19C1154 Chain Adjuster. Price, per pair....4c
If by mail, postage extra, 2 cents.

Bicycle Balls.

Steel Balls, highest grade, guaranteed true to gauge. Made of the finest tool steel.

No. 19C1170 ⅛-inch balls. Per dozen..1c
If by mail, postage extra, 2 cents.
No. 19C1171 5-32 inch balls. Per dozen..2c
If by mail, postage extra, 2 cents.
No. 19C1172 3-16 inch balls. Per dozen..3c
If by mail, postage extra, 2 cents.
No. 19C1173 ¼-inch balls. Per dozen..5c
If by mail, postage extra, 4 cents.
No. 19C1174 5-16 inch balls. Per dozen. 6c
If by mail, postage extra, 4 cents.

Standard Tire Repair Outfits.

No. 19C1190 Seroco Single Tube Outfit. Price....5c
No. 19C1195 Goodrich Jiffy Outfit. Price....14c
No. 19C1186 Morgan & Wright Double Tube Outfit. Price....10c
No. 19C1192 G. & J. Double Tube Outfit. Price....10c
No. 19C1193 Dunlop Double Tube Outfit. Price....10c
If by mail, postage extra, 3 cents.

Sureshot Solution.

For repairing punctures in single tube tires this cement is very satisfactory. Tubes, ¾x4 inches.

No. 19C1194 Sureshot Solution. Price, per tube....7c
If by mail, postage extra, 5 cents.

Valves for Single and Double Tube Tires.

No. 19C133 Morgan & Wright Valve and Stem complete. Price....7c
If by mail, postage extra, 2 cents.
No. 19C134 Metal Valve only. Price..5c
If by mail, postage extra, 2 cents.
No. 19C135 Rubber Stem only. Price 3c
If by mail, postage extra, 2 cents.
No. 19C136 Shoe Valve for single tube tire. Price....10c
If by mail, postage extra, 3 cents.
No. 19C80 G. & J. Valve. Price....11c
If by mail, postage extra, 3 cents.

Acme Patching Rubber.

Acme Patching Rubber, made from pure Para rubber, 1 dozen sheets in package.

No. 19C1197 Acme Patching Rubber. Price, per package........15c
If by mail, postage extra, 3 cents.

The Cox Repair Outfit.

This is the best plug repair outfit made; by following directions anyone can quickly repair their own single tube tires and do it properly.

No. 19C1202 Cox Repair Outfit. Price....17c
If by mail, postage extra, 6 cents.

Acme Tire Tape.

Acme Tire Tape will mend those pin punctures that you get so often. No cyclist should be without this very useful part of a repair outfit. We have put the price where it is as low as it is possible to put it.

No. 19C1210 Acme Tire Tape. Price, per roll....2c
If by mail, postage extra, 3 cents.

Lacing Cord.

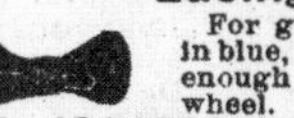

For guards on ladies' wheels, in blue, black, maroon or green; enough in a bunch to lace one wheel.

No. 19C1220 Lacing Cord. Price, per bunch....8c
If by mail, postage extra, 3 cents.

Neverleak Tire Fluid.

This is a compound invented for the purpose of making porous tires airtight, and is also a self healing puncture fluid. By injecting this fluid into tires you do not impair the resiliency, nor will it injure the rubber or fabric. Put up in ⅛-pint cans only.

No. 19C1222 Neverleak Tire Fluid. Price, per ⅛-pint....26c
Not mailable.

Pure Rubber Cement.

Pure Rubber Cement; the best that can be made.

No. 19C1226 Rubber Cement. ¾x4-inch tube. Price....3c
If by mail, postage and tube extra, 9 cents.
No. 19C1227 Rubber Cement. 1x6-inch tubes. Price....4c
If by mail, postage and tube extra, 10 cents.
No. 19C1232 Rubber Cement. In 4-ounce cans. Price....6c
If by mail, postage and tube extra, 15 cents.
No. 19C1233 Rubber Cement. In ½-pint cans. Price....11c
Not mailable.

Wood Rim Liquid Cement.

No. 19C1240 Wood Rim Liquid Cement. In 1x6-inch tubes. It sticks. Price....5c
If by mail, postage and tube extra, 10 cents.
No. 19C1241 Wood Rim Liquid Cement. In 4-ounce cans. Price....6c
If by mail, postage and tube extra, 15 cents.
No. 19C1242 Wood Rim Liquid Cement. In ½-pint cans. Price....9c
Not mailable.

Hard Tire Cement.

For re-cementing tires, grips, etc.

No. 19C1247 3-ounce cakes. Price....4c
If by mail, postage extra, 6 cents.

No. 19C1248 1-pound cakes. Price 17c
If by mail, postage extra, 18 cents.

Aluminum Lacquer.

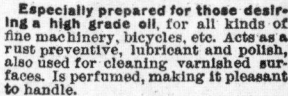

Sometimes called Nickelplater, for coating and retouching rusty parts of a bicycle. Not an enamel. Easily applied by anyone.

No. 19C1270 Aluminum Lacquer. Price, per bottle....8c
If by mail, postage and tube extra, 12 cents.

Chain Lubricant.

All chains require frequent cleaning and lubricating. In our lubricant is found an acceptable substitute for oil, it is more cleanly and will not catch the dust.

No. 19C1284 Chain Lubricant. Price....3c
If by mail, postage extra, 3 cents.

Bicycle Enamel.

This enamel is air drying and does not require baking; can be applied by anyone. Put up in 4-ounce cans in the following colors: Blue, black, green, maroon, vermilion, yellow or white. Specify color.

No. 19C1280 Bicycle Enamel. Price, per can....8c
If by mail, postage and tube extra, 15 cents.

Enamel Varnish.

To be applied over enamel to preserve it and to brighten old enamel.

No. 19C1276 Enamel Varnish, in ¼-pint can. Price, per can 10c
If by mail, postage and tube extra, 15 cents.

Acme Oil.

Especially prepared for those desiring a high grade oil, for all kinds of fine machinery, bicycles, etc. Acts as a rust preventive, lubricant and polish, also used for cleaning varnished surfaces. Is perfumed, making it pleasant to handle.

No. 19C1259 Acme Oil, 3-ounce bottle. Price....11c
Not mailable.

Bicycle Lubricating Oil.

A very necessary article in taking proper care of a bicycle and its bearings.

No. 19C1288 Lubricating Oil. ⅛-pint can. Price....6c
If by mail, postage and tube extra, 17 cents.
No. 19C1292 Lubricating Oil. ½-pint can. Price....11c
Not mailable.

OUR CROCKERY AND GLASSWARE DEPARTMENT.

Our Beautiful Crockery Catalogue, Printed in Seven Colors and Gold, is Free for the Asking.

WE ISSUE A VERY HANDSOME and complete Special Crockery Catalogue, showing our entire line of dinner sets and toilet sets in their actual natural colors, the finest crockery catalogue ever published, and this book will be sent to anyone by mail postpaid, free on application. While we recommend that you send your order for a dinner set or toilet set, direct from this catalogue without delaying to first write for the free Special Catalogue, because our entire line and our lowest prices and best offers are made in this book, nevertheless, if you want more information regarding the sets, or better, larger and handsomer colored illustrations, write for the free Crockery Catalogue, as illustrated hereon. Understand, you take no risk whatever in ordering direct from these pages, for our newest goods and best values are here displayed, and you can order any dinner set or toilet set from this catalogue with the understanding and agreement, that if it does not prove perfectly satisfactory in every way, we will return your money and pay transportation charges both ways. However, you are welcome to our free Special Crockery Catalogue, a beautiful book printed in seven colors and gold, and if you want the most complete book of information on crockery ever published, write and ask for this catalogue. Simply say: "Please send me your free Crockery Catalogue," and it will go to you by return mail, postpaid.

ABOUT FREIGHT CHARGES. Nearly all railroad companies carry crockery and glassware at second class rate, and sometimes as low as third class, depending on the section of the United States to which it is shipped. The second class rate averages from 40 to 50 cents per 100 pounds for 500 miles. The weights of the different dinner sets and glassware sets are all plainly given in the catalogue, and by referring to the freight rates in the front of this book you can get the freight rate to your railroad station and thus figure very close to what your freight will amount to, and you will find that it will amount to next to nothing as compared to what you will save in the price.

OUR BINDING GUARANTEE. We guarantee that if you order one of our sets of dinnerware or glassware, and do not find it in every respect better in quality and lower in price than what you could procure the same grade of ware for from any other dealer, upon return of the goods we will refund your money in full. We furthermore guarantee that our dinnerware will not craze, and will agree to replace, free of charge, any piece that may prove defective in material or workmanship. All the glassware listed is of the best grade it is possible to procure, and will, with ordinary care, stand the test of a lifetime.

UNDER THE ILLUSTRATION AND DESCRIPTION OF EACH STYLE OF DINNERWARE will be shown the combination which can be furnished of that kind, and in every case it would be advisable for the customer to **REFER TO THIS PAGE** to see exactly what pieces are contained in each set.

100-Piece Dinner Set.

12 Tea Cups	1 Oval Open Vegetable Dish	1 Sauce Boat
12 Tea Saucers	1 Round Open Vegetable Dish	1 Pickle Dish
12 Dinner Plates	1 Covered Vegetable Dish (2 pieces)	1 Covered Butter Dish (3 pieces)
12 Tea Plates	1 Covered Sugar Bowl (2 pieces)	1 Bowl
12 Pie Plates		1 Cream Pitcher
12 Sauce Dishes		1 Pitcher, quart size
12 Butter Plates		
1 Platter, 12-inch		
1 Platter, 14-inch		

Shipping weight, 90 pounds.

101-Piece Dinner Set.

12 Tea Cups	1 Round Open Vegetable Dish	1 Cream Pitcher
12 Tea Saucers	2 Covered Vegetable Dishes (4 pieces)	1 Pickle Dish
12 Dinner Plates	1 Platter, 12-inch	1 Bowl
12 Tea Plates	1 Platter, 14-inch	1 Covered Butter Dish (3 pieces)
12 Soup Plates	1 Covered Sugar Bowl (2 pieces)	1 Sauce Boat
12 Sauce Dishes		
12 Butter Plates		
1 Oval Open Vegetable Dish		

Shipping weight, 90 pounds.

56-Piece Dinner Set.

6 Tea Cups	1 Platter, 10-inch	1 Covered Butter Dish (3 pieces)
6 Tea Saucers	1 Platter, 12-inch	1 Sugar Bowl (2 pieces)
6 Dinner Plates	1 Oval Baker	1 Cream Pitcher
6 Tea Plates	1 Covered Vegetable Dish (2 pieces)	1 Bowl
6 Pie Plates	1 Sauce Boat	
6 Sauce Dishes	1 Pickle Di[sh]	
6 Butter Plates		

Shipping weight, 50 pounds.

80-Piece Dinner Set.

12 Tea Cups	1 Platter, 12-inch	1 Covered Vegetable Dish (2 pieces)
12 Tea Saucers	1 Platter, 14-inch	1 Sauce Boat
12 Dinner Plates	1 Round Open Vegetable Dish	1 Pickle Dish
12 Pie Plates	1 Oval Open Vegetable Dish	
12 Sauce Dishes		
12 Butter Plates		

Shipping weight, 65 pounds.

NOTE—ALL PLATTERS ARE MEASURED FROM EDGE TO EDGE.

FOR FIVE CENTS EACH WE WILL FURNISH, POSTPAID, AN INDIVIDUAL BUTTER PLATE OF ANY SET, WHICH WILL SHOW DECORATION OF THE SET.

OUR 100-PIECE AMERICAN MADE SEMI-VITREOUS CHINA DINNER SET, $4.49

ENTIRELY NEW. OUR ANGELUS PLAIN WHITE, SEMI-VITREOUS DINNER SET is, without doubt, the finest plain white dinner set on the market. It is made by America's best potter and is guaranteed not to craze. Its wearing qualities are unsurpassed, as the body is composed of the finest grades of clay, fired to a flint hardness and covered by a deep glossy milk white glaze, heretofore only to be found in the most expensive sets. As the illustration shows, this set is extremely handsome, as it is very light and thin and most gracefully modeled, and neatly embossed.

We positively guarantee the ware to be the finest selection, perfect in every way, without misshapes or small impractical sizes.

This set is carefully packed in a barrel and shipped direct from the pottery at East Liverpool, Ohio, from which point customer pays freight. We can furnish this set in a regular 100-piece combination as shown above. Shipping weight, 90 pounds.

No. 2C200 100-piece Dinner Set. Price..........$4.49

We can furnish the following pieces if ordered with a set:

Soup Plates, new coupe shape. Price, per dozen......$0.85

Coffee Cups and Saucers. Price per dozen...... 1.20

OUR WAVERLY SEMI-PORCELAIN DINNER SET.

$4.55 AND $5.98

FOR A HANDSOME MEDIUM PRICED DINNER SET we recommend our Waverly Set, which is made of the highest grade semi-porcelain pure white in color, and with a soft glossy glaze, which gives it a handsome appearance and will not craze. It has a neat and attractive shape and is decorated with a floral and scroll design, consisting of large petal flowers on a background of ferns. The decoration can be furnished in green, blue or pink, as desired. It is placed on the ware by a stencil process after the glaze is put on the clay and is then thoroughly baked in the glaze, so that it will never fade or wear off. It is made by the best known and oldest American pottery in East Liverpool, Ohio, whose trade mark stands for the very best quality of ware, both as to the glaze and decoration, and anyone purchasing one of these sets will be perfectly satisfied with it. Be sure to state the color you desire when ordering.

For number and style of pieces included in the dinner sets quoted below, see list above. Each set is carefully packed and shipped direct from the pottery in East Liverpool, Ohio, from which point the customer pays the freight. Shipping weight, 90 pounds.

No. 2C204 Our Waverly Semi-Porcelain Dinner Set, furnished in either of the following combinations:

56-piece Dinner Set. Price..........$4.55

100-piece Dinner Set. Price.......... 5.98

When ordered with the regular sets quoted above, we can furnish the following pieces:

Coffee Cups and Saucers. Price, per dozen..........$1.25

Individual Vegetable or Side Dishes. Price, per dozen.......... 1.25

Soup Plates, new coupe shape. Price, per dozen.......... .85

THE AZALIA DINNER SET, $4.45

THE DECORATION consists of neat floral sprays of dainty white azalias and green leaves, so delicately shaded and so perfect in workmanship that the flowers and foliage are true to life. It is applied by the new decalcomania process, which produces a much more perfect decoration than if decorated in the ordinary way. To produce the desired effect it is necessary to give the ware a double glaze, and a decoration of this sort will wear a lifetime and never fade, and is a much stronger ware on account of the extra length of time required in the firing. This set is made of a very fine quality of semi-porcelain, made by the famous Homer-Laughlin China Co., America's best potters, and is fully guaranteed in every respect. The shape used in the set is known as the new colonial pattern, which is the most artistic shape made. The ware is exceedingly thin and light and resembles the finest French china. Every piece is artistically embossed with a beautiful scroll, which forms a complete border. All plates, saucers, platters, etc., have scalloped festoon edges and are branded on the back by the famous makers' trade mark.

These sets are shipped direct to our customers from East Liverpool, Ohio, and are carefully packed by expert packers, which insures safe delivery.

No. 2C212 Our Azalia Semi-Porcelain Dinner Set.
56-piece Dinner Set. Ship'g wt., 55 lbs. Price, $4.45
80-piece Dinner Set. Ship'g wt., 65 lbs. Price, 4.98
100-piece Dinner Set. Ship'g wt., 90 lbs. Price, 6.49
101-piece Dinner Set. Ship'g wt., 95 lbs. Price, 7.48

For number and style of pieces quoted above, see page 560.

In ordering, please mention number of pieces desired.

OUR FLORENCE ROSE DINNER SET.

MADE BY THE EDWIN M. KNOWLES CHINA CO.

$4.98 TO $8.95

THE GREATEST VALUE EVER OFFERED. Our Florence Rose Dinner Set is one of the prettiest and most dainty patterns on the market. The decoration is applied by the new decalcomania process and is an exact reproduction of one of the most popular Haviland China patterns. The decoration consists of a delicate spray border of pink roses, with background of small white daisies with pink tinted petals and green foliage, with small clusters of roses artistically arranged to form a border. It is made by the celebrated Edwin M. Knowles China Company, one of the best known potteries in America. The ware is made from the best quality of semi-porcelain, being handsomely modeled and embossed and covered with a heavy milk white glaze. We fully guarantee the ware to be of the finest selection, perfect in every respect. Each set is carefully packed in a barrel and shipped from the pottery in East Liverpool, Ohio.

No. 2C217 Our Florence Rose Dinner Set.
56-piece Dinner Set. Shipping weight, 55 pounds. Price.. $4.98
80-piece Dinner Set. Shipping weight, 65 pounds. Price.. 5.89
100-piece Dinner Set. Shipping weight, 80 pounds. Price.. 7.48
101-piece Dinner Set. Shipping weight, 90 pounds. Price.. 8.95

For number and style of pieces, see page 560.

When ordered with above sets, we can furnish the following pieces:

Coffee Cups and Saucers. Price, per dozen............ $1.39
Individual Vegetable Dishes. Price, per dozen............ 1.20
Bone Dishes. Price, per dozen............ 1.10
Soup Plates, new coupe shape. Price, per dozen............ .98

OUR FLORAL BORDER DINNER SET, $6.98.

MADE IN ENGLAND.

FURNISHED IN TWO COLORS, CANTON BLUE OR RICH SAGE GREEN.

OUR FLORAL BORDER DINNER SET is the best value ever offered in good quality English ware. It is made by the celebrated W. Hulm Pottery, Burslem, Eng., and is guaranteed never to craze. The body of the ware is thin and light in weight and has a deep glossy glaze of milk whiteness. This set is superior in every respect to the average makes of medium priced English dinnerware and must be seen to be fully appreciated. The shape is new and attractive, having fancy scalloped edges, all covered pieces, including covered dishes, sugar, creamer, butter dish, etc., are very gracefully embossed.

THIS IS AN ENTIRELY NEW underglazed print decoration. It consists of a border of flowers and foliage, as shown in illustration, and can be furnished in CANTON BLUE or RICH SAGE GREEN.

The set consists of 100 pieces as follows:

12 Teacups	12 Individual Butters	1 Covered Sugar Bowl
12 Saucers	1 Platter, 10-inch	1 Creamer
12 Dinner Plates	1 Platter, 14-inch	1 Pickle Dish
12 Tea Plates	1 Baker, 8-inch	1 Sauce Boat
12 Pie Plates	2 Covered Dishes, 10-inch	1 Covered Butter Dish
12 Sauce Dishes	1 Bowl	

Each set is carefully packed in a barrel and is shipped from Chicago to our customers in Central and Western States, and from our warehouse in Boston, Mass., to eastern customers, thus assuring the lowest freight charges.

No. 2C243 100-Piece Dinner Set. Price............ $6.98
Shipping weight, 85 pounds. In ordering, please mention the color you desire.

JOHNSON BROS.' SILVER SHAPE SEMI-PORCELAIN WARE.

MADE IN ENGLAND.

JOHNSON BROS.' CELEBRATED ENGLISH SEMI-PORCELAIN WARE

for prices less than dealers usually ask for the stone china. Johnson Bros., like all potters, make two distinct grades of ware, iron stone china and semi-porcelain ware. Iron stone china is heavier, cheaper and not as white as semi-porcelain. Johnson Bros.' semi-porcelain is the finest quality of semi-porcelain made. It is superior in body, style and general finish and is no comparison to stone china. Owing to an extremely large contract made with this well known pottery we are able to furnish you this high grade semi-porcelain at prices much lower than usually asked for the cheap grades of stone china. Johnson Bros. are universally recognized as the world's best potters and bear equally as good a reputation to the English ware as Haviland does to the French china. The body of this fine ware is very carefully selected and is of extra quality and strength. It is much whiter than other semi-porcelain wares and is modeled on most graceful lines, every piece being extra thin and light in weight. The shape we offer is the latest and most handsome ever produced by any pottery (**known as the silver shape.**) Your attention is particularly drawn to the dainty, yet useful shapes of every piece, the graceful outlines of **handles** on all covered dishes, the handsome and attractive embossing on all flat pieces, such as plates, platters, etc. In fact, every piece is of the most tasty shape and is sure to win the admiration of all users of dinner ware.

No. 2C245 Johnson's English Semi-Porcelain Dinner Set.

Dinner Set.	Shipping wgt.	Price
56-piece Dinner Set	55 lbs.	$4.85
80-piece Dinner Set	65 lbs.	5.85
100-piece Dinner Set	90 lbs.	7.65
101-piece Dinner Set	95 lbs.	8.45

In ordering state the number of pieces desired.

For number and style of pieces quoted above see page 560.

No. 2C245 **Johnson Bros.' Silver Shape White Semi-Porcelain Ware sold in open stock.** For the convenience of our customers we also offer this fine ware (**as described above**) as an open stock pattern. Choose the number of pieces you desire at prices **mentioned below.** No orders will be accepted amounting to less than $2.00.

THE FOLLOWING IS A LIST OF PRICES FOR JOHNSON BROS.' WHITE ENGLISH SEMI-PORCELAIN, AS QUOTED IN OPEN STOCK.

	Actual Size	Each	Per Doz.
Tea Cups and Saucers	8 ounces capacity	$0.10	$1.10
Coffee Cups and Saucers	10 ounces capacity	.12	1.32
Bread and Butter Plates	6⅝ inches	.05	.60
Pie Plates	6¾ inches	.06	.64
Tea Plates	7¾ inches	.07	.78
Dinner Plates	8¾ inches	.08	.92
Dinner Plates, extra large	9¾ inches	.10	1.08
New Coupe Soup Plates	8 inches	.09	.96
Soup Plates	8¾ inches	.09	.92
Sauce Dishes	5¼ inches	.04	.42
Oat Meal Dishes	6¼ inches	.07	.75
Individual Butters	3 inches	.03	.28
Bone Dishes	7x3½ inches	.09	.95
Oval Covered Dishes	8½ inches	.48	
Oval Covered Dishes	9½ inches	.58	
Round Covered Casseroles	8½ inches	.65	
Sauce Tureens with Ladle and Stand	6½x5½ inches	.72	
Sauce Tureens without Ladle and Stand		.53	
Gravy and Sauce Boats	1 pint capacity	.19	
Soup Toureens with Ladle and Stand	10x8 inches	2.65	
Round Ope Nappies	8½ inches	.20	
Round Open Nappies	9½ inches	.24	

	Actual Size	Each	Per Doz.
Individual Vegetable Dishes or Bakers	5¼ inches	$0.08	$0.90
Oval Open Vegetable Dishes	9 inches	.14	
Oval Open Vegetable Dishes	10½ inches	.22	
Platters (small)	9⅝ inches	.11	
Platters (medium)	13½ inches	.21	
Platters (medium large)	14 inches	.33	
Platters (large)	14⅞ inches	.50	
Platters (extra large)	16⅞ inches	.78	
Oyster Bowls	1 pint capacity	.10	1.08
Pitchers	1 pint capacity	.11	
Pitchers	1¾ pint capacity	.15	
Pitchers	1¼ quart capacity	.17	
Pitchers	2 quarts capacity	.27	
Pitchers	2½ quarts capacity	.42	
Bowls	½ pint capacity	.07	
Bowls	1 pint capacity	.09	
Bowls	1 quart capacity	.11	
Creamers	⅞ pint capacity	.15	
Covered Sugar Bowls	¾ quart capacity	.33	
Covered Butter Dishes and Drainers	5½ inches	.43	
Covered Tea Pots	1 quart capacity	.38	
Cake Plates	10 inches	.20	
Pickle Dishes	8x5½ inches	.15	

THE ADELPHI DINNER SETS.

MANUFACTURED BY W. H. GRINDLEY & CO., TUNSTALL, ENGLAND.

THIS SET IS PURE WHITE and rivals Haviland French china in thinness, color and weight. In fact, the only way it can be told from Haviland china is by examining stamp on ware. It also has the extra advantage of durability in its favor, as one of these sets will wear equal to the French china. The shapes are the best that art and scientific pottery have ever devised. Plain white ware is becoming more popular every year, and it is hard to improve upon the appearance of a dinner table laid with a handsome plain white set; but before our Adelphi set was made, it was beyond the reach of ordinary pocketbooks to procure a handsome white dinner set, as only the most expensive ware had the beauty of our Adelphi dinner set. This set is pure white with a brilliant glaze. Every piece modeled in beautiful outlines. The ware is embossed with a dainty scroll design, which has heretofore been the distinguishing feature of Haviland china.

No. 2C253 Adelphi English Semi-Porcelain Dinner Set.

56-piece Dinner Set. Shipping weight, 55 pounds. Price........$4.95
80-piece Dinner Set. Shipping weight, 65 pounds. Price........5.95
100-piece Dinner Set. Shipping weight, 80 pounds. Price........7.75
101-piece Dinner Set. Shipping weight, 90 pounds. Price........8.65

In ordering please state number of pieces desired.

For number and style of pieces included in the dinner sets quoted above, see page 560. In addition to the regular sets quoted above, we can furnish the following pieces if ordered with a complete set:

Coffee Cups and Saucers. Price, per dozen........$1.40
Bone Dishes. Price, per dozen.........95
Soup Plates, new coupe shape. Price, per dozen.........98

Each set is carefully packed and shipped from Chicago to customers living in the Central and Western states, and from our warehouse in Boston, Mass., to eastern customers, thereby insuring the lowest freight charges in every shipment.

OUR KENSINGTON DINNER SET.

MADE BY THE CELEBRATED MAYER POTTERY CO.

THIS HANDSOME DINNER SET closely resembles the best quality of English semi-porcelain ware. It is so perfect in workmanship, quality and finish that it equals most high grade English dinner sets. It is made by the celebrated Mayer Pottery Co. and guaranteed never to craze. **The decoration is something entirely new** and consists of beautiful pink apple blossoms and sprays of green leaves and foliage, made by the new French decalcomania process and will never wear off. All knobs and handles are artistically traced in rich gold, which greatly adds to the attractiveness of the set. The shape is elaborately embossed with lace effect border design, as shown in illustration, and the ware is very thin and light in weight. This set is carefully packed in a barrel and shipped from the pottery in western Pennsylvania.

No. 2C263 56-Piece Dinner Set. Shipping weight, 55 lbs. Price... $5.49
80-Piece Dinner Set. Shipping weight, 65 lbs. Price... 6.48
100-Piece Dinner Set. Shipping weight, 80 lbs. Price... 7.98
101-Piece Dinner Set. Shipping weight, 90 lbs. Price... 9.39

No. 2C264 Same set as above, but decorated with violet rose sprays and French scrolls with green foliage, **a most handsome pattern.**

56-Piece Dinner Set. Shipping weight, 55 lbs. Price... $5.55
80-Piece Dinner Set. Shipping weight, 65 lbs. Price... 6.75
100-Piece Dinner Set. Shipping weight, 80 lbs. Price... 8.25
101-Piece Dinner Set. Shipping weight, 90 lbs. Price... 9.48

For number and style of pieces included in dinner sets above, see page 560.

OUR PARISIAN ROSE DINNER SET, $8.48.

MADE BY THE SMITH-PHILLIPS CHINA CO.

THIS IS THE PRETTIEST DECORATED DINNER SET for the price on the market. It is made by the celebrated Smith-Phillips China Co., one of the best known potteries in America, whose trade mark stands for the highest grade pure white semi-porcelain, guaranteed never to craze. The glaze is very deep and glossy. The decorations consist of dainty pink roses in panels formed by handsomely embossed scrolls. The rose is the most popular pattern used in decorating and in this set we have selected a rose which is bright and attractive and yet small and neat. Every piece is trimmed with gold lines on the edges and all embossed scrolls are traced by hand with bright gold, making this set one of the most attractive patterns ever turned out by any pottery. The shape of this set is an exact reproduction of Havlland china, and is thinner and of more graceful shape than the ordinary American china dinner sets. The decoration is **not gaudy**, but is very rich in appearance, and is sure to suit the most refined taste.

No. 2C265 Parisian Rose Dinner Set. Shipping weight, 90 pounds. Price.. $8.48

Shipped from the pottery in Eastern Ohio.

OUR HOLLY DINNER SET.

AMERICAN MADE, SEMI-PORCELAIN.

Shipped direct from our pottery in Ohio.
Shipping weight, 90 pounds.

THE HOLLY DINNER SET is of the best quality semi-porcelain. Made by the Homer-Laughlin China Co. The body is pure white with the deep glossy glaze which is characteristic of all high grade semi-porcelain ware. The shapes are artistic, being of the latest Colonial pattern. All pieces are neatly embossed and decorated with red holly berries with deep green foliage forming a handsome contrast. The handles and knobs of the cups and all large pieces are stippled with bright gold, which together with the floral decoration gives the set a striking appearance.

We furnish this set in the 100-piece combination, as shown on page 560.
No. 2C266 Our Holly Pattern 100-piece Dinner Set.
Price.. $8.70

When ordered with the regular set quoted, we can furnish the following pieces:

Coffee Cups and Saucers. Price, per dozen $1.48
Individual Vegetable Dishes. Price, per dozen 1.29
Soup Plates, new coupe shape. Price, per dozen........................ 1.20

CANTON BLUE MINTON AND GREEN EXETER DINNER SETS.

CANTON BLUE MINTON AND GREEN EXETER DINNER SETS, are furnished in two decorations CANTON BLUE and EXETER GREEN, both being decorated on good quality English semi-porcelain ware.

THE EXETER GREEN is made by Alfred Meakin, Tunstall, England. The decoration consists of light green vines and floral border patterns, which are decorated under glaze, and of very pleasing design.

THE CANTON BLUE is made by Bourne & Leigh who bear equally as good reputation as the famous Meakin pottery and is one of the most popular blue patterns on the market. The decoration is a Canton Flow Blue, which is a shade between a blue and gray. This is an underglaze decoration and exactly same shape, style and quality as the Green Exeter and is guaranteed to be the best set on the market for the price.

No. 2C271 Canton Blue and Exeter Dinner Set.
55-piece. Shipping weight, 55 pounds. Price...$5.95
80-piece Dinner Set. Shipping wgt., 65 lbs. Price, 7.10
100-piece Dinner Set. Shipping wgt., 80 lbs. Price, 8.85
101-piece Dinner Set. Shipping wgt., 90 lbs. Price, 10.25

In ordering please mention number of pieces desired.

For number and style of pieces included in the dinner sets quoted above, see page 560.

In addition to the regular sets quoted we can furnish the following pieces:

Coffee Cups and Saucers. Price, per dozen........$1.75
Bone Dishes. Price, per dozen.......... 1.25
Soup Plates, new coupe shape. Price, per dozen.. 1.35

ARBUTUS WHITE AND GOLD SEMI-PORCELAIN DINNER SETS.

ARBUTUS WHITE AND GOLD DINNER SET is made by the Homer Laughlin China Co., and is a dainty and most beautiful dinner set which is exceedingly low in price. Lovers of dainty china will most appreciate this rich dinner service, as the decoration consists of gold arbutus wreaths which form a complete border pattern encircling all pieces and has rich gold lace medallion centers. All handles and knobs are hand traced in gold.

Your particular attention is drawn to the beautiful shape known as the King Charles pattern which is much thinner than the ordinary dinner ware and closely resembles Haviland china. It is richly embossed and equal in quality and finish to the best grade of English porcelain ware. In fact this is of such a superior quality that we positively guarantee every piece against crazing even when put to extremely hard usage. Being carefully packed by expert packers we guarantee safe delivery.

This set is shipped from the pottery in Eastern Ohio.

We quote below four special sets at greatly reduced prices, but will furnish both plain white or white and gold in open stock.

No. 2C276 Arbutus White and Gold Dinner Set.
56-piece Dinner Set. Shipping weight, 60 lbs. Price....$6.85
80-piece Dinner Set. Shipping weight, 70 lbs. Price.... 7.95
100-piece Dinner Set. Shipping weight, 90 lbs. Price.... 8.95
101-piece Dinner Set. Shipping weight, 100 lbs. Price.... 9.85

In ordering please mention the number of pieces desired.

For number and style of pieces included in the dinner sets quoted above, see page 560.

No. 2C276 Open Stock Trailing Arbutus WHITE and GOLD. (Choose your own assortment.)

	Actual Size	Per Doz.
Tea Cups & Saucers, capacity	8¼ oz.	$1.33
Coffee Cups & Saucers, capacity	10½ oz.	1.58
Pie or Breakfast Plates	7½ in.	.85
Tea Plates	8⅝ in.	.94
Dinner Plates	9⅝ in.	1.15
Dinner Plates (extra large)	10¼ in.	1.33
Soup Plates	9⅝ in.	1.15
Coupe Soup Plates	8 in.	1.15
Sauce Dishes	5¼ in.	.60
Oat Meal Dishes	6¼ in.	1.35
Individual Butters	2¾ in.	.36
Bone Dishes	6x3 in.	1.10
Oyster Bowls	1¼ pin	1.39
Individual Vegetable Dishes	5½ in.	1.23

	Actual Size	Each
Pitchers	⅝ pint	$0.12
Pitchers	1½ pint	.15
Pitchers	1 quart	.23
Pitchers	2 quart	.28
Pitchers	3 quart	.35
Tea Pots	3 pints	.63
Gravy or Sauce Boats	¾ pint	.26
Sauce Tureens and Stands	9¾ in.	.65
Pickle Dishes	9½ in.	.19
Round Bakers Vegetable Dishes	8½ in.	.21
Round Bakers Vegetable Dishes	9½ in.	.28
Cake Plates	9⅞ in.	.23
Oval Bakers	9¼ in.	.21
Oval Bakers	10¼ in.	.28

	Actual Size	Each
Platters	10¾ in.	$0.12
Platters	11½ in.	.17
Platters	13½ in.	.29
Platters	15¼ in.	.55
Platters	18 in.	.69
Covered Dishes	9 in.	.62
Covered Dishes	9¾ in.	.79
Covered Casseroles	9¼ in.	.39
Soup Tureens and Stands	15¼ in.	2.25
Creamers	⅞ pint	17
Sugar Bowls, Covered	¾ quart	.39
Covered Butter Dishes	5½ in.	.55
Bowls	1¼ pint	.12

No. 2C277 Open Stock. Same as No. 2C276, only in PLAIN WHITE. (Not decorated.)

	Actual Size	Per Doz.
Tea Cups and Saucers	8¼ oz.	$0.85
Coffee Cups and Saucers	10½ oz.	1.10
Pie or Breakfast Plates	7½ in.	.55
Tea Plates	8⅝ in.	.65
Dinner Plates	9⅝ in.	.75
Dinner Plates	10¼ in.	.89
Soup Plates	9⅝ in.	.75
Coupe Soup Plates	8 in.	.75
Sauce Dishes	5¼ in.	.33
Oat Meal Dishes	6¼ in.	.73
Individual Butters	2¾ in.	.24
Bone Dishes	6x3 in.	.72
Oyster Bowls	1¼ pint	.93
Individual Vegetable Dishes	5½ in.	.83

	Actual Size	Each
Pitchers	⅞ pint	$0.08
Pitchers	1½ pint	.10
Pitchers	1 quart	.12
Pitchers	2 quart	.15
Pitchers	3 quart	.23
Tea Pots	1½ quart	.33
Sauce or Gravy Boats	¾ pint	.16
Sauce Tureens and Stands	9¾ in.	.33
Pickle Dishes	9½ in.	.12
Round Vegetable Dishes	8½ in.	.12
Round Vegetable Dishes	9½ in.	.18
Cake Plates	9⅞ in.	.16
Oval Bakers	9¼ in.	.10
Oval Bakers	10¼ in.	.17

	Actual Size	Each
Platters	10¾ in.	$0.10
Platters	11½ in.	.12
Platters	13½ in.	.15
Platters	15¼ in.	.32
Platters	18 in.	.39
Covered Dishes	8½ in.	.42
Covered Dishes	9¾ in.	.45
Covered Casserole	9¼ in.	.55
Soup Tureens	15¼ in.	1.45
Creamers	⅞ pint	.11
Sugar Bowls, Covered	¾ quart	.24
Covered Butter Dishes	5½ in.	.35
Bowls	1¼ pint	.07

No orders for Trailing Arbutus or Plain White Open Stock Patterns amounting to less than $3.00 will be accepted. The above prices are for these two patterns only.

$8.98

OUR EDGEWOOD GOLD STIPPLED DINNER SET.

MADE BY ONE OF THE LARGEST AMERICAN POTTERIES.

OUR EDGEWOOD DINNER SET is the highest grade American semi-porcelain, clear, white and glossy, made of the best quality of material, and decorated in the most artistic manner. It is made by the Homer-Laughlin China Co., whose trade mark stands for the highest grade American semi-porcelain, guaranteed not to craze. The shapes of the pieces are of the latest style and of large practical sizes. This set has a beautiful violet and green floral decoration. It is also elaborately decorated with gold, not of the ordinary kind, but has gold tracings on every cover, as shown in the illustration, while the knobs, handles and edges of all pieces are heavily stippled with gold, giving the set a very rich appearance. **We guarantee every piece to be of the very best quality, especially selected to** wear and if not found entirely satisfactory it can be returned at our expense of freight charges both ways.

This set is carefully packed in a barrel and shipped from the pottery at East Liverpool, Ohio. Shipping weight, about 90 pounds. We can furnish the set in the regular 100-piece combination, shown on page 560.

No. 2C292 100-piece Dinner Set. Price.. **$8.98**

When ordered with the regular set quoted above, we can furnish the following pieces:

Coffee Cups and Saucers. Price, per dozen.... **$1.75**
Soup Plates, new coupe shape. Price, per doz. **1.35**

THE OXFORD DINNER SET.

MADE BY JOHNSON BROS., ENGLAND.

$10.65

THIS HANDSOME DINNER SET is made by the celebrated Johnson Bros.' Pottery of England. The special combination of clays used, together with the deep glaze produce a quality of ware which will stand more service without cracking or chipping than the hard, brittle ware of some other potteries. The decorations of this pottery equal, and in some cases excel, those of the best French manufacturers. This set is decorated with delicate sprigs of dainty blue and white flowers and green leaves tied with double bowknot of pink ribbon and is put on under the glaze of the ware so that it will never fade or wear off. We call particular attention to the neat and original shape of the pieces of this set and the beautiful scroll work following the margin of the rococo edges which no one can fail to admire. Anyone ordering this dinner set will be more than pleased with both the wear and decoration. It is well known in this country that Johnson Bros. is one of the standard potteries of England, and anyone selecting a set made by them is at once assured of receiving a set made from the highest grade materials and with the latest and most delicate shapes and decorations.

Each set is carefully packed and shipped from Chicago to customers living in Central and Western states, and from our warehouse in Boston, Mass., to Eastern customers, thus insuring the lowest freight charges on every shipment. Shipping weight, 90 pounds.

We can furnish this set only in the 100-piece combination, shown on page 560.

No. 2C301 100-piece Dinner Set, complete. Price.................... **$10.65**
Coupe Soup Plates. Price, per dozen, **1.65**

OUR HASTINGS ROSE DINNER SET.

MADE BY W. H. GRINDLEY & CO. ENGLAND.

OUR HASTINGS ROSE DINNER SET presents Grindley & Co.'s latest pattern. It is considered by china experts to be one of the most clever and dainty English rose patterns ever produced and is sure to please. The famous Grindley's semi-porcelain ware is noted for its fine pure milk white body and its pure deep white glaze, and is fully guaranteed never to craze. **THE WARE IS LIGHT AND THIN AND HANDSOMELY MODELED,** being one of the very latest shapes made by this well known pottery. The decoration consists of dainty little rose scrolls on green foliage, forming a very pretty as well as attractive design, which is difficult to properly illustrate and which must be seen to be appreciated. **Each set is carefully packed in a strong barrel**, packed by experienced packers, which insures safe delivery, and is shipped from Chicago to customers living in Central and Western States, and from our warehouse in Boston, Mass., to our eastern trade.

No. 2C309 Our Hastings Rose Dinner Set.

56-piece Dinner Set. Shipping weight, 55 pounds. Price.................... **$7.20**
80-piece Dinner Set. Shipping weight, 65 pounds. Price.................... **8.25**
100-piece Dinner Set. Shipping weight, 80 pounds. Price.................... **10.70**
101-piece Dinner Set. Shipping weight, 100 pounds. Price.................... **11.98**

In ordering, please mention the number of pieces desired.

ENCHANTRESS DINNER SET.

MADE BY WOOD & SONS, BURSLEM, ENGLAND.

OUR ENCHANTRESS DINNER SET is made by the noted firm of Wood & Sons. The quality of the ware is the very best made in England, and that means the best in the whole world. New and handsome shape, decorated with a transfer decoration consisting of apple blossoms in delicate pink and white coloring, relieved with green leaves and twigs. The effect produced is as fine as hand work, and few people could tell the difference. Heavy gold trimmings on all the embossed parts of the large pieces, such as covered dishes, sugar bowl, platters, etc., add very materially to the beauty of this set. We wish to call special attention to the embossed circle on all rococo edges which adds strength to the wear as well as greatly enhancing the beauty of decoration.

This set is carefully packed in a barrel and shipped from Chicago.

No. 2C312 Enchantress English Semi-Porcelain Dinner Sets.

56-piece Dinner Set.	Shipping weight, 55 pounds.	Price............$7.25
80-piece Dinner Set.	Shipping weight, 65 pounds.	Price............8.30
100-piece Dinner Set.	Shipping weight, 90 pounds.	Price............10.75
101-piece Dinner Set.	Shipping weight, 95 pounds.	Price............11.85

For number and style of pieces quoted above, see page 560. In ordering, state number of pieces desired. When ordered with any of the sets quoted above, we can furnish the following pieces:

Coffee Cups and Saucers. Price, per dozen............$2.18
Bone Dishes. Price, per dozen............1.48
Soup Plates, new coupe shape. Price, per dozen............1.88

THE NEW TERESA DINNER SET.

MADE BY JOHNSON BROS., ENGLAND.

THIS IS ONE OF THE MOST HANDSOME DINNER SETS ever made by any pottery. Its decoration is strikingly beautiful, yet very delicate and dainty, as it consists of a dainty little border spray of pink roses artistically entwined with forget-me-nots. The background of the decoration is formed by green vines and leaves, which, combined with the roses and forget-me-nots make a most pleasing effect which must be seen to be appreciated. Its shapes and general outlines, as you will note, are something entirely new. The graceful shapes and handles of covered dishes, and artistic yet useful shapes of cups and saucers, the beautiful embossings on all pieces, combined with the dainty decoration, makes this set the most beautiful set on the market regardless of price.

This set is very carefully packed in a barrel by experienced packers and shipped from Cleveland, Ohio.

No. 2C320 The New Teresa English Semi-Porcelain Dinner Set.

	Shipping Weight	Price
56-piece Dinner Set.	55 pounds.........	$7.59
80-piece Dinner Set.	65 pounds.........	8.58
100-piece Dinner Set.	90 pounds.........	10.98
101-piece Dinner Set.	95 pounds.........	11.98

For number and style of pieces quoted above, see page 560.

LORRAINE WHITE AND GOLD DINNER SETS.

MADE BY JOHNSON BROS., ENGLAND.

THIS DINNER SET is one of the most handsome white and gold dinner sets ever produced by any pottery. You will observe by the illustration, that the shape of this set is something entirely new; one which no one can fail to admire. Every piece is modeled in a most artistic manner. The handsome embossings are very gracefully planned, and the gold is hand traced in such a manner as to outline the edges of embossment. Great care has been taken to full trace all edges, handles and knobs, giving you a full hand traced white and gold dinner set which is hard to equal at double the price. Johnson Bros. are reputed as producing the best grade of semi-porcelain ware in the world. The cups and saucers, the plates, in fact, every piece contained in this high grade set is nearly as thin as the finest grades of fine china. The ware is clear and white and has deep heavy glaze. We fully guarantee the wearing qualities of this dinner set in every respect, and with ordinary care it will last a lifetime.

This set is very carefully packed by experienced packers and shipped from Cleveland, Ohio.

No. 2C326 Lorraine White and Gold English Semi-Porcelain Dinner Set.

	Shipping weight	Price
56-piece Dinner Set............	55 lbs.	$7.75
80-piece Dinner Set............	65 lbs.	8.75
100-piece Dinner Set............	90 lbs.	11.25
101-piece Dinner Set............	95 lbs.	12.48

For number and style of pieces quoted above, see page 560. In ordering, state number of pieces desired.

OUR $11.39 FLOW BLUE WELLINGTON DINNER SET.

MANUFACTURED BY W. H. GRINDLEY & CO., ENGLAND.

$11.39

THIS HIGH GRADE ENGLISH SEMI-PORCELAIN SET is as thin and light as china and is entirely new in shape, having a neat embossed scroll edge on the scallops. It is decorated under the glaze in a beautiful deep flow blue color which forms a rich and striking contrast against the milk white body. The design consists of a large six-petal flower with bud and leaves in panels between lattice designs. The blue decoration is on the rims only, of the different pieces, leaving the pure white centers as shown in the illustration. This set is a plain, rich Colonial design and will please all lovers of cobalt flow blue dinner ware. The price we quote is lower than small dealers can purchase it at wholesale and is within the reach of all desiring a strictly high grade English dinner set.

Each set is carefully packed and shipped from Chicago to customers living in Central and Western states, and from our warehouse in Boston, Mass., to eastern customers, thus insuring the lowest freight charges on every shipment. Shipping weight, 90 pounds.

We can furnish this set in the regular 100-piece combination shown on page 560.

No. 2C328 **100-piece Dinner Set.** Price.................. **$11.39**

When ordered with the regular 100-piece set quoted above, we can furnish the following pieces:

Coffee Cups and Saucers. Price, per dozen.................. $2.10
Soup Plates, new coupe shape. Price, per dozen.................. 1.55

NARCISSUS DINNER SET.

MADE BY W. H. GRINDLEY & CO., TUNSTALL, ENGLAND.

THIS SET is the daintiest ever produced by W. H. Grindley & Co. This pottery is especially noted for the thinness of their wares, the rich elegant glaze, and the artistic models and elegant decorations. The Narcissus is their newest creation, and is the prettiest set we have ever shown. The decoration consists of dainty clusters of pink Narcissus with background of delicate green ferns arranged in graceful festoons. The body of the ware is finished with a beautiful embossed edge, which adds considerably to the appearance of this set. Every piece is trimmed with a heavy gold line, which adds the crowning feature to this beautiful set. As rich in appearance as the best grades of French china at a fraction of the cost. We cannot recommend this set too highly.

No. 2C347 Narcissus English Semi-Porcelain Dinner Set.

56-piece Dinner Set.	Shipping weight, 55 lbs.	$7.65
80-piece Dinner Set.	Shipping weight, 65 lbs.	9.23
100-piece Dinner Set.	Shipping weight, 80 lbs.	11.90
101-piece Dinner Set.	Shipping weight, 90 lbs.	13.40

Shipped from Chicago to our customers living in Southern and Western states, and from our warehouse in Boston to our eastern customers, thereby insuring lowest freight charges on every shipment. For number and style of pieces in sets quoted above, see page 560. When ordering mention number of pieces desired.

If ordered with above sets, we can furnish the following pieces:

Coffee Cups and Saucers. Price, per dozen.................. $2.25
Individual Vegetable Dishes. Price, per dozen.................. 1.69
Soup Plates, new coupe shape. Price, per dozen.................. 1.65

GENUINE CARLSBAD CHINA DINNER SET.

$12.95

AT $12.95 we offer our customers a fine Carlsbad china set, which we consider the greatest china dinner set ever offered by any house at so low a price. Do not judge this high grade ware by the low price we quote, as sets of this quality usually sell for double the price we ask. This set is made of a very fine quality of translucent china, which is thinner than Haviland china. The shape used in this set is entirely new, being beautifully embossed and gracefully outlined. The cups, sugars, creamers, etc., modeled so light and thin in shape that they are termed egg shell china, yet are very strong and durable. The decoration is something entirely new and consists of dainty pink floral spray with green leaves and vines which form a background which greatly adds to the beauty of the set. The decoration is put on by the new decalcomania process, which produces the beautiful flowers and foliage in their natural colors and is guaranteed never to wear off. Besides this beautiful decoration, pieces are full gold traced on knobs and handles.

This 100-piece set is carefully packed in a box and shipped direct from Chicago. Shipping weight, 100 pounds.

This set is furnished in the following composition:

12 Tea Cups and Saucers	1 14-inch Platter
12 Large Dinner Plates	1 16-inch Platter
12 Pie or Tea Plates	1 Gravy Boat
12 New Coupe Soup Plates	1 Covered Vegetable Dish
12 Sauce Dishes	1 Round Casserole
12 Individual Butters	1 Baker
1 Covered Sugar Bowl	1 Covered Butter Dish and Drainer
1 Cream Pitcher	1 Pickle Dish

No. 2C371 **100-piece Dinner Set, complete.** Price, **$12.95**

IMPERIAL AUSTRIAN CHINA DINNER SET.

MADE IN AUSTRIA.

$14.48

GENUINE IMPERIAL AUSTRIAN CHINA DINNER SET. The highest grade china made in Austria. Very light in weight and very translucent, so much so that the light will readily pass through even the larger pieces, such as covered dishes and platters, thus showing it to be as thin as the best French china. It is the equal of any of the French makes and is sold at one-third less. This particular pattern is one of the choicest made by this noted factory, and we flatter ourselves that we have selected the very best design that it was possible to get. This shape is considered by china critics to be the best modeled and most graceful ever made. The decoration is an elegant transfer of pink flowers with green leaves, gracefully arranged in dainty sprays. The pink decoration is the daintiest color made and is the most difficult to place upon dinner ware.

Shipped from Chicago to customers living in the Central and Western States, and from our warehouse in Boston, Mass., to Eastern customers, thereby insuring the lowest freight charges. Shipping weight, 100 pounds.

It is sold only in our 100-piece combination, as follows:

- 12 Dinner Plates
- 12 Breakfast Plates
- 12 Tea Plates
- 12 Sauce Dishes
- 12 Teacups
- 12 Tea Saucers
- 12 Individual Butters
- 1 Covered Sugar (2 pcs.)
- 1 Cream Pitcher
- 1 Sauce Bowl with Stand
- 1 Covered Butter Dish and Drainer (3 pieces)
- 1 Oval Covered Vegetable Dish (2 pieces)
- 1 Round Covered Vegetable Dish (2pcs)
- 1 Platter, 10 inches
- 1 Platter, 14 inches
- 1 Open Vegetable Dish
- 1 Pickle Dish

No. 2C374 100-piece Dinner Set, complete. Price............ **$14.48**

When ordered with the regular set quoted above, we can furnish the following pieces extra:

Coffee Cups and Saucers. Price, per dozen........................ **$2.95**

Soup Plates, new coupe shape. Price, per dozen........................ **2.49**

Soup Plates, regular deep shape. Price, per dozen........................ **2.43**

THE ELITE BAVARIAN CHINA DINNER SET.

$16.85

COMPARE THIS $16.85 GENUINE BAVARIAN China Dinner Set with those offered at $25.00 and you will fully appreciate that this is the greatest value ever offered in high grade dinner ware. It is made from the finest quality of thin translucent china, which is lighter and equally as finely selected as the best grades of Haviland china, and is made by the most celebrated factory in Europe. The shape, you will note, is most cleverly modeled, each piece being finely embossed, as the illustration shows. No expense has been spared to elaborately hand trace all pieces with double gold lines on each side of the Grecian border, and all covered pieces, including sugar bowls, covered dishes and cups and saucers, have hand gold traced handles. The decoration consists of dainty little garlands of pink roses and green foliage, forming a neat border design much sought for by lovers of beautiful china. The covered dishes, cups and saucers are decorated both in and outside and all flat pieces have a floral wreath in the center, producing a most artistic effect.

We can furnish this set in the following combination, consisting of 100 most useful pieces, as follows:

- 12 Teacups
- 12 Saucers
- 12 Dinner Plates
- 12 Breakfast Plates
- 12 Tea or Pie Plates
- 12 Sauce Dishes
- 12 Individual Butters
- 1 Platter, 11½ inches
- 1 Platter, 15½ inches
- 2 Open Vegetable Dishes
- 1 Covered Vegetable Dish (2 pieces)
- 1 Covered Sugar Bowl (2 pieces)
- 1 Sauce Boat and Stand (2 pieces)
- 1 Covered Butter Dish (3-pieces)
- 1 Cream Pitcher
- 1 Pickle Dish
- 1 Large Salad Bowl

No. 2C378 100-piece Dinner Set, complete. Price.... **$16.85**

Shipped from Chicago. Shipping weight, 90 pounds.

For those desiring to make their own selection of pieces, we quote this beautiful dinner pattern in open stock, giving you the advantage of selecting every conceivable piece made which goes to make up a complete dinner service, at the following prices:

SHIPPED FROM CHICAGO.

Elite Bavarian Open Stock Dinner Ware	Actual Size	Price, each	Per doz.
Tea Cups and Saucers	6 ounces	$0.23	$2.39
Coffee Cups and Saucers	8 ounces	.28	3.25
Chocolate Cups and Saucers	4 ounces	.25	2.75
After Dinner Cups and Saucers	3 ounces	.23	2.39
Dessert or Bread and Butter Plates	5⅝ inches	.15	1.48
Breakfast Plates	7½ inches	.18	1.73
Tea Plates	8¼ inches	.19	2.23
Dinner Plates	9½ inches	.23	2.59
Soup Plates, New Coupe Shape	7½ inches	.23	2.28
Sauce Dishes	4⅜ inches	.12	1.35
Oatmeal Dishes	5⅞ inches	.15	1.65
Individual Butters	3¼ inches	.07	.73
Bone Dishes	7 inches	.19	2.10
Egg Cups	5 ounces	.15	1.75
Cake Plates	10 inches	.48	5.50
Chop Dishes	11½ inches	.98	11.50
Cream Pitchers	½ pint	.23	2.75
Sugar Bowls	1 pint	.48	5.50
Covered Butter Dishes	7 pints	.55	6.40
Spoon Holders		.15	1.75
Tea Pots	3¼ pints	.98	11.00
Chocolate Pots	3 pints	.98	11.00

Elite Bavarian Open Stock Dinner Ware.	Actual Size	Price, each	Per doz.
Pickle Dishes	8¾ inches	$0.35	$4.00
Bowls	1½ pints	.45	5.00
Celery Trays	12¾ inches	.48	6.50
Toothpick Holders		.10	1.10
Salt and Pepper Shakers		.15	1.75
Platters, small size	11½ inches	.45	5.25
Platters, medium size	13½ inches	.73	8.70
Platters, large size	15½ inches	.98	11.50
Platters, extra size	17½ inches	1.95	23.20
Open Vegetable Dishes	8 inches	.43	4.90
Open Vegetable Dishes	9 inches	.49	5.75
Round Salad Bowls	9⅞ inches	.69	8.25
Oval Covered Dishes	9 inches	1.68	20.00
Round Casseroles (covered)	9 inches	1.75	20.50
Sauce Boats with Stands	9 inches	.95	11.25
Soup Tureens	11 inches	2.95	34.50
Covered Sauce Tureens	11 inches	1.75	20.50
Mustard Pots with Spoons		.23	2.75
Large Pitchers, No. 3	1 quart	.89	10.00
Syrup Pitchers with Plates	3 ounces	.48	5.75
Tea Pot Stands	6 inches	.15	1.60
Pudding Sets with Lining and Stands		1.98	23.50

The above prices are for ELITE BAVARIAN CHINA only. Orders amounting to less than $2.00 will not be accepted.

Our Genuine Haviland French China Dinner Sets.

THE EXTREMELY LOW PRICES which we quote for these three latest patterns of genuine Haviland French China Dinner Sets are made possible by reason of the very large contract we placed with Theodore Haviland, at an especially low price, to which we have added only our usual one small margin of profit. It is impossible for other dealers to purchase these sets, even at wholesale, at the extremely low price which we quote. On account of our low price a great many dealers try to convince our customers that our sets are not the genuine Haviland China; but do not allow yourself to be misled by what anyone may say of these sets, for we guarantee them to be made by Theodore Haviland, Limoges, France, with his trade mark stamped on the back of each piece. We cannot furnish individual butters as samples for we have imported these sets in complete 100-piece combinations and cannot break them even for samples.

The combinations of each of the three dinner sets listed below consist of the following 100 pieces:

12 Coupe Soup Plates	12 Fruit Plates	1 Pickle Dish
12 Plates, 8½-inch	1 Platter, 14-inch	1 Covered Butter Dish (3 pieces)
12 Plates, 6½-inch	1 Platter, 16-inch	
12 Cups	1 Baker	1 Sugar Bowl (2 pieces)
12 Saucers	1 Round Cov'd Dish, 2 pcs.	1 Cream Pitcher
12 Individual Butters	1 Oval Cov'd Dish, 2 pcs.	1 Sauce Boat (2 pieces)

Each set is carefully packed by expert packers and shipped direct to our customers in the west from Chicago and from our bonded warehouse in Boston to our eastern customers, thus insuring lowest rate of freight.

$19.45 OUR $19.45 HAVILAND 100-PIECE DINNER SET.

THIS GENUINE HAVILAND SET is of a new and handsome shape, in that pure translucent white, delicately decorated, and made only by Theodore Haviland of Limoges, France. Haviland china is always very thin, light in weight, perfect in color, great in strength, perfect in finish and beautiful in decoration. The decoration of the above set consists of a very delicate pink wild crab apple blossom with light green moss fern background. It has the genuine coin gold knobs and handles, adding richness to the set. The above illustration will give you some idea of the beautiful shape, but no picture can do justice to a Haviland French China Dinner Set, as it does not show the delicate decorations nor the thinness of the ware. This kind of ware must be seen to be appreciated.

No. 2C380 Price for full 100-piece Dinner Set as listed above.. **$19.45**

OUR HAVILAND ROSE 100-PIECE DINNER SET, $24.95.

OUR HAVILAND ROSE PATTERN. This is the most popular dinner set ever offered by this famous manufacturer. The decoration consists of dainty sprays of pink roses, artistically arranged on all pieces with faint green foliage and French scrolls. This decoration has heretofore only been displayed on sets sold at double the price we ask. This set is sure to please the most critical china buyer, as the decoration is not loud or gaudy, but very delicate and neat, yet strikingly beautiful. Pure coin gold adorns all pieces, such as cups, covered dishes, platters, bakers, etc., greatly adding to the richness of the set. The shape is known as the Vincennes shape, Haviland's newest and best pattern. Each piece is neatly embossed, as illustration shows, being a fancy festoon shape.

The ware is the finest made. It is light and thin, made from the choicest translucent china body, only obtainable in Limoges, France.

No. 2C384 100-Piece Haviland Dinner Set. Shipping weight, 100 pounds. Price.................. **$24.95**

OUR ROSE WREATH HAVILAND CHINA DINNER SET, $27.50.

THIS IS THE PRETTIEST HAVILAND ROSE BORDER PATTERN MADE, REGARDLESS OF PRICE, AND THE BEAUTY OF THIS SET IS BEYOND DESCRIPTION.

THE DECORATION consists of dainty little climbing roses, entwined with very faint and delicate green foliage and leaves, so gracefully arranged, forming one complete border encircling the edges of each piece. All pieces are adorned with a beautiful jewel center with four rose sprays. This decoration appeals to the most refined taste as it is very delicate and dainty. Pure coin gold adorns all pieces, such as cups, covered dishes, platters, bakers, etc., greatly adding to the beauty of the set. This set usually retails for $40.00.

The shape, known as Lambelle pattern, is the newest creation of Haviland. Each piece is artistically embossed with festoons of bow knot design, and bottom edges of each piece are embossed in rich lace effect.

The ware is the finest made, being very light and thin, and made from the very best quality white translucent china, only to be found in Limoges, France. Shipping weight, 100 pounds.

No. 2C386 100-piece Haviland Dinner Set. Price.................. **$27.50**

THIS BEAUTIFUL LINE OF TOILET SETS

is comprised of the choicest patterns selected from only the best potteries. As we furnish these in **first quality only,** we can guarantee the ware to be perfect in every respect and not to craze. The prices quoted, are in many instances lower than regular wholesale prices. All sets, excepting plain white, are furnished in two combinations, as follows:

10-piece Sets: Wash Bowl and Pitcher, Covered Chamber (two pieces), Covered Soap Dish and Drainer (three pieces), Hot Water Pitcher, Brush Vase and Mug.

12-piece Sets contain all the above mentioned pieces with large slop jar and cover added.

OUR UTILITY TOILET SET, $1.48.

This toilet set is made from the finest quality of selected white stone china, will withstand extremely hard usage and is especially recommended to those desiring a good set at a low price. It is made by America's best potter and is fully guaranteed not to craze.

No. 2C416 6-piece Toilet Set, consisting of wash bowl and pitcher, chamber and cover, soap dish and mug. Shipping weight, 40 pounds. Price $1.48

No. 2C417 7-piece Toilet Set, consisting of same pieces as No. 2C416, with slop jar added. Shipping weight, 55 pounds. Price 2.39

If ordered with the toilet set, **extra wash bowl with pitcher** can be furnished for 69 cents

OUR ARDMORE TOILET SET, $1.99.

Our Ardmore Toilet Set is made of absolutely the best grade of American semi-porcelain ware. The ware is equal to sets sold at double the price. The decoration consists of very **large and beautiful** Jack roses, prettily entwined with foliage. We can furnish it in green, blue or pink and it will therefore harmonize with the interior of any room. **Be sure to specify color** of decoration desired. Furnished in two combinations, securely packed in barrels. Shipped from our pottery in Eastern Ohio

No. 2C420 10-piece Toilet Set, all pieces as illustrated, less slop jar. Shipping weight, 65 pounds. Price $1.99

No. 2C421 12-piece Toilet Set, as illustrated, with jar. Shipping weight, 80 pounds. Price 3.69

OUR HARVARD TOILET SET, $2.59.

This is without exception the very best toilet set ever offered at so low a price. It is most handsomely tinted in light blue, light green or pink, at both upper and lower extremities of each piece, indicated by the dark shading in the illustration, and decorated with rich gold medallions, composed of pretty sprigs of wild roses, artistically placed between these tinted edges. This set is sure to harmonize with the furnishings of any room. It is made from the finest quality of semi-porcelain, in one of the newest shapes. These sets are well packed in a barrel and shipped from our pottery in Eastern Ohio.

No. 2C430 10-piece Toilet Set, all pieces as illustrated, less slop jar. Shipping weight, 60 pounds. Price $2.59

No. 2C431 12-piece Toilet Set, as illustrated, with jar. Shipping weight, 80 pounds. Price 3.98

BRIDAL WREATH TOILET SET, $2.95.

This set is richly decorated with a broad, rich gold vine and floral wreaths which are artistically arranged so as to encircle each piece near the top and bottom. It has a neat, bright gold medallion center figure between the wreaths. The edges, as well as the handles, are hand traced in bright gold to match, which makes this set one of the most attractive white and gold toilet sets ever produced. Shipped from our pottery in Eastern Ohio.

No. 2C440 10-piece Toilet Set, all pieces as illustrated, less slop jar. Shipping weight, 60 pounds. Price $2.95

No. 2C441 12-piece Toilet Set, as illustrated, with jar. Shipping weight, 80 pounds. Price 4.75

OUR YALE TOILET SET, $3.23.

Entirely new. The decoration is applied by the French decalcomania process, producing an exceptionally handsome pattern, consisting of large clusters of purple, blue and pink narcissus and tube roses, beautifully shaded, with a background of delicate ferns and green lily leaves. **All handles** are elegantly **stippled with bright gold.** These sets are beautifully tinted in **blue, maroon** or **pink** and therefore will harmonize with any room. In ordering, **please mention color of tinting desired.** Each set is carefully packed in a barrel. Shipped from our pottery in Eastern Ohio.

No. 2C455 10-piece Toilet Set, all pieces as illustrated, less slop jar. Shipping weight, 65 pounds. Price $3.23

No. 2C456 12-piece Toilet Set, as illustrated, with jar. Shipping weight, 80 pounds. Price 4.95

IRIS LILY TOILET SET, $3.45.

The decoration of this set consists of iris lilies in their natural colors of rich purple and dark crimson, with large green leaves, making a very highly attractive set which will harmonize with the colors of any sleeping apartment. We wish to call particular attention to the beauty of this decoration, for it cannot fail to give entire satisfaction. Each set is carefully packed in a barrel and shipped direct from our pottery in East Liverpool, Ohio.

We furnish this set in two assortments as follows:

No. 2C460 10-piece Toilet Set, all pieces as illustrated, less slop jar. Shipping weight, 65 pounds. Price $3.45

No. 2C461 12-piece Toilet Set, as illustrated, with jar. Shipping weight, 80 pounds. Price 5.25

NEWPORT TOILET SET, $3.98.

This handsome set is beautifully decorated with yellow and pink chrysanthemums and foliage, in addition to which, every piece is heavily stippled in rich gold, as shown by the dark shading in illustration. This gold treatment is very expensive and produces a rich and striking effect. It is made by one of the best potteries in America and is guaranteed strictly high grade and equal to sets sold for double the price we ask. Each set is carefully packed in a barrel and shipped from Eastern Ohio.

No. 2C470 10-piece Toilet Set, all pieces as illustrated, less slop jar. Shipping weight, 65 pounds. Price $3.98

No. 2C471 12-piece Toilet Set, all pieces as illustrated, with jar. Shipping weight, 80 pounds. Price 5.98

FLORIAN TOILET SET, $4.45.

In offering our Florian Toilet Set we aim to give the finest toilet set made. This set usually retails for $7.00 and $8.00. Owing to the large contract made with the maker we are able to quote the set far below the regular price. It is made by the famous Haynes Art Pottery and fully guaranteed. It is heavily embossed in artistic floral design, each embossing being very carefully hand traced in bright gold, also all edges, knobs and handles are very elaborately and full traced in gold, as shown by dark lines in illustration. Shipped from Chicago to our customers in the west, and direct from our pottery in Baltimore to **customers** living in the east, giving you the advantage of the lowest freight rates.

No. 2C480 10-piece Toilet Set, all pieces as illustrated, less slop jar. Shipping weight, 60 pounds. Price $4.45

No. 2C481 12-piece Toilet Set, all pieces as illustrated, with jar. Shipping weight, 80 pounds. Price 6.45

43 Pieces ANONA ASSORTMENT. Price, $2.49

THE ANONA ASSORTMENT is an exact reproduction of one of the finest and most popular cut glass patterns. It is made by one of America's foremost glass manufacturers, who has so successfully imitated the original models, that only experts can detect that it is not genuine cut glass. The glass used in this set is very brilliant and perfect in design and finish, as it is made by glass experts only. It is all hand finished and doubly annealed, which makes it exceedingly strong. All pieces contained in this assortment are full size and are sure to give entire satisfaction.

No 2C510 Consists of 43 pieces, as follows:

1 Water Pitcher (½ gallon)	1 Salt Shaker (nickel top)
12 Water Tumblers	1 Pepper Shaker (nickel top)
1 Cream Pitcher	1 Vinegar Cruet
1 Spoon Holder	1 Large Celery Tray
1 Covered Sugar Bowl	1 8¾-inch High Footed Bowl
1 Covered Butter Dish	1 5-inch Footed Jelly Dish
1 Large 9-inch Sauce Bowl	6 Individual Salt Cellars
12 Individual Sauce Dishes	1 5-inch Hand'ld Olive Dish

Neatly packed in a wood box. Shipping weight, 46 pounds. Price, complete $2.49

THIS BEAUTIFUL imitation cut glass design is the very latest pattern. The glass is of the very best quality, being of the same high grade as used in the finest cut glassware, so that it so closely resembles genuine cut glass that it is with difficulty that the pressed cut can be detected. We furnish this set with GENUINE SOLID STERLING SILVER TOPS to the salt and pepper shakers, and also on the syrup jug, so that the workmanship and material are of the highest class, and are nice enough to adorn a table set with the finest of dishes.

No. 2C531 18-piece glass set, consisting of:

1 Covered Butter Dish	1 Cream Pitcher	1 Half Gallon Pitcher
1 Large Berry or Salad Bowl	6 Sauce Dishes	1 Covered Sugar Bowl
	1 Spoon Holder	6 Water Tumblers

Price........ $1.39

Shipping weight, 30 pounds.

No. 2C532 This assortment of 35 pieces includes:

1 Water Pitcher (half gallon)	1 Cream Pitcher	1 Sugar Bowl
1 Butter Dish	12 Nappies	1 Vinegar Cruet
1 Salt Shaker	1 Berry Bowl	1 Syrup Jug
1 Celery Tray	12 Tumblers	1 Spoon Holder
		1 Pepper Shaker

Price, complete........ $2.89

Shipping weight, 40 pounds.

35 Pieces VICTORIA ASSORTMENT. Price, $2.89

37 Pieces DESPLAINES ASSORTMENT. Price, $2.98

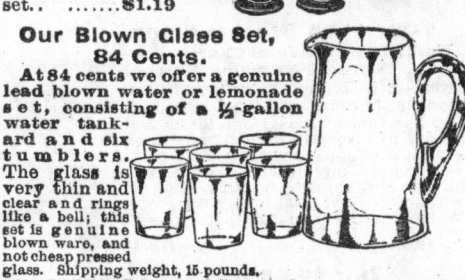

THIS SET is made of the very finest quality of pressed glass. The convex panel design brings out all the fire and brilliancy so characteristic of high grade crystal glass. The pattern is the newest produced this year. It is exceedingly heavy and handsome, and the tops of the salt and pepper shakers are of solid silver. A new but massive design which will attract the eye of the most particular.

No. 2C538 We can furnish the following assortment of 37 pieces:

1 Water Pitcher (½ gallon)	12 Nappies
12 Tumblers	1 Celery Tray
1 Cream Pitcher	1 Jelly Glass
1 Butter Dish	1 Syrup Jug
1 Spoon Holder	1 Vinegar Cruet
1 Sugar Bowl	1 Salt Shaker
1 Berry Dish	1 Pepper Shaker
	1 Fruit Stand

Packed complete in box. Shipping weight, 40 pounds. Price $2.98

Water Tumblers.

Our Water Tumblers are made of the highest grade clear crystal pot glass with perfectly smooth tops and bottoms. We can ship these tumblers direct from factory in Indiana in barrel lots of 20 dozen each at 2 cents less per dozen than prices quoted below.

No. 2C564 Plain Water Tumblers of heavy glass. Half-pint size. Price, per dozen........24c

No. 2C563 Plain Water Tumblers of heavy glass, with fluted bottoms. Half-pint size. Price, per dozen........36c

No. 2C564 No. 2C563

No. 2C566 Half-Pint Heavy Water Tumblers, with fluted bottoms and engraved bands. Price, per dozen........45c

No. 2C567 Half-Pint, Pure Flint, Lead Blown Tumblers, with neatly engraved bands. Price, per dozen........56c

No. 2C566 No. 2C567

No. 2C568 Half-Pint, Pure Flint, Lead Blown Water Tumblers, with elegant hand engraved floral decoration. This glass is very thin and dainty. Just the glass where a high grade tumbler is desired. Price, per dozen........75c

No. 2C570 Our Iced Tea Tumbler is just the thing for iced tea or any other drink requiring a small piece of ice in the glass, because it is much larger and taller than an ordinary tumbler. It is beautifully designed, as illustrated, and made of the very best crystal glass. Per dozen........$1.20

No. 2C568 No. 2C570

Jelly Tumblers.

No. 2C571 A long felt want has been a jelly tumbler which could be used as a drinking glass when not filled with jelly. The tumbler illustrated fills this want as it is a regular size tumbler with smooth top and bottom and a closely fitting tin top. Per doz........22c

No. 2C571

No. 2C579 Jelly Tumblers, tin top, holds ⅓-pint each, good quality. Price, per dozen........17c

No. 2C579

7-Piece Wine Set, $1.19.

This Handsome Set is made of the best quality of nile green glass, beautifully decorated and full gold trimmed by hand. The decoration is burnt on and will never wear off. The set consists of a large quart-sized handled decanter, with large ornamental imitation cut glass stopper, and six wine glasses to match. It has full gold line tracings and is very elaborate in decoration. Retails regularly for double the price we ask. Shipping weight, 10 pounds.

No. 2C569 Wine Set. Price, per set........$1.19

Our Blown Glass Set, 84 Cents.

At 84 cents we offer a genuine lead blown water or lemonade set, consisting of a ½-gallon water tankard and six tumblers. The glass is very thin and clear and rings like a bell; this set is genuine blown ware, and not cheap pressed glass. Shipping weight, 15 pounds.

No. 2C572 Price, carefully packed........84c

Water Set, 72 Cents.

No. 2C576 This beautiful and useful water set consists of one 1-quart water bottle and six drinking glasses. The pattern is the very latest style of a deep cut glass design. It is made of the highest grade crystal glass with a special design which brings out all the fire of the glass, giving it the appearance of genuine cut glass. Carefully packed to insure safe delivery. Shipping weight, 15 pounds. Price, complete........72c

7-Piece Water Set, 95 Cents.

No. 2C573 This Handsome Water Set is made of hand finished nile green glass, and is hand decorated in three delicate tints, which are fully burnt on and will not wear off. The set is composed of an extra large 12½-inch tankard pitcher, which has a fancy fluted top and is decorated with a wide amethyst band, covered with white enamel scroll pattern, and six handfinished tumblers, which are decorated to match, being a reproduction of a very high priced imported set. Shipping weight, 15 lbs. Price........95c

No. 2C575 Ruby Glass Water Set. This beautiful hand painted water set is made of finest quality ruby glass, which is artistically decorated with wild roses in their natural colors, every piece being traced in bright gold. The large tankard used in this set is blown in a new octagon colonial fluted shape. The six tumblers are very finely hand finished and decorated to match the pitcher, being beautifully decorated in seven different shades. Shipping weight, 15 pounds. Price........$1.85

Covered Chambers.

No. 2C591½ Made of yellow ware; child's size. Price........23c

No. 2C592 Made of yellow ware; medium. Price........28c

No. 2C593 Made of yellow ware; large. Price........33c

No. 2C593½ White semi-porcelain; child's size. Price........40c

No. 2C594 White semi-porcelain; medium. Price........50c

No. 2C595 White semi-porcelain; large. Price, 65c

Bed Pans.

No. 2C596 Made of best grade of white semi-porcelain. Regular size. Weight, 4½ pounds. Price........85c

LAMP DEPARTMENT.

WE TAKE PLEASURE IN INTRODUCING AN ENTIRELY NEW LINE OF ALL DIFFERENT STYLES OF LAMPS.

THESE LAMPS were selected as the very best of the different grades which they represent after long and earnest investigation. We know that our prices cannot be duplicated by any other firm, style, quality and workmanship of the lamps taken into consideration. They are all packed very carefully so that we can guarantee their arrival in perfect condition. If the best of oil is used and the wick is kept clean, we guarantee the lamps to give perfect satisfaction.

Sun Belgian Rochester

All Lamp Chimneys herein quoted are made by the famous Macbeth factories and are universally known as the best in the world. They are furnished in the following grades:

Anchor Brand, made from the first quality flint glass and is the best medium price chimney made.

Zenith Brand, made of fine lead glass, oil finished and annealed. Recommended as a high grade chimney.

Macbeth Pearl Glass Chimneys, universally recognized as absolutely the best chimney made, finely annealed and oil tempered, guaranteed to stand extreme heat. Each stamped with the maker's name and number for future reference.

Alabaster Chimneys, known as the unbreakable chimney, made from extra heavy especially prepared glass and guaranteed to stand exceedingly tough usage.

All our chimneys are packed in square cartons.

Catalogue No.	Anchor Brand.	Outside Measure. Bottom, inches	Height, inches	Price, per doz.
2C600	No. 0 Sun Crimp.......	2	7	$0.40
2C601	No. 1 Sun Crimp.......	2⅛	7½	.48
2C602	No. 2 Sun Crimp.......	3	8½	.59
	Zenith Brand.			
2C604	No. 1 Sun Crimp.......	2⅛	7½	.63
2C605	No. 2 Sun Crimp.......	3	8½	.77
2C607	No. 1 Sun Hinge Crimp	2⅝	7½	.70
2C608	No. 2 Sun Hinge Crimp	2⅝	8¼	.90
2C609	No. 1 Rochester........	2	8	.85
2C610	No. 2 Rochester........	2⅝	10	.90
2C611	No. 2 Rochester..... ..	2⅝	12	1.40
2C612	No. 2 Electric..........	3	10	.88
	Macbeth Pearl Top and Pearl Glass.			
2C614	Macbeth No. 500 (0 Sun)................			.79
2C615	Macbeth No. 502 (1 Sun)................			.83
2C616	Macbeth No. 504 (2 Sun).....			.95
2C640	Macbeth No. 4 (Jr. Rochester)........			.85
2C620	Macbeth No. 6 (1 Rochester)...........			.92
2C621	Macbeth No. 12 (2 Rochester, 10 in.).....			1.09
2C621½	Macbeth No. 9 (2 Rochester, 12 in.).....			1.55
2C626	Macbeth No. 10 (3 Rochester)............			1.95
2C624	Macbeth No. 40 (2 Electric, 10 in.)......			1.10
2C625	Macbeth No. 63 (2 Electric, Slim, 10 in.).			1.12
2C630	Macbeth No. 32 (1 Belgian).............			1.20
2C631	Macbeth No. 36 (00 Belgian)......... ..			1.70
2C632	Macbeth No. 50 (1 Student)........			.90
2C633	Nutmeg, 3½ in. tall, 1⅛-in. bottom....			.20
2C634	Gem, 4¾ in. tall, 1⅛-in. bottom.....			.25
	Alabaster Chimneys, extra heavy.			
2C641	No. 1 Sun, plain top			1.10
2C642	No. 2 Sun, plain top			1.30

BURNERS AND WICKS.

Genuine Banner Burner, made of solid brass. This is the best sun burner made.

No. 2C650 No. 0 Banner Burner, takes No. 0 wick and No. 0 Sun chimney. Price..............................4c

No. 2C651 No. 1 Banner Burner, takes No. 1 wick and No. 1 Sun chimney. Price.....................5c

No. 2C652 No. 2 Banner Burner, takes No. 2 wick and No. 2 Sun chimney. Price....................6c

GENUINE CLIMAX BURNER.

No. 2C656 Made of solid brass. Has double thread to fit either No. 2 or No. 3 lamp collar. Takes No. 3 wick, 1½ inches wide, and No. 2 Electric chimney. This is the most powerful single wick burner made. Price 15c

AMERICAN DUPLEX BURNER.

No. 2C658 Made of solid brass. Has double thread to fit No. 2 and No. 3 lamp collar. This is a double wick burner, using two No. 3 wicks 1½ inches wide and a No. 2 Electric chimney. Gives a strong, steady light and is perfectly safe. Price........25c

WICKS.	No.	Size		Price
No. 2C661	0	⅝-inch.	Per dozen................	3c
No. 2C662	1	⅝-inch.	Per dozen................	4c
No. 2C663	2	1 -inch.	Per dozen................	5c
No. 2C664	3	1½-inch.	Per dozen................	8c

No. 2C669 Lamp Wicks, Junior Rochester, round, 1¼ inches when flat. Price, per dozen.....14c

No. 2C670 Lamp Wicks, No. 1 Rochester, round, 1⅝ inches when flat. Price, per dozen.....16c

No. 2C671 Lamp Wicks, No. 2 Rochester, round, 2⅛ inches when flat. Price, per dozen.....19c

No. 2C672 Lamp Wicks, No. 3 Rochester, round, 4¼ inches when flat. Price, per dozen.....78c

No. 2C673 Lamp Wicks, No. 1 Belgian, round, 2 inches when flat. Price, per dozen......50c

Brass Night Lamps.

No. 2C701 Brass Night Lamp. 7¾ inches high, complete Gem burner, chimney and wick. Price...........15c

No. 2C703 Brass Night Lamp. This is the most practical night lamp made. The lamp is fitted with a revolving reflector and a bracket which enables you to hang lamp on wall. Height, 7¾ inches.

Price, complete........23c

Wall Lamps.

No. 2C705 This Very Useful Lamp became popular at once because of its great utility and low price. It has removable glass fount and reflector, No. 2 Sun burner and chimney. Is made to hang on a wall or rest on a table, and reflector can be taken off if desired. Shipping weight, 8 pounds. Price...25c

Hand Lamps.

No. 2C707 Plain Footed Glass Hand Lamp, complete with chimney, No. 1 Sun burner and wick. Safely packed so that it can be shipped without danger of breakage. Just the thing for carrying about the house. Guaranteed perfect in every way. Price......................24c

Large Stand Lamp made of clear pressed glass, complete with Sun burner, wick and chimney. Just the thing for bedrooms or to carry around the house.

No. 2C709 Crystal Stand Lamp, with No. 1 burner, chimney and wick. Price...35c

No. 2C711 Large Stand Lamp, like No. 2C709, with No. 2 Burner, wick and chimney. Price....43c

No. 2C713 Our Heavy Imitation Cut Glass Footed Hand Lamp complete with No. 1 Sun burner, wick and chimney. Price..33c

Bracket Lamps.

No. 2C722 Kitchen or Dining Room Bracket Lamp, finished in French bronze, has glass fount, No. 2 Banner burner, and 7-inch silvered glass reflector; complete with chimney as shown. Shipping weight, about 15 pounds. Price.....................45c

No. 2C724 Dining Room or Hall Lamp. Is the strongest and best finished on the market. We furnish it complete with glass fount, 8-inch silvered glass reflector, No. 2 Banner burner and chimney. The bracket is made of cast iron, fancy design, bronze finish. Shipping weight, 15 pounds. Price, complete, 65c

Our $1.85 Bracket Lamp.

No. 2C728 Two-Joint Church, Parlor or Bedroom Swinging Bracket Lamp, with 20-inch rope design arm. Is made of bronze metal, gold finished and has fancy crystal oil fount and shade, handsomely etched body with genuine cut glass crown design edge. Furnished complete with No. 2 Unique burner and chimney. Can be lighted without removing chimney or globe. Weight, securely packed, 20 pounds.

Price...........................$1.85

Our $2.45 Bracket Lamp.

No. 2C750 Where a strong light is needed we recommend this attractive and serviceable lamp. The bracket is made of cast iron and is finished in French bronze, fount is the celebrated Royal center draft burner, giving a light equal to 100 candle power, is made of brass, highly polished, and will hold enough oil to burn eight hours. The silvered glass reflector is 10 inches in diameter and can be so adjusted as to throw light wherever needed. Shipping weight, 25 pounds.

Price, complete.........$2.45

Wonderful Value for 79 Cents.

No. 2C730 At 79 cents we offer a lamp which has usually sold for twice this amount. The base is of brass, heavily nickel plated. It has a nickel plated No. 2 burner of extraordinary capillary power. It is furnished complete with wick, chimney, shade ring and a 7-inch imported white dome shade, making the best and cheapest reading lamp on the market. Shipping weight, 20 pounds. Price...................79c

No. 2C731 Nickel Lamp, exactly like above, with 7-inch imported green shade. Price.........$1.19

Reading or Table Lamps.

No. 2C734 Our Polished Nickel Reading or Table Lamp with one of the best center draft burners on the market. It will give as good light as a gas burner. It is complete with a 10-inch opal dome shade, holder, wick and chimney. This lamp is well made and shapely throughout. It gives a strong, steady, bright light and the wick can be raised or lowered instantly. It is made of plain polished metal with neat embossing at base, giving it a handsome appearance. Shipping weight, 20 pounds. Price......................$1.48

No. 2C735 Nickel Lamp, exactly like above, with 10-inch imported green shade. Price..... ..$1.99

No. 2C738 Parlor or Reading Lamp. This handsome, nickel center draft lamp is superior to all others because it is suitable for a parlor as well as a sewing lamp. It is very rich in pattern and for burning qualities it is unequaled. It is richly embossed and has two handles at the sides which greatly add to the appearance of the lamp. This lamp is made from solid brass and is full nickel plated throughout, and equipped with a large, high grade Royal Burner which is of an improved center draft type and is considered to be the best made. It is so simple in construction that the lamp can be easily taken apart, re-wicked and cleaned with no trouble. It is complete with a 10-inch imported white opal shade, 10-inch tripod and No. 2 Rochester chimney. Shipping weight, 20 pounds. Price.......................................$2.25

No. 2C739 Nickel Lamp, exactly like above, with 10-inch imported green shade. Price...$2.75

This Handsome Embossed Nickel Lamp, $1.95.

No. 2C736 Our New Embossed Nickel Lamp is one of the best made. It is smokeless and odorless, being built on the most scientific principles and is sure to give entire satisfaction. It is fitted with celebrated Juno center draft burner, which gives a strong, steady white light. It is complete with a 10-inch imported reading shade, No. 2 Rochester chimney, shade holder and No. 2 round Rochester wick. Shipping weight, when packed, 18 pounds.

Price..........................$1.95

No. 2C737 Nickel Lamp, as illustrated and described above, but with imported 10-inch green dome shade. Price..................$2.39

STUDENT LAMPS.

Student Lamps are universally recognized as the most perfect lamp for reading and sewing, because they can be adjusted to any height and the powerful light is thrown directly upon the work, and as the oil fount is at one side there is no shadow underneath the lamp. We have handled different makes of Student Lamps for years and we find that the ones we offer below are absolutely the best upon the market, as the mechanism is so perfect that they give no trouble.

This Student Lamp is nickel plated, has center draft burner with removable fount and perfect wick attachments, Junior Rochester wick and chimney, 7-inch dome shade. It will burn nine hours with one filling. Height to top of rod 21 inches. Is perfectly safe and reliable. Packed complete in a box for shipment. Weight, 16 pounds.

No. 2C756 With white shade. Price.......$2.89

No. 2C757 With green shade. Price....... 3.14

We also furnish a student lamp same style as No. 2C756, only much larger in size, which is equipped with No. 1 Rochester burner, wick and large 10-inch imported dome shade. This lamp is recommended to give double the light of the smaller size and is well worth the difference in price.

No. 2C759 Ideal Student Lamp. Price...$4.45

No. 2C760 Same as No. 2C759, with 10-inch imported green shade. Price...............$4.75

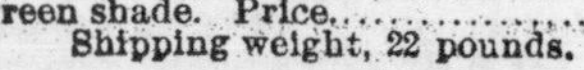

Shipping weight, 22 pounds.

HALL, STORE AND LIBRARY LAMPS.

WE DESIRE TO CALL SPECIAL ATTENTION TO OUR ASSORTMENT OF LAMPS,

AND TO THE FACT THAT

ALL METAL PARTS OF OUR LAMPS ARE MADE OF SOLID BRASS

WITH HANDSOME LACQUERED BRONZE FINISH.

A great many dealers advertise library lamps which in appearance are similar to ours, but are made of bronze metal, which is oftentimes mistaken for brass when the lamps are new, but will not stand the wear and retain the handsome appearance of a solid brass lamp. We guarantee every one of our lamps to stand the wear of a lifetime, and guarantee them not to tarnish. Each lamp carefully packed to insure safe delivery.

HALL LAMPS.

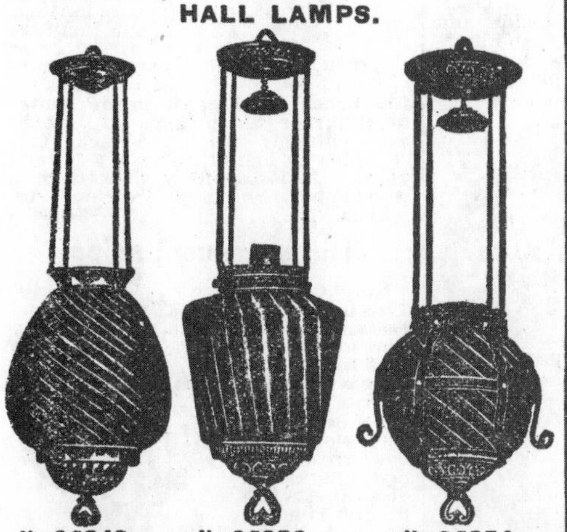

No. 2C849 No. 2C852 No. 2C854

No. 2C849 Hall Lamp, with a rich opal globe. Just the light for a hall. This is the cheapest and best hall lamp in the market. Length, 29 inches. Made of solid brass, finished in rich bronze. Packed carefully in box, with oil fount, burner and chimney complete. Ship'g weight, about 12 lbs. Price....**$1.10**

No. 2C850 Hall Lamp, exactly like No. 2C849, with rich ruby globe, which produces a rich mellow light. Shipping weight, 12 pounds. Price......................................**$1.23**

No. 2C852 Hall Lamp, with rich ruby globe, complete with oil fount, burner and chimney. Finished in rich bronze metal. Length, 29 inches. Makes a soft red light, and very attractive in hall. Weight, about 14 pounds. Price....................**$1.59**

No. 2C854 Hall Lamp. A new design in hand wrought black iron frame and rich ruby globe. Just the thing for halls and dens. Length, 29 inches. Complete with oil fount, burner and wick. Packed carefully to insure safe delivery. Shipping weight, 17 pounds. Price....................................**$1.98**

Store Lamps.

Juno Store Lamp. For large areas and where good light is required, only the best lamps should be procured. We guarantee every lamp we sell to give perfect satisfaction. The Juno gives a steady white light. Just the thing to throw light on a window display. Complete as illustrated with 15-inch tin shade, suitable for store or window lights, 85-candle power. Shipping weight, 40 pounds.

No. 2C856 Price, brass finish.........**$2.00**

No. 2C857 Price, nickel finish..............**$2.25**

$3.20 TO $4.95

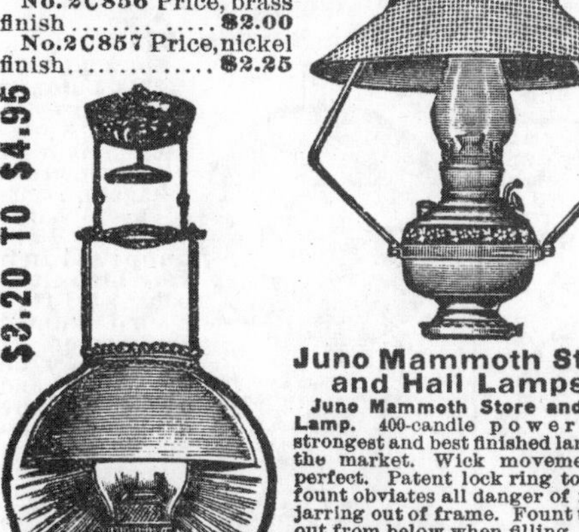

Juno Mammoth Store and Hall Lamps.

Juno Mammoth Store and Hall Lamp. 400-candle power, the strongest and best finished lamp on the market. Wick movement is perfect. Patent lock ring to hold fount obviates all danger of fount jarring out of frame. Fount taken out from below when filling. You are taking no chances with this lamp, as we guarantee every one to give perfect satisfaction or we will replace them and pay all expenses. Complete, as illustrated, with 14-inch plain dome shade suitable for churches, halls, stores, etc., and fitted **with automatic spring extension so that it can be lowered for cleaning and lighting of lamp.** Closed, 42 inches; fully extended, 78 inches. Money cannot buy a finer constructed lamp. It is very handsome in appearance. Shipping weight, 50 pounds.

No. 2C860 Price, complete, brass finish............**$4.70**

No. 2C861 Price, complete, nickel finish............**4.95**

Same lamp as above, but without automatic spring extension. You get the same service from this lamp, but you are obliged to use a step ladder or chair for lighting. Shipping weight, 40 lbs.

No. 2C862 Price, complete, brass finish............**$3.20**

No. 2C863 Price, complete, nickel finish............**3.35**

Our Leader at $1.79.

No. 2C785 This Lamp has 14-inch plain white dome shade with No. 3 Climax burner and No. 2 chimney; wick, 1½ inches; **solid brass frame and patent spring extension.** Length, closed, 27 inches; extended, 63 inches. **This frame being of solid brass will give much better service than the common polished bronze metal lamps, and is equal in every respect to lamps your dealer will ask $3.50 for.** Weight, 40 pounds. Price, **$1.79**

No. 2C786. Same Lamp as above described, but with a beautiful 14-inch hand decorated dome shade. Shipping weight, securely packed, 40 pounds. Price, **$2.21**

No. 2C785

No. 2C787 Library Lamp. Has extra heavy reinforced frame, made of solid brass, which will give far better service and will last longer than the ordinary bronze metal so commonly used in lamps of this style. Crystal oil fount and 14-inch plain dome shade, making a very beautiful and attractive lamp. Extra large No. 3 Climax burner and No. 2 Electric chimney; wick, 1½ inches. High grade automatic spring extension; length when closed, 30 inches; extended, 61 inches. The spring extension makes the lamp suitable for high or low ceiling. Shipping weight, about 40 pounds.
Price........................**$2.45**

No. 2C788 Same Lamp as described above, but with handsome decorated dome shade.
Price........................**$2.95**

No. 2C789 Solid Brass Library Lamp with No. 2 Juno center draft fount, 85-candle power. Fount removable for filling and cleaning. Automatic spring extension. Length, closed, 33 inches; extended, 69 inches. The base of the lamp is of beautiful embossed metal and finished in rich bronze to match the frame. This is a new design and is up to date in every way. Complete with 14-inch white dome shade. Takes No. 2 Rochester chimney and wick. Shipping weight, about 4 pounds. Price..**$3.48**

No. 2C793 Library Lamp with automatic spring extension. Length, closed, 30 inches; extended, 66 inches. Plain white dome shade, fancy glass oil fount with No. 3 Climax burner, No. 2 electric chimney and 1½-inch wick. **Solid brass frame,** not the common bronze metal. Has 30 cut glass pendants suspended from shade band. Shipping weight, about 40 pounds.
Price **$3.49**

No. 2C794 Same lamp as above, but furnished with beautifully decorated dome shade. Shipping weight, about 40 pounds.
Price **$3.95**

No. 2C797 Library Lamp. Has elaborate frame made of solid brass; not the bronze metal used on similar lamps of cheaper grade. The frame is extra heavy and reinforced, ornamented with fancy castings of solid brass. Has 14-inch dome shade with 30 cut glass pendants suspended from the shade band. Fancy crystal fount, No. 3 Banner burner takes 1½-inch wick, Shipping weight, about No. 2 Electric chimney. 40 lbs. Price.......**$4.25**

No. 2C798 Same Lamp as No. 2C797, described above, excepting the dome shade is handsomely decorated with flower design on tinted background.
Price **$4.48**

No. 2C799 Parlor Extension Lamp, fitted with No. 2 center draft burner, 85-candle power; takes No. 2 round wick, No. 2 Rochester chimney. Fount can be removed from vase for filling. Automatic extension. Length, closed, 40 inches; extended, 76 inches. Can be used in room with either high or low ceiling. All metal parts are solid brass. Fancy collar at top of fount holder. Vase and globe are beautifully decorated with hand painted floral decorations on rich tinted background. Shipping weight, about 40 lbs. Price......**$4.36**

No. 2C801 Library Lamp with automatic spring extension. Length, closed, 30 inches; extended, 73 inches. The celebrated No. 2 Juno fount and center draft burner giving 85-candle power light. Fount can be removed for filling and cleaning. No. 2 round wick, No. 2 Rochester chimney. Extra heavy collar at top of oil fount holder. Heavy reinforced solid brass frame and beautifully decorated and tinted fount and dome with 30 cut glass prisms suspended from dome band, make this one of the most attractive lamps in our line. Shipping weight, about 40 lbs.
Price.......................**$5.75**

Polka Dot Cerise Lamp

This is the latest style in a Library or Parlor Lamp. It has a fancy ruby metal vase with gold plated cupid ornaments and solid brass embossed frame, and a beautiful 14-inch ruby polka dot dome. It is constructed so as to cast a rich ruby glow in the upper part of the room, and at the same time produces a bright steady light beneath for sewing or reading purposes. It has the latest improved No. 2 center draft burner, chimney and wick and produces 100 candle power light. It is one of the most ornamental lamps made, and is trimmed with 30 cut glass prisms or pendants which greatly add to the striking beauty of the lamp.

No. 2C802 Library Lamp. Weight, 40 pounds. Securely packed in a barrel and shipped to eastern customers from our factory in Connecticut, and to western customers from Chicago.

Price..................**$5.98**

No. 2C803 Library Lamp. Has solid brass frame of most beautiful design with ornamental heavy castings. Has automatic spring extension; length, closed, 30 inches; extended, 73 inches. The part of the frame on which the lamp is suspended is made of twisted brass instead of chains. Has No. 2 Juno fount and center draft burner, giving 85-candle power light; can be removed for filling and cleaning. Has No. 2 round wick and No. 2 Rochester chimney. The fount and dome are beautifully decorated with hand painted carnations. A heavy brass collar strengthens the top of oil fount holder. Thirty cut glass pendants are suspended from the dome band. Shipping weight, 40 lbs. Price.......**$6.85**

SPECIAL BARGAINS IN BANQUET LAMPS.

Customers living in the Central and Eastern states who order one of our lamps only will receive it shipped direct from our factory in Pennsylvania, thus effecting a saving in transportation charges.

The Rustic Parlor Lamp, 89c.

No. 2 C 950 **This Handsome Banquet Lamp is an entirely new style of decoration this year,** being of shaded myrtle green and pink. It is heavily embossed, as shown in the illustration, which adds strength to the lamp as well as enhancing its appearance. It has a solid brass No. 2 burner, shade ring and No. 2 chimney. It is 17 inches high and has an 8-inch globe. At the extremely low price there is no reason why any home should not be decorated with this useful as well as ornamental lamp. Carefully packed to insure safe delivery. Shipping weight, 15 pounds.
Price.......................................89c

The Carmen, $1.09.

No. 2C955 **This Banquet Lamp has unusually handsome decorations,** consisting of large red flowers with dark green foliage on a tinted pink and white background. The bowl is heavily embossed, thus adding strength as well as attractive appearance to the lamp. It is 19 inches high and has an 8-inch globe. The metal foot is of cast brass. It is furnished with No. 2 brass Banner burner and takes a No. 2 chimney and 1-inch wick. Shipping weight 8 pounds. Price..............$1.09

The Victor, $1.89.

No. 2 C 965 **This Lamp is a handsome embossed design, as illustrated.** The embossing is of dark green forming panels of white, which have a large red flower and foliage in the center of each. This same embossing makes the lamp very strong. The metal base of the lamp is of cast brass. It has a removable oil fount of brass which can be taken from the bowl of the lamp to be filled. It is also furnished with a No. 2 brass burner and takes No. 2 chimney and 1½-inch wick. Owing to the removable fount this lamp is one of the best bargains which we furnish. It is 20 inches high and has an 8-inch globe. Shipping weight, 20 pounds. Price..............$1.89

Our Poppy Lamp, $1.98.

No. 2C967 **This Beautiful Reception or Parlor Lamp is exceptionally large and attractive.** It is complete with 9-inch globe and 9-inch vase, and measures 21 inches high. The decoration consists of large hand painted poppies in pink, purple and white. The globe and also the vase are delicately tinted at the top in light green and the bottom in pink. It has a heavy brass plated metal foot of scroll design. It is equipped with No. 3 Climax burner, No. 3 wick and No. 2 electric chimney, and produces 60-candle power light. This lamp, without doubt, is the greatest value ever offered. Carefully packed in wood box. Shipping weight, 20 pounds. Price..................$1.98

Art Nouveau Lamp, $2.89.

No. 2C903 **Entirely new. This Beautiful Lamp is a work of art.** It is a reproduction of a celebrated piece of **French Art,** being beautifully modeled and embossed and hand decorated. It is delicately tinted in purple and embossing is decorated in dark green with beautiful hand painted art figures on both sides of lamp and globe. It has the latest improved Success central draft burner (100-candle power) with large removable brass oil fount. All metal parts are made from brass and finished in satin finish art brass, to correspond with balance of lamp. Shipping weight, 30 lbs. Exceptional value. Price...$2.89

Cerise Beauty, $2.95.

No. 2C985 **This Banquet Lamp is entirely different from the ordinary decorated lamp, inasmuch as it has no floral decoration on the globe or vase, but instead the beautiful cerise color entirely covers both, and will not fade or wear off, for the color is mixed in the glass before being moulded. This gives a beautiful effect to the room when the lamp is lighted.** All metal parts are of polished brass. It has a removable oil fount for cleaning and filling and a No. 2 center draft burner and chimney. The lamp stands 26 inches high and has a 10-inch globe. Shipping weight, 25 pounds. Price......$2.95

The American Beauty Lamp.

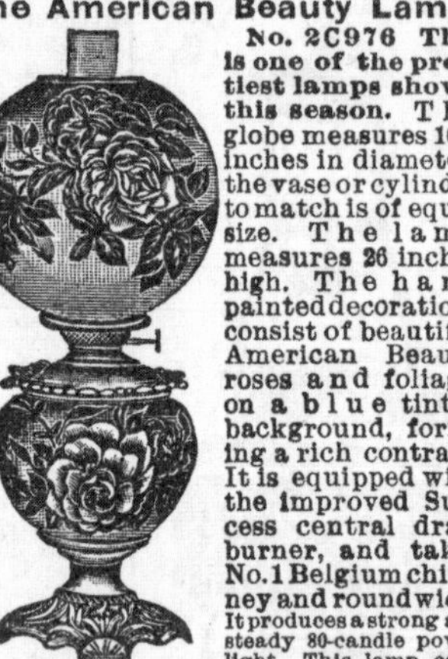

No. 2C976 **This is one of the prettiest lamps shown this season.** The globe measures 10½ inches in diameter, the vase or cylinder to match is of equal size. The lamp measures 26 inches high. The hand painted decorations consist of beautiful American Beauty roses and foliage, on a blue tinted background, forming a rich contrast. It is equipped with the improved Success central draft burner, and takes No. 1 Belgium chimney and round wick. It produces a strong and steady 80-candle power light. This lamp compares favorably with those sold by crockery dealers at $4.50 and $5.00. Carefully packed in strong wood box. Shipping weight, 25 pounds. Price..................$2.98

No. 2C980 **This Beautiful Lamp is particularly attractive owing to the beautiful dark red American Beauty roses which form the floral decorations.** These roses with the green foliage are printed on the tinted green background before the last firing of the lamp in the kiln and then the large roses are put on by hand in the deep red color, making the flowers stand out distinct from the lamp. The base is of solid cast brass and the fount holder has a solid brass drawn ring. The removable oil fount is of brass and has the No. 2 100-candle power center draft burner, taking No. 2 Rochester chimney and round wick. Shipping weight, 30 pounds. Price..................$3.20

No. 2C993 **This is a High Grade Metal Lamp, which is so popular at the present time.** The base is of solid brass with the fount holder of variegated brass finish and polished brass handles and top ring. The fount holder is ornamented by solid brass feather, securely riveted. The removable oil fount is of brass with large center draft burner and perfect wick attachment. It takes a No. 2 Rochester chimney and round wick. The 9-inch globe is of etched white glass, carefully ground on the inside and neatly trimmed with the stylish Fleur-de-lis design. It is 20 inches high. A lamp which cannot fail to please.
Price.................................$3.48

Seaside.

No. 2C995 **This is one of the latest patterns of Banquet Lamps and is entirely different from any other of our line.** Instead of the metal parts being of solid brass with the bronze finish they are oxidized or gun metal finish. The lamp itself is one of the neatest patterns on the market, having a tall, slender vase with 10-inch globe to match. It stands 27 inches high. The decoration consists of a rich dark seal brown in a cloud effect, having the sea view with ships, etc. When lighted the lamp gives a very dainty tint to the room. Shipping wgt., 25 lbs. Price, $3.65

Canary Metal Lamp, $3.78.

No. 2C1005 **Metal Lamp. Complete base is of solid brass in the old copper finish,** with polished brass handles and top ring. It has removable oil fount with 100-candle power center draft burner, and perfect attachment for raising and lowering the wick, which can be removed and renewed with no difficulty. The globe is of bright canary, ground on the inside so that it gives a very soft light and is just the lamp for reading, sewing, etc. It has No. 2 Rochester chimney and round wick. It is 20 inches high and has a 9-inch globe. Shipping weight, 30 pounds. Price..............$3.78

Cerise Lion Lamp, $3.95.

No. 2C1030 **This Lamp is made from rich, ruby glass and produces a rich, mellow, ruby glow.** It has the best 100-candle power No. 2 Royal center draft burner with a removable brass oil pot, which holds 1 quart of oil. All brass parts are gold plated and lacquered and will never tarnish. This lamp measures 26 inches high, globe and vase measure 10½ inches in diameter. One of the greatest values ever offered. Carefully packed in a strong box. Shipping weight, 30 pounds. Price..........................$3.95

The Brown Lion, $3.98.

No. 2C1016 **The body of this lamp is of brown, shaded from a dark seal brown to a light tan. The eight lions' heads stand out prominently from the lamp, and, together with the embossing, form the eight panels which contain the Oriental landscapes, which are far beyond description or illustration.** The mountings of this lamp are of solid brass and the removable brass oil fount has the highest grade center draft burner, which takes No. 2 Rochester chimney and round wick. It is 26 inches in height and has a 10-inch globe. It is carefully packed in a wooden box. Shipping weight, 30 lbs.
Price.......................................$3.98

The Princeton, $5.95.

No. 2C1025 **This is the largest lamp in our line, and is perfect in outline, decoration, construction and material.** The globe and bowl are of deep myrtle green decorated with highly tinted red and pink flowers and green foliage. These flowers are placed on the lamp after first removing the green decoration from the background only where the flower is to appear, and then painting the decoration on the body by hand, so that when lighted the light shows clearly and brightly through the flower, thus showing off the lamp to the very best advantage. The base and crown are of solid cast brass, highly polished. The removable oil fount is of brass and has large center draft 100-candle power burner with perfect wick attachment. It comes complete with No. 2 Rochester chimney and round wick. It is 30 inches high and has 11-inch globe. It is very carefully packed in a wooden box. Shipping weight, 35 pounds.
Price...........................$5.95

The Nevada, $7.95.

No. 2C1045 **This Lamp is** decorated with beautiful variegated pink roses with deep green foliage on a tinted green background. This decoration is very high class, being strictly hand painted throughout. It is not only on the front and back of the lamp, but completely covers all parts. When lighted it looks very beautiful, giving tone and elegance to the beautiful roses. The base and crown are of solid cast brass, highly polished and plated with gold. It has a removable brass oil fount, center draft 100-candle power burner and perfect wicking device. It is furnished with No. 2 Rochester chimney and round wick. It is 28 inches high and has 11-inch globe and bowl. It is packed carefully in a barrel. Shipping weight, 50 pounds.
Price...........................$7.95

ALL METAL PARTS OF OUR CHANDELIERS

ARE OF SOLID BRASS (NOT BRONZE METAL), WITH A HANDSOME BRONZE FINISH.

A great many dealers advertise chandeliers which, in appearance, are similiar to ours, but are made of bronze metal or plated steel, which is often mistaken for brass when the lamps are new, but will not stand the wear and retain the handsome appearance of solid brass. We GUARANTEE every one of our chandeliers to stand the wear of a lifetime and warrant them not to tarnish.

Two-Light Chandelier for only $6.89.

This Beautiful Chandelier is made of solid brass, finished in rich gold bronze, complete with fancy glass oil founts, etched globes of very popular shape. The No. 2 Unique burner is of a new design that can be lighted and filled without removing chimney or globe, thus avoiding all possibility of breakage in handling them. Takes 1-inch wick and No. 2 hinge chimney. It has the best patent automatic extension for raising and lowering so that it can be used with high or low ceilings. Packed complete in box to insure safe delivery. Shipping weight, 50 to 75 pounds

No. 2C810 Price, two lights complete..... $ 6.89
No. 2C811 Price, three lights complete... 8.65
No. 2C812 Price, four lights complete ... 10.85

Patent Extension Chandelier.

This Beautiful Chandelier has patent automatic extension for raising and lowering. It is made of solid brass, finished in rich gold bronze, with a center band studded with 12 beautifully colored cut glass jewels and 30 cut glass prisms suspended from same. This gives a very brilliant effect when lighted. Has fancy glass founts, best grade of No. 2 Unique burners and handsomely etched shades. The burners can be lighted without removing chimneys or shades, which is a great convenience. Takes 1-inch wick and No. 2 hinge chimney. The fancy rope shaped arms and standard make it very neat and attractive and it is an ornament as well as a fixture. Shipping weight, 70 to 100 pounds.

No. 2C826 Chandelier with two lights complete. Price $9.45
No. 2C827 Chandelier with three lights complete. Price..... $10.65
No. 2C828 Chandelier with four lights complete. Price..... $13.95

Three and Four-Light Chandeliers for Church, Hall or Dwelling Use.

Patent Extension Chandelier. Extended 57 inches. This chandelier is solid brass, elegantly finished in rich gold, with large ball and cast ornaments in bright silver finish. The No. 2 Unique burners can be trimmed and lighted without removing the chimney or globe. Takes 1-inch wick and No. 2 hinge chimney. Furnished with fancy glass oil founts and etched crystal globes. Shipping weight of three lights, about 75 lbs.; four lights, about 90 lbs.

No. 2C841 Chandelier with three lights complete. Price..... $11.35
No. 2C842 Chandelier with four lights complete. Price..... $13.95

Church or Hall Chandelier. Same chandelier as above except founts. This fixture is trimmed with celebrated No. 1 Miller fount, with center draft 55-candle power burner, making a very strong light for church or hall use.

No. 2C843 Chandelier with three lights complete. Price..... $13.45
No. 2C844 Chandelier with four lights complete. Price..... $16.85

Pedestal and Jardiniere, $1.95.

No. 2C1100 The Acacia Jar and Pedestal is one of the most popular patterns we show, especially when considering the low price. It measures 22 inches in height and is completed with a 9-inch jardiniere which will easily contain an 8-inch flower pot. It is beautifully embossed with the Acacia design, and artistically blended in blue-green with wine color mottlings. Shipped from Eastern Ohio. Weight, 40 pounds. Price..... $1.95

We also quote special prices on jardinieres separately.

No. 2C1101 7-inch Jardiniere, exactly like No. 2C1100 jardiniere. Measures 6¼ inches high and takes a 6-inch pot. Weight, 7 pounds. Price..... 23c

No. 2C1102 8-inch Jardiniere, exactly as above. Measures 7¼ inches high and takes a 7-inch pot. Weight, 8 pounds. Price..... 45c

No. 2C1103 9-inch Jardiniere, as above, measures 8 inches high and takes an 8-inch pot. Weight, 12 pounds. Price..... 65c

$2.95 Jardiniere and Pedestal.

No. 2C1105 This Beautiful Jardiniere and Pedestal is made by the celebrated Rozane pottery and is one of the most popular designs on the market. It is made from a china clay body which is superior to the clay usually used in the manufacture of this class of ware. It is artistically embossed with a fern leaf design and has a lovers' knot border, colored in rich blue, which is gradually blended into a rich Rookwood effect at the bottom of the jardiniere and the pedestal is decorated to match. The jardiniere has a pale olive green lining which greatly adds to its appearance. It measures 25 inches high and has a 10-inch jardiniere which will easily contain a 9-inch flower pot. Shipped from Eastern Ohio. Weight, 50 pounds. Price..... $2.95

$3.95 Jardiniere and Pedestal.

No. 2C1110 This Very Attractive Jardiniere and Pedestal is made by the celebrated Rozane pottery. It is beautifully embossed in a Grecian scroll pattern and blended from a light brown at the top to a dark grass green at the bottom, and has embossed dark royal blue shields which are artistically placed in the panels, forming a very rich contrast and making it agreeably attractive. It measures 26 inches high and is complete with a large 11-inch jardiniere to match, and will easily contain a 10-inch flower pot. Shipped from Eastern Ohio. Weight, 80 pounds. Price..... $3.95

No. 2C1112 8-inch Jardiniere, exactly like No. 2C1110, jardiniere measures 8 inches high and takes a 7-inch flower pot. Weight, 12 pounds. Price..... 48c

No. 2C1113 9-inch Jardiniere, like above, measures 9½ inches high and takes a 9-inch flower pot. Weight, 18 pounds. Price..... 65c

No. 2C1114 11-inch Jardiniere, like above, measures 10½ inches high and takes a 10-inch flower pot. Weight, 25 pounds. Price..... $1.25

15-Cent Rozane Cuspidor.

No. 2C1143 This High Grade Cuspidor is made from a stone china body which is beautifully colored in a dark green glazed effect, and highly embossed with scroll and ivy leaf with shield design. It is glazed both inside and out. It is an entirely new French shape with a very artistic scalloped top. A usual 30-cent value. Price..... 15c

Rookwood Effect Cuspidor, 23 Cents.

No. 2C1144 This cuspidor is of extra large size, being somewhat taller than the ordinary and is made from hard stone china body and is colored a rich, dark green, gradually blended into a deep shade of orange. It has a double glazed finish and richly embossed in a scroll design. A remarkable value. Price..... 23c

A Beautiful Hand Painted Jardiniere and Pedestal at $7.95.

No. 2C1120 At $7.95 we offer the finest Jardiniere and Pedestal on the market. The decoration is of the very latest, being an azalea pattern and is a genuine hand painted ware, which can only be done by the most skilled artists. The beautiful white azaleas and the dark foliage on a dark orange brown background, form a decided contrast, and can only be appreciated when seen. The general shape and pattern is very striking, being an exact reproduction of a celebrated French piece of art. The edges of the jardinieres are artistically scalloped, and are heavily treated with gold, and the inner part is decorated with a heavily stippled gold effect. It measures 29 inches in height, and has a 12-inch jardiniere which will easily contain an 11-inch flower pot. Shipped from Eastern Ohio. Weight, 75 pounds. Price..... $7.95

We also furnish jardinieres exactly like No. 2C1120 at the following prices:

No. 2C1121 8-inch Jardiniere, hand painted like illustration, measures 7¼ inches high and takes a 7-inch flower pot. Shipping wgt., 18 lbs. Price, $1.45

No. 2C1122 10-inch Jardiniere, hand painted like illustration, measures 9½ inches high and will take a 9-inch flower pot. Shipping wgt., 20 lbs. Price, $1.95

No. 2C1123 12-inch Jardiniere, hand painted like illustration, measures 10½ inches high and will contain an 11-inch flower pot. Shipping wgt., 30 lbs. Price..... $2.95

$1.59 Umbrella Stand.

No. 2C1124 Umbrella Stand. Made by the Rozane pottery, and is the best on the market for the price. This particular pattern is an exceptionally clever design, which represents a stork and cat tails, and is beautifully embossed, and has a double glaze finish. The top and bottom are neatly embossed in Gothic design, its colors are rich dark green and blue at the top, and gradually blended into a rich brown Rookwood effect at the base. It measures 18½ inches high, with 8½-inch opening at the top. Shipped from Eastern Ohio. Weight, 40 pounds. Price..... $1.59

$2.75 Rozane Umbrella Stand.

No. 2C1125 Umbrella Stand. Is of extra large size, measuring 22 inches across the opening at the top, and will accommodate a great many umbrellas. It is made from a fine clay china body, being richly embossed in shell and scroll design, and has a fancy scalloped top. The colorings are rich, dark pink underglazed, blended into pale green stripes, and the base is blended into a rich Rookwood effect. This umbrella stand readily retails at more than double the price we ask for it. Shipped from Eastern Ohio. Weight, 60 pounds. Price..... $2.75

Hand Painted Umbrella Stand, $7.95.

No. 2C1130 Iris Lily Umbrella Stand. This beautiful hand painted umbrella stand is recognized by artists and china painters as being a work of art. The purple colorings of the iris lily are delicately shaded in pink and red and has rich, green leaves, which form a background for this beautiful decoration. It is an exact reproduction of a very high priced French model. This stand is of extra size, measuring 23 inches high and has a 10½-inch opening at the top, which is heavily stippled in rich gold, and is made from an exceptionally fine white china body which is guaranteed not to craze. Shipped from Eastern Ohio. Weight, 75 pounds.

Price..... $7.95

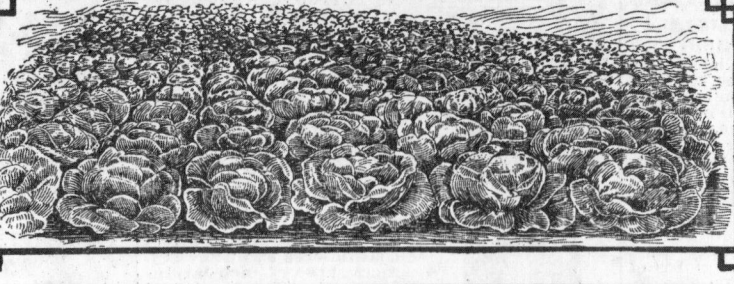

OUR SEED DEPARTMENT

We present to our customers our newly organized Seed Department, a department which we have been compelled to establish at the urgent demand of our customers who were daily sending us inquiries for seeds and plants from all parts of the country. We have therefore inaugurated this new department of seeds, in which we sell all kinds of farm seeds and field grasses, **all kinds** of trees and shrubs and all kinds of flower and vegetable seeds. We have made close and very favorable **arrangements** with the largest and most reliable seed farms in America, and in accordance with our established policy of asking **only a** small, narrow margin of profit above our cost, we are able to furnish to our customers the very best in this line **at the** lowest possible prices, lower prices than can be had from any other seed house.

We are able to fill any order, no matter how large, for FARM SEEDS, GARDEN and FLOWER SEEDS of any description.

WE ARE DETERMINED TO HANDLE ONLY THE BEST AND MOST RELIABLE SEEDS.

We have the unlimited confidence of our millions of customers throughout the entire country, and we could not afford to risk losing the confidence of any single one of our customers by sending out poor and unreliable seeds. Not only that, but the majority of our customers depend on reliable seeds for their living, and we would not solicit orders for this department unless we would be absolutely sure that the seeds we send out and the trees and shrubs we furnish from this department would prove a good advertisement for us and would be a means of strengthening the hold we have on our trade. We can assure you that the seeds we offer are the same kinds and varieties that have been used for years by farmers and market gardeners in all parts of the country, people who depend on reliable seeds for their means of livelihood, and who use nothing but the best seeds that grow.

OUR FREE SEED CATALOGUE.

Our Free Seed Catalogue is a complete book showing everything **in the** line of vegetable and flower seeds, field grasses, trees and shrubs **as well as** garden material, and we ask everyone who is interested in this line, as a **special** favor, to please write and get our free Seed Catalogue. Before you make **up your** spring order for seeds, or even if you intend to buy only one dollar's **worth of** flower seeds or vegetable seeds, send us a postal, ask for the free Seed **Catalogue,** and we will send it to you immediately by return mail, postpaid.

Our Free Seed Catalogue shows lower prices, more liberal offers than any other seed catalogue published. It is interesting from cover to cover. **We** can sell you the very best to be had in every variety at a lower price **than you** can find offered by any other concern, and we can save you a great deal of **money** in this line. **Please write for our Special Free Seed Catalogue.**

FLOWERS.

In our Free, Special, Descriptive Seed Catalogue, you will find a selection of the most popular and easily grown Flower Seeds.

Our selected varieties of flower seeds come from strictly first class **stock** of highest vitality and we know that in ordering from us you will get the **most** satisfactory results with your seeds for annual and perennial plants.

SEND FOR OUR SPECIAL SEED CATALOGUE. IT'S FREE

VEGETABLE SEEDS.

Seroco Reliable Vegetable Seeds Cheap.

NONE BETTER. NONE CHEAPER. ALL TESTED.

Our stock of vegetable seeds, we are sure, cannot be excelled either in quality or selection by any firm in the country. Every variety listed is desirable and has our recommendation. Our packets are, we believe, as well filled as any reliable dealer's in the United States, and in fact, a comparison has shown that they contain more seeds on the average than those of any other firm whose packets we have secured.

Write for our Special Free Seed Catalogue and get our low prices on the best garden seeds in the best selected varieties ever grown.

SEROCO SUPERIOR NORTHERN GROWN FARM SEEDS.

YIELD SUPERIOR PRODUCTS.

We are American headquarters for all kinds and varieties of farm seeds. Our contracts with some of the most reliable northern seed farms in America enables us to sell the best strains of all standard varieties, thoroughly dried and tested seeds. Send for our new Special Descriptive Seed Catalogue, and you can, from this special catalogue, make up your order for the best and most reliable seeds at the lowest prices.

The price on some farm and field seeds is subject to the fluctuation of the market and while the prices in our Special Seed Catalogue are correct according to market conditions at the date of the catalogue, we reserve the right to **change these prices without notice,** charging you the difference, which advance represents only the difference in cost to us. If the prices decline so that we can fill your order at a lower price than those printed in our Special Seed Catalogue, you will always get the benefit of such prices and the difference will be returned to you in cash.

TREES, SHRUBS AND PLANTS.

For the convenience of those of our customers who send to us for nearly all they buy, we have made arrangements with some of the largest and most reliable nurseries for our supply of trees, shrubs and perennial plants. From our Special Seed Catalogue, you can make your selections of trees, shrubs, etc., and send your order to us and we will have the stock sent you direct from the nursery.

REMEMBER.

We ship all orders for trees and shrubs direct from the nursery, fresh dug and carefully packed.

WRITE FOR OUR SPECIAL SEED CATALOGUE.

THESE TWO PAGES ARE MERELY TO INTRODUCE OUR NEW SEED DEPARTMENT to everyone who receives this catalogue. Our variety of seeds is so great that we cannot devote space to them all in this catalogue. We have prepared a very attractive and complete Special Seed Catalogue, and this catalogue will be sent to anyone by mail, postpaid, on application. **Write for our Free Seed Catalogue.** If you are interested in this line, if you use any seeds of any kind, don't fail to first write and get our Free Seed Catalogue before you place your order. We are sure that we can save you just as much money on your seed purchases as we can save you on any other line of merchandise, such as stoves, sewing machines, clothing, etc., depending on the amount of the purchase. You will find our prices throughout our Special Seed Catalogue just as much lower than the prices asked by seed houses generally or by retail dealers, as our prices on other lines of merchandise are lower than the prices asked by all other dealers.

YELLOWSTONE FLOWER SEED COLLECTION, 29 CENTS.

THE GREATEST BARGAIN IN FLOWER SEEDS EVER OFFERED.

Eighteen Varieties of the Most Beautiful Flowers of the Best and Most Popular Varieties, only 29 Cents.

1 package **Alyssum.**
1 package **Astor.**
1 package **Bachelor's Button.**
1 package **Butterfly Flower.**
1 package **Calliopsis.**
1 package **Foxglove.**
1 package **Marigold.**
1 package **Mignonette.**
1 package **Mourning Bride.**
1 package **Nasturtium.**
1 package **Pansy.**
1 package **Petunia.**
1 package **Phlox.**
1 package **Pink.**
1 package **Poppy.**
1 package **Snap Dragon.**
1 package **Sweet Peas.**
1 package **Verbena.**

REMEMBER—For only **29 cents**, we will send you these eighteen separate packets of flower seeds as named above. This collection of pretty and easily grown annuals is made up of fresh, high grade seeds, packed in a neat lithographed carton. This collection cannot be broken under any condition.

No. 56C100 Yellowstone Flower Seed Collection. Price................29c
If by mail, postage extra, 3 cents.

OUR ASTONISHING VEGETABLE SEED OFFER, YOUR GARDEN PLANTED FOR 33 CENTS.

REMEMBER, WE DO NOT ACCEPT ORDERS FOR LESS THAN 50 CENTS.

(SEE PAGE 2.)

If you want to take advantage of these three great bargains in seeds be sure to make your order 50 cents or more. Look over our other departments and include other needed goods with your order if you can use only one of these three seed offers.

SEROCO EXCELSIOR 33-CENT COLLECTION OF VEGETABLE SEEDS. Eighteen Varieties of Vegetable Seeds, 33 Cents. This Astonishing offer of the following:

1 package **Beet**, Crimson Globe.
1 package **Cabbage**, Early Jersey Wakefield.
1 package **Cabbage**, Holland Favorite.
1 package **Celery**, Golden Self Blanching.
1 package **Carrot**, Guerand or Oxheart.
1 package **Cucumber**, Evergreen, White Spine.
1 package **Lettuce**, Hanson.
1 package **Melon**, Osage or Water Ice Cream.
1 package **Melon**, Musk, Rocky Ford.
1 package **Onion**, Yellow Globe Danvers.
1 package **Onion**, Prize Taker.
1 package **Parsnip**, Long White Dutch or Sugar.
1 package **Radish**, Non Plus Ultra.
1 package **Spinach**, Victoria.
1 package **Squash**, Hubbard.
1 package **Tomato**, Sparks' Earliana.
1 package **Tomato**, Ponderosa.
1 package **Turnip**, Early White Milan.

THIS COLLECTION is made up of our highest grade seeds and costs more than double this amount if bought elsewhere. We cannot make any changes in this collection.

No. 56C110 Seroco Excelsior Vegetable Seed Collection. Price..........33c
If by mail, postage extra, 5 cents.

COMBINATION FLOWER AND VEGETABLE SEED COLLECTION, 43 CENTS.

TWENTY-FIVE VARIETIES Valuable Vegetable and Beautiful Flower Seeds, for only 43 cents. Our special vegetable and flower collection. Never were reliable seeds offered at such a low price. It would cost you three times as much to buy these seeds elsewhere. Take advantage of this unusual offer by ordering now, twenty-five varieties of the best vegetable and flower seeds, at our low price, 43 cents. Seeds that grow.

VEGETABLES.

1 package **Beet,** Early Egyptian.
1 package **Cabbage,** Early New Jersey Wakefield.
1 package **Celery,** White Plume.
1 package **Carrot,** Improved Long Orange.
1 package **Cucumber,** Early Cluster
1 package **Lettuce,** Prize Head.
1 package **Melon,** Champion Market.
1 package **Onion,** Large Red Wethersfield.
1 package **Parsnip,** Hollow Crown.
1 package **Radish,** Early Scarlet, Wide Tipped.
1 package **Spinach,** Long Standing.
1 package **Squash,** Mammoth Bush.
1 package **Turnip,** Early Snowball
1 package **Tomato,** Dwarf Champion.

FLOWERS.

1 package **Aster.**
1 package **Marigold.**
1 package **Petunia.**
1 package **Phlox.**
1 package **Snap Dragon.**
1 package **Calliopsis.**
1 package **Pansy**
1 package **Pink**
1 package **Poppy.**
1 package **Sweet Peas.**
1 package **Verbena.**

All of these twenty-five Vegetable and Flower Seeds only 43c.

REMEMBER—We cannot make a single change in this collection and no other varieties can be sold so cheap.

No. 56C120 Our Combination Flower and Vegetable Seed Collection. Price..........43c
If by mail, postage extra, 6 cents.

DRUG DEPARTMENT

OUR QUALITY GUARANTEE.

EVERY REMEDY, every proprietary medicine put up in our own laboratory or sold by us and prepared at the Seroco Chemical Laboratory is guaranteed absolutely pure, made from the very highest grade ingredients, positively free from any adulteration or alloy, never cheapened in any way at the expense of efficiency, and positively the best known prescription in each case for the ailment for which it is intended; and every patent (or proprietary) medicine of other makes offered in this catalogue, to the best of our knowledge and belief, is of standard quality, made by concerns of established and proven reliability; every drug, every article of merchandise shown in this catalogue is of the highest grade, never cheapened, efficiency never sacrificed for cost.

WITH OUR FACILITIES, with the most skilled chemists, the most skilled pharmacists, with the facilities afforded in our big laboratory, we are in such a position that no retail druggist can possibly be in a better position to thoroughly test, carefully analyze the goods we buy and sell, to know they are strictly pure and of the highest potency. You have our guarantee for this backed by our reputation known everywhere. You are sure of getting not only the highest quality, but you are also sure of getting the lowest price, one-half the price charged by others, and many times even much less.

WHY WE CAN GIVE SO MUCH MORE IN QUALITY.

WITH NEARLY ALL THE EXPENSE common to other dealers eliminated, where it is only necessary to ask our customers to pay a price that barely covers the cost of material and labor in our own laboratory, with but our one small percentage of profit added, there is not the slightest necessity of sacrificing quality for price, since we can make the price attractively low on the highest grade of goods obtainable.

FIRST, our reputation alone will preclude us from using anything but the very best, and secondly, it is very easy with our facilities to give our customers the very best, and then furnish them the goods for at least one-half the price others must get for inferior goods. If in our laboratory the remedy requires any spirits for its preservation, we do not consider price in the purchase. We only look to the quality, the very best obtainable, and the same applies to every ingredient, every formula we have. So, in ordering anything from this catalogue, and particularly remedies put up in our Seroco Chemical Laboratory, by comparison you will find them in every way better, more efficient, more satisfactory, not to mention very much lower in price than any similar remedy or article you can buy from any dealer anywhere.

SPECIAL ADVANTAGES TO AGENTS, DRUGGISTS, MERCHANTS AND HANDLERS OF DRUGS AND PROPRIETARY REMEDIES (PATENT MEDICINES.)

WE HAVE ON OUR BOOKS thousands of customers who make a business of buying goods from this department to sell again, particularly our own special remedies, made in our own laboratory, the Seroco Chemical Laboratory, and make a nice income at this work.

AGENTS MAKE FROM $5.00 TO $10.00 A DAY by devoting their time to selling our Seroco Chemical Laboratory remedies. Druggists, merchants and others often double their income by carrying a stock of these goods, supplying their customers with the highest grade goods made, and at a liberal profit to themselves.

THE ADVANTAGES WE OFFER over any other line of remedies made are many. First, every remedy put up in our own laboratory is put out under the manufacturing name of Seroco Chemical Laboratory, Chicago, and does not bear the name of Sears, Roebuck & Co., in any place, hence you can buy these goods and offer them for sale without any indication on the goods that they were purchased from us and in this way you haven't even the slightest competition from our house.

SECOND, every remedy is plainly priced on the outside of the package (without any reference whatever to our selling price), at the usual price at which similar remedies are retailed. For example, our sarsaparilla, the intrinsic value of one bottle of which is worth two of any other sarsaparilla made, bears the name on the outside of the carton "Seroco Chemical Laboratory, Chicago. Price, $1.00," whereas our price in single bottles is 50 cents or when you order a dozen of remedies together, only 40 cents a bottle. Therefore you can buy a bottle of Dr. Hammond's Sarsaparilla under the name Seroco Chemical Laboratory of which the price is plainly $1.00, for only 40 cents, if included in an order of one dozen or more of the different remedies, whereas any other widely advertised sarsaparilla of one-half the strength or efficiency would cost at least $8.00 per dozen if bought from the largest wholesale drug house, or nearly twice the price at which we sell Dr. Hammond's Sarsaparilla, so the agent, canvasser, druggist or retailer selling Dr. Hammond's Sarsaparilla who can sell it for $1.00 per bottle and make 60 cents, or can cut the price as much as he likes, making for his profit the difference between 40 cents per bottle and the price he chooses to ask for it. The same applies to other of our preparations. The name Sears, Roebuck & Co. appears on no package. Every package bears the name Seroco Chemical Laboratory. You can buy these goods direct from us in quantities of one dozen or more of the different remedies or assorted, at about one-half the price at which wholesale dealers sell inferior goods, you can offer them to your trade at cut prices and make a far bigger profit than on any other line of remedies offered to your trade. You can get the benefit of our dozen prices by ordering six or more packages. You need not order six of one kind, but as long as your order is for six or more packages you can take advantage of the dozen price.

ANOTHER ADVANTAGE.

OUR GOODS ARE PUT OUT IN HANDSOMER, far more attractive, better selling and more satisfactory packages than any other remedy made. Every package is of most convenient size. We use the handsomest, best shaped and most attractive boxes, bottles, cartons, wrappers, and general package material that is in any line of remedies made. The packages are in strict keeping with the contents of the same. As a rule, all packages are beautifully lithographed in colors in handsome designs, all bear the name of Seroco Chemical Laboratory, Chicago, and the usual retail selling price is plainly printed on each package. Each package carries with it the laboratory's binding guarantee for quality, a very essential point to the customer buying.

THE BOOK OF INSTRUCTIONS which we furnish with each remedy is far more complete and instructive than is furnished with any other remedy made. It is a complete treatise on the diseases for which the particular remedy is a specific, gives the patient much more information and enables him to use the remedy to far better advantage than if we were to furnish only the stereotyped information that usually goes with the ordinary patent remedy.

THE PRICES ASKED by the manufacturers for most patent medicines make it impossible for us to save you more than from 25 to 50 per cent, whereas, from our own laboratory, the Seroco Chemical Laboratory, we can furnish you higher grade remedies on the basis of the actual cost for the ingredients, compounding, package, etc., with but our one small percentage of profit added. As a rule, the price is from one-third to one-half that charged by retail dealers for inferior goods.

OUR POSITION ON THE PATENT MEDICINE QUESTION.

WE SELL NEARLY ALL OF THE ADVERTISED or so called patent medicines without adding our recommendation to any particular preparation. We simply furnish our customers such advertised patent medicines as they may want and which they would buy anyway, just the same as we supply any other merchandise, giving our patrons, however, the advantage of our buying facilities and supplying this class of goods at from 25 to 40 per cent lower prices than the prices which they would have to pay at any drug store. It must be understood, however, that we know nothing about the formulae or ingredients and we can, therefore, say nothing for or against the merit of such patent medicines.

IN ADDITION we furnish to our customers a selected line of household remedies, not only for the minor ills, but also for chronic diseases, and these remedies, being prepared in our own laboratory, under our own supervision, every ingredient going into these remedies being known to us and the formula itself being in every instance one used by thousands of physicians as the most reliable and efficient for the treatment of symptoms for which they are intended, we do not hesitate to guarantee them absolutely pure and harmless and to highly recommend these remedies, feeling confident that they will meet all reasonable hopes and expectations of the customer.

THESE HOUSEHOLD PREPARATIONS of ours, put up in the Seroco Chemical Laboratory, are preparations that are the result of a great deal of experience and are based on the most successful formulas and prescriptions that are recognized by practitioners as the most successful in the treatment of these certain symptoms and for the relief and cure of the disorders and diseases for which they are intended.

IN ALL CASES OF ACUTE SICKNESS, it is usually necessary, and in many cases of chronic diseases it is advisable, to employ the services of a skilled physician. The patient may not know what is ailing him; he may not be able to judge as to the nature of his symptoms, and a careful diagnosis should be made and the treatment employed should be suitable to his condition as ascertained by the physician's examination and as determined by his judgment. When you know, however, that you are suffering from indigestion or stomach trouble; when it is a question of saving for yourself inconvenience, time and expense; when you know that your ailment is a catarrh trouble which may have become chronic and which neither by treatment of the physician or by the use of so called patent medicines has been benefited, you need not hesitate to give our household remedy for indigestion or for catarrh, as the case may be, a fair test, as it may be just the remedy that covers your condition exactly, affording quick relief and a possible cure within a comparatively short time.

EVERY ONE OF OUR HOUSEHOLD REMEDIES is considered one of the best, if not the best prescription employed by the most successful medical practitioners for the treatment of the condition for which we supply them. Of this fact you may be certain. We also wish to emphasize the fact that these remedies are prepared in our own laboratory, that we know every ingredient that goes into the preparations and we consequently know and can assure you that they are absolutely harmless. You are not taking the slightest risk in giving our household remedies a thorough trial.

WE DO NOT CLAIM that any one of our household remedies is a "Cure All," nor do we wish you to understand that we (or anybody else) can claim that without a diagnosis of your case we know beforehand that our remedy will cure you. This would be unreasonable and you would have a perfect right to question our sincerity. What we do know is that our household remedies comprise the most valuable and highly successful prescriptions for the different ailments which they cover. We know that there is nothing harmful in any single one of our preparations. We know that they have afforded relief and even permanent cure in hundreds and thousands of cases. We know that they are prepared with the greatest care and we know that we are able to and do offer these remedies for a fraction of the cost of what the same prescription would cost put up in any drug store.

YOU CAN EASILY ASCERTAIN whether any one of the household remedies we recommend is suitable for the treatment, relief and cure of your case. You are taking no risk, for we do not ask, nor do we expect that you should risk a single penny when making a test of these remedies. They may be the best remedies made, they may have relieved and cured thousands of men and women, which fact would ordinarily be sufficient to secure your confidence. No matter how good a remedy may be, no matter how much it has done for others, the question for you to determine is "What will it do for me?" Is it at all suitable for your particular case? To learn whether it is or not you have the privilege of ordering the first bottle or package of our household remedies with the understanding that after you have used it you find that it has not benefited your case, upon receipt of your report to that effect and the statement that you have never ordered or used the same remedy before, we will refund you the entire amount you have paid for the first package. We shall not expect you to be put to any expense or to proceed with the treatment, unless you find that the medicine is helping you and seems to be just what you need for obtaining relief and a cure.

PRESCRIPTION DEPARTMENT.

OUR PRESCRIPTION DEPARTMENT is under the direct charge of one of the most able chemists and pharmacists in the country. Every prescription is compounded with the greatest care, only the very best drugs are used, and yet we are able to save our customers in nearly all cases one-half in price. If you send your doctor's prescription, or any other prescription, to us, you can rest assured it will be given professional care. There will not be any substitutions such as local druggists are often compelled to make for want of certain drugs. The prescription will be compounded in the most scientific manner and returned to you immediately and at a saving in price on an average of more than one-half.

REGARDING SPIRITUOUS LIQUORS.

WE DO NOT HANDLE OR SELL SPIRITUOUS LIQUORS.

POISONOUS, INFLAMMABLE OR EXPLOSIVE MATERIALS CANNOT BE MAILED.

WE ISSUE A SPECIAL CATALOGUE of Surgical Instruments and Physicians' Supplies, which will be mailed to any physician or surgeon, free on application.

DR. WILDEN'S QUICK CURE FOR INDIGESTION AND DYSPEPSIA.

DO YOU SUFFER FROM INDIGESTION? DO YOU HAVE DYSPEPSIA? DOES YOUR FOOD DISTRESS YOU?

Do you suffer from a stuffed up, choking feeling, a difficulty in breathing, pain in the chest, as if a lump were there, after your meals? These are the easily recognized and sure symptoms of indigestion. Send for Dr. Wilden's Quick Cure for Indigestion and Dyspepsia, the great stomach remedy, the enemy of indigestion in any form.

A GREAT PRESCRIPTION. Put up in the form of plain, easily taken tablets and highly recommended as a cure for dyspepsia. If you suffer from only an occasional attack of indigestion, even though your stomach is out of order but seldom, keep Dr. Wilden's Quick Cure on hand, take a tablet after your meals and you will not be troubled. You can then enjoy your meals and never suffer one particle of distress, you won't know you have such an organ as a stomach.

ONLY 38 CENTS PER BOX CONTAINING 50 DOSES, enough for 50 treatments. For 38 cents we furnish a box of Dr. Wilden's Quick Cure for Indigestion and Dyspepsia containing almost double the number of tablets or treatments, found in boxes of other so called dyspepsia tablets that retail at 50 cents everywhere.

FOR 58 CENTS we furnish a large box containing as much as three small ones and more tablets than are contained in dyspepsia remedies that retail at $1.00. Don't wait until your indigestion or occasional stomach trouble has become chronic. Don't think that because you suffer from distress after meals only once in a while that you should overlook it. With Dr. Wilden's tablets at hand for convenient use, you can check the trouble at once and at the slightest intimation of indigestion, the least fullness, stiffness or uncomfortable feeling after eating, take a tablet (they are small and dissolve easily), and in a short time you will be completely relieved. At the same time the stomach is toned and strengthened, better able to perform its natural functions and you are insuring yourself against after dangerous complications.

ONE TABLET OF DR. WILDEN'S QUICK CURE FOR INDIGESTION AND DYSPEPSIA HELPS THE STOMACH TO DIGEST FOOD. There is wonderful digestive power in a single tablet of this great stomach remedy and yet this splendid remedy does not contain one single particle of opium, calomel or any harmful ingredient, but it digests food, assists the stomach and strengthens the digestive organs.

WE EARNESTLY ASK YOU TO GIVE THIS DYSPEPSIA PREPARATION A FAIR TRIAL. We do not believe there is a preparation on the market that possesses more of the valuable digestive properties found in Dr. Wilden's Quick Cure for Indigestion and Dyspepsia. We are willing that you should send for a box of Dr. Wilden's Quick Cure for Indigestion and Dyspepsia with the understanding that you can give it a trial and if it does not benefit you and you will simply tell us that you received no benefit and that this is the first package you have tried, we will immediately return your money. We have great confidence in this remedy, and we do not want any of our customers to suffer, if we are able to offer them means of relief and cure.

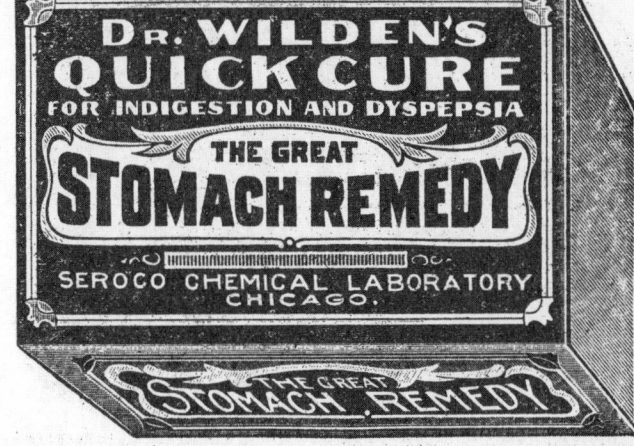

No. 8C1 Price, per dozen boxes, **$3.60**; regular size box..**38c**
No. 8C2 Price, per dozen boxes, **$4.80**; large box..**58c**
If by mail, postage extra, per small box, 2 cents; large box, 8 cents.

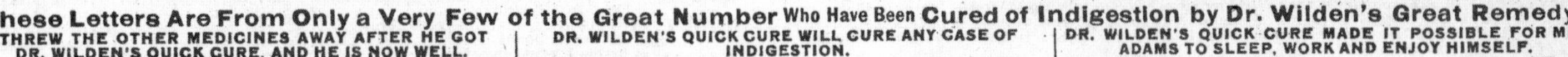
These Letters Are From Only a Very Few of the Great Number Who Have Been Cured of Indigestion by Dr. Wilden's Great Remedy.

THREW THE OTHER MEDICINES AWAY AFTER HE GOT DR. WILDEN'S QUICK CURE, AND HE IS NOW WELL.

Sears, Roebuck & Co., Chicago, Ill. Alexandria, S. D.

Gentlemen: In regard to Dr. Wilden's Quick Cure for Indigestion and Dyspepsia, I believe it to be the best remedy for indigestion on the market today. I had been suffering from indigestion for some time and I was getting worse instead of better under the treatment I was taking. I sent for some of your cure and threw the other medicine away when I received yours. I noticed a decided improvement after I had taken only two or three doses and I continued to improve steadily until I was entirely relieved and I do not suffer or have the least trace of indigestion left. I am very glad that I was able to find a remedy for this dreaded disease before it got so bad or developed into some worse disease that would be impossible to cure.

Yours very truly, WM. OVERMAN.

DR. WILDEN'S QUICK CURE WILL CURE ANY CASE OF INDIGESTION.

Sears, Roebuck & Co., Chicago, Ill. Newark, Ohio.

Gentlemen: Dr. Wilden's Quick Cure for Indigestion and Dyspepsia is indeed as you claim for it, a quick cure, and it not only cures quickly but cures completely any case of indigestion for which it may be taken. This seems like a strong statement, but I know that it is true because I have taken the cure myself and have given it to two of my children and a nephew, all of whom were suffering from stomach trouble and were not able to find relief from the medicines which they were taking. Your wonderful preparation effected a sure and quick cure in every case and you may well believe that we do not fail to give you the proper credit and to recommend your medicine whenever we can. Everything that we have ever received from your store has been the best we had ever bought any place and we have been treated fairly and honorably in all of our transactions with you.

Yours respectfully, JAS. A. PAGELS.

DR. WILDEN'S QUICK CURE MADE IT POSSIBLE FOR MR. ADAMS TO SLEEP, WORK AND ENJOY HIMSELF.

Sears, Roebuck, & Co., Chicago, Ill. Lebanon, Ky.

Gentlemen: I feel that I have been helped more by your Dr. Wilden's Quick Cure for Indigestion and Dyspepsia than I ever have by any other medicine or cure which I have taken for any disease. I suffered so much from indigestion that I was not able to sleep at night and I could not do my work properly in the daytime, and I was so nervous and irritable from my stomach trouble that I was becoming a burden both to myself and to my friends. I sought relief everywhere and took all the medicines and so-called cures that were recommended to me, but none of them did me any good until I took your Dr. Wilden's Quick Cure for Indigestion and Dyspepsia, which I read about in your big catalogue. I speedily began to grow better under your treatment and it was not long before all my suffering was gone and I was able to sleep and work and enjoy myself as I had done before I was afflicted with that awful disease.

Yours truly, THOMAS ADAMS.

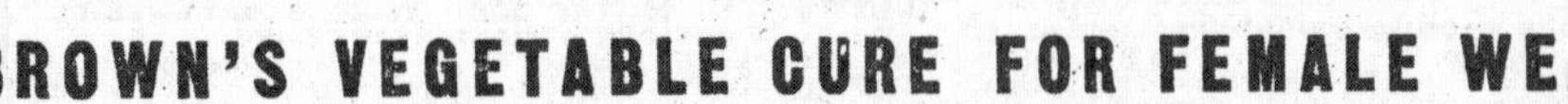
BROWN'S VEGETABLE CURE FOR FEMALE WEAKNESS.

LARGE COMMERCIAL SIZE QUART BOTTLES. RETAIL PRICE $1.00. OUR PRICE, EACH, 55c; PER DOZEN, $5.10.

A Very Effective Vegetable Tonic to be Used in the Treatment of Female Weakness, Falling of the Womb, Leucorrhea, Irregular or Painful Menstruation, Inflammation and Ulceration of the Womb, Flooding and all Female Disorders.

WOMEN, BROWN'S VEGETABLE CURE is most highly recommended for female disorders. If you have any of the following symptoms take this remedy at once, it may afford you an easy and lasting cure: Nausea and bad taste in the mouth, sore feeling in lower part of bowels, an unusual discharge, impaired general health, feeling of languor, sharp pain in region of kidneys, backache, dull pain in small of back, pain in passing water, bearing down feeling, a desire to urinate frequently, a dragging sensation in the groin, courses irregular, timid, nervous and restless feeling, a dread of some impending evil, temper wayward and irritable, a feeling of fullness, sparks before the eyes, gait unsteady, pain in womb, swelling in front, pain in breastbone, pain when courses occur, hysterics, temples and ears throb, sleep short and disturbed, whites, impaired digestion, headache, dizziness, morbid feeling and the blues, palpitation of the heart, nerves weak and sensitive, appetite poor, a craving for unnatural food, spirits depressed, nervous dyspeptic symptoms, a heavy feeling and pain in back upon exertion, fainting spells, difficulty in passing water, habitual constipation, cold extremities. If you have any of these symptoms send for a bottle of Brown's Vegetable Cure and give this preparation a trial. It will be sufficient to show you that Brown's Vegetable Cure is just the remedy you need—the remedy that will bring you not only relief but a cure, as it has in thousands of cases of suffering women who have given this medicine a fair test. Invalids have been made well and strong. Do not delay, one bottle will help and convince you.

UNDER THE GENERAL HEADING OF FEMALE WEAKNESS are included a vast array of systemic troubles, including leucorrhea or whites, prolapsus, or falling of the womb, irregular and painful menstruation, inflammation and ulceration of the womb, kidneys, bowel and liver troubles and ovarian difficulties. The term "female weakness" itself has no specific meaning and covers a multitude of ailments; in fact, given six different women with six different ailments peculiar to their sex, each one of them would be pretty sure to characterize her trouble as female weakness. **Brown's Vegetable Cure is very effective in the treatment of all of these diseases peculiar to women.**

BROWN'S VEGETABLE CURE FOR FEMALE WEAKNESS is a prescription that has proven highly efficient in a very large number of cases. It is one of our household remedies put up in our own laboratory, guaranteed to contain nothing harmful, but made up of those ingredients which are known to have the best effect in cases where the symptoms of female weakness are present. We offer it with every confidence and if you are suffering you can give this remedy a trial. If it affords you no relief, it will positively not harm you, and we will return to you your money if you have not used this remedy before.

Our Booklet, "The Woman's Friend," Valuable and Instructive, Sent Free with Every Bottle of Brown's Vegetable Cure.

No. 8C4 Price, per dozen bottles, **$5.10**; per bottle..**55c**
Cannot be mailed on account of weight.

READ THESE LETTERS FROM GRATEFUL WOMEN.

MRS. FULLER ENTIRELY CURED OF FEMALE WEAKNESS BY BROWN'S VEGETABLE CURE.

Emmet, Ark.
Sears, Roebuck & Co., Chicago, Ill.

Gentlemen: I received the Brown's Vegetable Cure which I ordered from you some time ago and I want to tell you that it has been a remarkable cure in my case. I have used it for female weakness and have been entirely cured. I had tried several cures which my friends had recommended before I used Brown's Vegetable Cure, but I did not receive any permanent relief. I think that this is the very best remedy of its kind on the market today and I do not hesitate to tell all of my friends about its remarkable properties. I think Mrs. Jones, who lives about three miles from me, will order some of the cure in a few days.

Yours sincerely,
MRS. CYNTHIAN FULLER.

BROWN'S VEGETABLE CURE IS THE BEST REMEDY OF ITS KIND ON THE MARKET.

Warsaw, Minn.
Sears, Roebuck & Co., Chicago, Ill.

Gentlemen: I feel that it is my duty to write and tell you of the remarkable cure which has been effected in my case by using your Brown's Vegetable Cure. I was a sufferer for a number of years from kidney and bladder troubles, but all of these troubles are now a thing of the past and I am once more a well woman, able to do all of my work and take care of my house as it should be taken care of. I certainly think that Brown's Vegetable Cure is the best remedy of its kind on the market. I had been taking medicine and was, when I received your medicine, taking medicine from a doctor here in Warsaw, but your Cure produced such an immediate and favorable result that I threw away all of the doctor's medicine and used nothing but Brown's Vegetable Cure.

Yours very truly,
MRS. C. C. CLAYTON.

BROWN'S VEGETABLE CURE DOES MORE GOOD THAN ALL OTHER MEDICINE PUT TOGETHER.

Sears, Roebuck & Co., Chicago, Ill. Leon, Iowa.

Gentlemen: It gives me much pleasure to tell you of the great good I have obtained from your excellent remedy, Brown's Vegetable Cure. I used the Cure for female weakness and I have received more help and benefit from it than I have ever received from any other medicine that I have tried. I have been a constant sufferer for a number of years and have tried a great number of remedies and have doctored for all of these years, but did not seem to get any stouter until after using Brown's Vegetable Cure, which is invaluable for female weakness or change of life. I am 46 years of age and have been quite poorly for some time, but since I received such great benefits from your medicine I am stronger than I have been for years. I am going to send to you for some more of your medicine. I was just telling my husband the other day that Brown's Vegetable Cure had done me more good than all of the rest of the medicine I have taken put together. I will continually praise your medicine for the great benefit I have received.

Yours very truly, MRS. W. L. ARNOLD.

A CURE FOR WEAK HEARTS — WONDER HEART CURE — DR. ECHOLS' AUSTRALIAN AURICLO,

42 CENTS AND 75 CENTS PER BOX, ACCORDING TO SIZE.

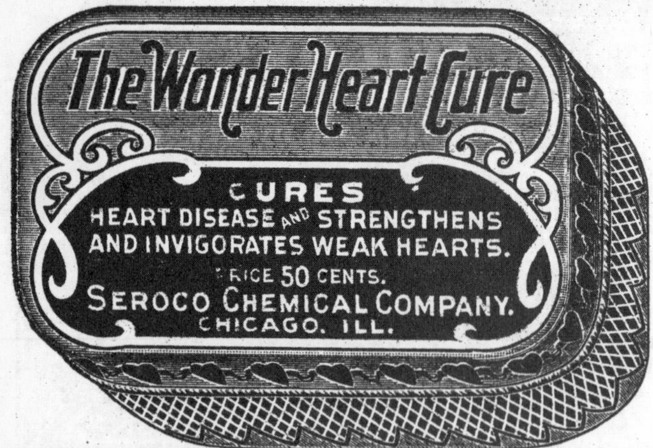

A Most Important Preparation. Recommended for Complications Indicating Heart Trouble.

THE HEALTH OF THE HEART IS MOST IMPORTANT. The heart is the great human pump, that sends the life giving blood to every part of the body. The amount of labor it performs day and night, working incessantly year after year, is almost beyond belief. All this vast amount of work must be done, and done well each day; if not, your health will surely suffer in consequence of the least failure of the heart to properly perform its duties.

SYMPTOMS OF HEART TROUBLE. In order that one may determine if the heart is affected, we ask attention to the following list of symptoms which denote heart disease: Flutttering of the Pulse, Palpitation of the Heart, Shortness of Breath, Tenderness and Sudden, Sharp Pains in the Left Side, Dreaming of Falling from a Height, Inability to Sleep Upon the Left Side, Fainting or Smothering Spells, Unconscious Spells, Dropsy, Sudden Starting in the Sleep and Noises in the Ears. In the simple descriptions of these symptoms, we have included the facts whereby heart trouble is recognized.

If you have the slightest suspicion of heart trouble, it would be advisable to take the Wonder Heart Cure immediately. You cannot make a mistake. The preparation will not harm a well heart and it may relieve and cure a disordered heart. The Wonder Heart Cure is a safe, scientific, carefully prepared remedy which acts upon the nerves, muscular tissues, membraneous linings and valves of nature's life pump, the heart. It is based on a prescription that has relieved hundreds of cases. It may fit your case exactly and you would receive wonderful benefit. If you are suffering from heart trouble, you should not overlook the opportunity of getting relief at a small expense and we are willing that you make a trial of Dr. Echol's Australian Auriclo. If you find that you have not received any benefit, simply write us to that effect and tell us that this is the first package of this remedy that you have tried, and we will cheerfully refund your money. We do not want to sell our customers anything, whether it is a sewing machine or a medical preparation or any other merchandise, unless we know that they get value received for their money; in fact, it is our aim to give them a great deal more value for their money than any other firm does. The price of this household remedy is very small indeed, but that does not mean that it has no efficiency; it means simply that we are willing so sell it on a small margin of profit. If you know that you are a sufferer from heart weakness or other heart complications, we recommend to you giving a trial to the Wonder Heart Cure. It has offered many a sufferer a means for relief and cure, and may accomplish the same for you. Under our liberal terms, you can find out whether the Wonder Heart Cure is suitable for the treatment of your case, without the slightest risk on your part. First, it cannot harm you, for we know the ingredients; and, secondly, if you try this remedy, if it does not help you, you need only notify us that the first box you have used of this remedy has not benefited your condition, and we will return to you every cent you have paid us for same.

WONDER HEART CURE is prepared in the form of a tablet and the remedy can be carried in the pocket without inconvenience. We furnish a box, containing 40 doses, for only 42 cents, larger boxes, containing 100 doses, for 75 cents. The price of the remedy is insignificant compared to its value, and no one who has the least indication of heart trouble should be without a box of this valuable remedy.

No. 8C6 Price, per box, containing 40 doses........ $0.42
Per dozen boxes........ 3.90
No. 8C7 Price, per box, containing 100 doses........ .75
Per dozen boxes........ 6.60
If by mail, postage extra, per small box, 3 cents; large box, 6 cents.

THOSE WHO HAVE TRIED WONDER HEART CURE ARE CERTAINLY THE BEST JUDGES. READ WHAT THEY SAY.

SUFFERED FOR YEARS FROM HEART TROUBLE, BUT WONDER HEART CURE CURED HER.

Sears, Roebuck & Co., Chicago, Ill. Kaufman, Texas.

Gentlemen: I am glad to say that I feel much relieved since taking your Wonder Heart Cure. I do not suffer any more from fluttering of the heart or from shortness of breath. I believe I will soon be completely cured, I have been suffering from heart trouble for a number of years and have tried a number of remedies without success until a neighbor friend of mine, who has bought a great many goods of you, told me of your Wonder Heart Cure. I immediately sent for some of the tablets, and began to feel better within two or three days after I first commenced taking them. I have steadily improved in health and I am now almost cured. Your Wonder Heart Cure is certainly a great remedy. Yours truly, MRS. R. E. SCOTT.

WONDER HEART CURE PRODUCES WONDERFUL RESULTS.

Sears, Roebuck & Co., Chicago, Ill. Five Mile, Ohio.

Gentlemen: I received the box of Wonder Heart Cure Tablets, and I am very much pleased with the results obtained from taking them, and want you to send me another box, for which please find enclosed the money. The tablets have done all you recommend for them, and I am indeed grateful to you for a medicine which has helped me like your Wonder Heart Cure Tablets. I do not have fainting or smothering spells as I used to have, and I now feel better than I have felt for several years. Your Wonder Heart Cure Tablets are certainly a grand remedy for anyone suffering from any kind of heart trouble.
Yours truly, MRS. JOSEPH WARLAIMONT.

OUR WONDER HEART CURE A GODSEND.

Sears, Roebuck & Co,, Chicago, Ill. Joppa, Ala.

Gentlemen: Regarding the Wonder Heart Cure which I ordered and received from you some time ago, will say that I have taken it with wonderful results. I was bothered with the palpitation of the heart and had very great pains in the left side. At first your medicine did not seem to help me, but by following the directions closely and taking it just as you advised, I soon began to be better and am now cured. Your Wonder Heart Cure is indeed a godsend to suffering humanity and anyone suffering from palpitation of the heart or troubled with fainting spells will be cured as I have been by using your Wonder Heart Cure. I cannot praise it too highly. Yours respectfully,
JAMES WARREN.

GLAD TO TELL OF THE GOOD RESULTS OBTAINED BY USING OUR WONDER HEART CURE.

Sears, Roebuck & Co., Chicago, Ill. Canon Diablo, Ariz.

Dear Sirs: It gives me great pleasure to tell you of the good results that I have obtained by using your Wonder Heart Cure Tablets. I was in very poor health, due, so my doctor told me, to heart trouble. I had fluttering of the heart and sinking spells at intervals. Reading the description of your Wonder Heart Cure Tablets and thinking that they would help me, I ordered some of them, and am pleased to say that they have cured me and I no longer suffer from heart trouble as I did. Thanking you for what the Wonder Heart Cure has done for me, and trusting that my suffering sisters may be relieved in the same manner, I remain,
Very gratefully yours, MRS. W. L. JONES.

CELERY MALT COMPOUND.

A HIGH CLASS PREPARATION. LARGE REGULAR $1.00 SIZE BOTTLES—COMMERCIAL QUART SIZE— OUR PRICE ONLY 56 CENTS.

THE GREAT NERVE BUILDER, BRAIN TONIC AND STIMULANT.

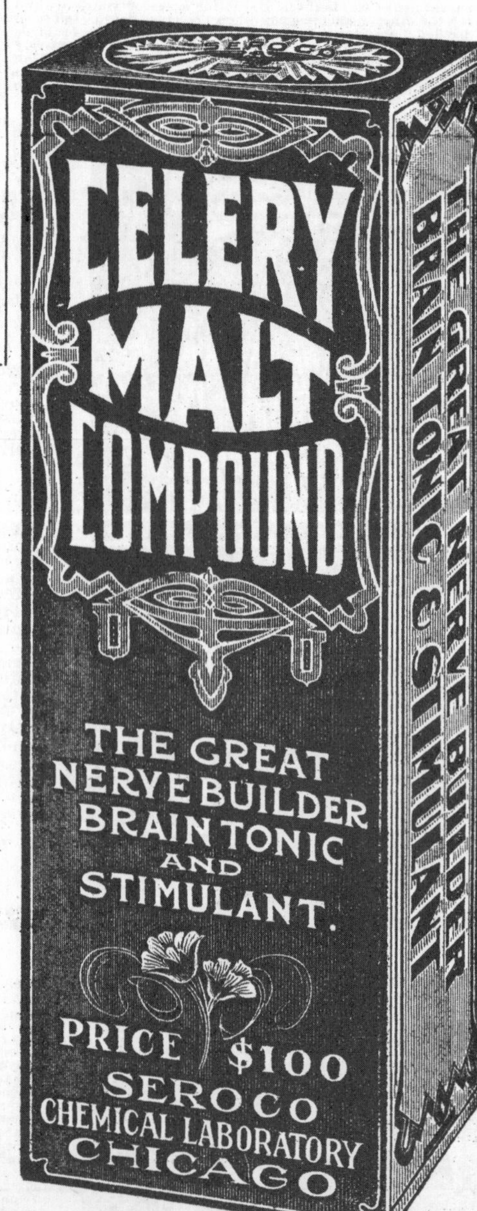

Celery Compound has for years been recognized as one of the best possible health tonics. Our Celery Compound is improved by the addition of malt, making it far superior to other similar remedies. We guarantee our Celery Malt Compound to be absolutely pure and unadulterated. It is regarded as superior to any other celery compound on the market, regardless of name or price.

IT IS A TRUE NERVE TONIC, a genuine appetizer, a stimulant both for the young and old. We do not claim that Celery Malt Compound is an absolute specific for any chronic disease, but it has a much wider range of usefulness, as it is just the preparation required in hundreds of cases, and where no chronic disease has taken hold, it is very beneficial in hundreds of the ills that flesh is heir to. It is a preparation of such usefulness that in many houses it is regarded as standard and is always kept on hand for immediate use.

CELERY MALT COMPOUND IS A RECOGNIZED NERVE AND BRAIN MEDICINE. It combines the tonic and quieting effects of celery with the nutritive and digestive elements of malt, and thereby gives immediate relief in nearly every form of nerve trouble. This great preparation contains in a concentrated form the active medicinal properties of the Italian celery seed, well known to the physicians as one of the best and most active controlling and strengthening agents for the nerves, also the phosphates in the same state as found in the strong, healthy, vigorous, natural body, and in quantities approved of by the medical profession, the value of which has been so thoroughly demonstrated in all brain and nervous affections and in emaciated conditions. In addition it contains a large percentage of malt, which is very strengthening and fattening. All this makes it an ideal combination, and it is not only a useful tonic and stimulant, but an extremely pleasant tasting preparation as well. As a brain and nerve tonic, appetizer and stimulant it has few equals in the realm of medicine. For insomnia, nervousness, mental or physical exhaustion, loss of appetite, impoverished blood and for that tired feeling that comes from close confinement or sedentary habits, it is very effective and infinitely better than all stimulants of an alcoholic nature.

IF YOU ARE NERVOUS, EXHAUSTED, CANNOT SLEEP, DIGESTION IMPERFECT, or if you are out of sorts generally and in a low physical condition, we earnestly recommend a trial of Celery Malt Compound. As a rule it will give new life and vigor and build up the entire system.

IF YOU ARE SUFFERING, make a trial of this great preparation, Celery Malt Compound, under our liberal offer as explained on the first page of this department. It is likely that this remedy will cover your case exactly and you will be surprised and delighted at the benefit you will receive. You can depend on it that the preparation will not do you a particle of harm. You assume not the slightest risk in making your test as to whether the Celery Malt Compound is the proper remedy indicated for the treatment of your condition.

LARGE SIZE BOTTLES, A big supply of medicine in each bottle. The dose is a teaspoonful, and a bottle will cover about two months' treatment. Considering price, the quantity, and its high efficiency, this preparation is indeed a wonder of value.

WITH EVERY BOTTLE OF CELERY MALT COMPOUND we send free of charge our interesting and instructive booklet, "How to Have Strong Nerves." A practical treatise on nerves and their disorders.

No. 8C8 Price, large bottle, each........ $0.56
Per dozen........ (Cannot be mailed on account of weight.)........ 5.10

READ WHAT OTHERS THINK OF CELERY MALT COMPOUND.

CELERY MALT COMPOUND A PERFECT SUCCESS. MR. CHAMPION CURED.

Sears, Roebuck & Co., Chicago, Ill. Forest, Ohio.

Gentlemen: I am going to write to you and tell you what my experience has been and how much good I have received from using your Celery Malt Compound. I have been using this compound for a little over two months now, and I can truthfully say that I am deriving a very great benefit from its use. I have tried several nerve preparations before, but have never been able to obtain the satisfactory results that I have obtained by using your Celery Malt Compound. In additon to toning up my nervous system, it has also aided my digestion wonderfully and has cured my entire system of all its ailments. Anybody suffering from nervousness could not do better than use your Celery Malt Compound. Respectfully yours, C. CHAMPION.

IS VERY THANKFUL FOR SUCH A VALUABLE REMEDY AS CELERY MALT COMPOUND.

Sears, Roebuck & Co., Chicago, Ill. Mt. Vernon, Ark.

Gentlemen: The Celery Malt Compound which I ordered and received from you some time ago, I have taken with very beneficial results. I feel that it has done me a great deal of good, and my health is about 100 per cent better than it has been at any time within the last six years. I was very nervous and could not eat with any degree of satisfaction, but now I do both to perfection, Celery Malt Compound gives perfect satisfaction, and I am very thankful to you for such a valuable remedy.
Yours very truly, A. J. TROBAUGH.

CELERY MALT COMPOUND CURES A NERVOUS CASE OF TEN YEARS' STANDING.

Sears, Roebuck & Co., Chicago, Ill. Mondamin, Ia.

Gentlemen: I want to add my testimony to hundreds of others who have used your valuable remedies, and I want all to know of the valuable and permanent results that I have obtained by using your Celery Malt Compound. My life was almost unbearable on account of my severe nervous disorders and my stomach troubles which came from my nervous condition. I could not do any work around the house and had been in a nervous state almost bordering on collapse for ten years. I used scores of remedies, each one guaranteed to cure me, but none of them produced any permanent effect. Your Celery Malt Compound began to help me after I had taken only half a bottle, and by the time I had taken two bottles, my sleeplessness was a thing of the past and I am now able to sleep well and I feel in excellent condition all of the time. I had not been able to eat or sleep good for ten years before I took your valuable medicine. It is a grand preparation and should be used by all who need a like remedy. Yours respectfully, MARY J. ROBINSON.

WINE OF LIFE — VIN VITAE — WINE OF LIFE

A NEW TONIC STIMULANT FOR THE TIRED, WEAK AND SICK OF ALL CLASSES. A RENEWER OF ENERGY. A STIMULANT FOR THE FATIGUED.

Retail Price, per Bottle, $1.25
OUR PRICE, **69 Cents**

A STRENGTHENER FOR THE WEAK, AN EFFECTIVE AND AGREEABLE FOOD FOR THE BLOOD, BRAIN AND NERVES.

NOT A MEDICINE, BECAUSE it is DELIGHTFUL to the TASTE AND TO THE STOMACH. | **NOT MERELY A STIMULANT,** BUT A GENUINE TONER AND STRENGTHENER.

A TONIC WHICH WE FIND IS AS YET UNEQUALED.

WHAT IS VIN VITAE? VIN VITAE (WINE OF LIFE) is a preparation combining through highest medical skill the curative, healing and strengthening powers of celebrated vegetable elements, with the invigorating tonic effects of the purest and finest wines of sunny California. The herbs supply the needed food strength for the blood and nerves, the wine element counteracts the disagreeable, nauseous properties of the herbs and gives just the right fire and life to the preparation. It is a combination producing a wonderful medical tonic.

VIN VITAE contains all the good properties of all the well known sarsaparillas, blood purifiers, regulators for men and women, nerve tonics, etc., without their disagreeable and distasteful ingredients. It is an ideal tonic and strengthener for all, combining all the best elements of similar medicine with distinctive and peculiar advantages of its own that make it enjoyed and appreciated by all who try it. It produces a wonderfully exhilarating result, and leaves no ill effects. As a pleasant medical tonic to strengthen and tone up the nerves, purify and enrich the blood, invigorate brain, body and muscles, regulate the system,

VIN VITAE—surpasses any preparation on the market. IT IS IN A CLASS BY ITSELF.

Are you Easily Tired? Do you Sleep Badly? Are you Nervous? Do you Feel Exhausted?	Have you Lost your Appetite? Is your Stomach Weak? Are you Thin?	Is your Circulation Poor? Are you Weak, either constitutionally or from recent sickness.

YOU SHOULD TAKE

VIN VITAE REGULARLY IF YOU MUST ANSWER YES TO ANY ONE OF THESE QUESTIONS.

TAKE VIN VITAE and the good effects will be immediate. You will get strong, you will feel bright, fresh and active; you will feel new, rich blood coursing through your veins, your nerves will act steadily, you will feel health and strength and energy at once coming back to you. If you are easily tuckered out, if some especially hard task has exhausted your vitality, or if you have undergone any kind of a strain, mental or bodily, Vin Vitæ will act quickly, put new life into you, and banish fatigue and a feeling of dullness within a very short time.

VIN VITAE is agreeable to the taste and acceptable to the most delicate stomach. For tired nerves in men and women, exhaustion, overwork, weakness, weak stomach or dyspepsia, loss of sleep, nervous trouble of any kind, for those recovering from a period of sickness, for all who feel tired, weak, worn out, Vin Vitæ, taken according to directions, acts with quick and satisfactory results. It puts new blood into the veins, new life into the body, and aids in filling every nerve cell with vibration and energy, in renewing wasted tissues, gives one the power to do double the ordinary amount of work without fatigue.

VIN VITAE MAKES WOMEN STRONG. Weak women, easily tired, worn out by ordinary household duties, should take Vin Vitæ, the Wine of Life, regularly as a tonic. Women sufferers from the diseases and troubles peculiar to their sex will realize more benefit from the strengthening and tonic effects of Vin Vitæ than from most of the "female regulators" extensively advertised, put together. It is a wonderful tonic for ailing and suffering women. Vin Vitæ is giving thousands of women health, beauty and freedom from the dragging pains which have made their lives so miserable. Those terrible backaches, headaches, aching sides and limbs, that torture some women every month, that make women old before their time, disappear if Vin Vitæ is taken as a tonic regulator. Vin Vitæ corrects all derangements peculiar to the sex, regulates the system, stops the pains, tones up the nervous organism, brightens the eye, clears the complexion, rounds out the figure and restores health.

WHAT DOES VIN VITAE DO FOR CHILDREN? Delicate children, undeveloped, puny boys and girls, should be given Vin Vitæ regularly. It builds up the growing system, gives needed nourishment to the muscles, makes bone and tissue. Children with delicate stomachs, unable to retain the strong and nauseous children's preparations with which the market is flooded, accept Vin Vitæ with relish. It is a splendid medicinal tonic for children.

69c BUYS A LARGE BOTTLE OF VIN VITAE. The illustration shows the appearance of the bottle, except that it is a large, full size bottle, containing a commercial pint, a quantity sufficient for all ordinary cases. Vin Vitæ is handsomely put up in keeping with the splendid preparation that it is.

VIN VITAE is compounded in our own laboratory, under the direction of our own skilled chemists, after a strict formula to which we have the exclusive right. Every ounce is carefully tested for strength and purity, so that we can offer it to our customers with our highest recommendation, for Vin Vitæ has been known for years, as the finest tonic wine stimulant, the most pleasant and powerful strengthener and rejuvenator. It can be taken with perfect safety. It is recommended by every physician who has made a test of it, and if it is subjected to analysis it will be found to contain only the best ingredients, and pure products that are noted for their stimulating, nourishing and strengthening properties, combined in such a way as to form a most agreeable tasting and effective preparation.

FOR LACK OF APPETITE, general lassitude, worn out nerves, Vin Vitæ is just what is needed. It improves the appetite, assists digestion, purifies and enriches the blood, carries life and strength to every nerve and fibre in the body, and induces a vigor and tone not usually obtained by the use of ordinary medicines. If you are not enjoying your usual good health, if you feel the need of a powerful tonic that ordinary medicines would never give.

No. 8C12
Price, per bottle.......69c

ORDER ONE BOTTLE as a test of this splendid preparation. We offer it on its merits, offer it to our customers as an excellent preparation. Everyone who is in need of a tonic should try Vin Vitae. We offer it feeling confident that if you try it you will be pleased with its agreeable and strengthening effects, and you will not fail to recommend Vin Vitae to your friends and neighbors. Almost everyone needs a tonic at some time or other. Keep a supply of Vin Vitae on hand. You will find a constant demand for it.

No. 8C12 Price, per dozen bottles for Vin Vitæ, the Wine of Life, $6.60

IN FAIRNESS AND AS A PROTECTION to you, you are permitted under the terms governing the sale of our household remedies, to order a bottle of Vin Vitae, take it according to directions and if you do not feel a decided improvement within a few days, if you do not feel that it renews your energy, sooths the nerves, improves digestion, induces restful sleep, brings back former strength, in fact, if you do not find that it does you more good than any medicinal tonic you have taken before, notify us, and we will not hesitate to refund to you on the first bottle we ever supply to you, the full amount you have paid for it.

per bottle.............. (Unmailable on account of weight.)............69c

DR. HAMMOND'S NERVE AND BRAIN TABLETS.

THE GREAT REMEDY FOR WEAK MEN.

A SPECIAL PRESCRIPTION IN A PREPARED FORM FOR THE TREATMENT AND CURE OF MEN'S SPECIAL DISEASES AND ALL DISTURBANCES OF THE NERVOUS SYSTEM.

Our Price, Per Box, Only 60 Cents; Six Boxes for $3.00

DR. HAMMOND'S NERVE AND BRAIN TABLETS are designed for the use of weak men and will not disappoint those who will use this treatment systematically and for a reasonable length of time, and a test of one single box of these tablets will be entirely sufficient to show the actual merit which they possess.

THOUSANDS OF MEN IN ILL HEALTH, or only slightly sick from other causes, yes, thousands of men who otherwise are strong and well, are suffering from a weakness which they are desirous and anxious to overcome. In some cases, owing to the peculiar cause of the weakness, it may require the personal supervision and treatment by a reliable physician. In such cases we warn you to be careful and under no circumstances place yourself in the hands of a so called advertising physician. Be sure that you personally know the physician as a man of standing, skill and reliability. To such a man explain your case freely and without reserve, without false pride and he will either do for you what medical science can do in such cases or else will frankly give you the very best advice.

IN MANY CASES OF MEN'S WEAKNESS it requires, however, only a safe yet powerful stimulant; a remedy that will reach the nervous system and build up the former strength and endurance without having a disturbing effect upon the digestive organs. There is one prescription that has been tested for many years that will do this; but one remedy that will meet in the majority of cases the expectations of those who require a medical treatment of this kind; a prescription which we have sold for many years—**Dr. Hammond's Nerve and Brain Tablets.**

THE MERIT OF DR. HAMMOND'S NERVE and BRAIN TABLETS is perhaps best illustrated by the fact that their sale has steadily increased from year to year. Millions of these tablets are used today by men who have convinced themselves by actual test that these tablets are the best medicine for the treatment of that condition for which they are intended.

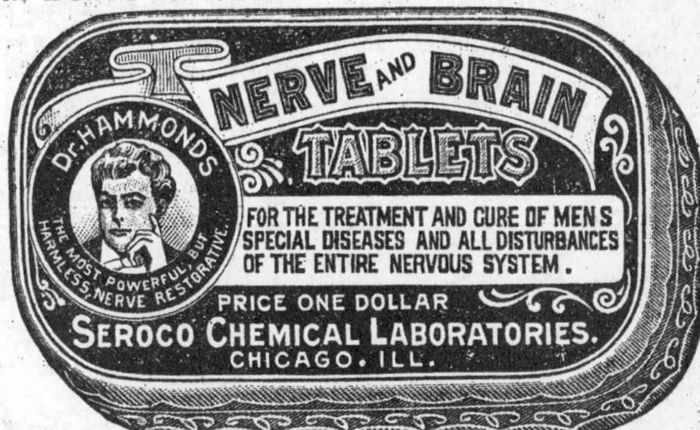

Illustration Shows Actual Size of the Box.

IF YOU HAVE USED THIS MEDICINE BEFORE, you will, of course, reorder it whenever you need the stimulating benefit they afford. If you have never tried **Dr. Hammond's Nerve and Brain Tablets,** you have the privilege of sending for one regular size box, containing about three or four weeks' treatment, use them as directed and if you are not entirely satisfied with the results, write us and we will refund to you at once the price of 60 cents which you have paid for same

DR. HAMMOND'S NERVE AND BRAIN TABLETS is a carefully compounded remedy; a preparation that took years of study and experimenting to perfect, in order to combine the elements that would restore vital force and revitalize the weakened sexual organism, and at the same time strengthen the heart action, and tone up the stomach, liver and kidneys.

No. 8C22 Dr. Hammond's Nerve and Brain Tablets Per box......$0.60
Per six boxes...3.00
Per dozen boxes. (If by mail, postage extra, per box, 3 cents)......6.00

SEROCO TOBACCO SPECIFIC

FOR THE TOBACCO HABIT.

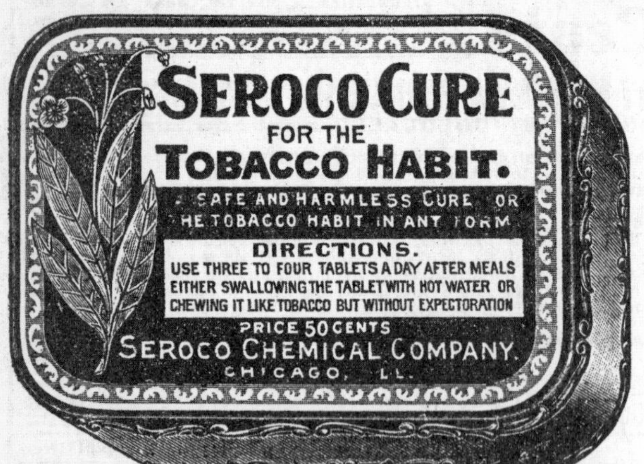

No Matter in what Form You are Using Tobacco, if You Want to Stop the Habit, Seroco Tobacco Specific is the Preparation You Should Try.

THIS TOBACCO SPECIFIC OR CURE FOR THE TOBACCO HABIT is a preparation that is a result of ong experience in the treatment of the tobacco habit. It has proven more successful than any other medical preparation or any treatment ever designed to help men break this disagreeable habit. It relieves without upsetting the nerves, without taking away your capacity for work, and without disarranging your physical system. It is a preparation, that, taken as directed, in many cases almost immediately overcomes the craving for tobacco and, not only this, but repairs the ill effects of the weed by upbuilding the stomach and nervous system. It is therefore a tonic as well as a tobacco specific cure. We can confidently say, that of all the tobacco specifics on the market, there seems none that compares with Seroco Cure for the Tobacco Habit. It is in a class by itself and we do not hesitate to offer it to our customers under the liberal terms governing the sale of our household remedies. We believe many of our customers could get relief by giving this preparation a trial and, while we do not pretend to guarantee a cure in every case, we offer the remedy for exactly what it is and nothing else. So much benefit has been derived from its use, that we give everyone the opportunity of making a trial and test for himself and if no benefit is received and it is the first package you have tried, we will gladly refund your money.

WITH EVERY PACKAGE, we send a booklet treating on the tobacco habit and how to get the best results from the use of Seroco Tobacco Specific, all of which is very valuable and helps wonderfully in getting relief and effecting a cure.

No. 8C16 Price, regular size box, per dozen, **$3.90**; each........ **42c**
No. 8C17 Price, large box, per dozen, **$6.60**; each........ **75c**
If by mail, postage extra, per box, 3 cents; large box, 4 cents.

THESE LETTERS SHOW THE GREAT VALUE OF SEROCO CURE FOR THE TOBACCO HABIT.

CURED AFTER USING THE FILTHY WEED FOR FORTY-SIX YEARS.

Sears, Roebuck & Co., Chicago, Ill. Linesville, Pa.

Gentlemen: The Seroco Cure for the Tobacco Habit did all that you claimed it would do. I have used tobacco for forty-six years, and although I tried numerous cures none of them helped me. I got one sample box and a 75-cent box of your Seroco Cure and it has cured me entirely. I have not taken a chew of tobacco for several months and now have no more desire for it. I will let any of my friends or anyone else have a sample of this wonderful cure and will help you all I can to get new customers. If you wish to use this in your testimonials, you are at liberty to do so.

Very truly yours, R. H. PEABODY.

TAKES GREAT PLEASURE IN RECOMMENDING OUR TOBACCO CURE.

Sears, Roebuck & Co., Chicago, Ill. McClure, Ohio.

Gentlemen: It is with pleasure that I write these few lines to say that your Seroco Cure for the Tobacco Habit has cured my husband of chewing tobacco. It has also cured him of nervousness. His appetite is better, and he has a better color in his face. MRS. JOHN CUNNINGHAM.

CURED AFTER MANY YEARS' INDULGENCE—WORTH ITS WEIGHT IN GOLD.

Summit, South Dakota.

Sears, Roebuck & Co., Chicago, Ill.

Gentlemen: Your Seroco Cure for Tobacco came duly to hand, and it has cured me of all desire for tobacco, after many years of hard chewing and smoking. It certainly is worth its weight in gold. You may use this as a testimonial with my full name and address if you wish. Yours respectfully,

HENRY HERREID.

AFTER USING ONE BOX OF SEROCO CURE FOR THE TOBACCO HABIT ALL HIS APPETITE FOR TOBACCO IS GONE.

Sears, Roebuck & Co., Chicago, Ill. Riverton, Neb.

Gentlemen: Your Seroco Cure for the Tobacco Habit has given me relief and I have no more desire to use tobacco. It had become a confirmed habit with me, and my friends were continually telling me what a disgusting habit it was, and I soon began to believe that there are not many worse things on earth than the use of tobacco. The Seroco Cure for the Tobacco Habit being recommended to me, I sent for a box, and followed this one with two more boxes. I am very glad to report that I am wholly without any desire for tobacco in any shape or form, and that this medicine is really a wonderful remedy, as has been very well proven in my case. Yours very truly,

T. F. MEADE.

CAN SAVE MONEY AS WELL AS HAVE BETTER HEALTH BY USING SEROCO CURE FOR THE TOBACCO HABIT.

Sears, Roebuck & Co., Chicago, Ill. Rocks, Md.

Gentlemen: I have been using your Seroco Cure for the Tobacco Habit for two months and can truthfully say that it indeed destroys all craving for tobacco. I had been addicted to the filthy weed, both chewing and smoking, for a number of years, but now after my using the Tobacco Cure for only eight weeks I have no more desire for it. I find that my general health is very much improved, and in addition to this, I am able to save quite a good deal of money which before I spent for tobacco. The Tobacco Cure is indeed a Godsend and users of tobacco should not hesitate to use this great remedy.

Yours very truly, LAWRENCE STREET.

HAVE YOU CATARRH?

CATARRH OF THE THROAT? NASAL CATARRH?
CATARRH OF THE STOMACH?

Or do you Suffer from Catarrh of any Kind in any of its Stages or from any of its Effects, such as Deafness, Indigestion or Weakness of any Kind? Try Dr. Hammond's Internal Catarrh Cure.

Retail price..........$1.00 Our price, per dozen........$5.10 Our price, each............55c

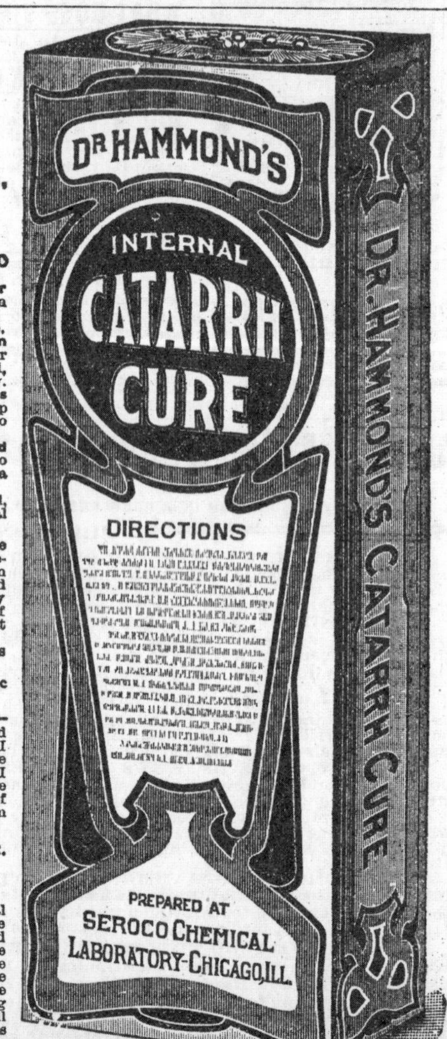

THOUSANDS OF THOSE WHO HAVE BEEN CURED WRITE US of the prompt and permanent relief derived from the use of our splendid catarrh remedy. Thousands more afflicted with this alarmingly prevalent and exceedingly offensive disease will be more than pleased to know the merits of this new remedy.

SYMPTOMS OF CATARRH are numerous. Among them are mucous discharge from the nostrils, a coated tongue, foul breath, slight deafness, watery eyes, throat troubles, indigestion, and in fact, catarrh has been mistaken in throat troubles, for tonsilitis and in the stomach for dyspepsia. Its effects are quite similar in these instances, and often deceive those so afflicted. If you have any one or more of these symptoms, you will never regret having read this announcement and giving **Dr. Hammond's Internal Catarrh Cure** a trial, because it goes straight to the root of the malady and enables tissues affected to throw off poisons and perform their functions perfectly.

DR. HAMMOND'S INTERNAL CATARRH CURE is a preparation which has met with decided success in the treatment of this disease. It is a highly efficient remedy and composed of a prescription that is used by the best physicians generally, but which, put up by any drug store, would cost you three times our price, not to mention that the druggist would not give you permission, as we do, to use the first bottle and if it does not benefit you, to refund your money.

IF YOU KNOW THAT YOU ARE A SUFFERER FROM CATARRH, send for a bottle of Dr. Hammond's Internal Catarrh Cure and give it a thorough trial according to directions. Your experience, no doubt, will be the same as that of hundreds of other customers who have received benefit by the use of this remedy right from the start and obtained final relief and cure by continuing the treatment a reasonable length of time.

DR. HAMMOND'S REMEDY is designated as an Internal Catarrh Cure because it reaches all kinds of catarrh, whether in the head, stomach, or elsewhere, for it works through the blood, enables it to throw off all poisons and fortifies the entire system against catarrhal trouble of every description.

WE HAVE SUPPLIED DR. HAMMOND'S CATARRH CURE during many years to thousands of customers, located in every State in the Union and particularly to those residing in the localities where catarrhal diseases are most prevalent and, judging from the reports received from those who have learned of the merit of Dr. Hammond's Internal Catarrh Cure by its use and the benefit derived from it we feel justified in saying to you: If you need a remedy of this kind, send for a bottle, use it in the proper manner and if not found suitable for your particular case, if the first bottle does not benefit you to a noticeable extent, do not proceed with the treatment; notify us and we will pay you back every cent that you have paid to us for this remedy. We believe, however, you will, as have thousands of others, have occasion to send for a few more bottles of Dr. Hammond's Internal Catarrh Cure, so that by following up this treatment you can bring the beneficial change in your condition produced by the first bottle's treatment, if possible, to an established cure.

PLEASE UNDERSTAND, however, that we want you to be the judge, we want you to know, beyond a reasonable doubt, that this remedy is really benefiting you before you are expected to proceed with the treatment.

No. 8C20 Price, per dozen bottles, **$5.10**; per bottle **55c**
Unmailable account of weight.

DR. HAMMOND'S CATARRH CURE IS THE BEST REMEDY ON THE MARKET FOR CATARRH.

Webster Grove, Mo.

Sears, Roebuck & Co., Chicago, Ill.

Gentlemen: I have used Dr. Hammond's Internal Catarrh Cure and I think it has done me a great amount of good. I think it is the best catarrh cure on the market, as it has been the means of my hearing being restored to me. I suffered for a number of years with catarrh, and in spite of the various medicines, or so called catarrh cures, which I tried, I did not receive any relief until I received Dr. Hammond's Internal Catarrh Cure. I thank you very much for your prompt and square dealing. Everything which I have ordered from you has been received O. K. and has been in every way just as you have guaranteed it to be.

Yours respectfully, W. H. MAXWELL.

DR. HAMMOND'S CATARRH CURE BETTER THAN ANY OTHER REMEDY.

Yellville, Ark.

Sears, Roebuck & Co., Chicago, Ill.

Gentlemen: I will say that Dr. Hammond's Internal Catarrh Cure, which I ordered from you sometime ago, has entirely cured my catarrh and has given me more relief than any other remedy that I have ever taken. I was very bad with catarrh of the head and nasal passages. This catarrh was so bad that it had affected my hearing and I was almost unable to hear anything except the loudest noises. Since taking the Dr. Hammond Internal Catarrh Cure, however, this has all been relieved and I am not afflicted with bad hearing any more. I still have a little bit of trouble with my nose once in a while, but I know that I will be completely cured by the time I have used all the medicine which I have. I will order another bottle or two in a couple of days, and when I have taken them I will write you just how I am getting along. Yours very truly, W. J. LANE.

MR. PRICE'S YOUNG SON COMPLETELY CURED BY DR. HAMMOND'S INTERNAL CATARRH CURE.

Ree Heights, S. D.

Sears, Roebuck & Co., Chicago, Ill.

Gentlemen: I write you in regard to the Dr. Hammond Internal Catarrh Cure, which I ordered and received from you some time ago. I ordered the medicine for my little boy, who was very bad with catarrh, and it helped him a great deal. Before he took the medicine, in the night when he was asleep he would breathe through his mouth, not being able to breathe through his nose because it was all stopped up with mucous; but after he took the medicine his nose was cleared up and he stopped breathing through his mouth entirely. I am very well satisfied and will advise anyone bothered with catarrh to use the Dr. Hammond's Internal Catarrh Cure sold by you. Yours very truly,

W. H. PRICE.

EVERY LADY IN THE LAND CAN HAVE A BEAUTIFUL COMPLEXION.

DR. ROSE'S ARSENOUS COMPLEXION TABULES ACT LIKE MAGIC

Per Box of 50 Treatments, 38 Cents. Per Box of 100 Treatments, 67 Cents.

GUARANTEED PERFECTLY HARMLESS.

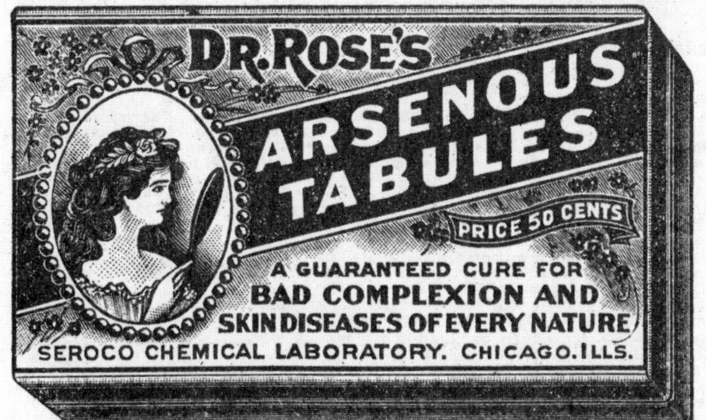

DR. ROSE'S ARSENOUS COMPLEXION TABULES ARE PERFECTLY SAFE. Taken as we direct, they will, honestly, not only beautify the skin, but will round out the features, improve the figure, and contribute greatly to the general good health by driving impurities from the blood.

IN THESE TABULES EVERY ELEMENT IS SELECTED with the greatest care, and nothing but the safest and very best materials are used. By their use according to our directions, a clear, dainty, transparent and altogether beautiful complexion is assured. It is hard to realize the wonderful properties of these little tabules until you have used them. The most marvelous transformation goes forward from the very first day of their use, and never ceases until you are willing to admit to yourself that your complexion is all that can be desired.

COARSE, RED SKIN BECOMES FINE IN TEXTURE, and delicate as a wild rose in coloring. Freckles, moth patches and skin blemishes of all kinds disappear. Facial eruptions that have defied the efforts of years disappear as though by magic, and the unsightly hollows of the face and figure round themselves out to beauty's perfect standard.

DR. ROSE'S SPLENDID TABULES produce a beautiful, transparent and pellucid complexion, a soft and smooth skin, brilliant, expressive eyes. The effect of these arsenous tabules upon the skin and the muscular tissues of the body, is to drive out impurities, banish unnatural oiliness and give it a transparent texture and beauty. Many ladies object to the use of cosmetics, no matter how superior they may be, because many of them conceal rather than permanently relieve skin imperfections. It is for this very large class that these marvelously effective little tabules are intended. This remedy clears and beautifies the skin by its action through the blood. There is nothing to apply externally—no sign that the most practiced eye can detect to tell that the beautiful complexion is not solely the work of nature.

IF YOU WANT TO IMPROVE YOUR COMPLEXION, send at once for a box of Dr. Rose's Arsenous Complexion Tabules, and watch the results. Better still, order a dozen boxes, follow our directions carefully, and be sure of the best results—a complete transformation. The expense is little, the improvement in your personal appearance, your attractiveness, your popularity, will be extremely gratifying to you, and worth fifty times the small cost of the preparation.

VALUABLE HINTS ON THE CARE OF THE COMPLEXION AND SKIN SENT WITH EVERY BOX

WE SEND FREE OF EXTRA CHARGE with every box of Dr. Rose's Arsenous Complexion Tabules a booklet containing plain directions for their use, also instructions how to care for the skin and complexion. A very valuable booklet, written by an expert and authority on this subject. This booklet alone is worth the price we ask for the tabules. It is your duty to make your personal appearance as attractive as possible. You can have a beautiful complexion by using Dr. Rose's Arsenous Complexion Tabules, and nothing adds so much to one's attractive appearance as a clear skin.

No. 8C25 Price, per dozen boxes, $3.60; per box of 50 treatments............38c
No. 8C26 Price, per dozen boxes, $6.00; per box of 100 treatments............67c
If by mail, postage extra, per box, small, 2 cents; large, 3 cents.

DR. ROSE'S ARSENOUS COMPLEXION TABULES HAVE RECEIVED THE HIGHEST PRAISE AS THESE LETTERS SHOW.

TABULES A GREAT HELP.

Ottumwa. Iowa, R. R. No. 5.

Sears, Roebuck & Co., Chicago, Ill.

Gentlemen: I believe that the tabules are a good thing. I feel sure they helped me. Respectfully, C. I. PETERS.

MISS LEE PRAISES DR. ROSE'S ARSENOUS TABULES VERY HIGHLY.

Webberville, Texas.

Sears, Roebuck & Co., Chicago, Ill.

Gentlemen: I have given your famous Dr Rose's Arsenous Complexion Tabules a thorough trial and will say that they are perfectly exquisite. I am an actress, and as you know from our using grease paint and other preparations upon our face, we are sometimes troubled with rough, red and coarse skin. I had tried numerous medicines and preparations which were said to keep the skin soft and tender, but I am sorry to say that they all failed to do this until I used your Dr. Rose's Arsenous Complexion Tabules. My face seemed to get better at once, and the roughness and redness left the skin and it was tender and soft as it should be. I know that this is a good trial for your medicine, both because I was afflicted very badly and because we give two performances daily, thus requiring the use of considerable grease paint, this having the tendency to keep the face rough, but I am happy to say that such is not the case since I commenced using your grand remedy. My sister and my father also use the remedy and both say that they have never used anything which does the work like your wonderful tabules. I can say they are the best I have ever used. Very sincerely yours, GERTRUDE LEE.

WOULD NOT BE WITHOUT DR. ROSE'S WONDERFUL TABULES.

Sears, Roebuck & Co., Chicago, Ill. Dorly, Texas.

Gentlemen: I am more than pleased with the wonderful results obtained from using your Dr. Rose's Arsenous Complexion Tabules. They have taken pimples off my face which have been there for a number of years, defying all the other various preparations which I used for them. I would not be without these wonderful tabules as long as it is possible to secure them, as I think they are the very best tabules on the market.

Very truly yours, JOE RILEY.

PIMPLES AND BLACKHEADS ALL GONE—THANKS TO DR. ROSE'S ARSENOUS COMPLEXION TABULES.

Fostoria, Ohio.

Sears, Roebuck & Co., Chicago, Ill.

Gentlemen: I have been troubled for three years with pimples and blackheads, and my skin was rough and coarse. I used preparations which I obtained from the local druggists, preparations which they said would cure me so that I would stay cured. I used these medicines one after another, but could find none that would do me the least bit of good. It was indeed a fortunate thing when I heard of your wonderful Dr. Rose's Arsenous Complexion Tabules, as I had almost given up hopes of my face ever being soft and smooth again, but now, after using your wonderful tabules for only about three or four weeks, my face is clear, and the pimples and blackheads have entirely disappeared. These tabules are indeed a wonderful medicine, and I thank you very much for making it possible for me to be relieved of those disagreeable pimples and blackheads.

Yours truly, D. C. STEVENS.

DR. WORDEN'S FEMALE PILLS

Female diseases and troubles peculiar to the sex relieved and woman's delicate system regulated by the use of DR. WORDEN'S FEMALE PILLS

SOLD ONLY BY US. 38 CENTS PER BOX.

THOUSANDS OF WOMEN suffering from the nerve and health racking ailments peculiar to their sex, have been restored to full health and strength by this great remedy after they had despaired of ever being well and strong again.

FEMALE TROUBLE. What a world of misery is expressed in those two words. What headaches, nausea, weakness, sickness, depression, etc., is the direct result of a derangement of the delicate female organism and nature's regular functions. Every woman well understands, far better than pen can write or words can tell, the suffering her sex must undergo by what is known as female trouble; suffering which is usually borne in silence, because only a woman can be confided in.

DR. WORDEN'S FEMALE PILLS will cure female troubles. They contain nothing that will injure the most delicate woman. They are not cure-alls. They are intended to relieve only the troubles peculiar to women. They cure leucorrhea, irregular, suppressed or painful periods (menstruation), thin blood, nervousness, sleeplessness (insomnia), sick headache, weakness, anemia, chlorosis or green sickness, hysteria, numbness of the hands and feet, ovarian difficulties, etc.

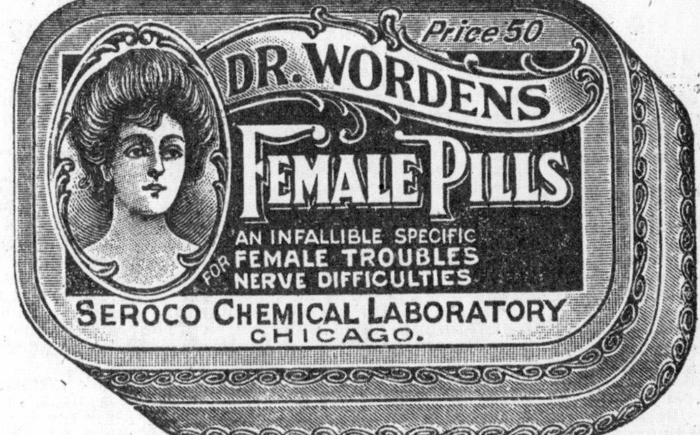

DR. WORDEN'S FEMALE PILLS ARE SAFE. Unlike drug compounds which depend upon violent minerals to force action, they relieve and cure by their splendid tonic effect. These little pills have a most marvelous effect upon weak and run down systems. No harmful element is contained in them, and they embody only those ingredients which make for the upbuilding of the entire nervous system, the purifying of the blood and the regulation of the entire female organism. If there were any possible way to better this remedy, no matter what the expense might be, we would adopt it. It is an honest fact that nothing ever offered to the women of the world before, has given even a small part of the satisfaction that this remedy has in every form of female trouble. It is recognized by physicians as embodying the very best prescription ever intended for these symptoms.

IMPORTANT. With every box of Dr. Worden's Female Pills we send free a booklet, containing valuable information on women's peculiar ills, as well as full instructions for Dr. Worden's remedy. Also helpful suggestions which will do much toward keeping the health and the wonderful female system in perfect order. If you are a woman and are suffering, send for this remedy. You are not doing yourself justice unless you try it. You owe that much to your family, to future generations, to nature and to yourself.

No. 8C29 Price, per dozen boxes, $3.30; per box............38c

If by mail, postage extra, per box, 2 cents.

GRATEFUL WOMEN EVERYWHERE WRITE US OF THE VIRTUES OF DR. WORDEN'S FEMALE PILLS.

NOTHING ON EARTH BETTER FOR FEMALE COMPLAINT THAN DR. WORDEN'S FEMALE PILLS.

Sears, Roebuck & Co., Chicago, Ill. Athens, Ala.

Gentlemen: I have received the greatest of benefit from the use of Dr. Worden's Female Pills. I had intended to write you and tell you of my experience before this, but I wanted to wait until I had given the medicine a thorough trial and had proved its worth. I took the pills according to directions and I am very happy to tell you that I have never felt better in my life than I have since I took your wonderful remedy. It is certainly a godsend to ailing and suffering women and it is my honest opinion that there is nothing on earth better for female complaint than Dr. Worden's Female Pills. Yours very truly,

MRS. E. D. WALKER, Box 334.

DR. WORDEN'S FEMALE PILLS HAVE NO EQUAL FOR FEMALE TROUBLES.

Sears, Roebuck & Co., Chicago, Ill. Clarence, Iowa.

Gentlemen: I wish to say a few words in praise of your great remedy, Dr. Worden's Female Pills. It is positively the best remedy that I have ever used or have ever heard of for female troubles. I suffered for a number of years more or less severely at times and I was not able to procure any remedy or any preparation which would help me. I heard of your prescription from a cousin of mine who lives in Ottumwa and who had used it with grand results. I am glad that she told me of the medicine, as it has been the means of my being restored to perfect health and I am not a sufferer as I used to be. I recommend with pleasure Dr. Worden's Female Pills to all ailing women.

Yours with gratitude, MISS MAE BARTLEME.

DR. WORDEN'S FEMALE PILLS DID HER MORE GOOD THAN ANY OTHER MEDICINE SHE EVER TOOK IN HER LIFE.

Sears, Roebuck & Co., Chicago, Ill. Awin, Ala.

Gentlemen: I take very great pleasure in recommending Dr. Worden's Female Pills which I ordered and received from you some time ago. I can truthfully say that they did me more good than any other medicine that I have ever taken in my life. I would advise anyone suffering as I suffered to use them. I am in better health now than I have ever been in at any time during the last three years. My appetite has increased greatly and I am not nearly so nervous as I was before I took the medicine.

I think that your company has at last found the medicine which will relieve womankind of their terrible sufferings if they would only learn about your medicine and take it.

Respectfully yours, MISS DAISY AUSTIN.

A NEW AND SUCCESSFUL BLOOD REMEDY.

DR. McBAIN'S FAMOUS BLOOD PILLS.

29 CENTS PER BOX. $2.40 PER DOZEN BOXES.

KEEP THE BLOOD PURE AND YOU CANNOT BE SICK, IS AN OLD BUT TRUE SAYING.

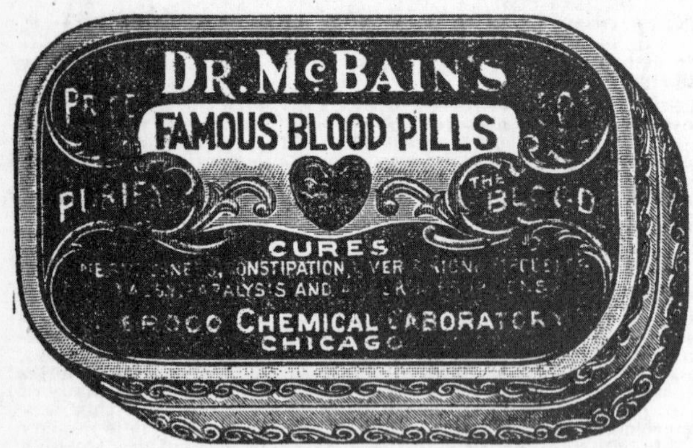

ONE-HALF OF ALL THE SICKNESS OF THE WORLD is due to impure blood. The results of impure blood are far reaching, as the blood is the medium through which every tissue of the body is fed and renewed. Therefore, impure blood, thin blood, poor blood, means starvation of the flesh, starvation of the nerves and brain, starvation of the very bones of the body, a general disorganization and decay of the entire physical system.

GENERAL DEBILITY, GENERAL WEAKNESS, sallow or pale complexion, loss of appetite, pain in the back, palpitation of the heart, nervous headaches, paralysis, etc., are all troubles and diseases arising from humors or impurities in the blood and the impurities become worse from day to day and aggravate the troubles until the blood and entire system are thoroughly disorganized.

DR. McBAIN'S FAMOUS BLOOD PILLS are a wonderful blood cleanser and purifier. The effect of these little blood pills is very beneficial. These pills are not of the cathartic nature; they do not upset the system by violent purging, but they act immediately on the blood, the seat of the trouble, vitalize it, renew the red corpuscles by feeding the proper nourishment to these red corpuscles, thus permitting the blood to purify itself. The elements of which these famous pills are compounded, not only enrich the blood, but also assist digestion, regulate the bowels, enliven the torpid liver and sluggish kidneys and send the thrill of new, fresh life quivering throughout every nerve and fibre of the being. Dr. McBain's Famous Blood Pills are invaluable to men and women alike. They act with the same precision on either sex as they affect the life giving current, the blood, whether in man or woman.

THESE BLOOD PILLS are offered by us to our customers for a fair trial and no one should overlook the opportunity we offer where so much is at stake and so much benefit can be derived. If you are not benefited, it will not cost you one cent, but there is no preparation offered for so little money that will effect such great changes for the better in any sufferer. If you have any trouble arising from impure blood, we earnestly recommend that you give this preparation a fair trial and convince yourself of the good it will do in your case.

FOR FEMALE TROUBLES, the disorders peculiar to women, Dr. McBain's Famous Blood Pills are especially recommended. Our blood pills can be taken according to directions without any danger, by either sex, and if carefully followed will give splendid results. Weakness, poor, thin blood, giving a sallow or pale complexion, loss of appetite, chlorosis or green sickness, pain in the back, palpitation of the heart, nervous headaches, suppression of menses, leucorrhea, tardy or irregular periods, hysteria, paralysis, and all diseases resulting from humors in the blood, which cause erysipelas, sores, swellings, are all benefited and often entirely cured by this remedy.

ONLY 29 CENTS A BOX, $2.40 FOR A DOZEN BOXES is our price for this great remedy. In retail drug stores pills of a similar nature, though not to be compared with Dr. McBain's for effectiveness, sell always at from 50 cents to $1.00 per box. We too, could of course, double our price for these pills if we were so inclined, and those who would pay us $1.00 to $2.00 per box, after using the pills, would even say they are worth any price, but following our policy of the lowest possible price, regardless of how valuable the article may be to others, we figure the cost of these pills made in our own laboratory with the smallest possible margin of profit and give our customers the benefit of every advantage we have.

THE PRICE OF THIS REMEDY is extremely low. Don't think that this affects the value of the remedy, for Dr. McBain's Famous Blood Pills is a high class blood remedy. With every box of these famous pills we send a valuable booklet, "How to Have Pure Blood," which is a short treatise on the blood and its diseases, with a safe, sure and convenient method of treatment for men, women and children.

No. 8C31 Price, per dozen boxes, **$2.40**; each..**29c**

If by mail, postage extra, per box, 3 cents.

These Letters are Expressions from Grateful Customers and we have Hundreds of other Letters Fully as Convincing.

THINKS DR. McBAIN'S FAMOUS BLOOD PILLS THE BEST BLOOD PILLS ON THE MARKET.

Toltec, Ark.

Sears, Roebuck & Co., Chicago, Ill.

Gentlemen: I have been intending for the past two or three weeks to write to you and tell you how much good my husband received from Dr. McBain's Famous Blood Pills which we ordered and received from you some time ago. My husband has been taking them for his blood and they have done him a great amount of good. His appetite has increased and in every way he feels much better. His blood flows freely and is not slow and sluggish as it was. I think Dr. McBain's Famous Blood Pills the best blood pills on the market.

Yours very truly, MRS. J. C. DOCKERY.

GIVES DR. McBAIN'S FAMOUS BLOOD PILLS FULL CREDIT FOR HIS RESTORED HEALTH.

Otterbein, Ind.

Sears, Roebuck & Co., Chicago, Ill.

Gentlemen: I am now free from disease and once more a well man and all due to Dr. McBain's Famous Blood Pills. My blood was very impure, my face was white and almost as pale as death with no color at all to my skin any place. Dr. Russell told me that I needed something to clear my blood of impurities, thus allowing the blood to have its proper nourishment, which in turn would be imparted to the various parts of my body, and thus restore my former good health. Reading of the wonderful cures of Dr. McBain's Famous Blood Pills and believing that they would help me, I sent for a box of them. After I had finished taking the second box I was not bothered any more with impure blood and all of my previous sickness and ill health disappeared. I was able to do all my work and did not have to have any help. My condition is now first class and I can give Dr. McBain's Famous Blood Pills all of the credit for curing me.

Very sincerely yours, JOSEPH NAGLE.

NOT BOTHERED ANY MORE WITH BAD BLOOD SINCE TAKING DR. McBAIN'S FAMOUS BLOOD PILLS.

Sycamore, Mo.

Sears, Roebuck & Co., Chicago, Ill.

Gentlemen: I have used your Dr. McBain's Famous Blood Pills with good results. I was very anemic and my face and skin were disfigured with unsightly eruptions. I knew that this condition was due to my blood being out of order and I determined to correct this condition, which, I am pleased to say, I was successful in doing after taking Dr. McBain's Famous Blood Pills. The benefit derived from them is almost past belief, as I am no more bothered with skin trouble and my blood supplies a fine rosy color to my cheeks and face. Dr. McBain's Famous Blood Pills are indeed a great remedy.

Yours very truly, ROBERT HISAN.

PURE BLOOD IS THE KEY TO HEALTH.

DR. BARKER'S BLOOD BUILDER

IS THE KEY TO PURE BLOOD. LARGE SIZE BOTTLE ONLY 60 CENTS.

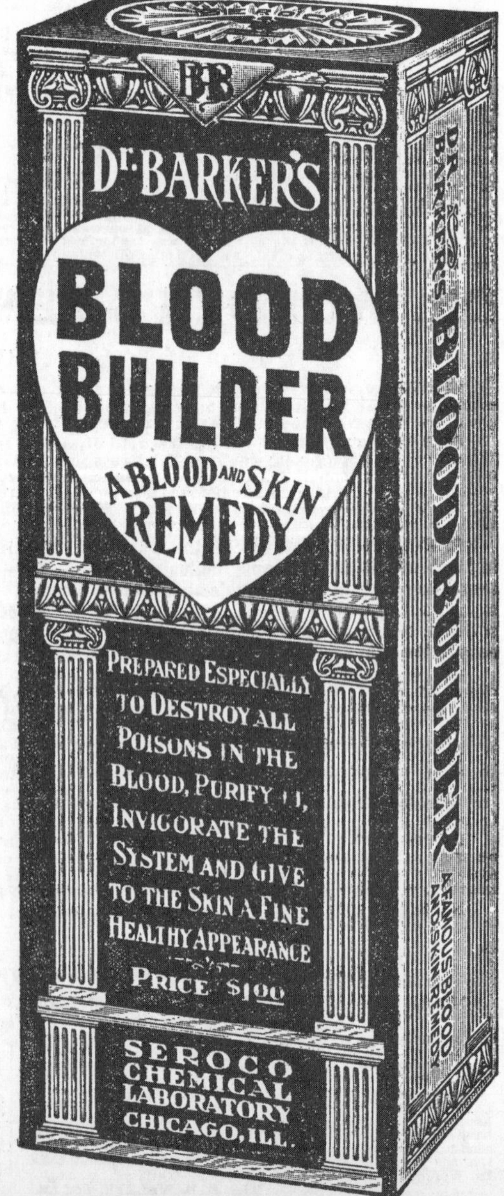

ARE YOU SATISFIED WITH YOUR HEALTH? **If not, do you know that 75 per cent of all diseases to which mankind is heir are directly traceable to impurities in the blood, poisons entering the system from impure food and air or the imperfect workings of the organs of the body?**

IF YOU ARE FEELING POORLY, and are not quite able to define what the trouble is, send for a bottle of Dr. Barker's Blood Builder. It is very likely your blood needs nourishment and Dr. Barker's Blood Builder contains the elements the blood requires. It is certainly a wonderful remedy and it purifies the blood, builds up the system, tones and strengthens every organ. It eradicates and even prevents these disorders becoming chronic, namely, scrofula, cancer, rheumatism, especially that originating from mercurial poisoning, nasal catarrh, pimples, chronic ulcers, boils and all other painful and disfiguring maladies which show themselves so offensively on the surface of the body or create serious disorders within. It purges the blood and is a remedy of the greatest merit for all forms of blood disorders, has been put to the test and we have reports of many cases that have yielded to its beneficial and curative influence. Dr. Barker's Blood Builder is of great value in eradicating all eruptions of the skin and face by improving the blood, and by its effect on skin imperfections helps to attain a perfect complexion. It has been found that Dr. Barker's Blood Builder is of great benefit to disorders originating from the stomach and wherever impure blood is the source of the trouble, whether it results in stomach trouble, constipation, kidney disease or otherwise, Dr. Barker's Blood Builder is of great value. We ask you to give this remedy a fair trial. Remember, it is compounded in our own laboratory and we can guarantee its purity. We can also assure you there is absolutely nothing harmful in this preparation and while it is very likely that you will receive the greatest benefit from its use, at the same time, if you do not, you will not receive the slightest harm. Order a bottle under our liberal proposition that enables our customers to receive the greatest benefit from our splendid line of household remedies, namely, with the understanding that if results are not entirely satisfactory, you can write us to this effect and if this is the first bottle you have tried, we will gladly refund your money. We have received great numbers of testimonials of the benefits derived by those who have suffered for years with these dangerous and sometimes fatal troubles, and who have tried many other remedies without any satisfactory results. **With every bottle** of Dr. Barker's Blood Builder we send free our valuable booklet, "How to Have Pure Blood," which explains in detail the action of this remedy and also gives important hints on the care and upbuilding of the system.

No. 8C34 Price, per dozen bottles, **$6.00**; per bottle, large size, each..**60c**

Unmailable on account of weight.

Letters of Praise for Dr. Barker's Blood Builder, the Best Evidence We Can Offer.

HER HEALTH 100 PER CENT BETTER SINCE USING DR. BARKER'S BLOOD BUILDER.

Toltec, Ark.

Sears, Roebuck & Co., Chicago, Ill.

Gentlemen: Dr. Barker's Blood Builder is indeed all that you claim for it. I used the remedy for bad blood as the doctors told me that this was what was the matter with me, but their medicine did not help me. It seemed as though my blood did not give the proper amount of nourishment to the various organs and in consequence I was very weak and not able to attend to my work. Since using Dr. Barker's Blood Builder, however, my blood is able to make up and to conduct a sufficient amount of nourishment to all parts of my body and my health has increased fully 100 per cent. I can recommend Dr. Barker's Blood Builder to all because it is strictly O. K. Yours very truly, MRS. RUDOLPH SCHOLTZ.

DR. BARKER'S BLOOD BUILDER CURES WHEN OTHER REMEDIES PROVE FAILURES.

Prattsburg, N. Y.

Sears, Roebuck & Co., Chicago, Ill.

Gentlemen: I thought you would like to hear how I am getting along and how I have improved since I began to take Dr. Barker's Blood Builder. I have taken two bottles and have improved until I am not bothered any more to amount to anything. I was troubled with eczema and erysipelas and had only temporary relief from the medicine which my doctor gave me. I thought that what I needed was some good blood remedy and decided to try your Blood Builder. I am very glad that I did, because now I am not troubled any more with my afflictions and my face, on which the eczema showed very badly, is now clear and smooth.

Yours truly, MRS. HARRY BROWNELL.

THIS LARGE ILLUSTRATION is reproduced direct from a photograph of a bottle of Dr. Hoffmann's Malt Extract. It is a strengthener and a flesh and tissue builder.

PUTS FLESH ON THIN PEOPLE.

DRINK IT AT YOUR MEALS,

If You are Well, to Keep Well; if You are Sick, to Regain Your Health and Strength.

BUILDS TISSUE AND MUSCLE, FILLS OUT THE HOLLOW PLACES, MAKES GRACEFUL CURVES INSTEAD OF SHARP ANGLES, AND ADDS FLESH TO THIN, BONY FIGURES, AND STRENGTHENS AS IT BUILDS.

DR. HOFFMANN'S MALT EXTRACT.

Guaranteed the Genuine Malt and Hops Extract, now offered for { **$1.45** per dozen bottles. **$2.60** per case containing two dozen bottles.

WHAT IS MALT EXTRACT?

Malt is barley that has been allowed to partially sprout and germinate and then dry, which develops the rich kernel into easily digested food. Hops are the female flowers of the Humulus Lupulus and add the soothing tonic and stimulating properties. Malt and hops are recognized as the greatest flesh building, strengthening combination ever produced in a liquid.

IT IS AMONG DRINKABLES WHAT BEEFSTEAK IS AMONG MEATS.

DR. HOFFMANN'S MALT EXTRACT **is made from malt, the concentrated liquid food, and hops, the gentle nerve tonic.** If you will order a dozen bottles or a case of Dr. Hoffmann's Malt Extract, take a glass at your meals and another glass before retiring, you will bring yourself up to a condition of health and strength that will be a wonderful surprise to you. **Makes thin, pale women the very picture of health.**

FOR INVALIDS AND CONVALESCENTS, **for those recovering from wasting fevers,** for those whose system is run down, who want an agreeable, nourishing tonic to drink at their meals, and who dislike and fear to use an alcoholic drink, **there is nothing to equal Dr. Hoffmann's Malt Extract.** It is very nutritious, it stimulates the appetite, it is a food as well as a tonic, and there is no preparation that so builds up the system after fevers or other wasting diseases.

FOR INVALIDS AND CONVALESCENTS IT IS ESPECIALLY RECOMMENDED.

IF THERE BE A NEW BABY IN THE HOUSE, **or one is expected, it will supply to the mother just the right nourishment, and plenty of it, so that baby will be strong and healthy, and no nursing bottle needed.** Dr. Hoffmann's Malt Extract contains the very best nourishment; concentrated, palatable and easily digested. Nurses and doctors use it to keep up the strength of their patients. **It will renew your energies, your strength and spirits.** If you suffer from sleeplessness, it will quiet the nerves and induce restful slumber. It helps the stomach in its work, gives new appetite, produces rich red blood and makes the thin stout.

FOR MAKING THIN PEOPLE HEAVIER AND STOUTER IT HAS NO EQUAL.

IF YOU ARE WEAK **or recovering from illness, or under weight,** ask your own doctor if he would advise you to drink a good malt extract at your meals. If he is fair he will answer, there is nothing better, provided, of course, you get a good, carefully prepared extract. Malt extract is recommended by the highest authorities. **Dr. Hoffmann's Malt Extract** is the best the market affords, the best that skill and care can produce.

Dr. Hoffmann's Malt Extract is Especially Recommended.

FOR LOSS OF APPETITE. **Take a small glassful half an hour before meals.** It is a wonderful appetizer.

FOR SLEEPLESSNESS **take a glassful on retiring at night.** It soothes the nerves and produces refreshing sleep.

FOR OBSTINATE COLDS, **coughs and bronchial and lung affections,** the Malt Extract is especially healing.

FOR DYSPEPSIA AND INDIGESTION **take the Malt Extract regularly at meals** in place of coffee, tea, milk, alcoholic or other drinks.

FOR INVALIDS **and convalescents when ordinary food is entirely indigestible** and the stomach in very weak condition, Dr. Hoffmann's Malt Extract is the ideal food and drink in one.

FOR THIN PEOPLE, **pale, angular women, Dr. Hoffmann's Malt Extract improves the appetite,** will add to the weight, build flesh, round out the figure, make rosy cheeks and give a new zest to life.

FULL DIRECTIONS GO WITH EACH BOTTLE.

The usual quantity is a glassful at each meal and one before retiring at night.

No. 8C36

Price, per dozen bottles............ **$1.45**
Price, per case, containing two dozen bottles.......................... **2.60**
Price, per cask containing 10 dozen. **11.50**

CONSUMPTIVES **and sufferers from wasting diseases should drink** the Malt Extract freely. It builds up and strengthens.

IMPORTANT TO USERS OF DR. HOFFMANN'S MALT EXTRACT

Dr. Hoffmann's Malt Extract is not a medicine, but a food which should be taken as a beverage in accordance with directions furnished with each bottle. In order to strengthen the results it may occasionally be advisable for the patient to use the proper kind of medicine in connection with Dr. Hoffmann's Malt Extract, and we can furnish for this purpose **concentrated extracts in the combinations as named below, which should be taken according to directions,** together with Dr. Hoffmann's Malt Extract.

DR. HOFFMANN'S PREDIGESTED CONCENTRATED EXTRACT OF MALT WITH PEPTONATE OF IRON AND MANGANESE. **This combination will act as a nutrient and digestant.** It is particularly used and recommended to overcome the green sickness of young women. This green sickness is known by the medical profession as chlorosis. It will assist in building up those who are recovering from any sickness, especially in diseases that are long continued, such as typhoid and scarlet fevers, smallpox, diphtheria, pneumonia and all diseases where fever is present. **IT IS A GREAT FLESH PRODUCER.** It is prescribed in all those conditions which are generally known as anemic; in other words, in cases where the blood supply or the richness of blood is low. Should be used in all cases of deficient digestion, in nervous trouble, lack of sleep, as it will purify the blood and strengthen it very quickly. The number of red corpuscles usually increases more than ten per cent in a few weeks. The dose is a teaspoonful to a tablespoonful.

No. 8C37 **Dr. Hoffmann's Predigested Concentrated Extract of Malt with Peptonate of Iron and Manganese.** Price, large bottles, each. **60c**

DR. HOFFMANN'S PREDIGESTED CONCENTRATED EXTRACT OF MALT WITH HYPOPHOSPHITES **is a combination which has long been recognized as of the highest value in the treatment of diseases due to defective nutrition of the nerves, muscular tissue or bone structure; is easy of assimilation and very palatable.** Should be taken in tablespoonful doses before meals.

No. 8C38 **Dr. Hoffmann's Predigested Concentrated Extract of Malt with Hypophosphites.** Price, large bottles, each............ **60c**

WHAT CHICAGO PHYSICIANS THINK OF DR. HOFFMANN'S MALT EXTRACT.

The most careful and scientific investigation and comparative tests of the genuine Dr. Hoffmann's Malt Extract with other similar preparations on the market shows that the genuine Dr. Hoffmann's Malt Extract is the purest and most palatable, containing more health giving properties than all the others combined.

Attested to April 14, 1902

Ernest Hoernig Ph. G

Registered, Chicago, Cook County, Illinois.

Although it is not customary for a physician to recommend so called prepared remedies, and while I have never allowed my name to be used in any advertisement of any kind, I am glad to have an opportunity of endorsing publicly the genuine Dr. Hoffmann's Malt Extract as the best tonic and flesh builder in existence. It is far superior to all other imported or domestic Malt Extracts, and, as it combines with its health giving properties a pleasant flavor, it is today, as shown in my extensive practice and experience, the most palatable and most valuable reconstructive tonic, and will unfailingly assist a conscientious practitioner to build up the general health of his patient to a degree not obtainable by any other means at his disposal.

R. J. Walter M. D.

IMPORTANT NOTICE.

During the winter months, December, January and February, and when the weather is extremely cold Dr. Hoffmann's Malt Extract is liable to freeze, and during that period we can accept orders and ship same only at customer's risk. It will be perfectly safe to ship same during ordinary cold weather.

OUR OWN COUGH CURE.

SOLD UNDER A POSITIVE GUARANTEE.

Retail price .... 50c and $1.00
Our price, 50-cent size, each $0.35
Our price, 50-cent size, per dozen 3.00
Our price, large $1.00 size, each .... .59
Our price, large $1.00 size, per dozen 5.40

NEGLIGENCE ON THE PART OF PARENTS, negligence on your own part, very often permits serious sickness to overtake the children or yourself when a little caution, a trifling expense, would have saved all the worry, trouble and not infrequently spared a dear life. We positively believe that there is among household remedies none that can prevent slight indispositions and serious illness so quickly, providing it is kept on hand, not sent for after the trouble has already developed to a certain degree, and also providing you secure the right preparation, a remedy that will not only relieve, but positively cure. We mean **OUR OWN COUGH CURE.**

WE RECOMMEND OUR OWN COUGH CURE knowing that it is without question the only cough remedy that will act quickly and at the same time is perfectly safe. What we recommend, however, still more is that you under no consideration delay ordering this remedy until you actually need it. **Order it at once, see that you have a supply of same always on hand,** so that it can be administered the moment the first signs of a cough are apparent. **A few doses will then do the work,** will prevent the cough from developing into bronchitis, pleurisy, pneumonia and other diseases of the lungs and pulmonary organs.

THERE IS DANGER indicated in the slightest cough. Don't neglect it. You owe it to yourself, to your relatives and friends to have the best means, that is, Our Own Cough Cure, ready at hand as soon as the cough makes its appearance. We cannot express it too strongly. We can't point out the danger too forcibly, and again ask you to consider the consequences of neglecting the first symptoms of a cough, and the necessity of immediate treatment to prevent the cough from developing into something worse, something that cannot be easily cured, something that may finally lead into consumption—incurable.

> There is no city, no town, no hamlet, nor a single household where you cannot sell Our Own Cough Cure. Everyone needs this remedy and will keep it on hand. You will need large quantities of both sizes. Be sure and order enough. . . . . . .

OUR OWN COUGH CURE is not only the best to stop the cough immediately, it is not only the best cough remedy for infants and children, it is practically the only safe and sure cure where a cough has become chronic; and we know of no medicine in existence that will do what **Our Own Cough Remedy does in chronic cases,** affording relief, always promptly allaying the inflammation of the bronchial tubes, and by its healing influence upon the organs that are always affected in such cases, it will gradually restore them to normal and healthy functions and assist in removing the chronic condition within the shortest possible time.

OUR OWN COUGH CURE is sold under a positive guarantee to be non-poisonous, to possess all the elements necessary for preventing the development of a cough, and where it has already taken hold of the patient, to quickly cure it. We personally guarantee it to be perfectly safe and harmless and to be the only cough remedy in existence that we can conscientiously recommend as being not only the cheapest but the best that can be produced. We supply Our Own Cough Cure in two sizes, the regular 50-cent size for 35 cents, the large $1.00 size for 59 cents.

DO NOT FAIL to include in your next order a supply of Our Own Cough Cure. You should never be without it. It is one of the greatest sickness preventers—a life saver.

No. 8C42 Price, per dozen, regular 50c size, $3.00; each 35c
No. 8C43 Price, per dozen, regular $1.00 size, $5.40; each 59c
Unmailable on account of weight.

Our Twenty-Minute Cold Cure.

NEVER FAILS.

Retail price $0.25
Our price, per dozen, $1.50; each 17c

OUR TWENTY-MINUTE COLD CURE is not only what its name implies, but a gentle laxative and a powerful tonic. It acts gently on the bowels without griping, induces the liver to healthy action and assists in restoring your general health. It is a splendid tonic for the nervous system, and if once used you will never be without it. It promptly cures colds, la grippe, headache and all the symptoms usually present in a severe cold.

YOU MAY SIT IN A DRAFT, or get your feet wet, may become chilled and soon notice that the pores are stopped up, perhaps a slight fever starts, you begin to snuffle. These are the signs of your getting down with a cold. This is the time to use our Cold Cure. Use one or two doses, follow it up by another dose or two in twenty minutes, and you may have cured your cold in its incipiency. There is no good reason why you should suffer with a cold for days, for weeks. There is absolutely no reason why you should take any chances of having the cold proceed and perhaps get down with a more serious disease after letting the cold reach a stage where it will require the services of a physician on account of the development of a very dangerous disease.

> Don't forget that Our Twenty-Minute Cold Cure is a good seller. It is an extraordinary low priced remedy and yields you a big profit. It can conveniently be carried by the patient and will always be ready for use.

TWENTY MINUTES' TREATMENT with our Cold Cure will oft times be sufficient to stop the cold, to prevent it from getting any further. A few doses of this grand preparation taken right at the beginning of the first symptoms of a cold will do the work. Don't wait a day or even an hour. Take Our Cold Cure at once. Promptness is the important part.

HAVE OUR COLD CURE in the house and if away from home carry a box with you in your vest pocket. The remedy is supplied in tablet form, in neat boxes, convenient to be carried in that manner. Nothing else will be needed to prevent a cold. **Our Twenty-Minute Cold Cure will save all the dangerous results of a cold.** All that is necessary is that you take it in time. In cases where the cold has already become seated before our cold cure could be obtained and used, be sure and get same as quickly as possible, use it in accordance with directions supplied with the remedy, and in connection with it Our Own Cough Cure, and you may feel assured that the combination of these two medicines will break up and cure the most severe cold and cough in the very shortest time.

No. 8C45 Our Twenty-Minute Cold Cure. Per dozen, $1.50; each...17c
If by mail, postage extra, per box, 2 cents.

Cure for the Opium and Morphine Habit.

Retail price $1.50
Our price, each $0.69
Our price, per dozen 6.80

WE HERE OFFER A PERFECTLY SAFE AND RELIABLE CURE to those addicted to the habit of using opium or morphine in any form or manner whatever. We guarantee this preparation to be absolutely harmless, to contain no poisonous narcotics. Can be taken freely without producing any of the deleterious effects on the system, such as are caused by the use of opium and morphia. Soon after taking a dose of this remedy a calming and soothing effect is produced. It acts as a tonic to the nerves; its use will completely destroy that terrible craving for morphine and opium in those who are victims to the deadly habit of taking these poisonous drugs, and free them from their bondage, restoring their health and making them feel like living again. A dose can be taken whenever a craving for morphine or opium exists; it will act at first as a perfect substitute, rendering the patient independent of these poisonous drugs, and after continued use for a short period the nerves will become strong and the general health improved, so that the remedy can be taken at longer intervals and soon altogether discontinued; then the cure is complete.

No. , C48 Price, per dozen bottles, $6.80; each 69c
Cannot be sent by mail on account of weight.

FAT FOLKS, TAKE DR. ROSE'S OBESITY POWDERS

THEY REDUCE YOUR WEIGHT 15 TO 40 POUNDS IN A COMPARATIVELY SHORT TIME

Retail price, $1.00. **Our price, per dozen, $5.40; each** 60c

TOO MUCH FAT IS A DISEASE and a source of great annoyance to those afflicted. It impairs the strength and produces fatty degeneration of the heart, which sometimes leads to a premature death. All people who have obesity are troubled with **sluggish circulation and labored action of the heart.** The patient feels lazy and burdensome. There is a

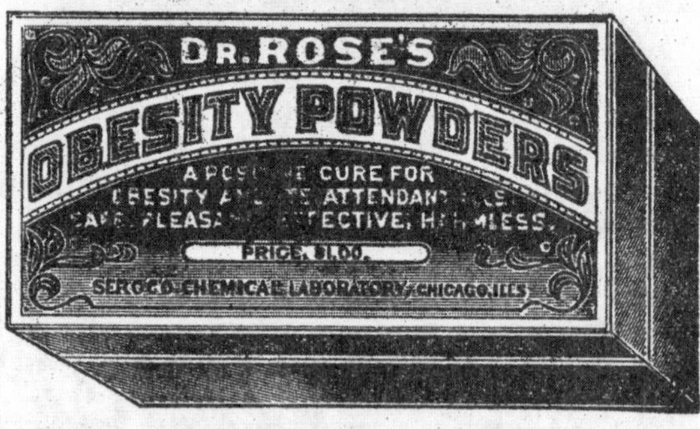

SLUGGISH CONDITION OF THE WHOLE SYSTEM

while they are not exactly sickly, there is a feeling that all is not right. Nervousness, rheumatism, headache, dropsy and kidney diseases are frequent complications of obesity, and, more cause to be alarmed, the heart is always affected.

> A boon to fat people who will be glad to obtain this remedy at home when they know you keep it on hand . . . .

—SEND AT ONCE FOR A BOX OF—
DR. ROSE'S OBESITY CURE

It will reduce corpulency in a safe and agreeable manner, perfectly harmless. No bad results follow its use, as is the case with many other preparations. Explicit directions and valuable information for fat folks enclosed in each box.

No. 8C52 Price, per dozen boxes, $5.40; per box 60c
If by mail, postage extra, per box, 7 cents.

Mexican Headache Cure.

Retail price.... 25c
Our price, each.. $0.19
Our price, per doz. 1.60

A SPLITTING HEADACHE CURED IMMEDIATELY by our positive Headache and Neuralgia Cure. Almost everyone is more or less troubled with a headache at some time or other. Some persons are hardly ever free from them, and suffer martyrdom. We confidently say to our customers that it is not necessary to suffer longer than the time it takes to get a package of our **Mexican Headache Cure. We can promise relief within a short time after the first dose has been taken.** A second dose is not required except in very obstinate cases. No matter from what cause, whether a nervous headache, or from the stomach, or a severe case of neuralgia, **you will usually obtain complete relief.** It is perfectly harmless, no bad results follow its use. Give it a trial when you suffer, and you can easily convince yourself that the Mexican Headache and Neuralgia Cure is the best and most uniformly successful headache remedy in existence.

> Who does not suffer from headaches occasionally? You can sell this cure to everybody you meet. Many customers who are now in charge of a distributing point for our remedies are sending twelve dozen orders at one time. . . . .

No. 8C55 Price, per box $0.19
Per dozen boxes 1.60
If by mail, postage extra, per box, 3 cents.

WE ARE WILLING for you to make a trial of any of our household remedies under these conditions. Send for a bottle or package, as the case may be, give the remedy a fair trial according to the directions and if you do not receive any benefit we will refund your money. All you need to do is to write us and state that you have received no benefit and that this is the first bottle or package that you have tried. We do not want to take anyone's money for the preparation, unless you get value received and unless you receive benefit from its use.

Old Reliable Eye Salve.

FOR SORE, WATERY AND DISEASED EYES, STYES, INFLAMMATION AND ULCERATIONS, FOR GRANULATED EYELIDS, there is nothing better than Old Reliable Eye Salve. Has been in use for hundreds of years and nothing better has ever been found. Our Old Reliable Eye Salve is today the only reliable eye salve which will give uniform and good results. Heals quickly and permanently. Can be easily applied. Is soothing, cooling and especially valued as a quick pain reliever in cases of sore and inflamed eyes. Furnished in air tight tin boxes with full directions.

No. 8C61 Old Reliable Eye Salve. Price, per dozen, $1.60; each......18c

If by mail, postage extra, per box, 4 cents.

Lloyd's English Boil Remedy.

A new remedy—a specific for curing boils.

LLOYD'S ENGLISH BOIL REMEDY is a discovery by an eminent English chemist of certain peculiarities in the poison which causes the formation of boils and his further discovery of the antidote which destroys this poison in the blood. It removes almost invariably the soreness in a few hours. The remedy is perfectly safe and it seems certain in its cure. No trouble, easy to take, the results are all that can be expected. The entire supply of his remedy to be sold in the United States is distributed to physicians and the general public by us, sole agents for the United States and Canada. **Don't wait until you are tortured with a boil! Be ready for the enemy! Keep a package on hand! It never spoils!**

No. 8C64 Retail price, 50c; our price, each......$0.28
Per dozen......2.50

If by mail, postage extra, per package, 5 cents.

Cathartic Pills, Only 10 Cents per Box.

Retail price......25c
Our price, per box......10c
Our price, per dozen boxes......90c

THIS IS THE OLD FASHIONED SUGAR COATED CATHARTIC PILL of the U. S. Pharmacopœia, the same as Ayer's, Brandreth's, Jaynes' and other much advertised pills. They act principally on the liver, and move the bowels gently without griping. **These pills are carefully prepared from fresh vegetable extracts, and can be thoroughly relied upon.** For this reason they are much superior to many others sold at double their price.

No. 8C67 Price, per dozen boxes, 90c; per box containing 25 pills......10c

If by mail, postage extra, per box, 2 cents.

Wonderful Little Liver Pills.

Retail price......25c
Our price, each......$0.13
Our price, per dozen......1.00

Entirely vegetable in their composition. These wonderful little pills operate without disturbance to the system, diet or occupation.

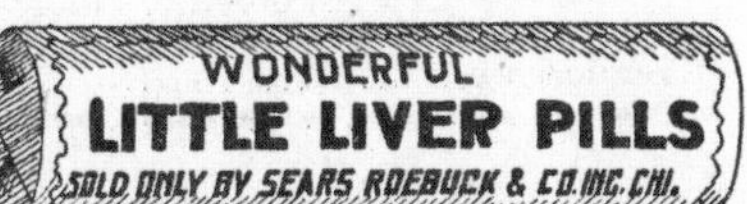

CONSTIPATION is an easy enough thing to cure if you will only persist in taking proper treatment. It is one of the commonest troubles and often thought to be a very little thing. Yet it is a well known fact that a large proportion of all human sickness is due to this one thing. When the bowels do not move regularly the natural drainage tract in the human system is dammed up, **decomposition ensues and poisonous gases and liquids are carried all through the system. The result is jaundice, torpid liver, biliousness, sallow skin, indigestion, foul breath, coated tongue, loss of appetite, pimples, belching foul gases, blotches, boils, dizziness, headache, cramps, colic, etc.** You can easily avoid all these troubles and keep your system pure and healthy by taking from time to time one or two of our **WONDERFUL LITTLE LIVER PILLS.** Some of our customers call them **"LITTLE GIANTS,"** they are so small in size and so easy to swallow, yet so effective and mild in their operation. Whenever your stomach, liver and bowels get out of order take one or two of our **LITTLE WONDERS** and notice the quick effect and great relief you will experience. Keep a box always beside you. Use them occasionally and they will keep you regular and well conditioned.

No. 8C70 Price, per dozen boxes, $1.00; each......13c

If by mail, postage extra, per box, 2 cents.

Purple Pills.

FOR SPECIAL USES. Every woman should be regular in the systemic functions peculiar to her sex. In all cases of irregularity and delays the celebrated Purple Pills will afford the necessary relief within a very short time. Purple Pills are made in the most scientific manner and contain the only emmenagogue compound prescribed by physicians as perfectly safe and certain in results. Instruction circular with each box.

No. 8C71 Price, extra large boxes, per dozen, $8.00; each......85c

If by mail, postage extra, per box, 5 cents.

Hammond's Sarsaparilla.

Guaranteed the Best on the Market.

Retail price......$1.00
Our price, each......$0.50
Our price, per dozen......4.80

There is no other Sarsaparilla made that will compare with it.

DR. HAMMOND'S SARSAPARILLA combines in an agreeable form the medicinal properties of the most approved alterative and blood purifying remedies of the vegetable kingdom. Dr. Hammond's Sarsaparilla will not cure everything, but the fact that on the purity and vitality of the blood depends the vigor and health of the whole system, and that disease of various kinds is often only the sign that nature is trying to remove the disturbing cause, lead to the conclusion that a remedy which gives life and vigor to the blood and eradicates **scrofula** and other impurities, as this preparation undoubtedly does, **must cure and prevent many diseases.** Hence the field of its usefulness is an endless one, and we are warranted in recommending it for all derangements caused by an unnatural state of the blood.

FOR SCROFULA Dr. Hammond's Sarsaparilla is especially recommended. It has been found to be the ideal remedy for kidney and liver troubles, eruptions and eruptive diseases of the skin, ulcers, tumors, erysipelas and other disorders arising from a low condition of the system or impure state of the blood. There are many sarsaparilla preparations on the market, but none of them will excel in strength and merit the one we offer. We know exactly what goes into it, for it is compounded in our own laboratory. We know that it contains only the purest and best ingredients and we can offer it to our customers with every confidence and every assurance. It has a long splendid record of cures to its credit and if you feel that you need a preparation of this kind, we certainly recommend that you give it a trial. Remember, that you can send for a bottle of Dr. Hammond's Sarsaparilla and give it a trial, and if you do not receive benefit, you can simply write us to this effect, state that this is the first bottle you have tried and we will cheerfully refund your money. This is a fair proposition and enables everyone to get the benefits of our meritorious line of household remedies.

OUR SARSAPARILLA is a purely scientific preparation. It is carefully prepared from the most powerful, yet perfectly safe and harmless alteratives and blood purifying agents, selected from the vegetable kingdom. This preparation **does not contain mercury** or arsenic in any form or combination whatever. It combines the merits of all other sarsaparilla compounds with defects of none. **For blood making, blood cleansing, flesh and appetite producing, our Sarsaparilla is unequaled. No family can afford to be without it. For infants, children, grown people, it should be taken regularly. Our prices are very low.**

> **Sarsaparilla is a household remedy everywhere. Those widely advertised retail for $1.00. Dr. Hammond's is better. You can save everybody money, give them the best Sarsaparilla at a lower price than they can buy inferior qualities, and yet the sale will net you a nice profit on every bottle that you dispose of.**

No. 8C73 Price, large bottle, each......$0.50
Per dozen......4.80

NEVER RETAILED AT LESS THAN $1.00.

Unmailable on account of weight.

Dr. Rowland's System Builder and Lung Restorer.

Large Commercial Quart Bottles.

Retail price......$1.00
Our price, each......$0.55
Our price, per dozen......5.10

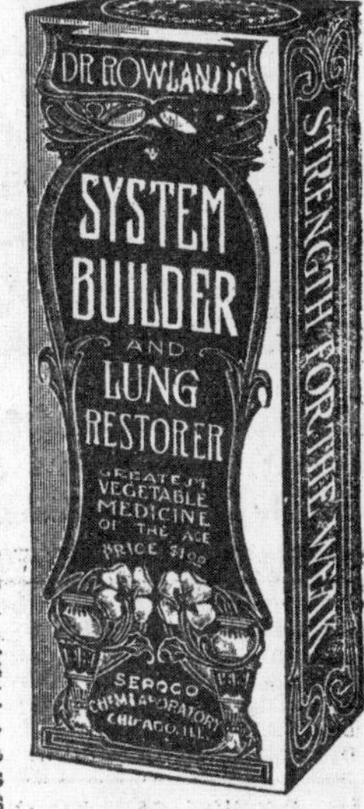

A Powerful Vegetable Medicine for the thousand ailments common to the masses.

FOR THE RELIEF OF COUGHS of all kinds, chronic and lingering, especially bronchitis, laryngitis, consumption, ulcerated throat, ministers' or public speakers' sore throat, hoarseness and suppression or loss of voice. It does not nauseate or debilitate the stomach or system, but improves digestion, strengthens the stomach, builds up solid flesh when the system is reduced below a healthy standard, **and invigorates and cleanses the whole system.**

As a remedy for torpor of the liver, generally termed liver complaint or biliousness, and for habitual **constipation of the bowels** it has no equal. For **loss of appetite, indigestion and dyspepsia, and for general or nervous debility or prostration,** in either sex, **it is especially recommended.** As an alterative or blood purifier, this medicine is far **superior** to any preparation of sarsaparilla, **iodide of potassium,** or any other medicine now offered for general sale. It is, therefore, very valuable in all forms of scrofulous and other **blood diseases,** also for all **skin diseases, eruptions, pimples, rashes and blotches, boils, ulcers, sores and swellings,** arising **from impure blood,** and usually cured by the use of a few bottles of this compound. **Unlike other alteratives** or blood cleansing medicines, it does not debilitate, but strengthens the entire system. **This is a very concentrated vegetable extract.** The dose is small and pleasant to the taste. Full directions accompany each bottle.

BUILD UP YOUR ENTIRE SYSTEM by using a few bottles of this remedy. **Is your health impaired, are you overworked,** do you need a general toning up? If so, we earnestly recommend a trial of this preparation.

No. 8C76 Price, large bottle, per dozen, $5.10; each......55c

Unmailable on account of weight.

Dr. Ross' Rheumatic Cure.

Retail price.. $1.00
Our price, each.. $0.65
Our price, per dozen.. 6.00

WHAT IS RHEUMATISM? **This dreadful disease, this scourge of humanity, is a blood disease,** always due to one cause; namely, the presence in the system of urea and uric acid, which poisonous elements could not be retained unless there was a defective kidney action underlying the rheumatic disease.

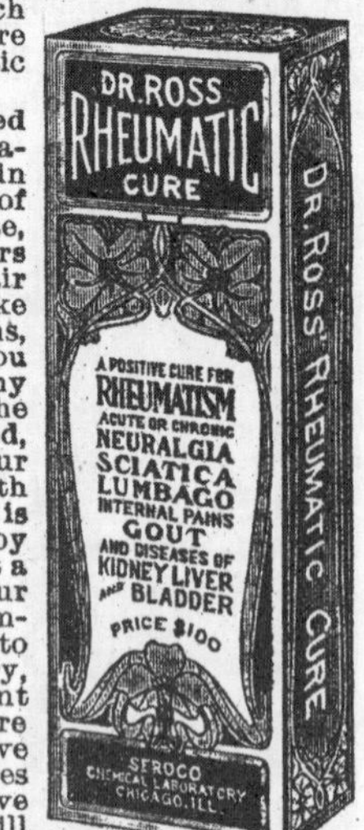

DR. ROSS' RHEUMATIC CURE **is an old and time tried preparation,** a combination of elements that has had wonderful success in relieving and curing this terrible disease. So many of our customers have received great benefit from its use, that we consider it the **duty** of everyone who suffers from rheumatism in any form to give this remedy a fair trial. We are willing that you should send for it, take it according to directions, and then if you find you have not received any benefit and this is the first bottle you have tried, we will gladly refund your money. It has met with such great success and is so highly recommended by those who have given it a fair trial, that it is our duty to bring it to the attention of those of our customers who may suffer from rheumatism, and ask them to give it a trial. It is put up in our own laboratory, under our own supervision. We know every ingredient that goes into it, we can guarantee it absolutely pure and harmless, and, from our long experience, we have found that there is no other preparation that compares with it in effectiveness. Even though you may have been suffering with rheumatism for years, still we recommend that you give Dr. Ross' Rheumatic Cure a fair trial. If you have rheumatic pains occasionally, it is all the more important that you take this remedy in time, for it will, in all probability effect a permanent cure. Dr. Ross' Rheumatic Cure acts on the blood and removes from the system a uric acid upon which the disease feeds. We have many letters on file, describing the benefit received from the use of this preparation, and in many families it has been in use for years with uniformly good results.

> **Our RHEUMATIC CURE is in great demand. If you handle our medicines you will need a good supply. Do not fail to order a sufficient quantity.**

No. 8C79 Price, per dozen, **$6.00;** per bottle........................ **65c**
Unmailable on account of weight.

Pure Norwegian Cod Liver Oil.

Retail price.. $1.00
Our price, each.. **46c**

GUARANTEED ABSOLUTELY PURE. **Highest grade made.** **You will save one-half in price and get the best goods** possible to put up if you place your order with us. **You can't afford to buy Cod Liver Oil unless you know it is absolutely pure. If you** buy from us you will have our guarantee and know it is absolutely pure and fresh, **imported direct from Norway,** in original packages, where it is prepared from strictly fresh livers, pure and sweet.

IN THE TREATMENT **of wasting diseases where the body has become emaciated,** where patients are losing flesh, where the system is constantly weakening and reaches a state of debility, our Pure Norwegian Cod Liver Oil will not only act as a food, increasing properly the assimilation of all food partaken of, but the medicinal properties which it contains will at the same time produce a quick restoration to general health; in fact, a lasting cure.

For consumption, severe colds, lung and throat troubles, NORWAY COD LIVER OIL should be taken regularly.

No. 8C83 Price, per pint bottle........ **46c**
Unmailable on account of weight.

Somone, for Sweet, Refreshing Sleep.

Retail price.. $1.50
Our price, each.. $0.72
Our price, per dozen.. 6.40

A RELIABLE REMEDY FOR SLEEPLESSNESS. **We ask any of our customers who may be troubled with insomnia, who cannot sleep at night, to give this valuable remedy a trial.** No matter from what cause the sleeplessness arises, a sound sleep will be procured by its use, and you will awake in the morning refreshed, strengthened and cheerful; no bad effects from its use. It is a vegetable preparation composed of herbs soothing and healing to the entire system. It can be used in safety by the weakest and most delicate and is a boon to those of nervous dispositions. A single dose will strengthen and invigorate. Ladies troubled with nervous spells should always have a bottle at hand. A dose or two in time will save them many hours of agony and serious discomfort and often prevent a more serious condition of the nervous system. Give this remedy a fair trial. The ingredients are absolutely pure and we offer it with the understanding that if you do not receive any benefit, and will write us to this effect, and this is the first bottle you have used, we will cheerfully refund your money. Full directions accompany each bottle how to use it both for sleeplessness and nervous troubles.

> **DO NOT FAIL TO INCLUDE THIS REMEDY IN YOUR QUANTITY ORDER. THOUSANDS OF PATIENTS NEED IT AND BUY IT.**

No. 8C85 Price, per dozen bottles, **$6.40;** each........................ **72c**
Cannot be sent by mail on account of weight.

Our Cod Liver Oil Emulsion.

Retail price.. $1.00
Our price, each.. $0.55
Our price, per dozen.. 5.40

Pure Cod Liver Oil with Hypophosphites of Lime and Soda.

OUR COD LIVER OIL EMULSION **is highly recommended in cases of consumption.** This preparation is of greatest value in the treatment of consumption, and it is endorsed by physicians generally. 55 cents is the lowest price at which the highest quality of Cod Liver Oil Emulsion was ever sold, and we feel sure our customers will appreciate this opportunity for giving them for 55 cents what they have heretofore been compelled to pay $1.00 or more for. This is a really great remedy for the treatment of phthisis or consumption, colds and chronic coughs, scrofula in its various forms, rheumatism, puny children, anemia or poor condition of the blood, and general debility. For consumption there is nothing that is more highly recommended than Cod Liver Oil Emulsion, and even in the first and second stages of consumption it often effects a quick and permanent cure. This preparation is without an equal for coughs and chronic colds, and serious complications and unnecessary expense can be avoided and often lung fever and other diseases averted by the use of Cod Liver Oil Emulsion. We would advise every household to have a bottle on hand always. It is invaluable for general debility and emaciation. **Our Cod Liver Oil Emulsion, taken regularly after meals, will build you up to renewed strength and vigor.**

> **An unusually good seller throughout the year. In making up your quantity order you ought not to overlook ordering a supply of EMULSION OF COD LIVER OIL.**

No. 8C91 Price, large bottles, each.......... **$0.55**
Per dozen.. **5.40**
Unmailable on account of weight.

Curtis' Consumption Cure.

Retail price.. 50c and $1.00
Our price, 50c size, each.. $0.29
Our price, 50c size, per dozen.. 2.40
Our price, $1.00 size, each.. .48
Our price, $1.00 size, per dozen.. 4.20

CURTIS' CONSUMPTION CURE

Is an Old and Time Tried Preparation, Compounded after a Prescription of a High Authority on the Diseases of the Lungs.

WHEN TAKEN IN TIME IT IS REGARDED AS A CURE FOR INCIPIENT CONSUMPTION.

THIS REMEDY CURES COUGHS AND COLDS **and arrests at once the progress of consumption** by preventing a further increase of tuberculous matter and while the system is under the influence of this remedy all nourishment is assimilated. It controls coughs, expectoration, night sweats, hectic fever and all other characteristics of consumption. We advise **you to try Curtis' Consumption Cure in the first stages of** the disease—in fact, if your lungs are at all affected by a cold, Curtis' Consumption Cure is a great protection. Understand, you can give this remedy a fair trial, and if it does not relieve, and you will so inform us, we will gladly return your money for the first bottle you tried.

No. 8C94 Price, regular size, each........................ **$0.29**
Per dozen.. **2.40**
Price, large size, each.. **.48**
Per dozen.. **4.20**
Postage and tube extra, small bottle, 12c; large bottle, unmailable.

Dr. Hammond's Tar Expectorant.

Retail price.. 50c
Our price, each.. $0.30
Our price, per dozen.. 2.70

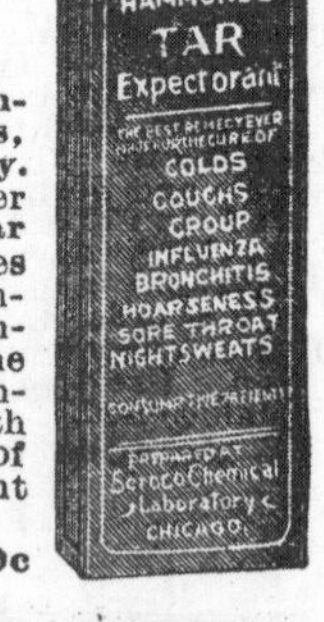

FOR THE TREATMENT OF COUGHS, **colds, influenza, bronchitis, laryngitis, hoarseness, sore throat and affections of the lungs generally.** Many cases of consumption have been prevented and other mild cases cured by the timely use of **Dr. Hammond's Tar Expectorant.** It is especially beneficial in those diseases which are too often regarded as simply annoying, such as common coughs and colds, which are really dangerous in their tendencies and demand prompt and active treatment. For the more serious forms of throat and lung troubles, its value cannot be overestimated, and to anyone worn out with constant coughing and loss of sleep. In cases of pulmonary disease, Dr. Hammond's Tar Expectorant almost always brings relief and prompt cure.

No. 8C95 Price, per dozen, **$2.70;** per bottle..**30c**
Unmailable on account of weight.

Dr. Walter's Celebrated Eye Water.

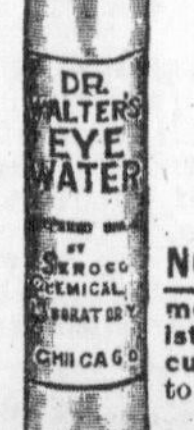

Retail price.. $0.25
Our price, each.. $0.14
Our price, per dozen.. 1.20

NO MORE WEAK OR SORE EYES. **Wherever this remarkable Eye Water has been introduced a marked improvement in the health of the eyes has been the result. Dr. Walter, a celebrated specialist on eye diseases, used this water 25 years in his practice, performing wonderful cures.** For weakness or inflammation of the eyes it has no equal; absolutely harmless to the youngest child.

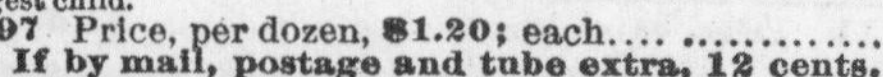

No. 8C97 Price, per dozen, **$1.20;** each........................ **14c**
If by mail, postage and tube extra, 12 cents.

Peruvian Wine of Cocoa.

Retail price..$1.00
Our price, each..**$0.68**
Our price, per dozen...**6.00**

A GENUINE RICH WINE IMPORTED BY OURSELVES and well known throughout Europe for its strengthening and nourishing qualities. It sustains and refreshes both the body and the brain and has deservedly gained its excellent reputation and great superiority over all other tonics. It is more effective and rapid in its action. It may be taken for any length of time with perfect safety, without causing injury to the system, the stomach and gastric juices. On the contrary, **Peruvian Wine of Cocoa aids digestion, removes fatigue and improves the appetite, without causing constipation.** For many years past it has been thoroughly tested and has received the endorsement of hundreds of the most eminent physicians who assureus of their utmost satisfaction with the results obtained by using it in their practice. They urgently recommend its use in the treatment of **anemia, impurity and impoverishment of the blood, consumption, weakness of the lungs, asthma, nervous debility, loss of appetite, malarial complaints, biliousness, stomach disorders, dyspepsia, languor and fatigue, obesity, loss of forces and weakness caused by excesses, and for similar diseases of the same nature.** It is especially adapted for persons in delicate health and convalescents. It is very palatable and agreeable to take and can be borne by the most enfeebled stomach where everything else would fail.

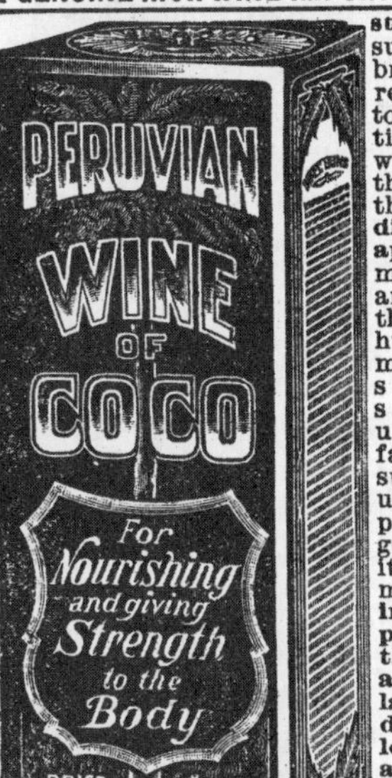

Wine of Cocoa is supplied in large quart bottles and represents a finer and more exquisite stimulant, strengthener and rebuilder than other tonics, which sell for $1.25 small pint bottles. We furnish quart bottles for one-third the price. . . . .

It is used in most of the hospitals in Europe, and many of our American public institutions are adopting it. After many severe tests it has been effectually proven that in the same space of time more than double the amount of hardship and work could be undergone when **Peruvian Wine of Cocoa** was used and no fatigue experienced.

No. 8C101 Price, per dozen, **$6.00**; per bottle............................**68c**
Unmailable on account of weight

Nutritive Tonic. Beef, Iron and Wine.

AN UNRIVALED STRENGTHENER FOR WORKERS, FOR ATHLETES, FOR THIN-BLOODED PEOPLE. SPLENDID FOR PUNY CHILDREN.

Retail price, pints,...$1.00
Our price, pints, each..**$0.30**
Our price, pints, per dozen...**3.20**
Our price, per half-gallon, each..**1.15**
Our price, per gallon, each...**2.10**

GUARANTEED HIGHEST GRADE ever produced No family should be without a bottle of Beef, Iron and Wine. This is an old time tonic, universally known for its great **strength giving and flesh producing qualities.**

THE GREAT TROUBLE with most of the beef, wine and iron found in the market at the present day is the poor quality of materials used in making it. It is often found in a state quite unfit for use on that account. **We take great pains with this preparation,** using only **Liebig's Extract of Beef** freshly prepared, the finest imported **sherry wine and pure iron** in a form specially prepared for assimilating with and enriching the blood.

THE BEST TONIC KNOWN to be used when suffering from extreme exhaustion, produced by overwork or other causes, brain fatigue, debility of all kinds, blood disorders, salt rheum, eruptions, anemia, scrofula and cancer. It stimulates digestion, improves the condition of the blood. Enriches it and enables it to throw off accumulated humor, and it will give tone and vigor to the entire system. **We have a great number of testimonials testifying to the great good this medicine has done for those who are weak, nervous and debilitated. Our prices are very low.** Inferior goods are sold everywhere at nearly double our prices. **Unmailable on account of weight.**

Keep a supply of our Beef, Iron and Wine always on hand. Your neighbors constantly use this household remedy. A good seller all the year round.

No. 8C102 Price, full pint bottles, each...................**$0.30**
Price, pint bottles, per dozen...................3.20
Price, ½ gallon bottle...................1.15
Price, 1 gallon jug...................2.10

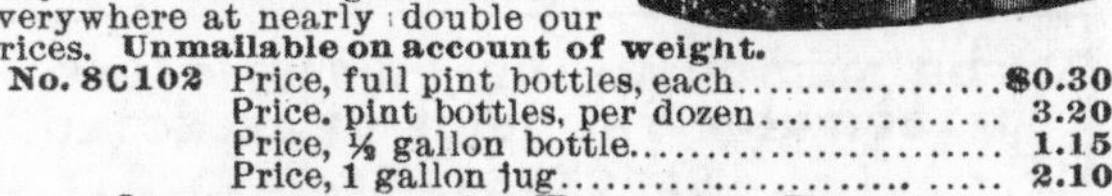

Instantaneous Earache Drops.

A FEW DROPS APPLIED ON A PIECE OF MEDICATED COTTON and inserted into the ear will promptly cure earache in a comparatively short time, removing the cause of the pain. INSTANTANEOUS EARACHE DROPS ARE VERY PENETRATING and, when properly applied, will reach all parts of the inner ear organism, removing and healing every portion in a diseased state. It should, therefore, not only be used for stopping earache, but also in deafness resulting from nasal catarrh, inflammation of the ear drums, necrosis of the inner ear bones, unusual discharges and for removal of hardened ear wax deposits.

INSTANTANEOUS EARACHE DROPS ARE PENETRATING, HEALING, SOOTHING AND EMOLLIENT.

No. 8C104 Instantaneous Earache Drops, 2-dram vials. Price, per dozen, **$1.80**; each..(If by mail, postage extra, per vial, 2c)...**20c**

ORANGE WINE STOMACH BITTERS.

Retail price...$1.00
Our price, each...**$0.65**
Our price, per dozen..**6.00**

GUARANTEED ABSOLUTELY PURE, AND THE HIGHEST GRADE ON THE MARKET.

Put up in extra large bottles holding a full commercial quart.

DO NOT COMPARE our Orange Wine Stomach Bitters with the bitters that are being sold by retail druggists generally at $1.00 to $1.50 a bottle, bitters that are made from the very cheapest ingredients. **Our Orange Wine Stomach Bitters** are made from wine distilled from the fruit of the Seville orange tree in combination with herbs well known for their tonic and healing effect on the stomach. **Order a dozen bottles.** You can sell them at $1.00 each with profit enough so that several bottles will cost you nothing.

THIS IS A PLEASANT BITTERS. As before explained, it is made from a wine distilled from the fruit of the Seville orange tree in combination with herbs well known for their tonic and healing effects on the stomach. As an appetizer there is no bitters made that will equal it, and it is a recognized cure for dyspepsia when its use is continued for some time. As a general bracer up of the whole system it has no equal, and the taste is so delicious that the most fastidious enjoy taking it. **Owing to the intrinsic and widely established therapeutic value of its** chief constituents, which are necessary to good digestion, this preparation stands unequaled. While furnishing admirable means for treating **gastric ailments, indigestion, want of appetite, malarial diseases, low spirits, and nervousness, it removes that tired feeling. It exerts a most wonderful power in sustaining the system during arduous labors and journeys. It is an agreeable and wholesome stimulant,** and imparts a pleasant taste with an agreeable sense of warmth which permeates the entire system. **Don't buy bitters from your local druggist** unless you are acquainted with the reputation of the manufacturers, and thus know that the ingredients contained are of the highest grade.

THE FINEST STOMACH BITTERS ON EARTH. LARGE BOTTLES, IMMENSE SALES, BIG PROFITS. ORDEP IN QUANTITIES. IT WILL PAY YOU IMMENSELY.

No. 8C105 Price for bottles holding full commercial quart, per dozen, **$6.00**; per bottle...**65c**
Unmailable on account of weight.

The Genuine German Herb Laxative Tea.

Retail price...25c
Our price, each..**$0.14**
Our price, per dozen...**1.10**

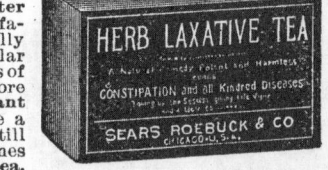

A HARMLESS VEGETABLE REMEDY and a positive cure for constipation, with no bad after effects. It is composed of herbs and roots familiar to the peasants of Germany, especially those who nurse the sick. Through irregular living, poorly cooked food, improper habits of eating, nearly all persons are suffering more or less from **constipation and the resultant sick headaches;** although there may be a daily movement of the bowels, there is still much fecal matter adhering to the intestines **and poisoning the blood. Our Herb Tea,** made of the simple, harmless herbs, will, when taken regularly for a short time, **thoroughly cleanse the stomach and bowels of all unclean matter.** The blood becomes purified and the person greatly improved in health.

No. 8C107 Price, per dozen, **$1.10**; per box...........................**14c**
If by mail, postage extra, per box, 7 cents.

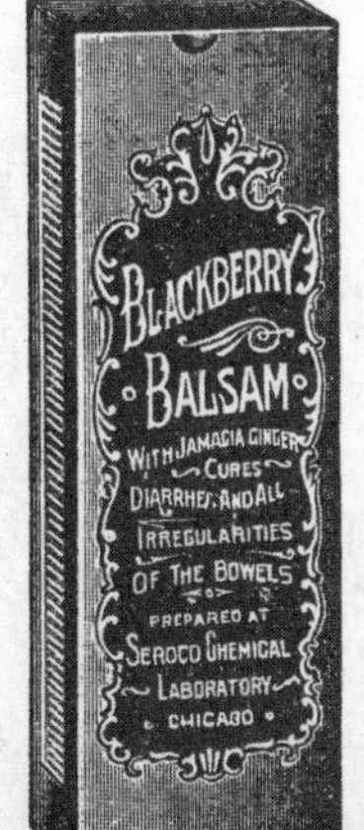

Blackberry Balsam.

Retail price...50c
Our price, each..**$0.20**
Our price, per dozen...**1.80**

A REMEDY which should be kept constantly on hand. The poorest in the land can afford it at only 20 cents a bottle. It will prevent serious illness if used promptly, and often be the means of saving life. It is a pleasant, safe, speedy and effectual remedy for **Dysentery, Diarrhea, Looseness, Asiatic Cholera, Cholera Morbus, Cholera Infantum, Summer Complaint, Colic, Cramps, Griping Pains, Sour Stomach, Sick and Nervous Headache, Pain or Sickness of the Stomach, Vomiting, Restlessness and Inability to Sleep, Wind in the Stomach and Bowels, Hysterics,** and for all bowel affections. We have received thousands of certificates from physicians, clergymen and families of the first respectability bearing the strongest testimony in its favor.

Our Blackberry Balsam is a household remedy in the fullest sense of the name, and will be found helpful for the above named symptoms in infants, children and adults.

No. 8C108 Price, per dozen, **$1.80**; per bottle...**20c**
If by mail, postage and tube extra, 16 cents.

GOLD SEAL GRAPE JUICE

UNFERMENTED. NON-ALCOHOLIC.

The Finest Product, the Purest Juice, Made by the Celebrated "Cold Expressed" Process, as Preferred and Prescribed by Physicians Generally.

GOLD SEAL Unfermented Grape Juice is non-alcoholic, absolutely pure, and without the slightest adulteration in any form. Gold Seal is not only a good grape juice, but is indisputably **THE VERY BEST GRAPE JUICE ON THE MARKET**, because it is the only grape juice made by the so-called "cold expressed" method, while nearly every other kind of grape juice is made by the boiling process, which easily can be and usually is adulerated to a considerable extent by the addition of sugar and water. Our Gold Seal Grape Juice is guaranteed to be the genuine article, and to give our customers an opportunity to compare the same with any other kind of grape juice, we make the following special offer: **Gold Seal Grape Juice, per single quart, $1.00.** We furnish it in original cases at $5.80 per dozen quarts, but those who wish to convince themselves first of the fact that Gold Seal Grape Juice is better than any other kind, may order as a trial one single bottle at the case price, or 54 cents for a quart. We know you will never use any other grape juice but Gold Seal.

GOLD SEAL Grape Juice is a household and health beverage of the highest order, a pleasant drink and food in sickness and convalescence, in summer and winter, for the young and the aged. Not a stimulant, but nature's own true tonic, the best that money can buy.

RECIPES for making Gold Seal Grape Lemonade, Gold Seal Grape Punch, Gold Seal Grape Gelatin, Gold Seal Grape Sherbet (frozen), Gold Seal Grape Ice and Gold Seal Grape Ice Cream will be furnished with every package of Gold Seal Grape Juice.

No. 8C110 Price, one only, quart trial bottle........$0.54
Price, per case, containing 12 pints........................ 3.80
Price, per case, containing 12 quarts...................... 5.80

Unmailable on account of weight.

Reliable Worm Syrup and Worm Cakes.

Retail price, each...50c
Our price, each...$0.22
Our price, per dozen..1.80
Our price for Worm Cakes, per box..........................20
Our price for Worm Cakes, per dozen boxes..............1.40

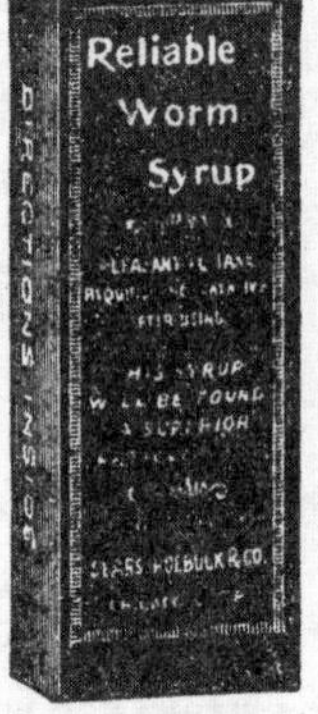

YOU CAN SAVE YOUR CHILDREN from much suffering and in many cases save their lives. No other disease is so fatal to children as worms. Unfortunately they are seldom free from them, and as the symptoms resemble those of almost every other complaint, they often produce alarming effects without being suspected. Worms are not only a cause of disease in themselves, but by their irritation aggravate all other diseases, wandering from one part of the body to another, winding themselves up into large balls, obstructing the bowels and frequently the throat, causing convulsions and too often death.

OUR RELIABLE WORM SYRUP effectually destroys the worms and removes the nest in which their young are deposited. It moves the bowels very gently, the worms being to a greater or less extent dissolved by the action of the medicine, can scarcely be recognized in the stools, but the improvement in the health of the child will be sufficient evidence of the beneficial effects of the medicine.

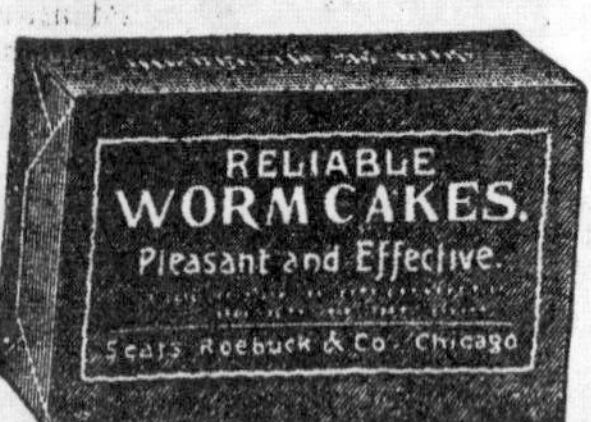

EVERY MOTHER ought to have a bottle of the syrup or a box of the cakes always in the house. The syrup and the cakes are the same medicine in different forms. The syrup is more pleasant to the taste and more suitable for very young children. The cakes can be given to older people; even adults can be benefited by using them, as grown up folks, as well as children, often suffer from worms. **These reliable worm medicines are not only worm destroyers, but act as a general tonic,** destroying sourness of the stomach and producing a healthy appetite. **Mothers, keep your children healthy.**

No. 8C111 Worm Syrup. Price, per dozen bottles, $1.80; per bottle..22c
If by mail, postage and tube extra, per bottle, 16 cents.

No. 8C112 Worm Cakes. Price, per dozen boxes, $1.40; per box......20c
If by mail, postage extra, per box, 2 cents.

Electric Liniment.

Retail price...50c
Our price, each.......................................$0.25
Our price, per dozen...................................2.10

THIS LINIMENT is an excellent remedy in cases of rheumatism, cuts, sprains, old sores, wounds, galls, bruises, growing pains, contracted muscles, lame back, stiff joints, frosted feet, chilblains, etc. Persons suffering from partial paralysis of arms and legs will be rendered great benefit by its use, frequently regaining complete use of those members; also as an application for the throat and chest and externally for lung trouble great relief will be experienced by rubbing the chest with this, one of the most penetrating and best liniments ever made. We call this remedy Electric Liniment because its application produces a feeling similar to the feeling produced by a mild charge of electricity. This is a liniment that should find a place in every family. It will offer relief in hundreds of different cases. It is one of the best remedies among our household preparations.

No. 8C115 Price, per dozen, $2.10; per bottle....25c
Not mailable.

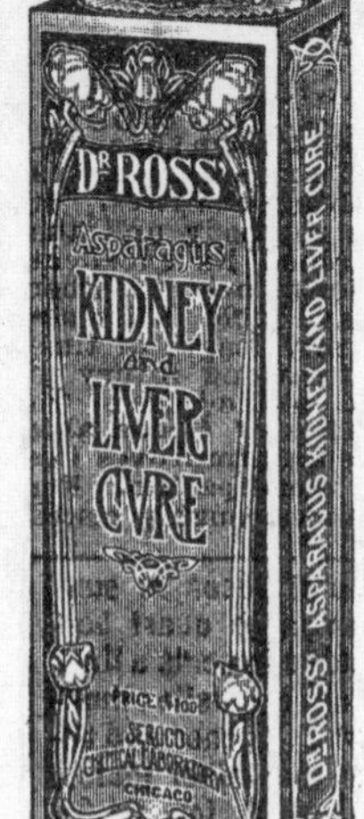

Dr. Ross' Kidney and Liver Cure.

Retail price...$1.00
Our price, each.......................................$0.65
Our price, per dozen..................................6.00

THIS IS THE FIRST TIME Dr. Ross' remedy has been offered direct to the patient. Heretofore it has been prescribed by doctors and then sold at $1.50 to $2.00 per bottle. Gives relief in disorders of the kidneys and liver. This is a great remedy, which will often effect a cure where all other remedies fail. **For all diseases arising from disordered kidneys, liver or bladder, Dr. Ross' Kidney and Liver Cure is highly recommended.** The medicine acts directly on the organs, its cleansing properties add vigor and tone to the whole system. **If you have kidney, liver or urinary trouble of any nature don't delay,** order a bottle and you will be surprised at the results.

WE WANT YOU TO GIVE Dr. Ross' preparation a trial and you can do so without risk. There is absolutely nothing harmful in this remedy, so you need not hesitate to give it a trial. If you do not receive any benefit from it, and will write us to this effect, we will gladly refund the price paid for the first bottle.

No. 8C121 Price, per bottle.......................$0.65
Price, per dozen..6.00

Unmailable on account of weight.

Our Laxative Fig Syrup.

Retail price......................25c and 50c
Our price, 25c size, each.............$0.18
Our price, 25c size, per dozen........1.80
Our price, 50c size, each...............35
Our price, 50c size, per dozen........3.30

FOR CONSTIPATION. The great remedy of the age for above trouble. **Laxative Fig Syrup was never retailed for less than 50 cents. Our special price is 18 cents. If you suffer from constipation,** order a large bottle of **Laxative Fig Syrup** and you will find immediate relief and a speedy and permanent cure. **Laxative Fig Syrup** is nature's own remedy for restoring the bowels to a healthy and normal condition. Unlike pills and purgatives, it strengthens instead of weakening and enfeebling their action. **For chronic constipation,** to effect a permanent cure a remedy is required that will not only act quickly on the bowels, but will produce a tone and stimulating effect upon the inner coating of the intestines, strengthen the muscular action and restore the paralyzed functions. **Laxative Fig Syrup,** if taken regularly, will cure constipation with its attending ills. **Laxative Fig Syrup** is perfectly harmless. It is a liquid made from **fruits, plants and herbs,** is mild in form and easy to take, and in all cases of **bowel, stomach, kidney and liver complaints** its effect upon the system is marked. Patients needing this remedy will buy of you not only single bottles, but often three or more bottles at one time; sufficient for a complete cure. You can make a good profit on every bottle you sell.

No. 8C124 Price, regular size bottle, per dozen, $1.80; per bottle...18c
Price, large size bottle, per dozen, $3.30; per bottle......35c

If by mail, postage and tube extra, small, 16 cents.
Large size unmailable on account of weight.

Speedy Cure Pile Remedy.

Retail price..50c
Our price, each...$0.22
Our price, per dozen....................................1.80

WHY SUFFER from Piles when 22 cents spent for our Speedy Cure Pile Remedy will give relief and may perform a cure. This preparation affords immediate relief and a prompt cure in many cases. It allays at once the extreme soreness and tenderness of all parts, reduces the inflammation and heals all ulcerative conditions. It is equally serviceable for itching piles. We have sold thousands of boxes and have received splendid reports. If you have tried other remedies without getting relief, try our Speedy Cure; you will find results satisfactory.

No. 8C130 Price, per dozen, $1.80; per box.....22c
If by mail, postage extra, per box, 4 cents.

BRANDY CORDIAL.

**FOR MEDICINAL AND DOMESTIC USE.
MADE FROM THE JUICE OF SELECTED BLACKBERRIES.
ABSOLUTELY PURE.**

This is not an ordinary blackberry wine, but a sweet, wholesome cordial of the finest quality, equally useful as a medicine for bowel complaints. Also used for flavoring pastry and fruit sauces.

A VALUABLE ARTICLE FOR EVERY HOME. EXTRA FINE QUALITY AND FULL STRENGTH.

No. 8C132 Brandy Cordial.
Price, per pint bottle...................................$0.30
Per quart bottle...50
Original cases of 12 pints...............................3.00
Original cases of 12 quarts.............................5.00

...s mailable on account of weight.

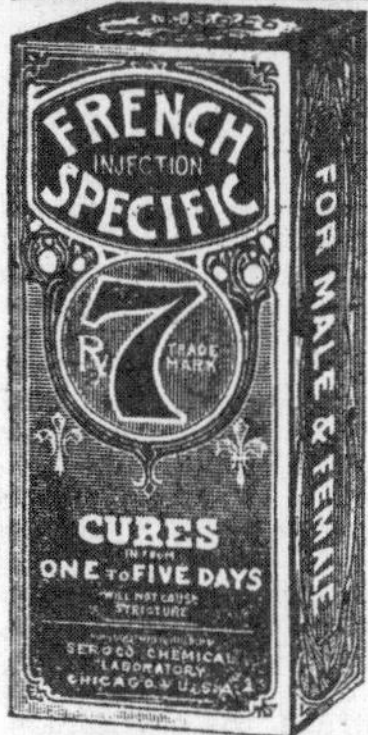

Injection No. 7.

Retail price......$1.00
Our price, each......$0.64
Our price, per dozen......6.00

CURES IN ONE TO FIVE DAYS. No other medicine required. No fear of stricture. No bad results. A French specific having a great reputation abroad as a reliable cure for all troubles of the urinary organs in either male or female; has a very quick effect and leaves no bad result, no matter how severe the case. Either gonorrhea or gleet quickly and easily cured. Full instructions and valuable information with each package.

No. 8C133 Price, per dozen, $6.00; per bottle....64c
If by mail, postage and mailing case extra, 18 cents.

No. 8C822 Hard Rubber Syringe, to be used with this remedy. Price, 16c

Bromo Vichy.

Retail price......10c and 25c
Our price, 10c size, each......$0.08
Our price, 10c size, dozen.......85
Our price, 25c size, each.......20
Our price, 25c size, dozen......1.60

A Morning Bracer. A Headache Reliever.
A Brain Clearer. A Nerve Steadier.

THIS IS BY FAR THE BEST "BROMO" preparation at present offered to the public. One or two teaspoonfuls taken in half a tumbler of cold water will instantly dispel any sickness of the stomach, relieve a severe headache, clear up the brain and steady the nerves. It is a thirst quencher, and causes a pleasant feeling to prevail all through the body. It is a quick remedy for nervous headaches, neuralgia, sleeplessness, over brain work, depression following alcoholic excesses, and all nervous troubles. A little should always be on one's bureau table for use in the morning or at night.

No. 8C136 Price, 10c size, per dozen, 85c; each......8c
Price, 25c size, per dozen, $1.60; each......20c
If by mail, postage extra, small size, 4 cents; large size, 8 cents.

Corns, Bunions and Warts.

Retail price......25c
Our price, each......10c
Our price, per dozen......90c

THE GREAT CHINESE CORN, Bunion and Wart Remover, never fails to give immediate relief, and a complete cure is certain when directions are faithfully followed. No one suffering from corns, bunions or warts should fail to give our great Chinese Corn, Bunion and Wart Remover a trial. We have tried it ourselves and found relief, therefore can testify knowingly as to its great merits.

No. 8C139 Price, per dozen, 90c; each......10c
If by mail, postage extra, 3 cents.

Angel's Oil.

The Greatest Cure on Earth for Pain.

Retail price......50c
Our price, each......$0.28
Our price, per dozen......2.70

COMPOSED OF VEGETABLE OILS. Offers great relief in cases of bronchitis, rheumatism, neuralgia, gout, sciatica, pleurisy, backache, quinsy, sore throat, stiffness of the neck and joints, sprains, cuts and wounds, lumbago, scalds and burns, headache, toothache, earaches, eruption, sores and swellings, inflammations, chilblains, frostbites, frosted feet, chapped hands and face, bites and stings of poisonous insects, weak ankles and joints, sore feet, pain in the back and limbs, ulcerated sores, or any other bodily pain or ailment.

THIS LINIMENT is worth its weight in gold and well named Angel's Oil, as it seems really a gift from the angels. Its uses are more numerous than we can mention here. Send for a bottle and try it. We are confident that you will never be without a bottle in the house. We make the price very low so that every one of our customers may afford to have a bottle constantly at hand.

No. 8C142 Price, per dozen, $2.70; per bottle......28c
If by mail, postage and tube extra, per bottle, 14 cents.

Every Mother Who Has Used It Proclaims Castroline Better than Castoria.

1100 Drops for Only 18 Cents.

Retail price......35c
Our price, each......$0.18
Our price, per dozen......1.80

KEEP YOUR CHILDREN HEALTHY and cheerful by using Castroline only. You need not have any other medicine in the house for your children. It is unquestionably the best thing for infants and children the world has ever known. It is harmless, and children like it. It gives them health and may save their lives. Mothers, keep it beside you, and you will always have something absolutely safe, pleasant to take, and the acme of perfection as a child's medicine for every ailment they are subject to.

CASTROLINE WILL DESTROY WORMS, allay fever, prevent vomiting, cures diarrhea and wind colic, relieves teething troubles. Cures constipation and flatulency. It assimilates the food, regulates the stomach and bowels, and gives to the child a healthy and natural sleep. When your baby cries give it a dose of CASTROLINE, its effect will be soothing to the baby and pleasant to you. It contains neither morphine nor opium nor any other narcotic properties. It is much superior to the so called soothing syrups which are being advertised daily. It will cause the baby to sleep when fretful, giving the mother her much needed rest. One size bottle only.

No. 8C143 Price, per dozen, $1.80; per bottle......18c
If by mail, postage and tube extra, per bottle, 16 cents.

Dr. Walker's Celebrated Skin Ointment.

Retail price......50c
Our price, each......$0.29
Our price, per dozen......2.70

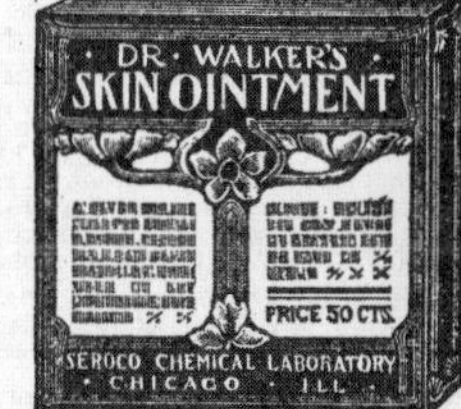

A positive cure for all skin diseases and blemishes and superior to every other skin ointment in the market, and furnished by us at less than one-half its selling value. This skin ointment is guaranteed to cure all eruptive and skin diseases, pimples, blotches, boils, eczema, salt rheum, erysipelas, ringworms or any scaly or scabby eruptions, often healing cracked or rough skin on the hands, face or any part of the body by a single application. We are in a position to furnish this grand cure for skin diseases and blemishes for only 29 cents a box. You could obtain no remedy that is better or can equal it in healing qualities if you were to pay $1.00 per package.

Dr. Walker's Skin Ointment is another preparation that is needed by thousands of sufferers. This remedy is already well known in every section of the country, and those who have tried it will accept no other ointment under any circumstances. You will find a ready sale for this article and it will yield you a good profit.

No. 8C157 Dr. Walker's Skin Ointment. Price, per dozen, $2.70; per box......(If by mail, postage extra, 3 cents.)......29c

WHITE STAR SECRET LIQUOR CURE.

Drunkards Cured Without their Knowledge.

Regular retail price......$2.50
Our price, complete box, 30 treatments......$1.10
Our price, complete box, 30 treatments, per dozen......9.60

AN EXCEEDINGLY SUCCESSFUL DRINK CURE. A treatment to be administered without the knowledge of the drinker. White Star Secret Liquor Cure, only $1.10 per box, 30 complete treatments. It is claimed that this remedy has saved many from that awful monster, Drink, and has protected thousands against a life of disease, poverty and degradation; that it has the power to release man from the bondage of whiskey, to reform even obstinate drunkards and to prevent the whiskey habit from taking a hold on only moderate drinkers.

WHITE STAR SECRET LIQUOR CURE is odorless, colorless and tasteless; a powder that can be given secretly in tea, coffee or food, and by its action on the system removes the taste, desire or craving for intoxicating liquors. Anyone can give the powder, no preparation required, absolutely no danger. Can be given to any man, young or old, without his knowledge, and whether he is a regular drinker or only a mild tippler it removes the desire for liquor and stops the terrible habit in due time. White Star Secret Liquor Cure stays the weak and flagging nerves, the mind becomes clear, the brain active, the flush of the face subsides, the step becomes steady, new health and strength are imparted, a higher moral tone is upheld; in a word, it makes him a man among men.

DRUNKENNESS IS A DISEASE and must be fought and counteracted by proper medical methods, the same as any other disease. The desire for liquor once established, the system requires its stimulus, and unless this appetite is counteracted it must be satisfied and the victim is powerless against its demands. Pledges and prayers often prove powerless after the appetite for intoxicants is once established. The system craves liquor with an insatiable demand that the average strength of the drinker cannot resist, and every time this desire is satisfied it means that the next time it comes on with redoubled force.

SEND FOR A BOX OF THE WONDERFUL WHITE STAR SECRET LIQUOR CURE, give it according to directions, a small powder in his tea or coffee. He cannot tell any difference, but it will work just the same. The effect will surprise and delight you. You will soon notice the improvement. The remedy will not only stop drinking, but it usually produces a dislike for liquor. The normal health will return, eyes become bright, step elastic, appetite good, sleep sound and natural—he is a saved man.

CAN THERE REALLY BE A CURE FOR DRUNKENNESS, or is it a habit that cannot be shaken off but grows stronger every day? Does it not seem reasonable that drunkenness is curable? Drunkenness is a disease more than a habit and as such is subject to treatment. If the proper medical elements necessary to counteract the effect of liquor and destroy the appetite for it are combined, there is no reason why it is not curable. White Star Secret Liquor Cure is the most successful and considered a perfect secret liquor cure. It is made expressly for us according to the celebrated original formula in our possession and we know just what it is and can offer it to our customers with every assurance that they will receive the genuine Secret Liquor Habit Cure. It is prepared in the form of this odorless and tasteless powder so that it can be given secretly without the patient's knowledge.

MAKE A TRIAL OF THIS REMEDY.

SEND FOR IT ACCORDING TO OUR OFFER AND AFTER GIVING IT A FAIR TRIAL ACCORDING TO DIRECTIONS, IF THERE IS NO BENEFIT DERIVED, WE WILL REFUND YOUR MONEY. If you buy it and do not receive benefit, write us so, state that this is the first box that you have tried and we will promptly refund your money. Remember, the price is only $1.10 per box (30 complete treatments). Full directions sent with each box. Medicine is sent in plain sealed package. All correspondence confidential.

No. 8C151 Price, per dozen boxes, $9.60; per box......$1.10
If by mail, postage extra, 12 cents.

Wine of Cod Liver Oil with Lime, Iron and Cherry Bark.

THIS IS A PLEASANT, ELEGANT PREPARATION, recommended and prescribed by physicians for the treatment of pulmonary affections and consumption.

WINE OF COD LIVER OIL contains the active medicinal principles of cod liver oil in a palatable form, avoiding the nauseating effect of the oil. It produces better results than plain cod liver oil, and at the same time admits of combining with it the very best tonics, tissue and blood builders, making the Wine of Cod Liver Oil with Lime, Iron and Cherry Bark **the most satisfactory codliver oil preparation obtainable.**

WINE OF COD LIVER OIL with Lime, Iron and Cherry Bark is a remedy that should always be used by patients who are constantly weakening and who are debilitated and wasting away. It is undoubtedly very valuable in the treatment of all lung troubles and consumption, colds and chronic coughs, scrofula, blood disorders and skin affections, as well as diseases of the joints and spine. It will build up the strength of the entire system, giving renewed health and vigor to the weak and debilitated, increasing the functional activity of every organ of the body.

WINE OF COD LIVER OIL with Lime, Iron and Cherry Bark is especially valuable for the treatment of women's complaint and children. Its pleasant taste makes it very palatable. It is easily taken by the patient, who will like it and relish it. It is quickly assimilated and taken up by the system, consequently it will improve the patient's condition almost from the first dose taken.

No. 8C160 Wine of Cod Liver Oil with Lime, Iron and Cherry Bark. Per bottle...$0.40
Per dozen....4.20
(Unmailable on account of weight)

Genuine English Pile Cure.

Retail price.... 50c
Our price, each....$0.34
Our price, per dozen....3.30

A scientifically prepared pile remedy in suppository form, soothing, healing and for the most effective curing of blind, itching or bleeding piles. Instant in relief, safe in its action, permanent in its cure. No matter what you may have employed for the treatment of this trouble, if all else has failed to afford you relief and cure, you should send for the Genuine English Pile Cure at once. You may have the same experience as have thousands of other sufferers troubled with different forms of this ailment, that is, you will find that the Genuine English Pile Cure will not only promptly relieve, but establish a cure in due time. The remedy having been prepared in the form of suppositories, admits of easy and convenient application, and will in this manner thoroughly reach the affected parts, and by its prompt healing action will prove more satisfactory than almost any mode of treatment of piles. The preparation is furnished in regular 50-cent size boxes, which we, however, supply to our customers at the exceedingly small price of only 34 cents per box.

An extraordinarily good seller. Don't omit to include in your quantity order a large supply of Genuine English Pile Cure. There are millions of men and women requiring this remedy, and as it is almost the only sure cure for piles, you can readily understand that you can dispose of very large quantities of same. The margin of profit on this remedy is very large. . .

No. 8C163 Genuine English Pile Cure.
Price, per dozen, $3.30; per box....34c
If by mail, postage extra, per box, 3 cents.

Cascara Cathartic Tablets.

FOR CONSTIPATION AND ALL GENERAL STOMACH, LIVER AND BOWEL COMPLAINTS.

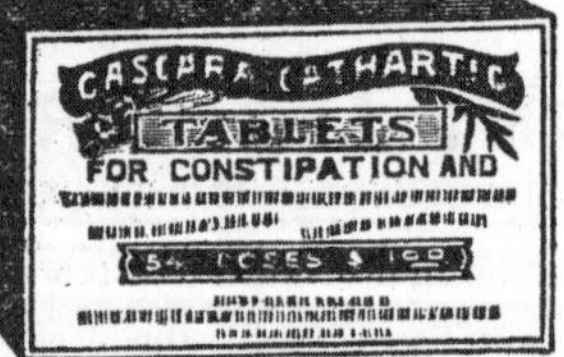

The grandest antiseptic laxative and stimulative tonic, the most effective remedy for the quick relief and cure of constipation, headache, jaundice, nausea, dyspepsia, female complaint, biliousness and all complications resulting from a disordered condition of the stomach and bowels. **Our Cascara Cathartic Tablets are really a wonderful combination of the most successful,** yet perfectly harmless remedies, recommended and used by the most eminent physicians, and a positive laxative and tonic. On account of their mild action on the bowels they are not only a valuable cathartic, but at the same time the most pleasing treatment for the cure of symptoms for which they are intended. **You will never know how easy it will be to keep yourself in a perfect and regular condition,** how quickly you can dispel those apparently unimportant yet exceedingly distressing little troubles resulting from a disturbed digestion or ar rregularity of the bowels. Using two or three Cascara Cathartic Tablets for a few days will tone up the entire system, strengthen the digestive organs and bowels connected with the function of digestion and the elimination of waste matter. You will feel lighter, brighter, more restful and cheerful and free from the nervous and painful state which always follows indigestion and bowel trouble. Less valued remedies of this kind are usually sold at 50 cents in boxes containing 30 to 35 doses. Our price for 50 doses is 30 cents. **We guarantee our Cascara Cathartic Tablets to give satisfaction.**

No. 8C165 Price, per box, large size, containing 54 doses....$0.30
Price per dozen boxes....(If by mail, postage extra, single boxes, 4 cents)....2.80

Dr. Allen's Asthma Cure.

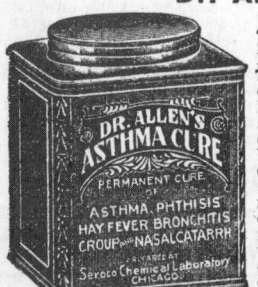

DR. ALLEN'S ASTHMA CURE is for the relief and permanent cure of all forms of Asthma, Phthisis, Hay Fever, Bronchitis, Croup and Nasal Catarrh. It is a scientific combination of oxygenating chemicals with such herbs, barks and gums, as have proven themselves effective for the relief of asthma and other affections of the respiratory organs, attended with short, difficult or spasmodic breathing. It is the result of many years' study and experiment in the treatment of diseases of the lungs and air passages, and all stages of asthma, that has **never failed to give some relief or effect a cure when a fair trial was given** and used according to directions. This remedy is used by inhalation and as its virtues reach the air passages direct, the relief obtained is instantaneous. **Plain directions and valuable information enclosed in each box,** and if the sufferer will follow these directions carefully, mild forms of asthma, hay fever, etc., **are often cured in a week or two;** but if the disease is old and deep seated and has obtained a firm hold on the system, the treatment ought to be continued for several months, even though the patient may believe himself entirely cured.

No. 8C169 Full size box. Price....$0.65
Per dozen boxes....6.20
If by mail, postage extra, per box, 5 cents.

Dr. Walters' Malaria, Ague and Chill Cure.

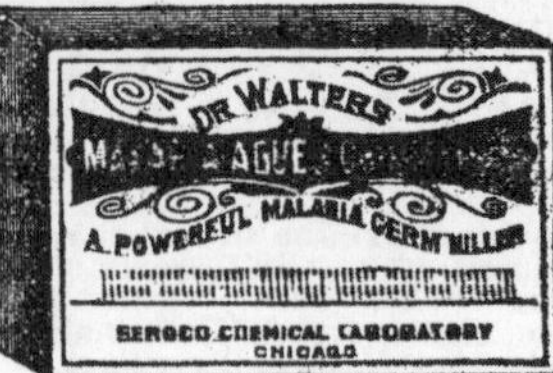

DR. WALTERS' WELL KNOWN MALARIA, AGUE AND CHILL CURE is a specific remedy for the cure of all diseases due to malaria poisoning. It will promptly relieve intermittent fever or fever and ague, remittent fever, dumb ague, periodic headache or malaria. It completely destroys the germs of malaria in the blood, thus removing the cause of the disease from the entire system. Dr. Walters' Malaria, Ague and Chill Cure should be used by persons living in a malarial district. It will protect them and act as a preventive and protector from malarial diseases. There is no reason why you should suffer from malaria poisoning when you can secure Dr. Walters' Malaria, Ague and Chill Cure, a positive and never failing remedy for all malarial diseases. This remedy will quickly restore the blood to a normal and healthy condition. It will quickly cure you of malaria, backache, headache, general debility, aching bones or any ailment due to malaria. It will act as a powerful tonic, appetizer and general invigorant for the entire nervous system. Those living in a malarial country can protect themselves from malaria germs by taking a few doses daily for a short time.

No. 8C171 Dr. Walters' Malaria, Ague and Chill Cure.
Price, per dozen boxes, $3.60; each....38c
If by mail, postage extra, per box, 4 cents.

CATARRH-OL SOLUTION.

THE LATEST AND GRANDEST SUCCESS IN CURING CHRONIC CATARRH.

This new local treatment for the cure of catarrh in the head or nose and throat, as well as all affections of the bronchial tubes and lung diseases, consists of a combination of the most powerful antiseptic and germ destroying ingredients, prepared for the purpose of preventing infectious diseases of the breathing organs and for the cure of catarrhal diseases of the head and lungs, and when applied with the newly invented and patented Catarrh-ol Nebulizer or Vaporizer will positively cure catarrh in all its different forms. **Catarrh-ol is cleanly, inexpensive and guaranteed to cure.** Its antiseptic and curing influences when it is properly used are simply marvelous. It does not cause even the slightest irritation. It is prompt in its relief and quick cures can always be assured. Catarrh-ol Solutions are furnished only in double and triple strength, known as Solution No. 1 and Solution No. 2. The first is of especial value in the treatment of catarrh of the nose and throat, while No. 2, or triple strength, is intended for bronchial trouble and lung diseases. **The Catarrh-ol Vaporizer** is the only instrument of its kind on the market, and, on account of its peculiar construction and patented features, will nebulize the solutions and carry the same over the entire surface of the mucous membrane, the seat of all catarrhal trouble, reaching every portion of the nasal passages and the air passages, the bronchial tubes and, through them, the lungs, soothing, healing and curing.

No. 8C172 Catarrh-ol No. 1. For catarrh of nose and throat. Price, 50c
No. 8C173 Catarrh-ol No. 2. For bronchial and lung trouble. Price, 50c
No. 8C174 Catarrh-ol Vaporizer. Price....95c
No. 8C175 Catarrh-ol Solution Treatment, including one bottle Catarrh-ol No. 1, one bottle Catarrh-ol No. 2, sufficient for three months' treatment, and one patent Vaporizer, all complete. Price....$1.65
Unmailable on account of weight.

Free Samples of Wall Paper.

WE SELL WALL PAPER, all the latest patterns, at astonishingly low prices, and we will send to anyone, free on application, a complete sample book, showing samples of our entire line of wall paper patterns, from the cheapest to the best, and if you need anything in the line of wall paper you can buy from us at about one-half the price you would pay any other dealer. We make all our own wall paper in our own wall paper mill, and the prices we ask are based on actual manufacturing cost with but our one small percentage of profit added. With each free sample book we send full instructions and directions showing how anyone, without any previous experience, can hang wall paper and do a fine job. We also give free and simple instructions how to order, how to calculate the quantity of paper you need, everything necessary. If you expect to do any papering this season and want to save about one-half the cost, **don't fail to write for our Free Wall Paper Sample Book.**

PAINT SAMPLES FREE.

Our Complete Book, How to Paint, also Free.

IF YOU HAVE A HOUSE, barn, fence, buggy, implements, or anything that would be improved by a coat of paint, or if you expect to do any painting or varnishing, don't spend one cent in this line until you first write for our Free Paint Sample Book. We send, free on application, a big book containing eighty-five different samples showing the actual natural colors of all of our paints, and we will also send you a complete book, "How to Paint," which explains everything and shows how anyone can do a good job of painting. You will also find simple directions how to order and how to calculate the quantity of paint you need. In fact, everything will be made plain so that you can order and also do the job yourself. All of our paint is made in our own factory, under the most economical methods, made of the highest grade materials that money can buy; our paint is ready mixed, ready to use, and we would certainly advise you to get our free sample book and free instruction book if you are interested in this line. **Just send a postal, ask for the Free Paint Sample Book and everything will go to you by return mail immediately, postpaid.**

Free Samples of Men's Ready Made Clothing.

WE SEND TO ANYONE, FREE ON REQUEST, a complete book showing cloth samples of our entire line of Men's Ready Made Clothing, which we sell at prices less than dealers pay at wholesale. With the sample book, we also send a tape measure and our plain and simple rules for taking your own measure and for ordering, and by which we guarantee a perfect fit and we take all the risk. If the suit or other garment we send you is not perfectly satisfactory in fit, quality or value, you are at liberty to return it to us at our expense, and your money will be promptly refunded. You will be surprised how much you can save on your clothing by sending to us. **If you have never investigated, don't put it off, but write today and ask for a Free Sample Book of Men's Ready Made Clothing.**

ANTI-CONGESTION PLASTIC DRESSING.

THE GREAT REMEDY FOR INFLAMMATORY RHEUMATISM, INFLAMMATION, FEVER.

AS RECOMMENDED, USED AND PRESCRIBED TODAY BY EVERY PHYSICIAN IN THE CIVILIZED WORLD, in the treatment of diseases accompanied by external or internal inflammation or congestion.

SOLD UNDER OUR PERSONAL GUARANTEE.

IF USED AND FOUND NOT SATISFACTORY, we will return every cent you have paid us for same. NO HOUSEHOLD, whether rich or poor, should be a single day without a sufficient quantity of ANTI-CONGESTION PLASTIC DRESSING.

Order a supply without a moment's delay. Send for it even before you send for a physician, for it is a real godsend, a remedy for any and all cases, acute or chronic, where superficial or deep seated congestion exists. **DO NOT UNDER ANY CIRCUMSTANCES FAIL TO PROVIDE YOURSELF with a package of ANTI-CONGESTION PLASTIC DRESSING** and keep it in the house ready for instant use. **DO NOT WAIT until you need it and then send for it. IT MAY BE TOO LATE WHEN IT ARRIVES** to give you the protection it would have afforded you if it had been kept for ready use.

ALTHOUGH IN CASES LIKE pneumonia, bronchitis, pleurisy, peritonitis, erysipelas, and poisoned wounds a physician should be called in, you should have Anti-Congestion Plastic Dressing on hand. In nine cases out of ten he will surely make an immediate application of an Anti-Congestion Plastic Dressing to reduce and remove the inflammation. You will, therefore, save money, worry, and perhaps the life of the patient by having this remedy on hand to meet the emergency without any delay.

BUT THIS IS NOT ALL. Simple instructions are furnished with this remedy and any one can make the application, so that you can in critical cases apply the Plastic Dressing and do for the patient, long before the doctor arrives, the exact thing he would have advised you to do as the first step after his examination of the patient. **In anticipating the action of the physician, you have aided him as much as may lie in your power in making the sufferer comfortable and in saving the life of the sick one.**

WHAT ANTI-CONGESTION PLASTIC DRESSING WILL DO:

It is the only bland and non-irritating remedy which allays and heals inflammation and congestion. It absorbs from the tissues over which it is placed, the moisture resulting from the inflamed condition. **It is applicable in all stages and in all varieties of inflammation.**

It acts as a complete dressing, furnishing compression, support, rest and protection for that part of the body to which it is applied; it acts as a poultice, does all any poultice can do, supplying heat and moisture, but it goes a great deal further, as it is absorbent, antiseptic, anodyne and nutrient, lasting from twelve to forty-eight hours. It does not annoy and irritate the patient, which nearly always is the case where irregular and too frequent poultice applications are made. **Anti-Congestion Plastic Dressing does not interfere with internal remedies of any kind.**

ANTI-CONGESTION PLASTIC DRESSING WILL GIVE INSTANT AND CERTAIN RELIEF IN ALL CASES OF

PNEUMONIA, PELVIC INFLAMMATION, TUMORS, FELONS, BURNS, TONSILITIS, BOILS, POISONED WOUNDS, INFLAMMATORY RHEUMATISM, BRONCHITIS, INFLAMED BREASTS, PERITONITIS, SPRAINS, CHRONIC ULCERS. ERYSIPELAS, PILES, DYSMENORRHOEA, FROSTBITES, SUNBURN AND OPEN WOUNDS IN WHICH INFLAMMATION OR CONGESTION IS A FACTOR. HEED OUR WELL MEANT ADVICE AND KEEP IT ON HAND READY FOR IMMEDIATE USE.

No. 8C177 12-ounce can Anti-Congestion Plastic Dressing. Price **$0.22**
No. 8C178 1-pound collapsible tubes Anti-Congestion Plastic Dressing. Price .... **.32**
No. 8C179 5-pound package Anti-Congestion Plastic Dressing. Price **1.20**
If by mail, postage extra, 12-ounce package, 22 cents. Larger sizes unmailable on account of weight.

COMPLETE INFORMATION AND INSTRUCTIONS will be furnished with each package.

Our Great Offer. Absolutely Free.

A very handsome, substantially made, cloth covered Medicine Case and our valuable book, "The Family Doctor," absolutely FREE.

WITH EVERY ORDER for twelve of the following 13-cent remedies we will send "The Family Doctor," a book giving full instructions how to use these remedies and containing other valuable information for the cure of the sick, **free.** We also supply these remedies in a well made medicine case for which there will be no extra charge. You can select any twelve of the following named remedies at **13 cents** each, and a black cloth covered case will be furnished with the same **without extra cost. For $1.50, covering the price of 12 bottles of the following listed household remedies, we will send the medicine at once, together with medicine case and medicine book free.**

No. 201. **COLD IN THE HEAD.**—Will cure quinsy, tonsilitis, cold in the head, influenza, and many of the milder troubles arising from cold. Price........ **13c**
No. 202. **COLIC**—Very useful for all childish pains, such as cramps, colic, or for the restlessness of teething, diarrhea, etc. Price........ **13c**
No. 203. **COUGH**—Valuable in coughs, bronchitis, hoarseness and any trouble in throat and chest arising from cold. Price........ **13c**
No. 204. **CONSTIPATION**—Will relieve obstinate cases of constipation, which are often the cause of headache, billousness, offensive breath, etc. Price........ **13c**
No. 205. **DIARRHEA**—Useful and a sure cure for any form of diarrhea, cholera morbus, cholera infantum, sour stomach, etc. Price........ **13c**
No. 206. **HEADACHE**—Good for headache of any sort, fever, cold, nervousness, la grippe, etc. Price........ **13c**
No. 207 **TONIC**—For any weakened condition of the system. Price........ **13c**
No. 208. **ALTERATIVE**—For impure blood, boils, scrofula, ulcers, eczema, etc. Price........ **13c**
No. 209. **DYSPEPSIA**—From any of the ordinary causes. Price........ **13c**
No. 210. **KIDNEY AND LIVER**—To remove or cure all diseases of the organs. Price........ **13c**
No. 211. **MALARIAL**—To be used when quinine fails, or when the patient cannot take it. Price **13c**
No. 212. **RHEUMATIC**—A true remedy. Price........ **13c**
No. 213. **NERVOUS TROUBLES**—Calms and soothes; will relieve nervousness in any form. Price........ **13c**
No. 214. **HEART REGULATOR**—A splendid tonic for the heart. Price........ **13c**
No. 215. **LIVER CORRECTOR**—For biliousness, jaundice, sallow complexion, sour stomach, etc. Price........ **13c**
No. 216. **KIDNEY DISORDERS**—Gently stimulates the kidneys and relieves urinary troubles in both old and young. Price........ **13c**
No. 217. **BRONCHIAL**—For difficult breathing, pain in the chest, cold in the bronchial tubes Price........ **13c**
No. 218. **THROAT**—For hoarseness, tickling in the throat; useful for speakers and singers. Price........ **13c**
No. 219. **NEURALGIA**—For the relief of neuralgia, sciatica, etc. Price........ **13c**
No. 220. **FEVER**—For all kinds of fever, especially that arising from cold. Price........ **13c**
No. 221. **CROUP**—For children; to be given when the first symptom appears. Price........ **13c**
No. 222. **MUMPS**—Give regularly and follow instructions in our Medical Guide. Price........ **13c**
No. 223. **PLEURISY**—For pain in the chest on breathing and coughing. Price........ **13c**
No. 224. **PIMPLES**—For skin blemishes. Price........ **13c**

HANDY POCKET TABLET REMEDIES. Twenty-four different remedies in large glass vials with metal screw top, will keep in every climate for years, a cure for almost every disease for only 13 cents. For 13 cents each, 2 cents extra for postage, we offer twenty-four different remedies, put up in neat tablet form, easy to take and convenient to be carried in vest pocket. These remedies are compounded in our own laboratory, and represent the best prescriptions of the highest medical authorities in the land, **are absolutely harmless, prepared from vegetable tinctures, herbs and roots. No mineral, mercury or poison.** These handy pocket tablet remedies will save you doctor bills and much suffering. **No family can afford to be without a supply of these remedies, and the price has been fixed so low, only 13 cents each vial, that all may be supplied.**

No. 8C199 12 Bottles of any of the above........ **$1.50**
Medicine Case and Medical Book free.
No. 8C200 24 Bottles of any of the above........ **2.50**
Medicine Case and Medical Book free.

A Few Handy Pocket Goods in Screw Top, Air Tight Glass Vials.

No. 8C275 Aromatic Cachou Lozenges, for perfuming the breath. Make a delicious confection. Price........ **6c**
No. 8C276 Silver Cachous, for perfuming the breath, vest pocket size **6c**
No. 8C278 Chlorate Potash Tablets. 5 grains each. For sore throat, hoarseness, etc. Price........ **5c**
No. 8C280 Soda Mint Tablets, for sour stomach, flatulency, nausea, etc.. **5c**
No. 8C282 Bronchial Troches, for coughs, colds, sore throat, hoarseness. **5c**
No. 8C284 Licorice Lozenges, pure, very soothing to the throat and bronchial tubes. Price........ **5c**
No. 8C286 Slippery Elm Lozenges. Demulcent, for roughness in the throat and irritating cough. Price........ **5c**
No. 8C288 Paregoric Tablets. Each tablet equals 15 drops of paregoric; dose 1 to 4, according to age. Price........ **5c**
No. 8C290 Pepsin Tablets, made from pure pepsin, for dyspepsia, indigestion, etc. Price, per bottle........ **15c**
No. 8C292 Trix, for the breath. Price, per package........ **3c**
No. 8C294 Sen-Sen. Price, per package........ **3c**
If by mail, postage extra, 2 cents.

Our Homeopathic Remedies.

12 bottles of different Homeopathic Remedies, your own selection........ $1.50
A nice, black cloth covered Medicine Case and Instruction Sheet free.

OUR HOMEOPATHIC SPECIFICS are prepared under the supervision of an old, experienced homeopathic physician. Great care is taken in preparing them according to the rules laid down by the **highest authorities on homeopathy,** and only the purest drugs used. Every one of the following specifics is **a special cure** for the diseases named on it. **Adults take 6 pellets, children from 1 to 3, according to age,** and from two to four doses are to be taken every day, according to the severity of the case. We ask the special attention of all our customers to these **high grade remedies. If you have them near at hand,** we guarantee they will **save you many a doctor's bill,** and what is of more consequence, quickly relieve any suffering member of the family and ward off more serious sickness.

No. 8C230 12 bottles, any selection........ $1.50
No. 8C232 24 bottles, any selection........ 2.50
No. 8C234 36 bottles, any selection........ 3.00
Medicine Case and Instruction Sheet free.

A SPECIAL OFFER. As an inducement to give these remedies a thorough trial, we will allow you to select 12 cures, including the 60-cent ones. Make your own selection, one or more of any kind, and we will put them in a neat case, such as we represent here, and only charge you $1.50. **No family can afford to neglect this great offer.**

A 12-Box Case will save you many dollars doctors' bills in a year and may save your life.

No family should be without a case of our Homeopathic Remedies.		Usual Price	Our Price
No. 8C235	Cures rheumatism or rheumatic pains	$0.25	$0.15
No. 8C236	Cures fever and ague, intermittent fever, malaria, etc.	.25	.15
No. 8C237	Cures piles, blind or bleeding, external or internal	.25	.15
No. 8C238	Cures ophthalmia, weak or inflamed eyes	.25	.15
No. 8C239	Cures catarrh, influenza, cold in the head	.25	.15
No. 8C240	Cures whooping cough, spasmodic cough	.25	.15
No. 8C241	Cures asthma, oppressed or difficult breathing	.25	.15
No. 8C242	Cures fevers, congestions, inflammations	.25	.15
No. 8C243	Cures worm fever or worm diseases	.25	.15
No. 8C244	Cures colic, crying and wakefulness of infants teething	.25	.15
No. 8C245	Cures diarrhea of children and adults	.25	.15
No. 8C246	Cures dysentery, griping, bilious colic	.25	.15
No. 8C247	Cures cholera, cholera morbus, vomiting	.25	.15
No. 8C248	Cures coughs, colds, bronchitis	.25	.15
No. 8C249	Cures toothache, faceache, neuralgia	.25	.15
No. 8C250	Cures headache, sick headache, vertigo	.25	.15
No. 8C251	Cures dyspepsia, indigestion, weak stomach	.25	.15
No. 8C252	Cures suppressed or scanty menses	.25	.15
No. 8C253	Cures leucorrhea, or profuse menses	25	.15
No. 8C254	Cures croup, hoarse cough, difficult breathing, laryngitis	.25	.15
No. 8C255	Cures salt rheum, eruptions, erysipelas	.25	.15
No. 8C256	Cures ear discharge, earache	.25	.15
No. 8C257	Cures scrofula, swellings, ulcers	.25	.15
No. 8C258	Cures general debility, physical weakness, brain fag	.25	.15
No. 8C259	Cures dropsy, fluid accumulations	.25	.15
No. 8C260	Cures seasickness, nausea, vomiting	.25	.15
No. 8C261	Cures kidney disease, gravel, calculi	.25	.15
No. 8C262	Cures nervous debility, vital weakness	1.00	.65
No. 8C263	Cures sore mouth and canker	.25	.15
No. 8C264	Cures urinary incontinence, wetting bed	.25	.15
No. 8C265	Cures painful menses, pruritus	.25	.15
No. 8C266	Cures diseases of the heart, palpitation	1.00	.60
No. 8C267	Cures epilepsy, St. Vitus' dance	1.00	.60
No. 8C268	Cures sore throat, quinsy or ulcerated sore throat	.25	.15
No. 8C269	Cures chronic congestions, headache	.25	.15
No. 8C270	Cures grip and chronic colds	.25	.15

If by mail, postage extra, per case, 26 cents; per bottle, 2 cents.

WE ARE PREPARED TO FURNISH ANYTHING in the line of Homeopathic Supplies, and guarantee them to be full strength and in fresh condition. We mention a few of the more prominent. When ordering the following remedies please specify what form you wish them in—pills, powders, discs or liquid.

Name	Strength	Name	Strength	Name	Strength	Name	Strength
Aconite	3x	Cinna	2x	Hydrastis	1x	Phosphorus	3x
Antimon. crud	3x	Cocculus	3x	Hyoscyamus	3x	Phosphorus aci	3x
Apis mel	3x	Coffea crud	3x	Ignati	3x	Phytolacca	0x
Arnica	3x	Colchicum	3x	Iodium	3x	Podophyllin	3x
Arsenic alb	3x	Colocynthis	3x	Ipecac	3x	Pulsatilla	3x
Baptisia	1x	Cuprum met	3x	Kali bichr	3x	Rhus tox	3x
Belladonna	3x	Digitalis	2x	Lachesis	6x	Sanguirnaria	2x
Bryonia alba	3x	Drosera	2x	Lycopodium	3x	Secale cor	1x
Calcarea carb	3x	Dulcamara	3x	Mercurius bnod	3x	Sepia	3x
Cantharis	3x	Eupatorium p'r	1x	Mercurius corr	3x	Silicea	6x
Carbo veg	3x	Ferrum phos	3x	Mercurius sol	3x	Spigelia	3x
Caulophyllum	1x	Gelsemium	1x	Mercurius viv	3x	Spongia	3x
Causticum	3x	Glonoine	3x	Natrum mur	6x	Staphysagria	3x
Chamomilla	3x	Graphites	6x	Nitric acid	6x	Sulphur	3x
China	2x	Hamamelis	1x	Nux vomica	3x	Tartar emetic	3x
Chinnin, arsen	2x	Hepar sulph. tr	3x	Opium	3x	Veratrum alb	3x
Cimicifuga	1x						

No. 8C300 ¼-ounce vials, each, **10c**; by mail........ **15c**
No. 8C302 ½-ounce vials, each, **15c**; by mail........ **20c**
No. 8C304 1-ounce vials, each, **20c**; by mail........ **25c**
No. 8C306 2-ounce vials, each, **40c**; by mail........ **45c**

LIQUID IROZONE (FERROUS LIQUID OXYGEN)

A GERM KILLER. AN OXYGEN SUPPLIER.

Cures Germ Diseases. Strengthens, Invigorates and Cures by Furnishing that Great Life Property, Oxygen to the Blood.

No. 8C309 Price, per bottle (commercial pint size)..46c

A WONDERFUL DISCOVERY.

LIQUID IROZONE (Ferrous Liquid Oxygen or Ozone Liquefied) is a harmless but powerful preparation for the prompt and effectual cure of all germ diseases. It cures by supplying oxygen (or ozone liquefied) to the blood and thus creating healthy tissue. Germs cannot thrive or live in healthy oxygenized tissue.

MANY DISEASES are directly caused by germ infection. In all such cases Liquid Irozone is an ideal, positive remedy because it kills the germs, it purifies the blood by supplying oxygen and it does all this without harming tissue or organ.

GREAT BENEFIT IS DERIVED by taking Liquid Irozone even if you are not positively sick, because it strengthens, invigorates and purifies the blood by supplying an extra quantity of oxygen, the life-giving principle of the atmosphere. It is perfectly safe, wonderfully effective and positively certain, a complete destruction of all germ life wherever germs may be the real cause of disease. It is nature's own tonic, supplying to the blood that substance that the human body most vitally requires in health and in sickness, namely, oxygen, and it supplies this great life principle in a new and scientific way.

YOU KNOW, OF COURSE, that without oxygen no human being can live. Every second of your life you need oxygen. Nature supplies it to you in every breath of air you inhale. It reaches the blood through the lungs. It is at this stage of the circulation of the blood through the body that the oxygen is taken into the blood, immediately changing the impure dark venous blood (vein blood) into purified, healthy, bright red or arterial blood. The blood after being ozonated with oxygen becomes purified and then passes into the heart and finally into the circulation, supplying to the weakened, impoverished and diseased tissues, cells and organs an abundance of that life sustaining fluid, pure, rich and healthy blood. If the blood is liberally supplied with oxygen, in its travel through the system it destroys germ life and at the same time revitalizes every organ, every part of the body, acting as a stimulative, tonic and invigorator, sustaining life and the healthy condition of the body.

THE NORMAL QUANTITY OF OXYGEN needed is supplied in nature by our breathing pure, fresh air. A lack of fresh air means a diminishing of the supply of oxygen for your body. Those that live constantly in the pure, open air, feed their lungs with all the oxygen needed to maintain life and to protect them against germ diseases, but millions of men, women and children, under the modern system of living, suffer from an insufficient supply of oxygen and therefore their systems are not immune from the attack of germs, and they may already be troubled with a germ disease in some form, or from the lack of pure air, or oxygen, they are unable to resist an attack if exposed to germ infection, no matter in what manner the infection may present itself.

BY TAKING LIQUID IROZONE you fortify your system against sickness, you ward off and cure all germ diseases by furnishing your system with a liberal and greater supply of oxygen. In Ferrous Liquid Oxygen we have the only liquefied oxygen that will destroy germs without destroying the tissues of the body and without creating a disturbing or distressing effect upon the digestive organs. Oxygen, as every one knows, is the vital part of air. It is the very source of vitality, the most essential element of life. **Oxygen is also nature's greatest tonic, the blood food, the nerve food, the scavenger of the blood.** It is oxygen that turns the blue blood to red in the lungs, it is oxygen that eliminates the waste tissue and builds up the new. You can therefore realize what a wonderful and valuable preparation Liquid Irozone is, how important it is that every one should avail himself of this great chemical product, Ferrous Liquid Oxygen or Ozone Liquefied.

LIQUID IROZONE supplies to weakened, exhausted and anemic subjects, a soluble, tasteless and non-constipating form of iron, which is so combined with purified ozone (or concentrated oxygen), as to produce a pleasant and palatable blood and tissue building tonic.

LIQUID IROZONE quickly restores to the impoverished blood an abundance of bright, red, healthy corpuscles.

BY THIS TREATMENT iron and ozone are carried to the tissues and cells, thus, the whole body shares in the benefit from this treatment of Liquid Irozone.

LIQUID IROZONE should be freely used as protection against germ infection and for the treatment and cure of so called germ diseases, especially all diseases of the blood: Anemia, blood poison, erysipelas, impure blood, running sores, skin diseases, scrofula, syphilis, salt rheum, tumors, ulcers; also in catarrh, consumption, cancers, dropsy, hay fever, la grippe, sore throat, tuberculosis, tonsilitis, malaria, pneumonia, pleurisy, bronchitis.

LIQUID IROZONE may be employed with great success in the treatment of all stomach, kidney, liver and bowel complications.

LIQUID IROZONE is exhilarating, vitalizing and purifying. Its effects are immediate. It gives to every organ the needed stimulation and without reaction. It positively purifies the blood. Liquid Irozone should be in every home. It is a universal necessity, applicable to each and every individual. There is no one who will not be benefited by its use.

No. 8C309 Liquid Irozone, commercial pint bottles, dollar size, each........................46c
Not mailable on account of weight.

Essence of Pepsin.

A preparation regularly prescribed by physicians, and usually recommended for the treatment of indigestion, and in complications resulting therefrom. A teaspoonful before or after meals will aid digestion and assimilation of food, and affords prompt relief when suffering from indigestion, as well as the distressing attacks to which chronic sufferers of dyspepsia are subject.

No. 8C435 Price, 8-oz. bottles. $0.50
Per dozen.......................5.40

Neutralizing Cordial.

A well known household remedy. Useful in treatment of diarrhea, dysentery and cholera morbus. Also a great remedy for dyspepsia, a general corrector of the stomach and bowels.

No. 8C438 Price, 4-ounce bottle..16c
Postage and tube extra, 16 cents.

Castor Oil.

Cold pressed and almost tasteless.

No. 8C440 Price, 2-oz. bottle.................. 8c
Price, 4-oz. bottle..12c
Price, 1-pt. bottle..25c
If by mail, postage and tube extra, 16 cents
Pints, unmailable.

Olive Oil (Sweet Oil).

This is a fine domestic oil considered equal to imported olive oil made from olives grown in vineyards of Italy. For either internal or external use. Anyone wishing to use an absolutely pure olive oil should send for this.

No. 8C442 Price, 2-oz. bottle....... 7c
Price, 4-oz. bottle..................10c
Price, ½-pt. bottle.................17c
If by mail, postage and tube extra, 16c. ½ pints unmailable.

Spirits of Camphor.

Made from pure Gum Camphor, imported by ourselves from Kobe, Japan.

No. 8C444
Price, 2-ounce bottles...... ..... 10c
Price, 4-ounce bottles........... 16c
Price, 1-pint bottles............. 60c
If by mail, postage and tube extra, 2-oz., 12 cents; 4-oz., 16 cents.
Pints unmailable on account weight.

Camphorated Oil.

An excellent article for rubbing on children's and grown up persons' chests and throats in cases of croup, difficulty in breathing, sore throat, coughs. A small quantity of pure spirits of turpentine added to it will increase its effectiveness in many cases.

No. 8C446 Price, 4-oz. bottles. 18c
Price, 8-oz. bottles..............................28c
Postage and tube extra, 4-ounce bottle, 16 cents.
8-ounce bottle unmailable on account of weight.

DEPARTMENT OF FAMILY REMEDIES AND HOUSEHOLD PREPARATIONS.

Prepared and put up by careful and experienced pharmacists and chemists in our own laboratory and sold under an absolute guarantee of highest strength and purity.

Borax.

The housekeeper's friend; has more uses about the home than even that of common salt. For the laundry, the kitchen, the bath and for various medicinal uses it is indispensable. Chemically pure and finely powdered. We put it up in 1-pound boxes with complete directions for using in washing, starching, keeping away moths, killing cockroaches, dressing wounds and bruises, arresting fermentation, cleaning clothes, etc. You can rely on getting from us the pure powdered borax, which will be a source of satisfaction to you, as it is a much adulterated article.

No. 8C420 Price, per 1-pound box.. ....10c

Laudanum.

(Tinct. Opium.)

U. S. P. Strength. Directions on each bottle for young and old.

No. 8C424 Price
1-ounce bottle.......... 8c
2-ounce bottle..........15c
4-ounce bottle..........25c
Unmailable.

Paregoric.

Always useful, both for children and adults. One of the best known and most extensively used house remedies. Full directions.

No. 8C426 Price, 2-ounce bottle..10c
Price, 4-oz. bottle.........................15c
If by mail, postage and tube extra, small, 12 cents; large, 16 cents.

Sweet Spirits of Nitre.

This article is more liable to adulteration than any other medicine. You seldom can get it pure and full strength from a drug store. It is a valuable medicine when fresh and unadulterated. We guarantee what we sell to be absolutely pure.

No. 8C429 2-ounce bottle 10c
4-ounce bottle... ......18c
1-pint bottle............75c
If by mail, postage and tube extra, 2-oz., 12 cents; 4-oz., 16 cents. Pints unmailable on account of weight.

Essence Peppermint.

Pure and strong. Best quality for medical use.

No. 8C431 Price, 2-ounce bottle..18c
Price, 4-ounce bottle...............30c
If by mail, postage and tube extra, 2 oz., 12 cents; 4 oz., 16 cents.

Essence Jamaica Ginger.

Prepared of great strength from the finest quality of Jamaica ginger, imported by ourselves. Ginger has healing properties peculiar to itself; many preparations are offered for sale which are represented as containing ginger, when generally they owe their hot taste to pepper alone. Buy our genuine essence and get the full benefit of its valuable properties.

No. 8C433 Price, 2-oz. bottle......................12c
Price, 4-oz. bottle..............................20c
Postage and tube extra, small, 12 cents; large, 16c.

Spirits of Turpentine.

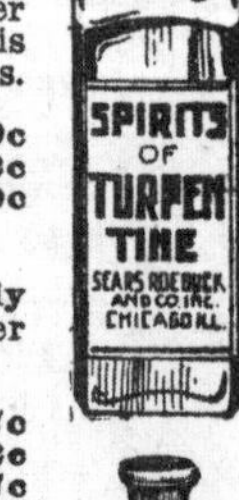

Pure, for internal or external use. When you wish to use turpentine as a medicine, whether internally or externally, always get a pure article. Never use the common oil of turpentine that is generally sold for mixing with paints. We sell the pure.

No. 8C448 Price, 4-ounce bottles, 9c
Price, 8-ounce bottles 12c
Price, 16-ounce bottles.................20c

Glycerine.

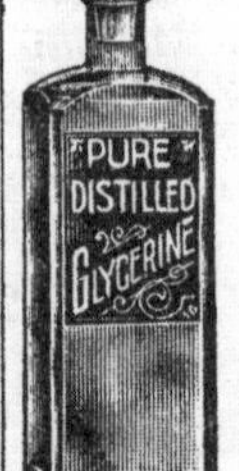

Warranted absolutely pure. Can be used either externally or internally.

No. 8C450
Price, 2-ounce bottles...7c
Price, 4-ounce bottles..12c
Price, ½-pound bottles17c
Price, 1-pound bottles.28c

Carbolic Acid.

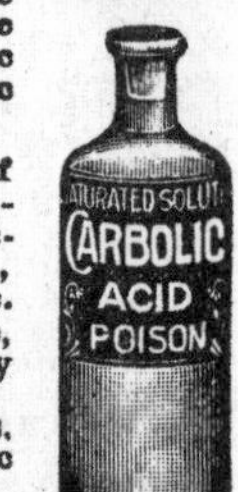

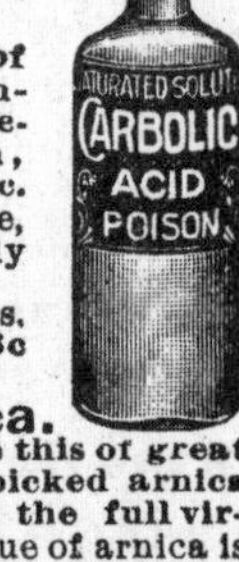

A saturated solution of Carbolic Acid for disinfecting purposes, destroying contagion, cleansing purposes, etc. Excellent for keeping away disease, destroying bad smells. Put up expressly for household use.

No. 8C452 Price, 1-pound bottles, each..18c
Unmailable on account of weight.

Tincture of Arnica.

We are careful to make this of great strength from recently picked arnica flowers, thereby getting the full virtues of the herb. The value of arnica is well known as an application to bruises, sprains, cuts, swellings, etc., but to secure any benefit it is necessary to have a strong, well prepared tincture such as ours.

No. 8C454 Price, 4-oz. bottles$0.12
Price, ¼-pint bottles .... .20
Price, 1-pint bottles .... .35
Price, per gallon.................. 3.00

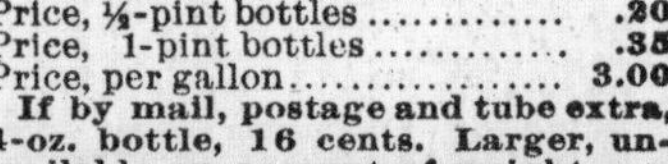

If by mail, postage and tube extra, 4-oz. bottle, 16 cents. Larger, unmailable on account of weight.

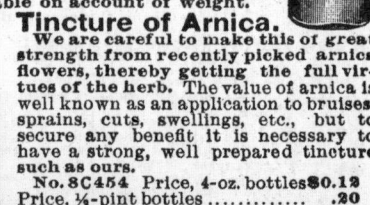

Ammonia.

Standard quality. Extra purity and strength. Put up expressly for home use. It lightens work and brightens the home. Makes the washing cleaner and polishing easier.

In pint bottles, with full directions for using in the laundry, for the toilet, and for cleaning glass, crockery, paint, taking out stains, etc.

No. 8C456 Price, per bottle........7c
Unmailable on account of weight.

Violet Ammonia.

For the Toilet and Bath. Violet Ammonia is a comparatively new article for toilet and bathing purposes, which has won the favor of every lady and gentleman who has given it a trial. They will never be without it. We furnish Violet Ammonia in liquid form and in the very best of condition for toilet and bath. It is inexpensive and a few drops added to the water before washing will be sufficient to purify and perfume it, and to whiten the skin of the user to perfection. A small quantity added to the bath will intensify the cleaning and invigorating effects greatly, leaving a mild but lasting odor always pleasing and refreshing.

No. 8C458 Violet Ammonia. 1-pint bottle. Price 18c
Not mailable on account of weight and size.

Genuine Witch Hazel Extract.

Buy Direct and Save All Retail Profits. We can save you money, save you one-half on anything in this line, and guarantee highest grade goods on the market. Our Extract of Witch Hazel, you will find even better than Pond's Extract; **a universal all healing remedy. Should be in every household;** useful for sore throat, hemorrhage, wounds, sprains, bruises, sore eyes, stiff joints, burns and in nearly every accident that one can have. **We guarantee this to be pure,** full strength and such as is not often found in retail stores. **Our price is so low that** every family can afford to keep a supply in their homes. **Look at our prices.**

No. 8C460
½-pint bottle, retail price, 40c; our price....12c
1-pint bottle, retail price, 50c; our price....22c
1-quart bottle, retail price, $1.00; our price..33c
½-gallon, retail price, $1.75; our price........60c
1-gallon, retail price, $2.50; our price........95c
Unmailable on account of weight.

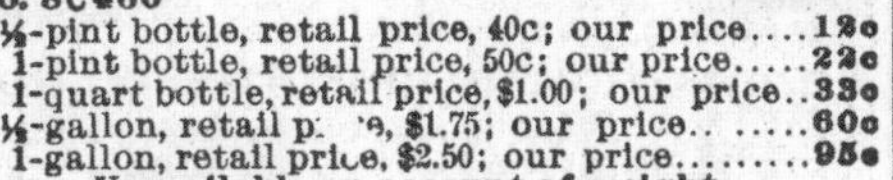

Arnicated Carbolic Salve.

The best in the world for burns, flesh wounds, chilblains, boils, felons, sores, piles, ulcers and fever sores. Excellent for salt rheum, eczema and ringworm.

No. 8C462 Price, box....18c
If by mail, postage extra, per box, 4 cents.

Refined Camphor.

(GUM CAMPHOR). We carry only the best and purest refined camphor, imported direct from Kobe, Japan, and **guarantee it to be the** highest grade of camphor obtainable, both for domestic and medicinal purposes.

No. 8C464 Price, 1-ounce cakes...........8c
No. 8C465 Price, 1-pound packages.....79c

Boric Acid—Pure.

(BORACIC ACID).

Guaranteed highest purity powder—a popular, valuable and aseptic healing dressing and protective for cuts, wounds, ulcers, sores, bruises and all inflamed and irritated surfaces, a healing and soothing application for chafed and harsh dry or rough skin. Absorbs the odor of perspiration and renders antiseptic and agreeably smelling all diseased parts to which it may be applied. A can of boracic acid should be in every well regulated home. It will come in handy and can be used in many cases with great advantage and excellent results.

No. 8C468 Price, 1-pound air-tight containers 23c

Pure Alcohol.

94 PER CENT, or 188 PROOF.

Guaranteed absolutely pure and full strength; distilled from the finest selected grain and recommended for every purpose for which pure grain alcohol is required. Our pure alcohol is undiluted, of full strength and of the highest quality.

No. 8C472 Price, per pt. bottle..$0.40
No. 8C473 Price, per qt. bottle.. .75
No. 8C474 Price, per gallon, can inclusive........................2.95

Wood Alcohol.

95 PER CENT.

Guaranteed full strength. Wood alcohol is also known as wood spirit and wood naptha. It is used for burning in alcohol stoves and lamps and by painters and others for cutting and dissolving shellac, paint and varnish. It is poisonous if taken internally, but perfectly harmless if used for mechanical purposes and considerably cheaper than grain alcohol.

No. 8C476 Price, per pt. bottle..$0.18
No. 8C477 Price, per qt. bottle.. .30
No. 8C478 Price, per gal., can inclusive.........................1.10

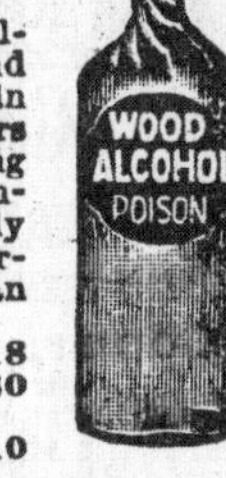

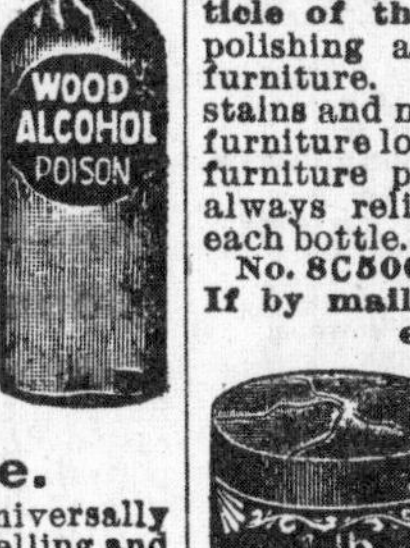

Tincture Iodine.

For external use only. Universally recommended for reducing swelling and inflammation, resulting from sprains and bruises, also highly endorsed by physicians for the treatment of goitre and erysipelas. Always apply by painting the affected parts with a camel's hair brush.

No. 8C480 Price, 2-oz. bottles....12c
No. 8C481 Price, 4-oz. bottles....20c
Not mailable.

Chloroform Liniment.

Highly recommended and always used by the old school physician for the external home treatment of swelling joints, neuralgia, rheumatism, lumbago, sprains and bruises. Chloroform liniment is one of the best liniments for removing inflammation quickly and is recognized as one of the most reliable counter irritants, and possesses great merit. Complete directions furnished with each bottle.

No. 8C484 Price, 2-oz. bottle......12c
No. 8C485 Price, 4-oz. bottle......20c

If by mail, postage and mailing tube extra, 16 cents.

Liquid Hickory Smoke.

FOR SMOKING AND CURING MEAT AND FISH In a simple and inexpensive manner.

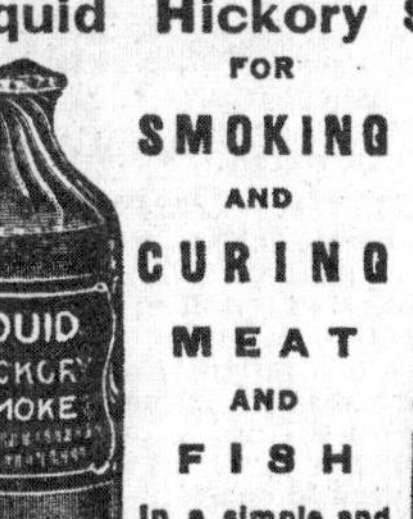

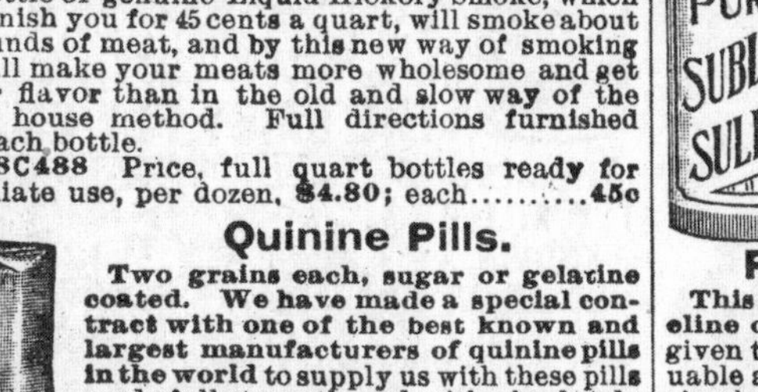

Our genuine Liquified Hickory Smoke is not only the most perfect, reliable and absolutely harmless modern vegetable liquid meat smoker, but it imparts a true and delicious hickory smoke flavor to meats, dried beef, sausages, fish and game, which renders them at the same time wholesome and palatable. Liquid Hickory Smoke is not only a meat smoker, but a meat preserver. By using Liquid Hickory Smoke you can keep your meat solid and sweet for any length of time. Liquid Hickory Smoke will accomplish the work of weeks of smoke-house smoking in a few minutes. No more smoke-houses needed. A brush and a bottle of Liquid Hickory Smoke will do it better and quicker and the cost is almost nothing. One bottle of genuine Liquid Hickory Smoke, which we furnish you for 45 cents a quart, will smoke about 300 pounds of meat, and by this new way of smoking you will make your meats more wholesome and get a finer flavor than in the old and slow way of the smoke house method. Full directions furnished with each bottle.

No. 8C488 Price, full quart bottles ready for immediate use, per dozen, $4.80; each..........45c

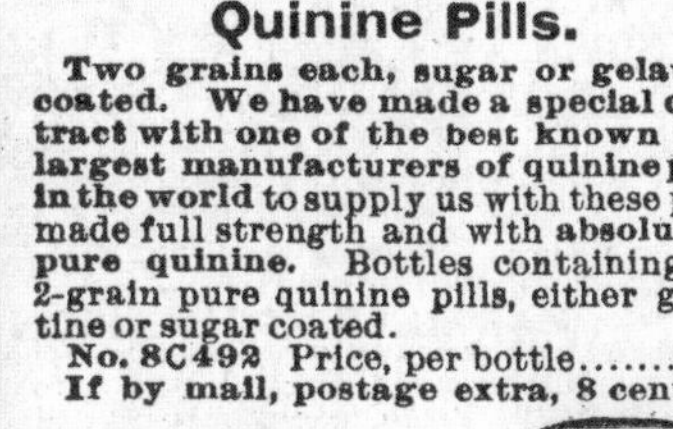

Quinine Pills.

Two grains each, sugar or gelatine coated. We have made a special contract with one of the best known and largest manufacturers of quinine pills in the world to supply us with these pills made full strength and with absolutely pure quinine. Bottles containing 100 2-grain pure quinine pills, either gelatine or sugar coated.

No. 8C492 Price, per bottle.......18c
If by mail, postage extra, 8 cents.

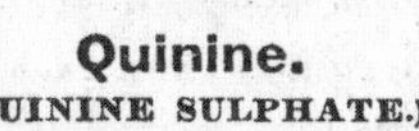

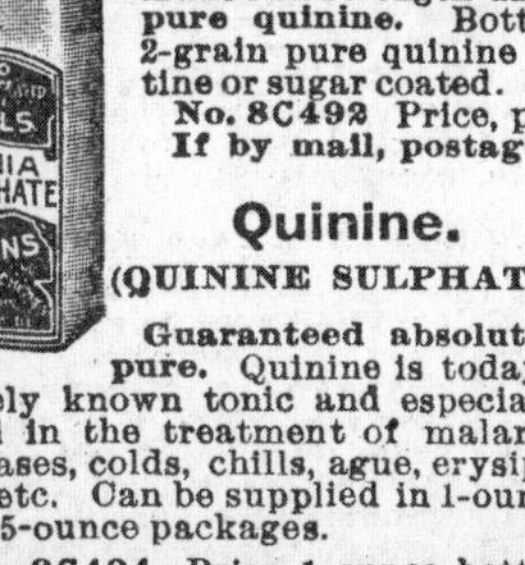

Quinine.

(QUININE SULPHATE.)

Guaranteed absolutely pure. Quinine is today a widely known tonic and especially used in the treatment of malarial diseases, colds, chills, ague, erysipelas, etc. Can be supplied in 1-ounce and 5-ounce packages.

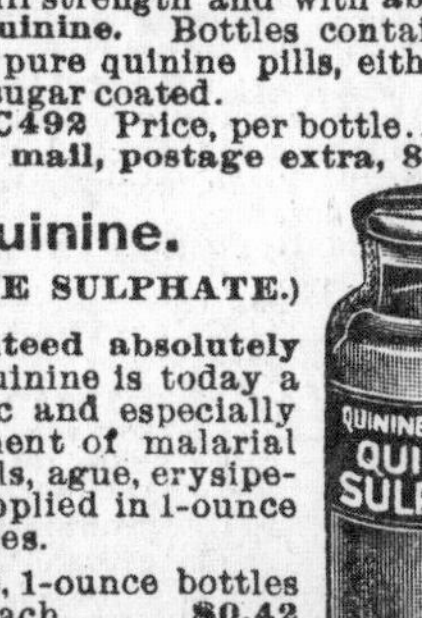

No. 8C494 Price, 1-ounce bottles or screw cap tins, each.........$0.42
No. 8C496 Price, 5-ounce screw cap tins, each..................2.00

Superfine Furniture Polish.

A handy and valuable household article of the greatest perfection for polishing and restoring all kinds of furniture. Quickly removes scratches, stains and marks of wear and makes the furniture look as good as new. Superfine furniture polish is easily applied and always reliable. Full directions with each bottle.

No. 8C500 Price, per bottle.......14c
If by mail, postage and mailing tube extra, 16 cents.

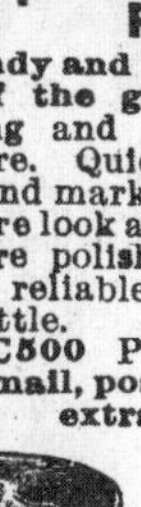

Milk Sugar—Pure.

(SUGAR OF MILK.)

Especially recommended for making modified milk as a food for infants. Practically indispensable in all cases where babies are brought up by the bottle. It is free from cane sugar, glucose, acids and other substances which might be disturbing or injurious. Full directions for infant feeding on each package. Furnished in airtight one-pound packages.

No. 8C502 Price, per 1-pound package.........................25c

Seidlitz Powders.

We always make our Seidlitz Powders fresh when we receive the order for them. Most of the powders bought in stores are worthless from being kept too long; they lose their strength. **We guarantee all Seidlitz Powders we send out to be made from pure materials and to be full strength. Put up in tin boxes, containing in each 10 blue and 10 white papers.**

No. 8C504 Price, per box......................16c
If by mail, postage extra, per box, 5 cents.

Epsom Salts.

These salts lose their strength when kept long in open drawers and boxes, as is the custom in most retail stores. **We furnish this salt always fresh and its valuable qualities unimpaired by exposure to the atmosphere.**

No. 8C506 Price, freshly put up to order, per 1-pound package...4c
Not profitable to mail.

Rochelle Salts.

When pure this salt is almost tasteless. We are particular to get it straight from the manufacturer and know that it is of pure quality.

No. 8C508 Price, ¼-pound package 13c
Price, ½-pound package......18c
Price, 1-pound package.......34c

Our Mexican Gulf Sea Salt.

For taking a genuine ocean bath at home. We have found this salt remarkable for strengthening the nerves and muscles. Toughens the skin, makes it clear and healthy, renders it impervious to skin troubles, and we can **highly recommend it in the physical development of both adults and children. We put it up.**

No. 8C510 Price, 5-pound bag, 15c
Price, 10-pound bag............25c

Sublimed Sulphur.

Can be used either internally or externally. The finest flowers of sulphur, prepared especially for medicinal use and packed by our chemist.

No. 8C512 Price, 1-pound pkg..5c

Petroleum Jelly.

This is another name for pure vaseline or cosmoline, and other titles given to it. It is one of the most valuable and also the most harmless and simple articles to have at hand in cases of **bruises, cuts, burns, chaps, roughness of the skin, etc.** For convenience, we put it in 2-oz. screw top glass jars.

No. 8C514 Price, 2-ounce glass jars.... ....4c
Price, 1-pound cans..........................16c
If by mail, postage extra, each, small, 8 cents; large, 20 cents.

Carbolized Petroleum Jelly.

This is the same as the above, with the addition of pure carbolic acid, which increases to a great extent its powers of healing.

No. 8C516 Price, per 2-ounce bottle.........8c
Price, 1-pound cans............................25c
If by mail, postage extra, each, small, 8 cents; large, 20 cents.

Don't forget postage when ordering goods to be sent by mail.

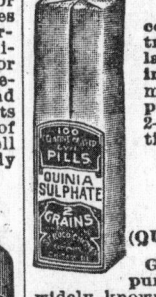

DYES

The Finest Household Colors in the World are the Seroco Stainless Dyes.

LIST OF COLORS WE FURNISH

Turkey Red	Olive Green
Cardinal	Myrtle Green
Wine	Emerald Green
Brown	Light Green
Seal Brown	Royal Purple
Cerise	Heliotrope
Navy Blue Old Rose	Drab
Royal Blue Pink	Yellow
Pale Blue Lemon	Salmon
Tan Tan also makes ecru	Black

There are any number of household dyes on the market, but if you will try them all you will find that the Seroco Dyes are the very best. These dyes are made in our own laboratory and are guaranteed by us. They are so simple a child can use them. Will not stain the hands or the vessel in which they are used. Our Seroco Dyes will dye cotton, silk and wool in the same bath. They wash as well as dye and are the only absolutely antiseptic dyes on the market. They dye a beautiful fast, permanent and fadeless color. Many dollars can be saved by using them. Old, worn and faded dresses and ribbons, feathers, etc., made to look new and fresh again. We can send any color or shade you desire. Come put up in envelopes each containing a separate dye, **with full directions** for use. Send sample that you want matched or state the color you wish.

No. 8C518 Price, each.......8c
Postage extra, each, 2 cents.

We can furnish cheaper dyes to compete with the cheap dyes that are universally sold. We recommend our Seroco Dyes.

No. 8C520 Angel Dainty Dyes, all colors. Price, each.... ......6c
Postage extra, each, 2 cents.

Cleanit Liquid.

The only preparation that removes fresh paint, grease, oils, syrup, beer or wine stains from carpets, dress goods, silks and all kinds of clothing, etc., without injury to the finest fabric. It leaves the goods soft and clean, free from marks or creases. It also removes all gloss or shine caused by wear, restoring the natural luster. A preparation that is indispensable in every household.

No. 8C525 Price, 4-ounce bottle..........15c
Price, 8-ounce bottle..........25c
Price, 16-ounce bottle..........40c
Unmailable on account of weight.

China Cement.

Sears, Roebuck & Co.'s China Cement. The best cement for mending glass, china, ivory, shell, marble, fur, terra cotta, meerchaum, porcelain, plaster of paris, wool, alabaster and leather. Does the work well and quickly.

No. 8C528 Price, per bottle......... 9c
If by mail, postage and tube extra, 8c.

Liquid Skin.

A newly invented preparation to be used for all cuts, bruises and abrasions. Acts instantaneously. Better, cheaper and quicker than any other antiseptic bandage, court plaster or other method usually applied for stopping loss of blood in any open, bleeding wound. Can be applied in a few seconds, forming at once a new skin over the cut, bruise or abrasion, protecting the wound from all foreign matter and healing it without a moment's delay or danger. If promptly applied it will positively prevent forming of pus or the setting in of blood poison. No person should be without this valuable yet inexpensive remedy. It may save your life or that of your friends most any day. Put up neatly in small vials, so it can be carried in the vest pocket, ready for immediate use.

No. 8C530 Liquid Skin, vest pocket size only. Price, per dozen, **$1.00**; each..................10c

Sulphur Candles.

For fumigating infected rooms and clothing in times of cholera, diphtheria, typhoid and scarlet fevers and all contagious diseases. The most powerful disinfectant known. Kills all insects. **Destroys noxious vapors.** When you wish to fumigate with sulphur, use these; no danger of fire, easily lighted, burns steady, a most convenient article to have.

No. 8C532 Price, per candle. ..8c
If by mail, postage extra, 5 cents.

Lightning Carpet Cleaner

For cleaning and whitening carpets and rugs. Will quickly clean the carpet, restore its color, remove grease spots and at the same time acts as a powerful, invaluable disinfectant and germicide. It not only leaves a freshness upon the carpet with but little work, but will also destroy disease germs very effectively without the slightest injury to the carpet or rug. Furnished in ½-pound boxes with full directions, sufficient for cleaning two small or one extremely large carpet.

No. 8C534 Price, per box..........................23c

Magic Kid Glove Cleaner.

A great money saver. Will make kid gloves almost like new. Requires but little work and always gives satisfactory results. Put up in paste form and tin boxes so it can easily be used and always handy.

No. 8C535 Price........14c

Copper, Brass and Silver Polish.

Put up in paste form. No dust, no dirt, no grit, but a reliable and inexpensive preparation for cleaning and polishing copper, brass and silver. A necessity to every particular housekeeper. Put up convenient for use in 1 and 2-ounce tin boxes.

No. 8C537 Price, per 1 oz...(Postage extra, 3c)...15c
No. 8C538 Price, per 2 oz...(Postage extra, 5c)...25c

Spots and Stain Eradicator.
(NON-INFLAMMABLE.)

An absolute necessity for the careful housekeeper. The most efficient and safest liquid preparation for the prompt removal of spots and stains from clothing, carpets, linen, woolens and all kinds of fabrics. Will remove stains caused by iodine, paint, iron rust, fruit, etc. It is colorless, odorless and non-inflammable. Guaranteed to do the work quickly and thoroughly. Complete directions with each bottle.

No. 8C540 Spots and Stain Eradicator, 2-ounce bottles, per dozen, **$1.20**; each..........12c
If by mail, postage extra, 12 cents.

Flake Tar Moth Destroyer.

A chemically pure product of coal tar for the preservation of furs and clothing, etc., from moths. It will not injure the most delicate fabrics and is a certain preventive of moth attacks which are so destructive to winter clothing, woolen goods especially.

No. 8C542 Price, 1-pound package............12c
If by mail, postage extra, 18 cents.

Insect Powder Gun.

For using Insect Powder No. 8C562.

No. 8C544 Price.......................................5c
If by mail, postage extra, 7 cents.

Large or Jumbo Powder Gun, holds ¼-pound of powder, button and spout screw off. Large opening for filling.

No. 8C545 Price.. ....16c
Postage extra, 6 cents.

Bed Bug and Roach Exterminator.

This preparation is in liquid form and furnished in a patent can with large spout, which makes its application easy and sure to reach the smallest opening. Golden Liquid will not only exterminate every bed bug and roach, but rid a room or building from these little pests entirely. Full descriptions with each can.

No. 8C548 Golden Liquid. ½ pint can. Price.20c
No. 8C550 Golden Liquid. One gallon.
Price............(Not mailable).............$1.55

Strangle Food.

The surest and quickest death to bugs. It instantly strangles. Kills cockroaches, bedbugs, croton bugs, ants, moths, fleas, lice and all other vermin. Harmless to man, beast or bird.

No. 8C551 Price, per can.......22c
If by mail, postage extra, 8 cents.

THE DAISY FLY KILLER.

THE BEST
FLY KILLER
KNOWN.
IT IS A
BEAUTY.

Will not injury or soil anything. Will effectually kill flies in a room.

HARMLESS TO PERSONS.

Will last all the season. It is cheaper than fly paper. Clean, neat, ornamental. Try it.

No. 8C556 Price, each, only.......................**12c**
Price, per dozen..............................$1.40
If by mail, postage extra, each, 9 cents.

Rat Killer.

The Great Vermin Destroyer.

The most efficient poison for rats, mice, cockroaches, ants, flies, squirrels, crows, bed bugs, and all kinds of troublesome vermin. This is a sure destroyer. Rats and mice do not die in the house after eating it, but go outside for air and water.

No. 8C559 Price, per box...(Unmailable)... 11c

Insect Powder.

A true Dalmatian Insect Powder, warranted free from all adulterations. **Fresh and strong.** Sure death to **bed bugs, croton bugs, potato bugs, cockroaches, fleas, lice, moths, flies, ants and all insects.** This article is very much subject to adulteration. **Buy** from us and get it pure.

No. 8C562 Price, put up in ¼-pound tin boxes, 10c; 1-pound boxes..30c
Unmailable.

NURSERY DEPARTMENT.

Baby Scales.

No. 49C2998 Spring Baby Scales. Capacity, 15 pounds. For the small sum of only 35 cents we furnish the well known baby scale, which will last a lifetime. This scale offers the means to ascertain and watch the weight, improvement and actual development of the little baby in a very convenient manner.

35c

Price..................35c
If by mail, postage extra, 4 cents.

Borated Talcum Baby Powder.

For the toilet and nursery. Preserves, softens and whitens the skin. For chafing it is an excellent powder. Absorbs moisture and keeps the skin cool and soft. Nicely perfumed and put up in handsomely decorated metal boxes, with sprinkler top.

No. 8C564 Price, per box..............8c
If by mail, postage extra, 4 cents.

No. 8C566 Excelsior Borated and Perfumed Talcum Powder. Tin boxes. Price, per box..........................5c
If by mail, postage extra, 4 cents.

Verona Violette and Crushed Rose

Eastman's Celebrated Antiseptic Talcum Powder. We furnish you the celebrated Eastman's antiseptic talcum powder, Verona Violette and Crushed Rose, in 4-ounce glass jars with perforated, nickel plated screw cap. The finest talcum powder on the market, thoroughly borated and delicately perfumed. This talcum powder is absolutely antiseptic, and beyond question the acme of perfection.

No. 8C568 Verona Violet, 4-ounce glass jar, screw cap. Price.......12c
No. 8C569 Crushed Rose. Price.12c
Not mailable.

Favorite Foot Powder.

This powder is particularly beneficial to those inclined to perspiration. For destroying bad odors and giving comfort to sore feet nothing like it has hitherto been put on the market. A little shaken in the shoes keeps the feet comfortable at all times.

No. 8C572 Price, per box.. .. ..12c
If by mail, postage extra, 3 cents.

Baby Soothing Syrup.

A blessing to parents, harmless and effectual in soothing and quieting children of any age. We guarantee it to contain no opium or morphine; prepared from simple herbs and has a wonderful effect in soothing and quieting a child who may be cross, no matter from what reason. A remedy for colic, excellent during teething time.

No. 8C574 Price, per bottle..................15c
If by mail, postage and tube extra, 12 cents.

Rubber Teething Rings.

No. 8C576 Rubber Teething Rings, seamless, full size, best white rubber. Price...............3c
No. 8C577 Rubber Teething Rings, full size, seamless, best black rubber. Price..............4c
No. 8C580 Bone Teething Ring, 1¾ inches, nicely finished. Price...............................4c

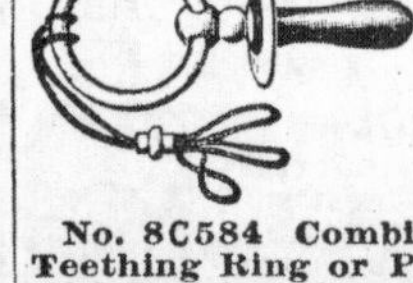

No. 8C582 New Style Teething Ring or Pacifier. The new style teething ring or pacifier is a bone ring and bone guard with a soft rubber nipple, having a silk cord for attaching to the baby's arm so the ring cannot be lost. Price..............8c

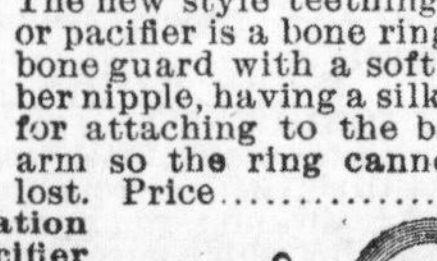

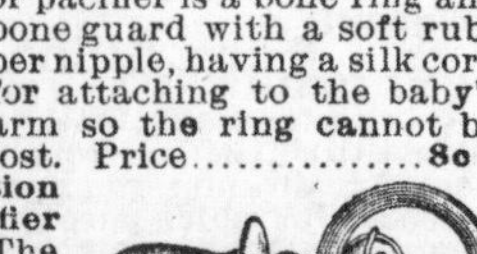

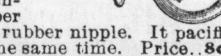

No. 8C584 Combination Teething Ring or Pacifier with Bell Attachment. The combination teething ring or pacifier with bell attachment consists of a rubber ring, bone guard and soft rubber nipple. It pacifies and amuses the baby at the same time. Price..8c
If by mail, postage extra, 2 cents.

Rubber Nipples.

Rubber Nipples for tube fittings. White, black or maroon.
No. 8C588 Price, each .2c
Per dozen..............20c

Rubber Nipples to fit over bottle, white, black or maroon.
No. 8C590 Price, each, 3c
Per dozen..............25c

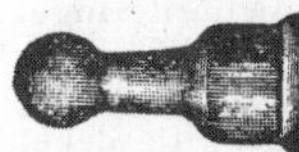

Health Nipples. Made from the finest Para rubber, is constructed so that the infant can obtain a strong hold and renders nursing easy.
No. 8C592 Per dozen, 45c; each 4c

Mizpah Valve Nipple. Making nursing easy. Allows the food to flow easily. Prevents colic.

No. 8C594 Price, per dozen, 45c; each........4c
If by mail, postage on rubber nipples extra, per dozen, 6c; each, 1c

Nursing Flasks.

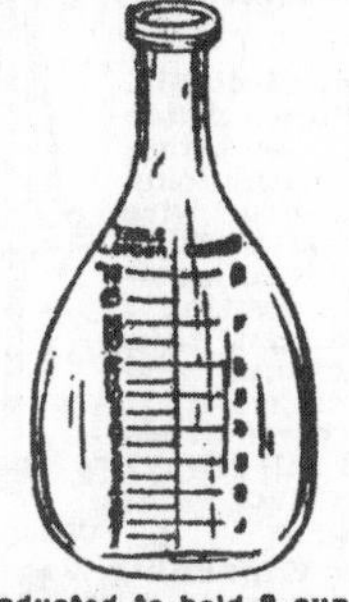

Graduated, to hold 8 ounces, oval shape, straight with sloping sides. No corners, therefore easy to clean. Weight, 14 ounces
No. 8C596 Price........4c

S., R. & Co.'s Complete Nurser.

S., R. & Co.'s Nurser No. 1. Fitted with white, black or maroon fittings, Complete with two brushes in each box. Weight, 16 ounces.
No. 8C603 Price ... 14c

Graduated Nursing Bottle.

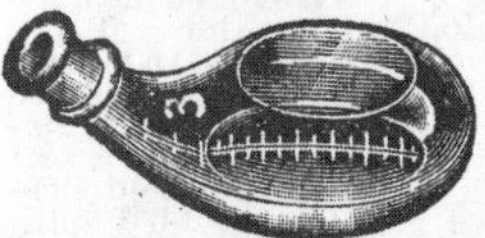

No. 8C598 Graduated Nursing Bottle, bent neck for tube fittings. Price..............5c
If by mail, postage extra 14c.

Glass Nipple Shields.

Glass Nipple Shield with white rubber nipple and bone guard.
No. 8C605 Price......8c
If by mail, postage extra, 5c

Nursing Bottles.

Nursing Bottles. Burr patent, white rubber fittings.
No. 8C600 Price.......8c
If by mail, postage extra 15c.

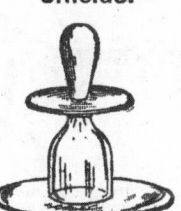

Glass Nipple Shield with long flexible rubber tube, mouth guard and rubber nipple. Weight, 8 ounces.
No. 8C607 Price...10c

Nursing Bottle Fittings.

Best quality, all complete, in white, black or maroon.
No. 8C610 Price..............................4c

English Breast Pump.

English Breast Pump, with white rubber bulb. One in box.
No. 8C614 Price..............15c
If by mail, postage extra, 8 cents.

Toilet Powder Puffs.

No. 8C616 For ladies' and infants' use. Satin tops, ivory handle.
Price..15c
If by mail, postage extra, 2 cents.

Puff Boxes.

Celluloid, in ivory, pink or blue. Very light and handsome.
No. 8C618 Price.............40c

White metal, handsome covers, ornamental tops.
No. 8C620 Price...........22c
If by mail, postage extra, 8 cents.

Chamois Skin.

Chamois skins are used as follows: Ladies use them for toilet purposes, for cleaning glass, woodwork of all kinds, carriages, silverware, or any metal, lining pockets and for chest protectors.

Our Very Fine Toilet Chamois, for applying powder, etc., to the face. Size, about 5x6 inches.
No. 8C638 Price..5c

Style	A	B	C
Size, inches	6½x8¼	9x11	11x13½
Price	5c	9c	15c
Style	D	E	F
Size, inches	15x20	26x23	28x32
Price	28c	50c	75c

Note—If a chamois about size 11x13½ inches is wanted, order No. 8C738 Style C.

Sponges.

Note Our Special Prices.

No. 8C642 Very fine, "small eye" Sponge. For surgical and nursery use. Price..............6c
No. 8C644 Small Toilet Sponge, for toilet use or can be used in shaving. Price..............6c
No. 8C646 Medium size Sheep's Wool Sponge, tough and durable. Price..............12c
No. 8C648 Large Toilet Sponge, suitable for the bath. Price..............18c
No. 8C650 Large Size Sheep's Wool Sponge. A very durable sponge. Price..............22c
No. 8C652 Cleaning Sponge. When wet they are about 15 to 24 inches in circumference. Suitable for carriage, woodwork, etc. Price..............10c
No. 8C654 Ladies' Silk Sponge, very fine, regular form. Price..............20c
No. 8C656 Extra fine, small medium; ladies' cup shaped silk sponge. Price..............35c
No. 8C658 Superfine, ladies' large cup shaped sponge, specially selected forms and shapes. Price..............50c

Bleached Mediterranean Sponges, for toilet and bath.
No. 8C660 Small. Price..............8c
No. 8C662 Medium. Price..............15c
No. 8C664 Large. Price..............25c
No. 8C666 Extra large bath sponge. Price.....40c

Unbleached Sheep's Wool Sponges. A choice grade of fine, soft sponges; strong and durable, for either bathing purposes or cleaning fine carriages.
No. 8C668 Medium. Price..............40c
No. 8C670 Large, bleached. Price..............60c

Cleaning Sponges. Suitable for cleaning buggies, woodwork, walls, etc. A strong, natural, unbleached sponge.
No. 8C672 Small. Price..............20c
No. 8C674 Large. Price..............35c

Patent India Rubber Bath Sponges.

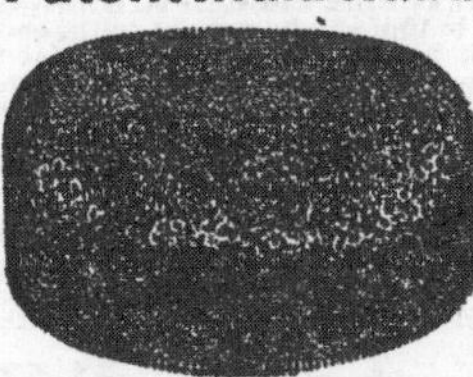

The Finest, Most Durable Bath Sponge in existence. Made of pure rubber, will take water like an ordinary sponge and gives a gentle friction to the skin, therefore being justly designated the most perfect toilet sponge ever made. It makes a fine lather when used with soap. It is hygienic and very durable; will last for years.

We offer these sponges at nearly one-half the prices at which they are sold elsewhere, and guarantee them to be the genuine patented article.
No. 8C676 Small. Price..............34c
No. 8C678 Medium. Price..............48c
No. 8C680 Large. Price..............68c
If by mail, postage extra, 4 cents.

Combination Sponge Bag.

Made of a high grade rubber lined satin, escalloped top, flap trimmed with red silk and fitted with patent button clasps. One side pocket for tooth brush, extra side pocket for comb, extra center pocket for brushes, extra pocket for soap holder. Size, 9x10 inches. A handsome article for bath or wash room equipment, and very handy when traveling.
No. 8C682 Combination Sponge Bag. Each..44c
If by mail, postage extra, 4 cents.

Bath Thermometer.

No. 49C1992 Bath Thermometer, in wood frame.
Price.........(Postage extra, 4 cents).......17c

Japanese Loofah Flesh Brush.

The Loofah is the fibrous part of a gourd that grows in the south of Japan. Their use gives a healthy glow to the body, removes all accumulations from the pores of the skin, increases the circulation of the blood, and leaves a pleasant sensation.

DIRECTIONS—The loofah may be used as a sponge just as it is, or to make it a trifle more handy, soak in water until it expands full size; cut lengthwise and remove the inner substance so that the loofah opens out like a cloth.
No. 8C685 Price, large size..............8c
If by mail, postage extra, 3 cents.

Loofah Bath Mitten.

Loofah front, with Turkish toweling back. The best bath mitten in the market.
No. 8C687 Price......15c
If by mail, postage extra, 2 cents.

Bath, Spray and Friction Brush Combined.

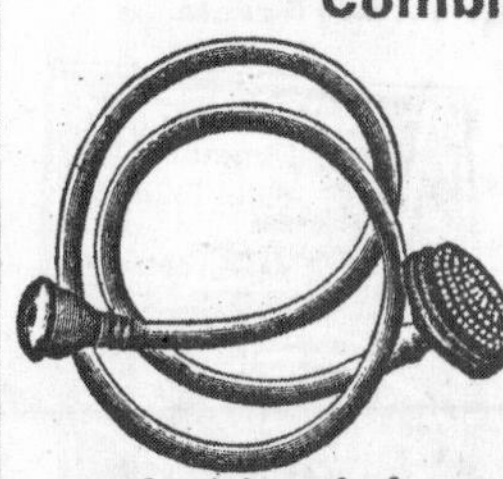

This combination of bath spray, friction and shampooing brush is one of the few articles that fills a long felt want. The Bath, Spray and Friction Brush is the latest improved combination brush for spraying and shampooing, doing this work in a perfect manner. It is used and recommended by every physician who has seen it and is made part of a bath room equipment in the leading hospitals. Of simple construction, it can be attached to any standard size bath tub or wash room faucet.
No. 49C89 Bath, Spray and Friction Brush.
Price (If by mail, postage extra, 24 cents).$1.55

Effervescing Bath Tablets.

ANTISEPTIC, PERFUMED.

The most perfect and delightful bath tablets made, which, owing to their antiseptic qualities and pleasant perfume, add value and pleasure to your bath, by making it more agreeable and refreshing, neutralizing germs and impurities in the water, toning and invigorating the system like an ocean bath, at the same time giving a delightful perfume to the body. Sold in original bottles only, containing 25 tablets, for 18 cents, a little more than ¾ cent for each bath.
No. 8C689 Effervescing Tablets, for the bath, 25 in bottle. Price..............18c
If by mail, postage extra, 12 cents.

Nursery Rubber Sheeting.

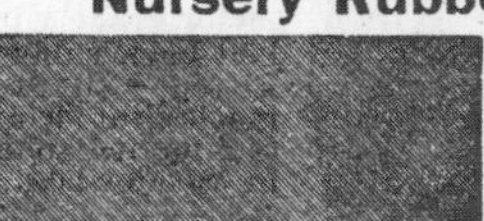

No. 8C690 White Rubber Sheeting. Heavy weight.

Width, inches	Price, per yard
27	35c
36	48c
45	62c
54	75c

No. 8C691 Tan Rubber Sheeting, soft as silk, very light in weight, strong and absolutely waterproof. For hospital and nursery use, also for making bathing caps, diapers, etc. 36 inches wide.
Price, per yard..............65c

Rubber Tubing

No. 8C692 Smooth or corrugated, white, for bulb and fountain syringes.
Price, per foot, ¼-inch..............5c
No. 8C693 White, black or maroon rubber tubing for feeding bottles. Price, per foot..........3c
No. 8C694 Glass tubes for nursing bottle fittings. Price, per dozen..............10c

The Rochester Milk Sterilizer.

A very simple and inexpensive apparatus that can be used either for steam or hot water sterilizing. It consists of a nicely finished tin sterilizing vessel with convenient handles and cover. A rack, holding eight graduated bottles and a brush for cleaning. Beads around the sterilizing chamber mark points to which water should be filled when in use.
No. 49C8097 Complete.
Price..............$1.70

The Arnold Milk Sterilizer and Pasteurizer.

The latest and most approved mode of sterilizing milk for infants. Prescribed by prominent physicians. Made of heavy tin, copper bottom, with rack for bottles, also brush for cleaning same.
No. 49C8095 Seven-bottle outfit. Price...$2.70

RUBBER GOODS.

Syringes, Etc.

The S., R. & Co.'s Gem Fountain Syringe, made from good quality rubber, with hard rubber fittings, three hard rubber pipes, including large irrigating pipe, in a neat box, long rubber tubing with patent shut off.

No. 8C753 2 quarts. Price......52c
No. 8C756 3 quarts, with three pipes. Price........62c
No. 8C759 4 quarts, with three pipes. Price..72c
If by mail, postage extra, 16 cents.

Reliable Fountain Syringe.

A Five-Pipe Syringe, including the infant, vaginal, rectal, irrigator and nasal pipes and fine heavy rubber reinforced seam ribbed bag. Patent shut off and strong tubing. All packed in fine wooden box.

No. 8C762 2 quarts. Price................$0.88
No. 8C765 3 quarts. Price.................97
No. 8C768 4 quarts. Price.................1.08
If by mail, postage extra, 21 cents.

Monarch Syringe.

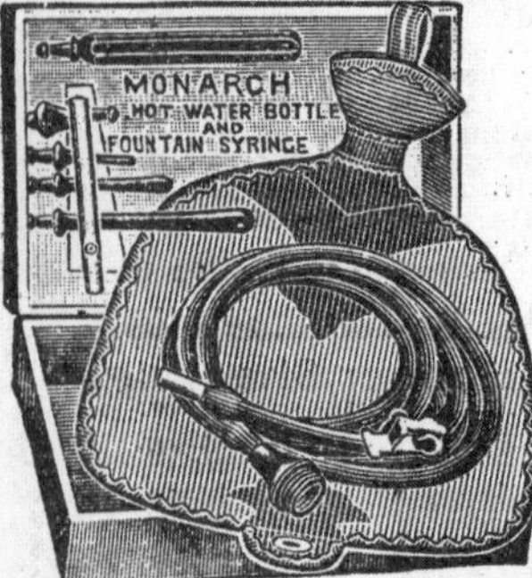

A Combination Syringe and Water Bottle, including hard rubber connections and infant, vaginal, rectal, irrigator and nasal pipes and six feet of pure rubber tubing and water bottle of very superior grade, ribbed back rubber. Fitted with automatic shut off attachment. Packed in wooden box.

No. 8C771 2 quarts. Price, complete.......$1.20
No. 8C774 3 quarts. Price, complete.......1.30
No. 8C777 4 quarts. Price, complete.......1.40
If by mail, postage extra, 28 cents.

Our Guaranteed Rapid Flow Perfection Fountain Syringe.

Rapid Flow Fountain Syringe, with flushing size rubber tubing, which admits of a rapid flow of water; made of extra quality white rubber, the simplest and best syringe made, hard rubber infant, rectal, irrigator and vaginal screw pipes, packed in handsome platform box, at half drug store prices.

No. 8C780 2 quarts. Price..................95c
No. 8C781 3 quarts. Price..................$1.05
No. 8C782 4 quarts. Price..................$1.15
If by mail, postage extra, 27 cents.

Acme Bulb Syringe.

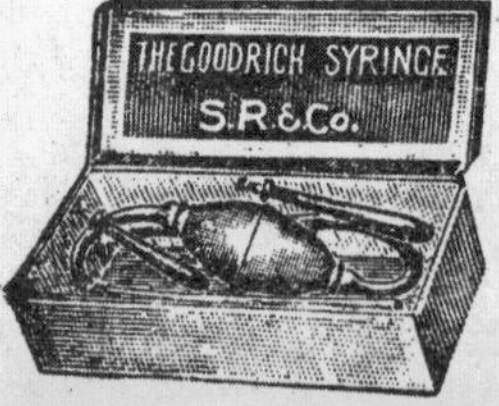

No. 8C783 S., R. & Co.'s Acme Bulb Syringe. Put up in nice pasteboard box. Good quality rubber, two hard rubber pipes. Drug store price, 50 cents for same quality. Our price..........25c
If by mail, postage extra, 10 cents.

Our 52-Cent Ideal Syringe.

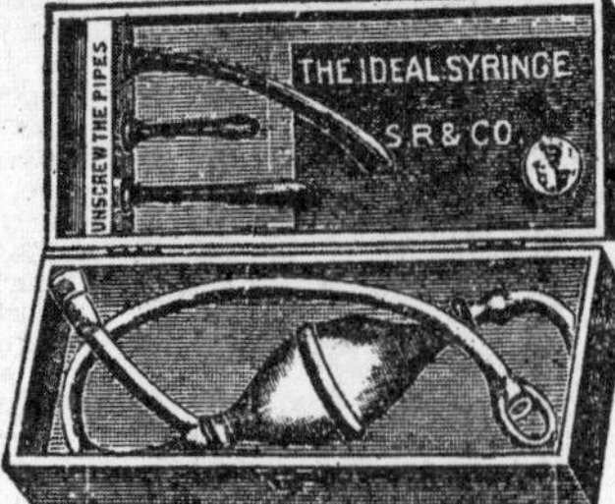

No. 8C786 The Celebrated Ideal Syringe, with three hard rubber pipes, put up in a neat wooden box. Druggists ask $1.00 for this syringe. Our price..........52c
If by mail, postage extra, 12 cents.

Ladies' Perfect Syringe.

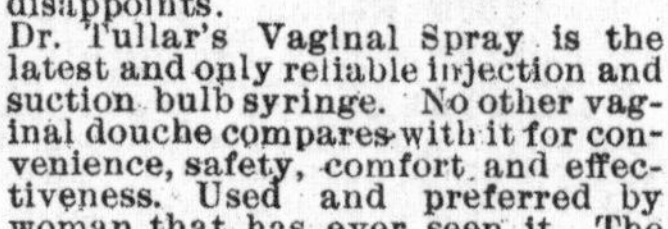

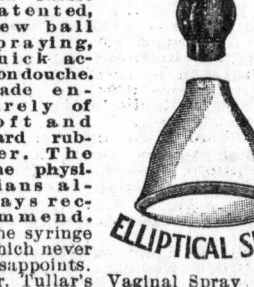

No. 8C792 The S., R. & Co.'s Ladies' Perfect Syringe, the best female syringe. Constructed on the latest scientific principles—injection and suction. Cleanses the vaginal passages thoroughly of all discharges. Recommended by the medical profession as one of the best and most efficient of any syringe ever made. Especially adapted for injections of hot water without soiling the clothing. Made of one piece of fine soft rubber. Price....55c
If by mail, postage extra, 17 cents.

Dr. Tullar's Vaginal Spray.

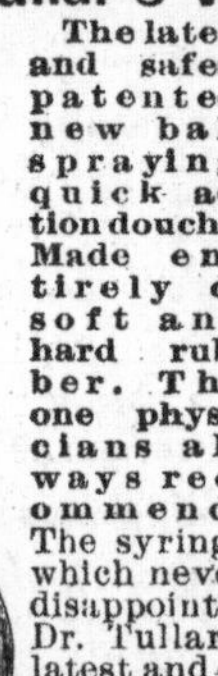

ELLIPTICAL SHIELD

The latest and safest patented, new ball spraying, quick action douche. Made entirely of soft and hard rubber. The one physicians always recommend. The syringe which never disappoints.

Dr. Tullar's Vaginal Spray is the latest and only reliable injection and suction bulb syringe. No other vaginal douche compares with it for convenience, safety, comfort and effectiveness. Used and preferred by every married woman that has ever seen it. The new patent ball tip discharges a hollow or cup-shaped spray. The only instant cleansing spray ever invented. This is Dr. Tullar's new invention. In this syringe the nozzle or discharge pipe is only ⅜ inch in diameter, and 5 inches long. It is made with a highly polished ball-shaped tip which allows its insertion under all conditions without the slightest discomfort or harm. It is long enough to allow a ball-spraying injection to come in immediate contact with, and remove all secretions and discharges that have become lodged in the folds about the neck or mouth of the womb. It is furnished with a soft rubber shield which is so shaped that it will fit correctly and properly and close the vaginal entrance, allowing the passage to be thoroughly flushed. It prevents spilling of the fluid and soiling of the clothes. The regular price of the Dr. Tullar's Ball-Spraying quick action douche everywhere is $3.00. We furnish the same to our customers with a positive guarantee that we supply the genuine Dr. Tullar's Ball-Spray Vaginal Spray and Douche for women at $1.57. Dr. Tullar's interesting folder, containing complete instructions and advice sent with every Dr. Tullar's syringe free.

No. 8C794 Price..................................$1.57
If by mail, postage extra, 20 cents.

Hard Rubber Stem Syringe.

For Females.

Superior to other syringes of this class and a most perfect syringe for a far reaching vaginal douche. Made with soft rubber bulb and hard rubber stem. Has no valves. Cannot corrode or get out of order. This is one of the most efficient syringes for cleansing the vagina, and is highly recommended by the best physicians to married ladies for that purpose, and for the treatment of any local disorder and female complaints.

No. 8C801 Price..................................56c
If by mail, postage extra, 10 cents.

Omega Syringe-Continuous Flow.

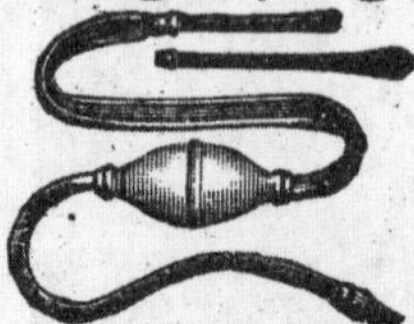

No. 8C804 Made of pure Para rubber. Omega Syringe No. 5, continuous flow, with hard rubber vaginal and rectal pipes. The valves are secured and cannot be lost. The continuous flow is the correct principle on which a syringe should be made. Packed in neat maroon box.
Price.........................36c
If by mail, postage extra, 10c.

No. 8C807 Omega Syringe No. 4, continuous flow. Hard rubber vaginal and rectal pipes, valves secured and cannot be lost. Omega No. 4, has a flattened outlet tube which is made by a specially invented process, that produces the continuous flow. Packed in neat octagonal box. Price..........62c
If by mail, postage extra, 15 cents.

No. 8C810 Omega Syringe No. 3, continuous flow. Has hard rubber vaginal, rectal and infant pipes, noiseless and non-corrosive sinker, patented screw joint socket, by which pipes are quickly attached without use of threads or washers. Packed in oval box. Price..................................82c
If by mail, postage extra, 10 cents.

Alpha Continuous Flowing Syringe.

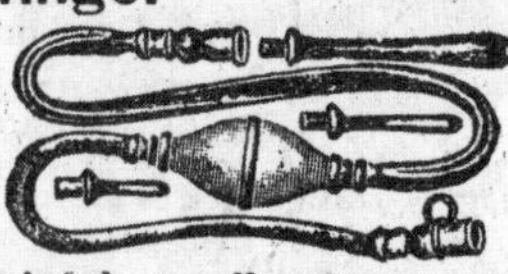

Made of best Para rubber. All intermittent syringes inject more or less air, which is invariably drawn back into the tube while the bulb is expanding and refilling; **this is often painful as well as dangerous. Not so with the Alpha Continuous Flowing Syringe.**

No. 8C811 Alpha E Syringe, continuous flow, hard rubber vaginal, rectal and infant pipes, noiseless and non-corrosive sinker, valves cannot be lost. Packed in handsome cloth covered case with nickel plated clasp. Price..............................$1.35
If by mail, postage extra, 15 cents.

No. 8C812 Alpha D Syringe, continuous flow, fitted with extra large valve chambers, hard rubber vaginal rectal, infant and nasal pipes and improved vaginal irrigating spray, noiseless and non-corrosive sinker. Packed in nice cloth covered case. Price. (If by mail, postage extra, 15 cents)..$1.65

Dr. Thiebaud's Expanding Vaginal Bath Speculum and Douche.

Expanded.

Collapsed

Can be used with either our Reliable, Monarch, Rapid Flow, Acme Bulb, Gem, Omega or Union Syringes. Is made with nickel plated, highly polished wire frame, with metal nozzle, and so constructed to make it collapsible. When placed in position it can be easily expanded, thus acting as a speculum and syringe at the same time. It will do what no other syringe will accomplish and will always insure a thoroughly successful douche.

No. 8C814 Dr. Thiebaud's Expanding Vaginal Bath Speculum and Douche. Price..........35c
If by mail, postage extra, 4 cents.

Bath Speculum and Douche.

No. 8C815 Expanding Return Flow Bath Speculum and Douche. This expanding bath speculum is fitted with latest improvements, a soft rubber shield preventing the spilling of fluid, also metal base with outlet tube and is recognized today as the most hygienic, convenient and always satisfactory appliance for vaginal irrigation. Can be used with fountain syringe or irrigator. Price, per dozen, $5.60; each..........55c
If by mail, postage extra, each, 5 cents.

Ear and Ulcer Syringe.

No. 8C817 Eye, Ear, Ulcer and Abscess Syringe. Capacity, 1 ounce; injection pipe; is made of soft and flexible rubber. Will not injure or pain the inflamed parts. Price..............16c
If by mail, postage extra, 3 cents.

Goodyear Infants' Syringe.

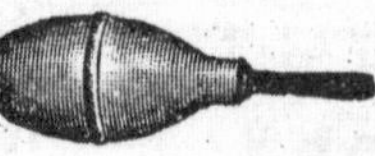

No. 8C818 Infants' Syringe. Holds one ounce and is made of a soft rubber bulb, with hard rubber infants' rectal pipe. Price............16c
If by mail, postage extra, 5 cents.

Hard Rubber Syringes.

Rectal Syringe, hard rubber, ring handle.
No. 8C820 2-ounce. Price.....................72c
If by mail, postage extra, 5 cents.
No. 8C821 3-ounce. Price.....................82c
If by mail, postage extra, 6 cents.

No. 8C823 Urethral or Male Hard Rubber Syringe. Capacity, ½ ounce. Price.......(If by mail, postage extra, 2c)....16c

No. 8C825 Vaginal Hard Rubber Syringe. Capacity, 2 ounces. Price.....................45c
If by mail, postage extra, 4 cents.

INCLUDE ALL THE GOODS YOU NEED IN ONE ORDER.

Look through our other departments and see if you cannot make up an order large enough to go by freight, which is the lowest cost of transportation. If you cannot use any other goods, perhaps some of your friends or neighbors would be glad to send in their order with yours and let all the goods come together by freight.

Flannel and Foulard Covered Water Bottles.

We have a complete line of the well known Faultless Water Bottles with beautiful French flannel and foulard covers, guaranteed to be the handsomest and best, and, therefore, the most satisfactory covered water bottles on the market, which we can furnish you at the following low prices. Our prices on the Faultless covered water bottles are less than what others charge for the common covered water bottles. Please compare these prices.

No. 8C827 Flannel Covered Water Bottles.	Price	No. 8C829 Foulard (silk) Covered Water Bottles.	Price
½ pint	$0.55	½ pint	$0.45
1 pint	.70	1 pint	.55
1 quart	.90	1 quart	.65
2 quarts	1.10	2 quarts	.80
3 quarts	1.35	3 quarts	.95
4 quarts	1.60	4 quarts	1.20

If by mail, postage extra, 20 cents.

Excelsior Hot Water Bottles.

Every one warranted; special prices.
No. 8C830 Price, 2 quarts.......60c
No. 8C832 Price, 3 quarts.......65c
No. 8C834 Price, 4 quarts.......70c
If by mail, postage extra, 2-quart, 11c; 3-quart, 13c; 4-quart, 15c.

Fleur de Lis Hyperion Standard Shape Water Bottles.

Handsome in appearance, of highest quality, with new patent stopper holder. Practically impossible to lose the holder. The latest improvement. Can be furnished in white, slate or Venetian color.
No. 8C837 Price, 2 quarts.......$0.90
No. 8C838 Price, 3 quarts....... 1.00
No. 8C839 Price, 4 quarts....... 1.10
If by mail, postage extra, 2-quart, 12c 3-quart, 14c; 4-quart, 16c.

Invalid Air Cushions.

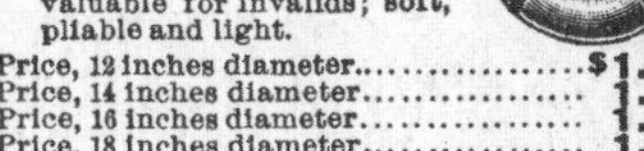

For use in the sick room, for bed sores, etc., it is invaluable for invalids; soft, pliable and light.
No. 8C843 Price, 12 inches diameter.......$1.00
No. 8C846 Price, 14 inches diameter....... 1.10
No. 8C849 Price, 16 inches diameter....... 1.25
No. 8C852 Price, 18 inches diameter....... 1.40
If by mail, postage extra, 20 cents.

Hospital Rubber Chair Cushions.

Strong and useful for persons engaged in sedentary occupations. Regular size, 17½ inches in diameter. Opening in center of cushion, when inflated, 6¼ inches.
No. 8C855 Price.......$2.50
If by mail postage extra, 35 cents.

Soft Rubber Bed Pans.

Round Bed Pans with outlet tube, soft rubber, substantial and convenient. Should be on hand in every well regulated household.
No. 8C858 Price.......$1.95
If by mail, postage extra, 35 cents.

Oval Bed Pans.

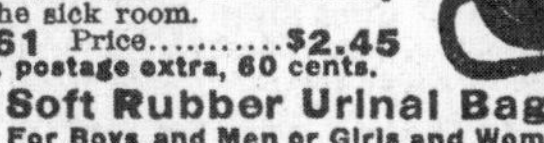

Oval Bed Pans, with outlet tube, soft rubber. The highest grade made. For ladies and men. A necessary article for the sick room.
No. 8C861 Price.......$2.45
If by mail, postage extra, 60 cents.

Soft Rubber Urinal Bags.

For Boys and Men or Girls and Women.

For bed wetting and general incontinence of urine. For male and female children and adults. For day and night use.

Soft Rubber Urinal Bag, the most comfortable pattern made, of the best material, for male, day or night use.
No. 8C943 Price.......$1.10
No. 8C946 Short, for boys....... .80
If by mail, postage extra, 12 cents.

Soft Rubber Urinal Bag, most improved pattern, made of the very best material, for female use.
No. 8C949 Price.......$1.10
If by mail, postage extra, 12 cents.

Pure Gum Soft Rubber Bag, for male. Large size, convenient pattern.
No. 8C952 Price.......90c
If by mail, postage extra, 12c.

No. 8C955 Soft Rubber Urinal Bag, improved French pattern; day and night use for females.
Price.......$1.85
If by mail, postage extra, 20c.

No. 8C958 Soft Rubber Urinal Bag, day and night use for male; improved French pattern, with waist belt ready to use without other attachments.
Price.......$1.95
If by mail, postage extra, 20c.

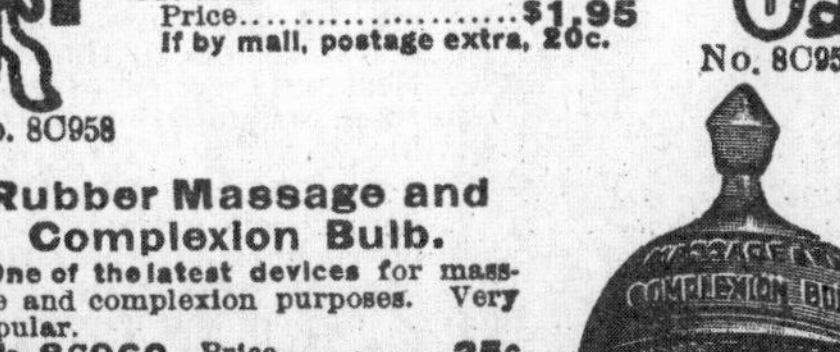

No. 8C955

No. 8C958

Rubber Massage and Complexion Bulb.

One of the latest devices for massage and complexion purposes. Very popular.
No. 8C960 Price.......25c
If by mail, postage extra, 2 cents.

The Automatic Cupper.

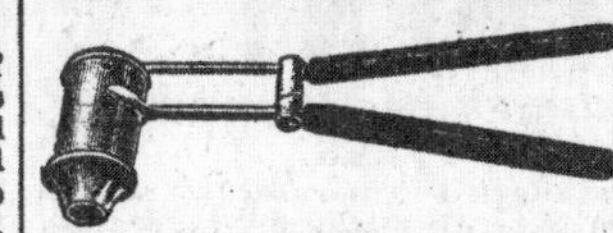

A new invention for massage purposes and for the removal of skin blemishes of every description.

The automatic cupper is simple in construction, but it is to-day the only instrument working on strictly scientific principles and which can be used for massaging the face and other parts of the body and also for the removal of blackheads, wrinkles and facial blemishes of any nature. When properly used, it will produce a healthy circulation in the most perfect and satisfactory manner. It will last a lifetime. Full instructions furnished with each instrument.
No. 8C962 Price.......$1.68
If by mail, postage extra, 10 cents.

The Improved Triplex Massage Roller for Self-Massage.

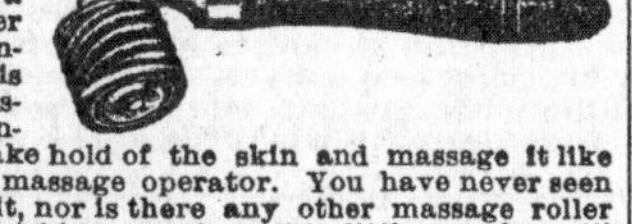

With the Triplex Massage Roller you can massage your face, neck and bust, in fact, any part of the body in a really scientific manner without the aid of another person. This is not an ordinary massage roller, but an instrument which will take hold of the skin and massage it like the hands of a skilled massage operator. You have never seen or used anything like it, nor is there any other massage roller that will accomplish quickly so much as this little wonder will do. It is a handsome instrument and works like a charm. Shipped in a neat box together with complete instructions.
No. 8C965 Improved Triplex Massage Roller.
Price.......75c
If by mail, postage extra, 10 cents.

Wrinkle Eradicator.

This convenient little article will remove wrinkles from around the eyes and nose and any part of the face. It invigorates the skin and keeps a perfect contour of the face.
No. 8C967 Price.......25c
If by mail, postage extra, 6 cents.

Magic Flesh Builder and Cupper.

An entirely new and scientific invention. Has no equal as a developer. Makes it possible for every lady to possess a well rounded, plump, beautiful figure. Rebuilds sunken tissues of the bust, neck, arms, and the only method which permanently removes wrinkles and makes the sunken cheeks smooth, full and developed.
No. 8C969 Price.......50c
If by mail, postage extra, 9 cents.

The Toilet Mask.

The Art of Beautifying the Complexion.

Every lady knows the value of a mask made of transparent rubber, acid cured, for the removal of freckles, liver spots, and other facial blemishes. As a bleacher it cannot be excelled, and will give any lady the fine, soft, velvety skin of a child. It is safe, simple, cleanly and effective for beautifying purposes, and never injures the most delicate complexion. Usually sold for $5.00.
No. 8C972 Price.......$1.55
If by mail, postage extra, 4 cents.

Seamless Para Gloves.

Seamless Para Gloves. By wearing them at night during sleep, you will obtain a hand as fair as an infant's, without the least injury. They will remove wrinkles, callouses, tan, sallowness, freckles and discolorations as if by magic. With care they will last for years. Made of the pure transparent rubber, same as face mask. State size when you order.
No. 8C974 Price, per pair.......95c
If by mail, postage extra, 6 cents.

Noparallel Household Rubber Gloves.

Noparallel Gloves keep the hands soft and white and are unequaled for ladies' use in doing housework. They are strong, soft and pliable, and can be worn without the slightest inconvenience in doing work of the most delicate nature. Every pair fully guaranteed. Order a half size to one size larger than your kid glove number.
No. 8C976 Price, per pair.......78c
If by mail, postage extra, 3 cents.

Rubber Gloves.

No. 8C978 Ladies and Men's Short Rubber Gloves. Colors, tan or black.
Ladies' sizes, 7, 8, 9. Price, per pair..75c
Men's sizes, 10, 11. Price, per pair....95c
If by mail, postage extra, 12 cents.

No. 8C980 Ladies' and Men's Gauntlet Rubber Gloves. Black and tan. Sizes, 7, 8, 9. Per pair..$1.05
Sizes, 10 and 11. Per pair.... 1.25
If by mail, postage extra, 15 cents.
Always order a size larger in rubber gloves.

Men's Heavy Rubber Mittens.

No. 8C982 Men's Heavy Rubber Mittens. Lined with sheeting. Black only. Price, per pair....95c
If by mail, postage extra, 8 cents.

Goodyear Plant Sprinkler.

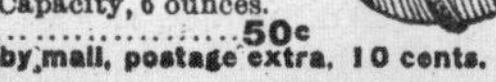

Plant Sprinkler for spraying plants and flowers without injury, for sprinkling clothing in the laundry, spraying carpets and clothing to prevent moths, spraying disinfectants in the sick room, etc.
No. 8C984 Capacity, 6 ounces.
Price.......50c
If by mail, postage extra, 10 cents.

Stomach Tubes.

No. 49C1657 Very Fine Maroon Soft Rubber Stomach Tubes with funnel ends. Price.......88c
If by mail, postage extra, 10 cents.

No. 49C1658 Extra Fine Maroon Soft Rubber Stomach Tube, with funnel end and bulb.
Price.......$1.05
If by mail, postage extra, 10c.

Rubber Finger Cots and Tips.

No. 49C1663 Antiseptic Finger Cots. Made of pure rubber; very light in weight.
Price, each.......3c
If by mail, postage extra, 1 cent.

Catheters.

No. 49C167 Male Catheter, olive tip, silken linen. English scale, 3 to 18. Price.......33c
No. 49C169 Male Catheter, conical tip, silken linen. English scale, 3 to 18. Price.......33c
No. 49C170 Male Catheter, cylindrical tip, silken linen. English scale, 3 to 18. Price.......33c
No. 49C171 Male Catheter, lisle thread. English scale, 3 to 18. Price...23c
No. 49C174 Soft Rubber Catheter, Patent velvet eye. American scale, 6 to 15. Price.......15c
No. 49C190 English Catheter, with wire stilet. Price.......15c
All catheters, if by mail, postage extra, 2 cents.

Bougies.

		Price, each.
No. 49C125	Urethral Bougie, olive tip, silken linen.	32c
No. 49C126	Urethral Bougie, olive tip, lisle thread.	23c
No. 49C127	Urethral Bougie, cylindrical tip, silken linen.	27c
No. 49C128	Urethral Bougie, cylindrical tip, lisle thread.	21c
No. 49C129	Urethral Bougie, conical tip, silken linen,	30c
No. 49C130	English Bougie	10c

All bougies, if by mail, postage extra, 2 cents.

Toilet or Medicinal Atomizers.

Atomizer for either Toilet or Medicinal Use. Hard rubber nozzle rubber bulb of fine quality. Continuous spray.
No. 8C989 Price.......35c
If by mail, postage extra, 14 cents.

The Most Reliable and Useful Atomizer in the world. Has three hard rubber tips. Can be used for spraying perfume, or disinfecting a sick room, or applying medicine to the throat or in the nose. It is made of the best materials, and with care will last a lifetime.
No. 8C991 Price.......78c
If by mail, postage extra, 12 cents.

Success Atomizer.

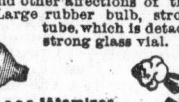

For liquifying and spraying; especially for atomizing medicines and medicated oils of every description for the treatment of catarrh, bronchitis, and other affections of the respiratory organs. Large rubber bulb, strong hard rubber tube, which is detachable; metal cap, strong glass vial.

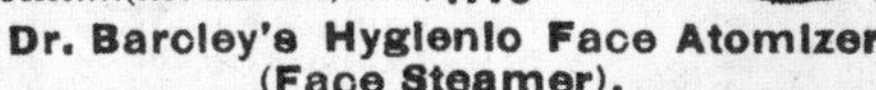

No. 8C994 Success Atomizer.
Price.......45c
If by mail, postage extra, 8 cents.

Hand Nebulizer.

No. 8C996 Hand Nebulizer. This is the latest improved and most useful hand nebulizer offered to the public. It throws a light or profuse spray of vapor, excelling that of any other instrument of its kind on the market. Removable throat and nasal tips of hard rubber.
Price....(Not mailable)......$1.10

Dr. Barcley's Hygienic Face Atomizer (Face Steamer).

For the rational and common sense treatment of the skin for the attainment of a clear, beautiful complexion. Dr. Barcley's Hygienic Face Atomizer (Face Steamer) is a handsome apparatus built on the same model as the large and expensive steaming apparatus used by dermatologists all over the country, but adapted in every detail for home use. The treatment with Dr. Barcley's Hygienic Face Atomizer, will accomplish for you better results in a few weeks than you could obtain with any other steaming method in months or years. It will make the skin firm and elastic, and gives the complexion a freshness, purity, transparency, brilliancy and harmonious coloring, which could not be gained in any other way. Dr. Barcley's Face Atomizer will successfully remove blackheads, liver spots, freckles; in fact, every known facial blemish, and bring back oily and dry skins to a normal condition, make them firm, pliable and velvety, establishing at the same time that healthful hue usually designated as a natural fine complexion. Dr. Barcley's Hygienic Face Atomizer (Face Steamer) has never been sold for less than $3.50; we furnish the same to our lady customers for 95 cents, with a guarantee that we supply at this special price the genuine Dr. Barcley's Hygienic Face Atomizer complete, with full directions and instructions.
No. 8C998 Dr. Barcley's Hygienic Face Atomizer, complete. Price.......95c

PERFUMERY DEPARTMENT.

WE OFFER THIS SEASON THE FINEST IMPORTED PERFUMES IN THE NEWEST, LATEST AND GRANDEST STYLES OF FANCY BOTTLES.

WE IMPORT the bulk of our perfume extracts direct from the flower gardens of France and the southern parts of Europe, receiving them in sealed copper vessels fresh from the producer. By this method we are enabled to save our customers one-half to two-thirds the usual profit made by other concerns on perfumes. **We furnish these high grade perfumes for little money compared to what is usually charged for even an inferior class of goods.** We can truthfully state that there is hardly another line of goods in which so much subtitution and adulteration is practiced as in perfumery. We guarantee that if you order from us, **you will receive the pure perfume extracts, lasting odors, and the perfume exatly as represented by us and as called for by you.**

THE ILLUSTRATIONS will give you a very accurate idea of the handsome packages or bottles in which our perfumes are supplied. In sending your order, select the size and style bottle desired, state the name of the odor which you wish to receive, and we will execute your order carefully. We feel confident you will be pleased with the perfumes when you receive them.

REMEMBER that a handsome bottle of high grade perfume always makes a welcome and dainty gift.

Kindly remember that you can get your favorite perfume in Triple Extract, Climax or Seroco grades, and that we guarantee them all to be strictly as represented. While the bottle, of course, will add nothing to the quality of the perfume, the handsome appearance of the perfume container serves a double purpose in making the package pleasing to the eye and later the bottle can be used for different toilet purposes, if desired. **Although we supply our 1-ounce perfume packages at extremely low prices, you can obtain an additional and considerable saving by ordering two ounces, four ounces, or, still better, ½-pound bottles. Wherever it is stated that perfume packages can be sent by mail, the amount of postage as stated with each item must be included, together with the price of the perfume, providing the customer wishes them forwarded in that manner.**

LIST OF ODORS WHICH WE ALWAYS CARRY IN STOCK:

Hyacinth,	Lilac Blossoms,	Shandon Bells,
Jessamine,	Carnation Pink,	Indian Violet,
Tuberose,	Rose Geranium,	Wood Violet,
Moss Rose,	Lily of the Valley,	Alpine Sweets,
Crab Apple,	Meadow Blossom,	Sweet Clover,
Violet,	Columbia Bouquet,	Ylang Ylang,
Wild Rose,	La France Rose,	White Rose,
Sweet Pea,	White Heliotrope,	Jockey Club,
Tea Rose,	New Mown Hay,	Mignonette,
Musk,	Peau d'Espagne,	Frangipani.

Triple Extract of any Odor.

This 1-ounce genuine round Lubin bottle, with ball glass stopper, only 25 cents.

The bottle, although of simple design, is one of quiet beauty, and, in combination with the fine quality of perfume it contains, giving you selection of our entire list of triple extracts, we offer you in our genuine round Lubin bottle one of the best and cheapest perfume packages for only 25 cents. Cannot be duplicated anywhere for less than 50 cents.

No. 8C1000 Price, 1-ounce round Lubin bottle......25c

If by mail, postage and mailing tube extra, 7 cents.

Your choice of any triple extract perfume of odors above listed, with genuine 1-ounce square Lubin bottle and sprinkler top, only 25 cents.

Usually sold in drug stores at 50 and 60 cents per ounce. Sprinkler top bottles are extremely convenient and many will prefer this style. 25 cents for this 1-ounce sprinkler top bottle and the high grade triple extract perfume supplied with same is a remarkably low price, quality of perfume and convenient style of bottle considered.

No. 8C1003 Price, 1-ounce square Lubin bottle, sprinkler top, each......25c

No. 8C1006 Price, 2-ounce square Lubin bottle, silvered sprinkler top, each......45c

If by mail, postage and mailing tube extra, small, 7c; large, 12c.

We will send you our celebrated Climax grade of perfume, worth 50 cents an ounce, for only 30 cents, and with it your choice of either one of the handsome and attractive Climax Bottles Nos. 1 and 2, as illustrated, without extra charge. We will supply you same packed in a nice paper box. These packages make a very acceptable present, welcome to and appreciated by every lady. The Climax grade perfumes are furnished in any odor above enumerated.

No. 1 1-oz. No. 2 1-oz.

No. 8C1009 The Climax Perfumes in Climax Bottles Nos. 1 and 2, as may be selected by you. Price, 1-ounce bottles in neat paper cases, each......30c

If by mail, postage and mailing tube, extra, 15c

This handsome cut glass stoppered bottle with one ounce of our fragrant and exclusive dainty Seroco Perfume, which you cannot obtain elsewhere in this country at any price, and which retails in foreign countries for $1.00 an ounce, you can obtain from us for the small sum of 40 cents.

Seroco Perfumes are the finest that can be produced. You will like them. You will enjoy them better than any other odors. This beautiful cut glass stoppered bottle, with fine Seroco perfume, for only 40 cents per bottle, is exceptional value. Shipped in neat paper boxes without extra charge.

No. 8C1012 Price, 1-ounce bottle......40c

If by mail, postage and mailing tube extra, 8 cents.

Two Ounce Bottle of Triple Extract Perfume, any odor you may wish, with this handsome glass stoppered bottle, only 45 cents. Splendid value at this price and very popular with our customers. An exceedingly attractive package and extremely ornamental for the dressing table of ladies. The best perfume and the nicest display bottle ever sold at the very low price.

If you were to buy the perfume alone, without this handsome and ornamental container, you could not secure a perfume to equal it and the same quantity for less than $1.00. This means a saving to you of more than half the cost of the perfume alone. A number of our customers order this style of bottle and our high grade perfume in quantities, supplying their friends with this article at 70 and 80 cents per bottle, thereby making a nice profit on their sales.

No. 8C1015 Price, 2-ounce bottle......45c

If by mail, postage and mailing tube extra, 13c.

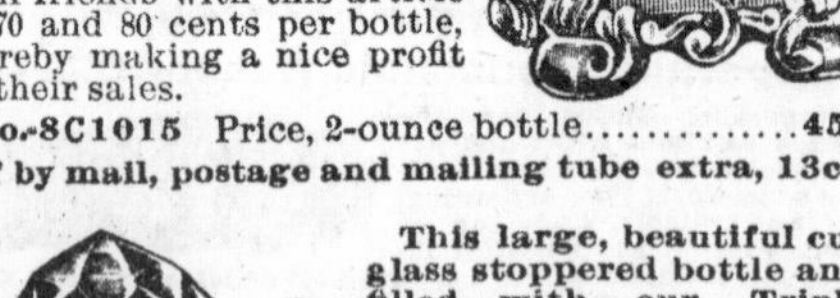

This large, beautiful cut glass stoppered bottle and filled with our Triple Extract Climax Perfume, worth 50 cents an ounce, or $1.00 value, for 55 cents. Almost one-half the price others would ask for the perfume alone, not mentioning the costly bottle in which the perfume is supplied. After using our Climax Perfume once you will surely order it again You may as well order a 2-ounce bottle on the start. There is nothing that can please people of good taste and refinement more than a faint trace of true odors of favorite flowers. Avoid cheap, coarse, diluted extracts. They have no lasting qualities and sometimes prove offensive. **The Climax Triple Extracts are always pleasing, elegant, lasting.** Our 2-ounce cut glass stoppered triple extract Climax Perfumes, any odor you may select.

No. 8C1018 Price, 2-ounce bottle......55c

Unmailable on account of weight.

Our Special Violette France.

Our Special Violette France Perfume, put up in magnificent 2-ounce cut glass stoppered bottle, for only 60 cents. A handsome package. Contains **society's latest, most exclusive odor.** People of fashion and all those who usually are referred to as **"swell" people prefer Violette France.** Sells as high as 75 cents and $1.00 an ounce. With a touch of this sweet, elegant and dainty perfume you can make the most simple as well as the most stylish and fascinating toilet complete. Its odor is often recognized as the perfume of gentility and good breeding.

60c

No. 8C1021 Price, 2-ounce bottle......60c

If by mail, postage and mailing tube extra, 11c.

American Beauty Buds and Violette France.

$1.65

Two of the most favorite extracts of all the odors of perfumes. Either one of these two odors will please more people than any other perfume in existence. We can furnish you the Violette France or if you prefer the American Beauty Buds in an Italian cut glass bottle and cut glass stopper as shown in this illustration. This makes this package especially desirable for presents. Handsome, beautiful design, large cut glass bottle and cut glass stopper, a highly appreciated ornament for the dressing table, containing an always welcome favorite perfume pleasing to all.

No. 8C1025 Commercial one-half pound cut glass bottle and cut glass stopper of either American Beauty Buds Perfume or Violette France, in paper box. Price, per box......$1.65

Unmailable on account of weight. Always mention in your order what odor is wanted.

Seroco Perfumes.

95c

Seroco perfumes, in all exquisite odors, represent the fine art of the most expert perfumers. They are in a class by themselves, often imitated but never equaled in any country. Seroco perfumes cannot be sold by any other house in the United States. We have the exclusive control. They have never been approached in fragrance distribution in daintiness and in lasting qualities. **We guarantee them genuine and finer than any other perfume,** regardless of price charged. Elegantly finished 4-ounce cut glass ground stopper bottle, admired and appreciated by every woman of taste and elegance, furnished to our customers at the astonishingly small price of 95 cents.

No. 8C1027 Our grandest Seroco Perfumes, all odors, in 4-ounce cut glass and ground stoppered bottles, sufficient for a six months' supply. Price......95c

Unmailable on account of weight.

$1.85 Buys Half-Pound Bottle, Any Odor Desired.

$1.85

For only $1.85 we will send a ½-pound bottle, sufficient for a year's needs, of either our Triple Extracts, our Climax or Seroco Perfume, any odor you may select, including Violette France and Wild Red Rose Extracts, in beautiful 8-ounce cut glass bottle with cut glass stopper, as shown in this illustration.

A year's supply for such a small price. The bottle is of heavy cut glass pattern and practically indestructible, and afterward may be used as a receptacle for fine toilet waters and forms one of the prettiest and loveliest dressing room ornaments imaginable.

No. 8C1030 One-half pound cut glass pattern bottle with cut glass stopper, containing any odor of any of our perfumes, $6.00 value, only...$1.85

Unmailable on account of weight.

TOILET PREPARATIONS

RECOGNIZING THE FRENCH TOILET PREPARATIONS as the standard and in many cases far superior to the preparations of like kind manufactured in any other country, the United States not excepted, we have at all times carried a very extensive line of French toilet preparations; but in order that our customers may have an opportunity to obtain from us all the latest standard toilet novelties and the newest articles in this line, we have added to our list of toilet preparations every article that has met with a favorable reception among the fashionable ladies in Europe and this country, and you will find in the assortment which we present to you in the following pages almost everything in the toilet line that is worth while having. You will please note that in addition to the well known preparations that have been imported and sold by us for years and which have, owing to their merit, secured many friends among our customers, we can supply you other toilet articles that have become the fashion in Paris, London and almost every city in the United States during recent years. While it is without doubt of importance that our lady customers should have a large selection for this class of articles, you will kindly observe by comparing our prices on these goods that we furnish them at prices which are nearly always only one-half of what others charge for similar preparations, and in many cases our prices are but one-third of the prices prevailing in drug stores and with other firms selling toilet preparations. **We also beg to call your attention to the fact that every article as presented in the following pages is fully guaranteed to come up to the standard under which it is listed, and it will give satisfaction** when used for the purpose for which it is intended. **Our toilet preparations are scientifically prepared, up to date, and will always please even the most exacting and fastidious of society ladies;** and we can give all our customers the positive assurance that in making their selection from the following listt hey will obtain not only the latest and the best toilet preparations, but they will save from fifty to sixty per cent in price on nearly every article.

Double Distilled Toilet Waters.

We carry the finest grade of toilet waters, made from first extraction, but supply them in both single and double distilled odors. Our single distilled toilet waters are guaranteed better and stronger than the best grade usually sold in drug stores, while the double distilled odors are in such a concentrated form and produced with the purest and finest white spirits that they can be diluted with the addition of distilled water, two bottles of our double distilled toilet water making three bottles of the purest and more than average strength toilet water. Both kinds are furnished in violet, carnation, lilac and rose. Beautiful in color, sweet odors, handsome bottles, in fact, the grandest perfumed waters for toilet and bath. The occasional sprinkling of a few drops of any of these waters on furniture, clothing, linen, etc., will keep these articles fresh, and owing to the highest purity and strength of the perfumes used in these waters their lasting quality is fully equal to their fragrance, thus making them more desirable and of greater value for toilet requisites than any other toilet preparations of this kind.

No. 8C1050 Toilet Water, single distilled, violet, carnation, lilac or rose.
Price, 4-ounce bottle..........24c
Price, 8-ounce bottle..........36c

No. 8C1053 Toilet Water, double distilled, violet, carnation, lilac or rose.
Price, 4-ounce bottle..........30c
Price, 8-ounce bottle..........45c

Always state plainly in your order the odor desired.
Unmailable on account of weight.

Extract Vegetal.

This latest perfumed water for the toilet is prepared for us in the original Paris style and recommended as one of the most delightful, refreshing toilet preparations for special occasions—elegant, sweet odors that please everybody. Put up in French taper bottles with sprinkler top; three odors.

No. 8C1056 Vegetal, lilac, large bottle. Price......................31c
No. 8C1059 Vegetal, violet, large bottle. Price......................31c
No. 8C1062 Vegetal, carnation, large bottle. Price..............31c
Unmailable on account of weight.

Sears, Roebuck & Co.'s Cologne Water.

Especially prepared by us for the toilet and handkerchief, and equal to the finest colognes in the market. It is very refreshing and of great value in the sick room, where it can be used as a **disinfectant by destroying bad odors and rendering the air in the room fresh and pleasant,** giving it a nice perfume.

No. 8C1065
Price, 8-ounce bottle, 55c; 4-ounce bottle...30c
If by mail, postage and tube extra, small, 16c; large, unmailable on account of weight.

Genuine Florida Water.

This is the finest toilet water manufactured. Can be used as a perfume, or mixed with water as a cooling and refreshing lotion for the skin. In the bath it is a luxury only known to those who have tried it. There are many imitations. Send to us and get the **only genuine quality.**

No. 8C1068
Price, regular size bottle..........25c
Price, ½-pint bottle....... ....40c
Unmailable on account of weight.

Genuine Imported Bay Rum.

No. 8C1071 This is a fine quality of **Bay Rum,** imported by ourselves from the Island of St. Thomas, in the West Indies. We import it in casks and bottle it as our customers require. Being a pure article it is very useful for toilet purposes. A refreshing lotion for the skin.

Price, ½-pint bottle............ 16c
Price, 1-pint bottle............ 26c
Price, 1-quart bottle............ 45c
Unmailable on account of weight.

Almond Nut Cream.

An excellent face cream, cleansing and cooling. Clears the skin from wrinkles, tan, freckles and other facial blemishes, rendering the face soft and white. This Almond Nut Cream is a pure preparation made from bleached almonds with the addition of other properly selected ingredients, making it one of the **most effective creams obtainable for freckles, pimples, scaly or scabby skin.** It is non-poisonous and does not contain any bleaching chemicals, which are always dangerous when used in face preparations.

No. 8C1074 Price......40c
Unmailable on account of weight.

Secret De Ninon.

This new French preparation is especially recommended for removing freckles, redness, blotches, tan and all imperfections of the skin, leaving same clear, soft and rich in appearance. By using Secret de Ninon you can secure a healthy, blooming complexion. Ladies exposed to the sun, wind and sudden changes of weather frequently find their delicate complexions injured from these causes, but **Secret de Ninon will quickly remove such imperfections and a satin like, smooth skin of great beauty can soon be acquired,** a complexion which will be admired by everyone. The preparation is positively harmless, nc ill effects. There is no preparation that will give better general satisfaction than does the Secret de Ninon, which always clears the complexion and enhances the beauty of the user in a marvelous manner.

No. 8C1077 Secret de Ninon. Per bottle.....55c
Unmailable on account of weight.

Witch Hazel Toilet Balm.

This is an elegant preparation for the skin when it is chapped and rough. A few applications well rubbed in makes the skin soft and velvety. It is also recommended for removing sunburn and freckles. It will prevent the skin from chapping or coloring when exposed to the cold if used before going out. It does not leave the skin greasy or sticky. Gloves can be used immediately after each application, the balm being absorbed by the skin very quickly. The Witch Hazel Balm is a very popular healing and soothing toilet requisite for harsh, dry, cracked or rough skin. Gentlemen find it a lotion more satisfactory for use after shaving than anything else.

No. 8C1080 Price, per bottle.18c
If by mail, postage and tube extra, each, 16 cents.

La Dore's Nail Powder.

A celebrated French preparation for giving color and brilliancy to the nails. A very desirable toilet article, used by ladies of fashion and good taste. Furnished in neatly decorated boxes.

No. 8C1083 Price, per box..................15c
If by mail, postage extra, 2 cents.

La Dore's Emery Nail Files.

Extra Quality La Dore's Emery Nail Files, unequaled for finishing, smoothing and beautifying the nails. One-half dozen in a box. Regular selling price, 25 cents. Our price only 12 cents.

No. 8C1086 Emery Nail Files, one-half dozen in a box. Price.**(If by mail, postage extra, 2 cents)**..12c

Sachet Powders.

The well known Genuine Eastman Sachet Powders in beautiful air tight sealed envelopes, the most fragrant, delicate odors, lasting and refined. Size of envelope, 3x4 inches; furnished in the following favorite odors: Verona Violette, Crushed Roses, Crushed Heliotrope, Crushed Carnation and the grandest of all — "Chic," a new and delightful perfume.

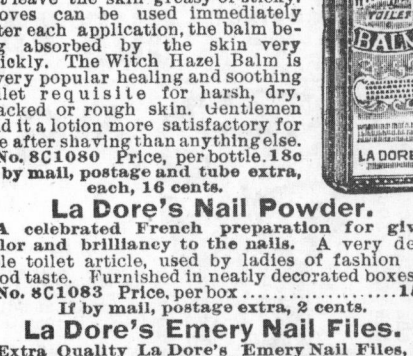

No. 8C1087 Sachet Powders in fancy envelope. Price, 8c
If by mail, postage extra, 2 cents.

Genuine Eastman Sachet Powders in medium size Screw Cap Glass Jars. We furnish the genuine Eastman Sachet Powders in medium size glass jars, with metal screw caps. Absolutely air tight, so the Sachet Powder will remain fresh and fragrant for a very long time. Selection in the following odors: "Chic," the latest, most delightful perfume, Verona Violette, Crushed Carnation, Crushed Roses and Crushed Heliotrope.

No. 8C1090 Sachet Powder, in medium size screw cap glass jars. Price..........................22c
If by mail, postage extra, 8 cents.

OUR WHITE LILY FACE WASH — 40c PER BOTTLE

THE LADIES' FAVORITE TOILET PREPARATION.

No. 8C1092

Per Bottle, 40c.

An Invaluable Remedy for Pimples, Freckles, Sallowness, Roughness, Wrinkles, Tan, Blackheads and All Irritations and Imperfections of the Skin.

Retail Price, 75c. Our Price, 40c; Per Dozen, $4.20.

Recommended By Thousands of Beautiful Women.

DIFFERENT FROM MOST COMPLEXION PREPARATIONS, our White Lily Face Wash contains not a particle of lead, silver, sulphur, arsenic, mercury or other poisonous mineral by which most complexion remedies, and particularly the advertised ones, produce a temporary smoothness and brilliancy of the skin. White Lily Face Wash is clear and harmless as water, contains no poison, no sediment, nothing to hurt the most tender and delicate skin. Its effect in quickly removing pimples, blackheads, freckles, roughness and tan is simply wonderful. White Lily Face Wash smoothes out wrinkles and roughness, all imperfections and irritations of the skin disappear, restores the delicate tint of girlhood and youth, leaving the skin soft and velvety. Nothing is more attractive than a lovely complexion.

DO YOU WANT TO BE BEAUTIFUL? Do you want a spotless skin, a matchless complexion, the envy and pride of everyone? Send for a bottle of White Lily Face Wash, use it according to directions and give it a fair trial. You will be surprised at its good results.

WHITE LILY FACE WASH has a wonderful sale. The market is full of injurious complexion preparations. Many, in fact most, of these preparations contain lead, arsenic, bismuth or mercury and are really dangerous in their effects. You can protect yourself from serious skin diseases by using our White Lily Face Wash. Take no chances. Avoid all danger. Use only a preparation that is absolutely harmless, one that you can depend on for a spotless skin, a positive beautifier that has been recommended by thousands of ladies.

USE ONLY THE GENUINE WHITE LILY FACE WASH, PREPARED AND SOLD BY US.

No. 8C1092 Regular retail price, per bottle, 75c; our price, per dozen, $4.20; each 40c
If by mail, postage and tube extra, 19 cents.

FOR REMOVING SUPERFLUOUS HAIR

OUR FAMOUS PARISIAN DEPILATORY

FOR REMOVING SUPERFLUOUS HAIR

Regular retail price, each ..$1.50
OUR PRICE, EACH......$0.65
OUR PRICE, PER DOZEN 6.60

At 65c Per Bottle We Offer Our Celebrated PARISIAN DEPILATORY. A Harmless and Successful Preparation for Removing Unsightly Hair from the Face, Neck and Arms.

WE POSITIVELY GUARANTEE OUR PARISIAN DEPILATORY NOT TO HARM THE MOST SENSITIVE SKIN OR MAR THE MOST DELICATE COMPLEXION.

Hair on the face, neck or arms, so embarrassing to ladies of refinement, can be removed without danger or chance of failure. The Parisian Depilatory instantly dissolves the hair wherever applied and removes it entirely.

THE GREATEST DRAWBACK TO PERFECT LOVELINESS in woman is a superfluous, unnatural growth of hair where nature never intended it. The prettiest face is marred and disfigured by hair on the lips, cheeks or chin. By means of our Parisian Depilatory every vestige of hair can be removed, a perfect clean, smooth, soft, beautiful skin is assured.

NO UNPLEASANT EFFECTS. The Parisian Depilatory is not only perfectly harmless, but it has the additional effect of a fine cosmetic, softening the skin and improving the complexion. It leaves no burning sensation, it is entirely painless, easily applied; one application is usually sufficient.

FAR SUPERIOR TO THE ELECTRIC NEEDLE. The electric needle will remove superfluous hair by destroying the roots, but it is a very painful operation. Serious results have often followed the use of the electric needle. Parisian Depilatory is highly recommended. No matter what you have tried before or how stubborn the growth of hair is, you ought to give Parisian Depilatory a trial.

A WONDERFUL PREPARATION. Compounded in our own laboratory by a competent chemist. Every ounce is prepared under his personal supervision. The ingredients are the best and purest, carefully selected. OUR PRICE of 65 cents per bottle is the lowest price ever heard of for a genuine depilatory.

DON'T PAY $1.00, $2.00 AND $3.00 for a so called hair remover. Be careful about using the preparations of unknown concerns. Some of the hair removers widely advertised are very powerful, very corrosive; they remove the hair and often burn the skin. You can use our Parisian Depilatory with perfect safety. Leaves no marks, no ill effects, no one can tell that you are using a hair remover. No one will know the difference except in your improved appearance, the enhanced loveliness of the skin and complexion.

NO TOILET IS COMPLETE without the famous Parisian Depilatory. Ladies of refinement everywhere find the Parisian Depilatory an invaluable toilet requisite. It removes the hair only where it is applied, does not interfere with the use of cosmetics, washes; has no effect whatever on the blood, complexion, health or hair, or any part of the person, except where it is applied. If you are bothered by superfluos hair, whether on face, neck or arms, if you want perfectly smooth, clean clear skin, send for a bottle of our celebrated 65-cent Parisian Depilatory, the only absolutely harmless hair remover ever compounded.

Our Celebrated Parisian Depilatory removes all superfluous hair and other imperfections, and leaves the skin soft, smooth and velvety.

One bottle is usually sufficient for any case.

No. 8C1095 Our price, per dozen bottles, $6.60; each....... ....(If by mail, postage and mailing tube extra, 8 cents) 65c

THE PRINCESS BUST DEVELOPER AND BUST CREAM OR FOOD

Regular retail price, each..............$5.00
OUR PRICE, EACH 1.50
With one bottle Bust Expander, and one jar Bust Food FREE.
OUR PRICE, PER DOZEN.........$16.00

WILL ENLARGE ANY LADY'S BUST FROM 3 TO 5 INCHES. PRICE FOR DEVELOPER, BUST EXPANDER AND BUST FOOD, COMPLETE - - - - - - - - $1.50

With every order for Princess Bust Developer and Bust Food, we furnish FREE one bottle of the GENUINE FLEUR DE LIS BUST EXPANDER and TISSUE BUILDER (retail price, 75 cents) without extra charge.

THE PRINCESS BUST DEVELOPER

IS A NEW SCIENTIFIC HELP TO NATURE.

COMBINED WITH THE USE OF THE BUST CREAM OR FOOD, FORMS A FULL FIRM WELL DEVELOPED BUST.

It will build up and fill out shrunken and undeveloped tissues, form a rounded, plump, perfectly developed bust, producing a beautiful figure.

THE PRINCESS BUST DEVELOPER AND CREAM FOOD is absolutely harmless, easy to use, perfectly safe and the only successful bust developer on the market.

IF NATURE HAS NOT FAVORED YOU with that greatest charm, a symmetrically rounded bosom full and perfect, send for the Princess Bust Developer and you will be surprised, delighted and happy over the result of one week's use. No matter what you have tried before, no matter if you have used other so called bust developers (paying $4.00, $5.00 or $6.00) the Princess Developer will produce the desired result in nearly every case. If you are not entirely satisfied with the result after giving it a fair trial, please return it to us and we will gladly refund your money.

Unmailable on account of weight.

PRINCESS BUST DEVELOPER.

Comes in two sizes, 4 and 5 inches in diameter. State size desired. The 4-inch Developer is the most popular as well as the most desirable size.

THE DEVELOPER is carefully made of nickel and aluminum, very finest finish throughout. Comes in two sizes, 4 and 5 inches diameter. In ordering please state size desired. The developer gives the right exercise to the muscles of the bust, compels a free and normal circulation of the blood through the capillaries, glands and tissues of the flabby, undeveloped parts, these parts are soon restored to a healthy condition, they expand and fill out, become round, firm and beautiful.

THE BUST CREAM OR FOOD

IS APPLIED AS A MASSAGE.

It is a delightful cream preparation, put up by an eminent French chemist, and forms just the right food required for the starved skin and wasted tissues. The ingredients of the Bust Food are mainly pure vegetable oils, perfectly harmless, combined in a way to form the finest nourishment for the bust glands. It is delicately perfumed and is

UNRIVALED FOR DEVELOPING THE BUST, ARMS AND NECK,

making a plump, full, rounded bosom, perfect neck and arms, a smooth skin, which before was scrawny, flat and flabby.

FULL DIRECTIONS ARE FURNISHED, SUCCESS IS ASSURED.

You need no longer regret that your form is not what you would like it to be. Ladies everywhere welcome the Princess Bust Developer and Cream Food as the greatest toilet requisite ever offered. We have letters from many of our lady customers, telling us the good results of the Princess Developer, how their busts enlarged from two to six inches, and expressing their gratitude for the big benefit derived.

THE PRINCESS BUST DEVELOPER AND FOOD is the only treatment that will actually develop and enlarge the bust, cause it to fill out to nature's full proportions, give that swelling, rounded, firm bosom, that queenly bearing, so attractive to the opposite sex. It brings a thin, awkward, unattractive girl or woman nearer to an exquisitely formed, graceful, fascinating lady, and absolutely without harm.

$1.50 is our Special Introductory Price for the PRINCESS DEVELOPER and BUST FOOD, Complete, the Lowest Price Ever Made on this Article.

DON'T PAY an extravagant price for a so called bust developer. Be careful of the medicines and treatments offered by various irresponsible companies. Send for the Princess Developer, complete with the Bust Food, at our special introductory price of $1.50, state whether you wish the 4 or 5-inch developer, and if you are not entirely satisfied with the results, if it does not meet your expectations, without the slightest harm or inconvenience, return it, after giving it a trial, and we will refund your money. Don't put off ordering. Nowhere else can you buy a Princess Bust Developer for only $1.50.

No. 8C1098 Our Princess Bust Developer, with one bottle Bust Expander, and one jar Bust Food, FREE. Price, complete....................$1.50

FLORAL MASSAGE CREAM.

COMPLETE COURSE OF INSTRUCTIONS FOR FACIAL MASSAGE SENT WITH EACH ORDER.

Floral Massage Cream (antiseptic). Regular 50-cent size jars, - - - - - 39c
Extra large size jar (½-lb.), enough for 60 treatments, only - - - - - 67c

A new, purifying, antiseptic, cleansing and beautifying massage cream, a most excellent preparation. Makes the old young, makes the plain beautiful, removes the telltale marks of time.

FULL DIRECTIONS for taking a complete course of massage treatment sent with each jar, the same course of treatment and the same preparation that society ladies receive in the fashionable city massage parlors at $1.00 per treatment. This is our latest and most improved toilet preparation, a high grade and perfectly satisfactory facial massage cream, to be used by anyone according to the plain and simple instructions for the course of massage treatment sent with every package.

FOR REMOVING HORIZONTAL LINES ON THE BROW, laughing wrinkles and crows' feet, wrinkles under the eyes, to make the cheeks plump and round, and to make your complexion just what you want it to be, healthy, clear and rosy. Floral Massage Cream is a toilet luxury which no woman, young, middle aged or old should deny herself. Our Floral Massage Cream contains no grease of any kind. It is composed of the purest ingredients, perfectly harmless to the most delicate skin. Its emollient effects are greater, its cleansing and beautifying results more marked than could be obtained from any other combination prepared for massaging purposes.

OUR FLORAL MASSAGE CREAM is the genuine massage preparation used so successfully by all massageurs of prominence in the massage parlors of every large city in this country and Europe, and is supplied by us exclusively to our customers for home massaging.

HAVE YOU EVER TRIED FACE MASSAGE? Have you ever experienced the peculiarly delightful, stimulating and exhilarating effects upon the facial nerves and muscles produced by a scientifically prepared and properly applied massage cream? Do you know that massaging the face is now considered a function which no progressive lady omits in order to produce and preserve that healthy glow, that pink of complexion which makes the beautiful features more beautiful, and adds to irregular ones attractions, the effect of which is really remarkable. We all know that exercise means increased circulation of the blood, but generally exercise is not entirely sufficient to produce the right results in the fullest measure for the facial perfection. Local exercise, in other words massage of the face, becomes necessary to induce increased circulation through the facial blood vessels, but even this is incomplete unless you use in connection with it the famous Floral Massage Cream which cleanses and clears the skin, arouses to activity every facial nerve and muscle, stimulates and feeds them, removes wrinkles under the eyes, on the brow, fills out the cheeks, making them plump and round, and insures a beautiful complexion in all cases. It is not surprising that the foremost professional massageurs will use nothing else in their work but Floral Massage Cream, which can be found in every fashionable massage parlor, where it is used almost exclusively.

IT IS NOT GREASY, it does not contain any animal fats, and therefore is not subject to decomposition. It is absolutely pure, therefore harmless and cleanly. It is prepared in the most scientific manner, therefore reliable and certain in results. It is, however, not necessary that you should employ the services of a professional massageur, for with our Floral Massage Cream you can massage your face in the privacy of your home, and at an expense of only a few cents. We supply the regular large $1.00 size jar of the genuine Floral Cream to our customers for 67 cents, sufficient for many months of facial massage treatment. Complete instructions are sent with each jar.

FLORAL MASSAGE CREAM HEALS THE SKIN, removes from the pores the impurities that make the skin rough and unwholesome. Its use renders the skin soft, white and beautiful It is antiseptic and eradicates the germs of disease, yet it is perfectly harmless to the most delicate skin. Floral Massage Cream is non-irritating, purifies and invigorates the pores of the skin, giving at the same time activity to the glands, which is always very desirable.

FLORAL MASSAGE CREAM IS A DELIGHTFUL PREPARATION and speedily renders facial muscles firm and healthy, clarifying the complexion quickly and permanently. Soothes and rests the nerves of the face, and produces a healthy glow and a sensation of ease and comfort.

No. 8C1099 Floral Massage Cream. Price, regular 50-cent jars, per dozen, $3.90; each.................39c

If by mail, postage extra, 14 cents.

No. 8C1100 Large size (holding three times the quantity of 50-cent jars). Price, per dozen, $6.00; each.........(Not mailable)..........67c

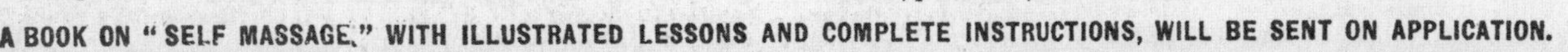

A BOOK ON "SELF MASSAGE," WITH ILLUSTRATED LESSONS AND COMPLETE INSTRUCTIONS, WILL BE SENT ON APPLICATION.

OUR 60-CENT PRINCESS TONIC HAIR RESTORER.

No. 8C1101

Per Bottle, 60c.

A WONDERFUL NEW HAIR TONIC AND PRODUCER.

Restores the Natural Color, Preserves and Strengthens the Hair for Years, Promotes the Growth, Arrests Falling Hair, Feeds and Nourishes the Roots, Cures Dandruff and Scurf, and Allays all Scalp Irritations.

THE ONLY ABSOLUTELY EFFECTIVE, UNFAILINGLY SUCCESSFUL, PERFECTLY HARMLESS, POSITIVELY NO-DYE PREPARATION ON THE MARKET

that restores gray hair to its natural and youthful color, removes crusts, scales and dandruff, soothes irritating, itching surfaces, stimulates the hair follicles, supplies the roots with energy and nourishment, renders the hair beautifully soft, and makes the hair grow.

THE WORLD FAMED Princess Tonic HAIR RESTORER SEROCO CHEMICAL LABORATORY CHICAGO ILL

EVERY SINGLE BOTTLE OF PRINCESS TONIC HAIR RESTORER is compounded especially in our own laboratory by our own skilled chemists, and according to the prescription of one who has made the hair and scalp, its diseases and cure, a life study.

Regular Retail Price, per bottle,	$1.00
Our Price, per bottle, . . .	.60
Our Price, per dozen bottles, . .	6.00

Unmailable on account of weight.

PRINCESS TONIC HAIR RESTORER IS NOT AN EXPERIMENT, not an untried, unknown remedy, depending on enormous, glittering advertisements for sales, but it is a preparation of the very finest and most expensive ingredients, that will positively cure any case of falling hair, stimulate the growth of new hair on bald heads, cure dandruff and other diseases of the scalp.

ARE YOU BALD?
Is your hair thin or falling out?
Does your hair come out easily and gather on the comb and brush when you brush it?
Does your head itch?
Do you have dandruff or scurf and do white, dust-like particles settle on your coat collar?
Is your hair stiff and coarse and hard to brush?
Is your hair fading or has it turned prematurely gray?

IF YOUR HAIR SUFFERS in any one or more of these particulars, we would urge you by all means to order a bottle of Princess Tonic Hair Restorer as a trial, for speedy relief. Use it according to directions and you will be surprised and delighted at the wonderful results. It acts direct on the tiny roots of the hair, giving them required fresh nourishment, starts quick, energetic circulation in every hair cell, tones up the scalp, freshens the pores, stops falling and sickly hair, changes thin hair to a fine heavy growth, puts new life in dormant, sluggish hair cells on bald heads, producing in a short time an **absolutely new growth of hair. If your hair is fading or turning gray,** one bottle of Princess Tonic Hair Restorer will give it healthy life, renew its original color and restore it to youthful profusion and beauty.

Princess Tonic Hair Restorer Grows Hair Like This.

USE IT ALWAYS IF YOU WANT A HEAD OF FINE, SILKY, GLOSSY HAIR, THE PRIDE OF EVERY WOMAN.

PRINCESS TONIC HAIR RESTORER IS GOOD FOR BOTH MEN AND WOMEN. IS EQUALLY EFFECTIVE ON MEN'S, WOMEN'S AND CHILDREN'S HAIR.

AS A CURE FOR DANDRUFF, as a tonic for thin and scanty hair, Princess Tonic Hair Restorer acts with quick and wonderful success. It removes crusts and scales, keeps the scalp clean and healthy, the roots at once respond to its vigorous action, dandruff is banished and a thick and healthy growth of hair is assured.

FOR A TOILET ARTICLE, as a fine hair dressing, no one who takes any pride in a nice head of hair can afford to be without a bottle always on the dresser. Princess Tonic Hair Restorer is delicately perfumed, and one light application imparts a delightful, refined fragrance. Neither oils, pomades, vaseline or other greases are required with our preparation.

DON'T SEND AWAY TO A CHEAP SPECIALIST and pay $1.00, $1.50 or $2.00 a bottle for a worthless and perhaps injurious preparation. Don't be misled by catchy advertisements with baits of free trial sample bottle and fake examination offers—such people will draw you in, make you believe something awful is the matter and scare you into paying enormous prices for alleged remedies, when you can get the genuine, tried, tested Princess Tonic Hair Restorer at 60 cents a bottle, the actual cost of the ingredients and labor of bottling, with our one small profit added.

PRINCESS TONIC HAIR RESTORER IS ABSOLUTELY HARMLESS. IT IS NOT A DYE. It will not injure the most delicate hair, it will not stain the daintiest head dress. Princess Tonic Hair Restorer works wonders with the hair. We get letters daily from people telling how much good it has done for them. It will do the same for you. You can sell a dozen bottles at a profit to yourself in your immediate neighborhood to people who see the good it has done and the wonderful results on your hair.

ORDER A BOTTLE AT 60 CENTS

which you can easily sell at $1.00, and if you do not find it all and more than we claim for it, if you do not find it is just the hair tonic you want, stimulating the growth, cleansing the scalp, stopping hair from falling out, restoring natural color, curing dandruff or promoting a new growth of hair on a bald head, return it to us at once **AND WE WILL CHEERFULLY REFUND YOUR MONEY.**

This Label is your Protection.

It shows that only the purest and finest ingredients are used.

EVERY BOTTLE OF OUR GENUINE PRINCESS TONIC HAIR RESTORER IS STAMPED WITH THIS LABEL AS SHOWN IN THE ILLUSTRATION,

OUR GUARANTEE OF HIGHEST QUALITY.

YOU WILL FIND VARIOUS SO CALLED HAIR TONICS and hair restorers widely advertised in the newspapers and magazines. Some of them possess merit and others do not. Those that possess merit are sold for two and three times the price we ask for the genuine Princess Tonic Hair Restorer, and are not equal to the preparation we put out under our binding guarantee for quality. If you have any doubt as to the merit of the Princess Tonic Hair Restorer as against the preparations advertised and offered by others, we would be willing for you to order our preparation, and then send for any other preparation in the market, give both preparations a fair and honest trial, and if you do not find the Princess Tonic Hair Restorer better by far than any other hair tonic, you need only write us to this effect and we will return your money. We reproduce herewith a few of the many letters we have received from pleased customers, telling us of the good they have received from the Princess Tonic Hair Restorer.

No. 8C1101 Price, per dozen bottles, **$6.00;** per bottle **60c**

CURES ITCHING SCALP, FALLING AND GRAY HAIR.

Maynard, N. Y.

Sears, Roebuck & Co., Chicago, Ill.

Dear Sirs:—In regard to the Princess Tonic Hair Restorer, I will say that it was used for itching scalp and falling hair, and also gray hair, and it cured these troubles. I think your remedy is all right.

Yours truly,
A. L. VAN HATTERS.

ONE BOTTLE OF PRINCESS TONIC HAIR RESTORER GIVES WONDERFUL RESULTS.

Sweetwater, Neb.

Sears, Roebuck & Co., Chicago, Ill.

Dear Sirs:—My wife used your Princess Tonic Hair Restorer for hair falling out, and it gave wonderful results, the hair stopped falling out and grew thicker after using one bottle of your famous Hair Restorer. We keep a bottle on hand all the time. I would recommend this Restorer to everybody who has trouble with their hair. Respectfully yours,
REV. E. HERZBERG.

THE BEST HAIR TONIC EVER USED.

Royal, Iowa.

Sears, Roebuck & Co., Chicago, Ill.

Dear Sirs:—Should you wish to know if the Princess Tonic Hair Restorer did any good towards the purpose for which it was bought, I would say that I bought it for falling hair and it stopped the trouble at once. Princess Tonic Hair Restorer is the best hair tonic I ever used.

Respectfully yours,
C. TOELLE.

English Lavender Smelling Salts.

REFRESHING AND INVIGORATING.

For faintness, headache, etc. In pretty, glass stoppered bottles, a useful and handsome ornament for the dressing table.

No. 8C1104 Price, per bottle, **18c**

If by mail, postage and tube extra, 10 cents.

Malaga Almond Meal.

This is the genuine Oriental meal; much more emollient than the meal usually sold in this country. We import it direct in original bags and put it up in nice packages. It is splendid for the skin and can be used in place of soap. **Malaga Almond Meal is highly recommended to ladies who have a very sensitive skin;** one that is easily affected even by the slightest presence of acid in a toilet preparation.

No. 8C1107 ¼-lb. size. Price..**15c**
½-lb. size. Price..**25c**

If by mail, postage extra, small size, 8 cents; large size, 12 cents.

Milk of Roses for the Complexion.

A great beautifier used by the most fashionable ladies in Europe, and prepared from fresh white and pale colored roses by a simple process, which, however, secures and obtains by a superior extraction, the finest odor and other portions which always have a pleasant and softening effect on the skin when used for the treatment of same, especially when the same is not entirely free from blemishes. The process for preparing this toilet article has been secured from the French manufacturer and chemist for our exclusive control in the United States.

No. 8C1110 Price............................**32c**

Unmailable on account of weight.

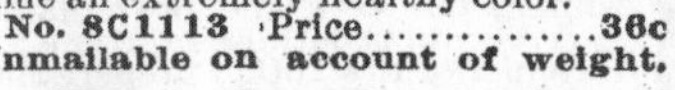

Genuine Juice of Lily Bulbs.

After many futile efforts we finally succeeded in obtaining the genuine and pure juice of the fresh bulbs of pond lilies, so that our customers are in a position to obtain from us the real, genuine article of this toilet preparation, recognized as one of the best in the world. When used for a limited time only this preparation always assures a clear complexion, soft and transparent, giving at the same time an extremely healthy color.

No. 8C1113 Price..............**36c**

Unmailable on account of weight.

Creme de Marshmallow.

A very fine, fragrant, dainty toilet lotion, bland and soothing, for preserving the complexion. Especially recommended for an inflamed and irritated condition of the skin. Ladies doing domestic work will find it a perfect lotion for the skin. May be applied at any time. Quickly absorbed by the skin. **Unmailable.**

No. 8C1116 Price...............**26c**

Milk of Cucumber.

An astringent wash, scientifically prepared from the fresh juice of green cucumbers. Cannot be equaled for the treatment of coarse pores and oily skin. Always gives a freshness to the skin, so much desired. **Purely vegetable and perfectly harmless.** This toilet article has been in great favor the past few years, and is highly recommended by ladies having used the wash constantly, and always with the very best results. **Unmailable.**

No. 8C1119 Price...............**25c**

Orange Flower Skin Food.

QUI VIVE.

This celebrated preparation has quickly grown into popular favor, and is today, by ladies of fashion, considered an indispensable toilet article. It acts as a skin nourisher and wrinkle remover, smooths roughness and fills out hollow cheeks, giving the natural healthy glow and beauty to the skin. Orange Flower Skin Food is today often preferred and used instead of preparations that would cost three and four times the price at which we can furnish same to our lady customers.

No. 8C1122 Regular sized jar. Price...........**21c**
4-ounce jars. Price......(Not mailable).........**35c**

If by mail, postage extra, regular size, 15 cents.

Creme Marquise.

QUI VIVE.

This cream is equally as popular as the Orange Flower Skin Food, and while it can be used successfully alone, most society ladies employ it together with the Orange Flower Skin Food. **It is especially effective for whitening, softening and preserving the skin.** When Orange Flower Skin Food and Creme Marquise are used together, they should be alternated by changing every other night.

No. 8C1125 Regular sized jar. Price.........**20c**
4-ounce jars. Price..........(Not mailable).........**37c**

If by mail, postage extra, regular size, 15 cents.

Mme. Qui Vive Complexion Powder.

This is an equally well known toilet article, prepared from the famous Qui Vive formulas, is non-irritating, contains no mineral poisons and may be applied without danger to the most delicate skin. Three shades, flesh, brunette and white.

No. 8C1129 Price, per box..................**18c**

If by mail, postage extra, per box, 3 cents.

Always state which color is wanted.

Floral Complexion Powder.

Floral Complexion Powder is one of the very best powders the market affords, is delicately perfumed, fragrant with natural flower odors, and is composed of carefully selected ingredients of the purest kind, and cannot under any conditions whatever cause inflammation or the slightest irritation of the skin as many other complexion powders often do.

No. 8C1131 Price, per box......................**25c**

If by mail, postage extra, per box, 7 cents.

La Dore's Powder de Riz.

Made from fine rice flour and exquisitely perfumed. This powder is very popular and preferred by many to any other complexion powder used for the purpose for which it is intended. Furnished in three shades, white, cream and flesh.

No. 8C1134
Price, per box......**15c**

If by mail, postage extra, per box, 3 cents.

Rouge de Theatre.

This is positively the best, giving a natural and lifelike glow, never injures the skin, is today considered by the theatrical profession the only safe and satisfactory rouge, and used by them almost exclusively owing to the fine distributive qualities which it possesses so that it can never be noticed or detected.

No. 8C1137 Price, per box...........**12c**

If by mail, postage extra, per box, 6 cents.

Liquid Rouge.

A harmless liquid preparation for giving color to the cheeks and lips, making them a perfectly natural, pretty color.

No. 8C1140 Price, per bottle.......**25c**

If by mail, postage extra, per bottle, 10c

Le Maire's Rubyline.

Rubyline is a refined and harmless rouge prepared in the form of a cream for tinting the cheeks, lips and fingers, leaves a perfectly natural stain or glow and can never be detected. The majority of ladies prefer rouge in this form, as it is put up in a very convenient manner and easily applied.

No. 8C1141 Price, per box..................**18c**

If by mail, postage extra, 5 cents.

Camphor Cold Cream.

Retail price.......................................25c
Our price, each..............................**$0.16**
Our price, per dozen.........................**1.50**

A SALVE OF REMARKABLE HEALING QUALITIES. Of great value when the skin is chapped from cold; it will heal up the cracks and **make the skin soft and smooth** again, also it cannot be excelled **as a soothing and healing application to burns,** and dressing for abrasions of the skin, pimples, boils, etc.

No. 8C1145 Price, per dozen, **$1.50**; each **16c**

If by mail, postage extra, per box, 6 cents.

HAIR PREPARATIONS.

Danderof.

The Great Scalp Cleaner and Tonic. Permanently cures dandruff, eczema, itching, hair falling out, humors, and all troubles of the scalp and hair. Will positively clear the scalp from dandruff and render it healthy, promoting the growth of the hair. It is recommended to ladies who desire long, glossy hair. It keeps the hair soft and glossy; prevents baldness; makes the hair grow stronger.

Price, **No. 8C1150** per bottle.. .....**42c**

Unmailable on account weight.

Hair Elixir.

A beautiful dressing for the hair, making it soft and glossy; prevents it from splitting and falling out. Cures dandruff and makes the hair grow. **Our Hair Elixir is used and recommended by every professional hair dresser in large cities.** It is the only safe hair preserver known, and should be used especially for protecting and promoting a fine growth of hair.

No. 8C1151 Price, per bottle **45c**

Unmailable on account of weight.

Eau De Quinine Hair Tonic.

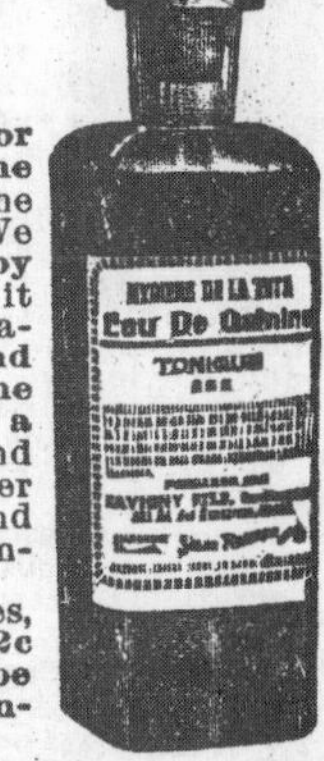

Excellent preparation for strengthening and dressing the hair; much used in Europe by the ladies of the best society. We have **the genuine, imported by ourselves from France,** where it **has gained a much deserved reputation as a valuable hair dressing and tonic. The genuine Eau de Quinine is recognized the world over as a stimulant to the hair nerves and roots, a strengthener and builder** where the natural strength and growth of the hair has become impaired.

No. 8C1152 Price, 8-ounce bottles, 35c; 4-ounce bottles.............**22c**

If by mail, postage and tube extra, small, 16 cents; large, unmailable on account of weight.

Barbers' Egg Shampoo.

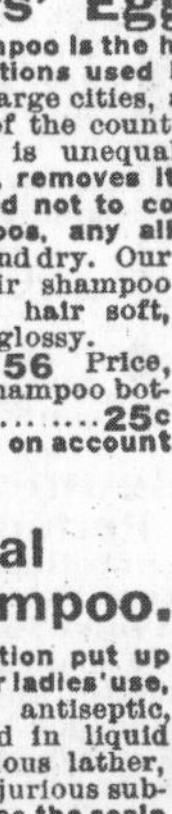

This shampoo is the highest grade of shampoo preparations used by the first class barbers in the large cities, and is very popular in every part of the country. As a gentleman's shampoo it is unequaled, makes clean and healthy hair, removes itching of the scalp, and is guaranteed not to contain, like most other egg shampoos, any alkali, which leaves the hair harsh and dry. Our barbers' hair shampoo renders the hair soft, smooth and glossy.

No. 8C1156 Price, 8-oz. round shampoo bottle...............**25c**

Unmailable on account of weight.

Imperial Shampoo.

A preparation put up especially for ladies' use, thoroughly antiseptic, and supplied in liquid form, making a soft and copious lather, free from alkalies and any injurious substances whatever. **It stimulates the scalp and leaves the hair soft and luxuriant,** and should be used once or twice a month freely. The Imperial Shampoo represents the highest art of shampoo preparations and is put up in handsome eight-ounce sprinkler top bottles, making it very convenient for use. The genuine Imperial Shampoo is never sold for less than $1.00 per bottle.

No. 8C1159 Price, 8-ounce sprinkler top bottle......(Unmailable.).......**32c**

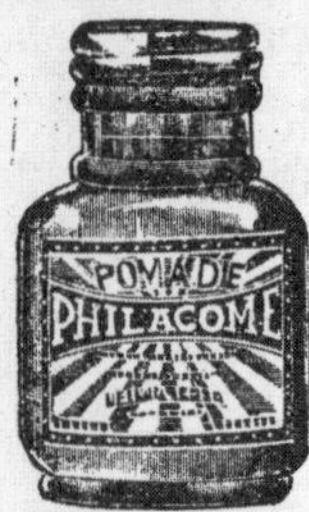

Pomade Philacome.

An exquisite dressing for the hair and mustache, nicely perfumed, and highest quality, in 2-ounce, large mouthed screw top bottle, very convenient for making application. This pomade is far superior to any other pomade usually retailing for 25 cents and even 50 cents per bottle.

No. 8C1162 Pomade Philacome. Price, 2-ounce screw top bottle....................14c
If by mail, postage extra, 5 cents.

Olive Wax Pomatum.

For fixing and laying the hair, whiskers and mustache. Highly perfumed, each stick wrapped in tin foil.

No. 8C1165 Price, per stick.......7c
If by mail, postage extra, 4 cents.

French Cosmetique.

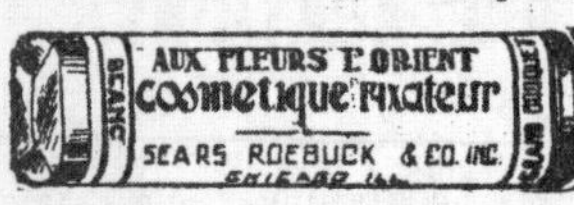

Wrapped in foil; black, pink or white. Retail price, 10 cents.

No. 8C1168 Price, per stick.........5c
If by mail, postage extra, 1 cent.

Magnesium Carbonate.

Rose Perfume Lump Magnesia. Used after shaving by some, who prefer it to Talcum Powder.

No. 8C1169 Price............5c
If by mail, postage extra, 2 cents.

Styptic Pencils.

Used at shaving. Will instantly stop bleeding. Should be kept on hand by everyone shaving himself.

No. 8C1170 Price,..............................6c
If by mail, postage extra, 2 cents.

Hair Curling Fluid.

This preparation will keep the hair in curl during the dampest or warmest weather; quite harmless to the hair; directions on each bottle.

No. 8C1171 Price, per bottle..15c
If by mail, postage and mailing tube extra, 17 cents.

Blondine.

The Famous Hair Bleach. This is a perfectly harmless preparation that will gradually turn the hair from any color to a beautiful blonde color. Any shade of color can be obtained, from light brown to golden by following the simple instructions which go with each bottle. We guarantee that no harm to the hair will result in using it, but **rather it is cleansing and strengthening.**

No. 8C1177 Price, small trial size bottle..42c
Price, large bottle.......................................70c
If by mail, postage and mailing tube extra, small, 16 cents; large, unmailable on account of weight.

Shampoo Paste.

Removes dandruff, leaves the hair soft and keeps the scalp in a healthy condition; produces the finest foam, is the most economical shampoo and is unexcelled as a cleanser.

No. 8C1180 Price, per small jar........................14c
Price, per large jar (50-cent size)..............................22c

If by mail, postage extra, small, 12 cents; large, 22 cents.

Petroleum Pomade.
Perfumed.

This is an excellent toilet article for chapped or rough skin, blotches, pimples. Also as a salve for sore lips. As a hair dressing it is much superior to the old style pomades and hair oils.

No. 8C1183 Price, per bottle..13c
If by mail, postage extra, per bottle, 8 cents.

Brilliantine.

An Imported French Hair Oil for making the hair soft and glossy. Gentlemen use it with advantage on the mustache to keep the hair in place and make it glossy.

No. 8C1186 Price, per bottle.....16c
If by mail, postage and tube extra, 15 cents.

Perfect Combination Hair Dye.
Black or Brown.

The Perfect Combination Hair Dye is a really perfect dye for dyeing the hair, mustache or whiskers, quickly, all shades of brown to a deep black.

Consists of two different preparations, which when used in combination will always insure satisfactory results. Explicit and complete directions are furnished with each package.

No. 8C1188 Price............40c
By mail, postage extra, 16 cents.

Cranodoform Hair Tonic.

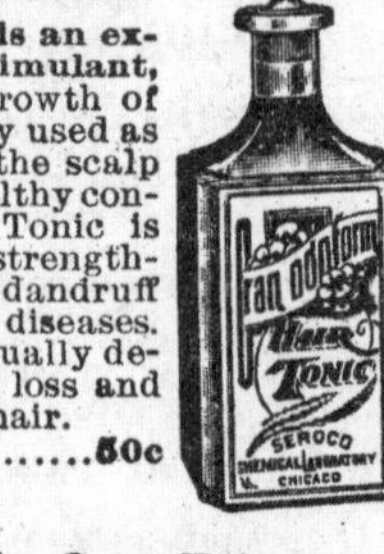

Cranodoform Hair Tonic is an excellent hair and scalp stimulant, and will greatly aid a new growth of the hair. When systematically used as a hair dressing, it will keep the scalp and the hair in a perfectly healthy condition. Cranodoform Hair Tonic is especially recommended for strengthening the hair and as a cure of dandruff as well as other cranial scalp diseases. It will always and very effectually destroy parasites, and stop the loss and the slow destruction of the hair.

No. 8C1190 Price..............50c
Not mailable.

Merigold's Sea Foam.
(DRY SHAMPOO.)

An Elegantly Perfumed Sea Foam, made under the well known Merigold process.

Cools and cleanses the scalp and benefits the hair.

An excellent hair dressing.

No. 8C1192 Price, 8-ounce bottle, **32c**
Not mailable.

TOOTH BRUSHES AND TOOTH PREPARATIONS.

Tooth Brushes.

If by mail, postage on tooth brushes, 2 cents extra.

No. 8C1216 A Good Four-Row Tooth Brush, good bristles, nice white handle. Price............4c

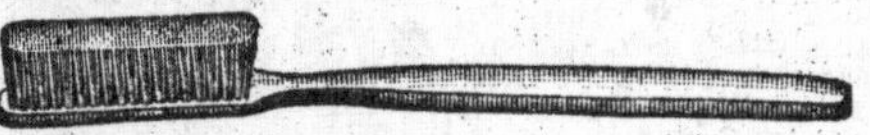

No. 8C1219 A Very Large, Good Quality Tooth Brush, pure white French bristles. Worth 20 cents, and usually sold at that price. Our price.........8c

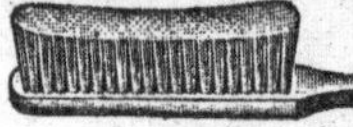

No. 8C1222 A Very Fine Imported Tooth Brush, our own importation, superior quality, usually sold by retail dealers at from 30 to 35 cents. Our price...12c

No. 8C1225 This is one of the finest imported Tooth Brushes to be had, finest French imported bristle. Especially suitable for ladies. Price....19c

No. 8C1227 The highest grade of fine, imported French Tooth Brushes, four rows, extra quality, new style, square handle. Price......................25c

No. 8C1228 Florence Dental Plate Tooth brushes for cleaning artificial teeth. Price......24c

The Genuine Prophylactic Tooth Brush.

The Prophylactic Tooth Brush, Adults' and Youths' Size, is the most perfect tooth brush made, and considered indispensable as a cleanser of the teeth. Constructed upon new principles of dental science and recommended very highly by dentists and physicians. Directions for use are given with each brush. It is furnished with new style patent hanger, so that the bristles may dry quickly and keep sweet and clean.

No. 8C1229 Prophylactic Tooth Brush, with patent hanger complete, each in a box. Price........20c
If by mail, postage extra, 3 cents.

The Rational Tooth Brush.

Prophylactic style. Made of light French bristles.
No. 8C1230 Price................................9c

Nail Brushes.

No. 8C1231 Extra Fine Nail Brush, four rows of imported bristles, white bone handle; a brush that druggists and retail dealers usually ask 15 cents for. Price......(If by mail, postage extra, 2c)......7c

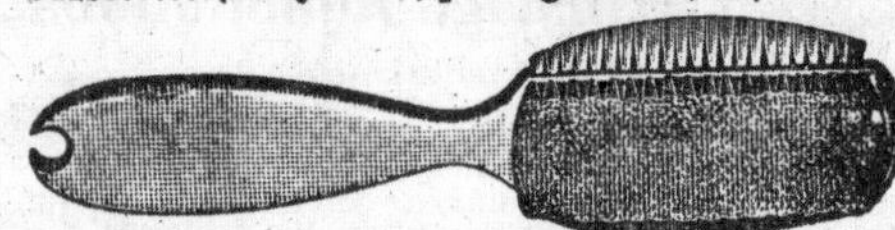

No. 8C1234 A very fine eight-row, Winged Nail Brush, with nail cleaner and scourer; dealers ask 50 cents for brushes of this quality. Price.......24c
If by mail, postage extra, 2 cents.

Ear Cleaner.

Improved Ear Cleaner, spoon and ear sponge combined. A very useful and pretty ivory toilet article.

No. 8C1237 Price.......8c
If by mail, postage extra, 1c.

Oriental Liquid Dentifrice.

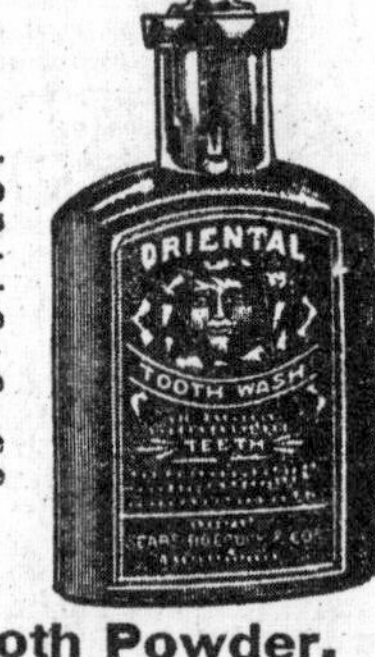
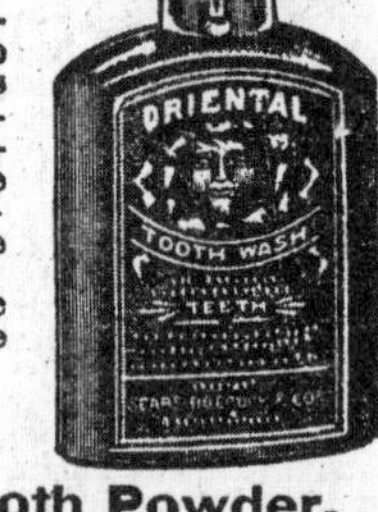

The most perfect preparation for the teeth. Will keep them entirely **free from stains or discolorations.** It will effectually remove the tarter, harden the gums and keep the teeth as lovely as pearls, leaving a delicious after taste in the mouth for hours.

No. 8C1239 Per bottle...15c
If by mail, postage and tube extra, 12 cents.

Pearl Tooth Powder.

In patent silver finish metal can. Dustproof and dampproof and most convenient.

Pearl Tooth Powder is prepared in accordance with the most valuable formula for beautifying and preserving the teeth. Approved, recommended and used by dentists and physicians. Cleanses, brightens, whitens the teeth and prevents decay. Contains nothing injurious; is far superior to all other preparations owing to its highly antiseptic properties, not found in any other tooth powder on the market.

No. 8C1241 Pearl Tooth Powder. Price....16c
If by mail, postage extra, 6 cents.

Sanitary Tooth Soap.

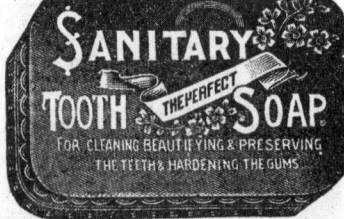

The Perfect Tooth Soap, for cleaning, beautifying and preserving the teeth, hardening the gums, and keeping the breath sweet; warranted not injurious; in metallic box. Retail price, 25 cents.

No. 8C1243 Our price, per box...............12c
If by mail, postage extra, 3 cents.

Dr. Lenny's Sanative Tooth Paste.

This well known tooth paste is without question the finest preparation furnished in metal tubes, and whitens, preserves and beautifies the teeth in the most satisfactory and effective manner. The metal tube style is a very convenient way of using a tooth preparation and is favored by many ladies and gentlemen who prefer it to tooth powders and tooth washes. This splendid preparation is superior to those that always retail at 25 cents.

No. 8C1245 Dr. Lenny's Tooth Paste in tubes. Regular 25-cent size. Price, 15c
If by mail, postage extra, 8 cents.

Toothache Wax.

For the cure of toothache. Easy to apply and gives almost instant relief. It is only necessary to break a small piece off and press it into the decayed part of the tooth.

No. 8C1247 Price, per vial......................9c
If by mail, postage extra, 1 cent.

SOAP DEPARTMENT.

FINE TOILET AND LAUNDRY SOAPS at prices that mean a BIG SAVING. Please note our splendid line of toilet soap—every good brand on the market, every kind that we can recommend to our customers. We guarantee the purity of these soaps, and we know that each is the best kind for the purpose recommended. Don't fail to include soap with your order. Nice soap is such a pleasing, refined addition to the toilet, adds so much to one's comfort and appearance, and costs so little that no one should overlook these offerings. Our **SEROCO LAUNDRY SOAP** is the greatest bargain ever heard of in the line of laundry soap. It is put out under our guarantee for quality and as the best value ever offered. In our Free Grocery Catalogue, sent to anyone on application, we show a complete line of other brands of laundry soap.

Dr. Lenny's Skin Soap.

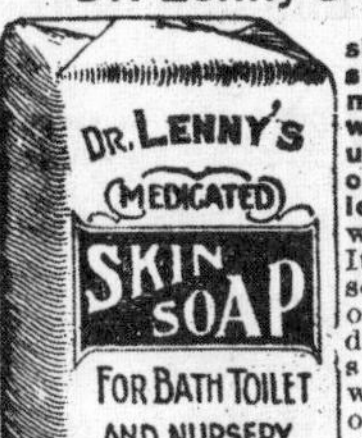

A true medicated skin soap which is superior, for the treatment of any skin trouble where a soap is to be used, to anything else on the market regardless of the price at which it may be sold. It is a medicinal soap in the true sense of the meaning of this designation, and thousands of physicians would today use no other soap for the purpose for which this soap is intended. It is also very desirable and valuable for the general toilet, bath and nursery.

No. 8C1249 Price, per bar 12c
Per box of three bars 30c
If by mail, postage extra, single bar, 4 cents; per box, 14 cents.

Healthy Complexion Soap.

"Necessaire" (the needful) is the name given to this soap by a celebrated French physician and chemist, and which is specially prepared according to his formula for Sears, Roebuck & Co. It is a combination of the purest soap making ingredients, combined with the latest discoveries in antiseptics and preservatives known to chemists. It is the perfection of soap to give the skin a healthy tissue and free it from all poisonous germ organisms which are so irritating, annoying and disfiguring. Its copious, abundant lather not only kills these organisms, but also detaches same from the surface to which they cling tenaciously. **It is the ne plus ultra of germ destroyers, and the greatest promoter of health, beauty and comfort. We guarantee its continual use to cure all skin diseases,** no matter how severe; also to make a beautiful, healthy complexion if used to the exclusion of all other soaps.

No. 8C1251 Price, per cake 10c
Per box of 3 cakes 25c
If by mail, postage extra, per cake, 4 cents; per box, 14 cents.

Genuine Witch Hazel Toilet Soap.

Prepared in accordance with the celebrated formula. We can guarantee our genuine Witch Hazel Soap to be without a peer amongst the soaps for toilet purposes. Our Witch Hazel Soap is absolutely pure and is highly recommended as the safest and best toilet soap. Physicians and complexion specialists are using Witch Hazel Toilet Soap almost exclusively.

No. 8C1253 Price, per large cake 9c
Per box of 3 cakes 20c
If by mail, postage extra, per cake, 3 cents; per box, 10 cents.

Seroco Cocoanut Oil.

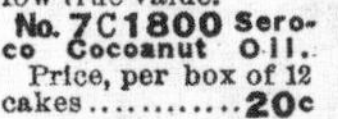

This soap is cut in 2-ounce cakes and is the best cheap soap on the market. Our price, too, is way below true value.

No. 7C1800 Seroco Cocoanut Oil. Price, per box of 12 cakes 20c

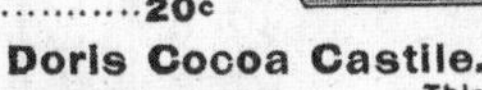

Doris Cocoa Castile.

This is a large 5-ounce oval cake of pressed castile. One of the largest and best regular 5-cent sellers.

No. 7C1801 Doris Cocoa Castile. Price, per box of 12 cakes 45c

Seroco Witch Hazel.

One of our best sellers. Combination of witch hazel and butter milk. Packed three cakes to the box.

No. 7C1803 Seroco Witch Hazel. Price, per box, 3 cakes, 10c

Seroco Oatmeal.

This is the best piece of oatmeal soap on the market. Packed three cakes in a box.

No. 7C1805 Seroco Oatmeal. Price, per box of 3 cakes 12c

WE DO NOT BREAK BOXES OF SOAP WHEN LISTED BY THE BOX ONLY. WHERE SINGLE CAKE PRICE IS NAMED, WE SELL LESS THAN A BOX.

Remmer's Best.

This is a large cake of first class toilet soap. Nicely perfumed, and very cheap at price quoted.

No. 7C1806 Remmer's Best. Price, per box of 3 cakes ... 10c

Garland Turkish Bath Soap.

This is a genuine Turkish bath soap, made from pure stock, nicely perfumed. Packed 12 cakes in neat pasteboard box.

No. 7C1808 Garland Turkish Bath. Price, per box of 12 cakes 40c

Iris Bouquet.

This is one of our best soaps. Made from best stock, well aged and the perfume used is of superior quality. Packed 6 cakes in box.

No. 7C1809 Iris Bouquet.
Price, less than box, per cake 9c
Per box of 6 cakes 50c

Baby's Bath.

This is one of the best toilet soaps on the market. Particularly well adapted for the baby's bath. Equally good for general use. Packed 3 cakes in box.

No. 7C1816 Baby's Bath
Price, less than box, per cake 10c
Per box of 3 cakes 27c

Colgate's Cashmere Bouquet.

Colgate's Cashmere Bouquet is par excellence of all, undoubtedly the very finest grade scented toilet soap made.

No. 7C1817 Price, less than box, per cake 21c
Per box of 3 cakes 61c

California Lemola.

Unexcelled for the toilet. As a complexion soap it has no equal. Peculiarly adapted for the scalp and hair. Cures sunburn and tan and is one of the best toilet soaps on the market for general use.

No. 7C1818 Price, per box of 3 cakes .. 24c

Cuticura.

We offer the Cuticura Toilet Soap, a soap that everybody knows, goods that are sold in almost every drug store in the civilized world, and where it is sold at 25 cents per cake.

No. 7C1820 Price, per cake 20c
Per box of 3 cakes 58c

Carbolic.

We guarantee this the highest grade carbolic acid soap on the market.

No. 7C1821 Price, per box of 3 cakes ... 19c

Sulphur.

Our Sulphur Soap we guarantee the highest grade sulphur toilet soap on the market. It is wrapped and put up in boxes of 3 cakes.

No. 7C1822 Price, per box of 3 cakes .. 19c

Garland Transparent Tar.

This soap is particularly adapted for a shampooing soap. If used regularly will keep the scalp free from dandruff and will keep the hair soft, and in good condition. Also a first class toilet soap for general use. Packed 3 cakes in box.

No. 7C1825 Garland Transparent Tar. Price, per box of 3 cakes 24c

Garland Glycerine Tar Soap.

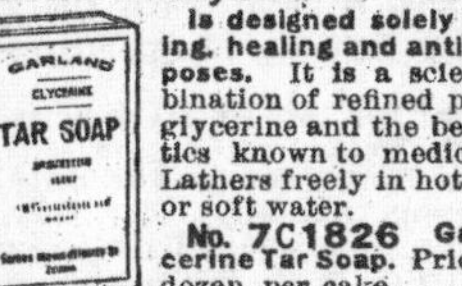

Is designed solely for cleansing, healing and antiseptic purposes. It is a scientific combination of refined pine tar and glycerine and the best antiseptics known to medical science. Lathers freely in hot, cold, hard or soft water.

No. 7C1826 Garland Glycerine Tar Soap. Price, less than dozen, per cake $0.04½
Per dozen cakes .... .50
Per box of 100 cakes 3.90

Pumine.

The mild yet positive action of Pumine Soap makes it especially adapted to the use of engineers, machinists, firemen, farmers, painters, miners, blacksmiths, bookkeepers and all factory employes, as it quickly removes grease, ink, paint and all other adhesive stains, without injury to the most delicate skin.

No. 7C1827 Pumine Soap
Price, less than full box, per cake ... $0.04½
Per box of 100 cakes 3.90

Seroco Transparent.

This is a marvelous value and we shall look forward to many repeated orders. This soap is never sold in a retail way at less than 5 cents.

Packed 12 cakes in a box.
No. 7C1828 Seroco Transparent. Price, per box of 12 cakes 40c

Pears' Unscented.

Pears' Soap has been on the market for more than 100 years. We feel that no extended description is needed.

Packed 12 cakes in a box.
No. 7C1831 Pears' Unscented.
Per single cake $0.12
Price, per box of 12 cakes 1.40

Pears' Scented.

This is the same soap as our No. 7C1831 except it is finely perfumed. Packed 3 cakes in a handsome cardboard box.

No. 7C1832 Pears' Scented.
Price, per single cake 15c
Per box, 3 cakes 43c

Levento Pressed Castile.

This is a strictly high grade domestic castile soap. The bars are cut 4 ounces each. When thoroughly dried out they weigh about 3½ ounces. Packed 12 cakes to the box.

No. 7C1835 Levento Castile. Price, per box of 12 cakes 40c

Conto-Elroy Pressed Castile.

This is a genuine olive oil castile soap, 3½-ounce cakes. Packed 12 cakes to the box, 6 white and 6 green. The kind that you pay 10 cents per cake for generally.

No. 7C1836 Conto-Elroy Castile. Price, per box of 12 cakes 50c

La Lune Castile.

This is the genuine imported La Lune brand of French Castile. Used in many of the best hospitals in this country and acknowledged by all to be the highest grade of castile soap on the market. We furnish this soap in white and pale green only. Bars weigh 3 pounds each, and we do not sell less than single bars.

No. 7C1837 La Lune Castile. Price, per bar, about 3 pounds 48c

La Peria Castile.

This is a genuine olive oil castile manufactured in this country and is considered by many to be the equal of the imported. We furnish this soap in white, mottled or pale green, in bars weighing about 2 pounds. We do not sell less than single bars. Be sure to state if white, mottled or pale green is wanted.

No. 7C1838 La Peria Castile. Price, per bar, about 2 pounds 27c

Levanto Castile.

This is the best medium priced castile soap on the market and we guarantee it to give perfect satisfaction. Furnished in white, mottled or green. Bars weigh about 2 pounds. We do not sell less than single bars.

No. 7C1839 Levanto Castile. Price, per bar, about 2 pounds 17c

Green Oil Soap.

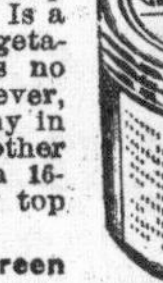

This soap is unequaled for general toilet purposes. Is highly recommended as a soap for shampooing. Is a strictly pure vegetable soap; contains no animal fats whatever, and is used by many in preference to all other soaps. Put up in 16-ounce glass screw top jars, as illustrated.

No. 7C1840 Green Oil Soap.
Price, per 16-ounce jar $0.19
Per case of 12 jars 2.00

SEROCO FAMILY LAUNDRY SOAP.

FOR ONLY $2.95 for a box of 100 bars, a little less than 3 cents a bar, we offer our celebrated Seroco Family Soap as the equal of laundry soaps that sell everywhere at 5 cents a bar, and even more. At our $2.95 price per box of 100 bars we feel confident we are giving such value in laundry soap as is offered by no other house.

OUR SEROCO FAMILY SOAP is put up for us under contract by one of the best soap manufacturers in Chicago, a manufacturer who sells the same soap under another name at almost double our price. The cost of our family soap is figured on very large quantities, on the basis of actual cost of the material and the labor, to which we add the narrowest kind of a margin of profit, **making our Seroco Family Soap the special leader of our soap department.**

We put up Seroco Family Soap in boxes containing 30 bars and 100 bars respectively. You can add a box to your next order, and as laundry soap takes the lowest possible freight rate, it will add next to nothing to the transportation charges. If 100 bars are more than you need, we are sure that you can readily dispose of it by dividing it up among your neighbors, as they cannot possibly buy as good soap for as little money, and you can even make a profit on the soap and still give them extra good value for their money.

THIS ILLUSTRATION gives you an idea of the appearance of a single bar of our **Seroco Family Soap.** Every bar is nicely wrapped, and in appearance and quality is the equal of any laundry soap sold, regardless of price. **We especially recommend our customers in making up their orders not to overlook the extremely low prices we quote on this, our celebrated Seroco Family Soap, the great leader of our soap department.** You will be getting laundry soap at about the actual cost to manufacture it, you will be getting absolutely the very best laundry soap it is possible to manufacture, **and at our special $2.95 price for a box of 100 bars, you will make a saving of at least 20 per cent.**

No. 7C1751 Our special price, per box of 100 bars $2.95
Price per box of 30 bars, 95c; less quantity, per bar .... .03¼

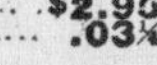

THE NEW IMPROVED RATIONAL BODY BRACE REDUCED FROM $1.69 to $1.19

SOLD UNDER OUR PERSONAL GURANTEE.

The Highest Grade, Most Perfect Woman's Brace for only $1.19. Guaranteed to be Not Only Equal, but Far Superior to Any Other Body Brace, Regardless of the Price at which they are Sold.

DO NOT PAY $8.00, $10.00 OR $12.00 for an inferior body brace when you can obtain from us the New Improved Rational Body Brace for only $1.19, guaranteed to render equal and better service than any other body brace, no matter what price you would be willing to pay for the same. You will never know what a Rational Body Brace means to a woman, as regards her comfort, general health and well feeling, until you possess one of these genuine New Improved Rational Body Braces, the greatest boon to weak, suffering womankind.

A WOMAN'S GENERAL HEALTH, strength, grace, erectness and beauty of form are regained and retained by wearing a properly adjusted Rational Body Brace. It will, in the most natural and always successful manner, cure the complaints of women. It will meet and remove the cause of weaknesses and organic displacements by applying its strengthening influence and natural support to parts of the body where it is most needed.

THE FRONT PAD, as illustrated, and abdominal supporter is fitted with the new hygienic, sanitary perforated, nickel plated shield, and made of specially prepared scientifically and correctly tempered brass perforated plates, which makes them pliable and strong. They quickly adjust themselves, and fit all figures. The springs used in this brace are silver plated and welded, the recently discovered Bessemer process being employed for this purpose, which makes them practically indestructible. Four nickel plated pads form a joint attachment to these springs, arranged in a manner so as to make the hips the main part upon which the supporting power of the New Improved Rational Brace rests, thus relieving the weakened internal organs, muscles and nerves from all unnatural strain. The effect is an immediate feeling of relief to the wearer, followed by regular and natural functions of every organ of the body involved.

THE IMPROVED RATIONAL BODY BRACE is highly recommended by physicians for all persons suffering from general weakness, to persons whose shoulders droop and whose posture is neither natural nor correct. It is the proper and only comfortable brace for fat people. A large abdomen is often reduced a few inches per month as a result of relief afforded by the brace to the stretched and overloaded muscles.

IT IS THE ONLY APPLIANCE that should be used by women troubled with falling of the womb or other irregularities of the female organism, including unnatural discharges, painful, delayed or profuse menstruation; also for all affections of the bladder. For the removal of pains in the shoulders, backache, headache, pains in the chest and weakness of the lower limbs nothing will equal it.

THE IMPROVED RATIONAL BODY BRACE is an abdominal supporter and shoulder brace combined, constructed so as to form a natural support to every organ of the body, including the spine, ribs, lungs, heart, liver, bowels, womb; in fact, every organ, bone and muscle of the human body. The supporting, strengthening and healing influence of the Rational Body Brace has never been approached by any other appliance. It assures to the wearer comfort, vigor, health, elasticity, ease; all of the utmost importance to women subject to physical changes, in all conditions and in every walk in life. **The Improved Rational Body Brace is made of specially prepared material** and is adjustable, thus always insuring a perfect fit. The upper portion of belt and shoulder pads consists of strong elastic webbing. The lower belt is non-elastic and as a result you will find in this appliance perfect support, yet absolute freedom for every movement of the body

WHITE MATERIAL is used throughout, which can easily be laundered and kept clean and in a sanitary condition. Every part of the belt and straps is treated by a special process, so as to reduce absorption of perspiration to a minimum.

YOU CAN WEAR the Improved Rational Body Brace to suit your own convenience and as you may prefer, either under corset, over vest, under closed drawers, over open drawers. The adjustable features of this brace make it possible to wear the same appliance at all times; whether before or after confinement will make no difference.

WOMEN SHOULD NOT under any circumstances cease wearing the genuine newly Improved Rational Body Brace before and after confinement. It will not only support them better than anything else, but will preserve their figure, and, what is still more important, it may be the means of saving their life.

HOW TO ORDER. Take measure over vest and drawers; state size around body about two inches below tops of hip bones. Mention if extra large adjustment is desired, giving height and weight at the same time.

An extra set of understraps is furnished with each body brace, free of charge, to be used when the first set is in the laundry, thus enabling the wearer to use the **Rational Body Brace** without interruption during the time when it is most needed.

No. 8C1260 The Improved Rational Body Brace complete, only **$1.19**
If by mail, postage extra, 20 cents.

EVERY RATIONAL BODY BRACE IS FURNISHED BY US UNDER OUR PERSONAL GUARANTEE.

THE VENUS OR SANITARY PROTECTOR.

NOW ONLY 23c EACH!

No woman who values comfort, cleanliness and health should be without it. The only practical protector. Perfect in fit. Safe in use.

THE ENORMOUS SALE of this grand protector has enabled us to manufacture it in such immensely large quantities, to reduce the cost of production to such an extent, that we are today in a position to offer this valuable appliance for the never heard of low price of 23 cents each.

THE VENUS PROTECTOR is made of a transparent India rubber sack which is very silky, soft and pliable and also very strong. This sack readily admits a napkin or any other soft substance like cheesecloth or cotton, and will hold it securely in the proper position. The belt is made of the very best lisle, non-elastic. The strap to which the sack is buckled is made of a superior grade of lisle elastic, which gives with the different movements of the body, thus keeping the protector always in the right place.

THE VENUS OR SANITARY PROTECTOR will save many times its cost in washing and bleaching. It is absolutely waterproof and thereby positively prevents soiling of the underwear. Each protector comes put up in a neatly finished box with full and explicit directions. With proper use will last a lifetime. After use each month all that is necessary is to clean it with a damp cloth or sponge. In ordering give waist measure.

POINTS OF EXCELLENCE in the Venus or Sanitary Protector. It is perfectly sanitary, comfortable, pliable and non-irritating; easily adjusted and readjusted, and indispensable to women walking, riding or traveling. Always clean and ready for use. Feels cool in summer and protects the wearer from cold in inclement weather. Retail price of the Venus or Sanitary Protector, $1.50 each.

Engraving shows the napkin in place, ready for use.

No. 8C1262 Price, each........................ 23c
If by mail, postage extra, each, 3 cents.

Absorbing Pads or Napkins for the protector, made of especially prepared muslin and medicated cotton.
No. 8C1264 Price, per dozen.................. 25c
If by mail, postage extra, 6 cents.

A bottle of Sanative Wash in concentrated form, sufficient for six months' supply, put up especially to be used in connection with the celebrated Venus or Sanitary Protector.
No. 8C1266 Sanative Wash. Price, per bottle.................. 20c
Unmailable on account of weight.

LADYLINE ANTISEPTIC SUPPOSITORIES.

THE NEVER FAILING LOCAL TREATMENT for the cure of inflammation, congestion and falling of the womb, antiversion, retroversion and prolapsus, dropsy of the womb, ulceration, polypus, tumor, leucorrhea (whites), profuse, difficult and delayed menstruation, ovarian tumors, fibroid tumors, inflammation and congestion of the ovaries, and cancers in the early stages. The Ladyline Antiseptic Suppositories are soothing, healing and curing.

Retail Price, $1.50 to $2.00.

No. 8C1268 Our price, regular size box, containing full month's treatment, only.............. 60c
Additional information and explicit instructions will be sent with each box.
If by mail, postage extra, 6 cents.

SPECIAL DEPARTMENT OF TRUSSES

IMPORTANT REDUCTION IN TRUSS PRICES.

HAVING COMPLETED OUR NEW TRUSS FACTORY and employing the most expert operators in producing these appliances, we are today not only in a position to place at the disposal of our customers the finest grades, the most substantial made trusses, but in addition by installing many labor saving devices and the latest improved machinery for the manufacture of trusses, it has given us an opportunity to still further reduce our already very low prices on nearly every style of our trusses. **We can now sell our trusses at lower prices than others can manufacture them, ours being always superior in quality, finish and workmanship. Being made by expert truss operators, we can always guarantee a perfect fit and comfortable appliances.**

THE GENTLEMAN IN CHARGE OF THIS DEPARTMENT alone has made the supplying of trusses by mail possible, and by following our rules for measurement he can not only fit you as accurately as you could be fitted by a physician at home, but, different from your physician or your druggist, who may not have your exact size or shape, he is able to have the truss made and adjusted to your exact requirements, and from his long experience, as soon as your order is received and examined, he understands your case thoroughly, can furnish you the exact size required, knows just what readjustment or changes are necessary, and as a result our customers really get in addition to receiving a truss at lowest factory price a professional service, which for comfort, health, money saving and general satisfaction is worth five times the price of the truss.

FROM THE LIMITED STOCK carried by the average druggist a professional man could not honestly fit and adjust a truss for one man in ten, for he would be unable to find the exact size, the exact shape and the proper adjustment, but the druggist or his clerk, in his eagerness to make the sale and get your money, will furnish you a truss which he claims is a fit at from $2.00 to $10.00, and for want of a professional man to study your case, select or make a truss to your exact size and adjust it to your case perfectly, you are compelled to pay this druggist three or four prices for a truss that is little better than nothing and very dangerous at the best.

WE MAKE A SPECIALTY OF FITTING TRUSSES and are prepared to offer to our customers unusual advantages in these goods. We employ only expert and thoroughly competent truss manufacturers, and we guarantee to send to any of our customers a perfectly fitting truss that will give satisfaction. A most important point is that we will save you from one to two hundred per cent on any truss you purchase. **You take no risk in sending to us for a truss.** You can try on our trusses, and if you are not satisfied, both as regards quality, comfort in wearing it, and saving in money, **simply return the truss to us and we will PROMPTLY RETURN YOUR MONEY.**

... HOW TO ORDER ...

STATE YOUR HEIGHT AND WEIGHT, HOW LONG YOU HAVE BEEN RUPTURED, WHETHER RUPTURE IS LARGE OR SMALL,

also state number of inches around the body on a line with the rupture, say whether rupture is on RIGHT OR LEFT SIDE, OR BOTH.

SELECT TRUSS WANTED BY NUMBER.

OUR UNQUALIFIED GUARANTEE.

WE GUARANTEE EVERY TRUSS SENT OUT BY OUR FIRM TO BE STRICTLY AS REPRESENTED AND OF THE HIGHEST GRADE OF ITS KIND. . . .

WE GUARANTEE that our prices are one-fourth to one-tenth of the prices charged by others and that, taking each style as a class, you cannot get a higher grade, finer or more substantial material or better fitting truss, no matter what price you would be willing to pay. We will send any of our trusses on request for comparison with trusses of other houses, and, if you do not find that our appliances are better in material, workmanship and fit, if you cannot see at a glance that you can save from $2.00 to $10.00 on our trusses (the saving depending on the style of truss you wear)

You can Return our Truss at our Expense and the full Amount you have paid for it will be Refunded to you for the asking.

THERE IS PROBABLY NO OTHER ARTICLE OF MERCHANDISE, nothing in the medical or surgical line which sells at such an exorbitant price as trusses, nothing on which the original cost to manufacture has been so utterly disregarded in arriving at the selling price. It seems ever since trusses have been made it has been the custom of everyone whose hands they pass through, from the original manufacturer to the final retailer, to exact an exorbitant profit, until a truss that really costs from **60 cents to $1.00** to make, has and **is now being retailed everywhere at from $2.50 to $10.00 and even upwards.**

WE CHANGE ALL THIS. We quote you the very highest grade trusses on the market, put every truss out under our binding guarantee, and name a price barely covering the actual cost to manufacture, manufactured under the direct supervision of our own professional man, thus insuring for you the very best grade of goods possible to manufacture, and saving you all the profit that the manufacturer, jobber, retailer and physician have heretofore added to make up a

BIG FANCY PRICE.

ELASTIC TRUSSES.
The Genuine New York Elastic Truss.

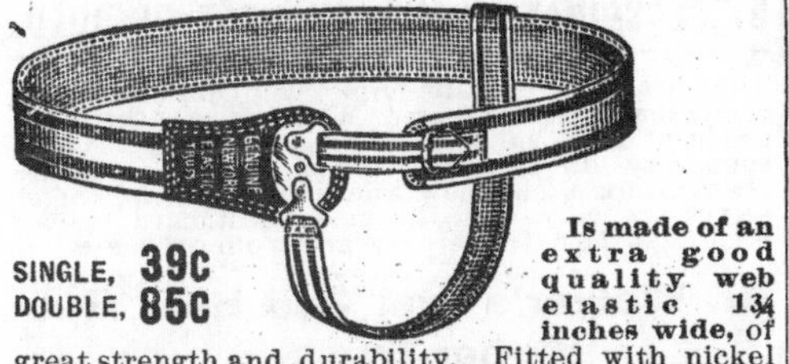

SINGLE, **39c**
DOUBLE, **85c**

Is made of an extra good quality web elastic 1¼ inches wide, of great strength and durability. Fitted with nickel fastenings, solid front and fine enamel pad, which is reversible, so it can be arranged for either right or left side. The price of this style of truss elsewhere is from $2.00 to $2.50. We guarantee it to be superior in quality, workmanship and finish, and it will cost you but 39 cents.

No. 8C1302 New York Elastic Truss, reversible, single. Price........................39c
No. 8C1304 New York Elastic Truss, reversible, double. Price........................85c

The above truss can be furnished in youths' and adults' sizes at the prices quoted. **Be sure and send with your order measurement around body on a line with rupture.**

If by mail, postage extra, 20 cents.

DO NOT FAIL to state on which side the rupture is located and give measurement around body on a line with the rupture.

Dr. Walker's Approved French Pad Single Elastic Truss, $1.45.

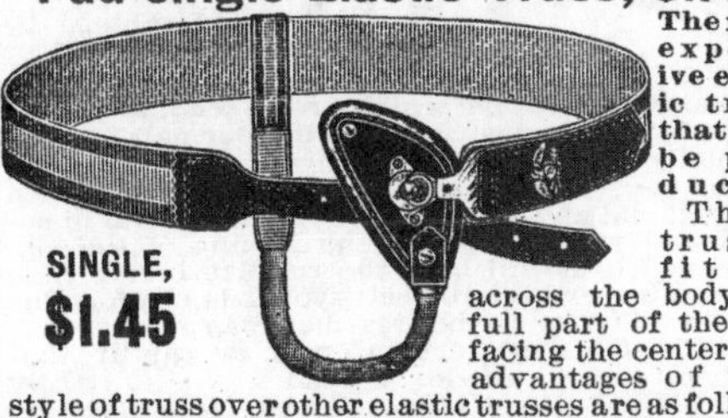

SINGLE, **$1.45**

The most expensive elastic truss that can be produced. This truss is fitted across the body the full part of the pad facing the center. The advantages of this style of truss over other elastic trusses are as follows:

First—By fitting across the body and fastening on the center steel posts on the back of pad a center draft over the top of pad is produced, insuring, in all cases, the right kind of pressure.

Second—By hooking on the tie strap the pad tips produce upward and inward pressure at the same time. **Dr. Walker's Approved French Pad Elastic Truss is, therefore, especially adapted for rupture which comes out egg shape, usually known as inguinal hernia, or light cases of scrotal rupture, where the intestines go down in the scrotum, called inguinal scrotal rupture.** Fitted with rubber tubing understraps. Can be furnished in stuffed pad or water pad. Made of the finest, extra wide and heavy web elastic. Handsomely trimmed and stitched. This truss is reversible and adjustable.

No. 8C1306 Dr. Walker's Approved French Single Elastic Truss. Price....................$1.45
No. 8C1307 Dr. Walker's Approved Truss, with Special Radical Cure Center Spring Pad. Price, $2.65

If by mail, postage extra, 20 cents.

Dr. Walker's Approved French Pad Double Elastic Truss, $1.95.

DOUBLE, **$1.95**

Has all the advantages, as explained in the description of the single truss, and is furnished with double rubber tubing under straps. It is adjustable in width, and also enables you to get the proper angle in the groin, thus making this double elastic truss the easiest and most comfortable in existence.

No. 8C1318 Dr. Walker's Approved French Pad Double Elastic Truss. Price....................$1.95
No. 8C1319 Dr. Walker's Double Elastic Truss, with Radical Cure Center Spring Pad. Price, $3.75

If by mail, postage extra, 20 cents.

The Genuine Lever Elastic Truss.

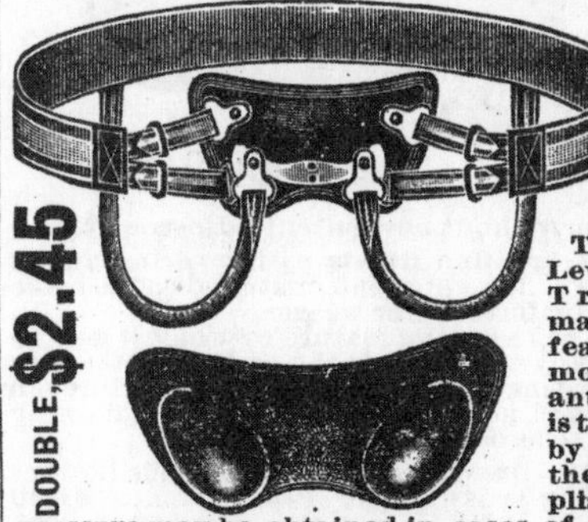

DOUBLE **$2.45**

The Genuine Lever Elastic Truss has many valuable features, the most important of which is the fact that by means of the lever appliance, extra pressure may be obtained in cases of severe rupture. The Lever Elastic Truss always gives satisfaction. Can be used for both single and double rupture. The belt is 2 inches wide, made of the very best web elastic. Solid leather casing and brass trimmings. Fine enamel finished double pads on one plate, as shown in illustration.

No. 8C1320 The Genuine Lever Elastic Truss. Price complete....................$2.45
No. 8C1321 Genuine Lever Elastic Truss, with water pads. Price....................$3.20
No. 8C1323 Genuine Lever Elastic Truss, with Radical Cure Center Spring Pad. Price.....$4.30

If by mail, postage extra, 20 cents.

Sold under a positive guarantee that no better truss of this style could be obtained anywhere, no matter what price you would be willing to pay.

Lea's Special Elastic Truss.

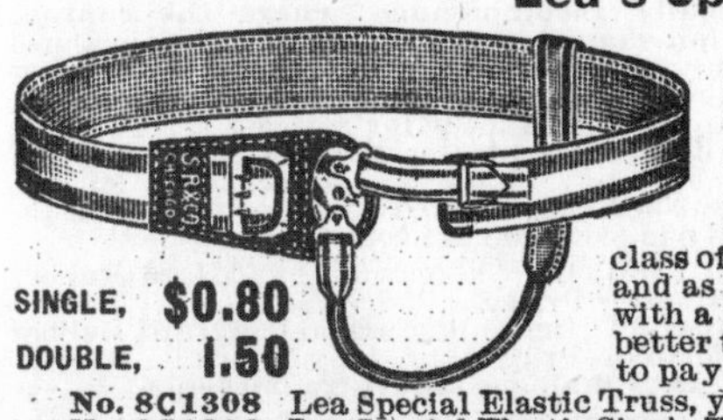

SINGLE, **$0.80**
DOUBLE, **1.50**

A superior quality of a high grade elastic truss, made of the finest quality of heavy web elastic. It has a new style belt, adjustable at both ends so it can be lengthened or shortened as may be desired. It is fitted with improved safety clutch fastenings. Complete with the celebrated water pads, which can be supplied either leather or silk covered. These water pads are very popular, comfortable, are reversible, so that they can be arranged for either right or left side. This class of truss is never sold by others for less than $4.00 or $5.00, single, and as high as $8.00 or $10.00 for the double truss. We furnish them with a positive guarantee to our customers that they cannot get a better truss of this style, no matter how much they would be willing to pay at the following low prices.

No. 8C1308 Lea Special Elastic Truss, youths' or adults' sizes, single. Price....................$0.80
No. 8C1309 Lea Special Elastic Single Truss, with Special Radical Cure Center Spring Pad..... 1.95
No. 8C1312 Lea Special Elastic Truss, youths' or adults' sizes, double. Price.................... 1.50
No. 8C1313 Lea Special Elastic Double Truss, with Special Radical Cure Center Spring Pad... 2.80

Be sure and send with your order measurement around the waist on a line with rupture.

If by mail, postage extra, 20 cents.

SPRING TRUSSES.

Plain Leather Covered French Spring Truss.

Single, **45c**

Double, **90c**

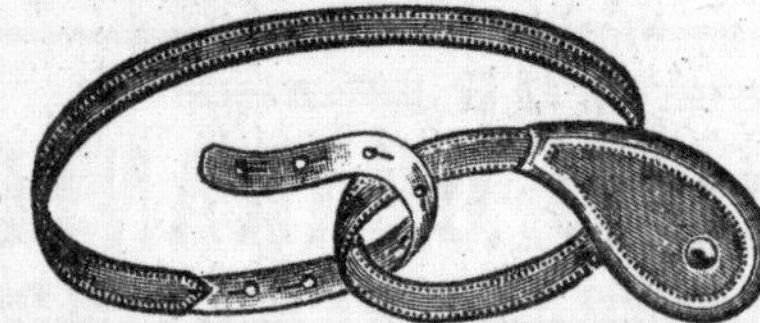

This illustration will give you an idea of the appearance of our single plain leather covered French truss, which we can furnish you at the extremely small price of 45 cents. The double plain leather covered French truss costs only 90 cents. These trusses cannot be duplicated at three and four times the price if bought elsewhere, and, although we supply them to our customers at a nominal figure, they are high grade, well made, leather covered spring trusses and give good satisfaction. Even at our low prices we sell this truss with a guarantee that it will fit perfectly, and, if not entirely satisfactory when you receive it, you can return it at our expense and we will cheerfully refund your money.

No. 8C1326 Plain Leather Covered Spring French Truss, single. Price 45c

No. 8C1328 Plain Leather Covered Spring French Truss, double. Price.................. 90c

If by mail, postage extra, 20 cents.

In ordering the single truss, be sure and state where the rupture is located (if on the right or left side). **Also give in all cases the measurement around body on a line with rupture.**

Fine French Leather Covered Truss.

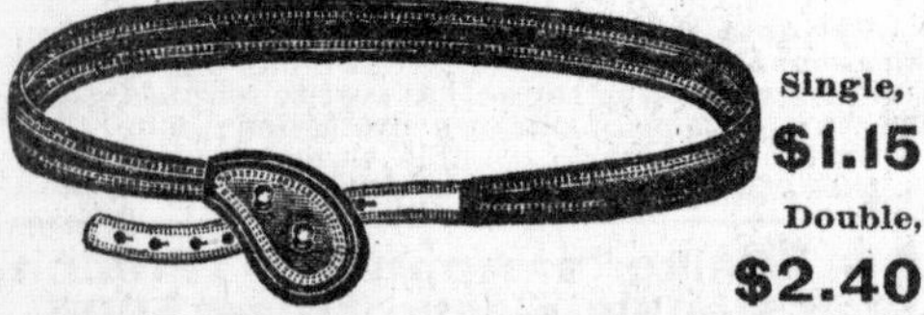

Single, **$1.15**

Double, **$2.40**

Contains the very best new process tempered steel springs, the finest quality of heavy orange calfskin cover, silk double stitching, extra wide and soft edges, hand made hair pad, white casing padded inside. The handsomest, most substantial and comfortable fine French spring truss that money can produce. Not reversible. **When ordering be sure to state side on which the rupture is located (right or left); also measurement around body on a line with rupture.**

No. 8C1334 Fine French Leather Covered Spring Truss, single. Price.................. $1.15

No. 8C1336 Fine French Leather Covered Spring Truss, double. Price.................. 2.40

If by mail, postage extra, 20 cents.

Sold under a positive guarantee that no better truss of this style could be obtained anywhere, no matter what price you would be willing to pay.

Dr. Walker's Approved Fine French Leather Covered Spring Truss.

Single **$1.20**

With or without new patent adjustment.

This truss has fine Russia calf covering and is furnished with fine water pad or stuffed pad to make it soft and comfortable for wearer.

This truss has a special feature by which it may be adjusted to any angle to suit the position of the rupture, by releasing the thumbscrew that goes through the nickel steel neck into the pad, thereby allowing pad to revolve as on a pivot.

No. 8C1340 Dr. Walker's Approved Fine Leather Covered Spring Truss, single. Price.......... $1.20

If by mail, postage extra, 20 cents.

In ordering, state side on which rupture is located (right or left); also give measurement around body on line with rupture.

Sold under our positive guarantee that no better truss of this style could be obtained anywhere, no matter what price you would be willing to pay.

Unless otherwise specified by the customer we will send the leather covered stuffed pads in all cases.

DO NOT FAIL TO STATE

ON WHICH SIDE RUPTURE IS LOCATED

(RIGHT OR LEFT)

And give measurement around body on a line with the rupture.

An Extra Fine Scrotal Truss.

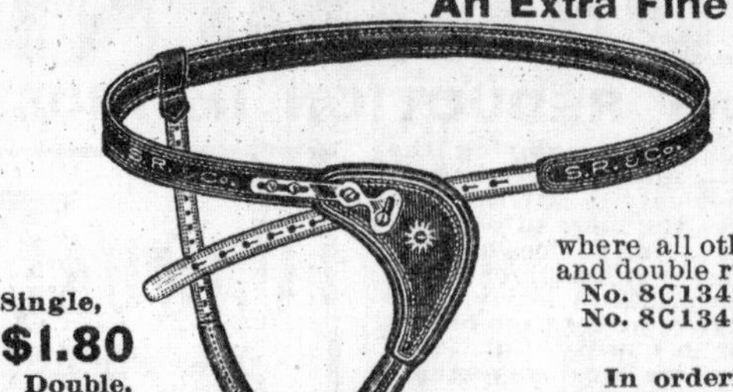

Single, **$1.80**

Double, **$2.95**

This Scrotal Truss is extra fine and most carefully made, complete in every respect and is highly recommended for that class of rupture, which is difficult to hold. Even the worst cases can be made comfortable for the patient by wearing this truss. It will always give satisfaction. The fine steel springs are covered with Russia leather; pads are soft and adjustable and in many cases will hold the rupture where all other styles of trusses have failed. Furnished for single and double rupture.

No. 8C1342 Extra Fine Scrotal Truss, single. Price... $1.80

No. 8C1344 Extra Fine Scrotal Truss, double. Price... 2.95

If by mail, postage extra, 20 cents.

In ordering, please give side on which rupture is located; also measurement around body on a line with the rupture.

Sold under a positive guarantee that no better truss of this style could be obtained anywhere, no matter what price you would be willing to pay.

Unless otherwise specified by the customer, we will send leather covered stuffed pads in all cases.

Dr. Walker's Approved Fine French Leather Covered Spring Double Truss.

Double, **$2.50**

The style, material and finish of this appliance is the same as the single Dr. Walker's Fine Leather Covered Truss, but with the additional spring back pad, as shown in illustration, which is soft, pliable, and makes this double truss very comfortable. The regular selling price of this style double truss is from $6.00 to $9.00.

No. 8C1350 Dr. Walker's Approved Fine French Leather Covered Spring Double Truss. Price. $2.50

If by mail, postage extra, 20 cents.

Sold under a positive guarantee that no better truss of this style could be obtained anywhere, no matter what price you would be willing to pay.

Unless otherwise specified by the customer, we will send leather covered stuffed pads in all cases.

Fine German Truss.

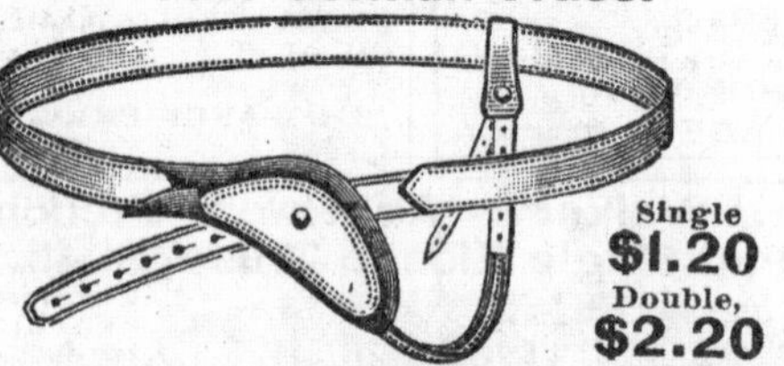

Single **$1.20**

Double, **$2.20**

In cases of rupture which are exceedingly difficult to be held in position the Fine German Truss is especially recommended. This is a spring truss, leather covered, with scrotal pad. It is fitted with an additional understrap, which holds the pad in position and which prevents the moving of the pad. Consequently it will hold the rupture better than most any other style of belt, yet it is comfortable and very effective in the treatment of rupture.

No. 8C1352 Fine German Truss, for rupture that is difficult to hold, single. Price.............. $1.20

No. 8C1354 Fine German Truss, for double rupture, double. Price.............. $2.20

If by mail, postage extra, 20 cents.

In ordering the Single Fine German Truss be sure and state the side on which the rupture is located, whether right or left; also give measurement around body on a line with rupture in all cases.

Sold under a positive guarantee that no better truss of this style could be obtained anywhere, no matter what price you would be willing to pay.

Unless otherwise specified by the customer, we will send leather covered stuffed pads in all cases.

The Peerless Improved French Extension Spring Truss.

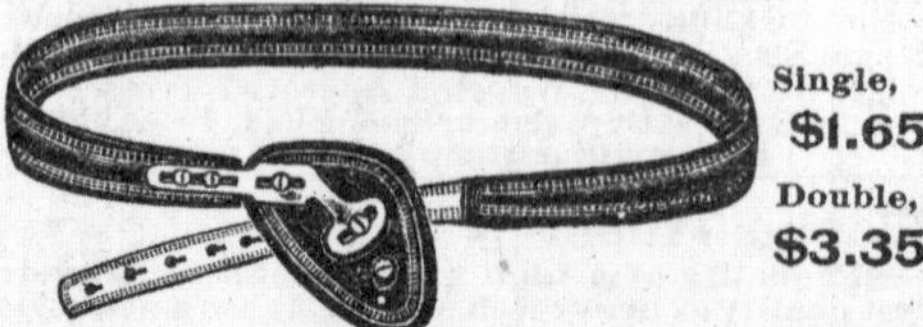

Single, **$1.65**

Double, **$3.35**

This truss is manufactured of heavy orange calfskin, padded inside, and tire casing, double silk stitched, with hand made hair pad. The belt is of the finest spring steel, leather covered, easy and comfortable. Pad can be extended and placed exactly in the proper position. Fine nickel trimmings. The pad is not reversible, but adjustable. Always state where rupture is located (right or left side) and give measurement around body on a line with the rupture. Sold under a positive guarantee that no better truss of this style could be obtained anywhere, no matter what price you would be willing to pay.

No. 8C1360 Peerless Improved French Extension Spring Truss, single. Price.............. $1.65

No. 8C1362 Peerless Improved French Extension Spring Truss, double. Price.............. $3.35

If by mail, postage extra, 20 cents.

Ball and Socket Truss.

Single, **$1.55**

Double, **$2.95**

Ball and Socket Truss or Set Screw Imperial. Made of the finest tested steel springs, covered with Russia leather; highly polished nickel mountings; is reversible; can be arranged for either right or left side, and the pads can be placed in any position desired, and when so placed are held firmly by a perfect fastener. This style of truss has in late years found many admirers, and those who have given same a trial prefer it often to any other style of appliance for the treatment of rupture. The fact that the pad can be placed in almost any position is a very good feature, appreciated by all.

No. 8C1367 Ball and Socket Truss, single $1.55

No. 8C1368 Ball and Socket Truss, double 2.95

If by mail, postage extra, 20 cents.

In ordering, always give measurement around body on line with rupture.

HARD RUBBER TRUSSES.

HARD RUBBER TRUSSES HAVE MANY ADVANTAGES, AND A LARGE NUMBER OF OUR CUSTOMERS PREFER THIS STYLE OF APPLIANCE.

THEY ARE ALWAYS CLEAN, ARE NOT AFFECTED BY PERSPIRATION NOR BY HEAT OR COLD.

They are free from any unpleasant odor and can be easily shaped and adjusted. We carry only the finest grade of hard rubber trusses and supply them at such very low prices that even those in moderate circumstances can now afford to secure for themselves the very best, the very finest hard rubber trusses at the extremely low prices offered below.

Dr. Walker's Oval Pad Hard Rubber Truss.

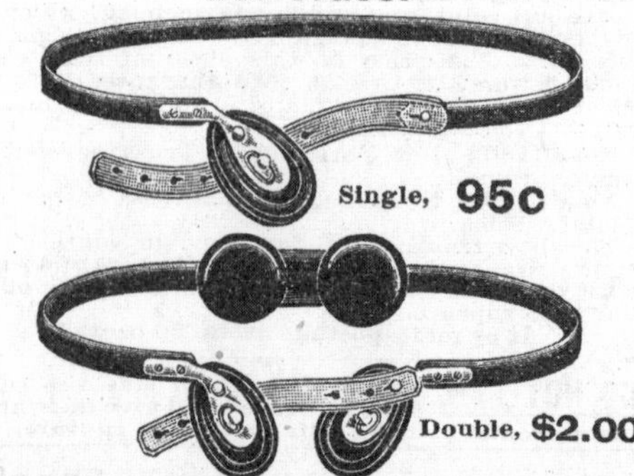

Single, **95c**

Double, **$2.00**

Especially recommended where the rupture comes out shaped like an egg. This small oval pad will easily fit in the right place, and will retain that class of ruptures better than any other style of pad. When applied constantly for at least a reasonable length of time a complete cure can be established. Adjustable pad; high grade hard rubber spring; finely finished nickel plated attachments; hard rubber oval pad, with two set screws.

No. 8C1380 Dr. Walker's Oval Pad Hard Rubber Truss, single. Price.............. 95c

No. 8C1382 Dr. Walker's Oval Pad Hard Rubber Truss, double. Price.............. $2.00

If by mail, postage extra, 20 cents.

When ordering, state location of rupture, whether on right or left side, also give measurement around body on line with rupture.

Sold under a positive guarantee that no better truss of this style could be obtained anywhere, no matter what price you would be willing to pay.

Dr. Walker's Hard Rubber French Pad Truss.

With or without new Patent Adjustment.

Dr. Walker's Hard Rubber French Pad Truss for Scrotal Rupture. The pad can be adjusted to any angle; raised and lowered to reach the conditions of the patient. The shank attachment is so-called malleable, and can be bent to suit. Fine hard rubber springs; highly finished nickel plated attachments; hard rubber French pad. Clean and comfortable.

Single, **95c**

No. 8C1386 Dr. Walker's Hard Rubber French Pad Truss, single....95c

No. 8C1388 Dr. Walker's Hard Rubber French Pad Truss, double.....$1.95

If by mail, postage extra, 20 cents.

Sold under a positive guarantee that no better truss of this style could be obtained anywhere, no matter what price you would be willing to pay.

In ordering, state location of rupture, whether on right or left side, also give number of inches around body on a line with the rupture.

Double **$1.95**

The Solid Comfort (Hood's) Hard Rubber Truss.

$1.90

This is an elegant hard rubber single truss, especially recommended by all truss experts and scientific truss fitters of the world. Before putting on this truss, the rupture should always be returned into the inguinal ring, placing truss in position, the pad right over the spot where the rupture is located. Then fasten the truss at the back. This truss not only cures rupture quicker than any other appliance, but prevents a breach or rupture on the opposite side. It has a small flat pad on the opposite side from the rupture, known as a "blind" pad, which will save you from a double rupture. Once adjusted it usually proves to be the most comfortable and safest truss for single rupture.

No. 8C1392 The Solid Comfort Hard Rubber Truss, for single rupture. Price................$1.90

No. 8C1393 Double Truss.................. 2.60

If by mail, postage extra, 20 cents.

Sold under a positive guarantee that no better truss of this style could be obtained anywhere, no matter what price you would be willing to pay.

In ordering, state location of rupture, whether on right or left side, also give number of inches around body on a line with the rupture.

The Solid Comfort Truss with Radical Cure Pads.

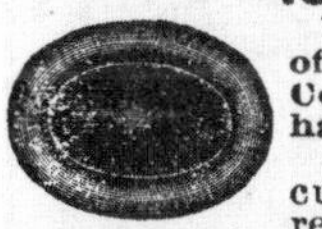

We now supply the best truss ever offered. A combination of the Solid Comfort truss with Radical Cure hard rubber center spring pad.

This new Radical Cure pad will cure almost any rupture within a reasonable length of time and the patient, if moderately careful after he is cured, will remain cured beyond question.

No. 8C1395 Solid Comfort Truss with Radical Cure center spring pads, for single rupture. Price...$3.35

No. 8C1396 Solid Comfort Truss with Radical Cure center spring pads, for double rupture. Price...$3.95

The Genuine Radical Cure Truss.

There are many so called Radical Cure trusses on the market but very few possess the merit claimed for them and that can positively be found in our genuine Radical Cure Truss. Owing to the wonderful influence of the pad, which is constructed on the most advanced ideas of truss experts, the Radical Cure truss will not only serve the purpose of holding up the rupture better than any other similar appliance but it will, even in cases of old standing, reduce the rupture and gradually affect an absolute cure in many of the most difficult cases, if worn properly for a reasonable length of time.

The Radical Cure Truss is made of best spring steel with a wide orange calf skin leather cover padded inside, top and bottom edges of the new style roll finish, that will prevent the edges from cutting into the skin. A handsome practical truss made of the best material, in the most approved manner, for which truss fitters everywhere charge from $15.00 to $25.00. We furnish it to you for $2.90, with full adjustment, so that the pad can be placed in the exact position required; that is, higher up, or lower down, or more towards the right, or more towards the left, making it possible for the patient to shift the pad to any position within reasonable limits, so that you can fit yourself to perfection and save for yourself from $10.00 to $20.00, which truss fitters usually charge for this service.

This Radical Cure Pad has a soft leather covered outer rim with a stationary hard rubber inner pad on metal plate back, adjustable in every direction and can be used for either the right or left side.

No. 8C1398 Radical Cure Truss with stationary hard rubber center pad, single. Price....................$2.90

No. 8C1399 Radical Cure Truss with stationary hard rubber center pad, double. Price....................$4.15

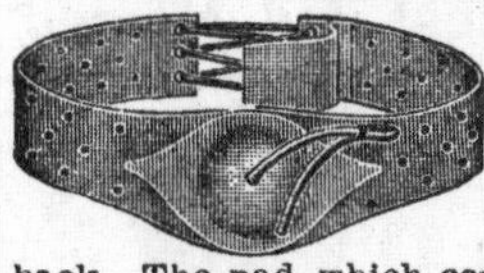

Infants' Soft Rubber Umbilical Truss with an inflatable pad. An excellent truss for very young infants. Sizes, 10 to 17 inches inclusive. It consists of a soft rubber belt which laces in the back. The pad, which covers the navel, is inflated through the rubber tube and when filled, the tube is tied with a soft string to prevent the escape of air from the pad. Give the circumference of the patient's body when ordering.

No. 8C1401 Price..................................50c

If by mail, postage extra, 3 cents.

Umbilical Trusses.

Regular $5.00 Truss for $1.75.

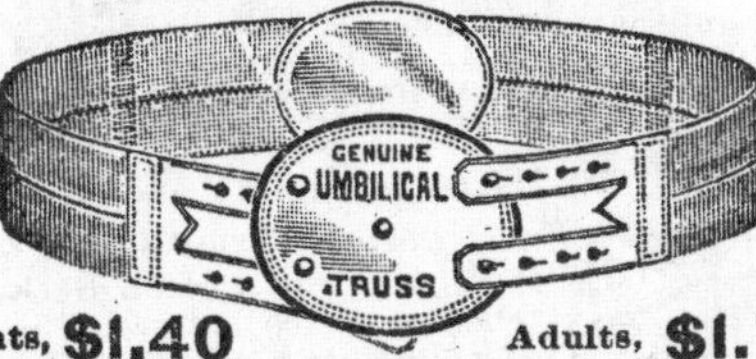

Infants, **$1.40** Adults, **$1.75**

We show in this illustration our Genuine Elastic Umbilical Truss, which is recommended by physicians as the very best truss for umbilical rupture. It is made of the strongest quality of elastic truss webbing, calf and kid pads. A more comfortable truss cannot be found to wear. An inferior quality of this truss is found in the market selling for $6.00 each. If in need of such a truss send to us for it and examine it. You will be satisfied and save lots of money.

No. 8C1404 Price, adults' size..................$1.75

No. 8C1405 Price, infants' size 1.40

If by mail, postage extra, 20 cents.

Heavy Elastic Truss Webbing.

Heavy elastic, for trusses, artificial limbs, etc.

No. 8C1413 Width, ¾-inch. Price, per yard .. 8c
No. 8C1414 Width, 1 -inch. Price, per yard ..12c
No. 8C1415 Width, 1¼-inch. Price, per yard ..18c
No. 8C1416 Width, 1¾-inch. Price, per yard ..22c
No. 8C1417 Width, 2 -inch. Price, per yard ..28c

Covered Elastic Bandages.

This is made of rubber thread and soft lisle thread; best quality, making a soft bandage that is light and porous.

No. 8C1432

2 in. wide by 9 ft. long (stretched). Price....$0.25
2 in. wide by 15 ft. long (stretched). Price.... .40
2 in. wide by 24 ft. long (stretched). Price.... .55
2½ in. wide by 9 ft. long (stretched). Price.... .30
2½ in. wide by 15 ft. long (stretched). Price.... .45
3 in. wide by 9 ft. long (stretched). Price.... .40
3 in. wide by 15 ft. long (stretched). Price.... .55

If by mail, postage extra, 2 cents.

Surgeons' Bandages.

Surgeons' Bandages, made of pure gum rubber, carefully selected and thoroughly seasoned. They will retain their strength and elasticity for years.

No. 8C1433

Width	Length	Price	Width	Length	Price
2 in.	9 ft......	$0.40	2½ in.	12 ft......	$0.75
2 in.	12 ft......	.55	2½ in.	15 ft......	.95
2 in.	15 ft......	.70	3 in.	9 ft......	.60
2 in.	18 ft......	.90	3 in.	12 ft......	.90
2½ in.	9 ft.....	.48	3 in.	15 ft......	1.15

Weight, per roll, from 3 to 6 ounces.

Randolph Umbilical Belt.

Made of strong covered elastic thread, with pad. Give measurement around the body.

No. 8C1434 Infants' sizes, up to 19 inches.......68c

No. 8C1435 Youths' sizes, up to 29 inches.....$1.10

No. 8C1436 Adults' sizes, up to 70 inches.. 1.58

If by mail, postage extra, 20 cents.

Our Elastic Stockings, Bandages, Suspensories and Abdominal Belts.

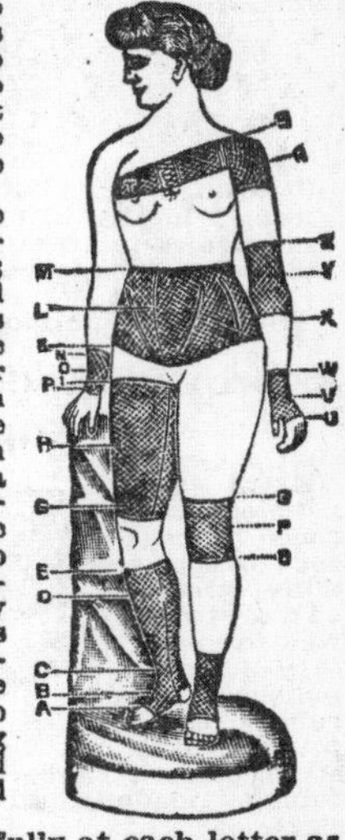

Cost only from one-half to one-third what other firms charge. We guarantee quality and workmanship to be the best. You can get nothing better at double the price at which we sell these goods.

For the relief of varicose veins; weak, swollen or ulcerated limbs; corpulency; abdominal weakness and tumors. As rubber goods spoil with age, these Elastic Stockings and Belts to wear well should be made of fresh material. We make these goods only to order. As soon as we receive an order from a customer for elastic stockings, belts or other elastic goods, we at once send it to our factory and have the article manufactured exactly according to measurements given. We guarantee perfect fit and goods that are actually fresh. Anyone who has had trouble in obtaining either serviceable or good fitting stockings is requested to give us a trial.

Take measurements carefully at each letter as indicated in the illustration; also give the length from the lowest letter to the highest. For example: A garter stocking you would take circumference at A, B, C, D and E; also the length from floor to E inside limb. For stockings extending above and below knee be sure to take size at F, also length from lowest point to F, and from F to highest point. Give us the exact measurements, which should be taken, if possible, in the morning. We allow for expansion.

Prices for Single Stocking or Pieces.

No.	Article	Fine Silk	Cotton
No. 8C1419	Shoulder Piece, S to U.......	$4.00	$3.20
No. 8C1420	Thigh Stocking, A to I.......	4.95	3.85
No. 8C1421	Thigh Legging, C to I.......	3.85	2.80
No. 8C1422	Thigh Piece, G to I..........	1.40	1.00
No. 8C1423	Knee Stocking, A to G.......	3.75	2.40
No. 8C1424	Knee Legging, C to G.......	2.90	2.35
No. 8C1425	Knee Cap, E to G...........	1.60	1.10
No. 8C1426	Garter Stocking, A to E.....	1.95	1.35
No. 8C1427	Garter Legging, C to E.....	1.45	1.05
No. 8C1428	Anklet, A to C..............	1.45	1.05
No. 8C1429	Wristlet, N to P.........	.75	.50
No. 8C1430	Abdominal Belt, K to M.....	5.25	4.50

If by mail, postage extra, 5 cents.

Abdominal Belt.

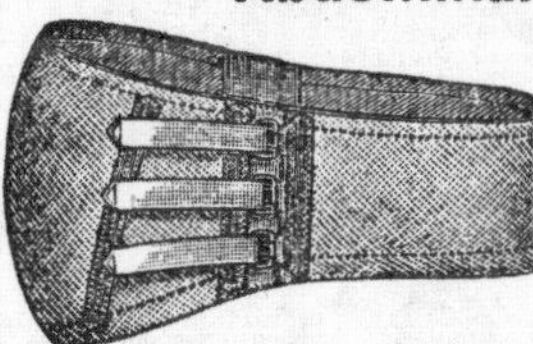

Abdominal Belt, made of strong silk elastic, with soft material trimmings and bracings. Give measurements at K, L and M. We guarantee to fit. Only made to order.

No. 8C1437

Price............$2.75

If by mail, postage extra, 13 cents.

Abdominal Supporter, No. 1.

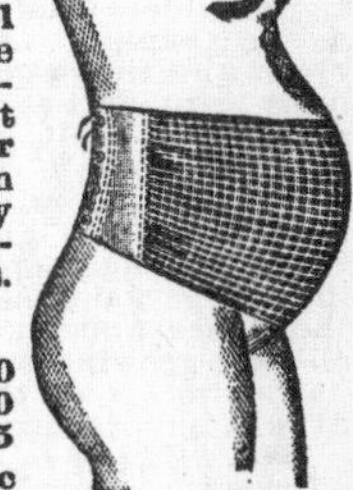

Covered Elastic Abdominal Supporter, made of soft lisle thread, interwoven with protected rubber thread, making it superior to any other supporter of its kind; may be washed in lukewarm water and thereby kept clean; is very light and comfortable. Weighs about 2 ounces. Made in all sizes to order.

No. 8C1438

Price, 8 in. wide..............$0.90
Price, 10 in. wide.......... 1.00
Price, 12 in. wide.......... 1.15

If by mail, postage extra, 10c

Our New Style Abdominal Belt.

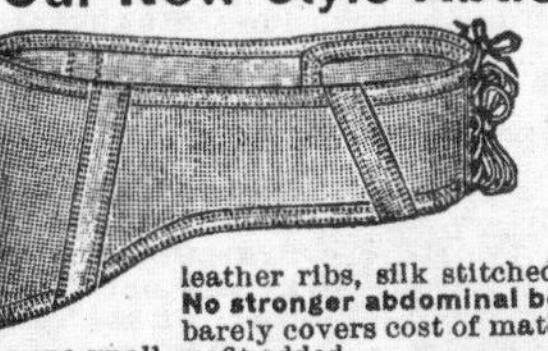

This, our new style abdominal belt as illustrated, is made of finest Sarden's medicated belt canvas cloth, nicely bound, stayed with heavy leather on outside and soft chamois skin strips on inside, leather ribs, silk stitched, metal eyelets to lace. **No stronger abdominal belt made,** and our price barely covers cost of material and labor, with but our one small profit added.

No. 8C1440 Price..78c

If by mail, postage extra, 10 cents.

Favorite Obesity Belt.

Made of strong moleskin cloth that yields sufficiently to assist shaping to the abdomen, thereby giving comfort and the support required. Our obesity belts are used to advantage by corpulent people, both ladies and gentlemen, and will reduce corpulency quickly and permanently. They will give shape to the pendulous or relaxed abdomen. They are fitted with strong elastic side straps and stays. In sending your order be sure to give your measure at the largest circumference around the abdomen.

No. 8C1442 Our Favorite Moleskin Cloth Obesity Belt. Price..$1.30

If by mail, postage extra, 12 cents.

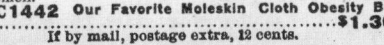

Abdominal Supporter.

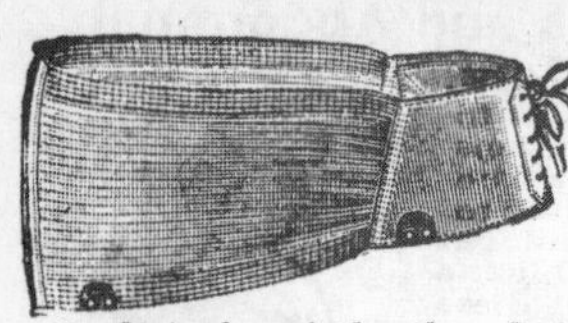

Abdominal supporter. Made with covered elastic front and firm sateen back, giving excellent support. A very comfortable supporter in case of corpulency and pregnancy. Sizes, to 30-inch girth the depth of supporters in front, 7 inches; 32 to 38-inch girth, the depth of supporters in front, 8 inches; 40 to 44-inch girth, the depth of supporters in front, 9 to 10 inches.

No. 8C1444 Egyptian Thread. Price $1.10
No. 8C1445 Silkoline. Price 1.30

Improved Abdominal and Uterine Supporter.

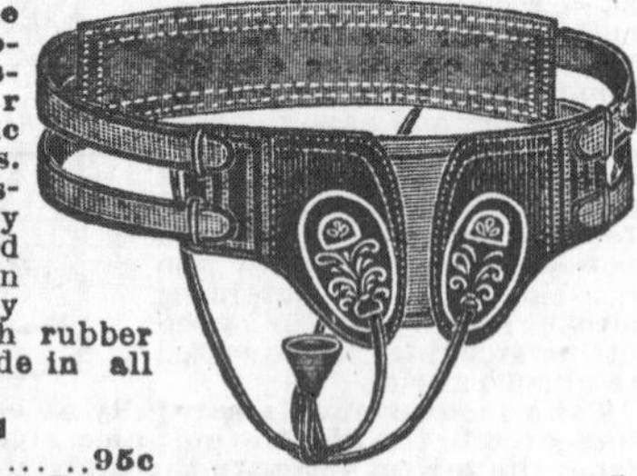

Extra fine pebbled morocco or russet leather with elastic side straps. New form pessary of highly polished hard rubber held in position by strong smooth rubber tubing; made in all sizes.

No. 8C1471
Price 95c
Extra tubes. Price, per pair.... 25c
Extra hard rubber pessaries. Price, each.... 40c
If by mail, postage extra, 20 cents.
When ordering, give circumference of abdomen at largest part.

The London Abdominal Supporter.

Well known as the best and strongest supporter in the market. We guarantee it to be made from the finest and stoutest materials procurable. Every part perfect.

No. 8C1472
Price, all sizes......69c
If by mail, postage extra, 30 cents.
When ordering, give circumference of abdomen at largest part.

Corset Shoulder Brace.

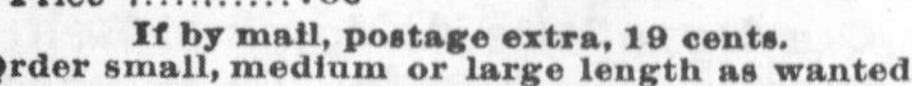

This is a perfect brace for supporting the back, and at the same time drawing the shoulders back so as to expand the chest and throw the body into an erect, graceful position. All tendency to round shoulders is thus avoided, and this to young people in the period when the bones and muscles are growing and hardening, is of the utmost importance.

No. 8C1476
Price 78c
If by mail, postage extra, 19 cents.
Order small, medium or large length as wanted.

S., R. & Co.'s Improved Washington Shoulder Brace.

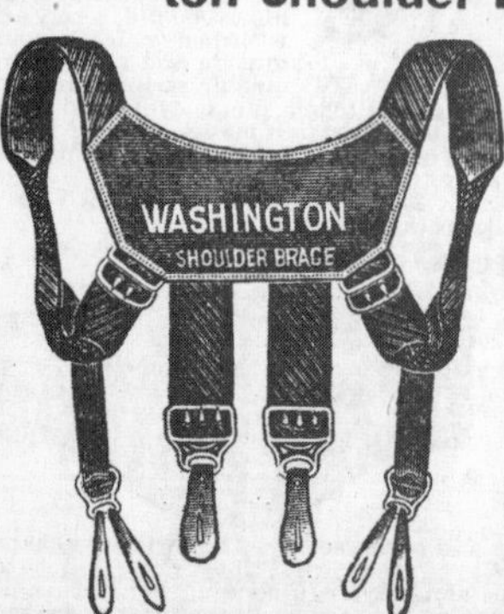

This brace is well arranged to draw the shoulders gently back without cutting or chafing under the arms, thus inclining the body to a graceful, correct position, expanding the chest and correcting all tendency to stooping or round shoulders. Made of strong silk webbing, calf back; webbing rolled under arms so as not to cut. Suspender attachment is of the strongest and finest material.

No. 8C1473 Price..... 68c
If by mail, postage extra, 15 cents.
Order small, medium or large length as wanted.

The Gamble Shoulder Brace for Men and Youths.

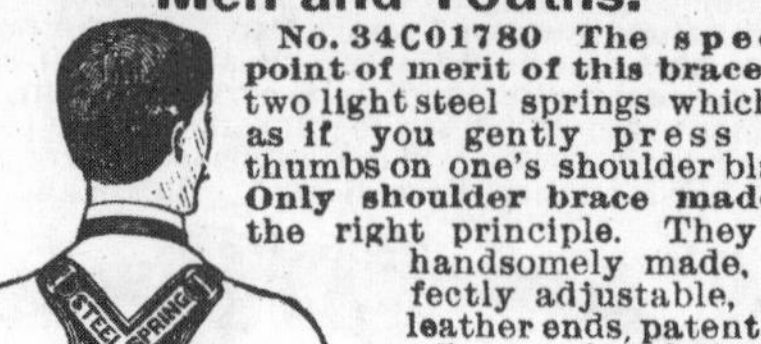

No. 34C01780 The special point of merit of this brace is in two light steel springs which act as if you gently press your thumbs on one's shoulder blades. Only shoulder brace made on the right principle. They are handsomely made, perfectly adjustable, roll leather ends, patent cast off snaps, best hair pads, leather lined in front of arms; most comfortable brace made. Sizes, 30 to 40 inches chest measure.
Price, per pair... $1.25
If by mail, postage extra, per pair, 12c.

The Gamble Ladies' and Misses' Shoulder Brace.

Perfect Shoulder Brace and Skirt Supporter Combined.

No. 34C01784 The Gamble Shoulder Brace for Ladies. Fine light drab jean web, adjustable to any position, finest hair padding, leather lined in front of arms, soft and pliable, will not chafe or irritate the skin. The principle is the same as in the men's brace, No. 34C01780. Sizes, 26, 28, 30, 32, 34 and 36 inches bust measure. Measure close under arms and above breasts. Per pair......95c
If by mail, postage extra, per pair, 8 cents.

Suspensory Bandages.

Chicago Army and Navy.

No. 8C1482 Cotton Sack, non-elastic. Price 15c
No. 8C1484 English Web Sack, elastic bands. Price...... ....38c
No. 8C1486 Bolting Silk Sack, elastic bands. Price..... .....45c
If by mail, postage extra, 5c.

O. P. C. Suspensory.

Automatically adjustable and never fails to fit and give satisfaction; for comfort, security, durability and elegance, the best in the world. Order by number. Give size, large, medium or small.

No. 8C1488 No. 2, lisle. Price..... 60c
No. 8C1490 No. 3, silk. Price. 90c
No. 8C1492 No. 4, all silk. Price..$1.25
No. 8C1494 No. 5, all silk, fancy colors. Price.......... $2.00
If by mail, postage extra, 5 cents.

J. P. Suspensory, Single Band.

Large, Medium and Small.
No. 8C1496 Cotton sack. Price...........16c
No. 8C1498 Silk sack. Price 29c
If by mail, postage extra, 4 cents.

Safety Suspensory.

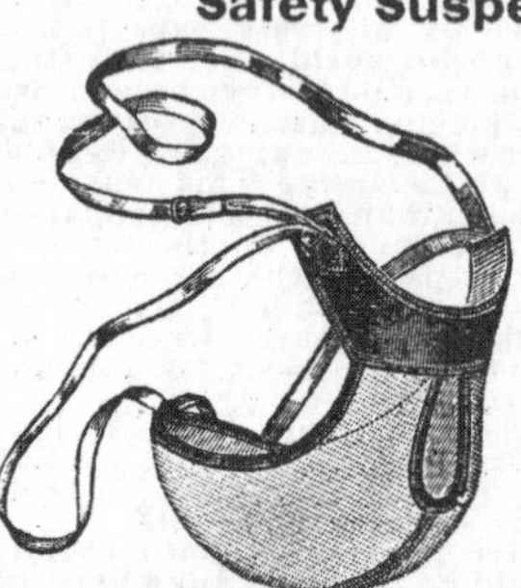

The construction of the Safety secures a perfect self adjusting sliding loop suspensory, which enables the sack to be detached for washing; no buckles on sack. Assorted sizes: large, medium and small.

No. 8C1500 Safety English web sack, elastic band.
Price........46c
No. 8C1502 Safety bolting silk sack, elastic band.
Price.........56c
No. 8C1504 Safety knitted silk sack, elastic band. Price....(If by mail, postage extra, 2 cents)....66c

NO MORE COUGHS AND COLDS.

Wear a Royal Frost Proof Chamois Jacket, sure protection against coughs, colds, pneumonia and all chest and lung troubles.

Only $1.20 for the genuine Royal Frost Proof Chamois Jacket, warm, light and comfortable, the most sensible garment ever devised. You cannot make a better investment during the fall and winter season.

The Royal Frost Proof Chamois Jacket is made for either men or women. The vest is made of the very best grade of chamois skin, which is the best cold resister known, and it is lined with the finest grade of fine flannel. It is carefully made and will last season after season. The seams, buttonholes and all parts of the vest are made in the most workmanlike manner. It is easy to wear, light, soft, pliable and comfortable, and does not interfere in any way with the wearing of other garments.

The knitted self adjusting sides insure a perfect fit. Each jacket nicely put up in a handsome carton. Look out for imitations. The Royal Frost Proof Chamois Jacket is extensively imitated, but the Royal is the best of them all. It is the lowest in price and yet the best in quality.

The Royal Frost Proof Chamois Jacket is handsome in appearance. It is a thorough protection to the lungs and chest, and at our extremely low price of $1.20 is an extraordinary value.

No. 8C1505 Royal Frost Proof Chamois Jackets for Men. Sizes, 34 to 44 in. chest measure. Price. $1.20
No. 8C1517 Royal Frost Proof Chamois Jackets for Women. Sizes, 32 to 38 in. bust measure. Price 1.20
Be sure to state size wanted, the number of inches around chest. If by mail, postage extra, 8 cents.

PLASTERS, POROUS AND PLAIN, SURGICAL DRESSINGS, ABSORBENT COTTON, LINT, OILED SILK, ANTISEPTIC GAUZES, ETC.

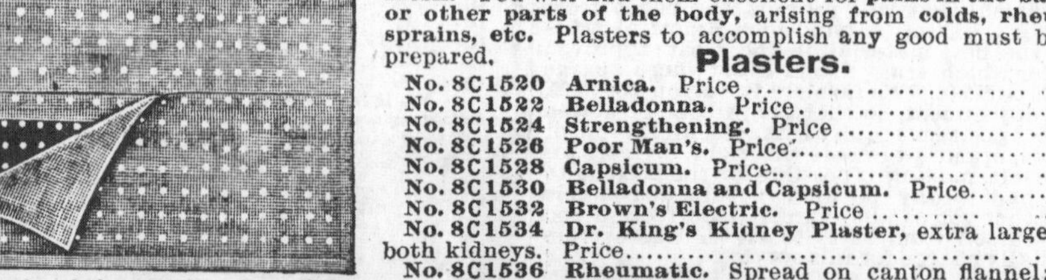

WE GUARANTEE all our Plasters to be full strength and fresh. You will find them excellent for pains in the back, chest or other parts of the body, arising from colds, rheumatism, sprains, etc. Plasters to accomplish any good must be freshly prepared.

Plasters.

No. 8C1520 Arnica. Price 7c
No. 8C1522 Belladonna. Price.......... 7c
No. 8C1524 Strengthening. Price 7c
No. 8C1526 Poor Man's. Price.......... 7c
No. 8C1528 Capsicum. Price.......... 7c
No. 8C1530 Belladonna and Capsicum. Price.......... 7c
No. 8C1532 Brown's Electric. Price 20c
No. 8C1534 Dr. King's Kidney Plaster, extra large to cover both kidneys. Price.......... 25c
No. 8C1536 Rheumatic. Spread on canton flannel; a great relief in local rheumatic pains. Price........(If by mail, postage extra, per dozen, 5 cents)....... 20c
No. 8C1538 Mustard Plasters on Cloth. 3 leaves in envelope. Price.......... 10c
No. 8C1539 Ten leaves in box. Price, per box.......... 25c
No. 8C1542 Absorbent Cotton, in cartons. Sterilized, 1 ounce. Price.......... 5c
No. 8C1544 Corrosive Sublimate Cotton, 1 ounce cartons. Price.......... 5c
If by mail, postage extra, 1 cent.

Court Plaster.

No. 8C1546 Balsamic Court Plaster in Case, 3 colors: black, white and flesh. Price, per case....3c

No. 8C1548 Fine Quality of Silk Court Plaster, three colors in red and gold tablet case. Price....5c

If by mail, postage extra, per dozen, 3 cents.

Mechanics' Court Plaster.

No. 8C1550 On kid, will not wash off, 1 piece, 2x3 inches in case. Price...(Postage extra, 1 cent)...5c

Electric Battery Plasters.

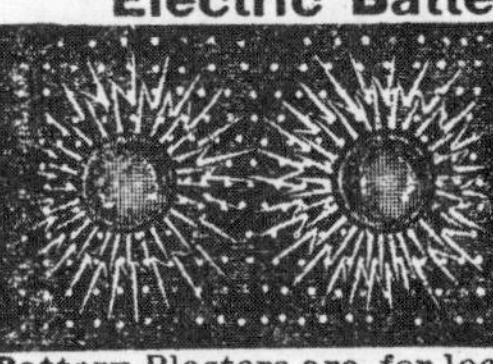

Actual electric current, not mere plates. Positive relief to women from the common and distressing backache incident to the sex at periods; also for rheumatic, kidney and muscular pains in back. These Battery Plasters are for local application only, and should be worn over the region of the pain. They will relieve all pains and weakness that can be reached by an external application of an electric current. If used according to instructions, the battery on this plaster will generate a strong galvanic current, which makes the plaster effective.

No. 8C1552 Price.......................40c

If by mail, postage extra, 3 cents.

Electric Insoles.

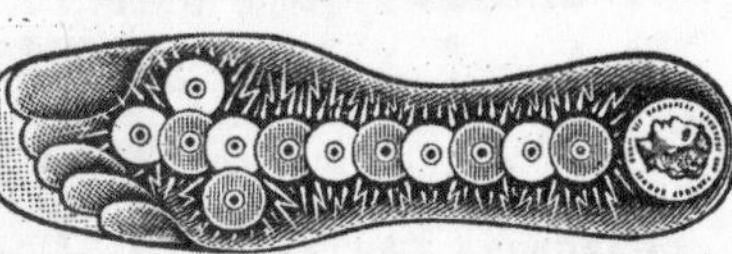

A boon to those troubled with poor circulation and cold feet. If the feet are kept warm, the body will be less subject to the various complaints arising from colds. **These Electric Insoles** contain the pure polished metals arranged in such a manner that a mild, pleasant current is produced along the soles of the feet, which stimulates the blood and keeps it circulating constantly. **They are worn with good results for cold feet, and to keep the feet dry.**

No. 8C1554 Price, per pair.......................18c

If by mail, postage extra, 10 cents.

Electric Ring for Rheumatism.

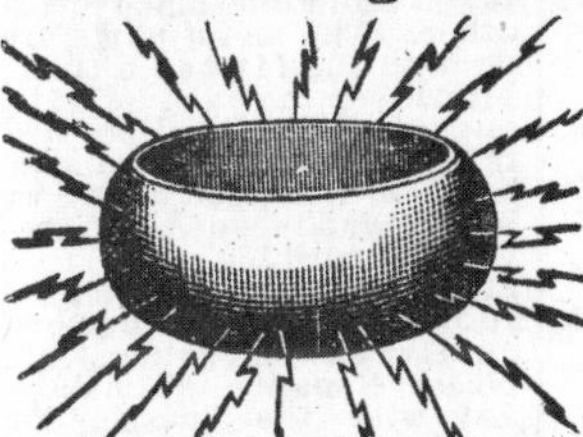

These are the first rings introduced into the United States, all others being imitations. Their popularity has caused many rings to be placed on sale that are without any curative properties.

No. 8C1556 Gray metal, polished. Price..30c

No. 8C1557 Gray metal, gold plated on outside. Price...(If by mail, postage extra, 2 cents)....55c

CRUTCHES.

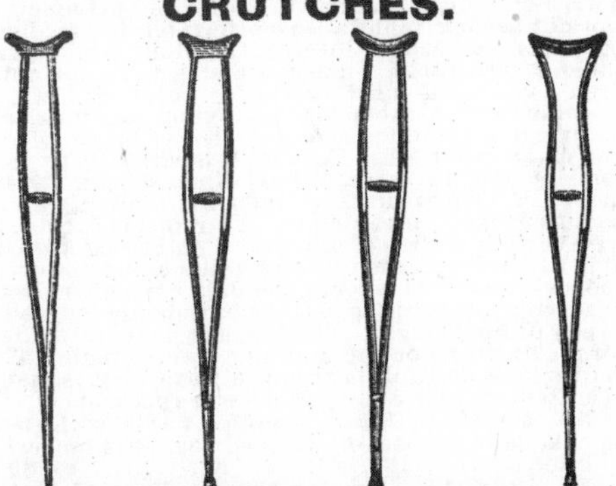

No. 8C1560 No. 8C1562 No. 8C1564 No. 8C1566

No. 8C1560 Plain, made of maple. The staff is split two-thirds its length from the top, bent to shape and held in shape by a hardwood hand piece, riveted and mortised to the arm piece, no ferrule. Made in sizes from 30 to 58 inches, every inch.

Price, per pair.......................69c

No. 8C1562 Selected maple stock, made of two pieces, glued together at lower third of crutch and reinforced by ferrules. Bent and held in shape by hardwood hand piece, riveted and mortised arm piece. Nickel plated screw ferrule at the bottom and supplied with a screw rubber tip. Made in sizes from 42 to 56 inches, every inch. Price, per pair.$1.60

No. 8C1564 Selected shaped maple stock, made similar to No. 8C1562. The staff is shaped and finely finished. The arm piece is well rounded and most comfortable; known as the "Cow Horn" crutch. Nickel plated screw ferrule and screw rubber tip. Made in sizes from 42 to 56 inches, every inch.

Price, per pair.......................$2.25

No. 8C1566 Extra selected maple stock, made similar to No. 8C1562, except instead of having a hardwood arm piece, it is supplied with an elastic leather arm piece filled with curled hair. The wood is of highly polished natural finish. At the lower end is supplied a clutch socket into which a special rubber tip is secured. Made in sizes 46 to 56 inches, every inch.

Price, per pair.......................$4.00

No. 8C1568 Selected rosewood stock, otherwise the same as No. 8C1566. Price, per pair........$7.50

Rubber Crutch Bottoms.

For use on Crutch No. 8C1560.

No. 8C1570 Rubber rasp style. Crutch tips or bottoms. Made in ¾, ⅝ and 1 inch diameter.

Price, per pair.......................18c

If by mail, postage extra, 5 cents.

Screw Socket Crutch Rubbers.

For use on Crutches No. 8C1562 and No. 8C1564.

No. 8C1572 Diameter screw, ⅜ inch; diameter base, 1¾ inches; length, 1½ inches. Price, per pair.......................18c

If by mail, postage extra, 4 cents.

Jaw Socket Crutch Rubbers.

No. 8C1574 To use on Crutches No. 8C1566 and No. 8C1568.

Size	Diameter	Length	Per pair
Small	¾ inch	1 inch	9c
Medium	1 inch	1¼ inches	18c
Large	1⅜ inches	1⅜ inches	22c

If by mail, postage extra, 4 cents.

Metal Crutch Sockets.

No. 8C1576 Metal Crutch Sockets, nicely finished, medium size. Price, per pair...........95c

No. 8C1578 Whitmore's Patent Crutch Sockets, nickel plated. Price, per pair...........$1.90

If by mail, postage extra, 4 cents.

Arrowsmith Arch Prop.

For Flat Feet.

Are you troubled with flat feet or from broken joint arch or instep? With the Arrowsmith Arch Prop, for flat feet, you cannot only walk with ease and comfort but this arch prop will positively remove the trouble entirely. The Arrowsmith Arch Props are adjustable and when once adjusted will retain the shape required. When ordering, state whether for men, women or children and also if you wear a wide, extra wide or narrow shoe. Single prop one-half of the price quoted below. If only one prop is ordered, always state whether for right or left foot.

No. 8C1580 Men's size. Price, per pair......$2.40

No. 8C1582 Women's and misses' size. Price, per pair.......................$2.25

No. 8C1584 Children's and infants' size. Price, per pair.......................$2.00

Artificial Legs.

Do not buy an artificial leg until you have sent for our Special Artificial Leg Pamphlet. It will give you plain and complete information on the latest and most improved artificial leg. We can save you from $40.00 to $60.00 on the best artificial leg made.

Write for our Special Artificial Leg Pamphlet. It is free.

Steel Extension for Short Legs.

Consists of a steel frame or support with leather covered sole and heel. The shoe rests on steel plates at toe and heel, supported by steel posts.

Directions for taking measurements. Have the patient stand erect (both feet bare), place books or blocks under the short foot until shoulders and pelvis are on a horizontal plane, then measure these books or blocks, which will be the height required for extension. State whether for right or left foot. Send a shoe which fits the patient.

Steel Extension for Short Leg.

No. 49C6784 Steel Extension for Short Legs.
Price, for child.......................$4.10
Price, for adult.......................4.50

Wood Extension for Short Legs.

The wood extension is made of English willow properly fitted to the shoe. This wood is light and strong.

Directions for taking measurements. Same as No. 49C6784.

No. 49C6785 Wood Extension for Short Legs. Price for child, 1½ to 2½ inches shortening, each...........$2.40

Price, for adult, 1½ to 2½ inches shortening, each...........$2.90

Price, for adult, 3 to 5 inches shortening, each...........$3.90

Cork Extension for Short Legs.

The cork used in these extensions makes a very light extension. The cork is attached to the shoe and is neatly covered with fine leather. A leather sole is attached to the cork, making a very durable article. This leather sole can be renewed from time to time as necessity requires. **Directions for taking measurement.** Same as No. 49C6784.

No. 49C6786 Cork Extension for Short Legs. Cork sole for 1 inch shortening. Price, each.......$3.65

Cork sole for 2 inches shortening. Price, each. 4.75
Cork sole for 3 inches shortening. Price, each. 5.85
Cork sole for 4 inches shortening. Price, each. 6.75
Cork sole for 5 inches shortening. Price, each. 8.50

Improved Extension Shoe for Short Leg.

OUR LATEST IMPROVED EXTENSION FOR SHORT LEG MAKES BOTH FEET LOOK ALIKE.

Foot, instep and ankle look like the perfect one. You can wear ready made shoes, high or low cut, any style, same as anyone. You stand and walk erect. Men can wear trousers legs of equal length. Ladies can pick up their skirts without showing deformity.

No. 49C6800 Price, for Extension for 5-inch shortening.......................$17.40

No. 49C6801 Price, for Extension for 5¼-inch to 6¾-inch shortening.......................19.80

No. 49C6802 Price, for Extension for 7-inch to 8-inch shortening.......................23.80

No. 49C6803 Price, for Extension for 8¼-inch to 10-inch shortening.......................25.75

No. 49C6804 Price, for Extension for 10¼-inch to 12-inch shortening.......................28.75

Hypodermic Syringes.

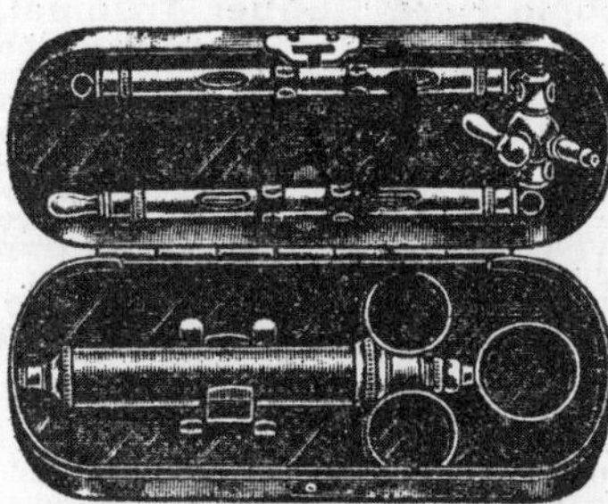

No. 49C1505 Aspirating Hypodermic Syringe, glass barrel, with three way stop cock, trocar, three aspirating needles in metal case. Price, ...$1.60

No. 49C1506 All Metal Aseptic. Price..$1.95

If by mail, postage extra, 8 cents.

No. 49C1507 Hypodermic Syringe, glass barrel, in aluminum case, four vials, two needles, expanding plunger and lubricating valve. Price......95c

If by mail, postage extra, 5c.

No. 49C1508 Hypodermic Syringe, in aluminum case, six vials, two needles, solid piston. Can be thoroughly sterilized as entire syringe is made of metal. Will take P. D.'s or standard gauge needles.

Price.......................$1.15

If by mail, postage extra, 5 cents.

No. 49C1511 P. D's Style Hypodermic Syringe, in aluminum case, glass barrel, six vials, lubricating valve and expanding plunger.

Price.......................$1.20

If by mail, postage extra, 5 cents.

No. 49C1509 Hypodermic Syringe, all metal, expanding plunger, in aluminum case, six vials. Price...........$1.25

If by mail, postage extra, 5 cents.

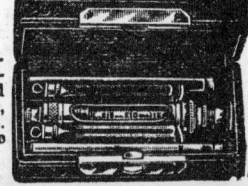

No. 49C1510 Hypodermic Syringe, in morocco leather covered case, leather plunger, two needles, two vials.

Price.......................70c

If by mail, postage extra, 5 cents.

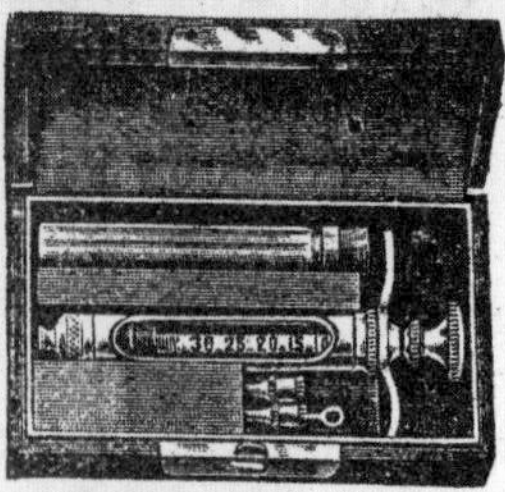

Dental Syringe.

No. 49C1512 Dental Syringe, heavily constructed throughout, glass barrel, with leather plunger, two needles, reinforced close to point and one vial.
Price..........$1.10
If by mail, postage extra, 5 cents.

No. 49C1495 Hypodermic Needles, standard gauge thread. Needle gauges: 23, 24, 25, 26, 27. State gauge wanted.
Price, per dozen..........30c
If by mail, postage extra, per dozen, 3 cents.

No. 49C1496 Hypodermic Needles, standard gauge thread. Screw stem. Needle gauges: 23, 24, 25, 26, 27. State gauge wanted. Price, per dozen..........35c
If by mail, postage extra, per dozen, 3 cents.

No. 49C1497 Hypodermic Needles, standard gauge thread. Reinforced. Same gauges as above.
Price, per dozen..........40c
If by mail, postage extra, per dozen, 3 cents.

No. 49C1498 P. D.'s Pattern Hypodermic Needles. Price, per dozen..........60c
If by mail, postage extra, per dozen, 3 cents.

The Telescopic Hard Rubber Trumpet.

Extended.

This Trumpet can be conveniently carried in the pocket or small hand bag, as it is so constructed in three sections as to telescope together, making it less bulky to carry. When ready to use it, the sections are drawn out and adjusted to the ear. It is a very powerful conductor of sound, the bell being cut away so as to gather in sounds and convey them strongly to the ear. Made of hard rubber with bright polished surface and being of good length can be held to the ear without the arm being raised and becoming tired.

Telescoped or folded

No. 49C2334 Telescope Trumpet, three sections.
Price. ......(Postage extra, 12 cents)........$1.55

Tooth Forceps (Human).

No. 49C648 No. 15 Lower Molar Forceps. Either side.
Price..........88c
If by mail, postage extra, 7 cents.

No. 49C650 No. 8 Universal Forceps. Straight handles.
Price..........88c
If by mail, postage extra, 7 cents.

No. 49C652 No. 24 Upper Molar Forceps. Either side.
Price..........88c
If by mail, postage extra, 7 cents.

No. 49C654 No. 35 Upper Root Forceps, bayonet shape.
Price..........88c
If by mail, postage extra, 7 cents.

No. 49C656 N 1 Upper Root Forceps, front.
Price..........88c
If by mail, postage extra, 7 cents.

No. 49C658 No. 7 Universal Root Forceps.
Price..........88c
If by mail, postage extra, 7 cents.

Manicure Instruments.

No. 49C1445 Corn Knife.
Price..........38c
If by mail, postage extra, 3 cents.

No. 49C1446 Corn Knife, round blade. Price..........38c
If by mail, postage extra, 3 cents.

No. 49C1447 Corn Knife, crescent shape blade. Price....45c
If by mail, postage extra, 3 cents.

No. 49C1448 Corn Chisel, double end. Price..........25c
If by mail, postage extra, 2 cents.

No. 49C1449 Folding Corn Knife. Price..........45c
If by mail, postage extra, 3 cents.

No. 49C1450 Cuticle Knife, long handle. Price........35c
If by mail, postage extra, 3 cents.

No. 49C1451 Cuticle Knife, short handle. Price..........25c
If by mail, postage extra, 2 cents.

No. 49C1452 Nail File, stiff, with bone handle.
Price..(If by mail, postage extra, 2 cents)...35c

No. 49C1453 Nail File, stiff, with nail cleaning point. Length, 5 inches. Price..........35c
If by mail, postage extra, 2 cents.

No. 49C1454 Flexible Nail File, length, 5 inches. Price........20c
If by mail, postage extra, 2 cents.

No. 49C1455 Cuticle Scissors, best quality steel, 3-inch.
Price..........40c
If by mail, postage extra, 6c.

No. 49C1456 Cuticle Scissors, 4-inch. Price........45c
If by mail, postage extra, 2c.

No. 49C1457 Nail Nipper, with spring. High grade steel.
Price..........50c
If by mail, postage extra, 5 cents.

No. 49C1458 Nail Nipper. Heavy, with patent spiral spring. Best grade steel.
Price..........$1.20
If by mail, postage extra, 7 cents.

No. 49C1459 Una's Comodone or Blackhead Extracting Curette and Lance. Price..........40c
If by mail, postage extra, 3 cents.

No. 49C1460 Una's Double Comodone or Blackhead Extracting Curette. Price..........40c
If by mail, postage extra, 3 cents.

No. 49C1545 Glass Nasal Douche.
Price per doz. $1.00; each, 10c
If by mail, postage extra, 2 cents.

Eye Baths.

No. 49C2294 Eye Baths, glass.
Price, per dozen, 35c; each..........5c
If by mail, postage extra, each, 2 cents.

Medicine Droppers.

No. 49C2296 Medicine Droppers, straight.
Price, each..........(Postage extra, 4 cents).....3c
No. 49C2297 Medicine Droppers, curved.
Price, each.......(Postage extra, 4 cents).......3c

Spring Bleeding Lance.

No. 49C2098 Spring Bleeding Lance. The only practicable, safe and convenient instrument for bleeding on the market. Used almost exclusively by old school physicians for the purpose in question.
Price........(Postage extra, 4 cents)..........55c

The Favorite Medicine Glass.

A valuable and important article for the sick room. The cover of the glass is so arranged that it prevents all impurities from polluting the medicine, at the same time preserves its full strength and effectually prevents decomposition of the ingredients in the medicine. The cover of dial glass has an indicator which can be set to indicate the time the next dose is to be taken, therefore making it unnecessary for the attendants to tax their memory when giving several different medicines. All the attention the dial requires is the resetting of the indicator after a dose has been given. The glass is provided with a clip which holds the spoon in such a position that it prevents it from staining or collecting lint, dust or other impurities, which it certainly does when laid down. The glass can be used for all forms of medicines, such as liquids, powders, pills, etc.
No. 49C2392 Price, without spoon..........20c

The Perfection Rectal Dilator and Irrigator.

Three in set, made of fine glass, perfectly smooth and easily sterilized. Considered the best rectal dilating and irrigating set on the market. Inexpensive, yet durable, and always effective. Our price for complete set, only 48c. We furnish the Perfection Rectal Dilator and Irrigator in sets of three, each one a different size. These dilators are made of very fine and smooth lead glass, and are highly endorsed by many physicians who have successfully employed this dilating and irrigating set in the treatment of constipation and hemorrhoids (piles). On account of its extremely low price, it offers an advantage over all dilators, as the patient will be in a position to use the set himself at his home without any difficulty and very successfully. In this way the patient himself can obtain quickly the very best of results, and establish a satisfactory cure in such cases where proper dilation and irrigation is all that is required to secure a cure. The set of three is furnished by us in cardboard box, with printed instructions for using same, so that the patient can aid you as much as possible to make your treatment of the case absolutely successful. The set consists of one small, one medium dilator, and one large dilator and irrigator fitted with cork and tube to which the tubing of the fountain syringe may be attached, making irrigation easy and effective. There is nothing better for the treatment of constipation, piles, fissures and nervousness.
No. 49C270 Set of Three Perfection Dilators. Price....(Postage extra, per set, 10 cents)....48c

No. 49C8265 Urinal, male, glass, not graduated.
Price..........42c
No. 49C8266 Urinal, male, glass, graduated.
Price..........55c

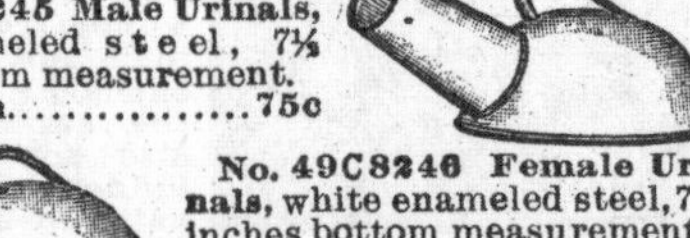

No. 49C8267 Urinal, female, glass, not graduated.
Price..........42c
No. 49C8268 Urinal, female, glass, graduated.
Price..........55c

No. 49C8245 Male Urinals, white enameled steel, 7½ inches bottom measurement.
Price, each..........75c

No. 49C8246 Female Urinals, white enameled steel, 7⅛ inches bottom measurement.
Price..........90c

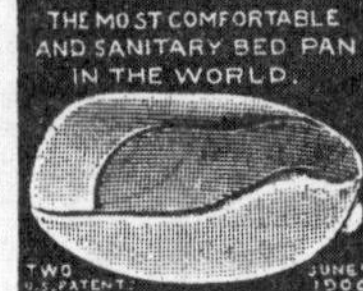

No. 49C8126 Bed Pan, 15x12¼ inches. Mottled pearl enamel inside and outside.
Price..........$1.50

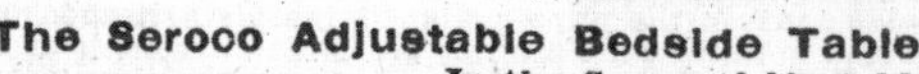

No. 49C8128 Douche Pan, 16x11x3 inches. Mottled pearl enamel inside and outside. Price..........95c

The Perfection Combined Bed and Douche Pan. Made of porcelain.

THE MOST COMFORTABLE AND SANITARY BED PAN IN THE WORLD.

No. 49C8123 Adult size.
Price..........$2.35
No. 49C8124 Child's size.
Price..........$2.00

The Seroco Adjustable Bedside Table.

In the Seroco Adjustable Bedside Table we offer to the public the most useful piece of furniture ever made. It can not only be used in the greatest number of ways, but can readily be taken from one place to another. The metal parts are done in the finest black, bronze or cream white enamel, nicely decorated in gold or plated and oxidized with copper, nickel or bronze, and lacquered to prevent tarnishing. The tops are of golden oak, hand rubbed; highly finished quarter sawed golden oak, birdseye maple and mahogany with the finest piano finish. When folded and not in use it occupies less than four inches of floor space. Adapted to use as a table for serving meals in bed, a table for reading in bed, a bolster or prop in bed, a writing table, a reading table for old or young, a work or sewing table, an aseptic table for medical purposes, a screen for intercepting light, a manicure table, a card table, a music stand, a table for children's games, a lunch table for porch or lawn, a drawing table, a table for displaying drawings and paintings, a stand for reference books in the office, and many other uses. Each table is carefully packed for shipment in a single box, dimensions 19x29x4½ inches, weighs about 22 pounds net, and about 35 pounds packed for shipment. A wrench is furnished with each table free of charge. The Seroco Adjustable Bedside Table is of great value and comfort in the sick room. It affords the only convenient way of serving meals to the patient, and can be adjusted to any desired height. The top may be readily tilted for reading book or paper at any desired angle. The Seroco Bedside Table is absolutely sanitary, is easily operated, durable and attractive in appearance.

No. 49C8010 Black Enamel Parts, with golden oak, hand rubbed, oil finished top, 18x24 inches.
Price..........$2.85
No. 49C8011 Bronze Brown Enamel Metal Parts, with golden oak, hand rubbed, oil finished top, 18x27 inches. Price..........$3.25
No. 49C8012 Cream White Metal Parts, with birdseye maple top, 18x27 inches. Price......$3.75
No. 49C8013 Oxidized Copper Metal Parts, with finely finished quarter sawed top, 18x27 inches.
Price..........$4.75
No. 49C8014 Full Nickel Plated Metal Parts, with quarter sawed oak or birdseye maple top, 18x27 inches. Price..........$5.60
No. 49C8015 Brass Metal Parts, mahogany or birdseye maple top, 18x27 inches. Price......$5.80

The New Ease and Comfort Back Rest.

The New Ease and Comfort Back Rest, as illustrated here, is of the most simple construction, but durable and convenient, and should be on hand in every home to be used in the sick room.

Others ask from $2.50 to $4.00 for back rests which are not made in as substantial and convenient a manner as the well known Ease and Comfort Back Rest. The Ease and Comfort Back Rest relieves much of the discomfort of persons confined to the bed, and is really indispensable to those who are compelled to endure a prolonged siege of illness, also to invalids who have to spend most of their time in bed, and in addition it will relieve the attendant waiting on the sick, of much arduous labor. The construction of the Ease and Comfort is very simple. Made of a stout wood frame with a ratchet underneath the back, so that the back rest can be placed in any inclined position to make the patient entirely comfortable. The cover is made of stout linen duck, laces in back, so that it can easily be removed and washed thus giving an opportunity to keep the back rest always in a clean and sanitary condition. The new Ease and Comfort Back Rest is cool and elastic, can be used with or without a pillow, or it can be placed under a mattress if preferred.

No. 49C8020 **Ease and Comfort Back Rest.** Price......................**$1.15**

INVALID RECLINING AND ROLLING CHAIRS

ARE YOU AN INVALID, **or have you a relative or friend who needs a reclining or rolling chair,** built especially for the comfort of invalids? We carry a complete line of standard styles of invalid chairs which are supplied to our customers at about half the prices at which these chairs have heretofore been sold. You need not pay from $40.00 to $60.00 for an invalid chair. We show you below a few styles with prices so low that you might think the chairs must be of inferior quality. We furnish these invalid chairs, however, under a binding guarantee that they are the highest grade of invalid chairs made; that their style, arrangement, adjustment, workmanship and finish is equal to, and in **many cases better** than that of any invalid chairs sold at two and three times our special low prices. We have a special **Invalid Chair Catalogue.** If you care for a larger selection, send for it, it is free.

IF YOU DESIRE **you need not wait to write for this special free catalogue of invalid chairs, for you can send your order direct from this catalogue from the styles illustrated herein** with the assurance that you will get the very best values we have to offer. We show on this page our leading and most popular styles of chairs, representing the very best values in the entire department, and if you find a chair among the following styles that pleases you, send us your order immediately. However, if there is any other style which you want (not shown herein), do not fail to write for the special **Free Catalogue of Invalid Chairs.**

AT OUR NEVER HEARD OF LOW PRICES, **every home that needs one, can afford an invalid chair.** For a comparatively small outlay you can brighten the hours and days of an invalid sufferer, make his condition less burdensome, supplying comforts which cannot be had, without these specially designed invalid chairs, and thus contribute in the greatest measure possible to the relief, comfort, contentment and happiness of the patient. **Special Invalid Chair Catalogue free on application.**

Reclining Rolling Chair.

Swivel wheel of large diameter.

It is one of the most popular styles of invalids' chairs. We particularly recommend it as being the easiest running because of its large swivel wheel. The chair is very comfortable, being a perfect fit to the human body and well proportioned. It is made of the best hardwood, finished in oak, rubbed and polished, with cane work as shown in illustration. The footboard folds up when not in use. It is furnished regularly with stationary push handle without extra charge.

The above is but one illustration and description of reclining rolling invalids' chairs. We issue a special **Invalid Chair Catalogue,** giving large illustrations, complete descriptions of every up to date, practicable, comfortable invalid's chair, at prices about one-half to one-third what other houses charge for same. If interested send for special **Invalid Chair Catalogue. It will be sent free on application.**

DIMENSIONS.

	Wide	Narrow
Height of back from seat	31 inches	31 inches
Height of seat from floor	22½ inches	22½ inches
Height of seat from footboard	17 inches	17 inches
Height of arms from seat	9½ inches	9½ inches
Depth of seat	20 inches	20 inches
Width of seat	19 inches	17 inches
Diameter of large wheels	28 inches	28 inches
Diameter of small wheel	10 inches	10 inches
Width over all	29 inches	27 inches

No. 49C14012 With oval steel rim and plain bearing wheels. Price......................**$13.95**

No. 49C14014 With ⅝-inch cushion rubber tires and plain bearing wheels. Price..............**$18.50**

No. 49C14015 With 1-inch cushion rubber tires and plain bearing wheels. Price..............**$23.20**

Weight, crated for shipment, about 100 pounds.

Ball bearings in both front and rear wheels, extra......................**$2.25**

In determining whether to order the narrow or wide pattern, measure the width of the doorways through which the chair is to pass.

Reclining Rolling Chair.

WITH COMMODE ATTACHMENT.

Supplied with a removable sliding seat, two steel elliptic springs and two swivel rear wheels. The chair is very comfortable, being a perfect fit to the human body and well proportioned. It is made of the best hardwood, finished in oak, rubbed and polished with cane work, as shown in illustration. The footboard is carpeted and folds up when not in use. It is furnished regularly with stationary push handle without extra charge.

DIMENSIONS:

	Wide	Narrow
Height of back from seat	31 inches	31 inches
Height of seat from floor	23½ inches	23½ inches
Height of seat from footboard	18 inches	18 inches
Height of arms from seat	9½ inches	9½ inches
Depth of seat	20 inches	20 inches
Width of seat	19 inches	17 inches
Diameter of large wheels	28 inches	28 inches
Diameter of small wheel	10 inches	10 inches
Width over all	29 inches	27 inches

Specify whether wide or narrow is desired.

No. 49C14038 With oval steel rim and plain bearing wheels. Price......................**$17.45**

No. 49C14039 With ⅝-inch cushion rubber tires and plain bearing wheels. Price..............**$22.35**

No. 49C14040 Same, with bicycle ball bearing wheels. Price......................**$24.35**

No. 49C14041 With 1-inch cushion rubber tires and plain bearing wheels. Price..............**$26.40**

No. 49C14042 Same with bicycle ball bearing wheels. Price......................**$28.40**

Weight, crated for shipment, about 100 pounds.

In determining whether to order the narrow or wide pattern, measure the width of the doorways through which the chair is to pass.

Fixed Rolling Chair.

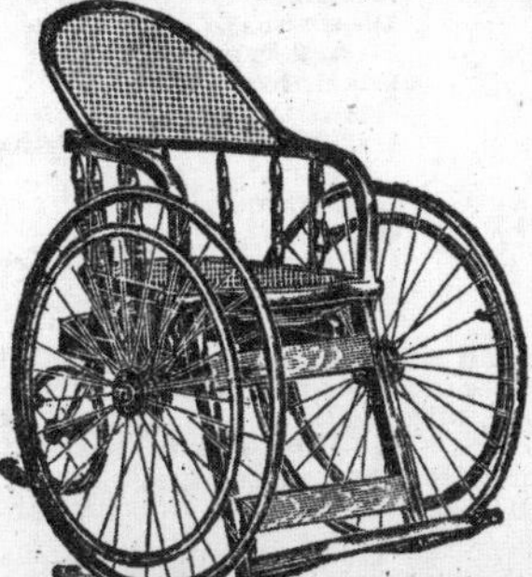

This chair has a bent oak frame filled in with open cane seat and back. The back of the chair is made to fit comfortably to the patient. It is a good substantial non-reclining chair.

DIMENSIONS.

Height of arms from seat	9¾ inches
Height of back from seat	20½ inches
Height of seat from floor	21 inches
Height of seat from footboard	17¾ inches
Depth of seat	18 inches
Width of seat between arms	18¾ inches
Diameter of front wheels	28 inches
Diameter of rear wheel	10 inches
Width over all	29 inches

No. 49C14066 With oval steel rim wheels, plain bearings......**$11.80**

No. 49C14067 With ⅝-inch cushion tires on front and rear wheels, plain bearings......................**$17.25**

No. 49C14068 With 1-inch cushion tires on front and rear wheels, plain bearings......................**$18.40**

For steel elliptic springs on the above chair, extra......................**3.00**

Weight, crated for shipment, about 100 pounds.

SEND FOR OUR SPECIAL INVALID CHAIR CATALOGUE.

Self-Propelling Rolling Chair.

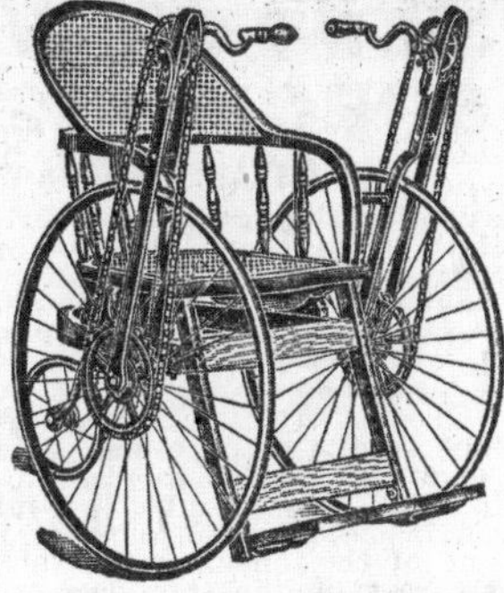

This chair is made in the same style and manner as chair No. 49C14066. But in addition it has the self propelling device which gives the patient greater independence of movement. The chair is propelled easily and it is especially intended for persons who are paralyzed in the lower limbs.

DIMENSIONS.

Height of arms from seat	9¾ inches
Height of back from seat	20½ inches
Height of seat from floor	21 inches
Height of seat from footboard	17¾ inches
Depth of seat	18 inches
Width of seat between arms	18¾ inches
Diameter of front wheels	28 inches
Diameter of rear wheel	10 inches
Width over all	30 inches

No. 49C14063 With oval steel rim wheels, plain bearings......................**$15.95**

No. 49C14064 With ⅝-inch cushion tire wheels, front and rear, plain bearings..............**$21.90**

No. 49C14065 With 1-inch cushion tires on front and rear wheels, plain bearings..............**$24.85**

For steel elliptic springs on the above chair, extra......................**$3.00**

Weight, crated for shipment, about 100 pounds.

SEND FOR OUR

SPECIAL INVALID CHAIR CATALOGUE

IF YOU WANT ANY KIND OF AN INVALID CHAIR NOT SHOWN ON THIS PAGE.

Rolling Chair.

WITH SPRINGS AND STEEL EXTENSION PUSH HANDLE. REED WORK IS FINISHED, SHELLACED AND VARNISHED.

This chair is similar to the World's Fair Rolling Chair, but far superior to that famous chair in many respects. It is lighter, and has 10-inch front wheels that run in a straight line. Body is made of the best grade of prime India reeds, and has a hygenic close woven cane seat. It has two elliptic springs, made of the best quality of spring steel, and steel extension push handle, with a turned hardwood cross bar furnished free of charge. Push handles are so constructed that a little pressure on same clears the front wheels from the ground, and allows the chair to be turned in a very small space and to go over crossings and obstructions very easily.

DIMENSIONS.

	Adult's size, inches	Child's size, inches
Height of back from seat	27	24
Height of seat from floor	22	19
Height of seat from footboard	15½	14
Height of arms from seat	11	9
Depth of seat	17	14½
Width of seat	19	15½
Diameter of rear wheels	26	24
Diameter of front wheels	10	8
Width all over	29	26

ADULT'S SIZE.

No. 49C14092 With oval steel rim wheels. Price......................**$13.70**

No. 49C14093 With ⅝-inch cushion rubber tires on rear wheels and ½-inch rubber tires on front, plain bearings. Price......................**$16.90**

No. 49C14096 With ⅝-inch cushion rubber tires on rear wheels and ½-inch on front, with bicycle bearings in both front and rear wheels. Price, **$18.70**

Weight, crated for shipment, about 100 pounds.

CHILD'S SIZE.

No. 49C14097 With oval steel wheels. Price......................**$11.50**

No. 49C14098 With ⅝-inch cushion rubber tires on rear wheels and ½-inch rubber tires on front wheels, plain bearings. Price..............**$14.90**

No. 49C14099 Same as No. 49C14098, except with bicycle ball bearings in both front and rear wheels. Price......................**$17.20**

Weight, crated for shipment, about 100 pounds.

SEND FOR OUR SPECIAL INVALID CHAIR CATALOGUE.

SPECIAL DEPARTMENT OF VAPOR BATH CABINETS.

OUR SPECIAL $2.19 PEERLESS VAPOR BATH CABINET.

THE CHEAPEST FOUR-WALL RUBBER LINED BATH ROOM, WITH IMPROVED FULL DOOR OPENINGS.

FOR ONLY $2.19 we offer this genuine Peerless Vapor Bath Cabinet as the only good and practical low priced bath cabinet made. We offer the $2.19 Peerless Vapor Bath Cabinet as the equal of cabinets you will find advertised in thousands of papers at $4.00 and $5.00.

THE ILLUSTRATION will give you a good idea of the appearance of our $2.19 Vapor Bath Cabinet in use, but you must try it to appreciate the convenience of the cabinet and the excellent value we are offering. **It is made of strong woven goods,** impervious to the vapor, as it is rubber lined throughout. It is made with a square galvanized steel frame, regular four-wall room construction, and is not one of the cheap collapsible or crush cabinets which merely rest on the shoulders of the party using them.

WITH EVERY $2.19 VAPOR BATH CABINET we furnish a complete alcohol heater and vaporizing pan as illustrated. With a small quantity of wood alcohol, which can be purchased at any drug store at a very small expense, to burn in the alcohol heater, and our $2.19 Bath Cabinet, you are in position to take any of the Turkish, Russian, vapor or medicated baths so highly recommended by physicians, and which cost $1.00 or $2.00 in regular bath houses.

THE IMPROVED Peerless Turkish and Vapor Bath Cabinet at $2.19 represents a four-wall room, rubber lined, with galvanized steel wire frames, and it will fold into the smallest space of any square folding bath cabinet. The cover material is of the best rubber coated muslin. Size, 28x30½x42 inches. Weight, complete, 11½ pounds.

WE FURNISH FULL DIRECTIONS and complete formulas how to prepare and take Turkish, Russian, hot air, steam or vapor baths, perfumed or medicated, in your own home with our $2.19 cabinet, at a cost of less than 3 cents a bath.

AS THE LOWEST PRICE HOME BATHING APPLIANCE our $2.19 Peerless Bath Cabinet is without an equal. While we recommend the purchase of one of our higher priced cabinets, our Peerless is fully guaranteed in every respect, will give entire satisfaction, and is the lowest priced bath cabinet ever offered. Many people go to Hot Springs, Mineral Springs and other health resorts for the purpose of taking a bath.

OUR $2.19 CABINET brings these baths within the reach of the poorest person in the country. With this cabinet you can receive in your own room all the beneficial treatment offered at such health resorts or sanitariums at an expense that is almost nothing. There isn't a man, woman or child that vapor baths will not benefit. Everyone, whether in health or in disease, should use a vapor cabinet bath. It is a perfect and natural way of freeing the skin and tissues of the poisons that clog and injure the system and produce disease. **$2.19 is by far the lowest price ever made on a high grade square folding bath cabinet. $2.19 is a price based on the actual production cost of the cabinet, with the smallest margin of profit added.** It is a price much lower than you can buy a good bath cabinet from any other concern, and with the well known benefits from vapor baths, everyone should avail themselves of this price without delay.

No. 8C2000 Price.......... $2.19

OUR BROWN BATH CABINET No. 2, $3.84

The illustration shows the appearance of the Brown No. 1 and No. 2 Bath Cabinets closed in use.

WITH VAPOR BATH remedies for sixteen weekly treatments free.

OUR SPECIAL BROWN CABINET No. 2 is made of the very best material and made on the most scientific principles. It is a cabinet large enough to enable you to take a foot bath while you are taking a Turkish bath. **The top of the Brown Cabinet No. 2 is in two pieces.** The Brown top is a very great convenience in entering as well as in cooling off. The construction of our Brown Cabinet No. 2 is most substantial. The covering is of special cabinet material (rubber coating inside, checked drill outside), that never stretches, thoroughly vapor proof. **The frame never weakens.** Steel braces are so fitted to every corner that the cabinet when open is a solid and substantial room. **In cooling off, both sides of the top may be unbuttoned and thrown back.** The whole cabinet is so jointed and hinged it can be put away in the smallest possible space. When you have finished using the cabinet, simply loosen the braces, tip the frame and it folds up completely. **Any child can open and close it in a second.**

SPECIAL ADVANTAGES OF THE BROWN CABINET. You require no assistant—everything is so simple and convenient. You simply open the door, step in, close the door and you immediately get the full benefit of the high temperature. **Temperature can be regulated at the will of the bather.** Plenty of room in the cabinet to move about, sponge, towel and cool the body perfectly. A five-minute vapor bath in a Brown cabinet starts the millions of skin pores at work expelling the dirt, impurities and poisons from the system, **does more good than six months of drug taking. No other cabinet is so simple to operate,** to open and close, folds up into such small space; is more convenient, compact, strong, light, roomy, handsome, durable or gives such excellent satisfaction.

We furnish free with our BROWN CABINET No. 2 at $3.84, a supply of vapor preparations for four weekly medicated baths as follows:

A supply of vapor preparations for four weekly medicated baths for the treatment of muscular and chronic rheumatism, eczema, skin diseases, parasites, neuralgia, reducing inflammation.

A supply of vapor preparations for four weekly medicated vapor baths for the treatment of fevers, colds, nervousness, nervous diseases, nervous exhaustion, bronchial congestion, enlargement of the liver, general weakness, debility, bronchitis, pleurisy, inflammation of the air passages, urinary complaints, bronchial and laryngial troubles.

A supply of vapor preparations for four weekly medicated vapor baths for the treatment of influenza, la grippe, sleeplessness, nervousness, hysteria, nausea, spasms, vomiting.

A supply of vapor preparations for four weekly medicated vapor baths for the treatment of constipation, enlarged glands, gastric troubles, congestion of liver and kidneys, jaundice, dyspepsia, tonsilitis, quinsy, irregular menstruation, syphilis, chronic scrofula, profuse perspiration.

No. 8C2001 Price, complete with stove and vaporizer.......... $3.84

OUR HIGHEST GRADE BROWN BATH CABINET No. 1, $5.89

FOR $5.89 we offer the highest grade bath cabinet of the celebrated Brown make, as the very finest and highest grade bath cabinet made. There is no better bath cabinet construction possible.

THE FRAME of the Brown Bath Cabinet is made of the only wood that is serviceable. The wood is kiln dried in a very high degree of heat and especially treated. The frame is guaranteed to stand both dry heat and vapor heat without warping. The cover used on the Brown Cabinet is non-absorbent, germ-proof, antiseptic and odorless. This material is the result of years of experiment. It is not only perfect for the purpose, but practically lasts forever.

OUR $5.89 BATH CABINET is constructed with double walls of the best rubber coated material that can be made, everlasting and always new. This gives a black rubber coating inside and outside, with air space between. The top is of double faced material, rubber coated both sides and held firmly in place by snap buttons. **The construction of our special $5.89 Cabinet is without doubt the best ever shown.**

FACE STEAMER FREE. A celebrated Brown Face Steamer, improved style, as shown in this illustration, will be included with each No. 1 Brown Vapor Bath Cabinet free. For treatment of the complexion the Brown face steamer is one of the most important parts of a vapor bath cabinet. **If same is wanted with other cabinets, price is $1.00 extra.**

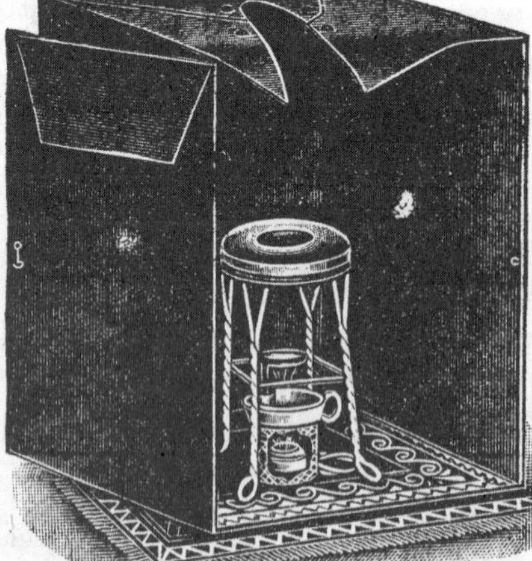

This illustration shows the appearance of the Brown No. 1 and No. 2 Bath Cabinets open.

A COLD IS CURED IN ONE NIGHT. Any kind of a cough or cold, throat trouble, affected bronchial tubes, cold on the chest or lungs is effectually cured with one good hot vapor bath taken according to directions. For nervous diseases, nervous debility, nervous prostration, nervous exhaustion, sleeplessness, overworked men and women of all classes, the Brown Bath Cabinet treatment is a grand relief. The vapor bath soothes the tired nerves, permits a more vigorous circulation of blood, thus restoring energy to the exhausted system.

AT OUR SPECIAL $5.89 PRICE we furnish this No. 1 Brown Cabinet complete with face steaming attachment, alcohol stove and vaporizer and complete instructions and formulas how to prepare and take any kind of a Turkish or vapor bath.

WE FURNISH FREE with this, our best BROWN BATH CABINET No. 1 at $5.89, the same supply of vapor preparations for the sixteen baths as given with the $3.84 Cabinet No. 2, and in addition, a number of the grandest special remedies, each covering a complete internal treatment for one month, to be used in connection with the bath, prepared each for the following complaints:

- Cold,
- Fevers,
- Coughs,
- Muscular and Chronic Rheumatism,
- Influenza,
- Grip,
- Muscular Pains and Soreness,
- Neuralgia,
- Tonsilitis,
- General Weakness,
- Debility,
- Pleurisy and Inflammation of air passages,
- General Tonic,
- Quinsy,
- Malarial Troubles,
- Enlarged Spleen,
- Constipation,
- Dyspepsia,
- Enlarged Glands,
- Gastric Troubles,
- Scrofula,
- Stimulating Skin and Kidneys,
- Syphilis,
- Parasites,
- Swelling of Feet or Hands,
- Eczema,
- Skin Diseases,
- Reducing Inflammation,
- Congestion of Liver and Kidneys,
- Jaundice,
- Biliousness,
- Colic,
- Nausea,
- Spasms,
- Vomiting,
- Sick Headache,
- Painful Menstruation,
- Acute Neuralgia,
- Pains in Back,
- Nervousness,
- Nervous Diseases,
- Nervous Exhaustion,
- Hysteria,
- Sleeplessness,
- Asthma,
- Weakness,
- Heart Troubles,
- Dizziness,
- Debility,
- Palpitation of the Heart,
- Gonorrhea,
- Gleet,
- Kidney and Urinary Troubles.

VAPOR BATHS are great for blood and skin diseases. For the relief and cure of scrofula, eczema, salt rheum, hives, pimples, ulcers, boils, carbuncles, barbers' itch, oily skin, poor complexion or the hundred other evidences of bad blood and skin imperfections, vapor baths are simply wonderful. For rheumatism and neuralgia, chronic, acute or inflammatory, our vapor baths have been known to cure where everything else had failed to give relief.

No. 8C2002 Price.......... $5.89

CANE SEAT CHAIRS or ordinary kitchen chairs can be employed in taking vapor baths in these cabinets. Customers wishing to order the fancy wire metal stool illustrated above can get the same from us at manufacturer's cost price.

No. 8C2003 Wire metal vapor bath stool. Price.......... $1.30

VETERINARY DEPARTMENT

Veterinary Instruments, Veterinary Medicines and Health Foods for Farmers and Raisers of Stock.

Hygroscopic Plastic Poultice.

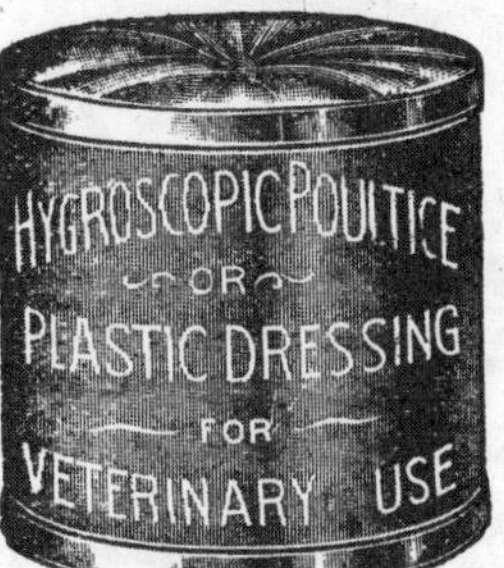

For veterinary use. Will save your horses and stock of all kinds, quickly cure inflamed joints, bruises, sprains, ulcers and wounds. Our wonderful Hygroscopic Plastic Poultice represents the latest scientific application in a method of treatment with earth dressings or poultices. It is prepared ready for use and is of greater medicinal value than any other similar preparation now on the market. Our Hygroscopic Plastic Poultice is today an absolute necessity to every owner of horses and stock. It will do better, quicker and more dependable service in the treatment of certain diseases in horses and cattle especially in the following conditions:

Sores of Any Kind	**Sprains**	**Ulcers**	**Inflamed Joints**
Carbuncles	**Wounds**	**Barb Wire Cuts**	**Erysipelas**
Bruises	**Inflamed Tendons**	**Burns**	**Sore Teats**
Quittor	**Inflamed Coronet**	**Canker**	**Galls**
Boils	**Mastitis,**		

After dehorning, castrating and docking and in all conditions of inflammation and congestion, deep or superficial, infected or non-infected. It does not in any way injure the hair or skin.

Full directions will be sent with each package.

No. 8C1701 **Hygroscopic Plastic Poultice,** in 1-pound cans. Price.......... **$0.30**
No. 8C1702 **Hygroscopic Plastic Poultice,** in 5-pound cans. Price.......... **1.20**

Veterinary Blister.

We have spent much time and made many experiments in preparing **a really practical and thoroughly reliable blister that can be applied easily, and good results follow. It is unexcelled for bone spavin, ringbone, splint, curb, bog spavin, blood spavin, thoroughpin, etc. Removes wind puffs, callouses, etc., from kicks and bruises, thickening of tendons, etc.** Full information how to use it and a description of bone spavin, etc., with each package.

No. 8C1704 Price, per box.......... **40c**

If by mail, postage extra, per box, 8 cents.

Veterinary Fever Remedy.

Give early in lung fever, pneumonia, bronchitis, pleurisy, laryngitis, sore throat, distemper, colds, etc. It is a positive cure, if given promptly, in an attack of laminitis, or founder, and accompanied by hot poultices to the horse's feet, it will remove the congestion and **effect a permanent cure in a few hours.** In case of inflammation of the bowels, given with **Star Crescent Colic Cure,** and hot applications to the belly, gives relief to the patient and **cures the disease in a few hours.**

No. 8C1705 Price, per bottle....... **40c**

Unmailable on account of weight.

Veterinary Wire Cut Remedy.

It will heal cuts and wounds in all parts of the body without leaving a scar. **It is the best remedy for cuts from barbed wire; it heals them the quickest.** In using this remedy it is not necessary to sew any cuts; if you have a flap that hangs down, **fasten it in place by a bandage, but don't close the sore—give it a free chance to** discharge. By applying this remedy it will soon heal. **It is an antiseptic, destroying all germs and foul odors.** It also protects the sores from flies and insects.

No. 8C1706 Price, per bottle....... **40c**

Unmailable on account of weight.

Star and Crescent Hoof Ointment.

For dressing horses' feet, curing and preventing dry and contracted feet, cures cuts, wounds, sores, bruises, prevents cracks and shelly hoofs, and keeps the hoof smooth, tough and black. It also makes the hoof healthy and polished.

No. 8C1715 Price, 1-pint can	**$ 0.60**
Price, 1-quart can..........	**1.00**
Price, 1-gallon can..........	**3.50**
Price, 5-gallon can..........	**13.50**

Unmailable on account of weight.

Milk Oil Sheep Dip.

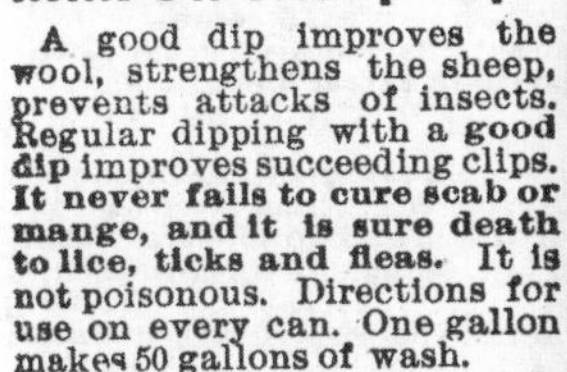

A good dip improves the wool, strengthens the sheep, prevents attacks of insects. Regular dipping with a good dip improves succeeding clips. **It never fails to cure scab or mange, and it is sure death to lice, ticks and fleas.** It is not poisonous. Directions for use on every can. One gallon makes 50 gallons of wash.

No. 8C1718 Price, per gallon.......... **$1.20**
Price, 5 gallons.......... **5.00**
Price, 10 gallons.......... **9.50**

Unmailable on account of weight.

Cooper's Sheep Dip,

Which almost every sheep grower knows. The genuine, imported by ourselves.

No. 8C1721

	25 gal.	100 gal.
Packet to make..........	**25 gal.**	**100 gal.**
Price, per packet..........	**40c**	**$1.50**

We will sell you any dip that is on the market and at the lowest possible prices.

Unmailable on account of weight.

Improved Condition Powder.

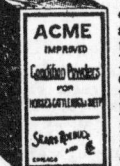

A Valuable Tonic Condition Powder carefully prepared by our veterinary surgeon from health giving, nutritious herbs, seeds, barks and roots. It therefore can be fed to the most delicate animal with perfect safety as a tonic. **This Tonic Condition Powder has valuable medicinal effects,** and may be given with great advantage in all cases of **loss of appetite, roughness of the hair or coat, stoppage of water and bowels, coughs, colds, inflammation of the lungs and bowels, recent founders, swellings of the glands of the throat, horse distemper, hidebound, and will also backen the heaves, and in recent cases effect a cure.** For cattle it ought to be fed once a day, for horses twice a day for two or three weeks at a time; the cost will only amount to one or two cents per day.

		Price
No. 8C1728	Put up in 1-pound packages...	**$0.15**
	Put up in 3-pound packages....	**.40**
	Put up in 5-pound packages....	**.60**
	Put up in 10-pound packages....	**1.00**
	Put up in 25-pound packages....	**2.00**
	Put up in 50-pound packages....	**3.50**
	Put up in 100-pound packages....	**6.00**

Veterinary Eye Water.

Apply to the eye three times a day by dropping three or four or several drops on the ball of the eye. If the eye is red or swollen on the inside of the lids, foment it several times a day with hot water, and keep the animal in a darkened and well ventilated stable. Feed on light and easily digested food, such as bran mash, carrots, etc.

No. 8C1730 Price, per bottle.......... **25c**

If by mail, postage and tube extra, 12 cents.

Veterinary Carbolic Salve.

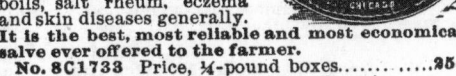

This is used with great success by horsemen wherever known for galls, no matter what they are caused from; for burns, cuts, wounds, scratches, old sores, abscesses, ulcers, speed cracks, hoof diseases, tetter, ringworm, itch, chapped and cracked skin, boils, salt rheum, eczema and skin diseases generally. **It is the best, most reliable and most economical salve ever offered to the farmer.**

No. 8C1733 Price, ¼-pound boxes.......... **25c**

If by mail, postage extra, 6 cents.

Chemical Dehorner.

A painless, simple, inexpensive remedy to prevent horns growing, which, if used for about two generations of cattle, a breed will be raised without horns. One bottle contains sufficient for one hundred horns, and it is so easily applied that a child may use it. It can be applied to **calves, sheep, goats, etc., soon after birth,** and no further care is necessary. We stand ready to guarantee that all trials made according to directions **will be successful,** and also that no harm will result to the calves from its use. It never spoils, so can be kept ready for use for years. In neat glass stoppered bottles; with very simple and clear directions.

No. 8C1736 Price, per bottle.......... **85c**

Unmailable on account of weight.

Creozone.

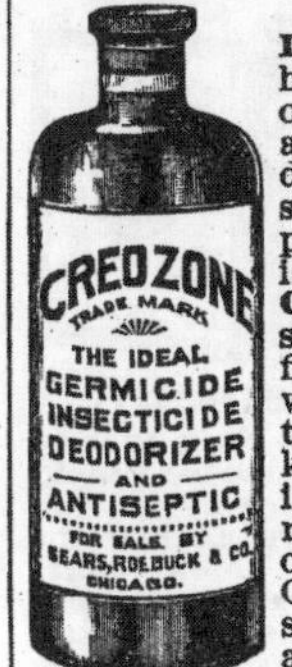

The Ideal Germicide, Insecticide, Deodorizer and Antiseptic. Perfectly harmless to man and the larger forms of animal life, but deadly to germs and insects. Creozone is the cheapest disinfectant to use on account of its strength, as one part to one hundred parts of water makes a solution which is death to all forms of germ life. **CATTLE:** Mange, screw worm, scratches, lice, inflamed udders, inflamed teats, galls, sores and wire cuts will heal quicker under Creozone treatment than any other treatment known. Try it and if you do not find it so, we will cheerfully refund your money. Lice will be entirely unknown on cattle if Creozone is used. **SHEEP:** Creozone will cure sheep affected with scab, foot rot, grubs in the head, anthrax, ticks, etc. If properly used as a preventive, your flock will not be affected with any of these diseases. **HORSES:** Creozone is the best remedy to use for bad hoofs, nail in the foot, scratches, galls, wire cuts, etc. It will keep flies off from affected parts, and will cure with remarkable rapidity. **HOG CHOLERA:** Do not wait and allow hog cholera to get into your herd, and kill off most of the hogs before you can effect a cure, but use Creozone in time, and prevent the disease from even getting a start. The expense of prevention is small, and it is a positive guarantee against hog cholera. **CHICKENS:** Can easily be cured of leukemia, pip, scaly legs, canker, cholera, limber neck and chicken pox if the Creozone treatment is used. Creozone is also the best lice destroyer and preventive. Where it is used lice will be unknown. **DOGS:** Creozone is positively guaranteed to cure mange. Fleas cannot live on dogs that are occasionally washed in water to which a small quantity of Creozone has been added. **INSECT PESTS ON PLANTS:** If plants are occasionally sprayed with a weak solution of Creozone such a thing as insects on them will be entirely unknown. **FOR URINALS AND CLOSETS:** Creozone is the best disinfectant and deodorizer, as it destroys all disease germs, and kills any bad odors which may be present. **Full directions sent with each package.** Order a bottle of Creozone, and if it does not do exactly as we claim for it, write us and we will send back your money.

No. 8C1737 Price, gallons..........	**$1.50**
Price, one-half gallon..........	**1.00**
Price, quarts..........	**.55**
Price, pints..........	**.40**
Price, one-half pint bottles....	**.20**

Unmailable on account of weight.

Hog Cholera Cure.

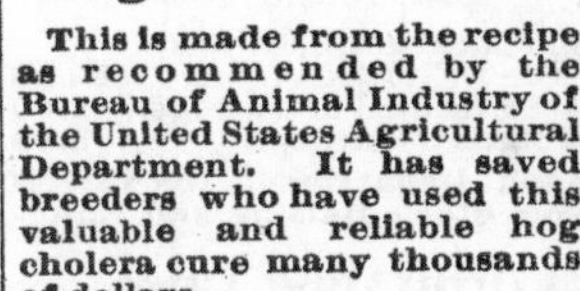
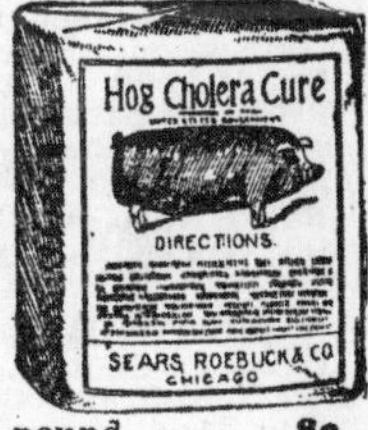

This is made from the recipe as recommended by the Bureau of Animal Industry of the United States Agricultural Department. It has saved breeders who have used this valuable and reliable hog cholera cure many thousands of dollars.

No. 8C1739 Price, 5 lbs.. **50c**
Price, 10 pounds.......... **95c**
Price, 25 to 50 pounds, per pound.......... **8c**
Price, 100 pounds or over, per pound.......... **7c**

Veterinary Liniment.

Very penetrating, cooling and healing. An article of great merit. Cannot be excelled as an application for sprains, bruises, cuts, scratches, spavin, grease heel, corns, thrush and other diseases of the foot, etc., also effective as an application in sore throat, distemper, pneumonia, bronchitis, lung fever, sweeney, etc.

No. 8C1742 Price, per bottle.. **25c**

Unmailable on account of weight.

Veterinary Colic Cure.

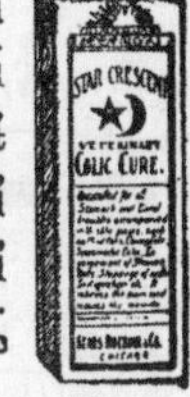

This remedy is unexcelled for all stomach and bowel troubles accompanied with colic pains, wind colic, spasmodic colic, cramp colic, engorgement of stomach, botts, stoppage of water, indigestion, etc. It relieves the pain and relaxes the muscular coat of stomach, bowels and bladder, causing a normal action and free evacuation of the organs.

No. 8C1745 Price, per bottle....... **75c**

Unmailable on account of weight.

Veterinary Worm Powders.

The standard English remedy for worms in horses, cattle, sheep, swine, dogs, etc.

Nearly all lambs, calves, colts and pigs have worms. When they begin to lose in condition, become hidebound, bloodless, or show great thirst and changeable appetite, or diarrhea, you can depend on it—they have worms. Our veterinary worm powders will cure them by giving one powder a day with the feed at the first symptoms.

No. 8C1751 Price, per package of powders.. **25c**

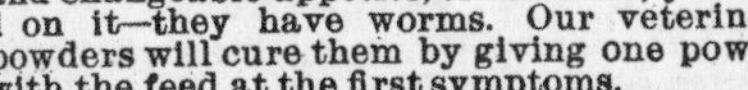

If by mail, postage extra, per package, 5 cents.

Dr. Heller's Powder Lice Killer.

The only powder vermicide on the market that is absolutely non-poisonous to fowls and eggs, and positive death to lice and fleas. It enjoys the largest sale of any powder vermicide in the United States, which alone is evidence of its merits.

No. 8C1753 Price, per 1 pound $0.18
Price per 6 pounds 1.00
Price, per 25 pounds 2.75

Veterinary Blackleg Remedy.

We guarantee this remedy to be a sure and positive cure for Blackleg in young calves or stock, and a positive preventive against the disease. **Blackleg, black quarters, bloody urine, extensive engorgement of shoulder, quarter, neck, side or breast.** It is most frequent in young or rapidly growing and thriving stock, attacking first the best of the herd, and rapidly running its way through. The first symptom **is dullness, quickly followed by lameness, and a swelling in some part of the body or limbs,** sore and painful, and crackling like paper or dry leaves, with a yellow or bloody substance oozing through the skin.

No. 8C1754 Price, per package, 25c.

Dr. Heller's Stock Food.

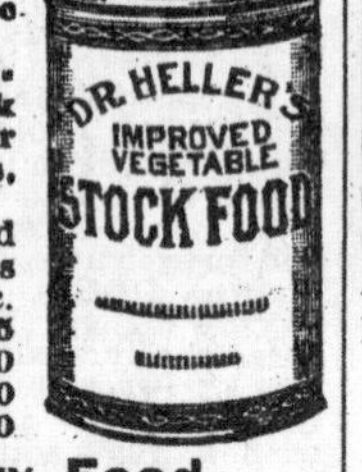

An improved vegetable stock tonic, which has no equal for growing and fattening horses, cattle, sheep and hogs.

It fattens beef cattle, and is good for calves and dairy cows. It cures garget, swelled bag, milk fever, etc.

No. 8C1760 Price, 5-lb. cans $0.65
Price, 25-pound drums..... 2.60
Price, 50-pound drums..... 4.50
Price, 100-pound drums..... 8.00

Dr. Heller's Poultry Food.

Guaranteed to Produce Eggs.

Dr. Heller's Poultry Food is used by the leading poultry fanciers of the United States, Canada and Europe.

Dr. Heller's Poultry Food is a wonderful egg producer, and makes large and healthy fowls. It will positively prevent and also cure chicken cholera, roup, gapes, and all diseases of the flock. It makes young chickens grow quickly and keeps them free from disease. It prevents having sickly broods of young chickens or droopy old ones, and it is positively guaranteed to increase the number of eggs at all seasons of the year.

No. 8C1766 1-pound packages, 1,800 feeds.
Price, per package $0.18
6-pound packages, 10,800 feeds. Per package... 1.00
25-pound kegs, 45,000 feeds. Per keg......... 3.25

REFER to our Book Department for Veterinary Works, Books on Stock Raising and Handling, etc.

Fleming's Lump Jaw Cure.

HOW IT CURES.—Fleming's Lump Jaw Cure is a liquid that is applied externally. It has remarkable penetrating qualities. Through the local absorbents and minor blood vessels it reaches and destroys every germ. When the germs are destroyed the tumor is dead, and nature proceeds to throw it off as it would any other foreign body. Some may judge that a remedy that will act as quickly as this is apt to be harmful, but instead of this it is absolutely beneficial. It protects the animal, for if a tumor were removed by ordinary methods there would be danger of blood poisoning, but **Fleming's Lump Jaw Cure is a powerful antiseptic and disinfectant.** It kills all poison, it stimulates a healthy growth of tissue, and a large tumor is often removed with not even a scar remaining.

No. 8C1767 Price, per bottle................ $1.49
If by mail, postage and tube extra, per bottle, 12c.

Dr. Heller's Germ Killer.

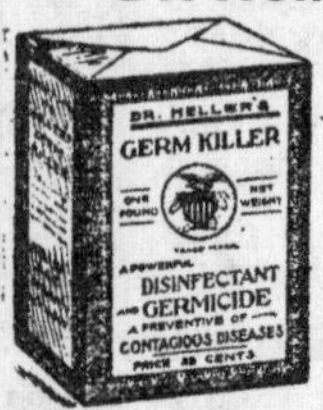

A powerful dry powder, germicide and disinfectant. An antiseptic of the widest range of usefulness and the only disinfectant that has been endorsed by the leading boards of health, physicians, and veterinary surgeons. Dr. Heller's Germ Killer is highly recommended to swine breeders to prevent all kinds of disease. For mange or skin disease on horses, cattle and hogs, it has no equal. It also destroys mites, jiggers, bed bugs, roaches, fleas, etc. For garbage boxes, cesspools, sinks, waste water basins, etc., it is highly recommended by boards of health for the sick room, and also for disinfecting patent closets. **For stable use,** Heller's Germ Killer acts instantly, destroying foul odors as soon as applied. It eradicates disease germs, insures pure air, and keeps the stock bright and full of life.

No. 8C1768 Price, 1-pound trial package... $0.15
Price, 6-pound cans.................................. .55
Price, 25-pound drums............................ 1.65
Price, 50-pound drums............................ 3.25

Brown's Lice Killer.

No disease known to the poultry fraternity can compare in its ravages to that wrought by the numerous family of insects known as "Chicken Lice." From the beginning to the end of the poultryman's career it is a continous fight against vermin. **We here present to our customers a lice killer which we guarantee to eradicate thoroughly, not only the mites and chiggers, but the body lice on fowls, by application to the roost and nest boxes, this being the simplest and best** method of treating a large number of fowls. All that is necessary is to paint with our lice killer the roosts, roost supports, nest boxes and all cracks or crevices that form a lodging place for the vermin. It is easily applied and does the work thoroughly, killing not only the lice, but also the mites and eggs. **For scaly leg it is invaluable** to the poultryman, as fowls that roost on poles that are occasionally painted with our lice killer will never have a sign of that unsightly disease.

No. 8C1799 Price, 1-gal. cans, 75c; ½-gal. cans......40c

Liquid Paris Green.

For spraying all kinds of fruit trees, vines and plants. Is sure death to potato bugs, chinch bugs, curculio, canker worms, etc. One can is sufficient for 180 gallons of water. Full instructions how to use it on every bottle.

No. 8C1802 Price, per can.......... 25c

Liquid London Purple.

For spraying all kinds of fruit trees, vines and plants. Is sure death to potato bugs, chinch bugs, curculio, canker worms, etc. Sufficient for 100 gallons of water. Directions how to use it to the best advantage.

No. 8C1804 Price, per bottle................ 25c
Not mailable on account of weight.

Purple Jack.

Sure death to the worm that eats the head of the cabbage or the fruit of the tomato.

No. 8C1805 Price, per bottle.................. 25c
Not mailable on account of weight.

Kerosene Emulsion.

For spraying and washing fruit trees, vines, plants, field crops and domestic animals. Destroys plant lice, red spiders, scales, mealy bugs, lice on cattle and hogs, tick on sheep. One can is sufficient for 50 gallons. **Not mailable on account of weight.**

No. 8C1808 Price, per can.................... 35c

Bordeaux Mixture.

Compounded from the old formula, but by an entirely new process. Prevents blight, rot, mildew and rust. Destroys all fungus growth on vegetation. One can is sufficient to dilute with 35 to 50 gallons of water. **Not mailable on account of weight.**

No. 8C1811 Price, per bottle.................... 25c

Improved Gall Cure.

A gall cure that can be depended upon. It will heal collar galls, bit galls, saddle galls, boot galls, and abrasions of the skin, while the animal is at work. Toughens the skin, stains the parts and makes a galled horse look respectable. Quickest cure, most economical and humane treatment.

No. 8C1815 Price, per 3-ounce box............ 12c
No. 8C1816 Price, 8-ounce box................ 20c
If by mail, postage extra, 3-oz. package, 6 cents 8-oz. package, 10 cents.

Blackleg Vaccine Outfit.

Complete and containing a mortar, pestle, funnel, graduate glass and filter paper to prepare the vaccine, also a fine hypodermic syringe, with needles, etc., to inject the same. This outfit will answer all requirements for the use of the vaccine distributed by the government or any other vaccine in powder form. The syringe is graduated for doses, and is complete and furnished alone or with extra needles if desired. The outfit is put up in a neat, polished hardwood case. Size, 7x6x4 inches. Weight, 4 pounds.

No. 8C1817 Complete vaccine outfit........ $3.65
No. 8C1820 Syringe only 2.35

Veterinary Instruments.

Wolf Tooth Forceps, bayonet pattern. Heavily nickel plated steel. Length, 10 in.
No. 8C1838 Price.............................. $2.35
If by mail, postage extra, 17 cents.

Wolf Tooth Forceps, curved. Heavily nickel plated steel. Length, 9 inches.
No. 8C1841 Price.............................. $2.00
If by mail, postage extra, 17 cents.

Molar Splinter Forceps. Heavily nickel plated.
No. 8C1844 Length, 12 inches. Price.... $2.65
If by mail, postage extra, 28 cents.

Straight Incisor Cutters. Heavily nickel plated.
No. 8C1847 Price.... $2.10
If by mail, postage extra, 17 cents.

Molar Extracting Forceps. Heavily nickel plated. Length, with handle, 18½ inches. Handle extra.
No. 8C1850 Price.............................. $4.95
If by mail, postage extra, 20 cents.

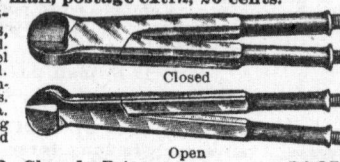

Molar Cutters, 2 styles, open and closed. Heavily nickel plated steel. Length, with handle, 18½ inches. Handles extra. When ordering mention the kind wanted.

Closed

Open

No. 8C1853 Closed. Price................ $4.95
No. 8C1854 Open. Price.................. 4.95

Handles for Cutters and Extractors. Can be used for open and closed molar cutters, also for molar extractors. No. 8C1856 Price, per pair, $2.15

Combination Horse Mouth Float. Jointed, copper plated, fine nickel finish and adjustable. Consists of three pieces, straight and angular, with two separate files. Can be used for upper and lower molars, also for first molar teeth.
No. 8C1862 Price, per set.............. $2.15
Extra blades can be furnished for this float. When ordering, state whether file or rasp is wanted.
No. 8C1863 Extra blades. Price, per doz., $1.65
Each..(If by mail, postage extra, 4 cents.) .15

Palmer's Dental File. Length, 12 inches.
No. 8C1865 Price.............................. 70c
If by mail, postage extra, 14 cents.

Plain Double File. 10 inches.
No. 8C1868 Price..... 45c
If by mail, postage extra, 15 cents.

Veterinary Thermometers, 5-inch, sensitive, self registering; in pocket case.
No. 8C1869 Price.............................. 90c
If by mail, postage extra, 4 cents.

Veterinary Thermometer, 6-inch, sensitive, self registering; in pocket case.
No. 8C1870 Price.............................. $1.50
If by mail, postage extra, 5 cents.

Veterinary Thermometer fenestrated case and chain.
No. 8C1871 Price.............................. $1.50
If by mail, postage extra, 8 cents.

No. 8C1873 **Separating Saw.** Price.............. 75c
If by mail, postage extra, 5 cents.
No. 8C1874 **Simmons' Pus Scoops.** Price.. 95c
If by mail, postage extra, 5 cents.

Pasteur Blackleg Vaccine.

We furnish the genuine Blackleg Vaccine, for protecting cattle against blackleg, either in powder form or in cord form. This Blackleg Vaccine has been used on over three million calves, which have thereby been successfully protected against blackleg. Both vaccines are supplied for single and double treatment.

No. 8C1821 **Pasteur Single Blackleg Vaccine** (powder form), per packet, sufficient for from ten to twelve head. Price.. $1.45

No. 8C1822 **Pasteur Double Blackleg Vaccine** (powder form), per double packet (first lymph and second lymph), sufficient for from ten to twenty head, according to age. Price........................ $1.95

No. 8C1823 **Pasteur Blackleg Vaccinating Outfit** (No. 2 syringe complete, and pestle, mortar, funnel, graduate and filters for preparing and using powder form of vaccine), complete in case. Price.. $5.90

No. 8C1824 **Single Blacklegine** (cord form of vaccine ready for use). No. 1, 10 doses. Price 1.45
No. 2 size, 20 doses.............................. $2.45 No. 3 size, 50 doses.............................. 5.90

No. 8C1825 **Double Blacklegine** (cord form of vaccine ready for use). Per packet of 10 doses (first lymph and second lymph, inclusive). Price.. $1.95

Blacklegine is applied with a needle, which is now very much improved and is provided with a handle. The handle with two needles is called the "Blacklegine Outfit," and the accompanying illustration shows this outfit with the dose attached to the needle and ready to be administered. Vaccination with Blacklegine is as simple as taking a stitch.

A booklet containing full particulars regarding Blackleg and its prevention with Pasteur Blackleg Vaccines, will be mailed upon application.

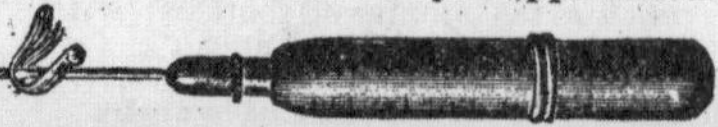

No. 8C1826 **Blacklegine Outfit** for using Blacklegine. The outfit consists of handle and two needles. Price........ 50c
If by mail, postage extra, 3 cents.
No. 8C1827 **Extra Blacklegine needles separately. Price, 20c.**

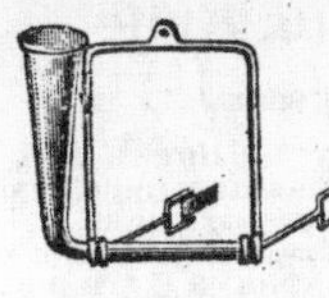

Burton's Drenching Bit.

Burton's Drenching Bit. No longer any trouble to give your horse medicine. One man can do it. Used by horsemen throughout the country. Weight, 1¼ pounds.
No. 8C1875 Price..................... $2.25

Trephine.

No. 8C1877 Trephine. Sizes, ½, ¾ and 1 inch. Price.........$1.30
If by mail, postage extra, 8 cents.

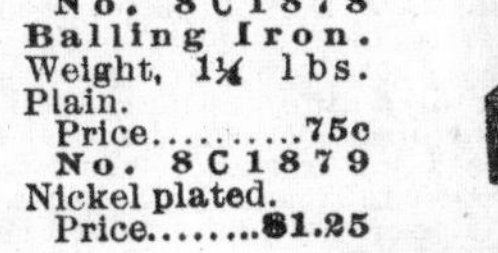

No. 8C1878 Balling Iron. Weight, 1¼ lbs. Plain. Price..........75c
No. 8C1879 Nickel plated. Price.......$1.25

Veterinary Trachea Tube.

Veterinary Trachea Tube, self retaining. Nickel plated.
No. 8C1880 Price...........$1.60
If by mail, postage extra, 5 cents.

Improved Self Retaining Trachea Tube With Sieve.

This tube, as can be readily seen by its shape, is self retaining, and contains sieve attachment to prevent dust from entering the trachea. Tube should be inserted when animal is to be speeded or worked hard. The insertion of this tube in a roarer or broken winded horse will transform him into a useful and profitable animal.
No. 8C1882 Improved Self Retaining Trachea Tube. Nickel plated. Price...................$2.00
If by mail, postage extra, 5 cents.

Folding Mouth Speculum.

This speculum is a new invention and has many advantages over all others. It is simple in construction and easily applied, and does not annoy or frighten the animal. It being a lever in itself, it does not require any mechanical appliance for opening the horse's mouth, and has no extra levers or other parts to injure the operator if the animal is fractious. It is the only speculum of its kind ever invented, and is small and convenient for the pocket or instrument case. It is so constructed as to allow access to the mouth from the front or either side without interfering with the use of any instrument that may be required. It is made of the best material and is more compact than any other on the market and weighs less than two pounds. The operator is absolutely safe when using this speculum.
No. 8C1884 Price, full nickel plated, with russet leather straps.................$4.20

Smith's Mouth Speculum.

The only speculum made by which the pressure of the horse's jaws is brought upon the front teeth instead of the soft tissues of the gums. It is very easily applied, and a special feature which can be found in no other speculum is the **curved side bars**, which expose the front molar teeth and afford an unobstructed view of the mouth from either side and the greatest possible space to operate in.
No. 8C1885 Price.....................$8.25

Improved Ecraseur.

This is one of the latest improved instruments. It can be held in the hand and the slack of the chain can be taken up at once by a simple movement with the thumb and finger without drawing out the screw or lengthening the instrument.
No. 8C1887 Price.....................$11.50
Farmer Miles' Castrating Ecraseur. Weight, 1 lb.
No. 8C1888 Price.....................$6.50

Spaying Emasculator.

Spaying Emasculator. This is the simplest, safest and quickest instrument made for castrating. Neither clamps, medicine nor cording are required. By means of this instrument the spermatic cord is severed by tortion, completely preventing the loss of blood. Length, 15 inches.
No. 8C1889 Price.....................$9.50

Eclipse Emasculator. A simple, strong, safe and quick instrument. No fear of hemorrhage after operations, as the blood vessels are completely closed.

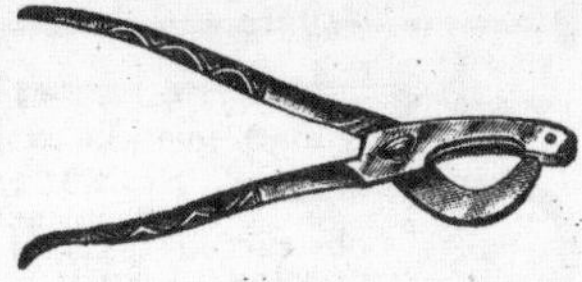

No. 8C1890 Straight. 12-inch long. Price, $5.95
No. 8C1891 Curved. 11-inch long. Price, 6.20

Castrating Knives.

Castrating Knife. Spring back.
No. 8C1892 Price.......65c
If by mail, postage extra, 2 cents.

Ziegler's Castrating Knife.
No. 8C1893 Price.....$1.15
If by mail, postage extra, 4 cents.

Horse Fleams.

Horse Fleams. Brass handle.
No. 8C1894
Price, one blade.............35c
Price, two blades...........45c
Price, three blades.........65c
If by mail, postage extra, 5 cents.

Spring Lancet.

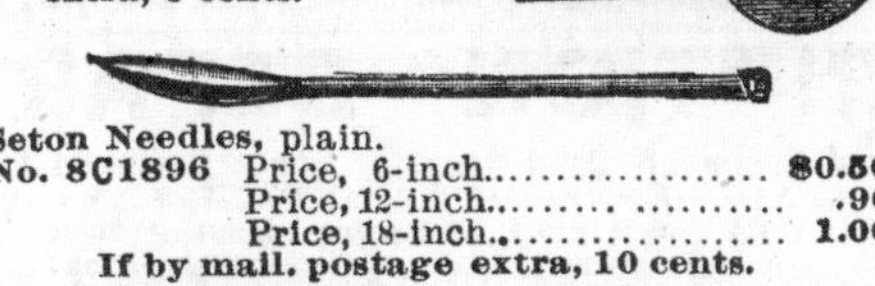

Guarded.
No. 8C1895 Price...........$2.25
If by mail, postage extra, 6 cents.

Seton Needles, plain.
No. 8C1896 Price, 6-inch.................. $0.50
Price, 12-inch.................. .90
Price, 18-inch.................. 1.00
If by mail, postage extra, 10 cents.

Seton Needles, jointed.
No. 8C1897 Price, 12-inch, 1 joint.........$1.50
Price, 18-inch, 2 joints.......... 2.00
If by mail, postage extra, 15 cents.

Horse Trocar, reversible.
No. 8C1900 Price.... (If by mail, postage extra, 8c)........95c

Horse Trocar, plain, reversible.
No. 8C1902 Price..............................55c
If by mail, postage extra, 3 cents.

Hoof Knife. Double edge, stiff handle.
No. 8C1904 Price..............................75c
If by mail, postage extra, 5 cents.

Hoof Knife, single edge, stiff handle.
No. 8C1906 Price.$1.00
If by mail, postage extra, 5 cents.

Fetlock Shears.
No. 8C1908 Price.$1.00
If by mail, postage extra, 2 cents.

Injection Syringes, metal.
No. 8C1910 16 ounces, weight, 1¼ lbs. Price $1.50
No. 8C1912 24 ounces, weight, 2¼ lbs. Price 1.85
No. 8C1914 36 ounces, weight, 3¼ lbs. Price 2.65

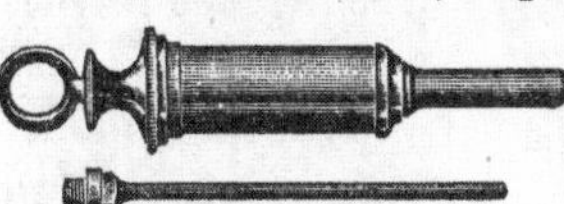

Veterinary Hard Rubber Horse Syringes, for administering medicine to horses and other animals. Quittor hard rubber, two pipes.
No. 8C1916 Price..............................$1.45
Syringe, same as preceding, but of metal, nickel plated, quittor, two pipes.
No. 8C1918 Price..............................$1.90
Veterinary Hard Rubber Horse Syringe, capacity, 24 ounces.
No. 8C1920 Price..............................$3.25

Horse Catheter, best quality.
No. 8C1922 Price..............................$1.75
Horse Catheter, domestic made.
No. 8C1924 Price..............................$1.10
If by mail, postage extra, 15 cents.

Combined Horse and Mare Catheter, metal.
No. 8C1926 Price..............................$1.80
If by mail, postage extra, 22 cents.

Mare Catheter, metal.
No. 8C1927 Price. $1.35
Mare Catheter, metal, jointed.
No. 8C1928 Price..............................$1.60
If by mail, postage extra, 8 cents.

Sutherland's Impregnating Syringe.
No. 8C1930 Price..............................$3.10
If by mail, postage extra, 15 cents.

Operating Scissors, straight, small.
No. 8C1931 Price........40c
Operating Scissors, straight, large.
No. 8C1932 Price..............................50c
Operating Scissors, curved, small.
No. 8C1933 Price..............................60c
Operating Scissors, curved, large.
No. 8C1934 Price..............................70c
If by mail, postage extra, 4 cents.

Artery Forceps, plain, 4¼-inch.
No. 8C1936 Price...........30c
Artery Forceps, plain, 6-inch.
No. 8C1938 Price.60c
If by mail, postage extra, 4 cents.

Operating Knives, plain folding, hard rubber handles, any style of blade.
No. 8C1940 Price..............................75c
Operating Knives, spring back, folding, hard rubber handles, any style of blade.
No. 8C1942 Price..............................$1.00
If by mail, postage extra, 3 cents.

Operating Knives, slide catch, folding, German silver handles, any style of blade.
No. 8C1944 Price..............................$1.50
Operating Knives, with stiff handle, small, plain.
No. 8C1946 Price..............................60c
Operating Knives, with stiff handle, small, aseptic.
No. 8C1948 Price..............................$1.00
Operating Knives, with stiff handle, large, aseptic.
No. 8C1950 Price..............................$1.95
If by mail, postage extra, 4 cents.

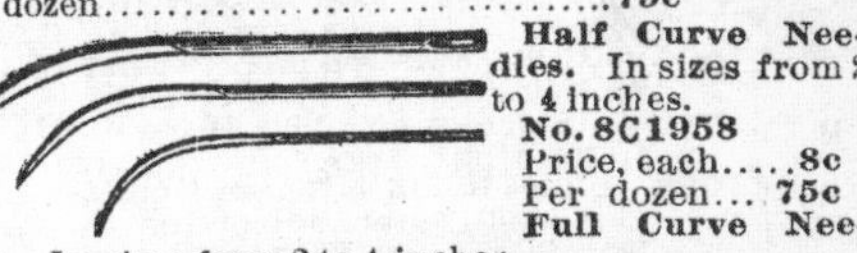

Braided Silk. Four sizes on card, white.
No. 8C1952 Price, per card..............42c
If by mail, postage, extra, 2 cents.

Twisted Silk. One size on card; white.
No. 8C1954 Price, per card..........9c
Four sizes on card.................25c
If by mail, postage extra, 2 cents.
Straight Needles. Sizes, 2 to 4 inches.
No. 8C1956 Price, each.............8c
Per dozen..........................75c

Half Curve Needles. In sizes from 2 to 4 inches.
No. 8C1958 Price, each.....8c
Per dozen... 75c
Full Curve Needles. In sizes from 2 to 4 inches.
No. 8C1960 Price, per dozen, 75c; each.......8c
If by mail, postage extra, 2 cents.

Veterinary Hypodermic Syringe and Aspirator.

Veterinary Hypodermic Syringe and Aspirator, in pocket case, fitted with three finger rings, adjustable cock, three sizes of needles, trocar and canula.
No. 8C1962 Price, complete...$2.00
Postage extra, 16c

No. 8C1964 The Boss Pig Extractor, with a treatise on the raising of the pig. This instrument was given first premium at the Iowa State Fair, 1895, and is the most valuable invention of the kind. The outfit is put up neatly in a box, and complete, weighs only 18 ounces. **Once tried always used, is the general prediction.**
Price of outfit, complete..............................79c
If by mail, postage extra, 22 cents.

No. 8C1965 The Improved Pig Forceps has points of excellence which make it a most practical instrument, and may be used upon either small or large sows with equal satisfaction. The instrument is made of malleable iron, tinned to prevent rusting; will not tear the sow or otherwise injure the animal in operation. Price..............................69c
If by mail, postage extra, 18 cents.

No. 8C1967 Perfection Calf Dehorner. So simple that it can be operated by anyone. So cheap it is within reach of all.
Price, nickel plated.............. $3.50

Keystone Dehorning Clippers. The latest improved and most powerful instrument for dehorning cattle manufactured.

No. 8C1968 The Keystone Dehorner Clipper, leader and rope, extra blades and screws. Price....... $9.20

No. 8C1969 Clipper alone. Price.......... $7.75

No. 8C1970 Dehorning Saw. Price.......... 95c

No. 8C1971 Dehorning Saw, nickel plated. Price. (By mail, postage extra, 32c). $1.35

No. 8C1973 Cattle Trocar and Canula (Bull Punch). For opening and draining abscesses, etc. Price......(By mail, postage extra, 8c)...... 40c

SOLID COIN SILVER.

No. 8C1975 Coin Silver Milking Tubes for sore and obstructed teats and hard milking cows; made of pure coin silver, and can be used with absolute safety. Set of four tubes, 2¼ inches long, in a neat box, with full directions for use.
Price, per set, silver.......... $1.25
Single tubes. Price, each.......... .35
Plain tubes, special lengths, inches....... 2¼ 3¼
Price, each. (By mail, postage extra, 2c)... 40c 45c

No. 8C1977 Teat Dilators. Price.... 60c
If by mail, postage extra, 2 cents.

No. 49C1978 Lead Probes, for treatment of stricture and obstructed teats, also for enlarging the opening in cows' teats; made in three sizes, small, medium and large; full directions for using with each probe.
Price... (If by mail, postage extra, 3c)....... 15c

No. 8C1980 Cow Teat Slitter, best implement steel; nickeled sheath, length, 5 inches.
Price.........(If by mail, postage extra, 3 cents)......... 80c

No. 8C1984 Stricture Cutter, for cows' teats; length, 7 inches, made of best implement steel. Price..... $1.20
If by mail, postage extra, 3 cents.

Poultry Instruments.

No. 49C1985 It is well understood that poultrymen can double their profits by caponizing their chicks. The operation is very simple, the instructions being so explicit that any one, after a careful reading, will be able to perform the operation with proper instruments. The demand for capons far exceeds the supply, even at an advanced price. The complete caponizing set contains the best instruments on the market, and at the price at which they are offered no one who keeps chickens can afford to neglect this opportunity of increasing their profits.
Price, per set, in velvet lined case, with book, "Instructions for Caponizing".....(If by mail, postage extra, 10c)..... $1.90

Angular Poultry Killing Knife.

No. 8C1989 Angular Poultry Killing Knife. The shape of this knife permits making incisions which are impossible with any other instrument.
Price.....(If by mail, postage extra, 5c)......45c

No. 8C1990 French Poultry Killing Knife. Every poultry raiser should have one. They are made of finely tempered instrument steel, with nickeled handle. Price.......... 36c
If by mail, postage extra, 5 cents.

No. 8C1991 The Philadelphia Poultry Marker. Do you keep a record of chickens? There is no better or quicker way than by this marker, as over two hundred different marks can be made by punching between the toes; for instance, between first and second toes of right foot can mean Wyandotte or Plymouth Rock; between second and third toes, White Leghorn or Langshan, etc.; so that hundreds of private marks can be made, not only to keep records, but by your private marks you can secure yourself from the chicken thief. They are well made, with steel spring and cutter, nicely nickel plated.
Price.....(If by mail, postage extra, 4c).....15c

No. 8C1992 Gape Worm Extractor. The disease commonly known as gapes is caused by a small worm in the windpipe of the fowls. When the chick seems to gasp frequently, it is a sure sign of gapes and it should receive attention at once. The only certain cure is to remove the worms by mechanical means. You will save time and money by having on hand a Gape Worm Extractor. The extractor quickly removes, without injury to the chick, the worms and the matter from the windpipe and effects an instant cure. One chick saved pays price of instrument. Price....(If by mail, postage extra, 2c)... 15c

PRESCRIPTION DEPARTMENT.

The Following are only a Few of the Most Commonly Used Drugs. For a Complete List send for our Special Drug Catalogue.

WE HAVE UNEQUALED FACILITIES FOR PREPARING PRESCRIPTIONS AND FAMILY RECIPES. In this branch of our Drug Department we employ only registered druggists having long experience. Our medicines are always fresh and of the best quality. Send your prescriptions and recipes to us—you can always feel well assured of having them prepared with the greatest care by competent and skillful druggists and chemists, using only the purest and freshest drugs, and at a price very much cheaper than you could have them prepared elsewhere. Orders for opium, morphine, cocaine and drugs of this class should be accompanied by a physician's prescription.

ACIDS, CHEMICALS AND DRUGS. All drugs that we offer for sale are guaranteed to be of standard quality, pure and unadulterated, and reliable in every way. All prices include vial or package necessary to contain the goods, unless otherwise specified. The mailing rates for liquids are, including tube, 8 cents for 1 ounce, 11 cents for 2 ounces and 17 cents for 4 ounces.

PRICES ARE SUBJECT TO MARKET CHANGES.

Articles	Per lb.	8-oz. Pkg.	4-oz. Pkg.	2-oz. Pkg.	1-oz. Pkg.
No. 8C7000 **Acetanilid**, 5-lb. lots or over, 45c per pound	$0 48	$0 25	$0 15	$0 10	$0 05
No. 8C7000½ **Wood Alcohol**, for mechanical or external use only, per gallon $1.00, can 15c extra; per pint 25c	....	....	....	....	....
No. 8C7000¾ **Alcohol**, pure grain, 94 per cent, per gallon $2.90, can 15c extra: subject to market fluctuations	....	....	....	....	....
No. 8C7038 **Alum**, lump, bbls., 2½c per lb. In 10 to 50-lb. lots, 4c per lb.; over 50 lbs., 3c per pound	4	....	....	....	....
No. 8C7039 **Alum**, powdered, bbls., 4c per lb. In 10-lb. lots or over, 7c per lb.	8	5	....	....	...
No. 8C7040 **Alum**, ground, bbls,, 4c per lb. In 10-lb. lots, 7c per lb.	8	5	....	....	....
No. 8C7088 **Blue Vitriol**, sulphate copper, 25 to 100-lb. lots, 8c per lb.; in 100 to 245-lb. lots, 6¾c per lb.; in barrels, 450-lb. lots, 6c per lb.	9	5	....	....	....
No. 8C7089 **Blue Vitriol**, powdered	15	10	8	5	....
No. 8C7090 **Borax**, refined crystals	9	5	....	....	....
No. 8C7091 **Borax**, powdered	10	5	....	....	....
No. 8C7093 **Brimstone**, bbls., 350 lbs., 3c; in 5 to 25-lb. lots, 3½c; 25 to 100-lb. lots, 3¼c	6	4	....	....	....
No. 8C7098 **Camphor**, refined, medicinal,	79	45	25	15	8
No. 8C7110 **Chalk**, French, powdered or glove powder, 10 to 25-lb. lots or over, 3½c per pound	7	5	....	....	....
No. 8C7111 **Chalk**, precipitated, English, 7-lb. bundles, 14c per lb.	20	15	10	....	....
No. 8C7112 **Chalk**, prepared, white	10	8	....	....	....
No. 8C7113 **Chalk**, prepared, pink	15	10	5	....	....
No. 8C7123 **Cocoa Butter**	70	40	20	12	8
No. 8C7133 **Copperas**, 520-lb. bbls., 1c; 5 to 50-lb. lots, 2c per lb.; 50 to 100-lb. lots, 1½c per lb.	3	....	....	....	....
No. 8C7134 **Copperas**, powdered for stock powders	8	....	....	....	....
No. 8C7139 **Creosote**	60	35	20	12	8
No. 8C7140 **Creosote**, pure, from beechwood	1 75	95	53	30	20
No. 8C7152 **Epsom Salts**, bbls., 1½c per lb.; 50 to 100-lb. lots, 2½c per lb.; 5 to 50 lbs, 3c per lb.	4	....	....	....	....
No. 8C7174 **Extract Witch Hazel**	25	15	....	....	...
No. 8C7184 **Glauber Salts**, 400-lb. bbls., 1c per lb.; in lots of 10 to 25 lbs., 3c per lb.; in lots of 25 to 100 lbs., 2c	4	....	....	....	....
No. 8C7185 **Glauber Salts**, powdered, for condition powders; in 50-lb. lots or over, 6c per lb.	8	4	....	....	....
No. 8C7204 **Gum Arabic**, best quality	75	40	20	10	8
No. 8C7205 **Gum Arabic**, medium quality	55	30	20	12	8
No. 8C7206 **Gum Arabic**, ordinary	35	20	12	8	5
No. 8C7207 **Gum Arabic**, powdered	80	40	20	10	7
No. 8C7208 **Gum, Asafœtida**, pure	50	30	18	10	5
No. 8C7209 **Gum, Asafœtida**, powdered	55	30	18	10	5
No. 8C7220 **Gum, Myrrh**	40	20	15	8	5
No. 8C7221 **Gum, Myrrh**, powdered	50	25	15	10	8
No. 8C7271 **Lead, Sugar**, powdered	35	20	15	10	8
No. 8C7308 **Mercury or Quicksilver**	90	50	30	20	12
No. 8C7316 **Moth Ball**, 10 lbs. and over, 6c per lb.	$0 08	$0 05	....	....	....
No. 8C7317 **Moth Camphor**	30	15	$0 10	$0 05	....
No. 8C7318 **Musk, Canton**	....	....	....	....	$0 35
No. 8C7319 **Musk**, true, 3-grain vials, 30c	....	....	....	....	30 00
No. 8C7324 **Nux Vomica**, powdered, 10-lb. lots and over, 18c per lb.	20	15	10	5	5
No. 8C7345 **Oil, Castor**, No. 1, pure, for medicinal use, per gal., $1.35, can extra; 5-gal. lots, $1.20 per gal., can included	28	....	15	10	....
No. 8C7346 **Oil, Castor**, No. 3, per gallon, $1.25; can extra	....	....	....	....	....
No. 8C7354 **Oil, Cod Liver**, Nor. white, per gallon, $3.30; can extra., 20c	60	....	....	....	....
No. 8C7380 **Oil, Lemon**	1 50	80	45	25	15
No. 8C7395 **Oil, Olive**, Malaga, yellow, per gal., $1.35; can extra	35	25	15	10	8
No. 8C7397 **Oil, Orange**	2 50	1 30	70	40	25
No. 8C7402 **Oil, Peppermint**, strictly pure	4 00	2 05	1 05	55	30
No. 8C7459 **Paris Green**	20	Subject to market change.			
No. 8C7460 **Paris Green**, in 14, 28 and 56-lb. kits	17				
No. 8C7461 **Paris Green**, in kegs of 100 to 175 lbs.	16				
No. 8C7483 **Potassium, Chlorate**, crystals, in 10 to 25-lb. lots, 18c per lb.; in kegs of 112 lbs., 16c per lb.	20	15	10	05	05
No. 8C7486 **Potassium, Iodide**, crystal	3 00	1 50	75	40	20
No. 8C7496 **Quinine, Sulphate**, 5-oz. tins, $2.00	....	....	....	....	42
No. 8C7500 **Resin**, common, bbls., 1¼c per lb.; 10-lb. lots, 4c per lb.; 50-lb. lots, 3c per lb.; 100-lb. lots, 2c per lb.	5	....	....	....	....
No. 8C7501 **Resin**, powdered, 100-lb. lots, 6c per lb.	10	....	....	....	....
No. 8C7506 **Sal Nitre**, crystals, bbls., about 400 lbs., 6c; 25-lb. lots and over, 7c per lb.	9	....	....	....	....
No. 8C7507 **Sal Nitre**, gran., 25-lb. and 50-lb. boxes, 7c per lb.	9	....	....	....	....
No. 8C7508 **Sal Nitre**, powdered	15	8	5	....	....
No. 8C7509 **Sal Rochelle**	30	15	10	8	5
No. 8C7531 **Seeds, Foenugreek**, ground, 50 to 100-lb. lots, 6c per lb.	10	8	5	....	....
No. 8C7561 **Soda, Caustic**, for making soap, 10-lb. lots, 9c per lb.; 50 to 100 lbs., 6c per lb.; 600-lb. drums, 3½c per lb.	10	....	....	....	....
No. 8C7570 **Sodium, Hyposulphite**, 112-lb. kegs, or over. 4c per lb.	5	....	....	....	....
No. 8C7591 **Strychnia**, crystals, ⅛-oz. vials, 18c; in 10-oz. lots, 1-oz. vials, 80c per oz.; in 100-oz. lots, 75c per oz.	....	....	....	....	85
No. 8C7592 **Strychnine**, Sulph. Pwd., ⅛-oz. vials, 18c	....	....	....	....	95
No. 8C7596 **Sulphur**, Flour of, bbls., 250 lbs., 2½c per lb.; bbls., 180 lbs., 3c per lb.; 25 to 100 lbs., 3½c per lb.	4	....	....	....	....
No. 8C7640 **Zinc, Sulphate**, in 5 to 10-lb. lots, 8c per lb.; 10 to 25-lb. lots, 7c per lb.; 25 lbs. or over, 6c per lb.; barrels, 350 lbs., 5½c per lb.	9	....	....	....	...

FOR COMPLETE LIST OF DRUGS AND CHEMICALS, SEND FOR SPECIAL DRUG CATALOGUE, FREE.

Proprietary and Patent Medicines.

The following list contains the principal patent medicines of the world. It is not possible for us to enumerate every single article that is manufactured, but we can and are willing to obtain for our customers any medicine or other article that they may wish. If you do not see the medicine you want mentioned here, write to us concerning it, or send us what you know it is worth and we will send it to you. With few exceptions the quantity prices on patent medicines when ordered in full dozen lots are as follows: $1.00 sizes, $8.00 per dozen; 50-cent sizes, $4.00 per dozen; 25-cent sizes, $2.00 per dozen.

No.	Name	Retail Price, each	Our Price, per doz.	Our Price, each
No. 8C9214	Antifebrin, 1-ounce boxes	$0 50	$ 1.75	$0.15
No. 8C9215	Antikamnia, powdered or tablets	1 25	12.00	1.00
No. 8C9218	Apioline, Chapoteaut's	1 00	8.00	.70
No. 8C9219	Arnold's Balsam, large	1 00	7.50	.65
No. 8C9220	Arnold's Balsam, medium	50	4.00	.40
No. 8C9228	Ayer's Ague Cure, regular size	1 00	4.50	.40
No. 8C9229	Ayer's Cherry Pectoral, regular size	1 00	8.75	.75
No. 8C9231	Ayer's Hair Vigor	1 00	8.00	.70
No. 8C9232	Ayer's Pills	25	2.25	.20
No. 8C9233	Ayer's Sarsaparilla	1 00	8.75	.75
No. 8C9242	Beecham's Pills, Eng	25	2.00	.18
No. 8C9275	Brandreth's Pills	25	2.00	.20
No. 8C9280	Bromo-Chloralum	50	4.00	.35
No. 8C9281	Bromo-Seltzer	10	.75	.08
No. 8C9282	Bromo-Seltzer	25	2.25	.20
No. 8C9283	Bromo-Seltzer	50	4.00	.35
No. 8C9284	Bromo-Seltzer	1 00	7.50	.65
No. 8C9298	Bucklen's Arnica Salve	25	2.00	.18
No. 8C9320	Carter's Iron Pills	50	4.00	.35
No. 8C9321	Carter's Little Liver Pills	25	1.60	.14
No. 8C9322	Carter's Nerve Pills	25	1.60	.14
No. 8C9323	Cascarets, small	10	1.00	.09
No. 8C9324	Cascarets, medium	25	2.40	.20
No. 8C9325	Cascarets, large	50	4.80	.40
No. 8C9326	Castoria	35	2.80	.24
No. 8C9376	Cuticura Ointment, large	1 00	9.50	.80
No. 8C9377	Cuticura Ointment, small	50	4.75	.40
No. 8C9378	Cuticura Resolvent	1 00	9.20	.80
No. 8C9379	Cuticura Plaster	25	......	.19
No. 8C9383	Damiana Wafers, pink for men	1 00	8.80	.80
No. 8C9384	Damiana Wafers, white for women	1 00	8.00	.75
No. 8C9387	Davis, Perry, Pain Killer	25	2.25	.20
No. 8C9388	Davis, Perry, Pain Killer	50	4.50	.40
No. 8C9471	Green's August Flower	75	5.75	.50
No. 8C9472	Green's Nervura Tonic	1 00	8.50	.75
No. 8C9481	Haarlem Oil, 3 hd's	15	.50	.06
No. 8C9492	Hall's Lung Balsam, large	1 00	7.50	.65
No. 8C9495	Hall's Catarrh Cure, F. J. Cheney's, Toledo	75	6.00	.50
No. 8C9496	Hall's Family Pills	25	2.00	.18
No. 8C9497	Hall's Hair Renewer	1 00	8.00	.70
No. 8C9498	Hamburg Drops, Koenig's	50	4.00	.35
No. 8C9500	Hamburg Breast Tea, genuine	25	2.00	.18
No. 8C9501	Hamlin's Wizard Oil, small	50	4.00	.35
No. 8C9502	Hamlin's Wizard Oil, large	1 00	8.00	.70
No. 8C9511	Hartman's Lacupia	1 00	8.00	.70
No. 8C9512	Hartman's Manalin	1 00	8.00	.70
No. 8C9513	Hartman's Peruna	1 00	8.00	.70
No. 8C9537	Hood's Sarsaparilla	1 00	8.75	.75
No. 8C9538	Hood's Olive Ointment	25	2.00	.18
No. 8C9539	Hood's Vegetable Pills	25	2.00	.18
No. 8C9548	Horsford's Acid Phosphate, large	1 00	8.00	.70
No. 8C9549	Horsford's Acid Phosphate, small	50	4.00	.35
No. 8C9550	Hostetter's Stomach Bitters	1 00	8.50	.73
No. 8C9582	Jayne's Alterative	1 00	8.00	.70
No. 8C9586	Jayne's Expectorant	1 00	8.00	.70
No. 8C9587	Jayne's Carminative Balsam	25	2.00	.18
No. 8C9588	Jayne's Liniment	50	4.00	.35
No. 8C9590	Jayne's Sanative Pills	25	1.75	.18
No. 8C9591	Jayne's Tonic Vermifuge, small	35	3.00	.25
No. 8C9607	Kendall's Spavin Cure, family use	50	4.00	.35

PROPRIETARY AND PATENT MEDICINES.—Continued.

No.	Name	Retail Price, each	Our Price, per doz.	Our Price, each
No. 8C9608	Kendall's Spavin Cure	$1 00	$ 8.00	$0.70
No. 8C9609	Kennedy's Medical Discovery	1 50	13.50	1.25
No. 8C9610	Kennedy's, Dr. David, Favorite Remedy	1 00	8.50	.75
No. 8C9613	Kennedy's Prairie Weed	1 00	8.00	.70
No. 8C9614	Kennedy's Rheumatic Dissolvent	1 50	12.50	1.15
No. 8C9516	Kennedy's Salt Rheum Ointment	50	4.00	.40
No. 8C9621	Kickapoo Indian Cough Cure	50	4.20	.40
No. 8C9622	Kickapoo Indian Oil	25	2.00	.18
No. 8C9623	Kickapoo Indian Sagwa	1 00	8.00	.70
No. 8C9624	Kickapoo Indian Salve	25	2.00	.18
No. 8C9625	Kickapoo Prairie Plant	1 00	8.00	.70
No. 8C9626	Kickapoo Worm Killer	25	2.00	.18
No. 8C9627	Kickapoo Pills	25	2.00	.18
No. 8C9640	Kilmer's Olive Branch for Females	1 00	......	.71
No. 8C9641	Kilmer's Prompt Parilla Pills	25	2.00	.20
No. 8C9642	Kilmer's Swamp Root, large	1 00	8.00	.70
No. 8C9643	Kilmer's Swamp Root, small	50	4.00	.35
No. 8C9644	Kilmer's U. & O. Ointment	50	4.00	.35
No. 8C9645	King's New Discovery, large	1 00	8.00	.70
No. 8C9647	King's New Discovery, small	50	4.00	.35
No. 8C9648	King's New Life Pills	25	2.00	.18
No. 8C9676	Lane's Family Medicine, small	25	2.00	.18
No. 8C9677	Lane's Family Medicine, medium	50	4.00	.35
No. 8C9688	Listerine, Lambert's	1 00	8.00	.70
No. 8C9705	Malted Milk Food, small (either powder or tablet form)	50	4.50	.40
No. 8C9706	Malted Milk Food, large (either powder or tablet form)	1 00	9.00	.75
No. 8C9707	Malted Milk Food, hospital size (either powder or tablet form)	3 75	....	3.00
No. 8C9724	McElree's Wine of Cardui	1 00	8.00	.70
No. 8C9725	McGill's Orange Blossom	1 00	7.50	.75
No. 8C9792	Paine's Celery Compound	1 00	8.00	.70
No. 8C9732	Pettitt's Eye Salve	25	....	.17
No. 8C9834	Pinkham's Blood Purifier	1 00	8.25	.70
No. 8C9835	Pinkham's Liver Pills	25	2.00	.18
No. 8C9836	Pinkham's, Lydia, Vegetable Compound, Liquid	1 00	8.25	.70
No. 8C9837	Pinkham's Compound Pills	1 00	8.25	.70
No. 8C9838	Pinkham's Sanative Wash	25	2.00	.18
No. 8C9840	Piso's Consumption Cure	25	2.00	.18
No. 8C9844	Pond's Extract, large	1 75	16.00	1.40
No. 8C9845	Pond's Extract, medium	1 00	8.00	.70
No. 8C9846	Pond's Extract, small	50	4.00	.35
No. 8C9860	Ripans Tabules	50	....	.34
No. 8C9895	Sage's Catarrh Remedy	50	4.00	.40
No. 8C9902	Sanmetto	1 00	8.00	.75
No. 8C9905	Schenck's Mandrake Pills	25	1.75	.15
No. 8C9911	Scott's Emulsion	1 00	8.00	.70
No. 8C9942	Shoop's Cough Cure, large	1 00	8.25	.70
No. 8C9943	Shoop's Cough Cure, small	25	2.00	.18
No. 8C9944	Shoop's Headache Cure	25	2.00	.18
No. 8C9945	Shoop's Laxative Pills	25	2.00	.18
No. 8C9946	Shoop's Restorative	1 00	8.50	.75
No. 8C9947	Shoop's Nerve Pills	25	2.00	.20
No. 8C9948	Simmons' Liver Regulator, liquid or powder	1 00	8.50	.70
No. 8C9949	Slocum's Psychine	3 00	25.00	2.25
No. 8C9950	Slocum's Ozomulsion	1 00	8.00	.70
No. 8C9975	St. Jacob's Oil	50	4.00	.35
No. 8C9979	Stuart's Dyspepsia Tablets	50	4.00	.35
No. 8C9980	Stuart's Dyspepsia Tablets, large	1 00	8.00	.75
No. 8C9998	Syrup of Figs	50	4.00	.35
No. 8C10029	Trask's Magnetic Ointment	25	2.00	.18
No. 8C10030	Trask's Ointment, large	40	3.25	.30
No. 8C10045	Wampole's Cod Liver Oil	1 00	8.30	.70
No. 8C10047	Warner's Safe Kidney and Liver Cure	1 25	8.00	.75
No. 8C10048	Warner's Safe Pills	20	1.50	.14
No. 8C10049	Warner's Safe Rheumatic Cure	1 25	10.50	.90
No. 8C10055	Warner's Lithia Tablets, Eff., 3-grain	25	2.00	.18
No. 8C10056	Warner's Lithia Tablets, Eff., 5-grain	50	3.00	.30
No. 8C10087	Winslow's Soothing Syrup	25	2.00	.20
No. 8C10089	Woodbury's Facial Soap	35	....	.20

FLUID EXTRACTS.

A fluid extract of a drug represents as nearly as possible the drug itself in a fluid form. TINCTURES are weaker preparations than fluid extracts, their general strength being from 10 to 33⅓ per cent of the crude drug, and consequently the dose is larger. Syrups are a more palatable form of administering drugs than either the fluid extracts or tinctures. Solid extracts are generally from two to five times stronger than the drug, and their dose is consequently smaller in proportion. In ordering these goods, please be careful to state just what you want, and always give the number. Each minum of our Fluid Extract represents the full strength of one grain of the pure drug, unless specified otherwise, so that the dose is the same in minums as in grains of the drug.

PRICES INCLUDE BOTTLES IN EVERY CASE.

When you wish us to mail to you any liquid, remember to allow us for the mailing boxes, as required by the postal authorities, also for postage. One ounce costs 8 cents, two ounces 11 cents, four ounces 17 cents. Four ounces is the largest bottle of liquid we can send by mail.

No.	Name	16-oz.	8-oz.	4-oz.	2-oz.	1-oz.
No. 8C8470	Aconite Root, U. S. P. (aconitum nap)	$1 35	70	40	25	15
No. 8C8471	Aconite Leaves	83	45	25	16	11
No. 8C8475	Arnica Flowers (arnica montana)	83	45	25	16	11
No. 8C8476	Arnica Root, U.S.P. (arnica montana)	1 35	70	40	25	15
No. 8C8484	Belladonna Leaves	90	49	26	16	11
No. 8C8485	Belladonna Root, U.S.P. (atropa bell)	1 13	61	34	20	13
No. 8C8494	Black Haw, U.S.P. (viburnum prunifolium)	1 58	84	45	25	16
No. 8C8496	Bladder Wrack (fucus vesi culosis)	1 01	55	30	18	12
No. 8C8502	Buchu, U. S. P. (barosma crenata)	1 40	75	40	25	15
No. 8C8512	Calendula Flowers (calendula officinalis)	1 75	90	50	30	18
No. 8C8513	Cantharides	3 75	1 92	1 00	53	30
No. 8C8514	Capsicum, U.S.P. (capsicum fastigiatum)	1 13	61	34	20	13
No. 8C8517	Cascara Sagrada (rhamnus purschiana)	94	51	30	18	12
No. 8C8518	Cascara Sagrada, bitterless, action on bowels same as regular extract	90	49	26	16	11
No. 8C8520	Catechu (acacia catechu)	90	49	26	16	11
No. 8C8521	Celery Seed (apium graveolens)	1 35	73	38	21	14
No. 8C8524	Cherry Bark, U.S.P. (prunus virginiana)	75	41	24	15	10
No. 8C8527	Cinchona, comp.	1 13	61	34	20	13
No. 8C8529	Cinchona, red, true	1 12	61	34	20	13
No. 8C8531	Clover Top (trifolium pratense)	90	49	26	16	11
No. 8C8532	Coca Leaves, U. S. P. (erythroxylon coca)	1 25	65	35	18	10
No. 8C8533	Cocculus Indicus (anamirta cocculus)	90	49	26	16	11
No. 8C8539	Colombo, U. S. P.	90	49	26	16	11
No. 8C8547	Cotton Root Bark, U.S.P. (gossypium herbaceum)	94	51	30	18	12
No. 8C8553	Damiana (turnera aphrodisiaca)	1 57	82	45	26	16
No. 8C8554	Dandelion Root, U. S. P. (taraxacum)	94	51	30	18	12
No. 8C8559	Ergot, U. S. P. (secale cornutum)	3 15	1 65	85	45	25
No. 8C8561	Foxglove, U. S. P. (digitalis purpurea)	$0.90	49	26	16	11
No. 8C8565	Gentian, U. S. P. (gentiana lutea)	75	41	24	15	10
No. 8C8566	Gentian Compound	86	47	28	16	11
No. 8C8567	Ginger, U. S. P. (zingiber officinalis)	1 13	61	34	20	13
No. 8C8569	Golden Seal, U. S. P. (hydrastis canadensis)	2 90	1 50	80	45	25
No. 8C8570	Golden Seal, without alcohol	2 25	1 20	65	35	20
No. 8C8571	Golden Seal, non-irritating, colorless, odorless, preferred to fluid extract for local use	1 60	85	45	25	18
No. 8C8585	Indian Hemp, U. S. P. (cannabis indica)	3 15	1 63	87	49	30
No. 8C8586	Ipecac, U. S. P. (ipecacuanha)	8 50	4 30	2 20	1 15	60
No. 8C8593	Kola Nut (sterculia acuminata)	1 87	97	52	29	16
No. 8C8600	Life Root (senecio grac)	67	37	22	14	10
No. 8C8614	Nux Vomica, U. S. P. (strychnos nux vom.)	90	49	26	16	11
No. 8C8617	Opium (for making laudanum), U.S.P.	4 00	2 00	1 05	60	35
No. 8C8619	Orange Peel (citrus aurantium)	90	50	26	16	11
No. 8C8623	Pennyroyal (hedeoma pulegioides)	67	37	22	14	10
No. 8C8635	Pulsatilla (anemone pulsatilla)	1 50	80	45	25	16
No. 8C8640	Rhubarb (rhuem palmatum)	1 50	79	44	25	16
No. 8C8641	Rhubarb, aromatic	1 25	65	35	20	14
No. 8C8643	Rhus Aromatica	2 02	1 05	57	27	16
No. 8C8644	Sarsaparilla, U. S. P. (smilax officinalis)	1 13	61	34	20	13
No. 8C8645	Sarsaparilla Comp., U. S. P. We use only the genuine Honduras sarsaparilla	1 13	61	34	20	13
No. 8C8646	Sarsaparilla Comp., for syrup	1 13	61	34	20	13
No. 8C8647	Sassafras (sassafras officinalis)	1 00	55	30	20	15
No. 8C8649	Saw Palmetto	1 35	73	38	21	14
No. 8C8652	Senna, U. S. P. (cassia acutiflora)	1 04	56	32	19	18
No. 8C8656	Soap Bark (quillaia saponaria)	90	49	26	16	11
No. 8C8662	Stillingia (stillingia sylvatica)	1 13	61	34	20	13
No. 8C8663	Stillingia Comp.	1 09	51	33	19	13

FOR COMPLETE LIST OF DRUGS AND CHEMICALS SEND FOR SPECIAL DRUG CATALOGUE, FREE.

FURNITURE OF EVERY KIND AT LOWER PRICES THAN EVER.

OUR FURNITURE DEPARTMENT for this year has been entirely revised, new and better lines of goods have been introduced, and all put on a price basis that will make our leadership unquestioned. **OUR FACILITIES FOR SUPPLYING OUR CUSTOMERS** with the best grades of furniture manufactured at the lowest possible prices were never so good as they are this season. Our manufacturing connections are such that in most lines our customers can buy from us for less money than retail dealers must pay for equal qualities.

WE INVITE A CAREFUL COMPARISON of our very handsome and complete lines of parlor suites, bedroom suites, iron beds, chairs, dining room furniture, etc., with those of other houses, AND ESPECIALLY OUR PRICES AS AGAINST THEIRS. All of our furniture is covered by OUR BINDING GUARANTEE, and your order is accepted by us with the understanding that the goods will please you in every way or you can return them at our expense of transportation charges both ways and we will refund your money.

FREIGHT RATES ON VARIOUS ARTICLES OF FURNITURE PER 100 POUNDS. We give below freight rates per 100 pounds on different articles of furniture to the central points in each state. Refer to the point nearest you, for the freight will be about the same to your town. From the list below you can tell exactly what the freight on nearly any article of furniture to your point will be, and save the trouble and time of writing to us for an estimate of freight. However, if you live in Oregon, California, Washington or Nevada, write for an estimate of the freight charges on furniture wanted.

FROM CHICAGO TO	Spiral Bed Springs	Glassware Iron Beds Wood Beds	Sideb'ds Dressers and Commodes, Chiffoniers	Mirrors	Extension Tables	Parlor Tables	Cane Seat Chairs Couches and Lounges	Hall Trees Wardrobes	Common Mattresses	Kitchen Cupboards and Bookcases
ALABAMA.										
Birmingham	$2.38	$1.03	$1.03	$1.19	$1.03	$1.79	$1.19	$1.79	$1.03	$1.79
Brewton	3.08	1.27	1.27	1.54	1.27	2.31	1.54	2.31	1.27	2.31
Montgomery	2.76	1.26	1.26	1.38	1.26	2.07	1.38	2.07	1.26	2.07
Ozark	3.92	1.68	1.68	1.96	1.68	2.94	1.96	2.94	1.68	2.94
ARIZONA.										
Benson	6.88	3.01	3.44	3.44	2.66	6.88	5.16	6.88	3.44	5.16
Flagstaff	7.80	3.40	3.90	3.90	2.70	7.80	5.85	7.80	3.90	5.85
Tucson	7.04	3.05	3.52	3.52	2.70	7.04	5.28	7.04	3.52	5.28
ARKANSAS.										
Knobel	1.90	.84	.95	.95	.68	1.90	1.43	1.90	.95	1.43
Little Rock	2.40	1.01	1.20	1.20	.77	2.40	1.80	2.40	1.20	1.80
Texarkana	2.60	1.15	1.30	1.30	.99	2.60	1.95	2.60	1.30	1.95
COLORADO.										
Denver	4.10	1.65	2.05	2.05	1.25	4.10	3.08	4.10	2.05	3.08
Grand Junction	7.40	3.15	3.70	3.70	2.50	7.40	5.55	7.40	3.70	5.55
Mancos	8.20	3.50	4.10	4.10	2.85	8.20	6.15	8.20	4.10	6.15
Sterling	3.62	1.58	1.81	1.81	1.25	3.62	2.72	3.62	1.81	2.72
CONNECTICUT.										
Bridgeport	1.64	.71	.82	.82	.71	1.23	1.23	1.64	1.23	1.23
Hartford	1.64	.71	.82	.82	.71	1.23	1.23	1.64	1.23	1.23
New London	1.64	.71	.82	.82	.71	1.23	1.23	1.64	1.23	1.23
DELAWARE.										
Dover	1.50	.65	.75	.75	.65	1.13	1.13	1.50	1.13	1.13
Newark	1.46	.63	.73	.73	.63	1.10	1.10	1.46	1.10	1.10
Wilmington	1.46	.63	.73	.73	.63	1.10	1.10	1.46	1.10	1.10
FLORIDA.										
Carrabelle	4.62	2.00	2.31	2.31	2.00	3.47	2.31	3.47	2.00	3.47
Jacksonville	2.70	1.14	1.14	1.35	1.14	2.03	1.35	2.03	1.14	2.03
Pensacola	2.20	.90	.90	1.10	.90	1.65	1.10	1.65	.90	1.65
Tallahassee	4.38	1.88	1.88	2.19	1.88	3.29	2.19	3.29	1.88	3.29
GEORGIA.										
Atlanta	2.94	1.26	1.26	1.47	1.26	2.20	1.47	2.20	1.26	2.20
Doerun	4.74	2.01	2.01	2.37	2.01	3.56	2.37	3.56	2.01	3.56
Thomasville	3.92	1.65	1.65	1.96	1.65	2.94	1.96	2.94	1.65	2.94
Waycross	3.50	1.50	1.50	1.75	1.50	2.63	1.75	2.63	1.50	2.63
IDAHO.										
Idaho Falls	6.60	2.80	3.30	3.30	2.20	6.60	4.95	6.60	3.30	4.95
Pocatello	6.60	2.80	3.30	3.30	2.20	6.60	4.95	6.60	3.30	4.95
Stites	7.90	3.40	3.95	3.95	2.85	7.90	5.93	7.90	3.95	5.93
ILLINOIS.										
Cairo	1.18	.48	.59	.59	.48	.59	.89	.89	.59	.89
Danville	.64	.27	.32	.32	.27	.32	.48	.48	.32	.48
Springfield	.94	.38	.47	.47	.38	.47	.70	.70	.47	.70
INDIANA.										
Elkhart	.50	.22	.25	.25	.22	.38	.38	.50	.38	.38
Evansville	.80	.34	.40	.40	.34	.60	.60	.80	.60	.60
Indianapolis	.64	.27	.32	.32	.27	.48	.48	.64	.48	.48
INDIAN TERRITORY.										
Atoka	3.00	1.29	1.50	1.50	1.07	3.00	2.25	3.00	1.50	2.25
Vinita	2.50	1.03	1.25	1.25	.83	2.50	1.88	2.50	1.25	1.88
Wyandotte	2.14	.88	1.07	1.07	.67	2.14	1.61	2.14	1.07	1.61
IOWA.										
Burlington	.94	.38	.47	.47	.29	.94	.71	.94	.47	.71
Council Bluffs	1.60	.65	.80	.80	.45	1.60	1.20	1.60	.80	1.20
Des Moines	1.36	.57	.68	.68	.40	1.36	1.02	1.36	.68	1.02
KANSAS.										
Ft. Scott	1.94	.81	.97	.97	.55	1.94	1.46	1.94	.97	1.46
Hartland	3.48	1.49	1.74	1.74	1.22	3.48	2.61	3.48	1.74	2.61
Topeka	2.18	.89	1.09	1.09	.64	2.18	1.64	2.18	1.09	1.64
Wichita	2.80	1.18	1.40	1.40	.91	2.80	2.10	2.80	1.40	2.10
KENTUCKY.										
Alexander (Fulton Co.)	1.60	.66	.66	.80	.66	1.20	.80	1.20	.66	1.20
Catlettsburg	.90	.39	.45	.45	.39	.68	.68	.90	.68	.68
Paducah	1.20	.50	.50	.60	.50	.90	.60	.90	.50	.90
LOUISIANA.										
Lake Charles	3.00	1.29	1.50	1.50	1.02	3.00	2.25	3.00	1.50	2.25
New Orleans	2.20	.90	.90	1.10	.90	1.65	1.10	1.65	.90	1.65
Shreveport	2.60	1.10	1.30	1.30	.92	2.60	1.95	2.60	1.30	1.95
MAINE.										
Augusta	1.88	.81	.94	.94	.81	1.41	1.41	1.88	1.41	1.41
Kennebunk	1.78	.77	.89	.89	.77	1.34	1.34	1.78	1.34	1.34
Portland	1.64	.71	.82	.82	.71	1.23	1.23	1.64	1.23	1.23
MARYLAND.										
Annapolis	1.60	.70	.80	.80	.70	1.20	1.20	1.60	1.20	1.20
Baltimore	1.44	.62	.72	.72	.62	1.08	1.08	1.44	1.08	1.08
Port Tobacco	1.50	.65	.75	.75	.65	1.13	1.13	1.50	1.13	1.13
MASSACHUSETTS.										
Boston	1.64	.71	.82	.82	.71	1.23	1.23	1.64	1.23	1.23
Jefferson	1.64	.71	.82	.82	.71	1.23	1.23	1.64	1.23	1.23
Springfield	1.64	.71	.82	.82	.71	1.23	1.23	1.64	1.23	1.23
MICHIGAN.										
Alpena	1.10	.45	.55	.55	.45	.83	.83	1.10	.83	.83
Lansing	.72	.31	.36	.36	.31	.54	.54	.72	.54	.54
Munising	1.50	.65	.75	.75	.48	1.50	1.13	1.50	.75	1.13
MINNESOTA.										
Crookston	2.80	1.18	1.40	1.40	.92	2.80	2.10	2.80	1.40	2.10
Milan	1.80	.77	.90	.90	.64	1.80	1.35	1.80	.90	1.35
St. Paul	1.20	.50	.60	.60	.40	1.20	.90	1.20	.60	.90
Tower	2.20	.94	1.10	1.10	.78	2.20	1.65	2.20	1.10	1.44
MISSISSIPPI.										
Natchez	2.20	.90	.90	1.10	.90	1.65	1.10	1.65	.90	1.65
Roxie	2.68	1.08	1.08	1.34	1.08	2.01	1.34	2.01	1.08	2.01
State Line (Wayne Co.)	3.08	1.32	1.32	1.54	1.32	2.31	1.54	2.31	1.32	2.31
MISSOURI.										
Chicopee	$2.82	$1.18	$1.41	$1.41	$0.89	$2.82	$2.12	$2.82	$1.41	$2.12
Hannibal	.94	.38	.47	.47	.29	.94	.70	.94	.47	.70
Springfield	1.80	.72	.90	.90	.50	1.80	1.35	1.80	.90	1.35
MONTANA.										
Billings	5.70	2.45	2.85	2.85	1.98	5.70	4.28	5.70	2.85	4.28
Glendive	4.30	1.76	2.15	2.15	1.46	4.30	3.23	4.30	2.15	3.23
Iron Mountain	6.80	2.95	3.40	3.40	2.44	6.80	5.10	6.80	3.40	5.10
NEBRASKA.										
Chadron	3.80	1.64	1.90	1.90	1.34	3.80	2.85	3.80	1.90	2.85
Crawford	4.40	1.76	2.02	2.02	1.43	4.04	3.03	4.04	2.02	3.03
Lincoln	1.70	.70	.85	.85	.49	1.70	1.28	1.70	.85	1.28
NEW HAMPSHIRE.										
Concord	1.64	.71	.82	.82	.71	1.23	1.23	1.64	1.23	1.23
Keene	1.64	.71	.82	.82	.71	1.23	1.23	1.64	1.23	1.23
Nashua	1.64	.71	.82	.82	.71	1.23	1.23	1.64	1.23	1.23
NEW JERSEY.										
Bridgeton	1.60	.70	.80	.80	.70	1.20	1.20	1.60	1.20	1.20
Newark	1.50	.65	.75	.75	.65	1.13	1.13	1.50	1.13	1.13
Pompton	1.50	.65	.75	.75	.65	1.13	1.13	1.50	1.13	1.13
NEW MEXICO.										
Albuquerque	4.64	2.06	2.32	2.32	1.80	4.64	3.48	4.64	2.32	3.48
Carlsbad	4.40	1.94	2.20	2.20	1.73	4.40	3.30	4.40	2.20	3.30
Lordsburg	5.44	2.46	2.72	2.72	2.27	5.44	4.08	5.44	2.72	4.08
NEW YORK.										
Albany	1.44	.63	.72	.72	.63	1.08	1.08	1.44	1.08	1.08
Buffalo	.90	.39	.45	.45	.39	.68	.68	.90	.68	.68
New York	1.50	.65	.75	.75	.65	1.13	1.13	1.50	1.13	1.13
NORTH CAROLINA.										
Clinton	2.80	1.20	1.20	1.40	1.20	2.10	1.40	2.10	1.20	2.10
Culberson	3.64	1.55	1.55	1.82	1.55	2.73	1.82	2.73	1.55	2.73
Newberne	2.20	.93	.93	1.10	.93	1.65	1.10	1.65	.93	1.65
NORTH DAKOTA.										
Bismarck	3.20	1.35	1.60	1.60	1.07	3.20	2.40	3.20	1.60	2.40
Jamestown	2.92	1.23	1.46	1.46	.97	2.92	2.19	2.92	1.46	2.19
Minot	3.50	1.49	1.75	1.75	1.21	3.50	2.63	3.50	1.75	2.63
OHIO.										
Caldwell	.90	.39	.45	.45	.39	.68	.68	.90	.68	.68
Cincinnati	.80	.34	.40	.40	.34	.60	.60	.80	.60	.60
Toledo	.74	.32	.37	.37	.32	.56	.56	.74	.56	.56
OKLAHOMA.										
El Reno	3.00	1.29	1.50	1.50	1.07	3.00	2.25	3.00	1.50	2.25
Guthrie	3.00	1.29	1.50	1.50	1.07	3.00	2.25	3.00	1.50	2.25
Woodward	3.00	1.29	1.50	1.50	1.37	3.00	2.25	3.00	1.50	2.25
PENNSYLVANIA.										
Erie	.90	.39	.45	.45	.39	.68	.68	.90	.68	.68
Harrisburg	1.44	.62	.72	.72	.62	1.08	1.08	1.44	1.08	1.08
Scranton	1.46	.63	.73	.73	.63	1.10	1.10	1.46	1.10	1.10
RHODE ISLAND.										
Bristol	1.64	.71	.82	.82	.71	1.23	1.23	1.64	1.23	1.23
Providence	1.64	.71	.82	.82	.71	1.23	1.23	1.64	1.23	1.23
Westerly	1.64	.71	.82	.82	.71	1.23	1.23	1.64	1.23	1.23
SOUTH CAROLINA.										
Abbeville	3.12	1.41	1.41	1.56	1.41	2.34	1.56	2.34	1.41	2.34
Charleston	2.70	1.14	1.14	1.35	1.14	2.03	1.35	2.03	1.14	2.03
Ehrhardt	2.64	1.65	1.65	1.95	1.65	2.93	1.95	2.93	1.65	2.93
SOUTH DAKOTA.										
Aberdeen	2.28	.95	1.14	1.14	.67	2.28	1.71	2.28	1.14	1.71
Belle Fourche	4.70	2.05	2.35	2.35	1.63	4.70	3.53	4.70	2.35	3.53
Yankton	1.82	.73	.91	.91	.51	1.82	1.37	1.82	.91	1.37
TENNESSEE.										
Charleston	3.00	1.29	1.29	1.50	1.29	2.25	1.50	2.25	1.29	2.25
Chattanooga	2.32	.99	.99	1.16	.99	1.74	1.16	1.74	.99	1.74
Memphis	1.70	.65	.65	.85	.65	1.28	.85	1.28	.65	1.28
TEXAS.										
Comanche	3.14	1.37	1.57	1.57	1.16	3.14	2.36	3.14	1.57	2.36
El Paso	3.38	1.59	1.69	1.69	1.34	3.38	2.54	3.38	1.69	2.54
Houston	3.14	1.37	1.57	1.57	1.10	3.14	2.36	3.14	1.57	2.36
Sanderson	3.88	1.66	1.94	1.94	1.48	3.88	2.91	3.88	1.94	2.91
UTAH.										
Colton	6.20	2.65	3.10	3.10	2.15	6.20	4.65	6.20	3.10	4.65
Frisco	7.30	3.18	3.65	3.65	2.66	7.30	5.48	7.30	3.65	5.48
Kelton	7.80	3.40	3.90	3.90	2.70	7.80	5.85	7.80	3.90	5.85
Terminus	6.80	2.92	3.40	3.40	2.40	6.80	5.10	6.80	3.40	5.10
VERMONT.										
Bradford	1.64	.71	.82	.82	.71	1.23	1.23	1.64	1.23	1.23
Montpelier	1.64	.71	.82	.82	.71	1.23	1.23	1.64	1.23	1.23
St. Albans	1.64	.71	.82	.82	.71	1.23	1.23	1.64	1.23	1.23
VIRGINIA.										
Lynchburg	1.44	.62	.72	.72	.62	1.08	1.08	1.44	1.08	1.08
Marion	1.68	.72	.84	.84	.72	1.26	1.26	1.68	1.26	1.26
Suffolk	1.44	.62	.72	.72	.62	1.08	1.08	1.44	1.08	1.08
WEST VIRGINIA.										
Charleston	.90	.39	.45	.45	.39	.68	.68	.90	.68	.68
Hinton	1.44	.62	.72	.72	.62	1.08	1.08	.44	1.08	1.08
Wheeling	.90	.39	.45	.45	.39	.68	.68	.90	.68	.68
WISCONSIN.										
Ashland	1.30	.55	.65	.65	.44	1.30	.98	1.30	.65	.98
Fond du Lac	.80	.33	.40	.40	.28	.80	.60	.80	.40	.60
Madison	.80	.35	.40	.40	.26	.80	.60	.80	.40	.60
WYOMING.										
Casper	5.40	2.35	2.70	2.70	1.90	5.40	4.05	5.40	2.70	4.05
Cheyenne	4.10	1.65	2.05	2.05	1.25	4.10	3.08	4.10	2.05	3.08
Evanston	6.20	2.65	3.10	3.10	2.15	6.20	4.65	6.20	3.10	4.65
Lander	8.00	3.65	4.00	4.00	3.20	8.00	6.00	8.00	4.00	6.00

55c

No. 1C49 Folding chair, made of hardwood, with slat seat and back. Folds into compact shape, size, when folded, 1¼x16x40 inches. Cannot fold accidentally when in use. Just the thing for card parties and entertainment halls. Weight, 10 pounds.

Price, each..........$0.55
Per dozen............ 6.00
Per hundred, shipped direct from factory....$45.00

40c

No. 1C51 This is a strong, serviceable chair, constructed of thoroughly seasoned hardwood, finished, golden, with seat, back spindles and posts neatly striped. Back is steam bent and has **four spindles.** Chair is especially adapted for use in lodge or entertainment halls. Weight, 10 pounds.

Price, each......$0.40
Per dozen........ 4.80

65c

No. 1C54 This attractive dining room chair is made of elm, selected stock, thoroughly seasoned and well finished in a rich golden color. Fancy spindles, top panel carved in a neat design. Wood seat, construction first class in every detail. **Shipping** weight, 8 pounds.

Price...............65c

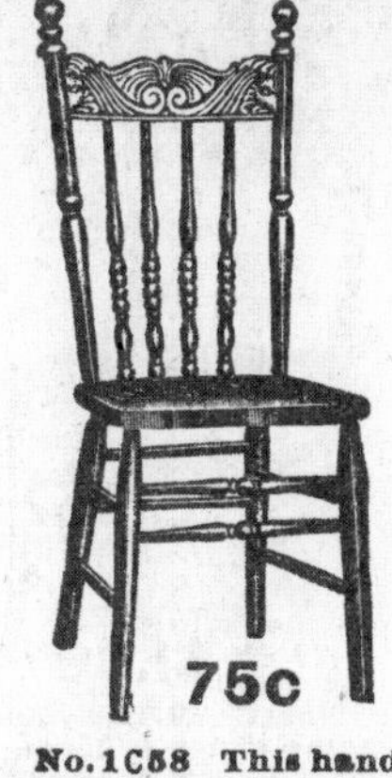

75c

No. 1C58 This handsome diner is made of selected elm, with a veneered wood seat. Top panel nicely carved, spindles and posts turned and well finished in imitation golden oak. Well constructed throughout, making a strong, durable and attractive chair. Shipping weight, 9 pounds.

Price...............75c

85c

No. 1C61 This handsome wood seat dining chair is made of selected rock elm, strongly constructed throughout. Has a neatly carved top panel and five fancy spindles in back. Front spindles and legs nicely turned. Wood seat securely braced to back posts. Golden finish only. Weight, 10 pounds.

Price...............85c

95c

No. 1C67 One of our most serviceable and comfortable dining room chairs. It is solid, yet rich and handsome in appearance; has a large, comfortable back, flat steam bent slats and back posts, upper back panel richly carved, has a full shaped seat. Golden finish only. Weight, 11 pounds.

Price...............95c

$1.05

No. 1C72 This attractive dining room chair, made of selected thoroughly seasoned elm, finished golden, has a broad roomy shaped seat, full braced arms and legs, making it as strong and durable as a chair can be made. Panels and spindles artistically ornamented, as shown in illustration. Weight, 12 pounds.

Price............$1.05

$1.25

No. 1C76 This is the latest thing out in a medium price veneered saddle seat diner, made of selected, thoroughly seasoned elm, golden finish. Back is neatly carved, as shown in illustration, and firmly braced to seat. Lower part of chair is strong and substantial. Weight, 12 pounds.

Price............$1.25

75c

No. 1C84 This handsome cane seat dining room chair is made of solid oak, golden finish. **Has** high back, firmly braced to seat, ornamented with fancy carving and spindles, as shown in illustration. Legs are solid and substantial. The equal of chairs sold by other dealers at double our price. Weight, 10 pounds.

Price...............75c

89c

No. 1C94 A special bargain in cane seat dining room chairs, made of selected oak, thoroughly seasoned, with dark golden gloss finish. Has large seat and high back handsomely carved. Legs and spindles are all turned and joined in a workmanlike manner, making a solid and substantial chair. Weight, 11 pounds.

Price...............89c

$1.15

No. 1C101 The best constructed and cheapest cane seat dining room chair on the market. Made of oak, with golden finish. Fancy back panel, beautifully carved legs and spindles, all hand turned. Back posts securely braced, seat wide and comfortable. Exceptional value at our very low price. Weight, 12 pounds.

Price............$1.15

$1.20

No. 1C103 An unusually attractive dining room chair, made of solid oak, golden finish with back panels quarter sawed. Has wide seat made of selected cane, thoroughly braced to back posts, as shown in the illustration. This is one of the most popular designs on the market. Weight, 12 pounds.

Price............$1.20

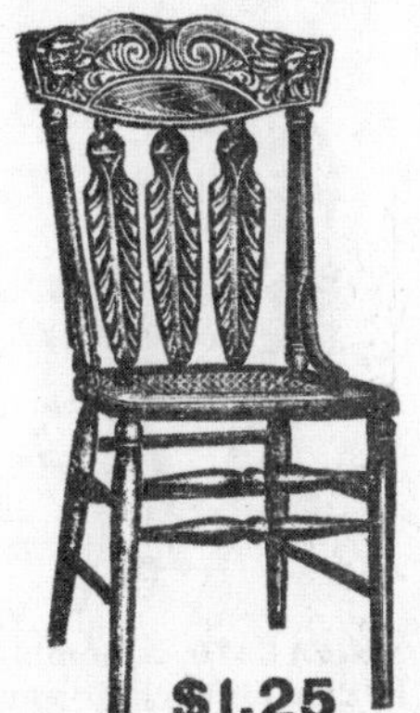

$1.25

No. 1C109 This is the very latest design in cane seat dining room chair. Made of selected rock elm, golden finish. Broad flat spindles and top panel, all deeply carved. Best cane seat and braced arms, solid and substantial. Weight, 12 pounds.

Price... ...$1.25

$1.30

No. 1C112 This cane seat chair is made of the best quality of oak, thoroughly seasoned, with a golden gloss finish. Has a shaped seat filled with best quality of cane. High back, with ornamented panels and spindles, securely braced. Entire chair is solid and well constructed. An exceptional value. Weight, 12 pounds.

Price............$1.30

$1.28

No. 1C117 An unusually attractive cane seat chair, with the latest style hand carved, heavy back panel supported by full braced and fancy turned posts and spindles; full cane seat made of best selected rock elm, golden finish. Weight, 12 pounds.

Price............$1.28

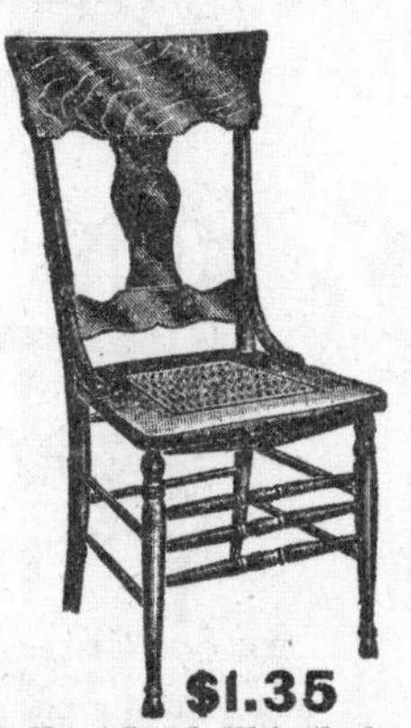

$1.35

No. 1C126 This chair is one of our most popular patterns. Made of oak, thoroughly seasoned, golden finish, panels quarter sawed. Wide cane seat with apron front, well braced to back posts. Legs firmly joined to seat, making a very solid and substantial chair. Weight, 12 pounds.

Price $1.35

$1.45

No. 1C129 The best chair ever shown for the money, made of seasoned oak, rich golden finish. Has a high back, handsomely carved panels and spindles, wide shaped seat covered with best quality of cane. Legs and back are strong and well braced. Just the chair to stand constant use. Weight, 12 pounds.

Price.. ... .$1.45

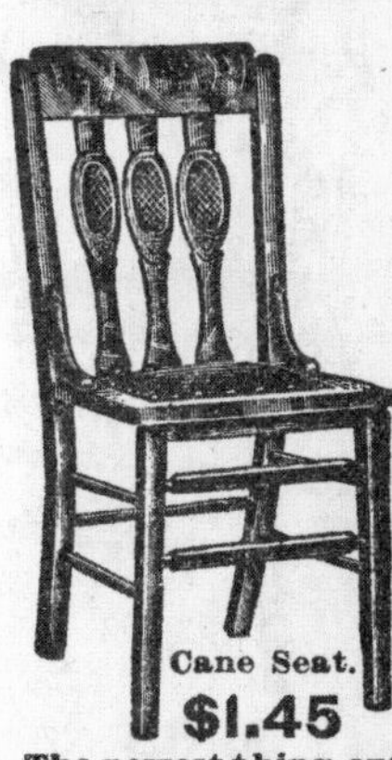

Cane Seat.

$1.45

The newest thing out in a solid oak diner, finished in a perfect imitation of quarter sawed oak, golden color, impossible to distinguish from the genuine. Panels artistically carved. Built on substantial lines and would be an ornament to any room. Weight, 13 pounds.

Price

No. 1C132 Cane seat...............$1.45
No. 1C133 Chase leather seat......$1.80

$1.49

No.1C135 **This veneered saddle seat dining room chair** has handsomely carved panels connected by flat spindles, giving it a handsome and attractive appearance. The best quality of veneering is used in the construction of the saddle seat. Back is firmly braced, making it very strong and durable. Weight, 12 pounds.
Price............$1.49

$1.55

No. 1C137 **The very latest design for 1905.** Veneered seat dining room chair, made of quarter sawed oak, golden finish. High back with three broad flat spindles and top panel deeply carved. Extra wide saddle seat with back posts securely braced to seat. Weight, 14 pounds. Price...$1.55

$1.89

No. 1C139 **This handsome diner** is made of solid oak thoroughly seasoned, finished golden and highly polished. Wide back panel is quarter sawed with just enough carving to give it an artistic effect. Seat is saddle shaped and made of best quality of veneer. Legs and back are strongly braced making it as durable as it is beautiful. Weight, 12 pounds. Price, $1.89

$1.85

Full box seat diner, of the latest pattern, made of quarter sawed oak, golden gloss finish. French shaped legs, flat spindles in back and square posts. Solid and durable. Cannot be beat for quality and price.
No. 1C145 Cane seat. Price..............$1.85
No. 1C146 Leather seat. Price.......$2.39

$2.15

This is one of the best values ever offered in a full box seat dining chair. Made of choice quarter sawed oak, hand polished, golden finish. The mortised frame seat and full braced French legs render it of the strongest possible construction. Weight, 13 pounds.
No. 1C154 Cane seat. Price..............$2.15
No. 1C155 Best leather seat. Price...$2.65

$2.85

Full box seat dining chair, made of selected quarter sawed oak, hand polished, golden finish. Mortised frame, shaped seat, French shaped legs and claw feet. Back panel carved as shown in illustration. A chair built for service as well as appearance. Weight, 15 pounds.
No. 1C161 Cane seat. Price..............$2.85
No. 1C162 Leather seat. Price.....$3.35

No. 1C208 Office chair. Is very comfortable, thoroughly well made, and handsome in appearance. The back posts are well bolted to seat. **Cane seat is hand woven,** and the spring may be adjusted to any degree of tension desired, while the chair may be raised or lowered by means of the screw in steel plate. This chair is made of the very finest rock elm and finished golden oak. Weight, 30 pounds.
Price............$3.25

No. 1C209 **A neat, comfortable office chair, made of selected elm, golden finish.** Back of chair is medium height and beautifully carved. Has steam bent arms, back posts and wood seat, fitted with latest style spring and revolving attachment.
Weight, 35 pounds.
Price............$4.25

No. 1C211 **Our $4.55 office chair is a large, comfortable, broad back chair.** Plain quarter sawed oak back panel and banister, shaped seat and wide comfortable arms; has the best patented screw and spring base, and is strong, durable and comfortable. Weight, 30 lbs.
Price..............$4.55

No. 1C214 **A large, comfortable and roomy high back office chair;** carved top and front, bent slats in back, made of best selected rock elm, finished golden; has the best patented screw and spring base, and is **strong and durable.** Weight, 38 pounds.
Price............$4.95

No. 1C216 **A strictly high class quarter sawed oak polished veneered saddle seat office chair,** made of the very best selected material, panels and arms shaped. It is fitted with the latest design screw and spring base, making it very strong and durable.
Weight, 35 pounds.
Price............$5.45

No. 1C221 **This office chair is made of selected quarter sawed oak, polished finish.** Has the best screw and spring attachment. Neatly shaped arms and back, strictly first class throughout. Will match any high grade desk. It has wood seat, saddle shape and very comfortable. Weight, 30 pounds
Price..........$5.85

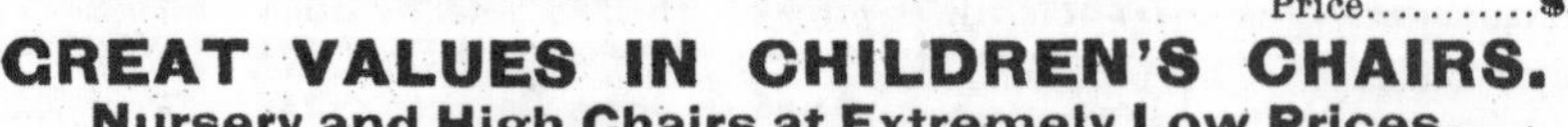

GREAT VALUES IN CHILDREN'S CHAIRS.

Nursery and High Chairs at Extremely Low Prices.

$1.65

No. 1C175 **This chair is thoroughly well made from a very fine selected oak.** The back and arms are extra well braced by means of iron rods passing through the seat. The chair is decidedly comfortable, and after being once used is considered an absolute necessity. Wood seat, perfectly finished. Weight, 14 pounds.
Price............$1.65

$1.95

No. 1C179 **A large, high back, comfortable office chair,** made of elm, finished golden. Steam bent arms, securely bolted to seat and back. Legs thoroughly braced, making it extra strong and durable. Just the thing for hotel use. Weight, 16 pounds.
Price............$1.95

This chair is really a **household necessity,** and no family with children should be without one. It is made up of the best rock elm, handsomely decorated, has full back with four spindles. It is strongly constructed, **and finished either in regular or antique oak or red.** Weight, 6 pounds.
No. 1C250 Without table. Price..........90c
No. 1C256 Same as No. 1C250, with table in front, as shown in illustration. Price....$1.10

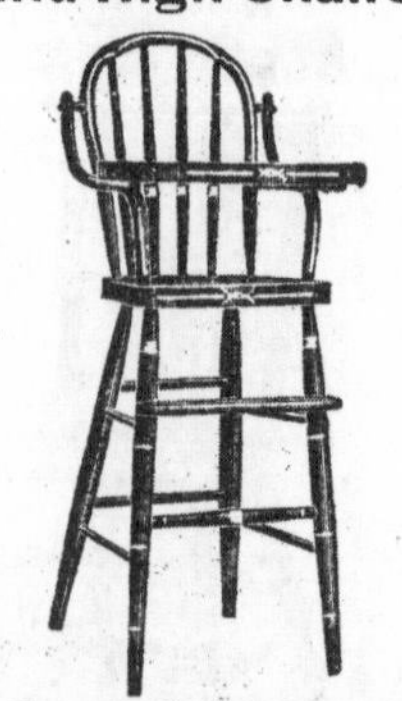

No. 1C275 **This chair is made of the best rock elm, kiln dried and thoroughly seasoned.** You will see from the illustration that it is strongly built and very handy. Adjustable table, which swings over child's head so that the child can be placed in the chair before adjusting the table. The chair is finished either in red or golden, as may be desired. Weight, 12 pounds.
Price..............$1.10

Our latest style child's high chair, as here illustrated, is made with either wood or cane seat. It has large drop table and is made of thoroughly seasoned golden elm, highly finished, making it one of the best grades on the market. The back panel is deeply and elegantly carved. Weight, 13 pounds.
No. 1C277 Wood seat. Price..............$1.69
No. 1C278 Cane seat. Price..............$1.90

No. 1C279 **A combination high chair and carriage that is perfect** and never gets out of order. Easily changed from a stationary high chair, which will not roll, to a low go-cart, making a very useful piece of furniture. This chair has wide back panel and has dark golden oak finish. Weight, 16 pounds.
Price..........$2.45

$1.10

No. 1C283 Our special cane seat ladies' sewing rocker. Made of oak, golden finish. Legs and back posts are firmly braced to seat, making it very strong and durable. Back is high with panels and spindles neatly ornamented. Constructed with a view of giving comfort and for durability. Weight, 12 pounds.
Price............ $1.10

$1.35

No. 1C284 An upholstered seat sewing rocker for $1.35. Made of oak, golden finish. Seat upholstered with a good quality of figured velour. Arm posts and spindles neatly turned and top panel handsomely carved. Back posts securely braced to seat. Shipping weight, 15 pounds.
Price............ $1.35

$1.65

Ladies' sewing rocker. Beautifully carved rocker with fancy shaped top, fancy turned posts and spindles, made of rock elm and finished in golden oak. A strong and serviceable rocker. Furnished in cane seat and wood seat. Weight, 14 pounds.
No. 1C294 With wood seat. Price........ $1.50
No. 1C295 With cane seat. Price...... $1.65

$1.75

No. 1C296 Our special cobbler seat rocker. Made of thoroughly seasoned oak, rich golden finish. High arm, high back, with solid posts securely braced, making a comfortable, durable rocker. Spindles are all turned and panels ornamented with a neat design in carving. Weight, 15 pounds.
Price............ $1.75

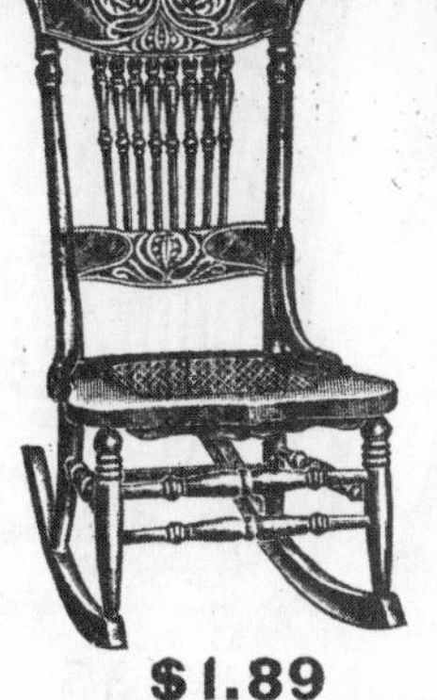

$1.89

No. 1C299 Ladies' sewing rocker. Made of seasoned oak, golden finish. High back, wide shaped seat, covered with best quality cane. Back posts and legs are securely braced to seat, making it extra strong and durable. Spindles and panels are ornamented as shown in illustration. Weight, 15 pounds.
Price............ $1.89

$2.05

No. 1C300 Ladies' or gents' cane seat rocker, wide seat, high back and bent arms. Substantial and comfortable, and presenting a pleasing appearance. Spindles are all nicely turned and carvings are neat and attractive. Finished in golden oak. Shipping weight, 18 pounds.
Price..... .....$2.05

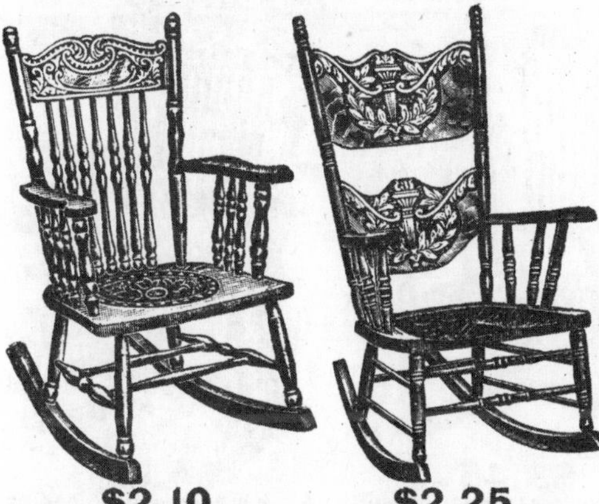

$2.10

An artistic high arm and high back rocker, with fancy embossed cobbler seat, made of quarter sawed oak, golden gloss and birch imitation, mahogany finish. Strongly constructed throughout and ornamented in artistic style.
No. 1C311 Golden oak. Price........ $2.10
No. 1C312 Mahogany finish. Price $2.15

$2.25

No. 1C314 A comfortable and roomy rocker, made of selected elm, golden finish. Wide saddle seat, high back, with broad panels, deeply embossed. Arms supported by three fancy spindles. For comfort it cannot be excelled. Weight, 18 pounds.
Price............ $2.25

$2.35

No. 1C315 The best and cheapest veneered wood seat rocker ever offered. This rocker is made of golden elm. Top panel is richly carved and connected with lower panel by ten turned spindles. Has wide seat and high back, insuring an easy and comfortable seat. Weight, 20 pounds.
Price............ $2.35

$2.38

No. 1C316 This large cobbler seat rocker is made of quarter sawed oak, golden finish, and is an exceptional bargain at the price offered. High arms, high banister back, neat designs of carving. Rocker is solidly constructed throughout of very best material, cannot be beat for comfort and style. Shipping weight, 20 lbs.
Price............ $2.38

$2.45

No. 1C317 Beautiful parlor rocker, made of golden oak with imitation leather seat and tufted top panel. Has a high back, wide roomy seat and high arms. Back is supported by five flat spindles, which is the very latest style of construction. Very comfortable and stylish in appearance. Shipping weight, 20 pounds.
Price............ $2.45

$2.55

No. 1C318 A veneered and shaped seat rocker. Made of golden elm. Handsomely carved panels. Arms are exceptionally well braced. Seat is made of specially selected veneering, broad and comfortable. Weight, 18 pounds.
Price............ $2.55

$2.65

No. 1C321 A high back shaped arm and saddle seat rocker made of solid quarter sawed golden oak. Large comfortable seat and back. Well constructed throughout of selected material and designed especially for comfort. Offered at a price that cannot be equaled. Furnished in golden oak only. Shipping weight, 20 pounds.
Price............ $2.65

$2.45

No. 1C326 A very attractive and serviceable sewing or nursing rocker, made of solid quartered oak with nicely embossed back panel supported by fancy turned and well braced posts. It is beautifully upholstered on both seat and back with fancy velour. Weight, 15 pounds.
Price............ $2.45

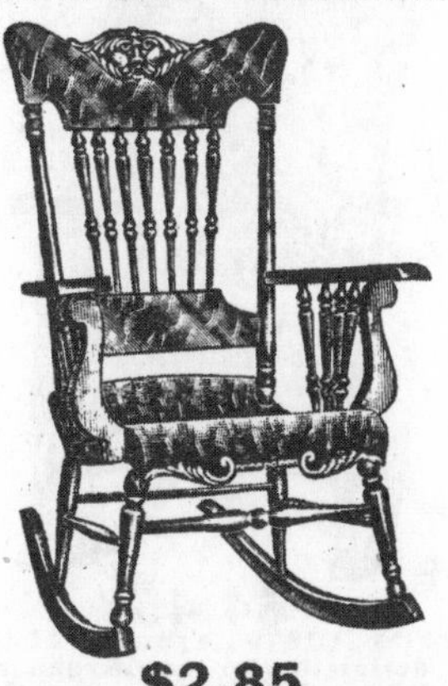

$2.85

No. 1C329 This is a large, roomy rocker, with a shaped, veneered seat. Made of selected rock elm, golden finish. High arms and high back with seven fancy turned spindles in back and four spindles supporting each arm. Top panel is shaped and neatly carved. Weight, 17 pounds.
Price............ $2.85

$2.95

The Farmer's Friend.

A high back, wide seat, comfortable rocker. Has heavy steam bent arms and slat spindles. Fancy carvings, as shown in illustration. Weight, 24 pounds.
No. 1C330 Price, wood seat............ $2.95
No. 1C331 Price, cane seat............ $3.40
No. 1C332 Price, leather seat............ $4.35

$2.95

No. 1C351 Our high back cobbler seat rocker. Made of oak, golden finished with cobbler seat, has wide top panel deeply carved, spindles and posts all handsomely turned. Arms are reinforced by iron rods firmly connected by two fancy turned spindles, making it very strong and durable. Weight, 22 pounds.
Price............ $2.95

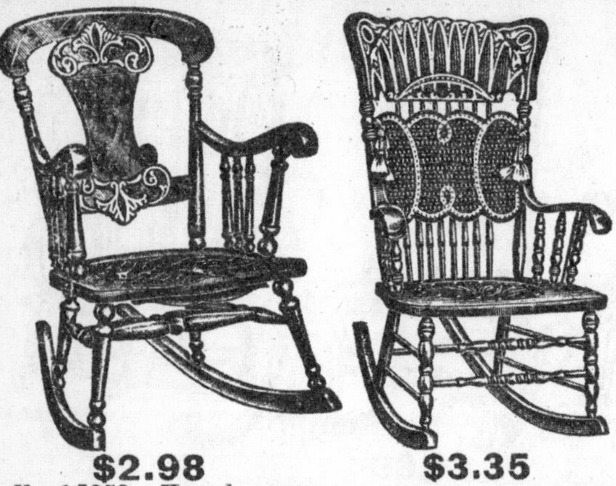

$2.98

No. 1C352 Handsome veneered seat rocker. Made of golden oak, gloss finish, with deeply carved lower panel and banister. High back and arms and saddle seat make it easy and comfortable. The veneering used in these seats is carefully selected and guaranteed by the manufacturers. Weight, 20 pounds. Price.......... **$2.98**

$3.35

No. 1C353 This handsome rocker has a high back, neatly carved, and upholstered with best quality of velour and trimmed with tassels. Has cobbler seat, with bent arms, rodded and bolted, making it doubly strong in every part. Weight, 20 lbs. Price, elm, golden finish...... **$3.35**
Price, mahogany finish 3.45

$3.15

No. 1C361 This latest design in a saddle shaped solid wood seat rocker is made of thoroughly seasoned oak, golden finish. Has high arms and high back. Spindles in back are flat and arms shaped. Richly ornamented with deep carving. Built for strength as well as comfort. Weight, 30 pounds. Price....... **$3.15**

$3.50

No. 1C359 A handsome roll seat, wide arm, high back rocker, made of oak. Panels and seat quarter sawed, finished in golden. Rocker is well constructed, put together with bolts and screws. Wide back panels and apron front neatly carved. Very comfortable. Shipping weight, 25 pounds.
Price, golden finish... **$3.50**

$3.55

Upholstered Rocker. Made of selected oak, or in birch, mahogany finish. It has a high back with a heavy hand carved panel on top, neatly curved arms, fancy shaped spindles and posts. The back and seat are upholstered in a choice quality of velour, ornamented with silk tassels. New in design and elegant in color and finish. Weight, 23 pounds.
No. 1C362 Price, golden oak.................. **$3.55**
No. 1C363 Price, mahogany finish.................. **$3.65**

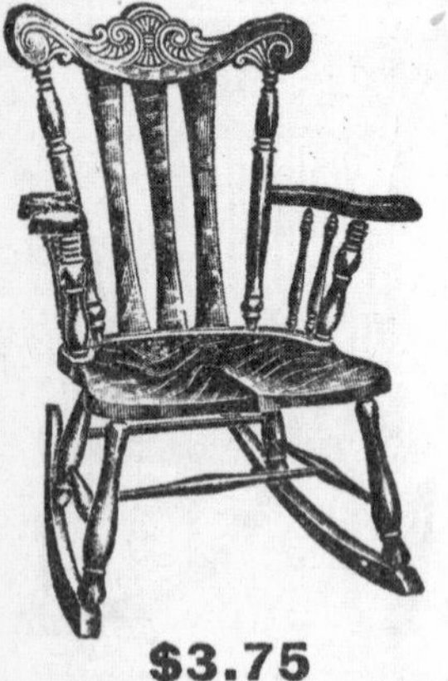

$3.75

No. 1C364 This beautiful parlor rocker is made of oak, quarter sawed, golden finish and polished. Shaped saddle seat, top panel handsomely carved, posts and spindles neatly turned. Solid, well constructed and comfortable. Shipping weight, 17 pounds.
Price.............. **$3.75**

$3.85

No. 1C365 Our special platform swing rocker with wide and deep roll seat. High arms, high back, two back panels and seat made of quarter sawed oak, finished golden. A good serviceable rocker that will be an ornament to any room. Shipping weight, 30 lbs.
Price.............. **$3.85**

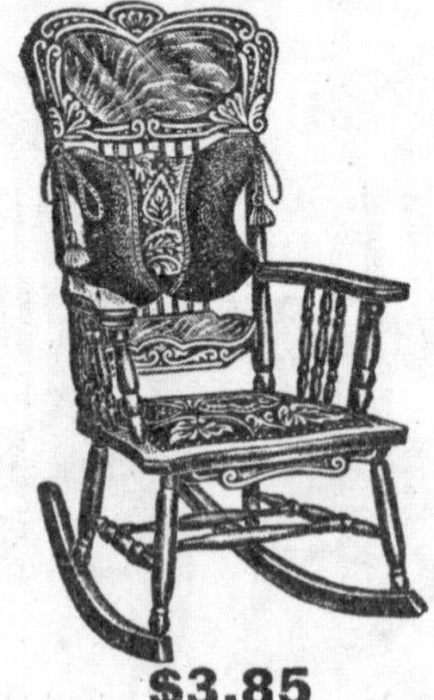

$3.85

Upholstered high back rocker, made of oak or birch with glossy golden or mahogany finish. Wide top slat with neat carving, fancy turned back posts, shaped arms, well braced by iron rods and three heavy spindles. Fully upholstered both seat and back with best velour and ornamented with silk tassels. Weight, 23 pounds.
No. 1C368 Price, golden oak.................. **$3.85**
No. 1C369 Price, mahogany finish.................. **$3.90**

$3.45

This rocker is made of well seasoned oak, golden finish or imitation birch, mahogany finish. High back and high arm; spring seat covered with a good grade of velour. Seat and legs well braced, making a strong and serviceable as well as ornamental rocker. Weight, 18 pounds.
No. 1C370 Price, golden oak.................. **$3.45**
No. 1C371 Price, mahogany finish.................. **$3.50**

$4.15

A handsome parlor rocker, made of choice golden oak or in mahogany finish. Upholstered in a choice quality of velour, hand biscuit tufted back and full stuffed upholstered seat. It is well braced in back and arms. Weight, 23 pounds.
No. 1C340 Price, golden oak.................. **$4.15**
No. 1C341 Price, mahogany finish.................. **$4.25**

$4.25

A magnificent large arm rocker. Handsomely carved back, fine shaped arms and large roll seat, firmly braced, making it very strong and durable. The back is upholstered in fine quality of velour, ribbed, puffed and tasseled. Weight, 25 pounds.
No. 1C346 Price, golden oak finish.............. **$4.25**
No. 1C347 Price, mahogany finish.............. **$4.35**

$5.20

Patent Rocker.

No. 1C372 A large, **comfortable rocker,** made of solid, golden quarter sawed oak throughout. The seat and back are veneered with the choicest quarter sawed stock. The arms are reinforced by five spindles and heavy hand carved posts. The new style platform base is the strongest possible construction, giving comfort and ease. It has a double curved roll seat. Shipping weight, 30 lbs.
Price.............. **$5.20**

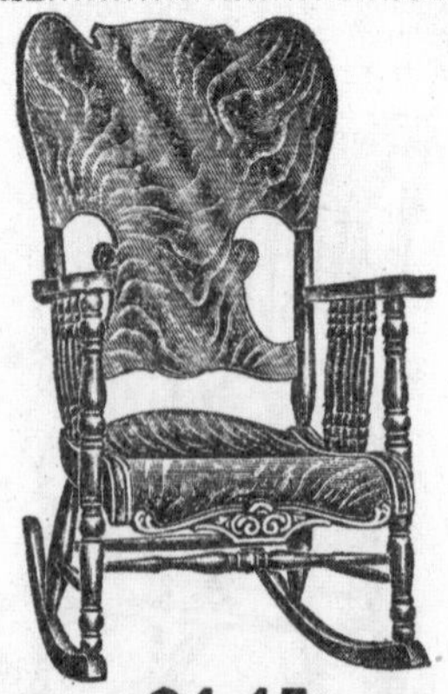

$4.45

No. 1C379 A beautiful design in a large arm rocker. It is made of the choicest quality of fine grained quarter sawed golden oak with a double curved roll seat. The construction and finish are the very best that skilled workmen can produce. Hand carving on front of roll seat. Broad, shapely panel in back and five spindles under each arm. Shipping weight, 30 pounds.
Price, golden oak, wood seat.................. **$4.45**

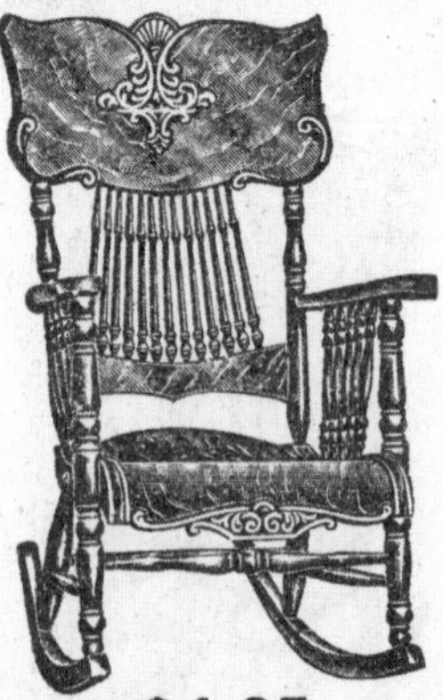

$4.65

No. 1C384 A comfortable ornamental rocker, made of quarter sawed oak with veneered full roll seat. High arms and high back. Beautifully carved back panel and turned posts and spindles. Strongly constructed throughout. Arms and front posts connected with bolts and screws. Finished golden. Shipping weight, 35 pounds.
Price.............. **$4.65**

$4.75

No. 1C385 A quarter sawed, polished and roll seat rocker. Made of quarter sawed and polished oak. Panels, hand carved, shaped arms and carved arm posts, roll on seat beaded and carved. The material in this rocker is especially selected, and it is constructed with special view to comfort and durability. Weight, 35 pounds.
Price.............. **$4.75**

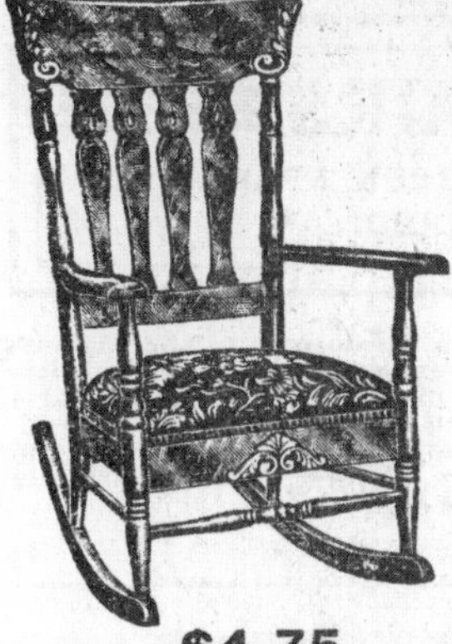

$4.75

This handsome upholstered seat rocker is made of selected material throughout, with wide back panels connected by flat carved spindles with posts handsomely turned. Has a spring seat, covered with high colored velour. Golden oak or mahogany finish. Weight, 22 pounds.

No. 1C398 Price, golden oak.............. ....$4.75
No. 1C399 Price, mahogany finish..............$4.85

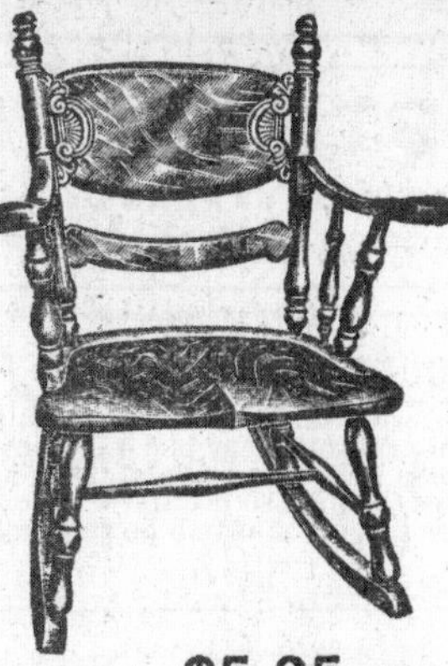

$5.25

No. 1C404 **One of the newest designs in a polished quarter sawed oak rocker.** Wood saddle seat, high arms, posts and spindles neatly turned, wide back panel neatly ornamented. Solidly constructed throughout and presenting a very artistic appearance. Finished in golden oak only. Shipping weight, 17 pounds.
Price..............$5.25

$5.95

This upholstered rocker is an exceptional value, made of selected quarter sawed oak, golden finish, or birch, imitation mahogany finish. Has high arms and back. Spring seat covered in best quality of velour. Strongly constructed throughout, it is especially designed for comfort and durability. Weight, 20 lbs.
No. 1C423 Price, golden oak..............$5.95
No. 1C424 Price, mahogany finish..............$6.00

$5.65

No. 1C425 **A massive arm rocker in selected quarter sawed golden oak, highly polished, not gloss finish.** Has heavy carved posts, finely curved arms, double curved seat and beautiful shaped back, with heavy spindle work. A very attractive design for the library, sitting room or parlor, at factory price. Strictly high grade in construction and finish. Shipping weight, 28 pounds.
Price.............. ....$5.65

$5.25

No. 1C432 **A handsome upholstered, roll seat rocker, spring seat, made of golden quarter sawed oak.** Fancy carved spindles, high bent arms and carved panels. Has a high back and wide seat upholstered in best quality of figured velour. Rocker is well constructed throughout. Weight, 25 pounds.
Price..............$5.25

$5.45

No. 1C433 **This handsome upholstered rocker is of the very latest design, made of quarter sawed golden oak.** Has a wide spring seat, roll front and upholstered in figured velour. Has a high back, wide carved panels in back and supporting the bent arms. Stock carefully selected and well constructed. Weight, 25 pounds.
Price..............$5.45

$5.80

No. 1C434 **This large parlor or library rocker is made** of quarter sawed golden oak or birch, mahogany finish, highly polished. Seat is 19x22 inches and upholstered in very best and latest pattern of velour. Back is 28 inches high, with top panel deeply carved and set with a number of turned spindles. Shipping weight, 40 pounds.
Price, golden oak.....$5.85
Price, mahogany finish 5.80

$5.95

No. 1C436 **This handsome wood seat rocker** is the very latest design, made of quarter sawed golden oak finish and highly polished. The material and workmanship on this rocker is first class in every particular. The seat, which is extra large, is 21 inches deep and the back is 27 inches high, making a model that insures comfort. Shipping weight, 35 pounds.
Price, golden oak......$5.95

$6.10

No. 1C438 **An odd design in parlor rocker** with solid wood seat, solid panel back neatly carved, made of quarter sawed oak, golden finish, or birch, imitation mahogany, highly polished. Back is 22 inches high and seat measures 20x22 inches, arm of medium height, making a combination that cannot be excelled for comfort and appearance. Shipping weight, 30 pounds.
Price, golden oak.....$6.15
Price, mahogany finish, 6.10

$6.20

No. 1C440 **This handsome rocker** is made of quarter sawed golden oak or birch, mahogany finish, highly polished. Seat is wide and deep, back high and upholstered in best quality velour. This rocker is solid, substantial and attractive in appearance, an ornament for either library or parlor. Shipping weight, 35 pounds.
Price, golden oak...$6.25
Price, mahogany finish.............. 6.20

$6.35

No. 1C442 **Parlor and library rocker** with upholstered seat and back, made of quarter sawed golden oak or birch, imitation mahogany finish, highly polished. Has extra wide seat and high back upholstered in best quality of velour. A massive, substantial chair. Material and workmanship of the very best. Shipping weight, 40 pounds.
Price, golden oak.....$6.45
Price, mahogany finish, 6.35

$6.85

No. 1C444 **This is a solid wood seat rocker** of exceptional beauty and entirely new design, made of quarter sawed oak, golden finish, or birch, imitation mahogany, highly polished. Roomy and comfortable seat, measures 19x22 inches and back 24 inches high. Carvings are deep and of artistic designs. Frame is extra heavy and presents a massive appearance. Shp'g wgt, 40 lbs.
Price, golden oak.....$6.95
Imitation mahogany.. 6.85

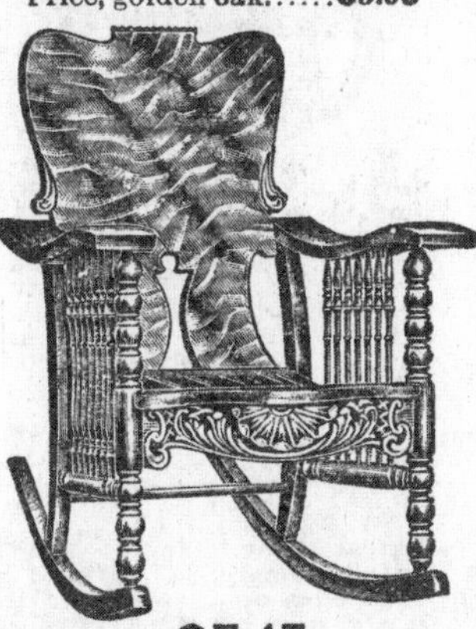

$7.15

No. 1C445 **This McKinley rocker** is the handsomest design of this style that has ever been offered. Seat, back and arms made of quarter sawed oak. Spindles, posts and front handsomely carved in rich designs, all hand polished, golden finish. **Big, roomy and comfortable.** Shipping weight, 30 pounds.
Price..............$7.15

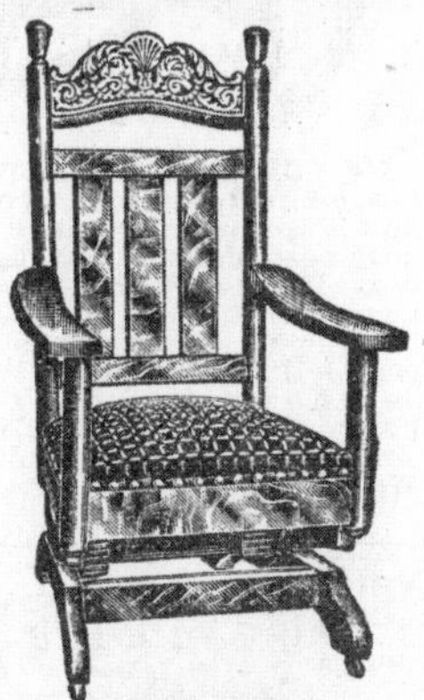

$7.35

No. 1C446 **Extra large platform rocker.** Seat upholstered in best quality of velour. Frame is made of quarter sawed oak, finished golden and highly polished. The back is handsomely carved and is 27 inches high. Seat extra large, measures 23x25 inches, fitted with best steel tempered springs. For comfort and elegance cannot be equaled. Shipping weight, 50 pounds.
Price..............$7.35

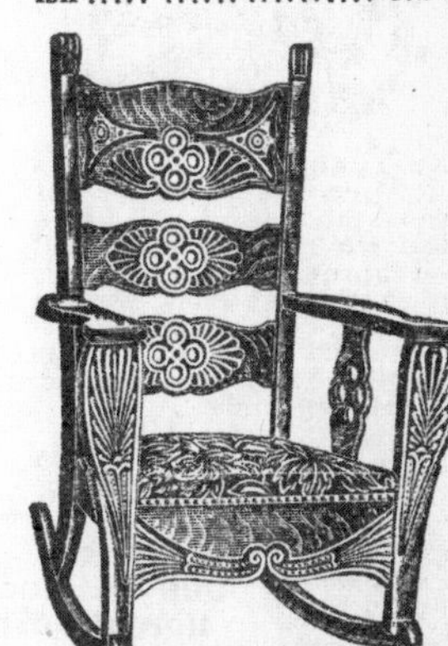

$8.25

No. 1C448 **This massive parlor or library rocker** is one of the handsomest designs that we have ever offered. It is made of quarter sawed oak or birch, mahogany finished, highly polished. Choice of seats upholstered in best quality of velour or **imitation Spanish leather.** High back with rich carving and the seat is extra large. Shipping weight 45 pounds.
Price, golden oak.....$8.35
Price, mahogany finish 8.25

REED ROCKERS AND RECEPTION CHAIRS

IN MAKING UP OUR LINE OF REED ROCKERS AND CHAIRS NO EFFORT OR EXPENSE HAS BEEN SPARED TO MAKE IT THE MOST ATTRACTIVE AND BEST CONSTRUCTED LINE EVER OFFERED.

WE GIVE YOU lower prices than any other concern can possibly make because we have purchased the entire output of one of the largest manufacturers in the world, and are giving you the benefit of this purchase with our one small percentage of profit added to the actual cost of making.

NOTHING BUT THE BEST imported reed is used in the manufacture of this line, and the material for the frame work is made from selected white maple, thoroughly dried and seasoned.

THE CONSTRUCTION of every article, from the lowest to the highest price is first class in every respect, every detail is looked after by a workman skilled in his particular line. The exposed parts of back posts and arms on every piece are covered by reed, closely wrapped, which not only adds to the strength of the chair, but gives it that finish and style which places this line so far above all others. Every rocker is perfectly balanced, which is a point that will be thoroughly appreciated.

No. 1C452 This porch or lawn rocker is made of best reed with high back and wide roll seat. The frame is made of maple finished with shellac or stained cherry. This is an exceptionally comfortable rocker at a price within reach of all. Shipping weight, 15 pounds.
Price....................$1.85

No. 1C456 A large size gents' or ladies' rocker, with high back and wide seat with full roll effect. Arms are a continuous roll and wrapped with reed. This rocker is well constructed and is the biggest bargain ever offered at the price. Shipping weight, 15 pounds.
Price....................$2.55

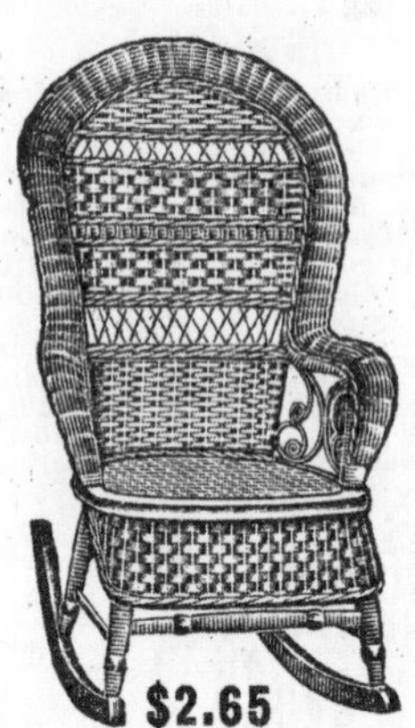

No. 1C458 Ladies' cane seat and reed rocker of the very latest pattern. It has a high back with continuous arms, full reed wrapped. Cane seat and a reed apron front. Frame is well constructed of well seasoned maple, finished in shellac. Shipping weight, 12 pounds.
Price....................$2.65

No. 1C461 This large size gents' or ladies' rocker is one of the latest designs and constructed with a view to comfort and durability. It has a wide roll seat, full wrapped continuous arms and posts and made over a maple frame, thoroughly seasoned. Shipping weight, 15 pounds.
Price....................$3.25

No. 1C463 This is without a doubt the best value in a ladies' rocker ever offered. It has the continuous roll arm, extending to the front and beneath the seat, forming a curtain or apron front. The seat is best hand woven cane and the woodwork of frame is maple, well seasoned. Weight, 12 pounds. Price......$3.45

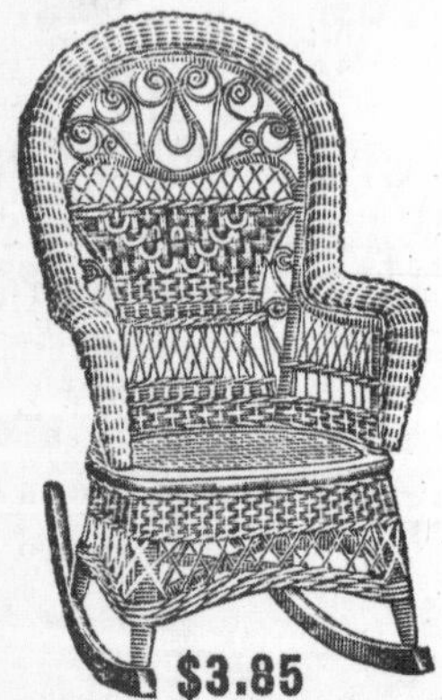

No. 1C469 A ladies' cane seat and reed rocker of handsome design. It has a hand woven cane seat, full reed apron front and sides and continuous arms. Frame is made of thoroughly seasoned wood and honestly constructed. Finished in shellac. Weight, 12 pounds.
Price....................$3.85

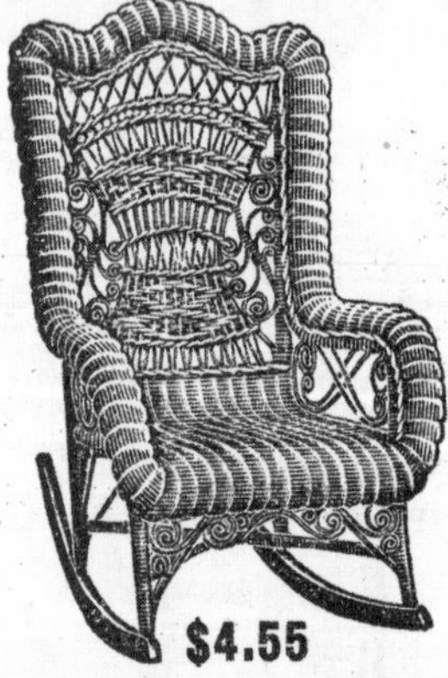

No. 1C471 Our special design gents' rocker, strong and comfortable, made of very best material throughout. It has the continuous arms with full roll effect, extending all the way around completing the basket seat, as shown in illustration. Fancy scroll front, posts full wrapped, finished in shellac. Weight, 15 lbs. Price...$4.55

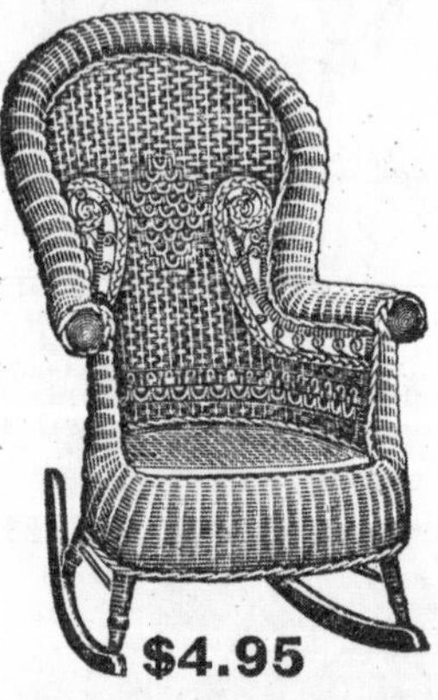

No. 1C472 For solid comfort this special pattern cannot be equaled. It has a hand woven cane seat, high roll arms and a full roll apron front. Back is high enough to form a comfortable head rest. Frame is made of the best maple, thoroughly seasoned. Weight, 15 pounds.
Price....................$4.95

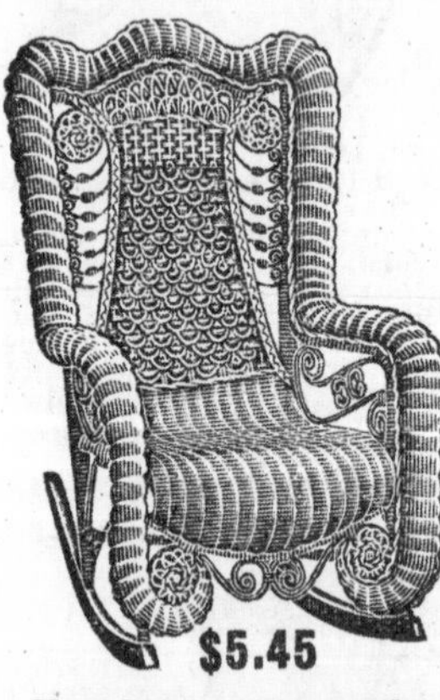

No. 1C475 This rocker was especially designed for us and nothing has been overlooked in the way of comfort, durability and attractiveness. It is made of the very best reed throughout, full roll seat, continuous arms with fancy scroll ornaments. Finished in shellac. Shipping weight, 15 pounds.
Price....................$5.45

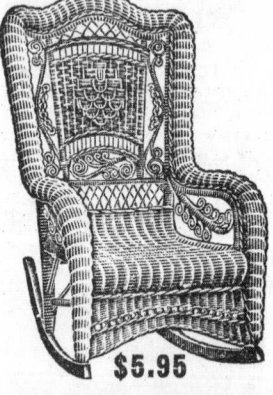

$5.95

No. 1C478 This handsome design in a reed rocker is well constructed of the very best reed, finished in shellac. Has a wide roll seat with full skirt front. The arms are full roll and all posts are wrapped with reed. Shipping weight, 15 pounds.
Price....................$5.95

Exceptional Values in Reception or Corner Chairs.

No. 1C465 Ladies' ornamented reception chairs made of the very best reed. Has a cane seat and finished in shellac. Posts and braces are all hand wrapped with reed, making altogether a very strong and durable chair, suitable for a parlor or reception room. Weight, 7 pounds.
Price....................$3.95

No. 1C467 Latest thing in fancy reed reception or corner chairs. Strong and comfortable, made of selected reed. Has a finely woven cane seat, and posts and legs are all wrapped by hand with best quality of reed. This is an exceptionally handsome chair and would be an ornament to any room. Wt., 12 lbs. Price..$4.25

Our New Reception Chair, Very Stylish and Only $6.25.

No. 1C474 Artistic reception chair, unusually graceful and pretty, yet very comfortable; well made of the finest reed, and is very strong; fit to adorn any parlor. In shellac finish.
Weight, 10 pounds. Price.........$6.25

Our $3.10 Turkish Divan.

No. 1C476 Turkish divan made of reed with cane seat, has high shaped arms and a fancy ornamented base; the entire piece is hand- somely ornamented and finished in shellac. It can be used in parlor or reception hall. Weight, 12 pounds.
Price....................$3.10

MORRIS CHAIRS

NEWEST DESIGNS, LATEST IMPROVEMENTS AT PRICES LOWER THAN EVER BEFORE

ON THE BASIS OF MANUFACTURING COST, with but our one small percentage of profit added, we offer you these high class Morris chairs, and you can buy them for less money than most retail dealers pay at wholesale. Never before have we been able to show such a splendid line of these popular chairs, or such fine, high grade chairs at such low prices.

THE MORRIS RECLINING CHAIR derives its name from the inventor, William Morris, a New England Yankee. It combines simplicity of construction with ease and comfort, as no other chair does. The spacious depth and width of the seat, the broad and high adjustable back, together with the broad arms, render the Morris chair the superior in ease and comfort of any chair devised. The frames are massive in design and are made to last a lifetime. The Morris chair has become so well known and the demand for them so great that the sale has jumped from the hundreds into thousands. No home can afford to be without one.

THE GREAT DEMAND for our Morris chairs enabled us to make a contract for an immense quantity of them at a very low price, and our customers reap the benefit. In fact the price which we quote is in almost every instance, much lower than the ordinary dealer can buy them.

DESCRIPTION OF OUR LINE OF MORRIS CHAIRS. The wood used in the construction of our Morris chairs is the best quality of highly figured oak, or fine wavey birch in imitation of mahogany, specially selected for the beauty of the grain of the wood. It is thoroughly air seasoned and kiln dried before being put through the factory. Every piece is guaranteed not to warp, shrink or check. The careful inspection and selection of the wood enables us to insure the best and most satisfactory results it is possible to obtain. Every chair is covered by our **binding guarantee**, and should it at any time prove defective or unsatisfactory we stand ready to refund the purchase price together with all transportation charges.

$3.95

THE CONSTRUCTION of our Morris chairs is strictly high grade in every detail. The joints are mortised and joined in the most perfect manner. The bars are highly ornamental, spindles are carefully framed and turned, the edges and corners rounded; the seats are upholstered with highly tempered steel springs, which are absolutely indestructible. The old fashioned string tied spring construction we have discarded. Our new, indestructible steel construction prevents the springs breaking loose and turning over. The seat of a Morris chair is the most essential part of it. We use the best grade of high carbon steel wire springs, intercoiled into steel band irons, which are crosswise on the bottom, and are fastened to the top of the side rails of the chair and can never get loose, besides being reinforced with a steel wire running lengthwise into which the coil springs are interlaced. Neat in appearance, sanitary and everlasting.

THE RATCHET ATTACHMENT. On each side of the chair is a simple ratchet attachment by which the back is raised or lowered, and locked into any position desired, automatically. It works very easily, and is absolutely guaranteed not to get out of order. This feature adds to the comfort and attractive appearance of the chair.

THE FINISH of our Morris chairs is strictly first class. The highest quality of material obtainable is used. Special care is taken to produce a smoother surface, a better luster and finish, that will not crack, peel or blister, that will look better after years of use than the ordinary finish will in one month. Each coating is thoroughly rubbed down and allowed to thoroughly dry and harden before applying the succeeding one. The oak is a beautiful golden color, and the birch is a perfect imitation of mahogany.

THE CUSHIONS of our Morris chairs are thoroughly well made. The velour coverings are the newest and best patterns. The colors are all guaranteed fast. They are closely stitched and button tufted. We furnish the cushions in any color desired, but especially recommend dark green, dark red or brown, as best adapted to harmonize with all surroundings. The full box edge, firm stitching and tufting of our cushions make them more shapely and lasting than any other cushion made.

THE VALUE WE ARE GIVING YOU cannot be fully appreciated unless you see, examine and compare our Morris chairs with those offered by others at 30 to 40 per cent higher than our prices. It is difficult for you, by illustration and description, to compare satisfactorily the real value, but if you will take any one of our Morris Chairs, that we illustrate and describe, and place it alongside of any Morris Chair offered by any other house, at anything approaching our price, you will at once see that with our facilities we are furnishing a much better design, a better finished and better made chair, at a much lower price than you can possibly buy elsewhere.

OUR TERMS OF SHIPMENT.

We accept your order with the distinct understanding and agreement that the Morris chair will reach you in perfect condition, and be perfectly satisfactory, otherwise, you can return it to us, and we will refund the purchase price, together with all transportation charges.

IF DESIRED we will ship any Morris chair by freight C. O. D., subject to examination, on receipt of only $1.00 deposit, the balance and freight charges payable when the chair is received and found satisfactory; but, we recommend that you send the full price with your order and thus save the extra charge of 25 to 50 cents that the railroad companies ask on C.O.D. shipments, for collecting the money and returning it to us. You take no risk whatever, for we will promptly return you all your money, and pay freight charges both ways, if you are not pleased with your purchase.

ABOUT FREIGHT CHARGES.

The freight charges on a Morris chair will amount to next to nothing as compared with what you will save in price. The Morris chairs are accepted by the railroad company at first class freight rates. The weight of each is given under each description, and by referring to page 630 you can calculate, almost to a cent, what the freight will amount to. For example, for many points within 400 to 600 miles of Chicago, the freight on a Morris chair will amount to 50 to 75 cents, whereas the saving will be from $2.50 to $6.00.

$3.95 BUYS THIS HANDSOME MORRIS CHAIR, MADE OF SOLID OAK, GOLDEN FINISH, SUCH A CHAIR AS DEALERS ASK $8.00 TO $10.00 FOR.

THIS MORRIS CHAIR, without doubt, is the most attractive in design, the handsomest in outline, and most comfortable and substantial chair it is possible to produce. We are offering the greatest value ever shown in this kind of a chair. You cannot fully appreciate the wonderful value we are giving in this chair unless you see it and compare it carefully with Morris chairs that others sell at double the price we ask. The frame is thoroughly well constructed in every detail, every joint perfectly fitted.

THE WOOD IS SOLID OAK, thoroughly air seasoned and kiln dried. The oak is a beautiful golden color. The highly ornamental and finely executed carvings on the front bar and posts add to the beauty and attractiveness of this handsome Morris chair. The seat is built of our indestructible solid Bessemer steel construction, intercoiled into steel bars, and fastened securely into the frame on the sides, besides being reinforced with a steel wire, running lengthwise, into which the coil springs are interlocked, making the most durable spring seat it is possible to produce.

THE SEAT of this Morris Chair is upholstered with our patent high carbon steel spring construction, guaranteed to last a lifetime. The seat and back are covered with the best quality imported velour cloth in plain or figured pattern, in dark green, red or brown colors, as desired.

We furnish this Morris chair in stationary cushions or with reversible cushions as desired.

THE BACK of this Morris chair is adjustable to four different reclining positions, by means of a solid brass rod and ratchet attachment guaranteed against breakage.

FITTED WITH HEAVY STEEL FRAME CASTERS, packed and shipped direct from our factory near Chicago, from which point customers pay the freight. Shipping weight, 50 pounds.

5,000 MORRIS CHAIRS AT $3.95. We expect to sell 5,000 of these special chairs at $3.95 in oak, during the following season. Our contract is made on that basis. We believe that all who want a Morris chair for little money and see this announcement, will send us their order, we believe they will recognize the extraordinary value we are offering. Furniture dealers will admit when they see the chair that it is indeed a bargain and a wonder of value. The prices are very little more than the actual cost of material and labor, on enormous quantity basis, with our very narrow margin of profit added. We illustrate this chair with a large picture, not only to direct attention to this Morris chair, but to emphasize the extraordinary values that our entire line of Morris chairs represent. You cannot afford to place your order elsewhere for a Morris chair if you will consider the values here illustrated and described.

WE SHIP this Morris chair with the distinct understanding and agreement, that, if it is not perfectly satisfactory in every respect, and exactly as represented and described; that if you are not satisfied that you have a better Morris chair than you can purchase elsewhere at double the price we ask, you can return it to us, and your money will be refunded, together with all transportation charges.

No. 1C5568 Golden Oak, Stationary Cushions. Price........ **$3.95**
No. 1C5574 Golden Oak, Reversible Cushions. Price........ **4.75**

A strictly high grade Morris Chair in fine quarter sawed oak, or in birch, mahogany finish, hand polished. It is a handsome design. Your choice of stationary cushions with full spring seat and back, or reversible genuine hair filled cushions in seat and back with full spring seat, with best quality of covering in green, red or brown velour. The back is adjustable to five different positions by our patent ratchet attachment. **See description on preceding page.** We challenge any retail store to duplicate this chair at double the price. Shipped direct from our factory near Chicago. Shipping weight, 55 lbs.

$6.45

No. 1C5575 Price, quarter sawed oak, stationary cushions $6.45
Price, mahogany finish, stationary cushions 6.40
No. 1C5576 Price, quarter sawed oak, reversible hair filled cushions 6.65
Price, mahogany finish, reversible hair filled cushions 6.60

This is one of our special designs. It is a very heavy, massive frame of fine flaky quarter sawed oak in golden finish, also in birch, mahogany finish, hand polished. Beautifully hand carved. It has broad, shapely arms. We furnish it with stationary cushions, spring seat and back, or with genuine hair filled reversible loose cushions, any color desired. It is fitted with our patent ratchet attachment, allowing five different adjustable positions for the back. **See further description on preceding page.** Shipped direct from factory in Chicago. Eastern points, from Western New York. Shipping weight, 55 pounds.

$6.85

No. 1C5590 Price, quarter sawed oak, stationary cushions $6.85
Price, mahogany finish, stationary cushions 6.80
No. 1C5592 Price, quarter sawed oak, reversible cushions 6.95
Price, mahogany finish, reversible cushions 6.90

This heavy hand carved claw foot Morris Chair is made of the choicest quarter sawed oak, or in birch, mahogany finish, piano polished. Broad, shapely arms, hand carving on front posts. We furnish this chair with stationary cushions, with full spring seat and back, or loose, reversible, genuine hair filled cushions in green, red or brown velour, best quality. The back is adjustable to five different positions by our atent adjustable ratchet attachment. **See further description on preceding page.** This chair sells for $12.00 to $15.00 in all retail stores. Shipped direct from our factory in Chicago. Eastern points from Western New York. Shipping weight, 65 lbs.

$7.35

No. 1C5618 Price, quarter sawed oak, stationary cushions $7.35
Price, in mahogany finish, stationary cushions 7.30
No. 1C5619 Price, quarter sawed oak, reversible cushions 7.45
Price, in mahogany finish, reversible cushions 7.40

This artistic and massive Morris Chair is made of the choicest quarter sawed oak, or in birch, mahogany finish, polished like a piano. We furnish it with stationary cushions with full spring seat and back, or with loose reversible hair filled cushions in the seat and back with full spring seat, covered in the best quality of imported velour in dark green, dark red or brown. By means of our patent ratchet you can adjust the back to five different positions. **See further description on preceding page.** Shipped direct from our factory in Western New York. Western shipments from Chicago. Shipping weight, 55 pounds.

$9.85

No. 1C5639 Price, quarter sawed oak, stationary cushions $9.85
Price, mahogany finish, stationary cushions 9.80
No. 1C5640 Price, quarter sawed oak, reversible hair filled cushions 9.95
Price, mahogany finish, reversible hair filled cushions, 9.90

This Massive Morris Chair is without question one of the best values ever offered. It is made of choice quarter sawed oak, or in birch, mahogany finish, piano polished. It has genuine hand carved, massive claw feet and heavy hand carved dragon heads on arms. It has our patent ratchet attachment for adjusting back to five different positions. Upholstered in the best quality of imported velour in dark green or dark red colors. We furnish it in full spring seat and back or with full spring seat with genuine hair filled reversible loose cushions. **See further description on preceding page.** Shipped direct from our factory in Chicago. Eastern points, from Western New York. Shipping weight, 55 pounds.

$8.25

No. 1C5630 Price, quarter sawed oak, stationary cushions $8.25
Price, mahogany finish, stationary cushions 8.20
No. 1C5631 Price, quarter sawed oak, reversible cushions 8.40
Price, mahogany finish, reversible cushions 8.35

No. 1C5632 For beauty of design, high quality of wood and finish, comfort and durability, this Morris Chair must be seen to be thoroughly appreciated. It is made of highly figured quarter sawed golden oak, or birch mahogany finish, highly polished. The broad, shapely arms are supported by shapely curved spindles. Front posts and bar decorated with finely executed hand carvings. It has reversible all hair filled cushions covered with best quality imported velour in brown, red or green colors, plain or figured as desired. Full spring seat, all steel construction. Back is adjustable to four different positions by means of a brass rod and ratchet. A chair that sells in stores at $12.00 to $14.00. Shipped direct from factory in Western New York. Shipping weight, 65 lbs.

$8.75

Price, quarter sawed oak, reversible hair filled cushions. $8.75
Price, birch, mahogany finish, reversible hair filled cushions 8.70

One of the most artistic Morris Chairs ever designed. Made in the finest quarter sawed oak, golden finish, or in birch, mahogany finish, hand polished. Elaborate hand carving on front posts. It has fine, shapely broad arms. It has our patent adjustable ratchet attachment, allowing five different positions for the back. We furnish it with full spring seat and back with stationary cushions or with full spring seat with loose reversible hair filled cushions in seat and back; covered in the best quality of velour in dark green or dark red colors. **See further description on preceding page.** Shipped direct from our factory in Chicago. Eastern points, from Western New York. Shipping weight, 65 pounds.

$9.35

No. 1C5636 Price, quarter sawed oak, stationary cushions $9.35
Price, mahogany finish, stationary cushions 9.30
No. 1C5638 Price, quarter sawed oak, reversible cushions 9.45
Price, mahogany finish, reversible cushions 9.40

No. 1C5642 This Magnificent Morris Chair is made of especially selected highly figured quarter sawed oak in a handsome golden finish, or birch mahogany finish, highly polished. Note the highly ornamental hand carvings on the posts and cross bar. It has full spring seat, all steel construction. The back is adjustable to four different reclining positions by means of a solid brass rod and ratchet. The reversible hair filled cushions are covered with the best quality plain or figured velour in brown, red or dark green colors as desired. This chair sells in retail stores for $16.00 to $18.00. Shipped direct from factory in Western New York. Shipping weight, about 65 pounds.

$10.65

Price, quarter sawed oak, reversible hair filled cushions $10.65
Price, birch, mahogany finish, reversible hair filled cushions 10.60

No. 1C5645 This large massive Morris Rocker we furnish in choice selected quarter sawed oak, or in birch, mahogany finish, piano polished. The cushions are stationary with our full steel construction spring seat upholstered in the best grade of velour in green, red or brown. The back is neatly tufted and is adjustable to five different positions by means of our patent ratchet attachment. See description of ratchet on preceding page. Shipped direct from our factory in Western New York or from Chicago. Shipping weight, 60 lbs.

$6.85

Price, golden quarter sawed oak, stationary cushions $6.85
Price, birch, mahogany finish, stationary cushions 6.75

No. 1C5649 This Morris Rocker combines elegance, comfort and durability. It has full steel construction spring seat and back. The wood is the very best flaked grain quarter sawed oak, or birch, in mahogany finish, finely polished. The seat is supported by full steel spring construction. Your choice of covering in red, dark green or brown velour, best quality. The hand carved dragon heads on the broad carved arms make it a very attractive design. Shipped direct from our factory in Western New York. Western points from Chicago. Shipping weight, 50 pounds.

$8.35

Price, golden oak, stationary cushions $8.35
Price, mahogany finish, stationary cushions. 8.30

THE IMPERIAL AUTOMATIC MORRIS CHAIR.

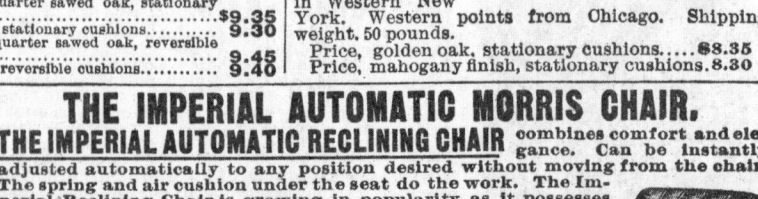

THE IMPERIAL AUTOMATIC RECLINING CHAIR combines comfort and elegance. Can be instantly adjusted automatically to any position desired without moving from the chair. The spring and air cushion under the seat do the work. The Imperial Reclining Chair is growing in popularity, as it possesses features not found in any other make. There are no rods or ratchets, a slight pressure of the body being all that is necessary to place it at any angle desired. We invite close comparison with similar chairs in the market and ours will be found better made, better finished and very much lower in price. The frame work of the two chairs illustrated, is made of quarter sawed oak, highly polished golden oak finish. The seat is 21½x23 inches and the back 21¼x29 inches, making the chair a very comfortable size and large enough to accommodate any person, large or small. Every chair is fitted with ball bearing casters and is shipped knocked down in a small crate and is easily set up. By shipping in this way the lowest transportation charges are assured. Shipping weight, 70 pounds.

No. 1C5659

No. 1C5658

Upholstered in	Velour	Tapestry	Fabricoid (Imitation Leather)	Crushed Plush	Genuine Leather
No. 1C5658 Price	$ 9.45	$ 9.65	$ 9.95	$10.75	$13.95
No. 1C5659 Price	10.45	10.65	10.95	11.75	14.95

GREAT VALUES IN EXTENSION TABLES

THE EXTENSION TABLES WHICH WE OFFER THIS SEASON ARE MADE BY THE LARGEST BEST KNOWN AND MOST RELIABLE MAKERS OF TABLES IN THE UNITED STATES.

THE FACTORIES devoted to the manufacture of our tables are factories that are thoroughly equipped with the latest type of machinery, employ only the highest class of workmen, and there are no factories in the country better equipped to turn out a higher quality of goods and at the same time at the very minimum of cost. Orders for plain oak tables from customers in the east and southeast will be filled direct from factory, located in the east. Orders for plain oak tables from western customers will be filled from our Chicago warehouse. Orders for quarter sawed oak tables will be filled from factory in Northern Indiana. By so doing the cost of unnecessary handling is eliminated and the lowest possible freight charges are secured to all customers. Every table is carefully crated with the legs detached and accepted by the railroad company at the lowest freight rate. The freight charges on an extension table are small compared with the great saving in price. The weight of every table, carefully packed for shipment, is given in the description and by referring to page 630, you can calculate almost to a penny what the freight charges will amount to. Don't be afraid of the freight charges.

REMEMBER that the customer pays the freight always, and that whether you buy from us or from your local dealer, you are paying the freight charges, because the dealer pays the same amount of freight as you do and must add the freight to his cost price when he figures his selling price.

OUR BINDING GUARANTEE FOR QUALITY. We guarantee the quality of each and every table we sell to be strictly high class in every particular. We guarantee the table to prove not only exactly as represented and described but perfectly satisfactory to you and we are ready to return your money and pay freight charges both ways if the table is not satisfactory in every way. If you do not find that the table we send you is better in material, construction, design and finish, and much lower in price than any table you can purchase elsewhere, you can return it to us and we will immediately refund your money, together with all transportation charges. Furthermore, we agree that should any table shrink, crack or in any way prove defective, we will repair it for you or refund your money.

ABOUT THE MATERIAL AND CONSTRUCTION OF OUR TABLES.

THE WOOD which is used in the construction of our tables is especially selected, thoroughly air seasoned and kiln dried and absolutely guaranteed not to warp, check or shrink.

THE CONSTRUCTION of our tables is absolutely the best that modern machinery and skilled workmanship can produce. Every part and piece is thoroughly well made, inspected and carefully fitted before being passed to the finishing department. The legs are fastened to the top by a very simple, strong and durable device. They are easily detached for convenience in moving or shipping.

THE FINISH of our tables is strictly first class and only the best grade of wood filler and varnish is used that is obtainable. The top of every table is rubbed until perfectly even and smooth which prevents the finish from being affected by hot plates or dishes which may be set upon it. The beauty of the finish must be seen to be fully appreciated. To obtain a smooth surface and better luster, and a finish that will not craze or check or blister, that will look better after years of use than tables offered by others do in two months, facilities are employed by which each coat of this finish is allowed to thoroughly dry and harden before applying the succeeding one.

OUR STYLES ARE UP TO DATE. The extension tables which we illustrate and describe on the following pages represent the newest and choicest designs of today. The selection represents the experience of years and careful study, and have been chosen with a view of giving our customers a line of tables as stylish in design, high grade in construction and finish as can be found anywhere, and to give them the privilege of sitting at home and selecting from our catalogue a table that is the equal in quality of any to be found in any store in the world, and at the same time give them the advantage of buying such a class of goods, usually sold at high prices, at the very low price of factory cost, with but one small percentage of profit added.

DON'T BE MISLED BY OUR LOW PRICES. Don't feel that because our prices are so very low the quality of our tables is not the very best. We sell these goods on an extremely narrow margin of profit, our facilities for buying and selling are much better than other firms, and while our prices are very low the standard and quality of our extension tables are strictly high grade. Our binding guarantee and refund offer protects you in every way, and you do not take any risk whatever in sending us your order.

OUR GREAT EXTENSION TABLE LEADER.

$4.25 for this Extension Dining Room Table is certainly the greatest value ever offered, the equal of dining room tables that retail generally at nearly double the price. This Extension Dining Room Table is made of solid oak, selected stock in a beautiful golden finish. The top is 3 feet 6 inches long, and can be extended to 6 feet; 3 feet 6 inches wide and is built with a heavy boxed rim with frame and mortised corners.

FOR EXTRA LENGTHS, SEE PRICE LIST BELOW.

$4.25

The lower edge of the boxed rim is nicely shaped and grooved. The top is supported by six legs, each 3 inches in diameter, joined together with heavy ornamental hand carved stretchers securely fastened into each leg. The legs are fastened to the top by the simplest, strongest and most durable construction possible. The legs can be easily detached for moving or shipping. The leaves are carefully fitted into each other by dowel pins. A firm and well constructed crate is furnished for this set of leaves. This table has an exceptionally beautiful golden finish which brings out perfectly the handsome grain of the wood. The filler and varnish used to fill the pores of the wood and to preserve and protect it are the best that can be produced. Our tables preserve their finish and color for a lifetime.

For strictly high grade construction and workmanship, attractiveness in design and beauty of color and finish, our tables cannot be excelled. We pack this table as well as all other tables in our line in a crate, the top, leaves and legs separately. Each table is furnished with a complete set of steel frame casters. Remember distinctly that we sell each table with the absolute guarantee and understanding that if upon receipt of the table you are not thoroughly satisfied, you can return the table to us and we will refund your money together with the transportation charges. This table weighs 165 pounds. Shipped direct from our eastern factory to our customers in the east or warehouse in Chicago to customers in the west.

No. 1C528
Price, 6-foot extension table $4.25
Price, 8-foot extension table 5.45
Price, 10-foot extension table 6.35
Price, 12-foot extension table 7.25

Our $1.15 Kitchen Table.

$1.15

No. 1C740 Kitchen Table. It is made of hardwood with basswood top and oak legs, has large roomy drawer. It is strongly constructed and has bolted leg fasteners. It can be taken apart for shipping, thus saving very largely on freight. Size of top, 27x42 inches. Shipped from factory in Chicago. Weight, about 40 pounds.
Price.........$1.15

A Solid Oak Drop Leaf Kitchen Table.

$2.65

No. 1C742 This table is one of the most practical and serviceable tables made for use in a kitchen. Has drop leaves so that it can be used as a regular sized kitchen table or extended as a dining table. Made of solid oak, finished golden. The top when open measures 39x48 inches. Shipping weight, about 90 pounds.
Price.......$2.65

Our $2.90 Solid Oak Drop Leaf Table.

$2.90

No. 1C744 This is one of the most desirable and necessary articles of furniture, and one that is convenient for general use. Not an extension table, but the leaves may be dropped so that the table will take up little space when not in use. It is made of solid oak with golden finish. The size of top is 39 inches wide by 48 inches long. Shipping weight, about 90 pounds.
Price.......$2.90

Our Great Bargain for $3.75.

No. 1C514 Extension Table. Is exceptionally massive, especially well constructed **of solid oak.** The legs are made with the bolt fastenings and are furnished complete with a set of casters. The size of the top is 42x42 inches when closed. Compare the size and quality of our tables with those offered by other dealers and you will readily recognize that our prices are unusually low. Shipping weight, 100 pounds.

Size	6-foot	8-foot
Price	**$3.75**	**$4.65**

Our $3.95 Solid Oak Extension Table.

No. 1C512 Table is made of golden oak, substantially built and exceptionally well finished. The legs are fastened with iron bolts at the corners, construction unusually strong and the table perfectly firm and solid. The dimensions of the top are 42x42 inches and it comes in 6 and 8 foot lengths. Complete with casters. Shipping weight, about 100 pounds.

Size	6-foot	8-foot
Price	**$3.95**	**$4.85**

Round Drop Leaf Extension Table.

No. 1C520 The Old Fashioned Round Drop Leaf Table, which we show in the illustration, is an old time favorite, and never goes out of date; nor does it lose any of its desirable features. **It is made of solid oak,** with an oval top, the size of which is 42x52 inches. It can be taken apart and shipped knocked down, thus saving very largely in the freight rate. It comes in three sizes, at the following prices. Complete with casters. Weight, about 100 pounds.

Size	6-foot	8-foot	10-foot
Price	**$4.45**	**$5.35**	**$6.25**

Wonderful Value at $4.95.

No. 1C531 This Extension Table is made of thoroughly air seasoned and kiln dried oak in a golden finish. The top is 42x42 inches with a full boxed rim. It has six legs, 3 inches in diameter securely fastened to the top and given additional strength and solidity by being joined with heavy stretchers, beautifully carved. Complete with best quality casters. Shipping weight, about 165 pounds.

Size	6-foot	8-foot	10-foot	12-foot
Price	**$4.95**	**$5.85**	**$6.75**	**$7.65**

OUR TABLES ARE CAREFULLY PACKED

To insure safe delivery. Read complete description on preceding page of HOW our tables are made.

Our $5.25 Solid Oak Extension Table.

No. 1C532 This Extension Table is made of solid oak, golden finish. The top measures 42x42 inches when closed. As shown in the illustration it has six massive, fancy turned legs, the end ones being joined by a handsomely carved stretcher, which adds greatly both to the appearance and strength of the table. Complete with casters. Shipping weight, about 165 pounds.

Size	6-foot	8-foot	10-foot	12-foot
Price	**$5.25**	**$6.15**	**$7.05**	**$8.95**

$5.35 For This Handsome Extension Table.

No. 1C533 This Extension Table has a top 42x42 inches with a heavy full boxed rim. The wood is thoroughly seasoned solid oak in a beautiful golden finish. The neatly turned and fluted legs are 3¼ inches in diameter. A substantial and well made table. Best quality casters. Shipping weight, about 160 pounds.

Size	6-foot	8-foot	10-foot	12-foot
Price	**$5.35**	**$6.25**	**$7.15**	**$8.05**

Exceptional Value, $5.65.

No. 1C535 This Extension Table is made of solid oak, golden finish. The top is 42x42 inches. It has six massive legs with hand carved claw feet, joined by handsomely carved stretchers giving it added strength and solidity. Compare this table with those offered by others at 30 to 40 per cent more than our price. High grade in construction in every detail. Shipping weight about 175 pounds.

Size	6-foot	8-foot	10-foot	12-foot
Price	**$5.65**	**$6.55**	**$7.45**	**$8.35**

□**No. 1C536 This Extension Table is made of thoroughly air seasoned oak, golden finish.** The top which is 42x42 inches has a heavy boxed rim. It is supported by five shapely turned and fluted legs, 4 inches thick, securely fastened to the top by a simple device which makes the strongest possible construction. Best quality casters. A table which sells in retail stores at $10.00 to $12.00. Shipped knocked down direct from factory in the East or Chicago. Shipping weight, about 175 pounds.

Size	6-foot	8-foot	10-foot	12-foot
Price	**$6.45**	**$7.35**	**$8.25**	**$9.25**

$6.85 Buys This 6-Foot Extension Table.

No. 1C541 This table is made from carefully selected extra heavy golden oak, exceptionally well finished. Has five large 5-inch hand turned and fluted legs; has a very large heavy top, 42x42 inches in size. It is a table you must see, examine and compare with others to appreciate its real worth. Complete with casters. Weight, packed for shipment, 175 pounds.

Size	6-foot	8-foot	10-foot	12-foot
Price	**$6.85**	**$7.75**	**$8.65**	**$9.55**

No. 1C544 You cannot fully appreciate the value of this table unless you see it. The top is 42x42 inches with a shapely full boxed rim. It has five massive hand turned and fluted 5-inch legs firmly fastened to the top. The wood is specially selected oak in a golden finish. Compare it with tables offered at double our price. Shipping weight about 175 pounds.

Size	6-foot	8-foot	10-foot	12-foot
Price	**$7.20**	**$8.10**	**$8.95**	**$9.85**

No. 1C548 This Dining Table is made of solid oak, in a beautiful golden finish. The full boxed top is 42x42 inches when closed. Supported by five massive fluted legs 5 inches in diameter, with hand carved claw feet. Fitted with best quality casters. Shipping weight, 175 pounds.

Size	6-foot	8-foot	10-foot	12-foot
Price	**$7.65**	**$8.60**	**$9.55**	**$10.50**

A 6-Inch Leg Table for $7.95.

No. 1C551 This is one of the handsomest tables in our line. For massiveness and solidity there is nothing to equal it. It is made of solid oak throughout. The top is 42x42 inches when closed. Has five turned and fluted 6-inch legs of beautiful design, fitted with best quality casters. Shipping weight, 175 pounds.

Size	6-foot	8-foot	10-foot	12-foot
Price	**$7.95**	**$8.90**	**$9.85**	**$10.80**

No. 1C552 Same table as No. 1C551, but with round top, **$1.00 extra.**

Wonderful Value.

No. 1C555 This Pillar Extension Table is made of solid oak, golden finish. It is the most wonderful value ever offered in a thoroughly well made table of this design. The massive pedestal base is firmly bolted to the top. The top is 42x42 inches and has a deep boxed rim. Shipped direct from factory in the East or Chicago. Shipping weight, 175 pounds.

Size	6-foot	8-foot	10-foot	12-foot
Price	$8.00	$8.95	$9.90	$10.85

Massive Golden Oak Extension Table.

No. 1C556 This Massive Solid Golden Oak Table has a full boxed top, size 42x42 inches. It has five hand carved legs, 5 inches in diameter, with heavy claw feet. Thoroughly well made in every detail of construction. Fitted with best quality casters. Shipping weight, 200 pounds.

Size	6-foot	8-foot	10-foot	12-foot
Price	$8.25	$9.20	$10.15	$11.10

Quarter Sawed Oak Extension Table.

No. 1C557 This Extension Table is made of solid oak golden finish. The perfectly round boxed top is 46 inches in diameter. It is supported by five massive turned and fluted legs, 5 inches thick. Legs are securely fastened to the top by a simple device which makes the firmest possible construction. Best quality casters. A table that sells in retail stores at $14.00 to $15.00. Shipped knocked down direct from factory in the East or Chicago. Shipping weight, about 190 pounds.

Size	6-foot	8-foot	10-foot	12-foot
Price	$10.25	$11.35	$12.45	$13.55

No. 1C558 Our Special Quarter Sawed Oak Extension Table. Top 45x45 inches, highly polished, made of the best quarter sawed oak. Fitted with handsomely turned legs, 5 inches in diameter. Best quality casters. The sharp corners noticed on nearly all tables are entirely done away with on these tables by fitting turned and polished blocks at each corner, giving to the table a finished and elegant appearance. Shipping weight, 200 pounds.

Size	8-foot	10-foot	12-foot
Price	$10.65	$11.75	$12.95

Our Special Extension Table.

No. 1C559 This beautiful high grade Extension Table. Top, 45x45 inches, highly polished, made of the best quarter sawed oak. Fitted with handsomely turned legs, 6 inches in diameter. Best quality casters. The sharp corners noticed on nearly all tables are entirely done away with on these tables by fitting turned and polished blocks at each corner, giving to the table a finished and elegant appearance. Shipping weight, 200 pounds.

Size	8-foot	10-foot	12-foot
Price	$11.95	$13.25	$14.45

Round Top Pillar Extension Table.

No. 1C560 The illustration shows a handsome design in a Round Top Pillar Extension Table. It is made of solid oak, beautifully finished. The top of the table measures 46 inches in diameter, and is beautifully ornamented with beaded moulding, while the legs are handsomely carved and ornamented, making it one of the most attractive tables which we can furnish. Shipping weight, about 175 pounds.

Size	6-foot	8-foot	10-foot	12-foot
Price	$11.45	$12.35	$13.25	$14.15

Quarter Sawed Oak Extension Table.

No. 1C574 A Massive Quarter Sawed Oak Extension Table. Size of top, 48 x 48 in. Made of the very best selected oak, quarter sawed and highly polished. Has massive legs, 6 inches in diameter, beautifully turned and carved and fitted with best quality casters. Ends rounded off and all corners finished off with turned and polished blocks. Shipping weight, 200 pounds.

Size	8-foot	10-foot	12-foot
Price	$13.25	$14.45	$15.65

A Bargain at $14.45.

No. 1C582 This handsome Table is made throughout of quarter sawed **oak,** best grade selected stock, exceptionally well made, with rounded corners, highly polished finish. Has 48x48-inch top; handsomely turned and fluted, massive 6-inch legs, with hand carved claw feet, best quality casters. A strictly high grade table. We invite comparison with other tables and ours will be found far superior in every way and the price lower. Shipping weight, 225 pounds.

Size	8-foot	10-foot	12-foot
Price	$14.45	$15.65	$16.95

A Fine Pillar Extension Table.

No. 1C586 This is the handsomest Round Top Pillar Extension Table in the market at anywhere near the price. It is made throughout of oak, with beautifully figured quarter sawed oak veneered pillar; quarter sawed oak top and rim. Made by the very best cabinetmakers to insure a strictly high grade piece of furniture, beautifully finished and highly polished throughout. Handsome, hand carved, ornamented claw legs, fitted with best quality casters. Has 45x45-inch top. We invite comparison with other tables at double our price. Shipping weight, 225 pounds.

Size	8-foot	10-foot	12-foot
Price	$14.95	$16.45	$17.95

No. 1C590 This Strictly High Grade Pillar Extension Table is made of highly figured quarter sawed oak, golden finish, highly polished. Heavy boxed rim top, 45x45 inches, supported by a massive pedestal 10 inches in diameter, with neatly rounded hand carved claw feet. Fitted with patent locking device to prevent spreading of the base. Compare this table with those sold by others at $20.00 to $25.00. Shipped knocked down, direct from factory in Northern Indiana. Shipping weight, about 225 pounds.

Size	8-foot	10-foot	12-foot
Price	$16.65	$18.25	$19.75

No. 1C595 This Strikingly Handsome Extension Table is made of highly figured quarter sawed golden oak, highly polished. The top is 48x48 inches, with rounded edges and a beautifully shaped boxed rim. Supported by a massive center pillar and four shapely curved legs with hand carved claw feet. A table that sells in retail stores for $25.00 to $30.00. High grade in construction, original and attractive in design, beautiful in finish. Shipped direct from factory in Northern Indiana. Shipping weight, about 250 pounds.

Size	8-foot	10-foot	12-foot
Price	$17.45	$18.95	$20.45

No. 1C596 This Magnificent Extension Table is made of specially selected quarter sawed oak in a beautiful golden polished finish. The extra large top, size 48x48 inches, has rounded edges and a full boxed rim. The massive pedestal is 12 inches in diameter. The shapely carved legs have hand carved lion's claw feet. Fitted with patent locking device. Handsome in design, high grade in construction, beautiful in wood and finish. Shipped knocked down from factory in Northern Indiana. Shipping weight, about 250 pounds.

Size	8-foot	10-foot	12-foot
Price	$17.95	$19.45	$20.95

KITCHEN CABINETS AND KITCHEN TABLES

AT PRICES LOWER THAN EVER BEFORE, WE OFFER AN ENTIRELY NEW LINE OF IMPROVED KITCHEN TABLES AND THE ATTENTION OF EVERY HOUSEWIFE IS INVITED TO THIS LINE OF GOODS.

KITCHEN CABINETS are an invention for assisting the housekeeper. A few years ago they were just being introduced and the sale was very limited. As soon as they were put on the market, however, and offered at popular prices, their usefulness was recognized and the sale of them has jumped from the hundreds to the thousands. The use of the kitchen cabinet has become so general that one is to be found in nearly every home in the United States. We know there is nothing more convenient and satisfactory for household use than a good kitchen cabinet. If you have not already purchased one of these economical and labor saving devices, don't fail to secure that much convenience for yourself without further delay. You will be surprised what a convenience a kitchen cabinet is, how many uses it can be put to, how nicely it takes care of the materials used in the kitchen and in such a convenient shape, helping to make a place for everything and keeping everything in its place.

OUR PRICES in every case are figured on factory cost. These cabinets are made for us under contract, by the largest and most representative manufacturers in this line. We have secured unusually advantageous prices which represent very little more than cost of raw material and skilled labor. Our selling prices on all of these goods represent the narrowest possible margin of profit above first cost to us and, as a result, you can buy a kitchen cabinet from us for about as little money as most furniture dealers pay at wholesale. Do not feel that because our prices are very low, that the quality of our cabinets are not the very best. Quality is a watchword with us and we never take one penny out of the quality to make a "catchy" price. The quality of these cabinets is strictly high grade and while dealers and others may advise you against sending your order to us and say we cannot furnish good furniture at such low prices, we want you to be the judge, we want you to give us the opportunity of proving our claim and at the same time relieve you of any risk whatever.

THEREFORE, we emphasize the fact that we accept your order and your money with the distinct understanding and agreement that if the cabinet or other article you get from us is not perfectly satisfactory in every way, in construction, quality and finish, if it does not represent extraordinary value, if you do not find you have made a big saving in price, you are under no obligation to keep the cabinet, but it can be returned to us at our expense and we will promptly return your money and pay freight charges both ways.

DESCRIPTION OF THE MATERIALS USED IN OUR KITCHEN CABINETS AND ABOUT THE WORKMANSHIP.

THE WOOD which we use in the construction of our kitchen cabinets is specially selected and thoroughly air seasoned and kiln dried. Absolutely guaranteed not to warp or shrink.

THE CONSTRUCTION of our Kitchen Cabinets in every detail is strictly high grade throughout. Every means has been used to make our kitchen cabinets as near perfection in detail of construction as modern science and skilled workmanship can make them. They are made of hardwood throughout, except the top of the base, which is white basswood, especially adapted for ease in cleaning.

THE DRAWERS AND BINS are so perfectly constructed as to be perfect fitting and frictionless. They can be easily taken out and cleaned, which is not the case with most cabinets of other manufacture.

EACH CABINET is fitted with one or two sliding, removable kneading and chopping boards, both sides smooth and even. Our kitchen cabinets are so constructed that the lower part of the legs can be removed and placed inside the cabinet for convenience in packing and shipping and can readily be put together by anyone. This adds to the safe handling of cabinets in transit and insures much lower rate of freight. Our kitchen cabinets measure full dimensions as described. The drawers and bins open and shut without a particle of friction and are securely built and will last a lifetime. The finish of our cabinets is strictly first class. We use the best wood filler and varnish to protect and preserve the wood. The top of the base and the kneading and chopping boards, which are placed above the small drawers in the base, are made of white basswood, unfinished for ease in cleaning.

FACTORY SHIPMENTS. To reduce our selling price to you to the lowest possible point by cutting out all intermediate expense of handling, we ship every cabinet direct to you from the factory where made. This means a big saving to you, for when we ship direct from factory to customer there is no extra freight handling or storage charges and as a result you save all that expense, and are thereby enabled to buy a kitchen cabinet from us for less than dealers can buy them in carload lots, in fact, as before stated, you cannot fully appreciate the values we are offering in this line until you have seen and compared them with other high grade cabinets at double the price we ask.

THE BASE OF OUR KITCHEN CABINETS without the top section makes a highly satisfactory, convenient and useful cabinet by itself. The flour, sugar and meal bins, the linen and cutlery drawers, pot and pan cupboards and the removable kneading and chopping board together with the roomy basswood top, will be fully appreciated by every housekeeper. We quote prices for the base alone (without the top section), in several of our cabinets described below.

Our Big Bargain Cabinet at $2.85.

No. 1C726 This cabinet is an illustration of this wonderful saving to our customers, not only in this article but in every other that we offer. We furnish this kitchen cabinet at a price considerably less than your retail furniture dealer can buy it in carload lots. Base is made of white maple, natural finish, with a white basswood table top, size, 25x45 inches. It has two dustproof flour bins with wooden bottoms, two drawers partitioned for cutlery and a removable carving and kneading board. Lower part of legs are detachable, and placed inside drawers for convenience in shipping. Top has a double paneled back, a roomy top shelf, below which are seven drawers for holding various commodities used in the kitchen. We furnish the base of this cabinet without the top section if desired. This cabinet is thoroughly well made in every detail of construction. Order one of our cabinets, place it beside any other cabinet offered at anywhere near our price and you will find our cabinet double the value of the other. Shipped direct from factory in Southern Michigan. Shipping weight about 140 pounds.

Price, complete cabinet........................$4.95
Price, without top section........................2.85

$7.45 Kitchen Cabinet.

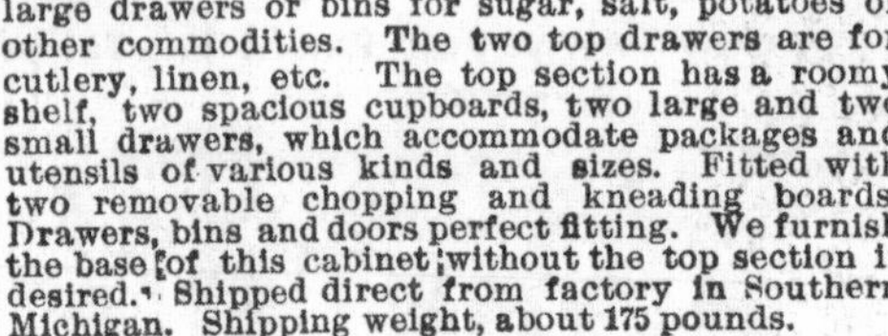

No. 1C729 This is one of the most convenient and useful Kitchen Cabinets ever designed. Made of thoroughly seasoned white maple, natural finish. The table top on the base is made of basswood with rounded edges, size 23x50 inches. It has two dustproof flour bins with wooden bottoms. In the center are two large drawers or bins for sugar, salt, potatoes or other commodities. The two top drawers are for cutlery, linen, etc. The top section has a roomy shelf, two spacious cupboards, two large and two small drawers, which accommodate packages and utensils of various kinds and sizes. Fitted with two removable chopping and kneading boards. Drawers, bins and doors perfect fitting. We furnish the base of this cabinet without the top section if desired. Shipped direct from factory in Southern Michigan. Shipping weight, about 175 pounds.

Price, complete cabinet........................$7.45
Price, without top section........................5.25

$8.35 Kitchen Cabinet.

No. 1C732 This Kitchen Cabinet at $8.35, is the equal of any cabinet offered by others at $12.00 to $15.00. Made of selected thoroughly seasoned northern hardwood, golden oak finish with a white basswood table top on the base section, size, 27x44 inches. It has a large dustproof sliding bin which holds 70 pounds of flour, a spacious cupboard for pots, pans, etc., a cutlery drawer, linen drawer and a removable carving and kneading board. Top section has a roomy cupboard, four small shelves, a large shelf and a combination shelf and plate rack on top. The construction is strictly first class throughout. The convenient and commodious arrangement will be fully appreciated by every housekeeper. It will save many weary steps. Carefully packed and shipped direct from factory in Northern Illinois. Shipping weight, about 160 pounds.

Price, complete cabinet........................$8.35
Price, without top section........................4.95

$8.75 Kitchen Cabinet.

No. 1C735 This Kitchen Cabinet is made of thoroughly seasoned hardwood, golden oak finish. Top of base is made of white basswood, size 26x48 inches. Bins have wood bottoms and will each hold 60 pounds flour. One of the drawers is for linen, the other partitioned for cutlery, etc. Fitted with removable kneading and chopping board. Top section has a broad upper shelf, four small drawers for salt, pepper, spices, etc., a tilting sugar bin and two roomy cupboards, below which is a broad shelf for coffee and tea cans, packages, etc. All drawers and bins can be removed for cleaning and airing. The wonderful utility of this cabinet will be appreciated by every economical housekeeper. Compare it with those offered by others at $12.00 to $15.00. Shipped direct from factory in Northern Illinois. Shipping weight, about 175 pounds.

Price, complete cabinet........................$8.75

Our Kitchen Cabinets are securely packed to insure safe delivery. Read what we say at top of this page about our Kitchen Cabinets.

THE ARTICLES DISPLAYED ARE NOT INCLUDED WITH THE CABINETS.

$8.85 Kitchen Cabinet.

No. 1C737 This Kitchen Cabinet is made of thoroughly seasoned white maple, natural finish. The base has a white basswood table top, with rounded edges, size, 25x48 inches. Entire cabinet is 60 inches high. Note the large, dustproof flour bin with wood bottom which holds 70 pounds of flour, the convenient pot and pan cupboard, above which is a cutlery drawer and linen drawer, to the right of which, are two small drawers and sugar bin. Fitted with two removable carving and kneading boards. Top section has a broad shelf, two roomy cupboards for bottles, packages and utensils. Four drawers in center for spices, small packages, and various commodities used in the kitchen. All drawers are perfect fitting and can be removed for cleaning and airing. Base and top have full paneled ends and back. This cabinet should be compared with those shipped by others at $11.00 to $12.00. We furnish the base of this cabinet without the top section if desired. Shipped direct from factory in Southern Michigan. Shipping weight, about 175 pounds.

Price, complete cabinet........................$8.85
Price, without top section........................5.65

$9.95 Kitchen Cabinet.

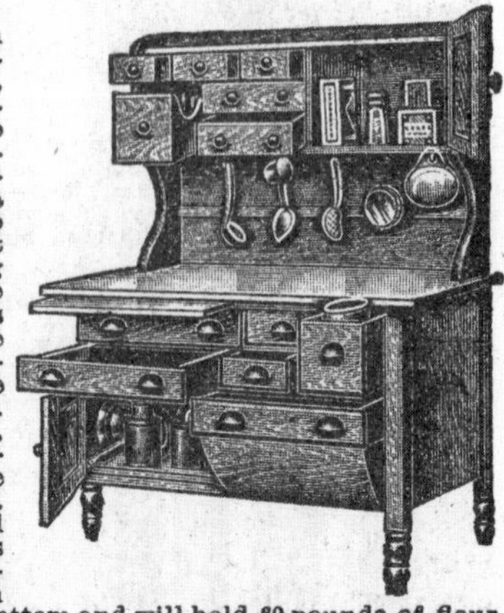

No. 1C741 In this high grade Kitchen Cabinet, we have provided in the many drawers and cupboards, for a storage place for almost everything used in the kitchen. It is made of white maple, natural finish. Base has a 26x48 in. table top, made of basswood for ease in cleaning. It has full paneled ends and back. Extra large bin has wooden bottom and will hold 60 pounds of flour. Note the five roomy drawers for linen, knives, forks, and various utensils and commodities. It has a removable kneading and chopping board. Top section has a broad shelf, below which are six drawers for sugar, spices, packages, etc., and a large cupboard for coffee cans, bottles, etc. All drawers can be removed for cleaning and airing. The high quality of cabinet construction, perfect fitting drawers and doors, the handsome wood and beautiful finish together with the wonderfully practical arrangement make this strictly high grade kitchen cabinet wonderful value at our price. It cannot be purchased in a retail store for less than $15.00 to $17.00. Shipped direct from factory in Grand Rapids, Mich. Shipping weight, about 200 pounds. Price $9.95

$10.15 Kitchen Cabinet.

The articles shown in pictures are not sent with the cabinets.

$10.15

No. 1C759 This Kitchen Cabinet is made of thoroughly seasoned hardwood, golden oak finish. Entire cabinet, 61 inches high. Base has a basswood top, size, 27x44 inches. Note the tilting dustproof bins with wood bottoms so constructed as to prevent friction, being balanced by metal attachments to the heavy cross bar beneath. One of the drawers above bins is for linen, the other partitioned for cutlery, etc. Top section has a convenient plate or pan rack above, below which are three spice drawers and two cutlery drawers. A broad lower shelf and swinging towel rack increase the utility of this cabinet. Every detail of construction first class. Shipped direct from factory in Central Indiana. Shipping weight, 140 lbs. Price, complete cabinet **$10.15**

$11.45 Kitchen Cabinet.

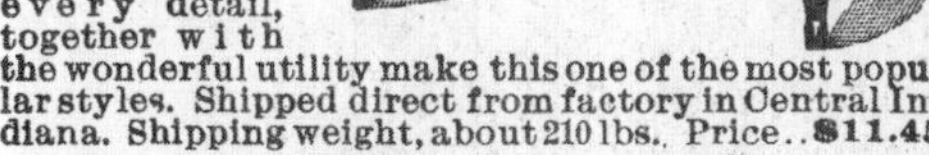

No. 1C765 This Cabinet is 83 inches high. Made of thoroughly seasoned northern hardwood, golden oak finish. Base exactly like No. 1C759. Extra large cupboard top has three broad shelves for dishes and utensils of all kinds. Fitted with double thick glass doors. Note the broad shelf below for packages, coffee cans, bottles, etc. All drawers and bins can be removed for cleaning. The perfect fitting dustproof drawers and doors, the high grade construction in every detail, together with the wonderful utility make this one of the most popular styles. Shipped direct from factory in Central Indiana. Shipping weight, about 210 lbs. Price..**$11.45**

$10.95 Kitchen Cabinet.

No. 1C758 The base of this Cabinet is exactly like No. 1C759, combining all the excellent features of that cabinet, wood bottom, dustproof swinging bins, linen and cutlery drawer, kneading and chopping board. The spacious cupboard top with perfect fitting panel doors, is subdivided into shelves and compartments that will accommodate dishes, all kinds of packages and kitchen utensils. Solid panel ends and back. Drawers removable for airing and cleaning. Entire cabinet, 84 inches high. High grade construction throughout. The economical housekeeper will fully appreciate the value we offer in this cabinet. Shipped direct from factory in Central Indiana. Shipping weight, about 200 pounds. Price.............**$10.95**

$12.45 Kitchen Cabinet.

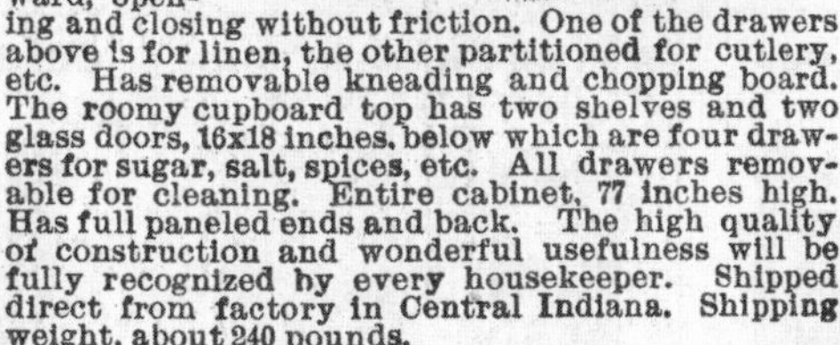

No. 1C766 This Cabinet is made of thoroughly seasoned northern hardwood, golden oak finish. Base has a white basswood top, 44 inches long, 27 inches wide. The dustproof wood bottom swinging flour bin which holds 60 pounds of flour, is perfectly balanced by metal attachments to a cross bar permitting it to swing forward, opening and closing without friction. One of the drawers above is for linen, the other partitioned for cutlery, etc. Has removable kneading and chopping board. The roomy cupboard top has two shelves and two glass doors, 16x18 inches, below which are four drawers for sugar, salt, spices, etc. All drawers removable for cleaning. Entire cabinet, 77 inches high. Has full paneled ends and back. The high quality of construction and wonderful usefulness will be fully recognized by every housekeeper. Shipped direct from factory in Central Indiana. Shipping weight, about 240 pounds.

Price, cabinet only..........................**$12.45**

$11.25 Kitchen Cabinet.

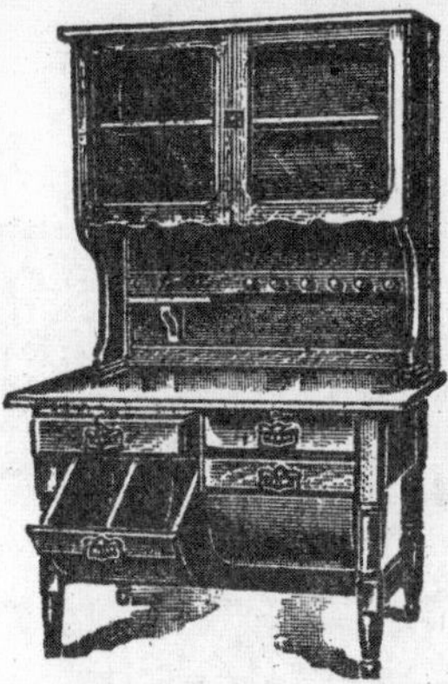

No. 1C762 This Cabinet has the same base as our No. 1C759. Entire cabinet is 70 inches high, 44 inches long, 27 inches deep. It is made of thoroughly seasoned northern hardwood, golden oak finish. Top section has a roomy cupboard with glass doors, below which is a bracket shelf and a row of brass hooks for hanging various utensils used in the kitchen. This cabinet is adapted to all the various demands of the model kitchen, and cannot be fully appreciated unless compared with other cabinets of the same style and quality at $15.00 to $18.00. Carefully packed and shipped direct from factory in Central Indiana. Shipping weight, about 200 pounds. Price............**$11.25**

$12.75 Kitchen Cabinet.

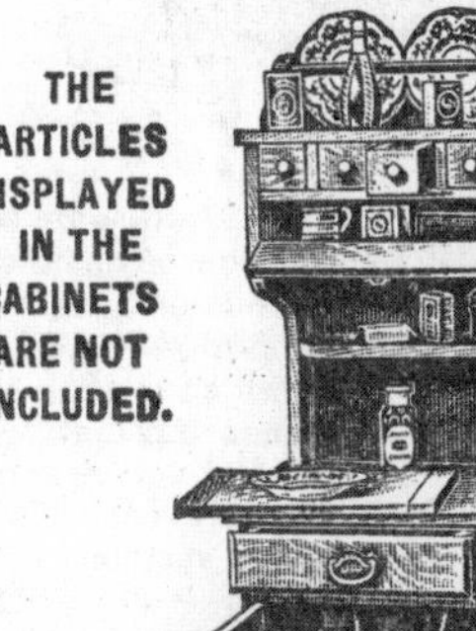

THE ARTICLES DISPLAYED IN THE CABINETS ARE NOT INCLUDED.

No. 1C768 In this Cabinet we have the same base as in No. 1C766. The top section has a convenient lower shelf for pepper and salt box, etc. Above this shelf is a roomy cupboard for bottles, coffee cans, tea cans, commodities in packages, etc. To the left of the cupboard are four drawers, below which is a small cupboard with drop hinged door. Above all is a large shelf for dishes. The drawers and bins are removable for cleaning. The ends of the base and doors are paneled to prevent warping. Every detail of construction is mechanically perfect. The wood is thoroughly seasoned hardwood in a golden oak finish. The high grade construction, perfect fitting drawers, doors and bin, the wonderful convenience of the various compartments will be fully appreciated by every housekeeper. This cabinet sells in retail stores at $18.00 to $20.00. Securely packed to insure safe delivery and shipped direct from factory in Central Indiana. Shipping weight, 200 pounds.

Price, cabinet only.........................**$12.75**

$14.45 Kitchen Cabinet.

No. 1C770 This illustration shows one of the most convenient Kitchen Cabinets ever devised. The wood is the best selected northern hardwood, thoroughly seasoned and kiln dried in a golden oak finish. The best wood filler and varnish is used to preserve and protect the wood. The base is 27x44 inches. It contains a spacious cupboard for storage of pots and pans, or other commodities which are kept in large packages. To the right of the cupboard is a dustproof swinging flour bin which will hold 50 pounds of flour, balanced on a cross bar by a simple metal attachment that permits it to swing forward, opening and closing without friction. Above these are two spacious drawers for cutlery, one of which is partitioned. The removable kneading and chopping board will be found convenient and serviceable. In the top section we have three spacious drawers in the center, both sides of which is a roomy shelf for commodities of various kinds and swinging doors, the inner side of which is a rack for bottles and small packages. The ornamental shelf at the top is a convenient receptacle for dishes, etc. Shipped direct from factory in Central Indiana. Shipping weight, 240 pounds. Price, cabinet only **$14.45**

$14.95 Kitchen Cabinet.

No. 1C773 The base of this Kitchen Cabinet is 44 inches long, 27 inches wide. It has a roomy cupboard for pots and pans or commodities contained in large packages. The dustproof swinging flour bin holds 50 pounds of flour. The bin is made entirely of wood which preserves the flour from moulding. The bin is perfectly balanced by means of metal attachments to a cross bar, permitting it to swing forward, opening and closing without a particle of friction. The base has two spacious drawers for cutlery, etc., one of which is partitioned. The chopping and kneading board which in the illustration is shown lying on top fits into the base above one of the drawers. In the top we have two roomy shelves convenient for dishes. On either side is a full paneled door, on the inside of which are convenient racks for dishes, bottles, spice cans, etc. In the center is a roomy drawer, below which is a shelf for soap, baking powder and other commodities. The drawer bins and doors are perfectly constructed and perfect fitting. Thoroughly seasoned northern hardwood in a golden oak finish is used in this cabinet, except the table top and kneading board which are white basswood for ease in cleaning. Shipped direct from factory in Central Indiana. Shipping weight, 240 lbs. Price, **$14.95**

Our $14.35 Kitchen Cabinet.

No. 1C775 This Convenient and Handsome Kitchen Cabinet is 44 inches long and 27 inches wide. The base contains two swinging bins, one holding 60 pounds of flour, the other partitioned for meal, sugar, etc. The bins are so placed in the cabinet as to rest on a lower cross piece which forms a brace, making the construction stronger. The bins swing open or shut without friction and can be readily removed for cleaning and airing. The bottoms are made of wood to prevent the contents from moulding. Above the bins are two spacious drawers, one of which is partitioned for cutlery, etc. Above each drawer is a removable kneading and chopping board. The top of this cabinet is entirely new in design and arrangement. In the lower part is a roomy shelf. The dustproof bread box is so constructed that it can be readily cleaned. On the right is a convenient towel rack. The upper shelf forms a convenient china and dish cupboard. To the right and left of this shelf are the doors, the inner side of which are arranged for spice cabinets, washing powder, small packages, etc. The wood is specially selected northern hardwood thoroughly air-seasoned and kiln dried in a golden oak finish. Shipped direct from factory in Central Indiana. Shipping weight, 185 pounds.

Price, cabinet only.......................................$14.35

THE ARTICLES DISPLAYED ARE NOT INCLUDED WITH THE CABINETS.

Our $15.95 Kitchen Cabinet.

$15.95

No. 1C778 This is the Most Complete Kitchen Cabinet ever constructed. It is made of thoroughly seasoned northern hardwood golden oak finish. The white basswood top of the base is 27 inches wide and 44 inches long. It contains a swinging flour bin, which will hold 50 pounds of flour, and a roomy cupboard for pots, pans, etc. The swinging bin is a very attractive and unique feature of this cabinet. The bottom of the bin is made of wood which keeps the contents perfectly dry. It is balanced on a lower cross bar by a simple metal attachment that permits it to swing forward, opening and closing without a particle of friction. The base has two spacious drawers, one of which is partitioned; also a large bread and chopping board. In the top we have a large cupboard for all cereals and commodities, as well as dishes used in the kitchen. On each side of the top is a swinging shelf for holding all the smaller size commodities, which are kept in the packages in which they come. The inside contains a tilting sugar bin which will hold 25 pounds of sugar, a convenient cupboard for bread, between which are a sliding spice can tray, and small tray for knives, forks, corkscrews and can openers. Below these we have a complete rack for pie pans, stew pans, etc. On the right hand side we have a towel rack. In the top we have a spacious shelf for dishes. Height of entire cabinet, 85 inches.

The drawers and bins are perfectly constructed, perfect fitting, and move without binding or friction. They can be easily taken out and cleaned. In this cabinet, as in all others of our line of kitchen cabinets, the best wood filler and varnish is used to preserve and protect the wood. The top of the base and kneading board are unfinished for ease in cleaning. You will never fully appreciate the wonderful amount of labor saved, the comfort and convenience of this kitchen cabinet, how nicely it takes care of all materials used in the kitchen, helping to make a place for everything and everything in its place, until you have used it. Shipped direct from factory in Central Indiana. Shipping weight, 270 pounds.

Price, cabinet only.......................................$15.95

$4.00 Kitchen Cupboard for $2.60.

No. 1C779 This Kitchen Cupboard is made of thoroughly air seasoned and kiln dried hardwood in a golden finish. It has two doors, three shelves inside, and one large drawer. Height, 4 feet 11 inches; width, 2 feet 10 inches. It has paneled ends. We furnish it with metal panels or wood panels, as desired. Thoroughly well made, and a very useful article in every household. Shipping weight, about 90 pounds.

Price, wood panels....$2.60
Price, metal panels.... 2.55

READ what we say about our KITCHEN CABINETS and KITCHEN CUPBOARDS on page 642.

Our $6.25 Oak Cupboard.

No. 1C780 This Handsome New Style Oak Front Cupboard is thoroughly well made in every detail of construction and finish. It stands 6 feet 11 inches high, 3 feet 4 inches wide and 14 inches deep. Fitted with double thick heavy glass doors, two drawers with brass pulls. Lower cupboard is made with heavy double doors, fitted with lock and key. Inside of cupboards have adjustable shelves. Shipped direct from our factory in Western Ohio. Shipping weight, 140 pounds.

Price.......................$6.25

A $12.00 Kitchen Cupboard for $6.45.

No. 1C784 An Attractive and Handsome Kitchen Cupboard with solid oak front, very large and roomy. Is 6 feet 11 inches high, 42 inches wide and 15 inches deep; has two drawers and shelves in top and cupboard. Panels, drawers and top beautifully carved. A very sensible and useful piece of furniture. Shipped direct from our factory in Western Ohio. Shipping weight, 140 pounds.

Price.......................$6.45

No. 1C788 Same as above, with glass doors.

Price.......................$6.95

Our Two-Piece Cupboard.

No. 1C794 This Cupboard is made in two pieces, the upper part containing shelves and glass doors; can be removed if desired. Solid oak front, golden finish; has two drawers and a roomy cupboard. Panels, drawers and top handsomely carved. Can be used in dining room for crockery or as a china closet. It is 7 feet 9 inches high and 41 inches wide; the base is 20 inches deep and the upper part 15 inches deep, leaving a shelf on top of the base 6 inches wide. Shipped direct from our factory in Western Ohio. Shipping weight, 150 pounds.

Price.......................$8.45

Combination Cupboard and Cabinet.

No. 1C796 This New Design and Useful Cupboard is made with solid oak front, golden finish. The base contains one cupboard, two large drawers, four spice drawers and flour bin 12 inches wide, 24 inches deep. Height, 6 feet 7 inches; width, 3 feet 2 inches; depth, 16 inches. Double thick glass in doors. Full paneled ends and back. Strictly first class in construction throughout. Shipped direct from our factory in Western Ohio. Shipping weight, 160 pounds.

Price.......................$8.95

OUR NEW AND ASTONISHING VALUES IN SIDEBOARDS FOR 1905.

WITH GREATER FACILITIES THAN EVER BEFORE, WITH NEW AND BETTER SIDEBOARD MANUFACTURING CONNECTIONS, WITH MANY NEW DESIGNS THROUGHOUT AND PATTERNS FROM OUR FORMER LINE IMPROVED AND STRENGTHENED, WE PRESENT TO OUR CUSTOMERS THIS SEASON : : : : : : : :

THE GREATEST VALUES IN SIDEBOARDS WE HAVE EVER BEEN ABLE TO OFFER.

WE HAVE LONG BEEN HEADQUARTERS on sideboards and other case goods, we have increased our output of these goods from year to year, thereby securing better and better manufacturing connections, we have been able to constantly improve the quality and reduce the price, and today we call more than ordinary attention to this magnificent line of sideboards, presented on this and the following pages, and do so with the assurance that we are in a position to furnish our customers greater values than were ever offered before, much better goods than they can secure from other dealers and all at prices about one-third less than goods of equal quality are sold in regular furniture stores. We have greatly strengthened our lines of sideboards as against any previous season. We are showing a larger variety, better selection and, whether you want a cheap sideboard or one of the best that money can buy, you can be suited from these pages, and no matter which sideboard you select, you may feel sure that you are saving about one-third in price. Our entire line of sideboards, from the cheapest to the best, every sideboard we handle is thoroughly well made from carefully selected material and extra well finished. You will find every sideboard we furnish to be of better material, better finish, better fitting, more lasting and in every way more satisfactory than what is turned out from the average factory and sold by the average retail dealer. You will find our designs strictly up to date, and, in fact, we offer you the same advantage in selection as if you were in one of the largest city furniture stores, with this difference, that the price you pay us is very much lower than the price the same quality sideboard would cost you in the city furniture store.

THESE SIDEBOARDS are manufactured for us under contract by one of the best manufacturers in the country, a manufacturer whose name alone in the trade is a guarantee for quality and our contract takes a large part of his entire product. Our contract is very large and it enables the manufacturer to produce his other goods at a lower cost, it enables him to contract for larger quantities of raw material, to run his factory at the highest capacity and in the most economical way, and we thereby secure really remarkably low prices. To our first cost, which is little more than actual manufacturing cost in the largest quantities, we add our uniform one small percentage of profit and we offer the sideboard to you on this basis, namely, cost of material and labor with but one small profit added. We put you in a position to own a sideboard for about as little money as most retail dealers pay at wholesale.

OUR QUALITY GUARANTEE.

EVERY SIDEBOARD in our entire line is covered by our binding guarantee for quality, guaranteeing the make, material and finish. We guarantee the sideboard to reach you in the same perfect condition that it leaves our factory and we guarantee that you will make a substantial saving in price by placing your order with us.

OUR MONEY REFUND OFFER.

WE ACCEPT YOUR ORDER with the understanding and agreement that you will be perfectly satisfied, that the sideboard will prove perfectly satisfactory to you in every way, and that you will positively save money by buying from us, otherwise, if you are not pleased with your purchase, you can return it to us and we will return your money and pay freight charges both ways. Our sideboards are substantially made and with ordinary care will last a lifetime.

ABOUT THE MATERIAL AND THE WORKMANSHIP.

THE WOOD used in the construction of our sideboards is thoroughly seasoned and kiln dried and absolutely guaranteed not to warp, check or shrink. Great care is taken in the selection of the wood, special attention being given to the grain of the wood.

THE CONSTRUCTION of our sideboards is the very best that skilled workmanship and modern machinery can produce. The drawer sides are all dovetailed and the bottoms grooved, the guides of the drawers are even and smooth. The panels are made of transverse layers of selected stock that prevents shrinking or warping. The frame work is mortised and joined in the most careful manner. The beautiful and highly ornamented carving is made by hand, skillfully executed in the most perfect manner.

THE FINISH. The very best grade of hardwood oil, varnish and glue that can be obtained is used in the finishing of our sideboards. Great care is taken in the entire process of finishing. Special attention being given to the preservation of the wood, to the bringing out of the fine flaky grain of the wood. The color is a beautiful golden. We guarantee every sideboard we ship to reach you in the same perfect condition in which it leaves the factory. To produce a higher grade of finish, a more perfect surface, better luster, and a finish that will not crack, peel, check, or become dull, that will look better after years of use than the ordinary finished sideboards do in one month, the best materials that can be obtained are used.

THE MIRRORS used in our sideboards are the best quality genuine French beveled plate, the thickest and heaviest grade made. The beveling finely executed and polished by hand to give as perfect a reflection as the flat surface of the mirror.

THE TRIMMINGS are the best quality of cast brass, highly burnished, full lacquered to prevent tarnishing. Locks, keys, knobs, and pulls are strictly first class and perfectly fitted.

ABOUT THE FREIGHT. To reduce handling as much as possible, and therefore, to reduce our selling prices, we ship these sideboards either from our North Carolina factory or from our warehouses in Southern Indiana and Louisville, Kentucky, whichever is nearer to the customer and in most cases we can, thereby effect quite a saving in freight.

OUR WONDER VALUE
SOLID OAK SIDEBOARD, $7.95.

$7.95 is our challenge price, our astonishingly low figure on a solid oak sideboard; such a sideboard would cost in a retail furniture store at least $15.00.

THIS HANDSOME SIDEBOARD is 44 inches long by 22 inches wide and is made of choice selected highly figured oak in a beautiful golden finish which brings out the grain of the wood perfectly. The highly ornamental top is fitted with a thick genuine French bevel mirror, size, 14x24 inches The base has two curved front top drawers, one of which is lined for silverware, one large roomy linen drawer, below which is a spacious cupboard, with double doors. The ends of the base, which are full paneled, are made of transverse layers of solid oak, which absolutely prevents warping, shrinkage or checking. The top is decorated with genuine hand carvings, finely executed. The wood is thoroughly air seasoned and kiln dried, guaranteed against warpage or shrinkage. The finish is strictly high grade, special care being taken to produce a perfectly smooth surface, a better luster, a finish that will not check or become dull, that will preserve the wood and look better after years of usage than the ordinary finish does in one month. The construction and workmanship are the very best. The frame is perfectly joined and mortised, the drawers dovetailed and grooved and move without friction or binding. All the drawers are fitted with locks and keys. The knobs and handles are the best quality of genuine cast brass, highly lacquered and burnished to prevent tarnishing. The sideboard cannot be purchased elsewhere for less than $15.00 or $18.00.

You cannot fully appreciate the wonderful value we offer you in this sideboard until you have seen it and compared it with sideboards offered by others at more than double the price.

We pack this sideboard carefully, the base is padded, the top crated, and we guarantee that it will reach you in a perfect condition. We ship from point nearest customer, thereby insuring lowest freight rates. Shipping weight, 175 pounds.

No. 1C899 Sideboard, shipped direct from factory in North Carolina, Southern Indiana or Louisville, Ky. Price.................**$7.95**

ORDER BY NUMBER.

No. 1C899 Price, $7.95

OUR OFFER SEND US YOUR ORDER for this $7.95 sideboard and when received, compare it with any sideboard you can buy at home or from any other dealer for $15.00 and if you do not find this sideboard equal to such in every way, we will not expect you to keep it, but you can return it to us at our expense and we will immediately return your money. This illustration will give you a good idea of the appearance of this handsome sideboard, of this wonderful value at $7.95, but it must be seen and compared with sideboards that sell at much higher prices to understand why it is such a remarkable bargain. It is beautifully made and finished, a fine piece of furniture in every way and if you think of buying a new sideboard, you will never have a better opportunity than this, or if any of your friends or neighbors are thinking of buying a piece of furniture like this, you will surely be favoring them by calling their attention to this sideboard at $7.95. Our profit on each sideboard we sell at $7.95 is extremely low. We are not looking for a large profit but it is our determination to furnish the greatest values possible to our customers. We want to give them good, substantial merchandise for less money than they can buy elsewhere. We want to save them every possible penny and we figure our price as low as we can. We know that every sideboard we send out at $7.95 will prove an advertisement for us, that the customer who receives this sideboard at $7.95 will be astonished at the quality we furnish. We confidently expect to sell 5,000 sideboards at $7.95 from this announcement, and if we do, it will mean 5,000 satisfied customers whose future trade we are likely to get.

REMEMBER, you take no risk whatever, if the sideboard is not all and more than you expect it to be, you are under no obligations to keep it but you can return it to us at our expense and we will return your money.

No. 1C906 This Sideboard is made of thoroughly air seasoned and kiln dried oak. High gloss, golden finish. The base has a 22x44-inch double top. It has two top drawers with serpentine fronts, one lined for silverware, a large linen drawer and cupboard with double doors below. Double panel ends. Fitted with locks, cast brass handles and best quality casters. Mirror is best quality French bevel plate, size, 16x28 inches. The roomy top shelf is supported by neatly curved standards. Compare this sideboard with those sold by others at $18.00 to $20.00 and it will be found a wonderful bargain. Shipped direct from factory in Central Indiana. Shipping weight, 175 pounds. Price.....**$10.95**

No. 1C910 At our price, $12.75, this solid golden oak sideboard with high gloss finish will be fully appreciated by every customer who buys it. Base has a 21x44-inch double top, full paneled ends and back. One of the curved front top drawers is lined for silverware. Mirror is best quality French bevel plate, size, 16x28 inches. Note the shapely curved standards supporting the two small bracket shelves and the broad and convenient top shelf. Crown is decorated with a heavy cross banded quarter sawed oak veneered roll. All carvings are finely cut and hand made. Fitted with locks, cast brass handles and best quality casters. Thoroughly well made and finished. Shipped direct from factory in Central North Carolina or Southern Indiana. Shipping weight, 175 pounds. Price.....**$12.75**

No. 1C914 This Sideboard is made of thoroughly seasoned oak, high gloss golden finish. Base has a shaped double top, size 21x44 inches, in a perfect imitation of quarter sawed oak grain. One of the top drawers is lined for silverware. Entire front is richly figured, quarter sawed oak. Double panel ends and hand carved claw feet. Mirror is best quality French bevel plate, size 16x28 inches. Broad top shelf supported by handsome curved standards. Decorated with finely executed hand carvings. Fitted with locks, cast brass handles and best quality casters. Thoroughly well made throughout. Compare this sideboard with those offered by others at $20.00 to $25.00. Shipped direct from factory in Western Pennsylvania. Shipping weight about 175 pounds. Price.....**$13.85**

No. 1C916 This Sideboard is made entirely of quarter sawed golden oak, beautifully finished and highly polished. The base is 45 inches long. Has three swell front top drawers, one lined for silverware. A large swell front drawer underneath, suitable for table linen, etc. Has two cupboards at the bottom. Fitted with cast brass fancy knobs, handles and locks. The mirror is French bevel plate, 16x26 inches. The sideboard is handsomely ornamented with raised carvings. Fitted with best quality casters. Shipped direct from factory in Western Pennsylvania. Shipping weight, 175 pounds. Price..**$14.95**

OUR SIDEBOARDS ARE CAREFULLY PACKED TO INSURE SAFE DELIVERY AND SHIPPED DIRECT FROM FACTORY.

No. 1C913 This large Sideboard is made throughout of oak, thoroughly air seasoned and kiln dried. High gloss golden finish. It has a 23x48-inch double top. The base has full paneled ends and double top drawers with curved fronts, one of which is lined for silverware. Below is a large linen drawer and a roomy cupboard with double doors. Fitted with locks, keys, cast brass handles and best quality of casters. The extra large mirror is the best quality of French bevel plate, size, 18x32 inches. The top shelf is supported by gracefully curved and hand carved standards with claw feet. The crown is ornamented with heavy roll. Genuine hand carvings on the top and base are finely executed. Thoroughly well made and well finished throughout. This sideboard should be compared with those offered by others at $25.00 to $30.00. Shipped direct from factory in Central North Carolina or Southern Indiana. Shipping weight, about 190 pounds. Price.....**$15.25**

No. 1C920 This Sideboard is made from carefully selected oak in a fine golden finish. The base is 22 inches wide by 48 inches long. It has two spacious cupboards, one large linen drawer and two full swell front top drawers, one of which is lined for silverware. The mirror is best quality French beveled plate, size 18x36 inches. The elaborate, ornamental and finely executed hand carvings, the massive posts and handsome design make this sideboard very attractive. Fitted with best quality casters. Shipped direct from our warehouse in Louisville, Ky., Southern Indiana, or from factory in North Carolina, thereby insuring lowest freight rates. Shipping weight, 190 pounds. Price.....**$15.65**

No. 1C926 This Sideboard is made of thoroughly air seasoned and kiln dried solid oak, with highly figured quarter sawed oak front. Finished throughout in the popular golden finish. Base has a 22x48-inch double top, shaped to correspond with the serpentine curved front of the drawers. One of the upper drawers is lined for silverware. Lower part of the base contains linen drawer and spacious cupboard with double doors. Top is fitted with best quality French bevel plate mirror, 18x32 inches. The carvings throughout are hand made and finely executed. Has best quality casters and cast brass knobs and handles. An exceptionally handsome and well made sideboard at a very low price. Shipped direct from our factory in Southern Indiana. Shipping weight, 200 pounds. Price.....**$17.25**

No. 1C928 This Sideboard is made of quartered oak, finished golden, rubbed and highly polished. It is 48 inches long. Has two full swell top drawers, one lined for silverware. Has roomy swell front drawer directly underneath, and two large closets below, with swell front doors, solid panel ends. The mirror is French bevel plate, 18x32 inches. The ornamentations are finely executed hand carvings. Strictly high grade throughout. Fitted with best quality cast brass knobs, handles and casters. Shipped direct from our factory in Western Pennsylvania, thereby insuring lowest freight rates. Shipping weight, 200 pounds. Price.....**$17.45**

No. 1C932 This Sideboard is made of solid golden oak, high gloss finish. The base is 23 inches wide and 46 inches long. Has two full, swell top drawers, one of which is lined for silverware, a roomy drawer and two cupboards below. The mirror is French bevel plate, 18x30 inches. The sideboard is handsomely ornamented with heavy hand carvings and is fitted with cast brass knobs and handles and best quality casters. Carefully packed and shipped direct from factory in Wisconsin. Shipping weight, 185 pounds. Price.....**$17.35**

No. 1C940 This Handsome Sideboard is an entirely new design. Made of solid oak throughout with full quartered oak front. Popular golden hand rubbed polished finish. The base is 4 feet long and 2 feet wide. Has three small top drawers, the middle one lined for silverware. Large linen drawer and double cupboard below. The mirror is the best French bevel plate, size 18x36 inches. Richly ornamented with hand carvings and trimmed with best cast brass knobs, handles and casters. In every respect a strictly high grade sideboard. Retail stores ask $35.00 for this article. Shipped direct from our factory near Grand Rapids, Mich. Shipping weight, 200 pounds. Price.....**$18.85**

No. 1C943 This exceptionally attractive high grade Sideboard is made of figured quarter sawed golden oak, highly polished. Base has a 23x46-inch double top and inclosed mouse and dust-proof bottom. Drawers are fitted with special guides, locks and best cast brass handles. Note the massive front corner posts with hand made claw feet and roll below cupboard. Mirror is the best quality French bevel plate, size, 18x30 inches. Spacious top shelf supported by double Corinthian columns, below which are bracket shelves resting on standards with claw feet, all hand carved. Crown is decorated with smooth, finely cut hand made carving. Cabinet construction is strictly high grade. This sideboard should be compared with those sold in retail stores at $35.00 to $40.00. Shipped direct from factory in Central Wisconsin. Shipping weight, about 175 pounds. Price.....**$19.95**

No. 1C952 This Sideboard is made throughout of the choicest selected, highly figured quartered oak, golden finish, highly polished. Base is 22 inches wide and 50 inches long. Has solid paneled ends, two top drawers, one lined for silverware, one large linen drawer, all full swell front. A spacious cupboard below. Ornamented with genuine hand carvings, and French beveled plate mirror, size, 18x40 inches. Handles are best quality of cast brass. Best quality casters. This sideboard retails in stores at $45.00. Shipped direct from our factory in Western Pennsylvania. Shipping weight, 200 pounds. Price.....**$20.85**

No. 1C948 This Sideboard is made of golden oak, highly figured quartered oak front, rubbed and polished, and is 48 inches long and 22 inches wide. Has two upper swell front drawers, one lined for silverware, and the lower drawer is serpentine in shape, large and roomy. Below this are two cupboards. Top has French bevel plate mirror, 18x36 inches. The handles are solid brass. Best quality casters. Shipped direct from our factory near Grand Rapids, Mich. Shipping weight, 200 lbs. Price..... **$21.35**

No. 1C960 This Sideboard is made of quarter sawed oak throughout, finished golden, rubbed and highly polished. Base is 48 inches long. Has two roll front top drawers, one lined for silverware. Full swell large drawer directly below, and two large cupboards at the bottom. Best quality cast brass knobs, handles and locks. Mirror is best French bevel plate, 18x36 inches. The sideboard is handsomely decorated and ornamented with beautiful and finely executed hand carvings. Shipped direct from our factory near Grand Rapids, Mich. Shipping weight, 225 pounds. Price..... **$22.45**

No. 1C962 This Sideboard is made of solid quarter sawed oak, finished golden, and highly polished throughout. It is 48 inches long, 24 inches wide and has two full swell upper drawers, one lined for silverware, a double swell drawer directly below and two large, roomy cupboards at the bottom. Top has three mirrors, one of which is 20x24 inches, and the two smaller ones each 8x12 inches. Shipped direct from our factory near Grand Rapids, Mich. Shipping weight, 225 pounds. Price............ **$23.45**

No. 1C964 Exceptionally High Grade Sideboard. The cabinet work throughout is of the very best and the finish unsurpassed; made throughout of selected quartered oak; thoroughly air and kiln dried, finished golden, highly polished. Base is 24x48 inches with full swell top drawers, one lined for silverware. Roomy drawer and cupboard below. Has claw feet, best quality casters. Best quality French bevel plate mirror, 18x40 inches. The carvings are all very finely executed hand work. Shipped direct from factory in Northwestern Indiana. Shipping weight, 225 lbs. Price... **$24.45**

No. 1C968 This Sideboard is made of choice selected quarter sawed oak, highly polished, in a rich, golden finish. It is 4 feet long, 2 feet wide. Has two serpentine swell front top drawers, the right hand one lined and divided for silver. Large linen drawer at bottom underneath two large closets. Best brass trimmings. The mirror is the best French bevel plate; size, 18x40 inches. The rich hand carvings on the top and front are highly ornamental; fitted with best quality casters. Shipped direct from our factory near Grand Rapids, Michigan. Shipping weight, 225 pounds. Price....... **$25.45**

No. 1C966 This Massive Colonial Style Sideboard is made throughout of specially selected, richly figured, quarter sawed, thoroughly seasoned golden oak, highly polished. The base has a 24x54-inch double top. Solid panel ends. Below is a large linen drawer with serpentine curved front and roomy cupboard, the doors decorated with hand carved dragons' heads; extra large mirror is best quality French bevel plate; size, 18x40 inches. The broad top shelf is supported by massive curved columns, resting on bracket shelves, supported by hand carved claw feet. The crown is decorated with a heavy, cross banded veneered roll, and finely executed hand made carvings. Fitted with best quality locks, cast brass handles and casters. Cabinet construction strictly high grade in every detail. This sideboard to be fully appreciated must be seen and compared with those offered by others at $50.00 to $60.00. Shipped direct from factory in Western Pennsylvania. Shipping weight, about 250 pounds. Price.............. **$29.75**

No. 1C967 Massive Colonial Style Sideboard. Made of richly figured quarter sawed golden oak, highly polished. The beautiful arched canopy top has a large French bevel plate mirror; size, 20x30 inches. The china closets on each side have French bevel mirrors; size, 12x18 inches, also inside glass panels and doors. Base has a double top; size, 25x50 inches. It has single panel ends and inclosed mouse and dust proof bottom. Drawers are fitted with special drawer guides, best quality locks, cast brass handles. One top drawer lined for silverware. Best quality casters. Decorated with smooth, finely executed hand made carvings. Perfect in every detail of construction and finish. This sideboard cannot be purchased in retail stores for less than $50.00 to $60.00. Shipped direct from factory in central Wisconsin. Shipping weight, about 300 pounds. Price........... **$35.75**

No. 1C969 This Combination Sideboard and China Closet is made of highly figured quarter sawed oak in a golden finish. Height, 67 inches; width, 46 inches. The china compartment has four grooved shelves, a double thick glass end and door. It has two roomy drawers, below which is a spacious cupboard with double doors. Mirror is best quality French bevel plate; size, 14x20 inches. A broad and convenient shelf extends entire length of top. Ornamented with genuine hand carvings. Fitted with locks, keys and best quality cast brass handles. Thoroughly well made in every detail of construction and finish. Sells in retail stores for $25.00. Carefully packed to insure safe delivery and shipped direct from factory in Northern Illinois. Shipping weight, about 175 pounds. Price.............. **$19.45**

No. 1C970 This Combination Sideboard and China Closet is a useful and ornamental addition to the dining room. Made of highly figured quarter sawed golden oak, highly polished. Height, 70 inches; length, 46 inches. The china cabinet has four adjustable grooved shelves, a double thick glass end and a full swell front glass door. It has two roomy drawers. The top one has a curved front and is lined for silverware. Below the drawers is a **spacious cupboard** with double doors. The mirror is the best quality French bevel plate, size, 14x20 inches. It has a broad top shelf. Decorated with finely executed hand carvings. Fitted with locks, keys and best quality cast brass handles. Strictly high grade in construction and finish. Shipped direct from factory in Northern Illinois. Shipping weight, about 190 pounds. Price.............. **$21.35**

No. 1C971 This Handsome Combination Sideboard and China Closet is made of specially selected, highly figured quarter sawed golden oak, highly polished. It is supported by hand carved French curved claw feet. China compartment has four grooved shelves, double thick glass end and full swell bent glass door with a top panel of highly ornamental genuine lead glass. It has two large drawers, the top one of which has a curved front and is lined for silverware. Below drawers, a roomy cupboard with double doors. It is 72 inches high, 50 inches wide. Mirror is best quality French bevel plate, size, 18x22 inches. It has a broad top shelf supported on the right hand corner by a beautiful column. Decorated with genuine hand carvings. Fitted with locks, keys and best quality cast brass handles. Carefully packed and shipped direct from factory in Northern Illinois. Shipping weight, about 200 pounds. Price.............. **$25.85**

No. 1C975 This Buffet Sideboard and China Cabinet Combination makes a very ornamental and useful addition to a dining room. The wood is highly figured quarter sawed golden oak, polished finish. Height, 52 inches; length, 38 inches. It has a large drawer, below which is a convenient and useful compartment for chinaware, silverware, etc., fitted with genuine leaded glass doors. The mirror on the top is the best quality French bevel plate, size, 10x34 inches. Note the shapely French curved front legs. Fitted with locks, keys and cast brass handles. Cabinet work and finish strictly high grade. Shipped direct from factory in Northern Illinois. Shipping weight, about 130 pounds. Price.. **$12.85**

No. 1C976 This illustration shows a new and very attractive design in a combination of Buffet Sideboard and China Cabinet. The wood is highly figured quarter sawed golden oak, polished finish. Height, 55 inches; length, 44 inches. The base has two top drawers for silverware, etc., and a large linen drawer at the bottom between which is a spacious china cabinet with beautiful leaded glass doors. The mirror on top is the best quality French bevel plate, size, 10x38 inches. The carvings are genuine hand made. Fitted with locks, keys, cast brass handles and best quality casters. Original in design, high grade in wood, construction and finish. Shipped direct from factory in Northern Illinois. Shipping weight, about 150 pounds. Price.............. **$14.75**

No. 1C977 This Buffet Sideboard is made of the finest selected quarter sawed oak with a beautiful highly figured grain and a highly polished finish. The base is 23 inches wide by 48 inches long, and has one large linen drawer, two spacious cupboards and two full swell top drawers, one of which is lined for silverware. The mirror in the top is the best quality French bevel plate, size, 14x36 inches. A high grade article in every detail of construction and finish. Shipped direct from our warehouses in Louisville, Ky., or Southern Indiana or from factory in North Carolina, thereby insuring lowest freight rates. Shipping weight, 175 pounds.

Price, quarter sawed oak........ **$14.95**

No. 1C978 This Buffet Sideboard is made of quarter sawed golden oak, highly polished. The base has a 22x44-inch double top with round edges and corners. It has two top drawers with swell fronts, one of which is lined for silverware. Below is a large linen drawer and a roomy cupboard with double doors. Fitted special guides with locks, keys and cast brass handles. Best quality casters. Supported by French curved legs with claw feet. Single paneled ends and inclosed mouse and dust proof bottom. Best quality French bevel plate mirror, size 14x36 inches. The convenient top shelf is supported by shapely curved standards with claw feet. Ornamented with deeply cut carvings on the top and base. Cabinet construction high grade. This buffet should be compared with those offered by others at $25.00 to $30.00. Shipped direct from factory in Central Wisconsin. Shipping weight about 160 lbs. Price, **$17.85**

No. 1C979 This Buffet Sideboard cannot be fully appreciated until seen. The wood is highly figured quarter sawed golden oak, highly polished. The base is 45 by 22 inches and contains two top small drawers, one lined for silverware, below which is a roomy cupboard with double doors. Base has solid panel ends supported with shaped French legs with hand carved claw feet. Handsome top, fitted with best quality French bevel plate mirror, size 12x36 inches, with a roomy shelf above it. Cabinet construction, wood, and finish the highest grade. Shipped direct from factory in Northern Indiana. Shipping weight, about 175 pounds. Price........ **$17.95**

No. 1C980 This Handsome New Design Buffet Sideboard is made of highly figured quarter sawed oak, hand polished, golden finish. The top is 43 inches long. The fine French beveled plate mirror in top section is 10x30 inches. The base contains two drawers, one of them lined for silverware and two closets. The shapely hand carved posts and claw feet, strictly high grade construction and beautiful finish makes this a very attractive and useful article. Shipped direct from our factory near Grand Rapids, Michigan. Shipping weight, 175 pounds.

Price, quarter sawed oak........ **$18.75**

No. 1C982 A new design made of choice flaky grained quarter sawed oak in a beautiful golden polished finish. The base is supported by full double curved French shaped legs with hand carved claws. Two cupboards, two swell front center drawers and two double curved top drawers fill the base, which is 23 inches wide by 48 inches long. The right hand top drawer is lined for silverware. The handsome top is hand carved and fitted with a genuine French plate mirror, 14x36 inches. Shipped direct from our warehouses in Louisville, Ky., Southern Indiana, or from factory in North Carolina, thereby insuring lowest freight rates. Shipping weight, 175 pounds.

Price........ **$18.95**

No. 1C986 This Combination Buffet China Cabinet is made of highly figured quarter sawed oak, in a golden polished finish. Height, 4 feet 4 inches; width, 3 feet 4 inches; depth, 16 inches. The china compartments in the ends, each have two shelves and full swell bent glass doors, size, 14x24 inches. It has two drawers and a spacious cupboard, fitted with lock, keys and best cast brass handles. Top ornamented with a shapely mirror of the best quality French bevel plate, size, 8x30 inches; supported by French curved legs. Thoroughly well made and a wonderful bargain at our price. Shipped direct from factory in Southern Indiana. Shipping weight, about 150 pounds. Price........ **$13.85**

CHINA CABINETS.

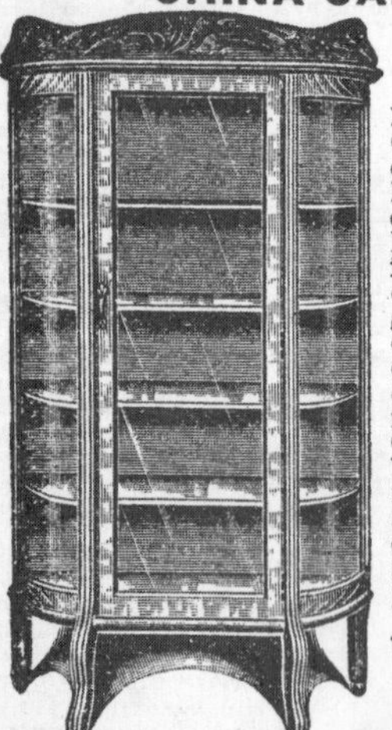

Our Leader.

No. 1C1043 This Handsome China Closet is made of thoroughly seasoned and kiln dried quarter sawed oak in a golden finish. It is 64 inches high, 36 inches wide and 14 inches deep. Fitted with four grooved shelves. It has double thick bent glass ends and large glass door. Thoroughly well made in every detail. Ornamental in design, beautiful in finish. It must be seen to be fully appreciated. Shipped direct from factory in Southern Indiana. Shipping weight, 150 pounds.

Price, as illustrated........ **$9.45**

This China Cabinet has full swell double thick bent glass ends and front. The wood is thoroughly air seasoned and kiln dried, specially selected, highly figured quarter sawed oak, polished golden finish. Height, 67 inches; width, 36 inches; depth, 16 inches. Mirror on top, 6x18 inches; mirror on back of top shelf, 9x30 inches, both best quality French plate. Finished back, double grooved shelves. Best quality French plate mirror for back of any shelf, $1.45 per shelf. Handsome in design, high grade in construction, beautiful in wood and finish. Shipped direct from factory in Central Indiana. Shipping weight, 175 pounds.

No. 1C1053 Price, as illustrated........ **$12.95**

No. 1C1057 Price, mirror in top decoration only........ **$11.50**

For beauty of design, high quality of finish and construction this China Cabinet cannot be excelled. Made of specially selected quarter sawed oak, golden finish, highly polished. It has full swell double thick glass ends, grooved shelves, hand carved claw feet. The ornamental hand carved canopy top has French beveled mirror, 8x36 inches. Height, 73 inches; width, 45 inches. French plate mirrors furnished for back of any shelf at $2.25 per shelf. Shipped direct from factory in Chicago. Shipping weight, 190 pounds.

No. 1C1058 Price mirror in top decoration only...... **$18.95**

No. 1C1059 Price, mirrors as illustrated........ **$20.45**

This China Cabinet is the most wonderful value ever offered. Made of thoroughly air seasoned and kiln dried quarter sawed oak in a beautiful golden finish, 70 inches high, 39 inches wide, supported by French shaped legs. It has hand carved top, finished back, grooved shelves, double thick glass ends. Mirror in top shelf best quality French plate, size 10x30 inches. Construction strictly first class. Best quality French plate mirror furnished for back of any shelf at $2.25 per shelf. Complete with casters. Shipped direct from factory in Chicago. Shipping weight, 175 pounds.

No. 1C1051 Price, without mirror........ **$10.95**

No. 1C1052 Price, as illustrated........ **12.95**

This China Cabinet is made of selected quarter sawed golden oak, thoroughly air seasoned and kiln dried. It is 69 inches high, 41 inches wide, fitted with best quality double thick bent glass ends. Mirror in top decoration 26x6 inches, mirror in top shelf 10x36 inches, both best quality of French plate. Grooved shelves, finished back. French plate mirrors furnished for back of any shelf at $2.25 per shelf. Shipped direct from factory in Chicago. Shipping weight, 175 pounds.

No. 1C1054 Price, without mirrors........ **$12.35**

No. 1C1055 Price, with mirror in top ornament only.... **$13.45**

No. 1C1056 Price, as illustrated, **$15.45**

This handsome China Cabinet is made of the choicest quarter sawed golden oak, piano polished. 79 inches high, 47 inches wide. The best quality French bevel mirror, 8x22 inches, in genuine hand carved canopy top decoration. It has massive round posts, heavy hand carved claw feet, grooved shelves and full swell double thick glass ends. French plate mirrors furnished for back of any shelf at $2.25 per shelf. Shipped direct from factory in Chicago. Shipping weight, 225 pounds.

No. 1C1060 Price, mirror in top decoration only........ **$24.85**

No. 1C1061 Price, mirrors as illustrated........ **$26.95**

SPECIAL DIVISION OF COMBINATION BOOKCASES.

WE HAVE MADE A SPECIAL DIVISION FOR COMBINATION BOOKCASES IN OUR FURNITURE DEPARTMENT as our sales on this line of merchandise have so increased in the last few years, and we have been able, by reducing the cost and improving the quality, to develop this line of case goods until it has become such an important branch of our Furniture Department that we have decided, in this issue of our catalogue, to devote more space to it than ever before and to let these goods form a special division of our Furniture Department. Moreover, we have completed an unusually advantageous contract with one of the largest and best manufacturers of case furniture in the United States, a contract that enables us to offer our customers greater values than ever before in this line, and we know that no one who has any idea of buying a combination bookcase and writing desk can afford to overlook the special values we offer.

OUR COMBINATION BOOKCASES this season, for beauty of design, high quality of construction and finish and convenience in arrangement and for extraordinary value, are positively unequaled. They embody all the new ideas in bookcase construction, the designs are greatly improved over any previous season and every one represents the product of the most up to date and modern machinery, the best material to be obtained and put together by the most skilled workmanship that money can buy.

A SAVING OF 35 TO 40 PER CENT in this line of combination bookcases. We effect a saving of 35 to 40 per cent for our customers in price as against the prices asked in retail furniture stores. We have made an investigation and we know the prices that small manufacturers, wholesalers, furniture jobbers and manufacturer's agents are asking of the retail trade for goods of this description. We have gone out and bought in retail furniture stores combination bookcases that compare with those we offer and we find that the bookcase that equals ours in quality is retailed at $5.00 to $12.00 more than our price; and in fact, we know that we are selling these goods direct to our customers for the same or less money than retail dealers pay at wholesale.

OUR PROTECTION TO OUR CUSTOMERS. In order that you need not feel that you are taking the slightest risk in sending to us for a combination bookcase, if you have any doubt as to the great values we offer, we wish to say that we stand ready to refund your money immediately and pay the freight charges both ways if the bookcase you get from us is not perfectly satisfactory in every way. We also guarantee these combination bookcases in every respect for quality of material, workmanship and finish, and if the bookcase you get from us is defective in any way return it, and your money will be refunded. In any case, if you are not perfectly satisfied we will see that your money is returned and the transaction will not cost you one cent.

FREIGHT CHARGES. In order to save handling expense, which helps to make our low prices possible, we ship these combination bookcases direct from the factory. The freight charges will amount to very little as compared with what you will save in price. The weight of each case is given in the description, and by referring to page 630 you can calculate almost to a cent what the freight will amount to. Always bear in mind that you pay the freight, whether you buy from us or from your local dealer, as your local dealer must figure the freight charges that he pays in fixing his selling prices.

HOW OUR COMBINATION BOOKCASES ARE MADE

and explaining why these goods are so much better than the ordinary class of combination bookcases sold in regular furniture stores.

THE WOOD used in the construction of our combination bookcases is specially selected, highly figured oak. It is thoroughly air seasoned and kiln dried before being put through the factory. Great care is taken to get the highest quality and the choicest flaky grained lumber.

THE CONSTRUCTION of our combination bookcases is strictly high grade, the best that modern machinery and skilled workmanship can produce. The framework is carefully joined and mortised evenly together, and grooves carefully fitted. The drawers all dovetailed on the sides, and grooved on the backs and bottoms. The panels are made of transverse layers of highly figured, flaky grained oak, which prevents warping or shrinkage. Every part and piece is carefully and perfectly fitted. The drawers all work smoothly without friction, and the doors close without binding. The hand carving is finely executed, and new and original in design.

THE MIRRORS used in our combination cases are the very best quality of genuine heavy thick French beveled plate, with a perfect beveled edge and a perfect reflection. We do not use any cheap domestic plate mirrors.

THE FINISH. The hardwood oil, the glue and the varnish used in the finishing of our combination case is of the highest grade obtainable. Special care is taken in the finishing of each case, plenty of time being given for each case to thoroughly harden and dry before rubbing and polishing down for the next coat. The color is a beautiful golden, which brings out the handsome flaky grain of the wood perfectly. A smooth surface, a better luster, and a finish that will not check or become dull; that will look better after years of use than the ordinary finished cases turned out by other factories do in one month, is guaranteed in every case we sell. You cannot fully appreciate the immense saving in price, the high quality of the materials and the finish of our cases unless you compare them with those offered by others at 30 to 40 per cent higher in price. It is difficult for you, by the illustrations and descriptions, to compare satisfactorily the real value, but if you take any case that we offer and place it alongside of any case offered by any other house at anything approaching our price, you will at once see that with our facilities we are furnishing you a much higher grade of goods at a great saving in price, much lower than you can possibly buy elsewhere.

THE WONDER OF OUR BOOKCASE LINE

OUR COMBINATION BOOKCASE AND WRITING DESK COMBINED OFFERED AT $7.35

No. 1C1102

$7.35 is our price for this handsome, high grade, Combination Bookcase and Writing Desk, a price that is possible only by reason of our advantageous and extremely large contract direct with the manufacturer and because we ask the narrowest kind of a profit above the actual cost of material and labor.

DESCRIPTION. This combination bookcase and writing desk is made of solid oak, golden finish, handsomely carved. The lid of the desk and glass frame of bookcase section are made of highly figured quarter sawed oak. This case is 72 inches high by 37 inches w de, and has a new and handsome design mirror made of the best quality heavy thick French bevel plate mirror, 12x12 inches in size. The writing desk is filled with pigeonholes, pen racks and compartments for envelopes and writing paper and stationery. Below the writing desk is a roomy cupboard for papers, magazines and other periodicals. The left hand side of the case is arranged for books. The glass door is made of clear double thick stock, firmly set into the rigid and well fitting frame. The door and desk lid are fitted with locks and keys. The back is full paneled to prevent warping. The entire case is made of thoroughly seasoned and kiln dried stock. **The frame is carefully constructed and fitted in a strictly first class manner.**

IF YOU PLACE YOUR ORDER WITH US for this special $7.35 combination bookcase and writing desk, you will be getting a wonderful value indeed, an article of furniture that is useful and ornamental, substantially built, highly finished, a piece of furniture wherein the price does not give a fair idea of the quality, and you will be getting it for really less money than the ordinary dealer pays at wholesale. This $7.35 combination bookcase and writing desk is a leader in this division of our furniture department. It is a piece of furniture that will astonish dealers as well as users when it is seen and examined. Dealers who are posted in the line will wonder how we can furnish it at the price, they will surely believe that we are offering it as a leader, below cost, which is not the case. It is a fair example of the values to be found throughout our entire furniture department, and the price is possible, by reason of our great advantages in buying, handling and selling the goods and our willingness to accept by far a smaller profit than any other dealer could afford to accept. **Send us your order for one of these handsome combination bookcases and writing desks, at our special $7.35 price,** show it to your friends and neighbors, let anyone, competent to judge, examine it carefully, **and if you and everyone does not admit that it is surely the greatest bargain in this line ever seen or heard of, you can return it to us and we will return your money and pay freight charges both ways,** and you will not be put to one penny's expense. Shipping weight, 150 pounds.

No. 1C1102 Combination Bookcase and Writing Desk. Price, $7.35

Wonderful Value at $8.95.

No. 1C1108 This Combination Bookcase is 72 inches high and 37 inches wide, is made of quarter sawed oak throughout, beautifully carved and highly polished. The handsomely shaped French bevel plate mirror is 12x12 inches in size. The case is trimmed with best quality brass handles, hinges and locks, and mounted on casters. Carefully packed and crated and shipped direct from our factory at Rockford, Ill. Shipping weight, 140 pounds.
Price........$8.95

No. 1C1107 This Handsome Combination Bookcase and Writing Desk is made of quarter sawed golden oak, thoroughly air seasoned. High gloss finish. It is 72 inches high and 38 inches wide. The desk has a convenient drawer and pigeonhole space inside, for letters, stationery, etc. Below desk is a large drawer and roomy cupboard. Bookcase has four adjustable shelves. Above the desk is a bracket shelf and a pattern shaped French bevel plate mirror, size, 12 by 12 inches. Desk lid and crown decorated with genuine hand carvings. Fitted with lock, keys, cast brass handles and best quality casters. Wonderful value at our price. Shipped direct from factory in Southern Indiana. Shipping weight, about 150 pounds.
Price..............$9.45

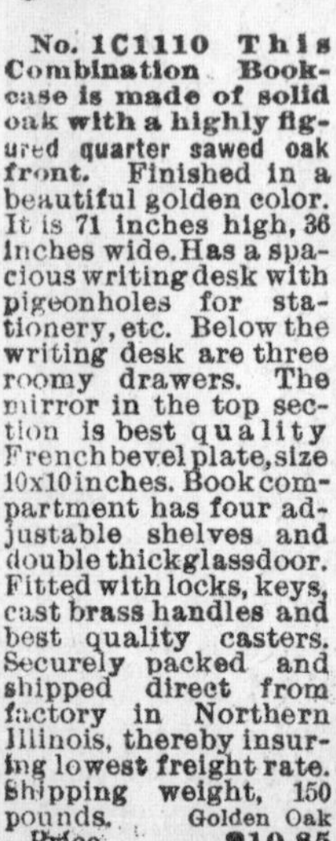

No. 1C1109 This Handsome Combination Bookcase and Desk is made of quarter sawed golden oak, excellently made and finished. It is 71 inches high and 39 inches wide and is fitted with a 12x12-inch handsomely shaped French bevel plate mirror. Inside of desk is provided with pigeonholes for envelopes and writing paper and other stationery. Below this is a roomy cupboard with door nicely ornamented, fitted with locks and keys, trimmings are of cast brass, with casters. Shipping weight, 150 pounds. Shipped direct from our factory at Rockford, Ill. Price, $9.95

No. 1C1110 This Combination Bookcase is made of solid oak with a highly figured quarter sawed oak front. Finished in a beautiful golden color. It is 71 inches high, 36 inches wide. Has a spacious writing desk with pigeonholes for stationery, etc. Below the writing desk are three roomy drawers. The mirror in the top section is best quality French bevel plate, size 10x10 inches. Book compartment has four adjustable shelves and double thick glass door. Fitted with locks, keys, cast brass handles and best quality casters. Securely packed and shipped direct from factory in Northern Illinois, thereby insuring lowest freight rate. Shipping weight, 150 pounds. Golden Oak
Price........$10.85

No. 1C1112½ This Solid Oak Combination Bookcase is one of the latest designs this season. The front is made of highly figured quarter sawed oak. Height, 75 inches; width, 38 inches. Interior of desk is fitted with pigeonholes for stationery. Below the writing desk are a drawer and spacious cupboard. Desk is ornamented with a French bevel mirror, 12x12 inches. Glass door is full swell. Thoroughly well made and well finished case, fitted with best cast brass handles, locks and keys. Packed and shipped direct from our factory at Rockford, Ill. Shipping weight, 150 pounds.
Price..........$11.15

No. 1C1114 This Combination Bookcase is one of the latest designs for this season, made of highly figured quartered oak. Height, 70 inches; width, 36 inches. Interior of desk is arranged for stationery and below the writing desk are three roomy drawers fitted with locks and keys. Desk is ornamented with a French bevel plate mirror, size 10x12 inches. This is an exceptionally well made and finished case and is fitted with best cast brass handles and best quality casters. Shipped direct from our factory at Rockford, Ill., thereby insuring lowest freight rate. Shipping weight, 150 pounds.
Price..........$11.75

No. 1C1123 This Combination Book Case and Writing Desk is made of highly figured quarter sawed golden oak or of birch in imitation of mahogany. Height, 72 inches, width, 39 inches. Book compartment has four adjustable shelves and full swell bent glass door. Interior of writing desk fitted with pigeonholes, pen racks, etc. Below writing desk is a swell front drawer and large cupboard. The highly ornamental top has a center bracket shelf and is fitted with a shapely French plate mirror, best quality, size 12x14 inches, fitted with locks, keys, cast brass handles and best quality casters. Shipped direct from factory in Northern Illinois. Shipping weight, about 150 pounds.

Quartered Oak Price............$12.50 Imitation Mahogany $12.45

No. 1C1132 This Handsome High Grade Combination Bookcase and Writing Desk is especially designed for us. This case is 71 inches high, 38 inches wide and is made of the best quality quarter sawed oak throughout; hand carved, highly polished. Handsome 12x14-inch French bevel plate mirror above the writing desk. Interior of desk is partitioned for stationery. The door of the bookcase has bent glass, trimmed with best quality cast brass handles, with casters. Carefully packed and shipped direct from our factory at Rockford, Ill. Shipping weight, 150 pounds.
Price, oak $13.85
Mahogany 13.75

No. 1C1133 This Combination Bookcase should be compared with those sold at retail for $20.00. It is made of highly figured quarter sawed oak, in a beautiful golden polished finish. Height, 73 inches; width, 39 inches. The ornamental hand carved top is fitted with pattern shaped French bevel plate mirror, size 14x14 inches. Book section has four adjustable shelves and double thick bent glass door, full swell. Writing desk is fitted with spacious pigeonholes for stationery, etc. Three roomy drawers below desk are fitted with locks, keys and best brass handles. Shipped direct from factory at Rockford, Ill. Shipping weight, 150 lbs. Quartered Oak
Price.........$13.95

No. 1C1120 This Handsome Combination Bookcase and Writing Desk is 72 inches high and 3 feet 2 inches wide, is made of solid quarter sawed oak, beautifully carved and highly polished throughout. 12x12-inch French bevel plate mirror; door is bent glass. The interior of the desk is provided with compartments for stationery, while the lower part of the writing desk forms a handsome cupboard. Fitted with best quality brass trimmings, complete with casters. Shipped direct from factory at Rockford, Ill. Shipping weight, 150 lbs. Price....$11.95

No. 1C1137½ This Handsome Combination Bookcase and Writing Desk is one of the best examples of the cabinet maker's art. The wood is highly figured quarter sawed golden oak or birch in a beautiful imitation of mahogany. Height, 74 inches, width, 39 inches. Book section has four adjustable shelves and full swell front glass door. Below the conveniently arranged writing compartment are three roomy drawers. The top drawer has a full swell front. The artistic and attractively designed top is hand carved and fitted with a genuine French bevel plate mirror; size, 12x16 inches. This case is wonderful value at our price. Shipped direct from factory in Northern Illinois. Shipping weight, about 150 pounds. Quartered Oak
Price.......$14.25
Imitation Mahogany
Price.....$14.20

No. 1C1139 This Combination Bookcase and Writing Desk is made of selected quarter sawed golden oak or birch, in a perfect imitation of mahogany. Highly polished. Height, 72 inches, width, 39 inches. Full swell bent glass door, with four adjustable shelves in book section. Writing compartment fitted with convenient arrangement of pigeonhole space and drawers. Above writing desk is a spacious compartment for magazines, papers, etc., fitted with best quality French bevel mirror; size, 10x16 inches. Below writing desk is a curved front drawer and roomy cupboard. The hand carved top is fitted with the best quality French bevel plate mirror; size, 6 x 18 inches. Fitted with locks, keys, cast brass handles and best quality casters. Shipped direct from factory in Northern Illinois. Shipping weight, about 150 pounds.
Golden Quartered Oak
Price.......$15.25
Imitation Mahogany
Price.......$15.20

Wonderful Value for $15.40.

No. 1C1140 Combination Bookcase and Writing Desk. Made of quartered golden oak, beautifully carved and highly polished. It is 74 inches high and 41 inches wide, has handsome shaped French bevel plate mirror, 12x14 inches, has shelf over the bookcase part and also over the writing desk. Interior of the desk is arranged with pigeonholes for envelopes, letter paper, etc. Below the writing desk is a handsome swell front drawer, and two straight front roomy drawers below. The glass in the bookcase door is double thick and all handles are solid brass, and the casters steel frame. Shipped direct from factory in Northern Illinois. Shipping weight, 175 pounds.

Price, quartered oak.............. **$15.45**
Price, mahogany finish........... **$15.40**

Great Value at $15.90.

No. 1C1141½ Combination Bookcase is 6 feet 5 inches high, and 3 feet 2 inches wide, fitted with the best quality French plate mirror, 12x16 inches. Made of selected quarter sawed oak or birch, imitation of mahogany, polished finish. It has a curved front, double thick bent glass door, with adjustable shelves in book section. Interior of desk has drawer and pigeonhole space, nicely arranged for stationery. Below the desk are three spacious drawers, the top one has curved front; fitted with locks, keys, cast brass handles, and best quality casters. The handsome and ornamental top is decorated with genuine hand carvings, finely executed. For beauty of design, choice grained wood and high class construction, this case cannot be excelled. Thoroughly well packed and shipped direct from factory in Northern Illinois. Shipping weight, 175 lbs.

Price, quartered oak.......... **$15.95**
Price, mahogany finish.............. **15.90**

No. 1C1154 Another New and Attractive Design Combination Bookcase and Writing Desk. Made of air seasoned quarter sawed golden oak or birch in perfect imitation of mahogany, highly polished. Height, 74 in.; width, 41 in. Book section fitted with four adjustable shelves and full swell bevel glass door. Writing desk compartment fitted with a convenient arrangement of pigeonholes, pen racks and drawers. Below writing desk are three large drawers with full swell front. Above desk a spacious cupboard for magazines, papers, etc., fitted with a genuine French bevel mirror; size, 8x16 inches, above which is a glass lattice panel. Fitted with locks, keys, cast brass handles and best quality casters. Shipped direct from factory in Northern Illinois. Shipping weight, about 175 pounds.

Price, quartered oak.... ....**$18.95**
Price, imitation mahogany......... **18.85**

No. 1C1155 This Combination Canopy Top Bookcase and Writing Desk is 6 feet 4 inches high, 3 feet 4 inches wide. It is made of choicest selected quarter sawed oak, or birch, in perfect imitation of mahogany, hand polished finish. Highly ornamental top, fitted with French bevel plate mirror, 8x36 inches. Interior of desk fitted with drawers and pigeonholes for stationery. Above the desk a spacious cupboard, with glass door lattice work front. The book section has a curved front double thick glass door. The shelves are adjustable to any size book. Below the desk are three roomy drawers. Desk lid, drawers and doors fitted with locks and best cast brass handles. Packed and shipped direct from our factory in Rockford, Ill. Shipping weight, 175 pounds.

Price, quartered oak.............**$19.75**
Price, mahogany finish.................. **19.70**

Double Combination Bookcase.

No. 1C1158 This Beautiful Double Combination Bookcase and Writing Desk is 73 inches high and 53 inches wide. Made of thoroughly air seasoned and kiln dried highly figured quarter sawed golden oak or of birch in a perfect imitation of mahogany, highly polished. Book compartments have eight adjustable shelves and fitted with double thick, full swell bevel glass doors. Interior of writing desk fitted with drawer, pigeonholes for stationery, pen racks, etc. Below writing desk are three roomy drawers. Mirror is best quality French bevel plate, size 14x18 inches, ornamental bracket shelf below mirror. Decorated with genuine hand carvings. Shipped direct from factory in Northern Illinois. Shipping weight, about 250 pounds.

	Quartered Oak	Mahogany Finish
Price..........................	**$21.25**	**$21.20**

Double Combination Bookcase.

No. 1C1159 This Magnificent Combination Bookcase and Writing Desk is made of specially selected high figured quarter sawed oak in golden finish, highly polished. Length, 57 inches, height, 73 inches. Book compartments have eight adjustable shelves and full swell bent glass doors. Writing desk is fitted with pigeonholes, drawers, pen racks, etc. Below writing desk are the roomy drawers, the top one of which has curved front. The mirror is the best quality French bevel plate, size, 14x14 inches. Above mirror is a convenient shelf supported by hand carved dragons' heads. Fitted with locks, keys, cast brass handles and best quality casters. The high grade construction, beautiful wood and finish must be seen to be fully appreciated. Sells for $35.00 to $40.00 in retail stores. Shipped direct from factory in Northern Illinois. Shipping weight, about 250 pounds.

	Quartered Oak	Mahogany Finish
Price........................	**$25.45**	**$25.35**

No. 1C1145 This Handsome Combination Bookcase and Writing Desk is made of highly figured, quarter sawed, golden oak, highly polished. height, 76 inches; width, 40 inches. Book section has four adjustable shelves and a full swell front bent glass door. Writing desk is fitted with pigeonholes, drawers, pen racks, etc. Below writing desk are three roomy drawers, the top one of which has a curved front. The mirror is the best quality French bevel plate, size, 16x18 inches. High grade in construction, handsome in design and beautiful in finish. Shipped direct from factory in Northern Illinois. Shipping weight, about 175 pounds.

Price, quartered oak **$16.95**
Price, mahogany finish...............**$16.90**

A Strictly High Class Piece of Furniture.

No. 1C1148 This double Combination Bookcase and Writing Desk is made of selected quarter sawed oak with highly figured, grain polished finish. Height, 6 feet 2 inches; width, 4 feet 9 inches. The hand carved and ornamental top is fitted with a genuine French beveled plate mirror, 14x14 inches. The desk in center is fitted with drawers and pigeonholes for stationery. Below desk are three roomy drawers. Book sections on each side have adjustable shelves for any size book. Best quality double thick glass doors. Well packed and shipped direct from our factory in Rockford, Ill. Shipping weight, 225 pounds.

Price, quartered oak.................................**$19.85**

No. 1C1142 This Combination Bookcase and Writing Desk is unusually handsome in design. Is 70 inches high and 39 inches wide, made of the very best selected highly figured quartered oak or genuine mahogany. Interior of writing desk is partitioned for stationery. Below are three drawers, the top one with full roll front, all fitted with best quality cast brass handles and locks. Above the writing desk is a spacious cupboard with French bevel plate mirror, 10x14 inches, in the door. Bookcase has swell front bent glass door. The top has a handsome shaped French bevel plate mirror, 6x34 inches, and the entire case is ornamented with sunken carvings of tasty design. A strictly high class piece of furniture. Shipped direct from factory in Northern Illinois. Shipping weight, 175 pounds.

	Quartered Oak	Mahogany Finish
Price.....	**$17.45**	**$17.40**

No. 1C1157 This Beautiful Combination Bookcase and Writing Desk is made of highly figured quarter sawed oak in a beautiful golden finish, highly polished. Height, 76 inches; width, 42 inches. Book compartment has four adjustable shelves and full swell bent glass door. Writing desk is partitioned for envelopes, papers, etc. Below writing desk are three spacious drawers with full swell front. The handsome top has a broad shelf and is fitted with one large French bevel plate mirror; size, 16x16 inches, and one French bevel plate mirror, 6x14 inches. Fitted with cast brass handles, locks and keys and best quality casters. A highly ornamental and useful addition to the home. Shipped direct from factory in Northern Illinois. Shipping weight, about 175 pounds.

Price, quartered oak...................**$20.25**
Price, mahogany finish................... **20.20**

Our $13.95 Combination Bookcase.

No. 1C1149 This Combination Bookcase and Writing Desk is made of solid oak in a fine golden finish. It stands 7 feet 10 inches high, 3 feet wide. The top section contains shelves adjustable to any size book. The base has three spacious drawers, The drop leaf of the writing desk is 16x34 inches. The roomy interior of the desk compartment is fitted with pigeonholes for stationery. The drawers and doors fitted with locks and keys and cast brass handles. The doors are fitted with double strength, clear glass doors. A convenient, substantial, thoroughly well made article throughout. Retail dealers ask double our price for such an article. Packed and shipped direct from our factory in Western Illinois. Shipping weight, 175 lbs.

Price, golden oak...................................**$13.95**

BOOKCASES.

No. 1C1156 This Bookcase, especially designed for hanging or standing is 25 inches high, 18⅛ inches wide and has three shelves, 5¾ inches deep. It will hold 50 average size books. Easily attached to wall or picture moulding. Made of thoroughly seasoned oak in a golden finish. Substantial in construction. Shipping weight, 25 pounds.
Price, golden oak.......45c

No. 1C1160 Neat, Attractive, Roomy Bookcase. Upper panel carved. Height, 52 inches; width, 24 inches; depth, 12 inches. Made of solid oak, golden or weathered finish or birch imitation mahogany; adjustable shelves, glass door. Takes up little room space. Weight, crated, 75 pounds. Shipped direct from factory in Chicago.
Price, golden oak.....**$4.95**
Price, weathered oak, 4.90
Price, mahogany finish 4.85

No. 1C1162 This Bookcase is made of beautifully figured, quartered oak, finished golden. Height, 57 inches; width, 24 inches. Has four adjustable shelves and door with double thick glass. Fitted with best quality casters, brass hinges, handle and lock. Guaranteed a strictly first class piece of furniture. Weight, 90 pounds. Shipped direct from factory in Northern Illinois. Price......**$5.35**

No. 1C1163 This is the greatest value in a Bookcase with two doors we have ever been able to show; the best constructed and most serviceable case of its kind on the market. Made of highly figured quartered golden oak or birch mahogany finish. It is 66 inches high and 31 inches wide. Has four adjustable shelves and double doors. It has a 12x6-inch French bevel plate mirror. Shipped direct from factory at Northern Ill. Weight, 90 pounds. Price, oak.....**$6.90**
Price, birch mahogany.. **6.95**

No. 1C1168 This Handsome Oak Bookcase is made from carefully selected stock, beautifully carved and ornamented. It stands 80 inches high, 41½ inches wide, 16 inches deep; has four strong, adjustable shelves, doors fitted with double thick glass, with lock and key. Has two drawers at bottom fitted with brass pulls; can also be used as a china closet and cupboard. Carefully crated to insure safe delivery and shipped direct from factory in Southern Indiana. Weight, packed for shipment, 140 pounds.
Price.................**$7.95**

Revolving Bookcase for $2.35.

No. 1C1184 This Revolving Bookcase is made of hard wood thoroughly seasoned and kiln dried, in a beautiful golden finish. The top section is attached to the base by steel ball bearings. Height, 3 feet; top is 19x19 inches; shelves, 16x16 inches. This case will accommodate 75 average books. Thoroughly substantial in construction. A splendid bookcase for the home or office. So constructed that it can be shipped knocked down, packed securely, shipped direct from factory in Chicago. Shipping weight, 35 pounds.
Price, golden birch....**$2.35**

Reduced to $9.45.

No. 1C1176 Bookcase is 5 feet 9 inches high and 38 inches wide, and made of quarter sawed oak, finished in a beautiful golden color; the shelves are adjustable and the doors are of extra double thick glass. This case has finest inside finish, the casters are best quality. It must be seen to be fully appreciated. Shipped direct from factory in Chicago. Shipping weight, 130 pounds.
Price.........**$9.45**

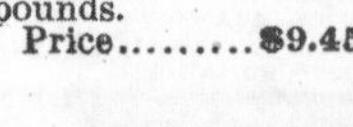

No. 1C1180 This is a Very Heavy, Richly Finished Bookcase; every bookcase made from carefully selected quarter sawed golden oak, with a high piano polish finish. Has three doors, as illustrated; doors are fitted with double thick glass; adjustable shelves; the bookcase is large and roomy; it is 61 inches wide and 54 inches high. Shipped direct from factory at Northern Illinois. Weight, complete, 175 pounds.
Price...**$15.95**

Improved Revolving Bookcase With Adjustable Dictionary Holder.

No. 1C1187 This is one of the most serviceable Bookcases on the market. It is 40 inches high, has 4 shelves 15x18 making 12 feet of shelf room enough for 100 or more volumes. It has adjustable book shelf 14x15 inches on which can be placed a dictionary, Bible, album or any large reference book at any angle desired. It is a handsome piece of furniture and an ornament to any office, library or parlor. It is constructed so that it can be shipped knocked down, thereby making a great saving in freight charges and is easily put together with 16 round head screws, instructions for putting together accompanying each case. Made of oak or birch finished in imitation mahogany. Shipping weight, 40 pounds. Price..... ....**$4.45**

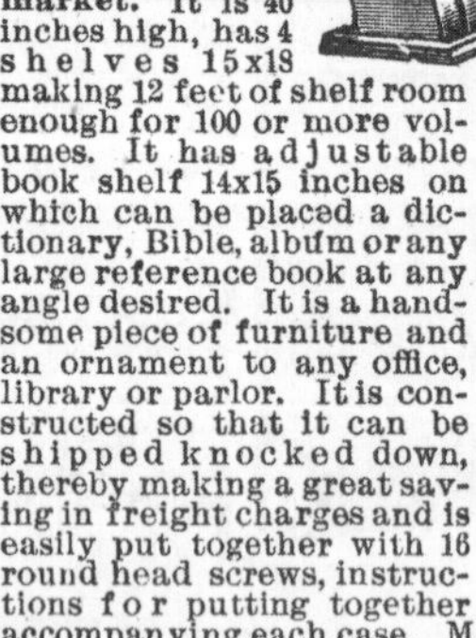

TABLE OF PRICES—SECTIONAL BOOKCASES.

Kinds with Doors	Depth, Inches	Height, Inches	Length, Inches	Order by Number	A Grade Solid Mahogany	B Grade Quartered Oak
Book Section..........	8	9½	34	1	$3.25	$2.35
Book Section..........	8	11	34	2	3.55	2.55
Book Section..........	9½	10¼	34	3	3.55	2.65
Book Section..........	9½	12¼	34	4	3.85	2.95
Book Section..........	12	13½	34	5	4.95	3.65
Book Section..........	9½	10¼	34	6	3.85	2.95
Book Section..........	9½	12¼	34	7	4.10	3.15
Book Section..........	12	13½	34	8	5.25	3.85
Top Section...........	8		34	9	2.10	1.50
Top Section...........	9½		34	10	2.12	1.50
Top Section...........	12		34	11	2.95	1.95
Base Section.	8		34	12	2.15	1.50
Base Section..........	9½		34	13	2.13	1.55
Base Section	12		34	14	2.15	1.60

Be sure to give number and dimensions in ordering sections.

Base section^ with drawers, any regular size, 90 cents extra.

SECTIONAL BOOKCASES.

No. 1C1193 This Perfection Sectional Bookcase is without question the best obtainable at any price. This popular style of bookcase is now conceded the only practical one for a growing library. Whether your collection of books is large or small, this case is easily adapted to it. No unfilled shelves, no surplus of books. The sectional bookcase also permits an artistic arrangement to fit almost any space. High quality of construction, specially selected wood of the choicest grain, and the piano polished finish, make this a desirable article for any home. Absolutely non-binding doors have at last been secured through the use of **ball bearings.** Sidewise and vertical expansion is limited only by the wall space. The end of each section is fitted with ornamental metal end plates that fit into the corresponding metal plates of the adjoining section and **lock the sections together in a perfect vertical alignment.** The door of each section is easily raised and slides back over the top of the books on four ball bearings, noiselessly and **without binding.** The air cushion construction allows the door to close without friction when released. We furnish our sectional bookcase in the choicest highly figured quarter sawed oak, or in genuine solid mahogany, the finest polished finish. Each section is 34 inches long, outside measurement. We furnish the book sections in three different depths, and five different heights, as noted in table below, which allows for the accommodation for any size book. Each size base section can be furnished with a drawer at 90 cents extra.

Single Section C.

This illustration shows one top section, one book section, one base section arranged one above the other, exposing the internal construction. The door is raised and pushed half way into position on four ball bearings. Each part is perfectly mortised and framed where joined, the wood is thoroughly air seasoned and kiln dried, finished inside and outside in a beautiful polish finish. Absolutely guaranteed not to warp, shrink or check. See prices in different sizes in table below.

Combination D. Price $12.70.

This illustration represents our Combination D; one top section, one base section and four book sections, in the different sizes, as noted in table which follows. This combination will accommodate 75 to 100 books, according to size of books. A favorite combination for the small library. Can be enlarged to fit your growing library. You take no risk when you buy the Perfection Sectional Bookcase, as we guarantee absolute satisfaction in every respect or your money will be cheerfully refunded. The high quality of the wood and finish and the perfect details of construction, with the very low price, make this unmatchable.

	Oak	Mahogany
1 Top Section, No. 9.............	$1.50	$2.10
3 Book Sections, No. 1. Each...	2.35	3.25
1 Book Section, No. 2...........	2.55	3.55
1 Base, No. 12....................	1.60	2.15
	$12.70	$17.55

Combination H.

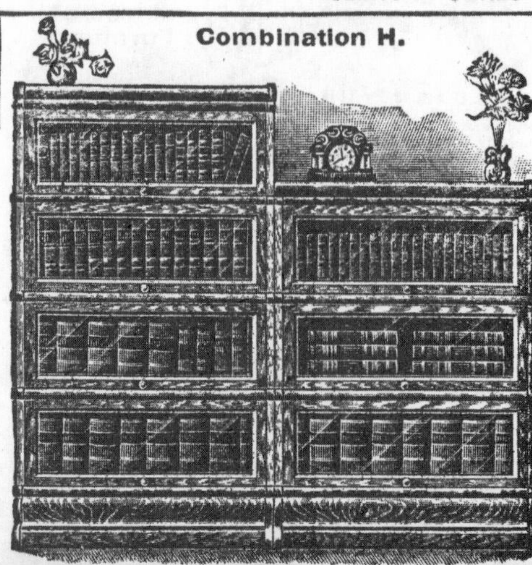

This illustration shows seven book sections, two base sections, two top sections expanded sidewise and interlocked.

WONDERFUL REDUCTION OF PRICES IN HIGH GRADE PARLOR TABLES.

No. 1C1196 Adjustable table, made with heavy malleable iron base and wood top, 18x24 inches, which can be tilted to any angle and adjusted to any height. Metal part finished in black or bronze enamel or oxidized copper with golden oak polished top. Adapted for reading, lunches, cards and sewing, as well as the most perfect bedside table ever devised. Be sure to state finish desired. Shipping weight, 26 pounds.

Price, black enamel **$2.95**
Price, bronze enamel 3.45
Price, oxidized copper 4.90

Folding Table.

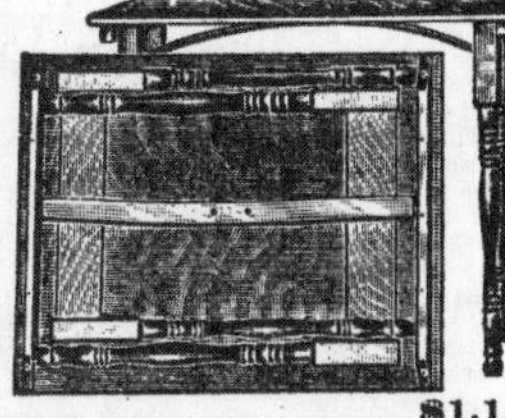

No. 1C1198 This folding table is made of wavy grained birch in a fine golden finish. The legs are hinged securely to the top, and when open are held in place with a strong flexible brace which extends entirely across the top. Size of top, 24x31 inches. Retails regularly at $2.25. Adapted for lunch, sewing, writing, card parties, etc. Shipping weight, 20 pounds.

Price, golden birch **$1.15**

No. 1C1199 This folding table is 26 inches long, 32 inches wide. The top is covered with the best quality of green baize cloth or chase leather, as desired. A removable rim attached by screws permits the detaching of the covering for cleaning. The legs are securely framed to a heavy stretcher which is fastened to the top by strong hinges. The metal folding brace is substantial in construction and perfect in operation. A general utility table. Shipping weight, about 20 pounds.

Price, green baize top **$2.35**
Price, chase leather top 2.45

No. 1C1200 This pretty parlor stand is an exceptionally useful piece of furniture, suitable for lamp or ornament. Made of oak, finished golden. Is 29 inches high with 12-inch top. Shipped knocked down, thereby greatly reducing the freight charges. Can be easily put together with screws, which are provided. Shipping weight, 15 pounds.

Price **56c**

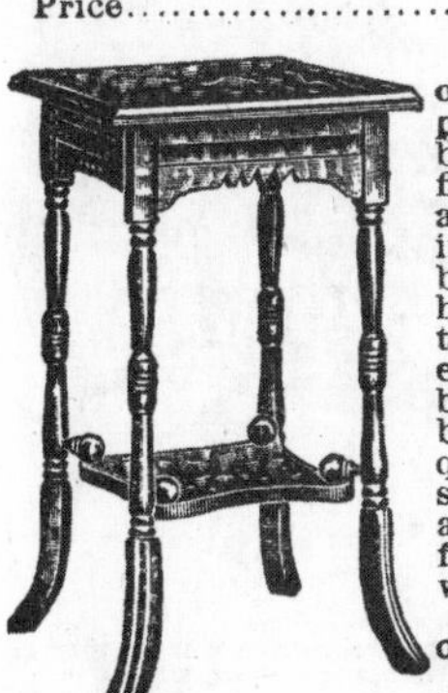

This parlor table is made of solid oak, in a hand polished golden finish, or in birch, mahogany polished finish. It is 32 inches high, and has a top 17x17 inches. The heavy, full boxed top is supported by handsome turned legs. Extra well constructed in every detail. It combines beauty, strength and durability, a combination of qualities hard to find in small parlor tables. Crated and shipped direct from our factory in Chicago. Shipping weight, 25 pounds.

No. 1C1201 Price, golden oak **$1.45**
No. 1C1203 Price, mahogany finish **$1.40**

This parlor table is made of solid oak, golden finish. Top is 24x24 inches. Has roomy lower shelf securely fastened to the neatly turned legs. Strictly first class in construction and finish. Shipped direct from Chicago. Shipping weight, 25 pounds.

No. 1C1204 Price, as illustrated **$1.15**
No. 1C1205 Price, with glass balls and brass claw feet .. **$1.45**

TABLES ON THIS PAGE, EXCEPT No. 1C1201, No. 1C1224½ AND No. 1C1225½, ARE SHIPPED KNOCKED DOWN TO INSURE LOWEST FREIGHT RATES.

Our Leader.

No. 1C1208 The best value ever offered in a parlor table at so low a price. Made of quarter sawed oak golden finish. Top, 24 x 24 inches. Broad, shapely lower shelf, smoothly turned, fancy designed legs securely fastened into the top. A table that sells in retail stores for $2.25 to $2.50. Shipped direct from factory in Western New York or Chicago. Shipping weight, 30 pounds.

	Oak
Price, as illustrated	**$1.20**

No. 1C1209 This parlor table is made of quarter sawed golden oak or birch, imitation mahogany, golden finish, highly polished. The top is 24x24 inches with rounded edges and beautifully embossed rim. The shapely turned legs are firmly attached to the top, strengthened by the spacious and neatly designed lower shelf. Shipped from factory in Western New York or Chicago. Shipping weight, 35 pounds.

	Quartered Oak	Mahogany Finish
Price, brass claw feet ...	**$1.95**	**$1.90**
Price, wood feet	1.65	1.60

No. 1C1216 This parlor table has a 24x24-inch shaped top, as shown in the illustration. Made of highly figured quartered golden oak or fine grain birch, finished imitation mahog'ny. Highly polished. Has neat beaded moulding underneath which is screwed to the top, thereby preventing it from warping; shaped lower shelf. Has turned legs with wood feet or brass feet with glass balls. This table sells in furniture stores at $3.50. Shipping weight, 25 pounds.

	Oak	Mahogany Finish
Price, brass claw feet ...	**$2.25**	**$2.20**
Price, wood feet	1.85	1.80

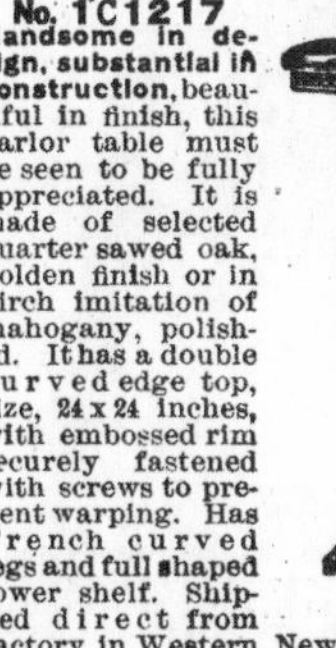

No. 1C1217 Handsome in design, substantial in construction, beautiful in finish, this parlor table must be seen to be fully appreciated. It is made of selected quarter sawed oak, golden finish or in birch imitation of mahogany, polished. It has a double curved edge top, size, 24 x 24 inches, with embossed rim securely fastened with screws to prevent warping. Has French curved legs and full shaped lower shelf. Shipped direct from factory in Western New York or Chicago. Shipping weight, 30 pounds.

	Oak	Mahogany Finish
Price	**$2.00**	**$1.95**

No. 1C1918 This parlor table has a round top 24 inches in diameter with full boxed rim. It is made of highly figured quarter sawed oak, golden finish or birch, in a perfect imitation mahogany finish, highly polished. The roomy shaped lower shelf is supported by neatly turned legs. Strictly high grade in construction; attractive in design and finish. Shipped from factory in Western New York or Chicago. Shipping weight 35 pounds.

	Quartered Oak	Mahogany Finish
Price, brass claw feet	**$2.50**	**$2.45**
Price, wood feet	2.15	2.10

No. 1C1222 This is one of the choicest patterns in a parlor table ever designed. The shapely curved 24x24-inch top, ornamented by broad shaped rim richly hand carved in a highly artistic manner. The spacious lower shelf is securely fastened to heavy rope shaped legs. We furnish it in specially selected quarter sawed oak, golden finish, or in choice grained birch in perfect imitation of mahogany, highly polished. Shipped direct from the factory in Western New York or Chicago. Shipping weight, 35 pounds.

	Oak	Mahogany
Price, brass claw feet	**$2.75**	**$2.70**
Price, wood feet	2.40	2.35

No. 1C1224 The wood in this parlor table is selected quarter sawed golden oak or birch finished in perfect imitation of mahogany, highly polished. It has a 24x24-inch top with curved rounded edges and a carved boxed rim. The shapely French legs are securely fastened to the top with patent bolt construction. Compare this table with those sold by others at $4.50 to $5.00. Shipped direct from factory in Western New York or Chicago. Shipping weight, 35 pounds.

	Quartered Oak	Mahogany Finish
Price	**$2.65**	**$2.60**

One of the best designs in a parlor table. It is made of choice selected golden oak, polished, fine grained, or in birch, mahogany finish, hand polished. The top is 22 inches wide and 30 inches long. Handsome carvings on the box edge. Thoroughly well made and very substantial. An exceptionally fine table. Carefully crated to insure against damage in shipping. Shipped direct from our factory in Chicago. Shipping weight, 40 pounds.

No. 1C1224½ Price, oak **$2.85**
No. 1C1225½ Price, mahogany finish 2.75

No. 1C1225 Another new and handsome design in a parlor table. Has 24x24-inch fancy shaped top, supported by broad rim designed to correspond with top. Has smoothly turned and fluted legs; broad shapely lower shelf. The wood is highly figured quarter sawed golden oak, or birch in imitation mahogany, highly polished finish. High grade in construction in every detail. A table that is sure to please. Shipped direct from the factory in Western New York, or Chicago. Shipping weight, 35 pounds.

	Quartered Oak	Mahogany Finish
Price, brass claw feet ..	**$3.15**	**$3.10**
Price, wood feet	2.80	2.75

No. 1C1228 You cannot fully appreciate the wonderful value we offer in this parlor table until seen. The wood is highly figured quarter sawed golden oak or birch, imitation of mahogany, highly polished. Note the serpentine curved top, size, 24x24 inches, with boxed rim and the beautiful feather design hand carvings on the legs. A spacious and shapely lower shelf is firmly framed into the legs. Shipped direct from factory in Western New York or Chicago. Shipping weight, 35 pounds.

	Quartered Oak	Mahogany Finish
Price, brass claw feet	**$3.30**	**$3.25**
Price, wood feet	2.95	2.90

No. 1C1230 This parlor table is made of highly figured quarter sawed golden oak or selected birch in imitation of mahogany. Highly polished. The handsome curved top, size, 24x24 inches, is reinforced by carved moulding artistic in design. Lower shelf matches the top and is securely fastened to the shapely French legs. Strictly first class in every detail. Shipped direct from factory in Western New York or Chicago. Shipping weight, 35 pounds.

	Quartered Oak	Mahogany Finish
Price	$3.25	$3.20

No. 1C1215 This is without question one of the handsomest parlor tables ever offered, a big bargain. Made of solid oak in a beautiful polished golden finish, fine grained, or in birch, mahogany finish, polished. The top is 24 inches by 24 inches. It has a heavy boxed top, beautifully fluted legs, and large lower shelf. Carefully crated to insure safe delivery. Shipped direct from factory in Chicago. Shipping weight, 50 lbs.

Price, oak, brass claw feet.... $3.35
Price, mahogany finished, brass claw feet.... 3.25

No. 1C1238 This parlor table should be compared with tables sold in retail stores for $5.00 to $6.00. The top is 24x24 inches and has neatly rounded edges. The wood is highly figured quarter sawed oak in a beautiful finish, or birch in a perfect imitation of mahogany. Highly polished. It has an ornamental hand carved boxed rim, handsome French shaped legs and a broad lower shelf. Construction and finish strictly high grade. An exceptionally fine table, shipped direct from factory in Western New York or Chicago. Shipping weight, 38 pounds.

	Quartered Oak	Mahogany Finish
Price	$3.45	$3.40

No. 1C1239 This is an unusually handsome parlor table. Has round top, which is 24 inches in diameter, rounded edges and full boxed rim. The fancy carved French shaped legs are firmly fastened to the top; the neatly shaped lower shelf adds strength and convenience to this beautiful table. The wood is quarter sawed golden oak or birch with a perfect imitation mahogany finish, both highly polished. Wonderful value at our price. Shipped direct from our factory in Western New York or Chicago. Shipping weight, 45 pounds.

	Quartered Oak	Imitation Mahogany
Price	$3.75	$3.65

No. 1C1240 This parlor table is graceful in design, substantial in construction, beautiful in wood and finish. Has handsome 24x24-inch curved top with rounded edges and full boxed rim. The full French curved hand carved legs are firmly attached to the top and given additional stability by the spacious and shapely lower shelf. The wood is highly figured quarter sawed golden oak or birch, mahogany finish, highly polished. Wonderful value at our price. Shipped direct from factory in Western New York or Chicago. Shipping weight, 35 pounds.

	Quarter Sawed Oak	Mahog. Finish
Price	$4.25	$4.15

No. 1C1242 This is without question one of the best values in a parlor table ever offered. It is made of beautiful flaky grained quarter sawed oak, or selected wavy grained birch, mahogany finish, highly polished. Brass claw feet holding large glass balls 4 inches in diameter. Heavy, full box curved frame top and broad lower shelf. Size of top, 26x26 inches. Strictly high grade. Carefully crated to insure safe delivery. Shipped direct from factory in Chicago. Shipping weight, 50 pounds.

	Oak	Mahogany
Price, brass claw feet	$4.85	$4.80
Price, wood feet	3.95	3.90

A Handsome Parlor Table for $4.90.

No. 1C1234 This is, without doubt, one of the handsomest parlor tables we have ever been able to furnish and a big bargain. Made of beautifully figured quartered golden oak or selected birch, in a beautiful mahogany finish. Highly polished. It is 29 inches high, 24x24-inch top. Hand carving, and legs of artistic design. Roomy lower shelf. A strictly high grade piece of furniture. Carefully crated to insure safe delivery. Shipping weight, about 50 pounds.

	Quartered Oak	Mahogany Finish
Price	$4.95	$4.90

No. 1C1244 For beauty of design, high quality of wood and finish, this handsome parlor table is without question one of the best values ever offered by any dealer. The wood is specially selected, highly figured quarter sawed oak in a beautiful golden finish or genuine mahogany, piano polished finish. It has a serpentine swell shaped full boxed top, size, 20x26 inches, genuine French shaped legs and spacious lower shelf. It combines artistic beauty with strength and durability. Shipped direct from factory in Western New York or Chicago. Shipping weight, 40 pounds.

	Quartered Oak	Genuine Mahogany
Price	$5.45	$6.25

No. 1C1241 This massive parlor table is made of thoroughly air seasoned and kiln dried highly figured quarter sawed oak in a beautiful golden finish, or selected birch, mahogany finish. Highly polished. The top, which is 28x28 inches, has a heavy full boxed edge with finely executed deep embossed rim. The massive, shapely and smooth turned legs are securely fastened to the top by our patent bolt construction and braced with a solid shaped shelf and are fitted with extra large glass ball brass claw feet. This table sells for $8.00 to $9.00 in retail stores. Shipped K. D. from factory in Western New York or Chicago. Shipping weight, 55 pounds.

	Oak	Mahogany Finish
Price, brass claw feet	$5.50	$5.45
Price, wood feet	4.55	4.50

No. 1C1243 This massive parlor table has a shapely double curved top, size, 28x28 inches, reinforced beneath with heavy moulding. The legs ornamented with finely executed feather design hand carvings and fitted with extra large glass ball brass claw feet and a broad shaped lower shelf. Made in highly figured quartered oak or birch, imitation mahogany. Shipped knocked down, to insure lowest freight rate. Shipped direct from factory in Western New York or Chicago. Shipping weight, 55 pounds.

	Quartered Oak	Mahogany Finish
Price	$6.25	$6.20

No. 1C1246 This round table is made of highly figured quarter sawed oak or birch imitation of mahogany. Highly polished. Top is 30 inches in diameter, with rounded edges and shapely moulding beneath. Legs are massive and hand carved in feathered design. Fitted with extra large glass ball brass claw feet. Spacious lower shelf. Shipped knocked down to insure lowest freight rate. Shipped direct from factory in Western New York or Chicago. Shipping weight, 65 pounds.

	Quartered Oak	Mahogany Finish
Price	$6.45	$6.40

No. 1C1247 This magnificent Colonial Style Parlor and Library Table is made in highly figured quarter sawed oak in a golden finish, or birch with genuine mahogany top, rim and shelf. Piano polished. The top is 36 inches in diameter with neatly rounded edges and full boxed rim. The massive curved legs have heavy hand carved claw feet. The broad and shapely lower shelf has veneered edges. High grade in material, construction and finish. A table for a lifetime. Shipped direct from factory in Western New York or Chicago. Shipping weight, 85 pounds.

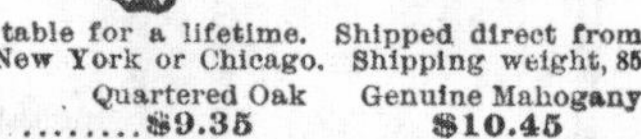

	Quartered Oak	Genuine Mahogany
Price	$9.35	$10.45

No. 1C1248 A very choice design in a solid golden oak library or sitting room table. The hand turned rope shaped legs, the roomy lower shelf, the hand polished finish and strictly high grade construction, make this table the greatest value ever offered at so low a price. The top is 2 feet by 3 feet. The spacious drawer has a hand carved pull. Don't be misled by the extremely low price quoted. Shipped from factory in Chicago. Shipping weight, 50 pounds.

Price.... $4.85

No. 1C1250 This library or parlor table is made of selected highly figured quarter sawed golden oak, or in birch imitation of mahogany. Highly polished. The top is 24x36 inches, containing a roomy drawer fitted with cast brass knobs. The shapely French legs are securely framed into the heavy boxed rim. Has a spacious lower shelf. Strictly high grade in construction. Shipped direct from our factory in Western New York or Chicago. Shipping weight, 60 pounds.

	Quartered Oak	Mahogany Finish
Price	$5.75	$5.70

No. 1C1251½ Another new design in a high grade library table. Made of highly figured quarter sawed golden oak, highly polished. The top is 26x42 inches. It has a swellshaped boxed rim with a large drawer. The shapely fluted and hand turned legs are securely framed into the top and given additional strength by a broad, lower shelf. Fitted with best quality casters. Every detail of construction strictly first class. Carefully packed and shipped direct from factory in Northern Indiana. Shipping weight, about 85 pounds.

Price.... $7.95

No. 1C1254 This Massive Library Table is made of highly figured quarter sawed oak, golden finish, highly polished. The top, which is 28x45 inches, has neatly rounded edges and corners, full boxed rim fitted with spacious drawer. Extra large shapely fluted legs and broad lower shelf. Best quality casters. A library table for a lifetime. Shipped direct from factory in Northern Indiana. Shipping weight, 100 pounds.

Price, quartered golden oak........ ....**$8.45**

No. 1C1257 This Library Table is made throughout of the very best quality of highly figured quartered golden oak. Also furnished in fine grain birch, finished imitation mahogany, with genuine mahogany veneered top. Highly polished. Top is 25x48 inches. Massive, handsomely turned and fluted legs. Roomy drawer, fitted with cast brass handles and lock. Ball bearing casters. This table would retail regularly at $18.00 to $20.00. Shipped direct from the factory in Northern Indiana. Shipping weight, 100 pounds.

Price, quartered oak **$9.85**
Price, birch mahogany.......... ....**9.80**

No. 1C1268 This Magnificent Library or Parlor Table is made of fine flaky grained quarter sawed oak, piano polished. The massive rope shaped legs are supported by heavy hand carved claw feet. It combines beauty and elegance with strength and durability. The top is 27 inches wide by 40 inches long. It has a large drawer and spacious lower shelf. The construction is strictly high grade throughout. This table sells at retail for $15.00 to $18.00. Shipped direct from factory in Chicago. Shipping weight, 70 pounds.

Price, quartered oak...................................**$10.65**

No. 1C1270 We offer this Magnificent Library Table, in the best selected quarter sawed oak, golden finish, or in birch with genuine mahogany top, rim and shelf; piano polished. The shapely curved top, size, 28x48 inches, has rounded edges, full boxed rim and a large drawer. The massive French legs are ornamented with hand carvings and claw feet. Has fancy shaped lower shelf. Attractiveness of design, massive and durable construction with beauty of wood and finish, all combined in this table. Shipped direct from factory in Western New York. Shipping weight, 100 pounds.

	Quartered Oak	Genuine Mahogany
Price....................	**$11.75**	**$12.95**

No. 1C1275 This Library Table is, beyond a doubt, one of the finest tables for the price in the market. Made of solid, highly figured quartered oak, or best quality birch, finished perfect imitation mahogany, with genuine mahogany veneer top. Has 32x50-inch top, massive and handsome legs with claw feet. The entire table is highly polished. Has a large drawer in top. A strictly high grade piece of furniture at a low price. Shipped direct from factory in Northern Indiana. Shipping weight, 125 lbs.

Price, quartered oak...........................**$12.95**
Price, birch mahogany.......................**12.85**

$5.85

No. 1C1301 This Parlor Cabinet is made of select birch finished in perfect imitation of mahogany. Height, 55 inches; width, 22 inches. The ornamented French beveled plate mirror in the top is 8x14 inches. Has three shapely shelves. Piano polish finish. Others ask double the price we ask for this cabinet. Shipped direct from factory in Northern Illinois. Shipping weight, crated, 50 pounds.

Price. **$5.85**

No. 1C1305 This handsome, artistic hand carved, piano polished cabinet is 55 inches high, 24 inches wide; fitted with two genuine French beveled plate mirrors 14x14 inches. Top section ornamented with two shapely brackets. It has two roomy fancy shelves. Shipping weight, 50 pounds. Shipped direct from factory in Northern Illinois.

Price.........................**$7.95**

$10.95

No. 1C1302 This is one of the choicest designs in Parlor Cabinets. No parlor is completely furnished if it does not contain a handsome parlor cabinet. Made of finest quality of selected birch, given the highest hand polished mahogany finish. It stands 54 inches high, 28 inches wide. The mirror in the ornamental top is 8x22 inches. The mirror beneath the top shelf is 12x20 inches. The mirror beneath the middle shelf is 10x20 inches. All the best quality of French beveled plate. Shipped direct from factory in Northern Illinois. Shipping weight, 50 pounds.

Price, without mirror back of lower shelf...............**$9.85**
Full mirror back, three mirrors as illustrated.....**$10.95**

No. 1C1306 This Handsome and Attractive Parlor Cabinet is made of the finest birch with a rich mahogany finish, with pretty ornamental shelves and two bevel plate French mirrors, one 7x26 inches and one 12x16 inches; is 60 inches high and 32 inches wide; is graceful in outline and a welcome and beautiful addition to a parlor. No parlor is properly furnished if it does not include one of our new and handsome cabinets. The illustration will give you some idea of the beautiful effect worked out in this new cabinet. Shipping weight, 50 pounds.

Price...............**$11.85**

$14.85

No. 1C1310 We offer this handsome new Parlor Cabinet as the equal of any parlor cabinet you can buy anywhere at $20.00 to $22.00. The wood is the finest wavy grained selected birch in the highest hand polished mahogany finish. It is 61 inches high, 32 inches wide. It has fine French beveled plate mirror of the best quality in the back. The mirror on the top is 8x24 inches; the mirror under the top shelf is 10x26 inches; the mirror in the center back of lower shelf is 18x21 inches; the two mirrors to the right and left of the mirror in the back of lower shelf are each 6x18 inches. For high quality of construction, beauty in finish and attractiveness of design this cabinet cannot be equaled at double the price. Thoroughly well packed and safe delivery guaranteed. Shipped direct from our factory in Northern Illinois. Shipping weight, 50 pounds.

Price, complete with five mirrors.........................**$14.85**

MUSIC CABINETS AND LADIES' DESKS.

Our new and up to date line of Music Cabinets and Desks, which we illustrate on this and the following page, are made by the largest, oldest and best known manufacturer of high grade goods of this kind in the United States. THE WOOD used in the construction is thoroughly air seasoned and kiln dried. Selected especially for the beauty of its grain and will please the most exacting and cultivated taste. **THE CONSTRUCTION** is strictly high grade in every detail. Every joint and tenon carefully and perfectly fitted. **THE FINISH.** This highly figured quarter sawed golden oak, the handsome birch and the rare and beautiful birdseye maple, are each given a high grade piano polish finish. No photograph or illustration can show the beautiful grain of this wood or the highly polished surface. **THE DESIGNS** are new, artistic and strikingly handsome, and at the prices we offer them represent a saving of 35 to 40 percent to our customers.

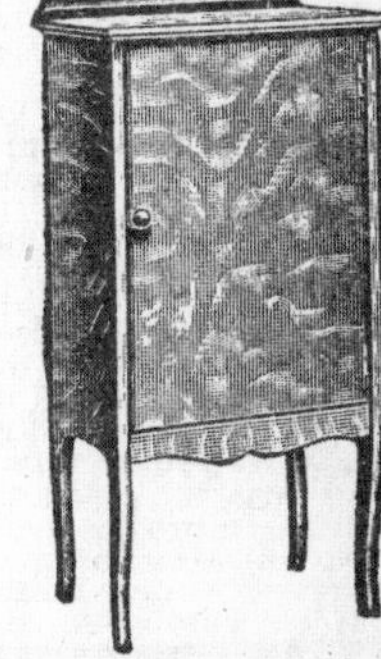

No. 1C1316 This is wonderful value in a High Grade Music Cabinet. We furnish it in solid golden oak with a highly figured quarter sawed oak front and top or in selected birch in a perfect imitation of mahogany, polished like a piano. Height, 41 inches; width, 19 inches. High grade in every detail of construction. Shipped direct from factory in Central Indiana. Shipping weight, about 50 pounds.

	Oak	Mahogany Finish
Price..	**$4.25**	**$4.15**

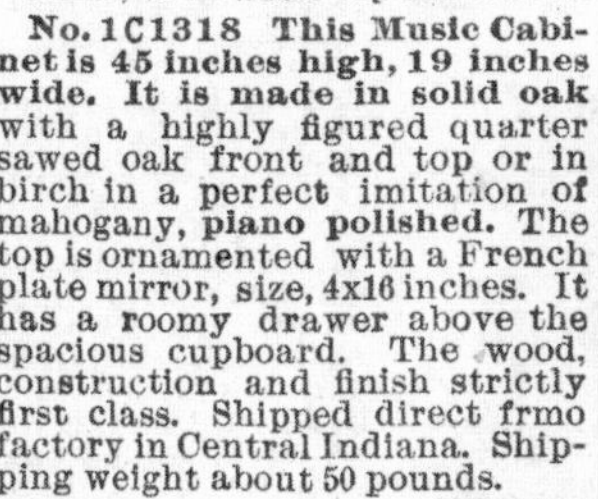

No. 1C1317 This Music Cabinet is made of thoroughly air seasoned and kiln dried birch in a perfect imitation of mahogany, polished like a piano. It stands 43 inches high and 19 inches wide. A spacious and convenient arrangement of shelves for music. Ornamented with a genuine French plate mirror; size, 4x16 inches. Thoroughly well made in every detail of construction and finish. A perfect match for mahogany piano. Shipped direct from factory in Central Indiana. Shipping weight, about 50 pounds.

Price, as illustrated.................................**$5.95**
Price, with wood top rail.............................**4.95**

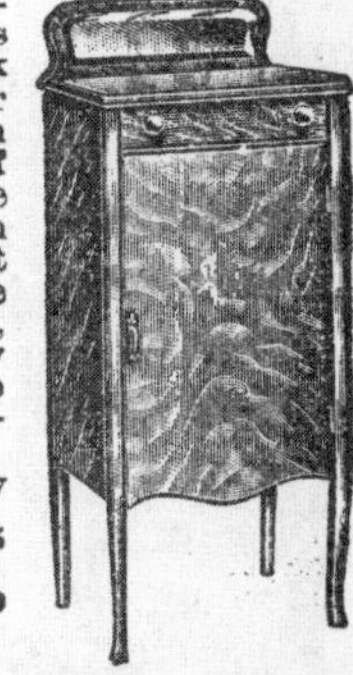

No. 1C1318 This Music Cabinet is 45 inches high, 19 inches wide. It is made in solid oak with a highly figured quarter sawed oak front and top or in birch in a perfect imitation of mahogany, **piano polished.** The top is ornamented with a French plate mirror, size, 4x16 inches. It has a roomy drawer above the spacious cupboard. The wood, construction and finish strictly first class. Shipped direct frmo factory in Central Indiana. Shipping weight about 50 pounds.

	Oak	Mahogany Finish
Price, as illustrated,	**$7.25**	**$7.15**
Price, with wood top rail..........	**6.30**	**6.20**

No. 1C1319 This Music Cabinet is made of highly figured black walnut or selected birch, with a genuine mahogany front and top. It stands 44 inches high, 20 inches wide. The pattern shaped mirror on the top is the best quality French band plate; size, 6x14 inches. It has genuine double curved French shaped front legs. Handsome in design, beautiful in material, high grade in construction and has a polished finish like a piano. Shipped direct from factory in Central Indiana. Shipping weight, about 50 pounds.

	Walnut	Mahogany
Price, as illustrated,	**$8.25**	**$8.30**
Price, wood top rail,	**7.35**	**7.65**

No. 1C1320 This Music Cabinet has a genuine mahogany front and top. Highly polished finish, a perfect match for mahogany piano. The height is 45 inches, the width 19 inches. It has double curved genuine French front legs. A full swell top drawer and a convenient arrangement of shelves inside. The door is decorated with genuine hand carvings, finely executed. The ornamental mirror is the best quality French bevel plate; size, 6x16 inches. Shipped direct from factory in Central Indiana. Shipping weight about 50 pounds.

Price, as illustrated......**$9.85**
Price, with wood top rail, **8.95**

$5.95

No. 1C1321 This Beautiful New Design Ladies' Desk is 45 inches high, 27 inches long, 15 inches deep. It is made in solid golden oak with a highly figured quarter sawed oak front and top, or in birch, mahogany finish or birdseye maple, highly polished. Inside has convenient arrangement of pigeonholes, pen racks, drawers, etc. The writing lid is 13x25 inches, below which is a roomy drawer. Top is decorated with a genuine French bevel plate mirror, size, 4x16 inches. To fully appreciate this desk it should be compared with desks offered by others at double our price. Shipped direct from factory in Central Indiana. Shipping weight, about 60 pounds.

	Oak	Mahogany Finish	Birdseye Maple
Price, as illustrated....	$5.95	$5.90	$7.50
With wood top rail......	4.85	4.80	6.50

$9.25

No. 1C1322 This New Design Ladies' Desk is made in solid golden oak with a highly figured quarter sawed oak front and top, in specially selected birch, in a perfect imitation of mahogany, in curly birch, natural golden finish, or in birdseye maple. The construction in every detail is strictly first class. Inside of desk is fitted with pigeonholes, pen racks and drawer. Below writing compartment a large drawer. It has double curved French shaped front legs. The mirror on top is the best quality French bevel plate, size, 4x20 inches. Height, 45 inches; depth, 16 inches; length, 28 inches. Desk lid, 13x28 inches. Shipped direct from factory in Central Indiana. Shipping wt., about 60 lbs.

	Oak	Mahogany	Curly Birch	Birdseye Maple
Price, as illustrated,	$9.25	$8.85	$9.50	$9.95
With wood top rail..	7.50	7.35	7.75	8.20

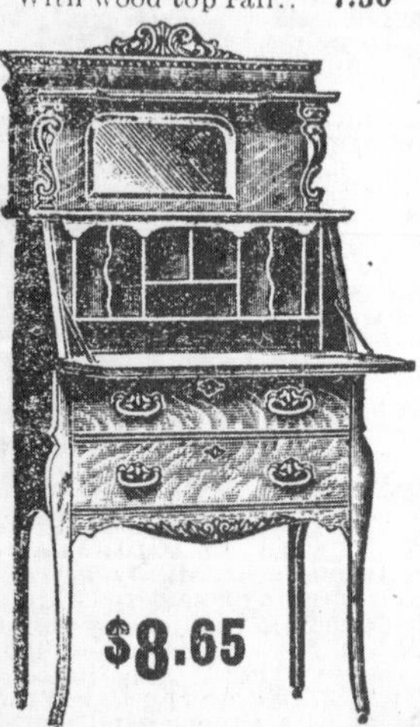

$8.65

No. 1C1323 Ladies' Desk; 4 feet 10 inches high, 29 inches wide, with 8x14-inch French bevel plate mirror. This desk is **made of solid oak,** with quartered oak front. Also made in birch, and is finished in a high gloss finish, either in golden oak or imitation mahogany. Fitted with roomy pigeonhole case. Has two large drawers and upper shelf. The **hand carving is beautiful, and the trimmings are of brass. Best quality casters.** Shipping weight, 100 pounds.

	Quartered Oak	Mah. Finish.
Price....	$8.65	$8.60

$10.75

No. 1C1324 This is another New Design in a Handsome Ladies' Desk. Made in three different woods, solid golden oak with a flaky grained quarter sawed oak front and top, birdseye maple or selected birch in a perfect imitation mahogany finish. All highly polished. Fitted inside with a convenient arrangement of pigeonholes, pen racks and drawer. Desk lid is 13x28 inches, below which is a curved front drawer. Height, 44 inches; depth, 17 inches; length, 30 inches. The mirror on top is the best quality French bevel plate, size, 4x20 inches. High grade in construction, beautiful in wood and finish. Shipped direct from factory in Central Indiana. Shipping weight, about 60 pounds.

	Oak	Mahogany Finish	Birdseye Maple
Price, as illustrated,...	$10.75	$10.65	$11.50

$10.50

No. 1C1325 This Strictly High Grade Ladies' Desk cannot be fully appreciated until seen and compared with those offered by others at double our price. It is 40 inches high, 30 inches long, 16 inches deep, with a hand carved writing lid 13x29 inches. Fitted inside with pigeonholes, pen racks and drawer. Also a large drawer below writing compartment. Double curved French shaped front legs and a spacious shelf below. We furnish it in solid oak with a higly figured quarter sawed oak front and top, or in birch in a perfect mahogany finish, highly polished. Cabinet work strictly first class. Shipped direct from factory in Central Indiana. Shipping weight, about 60 pounds.

	Oak	Mahogany Finish
Price..........................	$10.50	$10.00

No. 1C1328 This is one of best values in a desk for the home ever offered. It is 40 inches high, 30 inches wide and 17 inches deep with a writing lid 14x30 inches. It is made of solid oak with highly figured quarter sawed oak front and top in a beautiful golden finish, highly polished. Writing compartment fitted with convenient pigeonholes, two pen racks and drawer. The base has three large swell front drawers fitted with best cast brass handles. It has double curved French front legs and solid panel ends. Strictly high grade in every detail. Shipped direct from factory in Central Indiana. Shipping weight, about 100 pounds.
Price, golden oak.......................................$12.50

Wonderful Value for $3.95.

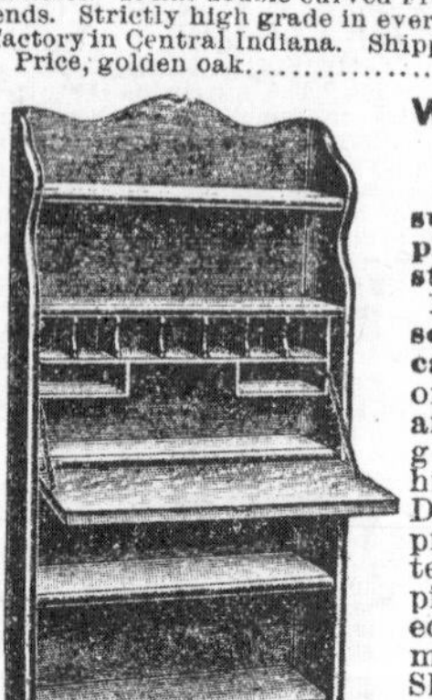

A Bookcase-Secretary, suitable for almost any place; can be used in the store, shop, office or home.
No. 1C1383 This Handsome Combination Bookcase and Secretary is made of solid oak, thoroughly air and kiln dried and finished golden. It is 60 inches high and 30 inches wide. Drop leaf and bookcase proper, 22 inches deep. Interior is partitioned with pigeonholes, as illustrated. Best case on the market at the price. Shipped direct from factory in Southern Indiana. Shipping weight, 75 pounds.
Price.......................$3.95

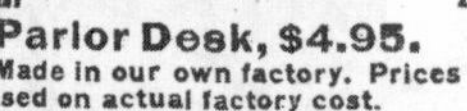

Parlor Desk, $4.95.

Made in our own factory. Prices based on actual factory cost.

No. 1C1386 Parlor Desk, neat design, well made of select golden oak, prettily hand carved and highly hand polished. Has large drop leaf fitted with lock, and inside is nicely partitioned with pigeonholes. The lower part can be used for books and has a brass rod for curtain; also has a French bevel plate mirror and a large shelf in upper part. Height, 5 feet; width, 2 feet 6 inches. Weight, about 60 pounds. Price............$4.95

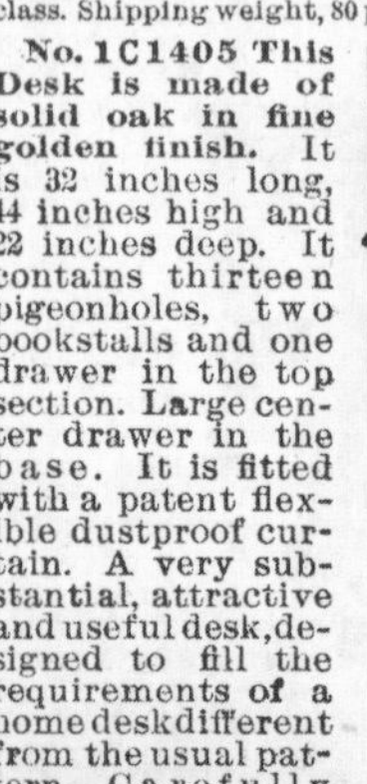

Our $5.95 Parlor Desk.

No. 1C1338 Parlor Desk. A graceful and good, sensible design. Made of select golden oak stock. Width, 30 inches; height, 63 inches. Inside is nicely partitioned with pigeonholes. Has a large drop leaf and the shelves below can be used for books. Has a brass rod and rings for curtain. **The top is ornamented with two shelves and a French bevel plate mirror. Shipped from factory in Western Michigan.** Weight, 70 pounds.
Price, in golden oak...$5.95

$5.95 Buys this Handsome Desk that Furniture Stores Ask $10.00 For.

No. 1C1390 This Handsome Desk is made of fine, carefully selected and thoroughly seasoned oak; has high golden finish; has three drawers with drop table to write on, and drawers and table are fitted with locks and brass pulls. The cabinet is conveniently divided; it has a compartment for books, papers and writing material and one pull drawer in center. The best construction throughout. The height of the desk is 4 feet 8 inches; width, 2 feet 6 inches. **It is beautifully polished and finished with scroll carvings, an extremely useful and ornamental piece of furniture. Shipped from our factory in Central Illinois.**
Shipping weight, 80 pounds. Price..........$5.95

A Handsome Parlor Desk for $6.95.

No. 1C1394 This Handsome Parlor Desk is made of oak and with quartered oak front, finished golden. Is 63 inches high, 30 inches wide and 13 inches deep. The mirror is 8x10-inch pattern French bevel plate. The top is of pretty design, ornamented with raised carvings. Has a small bracket at the left side and roomy shaped shelf supported by two turned columns at the right side on which bric-a-brac can be placed. **The lid of the writing desk is ornamented with raised carvings in scroll design.** The interior is arranged with pigeonholes for stationery. There is a brass rod with hooks, from which a curtain can be draped and ample space below for books or papers. This desk makes a handsome and useful piece of furniture. Shipping weight, 70 pounds. Price.........................$6.95

Our Prettiest Parlor Desk, $9.75.

No. 1C1399 This Desk is without doubt the most attractive and useful article of its kind on the market. Made of golden quartered oak. The interior is arranged for books and stationery, as illustrated. The lid of writing desk is supported, when open, by a brass arm at each side. The lower part of desk has one large drawer, two smaller drawers and a cupboard in which is a small drawer and three letter files. The drawers and cupboard are fitted with fancy cast brass handles, knobs and locks. The cabinet work and finish throughout are first class. Shipping weight, 80 pounds. Price, quartered oak.$9.75

$6.95

No. 1C1405 This Desk is made of solid oak in fine golden finish. It is 32 inches long, 44 inches high and 22 inches deep. It contains thirteen pigeonholes, two bookstalls and one drawer in the top section. Large center drawer in the base. It is fitted with a patent flexible dustproof curtain. A very substantial, attractive and useful desk, designed to fill the requirements of a home desk different from the usual pattern. Carefully packed and shipped direct from our factory in Southern Indiana. Shipping weight, 50 pounds.
Price, golden oak...$6.95

OUR NEW LINE OF HIGH CLASS GUARANTEED OFFICE DESKS

The office desks we display this season represent a line made for us under special contract by the largest, oldest and best desk manufacturers in this country, manufacturers whose long experience in the manufacture of desks enables them to give us the benefit of every good idea, whose modern machinery and skilled workmanship combine to produce better goods than are turned out by other manufacturers and whose contract with us, by which we take practically the entire output of the factory, enables us to offer these desks to our customers on the basis of manufacturing cost, the cost of material and labor with but our one small percentage of profit added. By this method and this connection we are able to eliminate from the selling price every unnecessary item and the price to you, the price printed in this catalogue, is as low or even lower than most retail dealers would pay at wholesale for these goods

OUR BINDING GUARANTEE. Every office desk shown on these pages is covered by our binding guarantee and shipped with the understanding and agreement that the desk is perfect in material, workmanship, finish, mechanical features, etc., and if the desk is found defective in any particular, it may be returned to us at our expense and your money will be refunded.

OUR REFUND OFFER. Every order for a desk is accepted by us with the understanding and agreement that when the desk is received, you can compare it with any desk you can get from any other concern at the same price and if you do not find that our desk is better quality in every way, that it represents a far better value for the money, we do not expect you to keep it, but it can be returned to us and we will refund your money and pay freight charges both ways.

SAFE DELIVERY GUARANTEE. We guarantee each and every desk to reach you in the same perfect condition that it leaves our factory. Every desk is carefully packed and shipped direct from our factory in Southern Indiana or North Carolina, or direct from Chicago and is sure to reach you in an absolutely perfect condition.

FREIGHT CHARGES are very reasonable, amounting to next to nothing, as compared with what you will save in price. Almost any desk can be shipped to points within 400 or 600 miles of Chicago at a cost of $1.00 to $1.75 freight charges and at many points the charges will only be 75 cents to $1.25.

THE WOOD used in our Office Desks is specially selected fine grained oak. It is thoroughly air seasoned and kiln dried. Absolutely guaranteed not to warp, shrink or check. The panels and polished writing bed are constructed of the three-ply wood, perfectly joined together with the grain crossing, thereby insuring great strength and preventing warping or shrinkage.

THE CONSTRUCTION of our Office Desks is the very best that skilled workmanship and modern machinery can produce. Every part of the frame work is perfectly fitted and joined by mortise and tenant. The drawers are dovetailed on the sides and grooved on the bottoms and backs, carefully and perfectly fitted with guides, making them easy moving and free from friction.

THE FINISH of our Office Desks is strictly high grade in every detail. The materials are the best obtainable from hardwood oil to the polishing coat of varnish. Special care is taken to bring out the highly figured grain of the wood. Plenty of time is given each coating and polishing process in order to produce a better and smoother surface, a brighter luster and a finish that will preserve its beauty for a lifetime instead of the ordinary finish produced by other makes that fade away in a few months.

THE COLOR is a beautiful shade of golden oak which brings out the highly figured grain of the wood perfectly and harmonizes with any surroundings.

OUR PATENT DUSTPROOF ROLL CURTAIN. The curtain has an unbroken, smooth outer surface, thereby preventing the catching and retaining of dust and grit, so detrimental and annoying to all other makes of flexible curtains; perfectly noiseless, free and easy action and graceful appearance while in motion, as though possessed of life. No friction caused by dust or grit accumulating in and between grooved slats. The outer surface is a solid sheet of veneering, showing beautiful grain of wood, lined with creases corresponding with the lower ribs to insure perfect flexibility and grace of motion; easily kept clean with an ordinary dusting brush. We guarantee the durability of our curtain and claim that no other curtain, now on the market, can be raised or lowered as easily and gracefully. No creaking, cracking noises or jerky motion while operating our curtain. THE PATENT DUSTPROOF CURTAIN used on all our roll top desks is undoubtedly superior to any other make, and an exceptionally desirable feature.

OUR LEADER OFFICE DESK AT $11.95

The Equal of Office Desks Sold Generally at $18.00. Note the Size and Description Carefully.

THIS OFFICE DESK is without doubt the most wonderful value ever offered in a roll top curtain desk. It is made of choice grained selected oak in a beautiful golden finish. It is 4 feet long, 30 inches wide and 46 inches high; it has four drawers in the left pedestal, each 20½ inches long, 10 inches wide and averages 4⅛ inches high. The right hand pedestal contains one drawer 20½ inches long, 10 inches wide and 4⅛ inches high and a spacious book cupboard containing two bookstalls for large books and four pigeonholes for stationery, etc. Above each pedestal is a sliding adjustable arm rest which adds to the convenience and table surface of the desk. The top section contains twelve pigeonholes for envelopes and stationery, etc., two drawers, two pen racks, blotter holder, etc. The spacious bed and splendid arrangement of pigeonhole case makes the desk the equal in comfort and convenience of desks at treble the price. It is fitted with dustproof flexible curtain, preventing the catching and retaining of dust and grit, so detrimental and annoying to all other makes of curtains. It is perfectly noiseless, free and easy of action and graceful in appearance, no friction caused by dust or grit accumulating in and between grooved slats, no creaking or cracking noises or jerky motion while operating the curtain.

$11.95

THIS DESK has a full paneled closed back and is finished all around. The drawers are dovetailed and the entire frame of the desk is mortised and joined in the most perfect manner possible. The easy moving and perfect fitting drawers, the flexible dustproof curtain, the spacious and convenient cupboard and pigeonholes together with handsome highly figured oak wood with beautiful golden finish makes this high grade desk one of the most wonderful bargains we have ever offered

THE CURTAIN is fitted with a Yale lock with two keys. The curtain locks the drawers in the left pedestal automatically. The door of the cupboard has a separate lock and key. This desk is mounted on patent chilled steel frame casters. Shipped direct from factory in Chicago, thereby insuring lowest freight rates. Shipping weight, 200 pounds.

No. 1C1430 Price.. **$11.95**

Solid Oak Flat Top Office Desk $8.95.

This Handsome Flat Top Office Desk is made of solid oak. It is 4 feet 6 inches long, 2 feet 6 inches wide and 30 inches high. The left pedestal contains three drawers, each 23 inches long, 11¼ inches wide, 3¼ inches high, and one drawer same length and width, 9 inches high. The right pedestal contains 1 drawer 23 inches long, 11¼ inches wide and 3¼ inches high, and a spacious cupboard containing five pigeonholes, each 4 inches wide by 3¾ inches high, and two bookstalls, 13¾ inches deep, 19 inches high and 4 inches wide. The distance between the pedestals in the 54-inch size desk is 24 inches, and in the 4-foot size 17½ inches. The top of this desk is made of transverse layers, insuring it against warpage or shrinkage. The ends and back are full paneled and the construction and finish are strictly high grade. Shipped direct from factory. Shipping weight, 150 pounds.

No. 1C1442 Price, 4 feet 6 inches long.....$9.85
No. 1C1444 Price, 4 feet long.....8.95

This Strictly High Grade Roll Top Desk For $12.45.

No. 1C1456 The illustration of this desk gives but a fair idea of the exceptional value which it represents. It is made of selected oak, in a beautiful golden finish. It is 48 inches long, 30 inches wide and 46 inches high. The left pedestal has three drawers, each 23 inches long, 9 inches wide and 3¼ inches deep, and one drawer 23 inches long, 9 inches wide, 9 inches high. The right hand pedestal contains one drawer 23 inches long, 9 inches wide and 3 inches high and a roomy cupboard containing four pigeonholes, each 4¼x3¼ inches, two bookstalls 13¾ inches deep, 19 inches high and 3 inches wide, besides a spacious cupboard in the rear for books and stationery. Distance between the pedestals, 22¾ inches. This desk has a full paneled closed back and ends, and is fitted with our patent flexible easy running dustproof curtain. The top section contains ten pigeonholes, 3x4⅛ inches, two drawers, pen racks, etc. Above each pedestal is an extension sliding arm rest. Note the roomy cupboard in rear of right pedestal Mounted on extra heavy patent chilled best quality casters. Shipped direct from factory in Southern Indiana. Shipping weight, 200 pounds.

Price, 4 feet long, solid oak.....$12.45

Wonderful Value at $14.95.

No. 1C1462 This Handsome High Curtain Office Desk is made of specially selected thoroughly air seasoned and kiln dried oak in a beautiful golden finish. It is 48 inches long, 30 inches wide, 45 inches high. The right hand pedestal contains a private drawer, with Yale lock. Dimensions, 9¼ inches long, 9½ inches wide and 3¾ inches high. A bookstall 19½ inches high, 12½ inches deep and 4 inches wide, two letter files with indexes 12¾ inches high 11 inches wide and 3 inches deep, and two pigeonhole compartments for stationery, etc. Four drawers, each 23 inches long, 12¼ inches wide and 4¼ inches high. The top section contains six wood front filing boxes, 9 inches long, 4 inches wide and 3 inches high, two bookstalls, 12 inches high, 9 inches deep and 3 inches wide, two compartments for stationery, above two drawers and two spacious pigeonholes, 9 inches deep, 5⅛ inches wide and 3 inches high. It is fitted with our patent dustproof flexible curtain. It has full paneled ends and back. The drawers run smoothly. Above each pedestal is a sliding arm rest. Retail dealers ask $25.00 for this desk. Thoroughly packed and shipped direct from factory in Grand Rapids, Michigan. Shipping weight, 200 pounds.

Price, 4 feet long, solid oak, golden finish.....$14.95

Extra Large High Solid Oak Roll Top Desk $18.95.

This High Roll Top Desk is 5 feet long, 33½ inches wide and 52 inches high. Made in solid oak, golden finish, walnut, natural finish and imitation mahogany. The left pedestal contains three drawers, each 24½ inches long, 11¼ inches wide and 3¼ inches high, and one drawer 24½ inches long, 11¼ inches wide and 9 inches high. The right pedestal has one drawer and spacious cupboard, containing five pigeonholes, 3x5⅝ inches, two bookstalls 19 inches high, 13¾ inches deep and 4 inches wide. Extension arm slide above each pedestal. The top section contains sixteen pigeonholes 3x4 inches, four pigeonholes 3x5⅝ inches, two bookstalls 17 inches high, 8¼ inches deep and 4 inches wide; four special compartments for stationery and two drawers This desk is fitted with our flexible dustproof curtain with Yale lock. Drawers in base lock automatically. This desk has a spacious cupboard in rear of right pedestal. Mounted on heavy patent chilled best quality casters. The high grade construction, choice grained wood and beautiful golden finish, make this desk exceptional value. Read what we say about how our desks are made. Thoroughly well packed and shipped direct from factory in Southern Indiana. Shipping weight, 275 pounds.

		Oak	Walnut	Imitation Mahogany
No. 1C1469	Price, 60 inches long......	$19.85	$20.45	$20.35
No. 1C1470	Price, 54 inches long......	18.95	19.85	19.45

Our Finest Office Desk For $20.85.

This Magnificent High Roll Top Desk is made of solid oak, the top and front highly figured quarter sawed, grain specially selected. The three upper drawers in each pedestal are each 24½ inches long, 11¼ inches wide and 3¼ inches deep. The two lower drawers in each pedestal are each 24½ inches long, 11¼ inches wide and 9 inches deep. The top section contains sixteen pigeonholes 3x4 inches, four pigeonholes 3x5½ inches, two bookstalls, each 17 inches high, 4 inches wide and 8¼ inches deep, four special pigeonholes for stationery and two drawers. This desk is fitted with our patent flexible dustproof curtain with Yale lock, which locks the drawers in the base automatically. Has an extension arm slide above drawers in each pedestal. The handsome columns on the front of the base, the beautiful hand carved drawer pulls, the full paneled closed back and ends, the strictly high grade construction and finish, make this desk, without doubt, wonderful value. We furnish this desk also in genuine walnut, or in birch, mahogany finish. Thoroughly well packed and shipped direct from our factory in Southern Indiana. Shipping weight, 300 pounds.

		Oak	Walnut	Imitation Mahogany
No. 1C1471	Price, 54 inches long......	$20.85	$22.45	$22.85
No. 1C1472	Price, 60 inches long......	21.95	23.85	23.95

Make your selection from these pages or
SEND FOR OUR

SPECIAL DESK CATALOGUE

showing the largest and most complete line of office desks, at factory prices.

BIG VALUES IN BEDROOM SUITES.

WITH OUR LINE OF BEDROOM SUITES **enlarged, greatly improved, brought right up to date to include the very newest styles for this season, and at greatly reduced prices,** we are prepared to save you so much money we feel you cannot afford to buy a bedroom suite elsewhere.

THE WONDERFUL GROWTH **of our furniture department has made it possible for us to make much larger contracts with the manufacturers than ever before,** thus reducing the cost to us, and enabling us to make lower prices to you. By a careful comparison of our prices with those of any other house or furniture dealer, we know, quality for quality, we can save you from $5.00 to $25.00 on a bedroom suite and can give you newer and more stylish patterns than you would likely be able to get from your local furniture dealers.

HOW WE ARE ABLE TO MAKE THE PRICES SO LOW, **and how it is possible for us to reduce our prices on bedroom suites below any previous quotations. Our bedroom suites are made for us under contract by the best manufacturers in this country,** and our output has increased to such an extent that we are able to contract in each case for a very large part of the output of the factory, and these factories, desiring to run at full capacity the year around, are willing to take our contract at the cost of material and labor, as it facilitates the working of their factory and enables them to run every working day at full capacity, and thus reduce the cost, not only on the suites they make for us, but on the suites they sell to other people. As a result, we obtain our bedroom suites this season, including all the newest designs, at about the cost of material and labor, to which we have added only our usual small percentage of profit.

TO APPRECIATE **the value we are giving in bedroom suites, you must see, examine and compare our suites with those offered by others at within 20 to 40 per cent of our prices.** Unfortunately, you cannot, by illustration and description, compare satisfactorily the real value, but if you take any suite that we advertise and place it alongside of any suite offered by any other house at anything approaching our price, you will at once see that with our facilities, we are furnishing a much higher grade of goods at a much lower price than you can possibly buy elsewhere.

ABOUT FACTORY SHIPMENTS. **To reduce our selling price to you to the lowest possible point,** you will note on a number of suites, we have reserved the right to ship either from our warehouse or direct from the factory. This means a big saving to you, for where we ship from the factory direct, there is nothing added for freight, handling or storage, and as a result, you can buy one bedroom suite from us for less than dealers can buy in carload lots.

QUALITY OF MATERIAL AND CONSTRUCTION. **Our suites, from the cheapest to the very best are all thoroughly well made,** from carefully selected material, extra well finished. We use nothing but the highest grade of thoroughly seasoned lumber. You will find every piece stronger, better fitting, better finished, more lasting and more satisfactory than is turned out of the average factory.

TERMS OF SHIPMENT. **Nearly all of our customers send the full amount of money with their orders, instead of having the goods shipped C. O. D.** We recommend this method, because it is a more satisfactory way for us to handle your order, and by sending the full amount of money with your order, you save the small extra charge of 25 to 50 cents that the express companies ask on all C. O. D. shipments for collecting the money and returning it to us. At the same time, if you prefer, we will, on receipt of a deposit sufficient to cover the freight charges, send any bedroom suite to you C. O. D., subject to examination, the balance and freight charges to be paid after the suite is received, examined and found perfectly satisfactory. If it is not satisfactory, pay nothing, the suite will be returned to us at our expense, and we will promptly return your money. Understand also, that if you send the full amount of money with your order, and the suite does not please you in every way, we are ready to immediately return your money and pay the freight charges both ways.

THIRTY DAYS' FREE TRIAL. **As a further guarantee that the bedroom suites that you get from us cannot be approached in extraordinary value** by any bedroom suites you can buy from any other dealer, we will allow you to keep the bedroom suite thirty days and at any time during the thirty days, if you are not perfectly satisfied with your purchase and the saving you have made, you are at liberty to return the suite to us and we will return your money and pay freight charges both ways.

ABOUT FREIGHT CHARGES. **The freight charges on a bedroom suite will amount to next to nothing as compared to what you will save in price.** The beds are accepted by the railroad companies at second class freight rate, the dressers and commodes at first class freight rate. The weight of each is given under each description and by referring to page 630 you can calculate almost to a penny what the freight will amount to, and you will find it will amount to next to nothing as compared to what you will save in price. **For Example:** From any points within 400 to 600 miles of Chicago the freight on an average three-piece bedroom suite will amount to $1.00 to $1.75, whereas the saving will be from $5.00 to $15.00, depending on the suite selected.

UNDERSTAND, **you take no risk in sending us your order and your money,** for we accept it with the understanding that if the bedroom suite does not reach you in perfect condition and is not in every way satisfactory and a much better suite than you can possibly buy elsewhere for the money, you are at liberty to return it to us at our expense of freight charges both ways, and we will immediately refund your money.

OUR PLATE GLASS IS ALL HIGH GRADE BEVEL GLASS. WE USE NONE OF THE CHEAP DOMESTIC PLATE.
OUR SUITES ARE ALL FULLY EQUIPPED, ALL CASTERED, ALL FULL FINISHED, EVERY PIECE GUARANTEED.

OUR THREE-PIECE BEDROOM SUITE FOR

$10.75

No. 1C1500
ORDER BY NUMBER.

FOR $10.75 **we offer this handsome high grade three-piece bedroom suite, a thoroughly reliable bedroom suite, made of good quality materials, well made in every respect, beautifully finished, such a bedroom suite as will retail at $20.00.**

Our $10.75 price is made possible only because we offer the suite at a very little more than first cost of material and labor. It is a value unapproached in bedroom suites, and establishes a new standard of value giving in this line throughout the trade. This bedroom suite is made for us under contract by one of the largest and best furniture manufacturers in the United States, made to match a certain standard of quality that we establish in a sample, and guaranteed by us and by the manufacturer in every way.

DESCRIPTION. **This suite is made of choice, specially selected, thoroughly air seasoned and kiln dried hardwood, in a beautiful golden oak finish.** The dresser is 19 inches wide and 40 inches long, and contains two large drawers and two top drawers with serpentine curved fronts. It has a shaped top. The mirror is the best quality of genuine French bevel plate, 20x24 inches. The bed is full size, 4 feet 6 inches wide by 6 feet 1 inch long (inside measurement) and stands 6 feet high. The dresser and bed have genuine hand carving, finely executed and very ornamental. The top rail on foot of bed is rounded and framed into the posts. The commode has single top drawer, with serpentine swell front and spacious cupboard below, and matches the dresser. This suite is heavy and massive, thoroughly **well made** and well finished.

SPECIAL TO FURNITURE DEALERS. **We realize that there are many furniture dealers throughout the country who do not buy goods in large enough quantities to secure the lowest possible price.** We know for such that this $10.75 bedroom suite represents a better value for them than they could secure from a manufacturer or wholesaler. We know that $10.75 is cheaper than they could buy such a bedroom suite for, and while we do not particularly solicit the trade of dealers, we accept orders from dealers for this bedroom suite on our regular terms, as plainly stated in this catalogue, but we cannot make any reduction in price regardless of quantity. There are many dealers who can make money by buying this bedroom suite from us at $10.75, putting it in their store and selling it again at a fair profit, and at the same time they will be giving their customers good value, and will be giving their rivals in trade good competition. This bedroom suite is well packed. Shipped direct from factory in Southern Indiana. Shipping weight is about 300 pounds.

No. 1C1500 Three-piece Bedroom Suite. Price, golden oak finish................................**$10.75**
Three-piece Bedroom Suite. Price, mahogany finish................................**10.95**

BIG VALUES IN BEDROOM SUITES.

Hotel Suite, $8.95.

No. 1C1503 A Chamber Suite of two pieces, suitable for hotels or for bedrooms that are too small for the larger size three-piece suites. **This suite is made of the best selected seasoned hardwood,** is thoroughly well put together and is finished golden. The bed is 6 feet high with 4-foot 2-inch slats. Top of headboard is fancy pattern shaped and decorated with heavy moulding, giving it a very neat appearance. **The combination washstand and dresser** is 17x33 inches, of a style which matches the bed perfectly. The top is handsomely carved. The dresser is fitted with large, roomy drawer and large compartment below. The mirror is excellent **bevel plate glass and is 14x24 inches in size.**

	Bed	Dresser	Suite
Shipping weight	90 lbs.	75 lbs.	165 lbs.
Price	$3.25	$5.75	$8.95

Hotel Suite, $10.70.

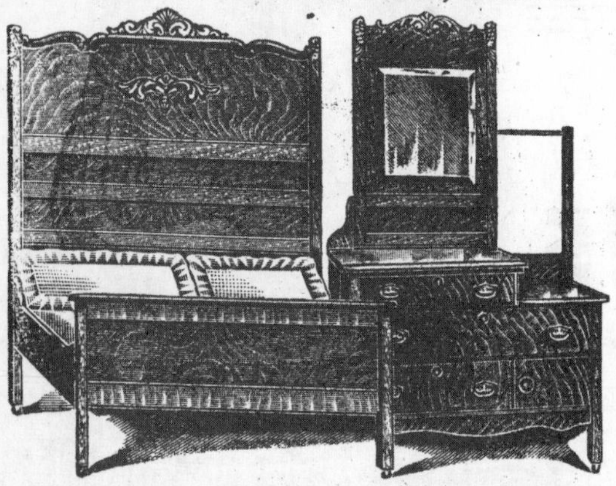

No. 1C1506 This Bedroom Suite is made of golden oak throughout, with the exception of the panels in the bed and drawer fronts, which are made of three-ply built up stock finished in a perfect imitation of quarter sawed oak. The bed is full size. The combination of dresser and commode economizes space. The base, which is 21x42 inches, contains three roomy drawers and a spacious cupboard. The mirror is an 18x20-inch high grade bevel plate. All drawers fitted with locks, keys and cast brass handles. Best quality of casters. A thoroughly substantial and well made suite. Securely packed and shipped direct from factory in Southern Indiana, thereby insuring lowest freight rate.

	Bed	Dresser	Suite
Shipping weight	90 lbs.	125 lbs.	215 lbs.
Price	$2.95	$7.75	$10.70

Our $13.25 Oak Bedroom Suite.

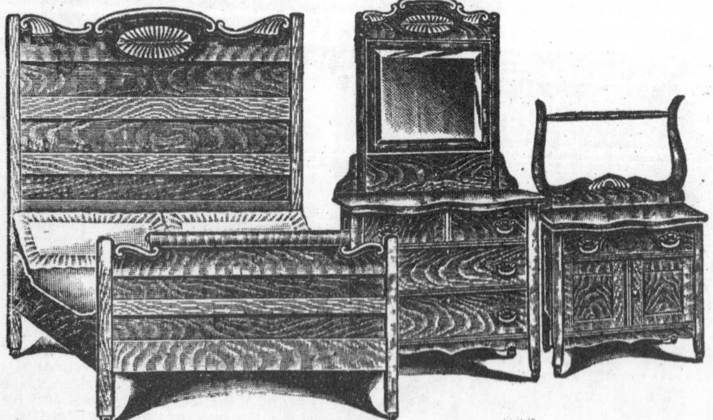

No. 1C1511 This is astonishing value in a solid golden oak Bedroom Suite. Entirely new in design, substantial in construction and handsome in finish. The bed is regular full size, 4 feet 6 inches wide, 6 feet long and 6 feet high, Decorated with hand made carvings on the head end and a massive roll on the foot end. The dresser is 40 inches long, 20 inches wide. It has two top drawers, beneath which are two large drawers fitted with locks, keys and best cast brass handles. Mirror is the best quality French bevel plate, size 20x24 inches. The washstand has a 17x30-inch top with single top drawer and spacious cupboard below. Carefully packed and shipped direct from factory in Southern Indiana. Shipping weight, 250 pounds.

Price, complete suite $13.25

ON THE FOLLOWING PAGES

We quote prices of Beds, Dressers and Washstands separately for those who do not want complete suites.

Read what we say about our Bedroom Suites on page 659. We invite the most careful comparison.

$13.45

No. 1C1512 This Bedroom Suite is made of the best selected northern hardwood, finished golden oak. It is a substantial and durable suite. The dresser is 42 inches long and contains three full size drawers, the top one full swell. The finely executed hand carvings on the bed and dresser are very attractive. The dresser is fitted with an extra quality of beveled plate mirror, 20x24 inches. Fitted with cast brass trimmings, locks and keys, complete with casters. Shipped direct from our factory in Southern Indiana. Shipping weight, 275 pounds.

Price, complete suite $13.45

$14.85

No. 1C1516 This Handsome Bedroom Suite consists of three pieces, as shown in the illustration, made of the best quality northern hardwood in a beautiful golden oak finish. The bed is full size, stands 6 feet 2 inches high and 4 feet 6 inches wide, by 6 feet 1 inch long, inside measurement. The bed and dresser are decorated with elaborate hand carvings; the dresser is fitted with the best quality beveled plate mirror, size 22x28 inches, and contains four drawers, the two top drawers having double serpentine swell. The washstand is made to match the dresser and is 17x32 inches; the dresser top is 19x42 inches; the drawers are all fitted with locks, knobs, handles and pulls, of the best cast brass. We ship this suite direct from our factory in Southern Indiana. Shipping weight, 285 pounds.

Price, complete suite $14.85

$15.45

No. 1C1520 In this solid oak Bedroom Suite we offer wonderful value. It must be seen to be fully appreciated. The bed is 6 feet 6 inches high, 4 feet 6 inches wide and 6 feet 1 inch long. The dresser has a shaped double top, 20x40 inches, solid oak panel ends, two swell front top drawers with two large drawers below, all fitted with best quality cast brass trimmings, locks and keys. The mirror is French bevel plate, size, 22x28 inches. Mirror frame and standards have rounded edges. The commode has 18x34-inch double top and matches the dresser. The massive hand carvings on bed and dresser are new in design and finely executed. The finish is beautiful golden, the construction first class, the design very attractive. Shipped direct from our factory in Southern Indiana. Shipping weight, 310 pounds.

	Bed	Dresser	Commode	Suite
Shipping weight	120 lbs.	14 lbs.	50 lbs.	310 lbs.
Price	$4.25	$8.25	$2.95	$15.45

Solid Golden Oak Bedroom Suite.

No. 1C1524 In this suite we offer a strictly first class bedroom suite, made of solid golden oak at $15.95. It is handsome in design, beautifully finished and decorated with tasteful carvings. The dresser and commode are fitted with best quality brass trimmings and all three pieces are fitted with best quality casters. The bed is full size, being 6 feet 4 inches high and 4 feet 6 inches wide. The dresser is 44 inches long and 20 inches wide, has double top and French bevel plate 22x28-inch mirror, handsome double swell top drawers, besides two full size roomy straight front drawers. The commode measures 18x34 inches, has a full swell top drawer to match the dresser, two lower drawers and a large roomy cupboard. **We ship this suite direct from factory in Southern Indiana.**

	Bed	Dresser	Commode	Suite
Shipping weight,	120 lbs.	150 lbs.	50 lbs.	320 lbs.
Price...........	$3.65	$8.95	$3.35	$15.95

No. 1C1532 This suite is made of solid oak, excellently finished and handsomely carved and decorated. The bed is 6 feet 5 inches in height; has 4-foot 6-inch slats. The dresser has a 20x44-inch double deck top, best quality French bevel plate, shaped mirror, 22x28 inches in size, and the latest design, swell top drawers. The commode measures 18x34 inches and the top drawer is double swell. The trimmings throughout are the best quality brass and each piece is fitted with casters. We ship this suite direct from our factory in Southern Indiana.

	Bed	Dresser	Commode	Suite
Shipping weight,	120 lbs.	150 lbs.	50 lbs.	320 lbs.
Price............	$3.85	$9.45	$3.45	$16.75

No. 1C1534 This suite should be compared with suites sold in retail stores at from $30.00 to $35.00. It is made of thoroughly air seasoned and kiln dried golden oak. The bed is 6 feet 6 inches high; 4 feet 6 inches wide; 6 feet 1 inch long. The base of the dresser is 22 x 44 inches. It has single panel ends. Drawers perfect fitting, move without friction. Fitted with locks, keys and best cast brass handles. The mirror is the best quality of French bevel plate, size 22x28 inches. The commode matches the dresser and has an 18x34-inch double top and a swell top drawer. The bed and dresser are decorated with beautiful hand carvings, original in design and finely executed. Note the massive roll on foot end of bed. Fitted with best quality casters. Shipped direct from factory in Southern Indiana.

	Bed	Dresser	Commode	Suite
Shipping weight,	120 lbs.	150 lbs.	50 lbs.	320 lbs.
Price.........	$5.15	$8.85	$3.45	$17.25

No. 1C1540 This suite should not be compared with suites offered by other dealers at anywhere near our price, as it is equal in quality and finish to suites that retail regularly at $28.00 to $35.00. It is made of golden elm or maple, mahogany finish, handsomely carved and decorated, as shown in the illustration. The trimmings are best quality brass, and each piece is fitted with casters. The bed is full size and measures 6 feet 4 inches in height and 4 feet 6 inches in width. The dresser measures 21x42 inches, and has double deck top, double swell top drawers and two large, roomy, straight front drawers. The mirror is French bevel plate, 24x30 inches. The commode is 18x34 inches, has splasher back and swell drawer to match the dresser, besides two lower drawers and a roomy cupboard. We ship this suite direct from our factory near Grand Rapids, Mich., thereby insuring the lowest freight rate.

	Bed	Dresser	Commode	Suite
Shipping weight,	120 lbs.	150 lbs.	50 lbs.	320 lbs.
Price...............	$3.95	$9.85	$3.75	$17.55

A Great Bargain at this Low Price.

No. 1C1544 This suite is entirely new in style of construction. It is made entirely of solid golden oak with the exception of the panels in the bed and the drawer fronts, which are made of selected three-ply built up stock, finished in perfect imitation of quarter sawed oak. The decorations on the bed and dresser are all elaborate raised carvings. The bed is 6 feet 1 inch high and 4 feet 6 inches wide. The dresser is 20 inches wide and 42 inches long. Has full swell front. The mirror is 24x30-inch imported bevel plate and is suspended in a handsome universal toilet. The handles and knobs are all cast brass and the dresser is fitted with locks, keys and casters. Shipped direct from our factory in Southern Indiana, thereby insuring the lowest freight rate.

	Bed	Dresser	Commode	Suite
Shipping weight,	120 lbs.	150 lbs.	50 lbs.	320 lbs.
Price..............	$3.75	$10.25	$3.75	$17.75

No. 1C1548 This Suite is made of the best selected northern hardwood in a beautiful golden oak finish. The dresser has a full double curved serpentine front with two top drawers and two large drawers beneath. The bed is 6 feet 3 inches high, 4 feet 6 inches by 6 feet 1 inch inside measurement. The dresser is fitted with the best quality bevel plate mirror, size 24x30 inches. The top of the dresser measures 20x42 inches, and the commode which is made to match the dresser, is 18x32 inches. All drawers fitted with locks and keys. The handles and pulls are the best cast brass. The equal of any suite offered for sale at $25.00 to $30.00. Shipped direct from our factory in Southern Indiana.

	Bed	Dresser	Commode	Suite
Shipping weight.........	100 lbs.	150 lbs.	50 lbs.	300 lbs.
Price.....................	$3.60	$10.90	$3.35	$17.85

A Wonder of Value. Such a Suite as Furniture Stores generally price at $24.00 to $28.00. Reduced to $17.95

No. 1C1552 This Suite consists of three pieces, as shown in the illustration, having a cheval dresser instead of the regular style generally offered by other dealers. All three pieces are made of the choicest golden oak, the wood being carefully selected and kiln dried. The design is one of the latest for this season, the dresser and commode having full swell top drawer, and all three pieces being elaborately carved and handsomely finished. The bed is full size, being 6 feet 4 inches high and 4 feet 6 inches wide. The dresser measures 20x44 inches, has French bevel plate mirror, 18x40 inches, and a very roomy cupboard, as shown in the illustration. The commode measures 18x34 inches and matches the dresser perfectly. Each piece of the suite is fitted with casters. We ship direct from factory in Southern Indiana.

	Bed	Dresser	Commode	Suite
Shipping weight	120 lbs.	135 lbs.	50 lbs.	305 lbs.
Price	$3.65	$10.95	$3.35	$17.95

$18.75

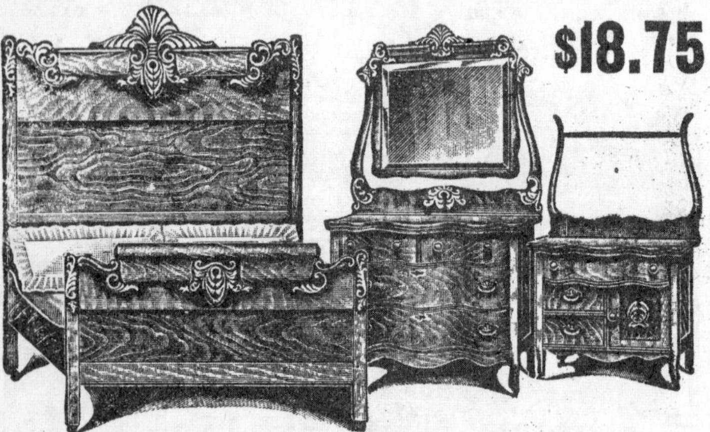

No. 1C1556 This Bedroom Suite is made of selected oak in a golden finish. The wood is thoroughly air seasoned and kiln dried. The base of the dresser is 22x44 inches and has a double serpentine swell front, double top, single solid panel ends and contains two top drawers and two large drawers fitted with locks, keys and the best quality cast brass handles. The mirror is the best quality French bevel plate, size, 24x30 inches, supported by shapely mirror frame and standards with rounded edges. The bed is 6 feet 6 inches high, 4 feet 6 inches wide and 6 feet 1 inch long. The commode has an 18x34-inch top, single solid panel ends and matches the dresser. The massive roll on the bed and the genuine hand carvings on bed and dresser are original in design and highly ornamental. This suite cannot be purchased in a retail store for less than $30.00 to $35.00. Shipped direct from our factory in Southern Indiana.

	Bed	Dresser	Commode	Suite
Shipping weight	120 lbs.	150 lbs.	50 lbs.	320 lbs.
Price	$5.15	$10.25	$3.35	$18.75

$19.85

No. 1C1560 This Bedroom Suite is one of the best values in our entire line and should be compared with suites generally sold at $35.00 to $40.00 by others. Made of thoroughly seasoned hard northern elm with a high gloss golden oak finish. The bed is regular full size, 6 feet 5 inches high, 4 feet 6 inches wide, 6 feet 1 inch long. Dresser has a shaped double top, size 23x43 inches. It has two top drawers below which are two large drawers all with full serpentine curved front, fitted with drawer guides, locks and cast brass handles. The handsome designed mirror is best quality French bevel plate, size 24x30 inches. Washstand has an 18x34-inch top and matches the dresser. Complete with casters. Construction and finish high grade throughout. Shipped direct from factory in Central Wisconsin.

	Bed	Dresser	Commode	Suite
Shipping weight	120 lbs.	150 lbs.	50 lbs.	320 lbs.
Price	$5.15	$11.25	$3.45	$19.85

REDUCED TO $21.95

No. 1C1564 This Suite is made of solid oak, handsomely decorated with fancy carvings and is beautifully finished throughout. The bedstead is 6 feet 8 inches in height and takes 4-foot 6-inch slats. The dresser is full swell front, of **large figured flaky quartered oak,** double deck top and measures 20x44 inches, handsomely shaped French bevel plate glass, 24x30 inches. The commode corresponds with the dresser and has 18x34-inch top with full swell top drawer. The dresser and commode are supplied with handsome cast brass handles and knobs and locks, and the entire suite is furnished complete with casters. Strictly high grade in every detail of construction, wood and finish. We ship from factory in Southern Indiana, thereby insuring lowest freight rates.

	Bed	Dresser	Commode	Suite
Shipping weight	120 lbs.	135 lbs.	50 lbs.	305 lbs.
Price	$5.70	$12.80	$3.45	$21.95

$23.25

No. 1C1577 This Bedroom Suite is made of the best solid quarter sawed oak, thoroughly seasoned and warranted against cracking or warping. The finish is of the best, being hand rubbed and highly polished. The illustration will give you some idea of the beautiful hand carving which decorates each piece of the suite. The bed is 6 feet 4 inches high and 4 feet 6 inches wide. It is very handsome in appearance, having highly figured quarter oak panels. The dresser is 21½ inches wide by 42½ inches long, has two swell top drawers and two large drawers beneath, 21¼ inches in depth. The top drawers are varnished inside. The mirror is the latest design French bevel plate, 24x30 inches. The commode is made to match the dresser and bed, has 34-inch top, two drawers, 18 inches deep and two roomy cupboards below. Best quality cast brass handles, knobs and casters. Shipped direct from our factory near Grand Rapids, Mich., thereby insuring lowest freight rate.

	Bed	Dresser	Commode	Suite
Shipping weight	120 lbs.	150 lbs.	50 lbs.	320 lbs.
Price	$5.95	$12.75	$4.55	$23.25

$24.75

No. 1C1568 This Bedroom Suite should be compared with suites sold in retail stores for $35.00 to $40.00. It is made of quarter sawed oak, specially selected stock with a highly figured grain, hand rubbed and highly polished golden finish. The bed is 78 inches high, 54 inches wide and 71 inches long. The dresser base has a double curved double top; size, 22x44 inches; serpentine swell front; solid single panel ends; two top drawers and two large drawers fitted with locks, keys and the best quality cast brass trimmings. The handsome pattern shaped mirror is the best quality French bevel plate, size, 24x30 inches. The commode has an 18x34-inch top; solid single panel ends and matches the dresser. The carvings are handsome, finely cut and highly ornamental. Construction strictly first class throughout. Shipped direct from factory in Southern Indiana.

	Bed	Dresser	Commode	Suite
Shipping weight	120 lbs.	150 lbs.	50 lbs.	320 lbs.
Price	$8.25	$12.25	$4.25	$24.75

$25.45

No. 1C1571 This Bedroom Suite is one of the very latest and handsomest designs in our entire line and represents astonishing value. It is made of selected highly figured ash with high gloss golden oak finish. The bed is 6 feet 6 inches high and 4 feet 6 inches wide. Is beautifully decorated with heavy hand cut carvings. The dresser is very large, being 22x42 inches. Has double swell front, round corner posts, shaped feet, double top. The drawers run unusually smooth, as they are fitted with patent drawer guides. The handles are all solid cast brass. One special feature of this dresser is the patent construction used in the bottom so that when the drawers are closed they are practically dust and vermin proof, a feature not found in any other dresser. The mirror is the best French bevel plate, 24x30 inches, rounded mirror frame and standards. The commode is made to correspond with the dresser and bed. All pieces are fitted with casters. Shipped direct from factory in Central Indiana, thereby insuring lowest freight rate.

	Bed	Dresser	Commode	Suite
Shipping weight	120 lbs.	150 lbs.	60 lbs.	330 lbs.
Price	$8.75	$12.45	$4.25	$25.45

$26.95

No. 1C1574 A new design in a strictly high grade solid oak bedroom suite. It is handsomely carved and beautiful in finish. The wood is almost entirely fine selected, flaky grained quarter sawed oak. The dresser has double top drawers, and the entire front is double swell serpentine shape. The mirror is the best French bevel plate, size 24x30 inches. The top of the dresser is 23 inches by 3 feet 7 inches. The top of the commode, which matches the dresser, is 18 inches by 2 feet 10 inches. The bed is 6 feet 7 inches high, 4 feet 6 inches wide and 6 feet 1 inch long inside, with finely executed carvings on the head and a very massive roll and beautiful carvings on the foot end. The suite sells for $45.00 to $50.00 in a retail store. See front pages for further information. Shipped from our factory in Central Wisconsin.

	Bed	Dresser	Commode	Suite
Shipping weight	120 lbs.	150 lbs.	60 lbs.	310 lbs.
Price	$7.50	$14.80	$4.65	$26.95

$29.45

No. 1C1578 This handsome bedroom suite is made of highly figured, thoroughly air seasoned ash, golden oak finish. The dresser has a shaped double top, 23x43 inches corresponding with the serpentine front. Dresser and washstand have double panel ends. Drawers move without friction, being fitted with special drawer guides, locks and best quality cast brass handles. Mirror is best quality French bevel plate, size, 24x30 inches. The bed is regular size, 6 feet 8 inches high, 6 feet long and 4 feet 6 inches wide. The massive roll on the front end of the bed and the corresponding part on the head of bed and the dresser are made of cross banded quarter sawed oak. Commode has an 18x34-inch top and matches the dresser. Bed and dresser elaborately decorated with hand made carvings. Cabinet work strictly first class throughout. Complete with best quality casters. Style of this suite is especially attractive and should be compared with those offered in retail stores at $40.00 to $50.00. Shipped direct from factory in Central Wisconsin.

	Bed	Dresser	Commode	Suite
Shipping weight	120 lbs.	150 lbs.	60 lbs.	310 lbs.
Price	$10.45	$14.65	$4.35	$29.45

$32.25

No. 1C1583 This Bedroom Suite is especially designed for us, it is made almost entirely of the best selected quarter sawed golden oak, hand polished. The bed is 6 feet 5 inches high, 4 feet 6 inches wide and 6 feet 1 inch long. Double swell front, full paneled ends. Large elegant shaped beveled French plate mirror, size 28x34 inches. The base of dresser is 43x23 inches. The handsome roll on head and foot of the bed and on the mirror frame are very effective and the carvings are beautiful. The commode matches the dresser and has an 18x34-inch top. The wide panels at the head and foot end of the bed are of especially selected quarter sawed oak, and the intervening panels of choice plain golden oak. The detail construction is strictly first class throughout. Shipped direct from factory in Central Wisconsin, thereby insuring lowest freight rate. See front pages for further information.

	Bed	Dresser	Commode	Suite
Shipping weight	125 lbs.	160 lbs.	60 lbs.	345 lbs.
Price	$9.75	$17.85	$4.65	$32.25

$32.75

No. 1C1585 This is one of the most attractive high grade bedroom suites which we furnish. The wood is choice highly figured thoroughly air seasoned northern elm, in a beautiful golden oak high gloss finish. Bed is regular size, 6 feet 6 inches high, 6 feet long, and 4 feet 6 inches wide inside. Note the massive hand made finely cut carvings on bed and dresser. Dresser is large, measuring 23x43 inches. It has a full serpentine curved front, and full panel ends. Drawers move without friction, being fitted with special drawer guides, locks and best cast brass handles. Extra large mirror is the best quality French bevel plate, size 28x34 inches. Commode has an 18x34-inch top and matches the dresser. This suite is well made in every detail of construction, and cannot be fully appreciated until seen and examined. It should be compared with suites offered by others at $45.00 to $50.00. Shipped direct from factory in Central Wisconsin.

	Bed	Dresser	Commode	Suite
Shipping weight	130 lbs.	160 lbs.	50 lbs.	340 lbs.
Price	$11.25	$16.85	$4.65	$32.75

$34.45

No. 1C1586 This magnificent Bedroom Suite must be seen to be fully appreciated. The wood is specially selected, highly figured quarter sawed oak in a beautiful golden color, highly polished. The bed is 6 feet 7 inches high, 4 feet 6 inches wide and 6 feet 1 inch long. The dresser base has a double top 21x44 inches and has a full serpentine swell front. The handsome designed mirror is the best quality French bevel plate, size 24x30 inches. The commode has a double top, 20x34 inches, and matches the dresser. The drawers are fitted with locks and the best cast brass handles. The bed and dresser ornamented with genuine hand carvings, new and original in design and finely executed. Strictly high grade in every detail of construction, wood and finish. Shipped direct from factory in Central Indiana.

	Bed	Dresser	Commode	Suite
Shipping weight	130 lbs.	160 lbs.	70 lbs.	360 lbs.
Price	$11.85	$17.75	$4.85	$34.45

No. 1C1591 This suite is one of the best and highest grade bedroom suites which we furnish. It is made of handsome, richly figured quarter sawed golden oak or genuine mahogany veneered, as desired, hand rubbed and highly polished, and finished so that the grain of the wood is most perfectly brought out, showing its full beauty. The bed is 6 feet 6 inches high, 4 feet 6 inches wide. It is elegant looking, having just enough carving to make it attractive. The dresser is very large, the top measuring 24x48 inches. Has handsome shaped front. The drawers are 24 inches in depth and are all varnished inside. The frame which holds the mirror is of artistic design and made to correspond with the bed. The mirror is the best French bevel plate, 28x34 inches. The commode corresponds with the dresser and the bed. It measures 18x36 inches. All the handles and knobs are best quality brass, and the casters steel frame. Each piece of the suite is carefully packed and we insure safe delivery. Shipped direct from our factory near Grand Rapids, Mich. Shipping weight, about 550 pounds.

	Quartered Oak	Mahogany
Price, complete suite........	**$49.85**	**$49.95**

READ WHAT WE SAY ABOUT
OUR BEDROOM SUITES
ON PAGE 659.

SPECIAL COMBINATION BEDROOM SUITES.

We illustrate below two Dressers, Chiffoniers and Washstands, which we furnish in four different woods, viz: Quarter Sawed Golden Oak, Curly Birch, Birdseye Maple and Genuine Mahogany.

THE QUARTER SAWED GOLDEN OAK is all specially selected, highly figured, flaky grained wood, carefully matched and finished in a beautiful golden color, which brings out the grain of the wood perfectly.

BIRDSEYE MAPLE is one of the handsomest grained woods of which furniture is made. The pores are very close, making a very hard and flinty surface when finished. This, together with the natural "Birdseye" grain of the wood when highly polished, makes a very beautiful, attractive and highly ornamental article of furniture. When finished, the color is a beautiful white, tinged slightly with yellow. This wood is specially adapted for guests' or young ladies' rooms.

THE GENUINE MAHOGANY used in the construction of these pieces grows in the forests of South America. This wood has always been highly desirable, because of the beauty of the grain and the high polish which can be given to its surface. One of its striking characteristics is, the older the wood the darker the reddish brown color becomes.

CURLY BIRCH has a beautiful curly or wavy grain. Its striking characteristic is the golden satin finish, slightly tinged with pink. It is considered by many experts as the choicest of all woods used in furniture.

THE CONSTRUCTION is strictly high grade throughout, every joint and panel perfectly fitted. Drawers have the best dovetail construction front and rear. All drawers finished inside.

THE FINISH. Each piece is given the best piano polished finish throughout. A smooth surface, a perfect luster, that will hold its surface for years is obtained by great care in the application of the several coatings of the finish, each coating being allowed to thoroughly harden and dry before being polished for the succeeding one. The finish of the pieces in all of the different woods is the best obtainable.

THESE COMBINATION SUITES, in any of the woods which you may select, when used with one of our metal beds, shown on pages 673 to 676, makes an ideal bedroom suite, of which, the attractiveness, high quality of construction and beauty of wood and finish cannot be fully appreciated until seen, examined and compared with those offered for sale by others at more than double the prices we ask.

No. 1C1592 This handsome high grade Special Combination Bedroom Suite, we furnish in suites or separately in any of the four woods described. The dresser has a 23x45-inch top. The chiffonier has a 21x33-inch top. The washstand has a 21x33 inch top. All have solid panel ends Dresser mirror is 26x32 inches. Chiffonier mirror is 16x20 inches. Both mirrors are best quality French bevel plate. Mirror frames and standards have neatly rounded edges. Drawers finished inside, fitted with locks, best cast brass handles and casters. In this suite, as well as in the others illustrated on this page, we offer exceptional value, and we solicit your order with the distinct understanding that if it is not all that we claim, all that you expect, you can return it and your money will be refunded with freight charges both ways. Shipped direct from factory in Western Pennsylvania. Shipping weight, dresser, 150 pounds; chiffonier, 150 pounds; washstand, 50 pounds.

	Quartered Oak	Curly Birch	Birdseye Maple	Genuine Mahogany
Price, Dresser....	**$23.35**	**$24.50**	**$24.85**	**$25.35**
Price, Chiffonier.	**18.00**	**19.15**	**19.45**	**19.85**
Price, Washstand	**7.35**	**7.75**	**7.95**	**8.10**

No. 1C1596 This Combination Bedroom Suite, in either of the four woods described, is exceptionally attractive in design. The dresser has a 24x48-inch double top. The chiffonier has a 21x34-inch top. The washstand has a 21x34-inch top. Each piece has solid panel ends and all drawers finished inside. Fitted with locks and best quality handles and casters. The extra large size dresser mirror is 28x34 inches, the chiffonier mirror is 16x22 inches. Both are the best quality French bevel plate. Mirror frame and standards are decorated with hand made carvings finely executed. This suite when used with one of our metal beds, shown on pages 673 to 676, makes a beautiful bedroom suite and must be seen to fully appreciate the wonderful value we offer at such extremely low prices. Separate pieces furnished if desired. Shipped direct from factory in Western Pennsylvania. Shipping weight; dresser, 200 pounds; chiffonier, 150 pounds; washstand, 60 pounds.

	Quartered Oak	Curly Birch	Birdseye Maple	Genuine Mahogany
Price, Dresser....	**$24.10**	**$24.25**	**$25.75**	**$26.25**
Price, Chiffonier.	**18.75**	**19.85**	**20.00**	**20.75**
Price, Washstand	**7.45**	**7.55**	**8.15**	**8.35**

WOOD BEDS.

WE QUOTE PRICES SEPARATELY ON WOOD BEDS IN THE BEDROOM SUITES. SEE PAGES 660 TO 664.

No. 1C2850 This Bed is made of hardwood, thoroughly air seasoned and kiln dried in a perfect imitation of quarter sawed golden oak. Height, 3 feet 6 inches. We furnish it in 3 feet 6 inches, or 4 feet 6 inches width. Substantial in construction. Shipped from factory in Southern Indiana. Shipping weight, 65 pounds.

Width....3½ feet	4½ feet
Price....**$1.85**	**$1.95**

No. 1C2854 Wood Bed, made of hardwood in a perfect imitation of quarter sawed golden oak, thoroughly seasoned and beautifully finished. Height, 4 feet; length, 6 feet; width, 3 feet 6 inches or 4 feet 6 inches. Construction first class. A bargain at our price. Shipped direct from factory in Southern Indiana. Shipping weight, 70 pounds.

Width....3½ feet	4½ feet
Price....**$2.20**	**$2.25**

No. 1C2856 Wood Bed, made of hardwood in a perfect imitation of quarter sawed oak. Height of head end, 4 feet 6 inches; width, 4 feet 6 inches. Head end decorated with genuine hand carvings. Foot end has broad top rail. Thoroughly well made and beautifully finished. Shipped direct from factory in Southern Indiana. Shipping weight, 57 pounds. Price.....**$2.75**

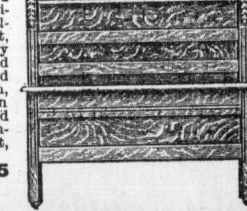

No. 1C2860 This Bed is made of thoroughly seasoned hardwood, in a perfect imitation of quarter sawed golden oak. Head end is 5 feet, 2 inches high and handsomely decorated with genuine hand carvings. Foot end has broad top rail. Length, 6 feet; width, 4 feet 6 inches. Construction strictly high grade. Shipped direct from factory in Southern Indiana. Shipping weight, 85 pounds.
Price................**$3.25**

No. 1C2864 This Wood Bed is 5 feet 8 inches high, made of hardwood, in a perfect imitation of quarter sawed golden oak. Head end is ornamented with a massive roll and genuine hand carvings. Length, 6 feet; width, 4 feet 6 inches. Foot end has broad top rail. Sells for double our price in stores. Shipped direct from factory in Southern Indiana. Shipping weight, 95 pounds.
Price...................**$3.75**

No. 1C2868 This Handsome Wood Bed is made of hardwood, in a beautiful and perfect imitation of quarter sawed golden oak. Height of head end, 6 feet 4 inches; width (slat), 4 feet 6 inches. Note the genuine and artistic hand carving on head and foot end. High grade in construction. Shipped direct from factory in Southern Indiana. Shipping weight, 100 pounds.
Price...................**$4.35**

NEW AND ASTONISHING VALUES IN DRESSERS.

THESE DRESSERS which we offer this season are made by the largest and most reliable manufacturers in the country. The designs are all new and up to date, they are shipped direct from the factory, enabling us to make the lowest price possible, based on the actual cost of manufacture with but our one small percentage of profit added. Almost every style of dresser made is illustrated on the following pages but we call your attention to the fact that we can furnish dressers from almost any of our large and handsome line of bedroom suites. The value we give you and the immense saving will only be fully appreciated when you compare these dressers with those offered by others at prices 30 to 40 per cent higher than we ask.

THE WOOD used in the construction of our dressers is thoroughly air seasoned and kiln dried before being put through the factory, it is carefully selected, special attention being given to the high quality of the grain.

HOW WE ARE ABLE TO MAKE THE PRICES SO LOW, and how it is possible for us to reduce our prices on bedroom suites and dressers below any previous quotation. They are made for us under contract by three of the best manufacturers in this country and our output has increased to such an extent that we are able to contract in each case for a very large part of the output of each factory, and these factories desiring to run at full capacity the year around, are willing to take our contract at a price very near the cost of material and labor, as it facilitates the working of their factory and enables them to run every working day at full capacity and thus reduce the cost, not only on the suites they make for us, but on the suites they sell to other people. As a result we obtain our dressers this season including all the newest designs, at about the cost of the material and labor and our price to you is but one small percentage of profit above the actual cost.

THE PRICES QUOTED are for the dressers, chiffoniers or washstands delivered on board the cars at the factory or our warehouse from which point customer pays the freight. You will find the freight charges will amount to next to nothing as compared to what you will save in price. Refer to page 630. Take the rate quoted to the point nearest you and from the weight of the article which we give under each description you can calculate almost to a cent what the amount of the freight charges will be to your town.

WE GUARANTEE that if you order one of our dressers, chiffoniers or washstands and do not find it in every respect better in quality, the design, the wood, the construction and the finish strictly high grade and lower in price than you can procure from any other dealer we will refund your money together with all transportation charges. We further agree that should any article that you purchase from us shrink, crack, check or in any manner become unsatisfactory we will at once replace the defective part or refund your money upon return of the article to us.

SAFE DELIVERY GUARANTEE. We guarantee the safe delivery of every dresser, chiffonier and washstand. Each article is carefully wrapped and packed in the best possible manner and is guaranteed to reach you in the same perfect condition it leaves the factory.

DEALERS may say our prices are too low for reliable goods. We know that our prices are very low, so low, in fact, that many of our customers are really in doubt whether to order from us. We wish to repeat most emphatically that every dresser, chiffonier and washstand we sell is strictly high grade, made from the best material, the best construction and finish and shipped to you under our binding guarantee for quality and safe delivery. Each article we sell is sent out with the idea that it must be an advertisement for us and our refund guarantee insures the customer against any possible risk in buying from us.

THE CONSTRUCTION of our dressers is strictly high grade throughout, the drawers all dovetailed, the panels built of transverse layers of 3-ply stock, the post and crossbars mortised and framed in the most perfect manner. In fact, every part and piece is thoroughly well made and fitted, the best that modern machinery and skilled workmanship can produce. All the drawers move easily. The bevel plate glass mirrors we use in our dressers are the very best obtainable. We use none of the cheap domestic plate. Every dresser is fully trimmed and castered and absolutely guaranteed in every detail of construction. **The very best quality of material is used in the finishing of our dressers.** The hardwood, oil, the glue and the varnish are the highest grade obtainable. Experienced and skilled workmen only are employed in the factory which makes these goods. The color is a beautiful golden which brings out the handsome grain of the wood.

$6.25

No. 1C1800 ORDER BY NUMBER

OUR $6.25 DRESSER.

A HIGH CLASS PIECE OF FURNITURE. THE WONDER OF THE FURNITURE WORLD.

$6.25 for this handsome dresser made of choice selected oak in a beautiful golden finish. Undoubtedly the most wonderful value in a strictly first class dresser that has ever been offered by any dealer. The base is 42 inches long by 19 inches wide and contains four roomy drawers. The mirror is the best quality of genuine hand polished French bevel plate; size, 18x20 inches. The frame which encloses the mirror is decorated with ornamental and finely executed genuine hand carvings. The drawers are all dovetailed and are fitted carefully to avoid binding or friction. The frame of this dresser is mortised and joined together in the best manner possible. The durability and construction we guarantee to be equal to any dresser made. The wood used in the construction of this dreser is specially selected from fine grained oak, thoroughly air seasoned and kiln dried and guaranteed not to warp, shrink or check. The finish is strictly high grade, special attention being given to the color to bring out the grain of the wood most effectively. The contract for a large quantity of these dressers enables us to offer them at a very low price, a price below what your retail dealer can buy them for in car lots.

WE EXPECT to sell 5,000 of these dressers this season at $6.25. We believe this page displaying this dresser and the low price of $6.25 will sell 5,000 of these dressers during the ensuing year. If it does we are well repaid in spite of the narrow margin of a few cents profit on each dresser. It will mean 5,000 well satisfied, enthusiastic customers, 5,000 people who will admit to themselves and most likely tell their friends that we certainly sell reliable goods below any kind of competition and that our descriptions and representations can be depended on. These customers will recommend us to their neighbors, when they want to buy other merchandise they will look in our catalogue and see what our price is before buying from some one else. In this way our trade grows and grows, one sale means another, one pleased customer is the means of getting another, and in return for this generous response on the part of our customers, we on our part are going to give them the benefit of every advantage we possess in buying and selling goods and always make our prices as low as possible, which will mean below all others.

No. 1C1800 DRESSER. Shipped direct from factory in Southern Indiana. Shipping weight, 100 pounds. Price........................ ......$6.25

No. 1C1804 This Dresser is made of solid oak, thoroughly air seasoned and kiln dried, in a golden finish. The base is 38 inches long and has three large drawers fitted with locks, keys and cast brass handles. It has full paneled ends. The mirror is the best quality French beveled plate, size, 18x20 inches. Best quality casters. Thoroughly substantial in detail of construction. Shipped direct from factory in Southern Indiana, thereby insuring lowest freight rates. Shipping weight, 100 lbs. Price..........$5.35

No. 1C1808 This Dresser is made of solid oak, golden finish, exceptionally well proportioned base and mirror. Has 38-inch top; handsome bevel mirror, 18x20 inches. Has upper full swell drawer and two roomy lower drawers trimmed with cast brass handles. Fitted complete with best quality casters. Mechanical construction first class in every detail. Shipped direct from factory in Southern Indiana, thereby insuring lowest freight rates. Shipping weight, about 100 pounds. Price..............$5.95

$6.95 for This $12.00 Dresser.

No. 1C1812 This Dresser is made of thoroughly seasoned oak in golden finish. Fitted with a shaped French bevel plate mirror, 20x24 inches; has serpentine shaped top, size, 19x40 inches. Two double curved top drawers and two large drawers fitted with locks and keys and fancy pulls, ornamented with hand carvings. Shipped direct from factory in Southern Indiana. Shipping weight, about 100 pounds. Price..............$6.95

No. 1C1816 This Beautiful Dresser is made of solid oak, finished golden. Has 20x42-inch double top. Serpentine swell top drawers and two large roomy lower drawers, fitted with cast brass knobs and handles. Has full panel ends. Beautiful diamond shaped French beveled large mirror, 20x20 inches. The toilet is ornamented with hand carvings. Shipped direct from our factory in Central Wisconsin. Shipping weight, 125 lbs. Price..........$7.95

$8.25 Combination Dresser and Washstand.

No. 1C1820 This Combination Dresser and Washstand is made of solid oak. The base is 20 inches long, 42 inches wide and contains three large drawers and closet. The mirror is 18x30 inches French bevel plate. Has double top, full paneled ends, brass trimmings. Packed and shipped direct from our factory in Southern Indiana. Shipping weight, 100 pounds. Price, golden oak..........$8.25

No. 1C1824 This is a Beautiful Hardwood White Enameled Dresser, considered very stylish and adapted for use with iron beds. Has handsomely shaped double top, 21 x 42 inches, and a bevel mirror, 20x24 inches. Has two upper full swell drawers and two roomy lower drawers trimmed with nice brass handles. Shipped from factory near Grand Rapids, Mich. Commode No. 1C1910 matches this dresser. Shipping weight, about 150 pounds.

Price, white enamel, $9.45
Price, golden oak finish.......... 8.35
Price, mahogany finish.......... 8.45

Cheval Dresser. $9.35

No. 1C1828 This Cheval Dresser is made of solid oak, golden finish. It is a large, roomy dresser. Has a cupboard and two small drawers at the right hand side and two large, roomy drawers below, all fitted with substantial brass knobs and handles. The mirror is fine beveled plate, 17x30 inches. Complete with set of best quality casters. Shipped direct from our factory in Central Wisconsin. Shipping weight, 150 pounds. Price..........$9.35

No. 1C1832 This Dresser is made from the best quality of highly figured oak in a fine golden finish. The base is 20 inches wide, 44 inches long and contains two double curved top drawers beneath which are two large straight front drawers. The mirror is the best quality of French beveled plate, 22x28 inches in size. The shapely standard and mirror frame have neatly rounded edges, ornamented with genuine raised hand carvings finely executed. Packed and shipped direct from our warehouses in Louisville, Ky., Southern Indiana or our factory in Central North Carolina, thereby insuring lowest freight rates. Shipping weight, 150 pounds.

Price, golden oak..........$10.75

No. 1C1836 This Dresser is made of thoroughly seasoned and kiln dried solid oak, in a beautiful golden finish. It has a double top; size, 22x44 inches, with rounded edges and shaped front to correspond with the full swell front of the drawers below. It has two top drawers and two large drawers. Drawer fronts are made of selected highly figured stock. It has single paneled ends. Mirror is the best quality French bevel plate, size, 22x28 inches. Supported by standards and frame with rounded edges and decorated with beautiful raised hand carvings. Fitted with locks, keys and best quality cast brass handles and casters. Thoroughly well made in every detail of construction and finish. Sells for $15.00 to $18.00 in retail stores. Shipped direct from factory in Southern Indiana. Shipping weight, 150 pounds.

Price, golden oak..........$10.85

No. 1C1840 This Dresser is made of solid oak, golden finish. It has single panel ends and a double top, size, 23x46 inches, with rounded edges, curved front and ends. It has two top drawers below which are two large drawers, all with double swell serpentine fronts of highly figured oak. Mirror is of the best quality French bevel plate, size, 22x28 inches. Standards and mirror frame have rounded edges and decorated with raised hand carvings finely executed. All drawers run smoothly without friction. Strictly high grade in every detail of construction. Shipped direct from factory in Southern Indiana. Shipping weight, 150 pounds.

Price, golden oak..........$11.25

No. 1C1844 Dresser. We recommend this dresser as one of the greatest values we have ever been able to offer. It is an entirely new design, very attractive and is sure to please. It is made of well seasoned, carefully selected golden oak with highly figured quarter sawed veneer facing on the drawers. It has 21x44-inch double top, full swell front; the cabinet work is exceptionally good and the details very carefully executed throughout. The mirror is 24x30-inch French bevel plate. The handles and knobs are all fancy cast brass. Shipped direct from the factory in Ohio. Shipping weight, 125 pounds. Price...$11.45

No. 1C1848 This Dresser is made of solid oak with a beautiful flaky grained quarter sawed oak swell front. The base has a double top, 20x44 inches. The beautiful pattern shaped mirror is the best quality French beveled plate, size, 24x30 inches. The standards and mirror frame have round edges, ornamented and with finely executed raised hand carvings. Two top drawers and two large drawers with the best burnished cast brass handles and locks. Retail dealers ask double our price for such a dresser. Shipped direct from our warehouses in Louisville, Ky., Southern Indiana or from our factory in Central North Carolina, thereby insuring lowest freight rates. Shipping weight, 150 pounds.

Price, golden oak..........$11.85

No. 1C1851 This Dresser is made of solid golden oak, thoroughly seasoned and kiln dried. The shaped double top is 23x46 inches. It has single panel ends, two top drawers, and two large drawers all with serpentine curved fronts made of highly figured specially selected stock. The mirror is the best quality French bevel plate, size, 24x30 inches, supported by standards and frame with rounded edges and decorated with genuine raised hand carvings, perfectly executed. Fitted with locks, keys and best quality cast brass handles and casters. Sells in retail stores at $18.00 to $20.00. High grade in construction, beautiful in wood and finish. A bargain at our price. Shipped direct from factory in Southern Indiana. Shipping weight, 150 pounds. Price..........$12.25

No. 1C1854 This Dresser is made of solid oak, thoroughly seasoned and kiln dried, in a beautiful golden finish. Single panel ends. It has a double top; size 23x46 inches, with curved ends and front and rounded edge. It has double top drawers, below which are two large drawers. Entire front is made of highly figured stock and has a double serpentine swell. Mirror is best quality French bevel plate; size, 24x30 inches. Note the shapely mirror frame and standards, with rounded edges, decorated with genuine raised hand carvings. This dresser must be seen to be fully appreciated. Strictly high grade in construction and finish. Shipped direct from factory in Southern Indiana. Shipping weight about 150 pounds.
Price..$12.50

No. 1C1857 This Beautiful Dresser is made of selected quarter sawed golden oak, birdseye maple or in genuine mahogany; highly polished. The base has a double top; size, 20x38 inches, with serpentine curved edge. It has solid panel ends and contains three large drawers with a double swell front. Fitted with locks, keys, cast brass handles and best quality casters. The shapely mirror is the best quality French bevel plate; size, 20x24 inches. The ornamental standards and mirror frame are made of the same kind of wood as the balance of dresser—not imitation finish. The carvings are hand made. This dresser matches chiffonier No. 1C1971, illustrated on page 669, and commode No. 1C1910½ on page 668 and is specially adapted for use in a young lady's bed room. Shipped direct from factory in Western Pennsylvania. Shipping weight, 125 pounds.

	Quarter Sawed Oak	Genuine Mahogany	Birdseye Maple
Price..	$12.75	$12.85	$12.95

No. 1C1860 This Dresser is made of solid oak, golden finish. The wood is thoroughly seasoned and kiln dried. The base has a shaped double top; size, 23 x 46 inches. It has single paneled ends. It has two top drawers and two large drawers, all with double curved serpentine fronts of highly figured oak. Mirror is the best quality of French bevel plate, size, 24x30 inches. Mirror frame and standards have rounded edges and decorated with genuine raised hand carvings perfectly executed. Drawers run smoothly. Construction throughout strictly first class. Wonderful value at our price. Shipped direct from factory in Southern Indiana. Shipping weight, 150 pounds.
Price........$13.25

No. 1C1863 This Handsome Dresser we furnish in highly figured quarter sawed golden oak, birdseye maple or selected birch in a perfect imitation of mahogany. All highly polished. The base has a double serpentine shaped top, size, 22x42 inches. It has two swell top drawers, below which are two large drawers. Fitted with locks, keys and the best quality cast brass handles and casters. The oval shaped mirror is the best quality French bevel plate; size, 24x30 inches, supported by shapely curved standards. This dresser matches No. 1C1975 chiffonier, illustrated on page 670, and commode No. 1C1910½ illustrated on page 668. Shipped direct from the factory in Western Pennsylvania. Shipping weight, about 150 pounds.

	Quartered Oak	Genuine Mahogany	Birdseye Maple
Price......	$14.75	$14.85	$14.95

No. 1C1866 This Dresser is made in specially selected highly figured quarter sawed golden oak, birdseye maple or in genuine mahogany, highly polished. It has a double top with a serpentine curve; size, 22 x 42 inches. The base has double top drawers, below which are two large drawers. It has a full swell front and solid panel ends. Fitted with locks, keys, cast brass handles and best quality French bevel plate mirror; size, 24x30 inches. The mirror frame and shapely standards ornamented with genuine hand carvings. Cabinet work, wood and finish strictly high grade. Shipped direct from factory in Western Pennsylvania. Shipping weight, about 150 pounds.

	Oak	Genuine Mahogany	Birdseye Maple
Price,	$15.25	$15.35	$15.45

No. 1C1872 This Dresser is strictly high grade in every detail of workmanship and finish. We furnish it in quarter sawed oak, birdseye maple or genuine mahogany, all highly polished. The base has a double top with serpentine curve, size, 22 x 42 inches, solid panel ends, a double swell serpentine front and contains two small drawers, below which are two large drawers. The shapely designed mirror is the best quality French bevel plate; size, 24x30 inches, supported by a highly ornamented hand carved frame. This dresser matches chiffonier No. 1C1980 illustrated on page 670 and commode No. 1C1913, illustrated on page 668. Shipped direct from factory in Western Pennsylvania. Shipping weight, about 150 pounds.

	Quartered Oak	Genuine Mahogany	Birdseye Maple
Price,	$15.75	$15.85	$15.95

No. 1C1875 This Dresser is made throughout of quarter sawed oak or birch mahogany, rubbed and highly polished. It has serpentine front and full swell ends. The top is 22x44 inches, and the drawers are very roomy, being 22 inches deep, varnished on the inside. Has beautifully shaped French bevel mirror, 24x30 inches, suspended in an open frame. The handles and knobs are cast brass and casters are best quality. Shipped from our factory near Grand Rapids, Mich. Shipping weight, about 150 pounds.

	Quartered Oak	Mahogany Finish
Price..................	$16.90	$16.95

No. 1C1877 This Beautiful Dresser we furnish in highly figured quarter sawed golden oak, birdseye maple or genuine **mahogany, highly polished.** The double top is 22x43 inches. The base has double top drawers. Fitted with locks, keys, and best quality cast brass handles and casters. It has solid panel ends. The handsome designed mirror is the best quality of French bevel plate; size, 24x30 inches. Note the shapely mirror frame and standards. The dresser matches chiffonier No. 1C1988 and commode No. 1C1913 illustrated on the following pages. Strictly high grade in material, construction and finish. Shipped direct from factory in Western Pennsylvania. Shipping weight, about 150 pounds.

	Oak	Birdseye Maple	Genuine Mahogany
Price..	$18.75	$18.85	$18.95

No. 1C1879 This Handsome Dresser is made of highly figured quarter sawed oak in a golden finish, highly polished. The top is 42 inches long and has a double curved front corresponding with the double swell front of the two large drawers below. It is supported by French curved legs. It has single panel ends. Two convenient curved front drawers resting on the top of the base add to the attractiveness of this dresser. Mirror is the best quality French bevel plate; size, 24x30 inches, and is supported by ornate and finely executed hand carved standards. Drawers finished inside. A strictly high grade dresser in every detail of construction and finish. Fitted with locks, keys and best quality cast brass handles and casters. Shipped direct from factory near Grand Rapids, Mich. Shipping weight, about 160 pounds.
Price..$21.50

No. 1C1880 This dresser is made of richly figured quarter sawed golden oak, thoroughly air seasoned and kiln dried, beautifully finished and decorated with genuine hand carvings, highly ornamental in design and finely executed. The base is 22x44 inches, with double top drawers, below which is a large drawer. All drawers have full swell serpentine fronts. It has single paneled ends and double top with serpentine curved edge corresponding with the drawer fronts. Fitted with locks, keys and best quality cast brass handles. The extra large size mirror is the best quality French bevel plate, size, 30x36 inches. Construction and finish first class throughout. Fitted with best quality casters. Shipped direct from factory in Southern Indiana. Shipping weight, about 160 pounds.
Price........$16.75

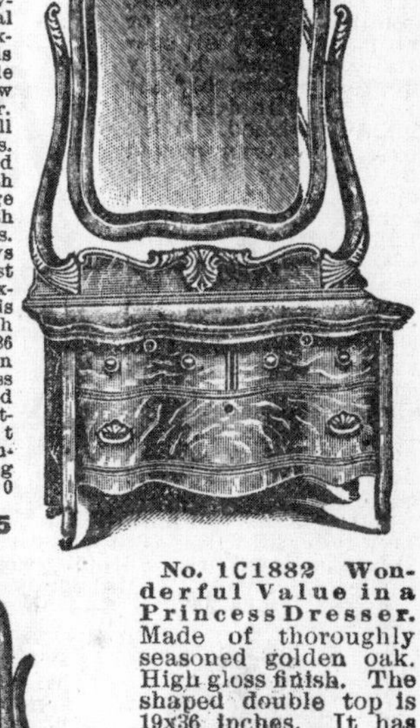

No. 1C1882 Wonderful Value in a Princess Dresser. Made of thoroughly seasoned golden oak. High gloss finish. The shaped double top is 19x36 inches. It has two roomy drawers, fitted with locks, keys and cast brass handles. Best quality of casters; double paneled ends. Mirror is the best quality French bevel plate; size, 18x30 inches. The mirror frame and standards are decorated with genuine hand carvings, finely executed. Thoroughly well made in every detail of cabinet construction and finish. Shipped direct from factory in Southern Ohio. Shipping weight, about 125 pounds.
Price... .....$8.45

No. 1C1881 This Elegant Princess Dresser has full swell front. It is made of selected quarter sawed oak of a fine flaky grain or in wavy birch in a beautiful mahogany color, hand polished. The base is 36 inches long, 21 inches wide. The handsome mirror is the best quality French beveled plate, 18x36 inches. The base contains two large drawers. Genuine cast brass trimmings. Sells for $18.00 to $20.00 in retail stores. Carefully packed to insure safe delivery. Shipped direct from factory in Southern Indiana, thereby insuring lowest freight rate. Shipping weight, 125 pounds. Price,
Quartered oak $10.95
Mahogany finish.............. 10.90

No. 1C1883 This Handsome Princess Dresser is made of the choicest highly figured quarter sawed oak or in genuine mahogany in beautiful polished finish. The base is 36 inches long, 20 inches wide and contains three drawers. This dresser measures 24 inches from the top of the base to the floor. It has full swell front and genuine cast brass trimmings. The mirror is the best French bevel plate, 18x36 inches. Especially convenient in the ladies' dressing room. Strictly high grade in every detail. Carefully packed and shipped direct from factory near Grand Rapids, Mich., thereby insuring lowest freight rates. Shipping weight, ... pounds.
Price, oak $14.40
Price, mahogany 14.45

No. 1C1885 This Beautiful Princess Dresser is 20x34 inches and stands 76 inches high. We furnish it in either of the three woods: quarter sawed golden oak, genuine mahogany or birdseye maple, all specially selected, highly figured, thoroughly air seasoned, kiln dried and highly polished. The base, which is supported by shapely French curved legs, has a double curved top. Has full panel ends, and contains two full swell serpentine shaped drawers, fitted with locks and keys and the best quality of cast brass trimmings. The mirror is the best quality of French bevel plate; size, 18x40 inches. The mirror frame and standards are highly figured as well as the base. Strictly high grade in wood, construction and finish. We guarantee it to be wonderful value. Shipped direct from factory in Western New York. Shipping weight, 140 pounds.

	Oak	Mahogany	Birdseye Maple
Price....	$14.75	$14.85	$14.95

No. 1C1886 This Princess Dresser at the price we quote represents astonishing value. We furnish it in highly figured quarter sawed golden oak, highly polished. It is 73 inches high and has 21x38-inch top. The drawers are perfect fitting, moving without friction, fitted with locks and best cast brass handles. It has solid panel ends. Mirror is best quality of French bevel plate, size, 18x36 inches. Mirror frame and standards have rounded edges. Has convenient small drawers in the top. Cabinet construction, high grade throughout. This dresser sells in retail stores at $25.00 to $30.00. Shipped direct from factory in Southern Ohio. Shipping weight, about 125 pounds.
Price, quarter sawed golden oak........$15.25

Ladies' Dressing Tables and Odd Commodes.

No. 1C1890 This Dressing Table we furnish in quarter sawed golden oak, birdseye maple or birch, mahogany finish. The base is 18x28 inches, supported by double curved French shaped legs and contains a roomy drawer. The mirror is the best quality French plate; size, 12x18 inches. Wonderful value at our price, shipped direct from factory in Western Pennsylvania. Shipping weight, about 40 pounds.

Price, oak $4.75
Price, mahogany.... 4.85
Price, birdseye maple 4.95

$4.75

Dressing Table With Oval Mirror.

No. 1C1892 This Ladies' Dressing Table is made in quarter sawed oak, genuine mahogany or birdseye maple, all specially selected, highly figured wood, thoroughly air seasoned, kiln dried and piano polished. The base, which is 18x29 inches, contains a spacious drawer, and is supported by shapely French curved legs. The oval French bevel plate mirror is 16x24 inches. The standards and mirror frame have rounded edges. High grade in construction, handsome in design, beautiful in finish. You pay elsewhere double the price we ask for this article. Shipped direct from our factory in Western New York. Shipping weight 60 pounds.
Price, quarter sawed oak.. $6.75
Price, genuine mahogany.. 6.85
Price, birdseye maple...... 6.95

$6.75

No. 1C1894 This Beautiful Ladies' Dressing Table is made of flaky grained quarter sawed oak in a golden finish. The base has a double curved serpentine shaped front and ends, and double top, size, 20x36 inches, supported by four double curved full French shaped legs. The mirror is the best quality French beveled plate, size, 16x28 inches. The roomy drawer is fitted with genuine burnished cast brass handles and lock. Shipped direct from our warehouse in Southern Indiana, Louisville, Ky., or from factory in Central North Carolina. Shipping weight, 65 pounds. Price $8.95

$8.95

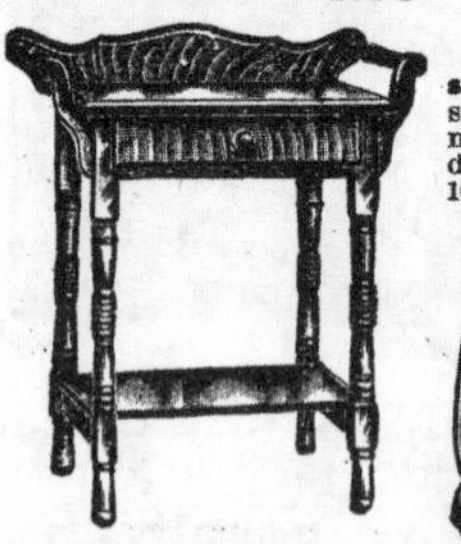

Our $1.35 Washstand.

No. 1C1900 This Washstand is made from thoroughly seasoned elm and ash wood mixed, golden oak finish, has one drawer and lower shelf. Top, 16x28 inches. Weight, 35 pounds.
Price $1.35

Our $2.75 Commode

No. 1C1902 This Commode is made of thoroughly seasoned hardwood, golden oak finish. It has one drawer and cabinet. Size of top, 18x32 inches. Drawer is fitted with fancy metal pulls. Shipped direct from factory in Southern Indiana, thereby insuring lowest freight rate. Weight, 50 pounds.
Price $2.75

White Enamel Commode, $4.15.

No. 1C1910 This Commode we furnish in white enamel, golden oak or mahogany finish: It is especially adapted for use with our iron beds, in white enamel, matches dresser No. 1C1824 on page 666. It has a double curved top, 18x33 inches, serpentine curved top drawer, two small drawers and spacious cupboard. Fitted with best quality cast brass trimmings and casters, strictly high grade in construction, wood and finish. Shipped direct from our factory near Grand Rapids, Michigan. Shipping weight, 65 pounds.
Price, oak $3.85
Price, mahogany.... 3.80
Price, white enamel. 4.15

No. 1C1910½ This Washstand matches No. 1C1857 dresser and No. 1C1971 Chiffonier. We furnish it in highly figured quarter sawed golden oak, genuine mahogany or birdseye maple. Highly polished. The double curved top is 18x28 inches. The base has solid panel ends and has serpentine shaped top drawer, below which is a roomy cupboard with two doors. The towel rack is made of same wood as base, and is **not imitation finish.** High grade in every detail of construction. Shipped direct from factory in Western Pennsylvania. Shipping weight, about 50 pounds.
Price, oak $5.10
Price, genuine mahogany........ 5.25
Price, birdseye maple 5.35

No. 1C1913 This Commode is strictly high grade in construction, wood and finish. We furnish it in quarter sawed golden oak, genuine mahogany or birdseye maple, specially selected, highly figured and highly polished. The base is 20x30 inches and contains two double serpentine swell drawers with a spacious cupboard below. The towel rack is made of same wood as the base, **not imitation finish.** Ornamental and finely executed hand carvings, solid panel ends and fitted with locks and keys and the best quality cast brass trimmings. Shipped direct from factory in Western Pennsylvania. Shipping weight, 65 pounds.

	Oak	Mahogany	Birdseye Maple
Price.....	$6.55	$6.75	$6.85

Elegant Toilet Washstand for $4.45.

No. 1C1914 This Toilet Washstand is especially adapted for small bedrooms and hotels. Made of best selected and well seasoned northern hardwood, golden oak finish and furnished with large, roomy drawer and large compartment below the drawer. Top is 18x32 inches. The mirror is excellent bevel plate glass and is 12x20 inches in size. Casters are best quality. Shipped direct from factory in Southern Indiana, thereby insuring lowest freight rate. Shipping weight, 70 pounds. Price........$4.45

Our $4.95 Hotel Stand.

No. 1C1915 This Stand is especially constructed for hotel use, but also makes a very attractive piece of furniture for the home. It is made of hardwood, finished imitation golden oak or mahogany. Has 17x33-inch double top and 14x24-inch bevel plate mirror. Serpentine shaped front drawer, roomy cupboard below. Cast brass handles and knob. Mounted on casters. Shipped direct from factory in Southern Indiana, thereby insuring lowest freight rate. Shipping weight, 60 pounds.
Price........ $4.95

Solid Oak Hotel Stand for $5.85.

No. 1C1917 This Hotel Stand is made of solid oak throughout, finished golden. Has full swell front top drawers with two drawers and a cupboard below. Has 18x34-inch double top. The mirror is best quality bevel plate, 14x24 inches. Knobs and handles are cast brass. Complete with casters. Shipped direct from factory in Southern Indiana, thereby insuring lowest freight rate. Shipping weight, 75 pounds.
Price $5.85

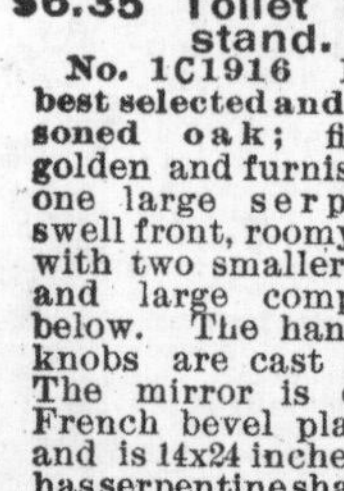

$6.35 Toilet Washstand.

No. 1C1916 Made of best selected and well seasoned oak; finished golden and furnished with one large serpentine swell front, roomy drawer, with two smaller drawers and large compartment below. The handles and knobs are cast brass. The mirror is excellent French bevel plate glass and is 14x24 inches in size; has serpentine shaped double top, 18x34 inches. Shipped direct from factory in Southern Indiana, thereby insuring lowest freight rate. Shipping weight, 70 pounds. Price........ $6.35

A Solid Oak Chiffonier for $3.60.

No. 1C1920 **This is without question the most wonderful value ever offered in a solid golden oak chiffonier.** The wood is thoroughly air seasoned and kiln dried, guaranteed not to warp, check or shrink. Top is 17x30 inches. The drawers are perfect fitting, moving without friction. It has full paneled ends and back. Fitted with locks, keys and cast brass trimmings. Complete with casters. Shipped direct from factory in Central North Carolina or Southern Indiana, thereby insuring lowest freight rate. Shipping weight, 100 pounds.
Price......................$3.60

Our $4.85 Chiffonier.

No. 1C1921 **This is another new design** which we are selling at a very low price. Made of **solid golden oak**, carved and nicely finished; top 17x30 inches. Has a genuine 12x20-inch French bevel mirror. The drawers are all very large and roomy, and are fitted with brass handles, locks and keys. Complete with casters. Shipped direct from factory in North Carolina, Louisville, Ky., or Southern Indiana, thereby insuring lowest freight rate. Shipping weight, 125 pounds.
Price......................$4.85

Wonderful Value, $6.25

A very ornamental and useful pattern; made of selected golden oak; has three large and two small drawers and one hat box; has handsome bevel French double mirror, 12x20 inches, a shaped top, 17x30 inches, and is well trimmed and finished. Fitted with best quality casters. Shipped direct from factory in Southern Indiana or North Carolina, thereby insuring lowest freight rate. Shipping weight, about 125 pounds.
No. 1C1923 Price, as illustrated......$6.25
No. 1C1922 Price, with wood top rail......$4.45

This Roomy Chiffonier is made of solid oak finished golden. The top is 19x33 inches. It has full paneled ends, five large drawers fitted with best quality cast brass handles, locks and keys. The mirror is the best quality French bevel plate, size, 12x20 inches. Workmanship and finish first class. Drawers run smoothly. Shipped direct from factory in Southern Indiana or Central North Carolina, thereby insuring the lowest freight rate. Shipping weight, 125 pounds.
No. 1C1928 Price, as illustrated......$5.45
No. 1C1929 Price, with wood top rail......$4.25

This Large Chiffonier is 19x33 inches, made of solid oak golden finish, thoroughly seasoned and kiln dried. It has three large drawers, two small drawers and convenient hat box. Mirror is the best quality French bevel plate, size, 12x20 inches. Fitted with cast brass handles, locks and keys. Thoroughly well made throughout. Sells for $8.00 to $9.00 in retail furniture stores. Shipped direct from factory in Southern Indiana or Central North Carolina, thereby insuring lowest freight rate. Shipping weight, 125 pounds.
No. 1C1932 Price, as illustrated......$6.45
No. 1C1931 Price, with wood top rail......$4.95

Extra Large Chiffonier, $7.10.

No. 1C1933 **This is an Exceptionally Large Chiffonier, made of golden oak.** Has 22x40-inch double top. Paneled ends. Five large drawers, fitted with cast brass fancy handles. The cabinet work is first class and drawers work perfectly. The casters are best quality. Shipped direct from factory in Southern Indiana, thereby insuring lowest freight rate. Shipping weight, about 125 pounds.
Note the extra large size of this chiffonier.
Price............$7.10

Extra Large Chiffonier with Mirror, $9.65.

No. 1C1934 **This Chiffonier is made of golden oak.** It is unusually large, having 22x40-inch double top. Paneled sides. Has five very large roomy drawers, fitted with cast brass fancy handles and locks. The upper three drawers are of equal size and the two lower ones are of equal size, but larger than the upper three. The toilet is handsomely decorated with raised carvings, and has beautifully shaped French bevel mirror, 14x24 inches. Casters are best quality. Shipped direct from factory in Southern Indiana. Shipping weight, 125 lbs.
Note the extra large size of this chiffonier.
Price......................................$9.65

With Mirror and Hat Box for $10.15.

This Chiffonier is made of solid oak in a golden finish. It is 22x40 inches with four panels in end. The base contains three large drawers, two small drawers and a spacious cupboard. Fitted with cast brass handles, locks, keys and casters. The handsome design, large bevel plate mirror is 14x24 inches. Construction and finish first class. Shipped direct from factory in Southern Indiana, thereby insuring the lowest freight rate. Shipping weight, 125 pounds.
Note the extra large size of this chiffonier.
No. 1C1937 Price, as illustrated.......$10.15
No. 1C1936 Price, with wood top rail, like No. 1C1933.........$7.75

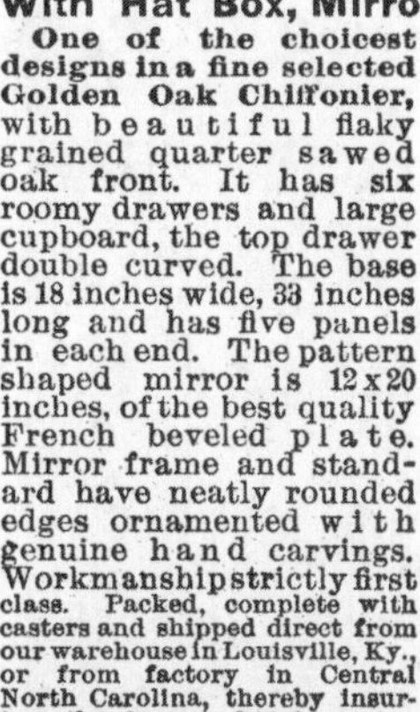

Six-Drawer Chiffonier with Mirror, $8.45.

A new design in a fine selected quarter sawed oak Chiffonier with six roomy drawers. The base is 18 inches wide, 33 inches long. It has five panels in the ends and a double top. The shapely mirror is the best quality French beveled plate, 12x20 inches. The mirror frame and standards have neatly rounded edges, surmounted with genuine hand carvings. All drawers fitted with locks and genuine burnished cast brass handles. The construction and finish strictly high grade throughout. Thoroughly well packed complete with casters and shipped direct from our warehouse in Louisville, Ky., or from our factory in Central North Carolina, thereby insuring lowest freight rate. Shipping weight, 150 pounds.

No. 1C1957 Price, as illustrated...........$8.45
No. 1C1956 Price, with wood top rail...... 6.95

With Hat Box, Mirror and Six Drawers.

One of the choicest designs in a fine selected Golden Oak Chiffonier, with beautiful flaky grained quarter sawed oak front. It has six roomy drawers and large cupboard, the top drawer double curved. The base is 18 inches wide, 33 inches long and has five panels in each end. The pattern shaped mirror is 12x20 inches, of the best quality French beveled plate. Mirror frame and standard have neatly rounded edges ornamented with genuine hand carvings. Workmanship strictly first class. Packed, complete with casters and shipped direct from our warehouse in Louisville, Ky., or from factory in Central North Carolina, thereby insuring the lowest freight rate. Shipping weight. 165 pounds.
No. 1C1959 Price, as illustrated......$8.95
No. 1C1958 Price, with wood top rail..... 7.45

Swell Front Quartered Oak Chiffonier, $8.85.

This illustration shows one of the best new designs in a Solid Oak Chiffonier, with a full swell, fine flaky grained quarter sawed oak in a beautiful golden polished finish. The base is 20x33 inches and has four large roomy drawers and two top drawers, fitted with locks and trimmed with the best quality burnished cast brass drop handles. The handsome pattern shaped mirror is the best quality of French beveled plate, size 12x20 inches. Well packed complete with casters and shipped direct from our warehouse in Louisville, Ky., or from factory in North Carolina, thereby insuring lowest freight rate. Shipping weight, 125 pounds.
No. 1C1966 Price, as illustrated........$8.85
No. 1C1965 Price, with wood top rail....... 7.35

Quartered Oak Chiffonier with Hat Box, $9.35.

A full swell front, strictly High Grade Chiffonier in solid golden quarter sawed oak, polished finish. The handsome shaped mirror is the best quality of French beveled plate, size 22x20 inches. The base is 20x33 inches and contains three large drawers, two small drawers and roomy cupboard and has five panels in the end. All drawers fitted with locks and genuine burnished cast brass drop handles. It has a double top with rounded edges. Thoroughly well packed, complete with casters and shipped direct from our warehouse in Louisville, Ky., or from factory in North Carolina, thereby insuring lowest freight rates. Shipping weight, 125 pounds.
No. 1C1968 Price, as illustrated.........$9.35
No. 1C1967 Price, with wood top rail..... 7.85

Chiffonier in Quartered Oak, Mahogany or Birdseye Maple.

No. 1C1971 **This Chiffonier is made of highly figured quarter sawed oak, birdseye maple or genuine mahogany,** all highly polished. The base has a double top, serpentine shape; size, 18x28 inches and solid panel ends. It has five large drawers with double swell front, fitted with locks, keys and best quality cast brass handles and casters. The mirror frame and standards are made of same kind of wood as base—not imitation finish. The mirror is best quality French bevel plate, 12x18 inches. High grade in quality of wood, construction and finish. This chiffonier matches dresser No. 1C1857, illustrated on page 667, commode No. 1C1910½ and dressing table No. 1C1890, illustrated on page 668. Shipped direct from factory in Western Pennsylvania. Shipping weight, about 125 pounds.
Price,
Quartered oak.........$11.00
Genuine mahogany.... 11.35
Birdseye maple....... 11.45

$11.90 Buys this Serviceable Chiffonier.

No. 1C1973 **This Handsome Chiffonier is made of golden oak or birch mahogany.** Has a 36-inch double top, two small drawers and hat box. Full swell front with three large drawers underneath, all fitted with best quality fancy cast brass knobs and handles. The mirror is 16x26 inches French bevel plate. French legs, complete with casters. Shipping weight, 120 pounds. Shipped from our factory near Grand Rapids, Mich.

Price, in golden oak..............$11.90
Price, mahogany finish..............$11.95

No. 1C1975 This Handsome Chiffonier we furnish in quarter sawed oak, birdseye maple or genuine mahogany. All highly polished. The base has a serpentine curved top; size, 20x33 inches, and three large drawers, two small drawers, and a spacious cupboard. The top drawer has a double swell front. The mirror frame and standards are highly figured wood like the base. Fitted with locks, keys and best quality cast brass handles and casters. The perfect oval shaped mirror is the best quality French bevel plate; size, 16x20 inches. High grade in every detail of construction. This chiffonier matches dresser No. 1C1863 and washstand No. 1C1910½. Shipped direct from factory in Western Pennsylvania. Shipping weight, about 150 pounds.

	Oak	Mahogany	Birdseye Maple
Price	$12.25	$12.65	$12.75

A High Grade Chiffonier for $13.45.

No. 1C1977 This is an Exceptionally Handsome Chiffonier. Especially designed to go with brass or iron beds. Made of selected quarter sawed oak, golden finish, birdseye maple or genuine mahogany as desired. Has serpentine shaped front, double top 20x34 inches, full panel ends. French legs. Best quality French bevel plate circular pattern mirror, 20x20 inches. Best quality cast brass handles and locks. Complete with casters. Throughout a strictly high class piece of furniture. Shipped direct from factory near Grand Rapids, Mich. Shipping weight, 140 pounds.

Price, quartered oak..$13.45
Price, genuine mahogany..........13.50
Price, birdseye maple..........13.55

Chiffonier in Quartered Oak, Birdseye Maple or Mahogany.

No. 1C1980 This Chiffonier has a double curved serpentine top; size, 20x30 inches. We furnish it in selected quarter sawed oak, birdseye maple or genuine mahogany, all highly polished. The mirror frame and standards are highly figured wood like the base. The base has solid panel ends and contains five large drawers fitted with locks, key and best quality of cast brass handles and casters. The beautiful pattern shaped mirror is the best quality French bevel plate; size, 16x20 inches. The shapely curved standards and mirror frame are hand carved. This chiffonier is thoroughly well made throughout and matches dresser No. 1C1872, illustrated on page 667, and commode No. 1C1913, on page 668. Shipped direct from factory in Western Pennsylvania. Shipping weight, 50 pounds.

	Quartered Oak	Genuine Mahogany	Birdseye Maple
Price	$13.95	$14.35	$14.45

An Exceptionally Fine Chiffonier for $14.95.

No. 1C1984 This is a strictly high class piece of furniture, made of solid golden oak with highly figured, quartered front. High gloss finish. The base measures 24x34 inches; has six drawers, with serpentine swell front. Best quality cast brass handles and locks; complete with casters. The mirror is best quality French bevel plate, 16x26 inches. The ornaments are all genuine hand carvings. Carefully packed and shipped direct from factory in Wisconsin. Shipping weight, 150 pounds.

Price..........$14.95

No. 1C1988 This strictly High Grade Chiffonier is made in three different woods, quarter sawed oak, genuine mahogany and birdseye maple, specially selected for beauty of the grain of the wood and highly polished. It is 34 inches long, 20 inches wide, 74 inches high. It has a full swell front, solid panel ends with two top drawers double curved. The mirror frame and standards are made of same kind of wood as the base, **not imitation finish.** The handsome designed mirror is the best quality of French bevel plate, size, 18x24 inches. The drawers are perfect fitting. Have locks, keys and the best quality cast brass handles. Complete with casters. This chiffonier matches dresser No. 1C1877. Shipped direct from our factory in Western New York. Shipping weight, 150 pounds.

Price, oak..........$16.45
Price mahogany....16.85
Price, birdseye maple..........16.95

No. 1C1999 This extra large, handsome chiffonier is made of highly figured quarter sawed golden oak or birch mahogany finish, thoroughly air seasoned and kiln dried, highly polished. The double top, size, 20x40 inches, is shaped to correspond with serpentine front. It has five large drawers, above which are two small drawers fitted with locks, keys and cast brass handles. It has massive round front corner posts and heavy hand carved claw feet. It has single panel ends. The pattern shaped mirror is the best quality French bevel plate, size, 16x26 inches. Mirror frame has rounded edges. The shapely curved standards are decorated with finely executed hand carvings. Complete with best quality casters. High grade in every detail of construction and finish. Sells in retail stores at $25.00 to $30.00. Shipped direct from factory in central Wisconsin. Shipping weight, 150 pounds.

Price, quarter sawed oak..........$19.45
Price, mahogany finish..........19.35

OUR LINE OF FINE WARDROBES

Shipped direct from our factory in Central Indiana. Knocked down, thereby insuring lowest freight rate.

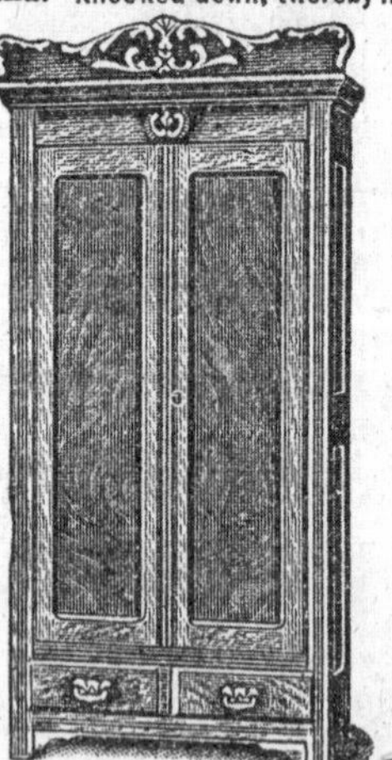

No. 1C2002 This Wardrobe is made with golden oak front thoroughly seasoned and finished; height, 7 feet 6 inches; width, 3 feet 3 inches; depth, 1 foot 4 inches. Two doors and two drawers. **This is by far the cheapest and best wardrobe on the market,** when you take into consideration the quality of material used in its construction and its good workmanship. **Will last a lifetime.** Weight, 140 pounds.

Price..........$7.45

No. 1C2003 Same Wardrobe as No. 1C2002 shown above, but larger size. Dimensions are 7 feet 6 inches high, 3 feet 9 inches wide and 16 inches deep. Shipping weight, 160 pounds.

Price..........$8.95

A $15.00 Wardrobe for $9.85.

No. 1C2010 One of our very best values in Wardrobes; made of selected golden oak front; is beyond criticism in construction and finish; no better can be had; has rich, heavy attractive carvings; is 7 feet 6 inches high, 3 feet 3 inches wide and 16 inches deep, making it very roomy; has two large paneled doors and two large roomy drawers; fitted with shelf and hooks. Can be shipped knocked down or set up. Weight, 140 pounds.

Price..........$9.85

No. 1C2011 Same Wardrobe as No. 1C2010 shown above, but is larger. Height, 7 feet 6 inches; width, 3 feet 9 inches. Weight, 160 lbs.

Price..........$10.95

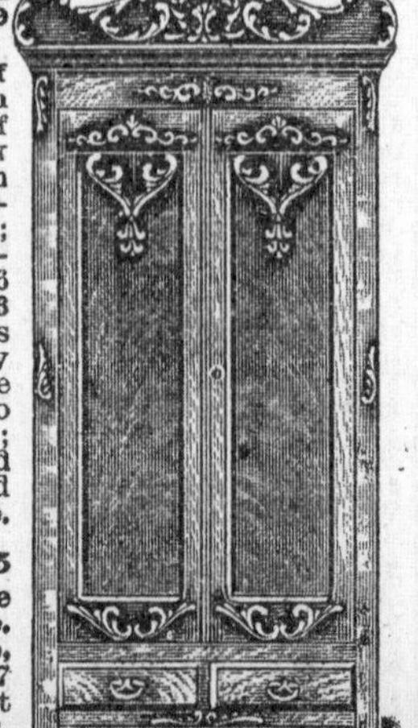

Our Latest Design in Wardrobes.

No. 1C2013 Made with golden oak front. Doors and top piece handsomely ornamented with rich carving. The base is extra heavy and is fitted with two drawers. Wardrobe is fitted with hooks and shelves. One of the best features of this wardrobe is that it sets solid on the floor and prevents the accumulation of dirt and dust underneath it. Dimensions, 7 feet 6 inches high, 39 inches wide and 16 inches deep. Weight, 150 pounds.

Price..........$9.95

No. 1C2014 Same Wardrobe as No. 1C2013 shown above, but is larger. Height, 7 feet 6 inches; width, 45 inches. Weight, 160 pounds.

Price..........$11.25

No. 1C2016 This High Grade Wardrobe is made of solid oak, thoroughly air seasoned and kiln dried. The double doors are fitted with three-ply panels to prevent shrinkage. The base contains two roomy drawers. This wardrobe is 7 feet 8 inches high, 3 feet 10 inches wide, 18 inches deep. Inside it is fitted with broad top shelf with double hooks. Top section and panels, decorated with finely executed hand carvings. Can be shipped knocked down, or set up. Well packed and shipped direct from factory in Western Ohio. Shipping weight, 155 pounds.

Price..........$13.85

This Strictly High Grade Solid Oak Wardrobe is a beautiful golden finish. Dimensions, 7 feet 5 inches high, 3 feet 4 inches wide, 16 inches deep. The extension base has two drawers. The double doors are fitted with best quality French beveled plate mirrors, 12x48 inches, or with three-ply oak panels. The handsome top is decorated with genuine hand carvings. The construction is strictly high grade. Can be taken apart for convenience in moving. Thoroughly packed and shipped direct from our factory in Western Ohio. Shipping weight, 160 pounds.

No. 1C2018 Price, panel doors..$10.95
No. 1C2019 Price, mirror doors..$18.45

This Handsome Wardrobe is made of choice grained oak with highly figured quartered oak panels, or with the best quality of French beveled plate mirrors, 14x48 inches, in the doors. The beautifully moulded base is fitted with two drawers. Inside of wardrobe is partitioned with three removable shelves on one side and single shelf with double hooks on other side. The ornamental top and side posts are hand carved. Absolutely dustproof and finished on the inside. Dimensions, 7 feet 10 inches high, 4 feet 4 inches wide, 18 inches deep. Knocked down construction. Strictly high grade in construction and hand polish golden finish. Well packed and shipped direct from our factory in Western Ohio. Shipping weight, 200 lbs.

No. 1C2022 Price, panel front..$18.95
No. 1C2023 Price, mirror front..$26.95

No. 1C2205 This hall rack is 64 inches high; width, 26 inches. The wood is selected quarter sawed oak in a golden glass finish. The pattern shaped mirror is best quality French bevel plate; size, 10x10 inches. Fitted with large double cast brass hat and coat hooks and umbrella rack. Useful, ornamental and wonderful value at our price. Shipping weight, about 50 pounds.
Price..................**$4.75**

No. 1C2207 This new design hall rack is made of highly figured quarter sawed oak, golden finish. Height, 66 inches; width, 24 inches. The mirror is the best quality French bevel plate; size, 10x14 inches. The double hat and coat hooks and umbrella holder are genuine cast brass. Decorated with genuine hand carvings. New in design, beautiful in wood and finish. Shipping weight, about 55 lbs.
Price..................**$5.50**

No. 1C2210 Artistic and highly ornamented hall rack. Made of selected quarter sawed golden oak with a beautiful finish. Height, 76 inches; width, 39 inches. The shapely new design mirror is the best quality French bevel plate; size, 10x17 inches. Roomy box with lid in seat, for rubbers, etc. Ship'ng wgt, 60 lbs. Pr..**$6.95**

No. 1C2212 Handsome in design, beautiful in wood and finish, this hall rack is 78 inches high, 32 inches wide. The oval shaped mirror is the best quality French bevel plate; size, 18x20 inches. The wood is specially selected highly figured quartersawed golden oak. Seat has a spacious box with lid for rubbers, etc. High grade in construction. Shipping weight, about 75 pounds.
Price..................**$8.85**

No. 1C2218 A new design, made of highly figured quarter sawed golden oak, handsomely carved. Height, 80 inches; width, 36 inches. The pattern shaped mirror is the best quality French bevel plate; size, 20x24 inches. Seat has spacious box with lid for rubbers, etc. Shipping weight, about 75 pounds.
Price..................**$10.75**

Each HALL RACK is fitted with large, double brass coat and hat hooks and umbrella holder like No. 1C2233.

Add 6 inches to width of each HALL RACK to include umbrella holder.

Each HALL RACK is fitted with large, double brass coat and hat hooks and umbrella holder like No. 1C2233.

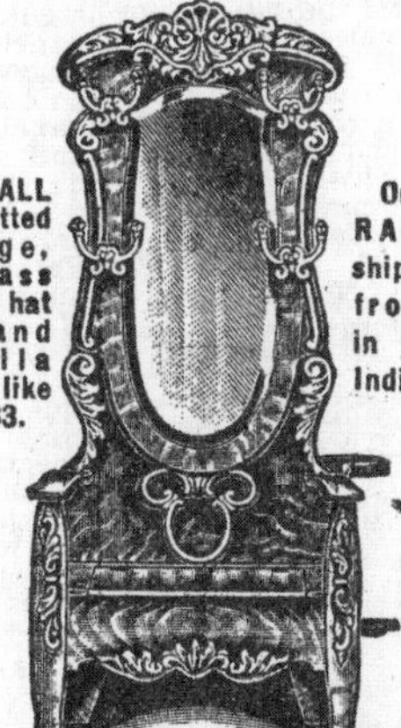

Our HALL RACKS are shipped direct from factory in Central Indiana.

No. 1C2224 **This massive hall rack is made of quarter sawed golden oak, with a highly figured grain.** The shapely designed mirror is the best quality French bevel plate; size, 18x30 inches. Decorated with genuine hand carvings. Height, 84 inches; width, 40 inches. Roomy box with lid in seat. Shipping wgt., about 100 lbs. Price.**$12.95**

No. 1C2226 **Another massive hall rack, made of selected, highly figured, quarter sawed oak,** golden finish, highly polished. Height, 84 inches; width, 42 inches. The oval shaped mirror is the best quality French bevel plate; size, 22x28 inches. Seat has a spacious box with lid. Shipping weight, about 100 pounds.
Price..................**$14.25**

No. 1C2228 **This handsome massive hall rack is 84 inches high, 44 inches wide.** Made of solid quarter sawed golden oak, highly polished. The beautiful pattern shaped mirror is the best quality French bevel plate; size, 24x30 inches. Large box with lid in seat. Shipping weight, 125 pounds.
Price..................**$16.35**

No. 1C2233 **The special features of this hall rack is the extra** large shapely French bevel plate mirror; size, 18x40 inches; the beautiful hand carved decorations. Made of selected quarter sawed golden oak, highly polished. Height, 80 inches; width, 36 inches. Spacious seat with box and lid. Shipping wgt., about 150 pounds. Price.. **$16.75**

No. 1C2239 **This extra large hall rack is 84 inches high, 48 inches wide.** The wood is highly figured quarter sawed golden oak, highly polished. The handsomely designed mirror is the best quality French bevel plate; size, 24x30 inches. Seat has roomy box with lid. Highly ornamented hand carvings. Shipping weight, 150 lbs. Price....**$18.85**

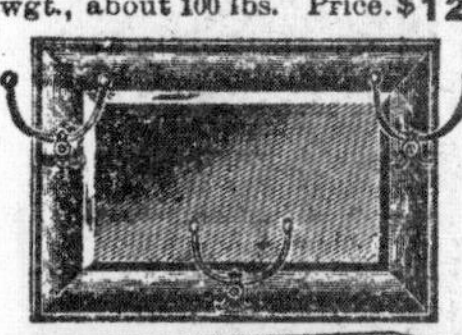

The wood of this hall seat and mirror is selected quartersawed golden oak, highly polished; seat is 32 inches long, 36 inches high, 18 inches deep; spacious compartment with lid in the seat for rubbers, etc. Mirror best quality French bevel plate. Attached to the frame are three double hat and coat hooks of solid brass. Shipping wgt., about 65 lbs.

No. 1C2234
Price, mirror 10x14.. **$1.65**
Price, mirror 12x26.. **$2.15**

No. 1C2250 Seat in golden oak..... **5.85**
No. 1C2252 Seat in weathered oak.. **5.75**

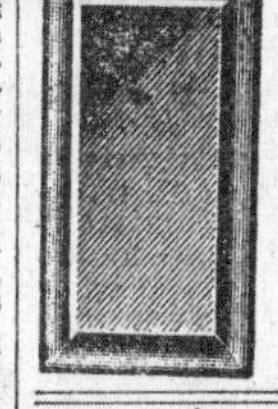

No. 1C2260 This mirror is made with heavy handsome solid oak frame, beautifully polished, and very finely fitted by the best workmen. We fit the frame with the best French plate made, in the following sizes, at the prices named below:

Size of Frame	Size of Plate	French Plain	French Bevel
1½-inch	7x 9 inches	$0.35	$0.45
1½-inch	9x12 inches	.45	.70
1½-inch	10x14 inches	.60	.90
1½-inch	10x17 inches	.80	1.00
2½-inch	12x20 inches	1.25	1.45
2⅛-inch	14x24 inches	1.40	2.05
3 -inch	16x28 inches	2.10	2.65
3 -inch	18x36 inches	3.05	3.95
3 -inch	18x40 inches	3.55	4.30

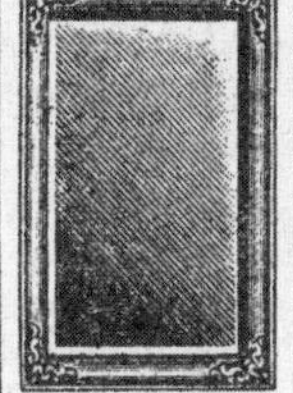

No. 1C2264 This beautiful parlor mirror is made of the best quality French bevel plate, with a heavy solid quarter sawed golden oak 1½-inch frame, decorated with four handsome brass ornaments on the corners. Wonderful value at our price. A strictly first class article.

Size of Plate	French Plain	French Bevel
7x 9 inches.........	$0.40	$0.55
8x10 inches.........	.50	.60
9x12 inches.........	.65	.75
10x14 inches.........	.75	.95
10x17 inches.........	.90	1.15
12x20 inches.........	1 30	1.60
13x22 inches.........	1.55	1.85
14x24 inches.........	1.75	2.25

No. 1C2268 Fancy pier mirror, for parlor, made of heavy 4-inch moulding, finely ornamented in Florentine design, carved and finished in gold, with shaded ornaments. Rich and ornamental. Frame 4 inches wide, finished in gold, cut out openings, fitted with French bevel plate.
Size, 18x20 inches. Price... **$2.95**
Size, 18x40 inches. Price... **$5.50**

No. 1C2272 **This handsome mirror** has a 6-inch frame, finished in green and gold or white and gold, with heavy raised ornamental stem and lining; both sides of stem are **finished fine green bronze or enamel.** Size of plate, 18x40 inches.
Price, French plate mirror, **$4.25**
Price, French bevel plate.. **5.50**

No. 1C2276 **Mirror.** Frame is 7 inches wide, finished in pearl green and tinted with gold; gold burnishes on the heavy ornamented corners. A beautiful parlor decoration. Fitted with the best imported French plate mirror, 18x40 inches.
Price, plain mirror.........**$4.95**
Price, bevel mirror..........**5.90**

No. 1C2280 **This ornamental parlor mirror** is made of the best quality genuine French bevel plate; size, 18x40 inches. Mounted in a handsome oak frame, decorated with beautiful raised carvings and finished in all gold or in black with gold ornaments. Price, all gold.......**$5.50**
Price, black and gold....... **5.45**

No. 1C2284 **This highly artistic parlor mirror is fitted with a beautiful oak frame,** finished in all gold with new raised carvings with tips highly burnished. Mirror is the best quality genuine French bevel plate; size, 18x40 inches. It must be seen to be fully appreciated. Sells for $10.00 in retail stores..... **$6.15**

Very best quality, very latest design.

No. 1C2288 **This mirror has a very heavy, solid golden oak frame, or imitation mahogany, with heavy top carving of rich pattern, and fluted columns on** frame and is very attractive and ornamental. Size of plate, 18x40 inches.
Price, imported French plate mirror...........**$6.10**
Price, imported French bevel mirror **$6.50**

OUR LINE OF WOOD FOLDING BEDS

is more complete this season than ever before and represents greater values than it has ever before been possible for us to offer to our customers. As a result of the very large increase in this department we have been able to make a contract with the largest and most reliable manufacturers in the country, makers of the highest grade folding beds, to supply our customers direct from the factory, thereby saving all of the intermediate expenses, such as freight and cartage, which we have deducted from our former prices and which places one of our beds in the hands of our customers at the actual factory cost, with but our usual one small percentage of profit added, making a price which is lower than what the average retail dealer throughout the country is obliged to pay for the same bed. **Don't use a so called wool mattress, they are made of ground rags and are very unclean and unsanitary.**

No. 1C2349 Mantel Folding Bed, made of hardwood, golden gloss finish. The bed is 48x72 inches when opened, and is fitted with the best woven wire spring with wire cable support, the finest construction for folding beds in the market. Has automatic end legs. Mattress to fit should be 3 feet 10 inches by 6 feet. Shipping weight, 160 pounds. Price, **$8.95**

This Folding Bed is made of hardwood, golden gloss finish. Built up front panels, ornamented with fancy carving. Top is fitted with a French bevel mirror, size, 10x12 inches, and side brackets. Woven wire spring with wire cable support, the finest construction for folding beds in the market, is furnished with the bed. Size of bed when open is 48x72 inches. A mattress to fit should be 3 feet 10 inches wide, 6 feet long and 2¼ inches thick, and to be flexible enough, should be made of cotton, hair or felt. Illustration shows bed with the mirror top. It can also be furnished with plain wood top. Shipping weight, 185 pounds.

No. 1C2354 Price, with mirror top......... **$10.95**
No. 1C2355 Price, with wood top.......... **9.85**

Oak front, built up oak panels, full paneled sides, finished in golden oak. Woven wire spring, with wire cable support, the finest construction for folding beds in the market. Size, closed, 65¼ inches high, 54 inches wide, 18⅛ inches deep. Size, open, outside, 54x75 inches; inside, 48x72 inches. Mattress to fit should be 3 feet 10 inches by 6 feet, with a 2¼-inch box, and to be flexible enough, should be made of felt, hair or cotton. Illustration shows top of bed with two fancy brackets. French bevel mirror, 8x16 inches. Shipping weight (full size), 193 lbs.

No. 1C2356 Price, with mirror top........ **$11.85**
No. 1C2357 Price, with plain top rail..... **10.75**

Mantel Folding Bed, made of thoroughly air seasoned northern hardwood, finished in a perfect imitation of highly figured quartered golden oak. The paneled front and ornamental top is decorated with attractive, finely executed hand carvings. The mirror is the best quality French bevel plate, size, 8x16 inches. On each side of mirror is a convenient bracket shelf. Bed when open for use is 48x72 inches. It is fitted with best quality woven wire spring with cable support, specially adapted for folding beds. Mattress to fit this bed should be 46x72 inches, with 2¼-inch box edge. We especially recommend cotton, hair or felt for this bed. We furnish this bed also with plain top rail. Shipping weight, 200 pounds.

No. 1C2358 Price, with mirror top........ **$12.35**
No. 1C2359 Price, with plain top rail..... **10.85**

This handsome Folding Bed has a solid oak front and full panel sides, golden gloss finish. The front and top are ornamented with heavy carvings, and a French bevel mirror, size 8x16 inches, with a neat bracket for ornaments on either side of mirror. The bed when opened out is 48 inches wide and 72 inches long and is furnished with a woven wire spring with wire cable support, the finest construction for folding beds in the market. Mattress is extra, and to fit should be 3 feet 10 inches wide by 6 feet long and 2¼ inches thick. Bed can also be furnished with a neat design wood top rail without mirror. Shipping weight, 180 pounds.

No. 1C2364 Price, with mirror top........ **$13.45**
No. 1C2365 Price, with plain top rail..... **12.15**

This Folding Bed is one of our latest designs; has full panel sides and quartered golden oak front panel. The top and front are ornamented with heavy carvings, and a French bevel mirror; size, 8x17 inches. The top also has a bracket on each side of the mirror, adding greatly to the finish of the top. The bed is 48x72 inches when opened for use, and is fitted with a woven wire spring with wire cable support, the finest construction for folding beds in the market. The mattress to fit bed should be 3 feet 10 inches wide, 6 feet long and 2½ inches thick, and to be flexible enough, should be made of cotton, hair or felt. This bed can also be furnished with a plain top rail. Shipping weight, 200 pounds.

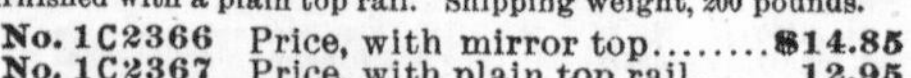

No. 1C2366 Price, with mirror top........ **$14.85**
No. 1C2367 Price, with plain top rail...... **12.95**

Quartered oak, golden finish, swell front. Built up veneered oak panels, full panel sides. Woven wire spring, with wire cable support, the finest construction for folding beds in the market. Size, closed, 68 inches high, 54 inches wide, 20 inches deep. Size, open, outside, 54x75 inches; inside, 48x72 inches. Mattress to fit should be 3 feet 10 inches by 6 feet, with a 2¼-inch box, and to be flexible enough, should be made of felt, cotton or hair. Top has two handsome brackets and shaped French bevel plate mirror. Shipping weight, 206 pounds.

No. 1C2377 Price, with mirror top...... **$18.95**
No. 1C2378 Price, with plain top rail..... **16.45**

This handsome Folding Bed is made of oak throughout, with quarter sawed oak front and top, full panel sides, highly polished, golden finish. The front is decorated with heavy carvings and has a full swell in center panel. The top is the very latest design. It has a large French bevel mirror, size 14x24 inches, supported by two elegantly carved standards, giving to the bed that artistic effect that has made it so popular. The bed is 48x72 in. and is furnished with the best woven wire spring with wire cable support, the finest construction for folding beds in the market. The mattress is extra, and to fit should be made 3 feet 10 inches wide, 6 feet long and 2¼ inches thick. We would recommend a cotton, hair or felt mattress. Shipping weight, 200 pounds.

No. 1C2379 Price, with mirror top........ **$19.85**
No. 1C2380 Price, with plain top rail..... **17.35**

WE GUARANTEE every bed to be strictly first class in every respect and made of thoroughly seasoned material. For workmanship, durability and general finish they cannot be excelled. All of our folding beds have the latest patent woven wire spring, with wire cable support, the best construction for folding beds in the market; patent mattress clamp to hold the bed clothes in place when the bed is open or closed. The legs on the foot end work automatically. When the bed is open they lock themselves and in closing the bed the legs swing back into the proper position without interfering with the bed clothes.

No. 1C2381 This Metal Folding Bed combines neatness, lightness, comfort and cleanliness. It is made entirely of steel except the top. Dimensions, closed, height, 45 inches, depth, 24 inches. Dimensions, open for use, length, 6 feet 2 inches, width, 4 feet. Fitted with the celebrated national spring. Front ornamented with large medallion of stamped steel. Top can be draped and ornamented with bricabrac, making an attractive article of furniture for the home. We furnish this bed also 3 feet 6 inches wide. Shipping weight, 80 pounds.

Price, with mirror top....................... **$10.50**
Price, with plain top, **9.25**

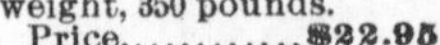

Showing Bed Open.

No. 1C2383 Golden oak, gloss finish, richly carved. Has 18x30-inch German bevel plate mirror. Self adjusting and locking metal swing legs. Fitted with fine woven wire spring with wire cable support, the finest construction for folding beds in the market. Will not tip the back. Size, closed, 78¼ inches high, 56 inches wide, 24 inches deep. Size, open, outside, 56x80 inches; inside, 50x74 inches. Mattress to fit should be 4x6 feet, with a 3-inch box. Shipping weight, 350 lbs. Price, **$18.95**

No. 1C2389 Our Solid Golden Oak Upright Folding Bed, with 18x40-inch bevel edge mirror. This bed is self adjusting and locking, and cannot close by accident. It is fitted with high grade woven wire spring with cable wire support, the finest construction for folding beds in the market. It is 81¼ inches high, 56¾ inches wide and 26 inches deep; when open, outside 50x74 inches, inside, 48x74 inches. The mattress to fit should be 4x6 feet with a 3-inch box. Shipping weight, 350 pounds.

Price............ **$22.95**

No. 1C2391 A Solid Substantial Upright Folding Bed, made with quarter sawed oak front, golden high gloss finish. The front is handsomely decorated with heavy carvings. The mirror is the best French bevel; size, 18x40 inches. The bed is 50 inches wide, 72 inches long and 82 inches high. Fitted with self adjusting lock, making it impossible for bed to close up by accident; with wire cable support, the finest construction for folding beds in the market. Mattress to fit bed should be 4 feet wide by 6 feet long with a 3-inch box. Shipping weight, 360 pounds. Iron weights separate, 150 pounds. Price.................. **$27.35**

ELASTIC FELT, COTTON OR HAIR MATTRESSES ARE BEST ADAPTED FOR FOLDING BEDS.

IRON AND BRASS BEDS OF NEWEST DESIGNS.

AT LOWER PRICES THAN EVER BEFORE.

THEY ARE INDESTRUCTIBLE AND WILL NEVER WEAR OUT.

THE METAL USED in the construction of our beds is strictly high grade throughout. No rusty scrap iron or corroded refused metals. The highest and best quality of malleable iron, rolled Bessemer steel and drawn brass tubing.

THE CONSTRUCTION of our metal beds is the best that modern machinery, science and skilled workmanship can possibly produce. Every part and parcel is carefully modeled, framed and joined. The joints and chills carefully founded and smoothed. The rails are made of Bessemer steel in angle shape and will not bend or break. Great care is taken in the fitting of the tongue and grooves by which the rail is fastened to the head and foot end. They stand firm and will support any weight of persons.

THE FINISH of our iron beds, we guarantee the best that can be made. The enamel which is used for the several coatings is the highest grade obtainable. Each coat after being carefully and thoroughly applied is baked in a large oven heated to a very high degree of temperature, then thoroughly smoothed and polished. This produces a finish that is impervious to water and all our iron beds can be cleaned of finger marks or other soiling by washing with soap and water.

THE BRASS TRIMMING which is used in the ornamentation and construction of our metal beds is of the highest quality of drawn brass tubing, highly polished and burnished, coated with the best quality of French lacquer, which absolutely preserves the polish and prevents tarnishing. Lacquer is to brass what varnish is to wood, it preserves the material.

DO NOT MISJUDGE the quality by the price: Because the prices are very low (much lower possibly than you have reason to expect), you run no risk of being dissatisfied with any bed or any other article of furniture you may order from us. The immense quantities we sell, the cost of handling being reduced and almost eliminated, the greatly reduced price at which we are able to purchase, the shipment direct from the factory to customer, together with the very small percentage of profit which we add, reduces the price at which we sell to almost one-half the price at which beds of equal quality are sold by others.

COLOR BEDS. We furnish all our iron beds in white enamel unless ordered otherwise. Under the especial description of each bed it specifically states whether furnished in "white enamel only." Many designs of beds are much more attractive in white enamel only and for that reason we furnish certain patterns in white enamel only. When beds are ordered in colors, shipment will be made direct from factory near Chicago and from three days to one week's time is required before shipment can be made.

HOW TO ORDER. When ordering a metal bed, be careful to state the width wanted, also the color. We illustrate our beds made up with bolster mattress and covering, but the price quoted is for the bed only. Springs, mattresses and pillows are illustrated and described on pages that follow.

OUR BIG BARGAIN IN IRON BEDS

A $3.50 IRON BED FOR ONLY

$1.98

$1.98 IS OUR PRICE FOR THIS HANDSOME IRON BED

LESS THAN RETAIL DEALERS CAN BUY SUCH BEDS IN WHOLESALE LOTS.

No. 1C2394

AT $1.98 we offer you this new and handsome design iron bed. The head of the bed is 54 inches high. The full width of the bed is 4 feet 6 inches wide by 6 feet 6 inches long, outside measurement. The posts are ⅞ inch in diameter. The filling rods are full $\frac{5}{16}$-inch stock. The rails and foot bar are made of highly tempered rolled steel, absolutely guaranteed not to bend or break. The posts and filling rods are made of fine malleable iron which renders the entire bed indestructible. This bed is full coated with pure white enamel, put on by a special process, and thoroughly baked and hardened. The handsome mountings on the posts are very attractive. The bed is strictly first class in every detail of construction and finish, and the special merit of the design is its simplicity and beauty of outline. You should also remember that our entire line of iron beds from the lowest price to the highest price are of highly artistic handwork and design.

WE ALSO furnish this bed 3 feet wide or 3 feet 6 inches wide. We guarantee for the bed a better finish, a better construction, more strength and durability than you will find in any bed to be found elsewhere at double the price. This bed with one of our handsome and moderate price dressers shown in the preceding pages will make a beautiful, attractive and up to date bedroom suite. Thoroughly well packed and shipped direct from Chicago.

IN ORDERING, be careful to state the width of the bed wanted.

No. 1C2394 Price.. **$1.98**

Special Iron Crib With Drop Sides, $4.25.

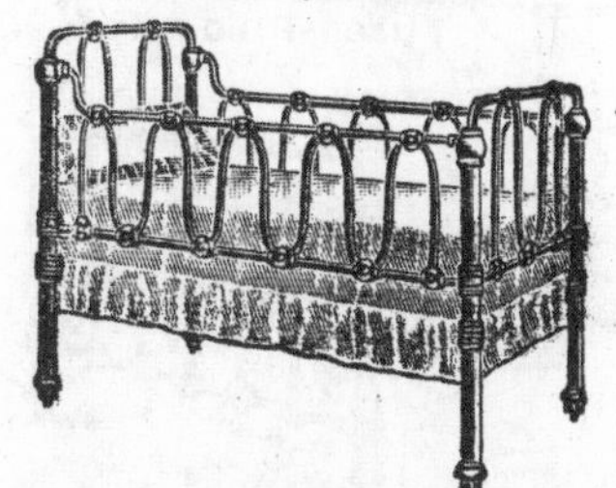

No. 1C2396 This Child's Iron Bed is made of the best quality malleable iron and high carbon steel. Height of head end, 42½ inches; height of foot end, 37½ inches. Corner posts are ⅞ inch thick. Filling rods between posts, ⅜ inch thick. Finished in white enamel with decorated gilt chills, or in any other color desired. It has hinged drop sides. Fitted with a strong woven wire spring. Shipped knocked down. Furnished in two sizes. Shipping weight, 105 pounds.

Size, 2 ft. 6 in. by 4 ft. 6 in. Price..... **$4.25**
Size, 3 feet by 5 feet. Price.......... **4.55**

Our $4.65 all Iron Crib, Drop Sides.

No. 1C2398 This Child's Iron Bed is in white enamel, or any color desired, with gilt decorated chills. Height, head end, 45½ inches; height, foot, 40½ inches. Corner posts, ⅞ inch. Filling rods, ⅜ inch thick. Made of best quality malleable iron and high carbon steel. Fitted with high grade woven wire spring. It has hinged drop sides. Sells in retail stores at $7.00 to $8.00. Shipped knocked down. Furnished in two sizes. Shipping weight, 115 pounds.

Size, 2 ft. 6 in. by 4 ft. 6 in. Price...... **$4.65**
Size, 3 feet by 5 feet. Price........... **4.95**

Our Massive $5.35 Iron Crib With Drop Sides.

No. 1C2400 This Child's Iron Crib has corner posts 1 1-16 inches thick; filling rods, ⅜ inch thick. Height, head end, 39 inches. Finished in white enamel or any other color desired, with gilt decorated chills. Fitted with best quality woven wire spring and casters. It has hinged drop sides; best quality malleable iron and high carbon steel used in the bed. Compare the bed with those for sale in retail stores at $8.00 to $10.00. Shipped knocked down. Furnished in two sizes. Shipping weight, 125 pounds.

Size, 2 ft. 6 in. by 4 ft. 6 in. Price..... **$5.35**
Size, 3 feet by 5 feet. Price........... **5.95**

Extra High Side Iron Crib, $5.95.

No. 1C2402 This Child's Iron Bed is 4 feet 6 inches long and 2 feet 6 inches wide. The main posts are 1 inch thick and the filling rods ⅜ inch thick. The head and foot are 48 inches high and sides 22 inches high, and the rods are 3¼ inches apart so that the child cannot stick its head through, climb over, fall out or otherwise harm itself. One side can be lowered. Fitted with woven wire springs and best quality casters. Finished in white enamel or any color desired, with gold decorated chills. Be sure to state color desired, otherwise white will be furnished. Shipped knocked down, well crated. Shipping weight, 125 pounds.

Size, 2 ft. 6 in. by 4 ft. 6 in. Price... **$5.95**
Size, 3 feet by 5 feet. Price......... **6.25**

Wonderful Value, $1.48.

No. 1C2404 This Iron Bed is made of the best quality malleable iron and high carbon steel. Height, head end, 48 inches; height, foot end, 38 inches; corner posts, ⅞ inch thick; filling rods, ⅜ inch thick; finished in baked white enamel. Wonderful value at our price. Furnished in 3 foot, 3 foot 6 inch, 4 foot and 4 foot 6 inch widths. Shipping weight, 55 pounds.
Price, all sizes..**$1.48**

Our $1.65 Iron Bed.

No. 1C2406 This Iron Bed has ⅞-inch pillars; top and bottom rods, ⅝ inch; other rods, ⅜ inch. Height of head, 51½ inches; foot, 45 inches. Comes in four widths, 3 feet, 3 feet 6 inches, 4 feet and 4 feet 6 inches. **Be sure and state the width wanted.** Complete with casters. Finished in baked white enamel. Shipping weight, 55 pounds. Price.............. **$1.65**

This Handsome Iron Bed, $3.15.

No. 1C2410½ This Iron Bed is made of malleable iron with steel side and cross rails. Height of head end, 48 inches. We furnish the bed in 3 feet, 3 feet 6 inches, and 4 feet 6 inches widths. White enameled finish. A strong, substantial and new design. Shipping weight, 80 pounds. Price, all sizes....**$3.15**

This Iron Bed Only $3.45.

No. 1C2411½ This Iron Bed is made of high grade malleable iron with solid steel filling rods and side rails. Height 61 inches. Posts are 1 1-16 inches in diameter. Vertical filling rods are 5-16 inch, and cross filling rods ⅜ inch in diameter. The heavy chills are gold decorated. Made in 4 foot 6 inch width only. Finished in white enamel finish only. Shipped direct from factory in Northern Indiana or Chicago. Shipping weight, about 90 pounds. Price................................**$3.45**

Our $3.75 Value.

No. 1C2412 This is an Impressive Looking Bed, standing 60 inches high; is made of selected materials and finished in the best white baked enamel. Posts, $1\frac{1}{16}$ inches; fillers, $\frac{5}{16}$ inch and ⅜ inch. Has brass caps and vases and full foot end. The construction and details are so perfect as to render it **practically indestructible.** This bed is made 4 feet 6 inches in width. **We are selling it at an astonishingly low price.** Complete with casters. Shipping weight, about 80 pounds. Price........................**$3.75**

$3.95 Iron Bed.

No. 1C2418 This Iron Bed has continuous pillars made of 1 1-16 inch iron tubes. Is 59½ inches high at the head and 40½ inches at the foot. The scrolls are 5-16-inch iron, the bottom rods are ⅜ inch. Finished in best quality baked white enamel. Ornamented with massive fancy gold decorated chills. Complete with best quality casters. Comes in four widths: 3 feet, 3 feet 6 inches, 4 feet and 4 feet 6 inches. Be sure to state width desired. Shipping weight, 100 pounds. Price............**$3.95**

This Massive Iron Bed $4.15.

No. 1C2420 This Handsome Iron Bed is made of high grade malleable iron with solid steel filling rods and side rails. Height of head end, 60 inches. Posts and top rods are $1\frac{1}{16}$ inch in diameter. Filling rods, ⅜ inch in diameter. Finished in best quality baked white enamel with gold decorations on chills. Made in 4 feet 6 inches size only. Shipped direct from factory in Northern Indiana or Chicago. Shipping weight, 95 pounds.
Price..**$4.15**

Our $4.25 Brass Trimmed Iron Bed.

No. 1C2424 Made of the best malleable iron. Baked white enamel finish and superior construction; 1 1-16-inch pillars; and has ⅛-inch **brass top rail on both head and foot.** Height of head, 58 inches; height of foot, 42 inches. Has brass spindles and top mounts and four brass vases. Fitted with best casters. Is made in the following sizes: 3 feet, 3 feet 6 inches, 4 feet, 4 feet 6 inches. Weight, 90 pounds. Price..**$4.25**

Patent Combination Bed.

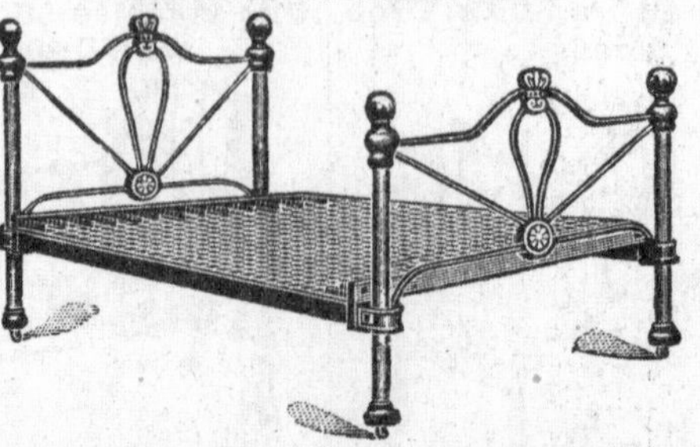

This Bed is composed of three parts only, head, foot and high grade spring, and has no side rails. The saving of the side rails makes the price of the bed much lower than one of the same grade with separate springs, and furthermore makes it possible to pack and ship the bed at less expense. The posts are 1 1-16-inch iron, mounted with four brass vases. The filling rods are ⅜ and 5-16 inch. The spring is exceptionally comfortable and guaranteed not to sag. Complete with casters. Shipping weight, 100 pounds.

No. 1C2426 Price, 3-foot 6-inch bed........**$4.30**
No. 1C2427 Price, 4-foot 6-inch bed........ **4.40**

Bow Foot Bed for $4.3

No. 1C2429 Head is 57 inches high; 45 inches at the foot; made of malleable iron, best baked white enamel finish. Posts, $1\frac{1}{16}$ inches; fillers, $\frac{5}{16}$ inch and ⅜ inch. Has brass caps, vases and rosettes and full extension foot end. Fitted with set of best casters. This bed is made in the following widths: 3 feet 6 inches and 4 feet 6 inches. Shipping weight, 100 pounds. Price........................**$4.35**

Our $4.85 and $4.95 Bed.

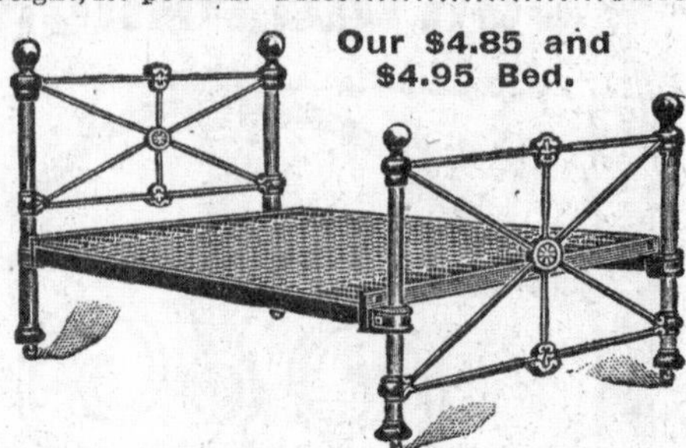

This Bed consists of head, foot and high grade spring, which, when put together, are exactly the same as regulation iron beds, but can be furnished at much less money than the iron bed with separate wire spring, on account of the saving of the side rails. **The beds are baked white enamel, made very strong, and are as durable as any other iron bed made.** The posts are made of $1\frac{1}{16}$-inch iron and are mounted with brass caps. The filling rods are ⅜ and $\frac{5}{16}$ inch, and are designed with a view of adding to the strength of the bed. The high grade spring is exceptionally comfortable and guaranteed not to sag. Complete with set of best casters. Shipping weight, about 100 pounds.

No. 1C2430 Price, 3-foot 6-inch bed.......**$4.85**
No. 1C2431 Price, 4-foot 6-inch bed....... **4.95**

Read what we say about our Iron Beds on page 673.

Our $5.25 Bed.

No. 1C2444 Head is 72 inches high, foot 59 inches high. The pillars are $1\frac{1}{16}$ inches in diameter, surmounted by handsome brass caps and vases; the spindles, cross rods and ornamental iron work $\frac{5}{16}$ inch in diameter, ornamented with brass tips and rosettes. The extended foot rail adds to its already handsome appearance. We furnish this bed 4 feet 6 inches wide by 6 feet long, finished white enamel of best quality. Complete with set of best casters. Shipping weight, 110 pounds. Price..........**$5.25**

Our Combination Three-Piece Bed.

This Bed is so constructed that the high grade spring forms the side rails and on account of this, the price will be found much lower than our regular iron bed of same grade with wire spring. This bed is exceptionally strong, having 1¼-inch posts and surmounted by handsome brass vases, and has brass top rails. We furnish it only in baked white enamel finish. The spring is exceptionally comfortable and guaranteed not to sag. Complete with set of best casters. Shipping weight, 100 pounds.

No. 1C2446 Price, 3-foot 6-inch bed...... **$5.40**
No. 1C2447 Price, 4-foot 6-inch bed...... **5.45**

ANY BED ON THIS PAGE

we furnish in any solid color desired with gilt decorated chills, or in the following combination of colors with gilt decorated chills: Maroon and white, pea green and white, pink and white, olive green and white, light blue and white, dark blue and white, emerald green and white, light blue and ivory white. In ordering be sure to state color desired, otherwise we ship white with gilt decorated chills. When finished in a combination of colors, the posts and top rods are finished in the first color mentioned above and the filling rods in white. If you are in doubt which color to order **send for our Free Special Furniture Catalogue,** in which we illustrate four beds decorated in combinations of colors which will aid you in making your selection.

$5.80

No. 1C2448 This bed is made with bow foot; the head is 63 inches high and the foot 48 inches high. The pillars are 1 1-16 inches, the brass vases 1¾ inches. It has brass top mounts ⅝ inch, and brass top rails, two brass rosettes. The iron top rod and scrolls are ⅝ inch and all other rods 5-16 inch. This is an exceptionally handsome bed, the brass top rail being especially ornamental as well as durable. Especially attractive, finished in dead black or white enamel or in our combination of pink and white with gilt chills. Fitted with best quality casters. Made in 4 foot or in 4 foot 6 inch widths only. Shipping weight, 88 pounds. **Be sure to state color and width desired.**

Price, one color with gilt chills........................$5.80
Price, two colors with gilt chills........................6.15

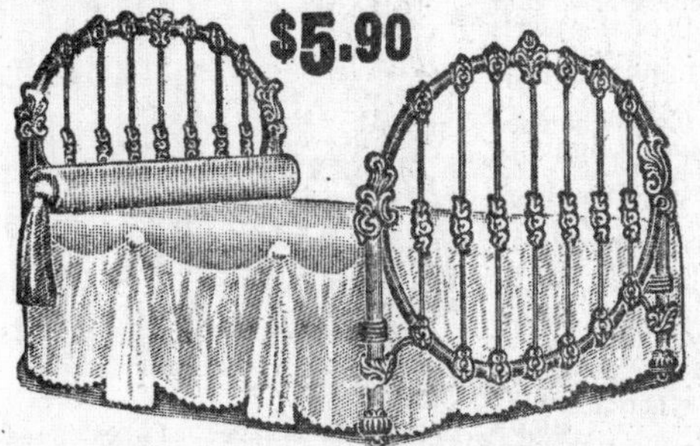

$5.90

No. 1C2452 Artistic Colonial Iron Bed. This pattern was designed to strongly appeal to lovers of the colonial style, and is offered at an extremely low price. The head end is 61½ inches high and the foot end 47½ inches; has 1 1-16-inch posts, ⅜-inch fillings and ⅜-inch bent tubes. Particular attention is called to the handsome chill work on this bed, which is decidedly artistic and renders the bed an ornament to any room. This bed is unusually attractive in our combination colors of pea green and white with gilt decorated chills. Made in 3½ foot and 4½ foot widths. Fitted with best quality casters. **Be sure to state size and color desired.** Shipping weight, 136 pounds.

Price, one color with gilt chills........................$5.90
Price, two colors with gilt chills........................6.25

$6.95

No. 1C2456 An Unusually Handsome Brass Trimmed Bed. Entirely new design. 65 inches high at head, 47 inches at foot. Has 1 1-16-inch corner posts and top rods, ⅜-inch bent tube, ⅜-inch filling rods. Handsome ⅜-inch brass spindles with husks in center of head and foot end. A beautiful bed when finished in either white enamel with gilt chills or in our combination colors of light blue and white with gilt chills. Made in 3 foot 6 inch and 4 foot 6 inch widths. Fitted with best quality casters. Shipping weight, 130 pounds. **Be sure to state width and color desired.** Price, one color with gilt chills..........$6.95
Price, two colors with gilt chills........................7.25

$7.35

No. 1C2460 Brass Trimmed Iron Bed. Strikingly handsome design. The pillars are made of 1 1-16-inch iron. Top tubes are ⅞ inch with ⅜-inch brass spindles and husks. The filling rods are ⅜ inch thick. This bed has unusually handsome and ornamental chills. Height of head, 71 inches; height of foot, 52 inches. An attractive design in white enamel as well as in combination colors of maroon and white with gilt chills. Fitted with best quality of casters. Made in 4 foot or 4 foot 6 inch widths. Shipping weight, 140 pounds. **Be sure to state width and color desired.** Price, one color with gilt chills..........$7.35
Price, two colors with gilt chills........................7.65

$7.65

No. 1C2461 This Iron Bed is made of the best quality malleable iron corner posts and solid steel filling rods. Posts and top rods are 1 5-16 inches thick, filling rods ⅜ inch thick, ornamented with handsome designed finely executed chills. Height of head end, 64 inches; height of foot end, 45 inches. Furnished in white enamel or combination colors, with gilt decorated chills. This bed is especially handsome, finished in emerald green, with gilt decorated chills. Made in 4 foot 6 inch width only. Fitted with best quality casters. **Be sure to state color desired.** Shipping weight, 185 pounds.

Price, one color and gilt chills........................$7.65
Price, two colors and gilt chills........................7.95

$7.95

No. 1C2464 This Iron Bed should be compared with what other dealers offer at $12.00 to $15.00, and it will be found handsomer in design, better made, better finished. It is 60 inches high, has massive posts made of 1 5-16-inch iron with full ⅜-inch filling rods. The top scroll is 1 1-16-inch steel tubing. The center rods in head and foot are made of ⅜-inch brass with gothic design husks and fancy brass rod ends. This bed is especially attractive in a combination of olive green and white, with gilt chills, or in maroon and white with gilt chills. Made in 4 foot 6 inch width only. Fitted with best quality casters. **Be sure to state color desired.** Shipping weight, 160 pounds.

Price, one color and gilt chills........................$7.95
Price, two colors and gilt chills........................8.25

$8.45

No. 1C2472 This Massive Gold Trimmed Iron Bed is without doubt one of the handsomest shown in our catalogue. In point of quality it is equal to beds offered by other dealers at from $12.00 to $16.00. It is 68 inches high, has 1 5-16-inch posts, 1 1-16-inch top rail and ⅜-inch fillings. The chills are exceptionally massive, of pretty design and are all decorated with gold, giving the bed an elegant and at the same time a modest appearance. Exceptionally handsome finished in emerald green, with gilt chills or in pea green and white with gilt chills. Made in 4 foot 6 inch width only. Fitted with best quality casters. **Be sure to state color desired.** Shipping weight, 175 pounds.

Price, one color and gilt chills........................$8.45
Price, two colors and gilt chills........................8.75

$9.35

No. 1C2474 In design and construction this bed cannot be equaled elsewhere at less than $15.00 to $20.00. The head is 68 inches high, the foot 49 inches high. The posts are 1 5-16 inches, the top rail 1 1-16 inches and the filling rods ⅜ inch. Strikingly attractive enameled in our combination of light blue and white with gilt chills, or in dead black with gilt chills. Fitted with best quality casters. Made in 4 foot 6 inch width only. Shipping weight, 175 lbs. **Be sure to state color desired.**

Price, one color with gilt chills........................$9.35
Price, two colors with gilt chills........................9.65

$9.65

No. 1C2476 This Massive Iron Bed is a very striking and artistic design, and should only be compared with beds that are sold elsewhere at $15.00 to $18.00. It is 62 inches high, has 1 5-16-inch posts and full ⅜-inch filling rods, 1 1-16-inch top steel tubing, with large, solid, 2⅜-inch cast brass vases. The center rods are ⅜-inch brass with gothic design husks and fancy brass rod ends. We recommend our combination of maroon and white enamel with gilt chills for this massive and exceptionally handsome bed. Fitted with best quality casters. Made in 4-foot 6-inch width only. Shipping weight, 165 pounds. **Be sure to state color desired.** Price, one color with gilt chills. $9.65
Price, two colors with gilt chills........................9.95

$9.95

No. 1C2477 This Massive Bed is a handsome new design. Height, head end, 68 inches. Posts and top rods are 1 5-16 inches thick, ornamented with extra large brass knobs. Filling rods are ⅜ inch thick. It has a beautiful leaf center design in head and foot end 10 inches long, made of non-breakable malleable iron. The scroll shaped filling rods have solid brass tips. This bed is especially attractive finished in pea green and ivory with gilt chills. Fitted with best quality casters. Shipping weight, 190 pounds. **Be sure to state color desired.**

Price, one color with gilt chills........................$9.95
Price, two colors with gilt chills........................10.25

$11.95

No. 1C2478 This Bed is one of the handsomest and most substantial combination iron and brass beds on the market. It has massive continuous pillars, made of 1 5-16-inch iron. Bottom tubes are ⅞ inch. Has 14 rods made of ⅜-inch brass tubing, with brass husks 4 inches long. Height of head, 61½ inches; foot, 47½ inches. The chills are extra large, feet massive and ornamental. This bed is especially attractive in dead black or in white with gilt chills. Made in 3 foot 6 inch, 4 foot, or 4 foot 6 inch widths. Fitted with best quality casters. Shipping weight, 185 pounds. **Be sure to state color desired.**

Price, one color with gilt chills........................$11.95
Price, two colors with gilt chills........................12.25

$10.45

No. 1C2479 This Iron Bed is a massive and strikingly handsome design. Head end, 64 inches high. Posts and top rods 1 5-16 inches thick. Extra heavy and highly ornamental chills attach the heavy filling rods to the top rods and posts. Corner posts mounted with finely executed dragon's heads. This bed is strikingly attractive, finished in our combination colors of maroon and white with gilt decorated chills. Made in 4-foot 6 inch width only. Fitted with best quality casters. Shipping weight, 210 pounds. **Be sure to state color desired.**

Price, one color with gilt chills........................$10.45
Price, two colors with gilt chills........................10.75

Wonderful Value All Brass Bed, $15.25.

No. 1C2484 This Brass Bed has continuous posts 1 inch thick, ⅝ inch filling rods, all ornamented with large brass husks. Height of head, 67 inches. New and attractive design. The best quality brass, highly polished and finished with the best French lacquer to prevent tarnishing. Wonderful value at our price. Furnished in 3½ feet, 4 feet and 4 feet 6 inches widths; length, 6 feet 6 inches. Shipping weight, 125 pounds. Price, any size..........**$15.25**

A Superb Brass Bed, Reduced to $17.95.

No. 1C2486 A Superb Brass Bed, made of the finest materials and guaranteed to wear and hold its finish for a lifetime. The pillars are 1 inch, vases 2 inches, top and bottom rails, ⅝ inch; head is 56 inches high and the swell end footboard, is 40 inches high. An unusually fine bed for little money. Finished with best quality French lacquer to prevent tarnishing. Furnished 3 feet, 3 feet 6 inches, 4 feet or 4 feet 6 inches in width. Weight, full size, packed, 109 pounds. Price....................**$17.95**

This Massive Brass Bed for $22.45.

No. 1C2487 This beautiful brass bed is so constructed that the heavy 1⅜-inch posts are merged into the top rails on head and foot end and made doubly strong and attractive by the addition of heavy and highly ornamented brass castings at the corners. The filling rods between the posts are ⅝ inch in diameter and fastened to the cross rails by genuine cast brass T ball castings. Height of head end, 60 inches. Foot end, 39 inches. Furnished in 3 feet, 3 feet 6 inches, 4 feet and 4 feet 6 inches width. The best quality brass tubing highly polished and preserved from tarnishing with the finest quality French lacquer. Shipped direct from factory in Chicago. Shipping weight, about 185 pounds. Price..........**$22.45**

An All Brass Bow Foot Bed for $22.95.

No. 1C2488 This Handsome Brass Bed has massive posts 2 inches in diameter. The filling between the posts is ⅝-inch stock, the cathedral knobs on top of posts, 3 inches in diameter. Head is 64 inches high. Foot end 44 inches high. Furnished 3 feet, 3 feet 6 inches, 4 feet and 4 feet 6 inches in width. Our brass beds are made of the best quality of brass tubing, that will not dent or bend. They are highly burnished with the highest grade of genuine French lacquer, that prevents tarnishings French lacquer is to brass what varnish is to wood, it preserve the finish. This quality of bed retails at $35.00 to $40.00 in stores. Shipping weight, 125 pounds. Price, any size..........**$22.95**

STEEL FOLDING BEDS AND STEEL COUCHES.

THE LINE SHOWN represents two of the most desirable patterns, being safe, sanitary, light, comfortable, durable and at popular prices.

THIS STYLE BED is built of light material throughout, thoroughly braced, supplied with woven wire fabric, which in turn is supported with National spring fabric across and lengthwise of the bed, making a strong and durable combination and absolutely prevents sagging. This bed, in its improved form, we guarantee to give perfect satisfaction to the purchaser. In its closed form the bed takes up very little space in the room. Light and easily handled. The finish will be in gold bronze with hardwood golden oak finished top. **We claim this bed, in its recently improved form, to be the best made and best appearing low priced bed on the market.**

No. 1C2502 OPEN.

FOR MATTRESSES TO FIT THESE BEDS, SEE PAGE 677.

No. 1C2502 CLOSED.
Height, 44 in. Depth, 20 in.

No. 1C2502 Size, 3 feet 6 inches by 6 feet 2 inches; weight, 55 pounds. Price................**$5.65**
No. 1C2503 Size, 4 feet by 6 feet 2 inches; weight, 60 pounds. Price................**6.10**

SPECIAL $9.95 STEEL FOLDING BED.

THIS STEEL FOLDING BED is made with a fine woven wire fabric supported with fifteen of the best tempered coil springs, making it impossible for the fabric to sag. The top is fitted with brass hooks ready to attach the curtains so that lower portion may be covered in the day time. The top of the bed is stationary and so arranged that when bed is opened it forms head piece. The foot piece folds under the top of the bed and in that position holds the mattress in place when bed is closed. There are no weights of any kind used in the bed, so it is impossible for it to close up when sleeping in same; at the same time it is so made that a child can operate it. Height when closed, 50 inches; depth, 24 inches; length, open, 6 feet 2 inches. Finished in bronze colors. Shipping weight, 125 pounds.

No. 1C2510

Price, 4-foot bed, without curtains..........................**$9.95**

This illustration shows bed when closed.

Heavy Cretonne Curtains for Iron Folding Beds, 90 Cents.

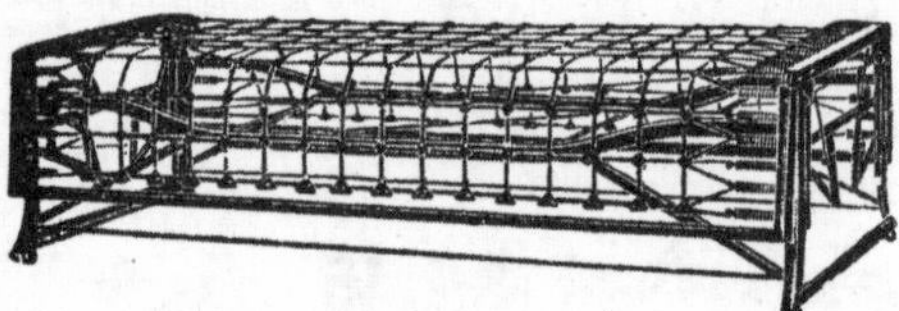
Illustration showing steel construction of couch.

Illustration showing couch when bolster and cover are used.

IN THE ILLUSTRATIONS we show our Folding Bed Couch, either used as a couch when the sides are dropped and covered with a couch cover, or when opened, to be used as a very comfortable, large size bed. **This couch is made of all steel,** making it practically vermin proof, and at the same time strong and durable. It is so constructed that the sides may be lowered and, covered with a mattress and couch cover, it then makes a very handsome and comfortable couch, just as shown in the illustration. The sides may be raised with ease and the folded couch becomes a very comfortable and extra large size bed. It is convenient, takes up little room, is comfortable and attractive. The size of the couch when the sides are dropped down is **74 inches long by 26 inches wide.** The size of the double bed when opened out to its full extent is **74 inches long by 50 inches wide.** Finished in gold bronze, complete with casters. Shipping weight, 70 pounds.

Illustration showing couch in bed position with mattress and bolster.

WE FURNISH THIS COUCH either with or without mattress, as shown in the illustration. We do not furnish the couch cover. By referring to our Dry Goods Department you will find a very complete line of draperies which can be furnished at a very small price.

No. 1C2530 Price, Steel Folding Bed Couch, without mattress..........**$3.65**
Mattress, Elastic Felt with Denim Covering..........**2.75**
Bolster, Elastic Felt with Denim Covering..........**1.15**

DAVENPORT–BED–COUCH, $5.95

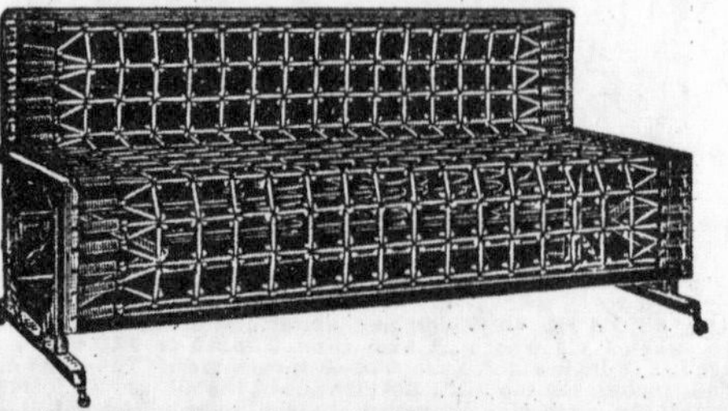

No. 1C2536 This Davenport—Bed—Couch is 6 feet long and 21 inches wide, as illustrated, 48 inches wide when open for use as a bed No. 1C2530, with the added feature of one wing or side forming a divan back. This wing when raised is firmly and automatically bolted in place and makes a perfectly rigid back. This is a new and original feature. To raise or lower the back, pull slightly on the ring at end of couch and then raise or lower as desired. **It will last a lifetime and is never out of repair, and will hold its shape and original form.** It will not sag, as soft edge couches do, after being used a short time. There are no locks, ropes, cords or string attachments used upon it. Its durability, appearance and simplicity are some of its strong features. It is the only piece of furniture manufactured entirely of steel that can be automatically, instantly and easily converted into four distinct useful pieces of furniture, namely, davenport, single bed, double bed and couch. Finished in gold bronze, complete with casters. Shipping weight, 60 pounds.

Price..........................**$5.95**

BED SPRINGS AND WIRE MATTRESSES.

OUR LINE of Bed Springs and Wire Mattresses has been carefully selected from the best line manufactured by the largest manufacturer of this class of goods, and buying in large quantities we are enabled to make prices that cannot be equaled by any other dealer in this class of merchandise. We guarantee every piece to be free from defect in material and workmanship, and sold with the understanding that if not found entirely satisfactory it can be returned to us at our expense and your money will be cheerfully refunded. We will make our springs any size desired, to fit any bed, without extra charge.

HOW TO ORDER. **When ordering a spring be sure and state whether spring is to be used on a wood or iron bed.** Springs for iron beds, as illustrated on this page (except No. 1C2814 and No. 1C2815) are made with extended sides, which rest on the side rail of bed and do not require bed slats. Springs for wood beds are made to fit inside bed rails and rest on the bed slats. **Give exact size of bed inside. State whether for a wood or iron bed.** If you want a spring 4 feet wide and 6 feet long, write it thus: 4-0 by 6-0, never write 4x6. Our woven wire mattresses measure 1 inch less in width and 1¼ inches less in length than marked. **We cannot fill orders for springs unless you give exact size and state whether for wood or iron bed.**

Our Patent Bed Slat for Iron or Brass Beds.

No. 1C2730 We call your attention to our Patent Bed Slat. This slat is adjustable and used to support steel spiral springs on iron or brass bedsteads. They are very strong and durable and can be adjusted to any size bed. Shipping weight, 35 pounds.
Price, per set, which includes four slats.........................**$1.35**

All our springs will fit iron beds without using slats, except No. 1C2814 and No. 1C2815.

Reduced in Price But Not in Quality.

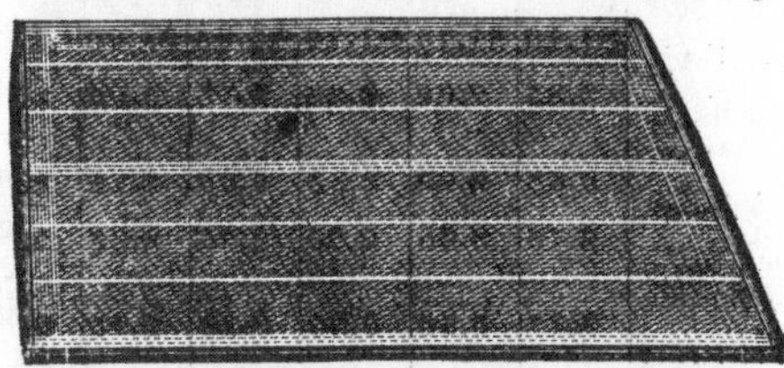

No. 1C2755 This Woven Wire Spring is the regular standard spring. Frame made of thoroughly seasoned hard maple, thick batten, perfectly tight joints between end rail and batten, batten crowning as shown, giving great strength. All our woven wire springs have patent end fastenings for the fabric, making it impossible for any of the wires to become loosened by any strain that will ever be put upon them. Shipping weight, 35 pounds. Price, all sizes..............................**99c**

A Bargain at $1.59.

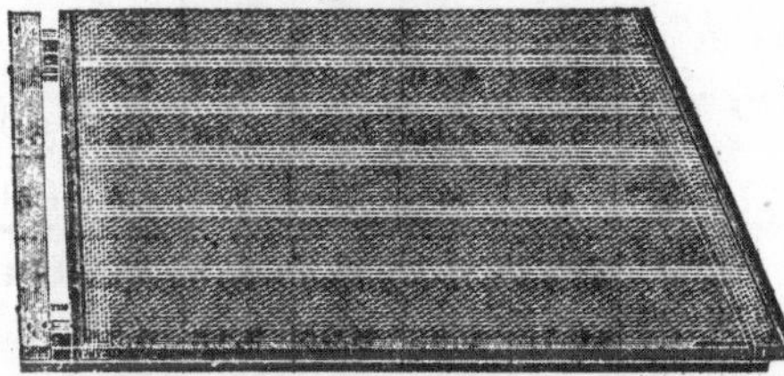

No. 1C2759 This is one of the very finest Woven Wire Springs made. The fabric is single pencil weave, iron cord edges and thirteen inner cords. The frame is made of selected hard maple, with corner blocks that elevate the fabric above the frame. Has a double end bar and bolt, extension device by which the weave can be tightened when necessary. The corners are strengthened with iron plates and the frame is coated with varnish, making an excellent finish. Shipping weight, about 58 pounds. Be sure to state size of bed for which spring is required when ordering. Price, all sizes..............**$1.59**

An Excellent Spring for $1.60.

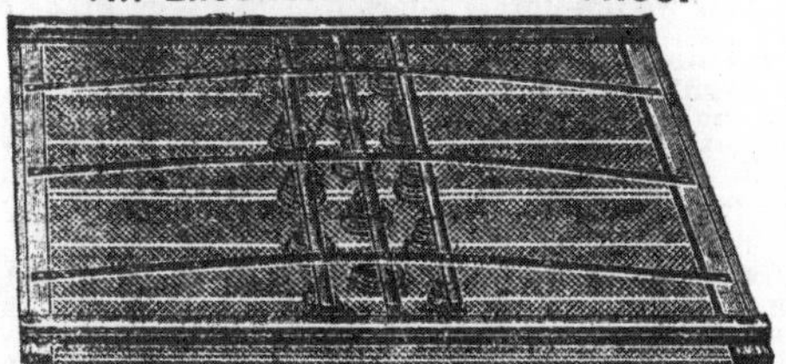

No. 1C2768 This is one of the very best low priced Bed Springs made. The fabric is double weave with cord edges and thirteen additional cords in the body of the fabric, as illustrated. The frame is made of hard maple and strengthened with steel corner plates. The center of the spring is strengthened by fourteen spiral springs resting on slats and fastened to the frame with iron bands. The construction is perfect for comfort and durability. Shipping weight, about 42 pounds. Be sure to state size of bed for which spring is intended. Price..........**$1.60**

Wonderful Value at $2.15.

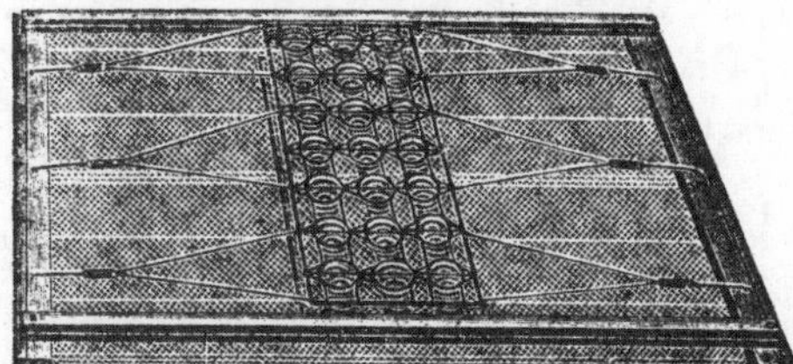

No. 1C2781 This Spring has a hard maple frame, bolted together. Strengthened with steel corner plates. The fabric is double weave with cord edges and fourteen inner cords and is supported by a small spiral spring bed, made of the best grade of wire, and attached to the frame with steel rods and helical springs in a manner that secures strength and elasticity. Shipping weight, 50 pounds. Price..**$2.15**

We cannot fill orders for springs unless you give the exact size and state whether for WOOD or IRON bed.

Angle Iron Frame, Woven Wire Spring.

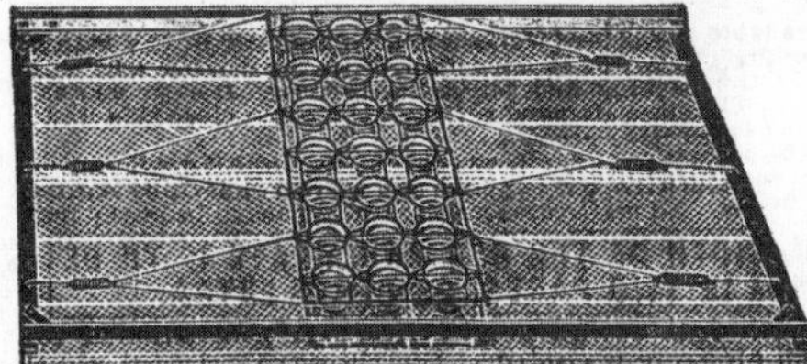

No. 1C2805 This Spring has angle iron end and side rail with corners braced at one end and improved cast corner connections that prevent twisting. The fabric is single and double weave, strongly corded. Has steel rod edges. The fabric is well elevated above the side rails and is supported by twenty-four steel spiral springs and six helical springs, making it impossible for it to sag. Shipping weight, about 56 pounds. Price, all sizes...........**$2.65**

Our $3.10 Metallic Woven Wire Spring.

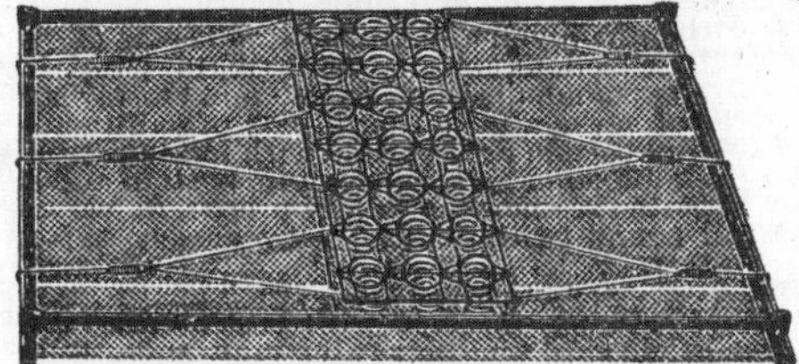

No. 1C2809 This Spring has tubular iron frame, high grade double weave fabric, with well corded rod edges. The tubes and side rails are 1⅛ inch in diameter, has angle steel ends. The fabric is well elevated above the side rails. Improved corner fastenings make the frame perfectly rigid. Has steel supporter of twenty-one spiral springs attached to the frame with six helical springs. Especially desirable for iron or brass beds. Shipping weight, largest size, 65 pounds. Price, any size..........**$3.10**

Our Best Tubular Iron Frame Spring.

No. 1C2813 The fabric in this spring is heavy tinned wire of best quality, fastened at each end to the steel end bars by 28 high carbon steel spiral springs. Side rails are 1¼-inch tubular iron. End bars 1¼-inch angle steel. Fabric raised three inches above side rails by heavy corner castings. Not excelled for comfort. Will last a lifetime. Shipping weight, about 10 pounds.
Price, any size...**$3.95**

Patent Interlocking Top.

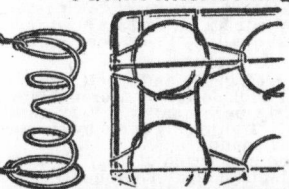

The Patent Interlocking Top is used exclusively on our All Wire Spring Beds. These illustrations show the construction of the spirals and how they are fastened together by continuous interlocking wire which so spreads the strain that no spiral or set of spirals is forced to support the whole of any weight. As a result these springs are more comfortable and last longer than any other all wire spring beds.

Reduced to $1.50.

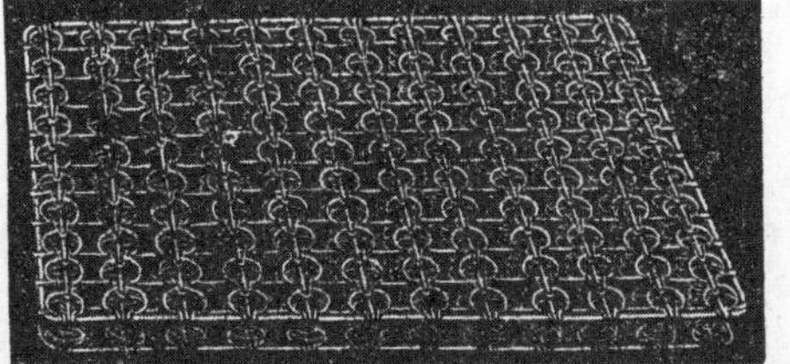

No. 1C2814 This Spiral Spring is thoroughly well made. The top and bottom surfaces are alike, the spiral spring being cone shaped so that the spring can be used either side up. This spring is made with the patent interlocking top, as described above, making it elastic and comfortable. It is finished in black japan and is clean and sanitary. The full size spring has 120 double coils. Shipping weight, about 25 pounds. State size of bed when ordering. To fit this spring to iron bed it is necessary to purchase a set of No. 1C2730 slats. Price..............**$1.50**

Our $2.85 All Steel Spring.

No. 1C2815 This Spiral Spring Bed is one of the finest on the market. It is made of best grade, high carbon steel wire, thoroughly oil tempered. The full size bed contains 120 reversed coil spirals, so that the bed can be used either side up. The spirals are joined with our patent interlocking top, as described above, which makes it exceptionally elastic and comfortable. The finish of this spring is black japan. Shipping weight, about 28 pounds. To fit this spring to an iron bed it is necessary to purchase a set of No. 1C2730 slats. Price..............**$2.85**

Our $3.45 All Steel Spring.

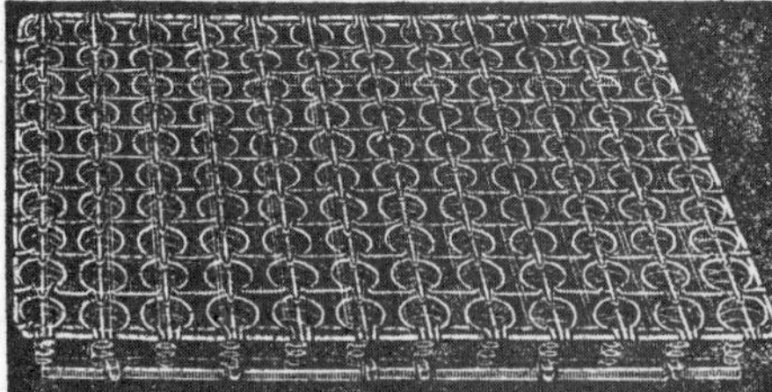

No. 1C2822 The special features of this Spring are the rigid base, unusual strength and extreme lightness in weight. The base is constructed with 12 steel bars joined together by three rows of steel braces. The top of the bed is composed of 120 highly tempered spiral springs bound together with our patent interlocking top, as illustrated and described above. The rigid base makes it impossible for the bed to get out of shape, and together with our interlocking top makes the most perfect spring bed ever placed on the market. **No slats are required with this spring when used on iron beds,** and only three slats when used on wood beds. Finished in black japan, which is exceptionally clean and sanitary. In ordering, be sure to state kind and size of bed for which you wish to use the spring. Shipping weight, about 47 pounds. Price..........................**$3.45**

Double Deck Spring.

No. 1C2824 This is called a double deck spring because the spiral springs are about one-third longer than the ordinary single deck spring, which gives the bed greater elasticity, consequently makes it the most comfortable bed on the market. There are 117 of these deep, highly tempered springs used and the edge springs rest on a steel bar directly over the side rail of the bed. All springs are securely attached to a rigid steel frame and steel slats. The entire spring is handsomely finished in black japan. Made for either iron or wood bed. Shipping weight, about 75 pounds.

Price, for metal bed..........................**$6.25**
Price, for wood bed...........................**4.75**

Upholstered Box Spring Mattresses.

This upholstered bed is made with 70 best oil tempered springs, interwoven with best Italian hemp twine, firmly tied eight ways, and fastened securely in a frame made of specially selected, clean hardwood, so that they can never work loose; full spring and rattan edge, all covered with a clean burlap, and then with the top material of tow or hair, as desired; and the whole upholstered with the finest quality of ticking. The illustration represents the mattress for metal beds, having a rabbet edge, the extended edges resting upon the side and end rails, thus entirely doing away with bed slats. The width of upholstered springs for metal bedsteads is always the same as the outside measure of the rails, 4-6, 4-0, 3-6, 3-0, and the regular length is 6-4. The corners are cut out for a bow foot bed at one end; for a straight foot the corners are round. Springs for a wood bed are regular 1-inch space all around. If the bedstead measures 4-6x6-4, the regular size of spring should be 4-4x6-2. Shipping weight, about 75 pounds.

No. 1C2832	Price, tow top..................................	**$ 8.75**
No. 1C2835	Price, hair top, excellent quality...	**11.45**
No. 1C2836	Price, hair top, best quality........	**13.95**

We cannot fill orders for springs unless you give the exact size and state whether for WOOD or IRON bed.

OUR GENERAL LINE OF MATTRESSES

The material used throughout our mattresses, from the lowest priced to the highest priced, is the very best that can be obtained and nothing has been left undone to give our customers a clean, sanitary, comfortable and durable bed that cannot be purchased elsewhere for less than double the price we ask. Our sales on every grade of mattresses are so large as to enable us to buy materials in such large quantities, as to secure them at a very low cost, and we give our customers the benefit of the saving. We handle nothing we cannot thoroughly recommend. Hence wool mattresses and shoddy mattresses are omitted from our list. We do not make or sell them.

THE TICKING. **However good the quality of the filling, a mattress will prove unsatisfactory if COVERED with an INFERIOR GRADE of TICKING.** The ticking must not stretch or tear and must be firm and strong enough to prevent a spreading of the mattress. We do not use a ticking that will not stand the **test.** The grades we use are very closely woven textile fabrics, guaranteed in **every mattress** to give absolute satisfaction.

THE HAIR **used in the construction of our mattresses, from the lowest grade to the highest grade, is put through a special washing, cleaning and purifying process,** which makes it absolutely pure, wholesome and sanitary. Hair varies in length from 1 inch to 2 feet, the longer the hair the more elastic and comfort giving the mattress. The medium length and longest hair is twisted and plaited by hand into ropes, allowed to remain so for months, and immediately before being placed within the ticking the hair ropes are untwisted, thus forming a very springy and elastic filling. Hair mattresses that are offered for sale by most dealers prove unsatisfactory, the customer being deceived as to **quality and cleanliness.** We absolutely guarantee **weight, quality and cleanliness** in every mattress we furnish.

SEA MOSS. **A pure vegetable fibre which grows on the bottom of the sea.** Being put through a special drying process the fibre curls into spirals. Being a product of the salt water it has many wholesome and hygienic properties and cannot be excelled for its sanitary and comfort giving qualities.

THE EXCELSIOR **which we use in the construction of our combination mattresses is made from choice selected white basswood, thoroughly seasoned and dried.** By a patented process it is cut and curled into a long spiral shaped fibre after which it is thoroughly screened and cleaned, every particle of dust being removed. The fibre thus prepared is very elastic and absolutely clean and sanitary and is placed within the ticking in alternating layers.

THE COTTON **used in the construction of our combination mattresses is guaranteed to be absolutely clean, new cotton.** We do not use any so called **wool,** which is nothing more than ground rags. Wool mattresses and wool combination mattresses are very **unclean and unsanitary,** get **lumpy** and are **worthless.** We do not sell them under any circumstances. The cotton used by us is thoroughly ginned, all dust and impurities removed and makes an absolutely clean, sanitary and comfortable bed.

THE HUSKS **which we use are clean selected corn husks,** the outer rough portion is discarded and the inner part only used. By a special process these are curled into spiral shaped strands and placed in the mattress in even layers, over which pure, clean cotton is spread, making a very comfortable, clean and lasting bed.

THE MAKING. **None but the most thoroughly experienced, reliable and skilled workmen are employed in the manufacture of our mattresses,** great care is used throughout the entire process of construction, from the sewing and binding of the **ticking,** thence to the filling process, the tufting and stitching and finally the packing and burlaping process. Money cannot buy a better made or a better finished article of the mattress product than our mattresses. The close diamond tuftings, the extra close side and end stitchings, and fine bindings on each mattress render it par excellence—no equal in its constructive process.

OUR GUARANTEE **means that every mattress is warranted to be perfect and exactly as represented, and if not found so and absolutely satisfactory in every respect, you are at liberty to return it at our expense and we will cheerfully refund the purchase price and transportation charges. We include EVERY MATTRESS listed below.** All mattresses are carefully packed in heavy paper and new burlap.

IN ORDERING MATTRESSES, STATE EXACT LENGTH AND WIDTH OF THE BED AND STATE IF TO BE MADE IN ONE OR TWO PIECES. MATTRESSES MADE IN TWO PARTS, 25 CENTS EXTRA.

	For Full Size Bed, 4 ft. 6 in. wide by 6 ft. long	For Bed 4 ft. wide by 6 ft. long	For Bed 3 ft. 6 in. wide by 6 ft. long	For Beds 3 ft. wide by 6 ft. long and 2 ft. 6 in. wide by 6 ft. long.	For Crib, Child's, Bed.	For Folding Bed
Guaranteed Minimum Weight, lbs.	45	40	35	30	20	30
No. 1C3100 Excelsior Cotton Top Mattress. Made with full bound heavy ticking, guaranteed not to stretch nor tear. Filled with pure white excelsior overlaid **with clean** new cotton. Leather tufted and closely stitched	$1.75	$1.75	$1.70	$1.65	$1.60	$1.70
No. 1C3108 Reversible Excelsior Mattress. Made with full bound heavy ticking, guaranteed not to stretch nor tear; overlaid **top and bottom** with clean new cotton; leather tufted and closely stitched. **Can be used either side up.**	2.35	2.30	2.25	2.15	1.90	2.28
No. 1C3110 Our Queen Combination Mattress. Filled with the best quality white **excelsior,** with heavy sheets of **clean, new cotton; top, bottom, sides and ends** diamond tufted with leather tufts, closely stitched; good quality, heavy ticking, firmly bound	2.65	2.60	2.55	2.45	2.15	2.58
No. 1C3111 Corn Husk Cotton Top Mattress. Choice, hand cleaned, selected husks; top covered with **thick layers of cotton;** diamond tufted with leather tufts, firmly bound, closely stitched; good quality, heavy twill ticking	2.75	2.65	2.60	2.55	2.35	2.63
No. 1C3118 Reversible Husk Cotton Top Mattress. Extra choice selected hand cleaned and hand stripped corn husks; covered **top and bottom** with heavy sheets of new clean cotton; superior quality, heavy, firmly bound ticking; close diamond tufting, leather tufts, close stitching. A good old fashioned corn husk mattress	3.35	3.30	3.20	3.15	2.75	3.25
No. 1C3126 Our Puritan Combination Mattress. Made with interwoven and alternating layers of excelsior, entirely surrounded with extra thick sheets of **clean, new cotton;** excellent quality **twill** ticking; top, bottom, ends and sides leather tufted; extra quality bed lace binding, firmly bound, diamond tufted and closely stitched	3.45	3.40	3.35	3.25	2.95	3.38
No. 1C3128 Home Favorite Combination Mattress. Made of seven alternating layers of sanitary sea moss; extra quality white excelsior and elastic felt; made so that top and bottom are overlaid with felted cotton and edged with sea moss; fine quality full bound twill ticking; extra close diamond tufting over top, bottom and sides	3.75	3.70	3.60	3.45	3.05	3.65
No. 1C3130 Sea Moss Mattress. Pure sanitary hygienic imported sea moss, specially prepared; very elastic, non-absorbent, comfortable and durable; excellent quality full bound twill ticking; very closely tufted and stitched, top, bottom and sides; leather tufts	3.95	3.90	3.80	3.70	3.25	3.85
No. 1C3135 Reversible Sea Moss Mattress. Highest grade, **sanitary sea moss** filling, with heavy layers of felted cotton laid over the top and bottom so it can be used either side up. Covered with best quality, extra heavy, twill ticking; full leather tufted top, bottom and sides; best grade twill binding; full bound and stitched. We highly recommend this mattress as being sanitary and very comfortable	4.45	4.40	4.35	4.30	3.65	4.38
No. 1C3132 Cotton Mattress. Made of special quality new cotton. Thoroughly ginned and cleaned. Covered with the best quality of satin finish ticking, firmly bound and closely stitched edges, closely tufted	6.25	6.10	5.95	5.45	3.45	5.95
HAIR MATTRESSES. Actual Weight of Mattress, pounds	40	36	33	30	18	30
No. 1C3148 Hair Mattress. Short black or gray curled hair, covered with best quality heavy Amoskeag ticking, close tufting, full bound and closely stitched. A very comfortable bed	$7.45	$7.35	$7.25	$7.10	$3.85	$7.05
No. 1C3156 Hair Mattress. A good quality of medium length gray or black curled hair, thoroughly washed and cleaned. Excellent quality of heavy Amoskeag sateen ticking. Thoroughly well made in every detail	10.75	9.65	8.95	8.15	4.85	8.10
No. 1C3158 Hair Mattress. This mattress is filled with a fine quality of gray or black curled hair. Specially cleaned, curled and prepared; extra closely tufted; special binding and stitching. Fine quality sateen ticking	13.45	12.10	10.95	9.85	5.25	9.80
No. 1C3160 Hair Mattress. Select quality of long black or gray hair, extra curled. Best quality heavy Amoskeag satin finish ticking; tufting, binding and stitching the best. **An exceptionally satisfactory mattress**	15.25	13.85	12.65	11.45	6.25	11.40

ELASTIC FELT, COTTON OR HAIR MATTRESSES ARE ESPECIALLY ADAPTED FOR FOLDING BEDS.

Feathers when taken from the fowl contain considerable quantities of oil and animal matter. If this is not entirely removed the decomposition which takes place renders the feathers foul smelling and unsanitary.

OUR SPECIAL PROCESS. **Every feather that we sell in bulk or in the pillow is put through a special process,** which consists in subjecting them to alternating currents of **steam, hot** and **cold** blasts of air, which absolutely removes every particle of foreign matter and renders the feathers odorless, wholesome, and hygienic. Renovating processes used by many others destroys the life and buoyancy of the feather. **By our special process, the life, resiliency and buoyancy** of the feathers is increased fully 50 per cent. This we absolutely guarantee in every grade of feathers we offer, from the lowest to the highest grade, whether in bulk or in the made up pillow. **You cannot fully appreciate the high standard of our feathers and feather pillows,** unless you make a close comparison with those offered by any other concern at fully 40 to 50 per cent higher in price than we ask. Should you favor us with an order, it will mean the sale of many more in your neighborhood.

OUR PILLOWS. **The ticking which we use on our pillows is the very best quality of heavy sateen or Amoskeag twill ticking.** We furnish them in a variety of sizes and weights. We especially recommend the 2½, 3 and 3½ pound weights. Each pillow is thoroughly filled and rounded out and will retain its life and buoyancy for years.

Steam Cured Feathers.

No. 1C2954 Grade C3. A very satisfactory graded mixture of duck and small selected turkey feathers and turkey down, absolutely odorless, steam dressed and air blast cured by our special process. Price, per pound....34c

No. 1C2956 Grade C2. A mixture of duck feathers, duck down and turkey down. Specially selected, steam dressed, air blast cured by our special process. Odorless and sanitary. A good combination. Price, per pound....42c

No. 1C2958 Grade C1. A mixture of pure, prime, live geese feathers with the best quality of specially selected choice duck feathers, free from coarse quills, cured by our special process. Sanitary, odorless and very resilient. Excellent value. Price, per pound....49c

No. 1C2960 Grade B3. Pure prime live geese feathers, blended with especially selected choice duck feathers, equal parts. Cold air blast cured, steam dried by our special process. Always satisfactory. Price, per pound....56c

No. 1C2962 Grade B2. Pure prime live geese feathers with a slight mixture of choice, specially selected duck feathers. Thoroughly cured by our special process. Exceptionally satisfactory. Price, per pound....64c

No. 1C2964 Grade B1. Pure prime live geese feathers. Steam dressed, air blast cured by our special process. Odorless, wholesome and sanitary. Very buoyant. Price, per pound....75c

No. 1C2968 Grade A2. The best quality of extra specially selected pure prime live geese feathers with down. Steam dressed and cured by our special process. Odorless, hygienic and wholesome. A very fine article. Price, per pound....80c

No. 1C2970 Grade A1. The very choicest pure white live geese feathers. Specially selected with the natural quantity of down retained. Specially cured by our steam and air blast process. Absolutely the best quality. Price, per pound....88c

Down.

No. 1C2982 A high grade and special mixture of live goose and live duck down. A thoroughly satisfactory and strictly pure quality. Very resilient and comfort giving. Thoroughly cured by our special process. Price, per pound....60c

No. 1C2983 The best grade of gray goose down. Pure and strictly high quality. Thoroughly cured by our special process of steam dressing and air blast. Price, per pound....85c

Pillows.

No. 1C3002 Special Brand. Extra specially selected prime white live geese feathers with extra quantity of down. Cured by our special process. The highest and best grade of feather pillows, best quality of sateen ticking.

Size	21x27	23x28	24x29	26x30	27x31
Weight, each	2 lbs.	2½ lbs.	3 lbs.	3½ lbs.	4 lbs.
Price, each	$1.60	$2.05	$2.40	$2.80	$3.20

No. 1C3003 Princess Brand. Extra quality of pure white live geese feathers, with natural quantity of down. Steam dressed, air blast cured by our special process. Best sateen ticking.

Size	21x27	23x28	24x29	26x30	27x31
Weight, each	2 lbs.	2½ lbs.	3 lbs.	3½ lbs.	4 lbs.
Price, each	$1.44	$1.80	$2.16	$2.52	$2.88

No. 1C3005 Our Reliable Brand. Selected, pure white, special steam dressed and blast cured prime live geese feathers. A fine quality, very soft and downy, strictly pure and high grade, best sateen ticking.

Size	20x27	22x27	23x29	24x29	26x31
Weight, each	2 lbs.	2½ lbs.	3 lbs.	3½ lbs.	4 lbs.
Price, each	$1.21	$1.50	$1.82	$2.12	$2.42

No. 1C3007 Our Famous Brand. Best quality of choice, live, white geese feathers, mixed with the best quality of specially selected choice down, live duck feathers, equal quantities of each. Best sateen ticking. A very fine pillow.

Size	20x26	21x27	22x29	24x30	25x30
Weight, each	2 lbs.	2½ lbs.	3 lbs.	3½ lbs.	4 lbs.
Price, each	98c	$1.22	$1.46	$1.70	$1.95

No. 1C3008 Our Peerless Brand. A very good quality of mixed geese and duck feathers, special steam dressed and blast cured. Absolutely odorless, wholesome and hygienic. A very satisfactory article, best sateen ticking.

Size	19x26	20x27	22x27	24x28	25x30
Weight, each	2 lbs.	2½ lbs.	3 lbs.	3½ lbs.	4 lbs.
Price, each	74c	93c	$1.12	$1.30	$1.49

No. 1C3012 Our Lily Brand. A good quality of duck feathers mixed with turkey down, special process steam dressed and blast cured, odorless, sanitary, free from coarse quills and very comfortable, best sateen ticking.

Size	20x26	21x27	22x28
Weight, per pillow	3 lbs.	3½ lbs.	4 lbs.
Price, per pillow	65c	75c	84c

No. 1C3014 Our Crown Brand. A very satisfactory quality of duck feathers, mixed with turkey down and small turkey feathers, cured by our special process, steam dressed and air blast, odorless, sanitary and wholesome.

Size	19x26	21x27	22x28
Weight, per pillow	3 lbs.	3½ lbs.	4 lbs.
Price, per pillow	45c	52c	61c

Down Cushions.

No. 1C3022 Java Brand. Made of imported Japanese silk floss, non-absorbent, verminproof, very resilient and elastic, odorless and hygienic. An ideal sofa cushion. Muslin covered.

Size	16x16	18x18	20x20	22x22	24x24	25x26
Price, each	21c	26c	35c	47c	59c	70c

No. 1C3024 Leader Brand. Filled with a mixture of duck and turkey down, steam dressed, air blast cured, odorless and sanitary. Muslin covered.

Size	16x16	18x18	20x20	22x22	24x24	26x26
Price, each	25c	32c	45c	58c	68c	59c

Elastic Felt Mattresses

$6.75 Grade B $8.35 Grade A $9.95 Grade AA

Sold under our personal guarantee as the equal of elastic felt mattresses universally advertised at $15.00.
Offered by us for a thirty nights' free trial. Sleep on it thirty nights, use it for a full month and convince yourself that we offer the most comfortable, sanitary and durable mattress made, otherwise the trial won't cost you one cent.

$9.95 Buys the Best GENUINE ELASTIC FELT MATTRESS in the world for the largest size bed, 4 feet 6 inches in width, by 6 feet 3 inches in length. Smaller sizes and different qualities at still lower prices according to the price list below.

THIS IS THE GENUINE ELASTIC FELT MATTRESS. **None better made; no other can surpass it in high quality of material or excellent workmanship.** Made of genuine elastic felt, which is the long, staple, white, fleecy cotton, thoroughly cleaned and purified, and woven and interlaced or felted so as to form sheets or layers the full size of the mattress; these sheets or layers are laid one upon the other, compressed and the ticking drawn over them; a mattress built up and enclosed (not stuffed); shapely, the same amount of "spring" in every spot, uniform everywhere never varies. An elastic felt mattress never becomes lumpy, never packs or spreads never requires renovating.

IT IS THE IDEAL BED. **Absolutely clean and sanitary, germproof, verminproof, non-absorbent,** as far in advance of the ordinary mattress as the electric light surpasses the tallow candle. You will never know what comfort is until you try an elastic felt mattress. You will never realize what a real night's rest means until you sleep on an elastic felt mattress.

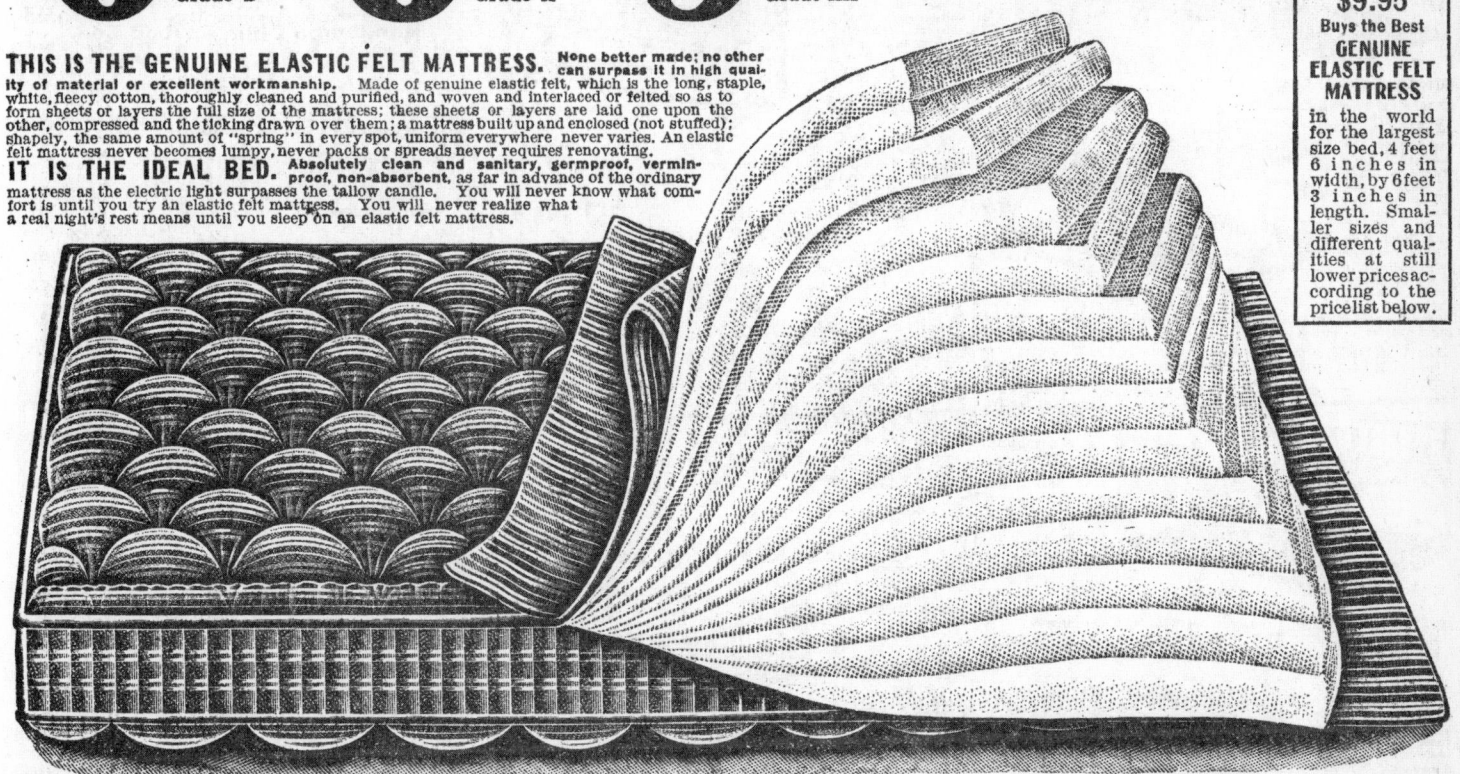

OUR CHALLENGE OFFER. **If you are thinking of buying a mattress let us induce you to place your order with us for one of our Genuine Elastic Felt Mattresses;** we want you to select this genuine elastic felt mattress purely in your own interest, for the greater and lasting satisfaction it will give you over any other make or style. **THIS IS OUR OFFER:**—Send us your order for this mattress, enclose our price; if you desire, send your order at the same time for any other mattress advertised by others at prices ranging from $12.00 to $15.00; compare them both carefully, note the material, construction, finish, etc., try both mattresses and if, after comparison, test and trial, you do not find our mattress the equal if not the superior, then you are under no obligation, return our mattress at our expense and we will promptly return your money, including transportation charges. Use our mattress a month, give it thirty nights' trial, and if you decide it is not as splendid as we led you to expect, just return the mattress to us and we will return your money and pay the freight charges both ways.

ABOUT THE FREIGHT CHARGES. **We do not quote this mattress "freight prepaid."** If we did, we would have to make higher prices, so as to cover freight charges to the most distant points, and the customer living 250 miles away would be helping to pay the freight to the customer living 350 to 1,000 miles away. You must pay the freight, but it is a very small matter. The mattress weighs, packed for shipment, about 50 pounds, and the freight for 100 to 300 miles will be about 25c to 50c; 500 miles, about 65c; greater or less distances in proportion; so you see the freight charges amount to practically nothing as compared with what you save in price by buying from us.

DESCRIPTION OF THE GENUINE ELASTIC FELT MATTRESS, the latest, most modern development of mattress making today. Our elastic felt mattress is made entirely from cotton, but it is the original and wonderful method of treating this cotton that results in its superior qualities. In the first place, we use only a superior quality of ripened cotton, a special quality which has exceptionally long, tough fibres of great strength and resiliency. Every pound of cotton we use is very carefully inspected and tested for that first great essential, elastic strength and necessary length of fibre. The cotton we use is absolutely pure and throughout the manipulation and treatment of this cotton we are extremely careful to preserve this original purity and keep the material free from every contaminating influence. The cotton is treated by special processes of air, dry heat and steam to properly age, cure, clean and prepare the fibres for successive handling. The carefully prepared material is then thoroughly worked and beaten into loose, flaky sheets and these sheets are slowly and evenly drawn and spun so that the fibres are stretched to their utmost tension and are then run over felting machines similar to the rotary printing presses, by which twin sheets are formed, one over the other, the fibres of which unite and interlace and join into a perfect single sheet. Before the sheets go over these machines they go through a certain action which naturally curls and curves the fibres, and at the end we have the wonderfully elastic, beautiful, light, airy, interlacing fibrous sheets which eventually form the filling of our genuine felt mattresses. These sheets are built up in layers, carefully fitted into the ticking and, unlike the ordinary hair mattress, the elastic felt mattress is not stuffed but is made just as you would make and pack a box. The felt sheets are laid one upon another very carefully until the required thickness is obtained and then compressed to a fraction of the original thickness and in this way the whole mass is interlaced into one sheet of uniform thickness throughout which is then enclosed in a tick entirely by hand. The pattern of the ticking is carefully matched, the softness is evenly distributed, every square inch possesses the same resiliency and it is impossible for the elastic felt mattress to bunch up, to mat down, to shift or fi.. in any way. The tufting also is very accurate. The tufts are the same distance apart and of the same tension. The stitching and boxing of border is carefully done. There is no mattress that will compare in thorough workmanship and in the splendid results obtained by this care and skill with our genuine elastic felt mattress.

This process and method of manufacture produces a mattress that is exceedingly soft and elastic, a mattress that is absolutely PURE, DUSTPROOF, GERMPROOF, VERMINPROOF, MOISTUREPROOF and NON-ABSORBENT, the most sanitary and most comfortable mattress on the market.

HOW DO WE MAKE THE LOW PRICES? **Because our margin of profit is very small;** because we ask you only enough money to cover the actual cost of material and only our one narrow profit added; because we sell this splendid article on the same small profit basis as we ask for all of our merchandise; because you are not paying us in each mattress about $5.00 to cover newspaper and magazine advertising expense; because our volume of sales is very large, our expenses of doing business very small and we can accept a smaller profit than any other dealer could afford.

YOU BE THE JUDGE. **Let us send you one of these Genuine Elastic Felt Mattresses.** Send us your order, enclose our price and try the mattress thirty nights. If at the end of that time, you are not still pleased and satisfied, convinced there is no better mattress made in the world, we will return your mone and pay freight charges both ways, as soon as you return the mattress to us. We know when you see and examine our mattress and try it, you would not part with it for double our price if you cou d not buy another.

WE MAKE THREE GRADES **of elastic felt mattresses, the difference in price being due to the relative cost of the felt and ticking,** but all three grades possess all of the good qualities of the best elastic felt mattresses made, such as softness, resiliency, etc.

SAMPLES **of the three grades of ticking and felt will be mailed free upon request.** If you are in doubt, send for samples, and convince yourself that our AA Dreamland grade mattress is the finest mattress of its kind in the world, regardless of name, make or price.

IN ORDERING MATTRESSES, STATE EXACT LENGTH, AND WIDTH OF THE BED AND STATE IF TO BE MADE IN ONE OR TWO PIECES. MATTRESS MADE IN TWO PARTS, 35 CENTS EXTRA.

	For Full Size Bed, 4 ft. 6 in. wide by 6 ft. long.	For Bed 4 ft. wide by 6 ft. long.	For Bed 3 ft. 6 in. wide by 6 ft. long.	For Beds 3 ft. wide by 6 ft. long and 2 ft. 6 in. wide by 6 ft. long.	For Crib, Child's Bed, 2 ft. 6 in. wide by 4 ft. 6 in. long.	For Crib, Child's Bed, 3 ft. wide by 5 ft. long.	For Folding Bed
ACTUAL WEIGHT OF MATTRESSES, UNPACKED, POUNDS	45	40	35	30	12	16	30
No. 1C3138 **B Grade, Elastic Felt Reliance Mattress.** This mattress is made of light brown or yellow colored felt, or what is generally known as unbleached stock. It is covered with a very good grade of ticking, is full bound, leather tufted and stitched, standard 4-inch border	$6.75	$6.50	$6.25	$6.00	$3.30	$3.95	$4.85
No. 1C3140 **A Grade Elastic Felt Our Sanitary Mattress.** This mattress is made of all pure white felt, covered with an excellent grade of satin finished ticking, full tufted with cotton tufts, bound and stitched in a most skillful manner, standard 4-inch border. The mattress should be compared with elastic felt mattresses offered generally throughout the country at from $10.00 to $15.00	8.35	7.95	7.55	7.15	4.10	5.25	6.35
No. 1C3142 **AA Grade Elastic Felt, Dreamland Mattress.** Our Dreamland Elastic Felt Mattress is without doubt the finest mattress of its kind in the world. This mattress should be compared only with very best elastic felt mattresses offered by other dealers and manufacturers at from $15.00 up and by close comparison, it will be found to be equal if not superior, to any mattress made, regardless of name, make or price. It contains only the very finest grade of elastic felt made from long staple, pure white cotton and covered with the best grade of satin finished ticking, tufted top with heavy cotton tufts, stitched sides, full bound with heavy twill binding, standard 4-inch border and made throughout by the most skilled workmen according to the highest art of mattress construction	9.95	9.45	8.95	8.45	4.95	6.25	7.85

All mattresses are carefully packed in heavy paper and new burlap, and safe delivery guaranteed.

COTS AND CRIBS

We call special attention to the construction of our Cradles, Cribs and Folding-Beds, as they are all made with screw construction so that when shipped they are packed in a condensed and small package, thereby greatly reducing the freight charges. Anyone can set up our cradles, cribs and folding beds without any difficulty, as the parts do not require special fitting. K. D. means knocked down, or in other words in parts. By shipping goods knocked down the freight charges are greatly reduced.

Universal Woven Wire Cot.

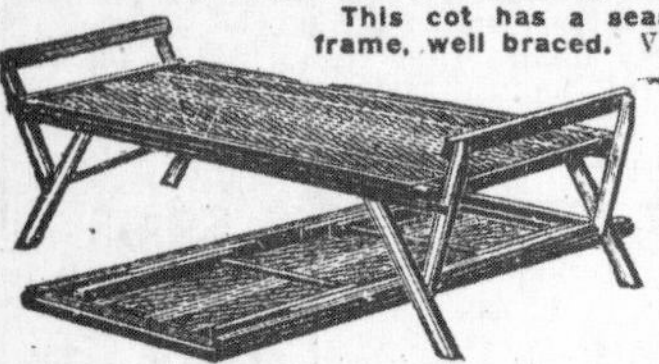

This cot has a seasoned hard maple frame, well braced. Varnish finish. The bed is made of strong single weave wire fabric. Head and foot are raised by opening legs. Shipping weight, about 30 pounds.

No. 1C2556 Size, 2 feet 6 inches wide by 6 feet long. Price........98c

No. 1C2557 Size, 3 feet wide by 6 feet long. Price........................$1.13

Wonderful Value at $1.10.

This is the best low priced, compact folding cot on the market. The frame is made of hard maple with upright posts, strongly braced. Varnish finish. The bed is made of strong single weave wire fabric, making the most comfortable and durable bed of its kind possible to produce. Shipping weight, about 35 pounds. Price.

No. 1C2560 Size, 2 feet 6 inches wide by 6 feet long $1.10

No. 1C2561 Size, 3 feet wide by 6 feet long.......... 1.25

An Excellent Cot for $1.75.

This cot is unusually attractive in design. Has a hard maple frame substantially made and well braced. Varnish finish. The bed is made of strong single weave wire fabric, which insures comfort and durability. Shipping weight, about 36 pounds. Price.

No. 1C2565 Size, 2 feet 6 inches wide by 6 feet long..$1.75

No. 1C2566 Size, 3 feet wide by 6 feet long.......... 1.87

No. 1C2567 Size, 3 feet 6 inches wide by 6 feet long. 1.99

Baby Gate.

This Adjustable Baby Gate is made of solid round steel rods. It is easily fastened to the **door or window frame** by a simple attachment, and can be made to fit several openings up to 3 ft. wide, by ordering an extra set of attachments for each opening. Opens and shuts like a door. Baby can't get it open. An absolute necessity for a home blessed with a lively and inquisitive baby. Shipping weight, 4½ pounds.

No. 1C2572 Baby Gate, complete. Price..............72c

Extra set of attachments, per set..........12c

Our $1.65 Cradle.

No. 1C2578 **This is a very handsome, substantial cradle, furnished complete with woven wire spring.** The frame is made of thoroughly seasoned selected white maple, finished in natural or imitation mahogany, as desired. Has shaped posts and panel head. It is well constructed and fully guaranteed. Size, 24x44 inches. Shipped knocked down in small package, thereby greatly **reducing freight** charges. Easily set up. Shipping weight, about 17 pounds. Price.. ....$1.65

Our $3.25 Cradle.

No. 1C2579 **This Cradle is made of thoroughly seasoned white maple, natural finish.** Length 43 inches, width, 24 inches. The body is fitted to a stationary base by a simple device which allows an easy, frictionless, rocking motion. It has shapely hand turned posts and spindles. Fitted with a high grade woven wire spring and best quality casters. Mechanical construction, strictly first class. Convenient, comfortable and durable. Shipped knocked down to insure lowest freight rate. Shipping weight, 30 pounds. Price..............................$3.25

Our $3.50 Patent Swing Bed.

It is so constructed that it remains level while rocking. The base is made of iron, well braced and perfectly rigid. Mounted on wheels. The frame is made of selected white maple, finished natural or imitation mahogany as desired. Has handsome rope turned posts, shaped head and foot and panel head with ornamental spool spindles. The spring is a woven wire fabric, especially adapted for children's beds and will be found exceptionally comfortable and durable. Size, 24x44 inches. Shipped knocked down in small package, thereby greatly reducing freight charges. Easily set up. Shipping weight, 33 pounds.

No. 1C2585 Price..............................$3.50

No. 1C2586 Same crib as No. 1C2585, but made of solid oak, finished golden. Price..............................$3.75

Our $5.45 Cradle.

No. 1C2589 **This Cradle is made of selected golden oak, high gloss finish.** Has full paneled closed sides and ends. Head end and foot end decorated with hand made carvings. Inside measurement, 20x36 inches. Base connected to bed by a perfect rocking attachment, permits a frictionless and noiseless swinging motion, no **tipping or rolling.** Best casters. Cabinet construction, first class. Shipped knocked down, thereby insuring lowest freight charges. Shipping weight about 55 pounds. Price..............................$5.45

Our $1.50 Folding Crib.

With woven wire spring. Size, 30x54 inches. Can also be furnished in 30x60 inches. Finished in maple, natural or mahogany, as desired. Fitted with our special folding device, making it impossible to fold by accident. It is one of the most durable and strongest child's beds made.

Open

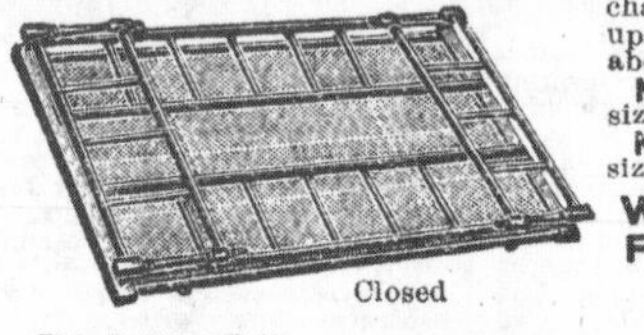

Closed

Shipped knocked down in small package, thereby greatly reducing freight charges. Easily set up. Shipping weight, about 25 pounds.

No. 1C2592 Price, size 30x54 in...$1.50

No. 1C2593 Price, size 30x60 in...$1.65

White Maple Folding Crib, $2.25.

This Folding Crib is made of selected white maple. Has shaped posts and legs. Extra high sides and ends. Constructed so as to fold with bedding in place. Adjustable braces for firmly holding legs in place when open. Castings are all made of malleable iron and the springs of special crib fabric. We can furnish this crib finished in natural or imitation mahogany. Be sure to state finish desired.

Open

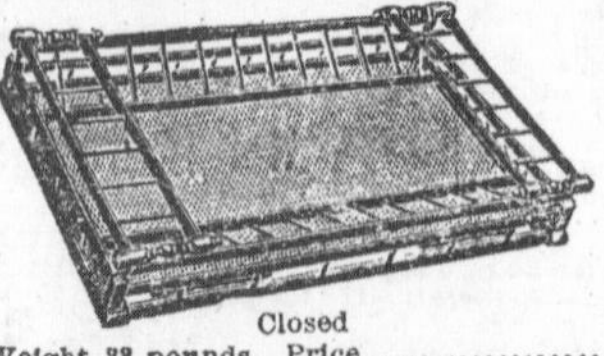

Closed

Shipped knocked down in small package, thereby greatly reducing freight charges. Easily set up.

No. 1C2596 Size, 30x54 inches. Weight, 28 pounds. Price.....$2.25

No. 1C2597 Size, 36x60 inches. Weight, 33 pounds. Price..............................$2.55

An Excellent Child's Bed for $1.90.

This Bed is made of selected white maple, finished in natural or imitation mahogany as desired. It is well constructed and guaranteed throughout. The spring is a woven wire fabric, especially adapted for children's beds, and will be found exceptionally comfortable and durable. Size, 30 inches wide, 60 inches long and 12 inches deep. Shipped knocked down in packages 4½ inches thick, thereby greatly reducing the freight charges. Easily set up. **Shipping weight, 25 lbs.**

No. 1C2604 Price..............................$1.90

No. 1C2605 Size, 40 inches wide, 60 inches long and 12 inches deep. Shipping weight, 28 pounds. Price.........$2.25

Child's Bed for $2.60.

This Child's Bed is made of selected white maple. Has handsome turned posts. Paneled head and foot. Spring of special crib fabric, comfortable and strong. The finish is natural color or imitation mahogany. Be sure to state finish desired. Shipped knocked down in package 4½ inches thick, thereby greatly reducing freight charges. Size, 30x60 inches. Shipping weight, 29 pounds.

No. 1C2612 Price..............................$2.60

No. 1C2613 Size, 40x60 inches. Shipping weight, 33 pounds. Price..............................$3.25

Handsome Child's Wood Bed.

This Child's Bed is made of white maple, natural finish or in solid oak, golden finish. It has ornamental spindles in head and foot end. Fitted with a high grade woven wire spring and best quality casters. Shipped knocked down, thereby securing lowest freight rate. Shipping weight, about 35 lbs.

No. 1C2614 Price, size, 30x60, Maple..........$3.50; Oak..............$3.95

No. 1C2615 Price, size, 40x60, Maple..........$3.75. Oak.............. 4.25

Be sure to state wood desired.

Child's Wood Bed, $3.75.

This Bed we furnish in white maple, natural finish or solid oak, golden finish. It has a curved top rail or head and foot end. Fitted with plain spindles in side rails and fancy spindles in head and foot ends. It has a high grade woven wire spring. Best quality casters. Shipped knocked down direct from Chicago. Shipping weight, 35 pounds.

No. 1C2616 Price, size, 30x60. Maple..........$3.75; Oak..............$4.25

No. 1C2617 Price, size, 40x60 Maple..........$4.25; Oak.............. 4.75

Be sure to state wood desired.

Excellent Child's Folding Bed for $3.75.

This Beautiful Child's Folding Bed is exceptionally well made of selected maple, has fancy turned posts and legs fitted with adjustable braces. The spring is made of special crib fabric, strong and comfortable. The finish is natural color or imitation mahogany. Be sure to state finish desired. Folds up without weights or springs, straps holding bedding in place when folded. Shipped knocked down in package 4½ inches thick, thereby greatly reducing freight charges. Easily set up.

No. 1C2622 Size, 30x40 inches. Shipping weight, crated, 59 pounds. Price..................$3.75

No. 1C2623 Size, 40x60 inches. Shipping weight, crated, 70 pounds. Price..................$4.15

Our Best Child's Folding Bed for $5.25.

This is the Best Child's Folding Bed in the market. Made of selected maple. Has fancy turned posts and legs and ornamental spool spindles. Neat, strong iron canopy, with rings for attaching drapery. Castings are all made of japanned malleable iron. The spring is made of special crib fabric. Two straps hold the bedding in place when bed is closed. Folds without weights or springs. Can be furnished in natural finish or imitation mahogany. Be sure to state finish desired. Shipped knocked down in small package, thereby greatly reducing freight charges. Easily set up.

Closed

Open

No. 1C2626 Size, 30x60 inches. Shipping weight, crated, 68 pounds. Price..............$5.25

No. 1C2627 Size, 40x60 inches. Shipping weight, crated, 76 pounds. Price..............$6.15

No. 1C2628 **This handsome child's bed is made of selected maple in either a natural or in a white enamel finish.** It is fitted with the best woven wire spring. Outside measurement, 3 feet 6 inches long, 2 feet 2 inches wide. It has extra high sides, one of which raises and lowers on perpendicular metal rods. Very strong and well made. It has 9 spindles on each side. Very smooth, round corners. Shipped knocked down for convenience in shipment. Retail stores ask $5.00 to $6.00 for child's bed like this. Carefully packed. Shipping weight, 25 pounds.

Price, in maple, natural finish..............$2.75

Price, in white enamel.............. 3.45

SEE PAGES 678 AND 679 FOR CRIB AND COT MATTRESSES.

DEPARTMENT OF UPHOLSTERED FURNITURE.

THIS DEPARTMENT has been greatly enlarged and improved, and following the very latest styles in upholstery, in frame work, covering and making, we present this new line of goods at prices based on the actual cost to produce, the cost of material and labor, with but our one small percentage of profit added.

OUR PARLOR SUITES are made for us under contract by one of the best makers in Chicago. Only the most skilled mechanics are employed. We have followed the very latest styles, to give our customers the same style and grade of goods that are handled by the most reliable city retail furniture dealers, where they are usually sold at fancy prices.

NEW DESIGNS IN HIGH GRADE COUCHES.

AT CUT PRICES, prices lower than ever before named by us or any other house, prices made possible by building these couches in a factory that is controlled by us, a factory located near the railroad tracks in a suburb of Chicago, equipped with every modern machinery for the manufacturing of frames, for the sewing, tufting, upholstering and making of couches, we are able to offer for this year an entirely new line of couches in all the very latest effects, in all the latest designs of frames and shapes, offer all the new materials at prices heretofore unknown, prices that barely cover the cost of material and labor, with but our one small percentage of profit added.

BY OUR WONDERFULLY LOW PRICES we have built up the largest upholstered furniture business in this country; we have become recognized everywhere as headquarters for everything in this line; leaders in prices with which no other maker or dealer will attempt to compete.

IN THE FRAME WORK, the coverings, the springs, the canvas and stuffing we use a higher grade of goods, a better class of material than is used by the average maker of upholstery, and you will find an upholstered couch, chair, divan, or other piece you may buy of us will have a distinctiveness in style, workmanship and finish not found in the ordinary grade of goods. You will find our goods more lasting, more satisfactory, and at least one-third lower in price than anything furnished by others that will approach our goods in general appearance and style.

OUR GUARANTEE AND REFUND OFFER. We will accept your order and money with the understanding that when you receive the goods, if they do not reach you in the same perfect condition they leave us, or if for any reason whatever you are not satisfied with your purchase, you are not convinced you have received from us such value as you could not possibly get elsewhere, you can return the goods to us at our expense of freight charges both ways and we will refund your money.

FREIGHT CHARGES. In order to save handling expense, which helps to make our low prices possible, we ship upholstered furniture direct from the factory. The freight charges will amount to very little as compared with what you will save in price. The weight of each article is given in the description, and by referring to page 630 you can calculate almost to a cent what the freight will amount to. Always bear in mind that you pay the freight, whether you buy from us or from your local dealer, as your local dealer must figure the freight charges that he pays in fixing his selling prices.

EVERY PIECE OF UPHOLSTERED FURNITURE IS MADE UP SPECIAL, and we therefore require from five to seven days after the order is received before we can make shipment.

THE COVERING MATERIALS.

To give our customers a better understanding of the materials which we use in upholstering our furniture, we give below a description of the texture of the different materials, which should give you an excellent idea of what you can expect. If desired, we will send free upon application samples of the materials used, though this should not be necessary. In sending for samples be sure to state kind of covering and whether for couch or parlor suite. When parlor suites are upholstered in Velour, Brocatelle or Silk Damask, each piece comprising the suite is upholstered in a different shade, but all shades are selected with great care so they will harmonize. We will furnish the entire suite in the same color throughout if desired, but we recommend a combination of colors except in materials which can be procured in only two colors, such as Brocaded Velour, Verona Plush, Crushed Plush and Car Plush. When these materials are used it is advisable to have the suite upholstered in the same color throughout.

FIGURED VELOUR.

Our high colored Velour is a cloth woven like velvet, but with a higher and heavier nap, is soft and has the velvet effect. The high colorings are put into the ground of the cloth by an extract process. The body colors are red, green or brown, and the pattern combinations of artistic colors which makes the total effect very striking. There are many grades of velour on the market and we use none which we cannot guarantee to give the best of satisfaction. Be sure to state color desired when ordering.

CORDUROY.

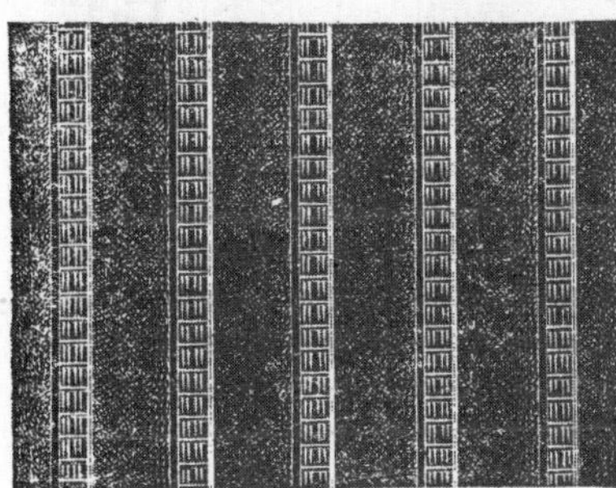

Corduroy is one of the best known and most staple upholstery coverings. Its wearing qualities cannot be excelled. It is woven like velvet, with parallel ridges instead of the plain surface which velvet has. There are many grades of corduroy. We use only the best imported grade. This illustration shows the figure design of our corduroy. The narrow corded, figured, parallel lines represent the background in red, myrtle green or tobacco brown. The broad gray lines represent the long raised nap of the cloth in deep red, myrtle or tobacco brown. A couch covered in this material will prove exceptionally satisfactory. Be sure to state color desired when ordering.

FLORAL BROCADED VELOUR.

nis cloth is exactly the same kind of material as the plain Brocaded Velour, but has a large floral pattern instead of the block pattern as illustrated in the description of plain Brocaded Velour. This cloth is one of the heaviest and best wearing materials used in upholstering furniture. We can furnish it only in deep red or myrtle green. Be sure to state color desired.

PLAIN BROCADED VELOUR.

This is an entirely new covering for upholstering purposes, and has thus far proven to possess most excellent wearing qualities. The body of the cloth is woven in fancy figure effects in a single solid color, into which is woven a fancy figured raised effect. It has a raised nap the same as plush. The illustration shows the figure design of our plain brocaded velour. The white part represents the terry background in a medium shade of red, myrtle green or tobacco brown. The dark part represents the raised long nap of the cloth in dark red, myrtle green or tobacco brown. Be sure to state the color when ordering.

FANCY BROCADED PLUSH.

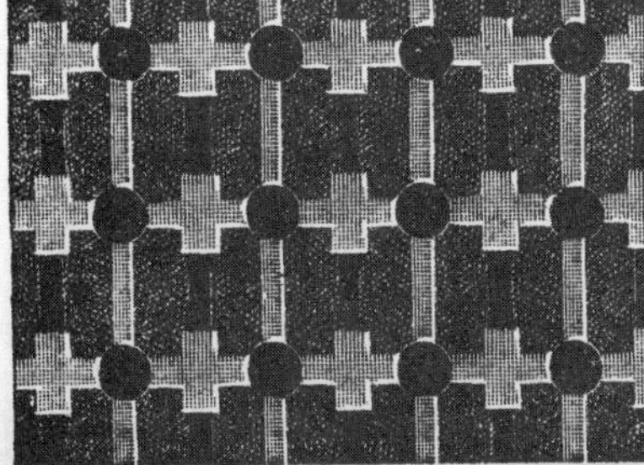

This material is made with a long raised nap similar to the plain brocaded velour, but the nap is woven in two colors. The white in the illustration represents the terry background in medium red or myrtle green. The long nap is represented by the black spots and lines and the dark shading; the dots and lines being black and the dark shading being either dark red or myrtle green. This is an exceptionally handsome and attractive material and is sure to please. Furnished by us at about one-half the price asked by other manufacturers and dealers. Be sure to state color desired when ordering.

BROCADED VERONA PLUSH.

This beautiful fabric is one of the most attractive coverings for high grade furniture which it is possible to procure. Only the strongest colors are used, giving the furniture when finished a most luxurious appearance. It is made with a raised figure in a floral design in a combination of red and black or green and black. The lightest part of the illustration represents the background in medium or myrtle green. The black and dark green in the illustration represent the long nap of the cloth, the black being black in the fabric and the dark gray being either red or green as desired. This goods is most attractive in myrtle green. Be sure to state color desired.

CRUSHED PLUSH.

Crushed Plush is universally known. It is made in many grades, but the quality which we use is not to be compared to what is offered by many other manufacturers and dealers. The crushed plush which we furnish, is made especially for us of a strictly high grade of fur which has an exceptionally silky, lustrous appearance and is guaranteed to hold its color; even the finest wool will not compare with it in this respect. After the fur is woven into the cloth the entire piece is put through the process of crushing, which brings out the rich shaded effects for which this cloth is so much sought. We can furnish crushed plush coverings in red, green, blue or brown, in solid colors only. Be sure to state color desired when ordering.

SILK BROCATELLE.

Silk Brocatelle is one of the most staple of all coverings known and used in upholstering parlor suites, fancy chairs and rockers, especially of the higher grades. This fabric, which is composed of the finest silk yarns, is woven in such a manner as to give the pattern or floral figures a raised effect, the ground work being of one color and the floral pattern of another color, thus giving a two toned effect with colors harmonizing. It is all silk and linen and the yarns are dyed before weaving, thus making the colors absolutely fast.

CAR PLUSH.

Car Plush is one of the oldest staple coverings that has ever been produced. It derives its name, Car Plush, from the fact that it is so exclusively used in covering car seats and is especially selected for this purpose on account of its durability. Fabrics that look well but do not wear well usually soon go out of style, but a couch covered with Car Plush is always in style and will wear like leather. There are many grades of Car Plush, some being made with the nap of the cloth of wool and mohair mixed, others with cashmere and mohair mixed or in other combinations which cheapen the cost of production. We use only the genuine all mohair, which is the only fabric which will hold its color absolutely, and there is no other fabric, even including wool, silk or linen, that will hold its color as well as mohair. We guarantee it not to fade. We can furnish it either in deep red, myrtle green or tobacco brown. Be sure to state color desired.

BROCADED SILK PLUSH.

This handsome material is made with a long nap, woven into fancy figures like the brocaded velour, with the exception that the nap of the cloth is made of all silk which gives it an exceptionally luxurious appearance. The silk nap and the yarns used in this cloth are dyed before being woven, which makes the colors absolutely fast. It is one of the handsomest coverings for high class parlor furniture. It is made in deep red, myrtle green, blue or tobacco brown

SILK DAMASK.

This covering has been in use for many years, and has proven one of the best materials for parlor suites, fancy chairs and rockers. This cloth is all pure silk and is the production of the skilled weaver and his loom. The handsome pattern and cloth effects are woven into the cloth, and not printed. The yarns are well selected and dyed before being woven into the tapestry, thereby producing fast colors. Silk damask is always in style, as the colors are bright and distinct, without being gaudy.

OUR $6.35 HEAVILY CARVED, SCROLL FRAME, ROCOCO UPHOLSTERED COUCH

At $6.35 We Offer This New Design, Handsome Couch, Heavy Hand Carved, Overstuffed Upholstering With Deep Biscuit Tufts. Undoubtedly and Without Question the Most Wonderful Couch Value Ever Offered. This New and Handsome Heavily Scrolled and Carved Frame, Over Stuffed Full Biscuit Tufted, Rococo Upholstered Couch, Must be Seen to be Fully Appreciated. It is the Equal of any Couch You Can Buy Elsewhere at $15.00 to $18.00.

From the illustration which has been engraved by our artist from a photograph of the couch, you can get some idea of the handsome appearance of the couch, but it must be seen to be appreciated.

THIS COUCH **weighs packed for shipment, about 100 pounds,** and the freight for 200 miles will average 40 to 60 cents; 400 miles, 60 to 90 cents. Greater or lesser distances in proportion. You will find the freight will amount to next to nothing compared to the saving in price.

HOW WE MAKE THE PRICE $6.35. **For some time we have utilized almost the entire capacity of one of the largest and best known couch factories in the United States,** in the building of our own magnificent line of couches, and to take care of the ever increasing volume of our business and keep us supplied, the factory has been compelled to constantly enlarge its facilities. Located in a suburb of Chicago, on the main line of one of the principal railroad tracks, where ground is cheap, they have been able to meet the situation, without a great outlay of money. The most modern machinery has been installed, and labor saving devices used. The high grade three-toned velour cloth upholstering is used in such large quantities that our factory is able to take the output of the largest New England mills. This three-toned velour cloth is shipped to us in carload lots. Year by year, with increasing capacity of the factory, we have been able to lower the cost of production, and we have all the time given our customers the benefit of this reduction, by making the couches cheaper and better. We are offering you this handsome couch, better made in every way, with the massive scroll carved frame, with large beautifully carved legs, at a less price than we have ever been able to offer such a couch.

No. 1C3400
ORDER BY NUMBER

$6.35

From this illustration which has been engraved by our artist, you can get some idea of the appearance of this handsome couch, but it must be seen to be appreciated. It has eight rows of full biscuit tufts instead of six as shown in the illustration.

It is positively the greatest couch value ever offered by any one. There is no other factory that can produce this couch in thousand lots at a cost of manufacture as low as the price we ask, $6.35.

THE CONSTRUCTION **of this handsomely designed, heavily scrolled, carved frame, full tufted couch, is exactly the same as we use on all of our couches.** The old way of tying the springs together with hemp twine we have discarded. We use nothing but the all steel indestructible construction on this couch, as well as on all the others we sell. We use 24 of the finest, highly tempered, very elastic Bessemer steel spiral springs in the body fastened at the top by interlacing steel wire, continuous bands and locked securely at the bottom into a steel frame, which in turn is fastened firmly into the side of the frame of the couch. This construction absolutely prevents the springs from breaking loose or turning over. The head is fitted with six spiral springs so placed as to produce the greatest comfort and wear.

THIS COUCH **is made on a handsome mahogany finished hardwood or in a golden oak frame of** the very latest rococo design, as illustrated, with large massive scroll carved effect and heavy carved scroll legs. This couch is extra large, being 30 inches wide and 75 inches long; one of the widest, longest, and in every way the strongest and most durable couches made. The upholstery covering is an extra high grade of figured velour, corduroy or crushed plush, as desired, all fast colors. The figured velour comes in a beautiful assortment of interwoven floral and scroll designs, with a body of green, red or brown, as desired. For full description of coverings used on this couch see page 681. It is extra deep button tufted, all the tufts are fastened with our patent steel Naper tufting buttons, making it impossible for the tufts to become loosened, as in the old style of tufting. There are eight rows of deep tufting, giving the couch a handsome, small, deep button tufted biscuit pattern effect, such as you will find on only the most expensive couches. Over the springs is drawn a heavy quality of canvas ticking, through which the patent Naper steel tufting buttons are passed from the top and clinched. All the tufts are firmly and evenly filled. A couch that is springy, soft, luxurious and everlasting.

OUR BINDING GUARANTEE. **While this couch as well as every other couch we sell is so built that it will give perfect satisfaction,** and last a lifetime, as a guarantee that everything is exactly as represented and described, and free from the slightest defect in material or construction, and that you will be perfectly satisfied, we will allow you to return to us the couch, if you find it otherwise, and we will at once refund your money together with the transportation charges.

SAFE DELIVERY GUARANTEED. **We guarantee the couch to reach you in the same perfect condition that it leaves our factory,** and should it through accident be damaged or broken, we will immediately ship you another one or refund your money.

COMPARE CAREFULLY. **Read the description of the couch and carefully compare it with those offered by others** at more than double our price, and you will quickly recognize the saving it is possible for you to make by placing your order with us.

DIRECT FROM FACTORY. **This couch is shipped direct from our factory near Chicago,** thereby cutting out all intermediate cost of handling and intermediate profits, which, together with favorable conditions outlined, enables us to quote such an extremely low price as $6.35.

	Figured Velour	Corduroy	Crushed Plush
No. 1C3400 Price......	**$6.35**	**$6.55**	**$8.05**

OUR GUARANTEED ALL STEEL SPRING CONSTRUCTION.

THIS ILLUSTRATION is a reproduction of a photograph of one of our couch frames and bodies, showing our celebrated all steel spring construction. This steel construction is used in all of our better couches, as you will find described under each number, and those not especially described as being made with this steel construction are made with common twine tied springs; but in our better couches you will find that we are using this steel construction, which is in many respects far superior to the common twine tied construction. The number of springs used is mentioned in the description of each couch and varies according to the style. In connection with the steel construction which is used in the body part of the lounge, we use a number of double cone steel springs in the head of the couch. **The springs,** the most essential part of a couch, are cone shaped and are drawn from the best high carbon steel wire obtainable. **The grade of wire used is alone a guaranty of the lasting** qualities of this construction. The elasticity and durability of the spring all depend on the shape, height and the weight of the steel wire used. Nothing has been spared in time or money, costly dies, etc., to construct this spring to give the best possible results. The springs on bottom side are intercoiled into steel band irons which run crosswise on bottom and are fastened to the top of side rail and can never get loose, besides being reinforced with a steel wire running lengthwise on the bottom, onto which the springs are also intercoiled. The top of spring is tied, as shown in illustration, every spring securely fastened with steel wire, no twine, and the edge wire is clinched into the springs in such a manner that it can never come off. Its neat appearance and sanitary features are especially desirable in a couch.

Our Leader at $3.75.

No. 1C3408

No. 1C3408 At $3.75 we offer a couch that is better made, better finished and handsomer in appearance than any couch offered by other dealers at from $5.00 to $7.00. While it is without doubt the most wonderful value ever offered at such a low price, and we guarantee it to give excellent service, we especially recommend our couches, ranging from $7.00 up, which are made with our all steel spring construction. This handsome couch is full size, 72 inches long and 26 inches wide. The frame is golden oak or embossed and made of hardwood, finished in imitation mahogany, as desired. This couch contains a full set of best oil tempered steel springs, drawn from high carbon cold rolled steel, 19 springs in all, securely tied. The springs are covered with heavy duck canvas where burlap is used by almost all other manufacturers. The upholstering is reliable and the covering is an excellent quality of highly colored velour in the latest patterns. We can furnish red, green or brown. Be sure to state color of upholstering and finish of wood desired, otherwise green covering and golden finished frame will be furnished. Complete with best quality casters. Shipping weight, 70 pounds.

Price, covered in velour...$3.75

Our Special $4.30 Overstuffed Couch.

No. 1C3416

No. 1C3416 As a leader, our all overstuffed tufted couch at $4.30 is without doubt the best couch of its kind in the market. It is 72 inches long, 27 inches wide, and made on a substantial hardwood frame, well braced to insure stability. It contains a full set of the best oil tempered steel springs, drawn from high carbon cold rolled steel, 19 springs in all, securely tied, insuring service as well as comfort. The springs are covered with heavy duck canvas instead of burlap, which is used by most all other manufacturers. The filling, tufting and upholstering is done in a thoroughly reliable manner. It is ornamented with tasseled fringe and fitted with best quality casters. The covering is an excellent quality of highly colored velour, guaranteed in quality and of the very latest design. Shipping weight, 75 pounds.

Price, covered in velour...$4.30

Our $4.75 Overstuffed Couch.

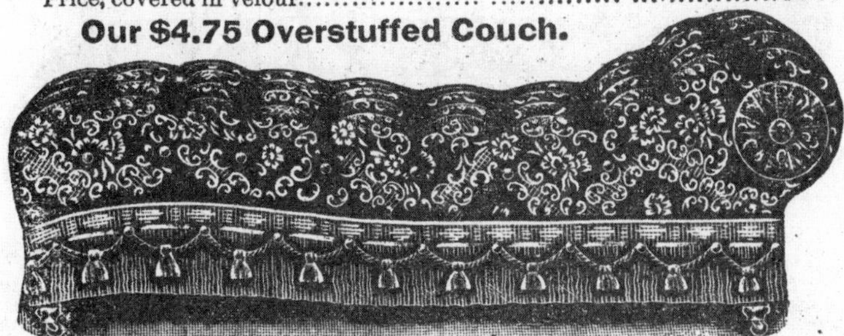

No. 1C3424

No. 1C3424 It is impossible to illustrate the exceptional value which this couch represents. It must be seen to be fully appreciated. The picture gives only a general idea of the style of the couch. It is full size, 74 inches long and 27 inches wide. The frame is built of thoroughly seasoned hardwood, well braced to insure durability. We use a full set of the best quality oil tempered steel springs, drawn from high carbon wire, 24 springs in all, securely tied. The springs are covered with good quality heavy duck canvas. The couch comes nicely shaped and tufted and trimmed with best quality fringe. On page 681 we describe the different upholstering materials we can furnish. Complete with casters. Shipping weight, 75 pounds.

The number of this couch is No. 1C3424. Always order by number and be sure to state the kind and color of covering desired.

Covering	Figured Velour	Corduroy	Plain Brocaded Velour
Price	$4.75	$4.95	$5.15

Our Fancy Biscuit Tufted Glenham Couch at $5.45.

No. 1C3432

No. 1C3432 This is a very handsome, stylish couch at an exceedingly low price. It is made at the same factory by the same workmen that make all our other couches and we consider it wonderful value. The frame is made of oak, finished golden, or birch, finished in imitation mahogany, as desired. It is beautifully ornamented with sunken carvings as shown in the illustration. The couch measures 73 inches in length and is 27 inches wide. Has spring edge, seat and head, made with our guaranteed steel spring construction, fully illustrated and described above, with 20 springs in the body and 4 in the head, 24 in all. By the use of this construction the bottom of the couch is left open for air and ventilation. The springs are covered with heavy duck canvas. Tow with cotton top is used as filling, which makes the tufts lasting and comfortable. The materials used in covering are fully described on page 681. Complete with best quality casters. Shipping weight, 80 pounds.

The number of this couch is No. 1C3432. Always order by number and be sure to state the kind and color of covering desired.

Covering	Figured Velour	Corduroy	Plain Brocaded Velour
Price	$5.45	$5.65	$5.85

Our $6.35 Biscuit Tufted Couch.

No. 1C3440

No. 1C3440 This couch is one which we have sold for the past two years, and it has given universal satisfaction. On account of the strikingly handsome design this couch has been copied by nearly all other manufacturers in every respect except quality. The frame is made of oak, finished golden, or birch, finished in imitation mahogany, as desired. It is 78 inches long and 30 inches wide and contains 30 of the best oil tempered steel springs, drawn from high carbon cold rolled steel, securely tied. The springs are covered with heavy duck canvas instead of the sheeting or burlap generally used by other manufacturers. It has 6 rows of deep tufting, put in with the celebrated Naper steel tufting buttons. The filling is the very best grade of fine tow with felted cotton top. The workmanship throughout is strictly first class. The upholstering material used is of the very best quality and the workmanship throughout is strictly first class. Read the description of the different covering materials on page 681. Fitted with best quality casters. Shipping weight, 100 pounds.

The number of this couch is No. 1C3440. Always order by number and be sure to state the kind and color of covering desired.

Covering	Figured Velour	Corduroy	Plain Brocaded Velour	Fancy Brocaded Plush
Price	$6.35	$6.55	$6.75	$6.95

A Handsome Turkish Overstuffed Couch for $6.95.

No. 1C3448

No. 1C3448 For handsome appearance and solid comfort there is not a couch in our entire line that will compare with this one when you consider the remarkable low price at which we are listing it. It is 75 inches long, 30 inches wide and made with eight rows of deep tufts stuffed with a special grade of tow and felted cotton top. The frame is made of hardwood, strongly braced to insure durability. We use our guaranteed indestructible all steel spring construction, as illustrated and described above. The springs are covered with heavy duck canvas and the bottom is left open so the inner construction can be plainly seen and which permits of air and ventilation. This couch is made with a full spring edge, an important feature for comfort. The lower part of the couch is trimmed with a handsome overskirt tassel wool fringe. Fitted with best quality casters. On page 681 we describe the quality and color of upholstering materials in which this couch is made. Shipping weight, 75 pounds.

The number of this couch is No. 1C3448. Always order by number and be sure to state the kind and color of covering desired.

Covering	Figured Velour	Corduroy	Plain Brocaded Velour	Fancy Brocaded Plush	Brocaded Verona Plush	Crushed Plush
Price	$6.95	$7.15	$7.35	$7.65	$8.45	$9.35

New Rococo Design Couch, $7.95.

No. 1C3454

No. 1C3454 This couch has an exceptionally substantial frame of striking design, handsomely carved claw feet. The design is entirely new and has been especially gotten up for us. The frame throughout is of hardwood, the mouldings, etc., are of select oak, in golden oak finish. The couch is very large, 78 inches long and 30 inches wide, made with eight rows of deep hand made tufts put in with all steel tufting buttons, which will not pull off. The spring construction is of our guaranteed all steel indestructible spring, as described on page 683. Has 28 springs in body and 6 in head, 34 in all, with spring edges, covered with heavy duck canvas where burlap is commonly used by other manufacturers, and the under side is left open for air and ventilation. The filling is of the very best quality of tow and felted cotton. On page 681 we describe the quality and color of upholstering materials which we can furnish. Complete with casters. Shipping weight, 100 pounds.

The number of this couch is No. 1C3454. Always order by number and be sure to state the kind and color of covering desired.

Covering	Figured Velour	Corduroy	Plain Brocaded Velour	Fancy Brocaded Plush	Brocaded Verona Plush	Crushed Plush
Price	$7.95	$8.15	$8.35	$8.65	$9.35	$10.45

Imperial Couch, $8.45.

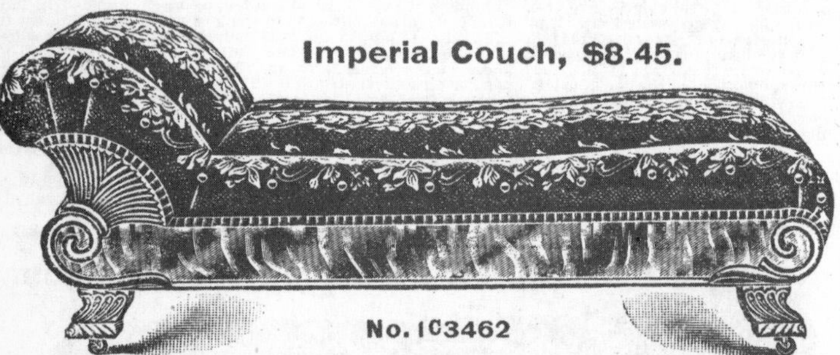

No. 1C3462

No. 1C3462 This smooth top couch, with imperial roll edge, is one of the very latest effects in smooth top upholstered couches. The frame and shape throughout is very stylish, the design has just been made and the style has never been shown before by anyone. It is a hardwood frame throughout and is veneered with selected, beautifully figured quarter sawed oak, finished in golden oak. It is ornamented with beautiful carvings and carved claw legs, as shown in illustration. The interior construction is of the very best, made with our guaranteed indestructible all steel springs, as fully described on page 683. Has 28 springs in body and 6 in head, 34 in all. Has spring edges with heavy duck canvas over the springs in place of burlap which is commonly used by other manufacturers. The bottom is left open so that the inner construction is in plain view which is an excellent sanitary feature. The couch is 78 inches long by 30 inches wide. The filling is of the very best quality of fine tow and felted cotton, and the couch is especially recommended for its wearing qualities, as well as being very easy to keep clean, and at the same time is very comfortable. On page 681 we describe the quality and color of upholstering material which we can furnish. The velour coverings for smooth top couches are especially made, having a handsome design pattern effect in center, as shown in illustration. Complete with casters. Shipping weight, 100 pounds.

The number of this couch is No. 1C3462. Always order by number and be sure to state the kind and color of covering desired.

Covering	Figured Velour	Corduroy	Plain Brocaded Velour	Brocaded Verona Plush	Crushed Plush	Car Plush
Price	$8.45	$8.65	$8.85	$9.95	$10.95	$13.45

Our $8.75 Turkish Couch.

No. 1C3470

No. 1C3470 This is one of the most comfortable and striking couches in our entire line, entirely up to date in design and construction. The frame is made of quartered oak, finished golden. The carvings are all hand made. The claw legs are fitted with best quality casters. The couch is 78 inches long and 30 inches wide and is made with our guaranteed indestructible all steel spring construction as described on page 683. **Has spring edges and heavy duck canvas covering over the springs.** Upholstered in eight rows of deep tufts, made with best quality tow and felted cotton filling, which insures wear and comfort. On page 681 we describe the quality and color of the upholstering materials which we can furnish. Shipping weight, 100 pounds.

The number of this couch is No. 1C3470. Always order by number and be sure to state the kind and color of covering desired.

Covering	Figured Velour	Corduroy	Plain Brocaded Velour	Fancy Brocaded Plush	Brocaded Verona Plush	Crushed Plush
Price	$8.75	$8.95	$9.15	$9.35	$10.25	$11.35

This Handsome Couch, $8.95.

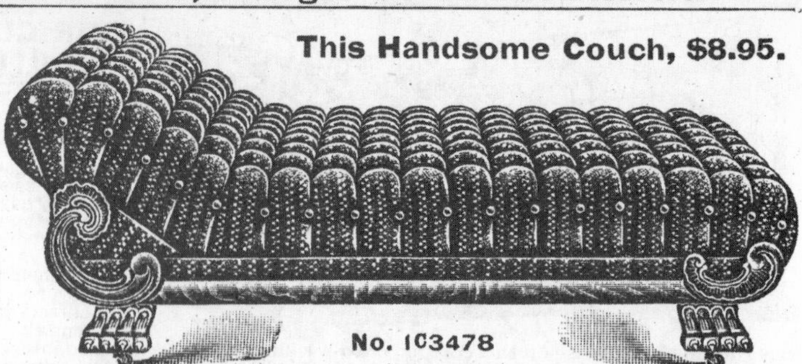

No. 1C3478

No. 1C3478 This luxurious couch is entirely new and up to date. The shell pattern effect is exceptionally handsome. Such effects as are illustrated on this couch can only be found in high priced couches. The frame is hardwood and the mouldings and carvings are of select quarter sawed oak, handsomely carved, as shown in illustration. Finished in golden oak, polished finish. It is 78 inches long and 30 inches wide and has eight rows of deep tufts made with all steel tufting buttons which will not pull off or pull through the cover; the inner construction is of our guaranteed indestructible all steel springs, as described on page 683. Has 28 springs in body and 6 in head, 34 in all; spring edges, heavy duck canvas over the springs and the filling is of the very best quality of fine tow and felted cotton. The very best quality of upholstering materials are used, as described on page 681. Complete with casters. Shipping weight, 115 pounds.

The number of this couch is No. 1C3478. Always order by number and be sure to state the kind and color of covering desired.

Covering	Figured Velour	Corduroy	Plain Brocaded Velour	Fancy Brocaded Plush	Brocaded Verona Plush	Crushed Plush
Price	$8.95	$9.10	$9.35	$9.60	$10.40	$11.40

A Handsome Smooth Top Couch for $9.25.

No. 1C3486

No. 1C3486 This couch is especially designed with a view of combining the most valuable points in consideration in the selection of a couch, namely, appearance, wearing qualities and comfort. Smooth top couches are considered by many to be more comfortable than the tufted ones. They are easier to keep clean, and as there is no strain on the surface of the goods they will wear better. This couch is 78 inches long and 30 inches wide. The frame is made of birch, finished imitation mahogany, or oak, finished golden, as desired. It is ornamented with beautiful carvings and has carved claw feet, fitted with best quality casters. The interior construction is of the very best. Made with our guaranteed indestructible all steel spring construction as fully described on page 683. Has 28 springs in the body, 6 in the head, 34 in all. Has spring edges with heavy duck canvas over the springs in place of the burlap which is commonly used by other manufacturers. The bottom is left open so that the inner construction is in plain view. This construction is also an excellent sanitary feature. It is double stuffed and the edges are double stitched. The center is made plain with tufted edges. On page 681 we describe the quality and color of the upholstering materials which we can furnish. The velour on smooth top couches is especially made, having a handsomely designed pattern in the center. Be sure to state finish of wood. Shipping weight, 115 pounds.

The number of this couch is No. 1C3486. Always order by number and be sure to state the kind and color of covering desired.

Covering	Figured Velour	Corduroy	Plain Brocaded Velour	Brocaded Verona Plush	Crushed Plush	Car Plush
Price	$9.25	$9.45	$9.65	$10.75	$11.85	$14.25

An Exceptionally Fine, Smooth Top Couch for $9.45.

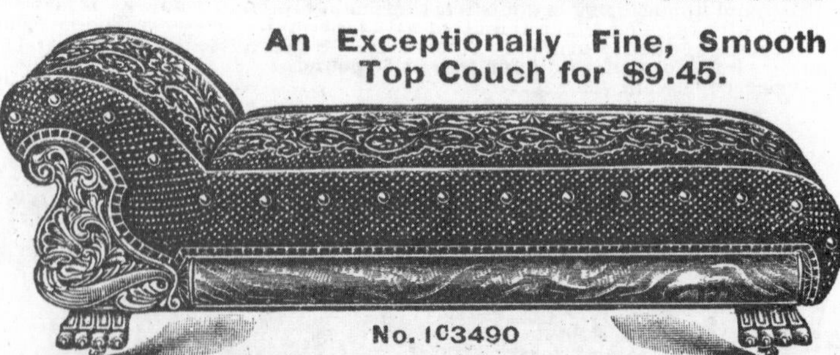

No. 1C3490

No. 1C3490 This couch is one of the handsomest and most comfortable couches in our line. Entirely new in design. The very latest smooth top construction. It measures 78 inches in length and 30 inches in width. The frame is made of quarter sawed oak, finished golden, and ornamented with raised hand made carvings. Has carved claw legs fitted with best quality casters. The spring construction is the same as we put in all our high grade couches, illustrated and described on page 683. Has 28 springs in body, 6 in head, 34 in all. Has full spring edges. The springs are covered with extra heavy duck canvas. Best grade fine tow and felted cotton filling. It is upholstered in the highest style of the art, with smooth top and roll edges so that it can be kept entirely free from dust. In point of construction, comfort, durability and appearance, this couch is all that could be desired. On page 681 we describe the quality and colors of upholstering material which we can furnish. Shipping weight, 110 pounds.

The number of this couch is No. 1C3490. Always order by number and be sure to state the kind and color of covering desired.

Covering	Figured Velour	Corduroy	Plain Brocaded Velour	Fancy Brocaded Plush	Crushed Plush	Car Plush
Price	$9.45	$9.60	$9.85	$10.05	$11.95	$14.45

A Handsome Turkish Couch for $9.55.

No. 1C3494

No. 1C3494 This couch is made of fine flaky grained quarter sawed oak, golden finish, hand polished. The beautiful gondola design with large massive head, heavy frame, and hand carvings, supported by hand carved claw feet, makes this one of the handsomest couches made. It is 78 inches long by 30 inches wide, and has eight rows of tufts. It is made with our guaranteed indestructible all steel construction, as described on page 683. It has full spring edges. The very best quality of upholstering materials are used, as described on page 681. Has 28 springs in the body, 9 in the head, 37 in all. Fitted with best quality casters. Shipping weight, 100 pounds.

The number of this couch is No. 1C3494. Always order by number and be sure to state the kind and color of covering desired.

Covering............	Figured Velour	Corduroy	Plain Brocaded Velour	Fancy Brocaded Plush	Crushed Plush	Car Plush
Price........	$9.55	$9.75	$9.95	$10.45	$11.95	$14.50

Handsome Gondola Couch, $9.65.

No. 1C3502

No. 1C3502 In this couch we have brought into effect the massive appearance which is so much desired and found only in high priced furniture, and have combined with it the full gondola effect. The frame is made of hardwood throughout and is veneered with beautifully figured quarter sawed oak, and is finished in golden oak with high polish. This couch is exceptionally comfortable on account of the shape. It is 80 inches long and 30 inches wide and is made with our all steel spring construction, as described on page 683, having 28 high tempered cold rolled clock steel springs in the body and 9 springs in the head, 37 in all. Full spring edges with heavy duck canvas over the springs. The inner side is left open for air and ventilation which prevents the gathering of dust, moths and germs. The upholstering is of the very latest style, having eight rows of deep hand made tufts. The filling is of the very best quality of tow and felted cotton and is made with steel tufting buttons, which will not pull off or pull through the cover. The upholstering materials are of the best grades especially selected, as fully described on page 681. Complete with best quality casters. Shipping weight, 115 pounds.

The number of this couch is No. 1C3502. Always order by number and be sure to state the kind and color of covering desired.

Covering.........	Figured Velour	Corduroy	Plain Brocaded Velour	Fancy Brocaded Plush	Brocaded Verona Plush	Crushed Plush
Price.....	$9.65	$9.85	$10.15	$10.35	$11.15	$12.25

This Couch is a Beauty for $9.95.

No. 1C3510

No. 1C3510 At $9.95 to $12.45, according to grade of upholstering used, this couch is certainly a beauty and a bargain. It is built on a very heavy, handsomely carved and decorated rococo hardwood frame with six turned pillars in the head and with very handsome turned legs. The frame is made of oak, finished golden. The couch is extra large, being 80 inches long and 30 inches wide, one of the largest, roomiest, and most comfortable couches made. Has our guaranteed, indestructible, all steel spring construction, illustrated and described on page 683. Has 28 springs in body, 9 in head, 37 in all. The springs are covered with extra heavy duck canvas and the under side is left open for air and ventilation, which is an excellent feature and will prevent the gathering of dust, moths and germs. It has spring edges all around and eight rows of hand made deep tufts, put in with the Naper steel tufting buttons, which will not pull out. The coverings include all the very latest effects for this season, as fully described on page 681. There is no stronger, more substantial, handsomer or more comfortable couch made at any price. Fitted with best quality casters. Shipping weight, 100 pounds.

The number of this couch is No. 1C3510. Always order by number and be sure to state the kind and color of covering desired.

Covering............	Figured Velour	Corduroy	Plain Brocaded Velour	Fancy Brocaded Plush	Brocaded Verona Plush	Crushed Plush
Price.......	$9.95	$10.25	$10.45	$10.55	$11.45	$12.45

Our Double Rococo Design Couch for $10.75.

No. 1C3526

No. 1C3526 This couch is double rococo design, brought out with raised carvings, mounted on a handsome figured panel of quartered oak, polished finished. This is a very large couch, measures 80 inches in length and 30 inches in width. Made with our guaranteed indestructible all steel spring construction, as described on page 683. Has 28 springs in body, 6 in head, 34 in all. Has full spring edges and heavy duck canvas over the springs. The under side of the couch is left open for air and ventilation, which is an excellent feature, as it prevents the gathering of dust, moths and germs. The upholstering is entirely new, namely, the plain center with tufted edge roll, making it more showy and comfortable than if entirely tufted and also easier to keep clean. Only the very best grades of upholstering materials are used, as fully described on page 681. The velour used is made especially for smooth top couches, as it has a handsome pattern design in the center. Shipping weight, 100 pounds.

The number of this couch is No. 1C3526. Always order by number and be sure to state the kind and color of covering desired.

Covering....	Figured Velour	Corduroy	Plain Brocaded Velour	Fancy Brocaded Plush	Crushed Plush	Car Plush
Price..................	$10.75	$10.95	$11.15	$11.35	$13.25	$15.75

This Massive High Grade Couch, $10.90.

No. 1C3534

No. 1C3534 This magnificent high grade couch must be seen and compared with those offered by retail stores at double our price to be fully appreciated. The massive frame is made of thoroughly air seasoned and kiln dried quarter sawed golden oak or selected birch in a perfect imitation of mahogany. Highly polished. Decorated with genuine hand carvings, deep cut and finely executed. Supported on handsomely carved claw feet. It is 80 inches long and 30 inches wide. The body of this couch has 28 and the head 6 double cone springs, 34 springs in all, of the best grade of high carbon bessemer steel, interlocked at the top and securely fastened at the bottom on a solid steel frame, as illustrated and described on page 683. The springs are covered with a heavy duck canvas, the under side left open for ventilation and to prevent the accumulation of dirt, moths, etc. It has spring edges all around and eight rows of hand made tufts, securely fastened with our Naper steel buttons, guaranteed not to pull out. Beauty, comfort and durability are combined in this strictly high grade couch. We furnish this couch in all the latest patterns in the best grades of upholstering materials, fully described on page 681. Fitted with best quality casters. Shipping weight, 100 pounds.

The number of this couch is No. 1C3534. Always order by number and be sure to state the kind and color of covering desired.

Covering..............	Figured Velour	Corduroy	Plain Brocaded Velour	Fancy Brocaded Plush	Brocaded Verona Plush	Crushed Plush
Price.	$10.90	$11.15	$11.45	$11.75	$12.45	$13.45

This Colonial Gondola Couch, $11.25.

No. 1C3542

No. 1C3542 This handsome new design, which has been especially designed for us and which is one of the very latest styles in upholstered couches contains all of the features of a colonial gondola and rococo effect. The frame is of hardwood throughout, thoroughly seasoned and kiln dried. The veneering is of the very finest select figured quarter sawed oak and is finished in golden oak, highly polished. It is 80 inches long; 30 inches wide and has an all steel spring construction, as described on page 683, having 28 high carbon steel springs in the base and 9 double cone steel springs in the head, making 37 in all. Full spring edges, heavy duck canvas over the springs, and the inner side is left open for air and ventilation and the tufting is nicely done with eight rows of hand made tufts with steel tufting buttons which will not pull off or pull through the cover. The filling is of the very best grade of fine tow and felted cotton. This couch is especially constructed for comfort, appearance and durability, and no couch of its equal in value can be purchased of anyone else at less than twice the price we ask for it. In fact this style is our exclusive pattern and cannot be bought elsewhere. The upholstering materials are of the very best grades, especially selected and fully described on page 681. Complete with casters. Shipping weight, 125 pounds.

The number of this couch is No. 1C3542. Always order by number and be sure to state the kind and color of covering desired.

Covering...	Figured Velour	Corduroy	Plain Brocaded Velour	Brocaded Verona Plush	Crushed Plush	Car Plush
Price................	$11.25	$11.60	$11.85	$12.75	$13.85	$16.25

SPECIAL VALUES IN LEATHER COUCHES.

OUR LEATHER COUCHES are made for us under contract by one of the best makers of leather couches in this country. We take the large part of the output of the factory and the cost to us is based on the actual cost of the material and labor with but a small manufacturers' profit added, **thus enabling us to offer an extra high grade of leather couch work at prices lower than ever before quoted.**

ABOUT THE LEATHER WE USE. Owing to the many qualities of leather which are made, it becomes necessary for us to explain the method of tanning and finishing of upholstering leather, so that our customers may not be deceived by any of the inferior qualities that are offered and which may easily be offered at as much as $5.00 a couch less, but such couches are not even worth as much as the cheapest cloth fabrics. For instance: Every hide taken from the "critter" is put through the tanning process and thereby becomes very thick and heavy and each hide is split into four parts. The top part is the very best of the hide and is termed No. 1 hand buffed. The next is the second grade, and is known as No. 1 machine buffed, it will do fairly well but is not as good as the other. The next cut is termed No. 2 machine buffed **and will not wear well.** The last cut, which is the part next to the flesh, is termed split leather **and is absolutely no good for** upholstering purposes. Great care is taken in selecting this leather to enable us to offer you something that will come up to your expectations when buying a leather couch.

CHASE LEATHER is one of the greatest inventions brought out in recent years. It serves as a substitute for leather in upholstering furniture, and can be produced at a very much lower cost. The body of the material is made of heavy drill, coated, finished and grained in exact imitation of the finest grade of hand buffed leather and is guaranteed by the manufacturers not to crack or peel off. Very much has been said about the lasting qualities of chase leather; in fact, the manufacturers of the material are so outspoken in the matter that they declare it will wear fully as well as genuine leather, and we do not hesitate to state that it will certainly wear far better than any of the inferior grades of leather, and in appearance it takes an expert to detect the difference between it and leather. We have used chase leather in the manufacture of our couches ever since it was first put on the market and have found it to give absolute satisfaction.

EVERY COUCH IS SENT OUT UNDER OUR BINDING GUARANTEE.
We guarantee it to reach you in the same perfect condition it leaves us, and to prove entirely satisfactory to you, otherwise you can return it to us at our expense of freight charges both ways and we will immediately refund your money. The leather couches weigh, crated for shipment, from 100 to 125 pounds, and you will find the freight will amount to nothing as compared with what you will save in price.

Wonderful Value, $10.85.

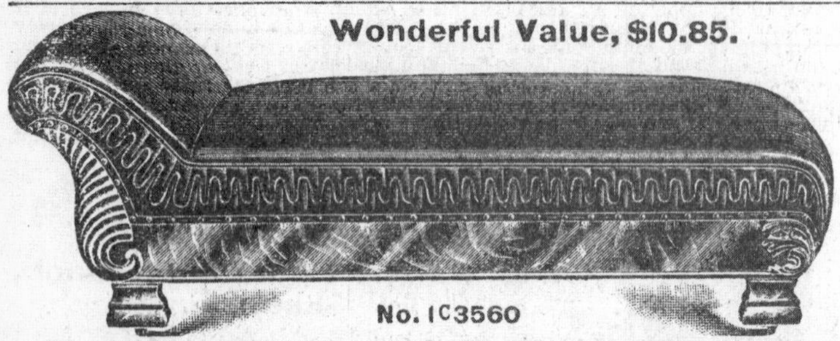

No. 1C3560

No. 1C3560 For $10.85, covered with the best quality of imitation leather, and for $19.85, covered with the best quality of hand buffed genuine leather, we furnish this massive solid golden quarter sawed oak couch (containing 30 springs) which cannot be had from a retail store at double the price. The frame is a new design and has a full spring edge. We use our celebrated indestructible all steel spring construction with 24 coil springs in the body and 6 in the head, as illustrated and described on **page 683. Read it.** The couch is 75 inches long by 30 inches wide. A very neat artistic design, made to wear and give satisfaction for a lifetime. Complete, with best quality casters. Shipped direct from our factory near Chicago. Shipping weight, 110 pounds.

Price, upholstered in chase leather $10.85
Price, upholstered in the best quality hand buffed genuine leather.. 19.85

A Bargain at $11.45.

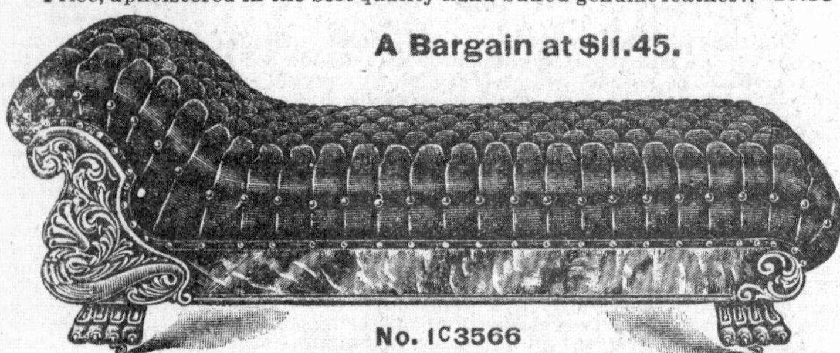

No. 1C3566

No. 1C3566 If you want a really first class couch and one that there is no wear out to, we especially recommend that you select a leather couch. At $11.45, covered with chase leather (the best imitation leather), or at $22.75, covered in the **best quality hand buffed leather,** we furnish this handsome couch as illustrated. **This couch is equal to couches that are generally retailed at nearly double the price.** The frame is select quarter sawed oak, finished in golden or imitation mahogany. Highly polished. Fitted with extra quality casters. This couch is made with 24 coil springs in the body and 6 in the head, our indestructible all steel spring construction, as described on page 683. Heavy duck canvas over the springs, stuffed with select washed hair. Small diamond tufts put in with our all steel Naper tufting buttons, as described on page 681. The couch is 76 inches long by 30 inches wide and weighs 110 pounds.

Price, upholstered in chase leather $11.45
Price, upholstered in best quality hand buffed leather.......... 22.75

Handsome Leather Couch.

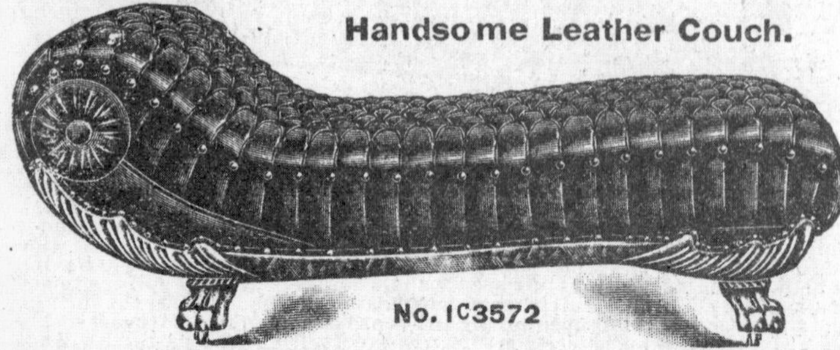

No. 1C3572

No. 1C3572 One of the choicest designs in a Turkish couch. It is mounted on a fine quarter sawed oak frame, supported by genuine hand carved claw feet. Has 28 spiral springs in the body and 9 in the head. Made with small and deep diamond tufting and with our guaranteed all steel spring construction and steel buttons, as described on **page 683.** Read it. Filling is select washed and curled hair filling. You will pay double our price in any retail store. The style, finish and construction are strictly high grade throughout, and the graceful dongola shape makes it a very attractive design. Length, 80 inches; width, 30 inches, and it contains 30 springs and a soft spring edge. Shipping weight, 100 pounds. Shipped from our factory near Chicago.

Price, upholstered in chase leather.......... $12.95
Price, upholstered in genuine hand buffed leather.......... 24.60

The Very Latest Product in Leather Furniture.

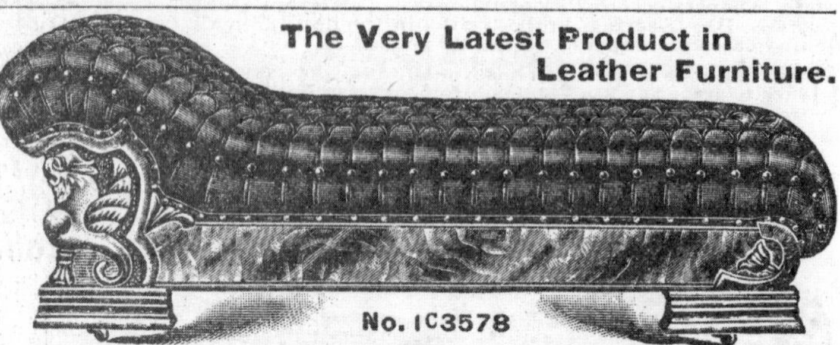

No. 1C3578

No. 1C3578 A large Turkish couch. A massive design, with very attractive hand carvings on the head, finely executed. The frame is made of the choicest grade of fine flaky grained quarter sawed oak in the hand polished finish. It is 80 inches long by 30 inches wide. Has 28 high carbon springs in body and 9 in head. It is made with our guaranteed all steel spring construction, as described on **page 683—read it.** With heavy duck canvas over springs, all steel buttons that absolutely will not come off or pull through cover, and will last a lifetime. Fitted with best quality casters. This couch sells in retail stores at double our price. Shipped from our factory near Chicago. Shipping weight, 145 pounds.

Price, upholstered in chase leather.......... $14.65
Price, upholstered in best quality hand buffed leather, with genuine all hair filling.......... 27.25

$28.95 Buys this Beautiful Extra Large Leather Overstuffed Couch.

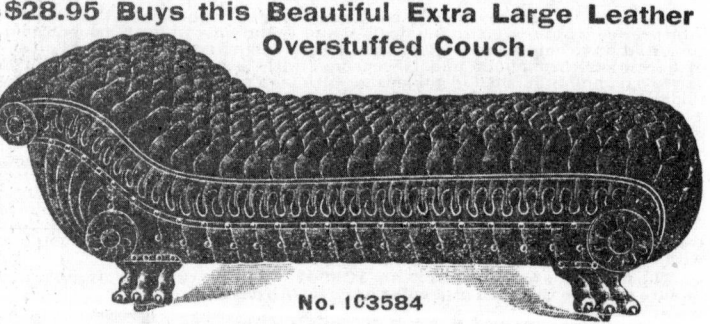

No. 1C3584

No. 1C3584 This handsome big overstuffed couch is covered in an extra high grade full finished hand buffed leather or chase leather, the best known imitation leather. One of the largest couches made, being 80 inches long and 30 inches wide. The frame is made of selected hardwood throughout, with very heavy carved legs, fitted with best quality casters. We furnish the frame either in golden oak or imitation mahogany, as desired. The upholstering is done in the best possible manner. Made with neat, small, deep diamond tufts; hand tufted throughout; made with the celebrated Naper steel tufting buttons that will not pull off. As will be seen from the illustration it is leather finished on the sides. **Nothing handsomer has been produced in a leather couch.** Made with our patent, guaranteed, all steel spring construction as described on page 683. Has 28 high carbon steel springs in body, 9 in head. Finished without any tying of twine. The springs are covered with a heavy duck canvas. **It is a couch that must be seen, examined and compared with other couches that sell at about double the price to appreciate the value given.** Shipping weight, 135 pounds.

Price, upholstered in chase leather and filled with select, clean, curled hair.......... $13.95
Price, upholstered in best quality leather and filled with select, clean, curled hair 28.95

This Massive High Grade Fine Leather Couch, $31.50.

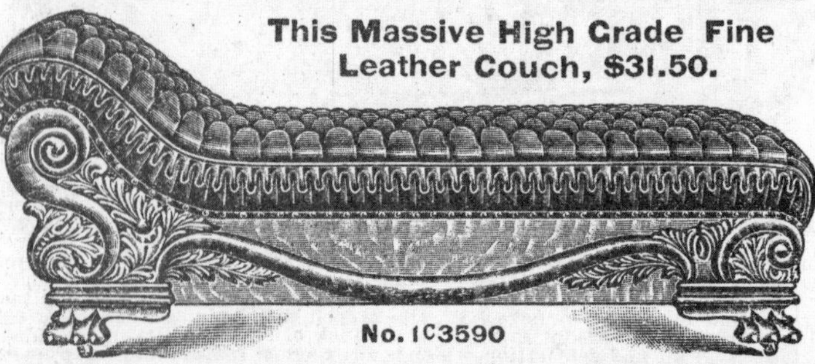

No. 1C3590

No. 1C3590 This magnificent couch is massive in design, high grade in construction, beautiful in finish. The frame is made of highly figured quarter sawed oak in a golden finish, highly polished. It is decorated with finely executed hand carvings and supported by hand carved claw feet. It is 33 inches wide, 79 inches long, 28 extra high steel springs in body and 9 in head. It is made with our guaranteed all steel construction with heavy canvas over springs, all steel buttons, that will not break off or pull through the cover, and guaranteed for a lifetime. All hair filled, full spring edge, close tufted top and beautifully ruffled edge. Shipped direct from factory in Chicago. Shipping weight, 125 pounds.

Price, upholstered in chase leather, all hair filled.......... $21.25
Price, upholstered in best quality leather, all hair filled.......... 31.50

BED COUCHES.

FOR A COMBINATION OF COMFORT AND PRACTICABILITY

the bed couch has proven one of the most satisfactory pieces of furniture made. It supplies the want of an extra bed where it would not be possible to have a bed standing permanently set up, and when not in use as a bed serves equally as well as a couch. **Our bed couches are far superior to those usually offered by other dealers**, as our factory has made a special study of the construction of bed couches to produce the best results, both when used as a couch and a bed.

OUR BED COUCHES are all constructed so that either side can be used as the front, being full finished on both sides, and can be used in the center of the room if desired.

NO MATTER WHICH BED COUCH YOU SELECT, it will be shipped with the distinct understanding that if not found entirely satisfactory, it can be returned to us at our expense of freight charges both ways and we will cheerfully refund the full price paid. As our couches are all shipped from the factory near Chicago, and no intermediate profits are added, the price will be found exceedingly low, and the couch equal to what other dealers sell at double our price.

Wonderful Value in a Bed Couch for $8.95.

No. 1C3602

No. 1C3602 This couch must be seen and examined to appreciate the value we are giving. It is built on a beautifully designed frame made of oak, finished golden, or birch, finished mahogany, as desired. It is made with full spring seat and six rows of small, deep tufts. The bed has an extra quality woven wire spring, supported by special steel coil springs on both sides and center of the bed, and covered with an extra quality of cotton top mattress and good quality of ticking. On page 681 we describe the upholstering materials which we can furnish. Be sure to state finish of frame desired. Complete with best quality casters. Shipping weight, 135 pounds.

The number of this couch is No. 1C3602. Always order by number and be sure to state the kind and color of covering desired.

Covering	Figured Velour	Corduroy	Plain Brocaded Velour	Fancy Brocaded Plush	Brocaded Verona Plush	Crushed Plush
Price	$8.95	$9.15	$9.35	$9.55	$10.45	$11.40

A Handsome Rococo Bed Couch for $9.25.

No. 1C3606

No. 1C3606 This couch is made in the new rococo design. Frame is oak, finished golden, or birch, finished mahogany, as desired. Has full spring seat, made with six rows of deep tufts. The bed is equipped with a special woven wire mattress, supported with steel coil springs on both sides and center of bed, and covered with good cotton top mattress and extra quality of ticking. The bed when open is 72 inches long and 50 inches wide, and when closed measures 72 inches in length and 24 inches in width. On page 681 we describe the upholstering materials which we can furnish. Be sure to state finish of frame desired. Fitted with best quality casters. Shipping weight, 135 pounds.

The number of this couch is No. 1C3606. Always order by number and be sure to state the kind and color of covering desired.

Covering	Figured Velour	Corduroy	Plain Brocaded Velour	Fancy Brocaded Plush	Brocaded Verona Plush	Crushed Plush
Price	$9.25	$9.45	$9.65	$9.85	10.75	$11.85

Victoria Bed Couch, $9.75.

No. 1C3612

No. 1C3612 This handsome bed couch is of the very latest design The frame is of oak, golden oak finish, and is ornamented with beautiful hand made carvings and claw feet, as shown in illustration. Both sides are alike. It is made with full spring seat and the bed is equipped with special woven wire mattress supported by steel coil springs on both sides and center of bed. Springs are covered with cotton top mattress, good quality of ticking. The size of bed is 72 inches long and 50 inches wide when open and when closed measures 72 inches in length and 24 inches in width. The upholstering is neatly done in small deep tufts. On page 681 we describe the upholstering material which we can furnish. Complete with casters. Shipping weight, 150 pounds.

The number of this couch is No. 1C3612. Always order by number and be sure to state the kind and color of covering desired.

Covering	Figured Velour	Corduroy	Plain Brocaded Velour	Fancy Brocaded Plush	Brocaded Verona Plush	Crushed Plush
Price	$9.75	$9.95	$10.15	$10.35	$11.25	$12.35

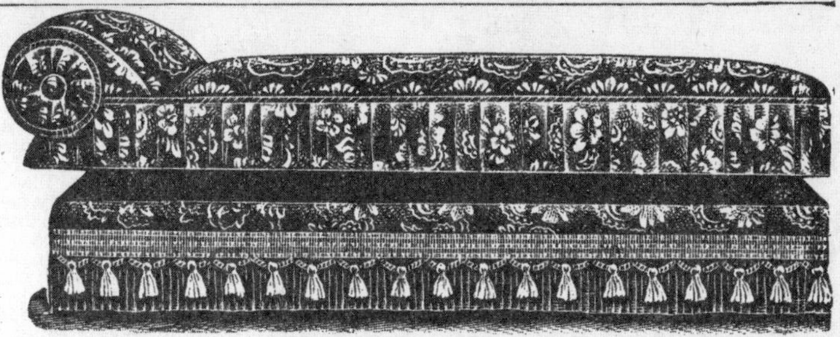

No. 1C3616

No. 1C3616 The illustration shows our large and handsome wardrobe couch with head rest. It is 78 inches long and 28 inches wide, the size of the box being 72 inches long, 25 inches wide and 8 inches deep. The wardrobe is very neatly finished and makes a splendid receptacle for wearing apparel. The frame is substantially built of hardwood. Has a full spring seat. Contains a full set of best steel springs, drawn from special high carbon wire. The bottom of the couch is covered with a deep fringe, so that there is nothing in its appearance when closed to indicate that it contains a wardrobe. **It is finished alike on both sides and is equipped with the very best automatic opener,** by the aid of which it can be opened very easily without drawing the couch from the wall, and will remain open without any support. Complete with best quality casters. Shipping weight, 150 pounds.

The number of this couch is No. 1C3616. Always order by number and be sure to state the kind and color of covering desired.

Covering	Denim	Figured Velour	Corduroy	Plain Brocaded Velour	Fancy Brocaded Plush	Crushed Plush
Price	$6.45	$7.95	$8.15	$8.35	$8.65	$10.45

No. 1C3620

No. 1C3620 This bed lounge is 70 inches long and 22 inches wide when closed, as shown in the illustration, and when open it is 72 inches long and 42 inches wide. The frame is substantially built of selected hard wood, golden finish. It is made up with the best quality woven wire springs supported by steel coil springs on both sides and in the center, making a very soft and comfortable bed. Has good quality cotton top mattress with good ticking. The lounge has full spring seat. The filling is fine quality tow with felted cotton top. Fully described on page 681. Complete with best quality casters. Shipping weight, 150 pounds.

The number of this couch is No. 1C3620. Always order by number and be sure to state the kind and color of covering desired.

Covering	Figured Velour	Corduroy	Plain Brocaded Velour	Fancy Brocaded Plush	Brocaded Verona Plush	Crushed Plush
Price	$7.45	$7.65	$7.85	$8.10	$8.45	$8.75

No. 1C3624

No. 1C3624 This bed lounge is one of the handsomest combination lounges in our entire line. It is built on an extra heavy, nicely carved and decorated frame made of oak, finished golden. Has heavy claw legs, fitted with best quality casters. It is 70 inches long, 22 inches wide and when open has a bed 72 inches long and 42 inches wide. Full spring seat and full upholstered back. The bed is fitted with woven wire mattress supported by steel coil springs on both sides and in the center of bed, covered with an excellent cotton top mattress. The ticking is good quality. The lounge has full spring seat. Shipping weight, 150 pounds.

The number of this couch is No. 1C3624. Always order by number and be sure to state the kind and color of covering desired.

Covering	Figured Velour	Corduroy	Plain Brocaded Velour	Fancy Brocaded Plush	Brocaded Verona Plush	Crushed Plush
Price	$8.45	$8.65	$8.85	$9.35	$9.85	$10.25

No. 1C3630

COMBINATION DIVAN AND COUCH.

No. 1C3630 This Roman Combination Divan, Sofa, Davenport or Couch is of the very latest design in this style of furniture. It is exceptionally serviceable on account of the number of ways in which it can be used. Illustration shows this piece of furniture in use as a sofa. Both ends can be lowered to any angle desired, and in so doing there are no strings to pull. The adjustments are automatic and operate very easily. When in use as a couch it is as comfortable as any couch can be made. The frame is of selected figured quarter sawed oak nicely finished and polished, is very beautifully decorated with carving, as shown in illustration. Carved claw legs. 27 inches wide, and measures 36 inches between the arms when ends are raised, and is 78 inches long when both ends are lowered. Made with small deep tufts and steel tufting buttons and the filling is of the very best quality of fine tow and felted cotton. Contains a full set of high carbon cold rolled steel springs with heavy duck canvas over the same, where burlap is commonly used by other manufacturers. To adjust the ends raise them to the highest point and a little beyond that and the head will drop to level and can then be raised to any position desired. On page 681 is described the color and upholstering which we can furnish. Complete with casters. Shipping weight, 150 pounds.

The number of this sofa is No. 1C3630. Always order by number and be sure to state the kind and color of covering desired.

Covering...........	Figured Velour	Corduroy	Plain Brocaded Velour	Fancy Brocaded Plush	Brocaded Verona Plush	Crushed Plush
Price...............	$10.75	$10.95	$11.15	$11.35	$12.45	$14.35

OUR COMBINATION ROMAN DIVAN, SOFA, DAVENPORT AND COUCH.

No. 1C3634

This illustration shows couch with back forming a regular davenport.

No. 1C3634

This illustration shows head and foot lowered, making a regular couch.

No. 1C3634 This beautiful piece of furniture is very attractive and serviceable. It is constructed so that both ends lower and either end can be used for head if desired, and the head can also be adjusted to almost any angle; or both ends can be lowered, making a beautiful and comfortable couch if desired to be used as such. The frame is made from selected figured quarter sawed oak, nicely finished and polished. Beautifully decorated with hand carvings as shown in illustration, and has carved Roman legs. It is 27 inches wide and measures 36 inches between the arms when ends are raised and 80 inches long when they are both let down. Made with small, deep tufts, put in with the celebrated Naper steel tufting buttons, which cannot pull out. The filling is of the best fine tow, with felted cotton top. It contains a full set of the best steel springs, well supported spring edges, and with a heavy duck canvas over the springs. Fitted with best quality casters. The attachments for adjusting the ends are very simple and are operated as follows: To place either end straight, raise the same to the highest point and a little beyond that and the head will drop down to level; it can then be raised to the different positions desired. There are no strings to pull, as the attachment is automatic. **There is no prettier or more serviceable piece of furniture in existence today.** On page 681 we describe the quality and colors of upholstering material which we can furnish. Shipping weight, 150 pounds.

The number of this divan is No. 1C3634. Always order by number and be sure to state the kind and color of covering desired.

Covering......	Figured Velour	Corduroy	Plain Brocaded Velour	Fancy Brocaded Plush	Brocaded Verona Plush	Crushed Plush
Price..........	$11.45	$11.65	$11.85	$12.15	$13.25	$14.95

OUR COMBINATION DAVENPORT, BED AND WARDROBE.

No. 1C3650 This piece of furniture is one of the latest inventions in the furniture line and is especially adaptable where room is scarce. It can be used as a wardrobe and spare bed if desired, as well as a handsome piece of parlor furniture. **The illustration shows the davenport when not in use as a bed and there is nothing about it that indicates that it is a wardrobe or that it can be used as a bed.** It is very neat in appearance and the idea of the bed and wardrobe have simply added to the value as a davenport. **It is so constructed that the back can be lowered and the ends extended, forming full head and foot ends, the same as a regular bed, as shown in the accompanying illustration.** The end gates, which swing open when the back lowers, are not noticeable when the back is raised, and there is nothing about it by which anyone can detect that it is a bed unless absolutely familiar with the combination. There are no hard edges or hard centers usually found in common bed couches and lounges; on the contrary, **it is an unusually soft and comfortable bed to sleep on. The wardrobe underneath is a handy receptacle for bed clothing, or if not used for that purpose can be used for any kind of wearing apparel or household articles.**

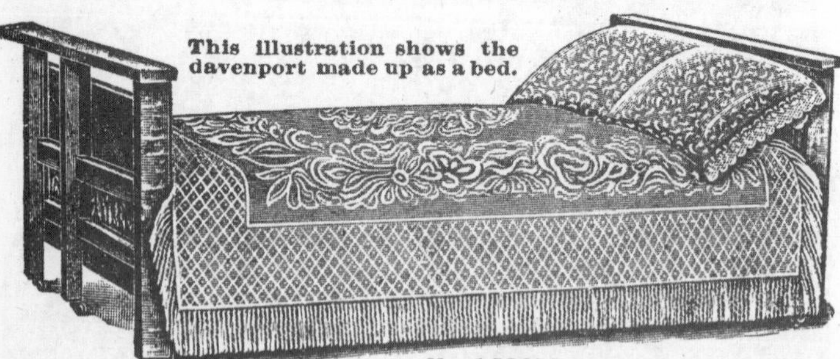

This illustration shows the davenport made up as a bed.

No. 1C3650

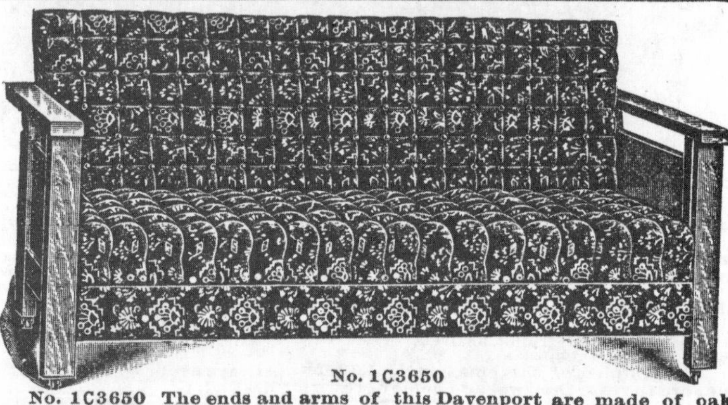

No. 1C3650

No. 1C3650 The ends and arms of this Davenport are made of oak finished golden or birch mahogany, high gloss finish. When the back is lowered for use as a bed it has a full head and foot end, the same as any regular bed, as shown in illustration. It is constructed with full spring edges seat and spring back, made with our guaranteed indestructible, all steel spring construction. This construction in both seat and back make it an exceptionally fine bed when the back is lowered. **The springs are covered with heavy duck canvas. The filling is the very best grade of fine tow, with felted cotton top. The tufts are put in with the Naper steel tufting buttons, which will not pull out.** On page 681, we describe the quality and color of materials we can furnish. Be sure to state finish of frame desired. Complete with best quality casters. This davenport is shipped knocked down, which insures the lowest possible freight rate. As easily set up as an ordinary bed. Shipping weight, 270 pounds.

The number of this davenport is No. 1C3650. Always order by number and be sure to state the kind and color of covering wanted.

Covering....	Figured Velour	Corduroy	Plain Brocaded Velour	Fancy Brocaded Plush	Brocaded Verona Plush	Crushed Plush	Car Plush
Price........	$15.65	$15.85	$16.10	$17.55	$19.45	$19.75	$25.50

No. 1C3656 This Davenport is the same in construction as No. 1C3650 excepting that the framework on the ends and lower front rail is made of solid oak, finished golden or birch mahogany, hand rubbed and polished. The inside and outside of the ends are upholstered with same material as seat and back. Shipping weight, 270 pounds.

The number of this davenport is No. 1C3656. Always order by number and be sure to state the kind and color of covering desired.

Covering..	Figured Velour	Corduroy	Plain Brocaded Velour	Fancy Brocaded Plush	Brocaded Verona Plush	Crushed Plush	Car Plush
Price......	$20.55	$20.85	$21.15	$22.25	$22.95	$24.85	$30.50

No. 1C3656

Fancy Parlor Chair.

No. 1C5708 Attractive in design, high grade in construction, beautiful in wood and finish, this arm chair is a wonderful bargain at our price. Made of birch in a perfect imitation mahogany finish. Note the shapely curved high arms and ornamental panel back. Upholstered all steel full spring seat. Substantial in construction. Shipped direct from factory in Chicago. Shipping weight, about 25 pounds.

	Figured Velour	Brocaded Verona Plush
Price....	$3.65	$3.90
	Damask	Silk Plush
Price....	$4.15	$4.40

Handsome Parlor Chair.

No. 1C5712 Handsome new design parlor arm chair. Made of selected birch in a perfect imitation of mahogany, polished finish. Upholstered with our all steel full spring seat. Extra high shapely arms with a hand carved, highly ornamental back and French shaped front legs. Cabinet construction strictly first class. Shipped direct from factory in Chicago. Shipping weight, about 30 pounds.

	Figured Velour	Brocaded Verona Plush
Price....	$3.75	$4.00
	Damask	Silk Plush
Price....	$4.25	$4.45

No. 1C5716 This parlor arm chair must be seen to be fully appreciated. It is made of selected birch in a perfect imitation of mahogany, highly polished. Seat is upholstered with our high carbon all steel construction. It has shapely high arms, broad panel back. Seat upholstered in best grades imported coverings. Sells in retail stores at double our prices. Shipped direct from factory in Chicago. Shipping weight, 30 pounds.

	Figured Velour	Brocaded Verona Plush
Price....	$4.00	$4.35
	Damask	Silk Plush
Price....	$4.75	$4.95

No. 1C5720 This parlor arm chair is made of selected birch in a perfect imitation mahogany polished finish. It has a full biscuit tufted seat, shapely curved, high arms and a broad hand carved panel back. Substantial in construction, attractive in design and beautiful in finish. Shipped direct from factory in Chicago. Shipping weight, about 30 pounds.

	Figured Velour	Brocaded Verona Plush
Price....	$4.85	$5.10
	Damask	Silk Plush
Price....	$5.45	$5.65

No. 1C5722 This parlor chair has a full spring seat, broad panel back decorated with genuine hand carvings. The wood is thoroughly air seasoned birch in a mahogany polished finish. It has high arms reinforced by six spindles and upholstered with our high carbon all steel full spring seat. A thoroughly well made, substantial and artistic piece for the parlor. Shipped direct from factory in Chicago. Shipping weight, about 30 pounds.

	Figured Velour	Brocaded Verona Plush
Price....	$5.35	$5.75
	Damask	Silk Plush
Price....	$6.15	$6.45

No. 1C5726 This rocker is a very ornamental piece of furniture built on such lines as to afford not only the greatest amount of strength, but also give unusual beauty. Has large seat, perfectly upholstered with our high carbon all steel construction. The frame is of solid birch, finished in a perfect imitation of mahogany. It is beautifully shaped, carved and decorated. Shipping weight, about 25 pounds. Our special prices are as follows:

	Price
Figured Velour	$4.75
Brocaded Verona Plush	5.10
Crushed Plush	5.25
Brocaded Silk Plush	5.45
Silk Damask	5.65

No. 1C5730 A new design, very ornamental and built on lines to afford not only the greatest amount of strength, but unusual beauty. It has a large spring seat made of our high carbon all steel construction. The frame is solid birch, The back is genuine mahogany veneer, handsomely carved. The finish is a perfect imitation of mahogany. Shipping weight, 35 pounds.

	Price
Figured Velour	$5.10
Brocaded Verona Plush	5.35
Crushed Plush	5.60
Brocaded Silk Plush	5.85
Silk Damask	6.05

No. 1C5734 This illustration represents our Student's Sleepy Hollow Chair. For solid comfort this chair has no superior. Nicely tufted. It is an ideal reading chair. The frame is made of solid oak, finished in a beautiful golden color. Shipping weight, 40 pounds.

	Price
Tapestry	$5.75
Figured Velour	6.95
Brocaded Verona Plush	8.45
Crushed Plush	8.95

No. 1C5736 same as No. 1C5734, but mounted on rockers at 75 cents additional to the above prices.

An Exceptionally Comfortable Reclining Swing Chair.

A Wonderful Bargain at $6.45

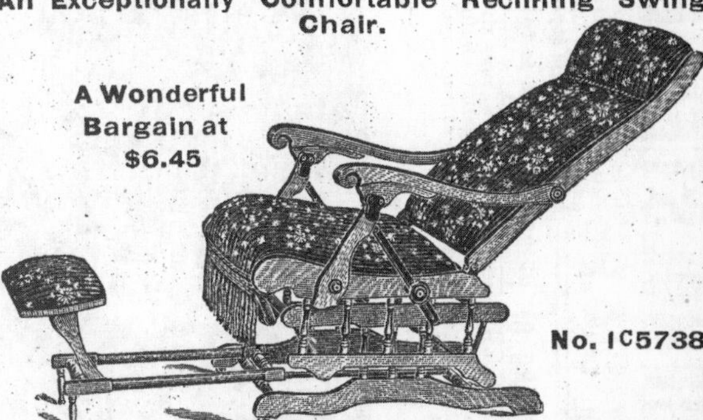

No. 1C5738

No. 1C5738 It is made entirely of oak, which insures strength and durability as well as a handsome finish. The seat is suspended on swings in such a manner that it gives a rocking motion. This, combined with the adjusting feature and foot rest, makes one of the most comfortable lounging chairs imaginable and an indispensable invalids' chair. The adjustment can be put at any position required and will stay where you put it. **The seat** is 20½ inches deep, 20½ inches wide, and the back is 30 inches high, with springs in both back and seat; upholstered with tow and cotton, covered with the best quality of figured velour, either red, green or brown. **The foot rest** is shown extended, but when not in use folds back underneath the chair, entirely out of sight.

WE FULLY GUARANTEE THIS ATTACHMENT IN EVERY PARTICULAR.

No. 1C5738 Price...**$6.45**

Shipping weight, 60 pounds.

Shipped direct from our factory in Central New York, from which point customer pays freight.

Our $5.95 Divan.

No. 1C5742 Selected birch finished in a rich dark mahogany with piano polish, full spring seat and edge, back being trimmed with tufted border. **Size, 34 inches long, 22 inches wide and 38 inches high. Weight, 45 pounds.**

Upholstered in	Figured Velour	Brocaded Verona Plush	Crushed Plush	Silk Brocatelle	Silk Damask
Price......	$5.95	$6.35	$6.85	$7.25	$7.55

Exceptional Value.

No. 1C5746 This divan is one of the prettiest, best made, and at the same time is the lowest priced divan in the market. It is especially designed with a view of strength in the frame as well as attractiveness in appearance. It is 40 inches long by 35 inches high and is made of selected birch, thoroughly well seasoned and finished in perfect imitation mahogany. The back is handsomely ornamented with scroll sawing and raised carvings; the upholstering is first class in every respect; the seat is supported by eight spiral springs, well tied and covered with best grades of upholstering material; the legs are graceful in design and fitted with ball bearing casters. Shipping weight, 65 pounds.

	Figured Velour	Brocaded Verona Plush	Crushed Plush	Silk Brocatelle	Silk Damask
Price.....	$7.95	$8.75	$8.95	$9.65	$9.85

This Handsome Divan $9.95.

No. 1C5750 This divan is one of the best values ever offered. It is 3 feet 4 inches long, 36 inches high. It is made of thoroughly air seasoned and kiln dried birch in a perfect imitation of mahogany, highly polished. It has a full steel spring seat, high arms and broad hand carved and decorated with marquetry inlaid work in top panel of back. Artistic is design, high grade in construction and finish. Shipped direct from factory in Chicago. Shipping weight, 65 pounds.

	Figured Velour	Fancy Brocaded Velour	Brocaded Verona Plush	Brocaded Silk Plush	Silk Damask
Price..	$9.95	$10.45	$10.95	$11.65	$11.85

SHIPPED DIRECT FROM OUR FACTORY, NEAR CHICAGO, FROM WHICH POINT THE CUSTOMER PAYS THE FREIGHT.

No. 1C5760

$14.95

BELOW WE QUOTE PRICES ON **SINGLE PIECES,** making it possible to order a **THREE-PIECE, FOUR-PIECE OR SIX-PIECE SUITE.**

OUR $14.95 5-PIECE UPHOLSTERED PARLOR SUITE.

AT $14.95 we offer this parlor suite as the greatest value ever furnished in this style.

HOW WE CAN MAKE THIS HERETOFORE UNHEARD OF PRICE of $14.95 is fully explained under the heading of new designs in High Grade Couches. It is made in the one factory that makes nothing but these suites and our upholstered couches. Our $14.95 price is below the lowest wholesale price, much lower than dealers can buy in the largest quantities.

THESE SUITES are made on the very latest style of thoroughly air seasoned and kiln dried hardwood frames. They are made extra strong, extra well braced throughout. Springs are the genuine Eagleton highest grade tempered steel springs. The suite is upholstered in the highest style of the art. We use the highest grade of upholstery covering as indicated below, and described on page 681. The colors in the different kinds of coverings harmonizing perfectly. Each piece is fully overstuffed, handsomely decorated and finished, with deep fringe, fancy binding, and decorated with a handsome rococo brass gimp ornamentation.

PRICES FOR COMPLETE SUITE OF FIVE PIECES:

The number of this Parlor Suite is No. 1C5760. Always order by number and be sure to state the kind and color of covering desired.

Covering	Figured Velour	Fancy Brocaded Velour	Floral Brocaded Velour	Brocaded Verona Plush
Price	$14.95	$15.90	$16.25	$18.15

PRICES FOR SINGLE PIECES:

	Figured Velour	Fancy Brocaded Velour	Floral Brocaded Velour	Brocaded Verona Plush
Sofa	$5.05	$5.30	$5.75	$6.05
Arm Chair	3.10	3.30	3.65	3.85
Rocker	3.50	3.80	4.15	4.35
Reception Chair	1.65	1.75	1.85	1.95

THIS SUITE CONSISTS OF THE FOLLOWING FIVE HANDSOME PIECES: One large sofa, 36 inches high, 23 inches wide and 52 inches long; one large rocker, 33 inches high and 28 inches wide; one large easy chair, 34 inches high and 28 inches wide; and two large parlor chairs, each 31 inches high and 20 inches wide. Weight, packed for shipment, 200 pounds.

OUR NEW $10.45 THREE-PIECE PARLOR SUITE.

No. 1C5764 In offering this three-piece parlor suite at $10.45 to $14.35 we assure our customers that they are buying these goods at less than dealers can buy in quantities. They come from our own factory in this city and you own them at the cost of material and labor with but our one small percentage of profit added. Compare this suite with anything you can buy from any other concern at from $12.00 up, and if you do not find it as good or better in every respect, we do not want you to keep it, but will cheerfully refund your money in full and pay all freight charges. In design this suite is entirely new, neat and attractive. The frame is made of birch with mahogany finish. It is massive and substantially built. The backs are handsomely scroll sawed and ornamented with raised carvings. The seats are made with our guaranteed all steel spring construction, excellently upholstered. Shipping weight, 150 pounds. Illustration shows velour covering.

PRICES FOR COMPLETE SUITE OF THREE PIECES:
The number of this Parlor Suite is No. 1C5764. Always order by number and be sure to state the kind and color of covering desired.

Covering......	Figured Velour	Fancy Brocaded Velour	Brocaded Verona Plush	Crushed Plush	Brocaded Silk Plush	Silk Damask
Price..........	$10.45	$11.20	$11.45	$11.65	$13.20	$14.35

PRICES FOR SINGLE PIECES:

	Figured Velour	Fancy Brocaded Velour	Brocaded Verona Plush	Crushed Plush	Brocaded Silk Plush	Silk Damask
Divan............	$5.25	$5.60	$5.70	$5.80	$6.55	$7.20
Arm Chair........	3.45	3.70	3.80	3.85	4.45	4.80
Reception Chair.	1.75	1.90	1.95	2.00	2.20	2.35

THIS MAGNIFICENT THREE-PIECE PARLOR SUITE, $18.75.

No. 1C5768 This magnificent strictly high grade three-piece parlor suite is the most wonderful value ever offered. This suite should be compared with suites offered by others at $25.00 to $30.00. The beauty of design, high quality of workmanship and elegance of finish can only be fully appreciated when you see it. The heavy and substantial frame is made of specially selected birch and finished in a perfect imitation of mahogany. The top bars and broad panels in the back are veneered with highly figured genuine mahogany. The back is decorated with genuine hand carvings, perfectly executed. Each piece has our guaranteed high carbon bessemer all steel construction. Furnished in the various high grade coverings by the single piece or full suite as noted below. Shipped direct from factory in Chicago. Shipping weight, about 175 pounds.

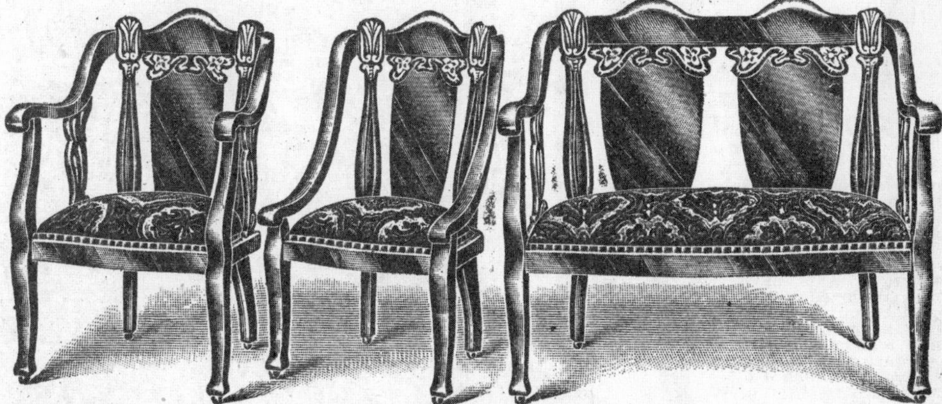

PRICES FOR COMPLETE SUITE OF THREE PIECES:
The number of this Parlor Suite is No. 1C5768. Always order by number and be sure to state the kind and color of covering desired.

Covering......	Figured Velour	Fancy Brocaded Velour	Brocaded Verona Plush	Crushed Plush	Brocaded Silk Plush	Silk Damask
Price...	$18.75	$19.45	$19.85	$20.65	$22.25	$23.35

PRICES FOR SINGLE PIECES:

	Figured Velour	Fancy Brocaded Velour	Brocaded Verona Plush	Crushed Plush	Brocaded Silk Plush	Silk Damask
Divan............	$9.25	$9.60	$9.85	$10.25	$11.15	$11.75
Arm Chair........	6.45	6.65	6.75	7.05	7.55	7.95
Reception Chair.	3.05	3.20	3.25	3.35	3.55	3.65

OUR NEW SPECIAL $13.95 FIVE-PIECE UPHOLSTERED PARLOR SUITE.

This illustration shows four pieces of our No. 1C5772 Parlor Suite. The fifth piece is a duplicate of the parlor chair, which has no arms.

NO. 1C5772 This five-piece suite consists of one large sofa, one large rocker, one large easy chair and two parlor chairs. The illustration shows the sofa, the rocker, the easy chair and one of the two parlor chairs.

THIS SUITE is made on new improved frames for this season, extra strong hardwood frames, finished in imitation mahogany which wears fully as good as genuine mahogany wood. Each piece is upholstered in a different coloring, five different shades to harmonize perfectly. Each piece has spring seat, the springs being made of the best tempered steel. The finish is unusually high for a suite at so low a price.

OUR PRICES represent the actual cost of these suites at the factory with but our one small margin of profit added. Every suite is made to order, which requires from 7 to 10 days after the order is received, and is shipped direct from the factory, thereby saving all expense of handling, which enables us to quote such low prices.

PRICES FOR COMPLETE SUITE OF FIVE PIECES:
The number of this Parlor Suite is No. 1C5772. Always order by number and be sure to state the kind and color of covering desired.

Covering......	Figured Velour	Fancy Brocaded Velour	Brocaded Verona Plush	Crushed Plush	Brocaded Silk Plush	Silk Damask
Price	$13.95	$14.75	$16.05	$16.50	$18.20	$19.40

PRICES FOR SINGLE PIECES:

	Figured Velour	Fancy Brocaded Velour	Brocaded Verona Plush	Crushed Plush	Brocaded Silk Plush	Silk Damask
Sofa..............	$4.75	$4.95	$5.35	$5.50	$6.10	$6.45
Arm Chair.......	2.85	3.05	3.35	3.45	3.70	3.95
Rocker...........	3.35	3.55	3.85	3.95	4.20	4.45
Reception Chair.	1.50	1.60	1.75	1.85	2.10	2.25

THIS BEAUTIFUL FIVE-PIECE $30.00 PARLOR SUITE FOR $16.45

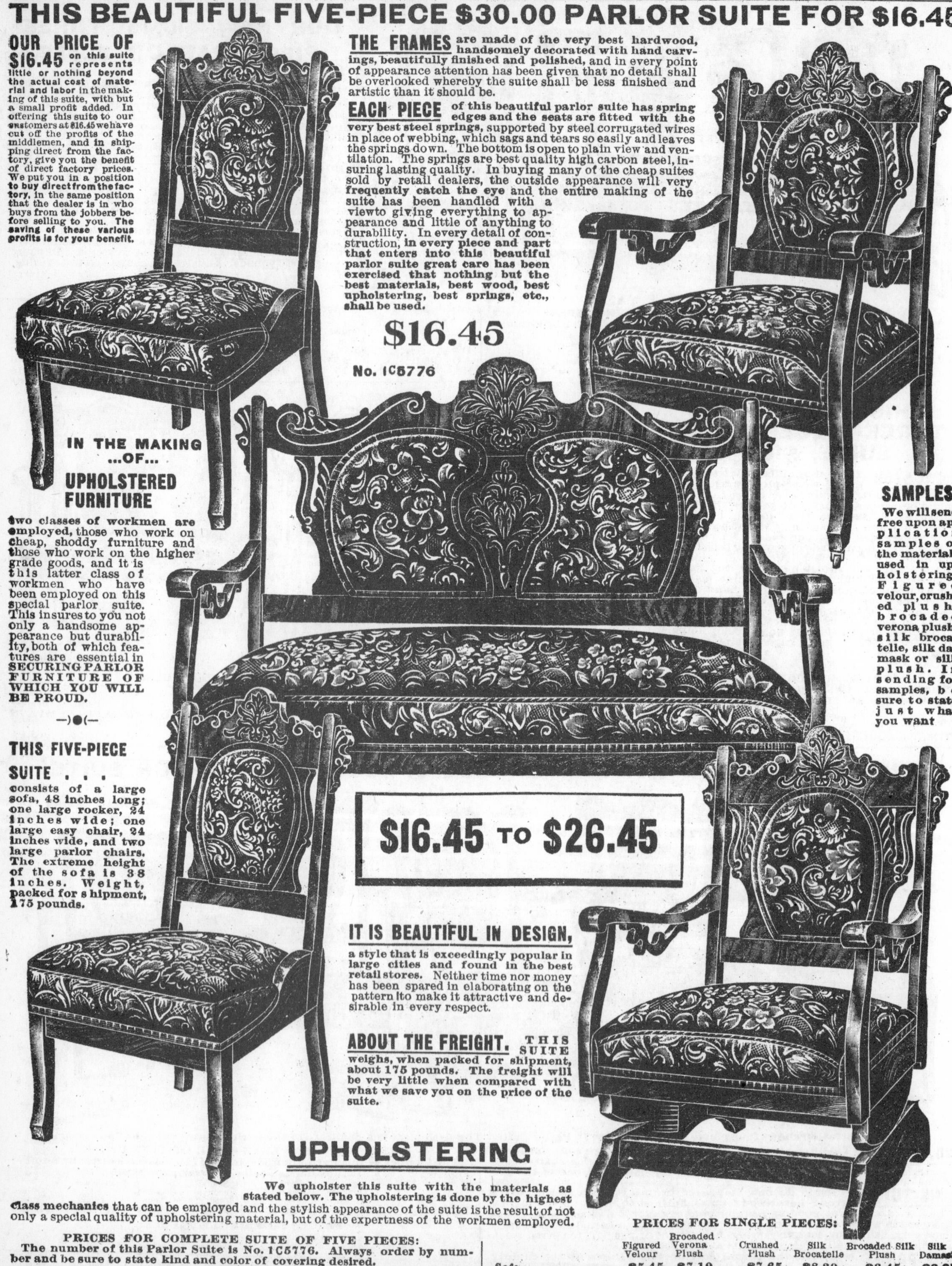

OUR PRICE OF $16.45 on this suite represents little or nothing beyond the actual cost of material and labor in the making of this suite, with but a small profit added. In offering this suite to our customers at $16.45 we have cut off the profits of the middlemen, and in shipping direct from the factory, give you the benefit of direct factory prices. We put you in a position to buy direct from the factory, in the same position that the dealer is in who buys from the jobbers before selling to you. The saving of these various profits is for your benefit.

THE FRAMES are made of the very best hardwood, handsomely decorated with hand carvings, beautifully finished and polished, and in every point of appearance attention has been given that no detail shall be overlooked whereby the suite shall be less finished and artistic than it should be.

EACH PIECE of this beautiful parlor suite has spring edges and the seats are fitted with the very best steel springs, supported by steel corrugated wires in place of webbing, which sags and tears so easily and leaves the springs down. The bottom is open to plain view and ventilation. The springs are best quality high carbon steel, insuring lasting quality. In buying many of the cheap suites sold by retail dealers, the outside appearance will very frequently catch the eye and the entire making of the suite has been handled with a viewto giving everything to appearance and little of anything to durability. In every detail of construction, in every piece and part that enters into this beautiful parlor suite great care has been exercised that nothing but the best materials, best wood, best upholstering, best springs, etc., shall be used.

$16.45

No. 1C5776

IN THE MAKING ...OF... UPHOLSTERED FURNITURE

two classes of workmen are employed, those who work on cheap, shoddy furniture and those who work on the higher grade goods, and it is this latter class of workmen who have been employed on this special parlor suite. This insures to you not only a handsome appearance but durability, both of which features are essential in SECURING PARLOR FURNITURE OF WHICH YOU WILL BE PROUD.

—)●(—

THIS FIVE-PIECE SUITE . . . consists of a large sofa, 48 inches long; one large rocker, 24 inches wide; one large easy chair, 24 inches wide, and two large parlor chairs. The extreme height of the sofa is 38 inches. Weight, packed for shipment, 175 pounds.

SAMPLES. We will send free upon application samples of the materials used in upholstering: Figured velour, crushed plush, brocaded verona plush, silk brocatelle, silk damask or silk plush. In sending for samples, be sure to state just what you want

$16.45 TO $26.45

IT IS BEAUTIFUL IN DESIGN, a style that is exceedingly popular in large cities and found in the best retail stores. Neither time nor money has been spared in elaborating on the pattern to make it attractive and desirable in every respect.

ABOUT THE FREIGHT. THIS SUITE weighs, when packed for shipment, about 175 pounds. The freight will be very little when compared with what we save you on the price of the suite.

UPHOLSTERING

We upholster this suite with the materials as stated below. The upholstering is done by the highest class mechanics that can be employed and the stylish appearance of the suite is the result of not only a special quality of upholstering material, but of the expertness of the workmen employed.

PRICES FOR COMPLETE SUITE OF FIVE PIECES:

The number of this Parlor Suite is No. 1C5776. Always order by number and be sure to state kind and color of covering desired.

Covering....	Figured Velour	Brocaded Verona Plush	Crushed Plush	Silk Brocatelle	Brocaded Silk Plush	Silk Damask
Price....................	$16.45	$21.30	$22.95	$24.75	$25.40	$26.45

PRICES FOR SINGLE PIECES:

	Figured Velour	Brocaded Verona Plush	Crushed Plush	Silk Brocatelle	Brocaded Silk Plush	Silk Damask
Sofa................	$5.45	$7.10	$7.65	$8.20	$8.45	$8.85
Arm Chair..........	3.40	4.45	4.85	5.30	5.40	5.60
Rocker..............	3.90	4.95	5.35	5.75	5.95	6.10
Reception Chair...	1.85	2.40	2.55	2.75	2.80	2.95

OUR $18.95 FIVE-PIECE PARLOR SUITE.

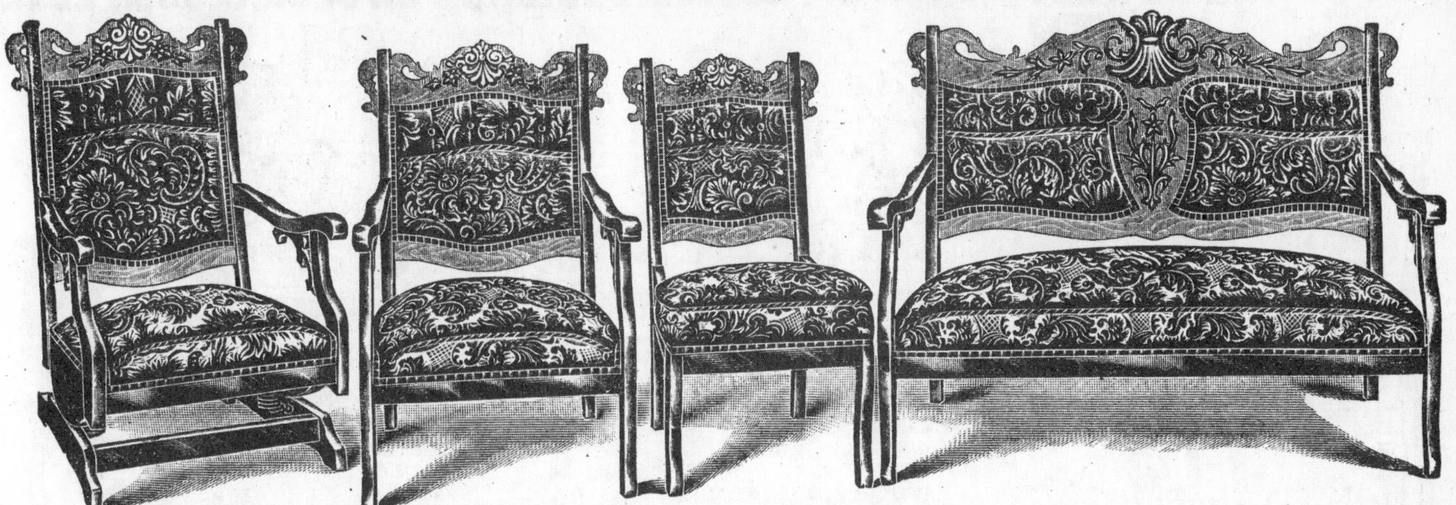

This illustration shows four pieces of our No. 1C5780 Parlor Suite. The fifth piece is a duplicate of the parlor chair without arms.

No. 1C5780 At $18.95 we offer this Five-Piece Parlor Suite as a rare bargain. It is complete in every detail of workmanship, material and finish, and guaranteed to please the most exacting, when the price is considered in connection with the quality.

THE FRAMES OF THESE PIECES are made of hard birchwood in mahogany finish. As seen from the illustration, the decoration in the way of carving, etc., is very handsome, and anyone ordering this suite is bound to be pleased, not only with the beautiful appearance of each piece, but the very evident **durability of the suite.**

WE UPHOLSTER EACH PIECE in the very best possible manner, with various qualities of coverings at the prices quoted. Each piece has full spring seat and spring edges, the springs being made of the best Bessemer steel wire, with the latest steel wire support on the bottom, instead of webbing, as used by others. This new construction is in plain view from the bottom, and there is no webbing to tear or sag. We fit the suite complete with the best casters.

OUR PRICES represent the actual cost of these suites at the factory with but our usual one small margin of profit added, and by shipping direct from the factory we save all extra expense of handling, which enables us to quote such low prices. We require from 7 to 10 days after an order is received before we can make shipment, as every suite is made to order.

Weight of suite complete, packed in burlap for shipment, about 175 pounds.

PRICES FOR COMPLETE SUITE OF FIVE PIECES.

The number of this Parlor Suite is No. 1C5780. Always order by number and be sure to state the kind and color of covering desired.

Covering	Figured Velour	Fancy Brocaded Velour	Floral Brocaded Velour	Brocaded Verona Plush	Crushed Plush	Silk Brocatelle
Price	$18.95	$19.35	$20.25	$21.50	$22.25	$25.90

PRICES FOR SINGLE PIECES:

	Figured Velour	Fancy Brocaded Velour	Floral Brocaded Velour	Brocaded Verona Plush	Crushed Plush	Silk Brocatelle
Sofa	$6.35	$6.45	$6.70	$7.05	$7.20	$8.65
Arm Chair	3.95	4.05	4.25	4.60	4.75	5.50
Rocker	4.45	4.55	4.80	5.15	5.30	6.05
Reception Chair	2.10	2.15	2.25	2.35	2.40	2.85

THIS HANDSOME FIVE-PIECE PARLOR SUITE, $26.30.

No. 1C5784 The exceedingly low price of $26.30 which we are able to make on this regular $50.00 parlor suite, is only made possible by large contracts with a leading manufacturer. This suite is made up in accordance with our own design, and from the illustration you can form some idea of the general **elegance and richness of effect of this beautiful suite. The five pieces of this suite are as follows:**

Large sofa, large arm chair, large rocker and two handsome reception chairs, both of which are alike, but only one of which is shown in the illustration. Without making undue comparisons with our other upholstered furniture, we can scarcely avoid saying **that nothing else in the line of upholstered goods has ever been offered by us** which combines the same elegance, durability, finish and quality as shown in this beautiful suite.

IT IS MADE OF SELECTED BIRCH RICHLY FINISHED IN MAHOGANY.

THE FINISH IS NOT MERELY LAID ON, as is the case with very cheap furniture, but it is beautifully hand polished. The daintiness of the design is greatly added to by the rich, hand made carving with which the backs of the pieces are decorated. **The greatest skill of cabinet makers** is brought into effect in this beautiful suite, and we offer it as the best example of great value which can be obtained from us in this line of goods.

EACH PIECE has easy spring seat and spring edges, **the springs being made of the best high carbon steel wire,** supported by steel corrugated wires in place of the webbing which is usually used in manufacturing suites. Webbing tears and sags, which is, however, entirely overcome by using these steel wire supports instead. We use a heavy duck canvas over springs where others use cheap burlap. Each piece is left open from the bottom to air and ventilation, which will **prevent breeding of germs and moths. The fronts are ruffled,** and the top of the back is finished with biscuit tufts, which gives a wonderfully beautiful effect to the suite. Every piece is double stuffed and has stitched fronts.

This illustration shows four pieces of our No. 1C5784 Parlor Suite. The fifth piece is a duplicate of the parlor chair, which has no arms.

PRICES FOR COMPLETE SUITE OF FIVE PIECES:

The number of this Parlor Suite is No. 1C5784. Always order by number and be sure to state the kind and color of covering desired.

Covering	Figured Velour	Fancy Brocaded Velour	Brocaded Verona Plush	Crushed Plush	Silk Brocatelle	Brocaded Silk Plush	Silk Damask
Price	$26.30	$27.50	$29.00	$29.55	$32.45	$34.80	$35.85

PRICES FOR SINGLE PIECES:

	Figured Velour	Fancy Brocaded Velour	Brocaded Verona Plush	Crushed Plush	Silk Brocatelle	Brocaded Silk Plush	Silk Damask
Sofa	$8.75	$9.10	$9.60	$9.80	$10.80	$11.70	$12.05
Arm Chair	5.60	5.95	6.35	6.45	6.95	7.45	7.70
Rocker	6.05	6.35	6.75	6.90	7.50	7.95	8.20
Reception Chair	2.95	3.05	3.15	3.20	3.60	3.85	3.95

ONE OF THE NEWEST AND MOST EFFECTIVE DESIGNS FOR $23.85 COMPLETE

This illustration shows four pieces of our No. 1C5788 Parlor Suite. The fifth piece is a duplicate of the parlor chair, which has no arms.

No. 1C5788 We are only to anxious to have such furniture introduced into every neighborhood, for we know that anyone who examines this suite and learns the price which we quote will be fully persuaded that a large percentage can be saved by purchasing their goods from us. An example of actual money saving is worth more to us as an advertisement than hundreds of dollars spent in newspapers.

THIS BEAUTIFUL SUITE consists of five pieces, namely: One large sofa, one large rocker, one large easy chair and two large parlor chairs, both of which are alike and only one of which is shown in the illustration.

THE FRAMES ARE MADE OF HANDSOME SELECTED BIRCH with mahogany finish. The heavy carving on the back of each piece, combined with the stylish and effective upholstering, makes this suite distinctive from all others at anything like the price. Shipping weight, 225 pounds.

COMFORT IS LOOKED AFTER. Spring seats and edges fitted with the best high carbon steel springs, making each piece free and easy. Springs are supported by steel corrugated wire instead of the old fashioned webbing which sags or tears so easily. Bottom of each piece is left open to light and ventilation, which prevents moths.

YOU MUST SEE, examine and compare this suite with anything you can buy elsewhere at anything like the price to appreciate the value we are giving, and to make this possible we offer to send you this, or any other suite you may select, guaranteeing it to reach you in perfect order, with the understanding that you may use it in your own home for 30 days, and if for any reason you become dissatisfied with your purchase or do not feel that you have received a much better suite than you could have obtained elsewhere, even at much more money, you may return the suite to us at our expense and we will immediately refund your money, together with any freight charges you may have paid.

WE CAN FURNISH THIS SUITE in any combination desired. On account of limited space we illustrate only four pieces, but list below the price of the five-piece suite in different grades of upholstering material; give the price of single pieces, and whether you order one, three or five pieces, you will be paying the same proportionate price.

ON PAGE 681 we fully describe the colors and quality of upholstering material we can furnish. The illustration shows silk damask covering of beautiful pattern and combination.

WE HAVE NO FEAR OF ANY COMPARISON that may be made between this suite and those carried by local furniture dealers. Our facilities for turning out high grade furniture at marvelously low prices are unequaled and we will be only too glad to have you compare our prices with any other that you may be able to secure.

The number of this Parlor Suite is No. 1C5788. Always order by number and be sure to state the kind and color of covering desired.

PRICES FOR COMPLETE SUITE OF FIVE PIECES:

Covering	Figured Velour	Floral Brocaded Velour	Brocaded Verona Plush	Crushed Plush	Brocaded Silk Plush	Silk Damask
Price	$23.85	$26.25	$27.65	$28.40	$32.25	$34.20

PRICES FOR SINGLE PIECES:

	Figured Velour	Floral Brocaded Velour	Brocaded Verona Plush	Crushed Plush	Brocaded Silk Plush	Silk Damask
Sofa	$7.95	$8.80	$9.30	$9.50	$10.85	$11.40
Arm Chair	5.05	5.65	5.90	6.05	6.95	7.35
Rocker	5.55	6.10	6.40	6.55	7.45	7.85
Reception Chair	2.65	2.85	3.05	3.15	3.60	3.80

A GENUINE TURKISH THREE OR FIVE-PIECE PARLOR SUITE.

Arm Chair.

Sofa.

Reception Chair.

The sofa is upholstered with eighteen high carbon steel springs, the rocker and arm chair each have nine springs, the reception chair six springs.

No. 1C5792 This extra large, elegant Turkish Parlor Suite can be furnished in various combinations of pieces, according to requirements. We show in the above illustrations a gents' easy chair, sofa and parlor or reception chair, in addition to which we can furnish a rocking chair, constructed in the same style as the gents' easy chair. The three-piece suite, consisting of parlor chair, sofa and gents' easy chair, or a regular five-piece suite, consisting of two reception chairs, 34 inches high, 20 inches deep, 20 inches wide; sofa, 37 inches high, 24 inches deep, 52 inches long; gents' easy chair and rocker, each 37 inches high, 24 inches deep, 30 inches wide, make the best combinations. **All the pieces are made with large and comfortable seats and are constructed according to the very latest ideas in the art of upholstering.** We use only the very best grades of material for covering, made up in the newest designs or patterns, each piece being covered with a different color, but made to harmonize with the other pieces. The suite is beautifully upholstered with tufted plush bands on the upper backs; plush effect around the edges. The fringe is made of the very best heavy worsted, festooned with double rows of silk and wool cord in combination of colors to harmonize with covering. Every piece is made up with the best springs and has spring edges and spring back, built of the very best material and made up by the very best class of mechanics.

Each piece is carefully packed and burlapped to insure its reaching destination in good condition. Send us your order for one of these handsome parlor suites and if it is not entirely satisfactory in every respect it can be returned at our expense and we will cheerfully refund your money and pay all charges. Shipping weight, 120 pounds.

The number of this Parlor Suite is No. 1C5792. Always order by number and be sure to state the kind and color of covering desired.

PRICES FOR COMPLETE SUITE OF THREE PIECES:

Covering	Figured Velour	Brocaded Verona Plush	Crushed Plush	Silk Brocatelle	Brocaded Silk Plush	Silk Damask
Price	$22.35	$26.30	$27.70	$30.25	$31.15	$32.20

PRICES FOR SINGLE PIECES:

	Figured Velour	Brocaded Verona Plush	Crushed Plush	Silk Brocatelle	Brocaded Silk Plush	Silk Damask
Sofa	$11.25	$13.25	$13.90	$15.40	$15.75	$16.10
Arm Chair	7.75	8.60	9.10	9.75	10.15	10.40
Rocker	7.25	9.15	9.65	10.25	10.65	10.90
Reception Chair	3.85	4.45	4.70	5.10	5.25	5.35

GENUINE TURKISH OVERSTUFFED SUITE, $33.75.

Designed by one of the Best Furniture Artists in the World. Strictly High Class and Up to Date. Nothing Cheap about this Beautiful Suite but the Price.

FIVE-PIECE PARLOR SUITE.

SOFA.

ARM CHAIR.

ROCKER.

RECEPTION CHAIR.

This illustration shows four pieces of our No. 1C5796 Parlor Suites. The fifth piece is a duplicate of the parlor chair, which has no arms.

No. 1C5796 **THIS ELEGANT TURKISH PARLOR SUITE** consists of one tete-a-tete, one rocker, one gents' easy chair and two parlor or reception chairs, five pieces, and all these pieces are made in extra large size, with extra high backs and large comfortable seats, and are the very latest design. The upholstering or covering of this suite is the latest design or pattern of imported goods; each piece is covered with a different color; the suite is beautifully upholstered with tufted plush bands and backs in snake ruffles, as shown in illustration, and trimmed with a heavy worsted fringe. The suite is made with the best springs and spring edges, and every piece is made with spring back. This is, without doubt, one of the best parlor suites on the market at the price we ask, and will be an ornament to any home.

UNDERSTAND, there are five full pieces as listed above. The illustration shows four of the five pieces.

YOU MUST SEE, **EXAMINE, AND COMPARE** this suite with anything you can buy elsewhere at anything like the price to appreciate the value we are giving, and to make this possible we offer to send you this or any other suite you may select, guaranteeing it to reach you in perfect order, with the understanding that you may use it in your own home 30 days, and if for any reason you become dissatisfied with your purchase or do not feel that you have received a much better suite than you could have obtained elsewhere, even at much more money, you can return the suite to us at our expense and we will immediately refund your money together with any freight charges you may have paid. Shipping weight, 225 pounds.

PRICES FOR COMPLETE SUIT OF FIVE PIECES:

The number of this Parlor Suite is No. 1C5796. Always order by number and be sure to state the kind and color of covering desired.

Covering....	Figured Velour	Fancy Brocaded Velour	Brocaded Verona Plush	Crushed Plush	Brocaded Silk Plush	Silk Damask
Price	$33.75	$35.85	$37.75	$39.15	$45.85	$46.90

PRICES FOR SINGLE PIECES:

	Figured Velour	Fancy Brocaded Velour	Brocaded Verona Plush	Crushed Plush	Brocaded Silk Plush	Silk Damask
Sofa.............	$11.25	$12.15	$12.75	$13.25	$15.35	$15.70
Arm Chair......	7.25	7.65	8.10	8.40	9.90	10.15
Rocker.........	7.75	8.15	8.60	8.90	10.40	10.65
Reception Chair	3.75	3.95	4.15	4.30	5.10	5.20

A MASSIVE FRAME PARLOR SUITE FOR $30.50.

This illustration shows four pieces of our No. 1C5800 Parlor Suite. The fifth piece is a duplicate of the parlor chair, which has no arms.

No. 1C5800 **THE ABOVE ILLUSTRATION shows but four of the five pieces furnished with the suite. The illustration will give you a general idea of the appearance of this suite,** although it falls far short of doing justice to the carving, decoration and outline of the frames; you must see, examine and compare this handsome new design with suites sold generally at about double our price to appreciate the real value we are offering—one of the greatest values that we have ever shown, and such value as is not approached by any other house.

AS A GUARANTEE **that this suite will please you and that you will find it far greater value for your money than you could possibly get elsewhere,** we will gladly accept your order for this suite to be sent to you under our guarantee that it will reach you carefully packed and in perfect condition, allowing you the privilege of taking the suite to your own home, setting it up in your home and keeping it thirty days, during which time you can compare it with suites sold by others, and if you are not perfectly satisfied with your purchase you can return the suite to us at our expense and we will immediately refund your money, together with any freight charges paid by you.

THESE FRAMES **are entirely new for this season, made of carefully selected and thoroughly seasoned beautiful grain birch,** given a rich, deep mahogany finish, rubbed and fully polished. They are elaborately carved. The illustration will give you just a little idea of the shaping and carving. They are made extra strong and especially designed to accommodate our new, stylish upholstering effect.

UPHOLSTERING. **These five pieces are upholstered in the very latest style.** They have corrugated wire bottoms, highly tempered springs, eighteen springs in the sofa, nine in the easy chair, nine in the rocker and four in each parlor chair. The springs are covered with white duck canvas, they are full spring edges, plain seats and fancy tufted backs. On page 681 we give a complete description of the different upholstering materials which we can furnish.

PRICES FOR COMPLETE SUITE OF FIVE PIECES:

The number of this Parlor Suite is No. 1C5800. Always order by number and be sure to state the kind and color of covering desired.

Covering....	Figured Velour	Brocaded Verona Plush	Crushed Plush	Silk Brocatelle	Brocaded Silk Plush	Silk Damask
Price........	$30.50	$33.90	$35.65	$37.25	$38.45	$39.95

PRICES FOR SINGLE PIECES:

	Figured Velour	Brocaded Verona Plush	Crushed Plush	Silk Brocatelle	Brocaded Silk Plush	Silk Damask
Sofa.............	$10.15	$11.30	$11.85	$12.45	$12.80	$13.30
Arm Chair	6.55	7.25	7.70	7.90	8.25	8.65
Rocker..........	6.95	7.85	8.20	8.50	8.80	9.10
Reception Chair	3.40	3.75	3.95	4.20	4.30	4.45

OUR NEW EMPRESS DESIGN PARLOR SUITE, $31.85.

This illustration shows four pieces of our No. 1C5804 Parlor Suite; the fifth piece is a duplicate of the parlor chair, which has no arms.

No. 1C5804 This five-piece Parlor Suite as illustrated above, is offered in the new Empress design at $31.85 to $40.95, according to grade of cloth cover used in the upholstering, as the equal of suites sold by most fashionable city furniture dealers at about double our price.

OUR $31.85 PRICE is made possible by reason of our facilities for turning these frames out by the use of the highest type of automatic labor saving machinery, facilities for buying the raw material in large quantities for cash, and our ability to control the output of the most economically operated upholstering factory in the country; in short, at $31.85 to $40.95 we offer you every advantage we have gained in the furniture business. You get these five pieces at just what they cost us to produce, with but our one small percentage of profit added.

THE ILLUSTRATION shows four pieces, namely, sofa, easy chair, rocker and one parlor chair, while the suite consists of five pieces, sofa, rocker, easy chair and two parlor chairs. The illustration gives but a slight idea of the beautiful effect worked out in each of these five pieces; in short, you must see, examine and compare these five pieces with anything you could buy elsewhere at anything like the price to appreciate the value we are giving, and to make this possible and to guarantee you against any chance of loss, we offer to send you this or any suite, guaranteeing it to reach you in perfect order and giving you the privilege of using it in your own home for thirty days, and if for any reason you become dissatisfied with your purchase and do not feel that you have received a much better suite than you could have obtained elsewhere, even at much more money, you can return the suite to us at our expense and we will refund your money.

THESE FRAMES, the new Empress design, are made from carefully selected, beautifully grained, thoroughly seasoned birch, given a deep, rich, full mahogany finish; they are heavily carved, rubbed and fully polished, reinforced, braced, glued and stayed, the most substantial frames possible to produce.

UPHOLSTERED with full corrugated wire bottoms, extra highly tempered springs, sofa having eighteen springs, easy chair and rocking chair nine springs, and parlor chairs four springs each. They have full spring edges, ruffled fronts, top of backs handsomely biscuit tufted. Each piece is upholstered in a different color, carefully selected with a view to perfect harmony. On page 681 we give a complete description of the different upholstering materials which we can furnish.

PRICES FOR COMPLETE SUITE OF FIVE PIECES:

The number of this Parlor Suite is No. 1C5804. Always order by number and be sure to state the kind and color of covering desired.

Covering	Figured Velour	Brocaded Verona Plush	Crushed Plush	Silk Brocatelle	Brocaded Silk Plush	Silk Damask
Price	$31.85	$35.60	$37.20	$38.75	$39.40	$40.95

PRICES FOR SINGLE PIECES:

	Figured Velour	Brocaded Verona Plush	Crushed Plush	Silk Brocatelle	Brocaded Silk Plush	Silk Damask
Sofa	$10.65	$11.85	$12.40	$12.95	$13.10	$13.65
Arm Chair	6.80	7.65	8.10	8.35	8.40	8.85
Rocker	7.40	8.20	8.50	8.85	9.10	9.35
Reception Chair	3.50	3.95	4.10	4.30	4.40	4.55

OUR NEW FIVE-PIECE PARLOR SUITE, $32.75.

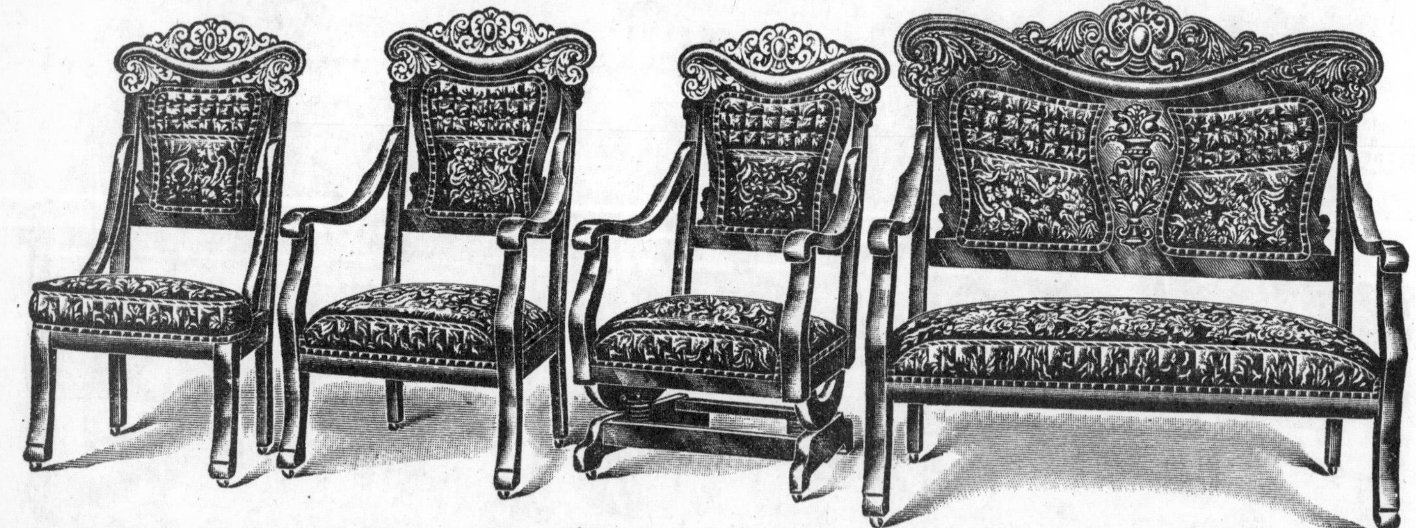

This illustration shows four pieces of our No. 1C5808 Parlor Suite; the fifth piece is a duplicate of the parlor chair, which has no arms.

No. 1C5808 The above illustration will give you just a little idea of the rich appearance, general style and beauty of this, our new $32.75 parlor suite. The illustration does not do the suite justice It fails to bring out clearly the rich pattern and the beautiful color effects or show the harmony of coloring which differs in each of the five pieces. However, you must see, examine and compare this suite with the commonplace suites usually retailed at $50.00 to $60.00 to appreciate the real value we are offering. The above illustration shows but four pieces, while the suite includes two reception chairs, making five pieces in all.

THESE FRAMES are entirely new designs, they are made of carefully selected birch, they are heavily carved, are given a full mahogany finish, rubbed and polished, made extra strong, reinforced at every joint and cannot in quality of material, style, workmanship or finish be compared with the many cheap frames with which the market is flooded.

THESE FIVE PIECES are beautifully upholstered in five different perfectly harmonizing colors and patterns. We use nothing but the best corrugated wire bottom, high tempered springs; we use an extra quality white duck canvas over the springs; they are made with full ruffled spring edge; tops and backs are handsomely biscuit tufted. The sofa has eighteen springs; easy chair, nine springs; rocker, nine springs and the two parlor chairs, four springs each. On page 681 we give a complete description of the different upholstering materials which we can furnish.

IN MAKING OUR PRICE OF $32.75 TO $42.00, according to the grade of covering, we have based our selling price on the actual cost of material and labor, with but our one small percentage of profit added, and we will gladly accept your order for one of these suites, to be sent to you with the understanding and agreement that it must reach you thoroughly packed and in perfect condition, we guaranteeing the delivery against any kind of damage in transit; and with the further understanding and agreement that you can take the suite home, keep it in your home for thirty days, during which time you can compare it with suites that sell generally at about double our price, and if for any reason you become dissatisfied with your purchase, you can return the suite to us at our expense and we will immediately refund your money, together with any freight charges paid by you. Shipping weight, 180 pounds.

PRICES FOR COMPLETE SUITE OF FIVE PIECES:

The number of this Parlor Suite is No. 1C5808. Always order by number and be sure to state the kind and color of covering desired.

Covering	Figured Velour	Brocaded Verona Plush	Crushed Plush	Silk Brocatelle	Brocaded Silk Plush	Silk Damask
Price	$32.75	$36.60	$38.20	$39.75	$40.40	$42.00

PRICES FOR SINGLE PIECES:

	Figured Velour	Brocaded Verona Plush	Crushed Plush	Silk Brocatelle	Brocaded Silk Plush	Silk Damask
Sofa	$10.90	$12.15	$12.70	$13.25	$13.40	$13.95
Arm Chair	7.05	7.90	8.35	8.60	8.65	9.10
Rocker	7.60	8.45	8.75	9.10	9.35	9.65
Reception Chair	3.60	4.05	4.20	4.40	4.50	4.65

BABY CARRIAGES AND GO-CARTS.

IN PRESENTING OUR LINE OF CARRIAGES AND GO-CARTS FOR THE YEAR 1905 **we are confident that we are offering the finest and most complete line of infants' vehicles which has ever been put on the market.** From the smallest folding cart to the usual full size reclining go-cart and baby carriage, our entire line of go-carts and carriages is supplied by the largest and best known manufacturer in the world, with facilities second to none and a reputation for making only the very highest grade of goods.

THE DESIGNS ARE ENTIRELY NEW **for this season and represent a most careful selection from a large number of sketches** submitted by the most expert designers who make a specialty of this class of work. They are designed with a view of producing the easiest riding and most comfortable vehicles on the market.

THE MATERIALS **used in our vehicles are the very best that can be obtained** and are subjected to a careful inspection before being made up.

THE DURABILITY **as well as the appearance of the carriage is always taken into consideration,** so that all carriages or go-carts, even the lowest priced ones, are guaranteed to give satisfactory wear.

THE ATTACHMENTS AND GEARS **which we furnish are strictly up to date in every respect** and possess many special qualities which are not found in the carriages or go-carts offered by other manufacturers or dealers.

THE WORKMANSHIP AND CONSTRUCTION **are guaranteed to be the very best throughout,** as only expert workmen are employed at our factories and every vehicle undergoes a most rigid inspection.

THE FINISH **throughout is in keeping with the high grade of material and workmanship** which enters into the construction of our vehicles.

EVERY GO-CART AND BABY CARRIAGE **is strongly crated in a small crate,** the wheels and gears off. By shipping in this way, the lowest transportation charges are obtained and safe delivery guaranteed. Our carriages and go-carts are so constructed that they can be easily assembled.

25 CENTS TO $1.50 **will pay the express or freight charges on a go-cart or carriage to any city in the United States located east of the Mississippi river.** All orders from customers living in the eastern states will be filled direct from our factory in Eastern Massachusetts, and from the central and western states direct from Chicago, thereby insuring the lowest transportation charges in every instance. We will be pleased to quote the exact freight or express charges to your railroad station on any vehicle you select, and you will find the charges to be but a very small amount as compared to what you will save in placing your order with us.

WE GUARANTEE PROMPT DELIVERY. **Every upholstered go-cart and carriage is made up special after the order is received by us,** which requires from three to six days, but under our contract with our manufacturers this year, we are able to guarantee that every order will be filled within eight days after it is received at the factory. While it will be possible in nearly every instance to fill the order within two to three days after it is received, you should allow at least eight days after the order is sent us for shipment to be made.

OUR LINE **for this year includes five distinct styles of vehicles,** the small folding cart, the small reclining, folding cart, the medium reclining go-cart, the large reclining go-cart and the regular baby carriage.

FREE SPECIAL CATALOGUE.

WE ESPECIALLY RECOMMEND **that you select your baby carriage or go-cart from the ones illustrated and described in this big catalogue,** rather than to delay to first write for our free special **Baby Carriage Catalogue** because we show our greatest values and best styles on these pages and we guarantee that any carriage you select from these pages will prove in every way satisfactory and that you will find it very much better than any you could buy elsewhere at anything like the price we offer. If you are unable to make a selection from the illustrations and descriptions shown on these pages, don't think of buying from anyone until you get our **Free Baby Carriage Catalogue,** in which we illustrate and describe our entire line, using large halftone illustrations which show every detail in the make-up of these carts even to the pattern of upholstery and the tuftings and patterns of the parasols.

SPECIAL PARTS AND REPAIRS **including wheels, rubber tires, springs, etc., fully described, with prices, in our Free Special Baby Carriage Catalogue.**

THIS CATALOGUE IS FREE FOR THE ASKING.

OUR CLIMAX GEAR **is the latest 1905 pattern.** It is very neat in appearance and strictly high grade in every respect, and is recommended as a very easy running gear. It has four 14-inch strong steel rubber tired wheels which are held to the axle by a patent detachable device and can be removed instantly by a simple adjustment of a patent lock. This overcomes the old difficulty of losing axle nuts or the loosening of wheels. The wheels are equipped with patent rubber hub caps and latest improved foot brake. Only the best grade material enters into the construction of this gear. It has four spiral springs made from fine oil tempered steel, arranged in such a manner as to produce the most elastic effect, causing the body of the cart to ride evenly without jolting. The axles are made from hard tempered steel. It is enameled in Brewster green and neatly striped.

OUR AUTOMOBILE CLIMAX GEAR, **as illustrated on our higher grade carts and carriages, is one of the best gears made.** In general construction it is the same as our regular Climax gear described above, only the wheels have extra heavy cushion tires, 5/8 inch thick, which makes the vehicle run extremely easy and absolutely noiseless.

THE AUTOMOBILE WHEELS **have extra wide rubber tires,** which prevent them from being caught in the cracks and crevices so commonly found in wood sidewalks and which is the main objection to the narrow rim wheels.

OUR ARTILLERY GEAR **is exactly the same in construction as our New Contracting Automobile Gear,** having all the very latest improvements, but is equipped with our heavy cushion tired wheels made from hard maple; handsomely ornamented in Brewster green and gilt stripes. The hub caps are made from brass, highly polished, and have strong brass ferrules on the inner part of the hub. Fully described on page 699.

BABY CARRIAGE AND GO-CART UPHOLSTERY.

We call special attention to our complete line of upholstering materials and indicate below the kind of materials, color and price, so that our customers can make a selection of any grade of upholstering desired other than the one regularly described under carriage or go-cart selected.

When a change in upholstering is desired, note the kind of upholstering in the carriage or go-cart you have selected, refer to the price list below to ascertain the value of the upholstering. Deduct this amount from the price of the go-cart or carriage regularly described and then add the price of the upholstering you wish to order. **For instance, if a go-cart is described with "D" cushions of Bedford Cord and you wish "E" cushions of Velour, deduct 70 cents from the price of the go-cart selected and add $2.20, which is the difference between "D" cushions in Bedford Cord and "E" cushions in Velour.** Under the descriptions of medium and large go-carts the wording "D" cushions means quilted seat and back with slumber roll and cords and tassels. "E" cushions are the same as "D" cushions, with the exception that they also have the **sides** upholstered. Upholstery described on small **Folding Go-Carts** is listed as **"F" and "G" cushions.** "F" cushions mean quilted seat and back, and dash with cord and tassels. "G" cushions are same as "F" cushions, with cushions covering both sides added. Carriages are all upholstered in seat, back and sides.

Material	MEDIUM AND LARGE RECLINING Go-Cart Cushions		SMALL FOLDING Go-Cart Cushions		CARRIAGE Upholstery. Furnished with seat, back and sides	COLORS
	"D"	"E"	"F"	"G"		
Denim	$0.60	$1.20	$0.50	$1.00	$1.25	Red, Blue, Myrtle, Golden Brown.
Bedford Cord	.70	1.40	.60	1.20	1.70	Red, Blue, Myrtle, Drab, Tan, Golden Brown.
Novelty Cloth	.75	1.50	.65	1.30	1.75	Red, Blue, Myrtle, Golden Brown.
Whipcord	.90	1.80	.75	1.50	2.25	Drab and Tan.
Velour	1.10	2.20	.80	1.60	2.85	Red, Blue, Green, Golden Brown.
Corduroy	1.15	2.30	.85	1.70	2.95	Red, Blue, Green, Golden Drab.
Simile Lambelle	1.25	2.50	.90	1.80	3.10	Red, Blue, Green, Golden Brown, Steel, Cerise.
Broadcloth	1.30	2.70	.95	1.90	3.15	Drab, Tan, Green.
Silk Damask	....	4.00	1.75	3.50	5.10	Red, Blue, Green, Steel, Cerise.
Silk Plush	....	4.25	1.80	3.60	5.30	Golden Brown, Nile, Cerise.

In every case be sure to state color of upholstering desired.

GRADES OF UPHOLSTERING.

DENIM. Good serviceable figured cotton fabric in bright colors.

BEDFORD CORD. Extra strong and serviceable ribbed material made of tightly woven cotton, furnished in solid colors.

NOVELTY CLOTH. Fancy figured, soft material in brocaded effect.

WHIPCORD. Similar to Bedford Cord, but of softer material and finish.

VELOUR. A sort of velvet plush, silk finished material, high colored floral figures with solid color background.

CORDUROY. Silk finished, closely woven ribbed material, solid colors.

SIMILE LAMBELLE. Mercerized Damask, beautifully figured with solid colored background. Very closely resembles silk.

BROADCLOTH. Fine quality of imported soft woolen material in solid colors.

SILK DAMASK. Beautiful silk brocaded figures of contrasting colors on pure silk background.

SILK PLUSH. Very similar to finest silk velvet, excepting material has extra long nap.

PARASOLS. **These parasols are complete with frame, but do not have the rod and top ball as shown in the illustration.** The parasol alone can be shipped by mail, in which case 16 cents must be allowed to cover prepayment of postage. When rod and top ball are ordered, they must be shipped by express or freight. Price of rod and top ball, **25 cents** extra.

No. 25C1 Percaline Parasol with fancy scalloped edge. Furnished in any color desired.
Price, without rod or top ball.....**39c**

No. 25C8 Extra quality Mercerized Sateen Parasol with fancy shirred ruffle, any color.
Price, without rod or top ball..**$1.29**

No. 25C2 Percaline Parasol, lined with percaline, fancy scalloped edge, any color.
Price, without rod or top ball.....**58c**

No. 25C15 Fine Satin Parasol lined with percaline with large fancy tucked ruffle, any color.
Price, without rod or top ball..**$1.98**

No. 25C5 Sateen Parasol with fancy scalloped ruffle. Any color desired.
Price, without rod or top ball....**89c**

No. 25C20 Liberty Silk Satin Parasol, lined with percaline, with two fancy scalloped ruffles and puff, any color. Price..........**$2.59**

LACE COVERS **are used on Parasols and do not have frames or linings.** You must have a parasol and frame to use a lace cover.

No. 25C25 Lace Cover, made of fly net, with two fancy ruffles and puff trimmed with ribbon, white only.
Price..........**49c**

No. 25C34 Lace Cover, made of fine quality point d'espirit and Bretonne net, with three ruffles and puff. Trimmed with fancy lace insertion. White only. Price......**$1.43**

No. 25C30 Lace Cover, made of fly net, with four fancy ruffles and puff, trimmed with three rows of fancy lace insertion, white only.
Price..........**87c**

No. 25C35 Lace Cover, made of extra quality fine Bretonne net, trimmed with three fancy tucked ruffles and a puff. Color, white only.
Price..........**$1.69**

No. 25C33 Lace Cover, made of good quality Bretonne, with two ruffles of fancy lace, trimmed with wide ribbon; white only.
Price..........**99c**

No. 25C37 Lace Cover, made of finest quality of Bretonne net lace, with double ruffles and a puff. Beautifully trimmed with two rows of fancy lace insertion. Color, white only. Price..**$1.98**

The Following Carts Are the Latest Inventions in Folding Go-Carts With Stationary Backs.

As shown in illustration, these carts can be very closely folded, demonstrating their usefulness, especially when traveling in trains or buggies, street cars, etc., or on the street. When folded all four wheels rest evenly on the floor, allowing it to stand alone whether open or closed. So compact are these carts that they can be folded to occupy the least possible space. They are very light, weighing about 11 pounds, yet very strongly constructed, making the most serviceable cart made for the least money. The materials used are the best money can buy. The gearing is made from tempered steel, finely enameled in Brewster green, and has rubber tired or steel wheels, insuring the most comfortable riding go-cart made for the price.

Our Unique Folding Go-Cart, $1.75.

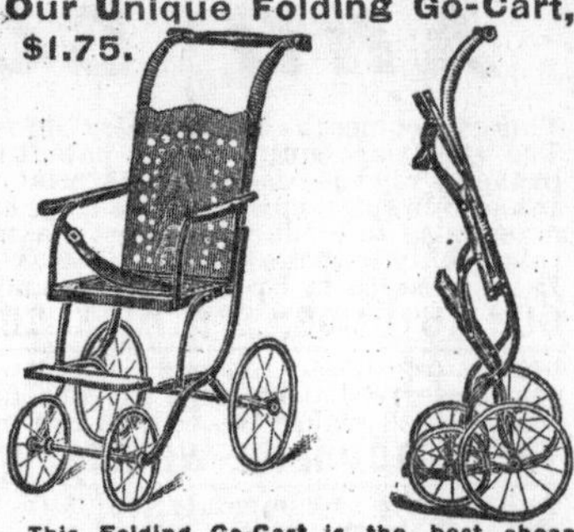

This Folding Go-Cart is the best cheap Go-Cart made. The seat and back are made from three-ply perforated veneer, and all wood parts are of finely selected hard maple, neatly varnished. The folding gear is the latest improved style, and is made from tempered steel enameled in Brewster green. It is fitted with strong steel tired wheels and is a very easy riding go-cart. Shipping weight, 10 pounds.

No. 25C7401 Folding Go-Cart...$1.75
Furnished with rubber tired wheels, 30c extra.

A Splendid Go-Cart for $2.89.

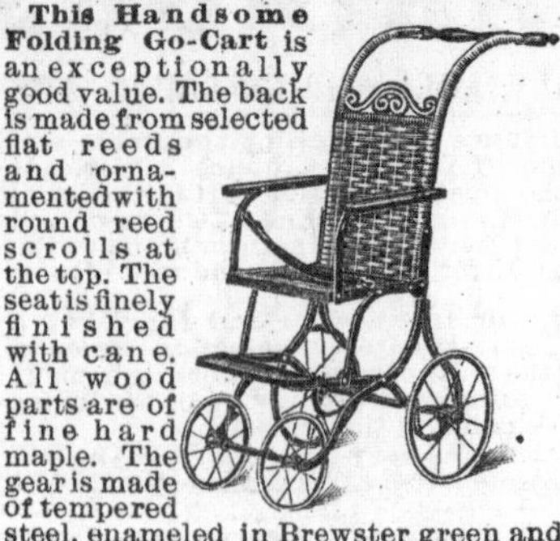

This Handsome Folding Go-Cart is an exceptionally good value. The back is made from selected flat reeds and ornamented with round reed scrolls at the top. The seat is finely finished with cane. All wood parts are of fine hard maple. The gear is made of tempered steel, enameled in Brewster green and striped. Shipping weight, 11 pounds.

No. 25C7421 Folding Go-Cart.
Price.......................... **$2.89**
Furnished with rubber tired wheels, 30 cents extra.

Wonderful Value for $3.43.

Exceptionally good value is given in this Handsome Folding Go-Cart. It is made from choice imported flat reeds, interwoven with round reeds, forming rolled edge, sides and back and has a strong cane seat. The handles are handsomely turned. The frame is made from hard maple in natural finish. The gearing is made from tempered steel and enameled in Brewster green and striped. It is completed with strong steel wheels. Shipping weight, 12 lbs.

No. 25C7431 Folding Go-Cart.
Price.......................... **$3.43**
Rubber tired wheels, 30 cents extra.

RECLINING AND FOLDING GO-CARTS.

This season's line of Reclining and Folding Go-Carts combines all the special features of the large reclining go-cart sleepers and folding go-carts. The back can easily be adjusted to an upright or reclining position, giving greatest comfort to the occupant. The dash can be raised or lowered as desired. In addition to these special features these carts can be compactly folded, therefore taking little room when not in use. They are light in weight and can easily be folded and carried when necessary. The material used in these carts is the best. The gearing is made from oil tempered steel, neatly enameled in Brewster green, neatly striped in yellow.

The seats on these carts are 13½ inches wide and 9½ inches long, excepting Nos. 25C7441 and 25C7451, in which the seat is 11x9½ inches. **These carts are completed with rubber tired wheels,** and are well worth the slight difference over the price asked for the stationary back folding carts.

SHIPPING WEIGHT ON UPHOLSTERED GO-CARTS AVERAGES ABOUT 40 POUNDS.

This Folding and Reclining Go-Cart is very substantially made from select hard maple. The back and seat are made from three-ply veneer in natural finish. The gearing has folding and reclining action and is very strong and well made, being tempered steel finely enameled in Brewster green neatly striped. This cart has strong steel wheels. Shipping weight, 15 pounds.

No. 25C7441 Go-Cart. Price.... **$2.98**
Furnished with rubber tired wheels, 30c extra.

This Folding and Reclining Go-Cart is substantially built and will withstand exceedingly hard usage. The body is made from imported flat reeds closely woven together forming back and dash, and has a strong cane seat. All wood parts are made from hard maple in natural finish. The gear has folding and reclining action and is made from tempered steel. It is enameled in Brewster green neatly striped. This go-cart is completed with strong steel wheels. Shipping weight, 15 lbs.

No. 25C7451 Go-Cart. Price.... **$3.69**
Furnished with rubber tired wheels, 30c extra.

Our $4.39 Folding and Reclining Go-Cart.

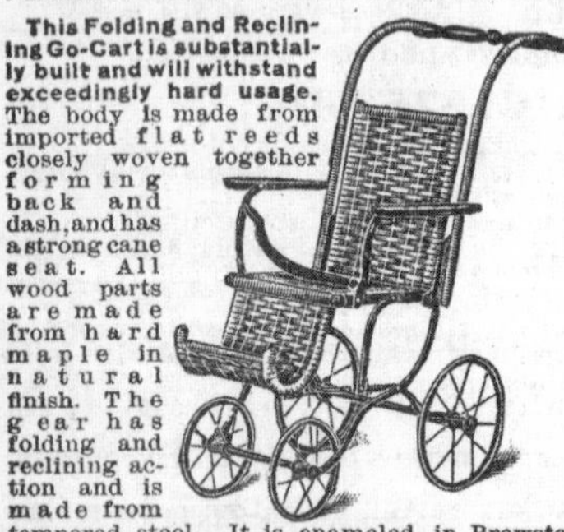

This Attractive Go-Cart is made from fine quality round and flat reeds. Has cane seat. It is finished in natural color, coated with transparent shellac. It has wrought steel handles with three walnut finished grips, the latest folding gear, enameled in Brewster green neatly striped, heavy steel wheels, with rubber caps, patent wheel fasteners and automatic foot brake.

No. 25C7461 Without upholstery and parasol. Price.......................... **$4.39**

No. 25C7462 Upholstered with **Novelty Cloth** ("F" cushions, see page 697). Has sateen parasol with fancy scalloped ruffle and adjustable parasol rod. Price, complete....... **$5.65**
Furnished with rubber tired wheels, 30c extra.

Shipping weight on upholstered Go-Carts average about 40 pounds.

Wonderful Value for $4.89.

The sides, dash and back of this cart are made from select round and flat reeds ornamented with hand turned wood balls. Has cane seat. Finished **throughout** with transparent shellac. Has steel push handles with three walnut finished grips. It has the latest folding and reclining gear, made from tempered steel, enameled in Brewster green, neatly striped, steel wheels with patent rubber hub caps, patent wheel fasteners and automatic foot brake.

No. 25C7471 Without upholstery and parasol. Price.......... **$4.89**

No. 25C7472 Upholstered with **Bedford Cord ("F"** cushions, see page 697). Has sateen parasol with scalloped ruffle and adjustable parasol rod.
Price, complete.................. **$6.32**
Rubber tired wheels, 30 cents extra.

A Bargain at $5.69.

This Handsome Reclining and Folding Go-cart is an exceptionally good value. The body and dash are made from selected round and flat reeds, woven by hand, and has a wheel guard edge ornamented with fancy scrolls. Has cane seat. Finished throughout in natural color and protected from weather by heavy coat of transparent shellac. It has the latest folding and reclining gear, made from finely tempered steel and enameled in Brewster green, neatly striped. Has rubber tired wheels with rubber hub caps, patent wheel fasteners and automatic foot brake.

No. 25C7481 Without upholstery and parasol. Price.......... **$5.69**

No. 25C7482 Upholstered with **Bedford Cord ("F"** cushions, see page 697). Has sateen parasol with fancy scalloped ruffle and adjustable parasol rod. Price, complete.......... **$6.98**

This is a new and striking design. The sides and back are made from flat reeds with fancy figured center and has full roll edge made from selected imported round reeds. The dash is **very strongly** made and is ornamented with hand turned balls. This cart has cane seat. It is coated with transparent shellac. It has the latest style folding and reclining gear; heavy rubber tired wheels with patent rubber hub caps and automatic foot brake, and is enameled in Brewster green, neatly striped.

No. 25C75 1 Without parasol and upholstery. Price.......... **$6.32**

No. 25C7522 Upholstered with **Tapestry ("F"** cushions, see page 697). Has percaline fancy scalloped edge parasol and adjustable rod.
Price, complete.................. **$8.19**

This Folding and Reclining Go-cart is an elaborate cart at a medium price. The body is made from imported round reeds, woven into a handsome design, and has full roll edge and a cane seat. Finished in light natural color and varnished with heavy coat of transparent waterproof shellac. It has the latest improved folding gear, finely enameled in green and neatly striped; heavy rubber tires with rubber hub caps and automatic foot brake.

No. 25C7531 Without parasol and upholstery. Price.............. **$6.87**

No. 25C7532 Upholstered with **Whipcord ("G"** cushions, see page 697). Has percaline scalloped edge parasol and rod. Price, complete....... **$9.46**

Very Elaborate Cart for $7.98.

The sides, back and dash are made from the finest quality of reeds, hand woven into a handsome full roll edge of round reeds with flat reed center. Has cane seat, finished throughout in light natural color and varnished with a coat of transparent **waterproof** shellac. It has the improved folding and reclining gear, finished in Brewster green enamel and neatly striped. Has heavy rubber tired wheels with rubber hub caps and patent foot brake.

No. 25C7561 Without upholstery and parasol. Price.......... **$7.98**

No. 25C7562 Upholstered with **Simile Lambelle ("G"** cushions, see page 697). Has extra quality mercerized sateen parasol with shirred ruffle and puff. Parasol rod. Price, complete. **$10.89**

This is the Best Folding and Reclining Go-Cart made. It is elaborate in design, and is woven by hand from the choicest imported round reeds and has a strong cane seat. The dash has closed sides, ornamented with scrolls and roll edge. It is finished in natural color and heavily coated with transparent shellac. It has the latest improved folding and reclining gear, enameled in Brewster green and striped. Steel handles with three ivory finished grips. The wheels have heavy cushion tires, patent rubber hub caps and a patent automatic foot brake.

No. 25C7581 Without parasol and upholstery. Price............ **$9.45**

No. 25C7582 Upholstered with first quality **Silk Damask ("G"** cushions, see page 697). Has satin parasol, percaline lined, with deep fancy ruffle and adjustable parasol rod.
Price, complete........ .....**$13.95**

MEDIUM SIZE RECLINING GO-CARTS.

THE EVER INCREASING DEMAND for smaller sizes of reclining go-carts has convinced all manufacturers and dealers that the sizes, heretofore offered and marketed were too large to suit the trade, and, therefore, they have in most instances discontinued the large size and have adopted the **medium size go-carts** (as shown on the two following pages) as **standard size**. We especially recommend this size cart to our trade as it is superior in every respect to the largest size go-carts. It is sufficiently large to meet all requirements; it is easier to handle, being less bulky, and equally as comfortable to the occupant. They include all the good features of the largest size carts with many new inventions added and are guaranteed to be the best on the market.

ONLY THE BEST MATERIALS enter into the construction of these carts. The gears are the latest improved patterns which can be furnished in either our **Climax** or **Automobile Climax Gears**—the easiest running gears made—and can be furnished with rubber or heavy cushion tires.

THE SIZE OF THE SEATS IN THESE GO-CARTS IS 14 INCHES IN WIDTH AND 11½ INCHES IN LENGTH.

OUR NEW CONTRACTING GEAR. We call particular attention to our New Contracting Gear, shown on next page, on Go-Cart No. 25C7221. This gear is the very latest invention and is covered by patents so that it can be made only by the manufacturer who furnishes our go-carts. This gear is especially designed for and adapted to our medium sized Reclining Go-Carts, as shown on the following page. It is so constructed that by the very simple operation of bringing the handles forward, the front and rear wheels are brought very closely together (see illustration of cart No. 25C7221). Where this gear is used, the go-cart can be greatly reduced in size, taking up one-third less room than the same style cart with the stationary gear, and therefore can be stored without difficulty in small halls or closets when not in use. **The springs in connection with this gear are so arranged that the cart will run smoothly, without jar or jolt.** Has four extra heavy cushion tires, ⅝ inch in diameter, patent attachment wheel fasteners, rubber hub caps and the latest improved automatic foot brake. It is highly finished in Brewster green enamel and neatly striped.

THE ILLUSTRATIONS of Carts No. 25C7191 and No. 25C7221 show how our medium sized Reclining Go-Carts can be folded up when not in use. Do not overlook the fact that on all our Reclining Go-Cart Sleepers the back and dash can be raised or lowered independently of each other to any position desired. **We quote nearly all of our Go-Carts and Carriages** with or without rubber tires as may be desired by our customers. The rubber tires used on our carriages are made of the very finest quality of rubber, guaranteed strictly high grade, and will outwear rubber tires usually furnished by other manufacturers. We call especial attention to the fact that our cushion tires are ⅝ inches thick, while most all other carts in the market are quoted with very **much smaller tires.** We invite comparison and guarantee to refund your money if you do not find our carts and carriages far better in every respect, and lower in price, than carts offered by any other dealer. Our manufacturer has given us a binding guarantee of prompt service, but as every cart is made to order, we advise you to allow seven to ten days for the cart to reach you after your order has been received by us, but where distances are short, your goods should reach you within five to seven days after the order is received.

Our Leader Go-Cart, Price, $3.95.

The best value ever offered in a cheap go-cart. This cart is very substantially built and of a graceful design. The body is made from selected maple, neatly turned, with sides and dash interwoven with flat reeds; all projecting edges are ornamented with turned wood balls. The foot and back can be adjusted to any angle desired. Has steel push handles, with three walnut finished hand grips. It has our **Climax Gear,** which is enameled in Brewster green and neatly striped. Has 14-inch patent detachable steel tired wheels with patent rubber hub caps and automatic foot brake.

No. 25C7001 Without upholstery and parasol. Price........$3.95

No. 25C7002 Upholstered with "D" cushions of **Denim,** see page 697. Has parasol with full sateen scalloped ruffle and patent parasol attachments, which can be adjusted to any angle. Price....**$5.45**

Furnished with rubber tired wheels, 65c extra.

Exceptionally Good Value for $5.35.

This is a very neat design. The body and dash is made from good quality interwoven flat and round reeds, which makes a solidly built cart. Has steel push handles, with three walnut finished hand grips. The frame is made from seasoned hard wood. It is finished in natural color and heavily coated with transparent shellac. This cart has our improved **ClimaxGear,** fully described on page 697; enameled in Brewster green and neatly striped. The wheels are 14 inches in diameter and are fitted with rubber tires, patent rubber hub caps and automatic foot brake. Both back and dash have automatic device for lowering or raising them to any desired position, and can instantly be converted into a sleeper.

No. 25C7011 Without upholstery and parasol. Price........$5.35

No. 25C7012 Upholstered with "D" cushions of good quality **Bedford Cord,** fully described on page 697. It has a handsome sateen parasol with deep fancy scalloped ruffle, and patent parasol attachments, which can be adjusted to any angle. Price, complete........**$6.85**

With plain steel tired wheels, 65 cents less.

A Bargain for $5.90.

A handsome sleeper cart for little money. The body is made from selected reeds, gracefully constructed with full round rattan scrolls and hand turned spindles and has a cane seat. Has steel push handles and three walnut finished hand grips. It is finished in natural light color fully protected by transparent shellac. This cart has the latest improved **Climax Gear,** fully described on page 697, enameled in Brewster green and fancy striped. It has detachable rubber tired wheels, 14 inches in diameter, patent rubber hub caps, and automatic foot brake.

No. 25C7021 Without upholstery and parasol. Price........$5.90

No. 25C7022 Upholstered with "D" cushions of **Novelty Cloth,** fully described on page 697, furnished with pretty fly net lace cover, with one large ruffle trimmed with ribbon; over durable percaline parasol with scalloped edge. Has attachments which can be adjusted to any angle. Price, complete........**$7.40**

With plain steel tired wheels, 65 cents less.

A New Design for $6.55.

A new and attractive design for a sleeper cart, made of imported reeds neatly woven into a pleasing pattern. Well made throughout and will give excellent service. Has steel push handles, with three walnut finished grips. Has cane seat. Finished throughout in natural color and coated with transparent shellac. Fitted with our Brewster green enameled **Climax Gear,** described on page 697, with four 16-inch rubber tired wheels, rubber hub caps, patent wheel fastener, automatic foot brake and has sleeper attachments.

No. 25C7041 Without upholstery and parasol. Price........$6.55

No. 25C7042 Upholstered with "D" cushions of **Novelty Cloth,** described on page 697. Has handsome sateen parasol with large scalloped edge and patent parasol attachments, which can be adjusted to any angle. Price, complete........**$8.15**

With plain steel tired wheels, 65 cents less.

Our $6.75 Sleeper Cart.

Wonderful value is given in this splendid cart. The body is made from finely selected flat cane reeds, ornamented with rows of round reed scrolls and has strong cane bottom. It is finished in natural color, coated with transparent shellac. Has steel push handles, with three walnut finished grips. Has our **Climax Gear,** fully described on page 697, enameled in Brewster green and fancy striped. It has rubber tired, detachable wheels, 14 inches in diameter, with patent rubber hub caps and automatic foot brake.

No. 25C7051 Without upholstery and parasol. Price........$6.75

No. 25C7052 Upholstered with "D" cushions of **Bedford Cord,** as fully described on page 697. Has handsome sateen parasol with fancy scalloped ruffle (any color), with attachments that can be adjusted to any angle. Price, complete........**$8.20**

With plain steel tired wheels, 65 cents less.

Special Value for $7.45.

This cart is very gracefully constructed from fine quality round and flat reeds and presents a new and novel design. It has full roll hard woven swelled sides, made from choicest whole reeds, and strong cane bottom seat, and finished with transparent shellac, producing a natural light color. Has steel push handles with three walnut finished hand grips. It has **our new Climax Gear,** fully described on page 697, neatly enameled in Brewster green, fancy striped. Wheels are 14 inches in diameter, with rubber tires and patent rubber hub caps. It has automatic foot brake.

No. 25C7071 Without upholstery and parasol. Price........$7.45

No. 25C7072 Upholstered with "D" cushions of **Bedford Cord,** fully described on page 697. Has percaline parasol with fancy scalloped edge, with fine net lace cover trimmed with large fancy ruffle and puff. With attachments that can be adjusted to any position. Price, complete........**$8.90**

With plain steel tired wheels, 65 cents less.

One of Our Best Values for $7.95.

This cart is made from fine quality of selected flat imported reeds closely woven in neat panel design and has a deep French wheel guard edge and heavy cane seat. It is finished in natural color and heavily coated with transparent shellac. Has steel push handles with three walnut finished grips. Has **Automobile Climax Gear,** the finest gear made, fully described on page 697. 14-inch heavy cushion rubber tired wheels with patent rubber hub caps and automatic foot brake. It is handsomely enameled in Brewster green and finely striped.

No. 25C7091 Without upholstery and parasol. Price........$7.95

No. 25C7092 Upholstered with "D" cushions of fine quality **Novelty Cloth,** fully described on page 697 and an extra quality mercerized sateen parasol with deep gathered ruffle and puff in any color. It has parasol attachments and can be adjusted to any angle. Price, complete........**$9.75**

With ordinary rubber tired wheels, $1.00 less.

SHIPPING WEIGHT ON ABOVE CARTS ABOUT 50 POUNDS.

A Wonderful Value at $8.95.

Handsome in appearance, strongly constructed, one of the greatest values offered. It has large rolled edges made from the finest quality of round reeds. The side panels are constructed from selected flat reeds and scrolls, forming a very artistic design. Has cane seat and steel push handles with three walnut finished grips. It is finished in natural color, coated with transparent shellac. It has **Automobile Climax Gear**, the finest made, fully described on page 697, and heavy 14-inch cushion tired wheels, with patent rubber hub caps and automatic foot brake, finished in Brewster green, fancy striped.

No. 25C7131 Without upholstery and parasol..$8.95

No. 25C7132 Upholstered with "D" cushions of **Bedford Cord.** (See page 697). Has percaline parasol with scalloped edge, with fine Bretonne net lace cover, with three deep tucked ruffles. It has parasol attachments and can be adjusted to any angle. Price, complete.......$10.95

With regular Climax Gear (smaller tires) $1.00 less.
With our new Contracting Gear, 60 cents extra.

Our New $7.95 Go-Cart.

As illustration shows, this is an entirely new and novel pattern. It is composed of fancy scrolls of selected reeds. All frame work is gracefully bent and securely glued, screwed and dovetailed. **Has cane seat.** It is finished in light natural color and heavily coated with transparent shellac. Has steel push handles with three walnut finished grips. It has the latest improved **Automobile Climax Gear**, fully described on page 697, with heavy 14-inch cushion tired wheels. It is enameled in Brewster green and fancy striped.

No. 25C7171 Without upholstery and parasol. Price.......$9.95

No. 25C7172 Upholstered with "D" cushions in **Velour**, fully described on page 697, and has fine satin percaline lined parasol with deep fancy ruffle, with parasol attachments that can be adjusted to any angle. Price, complete.......$12.75

Regular Climax Gear, with smaller tires, $1.00 less. Our new Contracting Gear, 60 cents extra.

Splendid Value For $11.50.

No prettier cart is shown this season at so low a price. It is made from selected round reeds which are closely woven, ornamented with fancy scrolls and wood bead trimming. Has cane seated bottom. All frame wood work is covered with rattan. The dash is heavy and well made and has closed sides. Has steel push handles with three walnut finished grips. It has two coats of transparent shellac, producing the natural light finish. It has **Automobile Climax Gear**, only used in the highest grade carts, being very elastic and easy riding. It is neatly enameled in Brewster green, fancy striped. The wheels are 14 inches in diameter and have cushion tires, patent rubber hub caps and automatic foot brake.

No. 25C7201 Without upholstery and parasol. $11.50

No. 25C7202 Upholstered with "E" cushions of **Simile Lambelle**, nicely tufted. (See page 697). Has satin, percaline lined parasol with deep tucked ruffle. It has attachments that can be adjusted to any angle. Price, complete.......$15.65

With our regular Climax Gear (smaller tires), $1.00 less than above prices.
With our new Contracting Gear, 60c more than above prices.

THE SEATS ON THESE GO-CARTS ARE 14 INCHES WIDE AND 11½ INCHES LONG.

Very High Grade Cart for $10.85.

Climax Gear Closed.

This cart is the highest grade in every detail. The body is very elaborate in design, made from selected round reeds, very closely interwoven into one large roll, with ornamental knobs and scrolls, producing a very striking effect. Has cane seat and steel push handles with three ivory enameled grips. It is finely finished with two coats of transparent shellac. It has the latest improved **Automobile Climax Gear**, used only on the highest grade carts. It is very elastic and easy riding. Neatly enameled in Brewster green and fancy striped. The wheels are 14 inches in diameter, and have heavy cushion tires and patent rubber hub caps, automatic foot brake.

No. 25C7191 Without parasol and upholstery. Price.......$10.85

No. 25C7192 Upholstered with **Simile Lambelle Silk**, which is very rich and handsome, ("E" cushions, see page 697) and percaline parasol and fine lace cover with adjustable parasol rod. Price, complete.......$15.25

Our regular Climax Gear, with smaller tires, $1.00 less.
With our new Contracting Gear, 60 cents more than above prices.

This New and Nobby Go-Cart only $12.15.

The body is made from finest quality imported reeds, very closely woven together, forming large shield shaped panels with ornamental rolls and neat mosaic centers. Has cane seat, steel push handles with three ivory enameled grips. It is finished in natural light finish and is coated with waterproof transparent shellac. It has the latest improved **patented contracting gear**, fully described on page 699, finished in Brewster green, enameled neatly, striped, and has 14-inch cushion tired detachable wheels.

Contracting Gear Closed.

No. 25C7221 Without upholstery and parasol. Price.......$12.15

No. 25C7222 Upholstered with fine quality **Corduroy** (choice colors), "E" cushions, quoted and described on page 697. It has a percaline parasol with fancy Bretonne net lace cover, trimmed with three ruffles and two rows of insertion. Parasol attachment can be adjusted to any angle. Price, complete.......$16.45

On this cart we furnish the **New Contracting Gear**, as shown in the illustration. This gear is so constructed that by the simple operation of bringing forward the handle the front and rear wheels can be brought closely together, as illustrated as opened and closed, taking but little room, thus having the same advantages as the folding go-cart.

Automobile Climax Gear, 60 cents less than the above prices.

Special Value for $13.75.

This handsome go-cart is one of the best constructed vehicles on the market and presents an exceptionally handsome appearance. The body is made of imported reeds beautifully woven by hand into a rich shell design. Back and seat are made of closely woven cane. Has steel push handles with three ivory enameled grips. A coat of transparent shellac gives the cart a bright and pleasing appearance. It has our new **Automobile Climax Gear**, fully described on page 697, finished in Brewster green enamel, fancy striped. Has four 14-inch cushion tired wheels, patent wheel fasteners and rubber hub caps. Complete, with brake and automatic sleeper attachments for the back and dash.

No. 25C7251 Without parasol and upholstery. Price.......$13.75

No. 25C7252 Upholstered with "E" cushions of **Simile Lambelle** (see page 697); fitted with a handsome satin parasol, percaline lined, with two tucked ruffles. Has patent parasol attachments, which can be adjusted to any angle. Price, complete.......$17.95

With our new Contracting Gear, 60 cents extra.

This cart furnished with our regular Climax Gear for $1.00 less than above prices.

A New French Design in Go-Carts for $21.95.

As illustration shows, this cart is a work of art, made only by the most skilled weavers. The body is very artistically designed, consisting of large French rolls of the finest selected, closely woven reeds and rattan, and has cane seat. Has steel push handles with three ivory enameled grips. It is finished in natural color and double coated with the best quality of transparent shellac. The seat, back and sides are upholstered with fine **Silk Damask** in choicest patterns (all colors, quoted on page 697). It has fancy percaline lined parasol, with finest quality white Bretonne net lace cover, with four double ruffles and puffs, trimmed with fancy lace insertion. Has patent parasol attachments and can be adjusted to any angle.

No. 25C7272 Go-Cart, as above described, with latest **Automobile Climax Gear**, fully described on page 697, 14-inch heavy cushion tired steel wheels, best oil tempered springs, enameled in Brewster green and fancy striped. Price..$21.95

Same cart as above, but with new artillery rubber tired wooden wheels, highly enameled and fancy striped, with brass hub caps and detachable wheel device. Price.......$22.95

Either gear as above mentioned, with new contracting device, 60 cents extra.

The Most Handsome Go-Cart Made for $24.85.

This is the finest go-cart ever shown regardless of price. The body and dash are made from the finest imported round reeds, every one of which is sanded and finished by hand. All edges are firmly bound by an ornamental rattan braid, greatly adding to the durability and attractiveness of the cart. It is constructed with covered automobile baskets on each side, a very convenient place for carrying baby's wraps, packages, etc. It is handsomely finished in natural light color, doubly coated with transparent shellac. The handle grips are neatly finished with ivory enamel. Seat, back and sides are elaborately upholstered with tufted cushions of **Silk Damask** in choicest patterns. It has a handsome parasol of Liberty silk satin, percaline lined, with two deep ruffles and puff, patent parasol attachments and can be adjusted to any angle. Has patent contracting gear, with artillery wood wheels, highly enameled in Brewster green, handsomely striped. Steel rims and very heavy cushion tires, brass hub caps and patent detachable wheel device.

No. 25C7282 Price, complete as illustrated and described.......$24.85

With Automobile Climax Gear, $1.65 Less.

ALL SLEEPER GO-CARTS HAVE AUTOMATIC SLEEPER ATTACHMENT by which the back and dash can be independently adjusted to any position desired.

OUR LARGEST SIZE
RECLINING GO-CARTS

FOR THE CONVENIENCE OF OUR CUSTOMERS desiring the largest size Go-Cart we have selected eight of the choicest and best patterns of a vast number of designs, especially made and submitted to us, and are positive that no dealer in this country can offer such a fine variety of carts which can equal ours in style, finish, general excellence and construction. The seats on these Go-Carts are 14 inches wide and 16 inches long.

SHIPPING WEIGHT ON THESE GO-CARTS IS ABOUT 60 POUNDS.

Our Leader, $4.95 Sleeper Cart.

This cart is of neat design and constructed in a very strong manner. It has our Climax Gear, enameled in Brewster green, fancy striped. It has steel wheels, 16 inches in diameter, fitted with patent wheel fasteners, rubber hub caps and automatic brake. The body is made of wood with closely woven flat reeds in dash and sides. It has reclining back and raising foot. Finished in natural color, coated with transparent shellac.

No. 25C6401 Without parasol or upholstering. Price.......................... **$4.95**

No. 25C6402 Upholstered with "D" cushions of **Bedford Cord**, fully described on page 697; handsome sateen parasol with fancy scalloped ruffle. Has parasol attachments, which can be adjusted to any angle.
Price, complete **$6.45**

Furnished with rubber tired wheels, 65 cents extra.

Our Special for $6.30.

Made of the finest imported reeds in a very neat pattern. Solid basket woven dash, sides and back. Cane seat. Finished in natural color, coated with transparent shellac. Has our **Climax Gear,** enameled in Brewster green and striped; 16-inch rubber tired wheels, rubber hub caps, patent wheel fasteners and automatic brake. Adjustable back and foot.

No. 25C6411 Without parasol or upholstering. Price.......................... **$6.30**

No. 25C6412 Upholstered with "D" cushions of **Bedford Cord**, fully described on page 697. Furnished with percaline parasol with fly net lace cover, trimmed with two ruffles and puff. Has parasol attachments, which can be adjusted to any angle.
Price, complete **$7.95**

With plain steel wheels, 65 cents less.

Our $6.95 Go-Cart.

This go-cart is made of imported flat and round reeds and has full roll sides, closely woven back and dash, and cane seat. All posts are tipped with turned wooden balls. Finished in natural color, coated with transparent shellac. Has our **Climax Gear,** finished in Brewster green enamel, fancy striped; rubber tired wheels are 16 inches in diameter, put on with patent clamp and fitted with rubber hub caps and automatic brake. Adjustable reclining device for back and dash.

No. 25C6421 Without upholstering or parasol. Price.......................... **$6.95**

No. 25C6422 Upholstered with "D" cushions of **Novelty Cloth,** fully described on page 697; sateen parasol with fancy scalloped ruffle; complete. Has parasol attachments, which can be adjusted to any angle.
Price, complete.......................... **$8.85**

With plain steel wheels, 65 cents less.

Our $7.95 Sleeper Cart.

An original and novel design in a sleeper cart, made with imported reeds woven into an artistic pattern. The handle forms the frame of bed of cart, to which the sides are securely fastened with reeds and screws, making it very strong. The shell design forming sides is one of the neatest of this season. Has closely woven back and cane seat. Finished in natural color, coated with transparent shellac. **It is furnished with our Climax Gear, Brewster green enameled, fancy striped,** and has sleeper attachment for back and dash. The rubber tired wheels are 16 inches in diameter, put on with patent clamp and are fitted with rubber hub caps and automatic brake.

No. 25C6431 Without upholstering or parasol. Price.......................... **$7.95**

No. 25C6432 Upholstered with "D" cushions of **Novelty Cloth,** fully described on page 697. Has percaline parasol with scalloped edge and lace cover of fly net with two fancy ruffles and puff, trimmed with ribbon. Has parasol attachments, which can be adjusted to any angle.
Price, complete.......................... **$9.55**

With plain steel wheels, 65 cents less.

PRICES ON TWIN GO-CARTS QUOTED ON APPLICATION.

Sleeper Cart With Automobile Gear, $9.45.

This is an attractive design, made of the best grade of selected reeds. The seat and back are of closely woven cane. Entire body is finished in natural color, with coating of shellac to protect the reeds. Has our automatic sleeper attachment by which the back and dash can be independently adjusted to any position desired. It is fitted with our celebrated **Automobile Climax Gear,** with 16-inch heavy cushion tired wheels, rubber hub caps, patent wheel fasteners and automatic foot brake. Enameled in Brewster green and decorated with stripes.

No. 25C6441 Without parasol or upholstering. Price.......................... **$9.45**

No. 25C6442 upholstered with "D" cushions of **Novelty Cloth,** fully described on page 697. Handsome satin parasol, percaline lined, with deep fancy ruffle to match upholstering. Has parasol attachments, which can be adjusted to any angle.
Price, complete.......................... **$11.55**

Furnished with regular rubber tired wheels, $1.00 less.

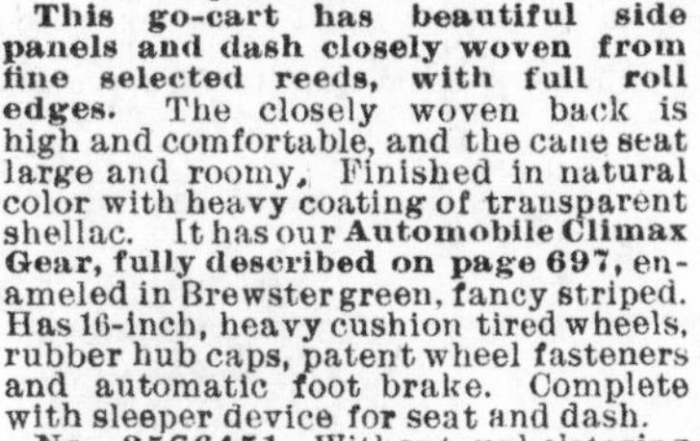

Sleeper Cart With Automobile Gear, $11.65.

This go-cart has beautiful side panels and dash closely woven from fine selected reeds, with full roll edges. The closely woven back is high and comfortable, and the cane seat large and roomy. Finished in natural color with heavy coating of transparent shellac. It has our **Automobile Climax Gear, fully described on page 697,** enameled in Brewster green, fancy striped. Has 16-inch, heavy cushion tired wheels, rubber hub caps, patent wheel fasteners and automatic foot brake. Complete with sleeper device for seat and dash.

No. 25C6451 Without upholstering or parasol. Price.......................... **$11.65**

No. 25C6452 Upholstered with "E" cushions of **Corduroy,** fully described on page 697, and with handsome satin parasol, lined with percaline, with a deep fancy hemmed ruffle. Has parasol attachments, which can be adjusted to any angle.
Price, complete **$15.65**

Furnished with regular rubber tired wheels, $1.00 less.

Sleeper Cart With Automobile Gear for $11.95.

Our handsome shell design, made of imported reeds, with fine, closely woven, high, comfortable back and closed foot. Cane seat. Entire body is finished in natural color, and protected by a heavy coat of transparent shellac. The handle forms part of the frame, giving strength and durability. It has our new **Automobile Climax Gear, fully described on page 697,** finished in the Brewster green enamel, fancy striped. Four 16-inch, heavy rubber cushion tired wheels, patent wheel fasteners and rubber hub caps. Complete with brake and sleeper device for back and dash.

No. 25C6461 Without upholstering or parasol. Price.......................... **$11.95**

No. 25C6462 Upholstered with "E" cushions of **Velour,** fully described on page 697, with handsome satin lined parasol, with one deep hemmed ruffle. Has parasol attachments, which can be adjusted to any angle.
Price, complete **$15.95**

Furnished with regular rubber tired wheels, $1.00 less.

One of Our Handsome Sleeper Carts.

This beautiful scroll design is one of the handsomest patterns shown this season. It has high, closely woven, comfortable back, and roomy seat and dash. **Cane seat.** The handles form part of the bed, making it very strong and durable. Entire body is finished in natural color and protected by a heavy coat of transparent shellac. **It has our new Automobile Climax Gear, fully described on page 697,** enameled in Brewster green, fancy striped. Has 16-inch heavy rubber cushion tired wheels, patent wheel fasteners, rubber hub caps and automatic foot brake. Complete with sleeper attachment for back and dash.

No. 25C6471 Without upholstering or parasol. Price.......................... **$13.85**

No. 25C6472 Upholstered with "E" cushions of **Velour,** fully described on page 697. Has percaline lined parasol with fancy scalloped edge and lace cover of fine Bretonne net with two large tucked ruffles and puff trimmed with two rows of insertion. Parasol any color; lace cover, in white only. Has parasol attachments, which can be adjusted to any angle.
Price, complete **$17.95**

Furnished with regular rubber tired wheels, $1.00 less.

THE BACK AND DASH OF THESE GO-CARTS CAN BE INDEPENDENTLY ADJUSTED TO ANY POSITION DESIRED.

BABY CARRIAGES.

IN PRESENTING OUR NEW LINE OF BABY CARRIAGES we are confident that we are showing the best baby carriages ever offered, at about two-thirds the usual price quoted by other dealers. The numbers shown on this page represent a most careful selection of the newest and most up to date 1905 models, made by the world's most famous manufacturer of children's vehicles.

ALL OUR CARRIAGES are built very substantially of the best materials and have all the latest devices, such as patent automatic foot brakes, steel handles with polished wood grips, patent rubber hub caps, and can be furnished with our Climax, Automobile Climax or Artillery Gears, the easiest running gears made. All our carriages are upholstered with cushion seats, back and two sides with material to harmonize with the balance of the carriage and have latest style parasols with rod and top ball, in fact, they are the best carriages made and are fully guaranteed in every respect.

Our $4.10 Baby Carriage.

No. 25C7602 This carriage is made of good material throughout, having a heavy maple frame glued and fitted at the corners, well finished in every way. It is upholstered with extra good grade of **Denim**, fully described on page 697, making a substantial covering. It has a carved bottom, and steel push handles with three walnut stained and polished grips and neatly shellaced. **The running gear is enameled in Brewster green and is tastily striped.** Has our **Climax Gear** with 16-inch steel wheels—rubber hub caps, patent wheel fasteners, automatic foot brake. The parasol is made of good quality of percaline with fancy scalloped edge, as illustrated. It can be adjusted to any angle. Price..................**$4.10**

Rubber tired wheels, 65c extra.

Our $5.95 Special Bargain.

No. 25C7612 This carriage is designed especially for us. The frame is made of seasoned maple with best grade of rattan scroll work, as illustrated. It is upholstered in extra good quality of **Denim**, fully described on page 697. It has our **Climax Gear**, enameled Brewster green and striped. Has 16-inch rubber tired wheels fitted with patent wheel fasteners, rubber hub caps and patent automatic foot brake. **Constructed so as to give the greatest strength and durability.** Has steel push handles with three walnut finished grips and neatly shellaced. The parasol is made of sateen with fancy scalloped deep ruffle. Color to match upholstering. It has parasol attachments, which can be adjusted to any angle. Price..................**$5.95**

With steel wheels, 65 cents less.

Our Great Value at $6.65.

No. 25C7622 This carriage has a specially constructed body with carved bottom, and built up of best grade of round and flat reeds in such a manner as to give a strong as well as handsome appearance. It has steel handles with three polished walnut grips, and neatly shellaced. The upholstering consists of extra good grade of **Denim** on seat, back and sides, fully described on page 697. It has our **Climax Gear**, enameled Brewster green and striped. Has 16-inch rubber tired wheels, with patent wheel fasteners and rubber hub caps. Complete with our automatic foot brake, which makes the carriage up to date in every respect. Has percaline parasol with fancy, scalloped, deep ruffle and lace cover of fly net, two fancy ruffles and puff, trimmed with ribbon. The parasol can be furnished in any color, but the lace cover in white only. Complete with parasol fixtures, which can be adjusted to any angle. Price..................**$6.65**

With steel wheels, 65 cents less.

Our $7.20 Baby Carriage.

No. 25C7642 This is one of the finest low priced carriages shown this season. The bed is made of best selected light maple with carved bottom and built up of the best grade of round and flat reeds. It has the latest improved steel handles with three polished walnut grips and neatly shellaced. Upholstering is of best grade of **Denim**, fully described on page 697. This makes a very neat and substantial covering for cushions. It has the latest style Brewster green enameled and striped **Climax Gear**, with 16-inch wheels, held to the axle by patent wheel fasteners. Has automatic foot brake. Hubs are fitted with rubber hub caps. Parasol is of sateen with scalloped ruffle. Color to match upholstery. Complete with parasol attachments, can be adjusted to any angle. Price..................**$7.20**

With steel wheels, 65 cents less.

Our Leader at $7.50.

No. 25C7662 Our competition carriage. We have made arrangements with the manufacturer for a large number of these carriages, made up with extra good grade of running gear, upholstering and parasol, and have obtained a price on this first class article that we feel is impossible for competition to meet, considering the material and workmanship put into the construction. **It has a full size reed body with carved bottom. Finished in natural color and heavily coated with transparent shellac. Upholstered in Novelty Cloth, any color, with silk plush roll head rest,** fully described on page 697. Has our **Climax Gear**, finished in Brewster green enamel, fancy striped, with 16-inch wheels fitted with patent wheel fasteners, automatic foot brake, rubber hub caps, and is much more elastic and easy riding than the old style gear. It has a steel handle with fancy walnut grips, which are very strong and durable, giving full control of the carriage. The parasol is of mercerized sateen, having the appearance of silk satin, with scalloped deep ruffle and finished in any color desired. Complete with parasol attachments, which can be adjusted to any angle. Price..**$7.50**

With steel wheels, 65 cents less.

Automobile Sleeper Carriage, $12.95

No. 25C7702 This is a very pretty design, worked out with flat and round reeds, with French rolls on the arms and back. Entire woodwork finished in natural wood, protected by a heavy coat of transparent shellac. It is fitted with our **Automobile Climax Gear**, enameled in Brewster green with fancy stripes. The handles are made of steel and are fitted with three polished walnut grips. Has four 16-inch rubber cushion tired wheels, rubber hub caps, patent wheel fasteners and automatic foot brake. Upholstered in fine **Velour**, fully described on page 697. The parasol is percaline, lined with percaline, scalloped edge, with lace cover of fine Bretonne net. Three fluted ruffles. Parasol can be furnished in any color desired. Cover in white only. Complete with parasol attachments, which can be adjusted to any angle. Price..**$12.95**

With regular rubber tired wheels, $1.00 less.

A Handsome Automobile Carriage for $16.45.

No. 25C7772 This is one of our handsomest carriages. The body is made of closely woven imported round and flat reeds, very best quality. Has cane bottom, high back and front with high French roll arms. Finished in natural color and heavily coated with transparent shellac. The handles form part of the bed, making the carriage extra strong. It has our latest, **Automobile Climax Gear**, finished in Brewster green enamel with fancy stripes. Has four 16-inch, heavy cushion tired wheels, patent wheel fasteners, rubber hub caps and automatic foot brake. Upholstered in **Simile Lambelle**, fully described on page 697. Has percaline lined parasol to match shade of upholstering and fine white Bretonne net lace cover with four large ruffles trimmed with ribbon. Complete with parasol attachments, which can be adjusted to any angle. Price..................**$16.45**

With regular rubber tired wheels, $1.00 less.

Our Finest Carriage.

No. 25C7792 Such a carriage will be found only in the finest stores in large cities. It has an extra high back and scroll design body, made of closely woven, imported round reeds and hand woven cane bottom. Finished in natural color and heavily coated with transparent shellac. Has our **Automobile Comfort Gear**, in which the handle forms a part of the gear, making it easy to guide. Has four 16-inch, heavy cushion tired wheels, with patent wheel fasteners, rubber hub caps and automatic foot brake, finished in Brewster green enamel, with fancy stripes. Upholstered in **Silk Damask**, full described on page 697. Handsome lined percaline parasol to match and extra fine, white Bretonne net lace cover, trimmed with six ruffles and with two rows of insertion and puff. Complete with parasol attachments, which can be adjusted to any angle. Price..................**$19.85**

With regular rubber tired wheels, $1.00 less.

BOOT AND SHOE DEPARTMENT.

HOW TO ORDER. Be sure to state the size and width you want. It is cheaper to send ladies' shoes, slippers, etc., by mail than by express. The postage rate is 1 cent an ounce. When you wish goods sent by mail, always send cash in full, including enough extra to pay postage, and we will ship by mail, postpaid. Be sure and enclose enough extra to pay postage. If you send too much we will promptly return what is over. Weight is given under each description that you may know the amount necessary to send. The widths run: AA, extremely narrow; A, extra narrow; B, very narrow; C, narrow; D, medium; E, wide; EE, very wide.

WE RECOMMEND GOOD SHOES. Poor shoes cost less, but do not wear so well, hence the BEST SHOES ARE CHEAPEST IN THE END.

ANY SHOES PURCHASED FROM US which are not fully up to your expectations, and BETTER VALUE than you can possibly obtain elsewhere, may be returned to us and the purchase price, together with all transportation charges, WILL BE PROMPTLY REFUNDED TO YOU.

THE EDUCATOR SHOE, $3.50 VALUE, OUR PRICE, $2.50.

THE EDUCATOR SHOE, BOTH WOMEN'S AND MEN'S, is made in all leathers, all styles, has a grace of outline, an individuality, and above all a quality of materials and workmanship never found under $3.50 to $4.00.

WE HAVE SPENT MUCH TIME in designing the styles shown below, and we really have never shown a line so handsome, so complete, and never a better shoe at any price. If you don't find the Educator Shoe the equal of any you have ever seen offered at from $3.50 to $4.00, return them at our expense. We refund every cent paid including transportation charges.

Ladies' EDUCATOR Dress Boot, $2.50.

The vamp of this boot is made of high quality guaranteed patent colt stock, the soles are rock oak leather, hand turned. Heel is the very latest full 12-8 Louis XIV style, and being made of leather will outwear any Louis heel ever made. The top of this shoe is made of fine quality mat kid, the eyelets are hand worked with silk thread. The patent leather back stay on the dull top makes a handsome contrast and the EDUCATOR stamp on sole insures quality. Sizes and half sizes, 2½ to 8. Widths, C, D, E and EE. Weight averages 25 ounces.

No. 15C1 Price, per pair...... $2.50

Ladies' EDUCATOR Kid Turn, $2.50.

The finest selection of satin finished vici kid is used in the vamp of this shoe, while the top is cut of the best dull mat kid. Latest style dress last, with patent leather tip, the latest full 12-8 Cuban heel, and genuine rock oak soles, hand turned. The shoe is fitted with fast color eyelets, trimmed in the best possible manner throughout and is the equal of the $3.50 and $4.00 kind usually found at retail. Sizes and half sizes, 2½ to 8. Widths, C, D, E and EE. Weight, 26 ounces.

No. 15C2 Price, per pair...... $2.50

Ladies' EDUCATOR Enamel Welt, $2.50.

AN IDEAL STREET BOOT.

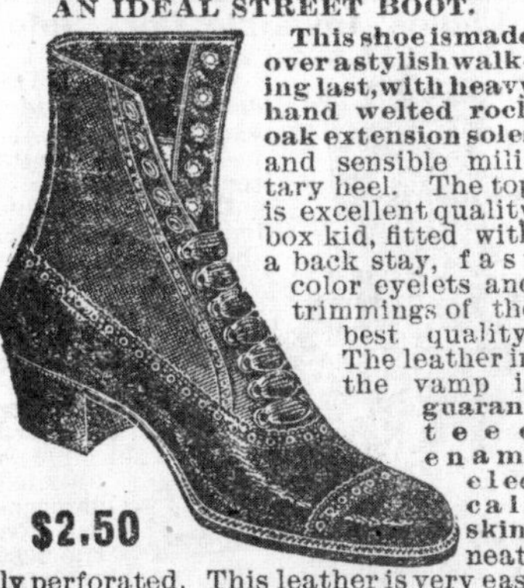

This shoe is made over a stylish walking last, with heavy hand welted rock oak extension soles and sensible military heel. The top is excellent quality box kid, fitted with a back stay, fast color eyelets and trimmings of the best quality. The leather in the vamp is guaranteed enameled calf skin neatly perforated. This leather is very easily polished, and with very little effort can always be kept bright and dressy. Every pair stamped EDUCATOR and guaranteed. Sizes and half sizes, 2½ to 8. Widths, C, D, E and EE. Weight, 32 ounces.

No. 15C3 Price, per pair...... $2.50

Our New EDUCATOR, $2.50.

LADIES' VELOUR CALF LACE. GOODYEAR WELT SEWN SOLES.

One of the hardest things in the shoe business is to make a shoe that will stand hard wear and still be good looking, neat and dressy. We have accomplished it in this shoe. It is suitable for either dress or street wear. Velour calf leather is a light weight, smooth, silky calfskin. Contains a wearing quality of the coarse kind, but is as soft and easy on the foot as the finest vici kid. The soles are heavy weight of clear oak leather, sewn by the Goodyear welt process. Medium height heel. The pattern is cut Blucher style with calf top, fancy perforated, velour calf lace stay and heel foxing. Dull calf top, medium round toe over a well fitting and comfortable last. EDUCATOR stamped on every pair. Sizes, 2½ to 8. Widths, C, D, E and EE.

No. 15C4 Price, per pair........... $2.50

Ladies' EDUCATOR Patent Colt Elastic Instep Lace, $2.50.

AN UP TO DATE STYLE AND A $3.50 QUALITY.

We quote elsewhere the Elastic Instep Shoe, made of kid, at $1.35, and have added this patent corona colt shoe for those who appreciate the comfort and style to be found only in this new patent leather. This patent leather is soft as kid, will not crack or draw the feet and can be kept bright as new by rubbing with a flannel cloth. The elastic gore instep fits high or low instep, conforms to every movement of the foot, and is becoming very popular. EDUCATOR stamped on sole—you know what that means. Sizes and half sizes, 2½ to 8. Widths, C, D, E and EE. Weight, 25 ounces.

No. 15C5 Price, per pair...... $2.50

Ladies' EDUCATOR Kid Boot, $2.50.

The handsomest pattern we have yet shown, combining the late high vamp, giving the high arch instep effect, with the patent colt tip and heel foxing. The upper stock is the finest mellow vici kid, while the sole is the very best rock oak, sewn on by hand, producing at once one of the most fashionable and comfortable light weight boots we have ever offered. Every pair stamped EDUCATOR, which means a guaranteed $3.50 value. Sizes, 2½ to 8. Widths, C, D, E and EE. Weight, averages 25 ounces.

No. 15C7 Price, per pair....... $2.50

Ladies' EDUCATOR Patent Colt Blucher, $2.50.

ANOTHER ONE OF OUR GREAT VALUES IN THE EDUCATOR LINE, SUCH AS RETAILS FOR $3.50.

Made of best guaranteed corona colt patent leather, with medium width tip toe and dull box kid top. The style is the very latest blucher pattern, with patent leather lace stay and sensible walking heel. The sole is cut from best rock oak sole leather, and being sewn on by the Goodyear welt process, insures a perfectly smooth insole and the most comfortable and serviceable patent shoe it is possible to make. This is the handsomest style we have seen and is extraordinary value. Sizes and half sizes, 2½ to 8. Widths, C, D, E and EE. Weight, 30 ounces.

No. 15C8 Price, per pair........... $2.50

Ladies' EDUCATOR Patent Colt Button, $2.50.

There is nothing in ladies' footwear quite so snappy and thoroughly up to date, and so universally popular, as the boot herewith illustrated. This boot is made from the very best selection of patent corona colt—the most satisfactory bright leather ever tanned—is made over the fashionable university last, with tip toe and full Cuban heel. The top is of dull mat calf, fitted with dull buttons; black satin inside facing and custom outside back stay. The soles are of medium weight, cut from first quality white oak sole leather; Goodyear welt sewn, producing a flexible and a perfectly smooth inner sole (no tacks or thread to hurt the foot). We guarantee the EDUCATOR equal to shoes generally sold at $3.50. Sizes and half sizes, 2½ to 8. Widths, B, C, D, E and EE. Weight averages 27 ounces.

No. 15C9 Price, per pair........... $2.50

Women's EDUCATOR Patent Colt Welt, $2.50.

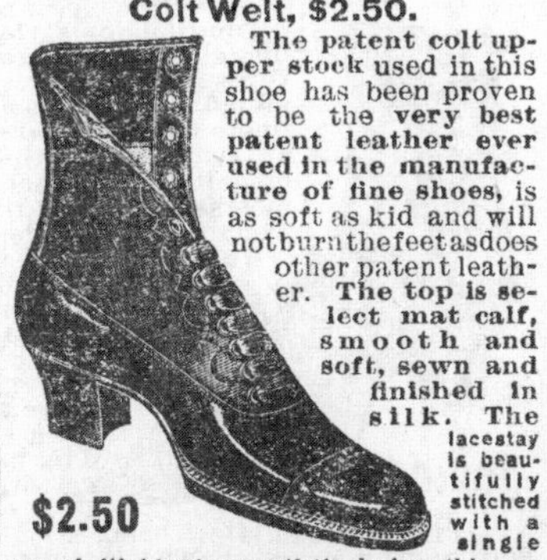

The patent colt upper stock used in this shoe has been proven to be the very best patent leather ever used in the manufacture of fine shoes, is as soft as kid and will not burn the feet as does other patent leather. The top is select mat calf, smooth and soft, sewn and finished in silk. The lacestay is beautifully stitched with a single row of stitching in an artistic design; this may well be called a perfect shaped shoe, having a medium round toe with straight tip and the latest heel. Sizes and half sizes, 2½ to 8. Widths, C, D, E and EE. Weight, 24 ounces.

No. 15C13 Price, per pair........... $2.50

For postage rate see page 4.

Ladies' EDUCATOR Patent Colt Welt, $2.50.

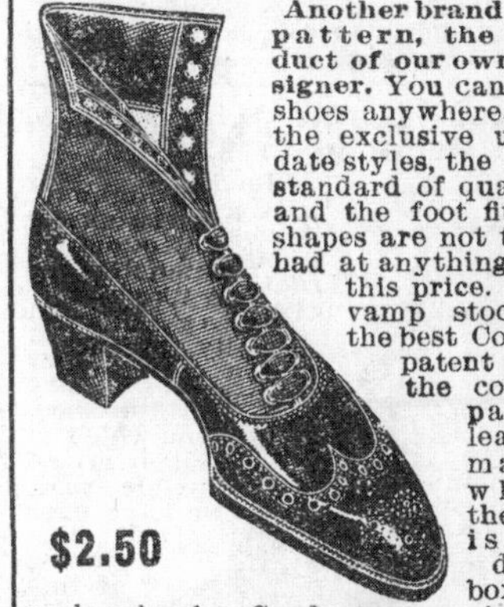

Another brand new pattern, the product of our own designer. You can buy shoes anywhere, but the exclusive up to date styles, the high standard of quality, and the foot fitting shapes are not to be had at anything like this price. The vamp stock is the best Corona patent colt, the coolest patent leather made, while the top is of dull boxkid, rock oak soles, Goodyear sewn, insure flexibility, and the EDUCATOR stamp on each pair guarantees the wear, workmanship and general high quality, the equal of any $3.50 shoe, and many at even higher prices. Sizes, 2½ to 8. Widths, C, D, E and EE. Weight averages 28 ounces.

No. 15C14 Price, per pair.. $2.50

Ladies' EDUCATOR Kid Welt, $2.50.

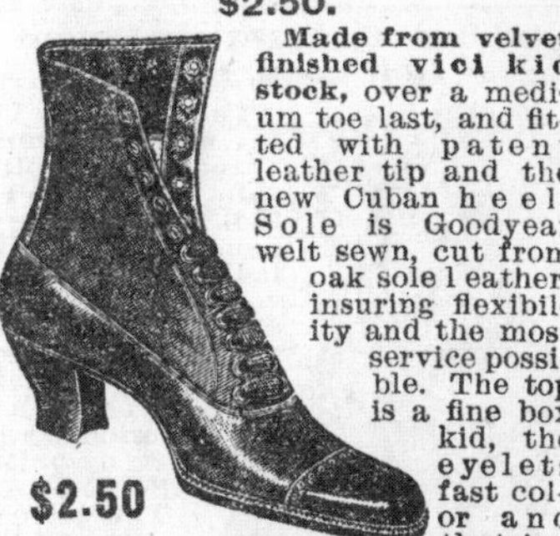

Made from velvet finished vici kid stock, over a medium toe last, and fitted with patent leather tip and the new Cuban heel. Sole is Goodyear welt sewn, cut from oak sole leather, insuring flexibility and the most service possible. The top is a fine box kid, the eyelets fast color and the trimmings of the best. No detail overlooked, and the name EDUCATOR insures the foot fitting, shape retaining qualities so much desired and never found at this price. Sizes and half sizes, 2½ to 8. Width, C, D, E and EE. Weight averages 29 ounces.

No. 15C15 Price, per pair.. $2.50

Ladies' EDUCATOR High Cut Velour Calf, $2.50.

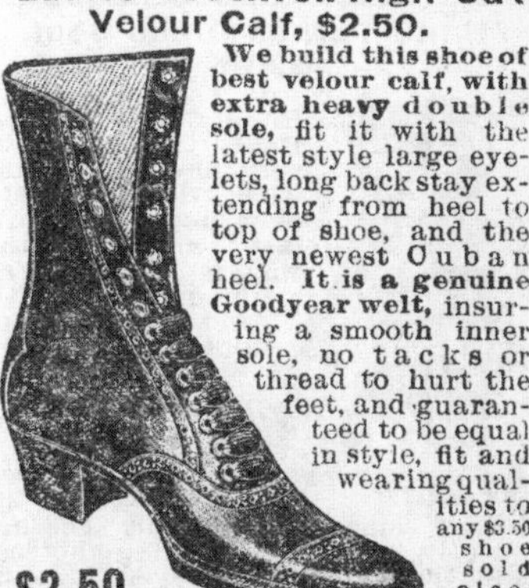

We build this shoe of best velour calf, with extra heavy double sole, fit it with the latest style large eyelets, long back stay extending from heel to top of shoe, and the very newest Cuban heel. It is a genuine Goodyear welt, insuring a smooth inner sole, no tacks or thread to hurt the feet, and guaranteed to be equal in style, fit and wearing qualities to any $3.50 shoe sold elsewhere. Sizes and half sizes, 2½ to 8. Widths, C, D, E and EE. Weight averages 32 ounces.

No. 15C16 Price, per pair....... $2.50

For postage rate see page 4.

The Elite, $2.00.

Ladies' Up to Date Congress Shoe. Made from finest chrome vici kid, over the late style coin toe last, with fancy patent leather tip and front stay. The sole is cut from flint-stone oak sole leather, is very flexible, and will outwear any sole tanned. It fits like a glove, has no buttons or laces to annoy you, can be put on or taken off in an instant, is suitable for house or street wear, and is 50 per cent cheaper than any similar shoe of the same quality. Sizes and half sizes, 2½ to 8. Widths, D, E and EE. Weight averages 32 ounces.

$2.00

No. 15C18 Price, per pair....$2.00

For postage rate see page 4.

Ladies' Leather Lined Shoe, Reduced to $2.00.

Lined throughout with genuine kid, thereby producing a shoe which fits the foot just like a silk stocking. Has an especially prepared cushion cork inner sole, making a very comfortable shoe, and one which is much more flexible than we have ever been able to offer at this price. The stock is a soft, plump vici kid, the style of last is a medium coin toe (not extreme), while the heel is a medium military style. Sizes and half sizes, 2½ to 8. Widths, D, E and EE. Weight averages 30 ounces.

$2.00

No. 15C21 Price, per pair....$2.00

For postage rate see page 4.

Ladies' Guaranteed Patent Colt Lace, $2.00.

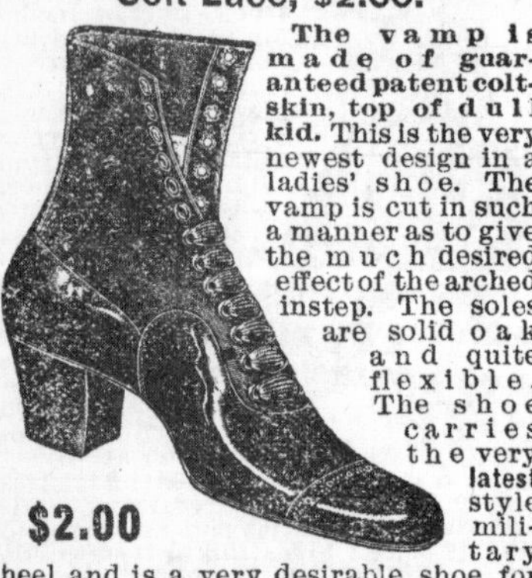

The vamp is made of guaranteed patent colt-skin, top of dull kid. This is the very newest design in a ladies' shoe. The vamp is cut in such a manner as to give the much desired effect of the arched instep. The soles are solid oak and quite flexible. The shoe carries the very latest style military heel and is a very desirable shoe for dress wear. Sizes and half sizes, 2½ to 8. Widths, D, E and EE. Weight averages about 25 ounces.

$2.00

No. 15C25 Price, per pair.....$2.00

Hand Turned Dress Boot, $2.25.

A Ladies' Strictly Hand Sewed Turned Boot. Made from a very fine, velvet finished vici kid stock, over our New York last (which, by the way, is our newest production), with kid tip, medium opera heel and the latest full outside back stay; materials which enter into the construction of this shoe are strictly first class, including the best silk thread, fast color eyelets, genuine white oak sole leather. Sizes and half sizes, 2½ to 8. Widths, C, D, E and EE. Weight averages 19 ounces.

$2.25

No. 15C26 Price, per pair $2.25

For postage rate see page 4.

Ladies' Box Calf Blucher, Reduced to $1.75.

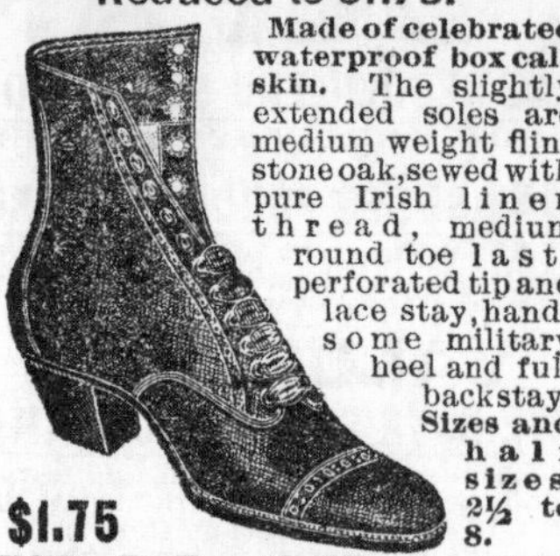

Made of celebrated waterproof box calf skin. The slightly extended soles are medium weight flint stone oak, sewed with pure Irish linen thread, medium round toe last, perforated tip and lace stay, handsome military heel and full backstay. Sizes and half sizes, 2½ to 8. Widths, D, E, and EE. Average weight per pair, 25 ounces.

$1.75

No. 15C27 Price, per pair....$1.75

For postage rate see page 4.

Ladies' Fancy Vesting Top Lace, $1.50.

We make this shoe of a fine velvet finished vici kid stock with fancy, good wearing vesting top. Leather heel and foxed, in an artistic design. This shoe is fitted with genuine oak soles which are very flexible. The inner sole and counter are absolutely all solid sole leather. Sizes and half sizes, 2½ to 8. Widths, D, E and EE. Weight averages 25 ounces.

$1.50

No. 15C28 Price, per pair... $1.50

For postage rate see page 4.

Ladies' Swell Vici Blucher, $2.25.

GOODYEAR WELT.

This is a very neat and dressy shoe, made from an extra fine selection of vici kid with the patent tip and up to date military heel. No better wearing material can be used for a ladies' shoe than kidskin, and when made over a stylish last and a well fitting pattern, as illustrated, it makes a very attractive shoe. It is a genuine Goodyear welt, with a medium weight flexible sole and is extraordinary value. Sizes, 2½ to 8. Widths, C, D and E. Weight averages 28 ounces.

$2.25

No. 15C34 Price, per pair....$2.25

Ladies' Patent Leather Blucher, $2.00.

The Blucher style being all the rage this season, we have added this shoe made from a guaranteed patent leather colt, which is the most serviceable patent leather made. We fit this shoe with dull mat calf top, Cuban heel and good wearing soles of medium weight. The style of last is the latest, being a medium width toe, and the shoe is stylish enough and good enough to sell at a much higher price. Sizes and half sizes, 2½ to 8. Widths, D, E and EE. Weight, 28 ounces.

$2.00

No 15C35 Price, per pair....$2.00

The Stage Favorite, $2.25.

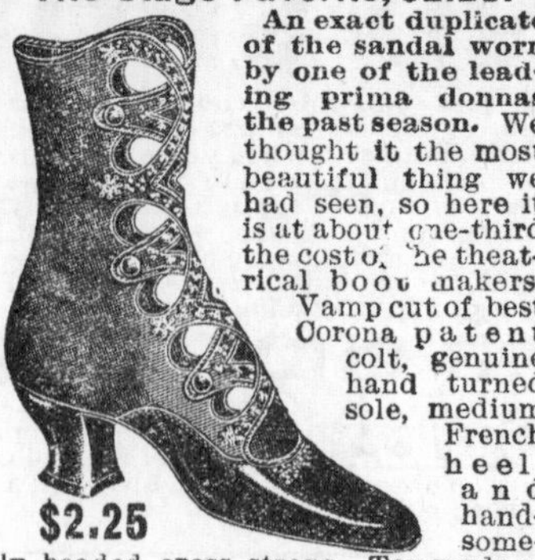

An exact duplicate of the sandal worn by one of the leading prima donnas the past season. We thought it the most beautiful thing we had seen, so here it is at about one-third the cost of the theatrical boot makers. Vamp cut of best Corona patent colt, genuine hand turned sole, medium French heel, and handsomely beaded cross straps. Top made of best box kid, producing a novelty for house party or dancing, at a price within the reach of all. Sizes and half sizes, 2½ to 8. Widths, C, D, E and EE. Weight, averages 18 ounces.

$2.25

No. 15C37 Price, per pair....$2.25

Ladies' Fancy Scroll Lace, $2.00.

Patent leathers have become so popular that we have, in the boot herewith illustrated, combined the patent leather with a fine selection of vici kid. This shoe is made with a light, flexible sole, fitted with latest Cuban heel, outside custom back stay, perfectly smooth inner sole, and while it is more comfortable to the wearer than the all patent leather shoe, it is also one of the handsomest styles we have ever seen. Sizes and half sizes, 2½ to 8. Widths, C, D, E and EE. Weight averages 27 ounces.

$2.00

No. 15C41 Price, per pair....$2.00

Ladies' Goodyear Welt Lace Reduced to $2.00.

This shoe is a genuine Goodyear welt vici kid, made over our handsome Beloit last, fitted with genuine patent calf tip and the latest military heel. Being a genuine Goodyear welt shoe, the wearer is insured a perfectly smooth inner sole, no tacks or thread to hurt the foot. A special value and warranted. Sizes and half sizes, 2½ to 8. Widths, D, E and EE. Weight averages 25 ounces.

$2.00

No. 15C45 Price, per pair....$2.00

Ladies' Kid Welt, $2.00.

A modern swing last, one that is designed to fit the foot and at the same time look neat. Fine vici kid is used in the vamp, while the top is of dull box kid. Fitted with patent leather tip, custom outside back stay and plump Goodyear welt sewn soles. This shoe is very stylish and is guaranteed to give satisfactory service and more comfort than you ever realized could be had for this price. Sizes, 2½ to 8. Widths, D, E and EE. Weight averages 26 ounces.

$2.00

No. 15C46 Price, per pair....$2.00

Ladies' Box Calf, Goodyear Welt Lace, $2.00.

Box calf stock is especially desirable from the fact that it can be polished by simply applying patent leather paste and rubbing with a flannel cloth. In this, our highest grade Goodyear welt box calf shoe, we use only the very best materials throughout. The stock is medium weight, as easy as kid, and twice as durable. Sizes and half sizes, 2½ to 8. Widths, C, D, E and EE. Weight averages 33 ounces.

$2.00

No. 15C47 Price, per pair..$2.00

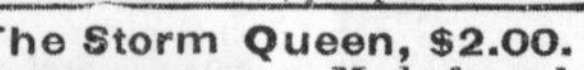

The Storm Queen, $2.00.

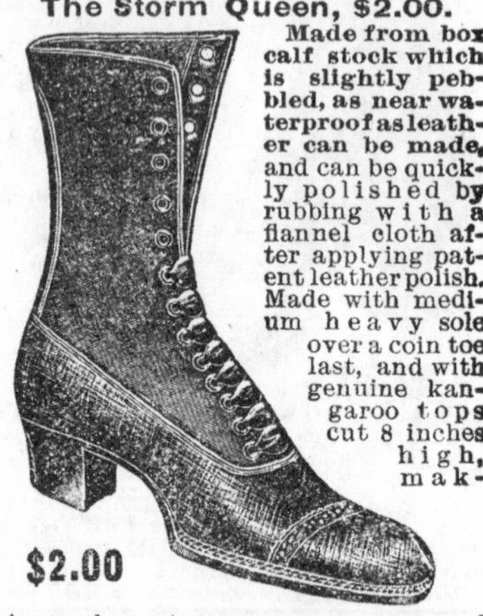

Made from box calf stock which is slightly pebbled, as near waterproof as leather can be made, and can be quickly polished by rubbing with a flannel cloth after applying patent leather polish. Made with medium heavy sole over a coin toe last, and with genuine kangaroo tops cut 8 inches high, making a shoe at once warm, snowproof and a splendid ankle support for those who skate. Warranted. Sizes and half sizes, 2½ to 9. Widths, D, E and EE. Weight averages 33 ounces.

$2.00

No. 15C50 Price, per pair..$2.00

Ladies' Fancy Scroll Lace, $2.00.

A handsome shoe, solid throughout, a perfect fitter, a fine vici kid upper and vamp stock, genuine McKay turned sole, very flexible, latest style perforated patent calf tip, medium coin toe (not extreme), fancy folded edge heel foxing and back stay, fast color eyelets, sewed throughout with silk, inside fitted with leather top band and lace stay, and price extremely low. Sizes and half sizes, 2½ to 8. Widths, C, D, E and EE. Weight averages 24 ounces.

$2.00

No. 15C54 Price, per pair. $2.00

Ladies' Invisible Cork Sole Lace, $2.00.

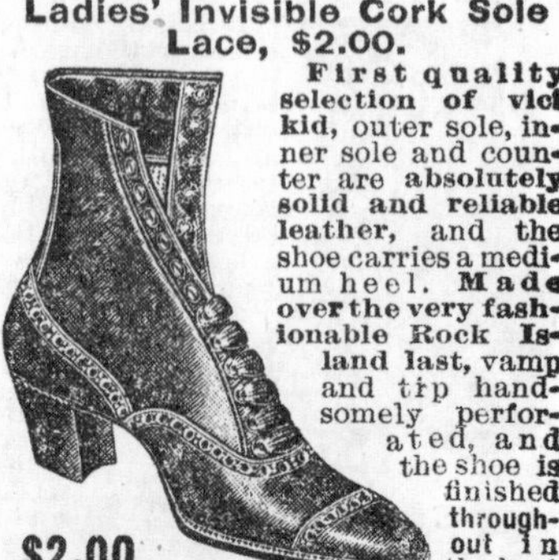

First quality selection of vici kid, outer sole, inner sole and counter are absolutely solid and reliable leather, and the shoe carries a medium heel. Made over the very fashionable Rock Island last, vamp and tip handsomely perforated, and the shoe is finished throughout in the best possible manner. The cushion cork invisible sole produces one of the most comfortable shoes it has ever been our pleasure to offer. Sizes and half sizes, 2½ to 8. Widths, D, E and EE. Weight averages 29 ounces.

$2.00

No. 15C58 Price, per pair...$2.00

For postage rate see page 4.

Elastic Instep Lace, $1.35.

Ever since we first offered the Elastic Instep Shoe we have been below all others in price, with the result that we sell more than all other dealers combined. Vici kid stock, latest style foxing, protected elastic goring at the instep, yields to every action of the foot. Fits high on low instep. Absolutely all solid and serviceable. The equal of shoes sold from $1.48 to $2.00. **Sizes and half sizes, 2½ to 8. Widths, D, E and EE.** Weight averages 28 ounces.

$1.35

No. 15C66 Price, per pair. ..$1.35

Ladies' NINE-STRAP Sandals, Reduced to $1.50.

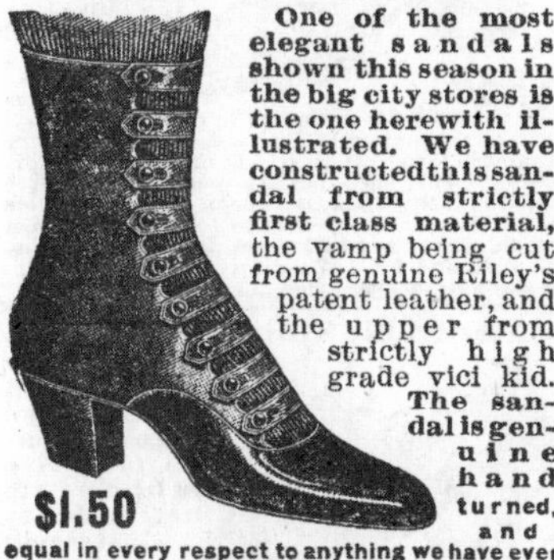

$1.50

One of the most elegant sandals shown this season in the big city stores is the one herewith illustrated. We have constructed this sandal from strictly first class material, the vamp being cut from genuine Riley's patent leather, and the upper from strictly high grade vici kid. **The sandal is genuine hand turned, and equal in every respect to anything we have ever seen offered at double our price.** Especially designed for party and house wear. **Sizes and half sizes, 2½ to 8. Widths, C, D, E and EE.** Weight averages 18 ounces.

No. 15C70 Price, per pair..........$1.50

For postage rate see page 4.

Ladies' Patent Colt Blucher, $2.00.

$2.00

The Blucher style is one of the most popular shoes we have ever offered, is all the rage in the large cities, and is a style which is at once comfortable and foot fitting. This shoe is made of the very best patent corona colt, with fancy **patent leather** lace stay and dull box kid top, which with the **patent leather trimmings, produces a very pretty contrast.** The style of last is the latest, the heel is of the full military shape, the sole of the good quality union sole leather, and altogether, we consider this one of the greatest values we have ever been able to offer. **Sizes and half sizes, 2½ to 8. Widths, D, E and EE.** Weight, 24 ounces.

No. 15C75 Price, per pair..... .....$2.00

For postage rate see page 4.

The Latest Style Common Sense Lace $1.85.

$1.85

We make this shoe from a fine soft vici kid, over a handsome round toe common sense last and with straight perforated patent leather tip. The soles are cut from good oak sole leather, flexible as a hand turn and much more durable than those usually found on a shoe at this price. The back stay is of the very latest pattern, making it absolutely rip proof, and to add all the comfort possible, we fit the shoe with the very latest style low heel, which is the most comfortable made. Sizes and half sizes, 2½ to 9. Widths, D, E and EE. Weight averages 29 ounces.

No. 15C79 Price, per pair..........$1.85

For postage rate see page 4.

Ladies' Patent Colt $1.50.

The shoe herewith illustrated is something never before offered at anything like this price, but we were enabled to purchase a very large quantity of this excellent patent colt and have made it into the shoe herewith illustrated, producing it at the unheard of price of $1.50. The style of last is the medium round toe. The shoe is fitted with mat calf top, the latest style heel flexible sole, custom outside back stay, and is reliable. **Sizes and half sizes, 2½ to 8. Widths, D, E and EE.** Weight averages 20 ounces.

$1.50

No. 15C82 Price, per pair.........$1.50

For postage rate see page 4.

Ladies' Low Heeled Shoes, $1.75.

$1.75

This shoe is made from genuine vici kid, on a medium coin toe last, with medium weight sewn sole, slightly extended edges, and the low heel so comfortable and so much in demand.

This is one of the best shoes we quote in the low heel style, is made in a thoroughly first class factory, absolutely all solid counter and inner sole, will give excellent satisfaction, at the same time being very dressy. **Sizes and half sizes, 2½ to 7. Widths, full.** Weight averages 30 ounces.

No. 15C84 Price, per pair....$1.75

Ladies Dongola Lace, Suitable for Street Wear, $1.60.

$1.60

This shoe is made of good quality vici kid stock, made over the latest Newark last; patent tip. Outer and inner sole and counter are absolutely solid and reliable leather. The vamp is high cut in a new and handsome arched instep pattern. The heel is a medium height. It is especially desirable for street wear. **Sizes, 2½ to 8. Widths, D, E and EE.** Weight, 30 ounces.

No. 15C86 Price, per pair...$1.60

Ladies' Vici Kid Lace, $1.50.

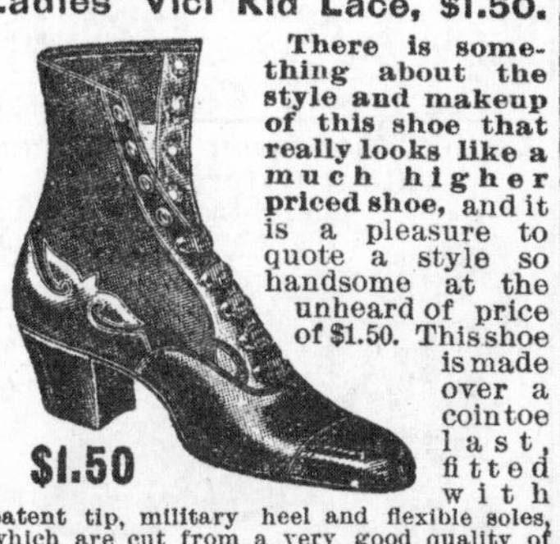

$1.50

There is something about the style and makeup of this shoe that really looks like a much higher priced shoe, and it is a pleasure to quote a style so handsome at the unheard of price of $1.50. This shoe is made over a coin toe last, fitted with patent tip, military heel and flexible soles, which are cut from a very good quality of union leather. The vamps are of good vici kid, the top being a dull box kid, splendidly trimmed throughout. **Sizes and half sizes, 2½ to 8. Widths, D, E and EE.** Weight averages 22 ounces.

No. 15C91 Price, per pair....$1.50

For postage rate see page 4.

Ladies' Genuine Box Calf Leather Lined Lace, $1.50.

$1.50

This shoe is made of box calfskin; the soles are of extra quality leather and are very serviceable. The seams are stitched with a double row of stitching which is practically rip proof. Carries a full back stay, medium heel, and is lined throughout with leather. While this shoe is built with the intention of being one of the best wearing shoes that we carry, it is, at the same time, a neat appearing shoe. **Sizes, 2½ to 8. Widths, D, E and EE.** Average weight about 24 ounces.

No. 15C97 Price, per pair....$1.50

Ladies' Spring Heel Lace, $1.50

$1.50

Ladies' spring heel shoes to fit well should be made over lasts made especially for spring heels, and we wish to call special attention to the fact that these, **our $1.50 shoes are made over our own lasts,** made by us with the one desire to produce, at a price within the reach of all, a shoe which would tread square and fit the foot in the same manner as the very best shoe made. **This shoe is cut from a good plump dongola kid, bright finish and serviceable. The last is the popular coin, which is the very latest style,** is round and about the width of a half dollar across the toe. **The tip** is of the newest design and cut from imported patent leather. **The bottoms** are cut from fine Union sole leather, sewed on by the McKay process, **very flexible and durable. Sizes, 2½ to 8. Widths, D, E and EE.** Weight, 19 ounces.

No. 15C99 Price, per pair....$1.50

Ladies' Vici Kid Lace, $1.50.

$1.50

Made of good soft vici kid stock over a medium broad toe last, with patent leather tips, slightly perforated vamp and sensible heel.

The soles are medium heavy, fair stitched edges, so that the shoe really looks like Goodyear welt.

Counter and inner sole are solid sole leather, and the shoe is built for service. **Sizes and half sizes, 2½ to 8. Widths, D, E and EE.** Weight, 29 ozs.

No. 15C101 Price, per pair ...$1.50

Ladies' Kid Lace, $1.35.

$1.35

Many of our customers have been surprised to buy a shoe for so little money and still get excellent wear. The service which this shoe gives does not surprise us, from the fact that we cut a **good selection of chrome kid,** use a splendid sole leather and have it made by shoemakers **who have a reputation for turning out wear resisting shoes. The style of last is a medium coin,** kid tip and lace stay, and it is a desirable shoe for the money. **Sizes and half sizes, 2½ to 8. Widths, D, E and EE.** Weight averages 29 ounces.

No. 15C103 Price, per pair....$1.35

For postage rate see page 4.

Ladies' Kid Congress Comfort Shoe, $1.50.

$1.50

We make this Ladies' Congress Shoe from a fine dongola kid stock, which is very much finer than we have ever been able to offer. Made over a common sense last, with heavy hand turned soles, which are very **flexible and being specially selected from Rock Oak, will outwear any turn shoe we have ever offered. To give the shoe more style than ordinarily found,** we fit with it the late style back stay. **Bear in** mind the fact that the materials are all specially selected, and quality the aim, rather than price. **Extraordinary value. Sizes and half sizes, 2½ to 9. Widths, EE.** Weight averages 29 ounces.

No. 15C105 Price, per pair.....$1.50

Ladies' Box Calf Lace, $1.50.

$1.50

We make this shoe over the St. Louis common sense last, with low, sensible heel, absolutely **solid** sole leather counter and inner sole, and suitable for hard wear. **The shoe is made in the same factory as our higher grade shoes, hence fits better and shows a good deal more style than is usually found in this kind of a shoe. Sizes and half sizes, 3 to 8. Full widths.**

Weight averages 28 ounces.

No. 15C107 Price, per pair.....$1.50

Ladies' Patent Colt Bluchor, $1.50.

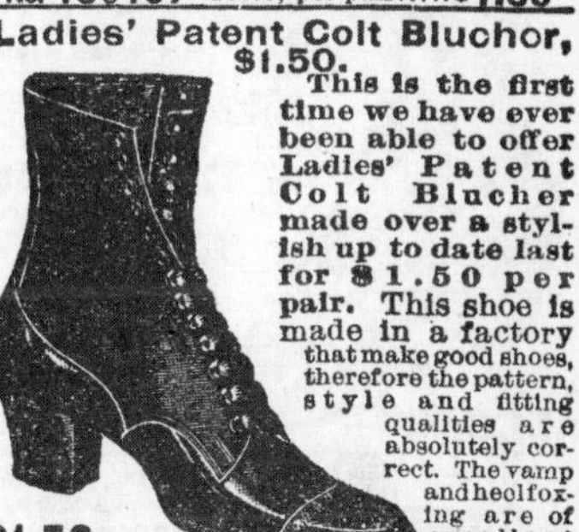

$1.50

This is the first time we have ever been able to offer Ladies' Patent Colt Blucher made over a stylish up to date last for $1.50 per pair. This shoe is made in a factory that make good shoes, therefore the pattern, style and fitting qualities are absolutely correct. The vamp and heel foxing are of excellent quality patent colt, the top is of dull mat calf, cut in the Blucher style which is all the rage this season. This shoe carries a medium weight slightly extended sole and a medium height Cuban heel. This shoe has the appearance of a high priced shoe and will give satisfactory wear. **Sizes and half sizes, 2½ to 8. Widths, D, E and EE.** Wt. averages 28 ozs.

No. 15C110 Price, per pair......$1.50

Ladies' Vici Kid Lace, $1.35.

$1.35

This boot is made over the fashionable Rochester last, with patent leather tip, medium weight, imitation welt sole, and suitable for dress or street wear. **The stock is a velvet finished vici kid, and mat calf top. Counter and inner sole are of one piece of sole leather** and the shoe is very serviceable. **Sizes and half sizes, 2½ to 8. Widths, D, E and EE.** Weight, 28 ounces.

No. 15C111 Price, per pair.... $1.35

Women's Box Calf Lace, $1.50.

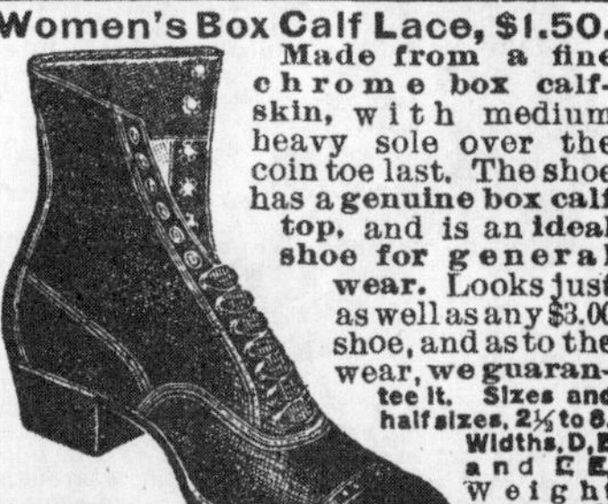

$1.50

Made from a fine chrome box calfskin, with medium heavy sole over the coin toe last. The shoe has **a genuine box calf top, and is an ideal shoe for general wear.** Looks just as well as any $3.00 shoe, and as to the wear, we guarantee it. **Sizes and half sizes, 2½ to 8. Widths, D, E and EE.** Weight averages 38 ounces.

No. 15C114 Price, per pair.....$1.50

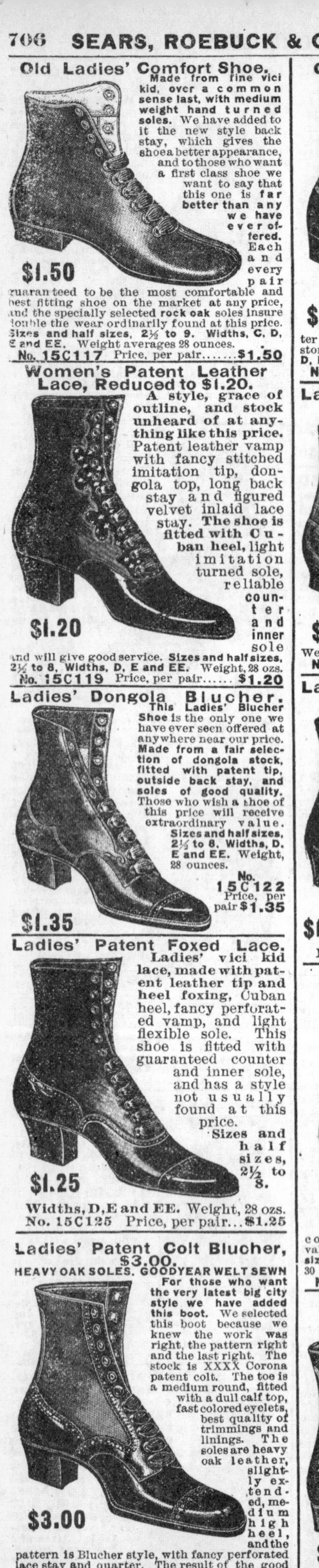

Old Ladies' Comfort Shoe.

Made from fine vici kid, over a common sense last, with medium weight hand turned soles. We have added to it the new style back stay, which gives the shoe a better appearance, and to those who want a first class shoe we want to say that this one is far better than any we have ever offered. Each and every pair guaranteed to be the most comfortable and best fitting shoe on the market at any price, and the specially selected rock oak soles insure double the wear ordinarily found at this price. Sizes and half sizes, 2½ to 9. Widths, C, D, E and EE. Weight averages 28 ounces.

$1.50

No. 15C117 Price, per pair....... $1.50

Women's Patent Leather Lace, Reduced to $1.20.

A style, grace of outline, and stock unheard of at anything like this price. Patent leather vamp with fancy stitched imitation tip, dongola top, long back stay and figured velvet inlaid lace stay. The shoe is fitted with Cuban heel, light imitation turned sole, reliable counter and inner sole and will give good service. Sizes and half sizes, 2½ to 8. Widths, D, E and EE. Weight, 28 ozs.

$1.20

No. 15C119 Price, per pair $1.20

Ladies' Dongola Blucher.

This Ladies' Blucher Shoe is the only one we have ever seen offered at anywhere near our price. Made from a fair selection of dongola stock, fitted with patent tip, outside back stay, and soles of good quality. Those who wish a shoe of this price will receive extraordinary value. Sizes and half sizes, 2½ to 8. Widths, D, E and EE. Weight, 28 ounces.

$1.35

No. 15C122 Price, per pair $1.35

Ladies' Patent Foxed Lace.

Ladies' vici kid lace, made with patent leather tip and heel foxing, Cuban heel, fancy perforated vamp, and light flexible sole. This shoe is fitted with guaranteed counter and inner sole, and has a style not usually found at this price. Sizes and half sizes, 2½ to 8. Widths, D, E and EE. Weight, 28 ozs.

$1.25

No. 15C125 Price, per pair... $1.25

Ladies' Patent Colt Blucher, $3.00.

HEAVY OAK SOLES. GOODYEAR WELT SEWN

For those who want the very latest big city style we have added this boot. We selected this boot because we knew the work was right, the pattern right and the last right. The stock is XXXX Corona patent colt. The toe is a medium round, fitted with a dull calf top, fast colored eyelets, best quality of trimmings and linings. The soles are heavy oak leather, slightly extended, medium high heel, and the pattern is Blucher style, with fancy perforated lace stay and quarter. The result of the good qualities is a shoe that gives to the wearer the kind of service she wants and more comfort than she expects. Sizes, 2½ to 8. Widths, B, C, D, E and EE. Average weight, about 32 ozs.

$3.00

No. 15C131 Price, per pair $3.00

Grand Leader Lace, $1.25.

Made from a special selection of genuine dongola kid, over the beautiful Rochester round toe last with patent leather tip. We have this shoe made with solid one-piece sole leather counter and inner sole, flexible machine sewed outer sole, and we actually believe it better than those usually sold at $1.75 by the retail stores. Sizes and half sizes, 2½ to 8. Widths, D, E and EE. Weight averages 28 ounces.

$1.25

No. 15C132 Price, per pair....... $1.25

Ladies' Everyday Shoe, $1.25.

Genuine Chrome Kangaroo Calf. Quite plump, has a slightly pebbled surface, and will give splendid service. The shoe is made over a handsome mannish last, cut with half seamless vamp, and fitted with the latest English back stay. The soles are fairly plump in weight. Sizes and half sizes, 2½ to 8. Widths, D, E and EE. Weight averages about 32 ounces.

$1.25

No. 15C136 Price, per pair........ $1.25

Ladies' Velvet Stay Kid Lace, Scroll Design, $1.25.

The design is pretty, the shoe is built by first class workmen, will give a great deal of service, as the kid stock is firm, the counter and insole reliable, and we are enabled to offer it to you at the unheard of price of $1.25. Sizes and half sizes, 2½ to 8. Widths, D, E and EE. Weight averages 23 ounces

$1.25

No. 15C138 Price, per pair. ..$1.25

Ladies' Heavy Kangaroo Grain, $1.00.

This shoe is made from Kangaroo grain leather, sometimes quoted as kangaroo calf. It is one of the strongest leathers made, yet soft and flexible. This shoe is made for those desiring a shoe for hard, heavy wear, is built with heavy soles, guaranteed counter and insole, and an exceptional value for the price quoted. Sizes and half sizes, 2½ to 8. Widths, full. Weight averages 30 ounces.

ALL SOLID

$1.00

No. 15C141 Price, per pair........ $1.00

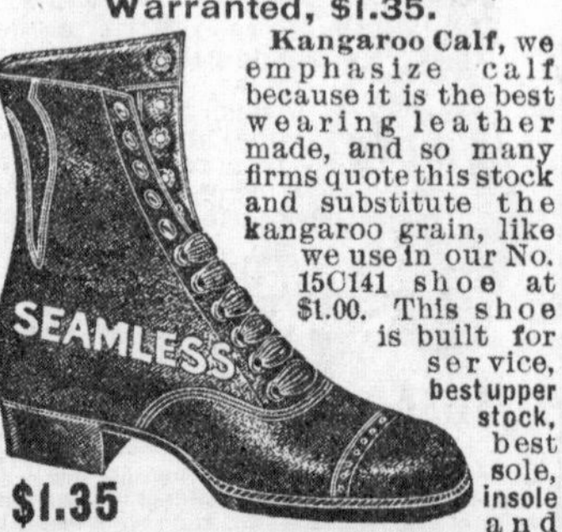

Ladies' Kangaroo Calf, Warranted, $1.35.

Kangaroo Calf, we emphasize calf because it is the best wearing leather made, and so many firms quote this stock and substitute the kangaroo grain, like we use in our No. 15C141 shoe at $1.00. This shoe is built for service, best upper stock, best sole, insole and counter we can buy. Seamless pattern (no rip), standard screw fastened, and absolutely built on honor. Sizes and half sizes, 2½ to 8. Widths, full. Weight averages 30 ounces.

$1.35

No. 15C145 Price, per pair........ $1.35

Ladies' Kangaroo Grain, Lace, $1.00.

Ladies' Kangaroo Grain, Lace. A soft stock which will turn water and wear like iron. Broad plain toe, and all solid leather, heavy sole, and made especially for hard, heavy wear. Sizes, 3 to 9. No half sizes. Full widths. Weight averages 30 ozs.

$1.00

No. 15C163 Price, per pair... $1.00

Old Ladies' Kid Lace Shoe, $1.00.

Old Ladies' Kid Lace Shoe, cut from a good plump dongola kid, and made over a broad, common sense last, which insures the wearer solid comfort. This shoe carries a good plump sole; is a genuine hand turn and low, broad heel. Sizes, 3 to 8. Full widths. Weight, averages 24 ounces.

$1.00

No. 15C167 Price, per pair... $1.00

Ladies' Dongola Leader, $1.00.

We prefer to sell better shoes, but for those who buy a shoe at from $1.25 to $1.50, we add this one. Genuine dongola stock, two-piece leather inner sole, counter guaranteed to outwear the shoe and good, firm outer sole. A shoe never sold by any factory or at wholesale under $1.00 and generally retailed from $1.25 to $1.50. Sizes and half sizes, 2½ to 8. Widths, full. Weight, 28 ounces.

$1.00

No. 15C169 Price, per pair... $1.00

LADIES' OXFORDS.

Ladies' Patent Corona Colt Blucher Oxford, $2.00.

This shoe is cut from the very best selection of this famous patent leather —is made over a medium round toe last, with perforated tip and fitted with the latest full military heel. The Blucher pattern is one of the handsomest we have seen, and is especially attractive when fitted with the dull mat calf top which is used in this shoe. The lace stay and heel foxing are slightly perforated, the shoe carries fast color eyelets, is genuine Goodyear welt sewn, producing flexibility and a perfectly smooth inner sole. Sizes and half sizes, 2½ to 8. Widths, C, D, E and EE. Weight averages 26 ounces.

$2.00

No. 15C172 Price, per pair......... $2.00

Ladies' Goodyear Welt Patent Leather Oxford, $1.75.

Made from a splendid quality of patent leather, over a medium round toe last, with perforated tip and dull mat kid top. This shoe is genuine Goodyear welt sewn, carries the latest full Cuban heel, is trimmed throughout in the very best manner, and to those who wish a snappy, foot fitting, shape retaining Oxford at a medium price, we recommend it. Sizes and half sizes, 2½ to 8. Widths, C, D, E and EE. Weight averages 26 ounces.

$1.75

No. 15C173 Price, per pair........ $1.75

Ladies' Patent Colt Oxford, $1.50.

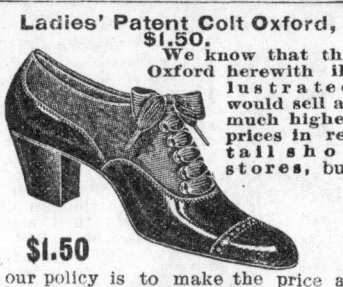

We know that the Oxford herewith illustrated would sell at much higher prices in retail shoe stores, but our policy is to make the price as low as possible. This Oxford is made from a good quality of genuine corona patent colt, over a handsome narrow round toe last; it is fitted with dull mat calf top, latest style heel foxing, flexible sole and serviceable. Sizes and half sizes, 2½ to 8. Widths, C, D, E and EE. Weight averages 25 ounces.

$1.50

No. 15C175 Price, per pair...... $1.50

Ladies' Dress Oxford, Reduced to $1.50.

Fine vici kid vamp, patent leather tip and quarter, and dull box kid top. This shoe is made with flexible hand turned sole, and being hand lasted and made in our best factory, will fit the foot and hold its shape much better than the lower priced goods usually sold in oxfords. This shoe carries a medium concave heel, slightly perforated quarter, and as a whole is a handsome, genteel shoe for street or dress wear. Sizes and half sizes, 2½ to 8. Widths, C, D, E and EE. Weight averages 18 ounces.

$1.50

No. 15C179 Price, per pair... $1.50

Patent Colt Ribbon Tie, $1.50.

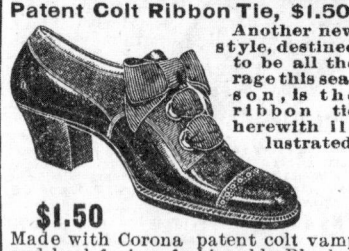

Another new style, destined to be all the rage this season, is the ribbon tie herewith illustrated.

$1.50

Made with Corona patent colt vamp and heel foxing, fashionable Blucher pattern and dull mat calf top, fitted with large eyelets and ribbon tie. The sole is of medium weight, fair stitched, cut of first class leather, and to those wishing the latest style, a good, serviceable, foot fitting low shoe, one at an unheard of price, we recommend it. Sizes, 2½ to 8. Widths, D, E and EE. Weight, averages 20 ounces.

No. 15C181 Price, per pair. $1.50

Ladies' New Colonial Ties, $1.50.

The latest style in Colonial Oxfords, is the one herewith illustrated, showing the fancy fleur de lis pattern, and a black bow at the instep. This shoe is made from a very fine selection of vici kid, light weight, flexible soles, is fitted with medium heel, and we consider it one of the most fashionable low shoes we have ever offered. Sizes and half sizes, 2½ to 8. Widths, C, D, E and EE. Weight averages 18 ounces.

$1.50

No. 15C183 Price, per pair $1.50

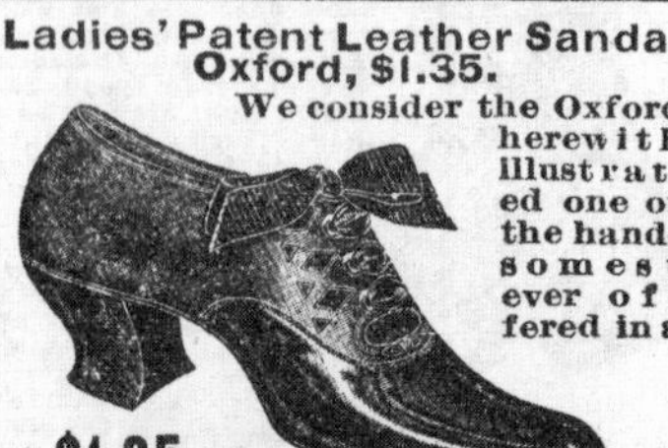

Ladies' Patent Leather Sandal Oxford, $1.35.

We consider the Oxford herewith illustrated one of the handsomest ever offered in a medium priced shoe. Made with good patent leather vamp, bright dongola quarter, with fancy open work lace stay and medium opera heel; a beautiful shoe for dress or party wear. Sizes and half sizes, 2½ to 8. Widths, C, D, E and EE. Weight averages 20 ounces.

$1.35

No. 15C187 Price, per pair...... $1.35

Ladies' Fancy Inlaid Oxford, $1.35.

Ladies' Genuine Dongola Oxford, made over a medium round toe last, with patent tip, and fitted with full

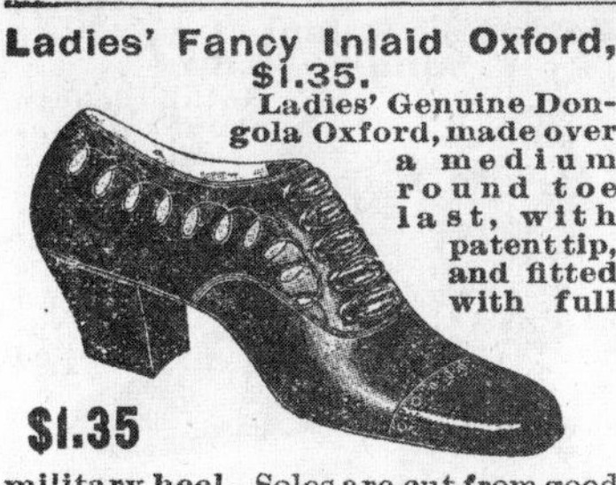

$1.35

military heel. Soles are cut from good quality sole leather, are flexible, and the quarter is a beautiful design, showing the effect of open work, at the same time being inlaid with silver leather. This is one of the most beautiful low shoes we have ever offered, and at the price quoted, is a rare value. Sizes and half sizes, 2½ to 8. Widths, D, E and EE. Weight averages 19 ounces.
No. 15C193 Price, per pair...$1.35

Ladies' Turn Vici Kid Blucher, $1.50.

Ladies' Vici Kid Blucher, fine velvet finished stock, with patent colt tip, heel foxing and lace stay,

$1.50

producing a handsome panel effect, the top being a dull mat calf. Fitted with fine oak hand turned sole, medium height Cuban heel, trimmed in the best manner throughout, and besides being an exclusive style, is a value you cannot duplicate elsewhere. Sizes and half sizes, 2½ to 8. Widths, C, D and EE. Weight averages 18 ounces.
No. 15C194 Price, per pair...$1.50

Ladies' Kid Blucher $1.50.

A Fine Mellow Vici Kid Vamp and perforated foxing, with dull mat calf top, patent leather tip and lacestay.

$1.50

Fitted with half double sole, black fair stitched, producing the effect of a Goodyear welt, medium Cuban heel and solid leather throughout. Built for style and fitting qualities. with the wearing points always in mind. Sizes and half sizes, 2½ to 8. Widths, D, E and EE. Weight averages 18 ounces.
No. 15C211 Price, per pair...$1.50

Latest Style Button Princess, $1.25.

We have made this front gore slipper from fine vici kid over a medium round toe last, with patent tip and me-

$1.25

dium heel. To increase the beauty of the shoe, we have made it with clasp buttons, although with the elastic goring over the instep it is not absolutely necessary that the buttons be used. Sizes and half sizes, 2½ to 8. Widths, D, E and EE. Weight averages 21 ozs.
No. 15C219 Price, per pair...$1.25
For postage rate see page 4.

Ladies' Four-Strap Black Kid Beaded Sandal, $1.35.

We have designed this slipper for those who wish a strictly up to date dress shoe, made of fine qual-

$1.35

ity of kid, handsomely lined, straps and edge neatly bound. Genuine hand turned sole, making it very light weight and especially suitable for party wear. Fancy beaded jet ornament on straps. Sizes and half sizes, 2½ to 8. Widths, C, D, E and EE. Weight averages 21 ounces.
No. 15C221 Price, per pair...... $1.35

Ladies' Ribbon Tie Sandal, $1.35.

Brand new in every particular is the sandal herewith illustrated. Fine vici kid, gen-

$1.35

uine hand turned sole, open work effect on vamp, which shows a handsome lace backing. Fitted with Cuban heel, large silk ribbon tie, kid stock lining and good in quality as it is original in design. Sizes, 2½ to 8. Widths, C, D, E and EE. Weight averages 15 ounces.
No. 15C223 Price, per pair...$1.35

Ladies' All Patent Leather Sandal Reduced to $1.25.

While this sandal is intended for dress wear, a great many are being used for street wear this season. The soles are hand turned and very flexible,

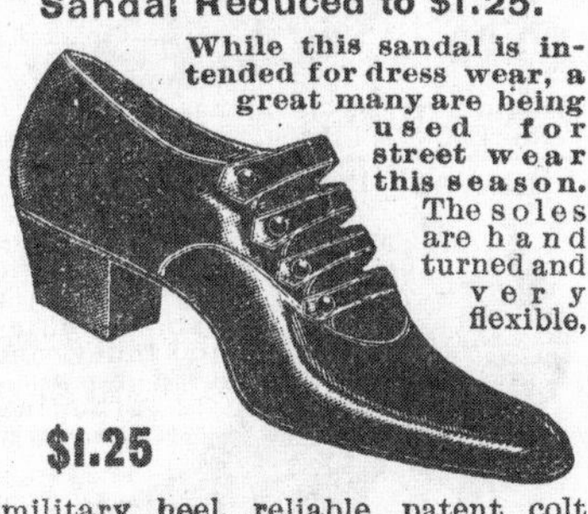

$1.25

military heel, reliable patent colt stock, and a value unequaled. Sizes and half sizes, 2½ to 8. Widths, D and E. Average weight, 21 ounces.
No. 15C225 Price, per pair...$1.25

Ladies' Half Congress, $1.35.

Desirable features of this handsome half Congress Shoe. It can be worn in the house or on the street, it can be put on or taken off quickly, no shoe laces to break, no button hook to be used. The best goring is used and the shoe is made of choice vici kid over a neat coin toelast

$1.35

with diamond patent leather tip. The soles are strictly hand turned. Sizes and half sizes, 2½ to 8. Widths, C, D, E and EE. Weight about 22 ounces.
No. 15C231 Price, per pair...$1.35

Ladies' Patent Colt Ribbon Tie, $1.25.

Fashion says the sandals must be tied with silk ribbon, so here it is. Patent colt vamp, dongola quarter, genuine hand turned

$1.25

sole, Cuban heel, nicely trimmed throughout, and a real silk ribbon tie. The value is exceptional. Sizes, 2½ to 8. Widths, D, E and EE. Weight averages 14 ounces.
No. 15C232 Price, per pair....$1.25

Ladies' Sandal Oxford, $1.15.

This Oxford is made of fine vici kid, with open work lace stays, thereby exposing the stocking just

$1.15

enough to produce one of the daintiest effects yet seen in a summer oxford. The soles are cut from the very best of leather and flexible. Sizes and half sizes, 2½ to 8. Widths, D, E and EE. Weight averages 21 ounces.
No. 15C234 Price, per pair....$1.15

Ladies' Patent Leather Oxford, $1.45.

Made of good patent leather stock, medium wide sole, with extension edges, and full perforated vamp, tip and heel foxing. Sizes and half

$1.45

sizes, 2½ to 8. Widths, D, E and EE. Weight averages 25 ounces.
No. 15C236 Price, per pair...$1.45
For postage rate see page 4.

Ladies' Tuxedo Kid, Four-Strap Sandal, $1.00.

The price, $1.00, does not indicate anywhere near the real value of the sandal. Tuxedo kid is very

$1.00

pliable and durable. This sandal is genuine hand turned, fitted with military heel, full kid quarter trimmed, and would be cheap at a much higher price. Sizes and half sizes, 2½ to 8. Full widths only. Weight averages 16 ounces.
No. 15C239 Price, per pair..$1.00

Ladies' Vici Mannish Oxford, $1.35.

We make this Oxford from fine, soft vici kid stock, which is very durable, and at the

$1.35

same time easy to the foot. The style of last is the medium mannish shape. Sizes and half sizes, 2½ to 8. Widths, D, E and EE. Weight averages 26 ozs.
No. 15C241 Price, per pair...$1.35
For postage rate see page 4.

Ladies' Tuxedo Kid Colonials, $1.00.

Made from fine tuxedo kid, genuine hand turned sole, latest full military heel, and fancy bow front.

$1.00

Suitable for street or house wear, and extraordinary value at price quoted. Sizes, 2½ to 8. Widths, D, E and EE. Weight averages 16 ounces.
No. 15C245 Price, per pair..$1.00

Patent Leather Oxford, $1.15.

A design that is attractive, and one we feel sure will please our patrons. Patent leather vamp, lace stay and cuff around top, with dull

$1.15

kid quarter. The Oxford is McKay sewn, flexible sole, Cuban heel and carries more style than is usually found for the price. Sizes, 2½ to 8. Widths, D, E and EE. Weight averages 17 ozs.
No. 15C247 Price, per pair..$1.15

Women's Extra Quality White Kid Sandal, $1.00.

We have had numerous calls for a White Kid Sandal of extra quality. This shoe is made of the very

$1.00

best quality white kid stock, fitted with high wood heel and a very beautiful satin cross strap bow at instep and vamp. This sandal is full kid trimmed, has the most beautiful strap, and, in fact, is the handsomest thing we have ever seen in a ladies' white sandal. The soles are genuine hand turned. Sizes and half sizes, 2½ to 8. Widths, D, E and EE. Weight, averages 14 ounces.
No. 15C250 Price, per pair.....$1.00
For postage rate, see page 4.

Ladies' Patent Colt Oxford, $1.00.

We know it is a ridiculous price, but we must keep the factory busy and have determined to sell a

$1.00

big lot. Genuine patent colt, Blucher pattern, half double sole, fair stitched, Cuban heel, leather insole and counter, large eyelets and big laces. Built to beat the world on price, but also to give satisfactory wear. Sizes, 2½ to 8. Widths, full. Weight averages 17 ounces.
No. 15C253 Price, per pair.$1.00

Ladies' Serge Buskin Slippers.

Ladies' Serge Buskin Slippers, turned soles, low, flat heels, fine quality. Sizes, 3 to 8. Full

$0.60

widths. Weight averages 18 ounces.
No. 15C254 Price, per pair.$0.60
For postage rate see page 4.

Women's Patent Leather Sandal, $0.95.

Made with patent leather vamp, kid quarter, French heel and bow strap. Strictly hand turned. We quote the regular heel and regular $1.00 sandal elsewhere at $0.69. This one is the $1.50 grade found elsewhere. Sizes, 2½ to 8. Widths, C, D, E and EE. Weight averages 18 ounces.

$0.95

No. 15C255 Price, per pair.$0.95

Ladies' White Kid Sandal, $0.80.

Ladies' White Kid Strap Sandals, made from a good selection of stock, medium narrow toe, strictly hand turned sole, and fancy bow over instep. White kid quarter trimmed and splendid value.

$0.80.

Sizes, 2½ to 8. Widths, D, E and EE. Weight averages 18 ounces.
No. 15C256 Price, per pair. $0.80

Ladies' Tuxedo Kid Sandal, $0.95.

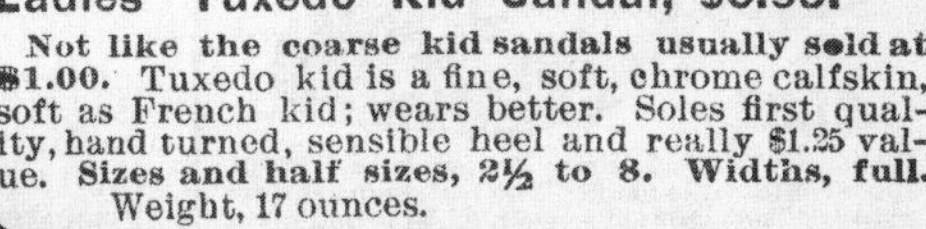

Not like the coarse kid sandals usually sold at $1.00. Tuxedo kid is a fine, soft, chrome calfskin, soft as French kid; wears better. Soles first quality, hand turned, sensible heel and really $1.25 value. Sizes and half sizes, 2½ to 8. Widths, full. Weight, 17 ounces.

No. 15C248 Price, per pair......$0.95
For postage rate see page 4.

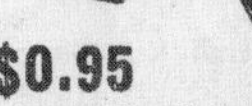

$0.95

$0.95

Ladies' Common Sense Oxford, $0.95.

Ladies' Common Sense Oxford, made from good dongola kid stock, with wide, plain toe, low broad heel and flexible sewed sole. This shoe is very neat and comfortable for house wear. **Sizes, 2½ to 8. Full widths.** Weight averages 25 ounces.

No. 15C258 Price, per pair............**$0.95**

For postage rate see page 4.

Ladies' Velour Calf Blucher, $1.00.

$1.00

Doesn't look possible, does it? Fact is, we control the production of this shoe and make the price to get rid of them as fast as produced.

Blucher cut, velour calf stock (we never saw it in a shoe under $1.50), half double sole, fair stitched, patent tip, military heel and sole leather counter and insole. The fashionable big eyelets and big laces, and a satisfactory Oxford. Far more than you would expect for the price. **Sizes, 2½ to 8. Widths full.** Weight averages 18 ounces.

No. 15C259 Price, per pair...**$1.00**

Ladies' Dongola Oxford, $1.00.

Genuine dongola stock, flexible sole, military heel, and fancy patent leather tip and

$1.00

patent inlaid quarter. A pretty pattern and the best we have ever been able to offer at this price. **Sizes and half sizes, 2½ to 8. Widths, full.** Weight averages 20 ounces.

No. 15C260 Price, per pair...**$1.00**

Ladies' Low Heel Sandal, $1.00.

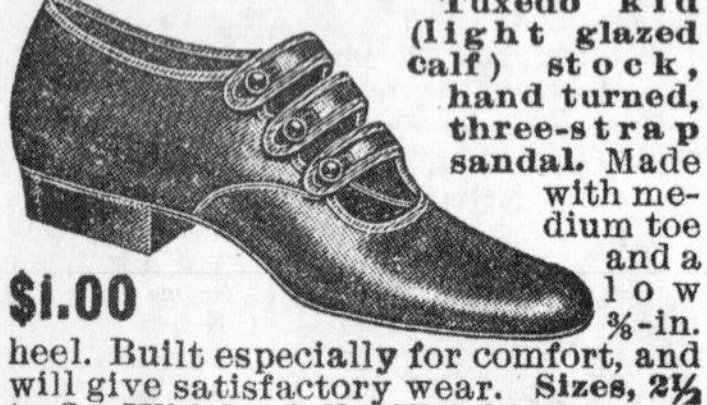

$1.00

Tuxedo kid (light glazed calf) stock, hand turned, three-strap sandal. Made with medium toe and a low ⅜-in. heel. Built especially for comfort, and will give satisfactory wear. **Sizes, 2½ to 8. Widths, full.** Weight averages 17 ounces.

No. 15C263 Price, per pair..**$1.00**

Ladies' Front Gore Oxford, $1.00.

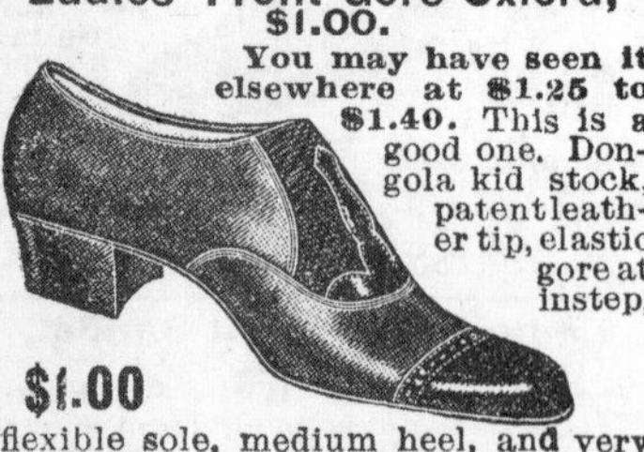

$1.00

You may have seen it elsewhere at $1.25 to $1.40. This is a good one. Dongola kid stock, patent leather tip, elastic gore at instep, flexible sole, medium heel, and very comfortable. **Sizes, 2½ to 8. Widths, full.** Weight averages 17 ounces.

No. 15C267 Price, per pair..**$1.00**

Women's Genuine Western Made Kangaroo Calf Oxford, $1.00.

Stock in this shoe is not the hard kangaroo grain used generally in shoes of this kind, but made of

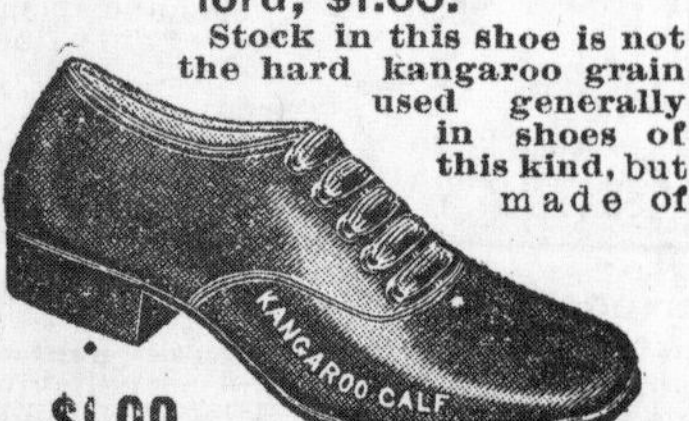

$1.00

Pfister & Vogel's famous kangaroo calf stock, the most durable made. The last and heel are made on the common sense plan, sole and inner sole are of the best wearing leather that can be secured. A very suitable garden Oxford. **Sizes 3 to 8. Widths, E and EE.** Weight averages 25 ounces.

No. 15C268 Price, per pair....**$1.00**

Ladies' White Canvas Ribbon Tie, $1.00.

This will be a white season. We anticipated it, and built this handsome Blucher, large eyelet ribbon tie. Made of fine white canvas, one-half double fair stitch. Cuban heel and guaranteed leather insole and counter, insuring all the wear found in shoes at double this price. **Sizes, 2½ to 8. Widths, D, E and EE.** Weight averages 16 ounces.

No. 15C269 Price, per pair..**$1.00**

Ladies' Black Kid Oxfords, $1.00.

$1.00

Made from good, plump dongola kid, medium weight, opera toe, with patent leather tip. In this shoe we give extra good value. Sizes, 2½ to 8. Full widths. Weight averages 22 ounces.

No. 15C271 Price, per pair...**$1.00**

For postage rate see page 4.

SEE OUR COLORED SHOES ON PAGES 713 AND 714 THEY'RE ALL THE RAGE NOW

Ladies' Pebble Grain Slippers, $0.55.

Ladies' Grain Slippers. Dampproof, sewed strong and durable, for out or in door wear.

$0.55

Sizes, 3 to 8. Full widths. No half sizes. Weight averages 22 ounces.

No. 15C272 Price, per pair..**$0.55**

For postage rate see page 4.

Ladies' Carpet Slippers, $0.20.

Made from Brussels carpet, leather sole and heel, good quality, bound and stayed. No better made. **Sizes, 3 to 8. No half sizes.**

$0.20

Weight averages 18 ounces.

No. 15C274 Price, per pair..**$0.20**

Ladies' Dongola Oxford, $0.80.

Made of genuine dongola stock, patent leather tip, thoroughly reliable counter and inner sole, and notwithstanding the low

$0.80

price, a surprisingly durable shoe. **Sizes and half sizes, 2½ to 8. Widths, full.** Weight averages 16 ounces.

No. 15C282 Price, per pair....**$0.80**

Ladies' Common Sense Lap Slipper, $0.75.

Good dongola stock, made over a common sense last, with low, broad heel, hand-turned sole.

$0.75

Very comfortable and durable for a house shoe. **Sizes, 3 to 8. Widths, full**

No. 15C284 Price, per pair....**$0.75**

Women's Patent Leather Sandal, $0.69.

$0.69

Nothing cheap about this sandal but the price. The patent leather is of good quality, hand turned sole, concave heel, kid quarter lined, and a sandal we have never before seen offered under 95 cents. **Sizes and half sizes, 2½ to 8. Full widths only.** Weight averages 14 ounces.

No. 15C288 Price, per pair..**$0.69**

Ladies' Two-Strap Sandal, $0.69.

Ladies' two-strap Cabretta Kid Sandal, sensible heel, sole leather counter and genuine hand turned sole. An unusual value. **Sizes, 2½ to 8. Widths, full.** Weight averages 14 ounces.

No. 15C290 Price, per pair, **$0.69**

$0.69

Ladies' White Canvas Oxford, $0.50.

Made of white canvas over a coin toe last, medium heel, good fair stitched sole, and serviceable. **Sizes, 2½ to 8. Widths, full.** Weight averages 14 ounces.

No. 15C292 Price, per pair, **$0.50**

MISSES' AND CHILDREN'S OXFORDS AND SHOES.

Misses' and Children's Patent Colt Bluchers.

Genuine patent colt, blucher cut Oxford, made with half double sole, fair stitched, sole leather counter and inner soles, low heels, and the latest big eyelets and wide laces. These oxfords are exceptional value. **Widths, full.** Weight varies according to size.

No. 15C302 Girls' sizes, 11½ to 3. Price, per pair..........**$1.00**

No. 15C303 Children's sizes, 8½ to 11. Price, per pair..........**$0.85**

No. 15C304 Children's sizes, 5 to 8. Price, per pair..........**$0.75**

Misses' and Children's All Patent Three-Strap Sandals, $0.95, $0.85 and $0.75.

Just as much style as any ladies' sandal, and why should they not have? All patent leather, spring heel, three straps, hand turn soles and suitable for dress wear. **Widths, full.** Weight varies according to size.

No. 15C305 Girls' sizes 11½ to 2. Price, per pair..........**$0.95**

No. 15C307 Children's sizes, 8½ to 11. Price, per pair..........**$0.85**

No. 15C309 Children's sizes, 5 to 8. Price, per pair..........**$0.75**

Misses' and Children's Vici Kid Blucher, $1.00 and $0.90.

We make this shoe after the same pattern as our ladies' fine shoes. We have never before seen this high class pattern made in misses' or children's shoes. The stock is fine vici kid, very dressy in appearance, and at the same time will give good service. The shoe is made over a medium broad toe last, patent leather tip. The soles are of the best quality of solid leather, slightly extended and carries a low heel. The Blucher pattern, handsomely stitched and perforated. Average weight about 14 ounces.

No. 15C308 Misses' sizes, 11½ to 2. Price, per pair..........**$1.00**

No. 15C310 Children's sizes, 8½ to 11. Price, per pair..........**$0.90**

Misses' and Children's Patent Quarter Shoes, $1.00.

A strictly dress shoe, made of extra quality of dongola leather. Soft and silky, a handsome shoe for dress or street wear. The very best of everything used in the making of this shoe. The oak soles are slightly extended, thus protecting the upper from being scuffed. Heel foxing and tip are patent leather. For those who wish a high class, genteel shoe, neat and dressy, we recommend this shoe. **Sizes, 8 to 2. Widths, full.**

No. 15C322 Price, per pair......**$1.00**

Misses' and Children's Fancy Kid Lace, $0.95 and $0.85.

A snappy, up to date pattern, patent leather tip, long outside back stay, and fancy perforated vamp. This shoe is cut from good plump dongola kid stock, good quality sole, counter and inner sole. Low ⅜-inch heel now so much in vogue in small shoes, and thoroughly reliable in every way. **Widths, D, E and EE.** Weight averages 18 ounces.

No. 15C330 Misses' sizes, 11½ to 2. Price, per pair..........**$0.95**

No. 15C332 Children's sizes, 8 to 11. Price, per pair..........**$0.85**

Misses' and Children's Box Calf Lace Shoes.

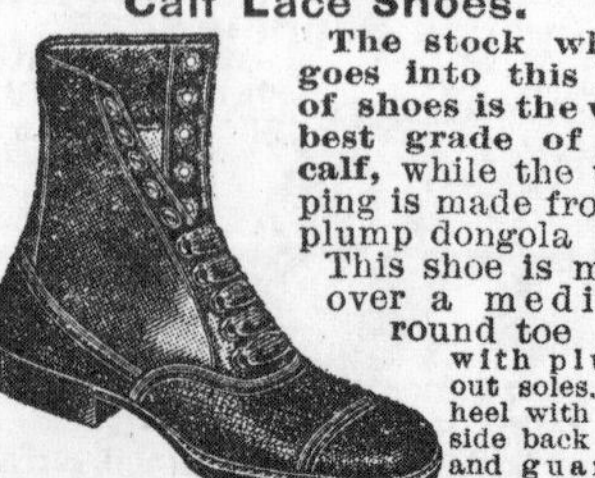

The stock which goes into this line of shoes is the very best grade of box calf, while the topping is made from a plump dongola kid. This shoe is made over a medium round toe last with plump out soles, low heel with outside back stay and guaranteed leather counter and inner sole. **Widths, D, E and EE.** Weight averages about 24 ounces.

No. 15C335 Misses' sizes, 11½ to 2. Price, per pair..........**$1.00**

No. 15C337 Children's sizes, 8 to 11. Price, per pair..........**$0.90**

Our Best School Shoes.

These School Shoes are made of the best kangaroo calf stock which has a pebbled surface; is soft and pliable and as near waterproof as leather can be made. We make this shoe with extremely low heel and plump bottom cut from finest oak sole leather. Nothing but the best solid leather counters and inner soles are used. Warranted. Full widths. Weight averages 30 ounces.

No. 15C358 Ladies' sizes, 2½ to 7. Price, per pair, reduced to............$1.50
No. 15C360 Misses' sizes, 11½ to 2. Price, per pair............$1.30
No. 15C362 Children's sizes, 8 to 11. Price, per pair............$1.20

Misses' and Child's Sandals, $1.00, $0.90 and $0.80.

The latest creation is the high cut sandal herewith illustrated, made with patent leather vamp, kid quarter and low heel. The misses' sizes have seven straps, child's sizes, 8½ to 11, have six straps and the little sizes, 5 to 8, are made with five straps. Nothing handsomer on the market, and take our word for it, the price does not nearly indicate the quality. Widths, full.

No. 15C374 Sizes, 11½ to 2, seven straps. Price, per pair............$1.00
No. 15C376 Sizes, 8½ to 11, six straps. Price, per pair............$0.90
No. 15C378 Sizes, 5 to 8, five straps. Price, per pair............$0.80

Misses' and Children's Patent Ribbon Ties, $1.00, $0.90 and $0.80.

Ribbon ties are all the rage, so here they are for the misses and children. Patent leather vamp, hand turnsole, spring heel, kid quarter with fancy openwork and silk ribbon tie, strictly up to date, and a beautiful dress sandal. Widths, full. Weight varies according to size.

No. 15C380 Misses' sizes, 11½ to 2. Price, per pair............$1.00
No. 15C381 Children's sizes, 8 to 11. Price, per pair............$0.90
No. 15C382 Children's sizes, 5 to 8. Price, per pair............$0.80

Women's, Misses' and Children's Fancy Kid Lace.

The fancy scroll pattern with inlaid plush produces a very pretty effect. Made from fine dongola stock, with patent leather tip. We consider this shoe equal to anything we have ever seen offered at one-half as much again. Widths, D, E and EE. Weight averages 16 ounces.

No. 15C402 Women's sizes, 2½ to 8. Price, per pair............$1.20
No. 15C404 Misses' sizes, 11½ to 2. Price, per pair............$0.95
No. 15C406 Children's sizes, 8 to 11. Price, per pair............$0.85

Misses' and Children's Dongola Lace, $0.80.

Misses' and Children's Shoes made from good genuine dongola kid stock. Sole leather counter and inner soles, medium heavy out soles and suitable for general wear, lots of it and extraordinary value at the prices quoted. Sizes and half sizes, 8 to 2. Widths, D, E and EE. Weight averages 15 to 22 ounces.

No. 15C410 Price, per pair..$0.80

Women's, Misses' and Children's Grain School Shoes, $1.00, $0.90 and $0.80.

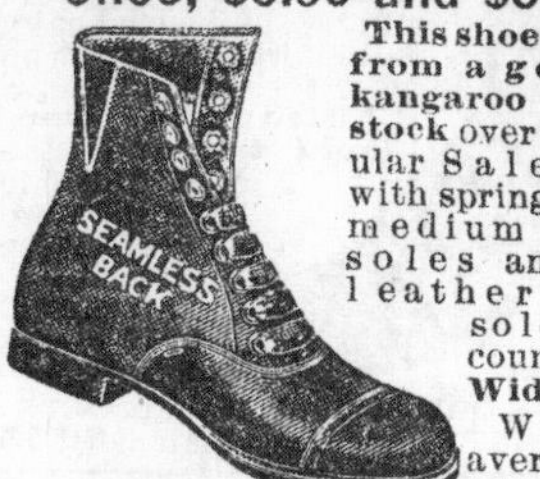

This shoe is made from a genuine kangaroo grain stock over the popular Salem last, with spring heels; medium plump soles and solid leather inner sole and counter. Widths, full. Weight averages 28 ounces.

No. 15C417 Women's sizes, 2½ to 8. Price............$1.00
No. 15C418 Misses' sizes, 11½, 12, 12½, 13, 13½, 1, 1½ and 2. Price, per pair..$0.90
No. 15C420 Children's sizes, 8, 8½, 9, 9½, 10, 10½ and 11. Per pair...$0.80

Misses' and Children's Patent Leather Shoes, $0.98 and $0.88.

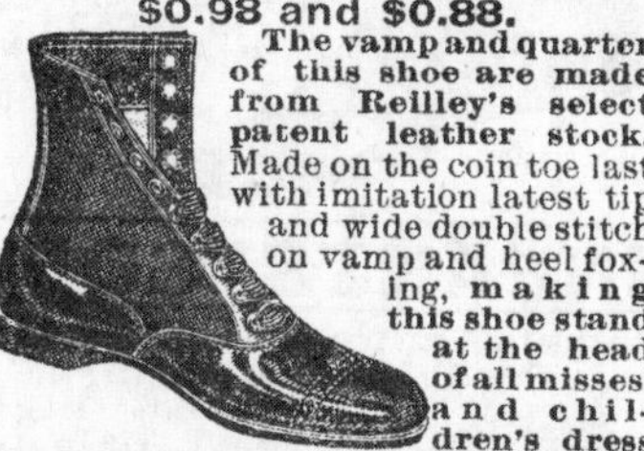

The vamp and quarter of this shoe are made from Reilley's select patent leather stock. Made on the coin toe last with imitation latest tip and wide double stitch on vamp and heel foxing, making this shoe stand at the head of all misses' and children's dress shoes. Widths, D, E and EE. Weight averages 16 ounces.

No. 15C422 Misses' sizes, 11½, 12, 12½, 13, 13½, 1, 1½ and 2. Per pair...$0.98
No. 15C424 Children's sizes, 8½, 9, 9½, 10, 10½ and 11. Per pair............$0.88

Special Bargains in Misses' and Children's Dongola Lace, $0.59, $0.49 and $0.39.

Made of good quality Dongola leather, over a medium broad toe last. Patent tip. Sole, insole and counter are solid leather. Low heels. This shoe is well made of substantial material and will give more wear than the price would indicate. Wide widths only. Average weight about 16 ounces.

No. 15C430 Misses' sizes, 11½ to 3. Price, per pair............$0.59
No. 15C431 Children's sizes, 8½ to 11. Price, per pair............$0.49
No. 15C432 Children's sizes, 5 to 8. Price, per pair............$0.39

Misses' and Children's Kid Blucher Oxfords, $0.69, $0.59 and $0.49.

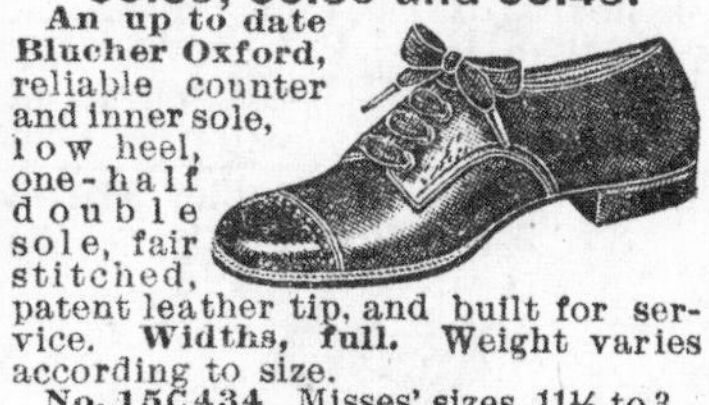

An up to date Blucher Oxford, reliable counter and inner sole, low heel, one-half double sole, fair stitched, patent leather tip, and built for service. Widths, full. Weight varies according to size.

No. 15C434 Misses' sizes, 11½ to 3. Price, per pair............$0.69
No. 15C435 Children's sizes, 1½ to 11. Price, per pair............$0.59
No. 15C436 Children's sizes, 5 to 8. Price, per pair............$0.49

Misses' and Children's White Canvas Blucher Oxfords. $0.69, $0.59 and $0.49.

Neatest and latest thing in summer footwear is the white canvas Blucher cut Oxford with large eyelets and large laces. Made half double sole, fair stitched, low heel and durable. Widths, full. Weight varies according to size.

No. 15C457 Misses' sizes, 11½ to 3. Price, per pair............$0.69
No. 15C458 Children's sizes, 8½ to 11. Price, per pair............$0.59
No. 15C459 Children's sizes, 5 to 8. Price, per pair............$0.49

Misses' and Children's Strap Sandals, $0.80 and $0.70.

We herewith illustrate our Misses' and Child's Dongola Strap Sandal, made over a medium last with fancy patent leather tip; suitable for street or dress wear. This sandal is genuine McKay sewed, and will give splendid service. Widths, full. Weight averages 14 ounces.

No. 15C460 Misses' sizes, 11½ to 2. Price, per pair............$0.80
No. 15C462 Children's sizes, 8 to 11. Price, per pair............$0.70
No. 15C463 Infant's sizes, 5 to 8. Price, per pair............$0.60

Misses' and Children's Patent Leather Sandals, $0.69, $0.59 and $0.49.

Beats the world and seems almost impossible to furnish a sandal so stylish at the unheard of price we mention. Patent leather vamp, genuine carbaretta quarter, spring heel, McKay turned sole, kid quarter lining and bow strap. Nothing like it has ever been quoted at a price under $1.00. Widths, full. Weight averages 12 ounces.

No. 15C464 Misses' sizes, 11½ to 2. Price, per pair............$0.69
No. 15C465 Children's sizes, 8½ to 11. Price, per pair............$0.59
No. 15C466 Children's sizes, 5 to 8. Price, per pair............$0.49

Misses' and Children's White Kid Sandals $0.69, $0.59 and $0.49.

These sandals are made of the very best quality white kid stock, spring heel, fancy bow at instep, and genuine McKay turned sole. Our one profit plan enables us to quote them to you at an unheard of price; therefore, when anticipating a purchase please remember that the price is the only thing cheap about them. The correct thing for graduation exercises, confirmation, or for party wear. Widths, full. Weight averages 14 ounces.

No. 15C468 Misses' sizes, 11½ to 2. Price, per pair............$0.69
No. 15C469 Children's sizes, 8½ to 11. Price, per pair............$0.59
No. 15C470 Children's sizes, 5 to 8. Price, per pair............$0.49

Little Gents' Vici Kid Bal, $1.00.

$1.00

A nice soft finished vici kid stock is used for this shoe, making a fine shoe for those boys with tender feet. Made over a full round toe last, perforated tip, short outside back stay, low heel, good durable sole, an exceptional value at the price quoted. Sizes and half sizes, 9 to 13½. Widths, full. Weight averages 22 ounces.

No. 15C473 Price, per pair...$1.00

Little Gents' Seamless Bal, $1.00.

$1.00

Made from genuine kangaroo grain leather, over coin toe last, with best sole leather counter and inner sole, durable out sole, and the low two-lift heel. This shoe is made in practically seamless pattern, will not rip, the soles being fastened on with the McKay machine, making the shoe practically indestructible. Sizes and half sizes, 9 to 13½. Widths, full. Weight averages 20 ounces.

No. 15C475 Price, per pair..$1.00

For postage rate see page 4.

Little Gents' Kangaroo Box, $0.80.

This Little Gents' Shoe is made of genuine kangaroo box stock, sometimes called box calf. Has all solid leather insole and counter, outside back stay, and will give much service for the price. Sizes and half sizes, 9 to 13½. Widths, full. Weight, 24 ounces.

No. 15C479 Price, per pair..$0.80

Misses' Vici Kid Blucher, $1.00.

Cut from a fine grade of vici kid with a good wearing but flexible sole. The scroll pattern is a very pretty and recent design, and the shoe is intended for a serviceable light weight dress shoe for spring and summer. Sizes and half sizes, 8 to 2. Widths, full. Weight, 16 ounces.

No. 15C480 Price............$1.00

Shoes for Little Men. Just Like Papa's, Reduced to $0.90.

$0.90

This Little Men's Shoe is not intended for grown up people, but for children, and we cannot furnish it in any size not quoted here. The stock in the vamp is of a good quality of satin calf. The top is made of fine dongola. All seams are protected from ripping by an extra row of stitching, while the back seam is reinforced with a back stay. The soles, inner soles and counters are of solid leather. The style of last is exactly like that of men's shoes, hence it is liked by the little folks. Sizes and half sizes, 7 to 13½. Widths, D, E and EE. Weight averages 22 ounces. We carry this shoe in black only.

No. 15C484 Price, per pair..$0.90

For postage rate see page 4.

Little Gents' Patent Blucher, Just Like Dad's, $1.20.

$1.20

This shoe is made in the same pattern as is sold in men's $3.50 shoes. Made of patent leather, vamp, quarter and lace stays, cut Blucher style, top of dull calfskin, making a very pretty contrast. While this shoe is intended for a dress shoe only, we use the same patent leather as is found in our high priced men's shoes, which will give excellent satisfaction. Sizes, 9 to 13½. Widths, D, E and EE. Wgt. averages 22 ounces.

No. 15C485 Price, per pair..$1.20

Baby Boy Box Calf Lace, $0.75.

LIKE BIG BROTHERS'.

Made on the same style as the little gents' shoe. Made of genuine box calf, fine quality soft leather, medium toe, dongola top, good quality oak sole and low heel. Made to give double the wear usually found in little shoes. Sizes, 5 to 8. Widths, E and EE. Weight, averages 22 ounces.

No. 15C488 Price, per pair..$0.75

Children's Velour Calf Blucher, $0.75.

JUST LIKE MAMMA'S.

Our aim in getting up this shoe is to offer our customers a child's shoe made over the very newest last, pattern and design the same as found in the ladies' highest priced shoes. The Blucher style; is handsomely stitched and perforated. This shoe is not only stylish in appearance, but is made from genuine velour calfskin, light and easy on the feet. It will give the same amount of wear as found in the heavy coarse leather. The soles are extra quality oak leather, hand turned and carry a low heel. **Sizes and half sizes, 5 to 8. Widths, D, E and EE.** Average weight, about 10 ounces.

No. 15C490 Price, per pair........**$0.75**

Child's Patent Leather Scroll, Reduced to $0.90.

This is the finest little shoe for dress wear we have ever offered. Made from best patent leather, fancy scroll pattern with inlaid figured velvet top. **Genuine oak hand turned** sole, spring heel and trimmed in the best possible manner. The $1.50 kind found elsewhere. **Sizes and half sizes, 5 to 8. Widths, D, E and EE.** Weight, 11 ounces.

No. 15C500 Price, per pair........**$0.90**

Children's Kid Lace, $0.75.

A merit made vici kid shoe, half double sole, fair stitched, spring heel. This shoe is made alongside our fine misses' goods and is serviceable. **Sizes, 5 to 8. Widths, full.** Weight, 14 ounces.

No. 15C502 Price, per pair **$0.75**

Infants' Patent Vamps, Three-Strap, $0.55.

The price is usually from 75c up, but we're always lower. Patent vamp, turn sole, kid quarter and a sandal that will outwear a half dozen pairs of soft soles. **Sizes, 2 to 5.** Weight, 8 ozs.

No. 15C541 Price, per pair... **$0.55**

Children's Vesting Top Lace, Red, Tan or Black, $0.80.

We herewith illustrate one of our very latest patterns in a child's scroll vesting lace shoe. We make this shoe from a very fine selection of genuine chrome vici kid in bright red, tan or black, with fancy imported vesting top to match. The soles are strictly hand turned, the shoe is stitched with silk thread and in fact nothing has been omitted to make it strictly high grade in every particular. **Sizes, 4, 4½, 5, 5½, 6, 6½, 7 and 8. Widths, C, D, E and EE.** Average weight, 12 ounces.

No. 15C543 Bright Red. Vesting to match. Price, per pair........**$0.80**

No. 15C545 Tan Color. Price, per pair........**$0.80**

No. 15C547 Black. Vesting to match. Price, per pair........**$0.80**

For postage rate see page 4.

Infants' Dress Shoe, Velvet Top, $0.60.

The best little infants' no heel shoe we carry. Built for those who have paid from $1.00 to $1.25 for similar shoes and who want the best. **Finest vici kid,** with patent leather tip, imported velvet top, and hand turned oak soles. Hard to find a more dressy shoe at any price, and besides this one is very durable. **Sizes and half sizes, 2 to 5. Widths, full.** Weight, 10 ounces.

$0.60

No. 15C551 Price, per pair...**$0.60**

Child's Paris Kid Lace, $0.65.

Child's Very Fine Paris Kid Lace Shoe, pretty coin toe last, patent leather tip and heel foxing. Soles hand turned, fitted with wedge heel, and a very dressy and durable little shoe. Used to be $0.65, but was not our standard of quality. We added 10 cents to the cost, knowing you would gladly pay it and get a really fine shoe. **Sizes and half sizes, 4 to 8. Widths, full.** Weight, 12 ounces.

No. 15C556 Price, per pair...**$0.65**

Children's and Infants' Panel Shoe, $0.65 and $0.45.

Different from the shoes ordinarily found at this price, are they not? Something about the pattern that suggests a fine article, and in reality they are better shoes than we have heretofore offered at these prices. **Fine kid, patent leather tip,** figured velvet top, and kid lace stay and top band. **Made in wedge heel sizes, 4 to 8, and no heel sizes, 2 to 5. Widths, full.** Weight averages 12 to 15 ounces.

No. 15C560 Wedge Heel. Sizes, 4 to 8. Price, per pair......**$0.65**

No. 15C561 No Heel. Sizes, 2 to 5. Price, per pair...... **.45**

Our Special Bargain in Child's Shoe, $0.35.

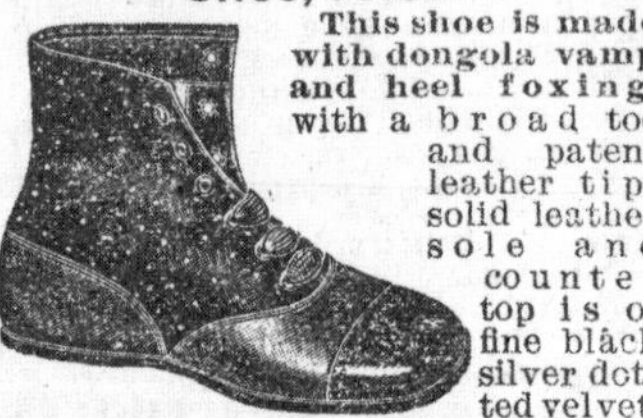

This shoe is made with dongola vamp and heel foxing, with a broad toe and patent leather tip, solid leather sole and counter top is of fine black silver dotted velvet. We are selling this shoe at a price much below any wholesaler on earth. **Sizes, 2 to 5. Widths, full.** Weight, 10 to 12 ounces.

No. 15C565 Price, per pair...**$0.35**

Children's Kid Button Shoes, $0.55 and $0.45.

Child's Kid Button, made from soft, glove like stock, spring heel, flexible soles, patent leather tip, all solid and durable. **Widths, full.** Weight, about 13 ounces.

$0.55

No. 15C568 Sizes, 4 to 8. Spring heel. Price, per pair........**$0.55**

No. 15C568½ Sizes 2 to 5. No heel. Price, per pair........**$0.45**

For postage rate see page 4.

Child's Kid Lace, $0.55.

Made from soft kid stock, patent leather tip, spring heel, hand turned sole, solid counter, and a durable shoe. Sizes and half sizes, 4 to 8. Widths full. Weight, 12 ounces

No. 15C569 Price, per pair...**$0.55**

Child's Box Calf Lace, $0.75.

This shoe, made from box calf stock, broad tip toe, and with heavy sole for children who give a shoe hard wear. **Fitted with dongola top,** and the most durable little shoe we have ever offered. **Sizes and half sizes, 5 to 8.**

$0.75

Widths, full. Weight, 16 ounces.

No. 15C571 Price, per pair...**$0.75**

Children's Silvered Velvet Top Lace.

Made of fine patent leather, no tip, hand turned sole, and finest silver dotted velvet top. The handsomest thing ever offered at this price.

No. 15C572 Sizes, 5 to 8. Price, per pair......**$0.75**

No. 15C573 Sizes, 2 to 5. No heel. Price, per pair, **$0.55**

Infants' Tan or Red Kid Lace, $0.45.

This Infants' Shoe is made from fine chrome lamb, the latest dark chocolate color, or the fashionable red; hand sewed, medium coin toe with tip, and no heel. **Sizes, 2, 2½, 3, 3½, 4, 4½ and 5.** Weight, about 10 ounces.

No. 15C574 Tan color. Price, per pair...............**$0.40**

No. 15C575 Red. Per pair. **.40**

Infants' Genuine Vici Kid Lace $0.45.

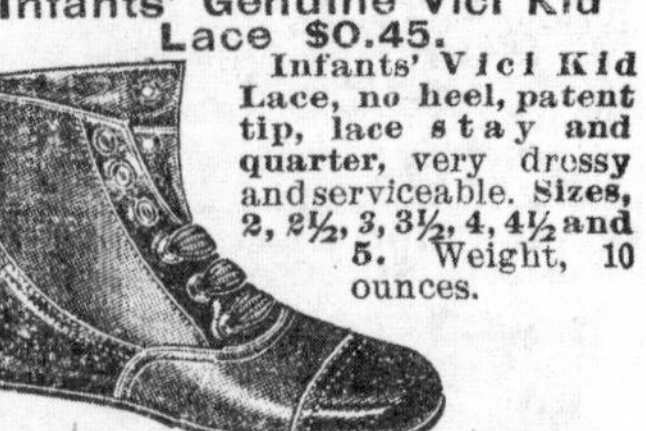

Infants' Vici Kid Lace, no heel, patent tip, lace stay and quarter, very dressy and serviceable. **Sizes, 2, 2½, 3, 3½, 4, 4½ and 5.** Weight, 10 ounces.

No. 15C576 Price, per pair, **$0.45**

INFANTS' SOFT SOLE SHOES.

Infants' Figured Velvet Bootee, Fur Trimmed, $0.35.

Infants' Figured Velvet Bootee. Made from fancy blue velvet with gilt figures, soft kid sole, fancy fur trimmed top; the kind usually sold at $0.75 to $0.80. **Sizes, 1 to 5.** Weight, averages 7 ounces.

No. 15C577 Price, per pair...**$0.35**

Per dozen pairs................ **4.00**

Three Pairs Assorted Colors for $0.60.

Patent leather, soft soles, ornament on vamp. Blue, pink and white stitched tops, so baby will have shoes to match dresses. The usual price is much more. Packed three pairs of one size to the box. We cannot change assortment. **Sizes, 1 to 4.** Weight, per three pairs, 9 ounces.

No. 15C578 Price, 3 pairs for. **$0.60**

Per dozen pairs, assorted........ **2.25**

Blue, Tan and Black; Three Pairs for $0.60.

Blue, tan and black stitched tops, patent leather vamp and foxing, ornament on vamp, soft soles. Usually cost from 25 cents to 40 cents per pair. We cannot furnish different colors from the ones named. **Sizes, 1 to 4.** Weight, per three pairs, 9 ounces.

No. 15C580 Price, 3 pairs for **$0.60**

Per dozen pairs, assorted........ **2.25**

A New Soft Sole, $0.30.

Patent leather vamp, heel foxing and lace stay, imported figured velvet top, soft sole. The handsomest thing we have seen. Sizes, 1 to 4. Weight, 4 ounces.

No. 15C583 Price, per pair...**$0.30**

Per dozen pairs.................. **3.25**

Infants' Inlaid Patent Leather Sandal, Soft Sole.

Made of patent leather, handsomely inlaid with gold tinsel cloth, fancy bow and buckle. The prettiest soft sole shoe ever made.

$0.35 **Sizes, 1 to 4.**

No. 15C585 Price, per pair. **$0.35**

Per dozen pairs............... **4.00**

Infants' Soft Sole Tan, $0.17.

This shoe is made from a choice selection of genuine kid, fancy stitched, has kid sole. Cut very full so you will have no trouble to put them on.

Color, tan. Sizes 1, 2, 3 and 4.

No. 15C588 Price, per pair **$0.17**

Per dozen pairs.............. **2.00**

Little Pets, Blucher Style. Three Pairs for $1.00.

Just like Mamma's in style. Nothing too good or too stylish for the sweet little babies. These little shoes are made first quality throughout, of best patent leather, best kid tops in blue, white and pink, latest style Blucher pattern and packed three pairs assorted to the box. Weight, per box, 9 ounces. **Sizes, 1 to 4.**

No. 15C589 Price, 3 pairs... **$1.00**

Per dozen pairs............... **3.75**

Infants' Fancy Patent Leather Sandals, $0.35.

Pink, White or Blue Tops.

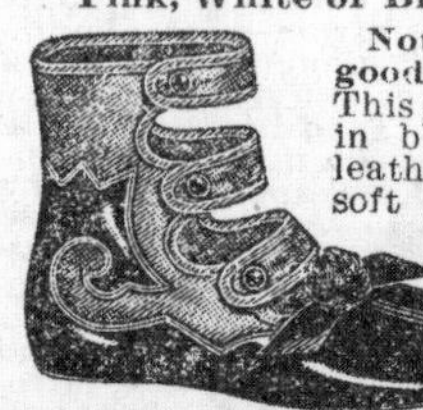

Nothing is too good for the baby. This sandal is made in black patent leather, having the soft sole, three straps and buckle ornament at instep. Such shoes usually bring from 50 to 75 cents per pair. **Sizes, 1 to 4.** Weight, 4 ounces.

No. 15C590 Price, per pair... **$0.35**

Per dozen pairs............... **4.00**

Infants' Wool Lined Tan Moccasins.

Just the thing for the baby. Made of soft leather, eiderdown lined, well made, nicely stitched and a good fitter. Easy to put on. Sizes, 1 to 4.

$0.15

No. 15C592 Price, per pair...$0.15
Per dozen pairs............ 1.60

Infants' Patent Leather Lace, $0.36.

We herewith illustrate our Infants' Patent Leather, Soft Sole Lace Shoe. Made with fancy pink silk top and patent scroll heel foxing. Sizes, 1, 2, 3 and 4. Full widths only. Weight, 7 ounces.

$0.36

No. 15C593 Price, per pair..$0.36
Per dozen pairs 4.00

A Treat for Baby—Three Pairs, Assorted, for $1.00.

The handsomest little shoes we have ever seen and the best quality. We quote elsewhere the ordinary kind, 3 pairs for 60 cents. Patent leather, with pink, white and blue kid, fancy stitched tops and soft soles. A splendid present for baby, as the assortment of colors goes nicely with dresses of colors to match. We pack these shoes three pairs to the box, any size, and though they are 40-cent shoes we sell three pairs for $1.00. **Sizes, 1 to 4.** Weight, 4 ounces.

No. 15C595 Price, three pairs for...................$1.00

No. 15C595½ Price, per single pair.................. .40

No. 15C596 Job lot, black top. Price, per pair.............. .21

Infants' Soft Sole Lace, Red, Tan or Black, $0.16.

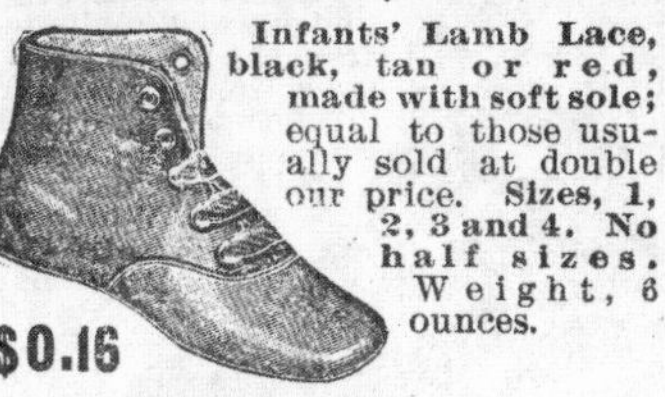

Infants' Lamb Lace, black, tan or red, made with soft sole; equal to those usually sold at double our price. Sizes, 1, 2, 3 and 4. No half sizes. Weight, 6 ounces.

$0.16

No. 15C597 Price, per pair...$0.16
Per dozen pairs.................. 1.75

Infants' Moccasins, $0.08.

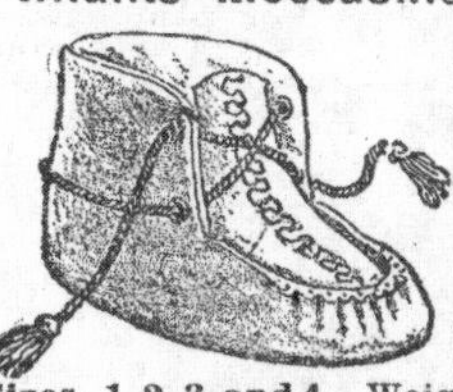

Infants' Lamb Moccasins, tan color only. We do not exchange these moccasins, as the profit will not admit of it. Sizes, 1, 2, 3 and 4. Weight, 3 ounces.

No. 15C598 Price, per pair....$0.08
Per dozen pairs.............. .95

Infants' Felt Nullifiers, $0.35.

This nullifier is made of a fine quality red felt trimmed with white fur. This is one of the neatest shoes for baby that can be desired. Sizes, 1, 2, 3 and 4. Average weight, about 5 ounces.

No. 15C599 Price, per pair.....$0.35

Infants' Red Felt Lace, $0.65 and $0.50. LEATHER SOLE.

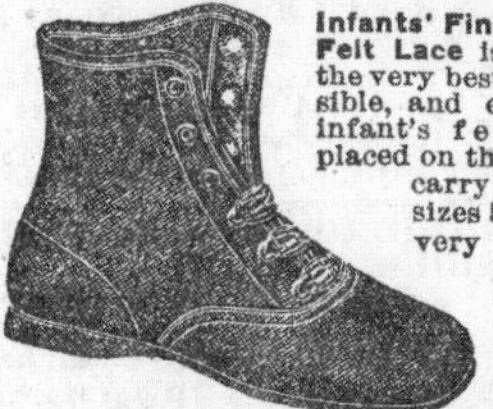

Infants' Fine Beaver Red Felt Lace is made up in the very best manner possible, and equal to any infant's felt shoe ever placed on the market. We carry this shoe in sizes 5 to 8, with a very slight half spring heel, while the sizes, 2 to 5, are made with no heel. Widths, full.

Average weight about 10 ounces.

No. 15C645 Sizes, 5 to 8, with spring heel. Price, per pair.................$0.65

No. 15C646 Sizes, 2 to 5, no heel. Price, per pair.................$0.50

FELT SHOES BELOW WHOLESALE.

Men's High Cut Wool Sheep Lined Lace, $1.85.

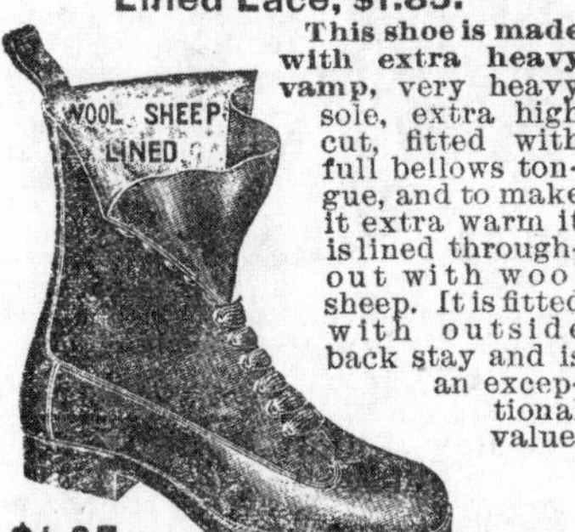

This shoe is made with extra heavy vamp, very heavy sole, extra high cut, fitted with full bellows tongue, and to make it extra warm it is lined throughout with wool sheep. It is fitted with outside back stay and is an exceptional value.

$1.85

Sizes, 6 to 12. No half sizes. Widths full. Weight averages 38 ounces.

No. 15C600 Price, per pair..$1.85

Men's High Cut Felt Bluchers, Fine Quality, $2.00.

This blucher is made from a good quality of felt, cut 10½ inches high, fitted with large black eyelets, wide felt tongue and is felt lined throughout. We make this blucher with vici kid tip, heavy leather sole and fitted with a rubber heel of good quality. This is a shoe handsome in appearance and at the same time very warm and comfortable. Sizes, 6 to 11. No half sizes. Widths, full. Weight averages 48 ounces.

$2.00

No. 15C602 Price, per pair...$2.00

Plush Lined Bluchers, Reduced to $1.65.

Made with satin calf foxing, heavy weight leather sole and heel. Blucher cut, with heavy ribbed felt front, quilted top and heavy plush lined throughout. One of the most durable and comfortable shoes ever made. Sizes, 6 to 11. No half sizes. Widths, full. Weight averages 48 ounces.

$1.65

No. 15C604 Price, per pair...$1.65

Men's Plush Lined, Reduced to $1.85.

This shoe is cut extra high, has heavy oak soles, solid sole leather counter and inner sole, wearproof calf foxing and tip, genuine dongola quilted top with full bellows tongue, and is lined with heavy plush to the top. We couldn't build a higher grade, more durable, warm lined shoe at any price.

$1.85

Sizes, 6 to 12. No half sizes. Widths, full. Weight, 43 ounces.

No. 15C605 Price, per pair...$1.85

Ladies' High Cut Felt Lace, $1.25.

A SURE CURE FOR RHEUMATISM.

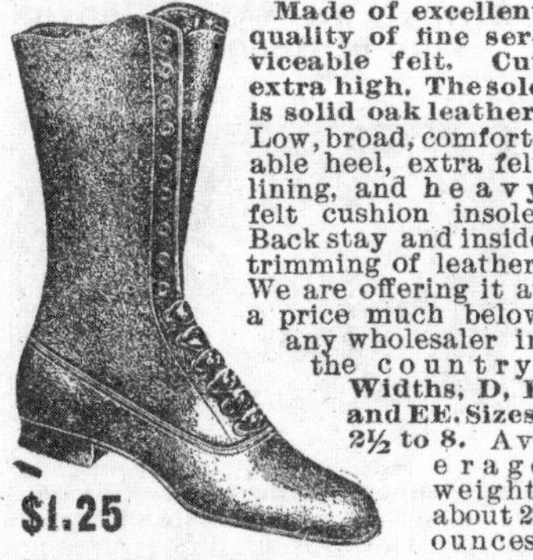

Made of excellent quality of fine serviceable felt. Cut extra high. The sole is solid oak leather. Low, broad, comfortable heel, extra felt lining, and heavy felt cushion insole. Back stay and inside trimming of leather. We are offering it at a price much below any wholesaler in the country. Widths, D, E and EE. Sizes, 2½ to 8. Average weight, about 27 ounces.

$1.25

No. 15C606 Price, per pair...$1.25

Men's Plush Lined Shoes, Reduced to $1.75.

This shoe is made from a soft kangaroo grain leather, especially adapted to wet weather. Made over a broad toe last, neat, yet full, and lined with heavy plush cloth, making it one of the warmest shoes that can be built. Sole leather counters and inner sole are used, while the outsole is cut from the best hemlock leather. We consider it the ideal warm shoe. Sizes and half sizes, 6 to 11. Widths, full. Weight, 43 ounces.

$1.75

No. 15C607 Price, per pair $1.75

Men's All Felt Lace, $1.00.

Men's extra heavy 36-ounce felt lace, made with heavy felt sole and heel and designed especially to wear inside of arctics or as a comfortable house shoe. Sizes, 6 to 12, no half sizes. Weight, averages 25 ozs.

No. 15C609 Price, per pair.......$1.00

Men's Fine Felt Lace, $1.50.

This shoe is made from a very fine felt, is felt lined throughout, fitted with outside back stay and fine dongola tip and heel foxing. This shoe is fitted with the very best of white felt sole and between the inner sole and the outer sole is fitted a full rubber sole of extraordinary value. Sizes, 6 to 12, no half sizes. Widths, full. Weight, averages 33 ounces.

No. 15C610 Price, per pair $1.50

Men's Leather Sole Felt Nullifier $0.85.

This nullifier is made of good quality felt with gore side, felt lined throughout and fitted with combination felt and harness leather sole, making it at once the most durable and comfortable felt shoe we have ever offered. Sizes, 6 to 12, no half sizes. Weight, averages 24 ounces.

No. 15C611 Price, per pair.......$0.85

Men's Hand Sewed Felt Slippers, $0.75.

Made from a fine beaver felt, all wool, with a felt sole sewed on by hand, and a leather outer sole made from harness leather. The outer sole is sewed on by hand, making it very flexible and easy. Don't be surprised if they last three winters. We positively guarantee them to outwear any felt slipper ever made. Order by number. Men's sizes, 6 to 12. Weight, about 25 ounces.

$0.75

No. 15C612 Price, per pair.......$0.75

Ladies' Blue Beaver Slippers, $0.85.

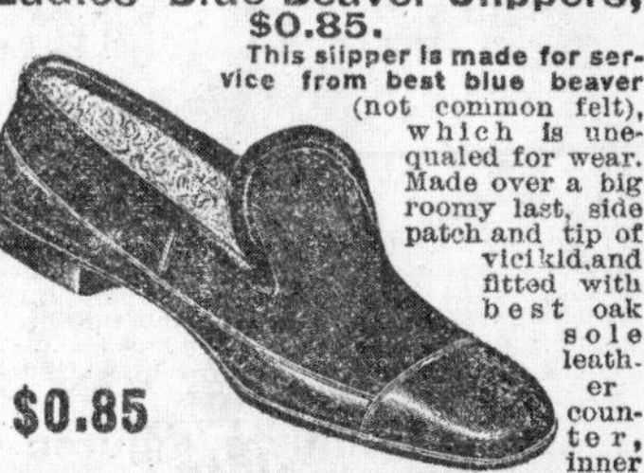

This slipper is made for service from best blue beaver (not common felt), which is unequaled for wear. Made over a big roomy last, side patch and tip of vici kid, and fitted with best oak sole leather counter, inner sole and outer sole. Couldn't make a more durable slipper at any price. Sizes and half sizes, 2½ to 8. Widths, full. Weight, 25 ounces.

$0.85

No. 15C615 Price, per pair.....$0.85

Ladies' Fancy Nullifier, $1.20.

This Nullifier is made with fine dongola vamp, genuine hand turned sole and a fine wine velvet top which is fur trimmed. Fleece lined throughout, fancy vamp and a value such as we have never before offered. Sizes and half sizes from 2½ to 8. Widths, full. Weight, averages 23 ounces.

$1.20

No. 15C619 Price, per pair.....$1.20

Ladies' Felt Lace Leather Sole, $0.48.

This shoe is made of a good grade of felt, reinforced with dongola side patchings, leather sole and heel and warm lined throughout. A shoe which we have never before been able to offer under 60 cents. Sizes, 3 to 8. No half sizes. Widths, extra full. Wt., 27 ozs.

No. 15C620 Price, per pair.....$0.48

Women's Felt Nullifiers, $0.85.

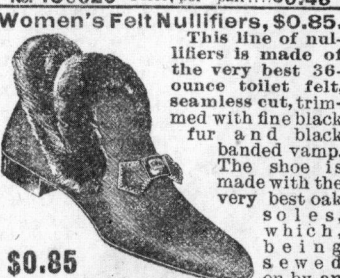

This line of nullifiers is made of the very best 36-ounce toilet felt, seamless cut, trimmed with fine black fur and black banded vamp. The shoe is made with the very best oak soles, which, being sewed on by an entirely new process, are very flexible and easy for the feet. Sizes, 2½ to 8. Widths, D, E and EE. Weight averages 27 ounces.

$0.85

No. 15C623 Price, per pair.....$0.85

For postage rate see page 4.

Ladies' Patent Vamp Dress Nullifiers, $1.15.

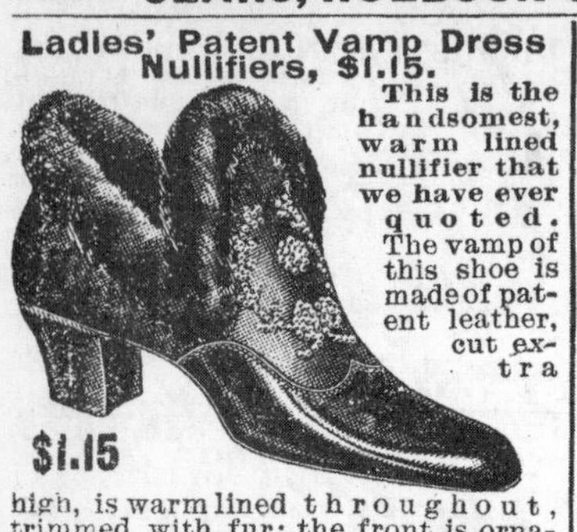

$1.15

This is the handsomest, warm lined nullifier that we have ever quoted. The vamp of this shoe is made of patent leather, cut extra high, is warm lined throughout, trimmed with fur; the front is ornamented with a handsome design of beadwork. Sizes, 2½ to 8. Widths, D, E and EE. Average wt. about 27 ozs.
No. 15C625 Price, per pair..$1.15

Women's Dongola Vamp Felt Nullifiers, $1.00.

$1.00

The vamp is made of fine soft dongola, patent tip neatly stitched on an artistic open work design. Is warm lined throughout, with heavy black felt top. Ornamented with steel cut bead work and trimmed with fur. The soles are oak leather hand turned and very flexible. Low style medium heel; combining style, warmth, service and comfort. Sizes, 2½ to 8. Widths, full. Average wt. 26 ozs.
No. 15C627 Price, per pair......$1.00

Ladies' Nullifiers, Figured Velvet, $0.69.

IMPORTED FIGURED VELVET.

$0.69

Sole is of good quality, serviceable counter, low sensible heel, fur bound, full fleece lined and a world beater for the money. Sizes and half sizes, 2½ to 8. Widths, full. Weight, 25 ounces.
No. 15C628 Price, per pair..$0.69

Ladies' Warm Nullifier, $1.00.

Made with fine and silky kid vamp, cut and stitched in artistic open work design. The top is dark red velvet cut extra high and trimmed with fine quality black fur. The soles are oak leather, hand turned and very flexible. This slipper is fleece lined throughout, and is very pretty and comfortable for house wear. Sizes, 2½ to 8. Widths, D, E and EE. Average weight about 27 ounces.
No. 15C629 Price, per pair...$1.00

Old Ladies' Wool Fleece Lined Bal $1.20.

A REDUCTION IN PRICE, BUT NO REDUCTION IN QUALITY.

$1.20

This shoe is designed for those wanting a roomy, sensible shoe with warm lining. Made of fine, soft vici kid stock, common sense toe and heel, flexible sole and lined throughout with felt, making the most thoroughly comfortable old ladies' shoe we have ever seen. Sizes and half sizes, 2½ to 8. Widths, full. Weight, 28 ounces.
No. 15C636 Price, per pair...$1.20

Ladies', Misses' and Children's Fine Felt Lace, $1.20 $0.90 and $0.80.

Is made from a very fine felt and foxed with a first class dongola kid. Solid leather extension soles. You will observe from the illustration that it has a nice kid tip, and being made over the new coin last, looks fully as well as the high priced cloth top shoes. Those who require a felt shoe and at the same time prefer a **dressy and good fitting boot**, will find this one just what they are looking for. **Sizes and half sizes. Widths, D, E and EE.** Weight averages 27 ounces.

Order by Number.

No. 15C637 Ladies' sizes, 2½ to 8.
Price, per pair....................................$1.20
No. 15C633 Misses' sizes, 12½ to 2, low heel.
Price, per pair....................................90
No. 15C635 Children's sizes, 9 to 12.
Price, per pair....................................80

For postage rate see page 4.

Ladies' Extra Wide Felt Lace, $1.00.

$1.00

For people who desire a felt shoe made on an extra broad toe last we have added this shoe to our line. It is made with a dongola vamp and heel foxing, extra quality, flexible sole, low broad heel, extra wide toe, made of heavy fine quality felt, nicely trimmed with velvet. This shoe is warm lined throughout. Sizes, 2½ to 8. EE width only. Average weight, 28 ounces.
No. 15C638 Price, per pair......$1.00

Ladies' All Felt Shoe, $1.00.

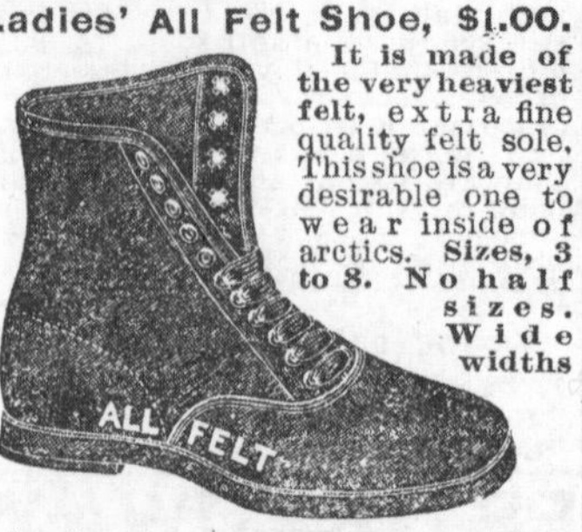

It is made of the very heaviest felt, extra fine quality felt sole. This shoe is a very desirable one to wear inside of arctics. Sizes, 3 to 8. No half sizes. Wide widths only. Average weight about 27 ounces.
No. 15C644 Price, per pair...$1.00

Women's Dongola Wool Lined Lace, $1.35.

WOULD SELL AT RETAIL FOR $1.75.

$1.35

For people who do not like to wear a felt shoe, but wish a shoe that will keep their feet warm in the coldest weather, this shoe answers the purpose. It is made of fine dongola, over a handsome last, patent leather tip, full extension back stay, solid oak slightly extended sewed soles, military heel, is lined with pure wool, has cushion insole. You get all the warmth and comfort of a felt shoe and the style and service of a good dongola dress shoe. Sizes, 3 to 8. Widths, full. Weight averages 30 ounces.
No. 15C639 Price, per pair......$1.35

Women's Silver Figured Velvet Nullifiers, $0.69.

$0.69

An up to date common sense slipper, ornamented with handsome buckle, high cut in front and back and trimmed with good quality black fur, low, broad, comfortable heel. Made over the broad, common sense, easy fitting last. Sizes, 3 to 8. Widths, full. Weight averages 24 ounces per pair.
No. 15C647 Price, per pair...$0.69

QUALITY COUNTS. BUY GOOD SHOES.

Women's Felt Slippers, $0.35.

$0.35

Made of heavy, fine quality all felt, sewed sole, lined throughout. Sizes, 3 to 8. Widths, full. Weight averages 16 ounces.
No. 15C650 Price, per pair.$0.35

Ladies' Medicated Flannel Lined Lace, $1.00.

$1.00

Ladies' Fine Felt Lace Shoe, made over a broad toe last, medicated red flannel lined and foxed with dongola kid. A shoe which is extremely comfortable and at the same time will give splendid service. Sizes, 2½ to 8. Widths, full. Weight averages 30 ozs.
No. 15C653 Price, per pair $1.00

Ladies' Seamless Nullifiers, $0.48.

$0.48

This is the only seamless front fur trimmed felt nullifier ever offered for anything like the price we have quoted. Made with leather sole and heel over a full last and a shoe which for actual wear is the equal of anything we have ever seen quoted up to 75 cents per pair. Sizes, 2½ to 8. Full widths. Weight averages 26 ounces.
No. 15C655 Price, per pair.$0.48

Ladies' Plush Bound Felt Slippers, $0.35.

This slipper is made from a fair quality of felt, is felt lined throughout, has felt inner sole, leather side patch. Really a 50-cent value. Sizes, 3 to 8. Widths, full. Weight averages 18 ozs.
No. 15C657 Price, per pair....$0.35

OUTING AND SPORTING SHOES.

Snow Shoes.

Genuine Indian made. The frame is first selected from second growth split ash, reinforced by two strong cross-pieces and riveted securely at the tail end. It also has the most desirable curved toes, which greatly assist even the amateur user. Strung with the very best cariboo gut and furnished with the tough moosehide thongs, we are offering this top notch snow shoe, the best made anywhere, for $3.00. Men's sizes only, 42 inches long, 14 inches wide.
No. 15C668
Price, per pair, $3.00

Men's Kangaroo Calf Bicycle Shoe, $1.25.

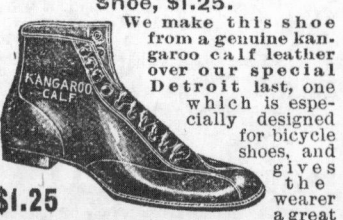

$1.25

We make this shoe from a genuine kangaroo calf leather over our special Detroit last, one which is especially designed for bicycle shoes, and gives the wearer a great deal of solid comfort. The shoe is absolutely all solid leather and durable. Sizes and half sizes, 5 to 11. Widths, full. Weight averages 35 ozs.
No. 15C663 Price, per pair...$1.25

Men's Fine White Canvas Outing Shoes, $1.25.

This shoe is made from a fine quality of white canvas, Blucher style, fitted with white agatine eyelets and the very best quality of rubber sole. This oxford is extra quality throughout, and should not be compared with those ordinarily found at the price we are quoting. Designed for those who wish an especially good outing shoe. Sizes and half sizes, 5 to 11. Widths, full. Weight averages 26 ounces.
No. 15C665 Price, per pair...$1.25

Men's, Boys', Youths,' Women's, Misses' and Children's Tennis or Outing Bals.

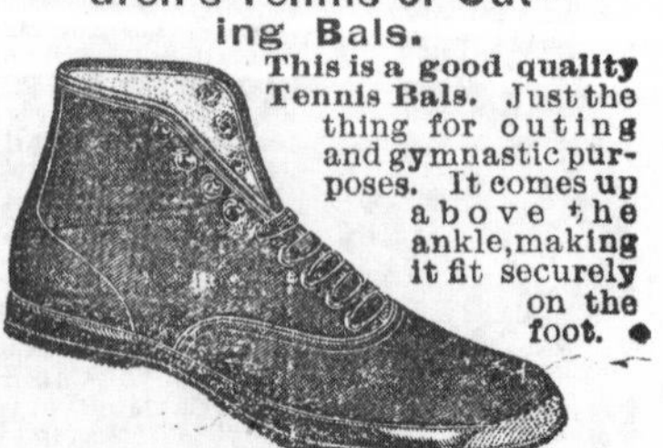

This is a good quality Tennis Bals. Just the thing for outing and gymnastic purposes. It comes up above the ankle, making it fit securely on the foot. Sizes and half sizes. Weight, 12 to 24 ounces.

No. 54C1512 Men's sizes, 6 to 12. Price, per pair....$0.60
No. 54C1514 Boys' sizes, 1 to 5½. Price, per pair.... .55
No. 54C1516 Youths' sizes, 11 to 13½. Price, per pair.... .50
No. 54C1518 Women's sizes, 3 to 8. Price, per pair.... .55
No. 54C1520 Misses' sizes, 11 to 2. Price, per pair.... .50
No. 54C1522 Children's sizes, 6 to 10½. Price, per pair.... .45

Men's, Women's, Boys', Youths', Misses' and Children's Tennis or Outing Oxfords.

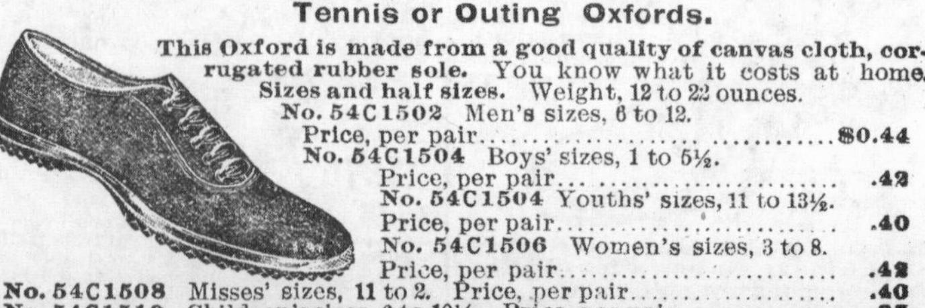

This Oxford is made from a good quality of canvas cloth, corrugated rubber sole. You know what it costs at home. Sizes and half sizes. Weight, 12 to 22 ounces.

No. 54C1502 Men's sizes, 6 to 12. Price, per pair....$0.44
No. 54C1504 Boys' sizes, 1 to 5½. Price, per pair.... .42
No. 54C1504 Youths' sizes, 11 to 13½. Price, per pair.... .40
No. 54C1506 Women's sizes, 3 to 8. Price, per pair.... .42
No. 54C1508 Misses' sizes, 11 to 2. Price, per pair.... .40
No. 54C1510 Children's sizes, 6 to 10½. Price, per pair.... .35

Men's and Boys' Canvas Outing Shoes, $0.48 and $0.45.

Men's Canvas Bal. Made with fair quality leather sole and heel, and suitable for bicycling and other similar sports. **Widths, full. No half sizes.** Weight averages 20 ounces.

$0.48

No. 15C692 Men's sizes, 6 to 11. Price, per pair......**$0.48**
No. 15C693 Boys' sizes, 1 to 5. Price, per pair...... **.45**

Vacation Oxford, $0.48.

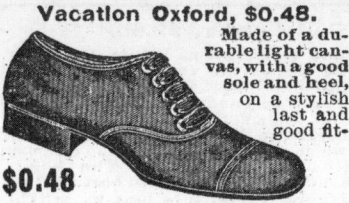

Made of a durable light canvas, with a good sole and heel, on a stylish last and good fitting pattern, neatly bound at top of vamp and tip, giving it just as much style as the high grade make, and we know it will stand the test against any offered elsewhere at double the price. **Sizes, 6 to 11, no half sizes. Full widths.** Weight, 15 to 20 ounces.

$0.48

No. 15C694 Price, per pair...**$0.48**

Men's Oxford Boot, $6.00 Value for $4.00.

We say a $6.00 value, and we might add that this exclusive pattern you probably have not seen at any price. It's the best piece of work produced by the most artistic shoe designer in America, and every part of the shoemaking is of the same high quality as the designing. The lower part of the shoe is made of specially selected patent corona colt, while the top is of velvet finished glove calf, producing the fitting qualities of the boot and the stylish effect of the Oxford. Velvet finished white oak sole of specially selected stock, hand sewed welt, a light flexible shoe, unequaled as to style, foot fitting and shape retaining qualities. To fully appreciate it you must see it and fit it on the foot, remembering our motto—Price paid and all transportation charges refunded, if unsatisfactory to you. **Sizes and half sizes, 5 to 11. Widths, C, D, E and EE.** Weight averages 30 ounces.

$4.00

No. 15C714 Price, per pair.......**$4.00**

Men's Fine Dress Oxford, $3.45.

The very latest style shown in all of the big city custom shoe shops is the button blucher Oxford, illustration of which is herewith shown. **This Oxford is made** of the very best patent corona colt stock, **over a handsome drop toe last, with oak soles, the** latest full military heel, and genuine **hand sewed welt.** This Oxford **has a** quality, **a style** and fit which it is impossible to obtain **in the** cheaper grade of shoes. **Sizes and half sizes, 5 to 11. Widths, B, C, D, E and EE, Weight** averages 28 ounces.

$3.45

No. 15C719 Price, per pair......**$3.45**

Men's Baseball Shoes, $1.85.

To play good ball you must have regulation baseball shoes. At this price every club can afford to have them. **Made from a good selection of kangaroo calf stock;** best of oak sole leather, fitted with genuine league toe and heel plates. **Sizes and half sizes, 5 to 11. Full widths only.** Weight averages 28 ounces.

$1.85

No. 15C696 Price, per pair..........**$1.85**

For postage rate see page 4.

Men's EDUCATOR Corona Colt Bal, $2.50.

This shoe is made from patent colt skin, which is very soft and pliable and does not cause the feet to become overheated, as the old fashioned patent calfskin, and at the same time **is fully as durable. This shoe**

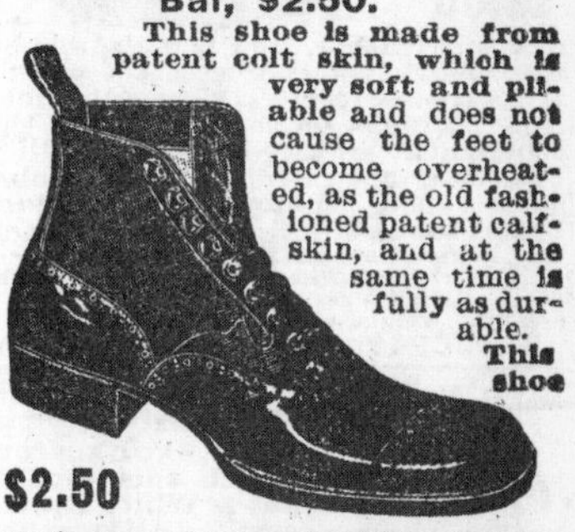

$2.50

is made over a medium English toe last; is a genuine Goodyear welt and has a box calf top, the very best linings and trimmings **and is** strictly high grade in every particular. **The** name **EDUCATOR** guarantees **$3.50** to **$4.00 in** shoe value. **Sizes and half sizes, 5 to 11. Widths, C, D, E and EE.** Weight averages **35** ounces.

No. 15C721 Price, per pair......**$2.50**

For postage rate, see page 4.

MEN'S FINE SHOES.

Men's Superfine all Patent Colt Blucher, Reduced to $3.00.

The shoe herewith illustrated is one of the handsomest things we have ever shown in men's fine footwear. One of the styles seen only in the very best big city stores, and there at $6.00 to $7.00 per pair. Made of the best patent corona colt stock (the most durable patent leather made), over a medium last, with tip toe and panel stitched quarter, quarter and top all being patent colt. The soles are of medium weight, genuine **hand sewn,** and will give the best of satisfaction, at the same time being flexible and easy. Fitted with fast color hooks and eyelets, best inside trimmings, and in fact the best shoe that the best shoemaker in America can produce. **Sizes and half sizes, 5 to 11. Widths C, D, E and EE.** Weight, 34 ounces.

$3.00

No. 15C705 Price, per pair....**$3.00**

The Lipton, $3.00.

OUR LATEST PRODUCTION.

A full page would not hold all the good qualities contained in this shoe, as it is the result of many months' careful study. The vamp is cut from the very best of plump, mellow vici kid and the tops from dull calf, while the trimmings, including the tip and heel foxing, are of the finest **patent coltskin.** The lace stay and collar are so arranged that together with the heel foxing a very handsome panel effect is formed. The soles are fine oak sole leather and it is a genuine bench made production that cannot be put on sale by any retailer for less than $5.00, but by guaranteeing to take all of the manufacturer's season production we are able to offer it at $3.00. **Sizes and half sizes, 5 to 11. Widths, C, D, E and EE.** Weight averages 35 ozs.

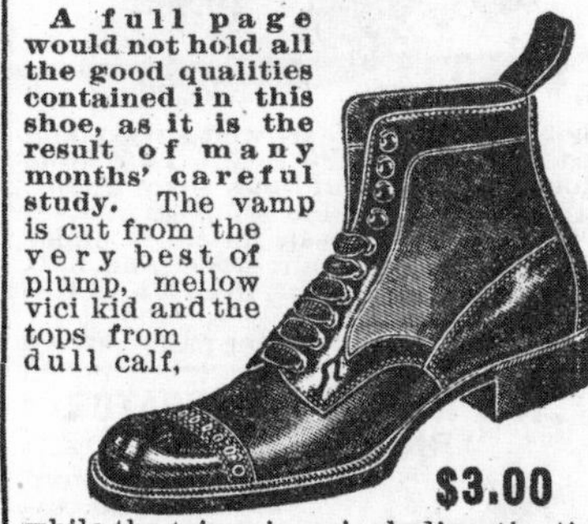

$3.00

No. 15C708 Price, per pair...**$3.00**

Our Very Best Dress Shoe, $3.45.

The maker of this shoe is known the world over as the best manufacturer of men's fine shoes, to retail at from $5.00 to $7.00 per pair. **Best patent corona colt stock hand sewed welt soles,** swell Newark last and pattern, and, while the illustration cannot be made more explicit, there is **a different fit, a snap, a comfort** in this make of shoe which we have never been able to duplicate in the west. The stock and wear is no better than our own shoes, but the difference in price goes for **that elegance of fit** and style, which is indescribable, but strikes the eye instantly when the shoe is seen. **Sizes and half sizes, 5 to 11. Widths, B, C, D, E and EE.** Weight averages 32 ounces.

$3.45

No. 15C715 Price, per pair........**$3.45**

Men's EDUCATOR Genuine Shell Cordovan Lace, Goodyear Welt, $2.50.

It is an established fact that cordovan leather is the most durable leather ever used in the manufacture of shoes. The fine texture of this leather renders it **waterproof. It is extremely firm, and the shoe** made of this leather **will retain** its shape longer than any material **that** can be used. The handsome perforated **tip** covers a medium wide coin toe. The **half** double sole is made of solid oak leather **with** modest extension soles, and Goodyear **welt** sewed. The eyelets are **fast** color. **Sizes, 5½ to 11. Widths, C, D, E and EE. Average** weight, 30 ounces.

$2.50

No. 15C723 Price, per pair......**$2.50**

Young Men's EDUCATOR, Patent Colt Lace, $2.50.

This shoe is something entirely out of the ordinary in the way of fine footwear. This shoe is made with best of oak soles, edges extended, dull box kid top, and in fact nothing has been omitted that is ordinarily found in the six and seven dollar fine shoes. Made by a manufacturer known the world over as producing the very highest grade of men's shoes manufactured, a shoe that will retain its shape, fit the foot, and give more ease and grace to the foot than any other make. The patent corona colt stock used in this oe is of the very best quality, and ing classed in our **EDUCATOR** line eans an excellent wearing shoe. **Sizes nd half sizes, 5 to 11. Widths, C, D, E and EE.** Weight averages 32 ounces.

$2.50

No. 15C707 Price, per pair... **$2.50**

For postage rate see page 4.

Men's Swell Blucher Colonial, $3.00.

The very latest style in men's low shoes is the plain toe, blucher colonial tie, herewith illustrated. Shown in all the exclusive city shoe shops at from $5.00 to $6.00 per pair and will surely be the rage with the up to date dressers. Stock is patent corona colt, will not draw the feet, and outwears any patent leather ever put on the market. Genuine hand sewed welt soles, military heel, outside back stay, and a style designed for the swellest dressers. **Sizes and half sizes, 5 to 11. Widths, C, D, E and EE.** Weight averages 29 ounces.

$3.00

No. 15C710 Price, per pair... **$3.00**

New Potay Toe, EDUCATOR, Patent Colt Button, $2.50.

For style, grace of outline and foot fitting qualities, this shoe surpasses anything we have ever seen. Guaranteed corona patent colt stock, with dull box kid top, and large dull buttons, and besides is all the rage with the swell dressers in New York, which means it must be correct. Welted oak soles; best of everything; new military heel. **Sizes and half sizes, 5 to 11. Widths, C, D, E and EE.** Weight, 29 ounces.

$2.50

No. 15C717 Price, per pair **$2.50**

Men's Russian Coltskin Bootee, Prime Oak Sole, Hub Core, $3.25.

GOODYEAR WELT.

The vamp stock is made of a box calf over a medium wide, soft box toe, combining style, durability, comfort and wear. The extension rock oak soles are sewed by the Goodyear welt process, making the inner soles perfectly smooth. The top is of the very best quality of Russian colt skin, 14 inches high. Outside back **stay** runs the entire length of the bootee, **is lined throughout with leather** and standard drill lining. **The** elastic **goring** in the side, as shown in **the illustration, makes** this the most desirable, comfortable **and perfect** fitting boot made. Very easy to **slip on or** off. Is thoroughly guaranteed in every **particular. Sizes, 6 to 11. Widths, D, E and EE.** Average weight, 42 ounces.

$3.25

No. 15C741 Price, per pair.. ...**$3.25**

Superfine Box Calf Lace, Reduced to $3.00.

New style, patent leather lace stay, and made in a factory turning out the finest, highest grade shoes in America, and we must admit that there is something indescribable about it, a fit, ease, and satisfied feeling in wearing it that does not go with the ordinary $3.50 and $4.00 kind. **Best box calf stock,** hand sewed, **heavy oak soles,** extension edges, new military heel, agatine hooks and eyelets, best linings and trimmings. **Honest all through. Sizes and half sizes, 5 to 11. Widths, C, D, E and EE.** Weight, 39 ounces.

$3.00

No. 15C713 Price, per pair...... **$3.00**

THE EDUCATOR SHOE

Has no equal in the world for the price.

Men's Box Calf Storm Shoe, $3.00.

GOODYEAR WELT. FULL LEATHER LINED.

$3.00

This shoe is made from a plump box calf leather, especially adapted to heavy weather, being extra high cut and fitted with snow excluding bellows tongue. Soles are cut from best California oak sole leather, and being sewed by the Goodyear welt process, the wearer is insured a perfectly smooth inner sole, no tacks or thread to hurt the foot, and at the same time a flexibility and ease not possible in a machine sewed shoe. **Made over a medium** broad toe last with tip, outside back stay, large eyelets, and first class materials and full leather lined to the toe. **Honest all through. Sizes and half sizes, 5 to 11. Widths, C, D, E and EE.** Weight, averages 40 ounces.

No. 15C748 Price per pair.......**$3.00**

Men's Plump Box Calf Welt Blucher, $2.95.

$2.95

The stock from which this shoe is cut is White Brothers' genuine box calf, which is known as the best. High grade oak sole leather, and made with extension edge and the latest style of rope stitching. **This shoe is fitted with large nickel hooks and eyelets,** outside back stay extending from heel to top of shoe, fine kid inside lace stay and top band, and stitched throughout with silk thread. **Genuine hand sewed welt and the best we know how to make at any price. Sizes and half sizes, 5 to 11. Widths, C, D, E and EE.** Average weight, 45 ounces.

No. 15C770 Price, per pair.......**$2.95**

Men's Extra High Cut Double Vamp Bluchers, $2.75.

DESIRABLE FOR HUNTERS, PROSPECTORS, ETC.

Reliable in every particular. This shoe is so made as to resist the strain of the hardest kind of wear. In getting up this shoe, every part has been carefully selected, and only first class leather used. The stock is kangaroo calf, tanned in such a manner as to make it as near waterproof as leather can be made. Seams stitched, restitched and riveted, making it absolutely rip proof. **The full extension back stay runs entirely to the top of the shoe. Is Blucher cut and full bellows tongue,** so arranged as to exclude all dirt, etc. A tip, extending to the heel, forms a double vamp, thereby insuring double the service found in the ordinary single vamp shoe. The soles are rock oak leather and filled with brass slugs, which increases the wear, are extended so as to protect the upper and sewed with the best Irish linen thread. **Large Klondike eyelets, rawhide laces. Sizes, 5 to 12. Widths, full.** Weight, about 55 ounces.

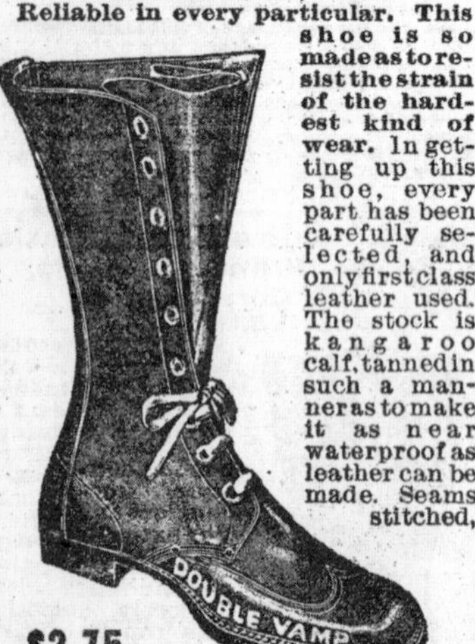

$2.75

No. 15C779 Price, per pair........**$2.75**

For postage rate see page 4.

Our Box Calf Leader, $2.95.

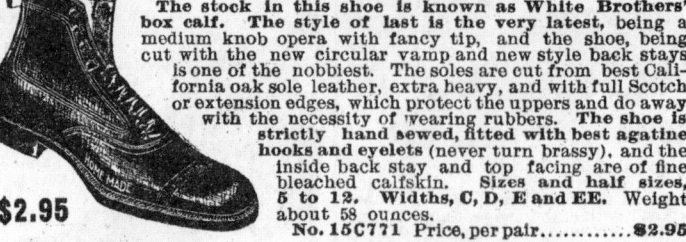

The stock in this shoe is known as White Brothers' box calf. The style of last is the very latest, being a medium knob opera with fancy tip, and the shoe, being cut with the new circular vamp and new style back stays is one of the nobbiest. The soles are cut from best California oak sole leather, extra heavy, and with full Scotch or extension edges, which protect the uppers and do away with the necessity of wearing rubbers. **The shoe is strictly hand sewed, fitted with best agatine hooks and eyelets** (never turn brassy), and the inside back stay and top facing are of fine bleached calfskin. **Sizes and half sizes, 5 to 12. Widths, C, D, E and EE.** Weight about 58 ounces.

$2.95

No. 15C771 Price, per pair............**$2.95**

EDUCATOR Ironoa Calf Bal $2.50.

$2.50

This is an entirely new shoe and is sold at a remarkably close margin when we put it in our EDUCATOR line at $2.50. It has a full double extra wide sole of the best Forest oak sole leather, and the upper is not only wearproof, but waterproof. We have added the high grade **Nojap** rubber heel. It might be termed a policeman's or letter carrier's friend, for it is light in weight, considering the amount of leather used. It is neat to look at and simply indestructible as a walking shoe. **Sizes and half size, 5½ to 12. Widths, full.** Weight, 35 ounces.

No. 15C776 Price, per pair...**$2.50**

Men's EDUCATOR Vici Kid Welt, $2.50.

$2.50

This shoe is made over a medium round toe last, single sole, with perforated tip, fitted with the everlasting English back stay, genuine Goodyear welt sewed, and carries all the style usually found in much higher priced lines. The name **EDUCATOR** is a guarantee that everything entering into the construction of this shoe is of the very best, including genuine oak soles, the best of thread and best of inner soles. **Sizes and half sizes, 5 to 11. Widths, C, D, E and EE.** Weight averages 32 ounces.

No. 15C781 Price, per pair..**$2.50**

Men's EDUCATOR Velour Calf Dress Blucher, $2.50.

$2.50

The swell blucher pattern herewith illustrated is one of the handsomest styles shown this season. This shoe is made from the best selection of velour calf—a leather which has the softness of vici kid, takes a polish like cordovan, and still retains the toughness of calfskin. The sole is of medium weight, Goodyear welt sewed, insuring a perfectly smooth insole and a comfort to the wearer not found in the ordinary kind sold at this price. **Sizes and half sizes, 5 to 11. Widths, C, D, E and EE.** Weight averages 35 ounces.

No. 15C783 Price, per pair...**$2.50**

Men's EDUCATOR Guaranteed Patent Colt Blucher, $2.50.

WE CLAIM IT TO BE AS GOOD AS ANY SHOE THAT RETAILS FOR $3.50.

Bluchers are all the rage and in this, our guaranteed patent leather colt shoe, we have a style never seen at anything like this price. Made of best dull calf top, California oak soles, natural finished bottoms. Goodyear welt sewed and the latest military heel. **This shoe has best of trimmings throughout,** and is special value at price quoted. We have never seen its equal under $3.50 to $4.00 per pair. **Sizes and half sizes, 5 to 11. Widths, C, D, E and EE.** Weight, 35 ounces.

$2.50

No. 15C785 Price, per pair. ..**$2.50**

The Roosevelt EDUCATOR Blucher, $2.50.

$2.50

This is bound to be a successful shoe no matter who buys it, for the pattern came into existence election day. Though intended only for higher priced shoes, we decided to put it **in our EDUCATOR** line, and that means it must be a good shoe. A vici kid vamp, tip and heel foxing, tooth glove, calf top and a nice medium, bright pure oak sole, finished in its natural color. It is a handsome shoe and will give the best of satisfaction. **Sizes, 5 to 11. Widths, C, D, E and EE.** Weight, 35 ounces.

No. 15C786 Price, per pair..**$2.50**

Men's EDUCATOR Guaranteed Patent Colt Kid, $2.50.

A WONDER OF VALUE.

$2.50

We make this shoe over the popular Brockton last with fancy perforated tips, genuine Goodyear welt soles and good quality dull calf tops. Sole leather is of the very best white oak stock, natural finished, so you can see the quality at a glance. We fit the shoe with fast color eyelets, silk thread, black kid inside top facing and, in fact, have omitted nothing to make it as dressy as possible. **Sizes and half sizes, 6 to 11. Widths, B, C, D, E and EE.** Weight averages about 35 ounces, according to size.

No. 15C787 Price, per pair...**$2.50**

Men's EDUCATOR Heavy Sole Box Calf, $2.50.

$2.50

It is made from White Bros.' box calf leather. The soles are cut from genuine California oak sole leather, made extra heavy and with full extended edges. This shoe is genuine Goodyear welt sewed and a custom outside back stay. It is a good fitting, dressy last, and every pair is stamped "EDUCATOR," insuring a $3.50 value. **Sizes and half sizes, 5 to 12. Widths, D, E and EE. Average weight,** 38 ounces.

No. 15C790 Price, per pair.....**$2.50**

Men's EDUCATOR Box Calf Blucher, $2.50.

$2.50

Made of White Brothers' box calf stock. One of the most serviceable leathers tanned; has a slightly pebbled surface, and is as near waterproof as leather can be made. **Late style Blucher pattern with perforated** tip and quarter, long outside back stay and new military heel. Soles are best oak, natural finish, so you can see the quality. Goodyear sewn and every pair stamped **EDUCATOR,** which guarantees a $3.50 value. **Sizes and half sizes, 5 to 11. Widths, D, E and EE.** Weight averages 43 ounces.

No. 15C800 Price, per pair......**$2.50**

Men's EDUCATOR Chrome Wax Calf Bal, Patent Saw Tooth Lace Stay, $2.50.

$2.50

No new make of leather has as yet been able to give better wearing results than wax calf, and by adding the Chrome or softening process to the Wax calf leather, we are able to offer a shoe that is good for all times, all weathers, and all kinds of service. Our illustration represents a shoe into which every good feature is embodied that our name "EDUCATOR" will stand for, and has an extra finish. We have put on a neat patent calf lace stay with a saw tooth edge. **Sizes and half sizes, 5 to 11. Widths, D, E and EE.** Average weight, 36 ounces.

No. 15C808 Price, per pair.....**$2.50**

Men's EDUCATOR Box Calf High Cut Lace, $2.50.

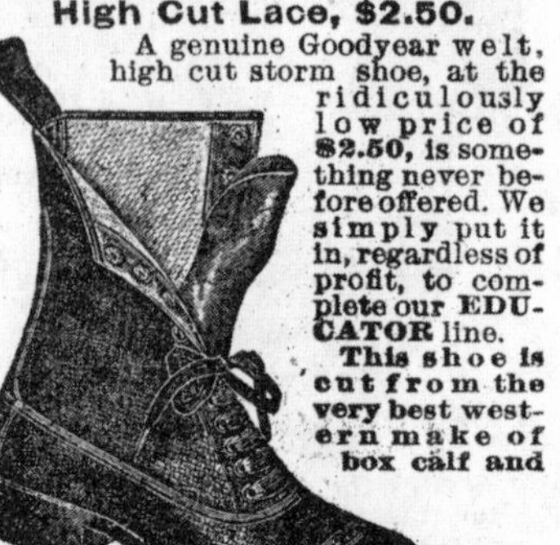

$2.50

A genuine Goodyear welt, high cut storm shoe, at the ridiculously low price of **$2.50,** is something never before offered. We **simply put it** in, regardless of profit, to complete our **EDUCATOR** line. **This shoe is cut from the very best western make of box calf and** sole leather, and will compare favorably with any $3.50 shoe you can buy elsewhere. Genuine Goodyear welt soles, heavy weight and slightly extended edges. By placing our **EDUCATOR** stamp on it we mean to imply "good as gold." **Sizes, 5 to 12. Widths, D, E and EE.** Average weight, 45 ounces.

No. 15C815 Price, per pair......**$2.50**

Men's EDUCATOR Kangaroo Lace, Goodyear Welt, $2.50.

Genuine kangaroo leather, very soft and pliable, and while it is the ideal leather for those with tender feet, it is more durable than many heavier leathers, and makes a splendid dress shoe

$2.50

at any season. We make this shoe alongside our best goods, over the fashionable Boston last, with tip toe. It is fitted with custom back stay, wearproof lining trimmed in the best possible manner, has white oak soles sewed on by the Goodyear welt process, making them at once flexible and producing a perfectly smooth inner sole. **Sizes and half sizes, 5 to 11. Widths, D, E and EE.** Weight averages 40 ounces.

No. 15C817 Price, per pair...**$2.50**

For postage rate see page 4.

Men's EDUCATOR Kangaroo Congress, $2.50.

GENUINE GOODYEAR WELT.

This shoe is made over the globe last and is especially desirable for those having tender feet. **The kangaroo stock is very soft and pliable,** and at the

$2.50

same time as tough as any leather tanned. **The soles are cut from oak sole leather, being sewed on by the Goodyear welt process; are very flexible** and much more comfortable than it is possible to make a machine sewed shoe. This shoe is fitted with wearproof lining, which is the best made, and alone will save one-half your present bill for socks. **Sizes and half sizes, 5 to 12. Widths, D, E and EE. Home made.** Weight averages 40 ozs.

No. 15C819 Price, per pair...**$2.50**

For postage rate see page 4.

Men's EDUCATOR Kangaroo Blucher, $2.50.

Our EDUCATOR line of shoes has become so wonderfully popular, that we have felt it necessary to add this fancy blucher pattern shoe to the line. The stock from which this shoe is

$2.50

made is a genuine kangaroo, but is finished bright, making one of the handsomest leathers we have ever seen, at the same time retaining all of the toughness that the genuine kangaroo has always been noted for. This shoe is made over a medium English last, with tip toe, best of oak sole leather, genuine Goodyear welt, and trimmed in the best manner throughout. The name **EDUCATOR** implies $3.50 value for $2.50. **Sizes and half sizes, 5 to 11. Widths, C, D, E and EE.** Weight averages 31 ounces.

No. 15C821 Price, per pair...**$2.50**

For postage rate see page 4.

Leather Lined EDUCATOR $2.50

For $2.50 who ever heard of a shoe with a genuine Goodyear welt cork filled sole, leather lined, solid double oak sole, popular **box calf** stock as near waterproof as leather can be made. But in this shoe we offer you even more, a shoe made

$2.50

over a stylish and up to date last, with modern toe and tip, seams sewed with silk and linen thread, **will not rip.** The box calf stock is the result of science in the process of tanning calfskin. It is easy to take care of, and an occasional application of box calf or patent leather paste will keep it like new. **Sizes and half sizes, 5 to 12. Widths, C, D, E and EE.** Weight averages 45 ounces.

No. 15C829 Price, per pair....**$2.50**

Men's VELOUR CALF Welt, Reduced to $2.00.

Don't judge the quality of this shoe from the price. It is made of Velour Calf, sometimes called Tuxedo kid, which in reality is a bright finished calfskin; genuine Goodyear welt, light soles, outside back

stay, perfectly smooth inner sole and is the equal of shoes usually sold at $3.00 to $3.50. We simply name $2.00 per pair, determined as we always are, to demonstrate our ability to undersell all others. **Sizes, 5 to 11. Widths, D, E and EE.** Weight, 33 ounces.

No. 15C830 Price, per pair, reduced to.............................**$2.00**

For postage rate see page 4.

Goodyear Welt Box Calf Blucher, $2.00.

Good box calf vamp, pebble calf top, and heavy soles sewed on by the Goodyear welt process, insuring a smooth inner sole, no tack or thread to hurt the foot. A

shoe that will compare favorably with the $3.00 kind found elsewhere. **Sizes and half sizes, 5 to 11. Widths, D, E and EE.** Weight, 39 ounces.

No. 15C831 Price, per pair...**$2.00**

Men's EDUCATOR Kangaroo Lace, $2.50.

It is a well-known fact that genuine Australian kangaroo leather is the most comfortable for tender feet and also more tough than many leathers twice as heavy. This shoe is made especially for those who want a soft, comfortable shoe, over the plain toe globe last and genuine Goodyear welt, oak soles, of medium weight. The shoe is stitched throughout with silk and linen, fitted with calf inside lace stay and top band, wearproof lining and every pair stamped **EDUCATOR** on the sole. **Sizes and half sizes, 5 to 12. Widths, C, D, E and EE.** Weight averages 40 ounces.

$2.50

No. 15C825 Price, per pair, **$2.50**

For postage rate see page 4.

Men's Patent Colt Button, $2.00.

We make this shoe from **best patent colt** leather over medium coin toe, **with perforated tip and with light single sole. THE TOPS are cut from dull mat calf,** and to make

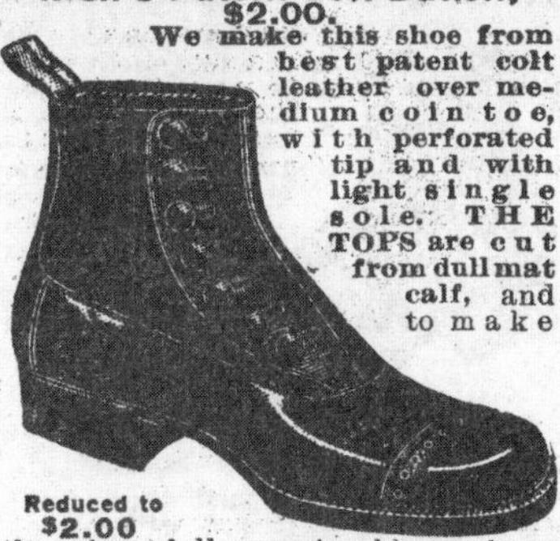

the shoe fully serviceable, we have reinforced both the buttons and the button fly with genuine **Napa Tanned Kid. Sizes and half sizes, 6 to 11. Widths, D, E and EE.** Average weight, 36 ounces.

No. 15C835 Price, per pair...**$2.00**

The Breadwinners' Goodyear Welt Lace Shoe. Reduced to $1.60.

Made of the famous C. F. J. leather, tough as cowhide, soft as a glove, medium weight Goodyear welt soles, insuring a smooth inner sole, no tacks or thread to hurt the foot, broad comfortable last, sensible heel

outside back stay, and shank reinforced with standard screw fastening. Especially suited to carpenters, painters, teamsters, and all who wish a durable shoe, and at the same time all the comfort found in the $3.00 kinds. **Sizes, 6 to 11. Widths, full.** Weight, 45 ounces.

No. 15C839 Price, per pair...**$1.60**

The Week Day Goodyear Welt Blucher, $2.00.

The first practical Goodyear welt workingmen's shoe ever offered at a low price. Blucher cut, made of the famous C. F. J. leather, soft, and as tough as cowhide. Goodyear welt, heavy oak soles no tacks or threads

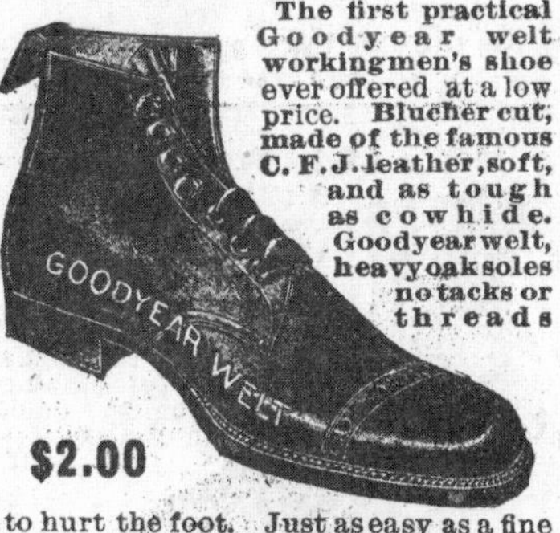

to hurt the foot. Just as easy as a fine $4.00 shoe, and shank reinforced with standard screw fastening. Broad tip toe last, outside back stay, sensible heel, and designed for carpenters, teamsters, painters, trainmen, and all those having heavy work who appreciate the style and comfort usually found in the best welt shoes. **Sizes, 6 to 11. Widths, full.** Weight, 45 ounces.

No. 15C840 Price, per pair...**$2.00**

Men's Seal Vamp High Cut Lace, Bellows Tongue, $2.00.

Seal leather is a stock of extreme durability, and will resist the hardest kind of wear. Tanned by the best known process to give strength. This shoe has a solid oak sole, standard screw fastenings. A top made of kangaroo calf stock, has leather outside and inside;

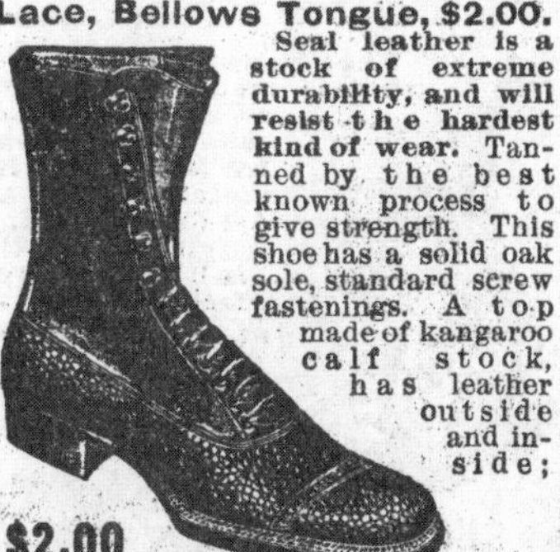

back stay extending all the way to the top of the shoe, and full bellows tongue of heavy dongola, made seamless. **Sizes, 6 to 12. Widths, D, E and EE.** Average weight, 45 ounces.

No. 15C843 Price, per pair...**$2.00**

Men's Coltskin NINE WIDE Lace, $2.00.

This shoe is made of the genuine Russia coltskin, over a special last, which is a full 9-wide standard measurement; in other words,

would be **EEEEE** in width. Made with half double sole, and is especially designed for those desiring a shoe made extra wide and roomy. **Sizes and half sizes, 6 to 12. Width, EEEEE.** Weight averages 37 ounces.

No. 15C845 Price, per pair.**$2.00**

For postage rate see page 4.

Genuine Box Calf, Goodyear Welt, $1.85.

All of our former offers are surpassed by this, and we offer you here a shoe as described above, at a price the wholesale jobbers would be pleased to buy them in case lots at. We guarantee this shoe in every respect, fit, quality and style, the equal

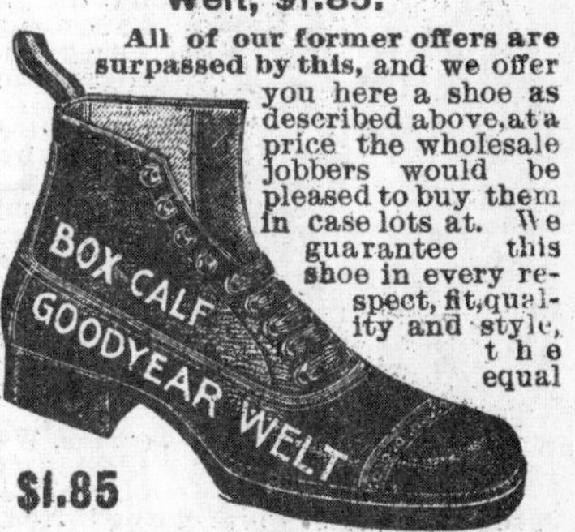

of any $3.00 shoe in the market. It is snappy and dressy enough for any Broadway gentleman, yet has the wearing quality of a first class every day knockabout shoe. **Sizes and half sizes, 5 to 11. Widths, D, E and EE.** Weight averages 38 ounces.

No. 15C847 Price, per pair.**$1.85**

The R. R. Life Saver, Men's Box Calf Lace Congress, $1.75.

Cut from the very best western make of box calf and sole leather and a western product throughout, which signifies the best of durability, and we challenge any one to produce

its equal at anywhere near our price, which is only $1.75. **Sizes, 5 to 11. Widths, D, E and EE.** Average weight, 36 ounces.

No. 15C849 Price, per pair.**$1.75**

Men's Goodyear Welt, Vici Kid Blucher, $2.00.

This Vici Kid Shoe is cut from a very good quality of velvet finished kid is made over a medium English last, with half double sole and absolutely all solid sole

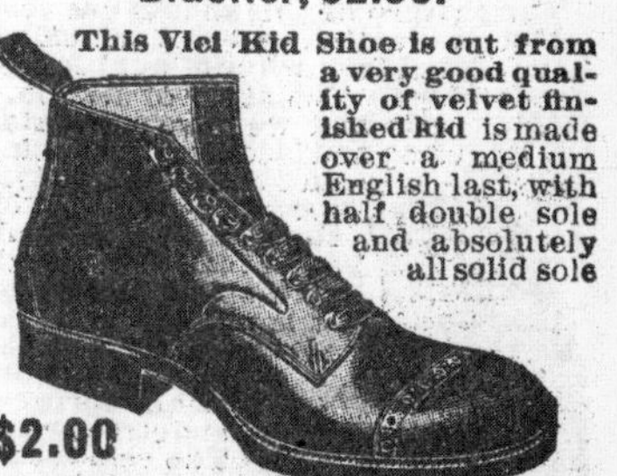

leather counter and inner sole. The shoe is fitted with outside back stay, perforated tip toe, and is genuine Goodyear welt sewn, insuring a comfort unusual in a fine dress shoe for this price. **Sizes and half sizes, 6 to 11. Widths, D, E and EE.** Weight averages 39 ounces.

No. 15C850 Price, per pair.**$2.00**

For postage rate see page 4.

The Mikado, $1.85.

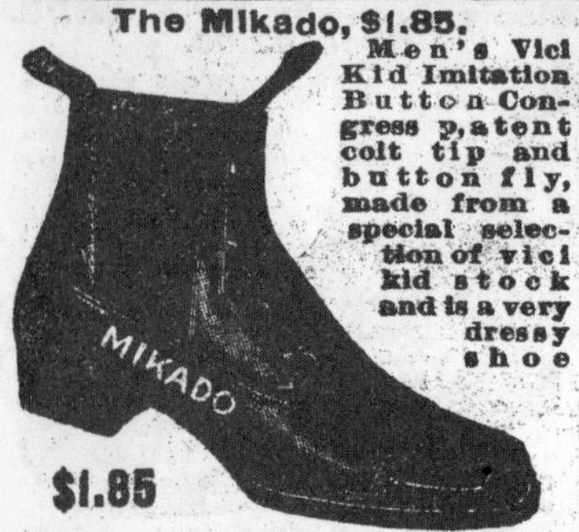

Men's Vici Kid Imitation Button Congress patent colt tip and button fly, made from a special selection of vici kid stock and is a very dressy shoe with good flexible sole. It is exceptionally light and easy on the foot, yet will give good service on account of the special selection of material from which it is made. Sizes, 5 to 11. Widths, D, E and EE. Weight, averages 35 ounces.

No. 15C852 Price, per pair...$1.85

Steel Shod Police Lace, $1.75.

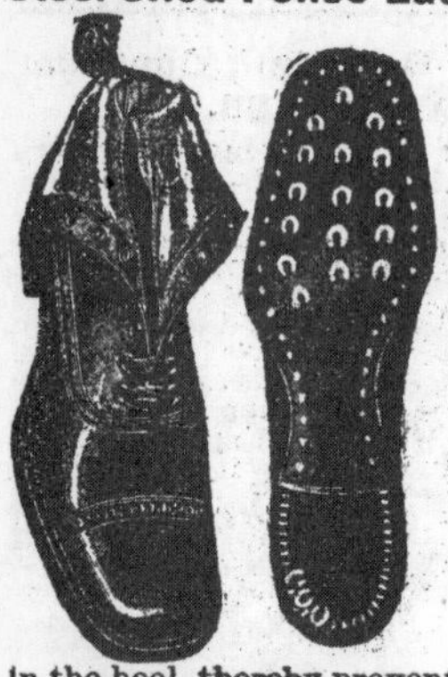

Badger calfskin, made with double soles, extension edges, and the sole being filled with the famous hardened steel Perfection circlettes, will render twice the service found in any otners. We also put circlettes in the heel, thereby preventing it from wearing down on one side. Especially designed for teamsters, police, railroad men and all those who need a heavy, serviceable shoe. Home made. Sizes and half sizes, 5 to 12. Widths, D, E and EE. Weight averages 48 ounces.

No. 15C854 Price, per pair...$1.75

Featherweight Vici Kid Lace, $1.95.

We illustrate herewith our latest genuine vici kid shoe, made with circle seam, fancy stitched panel and outside back stay from heel to top of shoe. It is especially designed for those wishing a light weight and yet durable shoe. The soles are cut from the best of leather, and being made in our new 20th Century shoe plant, it has the appearance and in fact is equal to many shoes sold for much more money. HOME MADE. Sizes and half sizes, 6 to 11. Widths, D, E and EE. Weight averages 35 ounces.

No. 15C858 Price, per pair...$1.95

For postage rate see page 4.

Men's Velour Calf Lace, Reduced to $1.75.

The pattern of this shoe is our very latest production and one which we have copied from some of our highest grade shoes. The style of last is a medium coin and we have perforated the tip, vamp and lace stay, producing an extraordinary style for this price. The shoe is absolutely all solid leather and will give splendid service. It is not, however, intended for a working shoe, but more especially for dress and street wear. The velour calf stock is one of the handsomest leathers ever produced. Sizes and half sizes, 6 to 11. Widths, D, E and EE. Weight, about 33 ounces.

No. 15C861 Price, per pair...$1.75

Men's Cork Sole Lace, $2.00.

We have made it with a full sheet cork sole placed between the inner and the outer sole and extending from toe to heel. The outer sole is cut from the best union sole leather, and will wear like iron. Stitched throughout with silk thread, fitted with plump dongola top and genuine calfskin inside trimmings. If you are looking for a shoe at this price, you cannot secure the equal of this one in the United States. Sizes and half sizes, 5 to 12. Widths, D, E and EE. Weight averages 38 ounces.

No. 15C864 Price, per pair...$2.00

Men's Patent Colt Blucher, $2.00.

This Blucher is made of good quality genuine patent colt stock—the style of pattern being used in many shoes sold up to four and even five dollars per pair. Made over a medium round toe last, with perforated tip and quarter foxing, and to make it even more desirable, we fit it with the patent leather lace stay, which is also perforated. The soles are good quality, the shoe is well trimmed and exceptional value for the price quoted. Sizes and half sizes, 5 to 11. Widths, D, E and EE. Weight averages 38 ounces.

No. 15C868 Price, per pair....$2.00

For postage rate see page 4.

Men's Light Weight Vici, $1.75.

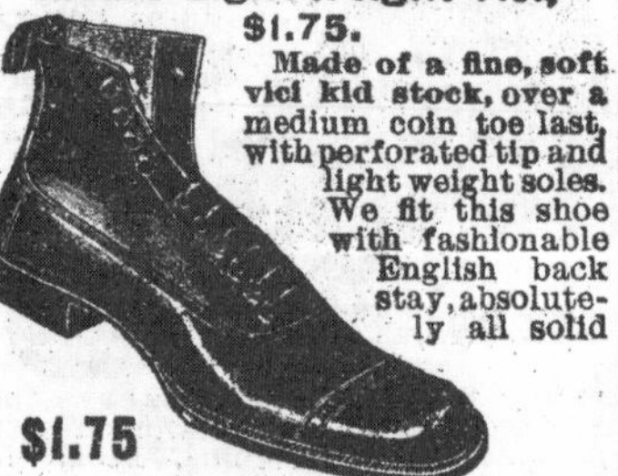

Made of a fine, soft vici kid stock, over a medium coin toe last, with perforated tip and light weight soles. We fit this shoe with fashionable English back stay, absolutely all solid sole leather counter and inner sole, making a very dressy, and at the same time durable shoe. Sizes and half sizes, 5 to 11. Widths, D, E and EE. Weight, 35 ounces.

No. 15C871 Price, per pair...$1.75

For postage rate see page 4.

Men's Glaced Coltskin Lace.

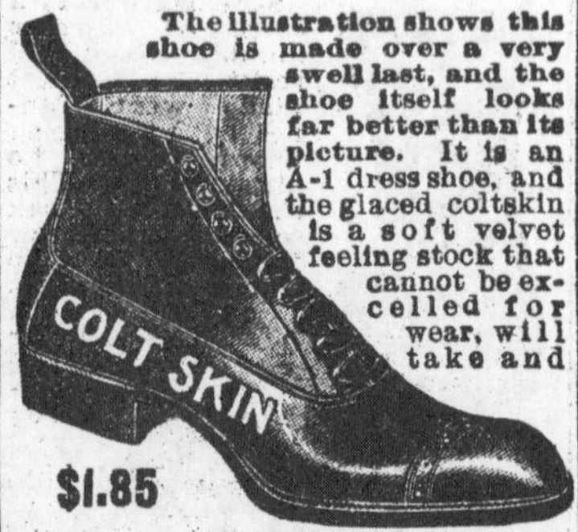

The illustration shows this shoe is made over a very swell last, and the shoe itself looks far better than its picture. It is an A-1 dress shoe, and the glaced coltskin is a soft velvet feeling stock that cannot be excelled for wear, will take and retain a bright polish and does not scuff off so easily as the kidskin. Widths, D, E and EE. Sizes and half sizes, 5 to 11. Weight, 35 ounces.

No. 15C874 Price, per pair...$1.85

Men's Patent Colt Lace, $2.00.

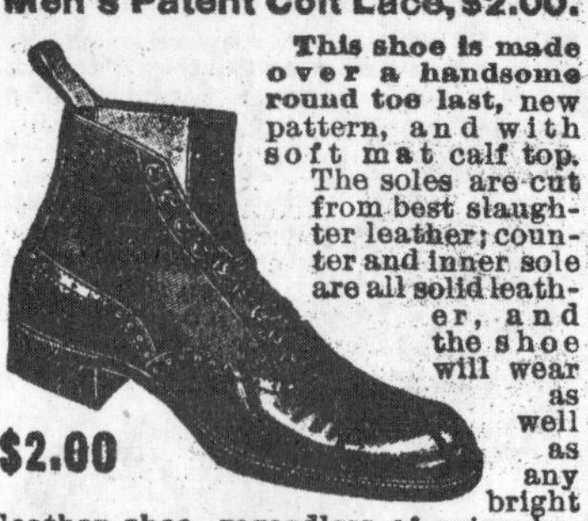

This shoe is made over a handsome round toe last, new pattern, and with soft mat calf top. The soles are cut from best slaughter leather; counter and inner sole are all solid leather, and the shoe will wear as well as any bright leather shoe, regardless of price, besides having the style and foot fitting qualities usually found only in the higher grades. Sizes and half sizes, 5 to 11. Widths, D, E and EE. Weight averages 35 ounces.

No. 15C875 Price, per pair...$2.00

Men's Satin Calf Lace, Reduced to $1.20.

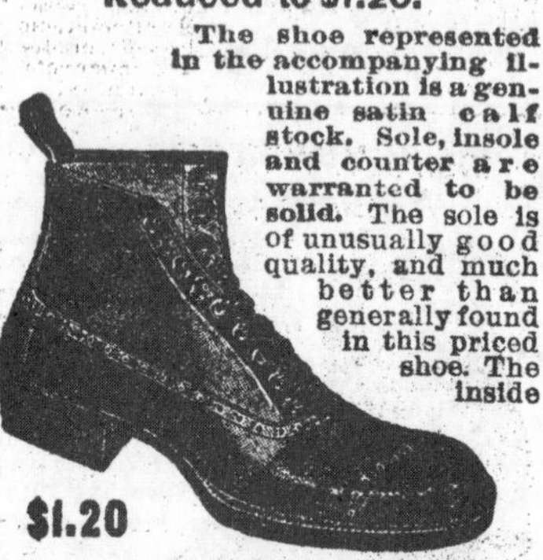

The shoe represented in the accompanying illustration is a genuine satin calf stock. Sole, insole and counter are warranted to be solid. The sole is of unusually good quality, and much better than generally found in this priced shoe. The inside trimmings are of leather. Sizes, 5 to 11. Widths, D, E and EE. Average weight, 48 ounces.

No. 15C878 Price, per pair...$1.20

Men's Patent Colt Blucher, $1.60.

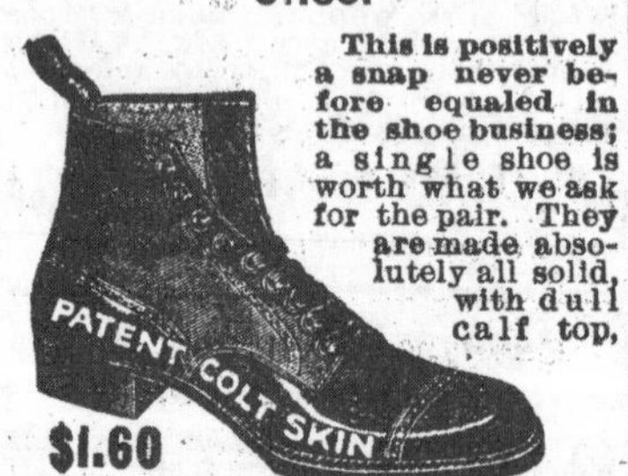

This is positively a snap never before equaled in the shoe business; a single shoe is worth what we ask for the pair. They are made absolutely all solid, with dull calf top, on the same last and pattern as the high grade shoes by a manufacturer who does not know how to make poor goods. Remember our motto, "Satisfaction guaranteed or money refunded with all transportation charges." This will make you feel like ordering several pairs at this ridiculously low price of $1.60. Sizes and half sizes, 5 to 11. Widths, D, E and EE. Weight, 26 ounces.

No. 15C880 Price, per pair...$1.60

Men's Box Calf Lace, Reduced to $1.60.

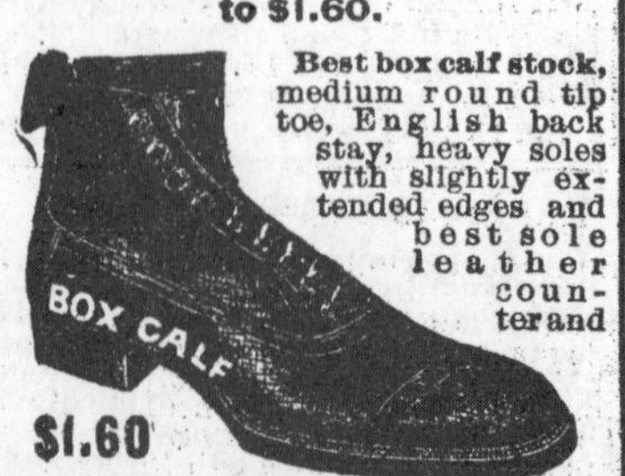

Best box calf stock, medium round tip toe, English back stay, heavy soles with slightly extended edges and best sole leather counter and inner sole. This shoe is very neat in appearance, and will give all the wear usually found in a $2.50 kind. Sizes and half sizes, 5 to 11. Widths, D, E and EE. Weight, 39 ounces.

No. 15C882 Price, per pair...$1.60

Men's Leather Lined Lace, $1.75.

Made from a first selection of badger calfskin, full leather lined, with double soles, extension edge and a genuine seal calf top, and fancy perforated tip and vamp. Should you order this shoe and not consider it the greatest bargain you ever saw, return it and we will immediately refund purchase price together with all transportation charges. Sizes and half sizes, 6 to 12. Widths, D, E and EE. Weight averages 42 ounces.

No. 15C884 Price, per pair...$1.75

Men's Heavy Split High Cut, Three-Sole Lace, $1.50.

No manufacturer has ever dared to put out so much good material at this figure. It is made of a good quality heavy split, with two full soles and a slip sole, solid leather counter and inner sole, and to those who have use for such a shoe it is a phenomenal bargain at $1.50. Sizes, 6 to 12. No half sizes. Full widths. Weight, 50 ounces.

No. 15C886 Price, per pair...$1.50

Men's Seamless Lace, Reduced to $1.35.

The shoe herewith illustrated is made of the famous C. E. J. French Kang-kip leather, which is superior to any ever tanned for a heavy working shoe. It is plump, soft, mellow, and is practically seamless, the only seam being in the back, which is reinforced, making a practically rip proof shoe. Fitted with double sole, pegged, all leather heel, solid sole leather counter, and dirt excluding bellows tongue. The shoe is unlined. We simply never have seen anything like it for the price quoted. Sizes, 6 to 11. No half sizes. Widths, full. Weight averages 45 ounces.

No. 15C887 Price, per pair $1.35

For postage rate see page 4.

Men's Seal Calf Seamless, Reduced to $1.50.

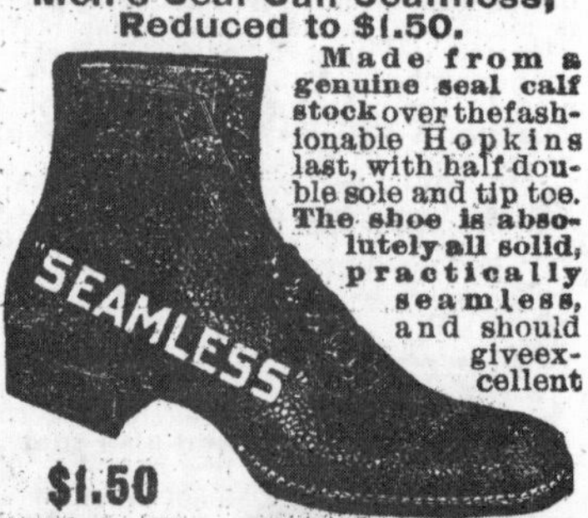

Made from a genuine seal calf stock over the fashionable Hopkins last, with half double sole and tip toe. The shoe is absolutely all solid, practically seamless, and should give excellent service. The price which we are naming on this shoe barely covers the actual cost of material and labor with our one small profit added, hence in considering the value of the shoe, please remember that while the price is $1.50, the value is really much more. Sizes and half sizes, 6 to 11. Widths, full. Weight averages 43 ounces.

No. 15C891 Price, per pair. $1.50

Boys' Never Rip Seamless Lace, Reduced to $1.20.

Made of very best selection of kangaroo grain, which is soft, durable and as near waterproof as it is possible to make leather. This shoe is seamless on the sides and back, the only seam being under the tip, which is securely riveted, and the soles being put on with invisible screws, makes a shoe absolutely rip proof. Sizes and half sizes, 1 to 5½. Full widths. Weight averages 30 ounces.

No. 15C892 Price, per pair...$1.20

Seamless Kangaroo Calf Bal, $1.85.

In adding this to our line we are complying with a request from all parts of the country. There is something about this leather that enables a man to wear it all day and yet not have a tired feeling when taken off at night.

SEAMLESS KANGAROO CALF

$1.85

The last, while neat and stylish, has a full roomy tread, and the sole, counter and insole are of the best western slaughter leather, insuring the best wear to be had, regardless of price. Widths, full. Sizes and half sizes, 6 to 12. Weight, 38 ounces.

No. 15C893 Price, per pair..$1.85

Boys' Seamless Kangaroo Calf Bal, $1.50.

In every way the same as the men's shoe No. 15C893. We quote cheaper shoes, but quality was our whole thought in building this one. Sizes, 1 to 5½. Widths, full. Weight 32 ounces

No. 15C894 Price, per pair..$1.50

Men's Extra Heavy Satin Shoes Reduced to $1.35.

Extra Heavy Satin Calf Bals, pebble calf top, absolutely all solid, with two full soles and slip, making an extra heavy, practically indestructible shoe. Vamps triple stitched, soles standard screw fastened and reinforced with best waxed thread. Sizes, 6 to 12. No half sizes. Widths, full. Weight averages 48 ounces.

$1.35

No. 15C895 Price, per pair..$1.35

Boys' Box Calf Lace, Reduced to $1.25.

A genuine western product, both in material and labor, and equal to any shoe we have ever seen offered at one-half as much again. Box calf stock, solid sole leather counter and inner sole, no cut off vamp under tip, and the very best slaughter outsole. Sizes and half sizes, 1 to 5½. Widths, D, E and EE. Weight averages, 30 ounces.

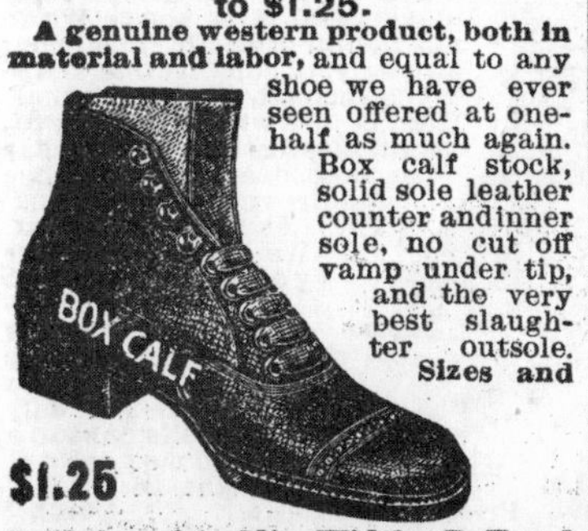

No. 15C897 Reduced price, per pair..........$1.25

For postage rate see page 4.

Boys' Box Calf Blucher, Reduced to $1.35.

This shoe is made from a genuine box calf leather, known the world over as the most durable and satisfactory. The shoe is absolutely all solid sole leather counter and inner sole, medium weight outsole. The vamp extends under the tip, and will give exceptional wear. The style is better than the average boys' shoe and to those wishing a strictly up to date shoe which will also give splendid service, we recommend it. Sizes and half sizes, 1 to 5½. Widths, D, E and EE. Weight averages 34 ounces.

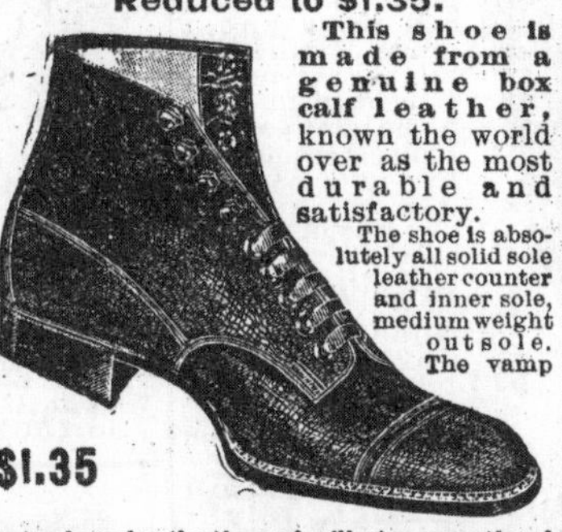

No. 15C899 Reduced price, per pair..........$1.35

For postage rate see page 4.

Men's Combined Congress and Lace, $1.35.

Made from a good selection of badger calfskin, medium full coin tip toe and plump soles. It is fitted with seal calf top, absolutely all solid sole leather counter and inner sole, and to those who wish a serviceable shoe at a low price we recommend it. Sizes and half sizes, 5 to 11. Widths, D, E and EE. Weight averages 38 ounces.

No. 15C901 Price, per pair......$1.35

For postage rate see page 4.

Boys' and Youths' Storm Shoes, $1.50 and $1.40.

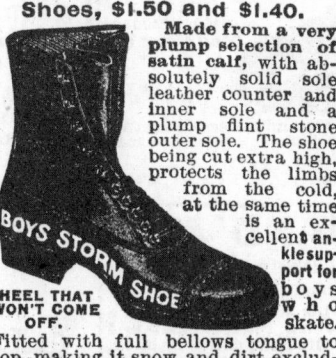

Made from a very plump selection of satin calf, with absolutely solid sole leather counter and inner sole and a plump flint stone outer sole. The shoe being cut extra high, protects the limbs from the cold, at the same time is an excellent ankle support for boys who skate. Fitted with full bellows tongue to top, making it snow and dirt excluding. Widths, D, E and EE. Weight averages from 20 to 35 ounces.

BOYS STORM SHOE

HEEL THAT WON'T COME OFF.

No. 15C903 Boys' sizes, 2½ to 5½. Price, per pair..........$1.50

No. 15C904 Youths' sizes, 11½ to 2. Price, per pair..........$1.40

For postage rate see page 4.

Men's Coin Toe Satin Calf Lace, A Leader, $1.00.

This shoe is made of fine satin calf, made on the latest coin toe last, and fitted with durable top. Stitched and perforated tip. The sole is made of solid and durable leather. Counter and inner sole also are made solid. This shoe is lined, trimmed and fitted in a manner seldom found in this priced shoe. Sizes and half sizes, 6 to 11. Widths, D, E and EE. Weight, 40 ounces.

$1.00

No. 15C909 Price, per pair......$1.00

For postage rate see page 4.

Men's Satin Calf Congress, $1.20.

The stock from which it is made is a good selection of satin calf, and will wear well. Fitted with seal calf top, plump hemlock soles, and genuine sole leather counter and inner sole. No shoddy enters into this shoe. Sizes, 6 to 12; no half sizes. Widths, D, E and EE. Weight averages 45 ounces.

SOLID LEATHER

$1.20

No. 15C910 Price, per pair......$1.20

For postage rate see page 4.

Boys' Steel Shod Lace, Reduced to $1.25.

London toe last with full perforated tip, genuine dongola top, satin calf vamp and best sole leather bottoms. The shoe is fitted with custom back-stay, stitched with silk and linen, and the plump outsole filled with brass slugs; heel is a new specialty, entirely our own, and is constructed so that the top lift will not fall or be knocked off with any ordinary wear, making a shoe practically indestructible. Weight averages 25 to 36 ounces. Widths, D, E and EE.

No. 15C911 Boys' sizes and half sizes, 13 to 5½. Price, per pair..........$1.25

Boys' Satin Shoe, $1.00.

Outer soles, inner soles and counters are of solid leather. The back of this shoe is reinforced by a full back stay, medium coin toe, perforated vamp and tip. While this shoe is intended for hard wear, as the material is of the very best quality, at the same time it has a very neat and dressy appearance. Sizes and half sizes, 1 to 5½. Widths, D, E and EE. Weight averages 30 ounces.

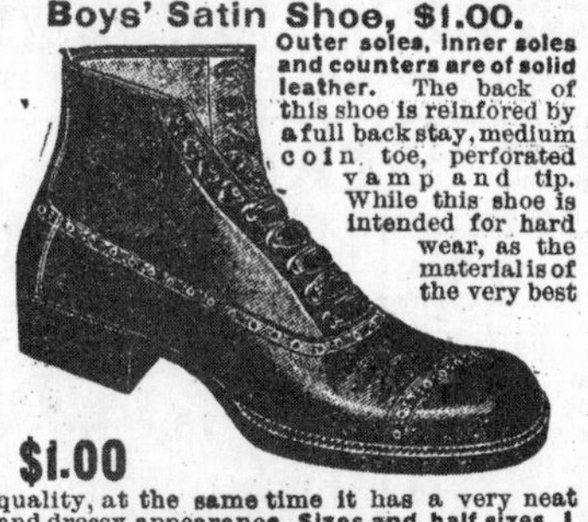

No. 15C914 Price, per pair.. ....$1.00

Men's Satin Calf Lace, Reduced to $1.00.

This is the same fine Satin Calf Shoe that usually sells at $1.50, and while we really cannot afford to make the price $1.00, we do so rather than offer those who want a shoe at this price an inferior article. Made over a plain globe last, with plump soles, and absolutely solid one piece sole leather counter and inner sole. The shoe is stitched well, fitted with fine top, and on today's market is an exceptional bargain. Sizes, 6 to 12; no half sizes. Widths, D, E and EE. Weight averages 40 ounces.

$1.00

No. 15C908 Reduced price, per pair..........$1.00

For postage rate see page 4.

Boys' Patent Colt, Goodyear Welt Blucher, $1.60.

LIKE PAPA'S DRESS SHOE.

This is really a men's fine dress shoe made in boys' sizes. Made in our EDUCATOR factory, and a better quality than we have ever carried at any price.

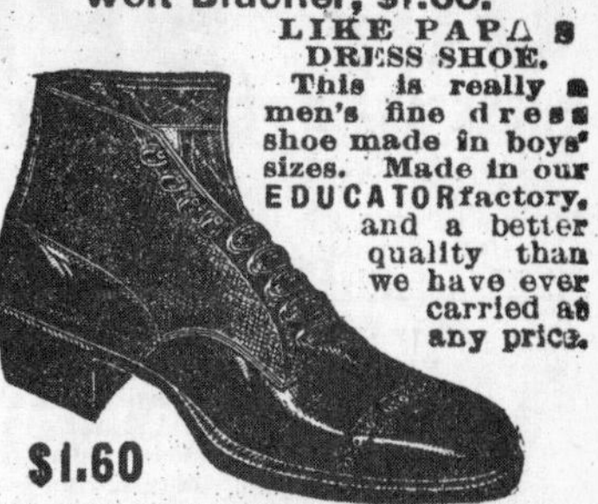

There is the best of sole leather and patent coltskin in this shoe and it is made just as well as any men's $4.00 shoe. A genuine Goodyear welt, oak sole, patent colt dress shoe that cannot be beat for either looks or wear no matter where you go. Sizes, 1 to 5½. Widths, D, E and EE.

No. 15C915 Price, per pair..$1.60

Boys' Patent Colt Lace, $1.50.

We have endeavored for some time to obtain a boys' genuine patent Corona colt shoe, which we could furnish to our patrons at a price reasonable enough to insure a large sale, and have succeeded in obtaining such a shoe. The shoe has all the style found in our best men's shoes, made with medium weight sole, dull kid top, English back stay, fancy perforated tip, and in fact a strictly high grade shoe throughout. Nothing cheap about it but the price. Sizes and half sizes, 1 to 5½. Widths, D, E and EE. Weight averages 34 ounces.

PATENT COLT

$1.50

No. 15C917 Price, per pair.$1.50

For postage rate see page 4.

Men's C. F. J. Work Shoe, $1.65.

The shoe herewith illustrated is one known the country over for its wearing qualities, and sold by almost every reputable dealer at from $2.25 to $2.50. Made of the famous C.F.J. leather. Soft as a glove, yet tough as cowhide. Heavy sole fastened on with standard screws, outside back stay. All solid leather counter and inner sole and built on honor. Each and every pair stamped Long Life on the sole, which means exactly what it says. Sizes, 6 to 12. No half sizes. Widths, D, E, EE. Weight, 48 ounces.

No. 15C920 Price, per pair.$1.65

Men's Choice Vici Kid Blucher, $1.35.

Made from a very serviceable grade of leather by a manufacturer who makes only high grade goods, consequently these will have the fit and style of a regular $3.00 to $4.00 shoe. You will notice both the pattern and style of the last have a nice light and airy appearance. Sole leather counter and inner sole. Sizes and half sizes, 5 to 11. Widths, D, E and EE. Weight averages 32 ounces.

No. 15C922 Price..........$1.35

Our SPECIAL MERIT Selections.

THERE ARE A FEW PLAIN FACTS that we want those who are using our shoes to know: **First**—That we are supplying to the customer direct more pairs of shoes than any other house in the world, either mail order or otherwise, as our daily output is now nearly 20,000 pairs, every day for the six days of the week. **Second**—That in having this enormous shoe business we naturally see all makes and styles, and when we call your attention to a **Special Merit Selection** it is done with a view of bringing to your especial notice a few lines that have been manufactured under our own guidance, using materials and labor that are best adapted for good service, as it has been very clearly demonstrated that no matter how handsome, how low priced, or what other qualifications a shoe may possess, if it does not give serviceable wear it cannot be satisfactory. With this idea always before us we make it a maxim to be sure of the quality and figure the price as close as it can be made.

Our Double Star Napa, $2.50.

The quality of Napa tanned upper leather is unquestionable, and this shoe is cut from the highest grade and plumpest selections of it. This material has stood the test in the Rocky Mountain regions and gritty sand states for many years past, and where absolute rough usage is necessary, we cannot recommend anything better. Weather will not penetrate, and the very best sole leather used in the soles, heels, insoles and counters render it as near waterproof as a shoe can be made, has standard screw fastening with strongly reinforced shank and has a row of wax thread stitching around vamp. The last is a very easy fitting one, making it most desirable for railroad men, letter carriers, policemen and those whose duty keeps them on their feet and exposed to all weathers. **Sizes, 5 to 13, in half sizes. Widths, full.** Weight, averages 55 ounces.

WESTERN MADE

$2.50

No. 15C805 Price, per pair..........$2.50

Viscolized Pebble Calf, 12-inch, Two-Buckle Blucher, Reduced to $4.50.

The soles of this shoe are **double stitched** around the forepart, and there is also a full row of stitching around the extension heel. Above the heel is a solid sole leather counter on the outside, put on very neatly. As a whole, this shoe, a genuine hand-sewed, Goodyear welt stitched, with its full bellows tongue, imported upper stock, full double sole of the very best prime oak sole leather, outside sole leather counter, two steel buckles, and rawhide laces, makes a combination that will stand either fire or water. No custom shoemakers can make this shoe for less than $10.00 to $12.00. **Sizes and half sizes, 5 to 12. Full widths.** Weight, about 4½ pounds.

No. 15C704 Price, per pair..........$4.50

Our New Huntsman, Reduced to $4.50.

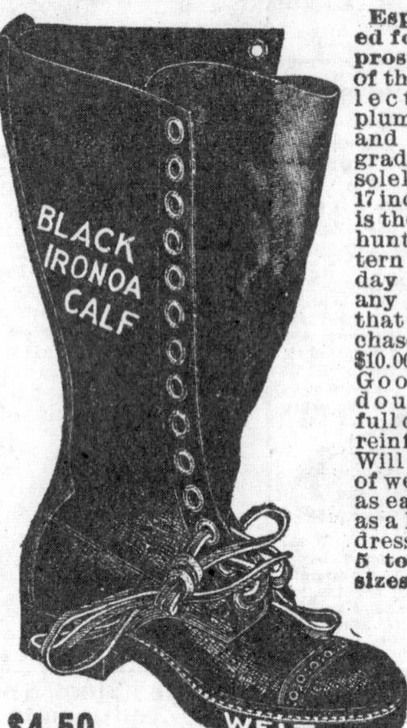

Especially adapted for hunters and prospectors. Made of the very best selection of extra plump chrome calf and the highest grade of pure oak sole leather, cut full 17 inches high. This is the most popular hunting boot pattern in demand today and equal to any custom shoe that can be purchased for $8.00 to $10.00. The shoe is Goodyear welt, double stitched, full double sole and reinforced shank. Will resist any kind of wear and yet be as easy on the foot as a lightweight dress shoe. **Sizes, 5 to 12, in half sizes; D, E and EE widths.** Shipping weight, 4 pounds.

No. 15C702 Price, per pair..........$4.50

The Stockyards' Favorite, $2.50.

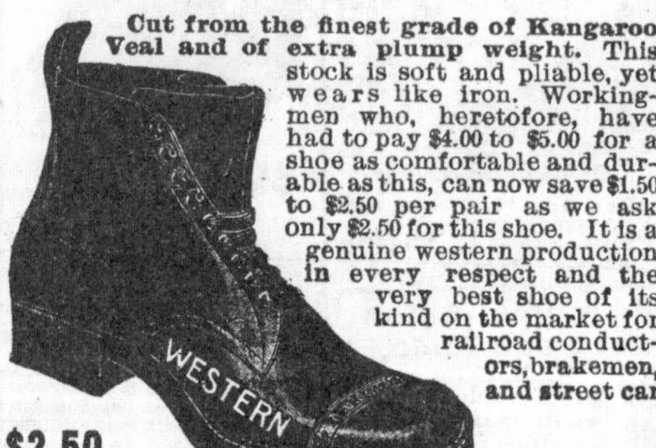

Cut from the finest grade of Kangaroo Veal and of extra plump weight. This stock is soft and pliable, yet wears like iron. Workingmen who, heretofore, have had to pay $4.00 to $5.00 for a shoe as comfortable and durable as this, can now save $1.50 to $2.50 per pair as we ask only $2.50 for this shoe. It is a genuine western production in every respect and the very best shoe of its kind on the market for railroad conductors, brakemen, and street car men. Full double sole and standard screw fastening. **Sizes, 5 to 12 in half sizes. Widths, full.** Weight, 50 to 58 ounces.

No. 15C797 Price, per pair..........$2.50

MEN'S SPECIAL WESTERN SHOES.

Genuine Porpoise Hide Lace Shoes, $2.50.

These shoes are made from the genuine North Sea porpoise hide, soft and easy on the foot, strong as tempered steel. Nothing better on earth in the way of shoe leather for water shedding qualities. Made on a broad and easy fitting wide toe last, allowing perfect freedom and action of the foot. These shoes have triple flint stone **slaughter soles. Scotch extension edges,** and low, broad heels. **Stitched and restitched with three rows of linen** thread and as near rip proof as it is possible to make a shoe. **Sizes, 6 to 12. Extra wide widths only.** Weight, 43 to 52 ounces, according to size.

No. 15C795 Price, per pair..........$2.50

California Napa Tanned River Shoe, $3.75.

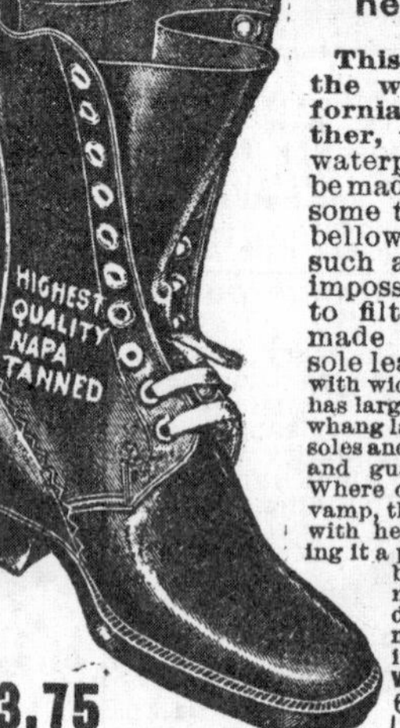

This shoe is made from the world famous California Napa tanned leather, which is as nearly waterproof as leather can be made, and is claimed by some to be fireproof. The bellows tongue is fitted in such a manner that it is impossible for dirt or water to filter through. It is made with heavy outside sole leather counter, fitted with wide outside back stay, and has large Klondike eyelets and whang laces. Made with two full soles and a No. 1 hard leather tap, and guaranteed to hold calks. Where quarters are stitched to vamp, they are stayed by hand with heavy waxed thread making it a perfect river shoe. Made by a western factory making exclusively driving shoes, and noted for their high quality. **Sizes, 6 to 11. Widths, full.** Weight, 65 ounces.

No. 15C1079 Price, per pair..........$3.75

THREE STRICTLY HAND MADE SHOES.

Hand Made Seamless Bal, $2.25.

Hand nailed, hand lasted, hand crimped. With a medium plump selection of the very best upper and sole leather, the price we quote looks ridiculously low, but we have contracted for all the manufacturer could make of this special shoe and we give you the benefit of our great purchase. They are made by a western factory, which means that A1 wearing material is used. **Sizes, 5 to 12, in half sizes. Full widths only.** Weight, 48 ounces.

HAND MADE SEAMLESS

$2.25

No. 15C803 Price, per pair....$2.25

Light Weight Seal Cruiser, $2.50.

STRICTLY HAND MADE.

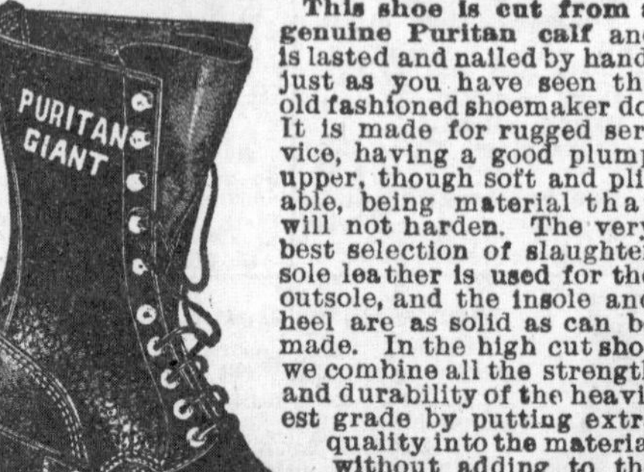

This shoe is cut from a genuine Puritan calf and is lasted and nailed by hand, just as you have seen the old fashioned shoemaker do. It is made for rugged service, having a good plump upper, though soft and pliable, being material that will not harden. The very best selection of slaughter sole leather is used for the outsole, and the insole and heel are as solid as can be made. In the high cut shoe we combine all the strength and durability of the heaviest grade by putting extra quality into the material without adding to the weight, for it is practically what we call it, "A Light Weight Cruiser," as the average weight is only 38 ounces. **Sizes, 6 to 12. No half sizes. Made in full widths.**

No. 15C1096 Price, per pair..........$2.50

Farm Special. Western Hand Made Foot Form Shoe, $2.25.

Genuine kangaroo calf, hand lasted, hand crimped, hand nailed. Outclasses any shoe made for a **high grade farm** and general work shoe. We do not follow the old idea that any ugly, uncomfortable shape is good enough for a work shoe. Here is just where **perfect fit,** solid comfort and good wear are most needed. This shoe requires no "breaking in." They fit from the first. We are working for your permanent trade and we offer you the best. We care nothing for a shoe that only sells once to a customer. **Sizes, 6 to 12. Widths, full.** Weight, 38 ounces.

HAND MADE SEAMLESS

$2.25

No. 15C1098 Price, per pair..........$2.25

SEE OUR

TAN SHOES

FOR SUMMER WEAR

Colored Pages 713 and 714.

DON'T FAIL

TO STATE SIZE WANTED.

Men's Seal Calf Seamless, Reduced to $1.60.

This home made shoe is built from best seal calf stock, as near waterproof as it is possible to make leather, and with extra

$1.60

heavy double soles. The soles are cut from best leather, fastened on with standard screws, and we fit it with absolutely all solid sole leather insole and counter of best quality. **Sizes, 6 to 11. No half sizes. Widths, full.** Weight, about 45 ounces.

No. 15C925 Price, per pair...... **$1.60**

Men's Satin Calf Blucher, $1.35

A Satin Calf Shoe made over a medium round toe last, cut blucher pattern, making the neatest shoe ever seen at this price. Top is cut from seal calf, sole and counter fully reliable and a shoe which looks double value

$1.35

and will give good service. **Sizes and half sizes, 6 to 11. Widths, D, E and EE.** Weight averages 36 ounces.

No. 15C929 Price, per pair...... **$1.35**

High Grade Bengal Calf Bal, $1.50.

This shoe is cut from the very choicest of Bengal calf and dull dongola, and the pattern is a duplicate of that used in our high priced goods. Made absolutely all solid, plump outsole,

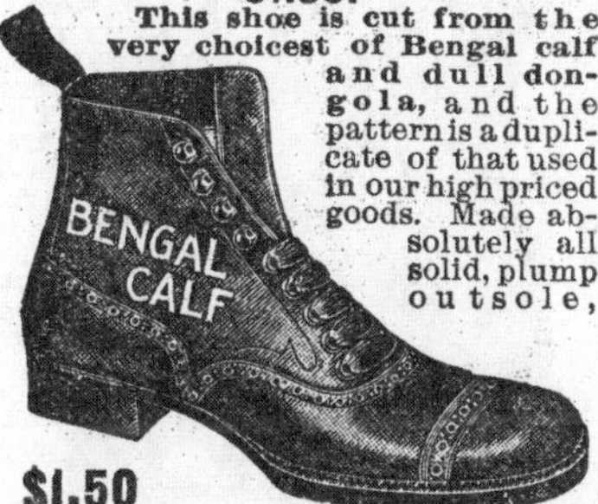

$1.50

short back stay fitted with "the heel that won't come off," and very serviceable. **Sizes and half sizes, 6 to 11. Widths, D, E and EE.** Average weight, 39 ounces.

No. 15C931 Price, per pair...... **$1.50**

Men's Kangaroo Calf Lace, $1.50.

A light weight shoe with unusual wearing qualities. Made of kangaroo calf stock with half double sole, sole leather counter and insole, standard natural grain finished sole (quality shows there) and a shoe buil to make and keep friends.

Sizes, 6 to 12. Widths full.

No. 15C933 Price, per pair...... **$1.50**

Boys' Hardware Shoe, $1.50.

We have had numerous calls for a boys' shoe which would positively stand the hard knocks which the average western boy knows how to give a shoe. This shoe is built—not for style—but for the

WESTERN MAKE

$1.50

purpose of giving satisfactory wear. It is made of a genuine kangaroo grain leather, fitted with full double sole, the highest grade counter, inner sole and lining. The quarter foxing and back stay being one piece makes it practically ripproof, and the soles, being standard screw fastened, produces a shoe which is practically indestructible. **Sizes and half sizes, 1 to 5½. Widths, full.** Weight averages 35 ounces.

No. 15C934 Price, per pair...... **$1.50**

For postage rate see page 4.

Boys' Heavy Knock About Shoe, $1.25.

Especially gotten up for boys who are hard on their shoes. There are too many shoddy, worthless shoes on the market today. Our object in offering our customers this shoe, so carefully made of extra heavy satin calf, thick, double soles,

FOR HEAVY WEAR

$1.25

sewed and nailed, solid leather counter and sensible tip toe last, is to give them a shoe that will resist the wear and tear such as most boys are sure to give a shoe. **Sizes, 1 to 5½. Widths, full.** Weight, 35 ounces.

No. 15C936 Price, per pair... **$1.25**

Our Best Plow Shoe, $1.35.

We quote the usual $1.35 plow shoes elsewhere at from $1.00 to $1.10, but for those who wish the very best that money can buy, the kind our forefathers used to

$1.35

wear, we offer this shoe. Western made, best Milwaukee oil grain leather, pegged sole, best sole leather counter, inner sole and outer sole. In short, a better shoe than we have seen in recent years. One that would retail at $1.75 to $2.00. **Sizes, 6 to 12. Widths, full.** Weight, 45 ounces.

No. 15C945 Price, per pair........ **$1.35**

Oil Grain Stitchdown, $1.20.

The time honored name of Stitchdown is recognized throughout the country as the farmers' friend. It is strictly a solid shoe in every respect, yet light and flexible and combines

$1.20

durability and comfort. It has a good selection of medium weight oil grain in the upper and the soles are of slaughter sole leather. **Sizes, 6 to 12; no half sizes. Full widths.** Weight, 30 ounces.

No. 15C966 Price, per pair, **$1.20**

MEN'S OXFORDS AND SLIPPERS.

Men's Patent Colt Goodyear Welt Oxfords, $2.00.

The very best of corona colt patent leather is used in the vamp of this Oxford. The top is cut

$2.00

from first quality dull box kid, the style of last is the very latest, military heel, and being Goodyear welt sewn, insures ease, and foot fitting qualities unusual at the price. **Sizes and half sizes, 5 to 11. Widths, C, D, E and EE.** Weight averages 28 ounces.

No. 15C974 Price, per pair... **$2.00**

Men's Patent Leather Dress Oxfords, $1.50.

Made over a medium round toe last, with a light single sole, fancy

$1.50

perforated tip, inlaid vesting top, and while designed especially for dress wear, the patent leather is of good quality and will give as much wear as could reasonably be expected from a bright leather shoe. **Sizes and half sizes, 5 to 11. Widths, D, E and EE.** Weight averages 25 ounces.

No. 15C976 Price, per pair.... **$1.50**

Men's Patent Leather Blucher Oxfords, $1.50.

The beautiful Blucher patent leather Oxford herewith illustrated is special value at the

$1.50

price quoted. Made over a medium round toe last, dull box kid top, fitted with outside back stay, good, durable soles, and a snappy, good fitting low shoe. **Sizes and half sizes, 5 to 11. Widths, D, E and EE.** Weight averages 29 ounces.

No. 15C978 Price, per pair... **$1.50**

Men's Vici Southern Tie, $1.50.

Made of good vici kid stock, half double sole, absolutely

$1.50

all solid, plain globe toe, and a shoe designed especially for those wishing comfort. Exceptional value at the price quoted. **Sizes and half sizes, 6 to 12. Widths, full.** Weight averages 28 ounces.

No. 15C980 Price, per pair.... **$1.50**

For postage rate see page 4.

Men's Vici Kid Oxfords, $1.35.

This Oxford is made to our order from a fine quality of vici kid, with tip,

VICI KID

$1.35

and when on the foot it has the appearance of a fine shoe. The soles are of good stock, sewed on by the McKay process and besides being a very neat shoe, it will give the wearer a great deal of service and solid comfort. **Sizes and half sizes, 5 to 12. Widths, D, E and EE.** Weight, 28 ounces.

No. 15C982 Price, per pair... **$1.35**

For postage rate see page 4.

Men's Tuxedo Kid Nullifiers, $1.35.

Made from good quality of Tuxedo kid, which is really a fine, bright, finished calfskin, light hand turned flexible soles, medium heel and toe, the best elastic gore, and a slipper which will be very

$1.35

comfortable, and can also be worn on the street if desired. Especially suited for house wear, as it protects the ankles from drafts thereby preventing many colds. **Sizes and half sizes, 5 to 12. Widths, full.** Weight, 28 ounces.

No. 15C984 Price, per pair... **$1.35**

For postage rate see page 4.

Men's Dongola Oxfords, $1.15.

This shoe is made from a fine dongola kid, light sole, which is very flexible, medium heel, medium common sense toe, and is very

COMFORT

$1.15

durable. Nothing cooler or more comfortable for summer wear. **Sizes and half sizes, 5 to 12. Widths, D, E and EE.** Weight, 28 ounces.

No. 15C986 Price, per pair... **$1.15**

For postage rate see page 4.

Colt Patent Leather Oxfords, $1.35.

Made from a good grade of stock over a medium plain toe. The bottoms are light hand turn, very flexible and especially desirable for dancing.

$1.35

Fitted with cloth lace stay, and splendid value at the price. **Sizes and half sizes, 5 to 12. Widths, C, D, E and EE.** Weight, 20 ounces.

No. 15C988 Price, per pair.. **$1.35**

For postage rate see page 4.

Men's Patent Leather Oxfords.

Stock is a good selection of patent leather; style of last is latest English; the soles are of good quality leather, with full extension edges and full

$1.35

perforated vamp. Is all the rage in large cities, and is something that cannot ordinarily be obtained in shoes offered at this price. **Sizes and half sizes, 5 to 12. Full widths.** Weight, 30 ounces. **Order by number.**

No 15C989 Price, per pair, **$1.35**

For postage rate see page 4.

Men's Grain Slippers, $0.80.

Men's Heavy Slippers, made from good grain stock, machine sewed, and all solid. This slipper is dampproof and very serviceable, and should not be compared with the cheap slippers usually sold at this price. **Warranted. Sizes, 6 to 12; no half sizes. Full widths.** Weight, 28 ounces.

No. 15C990 Price, per pair, **$0.80**

For postage rate see page 4.

Men's Patent Leather Oxfords, $1.00.

This shoe is genuine machine sewed, kid quarter lined, and

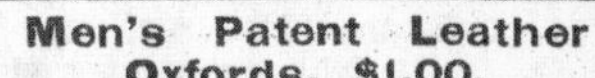

$1.00

while we cannot warrant patent leather, we assure you it is exceptional value. **Sizes and half sizes, 6 to 11. Widths, full.** Weight averages 25 ozs.

No. 15C992 Price, per pair, **$1.00**

For postage rate see page 4.

Men's Carpet Slippers, $0.25.

Made from Brussels carpet, bound and stayed, leather sole and a slipper which will give good wear and lots of comfort. **Sizes, 6 to 12; no half sizes.**

$0.25

Weight, 20 ounces.

No. 15C996 Price, per pair, **$0.25**

For postage rate see page 4.

FOR

TAN SHOES

SEE PAGES 713 AND 714

Men's Tuxedo Kid Opera Slipper, $1.00.

It is made of genuine tuxedo kid, vamp handsomely inlaid with patent leather under a beautiful new scroll pattern. The soles are hand turned, and counters are of solid leather. A slipper unexcelled for beauty, service and comfort. Sizes, 6 to 11. Widths, C, D, E and EE. Weight, 14 ounces.

$1.00

No. 15C997 Price, per pair...$1.00

For postage rate see page 4.

Men's Dongola Nullifiers, $1.00.

Made over a broad toe, sensible last, and unlike most nullifiers, it is made with one-half double sole, fair stitched, making it suitable for outdoorwear as well as a house slipper, designed especially for southern trade, but made with sole leather counter, fairly good quality sole, and will give much better wear than would ordinarily be expected, price considered. Sizes, 6 to 12. Width, EE only. Weight averages 26 ounces.

$1.00

No. 15C999 Price, per pair ..$1.00

Men's Tuxedo Kid Everett Slipper, $1.00.

The name Tuxedo kid is given to a fine light weight selection of glazed calfskin and gives great wearing service, yet is light and airy. Hand turned sole, leather counter, patent leather trimmed. Sizes and half sizes, 5 to 12. Widths, full. Weight, 18 ounces.

$1.00

No. 15C1004 Price, per pair, $1.00

Men's Imported Velvet Everett, $0.50.

The greatest value we have ever offered. Made with blue and white figured imported velvet, with alligator quarter. Sizes, 6 to 11; no half sizes. Full widths. Weight, 14 ounces.

$0.50

No. 15C1016 Price, per pair, $0.50

New Idea Plow Shoe, $1.10.

Made from Milwaukee oil grain leather, half double sole, absolutely solid sole leather counters and inner soles, and will wear much better than any plow shoe offered at near this price. The principal feature, however, is the crimped tongue, which hugs the instep closely, and the large brass eyelets and strong buckskin laces, which will outwear the shoe. Sizes, 6 to 12; no half sizes. Widths, full. Weight averages 47 ounces.

$1.10

No. 15C1029 Price, per pair, $1.10

For postage rate see page 4.

$0.95 and $0.90 Oil Grain Creole.

Made from the best Milwaukee oil grain stock, is very soft and pliable, has sole leather counter and inner sole and a good heavy outer sole, cut from the best stock. When we say sole leather counter, we mean it. Quality counts. No half sizes. Weight, about 42 ounces.

No. 15C1030 Men's sizes, 6 to 12. Price, per pair..................$0.95
Sizes 13 and 14, 25 cents extra.

No. 15C1031 Boys' sizes, 1 to 5. Price, per pair....................$0.90

For postage rate see page 4.

$0.95 and $0.90 Oil Grain Dom Pedro.

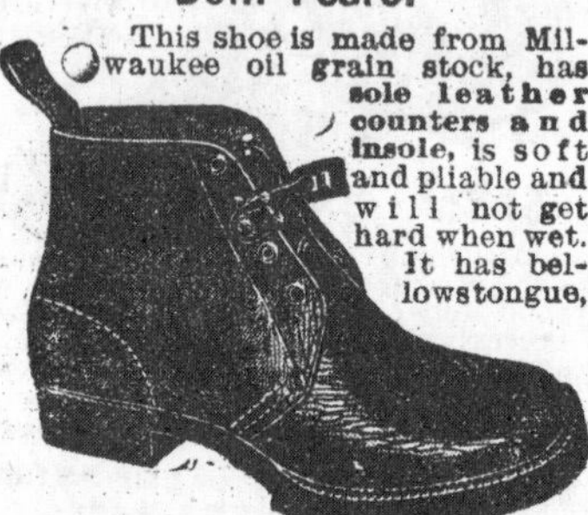

This shoe is made from Milwaukee oil grain stock, has sole leather counters and insole, is soft and pliable and will not get hard when wet. It has bellows tongue, which makes it dirtproof. Widths, full. Weight, about 42 ounces.

No. 15C1032 Men's sizes, 6 to 12. Price, per pair..................$0.95

No. 15C1033 Boys' sizes, 1 to 5. Price, per pair..................$0.90

For postage rate see page 4.

Kangaroo Kip Creedmoor, $1.35.

This shoe is cut from the very best selection of kangaroo kip and slaughter sole leather, with an outside top, making a full double sole to shank. The shank is also reinforced and the soles are fastened on with second growth hickory pegs. It is well worth $2.00, but our price is $1.35. Sizes, 5 to 12. No half sizes. Full widths.

$1.35

No. 15C1035 Price, per pair, $1.35

Men's Kangaroo Calf Blucher, $1.75.

We herewith illustrate our latest production in a men's neat appearing shoe, which at the same time will wear well. Made from a plump kangaroo calf stock, Blucher style cut, broad tip toe, and heavy half double soles. This blucher cut shoe fits the ankle closely, is dirt excluding, crimped and very satisfactory for general heavy wear. Sizes, 6 to 11; no half sizes. Widths, full. Weight averages 45 ounces.

$1.75

No. 15C1037 Price, per pair $1.75

Men's Seal Bellows Tongue Blucher, $1.35.

Made from seal calf, with bellows tongue and full double soles, fastened on by the newest process, known as the double clinch. Two rivets are used where the vamp and quarters meet making ripping next to impossible, so the shoe is especially built for hard usage, yet made over a last that is as easy fitting as a high priced shoe would be. Sizes, 5 to 12. Full widths. Weight, 42 ounces.

$1.35

No. 15C1042 Price, per pair. $1.35

Men's Oil Grain Wood Sole Shoe, $1.10.

The shoe is made from best Milwaukee oil grain leather, and the sole is put on in such a manner as to make it absolutely waterproof.

The wood sole being a nonconductor, is much drier, much warmer, than any leather made, besides being lighter. The sole is shaped to the foot, making an easy shoe and one especially desirable for those working in wet places. Sizes, 5 to 12; no half sizes. Widths, full. Weight averages 39 ounces.

No. 15C1047 Price, per pair.. $1.10

Armored Shank, $1.25.

Thousands of feet have been ruined by the use of the spade for the lack of some stout protection to the foot, and this illustration shows you a shoe that is especially adapted for just such cases, fitted with outside iron counter and heavy sole leather shank pieces riveted on. A shoe designed for all kinds of heavy wear. An extraordinary value. Sizes, 6 to 12; no half sizes. Full widths. Weight averages 50 ounces.

$1.25

No. 15C1052 Price, per pair. $1.25

Men's Mining Shoe, $1.50.

Made from a good selection of stock, with full double soles and thoroughly nailed heel and sole. At an additional cost we have fitted this shoe with a heavy iron toe plate, and also encircled the heel with a heavy iron plate, thereby making it practically indestructible. Sizes 6 to 12; no half sizes. Widths, full. Weight averages 65 ounces.

No. 15C1076 Price, per pair.....$1.50

For postage rate see page 4.

Men's River Boot, $2.95.

Strictly Western Made, Oil Grain River Boot, cut from the best Milwaukee grain stock. Made with half double sole and extra heavy tap, which is cut from selected sole leather, guaranteed to hold calks. Heels are low and broad. The boot is made with strap top, is absolutely all solid leather, and is as nearly waterproof as it is possible to make.

Sizes, 6 to 12, no half sizes.

Weight, about 50 ounces.

No. 15C1080 Price, per pair. $2.95

For postage rate see page 4.

The New Light Weight Hunter, $3.50.

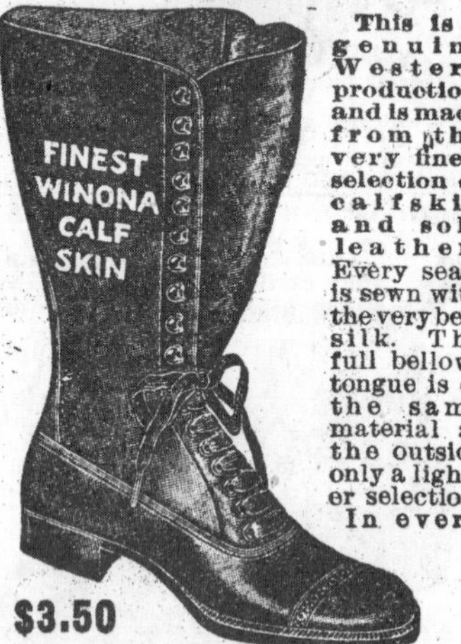

This is a genuine Western production, and is made from the very finest selection of calfskin and sole leather. Every seam is sewn with the very best silk. The full bellows tongue is of the same material as the outside only a lighter selection. In every way it is built on honor and would be cheap at $5.00, and it is only by contracting for all the manufacturer can make that we are enabled to offer them at the prices we do. Sizes and half sizes, 5 to 11. Widths, D, E and EE. Weight, 45 to 65 ounces.

$3.50

No. 15C1087 Price, per pair.. $3.50

Men's Kangaroo Calf Logging Shoe, $2.50.

This shoe is made from the genuine kangaroo calf stock, extra high cut, blucher style, and the tongue being crimped fits the ankle closely, producing a shoe which will shed water and is much more practical for loggers' use than the ordinary pattern. This shoe is made with two extra heavy soles, and the regulation long outside tap; has an extra heavy outside sole leather counter and is fitted with the large Klondike brass eyelets and rawhide laces. Sizes, 6 to 11; no half sizes. Width, EE only. Weight, 59 ounces.

$2.50

No. 15C1093 Price, per pair.. $2.50

We save you all the retailer's profits and more too on the goods you buy from us - - - - - -

King Comfort. Leather Sole Wool Lined Sheep Boot, $1.95.

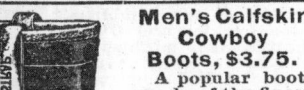

This boot displaces the old pac at a much less cost but increased value and it entirely supersedes the sheep boot made without the sole leather sole and heel. It can be worn with any kind of an overshoe and takes the place of both legging and German sock. The most practicable, serviceable and comfortable winter footwear made. **Full sizes only, 5 to 12.** Weight 42 ounces.

$1.95

No. 15C1116 Price, per pair..**$1.95**

Men's Llama Calf Boots, $2.95

The stock from which this boot is made has a pebbled surface similar to the kangaroo skin, is very soft and pliable and contains enough oil to make it practically waterproof. **This boot is made with full double sole** and outside tap cut from the very best of sole leather and for those who want a thoroughly soft, yet durable boot. **Sizes, 6 to 11. No half sizes. Full widths.** Wt., 50 ounces.

No. 15C1134 Price, per pair..**$2.95**

Men's Calfskin Cowboy Boots, $3.75.

A popular boot, made of the finest quality kangaroo calf. Has a medium round toe and is one of the best fitting boots ever manufactured. Although it is light and dressy, the leather is so tanned as to give it strength unusually found in this style of boot. The leg and vamp, as shown in illustration, are very handsomely stitched in artistic designs. This boot is made with calfskin side lining, oak soles, 18-inch leg, 1¼-inch solid leather heel. **Sizes, 5 to 11. No half sizes. Widths, full.** Made with a new jack strap. Average weight, 50 ounces.

No. 15C1152 Price, per pair...**$3.75**

Soudan Calf Cowboy Boot, $4.50.

This boot is made of the genuine Soudan calf stock, which is very soft and pliable, and is by far the most practical stock for riding boots. Made with 20-in. leg, fancy stitched and ribbed, hand sewed oak soles, and the 2-inch regulation concave heel. Those wishing the very best cowboy boot to be had at any price will do well to order this one. Our price is below all others **Sizes, 4 to 11. No half sizes.** Shipping weight averages 50 ozs.

No. 15C1155 Price, per pair...**$4.50**

The Western, $2.50.

Made of genuine calfskin, is all solid and a most popular cowboy boot. It has extra high heel, medium toe, and is extremely durable for all kinds of wear. **Every pair warranted to be better value than can possibly be obtained elsewhere.** Note reduction. **Sizes, 5 to 11; no half sizes.** Weight, 56 ounces.

No. 15C1157
Price, per pair, **$2.50**

For postage rate see page 4.

Our $2.75 Calfskin Boots.

A WONDER OF VALUE.

We make this boot from a fine calfskin, over a medium last, and with low, broad heel. The soles are cut from good, **plump sole leather,** are of medium weight and durable. We fit this boot with **a fine goat leg,** and to those who wish a durable, neat dress boot we recommend it. **We have never seen anything like it for the price. Sizes, 6 to 11; no half sizes.** Weight, 45 to 60 ounces.

No. 15C1158 Price, per pair, **$2.75**

For postage rate see page 4.

The Easy Farmer Boot, $1.75.

NO MORE TIRED FEET.

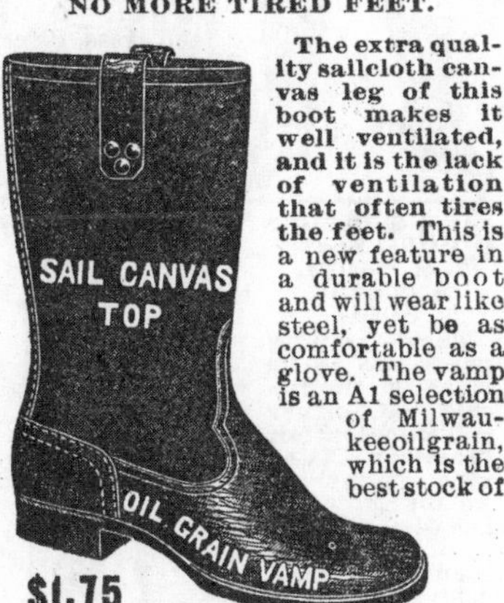

The extra quality sailcloth canvas leg of this boot makes it well ventilated, and it is the lack of ventilation that often tires the feet. This is a new feature in a durable boot and will wear like steel, yet be as comfortable as a glove. The vamp is an A1 selection of Milwaukee oil grain, which is the best stock of its kind made. **Western made.** Warranted. **Sizes, 5 to 12,** in full sizes only. **Width, EE.** Average weight, 35 ounces.

No. 15C1160 Price, per pair. **$1.75**

Men's Calf Peg Boot, $2.40.

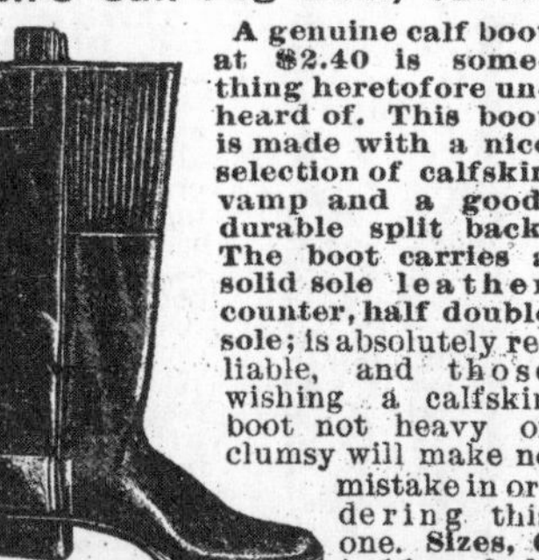

A genuine calf boot at $2.40 is something heretofore unheard of. This boot is made with a nice selection of calfskin vamp and a good, durable split back. The boot carries a solid sole leather counter, half double sole; is absolutely reliable, and those wishing a calfskin boot not heavy or clumsy will make no mistake in ordering this one. **Sizes, 6 to 11; no half sizes.** Weight averages 40 to 55 ounces.

No. 15C1165 Price, per pair. **$2.40**

For postage rate see page 4.

Men's All Rubber Arctics, $1.32

Men's All Rubber Arctics, made from heavy duck and covered with rubber, making the most durable arctic yet produced and one that can be cleaned with sponge and water. **Sizes, 6 to 12.** No half sizes. Weight, 44 ounces.

No. 54C1298 Price, per pair. **$1.32**

For postage rate see page 4

Men's, Women's, Misses' and Children's Storm Slippers.

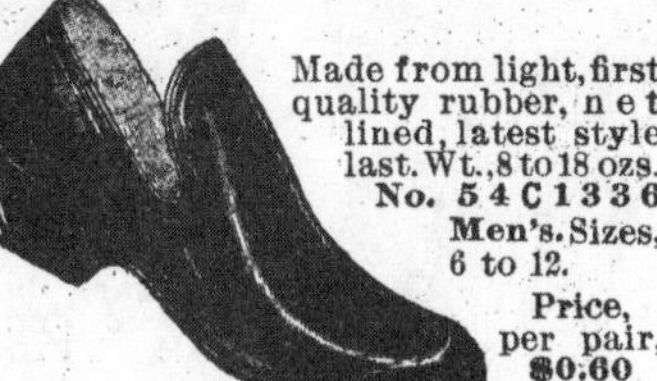

Made from light, first quality rubber, net lined, latest style last. Wt., 8 to 18 ozs.

No. 54C1336 Men's. Sizes, 6 to 12. Price, per pair **$0.60**

No. 54C1338 Women's. Sizes, 2½ to 8. Price, per pair....**$0.45**

No. 54C1338½ Women's. Spring heel. Sizes, 2½ to 8. Per pair.....**$0.45**

No. 54C1339 Misses'. Spring heel. Sizes, 11 to 2. Price, per pair....**$0.39**

No. 54C1339½ Child's. Spring heel. Sizes, 5 to 10½. Price, per pair....**$0.33**

For postage rate see page 4.

Men's and Boys' Self Acting Sandals and Women's Light Croquets.

First Quality Self Acting Sandals, made to fit the new style shoes. Weight, 10 to 23 ounces.

No. 54C1340 Men's. Sizes, 6 to 12. Price, per pair....**$0.58**

No. 54C1342 Boys'. Sizes, 1 to 5½. Price, per pair....**$0.48**

No. 54C1343 Ladies' Croquets. round toe only. Sizes, 2½ to 8. Width, F. Price, per pair....**$0.42**

Men's and Women's Extra Heavy Rubbers.

Made from first quality pure gum, extra heavy, net lined and especially designed for hard wear. **Broad toe only.** Weight, 28 ounces.

No. 54C1344 Men's. Sizes, 6 to 13. Price, per pair....**$0.77**

No. 54C1345 Women's. Sizes, 2½ to 8. Weight, 12 ounces. Price, per pair....**$0.40**

For postage rate, see page 4.

Men's Pebble Leg Short Boots, Fine Quality. $2.64

Men's Pebble Leg Short Boots, bright finish. Nothing better made. **Sizes, 6 to 12. No half sizes.** Weight, 64 ounces.

No. 54C1360 Price, per pair....**$2.64**

Boys', Youths', Ladies', Misses' and Children's Pebble Leg Short Boots. Good Quality.

These boots are made bright finish, are neat looking and something every woman and child should have. Weight, 24 to 38 ounces.

No. 54C1361 Women's. Sizes and half sizes, 2½ to 8. Price, per pair....**$1.32**

No. 54C1362 Boys' Sizes 1 to 6, no half sizes. Price per pair....**$1.79**

No. 54C1363 Misses'. Sizes and half sizes, 11 to 2. Price, per pair, **$1.10**

No. 54C1364 Youths'. Sizes, 10 to 13½. Price, per pair....**$1.32**

No. 54C1464½ Children's. Sizes and half sizes, 5 to 10½. Price, per pair....**$0.92**

Men's Gum Hip Boots, $3.74.

Men's Dull Finish Hip Boots. Made from strictly first quality rubber, very serviceable. Every pair warranted to be as good as any on the market. Friction lined only. **Sizes, 6 to 12. No half sizes.** Weight, about 6¼ lbs.

No. 54C1366 Price, per pair, **$3.74**

Boys' Storm King Boots, $2.21.

Boys Storm King Boots. Dull finish; they are made to buckle just above the knee and are better than the ordinary short boot, as they keep the snow and water from entering at the top. Net lined only. **Sizes, 1 to 6. No half sizes.** Weight, 64 ounces.

No. 54C1367 Price, per pair..**$2.21**

Men's Gum Sporting Boots, $3.74.

Men's Dull Finish Thigh or Sporting Boots, made from strictly first quality rubber; just the thing for fishing and hunting and all purposes where a high top boot is wanted. Net lined only. **Sizes, 6 to 12. No half sizes.** Weight, 6¼ pounds.
No. 54C1368 Price, per pair.. **$3.74**

Men's Duck Foot Hip Boots, Woonsocket Brand $3.95.

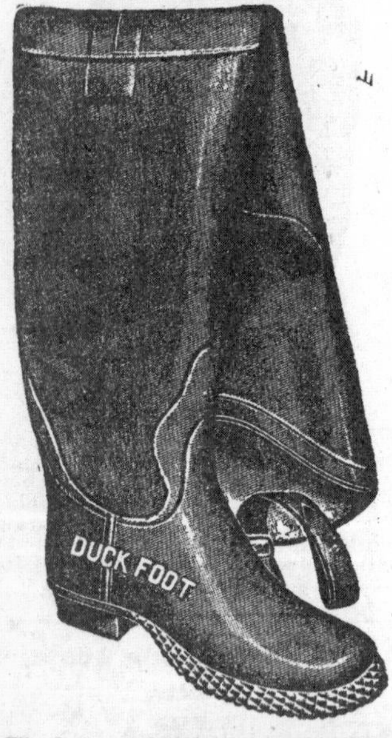

We herewith illustrate our Men's Duck Foot Hip Boot, without a doubt the most durable made, regardless of price. It is made from strictly first quality pure gum rubber, over a heavy duck foot, which makes it as near puncture and snag proof as it is possible to make it. The leg is made from pure gum rubber and will not crack like the all duck boots. We build it with rolled soles, thereby protecting the uppers and making it much more durable. Friction lined only. Should you desire more warmth, we recommend the arctic socks, which cost but 8 cents per pair and are much better than a felt lined boot, since they can be taken out at night and dried. **Sizes, 6 to 13; no half sizes. Widths, full.** Weight, 104 to 116 ounces.
No. 54C1368½ Price, per pair. **$3.95**

Men's Duck Foot Short Boot, Rolled Soles, $2.75.

YOU SAVE AT LEAST
75 CENTS
ON EVERY PAIR.

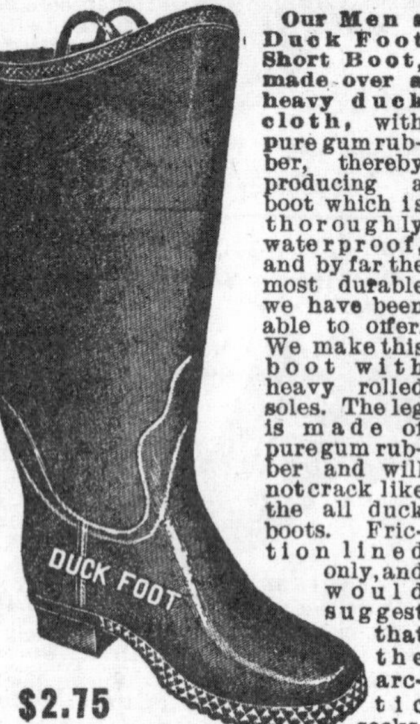

Our Men's Duck Foot Short Boot, made over a heavy duck cloth, with pure gum rubber, thereby producing a boot which is thoroughly waterproof, and by far the most durable we have been able to offer. We make this boot with heavy rolled soles. The leg is made of pure gum rubber and will not crack like the all duck boots. Friction lined only, and would suggest that the arctic socks, which costs but 8 cents per pair, be used in case a warmer boot is required. This sock can be removed at night and thoroughly dried and will give, together with this boot, much better satisfaction than the old fashioned felt lined boot. **Sizes, 6 to 13. No half sizes.** Weight, 90 ounces.
No. 54C1369 Price, per pair. **$2.75**

Boys' Dull Finish Short Boots, $1.79.

Boys' Dull Finish Rubber Boots, 15-inch leg. At this price every boy should own a pair of rubber boots, for at times they are indispensable. Friction lined only.
Sizes, 1 to 6. No half sizes. Weight, 54 ounces.
No. 54C1406 Price, per pair.......... **$1.79**

Lumbermen's Over, Oil Grain Top, 10 Inches High, $1.80.

This Lumbermen's Over is made of best quality of pure gum rubber. Top of best oil grain leather, securely stitched to vamp, and fitted with full bellows tongue. Height from heel to top of pac is 10 inches. Large eyelets, with strings of rawhide. This shoe is made with a heavy rolled edge sole, with seams reinforced throughout by double stitching. Strictly first quality. **Sizes, 6 to 12.** Weight averages 48 ounces.
No. 54C1410 Price, per pair, **$1.80**

Men's, Boys', Women's, Misses' and Children's Rolled Sole Rubbers.

Extra Heavy Rolled Sole and Heel. Although made to stand hard wear, is at the same time neat appearing. Made of pure gum rubber. Reinforced heel and edge with double thickness of rubber. Medium broad toe. **Fine quality.** Weight, 15 ounces.

No. 54C1384	Men's sizes, 6 to 12. Price, per pair	$0.64
No. 54C1385	Boys' sizes, 1 to 5½. Price, per pair	.54
No. 54C1386	Women's sizes, 2½ to 8. Price, per pair	.48
No. 54C1387	Misses' Spring Heel. Sizes, 11 to 2. Price, per pair	.40
No. 54C1388	Children's Spring Heel. Sizes, 5 to 10½. Price, per pr.	.35

Men's Leather Sole Rubber Boots, $3.95.

GOODYEAR WELT. **Men's Leather Sole Rubber Boots,** made from first quality pure gum rubber, with leather insole, and heavy leather outsole and heel, slightly extended, thereby protecting the uppers. **Just the thing for miners, dairymen and railroad work.** The welt sole produces flexibility and the ease of a fine shoe. Usual price is $5.00.

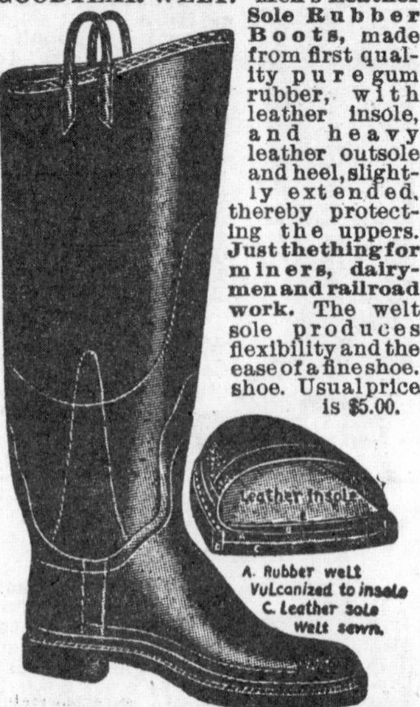

Warranted. A desirable boot for dairymen, miners, etc. Sizes, 6 to 12. No half sizes. Weight, 90 ounces.
No. 54C1424 **Men's Gum Short Boot.** Price, per pair.......................... **$3.95**

Men's Wading Pants, Boot Feet, Dull Finish and Mackintosh.

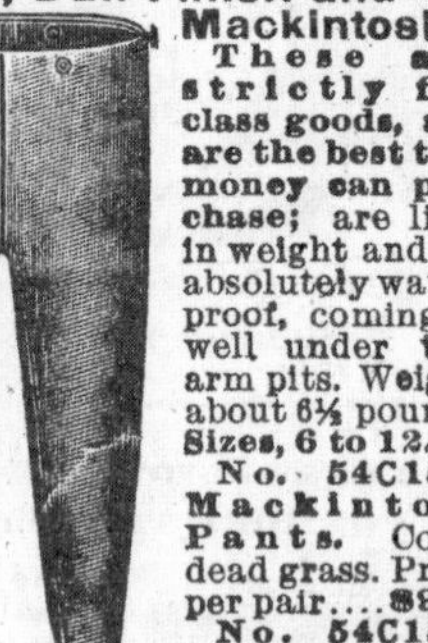

These are strictly first class goods, and are the best that money can purchase; are light in weight and are absolutely waterproof, coming up well under the arm pits. Weight, about 6½ pounds. **Sizes, 6 to 12.**
No. 54C1530 **Mackintosh Pants.** Color, dead grass. Price, per pair.... **$9.75**
No. 54C1532 **Dull Finish Pants.** Color, black. Price, per pair........ **$6.75**

Men's Mackintosh Wading Pants, Stocking Feet.

These wading pants are to be worn on the inside of either rubber or leather footwear. Are very light in weight and absolutely waterproof, making them an ideal fishing or hunting pants. Color, dead grass only; weight 76 ounces. **Sizes, 6 to 12.**
No. 54C1534 Price, per pair....... **$6.75**

Men's Mackintosh Hip Boots, Boot and Stocking Feet.

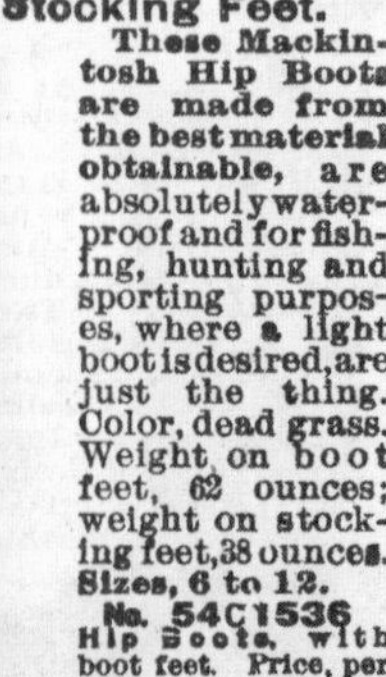

These Mackintosh Hip Boots are made from the best material obtainable, are absolutely waterproof and for fishing, hunting and sporting purposes, where a light boot is desired, are just the thing. Color, dead grass. Weight on boot feet, 62 ounces; weight on stocking feet, 38 ounces. **Sizes, 6 to 12.**
No. 54C1536 **Hip Boots, with boot feet.** Price, per pair........ **$7.50**
No. 54C1538 **Hip Boots, with stocking feet.** Price, per pair...... **$5.50**

Lumbermen's Combination Sock and Canvas Leggings, $0.80.

No. 54C1199 Probably the most valuable improvement for lumbermen's socks ever thought of is the canvas top. It combines all the good qualities of the sock and the canvas legging, the canvas being attached to the sock in such a manner as to extend down over the rubber overshoe, thereby excluding all snow. This sock is made from heavy pure wool, the foot being tufted, while the canvas top is very heavy; absolutely waterproof and felt lined to top. It is fitted with four leather straps and buckles. Sizes, 14 to 18 inches calf measure. Weight, 25 ounces. Price, per pair........ **$0.80**
Per dozen pairs.............. **8.75**
For postage rate see page 4.

Ladies' Jersey Leggings.

No. 54C1201 Ladies' Jersey Leggings, knee length, with 10 buttons and buckle at top. The jersey cloth legging fits like a stocking, and being all wool, is warm and comfortable. Color, black. Shoe sizes, 3 to 7. Weight, 8 ounces.
Price, per pair.. **$0.49**
Per doz. pairs.. **5.75**
For postage rate see pg. 4.

Ladies' Melton Leggings.

No. 54C1203 Ladies' Fine Wool Black All Melton Leggings, knee length, with 10 buttons and buckle at top. Nothing like it ever offered at this price. **Shoe sizes, 3 to 7.** Weight, 8 ounces. Price, per pair.... **$0.48**
Per dozen pairs.................... **5.50**
For postage rate see page 4.

Combination Thigh Leggings.

Ladies', Misses' and Children's.

This is a very good illustration of our Combination Legging and Overgaiter. It is without a doubt the best fitting, warmest and most comfortable legging that can be produced. Being made from a fine black jersey cloth, it fits as closely as a stocking and conforms to every movement of the limb. Has six buttons up side and ribbon top. Weight, 9 ounces.
No. 54C1205 **Ladies' sizes, 3 to 7.**
Price, per pair.......................... **$0.60**
Per dozen pairs.......................... **6.50**
No. 54C1207 **Misses' sizes, 11 to 2.**
Price, per pair.......................... **$0.50**
Per dozen pairs.......................... **5.50**
No. 54C1209 **Children's sizes, 8 to 10.**
Price, per pair.......................... **$0.40**
Per dozen pairs.......................... **4.50**
For postage rate see page 4.

Ladies' and Men's Overgaiters.

No. 54C1211 Ladies' Fine Overgaiters, made heavy for fall and winter wear. Shoe sizes, 3 to 7. Weight, 8 ounces.
Price, per pr. **$0.19**
Per doz. prs. **2.09**
No. 54C1215 Ladies' 7-button imported kersey, the nobbiest and unexcelled overgaiter. Sizes, 3 to 7.
Price, per pair.......................... **$0.35**
Per dozen pairs.......................... **3.75**
No. 54C1219 **Men's heavy 5-button Melton. Sizes, 6 to 11.** Price, per pair.. **$0.19**
Per dozen pairs.......................... **2.00**
No. 54C1223 **Men's heavy 5-button imported kersey. Sizes, 6 to 11.**
Price, per pair.......................... **$0.35**
Per dozen pairs.......................... **3.75**
For postage rate see page 4.

Men's Extra High Cut Felt Lined Overgaiters, $0.45.

No. 54C1226

Men's Extra High Cut Felt Lined Ten-Button Overgaiter, made from heavy weight kersey, very warm and comfortable for winter wear. **This is the best overgaiter ever placed upon the market. Sizes, 6 to 11.**
Weight, 8 to 12 ounces, according to size.
Price, per pair.......................... **$0.45**
Per dozen pairs.......................... **5.25**

Men's Napoleon Leather Leggings, $1.25.

No. 54C1227 Made from the best grade of black grain leather. Napoleon style with the latest style spring fastener. This legging is very popular; can be put on much quicker than any other style and is very durable. Sizes, 14 to 18 inches calf measure. Weight, per pair, averages 18 ounces.
Price, per pair......$1.25

For postage rate see page 4.

15-Ounce Army Style Leggings.

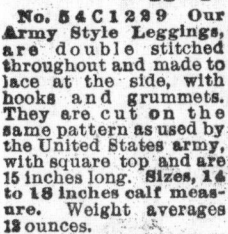

No. 54C1229 Our Army Style Leggings, are double stitched throughout and made to lace at the side, with hooks and grummets. They are cut on the same pattern as used by the United States army, with square top and are 15 inches long. Sizes, 14 to 18 inches calf measure. Weight averages 12 ounces.

Price, per pair..$0.44
Per dozen pairs.. 5.00

Men's Mackintosh Leggings, $0.48.

No. 54C1231 This legging is known as the army legging. It is made of gray mackintosh cloth, and felt lined throughout. Fastened with automatic snap buckle. Instep strap of fine quality leather, fastened to the legging by means of rivets. It is one of the strongest leggings manufactured, and is absolutely waterproof. Men's sizes only, 14 to 18 inches calf measure. Weight, 20 ounces.
Price, per pair..................$0.48
Per dozen pairs................. 5.50

For postage rate see page 4.

Our Waterproof Covert Lace Leggings.

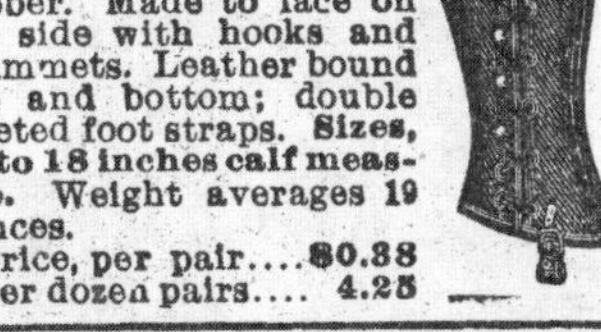

No. 54C1232 These leggings are made similar to the mackintosh cloth, outside facing of covert, felt lined throughout, with an interlining of rubber. Made to lace on the side with hooks and grummets. Leather bound top and bottom; double riveted foot straps. Sizes, 14 to 18 inches calf measure. Weight averages 19 ounces.
Price, per pair....$0.38
Per dozen pairs.... 4.25

24-ounce Canvas Buckle Knee Leggings.

No. 54C1259 These leggings are made from extra heavy canvas, leather bound at the top and bottom, with five buckle straps and reinforced heel. The straps and buckle billets are sewed between the canvas; and the foot straps are double riveted. Sizes, 14 to 18 inches calf measure. Weight averages 20 ounces.
Price, per pair.....$0.67
Per dozen pairs..... 7.75

Lanz Patented Men's Canvas Knee Leggings.

No. 54C1260 This legging is one which has the advantage over all other canvas lace leggings which are used for going through bushes, forests or other places where the hooks on the leggings are apt to be caught. We have had these made up for us in extra heavy canvas intended for hard service, leather bound top and bottom, all seams flat felled and double rows of stitching, foot straps of extra quality, double riveted and with grummet eyelets used on all army lace leggings. Calf measure over trousers, 14, 15, 16, 17 and 18 inches. What size do you wear?
Price, per pair........$0.50
Per dozen pairs........ 5.50

24-ounce Waterproof Knee Leggings.

No. 54C1261 These leggings are made from 24-ounce canvas, lace style, with hooks and grummets. They are leather bound at the top and bottom, and have a reinforced heel. The seams are double felled and stitched, heavy leather footstraps. Sizes, 14 to 18 inches, calf measure. Weight averages 22 ounces.
Price, per pair.....$0.65
Per dozen pairs.... 7.50

Men's Excluder Canvas Lace Leggings, $0.45.

Excludes Snow and Dirt.

No. 54C1262 A high grade extra heavy Tan Canvas Legging that prevents and keeps out snow and dirt. Equal in every respect to leggings sold at nearly double our price. The excluder is made of the same grade canvas as the legging itself and is 9 inches wide. Some leggings on the market in this style have a much narrower excluder, making it difficult to put on. Full size 17-inch knee legging that will give excellent wear. Sizes, 14, 15, 16, 17 and 18 inches. Be sure and state size of calf measure over trousers.
Price, per dozen pairs, $4.80; per pair..45c

15-ounce Canvas Spring Riding Leggings.

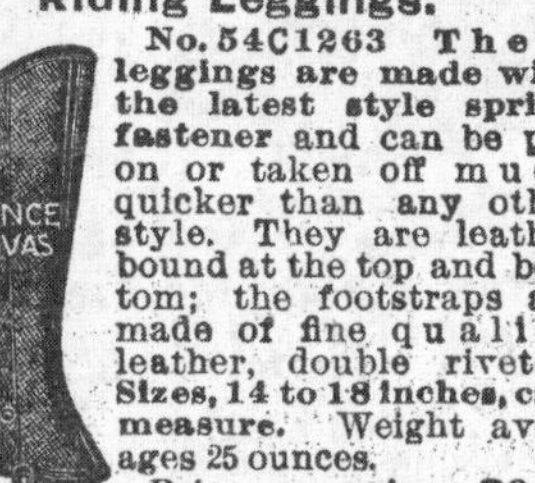

No. 54C1263 These leggings are made with the latest style spring fastener and can be put on or taken off much quicker than any other style. They are leather bound at the top and bottom; the footstraps are made of fine quality leather, double riveted. Sizes, 14 to 18 inches, calf measure. Weight averages 25 ounces.
Price, per pair....$0.50
Per dozen pairs.... 5.75

Mackinaw Blanket Lined Spring Riding Leggings, $0.45.

No. 54C1264 Mackinaw Blanket Lined Leggings have been very popular the past few years. These leggings are not only warm but absolutely waterproof. They are made of a fabric composed of three parts as follows: Outside is of covert cloth and inside of blanket fleece lining with an interlining of rubber. Leather bound top and bottom, seams flat felled and double stitched, with steel springs riveted on side. Sizes, 14 to 18 inches, calf measure.
Price, per pair..................$0.45
Per dozen pairs................. 4.80

8-ounce Lace Knee Leggings.

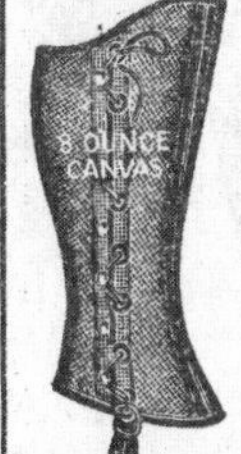

No. 54C1265 These leggings are made to lace at the side, by means of hooks and grummets. They are double stitched throughout, and are leather bound at the top and bottom. Sizes, 14 to 18 inches, calf measure. Weight averages 10 ounces.
Price, per pair....$0.35
Per dozen pairs.... 3.95

Campaign Leggings, $0.19.

No. 54C1266 We call it a Campaign Legging on account of the cheapness. This is not the usual flimsy legging so often sold for campaign purposes and which are practically worthless. Has grummet eyelets and hooks to match, and good quality russet leather straps. This is a first class legging to use as a trouser protector when riding a bicycle. Largely used by political marching clubs. Made in all sizes, 14, 15, 16, 17 and 18 inches, calf measure over trousers.
Price, per pair..................$0.19
Per dozen pairs.... 2.00

18-Ounce Heavy Waterproof Canvas Leggings.

No. 54C1267 This Legging is the most practical and serviceable legging on the market, as it laces down the front like a shoe, which makes it very convenient to put on and take off. It is also waterproof, has a snow or water guard. The seams are double felled and stitched; heavy leather foot straps. Sizes, 14, 15, 16, 17 and 18 inches calf measure.
Price, per pair..................$0.55
Per dozen pairs.................. 6.00

18-Ounce Men's Canvas Thigh Leggings.

No. 54C1269 These are the most practical leggings for hunting, as they are 23 inches long, and protect the trousers when going through bushes. Made with 5 buckle straps, to the knee, and lace from knee to the top. Leather bound at the top and bottom. Sizes, 14 to 18 inches calf measure. Weight averages 30 ounces.
Price, per pair.......$0.63
Per dozen pairs...... 7.00

Boys' Canvas Thigh Leggings.

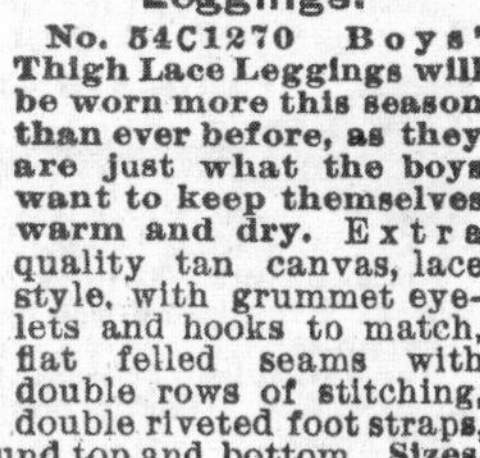

No. 54C1270 Boys' Thigh Lace Leggings will be worn more this season than ever before, as they are just what the boys want to keep themselves warm and dry. Extra quality tan canvas, lace style, with grummet eyelets and hooks to match, flat felled seams with double rows of stitching, double riveted foot straps, leather bound top and bottom. Sizes, 10, 11, 12 and 13 inches calf measure.
Price, per pair..................$0.40
Per dozen pairs.. .... 4.05

18-Ounce Canvas Spring Fastener Thigh Leggings.

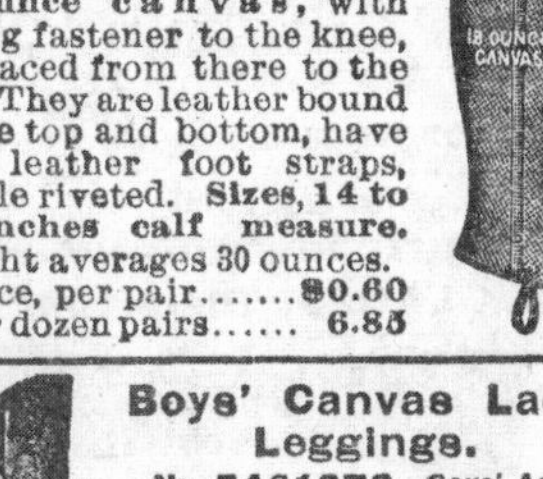

No. 54C1271 Made from 18-ounce canvas, with spring fastener to the knee, and laced from there to the top. They are leather bound at the top and bottom, have fine leather foot straps, double riveted. Sizes, 14 to 18 inches calf measure. Weight averages 30 ounces.
Price, per pair.......$0.60
Per dozen pairs...... 6.85

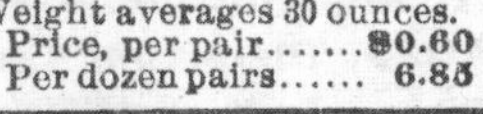

Boys' Canvas Lace Leggings.

No. 54C1272 Boys' Army Lace Leggings with grummet eyelets and hooks to match. Made from extra heavy tan canvas, all seams flat felled and double row of stitching, leather bound top and bottom, double riveted russet leather foot straps, full size knee length. A very serviceable legging for a boy. Sizes, 10, 11, 12 and 13 inches calf measure. Be sure and state size. Price, per pair.....$0.35
Per dozen pairs....... 3.75

Smith's Jet Black Dressing, $0.07.

FOR LADIES' AND CHILDREN'S SHOES.

No. 54C2008 Jet Black Shoe Dressing is the most perfect dressing made; without a rival. It dries quickly, and is known the world over for producing a jet black and lustrous finish, especially on vici kid shoes. Each bottle put up in attractive carton.
Price, each..........$0.07
Per dozen.......... .75
Unmailable on account of weight.

Gilt Edge Dressing, $0.15.

Sold everywhere for 25 cents.
No. 54C2010 Ladies' Gilt Edge Shoe Dressing is very useful for a great many things besides shoes. It will make your old rubbers, shopping bags and black kid gloves look equal to new.
Per bottle.......$0.15
Per dozen....... 1.75
Unmailable on account of weight.

Combination Dressing for Black and Russet Shoes.

No. 54C2012 Consists of a bottle of cleaner and a box of polish, put up in a handsome carton. This is a polish that not only produces a handsome luster, but at the same time softens and preserves the leather.
Price, each.......$0.06
Per dozen......... .65
No. 54C2013 For Tan Shoes. Price, each.$0.06
Per dozen.........................$0.65
Unmailable on account of weight.

Smith's Waterproof Polish, $0.10.

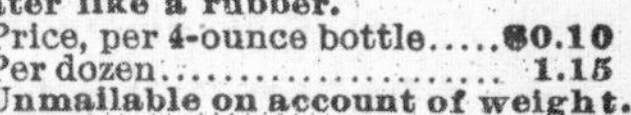

For Men's and Boys' Shoes.
No. 54C2016 Produces a brilliant jet black polish without brushing, thus saving time, labor and money. It is waterproof in rain or snow, is largely used in winter to keep the feet dry, thus preventing cold and rheumatism. Men or boys who dislike to wear rubbers should use this, as it sheds water like a rubber.
Price, per 4-ounce bottle.....$0.10
Per dozen........................ 1.15
Unmailable on account of weight.

Frank Miller's Leather Preservative and Waterproof Oil and Blacking.

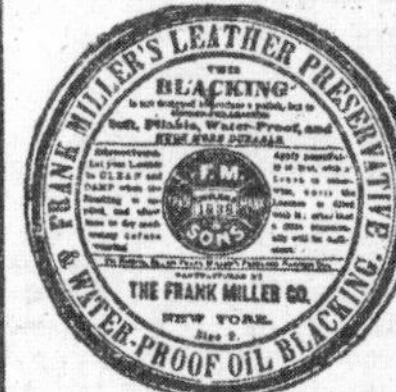

25-Cent Size at $0.10.
No. 54C2018 For over fifty years it has been in use. This blacking is not designed to produce a polish, but renders the leather soft and pliable and makes it absolutely waterproof.
Per dozen, $1.10; per box. $0.10

Shine-M-Up Cabinet.

No. 54C2005 The latest, easiest and most satisfactory shoe shiner ever offered, because it has transformed a very irksome job into a pleasant pastime. It is not necessary to bend the back in operating this shiner, but stand in an almost natural position when polishing the shoes. Weathered oak finish, a handsome piece of furniture. Cabinet complete, containing one pure bristle shoe brush, one bottle of cleaner, one box polishing paste and a polishing cloth. Height, 15 inches; width, 14 inches; length, 11 inches.
Price, only........ ....$1.50

POLISHING PASTE.

For all enamel and patent leather shoes. Also used as a finishing paste for producing a higher luster on ladies' and children's shoes and men's and boys' velour calf, kangaroo, vici kid and all calfskin shoes.

Patent Leather Polish, $0.03.

Large 10-cent size.
No. 54C2028 Black.
Price, per box $0.03
Per dozen...... .30

No. 54C2030 Patent Leather Polish for boot blacks, in ¼-pound boxes.
Price, per box...................$0.10
Per dozen....................... 1.00

Shushine Shoe Polish.

You Can't Spill It.

No. 54C2034 Not necessary to use any other paste in connection with Shushine, as it blacks and shines at the same time and produces a patent leather finish on all dry leather shoes and keeps patent and enamel leather shoes looking just like new. Put up in metal tube, each in carton with directions. Weight, 3 ounces.
Price, each..........$0.07
Per dozen........... .75
If by mail, postage and tube extra, 10 cents.

SHOE LACES.

Neverbreak Shoe Laces.

A patented shoe lace adopted by the War Department for the U. S. army.

No. 54C2044 36 inches. For men's and boys' shoes. Dozen pairs.... $0.23
Per gross laces................. 1.25
Postage extra, per doz. pairs, 4 cents.

Make Your Own Shopping Bag.

Three dozen shoe laces of the best quality and just the proper weight for shopping bags. These bags are all the rage and very handsome. See illustration. Please understand, we are not quoting a price on this bag, simply on the laces with which to make it. We furnish complete instructions how to make bag with each order.

No. 54C2052 Price, for three dozen laces, best quality...............$0.18
Price, per gross laces.......... .65

Special Basket Weave Shoe Laces.

For Making Belts, Etc.

No. 54C2054 Instructions how to make shopping bags and belts from laces with each order for laces. Basket weave shoe laces are the very latest and are used for making belts, collars, neckties, etc. They are made in different combination of colors, such as black and white mixed, red and black mixed, and in solid colors as follows: white, red, pink, green, lavender, blue and black. One dozen shoe laces are enough for making a belt. Price, per dozen laces....$0.09
Per gross laces.............. 1.00
Postage, per dozen laces, 2 cents.

Waterproof Army Shoe Lace.

No. 54C2058 This lace is made from the best of linen, woven very close, is about ½-inch wide, 1 yard long, with brass spiral tags. It is without a doubt the best lace ever made for men's shoes as it has the strength and wearing qualities of the porpoise lace. Used by the U. S. Government.
Price, per dozen pairs..........$0.16
Per gross laces.................. .90
If by mail, postage extra, per dozen pairs, 4 cents.

Best Porpoise Laces.

Best English Porpoise Laces, with spiral tags, the strongest and best made at any price.
No. 54C2060 36-inch.
Price, per dozen pairs..........$0.33
Per gross laces................. 1.85
No. 54C2062 45-inch.
Price, per dozen pairs..........$0.43
Per gross laces................. 2.45
Postage extra, per dozen pairs, 6c.

Men's, Ladies', Boys' and Misses' Flat Tubular Laces.

These laces are guaranteed 88 thread and full lengths. The best domestic tubular lace made, and usually sold at 5 cents per pair. Black or tan.
No. 54C2066 27-inch for children's shoes. Black only.
Per gross, $0.55; per dozen pairs $0.10
No. 54C2068 36-inch tan.
Per gross, $0.70; per dozen pairs .12
No. 54C2070 45-inch tan.
Per gross, $0.80; per dozen pairs .14
No. 54C2072 36-inch black.
Per gross, $0.70; per dozen pairs .12
No. 54C2074 45-inch black.
Per gross, $0.80; per dozen pairs .14
No. 54C2076 54-inch tan.
Per gross, $0.95; per dozen pairs .17
No. 54C2078 54-inch black.
Per gross, $0.90; per dozen pairs .16
Postage extra, per dozen pairs, 4c.

Round Cord Laces.

No. 54C2082 36-inch Men's Black.
Per gross, $0.35; per dozen pairs $0.06
No. 54C2084 54-inch Ladies' Black.
Per gross, $0.52; per dozen pairs $0.09

Himalaya Laces.

Flat wide laces for Ladies' and Men's Oxfords and Ladies' Shoes.
No. 54C2090 27-inch for Oxfords, Black. Price, per dozen pairs...$0.10
Per gross........................ .55
No. 54C2094 54-inch for Ladies' Shoes, Black. Per dozen pairs..$0.19
Per gross....................... 1.05
If by mail, postage, per doz. pairs, 4c

Men's and Women's Medium Tubular Laces.

A Medium Grade Heavy Tubular Lace, the kind made for service and usually put in fine shoes at the factory. A special value at the price quoted. Black only.

		Per gross	Per doz. pairs
No. 54C2096	36 in. long.	$0.44	$0.08
No. 54C2097	45 in. long.	.54	.10
No. 54C2098	54 in. long.	.64	.12

Postage extra, per doz. pairs, 5 cents.

SILK LACES—Black and Tan.

Wide Flat Pure Silk Shoe Laces, are all the rage for women's shoes and especially for men's and women's oxfords.
No. 54C2100 Women's Silk Shoe Lace, 54 inches long.
Price, per pair.................$0.11
No. 54C2102 Men's and Women's Silk Oxford Lace. Length, 30 inches.
Price, per pair..................$0.09
No. 54C2103 Men's and Women's Tan Silk Oxford Lace. Length, 30 inches. Price, per pair....... $0.13
If by mail, postage extra, 1 cent.

Rawhide Laces.

		Price, per 100 laces	Price, per doz. pairs
No. 54C2107	36-inch.	$1.50	$0.40
No. 54C2108	45-inch.	1.75	.50

Postage, per dozen pairs, 12 cents.

"Money Maker" Boot Black Stands.

No. 54C2134 Boot Black Stand, imitation mahogany, finished in the best up to date style, fancy brass covered and trimmed (as shown in illustration), extra heavy carved supports with two bronze fancy foot rests, large drawer for supplies, one small drawer and step. Weight, 100 pounds.
Price......................$5.95

No. 54C2136 Boot Black Stand, zinc covered and trimmed instead of brass, not as fancy and has no extra step, otherwise as No54C2134. Shipping weight, 100 pounds.
Price..........................$4.20

Shoe Stretchers, $0.45.

No. 54C2142 Wood Shoe Stretcher, made in four sizes, men's large and medium size, ladies' size and children's size. Has corn and bunion attachments, and is an article which every family should have in the house. Weight, 30 ounces. Price........$0.45

Lightning Shoe Stretcher, $0.50.

Corn and Bunion Cure.

No. 54C2144 It reaches any part of the shoe without stretching the whole shoe. A sure cure for corns and bunions. Made of japanned iron. Weight, 24 ounces. Price.......$0.50

Best Heel Stiffeners.

No. 54C2150 The best in the world. Easily put on, and will fit any shoe. Prevents boots and shoes from running over. Nails and screws free.
Price, per dozen pairs..............$0.20
If by mail, postage extra, per pair, 2c.

Out of Sight Ice Creepers.

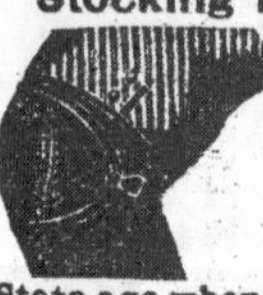

No. 54C2160 Out of Sight Ice Creepers, positively prevent one from slipping, and are the only practical ice creepers which can be turned down out of the way when not in use, as per illustration. Made to fit any size boot or shoe.
Price, per pair..................$0.10
Per dozen pairs................. 1.10
Postage extra, per pair, 5 cents.

Stocking Knee Protectors.

Stocking Knee Protectors are very desirable for boys and girls who wear their stockings out quickly at the knees. We quote below both cloth and leather. State age when ordering.
No. 54C2164 Jersey Cloth.
Price, per pair...................$0.14
Per dozen pairs.................. 1.60
No. 54C2166 Leather.
Price, per pair...................$0.16
Per dozen pairs.................. 1.75
Postage extra, per pair, 2 cents.

Stocking Heel Protectors, $0.09.

Made from a good grade of leather and will save many times its cost every month.
No. 54C2168 Men's.
Sizes, 6 to 11.
Per pair $0.09
Per dozen pairs......$1.00
No. 54C2170 Women's and Children's. Sizes 2 to 7.
Price, per pair..................$0.09
Per dozen pairs.................. 1.00
Postage extra, per pair, 1 cent.

SHOE BRUSHES.

No. 54C2210 Pure Bristle Shoe Brush. Seven rows of strictly pure bristles, 1 inch long. Block 7½ inches long. **This is a handsome, well filled, durable brush that will always give satisfaction to the user.** Weight, 10 ounces.
Price, per dozen, $2.75; each...$0.25

Marvel Shoe Polisher, $0.17.

No. 54C2256 The Marvel Shoe Polisher is a combination bristle and felt brush and imitates the action of a cloth as used by bootblacks. The bristles keep the felt in the proper position and readily cleans and polishes shoes in all parts. Unequaled for patent leather, box calf and all dry leather shoes. Weight, 12 ounces.
Price, per dozen, $1.95; each. $0.17

American Shoe Holder.

No. 54C2260 For holding the shoe while being cleaned and polished off the foot, leaving both hands free to polish. Adjustable to any size shoe, detachable when not in use. Perfectly rigid and indestructible. Complete outfit with three lasts, men's, women's and children's shoes. Furnished complete with one box of polish and polishing cloth.
Price, per dozen, $6.50; each $0.60

A FEW FACTS ABOUT LEATHER HALF SOLES.

As a safeguard to the consumer when buying leather cut soles, or half soles, we hereby state a few facts about the different selections these half soles are made in.

The best quality soles are always stamped on the top of every dozen, F, or Fine; the second quality (sometimes sold by other firms as the best quality), are stamped M, or medium, and the third selection are all stamped C, or coarse.

We call your attention to the above facts in order that you may know positively what you are getting, no matter where you buy.

Hemlock Tanned Half Soles.

All our hemlock half soles and heel top pieces are cut from slaughter sole leather made from packer hides. We do not handle dry hide soles on which it is easy to quote low prices.

Each pair carefully selected. Assorted sizes in dozens. Will cover wide shoes.

MEN'S HEMLOCK HALF SOLES.

No. 54C2306 Best Quality, 6 inches thick, per dozen pairs.
Price, per pair.................$0.30
Per dozen pairs................. 3.25
No. 54C2309 Best Quality, 5½ inches thick, per dozen pairs.
Price, per pair.................$0.25
Per dozen pairs................. 2.90
No. 54C2312 Good Quality, 5-inch thickness. Price, per pair.....$0.18
Per dozen pairs................. 2.00
No. 54C2313 Medium Quality, 4½-inch thickness. Per pair.....$0.12
Per dozen pairs................. 1.40

Continued on following page.

Capitol Wool Slipper Soles.

The Capitol Wool Slipper Soles are the best ever produced and preferred by most women for crocheted and knit toilet slippers. Unlike all others, the stitch or cord of the Capitol is exactly on the upper edge. The needle can thus be thrust directly through the meshes of the stitch and not on an angle, with the risk of breaking the needle as with other soles where the cord is too far over the edge.

No. 54C2176	Men's. Sizes, 6 to 11.	Price, per pair	$0.27
No. 54C2178	Women's. Sizes, 3 to 7.	Price, per pair	.18
No. 54C2180	Misses. Sizes, 11 to 2.	Price, per pair	.16
No. 54C2182	Child's. Sizes, 5 to 10.	Price, per pair	.14

If by mail, postage extra, per pair, 3 cents.

BOYS' HEMLOCK HALF SOLES.

No. 54C2319 Best Quality, 5-inch thickness. Price, per pair $0.20
Per dozen pairs, $2.10

WOMEN'S HEMLOCK HALF SOLES.

No. 54C2324 Best quality, 4½-inch thickness. Price, per pair $0.15
Per dozen pairs 1.60

No. 54C2328 Good quality, 3½-inch thickness. Price, per pair $0.08
Per dozen pairs .... .80

Men's Best Oak Tanned Half Soles.

Our Oak Half Soles are cut from the best white oak sole leather. They are suitable for sewed or nailed work and will wear a long time. See prices.

No. 54C2330 Best quality, extra 5-inch thickness. Price, per pair, $0.30
Per dozen pairs 3.25

No. 54C2331 Best quality, 4½-inch thickness. Price, per pair $0.20
Per dozen pairs 2.20

No. 54C2332 Medium quality, 4½-inch thickness. Price, per pair, $0.15
Per dozen pairs 1.60

No. 54C2334 Women's Oak, best quality, 4-inch thickness. Per pr. $0.12
Per dozen pairs 1.35

Square Cut Soles.

Our Squares are all cut 6½ x 8½ inches. This size is suitable for men's, women's or children's shoes.

No. 54C2335 Good quality, 5 inches to the doz. Price, per piece $0.20
Per dozen pieces 2.10

OAK TANNED SQUARE SOLES.

No. 54C2338 Good quality, 5 inches to the dozen. Price, per piece .. $0.20
Per dozen pieces 2.10

White Oak Jumbo Soles.

Sizes, 8¼ x 12½ inches. Each piece will cut two large pairs of men's half soles or three pairs of women's half soles. Also used for making heel top pieces.

No. 54C2344 Best Grade. Heavy substance, weighing 9 pounds to the dozen. Price, each $0.40
Per dozen pieces 4.50

No. 54C2345 Best Grade. Medium substance, weighing 8 pounds to the dozen. Price, each $0.35
Per dozen pieces 4.00

No. 54C2346 Best Grade. Light substance, weighing 7 pounds to the dozen. Price, each $0.30
Per dozen pieces 3.50

Hemlock Heels.

No. 54C2347 Good Quality, 5-inch thickness. Per doz. pairs, $0.43

No. 54C2348 Boys' Best Quality, 5-inch thickness. Per doz. pairs, $0.40

No. 54C2349 Women's Best Quality, 4½-inch thickness. Per doz. pairs, $0.39

Our $1.25 and $0.70 Leather Outfits.

No. 54C2900 For only $1.25 we offer you this Outfit, made from best quality hemlock half soles and heel lifts, also enough patching leather to do the cobbler work of the entire family.

Notice the large sizes of soles and the big variety.

1 pair men's boot taps, size 14.
1 pair men's best half soles, size 12.
1 pair boys' best half soles, size 7.
1 pair women's best half soles, size 7.
1 piece square cut sole, size 6½x8½.
1 pair men's best largest size heel lifts.
1 pair boys' best largest size heel lifts.
1 pair women's best largest size heel lifts.
1 package each of 4-8 and 5-8 clinch nails and 1 package 5-8 heel nails, also a small quantity of patching leather.

Price, for complete outfit as described, put up in a neat pasteboard carton **$1.25**

Our Bargain $0.70 Outfit.

No. 54C2300 Like our $1.25 Outfit, only made from medium quality leather; instead of the boot tap, one pair large men's half soles, size 13. **The biggest bargain ever offered.** Price, each, only $0.70

SOLE LEATHER SIDES.

No. 54C2354 Prime Selection Rumsey Slaughter Sole Leather, plump weight, clear, no brands, measures 15 to 20 square feet to a side weighing from 18 to 26 pounds. Price, per pound $0.30

SOLE LEATHER STRIPS.

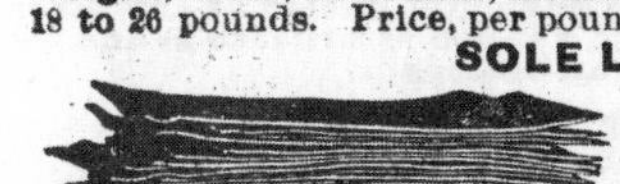

These Strips are cut from firm sole leather sides and are in every way the most practical for family shoe repair work. All the various shaped soles and heel top pieces can be cut from these strips to good advantage. Each strip is about 8 inches wide and varies in length from 1⅓ to 2⅓ feet. Prices quoted are for average strips. **We will charge you only for exact weight at the lowest market price.** Shipping weight averages from 1 to 2¾ pounds per strip.

Hemlock Sole Leather Strips.

No. 54C2368 Best quality, heavy thickness. Per piece, about $0.60
No. 54C2369 Best quality, medium thickness. Per piece, about .... .50
No. 54C2370 Good quality, light thickness. Per piece, about .... .40

Oak Sole Leather Strips.

No. 54C2371 Best quality, heavy thickness. Per piece, about $0.65
No. 54C2372 Best quality, medium thickness. Per piece, about .... .55
No. 54C2373 Best quality, light thickness. Per piece, about .... .45

INSOLES.

Our Non-Crumpling Hair Insoles.

Made of genuine horsehair, well covered and stitched. Has a patent fine steel stay running the entire length of sole, causing it to retain its proper shape and to lie perfectly smooth in the shoe. **This sole is considered the most healthful insole ever manufactured.**

No. 54C2402 Men's sizes, 6 to 11. Price per pair. $0.06
Per dozen pairs .... .65

No. 54C2404 Woman's sizes, 3 to 7. Price, per pair $0.06
Per dozen pairs .... .65

If by mail, postage extra, per pair, 3 cents.

Cork Hair Cushion Insoles, $0.07.

Something new in insoles, a combination of cork and hair. Can be used as a cork cushion insole by having the cork side of the insole next the foot, the hair side acting as a cushion and the cork keeping the foot dry.

No. 54C2406 Men's sizes, 6 to 11.
Price, per pair $0.07
Per dozen pairs .... .75

No. 54C2408 Women's sizes, 3 to 7.
Price, per pair $0.07
Per dozen pairs .... .75

If by mail, postage extra, per pair, 3c.

Polar Socks, $0.06.

For Inside of Rubber Boots.

No. 54C2420 Fleece lined Polar Socks for house, chamber, bath room, and especially desirable for inside of rubber boots. Men's sizes, 6 to 11.
Price, per pair $0.06
Per dozen pairs .... .70

If by mail, postage extra, per pair, 4c.

Canvas Slippers, $0.08.

For Inside of Rubber Boots.

No. 54C2422 Men's First Grade Canvas Slippers, with sheepskin bottoms, used for inside of rubber boots. Sizes, 6 to 11.
Price, per pair $0.08
Per dozen pairs .... .85

If by mail, postage extra, per pair, 3c.

Parker's Arctic Socks, $0.17.

Fleece lined, unequaled for house, chamber, bath room, and especially desirable for inside of rubber boots.

No. 54C2424 Men's sizes, 6 to 11.
Price, per pair $0.17
Per dozen pairs 1.85

No. 54C2426 Ladies' sizes, 3 to 7.
Price, per pair $0.17
Per dozen pairs 1.85

If by mail, postage extra, per pair, 2c.

RUBBER HEELS.

We do not put on rubber heels.

Seroco Cushion Heels, 10 Cents per Pair.

Equal to many heels sold at 25 cents per pair.

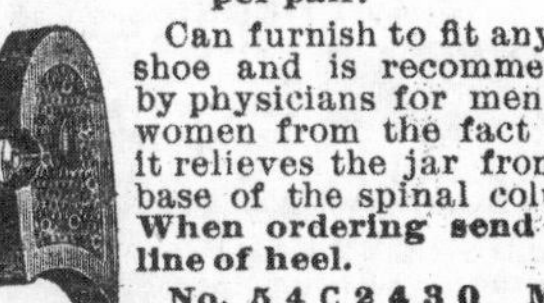

Can furnish to fit any size shoe and is recommended by physicians for men and women from the fact that it relieves the jar from the base of the spinal column. **When ordering send outline of heel.**

No. 54C2430 Men's sizes. Price, per pair $0.10
Per dozen pairs 1.10

No. 54C2432 Women's sizes.
Price, per pair .... .09
Per dozen pairs $1.00

If by mail, postage extra, per pair, 5c.

Whole Rubber Heels.

Thousands of people, obliged to do a great deal of walking, find rubber heels indispensable. They give a spring and buoyancy to the step, remove all jar, and prevent slipping. **Nervous persons** should wear them. Quickly and easily fastened to any style of shoe. Weight, 7 ounces. **When ordering, send outline of heel.**

No. 54C2434 Men's sizes.
Price, per pair $0.18
Per dozen 2.00

No. 54C2436 Women's sizes.
Price, per pair $0.17
Per dozen 1.90

OUR PRICES ON
SHOE FINDINGS
ARE OF SPECIAL INTEREST TO DEALERS AND COBBLERS.

SOLE AND HEEL PROTECTORS.

Metal Sole and Heel Protectors at 23 Cents per Set.

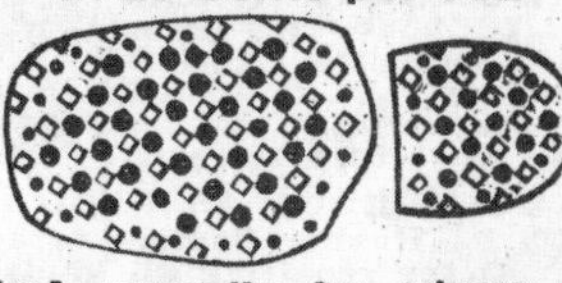

Used generally by miners and foundry men. Set comprises two metal taps and two metal heel top pieces. Weight averages 2 pounds.

No. 54C2452 Men's sizes, 6 to 11.
Price, per set $0.23

Steel Heel and Toe Plates.

Crescent Heel and Toe Plates, cut out of hardened sheet steel, cannot break. Will outwear any plate on the market, and at the same time, the price is lower than many others. No. 2, for women's shoes. No. 3 for men's shoes. Weight, 7 ounces.

No. 54C2460 Price, per box of 1½ dozen pair, No. 2 .... $0.07

No. 54C2462 Price, per box of 1 dozen pair, No. 3 .... $0.05

SHOE NAILS.

Remember, our price is per pound. Some concerns quote theirs per package which means per half pound.

HOLD FAST.

Genuine Brass Clinch Nails.

No. 54C2466 In half pound packages. Latest Improved Brass Clinching Nails. Sizes, 3-8, 3½-8, 4-8, 4½-8, 5-8, 5½-8, 6-8, 6½-8 and 7-8.
Price, per pound $0.19

Baker's Celebrated "Hold Fast" Nails.

In Half Pound Packages.

No. 54C2468 Baker's Patent Wire Clinch Nails. Sizes, 3-8, 3½-8, 4-8, 4½-8, 5-8, 5½-8, 6-8, 6½-8 and 7-8.
Price, per pound $0.10

Cobbler's Iron Clinch Nails.

No. 54C2472 Iron Clinch Nails, in half pound packages, same as used by most cobblers, 3-8, 3½-8, 4-8, 4½-8, 5-8, 5½-8, 6-8.
Price, per pound $0.06

Iron Heel Nails.

No. 54C2474 Common Iron Heel Nails, in one pound packages, 3-8, 4-8, 5-8, 6-8.
Price, per pound $0.05

Hob Nails.

No. 54C2478 Grooved Head Hob Nails. One-half pound packages. All lengths, 3-8 to 5-8.
Price, per pound $0.06

Hungarian Nails.

No. 54C2480 Hungarian Nails, in half pound packages, for bottom of miners' boots and shoes. Sizes, 3-8, 4-8, 5-8. Price, per pound $0.06

SAMPSON SEAM FASTENER OR HAND STAPLING TOOL.

By means of small staples especially made for this seam fastener, shoes are prevented from ripping in the seams. These staples when clinched are almost invisible and will outwear the shoe. **The staples are the most perfect made and will not tear the threads as other kinds do if put directly over the seams or stitching. No family should be without one of these tools and a box of staples to prevent and repair ripped seams.**

No. 54C2516 Seam Fastener.
Price $0.85

No. 54C2517 Staples or Fasteners to be used with No. 54C2516. Made in three sizes, short No. 1, medium No. 2 and long No. 3. Medium or No. 2 is the size mostly used. 576 staples in box.
Price, per box $0.20

Best Leather Cement.

No. 54C2522 1 ounce. Price per bottle..............$0.05
Per dozen.............. .55
If by mail, postage and tube extra, per bottle, 10 cents.
No. 54C2524 2 ounces. Price, per bottle.......$0.09
Per dozen.............. 1.00
If by mail, postage and tube extra, per bottle, 12 cents.

Best Rubber Cement.

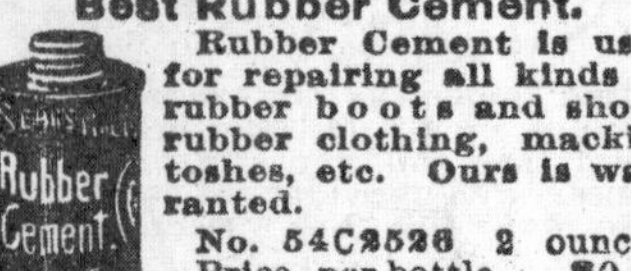

Rubber Cement is used for repairing all kinds of rubber boots and shoes, rubber clothing, mackintoshes, etc. Ours is warranted.
No. 54C2526 2 ounces. Price, per bottle.....$0.05
Per dozen .... .55
No. 54C2528 4 ounces.
Price, per can..................... .08
Per dozen........................ .90

Elastic Goring.

No. 54C2550 Hub Goring, 5-inch. Price, per yard..................$0.50

Witham's Boot Calks and Calk Sets.

For Lumbermen's Boots and Shoes.
No. 54C2552 Ball Calks.
Per dozen, $0.05; per 100.......$0.40
No. 54C2554 Heel Calks.
Per dozen, $0.05; per 100......$0.40
No. 54C2556 Calk Sets. Weight, 4 ounces. Price..................$0.12

Shoemakers' Wax.

No. 54C2560 Price, per doz.....$0.05
Shipping weight, 1 lb. per doz. balls.

Shoemakers' Bristles.

No. 54C2562 Price, per ¼ oz., $0.10

Barbour's Shoe Thread.

Barbour's Best Irish Flax Shoe Thread, half bleached, is used for hand sewing and is the best on the market at any price.

2-ounce balls.

	No.	Per lb.	Per ball
No. 54C2568	12	$1.25	$0.16
No. 54C2570	8	1.05	.14
No. 54C2572	10	.95	.12
No. 54C2574	10 (Am. Standard)		

Per ball, $0.09; per pound.....$0.65
No. 54C2576 No. 10 (Columbia)
Per ball, $0.07; per pound......$0.52
No. 54C2578 Best Yellow Irish Flax. Per ball, $0.18; per lb....$1.40

TOOLS FOR REPAIRING.

The Perfecto Improved German Repair Machine.

No. 54C2690 The arm being the smallest of any machine, it will stitch closer to the toe of a shoe than any other machine made. This machine can be so adjusted as to be used for the very finest of work, as well as the heaviest coarse work. By means of the improved feedbar, you may sew all around in any direction. This machine has no equal in the world, and is fully guaranteed in every part. At the extremely low price we offer this machine, parties who have never before been able to own a machine may have the very best at a price below any other machine made. Set up ready for immediate use, with catalogue of parts and complete directions for using. The following extra parts go with every machine: 1 package assorted needles, 1 wrench, 1 pair tweezers, 1 stitch gauge, 1 foot hemmer for fine work, 1 needle plate, 1 cam roller, 4 bobbins, 2 pressure springs, 1 screwdriver, 1 oil can. Weight, 90 pounds.
Price..........................$34.95

N. B.—Prices of separate parts for the above machine, sent upon request.

Iron Lap Lasts.

Made of iron and very handy to have in the house.
No. 54C2692 Men's large.....$0.17
No. 54C2694 Men's medium... .12
No. 54C2696 Ladies' medium. .07
Shipping weight averages 4 lbs. each.

Iron Shoe Lasts and Stand.

No. 54C2698 Reversible Iron Stand, medium height, with three lasts, small, medium and large.
Price, per set, complete.$0.30
Per dozen sets.......$3.25
Weight, 5½ pounds.
No. 54C2700 24-inch stand with four lasts. Reversible.
Price, per set.........$0.45
Per dozen sets.........$5.40
Weight, 14½ pounds.

24-inch Malleable Stand.

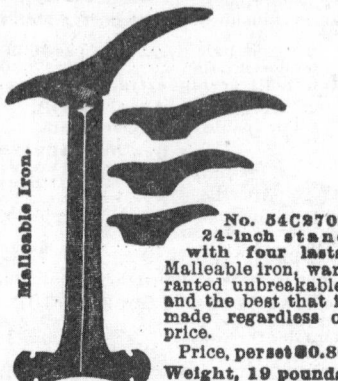

Malleable Iron.

No. 54C2702 24-inch stand with four lasts. Malleable iron, warranted unbreakable, and the best that is made regardless of price.
Price, per set $0.80
Weight, 19 pounds.

Shoemakers' Hammers.

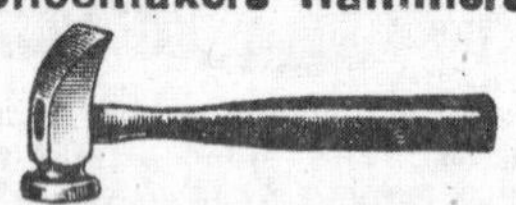

No. 54C2706 Shoemakers' Steel Hammer, No. 0, 15-ounce. Price.$0.23

Shoemakers' Rasps, Best Quality.

No. 54C2714 8-inch half round; weight, 6 ounces. Price..........$0.19
No. 54C2716 9-inch half round; weight, 9 ounces. Price.........$0.25

Awl Handles.

No. 54C2722 Patent Peg Awl Handles with wrench. Price, each.....$0.04
Per dozen........................ .45
If by mail, postage extra, each, 4c.
No. 54C2724 Common Sewing Awl Handles.
Price, per dozen...............$0.09
If by mail, postage extra, each, 2c.

Awl Blades.

No. 54C2730 Sewing Awl Blades, assorted.
Price, per dozen $0.09
No. 54C2732 Peg Awl Blades, assorted sizes. Price, per dozen..$0.04
Postage extra, per dozen, 1 cent.

Needles.

No. 54C2734 Shoemakers' Sewing Needles, assorted.
Price, per paper..............$0.05
Postage extra, per dozen, 1 cent.

Shoemakers' Knives and Skivers.

Warranted Theo. Harrington's Best.

Best steel, knives on the market. Square point good for kitchen use. Regardless of where you buy, be sure to get Theo. Harrington's make, which is the best in the world.
No. 54C2746 Square Point. 1½-ounce. Price, each............$0.06

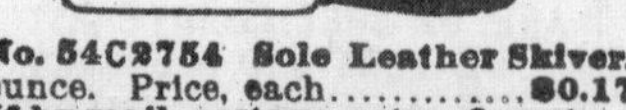

No. 54C2754 Sole Leather Skiver. 2-ounce. Price, each...........$0.17
If by mail, postage extra, 6 cents.

COBBLER OUTFITS.

WHY NOT BUY THE MOST COMPLETE AND RELIABLE OUTFIT FROM US?

WE HAVE PROFITED BY OUR PAST EXPERIENCE, and no doubt you have too, that it is a foolish waste of money to buy an outfit that is incomplete and has stand and lasts which go to pieces on the first blow of the hammer, and contains a cheap iron hammer which is not much better, in fact, every article is worthless when it comes to practical service.

OUR AIM is not to give you an outfit containing the most articles for the smallest amount of money, but one which is better than any other outfit on the market and cheapest for value received, an outfit that you need not be ashamed of.

Combination Shoe, Harness and Tinners' Outfit, $1.98

$1.98 BUYS THE BEST EVER BUILT. Order this outfit at $1.98 and if you do not say it is for all practical uses worth a dozen of any other outfits on the market, you can return it at our expense and we will refund your $1.98. Before getting out this big high grade outfit, we purchased the best outfits advertised by other leading houses at $1.75 to $2.50, and we found the best outfit in the lot compared with our big $1.98 outfit about as follows:

OUR HAMMER is made of the best forged steel. The other outfit contained a worthless cast iron hammer, costing 48 cents a dozen.
OUR KNIFE costs as much as two of the other knives.
OUR SOLDERING IRON is extra heavy, the other light and worthless.
OUR RIVETING MACHINE is high grade and practical, the other is almost worthless. We found the same comparison on almost every item that went into the outfit. The best outfit we found put up in a cheap, common box, while ours goes into a handsome stained hinged tool chest.

OUR BIG $1.98 OUTFIT is the only thoroughly reliable and practical outfit on the market for the repairing of boots, shoes, harness and tinware, all high grade, standard tools and furnishings.

Every article contained in this outfit is the best money can buy suitable for the best shoemakers', tinners' and harness makers' use. We guarantee each and every tool to be of the best quality and to give the best of satisfaction. The tools are made by the best manufacturers of the highest grade of tools. The outfit is not composed of worthless cast iron hammers, worthless riveters, knives that will not keep an edge, soldering irons too light to hold the heat and do the work. It is put up on honor, containing only carefully selected tools of the highest standard offered in any combination outfit.

Our special price of $1.98 barely covers the cost of material and labor, with but our one small percentage of profit added.

We urge you to order this, the highest grade outfit made, and when you get it, if you do not say that our forged steel hammer, knife, riveter and soldering iron are worth a dozen of the same tools furnished by others, if you do not say that our outfit at $1.98 is cheaper than any outfit offered by any other house, even at half their present selling price, you can return it to us and we will immediately refund your $1.98. Weight, 28 pounds.

CONTENTS.

1 Extra Heavy Iron Stand,	1 Package of Shoe Pegs,
4 Extra Heavy Lasts,	1 Pound of Iron Heel Nails,
1 Best Riveting Machine,	¼ Pound 4-8 Clinch Nails,
1 Nickel Plated Steel Shoemakers' Hammer,	¼ Pound 5-8 Clinch Nails,
1 Best Steel Shoe Knife,	4 Pairs Best Heel Plates,
1 Patent Peg Awl Handle,	6 Shoe and Harness Needles,
1 Peg Awl,	1 Improved Saw and Harness Clamp,
1 Sewing Awl Handle,	1 Box Harness and Belt Rivets,
1 Sewing Awl,	1 Steel Punch,
1 Harness Awl Handle,	1 Soldering Iron, Extra Heavy,
1 Harness Awl,	1 Bar Solder,
1 Wrench for Peg Awl Handle,	1 Box Rosin,
1 Ounce Best Leather Cement,	1 Ounce Soldering Fluid,
2 Ounces Best Rubber Cement,	1 Copy of Directions for Soldering,
1 Bunch Bristles,	1 Copy of Directions for Shoe Repairing.
1 Ball of Thread, 2-ounce,	
1 Ball of Wax,	

This outfit is actually worth four times as much as any outfit ever placed upon the market.
No. 54C3001 Price.......................................$1.98

ORDER THIS OUTFIT AT $1.98 and if you do not say it is, for all practical purposes, worth a dozen of any other outfits on the market, you can return it at our expense and we will refund your $1.98.

DEPARTMENT OF MEN'S, WOMEN'S AND CHILDREN'S HOSIERY.

OUR COMPLETE HOSIERY DEPARTMENT. In no other department of our house is our strong buying power more in evidence than in this, our very complete department of men's, women's and children's hosiery. Our contracts direct with the leading hosiery mills in the world for quantities larger than are used by the biggest jobbers, enables us to reduce the cost of production, the cost to us and the cost to our customers to figures that no other concern attempts to meet. In everything in the line of hosiery we are giving the people values that are the same as lasting advertisements for us. **WE GUARANTEE to furnish you a better article in hosiery than you will get from any other house at the same price.** On many numbers our prices to you are about the same as these goods sell at wholesale. **On the basis of the very best possible value for your money, we ask your careful consideration for this department, and your orders for anything you need in this line.**

POSTAGE—WHEN ORDERING SHIPPED BY MAIL DO NOT FAIL TO INCLUDE POSTAGE.

Do not forget the importance of giving correct size that you may have a comfortable and proper fit.

How to Order Sizes Correctly. Scale of Sizes for Men's Hose.						
Shoe	5-5½	6-6½	7-7½	8-8½	9-9½	10-10½-11
Hose	9	9½	10	10½	11	11½

MEN'S COTTON SOCKS

ROCKFORD SOCKS.

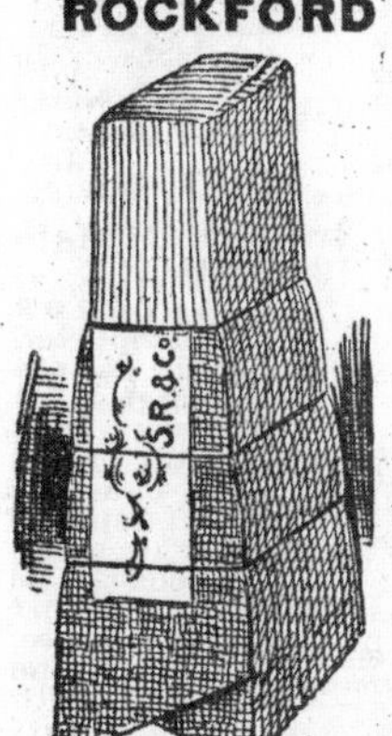

Made by the Nelson Knitting Co.

No. 16C2000 Men's Full Seamless Knit Socks in assorted gray mixtures. Good weight; suitable for wear all the year round. Extra good value.

Price, per doz. pairs, 60c

If by mail, postage extra, per dozen, 32 cents.

Men's Rockford Socks.

The Nelson Knitting Co.'s Seamless Rockford Socks.

No. 16C2004 The Nelson Knitting Co.'s Seamless Rockford Socks. Blue or brown mixed. Heavy double heels and toes, and fine finished ribbed tops. Every pair warranted.

Per dozen pairs....80c

If by mail, postage extra, per dozen pairs, 35 cents.

Boys' Rockford Socks.

No. 16C2006 Boys' Heavy Cotton Rockford Socks. Blue or brown mixed. Good socks for all year round wear. For boys and youths from 10 to 15 years of age.

Price, per dozen pairs..........65c

If by mail, postage extra, per dozen pairs, 34 cents.

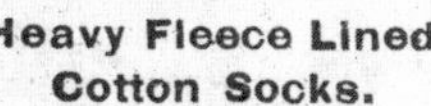

Heavy Fleece Lined Cotton Socks.

No. 16C2007 Men's Heavy Cotton Fleece Lined Socks, made of extra heavy cotton yarn, with a fine soft fleecing on the inside, which makes a very warm cotton sock for winter wear. Mixed colors Sizes, 10, 10½, 11 and 11½.

Per pair...$0.09

Dozen pairs..1.00

If by mail, postage, extra, per pair, 4 cents.

Clouded Colored Cotton Socks.

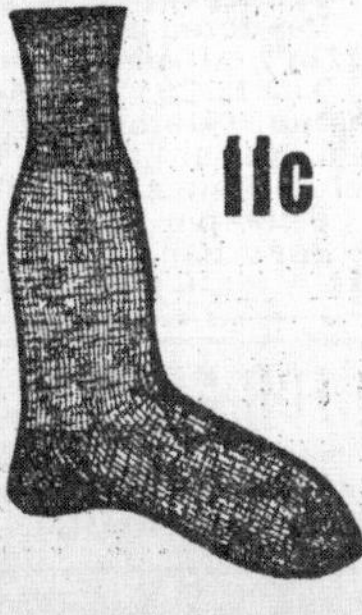

No. 16C2008 [M]en's Fine Full [Se]amless Socks, in [ne]w and handsome [br]own and olive mixes, also neat gray [mi]xtures; extra fine [qu]ality, with finely [fini]shed feet with [mer]cerized heels and [toe]s. The equal of [any] 20-cent hose in [the] market. Weight, [abou]t 17 ounces to the [doze]n. Sizes, 9½, 10, [10½,] 11 and 11½.

11c

[Per] pair....$0.11

[Doz]en pairs 1.25

[If by] mail, postage [extra,] per pair 2 cents.

Men's Unbleached Hose, 12 Cents.

No. 16C2016 Men's Genuine Cream Brown British Seamless Socks. Fine elastic ribbed tops, double heels and toes; **knit to wear long and well and guaranteed to do so.** Fits like a glove and has no seams across the toe to cripple the foot. Sizes, 9½, 10, 10½, 11 and 11½.

Price, per pair..................$0.12

Per dozen pairs...............1.35

If by mail, postage extra, per pair, 2c.

Men's Genuine British Socks, 20 Cents.

No. 16C2020 Our Great 40-Gauge Genuine British Socks. Medium weight; full seamless, with elastic ribbed tops and spliced heels and toes; ecru or cream brown color; **strong and dependable.** Sizes, 9½, 10, 10½, 11 and 11½.

Price, per pair........$0.20

Per dozen pairs........2.35

If by mail, postage extra, per pair, 2 cents.

Men's Plain Color Socks.

No. 16C2024 Men's Extra Finish Egyptian Socks. These goods are made from a fine comb Egyptian cotton with finished seamless feet, mercerized toes and heels of contrasting colors. These socks come in fawn or steel blue colors. Sizes, 9½, 10, 10½ and 11.

12c

Price, per pair..............$0.12

Per dozen pairs...............1.35

If by mail, postage extra, per pair, 2c.

Men's Tan or Brown Color Socks, 11 Cents.

No. 16C2025 Men's Plain Tan or Brown Socks, made of double thread Maco cotton, full seamless double heels and toes. Our special value. Colors, tan or brown. Sizes, 9½, 10, 10½ and 11.

Price, per pair..$0.11

Per dozen pairs........1.25

If by mail, postage extra, per pair, 2 cents.

MEN'S BLACK SOCKS.

Men's Heavy Cotton Black Socks, 10 Cents.

No. 16C2064 Men's Fine Gauge Absolutely Fast Black, Seamless Heavy Cotton Socks. Knit from fine combed Egyptian cotton, double heels and toes. **Very soft and comfortable on the feet. Strong and full of good wearing qualities.** Sizes, 9½, 10, 10½, 11 and 11½.

10c

Price, per pair..................$0.10

Per dozen pairs..................1.10

If by mail, postage extra, per pair, 2c.

Men's Black Socks with Ecru Soles.

No. 16C2065 Men's Black Socks. Made of good quality cotton yarn; fast black with ecru soles and heels. Sizes, 9½, 10, 10½, 11 and 11½.

12c

Price, per pair..........$0.12

Per dozen pairs..........1.35

If by mail, postage extra, per pair, 2 cents.

Men's Black Cotton Socks, 11 Cents.

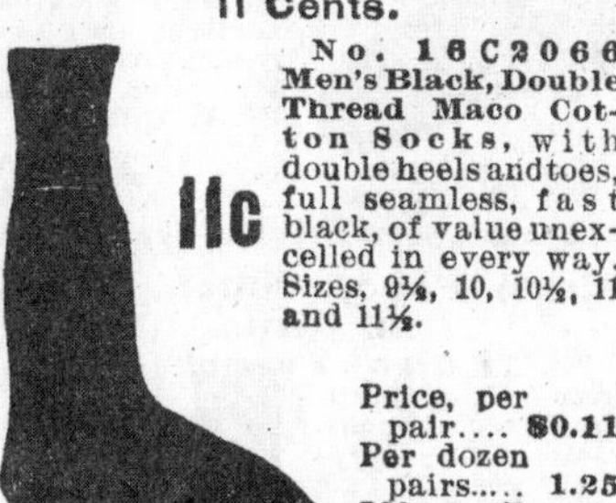

No. 16C2066 Men's Black, Double Thread Maco Cotton Socks, with double heels and toes, full seamless, fast black, of value unexcelled in every way. Sizes, 9½, 10, 10½, 11 and 11½.

11c

Price, per pair.... $0.11

Per dozen pairs..... 1.25

If by mail, postage extra, per pair, 2 cents.

Men's Black Socks with Ecru Feet.

No. 16C2067 Men's Fine Egyptian Combed Yarn Hose, seamless, made with black leg and natural ecru foot. Durable and easy on the feet. Our low price on this hose represents the cost to your local merchant. Elastic ribbed tops. Sizes, 9½, 10, 10½, 11 and 11½.

DON'T FAIL TO GIVE SIZE

12c

Price, per pair..........12c

Per dozen pairs................$1.35

If by mail, postage extra, per pair, 2c.

OUR GREAT LEADER.

Fast Black Genuine Maco Socks, 15 Cents.

No. 16C2068 Men's Extra Quality Fast Black Genuine Maco Cotton Socks, with three-ply heels and toes and fine elastic ribbed tops. **Strictly high grade in every respect.** Regular retail value, 20 to 25 cents. Sizes, 9½, 10, 10½, 11 and 11½. Plain fast black. Price, per pair. $0.15

Per dozen pairs........ 1.75

If by mail, postage extra, per pair, 2 cents.

For a FULL LINE of

HEAVY WINTER HOSIERY

Write for

OUR FREE SPECIAL HOSIERY CATALOGUE.

Men's Fine Mercerized Socks, 18 Cents.

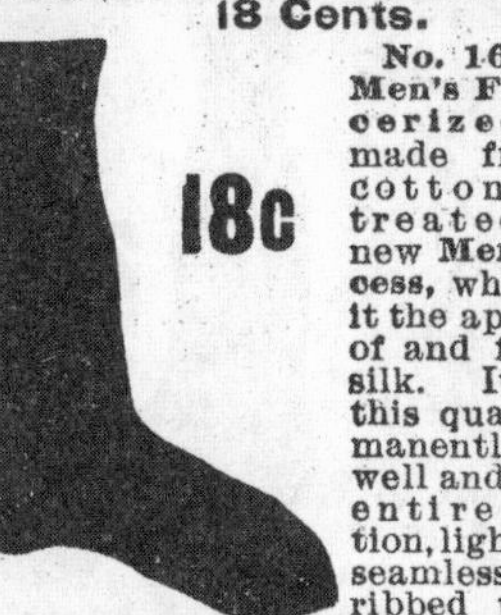

18c

No. 16C2069 Men's Fine Mercerized Hose, made from fine cotton yarn, treated by the new Mercer process, which gives it the appearance of and feels like silk. It retains this quality permanently, wears well and will give entire satisfaction, light weight, seamless, elastic ribbed tops and will fit the foot perfectly. Color, black. Sizes, 9½, 10, 10½ and 11.

Price, per pair...............$0.18

Per dozen pairs..............2.00

If by mail, postage extra, per pair, 2c.

Men's Tan Cotton Socks.

No. 16C2070 Men's Extra Fine Maco Cotton Socks, made of the finest quality Egyptian cotton. Special German dye. These goods are our own importation from Chemnitz, Germany, and we recommend them to give excellent wear. Sizes, 9½, 10, 10½, 11 and 11½.

20c

Price, per pr. 20c

Per dozen pairs...............$2.25

If by mail, postage extra, per pair, 2c.

Black Socks with Ecru Soles.

20c

No. 16C2071 Men's Medium Weight Fast Black Cotton Hose, with ecru heels and toes and ecru soles, double heels and toes, and fine ribbed elastic tops; **made from extra fine real Maco cotton;** our own importation. Sizes, 9½, 10, 10½, 11 and 11½.

Price, per pair.......$0.20

Per dozen pairs 2.25

If by mail, postage extra, per pair, 2c.

Always state size wanted when ordering hosiery.

OUR SPECIAL VALUE AT 20 CENTS.

No. 16C2072 Men's Extra Fine Real Three-Thread Maco Egyptian Cotton Socks. Plain black, with double heels, toes and spliced soles. Long elastic ribbed tops. **Absolutely fast color. Strictly fine and high grade. If you want something extra fine, one of the best fine gauge cotton socks made, order this number and the value will please you.** Sizes, 9½, 10, 10½, 11 and 11½. Price, per pair............$0.20

20c

Per dozen pairs.............2.25

If by mail, postage extra, per pair, 2c.

Men's Silk Clocked Hose, 25 Cents.

No. 16C2073 Men's Fine Maco Egyptian Yarn Hose, double soles and heels, very fine gauge, embroidered with silk clock work stitch up the sides as shown in illustration. **This is a superfine quality hose that invariably meets the approval of well dressed men.** Sizes, 9½, 10, 10½ and 11.

Price, per pair....$0.25

Per dozen pairs.... 2.85

If by mail, postage extra, per pair, 2c.

MEN'S COTTON SOCKS.

Men's Black Lisle Socks, 25c.

No. 16C2075 Men's Full Fashioned Imported Black Lisle Socks. These goods are of the finest quality and exceptional value at our price. Fast black. Sizes, 9½, 10, 10½ and 11.
Price, per pair........$0.25
Per dozen pairs........ 2.85
If by mail, postage extra, per pair, 2 cents.

Men's Black Lisle Socks, 35 Cents.

No. 16C2077 Men's Super Quality, Extra Fine Gauge Lisle Socks, made of genuine French brilliant lisle, full fashioned double heels and toes, which is an advantage as to the wear. We cannot recommend this number too highly. Fast black. Sizes, 9½, 10, 10½ and 11. Price, per pair, $0.35
Per dozen pairs....... 4.00
If by mail, postage extra, per pair, 2 cents.

Men's Fancy Oxford Gray Socks, 11 Cents.

No. 16C2080 Men's Fancy Oxford Gray Socks, made of good quality cotton yarn with black printed figures. Oxford gray socks are the very latest designs for men's wear. This quality is good value. Sizes, 9½, 10, 10½, 11 and 11½.
Price, per pair........$0.11
Per dozen pairs........ 1.25
If by mail, postage extra, per pair 2c.

Men's Fancy Embroidered Socks, 11 Cents.

No. 16C2082 Men's Fine Cotton Hose. Made from fine cotton yarn, fast black with colored embroidered figures, as shown in illustration. This hose is seamless, close knit, elastic ribbed tops. Color, black. Sizes, 9½, 10, 10½, 11 and 11½.
Price, per pair...$0.11
Per dozen pairs.. 1.25
If by mail, postage extra, per pair, 2 cents.

Men's Fancy Tan Cotton Socks

No. 16C2083 Men's Fancy Tan Socks, made of good quality Egyptian cotton. The ground work is tan with fancy stripes and dots, as shown in illustration. Sizes, 9½, 10, 10½, 11 and 11½. Price, per pair........$0.11
Per dozen pairs........ 1.25
If by mail, postage extra, per pair, 2 cents.

Men's Fancy Black Cotton Socks, 11 Cents.

No. 16C2084 Men's Fancy Black Socks, made of good quality cotton yarn; the ground work is black with fancy white stripes or dots. Sizes, 9½, 10, 10½, 11 and 11½.
Price, per pair........$0.11
Per dozen pairs........ 1.25
If by mail, postage extra, per pair, 2 cents.

Men's Fancy Cotton Socks, 11 Cents.

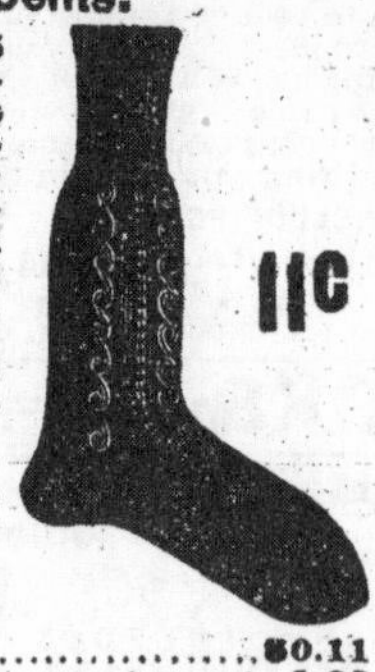

No. 16C2085 Men's Fancy Cotton Hose, made with close knitted tops, seamless. Embroidered in fancy scroll design, as shown in illustration. A new novelty. This hose will give entire satisfaction. Color, black. The embroidery will be of contrasting colors. Sizes, 9½, 10, 10½, 11 and 11½.
Price, per pair........$0.11
Per dozen pairs........ 1.25
If by mail, postage extra, per pair, 2c.

Men's Fancy Cotton Socks.

No. 16C2086 Men's Extra Quality Fancy Socks, made of fine quality Egyptian cotton, ground work is tan color with silk embroidered figures of contrasting colors. We can recommend this sock to give excellent wear. Dye absolutely fast. Sizes, 9½, 10, 10½, 11 and 11½.
Price, per pair........$0.20
Per dozen pairs........ 2.35
If by mail, postage extra, per pair, 2c.

Men's Fancy Cotton Socks, 20 Cents.

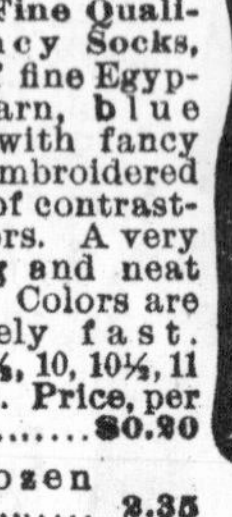

No. 16C2087 Men's Fine Quality Fancy Socks, made of fine Egyptian yarn, blue mixed with fancy silk embroidered figures of contrasting colors. A very pleasing and neat design. Colors are absolutely fast. Sizes, 9½, 10, 10½, 11 and 11½. Price, per pair........$0.20
Per dozen pairs........ 2.35
If by mail, postage extra, per pair, 2c.

A Special Novelty in Men's Lace Hose.

No. 16C2088 These goods are made of a fine Egyptian cotton, lisle finish with a narrow open work down to the toe with colored embroidery, giving it a very stylish effect. Double heels and toes. Close fitting ribbed tops. Color, black, slate or fawn, colored embroidery. Sizes, 9½, 10, 10½ and 11.
Price, per pair........20c
Per dozen pairs....$2.35
If by mail, postage extra, per pair, 2c.

Men's Fancy Tan Socks 25c.

No. 16C2090 Men's Extra Quality Fancy Socks, made of the finest quality Egyptian cotton yarn. Ground work is tan mixed with fancy silk embroidered figures of contrasting colors. Fancy socks will be much worn this year and this neat pattern, we feel confident will please you. Sizes 9½, 10, 10½, 11 and 11½.
Price, per pair........$0.25
Price, per dozen pairs........ 2.85
If by mail, postage extra, per pair, 2c.

Men's Silk Embroidered Hose.

No. 16C2091 This number is made of two-thread pure Egyptian cotton high spliced heels and toes with colored silk embroidered clockwork stitch up the sides, as shown in illustration. Black only. Sizes, 9½, 10, 10½ and 11. Price, per pair....$0.20
Per dozen pairs........ 2.35
If by mail, postage extra, per pair, 2c.

Men's Embroidered Black Socks at 25 Cents.

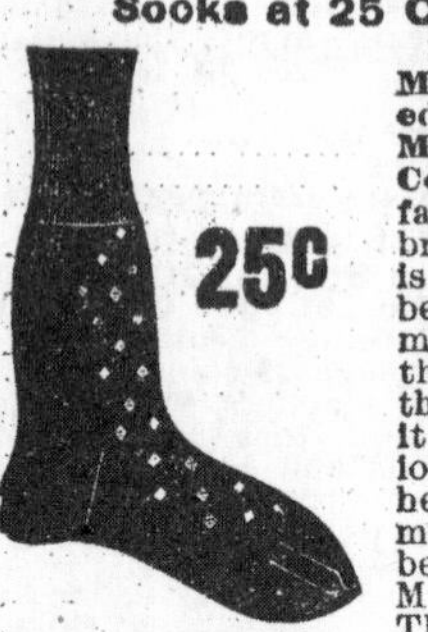

No. 16C2092 Men's Imported Genuine Maco Black Cotton Sock, fancy silk embroidered. This is one of the best quality men's socks that we have this season, as it is a full fashioned double heels and toes, made of the best quality Maco yarn. The embroidery is red, white or green figured designs. Color, black only. Sizes, 9½, 10, 10½, 11 and 11½. Price, per pair......$0.25
Per dozen pairs........ 2.85
If by mail, postage extra, per pair, 2c.

Our Leader—Men's Fancy Hose, 20 Cents.

No. 16C2093 Men's Fancy Hose, fashioned and shaped to fit the foot perfectly. Made of fine Egyptian yarn and will give good service; elastic tops and fast colors. A first class article that will give good satisfaction. Stripes in all colors. Sizes, 9½, 10, 10½ and 11.
Per pair....$0.20
Dozen pairs.. 2.35
If by mail, postage extra, per pair, 2c.

Men's Black Lace Hose.

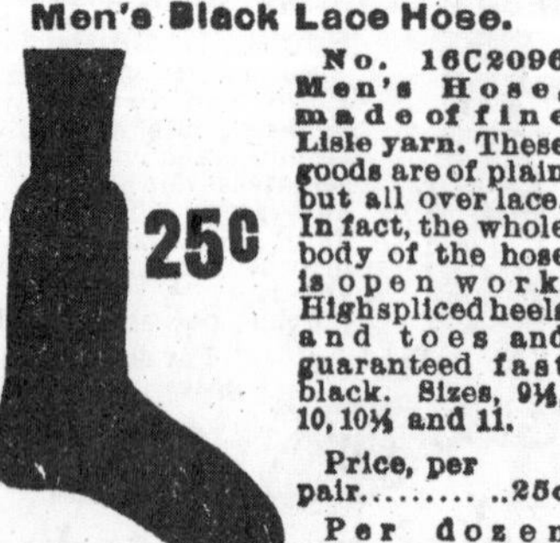

No. 16C2096 Men's Hose, made of fine Lisle yarn. These goods are of plain but all over lace. In fact, the whole body of the hose is open work. High spliced heels and toes and guaranteed fast black. Sizes, 9½, 10, 10½ and 11.
Price, per pair.........25c
Per dozen pairs.......$2.85
If by mail, postage extra, per pair, 2c.

Men's Embroidered Lace Hose

No. 16C2097 This Men's Hose we have imported direct from Chemnitz, Germany. Is made of the best lisle thread, high spliced heels and toes, lace work down to the toe with small colored figured embroidery. This is a new effect, and is very much in demand. Black only. Sizes, 9½, 10, 10½ and 11.
Price, per pair........$0.35
Per dozen pairs........ 4.00
If by mail, postage extra, per pair, 2c.

Men's New Stripe Hose.

No. 16C2102 We illustrate herewith Men's New Style Stripe Fine Black Lisle Hose. This is a new effect, embroidered directly on the surface of the hose after it has been dyed and knit and stands out in strong relief. The stripes are white, blue, light blue, dark blue or red. Sizes 9½, 10, 10½ and 11.
Price, per pair........$0.25
Per dozen pairs........ 2.85
If by mail, postage extra, per pair, 2c.

Men's Fancy Imported Lisle Socks, 39 Cents.

No. 16C2103 Men's Imported Fancy Lisle Socks, high spliced heels and toes. Under this number we can furnish you a special novelty in men's fancy socks. The combination of colors are white, green, red or blue background with embroidery of contrasting color. These goods are made of the finest French brilliant lisle and will give excellent wear. Sizes, 9½, 10, 10½ and 11.
Price, per pair........$0.39
Per dozen pairs........ 4.50
If by mail, postage extra, per pair, 2c.

Extra Heavy Baseball Stockings.

No. 16C2104 Baseball Stockings. Extra heavy, long ribbed cotton stockings, double spliced heels and toes. Made full length and reach above the knee. Plain black only. All sizes, from 9½ to 11½.
Price, per pair..$0.20
Per dozen pairs.. 2.25
If by mail, postage extra, per pair, 5 cents.

BICYCLE OR GOLF HOSE.

No. 16C2105 Men's Fine Ribbed Leg Woolen Bicycle Hose, footless, roll down tops. Will give good satisfaction. Colors, black or brown.
Price, per pair........$0.45
Per dozen pairs........ 5.40
If by mail, postage extra, per pair, 3c.

MEN'S GARTERS.

"The Sun" GARTER

No. 16C2175 Men's Elastic Web Garters, made in neat, fancy striped patterns. Assorted colors. See illustration for style.
Price, per pair.....7c
Per dozen pairs..80c
If by mail, postage extra, per pair, 3 cents.

No. 16C2176 Men's Fine Mercerized Web Garters, made same style as shown in illustration. Very fine. Colors, black, white, old gold, blue or red, 20-cent quality.
Price, per pair........$0.1
Per dozen pairs........ 1.7
If by mail, postage extra, per pair,

No. 16C2177 Men's Silk Garte same style as shown in illustrati Put up one pair in a box. Colors, bla blue, orange, white or red.
Price, per pair........$0.2
Per dozen pairs........ 2.2
If by mail, postage extra, per pair,

LADIES' COTTON HOSIERY.

SPECIAL NOTICE.—In ordering Ladies' Hose please refer to the following scale of sizes:

		Takes about
No. 2	Ladies' shoe	8 -inch hose
No. 2	Ladies' shoe	8½-inch hose
No. 3 & 4	Ladies' shoe	9 -inch hose
No. 6 & 6	Ladies' shoe	9½-inch hose
No. 7	Ladies' shoe	10 -inch hose

If by mail, postage extra, per dozen pairs, 22 to 34 cents on ladies' hose.

Always give correct size in order. Always include sufficient postage when ordering hosiery shipped by mail.

Ladies' Oxford Mixed Hose, 9 Cents.

No. 16C2298 Ladies' Extra Quality Dark Oxford Gray Mixed Seamless Cotton Hose. Fine gauge and good medium weight for all the year round wear. Made by the famous Nelson Knitting Mills. We sell tons of them every year and have never had a single complaint in regard to them. They are soft and close knit, very strong and durable.

Price, per dozen pairs, $1.00; per pair 9c

If by mail, postage extra, per dozen, 45 cents; per pair, 4 cents.

LADIES' BLACK HOSIERY.

A Satisfactory Stocking at 10 Cents.

No. 16C2302 Genuine Lawrence Mills Fast Black Cotton Hose. Made full size and length. Medium weight. Strong and reliable.

Price, per dozen pairs, $1.10; per pair........10c

If by mail, postage extra, per pair, 3 cents.

A Good Stocking for 12 Cents.

No. 16C2308 Ladies' Fast Black Cotton Hose. Made heavier weight and finer than the above. Very durable and sure to satisfy. Double soles and heels. Sizes, 8½, 9, 9½ and 10. Price, per pair........$0.12

Per dozen pairs........1.35

If by mail, postage extra, per pair, 3 cents.

Black Stockings at 15 Cents.

No. 16C2309 Full Seamless Hose. Warranted absolutely fast black and stainless. Soft, smooth finish with elastic hemmed tops, double heels and double toes. 20-cent quality when bought at retail. Sizes, 8½, 9, 9½ and 10. Price, per pair........$0.15

Per dozen pairs........1.75

If by mail, postage extra, per pair, 3 cents.

Ladies' Black Hose, Extra Quality, for 20 Cents.

No. 16C2311 Ladies' Extra Fine Cotton Hose, made of pure combed Maco cotton yarn. These hose are full fashioned, with shapely ankle and foot, and elastic leg, absolutely fast black and stainless. We cannot recommend this hose too highly. It is correct in size, knitted to fit and reliable in yarn, dye and wear. Sizes, 8½, 9, 9½ and 10. Price, per pair. $0.20

Per dozen pairs........2.35

Postage extra, per pair, 3 cents.

OUR FAMOUS BERENICE LADIES' BLACK HOSE, 25 CENTS.

Unequaled Anywhere.

No. 16C2312 Extra Fine Silky Finished Real Maco Cotton Hose. Plain black, with three-thread heels and toes; made from extra selected combed yarn, full seamless, finely shaped full fashioned hose. Guaranteed absolutely fast black and stainless. Nothing better ever sold for less than 35 cents retail. The Berenice brand of hosiery is the best made. Sizes, 8½, 9, 9½ and 10.

Price, per dozen pairs, $2.85; per pair........25c

If by mail, postage extra, per pair, 3 cents.

Ladies' Fine Black Hose, 35 Cents.

No. 16C2313 Ladies' Fast Black Hose. Plain black, full seamless, with high spliced heels and toes and double soles. Knit from finest imported Maco cotton. Extra fine gauge, medium light weight, 1¾ pounds to the dozen; soft as silk and absolutely fast color and stainless. Sizes, 8½, 9, 9½ and 10. The dependable kind.

Price, per dozen pairs, $4.00; per pair........35c

If by mail, postage extra, per pair, 3 cents.

PLAIN BLACK LISLE HOSIERY. 25 and 35 Cents.

No. 16C2314 Ladies' Plain Black Lisle Imported Hose, made from fine lisle thread. Fine fashioned and perfectly shaped spliced heels and soles. Lisle hose are cool. Do not forget size. Sizes, 8½, 9, 9½ and 10. Price, per pair........$0.25

Per doz. prs. 2.75

If by mail, postage extra, per pair, 3 cents.

No. 16C2315 Ladies' Plain Black Lisle Imported Hose, finer quality than the above, very light weight, full fashioned, spliced heel and double soles. Sizes, 8½, 9, 9½ and 10.

Per pair....$0.35

Per doz. prs. 4.00

Postage extra, per pair, 3c

Ladies' Fine Ribbed Black Hose, 20 Cents.

No. 16C2316 Ladies' Fine Ribbed Leg Hose. Made from good quality cotton yarn. Medium weight, seamless fast black, and closely knit plain foot. Sizes, 8½, 9, 9½ and 10.

Per pair. $0.20

Per doz.. 2.35

If by mail, postage extra, per pair, 3 cents.

Ladies' Stockings, with Ecru Cotton Foot, 12 Cents.

No. 16C2318 Ladies' Seamless Plain Cotton Hose, fast black legs, made with all ecru foot, as shown in illustration; an excellent hose, wearing better than all black, and easy to darn. These stockings are knitted fine gauge, and retail at 20 cents per pair. Color, black. Sizes, 8½, 9, 9½, and 10.

Price, per pr., $0.12

Per dozen prs., 1.35

If by mail, postage extra, per pair, 3c; per dozen pairs, 30c.

If you fail to give size, we cannot fill your order.

Berenice Fast Black Cotton Hose, 20c. With Ecru Color Soles.

No. 16C2319 Fast Black Hose, with cream colored, unbleached heels, toes and soles; made from extra selected real Maco cotton, easy on the feet, warranted to give lasting satisfaction in looks and wear. Soft, smooth and very strong and durable. Berenice Hosiery we warrant absolutely fast black and stainless. Can be used with slippers, as the white sole will not show above the top. Sizes, 8½, 9, 9½ and 10.

Per pair... $0.20

Per dozen, 2.35

If by mail, postage extra, per pair 3 cents.

IN ORDERING DON'T FAIL TO STATE THE SIZE YOU WANT.

Ladies' White Cotton Hose, 12c and 25c.

No. 16C2385 Ladies' Plain White Hose, made of good quality cotton yarn. Sizes, 8½, 9, 9½ and 10.

Price, per pair $0.12

Per doz. pairs 1.35

If by mail, postage extra, per pair, 3c.

No. 16C2386 Ladies' Extra Quality Plain White Cotton Hose. Fine gauge, full seamless, soft and smooth. Sizes, 8½, 9, 9½ and 10. Price, per pair, 25c

If by mail, postage extra, per pair, 3c.

Ladies' Opera Length Hose, 35 Cents.

No. 16C2406 Ladies' Opera Length Hose, fast black. Sizes, 8½, 9, 9½ and 10. Per pair........$0.35

Dozen pairs........4.00

If by mail, postage extra, per pair, 4 cents.

Ladies' Fancy Hose.

No. 16C2410 Ladies' Fancy Hose, made of good quality cotton yarn, black with white stripes from top down to toe, as shown in illustration. This stocking is fast color, full of good wearing qualities and will give satisfaction. Sizes, 8½, 9, 9½ and 10.

Per pair....$0.11

Doz. pairs....1.25

If by mail, postage extra, per pair, 2 cents.

Ladies' Fancy Tan Hose.

11c

No. 16C2411 Ladies' Fancy Hose, made of good quality of cotton yarn, tan ground with fancy stripes and figures in white. This is something new in fancy hose, right up to date and nobby. Fast colors. A good, durable stocking. Sizes, 8½, 9, 9½ and 10.

Per pair....$0.11

Dozen pairs..1.25

If by mail, postage extra, per pair, 3 cents.

Ladies' Fancy Dot Hose, 11 Cents.

No. 16C2412 Ladies' Fancy Dot Hose, made of a fine quality of cotton yarn, seamless leg. The ground work of this stocking is black, with white dots or figures, as shown in illustration; special value at our low price. Sizes, 8½, 9, 9½ and 10.

Per pair........$0.11

Doz. pairs........1.25

If by mail, postage extra, per pair, 3 cents.

Ladies' Fancy Hose, 11 Cents.

11c

No. 16C2413 Our illustration gives a fair representation of this new design in ladies' hose, knitted from clean cotton yarn. An astonishing value at our low price. Color, black with white figures and stripes. State size in your order. Sizes, 8½, 9, 9½ and 10.

Per pair..$0.11

Doz. pairs.. 1.25

If by mail, postage extra, per pair, 3 cents.

Ladies' Embroidered Hose, 20 Cents per Pair.

No. 16C2420 This hose is made of a fine Egyptian cotton with a spliced heel and toe, fast black color. Embroidered in red, blue or white. Sizes, 8½, 9, 9½, 10.

Pair, $0.20

Doz. pairs... 2.25

If by mail, postage extra, per pr., 3 cents.

Silk Embroidered Hose, 40c.

No. 16C2422 Ladies' Fine Black Cotton Hose, full fashioned and elastic knitted; made with fancy silk embroidery, which work is done by hand. The illustration gives a fair representation. The embroidery comes in blue, red, green, etc. We always assort them when several pairs are ordered, unless otherwise stated. Sizes, 8½, 9, 9½ and 10.

Per pair........$0.40

Dozen pairs........4.50

If by mail, postage extra, per pair, 3 cents.

LADIES' LACE HOSIERY.

Ladies' Lace Hose, 11c per Pair.

No. 16C2424 Ladies' Good Quality Seamless Lace Hose, of fine cotton and an exceptional value at this low price. Color, black only. Sizes, 8½, 9, 9½ and 10.

Per pair....$0.11

Doz. pairs.. 1.25

If by mail, postage extra, per pair, 3c.

Our New Lace Hose, 20c per Pair.

No. 16C2429 Ladies' New Style Lace Hose. Made in fancy knitted lace down to ankle. A stocking that looks particularly well worn with low shoes. Knitted from fine quality yarn, and have perfect fitting seamless feet. Few stores sell this quality for 25 cents and most of them would ask you more. You can save at least 5 cents a pair, 60 cents per dozen, if you buy them from us. Color, black. Sizes, 8½, 9, 9½, 10.

Per pair........$0.20

Dozen pairs..... 2.35

If by mail, postage extra, per pair, 3 cents.

Imported Lace Effect Lisle Hose, 35 Cents.

No. 16C2436 A Perfect Hose in every respect. Strictly high grade; our idea of what a par excellence hose should be. Warranted absolutely stainless. They are full fashioned and have extra spliced heels. Imported by us and guaranteed to be all that we claim for them—and more. Color, black. Sizes, 8½, 9, 9½, 10.

Pair........$0.35

Doz. pairs.. 4.00

If by mail, postage extra, per pair, 3c.

Ladies' Lace Hose, 40 Cents per Pair.

No. 16C2440 Ladies' Fine Lace Front Hose. This is the latest novelty in ladies' lace hose. Made from a fine lisle thread yarn, plain down to the ankle with lace open work effect from ankle down to the toe. This stocking is very much in favor to wear with low shoes. Absolutely fast black. High spliced heels and toes. Sizes, 8½, 9, 9½, 10.

Per pair........$0.40

Dozen pairs, 4.50

If by mail, postage extra, per pair, 3c.

Ladies' Lace Tan Hose, 40 Cents.

No. 16C2442 Ladies' Extra Fine Quality Lisle Lace Hose, our own importation from Chemnitz, Germany. Lace designs are the latest effect, as shown in illustration. Colors, assorted tan. Sizes, 8½, 9, 9½ and 10.

Price per pair........$0.40

Doz. pairs..4.50

If by mail, postage extra, per pair, 3 cents.

LADIES' EXTRA WIDE LEG COTTON HOSE.

No. 16C2460 Ladies' Seamless Extra Wide Leg, Black Hose, made of fine cotton, seamless leg, high spliced heels and toes, and warranted fast black. Sizes, 8½, 9, 9½ and 10.

Price, per pair........$0.12

Per dozen pairs........1.35

If by mail, postage extra, per pair 3c

No. 16C2464 Ladies' Extra Wide Leg Hose, made with extra wide legs. Fast black, heavy cotton, with double heels and toes. Sizes, 8½, 9, 9½ and 10.

Price, per pair........$0.18

Per dozen pairs........2.00

If by mail, postage extra, per pair 3c.

Ladies' Out Size or Extra Wide Leg Hosiery.

No. 16C2466 Ladies' Fast Black, Extra Wide Leg Cotton Hose, made with extra wide legs and tops, spliced heels and double soles. Sizes, 8½, 9, 9½ and 10.

Price, per pair........$0.25

Per dozen pairs........2.85

If by mail, postage extra, per pair, 3c.

FOR LADIES' HEAVY WINTER HOSE SEND FOR FREE CATALOGUE OF HOSIERY.

BOYS', MISSES' AND CHILDREN'S COTTON HOSIERY.

Size of Shoes	4-5	6-7	8-9	10-11	12-13	1-2	2-3	3½-4½	5-6	6-7
Size of Hose	5½	6	6½	7	7½	8	8½	9	9½	10

Children's Cotton Ribbed Hose

No. 16C2600 Children's Fine Ribbed Cotton Hose, full seamless, with long legs and nicely shaped feet. Warranted fast black and stainless, good strong stockings.

Sizes	5½	6	6½
Price, per pair	7c	8c	8c
Per doz. pairs	80c	90c	90c
Sizes	7	7½	8
Price, per pair	9c	9c	$0.10
Per doz. pairs	95c	95c	1.10
Sizes	8½	9	9½
Price, per pair	$0.11	$0.11	$0.12
Per doz. pairs	1.25	1.25	1.35

If by mail, postage extra, per pair, 3c.

Children's Black Cotton Hose

No. 16C2604 Children's Fine Gauge Ribbed Cotton Hose, extra well made with double knees. Warranted absolutely fast black and stainless. The best cheap hose ever made. Always state size.

Sizes	Price, per pair	Per dozen pairs
5½	10c	$1.10
6	10c	1.10
6½	11c	1.25
7	11c	1.25
7½	12c	1.35
8	12c	1.35
8½	13c	1.45
9	13c	1.45
9½	14c	1.60

If by mail, postage extra, per pair, 4c.

Wear Well Stockings.

No. 16C2608 Children's Special Wear Well Stockings. Heavy ribbed legs and full seamless feet. Warranted absolutely fast black and stainless. Knit from specially prepared Egyptian cotton. Soft, smooth, very dressy and perfect fitting. Finely shaped and made with double spliced knees and three thread heels and toes; good wearing hose.

Sizes	6	6½	7
Price, per pair	$0.13	$0.14	$0.14
Per dozen pairs	1.45	1.60	1.60
Sizes	7½	8	8½
Price, per pair	$0.15	$0.15	$0.16
Per dozen pairs	1.70	1.70	1.80
Sizes	9	9½	
Price, per pair	$0.17	$0.18	
Per dozen pairs	1.90	2.00	

If by mail, postage extra, per pair, 5 cents.

S., R. & Co.'s Special Warranted Boys' Stockings, 20c per Pair.

No. 16C2612 We present herewith the best heavy cotton stocking, for boys (girls wear them, too), made in the United States. This special stocking made for us excels all others for wear, strength and elasticity. Instead of simply making the leg of the usual weight with double knee, the entire leg is made extra or what is called triple weight throughout, and the entire foot is extra heavy and closely knit, making a wear resisting stocking never before equaled. The tops are perfectly finished and will not ravel out in any way. Every pair is accurately sized. You will be satisfied with no other stocking after buying this one. We want your order, because you will find it better than any stocking sold at from 25 to 35 cents a pair. Color, black only. Sizes, 6, 6½, 7, 7½, 8, 8½, 9, 9½ and 10. Don't forget sizes.

Price, per pair......$0.20
Per dozen pairs..... 2.25

By mail, postage extra, per pair, 5c; box of 6 pairs, 24c.

EXTRA STRONG AND HEAVY TRIPLE KNIT LEG

DOUBLE KNIT FOOT

Misses' Special Mercerized Silk Hose.

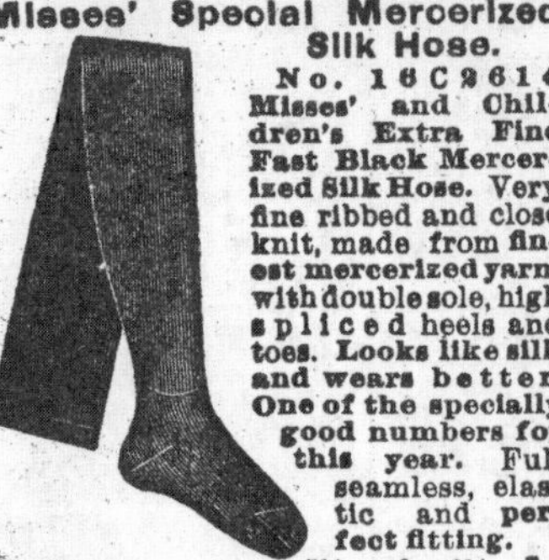

No. 16C2614 Misses' and Children's Extra Fine Fast Black Mercerized Silk Hose. Very fine ribbed and close knit, made from finest mercerized yarn, with double sole, high spliced heels and toes. Looks like silk and wears better. One of the specially good numbers for this year. Full seamless, elastic and perfect fitting.

Sizes	5½	6	6½	7
Price, per pair	17c	18c	19c	19c
Sizes	7½	8	8½	9
Price, per pair	20c	20c	21c	21c

If by mail, postage extra, per pair, 3c.

S., R. & Co.'s Special Warranted Light Weight Ribbed Cotton Stockings, 21 Cents per Pair.

No. 16C2616 This is another of our especially good things in children's hosiery. Made from strong, fine, smooth Egyptian lisle yarn, which is the most durable of light weight yarns. We want your order for this quality; smooth, perfect fitting hose, equal to the best 25c hose at retail. Color, black. Sizes, 5½, 6, 6½, 7, 7½, 8, 8½ and 9. Don't forget to give size.

Price, pair....21c

If by mail, postage extra, per pair, 3c.

Misses' and Children's Cotton Stockings.

No. 16C2618 Children's very fine quality Mercerized Lace Stockings. New design for children that will be much worn this season, knitted from a fine mercerized yarn, which is treated by a patented process which makes it resemble silk. We will charge you according to the size. Black only.

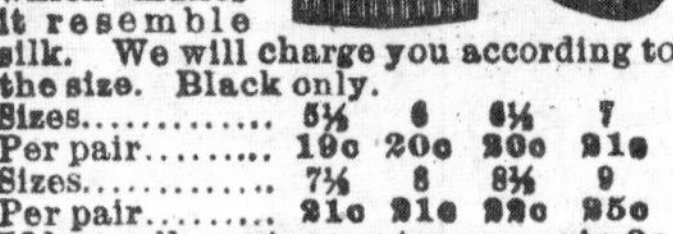

Sizes	5½	6	6½	7
Per pair	19c	20c	20c	21c
Sizes	7½	8	8½	9
Per pair	21c	21c	22c	25c

If by mail, postage extra, per pair, 3c.

Misses' and Children's White Mercerized Lace Stockings.

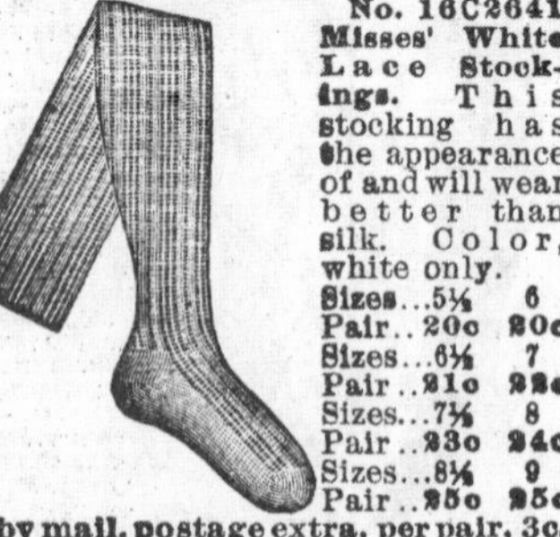

No. 16C2641 Misses' White Lace Stockings. This stocking has the appearance of and will wear better than silk. Color, white only.

Sizes	5½	6
Pair	20c	20c
Sizes	6½	7
Pair	21c	22c
Sizes	7½	8
Pair	23c	24c
Sizes	8½	9
Pair	25c	25c

If by mail, postage extra, per pair, 3c.

Misses' and Children's Tan Cotton Ribbed Hose.

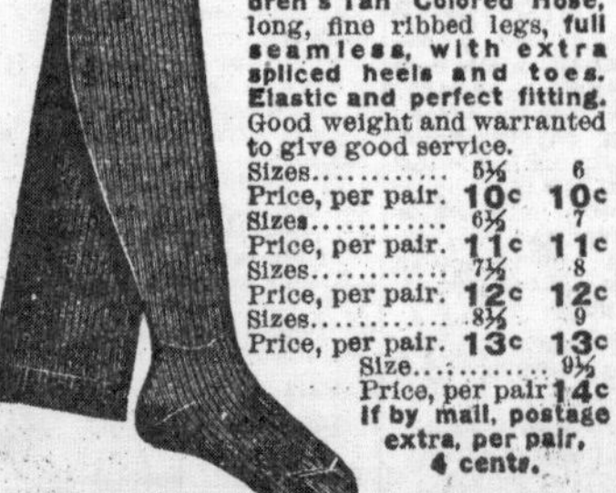

No. 16C2654 Children's Tan Colored Hose, long, fine ribbed legs, full seamless, with extra spliced heels and toes. Elastic and perfect fitting. Good weight and warranted to give good service.

Sizes	5½	6
Price, per pair	10c	10c
Sizes	6½	7
Price, per pair	11c	11c
Sizes	7½	8
Price, per pair	12c	12c
Sizes	8½	9
Price, per pair	13c	13c
Size		9½
Price, per pair		14c

If by mail, postage extra, per pair, 4 cents.

INFANTS' COTTON AND WOOL HOSIERY.

INFANTS' SCALE OF SIZES.

Size of Shoe	1	2-3	4	5	6-7
Size of Hose	4	4½	5	5½	6

No. 16C2710 Infants' Ribbed Fast Black Cotton Hose. Fine soft finish, close knit and full seamless. Sizes, 4½, 5, 5½ or 6.

Per pair..$0.09
Dozen..... 1.00

No. 16C2714 Infants' Fine Ribbed Cotton Hose, made of fine yarn with fashioned feet. One of our strongest values. Colors, black, sky blue, pink, tan, red or white. Sizes, 4½, 5, 5½ and 6.

Price, per pair..........$0.11
Per dozen pairs.......... 1.25

If by mail, postage extra, per pair, 1c.

Infants' Mercerized Hosiery at 18 Cents per Pair.

No. 16C2720 Infants' Fine Mercerized Cotton Hose, fine ribbed legs, perfectly shaped feet. The mercerized process is that of making a fine Egyptian cotton yarn feel like silk; looks like silk and will wear better. An especially fine number made in the following colors: Black, sky blue, white, red or pink. State color and size when ordering. Sizes, 4½, 5, 5½ and 6. Per pair....$0.18
Per dozen pairs.......... 2.00

If by mail, postage extra, per pair, 2 cents.

Infants' Lace Effect Stockings.

No. 16C2728 Infants' Fine Cotton Stockings, in new style; drop stitch lace effect; made of smooth, soft, clean yarn, warranted to give entire satisfaction; perfectly shaped feet and legs. Retail price, 15 to 20 cents. Colors, black, white, red, pink or sky blue. Sizes, 4½, 5, 5½ and 6.

Price, per pair........$0.11
Per dozen pairs........ 1.25

If by mail, postage extra, per pair, 2 cents.

Infants' Mercerized Lace Stockings.

No. 16C2729 Infants' Fine Mercerized Stockings. By mercerized, we mean a process of treating cotton yarn which makes it resemble pure silk. This stocking is lace open work effect down to the ankle. Plain, seamless foot. Colors, black, white, sky blue, pink or red. Sizes, 4½, 5, 5½ and 6.

Price, per pair.............$0.18
Per dozen pairs............ 2.00

Postage extra, per pair, 2c.

INFANTS' WOOL RIBBED HOSE.

No. 16C2735 Infants' Cashmere Hose, wool ribbed, an excellent value. Colors, black, cardinal, pink, light blue or white. Sizes, 4, 4½, 5, 5½ and 6.

Price, per pair..........$0.12
Per dozen............... 1.35

If by mail, postage extra, per pair, 2 cents.

Infants' Worsted Ribbed Hose, 15 Cents.

No. 16C2740 Infants' Fine Worsted Ribbed Hose, with fine smooth worsted feet and merino tipped heels and toes. A special value at our low price. Black, red, blue, pink or white. Sizes, 4, 4½, 5, 5½ and 6.

Price, per pair........$0.15
Per dozen pairs....... 1.75

If by mail, postage extra, per pair, 2 cents.

Our Extra Quality Ribbed Wool Hose, 20 Cents.

No. 16C2744 Infants' Superfine Cashmere Hose, made of pure Australian yarn of choice quality, with silk heels and toes; strictly high grade. Fine elastic knitted; easily put on or off. Colors, black, white, pink, red or blue. Be sure to state color and size in order. Sizes, 4, 4½, 5, 5½ and 6.

Price, per pair.........$0.20
Per dozen pairs......... 2.35

If by mail, postage extra, per pair, 2 cents.

MEN'S SUMMER UNDERWEAR.

HOW TO ORDER UNDERWEAR.

Instructions on Taking Measurements.

FOR BREAST AND WAIST.

A close, firm (but not too tight) measure should be taken over vest with coat off, observing that you do not expand the chest. Take close breast measure and see that the tape is close up under the arms, and over the shoulder blades. For waist, measure under the vest just above the hips.

POSTAGE: Always include postage when ordering shipped by mail.

Men's Balbriggan Underwear, 20 Cents.

No. 16C5024 Men's Summer Weight Balbriggan Undershirts. Fancy stitched collarette neck, ribbed cuffs and taped front. Sizes, 34 to 46 breast measure. Price, each....$0.20
Per dozen.......... 2.35

No. 16C5025 Men's Drawers, to match above shirts. Sizes, 30 to 44 waist measure. Price, per pair.........$0.20
Per dozen pairs............ 2.35

If by mail, postage extra, each, 9c.

Men's Plain Balbriggan Underwear, 30 Cents.

30c

No. 16C5028 Men's Fine Gauge French Balbriggan Undershirts. Fancy collarette neck, pearl buttons and ribbed, close fitting cuffs; fine, soft silk finish. Ecru color only. Sizes, 34 to 44 inches breast measure only.

Each.....$0.30
Per dozen 3.40

No. 16C5029 Drawers to match above shirts. Sizes, 30 to 42 waist measure.

Per pair..$0.30
Doz. pairs 3.40

If by mail, postage extra, each 9c.

Men's Honeycomb Knit Underwear, 40 Cents.

40c

No. 16C5030 Men's Fine Egyptian Cotton Undershirts, summer weight, knitted in fancy honeycomb or mesh style, as illustrated. A cool, comfortable summer undergarment. Ecru color. Sizes, 34 to 44 inches breast measure. Price, each, 40c

Per doz. $4.50

No. 16C5031 Men's Drawers to match above shirts. Sizes, measure, 30 to 42.

Price, per dozen pairs, $4.50; each....40c

If by mail, postage extra, each, 10 cents.

Men's Combed Egyptian Balbriggan Underwear, 40c.

Our Special Leader.

40c

No. 16C5032 Men's Extra Quality Fine French Balbriggan Undershirts. A very fine summer undergarment, with soft smooth surface. A strictly high grade, first class, undergarment, equal to the best made retailing at 65 cents. Made from fine combed Egyptian yarn, and both shirts and drawers are stitched with the Union special covered elastic seams that will not rip or irritate. Plain ecru color only. Sizes, 34 to 44 inches breast measure.

Price, each $0.40
Per dozen............ 4.50

No. 16C5033 Men's Drawers, to match above shirts. Sizes, 30 to 42 waist measure.

Price, per doz. pairs, $4.50; per pair, 40c

If by mail, postage extra, each, 9 cents.

MEN'S SUMMER UNDERWEAR.

FOR MEN'S WINTER UNDERWEAR, SEND FOR SPECIAL CATALOGUE OF UNDERWEAR.

Men's Balbriggan Summer Underwear, 40 Cents.

Colors, Light Blue or Pink.

No. 16C5034 Men's Fine Quality Balbriggan Undershirt, made of pure combed Egyptian yarn. Fancy collarette neck and trimmed with fine pearl buttons. Colors, light blue or pink. Sizes, 34 to 44 breast measure. Price, each..$0.40 Per dozen.. 4.50

No. 16C5035 Men's Fine Light Weight Balbriggan Drawers, to match above shirt. Sizes, 30 to 42 waist measure. Price, per pair........$0.40 Per dozen pairs................. 4.50 If by mail, postage extra, each, 9c.

Men's Light Weight Balbriggan Summer Underwear, 40 Cents.

Color, White.

No. 16C5036 Men's Fine Quality Balbriggan Undershirt, very fine light weight garment, made of pure combed Egyptian yarn, and for a light weight summer garment we consider it one of the best garments; in fact, it is more like a gauze weight. Fancy collarette neck and trimmed with fine pearl buttons. Color, white. Sizes, 34 to 44 breast measure. Price, each...........$0.40 Per dozen........................ 4.50

No. 16C5037 Men's Fine Light Weight Balbriggan Drawers, to match above shirt. Sizes, 30 to 42 waist measure. Price, per pair........$0.40 Per dozen pairs................ 4.50 If by mail, postage extra, each, 9c.

French Balbriggan, 65 Cents.

65c

No. 16C5038 Men's High Grade Genuine French Balbriggan Undershirts. Shaped shoulders, tailor cut. For more than forty years these shirts have been recognized as the best manufactured. Underwear of very fine texture. Ecru color. Sizes, 34 to 44 breast measure. Price.. ..$0.65 Per dozen. 7.50

No. 16C5039 Men's Drawers, to match above shirts. Sizes, 30 to 42 waist measure. Price, per pair..$0.65 Per dozen pairs............... 7.50 If by mail, postage extra, each, 10c.

Our Special Leader in Fine Mercerized Underwear, 85c.

85c

No. 16C5040 Men's Fine Plain Knitted Undershirts, made of the new yarn called American mercerized silk, which is a very fine Egyptian cotton yarn treated by a special process, which gives the appearance of and many of the properties of silk. It will wear better than a silk garment, and we guarantee every garment to be entirely satisfactory in every particular. You have a choice of colors as follows: Fawn or light blue. Be sure to state the color in your order. Sizes, breast measure, 34 to 46. Price.......................................85c

No. 16C5041 Men's Drawers, to match above undershirts. Sizes, waist measure, 30 to 44 inches. Price, per pair..........................85c If by mail, postage extra, each 9 cents.

FOR MEN'S WINTER UNDERWEAR send for free Special Catalogue of Underwear

Black Balbriggan Underwear.

40c

No. 16C5042 Men's Fine Black Balbriggan Undershirts, made of Egyptian cotton. Color, absolutely fast black. Sizes, 34 to 44 breast measure. Price, each......$0.40 Per doz.. 4.50

No. 16C5043 Men's Drawers, to match above shirts. Sizes, waist measure, 30 to 42 inches. Price, per pair....................$0.40 Per dozen pairs........................ 4.50 If by mail, postage extra, each, 9c.

MEN'S FANCY UNDERWEAR.

Men's Cadet Blue and White Striped Balbriggan Underwear, 40 Cents.

40c

No. 16C5078 Men's Fine Fancy Balbriggan Undershirts, knit from fine Egyptian cotton, made in a very narrow ⅛-inch alternating white and blue stripe. A very pretty garment that never fails to give satisfaction. Fast color. Never retails for less than 50 to 65 cents. Stitched throughout with never rip seams. Sizes, 34 to 44 breast measure. Price, per dozen, $4.50; each... 40c

No. 16C5079 Men's Drawers to match above shirts. Waist measure, 30 to 42 inches. Price, per doz., $4.50; per pair, ..40c If by mail, postage extra, each, 9c.

Men's Fancy Tan Mixed Underwear, 40 Cents.

40c

No. 16C5080 Men's Fancy Honeycomb Undershirts, summer weight, made of fine balbriggan. This is woven in a fancy style of tan and white mixed, and makes a very desirable garment in fancy underwear. Sizes, 34 to 44 breast. Price, each, $0.40; per dozen...$4.50

No. 16C5081 Men's Drawers, to match above shirts. Sizes, 30 to 42 inches waist measure. Price, per doz., $4.50; per pair, ..40c If by mail, postage extra, each, 9c.

Men's Ecru Jersey Ribbed Underwear, 40 Cents.

40c

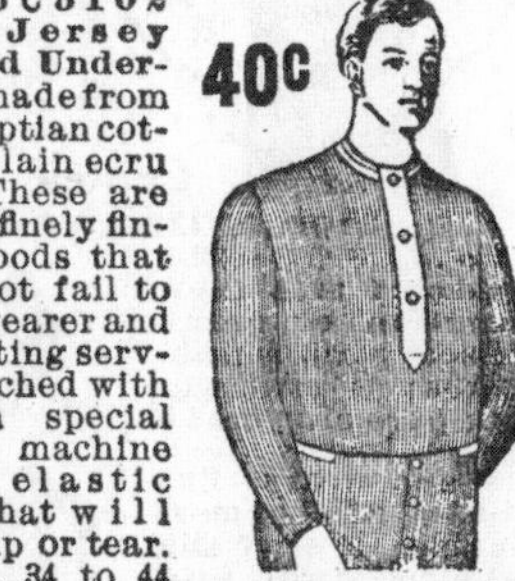

No. 16C5102 Men's Jersey Ribbed Undershirts, made from fine Egyptian cotton in plain ecru color. These are strictly finely finished goods that will not fail to please wearer and give lasting service. Stitched with Union special sewing machine covered elastic seams that will never rip or tear. Sizes, 34 to 44 breast measure. Price, each.....$0.40 Per dozen.............................. 4.50

No. 16C5103 Men's Drawers, to match above shirts. Sizes, waist measure, 30 to 42 inches. Price, per dozen, $4.50; per pair, 40c If by mail, postage extra, each, 9c.

ALWAYS STATE SIZE WANTED.

Fish Net Shirts, 35 Cents.

Fish net garments are made in shirts only.

35c

No. 16C5112 Men's Extra Quality Fish Net Undershirts. White or Ecru. Short sleeves. The coolest undershirts made. Sizes, 34 to 44 breast measure. Price, per dozen, $4.00; each.... 35c If by mail, postage extra, each, 6c.

Men's Jean Drawers, Stretchy Seam, 40c.

No. 16C5116 Men's Fine Jean Drawers, made with stretchy seams down each side of the leg, giving easy motion and greater comfort. The seams are of wide elastic ribbed balbriggan on the sides of the legs and in back, are self adjusting, easy and comfortable. Ribbed anklets. Sizes, 30 to 44 waist measure and 30 to 34 inseam. Color, white. Price, per pair..........$0.40 Per dozen pairs........ 4.50 If by mail, postage extra, per pair, 11c.

Men's Extra Size Underwear, 50 Cents.

No. 16C5118 Men's Extra Size Balbriggan Undershirts, very fine summer undergarment. Strictly high grade, first class undergarment. Made from fine combed Egyptian yarn, stitched with the Union Special. Covered elastic seams. Will not rip or irritate; ecru color. Sizes, 46 to 52 inches chest measure. Price, each...........$0.50 Per dozen.............. 5.75

No. 16C5119 Men's Drawers, to match above shirt. Sizes, 46 to 50 waist measure. Price, per pair....$0.50 Per dozen pairs.... 5.75 If by mail, postage extra, each, 12 cents.

MEN'S SUMMER WEIGHT UNION SUITS.

Instructions for Taking Measurements, FOR BREAST AND WAIST.

A close, firm (but not too tight) measure should be taken over vest with coat off, observing that you do not expand the chest. Take close breast measure and see that the tape is close under the arms and over the shoulder blades.

80-Cent Union Suits.

No. 16C5120 Men's Summer Weight Ribbed Egyptian Cotton Union Suits. This garment is carefully proportioned on scientific principles and will be found perfect fitting in every particular. They are made with fine pearl buttons, silk tipped cuffs and silk finished all the way down the front. A special value at our low price. Color ecru. Sizes, 34 to 44 breast measure. Each.....$0.80 Per dozen......... 9.00

Men's Extra Sizes.

No. 16C5122 Men's Extra Sizes. Same as above. Ecru color only. Sizes, 46, 48, 50 and 52 breast measure. Price, $1.00 Postage extra, 19 cents.

Men's Fine Lisle Union Suits, $1.15.

No. 16C5124 Men's Fine Lisle Thread Union Suits, ecru color, summer weight. Fine quality, high grade in every particular. Silk trimmed around neck; pearl buttons; perfect buttonholes; silk tipped cuffs and stitched throughout with Union special sewing machine; never rip elastic covered seams. Sizes, 34 to 44 only. Price, each. $ 1.15 Per dozen....... 13.00 If by mail, postage extra, 19 cents.

Men's Mercerized Union Suits, $1.75.

No. 16C5131 Men's Fine Ribbed Mercerized Union Suits, summer weight. A superior quality, high grade union suit knitted from fine mercerized yarn in two colors, flesh or light blue. These garments are made with a perfect fitting neck that will not lose its shape and silk overstitched all around edging on cuffs and ankles. By mercerized we mean fine Egyptian cotton, treated by the new Mercer process, by which the yarn is made to look like and feel like silk, retaining this surface permanently. Sizes, 34 to 44 breast measure. State your height, weight and breast measure and the color desired when you order. Price, each...$ 1.75 Per dozen...... 20.00 If by mail, postage extra, each, 18c.

MEN'S LIGHT WEIGHT WOOL UNDERWEAR.

Summer Weight Merino Underwear, 40 Cents.

40c

No. 16C5150 Men's Light Weight Natural Gray Mixed Summer Merino Undershirts. Soft wool finish, a good spring or fall underwear but preferred by many for summer wear. Retail value, 50 cents. Fine pearl buttons. Sizes, 34 to 44. Price, ea. $0.40 Per doz.. 4.50

No. 16C5151 Men's Drawers, to match above shirts. Sizes, 30 to 42 waist measure. Price, per pair, $0.40 Per dozen pairs .... 4.50 If by mail, postage extra, per pair, 11c.

Men's Light Summer Weight Wool Underwear, 80 Cents.

80c

No. 16C5160 Men's Fine Superior Light Weight Undershirts, natural gray in color, about 90 per cent pure wool. This is a soft, fine garment, made partly of Australian wool, suitable for all the year round wear. We strongly recommend goods of this character because of their great merit, and they never fail to give satisfaction. Color, natural gray only. Sizes, 34 to 46 inches breast measure. Price, each, $0.80; per dozen.....$9.00

No. 16C5161 Men's Drawers, to match above undershirts. Sizes, 30 to 44 inches waist measure. Price, per pair...........$0.80 Per dozen pairs................. 9.00 If by mail, postage extra, each garment, 11c.

Our Special S., R. & Co. Light Summer Weight Wool Underwear.

$1.40

No. 16C5170 S., R. & Co.'s Finest Grade Medium Weight Health Undershirts, flat knit, fine soft surface. Made from pure Australian lamb's wool. These are the kind your physician would recommend particularly to those whose physical condition makes it imperative that fine pure woolen underwear should be worn. Natural sanitary gray color. Sizes, 34 to 46 breast measure. Price, each, $1.40; per dozen..$15.00

No. 16C5171 Drawers, to match above shirts. Sizes, 30 to 44 waist measure. Price, per pair...................$ 1.40 Per dozen pairs.................. 15.00 If by mail, postage extra, each 11 cents.

LADIES' SUMMER UNDERWEAR.

LADIES' KNITTED CORSET COVERS.

No. 16C6690 Ladies' Knitted Corset Covers, made of good quality cotton yarn, shaped waist, silk trimmed, pearl buttons down the front. Sizes, 4, 5 and 6. Color, white.
Price, each......$0.20
Per dozen........ 2.25
If by mail, postage extra, each, 6 cents.

No. 16C6694 Ladies' Extra Quality Knitted Corset Covers, made of the finest combed Egyptian cotton yarn, shaped waist, silk trimmed, pearl buttons down the front, long sleeves. This style of corset cover is very much in favor. Color, white only. Sizes, 4, 5 and 6.
Price, each......$0.35
Per dozen........ 4.00
If by mail, postage extra, each, 6 cents.

LADIES' SUMMER UNION SUITS.

TABLE OF SIZES.

Size 4 is for	32-inch bust
Size 5 is for	34 to 36-inch bust
Size 6 is for	38 to 40-inch bust

Ladies' Summer Union Suits, 40 Cents.

No. 16C6861 Ladies' New Lisle Finish Ribbed Summer Union Suits, square neck, sleeveless, silk finish neck and armholes, silk tape all around neck and armholes, and closed front. Knee length and form fitting waist. Color, white. Always give size. Sizes, 4, 5 and 6.
Price, each.........$0.40
Per dozen.......... 4.50
If by mail, postage extra, each, 6 cents.

Ladies' Union Suits, Long Sleeves, Ankle Length.

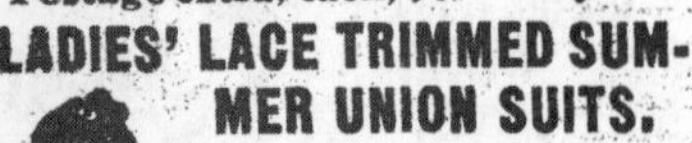

No. 16C6865 Ladies' Ribbed Summer Weight Union Suits, made of fine grade cotton yarn, buttons across the bust, as shown in illustration. These suits are made to fit, and you will find this to be an exceptional value for the price. Long sleeves, ankle length. Color, white only. Sizes, 4, 5 and 6.
Price, each......$0.40
Per dozen........ 4.50
Postage extra, each, 9c.

Ladies' Summer Union Suits, 40c. LONG SLEEVES.

No. 16C6869 Ladies' Jersey Ribbed Union Suits, pure white Sea Island cotton, one of the best union suits we have ever offered. No detail is spared to make this one of the finest. Crochet trimmed neck, shaped form fitting waist, long sleeves. This suit opens all the way down the front. They are easily put on and taken off. Ankle length. Color, white. Sizes, 4, 5 and 6. Price, each, $0.40
Per dozen.......... 4.50
Postage extra, each, 9c.

LADIES' LACE TRIMMED SUMMER UNION SUITS.

Ladies' New Style Trimmed Summer Union Suits.

No. 16C6903 Ladies' New Style Summer Union Suits, made from a fine Egyptian cotton, lace trimmed neck and arms, umbrella style leg, trimmed with torchon lace about 2 inches wide. Color, white.
Price, each........$0.21
Per dozen.......... 2.50
If by mail, postage extra, each, 8 cents.

Ladies' Lace Trimmed Summer Union Suits.

No. 16C6905 Ladies' New Style Summer Union Suits, light weight, Jersey ribbed, silk trimmed around neck with silk tape, silk tape trimmed around armholes. Fancy lace trimmed bottoms, as shown in illustration. A new style, comfortable undergarment that is meeting popular favor everywhere. Our low price of 40 cents is made possible by buying these goods direct from the manufacturer, and at the same time we are able to give you a better garment than is sold at retail at double our price. White only. Sizes, 4, 5 and 6.
Price, each....$0.40
Per dozen...... 4.50
If by mail, postage extra, each, 12c.

Ladies' Lace Trimmed Union Suits.

No. 16C6906 This Union Suit is made of fine lisle cotton, lace trimmed neck and arms, silk tape, large umbrella leg trimmed with a fine torchon lace about 2½ inches wide. Lace bottom union suits in summer weight goods are very much in demand. Color, white. Sizes, 4, 5 and 6.
Price, each.......$0.70
Per dozen......... 8.00
If by mail, postage extra, each, 12 cents.

LADIES' SUMMER VESTS

TABLE OF SIZES.

Size 4 is for	32-inch bust
Size 5 is for	34 to 36-inch bust
Size 6 is for	38 to 40-inch bust
Size 7 is for	40 to 42-inch bust
Size 8 is for	42 to 44-inch bust
Size 9 is for	46 to 48-inch bust

Instructions on Taking Measurements.

BUST MEASURE—All around body under the arms, over fullest part in front, and well up over the shoulder blades.

NOTE—Do not fail to allow postage when ordering goods shipped by mail.

LADIES' SLEEVELESS VESTS.

Ladies' Vests, 8 Cents.

No. 16C6915 Ladies' Vests. This is a ribbed summer vest, sleeveless. Trimmed neck and arms. Special value. Color, white. Sizes, 4, 5 and 6.
Price, each....8c
Per dozen.....92c
If by mail, postage extra, each, 5c.

Ladies' Vests, 10 Cents.

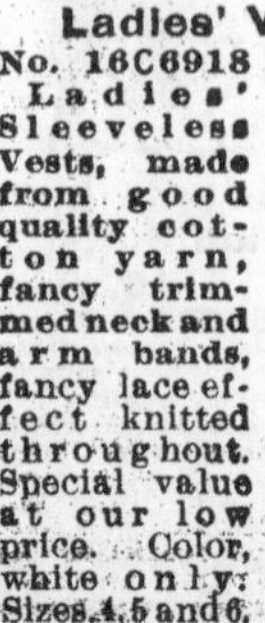

No. 16C6918 Ladies' Sleeveless Vests, made from good quality cotton yarn, fancy trimmed neck and arm bands, fancy lace effect knitted throughout. Special value at our low price. Color, white only. Sizes, 4, 5 and 6.
Price, each..........$0.10
Per dozen............ 1.15
If by mail, postage extra, each, 5c.

Ladies' Sleeveless Vests, 14c.

No. 16C6920 Ladies' Sleeveless Vests, fancy lace trimmed arm bands and lace inserted front and back. A very pretty summer vest at an exceedingly low price. Color, white only. Sizes, 4, 5 and 6. Busts, 30 to 38 inches.
Price, ea..$0.14
Per doz.. 1.50
If by mail, postage extra, ea., 5c.

Ladies' Lace Trimmed Vests, 21 Cents.

No. 16C6922 Ladies' Fancy Lace Trimmed Vest, Swiss ribbed, made of fine lisle cotton, trimmed with torchon lace, front and shoulder, silk tape. The newest design for summer wear. Color, white only. Sizes, 4, 5 and 6.
Each,...... $0.21
Per dozen .. 2.35
If by mail, postage extra, each, 5c.

Ladies' Black Ribbed Vests.

No. 16C6923 Ladies' Fine Cotton Ribbed Vests, lace trimmed, silk tape neck and arms, Richelieu ribbed. Color, black only. Sizes, 4, 5 and 6.
Each ...$0.21
Dozen... 2.35
If by mail, postage extra, each, 7 cents.

No. 16C6926 Ladies' Mercerized Vests. Sleeveless. Fine mercerized vests with silk crocheted neck and armholes and silk tape. Sizes, 4, 5 and 6 to fit busts 30 to 40. White only. This is special value at our low price.
Price, each, $0.22
Per dozen.. 2.50
If by mail, postage extra, each, 5c

Ladies' Lace Trimmed Vests, 21 Cents.

No. 16C6928 Ladies' Swiss Ribbed Vests, trimmed with Nottingham torchon lace. These goods are made from a fine lisle cotton, Swiss ribbed, silk tape neck and arms. White only. Sizes, 4, 5 and 6.
Each... $0.21
Per doz... 2.50
If by mail, postage extra, each, 5c.

Ladies' Fine Mercerized Vests.

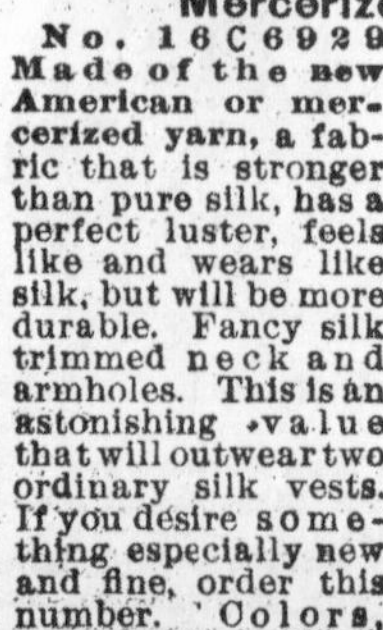

No. 16C6929 Made of the new American or mercerized yarn, a fabric that is stronger than pure silk, has a perfect luster, feels like and wears like silk, but will be more durable. Fancy silk trimmed neck and armholes. This is an astonishing value that will outwear two ordinary silk vests. If you desire something especially new and fine, order this number. Colors, pink or blue. Sizes, 4, 5 and 6.
Price, per dozen, $2.85; each.......25c
If by mail, postage extra, each, 5c.

Wing Sleeve Vests, 8 Cents.

¼ Sleeves.

No. 16C6932 Ladies' Fine Ribbed Summer Vest, made of Egyptian cotton, with short wing sleeves, as shown in illustration.
Price, each. 8c
Per dozen .. 92c
If by mail, postage extra, each, 5c.

Wing Sleeve Vests, 11 Cents

¼ Sleeves.

No. 16C6933 Ladies' Fine Jersey Ribbed Summer Vests. New fancy ribbed Egyptian cotton, with square fancy crocheted neck and short wing sleeves. Color, white. Sizes, 4, 5 and 6. These are very desirable garments and usually retail for 25 cents. Our price is different.
Price, each...$0.11
Per dozen.... 1.25
If by mail, postage extra, each, 5c

Ladies' Wing Sleeve Vests, 15 Cents Each.

¼ Sleeves.

No. 16C6934 Ladies' Good Quality Wing Sleeve Vest, knit from fine Egyptian cotton yarn, with short wing sleeves, as shown in the illustration. Swiss ribbed, silk trimmed neck. Made in white only. Sizes, 4, 5 and 6.
Price, each $0.15
Per dozen.. 1.75
If by mail, postage extra, each, 4 cents.

LADIES' EXTRA SIZE VESTS.

¼ Sleeves.

No. 16C6937 Ladies' Extra Size Ribbed Vest, made of good quality cotton yarn, large, full sizes, low neck, Richelieu ribbed front with short wing sleeves. Cream white only. Sizes, 7, 8 and 9.
Each......$0.12
Per dozen 1.35
If by mail, postage extra, each, 5 cents.

LADIES' EXTRA SIZE SLEEVELESS VESTS.

No. 16C6939 Ladies' Extra Size Ribbed Vests, low neck, sleeveless, with crocheted neck and silk tape. Busts 42, 44 and 46.
Price, each $0.12
Per dozen.. 1.35
If by mail, postage extra, each, 5 cents.

Ladies' Lace Trimmed Vests, Extra Size, 22 Cents.

No. 16C6941 Ladies' Extra Large Size Ribbed Summer Vests. Knit of fine lisle yarn, best quality of cotton yarn that is made; sleeveless, crocheted neck, with silk tape and lace trimmed. Sizes, 7, 8 and 9, for busts 42, 44 and 46.
Price, each $0.22
Per dozen.. 2.50
If by mail, postage extra, each, 5c.

LADIES' LONG SLEEVE SUMMER VESTS, SUITABLE TO WEAR IN ALL SEASONS.

No. 16C6946 Ladies' Fine Combed Egyptian Cotton Vests, with high neck and long sleeves, shaped waist, crocheted neck with silk tape inserted. F..e pearl buttons. Color, white. Sizes, 4, 5 and 6, to fit busts 30 to 40 inches.
Price, each. $0.20
Per dozen.. 2.35
Postage extra, each 6 cents.

Ladies' Extra Size Vests.
LONG SLEEVES.

No. 16C6947 Ladies' Fine Cotton Ribbed Vests. Same quality as above. In extra sizes, 7, 8 and 9.
Price, each........................ $0.21
Per dozen........................ 2.50
If by mail, postage extra, each, 6c.

Ladies' Ribbed Vests.
SHORT SLEEVES.

No. 16C6950 Ladies' Fine Egyptian Cotton Vest, shaped to fit the form. Same quality as above, but with short sleeves. Silk crocheted neck with silk tape inserted. Pearl buttons. Color, cream white. Sizes 4, 5, 6, 7, 8 or 9, to fit busts 30 to 44.
Price, each... $0.20
Per dozen.... 2.35
If by mail, postage extra, each, 6c.

Ladies' Lisle Long Sleeve Vests, 39 Cents.

No. 16C6954 Ladies' Fine Ribbed Lisle Vests, light weight, shaped waist and long sleeves, silk crocheted neck, pearl buttons. Color, cream white only. Sizes, 4, 5 and 6.
Each..... $0.39
Per dozen 4.50
If by mail, postage extra, each, 8 cents.

LADIES' SUMMER RIBBED DRAWERS.

No. 16C6970 Ladies' Fine Jersey Ribbed Form Fitting Egyptian Cotton Drawers, knee length. Open back. Draw string and shaped waist. Color, cream white. Sizes, 4, 5, 6, 7, 8 and 9.
Price, per pair....... $0.23
Per dozen pairs..... 2.75

No. 16C6971 Ladies' Drawers, ankle length. Sizes, 32, 34, 36, 38, 40, 42.
Price, per pair.......... 50c
Postage extra, per pair, 6c.

Lace Trimmed Drawers, 22c.

No. 16C6980 Ladies' Jersey Ribbed Egyptian Cotton Drawers. Knee length, trimmed with lace, as shown in illustration. Preferred by many to the close knit ends. These are extremely popular goods, being cool and comfortable for summer wear. White only, Sizes, 4, 5, 6, 7, 8 and 9.
Per pair.... $0.22
Per doz. prs. 2.50
Postage extra, per pair, 6 cents.

Lace Trimmed Drawers, 39c.

No. 16C6981 Ladies' Lace Trimmed Drawers, extra quality, made of fine Egyptian cotton yarn with wide fancy lace bottoms, of durable quality. Retail everywhere at 50 cents. White only. Sizes, 4, 5, 6, 7, 8 and 9.
Per pair.. $0.39
Doz. pairs 4.50
Postage extra, per pair, 6 cents.

Ladies' Lace Trimmed Drawers, 42 Cents.

No. 16C6982 Ladies' Lace Trimmed Drawers, made from fine lisle yarn with a French band, large umbrella leg with torchon lace trimming about 2½ inches wide. Color, white. Sizes, 4, 5 and 6.
Price, per pair.................. $0.42
Per dozen pairs.................. 5.00
If by mail, postage extra, per pair, 6c.

INFANTS' UNDERWEAR.

INFANTS' UNDERVESTS.

Table of Sizes for Infants' Shirts.

	Length inches	
Size 1	9	suitable for....1 to 3 months
Size 2	10	suitable for....3 to 6 months
Size 3	12	suitable for....6 to 9 months
Size 4	14	suitable for....9 to 12 months
Size 5	15	suitable for....1 to 2 years
Size 6	16	suitable for....2 to 3 years
Size 7	18	suitable for....3 to 4 years

Postage on Infants' Vests, 3c extra.

The Rubens Infants' Shirts.

THE RUBENS SHIRT is simplicity itself. Is made without any buttons whatever, and is so constructed that DOUBLE PROTECTION is given to the vital parts, the chest, lungs and abdomen. This is by all odds the most sensible and practical infants' shirt ever made. The highest medical authorities pronounce it healthful, and as being particularly desirable for infants.

No. 16C7000 The Rubens Infants' Shirt, made of Egyptian cotton. The straps fasten at back with small safety pin, and can be adjusted in an instant. Fine Jersey ribbed and very soft.

Sizes....	1	2	3	4	5	6	7
Price....	23c	26c	29c	32c	35c	38c	41c

No. 16C7005 The Rubens Shirt. Made of all pure, soft cream white Saxony wool. Fine Derby ribbed.

Sizes....	1	2	3	4	5	6	7
Price....	38c	41c	44c	47c	50c	53c	56c

No. 16C7010 The Rubens Infants' Shirt. Made from finest and softest all wool cream white worsted yarn, fine Derby ribbed with fancy silk braid trimming all around, collarette neck, silk stitching all around straps, skirt, sleeves, cuffs, and over all edges.

Sizes....	1	2	3	4	5	6	7
Price....	44c	47c	50c	53c	56c	59c	62c

Infants' Summer Cotton Vests.

No. 16C7015 Infants' Fine Cotton Vests or Wrappers, open down the front, light weight, nicely trimmed. Color, white. Sizes, 1, 2, 3, 4 and 5. Price.......... 12c

Infants' Winter Cotton Vests.

No. 16C7020 Infants' Heavy Cotton Vests or Wrappers, full winter weight, soft fleecing on the inside; open down front. Color, cream white. Sizes, 1, 2, 3, 4 and 5. Price.......... 12c

Infants' Wool Vests.

No. 16C7025 Infants' Fine Derby Ribbed Cream White Merino Vests (wool and cotton mixed), buttoned all the way down front, with overcast stitching on the neck, cuffs and tail. Soft and comfortable, and non-shrinkable.

Sizes..........	1	2	3	4	5	6
Price..........	20c	22c	23c	24c	25c	25c

No. 16C7035 Infants' Fine Derby Ribbed Cream White Saxony Wool Knit Vests. Buttons all the way down the front. Very easily put on and taken off. Neck, front and tail all overcast with silk cross stitch and embroidery. Same style as illustration of wool vests above.

Sizes..........	1	2	3	4	5	6
Price..........	25c	28c	30c	35c	35c	40c

No. 16C7040 Infants' Extra Fine Quality Jersey Ribbed Cream White Lamb's Wool Vests. Buttons all the way down the front. Fine white pearl buttons and silk trimming down the front, 90 per cent purest lamb's wool.

Sizes..........	1	2	3	4	5
Price..........	35c	38c	41c	44c	47c

If by mail, postage extra, 3 cents.

Infants' Fine Ribbed Bands.

No. 16C7055 Infants' Fine Jersey Ribbed Cashmere Wool Bands, with shoulder straps silk crocheted. Will fit perfectly and remain in place without the use of pins. This is accomplished by extra fine rib at bottom of garment; 90 per cent pure lamb's wool and very soft.

Length, 8 inches. Price.................. 20c
Length, 9 inches. Price.................. 22c
Length, 10 inches. Price.................. 24c
Length, 11 inches. Price.................. 26c
Length, 12 inches. Price.................. 28c
If by mail, postage extra, each, 3 cents.

Child's Ribbed Seamless Waist and Shirt Combined.

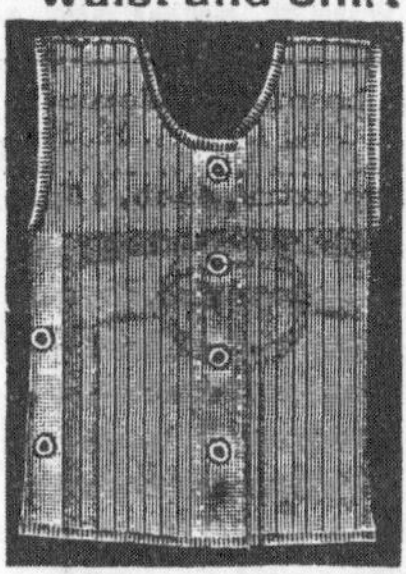

No. 16C7060 This is a Combination Waist and Shirt Combined, for boys and girls, and can be worn either with or without regular undershirt. It is made of fine Jersey ribbed cotton, ecru color. For children from 2 to 12 years of age. Give age of child when ordering.
Price, per dozen, $1.25; each..... 11c
If by mail, postage extra, each, 4c.

THE E. Z. WAIST.

The E. Z. Waist for Boys.

No. 16C7062 Boys' E. Z. Waist, made of fine combed Egyptian cotton yarn. This waist has the tubular bands crossed on the back like a man's suspenders which hold up pants and drawers. Well made, strong and durable. Sizes, from 2 to 13 years. State age of boy when ordering. Color, cream.

Back view of boys' style

Price, per dozen. $2.35; each.... 21c
If by mail, postage extra, each, 4c.

The E. Z. Waist for Girls.

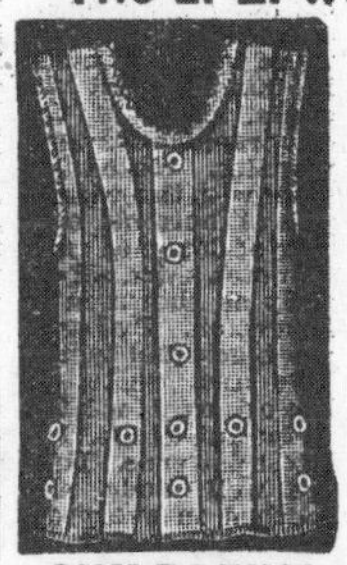

No. 16C7064 Girls' E. Z. Waist. The fabric is a pure Egyptian cotton put through the bleaching process, making the garment white and soft. This waist has the tubular bands up and down to hold up skirts and drawers, and may be buttoned down the back or front. A very satisfactory garment. Sizes, from 2 to 13 years. State age when ordering. Color, white.
Price, each... $0.21
Per dozen,...... 2.35
If by mail, postage extra, each, 4 cents.

CHILDREN'S AND MISSES' SUMMER UNDERWEAR.

Table of Sizes for Children's and Misses' Underwear.

VESTS		PANTALETS	
Sizes, inch	For Age	Sizes, inch	For Age
16,	1 year and under	16,	1 to 1½ years
18,	1 to 1½ years	18,	1½ to 2 years
20,	1½ to 2 years	20,	2 to 4 years
22,	2 to 4 years	22,	4 to 6 years
24,	4 to 6 years	24,	6 to 8 years
26,	6 to 8 years	26,	8 to 10 years
28,	8 to 10 years	28,	10 to 12 years
30,	10 to 12 years	30,	12 years
32,	12 to 13 years	32,	13 years
34,	13 to 14 years	34,	14 years

Girls' and Misses' Cotton Vests.

No. 16C7080 Girls' and Misses' Fine Cotton Vests, made Derby ribbed, sleeveless. Sizes, 20 to 28 breast measure. Color, white. Be sure to give age or size in ordering. Price, each.... 7c
If by mail, postage extra, each, 3 cents.

Girls' and Misses' Fine Ribbed White Vests.

No. 16C7082 Girls' and Misses' Summer Vests, ribbed; made with short sleeves and crocheted neck. Sizes, 20 to 28 breast measure. Price.... 7c
Postage extra, each, 5 cents.

Girls' and Misses' Summer Vests and Pants.

No. 16C7084 Children's Long Sleeve Fine Ribbed Summer Cotton Vests, made of good quality bleached cotton yarn. Sizes, 22 to 28 breast measure.
Price, each $0.13
Per dozen...... 1.35

If by mail, postage extra, each, 5c.

No. 16C7085 Children's Fine Ribbed Knee Pants, open at the sides, to match vests Nos. 16C7080, 16C7082, 16C7084. Order the same size pants as vest. Sizes, 22 to 28.
Price, each........ $0.12
Per dozen.......... 1.35
If by mail, postage extra, each, 5 cents.

Children's Gauze Undervests, Short Sleeves.

No. 16C7086 Children's Gauze Undervests. High neck and short sleeves, made from fine cotton.

Sizes......	18	20	22
Price......	12c	14c	16c
Sizes......	24	26	28
Price......	18c	20c	22c
Sizes......	30	32	34
Price......	24c	26c	28c

If by mail, postage extra, each, 4 cents.

Children's Gauze Undervests, Long Sleeves.

No. 16C7088 Children's Fine White Gauze Summer Vests or Shirts, same as No. 16C7086, but made high neck and long sleeves.

Sizes....	18	20	22
Price....	12c	14c	16c
Sizes....	24	26	28
Price....	18c	20c	22c
Sizes....	30	32	34
Price....	24c	26c	28c

Postage extra, each, 4 cents.

Children's Gauze Pants.

No. 16C7089 Children's Gauze Pants, to match above vests. Knee length. Color, white only.

Sizes..........	18	20	22
Price, each,	12c	14c	16c
Sizes..........	24	26	28
Price, each,	18c	20c	22c
Sizes..........	30	32	34
Price, each,	24c	26c	28c

If by mail, postage extra, each, 3 cents.

Children's Medium Weight Cotton Ribbed Underwear.

No. 16C7090 Children's Ribbed, Long Sleeve Undershirts, made from very best quality Sea Island cotton, Jersey ribbed. Color, ecru.

Sizes..	20	22	24
Price..	20c	22c	24c
Sizes..	26	28	30
Price..	26c	28c	30c

No. 16C7091 Children's Pants, open at side, to match above undershirts. Ankle length.

Sizes..........	20	22	24
Price..........	20c	22c	24c
Sizes..........	26	28	30
Price..........	26c	28c	30c

If by mail, postage extra, each, 5c.

BOYS' OR YOUTHS' SUMMER UNDERWEAR.

SIZES, 24, 26, 28, 30, 32 and 34.

Don't Fail to Give Breast and Waist Measure.

Boys' Balbriggan Summer Shirts and Drawers.

No. 16C7504 Boys' Fine Egyptian Cotton Balbriggan Undershirts, flat knit. This is a superior quality of fine cotton that will be appreciated for its fineness. Made high neck, long sleeves, and retails for 50 cents. Ecru color. Sizes, 24 to 34 breast measure.
Price, each.................. 25c

No. 16C7505 Boys' Fine Balbriggan Knickerbocker Knee Length Drawers, to wear with knee pants, nicely trimmed to match above shirts. Sizes, 24 to 34 waist. Price, per pair........ 25c

No. 16C7507 Boys' Fine Balbriggan Ankle Length or Long Drawers to match above shirts. Sizes, 24 to 34 waist measure.
Price, per pair.............................. 25c
If by mail, postage extra, 4 cents.

UNLAUNDERED WHITE SHIRTS.

Always State Size in Your Order.

No. 34C54 Men's Regular Length Bosom Unlaundered Shirts, made of New York Mills muslin, double back and front, continuous facings and gussets throughout, linen set in bosom. **Long bosom, open back style.** Sizes, 14, 14½, 15, 15½, 16, 16½, 17, 17½ and 18 neckband. Price, each.................**$0.50**
Per dozen.................(**If by mail, postage extra, each, 12 cents.**).................5.50

No. 34C58 Men's Short Bosom Fine Unlaundered Shirts, Short Bosom, open back only. Sizes, 14, 14½, 15, 15½, 16, 16½, 17, 17½ and 18 neckband. Price, per dozen, **$5.50**; each.................50c
If by mail, postage extra, each, 14 cents.

No. 34C62 Men's Regular Length Bosom Extra Quality Unlaundered White Shirts, made of the best heavy muslin, which insures durability; 2100 linen bosom. Reinforced gussets and facings. Double front and back. **Open back only.** Sizes, 14, 14½, 15, 15½, 16, 16½, 17, 17½ and 18 neckband.
Price, per dozen, **$9.00**; each.................75c
If by mail, postage extra, each, 14 cents.

MEN'S LAUNDERED WHITE SHIRTS.

WE SELL YOU A SHIRT AT 80c THAT OTHERS ASK $1.00 FOR.

Made from the finest Wamsutta Muslin, 2100 linen bosom reinforced; split neckband, all double stitched, flat felled seams and large full body. Sizes, 14, 14½, 15, 15½, 16, 16½, 17, 17½, 18, 18½, 19, 19½ and 20 neckband. Price, each.................**$0.80**
Per dozen.................(**If by mail, postage extra, each, 15 cents.**).................**9.00**

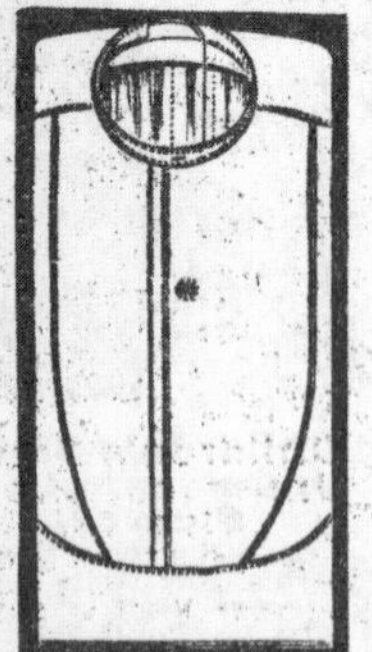

No. 34C86 Short bosom, open back only.

No. 34C88 Short bosom, open front and back.

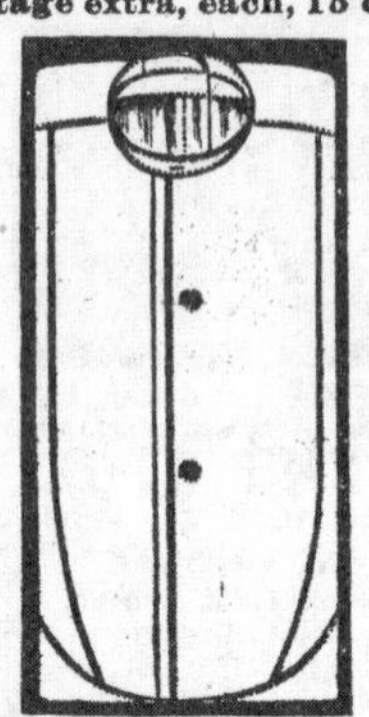

No. 34C104 Regular length bosom, open back only.

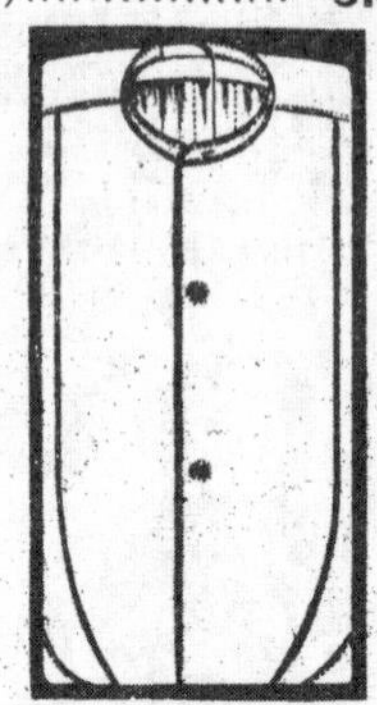

No. 34C102 Regular length bosom, open front and back.

MEN'S LAUNDERED COLORED SHIRTS.

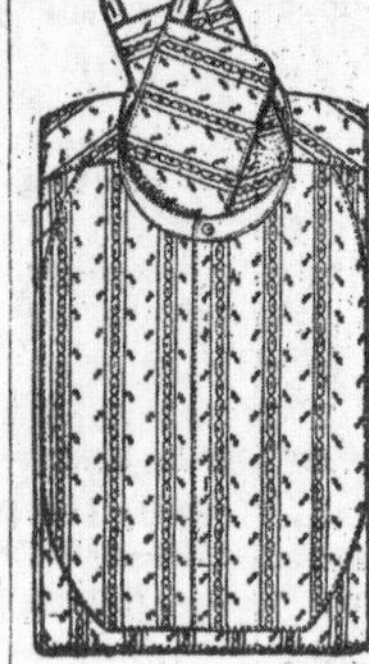

Men's Fancy Colored Shirts, 50 Cents.

No. 34C134 Men's Fancy Percale Shirts, made of good quality percale in combinations of white grounds, black, red or blue stripes, medium length bosom, open front and back, one pair of link cuffs to match. Sizes, 14, 14½, 15, 15½, 16, 16½ and 17.
Price, each.................**$0.50**
Per dozen.................**5.50**
If by mail, postage extra, each, 15 cents.

Men's Colored Shirts, 80 Cents.

No. 34C143 Men's Garner's Fine Percale Dress Shirts; made with medium length bosom, with pair of link cuffs; gusset facings with patent splice at back buttonhole to prevent collar button from rubbing the neck. We have these goods in blue and white, pink and white, red and white and narrow black and white stripes. Give color you prefer and you will be pleased with our selection. Open front and back. Sizes, 14, 14½, 15, 15½, 16, 16½, 17 and 17½. **What size do you wear?**
Price, each.................**$0.80**
Per dozen.................**9.00**
If by mail, postage extra, each, 13 cents.

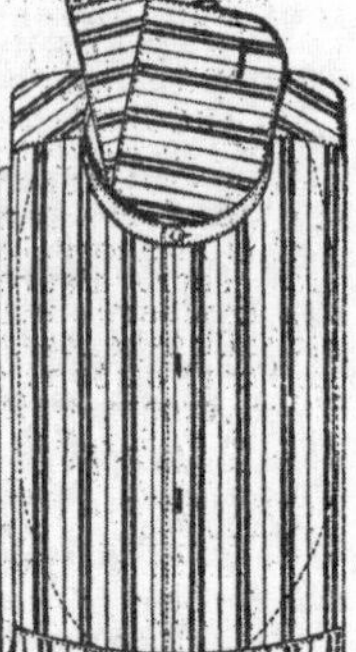

MEN'S NEGLIGEE SHIRTS

Men's Tan or Blue Plaited Bosom Madras Shirts, $1.00.

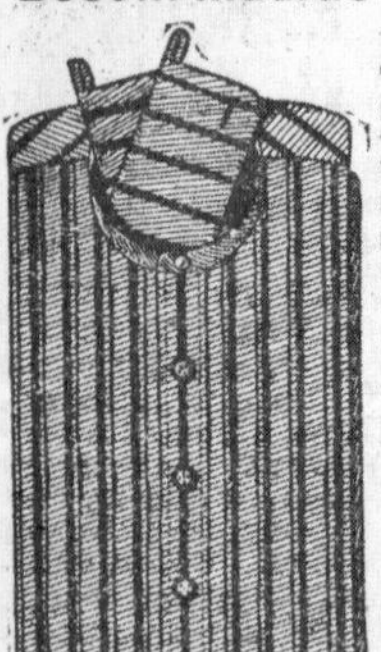

No. 34C146 Tan Shirts being much in demand this season, we have made a special effort to get a fine madras cloth for this number. This shirt has a flexible bosom with four plaits on either side, with a black stripe on the edge of each plait. The ground colors are tan or steel blue. One pair of link cuffs to match. Bosom closed with three large pearl buttons. Sizes, 14, 14½, 15, 15½, 16, 16½ and 17. Price, each.................**$1.00**
Per dozen.................**11.40**
If by mail, postage extra, each, 16 cents.

Our New Novelty Summer Shirts, 59 Cents.

No. 34C147 We offer herewith one of the newest shirts for this season, made as shown in the illustration, with fancy striped percale body and fancy inserted openwork bosom of a new French cloth, the special feature of which is a slightly open work design alternating with three rows of raised corded effects in a contrasting color. For instance, the corded effects are in either blue, red or black and the background is white. They are made open front only and close with three fine pearl buttons; one pair link cuffs. Sizes, 14, 14½, 15, 15½, 16, 16½ and 17. Price, each, **$0.59**
Per dozen.................**6.75**
If by mail, postage extra, each, 16 cents.

Men's Colored Negligee Shirts, at 39c

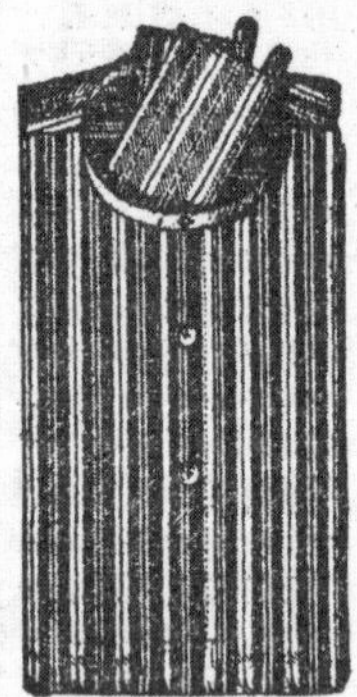

No. 34C148 We cannot say too much as to the wonderful value we are offering in this shirt at 39 cents. Made of the celebrated Garner's percales, closed in front with three large pearl buttons, one pair of detached cuffs to match shirt, all exactly as shown in illustration. Colors, are black and white, blue and white, ox blood and white stripes, also tans. The latest patterns. They are well made and finished in every detail. The equal of these shirts retail at 75 cents. Better lay in a supply. Sizes, 14, 14½, 15, 15½, 16, 16½ and 17.
Price, per dozen, **$4.50**; each.................39c
If by mail, postage extra, 10 cents.

Regular $1.00 Colored Negligee Shirts, 50c

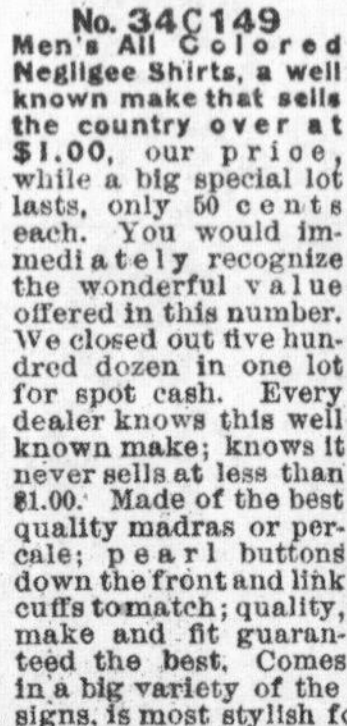

No. 34C149 Men's All Colored Negligee Shirts, a well known make that sells the country over at $1.00, our price, while a big special lot lasts, only 50 cents each. You would immediately recognize the wonderful value offered in this number. We closed out five hundred dozen in one lot for spot cash. Every dealer knows this well known make; knows it never sells at less than $1.00. Made of the best quality madras or percale; pearl buttons down the front and link cuffs to match; quality, make and fit guaranteed the best. Comes in a big variety of the newest, handsomest designs, is most stylish for the season, also plain white. Sizes, 14, 14½, 15, 15½, 16, 16½ and 17. Our 50-cent price is only guaranteed as long as this special lot lasts. Send us your order with the understanding that if the shirts do not prove perfectly satisfactory and are not regular $1.00 quality, you can return them at our expense and your money will be refunded.
Price, per dozen, **$6.00**; each.................50c
If by mail, postage extra, each, 10 cents.

Men's Plaited Bosom All White Negligee Shirts, 50 Cents.

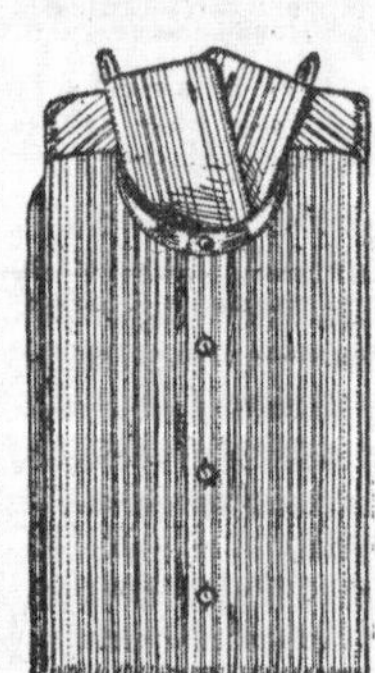

No. 34C151 This Shirt is made from a fine white corded madras. Made with a flexible bosom with six plaits on either side. Three large pearl buttons, and for a neat, genteel, negligee shirt we consider this one of our best numbers. One pair of link cuffs to match. Sizes, 14, 14½, 15, 15½, 16, 16½ and 17.
Price, per dozen, **$5.50**; each.....50c
If by mail, postage extra, each, 16c.

Men's Plain Colored Mercerized Madras Soft Shirts, $1.55.

No. 34C152 Men's Plain Colored Mercerized Madras Shirts, made of an imported mercerized madras cloth and has the appearance of an all silk shirt. Double stitched throughout with silk, yoke back, faced sleeves and pearl buttons. Perfectly made in every way. Colors, cream white or tan only. Sizes, 14½, 15, 15½, 16, 16½ and 17.
Price, per dozen, **$18.00**; each **$1.55**
If by mail, postage extra, 12 cents.

Men's White Mohair Soft Shirts, $1.55.

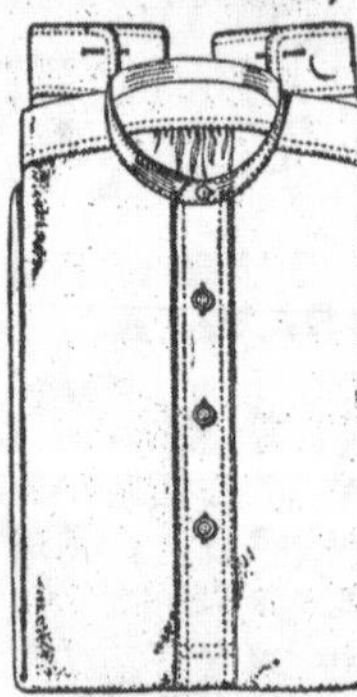

No. 34C153 Men's Extra Fine White Mohair Shirts, light weight, made of fine close texture mohair, superior quality. Double stitched throughout, faced sleeves, pearl buttons and cuffs attached. A fine, up to date outing shirt. Sizes, 14½, 15, 15½, 16, 16½ and 17.
Price, each...**$1.55**
Per doz...**18.00**
If by mail, postage extra, 12 cents.

Men's Linen Colored Pongee Shirts, $1.25.

No. 34C154 Men's Negligee Style Pongee Shirts, made of a light weight cloth. Double stitched throughout with silk, yoke back, faced sleeves, and pearl buttons, cuffs attached. Linen colored background with broken stripes, and figures of a darker shades, and also stripes and figures of cream color. A very handsome shirt, and strictly up to date. Sizes, 14½, 15, 15½, 16, 16½ and 17. Price, each.................**$1.25**
Per dozen.................**14.00**
If by mail, postage extra, each, 12c.

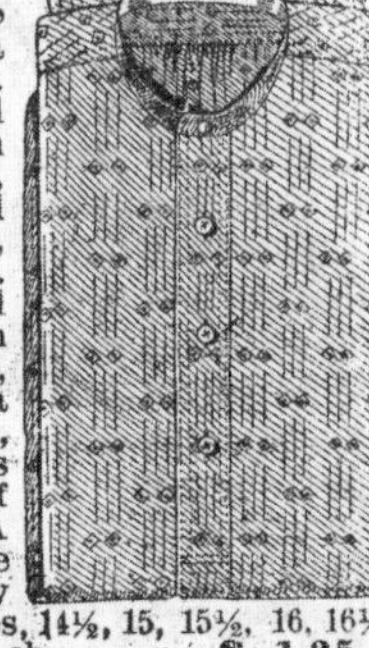

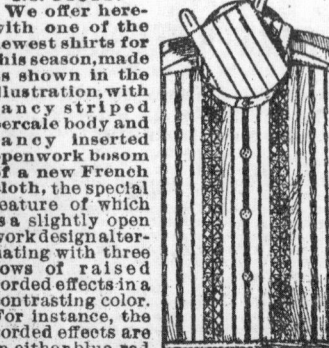

DON'T FAIL TO STATE SIZE WHEN YOU WRITE YOUR ORDER

OUR SPECIAL 80-CENT NEGLIGEE SHIRTS.

REGULAR $1.00 AND $1.25 SOFT BOSOM SHIRTS FOR 80 CENTS.

AS GOOD VALUE as you can buy elsewhere for $1.00 to $1.25. These shirts are made of extra fine quality percale in white grounds with colored or black stripes or figures, in woven madras cloth, colored grounds with stripes of contrasting colors. We also have these goods in plain white.

You will note the heading over each shirt describing the cloth, whether percale, madras or plain white muslin, also whether plain or plaited bosom.

They are made open front only, and close with three pearl buttons, double stitched throughout, yoke back.

NOTE THE BIG VARIETY OF STYLES AND PATTERNS BELOW. Any kind on this page 80 cents each. Pick out the kind you want from the illustration and description and order according to the number under the picture. ALWAYS STATE NECK SIZE WANTED.

OUR OFFER. Order as many as you want, but in dozen lots you save money. (Order by catalogue number.) State size around the neck, and whether light or dark shirts are required, and we will send you the shirts with the

UNDERSTANDING AND AGREEMENT, THAT IF THEY ARE NOT THE MOST ASTONISHING VALUE, THE GREATEST SHIRT BARGAIN YOU HAVE EVER SEEN OR HEARD OF,

YOU CAN RETURN THEM TO US AT OUR EXPENSE AND WE WILL PROMPTLY REFUND YOUR MONEY.

SIZES:
14, 14½, 15, 15½, 16, 16½ AND 17.

PRICE, EACH, 80 CENTS

PER DOZEN, $9.00

IF BY MAIL, POSTAGE EXTRA, EACH, 15 CENTS.

PLAITED BOSOM NEGLIGEE SHIRTS, 80 CENTS.

Colored Figure Percale. Sizes, 14 to 17.

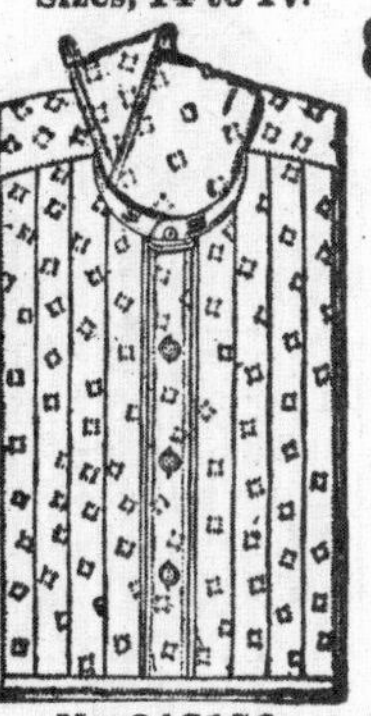

No. 34C176

80c

White Body Colored Pique Bosom. Sizes, 14 to 17.

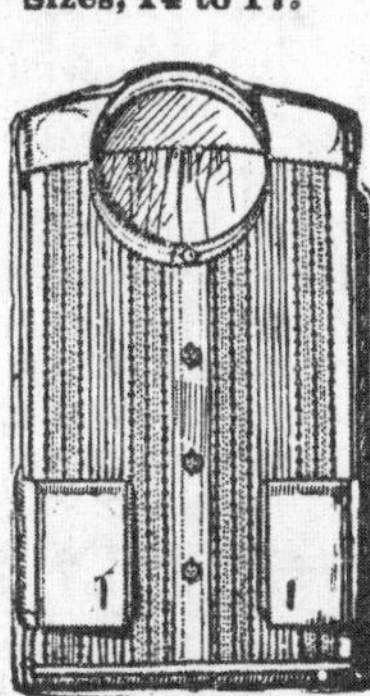

No. 34C180

Colored Striped Percale. Sizes, 14 to 17.

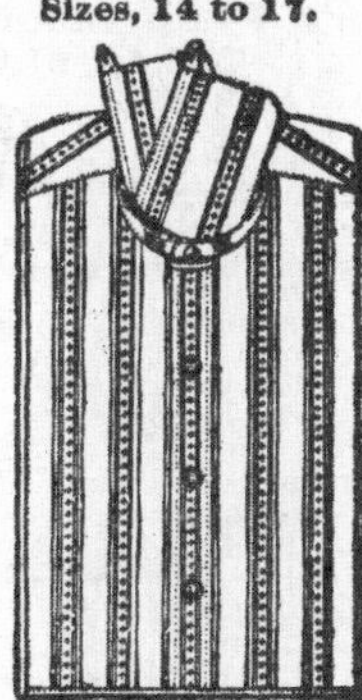

No. 34C181

All White Muslin. Sizes, 14 to 17.

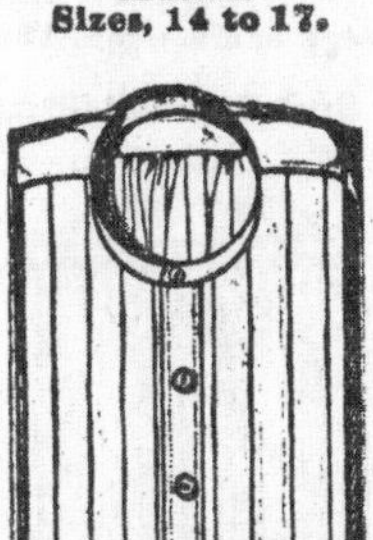

No. 34C189

All White Corded Madras. Sizes, 14 to 17.

80c

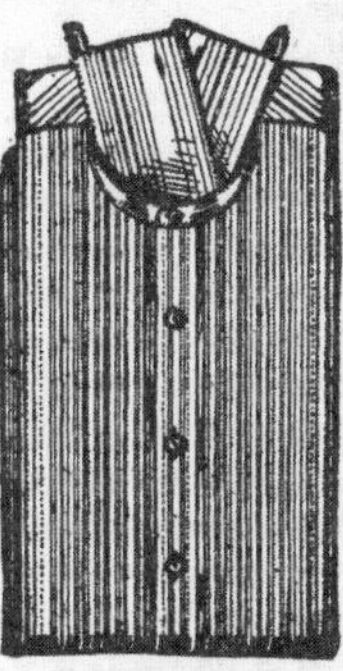

No. 34C190

White Muslin Body. Fancy White Pique Bosom. Sizes, 14 to 17.

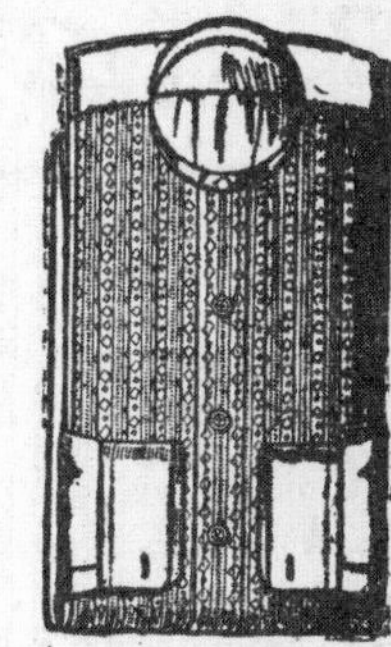

No. 34C192

PLAITED BOSOM NEGLIGEE SHIRTS.

Tan Colored Madras. Sizes, 14 to 17.

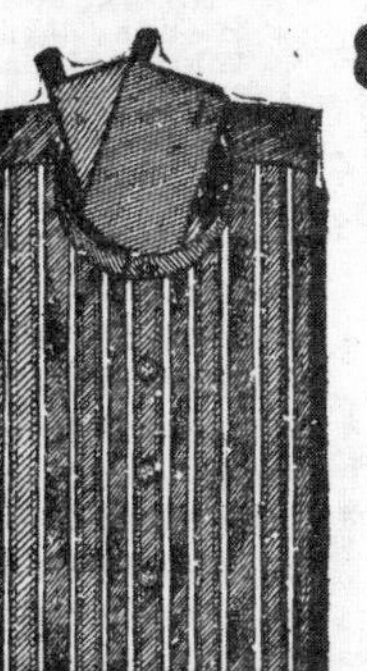

No. 34C193

80c

Colored Striped Percale. Sizes, 14 to 17.

No. 34C195

COLORED NEGLIGEE (SOFT BOSOM) SHIRTS, 80c.

All White Corded Madras. Sizes, 14 to 17.

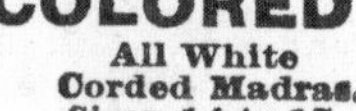

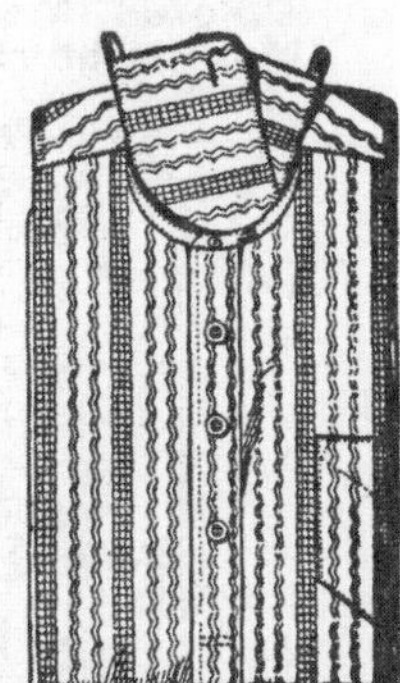

No. 34C211

Corded Madras. Colors, Tan, Blue or Slate. Sizes, 14 to 17.

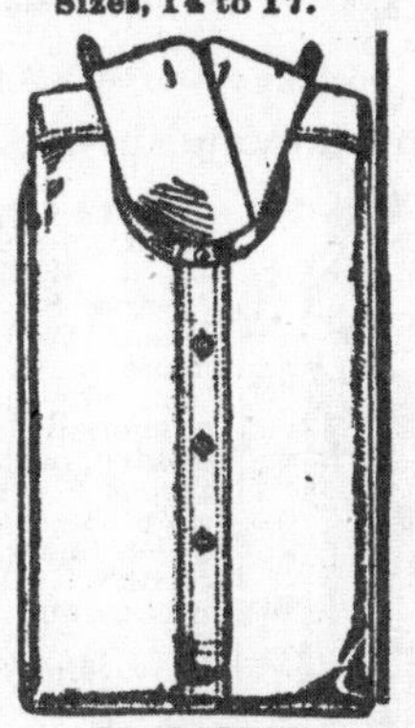

No. 34C213

Colored Striped Percale. Sizes, 14 to 17.

80c

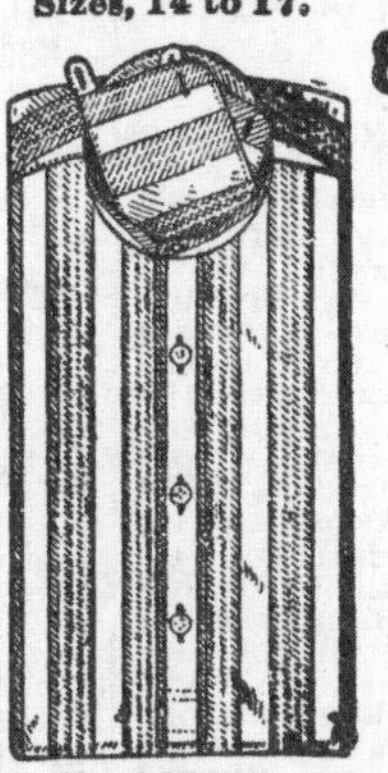

No. 34C214

Colored Striped Madras. Sizes, 14 to 17.

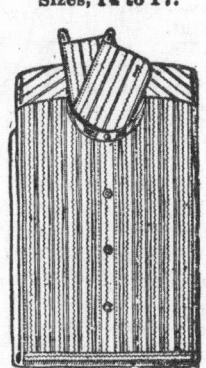

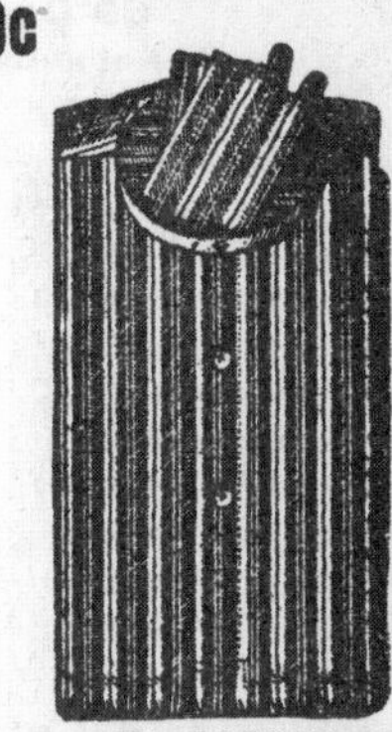

No. 34C216

COLORED NEGLIGEE (SOFT BOSOM) SHIRTS, 80 CENTS.

Colored Striped Percale. Sizes, 14 to 17

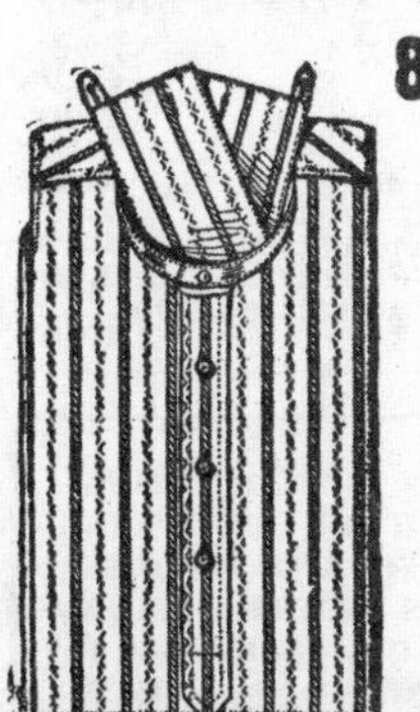

No. 34C221

80c

Colored Striped Percale. Sizes, 14 to 17.

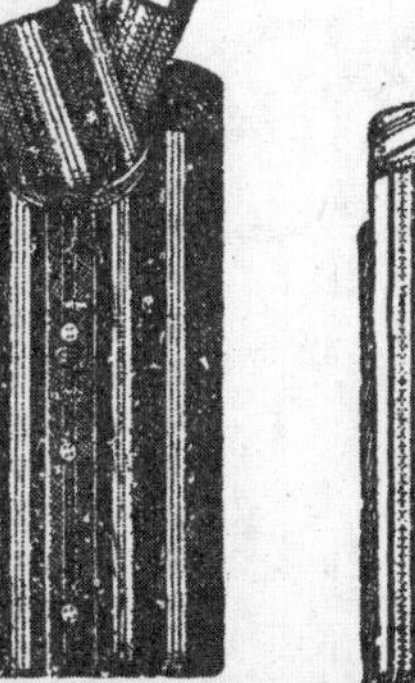

No. 34C223

Colored Striped Percale. Sizes, 14 to 17.

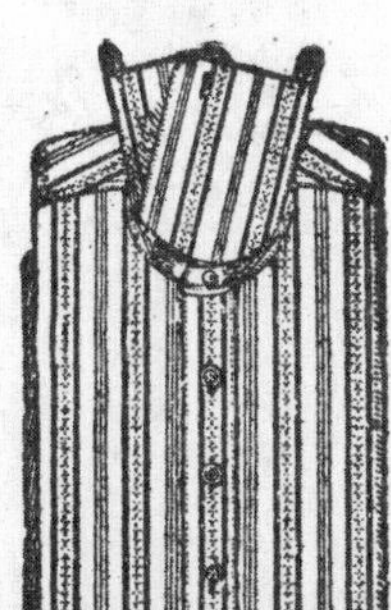

No. 34C224

Colored Figure Percale. Sizes, 14 to 17.

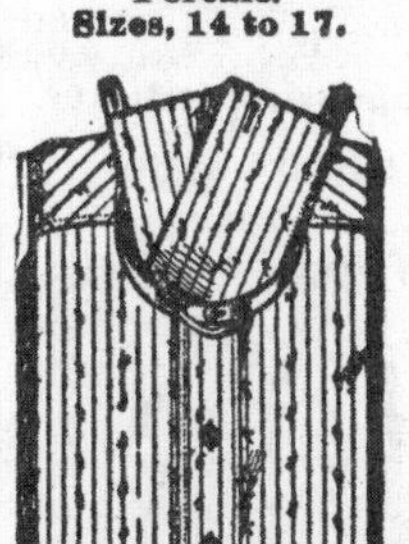

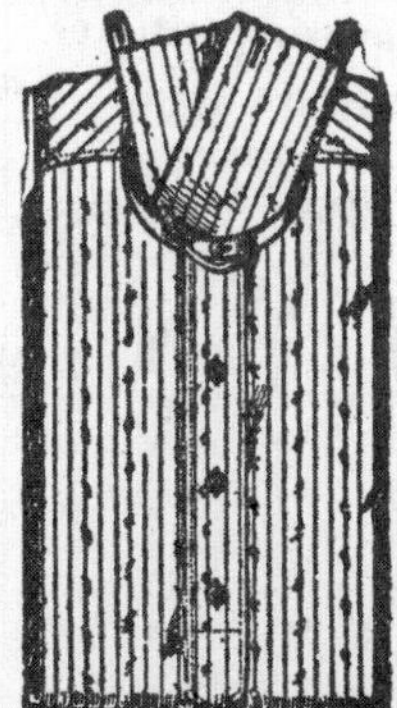

No. 34C226

Colored Striped Percale. Sizes, 14 to 17.

80c

No. 34C228

Colored Madras, 2 Collars, 1 pr. Cuffs. Sizes, 14 to 17.

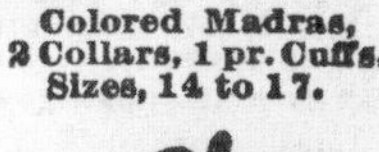

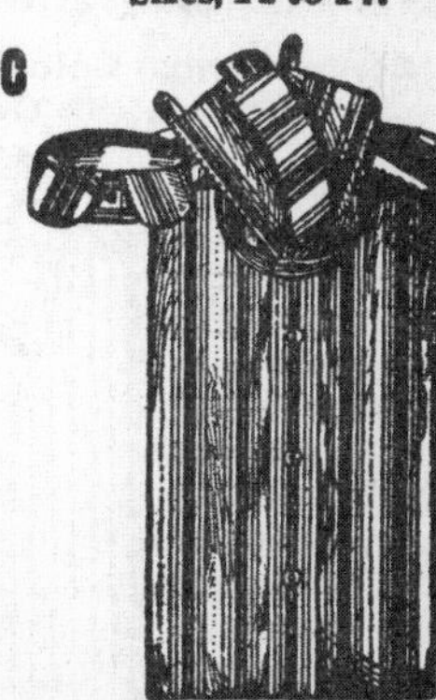

No. 34C244

ALL THE ABOVE SHIRTS ARE 80 CENTS EACH.

MEN'S NEGLIGEE SHIRTS—Continued.

Men's Colored Negligee Shirts, 39 Cents.

Starched collars and cuffs attached.

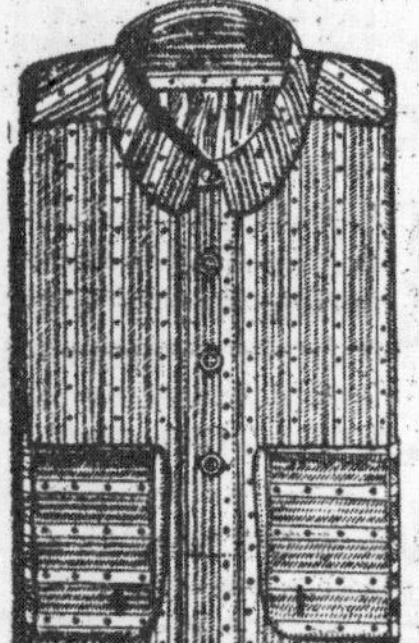

No. 34C250 Men's Good Quality Laundered Percale Shirts with attached collars and cuffs. An excellent shirt for our low price. A large variety of stripes in large assortment of colors. Sizes, 14, 14½, 15, 15½, 16, 16½ and 17. **What size do you wear?**

Price......39c

If by mail, postage extra, 12c.

Our Special Value, 80 Cents.

Sizes, 14, to 16½.

Starched collars and cuffs attached.

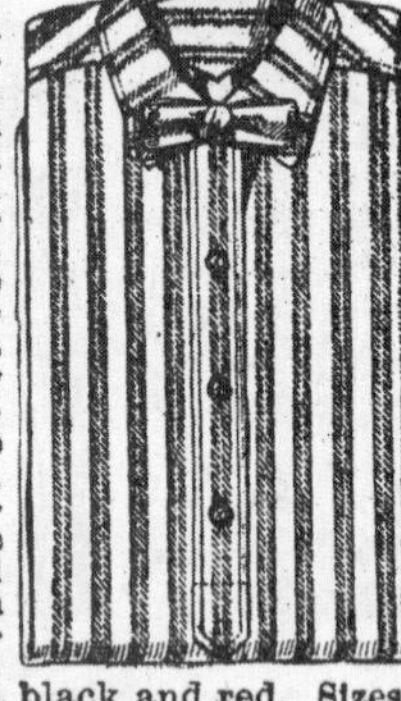

No. 34C258 Men's Fine Laundered Madras Negligee Shirts, made from fine imported woven madras. **They are extremely durable and the colors are absolutely fast.** Collar is finely shaped, designed to fit the neck properly, and cuffs are attached. Made in stripes and plaids in which the predominating colors are white, blue, black and red. Sizes, 14, 14½, 15, 15½, 16 and 16½.

Price......80c

If by mail, postage extra, 15c.

Men's Soft or Negligee Shirts, 39 Cents.

Not starched.

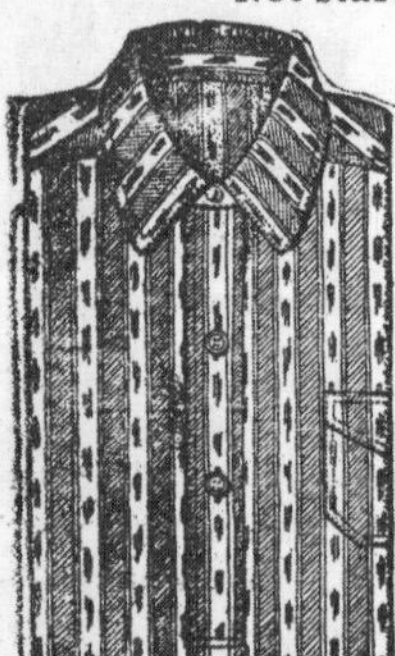

No. 34C262 This line of overshirts we have had made up for us in great quantities. They are made from **madras cloth**, the colors and patterns are woven **through and through** (not printed). Cut full 36 inches long and never retail for less than 50 cents. Made with yoke back, felled seams, shaped shoulders and extension neckband. We have them in neat stripes, assorted patterns and colors. Sizes, 14½, 15, 15½, 16, 16½ and 17 only. Each..$0.39

Per dozen......4.50

If by mail, postage extra, each, 12c.

Men's Fancy Colored Sateen Shirts, 39 Cents.

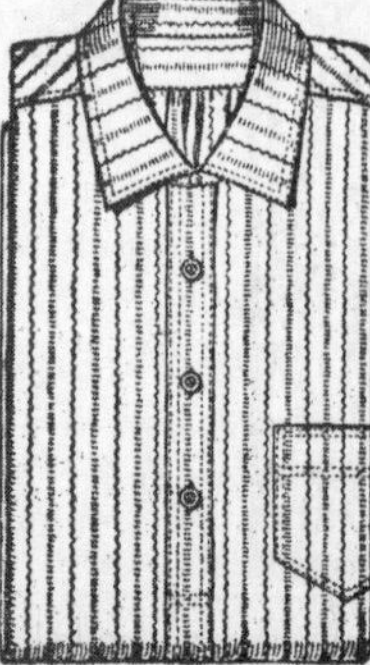

No. 34C264 Men's Good Quality Sateen Shirts, fast colors, in light colored stripes. Yoke back, pearl buttons, shaped shoulders, felled seams, gussets, extension neckband, and full 36 inches long. Double stitched throughout. Sizes, 14½, 15, 15½, 16, 16½ and 17. Price..$0.39

Per doz..4.50

If by mail, postage extra, each, 12c.

Men's Bedford Cord Shirts, 39 Cents.

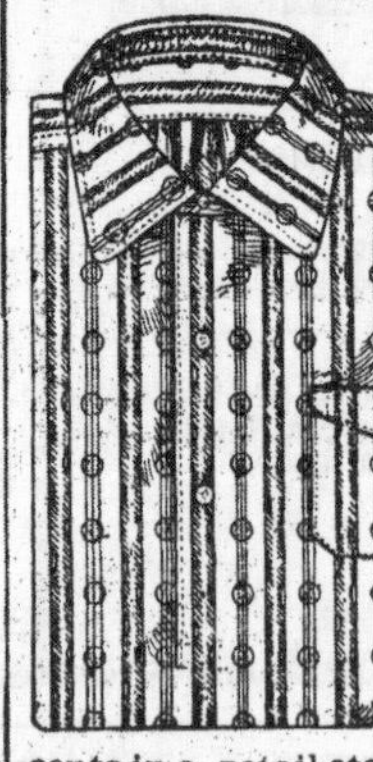

No. 34C268 Men's Fine Negligee or Soft Shirts, made of Bedford cord cloth that makes up in a very neat and desirable shirt. Light colors, stripes in very pleasing patterns. Yoked back, shaped shoulders, felled seams, extension neckband, full size and 36 inches long. A shirt of this material and the equal in make, fit and workmanship will cost you fully 75 cents in a retail store. Sizes, 14½, 15, 15½, 16, 16½ and 17.

Price, each......$0.39

Per dozen......4.50

If by mail, postage extra, each, 12c.

Our Special Soft Shirts, 65c.

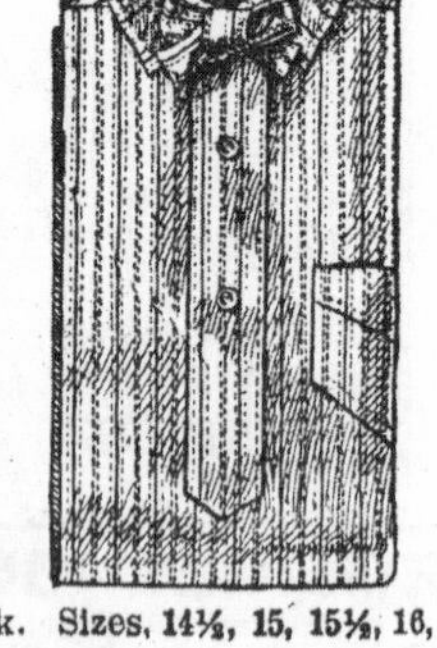

No. 34C270 Our New Negligee or Soft Shirt. Made large and full size, of fine, good weight madrascloth, colors woven in. The patterns in this shirt are especially pleasing, made in a combination of stripes with string ties to match. Pearl buttons, pocket on the side and yoke back. Sizes, 14½, 15, 15½, 16, 16½ and 17.

Price, each......$0.65

Per dozen......7.50

If by mail, postage extra, each, 14c.

Our Special Value at 80c.

No. 34C274 Men's Fine Light Weight Madras Shirts. Made in the best manner possible. Our new button down collar; necktie to match, which can be tied either in a knot or bow. One pocket, and cut large in the body. The color designs in these are pleasing to those desiring quiet effects. Made in stripes, blue, pink and black, etc. Sizes, 14½, 15, 15½, 16, 16½ and 17.

Price, each......$0.80

Per dozen......9.00

If by mail, postage extra, each, 10c.

Our Great $1.00 Leader.

No. 34C278 Men's Fine Cheviot or Heavy Madras Cloth. Made with yoke back, large full body and flowing end tie to match. One pocket on left side. Beautiful stripes, in which blue and white or black and white are the predominating colors. Sizes, 14½, 15, 15½, 16, 16½ and 17. Each..$1.00

Per doz. 11.40

If by mail, postage extra, each, 10c.

Oxford Cloth Shirts for $1.00.

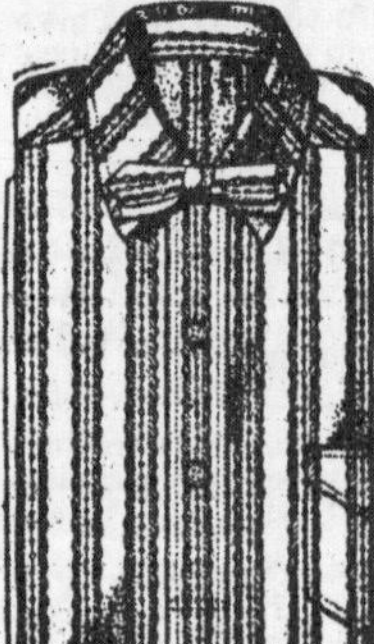

No. 34C292 Men's Fine Heavy Weight Oxford Cloth Shirts. The most durable of all cotton shirts made. Yoke back, large, full body, stitched with silk; an incomparable value and will outwear two or three ordinary shirts. One pocket and tie of same fabric. A most beautifully woven cloth, alternating in various colors over a light background, black, yellow, blue, green and pink stripes. Sizes, 14½, 15, 15½, 16, 16½ and 17. Regular retail price, $2.50.

Price, each......$1.00

Per dozen......11.40

If by mail, postage extra, each, 12c.

Men's Plain Colored Pongee Shirts, $1.00.

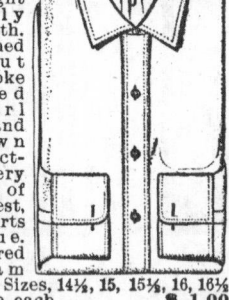

No. 34C293 Men's Plain Colored Cotton Pongee Shirts, made of a light weight, finely woven cloth. Double stitched throughout with silk, yoke back, faced sleeves, pearl buttons, and button down collar. Perfectly made in every way, and one of the handsomest, up to date shirts we catalogue. Linen colored and cream white, only. Sizes, 14½, 15, 15½, 16, 16½ and 17. Price, each......$1.00

Per dozen......11.40

If by mail, postage extra, each, 12c.

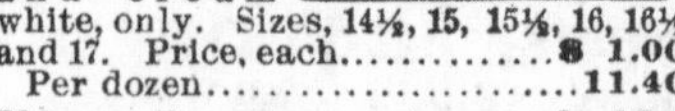

Men's Plain White or Tan Colored Mercerized Madras Shirts, $1.55.

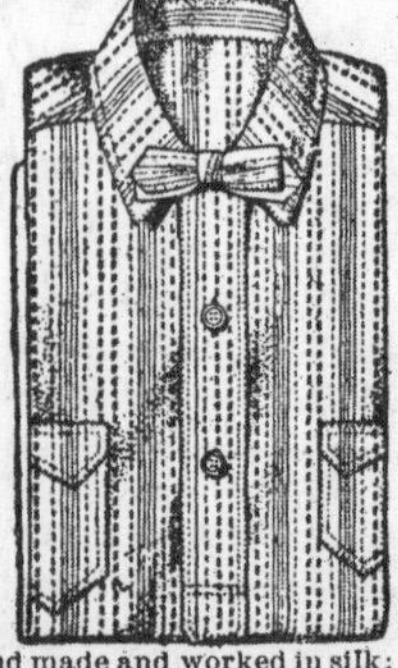

No. 34C294 Men's Plain Colored Mercerized Madras Shirts, made of a heavy madras cloth, and has all the appearance of a silk shirt. Double stitched throughout with silk, button down collar, yoke back, faced sleeves, pearl buttons and one pocket. Perfectly made in every way. Colors are plain tan or white. This is one of the newest up to date soft shirts. Sizes, 14½, 15, 15½, 16, 16½ and 17. Price, per doz., $18.00; each..$1.55

If by mail, postage extra, each, 12c.

Fine French Flannel Shirts for $1.55.

No. 34C296 Men's Fine Light Weight French Flannel Shirts. The cloth is shrunk before being made up, but should be carefully washed. All the colors composing the pattern stand out in strong relief. Attractive stripe effects in alternating colors of blue, black and green. Two rows of silk stitching around the collar and double silk stitching throughout the entire shirt. The tie to match is full length. The buttonholes are hand made and worked in silk; has pearl buttons in front and two pockets. Sizes, 14½, 15, 15½, 16, 16½ and 17.

Price, per dozen, $18.00; each, $1.55

If by mail, postage extra, each, 10c.

Fine Silk Shirts for $2.00.

No. 34C300 Men's Fine Silk Shirts. Made with button down collar and tie to match. Made from cloth about 75 per cent pure silk, and has all the appearance of a pure silk shirt and will wear better. The finest workmanship, stitched with silk, and has every improvement known to the trade. The usual retail price, $3.50. A large variety of new and stylish patterns of modest and delicate colorings. Sizes, 14, 14½, 15, 15½, 16, 16½ and 17.

Price, each......$2.00

Per dozen......23.00

If by mail, postage extra, each, 10c.

Extra High Grade Flannel Shirts, $2.25.

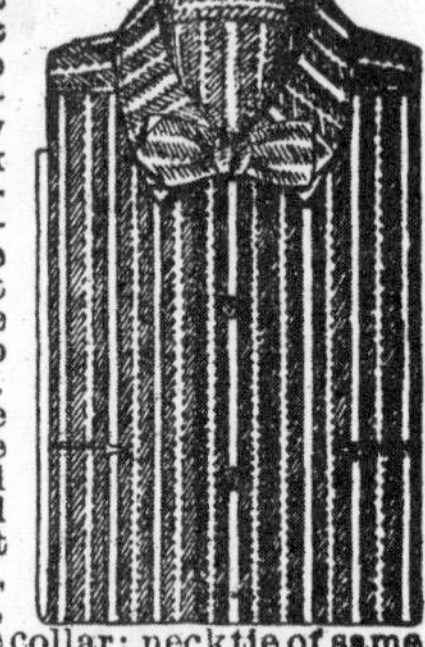

No. 34C304 The Finest Flannel Shirt on sale. The patterns are exclusive, new and neat, in silk stripes on medium color background. The handsomest shirt you have ever seen, no loud effects. Made with wide yoke; full size body, faced sleeves, felled seams, finest pearl buttons, button down, stay in its place collar; necktie of same material; two new style cut in pockets; silk finish, and stitched throughout with silk. Sizes, 14½, 15, 15½, 16, 16½ and 17. Price......$2.25

If by mail, postage extra, 18c.

White Mohair Shirts, $1.55.

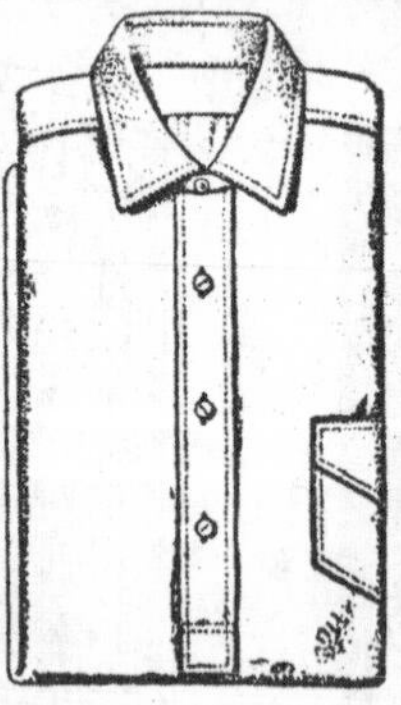

No. 34C305 Men's Fine White Mohair Shirts, light weight, made of fine, close texture mohair, superior quality, fine, soft cloth, one pocket, faced sleeves, felled seams, four pearl buttons down the front. Sizes, 14½, 15, 15½, 16, 16½ and 17.

Price..$1.55

If by mail, postage extra, 10 cents.

MEN'S BLUE FLANNEL OVERSHIRTS.

Sizes, 14½, 15, 15½, 16, 16½, 17.

No.		Price, each
34C535	Single breasted	$1.00
34C540	Single breasted	1.75
34C541	Single breasted	2.25
34C544	Double breasted	1.00
34C550	Double breasted	1.40
34C552	Double breasted	2.00
34C556	Double breasted, firemen's	2.00

FOR MEN'S AND BOYS' WINTER OVERSHIRTS, MEN'S, BOYS' AND LADIES' SWEATERS, MEN'S SMOKING AND CARDIGAN JACKETS, SEND FOR OUR SPECIAL FURNISHING GOODS CATALOGUE.

COTTON WORK SHIRTS, 38 CENTS.

THE KIND YOU PAY 50 CENTS FOR ELSEWHERE

Men's Colored Cheviot Working Shirts, 38 Cents.

No. 34C358 Men's Cheviot Working Shirts, medium stripes, all colors woven into cloth; a very neat working shirt; splendid wearing material, good honest value, fully deserving the name of "The Big Work Shirt." Yoke back, felled seams, extension neckband and gussets. Sizes, 14½, 15, 15½, 16, 16½ and 17.

Price, each..... $0.38
Per dozen..... 4.35

If by mail, postage extra, each, 15c.

Colored Flannelette Shirts, 40 Cents.

No. 34C362 Men's Shirts, made of French Domet Cotton Flannel. Popular because they are dependable. Of strictly first class manufacture, including extension neckband, shaped shoulders, and yoke back. They are cut 36 inches long, are made in light or medium colors, stripes, all neat, modest patterns. There is durability in these garments as well as good looks and solid comfort. Sizes, 14½, 15, 15½, 16, 16½ and 17.

Price, each..... $0.40
Per dozen..... 4.50

If by mail, postage extra, each, 15c.

Men's Plain Blue Chambray Overshirts, 38 Cents.

No. 34C363 Men's Plain Dutch Blue Woven Chambray Overshirts. One of the standard reliable cloths for working shirts. Made with felled seams, extension neckband, full size and 36 inches long. Sizes, 14½, 15, 15½, 16, 16½ and 17. What size do you wear?

Each... $0.38
Per doz. 4.35

If by mail, postage extra, each, 15c.

Men's Plain Tan Color Cotton Work Shirts, 38 Cents.

No. 34C364 Men's Plain Tan Color Twilled Cotton Work Shirt, box plait front with three rows of stitching, yoke back, double stitched seams throughout, extension neckband, one pocket. This is a regular army shirt. Color, tan only. Sizes, 14½, 15, 15½, 16, 16½ and 17.

Each..... $0.38
Per dozen 4.35

If by mail, postage extra, each, 15 cents.

Men's Fancy Stripe Chambray Work Shirts, 38 Cents.

No. 34C367 This shirt is made of a very heavy chambray in a cadet or bluish gray color, with fancy colored stripes; made double front and back, felled seams throughout, extension neckband and full 36 inches long. This cloth is one of the strongest and most durable materials for a work shirt. Sizes, 14½, 15, 15½, 16, 16½ and 17.

Price, per dozen, $4.35; each..... 38c

If by mail, postage extra, each, 15c.

Men's Plain Black Twilled Work Shirts, 38 Cents.

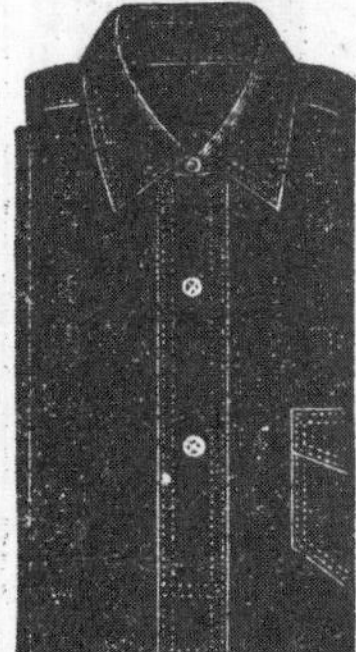

No. 34C372 Men's Plain Black Twilled Overshirts, made of heavy black drill, felled seams, extension neckband, one pocket, and full 36 inches long, double stitched. Sizes, 14½, 15, 15½, 16, 16½ and 17.

Each.... $0.38
Per doz... 4.35

If by mail, postage extra, each, 15 cents.

Men's Black and White Twilled Work Shirts, 38 Cents.

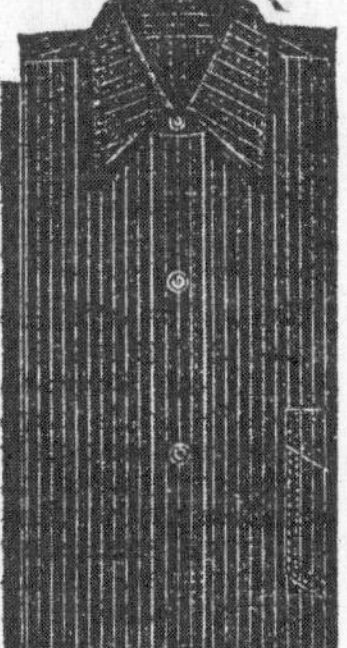

No. 34C373 Men's Black Twilled Overshirts, made of heavy black drill with neat white stripes. Yoke back, felled seams, gussets, extension neckband, one pocket, and full 36 inches long. Sizes, 14½, 15, 15½, 16, 16½ and 17.

Price, each, $0.38
Per dozen, 4.35

If by mail, postage extra, each, 15 cents.

Men's Black Heavy Twilled Cotton Overshirts, 38 Cents.

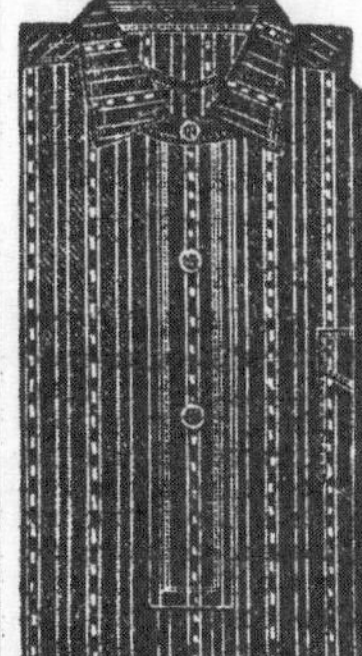

No. 34C374 Men's Heavy Twilled Cotton Overshirts, fancy stripes in blue, yellow or red; the background is black. These combinations make a very handsome shirt. Sizes, 14½, 15, 15½, 16, 16½ and 17.

Each..... $0.38
Per dozen 4.35

If by mail, postage extra, each, 15 cents.

—FOR—

HEAVY FLANNEL SHIRTS

Write for our FREE CATALOGUE OF SHIRTS.

Men's Black and White Twill Cotton Overshirts, 38 Cents.

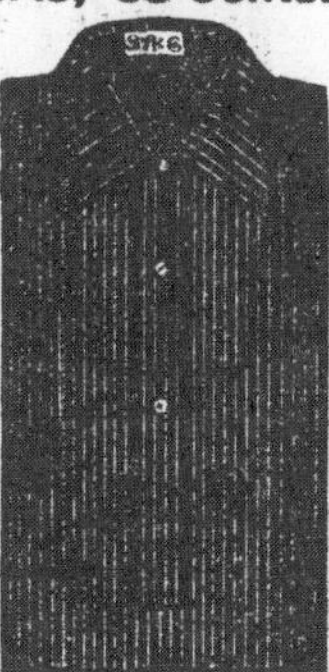

No. 34C378 Men's Black Cotton Overshirts, made of heavy black twill with white hairline stripes, extension neck band, yoke back, felled seams, 36 inches long and full size. Sizes, 14½, 15, 15½, 16, 16½ and 17.

Each..... $0.38
Per dozen 4.35

If by mail, postage extra, each, 15 cents.

Men's Extra Size Working Shirts, 40 Cents.

No. 34C379 Men's Extra Size Black and White Stripe Twilled Cotton Overshirts, made in extra size and very large bodies. Sizes, 17½, 18, 18½ and 19. Price, each..... $0.40
Per dozen..... 4.50

If by mail, postage extra, each, 16c.

Men's Black and White Shield Front Shirts, 38 Cents.

CORDED FRONT.

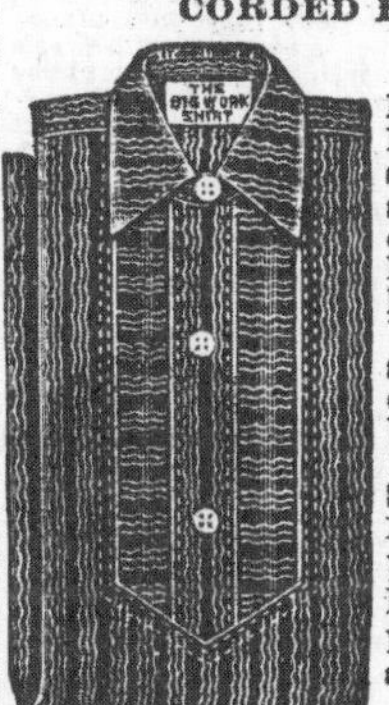

No. 34C380 Men's Corded Front Overshirts. Made of standard twill cotton, black only, with white hairline stripes. Yoke back gussets, felled seams, extension neckband, and full 36 inches long. Sizes, 14½, 15, 15½, 16, 16½ and 17.

Price, each, $0.38
Per dozen.. 4.35

If by mail, postage extra, each, 15 cents.

Men's Black and White Twilled Overshirts, 38 Cents.

DOUBLE FRONT AND BACK.

No. 34C381 Men's Black Twilled Overshirts with neat white figures. These goods are made of full standard cloth double front and back, felled seams, double cuffs, 36 inches long. Sizes 14½, 15, 15½, 16, 16½, and 17.

Price, each 38c
Per doz., $4.35

If by mail, postage extra, each, 15 cents.

Men's Black and White Working Shirts, 38 Cents.

DOUBLE FRONT AND BACK.

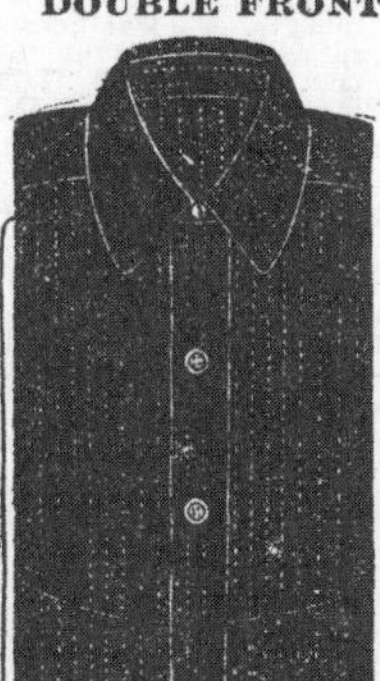

No. 34C383 Good Quality Heavy Woven Cotton Overshirts. Fast black, with neat small white stripes; double back and shoulders, extending down front, as shown in illustration; felled seams and double cuffs. Cut full size and guaranteed to wear long and well. Sizes, 14½, 15, 15½, 16, 16½ and 17.

Price, each..... $0.33
Per dozen..... 4.35

If by mail, postage extra, each, 15c.

MEN'S BLACK SATEEN SHIRTS.

Men's Figured Black Sateen Shirts.

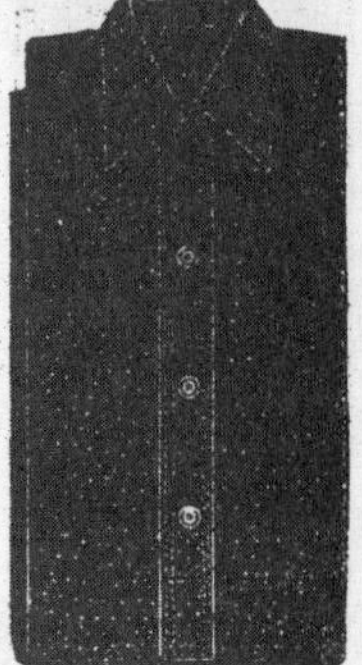

No. 34C392 Men's Fast Black Sateen Shirts, with small white polka dot. Made full size, felled seams, extension neckband, yoke back, one pocket, 36 inches long and double stitched. Sizes, 14½, 15, 15½, 16, 16½ and 17.

Each..... $0.40
Per doz... 4.50

Postage extra, 12 cents.

No. 34C393 Men's Fast Black Sateen Shirts. Made full sized, felled seams, extension neckband, yoke, pearl buttons and gussets; 36 inches long. Sizes, 14½, 15, 15½, 16, 16½ and 17.

Each.. $0.40
Per doz. 4.50

By mail, postage extra, each, 12 cents.

Our Leader. Men's Black Sateen Shirts, 80 Cents.

No. 34C395 Men's Extra Heavy and Fine Black Sateen Shirts. Finely made, shaped shoulders, double stitched throughout, felled seams, pearl buttons, extension neckband, faced sleeves, full size and 36 inches long, yoke back which is made in such a way as to make the shoulders double. Sizes, 14½, 15, 15½, 16, 16½ and 17.

Price, each..... $0.80
Per dozen..... 9.00

If by mail, postage extra, each, 15c.

Men's Extra Fine Black Sateen Shirts, $1.10.

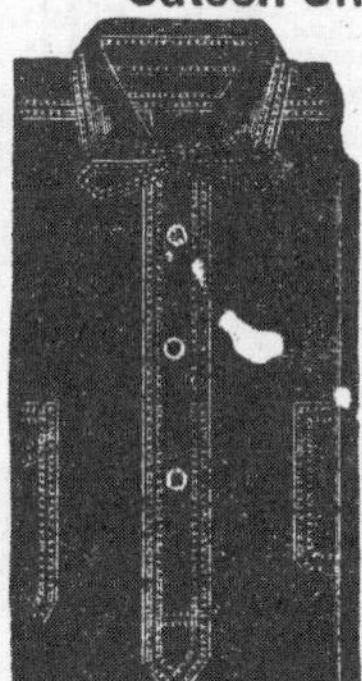

No. 34C397 Men's Extra Fine Black Sateen Overshirts. This number has every detail for making a shirt good fitting, strong and durable, such as felled seams and gussets, wide facings, shaped shoulders. Full 36 inches long. Sizes, 14½, 15, 15½, 16, 16½ and 17.

Each... $ 1.10
Per doz.. 12.50

If by mail, postage extra, each, 16 cents.

Fancy Figured Black Sateen Shirts, $1.10.

No. 34C398 Men's Extra Quality Black Sateen Shirts, made from a fine new black sateen cloth with a fancy effect throughout, double stitched throughout in white thread, shaped shoulders, pearl buttons, gussets, faced sleeves. A strictly first class shirt. Regular retail price, $2.00. Sizes, 14½, 15, 15½, 16, 16½ and 17.

Each... $1.10
Per dozen, $12.50

If by mail, postage extra, 16 cents.

Firemen's or Teamsters' Blue Twill Cotton Shirts, $1.00.

No. 34C391 Fireman's or Teamsters' Heavy Weight Blue Twill Cotton Shirts, made up in regular firemen's style, double breasted, large white pearl buttons, extra long pointed collar, deep cuffs, warranted first quality in every respect. Sizes, 14½, 15, 15½, 16, 16½ and 17.
Each......$ 1.00
Per doz... 11.00
If by mail, postage extra, each, 20 cents.

Buckskin Color Moleskin Shirts, 55 Cents.

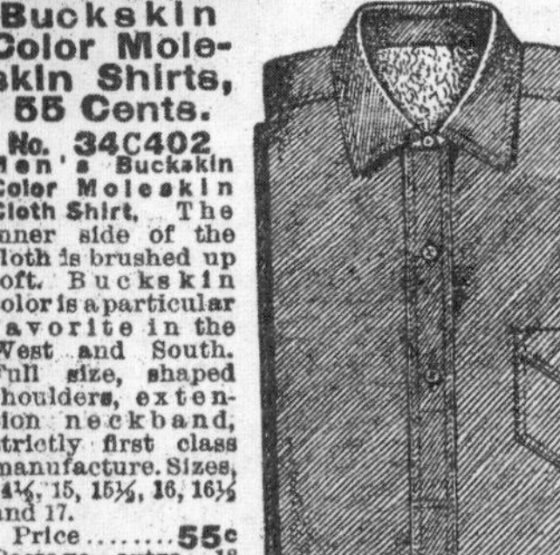

No. 34C402 Men's Buckskin Color Moleskin Cloth Shirt. The inner side of the cloth is brushed up soft. Buckskin color is a particular favorite in the West and South. Full size, shaped shoulders, extension neckband, strictly first class manufacture. Sizes, 14½, 15, 15½, 16, 16½ and 17.
Price........55c
Postage extra, 18 cents.

Pemberton Cloth Heavy Cotton Shirts, 70 Cents.

No. 34C405 Men's Pemberton Cotton Cassimere Overshirts. The Pemberton cloth is a heavy, closely twilled cotton, in plaid and stripe effects, about the same character as in woolen cashmere shirts. By a special machine the surface is brushed soft, but not fleeced. Very durable and will stand wear. Full size, felled seams, medium colors. Sizes, 14½, 15, 15½, 16, 16½ and 17. Price......70c
If by mail, postage extra, 18 cents.

MEN'S NIGHTSHIRTS.

SPECIAL NOTICE—Men's Nightshirts are not made in half sizes.

Muslin Nightshirts, 45c.

No. 34C606 Men's Fancy Front Nightshirt. Made from superior quality white muslin. Tastefully embroidered on collar and down the front in beautiful contrasting colors. Sizes, 14, 15, 16, 17 and 18.
Price, each.........$0.45
Per dozen........ 5.25
If by mail, postage extra, each, 14 cents.

Very Fine Muslin Nightshirts, 75c.

No. 34C612 Men's Superfine Nightshirts. Made of finest Utica Mills muslin. Collar and cuffs all handsomely trimmed with insertion and richly embroidered in silk of contrasting shades, cardinal, baby blue, rose, pink, opal, lavender, etc. Sizes, 14, 15, 16, 17 and 18. Price, each.$0.75
Per dozen......... 9.00
If by mail, postage extra, each, 14 cents.

Men's Extra Long Muslin Nightshirts.

No. 34C614 Men's Extra Long Plain White Nightshirts, made of the finest Utica Mills muslin. Extra large body, 60 inches long, yoke back, pearl buttons, patent facings. Sizes, 14, 15, 16, 17, 18 and 19.
Price..............85c
Postage extra, 18 cents.

No. 34C615 Men's Extra Fine Muslin French Neck Nightshirts; fancy trimmed, pearl buttons and double stitched throughout. This nightshirt is made without a collar, making a very cool garment for summer wear. Sizes, 14, 15, 16, 17 and 18. Price..$0.75
Per dozen... 9.00
If by mail, postage extra, 14 cents.

No. 34C618 Men's Extra Fine Muslin French Neck Nightshirts; made of the finest cambric muslin and embroidered in silk around the neck and down the front, as shown in illustration, one pocket. This nightshirt is made without a collar. Plain white only. Sizes, 14, 15, 16, 17 and 18.
Price..............95c
If by mail, postage extra, 14 cents.

Men's French Flannelette Nightshirts.

No. 34C620 Men's Good Quality Flannelette or Domet Nightshirts. Full size body and well made; fancy stripes. The soft smooth cloth is particularly pleasant for sleeping garments. Sizes, 14, 15, 16, 17 and 18. Price.......$0.40
Per dozen......... 4.50
Postage extra, each, 16 cents.

No. 34C626 Men's Extra Fine French Flannelette Cloth Nightshirts. Try them once and you will never wear any other kind. They are made in the best manner possible. Cut full length and have yoke back, white pearl buttons, handkerchief pocket, double stitched seams. Soft and fine in texture. Made in light colors, neat combination stripes. Sizes, 14, 15, 16, 17 and 18.
Healthful, durable and warm. Price..........75c
If by mail, postage extra, 18 cents.

Extra Heavy Flannelette Nightshirts, 95 Cents.

No. 34C628 Men's Flannel Nightshirts. Made of high grade extra heavy Domet flannel, cut 56 inches long, yoke back, white pearl buttons, handkerchief pocket and double stitched seams. They are soft and fluffy like swansdown, assorted colors in figures and stripes. Sizes, 15, 16, 17, 18, 19 and 20. Price......95c
Postage extra, 19 cents.

Extra Long Flannelette Nightshirts.

No. 34C632 Men's Extra Long Flannelette Nightshirts, of same quality as No. 34C628, but 60 inches in length. Just the thing for cold weather. A special comfort for tall men. Sizes, 15, 16, 17, 18, 19 and 20. Price, ..$1.00
Postage extra, 20 cents.

Boys' Muslin Nightshirts, 45 Cents.

No. 34C780 Boys' Muslin Nightshirts. Boys' good quality muslin nightshirts; full size and length. Sizes, 12, 13 and 14.
Price...........45c
If by mail, postage extra, 10 cents.

For Boys' Winter Shirts and Sweaters, send for our Special Furnishing Goods Catalogue.

BOYS' SHIRTS.

Sizes, 12, 12½, 13, 13½ and 14.

Boys' Laundered White Shirts.

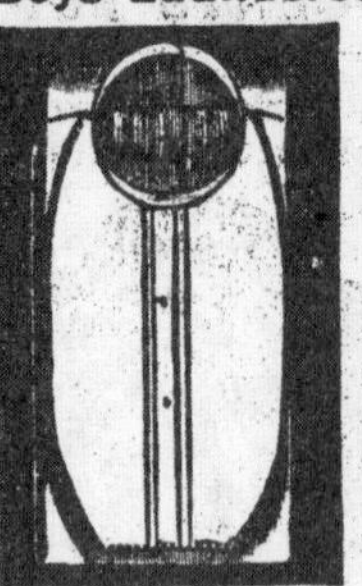

No. 34C664 An Extra Fine Quality Boys' Laundered White Shirt, made from specially selected muslin with all linen bosom. Thoroughly well made and reinforced. Fine dress finish; open back. Sizes, 12, 12½, 13, 13½ and 14.
Price.........65c
If by mail, postage extra, 10 cents.

Boys' Unlaundered White Shirts, 42 Cents.

No. 34C666 Boys' Unlaundered White Shirts, made of New York Mills muslin, double front and back, linen bosom. Sizes, 12½, 13, 13½, 14 neckband.
Price, per dozen, $4.75; each......42c
If by mail, postage extra, each, 10c.

BOYS' COLORED SHIRTS.

Boys' All Colored Percale Shirts, 43c.

No. 34C670 Boys' or Youths' All Colored Percale Shirts, with medium bosom, laundered, open back only; made of good quality percale, in large variety of stripes, plaids, blue, pink, red, etc. Sizes, 12, 12½, 13, 13½ and 14. What size do you wear?
Price, each...$0.43
Per dozen... 4.75
Postage extra, 10c.

Boys' Negligee Shirts, 35c.

No. 34C676 Boys' Negligee Shirts, made of good quality percale, large variety of stripes, black and white, blue and white, red and white, etc. One pair of link cuffs to match, three pearl buttons down the front, to be worn with white collars. Sizes, 12, 12½, 13, 13½ and 14. Each, $0.35
Per dozen.. 4.00
Postage extra, 12c.

Boys' Negligee Shirts, 39c.

No. 34C678 Made of French Percale, with two collars and one pair of cuffs to match. A sensible shirt that will give enduring satisfaction. The designs are in stripes on solid background, such as blue, pink or black and white; all pretty combinations. Never retails for less than 50 cents. Do not forget size. Sizes, 12, 12½, 13, 13½ and 14.
Price, each....$0.39
Per dozen...... 4.50
Postage extra, 10c.

Boys' Laundered Negligee Shirts, 38 Cents.

No. 34C682 Boys' Laundered Negligee Shirts. Made from fancy colored French percale, with attached turn down collar and cuffs, white ground with colorings of black, red, pink, blue, etc. Sizes, 12½, 13, 13½ and 14.
Always mention size worn.
Price, each 38c
Per dozen.......$4.25
If by mail, postage extra, each, 10c.

Boys' Soft or Negligee Shirts, Not Starched, 38 Cents.

No. 34C684 Boys' Good Quality Sateen Shirts, fast colors in light colored stripes. Yoke back, pearl buttons, shaped shoulders, extension neckband, felled seams, and double stitched. Sizes, 12, 12½, 13, 13½ and 14. Each..$0.38
Per dozen 4.25
Postage extra, each, 10 cents.

Boys' Soft Shirts 35c.

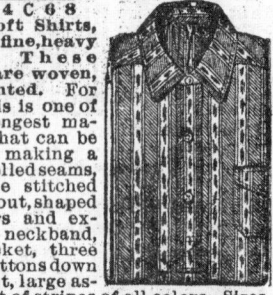

No. 34C68 Boys' Soft Shirts, made of fine, heavy madras. These goods are woven, not printed. For wear, this is one of the strongest materials that can be used in making a shirt. Felled seams, double stitched throughout, shaped shoulders and extension neckband, one pocket, three pearl buttons down the front, large assortment of stripes of all colors. Sizes, 12½, 13, 13½ and 14. Price, each.$0.35
Per dozen......... 4.00
If by mail, postage extra, each, 10c.

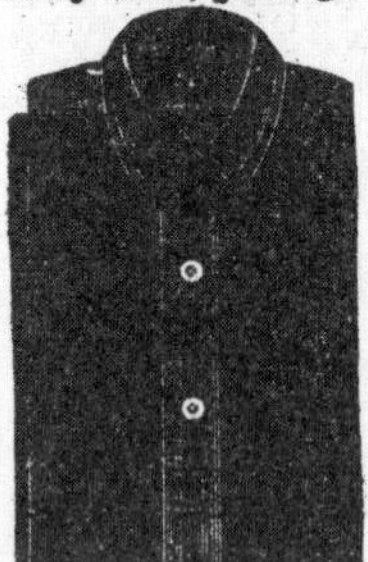

Boys' Black Sateen Overshirts, 40c.

No. 34C706 Boys' Fast Black Sateen Overshirts. Finely made and finished, yoke back and double stitched; reliable in every way. Sizes, 12, 12½, 13, 13½ and 14.
Each...$0.40
Per doz. 4.50
Postage extra, each, 6c.

Good Value at 35 Cents.

No. 34C710 Boys' black with blue, yellow or white stripes, Twilled Cotton Overshirts, made in first class manner, as illustrated. A good strong working shirt. Sizes, 12½, 13, 13½ and 14.
Price, each, $0.35
Per dozen.. 4.00
Postage extra, each, 10 cents.

Boys' Fancy Stripe Chambray Work Shirts, 35 Cents.

No. 34C711 Boys' Chambray Work Shirts, made of a very heavy chambray in a bluish color, with fancy colored stripes. Yoke back, extension neckband, and double stitched. Sizes, 12½, 13, 13½ and 14. Each...$0.35
Per dozen 4.00
Postage extra, each, 10 cents.

Boys' Woven Chambray Overshirts 35c.

No. 34C712 Boys' Plain Blue Woven Chambray Overshirts. One of the best fast color cloths that will stand repeated washing and hard wear; made in the same manner as No. 34C710. Sizes, 12½, 13, 13½ and 14.
Each.........$0.35
Per dozen... 4.00
If by mail, postage extra, each, 10 cents.

MEN'S LINEN COLLARS, 10 CENTS.

OUR COLLARS AT 10 CENTS ARE 4-PLY PURE LINEN AND WARRANTED TO BE SUCH. THEY ARE EQUAL TO ANY COLLARS RETAILING AT 15 CENTS EACH.

DO NOT FORGET TO GIVE SIZE FOR COLLARS.

If by mail, postage on collars extra, per dozen, 15 cents; each 2 cents.

No. 34C1062 Front, 1⅞-in. Back, 1½-in. Sizes, 14 to 18½. Each... $0.10 Per doz., 1.10

No. 34C1064 Front, 2¼-in. Back, 2 in. Sizes, 14 to 18. Each... $0.10 Per doz. 1.10

No. 34C1066 Front, 2⅝-in. Back, 2¼-in. Sizes, 14 to 17½. Each... $0.10 Per doz. 1.10

No. 34C1067 Front, 1¾-in. Back, 1½-in. Sizes, 14 to 18. Each... $0.10 Per doz. 1.10

No. 34C1068 Front, 2-in. Back, 1¾-in. Sizes, 14 to 17. Each... $0.10 Per doz. 1.10

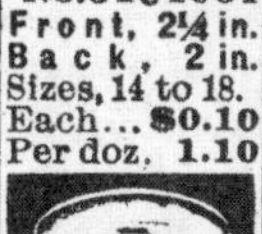

No. 34C1069 Front, 2-in. Back, 1¾-in. Sizes, 14 to 17. Each... $0.10 Per doz. 1.10

No. 34C1072 Front, 2½-in. Back, 2¼-in. Sizes, 14 to 18. Price... $0.10 Per doz. 1.10

No. 34C1074 Front, 2⅝-in. Back, 2¼-in. Sizes, 14 to 17½. Each.... $0.10 Per doz. 1.10

No. 34C1076 Points, 2¼-in. Back, 1¾-in. Space, ¾-in. Sizes, 14 to 18. Each... $0.10 Per doz. 1.10

No. 34C1084 Points, 2¼-in. Back, 1⅛-in. Space, 1¼-in. Sizes, 14 to 17½. Each... $0.10 Per doz. 1.10

No. 34C1088 Points, 2½-in. Space, ½-in. Back, 1¼-in. Sizes, 14 to 18. Each... $0.10 Per doz. 1.10

DO NOT FAIL TO STATE SIZE.

No. 34C1000 Front, 2-in. Back, 1⅝-in. Sizes, 14 to 18. Each... $0.10 Per doz. 1.10

No. 34C1004 Front, 2½-in. Back, 2¼-in. Sizes, 14 to 17. Each... $0.10 Per doz. 1.10

No. 34C1010 Front, 2⅝-in. Back, 2⅜-in. Sizes, 14 to 17. Each... $0.10 Per doz. 1.10

No. 34C1012 Front, 2½-in. Back, 2⅛-in. Sizes, 14 to 17½. Each... $0.10 Per doz. 1.10

No. 34C1038 Front, 2-in. Back, 1½-in. Sizes, 14½ to 18. Each... $0.10 Per doz. 1.10

No. 34C1042 Front, 1¾-in. Back, 1⅝-in. Sizes, 14½ to 19. Each... $0.10 Per doz. 1.10

No. 34C1048 Front, 2-in. Back, 1¾-in. Sizes, 14 to 17. Each... $0.10 Per doz. 1.10

No. 34C1054 Front, 2⅜-in. Back, 2⅛-in. Sizes, 14 to 17. Each ... $0.10 Per doz.. 1.10

No. 34C1056 Front, 2½-in. Back, 2¼-in. Sizes, 14 to 17. Each... $0.10 Per doz.. 1.10

No. 34C1060 Front, 2⅝-in. Back, 2½-in. Sizes, 14 to 17. Each... $0.10 Per doz. 1.10

WHAT SIZE DO YOU WEAR?

MEN'S LINEN CUFFS, 14 CENTS PER PAIR.

Sizes, 9½, 10, 10½, 11 and 11½ inches.

LET US REMIND YOU AGAIN that cuffs quoted herewith are made 4-ply of pure linen, goods that we warrant to be perfect and that retail at 20 cents a pair. If by mail, postage extra, per dozen pairs, 20 cents; per pair, 2 cents.

No. 34C1100 Width, 3¾-in. Men's Linen Cuffs. 9½ to 11½. Price, per pair, $0.14 Per dozen pairs.... 1.60

No. 34C1104 Width, 4-in. Men's Linen Cuffs. 9½ to 11½. Price, per pair, $0.14 Per dozen pairs ... 1.60

No. 34C1110 Width, 4-in. Men's Linen Cuffs. 9½ to 11½. Price, per pair, $0.14 Per dozen pairs..... 1.60

No. 34C1114 Width, 4-in. Men's Linen Cuffs. 9½ to 11½. Price, per pair, $0.14 Per dozen pairs..... 1.60

No. 34C1118 Width, 4¼-in. Men's Linen Cuffs. 9½ to 11½. Price, per pair, $0.14 Per dozen pairs..... 1.60

No. 34C1122 Width, 4¼-in. Men's Linen Cuffs. 9½ to 11½. Price, per pair, $0.14 Per dozen pairs..... 1.60

DON'T FAIL TO STATE SIZE WANTED WHEN YOU WRITE YOUR ORDER

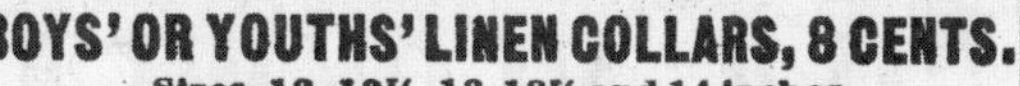

BOYS' OR YOUTHS' LINEN COLLARS, 8 CENTS.

Sizes, 12, 12½, 13, 13½ and 14 inches.

No. 34C1150 Back, 1¾-in. Points, 2-in. Boys' Collars. Sizes, 12 to 14 only. Price, each........8c Per dozen, 90c

No. 34C1151 Front, 1⅝-in. Back, 1⅜-in. Boys' Linen Collars. Sizes, 12 to 14 only. Price, each, 8c Per dozen, 90c

No. 34C1152 Front, 1⅞-in. Back, 1⅝-in. Boys' Linen Collars. Sizes, 12 to 14 only. Price, each, 8c Per dozen, 90c

No. 34C1154 Front, 2¼-in. Back, 2-in. Boys' Linen Collars. Sizes, 12 to 14 only. Price, each, 8c Per dozen, 90c

No. 34C1166 Front, 2¼-in. Back, 2-in. Boys' Linen Collars. Sizes, 12 to 14 only. Price, each. 8c Per dozen, 90c

No. 34C1168 Front, 2½-in. Back, 2⅜-in. Boys' Linen Collars. Sizes, 12 to 14 only. Price, each, 8c Per dozen, 90c

No. 34C1169 Front, 2-in. Back, 1¾-in. Boys' Linen Collars. Sizes, 12 to 14 only. Price, each, 8c Per dozen, 90c

DO NOT FAIL TO STATE SIZE.

BOYS' OR YOUTHS' LINEN CUFFS, 14 CENTS.

Sizes, 8, 8½, 9 and 9½ inches.

No. 34C1170 Width, 3⅜-in. Boys' Linen Cuffs. Sizes, 8 to 9½. Price, per pair...14c Per dozen pairs. $1.60

No. 34C1174 Width, 3⅝-in. Boys' Linen Cuffs. Sizes, 8 to 9½. Price, per pair...14c Per dozen pairs.. $1.60

No. 34C1182 Width, 3¼-in. Boys' Linen Cuffs. Sizes, 8 to 9½. Price, per pair .. 14c Per dozen pairs . $1.60

DO NOT FAIL TO STATE SIZE.

CELLULOID WATERPROOF COLLARS FOR MEN AND BOYS, 11 CENTS.

No. 34C1200 Front, 1⅞-in. Style Royal, Celluloid Collars. Sizes, 12½ to 20. Each... $0.11 Per doz. 1.20

No. 34C1202 Front, 1¾-in. Back, 1½-in. Style Tuxedo, Celluloid Collars. Sizes, 12 to 18½. Each... $0.11 Per doz. 1.20

No. 34C1203 Front, 1½-inch. Back, 1¼-inch. Style Claremont, Celluloid Collars. Sizes, 12½ to 18. Each... $0.11 Per doz. 1.20

No. 34C1204 Front, 2¼-inch. Back, 1¾-inch. Sizes, 12½ to 18. Each... $0.11 Per doz...1.20

No. 34C1205 Front, 2⅛-inch. Back, 1⅞-inch. Sizes, 12½ to 18½. Each.....$0.11 Per doz ..1.20

No. 34C1206 Front, 1½-inch. Back, 1⅜-inch. Celluloid Collars. Sizes, 12 to 19½. Each.....$0.11 Per doz ... 1.20

No. 34C1212 Front, 2-inch. Back, 1¾-inch. Celluloid Collars. Sizes, 13½ to 18½. Each.....$0.11 Per doz... 1.20

CELLULOID WATERPROOF CUFFS, 22 CENTS.

Sizes, 9½, 10, 10½, 11 and 11½.

No. 34C1216 Width, 3½-in. Style Fifth Avenue, Celluloid Cuffs. Sizes, 9½ to 11½. Price, per pair ... $0.22 Per doz. 2.40

No. 34C1218 Width, 3½-in. Style Excelsior, Celluloid Cuffs. Sizes, 9 to 11½. Price, per pair, $0.22 Per doz. 2.40

No. 34C1230 Men's Rubber Bosoms, 9¼ inches long, medium length, in polished or dull finish. Price........35c If by mail, postage extra, each, 4 cents.

RUBBER COLLARS FOR MEN AND BOYS, 15 CENTS.

In polished or dull finish. State kind in your order. Choice of any style, 15 cents each, or $1.65 per dozen.

No. 34C1234 Front, 2-inch. Back, 1¼-inch. Rubber Collar, polished or dull finish. Sizes, 12 to 18½. Price, each... $0.15 Per doz. 1.65

No. 34C1236 Front, 1¾-inch. Back, 1½-inch. Rubber Collar, polished or dull finish. Sizes, 12 to 18½. Price, each.... $0.15 Per doz. 1.65

No. 34C1238 Front, 2-inch. Back, 1⅝-inch. Rubber Collar, polished or dull finish. Sizes, 12½ to 18½. Price, each.. $0.15 Doz... 1.65

No. 34C1240 Front, 1¾-inch. Back, 1½-inch. Rubber Collar, in polished or dull finish. Sizes, 12 to 18½. Price, each... $0.15 Per doz. 1.65

No. 34C1242 Front, 2¼-inch. Back, 1¾-inch. Rubber Collar, in polished or dull finish. Sizes, 13½ to 17½. Price, each... $0.15 Per doz. 1.65

No. 34C1252 Front, 2¼-inch. Back, 2-inch. Rubber Collar, in polished or dull finish. Sizes, 13½ to 17½. Price, each.. $0.15 Doz .. 1.65

No. 34C1262 Front, 2-inch. Back, 1¾-inch. Rubber Collar, in polished or dull finish. Sizes, 12 to 18. Price, each.. $0.15 Per doz... 1.65

No. 34C1264 Front, 2-inch. Back, 1⅞-inch. Rubber Collar, in polished, or dull finish. Sizes, 13½ to 17½. Price, each, $0.15 Per doz... 1.65

RUBBER CUFFS FOR MEN AND BOYS, 30 CENTS.

No. 34C1270 Men's Rubber Link Cuffs, polished or dull finish. Sizes, 10, 10½, 11 and 11½. Per pair...... $0.30 Per doz...... 3.40

No. 34C1274 Men's Rubber Plain Cuffs, in polished or dull finish. Sizes, 9½, 10, 10½, 11, 11½. Per pair.... $0.30 Per doz.... 3.40

CELLULOID SHIRT FRONTS.

No. 34C1222 SHORT. Front, 7 in. Width, 6¾ inch. Celluloid Shirt Front, interlined. Short length. Price.............25c If by mail, postage extra, each, 2 cents.

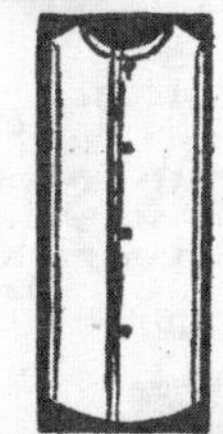

No. 34C1226 LONG. Front, 13 in. Width, 6⅞ in. Celluloid Shirt Front; made of extra quality celluloid, interlined. Long length. Price......42c If by mail, postage extra, each, 4 cents.

No. 34C1224 MEDIUM. Front, 9¼ in. Width, 7 in. Celluloid Shirt Front, interlined. Medium length. Price..35c If by mail, postage extra, each, 3c

OVERSLEEVES.

No. 34C1294 Men's Fast Black Sateen Oversleeves. Rubber top. Price, per pair........................18c If by mail, postage extra, 4 cents. Hose Supporters, see Index.

MEN'S ARM BANDS.

No. 34C1296 Men's Arm Bands. Colors, black, blue, red or white. Price, per pair.............................. 5c Per dozen pairs.............................. 55c

No. 34C1298 Men's Arm Bands, better quality than the above. Colors, black, blue, red or white. Price, per dozen pairs, $1.10; per pair.............................19c If by mail, postage extra, per pair, 2 cents.

WIZARD CUFF HOLDERS.

No. 34C1280 The Wizard Cuff Holders, improved, nickel plated. Price, per pair.......6c

If by mail, postage extra, 2 cents.

NECKTIE HOLDER.

No. 34C1288 Men's Necktie Holder, lever clamp, nickel plated. Price, each...............3c If by mail, postage extra, 1 cent.

OUR MEN'S SILK NECKWEAR DEPARTMENT.

OUR PRICE ON NECKWEAR IS JUST ABOUT ONE-HALF THE PRICE YOU PAY FOR THE SAME GRADE OF GOODS ELSEWHERE.

For 10c we sell you silk bows that others ask 20c for.	For 20c we sell neckwear that everyone else charges 50c for.	Our 30c neckties are the same kind you pay elsewhere 50c and 75c for.

WE ARE ABLE TO MAKE THESE LOW PRICES BECAUSE WE ARE THE LARGEST RETAILERS OF NECKWEAR IN THE COUNTRY. WE BUY OUR SILKS IN ENORMOUS QUANTITIES AND WE ARE ABLE TO MAKE PRICES THAT OTHERS CANNOT ATTEMPT TO MEET. SEND US YOUR ORDER FOR NECKWEAR AND YOU WILL REALLY BE SURPRISED AT THE SPLENDID QUALITY OF GOODS YOU WILL RECEIVE AT OUR LOW PRICES. ORDER ANY TIE FROM THIS PAGE AND IF YOU DO NOT AGREE THAT IT IS THE BEST VALUE YOU HAVE EVER SEEN, YOU CAN RETURN IT TO US AND WE WILL PROMPTLY RETURN ALL YOUR MONEY.

Always State Color You Prefer and Order By Number.

THE ILLUSTRATIONS SHOW THE STYLES ONLY. WE FURNISH THEM IN A BIG VARIETY OF PATTERNS AND COLORINGS.

If by mail, postage extra, on all neckwear, each, 2 cents.

MEN'S HIGH GRADE SILK TECK TIES.

Made of the best quality of silks, in the newest shapes, fine linings and wide bands. We can furnish you any pattern in any color combination you desire also plain black silk or satin. Kindly state color and pattern desired and we can please you.

Fancy Colored Silk.

No. 34C1306
Price, each............20c

Fancy Colored Silk, Shield Teck.

No. 34C1310
Price.........20c

Fancy Colored Silk.

No. 34C1318
Price, each..............................30c

Fancy Colored Silk.

In a box.
No. 34C1322
Price.......40c

Fancy Colored Silk.

No. 34C1326
Price......50c

Black Silk or Satin.

Different qualities according to price.

No. 34C1332 Price, 25c
No. 34C1334 Price, 40c
No. 34C1336 Price, 75c

MEN'S HIGH GRADE SILK PUFF TIES.

Silk lined, latest shapes, assorted colors and patterns, also plain black.

Plain Black.

No. 34C1344
Price.........40c

Fancy Colored Silk

No. 34C1352
Price.............40c

MEN'S FINE SILK FOUR-IN-HAND TIES.

Made reversible, can be worn on either side. Any color or pattern desired. Also plain black silk or satin.

Fancy Colored Silk.

No. 34C1366
Price..........20c

Fancy Colored Silk.

No. 34C1370
Price........30c

Fancy Colored Silk.

No. 34C1374
Price...........40c

Plain Black Silk or Satin.

No. 34C1376
Price.......40c

MEN'S FINEST QUALITY SILK IMPERIAL.

Can be tied as four-in-hand or puff. Beautiful design. Any color you prefer.

No. 34C1392
Price..................................75c

MEN'S SILK STRING TIES.

Made of the best grade of fancy silks, in a large assortment of colors. Also plain black silk or satin.

Fancy Colored Silk.

No. 34C1393
Price...................................10c

No. 34C1394
Price....................................20c

Plain Black Silk.

No. 34C1396
Price...................................25c

Plain Black Folded Tie.

No. 34C1398
Price....................................20c

MEN'S SILK BAND BOWS.

Made full shape and latest style bow, adjustable elastic and hook in the back to fit any size collar. Made of the finest silks in a large assortment of the latest up to date colors and patterns, in stripes, figures or Persian designs. Also plain black silk or satin. Always state color.

Fancy Colored Silk Bow.

No. 34C1428
Price.............15c

Plain Black Silk or Satin Bows.

No. 34C1440
Price.................15c

No. 34C1444
Price.........................25c

MEN'S SILK SHIELD BOWS.

To be worn with lay down collars, made of the finest silks in a large assortment of patterns and designs, in any color you desire. Also plain black silk or satin. Large or small shapes, as illustrated.

Plain Black Silk or Satin Bows.

No. 34C1400
Price... ....10c

No. 34C1402
Price 10c

No. 34C1404
Price..........19c

Fancy Colored Silk Shield Bows.

No. 34C1412
Price 12c

No. 34C1416
Price...............10c

No. 34C1418
Price 10c

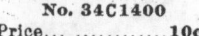

MEN'S COTTON SUMMER NECKWEAR.

Colored Madras Band Bows.

No. 34C1466
Price, each............5c

Colored Madras Shield Bows.

No. 34C1474
Price, each............5c

White Lawn Band Bows.

No. 34C1484
Price, each............4c

White Lawn Band Bows.

No. 34C1488
Price, each............10c

White Lawn Band Bows.

No. 34C1490
Price, each............19c

Embroidered White Lawn Band Bows

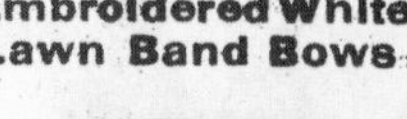

No. 34C1494
Price, each............8c

Embroidered White Lawn Band Bows.

No. 34C1496
Price, each............15c

White Lawn Shield Bows.

No. 34C1500
Price, each............3c

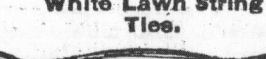

White Lawn String Ties.

No. 34C1508 Price, per doz....10c
No. 34C1510 Price, per doz....15c
No. 34C1512 Price, per doz....25c

Colored Percale String Ties.

No. 34C1518 Price, per doz....10c
No. 34C1522 Price per doz....18c

Colored Madras String Ties.

No. 34C1528 Price, per dozen 40c
No. 34C1530 Price, per dozen, 65c

Men's Washable Fancy Colored Madras.

No. 34C1560
Price, each.......10c

Four-in-Hands, White Duck, Embroidered Ends.

No. 34C1566
Price, each.......20c

Washable Stock Ties.

A collar and tie combined. Any color you prefer.

No. 34C1570
Price, each.......20c

Cotton Shield Teck Ties.

Assorted colored stripes.

No. 34C1572
Price, each.....12c

SILK WINDSOR TIES.

Plaids.

No. 34C1574
Price, each......20c

Blue Polka Dots.

No. 34C1576
Price, each..20c

Plain colors, black, white, navy, yellow or red.

No. 34C1578
Price, each...20c

Children's Fancy Colored Silk Plaid Bows.

No. 34C1582
Price, each............................25c

BOYS' FINE SILK NECKWEAR.

Silk Tecks. Silk Four-in-Hands. Silk Shield Tecks.

34C1586 Price.....17c
34C1588 Price..17c
34C1590 Price..20c

Made of the finest silks, and comes in a large variety of fancy colors, in stripes, figures and Persian designs. Made a special size for boys, in the shapes as shown in illustrations.

PLEASE STATE COLOR DESIRED.

String Tie.

No. 34C1592
Price....................12c

Silk Band Bows.

No. 34C1594
Price....................10c

Silk Shield Bows.

No. 34C1598
Price....................10c

SUSPENDER DEPARTMENT.

OUR LINE OF SUSPENDERS CANNOT BE EXCELLED FOR QUALITY AND WORKMANSHIP.

MEN'S EXTRA HEAVY OR FARMERS' SUSPENDERS.

Police Back Suspenders.

No. 34C1602 Made from heavy, strong 1½-inch elastic web, cushioned back. Extra strong, non-breakable clasps and buckles.
Per pair..$0.20
Per dozen 2.35
Postage extra, 5 cents.

Men's Extra Heavy Cross Back Suspenders.

25c

No. 34C1605 Made from heavy 2-inch elastic web, cowhide ends. Shirley buckle and an extra strong and durable cast-off. Leather trimmings. If by mail, postage extra, per pair, 5 cents.
Price, per pair............$0.25
Per dozen............2.75

Men's Extra Heavy Cross Back Suspenders.

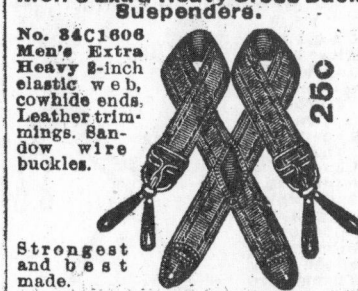

25c

No. 34C1606 Men's Extra Heavy 2-inch elastic web, cowhide ends. Leather trimmings. Sandow wire buckles.

Strongest and best made.
Price, per dozen, $2.85; per pair..25c
If by mail, postage extra, per pair, 5c.

Men's Extra Heavy Suspenders.

No. 34C1612 Men's Extra Heavy Suspenders. Made with self adjusting back; 2-inch elastic web, cowhide ends, wire buckles.
Per pr..$0.20
Dozen... 2.35
If by mail, postage extra, per pair, 7 cents.

Extra Strong Heavy Suspenders.

No. 34C1616 Men's Extra Heavy Strong Cross Back Suspenders, 2-inch elastic web, large sliding Shirley buckles, cowhide ends.
Pair 30c
Doz...$3.40
If by mail, postage extra, 8 cents.

The Shirley Hercules Brace.

No. 34C1620 Men's Extra Heavy, Strong Cross Back Suspenders, 2-in. elastic web, large sliding buckles, cowhide ends. Length, 40 inches.
Per dozen, $4.50; per pair....40c
If by mail, postage extra, per pair, 8 cents.

Extra Strong Police Back Suspenders.

No. 34 C 1624 Firemen's, Policemen's and Mechanics' Extra Stout Elastic Web Suspenders. Leather cushioned back and heavy rolled leather ends.
Per pair..$0.35
Per doz. 4.00
If by mail, postage extra, per pair, 5c.

MEN'S MEDIUM WEIGHT SUSPENDERS.

Men's Fancy Suspenders.

No. 34C1628 Men's Fancy Suspenders. 1½-inch elastic web, medium colors, with braided ends Nickeled cast off buckles.
Per pair..$0.12
Per dozen, 1.35
If by mail, postage extra, per pair, 5 cents.

Cross Back Suspenders, 20c.

No. 34C1632 Men's Cross Back Suspenders, 1¼-inch webbing, heavy leather trimmings and ends, snap button cast off, sliding buckles.
Per pr., $0.20
Per doz., 2.35
If by mail, postage extra, per pair, 5 cents.

Our New Cord Suspenders, 25 Cents.

No. 34C1648 A New Suspender designed to equalize the extreme movements of the body. No matter what position you assume the strain is practically the same on all buttons. The running cord is non-elastic, strong and durable.
Price, per pair $0.25
Per dozen 2.75
If by mail, postage extra, per pair, 6c.

Men's Suspenders, Lisle Web.

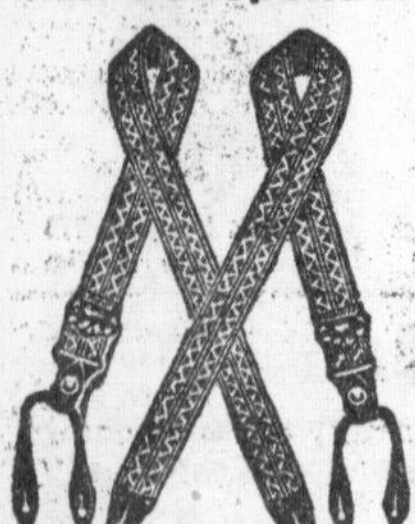

No. 34C1660 Men's Suspenders, made from lisle elastic webbing, about 1⅛ inches wide. Lisle web is lighter weight than the usual cotton webs or elastic and is cooler and very comfortable for summer wear. Nickel plated trimmings, leather ends and cast off snap buttons. Per pair. $0.18
Per dozen 2.00
If by mail, postage extra, per pair, 5c.

Our Special Elastic Web Cross Back Leather End Suspenders, 25 Cents.

No. 34C1664 Men's Elastic Web Cross Back Suspenders. Handsomely designed, colors woven in web, glove snap fasteners. Brass sliding buckles; fine leather ends.
Per pair.. $0.25
Per dozen 2.75
If by mail, postage extra, per pair, 5 cents.

Extra Fine Embroidered Suspenders, 20 Cents.

No. 34C1668 Men's Extra Fine Embroidered Suspenders. Braided lisle ends and drawer supporters. Light, medium and dark colors.
Per pair.. $0.20
Per dozen 2.35
If by mail, postage extra, per pair, 5c.

The Guyot Style, 35 Cents.

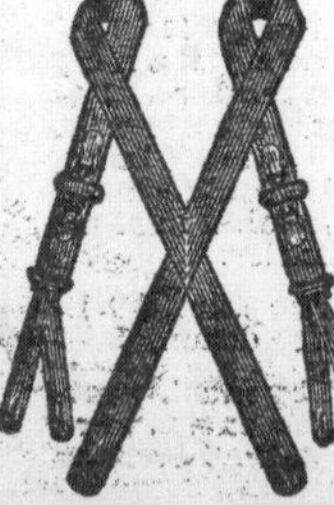

No. 34C1672 Bretelle's Universelles. The Famous French Sanitary Suspenders. Light weight, strong linen web with elastic in back pieces only. Light and dark colors.
Per pair. $0.35
Per doz. 4.00
If by mail, postage extra, per pair, 5c.

The Guyot Style, 19 Cents.

No. 34C1674 Guyot Style Non-Elastic Suspenders. Same style as No. 34C1672, only of a cheaper quality.
Per pair.. $0.19
Per dozen 2.25
If by mail, postage extra, per pair, 5 cents.

Guyot Style, 15 Cents.

No. 34C1676 Guyot Style Non-Elastic Suspenders. Colors, white, drab; also stripes, light or dark.
Price, per doz., $1.75; per pair.. 15c
If by mail, postage extra, per pair, 5c.

Men's Cross Back Suspenders, 35 Cents.

No. 34C1680 Men's Cross Back Suspenders, made from silk embroidered 1¼-inch wide webbing, brass sliding buckles, snap button cast off and genuine calf ends.
Per pair.. $0.35
Per dozen 4.00
If by mail, postage extra, per pair, 6 cents.

The President Suspenders.

No. 34C1688 A well known and greatly advertised Suspender, with improved back which equalizes the strain on all parts with every attitude. Relieves the strain on shoulders and not likely to pull off buttons.
Price, per dozen, $4.17; per pair. 45c
If by mail, postage extra, per pair, 5c.

Special 50-Cent Value.

No. 34C1696 Men's Silk Elastic Web Suspenders, 1⅜-inch web in very handsome stripes, sliding buckles, leather ends and snap button cast off.
Per pair.. $0.50
Per dozen. 5.50
If by mail, postage extra, per pair, 6c.

Men's Silk Suspenders, Non-Elastic Web.

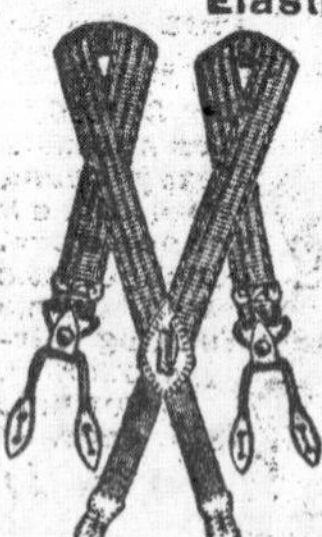

No. 34C1704 Men's Silk Non-Elastic Web Suspenders, with entirely new gold and filigree sliding buckles and snap button cast off. Pure silk elastic in back piece, tipped with kid. Fine kid trimmings.
Per pair.... $0.35
Per dozen.. 4.00
If by mail, postage extra, per pair, 5 cents.

Men's Silk Lisle Suspenders, 35 Cents.

No. 34C1708 Men's Fine Suspenders made from fine mercerized narrow silk elastic lisle webbing. They look like genuine silk but much better and are strong and durable. One of the very best new light weight suspenders offered this season. Medium light stripes, gilt buckles, fine leather ends and cast off.
Price, per dozen, $4.00; per pair, 35c
If by mail, postage extra, per pair, 5c.

Men's Silk Suspenders in Covered Boxes.

No. 34C1712 Men's Silk Non-Elastic Web Suspenders, with gilt sliding buckles, snap button cast off and fine kid ends, making a very handsome suspender. Assorted light colors. Packed one pair in a handsome box.
Price, per pair. 50c
Postage extra, per pair, 10 cents.

Men's Embroidered Satin Suspenders.

No. 34C1716 Fine Quality High Grade Men's Suspenders, made of fine satin, richly embroidered, beautiful floral sprays of contrasting colors embroidered down front. Colors, black, cream, blue, pink, lavender or garnet. Packed one pair in fancy box. A very handsome box. Per pair.... 85c
Postage extra, per pair, 10 cents.

Men's Silk Suspenders, 50c.

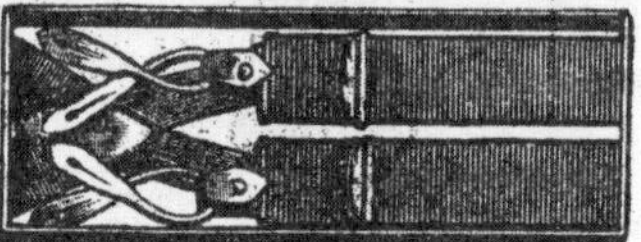

No. 34C1724 Men's Silk Non-Elastic Web Suspenders, made from a heavy quality of silk, 2 inches wide, finished with gilt buckles, snap button cast off and white kid ends, heavy elastic in back piece. Assorted colors, pink, blue, white, etc. Packed one pair in a very handsome box.
Price, per pair. .... [illegible]0c
Postage extra, per pair, 10 cents.

LEATHER SUSPENDERS.

Men's Self Adjusting Suspenders, 30 Cents.

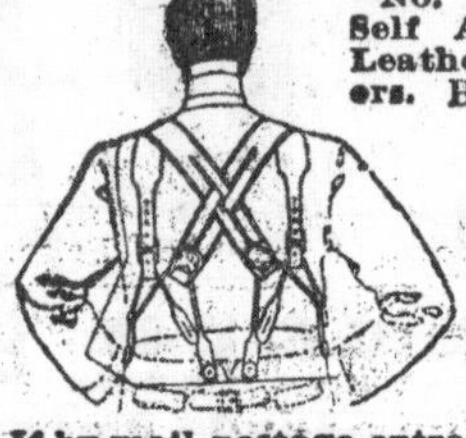

No. 34C1734 Self Adjusting Leather Suspenders. Best oak tan calfskin, and will not pull the buttons off. Comfort, ease and durability.
Price, per pair.. $0.30
Dozen 3.50
If by mail, postage extra, per pair, 5c.

Our Special Leather Suspenders, 50 Cents.

No. 34C1742 The latest and best of all Leather Suspenders. Made of grain leather with the new equalizing back which adjusts itself to every movement of the body. The ends are made of an extra heavy elastic cord.
Price, per pair $0.50
Per dozen 5.50
If by mail, postage extra, per pair, 7c.

BOYS' SUSPENDERS.

Fancy Striped Patterns, 10 Cents.

No. 34C1754 Boys' and Youths' Suspenders. Fancy striped patterns, leather back, strong elastic web. Woven ends and good strong buckles.
Per pair...... $0.10
Per dozen..... 1.10
If by mail, postage extra, per pair, 4 cents.

Embroidered Suspenders, 15 Cents.

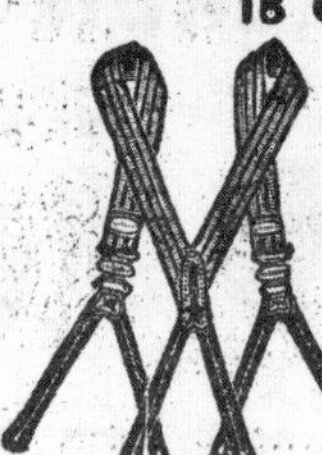

No. 34C1758 Boys' and Youths' Fancy Silk Embroidered Elastic Web Suspenders. Woven ends and sliding buckles.
Per pair. $0.15
Per dozen. 1.75
Postage extra, per pair, 5 cents.

Boys' Police Style Suspenders, 13 Cents.

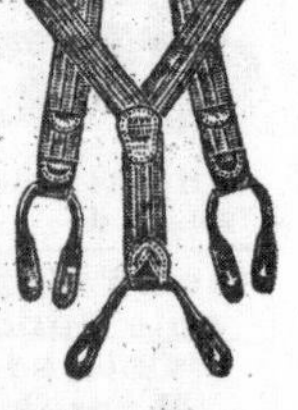

No. 34C1760 Made from a heavy 1¼-inch elastic cushion back web, sliding buckles and calf ends, regular police style.
Per pair $0.13
Per dozen 1.50
If by mail, postage extra, per pair, 5 cents.

Boys' Suspenders, 17 Cents.

No. 34C1764 Boys and Youths' Extra Quality Suspenders, elastic web, medium colors, cushion back, cast off buckles.
Price per pair.. $0.17
Per dozen 1.95
If by mail, postage extra, per pair, 5 cents.

Heavy Elastic Web Suspenders, 10c.

No. 34C1766 Boys' Heavy Strong Elastic Web Cross Back Farmer Suspenders. Web 1⅛ inches wide, heavy leather trimmings and ends, strong buckles.
Price per pair, $0.10
Per dozen..... 1.15
If by mail, postage extra, per pair, 5 cents.

Boys' Special Suspenders, 20 Cents.

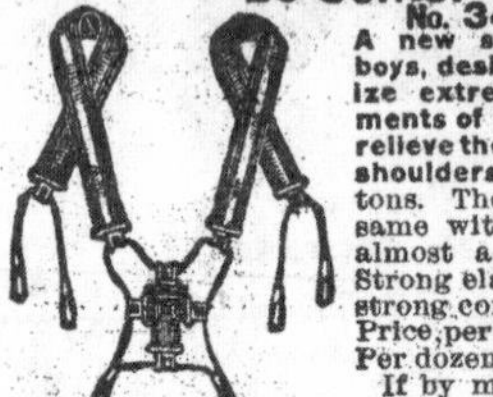

No. 34C1768 A new suspender for boys, designed to equalize extreme movements of the body and relieve the strain on the shoulders and the buttons. The strain is the same with the body in almost any position. Strong elastic web, with strong cord ends.
Price, per pair $0.20
Per dozen..... 2.25
If by mail, postage extra, 5 cents.

Shoulder Brace, 35 Cents.

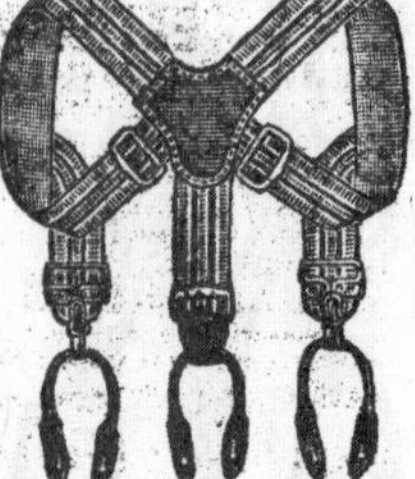

No. 34C1770 Men's Superior Shoulder Braces. Fancy overshot elastic web. Suspender attachment with fine leather ends. Light and medium colors.
Per pair, $0.35
Per doz., 4.00
By mail, postage extra, per pair, 7c.

Gamble Shoulder Brace for Men and Youths.

No. 34C1780 The special point of merit of this brace is in two light steel springs which act as if you gently press your thumbs on one's shoulder blades. They are perfectly adjustable, roll leather ends, patent cast off snaps, best hair pads, leather lined in front of arms, and will brace a man up. Sizes, 30, 32, 34, 36, 38 and 40 inches chest measure. Price, per pair $1.25
By mail, postage extra, per pair, 12c

The Gamble Shoulder Brace for Ladies and Misses.

A Perfect Shoulder Brace and Skirt Supporter Combined.

No. 34C1784 The Gamble Shoulder Brace for Ladies. Fine light drab jean web, adjustable to any position, finest hair padding, leather lined in front of arms. Sizes, 26, 28, 30, 32, 34, 36, 38, 40 inches bust measure.
Price, per pair........ 95c
By mail, postage extra, per pair, 8c.

Shoulder Brace for Men and Boys.

No. 34C1794 Men's Shoulder Brace, made of fine web. Give chest measure. Sizes, 32, 34, 36, 38, and 40 inches.
Price, per pair, $0.35
Per dozen..... 4.00

No. 34C1795 Boys' Shoulder Brace. Give chest measure. Sizes, 24, 26, 28, and 30 inches. Price, per pair........ $0.35
Per dozen........ 4.00
By mail, postage extra, per pair, 5c.

Ladies' Shoulder Brace and Skirt Supporter Combined.

No. 34C1796 Ladies' Shoulder Brace, non-elastic web, plain white or colored. Sizes, 32, 34, 36 and 38 inches. Give bust measure.
Per pair..... $0.35
Per dozen.. 4.00

No. 34C1797 Girls' Shoulder Brace, made same as ladies. Sizes, 24, 26, 28, and 30 inches. Give bust measure.
Price, per doz., $4.00; per pair,.. 35c
By mail, postage extra, per pair, 5c.

MEN'S AND BOYS' LEATHER BELTS.

Always Give Waist Measure When Ordering Belts. If by mail, postage extra, each, 7 cents.

No. 34C1800 Men's plain leather belts, 1¼ inches wide. **Colors, black or tan.** Sizes, 30 to 44 inches.
Price........ 15c

No. 34C1802 Men's grain leather belts, 1½ inches wide. Large metal eyelets. **Color, orange only.** Sizes, 30 to 42 inches. Price........ 20c

No. 34C1804 Men's fancy leather Belts, 1¼ inches wide. **Colors, black or brown.** Sizes, 30 to 50 inches.
Price........ 25c

No. 34C1808 Men's English calf leather belts, 1½ inches wide. **Colors, black or tan.** Sizes, 30 to 50 inches.
Price........ 35c

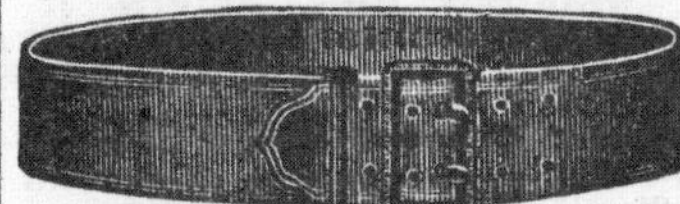

No. 34C1816 Men's extra wide, plain leather belts, 2⅜ inches wide. **Colors, black or tan.** Sizes, 30 to 44 inches. Price........ 25c

No. 34C1821 Men's braided imitation morocco leather belts, 1¼ inches wide. **Colors, black or tan.** Sizes, 30 to 42 inches. Price........ 35c

No. 34C1822 Men's calfskin leather belts, 1¼ inches wide. **Colors, black or brown.** Sizes, 30 to 42 inches. Price. 35c

No. 34C1828 Men's patent leather belts, 1¼ inches wide. **Color, black only.** Sizes, 30 to 42 inches. Price. 25c

No. 34C1834 Men's Turkish morocco leather belts, braided, 1½ inches wide. **Color, brown only.** Sizes, 30 to 42 inches. Price........ 75c

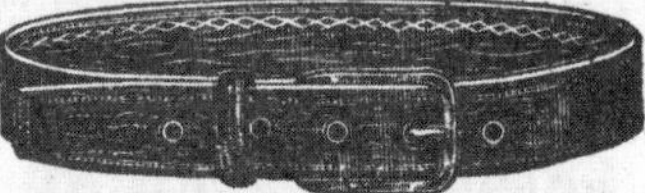

No. 34C1838 Men's Turkish morocco leather belts. **Colors, black or brown.** Sizes, 30 to 42 inches.
Price........ 75c

BOYS' BELTS.

No. 34C1850 Boys' leather belts, 1 inch wide. **Color, tan only.** Sizes, 24 to 30 inches. Price........ 12c

No. 34C1854 Boys' fancy leather belts, 1 inch wide. **Colors, black or brown.** Sizes, 24 to 30 inches.
Price........ 25c

Colored Corner Handkerchiefs or PILLOW TOPS at 7 Cents.

No. 34C1938 Men's Fine Cambric Hemstitched Handkerchiefs. Colored corners and borders.
Price, each... 7c
Per dozen... 75c

No. 34C1940 Fine Cambric Hemstitched Handkerchiefs. A reproduction of America's famous Indian.
Price, each... 7c
Per dozen... 75c

Men's Japanette Handkerchiefs.

No. 34C1958 Japanette Handkerchiefs; hemstitched, colored border.
Price, each... 7c
Per dozen... 75c

Plain White Japanette.

No. 34C1962 Men's Cream White Japanette Handkerchiefs, with 1-inch hemstitched border. Size, 18x18 inches.
Price, per dozen, 75c; each...... 7c
If by mail, postage extra, per doz., 14c.

No. 34C1964 Men's Fancy Excelda Japanette. Colored border in a variety of styles.
Each...... $0.18
Per dozen, 2.00

Men's Initial Handkerchiefs.

No. 34C1970 Japanette Initial Handkerchiefs, with 1-inch hem, cream white with handsome silk embroidered initial.
Each..... $0.09
Per dozen, 1.00

No. 34C1972 Men's Excelda Japanette Handkerchiefs, with handsome silk initial and 1-inch hemstitched border.
Each.... $0.18
Per dozen. 2.00

No. 34C1974 Gentlemen's Fine White Linen Hemstitched Initial Handkerchiefs; an elegant quality, full size and very durable.
Each...... $0.14
Per dozen, 1.50

No. 34C1978 Men's Pure Irish Linen Handkerchiefs, plain white with handsomely embroidered initial.
Each..... $0.23
Per dozen 2.75

No. 34C1982 Men's Fine Pure Linen Handkerchiefs, ¼-inch hemstitched border and embroidered with small finely worked initial.
Each........ $0.35
Per dozen.. 4.00

NOTE—Initial handkerchiefs are made in all initials except I, O, Q, U, V, X, Y, Z

HANDKERCHIEF DEPARTMENT.

MEN'S TURKEY RED HANDKERCHIEFS.

Sold by the dozen only.

No. 34C1900 Size, 18x18 inches.
Per dozen....... 25c

Standard Turkey Red Handkerchiefs.

Sold by the dozen only.
No. 34C1904

Size, 18x17 inches.
Price, per dozen........ 30c
If by mail, postage extra, per doz., 10c.

Size, 21x20 inches.
Price, per dozen........ 40c
If by mail, postage extra, per doz., 14c.

Size, 24x23 inches.
Price, per dozen........ 49c
If by mail, postage extra, per doz., 16c.

Size, 28x26 inches.
Price, per dozen........ 68c
If by mail, postage extra, per doz., 24c.

Indigo Blue Handkerchiefs.

No. 34C1908 Size, 21 inches.
Per dozen.... 49c
If by mail, postage extra, 14c.
Size, 24 inches.
Price, per dozen........ 65c
If by mail, postextra, 16c.

Men's Fancy Blue and Red Handkerchiefs.

Suitable for Pillow Tops, and can be made into Ladies' Kimonas.

Nos. 34C1905-1906
Price, per dozen........ 58c

No. 34C1906 Fancy Indigo Blue Handkerchiefs, 24 inches square.
Per dozen... 58c

No. 34C1905 Men's Fancy Turkey Red Handkerchiefs, 24 inches square.

If by mail, postage extra, per doz., 16c.

Sateen Handkerchiefs.

No. 34C1912 Imported Sateen Handkerchiefs; full size; fine soft finish.
Price, each... 7c
Per dozen... 80c
If by mail, postage extra, per doz., 14c.

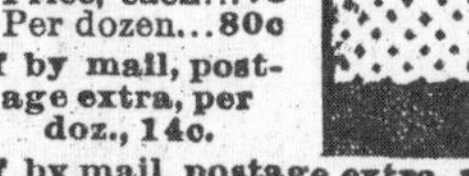

If by mail, postage extra, per dozen on all Men's Handkerchiefs, 14c.

Men's Hemstitched Handkerchiefs, Colored Border.

No. 34C1920 Men's Hemmed Colored Bordered Handkerchiefs, with woven tape borders.
Price, per dozen........ 45c

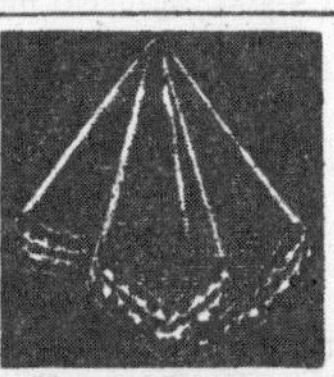

No. 34C1930 Fancy Colored Border Cambric Handkerchiefs. Assorted colors.
Price, per dozen........ 55c

No. 34C1934 Men's Fine Cambric Handkerchiefs. White center, with colored borders.
Price, each... 7c
Per dozen... 75c

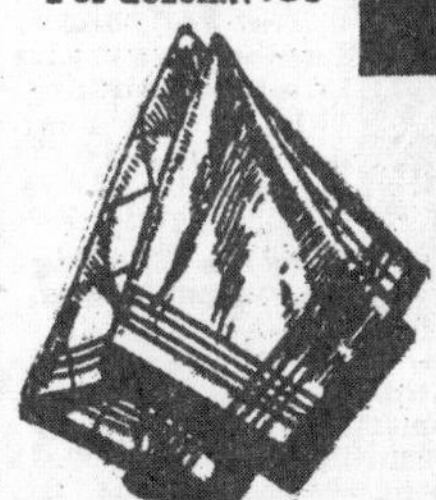

No. 34C1942 Men's Fine Cambric Hemstitched Handkerchiefs. With a colored border and plain white or colored center.
Each.... 10c
Per dozen...... $1.10

No. 34C1946 Men's Hemstitched Handkerchiefs, white centers with handsome and artistic fancy colored borders. Full size, soft and fine.
Each..... $0.15
Per dozen, 1.70

Men's White Cambric Handkerchiefs.

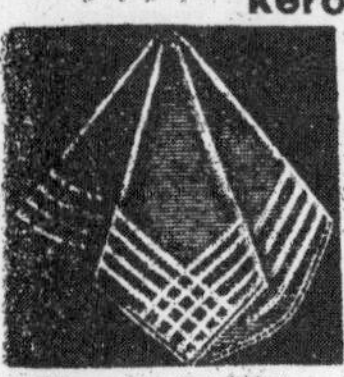

No. 34C1986 Men's Fine Plain White Linen Finish Cambric Handkerchiefs. Plain hem with rib effect tape border, medium size.
Price......4c
Per dozen...45c

No. 34C1990 Men's Large Size Plain White Cambric Handkerchiefs. Size, 21x21 inches. Ribbed pattern borders. A special value.
Price, per dozen, 75c; each.......7c
If by mail, postage extra, per doz., 14c.

No. 34C1994 Men's Hemstitched Handkerchiefs. Made with ½ inch hemstitched hem, with a woven satin border, medium size.

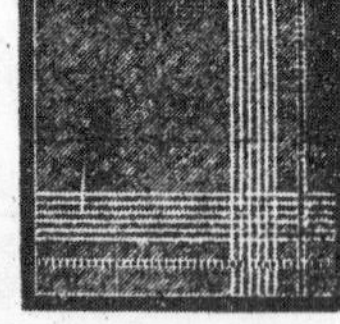

Price, each...8c
Per dozen...90c

MEN'S PLAIN WHITE HEMSTITCHED HANDKERCHIEFS.

No. 34C2012 Men's White Cambric Handkerchiefs. 1-inch hem, medium size, value exceptionally good.
Per dozen......45c
If by mail, postage extra, per doz., 12c.

No. 34C2016 Men's Fine White Cambric Cotton Handkerchiefs, made with 1-inch and ½-inch hemstitched border. Price, each..................6c
Per dozen............................65c
If by mail, postage extra, per doz., 12c.

Men's White Linen Handkerchiefs.

No. 34C2000 Men's Pure Irish Linen Handkerchiefs. Plain white, large size with finished tape borders, the best value possible at this low price.

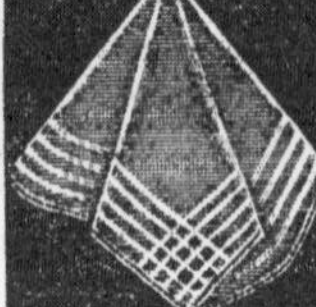

Price, each. $0.11
Per dozen.... 1.25

Extra Size Linen Handkerchiefs.

No. 34C2004 Men's Extra Size Pure Irish Linen Handkerchiefs, plain white, tape effect border and hem. Size, 20x21 inches.
Price, per dozen, $3.00; each....25c

No. 34C2008 Men's Extra Quality White Pure Linen Tape Border Handkerchiefs. Size, 21x21 inches. This is a special grade, light weight and fine.
Price, each $0.35
Per dozen....4.00

MEN'S PLAIN WHITE LINEN HEMSTITCHED HANDKERCHIEFS.

No.	Size	Price, each	Per dozen
34C2030	18x18 inches	$0.11	1.25
34C2032	Full size 18½x18½ inches	$0.15	1.70
34C2034	19x19 inches	$0.16	1.85
34C2038	17x17½ inches	$0.25	2.85
34C2040	18½x18½ inches	$0.25	2.85
34C2042	18½x18½ inches	$0.35	4.00
34C2046	19x19 inches	$0.45	5.00

If by mail, postage extra, 14 cents per dozen, on linen handkerchiefs.

LADIES' HANDKERCHIEFS.

Ladies' Fancy Cotton Handkerchiefs.

No. 34C2050 Ladies' Hemstitched Handkerchiefs, medium size, fancy colored borders, assorted designs, also plain colored borders. Per dozen, 40c
If by mail, postage extra, per doz., 8c.

No. 34C2054 Ladies' Cotton Handkerchiefs, with scalloped edges and printed floral design border.
Price, per doz. 35c
If by mail, postage extra, per dozen, 8 cents.

No. 34C2062 Ladies' Hemstitched Handkerchiefs, with fancy colored border. Printed floral designs in the corners. Price, per doz., 48c
If by mail, postage extra, per doz., 8c.

LADIES' MOURNING HANDKERCHIEFS.

No. 34C2066 Ladies' Black Border Mourning Handkerchiefs, hemstitched cambric.
Price, per doz. 45c
Postage extra, per dozen, 8 cents.

No. 34C2068 Ladies' Fine Imported Cambric Mourning Handkerchiefs.
Price, each... 6c
Per dozen.... 65c
If by mail, postage extra, per dozen, 8 cents.

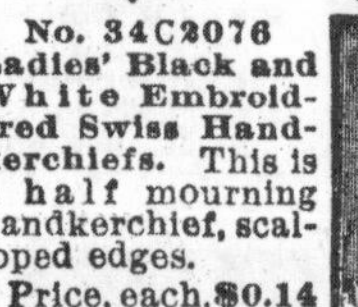

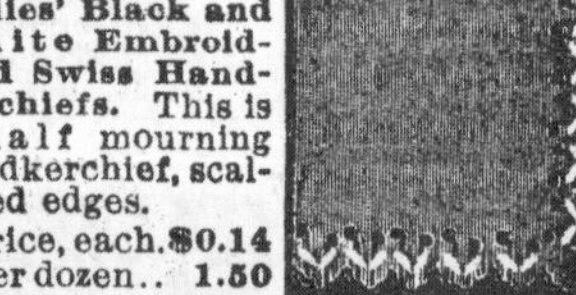

No. 34C2072 Ladies' Fine Imported Linen Mourning Handkerchiefs, with neat ⅛-inch fast black borders.
Price, each, $0.25
Per dozen.. 2.85
Postage extra, per dozen, 8 cents.

No. 34C2076 Ladies' Black and White Embroidered Swiss Handkerchiefs. This is a half mourning handkerchief, scalloped edges.
Price, each. $0.14
Per dozen.. 1.50
If by mail, postage extra, per doz., 8c.

LADIES' PLAIN WHITE HEMSTITCHED HANDKERCHIEFS.

No. 34C2080 Ladies' Fine White Cambric Handkerchiefs, with neat, narrow, hemstitched borders.
Price, per doz. 45c
If by mail, postage extra, per dozen, 7 cents.

No. 34C2084 Ladies' Fine Imported White Cambric Handkerchiefs, with ⅛-inch hemstitched border.
Price, per dozen, 65c; each.......6c
If by mail, postage extra, per doz., 8c.

No. 34C2088 Extra Fine Quality White Linen Finish Cambric Handkerchiefs, with ½-inch hemstitched border and fancy white corded design inside of the border.
Price, per doz. 45c
If by mail, postage extra, per doz., 8c.

LADIES' PLAIN WHITE, IRISH LINEN HEMSTITCHED HANDKERCHIEFS.

No.	Size	Price, each	Per dozen
34C2091	14x14 inches	7c	75c
34C2093	12½x12½ inches	$0.09	1.00
34C2096	13x13 inches	$0.15	1.75
34C2098	13x13 inches	$0.18	2.00
34C2100	13x13 inches	$0.25	2.85
34C2102	13½x13½ inches	$0.30	3.40

If by mail, postage extra, per doz., 8c.

Ladies' Fancy Linen Handkerchiefs.

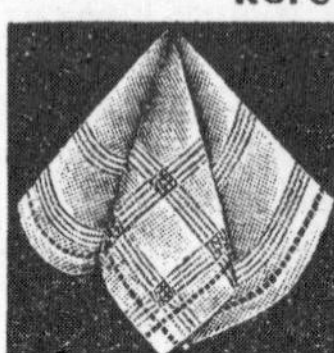

No. 34C2103 Ladies' Fine Pure Linen Hemstitched Handkerchiefs. Plain white with ¼-inch hem and corded design inside of border.
Price, each, $0.13
Per dozen.. 1.50
If by mail, postage extra, per doz., 8c.

Handkerchief Centers.

No. 34C2104 All Linen Handkerchief Centers, Two widths of hem, ⅛ and ¼ inch.
Size, inches. . 6x6
Price, each..... 7c
Per dozen.... 80c
Size, inches... 7x7
Price, each.....8c
Per dozen...... 90c
Size, 9x9 inches. Price, each...$0.09
Per dozen.......................... 1.05

No. 34C2105 All Linen Handkerchief Centers, finer quality than the above number.

Size, inches....	6x6	7x7	9x9
Price, each...	$0.10	$0.12	$0.16
Per dozen....	1.10	1.35	1.85

If by mail, postage extra, each, 1c.

LADIES' INITIAL HANDKERCHIEFS.

NOTICE—Initial Handkerchiefs are made with all letters of the alphabet except I, O, Q, U, V, X, Y and Z.

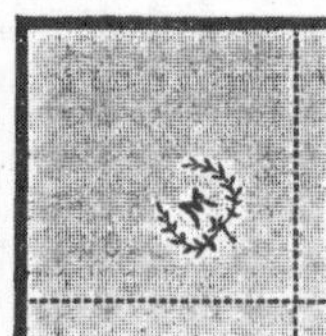

No. 34C2107 Ladies' Cambric Initial Handkerchiefs. One-half inch hemstitched border and a fancy embroidered initial in a wreath in the corner.
Price, each... 5c
Per dozen...55c

No. 34C2108 Ladies' Fine Cambric Initial Handkerchiefs, ⅛-inch hemstitched border and fancy initial.
Price, each...5c
Per dozen...55c

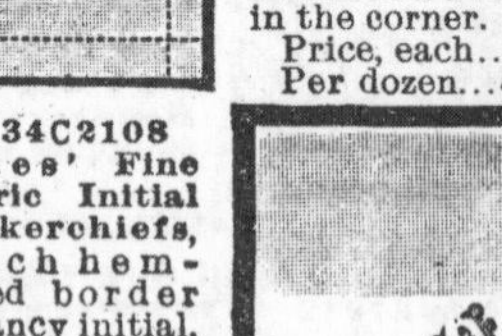

No. 34C2112 Ladies' Fine All Linen Initial Handkerchiefs. One-eighth inch hemstitched border. Each. $0.11
Per dozen.. 1.25

No. 34C2114 Ladies' All Pure Linen Initial Handkerchiefs. One-quarter inch hemstitched border.
Price, each..$0.18
Per dozen......2.00

No. 34C2116 Pure White Irish Linen Initial Handkerchiefs, hemstitched border with white embroidered initial in corner, ⅛-inch hem.
Price, each. $0.25
Per dozen... 2.75
If by mail, postage extra, on all ladies' initial handkerchiefs, per doz., 8c.

Ladies' Swiss Embroidered Handkerchiefs.

No. 34C2120 Ladies' Hemstitched Border Handkerchiefs, with fancy open work figures in corners. An excellent value at our low price.
Price, per doz. 55c

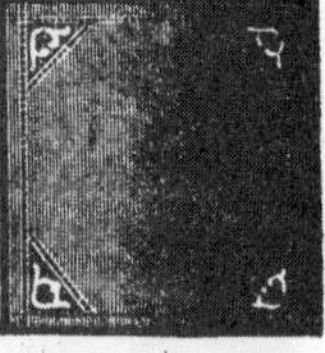

No. 34C2122 Ladies' Fine Swiss Embroidered Handkerchiefs. Hemstitched and embroidered all around edge.
Price, each. 8c
Per dozen. 90c

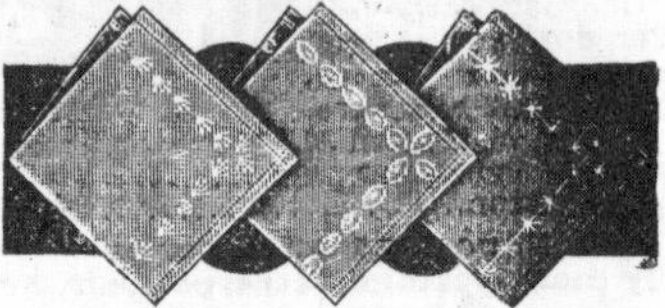

No. 34C2124 Made from Fine Imported Swiss Lawn, hemstitched, and beautifully hand embroidered figures inside border. Price, each........7c
Per dozen...........................80c

No. 34C2128 Ladies' Handkerchiefs, with Marie Antoinette embroidered edges, made in Switzerland.
Price, each.......................$0.12
Per dozen.............................1.35

No. 34C2130 Ladies' New Style Embroidered Lawn Handkerchiefs, ½-inch hem, with embroidery all around center and border.
Each.......$0.12
Per dozen.. 1.35

If by mail, postage extra on all ladies' emdroidered handkerchiefs, per doz., 16c.

Ladies' Fine Swiss Handkerchiefs.

No. 34C2132 Ladies' Fine Swiss Handkerchiefs. Price, each.. $0.15
Per dozen........................ 1.75

No. 34C2136 Ladies' Fine Swiss Embroidered Handkerchiefs, scalloped edges, each handkerchief has silk colored ribbon inserted through the embroidery. They can also be used for corset covers. Blue or pink ribbons.
Price, each..................$0.25
Per dozen........................2.85

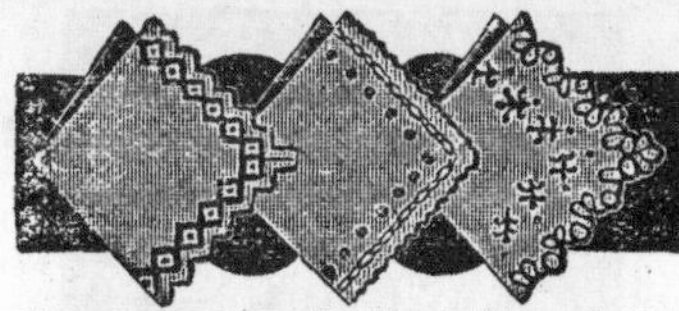

No. 34C2138 Ladies' Fine Swiss Handkerchiefs. Price, each.... $0.20
Per dozen.... 2.35

Something Extra for 35 Cents.

No. 34C2142 Ladies' Extra Fine Swiss Handkerchiefs. Price, each. $0.35
Per dozen.... 4.00

Ladies' Extra Quality Swiss Handkerchiefs.

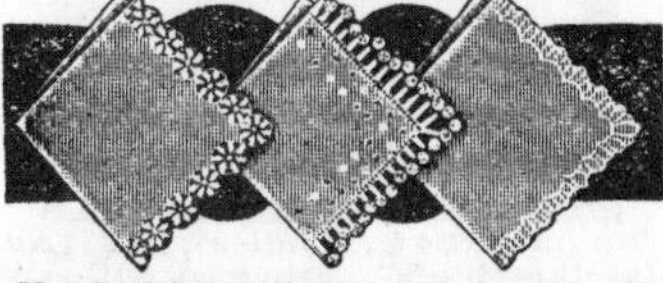

No. 34C2148 Ladies' Extra Quality Swiss Handkerchiefs. Price, each. $0.45
Per dozen.... 5.00

No. 34C2152 Ladies' Extra Quality Fine Swiss Cloth Handkerchiefs.
Price, each.... $0.50
Per dozen.... 5.75

No. 34C2156 Ladies' Extra Quality Fine Swiss Handkerchiefs.
Price, each.... 75c
If by mail, postage extra on all ladies' Swiss handkerchiefs, per doz., 16c.

LADIES' LACE HANDKERCHIEFS.

No. 34C2160 Ladies' Fine Swiss Handkerchiefs, with fancy hemstitched border and lace edge. A very pretty handkerchief. Price, per dozen.... 55c

No. 34C2164 Ladies' Fine Swiss Handkerchiefs, with Valenciennes lace insertion all around. An excellent value.
Price, each, $0.09
Per dozen.. 1.00
Postage, extra, per dozen, 16 cents.

No. 34C2168 Ladies' Fine Swiss Handkerchiefs, with lace all around hem and Valenciennes lace inserted corners.
Each.... 7c
Per dozen, 80c

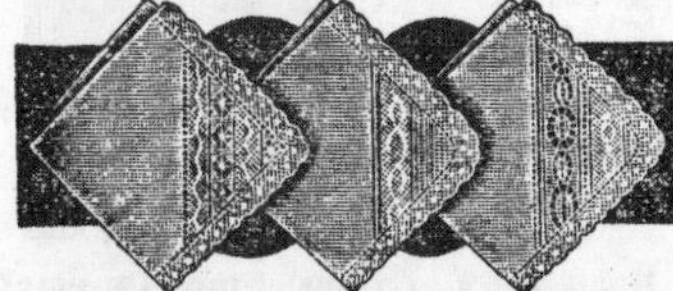

No. 34C2176 Ladies' Fancy Lace Edge and Valenciennes Lace Inserted Corner Handkerchiefs.
Price, per dozen, $1.70; each... 15c
If by mail, postage extra, per doz., 16c.

No. 34C2178 Ladies' Fancy Lace Edge Handkerchiefs.
Price, per dozen, $2.25; each... 20c
If by mail, postage extra, per doz., 16c.

No. 34C2180 Ladies' Fine All Linen Lace Handkerchiefs.
Price, per dozen, $2.75; each.... 25c
If by mail, postage, extra, per doz., 16c.

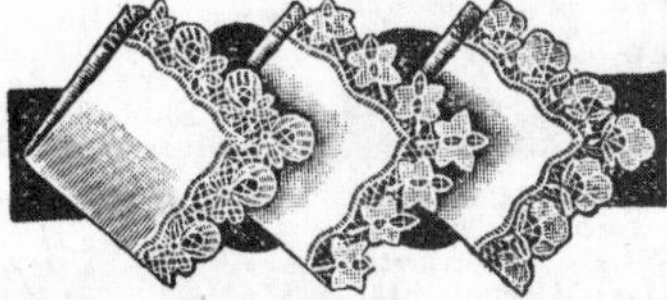

No. 34C2181 Ladies' All Linen Lace Handkerchiefs.
Price, per dozen, $4.50; each.... 40c
If by mail, postage extra, per doz., 16c.

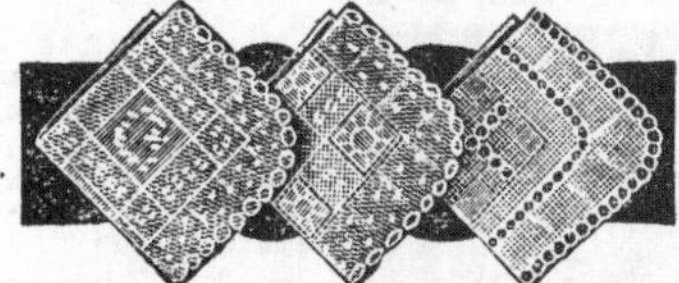

No. 34C2182 Ladies' Fine Swiss Lace Handkerchiefs. Price, each.... $0.35
Per dozen.... 4.00
If by mail, postage extra, per doz., 16c.

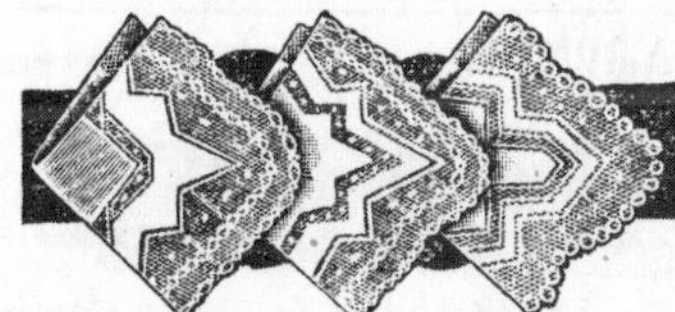

No. 34C2183 Ladies' all Pure Linen Lace Handkerchiefs.
Price, per dozen, $5.75; each.... 50c
If by mail, postage extra, per doz., 16c.

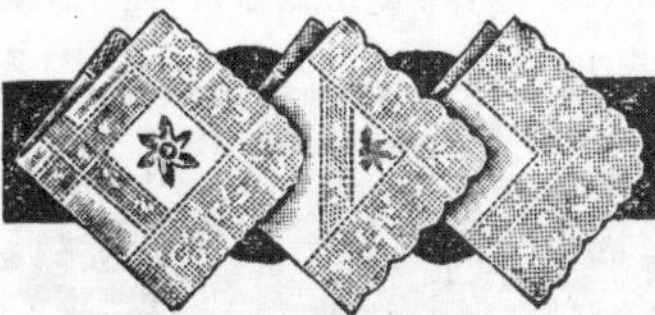

No. 34C2184 Ladies' All Pure Linen Lace Handkerchiefs.
Price, per dozen, $8.50; each.... 75c
If by mail, postage extra, per dozen, 16 cents.

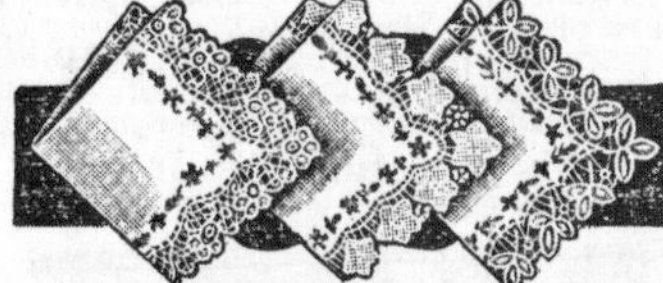

No. 34C2185 Ladies' All Linen Lace Handkerchiefs. Price, each.... $0.85
Per dozen.... 9.00
If by mail, postage extra, per dozen, 16 cents.

No. 34C2190 Ladies' Fine Lace Handkerchiefs. Price, each.... $0.85
Per dozen.... 9.00
If by mail, postage extra, per dozen, 16 cents.

CHILDREN'S HANDKERCHIEFS.

No. 34C2191 Children's Plain White Hemstitched. Cotton Handkerchiefs. Soft and fine with a very neat and narrow hemmed border. Put up three in a fancy box.
Price, per box.... 15c
If by mail, postage extra, per box, 7 cents.

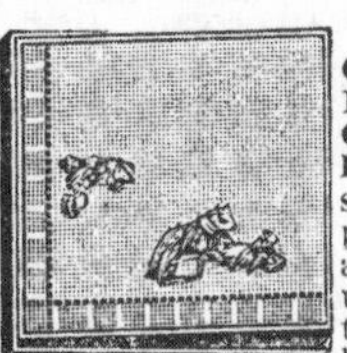

No. 34C2192 Children's Plain White Cambric Handkerchiefs, 1¼-inch hemstitched, soft and fine, closely woven. Good size.
Price, per dozen.. 55c
If by mail, postage extra, each, 1c.

No. 34C2193 Children's Fancy Border Hemmed Cambric Handkerchiefs. Handsome and comic picture designs around border. Put up three in a beautiful box with handsome picture on cover. Price, per box.... 10c
If by mail, postage extra, per box, 4c.

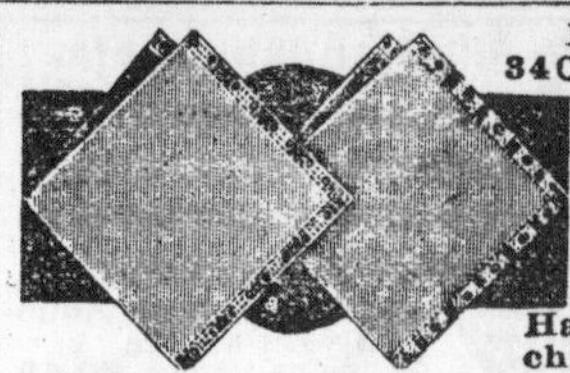

No. 34C2194 Children's Fancy Bordered Hemstitched Handkerchiefs.
Price, per half dozen.... 16c
If by mail, postage extra, 5 cents.

No. 34C2197 Children's Fancy Bordered Hemstitched Handkerchiefs with fancy embroidered initials. They come put up three in a fancy box.

Notice—Initial handkerchiefs are made in all initials except I, O, Q, U, V, X, Y and Z.
Price, per dozen, 90c; each.... 8c
If by mail, postage extra, each, 1c.

No. 34C2198 Children's Cambric Fairy Handkerchiefs, printed in fast colors in an assortment of pictures. Price, per dozen... 45c
If by mail, postage extra, each, 1 cent.

SILK HANDKERCHIEFS.

Postage extra, each, 2 cents; per dozen, 14 cents.
SPECIAL NOTICE—Initial handkerchiefs are made in all initials except I, O, Q, U, V, X, Y and Z.

Men's Initial Handkerchiefs.

No. 34C2206 Men's White Japanese Silk Handkerchief with 1-inch hem. Size, 16 inches.
Price, each, $0.22
Per dozen.... 2.75

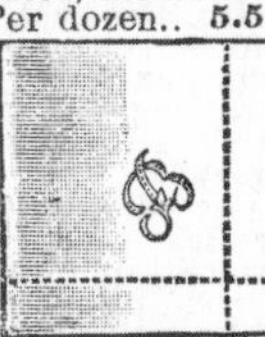

No. 34C2210 Japanese Silk Initial Handkerchiefs. Size, 18½ inches.
Each.... $0.35
Per doz.... 4.00

No. 34C2212 Men's Fine Quality White Japanese Silk Initial Handkerchiefs, Size, 21 inches.
Price, each. $0.50
Per dozen.. 5.50

No. 34C2214 Men's Extra Heavy Pure White Silk Initial Handkerchiefs. Size. 21 inches.
Price, each, $0.75
Per dozen.. 8.50

Men's Plain White Japanese Silk Handkerchiefs.

No. 34C2217 Men's Plain White Hemstitched Silk Handkerchiefs, Size, 15½ inches. with ¾-inch hem.
Price, each, $0.20
Per dozen.... 2.35
If by mail, postage extra, each, 2 cents.

No. 34C2218 Size, 18 inches, with 1-inch hem. Price, each.... $0.25
Price, per dozen.... 2.75
No. 34C2220 Size, 20 inches, 1-inch hem. Price, each.... $0.34
Per dozen.... 4.00
No. 34C2222 Size, 22 inches, 1½-inch hem. Price, each.... $0.50
Per dozen.... 5.50
No. 34C2226 Size, 20 inches, with 1-inch hemstitched border.
Price, per dozen, $5.00; each.... 43c
No. 34C2230 Size, 24 inches.
Price, per dozen, $8.00; each.... 70c

Men's Plain White Twilled Silk Handkerchiefs.

No. 34C2232 Men's Fine Twilled Silk Handkerchiefs. Size, 20 inches, ½-inch hem. Price, each.... $0.45
Per dozen.... 5.00
No. 34C2234 Men's Fine Twilled Silk Handkerchiefs. Size, 23¼ inches, 1½-inch hem. Price, each.... $0.75
Per dozen.... 8.50

Black Silk Handkerchiefs.

No. 34C2238 Men's Plain Black Silk Handkerchiefs, with hemstitched border. Size, 19 in. Price, each. $0.35
Per dozen.... 4.00

Men's Fancy Colored Border Silk Handkerchiefs.

No. 34C2244 Fine Japanese Silk Handkerchief, in 1-inch hemstitched fancy borders in all the latest colorings.
Price, each $0.20
Per dozen.. 2.35

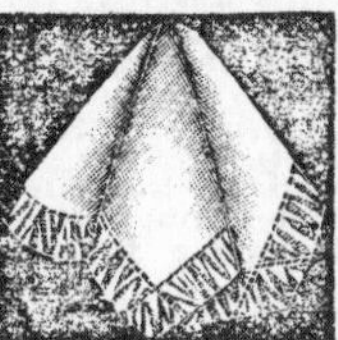

No. 34C2248 Men's Fine Japanese Silk Handkerchiefs, 1-inch hemstitched fancy colored borders.
Price, per dozen, $4.00; each.. 35c

No. 34C2250 Men's Fine Japanese Silk Handkerchiefs, in the latest fancy colored borders, extra heavy silk, 1-inch hem, large size. White center.
Price, ea. $0.50
Per dozen 5.75

No. 34C2252 Men's Japanese Silk Handkerchiefs. 1-inch hemstitched, fancy colored border with plain white centers.
Price, each... $0.40
Per dozen.... 4.50

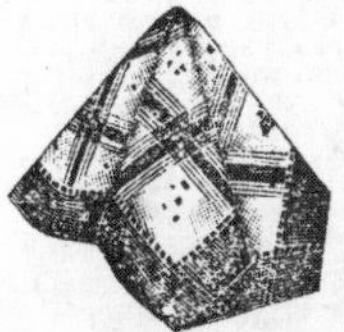

No. 34C2258 Men's Japanese Silk Handkerchiefs, colored plaid centers, red, purple, blue, etc., with hemstitched solid colored borders.
Price, ea. $0.25
Per dozen. 2.85

No. 34C2262 Men's Fancy Silk Handkerchief. fancy 1¼-inch hemstitched. Nicely colored striped centers, with fancy figures.
Price, each. $0.25
Per dozen... 2.85

Men's Silk Handkerchiefs.

No. 34C2264 Men's Fancy Japanese White Silk Handkerchiefs in beautiful fancy 1½-inch hemstitched, ring or polka dot effects in center. Color, blue only. Full size.
Price, each... $0.40
Per dozen.... 4.50

Men's Silk Bandana Handkerchiefs.

No. 34C2276 Men's Fine Japanese Silk Bandanas; red only; hemmed tape border in fancy Persian design, and figured centers. Size, 28 inches.
Price, each. $ 0.90
Per dozen.. 10.00

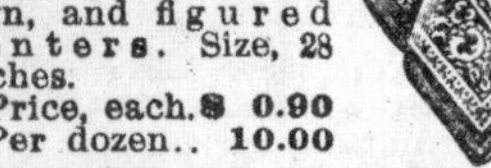

FANCY BROCADED SILK HANDKERCHIEFS.

No. 34C2280 Fancy Brocaded Silk Handkerchiefs, small size, assorted colors.
Price, each.. $0.19
Per dozen.... 2.25

No. 34C2284 Fancy Brocaded Silk Handkerchiefs, in large assortment of colors, blue, red, pink, green, etc.
Price, each.. $0.25
Per dozen.... 2.85

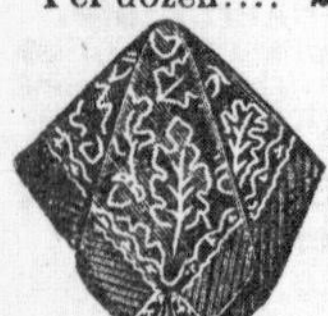

No. 34C2288 Fancy Brocaded Silk Handkerchiefs, in pretty new effects, in red, blue, green, pink, etc., and medium dark colors.
Price, each.. $0.35
Per dozen.... 4.00

No. 34C2292 Fine Silk Brocaded Handkerchiefs. Large size; richly brocaded in new and beautiful effects in fancy colors; also all black or all cream white.
Price, each.. $0.42
Per dozen... 5.00

No. 34C2296 Extra Fine Silk Brocaded Handkerchiefs. Large size, heavy, richly brocaded in new designs, including the combined floral and stripe effects.
Price, each.. $0.50
Per dozen.... 5.75

If by mail, postage extra, each, 1c; per dozen, 10 cents.

LADIES' SILK HANDKERCHIEFS.

If by mail, postage extra, each, 1 cent.

No. 34C2300 Ladies' White Japanese White Silk Handkerchiefs. ⅛-inch hemstitched. Size, 11 inches. All letters except I, O, Q, U, V, X, Y and Z.
Price, each. $0.14
Per dozen.. 1.50

No. 34C2304 Ladies' Japanese White Silk Handkerchiefs. Hemstitched border, size 16 inches. All letters except I, O, Q, U, V, X, Y and Z.
Price, each....... 23c
Per dozen.................... $2.75

Ladies' Fancy Silk Embroidered Handkerchiefs.

No. 34C2308 Fine Imported White Silk Handkerchiefs. Scalloped edges and contrasting colored silk embroidery, pink, blue, lilac, olive, cardinal, etc.
Price, each 7c
Per dozen 75c

No. 34C2312 Ladies' Pure Silk Handkerchiefs. Cream white, scalloped and embroidered borders, delicate colorings. 10 x 10 in.
Price, ea.. $0.15
Per dozen. 1.70

No. 34C2316 Very Rich and Attractive Pure Silk Handkerchiefs. Cream white silk embroidery, scalloped edges, artistic open work designs. Each, $0.20
Per dozen, 2.25

No. 34C2324 Ladies' Pure White Japanese Handkerchiefs. Scalloped edge. The embroidery is of silk. All pure white. Price, each $0.35
Per dozen, 4.00

No. 34C2334 Ladies' Fine White Silk Handkerchiefs, scalloped edges, in new and beautiful designs.
Price, ea. $0.40
Per doz... 4.50

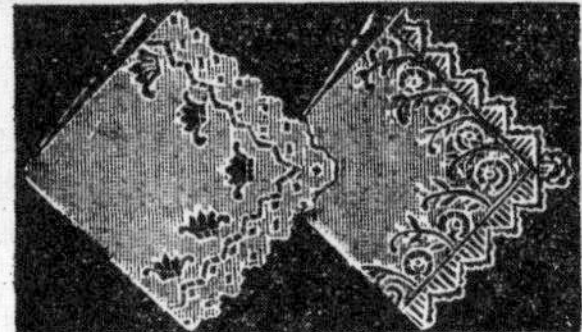

No. 34C2338 Ladies' Fine Quality White Silk Handkerchiefs in beautiful floral and scroll designs.
Price, per dozen, $5.75; each.. 50c

No. 34C2342 Ladies' Fine Quality Swiss Embroidered Silk Handkerchiefs. Embroidered in pure white. Openwork Swiss designs.
Price, ea. $0.75
Per doz.. 8.50

No. 34C2344 Ladies' Silk Lace Handkerchiefs. Trimmed with silk lace in most beautiful designs.
Price, per dozen, $8.50; each.. 75c
If by mail, postage extra, each, 2c.

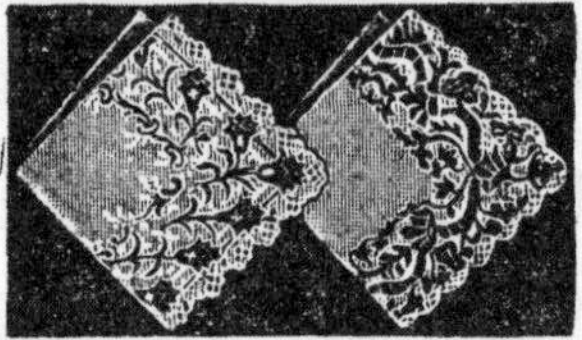

No. 34C2346 Ladies' Finest Quality White Silk Handkerchiefs, embroidered in elaborate floral effect and open work designs.
Price, per doz., $11.40; each, $1.00

GLOVE DEPARTMENT

OUR GLOVE DEPARTMENT IS ONE OF THE LARGEST IN THIS COUNTRY.

How to Fit a Kid Glove.

In order that satisfactory wear may be had from a kid glove, it is very necessary that it should be put on right the first time. First push the fingers in, leaving out the thumb, and work them into place by rubbing from the tips downward. **Do not press down between the fingers.** Insert the thumb and apply same method as used with fingers; then push the glove on up the hand. **Do not pull by taking hold at wrist, as this destroys the shape. Remember your gloves will give lasting service if fitted right the first time.**

How to Measure Hand for Size of Glove.

Draw a tape around the knuckles, as shown in the illustration. Ladies' kid gloves are not made in sizes larger than size 8, and in fancy colors or the finest qualities do not run larger than 7½.

Ladies' kid glove sizes are as follows: 6, 6¼, 6½, 6¾, 7, 7¼, 7½, 7¾ and 8. **Always give color and size.**

Ladies' F. W. L. French Kid Gloves, 95c.

No. 33C27 Ladies' F. W. L. French Kid Gloves, made with two clasps, perfect stitching and embroidered backs. Sizes, 6 to 8. Colors, black, white, reddish brown, tan, seal brown or gray. Price, per pair.................... 95c
If by mail, postage extra, per pair, 2 cents.

LA ROME FRENCH KID GLOVES.

No. 33C28 Ladies' La Rome French Kid Gloves; made with the new Paris filet hand made embroidery. Three clasps, gusseted fingers. The skins for the La Rome gloves are specially selected, being soft and pliable, and it has no superior in fit, wear and durability. Colors, black, tan, brown or white. Sizes, 6 to 8.
Price, per pair.................... $1.40
If by mail, postage extra, per pair. 2c.

BERENICE FRENCH KID GLOVES, $1.35.

No. 33C30 The Berenice Gloves have a world wide reputation as being the best of imported genuine kid gloves. Select light weight kid skins, extremely elastic and pliable, retaining their shape better than any other glove. **Finely stitched and finished;** embroidered backs. French gusseted thumbs, three clasps. Colors, black, white, seal brown, reddish brown, tan or gray. Sizes, 6 to 8 only.
Price, per pair.................... $1.35
If by mail, postage extra, per pair, 2c.

Genuine Chevrier Washable Kid Gloves for $1.50.

PIQUE SEWN.

No. 33C32 Ladies' Best Washable Kid Gloves. Made by Felix Chevrier of Grenoble, France, from the most select and best kid skins obtainable. Slightly heavier than the regular weight ladies' kid gloves. The best that we can obtain. Embroidered backs and full pique sewing, two clasps. A more perfect fitting or better wearing glove is not to be had. **Every pair warranted,** and we will replace with new gloves if found defective. Colors, white, tan or black. Sizes, 6 to 8 only.
Price, per pair.................... $1.50
If by mail, postage extra, per pair, 2c.

F. W. L. Foster Hook Lacing Kid Gloves 95 Cents.

No. 33C36 Ladies' Four-Hook Lacing Dressed Kid Gloves. Cable sewn. Foster lacing, made of fine quality French dressed stock and will give good satisfaction. Embroidered backs and French gusseted thumbs. Colors, black, white, seal brown or reddish brown, tan or gray. Sizes, 6 to 8.
Price, per pair.................... 95c
If by mail, postage extra, per pair, 2c.

LA ROME French Kid Gloves for $1.40.

No. 33C38 Ladies' La Rome Genuine French Kid Gloves, made with four-hook Foster lacing, cable sewn. Fine, selected stock. Will retain its shape better than any other glove. Embroidered backs, French gusseted thumbs. Color, black only. Sizes, 6 to 8.
Price, per pair.................... $1.40
If by mail, postage extra, per pair, 2c.

Our Special Ladies' Undressed Kid Gloves, 80 Cents.

No. 33C45 Ladies' Genuine Undressed Kid Gloves. Embroidered backs, two clasps. We warrant this glove to be perfect and give entire satisfaction. Colors, black, light or dark brown. Sizes, 6 to 8.
Price, per pair.................... $0.80
Per dozen pairs.................... 9.00
If by mail, postage extra, per pair, 2c.

Ladies' Genuine Undressed Kid or Mocha $1.10 Gloves.

No. 33C46 Ladies' Fine Quality Genuine Mocha Gloves, soft as silk velvet. One of the most satisfactory gloves made. Finest imported Mocha stock, similar to suede, but much heavier in weight. Three rows of silk embroidery in back, two snap buttons. Pique sewn, French gusseted thumbs. **Very stylish and dressy.** Colors, black, brown or gray. Sizes, 6 to 8. **Do not forget size.**
Price, per pair.................... $1.10
If by mail, postage extra, per pair, 2c.

For Heavy Winter Gloves and Mittens

Write for our free special Glove Catalogue.

Ladies' Chamois Gloves, 75 Cents.

No. 33C54 Ladies' Fine Imported Chamois Gloves, soft and durable, made with two snap buttons and delicate embroidery on backs. Colors, white or buff. Sizes, 6 to 8 only.
Price, per pair.................... 75c
If by mail, postage extra, per pair, 2c.

Ladies' Gauntlet Driving Gloves, 75 Cents.

No. 33C60 Ladies' Gauntlet Driving Gloves made of good quality domestic kid. Three point stitched backs and patent snap buttons. Colors, tan, brown or black. Sizes, 6 to 8½. One size larger than the regular kid glove, is most satisfactory for a driving glove.
Price, per pair.................... 75c
If by mail, postage extra, per pair, 4c.

Ladies' Kid Gauntlet Driving Gloves, $1.10.

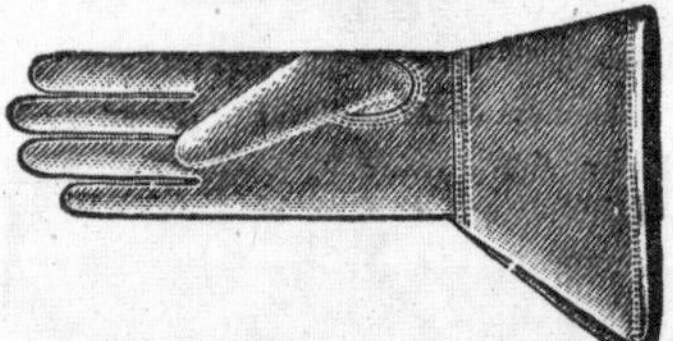

No. 33C62 Ladies' Fine Gauntlet Driving Gloves, made of fine imported stock. Embroidered backs. We expressly recommend this quality. Colors, tan, brown or black. Sizes, 6 to 8½. Price, per pair.......... $1.10
If by mail, postage extra, per pair, 4c.

Our $1.60 Ladies' Buckskin Gauntlet Driving Glove.

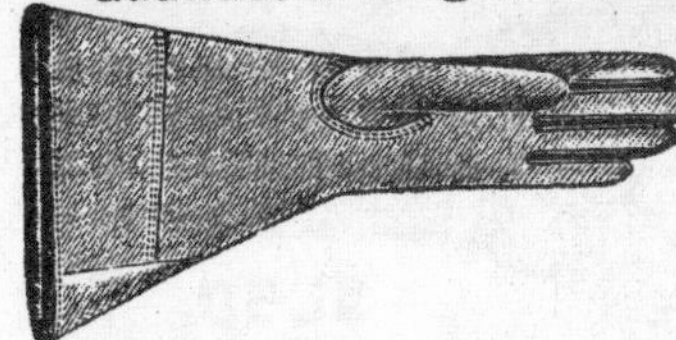

No. 33C64 Ladies' Fine Gauntlet Glove, made of select light weight Plymouth buckskin. Embroidered backs. This is the most stylish driving glove made for ladies' use; a fine fitting glove and one of the most durable kind. Sizes, 6, 6½, 7, 7½, 8 and 8½.
Price, per pair........ ....$1.60
If by mail, postage extra, per pair, 4c.

LADIES' SILK AND FABRIC GLOVES.

Sizes, 6, 6½, 7, 7½, 8 and 8½.

Our Special Silk Gloves, 75c.

No. 33C99 Ladies' Two-Clasp Pure Silk Glove. Guaranteed all pure Milanese silk. Genuine double tipped fingers. Embroidered backs. Colors, black or white. Sizes, 6 to 8½.
Price, per pair........................75c
If by mail, postage extra, per pair, 1c

Our 45c Leader Silk Glove.

No. 33C102 Ladies' Pure Silk Glove with two patent clasps, nice quality and **double tipped fingers.** Embroidered backs. Colors, black or white. Sizes, 6 to 8½ only.
Price, per pair........................45c
If by mail, postage extra, per pair, 1c.

Ladies' Lisle Thread Gloves.

No. 33C104 Ladies' Extra Fine Quality Lyonnaise Lisle Glove, made of finest imported lisle, embroidered backs, 2 pearl clasps. This is the best quality of lisle glove we carry. Colors, white, slate or mode. Sizes, 6 to 8½.
Price, per dozen, $4.50; per pair, 40c
If by mail, postage extra, per pair, 1c.

Ladies' Lisle Thread Gloves, 22 Cents.

No. 33C106 Ladies' Very Fine Lyonnaise Suede Lisle Gloves, with embroidered backs. An especial quality at this low price. Two clasps. Colors, black or white. Sizes, 6 to 8½ only. Price, per pair..............22c
If by mail, postage extra, per pair, 1c.

Ladies' Lisle Gloves, 12 Cents.

No. 33C107 Ladies' Lisle Gloves. Plain wrists, three rows of stitching on backs. Colors, black, white or gray only. Sizes, 6 to 8½; black, to size 9.
Price, per pair........................12c
If by mail, postage extra, per pair, 1c.

Ladies' Elbow Length Silk Gloves.

No. 33 C 108 Ladies' Pure Silk Glove, elbow length. Silk embroidered backs, elbow length. Colors, white or black only. Sizes, 6 to 8½.
Price, per pair........................45c
If by mail, postage extra, 2 cents.

No. 33 C 109 Ladies' Pure Silk Elbow Length Glove, double tipped fingers. Colors are plain black or white, with three rows of silk stitching on the back, elbow length, which will be very much in demand this season. Sizes, 6 to 8½. Price, per pair.....70c
If by mail, postage extra, 2 cents.

Girls' or Misses' Plain Lisle Gloves, 14 Cents.

No. 33C117 Girls' or Misses' Lisle Gloves. Plain wrists, three rows silk stitching in back. Colors, slate or white only. State age in order, or glove size measured as for kid gloves. For ages 6 to 14 years.
Price, per pair........ ....14c
If by mail, postage extra, per pair, 1c.

LADIES' PLAIN SILK MITTS.

No. 33C125 Ladies' Semi-Milanese Pure Silk Mitt, 10½ inches long, glove embroidery on back and inserted thumb. Colors, black or white; an especially strong value.
Price, per pair........................23c
If by mail, postage extra, 1 cent.

Ladies' Silk Mitts, 35 Cents.

No. 33C127 Ladies' Heavy Milanese Pure Silk Mitt, 11 inches long, glove embroidery on back and inserted thumb. Color, black only. This quality is equal to the regular 50-cent mitts at retail. Price, per pair........35c
If by mail, postage extra, 1 cent.

Ladies' Elbow Length Plain Silk Mitts, 50 Cents.

No. 33C131 Ladies' Pure Silk Mitts, elbow length, silk embroidery on the back, inserted thumb. Colors, black or white. Price, per pair....50c
If by mail, postage extra, 2 cents.

BOYS' UNLINED WORKING GLOVES.

Boys' Unlined Gauntlet Gloves.

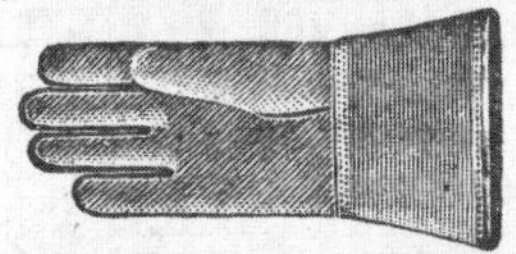

No. 33C344 Boys' Unlined Gauntlet Gloves. Calfskin palms, welted seams, large gauntlet cuffs. Ages, 8 to 14 years.
Price, per pair........................40c
If by mail, postage extra, per pair, 4c.

Boys' Unlined Sheepskin Gloves, 35 Cents.

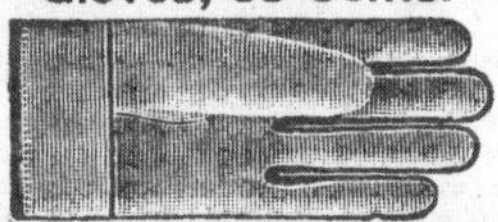

No. 33C346 Boys' Unlined, Band Top, Sheepskin Gloves, stitched backs, string fasteners. Ages, 8 to 14 years.
Price, per pair........................35c
If by mail, postage extra, per pair, 4c.

Boys' Unlined Buckskin Gloves, 50 Cents.

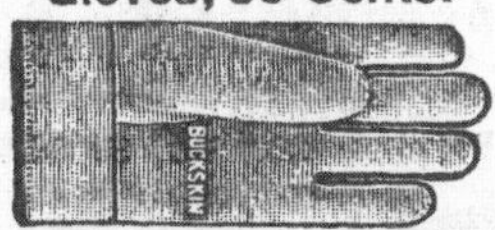

No. 33C348 Boys' Unlined Buckskin Gloves, band tops, string fasteners, embroidered backs. Ages, 8 to 14 years. Price, per pair..............50c
If by mail, postage extra, per pair, 4c.

MEN'S KID GLOVES.

How to Measure Size of Glove.

Draw a tape line around the knuckles, as shown in the illustration. Size is by inches.
Postage extra on men's kid gloves, 6 cents.

Men's Fine Kid Gloves, 85c.

No. 33C364 Men's Imported Stock Kid Gloves, fine dress finish, medium weight, with pique sewn back and patent buttons. **Stitched with silk throughout. All the new shades,** brown and tan. Sizes, 7¼ to 10½.
Price, per pair........................85c

Men's Fine Kid Gloves, $1.00.

No. 33C366 Men's Fine Kid Gloves, made from select imported stock. One clasp, pique sewn, gusset between fingers, three rows narrow stitching on back. **A staple glove.** Colors, black, brown or tan. Always state color and size in order. Sizes, 7¼ to 10½ only. Per pair...........$1.00

Men's Outseam Heavy Kid Gloves, $1.00.

No. 33C371 Men's Fine Heavy Cape Domestic Kid Gloves. This glove is a heavy kid glove. Outseam. Snap fastener at the wrist. Three rows of stitching on the back, and is what is called a gentleman's walking glove, being a heavier glove than the regular kid glove, and will give excellent satisfaction. Color, reddish brown. Sizes, from 7 to 10½. Price, per pair...$1.00
If by mail, postage extra, per pair, 4c.

MEN'S UNDRESSED KID OR MOCHA GLOVES.

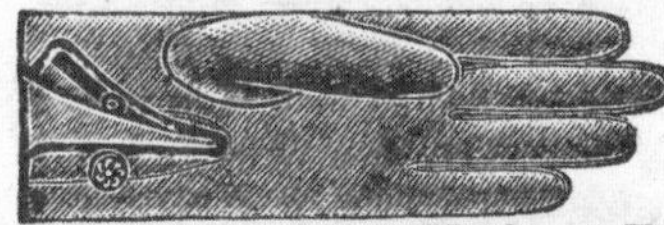

No. 33C376 Men's Mocha or Undressed Kid Gloves of good quality, **pique** sewn, three rows narrow stitching on back, one clasp. Colors, brown, tan or gray. Sizes, 7¼ to 10½ only.
Price, per pair....................$1.00
If by mail, postage extra, per pair, 4c.

Men's Genuine Undressed Kid or Mocha Gloves, $1.25.

No. 33C378 Men's Finest Genuine Mocha Gloves. The best quality mocha glove that you can buy. Real mocha skins remain soft always and have a fine velvet like surface. Three narrow rows of stitching on back, **pique sewn,** English thumb, one clasp. We warrant every pair against manufacturer's defects. Colors, brown, tan or gray. Sizes, 7¼ to 10½.
Price, per pair... ....$1.25
If by mail, postage extra, per pair, 4c.

Men's Fine Reindeer Mocha Gloves, $1.35.

No. 33C380 Men's Best Quality Reindeer Dress Gloves. Surface is the same as fine mocha, but skin is much heavier than No. 33C378. **Stitched outseam,** one clasp and spear back. Strictly high grade and every pair warranted against manufacturer's imperfections. A fine walking glove. Many use them for driving. Color, dark tan, or gray. Sizes, 7¼ to 10½ only.
Price, per pair....................$1.35
If by mail, postage extra, per pair, 4c.

MEN'S DRIVING GLOVES.

No. 33C390 Men's Medium Heavy Weight Driving Gloves, with silk stitched backs, patent snap buttons, outseams and silk sewed throughout. Sizes, 8 to 10½. **Medium dark color.** Price, per pair. **45c**
If by mail, postage extra, per pair, 3 cents.

Special Fire and Water Resisting Horsehide Driving Gloves, 79 Cents.

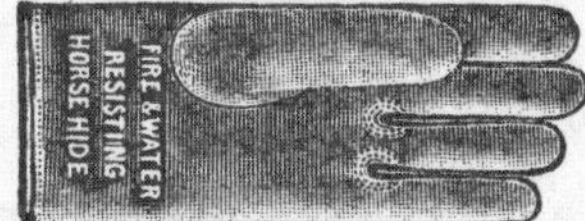

No. 33C391 Men's Genuine Horsehide Driving Gloves. The leather used in making this glove is of the best known fire and water proof tannage, and genuine horsehide of special selection. Warranted to remain pliable in any climate and to be proof against heat, steam, boiling or cold water. Inseams. **Every pair warranted.** Retail price is $1.00 for gloves that are frequently not as good. Sizes, 8, 8½, 9, 9½, 10, 10½. **We warrant every pair.**
Per pair........................$0.79
Per dozen pairs....................9.00
If by mail, postage extra, per pair, 4 cents.

Our Special Buckskin Driving Gloves, $1.25.

No. 33C392 Men's Highest Grade Genuine Plymouth Buckskin Gloves. Made from the most carefully selected buckskin obtainable; soft as velvet, medium weight, gussets between fingers, and snap button fasteners. **Superior to all others for driving and excelled by none in workmanship and fit.** Sizes, 8 to 10½.
Price, per pair....................$1.25
If by mail, postage extra, per pair, 4c.

MEN'S UNLINED WORKING GLOVES.

BUCKSKIN WORKING GLOVES.

All deerskins are more or less scarred. They become scratched while the animal is running wild, or by dragging over the ground after the deer has been killed. The scratch, break or crack is not usually very deep, only the outer grain is broken. The "true skin," or fibrous portion, is not injured, **so the wearing quality of the leather is not materially hurt.** It is, therefore, seldom that buckskin gloves do not bear scratches.

Genuine Saranac Drab Buckskin Gloves, 50 Cents.

No. 33C394 Men's Genuine Drab Buckskin Gloves. Steamproof, regular weight, welt seams and stitched backs, sewed with waxed linen thread and patent string fasteners. Guaranteed genuine buckskin.
Price, per pair........................50c
If by mail, postage extra, per pair, 7c.

Saranac Drab Buckskin Gloves

No. 33C396 Ira Parker's Medium Weight Drab Buckskin Gloves. Unlined, welt seams, sewed with waxed linen thread, patent string fasteners and stitched backs. Per pair... 80c
If by mail, postage extra, per pair, 7c

Men's Fine Saranac Drab Buckskin Gloves, $1.00.

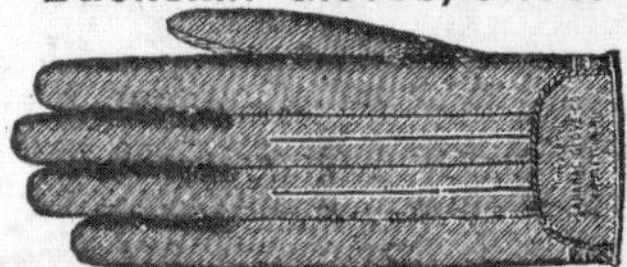

No. 33C398 Men's Fine Saranac Buckskin Gloves. Made from selected skins, medium weight, welt seams, stitched back, patent fasteners, warranted to remain soft and pliable. Sizes, 8 to 10½. Price, per pair. $1.00
If by mail, postage extra, per pair, 9c.

Genuine Saranac Yellow Buckskin Gloves, 60c.

No. 33C400 Ira Parker's Steam and Waterproof Guaranteed Saranac Buckskin Gloves. Regular weight and very strong; unlined. Sewed with waxed linen thread and fitted with string fasteners. Sizes, 8 to 10½.
Price, per pair....................$0.60
Price, per dozen pairs........ 7.00
If by mail, postage extra, per pair, 7c.

Genuine Saranac Yellow Buckskin Gloves, 80c.

No. 33C402 Heavy Weight, Ira Parker's Genuine Oil Tanned Unlined Saranac Heavy Buckskin Gloves. Stitched backs. Sewed throughout with waxed linen thread. Patent string fasteners, the best fasteners known. Sizes, 8 to 10½.
Price, per pair....................80c
If by mail, postage extra per pair, 7c.

Buckskin Gloves, 98 Cents.

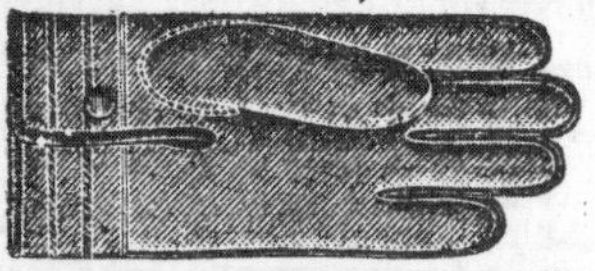

No. 33C404 Men's Fine, Soft Dressed Buckskin Gloves. Medium weight, fine welt stitched backs, set in thumbs and patent front snap buttons; soft and pliable and warranted in every way. Sizes, 8 to 10¼.
Price, per pair....................98c
If by mail, postage extra, per pair, 7c.

Heavy Plymouth Buckskin Gloves, $1.25.

No. 33C406 Men's Heavy Plymouth Buckskin Gloves, made with patent button fastener and welt seams. A strong, durable glove. Sizes, 8 to 10½ only. Price, per pair..$1.25
If by mail, postage extra, per pair, 7c.

Extra Heavy Buck Gloves, $1.15.

No. 33C412 Men's Extra Heavy and Thick Buck Gloves, made with durable riveted thumb and reinforced palm. A good glove to handle stone, hedges or any kind of rough work. Sizes, 9, 9½ and 10.
Price, per pair....................$ 1.15
Per dozen pairs....................13.00
If by mail postage extra, per pair, 10c.

Men's Canvas Gloves.

Owing to the low price we quote on canvas gloves we can furnish only by the dozen pairs.

Men's Heavy Canvas Gloves, made of bleached canvas, band wrist, full shape and well made.

No. 33C444 6-ounce Canvas Gloves. Price, per dozen pairs....60c

No. 33C445 8-ounce Canvas Gloves. Price, per dozen pairs....80c

Men's Leather Tipped Canvas Gloves.

No. 33C446 Men's Heavy Ten-ounce Canvas Gloves. Fingers and thumb tipped with leather reinforcing, making it a very durable glove.
Price, per dozen pairs.......$1.00
Postage extra, per dozen pairs, 30c.

Men's White Napa Goat Gloves

No. 33C452 Men's Extra Selected White Unlined Napa Tanned Goatskin Gloves, extra well made and sewed, cord backs and patent string fasteners. Soft and pliable, wide band tops. Price, per pair............$0.35
Per dozen pairs....................4.00
If by mail, postage extra, per pair, 5c.

HOGSKIN GLOVES.

New Process Tannage.

No. 33C453 Men's Heavy Hogskin Gloves, tanned under new process, making it one of the toughest gloves sold. We can recommend it for a strong, serviceable glove at a low price. Price, per pair..............40c
If by mail, postage extra, per pair, 5 cents.

Men's Heavy Calfskin Gloves, 40 Cents.

No. 33C454 Men's Heavy Working Glove with an all calfskin palm, with heavy muleskin back, welted seams throughout, double stitched and patented string fastener on the back. Good, durable glove, unlined.
Price, per pair....................$0.40
Per dozen pairs....................4.50
If by mail, postage extra, per pair, 6c.

Men's Horsehide Unlined Gloves, 50 Cents.

No. 33C456 Men's Horsehide Saranac tan, double stitched, welt seams and patent string fastener on the back. This glove is good weight, and we consider it one of our best values in a working glove. Price, per pair.........50c
If by mail, postage extra, per pair, 6c.

Men's Small Size Gloves.

No. 33C457 Men's Gloves. Small sizes for men with small or short, thick hands to fit. Sizes, 7½, 8, 8½. Fire and waterproof tannage; cord fasteners at wrists. A reliable glove at a low price.
Price, per pair....................45c
If by mail, postage extra, per pair, 4c.

Special Fire and Water Resisting Horsehide Gloves, 79c.

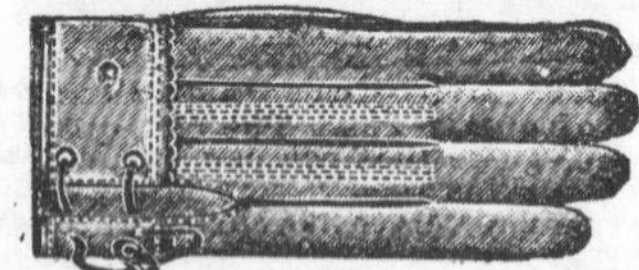

No. 33C464 Unlined Horsehide Gloves. Fire and water proof. This glove is made of the same quality of selected horsehide as our No. 33C482 gauntlet glove. **The best glove made for teamsters, railroad men, engineers, firemen, farmers, ranchmen and laborers.** A glove that has withstood the severest tests, and **we warrant every pair to give entire satisfaction.** Warranted to remain soft and pliable in any climate and to be proof against heat, steam, boiling or cold water. Welt sewn, banded wrists and cord fasteners. You will pay $1.00 for gloves at retail not as good as this one. Our price is the lowest, and quality the best. Sizes, 8, 8½, 9, 9½, 10 and 10½. Price, per pair..........$0.79
Per dozen pairs....................9.00
If by mail, postage extra, per pair, 6c.

Special Horsehide Gloves.

No. 33C468 Men's Special Horsehide Gloves, fire and waterproof and warranted to remain soft and pliable. Made with patent seamless fingers. Seams are on back and reinforced with extended welt. Band tops, string fasteners. Price, per pair..............$0.79
Per dozen pairs....................9.00
If by mail, postage extra, per pair, 6c.

Men's Horsehide Gauntlet Gloves, 80 Cents.

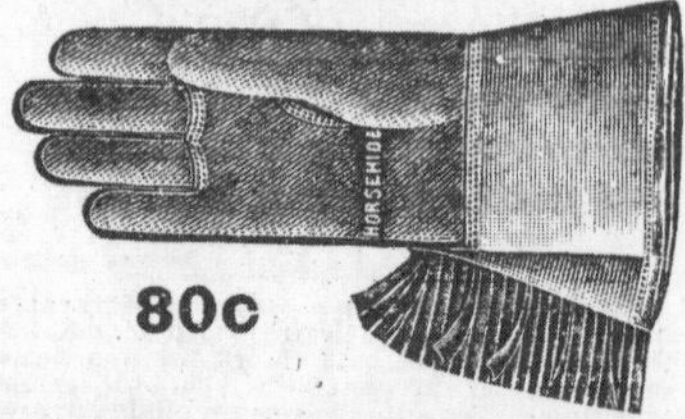

No. 33C474 Men's Horsehide Unlined Gauntlet Gloves. Made from selected stock of specially tanned horsehide, and warranted to remain soft and pliable, and will resist steam, and water. Gauntlets trimmed with fringe, and reinforced thumb. Sizes, 8 to 10½.
Price, per pair....................80c
If by mail, postage extra, per pair, 9 cents.

Men's Goatskin Gloves, 40c.

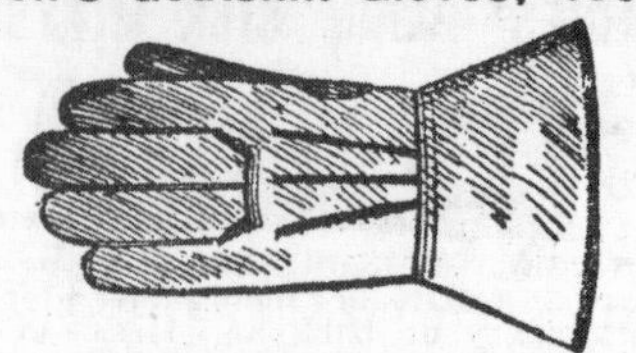

No. 33C476 Men's Goatskin Gloves. Genuine Napa tanned goatskin, fancy overstitched backs, wide gauntlet wrists. Price, per pair...40c
If by mail, postage extra, 8 cents.

Electric Tan Fireproof Gauntlets, 50 Cents.

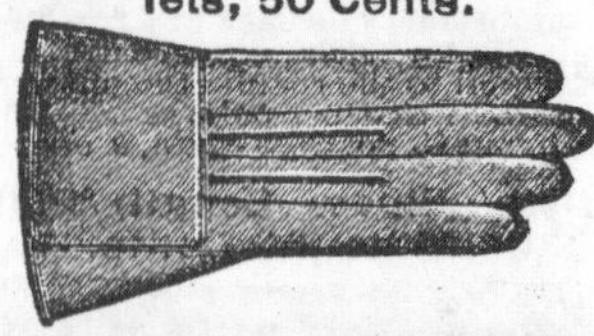

No. 33C480 Men's Fire and Waterproof Electric Tan Gauntlet Gloves. Medium heavy weight that will not get hard and stiff. **Extra reinforced around thumbs.** A very good glove that is sure to prove satisfactory. Sizes, small, medium and large.
Price, per pair....................$0.50
Per dozen pairs....................5.75
If by mail, postage extra, per pair, 8c.

SPECIAL FIRE AND WATER RESISTING HORSEHIDE GAUNTLET GLOVES, 79 CENTS.

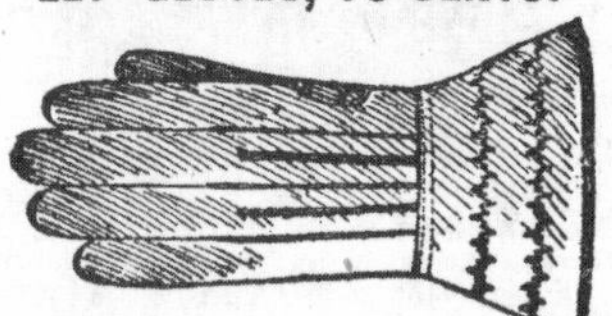

No. 33C482 Unlined Gauntlet Gloves; fire and water proof; genuine horsehide. Under this number we offer the best glove made for **teamsters, farmers, brakemen, engineers, firemen, ranchmen, laborers, everybody whose work is severe on the hands.** The leather used in making this glove is of the best known fire and water proof tannage and genuine horsehide of special selection. Warranted to remain pliable in any climate and to be proof against heat, steam, boiling or cold water. Welted sewn, reinforced thumbs. **Every pair warranted.** Retail price is $1.00 for gloves that are frequently not as good. Sizes, 8, 8½, 9, 9½, 10 and 10½. **We warrant every pair.** Price, per pair............$0.79
Per dozen pairs....................9.00
If by mail, postage extra, per pair, 9c.

Men's Horsehide Gauntlet Driving Gloves, $1.00.

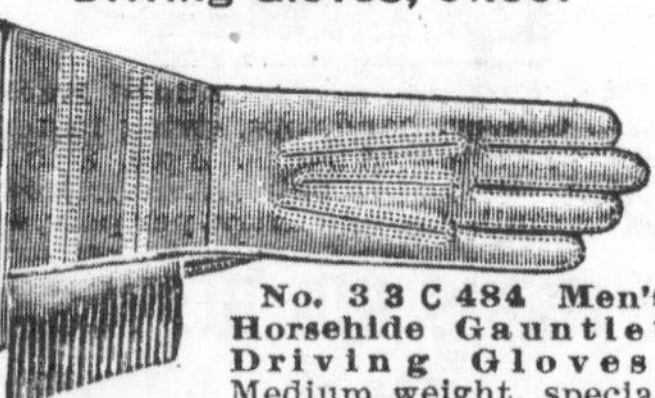

No. 33C484 Men's Horsehide Gauntlet Driving Gloves. Medium weight, special tannage and warranted to remain soft and pliable. Heavy silk embroidered cuffs and backs, and gauntlets trimmed with fringe. Sizes, 8 to 10½.
Price, per pair....................$1.00
If by mail, postage extra, per pair, 9c.

Men's Favorite Horsehide Gauntlets, $1.35.

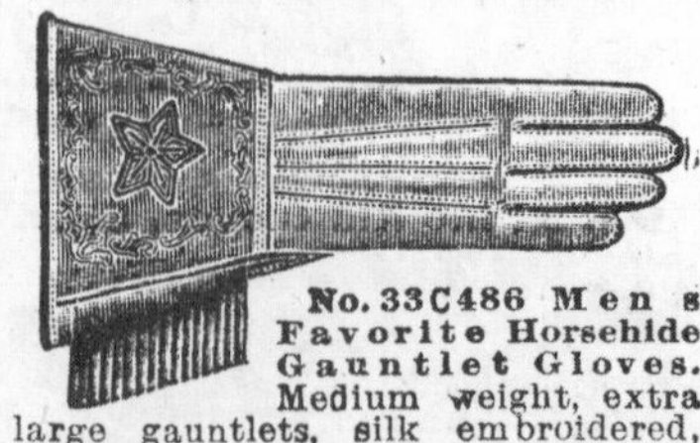

No. 33C486 Men's Favorite Horsehide Gauntlet Gloves. Medium weight, extra large gauntlets, silk embroidered, stitched backs, inseams, and cuffs trimmed with leather fringe. We warrant every pair to remain soft and pliable and to be proof against heat, steam and water. Sizes, 8 to 10½.
Price, per pair....................$1.35
If by mail, postage extra, per pair, 8c.

Cowboys' Gauntlet Regulation Gloves, $1.50.

No. 33C492 Cowboys' Buckskin Gauntlet Gloves. Indian tanned. Made from prime selected buck, medium weight and unlined. **Soft and smooth,** made with wide gauntlet wrists. Heavily stitched backs and richly embroidered gauntlets. **A great favorite with cowboys, ranchmen and cattlemen.** Also popular for horseback riding in all parts of the country. Sizes, 8 to 10½.
Price, per pair....................$1.50
If by mail, postage extra, per pair, 8c.

The Lone Star Buck Gauntlet Gloves, $1.50.

No. 33C494 The Lone Star Gauntlet Gloves, made from the finest quality table cut Indian tanned buckskin. Light yellow color, soft and fine. Fancy embroidered gauntlets, trimmed with buckskin fringe and **finished in very best manner throughout.** Sizes, 8 to 10½. Price, per pair.........$1.50
If by mail, postage extra, 8 cents.

Unlined Buck Gauntlet Gloves.

No. 33C496 Men's Unlined Plymouth Buck Gauntlet Glove. This glove is made of genuine Plymouth buck. Three rows of heavy stitching around the cuff, which is extra wide. This is an excellent driving glove, and we know it will give entire satisfaction. Sizes, 8 to 10½. Price, per pair, $1.25
If by mail, postage extra, 8 cents.

MEN'S UNLINED WORKING MITTENS.

For Choppers, Hedge Cutters, Lumbermen, Etc.

No. 33C702 Unlined Genuine Saranac Caribou Mittens. Made throughout from splendid quality of caribou tanned leather, **welted and wax thread sewed;** made especially to wear over a woolen mitten for wood chopping, etc.
Price, per doz., $4.50; per pair, 40c
If by mail, postage extra, per pair, 8c.

Men's Horsehide Unlined Choppers' Mittens, 50c.

No. 33C708 Men's Unlined Horsehide Choppers' Mittens. Band tap patent string fasteners.
Price, per pair....................50c
If by mail, postage extra, per pair, 8c.

Sears, Roebuck & Co.'s Special Horsehide Mittens

No. 33C710 Men's Genuine Fire and Waterproof Horsehide Mittens, made of genuine horsehide, double stitched and riveted thumb. Unlined. Price, per pair........$0.79
Per dozen pairs.................9.00
If by mail, postage extra, per pair, 8c.

Yellow Saranac Buckskin Choppers' Mittens for 80c.

No. 33C712 Men's Stout, Medium Heavy Weight Saranac Tan Buckskin Choppers' Mittens. Heavy welt seams. Sewed with waxed thread and warranted real buckskin.
Price, per pair......................80c
If by mail, postage extra, per pair, 8c.

Fine Jack Buckskin Mittens, $1.15.

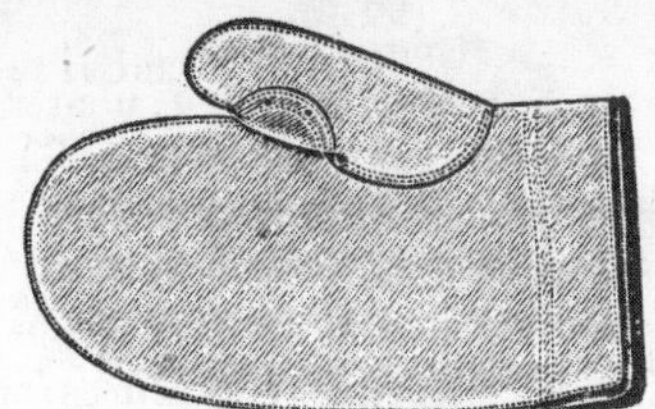

No. 33C714 Genuine Jack Buckskin Reversible Mitten. Strictly No. 1 selected stock, light drab double stitched and double thumb, made out seam and riveted thumb.
Price, per pair..................$1.15
If by mail, postage extra, 12 cents.

Men's Canvas Mittens.

Owing to the low price we quote on canvas mittens, we can furnish by the dozen pairs only.

No. 33C720 Men's Heavy Canvas Mittens, 8 ounces.
Price, per dozen pairs 65c

No. 33C722 Men's Canvas Mittens, made with double palms and double thumbs; no lining.
Price, per dozen pairs..............80c

Wrist Straps.

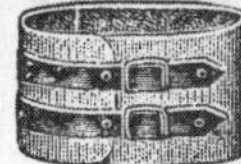

No. 33C910 Men's Heavy Calfskin Wrist Straps. Made 2½ inches wide and buckle around wrist with two small straps. Price, each.................6c
Per dozen pairs, $1.35; per pair..12c
If by mail, postage extra, each, 2c.

Men's Wrist Straps.

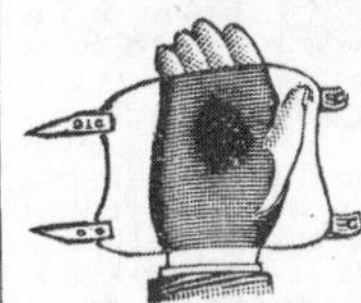

No. 33C912 Wrist Strap. Made from fine quality soft leather. Twice around wrist. One piece.
Price, each.....$0.12
Per pair.............................$0.24
Per dozen pairs.................. 2.70
If by mail, postage extra, each, 2c.

Horsehide Leather Palms.

No. 33C946 Leather Palm made of horsehide, strap and buckle fastener on the back making it adjustable for any size hand. State which is wanted, right or left hand.
Price, per dozen, $1.35; each....12c
If by mail, postage extra, each, 4c.

The Holloway Leader at $2.00.

No. 33C2095 Men's Fedora Style Holloway Hat. Bound edge. Crown is 6 inches; brim, 2¾ inches. Colors, black or pearl. Sizes are 6¾ to 7¾.
Price...............................$2.00
If by mail, postage extra, 25 cents.

The Holloway Raw Edge Fedora, $2.00.

No. 33C2096 Men's Celebrated Holloway Fedora Raw Edge Hat. Crown is 5¾ inches, brim is 3¾ inches. Made from finely selected nutria fur stock, silk band and fine leather sweatband. Colors, black or pearl. Sizes, 6¾ to 7¾. Price.................$2.00
If by mail, postage extra, 25 cents.

MEN'S HATS.

MEN'S, BOYS' OR CHILDREN'S HATS.

HOW TO MEASURE FOR A HAT.

Hat size	Inches around head	Hat size	Inches around head	Hat size	Inches around head
6⅛	19⅝	6¾	21½	7⅜	23⅝
6¼	19¾	6⅞	21⅝	7½	23¾
6⅜	20¼	7	22¼	7⅝	24
6½	20¾	7⅛	22½	7¾	24½
6⅝	21	7¼	23		

If you do not have a tape measure at hand, use a strip of paper for measuring and attach same to your order.

Young Men's Small Shape Derby or Stiff Hats, $1.50.

No. 33C2010 Young Men's Small Shape Stiff Hat. Crown, 5 inches; brim, 1⅞ inches. Color, black. Sizes, 6¾ to 7¾. What size do you wear?
Price..................................$1.50
If by mail, postage extra, 26 cents.

The Holloway Men's Stiff Hats for $2.00.

No. 33C2014 Young Men's Fashionable Stiff Hat. Crown, 5¼ in., brim, 1⅞ in. We warrant every hat to give satisfactory service. Sizes, 6¾ to 7¾. Color, black only. What size do you wear? Price..................$2.00
If by mail, postage extra, 26 cents.

Our Holloway Special, $2.00.

No. 33C2020 Men's Medium Shape Hat. Made of best quality fur stock Crown, 5½ inches; brim, 2 inches. Color, black. Sizes, 6¾ to 7¾.
Price..................................$2.00
If by mail, postage extra, 26 cents.

Men's Large Shape Stiff Hats.

No. 33C2040 A style particularly suited to large men. Crown, 5½ in.; brim, 2¼ inches. Sizes, 6¾ to 7¾. Color, black only. Price...$1.50
If by mail, postage extra, 26 cents.

The Holloway Men's Large Shape Hat, $2.00.

No. 33C2046 Men's Large Full Shape Stiff Hat. Crown, 5½ inches; brim, 2¼ in. Color, black only. Sizes, 6¾ to 7¾. Price....$2.00
If by mail, postage extra, 26 cents.

Dunlap Styles, $2.00.

No. 33C2060 Men's High Grade Stiff Hat, in the Dunlap styles. We furnish the latest styles or shapes as issued in the fall. Crown, 5½ inches; brim, 2 inches. Sizes, 6¾ to 7¾. Color, black only. Price $2.00
If by mail, postage extra, 26 cents.

Men's Silk Hat, $5.00.

No. 33C2062 Men's Very Fine Quality Silk Hat, made in the prevailing style, Dunlap or Knox blocks. Sizes, 6⅝ to 7½. Price.$5.00
If by mail, postage extra, 26 cents.

Dressy Fedora Hat for $1.00.

No. 33C2080 Men's Medium Shape Fedora Hat. Crown, 6 inches; brim, 2¾ inches. Color, black. Sizes, 6¾ to 7¾. What size do you wear? Price...................................$1.00
If by mail, postage extra, 25 cents.

Our Trebor Hat, $1.50.

No. 33C2090 Men's Fedora Hat. Crown, 6 inches; brim, 2¾ inches; raw edge. Colors, black or pearl. Sizes, 6¾ to 7¾. Price $1.50
If by mail, postage extra, 25 cents.

Special Soft Hat, $1.50.

No. 33C2092 Men's New Style Soft Fur Hat. Crown, 5½ inches; brim, 3 inches. The stylish and proper hat for young men and at the same time not too extreme. Color, black. Sizes, 6¾ to 7¾. Price...........................$1.50
If by mail, postage extra, 25 cents.

Men's New Style Holloway Hat, $2.00.

No. 33C2093 Men's New Style Holloway Hat. Crown, 5 inches; brim, 2⅞ inches, raw edge. Color, black. Sizes, 6¾ to 7¾. Price............$2.00
If by mail, postage extra, 28 cents.

The Holloway Special, $2.00

No. 33C2094 Young Men's Special Holloway Hat. Bound edge. Crown, 5¾ inches; brim, 2¾ inches. Color, black only. Sizes 6¾ to 7¾. Price.......$2.00
If by mail, postage extra, 25 cents.

Young Men's Latest Style Holloway Hat $2.00.

No. 33C2097 Young Men's Latest Style Holloway Hat. Crown, 5¼ inches; brim, 3¼ inches; raw edge. Colors, black, pearl or beaver. Sizes, 6¾ to 7¾. Price..................$2.00
If by mail, postage extra, 28 cents.

The Holloway Tourist Hat, $2.00.

No. 33C2098 This is the Celebrated Holloway, Young Men's Latest Style Tourist Hat, raw edge. Colors, black or pearl. Sizes, 6¾ to 7¾.
Price...................................$2.00
If by mail, postage extra, 28 cents.

J. B. Stetson Fedora Style, $2.95.

No. 33C2099 J. B. Stetson Fedora Style Hat. Crown, 6 inches; brim, 2⅝ inches; raw edge. This is a Stetson hat that others ask $3.50 for. We guarantee this to be the genuine Jno. B. Stetson hat, and positively Stetson's very best grade in this style. Color, black. Sizes, 6¾ to 7¾. Price.........$2.95
If by mail, postage extra, 25 cents.

The Holloway Western Fedora, $2.00.

No. 33C2100 A Hat for ranchmen, miners, planters, stockmen and farmers. The right style for large men. Dimensions: Crown, 6 inches; brim, 3¼ inches. Colors, black, fawn or beaver. Sizes, from 6¾ to 7¾. What size do you wear? Price..........................$2.00
If by mail, postage extra, 28 cents.

The Holloway, $2.00.

No. 33C2101 The Reliable Holloway Medium Shape Hat. Has 6-inch crown, 2¾-inch brim; raw edge. One of the newest blocks and warranted to retain its shape. Color, black only. Sizes, 6⅝ to 7¾. Price......$2.00
If by mail, postage extra, 25 cents.

Holloway Large Shape, $2.00.

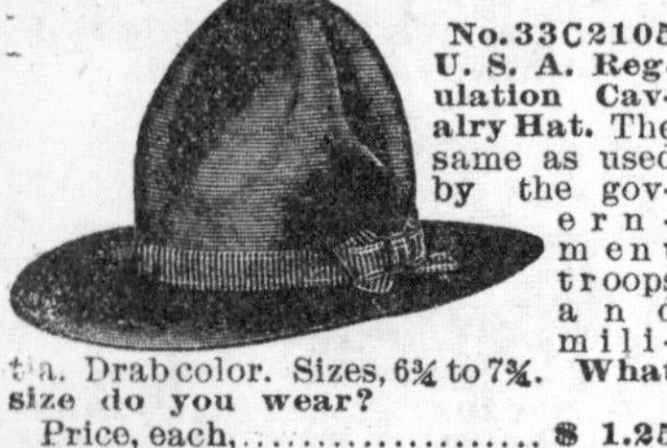

No. 33C2102 Holloway's Large Shape Hat. The right style for large men. Dimensions—Crown, 6 inches; brim, 3¼ inches; raw edge. Color, black only. Size, 6⅝ to 7¾. Price......$2.00
If by mail, postage extra, 28 cents.

U. S. Army Cavalry Hats, $1.25.

Adopted by the Government.

No. 33C2105 U. S. A. Regulation Cavalry Hat. The same as used by the government troops and militia. Drab color. Sizes, 6⅝ to 7¾. What size do you wear?
Price, each......$ 1.25
Per dozen......14.00
If by mail, postage extra, each, 25 cents.

The Roosevelt $1.00 Hat.

No. 33C2108 Men's Fur Hat, flat set brim, in a good quality fur stock, Crown, 6 inches; brim, 3⅛ inches, flat set. A fuller shape than the regulation cavalry hats. Colors, black or belly nutria. Sizes, 6⅝ to 7¾. What size do you wear? Price......$1.00
If by mail, postage extra, 30 cents.

The Holloway Roosevelt Style $2.00 Hat.

No. 33C2110 This is the Regulation Roosevelt Hat, 6-inch crown, 3¼ inch brim, made from finely selected nutria fur stock, raw edge. Color, black. Sizes, 6⅝ to 7¾. Price...$2.00
If by mail, postage extra, 30 cents.

Columbia Style, $1.40.

No. 33C2117 Columbia Style Hat, crown 5¾ inches, brim, 3 inches. Fine quality nutria fur. Color, black only. Sizes, 6⅝ to 7¾. Price......$1.40
If by mail, postage extra, 30 cents.

The Holloway Governor Style, $2.00.

No. 33C2118 Our Governor, $2.00. A hat made from fine nutria fur stock, beautifully proportioned, boss raw edge. crown, 6 nches; brim, 3¼ inches. Colors, black or belly nutria. Sizes, 6⅝ to 7¾. Price......$2.00
If by mail, postage extra, 30 cents.

The Holloway Governor Style Hat, $2.50.

No. 33C2119 The Governor Style Hat, of superior quality fine nutria fur stock, all hand made hat. Colors, black or belly nutria. Sizes, 6⅝ to 7¾.
Price......$2.50
If by mail, postage extra, 30 cents.

J. B. Stetson Columbia Style, $2.95.

No. 33C2121 John B. Stetson Columbia Style Soft Hat. The crown is 5¾ inches high and brim 3 inches wide; raw edge. You will always find Stetson's name on the sweatband. This is a Stetson hat that others ask $3.50 for. We guarantee this to be the genuine Jno. B. Stetson hat, and positively Stetson's very best grade in this style. Colors, black or belly nutria. Sizes, 6⅝ to 7¾. Weight, about 4⅛ ounces.
Price......$2.95
If by mail, postage extra, 30 cents.

J. B. Stetson Famous Big Four, $3.75.

No. 33C2125 John B. Stetson Big Four Hat. Crown, 6 inches; brim, 4 inches. Stetson's hats will keep their shape for years. This is a Stetson hat that others ask $5.00 for. We guarantee this to be the genuine Jno. B. Stetson hat. and positively Stetson's very best grade in this style. Colors, black and belly nutria. Sizes, 6⅝ to 7¾.
Price......$3.75
If by mail, postage extra, 30 cents.

The Big Four, $2.25.

No. 33C2126 The Big Four is a staple, broad brim hat that is a particular favorite in the South and West. The crown is 6 inches and brim 4 inches; exactly the same block and style as the famous Stetson hat of this name. You will pay $3.00 to $3.50 for no better hat. We warrant every hat to give entire satisfaction. Colors, black or belly nutria. Sizes, 6⅝ to 7¾.
Price......$2.25
If by mail, postage extra, 30 cents.

The Graeco Style, $1.50.

No. 33C2130 The Græco, Men's Light Weight, Medium Shape Fur Hat. Slightly curved, raw edge brim. Crown, 5 inches; brim 2⅝ inches. Colors, black, brown or belly nutria. Sizes, 6⅝ to 7¾.
Price......$1.50
If by mail, postage extra, 25 cents.

The Holloway Graeco Style, $2.00.

No. 33C2132 Men's Fine Quality Graeco Style Hat. Crown, 5 inches; brim, 2⅝ inches; medium shape. Colors, black or belly nutria. Sizes, 6⅝ to 7¾. Price......$2.00
If by mail, postage extra, 25 cents.

J. B. Stetson Graeco Style, $2.95.

No. 33C2142 J. B. Stetson Graeco Style. Crown, 4¾ inches; brim, 2⅝ inches, with slight roll, as shown in illustration. This is a Stetson hat that others ask $3.50 for. We guarantee this to be the genuine Jno. B. Stetson hat, and positively Stetson's very best grade in this style. Colors, black or belly nutria. Sizes, 6⅝ to 7¾. Price......$2.95
If by mail, postage extra, 25 cents.

The Holloway Crusher Hat, 90 Cents.

No. 33C2192 Men's Fine Grade Crusher. Narrow silk ribbon band, raw edge brim, medium curl. Colors, black or pearl. Be sure to state size and color. Sizes, 6⅝ to 7¾.
Price......90c
If by mail, postage extra, 24 cents.

The Holloway French Pocket or Crusher Hat, $1.35.

No. 33C2196 The finest, softest, lightest weight pocket hat ever produced. Made from finest French fur felt. Rolling up a hat of this quality to pack in grip or to put into pocket has very little effect on its shape or appearance. Colors, black or pearl. Sizes, 6⅝ to 7¾ only. Price......$1.35
If by mail, postage extra, 24 cents.

Holloway's Special Crusher, $2.00.

No. 33C2198 Holloway's Special Crusher, made from best quality fur, soft and flexible, and may be worn in any shape desired. Has fancy band. Color, black only. Sizes 6⅝ to 7¾.
Price......$2.00
If by mail, postage extra, 24 cents.

Men's Full Shape Crusher Hats, $1.35.

No. 33C2200 Our $1.35 Special Full Shape Crusher Hat. Extra fine soft finish, medium weight. Large full shaped crown that can be creased; full shape brim; made in black or nutria only. Sizes, 6⅝ to 7¾. What size do you wear? Price......$1.35
If by mail, postage extra, 24 cents.

A Good Hat for Driving.

No. 33C2206 Young Men's New Style Crusher. A comfortable, full shape crusher to wear instead of a stiff or fedora hat when driving, traveling or on an outing, etc. A hat in which you will feel well dressed. Raw edge brim. Colors, black or steel. Sizes, 6⅝ to 7¾. Price......$1.50
If by mail, postage extra, 25 cents.

The Raw Edge Railroad Hat, $1.00.

No. 33C2210 Clear Fur Railroad, Narrow silk cord band, raw edge brim, 2⅛ inches; crown, 4 inches. Colors, black or belly nutria. Sizes, 6⅝ to 7¾. What size do you wear? Price $1.00.
If by mail, postage extra, 24 cents.

The Holloway Special Railroad Hat, $2.00.

No. 33C2215 Clear Nutria Fur. A fine kettle finished hand made hat, fine silk band, raw edge; 4⅛-inch crown; brim, 2⅝ inches. Colors, black or belly nutria. Sizes, 6⅝ to 7¾. Price, $2.00
If by mail, postage extra, 24 cents.

J. B. Stetson Railroad Hats.

No. 33C2216 J. B Stetson Railroad Hat. Crown, 4⅛ inches by 2⅝ inches brim, raw edge. Every railroad man knows that the Stetson hat is just the right style and shape for his business. This is a Stetson hat that others ask $3.50 for. We guarantee this to be the genuine Jno. B. Stetson hat, and positively Stetson's very best grade in this style. Colors, black or belly nutria. Sizes, 6⅝ to 7¾. Price......$2.95
If by mail, postage extra, 24 cents.

Our Saxony Wool Ranch Hat, $1.00.

No. 33C2314 Men's Fine Grade Saxony Wool Cowboy Ranch Hat, with wide brim, single buckle, embossed leather band and leather binding. Calfskin or nutria color. Sizes, 6⅝ to 7⅛. Price......$1.00
If by mail, postage extra, 32 cents.

COWBOY SOMBREROS.

No. 33C2318 Cowboys' Extra Fine Heavy Weight Saxony Wool Sombrero, with 4⅛-inch crown and 4-inch brim, with wide single buckle, embossed leather band and leather binding. Band is embossed in beautiful floral and novelty patterns in variegated colors. Sizes, 6⅝ to 7⅛ only. Colors, belly nutria or light calfskin. What size do you wear? Price......$1.25
If by mail, postage extra, 32 cents.

Pine Ridge Scout, $2.00.

No. 33C2326 Cowboys' Favorite Sombrero Hat. Belly nutria color; crown, 4 inches; brim, 4 inches; raw edge, flat, stiff, knife blade brim; 1-inch silk ribbon band. Weight, 6 ounces. Sizes, from 6⅝ to 7¾. What size do you wear? Price......$2.00
If by mail, postage extra, 32 cents.

Never Flop, $2.50.

No. 33C2332 This is the Never Flop Hat. There are many so called Never Flop Hats on the market, but there is only one Never Flop that has proven to be all that its name implies. Has raw edge, scoop brim, 4 inches wide; 4½-inch crown. Weight, 8 ounces. Color, side nutria. Sizes run from 6⅝ to 7¾. What size do you wear?
Price, with a guarantee not to flop......$2.50
If by mail, postage extra, 32 cents.

ALWAYS STATE SIZE WANTED WHEN YOU WRITE YOUR ORDER.

Texas Steer, $2.75.

No. 33C2336 The Texas Steer Style Sombrero Hat. Crown, 4½ inches; brim, 5 inches. Fancy leather band with four silver stars. Fine nutria fur, never flop brim. Weight, 8 ounces. Color, side nutria. Sizes, 6¾ to 7¾. Price $2.75

If by mail, postage extra, 38 cents.

The Texan Chief, $3.25.

No. 33C2352 Texan Chief Cowboys' High Crown Mexican Style Sombrero Hat, 5-inch brim and 6½-inch crown; 1-inch silk ribbon band or tassel cord braided band, if desired. Flat, never flop brim with raw edge. One of the very best as well as the most popular sombreros ever made from best quality **clear nutria fur.** Color, belly nutria. Sizes, 6¾ to 7¾.

Price, with fancy cord band as illustrated $3.25

Price, without fancy cord band, 2.75

If by mail, postage extra, 38 cents.

MEN'S WARM WEATHER HATS.

Men's Imitation Panama Hat, 39 Cents.

No. 33C2361 Men's Fine Imitation Panama Crash Hat, regular Alpine or Fedora shape. Sizes, 6¾ to 7½.

Price, per dozen, $4.50; each....39c

If by mail, postage extra, each 25c.

Men's White Duck Hat, 37c.

No. 33C2363 Men's Fine White Duck Hat, medium shape, stitched brim, four-piece crown with taped seams. This is just the thing for boating and outing and one of the coolest hats for summer wear. Sizes, 6¾ to 7½.

Price, per dozen, $4.25; each....37c

If by mail, postage extra, each, 24c

Regulation Army Hat, 37c.

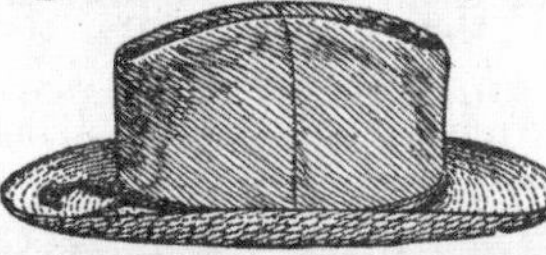

No. 33C2364 Serviceable Farm Hat for all kinds of weather. Made of brown twilled duck. Silk cord band, leather sweatband. Sizes, 6¾ to 7½. **What size do you wear?**

Price, each........$0.37

Per dozen........4.25

If by mail, postage extra, each, 25c.

BOY'S OR YOUTHS' HATS AND CAPS.

Sizes are 6½, 6⅝, 6¾, 6⅞, 7. Always state size in your order. If you do not know the size, measure as directed on first page of Hat Department.

Boys' Saxony Wool Hats, 40 Cents.

No. 33C2370 Boys' and Youths' Saxony Wool Hats, medium shaped crown and brim. Colors, black or gray. Sizes, 6½ to 7⅛ only. **What size do you wear?** Price........40c

If by mail, postage extra, 14 cents.

Boys' Wool Fedora, 45 Cents.

No. 33C2374 Boys' Latest Style Fedora Hats. Made from fine Saxony wool, with silk band and leather sweatband. Colors, black or gray. Sizes, 6¼ to 7⅛ only. Price........45c

If by mail, postage extra, 14 cents.

Boys' Wool Golf Style Hat, 45 Cents.

No. 33C2378 Boys' Golf Style Wool Hat, trimmed with narrow band and leather sweatband; raw edge. A good hat at a very low price. Colors, black or light gray. Sizes, 6½ to 7⅛ only. Price..45c

If by mail, postage extra, 14 cents.

Boys' Fine Fur Golf Style Hat $1.00.

No. 33C2390 Boys' Fine Fur Soft Hat in new golf style. Trimmed with silk band and leather sweatband. Raw edge. A stylish, correct hat, very becoming to most boys. Color, black. Sizes, 6½ to 7⅛ only.

Price........$1.00

If by mail, postage extra, 14 cents.

Boys' New Style Crusher Hat.

No. 33C2392 Our Boys' or Youths' New Style Crusher Hat, made from clear nutria fur and finished with black silk band, leather sweatband and raw edge. Colors, black or pearl. Sizes, 6½ to 7⅛.

Price........90c

If by mail, postage extra, 14 cents.

Boys' New Style Tourist Hat.

No. 33C2393 Boys' or Youths' New Style Tourist Hat, made from clear nutria fur, raw edge, narrow silk band and leather sweatband. Colors, black and pearl. Sizes, 6½ to 7⅛.

Price........90c

If by mail, postage extra, 14 cents.

Boys' Fine Fedora Hats.

No. 33C2394 Boys' Handsome Fedora Hat. Very latest fedora style, wide silk ribbon band and fine leather sweatband. Made from fine fur felt. Colors, steel and black. Sizes, 6½ to 7⅛ only. A medium shape, suitable for boys up to 16 years of age.

Price........$1.25

If by mail, postage extra, 25 cents.

Boys' or Youths' Latest Style Hat, $1.25.

No. 33C2396 Boys' or Youths' Latest Style Hat, made of clear nutria fur stock, can be worn creased or indented, raw edge, or finished with silk band and leather sweatband. Colors, black. Sizes, 6½ to 7⅛. Price........$1.25

If by mail, postage extra, 25 cents.

Boys' White Duck Hat, 35c.

No. 33C2400 Boys' Fine White Duck Hat. Double stitched, six-piece crown, stitched brim and taped seams, leather sweatband and finished with narrow black silk band. Sizes, 6½ to 7⅛. Price........35c

If by mail, postage extra, 14 cents.

Boys' Cowboy Hat, 45 Cents.

No. 33C2408 Rough and Tumble Saxony Wool Hat. Leather band and binding; leather sweatband. **Made to stand the rough usage that the schoolboy's hat is sure to receive.** Colors, belly nutria or gray. Sizes, 6½ to 7⅛. **What size do you wear?** Price....45c

If by mail, postage extra, 25 cents.

Boys' Fancy Yacht Cap, 45c.

No. 33C2545 Boys' Fancy Yacht Cap. Made of all wool cassimere, silk lined, leather sweatband, patent leather visor and finished with heavy silk cord and anchor buttons. Sizes, 6½ to 7⅛. Price........45c

If by mail, postage extra, each, 10c.

Boys' Plain Blue Yacht Caps.

No. 33C2546 Boys' Blue Yacht Cap. Made of blue German broadcloth. Heavy braid band, black patent leather visor, ornamented leather front strap, leather sweatband and silk lined. Sizes, 6½ to 7⅛. **What size do you wear?**

Price, per dozen, $5.25; each....45c

If by mail, postage extra, 10 cents.

Double Cover Yacht Caps.

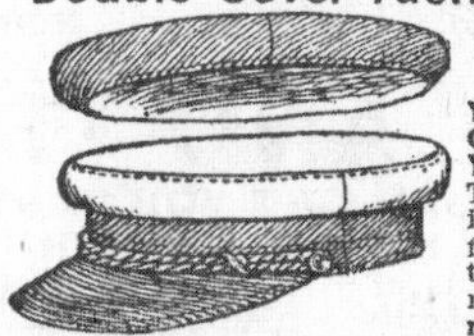

No. 33C2550 Boys' or Youths' Double Cover Fine Yacht Caps. The cap proper is made with a fine white duck top. The separate cover is made of blue serge and slips over the white top, making a regular style blue cap. The band, visor and blue detachable cover are made of fine blue wool serge. Navy blue only. Sizes, 6½ to 7⅛ only. Price, per dozen, $4.50; each........39c

If by mail, postage extra, each, 10 cents.

Boys' Leather Automobile Cap.

No. 33C2551 Boys' Leather Automobile Cap, made of fine quality black leather, soft and pliable, exceptionally well made, with leather sweatband, patent leather visor, hercules braid and finished with patent leather strap and anchor buttons. Sizes, 6½ to 7⅛. Price........48c

If by mail, postage extra, 10 cents.

Boys' Harvard Golf Cap, 37c.

No. 33C2558 The Harvard Golf Cap. Made from fine all wool fancy gray mixed cheviot suitings. Silk linings. Warranted first class in every way. Sizes, 6½ to 7⅛.

Price, per dozen, $4.25; each........37c

If by mail, postage extra, each, 6 cents.

Boys' Navy Blue University Cap, 39 Cents.

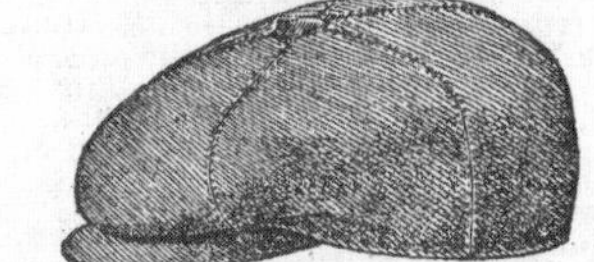

No. 33C2560 Boys' Fine Navy Blue Broadcloth Caps. Eight-piece top and lined with fancy twilled silk lining. Sizes, 6½ to 7⅛.

Price, per dozen, $4.50; each........39c

If by mail, postage extra, each, 6 cents.

Boys' Military Cap, 45 Cents.

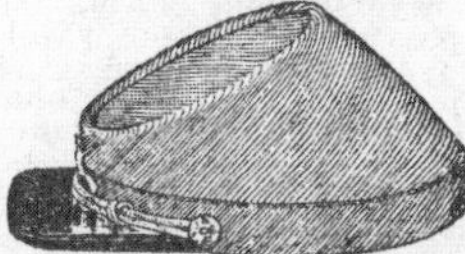

No. 33C2564 Boys' Fine Navy Blue Cadet or Military Cap. Made from regulation uniform cloth, with gilt cord and buttons. Always a great favorite with the boys. Sizes 6½ to 7⅛ only.

Price, per dozen, $5.25; each........45c

If by mail, postage extra, each, 10 cents.

CONDUCTORS' CAPS.

Made with patent wire frame. Never get out of shape.

No. 33C4005 Conductors' Extra Fine Navy Blue Broadcloth Cap, with patented wire frame and fine leather sweatband. **When lettering is desired we require cash in full with order.** Sizes, 6¾ to 7¾. Price. $1.35

Price, with "Conductor" in gold wire block letters $2.35

If by mail, postage extra, 18 cents.

No. 33C4010 Same cap as above in fine black grosgrain silk. Sizes, 6¾ to 7¾. Price........$1.45

If by mail, postage extra, 18 cents.

This price is for plain cap without lettering. Gold wire block embroidered letters will cost 10 cents per letter extra. Allow us one week for delivery. We always put letters like the word "Conductor" on detachable silk band.

No. 33C4015 Made from finest quality of fine bluebroadcloth with wire frame. Sizes, 6¾ to 7¾. Where lettering is desired we require cash in full with order. Price........$1.45

If by mail, postage extra, 18 cents.

Gold wire block letters cost 10 cents extra per letter.

No. 33C4020 Same cap as above, made of fine grosgrain silk, with wire frame. Color, black. Sizes, 6¾ to 7¾. Price........$1.45

If by mail, postage extra, 18 cents.

Army Caps, 75 Cents.

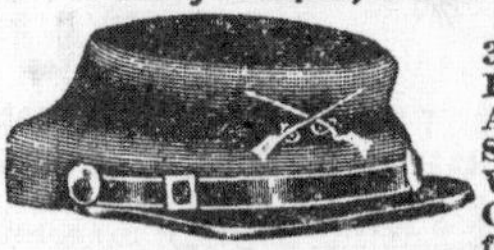

No. 33C4022 Regulation Army or Sons of Veterans Caps, made from blue broadcloth and finished with brass cross guns and buttons, patent leather strap and visor. Sizes, 6¾ to 7¾. Price........75c

If by mail, postage extra, 12 cents.

Letter Carriers' Caps.

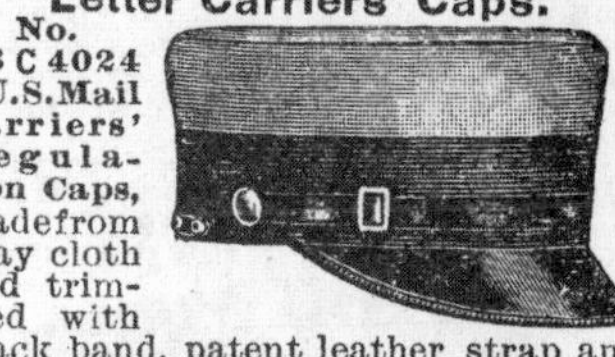

No. 33C4024 U.S. Mail Carriers' Regulation Caps, made from gray cloth and trimmed with black band, patent leather strap and visor. Sizes, 6¾ to 7¾. Price..$1.35

If by mail, postage extra, 18 cents.

Nickel Plated Cap Badges Made to Order.

The following badges are made from German silver, nickel plated. These badges are made to order with any lettering desired. They cannot be returned or exchanged unless we are clearly in error. **Always order by catalogue number and state plainly just what lettering you desire. Allow about five days for making.**

No. 33C4025 Official Stars, fourteen letters, such as City Marshal, Deputy, Police, etc. Price........75c

If by mail, postage extra, 3 cents.

No. 33C4030 Nickel Plated German Silver Badge. Size, ¾x3 inches. Conductor, Baggageman, Porter, News Agent, Expressman or any words not exceeding fifteen letters. Made to order. Price........50c

If by mail, postage extra, 2 cents.

No. 33C4035 Nickel Plated German Silver Badge, with fancy oval, 1-inch wide by 3 inches long. Suitable for such words as **Hotel Porter, Conductor, City Expressman, Baggageman and similar words not exceeding twenty-two letters. Always state what letters you want.**

Price........50c

If by mail, postage extra, 2 cents.

NOTE—Larger badges made to order at from $1.25 to $2.50, according to size and lettering. It requires about five days to have these badges made to order.

MEN'S SUMMER CAPS.

Men's sizes, 6¾, 6⅞, 7, 7⅛, 7¼, 7⅜ and 7½.

THE SIZE OF A CAP is very important, therefore when you make out your order don't forget to state just what size you want. We can then fill your order promptly and to your entire satisfaction.

No. 33C4040 Engineers' Black Leather Cap. Standard shape, well made and just the cap to wear on the engine. Sizes, 6¾ to 7¾.
Price, per dozen, $4.25; each......35c
If by mail, postage extra, each, 6c.

No. 33C4045 Engineers' Black Leather Cap, six-piece top, finely made and well lined. Sizes, 6¾ to 7¾.
Price....35c
If by mail, postage extra, 6 cents.

No. 33C4050 Engineers' Fine Black Silk Cap, with extra wide visor to protect the eyes. Handsomely satin lined. Sizes, 6¾ to 7¾.
Price, per dozen, $4.75; each.....42c
If by mail, postage extra, 6 cents.

Men's Extra Quality Blue Serge Golf Caps.

No. 33C4060 Made of extra quality navy blue wool serge, with heavy silk lining and hook down front. Six-piece top with double stitched seams and extra fine finish. Sizes, 6¾ to 7¾. What size do you wear?
Price, per dozen, $4.50; each.........39c
If by mail, postage extra, 6 cents.

Fancy Golf Caps.

No. 33C4070 Men's Extra Fine Quality Scotch Cheviot Golf Cap, handsome plaids and checks in light and dark colors, lined with heavy rich silk lining. Sizes, 6¾ to 7¾.
Price, per dozen, $4.50; each....39c
If by mail, postage extra, 6 cents.

Men's Double Cover Combination Yacht Cap.

No. 33C4080 Men's Double Cover Fine Yacht Cap. The newest and most practical yacht cap made. The cap proper is made with a fine white duck top. The separate cover is made of blue serge and slips over the white top, making a regular style blue cap. When the separate cover is attached, the point of the contact is invisible, having exactly the appearance of a regular blue yacht cap. Made in a strictly first class manner throughout, with fine leather sweatband. The band, visor and blue detachable cover are made of fine blue wool serge. The most practical cap introduced for many years. Sizes, 6¾ to 7¾ only.
Price, per dozen, $4.50; each.........39c
If by mail, postage extra, each, 12 cents.

Our Latest Style Yacht Cap.

No. 33C4090 The Latest Style Men's Yacht Cap, made of imported Scotch cheviot mixed plaids and checks in light and dark colors. The band and visor are made of same material, leather sweatband. Sizes, 6¾ to 7¾. What size do you wear?
Price, per dozen, $4.50; each.........39c
If by mail, postage extra, each, 12 cents.

Our Special Men's Silk Yacht Cap.

No. 33C4095 Our Men's Special Black Silk Yacht Cap, made of fine quality black grosgrain silk, and finished with black lining, full leather sweatband. Hercules braid, patent leather visor with silk cord and anchor buttons. Color, black only. Sizes, 6¾ to 7¾.
Price...49c
If by mail, postage extra, 12 cents.

Men's Plain Blue Yacht Caps.

No. 33C4100 Men's Plain Blue Yachting Cap, made of blue German broadcloth, leather sweatband, patent leather visor, and lined with silk. An unusually good value. Size, 6¾ to 7¾. What size do you wear?
Price, per dozen, $5.50; each.........48c
If by mail, postage extra, each, 12 cents.

FOR HEAVY WINTER CAPS

Write for our Free Special Hat and Cap Catalogue.

The Latest Men's Yacht Caps.

No. 33C4105 The Latest Men's Yacht Cap, Russian style, very nobby and attractive, made of imported fancy cheviot mixtures, plaids, checks and stripes, light and dark colors. This cap is finished with silk lining, leather sweatband and patent leather visor. This is decidedly a nobby cap. Sizes, 6¾ to 7¾. What size do you wear?
Price, per dozen, $5.50; each.........48c
If by mail, postage extra, each, 12 cents.

Leather Automobile Caps.

No. 33C4110 Men's Leather Automobile Cap. A decided novelty made of extra fine quality black leather, soft and pliable, made in a strictly first class manner throughout, with fine leather sweatband and patent leather visor. Just the cap for automobilists and cyclists. Sizes, 6¾ to 7¾. What size do you wear?
Price, per dozen, $5.50; each.......50c
If by mail, postage extra, each, 15 cents.

Men's Leather Automobile Cap.

No. 33C4115 Men's Fine Leather Automobile Cap, made of best quality soft pliable black leather, welted seams, one-piece top, Russian leather sweatband, heavy black mercerized lining. Hercules braid, patent leather visor, leather strap in front and anchor buttons. Sizes, 6¾ to 7¾. Price............75c
If by mail, postage extra, 15 cents.

TRUNKS AND TRAVELING BAGS.

WE SELL TRUNKS AT ALL PRICES. WE CAN SUIT YOU IN STYLE AND QUALITY. WE WANT YOUR ORDER, BECAUSE WE CAN SELL YOU GOOD TRUNKS AND BAGS CHEAPEST.

IN TRUNKS AND BAGS, as in most other kinds of merchandise, we recommend the better grades, for they are the cheapest in the end. A dollar or two added to the price of a trunk may mean many years of additional usefulness. The particular reasons why we deserve careful consideration and your order, is because we protect you from high prices, from dishonest quality and workmanship. While we sell the cheaper kinds as well as the better grades, each represents the best value of that kind at lowest possible prices. We do not offer one kind of trunk or bag at cost and then ask you to pay too much for another.

THERE IS INTEGRITY in trunks as in other merchandise. They should be made to stand the wear and tear which they are sure to get from time to time.

OUR TRUNKS AND BAGS are made under careful supervision; every nail, rivet, clamp, hinge and lock is attached with the exactness and skill of thorough workmen. THIS IS WHY WE WARRANT EVERY TRUNK AND BAG to be as represented and the best of its kind at the lowest possible price. If you do not see what you want, write to us for information and get our prices.

Crystallized or Fancy Metal Covered Trunks.

Cross Bar Slats, Iron Bottom.

No. 33C5002 Very substantially made; barrel stave top, iron bound, cross bar slats on top, body slats, set up tray with covered bonnet box, iron bottom.

Length	Width	Height	Weight	Price
26 in.	14½ in.	17½ in.	27 lbs....	$1.65
30 in.	16½ in.	19½ in.	34 lbs....	2.10
34 in.	18½ in.	21½ in.	41 lbs....	2.65
36 in.	19½ in.	22½ in.	46 lbs....	2.90

Crystallized Metal Covered Trunks, Flat Top.

No. 33C5010 Will stand the hard knocks that any trunk is sure to receive. Flat top, large shape, iron bound, cross bar slats on top; long slats on body, set up tray with covered bonnet box. Iron bottom.

Length	Width	Height	Weight	Price
26 in.	14½ in.	17 in.	28 lbs....	$1.75
30 in.	16½ in.	19 in.	35 lbs....	2.25
34 in.	18½ in.	21 in.	43 lbs	2.75
36 in.	19½ in.	22 in.	46 lbs....	3.00

Extra Quality Crystallized Metal Trunks.

Great Bargain, $2.25 Trunk.

No. 33C5014 Full finished cross bar slats, iron bottom, barrel stave top, cross bar slats on top and upright on front, iron clamps, brass Monitor lock, patent bolts, rollers, hinges, etc.; covered tray with bonnet box and side compartments; fall-in top. This is a handsome trunk, very wide and high and extra well made.

Length	Width	Height	Weight	Price
26 in.	14½ in.	17½ in.	30 lbs....	$2.25
30 in.	16½ in.	19½ in.	37 lbs....	2.75
34 in.	18½ in.	21½ in.	46 lbs....	3.25
36 in.	19½ in.	22½ in.	50 lbs ..	3.50

No. 33C5020 Fancy metal covered, flat top, with front and back rounded, hardwood reverse bent slats, metal corner bumpers, clamps, bottom rollers, etc. Monitor lock and patent bar bolts, heavy strap hinges, tray, with bonnet box. Fall-in top and side compartments, all separately covered and four slats on all sizes. Without a doubt this is the handiest and most substantial trunk ever built for our low price.

Length	Width	Height	Weight	Price
28 in.	16 in.	18½ in.	34 lbs.....	$3.00
32 in.	18 in.	20½ in.	44 lbs.....	3.50
36 in.	20 in.	22½ in.	55 lbs.....	4.00

Crystallized Metal Covered Trunk.

No. 33C5024 Cross bar slats, hinge tray, iron bottom, full finish, with parasol case. Barrel stave top, wide iron bound, five cross bar slats on top and upright on front, end slats, malleable iron corners and shoes, etc., stitched leather handles. Excelsior lock, patent bolts, fancy skeleton work, covered tray with bonnet box, parasol case and side compartment, fall-in top.

Length	Width	Height	Weight	Price
28 in.	16 in.	19½ in.	39 lbs....	$3.40
32 in.	18 in.	21½ in.	47 lbs....	3.90
36 in.	20 in.	23½ in.	58 lbs....	4.45
38 in.	21 in.	24½ in.	64 lbs....	4.85

New Shape Up to Date Trunk, Cross Bar Slats, Iron Bottom.

Crystal Covered Trunk, $3.95.

No. 33C5028 Handsome Silver Crystal Covered Trunk, fitted with parasol case. Excelsior lock, hinge tray and all of the conveniences to be found in high priced trunks. Large trunk, flat on top with corners rounded, hardwood slats on top and body, heavy bolts, malleable iron skeleton work, hinges, etc., full finished tray with hat box, side compartment, fall-in top, four slats on all sides.

Length	Width	Height	Weight	Price
28 in.	17 in.	19½ in.	39 lbs..	$3.95
32 in.	19 in.	21½ in.	47 lbs..	4.60
36 in.	21 in.	23½ in.	59 lbs..	5.20

Our Special for $4.00.

Iron Bottom and Rosewood Finish.

No. 33C5035 High Wide Trunk, covered with heavy iron, enameled, rosewood finish. Flat top, iron bottom, round corners. Hardwood bent slats over entire top, upright on front and end slats. All protected with heavy metal clamps and bumpers, cross strip clamps and fancy skeleton iron work on ends. Heavy Excelsior lock and side bolts, stitched leather handles, heavy hinges, covered tray, with bonnet and parasol compartments. Handsomely finished and one of the very best values we have ever offered.

Length	Width	Height	Weight	Price
28 in.	17 in.	19½ in.	39 lbs..	$4.00
32 in.	19 in.	21½ in.	47 lbs..	4.65
36 in.	21 in.	23½ in.	59 lbs..	5.25

Order all the goods you need from us and save money.

Black Enameled Iron Trunk for $4.00.

No. 33C5040 Black Enameled Iron Round Top Trunk, large size box covered with black enameled iron, flat top with **rounded corners**, hardwood bent slats on top with one extra slat in center full length of trunk, fancy clamps, rollers, leather handles, brass Excelsior lock; **patent bolts**, full covered hinged tray, with bonnet box, fall-in top, **all fancy trimmed. Iron bottom.**

Length	Width	Height	Weight	Price
28 in.	17 in.	20 in.	43 lbs.....	$4.00
32 in.	19 in.	22 in.	51 lbs.....	4.65
36 in.	21 in.	24 in.	62 lbs.....	5.25

Fancy Metal Covered Trunk for $5.30.

Excelsior Lock.

No. 33C5050 Extra High and Wide Trunk, barrel stave top, cross bar slats on top, upright on front, malleable iron bumpers. **Excelsior lock,** fancy chain work, malleable iron bolts, heavy hinges, stitched leather handles, covered tray with bonnet box, **parasol case** and other compartments, fall-in top, **crystallized metal,** handsomely trimmed and finished.

Length	Width	Height	Weight	Price
32 in.	19½ in.	24½ in.	54 lbs....	$5.30
34 in.	20½ in.	25½ in.	60 lbs....	5.70
36 in.	21½ in.	26½ in.	65 lbs....	6.20

Canvas Covered Trunk for $2.75.

No. 33C5052 A Good Canvas Covered Trunk at a very low price. Square top, painted canvas cover, hardwood slats on top and body, protected with heavy iron clamps, heavy bottom cleats, Monitor lock and patent bolts and heavy hinges. Set up tray with covered hat compartment. The best low priced canvas covered trunk sold.

Length	Width	Height	Weight	Price
32 in.	17¾ in.	20 in.	37 lbs....	$2.75
36 in.	19½ in.	22 in.	46 lbs....	3.25

Our $3.85 Trunk.

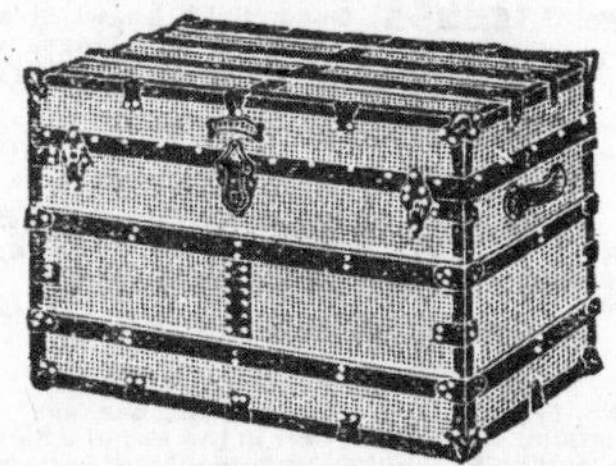

No. 33C5056 Cheapest Trunk in the market; large box, covered with heavy canvas, four heavy hardwood slats on top and two on body running full length of trunk, heavy japanned corners and steel strip clasp, heavy bolts, Monitor lock, hinge tray with hat box and side compartment separately covered, cloth faced. **An honest, strong trunk at a very low price.**

Length	Width	Height	Weight	Price
32 in.	18½ in.	20¾ in.	45 lbs....	$3.85
34 in.	19¼ in.	21½ in.	52 lbs...	4.15
38 in.	21 in.	23 in.	60 lbs....	4.75

Trunk for $4.30 and Up.

No. 33C5058 Large box, covered with heavy canvas, painted, four heavy hardwood slats on top and two on body running full length of trunk. Front and back of top and bottom and ends protected with our new steel binding, heavy japanned corners and steel strip clamps, with center band, heavy bolts, Monitor lock, hinge tray with hat box and side compartment separately covered, cloth faced. Dress tray.

Length	Width	Height	Weight	Price
30 in.	17⅝ in.	20 in.	45 lbs....	$4.30
32 in.	18½ in.	20¾ in.	48 lbs....	4.60
34 in.	19¼ in.	21½ in.	53 lbs....	4.90
36 in.	20¼ in.	22¼ in.	56 lbs....	5.20
38 in.	21 in.	23 in.	62 lbs....	5.50

Canvas Covered Trunk for $3.55.

No. 33C5060 Canvas covered, iron bottom, square top, corners double iron bound, four hardwood slats full length of trunk, **two slats all around body,** japanned steel bumpers and clamps, large brass plated Monitor lock, **heavy bolt locks,** tray containing hat box and packing compartment, fall-in top all covered. With dress tray.

Length	Width	Height	Weight	Price
28 in.	17 in.	19½ in.	40 lbs....	$3.55
32 in.	18½ in.	21 in.	46 lbs....	4.18
36 in.	20 in.	23 in.	56 lbs....	4.83

Special Value at $5.50 to $6.90.

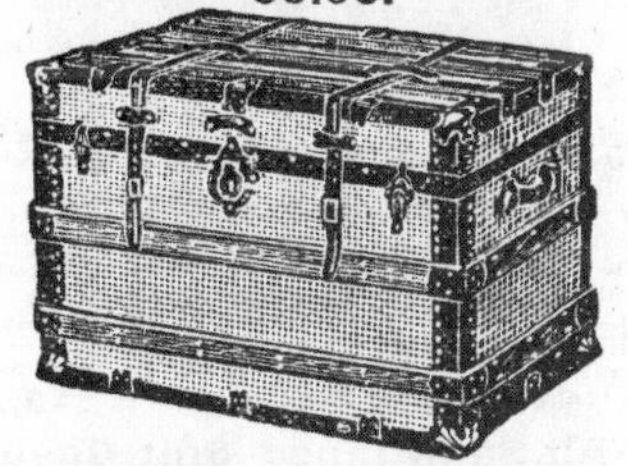

No. 33C5070 Large size box, covered with painted canvas, olive colored iron binding, four heavy hardwood slats on top, two slats running full length of trunk on body, with hardwood bottom cleats. Front and back of top and bottom protected with our **new steel binding** running entire length of trunk, heavy brass plated corner shoes and clamps, heavy brass plated bolts and Monitor locks. Sole leather straps.

Length	Width	Height	Weight	Price
30 in.	18 in.	19½ in.	44 lbs.	$5.50
32 in.	18¾ in.	20¼ in.	48 lbs.	5.85
34 in.	19½ in.	21 in.	53½ lbs.	6.20
36 in.	20¼ in.	22 in.	58½ lbs.	6.55
38 in.	21 in.	22½ in.	64½ lbs.	6.90

Canvas Covered Trunks, $6.25 to $8.75.

No. 33C5078 Large, Full Sized Trunk, covered with heavy waterproof canvas, bound with olive enameled iron binding; hardwood slats used entirely on this trunk, **all protected with brazed malleable clamps and corners of the latest pattern.** Heavy valance set buckle, bar bolts, Excelsior lock, stitched leather handles, two heavy sole leather straps. Inside arranged with roomy upper tray, with hat box and side compartments separately, covered with folding lids. Extra skirt tray below. Cloth faced. This is one of the best values ever offered to trunk buyers.

Length	Width	Height	Weight	Price
30 in.	18 in.	20½ in.	45½ lbs.	$6.25
32 in.	19 in.	21½ in.	50 lbs.	6.75
34 in.	20 in.	22½ in.	55 lbs.	7.25
36 in.	21 in.	23½ in.	58½ lbs.	7.75
38 in.	22 in.	24½ in.	63 lbs.	8.25
40 in.	22½ in.	25½ in.	70 lbs.	8.75

Leather Bound, All Riveted, Canvas Covered Trunk.

Of Stanch Construction.

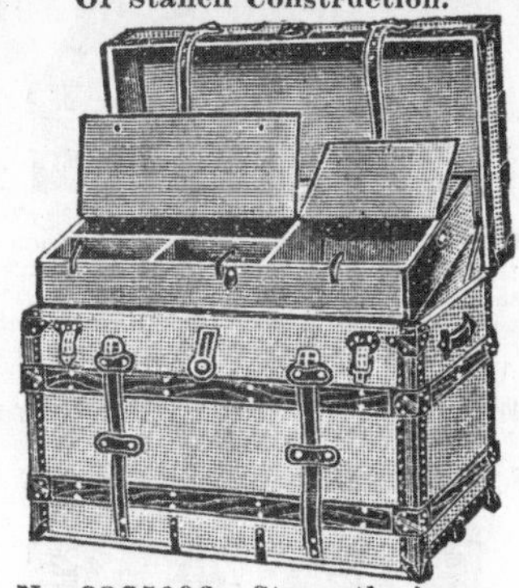

No. 33C5096 Strength in every feature. Covered with heavy canvas, painted; hardwood slats, all protected with heavy brassed clamps; edges bound with leather, heavy sole leather straps. Brass Excelsior lock, tray with hat box and other compartments, separately covered with folding lids; edge of tray bound with metal binding, **dress tray cloth lined.**

Length	Width	Height	Weight	Price
32 in.	19½ in.	23 in.	58 lbs....	$9.20
34 in.	20¼ in.	24 in.	62 lbs....	10.00
36 in.	21 in.	25 in.	67 lbs....	10.75
38 in.	22 in.	26 in.	75 lbs....	11.55

Our Sole Leather Bound Slatless Basswood Trunk.

No. 33C5100 Slatless Veneer Top Basswood Trunk, sole leather binding and straps, cloth lined, heavy riveted, large, very light weight and strong, covered with heavy duck, painted; equipped with brassed bumpers, clamps, corner shoes, rollers, extra heavy Excelsior lock, side bolts and heavy hinges; bound with leather all around edges, back and front, heavy sole leather straps, high set-up tray with hat box and side compartment, extra dress tray; cloth finished throughout; a quality seldom found in retail stores.

Length	Width	Height	Weight	Price
34 in.	20 in.	24½ in.	62 lbs....	$11.90
36 in.	21 in.	25½ in.	68 lbs....	12.80
38 in.	22 in.	26½ in.	73 lbs....	13.70

Wonderful Values in Bureau Trunks.

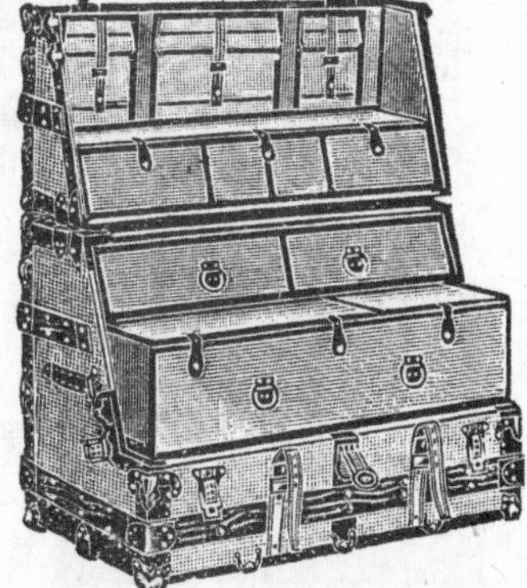

No. 33C5110 The Finest Bureau Trunk made. Steel trimmings, all riveted, Irish linen faced. Basswood box, canvas covered, olive colored steel binding on edges of top and bottom, trimmed with brass clamps and heavy corner bumpers; all riveted; brass Excelsior lock. Four steel hinges, Hagney bolts on ends; linen lined, with genuine Irish linen facing; all compartments are separately covered and easy of access, and arranged as shown in illustration. A veritable traveling chiffonier of great convenience.

Length	Width	Height	Weight	Price
32 in.	20 in.	24 in.	76 lbs...	$16.80
34 in.	20¾ in.	25 in.	82 lbs....	18.10
36 in.	21½ in.	26 in.	88 lbs..	19.45
38 in.	22¼ in.	27 in.	95 lbs....	20.80
40 in.	23 in.	28 in.	102 lbs....	22.15

Our $9.95 Dresser Trunk.

No. 33C5116 Riveted; all space can be utilized, and is accessible at **any** time; upper part contains three compartments, with three drawers in body. **An excellent trunk for skirts and dresses.** Covered with heavy painted canvas, hardwood slats on top and around body of trunk; Excelsior lock, heavy steel clamps and corners, patent lever bolts on front and heavy lock bolts on ends. A veritable traveling chiffonier of great convenience.

Length	Width	Height	Weight	Price
32 in.	19½ in.	22¾ in.	62 lbs..	$9.95
34 in.	20¼ in.	23½ in.	69 lbs..	10.75
36 in.	21 in.	24 in.	74 lbs..	11.75
38 in.	22 in.	24½ in.	80 lbs..	12.75

Special Quality Wagon or Steamer Trunk.

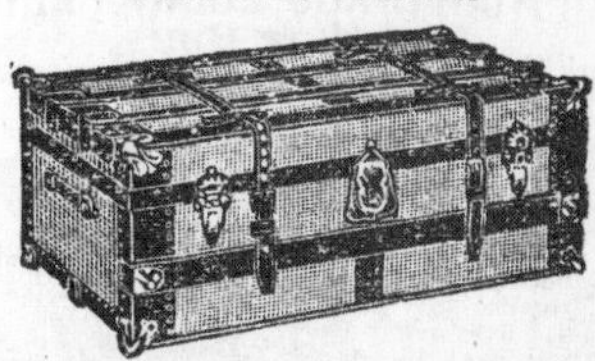

No. 33C5136 Our Special Quality Wagon or Steamer Trunk. Covered with heavy canvas, painted; four hardwood slats on top, one on body, with metal tips, all protected with heavy brass clamps and fancy corner bumpers; brass plated Monitor lock and side bolts.

Length	Width	Height	Weight	Price
32 in.	18¼ in.	11½ in.	34 lbs..	$5.50
36 in.	20 in.	11½ in.	38 lbs..	6.00
38 in.	21 in.	11½ in.	41 lbs..	6.25

SPECIAL VALUES IN BAGS, GRIPS AND VALISES.

Our line of these goods is very carefully selected, so that we may offer our customers only the most practical and convenient styles. All of these goods are high grade, guaranteed, and our prices are 30 to 50 per cent lower than the same class of goods is sold at retail.

Fine Grain Leather Bag at $2.50 to $4.05.

No. 33C5184 One of the most serviceable and best grade leather bags in the market, made of fine selected full stock grain leather, heavy grain leather straps all around, double flange frame, nickel plated long flat key lock, with handle combined, heavy nickel side catches, linen lined. Color, brown.

Length	Weight	Price
14 inches	4½ pounds	$2.50
16 inches	5 pounds	2.75
20 inches	6 pounds	3.35
24 inches	7½ pounds	4.05

Fine Pebble Leather Brown Club Bag.

No. 33C5208 Club Bag, selected pebble leather, large plated lock and side catches, leather handle with rings, cloth lined.

Lgth.	Wgt.	Price	Lgth.	Wgt.	Price
10 in.	1 lb.	65c	14 in.	2 lbs..	85c
12 in.	1½ lbs.	75c	16 in.	2¼ lbs..	95c

Deep Shape Club Bag.

No. 33C5228 One of the best, at a low price. Good genuine grain leather club bag, durably made, heavy japanned frame to match, plated trimmings, cloth lined. Color, brown.

Lgth.	Wgt.	Price	Lgth.	Wgt.	Price
14 in.	2½ lbs...	**$2.00**	18 in.	3¼ lbs...	**$2.40**
16 in.	3 lbs...	**2.20**			

Leather Lined Deep Club Bag.

No. 33C5232 This style of bag is now very popular. They will hold much more and are but a few ounces heavier than the smaller shapes. Full grain leather, heavy brass trimmings, leather covered steel frame, **full leather lined.** You buy it from us at the wholesale price. Color, brown.

Lgth.	Wgt.	Price	Lgth.	Wgt.	Price
14 in.	2¾ lbs.	**$3.00**	16 in.	3¼ lbs.	**$3.55**
16 in.	3 lbs.	**3.75**			

Genuine Alligator Club Bags.

No. 33C5234 You have perhaps read of such things in irresponsible advertisements, but we doubt if you ever bought a genuine **Alligator Bag** at this low figure, **$3.25. Leather lined,** hinge stay. Very handsome bag for ladies' use. **Your highest expectations realized.**

Lgth.	Wgt.	Price	Lgth.	Wgt.	Price
12 in.	2½ lbs.	**$3.25**	16 in.	3½ lbs.	**$4.25**
14 in.	3 lbs.	**3.75**			

Our High Grade, Leather Lined Traveling Bags.

No. 33C5239 English Bag, extra high and wide, heavy steel frame, leather covered, hand stitched, best lock and trimmings. English automatic catches and inside stay to hold bag open. English sunk lock. A bag especially adapted for gentlemen's or ladies' use. Leather lined, with three inside pockets. Color, dark brown.

Lgth.	Wgt.	Price	Lgth.	Wgt.	Price
14 in.	4¼ lbs..	**$5.00**	16 in.	4¾ lbs.	**$6.00**

A Good Cabinet Bag.

No. 33C5240 Cabinet Style Bag, made of genuine grain leather, japanned frame, brass lock and trimmings, heavy handle, cloth lining and inside pockets. This style of bag is roomy and will hold more than club bag styles. Color, brown.

Lgth.	Wgt.	Price	Lgth.	Wgt.	Price
14 in.	4 lbs....	**$2.75**	16 in.	4½ lbs..	**$3.25**

Selected Leather Cabinet Bag.

No. 33C5242 Best Selected Leather Cabinet Bag, leather covered frame, large brass lock with combination ring handle and top catches, full leather lined, inside pockets. Color, dark brown.

Lgth.	Wgt.	Price	Lgth.	Wgt.	Price
14 in.	4¼ lbs.	**$4.25**	18 in.	5½ lbs.	**$5.25**
16 in.	4¾ lbs.	**4.75**			

SUIT CASES.

AT PRICES far below what others ask for equal qualities, we furnish high class, guaranteed SUIT CASES for very little money. **A SUIT CASE** is a convenience; it enables you to carry clothing without wrinkling it and is easy to handle, in many respects more useful than a bag or valise.

Imitation Leather Suit Case, $1.10.

No. 33C5302 Olive Enameled Cloth, imitation of leather. Solid leather corners and handle. Brassed lock and bolts. Cloth lined. A good, durable case. Length, 24 inches. Weight, 6 pounds. Price.................**$1.10**

Our Special Keratol Suit Case.

No. 33C5304 Our Special Rain and Waterproof Suit Case, has the appearance of brown grain leather, heavy leather corners, cloth lined, brass lock and catches. Color, brown. Length, 24 inches. Weight, 6 pounds.
Price............................**$1.80**

Imitation Alligator Suit Case, $1.50.

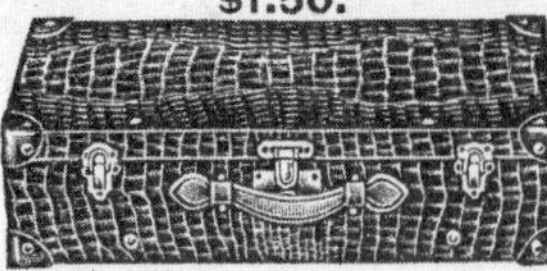

No. 33C5307 Imitation Alligator Suit Case, with genuine alligator corners, sole leather handles, brass plated bolt and lock, cloth lined and inside straps. Looks like leather and is equal to it for wear.
Length, 24 in. Weight, 7 lbs. Price..**$1.50**
Length, 26 in. Weight, 8 lbs. Price..**1.75**

Leather Dress Suit Case, $2.50.

No. 33C5310 Leather Dress Suit Case, steel frame, brass lock and catches, all leather, Vienna handle, solid cowhide riveted corners, linen lined, leather straps inside. This is the most remarkable value in all leather dress suit case on the market. Sole leather color only. Length, 24 in. Wt., 7 lbs. Price, **$2.50**

Leather Suit Case, $3.25.

No. 33C5311 Good Leather Suit Case, with double steel frame, brass lock. Solid cowhide rounded handle, linen lined and four leather straps inside. This is a beautiful and desirable suit case and worth much more than we ask. Length, 24 inches; weight, 7 pounds. Price.........**$3.25**

Leather Dress Suit Case, $4.35

No. 33C5312 A most excellent value. Heavy dark brown colored leather. Steel frame, brass spring lock. Cloth lined, with inside straps. Convenient to handle and exceedingly rich in appearance.

Length	Weight	Price	Length	Weight	Price
24 in.	7 lbs.	**$4.35**	26 in.	8 lbs.	**$4.70**

Leather Suit Case with Tray, $5.00.

No. 33C5314 Made of Heavy Cowhide Case Leather. Double steel frame, brass plated lock and catches, heavy round handle, linen lined and four heavy leather straps in body. Contains linen covered drum bottom tray which can be used to great advantage. Case is beautifully creased.
Length, 24 inches. Price......**$5.00**
Length, 26 inches. Price...... **5.50**

WHILE OUR PRICES ON TRUNKS AND SUIT CASES ARE VERY LOW,

don't make a mistake and think that our trunks and suit cases are not first class in quality. You will find that, quality considered, our prices are about 50 per cent below any kind of competition, and we can save you a great deal of money on a trunk or suit case.

Leather Suit Case, $4.90.

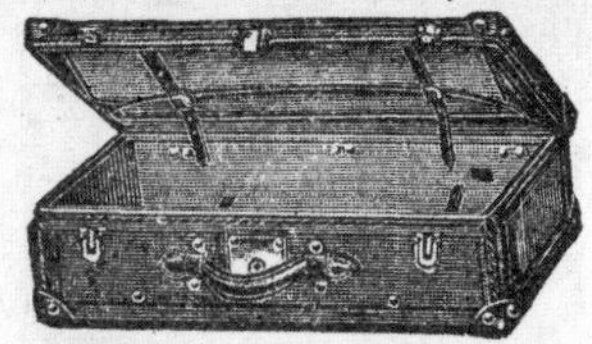

No. 33C5316 Made of heavy fine cowhide case leather. Steel frame, brass plated lock and catches, heavy round handle, duck lined with strap in body and shirt fold in top. For a sightly and durable case, this case cannot be excelled.
Lgth. 24 in. Wgt., 7½ pounds. Price....**$4.90**
Lgth. 26 in. Wgt., 8½ pounds. Price.... **5.50**

Fitted Leather Suit Case, $6.50.

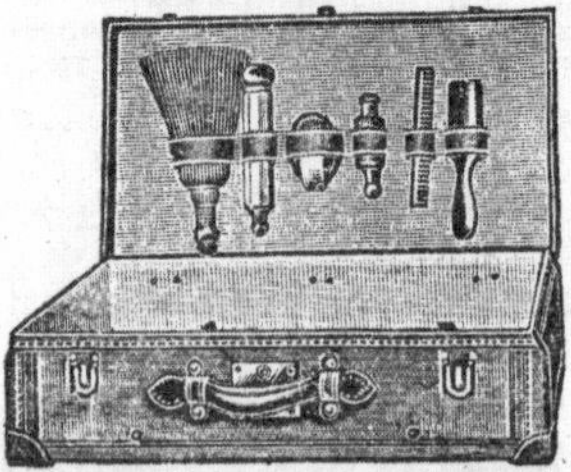

No. 33C5317 Made of Extra Quality Selected Cowhide. Solid cowhide handle and corners. New English rounded top, beautifully creased by hand and lined with the best Irish linen. Finest brass lock and catches. Fitted with whisk broom, hair brush, soap box, tooth and nail brush in glass case, perfume bottle and comb, each article firmly held in place by heavy loops. A most desirable and serviceable case and never before offered for such little money.
Length, 24 inches. Price.......**$6.50**

Three-Pocket Suit Case, $6.25.

No. 33C5318 A new Suit Case with three pockets in the lid suitable for holding collars, cuffs, handkerchiefs, etc., where easily accessible. Made from select cowhide case leather, heavy leather corners, newest brass catches and lock and steel frame. Holland linen pockets and lining and inside straps. A most practical case for convenience and durability. Color, brown.

Length	Weight,	Price
24 inches.	7 pounds.	**$6.25**

All Satin Lined Suit Case, $6.25.

No. 33C5319 Made of an extra quality selected cowhide, solid cowhide corners and handle. New English rounded top, beautifully creased by hand, finest brass lock and catches. Lined complete with rich satin, heavily padded and stitched with silk. Without exception this is the finest case ever brought out to be sold for the money. Length, 24 inches.
Price.......................................**$6.25**

Fine Leather Lined Suit Case, $6.95.

No. 33C5320 Fine Brown Leather Suit Case, heavy leather covered steel frame, fine rolled handle, etc., fine brass lock and catches. Heavy brass rivets, stitched ends, double corners, leather lined body and shirt fold. If you want the best and finest, this is the case you are looking for.
Length, 24 inches; weight, 7½ lbs. Price, **$6.95**
Length, 26 inches; weight, 8½ lbs. Price, **7.45**

English Bellows Case.

No. 33C5322 Up to Date English Bellows Case, made of brown cowhide leather. Heavy corners, with single accordion bellows side, reinforced with two heavy straps. Heavy roll handle attached to sole leather loops, securely riveted. Brass locks and bolts on this case. Selected Holland linen lined, with partition in the center. This is an exceptionally fine case and cannot help but satisfy those looking for a case of this character.

Length	Weight	Price
24 inches.	10¼ pounds.	**$11.00**
26 inches.	11¼ pounds.	**11.50**

CANVAS TELESCOPES.

25 to 75-Cent Telescopes.

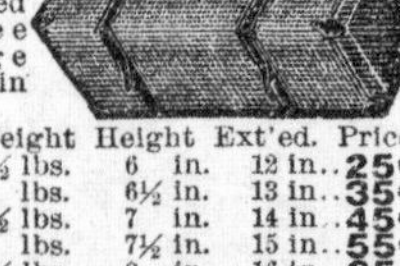

No. 33C5344 Riveted leather corners and bottom tips, heavy stitched handle; three straps on large sizes, heavy grain leather strap.

Lgth.	Width	Weight	Height	Ext'ed.	Price
14 in.	7 in.	1½ lbs.	6 in.	12 in..	**25c**
16 in.	8 in.	2 lbs.	6½ in.	13 in..	**35c**
18 in.	9 in.	2½ lbs.	7 in.	14 in..	**45c**
20 in.	10 in.	3 lbs.	7½ in.	15 in..	**55c**
22 in.	11 in.	3½ lbs.	8 in.	16 in..	**65c**
24 in.	12 in.	4 lbs.	8½ in.	17 in..	**75c**

Full Leather Bound Canvas Telescopes.

No. 33C5346 Heavy Canvas Leather Bound Telescope, hand sewed, heavy leather tips, grain leather straps all around.

Lgth.	Width	Wgt.	Height	Ext'd	Price
16 in.	8¼ in.	2 lbs.	6½ in.	12 in.	**$0.65**
18 in.	9¼ in.	2½ lbs.	7¼ in.	13 in.	**.75**
20 in.	10¼ in.	3 lbs.	8 in.	14 in.	**.85**
22 in.	11¼ in.	3½ lbs.	8¾ in.	15½ in.	**.95**
24 in.	12¼ in.	4 lbs.	9½ in.	17 in.	**1.05**
26 in.	13¼ in.	4½ lbs.	10¼ in.	18½ in.	**1.15**

Extra Heavy Canvas Telescopes.

No. 33C5350 Extra heavy canvas; edges bound all around with wide leather, very heavy corner protectors; two and three sole leather straps, best handle made.

Lgth.	Width	Wght.	Height	Ext'ed	Price
20 in.	11¼ in.	5 lbs.	8½ in.	15 in.	**$1.30**
22 in.	12¼ in.	5½ lbs.	9¼ in.	16 in.	**1.45**
24 in.	13¼ in.	6½ lbs.	10 in.	17 in.	**1.60**
26 in.	14¼ in.	8 lbs.	10¾ in.	18 in.	**1.75**

With patent lock straps, 50 cents extra.

CANVAS SUIT CASE.

No. 33C5352 Dress Suit Case, plain canvas, telescope style, leather straps and handles, and leather bound.
Lgth., 22 inches. Wgt., 5 lbs. Price...**$1.00**
Lgth., 24 inches. Wgt., 6 lbs. Price... **1.10**

Shoulder or Sling Straps.

No. 33C5354 Solid Grain Leather Shoulder or Sling Straps, for use on club bags, ⅝-inch wide with spring snaps. Price... **19c**
If by mail, postage extra, 4 cents.

Shawl Straps.

No. 33C5355 Good, Solid Shawl Straps, with heavy stitched handles and rings, with two straps. Price.......................**20c**
If by mail, postage extra, 6 cents.

No. 33C5356 Patent Lock Strap for Telescopes. Price..............................**50c**
If by mail, postage extra, 6 cents.

Trunk or Bag Name Tag.

No. 33C5357 Trunk or Bag Name Tag of brown grain leather. Strap and buckle fastener. Price, single panel, each..............**8c**
If by mail, postage extra, 2 cents.

Package Handles.

No. 33C5359 Handle your package with a handle. Something new in the way of a handle for satchels. Very convenient for carrying packages. Made exactly the same as a leather handle on a valise with snap at each end.
Price, per dozen, **$2.25**; each........**20c**
If by mail, postage extra, each, 4 cents.

Trunk Straps.

No. 33C5360 Very Heavy Strong Grain Leather Trunk Strap. 9 feet long, 1¼ inches wide. Price..............................**50c**
If by mail, postage extra, 14 cents.

Fibre Lunch Boxes.

No. 33C5361 This is something entirely new, and it is certainly the very best thing in the lunch box line ever produced. These boxes are made from a specially prepared fibre, **leather color and thoroughly waterproof.**
Price.......................................**20c**
If by mail, postage extra, 4 cents.

DRESS GOODS AND SILK DEPARTMENT.

WE ARE THE LARGEST DEALERS IN DRESS GOODS AND SILKS IN THE WORLD, selling direct to the consumer. The dress goods and silks shown in this catalogue embrace the most staple, up to date, plain weaves and plain colors, as well as the VERY LATEST STYLES FOR THIS SEASON; all the new novelties, all the latest shades, all the most desirable, new, up to date, handsome effects. The goods we show are the same grade, style and quality of goods as you will find in the finest city retail stores.

OUR PRICES are all based on the actual cost to us, with but our one small percentage of profit added. All foreign goods, including Japanese Silks, are imported by us direct from the foreign looms. Many of the domestic goods shown are bought by us direct from the manufacturer on season contracts for either part or all of the product of the different mills, and on the basis of manufacturing cost, with but our one small percentage of profit added, will mean a saving to you of fully one-half as against any price you could get similar goods elsewhere.

OUR BINDING GUARANTEE AND REFUND OFFER.

IF YOU SEND US AN ORDER for anything in dress goods or silks, even though the goods are cut from the piece (the number of yards you order), nevertheless we accept your order and send the goods to you with the understanding and agreement that if they are not perfectly satisfactory as to quality, style, color, price, in every way satisfactory, you can return the goods to us at our expense, and we will immediately refund your money, together with any express charges paid by you.

OUR PRICE GUARANTEE.

WE GUARANTEE EVERY ARTICLE listed in this department to be greater value, in other words (quality for quality) lower in price than you can buy elsewhere, and if you send us an order for anything in dress goods or silks, and if you do not find when the goods are received that they are better in quality and lower in price than you can buy elsewhere, we especially request that you return the goods to us at our expense and get your money back.

HOW TO ORDER.

SELECT THE GOODS wanted from the illustration and description, order by number, state the number of yards wanted and color desired. If you wish to leave the selection of shade or pattern to the judgment of an expert in our department, simply give us an idea of the pattern and shade wanted, and we will guarantee to select a color and pattern that is most suitable, always with the understanding that the goods can be returned to us at our expense if they are not satisfactory.

AS A MATTER OF ECONOMY we are compelled to represent this line with small illustrations and somewhat abbreviated descriptions. It is impossible with black ink on white paper to give any of the coloring, any of the beautiful shading, and but a very slight idea of the pattern effect in the many new and handsome numbers shown this season. If you are unable to make a selection from the illustrations and descriptions, we will cheerfully furnish samples free, but we advise that you do not delay to first write for samples, but rather try to make your selection from the illustrations and descriptions shown, as you take no chance whatever, for if the goods are not perfectly satisfactory when received, remember they can be returned to us at our expense, and your money will be promptly returned to you.

SAMPLES SENT FREE ON APPLICATION.

WE WILL SEND SAMPLES OF DRESS GOODS AND SILKS TO ANY ADDRESS BY MAIL, POSTPAID, FREE ON APPLICATION.

THE ACCOMPANYING ILLUSTRATION is a sample of our No. 14C420, 50-inch all Pure Wool Ladies' Cloth, which we furnish at **44 cents per yard,** and which you will find illustrated and described on page 758 in this book. This No. 14C420 is shown by us in twelve to twenty different shades, according to the condition of our stock, and if you should write for **a free sample** of this No. 14C420 you would receive a small card as illustrated, 5½ inches inches long, 3 inches wide, fully describing the goods and attached to this card by a metal staple would be twelve to twenty good sized cloth samples as illustrated, a sample of every shade we have in stock in this number at the time your order is received. **For example,** this particular number today is shown in tan mixtures, light gray, medium gray or dark gray mixtures, blue mixtures, brown mixtures, plain solid shadings of slate, tan, cardinal, garnet, myrtle green, brown, royal blue, navy blue or black.

OUR 50-INCH ALL PURE WOOL LADIES' CLOTH AT 44 CENTS PER YARD.
No. 14C420 Width, 50 inches.
IN OFFERING THIS 50-INCH CLOTH AT 44 CENTS PER YARD
WE WISH TO CALL YOUR ATTENTION
IN ORDERING,
Price, per yard,
44c
No. 14C420 Width, 50 inches. Price, per yard.......................44c
SEARS, ROEBUCK & CO., Chicago, Illinois.

THE ACCOMPANYING ILLUSTRATION is shown to explain the manner in which these goods are sampled, how every number is sampled separately and fully described, and how attached to the card is a good sized cloth sample of every shade furnished in the number referred to. **For example,** a plain black may be shown on a card as illustrated here and fully described, with but one sample attached; another number may be shown in twenty different shades or patterns, in which case there will be as many different samples attached to the card, so when you ask for a sample of any one number you get a fair sized cloth sample of every different shade or different pattern we have in stock in the particular number called for. You can get a full description of the goods and you are then enabled to order as intelligently and with just as much assurance of what you will receive as if you were in our store selecting the goods from stock.

The above illustration shows how we sample free each number of Dress Goods and Silks as shown in this catalogue.

IF YOU ASK FOR A FREE SAMPLE OF ANY NUMBER OF DRESS GOODS OR SILKS, AS SHOWN IN THIS CATALOGUE, you will receive a card as illustrated as shown above, and attached to the card will be a good sized cloth sample of every shade we have in stock of the particular number you asked for. above, on the card the particular goods called for will be fully described

ONE OR TWO NUMBERS FURNISHED FREE.

PLEASE CONFINE YOUR REQUEST FOR FREE SAMPLES TO ONE OR TWO NUMBERS IF POSSIBLE. While we want to send you free by mail, postpaid, on application, just the samples you want, and in every coloring and every pattern we have, as a matter of economy, we are compelled to ask our customers to confine their requests for free samples to only the particular numbers in which they are interested; therefore, as a rule you will get just the samples you want by first selecting the goods from this catalogue, decide on the one or two numbers in which you are interested, and then on a postal card or in a letter ask us to send you samples of this particular number or two numbers and the samples (as many as are required to show our complete line of coloring and patterns), attached to the card with full description as illustrated above, will go to you by return mail, postpaid free. **Understand, we do not make it compulsory that you confine your requests for samples to one or two numbers.** If you feel you must have samples of three, four or more numbers in order to make your selection, and will so state in the letter or a postal card, the samples you call for will be sent to you in the exact same style as shown in the illustration above, and will go to you by return mail, postpaid, free.

WE WOULD GLADLY FURNISH SAMPLES in unlimited quantities and without request to our customers to confine their application for samples to one or two numbers if it wasn't absolutely necessary as a matter of economy and to protect our incomparably low prices that we ask our customers to confine their requests as far as possible to one or two numbers, always with the understanding that if you request a sample of but one number you may receive a card with as many as twenty samples attached, for it may require this number of samples to show our entire line of colorings and patterns in the particular goods you ask for.

DON'T BUY A YARD of dress goods or silks until you have compared our prices, illustrations and descriptions in this catalogue with the prices charged by others, and then if in doubt, don't buy elsewhere until you have written for free samples of at least one or two of the numbers in which you are interested. When you have received a card with the full set of samples attached of the particular number or numbers you ask for, and have compared the goods (style for style, pattern for pattern, shade for shade, quality for quality) with the goods offered by any other house, you will decide that you cannot afford to buy elsewhere.

The following table may be found useful in determining quantities of material required for a waist or skirt for the average person:

	Amount required for a Waist.	Amount required for a Skirt.
If the goods are 18 to 21 inches wide, it requires..........	4 yards	10 yards
If the goods are 26 to 28 inches wide, it requires..........	3 yards	7⅞ yards
If the goods are 34 to 38 inches wide, it requires..........	2¼ yards	6 yards
If the goods are 42 to 46 inches wide, it requires..........	1⅞ yards	5¼ yards
If the goods are 50 to 54 inches wide, it requires..........	1⅝ yards	4½ yards

CASHMERES AND HENRIETTAS.

Wool Filled Cashmere at 12c.

No. 14C110 This is an extra fine quality of inexpensive Cashmere, strictly one-half wool, of good weight and texture, that will give the very best service. The colors are clear and perfect, as follows: Slate, myrtle green and purple. This fabric is retailed generally at 15 to 17 cents per yard. Width, 28 inches.
Price, per yard 12c

WE CALL ESPECIAL ATTENTION TO No. 14C768, WHICH IS A LEADER WITH US THIS SEASON.

Our Very Best Wool Filled Henrietta at 25 Cents.

No. 14C140 Silk Finished Wool Filled Henrietta. An excellent weight fabric with a handsome, silky surface, running in a line of perfect, clear, fast colors, as follows: Cream, pink, light blue, old rose, slate, tan, brown, myrtle green, reseda green, cardinal, wine, royal blue, navy blue or black. The light shades are much used for evening wear, graduating dresses, etc., as well as for children's wear. They will wash. This cloth will withstand hard usage. Width, 35 inches.
Price, per yard...................................25c

All Wool French Silk Finished Henrietta at 49 Cents.

No. 14C150 At 49 cents per yard we offer this high class, all wool, silk finished imported Henrietta as the equal of goods that retail generally at 60 to 70 cents. It is a good weight fabric made from the best long fibre wool yarns and finished with a handsome, silky luster. If you want style and durability, you will find it in this cloth. The colors are cream, pink, light blue, nile green, old rose, slate, tan, brown, reseda green, myrtle green, cardinal, wine, royal blue, navy blue or black. Width, 38 inches. Price, per yard...........................49c

Our Celebrated German Henrietta at 85 Cents.

No. 14C170 The very best quality, silk finished, all wool Henrietta; none better made. The texture, finish and colorings are the most perfect that can be produced. We are enabled to quote this especially low price only by reason of the fact that we import these goods ourselves direct from Germany and thereby do away with the wholesaler's profit. The colors are cream, pink, light blue, slate, tan, brown, myrtle green, cardinal, wine, royal blue, navy blue or black. We will guarantee every yard of this cloth. Width, 45 inches. Price, per yard..................85c

Our Famous Wool Henrietta at 20 Cents.

No. 14C130 Perfect Weave Henrietta. A fabric that is made from the very best materials, the filling being pure wool and the warp cotton, making a cloth of about 60 per cent wool to 40 per cent cotton. It has all the appearance and durability of the all wool goods and the colors are clear and fast. The colors are cream, pink, light blue, nile green, old rose, slate, tan, brown, purple, reseda green, myrtle green, cardinal, wine, royal blue, navy blue or black. This is one of our most popular henriettas and a cloth that we can recommend very highly. Width, 35 inches. Price, per yard..20c

Wide, All Wool Imported Henrietta at 65 Cents.

No. 14C160 This is an extremely fine silk finished Henrietta, absolutely perfect in weave and texture, and at our special 65-cent price is a remarkable value. The colors are cream, slate, tan, brown, cardinal, wine, myrtle green, royal blue, navy blue or black. We cannot recommend this cloth too highly. Width, 44 inches.
Price, per yard..65c

COLORED DRESS GOODS.

MOHAIRS, BRILLIANTINES AND SICILIANS.

These are the most popular fabrics of the season, and are growing stronger every day. The new champagne tan is a favorite, and together with cream is being used extensively this season. Mohair bathing suits are far superior to all others. For shirt waists and summer costumes, mohairs and sicilians are the correct things and many new and catchy effects are shown in fancy and brocaded mohairs. the small, neat designs being especially handsome.

Yard Wide Mohair at 23 Cents.

No. 14C175 Alpaca or Brilliantine. A nicely finished fabric of medium weight and quality. This is the best inexpensive number we ever offered. Comes in cream. brown, royal blue, navy blue or black. Width, 36 inches. Price, per yard........23c

Bright Mohair Brilliantine at 33 Cents.

No. 14C185 Colored Mohair Brilliantine. This is a perfect weave fabric with good luster and weight. A cloth that will give exceptional wear. Colors are navy blue, brown or black. Width, 36 inches. Price, per yard........33c

Lustrous Mohair Brilliantine at 43 Cents.

No. 14C190 Lustrous Colored Brilliantine. A fabric that we can guarantee for color, style and durability. This is a very good weight fabric and a quality generally sold at 60 cents per yard. Colors are light navy, dark navy, cardinal, tan, golden brown, gray mixed or cream white. Width, 38 inches. Price, per yard, 43c

Colored Mohair Brilliantine at 69 Cents.

No. 14C192 A wider, heavier and more lustrous cloth than the preceding number. Mohairs have the call this season, and this one in particular is very desirable. Colors are royal blue, navy blue, medium brown or cream. This is a beautifully finished, imported mohair, and one that will wear like iron. Width, 44 inches. Price, per yard........69c

50-inch Mohair Sicilian at 46 Cents per Yard.

No. 14C195 This is a medium weight bright Mohair fabric, and at the price quoted, will certainly be a leader with us. Comes in perfect shades of brown, light navy, dark navy or black. Width, 50 inches. Price, per yard, 46c

Heavy Weight Lustrous Sicilian at 69 Cents.

No. 14C200 Lustrous Colored Sicilian. The same weave as brilliantine, but of coarser grain and heavier weight. It is preferred by many on account of its heavy weight. It is a very desirable fabric for garments where great strength and durability are required. This is an extra value, being the equal of goods that retail generally at $1.00 per yard. The colors are navy blue or black. Width, 50 inches. Price, per yard........69c

Pekin Striped Mohair at 80c.

No. 14C201 Solid Color Pekin Striped Mohair, just like ordinary mohair brilliantines, only that it has a woven self color stripe, which adds novelty to its appearance. Those desiring a slight change from plain weave goods will appreciate this number. We can highly recommend it for style, color and durability. Comes in navy blue, cream or black. Width, 44 inches. Price, per yard........80c

Fancy Brilliantine at 43 Cents.

No. 14C202 The figure is small, clear and snappy, the narrow white dart giving added character to it. The designs are brought out with brilliancy and pronounce the fabric as a winner, a value that cannot be duplicated. Our fancy mohairs have been carefully selected from the entire English market. Colors are navy, garnet, brown or black. Width, 36 inches. Price, per yard........43c

Printed Warp Mohairs at 59 Cents Per Yard.

No. 14C203 Printed Warp Mohair is one of the newest, most stylish and desirable fabrics shown this season. Woven just like a brilliantine, very firm and wear resisting and about the same weight. The colors are solid shadings shot with variegated printed warp effects of beautifully contrasting colors, but so indistinct that the ground colors predominate. It is a bright, snappy material that will please any purchaser. The ground colors are cadet blue, light brown, reseda green, light gray or dark gray. Width, 42 inches. Price, per yard........59c

Fancy Mohair 69 Cents.

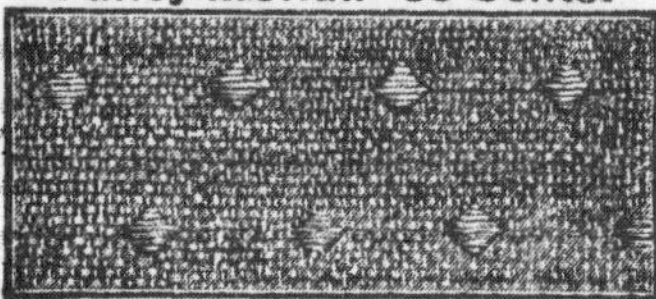

No. 14C204 This represents the pick of the English market on this up to date fabric, both as to quality and design. It is unequaled for year round wear for shirt waists or entire costumes. The figure is small and very brilliant and the delicate white splash effect is very pleasing and can only be appreciated when seen in the garment. Shades are medium navy, brown, garnet or black. Width, 42 inches. Price, per yard........69c

FRENCH SERGES.

All Pure Wool Fine French Serge at 45 Cents.

No. 14C230 At the price quoted, one would naturally expect a cloth this width to be a cotton warp fabric, but our guarantee goes with every yard of this number as being exclusively all pure Australian wool and possessing a beautiful, even twill. It is a fabric of extraordinary wear resisting qualities, combined with a very neat surface appearance. Colors are all pretty, clear shadings of tan, gray, myrtle green, brown, cardinal, wine, royal blue, navy blue or black. Nothing imparts more grace to the figure than a costume made of this stylish French serge. Width, 44 inches. Price, per yard........45c

All Worsted French Beige Suiting at 65 Cents.

No. 14C250 All Worsted Beige Suiting of firm and wiry texture, in soft, mixed colorings. This staple and durable fabric is too well known to require lengthy description other than to say that no more desirable dust defying fabric can be had at any price. These goods are of medium weight, are made from the purest of worsted, and at our special price of 65 cents they have no equal. Comes in mixtures of light, medium or dark gray, also navy blue mixtures or brown mixtures. Width, 41 inches. Price, per yard........65c

HEAVY SERGES.

Heavy Union Serge at 21c.

No. 14C252 For a popular priced serge of medium heavy weight, we have no better value to offer than this 40-inch cloth. This is a union, or cotton warp fabric, but the wool is thrown to the surface in such a manner as to make it appear almost as sightly as an all wool material, and the cotton greatly adds to the wearing qualities, in fact, it will wear better than a similar grade of all wool goods. It is very desirable for children's dresses as well as for ladies and misses. The colors are brown, myrtle green, cardinal, wine, royal blue, navy blue or black. Note the width, 40 inches. Price, per yard........21c

All Pure Wool Serge at 42c.

No. 14C254 All Wool Serge, a trifle heavier than a French serge, and the diagonal wale a bit narrower than a storm serge. A firm and durable cloth that will give almost everlasting service. Retail stores ask 50 cents and up for this quality. Colors are slate, brown, dark green, cardinal, wine, royal blue, navy blue or black. Cloths like this speak loudly in favor of our dress goods department. Width, 36 inches. Price, per yard........42c

All Wool Extra Quality Heavy Suiting Serge at 66 Cents.

No. 14C260 This is an excellent quality of all worsted Suiting Serge. A good weight, firm and wiry cloth that will shed dust and give the most excellent service. Colors are slate, tan, myrtle green, brown, cardinal, wine, royal blue, navy blue or black. This is a cloth that we can recommend very highly for tailor made suits, serviceable dresses, etc. Width, 46 inches. Price, per yard........66c

CHEVIOTS.

Of cheviots, very nearly the same may be said, as of the serges. They possess unequaled wearing properties, will please many who prefer something which is a little away from the smooth faced goods. In this connection we might add that soft browns and grays will be leaders this season in both serges and cheviots.

Yard Wide Suiting Cheviot at 20 Cents.

No. 14C290 This is an unusual value of medium weight Cheviot, woven from good stock, and of perfect, even twill, slightly resembling a high grade repellant. On account of its firm construction this fabric will stand hard usage. Comes in serviceable shades of dark gray, navy blue, myrtle green, seal brown, dark red or black. Width, 36 inches. Price, per yard........20c

All Wool Cheviot at 42 Cents.

No. 14C300 All Pure Wool Cheviot, not a cheap, loosely woven fabric, but a heavy, well made cheviot that retails ordinarily at 50 to 60 cents. It is one of the ideal suit and skirt materials, as it holds its shape and will wear almost everlastingly. Colors are gray, tan, brown, myrtle green, cardinal, wine, royal blue, navy blue, or black. Width, 36 inches. Price, per yard........42c

All Wool Cheviot at 65 Cents.

No. 14C320 Extra Width All Pure Wool Cheviot. A wider cloth and better quality than the preceding number. A good weight, perfect weave material that we can thoroughly recommend. At our 65-cent price this is a very attractive value. Colors are gray, brown, myrtle green, wine, royal blue, navy blue or black. Width, 50 inches. Price, per yard........65c

Pebble Cheviot at 82 Cents.

No. 14C350 Extra quality pebble cheviot. A splendid weight cloth made from the purest Australian wools. This weave differs from ordinary plain cheviot in the respect that the surface is pebbled and rather resembles a coarse weave granite. They are used extensively for all suiting purposes and make very neat, durable and becoming costumes. Comes in navy blue only. Width, 50 inches. Price, per yard........82c

FLANNELS AND BROADCLOTHS.

Flannels are put to endless different uses on account of being all wool and fast colors, while the cost is very reasonable. They are recognized as the ideal fabric for waists, dresses and suits for ladies, misses and children, for little boys' suits, men's tennis and golfing suits, and great quantities are made up every year into bathing suits.

Broadcloths are indispensable and are worn the year round. When converted into the popular tailor made suits they are becoming to everyone, and impart to the wearer a feeling of money well invested. The new mixtures will be exceedingly popular this season, meeting a long felt want for a medium light weight fabric, something a little different from anything we have yet had in this line.

All Wool Tricot Flannel at 22 Cents.

No. 14C380 All Wool Tricot Flannel. A very soft and pretty fabric, highly desirable for waists and for ladies', misses and children's dresses. It will wash. The colors are pink, light blue, reseda green, old rose, pearl gray, tan, myrtle green, brown, cardinal, wine, turquoise blue, royal blue, navy blue or black. Width, 28 inches. Price, per yard........22c

Yard Wide All Wool Ladies' Cloth at 32 Cents.

No. 14C400 Fine, All Wool, Yard Wide Ladies' Cloth. A good weight cloth of very perfect weave and clear, pretty, solid colors and mixtures. We aim to give our patrons exceptionally good value in this number. Colors are slate, cardinal, wine, brown, myrtle green, royal blue, navy blue or black, also mixtures of light, medium or dark gray, blue mixture, brown mixture or tan mixture. This is positively the best yard wide ladies' cloth manufactured. Width, 36 inches. Price, per yard, 32c

All Pure Wool Ladies' Cloth at 44 Cents.

No. 14C420 All Wool Ladies' Cloth or Dress Flannel. We buy this cloth in very large quantities direct from the weavers, and can, therefore, quote the wholesale price of 44 cents. This is a splendid weight cloth of nice, even weave. Its extra width makes it a very economical cloth to buy. The colors are tan mixtures, light gray, medium gray or dark gray mixtures, blue mixtures, brown mixtures, plain solid shadings of slate, tan, cardinal, garnet, myrtle green, brown, royal blue, navy blue or black. Note the width, 50 inches. Price, per yard........44c

All Wool Broadcloth at 72 Cents.

No. 14C430 A very nicely finished fabric, made from good stock, woven fine and close, producing a very good weight and stylish appearing material, appropriate for either suits, skirts, waists or dresses. It is a suiting that will give exceptional service. Colors are choice shades of slate, tan, brown, myrtle green, wine, royal blue, navy blue or black. Width, 50 inches. Price, per yard........72c

All Wool French Broadcloth at 85 Cents.

No. 14C440 This is a very desirable material for tailor made suits. It is a beautifully constructed cloth of very good weight and lustrous finish. It is made by one of the best French weavers and we cannot say too much in praise of its many good qualities. The colors are all solid shadings of slate, tan, brown, myrtle green, wine, royal blue, navy blue or black. Width, 50 inches. Price, per yard........85c

Superior Quality of All Wool French Broadcloth at $1.19.

No. 14C450 In offering this fabric we feel that we are giving a cloth that combines all the style and service of goods for which retailers generally ask $1.50. This is a finer quality and more lustrous finished cloth than the preceding number. There is nothing more dressy than broadcloth and no fabric made that will give better service. We especially recommend this number. The colors are cream white, slate, tan, brown, myrtle green, garnet, royal blue, navy blue, or black. Width, 50 inches. Price, per yard........$1.19

Fine Mirror Finish Broadcloth at $1.39.

No. 14C453 Fine Worsted Warp Broadcloth, of good weight and very superior luster. Only the purest of all wool and worsted yarns are used in its construction. This is the very best one we offer and a quality suitable for the highest grade garments. We have it in the stylish suiting shades of tan, brown, navy blue, or black. Bear in mind, there is no material made that is more stylish, or that will give better all around service than broadcloth. Width, 54 inches. Price, per yard........$1.39

50-Inch All Wool Broadcloth Mixtures, at 88 Cents.

No. 14C455 A new creation, which overtops all others this season. When you see the goods, if only in the small sample, you will wonder how we can offer them at less than $1.10 or more. This cloth is all wool, of pleasing broadcloth weight and will retain its dressy character through long service. Colors (all mixtures) are tan, castor, medium navy, brown, medium gray or dark gray. Width, 50 inches. Price, per yard........88c

VENETIAN CLOTHS.

All Wool Venetian at 42 Cents.

No. 14C480 Fine Quality and Heavy Weight all pure wool Venetian Cloth just like the high priced goods, only in the 36-inch width. The weave is close and firm and the finish lustrous. It is a superior quality to any 50-cent Venetian on the market. Colors are slate, tan, brown, myrtle green, medium cardinal, wine, reseda green, navy blue or new blue, also light, medium or dark gray mixtures, tan mixtures, brown mixtures, blue mixtures, green mixtures or wine mixtures. Width, 36 inches. Price, per yard........42c

Fine Suiting Venetian at 69c.

No. 14C490 Our cloth is a pretty, even weave, heavy weight fabric, and a better quality than we ever offered at this price. Venetian cloth is a very sensible suiting to buy. It possesses an abundance of style and wearing qualities, and the extra width makes it an inexpensive material. Colors are slate, tan, brown, wine, myrtle green, medium cardinal, royal blue, navy blue or black, also medium or dark gray mixtures, wine mixtures, tan mixtures, brown mixtures, blue mixtures or green mixtures. Width, 50 inches. Price, per yard 69c

Fine Imported Venetian at 95c.

No. 14C500 All Wool Venetian Cloth, an extra good one. A medium heavy weight, closely woven, compact cloth with even twill. One that will give very good service. Venetian cloths are much in demand now and this one in particular. Comes in solid colors of slate, tan, brown, wine, royal blue, navy blue or black. Retail stores ask much more money for this grade. Width, 48 inches. Price, per yd..95c

HEAVY SUITINGS AND SKIRTINGS.

Heavy Costume Cloth at 40 Cents.

No. 14C510 Heavy Costume Cloth. Not strictly all wool, but with just enough cotton in its construction to greatly add to its wearing qualities. It has all the appearance of an all wool melton that sells for twice the money. At our price it is one of the biggest bargains in our dress goods department. Last season we could hardly supply the demand for this cloth. It is much used for suits and dresses for ladies, misses and children and is a very good material for rainy day skirts. Colors are green mixed, wine mixed, brown mixed, medium gray mixed, dark gray mixed, solid navy blue or black. Note the width, 54 inches. Price, per yard........40c

Heavy Thibet Skirting at 69c.

No. 14C520 Heavy Wool Thibet, or Rainy Day Skirting. It is a very good weight cloth of close, firm weave. Can be made up without lining and will wear almost everlastingly. Colors are navy blue mixture, tan mixture, brown mixture, medium or dark gray mixture, or plain, solid, black. This is an exceptional value for the money. Width, 54 inches. Price, per yard........69c

Extra Heavy Weight Kersey Cloth at 80 Cents.

No. 14C530 Heavy Weight Kersey Cloth, close and firm in weave and will simply wear forever. Very popular for tailored suits and unlined skirts. It is the ideal fabric for rainy day skirts. Colors are black, navy blue, tan mixture, brown mixture or dark gray mixture. Width, 54 inches. Price, per yard........80c

Fine Melton Suiting at 80c.

No. 14C540 Fine All Pure Wool Melton Suiting. Not the very heavy goods, but a nice suiting weight. It is very closely woven and has a smooth finish, rather resembling a mixed broadcloth. Meltons make the neatest kind of tailored suits or skirts, either lined or unlined. Colors are tan mixture, light gray mixture, medium gray mixture, dark gray mixture, plain brown, navy blue or black. Width, 54 inches. Price, per yard........80c

COLORED DRESS GOODS.

PLAIN AND FANCY DRESS FABRICS.

Yard Wide Scotch Mixtures at 41 Cents per Yard.

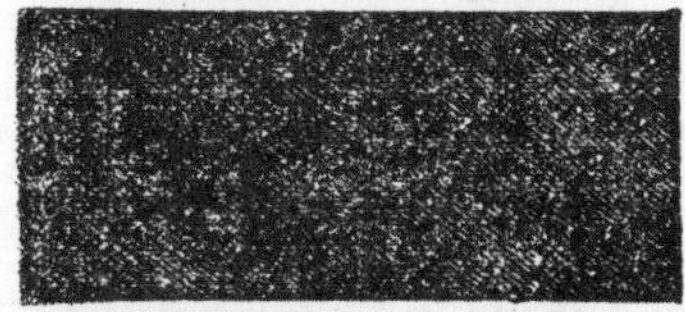

No. 14C550 This is a handsome, low priced cloth and one of which we are justly proud, and after you have worn it through one season, we know you will agree with us that it is a wonder at the price. Medium cheviot weave; firm, durable construction; absolutely all wool; up to date in character; these are among its leading features. Every suit pattern we sell of this number is bound to bring us another customer. Comes in mixtures of tan, brown, garnet, myrtle green, medium navy, black. Width, 36 inches.
Price, per yard....................41c

50-inch All Wool Mixtures at 69 Cents per Yard.

No. 14C555 This is a wider and higher grade fabric than the preceding number, and resembles very closely the imported effects to be seen on dress goods counters in New York's and Chicago's leading stores. The cloth, however, is not excessively mannish, but will make up into a charmingly neat costume. It represents one hundred per cent of good, honest wear, and we think that is enough said. We have it in appropriate suiting mixtures of tan, brown, myrtle green, navy blue or black. Width, 50 inches.
Price, per yard....................69c

Half Wool Florentine Brocade at 12½ Cents.

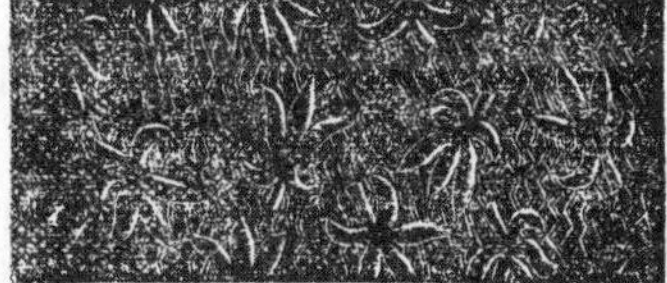

No. 14C590 Strictly Half Wool Bright Brocade Novelty. It is about the weight of a henrietta cloth and is a well made, durable cloth with perfectly fast colors. Comes in cardinal, wine, royal blue, navy blue or black. This fabric is much used for children's wear and gives very good satisfaction. Width, 27 inches.
Price, per yard....................12½c

Fine Wool Armure at 15 Cents.

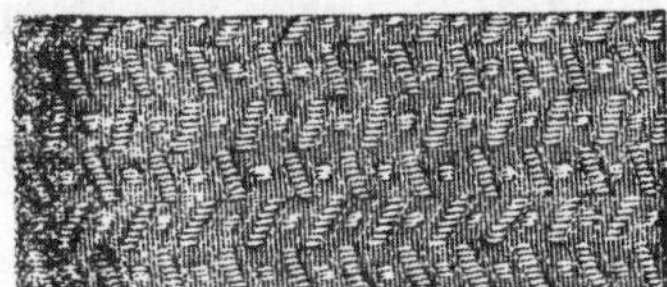

No. 14C630 This is one of the neatest and most genteel inexpensive fabrics shown. It is a trifle over half wool, is good weight, firm and durable. The ground weave is armure with small unpronounced set figures. It is so near a plain weave that it might be called a staple fabric. Colors are dark green, cardinal, wine, royal blue or navy blue. Width, 32 inches.
Price, per yard....................15c

Half Wool Jacquard Novelty at 15 Cents.

No. 14C640 This is an especially attractive value in a strictly half wool brocade. The ordinary retail price of this cloth is 22 cents to 25 cents. We placed a very large order and in consequence we can save you money on the purchase of every yard of this material. The ground weave resembles a poplin and is very well constructed. Comes in cardinal only. This will be found an excellent cloth for children's wear, as well as for ladies' and misses' dresses. Width, 40 inches.
Price, per yard....................15c

Mohair Brocades at 43 Cents.

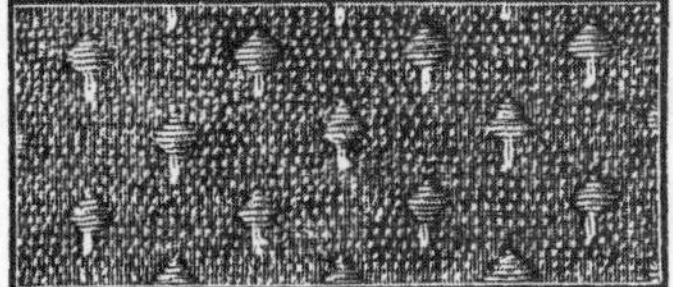

No. 14C642 Nothing newer or possessing more real merit will be seen this season. Exquisite design, brocaded in pure, bright mohair yarns on grounds of the same fabric and color. Just enough white woven into it to enliven it nicely. In a waist or suit made from it, it will look well until it wears out, and that will say a lot, for there is no wear out to it. We have it also in another equally pretty pattern. Either design is dressy. Colors are garnet, brown, navy or black. Width, 26 inches.
Price, per yard....................43c

Superfine Mohair Brocades.

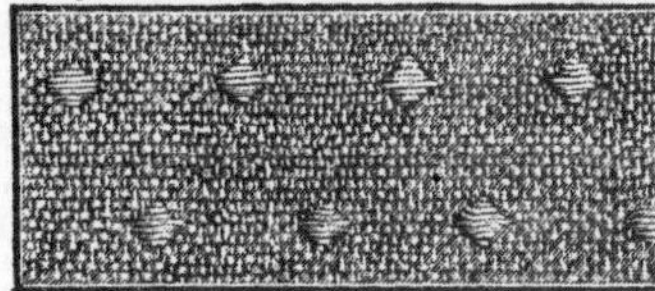

No. 14C646 Our highest grade mohair brocade, representing $1.00 worth of wear and beauty in every yard. The design is bright and exceptionally neat, slightly mixed with white, the choicest we have seen brocaded, one of the best, pure mohairs ever imported. Makes up handsomely into shirt waist suits or separate waists. Colors are garnet, brown, navy or black. Width, 42 in. Price, per yd., 69c

Poplar Cloth at 21 Cents.

No. 14C650 A fashionable half wool dress fabric. One of the best wearing materials made. Slightly heavier than a henrietta cloth and woven firmer and more wiry. Very desirable for ladies' wear and splendid for children. Comes in clear fast colors, cream, gray, tan, cardinal, brown, royal blue, navy blue or black. Poplar cloth is one of the neatest low priced weaves shown this season. Width, 36 inches.
Price, per yard....................21c

All Wool Granite at 39 Cents.

No. 14C660 This fabric is one of our most popular sellers and represents most excellent value for the money. Most granites quoted by other houses at this price, and even higher prices, are half cotton, but in this cloth you get a guaranteed pure wool fabric of pretty, fine weave and good weight. The colors are clear and perfect shades of pearl gray, slate, tan, brown, olive green, myrtle green, cardinal, wine, royal blue, navy blue or black. Width, 37 inches. Price, per yard......39c

Fine Weave Colored Wool Melrose at 39 Cents.

No. 14C670 Fine, pretty, even texture, Wool Melrose, a new fancy weave, but with so little of the fancy effect that it might be termed a plain cloth. About the weight of a henrietta and a pleasant change from plain staple weaves. It is very firm in construction and will wear for years. Colors are cream, slate, tan, brown, myrtle green, cardinal, wine, royal blue, navy blue or black. Width, 36 inches.
Price, per yard....................39c

English Coating Worsted at 69 Cents.

No. 14C725 English Coating Worsted, a bright new weave material of design as shown in the illustration. It is about the weight of a suiting serge and is made from hard twisted, all worsted yarns woven very closely, making a firm and wiry cloth that will shed dust and wear splendidly. This is a stylish and pleasing material, appropriate for either suits or dresses, and is an excellent value at the price. Colors are all solid shades of tan, brown, myrtle green, light navy or black. Width, 42 inches. Price, per yard....................69c

All Wool Roxanna Cloth at 69c.

No. 14C730 A medium weight dress or suit fabric, made from hard twisted worsted and mohair yarns woven very firm, making a wiry, wear resisting fabric of pretty, bright luster. It bears a slight resemblance to poplin, but is a trifle more fancy in weave than the latter material. It is one of the best dust shedding fabrics made and we can highly recommend it for all round service. Colors are tan, brown, dark green, wine, royal blue, navy blue or black. Width, 45 inches.
Price, per yard....................69c

All Wool Paquin Suiting at 85c.

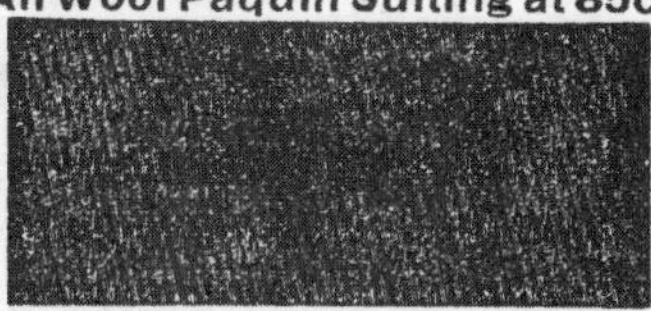

No. 14C765 A fabric constructed from the best worsted yarns and woven with a very genteel diagonal effect that makes up to such becoming advantage in tailored suits and skirts, as well as dresses. It is a well made material of firme texture and a trifle heavier than medium weight. It is an all the year round fabric and comes in pretty colorings of slate, tan, myrtle green, brown, cardinal, wine, royal blue, navy blue or black. This is one of our very best offerings this season. $2.00 to $3.00 saved on a dress or suit pattern by buying this number. Width, 45 inches. Price, per yard....................85c

All Wool Luxorine at 95 Cents.

No. 14C770 A new creation of exceptional merit, and one that will appeal strongly to you if you are looking for an all wool cloth of medium weight, one that will wear as long as a mohair fabric and keep its color clear and perfect through the hardest wear. Nothing more handsome made for traveling suits, as it sheds dust and insures the wearer a garment that will retain its shape. The weave is a medium fine granite effect, but by no means pronounced, and has just enough character to place it outside the plain class of goods. Colors are slate, tan, brown, myrtle green, wine, royal blue, navy blue or black. Width, 46 inches. Price, per yard....................95c

Colored Wool Peau de Soie at 89 Cents.

No. 14C790 All Worsted Peau de Soie. The same weave and similar in appearance to the silk goods of the same name. Just a nice medium weight material that will make up and drape nicely. Is made from rather hard twisted worsted yarns, woven in a pretty round peau de soie twill. It is finished smooth and lustrous. Colors are slate, tan, brown, myrtle green, wine, royal blue, navy blue or black. This is one of the best values we quote. Width, 45 inches. Price, per yard....................89c

LIGHT WEIGHT DRESS FABRICS.

Plain Wool Challie or Nuns' Veiling at 15 Cents.

No. 14C806 Plain Colored Nuns' Veiling or Challie. Strictly half wool. A medium light weight, soft and pretty fabric. In appearance it is almost identical to the all wool goods. It will wash and wear perfectly. It is a very desirable fabric for party and graduating dresses and waists. The texture of the cloth is close and fine and will make up and drape very gracefully. Colors are cream, pink, light blue or black. Width, 22 inches. Price, per yd., 15c

All Wool Albatross at 38 Cents.

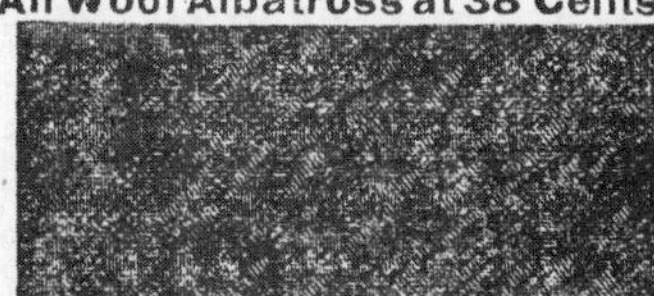

No. 14C810 This attractive crepe effect washable all wool fabric, will be very stylish again this season. Our cloth is a regular 50-cent retailer and is of very nice weave and quality. Colors are cream, pink, light blue, old rose, pearl gray, lavender, nile green, champagne tan, golden brown, royal blue, navy blue, cardinal, or black. Width, 36 inches.
Price, per yard....................38c

All Wool Batiste at 40 Cents.

No. 14C815 Plain, Solid Color, All Wool Batiste, or Nuns' Veiling, a pretty, soft fabric, about the weight of albatross, but woven flat and not quite so woolly in appearance. This is the correct material for light weight dresses and waists that are being worn so much at the present time. It is a very well made cloth of good, clear colorings and one that will wear fully as well as a henrietta. The colors are cream, pink, light blue, tan, light gray, old rose, reseda green, cardinal, royal blue, navy blue, medium brown, or black. Width, 38 inches. Price, per yard.....40c

Imported Silk Warp Sublime at 89 Cents.

No. 14C830 This fabric is made in France from the best raw materials possible to obtain. The warp is all pure silk and the filling long fiber wool, producing a medium weight fabric of beautiful texture and rich, silky sheen. It is used extensively for wedding and evening costumes, also for street waists and dresses. No fabric made that will make up and drape more gracefully. Colors are cream, pink, light blue, old rose, nile green, yellow, lavender, pearl gray, tan, royal blue, brown, cardinal or black. Width, 38 inches. Price, per yard........89c

Silk and Wool Eolienne at 75 Cents per Yard.

No. 14C835 Colored Silk and Wool Eolienne. A fine, sheer fabric that is highly desirable for this season's popular light weight dresses and waists. It is very firmly woven from pure silk and wool, the silk being thrown to the surface, giving it the appearance of an all silk material. This is a fabric that will drape very handsomely, and, in spite of its light texture, will wear very well. Colors are cream, tan, brown, navy or black. Width, 42 inches.
Price, per yard....................75c

Silk and Wool Eolienne at $1.15 per Yard.

No. 14C838 Colored Silk and Wool Eolienne, a finer and better quality than the preceding number, the same grade that is commonly sold for $1.50 to $1.75. Although light and airy in appearance, it is constructed so firmly as to outwear many heavier weight materials. Eoliennes make rich and silky waists and dresses that always please the wearer. Colors are cream, tan, brown, navy or black. Width, 44 inches. Price, per yard....$1.15

All Wool Etamine or Voile at 36 Cents.

No. 14C845 A very stylish, all wool fabric, rather light weight and semi-transparent. It is usually made over an independent lining, contrasting colored linings being frequently used. These etamine fabrics make up and drape very gracefully and represent one of the very newest styles. Colors are cream, white, tan, brown, royal blue, navy blue or black. Etamines of this quality retail at 50 cents and up. Width, 37 inches.
Price, per yard....................36c

All Wool Voile or Panama at 49 Cents.

No. 14C850 This is a very nobby weave of this new suiting, and one that will make up handsomely in any sort of a street, traveling or house dress. It is a semi-transparent fabric on the order of canvas. The yarns are hard twisted worsted, making a very firm and durable cloth that will not shrink. Colors are slate, tan, brown, wine, myrtle green, royal blue, navy blue or black. This is an exceptional value for the money. Width, 38 inches.
Price, per yard....................49c

Fashionable Colored Voile at 79 Cents.

No. 14C865 Imported All Worsted Colored Voile, a pretty, open weave fabric, much worn now. It is light weight, of fine, even mesh, woven very firm and wiry, and a material that will surely please the purchaser. The shadings are especially good this season, as follows: Tan, reseda green, medium brown, medium navy or black. Do not confuse this fine imported number with the inferior domestic goods offered at similar prices. Width, 44 inches. Price, per yard....................79c

PLAIDS AND WAISTINGS.

Heavy Worsted Plaid at 23 Cents per Yard.

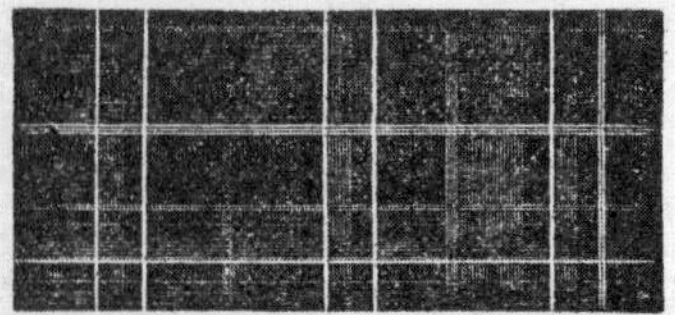

No. 14C1000 **This is a heavy weight, half wool, granite ground Plaid.** It is a very new idea in plaids and one of the choicest patterns ever shown for the money. It is very firm in weave and will wear like leather. We could not sell it at 23 cents if we had not bought an enormous quantity and made a saving of 30 per cent in the purchase price. Comes in a big variety of colors, including cardinal, green, blue, brown or wine, with appropriate and harmonious color combinations. Width, 33 inches. Price, per yard......................23c

Silk and Wool Plaid at 35 Cents per Yard.

No. 14C1010 **This is an unusually handsome and attractive wool Plaid of medium weight and close, firm texture.** There is quite a bit of silk in its construction, which adds considerable tone to the general effect. Retailers ask 50 to 60 cents for this grade. Comes in pretty color combinations of bright, medium and dark effects. Width, 36 inches.
Price, per yard......................35c

Stylish Check Suiting at 43c.

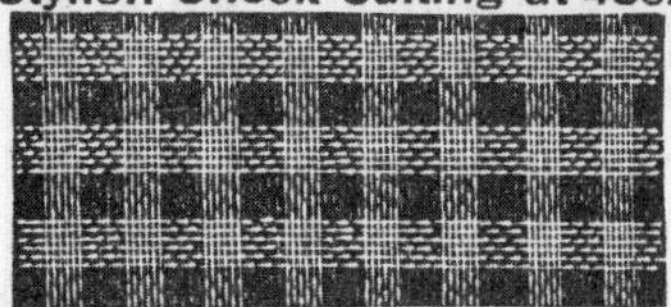

No. 14C1015 **Suiting Checks are very much in demand now for ladies' shirt waist suits,** as well as for children's dresses. This number is a very neat weave, not quite all wool, but with just enough cotton to greatly add to its wearing qualities. The colors are all clear, pretty shades and guaranteed fast, in fact, the cloth can be washed, if desired. The checks are the size shown in the illustration. Colors are black and white, blue and white, brown and white or red and black. Width, 38 inches. Price, per yard......................43c

Velour Novelty Waisting at 29c

No. 14C1035 **In offering this velour novelty waisting to our trade, we do not hesitate to say that it is absolutely in a class by itself,** both for handsome color combinations and assurance of satisfactory wear. The cloth is of medium weight, of firm construction, and the Persian design is exquisite. Some idea of its beauty can be had from the illustration. The ground colors are perfect shades of cream, pink, light blue, reseda green, cardinal, light navy or black, with the Persian design in charming contrast appropriate to each shade. This will produce a stunning waist and is sure to win favor from the start. Width, 30 inches.
Price, per yard......................29c

Jacquard Stripe Wool Waisting at 39 Cents per Yard.

No. 14C1045 **This striking Jacquard stripe waisting is offered in competition with goods shown by other houses at 50 cents per yard and upwards.** This waisting is of very firm weave, though not over medium weight, and will be found very appropriate for wear the year around. In construction it resembles a close grain granite cloth, and at intervals of one and a quarter inches beautiful Jacquard stripes of soothing combinations are interwoven, giving an effect that at once marks the cloth as a new departure. The ground colors are clear tints of cream, pink, light blue, gray, cardinal, royal blue or black. Width, 27 inches. Price, per yard......................39c

For plain colored all wool waisting see No. 14C380.

CREAM DRESS FABRICS.

No. 14C130 **Cream Half Wool Henrietta.** Width, 35 inches. Price, per yard..........20c

No. 14C140 **Cream Half Wool Henrietta.** Width, 34 inches. Price, per yard..........25c

No. 14C150 **Cream All Wool Henrietta.** Width, 38 inches. Price, per yard..........49c

No. 14C160 **Cream All Wool Henrietta.** Width, 45 inches. Price, per yard..........65c

No. 14C170 **Cream All Wool Henrietta.** Width, 45 inches. Price, per yard..........85c

No. 14C175 **Cream Mohair Brilliantine.** Width, 36 inches. Price, per yard..........23c

No. 14C190 **Cream Mohair Brilliantine.** Width 37 inches. Price, per yard..........43c

No. 14C192 **Cream Mohair Brilliantine.** Width, 44 inches. Price, per yard..........69c

No. 14C1255 **Cream Mohair Brilliantine.** Our best quality silk finished. Width, 44 inches. Price, per yard..........98c

No. 14C201 **Cream Pekin Stripe Mohair.** Self colored stripes. Very rich and stylish. Width, 44 inches. Price, per yard..........80c

No. 14C450 **Cream All Wool Broadcloth.** Fine finish; twilled back. 50 inches wide. Price, per yard..........$1.19

No. 14C650 **Cream Poplar Cloth.** 35 inches wide. Price, per yard..........21c

No. 14C670 **Cream Wool Filled Melrose.** Fine pretty weave. 36 inches wide. Price, per yard..........39c

No. 14C806 **Cream Half Wool Challie or Nuns' Veiling.** 22 inches wide. Price, per yard..........15c

No. 14C810 **Cream All Wool Albatross.** 36 inches wide. Price, per yard..........38c

No. 14C815 **Cream All Wool Batiste or Nuns' Veiling.** 38 inches wide. Price, per yard..........40c

No. 14C830 **Cream and Silk Wool Sublime.** 38 inches wide. Price, per yard..89c

No. 14C835 **Cream Silk and Wool Eolienne.** 42 inches wide. Price, per yard..........75c

No. 14C838 **Cream Silk and Wool Eolienne.** 44 inches wide. Price, per yard..........$1.15

No. 14C845 **Cream All Wool Voile.** 35 inches wide. Price, per yard..........36c

BLACK DRESS GOODS.

A REMARKABLE COLLECTION OF BLACK DRESS MATERIALS, COMPRISING EVERY THING OF A STAPLE AND FANCY NATURE IN SOLID BLACK.

WE HAVE MADE THIS DEPARTMENT **the subject of most careful study to bring it to its present state of perfection, and we were never before in a better position to suit the tastes of our host of customers.** We are constantly searching the markets for new weaves and can say without boasting that we can supply you with anything that is desirable in black goods, at prices that will make a dollar reach farther than at any other store.

CASHMERES AND HENRIETTAS.

Our Famous Black Wool Henrietta at 20 Cents.

No. 14C1390 **Perfect Weave Henrietta;** a fabric that is made from the very best materials, the filling being pure wool and the warp cotton, making the cloth about 60 per cent wool to 40 per cent cotton. It has all the appearance and durability of all wool goods. Comes in a perfect shade of fast black. This is one of our most popular henriettas, a cloth that we can recommend very highly. Width, 35 in. Pr yd 20c

Our Very Best Black Wool Filled Henrietta at 25 Cents.

No. 14C1400 **Silk Finished Wool Henrietta,** an excellent weight fabric with a handsome, silky surface in a perfect shade of rich black. This fabric will make up very stylishly and withstand hard usage. Width, 36 inches. Price, per yard......................25c

All Wool French Silk Finished Black Henrietta at 49 Cents.

No. 14C1410 **At 49 cents per yard we offer this high class, All Wool, Silk Finished, Imported Henrietta** as the equal of goods that retail generally at 60 to 70 cents per yard. It is a good weight fabric, made from the best long fibre wool yarns, finished with a handsome, silky luster. If you want style and durability, you will find it in this cloth. Comes in a rich, clear shade of black. Width, 38 inches.
Price, per yard......................49c

All Wool Imported Black Silk Finished Henrietta at 65c.

No. 14C1430 **This is an extremely fine Silk Finished Henrietta,** absolutely perfect in weave and texture and at our special 65-cent price is a remarkable value. Comes in a perfect shade of rich, lustrous black. We cannot recommend this cloth too highly. Width, 44 inches.
Price, per yard......................65c

Our Celebrated Black German Henrietta at 85 Cents.

No. 14C1440 **Extra fine quality Silk Finished All Wool Henrietta.** The texture, finish and color are the most perfect that can be produced. We are enabled to quote this especially low price only by reason of the fact that we import these goods ourselves direct from Germany and thereby do away with the wholesaler's profit. Comes in a perfect shade of lustrous black. We will guarantee every yard of this cloth. Width, 45 inches. Price, per yard...85c

Double Warp Silk Finished Black Henrietta at 98 Cents.

No. 14C1450 **Very good weight, fine quality of Silk Finished Double Warp Henrietta** in a rich, lustrous shade of black. This is a very economical cloth to buy, as it possesses exceptional durability and will retain its luster for years. Width, 44 inches. Price, per yard...98c

Imported Black Silk Warp Henrietta at $1.00.

No. 14C1480 **A nice weight, perfect twill Henrietta,** made with purest of wool filling and silk warp. It is very lustrous in finish and a cloth that will give extraordinary wear. Width, 43 inches. Price, per yard......................$1.00

Our Best Silk Warp Black Henrietta at $1.23.

No. 14C1490 **A Genuine Koehler German Henrietta,** famous for its lustrous finish. Made from finest wool, with [illegible] warp. The twill is very fine and the [illegible] absolutely perfect. Width, 44 inches. Price, per yard......$1.23

NUNS' VEILING.

Plain Black Wool Challie, or Nuns' Veiling, at 15 Cents.

No. 14C1500 **Plain Black Nuns' Veiling, or Challie,** strictly half wool, a medium light weight, soft and pretty fabric. In appearance it is almost identical to the all wool goods. The texture of the cloth is close and fine and will make up and drape very gracefully. Width, 22 inches. Price, per yard......................15c

All Wool Black Batiste at 40c.

No. 14C1505 **Plain All Wool Black Batiste or Nuns' Veiling,** a soft, pretty fabric about the weight of an albatross but woven flat and not quite so wooly in appearance. This is the correct fabric for the light weight dresses and waists that are being worn so much at the present time, and is an especially good value for the money. Width, 38 inches. Pr yd..40c

Fine Black Nuns' Veiling at 69 Cents.

No. 14C1520 **Wider and better than the preceding number.** We can guarantee it for perfect, even weave and lasting qualities. Width, 42 inches. Price, per yard..........69c

ALBATROSS AND SUBLIME.

All Wool Black Albatross at 38 Cents.

No. 14C1540 **This attractive, crepe effect, all wool fabric will be very stylish again this season.** Our cloth is a regular 50-cent retailer and is of very nice weave and quality. Comes in medium black. Width, 36 in. Pr yd. 38c

Black Gloria Silk at 60 Cents.

No. 14C1560 **Black Gloria Silk or Silk Sublime.** The warp is pure silk and the filling fine lisle thread. It is of medium light weight, rich and lustrous in finish and crisp and silky in texture. It is much used for waist and dress purposes, as well as for fine linings. It will give almost everlasting service. Width, 46 inches. Price, per yard......................60c

Imported Silk Warp Black Sublime at 89 Cents.

No. 14C1570 **This fabric is made in France from the very best raw materials possible to obtain.** The warp is all pure silk and the filling long fibre wool, the silk being thrown to the surface, giving it the appearance of an all silk fabric. There is no fabric made that will make up and drape more gracefully. Comes in a pretty shade of black. Width, 38 inches. Price, per yard......................89c

BLACK MOHAIR ALPACAS, BRILLIANTINES AND SICILIANS.

We have these popular and serviceable fabrics in a big variety of qualities at prices ranging from 23c to $1.10 per yard. We carry only the best imported goods and we guarantee any quality quoted below to give absolute satisfaction. We exercise unusual care in the inspection of these goods before accepting them and each and every number is perfect in weave, luster and color. These goods are imported direct by us from the European manufacturers in enormous quantities and we are thereby in a position to quote as low or lower prices than the dealer has to pay for the same grade of goods.

Black Mohair Alpaca at 23c.

No. 14C1580 **Black Mohair Alpaca.** A nicely finished fabric of medium weight and quality. This is the best inexpensive number we ever offered. Width, 36 inches.
Price, per yard......................23c

Bright Black Mohair Brilliantine at 33 Cents.

No. 14C1595 **Black Mohair Brilliantine.** This is a perfect weave fabric with good luster and weight. A cloth that will give exceptional wear. Width, 36 inches. Price, per yard, ..33c

Lustrous Black Mohair Brilliantine at 40 Cents.

No. 14C1600 **Lustrous Black Brilliantine.** A quality we can guarantee for color, style and durability. This is a very good weight fabric and a quality generally sold at 60 cents per yard. Width, 38 inches.
Price, per yard......................40c

Silk Luster Black Brilliantine at 45 Cents.

No. 14C1610 **This is a very high grade Silk Luster Brilliantine.** Comes in a perfect luminous black with silky surface that will shed dust. An exceptionally good value. Width, 38 inches. Price, per yard..........45c

Wide Bright Black Brilliantine at 49 Cents.

No. 14C1620 **Finished the same as the preceding number, but not quite so heavy.** Intended for those who desire wide fabrics for advantage in cutting. Width, 44 inches.
Price, per yard......................49c

Lustrous Black Mohair Brilliantine at 60 Cents.

No. 14C1630 **A new number this season and one of the biggest bargains ever offered.** Is fabric of good weight, having a rich, silky luster found only in the finest grade of goods. It is constructed from the best materials and will wear like leather. Width, 44 inches.
Price, per yard......................60c

Silk Finished Black Mohair Brilliantine at 85 Cents.

No. 14C1640 **This is an unusually brilliant finished fabric of perfect, even weave and appropriate brilliantine weight.** It is made from first quality, long, silky fibre mohair and for durability and rich, silky appearance we cannot speak too highly of it. Retailers generally ask $1.25 for the same grade of goods. Width, 44 inches. Price, per yard......................85c

Brilliant Tamise Mohair at $1.10.

No. 14C1650 **Tamise Mohair is a fabric woven exactly the same as a brilliantine,** but is a trifle lighter weight, has a finer grain and more of a silky sheen. In fact, it is rather hard to distinguish a tamise cloth from an all silk fabric. It is one of the firmest and most durable dress materials made and we know it will give the best of satisfaction. Width, 45 inches.
Price, per yard......................$1.10

Silk Luster Black Mohair Brilliantine at $1.00.

No. 14C1660 **Our very best quality of black silk finished Brilliantine.** This cloth has no equal for beautiful, even texture and rich, silky luster. It is made from the very finest quality of mohair, will wear for years and retain its rich appearance. Money could not buy a better brilliantine. Its exceptional width renders it an inexpensive material. Width, 50 inches. Price, per yard....$1.00

50-Inch Black Mohair Sicilian at 46 Cents per Yard.

No. 14C1665 **This is a medium weight, bright, pure Mohair fabric,** and at the price will certainly be a leader with us. Comes in a very perfect shade of black. Width, 50 inches.
Price, per yard......................46c

Beautiful Bright Black Mohair Sicilian at 69 Cents.

No. 14C1670 **Lustrous Black Sicilian,** the same weave as brilliantine, but of coarser grain and heavier. It is preferred by many on account of its heavy weight. It is a very desirable fabric for garments where great strength and durability are required. This is an extra value, being the equal of goods that retail generally at $1.00. Width, 50 inches.
Price, per yard......................69c

Heavy Weight Brilliant Black Sicilian at 80 Cents.

No. 14C1680 **Brilliant Black Sicilian,** the same as the preceding number, but wider, heavier and better quality. Considering the width, it is a very inexpensive fabric and one that will wear perfectly and shed dust. Width, 50 inches. Price, per yard..........80c

Our Best Lustrous Black Sicilian at 95 Cents.

No. 14C1690 **The very best grade of Lustrous Black Sicilian.** Has a perfect, even, heavy grain and a rich, silky surface. This cloth has no equal for durability, and we can guarantee the value unmatchable. Width, 59 inches. Price, per yard..........95c

Pekin Striped Black Mohair at 80 Cents.

No. 14C1691 **All Solid Black Pekin Striped Mohair,** just like the ordinary mohair brilliantines, only that it has a woven self color stripe, which adds novelty to its appearance. We highly recommend it for style, color and durability, and suggest it to those who desire a slight change from plain weave mohairs. Comes in a lustrous shade of black. Width, 44 inches.
Price, per yard......................80c

BLACK DRESS GOODS.

BLACK FRENCH SERGES

All Pure Wool Black French Serge at 45 Cents.

No. 14C1720 At the price quoted, one would naturally expect a cloth of this width to be a cotton warp fabric, but our guarantee goes with every yard that this number is all pure wool, very good weight and a beautiful clear black. Width, 44 inches. Per yard........45c

Extra Quality All Wool Black French Serge at 65 Cents.

No. 14C1730 This is a very economical fabric to buy. It is a very pretty weave of French serge, finer and better quality than the preceding number, and one that will give excellent service. Comes in a very pretty shade of black. Width, 46 inches. Per yd. 65c

Extra Fine Quality Black French Serge at 98 Cents.

No. 14C1750 This is one of the very best qualities of imported fine all worsted black Serge. It is a nice medium weight cloth, with exceedingly fine and perfect twill, is very rich in effect and will make up neater and wear better than almost any other black dress fabric. It is a quality that is generally retailed at $1.25. Width, 48 inches. Price, per yard 98c

HEAVY BLACK SERGES.

Heavy Union Black Serge, 21c.

No. 14C1754 It is the best fabric of its kind on the market at any price. Strictly one-half wool. Comes in a clear shade of black. Note the width, 40 inches. Price, per yard 21c

All Pure Wool Black Serge, 42c.

No. 14C1756 All Wool Black Serge, a trifle heavier than a French serge, and the diagonal wale a bit narrower than a storm serge. A firm and durable cloth that will give almost everlasting service. Retail stores ask 50 cents and up for this quality. Width, 36 inches.
Price, per yard..............................42c

All Wool Extra Quality Black Suiting Serge at 66 Cents.

No. 14C1760 This is an excellent quality of all worsted Suiting Serge, a good weight, firm and wiry cloth that will shed dust and give most excellent service. Comes in a nice shade of medium black. This is a cloth that we can recommend very highly for tailor made suits, serviceable dresses, etc. Width, 45 inches.
Price, per yard..............................66c

Black Suiting Serge at 79c.

No. 14C1770 50-inch Black Suiting Serge, made from pure worsted yarns, the same as a storm serge, but of more even twill, resembling a coating or clay worsted. Perfect in texture and finish, and a cloth that will prove almost indestructible. Width, 50 inches.
Price, per yard..............................79c

Our Best Waterproof Black Coating Serge at 95 Cents.

No. 14C1775 Black Storm or Coating Serge. The best quality we carry and a beauty for the money. Is a good heavy weight with medium sized twill, and is the firmest and most wiry worsted made. Will shed dust and water and wear like leather. Width, 50 inches.
Price, per yard..............................95c

BLACK CHEVIOTS.

Yard Wide Black Suiting Cheviot at 20 Cents.

No. 14C1776 This is an unusual value of medium weight cheviot, woven from good stock, and of perfect, even twill, slightly resembling a high grade repellant. On account of its firm construction, this fabric will stand hard usage. Comes in a serviceable shade of black. Width, 36 inches. Per yard........20c

All Wool Black Cheviot at 42c.

No. 14C1777 All Pure Wool Cheviot, not a cheap, loosely woven fabric, but a heavy, well made cheviot, that retails ordinarily at 50 to 60 cents. It is one of the ideal suit and skirt materials, as it holds its shape and will wear almost everlastingly. Comes in a perfect shade of black. Width, 36 inches. Per yard......42c

All Wool Black English Cheviot at 47 Cents.

No. 14C1780 Fine English Cheviot, made from best quality all pure wool. A nice weight and a splendid texture for suits and skirts where unusual durability is desired. The soft, unclipped, cheviot surface of these goods shows to advantage in the made up costume. Comes in a very pretty shade of black. Width, 42 inches. Price, per yard........................47c

All Wool Black Cheviot, at 65c.

No. 14C1790 Extra width, all pure wool black Cheviot, a wider cloth and better quality than the preceding number. A good weight, perfect weave material that we can thoroughly recommend. At our 65-cent price this is a very attractive value. Width, 50 inches.
Price, per yard..............................65c

HEAVY BLACK SUITINGS

Heavy Black Costume Cloth at 40 Cents.

No. 14C1860 Heavy Costume Cloth, not strictly all wool, but with just enough cotton in its construction to greatly add to its wearing qualities. It has all the appearance of an all wool melton that sells at twice the money. At our price it is one of the biggest bargains in our dress goods department. Last season we could hardly supply the demand for this cloth. It is much used for suits and dresses, and is a very good material for rainy day skirts. Comes in a perfect shade of black. Note the width, 54 inches. Price, per yard..........40c

Heavy Black Thibet Skirting at 69 Cents.

No. 14C1870 Heavy Wool Thibet or Rainy Day Skirting. It is a very good weight cloth of close, firm weave. Can be made up without lining and will wear forever. This is an exceptional value for the money. Width, 54 inches. Price, per yard..................69c

Extra Weight Black Kersey Cloth at 80 Cents.

No. 14C1880 Heavy Weight Black Kersey Cloth, smooth surface and almost invisible twill, close and firm in weave and will simply wear everlastingly. Very popular for tailored suits and unlined skirts. It is the ideal fabric for rainy day skirts. Width, 54 inches.
Price, per yard..............................80c

Fine Melton Suiting at 80c.

No. 14C1890 Fine All Pure Wool Melton Suiting, not the very heavy goods, but a nice suiting weight. It is very closely woven and has a smooth finish, rather resembling a broadcloth. Meltons make the neatest kind of tailored suits or skirts, either lined or unlined. Comes in a clear, perfect shade of black. Width, 54 inches. Price, per yard..........80c

BLACK FLANNELS, BROADCLOTHS AND VENETIANS.

You can order direct from this catalogue without writing for samples and be assured of satisfactory goods; however, we furnish samples free as explained on page 757.

All Wool Black Tricot Flannel at 22 Cents.

No. 14C1900 All Wool Tricot Flannel, a very soft and pretty fabric, highly desirable for ladies' and misses' waists and dresses. Comes in a very pretty shade of medium black. This is one of the best inexpensive black wool fabrics we have ever offered. Width, 28 inches.
Price, per yard..............................22c

All Wool, Fine Twilled Black Waisting at 29 Cents.

No. 14C1915 All Wool, Fine Twilled Black Waisting; a soft and clinging light weight fabric, highly desirable for waists and dresses, dressing sacques, wrappers, etc. We aim to give our customers an extra value in this number. Comes in a rich shade of black. Width, 27 inches. Price, per yard......................29c

All Wool Black Sacking at 32c.

No. 14C1920 Yard Wide, All Pure Wool Black Sacking, a good weight cloth of perfect weave in a pretty, clear shade of black. Sackings of this quality usually retail at 45 cents and upwards. We aim to give our patrons an exceptionally good value in this number. This is the best yard wide sacking made. Width, 36 inches. Price, per yard......................32c

All Pure Wool Ladies' Cloth in Black at 44 Cents.

No. 14C1930 All Wool Ladies' Cloth or Dress Flannel. We buy this cloth in very large quantities and therefore give you a great deal better value than retailers generally. This is a medium weight cloth of nice, even weave. Its extra width makes it a very economical cloth to buy. Comes in a perfect shade of black. Width, 50 in. Per yard...44c

All Wool Black Broadcloth at 72 Cents.

No. 14C1940 A very nicely finished fabric, made from good stock, woven fine and close, producing a good weight and stylish appearing material, appropriate for either suits, skirts, or dresses. It is a suiting that will give exceptional service. Comes in a perfect shade of medium black. Width, 50 inches. Price, per yard......................72c

All Wool Black French Broadcloth at 85 Cents.

No. 14C1950 This a very desirable material for tailor made suits. It is a beautifully constructed cloth of very good weight and lustrous finish. It is made by one of the best French weavers and we cannot say too much in praise of its many good qualities. Comes in a perfect shade of medium black. Cloths like this speak louder than words in praise of our dress goods department. Width, 50 inches.
Price, per yard..............................85c

Stylish Black Natte at 82c.

No. 14C1792 Medium Heavy Weight Black Natte, or Etamine. It is called natte, but is, in reality, almost as heavy as cheviot. It has a slight open weave. It is a material that will make a very stylish and durable suit or skirt; strictly all wool. Comes in a medium shade of black. Width, 50 inches. Price, per yard, 82c

Fine Quality, All Wool Black French Broadcloth at $1.19.

No. 14C1960 In offering this fabric we feel that we are giving a cloth that combines all the style and service of goods for which retailers generally ask $1.50 to $1.75. This is a finer quality and a more lustrous finished cloth than the preceding number. There is nothing more dressy than broadcloth and no fabric that will give better service. We especially recommend this number. Comes in a very pretty shade of black. Width, 50 inches.
Price, per yard..............................$1.19

Fine Twilled Back Black Broadcloth at $1.39.

No. 14C1970 This is an exceptionally fine quality of mirror finished Black French Broadcloth, with twilled back and one that will be appreciated by lovers of fine materials. It is of good weight and will make up handsomely. This is one of our very best numbers, and for value it cannot be equaled. It will not wear rough like some cloths do. Width, 50 inches.
Price, per yard..............................$1.39

Our Celebrated Delius Black Broadcloth at $1.69.

No. 14C1980 The combination of style, quality, value and beautiful appearance will be found in this excellent fabric. It is a splendid weight cloth, with a mirror finish, and we can guarantee it not to wear rough. We have sold this cloth for several seasons past at $1.98 per yard, but by buying a very large quantity we forced the price down, and we are pleased to give our customers the advantage. At $1.69 it will prove a good investment. Width, 50 inches.
Price, per yard..............................$1.69

All Wool Black Venetian at 69c.

No. 14C2000 Our cloth is a pretty, even weave, heavy weight fabric and a better quality than we ever sold before at this price. Venetian cloth is a very sensible suiting to buy. It possesses an abundance of style and wearing qualities and the extra width makes it an inexpensive material. Comes in a perfect shade of black. Width, 50 inches. Price, per yard. 69c

Fine Imported Black Venetian at 95 Cents.

No. 14C2010 All Wool Venetian Cloth, and an extra good one. Medium heavy weight, closely woven compact cloth with even twill. One that will give very good service. Venetian cloths are much in demand now and this one in particular. Comes in a lustrous, medium black. Retail stores ask much more money for this grade. Width, 48 inches.
Price, per yard..............................95c

FINE WEAVE DRESS AND SUIT FABRICS.

Black Poplar Cloth at 21 Cents.

No. 14C2028 A Fashionable Half Wool Fabric, slightly heavier than a henrietta cloth, and woven firmer and more wiry. This cloth is unequaled for durability, and the color is guaranteed not to fade or crock. Poplar cloth is one of the neatest low priced weaves shown this season. Width, 36 inches.
Price, per yard..............................21c

All Wool Black Granite at 39c.

No. 14C2030 This fabric is one of our most popular sellers and represents excellent value for the money. Most granites quoted by other houses at this and even higher prices, are half cotton, but in this cloth you get a guaranteed pure wool fabric of pretty, fine weave and good weight. Comes in a perfect shade of medium black. Width, 36 inches.
Price, per yard..............................39c

All Wool Black Granite at 46c.

No. 14C2040 Our next better grade of granite is the product of a celebrated mill and is a quality that will satisfy the demands of the very best dressers. Granite suitings are excellent cloths to buy. They combine style and genteel appearance with wonderful wearing qualities, and the result is a pleased customer. This is a heavier and better grade than the preceding number. Comes in a perfect shade of medium black. Width, 36 inches.
Price, per yard..............................46c

Heavy Black Granite Suiting at 69 Cents.

No. 14C2090 Extra weight and width Granite Suiting, a most desirable fabric for tailor made suits, skirts and trimmed dresses. The very firm, even texture and fine finish stamps this granite as a very high class article. Comes in a very clear shade of medium black. We know this cloth will please you and give excellent service. Width, 48 inches.
Price, per yard..............................69c

Black All Wool Roxanna Cloth at 69 Cents.

No. 14C2110 A medium weight dress or suit fabric made from hard twisted worsted and mohair yarns woven very firmly, making a very wiry, wear resisting fabric of pretty bright luster. It bears a slight resemblance to poplin, but is a trifle more fancy in weave than the latter fabric. It is one of the best dust shedding materials made and we can highly recommend it for all round purposes. Width, 43 inches.
Price, per yard..............................69c

New Black English Coating Worsted at 69 Cents.

No. 14C2112 English Coating Worsted, a bright new weave material, of design as shown in the illustration. It is about the weight of a suiting serge and is made from hard, twisted all worsted yarns woven very closely, making a firm and wiry cloth that will shed dust and wear splendidly. This is a stylish and pleasing material, appropriate for either suits or dresses, and is an excellent value at the price. Comes in a medium shade of lustrous black. Width, 42 inches. Price, per yard...............69c

Black Paquin Suiting at 85c.

No. 14C2113 A fabric constructed from the best worsted yarns and woven with a very genteel diagonal effect that makes up to such becoming advantage in tailored suits and skirts, as well as dresses. It is a well made material of firm texture and a trifle heavier than medium weight. It is an all the year around fabric and is unequaled for richness of color and stylish appearance. Comes in black only. This is one of our very best offerings this season. $2.00 to $3.00 saved on a dress or suit pattern by buying this number. Width, 45 inches.
Price, per yard..............................85c

Stylish Black Nub Natte at 89c.

No. 14C2115 Rich and handsome All Worsted Black Nub Natte. An exclusive dress and suit material that has found favor with the very best dressers among our customers. It is of medium heavy weight, is rich and lustrous in color and possesses a very distinctive style that will surely please all lovers of fine dress materials. At 89 cents per yard it is an extraordinary value. Comes in solid black only. Width, 50 inches.
Price, per yard..............................89c

Imported Black Bedford Cord at 40 Cents.

No. 14C2130 English Bedford Cord. A nobby and genteel suiting, appropriate for dresses or suits for any occasion. It is a medium weight fabric of firm texture and nice finish, with a well defined cord running lengthwise of the goods. Comes in a perfect shade of black. Width, 42 inches. Price, per yard, 40c

BLACK DRESS GOODS.

Fine Weave Black Wool Melrose at 39 Cents.

No. 14C2162 Fine, Pretty, Even Texture Wool Melrose, a new fancy weave, but with so little of the fancy effect that it might be termed a plain cloth. About the weight of a henrietta, and a pleasant change from plain staple weaves. It is very firm in construction and will wear for years. Comes in a pretty shade of black. Width, 36 inches. Per yd. **39c**

All Worsted Black Satin Venetian at 49 Cents.

No. 14C2164 Lustrous Satin Venetian, not the regular wool venetian, but a medium weight, bright finished, all worsted dress fabric. It is a closely woven, glossy material that will give excellent service and not wear rough. Comes in a lustrous shade of black. Retailers generally ask 90 cents for this grade. Width, 38 inches Price, per yard........................**49c**

Black Drap d'Alma at 89c.

No. 14C2166 This old reliable weave hardly needs a description other than to say that it is a medium weight, smooth finished, pure wool dress or suit material that has stood the test of many years of popularity and never disappointed a purchaser. The weave is an unpronounced diagonal effect. Comes in a rich shade of black. Width, 44 in, Price, per yd. **89c**

All Wool Black Peau de Shark at 85 Cents.

No. 14C2170 One of the latest plain effect weaves to be had. It is of medium weight, made from bright worsted yarns, and in effect is quite lustrous. It is a fabric that will withstand hard wear. The illustration is a good representation of the weave. Comes in a rich shade of black. Width, 44 in. Price, per yd. **85c**

All Wool Black Luxorine at 95c.

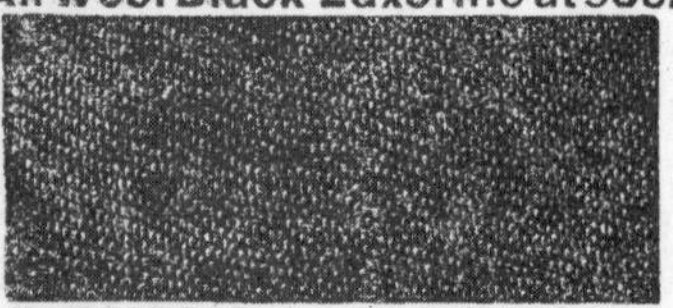

No. 14C2210 A new creation of exceptional merit, and one that will appeal strongly to you if you are looking for an all wool cloth of medium weight and one that will wear as long as any mohair fabric and keep its color perfect through the hardest wear. The weave is a medium fine granite effect, but by no means pronounced; has just enough character to it to place it outside the plain class of goods. Comes in a perfect shade of brilliant black. Width, 46 inches. Price, per yard..........**95c**

All Wool Black Peau de Soie at 89 Cents.

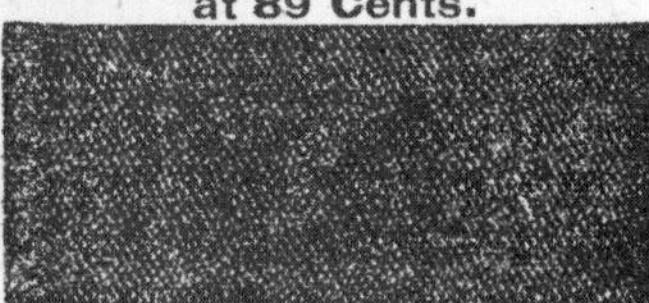

No. 14C2220 All Worsted Peau de Soie, the same weave and similar in appearance to the silk goods of the same name. Just a nice, medium weight material that will make up and drape nicely. It is made from rather hard twisted worsted yarns woven in a pretty, round peau de soie twill. It is finished smooth and lustrous. Comes in bright black. Width, 45 inches. Price, per yard.......................**89c**

Black Melrose at $1.10.

No. 14C2230 One of the newer, fancy weaves, but sufficiently plain to be classed among staple fabrics. It is a trifle heavier than a henrietta and made from harder twisted yarns, making a very firm texture. The small, seeded effect and the rich general appearance of the cloth will show up handsomely in the made up garment. It is strictly all wool and we will guarantee it to please. Width, 45 inches. Price, per yard.... ....**$1.10**

BLACK ETAMINES AND VOILES.

All Wool Black Etamine Canvas at 36 Cents.

No. 14C2265 A very stylish, all wool fabric of rather light weight and semi transparent. It is usually made over an independent lining, contrasting colored linings being frequently used. These etamine fabrics make up and drape very gracefully and represent one of the very newest styles. Comes in a perfect shade of medium black. Etamine of this quality retails at 50 cents and up. Width, 37 inches. Price, per yard...................**36c**

All Wool Black Voile or Panama at 49 Cents.

No. 14C2270 This is a very nobby weave of this new suiting and one that will make up handsomely into any sort of a street, traveling or house dress. It is a semi transparent fabric on the order of canvas. The yarns are hard twisted worsted, making a very firm and durable cloth that will not shrink. Comes in a perfect shade of black. This is an exceptional value for the money. Width, 38 inches. Price, per yard...........**49c**

Fashionable Black Voile at 79 Cents.

No. 14C2285 Imported All Worsted Black Voile, a pretty, open weave fabric, much worn now. It is light weight, of fine, even mesh and woven very firm and wiry. To be worn over black or colored foundations. This is a quality that will surely please the purchaser. Comes in medium blue black. Width, 44 inches. Price, per yard.........................**79c**

Black Twine Cloth or Etamine at 98 Cents.

No. 14C2288 A fabric like the preceding number, but a trifle more open in weave. It is made from the very best round, smooth yarns, and has none of the crepe effect, as seen in most etamines. It will wear as well as a serge or any staple weave and will not shrink. Width, 44 inches. Price, per yard..................**98c**

Black Silk and Wool Eolienne at 75 Cents per Yard.

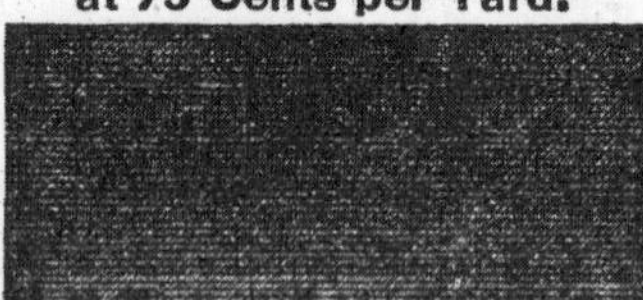

No. 14C2290 Black Silk and Wool Eolienne, a fine sheer fabric that is highly desirable for this season's popular light weight dresses and waists. It is very firmly constructed of pure silk and wool, the silk being thrown to the surface, giving it the appearance of an all silk material. This is a fabric that will drape handsomely and in spite of its light weight will wear very well. Comes in a pretty, lustrous black. Width, 42 inches. Price, per yard...**75c**

Black Silk and Wool Eolienne at $1.15.

No. 14C2295 Black Silk and Wool Eolienne, finer and better than the preceding number, a grade that commonly sells for $1.50 to $1.75. This is one of the richest and most stylish fabrics we are showing this season. The shade of black is clear, bright and lustrous. Width, 44 inches. Price, per yard......**$1.15**

Fine Black Wool Peau de Soie at $1.25.

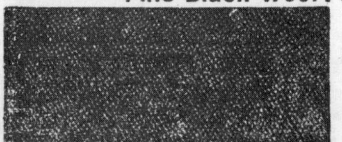

No. 14C2250 The finest kind of an imported worsted fabric, woven the same as an all silk peau de soie. It is medium weight cloth, of close, even texture, made from lustrous blue black, all worsted yarns. It is just the sort of a fabric that lovers of nice black goods will appreciate. It is one of the richest appearing materials made and is a quality that is retailed generally at $1.75. Width, 46 inches. Price, per yard.........................**$1.25**

SILKS.

DEPARTMENT OF PLAIN AND FANCY SILKS.

IN THIS DEPARTMENT will be found every new, staple and desirable weave of plain and fancy silks for dresses, waists, trimmings, linings, etc. We are constantly on the lookout for new ideas in patterns and weaves that we think would be of interest to our customers, and as a result our offerings at all times are strictly new and up to date. The great success of our silk department is due to the fact that we have entirely ignored the old custom of adding fancy profits to our prices. We mark all silks on our usual one small profit plan that prevails throughout our entire house. Thus you can buy silks on the same low price basis that you can sheeting or any other inexpensive material.

OUR GUARANTEE REFUND OFFER. You may select any silk from this catalogue, the same will be shipped to you with the distinct understanding and agreement that if the goods are not as good or better than represented, or if they are not thoroughly satisfactory to you in every way, you are under no obligation to keep them, but can return them to us at our expense and we will refund your money.

SEE PAGE 757 ABOUT FREE SAMPLES. WE DO NOT CUT SILKS ON THE BIAS.

COLORED TAFFETA SILKS.

Colored Taffetaline Silk at 30c.

No. 14C3000 All Silk Taffetaline, almost like taffeta. A pretty, medium weight material, much used for linings, as well as for inexpensive suits and shirt waists. It is very firm in weave, being almost impossible to tear it. It has that stylish rustle so desirable in drop skirt foundations. More than your money's worth promised with every yard of this silk. The colors are white, cream, light blue, pink, burnt orange, nile, gray, turquoise, tan, golden brown, dark brown, violet, reseda green, myrtle green, cardinal, royal blue, navy or black. Width, 19 inches. Price, per yard..........**30c**

Guaranteed Taffeta at 48c.

No. 14C3020 This is a new quality this season, and one of the best values we ever offered. It is a medium weight all silk taffeta that we can positively guarantee not to split, crack, tear or slip on the warp. It is a very desirable silk for waists and dresses and for linings it is superior to any fabric we ever offered. The colors are white, cream, light blue, pink, nile green, yellow, burnt orange, old rose, gray, tan, golden brown, dark brown, turquoise, reseda green, myrtle green, cardinal, wine, royal blue, navy blue or black. Remember, our guarantee goes with every yard. Width, 18½ inches. Price, per yard.....................**48c**

All Silk Chiffon Taffeta at 59c.

No. 14C3030 All Pure Silk Chiffon Taffeta. Not the rustling sort, but a rather soft, heavy silk that will drape nicely in waists and dresses and wear like leather for linings. Colors are white, cream, pink, light blue, nile, gray, tan, old rose, reseda green, golden brown, cardinal, royal blue, navy blue or black. Width, 19 inches. Price, per yard..................................**59c**

All Silk Guaranteed Taffeta, 69c

No. 14C3050 All Pure Silk, Heavy Weight, Wear Guaranteed Taffeta. It has the desirable velvet finish found only in the very best goods. This is by far the richest appearing silk we have ever been able to offer at this price. It is soft and delicate to the touch and slightly rustling. Colors are white, cream, yellow, light blue, pink, turquoise, lavender, nile, rose, tan, pearl gray, olive green, myrtle, cardinal, wine, golden brown, dark brown, royal blue or navy. Width, 19 in. Price, per yd. **69c**

27-inch Wide All Silk Taffeta at 85 Cents.

No. 14C3060 This is a very superior quality of imported All Silk Taffeta. It is very similar to the preceding number, but wider. It will compare favorably with silks offered by retailers as high as $1.25 per yard. Colors are white, cream, light blue, pink, turquoise, gray, lavender, nile, reseda green, old rose, cerise, royal blue, navy blue, tan, light brown, cardinal, garnet or myrtle green. Width, 27 in. Price, per yard...**85c**

Changeable Glace Taffeta Silk at 69 Cents.

No. 14C3070 All Pure Silk Glace Changeable Taffeta, a silk of very beautiful iridescent effect and one that will find favor with those who desire something slightly different from plain, solid colors. Comes in combinations of pink and white, brown and white, violet and black, green and black, cardinal and black, royal blue and black or brown and black. These stylish two-toned silks are much used now both for fancy waists, shirt waist suits and petticoats, as well as for fine linings. Width, 19 inches. Price, per yard........................**69c**

PLAIN COLORED JAPANESE SILKS.

社會式株練發布絹俣川

These dainty and desirable wash silks will be more popular than ever this season. The qualities we offer are perfect in weave, color and finish and are splendid values. See page 757 about free samples.

Our New Kioto Japanese Silk at 25 Cents.

No. 14C3075 A special bargain in an all pure silk fabric, pretty in texture and colorings, and to all appearances as good as some silks that sell for nearly twice the money. This is by far the best low priced silk we have ever offered. Comes in cream, scarlet or black only. Width, 18 inches. Price, per yard.................**25c**

20 and 23-inch Colored Japanese Silk at 35 and 39 Cents.

Plain Japanese Silk, a fine and beautifully woven all silk fabric. It is light in weight, although heavy for this class of goods, but woven so firmly that it will give the very best of service and will wash. The colors are clear and perfect shades of white, cream, light blue, turquoise, pink, old rose, nile, lilac, purple, yellow, bright cardinal, medium cardinal, wine, medium blue, royal blue, navy blue, emerald green, gray, ecru, brown or black.

No. 14C3080 Width, 20 inches. Price, per yard **35c**

No. 14C3090 Width, 23 inches. Price, per yard...............................**39c**

Natural Cream White Japanese Wash Silk.

These silks are in their natural state, just as they come from the weavers, without coloring of any kind, and are very dainty, soft and clinging. While they are light and airy in construction, they are none the less durable, in fact, they will wear much better than the same, or even heavier weight in a cotton fabric. They are a very pretty shade of cream, are all silk, and will wash like muslin.

No. 14C3100 Natural Cream White Habutai Silk. Width, 20 inches. Price, per yard. **31c**

No. 14C3110 Natural Cream White Habutai Silk. Width, 23 inches. Price, per yard. **35c**

No. 14C3120 Natural Cream White Habutai Silk. Width, 27 inches. Price, per yard. **40c**

No. 14C3130 Natural Cream White Habutai Silk. Width, 36 inches. Price, per yard. **53c**

Natural Tan Colored Pongee Silk at 55 Cents.

No. 14C3155 All Pure Silk Pongee in natural tan color. It is a heavy weight, firm and durable cloth that will wash and wear almost everlastingly. Is much used for waists and full costumes, as well as for raglans, sacques and even for fine underwear. It is a very sensible silk to buy, because it sheds dust and does not soil easily. Width, 22 inches. Price, per yard...........................**55c**

Free Samples of Men's Ready Made Clothing.

WE SEND TO ANYONE, FREE ON REQUEST, a complete book showing cloth samples of our entire line of Men's Ready Made Clothing, which we sell at prices less than dealers pay at wholesale. With the sample book, we also send a tape measure and our plain and simple rules for taking your own measure and for ordering, and by which we guarantee a perfect fit and we take all the risk. If the suit or other garment we send you is not perfectly satisfactory in fit, quality or value, you are at liberty to return it to us at our expense, and your money will be promptly refunded. You will be surprised how much you can save on your clothing by sending to us. **If you have never investigated, don't put it off, but write today and ask for a Free Sample Book of Men's Ready Made Clothing.**

WE DO NOT CUT SILKS OR VELVETS ON THE BIAS.

SILKS

WE DO NOT CUT SILKS OR VELVETS ON THE BIAS.

COLORED SATINS.

Plain Satin Duchesse at 35c.

No. 14C3190 **Plain, Solid Colored Satin Duchesse.** Has a very close, firm, all silk satin face and cotton mixed back. It is a grade that usually retails at 50 cents. The colors are white, cream, pink, light blue, turquoise, purple, pearl gray, old rose, cardinal, wine, navy, myrtle, tan, brown or black. Width, 18 inches. Price, per yard..........35c

All Silk Liberty Satin at 49c.

No. 14C3195 **All Pure Silk Twilled Back Liberty Satin,** in plain, solid colors, a silk of beautiful, soft, clinging texture that will make up with unusually rich and stylish effect. It is an extra good one for the money and one that is bound to please the most exacting tastes. The colors are white, cream, yellow, light blue, pink, turquoise, lavender, reseda green, old rose, tan, brown, gray, royal blue, navy, cardinal or black. Width, 20 in. Per yd...49c

All Silk Satin Duchesse at 85c.

No. 14C3210 **Heavy Weight, All Silk, Solid Color Satin Duchesse,** one of the very best qualities imported. It has a finish and luster that will stand hard usage. The colors are pure white, pink, light blue, yellow, nile green, reseda green, turquoise, old rose, lilac, violet or pearl gray. Width, 20 inches. Per yard...85c

MISCELLANEOUS SILKS, PLAIN COLOR WEAVES.

Chiffon Poplinette at 45 Cents.

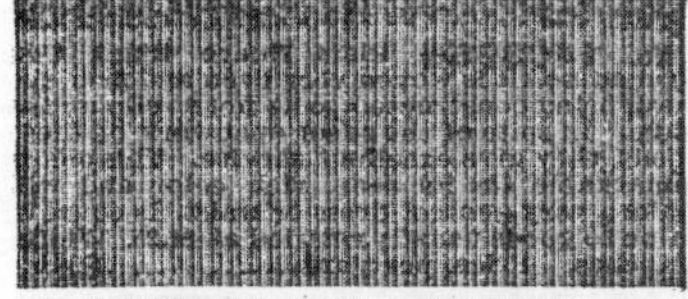

No. 14C3220 **Chiffon Poplinette,** a new creation this season. A medium weight, pin cord silk, woven beautifully soft and lustrous. One that we can guarantee for color and durability. This silk is reversible, both sides being finished equally well, and it is desirable, not only for waists, dresses, etc., but for linings as well. Colors are cream white, light blue, corn color, pink, champagne tan, reseda green, gray, cardinal, golden brown, myrtle green, royal blue, navy blue or black. Width, 18 inches. Price, per yard..........45c

All Silk Crepe de Chine at 65c.

No. 14C3250 **Beautiful, Fine, All Silk Crepe de Chine.** The ideal fabric for wedding gowns and evening wear. The darker colorings are used extensively for street costumes and waists. Ours is a very superior quality, being the equal of goods generally retailed at 90 cents to $1.00. It is soft and dainty and unusually lustrous. Colors are white, cream, pink, light blue, light yellow, nile, lavender, pearl gray, old rose, tan, cardinal, royal blue or black. Width, 23 inches. Price, per yard..........65c

Plain Colored Peau de Soie, 78c

No. 14C3270 **Plain, Solid Colored, All Silk Reversible Peau de Soie,** one of the most desirable plain weave silks at the present time. Ours is a medium heavy weight cloth of very fine construction and we can safely say that it will outlast almost any silk made. It is very luxurious in finish and the colors are choice shades of cream, light yellow, pink, light blue, nile, old rose, pearl gray, turquoise, tan, brown, reseda green, myrtle, cardinal, wine or navy. Width, 19¼ inches. Price, per yard........78c

FANCY STRIPE AND BROCADE COLORED SILKS.

Japanese Kai Ki Wash Silks at 25 Cents.

No. 14C3280 **This is the best quality we ever offered at the price.** Is good weight, close and firm. Comes in a very pretty line of cord stripe designs in a nice assortment of colors, including light blue, pink, red, green, tan or lavender combined with white, also plain solid white. These are sensible silks to buy; they wash like muslin and wear splendidly. Width, 18 in. Per yd....25c

Fancy Japanese Habutai Wash Silks at 35 Cents.

No. 14C3290 **Japanese All Silk Habutai,** similar to the preceding number, but a finer and better quality. The ordinary value of this silk is about 45 to 50 cents, but we contracted direct with the Japanese weavers for an unusually large lot and we made a big saving in price. Comes in beautiful cord stripe designs, in a large line of colors, including light blue, pink, reseda green, tan, cardinal, black or lavender combined with white, also plain solid white. It is a silk that we can recommend for wearing and washing qualities. Width, 18 in. Per yard....35c

Handsome Colored Silk Brocade at 35 Cents.

No. 14C3320 **Colored Brocaded Silk Novelties.** Good weight, well made, goods that will give exceptional service and prove in every way a satisfactory purchase. The designs are especially choice and colors very clear. We show white, cream, yellow, lilac, light blue, pink, nile green, also solid black. Width, 18 inches. Price, per yard..........35c

Fancy Taffeta Silk at 44 Cents.

No. 14C3331 **Here is a fancy taffeta silk without a peer.** The dotted white stripes are almost invisible and the combination of tints on each colored ground are superb. After covering the entire market, we are satisfied that this is easily the most perfect fancy taffeta silk shown this season. The ground colors are light navy blue, golden brown, myrtle green, garnet or black. Width, 18 inches. Price, per yard..........44c

Fancy Taffeta Silk at 65 Cents.

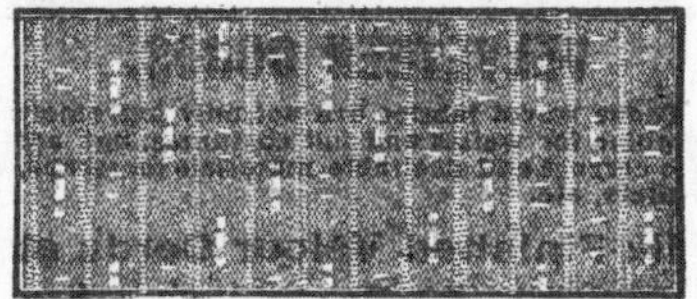

No. 14C3332 **Fancy silks will be worn to a larger extent this season than ever before.** The ground, plain color in each, and dainty, dotted hair line stripe of white, and small dart of white between, as shown, gives the material a nobby appearance without getting away from what is styled a quiet design. We have selected only the shades which are, without question, the latest for this season. They are garnet, brown, myrtle green, medium navy or black. Width, 18½ inches. Price, per yard..........65c

All Silk Printed Warp Taffeta at 69 Cents.

No. 14C3333 **Printed Warp Fancy Colored Taffeta,** an all pure silk novelty that is brand new this season. The ground colors in all are solid shades and can be had either in gray, brown, myrtle green, navy or black, with design as shown in the illustration. The spots or figures are in printed warp shot effects of beautifully contrasting colors, that harmonize nicely with the solid ground colors. It is not an extreme novelty, but a style that will appeal to modest dressers. Width, 19 inches. Price, per yard..........69c

Imported Chameleon Check Silk at 69 Cents.

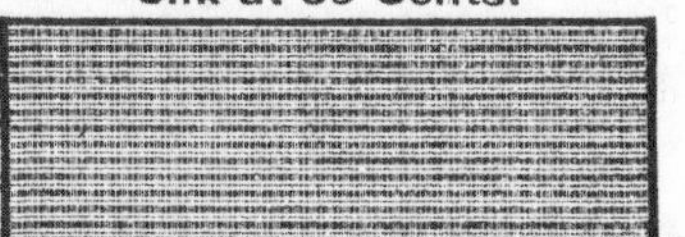

No. 14C3335 **This is one of the newest and richest all silk suiting materials we have to offer.** It is similar to a taffeta in weight and weave, but is much more lustrous than that silk. There being several shades in each color combination, makes the silk as changeable as the chameleon, from which it gets its name. The check is so small and unpronounced as to make the goods appear almost plain. The predominating colors are light blue, burnt orange, golden brown, green and blue or black and white. Width, 18 inches. Price, per yard..........69c

BLACK SILKS, PLAIN AND FANCY.

A MOST COMPLETE RANGE OF SOLID BLACK SILKS, **comprising everything new, staple and desirable in the foreign and domestic goods, both plain and fancy.** Your special attention is directed to the Japanese Black Silks, guaranteed Black Peau de Soie and the guaranteed Black Taffetas. These are by far the best goods in America for the money.

WE HAVE SPARED NO EXPENSE **in searching the markets of the world for the best styles and values to offer our customers and we solicit your orders with the understanding and agreement** that if the goods, when received, are not as good or better values than represented, or if they are not satisfactory in every way, they can be returned to us at our expense and we will refund your money, together with what you paid for freight or express charges.

SEE PAGE 757 ABOUT FREE SAMPLES. **WE DO NOT CUT BLACK SILKS ON THE BIAS.**

BLACK TAFFETA SILK.

Black Taffetaline Silk at 30c.

No. 14C3490 **All Silk Black Taffetaline, almost like Taffeta.** A pretty, medium weight material, much used for linings as well as for inexpensive suits and shirt waists. It is very firm in weave, being almost impossible to tear it. It has that stylish rustle so desirable in drop skirt foundations. Comes in a pretty bright black. Width, 19 inches. Price, per yard..........30c

36-inch Black Taffetaline Silk at 59 Cents.

No. 14C3495 **Yard Wide All Silk Black Taffetaline,** the same quality as the preceding number, only in the 36-inch width. This is a bright, firm, wear resisting silk that is much in demand now and will be found a very satisfactory material for linings, as well as for dresses and waists. Comes in black only. Width, 36 inches. Price, per yard..........59c

All Pure Silk Black Rustling Taffeta at 48 Cents.

No. 14C3510 **At this price one would naturally expect an ordinary grade of Taffeta,** but our guarantee goes with every yard of this silk as being of superior quality, exceedingly well made, of very lustrous finish and rich color and one that will wear and not break. It is one of our most popular numbers of black silk and will give absolute satisfaction, or we stand ready to refund your money. Width, 18 inches. Price, per yard..........48c

All Silk Black Chiffon Taffeta at 59 Cents.

No. 14C3520 **All Pure Silk Black Taffeta,** not the rustling sort, but a rather soft, heavy silk that will drape nicely in waists and dresses and wear like leather for linings. Width, 19 inches. Price, per yard..........59c

Yard Wide Black Rustling Taffeta at 95 Cents.

No. 14C3530 **Yard Wide Black Taffeta, medium weight and good quality.** Considering the price, it is one of the best numbers we have. We always advocate the purchase of better taffetas and offer this quality to satisfy the demand for a low priced, yard wide silk. Width, 36 inches. Price, per yard..........95c

GUARANTEED ALL SILK BLACK TAFFETA.

Scientific study applied to Taffeta has resulted in bringing out a most perfect quality of good weight, medium soft and lustrous rustling Taffeta. We positively guarantee these goods against tearing and cracking and you can buy any of the widths quoted below with the assurance that you are getting extraordinary value and that you run no risk, as we will refund your money if the silk is not entirely satisfactory. There are five strong arguments in favor of these taffetas. **They are all silk, inexpensive, unbreakable, everlasting and guaranteed.**

No. 14C3540 **19-inch guaranteed Taffeta.** Price, per yard..........65c
No. 14C3550 **21-inch guaranteed Taffeta.** Price, per yard..........72c
No. 14C3560 **23-inch guaranteed Taffeta.** Price, per yard..........79c
No. 14C3570 **26-inch guaranteed Taffeta.** Price, per yard..........90c
No. 14C3580 **36-inch guaranteed Taffeta.** Price, per yard..........$1.19

Heavy Weight, Guaranteed Black Waterproof Taffeta.

Our next better grade of all Silk Black Taffeta is a thoroughly waterproof and unspottable silk, a trifle heavier than the preceding numbers, is very well made of perfect pliable texture and guaranteed not to split, break, tear or crack. This silk is not only desirable for all purposes for which taffeta can be used, but is also very appropriate for outside garments, wraps, jackets, raglans, etc.

No. 14C3610 **36-inch Black Waterproof Taffeta.** Price, per yard..........$1.40

Stylish All Silk Novelty at 75 Cents.

No. 14C3338 **Just a little out of the ordinary, this will appeal to all who are looking for the best that is offered, and who recognize good values on sight.** Woven in a high grade, fine pure silk taffeta, possessed of exceptional durability and in height of luster it is unsurpassed. In this, the delicate, dotted lines appear in beautiful tints in contrasting colors, giving an appearance that at once gives the fabric the stamp of merit. Over all is brocaded, in brilliant silk of the same shade as the ground color, a neat leaf design, like the illustration. Ground colors are turquoise blue, golden brown, garnet, myrtle green or royal blue. Width, 19 inches. Price, per yard..........75c

BLACK JAPANESE SILKS.

Plain Black Japanese Habutai Silk.

Silks of our own importation at money saving prices. The qualities in all are excellent, being close and firm in weave, all silk and absolutely fast black. While they are medium light weight, they are heavy for this class of goods and will wear much better than the same weight of linen or cotton goods.

No. 14C3630 **Black Habutai Silk.** Width, 20 inches. Price, per yard..........35c
No. 14C3640 **Black Habutai Silk.** Width, 23 inches. Price, per yard..........39c
No. 14C3650 **Black Habutai Silk.** Width, 27 inches. Price, per yard..........46c
No. 14C3660 **Black Habutai Silk.** Width, 36 inches. Price, per yard..........67c

BLACK PEAU DE SOIE.

All Silk Black Peau Messaline at 49 Cents.

No. 14C3665 **All Pure Silk Peau Messaline, or Peau de Soie,** one of the new things in lustrous black silks. It is woven about the same as a peau de soie, but is softer and more brilliant, although about the same weight. This silk is made in Italy, dyed in France and is superior to similar weaves of domestic goods, and is also much cheaper. Comes in bright black only. Width, 18 inches. Price, per yard..........49c

All Silk Black Peau de Soie 69c.

No. 14C3670 **This is one of our leading numbers and one of which we sell hundreds of pieces.** It is lustrous in finish, perfect in weave and a heavy weight, reversible, all silk peau de soie, guaranteed to wear and not split. Retailers generally ask 90 cents to $1.00 for this grade. Width, 19 inches. Price, per yard..69c

Guaranteed All Silk Black Peau de Soie.

We quote below four widths of black Peau de Soie, all identical in quality. They are heavy weight but of soft and delicate touch, strictly all pure silk, of rich and lustrous finish, reversible and are **positively guaranteed to wear and not crack or split.** You can order any of the widths quoted below with the assurance that you will get extraordinary value for your money and if the goods do not please you, they can be returned to us at our expense and we will refund your money.

No. 14C3680 **20-inch Peau de Soie.** Price, per yard..........85c
No. 14C3690 **23-inch Peau de Soie.** Price, per yard..........95c
No. 14C3700 **27-inch Peau de Soie.** Price, per yard..........$1.12
No. 14C3710 **36-inch Peau de Soie.** Price, per yard..........$1.45

BLACK SATINS.

Black Satin Duchesse at 35c.

No. 14C3730 **Plain Black Satin Duchesse,** a good weight well made silk. Has a very close and fine all silk satin face and cotton mixed back. Width, 18 inches. Price, per yard..........35c

All Silk Black Liberty Satin at 49 Cents.

No. 14C3745 **All Pure Silk, Twilled Back Black Liberty Satin,** a silk of beautiful, soft, clinging texture that will make up in an unusually rich and stylish effect. It is an extra good one for the money and one that is bound to please the most exacting tastes. Width, 20 inches. Price, per yard..........49c

All Pure Silk Black Satin Duchesse at 60 Cents.

No. 14C3750 **All Pure Silk, Twilled Back Black Satin Duchesse.** This is positively the biggest bargain ever offered in satin duchesse, being the equal of goods sold generally at 90 cents per yard. It is one of our big leaders and a satin of which we sell hundreds of pieces in a season. It is a medium heavy weight fabric, constructed unusually fine and firm and has a most beautiful luxurious finish and color. Width, 19 inches. Price, per yard..........60c

Black Satin Duchesse at 75c.

No. 14C3760 **Twilled Back Black Silk Satin Duchesse** of unusually luminous finish and color. Heavier and wider than the preceding number and one that is bound to find favor with good dressers. Width, 21 inches. Price, per yard..........75c

Our Challenge Black Satin Duchesse at 95 Cents.

No. 14C3770 **We challenge competition on this Heavy, Wide Black Silk Satin Duchesse.** It is wider and heavier than the preceding number and is much favored, not only for waists and dresses, but for wraps, jackets, etc., as it is exceptionally fine and durable. Width, 24 inches. Price, per yard..........95c

Wide Black Lining Satin, 75c.

No. 14C3795 **Yard Wide Black Lining Satin,** heavier and much more durable than satin duchesse. It is constructed especially for lining purposes and will not rough up. Used extensively for lining wraps and jackets, as well as tailor made suits. A great value. Width, 36 inches. Price, per yard..........75c

SILKS. VELVETS. LININGS.

MISCELLANEOUS PLAIN WEAVES.

All Silk Black Crepe de Chine at 65 Cents.

No. 14C3820 **Beautiful, Fine, All Silk Black Crepe de Chine,** a very superior quality, being the equal of goods generally retailed at 90 cents to $1.00. It is soft and dainty and unusually lustrous. Width, 23 inches.
Price, per yard..........................65c

Black Grosgrain Silk at 95c.

No. 14C3840 **Heavy Weight Lustrous Black Grosgrain Silk.** Has a well defined round cord and is fine and well made. Grosgrain silks have stood the test of years of popularity and the demand for them never ceases. Width, 23 inches. Price, per yard..........................95c

Black Chiffon Poplinette at 45 Cents.

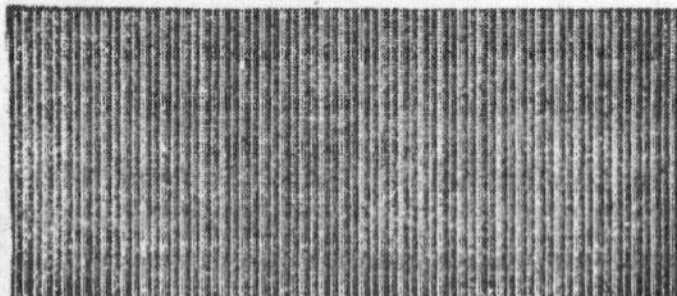

No. 14C3850 **Chiffon Poplinette,** a new creation this season. A medium weight, pin cord silk, woven beautifully soft and lustrous. One that we can guarantee for color and durability. This silk is reversible, both sides being finished equally well, and it is desirable, not only for waists, dresses, etc., but also for linings. Comes in a bright shade of lustrous black. Width, 18 inches, Price, per yard.45c

Black Silk Armuretta at 69c.

No. 14C3860 **A strikingly handsome, solid black, all pure silk material.** It is a good weight silk, very firm and well constructed and is so near a plain weave that it could almost be called a staple silk. Those desiring a silk that is neither a pronounced fancy nor decidedly plain weave will be suited with this number. The value is excellent. Width, 22 inches.
Price, per yard..........................69c

Black Ground Novelty Silk.

No. 14C3885 **A good weight silk of nice, pliable texture.** Black taffeta ground with black brocade designs, also colored figures as seen in illustration. The ground in all is black with figures of different colors, as follows: Rose, corn color, emerald, turquoise or cardinal. The general effect of the silk is black, the colors not being at all pronounced. Width, 19 inches. Price, per yard..........................69c

IMPORTED BLACK SILK GRENADINES.

Black Silk Grenadine at 69c.

No. 14C3920 **The illustration represents one of the patterns of this very popular dress and waist fabric.** They come in a variety of small, medium and large designs, also stripe patterns. This is a rich and lustrous silk grenadine, that will make up with handsome effect, either over a black lining or over one of a contrasting color. The mesh of these goods is exceedingly firm and superior to goods that we have heretofore sold as high as 98 cents. Width, 44 inches. Price, per yard..........................69c

Beautiful Black Silk Grenadine at 89 Cents.

No. 14C3930 **A very handsome quality of Black Silk Fancy Grenadine.** Comes in small and medium sized designs that are shown for the first time this season. Anyone desiring an exclusive style will find it in this number. These goods are not light weight nor extremely thin, like most grenadines, but are good weight and, although sheer, are unusually firm in construction, and will give as good service as many solid weave fabrics. Width, 44 inches.
Price, per yard..........................89c

High Class Black Silk Grenadine at $1.19.

No. 14C3940 **We cannot speak too highly in praise of this extra fine quality of Black Silk Fancy Grenadine.** The designs are new and exclusive, either floral or stripe patterns, and the weave is exceptionally firm, even and durable. Retailers generally make large profits on this character of goods, frequently asking as high as $1.75 for this grade. Width, 44 inches.
Price, per yard..........................$1.19

Plain Weave Black Silk Grenadine at 85 Cents.

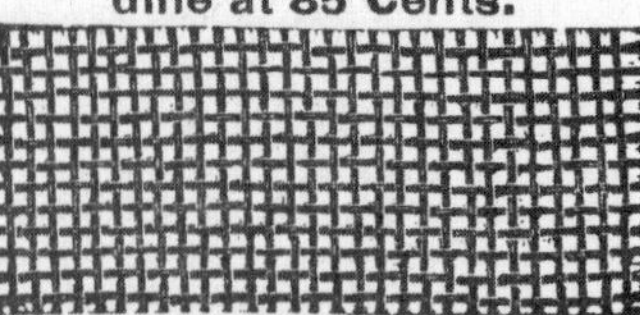

No. 14C3950 **Plain Weave Black Silk Grenadine.** It is woven very even and firm, the mesh being constructed so as not to slip on the warp. In spite of the sheer openwork of these goods, they give excellent service. This one is remarkable for its deep, rich color and will make a very genteel dress or waist. Is equal in value to goods usually retailed at $1.25. Width, 44 inches. Price, per yard..........................85c

DEPARTMENT OF

VELVETS, VELVETEENS AND VELOUR CORDS.

A WORD ABOUT OUR VELVETS AND VELVETEENS. We carry only the most perfectly made, dyed and finished goods to be had. They are unequaled for luster and depth of color, and values are better than obtainable elsewhere.

NOTE—We do not cut velvets, velveteens or cords on the bias.

COLORED VELVETEENS.

Dress Velveteen at 25 Cents.

No. 14C3960 **An excellent quality for the price.** We never before were able to offer such a good one. The colors are cream, light blue, pink, nile, old rose, gray, turquoise, tan, brown, violet, hunter's green, cardinal, wine, royal blue, navy blue or black. Width, 18 inches. Price, per yard..........................25c

Florodora Velvetta at 38c.

No. 14C3970 **This is an improvement over velveteens that have sold previous seasons.** Its depth of color and silky finish cannot be equaled in ordinary velveteens. Colors are white, cream, light blue, pink, nile, old rose, gray, turquoise, tan, brown, violet, myrtle, cardinal, wine, royal blue, navy blue or black. Width, 22 inches. Price, per yard..........................38c

Fine Silk Finished Velveteen.

No. 14C3980 **This is similar to the preceding number,** but is a shade better in quality and a greater value than we ever offered before at the price. It has an excellent silk finish and it simply will not wear out. Colors are white, cream, light blue, pink, nile, old rose, gray, turquoise, tan, brown, violet, myrtle, cardinal, wine, royal blue, navy blue or black. Width, 22 inches. Price, per yard..........................46c

Our Best Silk Finished Velveteen at 69 Cents.

No. 14C3990 **One of the best qualities made.** It is of remarkable brilliancy and beauty of coloring, and a quality that is frequently sold by dealers as high as $1.00. It is especially adapted for the finest kind of waists or full suits, as well as being very desirable for misses' cloaks and dresses and boys' suits. Colors are white, cream, light blue, pink, nile, gray, turquoise, tan, brown, lilac, myrtle, cardinal, wine, royal blue, navy or black. Width, 24 inches.
Price, per yard..........................69c

COLORED SILK VELVETS.

Croise Back Silk Velvet at 59c.

No. 14C4000 **An All Silk Close Pile English Velvet with croise back.** The term "croise back" means that there are additional threads twisted in with the pile which prevents the latter pulling out. Velvets of this weave and finish sell at much higher prices. Colors are pure white, cream white, pink, old rose, light blue, turquoise, lilac, yellow, gray, cardinal, wine, royal blue, navy, tan, light brown, dark brown, myrtle green or black. Width, 18 inches.
Price, per yard..........................59c

Croise Back Silk Velvet at 75 Cents.

No. 14C4010 **This is a very superior quality of Silk Velvet.** It has a deep, rich, all silk pile and a very handsome finish. This velvet is made by one of the leading weavers in France and is dyed by the best dyer in England, a combination that insures most perfect results in velvets. The colors are white, cream, light blue, sapphire blue, pink, old rose, gray, turquoise, tan, brown, light myrtle, dark myrtle, cardinal, wine, royal blue, navy or black. Width, 18 inches.
Price, per yard..........................75c

PLAIN BLACK VELVETEENS.

Black Velveteen at 25 Cents.

No. 14C4020 **An excellent, inexpensive quality of Black Velveteen.** Comes in a clear, perfect coloring. Width, 18 inches.
Price, per yard..........................25c

Black Florodora Velvetta at 38 Cents.

No. 14C4030 **This is an improvement over velveteens that have sold previous seasons.** Its depth of color and silky finish cannot be equaled in ordinary velveteens. Comes in a rich shade of black. Width, 22 inches.
Price, per yard..........................38c

Black Silk Finished Velveteen at 46 Cents.

No. 14C4040 **This is similar to the preceding number,** but is a shade better in quality. Has an excellent silk finish and comes in a perfect shade of lustrous black. Width, 22 inches.
Price, per yard..........................46c

Our Best Silk Finished Black Velveteen at 69 Cents.

No. 14C4050 **One of the best qualities made.** It is of remarkable brilliancy and beauty of coloring, and a quality that is frequently sold by dealers as high as $1.00. The shade of black is excellent. Width, 24 inches.
Price, per yard..........................69c

BLACK SILK VELVETS.

Black Silk Velvet at 59 Cents.

No. 14C4070 **Good Quality Black Silk Velvet,** deep pile and lustrous coloring. Width, 18 inches. Price, per yard..........................59c

Black Silk Velvet at 75 Cents.

No. 14C4080 **An All Silk, Close Pile English Velvet with croise back.** This is one of our most popular sellers and is a splendid value for the money. Comes in a lustrous shade of black. Width, 18 inches. Price, per yard..........................75c

Croise Back, Black Silk Velvet at 95 Cents.

No. 14C4090 **Handsome Silk Velvet with croise back,** a very choice quality. This is a very popular number with us and one that will give our customers the very best kind of service. Width, 18 inches.
Price, per yard..........................95c

Fine Silk Warp Black Velvet at $1.20.

No. 14C4100 **A better quality than the preceding number,** has a closer, finer, all silk pile and a croise back. This is one of the very best English dyed qualities, one that will make up beautifully and give good wear. Width, 19 inches. Price, per yard..........................$1.20

VELVETEEN CORDS.

These velvet fabrics are not only extremely popular for waists and full costumes, but are the correct and desirable materials for wraps, jackets, etc.

Silk Finished Velour Cords at 43 Cents.

No. 14C4120 **A very handsome and inexpensive quality of the intensely popular corded velvets.** The cloth is medium heavy weight and the cords are rather narrow and have a lustrous, silky finish. A strong argument in favor of velour cords is that they are almost everlasting. This number will be found an excellent one for children's wear. Colors are cream white, tan, cardinal, garnet, brown, navy or black. Width, 23 inches. Price, per yard..........................43c

Handsome Corded Velour at 59 Cents.

No. 14C4130 **Corded Velour for waists and full costumes.** A very lustrous and handsome quality, with moderately large cords. These goods have a deep, rich pile and make up with exceedingly genteel effect. Colors are cream white, gray, tan, medium brown, myrtle, cardinal, wine, light navy, dark navy or black. This is a very good value for the money. Width, 22 inches.
Price, per yard..........................59c

Metallic Printed Velvet at 55c.

No. 14C4150 **Fancy velvets are very stylish and much in demand for waists and full costumes.** The silver printings on the rich, dark background are most beautiful in effect and the durability of this material is too well known to need comment. Ground colors are myrtle green, dark cardinal, medium brown, black or navy blue with silver printings of dots or small set designs. Width, 22 inches. Price, per yard..........................55c

DEPARTMENT OF LININGS

This is one of our most important departments, and one that should not be overlooked by those ordering dress goods, silks, cloakings or cotton fabrics. We can save you at least 25 to 40 per cent on all linings.

WE DO NOT SAMPLE LININGS.

WAIST LININGS.

Best Sateen Twilled Waist Lining at 6½ Cents.

No. 14C4440 **A splendid heavy weight Waist Lining** in black, brown, drab or white. Width 27 inches. Price per yard......6½c

Good Quality Silesia at 8c.

No. 14C4450 **A very good quality of Silesia,** well made and durable. Comes in white, pink, light blue, cardinal, wine, olive, slate, myrtle green, brown, navy or black. Width, 36 inches. Price, per yard........8c

Roman Silesia at 11 Cents.

No. 14C4470 **Our Best Extra Fine Twilled Silesia,** a nice weight lining that will give excellent service. The colors are white, pink, light blue, pearl gray, medium gray, cardinal, wine, brown, myrtle green, navy or black. Width, 36 inches. Price, per yard, 11c

PERCALINES.

Kid Finished Percaline at 10c.

No. 14C4490 **This number of Percaline is kid finished,** a particularly fine, durable quality, and a leader with us. The colors are white, cream, pink, light blue, old rose, royal, pearl, lavender, nile green, myrtle green, yellow, tan, medium brown, heliotrope, reseda green, pearl gray, medium gray, cardinal, wine, navy or black. Width, 36 inches.
Price, per yard..........................10c

Best Waist Percaline at 13½c.

No. 14C4500 **This is an extra fine quality of Percaline,** a lining that retails generally at 18 to 20 cents. It is fine and even in weave, will wear well and not stretch. The colors are white, cream, pink, old rose, royal, tan, light blue, yellow, nile, reseda green, myrtle green, pearl gray, slate, cardinal, wine, medium brown, navy or black. Width, 36 inches.
Price, per yard..........................13½c

Carlisle Satin Moire Lining at 12 Cents.

No. 14C4510 **Moire Striped Effect Taffeta Lining.** A very fine quality, of nice, medium weight, and one that will give exceptional service. The rich moire effect on the bright black satin ground makes a handsome lining for the best dresses. Comes in black only. Width, 36 inches. Price, per yard........12c

Mercerized Spun Glass Rustling Lining at 8 Cents.

No. 14C4520 **This is one of the newest and most popular lining materials.** It resembles silk and is crisp and rustling. It is very perfect in weave, of medium weight, and has a beautiful silky finish. Colors are cream white, tan, dark gray, light gray, myrtle green, cardinal, wine, brown, navy or black. Width, 36 inches. Price, per yard..........................8c

Mercerized Spun Glass Rustling Lining at 12 Cents.

No. 14C4525 **A finer and better quality than the preceding number.** These rich, silky, rustling linings are very much in demand and we can recommend them for style and durability. Colors are white, cream, pink, light blue, old rose, light gray, slate, nile green, yellow, cardinal, myrtle green, navy, cerise, tan, brown, wine or black. Width, 36 inches.
Price, per yard..........................12c

Nearsilk or Shadow Silk, 15c.

No. 14C4540 **Nearsilk Dress Lining,** not silk, but closely resembling it, medium weight, very fine, well made, and used for lining the very best dresses. Can be had in white, cream, light blue, pink, lavender, lemon, turquoise, pearl, old rose, nile green, reseda green, myrtle, green, orange, tan, medium brown, cardinal, wine, cerise, purple, slate, navy or black. Width, 36 inches. Price, per yard..........................15c

LININGS.

SKIRT LININGS.

Best Quality Kid Finished Cambric at 3½ Cents.

No. 14C4550 Kid Finished Lining Cambric. Ours is the best 64x64 cloth. The colors are white, cream, yellow, nile green, lavender, pink, light blue, purple, light gray, slate, tan, brown, myrtle green, cardinal, wine, navy or black. Width, 25 inches. Price, per yard....3½c

Taffeta Skirt Lining at 8 Cents.

No. 14C4560 A good grade of Medium Weight Taffeta Skirt Lining, one that will wear well. Comes in black only. Width, 36 inches. Price, per yard....8c

Taffeta Skirt Lining at 10 Cents.

No. 14C4570 A very fine quality of Taffeta Skirt Lining. A desirable lining for better class of dress goods; comes in a very perfect shade of black. Width, 36 inches. Price, per yard....10c

CANVAS.

Elastic Canvas at 6 Cents.

No. 14C4620 Elastic Canvas, in good quality and nice weight. The proper thing for the bottom of skirts. Comes in black, tan, brown, gray or white. Width, 25 inches. Price, per yard....6c

All Linen Canvas Duck at 12c.

No. 14C4630 Elastic Canvas Duck, strictly all pure Irish linen; is heavy weight, stiff and durable, and one of the most popular linen canvases on the market. It insures a perfect shape to the garment. Comes in tan, gray, brown, white or black. Width, 25 inches. Price, per yard....12c

MERCERIZED SATEEN.

Heavy Mercerized Lining Sateen at 12 Cents.

No. 14C4690 A Heavy Weight Mercerized Lining or Skirting Sateen, highly desirable for lining purposes as well as for underskirts. It is a very firm and durable cloth and has a beautiful silky finish. The colors are tan, brown, royal blue, navy, cardinal, wine, turquoise, light gray, dark gray, pink, light blue, myrtle green, white, cream or black. Width, 30 inches. Price, per yard....12c

Heavy Mercerized Sateen Linings or Skirtings at 17c.

No. 14C4700 Heavy Weight Mercerized Sateen Linings. Guaranteed permanent finish. These goods are beautifully made and have a silky luster, unequaled in any other cotton fabric made. They are not only adapted for fine linings, but are used extensively for dress purposes and for petticoats. They will wear almost everlastingly. The colors are white, cream, yellow, light blue, pink, old rose, cerise, cadet, heliotrope, purple, nile green, olive green, tan, medium brown, pearl gray, slate, cardinal, wine, royal blue, navy blue or black. Width, 36 inches. Price, per yard....17c

Heavy Mercerized Black Skirting Sateen at 22 Cents.

No. 14C4710 A very handsome satin finished fabric, of heavy weight and perfect, even weave, used for petticoats as well as for best lining purposes. Comes in a rich and lustrous shade of black. Width, 36 inches. Price, per yard....22c

Heavy Mercerized Black Skirting Sateen at 29 Cents.

No. 14C4720 Mercerized Bright Black Skirting Sateen, same as the preceding number, but a better quality. It is the highest grade manufactured. Steaming or ironing cannot affect it in any way. Comes in a rich, silky black. Width, 36 inches. Price, per yard....29c

Imperial Moire at 22 Cents.

No. 14C4725 Rich and Silky Imperial Moire. For drop skirts and linings, as well as for jackets, capes, wraps, etc. A medium heavy weight material with beautiful moire or watered finish, that will not grow shiny or catch the dust. Colors absolutely fast and uncrockable. Comes in white, cream, light blue, old rose, slate, tan, brown, myrtle, garnet, royal blue, navy blue or black. Width, 33 inches. Price, per yard....22c

FOR BLACK SILK LINING SATIN SEE No. 14C3795, IN SILK DEPARTMENT.

BLACK AND COLORED HENRIETTA SATEENS.

Fast Black Henrietta Sateen at 10 Cents.

No. 14C4750 This is a very good quality of Fast Black Henrietta Sateen, good weight and perfect color. Width, 30 inches. Per yard, 10c

Fast Black Henrietta Sateen at 12 Cents.

No. 14C4760 This is a very fine quality of Fast Black Henrietta Sateen and one of our most popular numbers. Good weight and guaranteed fast color. Width, 31 inches. Per yd. 12c

Fast Black Silk Finished Sateen at 15 Cents.

No. 14C4770 This Handsome Silk Finished Henrietta Twilled Sateen has the appearance of an all wool henrietta that would cost double the money. Very good weight, guaranteed fast color. Width, 31 inches. Price, per yd....15c

Silk Finished Black Sateen at 18 Cents.

No. 14C4780 This is the very best make of Silk Finished Black Sateen. Has a fine, close henrietta twill, good weight and absolutely indelible color. This sateen retails in ordinary stores at 25 cents per yard. Width, 32 inches. Price, per yard....18c

Solid Black Brocaded Henrietta Sateen at 12 Cents.

No. 14C4790 This is a very fine quality of Lustrous Brocaded Sateen with new and stylish bright brocaded designs of large, medium or small size. Comes in solid fast black only. Width, 28 inches. Price, per yard, 12c

Silk Finished Brocaded Black Sateen at 16 Cents.

No. 14C4800 This is the very finest quality of Black Brocaded Sateen on the market. It has all the style and appearance of an all wool henrietta brocade. Comes in a very handsome line of bright brocaded designs of large, medium or small size. This is a superior quality of sateen and one that will give absolute satisfaction. Comes in solid guaranteed fast black only. Width, 29 inches. Per yard, 16c

Colored Dress Sateens at 11c.

No. 14C4810 Colored Dress Sateens are much in demand for all wash goods purposes, as well as for interlinings. This is one of our most popular numbers and comes in a perfect line of solid color shadings of pink, light blue, nile green, yellow, tan, slate, royal blue, navy blue, brown, turkey red, wine, cream white or pure white. The fabric is of medium weight, with perfect, even texture and good, clear shadings. It is an exceptional value for the money. Width, 31 inches. Per yard, 11c

Silk Finished Colored Sateen at 16 Cents.

No. 14C4820 This is the best quality of Colored Sateen, one that will give absolute satisfaction. It is of medium weight, with perfect, fine henrietta twill and in a texture highly desirable for interlinings as well as for wash dress purposes. The colors are pink, light blue, nile green, yellow, slate, tan, royal blue, navy blue, brown, turkey red, wine, cream white or pure white. This is a very high class fabric and at the price we defy competition. Width, 31 inches. Price, per yard....16c

DOMESTIC DEPARTMENT.

THIS SEASON finds us in a stronger position in the Domestic market than ever before and we can safely say without boasting that we are among the very largest dealers in the country in these staple goods, and we take this opportunity of again impressing upon you the fact that we are determined to undersell all kinds of competition, determined that no other concern in the country shall sell you domestics as low or give you as good, careful and conscientious service in the matter of filling your wants as we will.

Talk is cheap and we could cover pages with it, but values speak louder than words, and what we desire is that you send your orders to us and then let the merchandise do the talking.

OUR GUARANTEE OFFER. Send your order to us for any goods in this department and upon receipt of same, if they are not as good or better than represented or you expect, or if they are not entirely satisfactory to you in every way, and if you are not convinced that you are getting better value for your money than you could get elsewhere, you are under no obligations to keep the goods, but can return them at our expense of transportation charges both ways and we will refund your money. We know of no offer more liberal than this.

WE DO NOT SAMPLE DOMESTICS. REMEMBER, you have the assistance of an expert in this department in filling your order. You will find the goods perfectly satisfactory or we will refund your money.

UNBLEACHED SHEETINGS.

We handle none but the best brands, and each number may be depended upon as the standard of its class. Our prices are unapproachable. We do not recommend for sheeting purposes the first grade quoted. It is extensively used as a plant bed cloth, also as a wall covering, for those desiring something better and heavier than a cheese cloth.

No. 36C10 Width, 36 inches. Price, per yard....4½c
By the piece of about 60 yards, per yard, 4¼c

No. 36C14 Width, 36 inches. Price, per yard....4¾c
By the piece of about 60 yards, per yard, 4½c

No. 36C18 Width, 36 inches. Price, per yard....5½c
By the piece of about 60 yards, per yard, 5¼c

No. 36C22 Width, 36 inches. Price, per yard....6½c
By the piece of about 60 yards, per yard, 6¼c

No. 36C26 Width, 40 inches. Price, per yard....7½c
By the piece of about 55 yards, per yard, 7¼c

Wide Unbleached Sheetings.

This line of wide unbleached sheetings has no equal, at or near our prices, either in weight, durability or finish. The measurement given is the actual width.

No. 36C30 Width, 42 inches. Price, per yard....10½c
By the piece of about 45 yards, per yard, 10¼c

No. 36C34 Width, 45 inches. Price, per yard....11c
By the piece of about 45 yards, per yd...10⅝c

No. 36C38 Width, 54 inches. Price, per yard....12c
By the piece of about 45 yards, per yd..11½c

No. 36C42 Width, 69 inches. Price, per yard....16c
By the piece of about 45 yards, per yd..15½c

No. 36C46 Width, 78 inches. Price, per yard....18c
By the piece of about 45 yards, per yd..17¼c

No. 36C50 Width, 87 inches. Price, per yard....20c
By the piece of about 45 yards, per yd....19c

Best Qualities.

This is by far the most serviceable sheeting made. It is used extensively by hotels, boarding houses, etc., where unusual durability is required. Will surely please you when you see it and retain your confidence after long use.

No. 36C66 Width, 69 inches. Price, per yard....18c
By the piece of about 45 yards, per yd..17¼c

No. 36C70 Width, 78 inches. Price, per yard....20c
By the piece of about 45 yards, per yd....19c

No. 36C74 Width, 87 inches. Price, per yard....22c
By the piece of about 45 yards, per yd....21c

HALF BLEACHED MUSLIN.

Finished softer than the pure bleached cotton and will wear well.

No. 36C76 Half Bleached Muslin. Width, 36 inches. Price, per yard....7¼c
By the piece of about 60 yards, per yard...7c

Bleached Muslins.

Our domestic business has been built up on just such values as these. We offer this line of yard wide bleached cottons in competition with goods sold by others at 10 per cent more money and have no fear of the results.

No. 36C78 Width, 36 inches. Per yard....5c
By the piece of about 55 yards, per yard..4⅞c

No. 36C82 Width, 36 inches. Per yard, 5¾c
By the piece of about 55 yards, per yard 5½c

No. 36C86 Width, 36 inches. Per yard, 6¾c
By the piece of about 55 yards, per yard..6½c

No. 36C90 Width, 36 inches. Per yard. 7½c
By the piece of about 55 yards, per yard. 7¼c

No. 36C94 Width, 36 inches. Per yard....8c
By the piece of about 55 yards, per yard..7½c

EXTRA FINE WHITE CAMBRIC MUSLINS.

These goods are finished soft for the needle and we highly recommend them for ladies' and children's fine wear.

No. 36C98 Superior White Cambric, 36 inches wide. Price, per yard....7½c
By the piece of about 55 yards, per yard..7¼c

No. 36C102 Berkeley White Cambric, 36 inches wide. Price, per yard....8½c
By the piece of about 55 yards, per yard...8c

No. 36C106 Wamsutta White Cambric, 36 inches wide. Price, per yard....10½c
By the piece of about 55 yards, per yd....10c

BLEACHED INDIAN HEAD SHRUNK MUSLIN.

No. 36C108 Best Quality Bleached Indian Head Shrunk Muslin. Width, 36 inches. Price, per yard....11c
By the piece of about 50 yards, per yd..10½c

BEST WIDE HALF BLEACHED SHEETINGS.

These will give exceptional wear and wash white.

No. 36C112 Half Bleached Sheeting. Width, 69 inches. Price, per yard....20c
By the piece of about 45 yards, per yard..19c

No. 36C115 Half Bleached Sheeting. Width, 78 inches. Price, per yard....22c
By the piece of about 45 yards, per yard..21c

No. 36C117 Half Bleached Sheeting. Width, 87 inches. Price, per yard....24c
By the piece of about 45 yards, per yard..23c

WIDE BLEACHED SHEETINGS.

This is a good, honest value, and a trade retainer.

No. 36C119 Width, 42 inches. Price, per yard....11c
By the piece of about 45 yards, per yard 10⅝c

No. 36C121 Width, 45 inches. Price, per yard....12c
By the piece of about 45 yards, per yard 11½c

No. 36C122 Width, 54 inches. Price, per yard....14c
By the piece of about 45 yards, per yard 13½c

No. 36C126 Width, 69 inches. Price, per yard....18c
By the piece of about 45 yards, per yard 17¼c

No. 36C130 Width, 78 inches. Price, per yard....20c
By the piece of about 45 yards, per yard. 19c

No. 36C134 Width, 87 inches. Price, per yard....22c
By the piece of about 45 yards, per yard. 21c

Best Qualities Wide Bleached Sheetings.

No. 36C142 Width, 42 inches. Per yd, 12½c
By the piece of about 45 yards, per yard 12c

No. 36C150 Width, 54 inches. Per yard, 14c
By the piece of about 45 yards, per yard 13½c

No. 36C162 Width, 69 inches. Per yard, 21c
By the piece of about 45 yards, per yard 20c

No. 36C164 Width, 78 inches. Per yard, 23c
By the piece of about 45 yards, per yard 22c

BLEACHED PILLOW CASE CLOTH.

Thoroughly grass bleached and good texture.

No. 36C176 Width, 45 inches. Price, per yard....13c
By the piece of about 45 yards, per yard 12½c

No. 36C180 Width, 50 inches. Price, per yard....15c
By the piece of about 45 yards, per yard 14½c

BLEACHED TUBULAR SEAMLESS PILLOW CASING.

No side seams are required; a very satisfactory cotton.

No. 36C182 Width, 42 inches. Price, per yard....14½c
By the piece of about 45 yards, per yard 14c

No. 36C183 Width, 45 inches. Price, per yard....15½c
By the piece of about 45 yards, per yard 15c

UNBLEACHED DRILLING OR POCKETING.

No. 36C196 Width, 29 inches. Price, per yard....7c
By the piece of about 60 yards, per yard 6¾c

WHITE DUCK OR CANVAS.

No. 36C220 Eight ounces to the yard. Width, 29 inches. Price, per yard.... 9¾c
By the piece of about 60 yards, per yard, 9½c

No. 36C224 Ten ounces to the yard. Width, 29 inches. Price, per yard....12½c
By the piece of about 60 yards, per yd.. 12c

CHEESE, BUTTER OR DAIRYCLOTH

No. 36C228 Unbleached Cheese Cloth, 36 inches wide. Price, per yard....2¼c
By the piece of about 70 yards, per yard, 2⅛c

No. 36C232 Unbleached Cheese Cloth, 36 inches wide. Price, per yard....3¼c
By the piece of about 70 yards, per yard, 3⅛c

No. 36C236 Bleached Butter Cloth, 36 inches wide. Price, per yard....3¼c
By the piece of about 60 yards, per yard, 3⅛c

COLORED CHEESE CLOTH OR BUNTINGS.

For dresses and decoration. Come in a large range of colorings, in two widths. We can furnish in either width any of these shades: yellow, orange, lavender, violet, purple, pink, rose, cardinal, light blue, royal blue, navy blue, nile green, apple green, shamrock green, white, cream or black.

No. 36C240 Width, 25 inches.
Price, per yard....3½c
By the piece of about 40 yards, per yard, 3¼c

No. 36C244 Width, 36 inches.
Price, per yard....4½c
By the piece of about 40 yards, per yard, 4¼c

SEA ISLAND COTTON BATISTE.

This is a high grade bunting or batiste and is suitable for dresses. Is also used, to a large extent, for high class decorations, as well as comforter covers and draperies. Colors are pink, rose, cardinal, light blue, royal blue, navy blue, nile green, apple green, shamrock green, lavender purple, yellow, white, cream or black.

No. 36C248 Cotton Batiste. Width, 36 inches. Price, per yard....6½c
By the piece of about 40 yards. per yd., 6¼c

READY MADE SHEETS AND PILLOW CASES.

We are enabled to sell the ready hemmed goods at a price impossible to other houses. We offer our special brand, Leader, as the best value ever offered for sheets and pillow cases.

NOTE—Every sheet and pillow case is torn, not cut, and we can guarantee them true and perfect.

Ready Hemmed Leader Unbleached Sheets.

No. 36C250 Ready Made Unbleached Sheets, same quality of goods as in our No. 36C254, but not bleached.

Actual size, in.	60x86	68x86	80x86	86x86
Price, each.	$0.42	$0.46	$0.49	$0.57
Per dozen..	4.85	5.20	5.50	6.40

Leader Bleached Sheets.

No. 36C254

Actual size, in.	63x86	72x86	81x86	86x90
Price, each	$0.46	$0.49	$0.56	$0.62
Per dozen...	5.20	5.50	6.30	7.00

Leader Bleached Pillow Cases

These ready made bleached pillow cases match our bleached sheets, being made from the same grade of goods. We do not handle unbleached pillow cases.

No. 36C264 Leader Bleached Pillow Cases.
Size, 20½x34 inches. Price, each....$0.12
Per dozen.... 1.35
Size, 22x34 inches. Price, each.... .13
Per dozen.... 1.45

Extra Quality Hemstitched Bleached Sheets and Pillow Cases.

These have a double hemstitch and are of a very fine and heavy texture.

No. 36C280 Bleached Hemstitched Sheets. Size, 81x87 in. Price, each..$0.77
Per dozen.... 8.80

No. 36C282 Bleached Hemstitched Pillow Cases. Size, 22x34 inches.
Price, each....$0.18
Per dozen.... 1.95

BED TICKING.

These goods are made in blue and white stripes of various widths.

No. 36C286 Width, 29 inches.
Price, per yard....5½c
By the piece of about 60 yards, per yd., 5¼c

No. 36C290 Width, 30 inches.
Price, per yard....7c
By the piece of about 60 yards, per yd., 6¾c

No. 36C294 Width, 31 inches.
Price, per yard....9 c
By the piece of about 50 yards, per yd., 8¾c

Continued on next page.

Extra Quality Bed Ticking.

No. 36C298 Extra fine quality, firm, close weave, weight, 8 ounces per yard. Width, 32 inches. Price, per yard....12c
By the piece of about 50 yards, per yd...11½c

No. 36C302 Amoskeag Brand, A. C. A., 32 inches wide. Price, per yard....18c
By the piece of about 40 yards, per yard..17c

No. 36C306 Conestogo Brand, extra heavy, none better made. Width, 60 inches.
Price, per yard....30c

No. 36C310 Turkey Red Linen Finish German Ticking. Warranted fast color. It is oil boiled turkey red, sateen finished, medium weight. Width, 33 inches. Price, per yard....17c
By the piece of about 40 yards, per yard..16c

Striped Awning Duck.

No. 36C318 Striped Heavy Awning Duck, 31 inches wide, color absolutely fast; comes in blue and white, brown and white or red and white stripes. Weight, per yard, 8 ounces. Width, 31 inches. Price, per yard....16c
By the piece of about 45 yards, per yd...15½c

BLUE DENIMS.

No. 36C322 Blue Denim, strong and durable, fast color. Width, 28 inches.
Price, per yard....8c
By the piece of about 50 yards, per yard..7½c

No. 36C326 Blue Denim, extra heavy, width, 28 inches. Price, per yard....10½c
By the piece of about 50 yards, per yard..10c

No. 36C330 Blue Denim, extra heavy twill and will give exceptional wear. Width, 28 inches. Weight, 8 ounces per yard.
Price, per yard....13c
By the piece of about 45 yards, per yd...12½c

BROWN DENIMS.

No. 36C334 Brown Denim, good quality, close, firm weave. Width, 28 inches.
Price, per yard....10c
By the piece of about 50 yards, per yard 9½c

No. 36C342 Brown Denim, extra quality, strong and heavy. Width, 28 inches.
Price, per yard....13c
By the piece of about 45 yards, per yard 12½c

Checked and Striped Shirtings.

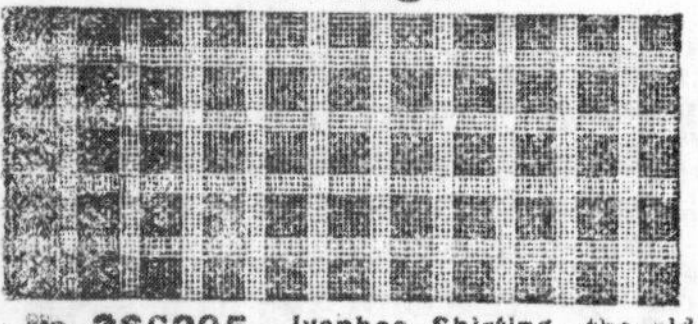

No. 36C395 Ivanhoe Shirting, the old standby, a great variety of checks, plaids and stripes, in blue, brown, red and combinations of green or black. Width, 25 inches.
Price, per yard....5c
By the piece of about 50 yards, per yard 4½c

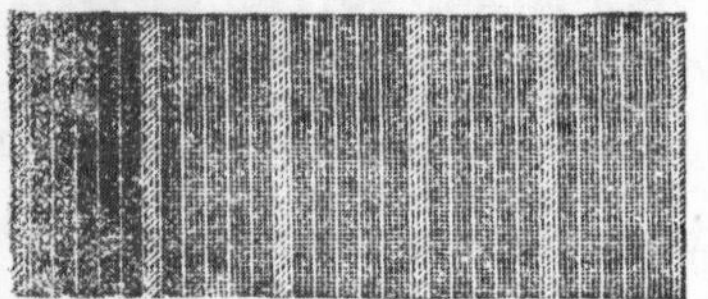

No. 36C405 Heavier and wider than the preceding number; comes in the same range of colorings and patterns. Width, 27 inches.
Price, per yard....6½c
By the piece of about 50 yards, per yard 6¼c

Cheviot Shirtings.

No. 36C415 We have greatly improved our line of Cheviot Shirtings this season, and are willing to let you be the judge of their fitness. This is a good, dependable fabric and at the price, has no equal. Comes in narrow and medium plain and fancy stripes in light blue and white, dark blue and white, pink and white or red and white. Width, 29 inches.
Price, per yard....8½c
By the piece of about 40 yards, per yard...8c

Extra Quality Fine Cheviot Shirting.

No. 36C425 Handsome Shirting Cheviots. This particular brand is used exclusively by many leading shirt manufacturers on account of its wearing qualities and fast colors. Comes in pink and white, red and white, light blue and white or dark blue and white, in new, fancy stripes and nobby checks. Width, 30 inches. Price, per yard....10½c
By the piece of about 40 yards, per yard 10c

Bull Hide Black and White or Blue and White Twill Shirting.

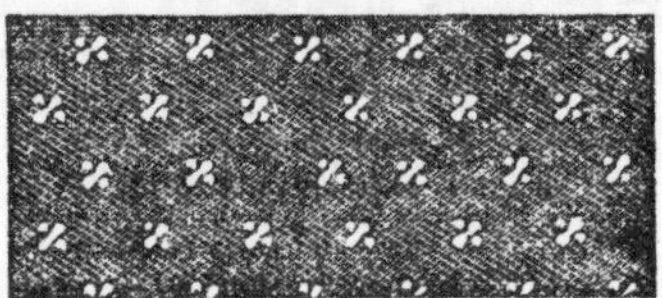

No. 36C435 Bullhide Shirting, strong and heavy and will wear like iron. Comes in black and white stripe or figure. This is the best aniline dye. Width, 28 inches.
Price, per yard....9c
By the piece of about 45 yards, per yard 8½c

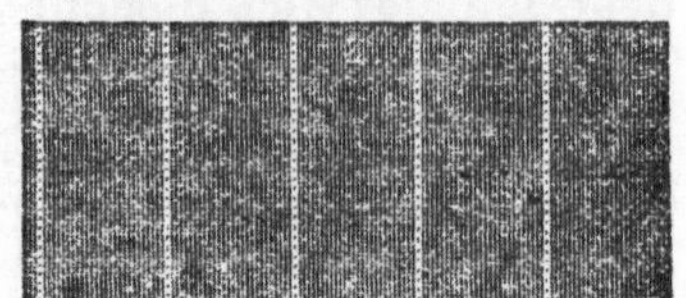

No. 36C445 Bullhide Shirting, same as above, but comes in blue and white, stripe or figure. This is the very best indigo dye. Width, 28 inches. Price, per yard....10c
By the piece of about 45 yards, per yard 9½c

GRAIN BAGS.

This has become a very important department with us, selling more than three million bags in a season.

No. 36C455 12-ounce, 2-bushel Seamless Grain Bag. Price, each....$0.15
Per bale of 100 bags....14.50

No. 36C485 Our Own Special 16-ounce, 2-bushel Seamless Grain Bag, a brand equal to any bag sold at 22 to 25 cents.
Price, each....$0.18½
Per bale of 100 bags....18.00

No. 36C495 Stark A, 16-ounce, 2-bushel Seamless Bag. Price, each....$0.20
Per bale of 100 bags....19.00

No. 36C505 American A, 16-ounce, 2-bushel Seamless Bag. Price, each $0.18½
Per bale of 100 bags....18.00

CARPET WARP.

No better warp made in construction or brightness of color. Has also a greater yardage than any other make. 8½ yarn, 90-inch reel. Cannot sell less than 5 pounds in white or any other one color in skein. Where a less quantity is desired, order No. 36C520 or No. 36C525 on spools.

No. 36C510 White Carpet Warp, 5-pound bundles only. Price, per pound....19c
In 100-pound lots, per pound....18c

No. 36C515 Colored Carpet Warp, in red, green, orange, brown, medium blue, yellow, slate or black. Price, per pound....21c
In 100-pound lots, per pound....20c

Carpet Warp on Spools.

These spools are ready for the warper. They save the weaver tedious hand winding. Put up in 5-pound boxes, containing 10 spools of ½ pound each.

No. 36C520 White Warp, on spools.
Price, per pound....20c
In 100-pound lots, per pound....19c

No. 36C525 Colored Carpet Warp, on spools, same colors as in No. 36C515.
Price, per pound....22c
In 100-pound lots, per pound....21c

COTTON BATTING.

No. 36C530 Cotton Batting, fair quality.
Price, per roll of 14 ounces....$0.08¼
Per bale of 50 pounds, or 57 rolls....4.30

No. 36C535 Cotton Batting, good quality, a clean bat and a good batting for the money.
Price, per roll of 16 ounces....$0.09
Per bale of 50 pounds....4.30

No. 36C540 Cotton Batting, a nice, clean article. Price, per roll of 16 ounces..$0.11½
Per bale of 50 pounds....5.50

No. 36C545 Cotton Batting, one of the best qualities made, pure white and clean.
Price, per roll of 16 ounces....$0.13
Per bale of 50 pounds....6.00

No. 36C550 Snow White Cotton Batting, much used for medical purposes.
Price, per roll of 16 ounces....$0.17½
Per case of 50 pounds....8.10

MOSQUITO NETTING.

No. 36C555 Mosquito Netting, sold by the piece only. Colors are pink, yellow, emerald green, blue, red, white or black. Width, 60 in.
Price, per piece of about 8 yards....38c

COTTON WADDING.

No. 36C565 Cotton Wadding, slate color only. Price, per sheet....2c
Per dozen sheets....22c

No. 36C570 Cotton Wadding, white.
Price, per sheet....2½c
Per dozen sheets....26c

Tinted Wadding.

No. 36C575 Fancy Tinted Wadding. Colors are light blue, pink, nile green or yellow.
Price, per sheet....3½c
Per dozen sheets....35c

TABLE OILCLOTHS.

We roll all oilcloths on sticks for shipment, and we guarantee the cloth to reach you in perfect condition. These goods cannot be sent by mail.

Marble Pattern.

No. 36C585 Best Quality Table Oilcloth, marble pattern. Blue or black vein. Width, 45 inches.
Price, per yard....$0.17½
Per piece of 12 yards....2.00

Plain White.

No. 36C590 Best Quality Plain White Table Oilcloth. Width, 45 inches.
Price, per yard....$0.17½
Per piece of 12 yards....2.00

Plain Black.

No. 36C593 Black Pebbled Enameled Oilcloth. Width, 45 inches.
Price, per yard....$0.18
Per piece of 12 yards....2.05

Fancy Patterns.

No. 36C595 Best Quality Table Oilcloth, fancy colors in a variety of patterns, width, 45 inches. Price, per yard....$0.17
Per piece of 12 yards....1.95

Shelf Oilcloth.

No. 36C600 Shelf Oilcloth, white or fancy wood pattern, 12 inches wide, scalloped edges, printed with pretty lace effects. Sold by piece only. Price, per piece of 12 yards....49c

NATIONAL DECORATIONS.

The National Flag Made of All Wool Bunting.

36C	Length	Width	Each	Per doz.
36C611	5 feet	27 inches	$1.05	$12.00
36C613	6 feet	38 inches	1.25	14.40
36C615	7 feet	41 inches	1.50	17.00
36C617	8 feet	48 inches	1.95	22.00
36C619	10 feet	60 inches	3.00	33.00
36C621	12 feet	71 inches	3.75	41.70

National Decorating Bunting.

No. 36C645 Fast Color Cotton Bunting, printed in red, white and blue stripes, either plain, or with stars. In ordering, mention which is desired. Absolutely fast colors. Width, 23 inches. Price, per yard....3½c
By the piece of about 60 yards....3¼c

DEPARTMENT OF TABLE LINENS, NAPKINS, TOWELS, CRASHES, ETC.

THIS IS ONE OF THE STRONGEST DEPARTMENTS IN OUR HOUSE.

ON TABLE LINENS AND NAPKINS of all kinds we are absolutely headquarters. We buy the goods direct from the very best manufacturers and bleachers of linens in Ireland, Scotland, Austria and Germany, the great linen producing countries, and we turn them over to our customers with but our one small percentage of profit added to the first cost of merchandise, with nothing added for the mill agents' and jobbers' profits, such as is done when buying goods in the regular way from retailers.

WE HAVE GREATLY IMPROVED THE LINEN DEPARTMENT this season by adding the very best values to be had in the newer creations of table sets, matched cloths and napkins, hemstitched cloths, towels, doilies, etc.

ON CRASHES, GLASS CLOTHS AND TOWELING OF ALL KINDS we are positively the best equipped house in the country. Our purchases were never larger or never placed more advantageously.

A WORD about the manner in which we cut table damasks. It is the custom of most houses to cut these goods regardless of the pattern, which entails a loss upon the customer of ⅛ to ⅜ of a yard when the cloth is straightened up to be hemmed. It is a positive rule with us to draw a thread in all damasks to use as a guiding line for cutting, thereby positively doing away with any loss in hemming and finishing the cloth.

Turkey Red Damask at 15c.

No. 36C655 Turkey Red Table Damask, comes in pretty floral and set designs; a good fabric for the money. Width, 50 inches.
Price, per yard....15c
By the piece of about 40 yards, per yard 14½c

Turkey Red Table Damask at 20 Cents.

No. 36C665 Fast Color Turkey Red Damask, in a variety of floral and set patterns. Excellent value at the price asked. Width, 58 inches. Price, per yard....20c
By the piece of about 40 yards, per yard 19½c

Dice Pattern Turkey Red Damask at 20 Cents.

No. 36C675 The same cloth as the preceding number, but in a dice pattern, like illustration. Width, 58 inches.
Price, per yard....20c
By the piece of about 40 yards, per yard 19½c

Fancy Checked Damask, 20c.

No. 36C685 Checked Damask in red and white or indigo blue and white. Small, medium or large sized checks, with jacquard figures woven in the checks and borders to match. In ordering, be sure and state whether red or blue is wanted. Width, 58 inches.
Price, per yard....20c
By the piece of about 35 yards, per yard 19½c

Oil Boiled Turkey Red Damask at 28 Cents.

No. 36C695 Oil Boiled Turkey Red Damask, fine satin finish, perfect weave. Comes in a variety of floral designs. Colors are perfectly fast. Width, 58 inches. Price, per yard....28c
By the piece of about 30 yards, per yard 27c

Dice Pattern Turkey Red Damask at 28 Cents.

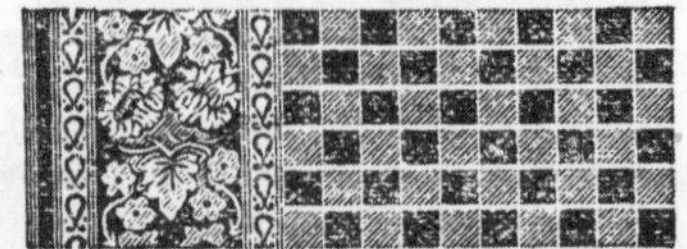

No. 36C705 The same cloth as the preceding number, but in a medium sized dice pattern like illustration. Width, 58 inches.
Price, per yard....28c
By the piece of about 30 yards, per yard 27c

Green and Red Damask, 35c

No. 36C715 Colored Table Damask of fine quality. The ground color is turkey red with green floral pattern or dice. Colors are guaranteed fast. Width, 58 inches. Per yd., 35c
By the piece of about 35 yards, per yd., 34c

Extra Fine Oil Boiled Turkey Red Damask at 39 Cents.

No. 36C735 For an exceptional value in Turkey Red Damask we recommend this number. The colors are guaranteed fast and the fabric has a beautiful satin finish. Comes in handsome floral design like and similar to the illustration. Width, 58 inches. Per yd., 39c
By the piece of about 30 yards, per yd., 38c

Extra Fine Quality Dice Pattern Turkey Red Damask at 39 Cents.

No. 36C745 The same quality as No. 36C735, but dice pattern only. Width, 58 inches. Price, per yard 39c
By the piece of about 30 yards, per yard, 38c

Red Border Cream Bleached Damask at 25 Cents.

No. 36C755 Red Border Union Table Damask, cream bleached, floral designs and fast color borders. Width, 54 inches.
Price, per yard 25c
By the piece of about 30 yards, per yd., 24½c

Half Bleached Table Damask at 27 Cents.

No. 36C765 Fine, Half Bleached Linen Table Damask, a good cloth for the money. Comes in a range of very pretty patterns. We do not believe in quoting cheaper grades than this, as they are very unsatisfactory to the user. This fabric will be found an excellent value for the money. Width, 54 inches. Price, per yard, 27c
By the piece of about 30 yards, per yard 26c

Half Bleached Damask at 27c.

No. 36C775 A Heavy Weight, Perfect Weave Damask in a large range of new patterns, one of which is like the illustration. This is a splendid quality for the price. Width, 54 inches.
Price, per yard 27c
By the piece of about 30 yards, per yard 26c

Fine, Half Bleached Linen Damask at 40 Cents.

No. 36C785 Fine Quality Half Bleached Linen Damask in close, perfect weave and heavy weight. Comes in handsome floral center patterns with borders to match. An excellent damask for general use. Width, 58 inches.
Price, per yard 40c
By the piece of about 30 yards, per yard, 39c

Wide, Half Bleached All Linen Table Damask at 45 Cents.

No. 36C795 This is an especially attractive number in Half Bleached Table Damask. It is a very finely woven cloth of good weight, and runs in a beautiful assortment of designs and very neat borders. Guaranteed all pure linen. Width, 64 inches. Price, per yard..45c

All Linen Half Bleached Damask at 65 Cents.

No. 36C805 This is our very best quality of wide, Half Bleached Damask and is made from all pure Irish linen and is an excellent weight cloth that will wash and wear perfectly. The designs are especially attractive this season. This is one of the best values in our linen department. Width, 70 inches.
Price, per yard 65c

BLEACHED TABLE DAMASK

Mercerized Pure White Satin Table Damask at 50 Cents.

No. 36C815 The newest and most correct thing in the damask line. A very highly finished, imported satin damask, running in a beautiful range of patterns. The cloth is made of long fibre Sea Island cotton, highly mercerized, giving it a rich, handsome, silky finish found only in the very best Irish and Scotch damasks. Will wash and retain the finish and color. Width, 66 inches. Price, per yard..50c

Bleached Table Damask at 21 Cents.

No. 36C825 Bleached Union Table Damask, in a variety of handsome designs. Width, 58 inches. Price, per yard 21c
By the piece of about 35 yards, per yard 20c

Bleached Union Table Damask at 24 Cents.

No. 36C835 Pure White Union Linen Table Damask, in a choice assortment of new patterns. This is really worth 15 per cent more money. Width, 64 inches. Price, per yard, 24c
By the piece of about 30 yards, per yard 23c

All Linen Bleached Table Damask at 43 Cents.

No. 36C845 Bleached All Linen Table Damask, strong and durable and splendid value for the money. Comes in a large assortment of new damask designs. This is a cloth that will give exceptional service. Width, 58 inches. Price, per yard 43c

All Linen Bleached Table Damask at 49 Cents.

No. 36C855 This is one of our most popular numbers in Bleached Table Damasks and is one of the best values we are offering in the linen department. It is a very heavy weight damask, made from pure Irish linen, running in a beautiful range of new patterns. The ordinary dealers will charge from 60 to 65 cents per yard for a similar grade of goods. Warranted all pure linen. Width, 60 inches. Price, per yard 49c

Bleached Table Damask at 60 Cents.

No. 36C865 Bleached Table Damask, guaranteed pure Irish linen, exceptional quality, good weight, beautiful satin finish and excellent variety of new designs and borders to match. One of our most popular sellers. Width, 70 inches. Price, per yard ...60c

WE DO NOT SEND SAMPLES of these goods.

BLEACHED TABLE DAMASKS AND NAPKINS TO MATCH.

We quote below four very strong numbers of pure white bleached damasks with napkins to match. The qualities are the very best the market affords. The selection of designs is well assorted, the newest and most artistic we are able to procure. These cloths and napkins will be sold together or separately.

Fine Bleached Table Damask with Napkins to Match.

No. 36C875 Beautiful Satin Finished, Heavy Weight, Pure Linen Table Damask, bleached snow white. This is an excellent quality and cannot be equaled for the price. Comes in a beautiful range of patterns and is a cloth that will give exceptional service. Width of damask, 70 inches.
Price, per yard 75c
No. 36C1305 Napkins to match this damask. Price, per dozen..$2.00

Extra Fine Quality Bleached Table Damask with Napkins to Match.

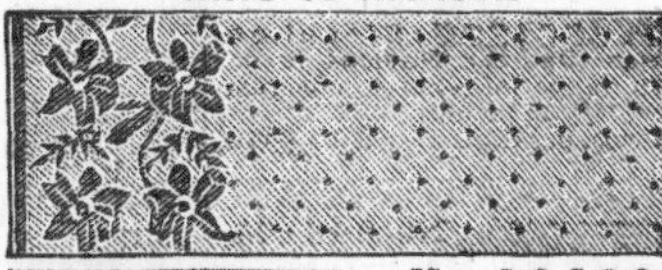

No. 36C885 Extra Fine Quality Bleached All Linen Table Damask in beautiful satin finish, a heavy weight cloth that will wear for years. Very handsome, new designs, either floral patterns, set figures or dot patterns like the illustration. Width of damask, 72 inches. Price, per yard 80c
No. 36C1315 Napkins to match this damask. Price, per dozen..$2.50

Extra Heavy Satin Bleached Damask with Napkins to Match.

No. 36C895 Extra Heavy Quality Satin Damask, bleached pure white. This cloth is made from the finest kind of pure Irish linen in rich and lustrous designs. This is a damask that we can recommend for durability. Width of damask, 70 inches. Price, per yard 98c
No. 36C1325 Napkins to match this damask. Price, per dozen..$2.75

Our Very Best German Satin Damask with Napkins to Match.

No. 36C905 Our very finest quality of pure German Linen Damask. These goods are the product of the best German manufacturers, whose reputation for fine table linen is world wide. Money could not buy a better article. Width, 70 inches. Price, per yard $1.10
No. 36C1335 Napkins to match this damask. Price, per dozen $3.25

TABLE FELT, OR SILENCE CLOTH, AT 33 CENTS.

For use on dining tables underneath the damask cloth to deaden the sound of the china and protect the finish of the table against hot dishes.

No. 36C915 Silence Cloth. We carry but one grade and that one the best the market affords. It comes in the very heaviest of cream white cotton, napped heavily on both sides; a cloth that sells ordinarily at 50 cents per yard. Width, 54 inches. Price, per yard 33c
By the piece of about 18 yards, per yd ...32c

Turkey Red Table Covers. Ready to Use.

No. 36C925 Size, 58x70 inches. Price, 55c
No. 36C930 Size, 58x85 inches. Price, 68c

Imported Turkey Red Table Covers.

No. 36C945 Size, 66x66 in. Price, $1.15
No. 36C950 Size, 66x86 in. Price, 1.50
No. 36C955 Size, 66x101 in. Price, 1.85

Ready to Use Table Cloths.

Half bleached with fast red border.

No. 36C965 Size, 48x66 inches. Price, 49c
No. 36C970 Size, 48x68 inches. Price, 59c
No. 36C975 Size, 48x95 inches. Price, 85c

All Linen Bleached Table Cloths with Red, Blue or All White Borders.

No. 36C985 Size, 54x60 in. Price, $0.85
No. 36C990 Size, 54x80 in. Price, 1.00

Pure Irish Linen Damask Table Cloths with Napkins to Match.

SOLD SEPARATELY.

Below we quote three all linen table cloths, identical in quality, weight and design, differing only in size. These are beautiful, all pure linen cloths, unrivaled for splendor of pattern, snowy whiteness and excellent wearing qualities. We show them in neat designs and can furnish good sized napkins, matching them in every way. These are exceptional values, and if you are seeking a dependable article in an all pure Irish Damask cloth and napkins for good service and appearance, permit us to suggest these numbers for your selection. We know they will please you. Either cloth or napkins sold separately.

No. 36C1045 Size, 66x68 inches. Price $1.39
No. 36C1050 Size, 66x86 inches. Price 1.80
No. 36C1055 Size, 66x104 inches. Price 2.19
No. 36C1330 Napkins to match above cloth, size, 22x22 inches. Price, per doz. $1.90

Bleached Linen Table Cloths.

With Napkins to Match Sold Separately.

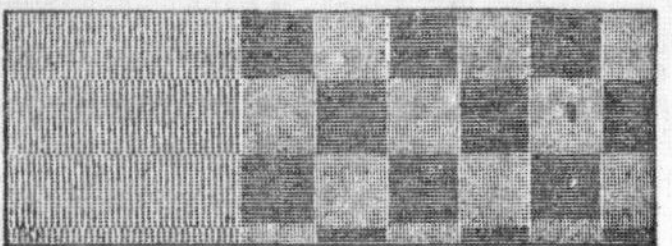

Extra Heavy Linen, Dice Pattern Table Cloths, bleached, with napkins to match, as quoted below. This is a cloth that will stand any amount of hard wear, is very nicely finished and will retain its appearance for years. Comes only in pattern as shown in the illustration.

No. 36C1125 Size, 62x66 inches. Price.......... **$1.10**
No. 36C1130 Size, 62x82 inches. Price.......... **$1.29**

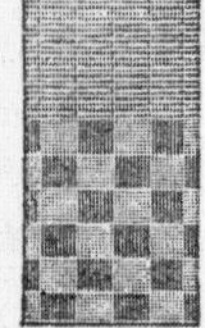

Extra Heavy Linen Napkins.

To Match Above Cloths.

No. 36C1140 Size, 16x16 inches. Price, per dozen..... **85c**
No. 36C1145 Size, 19x19 inches. Price, per dozen... **$1.19**

Fine All Linen Matched Table Set at $1.75.

No. 36C1155 Imported All Linen Matched Table Set, fully bleached, beautiful finish, long heavy fringe. Handsome center designs of solid white with fast color borders of red, blue or all white. Size, 54x86 inches. One dozen napkins to match, size, 15x15 inches. Price, complete set..... **$1.75**

All Linen Matched Table Set at $2.50.

EXTRA GOOD QUALITY.

No. 36C1165 Matched Table Set, fine quality of all pure bleached linen with perfect satin finish and long, heavy fringe. Heavy weight damask. The center is of solid white with artistic woven damask designs, bordered with either red, blue or solid white. Size, 58x92 inches. One dozen napkins to match, size, 15x15 inches.
Price, complete set.......... **$2.50**

Matched Hemstitched Table Sets at $3.95.

No. 36C1185 Hemstitched Bleached All Pure Linen Matched Table Sets in a beautiful assortment of designs with appropriate borders all around, also most perfect hemstitching all around; comes in solid white only and is a very nicely finished **heavy damask.** Size, 63½x80 inches. One dozen heavy napkins to match, size, 16x16 inches, also beautifully hemstitched all around. They come packed neatly, one set in a box.
Price, complete set.......... **$3.95**

Bleached Hemstitched Matched Table Set at $4.98.

No. 36C1195 All White Bleached Hemstitched Table Sets. These are imported direct from Belfast, Ireland, which is headquarters for the best linens in the world, and no nicer set could be had under $7.00. This set is made of very heavy satin damask, comes in a beautiful assortment of center designs and borders all around, with hemstitching as perfect as can be made. The hemstitching runs all around the cloth. Size of cloth, 62x93 inches. One dozen napkins to match, size, 18x18 inches; made of exactly the same cloth and finished in the same manner. Come packed one set in a neat box. Price, complete set... **$4.98**

TABLE NAPKINS.

No. 36C1235 Bleached Union Damask Napkins, come in a range of choice designs. Size, 14½x15 inches.
Price, per dozen.......... **50c**

No. 36C1255 Superior Quality Bleached Linen Napkins. Handsome floral patterns in new designs. Extra quality. Especially good wearing. If you do not think these the best napkins you ever bought for the price, you may return them to us and we will refund your money. Size, 17x17½ inches. Price, per doz., **75c**

No. 36C1265 Special Value, Extra Quality Bleached All Pure Linen Napkins, new and very handsome floral designs. They are handsome in pattern and finish and are dependable in every way. We warrant them to give satisfaction. Size, 18x19 inches.
Price, per dozen...... **95c**

No. 36C1275 Extra Fine Bleached All Linen Imported Napkins, with charming floral designs, good heavy weight, closely woven and extra fine finish. Size, 19½x19½ inches.
Price, per dozen... **$1.00**

Best Irish Linen Napkins.

No. 36C1285 This is one of our leading numbers. It is good, generous size, and is made of the **best Irish linen;** has a very fine finish. Comes in beautiful floral and set designs with handsome border. Size, 20x21 inches. Per dozen.. **$1.50**

No. 36C1305 Real Irish Bleached Satin Finished Napkins, heavy weight and closely woven. **All pure linen and thoroughly dependable;** handsome floral patterns, one of our specially clever values. **Will match our No. 36C875 table linen.** Size, 22x22 inches.
Price, per dozen.............. **$2.00**

No. 36C1315 Extra High Grade Imported Satin Finished Linen Napkins. Elegant quality and will wear for years. A superior value to any we have offered heretofore at the price. Size, 23x24 inches. **Will match our No. 36C885 table linen.**
Price, per dozen... **$2.50**

Irish Satin Damask Napkins at $2.75 per Dozen.

No. 36C1325 Our New 22x22 Bleached Satin Damask Pure All Linen Napkins will match our No. 36C895 table linen. Size, 22x22 inches.
Price, per dozen.... **$2.75**

Irsh Linen Napkins

No. 36C1330 Fine Irish Linen Napkins, matching exactly our damask cloths Nos. 36C1045, 36C1050 and 36C1055. Size, 22x22 in. Price, per doz. **$1.90**

German Satin Damask Napkins at $3.25 per Dozen.

No. 36C1335 Very Finest Grade of German Linen Napkins, nothing finer made. Bleached pure white. This napkin will last for years. Comes in pretty floral designs and will match No. 36C905 table linen. Size, 23x24 inches. Price, per dozen, **$3.25**

Fringed Bleached Napkins.

No. 36C1385 Extra Fine Quality Fringed Bleached Napkins, all linen, select stock, extra good value. Comes in plain white only. Size, 15x15 in. Price, per dozen... **60c**

We do not sample these goods

DEPARTMENT OF TOWELS.

This is one of our strongest departments and one of which we are justly proud. Each and every number quoted below is a value that cannot be equaled by retailers. The reason for this is that we buy direct from both the foreign and domestic manufacturers and thereby do away with the jobber's or middleman's profit. Several numbers below are priced by the dozen; in these instances we will sell no less quantity than a half dozen. Measurements of fringed towels include the fringe.

Checked Glass Towels.

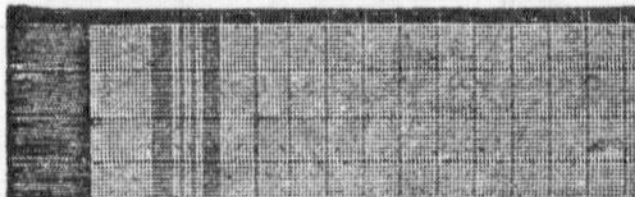

No. 36C1555 Cotton Glass Towels, blue or red checks. Fringed ends. Size, 15x27 inches. Price, per dozen.......... **30c**

Cotton Towels, Duck Weave.

Especially Recommended for Barbers' Use.

No. 36C1595 Full Bleached Cotton Towels, neat red borders, fringed ends, fine, firm weave, good value. Size, 14x28 inches.
Price, per dozen.......... **39c**

Hemmed Towels for Barbers' Use.

No. 36C1600 Pure Bleached Soft Cotton Towels with fast red border. A good value. Size, 14x28 inches. Price, per dozen......... **42c**

Cream Honeycomb Cotton Towels.

No. 36C1615 Cream Honeycomb Towels, neat colored borders, fringed ends, very fair weight and good value. Size, 16x36 inches.
Price, per dozen.......... **48c**

HUCKABACK TOWELS.

Towels of this weave are always desirable because of the extraordinary wearing and washing qualities. We quote below a very strong line of these popular towels, and we can conscientiously say that any number you select will give absolute satisfaction or we stand ready to promptly refund your money.

Hemmed Huck Towels.

No. 36C1675 Pure White Hemmed Cotton Huck Towels. Best towel on the market at the price. Comes in red or white borders. Size, 16x29 inches. Price, per dozen, **65c**; each........ **6c**

No. 36C1685 Pure White Hemmed Cotton Huck Towels, perfect weave and heavy weight, neat red borders. This towel is a wonder for the money. Size, 19x38 inches. Price, each........ **8c**
Per dozen.......... **88c**

Linen Huckaback Towels.

No. 36C1715 Linen Huck Towels. These come in red, blue or plain white borders. It is a good weight cream bleached towel, with hemmed ends, and one of our biggest sellers. Particularly adapted to hotel use. At 10 cents it is a remarkable value, Size, 17x31 inches.
Price, per dozen, **$1.05**; each.......... **10c**

Linen Huck Towels.

No. 36C1725 Linen Huck Towels, bleached, with hemmed ends and neat red, blue or white borders. Good, heavy weight and a towel that would ordinarily retail at about 18 cents. Size, 17x35 inches. Price, each........ **$0.12**
Per dozen.......... **1.33**

No. 36C1735 Linen Bleached Huck Towels. Firm and well made of extra heavy weight, with red or white borders and hemmed ends. A big attractive towel that you could not duplicate under 20 cents. Size, 18x36 inches.
Price, each.......... **$0.15**
Per dozen.......... **1.63**

DAMASK TOWELS.

Loom Damask Towels at 7c.

No. 36C1775 Loom Damask Linen Towels, cream bleached, with very pretty damask center, neat red borders both ends and sides, with fringed ends. Nothing like them ever sold for the money. Size, 14x26 inches. Price, each **7c**
Per dozen.......... **75c**

Loom Damask Towels at 9c.

No. 36C1785 Cream bleached. Fine damask pattern centers, red borders both ends and sides, with long fringe. These towels are strong and serviceable. Size, 16x32 inches.
Price, each.......... **9c**
Per dozen.......... **97c**

Loom Damask Fringed Towels at 12 Cents.

No. 36C1795 Damask Towels, with fine assortment of center patterns and pretty red borders on both ends and sides. Heavy fringed ends. These towels are cream bleached, extra heavy weight and an exceptional value for the money. Size, 18x36 inches.
Price, each.......... **$0.12**
Per dozen.......... **1.33**

All Linen Bleached Damask Towels at 13 Cents.

No. 36C1805 Good Quality All Linen Damask Towels. Long knotted fringe. Handsome borders of red, blue or plain white, damask design centers of the very newest patterns. Size, 17x34 inches. Price, each........ **$0.13**
Per dozen.......... **1.45**

All Linen German Damask Towels at 20 Cents.

No. 36C1815 Extra Large Size All Linen Towels, bleached pure white. Good weight with choice center designs, long knotted fringe and borders of red, blue or plain white. A towel that we can highly recommend. Size, 20x45 inches. Price, each....$0.20
Price, per dozen....2.20

German Satin Damask Towels at 27 Cents.

No. 36C1835 Extra Fine Quality Silver Bleached Satin Damask Towels, absolutely all pure German linen, long heavy knotted fringe and comes in neat borders of red, blue or solid white. These towels are extra large size and are used extensively for dresser and chair scarfs. It is a big, heavy towel for little money. Size, 22x48 inches. Price, each....$0.27
Per dozen....2.90

TURKISH BATH TOWELS.

We are very proud of the big values we offer in Turkish Bath Towels. Each and every number quoted below has been most carefully sought for and considered until we can conscientiously say that you could not possibly equal these values elsewhere.

Our Unbleached Towels are made from selected firm but soft cotton double and twist yarns, that will bleach out in two or three washings.

Our Bleached Towels are finished at the best bleachery in the country, and they are soft and absorbent and pure snow white.

Cream or Unbleached Turkish Towels.

No. 36C1885 Size, 15x30 inches.
Price, per dozen....$0.48

No. 36C1895 Size, 19x42 inches.
Price, each....:08
Per dozen....:90

No. 36C1905 Size, 21x52 inches.
Price, each....:13
Per dozen....1.40

No. 36C1915 Size, 24x54 inches.
Price, each....:18
Per dozen....2.00

Bleached Turkish Towels.

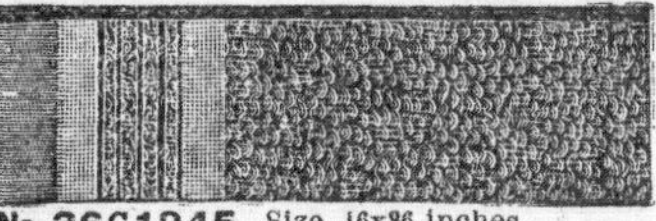

No. 36C1945 Size, 16x36 inches.
Price, each....$0.08
Per dozen....:90

No. 36C1955 Size, 22x45 inches.
Price, each....:12
Per dozen....1.35

No. 36C1965 Size, 22x48 inches.
Price, each....:17
Per dozen....1.90

TURKISH WASH CLOTHS, HALF BLEACHED.

No. 36C1985 Size, 8x9½ inches.
Price, per dozen....13c

No. 36C1995 Size, 12x12 inches.
Price, per dozen....22c

BLEACHED TURKISH TOWELING.

No. 36C2025 Turkish Toweling or Terry Cloth. Pure white bleached. Used extensively for hand and roller towels, bath robes and mittens, wash cloths, also for bureau covers. etc. Width, 18 inches. Price, per yard....12c
By the piece of about 20 yards, per yd. 11¼c

BLEACHED AND UNBLEACHED CRASH TOWELING.

No. 36C2045 Bleached Cotton Crash Toweling, with colored borders, is a good heavy close woven toweling. Width, 16 inches.
Price, per yard....4¼c
By the piece of 25 yards, per piece....99c

No. 36C2050 Unbleached Linen Crash, standard quality. Width, 15½ inches.
Price, per yard....5c
By the piece of about 50 yards, per yard..4¾c

No. 36C2055 Unbleached Linen Crash, all pure linen, a good firm cloth and splendid value for the money. Width, 15 inches.
Price, per yard....5½c
By the piece of about 50 yards, per yard.5¼c

No. 36C2060 Unbleached All Linen Crash. A good substantial toweling. Width, 17 inches.
Price, per yard....7½c
By the piece, about 50 yards, per yard....7¼c

No. 36C2065 Cream Bleached All Linen Crash, extra heavy, and will wear for years. Width, 15 inches. Price, per yard....8c
By the piece, about 50 yards, per yard....7¾c

No. 36C2070 Cream Bleached All Linen Crash Toweling. Much finer quality. Width, 17 inches. Price, per yard....9c
By the piece, about 50 yards, per yard....8½c

No. 36C2075 Cream Bleached All Linen, Extra Fine Crash Toweling, a very close weave. Width, 17 inches. Price, per yard....10c
By the piece, about 50 yards, per yard....9½c

HUCK TOWELING.

No. 36C2078 Bleached Cotton Huck Toweling. A better article than the price would indicate. Fast color, red border. Width, 16½ inches. Price, per yard....5c
By the piece of about 50 yards, per yard. 4¾c

No. 36C2080 Pure White Marseilles Weave Toweling, heavy and absorbent, with plain weave center and narrow, woven border. Used for fancy work, as well as for towels. A good value for the price. Width, 18 inches. Price, per yard....7c
By the piece, of 25 yds., per yd..6¾c

No. 36C2085 Bleached Linen Huckaback Toweling; no better wearing toweling made. Width, 18 inches. Price, per yard....11c
By the piece of about 40 yds., per yard..10½c

UNBLEACHED RUSSIA CRASH.

No. 36C2090 Width, 17 inches.
Price, per yard....5c
By the piece of about 40 yards, per yard....4¾c

No. 36C2095 Width, 17 inches.
Price, per yard....6¾c
By the piece of about 40 yards, per yard....6½c

No. 36C2098 Extra wearing quality. Width, 15 inches. Price, per yard....7¼c
By the piece of about 40 yards, per yard....7c

Bleached Russia Crash.

No. 36C2100 16-Inch All Pure Linen Extra Quality Fine Bleached Pure White Russia Crash. This crash is made on hand looms by Russian peasants and it is without argument the very best and most durable crash made.
Price, per yard....9c
By the piece, about 40 yards, per yard....8c

GLASS TOWELING.

No. 36C2105 Cotton Glass Toweling, assorted red and blue checks. Width, 17 inches.
Price, per yard....4¼c
By the piece of about 50 yards, per yard....4c

No. 36C2110 A better and stronger quality, in blue or red checks. Width, 17 inches.
Price, per yard....8c
By the piece of about 50 yards, per yard..7¾c

No. 36C2115 Pure White Glass Toweling in assorted red borders; of purest linen with a small amount of cotton and thoroughly bleached. Width, 17½ inches. Price, per yard....9c
By the piece of about 50 yards, per yard..8½c

PLAIN LINENS.

Irish Butcher Linens.

No. 36C2125 Bleached Irish Butcher Linen, 36 inches wide. Warranted pure linen. Price, per yard, 25c
By the piece of about 25 yards, per yard....24c

No. 36C2135 Extra Fine Quality Irish Butcher Linen; very firm, close weave; one of the best numbers to be had. Width, 40 in. Price, per yd..39c
By the piece of about 25 yards, per yard....37½c

White Irish Bosom or Fronting Linen.

No. 36C2140 Fronting or Bosom Linen, an extra fine quality, all pure linen. Width, 36 in. Price, yard..49c
By the piece, about 25 yds., per yard....46½c

White Handkerchief Linen.

No. 36C2150 Pure White Handkerchief Linen, nice quality, sheer and beautiful. Best Irish goods; strictly all linen. Width, 36 inches.
Price, per yard....39c
By the piece of about 25 yards, per yard....37½c

No. 36C2155 Similar to the preceding number, but a better quality. These goods will also make up into dainty waists. Width, 36 inches.
Price, per yard....50c

No. 36C2160 Handkerchief Linen, similar to preceding number, but the very best quality. Width, 36 inches.
Price, per yard....59c

White Art Linens for Embroidery.

We have the very best line of these all pure linen goods in every width. We have placed large orders with Irish and Scotch manufacturers for these goods, and can guarantee a saving of 25 to 33⅓ per cent on each purchase. **We sell them in any quantity which you may require.**

No. 36C2165 18-inch. Per yard...25c
By the piece of about 25 yds., per yard.., 24c

No. 36C2170 22-inch. Per yard...30c
By the piece of about 25 yds., per yd..., ..29c

No. 36C2175 36-inch. Per yard...45c
By the piece of about 25 yds., per yd..., 42½c

No. 36C2180 45-inch. Per yard...55c
By the piece of about 25 yds., per yd..., 52½c

DEPARTMENT OF BEDSPREADS.

This is one of the most important departments in the house, and it has taken years of labor to bring it up to its present state of perfection. We control the output of several mills that make nothing but bedspreads, and we thereby not only secure the best possible prices and terms, but are in position to give our customers new and exclusive patterns. We will guarantee to save our customers from 15 to 35 per cent on every bedspread purchased. In our collection will be found the most desirable numbers of **Crochet, Honeycomb, Marseilles Satin** and fancy colored **bedspreads,** both hemmed and fringed. If you are not pleased with your selection, you may return same to us, and we will refund your money and pay express charges both ways.

HEMMED CROCHET BEDSPREADS.

Fine White Crochet Bedspread at 59 Cents.

No. 36C2205 White Crochet Bedspread. A very large seller. Heavy bedspread in handsome range of patterns. Size, 66x76 inches.
Price, per dozen, $6.70; each....59c

Marseilles Pattern Crochet Bedspread at 73 Cents.

No. 36C2210 White Crochet Bedspread, Marseilles Pattern. A good weight spread, in nicely assorted patterns. A big bargain for the money. Size, 70x80 inches. Price, each, $0.73
Per dozen....8.25

Heavy Crochet Bedspread, 98 Cents.

No. 36C2215 White Marseilles Pattern Bedspread. Made from long staple cotton 3-ply yarns, both warp and filling. Comes in handsome center and border designs. A heavy weight bedspread that retails ordinarily at $1.25. Size, 76x84 inches.
Price, each....$ 0.98
Per dozen....11.25

FRINGED CROCHET BEDSPREADS.

These quilts have knotted fringe all around.

Fringed Crochet Bedspread at 98 Cents.

No. 36C2230 Fringed, White Crochet Bedspread, beautiful Marseilles pattern. Heavy knotted fringe, 5 inches long. This is one of our most popular spreads and a wonderful value for the money. Size, 74x84 inches.
Price, per dozen, $11.25; each....98c

Extra Heavy White Fringed Bedspread at $1.30.

No. 36C2235 Our Extra Heavy, White Fringed Marseilles Pattern Crochet Bedspread. This is a full size, heavy crochet quilt, with a very handsome line of new patterns. It has a long, heavy fringe and is a quilt that is sightly and rich in appearance. Size, 82x92 inches. Price, each....$ 1.30
Per dozen....14.90

Our New Cut Corner Crochet Bedspread at $1.50.

No. 36C2245 The above illustration will give you an idea of our New Cut Corner Bedspread. The lower corners of the spread are cut out perfectly to permit draping around the bed posts. The bedspread represented in the illustration is a white Marseilles pattern crochet spread with long heavy fringe. It is made from selected 3-ply cotton yarns and comes in a beautiful range of patterns. This is one of the most durable bedspreads we have to offer and for value it cannot be equaled. This is a style of bedspread that we can recommend very highly. Size, 88x92 ins. Price, each....$ 1.50
Per dozen....17.00

Cut Corner Crochet Bedspread at $1.75.

No. 36C2250 Cut Corner Crochet Bedspread. Pure white Marseilles pattern, extra heavy weight, long, heavy fringe. We recommend this style of quilt very highly, as it fits and drapes most perfectly. At $1.75 this bedspread is a most remarkable value, and one that will give the user absolute satisfaction. Size, 88x96 inches. Price, each....$ 1.75
Per dozen....19.80

SATIN BEDSPREADS.

Hemmed Patent Satin, Marseilles Design, Bedspread.

No. 36C2252 Give this quilt a trial and we guarantee you will be thoroughly pleased with it. Comes in several handsome patterns. Size, 76x88 inches. Price, each....$ 1.25
Per dozen....14.00

Fine White Satin Bedspread at $1.65.

No. 36C2255 White Satin Bedspread, full size and good weight. Beautiful new designs. This is a genuine **embroidered satin spread,** and the biggest bargain ever offered. We can guarantee it for style and durability. Size, 78x90 inches. Price, each....$ 1.65
Per dozen....18.80

Extra Heavy Satin Bedspread at $2.50.

No. 36C2265 Beautiful White Satin Bedspread. Extra heavy and large size and comes in a pretty line of new designs. This is an extraordinary value for the money. A spread that would cost $3.25 to $3.50 in city stores. We suggest this number to those who want an up to date durable bedspread. Size, 81x88 inches. Price....$2.50

Fringed Patent Satin, Marseilles Design, Bedspread.

No. 36C2270 The Handsome Satin Spread has passed the novelty stage and is a meritorious article. A very good spread for all purposes. Size, 80x92 inches, including fringe all around. Price, each....$ 1.55
Per dozen....17.50

Fringed Crochet Bedspreads in Colors at 93 Cents.

No. 36C2285 Colored Honeycomb Crochet Bedspread. Long, heavy fringe, heavy weight and full size. This is one of the most stylish colored spreads on the market and at 93 cents, represents a saving of at least 32 cents, as these bedspreads sell for $1.25 and upwards in the city stores. Can be had in the following colors: Pink, light blue, red, brown, or navy blue, combined with white, all perfectly fast and washable. Size, 86x94 inches.
Price, per dozen, $10.65; each........93c

Fringed Crochet Bedspreads in Colors at $1.07.

No. 36C2290 Our Extra Heavy Large Size Fringed Colored Crochet Bedspread. This is one of the heaviest and richest looking colored spreads on the market. Comes in pink, light blue, red, brown, or navy combined with white. Has a heavy, deep fringe all around. One of the biggest bargains that we have ever been able to offer. Size, 86x90 inches.
Price, per dozen, $12.25; each.....$1.07

Heavy Mitcheline Bedspreads at $1.19.

No. 36C2295 Large Size Heavy Weight Mitcheline Bedspread. One of the most durable spreads to be had. It is made from the best staple cotton, woven into heavy round yarns, producing a very pretty and pronounced pattern. The colors are red and white, dark blue and white, pink and white or light blue and white, and are perfectly fast and washable. An excellent spread for the money. Size, 72x88 inches. Price, each..................$ 1.19
Per dozen 13.35

WHITE WASH DRESS GOODS.

WE DESIRE TO CALL YOUR PARTICULAR ATTENTION to this department, which is a division of our general department of Wash Dress Goods, Linens, etc. The values offered herein are really wonderful and cannot be equaled; in fact, we solicit a comparison to convince you of the truth of our assertions. It is a well known fact that we are among the very largest handlers of cotton goods of all sorts, and particularly white goods. Our enormous buying capacity enables us to buy in the largest quantities and thereby secure the very lowest possible prices and terms, and we never fail to give our customers the advantage of these well made purchases. We control the entire output of several mills that make nothing but fine cotton fabrics and this fact lends force to our argument that we own our merchandise cheaper than other concerns. We could not occupy the enviable position which we do, were it not for the fact that we give our patrons the best sort of treatment and better value for their money than they could possibly secure elsewhere.

OUR MAMMOTH LINE OF WHITE GOODS is better selected and assorted this season than ever before, comprising the choicest productions of foreign and domestic looms in all the staple and new weaves of India Linons, Victoria Lawns, Persian Lawns, Organdies, Swisses, Mulls, Nainsooks in plain and fancy weaves, Piques, Corduroys and Dimities, as well as the highest class of mercerized or silk finished Waisting Damasks, Ottoman Cords and numerous other fancy and staple weaves.

OUR GUARANTEE OFFER. We are so positive that our prices and merchandise are absolutely right that we will allow you to select anything in this department with the understanding and agreement that if when the goods are received they are not as good or better than represented, or if they do not please you in every respect, and you do not think you are getting good value for your money, you are under no obligations to keep the goods, but can return them to us, at our expense of transportation charges both ways, and we will refund your money.

INDIA LINONS.

This fabric is commonly called India Linen, which is wrong and decidedly misleading, as there is no linen in its construction, but it is made of selected Sea Island cotton, very fine and sheer, with a smooth, glossy finish. It is a most popular fabric, and for washing and wearing qualities it cannot be equaled.

WHITE INDIA LINON.

No. 36C2325 Very good quality White India Linon, exceptional value for the money, 28 inches wide. Price, per yard............5½c
Full piece of about 24 yards, per yard....5¼c

No. 36C2330 Good, fine quality White India Linon, very sheer, 30 inches wide.
Price, per yard..............................7½c
Full piece of about 24 yards, per yard....7¼c

No. 36C2335 Extra fine quality White India Linon, a big bargain at the price, 30 inches wide. Price, per yard..................11c
Full piece of about 24 yards, per yard..10½c

No. 36C2340 Exceptionally good quality White India Linon, nice texture, very fine and sheer. This is one of our most popular linons, 32 inches wide. Price, per yard............15c
Full piece of about 24 yards, per yard....14c

No. 36C2350 The very finest grade of India Linon in our white goods department; very sheer and beautiful; 32 inches wide.
Price, per yard..............................20c
Full piece of about 24 yards, per yard....19c

LINEN COLOR INDIA LINON.

This fabric will be used more than ever this season. This is a color in India Linon that is sure to find favor with everyone who buys it, and the grades we quote below are ones that cannot be equaled for the price. It comes in a deep, rich ecru or linen color.

No. 36C2355 Plain Linen Color India Linon, very good quality, 31 inches wide.
Price, per yard..............................7½c
Full piece of about 24 yards, per yard....7¼c

No. 36C2360 Plain Ecru Linen Color India Linon, extra fine quality, 31 inches wide.
Price, per yard..............................10c
Full piece of about 24 yards, per yard.....9½c

No. 36C2365 Plain Ecru or Linen Color India Linon of very superior quality that we can highly recommend. 31 inches wide.
Price, per yard..............................14c
Full piece of about 24 yards, per yard....13c

BLACK INDIA LINON.

Positively fast color and will not crock or fade from exposure to the sun. We know of no fabric that will give better satisfaction to the wearer.

No. 36C2370 Very good quality fast black India Linon, 31 inches wide. Price, per yd. 7½c
Full piece of about 24 yards, per yard.....7¼c

No. 36C2375 Fine quality fast black India Linon, 31 inches wide.
Price, per yard..............................10c
Full piece of about 24 yards, per yard.....9½c

No. 36C2380 Extra fine quality fast black India Linon, 31 inches wide.
Price, per yard..............................14c
Full piece of about 24 yards, per yard....13c

No. 36C2385 Very finest quality fast black India Linon, nothing better to be had at any price, coloring rich and lustrous, 31 inches wide. Price, per yard..........................20c
Full piece of about 24 yards, per yard ...19c

WHITE VICTORIA LAWN.

40-Inch White Victoria Lawn at 16 Cents.

No. 36C2505 40-inch White Victoria Lawn. This is an exceptional value for the money. Is made of fine, long fibre Egyptian yarn and has a very perfect finish and texture. It is used extensively for dresses, waists and fine sheer undergarments. Width, 40 inches.
Price, per yard..............................16c
By the piece of about 40 yards, per yard..15c

WHITE PERSIAN LAWN.

These soft, sheer fabrics are really the finest and most beautiful in texture of anything shown in white goods. They are used extensively for children's dresses, young ladies' graduating dresses, and for ladies' fine white gowns and waists. The values we quote cannot be equaled and we stand ready to refund your money if you are not thoroughly satisfied with your selection. These goods are made in Ireland.

No. 36C2515 White Persian Lawn, very fine and sheer. Our most popular number and a quality that generally retails at from 25 to 35 cents per yard. Width, 32 inches.
Price, per yard..............................14c
Full piece of 24 yards, per yard...........13c

No. 36C2520 White Persian Lawn, beautiful sheer silky finish; warranted to give satisfaction. Width, 32 inches.
Price, per yard..............................17c
Full piece of 24 yards, per yard,..........16c

No. 36C2525 White Persian Lawn, one of the handsomest qualities we carry and a remarkable value. Width, 32 inches.
Price, per yard..............................20c
Full piece of 24 yards, per yard...........19c

BLACK PERSIAN LAWN.

No. 36C2540 Black Persian Lawn, a fine, silky finish and perfect weave. Warranted fast color. Width, 31 inches. Price, per yard....10c
Full piece of about 24 yards, per yard.....9½c

No. 36C2545 Black Persian Lawn, extra fine, even silky finish. The texture is light and airy. Guaranteed fast black in a rich shade. Width, 31 inches. Price, per yard. 12c
Full piece of about 24 yards, per yard..11½c

No. 36C2550 Guaranteed Fast Black Persian Lawn. The finest quality made. A most beautiful, lustrous, sheer and perfect weave. Width, 31 inches. Price, per yard.........16c
Full piece of about 24 yards, per yard....15c

WHITE INDIA MULL.

A very soft sheer fabric, with beautiful silky finish. Very desirable for ladies' and children's fine white dresses. The numbers quoted below are the best values obtainable.

No. 36C2570 White India Mull. Width, 30 inches. Price, per yard..................12½c
Full piece of 24 yards, per yard...........12c

No. 36C2571 White India Mull, extra fine. Width, 30 inches. Price, per yard..........15c
Full piece of 24 yards, per yard...........14c

No. 36C2572 White India Mull, finest quality made. Width, 32 inches.
Price, per yard..............................22c
Full piece of 24 yards, per yard...........21c

WHITE SWISS MULL.

A light and airy fabric of sheer and open weave, rather stiff finish. Highly desirable for dainty washable white dresses where graceful drapery is wanted. These goods are imported direct and the values we quote are unmatchable.

No. 36C2575 White Swiss Mull. A very popular number. Width, 29 inches.
Price, per yard..............................10c
Full piece of 25 yards, per yard............9½c

No. 36C2580 White Swiss Mull. A good quality, exceptional value. Width, 29 inches.
Price, per yard..............................11½c
Full piece of 25 yards, per yard...........11c

No. 36C2585 Good Quality White Swiss Mull. Width, 32 inches. Price, per yard..18c
Full piece of 25 yards, per yard...........17c

No. 36C2590 Extra Fine Quality White Swiss Mull. Width, 32 inches.
Price, per yard..............................21c
Full piece of 25 yards, per yard...........20c

WHITE DOTTED SWISS.

These sheer and dainty fabrics are always in demand for wash dresses and waists. The values quoted below are especially attractive.

No. 36C2605 White Dotted Swiss, comes in small and medium dots. Width, 23 inches.
Price, per yard.... 8c
By the piece of about 50 yards, per yard..7½c

No. 36C2610 White Dotted Swiss, much better than the above number, comes in small and medium dots. We can also furnish this swiss in small set figures, composed of a cluster of five pin dots. This is a new thing and highly pleasing. In ordering, please mention whether pin dots, medium dots or figures are desired. Width, 25 inches.
Price, per yard..............................11c
By the piece of about 50 yards, per yard 10½c

No. 36C2615 White Dotted Swiss, with pin dots, very fine and sheer. Width, 25 inches.
Price, per yard..............................14c

No. 36C2620 Extra Fine and Sheer Dotted Swiss. This is one of the best numbers made. It comes in medium or pin size dots. Width, 26 inches. Price, per yard.........20c

White French Organdie.

We are direct importers of these sheer, beautiful dress fabrics that are so popular for wedding, reception and graduating gowns and we are thereby in a position to make you a great saving in price.

No. 36C2630 White French Organdie, very sheer and fine. Perfect in color—a quality that ordinarily retails at 60 cents per yard. Width, full 66 inches. Price, per yard......35c

No. 36C2635 White French Organdie. A beautiful light and airy fabric and extra value for the money. Width, full 68 inches.
Price, per yard..............................50c

No. 36C2640 White French Organdie, extremely sheer and absolutely perfect in weave and one of the finest fabrics imported. Width, 68 inches. Price, per yard..........75c

No. 36C2645 Our very best White French Organdie. Nothing better imported at any price. This grade is the equal of fabrics sold by retail dealers as high as $1.50 per yard. Absolutely perfect in weave, finish and color. Width, 68 inches. Price, per yard.........95c

Long Cloths.

IN PLAIN WHITE.

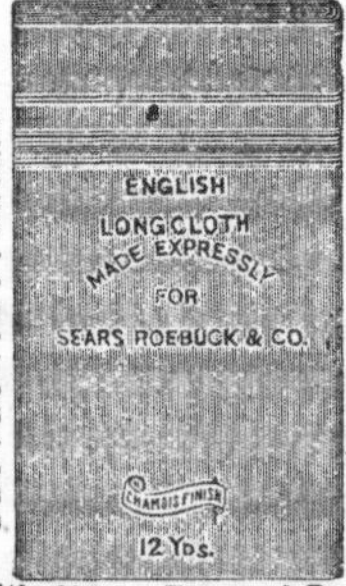

These fabrics are made from the finest Egyptian cotton, soft finish and of a weight that is very desirable for ladies' and children's white underwear, and preferable to glazed finished cambrics. We quote below four numbers, any one of which is the best value the market affords. These goods are made especially for us by one of the best mills in the country.

No. 36C2655 Width, 36 in. Per yard 8c
Full piece of 12 yards, per yard..........7½c
No. 36C2660 Width, 36 in. Per yard 9c
Full piece of 12 yards, per yard..........8½c
No. 36C2665 Width, 36 in. Per yard 11c
Full piece of 12 yards, per yard..........10½c
No. 36C2670 Width, 36 in. Per yard 13c
Full piece of 12 yards, per yard..........12c

Plain White Nainsooks.

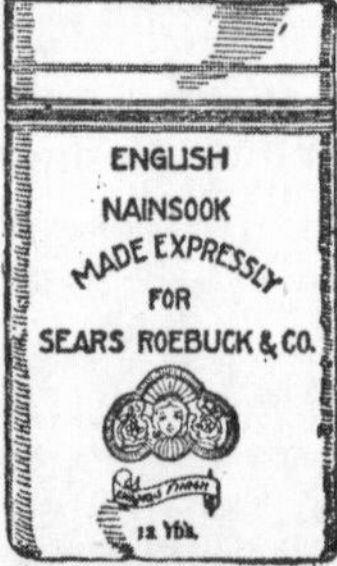

Similar to long cloth but of softer finish and lighter weight. A fabric of beautiful texture and much used for ladies' and children's fine underwear. These goods are made especially for us in enormous quantities and we are able to sell them to our customers at less money than the ordinary dealer has to pay. They are put up in 12-yard pieces and you can have them either by the full piece or by the yard. We challenge competition on the numbers quoted below.

No. 36C2680 Width, 36 in. Per yd....8c
Full piece of 12 yards, per yard..........7½c
No. 36C2685 Width, 36 in. Per yd.. 11c
Full piece of 12 yards, per yard..........10c
No. 36C2690 Width, 36 in. Per yd.. 14c
Full piece of 12 yards, per yard..........13c
No. 36C2695 Width, 36 in. Per yd.. 17c
Full piece of 12 yards, per yard...........16c

Maderia Nainsook.

Pure White, Fine Silky Finish, Soft and Sheer.

No. 36C2705 We sell enormous quantities of this beautiful and popular fabric. It is made from the very finest of selected Sea Island cotton yarns and is the equal of similar fabrics that sell in retail stores at 25 to 30 cents per yard. Sold only in full pieces of 10 yards. Width, 38 inches.
Price, per full piece of 10 yards..............$1.75

Cotton Diaper Cloth.

No. 36C2715 Cotton Diaper Cloth. We carry nothing but the very best goods to be had. Ours is a sanitary cloth and is chemically pure and absorbent. It is rendered soft by hygienic process of bleaching and finishing. Comes only in 10-yard pieces, put up in sealed paper bags. To be had in the following widths:

	Price,
Width, 18 inches, per piece......	50c
Width, 20 inches, per piece......	55c
Width, 22 inches, per piece......	60c
Width, 24 inches, per piece......	65c
Width, 27 inches, per piece......	70c

WHITE WELT PIQUE.

A medium heavy weight, pure white cotton fabric. An everlasting material that will wash beautifully.

No. 36C2735 White Pique or Corduroy, medium size cord. Width, 28 inches.
Price, per yard..............................12½c
By the piece of about 40 yards, per yd, 11½c

White Jacquard Nainsook Brilliantine at 7 Cents.

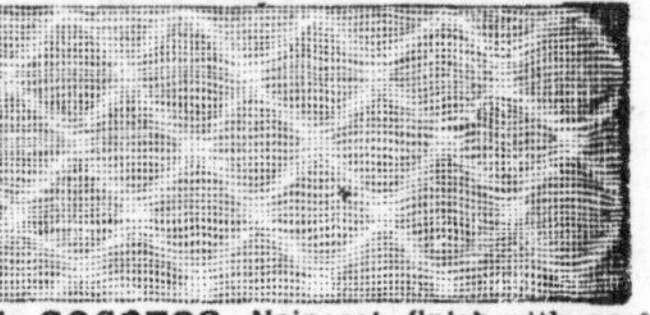

No. 36C2738 Nainsook finish with neat check designs in all white. Width, 25 inches.
Price, per yard..............................7c
By the piece of about 50 yards, per yd, 6½c

White Fancy Madras at 11c.

No. 36C2740 Pure White Fancy Figured Madras in patterns like and similar to illustration. Very appropriate in weight and appearance for waists, white wash dresses or men's warm weather shirts. Width, 36 inches.
Price, per yard..............................11c
By the piece of about 40 yards, per yd, 10½c

CHECK AND STRIPE NAINSOOK.

White Check Nainsook at 5c.

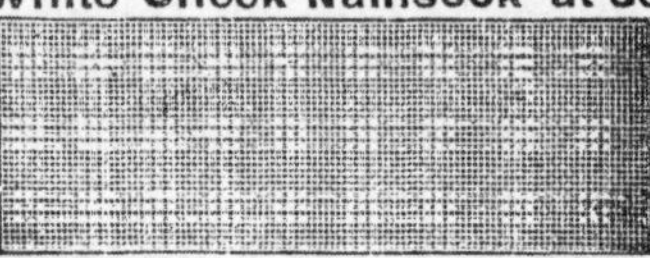

No. 36C2760 White Check Nainsook. Good weight, well made goods. Large, medium and small sized checks. This quality generally sells for 7 to 8 cents. Width, 24 inches.
Price, per yard..............................5c
By the piece of about 50 yards, per yd, 4½c

White Check Nainsook at 7c.

No. 36C2770 White Check Nainsook. Heavier and better than the preceding number. Comes in large, medium and small size checks. Width, 24 inches. Price, per yd, 7c
By the piece of about 50 yards, per yd, 6½c

White Check and Stripe Nainsook at 10 Cents.

No. 36C2780 Check and Stripe Nainsook in pure white. Good weight, perfectly woven fabric with handsome satin stripes and checks of all sizes. An excellent value for the money. Width, 27 inches. Price, per yd, 10c
By the piece of about 50 yards, per yd, 9½c

WHITE SKIRTING OR APRON LAWN.

These goods are much used for white skirts, aprons and infants' long dresses. They are full width for skirts or aprons and are hemmed and bordered at bottom. We do not sample apron pattern lawns.

Full Width White Apron Lawn at 12½ Cents.

No. 36C2820 White Apron Lawn, full 40 inches wide, which is the correct apron or skirt length, bordered with double texture fabric which gives the appearance of a hem 3½ inches deep, also three pretty double cord stripes. A very popular fabric and a big bargain at the price. Width, 40 inches.
Price, per yard..............................12½c
By the piece of about 40 yards, per yd, 11½c

White Check and Stripe Dimity at 9 Cents.

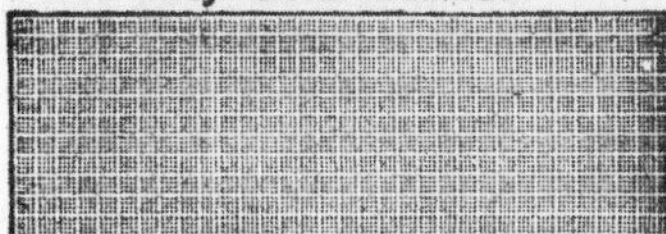

No. 36C2860 Check and Stripe White Dimity. Has a beautiful, soft, sheer finish. This is a very popular number with us and very good value for the money. For wearing and washing qualities it cannot be equaled. Width, 28 inches.
Price, per yard...........9c
By the piece of about 50 yards, per yard, 8½c

Mercerized Striped Lawn.

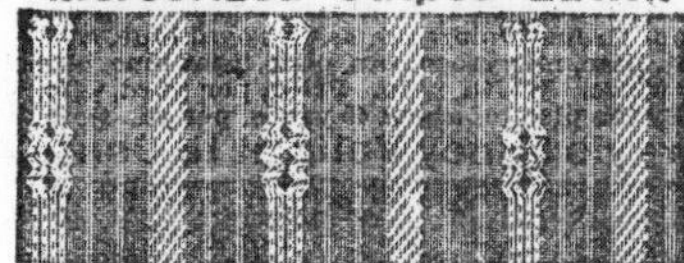

No. 36C2875 The illustration will give you some idea of the beauty of this Mercerized Striped Lawn. The stripes are neat and carefully mercerized, while the groundwork is a firm, even lawn texture. Comes in pure white only. Width, 27 inches. Price, per yard, 12c
By the piece of about 35 yards, per yd., 11½c

Mercerized Striped Madras.

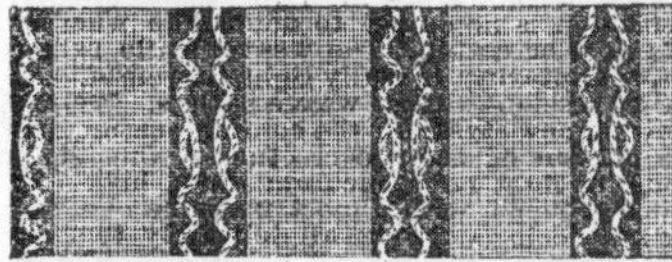

No. 36C2877 Pure White Madras, constructed from high grade yarns with fancy stripes as shown. The mercerization of these stripes is permanent and cannot wash out. This is an elegant summer suiting at a moderate price. Pure white only. Width, 27 inches.
Price, per yard...........12c
By the piece of about 40 yards, per yd.. 11½c

Imported Mercerized Striped Madras at 18 Cents.

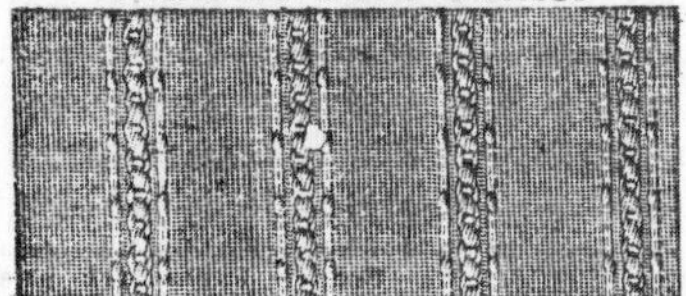

No. 362890 A much finer quality than the preceding number, being a genuine imported madras of superb texture and neat pleasing stripe combinations. Pure white only. Width, 27 inches. Price, per yard.........18c

Extra Quality Imported White Canvas Cloth at 23 Cents.

No. 36C2895 Imported Pure White, Fine Mercerized Canvas Cloth, the genteel fabric for two-piece suits, separate skirts, etc. Being mercerized in the yarn before weaving, the strength of the yarns has been increased to a large extent, while at the same time a suit of this canvas cloth may be worn a month longer time than any other white goods without soiling. Width, 27 inches. Price, per yard...23c

Mercerized White Satin Damasse at 25 Cents.

No. 36C2920 This Satin Damasse, being highly mercerized and woven from the finest Egyptian cotton on jacquard looms, has the appearance of an all silk satin damasse and is about the same weight. It comes in a variety of lovely patterns of medium size, any of which would please you. Width, 29 inches.
Price, per yard.........25c

Imperial Damask Satin in Pure Snow White at 33c.

No. 36C2930 This fabric looks like silk and is fully as rich appearing, notwithstanding was woven for us from selected Egyptian on and not a fibre of silk is used in its construction. The cotton is mercerized in the yarn re weaving, which renders the luster absoly permanent and washable. It is woven in small or medium designs or dice checks on ground, also block squares and floral de on pinhead dot ground. Width, 29 inches.
ce, per yard...........33c

Champagne or Linen Colored Mercerized Damasse at 23c.

No. 32C2944 The latest and most tasty fabric offered this season in the all popular shade of champagne. No color so appropriate and none which shows up to better advantage the neat ideas embraced in our new mercerized damasse. Like the white goods of this description, it is an imported article, and at the price we have been able to quote it we are confident of its success. Comes in tan or champagne ground with dots of small or medium sizes. Width, 28 inches.
Price, per yard...........23c

Champagne Color Mercerized Stripe Lawn at 10 Cents.

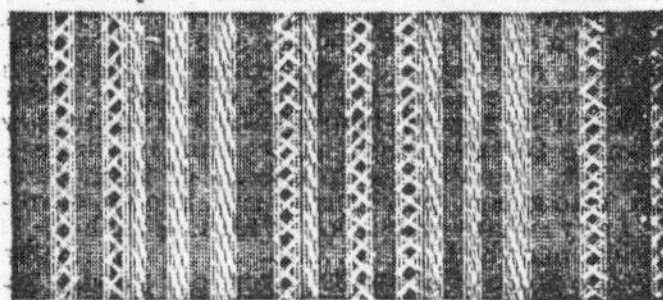

No. 36C2946 An unusually seasonable offering at a money saving figure. The lawn ground is woven of dependable yarn, while the mercerization of the stripes really stamps the fabric as a much higher priced production than our quotation would indicate. Comes in tan or champagne colored ground only, in narrow or medium stripes similar to illustration. Width, 28 inches. Price, per yard..10c
By the piece of about 40 yards, per yard...........9½c

Plain Black Figured or Dotted Swiss at 18 Cents.

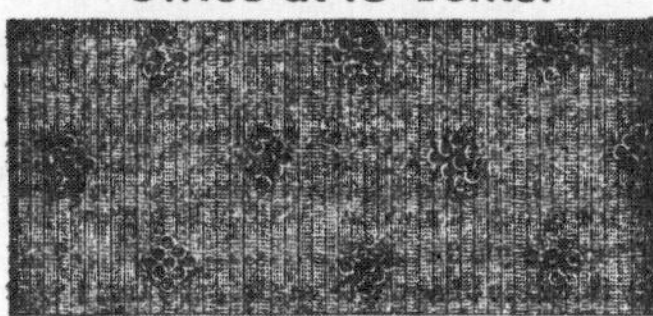

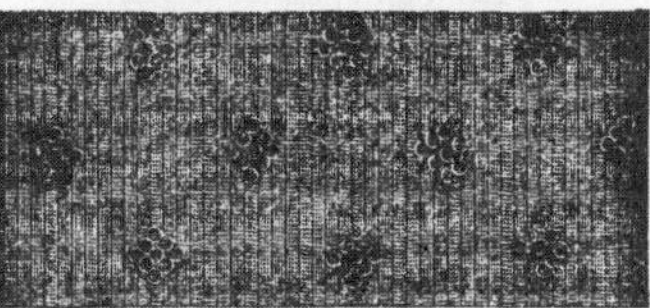

No. 36C2960 Of the newer creations in plain black goods, for this season, this particular fabric is destined to distance all other in its race to the goal of popular favor. Its color is a lustrous black, and will wash without crocking. Neither sun nor perspiration has any effect on this black swiss. Comes in solid black in medium size dot or small figure as desired. We can guarantee your satisfaction. Width, 28 inches.
Price, per yard...........18c

COLORED WASH DRESS GOODS

OUR COLORED WASH DRESS GOODS DEPARTMENT, has been completely reorganized for this season, our lines have been greatly enlarged, we have made exceedingly large contracts with foreign and domestic mills, and by the most economic handling, with but our one small percentage of profit added, we can safely say that you can buy one yard or one piece from us for as little, if not less than your storekeeper at home can buy in 100-piece lots. **The greatest values in entirely new, up to date, high class wash fabrics that ever went out of this or any other house.**

OUR SPECIAL OFFER. Do not wait for samples. (If you want samples first, ask for them as explained on page 757.) Select the goods you will want for a dress or shirt waist pattern. **Give us an idea of the color or pattern wanted.** We will send them to you with the understanding that if they are not perfectly satisfactory, and the greatest value ever shown in your section at anything like the price, if they are not new, handsome, and up to date, matchable only by the very newest effects, as shown in the choicest city stores, you can return the goods to us at our expense, and we will refund your money. **You must see and examine these goods, compare them with the goods offered by other dealers to appreciate the value we are giving.**

FREE SAMPLES--SEE PAGE 757 ABOUT FREE SAMPLES.

PERCALES, MADRAS WEAVES, ETC.

Heavy Printed Dress Percales at 8 Cents.

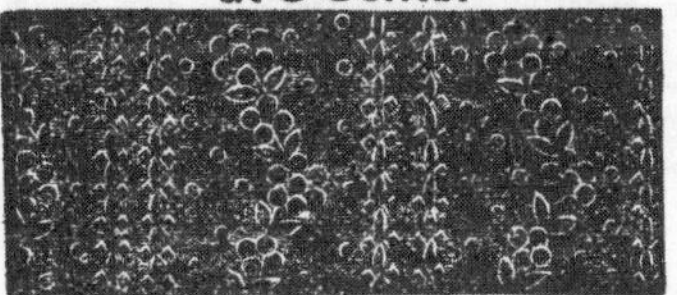

No. 36C2970 Dress Percales in dark effects. This is a heavy, well made percale. The ground colors are navy blue, black, wine or medium blue, with white extract printings of floral designs, stripes and polka dots. This is a standard percale and is excellent value for the money. Width, 31 inches.
Price, per yard...........8c
By the piece of about 50 yards, per yard, 7½c

Standard Dark Ground Percales at 10 Cents.

No. 36C2980 Standard Percales, extra heavy weight, fine even texture. Colors are absolutely fast and washable. To be had in dark effects only. The ground colors are black, navy blue, medium blue or wine with extract printings in white of floral designs, stripes or dots. This is the very best standard percale and at our special price cannot be equaled in value. Width, 36 inches.
Price, per yard...........10c
By the piece of about 45 yards, per yard, 9½c

Standard Percales in Light Effects at 10 Cents.

No. 36C2990 This is the very best Percale made. Extra heavy weight, even, close texture. To be had in light effects only. This is suitable for shirt waists, wash dresses and men's shirts. The colors are absolutely fast and washable. For durability, these goods cannot be equaled. The ground colors are white with printings of stripes and floral designs in the following colors: pink, light blue, red, black, green or tan. The designs are all new and up to date and sure to please you. Width, 36 inches. Price, per yard...........10c
By the piece of about 45 yards, per yard, 9½c

Delmar Printed Madras at 8c.

No. 36C3000 Heavy Printed Madras in firm, perfect texture. A very good fabric that will wash and not fade. It comes in white grounds with printed stripes or small figures in a great variety of colorings. This is a fabric of which we sell hundreds of pieces every season, and at our special 8-cent price represents a big saving. Width, 32 inches.
Price, per yard...........8c
By the piece of about 50 yards, per yard, 7½c

Printed Corded Madras at 11 Cents.

No. 36C3010 Heavy weight, perfect weave, printed Madras in beautiful designs, any one of which, like the illustration, is of the very newest. The body of the cloth is perfectly plain madras weave with alternate heavy cable cord and tape stripes. The ground colors in all are white, with printings of stripes and floral designs, in black, navy blue, light blue or red. This is a fabric that will wear and wash perfectly. Width, 36 inches.
Price, per yard...........11c
By the piece of about 45 yards, per yard, 10c

Striped Madras at 12 Cents.

No. 36C3020 This is a real Madras fabric of medium heavy weight. It is a fabric highly desirable for shirt waists, shirt waist suits, and is also used for men's shirts. The body of the cloth is perfect madras weave with heavy cord stripes. The colors are woven, not printed. Comes in stripes of black and white, navy blue and white, light blue and white or red and white. This fabric is calculated to give exceptional service and will wash without fading. Width, 32 inches. Price, per yard...12c
By the piece of about 40 yards, per yard, 11c

Fine Printed Lawns at 4c.

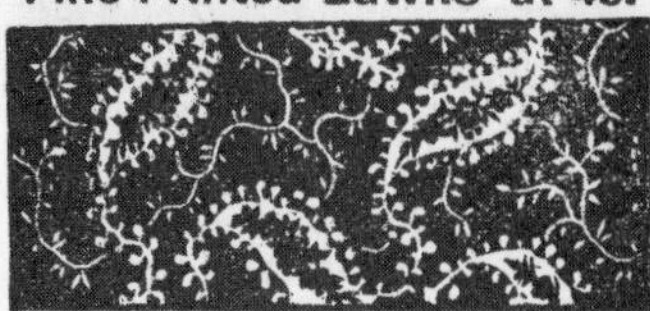

No. 36C3030 The ground colors are white, pink, light blue, navy blue, black, red, lavender, green or gray with various printed designs. In fact, we can give you almost any combination of colors you wish. Width, 28 inches. Price, per yard...........4c
By the piece of about 50 yards, per yd. 3⅞c

Primrose Printed Challie, 4c.

No. 36C3040 Printed Challie. The styles are cream grounds with neat floral designs in colors of pink, blue, red, green or black, also floral on ground colors of black, navy blue, green, brown, pink or light blue, also white dots on colored grounds. Width, 23 inches.
Price, per yard...........4c
By the piece of about 50 yards, per yd.. 3⅞c

Empress Batiste at 7 Cents.

No. 36C3050 A pretty, sheer and washable fabric, in texture similar to lawn, and at 7 cents it is an especially attractive value. One style is white ground with new and pretty floral designs of black, pink or light blue; another style is tinted ground of pink, light blue, light green, tan, navy blue, cardinal or black with neat floral printings of white. This fabric will wear and wash very satisfactorily. Width, 23 inches. Price, per yard...........7c
By the piece of about 50 yards, per yd.. 6⅞c

Lace Striped Lawn at 10 Cents.

No. 36C3060 This is a very pretty, sheer Lace Striped Lawn, and one of the most stylish medium priced wash fabrics in the department. It has very neat lace stripes about one inch apart. One style is black, navy, green or tan ground with fancy white stripes. Another is pink, green, light blue or tan ground with neat small floral designs of white. Colors are fast and washable and are very dainty and well selected. Width, 28 inches.
Price, per yard...........10c
By the piece of about 40 yards, per yd.. 9½c

Fine Pompadour Batiste at 9c.

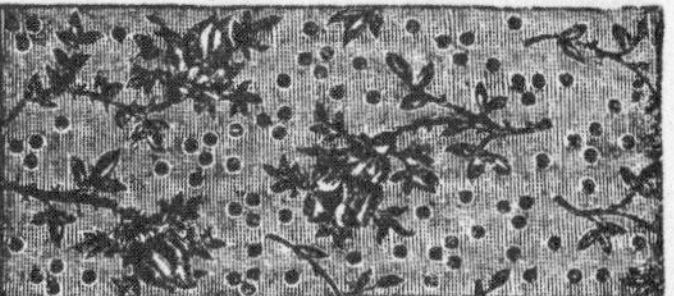

No. 36C3070 The illustration will give you an idea of one of the patterns in which this fine, sheer Batiste is to be had. The weave of the fabric is even and perfect and of rather sheer texture. The colors are washable and come in tan and black, gray and white, yellow and black, white and lavender, white and light blue, white and green, white and pink or white and black. This is a fabric that we can recommend very highly and is an exceptional value for the money. Width, 30 inches.
Price, per yard...........9c
By the piece of about 40 yards, per yd.. 8½c

Fancy Printed Dimity at 10½c.

No. 36C3080 Dimities are among the most desirable wash fabrics. The dainty hair line cord effects give the fabric a very neat appearance. This is a sheer, even, perfect weave fabric and possesses wonderful washing and wearing qualities. We have it in a large and well selected range of patterns and colors. One style is pink ground with black floral designs, blue ground with small black floral designs, white ground with small black floral designs, other styles are white ground with black, blue or red dots; white ground with pink, lavender or blue stripe and dot effects. This fabric is highly desirable for ladies' and misses' wash dresses, shirt waists, etc., and will be found a very economical cloth to buy. Width, 29 inches. Price, per yard...........10½c
By the piece of about 40 yards, per yd 10⅛c

29-Inch Olive Cords, 12 Cents.

No. 36C3100 A very nobby printed fabric of batiste or lawn nature, with pin cords interwoven at irregular intervals, leaving a plain lawn ground stripe, about an inch in width. The ground colors are in solid shades of light blue, medium blue, navy blue, pink, cardinal, nile green or black, with printings in white of either floral designs or small diamond and dot effects. It is a fabric that has wonderful washing and wearing qualities and is appropriate for any purpose for which wash dress goods are used. Width, 29 inches. Per yard.....12c
By the piece of about 40 yards, per yd..11½c

Tinted Ground Printed Splash Fancy at 15 Cents.

No. 36C3110 A tinted ground of variegated or Beige effect, entirely new this season and a pleasant change from solid color tints. The printings are also decidedly new, being of splash designs, the same in all except for the difference in the ground colors, which are light blue, navy, pink, black, tan or medium gray. The fabric is of lawn or batiste nature, very sheer and dainty, with leno and cord stripes intermingled in clusters about an inch apart, the stripes being of the same ground colors. Width, 28 inches. Price, per yard.....15c
By the piece of about 40 yards, per yard..14c

Mercerized Striped Novelty at 22 Cents.

No. 36C3130 This is one of the daintiest and most desirable wash waistings or dress fabrics to be had in our entire wash goods department. It has a very bright, fancy stripe, like the illustration, mercerized in colors; also, wide embroidered effects relieved by cords. It comes in plain solid colors of pink, light blue, tan, light green, gray, lavender, yellow, cardinal, navy or black. We also have it in white grounds with printings of floral designs in black, blue or cardinal. This is a highly desirable fabric for all wash goods purposes, and one that will give exceptional service. Width, 33 inches. Price, per yard.....22c

Solid Colored Embroidered Dotted Swiss at 11 Cents.

No. 36C3140 Embroidered Dotted Swisses are always desirable and are much used for street dresses and waists, as well as for evening gowns, graduating dresses, etc. This fabric is dainty and sheer, with well made embroidered dots of the same ground colors. It comes in black, navy, red, pink, light blue, tan, nile green, gray, yellow or cream solid colors. This fabric sells in ordinary retail stores at 15 to 18 cents per yard. Width, 28 inches.
Price, per yard.....11c
By the piece of about 45 yards, per yard. 10½c

Plain Solid Colored Dimities at 11 Cents.

No. 36C3150 Dimities are more desirable than ever, because of the tiny raised cords, producing a handsome effect on the fine, sheer ground. This is a very good value for the money and is a desirable fabric for evening and house wear, also for summer street costumes. The colors are light blue, pink, nile green, tan, navy, lavender, cardinal, purple, primrose yellow, medium blue or black, and are perfectly fast and washable. Width, 30 inches.
Price, per yard.....11c
By the piece of about 45 yards, per yard. 10½c

Dotted Cotton Crepe at 12c.

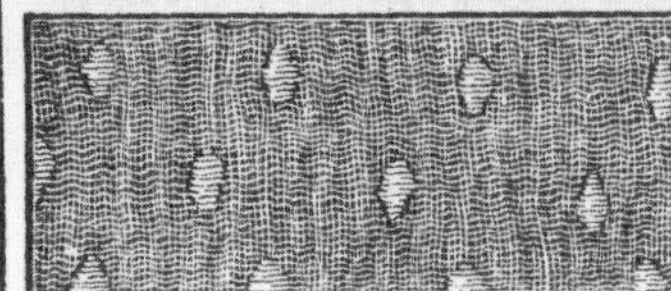

No. 36C3160 This is a most beautiful fabric, and has the appearance and finish of wool goods worth double and triple the money. The dotted surface is new and very attractive, possessing that highly desirable crinkled effect. Fine for party dresses or decorations. It is of medium weight, in a well selected line of washable colorings, as follows: Pink, light blue, lavender, nile green, yellow, violet, cardinal, navy blue, cream white, pure white or black. This fabric is much used for inexpensive evening dresses, also for children's wear. Width, 26 inches.
Price, per yard.....12c
By the piece of about 35 yards, per yard. 11½c

Plain Lawns or Organdies.

No. 36C3163 Plain Colored Lawns or Organdies in all the needed shades. Everyone is familiar with their many good features, and, in order to create a special demand for them, we have placed ourselves in an advantageous position with the manufacturers, whereby we can offer them to our customers at such extremely low prices as to make a reputation for ourselves on this class of goods. Colors: rose, pink, light blue, light navy, primrose, yellow, nile green, lavender, tan, cardinal, black or white. Width, 31 inches. Price, per yard.....6½c
By the piece of about 50 yards, per yard..6¼c

No. 36C3166 This is a finer quality than the previous number, and one that will readily appeal to those who have been accustomed to paying 15 to 18 cents for organdies. Particularly to such customers do we submit our claim as to the value of this organdie. Dainty in texture, yet firm. Colors clear and perfect, and is a pretty summer dress fabric at a money saving figure. This line of colored organdies will not be long in making friends. Fast, thoroughly washable tints of pink, light blue, nile green, lavender, yellow, tan, navy, cardinal, black or white. Width, 31 inches.
Price, per yard.....9c
By the piece of about 50 yards, per yard..8½c

Plain Sheer Linen Color Batiste at 11 Cents.

No. 36C3168 Ecru or Natural Linen Color Batiste, very sheer and dainty. A most stylish material for entire dresses or waists for ladies' and children's wear. It has the appearance of an all silk shantung or tussah silk. This fabric is exceptionally fine, sheer and beautiful and at the price is a marvel of cheapness. Width, 28 inches. Price, per yard.....11c
By the piece of about 40 yards, per yard. 10½c

Silk Mixed Batiste at 18c.

No. 36C3170 Sheer Silk and Cotton Batiste, a very new and desirable wash material, much resembling a shantung silk and highly desirable for wash dresses and waists. It is a very sheer and beautiful fabric, half silk and half cotton, in the natural linen color only. It is the product of the very best domestic weavers, and at 18 cents per yard represents a saving of 12 to 15 cents per yard, as this fabric sells in city stores at 30 and 35 cents per yard. Width, 28 inches. Price, per yard.....18c
By the piece of about 40 yards, per yard...17c

Plain Colored Silk Mull at 19 Cents.

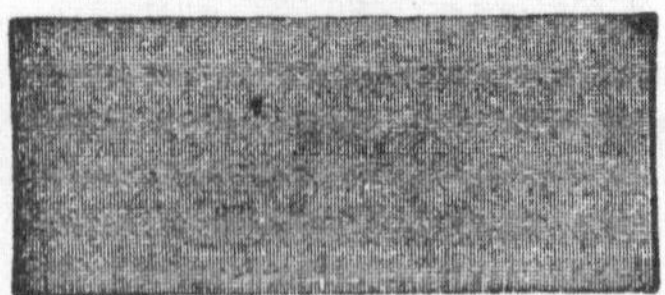

No. 36C3172 This dainty, sheer, half silk material is one of the most desirable fabrics in the wash goods line. It is highly desirable for house and street wear, as well as for evening and party dresses and waists or graduating dresses for young ladies. It comes in solid colors only, as follows: Pink, light blue, lavender, Primrose yellow, pearl gray, nile green, tan, cardinal, gray, navy blue, brown, black, cream or white. We are direct importers of this dainty silk mull and are thereby in a position to offer it to our customers at the same price the dealer has to pay. Width, 28 inches.
Price, per yard.....19c
By the piece of about 30 yards, per yard. 18c

Dotted Mousseline de Soie in Solid Colors at 24 Cents.

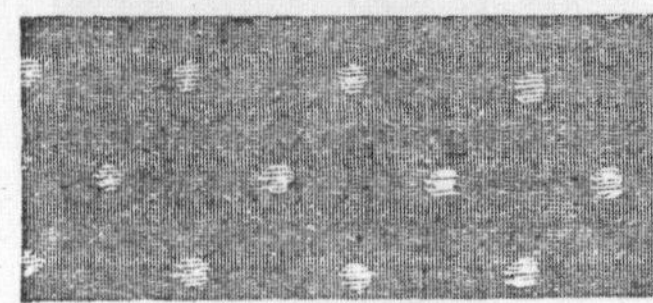

No. 36C3176 The dots are about ⅛ of an inch across and about 1 inch apart. The fabric, which is commonly called silk mull, is a very pretty, sheer and silky weave. The dots are more glossy than the ground and therefore show up very distinctly. This is an all the year round fabric and highly desirable for evening and graduation dresses or waists. We have it in shades of light blue, pink, nile green, pearl gray, tan, brown, cardinal, navy, white or black. Width, 28 inches.
Price, per yard.....24c
By the piece of about 30 yards, per yard. 23c

Fancy Silk Mull at 35 Cents.

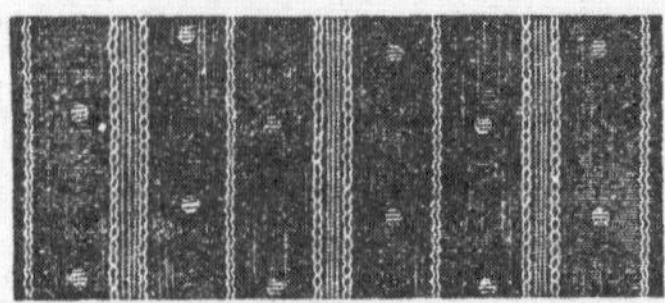

No. 36C3178 Beautiful Sheer Mousseline with silk lappet work, like illustration, also a few other choice effects. If you wish something just a shade better than the usual offering in mousseline or silk mull, this is it. Colors are pink, heliotrope, lavender, cream, light blue, nile green, rose, tan, gray, cardinal or black. Width, 27 inches.
Price, per yard.....35c
By the piece of about 30 yds., per yard. 33½c

Corded Wash Silk Novelties at 38 Cents.

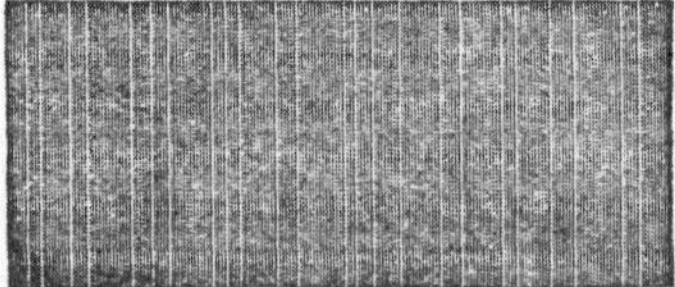

No. 36C3180 Here is submitted to you a new summer weave, and a smart one. There is nothing used in its construction but the purest silk, together with a small percentage of fine combed Egyptian cotton, making a sightly material and at the same time a dependable one at a small price. The narrow cords are of silk, raised from the body of the cloth just enough to display to the best advantage the lustrous sheen. Comes in perfect colors of black, navy blue, the new brown, tan, cream or white. Width, 27 inches.
Price, per yard.....38c

Wash Pongee Silks at 38 Cents.

No. 36C3182 These delightfully dainty Wash Pongee Silks are growing with us every season and are really an all year round cloth, though, when first introduced, was intended for summer use only. It has all the good qualities of real pure silk, and will outwear it at a fraction of the cost. Only the most perfect silk is used, representing the larger part of the material used, the balance being carefully selected and treated Egyptian cotton. To look at this creation and to handle it, one would think it to be all pure silk, so cleverly is it constructed. Washing and long wear has no effect whatever on color or luster, and the wearing quality is marvelous. Comes in pink, light blue, tan, gray, lavender or white. Width, 27 inches. Price, per yard.....38c

VOILE WASH FABRICS.

Argyle Plain Colored Voile at 15 Cents.

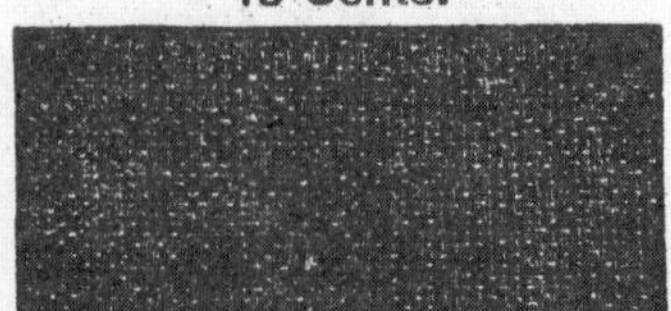

No. 36C3184 This is the same cloth as our No. 36C3188, which has proved itself such an immense favorite. The plain colors will, without question, be equally as strong. Our Argyle Plain Colored Voile carries the touch of the French Wool Voile, while the colors are as clear and perfect as any foreign dye, and are absolutely fast. Looks well, wears well, washes well and is a stayer. The colors are navy, cadet blue, light blue, pink, tan, brown, black or white. Width, 28 inches.
Price, per yard.....15c
By the piece of about 45 yards, per yard 14c

Fancy Nub Stripe Egyptian Voiles at 10 Cents.

No. 36C3186 For a low priced wash novelty this surpasses all its competitors. The weight is a trifle less than medium, and the construction, while sheer, is nevertheless of sufficient wiriness to withstand hard wear. The nubs are brought out in pure white on solid colored grounds to a charming degree of perfection. Ground colors are navy, royal blue, cardinal, lilac, nile green, tan, pink, light blue, black or white. Width, 28 in. Price, per yard, 10c
By the piece of about 45 yards, per yd.. 9½c

Argyle Fancy Voile at 15 Cents.

No. 36C3188 An exact copy of All Wool Voile or Etamine. In the made up suit, close inspection is necessary to determine whether it is wool or cotton. The weave, while rather heavy appearing, is really light in weight, and rather resembles loose weave batiste. We are showing new styles for the coming season, and are certain of their correctness. One style comes in light navy, medium navy, brown or black grounds, with almost invisible check of the same color and over all delicately touched here and there with small polka dots of contrasting tints, such as red and white on navy, green and white on black, black and white on brown, or black and white on navy. Another style is all tan colored ground with harmonious color combination in fetchy designs in red, blue, black, brown or green. Width, 28 inches.
Price, per yard.....15c
By the piece of about 45 yards, per yd., 14c

Voile Royalle at 17 Cents.

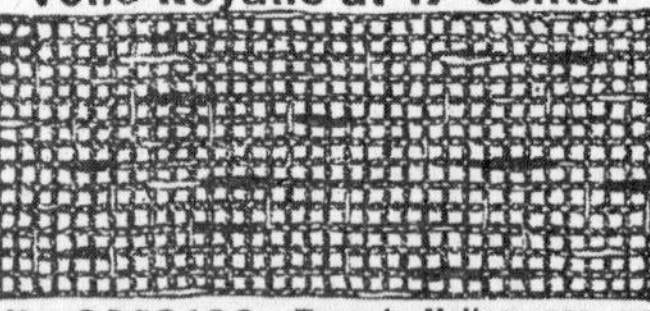

No. 36C3190 French Voiles are unquestionably the strongest favorites for spring and summer costumes. This Voile Royalle possesses the desirable features of the exclusive French wool voiles as to touch, color, and wear, and at a nominal cost. Comes in pure white with satin stripe, gray or black grounds with white, pink or blue neat splash effects, also in narrow or medium stripes of black and white, light blue and white, or pink and white. Width, 28 in. Price, per yd., 17c

Imported Voile Checks, 30c.

No. 36C3192 This Handsome Imported Checked Voile is woven in Europe from the finest Egyptian cotton obtainable and will wear better than the wool voiles, and will not pull. The check designs are neat and considered the cream of this year's work. The colors are clear and fast, in light blue, black, yellow, lavender, pink, light green or tan. Width, 28 inches. Price, per yard.....30c

Nub Zephyrs at 10 Cents.

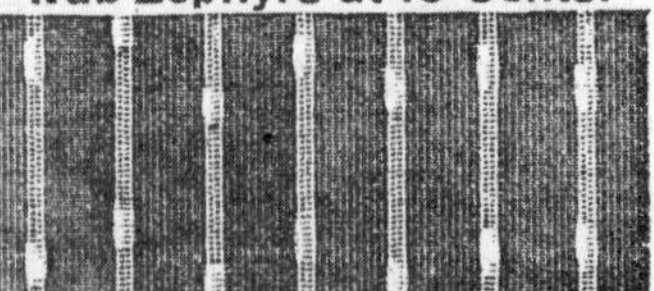

No. 36C3194 Handsome Chambray Zephyrs in this season's newest tints. The texture of the fabric is of chambray nature, but finished soft so as to drape gracefully and make up into charming shirtwaist suits or separate waists or skirts, also highly desirable for children's wear. Comes in brown, tan, light blue, light navy, nile green, pink, or dark gray. Width, 25 inches. Price, per yd., 10c
By the piece of about 40 yards, per yd., 9½c

DIVISION OF MEDIUM AND HEAVY WEIGHT SUITING EFFECT WASH FABRICS, IN PLAIN AND FANCY WEAVES.

New Canvas Dress Duck at 9c.

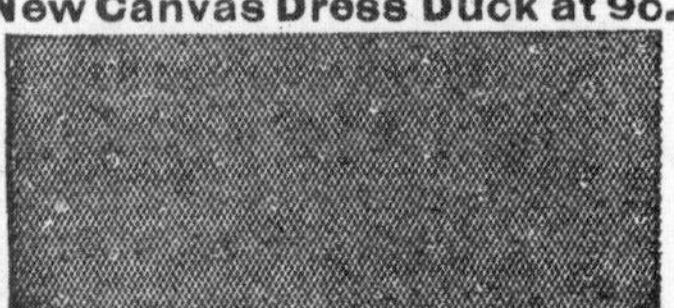

No. 36C3196 This well known fabric we have in a choice range of white figures and polka dots on navy blue or black grounds, also white polka dots on red grounds. Our cloth is full 28 inches wide and is a good heavy weight and a fabric much in demand for suits or separate skirts. The quality is the very best to be had. The figures are small, neat designs like and similar to the illustration, and polka dots are medium size. This fabric is used extensively for men's shirts and boys' suits. It is a marvel of durability. Width, 28 inches. Price, per yard.....
By the piece of about 45 yards, per yd.. 8

Printed Silk Fil de Soie at 21 Cents.

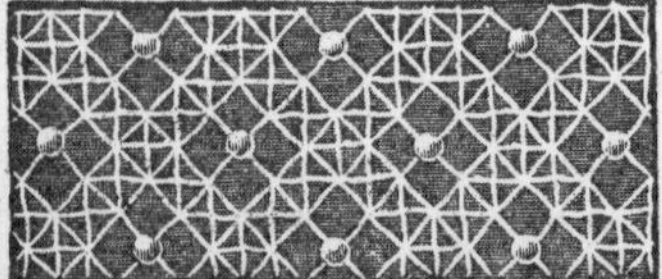

No. 36C3174 This handsome, light weight weave Fil de Sole comes in patterns like the illustration, namely, printings of white on groundwork of various shades of light blue, medium blue, lavender and navy blue. The texture of the cloth is very fine and sheer, and of a weight highly desirable for waists and full costumes where graceful drapery is wanted. It is a fabric that will be much used for all of the various wash goods purposes. Its silky luster and up to date designs, stamp it as one of the most stylish fabrics shown this season. It is a material that will wash and wear exceptionally well, and we have no hesitancy in recommending it to our customers. Width, 28 inches. Price, per yard.....21c
By the piece of about 30 yards, per yard.....20c

Solid Color Wash Duck at 8c.

No. 36C3198 This is a heavy, well made Duck of perfect, even texture. The colors are perfect, fast and washable. This fabric is much used for two-piece suits, odd skirts and waists, and also for little folks' suits. The colors are cardinal, tan, navy, white or black. Width, 28 inches. Price, per yard..................8c
By the piece of about 45 yards, per yard..7½c

Olivette Granitelle Cloth at 13c.

No. 36C3200 A new weave on the order of a granite, and will wear exceptionally well. Very serviceable for waists, separate skirts or men's shirts. Pure white ground with small neat designs in black. Width, 29 inches.
Price, per yard..............................13c
By the piece of about 40 yards, per yard..12c

Printed Corded Pique at 10c.

No. 36C3220 Printed Corded Pique is a very popular material for two-piece wash suits, odd skirts or waists, as well as for wash dresses, and has proved itself an excellent material. It is also used a great deal for children's dresses. The colors are absolutely fast, and of a wide variety. White ground with either stripes, dots or figures of black, red, blue or green. Also in colored grounds, such as navy, cadet blue, wine or black, with white dots. Width, 23 inches. Price, per yard..................10c
By the piece of about 40 yards, per yard..9½c

Heavy Covert Suiting at 10c.

No. 36C3250 This is a well made, nicely finished cotton suiting, that has all the appearance of a wool covert cloth and is highly desirable for all suiting purposes. It comes in very stylish mixtures of brown and white, tan and white, gray and white, medium navy and white, dark navy and white or black and white. The colors are absolutely fast, and the fabric will wash and retain its wool suiting effect. Width, 28 inches. Price, per yard..10c
By the piece of about 45 yards, per yard..9½c

Plain Colored Mercerized Canvas, 15 Cents.

No. 36C3260 The Exquisite Two-piece Suit Fabric, also appropriate for separate skirts or shirt waists. This is a light weight canvas cloth, just a trifle heavier than a voile, and not quite as open in construction. The mercerization is done in the yarn, consequently will not wash out, but will retain its luster. The wearing quality of this fabric is unsurpassed. Colors, pink, tan, light blue or white. Width, 28 inches.
Price, per yard..............................15c

German Linen Suiting at 11c.

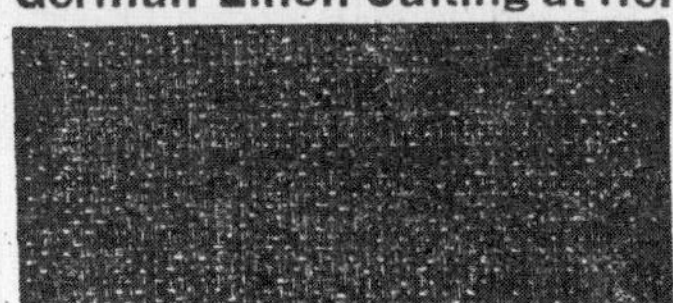

No. 36C3375 There is no linen used in the construction of this cloth else we could not sell it at the price, but it takes its name from the nature of the yarns used, which are hard and evenly twisted and closely woven, making a cloth which to all appearance is an imported linen suiting. Will give excellent service, particularly adapted to the making of two-piece suits. Colors, which are guaranteed fast, are navy, cadet blue, light blue, tan, black or white. Width, 32 inches. Price, per yard..........11c
By the piece of about 45 yards, per yd..10½c

Natural Tan Dress Linens.

Dress Linens are a very important factor in the wash goods line, this year greater than ever. The even texture and excellent washing and wearing qualities make them highly desirable for wash skirts, waists, two-piece suits, traveling costumes, children's wear or men's linen dusters. We quote one quality of medium weight in three widths.

No. 36C3380 Width, 27 inches.
Price, per yard..............................14c
By the piece of about 30 yards, per yd...13¼c

No. 36C3390 Width, 31 inches.
Price, per yard..............................17c
By the piece of about 30 yards, per yard..16c

No. 36C3400 Width, 36 inches.
Price, per yard..............................19c
By the piece of about 30 yards, per yard..18c

Pure White Dress Linens.

Bleached Irish Dress Linens. Pure snow white. Nice medium weight. Even texture and a record breaker for value. Comes in two widths, both the same quality.

No. 36C3415 Width, 27 inches.
Price, per yard..............................17c
By the piece of about 30 yards, per yard..16c

No. 36C3425 Width, 35 inches.
Price, per yard..............................21c
By the piece of about 30 yards, per yard..20c

Imported Linen Luster at 13c.

No. 36C3440 Irish Linen Lusters in a range of new and up to date shadings. This fabric is one of the newest creations for ladies' wash skirts, two-piece suits, shirt waists, etc. It is made by the best Irish linen weavers and is finished with a very silky sheen. It is not an all linen fabric, there being about 25 per cent cotton in its construction. It is of good suiting weight and can be had in the following colors: Light blue, navy blue, cadet blue, tan, brown, dark gray, red or olive green. We know of nothing more stylish or appropriate for an up to date wash suit or dress. Width, 27 inches.
Price, per yard..............................13c
By the piece of about 30 yards, per yd...12½c

DEPARTMENT OF APRON AND DRESS GINGHAMS.

We do not sample apron ginghams. We recommend that you order ginghams direct from the catalogue illustrations and descriptions without waiting for samples. However, if you prefer to see samples, we will furnish good size clippings of all dress ginghams from No. 36C3490 to No. 36C3540, as stated on page 757, which will include all the styles and colorings in each number.

Check Apron Ginghams at 4½ Cents.

No. 36C3460 Apron Ginghams in small and medium sized even checks of green, blue, black or brown. This is a well made fabric and an exceptional value for the money. Width, 25 inches.
Price, per yard..............................4½c
By the piece of about 50 yards, per yard...4⅜c

Staple Apron Check Gingham at 5 Cents.

No. 36C3470 This is a very strong number of Apron Ginghams. Comes in even checks, small, medium or large size, also small broken checks. Colors are brown, black, blue, green or pink. This cloth will give exceptional wear and will wash perfectly. Width, 26 inches.
Price, per yard..............................5c
By the piece of about 50 yards, per yard..4⅞c

Heavy Apron Ginghams at 5½c.

No. 36C3480 This is our very best quality of Apron Gingham, good, firm, heavy weight fabric, with perfect colorings. Comes in large, medium and small sized even checks of blue, brown, black, green or pink. This is one of the heaviest and best apron ginghams on the market and at the price is a remarkable value. Width, 27 inches. Price, per yard........5½c
By the piece of about 45 yards, per yard..5⅜c

Fancy Dress Ginghams at 5c.

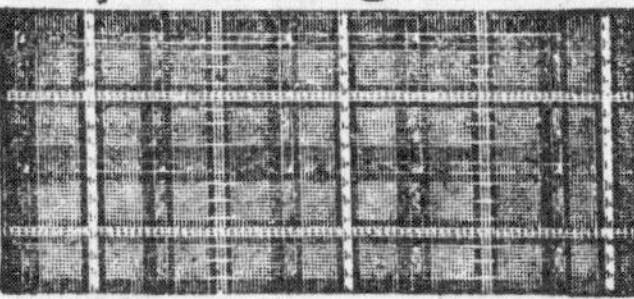

No. 36C3490 The accompanying illustration will give you a faint idea of one of the styles of this fabric, an inexpensive wash dress gingham. This is really one of the most remarkable values ever offered in dress ginghams. It is a strong, well made fabric in a large range of pretty, washable colors. Can be had in neat checks, small plaids and fancy stripes of medium size. Colors are pink, navy, brown, black, light blue and red. For an inexpensive dress gingham this number has no equal. Width, 23 inches. Price, per yard..5c
By the piece of about 45 yards, per yard..4⅞c

Fancy Dress Gingham at 7c.

No. 36C3500 This is a very fine quality Madras Effect Gingham, good weight fabric, perfect weave and texture. Colorings are well selected and washable. Can be had in checks, small plaids or medium size stripes of pink, light blue, gray, red or brown, combined with white. This is a very popular number with us and we know it will give absolute satisfaction. Width, 27 inches. Price, per yard..........7c
By the piece of about 42 yards, per yard..6⅞c

Our Linenized Gingham Suiting at 7 Cents.

No. 36C3510 This is a cotton fabric of madras or zephyr nature with various styles of stripes of woven colors on ecru or linen color grounds, and is a fabric that will wash and not fade. The cloth is finished by the new linenizing process, which renders it decidedly of the appearance of a natural Irish linen, and will be extremely popular this season. The colors are light blue on linen, dark blue on linen, white on linen, red on linen, black and blue on linen, black and red on linen or green on linen. It is appropriate for wash suits, dresses or waists and is an excellent cloth for little folks' dresses. Width, 27 inches.
Price, per yard..............................7c
By the piece of about 45 yards, per yard..6⅞c

27-inch Fancy Dress Gingham, at 8½ Cents.

No. 36C3520 This is one of the very best wearing and washing Ginghams made. It is constructed from the very best dyed yarns and woven in to a perfect, even texture, either in the plain solid zephyr weaves or in the corded effects. We have a very large range of styles and patterns, among which are small and medium sized even checks of pink and white, light blue and white or black and white. Fancy dress checks, plaids and dress and shirt waist stripes of pink and white, light blue and white, tan and white, gray and white, green and white, dark blue and white, red and white or black and white; also many other combinations. In addition to the fancy styles we also carry a range of plain chambray effects in pink, light blue, red, tan, nile green, dark blue, steel or gray. At 8¼ cents per yard we defy competition. Width, 27 inches. Price, per yard..........8½c
By the piece of about 40 yards, per yard..8⅜c

Seersucker or Nurses' Stripe Gingham at 9½ Cents.

No. 36C3540 Seersucker Ginghams are positively the most durable and best washing ginghams made. They are much used for wash dresses, shirt waists and men's shirts, and are also used very extensively in hospitals for nurses' costumes. Comes in stripes only. Colors are blue and white, or blue and white with red mixture, also in dark blue ground with narrow white stripes. These are the very best seersucker goods and at the price cannot be equaled. Width, 27 inches.
Price, per yard..............................9½c
By the piece of about 40 yards, per yard 9⅛c

Real Manchester Chambray at 8 Cents.

WE DO NOT SAMPLE CHAMBRAYS.

No. 36C3550 Chambrays are among the most desirable and durable wash fabrics made. This is a real Manchester chambray, the genuine yarn dyed goods, with perfect chambray finish. The colors are light blue, light pink, deep pink, cadet blue, dark blue mixed, steel gray, nile green, linen color, buff color or brown. For washing qualities this fabric has no equal. Width, 24 inches.
Price, per yard..............................8c
By the piece of about 45 yards, per yard, 7⅞c

32-inch Chambray, 12 Cents.

No. 36C3560 This is a wide, soft finished Chambray, of perfect, even texture. It is a most desirable fabric for all round wash goods purposes, dresses, shirt waists, men's shirts, etc. The colors are absolutely fast. Comes in pink and white, light blue and white, navy blue and white, nile green and white, linen and white or brown and white. It is hardly just to call it a mixture, because the general appearance of the fabric is almost solid color. For wearing and washing qualities it cannot be equaled. Width, 32 inches.
Price, per yard..............................12c
By the piece of about 40 yards, per yd. 11½c

Our Knickerbocker Effect Chambray at 6½ Cents.

No. 36C3570 We have nothing neater or more desirable to offer in an inexpensive wash fabric than this Knotted Yarn Chambray. The groundwork is solid color with irregular white Knickerbocker effect splashes. Colors are pink, light blue, medium blue, red, tan, brown, green or gray. It will be found an excellent fabric for little folks' wear, as well as for ladies' and misses' dresses and waists. This chambray will wear and wash beautifully. Width, 25 inches. Price, per yard........6½c
By the piece of about 50 yards, per yard 6⅜c

Fancy Chambray at 6½ Cents.

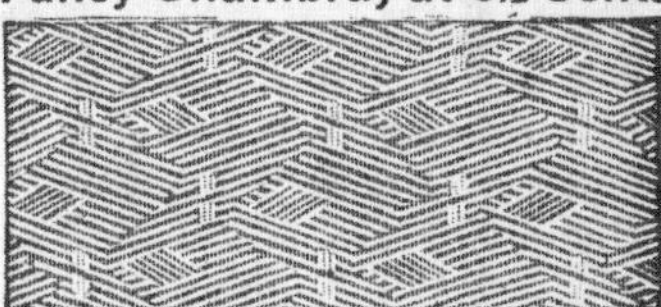

No. 36C3575 The same cloth as the preceding number, but shown in a neat figure like illustration. Comes in pink, light blue, light navy, dark gray or red. Width, 25 inches.
Price, per yard..............................6½c
By the piece of about 45 yards, per yard 6⅜c

Iris Changeable Sateen at 12c.

No. 36C3668 Beautiful Iris changeable effects in all the newest combinations. These novel sateen creations are the nearest approach possible to the popular imported changeable taffetas and can hardly be detected from them except upon critical examination. Real marvels of beauty, and at the price you cannot afford to pass them by. Comes in red and black, jasper gray, navy and black, green and black, brown and black or turquoise and black. Width, 27 inches. Price, per yard........12c
By the piece of about 40 yards, per yard. 11½c

Corded Scotch Zephyr Gingham at 12 Cents.

No. 36C3530 Corded Scotch Gingham in a beautiful line of designs like and similar to the illustration. It is of zephyr weave, with pretty madras cords at irregular intervals. This is a fabric that is highly desirable for shirt waists or wash dresses, as well as for men's shirts. It comes in medium sized stripes only. Colors are absolutely fast and washable. Comes in pink and white, light blue and white, green and white, gray and white or tan and white. This fabric is sold in the ordinary way by dealers at 15 to 18 cents per yard. Width, 30 inches. Price, per yard..........12c
By the piece of about 40 yards, per yd... 11½c

Black Printed Sateens.

No. 36C3670 Black ground, fine sateen, printed in white in neat designs. Shows up handsomely and will wear and wash well. Width, 29 inches. Price, per yard....11½c
By the piece of about 40 yards, per yard. 11c

Lyons' Gun Metal Sateen.

No. 36C3673 A very fine high grade mercerized sateen, printed in several beautiful patterns like and similar to illustration. The plain sateen itself is worth more than we ask for the printed fabric. Goods of sateen construction in neat small designs are to be more popular this season and next, than ever before. Comes in small check like illustration, in black and white with red, white or turquoise dots, navy and white check with turquoise dots, also in a variety of small neat patterns of exceptional beauty in jasper gray, light navy mixed or black and white. Width, 27 inches.
Price, per yard....12c
By the piece of about 40 yards, per yard. 11½c

DEPARTMENT OF STAPLE AND FANCY SHIRTING AND DRESS CALICOS.

WE DO NOT SAMPLE THIS LINE.

Light Effect Shirting or Dress Print at 4½ Cents.

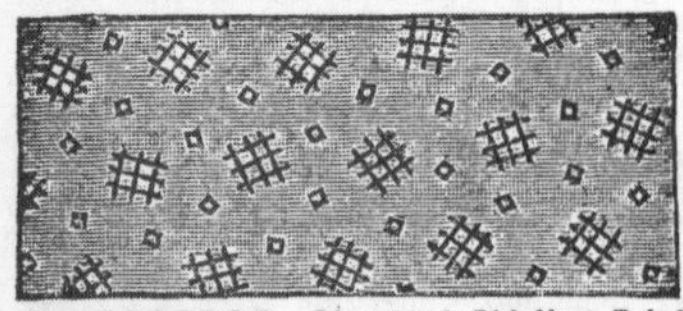

No. 36C3690 Standard Shirting Print. This is a very good quality of print. Colors are perfectly fast and washable. Comes in white ground, with stripes, small figures or polka dots. Colors are pink and white, red and white, blue and white or black and white. Special value at the price. Width, 25 inches.
Price, per yard....4½c
By the piece of about 50 yards, per yard. 4⅜c

Standard Dress Print at 4½c.

No. 36C3700 Standard Dress Print, in an endless variety of small, medium and large designs. It comes in dark and medium colors such as black, brown, dark blue, gray, purple dark green or dark red. This is a standard 64x64 cloth and at 4½ cents per yard is a big bargain. Width, 25 inches. Price, per yard....4½c
By the piece of about 50 yards, per yard..4⅜c

Red Ground Figured Dress Print at 4½ Cents.

No. 36C3710 This is an oil boiled fast color Print. The ground color is a handsome shade of cardinal. Comes with black printings of figures and stripes, also with white printings of stripes and floral designs. Patterns are all new and up to date and we can recommend this cloth very highly. Width, 25 inches.
Price, per yard....4½c
By the piece of about 50 yards, per yard..4⅜c

Garibaldi Print, Black Ground with Red Designs, 5½c.

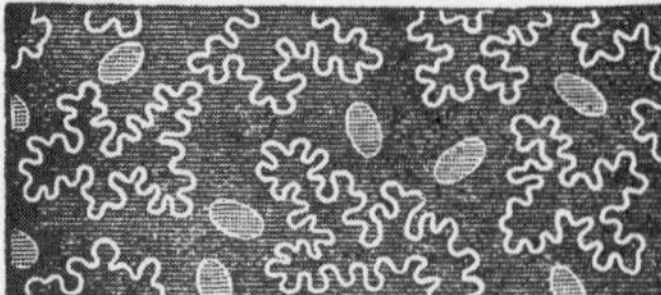

No. 36C3720 Garibaldi Print. This is a very handsome and popular black ground print. The printings are all of cardinal in various neat, small or medium sized figures, small stripes, also polka dots. This is a thoroughly fast color print and one that we know will please you. Width, 25 inches. Per yard..5½c
By the piece of about 50 yards, per yard..5¼c

Cadet Blue Print with White Printings at 5 Cents.

No. 36C3730 Cadet Blue Prints are always desirable. Colors are absolutely fast and will make up into neater and prettier effects than almost any other style of print. The ground in all is cadet blue, with printings in white of neat stripes, small and medium sized figures, dots and floral designs. A fabric that we can recommend very highly. Width, 25 inches. Price, per yard....5c
By the piece of about 50 yards, per yard..4⅞c

Black and White Mourning Print at 5 Cents.

No. 36C3740 Standard Mourning Print, one of the best selling prints on the market. Colors are absolutely fast and the fabric is very well made, of close, even texture. One style is ground color of black with white floral designs, either small, medium or large size, also neat stripes and hairline effects. Another style is gray ground with distinct black and white colorings. This is a standard 64x64 cloth and we guarantee it to give the user absolute satisfaction. Width, 25 inches.
Price, per yard....5c
By the piece of about 50 yards, per yard..4⅞c

Heavy Dark Dress Prints at 5½ Cents.

No. 36C3750 Dark Dress Prints. These are extra heavy weight and good quality and come in a large range of small, medium and large sized designs, also neat stripes. Ground colors are black, brown, blue, gray, purple or green. Nothing better made in dress print than this number. Width, 25 inches.
Price, per yard....5½c
By the piece of about 50 yards, per yard..5¼c

Indigo Blue Print at 5 Cents.

No. 36C3760 Indigo Blue Print. This is a standard cloth, thoroughly fast color, good weight and quality; firm texture. Comes in a big variety of neat stripes, figures and polka dots. A cloth that will wash well and give the best of service. Width, 25 inches.
Price, per yard....5c
By the piece of about 50 yards, per yard..4⅞c

Heavy German Indigo Blue Dress Print at 8½ Cents.

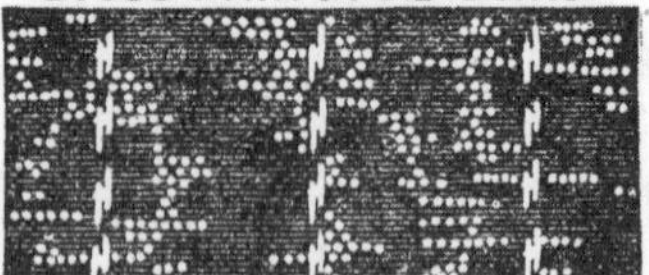

No. 36C3770 This is a genuine Indigo Blue German Print Cloth. Color is guaranteed fast, and for service this cloth cannot be equaled. It comes in a great variety of small and medium sized figures, stripes and polka dots. This cloth usually sells in the ordinary retail stores at 10 to 12½ cents per yard. Width, 29 inches. Price, per yard....8½c
By the piece of about 50 yards, per yard..8¼c

Extra Heavy German Indigo Blue Print at 9½ Cents.

No. 36C3780 This is the very heaviest and best made German Indigo Blue Print, guaranteed fast color, and for durability and washing qualities it has no equal. Comes in a large variety of styles, including small, medium and large sized figures, also neat stripes and polka dots. Width, 31 inches.
Price, per yard....9½c
By the piece of about 50 yards, per yard...9c

Plain Turkey Red Print at 5c.

No. 36C3790 This Plain Turkey Red Print is absolutely fast color. It is a fine, perfect weave and good weight cloth, one that usually sells at about 7 cents per yard. Comes in perfect turkey red coloring. Width, 25 inches. Price, per yard....5c
By the piece of about 50 yards, per yard..4⅞c

Oil Boiled Turkey Red Print at 8 Cents.

No. 36C3800 Oil Boiled Turkey Red Print. This is the finest grade of this popular cloth. It is a fabric of close, even texture and good weight. Color is a very pretty shade of bright cardinal. At 8 cents p r yard this represents excellent value. Width inches.
Price, per yard....8c
By the piece of about 50 yards, per yard..7½c

Solid Colored Prints at 5½c.

No. 36C3810 Solid Colored Prints. Standard quality and very best colorings. Come in turkey red, green, navy blue, orange, new blue or black. Width, 25 inches.
Price, per yard....5½c
By the piece of about 50 yards, per yard..5¼c

Fancy Robe Print at 4½ Cents.

No. 36C3820 Fancy Robe Print, much used for comforters, etc., comes in a very extensive range of patterns, scrolls, oriental and floral designs, and a big assortment of colors. This is a firm, well made print, and an exceptional value for the money. Width, 24 inches.
Price, per yard....4½c
By the piece of about 50 yards, per yard..4⅜c

Heavy Robe Print at 5 Cents.

No. 36C3830 This is one of the heaviest and best Robe Prints made. Comes in a very handsome line of fancy scroll, oriental and floral designs. The colors are brown, black, blue, green or purple, with medium large sized contrasting figures. Width, 24 inches.
Price, per yard....5c
By the piece, of about 50 yards, per yard. 4⅞c

Oil Boiled Robe Print at 5½c

No. 36C3840 Oil Boiled Robe Print. Thoroughly fast colors. Comes in red grounds, with combinations of black and white in scrolls and oriental medium large sized designs. This will prove a very serviceable comforter print, and one that we can very highly recommend. Width, 24 inches. Price, per yard, 5½c
By the piece of about 50 yards, per yard, 5¼c

Silkoline Comforter Coverings.

No. 36C3845 Yard Wide Printed Silkolines in handsome colorings and patterns. Come in green, red, yellow, rose, blue or tan grounds, with appropriate combinations of handsomely tinted floral work. Width, 36 inches.
Price, per yard....9c
By the piece of about 50 yards, per yard..8½c

OUTING FLANNELS.

WE DO NOT SAMPLE OUTING FLANNELS.

Fleeced Outing Flannel at 5½ Cents.

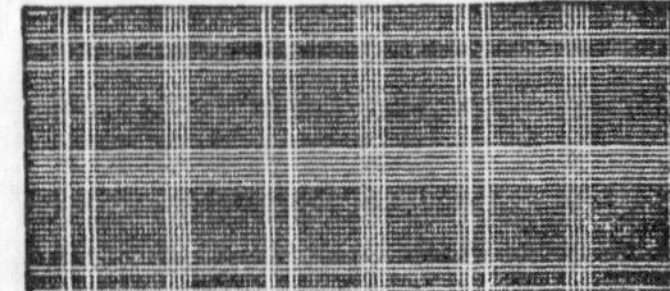

No. 36C3850 Fleeced Outing Flannel, fair quality and weight and very good finish, in a pretty range of colorings, either light or dark effects, in checks, plaids and stripes. This is the best outing flannel we ever offered at the price. Width, 25 inches. Price, per yard, 5½c
By the piece of about 50 yards, per yard, 5¼c

Fine Outing Flannel at 7 Cents.

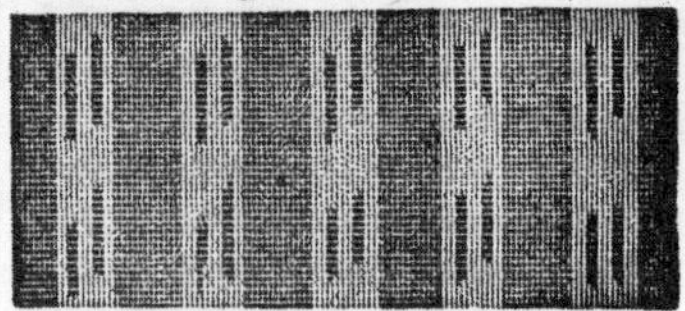

No. 36C3860 Outing or Tennis Flannel. This is a very good weight, closely woven fabric. It has a very good nap. Comes in handsome designs and colorings, either light or dark effects, in stripes, checks or plaids. This cloth will give exceptional service. Width, 27 inches.
Price, per yard....7c
By the piece of about 50 yards, per yard, 6¾c

Heavy Tennis Flannel at 9c.

No. 36C3870 Heavy Fleeced Tennis Flannel. This is one of the best numbers of tennis flannel to be had. Is a very good weight fabric, has a deep, soft nap, is woven firm and strong, and will give the best of service. Comes in a very choice line of colorings, either light or dark, checks, stripes or plaids. Colors are blue and white, pink and white, tan and white, cardinal and white, black and white, light effects, also dark effects in brown, navy blue, dark red or dark gray. It is a very desirable material for house wrappers, kimonas, waists, night dresses, etc. Colors are absolutely fast. Width, 28 inches. Price, per yard..9c
By the piece of about 50 yards, per yard, 8¾c

Heavy Outing Flannel at 9c.

No. 36C3880 Extra Quality Outing Flannel. This is one of the heaviest and best numbers made; in fact, it is a number manufactured especially for us. It is of exceptionally fine, firm texture and comes in a very pretty line of wash colorings in either light or dark effects. Colors are light blue and white, pink and white, tan and white, red and white, black and white, also dark effects of navy blue, brown, gray or dark red fancies. Width, 29 inches.
Price, per yard....9c
By the piece of about 50 yards, per yard, 8¾c

Daisy Cloth or Baby Flannel at 9 Cents.

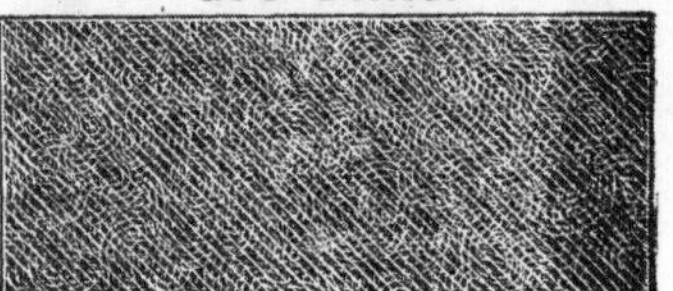

No. 36C3890 Baby Flannel, medium heavy weight, of beautiful soft texture. Has a well defined flannel twill, with pretty, soft nap on both sides. It bears a very close resemblance to an all wool French flannel and is one of our most popular selling numbers. Comes in solid colors only, cardinal, royal blue, pink, light blue, pure white or cream color. It is much used for babies' wear, as well as for ladies' dressing sacques, kimonas, tea gowns, night dresses, etc. At 9 cents per yard this is really an exceptional value. Width, 28 inches.
Price, per yard....9c
By the piece of about 50 yards, per yard, 8¾c

Guinea Hen or Mottled Fleeced Flannel at 6½ Cents.

No. 36C3900 Guinea Hen Flannel, heavier than outing flannel and has a deeper, softer nap. This is a special bargain at our price. Comes in mottled gray, brown, blue or pink mixtures. Width, 27 inches.
Price, per yard....6½c
By the piece of about 45 yards, per yard, 6¼c

Good Quality Mottled Fleeced Flannel at 8 Cents.

No. 36C3910 Mottled Fleeced Flannel, very good weight and extra heavy, deep, soft fleece on both sides. This flannel sells at 10 cents and upward in the ordinary retail stores. Comes in mottled gray, brown, blue or pink mixtures. Width, 27 inches.
Price, per yard....8c
By the piece of about 45 yards, per yard, 7½c

Extra Heavy Mottled Fleeced Flannel at 9½ Cents.

No. 36C3920 Guinea Hen or Mottled Fleeced Flannel. This is extra heavy and very fine quality of this popular cloth. Has a deep, heavy, soft fleeced nap on both sides. Comes in gray, blue, brown or pink mixtures. This cloth will give the user the very best of satisfaction. Width, 28 inches.
Price, per yard....9½c
By the piece of about 45 yards, per yard, 9c

DRESS FLANNELETTES.

WE DO NOT SAMPLE FLANNELETTES.

Fine Dress Flannelettes at 8c.

No. 36C3930 Fine Fleeced Back Flannelettes. This is one of our leading numbers for ladies', misses' and children's dresses, wrappers, kimonas, etc. It is a well made fabric with a fine serge face and fleeced back. Comes in dark and medium grounds with oriental and floral designs, small figures, polka dots, etc. Some of the colors are red and black, black and white, blue and white, tan and white, wine and white, gray and white, etc. The colors are fast and washable and the fabric will be found very durable. Width, 28 inches. Price, per yard..8c
By the piece of about 45 yards, per yard, 7¾c

Fancy Dress Flannelette 8½c

No. 36C3940 For this number we have secured a most complete and handsome selection of designs and colorings. The cloth is close and firm, with well napped back, making a very desirable material for wrappers, kimonas, waists, underskirts or children's dresses. Ground colorings are navy, garnet, tan, pink or light blue, also in black or gray with white small designs, and in navy or black grounds with white polka dots, either small or medium sized. Width, 28 inches. Price, per yard..8½c
By the piece of about 45 yards, per yard, 8c

Fine Flannelette at 11 Cents.

No. 36C3945 A higher grade and wider dress Flannelette, and one that will prove itself a winner. The cloth is a very fine twill, of nice, medium weight. The oriental design is a beauty. This fabric will make up into stylish waists or dresses, and is especially desirable for children's wear. Comes in ground colors of light blue, pink, tan, cardinal, navy or black. Width, 34 inches. Price, per yard..........11c
By the piece of about 45 yards, per yard, 10½c

Heavy Flannelette at 11 Cents.

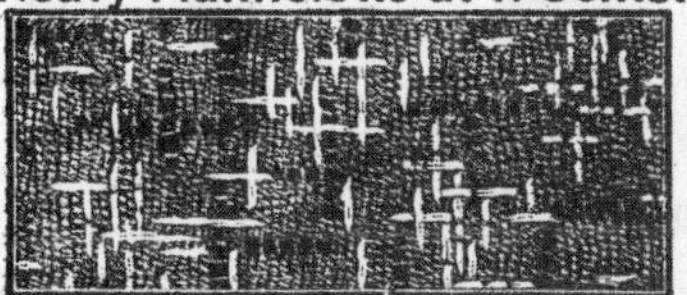

No. 36C3955 This number has a heavier fleeced back than the preceding one, and is not quite so wide, and is mostly used for wrappers and dressing sacques or underskirts. The colors are all dark and very appropriate for these purposes. The ground is a dainty, mottled effect, on which is printed in white the splash pattern as illustrated. Comes in tan, brown, garnet, navy or black. Width, 27 inches. Price, per yard..........11c
By the piece of about 45 yards, per yard, 10½c

SHAKER FLANNELS.

WE DO NOT SAMPLE SHAKER FLANNELS.

White Shaker Flannel at 5c.

No. 36C4000 White Shaker Flannel, fair weight and quality and exceptionally good value at our special price. Width, 24 inches.
Price, per yard..........5c
By the piece of about 50 yards, per yard, 4¾c

Plain White Shaker Flannel at 6¼ Cents.

No. 36C4010 White Shaker Flannel, very good weight and good fleece, one of the best Shaker flannels we ever sold for the money. Width, 27 inches. Price, per yard..........6¼c
By the piece of about 50 yards, per yard, 6c

Extra Value White Shaker Flannel at 8 Cents.

No. 36C4020 Plain White Shaker Flannel, very good quality with heavy nap. A big bargain at the price. Width, 28 inches. Per yd..8c
By the piece of about 50 yards, per yard, 7¾c

Plain White Shaker Flannel at 10 Cents.

No. 36C4030 Plain White Shaker Flannel, extra wide and good quality. Perfect nap. Width, 30 inches. Price, per yard..........10c
By the piece of about 50 yards, per yard, 9¾c

Pure White Bleached Shaker Flannel.

No. 36C4035 Pure White Shaker Flannel, thoroughly bleached and of good weight and serviceable construction. It is woven very close and is an excellent value. Width, 25 inches. Price, per yard..........10c
By the piece of about 50 yards, per yard, 9¾c

Yard Wide White Shaker Flannel at 12 Cents.

No. 36C4040 Extra Wide White Shaker Flannel. Exceptional quality heavy weight and nap. Width, 36 inches. Price, per yard..13c
By the piece of about 50 yards, per yd., 12¾c

UNBLEACHED CANTON FLANNELS.

We do not carry inferior qualities, but each and every number quoted below will be found good, clean merchandise, and from a standpoint of value, they are unapproachable.
WE DO NOT SAMPLE CANTON FLANNELS.

No. 36C4060 Unbleached Canton Flannel, fair weight, very serviceable. Width, 24 inches. Price, per yard..........5¼c
By the piece of about 40 yards, per yard, 5 c

No. 36C4070 Unbleached Canton Flannel, good weight and quality. Width, 27 inches.
Price, per yard..........7½c
By the piece of about 40 yards, per yard, 7¼c

No. 36C4090 Unbleached Canton Flannel. This is an especially good value and is a very good weight; has a long heavy nap. Width, 28 inches. Price, per yard..........9½c
By the piece of about 40 yards, per yard, 9¼c

No. 36C4100 Unbleached Canton Flannel, heavy weight, deep, long nap. The cloth will give exceptional service. Width, 30 inches.
Price, per yard..........11½c
By the piece of about 40 yards, per yard, 11c

No. 36C4120 Unbleached Canton Flannel, very heavy weight, twilled back, long, deep, heavy nap; one of the very best qualities made. Is used extensively for husking mitts, as well as for all other purposes. Width, 32 inches. Price, per yard..........15c
By the piece of about 40 yards, per yard, 14c

BLEACHED CANTON FLANNELS.

No. 36C4140 Bleached Canton Flannel. This is a good, medium weight flannel, with perfect nap. Width, 24 inches.
Price, per yard..........7 c
By the piece of about 40 yards, per yard, 6¾c

No. 36C4150 Bleached Canton Flannel. This is a very popular number and one that will give the best of satisfaction. Width, 25 inches.
Price, per yard..........8½c
By the piece of about 40 yards, per yard, 8¼c

No. 36C4160 Bleached Canton Flannel. Very good weight, long, perfect nap, exceptional quality. Width, 26 inches.
Price, per yard..........10 c
By the piece of about 40 yards, per yard, 9½c

No. 36C4170 Bleached Canton Flannel. This is extraordinary quality, heavy, perfect goods. Has a deep, heavy nap. Width, 29 inches.
Price, per yard..........12½c
By the piece of about 40 yards, per yard, 12 c

Colored Canton Flannels, 11½c

No. 36C4190 This is a very good quality of twilled back, heavy fleeced Canton Flannel. It is a fabric much used for drapings, linings, skirtings, dresses, etc. Colorings are very good and well selected, as follows: pink, orange, myrtle green, medium blue, gray, brown, olive, cardinal, wine or navy blue. Width, 28 inches.
Price, per yard..........11½c
By the piece of about 40 yards, per yard, 11c

EIDERDOWNS.

These beautiful, soft, deep fleeced fabrics are always much in demand and are highly desirable for ladies' house sacques, kimonas, tea gowns, bath robes, etc., as well as for children's cloaks. The numbers quoted below are the very best of their class to be had. We will guarantee to please you, and at the same time save you money on the selection of any one of the following qualities.

Plain Colored Eiderdown, 19c

No. 36C4360 Colored Eiderdown, a very good quality and good width. Colors are solid, and very good shades. Can be had in light blue, pink, cardinal, gray or cream white. An excellent value for the money. Width, 26 inches. Price, per yard..........19c

Deep Fleeced Eiderdowns at 25c and 39c.

This is a heavy, Soft Fleece Eiderdown, and comes in a good selection of colors and in two widths, both the same quality. Colorings are pink, light blue, cardinal, tan, gray or white.

No. 36C4370 Width, 27 inches. Price, per yard..........25c

No. 36C4380 Width, 36 inches, Price, per yard..........39c

PLAIN WHITE WOOL FLANNELS

WE DO NOT SAMPLE WHITE FLANNELS.

Half Wool White Shaker Flannel at 25 Cents.

No. 36C4445 Half Wool White Shaker Flannel, extra heavy weight and good, deep fleece. This cloth will give the very best of service. Strictly half wool. Width, 29 inches.
Price, per yard..........25c

White Half Wool Flannel, 14c

No. 36C4450 Plain White Half Wool Flannel, one of the most attractive values in the department. Medium weight and close texture. Width, 25 inches. Price, per yard....14c

Plain White Wool Flannels at 20 Cents.

No. 36C4460 Plain white, half wool, medium weight and firm texture. This flannel will give exceptional service. Width, 27 inches.
Price, per yard..........20c

Plain White Wool Flannels at 25 Cents.

No. 36C4470 Plain White Wool Flannel. This grade is generally called an all wool flannel, but it is in reality about 25 per cent cotton. It is a close, pretty, even weave and a fabric that will wear and wash perfectly. Width, 27 inches. Price, per yard..........25c

White All Wool Flannel at 35c.

No. 36C4480 All Wool White Flannel, very good quality and weight, one of the best values we ever offered for the money. Width, 30 inches. Price, per yard..........35c

Extra Quality White All Wool Flannel at 42 Cents.

No. 36C4490 This is an extra quality of All Wool White Flannel, good weight and perfect, even texture. A flannel that will give absolute satisfaction. Width, 31 inches.
Price, per yard..........42c

Best Quality Plain White All Wool Flannel at 50 Cents.

No. 36C4500 Plain White All Wool Flannel, a very superior quality. Perfect in weave, weight and texture. Unexcelled for wear. Width, 35 inches. Price, per yard..........50c

White Silk Warp Flannel at 80 Cents.

No. 36C4510 White Silk Warp Flannel. The filling of this flannel is pure, long fibre wool, with an all silk warp. It is a good medium weight and perfect, close, even texture. Is non-shrinkable. This flannel is generally sold by retail dealers for $1.00 per yard. Width, 31 inches. Price, per yard..........80c

EMBROIDERED FLANNELS.

WE DO NOT SAMPLE FLANNELS.

This is a very important division in our Dry Goods Department and one that we have been constantly improving, until we have reached perfection, both in the quality of the work and the artistic range of patterns. We use only the medium and best grades of cream all wool flannel, 33 inches in width, including hem. Each number, is beautifully hemmed. The embroidery is the very best procurable, each scalloped number being finished with buttonhole stitched edges, which renders it exceptionally durable. The patterns are new and exclusive, being embroidered especially for us from our own submitted designs, and ranging in width from 1 to 6 inches. Each and every number will wash beautifully. We wish to say regarding prices, that we are positively lower than the lowest. This is made possible only by the fact that these goods are embroidered for us in thousand piece lots and we thereby make a big saving in the cost price and we never fail to give our customers the benefit of any well made purchase. We will guarantee to please you and at the same time save you money on any number quoted below. We do not sample embroidered flannels. The patterns are all exactly as represented in the illustrations.

Silk Embroidered Flannel at 49 Cents.

No. 36C4520 Silk Embroidered Flannel. Very good quality of pretty cream all wool flannel, with handsome openwork hemstitched and floral silk embroidered design, exactly like the illustration. The design is new this season and is most beautifully finished. Width of flannel, 33 inches, with silk embroidery 1¼ inches wide. Price, per yard..........49c

Silk Embroidered Flannel at 49 Cents.

No. 36C4530 Scalloped Edge Silk Embroidered Flannel, in a very new and handsome design, exactly like the illustration. The flannel is very good weight and splendid quality in a pretty shade of cream. The embroidery is beautifully executed, the scallops being buttonhole stitched, thereby rendered doubly durable. The illustration will give you an idea of the beauty of this pattern. Width of flannel, 33 inches, with embroidery 1⅛ inches wide.
Price, per yard..........49c

Hemstitched Embroidered Flannel at 49 Cents.

No. 36C4540 Hemstitched Silk Embroidered Flannel, in one of the newest and handsomest openwork hemstitched and fancy ring designs, exactly like the illustration, with the very best quality of workmanship, that will wash perfectly. The flannel is of exceptionally good quality, good weight, in a perfect shade of cream. This is an especially attractive number for infants' wear and is a quality of which we sell thousands of pieces. Retailers generally pay as much or more for this pattern than we ask. Width of flannel, 33 inches, with embroidery 1 inch wide. Price, per yard..........49c

Scalloped Edge Embroidered Flannel at 59 Cents.

No. 36C4550 The accompanying illustration will show you the beauty of this new scalloped edge design, which is especially adapted for infants' wear and also for ladies' fine under garments. We have exercised unusual care in the selection of designs, and we think that this number is one of the handsomest shown. The flannel is a very good quality, perfect, even texture goods, in a medium shade of cream. The embroidery is the very best, with buttonhole stitched finished scallops. The illustration does not do justice to the heavy, wide embroidery. Width of flannel, 33 inches, with embroidery 1¼ inches wide.
Price, per yard..........59c

Scalloped Edge Silk Embroidered Flannel at 65 Cents.

No. 36C4560 This is a remarkably handsome design of embroidery, worked upon a very fine, all wool cream baby flannel. Too much cannot be said about the beauty of this embroidery. It is very new in pattern and of the very best workmanship. The edge is buttonhole stitched and durable. The illustration hardly does justice to the pattern, as it really appears a great deal heavier and wider. Width of the flannel, 33 inches, with embroidery 2¾ inches wide. Price, per yard..........65c

Extra Heavy Silk Embroidered Flannel at 95 Cents.

No. 36C4590 This is one of the handsomest and best executed Silk Embroidered Flannels we have ever been able to offer for the money. The embroidery is exceedingly heavy and the pattern strikingly new and very durable. The edge is wide embroidered and finished with a buttonhole stitch. The flannel is one of the very best qualities, of very good weight, strictly all wool and a pretty shade of cream. The accompanying illustration will give you a faint idea of the effect of the embroidery as it appears in the goods, but we wish to add that it does not do justice to the work, which, seen in the piece, is vastly handsomer. At 95 cents per yard this embroidered flannel is a big bargain. Width of flannel, 33 inches, with embroidery 3½ inches wide.
Price, per yard..........95c

Heavy Embroidered Flannel at $1.20.

No. 36C4610 The accompanying illustration is a correct picture of the widest and heaviest Embroidered Flannel we carry. This embroidery is 6 inches in width, of a very handsome and showy design of very well executed embroidery upon our very best quality of cream all wool flannel of exceptional weight and perfect, even texture. This embroidered flannel we will guarantee to give the best satisfaction for washing qualities and durability. Width of flannel, 33 inches, with embroidery 6 inches wide. Price, per yard..........$1.20

CARPET DEPARTMENT

WITH LOWER PRICES THAN EVER BEFORE, GREATLY REDUCED FROM PREVIOUS SEASONS; with an entirely new line of up to date and attractive patterns; with a larger and more carefully selected line than ever before; with improvements, advantages and inducements greater than we have ever been able to offer, we direct your attention to this new, enlarged and greatly improved Carpet Department.

FOR THE SEASON OF 1905 we have been able to eclipse all previous records in the way of value giving in this department, and whether you want 5 yards or 100 yards of carpet, whether you want the cheapest rag carpet or the very finest Axminster goods, we feel that we have a right to ask for your order, because we can certainly give you such carpet value for your money as you could not possibly receive elsewhere.

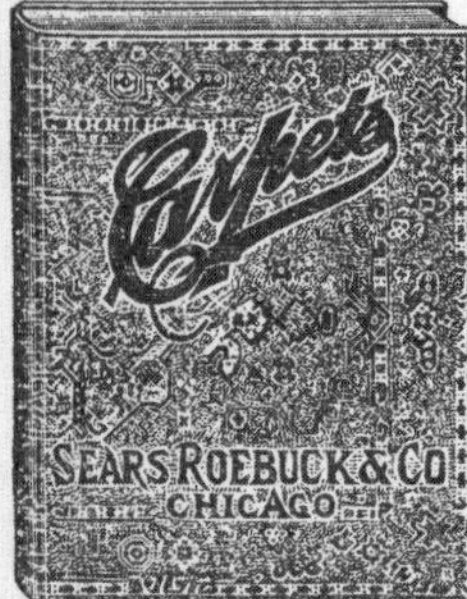

OUR FREE CARPET CATALOGUE. In the following pages of this, our General Merchandise Catalogue, by the small black and white illustrations, we are able to give you a very good general idea of our line of carpets, rugs and draperies, to enable you to order almost anything in the line intelligently, always, of course, with the understanding that if the goods are not perfectly satisfactory you can return them to us at our expense and we will immediately refund your money. While we always advise our customers to make up their orders direct from this, our general catalogue, if, however, you would like first to receive our Special Carpet Catalogue, showing our entire line of carpets, rugs, draperies, etc., in their actual natural colors, this catalogue will be sent to you by mail, postpaid, free on application.

OUR FREE SPECIAL CARPET CATALOGUE is the largest, handsomest and most complete carpet and drapery catalogue published. It shows all the Axminster, Moquette, Velvet and Brussels carpets, with borders to match; it shows also our complete line of Ingrain, Granite, Hemp and Rag Carpets in the exact colorings; beautiful small color plates of our entire line of carpets, art squares, rugs, mattings, linoleums, oilcloths and floor coverings of all kinds, curtains, draperies, etc. In this free Carpet Catalogue by large illustrations, reproduced by the new three-color photographic process, we show everything we handle in carpets, the most complete art color catalogue published.

THIS CARPET CATALOGUE will be sent to any address by mail, postpaid, on application, and yet we would advise you not to delay to first write for this free Carpet Catalogue, since you can order direct from the following pages of this, our big catalogue, under our guarantee that the carpet will please you, and if not found perfectly satisfactory, you can return it to us at our expense and we will immediately refund your money. If you are unable to make a selection from the pages in this catalogue don't buy a carpet, rug, matting, curtains or anything in carpets, rugs or draperies until you receive our Free Carpet Catalogue, for we can certainly save you a great deal of money on anything and everything in this line.

OUR QUALITY GUARANTEE, 30 DAYS' FREE TRIAL AND MONEY REFUND OFFER. Every article shown in this department is guaranteed as to quality and guaranteed to please. If you send us an order for any goods in this department your order will be accepted and the goods will be sent to you with the understanding and agreement that they must reach you in perfect condition, that they must prove entirely satisfactory to you, that you are to have the privilege of taking the goods to your own home, and if for any reason you become dissatisfied with your purchase at any time within thirty days, or if at any time within thirty days you feel that you have not made a big saving in cost by sending your order to us, you are at liberty to return the goods to us at our expense and we will immediately refund your money.

OUR CARPETS ARE ALL ENTIRELY NEW FOR THIS SEASON, all new numbers, all the very latest pattern and color effects. We are showing no old "carry-over" styles. We are offering only such carpets as you will find in the most fashionable city retail carpet stores and there at fancy prices; we are offering a line of carpets which for style, pattern and color effect will not be found in the ordinary retail store, and we are offering these carpets at very much lower prices than the old style carpets are being sold for generally.

OUR LIBERAL C. O. D. TERMS. While nearly all of our customers send cash in full with their orders, and we advise doing this, since it saves you an extra express charge of from 25 to 50 cents which the express companies always make for collecting the money and returning it to us, nevertheless, to those who wish to see and examine the carpet before paying for it, we will, on receipt of $1.00, send any carpet, rug or anything in the carpet department to any address east of the Rocky Mountains by freight or express C. O. D., subject to examination. You can examine the goods at your nearest railroad station, and if found perfectly satisfactory you can then pay the freight agent our price and freight or express charges, less the $1.00 sent with order, all this, of course, with the understanding that you are to have the privilege of returning the goods at any time within thirty days if for any reason you decide they are not what you want, we to immediately refund your money, together with any freight or express charges paid by you.

CARPETS THAT ARE MADE UP, that is, carpets that are matched and sewed will not be sent C. O. D. For all made carpets, cash in full must accompany your order; but understand, even then, if the carpet is not satisfactory when received, for any reason whatever, you are at liberty to return it to us at our expense at any time within thirty days and we will immediately refund your money, together with any freight or express charges paid by you.

BEAR IN MIND, we advise against shipping C. O. D. It is more economical and will be found more satisfactory to send cash in full, always, of course, with the understanding that we immediately refund your money if you are not perfectly satisfied.

HOW WE CAN FURNISH BIG SETS OF CARPET SAMPLES FREE.

TO SHOW SAMPLES OF OUR ENTIRE LINE OF CARPETS WE HAVE GOTTEN OUT THREE BIG SETS OF CARPET SAMPLES AS FOLLOWS:

SET NO. 1. This set comprises a good liberal sized sample of our entire line of Ingrain and Granite Carpets, a complete assortment of all the different grades and styles of Ingrain and Granite carpets we handle, from the cheapest to the very best.

SET NO. 2. This set comprises a good liberal sample of our entire line of Tapestry Brussels Carpets, a good sized sample of every style, color and grade of Tapestry Brussels we handle, everything from the cheapest to the best.

SET NO. 3. This set comprises a good liberal sized sample of our entire line of Axminster, Moquette and Wilton Velvet Carpets, all the different patterns and colorings, all the different styles, all the different fashions, from the highest to the lowest, in our complete line of Axminster, Moquette and Wilton Velvet carpets.

HOW TO GET ANY ONE OF THESE SETS FREE. State whether you want Set No. 1, Ingrain and Granite Carpets; Set No. 2, Tapestry Brussels Carpet, or Set No. 3, Axminster, Moquette and Wilton Velvet Carpets, enclose $1.00 with your application, state sample set wanted, and the samples will go to you by return express, they will go to you with the understanding and agreement that as soon as the samples are returned to us at our expense we will refund the $1.00 sent us; or, should you send us an order as taken from any one of the samples, you can return the samples and deduct the $1.00 from the amount of your order.

UNDERSTAND, we want to furnish these samples free, your choice of set Nos. 1, 2 or 3. We want you to get either set of these samples without cost to you, but as a necessary protection to ourselves, since these sets cost us considerably more than $1.00 each, we think it only fair to request that in asking for set Nos. 1, 2 or 3 that you send $1.00 with your request, since we give you the privilege of returning the samples to us at our expense, we agreeing to immediately refund your $1.00 as soon as the samples are received by us.

FROM THIS ILLUSTRATION we endeavor to merely give you an idea of the big line of samples we furnish in our complete sets. These samples are 9x18 inches, large enough to enable you to select intelligently and know just what you are going to get as to quality and pattern.

UNDERSTAND, we are not anxious to sell you a set of samples. They cost us more than $1.00 and we really make no charge for them at all. We send you your choice of set, Nos. 1, 2 or 3, with the understanding that as soon as the set is returned to us we will refund the $1.00 you sent us.

IT IS NOT NECESSARY to delay to first write for samples of carpet, since you can order from the illustrations and descriptions shown in this book, or you can write for our Free Carpet Catalogue and we will send it to you by return mail, postpaid. Whether you order from the following pages or from our Special Free Carpet Catalogue, any orders sent us for goods from this department—carpets, rugs, linoleums, coverings of any kind, or draperies—the goods will go to you with the understanding and agreement that they must reach you in perfect condition, they must prove entirely satisfactory to you, you must see that you have made a big saving in cost, and with the further understanding that you are at liberty to return the goods to us at any time within thirty days at our expense, we agreeing to immediately refund your money, together with any freight or express charges paid by you.

OUR VERY LOW PRICES FOR CUTTING, MATCHING AND SEWING CARPETS.

2 CENTS PER YARD FOR INGRAIN CARPET. At 2 cents per yard extra we will match and sew any 36-inch Ingrain, Rag or Granite Carpet to fit any room.

3 CENTS PER YARD FOR TAPESTRY, VELVET, MOQUETTE AND AXMINSTER CARPET. For 3 cents per yard, we will cut, match and sew any of our 27-inch carpets to fit any room.

10 CENTS PER YARD FOR BORDER CARPETS. At 10 cents per yard we will cut, match and sew any Tapestry, Velvet, Axminster or Moquette Carpet, where there is a border to match. For example, in making a rug from a Tapestry, Velvet, Moquette or Axminster carpet in which there is a border on four sides, or in making a border carpet to fit any size room, we make a charge of 10 cents per yard for matching, making and sewing.

OUR SPECIAL PRICES of 2, 3 and 10 cents per yard for matching, and sewing, according to the kind of carpet, are very much lower than the same work is being done by any other house, but the demand for made-up carpets has grown to where we are now doing this work by automatic machinery on so large a scale that we have been able to reduce the cost of matching, making and sewing, and we feel like giving our customers the benefit of this saving.

WASTAGE IN MATCHING CARPETS. Where you order a carpet cut, matched, sewed and made, you must make a little allowance for wastage in matching the patterns exactly. We require that you allow 1¼ yards wastage in matching for each 25 yards. For example, if you wish a carpet made for a room that measures 25 yards, you should pay for 26¼ yards, or if you wish a carpet made for a room measuring 12 yards, you should pay for 12¾ yards. We will cut with just as little waste as possible, and if we can make it up, wasting less than the amount you allow for—namely, 1¼ yards to every twenty-five, we will give you the benefit of the saving and return the difference to you in cash. **There will be less waste and better matching where we make the carpet for you,** even though you buy it and match and make it yourself, for the reason that where we are cutting up hundreds of rolls, we can always make a saving of waste by cutting and matching from several rolls, where we make the carpet for you we give you the benefit of this saving. Where there is any waste in matching we send you the waste pieces with the carpet, so that you can verify the wastage, and possibly make use of the small pieces for mats, coverings, etc.

HOW WE CUT, MATCH AND SEW CARPETS.

We have a large organization for doing this work, which alone makes possible our special 2, 3 and 10 cent per yard price. Only expert carpet sewers are employed in this department. We have several large special electric carpet sewing machines, where the carpets come edge to edge, insuring a perfect match, and preventing their having ridges which injures the appearance and wears out at the seam. **At our special prices of 2, 3 and 10 cents** per yard and with our facilities for making up and matching with the very minimum of wastage, **you** will find it cheaper to let us make the carpet for you than to buy it in the piece. **In ordering carpet cut,** matched and made for a square room it **is only** necessary to give the length and width of the room, but if the room is irregular in shape, such as a bay window, alcove, fireplace or like irregular lines, **you should** make a drawing on a piece of paper showing the dimensions, being sure to give exact measurements.

IN ORDERING CARPET MATCHED AND SEWED

BE CAREFUL TO GIVE THE EXACT SIZE OF ROOM OR ROOMS. If an odd size, having a fireplace, bay window or offset, be sure to send a diagram with exact measurements, also to allow one and one-half yards in every 25 yards for wastage in matching.

AMOUNT OF CARPET

A FEW INSTRUCTIONS THAT WILL MAKE IT EASIER TO ORDER CARPETS AND AVOID DELAYS

WE HEREWITH GIVE A LIST OF DIFFERENT SIZED ROOMS and have figured the number of yards of 36-inch ingrain carpet, 27-inch Brussels, velvet or Axminster carpets, made plain without border, also Brussels, velvet or Axminster carpets, made with border, that would be required. If the size of your room is not given in this list and you wish to order carpet at once we would advise you to allow enough money to pay for the next larger size and we will cut the carpet with the least possible waste and will only charge you with the exact amount of carpet used in the cutting. In figuring the amount of carpet used in fitting these rooms we have included the waste that would ordinarily be used, but if we can cut the carpet with less waste when your order is received we will do so and will refund whatever balance you have at the time the shipment is made. Perhaps you will wonder why there should be waste used in matching a carpet, and we wish to advise that the patterns of different style carpets do not match at exactly the same distance, some patterns being 30 inches apart, some 32, 34 and 36 inches. Take for instance a room size 14x15 feet, and you will readily see that it requires 5 widths of 36-inch ingrain carpet, each width being 14 feet long. This would be the actual amount of carpet used to cover the room. We find when we go to cut this carpet that the patterns will not match at 14 feet exact, but we find that this pattern cuts at 14 feet 9 inches, and you will readily see that each strip will have to be cut 14 feet 9 inches long to make the patterns match on every strip. On five widths of carpet we would be obliged to use 45 inches more carpet than is actually needed to cover the room and you would be charged with 1¼ yards waste used in matching. This also applies to rooms of different sizes and also applies to Brussels, velvet and Axminster carpets as well as ingrain carpets. Should your room be size 14x14 feet, you will see that we are obliged to use five widths of carpet to cover the room and there will be a strip of one foot on the side that you will either have to turn under or, in a great many cases, our customers use this extra amount of carpet used in matching to be placed at threshold, or will save these pieces to be used in case a hole is burned in the carpet, as quite often occurs. Remember, Brussels, velvets and Axminster carpets are only 27 inches wide; borders used on carpets are only 22½ inches wide. Ingrain carpets are 36 inches wide. If your room is odd shaped, having a bay window, fireplace or offset, and you do not feel that you can figure the exact amount of carpet in it, we would advise you to send us a diagram of the room, giving all measurements, and we will be pleased to quote you a price on any carpet you may wish. You will note that two rooms of different sizes will require the same amount of carpet. For example, a room 14x14 feet will require 24¼ yards of ingrain carpet. For a room size 15x14 feet it will require 24¼ yards of ingrain carpet. On each of these rooms we are obliged to use five widths of carpet, each width 14 feet long, which, of course, does not include the waste used in matching. You will readily see that for the room size 14x14 feet you will have 1 foot of carpet 14 feet long that you will either have to turn under or can cut it off and use at the threshold as above stated.

As we have placed several improved carpet sewing machines in our carpet department and each machine is in charge of an expert operator we are positive that the carpets will be sewed much better than you can have the work done yourself and can do it much cheaper for you than you can have the work done. **The cost of sewing carpets ordered from us is as follows:**

Ingrain carpets, per yard..**2c**

Brussels, velvet or Axminster carpets, without border, per yard..........**3c**

Brussels, velvet or Axminster carpets, with border, per yard............**10c**

Size of Room, Feet	Yards of Ingrain Carpet (36 inches wide) Needed	Yards of Brussels or Velvet (27 inches wide) Needed	Yards of Brussels or Velvet, Made With Border (including border), Needed	Size of Room, Feet	Yards of Ingrain Carpet (36 inches wide) Needed	Yards of Brussels or Velvet (27 inches wide) Needed	Yards of Brussels or Velvet, Made With Border (including border), Needed	Size of Room, Feet	Yards of Ingrain Carpet (36 inches wide) Needed	Yards of Brussels or Velvet (27 inches wide) Needed	Yards of Brussels or Velvet, Made With Border (including border), Needed	Size of Room, Feet	Yards of Ingrain Carpet (36 inches wide) Needed	Yards of Brussels or Velvet (27 inches wide) Needed	Yards of Brussels or Velvet, Made With Border (including border), Needed
9x 9	9½	12⅜	17⅛	10x18	21¾	28	33⅝	13x16	25	33¼	38⅛	17x17	35½	46¾	60
9x 9½	10	13⅛	18	11x11	15⅛	19¼	24½	13x16½	25⅜	34¼	39⅜	17x17½	36½	48	61¾
9x10	10½	14	18⅝	11x11½	15⅛	20	25½	13x17	26⅛	36¼	41	17x18	35½	49⅛	63½
9x10½	11	14⅝	19⅜	11x12	15⅛	20¾	26	13x18	28	37½	42⅝	17x19	39½	52	66¾
9x11	11½	15⅛	20½	11x12½	17⅛	21⅔	27	14x14	24¼	31¾	37	17x20	41	54¾	59
9x11½	12	16	21	11x13	18	22½	28	14x14½	24¼	32¾	38¼	17x21	43	57½	61½
9x12	12½	16⅝	21⅝	11x13½	18⅝	23⅓	29¼	14x15	24¼	33¾	39½	17x22	45	60	64
9x12½	13	17⅜	22⅜	11x14	19½	24¼	29¾	14x15½	26½	35	40½	17x24	49	65½	69½
9x13	13½	18	23⅛	11x14½	20	25	30⅜	14x16	27¾	36	41¾	18x18	37½	49½	56¾
9x13½	14	18⅝	24	11x15	20⅔	26	31⅔	14x16½	28¾	37	43	18x18½	38½	50¾	58
9x14	14½	19⅜	24⅔	11x15½	21⅓	26⅜	32½	14x17	29⅔	38	44	18x19	39½	52	59¾
9x14½	15	20	25⅝	11x16	22	27½	33½	15x15	26¼	36½	40	18x19½	40½	53½	61
9x15	15½	20⅝	26⅛	11x16½	22¾	28⅛	34	15x15½	27	37⅛	41¼	18x20	41½	54¾	62½
9x15½	16	21⅜	27	11x17	23¼	29¼	35⅛	15x16	28	39¼	42½	18x21	43½	57½	65½
9x16	16½	22	27⅝	11x18	24¾	31	37	15x16½	28¾	39¾	43½	18x22	46½	60	68
9x16½	17	22⅝	28½	12x12	16¾	23¼	28	15x17	29½	41	44¾	18x24	49½	65½	73¾
9x17	17½	23⅜	29¼	12x12½	17½	24	29⅛	15x17½	30½	42	46	19x19	42¾	55½	62¾
9x18	18½	24⅝	30⅝	12x13	18⅓	25	30	15x18	31¼	43¼	47¼	19x19½	44	57	64
10x10	12¼	16	20⅛	12x13½	18⅔	26	31	15x18½	32	44½	48¼	19x20	45¼	61	68¾
10x10½	13	16⅝	21¼	12x14	19½	27	32	15x19	33	45½	49½	19x22	49½	64	71¾
10x11	13½	17⅛	22	12x14½	20	27⅜	33	15x20	34⅜	48	52	19x23	51½	67	74¾
10x11½	14	18⅛	23	12x15	21	28¼	34	15x22	38	52½	56½	19x24	53¾	70	77¾
10x12	14¾	19	23⅝	12x15½	21½	29½	35	16x16	30¾	40½	45½	20x20	48½	61⅛	69½
10x12½	15⅛	19⅝	24½	12x16	22	30½	36	16x16½	31¾	41¾	46½	20x20½	49⅜	63	70¾
10x13	16	20⅛	25⅛	12x16½	22⅜	31⅛	37	16x17	32⅜	43	48	20x21	50¾	64½	73
10x13½	16½	21¼	26¼	12x17	23½	32¼	38	16x17½	33¾	44¼	49¼	20x22	53	67½	75¾
10x14	17¼	22	27	12x18	25¼	34	40	16x18	34⅜	45½	50½	20x24	58¾	73½	82
10x14½	17⅜	22⅜	27¾	13x13	20½	27¼	32	16x18½	35½	46¾	51½	21x21	50¾	68¼	76
10x15	18¼	23⅛	28⅔	13x13½	21	28¼	33	16x19	36½	43¾	53	21x22	53	71⅛	79½
10x15½	19	24¼	29½	13x14	22	29¼	34	16x20	38¼	50½	55½	21x24	58¾	78	86
10x16	19½	25	30⅛	13x14½	22½	30¼	35¼	16x21	40	53	58	22x22	57½	75	88
10x16½	20	25⅔	31¼	13x15	22½	31¼	36⅛	16x22	42	55¼	60½	23x23	63⅛	82½	91
10x17	20½	26⅛	32	13x15½	24¼	32¼	37⅛	16x24	45⅜	50½	65½	24x24	66	90	96

WHEN ORDERING CARPET MADE WITH A BORDER

be sure and allow enough money to pay for same, as it will avoid any delay in writing for money to cover cost of goods. Remember the border is only 22½ inches wide. The body of the carpet is 27 inches wide. The diagram shown on this page is of a room 10 feet 6 inches by 10 feet 6 inches and if you will follow instructions given we do not think you will experience any trouble in allowing enough to pay for carpet and border to fit the room.

Measure the distance around the room in yards, which gives the exact number of yards of border required. In this instance it would be four times 10 feet 6 inches or 42 feet, which is 14 yards of border.

To get the number of strips of carpet, deduct the width of two strips of border or 45 inches from 10 feet 6 inches, which leaves 6 feet 9 inches, or 81 inches. Divide by 27 inches, which is the width of one strip of carpet, which gives the number of strips of carpet needed.

To get the length of the strips, deduct the width of two strips of border or 45 inches from length of room or 10 feet 6 inches, which gives the length of strips, or 6 feet 9 inches. Three strips 6 feet 9 inches would be 20 feet 3 inches or 6¾ yards.

Allow 1½ yards for matching patterns, which would make the total amount of carpet and border to fit a room 10 feet 6 inches by 10 feet 6 inches—22¼ yards. The cost of sewing carpet with border is 10 cents per yard extra.

10 FT. 6 INCHES

BORDER 22½ INCHES

22½ INCHES

CARPET 27 INCHES

6 FT. 9 INCHES

CARPET 27 INCHES

6 FT. 9 INCHES

CARPET 27 INCHES

6 FT. 9 INCHES

BORDER 22½ INCHES

10 FT. 6 INCHES

BORDER

BORDER

10 FT. 6 INCHES

10 FT. 6 INCHES

If your room should require more than an equal number of strips and less than 13 inches in width you should allow for one-half width of carpet. If more than 13 inches is needed you should allow for one width.

When ordering carpet with border be sure to allow 1½ yards for matching and if we can cut the carpet with less waste we will do so and will only charge for the exact amount of carpet used in cutting. **Whatever waste is left** will be sent you with balance of goods.

BELOW WE GIVE AN EXAMPLE

of how we figure the amount of carpet and border for a room 10 feet 6 inches by 12 feet 6 inches.

10 feet 6 inches
10 feet 6 inches
12 feet 6 inches
12 feet 6 inches

46 feet border, or 15⅓ yards.

10 feet 6 inches, width of room, by 12 ft. 6 in., length of room.
3 feet 9 inches, width of 2 strips of border, by 3 ft. 9 in., width 2 strips border.

6 feet 9 inches, width of body of carpet — 8 ft. 9 in., length of strips.
12 inches — 3, No. of strips.

72 inches — 3 | 26 feet 3 inches
9 inches

27 | 81 inches, width of body of carpet.
3, number of strips of carpet required.

8¾ yds. carpet.
15⅓ yds. border,
1½ yds. for matching.
25$\frac{7}{12}$ yds. carp't and bor'r.

If you wish Brussels, velvet or Axminster carpet made without border get the width of the room in inches and divide by 27, which gives the number of strips of carpet.

Multiply the number of strips by the length of each strip in feet, which gives the number of feet of carpet. Divide by 3 which leaves the number of yards. Always allow 1½ yards for matching patterns.

If the room is odd shape, having a bay window, fireplace or offset, be sure to send a diagram, giving all measurements exactly.

To protect you against any possible dissatisfaction, any chance of loss, to save you time and the slightest disappointment in selecting any carpet from our big line, as shown in this catalogue, we accept any carpet order with this distinct understanding and agreement that if the carpet you receive from us is not even better value than you expected to get, **you are at** liberty to return it to us at our expense of transportation charges **both ways,** and we will promptly refund your money.

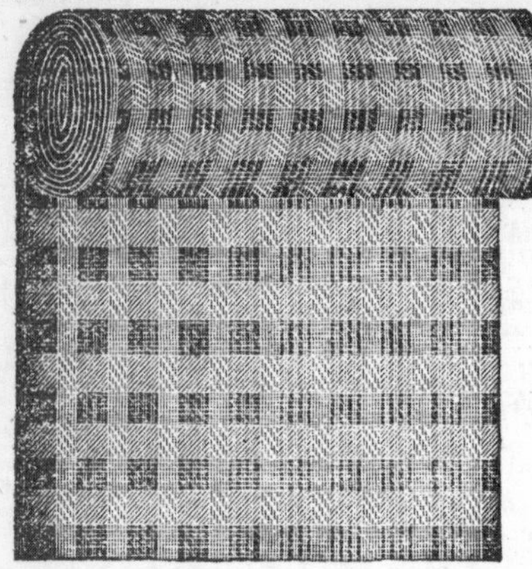

Our 10-Cent Hemp Carpet.

FOR 10 CENTS per yard we offer this 36-inch fancy Hemp Carpet, as the equal of carpet that retails everywhere at 15 to 18 cents a yard. From the illustration, engraved by our artist direct from a photograph, you can get an idea of the pattern. **This is new for this season,** woven for us under contract by one of the largest Southern mills, and while too much must not be expected of a 36-inch carpet at 10 cents per yard, and we always advise you to order a better grade, **we guarantee that in this we furnish such a carpet for 10 cents as never before was put out of any carpet house, wholesale or retail.** Width, 36 inches.
No. 37C1 Price, per yard, 10c

Our Special 15-Cent Hemp Carpet.

FOR 15 CENTS we offer this Hemp Carpet, 36 inches wide, in competition with carpets that sell everywhere at about 30 cents a yard. This is an extra fine quality Villa hemp, woven very carefully, a good, durable carpet that will give good satisfaction. This carpet is from one of the largest Southern makers of hemp carpet. It is extra strong, comes in all the latest stripe and check effects.

While we always advise our customers to order a high grade carpet, nevertheless, we promise you that if you order this hemp carpet you will get a carpet at 15 cents per yard, in 36-inch width, which in color, body, style and wearing qualities will excel anything you can buy elsewhere at anything like the price.

For exact color illustration of this carpet, see No. 37C5, on page 783.
No. 37C5 Width, 36 inches. Price, per yard.................... 15c

22 Cents Buys Our Best Hemp Carpet.

FOR 22 CENTS we offer this 36-inch extra super quality IXL Hemp Carpet, from one of the best Southern mills. **Our 22-cent price** is made possible by reason of taking the output of the mill, a mill located where it can turn out better carpets for less money than any other mill in the country. **This is one of the best hemp carpets made.** You must see it, examine it and compare it with other hemp carpets to appreciate the value we are giving. **It is a good, heavy, firm hemp in a fancy stripe weave. If you want an A1 hemp carpet we advise you by all means to order this, our highest grade.** It is a carpet the equal of carpets that are retailed generally at 35 to 50 cents.
No. 37C9 Width, 36 inches. Price, per yard.................... 22c

Our 27-Cent Rag Carpet.

FOR 27 CENTS we offer this new, handsome Rag Carpet as a special value, the equal of carpet that you have no doubt paid 40 to 50 cents for. From this illustration, engraved by our artist direct from a photograph, you can get some idea of the appearance of our new, high grade rag carpets, of which we have two numbers, one at 27 cents, and one at 34 cents per yard. Our special 27-cent price is below the lowest market today. This is a splendid quality of rag carpet at the price; is a pretty pattern, will give thorough satisfaction, comes 36 inches wide, and is a carpet you must see, examine and compare with other carpets to appreciate its value and exceptionally rich colorings. Give us an idea of the room you wish to carpet, order this, our special 27-cent rag carpet, and if you do not say that it is such value as you have never seen before, return it to us at our expense and we will refund your money.
No. 37C13 Width, 36 inches. Price per yard.................... 27c

Our Finest Rag Carpet at 34 Cents per Yard.

FOR 34 CENTS we offer this, our very best quality, extra heavy rag carpet, as the equal of carpets that sell generally at 50 cents and upward. This carpet is now one of our special values, made for us by a large Southern mill that makes a specialty of rag carpet, and we take practically their entire output of this one number.

THIS CARPET is extra heavy and extra strong, comes in a handsome bright pattern, and we can safely say that there is no better ¼ wool rag carpet of the kind on the market. The colorings are very handsome and we can guarantee the carpet for durability. Let us know the size of the room you wish to cover, give us an idea of the color wanted, and we will send you the carpet with a guarantee that it will be all and more than you expect or we will immediately return your money.

For exact color illustration of this carpet, see No. 37C17, on page 783.
No. 37C17 Width, 36 inches. Price, per yard.................... 34c

OUR GRANITE TERRY CLOTH.

Something New for Floor Covering, 28c per Yard.

THESE GOODS are used principally for border or filling where rugs are used. They come in very attractive shades of plain red, green, blue or brown. These goods are of a very substantial quality and make a very pretty floor furnishing.
No. 37C21 Width, 36 inches. Price, per yard.................... 28c

Our New Wool Terry Floor Covering.

THIS IS THE BEST QUALITY MADE in these very fashionable floor coverings and are principally adapted for fillings where rugs are used. They come in pretty shades of green, red or blue. They are 36 inches wide, and at our price, 60 cents per yard, are remarkable values.
No. 37C25 Width, 36 inches. Price, per yard.................... 60c

Carpet Linings.

No. 37C29 **Felt Carpet Lining,** or paper, in rolls of 50 yards. Weight, about 31 pounds. Price, per roll.................... 48c

No. 37C33 **Sewed Carpet Lining,** filled with jute. Keeps the floor nice and warm and protects the carpet. Width, 36 inches.
Price, per yard, 2½c; full bale of 200 yards.................... $4.00

No. 37C37 **Cotton Carpet Bindings,** 1 inch wide; 10¼ yards to roll.
Price, per roll.................... 15c

Our World Famous Heavy Floral Granite Carpet at 23 Cents per Yard.

AT 23 CENTS per yard we have sold thousands upon thousands of yards of this extraordinary quality of heavy floral design granite carpet, with universal satisfaction to each and every purchaser. We have established an output for this particular number that is astonishing, the marvel of manufacturers and dealers alike. We have been enabled to study and improve the quality of this granite carpet from season to season, and this season we offer a better grade than ever before at the reduced price of 23 cents, and we can assure everyone that there is nothing on the market that can possibly compete with this number. With a larger contract than ever before, enabling the mill to buy their raw materials to still greater advantage, with an improved quality and reduced price we expect to sell at least 350,000 yards of this particular number, and we know that each and every yard that we send out at this price will be an advertisement for us.

No. 37C41 Width, 36 inches. Price, per yard.... 23c

THE ACCOMPANYING ILLUSTRATION, engraved direct from a piece of the carpet, will give you some idea of the handsome floral design, but it is impossible to bring out the beautiful color effect. This is a design that secured a prize in a great carpet exhibition, and it comes in a variety of colorings in dark green, also in dark, rich red grounds with general harmonizing effects. The maple leaves in the green carpet are tan and oak, while in the red ground the design in maple leaf is bright empire green shading to nile green. The colors are lasting and we guarantee the durability of this pretty 23-cent heavy granite carpet. It is equal to the same class of granite carpets that are selling everywhere at 35 to 50 cents per yard.

HOW WE MAKE THE PRICE 23 CENTS. This carpet is manufactured for us under contract in North Carolina where labor and material are very cheap, and in a factory whose mill is run by water power, and where everything combines to make this extra heavy granite carpet at the minimum of cost. To carry out our contract the most rapid carpet making machinery has been employed, machinery that turns out three yards at the cost of one yard on an ordinary machine. It takes the entire output of the mill to fill our orders on this one number of carpet, and we are constantly adding to the number of looms as our demand increases. It has all the appearance of a wool carpet.

For exact color illustration of this carpet, see No. 37C41 on page 783.
No. 37C41 Width, 36 inches. Price, per yard.................... 23c

Our New Red and Green Heavy Ingrain Carpet at 29 Cents per Yard.

FOR 29 CENTS per yard we offer this brand new design for 1905, a heavy Union ¼ wool, reversible ingrain carpet, something entirely new in pattern effect, as the equal of carpet that will sell generally at 50 to 60 cents per yard.

THIS CARPET is a fair example of our wonderful price making power in the carpet line. It is made for us under contract by one of the largest Philadelphia mills, and under our contract we take every yard of this particular pattern that the mill turns out. In past seasons we have been able to offer some very special values in Union ¼ wool ingrain carpets, but we feel that we have eclipsed all former efforts with the pattern that we are able to show this season. If you could see this carpet and note the handsome color effects, compare it with carpet that is sold in your own city or by any other house at 25 to 35 per cent more than our price, you would better appreciate the value we are offering.

No. 37C45 Width, 36 inches. Price, per yard.... 29c

THE ILLUSTRATION will give you some idea of the beautiful design. It is a combination flower and leaf and scroll design, beautifully worked out in harmonizing colors. This carpet is suitable for any room and we know that you cannot help but be pleased with the design and color.

IF YOU WILL SEND US YOUR ORDER for as many yards as you require of this special Union ¼ wool, heavy ingrain carpet we will send the carpet to you with the understanding that if it is not all and even more than you expect, by far a greater value than you could possibly get from any other source, you are at liberty to return it to us and we will promptly refund your money.

REMEMBER that for 2 cents per yard extra we will cut, match and sew any ingrain carpet in our line. We would advise you to have your carpet sewed by us, as we sew all carpets on our electric sewing machines which bring them edge to edge and we do not have unsightly seams, so that it is as perfect on one side as on the other.

IF YOU WANT A LOW PRICED CARPET and yet a carpet that will brighten your room, show a handsome pattern effect and give unexcelled wear, send us your order **for this** special red and green Union ¼ wool ingrain carpet and you will receive **such value** as was never before offered.

For exact color illustration of this carpet, see No. 37C45 on page 783.
No. 37C45 Width, 36 inches Price, per yard.................... 29c

OUR WONDERFUL VALUES IN HEMP AND RAG CARPETS AT 15c AND 34c PER YARD. OUR NEW 1905 PATTERNS IN INGRAIN CARPETS AT LOWER PRICES THAN EVER BEFORE, 23c, 29c, 33c, 49c AND 63c PER YARD.

FOR BLACK AND WHITE ILLUSTRATIONS AND COMPLETE DESCRIPTIONS OF THESE CARPETS, SEE PAGES 782, 785, 786, 787 AND 788.

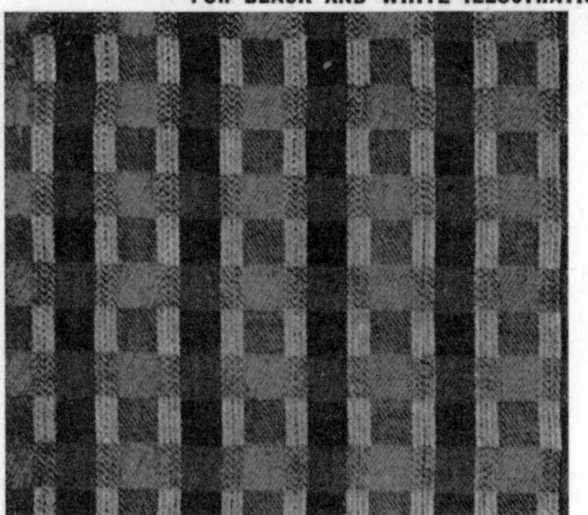

No. 37C5 For full description see page 782.
Width, 36 inches. Price, per yard..............**15c**

No. 37C17 For full description see page 782.
Width, 36 inches. Price, per yard..............**34c**

No. 37C41 For full description see page 782.
Width, 36 inches. Price, per yard.............**23c**

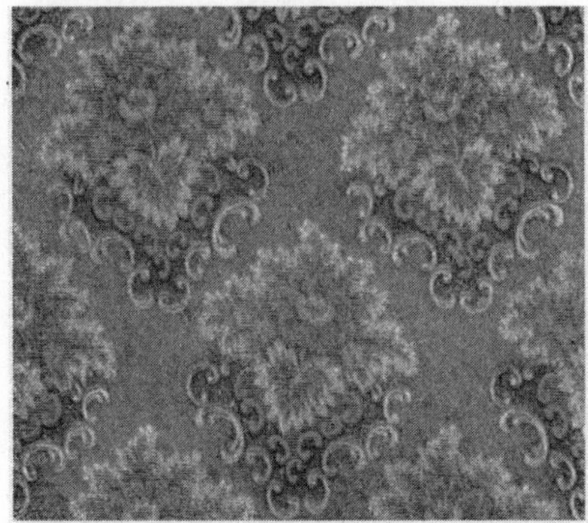

No. 37C45 For full description see page 782.
Width, 36 inches. Price, per yard..............**29c**

No. 37C49 For full description see page 785.
Width, 36 inches. Price, per yard..............**29c**

No. 37C61 For full description see page 785.
Width, 36 inches. Price, per yard..............**33c**

No. 37C53 For full description see page 785.
Width, 36 inches. Price, per yard..............**33c**

No. 37C69 For full description see page 786.
Width, 36 inches. Price, per yard.............. **49c**

No. 37C73 For full description see page 786.
Width, 36 inches. Price, per yard..............**49c**

No. 37C93 For full description see page 787.
Width, 36 inches. Price, per yard.............. **63c**

No. 37C97 For full description see page 788.
Width, 36 inches. Price, per yard.............. **63c**

No. 37C109 For full description see page 788. Width, 36 inches. Price, per yard....... **63c**

NEW DESIGNS IN 2-PLY and 3-PLY ALL WOOL INGRAIN CARPETS AT 63c and 82c PER YD. GREAT VALUES IN 8, 9 and 10-WIRE TAPESTRY BRUSSELS CARPETS AT 52c, 69c and 81c PER YD. BEAUTIFUL AXMINSTER CARPETS AT 91c and $1.17 PER YD. HIGH CLASS WILTON VELVET CARPETS AT 94c and 98c PER YD.

FOR BLACK AND WHITE ILLUSTRATIONS AND COMPLETE DESCRIPTIONS OF THESE CARPETS, SEE PAGES 787, 789, 790, 791, 792 AND 793.

No. 37C89 For full description see page 787. Width, 36 inches. Price, per yard.............63c

No. 37C113 For full description see page 789. Width, 36 inches. Price, per yard.............82c

No. 37C129 For full description see page 790. Width, 27 inches. Price, per yard.............52c

No. 37C141 For full description see page 790. Width, 27 inches. Price, per yard.............69c

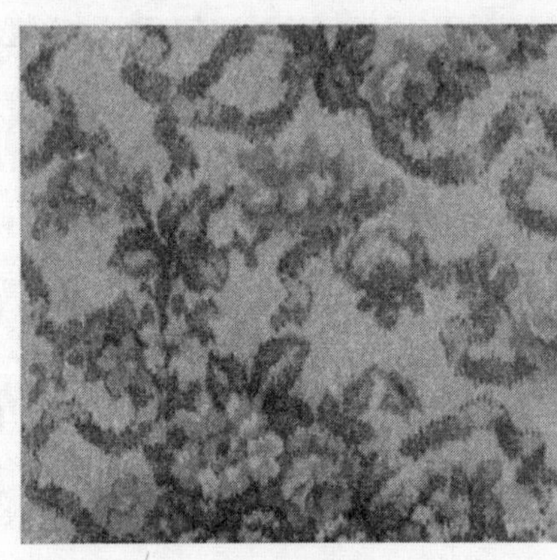

No. 37C137 For full description see page 790. Width, 27 inches. Price, per yard.............69c

No. 37C153 For full description see page 791. Width, 27 inches. Price, per yard.............81c

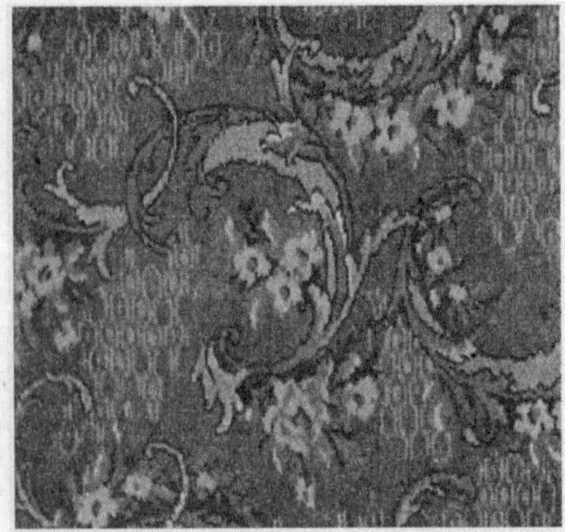

No. 37C149 For full description see page 791. Width, 27 inches. Price, per yard.............81c

No. 37C169 For full description see page 792. Width, 27 inches. Price, per yard.............94c

No. 37C177 For full description see page 793. Width, 27 inches. Price, per yard.............98c

No. 37C173 For full description see page 793. Width, 27 inches. Price, per yard........98c

No. 37C157 For full description see page 791. Width, 27 inches. Price, per yard.......91c

No. 37C189 For full description see page 793. Width, 27 inches. Price, per yard.....$1.17

Our New, Extra Heavy, Green and Oak, Union Wool Ingrain Carpet at 29 Cents Per Yard.

No. 37C49 Width, 36 inches. Price, per yard.... 29c

THIS IS ONE of the big values in our great line of Union ¼ wool ingrain carpet, one that we can highly recommend and offer in competition with carpet that retails generally at 50 cents per yard. This carpet is full 36 inches wide, an extra heavy quality and an entirely new design for 1905. The illustration, engraved from the carpet itself, will give you some idea of the pattern, but it must be seen in the full piece or made up into a fine parlor carpet to appreciate its full value. We guarantee this carpet to be strictly one-fourth wool, and we know that dealers cannot buy this grade of carpet from wholesalers and manufacturers at as low a price as we offer it direct to you. This carpet is made for us under contract, our order calls for an enormous quantity and the price we make is really based on manufacturing cost with only an extremely narrow margin of profit added.

THE PATTERN is a dark green ground effect with a leaf or floral pattern worked out in shades of tan, yellow, white, black and olive, giving the general effect of oak leaves. This is one of the prettiest designs in our entire line of Union ¼ wool ingrain carpet, one of the best values we have to offer, and is a carpet that will not only please you but will surprise you in the value it represents at this very low price.

WE HAVE BUILT UP A WONDERFUL TRADE ON INGRAIN CARPET.

By selling these goods at low prices, very close to actual cost, we have been able to distance any and all competition. This has given us a position among manufacturers and a price leverage, all of which our customers get the benefit of in the way of the lowest possible prices.

For exact color illustration of this carpet, see No. 37C49 on page 783.
No. 37C49 Width, 36 inches. Price, per yard 29c

Our Extra Heavy, Red and Tan, Half Wool Ingrain Carpet at 33 Cents per Yard.

No. 37C53 Width, 36 inches. Price, per yard.... 33c

THIS IS AN ENTIRELY NEW PATTERN and design for 1905, and we predict that it will be one of our greatest sellers. It is a carpet that is appropriate for use in any room, something that is bright, cheerful, and yet not too light in pattern effect to quickly grow old or dirty.

THE ILLUSTRATION will give you an idea of the design, and the colorings are exceptionally pretty. The main ground effect is tan, worked out by means of yellow and white, and the figure, which is a beautiful large floral design, is dark red, a combination of dark red, white, tan and black. This makes a very rich combination. The shading of the different colorings are really beautiful and all harmonize perfectly.

THIS IS ONE OF THE VERY BEST half wool ingrain carpets we have ever put on the market. It surpasses anything we have ever been able to offer in past seasons and those who have bought from this line in the past will recognize that this is a strong statement. Our carpet line for this season is entirely new, each and every pattern is new for 1905, and we know that we have strengthened our line and improved our values very materially. We have made better manufacturing connections and we can assure you that when you buy from us you are owning your carpet for really less money than your retail dealer could buy it. Our contract for this beautiful, heavy, red and tan, half wool ingrain carpet is direct with the mill, one of the largest mills of its kind in the world. We have an extremely advantageous contract and to our actual and lowest cost price on a long time, big quantity contract, we add our uniform one small margin of profit. We know that such value in ingrain carpet was never before offered at anything like the price.

WHILE WE FREELY FURNISH SAMPLES, as explained on page 780, we recommend that you send us your order direct from this description, under our positive assurance that if the carpet is not all and more than you expect and if you are not thoroughly pleased with your purchase, you can return it to us at our expense of transportation charges both ways, and we will promptly return your money.

For 2 cents per yard extra, we will cut, match and sew this carpet to fit any room.

For exact color illustration of this carpet, see No. 37C53 on page 783.
No. 37C53 Width, 36 inches Price, per yard 33c

This Beautiful Half Wool Ingrain, Light Green Parlor Carpet at 33 Cents per Yard.

No. 37C57 Width, 36 inches. Price, per yard....... 33c

THIS IS ANOTHER ONE of our great carpet leaders for 1905, an entirely new design; a pattern never before offered, and if you order it, you can feel sure of having a carpet entirely different from your neighbors' or, in fact, different from anything in your section. Not only that, but you may be sure that never before has a half wool ingrain parlor carpet been offered for 33 cents per yard that will compare in quality, style and durability with this special number. We have made a contract with the mill that produces this carpet for an extremely large quantity of the goods; a quantity that secures for us a liberal concession in price as against the price wholesalers pay the mill, and this advantage we give our customers the benefit of. At 33 cents per yard you may feel that you are buying this carpet for just as little money as your dealer would pay if he bought it at wholesale. We even question whether your dealer could get as good a quality as this carpet at the price we offer.

PLEASE NOTE THE DESIGN as shown in the illustration. It is a new and striking combination of floral, leaf, scroll and geometrical design on a bright green and light tan background with the pattern in bright green, black, white and tan. This carpet is thoroughly reversible and while we always urge our customers to buy the best grade of goods as far as their means will allow, nevertheless, we can recommend this grade at the price offered, as a carpet far superior to that which you will see offered at prices ranging up to 50 cents per yard. We can save you so much money on your carpet order that you really cannot afford to buy elsewhere.
No. 37C57 Width, 36 inches. Price, per yard 33c

SEE PAGE 780 ABOUT CARPET SAMPLES; ALSO OUR LOW . . PRICES FOR MATCHING AND SEWING CARPET . .

Our Extra Heavy, Half Wool Ingrain, Light Parlor Carpet at 33 Cents per Yard.

No. 37C61 Width, 36 inches. Price, per yard 33c

AT 33 CENTS PER YARD we offer this carpet, full 36 inches in width, as the equal of carpets that sell everywhere at 50 cents and upward. It is a beautiful new 1905 design, a carpet that will be very appropriate for sitting room or parlor, and comes in a medium light color ground of light tan with the pattern worked out in green, white, red and tan. The pattern is a beautiful leaf and flower and geometrical design, something entirely new, and we know it will please you. It is a design copied from a pattern of one of the highest priced carpets on the market. This carpet is extra strong and durable, carefully woven, made by one of the largest and best mills, where they make a specialty of heavy wool ingrain carpets, and we guarantee that for service and durability it has no equal.

WHILE WE RECOMMEND the purchase of as good a carpet as your means will allow, and there is always a great deal of satisfaction to be derived from the higher priced goods, nevertheless, we can gladly recommend this special heavy wool ingrain carpet at 33 cents, and you can buy it with every feeling that it will be perfectly satisfactory, and that it is equal to carpet that retails generally at 50 per cent more money. The illustration will give you some idea of the pattern effect, but we know that when you see the carpet you will realize that it is impossible by means of a picture or description to do it full justice.

WE CHARGE 2 CENTS per yard extra for sewing this carpet to fit any room. We recommend that you have your carpets made up by us as we charge only the actual cost of the labor, and you will find that the carpet we make up will be much nicer and cheaper than if you made it at home by hand or on an ordinary machine. We sew all our carpets on electric sewing machines, which makes a perfect seam on both sides of the carpet, rendering it thoroughly reversible.

WE RECOMMEND that you send your order direct from this description under our binding guarantee to please you or immediately return your money, but if you wish to see a sample of this carpet send us $1.00 and ask for Sample Set No. 1, and we will send you our entire line of ingrain samples. We will refund the dollar when the samples are returned to us, or if you send us your order you can return the samples and we will allow the dollar to apply on the order.

For exact color illustration of this carpet, see No. 37C61 on page 783.
No. 37C61 Width, 36 inches. Price, per yard 33c

Our Extra Heavy, Dark Green and Oak, Cotton Chain Ingrain Carpet at 49 Cents per Yard.

No 37C65 Width, 36 inches. Price, per yard.... 49c

THIS IS A CLOSELY WOVEN, two-ply, reversible ingrain carpet with a cotton chain and is as heavy and well made as any ingrain carpet on the market. It is an entirely new design for this season; a pattern that we know will prove very popular; modeled after one of our best sellers from last season with just enough difference to give an entirely new effect. The pattern is a leaf design worked out in an oak (a yellowish tan) background with dark green, white and yellow, a very pleasing effect, a pattern and coloring that will add to the cheerfulness of any room and at the same time one that will not soil easily or that you will soon get tired of. The colors harmonize beautifully and we know that this is a carpet that is sure to please.

WE GUARANTEE that you could not equal this splendid, heavy, dark green and oak ingrain carpet in any other store for less than 75 cents per yard. Our price represents only a little more than actual mill cost with an extremely narrow margin of profit added. It is our desire to furnish better carpet for less money than can possibly be had from any other stores and we are sure that a comparison of these qualities and our prices will show that we are succeeding in our ambition. Remember, that if you favor us with your order we guarantee that the carpet will please you in every way and will prove a better value than you could possibly purchase elsewhere, and if you are not thoroughly convinced of this after receiving the carpet and comparing it with anything sold by any other dealer, you are at liberty to return it to us at our expense and we will promptly return your money. **On the introductory pages we show plainly just how to order the carpet** you need and how to measure a room, and also our prices for matching and sewing so that you can send us your order direct from this catalogue with the assurance that everything will turn out very satisfactory.

No. 37C65 Width, 36 inches. Price, per yard 49c

Our New, Light Ground, Cotton Chain, Extra Heavy Ingrain Carpet at 49 Cents per Yard.

No. 37C69 Width, 36 inches. Price, per yard.... 49c

FOR 49 CENTS per yard we offer this entirely new design, one of the leading popular color effects for 1905, as the equal of ingrain carpet of this grade that will sell generally at almost double our price. **The general ground effect of this carpet is a very light tan.** The pattern is a large floral design brought out in light green, dark red, tan and white; a very beautiful pattern, a carpet that will look well in any parlor and in which the color effects harmonize perfectly. The illustration will give you a fair idea of the design, but the carpet must be seen to get the full benefit of the handsome color effect. This is another of our great values in ingrain carpets, a carpet that emphasizes our great position in the carpet market, by showing for how little money we furnish a strictly high class, durable carpet.

IF YOU FAVOR US with your order for this new, light ground effect, cotton chain, extra heavy ingrain carpet, you are at liberty to compare the goods we send you with carpet that you can buy at home for double the price, and if you do not find our carpet equal to such in every respect and by far a greater value than you could possibly get elsewhere, you can return our carpet to us and we will promptly return all your money, including what you paid for transportation charges.

WHILE WE FURNISH SAMPLES of all the carpets in our line, as fully explained on page 780, and while our Free Special Carpet Catalogue shows our entire line of carpets in their actual colorings, nevertheless you can easily send us your order direct from these pages, because we know that you will be more than pleased with any carpet you select. We are sure that this particular ingrain carpet will not only satisfy you thoroughly but will really delight you in the beauty of the pattern and design.

For exact color illustration of this carpet, see No. 37C69 on page 783.
No. 37C69 Width, 36 inches. Price, per yard.................... 49c

ABOUT SAMPLES. If samples of any carpet on this page are wanted, which is really unnecessary, as we guarantee our carpets to be exactly as represented, or refund your money, yet, if you desire samples you may **SEND US $1.00 AND ASK FOR OUR SAMPLE SET NO. 1,** and our entire line of ingrain carpets will be sent to you. The $1.00 will be refunded to you when the samples are returned to us or allowed on your carpet order.

Our New Tan, Green and Red Design, Cotton Chain, Ingrain Carpet at 49 Cents per Yard.

No. 37C73 Width, 36 inches. Price, per yard.... 49c

THIS IS CERTAINLY a new prize design for 1905, a very distinctive pattern effect, something entirely different than what will be shown in cheap carpets in retail stores, a pattern that is usually found only in carpets sold at much higher prices. While the illustration will give you an idea of the design, it is really impossible to properly describe the beautiful color effect. The background of this carpet shades from tan to light green and the pattern is a handsome, new style floral effect. On the tan ground, this pattern is worked out in green, yellow, tan and black, and on the light green background the pattern is worked out in bright red, light green and tan.

THIS IS A CARPET suitable for parlors, libraries, halls or bedrooms. It is a style and pattern that would cost, in a large city store, at least $1.00 per yard. It is a thoroughly reversible carpet, strongly woven, carefully made, one that we can most highly recommend for durability; a carpet that will so please and satisfy you that it will be a lasting advertisement for us.

WE ARE EXTREMELY ANXIOUS for your order for carpet. We feel that we can serve you in this line far better than any other concern can, we can give you a higher grade of goods, a more up to date line of patterns and designs and, above all, we can give you such quality at a low price as you cannot possibly find offered by any other dealer.

REMEMBER what we said about wastage in matching patterns, as explained on page 780, and also bear in mind that for 2 cents per yard extra, we will cut, match and make this carpet to fit any room.

For exact color illustration of this carpet, see No. 37C73 on page 783.
No. 37C73 Width, 36 inches. Price, per yard.................... 49c

Our New 1905 Floral and Medallion Pattern, in Dark Wine Background, Heavy Cotton Chain Ingrain Carpet at 49 Cents per Yard.

No. 37C77 Width, 36 inches. Price, per yard 49c

FOR ONLY 49 CENTS per yard, at least 30 per cent lower in price than will be offered by any other dealer, we present this absolutely new design, new, heavy cotton chain ingrain carpet and offer it to our customers as one of the best values that can be found in the entire carpet market. The pattern is particularly pleasing, being a new combination of a floral and medallion design formed by dark wine background and the large floral design worked out in dark red, light green, yellow and white, and a small medallion figure in a small combination of colors, all harmonizing perfectly and producing an agreeable pattern. This is certainly a wonder of values; a carpet that is strictly reversible; one side is always as handsome as the other, thereby giving practically double the wear of an ordinary carpet.

IF YOU WANT A SPLENDID FLOOR COVERING for your parlor, bedroom or sitting room; a carpet that is bright and cheerful; one of the very latest designs, up to date in every particular; a carpet that will give an unusual amount of wear on account of its splendid body, then send us your order for this special number and if you do not agree with us that it is unquestionably one of the greatest values ever offered in cotton chain ingrain carpets, we are willing to return your money and pay all transportation charges and the carpet can be returned to us.

WE BUY THIS NEW 1905 DESIGN floral and medallion pattern ingrain carpet from one of the very best carpet manufacturers in the country; a maker whose goods are standard and cannot be compared with the mills that supply the carpet for many dealers and mail order houses. It is the kind of carpet that will be an advertisement for us and that has helped to build up this department to its present enormous size. We recommend that you send us your order direct from this catalogue without waiting for further illustration or description, but if you desire, we will cheerfully send you free, on application, our special new, complete catalogue of carpets, which shows this as well as all of our carpets in their actual natural colors. The carpet catalogue is free, but you can **send your order immediately without waiting to write for it** and we will guarantee to please you or we will return your money. **On the preceding pages we give full information how to measure a room** and how to order a carpet, as well as our very low prices for matching and sewing.

No. 37C77 Width, 36 inches. Price, per yard.................... 49c

Our Extra Heavy, Green and Cardinal, Extra Super, Two-Ply, All Wool Ingrain Carpet at 63 Cents per Yard.

No. 37C81 Width, 36 inches. Price, per yard.... 63c

AT 63 CENTS we offer this rich new red and green design in heavy, all wool, two-ply reversible, 36-inch wide ingrain carpet. This carpet is closely woven and extra well made and finished. Our price of 63 cents covers the exact cost of manufacture with only our one small percentage of profit added. If you order one or more of these carpets from us and do not find them superior to anything you have seen at anywhere near our price, you may return them to us, at our expense, and we will immediately refund your money. This carpet has a very pretty ground of empire green, with floral effects and scrolls brought out in a bright shade of cardinal. This is one of the handsomest designs we have ever been able to present to our customers in these beautiful goods. The colors are absolutely fast and it is strictly all wool.

THIS ILLUSTRATION gives you a faint idea of the design of this carpet, but in our special carpet catalogue we reproduce it by the new photo color process, taken from a 1½-yard sample of the carpet itself. You will get a very good idea of the color and pattern in which we present this prize design. Still, it is almost impossible, through any photographic process to show it in all its richness, with its dark green background effect and the rich red heavy scroll effects. To realize its beauty it is absolutely necessary to see the carpet itself as it cannot be brought out in all its rich colors by any photo color procees. This carpet will add richness to any decorations in parlor or other rooms.

AT 2 CENTS PER YARD we sew our ingrain carpet to fit any room. All our carpets are reversible when sewed on our electrical machines, for there are no unsightly ridges, being finished perfectly on both sides.

IF SAMPLES ARE WANTED you can enclose $1.00 to us and ask for our Sample Set No. 1 and our entire line of ingrain carpets will be sent to you, the $1.00 to be returned to you when the samples are returned to us, or if a selection is made, we will apply the $1.00 on your order.

No. 37C81 Width, 36 inches. Price, per yard.......................... 63c

Our New Design in Dark Wine Ground Extra Super Ingrain at 63 Cents per Yard.

No. 37C85 Width, 36 inches. Price, per yard 63c

THIS IS A VERY HEAVY quality all wool reversible carpet, 36 inches wide. It is a new prize design. We guarantee this to be one of the highest grades of ingrain carpets. If you order one or more carpets of this special design all wool ingrain carpet, and after you have received it, you do not think it is better value than anything on the market for the money, you may return it to us and we will cheerfully refund your money. Remember, in pricing this carpet to you at 63 cents per yard we barely cover the cost of material and labor with our one small percentage of profit added. It is only from the fact that we handle carpets in larger quantities than any other house in America that makes it possible for us to sell this carpet at this phenomenally low price.

THE GENERAL COLOR EFFECT of this carpet is produced by a groundwork of a deep, rich shade of wine, and the floral effects are brought out in bright cardinal and rich emerald green; also bunches of foliage and flowers are brought out in colors of tan, yellow and white. This is one of the best and most popular designs that we are showing this season. The colors are guaranteed fast, and the carpet is strictly all wool. In our free Special Carpet Catalogue this carpet is reproduced by the new photo color process from a 1½-yard sample of the carpet itself, and will give you some idea of the color and pattern effect. But this carpet must be seen to be appreciated.

No. 37C85 Width, 36 inches. Price, per yard.......................... 63c

2 CENTS PER YARD FOR SEWING. At 2 cents per yard extra, we cut, match and sew any ingrain carpet in our line. We would advise you to have your carpet sewed by us, as we sew all carpets on our electric sewing machines which bring them edge to edge and we do not have unsightly seams, so that it really is as perfect on one side as on the other. Our seams are perfectly finished and your carpet will be thoroughly reversible.

Our Extra Heavy, Light Tan and Green, Extra Super, Two-Ply, All Wool Ingrain Carpet at 63 Cents per Yard.

FOR 63 CENTS we offer this rich, bright, new green and light tan design in a heavy, all wool, two-ply, reversible, 36-inch width ingrain carpet. This carpet is closely woven and extra well made and finished. Our price of 63 cents is about the actual cost to manufacture, with only our one small percentage of profit added. If you order this special carpet from us and do not find it superior to anything you have seen at anywhere near our price, you may return it to us at our expense, and we will immediately refund your money.

No. 37C89 Width, 36 inches. Price, per yard.... 63c

THIS CARPET has a very pretty ground of light green which also show on close inspection a dark red mixture. The pattern effect is composed of white, light green and red, harmonizing perfectly and producing a carpet that is appropriate for parlor or sitting room. The colors are absolutely fast and the carpet is strictly all wool. The illustration will give you a very good idea of the pattern itself, but no illustration can do the carpet justice.

WE WILL SEND a full set of samples of all our ingrain carpets, including this number, for $1.00, as explained on page 780, the $1.00 to be refunded when the samples are returned to us; but you can send us your order direct from this description without any hesitancy, because we know that you will be more than pleased; in fact, we guarantee that you will be thoroughly satisfied, and if you are not pleased with your purchase, you can return the carpet to us at our expense, and we will return all your money. We will take all the chances because we know that never before have such values been offered in carpet.

FOR 2 CENTS per yard extra we sew our ingrain carpet to fit any room. All our carpets are reversible when sewed on our electric machine, for one side is finished just like the other and there are no unsightly seams or ridges.

For exact color illustration of this carpet, see No. 37C89, on page 784.

No. 37C89 Width, 36 inches. Price, per yard.......................... 63c

Our Light Green Ground Effect, Heavy, All Wool, Extra Super, Two-Ply Ingrain Carpet at 63 Cents per Yard.

THIS IS ANOTHER one of the new designs that we are showing in our big line of extra super ingrain carpets. It is entirely new for 1905, a design that we selected as being the finest out of dozens of patterns that were offered us, a pattern that we know will please our customers and prove an ornament to any room. The colors harmonize beautifully and the design is new and distinctive. The illustration shows the style of the design—a big scroll and six-leaf floral pattern which is worked out as follows: The main effect of the background is of light green with a small mixture of red, the large scroll is worked out in green, red and white, and white predominates in the six-leaf floral design which is outlined in red, green and tan, all harmonizing perfectly, forming a most beautiful pattern as a floor covering.

No. 37C93 Width, 36 inches. Price, per yard.... 63c

WE GUARANTEE this to be the very highest grade of extra super two-ply ingrain carpet on the market. It is strong and well made, a better grade than is generally found in two-ply carpets; in fact it has all the wearing qualities and is nearly as heavy as three-ply carpets that sell for a great deal more money.

OUR SPECIAL PRICE of 63 cents per yard for this two-ply, full 36-inch width carpet, is a price made possible only by reason of our advantageous contract with the mill, by which we take every yard of this particular carpet that they turn out. We are more than pleased with our carpet contracts for this season; we are able to offer our customers still further inducements as against last season and we know that no one can compete with us. We ask for your order with the understanding that we will send you such goods for your money as you absolutely could not secure elsewhere.

For exact color illustration of this carpet, see No. 37C93 on page 783

No. 37C93 Width, 36 inches. Price, per yard.......................... 63c

Our Dark Tan Ground, Heavy, All Wool, Extra Super, Two-Ply Ingrain Carpet at 63 Cents per Yard.

No. 37C97 Width, 36 inches. Price, per yard.... 63c

AT 63 CENTS per yard, we present this new 1905 pattern as one of our very best values in two-ply Ingrain carpet, a carpet that has all the style and color effects that are found in much higher priced goods and one that will give exceptional wear, and is without question a greater value than we have ever before been able to offer in this line.

YOU CAN GET SOME IDEA of the pattern from the illustration. It is a large, liberal, free flowing scroll and floral design worked out in a wonderful combination of colorings, all harmonizing perfectly. The background of this carpet is light tan and green, neither too light or too dark, a pattern that is bright and cheerful and yet will not show dust and dirt very easily. The design is worked out in dark wine color, light green, dark green, tan, white and black, and must really be seen to be appreciated. It is one of the handsomest patterns that we were able to secure for this season, a real prize design, and we know will create a sensation wherever it goes, when our very low price is taken into consideration.

WE WERE NEVER BEFORE in a position to give such extraordinary carpet values. This season more than ever before, competition for us in the carpet line is really out of the question. We have eclipsed all previous efforts, obtained better designs, handsomer patterns, better wearing, better woven and more durable carpets, and we have been able to reduce the prices. If you expect to buy a carpet you cannot afford to place your order elsewhere, and you can order direct from these illustrations and descriptions without waiting either for samples or a special catalogue, with the understanding that the carpet we send you must please you in every way or we will immediately return your money

For exact color illustration of this carpet, see No. 37C97 on page 783.

No. 37C97 Width, 36 inches. Price, per yard.......................... 63c

Our Light Tan Ground, Heavy, All Wool, Extra Super Ingrain Two-Ply Carpet at 63 Cents per Yard.

No. 37C101 Width, 36 inches. Price, per yard.... 63c

THIS PATTERN is one of the new and popular designs of 1905; a carpet that we are sure will meet with a big sale. It is the style of carpet that is suitable to almost any room in the house. The body is extra heavy, closely woven, very durable and the carpet is strictly reversible, so that you get almost double the wear from this that you would out of the ordinary carpet. The illustration will give you some idea of the pattern, which consists of a light tan background effect with a large flower and leaf cluster worked out in light green, red, light tan and white. The colorings all harmonize perfectly and we are sure that any one who orders this handsome ingrain carpet, will be more than pleased when it is received.

THIS CARPET must be seen to be appreciated. It will look a great deal handsomer laid on the floor, covering an entire room, than it does in a small piece. It is one of the qualities we have selected after a most careful comparison of the representative carpet manufacturers' lines, and it is a wonderful value. We are safe in guaranteeing that the price at which we offer it is as low or even less money than most dealers will pay at wholesale for such an ingrain carpet. Our enormous carpet business has been built up by furnishing such values as this two-ply carpet at our special price. We have sold thousands of yards of carpet in every state and there are few towns in which you cannot find people who have bought carpet from us. You will probably find some of our carpet customers among your own neighbors and we gladly refer you to them as to the values we furnish and whether they advise you to send us your order. **This is a strictly high class ingrain carpet,** thoroughly reversible, extra super, two-ply, one of the latest designs for 1905, and a carpet that is positively unequaled at our price. **See page 781 about how to measure a room and our price for cutting, matching and sewing.**

No. 37C101 Width, 36 inches. Price, per yard.................. 63c

Our New Floral Design, Green and Oak, All Wool, Two-Ply, Ingrain Carpet at 63 Cents Per Yard.

No. 37C105 Width, 36 inches. Price, per yard.... 63c

THIS NEW, bright, heavy quality reversible 36-inch two-ply ingrain carpet, comes in a dark green effect background with a beautiful flower and leaf pattern worked out in oak, tan, red, black and white. It is a very handsome design in which the colors harmonize perfectly and it will make a very suitable carpet for parlor, sitting room or dining room. The illustration will give you a little idea of the pattern, but it is impossible to reproduce the colors to do full justice to the carpet. Our Free Special Carpet Catalogue illustrates this carpet in colors and will give you a better idea of the design, and if you desire you can first write to get this free carpet catalogue. At the same time we wish to say that you are not taking any chances whatever in sending us your order direct from this page, for we guarantee that you will be well pleased with the carpet and if you are not perfectly satisfied you can return the carpet at our expense and we will return your money.

DON'T THINK of buying one single yard of carpet from any other dealer as long as you have an opportunity of buying from us. We are offering so much greater values than you can get anywhere else; our designs are so much newer and up to date; our guarantees are so much more binding, that in your own interest alone we urge you to send us your order.

See page 780 about how to get samples, also our special prices for matching and sewing carpet to fit any room.

No. 37C105 Width, 36 inches. Price, per yard...................... 63c

This Rich, Light Green and White Ground, Extra Super, All Wool Ingrain Carpet at 63 Cents per Yard.

THIS IS positively one of the brightest, richest pattern effects in our entire line. It is a groundwork of bright green with a large scroll and pattern effect worked out in white and light green, making one of the most striking and handsome carpets in our entire line, strictly all wool and the colors are fast.

AT 63 CENTS per yard we offer this 36-inch extra heavy all wool ingrain carpet, a carpet that is made so heavy, is so firmly woven and made of such durable material that you get practically as much service out of this two-ply carpet as you would from the average three-ply carpets furnished by other dealers. We control the output of this particular carpet. We have a contract with the mill for all the carpet of this particular number that they will turn out. They are enabled to allow their looms to run constantly on this one carpet, this one pattern and without change, which helps to make economical production. This is all figured in our price, and as we add our uniform small percentage of profit, our customers get the benefit of every advantage that we have. We know that we are furnishing such value in this particular number as will be a revelation to every buyer. It is a carpet that will surprise dealers and customers alike in the value that it represents at our low price. In fact, we can say that we offer the carpet to you direct for less money than the average dealer pays at wholesale.

No. 37C109 Width, 36 inches. Price, per yard.... 63c

SEND US YOUR ORDER direct from this description with our promise that the carpet will prove all and even more than you expect. Put yourself in our hands and if you are not more than pleased with your purchase, we will immediately return your money and pay all transportation charges; but at the same time if you wish to see samples we will gladly send them (our entire line of ingrain carpets, Sample Set No. 1) on receipt of $1.00, the $1.00 to be returned to you when the samples are returned to us. If you send us an order you can return the samples and the $1.00 will be credited on your order.

For exact color illustration of this carpet, see No. 37C109 on page 783.

No. 37C109 Width, 36 inches. Price, per yard...................... 63c

Our 82-Cent Heavy Quality, Reversible, Closely Woven, 36-inch Width, All Wool, Three-Ply Ingrain Carpet.

No. 37C113 Width, 36 inches. Price, per yard. . 82c

THIS IS ONE of the wonders of our carpet line, a really extraordinary value; a carpet that is not only very harmonious in coloring and pattern effect, but a floor covering that is extremely durable and absolutely reversible. **It is strictly a fast color carpet** and has all the appearance of carpets that retail generally at $1.00 to $1.25 per yard.

THE PATTERN is entirely new for this season. It is a very rich green and red effect with a handsome floral design worked out in white, tan, green and red. The illustration will give you some idea of the pattern, but only the carpet itself can show the beautiful blending of the colors and what a new, stylish and satisfactory design is embodied in this 1905 pattern. The background of the carpet is light green, with large, heavy scrolls of dark red and a leaf made up of white, green and red; very pleasing and a combination that will not be duplicated in the cheap carpets shown by retail dealers generally. **We feel confident that we are offering in this number by far the greatest value we have ever been able to furnish in a three-ply ingrain carpet at anything like this price.** We cannot recommend it too highly, and if you will favor us with your order for this carpet, we will guarantee to send you such a satisfactory carpet, will give you such splendid value for your money, that you will be sure to call the attention of your friends and neighbors to the goods you bought from us.

REMEMBER that for 2 cents per yard extra, we will cut, match and sew this carpet to fit any room. Also remember that you should allow 1½ yards waste to every twenty-five yards that you order, to enable us to match the pattern correctly. We will send you the waste with the made up carpet. If you want one of the greatest values in an 82-cent ingrain carpet ever purchased, send us your order for this number with the understanding that if it is not all and more than we claim for it, return the carpet to us and we will immediately refund your money.

For exact color illustration of this carpet, see No. 37C113 on page 784.

No. 37C113 Width, 36 inches. Price, per yard........................82c

Our New, 36-inch Width, Rich, Dark Green, Red and Tan, Extra Heavy, All Wool, Three-Ply Ingrain Carpet, 82 Cents.

No. 37C117 Width, 36 inches. Price, per yard.... 82c

AT 82 CENTS PER YARD, a price lower than ever before, we offer this beautiful design in an extra heavy, 36-inch width, all wool, three-ply, reversible ingrain carpet, a carpet that will retail generally at $1.00 per yard. We know from a careful inspection of everything the market offers, that no such value has ever before been offered in the carpet line. We have never been able to place a handsomer pattern before our customers or a carpet that for wear, style, general appearance and durability will compete with this special number. The illustration will give some idea of the pattern effect, but the carpet must be seen to be appreciated. **We know that it will more than meet your requirements.** You will be more than pleased with the carpet when you receive it. The design is worked out on a dark, almost black background with bright green sprays and small leaves and a beautiful scarlet oak leaf as well as a large leaf worked out in yellow, tan, red and black.

THIS IS POSITIVELY one of the best three-ply all wool ingrain carpets ever placed on the market. We cannot recommend it too highly and it is offered the same as all of our carpets in this catalogue, with the understanding that if it is not all and more than we represent it to be, if you are not thoroughly pleased and satisfied that you received the greatest possible value for your money, you can return it and we will return your money, including what you paid for transportation charges.

WE ARE HEADQUARTERS ON CARPETS. We are in position to give you such values as you cannot secure from any other house. We place you on the same basis, as far as buying is concerned, as the largest retail dealers. You can buy carpet from us for one or more rooms for just as little money as your retail dealer pays at wholesale. In many cases you will be buying for less money. While we show this carpet in its actual natural colors in our Free Carpet Catalogue, sent to any one on application, you can order your carpet direct from this description with the positive assurance of being well pleased with your purchase. We guarantee the colors in this carpet to be absolutely fast. **See page 781 on how to measure a room and our prices for cutting, matching and sewing.**

No. 37C117 Width, 36 inches. Price, per yard........................82c

Our Extra Quality, Closely Woven, Reversible, 36-inch, All Wool, Three-Ply Ingrain Carpet at 82 Cents per Yard.

No. 37C121 Width, 36 inches. Price, per yard....... 82c

THIS IS AN EXTREMELY HANDSOME new 1905 design, something specially desirable; one of the greatest values we have ever seen in an all wool, three-ply ingrain carpet at anything like this price. It is equal in every respect to carpet that sells in retail stores at $1.00 per yard, and, in fact, we question if retail dealers will be able to offer such a beautiful, attractive pattern in any of their $1.00 carpets. The illustration will give you some idea of the beauty of this design, but it must be seen to be appreciated. **It is a magnificent large scroll and floral design consisting of a very attractive light green background effect with large green scrolls and a large floral design worked out in dark red, light green and white.** This carpet will surely add greatly to the appearance of any room; it will make a room very bright and cheerful and will give you a floor covering that cannot be equaled at much less than double our price. If you order this special number you will get a strictly all wool ingrain carpet, which for beauty of design, harmony of colors, strength, durability, wearing quality and all around good value, cannot be equaled anywhere at anything like our price.

WE ARE PARTICULARLY PROUD of this design; it is one of the leaders of our line; a product of one of the very best ingrain carpet mills and is offered to our customers on a basis of manufacturing cost with our one small percentage of profit added. **See page 781 how to measure a room.** Send us your order for as much of this carpet as you will require; let us cut, match and sew the carpet at the extra cost for this work as stated on page 780, and you will have a carpet that you will be proud to own; one that you will be complimented on, and we are sure that if your neighbors see it and learn the price, they will certainly give us their carpet business also. While our Free Carpet Catalogue, sent to any one on application, shows a handsome picture of this carpet illustrated in the actual colors that show on the carpet, yet you need not wait to write for this catalogue, but can order your carpet direct from this description and we will take all the chances of your being entirely pleased with your purchase. If you are not perfectly satisfied you can return the carpet to us and we will promptly return your money.

No. 37C121 Width, 36 inches. Price, per yard........................82c

52 Cents per Yard Buys This New, Dark Green, Eight-Wire, Genuine Tapestry Brussels Carpet.

No. 37C125 Width, 27 inches. No Border. Price, per yard.......... 52c

52 CENTS PER YARD for Genuine Tapestry Brussels Carpet in the full 27-inch width and new quality shown in this carpet, is a price that everyone will admit is not approached by anything offered in regular carpet stores. Our 52-cent price is made possible by reason of our contracting for the entire output of the mill, reducing the cost of the carpet to us to the actual cost of material and labor, to which we add our one small percentage of profit.

THIS IS A VERY NEW, rich and distinctive pattern, a color effect and design that has not been shown before and is positively exclusive with us. If you buy this carpet you will be getting a genuine tapestry Brussels carpet at an extremely low price and at the same time you will be getting a color effect and design entirely different from carpets shown by smaller dealers. The pattern consists of a dark green ground with a small light green six pointed star and large tan and red floral pattern harmonizing beautifully with the dark green ground work. You can see the exact coloring of this carpet in our special Free Carpet Catalogue which we will send to you on request, or you can get samples of our entire line of tapestry Brussels carpet, as explained on page 780. However, without waiting to get these samples or the special carpet catalogue, you can feel free to send us your order direct from this page for as much of this tapestry Brussels as you need (see page 781 how to measure a room) and we will send the carpet to you under our guarantee for quality, under our positive assurance that it is the greatest value that you have ever seen in this line and with the full understanding that if the coloring or the pattern does not please you in every way, you are at liberty to return the carpet to us at our expense and we will promptly return your money.

WE HAVE STRENGTHENED AND IMPROVED our line of tapestry Brussels carpets most wonderfully for this season. Never before have we been able to secure such splendid values in carpet to offer our customers at such low prices. No one can question our leadership in this department after seeing the goods we offer and knowing our prices.

No. 37C125 Width 27 inches. Price, per yard........................52c

This Beautiful, Tan Ground, Eight-Wire, Tapestry Brussels Parlor Carpet, Only 52 Cents per Yard.

No. 37C129 Width, 27 inches. No Border. Price, per yard....... 52c

WE OFFER in this brand new 1905 design in Eight-wire Tapestry Brussels Carpet for 52 cents per yard a pattern and color effect reproduced from one of the most expensive Wilton velvet carpets; in fact, this tapestry Brussels carpet has all the rich and exclusive appearance of Wilton velvet carpets that sell at twice the special price we ask. It is a beautiful new design, produced by means of a rich tan background with a beautiful rose and leaf pattern worked out in red and green. The colors harmonize beautifully and we doubt if another such a rich pattern can be shown by any retail dealer in his eight-wire tapestry Brussels line. This carpet is offered by us on the basis of almost exact manufacturing cost with only our one small percentage of profit added. It is really a most astonishing value and you will say so when you get the carpet.

IF YOU WILL SHOW IT TO ANY DEALER he will admit that at 52 cents it certainly is a bargain; in fact, our price is less than most dealers can buy at wholesale, as our contract covers the entire output of the mill—a season contract —and there is only a few cents difference between our cost price and this our 52-cent selling price. While we will gladly send you a full line of our samples of our Brussels carpets on receipt of $1.00, which will be returned to you when the samples are returned to us, and while you can see our entire line of carpets in their actual colors in our free carpet catalogue, nevertheless, you can order direct from this description and we will send the carpet to you and you will be well satisfied with it. We will take all the risk if you order direct from this description and will send the carpet to you with the distinct understanding that if it does not please and satisfy you in every way, you can return it to us at our expense and we will promptly return your money.

For exact color illustration of this carpet, see No. 37C129 on page 784.
No. 37C129 Width, 27 inches. Price, per yard.................. 52c

69 Cents per Yard Buys this New Handsome 1905 Pattern, Genuine Nine-Wire Tapestry Brussels Carpet.

No. 37C133 Width, 27 inches. Price, per yard 69c

THIS IS ANOTHER one of our prize winning designs, a floral pattern designed after several patterns that have proven the greatest sellers with us in the past, and yet combining new features, bringing it up to date to get in our new 1905 line of carpets. This is a carpet that is suitable for any room in the house —bedroom, sitting room, dining room or parlor; a carpet that will not show soil; a quality that will give exceptional wear. The illustration will give you a little idea of the design, which is a very large floral pattern. The general effect of the carpet is a medium tan ground with a large floral scroll in tan, edged with dark red and bright red cluster of red roses and green leaves in the center.

THE SPECIAL CARPET CATALOGUE shows a picture of this number, as well as all of our carpets, and if you would like to see these carpets illustrated in colors, just write for the Free Carpet Catalogue, and it will be sent by mail, postpaid. Nevertheless, we wish to say that you can order immediately, without first waiting to receive this catalogue, and we will accept your order for this or any other of our carpets with the understanding that if you are not thoroughly pleased with the goods when received, they can be returned to us at our expense and we will promptly return your money.

69 CENTS PER YARD for this genuine nine-wire new tapestry Brussels carpet, is a quality and price offer never before known in the carpet market. If you get this carpet, show it to your dealer, who will admit that the quality is certainly exceptional when the price is considered. It is a strictly high class, high grade tapestry Brussels carpet, a quality which usually retails at $1.00 to $1.25 per yard and far handsomer in design and more up to date in every way than carpets offered by small dealers. On the preceding pages you will find full instructions for measuring a room and for ordering and all about our special price for cutting, matching and sewing the carpet; also our offer regarding carpet samples. Everything is explained clearly so that you can place your order and be sure there will be no mistake and that the transaction will be perfectly satisfactory in every way.

SEND US YOUR ORDER for the carpet you need and let us show you how much greater values we can give you than any other concern and for how little money we can furnish you a strictly high class, up to date and durable carpet.

No. 37C133 Width, 27 inches. Price, per yard..................69c
Border to match. Width, 22½ inches. Price, per yard, 69c.

Our New Light Tan, Genuine Nine-Wire Tapestry Brussels Carpet, Only 69 Cents per Yard.

THIS IS AN ENTIRELY NEW DESIGN FOR 1905.

THE PATTERN and color effect worked out by the manufacturer is our own idea made especially for us and therefore a design that you will not see duplicated anywhere. We believe it is unquestionably one of the handsomest light effect tapestry Brussels carpets ever produced; a carpet that will look very handsome in any parlor and has all the style and appearance of carpet that is generally sold at two or three times our price. Our special price of 69 cents per yard barely covers the actual cost of material and labor with but our one small percentage of profit added and is by far a lower price than dealers can buy such a grade of Brussels carpet from wholesalers and jobbers.

No. 37C137 Width, 27 inches. Price per yard...... 69c

THE ILLUSTRATION will give you an idea of the design. The colorings are beautiful and harmonious. The background is a tan effect, not too dark and yet not too light. It combines a large flower and leaf pattern worked out in green, red, brown and black. The green shades from light to dark and all of the colorings blend beautifully. We question if another such handsome pattern can be found in any retail carpet store, or at least a pattern as rich as this in any carpet for less than $1.50 per yard. This carpet is suitable for parlors, libraries, halls, sitting room or wherever a rich, distinctive, serviceable floor covering is desired, and you and everyone will admit, when the carpet is received, that it is certainly an extraordinary value. We feel that with the line of carpets we are offering this season and the prices we are naming, that our position in this department is past all competition.

IF YOU FAVOR US WITH AN ORDER and do not consider that you have received such value in this beautiful light tan, genuine nine-wire Brussels carpet as was never offered and cannot be offered by any other dealer, we expect you to return the carpet to us and we will promptly return your money.

See page 780 about samples and our prices for cutting, matching and sewing.

For exact color illustration of this carpet, see No. 37C137 on page 784.
No. 37C137 Width, 27 inches. Price, per yard................... 69c
Border to match. Width, 22½ inches. Price, per yard, 69c.

69 Cents per Yard Buys this Genuine Nine-Wire New 1905 Design Tapestry Brussels Carpet.

THIS IS ONE of the Finest Nine-wire Tapestry Brussels Carpets ever produced. It is made by one of the best manufacturers of Brussels carpet in the country; a maker whose name is accepted in the trade as a symbol of the best quality and whose goods are found in the finest metropolitan carpet and drapery establishments. We have a special contract with this manufacturer for this one particular pattern which we selected from his entire line of nine-wire tapestry Brussels as being the very handsomest to offer to our customers, and the price we name on this carpet, namely, 69 cents per yard, is even lower than dealers pay wholesalers and jobbers for productions from this same mill.

No. 37C141 Width, 27 inches. Price, per yard...... 69c

THIS PATTERN must be seen to be appreciated. It is impossible to do it justice in a description or illustration. The illustration will give you an idea of the design, which is a very beautiful empire green background with also a light green effect and a large scroll and floral design, formed by rich red, light and dark green, tan, white and black. This is a strictly high class pattern, is suitable for the finest parlor carpet and will be an ornament and a credit to any room and will give exceptional wear. There is nothing to approach it for durability, service and, above all, in the rich coloring and pattern effect for less than $1.00 or $1.25 per yard as offered by retail dealers generally.

FOR 3C PER YARD EXTRA we will match and sew any 27-inch carpet to fit any room, and in this way you will get a perfect job, because we sew all of our carpets on electric sewing machines, bring the edges together perfectly and do not leave any unsightly edges or ridges.

For exact color illustration of this carpet, see No. 37C141 on page 784.
No. 37C141 Width, 27 inches. Price, per yard.................. 69c
Border to match. Width, 22½ inches Price, per yard, 69c

This Heavy, Medium Tan Ground, Genuine Ten-Wire Tapestry Brussels Carpet, Only 81c per Yard.

A NEW 1905 DESIGN.

No. 37C145 Width, 27 inches. Price, per yard..... 81c

IF YOU ORDER this Ten-wire Tapestry Brussels Carpet from us and then, when it is received, compare it with anything you can buy in your own town in this line at $1.00 or $1.25 per yard, you will better appreciate the value we are offering and it will convince you far more than anything we can say in this catalogue. This is an entirely new design and a new quality at this price; a quality much better than anything we have ever offered and far ahead of any tapestry Brussels that has sold at retail at higher figures. This illustration will give you a little idea of the design, which consists of a medium dark tan ground with a large flower design of red roses, green leaves and small flowers worked out in yellow, tan, brown, black and white, all the colors harmonizing absolutely. This is a carpet that will give most exceptional wear; will not show dust and dirt easily; is suitable for any room; is closely woven, thoroughly well made and is an unusual value for the money.

IT IS ONE OF THE LEADERS of our tapestry Brussels line and we have contracted for nearly the entire output of the mill on this particular number; securing a price which gives us an immense advantage and enables us to make this extremely low price to you. Dealers will find it impossible to buy a better carpet at wholesale at this price than the one we here offer. You can get this carpet made or unmade as desired, either the plain carpet or made up with a border which harmonizes perfectly with the carpet and you will positively find that we have furnished you with a carpet the equal of which generally retails as high as $1.50 per yard.

SEND US YOUR ORDER IMMEDIATELY, direct from this page under our guarantee that you will be entirely pleased with your purchase, or, if you wish a better illustration, write for our free Special Carpet Catalogue, which shows this and our entire line of carpets in their actual colors; or, if you wish, send $1.00 for samples, as explained on page 780. Most of our customers find that they can order direct from this catalogue and always receive perfectly satisfactory goods without waiting for samples or special catalogues.

No. 37C145 Width, 27 inches. Price, per yard 81c
Border to match. Width, 22½ inches. Price, per yard, **81c.**

81 Cents per Yard Buys this New, Heavy, Genuine Ten-Wire, Rich Imported Green Tapestry Brussels Carpet,

IN THE VERY LATEST PATTERN EFFECT AND AN ENTIRELY NEW DESIGN FOR THIS SEASON.

No. 37C149 Width, 27 inches. Price, per yard....... 81c

THE ILLUSTRATION will give you an idea of the design of this carpet, but it should be seen to be appreciated. The background is a very handsome and unusual shade of dark green, intermixed with a little white, and the figure, which is a large flower and scroll effect, consists of rich tobacco brown, black and red. This is an unusually striking color combination; a beautiful design, rich and attractive and will add beauty to any home. It is a quality that cannot be approached by any carpet sold in any retail store for less than 50 per cent higher price. It is one of our new patterns for this season and is sure to meet with universal approval.

THIS IS A BRUSSELS CARPET that there is practically no wear-out to; it is closely woven; has a perfect surface and is one of the prettiest parlor carpets on the market. The color effect will harmonize with most any house furnishings. If you will order this special number, you will be getting a Brussels carpet that will be a great deal more stylish than anything that will be shown in your section and a carpet that will probably not be equaled by anything in your neighbor's home.

FOR 3 CENTS PER YARD we cut, match and sew this carpet to fit any room. If you order this carpet with border and want the border matched and sewed, we will charge you 10 cents per yard extra. We recommend that you order direct from this catalogue without waiting to write for samples, although we furnish samples, as explained on page 780. We guarantee that the carpet we send you will please you thoroughly or we stand ready to immediately refund your money.

For exact color illustration of this carpet, see No. 37C149 on page 784. 81c
No. 37C149 Width, 27 inches. Price, per yard...........................
Border to match. Width 22½ inches. Price, per yard, **81c.**

81c per Yard Buys This Heavy, Medium Tan Ground, Genuine Ten-Wire Tapestry Brussels Carpet.

IN AN ENTIRELY NEW COLOR AND PATTERN EFFECT.

No. 37C153 Width, 27 inches. Price, per yard...... 81c

AT 81c PER YARD we offer this Genuine Ten-wire Tapestry Brussels Carpet as the equal of any carpet that you can buy in any retail carpet establishment up to $1.25 per yard. It is a new 1905 design; a pattern selected from ten-wire tapestry Brussels designs offered by a dozen representative manufacturers and we think it will please our customers better, give better service and look brighter after years of wear than anything we can offer them. The illustration will give you a little idea of the design. The color scheme is worked out by means of a beautiful medium tan background and a very large, heavy dark and light green and red rose and leaf scroll design; a very rich distinctive pattern, the same kind of a design that you often see in the finest Wilton velvet carpets for parlors or libraries. This will make an exceptionally handsome floor covering. We guarantee that there is nothing more durable in the line of carpet and nothing that will give the same pleasing effect.

IN BUYING YOUR CARPET from us you are not only securing the benefit of the lowest possible prices, prices that mean considerable saving to you, but you are also getting the benefit of exclusive patterns; the very best designs the market offers, selected by our carpet buyer from the representative manufacturers and positively a better class of goods than is generally offered in retail stores. Remember we cut, match and sew this carpet to fit any room for only 3 cents per yard extra; or with mitered border to match, 10 cents per yard extra. While we will gladly furnish samples as explained on page 780, you can send us your order without waiting to write for samples under our assurance that the carpet we send you will please you in every way, otherwise you can return it to us and we will immediately return your money.

For exact color illustration of this carpet, see No. 37C153 on page 784.
No. 37C153 Width, 27 inches. Price, per yard.................... 81c
Border to match. Width, 22½ inches. Price, per yard, **81c.**

This Heavy, Soft, Luxurious, Light Tan, Axminster Carpet, Only 91 Cents per Yard.

No. 37C157 Width, 27 inches. Price, per yard 91c

AT 91c PER YARD, a price that is very little more than the actual manufacturing cost with a narrow margin of profit added, we offer this very handsome, soft, deep nap, luxurious Axminster carpet. This Axminster carpet is one of the richest Axminster carpets made; a carpet that in quality and design is fully equal to carpets that retail as high as $2.00 per yard. We know that when you see this carpet, compare the coloring and especially the quality with what is offered by other dealers, you will really be surprised and wonder how we can furnish you such a carpet at the price.

WE ARE HEADQUARTERS in this line; our carpet contracts are something enormous and far ahead of any contracts the mills have ever handled. We are enabled to get such price concessions as enable us to make such extremely low selling prices. It is impossible to properly describe this rich, handsome Axminster carpet. We ask you to order it under our agreement, for it is the finest thing in this line ever shown; under our guarantee that it will more than please you, and under our offer to compare it with anything you can get from any other dealer at 50 per cent more money, and if it does not come up to all of these representations, if it is not superior to the carpets offered by others at 50 per cent higher price, you can return it to us and we will promptly return your money.

THIS CARPET has a beautiful light tan shading to dark tan background. The main design is a beautiful large flower and wreath effect worked out in light and dark green, red, pink, tan, yellow and olive. It is fit for the finest rooms in the finest houses; a carpet that will be a credit and advertisement to us. While we gladly furnish samples of this and our entire line of 27-inch carpets for only $1.00, and the $1.00 to be returned, as explained on page 780, nevertheless, you can just as well order this carpet direct from this description, with the understanding that it will be perfectly satisfactory to you in every way.

For exact color illustration of this carpet, see No. 37C157 on page 784. 91c
No. 37C157 Width, 27 inches. Price, per yard...........................
Border to match. Width, 22½ inches. Price, per yard, **91c.**

91 Cents per Yard Buys this New, Rich, Cardinal Ground Axminster Carpet.

No. 37C161 Width, 27 inches. Price, per yard 91c

THIS IS ONE of our new striking designs for 1905, a carpet in which the pattern is brought out in bold relief and in which the colors harmonize beautifully. It is one of our finest pattern effects and a quality that is most exceptional. Carpets inferior to this are very often sold by dealers as genuine Axminster carpets. This is a carpet made by one of the best Axminster carpet mills in the country, one of the finest patterns and is offered by us on the basis of actual mill cost with only our one small percentage of profit added, a carpet the equal of which is sold by retailers at $1.50 per yard. This most beautiful design consists of a bright, rich cardinal ground, with a very large rose in light red and a smaller flower in light blue with large green leaves, all harmonizing perfectly.

THE SMALL ILLUSTRATION will give you a general idea of the pattern and it can be seen to better advantage in our special free carpet catalogue which contains illustrations of all our carpets in their actual natural colors. We also furnish a sample of this in our line of Axminister carpet samples on receipt of $1.00, as explained on page 780, but it is really unnecessary to wait for samples, or for the free special carpet catalogue, because, if this carpet seems to please you, you need not hesitate to order direct from this catalogue. We will gladly accept your order for any amount of carpet with the understanding and agreement that the carpet must please you perfectly when received; must be equal or better than represented, and if you are not thoroughly satisfied in every way, you are at liberty to return the carpet to us at our expense and we will promptly return your money.

IN OFFERING THIS CARPET AT 91c PER YARD, we know that we are setting a pace for value giving in carpets that makes competition with us out of the question. We know that this is a lower price than any dealer can buy this carpet at wholesale; it is a price that represents very little more than the mill cost. This carpet will make up very nicely either as plain carpet or with a border to match. We are equipped to make up the carpet so that the pattern will match perfectly, so that it will fit your room and the seams will be perfect; the edges are joined perfectly and there will be no unsightly ridges. On page 781 you will find full instructions, how to measure a room and how to order, and you can send us your order for carpet, feeling sure that everything will prove perfectly satisfactory.

No. 37C161 Width, 27 inches. Price, per yard 91c
Border to match. Width, 22½ inches. Price, per yard, 91c.

Our Extra High Grade, Genuine Wilton Velvet Hall and Stair Carpet at 94 Cents per Yard.

No. 37C165 Width, 27 inches. Price, per yard...... 94c

THE ILLUSTRATION will give you some idea of the neat yet handsome design of this Hall and Stair Carpet, which comes in a medium tan background with a neat small figure worked out in red, green, yellow and tan. In the stair carpet the pattern carries a neat, finished border effect on each side. The pattern is especially desirable in carpet intended for halls and stairs and it is really one of the greatest values we have ever seen in this kind of a carpet. The quality is excellent, a grade that would retail at $1.50 to $1.75 in any fine carpet store. In fact, there are few Wilton carpets on the market that are any better in grade and none that are newer in pattern. In our free Special Carpet Catalogue, which we send to anyone on application, we show this carpet in exact colorings and give you a very fair idea of its appearance, but we wish to say, that it is really not necessary for you to get this special catalogue, if you do not care to wait for it, because you can send your order direct from this page with the understanding that if the carpet when received does not please you in every way, you can return it to us and we will promptly return your money.

IF YOU ARE IN NEED OF CARPET for hall or stairs and wish to get something strictly up to date and of the correct style, send us your order for this special number and we assure you that you will not only be well pleased with your purchase, but receive such value for your money as cannot be had from any other house. We are selling this carpet on extremely narrow marginal profit and we know that our price represents a value that dealers generally cannot possibly compete with. In ordering, state if you want hall or stair carpet.

No. 37C165 Width, 27 inches. Price, per yard 94c
Border to match. Width, 22½ inches. Price, per yard, 94c.

Only 94 Cents per Yard for This Rich Brown Background, Extra High Grade Wilton Velvet Carpet.

AT 94 CENTS PER YARD we offer this Genuine Wilton Velvet Carpet, an entirely new coloring and pattern effect for 1905; a beautiful high class grade carpet, the equal of any carpet that will sell in high class metropolitan carpet stores at $1.50 per yard. This is one of the greatest values in fine carpets that we show this season; a rich exclusive pattern, by far more stylish than the carpets that will be shown in retail stores generally, selected by our expert carpet buyer after a careful consideration of twenty different brown Wilton velvet carpets.

THE ILLUSTRATION will give you some idea of the pattern. The carpet itself must be seen to be appreciated. The background is made of a rich dark brown, shading to a light brown, with a scroll effect of tan and a beautiful green leaf and red rose outlined in black. This pattern is certainly exclusive in appearance; one that is sure to please and delight you. We are willing to accept your order for this carpet, cut it, make, match and sew it to fit any room and send it to you with the understanding that if you are not more than satisfied with it, if you do not consider that we have furnished you a value much better than you can possibly get elsewhere, you can return the carpet to us at our expense and we will promptly return your money. We take all the risk. We know that no other concern is

No. 37C169 Width, 27 inches. Price, per yard...... 94c

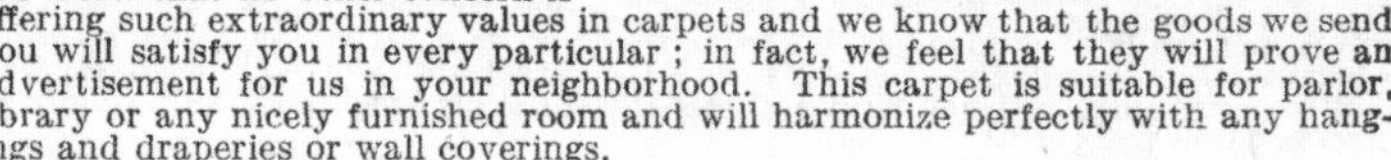

offering such extraordinary values in carpets and we know that the goods we send you will satisfy you in every particular; in fact, we feel that they will prove an advertisement for us in your neighborhood. This carpet is suitable for parlor, library or any nicely furnished room and will harmonize perfectly with any hangings and draperies or wall coverings.

ON PAGE 781 we give full instructions how to measure a room and how to order carpet and you need not hesitate to send us your order; just follow our plain and simple rules and we will guarantee to please you or refund your money at once. You will also note how we furnish a complete set of samples of all our Wilton carpets on receipt of $1.00, which will be refunded on return of samples to us or applied on your order.

For exact color illustration of this carpet see No. 37C169 on page 784.
No. 37C169 Width, 27 inches. Price, per yard 94c
Border to match. Width, 22½ inches. Price, per yard, 94c.

At 98 Cents per Yard You Can Buy this Rich, Dark Green, Extra High Grade Wilton Velvet Carpet.

No. 37C173 Width, 27 inches. Price, per yard 98c

NO ILLUSTRATION or description can do justice to the depth of color and the full beauty of this Wilton velvet carpet. It is a premium design; a pattern selected in competition with a dozen other beautiful green ground Wilton velvets and we offer it to our customers with the assurance that no handsomer carpet at this price has ever before been put on the market. The pattern is a rich, deep green ground with a beautiful flower and scroll design, worked out in bright red, light green and just a little tan effect. It will make a beautiful carpet for parlor, sitting room or library, and if you buy this number you can feel that you are getting the same value that is usually offered in $1.50 carpet sold in retail stores.

THIS CARPET will make up handsomely either in the plain carpet or with a border. If you want us to make up the plain carpet to fit your room, allow 3 cents per yard extra and we will cut, match and sew the carpet. If you want it made up with a handsome border in a rug effect, allow 10 cents per yard extra and we will make it up and miter the corners perfectly.

OUR 98c PRICE is based on the manufacturing cost and is an extremely low price for carpet of this quality; a price that cannot be duplicated and we are therefore willing that you order this carpet with the understanding that if it does not please you in every way, you can return it to us at our expense and we will return your money, even though the carpet has been cut and made to fit your room. If you need carpet you cannot afford to place your order elsewhere, because we are furnishing greater values than ever before this season, such bargains in carpet that can positively not be duplicated.

For exact color illustration of this carpet see No. 37C173 on page 784.
No. 37C173 Width, 27 inches. Price, per yard.................. 98c
Border to match. Width, 22½ inches. Price, per yard, 98c.

98 Cents per Yard Buys this Beautiful Light Brown Wilton Velvet Carpet.

No. 37C177 Width, 27 inches. Price per yard..... 98c

THIS IS ONE of the Handsomest Light Brown Wilton Velvet Carpets in our collection of genuine Wilton Velvets; it is a pattern that is entirely new for this season; a carpet that is made by one of the best manufacturers of high class Wilton velvets on the market; a manufacturer whose goods are handled generally in the finest metropolitan stores. We have an extremely advantageous contract for this special number; in fact, we inspected his entire line of Wilton velvet carpets; selected this as the most pleasing, richest effect, and made a contract whereby we take every yard of this number that his looms will turn out. We enable him to dispose of the product of these looms without any of the usual selling expense. We sell the carpet at almost manufacturing cost, adding a very small margin of profit to our first cost. We put you in position to own one of the most beautiful Wilton velvet carpets that will be offered this season by anyone at the lowest possible price, a price less than your own home dealer could buy at wholesale. We can furnish you with not only the cream of the market as far as style and pattern is concerned, but we save you so much money that there is no comparison between our prices and prices asked by others.

The pattern is a light tan and green background with a large scroll and flower design, worked out in dark brown, bright red and light green; a most pleasing combination; a pattern that is at once rich and distinctive.

LET US SEND YOU THIS Beautiful Wilton Velvet Carpet and you will own such a carpet as will not be duplicated in any neighborhood. For 3 cents a yard we will cut, match and sew this carpet to fit any room; or, for 10 cents a yard extra we will make it up with a border into a handsome rug.

For exact color illustration of this carpet, see No. 37C177 on page 784.

No. 37C177 Width, 27 inches. Price, per yard.................... 98c
Border to match. Width, 22½ inches. Price, per yard, **98c.**

98 Cents per Yard Buys This High Grade Genuine Wilton Velvet Carpet,

IN THE RICHEST NEW RED GROUND FLORAL PATTERN EFFECT EVER SHOWN.

No. 37C181 Width, 27 inches. Price, per yard...... 98c

THIS IS A HEAVY, deep, closely woven, genuine Wilton Velvet of the highest grade; one of the new designs for 1905, a rich shade of cardinal ground in a handsome scroll design. The color of the scroll is tan and the floral pattern consists of tan and red roses with leaves of a beautiful bright green shade, making a general pattern effect that is pleasing, as the colors all harmonize perfectly. The border pattern also matches the carpet pattern and this carpet will make up very beautiful with the 22½-inch border to match.

THE ILLUSTRATION will give you a little idea of the figure of which the design consists, but of course, it is impossible to reproduce the beautiful color effects on this page. In our Special Free Carpet Catalogue, sent to anyone on application, we show a very good reproduction of this carpet in colors which gives you a very clear idea of the pattern. While we are pleased to send this carpet catalogue to any one on application, still, we wish to say that you need not hesitate to send us your order immediately from this book if you do not care to write for the catalogue, for we are sure that you will be entirely pleased with your purchase. This carpet is such an exceptional value for the money that we are willing you should order it with the understanding that if it does not come up to your expectations in every way, you can return it and we will promptly return your money.

THIS NEW, HIGH CLASS, GENUINE WILTON VELVET CARPET is one of the richest and handsomest numbers in our entire line; a really fine piece of goods, something that is suitable for the very best rooms. It is a product of a mill whose goods are recognized far and wide as the leaders in their class and at our price you can feel sure that you are buying your carpet for just as little money as any dealer buys at wholesale. When you can secure a carpet of this quality, the very best and handsomest design, at the price we offer, it will surely pay you to consider this Wilton velvet very carefully before you place your order for any of the cheaper grades. This carpet will make up beautifully as a plain carpet, or made up with the 22½-inch border to match in the style of a rug. On page 780 you will find our prices for matching and sewing and also instructions how to measure a room.

No. 37C181 Width, 27 inches. Price, per yard.................. 98c
Border to match. Width, 22½ inches. Price, per yard, **98c.**

This New, Handsome, Dark Tan, Highest Grade Axminster Carpet, Only $1.17 per Yard.

THE CHOICE of the samples of six of the best carpet makers in the country is represented in this particular number. A beautiful high grade, genuine Axminster carpet in one of the richest color and pattern effects ever offered. This carpet is bound to be an advertisement for us wherever it is shown. If you want a carpet equal to the carpets that are sold in retail stores at $2.25 to $2.50 per yard--a strictly new 1905 design, suitable for the very finest parlors or sitting rooms--send us your order for this number and we will guarantee that you will be more than pleased with your purchase. The illustration will give you just a little idea of the beautiful, rich pattern.

No. 37C185 Width, 27 inches. Price, per yard..... $1.17

IN OUR FREE CARPET CATALOGUE we show this carpet illustrated in its actual natural colors and you can get a sample of this carpet by sending $1.00 for samples of the entire line of Axminster carpets as explained on page 780; but if you wish to order immediately, we would explain that the carpet consists of a very rich coffee color ground, worked with a large cluster of red roses and green leaves on a dark brown leaf and scroll design. This carpet cannot be compared with any of the cheap Axminster carpets on the market. It can only be compared with the very finest goods offered in large city stores at 50 per cent higher prices. It is a carpet that will please our large city trade as well as our customers in smaller towns. It is a quality that is unsurpassed; a pattern that we are particularly proud of, and there is nothing in the entire line that we can more highly recommend to our customers.

THIS CARPET comes with a very handsome border to match, but of course, you can order the carpet made up alone, or, order sufficient border to match and have the carpet made up with border into a handsome rug effect. We will cut, match and sew the carpet for 3 cents per yard extra, or, if made with a border, for 10 cents per yard extra. We will be glad to receive your order for this Axminster carpet direct from this catalogue, with the understanding that the carpet must please you in every way; be up to the representations in every respect, and if you are not thoroughly satisfied with your purchase and convinced that you have received the most astonishing value for your money, you can return it at our expense and we will promptly return your money.

No. 37C185 Width, 27 inches. Price, per yard.................. $1.17
Border to match. Width, 22½ inches. Price, per yard, **$1.17.**

$1.17 per Yard for this New, Handsome, Bright Moss Green, Highest Grade Axminster Carpet.

THIS IS the Highest Grade Genuine Axminster Carpet made, an entirely new pattern, something altogether out of the ordinary, the very latest out for this season. It has a very rich dark yet bright moss green ground with red roses and a beautiful foliage scroll effect in tan and brown. It is one of the softest, heaviest, most luxurious Axminster carpets we offer and is presented by us to compete with anything that the finest carpet stores have to offer in this line up to $2.00 per yard.

No. 37C189 Width, 27 inches. Price, per yard.... $1.17

THIS CARPET is produced by one of the finest carpet mills, which makes a specialty of high class Axminster carpets; it is the pick and choice of their entire line and a pattern that we know will please every customer. It is rich and distinctive and will give an unusual amount of wear; hold its color almost forever and at our special price of $1.17 per yard represents a value that is simply unequaled.

IF YOU WISH TO COVER A PARLOR, library, or other room with a beautiful fashionable shade of dark green carpet, a color that is very rich and will harmonize perfectly with almost any kind of wall covering or hangings; if you want to get a carpet that is strictly up to date, one of the handsomest that will be offered this season, we would especially recommend that you order this particular carpet. There is no illustration that will do this carpet justice and it must be seen to be appreciated.

REMEMBER that for 3 cents per yard extra, we will cut, match and sew this carpet to fit your room, or, for 10 cents per yard extra we will make it up with a handsome border to match. While you can get a sample of this and our entire line of Axminster, Moquette and Wilton velvet carpets, as explained on page 780, nevertheless, it is really unnecessary to wait for samples because you can order direct from the catalogue with every assurance of receiving a perfectly satisfactory carpet. We take all the risk and if you are not more than pleased we stand ready to return your money.

For exact color illustration of this carpet, see No. 37C189 on page 784.

No. 37C189 Width, 27 inches. Price, per yard.................. $1.17
Border to match. Width, 22½ inches. Price, per yard, **$1.17.**

$1.19 per Yard is Our Price for this New 1905 Design, Rich Dark Green Background, Extra High Grade Wilton Carpet.

No. 37C193 Width, 27 inches. Price, per yard... $1.19

WE CANNOT RECOMMEND this carpet too highly. It is a striking and beautiful design; a rich, deep, dark green ground with a very handsome red rose within a light green wreath. The pattern effect also embodies a beautiful black outline accentuating the red rose. In general pattern effect, harmony of colors, in wear and durability, we will match this Wilton carpet against any Wilton carpet that will sell in the finest carpet stores at $1.50 per yard. We know that we are selling these fine grades for less money than they were ever before offered. Dealers and customers alike will be surprised at the quality of Wilton carpet we furnish at this price. It is all due to the fact that we are the largest distributors of fine carpets in the world, selling direct to the consumer. Our contracts are the biggest individual contracts placed with the mills, and we are willing to accept a very much smaller margin of profit than any other dealer could afford to accept.

THE ILLUSTRATION shows in a general way, the design of this Wilton Carpet, and in our special carpet catalogue, sent free on application, all of these carpets are shown in their actual natural colors. If you would like to see this carpet printed in colors, send for the Free Carpet Catalogue. At the same time, we would like you to understand that it is really unnecessary to do this because you can order direct from this page and we will take all risk. We will assure you that you will be more than pleased with your purchase, and if everything does not turn out to your satisfaction, simply return the carpet to us and we will promptly return your money.

WHEN YOU GET THIS CARPET compare it with the finest value in your home town at $1.50 and if it is not richer in effect, and better quality in every way, we will return your money to you. If you want a fine carpet, something above the average; a carpet entirely out of the ordinary run, send us your order for this Wilton carpet and we are sure you will be more than pleased with your purchase. This carpet makes up nicely with the 22½-inch border to match, either as a carpet or made up into a rug to fit any room. **We only ask 3 cents per yard extra for cutting, matching and sewing the plain carpet,** or 10 cents per yard extra for the carpet made with a border.

No. 37C193 Width, 27 inches. Price, per yard.................. $1.19
Border to match. Width, 22½ inches. Price, per yard, **$1.19.**

$1.19 per Yard Buys This Beautiful Rich Red and Light Tan, Extra High Grade Persian Wilton Carpet.

No. 37C197 Width, 27 inches. Price, per yard..... $1.19

THIS IS A GENUINE American Wilton Carpet; positively one of the best makes on the market, a product of one of the finest carpet mills in the country, the kind of carpet that you do not find in the small retail stores, but a grade that can only be had in the large cities and sold at prices at least 50 per cent higher than what we ask. For a handsome parlor, library or sitting room carpet, or for a bedroom carpet far above the ordinary, we call particular attention to this number as one of the very richest patterns in our entire line and without question one of the very greatest values ever offered in Wilton carpet.

THE ILLUSTRATION gives you just a little idea of the pattern. It is really almost impossible to illustrate or describe it in a way that will do it justice. Our special free carpet catalogue, sent to anyone on application, shows a much larger illustration of this Wilton carpet and shows it in its actual natural colors, but at the same time, if you do not care to wait for the special carpet catalogue and want a particularly fine Wilton carpet, a wonderful value for the money, you can send us your order immediately from this catalogue and we will accept your money and your order with the understanding that if you are not more than pleased with the carpet when it is received, you need not hesitate to return it to us at our expense and we will promptly return your money.

THIS PATTERN is very intricate, consisting of floral and scroll design. The general effect of the carpet is red with just enough light tan to make it very bright and cheerful. The red is a particularly rich shade and the scroll is outlined in light green, the flowers in deep red with a black and tan center. We have seen a great many Wilton carpets, but none excel this particular one in richness of design or in the harmonizing blend of the colors.

No. 37C197 Width, 27 inches. Price, per yard.................. $1.19
Border to match. Width, 22½ inches. Price, per yard, **$1.19.**

Wonderful Stair Carpet Values.

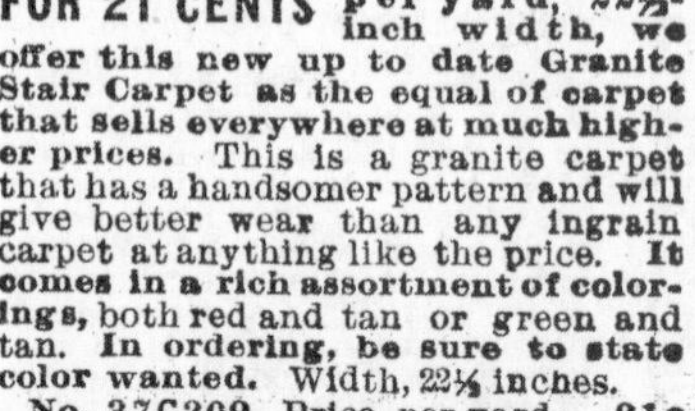

FOR 10 CENTS PER YARD we offer this 18-inch Hemp Stair Carpet as our leader for this season. From the illustration, engraved by our artist from a photograph, you can form some idea of the stripe pattern effect of this carpet, but unfortunately we cannot show you the colors. This carpet comes with a tan mixed center and red border. **While we always advise that in selecting a carpet you take one of our better numbers of high priced carpets,** and get something especially new and handsome, yet at the price, **10 cents per yard,** this 18-inch stair carpet cannot be duplicated in any market in this country. Width, 18 inches.

No. 37C205 Price, per yard........10c

Our Special 21-Cent Granite Stair Carpet.

FOR 21 CENTS per yard, 22½-inch width, we offer this new up to date Granite Stair Carpet as the equal of carpet that sells everywhere at much higher prices. This is a granite carpet that has a handsomer pattern and will give better wear than any ingrain carpet at anything like the price. **It comes in a rich assortment of colorings,** both red and tan or green and tan. **In ordering, be sure to state color wanted.** Width, 22½ inches.

No. 37C209 Price, per yard....21c

Extra Heavy Ingrain Stair Carpet for 36 Cents.

FOR 36 CENTS we offer this handsome, Extra Heavy Ingrain Stair Carpet, in 22½-inch width as the finest stair carpet we handle. A number entirely new for this season, from one of the best mills in this country, and if you order this carpet and do not find it equal to anything you can buy from your storekeeper at home at 60 cents per yard, we will cheerfully return your money. It comes in a beautiful combination of colorings. **Give us an idea of the coloring wanted and we will guarantee to please you.** Width, 22½ inches.

No. 37C213 Price, per yard..36c

Reversible Crexton Rugs, 82c.

This is an entirely new rug made especially for us. A very heavy fibre is used. It has a heavy wool fringe and comes in olive, tan and blue.

No. 37C217 Size, 30x60 inches. Price........82c

Reversible Heavy Cotton Bath Rugs, 89 Cents.

This is an entirely new innovation in our rug department; something needed in every home, a rug that is washable. **The illustration will give you some idea of the general effect. It is** of a Japanese design and comes in combinations of red, green and blue. **It has fringed ends.** Size, 30 inches wide by 60 inches long, including fringe.

No. 37C221 Size, 30x60 inches. Price................................89c

Our Big Jute Smyrna Rug Bargain, 97 Cents.

This full size 30x60-inch rug is one of the best bargains to be found in our carpet department. It is a rug that would be considered cheap in the ordinary retail store at $2.00 to $2.25. It comes in red, green and blue combinations. In ordering, give the general color effect wanted and we will pick out a rug that will be sure to please you.

No. 37C225 Size, 30x60 inches. Price..... ....97c

See Page 780 How We Furnish Carpet Samples;
full instructions for measuring a room and for ordering, and our special prices for matching and sewing.

Our New $1.38 Leader.

For $1.38 we offer this handsome Sheik Oriental Velvet Rug, entirely new for this season. It is an imitation of the popular Wilton or Axminster rug, and comes in a handsome combination of colorings, bright, medium, also rich dark styles. In ordering give us some idea of the coloring wanted and we guarantee to please you.

No. 37C229 Size, 27x54 inches. Price........$1.38

Our Animal Pattern Wool Smyrna Rug

This rug comes in beautiful color combinations of light and dark green, yellow, gray, black, scarlet and cardinal. We furnish this rug in both sizes, with dog as per illustration, also sheep or peacock.

No. 37C233 Size, 26x54 inches. Price.......$1.55
No. 37C237 Size, 30x60 inches. Price....... 1.89

Our New Big Line of Fringed Granite Floor Rugs.

This is the most popular line of inexpensive rugs on the market. The accompaning illustration will give you an idea of this heavy granite floor rug. It comes in a variety of colors in reds, greens, blues, cardinals, tans, etc. It has very handsome fringed ends and quite a variety of scroll, oriental, small, medium and large designs.

No. 37C245 Size, 20x36 inches. Price.........25c
No. 37C249 Size, 30x60 inches. Price..........45c
No. 37C253 Size, 36x72 inches. Price..........69c

A New Rug Sensation.

Our enormous cutting of Velvet, Brussels and Axminster carpets, necessarily leaves us with a lot of short ends from 1½ to 3 yards in length, that we are obliged to dispose of at a great loss at the end of the season. In order to give our customers the full benefit of this cut price, we have decided to make up the various ends of 22¼-inch borders, also the 27-inch wide regular carpets in these qualities into rugs, with wool fringe at the ends, and we propose to sell them at considerably less than the regular price per yard from the piece. Handsome rugs of all the beautiful styles shown in our color plate pages at a nominal price. Mention, when ordering, whether dark, medium or light color is wanted, and we will select the prettiest rug in the collection, and it will be sure to please you. These rugs are made of either border or carpet in uniform lengths, 54 inches long.

		Price
No. 37C257	8-wire Tapestry carpet only......	$0.75
No. 37C261	9-wire Tapestry carpet or border	.98
No. 37C265	10-wire Tapestry carpet or border	1.19
No. 37C269	Wilton Velvet carpet or border..	1.39
No. 37C273	Axminster carpet or border......	1.89

Our Elegant Extra Heavy Axminster Rug with Pattern of Animals, at $1.98.

This rug comes in very fine assorted colorings including green, cardinal and brown combinations with a pattern of a cat and dog like the accompanying illustration, also Newfoundland dog or peacock. Any of the patterns are like tapestry and as handsome as a picture.

No. 37C241 Size, 27x63 inches. Price......$1.98

BIG FUR RUG VALUES.

In fur rugs we are still maintaining our low prices in spite of the marked advance in the price of these goods. Skins have advanced in the market from 15 to 30 per cent, but under our arrangement for supply, we can for a time, at least, continue furnishing fur rugs at our present extremely low prices. Understand, every rug is covered by our guarantee, and if it is not found perfectly satisfactory and exactly as represented, you can return it to us at our expense and we will refund your money.

Our $2.49 White Chinese Goat Fur Rug.

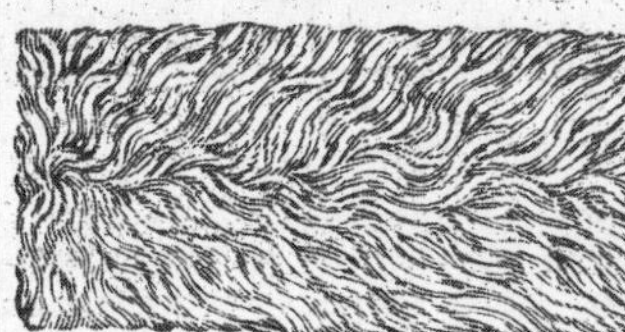

No. 37C277 This is a fine white Chinese Goat Rug, unlined. Size is 30x60 inches. It is thick and heavy, and is the equal of rugs that sell generally at about double our price. Price...............$2.49

Our $2.49 Fine Gray Chinese Goat Fur Rug.

No. 37C281 At $2.49 we offer this Goat Rug. This rug is made from selected Chinese goatskins, fine gray in color, and comes unlined. Size, 30x60 inches. Guaranteed the equal of rugs that sell at double the price. Price......................$2.49

Our Special $3.25 Black Goat Rug.

No. 37C285 For $3.25 we offer this handsome Jet Black Goat Fur Rug, colored to a jet black. Size, 30x60 inches. They come unlined; extra thick skin, heavy long fur and are most extraordinary value. Price... ....$3.25

Two-Toned Chinese Lined Goat Rugs.

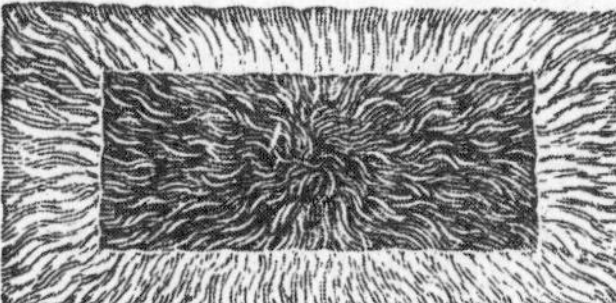

No. 37C289 Comes in black and white, black and gray, gray and white, brown and white, in either diamonds or square shaped centers, also in solid colors of white, black, gray or brown. Size, 30x60 inches. Price.............................$4.48

SPECIAL RUG VALUES.

98c, $1.98, $3.59 AND UP TO $21.25 AXMINSTER RUG LEADERS.

See and examine one of these rich Axminster Rugs to appreciate the values we are giving at 98 cents, $1.98 and $3.59. Do not fail to include one or more rugs with your order for carpet, draperies or other goods. Remember, it will add next to nothing to the freight. You will be surprised at the value you will receive, and if not, you can return the rugs to us at our expense and we will return your money. From the illustration, engraved by our artist from a photograph, you can form some idea of the beautiful designs worked out in these, our rich special Axminster rugs. It is an extra quality, made for us by one of the best rug makers in this country. Made from first class stock. The colorings are beautiful. They come in rich combinations of green, dark red, etc. In ordering, give us an idea of the colorings wanted and we will guarantee to please you. We furnish this rug in the following sizes:

No. 37C293	Price for rug 1½x3 feet..................	$ 0.98
No. 37C297	Price for rug 2 feet 3 inches by 5 feet 2 inches..........	1.98
No. 37C301	Price for rug 3x6 feet..................	3.59
No. 37C305	Price for rug 4 feet 6 inches by 6 feet 6 inches, seamless...	7.25
No. 37C309	Price for rug 6x9 feet, seamless..............	14.95
No. 37C313	Price for rug 8 feet 3 inches by 10 feet 6 inches, seamless..	19.00
No. 37C317	Price for rug 9x12 feet, seamed..............	21.25

OUR CELEBRATED DUCHESS SMYRNA RUGS, 79 CENTS TO $21.48.

At 79 cents to $21.48, according to size, we offer our new line of Smyrna Rugs in special and exclusive designs, entirely new for this season, direct from the mill, at prices that defy competition, prices that barely cover the cost of material and labor, with but our one small percentage of profit added. These are the celebrated Duchess Smyrna Rugs in all the very latest Oriental and Persian designs. They are gotten out for us under contract to imitate rugs that sell at five to ten times the price; extra heavy, very serviceable, a rich surface effect, a value that can only be appreciated by seeing, examining and comparing with rugs that your storekeeper sells at greatly advanced prices. To enhance the beauty of a room or hall, to add a richness to any effect you will get from any one of our fine carpets, in ordering a carpet, draperies or other goods do not fail to include one of these rugs. We guarantee the quality, we guarantee to please you, and if the rug does not prove all and even more than you expect, you can return it to us at our expense and we will return your money. The opposite illustration, engraved by our artist from a photograph, will give you but a faint idea of the endless number of rich Persian and Turkish pattern effects worked out in these handsome Duchess Smyrna Rugs. These rugs are reversible, one side is as handsome as the other. They have a strictly all wool fringe, the combinations of colorings are particularly handsome. They are rugs that are practically indestructible and they will give years of constant wear. The three largest sizes, 6x9 and up, are finished without fringe. Our special price of 79 cents to $21.48, according to size, as follows:

No. 37C321	Size, 1 foot 6 inches by 2 feet 10 inches........	$0.79
No. 37C325	Size, 1 foot 9 inches by 3 feet 9 inches..........	1.12
No. 37C329	Size, 2 feet 2 inches by 4 feet 6 inches..........	1.55
No. 37C333	Size, 2 feet 6 inches by 5 feet..............	1.89
No. 37C337	Size, 3 feet by 6 feet..................	$ 2.79
No. 37C341	Size, 4 feet by 7 feet..................	4.45
No. 37C345	Size, 6 feet by 9 feet..................	9.98
No. 37C349	Size, 7 feet 6 inches by 10 feet 6 inches........	15.00
No. 37C353	Size, 9 feet by 12 feet..................	21.48

WONDERFUL BARGAINS IN FLOOR RUGS OR ART SQUARES AT $1.80 UP TO $12.00.

OUR HEAVY REVERSIBLE $1.80 RUG.

FOR $1.80 TO $3.60, according to size, as listed below, we furnish this extra heavy ingrain or granite rug woven in one solid piece. A beautiful center with handsome, deep border to match, the border fringed on two ends with deep fringe. This is a heavy weight cotton granite, a closely woven goods, and offered at a price of $1.80 to $3.60 for the reasons explained below. This rug comes in the very latest patterns, handsome center and deep border, in a big variety of colorings, including wine, cardinal, blue and various shades of green. Understand, the rug is not made in solid colors, but in a handsome combination of colorings worked into a variety of beautiful patterns. Simply give us an idea of the coloring wanted and we will guarantee to please you. This illustration, taken from a small corner of the rug, showing how the border matches the center, will give you just a little idea of the appearance of the big rug with border complete. When you can use a made rug in place of a carpet for a fair sized bedroom at a cost of $1.80 or a good sized parlor rug, for from $2.70 to $3.60 and get all the quality and style that is shown in this heavy, reversible, serviceable, deep border floor rug or art square, we believe we are entitled to your trade.

HOW WE MAKE THE PRICE $1.80 TO $3.60. These rugs are made for us under contract by a North Carolina Granite Carpet Mill, a mill that runs exclusively on heavy cotton or granite carpets. This particular mill is located where materials are low, where they can command cheap labor, where everything combines to make possible the production of a heavy weight granite carpet at a low cost and we have for several seasons taken the entire output of this mill on granite carpets and recently we have induced them to put in looms for the weaving in one piece of our heavy reversible, deep border granite rugs in sizes from 6x9 feet to 9x12 feet, and by so doing we have gotten the cost of these finished rugs down to the same basis of cost as our granite carpets.

No. 37C357	Size, 6 x9 feet.	$1.80
No. 37C361	Size, 7½x9 feet.	2.25
No. 37C365	Size, 9 x9 feet.	2.70
No. 37C369	Size, 9x10½ feet.	$3.15
No. 37C373	Size, 9x12 feet.	3.60

WE GUARANTEE TO PLEASE YOU IN EVERY WAY OR REFUND YOUR MONEY.

THESE HANDSOME, HEAVY, TWO-PLY, WOOL FACE, REVERSIBLE, WIDE BORDER, LARGE BRUSSELETTE FLOOR RUGS AT $3.90 TO $7.80.

AT $3.90 for size 6 x 9 feet to $7.80 for largest size, 9 x 12 feet, we furnish you these handsome, heavy, wool, two-ply, genuine Brusselette floor rugs, woven in one piece without a seam, absolutely new design throughout, new coloring, square centers and wide border to match, a rug complete to cover any room and preferred by many in place of a carpet.

THE SMALL ILLUSTRATION showing a corner of the rug and showing the difference in design between the wide border and the center and showing also how these two designs harmonize perfectly, will give you a little idea of the general effect, but the rug must be seen to be appreciated. In our Special Carpet Catalogue, sent free to anyone on application, we show one of these rugs in its actual colors, but they come in a big variety of different color effects so that it is impossible to properly illustrate and describe all of them. We can furnish this beautiful, wool face, two-ply Brusselette rug in a big variety of absolute fast colors, all of which harmonize perfectly. We can give you red effects, green effects or tan effects and in each one the design is worked out in harmonizing colorings and all you need to do is to give us an idea of your preference with the general color effect that you prefer, say whether you like a large or small pattern or a medium design, advise us just what you want and we will send it to you with the understanding that if it does not please you in every way, you can return it to us and we will immediately return your money.

WE HAVE SELECTED THIS LINE of floor rugs as one of our big rug leaders. It is far above the ordinary in quality and we made a large contract, securing a very substantial reduction in price. These floor rugs are better than anything we have offered in previous seasons at these prices and our customers who have bought from us in this line from other catalogues will appreciate what this statement means. If you want a handsome floor rug, send us your order for one of these, tell us what you like in the way of color effect and we will send the rug to you and we are sure that you will be more than pleased with your purchase. We know that you will show the rug to your friends and neighbors and that it will prove a good advertisement for us and will please you so well that you will send us your future orders. Our prices are very little more than manufacturing cost; even lower than retail dealers can buy in any quantity at price list.

No. 37C377	Size, 6 x 9 feet.	$3.90
No. 37C381	Size, 7½x 9 feet.	4.88
No. 37C385	Size, 9 x12 feet.	7.80

$4.50 to $12.00 for These Handsome, Heavy Weight, Two-Ply, All Wool, Reversible, Wide Border, Deep Fringe, Large Floor Rugs.

AT FROM $4.50 FOR SIZE 7½ X 9 FEET TO $12.00 FOR SIZE 12 X 15 FEET, we furnish these handsome, heavy, all wool, two-ply rugs, woven in one piece without a seam; large, handsome square centers, with beautiful wide borders to match, a rug complete to cover any room; made to take the place of carpets.

THIS SMALL ILLUSTRATION showing a corner of the rug, showing how the wide border blends with the beautiful square center, showing the deep fringe on the border, is intended to give you a little idea of the effects worked out in these large floor rugs or art squares. These handsome rugs are entirely new for this season; all new designs. They come in a beautiful variety of fast colorings, including various shades of red, blue, green and tan. Give us an idea of the shade and pattern wanted, whether large, medium or small design and we will send you a rug that we guarantee will please you, and if not, you can return it to us at our expense and we will immediately return your money. With a view to furnishing our customers a handsome, wide bordered art square complete, woven in one piece, at about one-half the price at which such art squares have heretofore been furnished, we took the matter up with the mill that makes our ingrain carpets and had them introduce looms on which the same carpeting could be woven in the wide border rugs at practically the same cost as the weaving of carpets, and as a result, we are able to offer you these extra heavy, two-ply, strictly all wool reversible art squares or big floor rugs with beautiful centers and wide fringed borders, all in one piece, all in the very latest patterns and handsome colorings, at the heretofore unheard of prices of $4.50 to $12.00 according to size.

No. 37C393	Size, 7½x 9 feet.	$4.50
No. 37C397	Size, 9 x 9 feet.	5.40
No. 37C401	Size, 9 x10½ feet.	6.30
No. 37C404	Size, 9 x12 feet.	7.20
No. 37C409	Size, 10½x12 feet.	$ 8.40
No. 37C413	Size, 12 x12 feet.	9.60
No. 37C417	Size, 12 x15 feet.	12.00

Our Great Big 9x12 Wilton Velvet Rug Bargain at $20.95.

This is the biggest value that was ever offered in our carpet department. This rug is made for us by one of the biggest mills in this country. It is size 9x12 feet. It will fit a large room. It has a beautiful center, comes in medallion effects, also oriental small patterns. It is a velvet rug such as you would pay $40.00 for in any city retail store. These goods we offer to our patrons at a minimum price. It is a velvet rug that you could not have made of the carpet by the running yard for less than $30.00; in fact, we think that we are giving the biggest bargain that ever went out of our house in this handsome 9x12 Wilton velvet rug. The predominating colors are red, blue, tan and green. Mention whether you would like a small or large pattern, whether you wish a medallion center or oriental design. Leave it to us to pick out the pattern for you and we are sure that you will be pleased with this beautiful Wilton velvet rug. The accompanying illustration will give you an idea of the style of this handsome rug, as it is taken from a correct photograph.

No. 37C421 Size, 9x12 feet. Price..$20.95

Our Luxurious, Big Genuine Roxbury 9x12 and 7x9-Foot Fine Tapestry Brussels Carpet Rugs at $17.95 and $10.95.

THESE ARE TWO OF THE richest and most durable 10-wire tapestry rugs made. They have but three seams. They have a 22-inch border which is woven solid with a center and the colors and pattern blend and harmonize perfectly. These 9x12 and 7x9 rugs will cover any rooms ranging from 9x12 to 12x16 feet and 8x10 to 9x11 feet. In fact these big bordered rugs are large enough to fit any parlor, library or other rooms larger than 9x12 and 7x9 feet and the floor space between the carpet and the wall, if the floor is not polished hardwood, can be easily stained to give the effect of the most expensive city houses where they have highly polished hardwood floors.

THE ACCOMPANYING ILLUSTRATION showing one-fourth of the rug taken from a photograph gives you an idea of how perfectly the deep woven border matches the handsome center. Our prices of $17.95 and $10.75 are based on the actual cost of manufacture with our one small percentage of profit added. In fact we have gotten out these beautiful tapestry rugs in such large quantities that we are enabled to offer them at a price one-third less than the same rug can be purchased from any retail carpet store. This is an opportunity for you to get to all intents and purposes, a made up, complete 10-wire tapestry rug at less than the cost of a tapestry carpet not as heavy or durable. Simply roll out this rug on the floor and see the harmonious blending of colors that can only be produced where the border and center are woven to match the combination perfectly.

WE CAN FURNISH 9X12 RUGS in an endless variety of handsome, new designs and patterns, either small, medium or large, in a big line of colors, including tan ground with bright floral design, red and green ground with floral design, green ground with medallion figure, blue ground with floral figure, Persian, red and green ground, oriental designs of dark red and green grounds, with correspondingly beautiful colorings in the border. Size 7x9 comes in small designs only in tan, red, blue or green grounds.

SIMPLY GIVE US AN IDEA OF THE COLORING WANTED and we will send you the rug with the understanding that if not perfectly satisfactory when received, you can return it to us at our expense and we will refund your money. While nearly all of our customers send cash in full with their orders, thus saving the extra 25 or 50 cents which the express companies charge for collecting and returning money to us, and with the understanding that we are to return your money if the rug is not entirely satisfactory, if you wish to see and examine the rug before paying for it, we will, on receipt of $1.00 send either rug you may desire by freight or express C. O. D. You can examine it at your nearest railroad station and if found perfectly satisfactory and exactly as represented by us, pay your railroad agent our price and freight charges, less the $1.00 sent us. These two rugs are exactly the same quality, the only difference being in the size, one being 9x12 and the other being 7x9 feet.

No. 37C425 Size, 9x12 feet. Price..$17.95
No. 37C429 Size, 7x 9 feet. Price..10.75

Our Big 9x12 Ten-Wire Tapestry Brussels Rug at $14.95.

THIS RUG IS manufactured by the famous Sanford & Son, Amsterdam, N. Y., the biggest rug manufacturers in the world. We have closed a contract for a tremendous quantity of these rugs at a price so extremely low that we are enabled to sell them for about one-half their value. We know that rugs no better are being sold in retail stores in Chicago and New York as high as $30.00. This rug we can furnish in but one size, namely, 9x12 feet. It is suitable to take the place of a carpet to fit any room in sizes ranging from 9x12 to 12x16 feet. If your room is 9x12 feet this heavy Brussels rug will cover it completely. If the room is larger than 9x12 feet the bare floor between the rug and the wall can be finished by staining and varnishing the floor. If you do not care to do this, we can furnish a filling to harmonize with the colors in the rug. This rich 10-wire tapestry Brussels rug has three seams in the entire rug. The big 18-inch border is woven solid into the body or inner square of the rug, in beautiful harmonizing colorings. This makes a handsomer effect than can be produced by being made up with a Brussels carpet center and a Brussels carpet border.

THE ACCOMPANYING ILLUSTRATION is taken from a photograph of a corner of the rug. You can get some idea of how beautifully the border blends into the center, and the effect that we have been able to work out with this big 9x12-foot rug. This is a rug that you must see to appreciate the value we are giving you. We can furnish this rug in a variety of new, handsome prize designs in small, medium and large patterns and also in a big variety of handsome colorings, in which are green, red, blue, tan and oak effects. Simply give us an idea of the coloring wanted, say whether you want small, medium, or large pattern and we will send the rug to you, guaranteeing it to please you, guaranteeing it to be the equal of anything that you can buy at home at double our price, and if when received you do not find it entirely satisfactory you can return it to us at our expense and we will refund your money.

OUR $1.00 C. O. D. subject to examination, pay after received proposition. While we advise you to send cash in full with your order and thus save the extra express charge of 25 or 50 cents for collecting and returning the money to us, if you wish to see and examine this 9x12-foot heavy Brussels rug before paying for it you can send us $1.00 and we will send it to you by freight C. O. D. subject to examination, and you can pay the balance, $13.95 and freight charges, after the rug is received, providing it is perfectly satisfactory. Do not forget it is greatly to your advantage to send cash in full with your order, we, of course, agreeing to return your money if you are not perfectly satisfied in every respect.

No. 37C433 Size, 9x12 feet. Price..$14.95

Our Special Extraordinary Bargain in our One-Seam 9x12 Nine-Wire Tapestry Brussels Rug at $13.80.

NOTHING IN OUR CARPET department can equal this for value at our price. These rugs are made with but one seam and have a very handsome border 18 inches deep. These rugs come in handsome colorings of red, green, blue, tan and oak effects. The designs are all new, up to date and range from small, neat designs to the medium or large floral or scroll effects, also with medallion centers. We send these rugs on the same conditions and propositions as our other rugs. If you want an extra fine, beautiful, up to date, new style tapestry Brussels rug, a rug that will be most serviceable as well as a splendid ornament in the room, a quality that sells in retail carpet houses at prices ranging from $17.00 to $20.00, send us your order for this splendid 9x12 9-wire tapestry brussels rug at $13.80, and we guarantee that you will be more than pleased with your purchase. If you desire, the rug will be shipped on receipt of only $1.00 deposit, balance payable C. O. D., but we suggest that you send the full amount of cash with your order and thus save the small extra charge of 25 to 50 cents the express companies always ask on C. O. D. shipments.

No. 37C437 Size, 9x12 feet. Price..$13.80

Our New Extraordinary High Grade English Wilton Rugs.

WE HAVE added this grand quality of English Wilton Rugs to our collection of rugs, and we can positively say that this is absolutely the best English Wilton rug on the market. It has a very close deep pile, has a velvet surface effect and the pattern is entirely new. The accompanying illustration shows the handsome design in which we are presenting this special extraordinary quality of English Wilton rug. We have in this style rug four sizes only. The colorings are tan, red, green and blue, the combination in colors harmonizing perfectly. **This rug is shown in actual colors in our free Special Carpet Catalogue, sent on request.**

In order to appreciate this rug it is necessary for you to see it. We know that one of these rugs sold in a neighborhood will be the means of selling hundreds. This is a rug that will retail for more than double our price in city carpet stores. We have these rugs made up especially for us. **We claim for them that they are better English Wilton rugs than are shown by any other house.**

No. 37C441 Size, 27x54 inches. Price........ $3.25
No. 37C445 Size, 36x63 inches. Price........ 5.00
No. 37C449 Size, 8 feet 3 inches by 10 feet 6 inches. Price........ 29.95
No. 37C453 Size, 9x12 feet. Price........ 33.95

Our New 9x12 Special Extraordinary High Grade Axminster Rugs at $21.25 Each.

THIS HANDSOME, Deep, Rich Pile Axminster Rug is one of the newest in style and best in quality; richer in handsome colorings than anything we have added to our line this season. This rug is actually worth double the price we ask for it. It would be impossible for us to offer anything more beautiful in design or harmonious in colorings. The illustration accompanying this description gives a good idea of the design in which this rug comes. We furnish this rug in medallions and oriental styles. It comes in harmonizing colorings of greens, tans or reds.

This rug is shown in actual colors in our free Special Carpet Catalogue, sent on request.

We know that rugs of inferior pattern and quality are being sold in high class stores at $50.00 each and more. When ordering other goods do not forget to include one or more of these handsome rugs, and when they are received if they are not entirely satisfactory in every way and you do not find them equal in every way to rugs that are sold for twice our price, you can return them to us and we will refund your money.

No. 37C457 Size, 9x12 feet. Price........ $21.25

DEPARTMENT OF CHINA MATTINGS.

16c per Yard for 36-inch Goods.

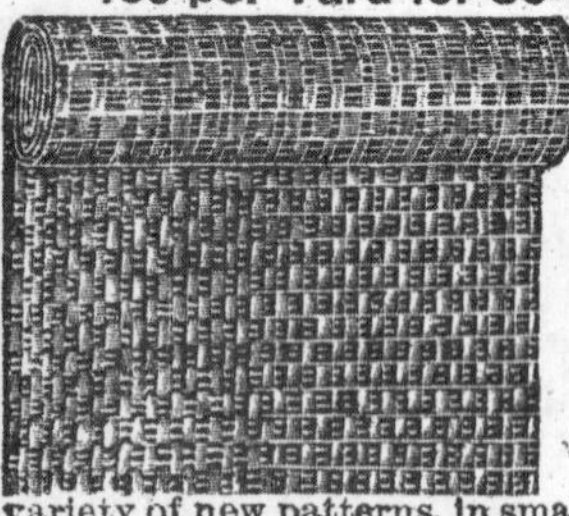

16 cents per yard buys this 36-inch goods, our new, good weight, firmly woven, jointless imported, genuine Chinese Fancy Matting. By the illustration we merely intend to give you an idea of the pattern in which we can furnish these goods. They come in a variety of new patterns, in small, medium and large designs; in a variety of colorings, including green, red or blue. Width, 36 inches.

No. 37C465 Price, per yard........ $0.16
Per roll of 40 yards........ 5.90

Our Special 19-Cent China Matting.

19 cents buys our new imported Canton, China, extra weight, closely woven fancy pattern 36-inch wide matting. The illustration will merely give you an idea of the pattern. These goods come in an endless variety of handsome, new patterns in small, medium and large designs in a variety of colorings, red, green or blue. Our 19-cent number is of extra quality, the equal of matting that sells generally at almost double the price. Our special price of 19 cents per yard barely covers the cost to us as direct importers, with our one small percentage of profit added.

No. 37C469 Width, 36 inches. Price, per yd. $0.19
Per roll of 40 yards........ 7.00

23 Cents Buys this Imported Matting.

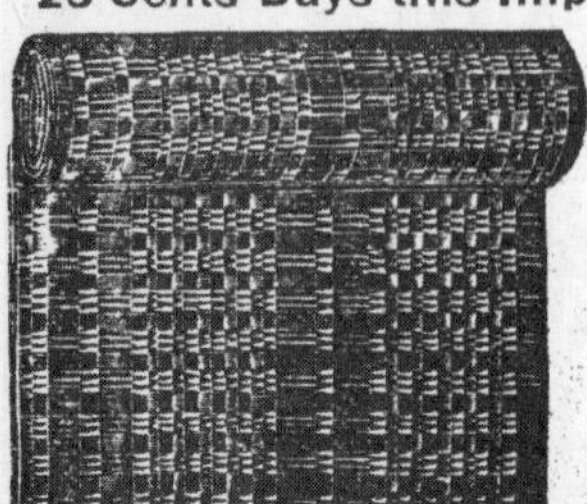

22 cents for this new, extra fine, heavy, firmly woven, genuine imported Chinese Matting. This matting we imported direct from Deacon & Co., Canton, China, a concern that has control of all the high grade Chinese mattings. You will find this matting we will furnish you at 23 cents per yard, the equal of mattings that sell generally at about double the price. The illustration merely gives you an idea of the pattern. These goods come in endless variety of patterns, in small, medium and large designs and a nice variety of colorings, including, red, green, blue or straw. A full roll would cost you only $8.40, and we always urge that our customers order in full rolls, but if you wish any particular length we will cut from the roll and fill your order for any quantity.

No. 37C473 Width, 36 inches. Price, per yd $0.23
Per roll of 40 yards........ 8.40

27 Cents per Yard for the Highest Grade Genuine China Matting.

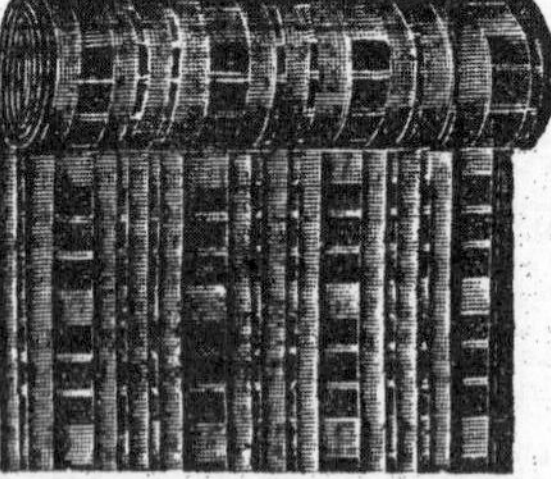

27 cents per yard buys the highest grade genuine imported Chinese Straw Matting we handle, the equal of any matting you can buy elsewhere at double the price. If you want the very finest imported Chinese matting, goods we import direct from Deacon & Co., at Canton, China, controllers of the highest grade fancy woven Chinese straw matting, a matting suitable for any room, for almost any purpose, matting that will give double the wear of any domestic matting, we especially recommend to you this, our highest grade matting. The illustration is shown only to give you an idea of the variety of patterns in which these are furnished. They come in an endless variety of handsome small patterns. We could not agree to furnish patterns exactly as illustrated, but always equally as desirable. The colorings include a large variety of red, blue or green. Remember our 27-cent price is the actual cost to us in China, transportation, duty, and our one small percentage of profit added.

No. 37C477 Width, 36 inches. Price, per yard........ $0.27
Per roll of 40 yards........ 10.00

ORDER ANY CARPET, MATTING, RUG or ART SQUARE FROM THIS DEPARTMENT, and if, when the goods are received, you are not more than pleased, if you and your friends don't say we have furnished you exceptional value for your money, you can return the goods to us and we will return your money and pay freight or express charges both ways.

SPECIAL VALUES IN FINE IMPORTED

FANCY WOVEN JAPANESE STRAW MATTING.

AT 21, 25 AND 27 CENTS PER YARD, for 36-inch width goods, we offer these fine imported Japanese mattings in competition with mattings that sell generally at about double the price.

WE ARE DIRECT IMPORTERS OF THESE GOODS. They come to us direct from the East Indies and from Kobe, Japan. We own them at the actual cost in Japan, duty and transportation charges, to which we add but our one small percentage of profit, and as a result you can buy these goods from us in any quantities at less than dealers can buy in ten-piece lots.

Special 21c Imported Japanese Matting.

This is a handsome, glossy finish, beautifully woven Japanese Straw Matting. Matting that will give excellent wear, the equal of matting that sells generally at about 50 cents per yard. The illustration is only shown to give you an idea of the pattern in which these mattings are furnished. The patterns vary somewhat. The colors are red, blue or green, interwoven with the straw color, the green, blue or red color predominating. These 36-inch mattings are suitable for all kinds of floor covering. They are used very largely in homes, hotels, for coverings for bedrooms, halls and other rooms and used almost exclusively in place of carpets in summer homes, summer hotels, etc. Width, 36 inches.

No. 37C481 Price, per yard........ $0.21
Per roll of 40 yards........ 7.80

Our Special 25-Cent Imported Matting.

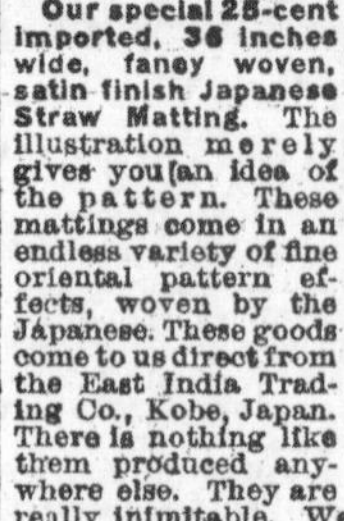

Our special 25-cent imported, 36 inches wide, fancy woven, satin finish Japanese Straw Matting. The illustration merely gives you an idea of the pattern. These mattings come in an endless variety of fine oriental pattern effects, woven by the Japanese. These goods come to us direct from the East India Trading Co., Kobe, Japan. There is nothing like them produced anywhere else. They are really inimitable. We own them at first cost and our price is less than dealers can buy in any quantity. For bedrooms, halls and other rooms, these coverings are becoming very popular. They are very much used in place of carpets. Comes in red, green or blue. Width, 36 inches.

No. 37C485 Price, per yard........ $0.25
Per roll of 40 yards........ 9.20

Our Fine 27-Cent Japanese Matting.

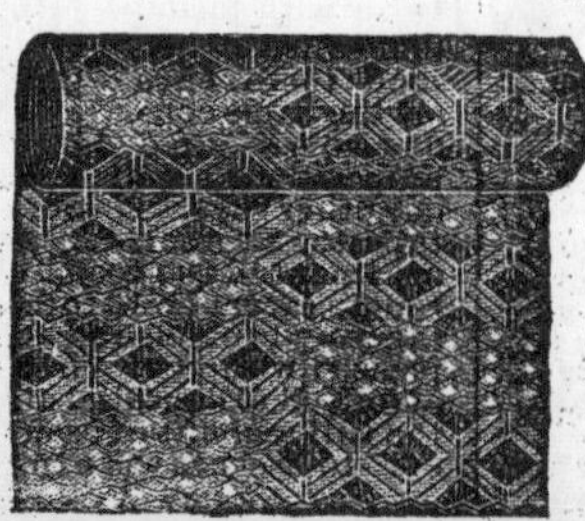

27 cents buys a heavy weight, extra closely woven, finely finished satin surface Imported Japanese Matting. This pattern merely gives you an idea of the big variety of patterns in which these mattings are furnished. This handsome, new cameo pattern is made of the finest warp, very smooth, of carefully selected straw, very closely woven, the highest grade matting made by the East India Trading Co. These goods come direct from Kobe, Japan, and you will find the matting equal to any matting you can buy elsewhere at double the price. Our special price of 27 cents barely covers the cost to us with but our one small percentage of profit added. These mattings come regularly in rolls of 40 yards and we prefer not to cut rolls and nearly all our customers order full rolls. However, if you desire, we will cut any length from the rolls that you wish at our special 27-cent price. Comes in red, green or blue. Width, 36 inches.

No. 37C489 Price, per yard........ $0.27
Price, per roll of 40 yards........ 10.00

Our Fine White or Light Tan Straw, Inlaid Figure Jap Matting at 27 Cents per Yard.

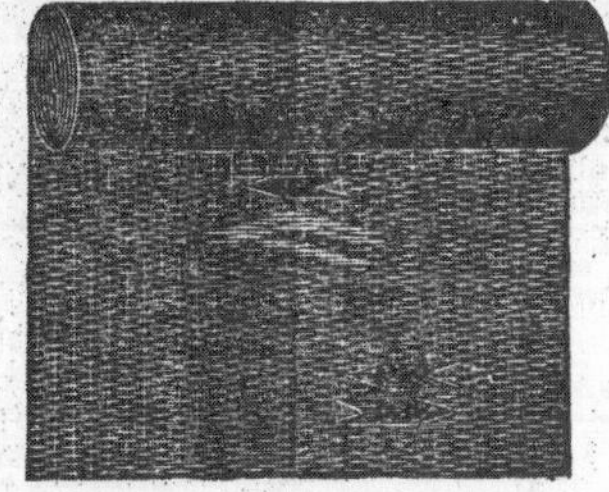

This is an extra quality of fine Japanese Matting, splendid weight, closely woven, fine finish, cotton warp matting, made of white straw (really light tan in color) with a small inlaid figure in red and green. This is a much better grade of matting than any we have ever before listed, entirely out of the ordinary, such a quality as would readily retail at 50 cents per yard. Our price of 27 cents per yard is based on our original first cost in largest quantities and is lower than retail dealers pay at wholesale. We highly recommend this number, and if you are looking for an especially good matting this is the one you want to buy. Width, 36 inches.

No. 37C493 Price, per yard.............. $ 0.27
Per roll of 40 yards.............. 10.00

Big Values in Napier or Rope Matting.

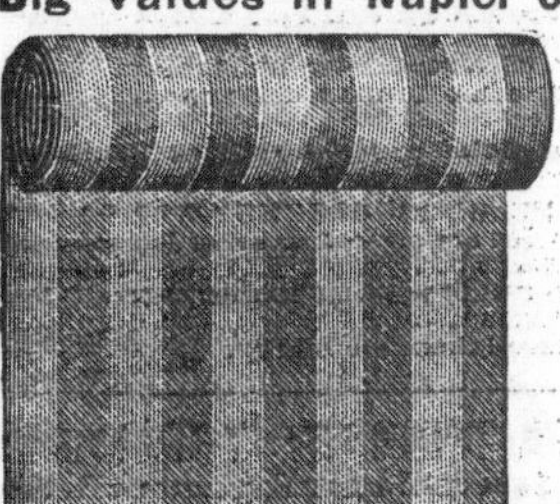

At from 12 to 35 cents per yard, according to width (widths running from 18 to 54 inches), we offer you these heavy genuine Napier or Rope Mattings in all the latest patterns and color designs, as the greatest values ever shown. From the illustration, engraved by our artist from a photograph, you can get some idea of the pattern furnished in our **12 to 35-cent Napier floor mattings.** They come in a variety of the latest stripes of narrow, medium and wide alternating. We can furnish it in red and tan stripes only. These mattings in the various widths are used almost exclusively for aisles in churches, halls and public buildings, in stores, schools, in halls and stairways in the home; many times used in place of carpets for bedrooms and other rooms, often used as rugs over carpets in muddy weather to protect the carpet. **Our prices of from 12 to 35 cents barely cover the cost to manufacture, with but our one small percentage of profit added.** We furnish this our special Napier matting in five different widths that we may be able to fit almost any aisle, and we especially recommend these goods for churches, and direct the attention of church committees to the exceptional values we have to offer in this line. These goods are extra heavy. They are firmly woven, heavy rope cord, they will give extra good wear, and are the equal of mattings that sell generally at about double the price.

No. 37C497 Width, 18 in. Price, per yard......12c
No. 37C501 Width, 27 in. Price, per yard......18c
No. 37C505 Width, 36 in. Price, per yard......25c
No. 37C509 Width, 45 in. Price, per yard......30c
No. 37C513 Width, 54 in. Price, per yard......35c

Extra Heavy, Genuine Imperial Napier Matting.

Extra Heavy, Double Woven, Genuine Imperial Napier Matting, the highest grade and heaviest weight made, at 18 to 50 cents per yard, according to width. From the illustration you can get an idea of the stripe pattern effect we furnish in our highest grade of Napier mattings. They come in stripes, small, medium and wide, and in colors of red and tan only. This is without doubt the most serviceable matting made, especially for public places, churches, halls, lodges, etc., a matting that can be subjected to far more than ordinary wear.

No. 37C517 Width, 18 in. Price, per yard......18c
No. 37C521 Width, 27 in. Price, per yard......25c
No. 37C525 Width, 36 in. Price, per yard......35c
No. 37C529 Width, 45 in. Price, per yard......42c
No. 37C533 Width, 54 in. Price, per yard......50c

Metal Ends.

We finish heavy napier or rope matting with metal ends at special prices when ordered. Illustration shows the style of this metal end.

No. 37C537 For 18-inch width.
Price, for each end.............. 12½c
No. 37C541 For 27-inch width.
Price, for each end.............. 19c
No. 37C545 For 36-inch width.
Price, for each end.............. 25c
No. 37C549 For 45-inch width.
Price, for each end.............. 32c
No. 37C553 For 54-inch width.
Price, for each end.............. 38c

FLOOR OILCLOTHS AND LINOLEUMS.

Our 25-Cent Fancy Floor Oilcloth.

Green figure on a tan background. For illustration, showing the exact coloring, write for our Free Carpet Catalogue. We offer this oilcloth at 25 cents per yard for 1 yard wide, 38 cents for 1½ yards wide, or 50 cents for 2 yards wide, **as one of the strongest floor oilcloths procurable and at this price it is a wonder of cheapness.** It is very low in price but the quality will prove to be extraordinary. We have enlarged our oilcloth and linoleum department to such an extent and the sales have been increased so that we can handle these goods in such enormous quantities that we are enabled to make a price very much lower than any competition. We have cut the cost to a minimum; in fact, to the exact cost to manufacture and our one small profit added.

Width, yards	1	1½	2
No. 37C557 Price, per yard	25c	38c	50c

Our New Mendoza Heavy Floor Oilcloth.

White and green body effect. For color illustration showing the exact coloring of this pattern write for our free Carpet Catalogue. We have reproduced in this, our extra quality of floor oilcloth, the patterns of some of the most expensive floor oilcloths imported, cloths that sell at double the price at which we offer this oilcloth, and we have effected in this our 27-cent oilcloth all the weight, pattern effect and lustrous coloring which you will get in the high grade of goods. We guarantee the wear of this floor oilcloth.

Width, yards	1	1½	2
No. 37C561 Price, per yard	27c	40c	54c

Our Handsome Medallion Pattern Oilcloth.

The accompanying illustration shows our very best grade of oilcloth. **This beautiful pattern, in tan ground, red, white and yellow figure, has an extra lustrous finish and is equal to the fancy imported oilcloth that sells at double the price.** In our free Carpet Catalogue you can see this pattern in the extra colors in which we have produced it, by the new photographic color process. We have effected in this grade the heaviest and best and most wear resisting floor oilcloths that it is possible to produce. We guarantee them in every respect. If you send us your order for this class of goods in any of our grades and if it does not prove thoroughly satisfactory when received you may return them to us at our expense and we will refund your money.

Width, yards	1	1¼	1½	2	2½
No. 37C565 Price, per yard	29c	36c	44c	58c	73c

Our New Small Floral Design Linoleum.

At $1.00, $1.25 and $2.50 per yard, according to width, we offer this handsome pattern in a green background, with a red and white figure. We guarantee this to be the genuine imported Scotch linoleum. We have made a contract with one of the largest manufacturers of this class of goods in the world and import it direct in large quantities. For quality and beautiful color effect these goods cannot be surpassed. For illustration showing the exact colorings and pattern in which this linoleum comes, write for our Free Carpet Catalogue.

Width, yards	2	2½	4
No. 37C569 Price, per yard	$1.00	$1.25	$2.50

Our New Extra Heavy Linoleum at $1.00 to $2.50 per Yard, According to Width.

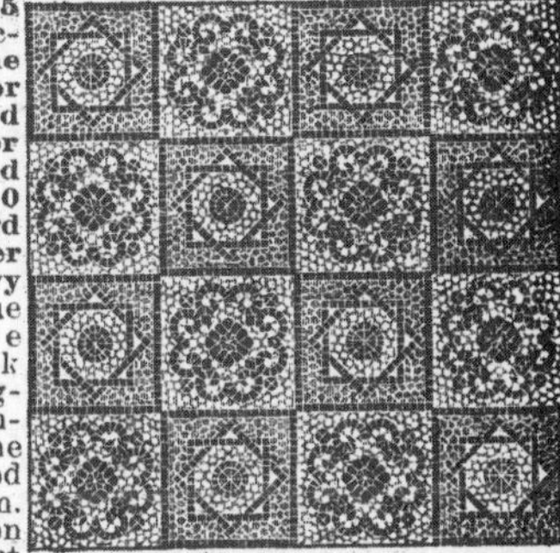

At $1.00, $1.25 and $2.50, according to the width, $1.00 for the 2-yard width, $1.25 for the 2½-yard width, and $2.50 for the 4-yard width, we offer this extra heavy linoleum. Blue and white ground, black and yellow figure. We guarantee this to be the genuine imported Scotch linoleum. For illustration showing the exact color effect and pattern as reproduced by the new photographic color process, write for our Free Carpet Catalogue.

Width, yards	2	2½	4
No. 37C573 Price, per yard	$1.00	$1.25	$2.50

This Up to Date Pattern in Heavy Linoleum is a Leader With Us for this Season.

Our extra heavy high grade linoleum should not be compared with the ordinary cheap American makes, as we guarantee this to be the genuine imported linoleum. Brown ground, green, red and yellow figure. For color plate showing the exact pattern and color combination effect in this high grade linoleum, write for our Free Carpet Catalogue.

Width, yards	2	2½	4
No. 37C577 Price, per yard	$1.00	$1.25	$2.50

Our Extra Quality $1.30 to $2.80 Heavy Linoleum.

New and Exclusive Patterns.

Our new, double weight, special quality of linoleum comes in 2½ and 4-yard widths. This is a linoleum heavier and better than anything we have ever shown before. White ground, light green and red figure. It is double the weight of ordinary linoleums, and made for us under special contract. For the pattern and colors in which this extra heavy linoleum comes, write for our Free Carpet Catalogue. It is reproduced by the new photographic process and is an exact copy of the original.

Width, yards....	2	2½	4
No. 37C581 Price, per yard	$1.30	$1.70	$2.80

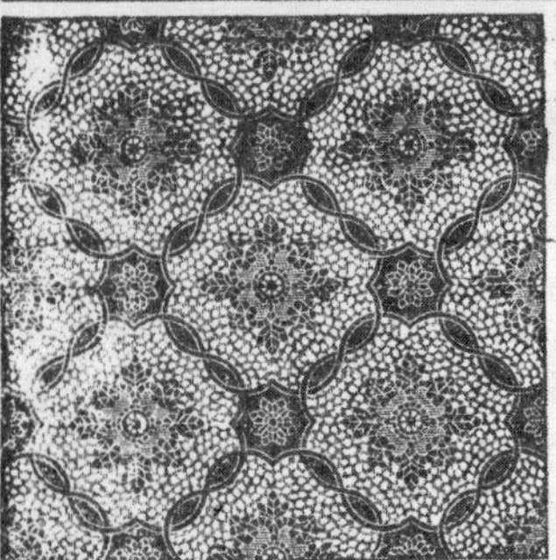

Our Best Quality of Linoleum at $1.30 to $2.80 per Yard.

The accompanying illustration shows the pattern of another of our double weight new linoleums and goods which we sell at less than one-half the price that you would be compelled to pay elsewhere. Comes in light gray ground, blue figure and dark scroll circle. For color illustration, showing pattern and color effects of this, one of our most handsome and reliable patterns of linoleum, write for our Free Carpet Catalogue.

No. 37C585

Width, yards	2	2½	4
Price, per yard	$1.30	$1.70	$2.80

Our Heavy Double Weight New Style Linoleum.

Gray Ground, with Yellow Scroll, Red, Green and White Flowers.

Write for our Free Carpet Catalogue, showing the exact colorings of the accompanying black and white illustration of our extra heavy, double weight linoleum. This is a pattern entirely new. Our extra heavy, double weight linoleum is made under our linoleum buyer's instructions as regards patterns, colors and weight, and we guarantee them as being uniform and the grade always kept up. We warrant them to wear.

No. 37C589 Width, yds.	2	2½	4
Price, per yard	$1.30	$1.70	$2.80

THREE NEW STYLES OF HANDSOME IMPORTED INLAID LINOLEUM.

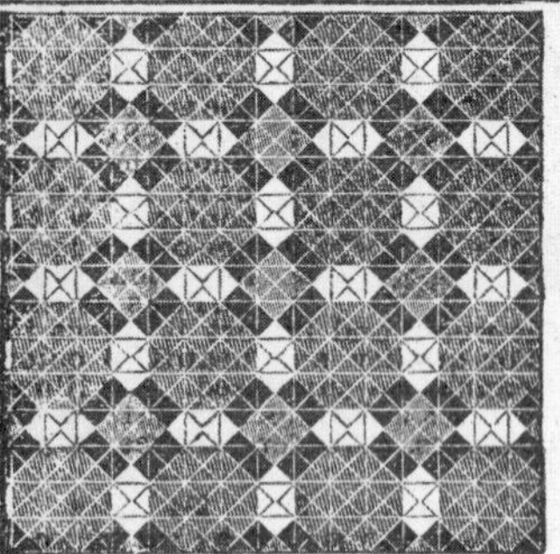

No. 37C597 Dark red ground, brown and yellow inlaid. Price, per running yard, 2 yards wide $2.58

No. 37C601 Green and white. Price, per running yard, 2 yards wide.... $2.58

No. 37C605 Same pattern as above, only blue and white. Price, per running yard, 2 yards wide.... $2.58

No. 37C609 Red and blue inlaid on light yellow ground. Price, per running yard, 2 yards wide $2.58

OUR THREE HANDSOME STYLES OF INLAID LINOLEUM, illustrated opposite. These goods can be seen in the original colors, just exactly as they will appear on your floor, by writing for our Special Carpet Catalogue, where the colors are reproduced by the new photographic color process. It is unnecessary for us to go into details with regard to these handsome linoleums. Inlaid linoleums are used extensively in the largest hotels, big billiard rooms, and public rooms generally. They are goods that are absolutely perfectly made, goods made under our contract and under the supervision of our expert linoleum and oilcloth buyer. They are goods that will wear clear through to the floor without losing the luster or color; in fact, they are almost indestructible. The three styles which we have selected we consider the newest and best things that are shown in these new, handsome, popular goods. They come 2 yards wide. The diamond pattern (center illustration) inlaid marble effect linoleum, comes in blue and white as well as green and white.

Our Free Special Carpet Catalogue show these linoleums in their actual colors.

OUR NEW HANDSOME INLAID LINOLEUMS AT $2.58 PER RUNNING YARD, 2 yards wide are offered by us as the greatest values ever shown in high grade linoleums. They are the equal of what dealers generally sell at 50 per cent higher price. They are the newest styles for this season, have a heavy, deep, surface and we cannot recommend them too highly.

OUR NEW DEPARTMENT OF RUBBER MATS, STAIR TREADS AND CORRUGATED BEST HEAVY RUBBER MATTING BY THE YARD.

We have formed a combination with one of the biggest of rubber concerns in the United States, and we have such a favorable arrangement with them that it will be possible for us to beat any competition prices on these goods.

Cocoa Door Mats.

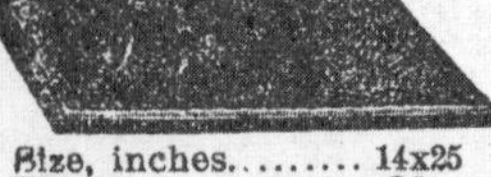

No. 37C613 The Very Best Cocoa Door Mats, in the following sizes:

Size, inches	14x25	16x27	18x30	20x33
Price	32c	39c	53c	75c

Our Very Heavy, Peerless, Reversible Cocoa Matting.

This is positively the best matting made. It is very heavy and durable for church aisles, halls and any floor subject to wear. Comes in following widths:

No. 37C617 Width, 18 inches. Price, per yard..20c
No. 37C621 Width, 27 inches. Price, per yard..30c
No. 37C625 Width, 36 inches. Price, per yard..40c
No. 37C629 Width, 45 inches. Price, per yard..50c
No. 37C633 Width, 54 inches. Price, per yard..60c

A roll of same contains about 70 to 72 running yards. Price for a full roll will be 3 cents per square yard less.

Our Fancy Corrugated Stair Treads.

This is a good, heavy, hard rubber tread with a very fancy corrugated surface in little figures, square and fancy geometrical styles.

No. 37C637 Size, 6x18 inches. Price.......... 23c
No. 37C641 Size, 7x24 inches. Price.......... 30c

Our Fancy Diamond Stair Treads.

These are heavier rubber than the first number quoted, and come in fancy effects only.

No. 37C645 Size, 6x18 inches. Price.......... 29c
No. 37C649 Size, 7x24 inches. Price.......... 39c

Our Corrugated Heavy Rubber Matting.

No. 37C653 This is a very heavy corrugated matting, comes 36 inches wide, 8 pounds to the yard, and is one of the most durable mattings ever shown on the market. Our price is fully one-half less than the lowest price quoted by dealers. Width, 36 inches. Price, per yard.......... 98c

Rubber Door Mats.

The accompanying illustration will give you an idea of the style of these mats. They come in extraordinary heavy rubber, are thick and durable.

No. 37C661 Size, 17x30 inches, heavy rubber door mats without scraper. Price.......... 89c

OUR NEW DEPARTMENT OF WIRE DOOR MATS.

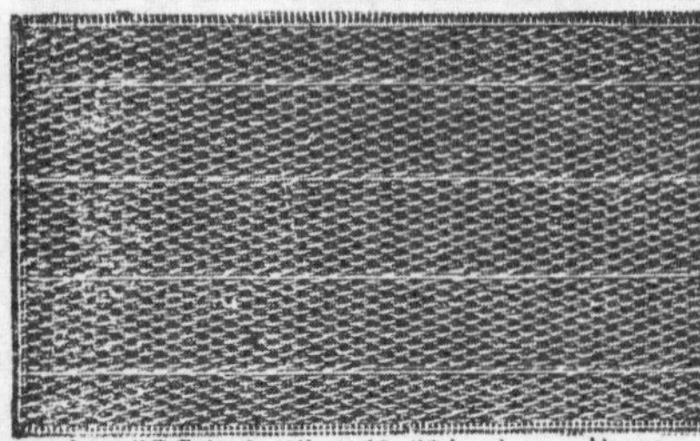

We use nothing but the strongest steel wire mats, made by the best steel manufacturer in the United States. They are made solid by cross pieces which hold them perfectly in shape. They are guaranteed to keep in perfect shape under any use. They are made of hard, galvanized steel wire and are the most strong and durable rigid frame mats on the market.

No. 37C665 Size, 16x24 inches. Price.......... $0.59
No. 37C669 Size, 18x30 inches. Price.......... .79
No. 37C673 Size, 22x36 inches. Price.......... 1.25

OUR EXTRA HEAVY FLEXIBLE STEEL MAT.

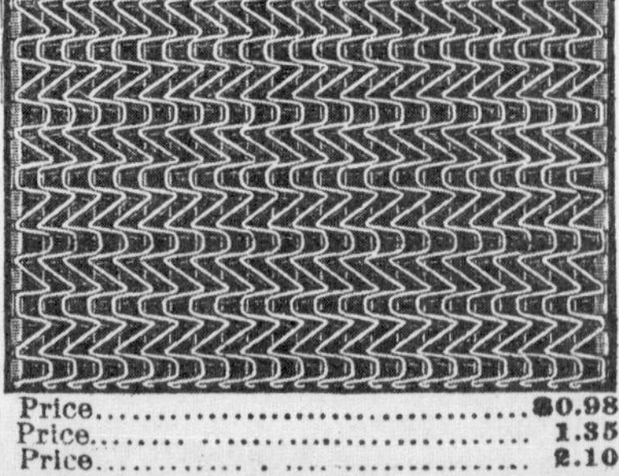

This mat can be seen in the city buildings, in street cars, elevators, barrooms and for halls and at thresholds in the finest residences. It is a smoothly made steel mat that will not scratch or injure the finest hard wood or marble floor. We keep a stock of popular sizes, as 16x24, 18x30 and 24x36 inches. However, we can furnish this mat in any size required on request. When wanting special sizes, always be sure to give us the correct measurements and we will make prompt shipment of same.

No. 37C677 Size, 16x24 inches. Price.......... $0.98
No. 37C681 Size, 18x30 inches. Price.......... 1.35
No. 37C685 Size, 24x36 inches. Price.......... 2.10

WE GUARANTEE SATISFACTION

In every transaction or Refund Your Money.

METALLIC OILCLOTH BINDING.

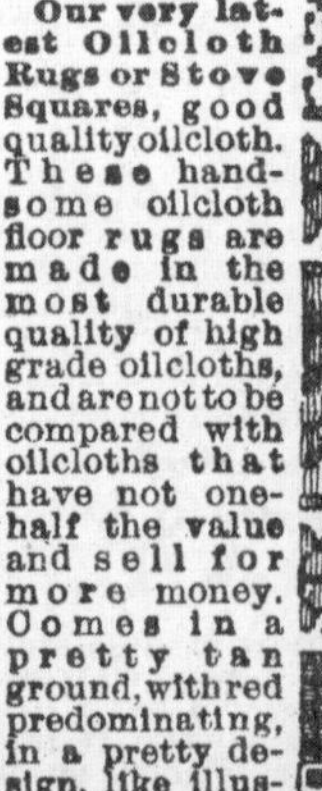

No. 37C697 Brass Oilcloth Binding to ornament, protect and fasten down the edges of oilcloth stove squares. Sold only in sets, complete with corners and tacks, as follows:

Set of 4 yards, weight, 4 ounces.......... 9c
Set of 5 yards, weight, 5 ounces.......... 12c
Set of 6 yards, weight, 6 ounces.......... 14c
Set of 8 yards, weight, 8 ounces.......... 18c

No. 37C701 Zinc Oilcloth Binding, put up in sets, same as above.

Set of 4 yards, weight, 4 ounces.......... 5c
Set of 5 yards, weight, 5 ounces.......... 6c
Set of 6 yards, weight, 6 ounces.......... 7c
Set of 8 yards, weight, 8 ounces.......... 10c

OILCLOTH RUGS.

Our very latest Oilcloth Rugs or Stove Squares, good quality oilcloth. These handsome oilcloth floor rugs are made in the most durable quality of high grade oilcloths, and are not to be compared with oilcloths that have not one-half the value and sell for more money. Comes in a pretty tan ground, with red predominating, in a pretty design, like illustration.

No. 37C689 1¼ yards square. Price.......... $0.75
No. 37C693 2 yards square. Price.......... 1.25

NOTE OUR LOW PRICES ON WINDOW SHADES.

IN ORDERING WINDOW SHADES an allowance of about 6 inches must be made from lengths quoted. Shades quoted size 3x6 feet are cut 6 feet long before they are mounted. The hemming and mounting take up about 6 inches. The 6-foot mounted shade will, therefore, measure but 5½ feet; the 7-foot shades will measure about 6½ feet. All of our shades are mounted and ready to hang; we do not sell them any other way.

THREE FEET WIDE is the regular stock size of window shades. Any shades narrower than three feet or wider than three feet will have to be made to order expressly, therefore costing more in proportion. **We require cash in full with orders for special made shades.**

OUR GUARANTEE FOR QUALITY. These goods come to us direct from two of the largest makers in this country. Every piece in this department is guaranteed to us by the manufacturer as to quality of material, workmanship and finish, and the same guarantee goes to you from us.

PRICES QUOTED include brackets and slats. Shade pulls, cords, etc., are extra and can be selected from our quotations in another column.

LETTERING. The price for lettering window shades with gold letters is 40 cents per running foot. Shade cloth 48 inches and wider is made of a heavy fabric and will not always exactly match colors in narrower and cheaper cloth.

IMPORTANT NOTICE. THE LENGTHS QUOTED ON WINDOW SHADES ARE MANUFACTURERS' MEASUREMENTS.

Plain Opaque Window Shades.

No. 37C705 Plain Water Color Opaque Window Shades. Mounted on patent spring rollers. Made plain without fringe or dado. Colors: Light olive, pea green, terra cotta, dark green, light buff, dark olive, slate or white. **Always state color desired.** Size, 3x6 feet (manufacturers' measurement). Price.......22c

No. 37C709 Plain Water Color Opaque Window Shades, same as above, but cut down less than 3 feet wide. Price.......27c

No. 37C713 Plain Opaque Shades, same quality and colors as above. Size, 3x7 feet (manufacturers' measurement). Price.......25c

No. 37C717 Same as No. 37C713, cut down, less than 3 feet wide. Price.......30c

No. 37C721 Plain Water Color Opaque Window Shades. Exact same quality as above. Size, 3x8 feet. Price.......35c

Fringed Window Shades.

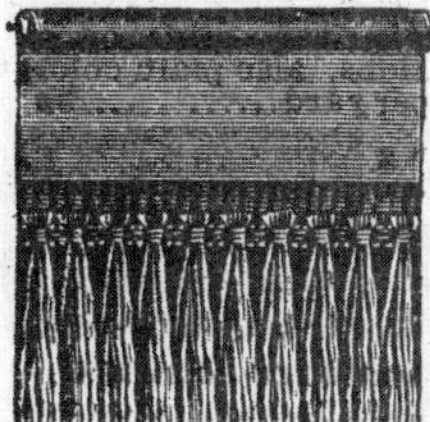

No. 37C725 Fringed Water Color Opaque Window Shades, with very handsome 3¼-inch fringe at bottom. Mounted on patent spring rollers. Colors same as No. 37C705. Size, 3x6 feet (manufacturers' measurement). Price...30c

No. 37C729 Fringed Water Color Opaque Window Shades, same quality as above, but cut down to less than 3 feet wide. Price.......35c

No. 37C733 Fringed Water Color Opaque Window Shades. Same quality as No. 37C725, but 7 feet long. Price.......35c

No. 37C737 Fringed Water Color Opaque Window Shades. Same as No. 37C733, but cut down to less than 3 feet wide. Price.......40c

No. 37C741 Fringed Opaque Window Shades. Same as No. 37C733, but size 3x8 feet. Price.......40c

All Window Shades from Nos. 37C705 to 37C741 inclusive are not made wider than 3 feet.

Best Quality Window Shades.

No. 37C745 Plain Opaque Shades. Made from very best grade oil opaque, and mounted on patent spring rollers. Plain, without fringe or dado. Colors: same as No. 37C705. Size, 3x6 feet. Price.......35c

No. 37C749 Plain Opaque Shades, same as above, cut down to less than 3 feet wide. Price.......40c

No. 37C753 Plain Opaque Shades, same quality as No. 37C745, but 3x7 feet. Price.......40c

No. 37C757 Same as No. 37C753, but cut down to less than 3 feet wide. Price.......45c

No. 37C761 Plain Opaque Shades, same quality as No. 37C745, but 3x8 feet. Price.......45c

Following are prices on the above shades made to order in the following widths and 6 feet long:

No. 37C765 Over 36 inches wide up to 42 inches wide. Price.......$0.90
Over 42 inches wide up to 45 inches wide. Price, .95
Over 45 inches wide up to 48 inches wide. Price, 1.05
Over 48 inches wide up to 54 inches wide. Price, 1.30
Over 54 inches wide up to 63 inches wide. Price, 1.55

Above sizes in 7 and 8 feet long, at 10 cents each extra for the 7-foot and 20 cents extra for 8-foot.

Fringed Oil Opaque Shades.

No. 37C769 Fringed Oil Opaque Window Shades, made from best quality oil opaque cloth, same fringe as illustrated in our cheaper shades. Colors, same as No. 37C705. Size, 3x6 feet. Price.38c

No. 37C773 Same shade as No. 37C769, but cut down to less than 3 feet wide. Price.......42c

No. 37C777 Fringed Oil Opaque Window Shades, made from best quality oil opaque cloth, same fringe as in No. 37C725 shades. Colors same as No. 37C705. Size, 3x7 feet. Price.......50c

No. 37C781 Same as No. 37C777, but cut down to less than 3 feet wide. Price.......55c

No. 37C785 Fringed shades, No. 37C777, made to order in the following widths and 7 feet long:
Over 36 in. wide up to 42 in. wide. Price.......$1.10
Over 42 in. wide up to 45 in. wide. Price....... 1.15
Over 45 in. wide up to 48 in. wide. Price....... 1.25
Over 48 in. wide up to 54 in. wide. Price....... 1.50
Over 54 in. wide up to 63 in. wide. Price....... 2.05

Above sizes in 8 feet long at 10 cents each extra.

No. 37C789 Fringed Oil Opaque Window Shades, same as No. 37C777, but 8 feet long. Price.......55c

Lace Trimmed Window Shades.

GENUINE HAND MADE.

No. 37C793 Lace Trimmed Window Shades, made from very best quality oil opaque shade cloth, **mounted on patent spring rollers.** Beautiful lace edging on bottom, 4¼ inches deep. Colors, same as No. 37C705. Size, 3x6 feet (manufacturers' measurement). Price.....50c

No. 37C797 Lace Trimmed Window Shades, same as No. 37C793, but cut down to less than 3 feet wide. Price.......55c

No. 37C801 Lace Trimmed Window Shades, same as No. 37C793, but 7 feet long. Price.......55c

No. 37C805 Same exactly as No. 37C801, but cut down to less than 3 feet wide. Price.......60c

No. 37C809 Lace Trimmed Window Shades. Same quality as preceding numbers, but size 3x8 feet. Price.......60c

Following are same quality as No. 37C809, made to order in the following widths and 6 feet long:

No. 37C813 Over 36 inches wide up to 42 inches wide inclusive. Price.......$1.20
Over 42 inches wide up to 45 inches wide.. 1.25
Over 45 inches wide up to 48 inches wide...... 1.40
Over 48 inches wide up to 54 inches wide...... 1.65
Over 54 inches wide up to 63 inches wide...... 2.05

We can furnish the above sizes in shades 7 and 8 feet long, at 10 cents each extra for the 7-foot and 20 cents each extra for the 8-foot.

Lace and Insertion Window Shades.

GENUINE HAND MADE.

No. 37C817 Best Quality Oil Opaque Window Shades with lace and insertion as per illustration. One of the richest things to be had in shades; looks very rich. Colors, same as No. 37C705. Size, 3x6 feet. Price.......65c

No. 37C821 Same shade as No. 37C817, but cut down to less than 3 feet wide. Price...70c

No. 37C825 Same Shade as above, but size 3x7 feet. Price...70c

No. 37C829 Same as above, cut down to less than 3 feet wide. Price.......75c

No. 37C833 Lace and Insertion Shades, same quality as No. 37C817, but size 3x8 feet. Price..75c

No. 37C837 Same Shade as No. 37C833, cut down to less than 3 feet wide. Price.......95c

Following are prices on Best Oil Opaque Window Shades with lace and insertion, same quality as preceding numbers, made to order in the following widths and 6 feet long.

No. 37C841	Price
Over 36 inches wide, up to 42 inches wide.....	$1.45
Over 42 inches wide, up to 45 inches wide.....	1.55
Over 45 inches wide, up to 48 inches wide.....	1.70
Over 48 inches wide, up to 54 inches wide.....	2.00
Over 54 inches wide, up to 63 inches wide.....	2.45

We can furnish the above sizes in shades 7 and 8 feet long, at 10 cents each extra for the 7-foot and 20 cents each extra for the 8-foot.

SPECIAL SIZE MADE TO ORDER SHADES.

FOR STORES, OFFICES AND RESIDENCES. The following shades we make to order from the very best quality hand made oil painted opaque shade cloth. It usually requires about four days to have special size shades made to order. We require the full amount of cash with the order in every instance.

SHADES MADE TO SPECIAL ORDER CANNOT BE RETURNED IF SENT AS ORDERED.

COLORS—Special size shades are made only in the following colors: Dark green, olive, terra cotta, stone, pea green and light buff.

State whether width you desire is width of cloth or roller measure. Roller measure means from end to end of tips. We quote the width of cloth complete.

Lettering.

Price for lettering window shades with Shaded Gilt Lettering is 40 cents per running foot, EXTRA. Shade cloth, 48 inches and wider, is made of **heavier fabric and will not always exactly match colors of smaller shades.**

If the exact size you wish is not given in the following schedule, the next larger size will be charged, but the shade will be cut the exact size you order.

No. 37C845 Order by number, size and price.

Finished Length in feet	Width of Shades in Inches											
	38 in.	42 in.	45 in.	48 in.	54 in.	63 in.	72 in.	81 in.	90 in.	100 in.	104 in.	120 in.
4 ft.	$0.51	$0.80	$0.84	$0.94	$1.10	$1.37	$1.78	$2.14	$2.48	$2.86	$3.04	$ 6.16
5 ft.	.60	.90	.94	1.06	1.25	1.52	1.97	2.38	2.75	3.32	3.40	6.90
6 ft.	.67	1.00	1.05	1.19	1.40	1.71	2.17	2.60	3.02	3.50	3.78	7.63
7 ft.	.74	1.10	1.16	1.31	1.55	1.87	2.36	2.84	3.30	3.82	4.15	8.37
8 ft.	.81	1.20	1.27	1.44	1.69	2.04	2.56	3.07	3.58	4.15	4.54	9.11
9 ft.	.88	1.37	1.40	1.64	1.97	2.34	2.91	3.45	4.06	4.70	5.12	10.08
10 ft.	1.06	1.47	1.57	1.75	2.13	2.51	3.11	3.70	4.34	5.04	5.50	10.83
11 ft.	1.13	1.58	1.68	1.87	2.27	2.67	3.30	3.92	4.62	6.69	7.19	11.57
12 ft.	1.20	1.75	1.88	2.10	2.52	2.97	3.65	4.30	5.08	7.25	7.81	12.53
13 ft.	1.54	1.96	2.08	2.27	2.95	3.27	3.99	4.53	5.36	7.57	8.19	13.27
14 ft.	1.60	2.06	2.20	2.39	3.10	3.43	4.17	4.77	5.64	7.91	8.55	14.00
15 ft.	1.75	2.24	2.38	2.66	3.36	3.72	4.55	5.16	6.12	8.44	9.14	14.99

The Sans Gene Perfection Window Shade Adjuster.

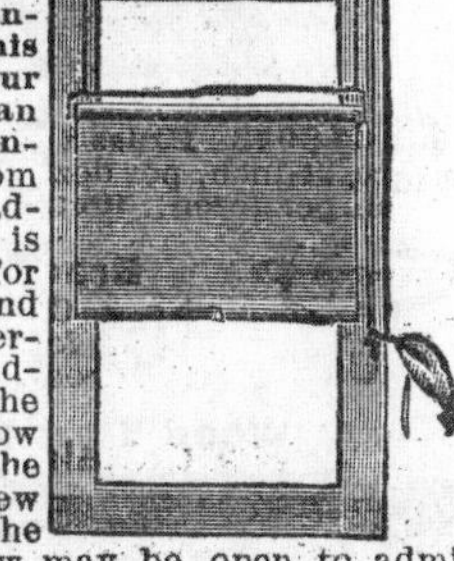

No. 37C849 The most simple and useful invention of the age. With this adjuster attached to your window shade you can shade any part of your window, either the top, bottom or the middle, without shading the balance of it. It is particularly adapted for bath rooms, bedrooms and toilet rooms. With the Perfection Window Shade Adjuster you can shade the lower part of your window so that the interior of the room is hidden from view from the outside, while the upper part of the window may be open to admit light, air, etc. **Can be adjusted to any shade in five minutes; can't get out of order; will last a lifetime.** Is so cheap that you can afford to have it on every window. Price.......14c

Shade Fringe.

No. 37C853 Extra Fine Quality Shade Fringe fancy knotted heading. Heavy and handsome. Width, 3¼ inches. Same pattern as used on shades No. 37C725 (see illustration). All staple colors. Price, per yard.......7c

Shade Lace.

No. 37C857 Very Handsome Shade Lace, same pattern and quality as used on No. 37C793 shades, as per illustration; all staple colors; new pattern. Width, 3¼ inches. Price, per yard.......15c

Shade Pulls.

No. 37C861 Ring Shade Pulls. Handsome silver and copper finish. Price.......5c

Shipping weight, 1 ounce each.

Spiral Bar Shade Pulls.

No. 37C865 Spiral Bar Shade Pulls with drop chains. Handsomely finished in silver effect. Price.......5c

No. 37C865

No. 37C869 Spiral Bar Shade Pulls. Same as above, with copper or gilt finish. Price.......5c

Vestibule Rods for Sash Curtains.

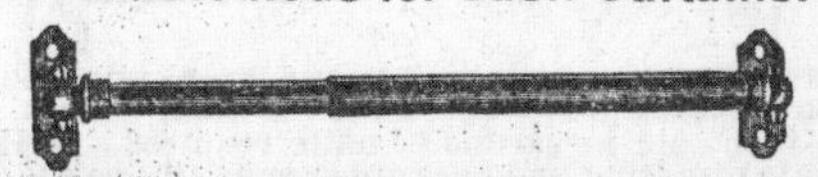

No. 37C873 Telescope Vestibule Rods. Made with brackets complete; can be adjusted inside or outside the rods; are made of two brass tubes, one sliding inside of the other, and will extend 24 to 44 inches. ⅜-inch rod. Price.......10c

Our Heavy Brass Telescope or Extension Rod, with Fancy Polished Brass Ends.

No. 37C877 This Rod is extremely durable and heavy, closed is 30 inches wide and can be extended to 54 inches. It comes with brackets complete. Price........12c

No. 37C881 Same rod as No. 37C877. Extends from 54 to 78 inches. Price, complete with brackets........17c

No. 37C885 Telescope Vestibule Rods. With pretty corrugated ball ends, as per illustration; a very fancy rod, complete with brackets. Will extend 28 to 54 inches. Price........15c

No. 37C889 Same rod as No. 37C885. Extends from 54 to 78 inches. Price, complete........20c

Our Brackets For 1½-Inch Brass or Wood Poles.

This is one of the most strongly made and durable brass brackets. They are used for extending the pole out from the window so that lace curtains may be hung from the window. They adjust 4 to 7 and 7 to 12 inches.

No. 37C893 Brackets, that adjust 4 to 7 inches. Price, per pair........13c

No. 37C897 Brackets, that adjust 7 to 12 inches. Price, per pair........16c

Brass Vestibule Curtain Rod Rings.

No. 37C901 This is one of the most serviceable brass rings on the market.

Size........	⅝ inch	½ inch	¾ inch	⅞ inch
Price, per doz.	8c	10c	12c	15c

No. 37C905 Fancy Telescope Vestibule Rods. Is made of heavy ½-inch brass tubing with fancy silver ends with brass band and tip like illustration, extends from 27 inches to 54 inches; complete with brackets. Price........25c

Stair Pads.

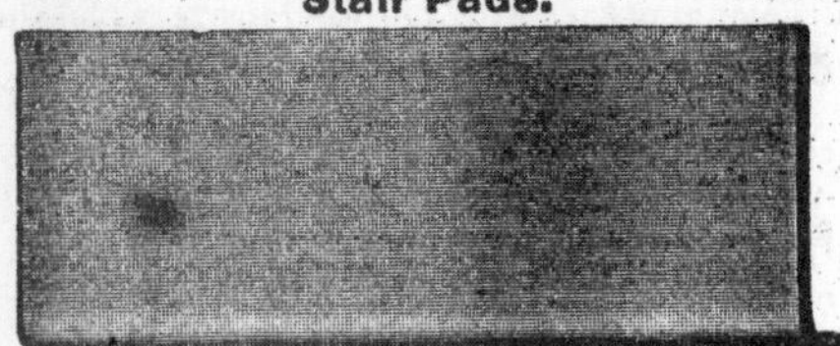

No. 37C909 Stair Pads, 22½ inches long. Price, per dozen........$1.20

Curtain Poles.

No. 37C913 Wood Trimmed Curtain Poles, 1⅜-inch, finished in California walnut, mahogany, oak or ebony. Price includes two turned wooden ends, two brackets for ends and sufficient quantity of rings for pole. **Don't fail to mention kind of finish wanted.**

Length	5 ft.	6 ft.	7 ft.	8 ft.	9 ft.
Price	25c	29c	32c	36c	40c

No. 37C917 Wood Pole Trimmings. Same as used with No. 37C913 poles. Price, per set........12c

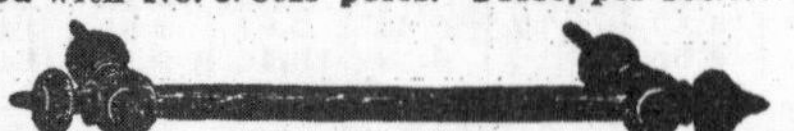

No. 37C921 Wood Curtain Poles, suitable for bedrooms or sash curtains, ¾-inch, finished antique oak only. Price includes brackets and ends. No rings included. Length, 4 feet. Price........10c
Length, 5 feet. Price........12c

No. 37C925 Brass Trimmed Curtain Poles, 1⅜-inch poles, finished in oak, mahogany, walnut or ebony, complete with two brass ends, two brass brackets and sufficient quantity of rings for pole.

Length	5 ft.	6 ft.	7 ft.	8 ft.	9 ft.
Price	19c	23c	26c	29c	32c

No. 37C929 Brass Pole Trimmings, same as used with No. 37C925 poles. Price, per set........13c

Curtain Poles and Sockets.

No. 37C933 Curtain Pole and Bracket or Socket, complete, as per illustration. A brass socket with 1⅜-inch pole, no screws or nails required. It fits on inside of casing and has rubber ends. Cut pole ¾-inch shorter than space between opening and attach brackets. Complete with poles.

Length	5 ft.	6 ft.	7 ft.	8 ft.	9 ft.
Price	22c	26c	29c	33c	36c

No. 37C937 Socket without pole. Price, pair........12c

White Enameled Curtain Poles.

No. 37C941 White Enameled Corrugated Cottage Curtain Pole. With fancy corrugated ball ends and also fancy rosette screws, as per illustration. This is the prettiest rod in the market and is sure to please. ¾-inch rod, 4 feet only. Complete with fixtures. Price........12c

Our New ¾-Inch Brass Curtain Poles at 29 Cents Each.

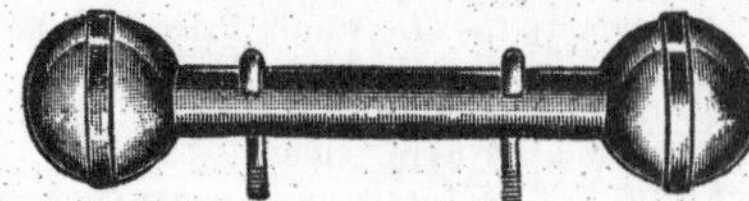

This is a very heavy brass pole with an elegant finish, and the heavy brass ends of this pole are 1½ inches in diameter. They come with brackets as per illustration. This is an entirely new pole and we consider it one of our most showy and serviceable poles. Size, ¾-inch pole, length, 4 feet.

No. 37C945 Price........29c

No. 37C949 Our Fancy White Enameled Pole, with silver end and polished gilt band and tip like illustration. The pole is ¾-inch and 4 feet long. Complete with trimmings. Price........20c

No. 37C953 Corrugated White Enameled Pole, 1⅜-inch in diameter. Complete with trimmings.

Length, feet........	4	5	6	7	8
Price	28c	32c	35c	39c	42c

Curtain Pole Trimmings.

No. 37C957 Corrugated Silver Ball Trimmings, with gilt tip, same as used with No. 37C953 poles, complete with brackets and rings. Per set....20c

No. 37C961 Our Fancy Pole Trimmings for 1⅜-inch pole like illustration, are finished in silver and have a polished brass band and tip. Complete with brackets and rings. Price, per set........25c

Stair Buttons.

No. 37C965 Stair Buttons, are 1⅜-inch in diameter and are finished in silver, copper or gilt. Price, per dozen........16c

Z Cut Brass Stair Corners.

No. 37C969 These corners prevent dust from accumulating in the corners of stairs where it is hard to sweep. It takes but one nail to fasten these corners. Price, per dozen...$0.15
Per gross........1.75

Brass Stair Rods.

No. 37C973 Brass Stair Rods. Price, 24-inch, per dozen........70c
26-inch, per dozen..80c; 30-inch, per dozen........95c

Brass Drapery Hooks.

No. 37C977 Like illustration. Price, for two dozen........5c
Per gross........25c

Wood Stair Rods.

No. 37C981

No. 37C981 Wood Stair Rods, acorn tip, finely finished. Come in antique oak only, in 27 and 30 inches long, with screws. Price........4c

Brass Tassel Hooks.

No. 37C985

No. 37C985 Nicely Polished. Price........5c

Three-Quarters Brass Plated Steel Rods.

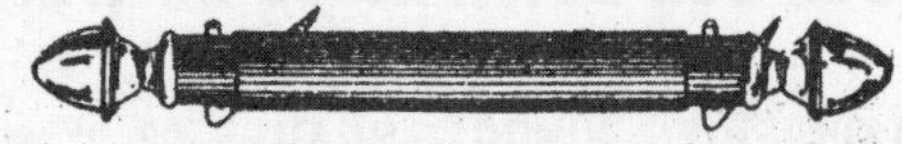

No. 37C989 Three-Quarters Brass Plated Steel Rods like accompanying illustration. They extend from 28 to 56 inches. This is a very solid rod and being brass plated on a steel foundation makes it a very permanent, strong rod for any drapery purposes. Price........28c

No. 37C993 The same rod as above, extends 56 to 80 inches. Price, each........35c

Picture Moulding Hooks.

No. 37C1001

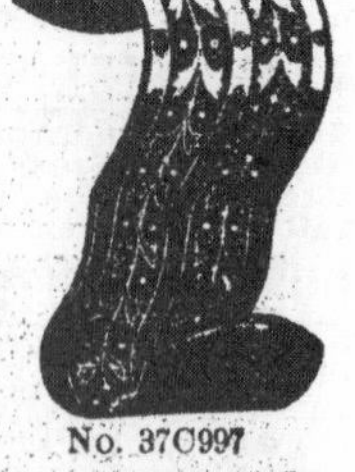

No. 37C997

No. 37C997 Brass Plate Picture Hooks. Price, per dozen........6c

No. 37C1001 This is the solid Brass Moulding Hook. Price, per dozen........15c

Rug Fasteners.

No. 37C1005 The New Patent Rug Fastener. Just the article to keep rugs and art squares fastened to the floor. Price, per dozen........30c

No. 37C1009 Picture Nails, with white porcelain heads, brass trimmed. Price, per dozen........10c

Curtain Loops, Etc.

No. 37C1013 A White Cotton Curtain Loop, cord and tassels. Price, per pair........8c

No. 37C1017 Curtain Loops, cord and tassels, to be used with tapestry curtains. Per pair..15c

No. 37C1021 Heavy Chenille Curtain Loops, cord and tassels. Price, per pair........19c

No. 37C1013

No. 37C1025 Brass Curtain Chain, a good strong chain usually sold for very much more money. Price, per pair........7c

No. 37C1025

No. 37C1029 Spiral Curtain Chains, pretty, strong and durable. Per pair..14c

No. 37C1033 Heavy Mercerized Curtain Loop, to match our mercerized portiere. Price, per pair........40c

Rug Fringes.

No. 37C1037 Wool Rug Fringe, with gimp heading 3 inches deep; tan, olive or red combinations, also plain colors. Price, per yard........6c

No. 37C1041 Knotted Rug Fringe, 4 inches wide, tan, olive or red, plain or combination. Price, per yard........11c

Furniture Fringe.

No. 37C1045 Cotton Furniture Fringe, heavy and durable. Comes in all combinations of colors to match furniture covering. A very pretty fringe for the money. Full width, 7 inches. Price, per yard........10c

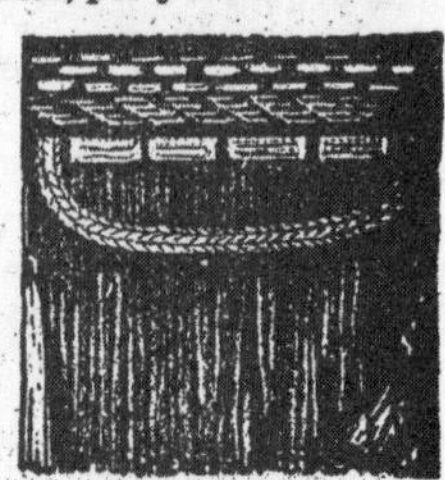

Worsted Furniture Fringe.

No. 37C1049 Comes in a very fancy heading and deep fringe, full width in combination of colors to match all furniture coverings. Full width, 7 inches. Price, per yard........15c

Our 20-Cent Heavy Furniture Fringe.

No. 37C1053 Extra High Grade Worsted Furniture Fringe, has beautiful heavy strands and tassels, with fancy deep heading on a good quality of fringe. We can furnish any combination of colors to match furniture coverings. Full width, 7 inches.

Price, per yard........20c

Hassocks and Foot Rests.

Children's Hassocks.

9x9 inches, 4 inches high. This serviceable and pretty little tapestry Brussels covered hassock, solidly made, is an ornament as well as a practical piece of furniture for any home.
No. 37C1057 Price........19c

No. 37C1061 Our Popular, Low Priced Hassock is 12 inches in diameter and 5½ inches high, covered with fine tapestry Brussels carpet. **Don't fail to order one of these comfortable and beautiful hassocks.**
Price.... ....39c
No. 37C1065 Same, covered with velvet or moquette carpet. Price.... .....59c

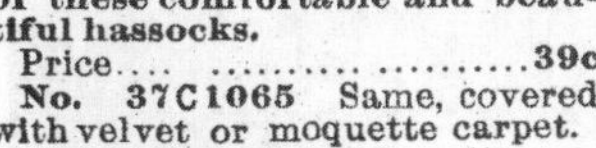

Our 49-Cent Hassock.

The illustration represents the choicest and most stylish original shape hassock in our collection. Size, 12x14 inches, 6 inches high. Covered with a good quality of Brussels carpet.
No. 37C1069 Price....49c

This illustration is exactly as the stool herein described will look. It made from a true photograph. It has wood frame with steel wire legs. It An ornament for any house. Covered with velvet. Size, 10x14 inches, inches high.
No. 37C1073 Price, 75c

The Star Hassock.

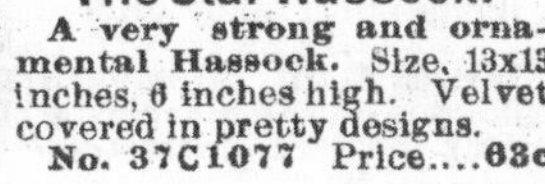

A very strong and ornamental Hassock. Size, 13x13 inches, 6 inches high. Velvet covered in pretty designs.
No. 37C1077 Price....63c

Something Entirely New in Parlor Ornaments.

Our Handsome Wicker Fancy Parlor Stool at $1.09 and $1.39.

This is the prettiest and most serviceable parlor stool to be used in parlors, libraries, children's rooms, in camping, tenting and for porches, lawns, etc. It is an ornament and a pretty house furnishing, good enough for the handsomest parlor or summer cottage. Top covered with satin printed velour, or with Wilton velvet carpet.

No. 37C1081

No. 37C1085

No. 37C1081 Size of top, 12 inches in diameter; height, 10 inches. Price..............$1.09
No. 37C1085 Size of top, 13½ inches in diameter; height, 14½ inches. Price............$1.39

The illustration gives a good idea of the handsome style of this durable and ornamental hassock. It is covered with a superior quality of Wilton velvet carpet. Size, 12x12 inches, 6½ inches high.
No. 37C1089 Price..... 75c

No. 37C1093 Our Octagon Ottoman Foot Rest. Comes 11x13 inches and 9¼ inches high. **This is a very beautiful home decoration.** It is something that should be in every parlor or sitting room. Covered with best tapestry carpet. Price.......63c
Covered with moquette or velvet carpet. No. 37C1097 Price........................75c

In ordering furniture, carpets, portieres or anything in these lines, **don't omit one of these beautiful ottomans.**

Special Extraordinary.

Extra Large Velvet Hassock. We are the originators of this grand sumptuous Oriental hassock. The design is exclusive with us. Size, 15x15 inches, 9 inches high.
No. 37C1101 Price, 85c

Our Great Bargain in Hassock and Slipper Box Combined.

No. 37C1105 This is strongly made and covered with the best tapestry or velvet carpet. Size, 9½x12½ inches and is 7 inches high. This is one of the most convenient, ornamental and comfortable foot rests that can be furnished.

The price makes it within the reach of all. This is certainly a great bargain and should be in every home. Don't fail to order one of these beautiful combination hassocks.
Price, each, covered with Brussels carpet....89c
No. 37C1109 Covered with velvet carpet. Price.......................98c

Our Parlor Stool or Foot Rests.

(Can also be used for children's low seats.)

No. 37C1113 These stools have wood frames, malleable iron legs, finished in gold bronze. They will certainly make an ornament for any house. They are covered with velvet carpet only, and the price is simply phenomenal, considering the value which we give you in one of these serviceable and convenient stools or foot rests. **Size, 11x11 inches, 7 inches high.** Price.......59c

Our Commode for Use in Bedrooms.

This is one of the most useful articles that could be in any house. Convenient for children or in case of sickness. **These commodes are made of fine imitation oak,** with a beautiful Brussels carpet covered top. Size, 15½ inches high and 14½ inches square. These commodes are something that should certainly be in every well regulated house. The convenience for one week would overcome the expense.
No. 37C1117 Price, each, without pan...$1.98
No. 37C1121 Price, with pan............ 2.48

OUR NEW CARPET AND RUG WEAVING MACHINERY AND ACCESSORIES.

OWING TO THE MANY INQUIRIES REGARDING THE PRICE of and the relative merits of carpet and rug machinery, we have this season inaugurated a department for this class of machinery and placed it in the hands of a competent expert in this line. We cannot afford space to adequately describe our steel frame fly shuttle carpet loom and the various parts and their prices but the following illustrations and brief descriptions will serve to present to your notice the loom and accessories, and upon application, if interested, we will give inside quotations on everything that goes with the machine described; also various parts that are not described or illustrated, or any information regarding this class of carpet machinery. We feel that in presenting our machine we are recommending the very best carpet weaving loom on the market. **Remember that upon application we will furnish any information that you may require regarding this thoroughly reliable carpet loom and weavers' supplies.**

OUR EXTRA STRONG, WELL MADE, STEEL FRAME FLY SHUTTLE CARPET LOOM.

This is acknowledged by carpet weavers generally to be the strongest and most durable loom on the market. We offer you this loom with the understanding that everything we claim for it will be substantiated, that we will send it to you on a guarantee that it is the strongest and best loom that is made. This loom, being almost entirely constructed of steel is practically indestructible. We are the originators of the steel frame looms, and ours is the only standard steel loom on the market today. It is better than looms that are quoted at more than double our price. We make this statement knowing exactly what we are talking about as we have had experience with looms that are sold at nearly double our price and that were not as good a loom. This loom is fully one-third stronger than any other loom on the market and has a wearing capacity unequaled. It weighs 400 pounds placed on the cars. A cast iron loom of equal strength would weigh from 200 to 300 pounds more. **A wood frame loom is not to be compared to it in any of its make up, and a light weight wrought iron frame loom is not worth buying.** Our price of $50.00 is based on the actual cost to manufacture with our one small profit added. These looms are made for us under contract in big lots. As we have such a large capacity it is possible for us to name this price. Ordinarily the loom should sell for $90.00. Practical carpet weavers cannot fail to see the strong points in this extra heavy well made, fly shuttle carpet loom. Included with this loom are all the new and modern improvements that are needed in weaving carpets and rugs, also full instructions for setting up and operating the loom. With this loom we send you one dozen shuttles, one warp reel, one spool rack, one reed, harness and heddles, and one shuttle filling machine. We feel satisfied that when one of these looms is sold in a neighborhood that a great many others will recognize its merits and will buy it.
No. 37C1125 Price, including accessories..............................$50.00

Our Hand Shuttle No. 1.

The accompanying illustration shows a perfect picture of our Hand Shuttle No. 1. This hand shuttle is made of three pieces. It is nearly two feet long, will hold one pound of filling and is, we believe, the best cheap hand shuttle on the market.
No. 37C1129 Price, per dozen..................50c

Our Hand Shuttle No 2.

This is a single chambered shuttle. Made out of a solid piece of hard maple wood and holds about three-quarters of a pound of filling. As the filling does not come in contact with the warp, it slips through as though it were greased.
No. 37C1133 Price, each..................25c

Spinning Wheel.

We take pleasure in submitting a beautiful spinning wheel with patent accelerating wheel head and cast steel spindle. This we consider a great addition to our weavers' supplies. The rim is 3 feet 10 inches in diameter.

No. 37C1137 Price, $4.90

Our Hand Carpet Bobbin Shuttle.

The accompanying illustration represents our hand carpet bobbin shuttle which is used very extensively. Some weavers use the bobbin shuttle. Some prefer a bobbin shuttle to put the binding in with. We furnish this hand shuttle as one of the best shuttles in the market. We charge $1.19, or a wholesale price, providing that this shuttle is ordered at the same time as the carpet loom. This shuttle is made of hard maple, is 13 inches long and well protected at sides, ends and bottom with wire and will last a lifetime.
No. 37C1141 Price........................$1.19

Our Heddles for Harness.

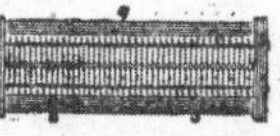

Our heddles for harness are 12 inches long and made of the best quality of bronzed No. 20 annealed steel wire, with special reference to heavy weaving, such as carpets, curtains, rugs, etc. Six hundred heddles are furnished with each harness.
No. 37C1145 Price, per pair.............$2.10
No. 37C1149 No. 20 annealed steel wire heddles, 12 inches long. Price, per hundred....16c

Weavers' Spools.

Our spools are of two sizes, like illustrations. The large size is nearly 2 inches in diameter, the small size is 1¼ inches in diameter. Both sizes are 6½ inches long and have a ¼-inch hole through them. Large size weaver's spools, 6½ inches long by 2 inches in diameter, hold about ¾ pound of warp.
No. 37C1153 Price, per dozen...............58c
Small spools, 6½ inches long by 1¼ inches in diameter.
No. 37C1157 Price, per dozen...............43c

Wool and Cotton Cards.

No. 37C1161 Wool Cards. Size, 9¼x4¼ inches.
Price, per pair.............$0.22
Per dozen pairs............ 2.33
No. 37C1165 Cotton Cards. Size, 10⅜x4⅜ inches.
Price, per pair...............$0.35
Per dozen pairs............. 3.80

Our Steel Carpet Reeds.

The accompanying illustration shows our steel carpet reeds. These reeds are very much heavier than the ordinary reeds in use, and are made with special reference to heavy weaving. They are 45 inches long and come with 9, 10, 11, 12, 13 and 14 dents to the inch. They weigh about 3½ pounds.
No. 37C1169 Price........................$1.25

OUR ENLARGED BLANKET DEPARTMENT.

WE HAVE ADDED LARGELY TO OUR POPULAR BLANKET DEPARTMENT for this season and although prices have advanced considerably we have by careful manipulation and early buying secured blankets so that we will be able to sell them at a big saving to our customers. We have several large blanket mills of which we control the output, and have reduced the cost to the very minimum. Our line of blankets includes all the popular grades from the lowest priced to the finest fleece wool blankets that are produced. We claim to be the largest distributors of blankets in the United States and this year we are prepared to double our sales of last year and feel confident that this will be accomplished. Our aim is to furnish blankets at less than any possible competitor. We have an expert blanket man who is thoroughly in touch with the manufacture and finish of blankets.

No. 37C1173 White or Gray Cotton Blankets. Gray, size, 50x72 inches. Price, per pair.........59c

No. 37C1177 White, size, 50x72 inches. Price, per pair.........59c

No. 37C1181 Our Special Extraordinary Value in White or Gray Blankets. Gray, size, 54x70 inches. Price, per pair.........69c

No. 37C1185 White, size, 54x70 inches. Price, per pair.........69c

No. 37C1189 Our Extra Quality White or Gray, with Fancy Colored Border Blankets. Gray, size, 62x76 inches. Price, per pair.........89c

No. 37C1193 White, size, 62x76 inches. Price, per pair.........89c

No. 37C1197 Our Special Extraordinary Value in Heavy Colored Bordered Blankets. Gray, size, 62x76 inches. Price, per pair.........$1.09

No. 37C1201 White, size, 62x76 inches. Price, per pair.........$1.09

No. 37C1205 Our Heavy Large Size White or Gray, Heavy Fleeced Blankets. Color, gray, size, 72x80 inches. Price, per pair.........$1.35

No. 37C1209 White, size, 72x80 inches. Price, per pair.........$1.35

No. 37C1213 Our Special Extraordinary Heavy, Extra Size Double Blanket. Gray, size, 70x78 inches. Price, per pair.........$1.48

No. 37C1217 Our Great Big Bargain in an All Pure Wool, Large Size, Perfectly Made Blanket. White, size, 63x76 inches. Price, per pair.........$3.19

No. 37C1221 Gray, size, 63x76 inches. Price, per pair.........$3.19

No. 37C1225 Scarlet, size, 63x76 inches. Price, per pair.........$3.19

No. 37C1229 Our Genuine All Wool, Fine Fleeced, Serviceable, Well Made Arctic, Full 5-pound Blankets. White, size, 70x80 inches. Price, per pair.........$3.98

No. 37C1233 Gray, size, 70x80 inches. Price, per pair.........$3.98

No. 37C1237 Scarlet, size, 70x80 inches. Price, per pair.........$3.98

No. 37C1241 Our Extra Heavy, Soft Wool Filled Finish, Fine Fleeced Blanket. White, size, 72x80 inches. Price, per pair.........$1.75

No. 37C1245 Our Extra Heavy, Soft Finish, Heavy Nap, Wool Filled Gray Blankets. Gray, size, 72x80 inches. Price, per pair.........$2.35

No. 37C1249 Our New, Especially Fine, Soft Fleeced, All Pure Wool Blankets. White, size, 70x80 inches. Price, per pair.........$4.98

No. 37C1253 Gray, size, 70x80 inches. Price, per pair.........$4.98

No. 37C1257 Scarlet, size, 70x80 inches. Price, per pair.........$4.98

No. 37C1261 Our Special Extra Value in a Large 11-4 Extra Heavy White Wool Blanket. Size, 72x80 inches. Price, per pair.........$3.15

No. 37C1265 Our Celebrated Lathrop, White Wool 11-4 Blankets. Size, 72x80 inches. Price, per pair.........$4.75

No. 37C1269 Our Extra Heavy Genuine California Fleeced Wool Blankets. White, size, 76x84 inches. Price, per pair.........$7.25

No. 37C1273 Gray, size, 76x84 inches. Price, per pair.........$7.25

No. 37C1277 Scarlet, size, 76x84 inches. Price, per pair.........$7.25

No. 37C1281 Our Special, Extraordinary, Pure Wool, Extra Size Blankets in White or Scarlet. White, size, 72x84 inches. Price, per pair.........$8.75

No. 37C1285 Gray, size, 72x84 inches. Price, per pair.........$8.75

No. 37C1289 Scarlet, size, 72x84 inches. Price, per pair.........$8.75

No. 37C1293 Our Luxurious, Extra Large, Finest, All Pure Wool, 7-pound Blankets. Size, 78x84 inches. Price, per pair.........$12.50

No. 37C1297 Our Celebrated, Heavy Jack Frost Wool Blankets. Size, 70x80 inches. Per pair...$2.98

No. 37C1301 Our Extra Heavy Blue Gray Klondyke Wool Camping Blanket. Size, 66x80 inches. Color, dark blue gray. Price, per pair.........$3.98

No. 37C1305 Our Great Big Scarlet Camping Blanket. Size, 70x82 inches. Price, per pair...$4.98

No. 37C1309 Our 10-pound, Dark Blue, Klondyke Camping Blanket. Size, 62x82 inches. Price, per pair.........$6.00

No. 37C1313 Regulation United States Army Blankets. Size, 66x82 inches. Color, silver gray with black border. Price, per pair.........$6.95

No. 37C1317 Our Especially Fine All Wool, Fleeced, Handsome Colored Border Blankets. White, size, 76x88 inches. Price, per pair.........$9.98

No. 37C1321 Gray, size, 76x88 inches. Price, per pair.........$9.98

No. 37C1325 Scarlet, size, 76x88 inches. Price, per pair.........$9.98

Fancy All Wool Plaid Blankets.

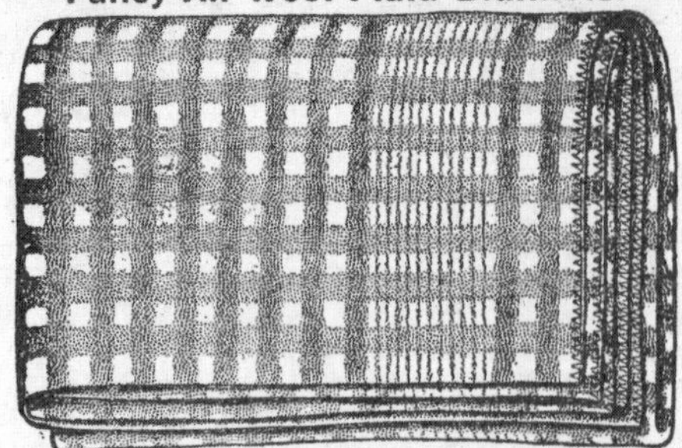

The accompanying illustration will give you some idea of the pattern of the plaids in which these heavy, all wool blankets come. We have them in a very handsome assortment and combination of colorings, including black and red, gray and black, green and white, pink and blue, and green, pink and white. These blankets are extra large size, 70 x 80 inches, and weigh fully five pounds to the pair. These are made at our mill at Louisville, Kentucky, and of the very finest of selected, perfectly scoured, clean wool. We guarantee them not to shrink. They are extra well finished and are equal to a great many plaid blankets in the market that sell as high as $10.00.

No. 37C1329 Size, 70x80 in. Price, per pair, $4.69

Our Extra Heavy Finest All Wool Fleeced Plaid Blankets at $6.98 per Pair.

Such blankets cannot be equaled in retail dry goods stores for less than $10.00 per pair.

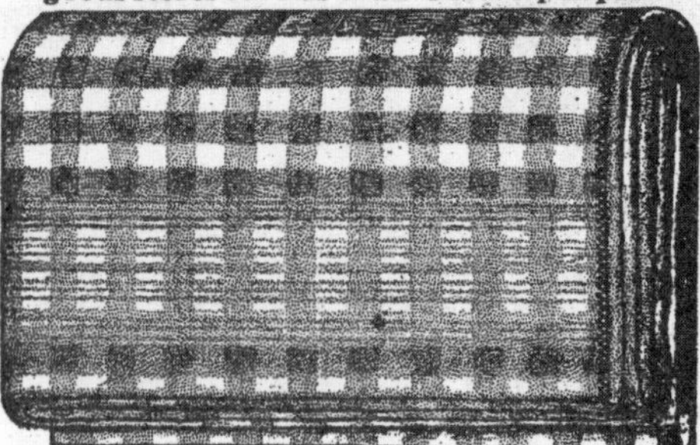

These are the swellest up to date plaid blankets on the market. They are not to be found except in the very high class blanket departments and there they sell from $12.00 up. They are goods we are able to make a very low price on from the fact that we control the mill in which they are manufactured and we have the cost cut down to a minimum and to this we add but our one small margin of profit. The wool used in constructing this blanket is of the very finest combed quality and is soft and luxurious. Nothing more handsome in colorings than these, our fancy plaid all wool fleeced 5½-pound blankets. They come in colors, black and red, brown and white, black and white, baby blue and white, pink and white, gray and white, also scarlet and white.

No. 37C1333 Size, 72x84 inches. Per pair..$6.9

DEPARTMENT OF BABIES' CRIB BLANKETS.

Our Pure, Fine, White Wool Filled, Mohair Bound and Fancy Colored Bordered, Size 30x40-inch Blanket at 80 Cents per Pair.

This is a very serviceable little blanket and a blanket that would sell ordinarily at about $1.25.

No. 37C1337 Size, 30x40 inches. Price, per pair.........80c

Our White Crib Blankets, Extra Fine Quality California Wool Filled at $1.49 per Pair.

This is a blanket well worth $2.25 per pair. Comes with fancy colored borders.

No. 37C1341 Size, 30x40 inches. Price, per pair.........$1.49

Our Very Finest Quality, All Pure Wool White Crib Blankets at $3.25 per Pair.

This is one of the most luxurious baby crib blankets on the market, a blanket that sells very often at as high as $5.00 and more. This blanket is fit for the very finest trade. Nothing better could be found in any of the city stores. It is good weight.

No. 37C1345 Size, 36x48 inches. Price, per pair.........$3.25

OUR NEW, ENLARGED DEPARTMENT OF QUILTED AND TUFTED UP TO DATE COMFORTERS.

WE HAVE PUT IN AN ENTIRELY NEW LINE of this very important class of house furnishings. We are giving the biggest values that we have ever given. We are giving styles that are new. We are giving qualities that have been carefully selected, in fact our entire line of comforters are made especially for us, and for price, style and quality are unapproached by any other house. This class of house furnishings has become such an important factor in our business that we have given it an entire department to itself. We handle more quilted and tufted comforters than any other three houses in the United States. We have placed very large orders with big Southern cotton producers, and our factories are located in the South, whereby we are enabled to get cotton at the very minimum of cost. We have gotten the manufacturing down to a point where it is a big saving to our customers. Our price is based on the exact cost to manufacture with a small margin for profit. We are selling comforters at a less price than any wholesaler or jobber, for one comforter or as many as desired. We have but one price for one or for quantity.

WE HAVE SELECTED FOR THIS SEASON some very strikingly pretty styles of coverings for our comforters. They certainly will be appreciated. We have comforters in various weights. Some are made especially for city trade and are light in construction, and others are made heavier for the rougher wear. You will find our styles prettier, and they have a newness and freshness and the colorings are generally more clean than found in the ordinary makes of comforters. The process of quilting and tufting is accomplished in our factories by the latest automatic electric machines which do the work evenly and perfectly and turn out a smooth, handsomely made, beautifully stitched, nicely shaped, full width, filling evenly distributed, and such a comforter as you must see, examine and compare with those furnished by others to appreciate the excellence of the comforters we are producing for this season. Our prices are extremely low. You can buy from us well finished, perfectly made comforters for considerably less money than you could buy common, ordinarily made, poorly covered comforters that are made by hand or by crude, old fashioned machinery.

WE AIM TO GIVE YOU the most perfectly constructed, best filled and handsomest covered comforter that it is possible to make and to save you at least one-third what you would pay to your home dealer or in ordinary city stores. We guarantee every comforter that we put out to be fully up to our description, and if, when you receive comforters from us, they do not prove thoroughly satisfactory, you are at liberty to return them to us at our expense and we will immediately return your money. When ordering blankets and other goods do not forget the long, cold winter ahead, and be sure to include one or more comforters with your order.

No. 37C1349 Fancy Print, Dark Colored, Floral Design Bed Comforters. Size, 52x68 inches. Price, each.........59c

No. 37C1353 Our Fancy Print, Reversible Bed Comforters. Size, 64x72 inches. Price, each.... 75c

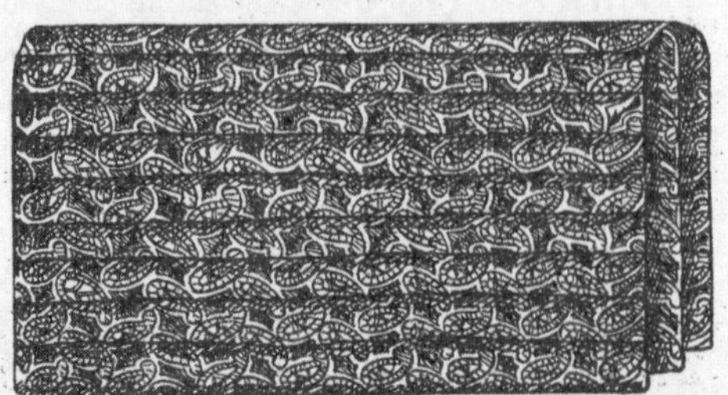

No. 37C1357 Our Reversible Handsome Chintz, Persian Print, 66x82-inch Comforter. Price, each.........89c

No. 37C1361 Our Heavy Fine Silkoline Tufted Fancy Medium Weight Comforter. Size, 66x76 inches. Price, each.........$1.00

No. 37C1365 Our Handsome Tufted Silkoline Covered, Reversible Comforter. Size, 68x78 inches. Price, each.........$1.25

No. 37C1369 Our New Design Handsome Silkoline Fancy Stitched Comforter. Size, 68x78 inches. Price, each.........$1.45

No. 37C1373 Our Extra Weight, Fancy Stitched, Reversible, Heavy Silkoline Covered Comforter. Size, 70x80 inches. Price, each.........$1.75

No. 37C1377 Our Specially Pretty Design of Fine Long Fibre Cotton Filled, Reversible, Tufted Comforter. Size, 70x82 inches. Price, each.......$1.98

No. 37C1381 Something New in a Beautiful Fancy Stitch Reversible Comforter. Size, 70x78 inches. Price, each.........$2.25

No. 37C1385 Our Extra Size, Reversible, Heavy India Cloth Covered, Fancy Stitch Comforter. Size, 78x86 inches. Price, each.........$2.50

No. 37C1389 Our Large Size, Handsomely Quilted, Reversible Sateen Comforter. Size, 70x80 inches. Price, each.........$2.75

Big Bargains in Down Comforters.

No. 37C1393 Our Big 70x80-inch, Down Filled, Handsome Style Comforter. Size, 70x80 inches. Price, each.........$5.25

No. 37C1397 Our Highest Grade, Handsomest Style, Mercerized Silk Covered Down Comforter. Size, 70x80 inches. Price, each.........$7.50

OUR NEW ENLARGED AND IMPROVED DEPARTMENT OF LACE CURTAINS.

FOR THIS SEASON we are able to place before our customers a larger, better and more exclusive variety of lace curtains than ever before. Every style illustrated and described is absolutely new, and many of these styles are exclusive with us, from designs made for us alone, and which you will not find copied in any of the cheaper curtains on the market.

WE DIRECT PARTICULAR ATTENTION to the handsome new styles we are showing in Nottinghams, in combination curtains, Lambrequin styles, also some very beautiful designs in Irish Point, Brussels Net, Cluny, Renaissance, Battenberg, French Embroidered and Tambour effects. The styles we show can be depended upon as representing the most popular and up to date designs; in fact, the same manufacturers that supply us, furnish goods for the curtain departments of some of the largest and most exclusive metropolitan retail curtain and drapery establishments.

OUR LACE CURTAIN GUARANTEE OFFER.

WE SOLICIT YOUR ORDER from this department with the understanding and agreement that if the curtains we send you do not prove perfectly satisfactory in every way, as good or even better than you expect from reading the description, and if you are not convinced when the goods are received that we have furnished you with better value than you could possibly get elsewhere, you are at liberty to return the curtains to us and we will refund your money and pay transportation charges both ways. We are sure that we are furnishing, this season particularly, the greatest values in lace curtains that ever went out of any house. We have given most careful attention to the styles here selected, with the idea of not only furnishing our customers with the most up to date designs to be had, but also that we may offer these goods as representing matchless values, and we know that if you wish to buy lace curtains and will compare our prices and our goods, we will be sure to receive your order.

WE DO NOT SAMPLE CURTAINS.

IT IS IMPOSSIBLE TO SEND SAMPLES of these goods, but every curtain is sent out under our binding guarantee as to quality, and under our binding guarantee that it will please you, and if you are not perfectly satisfied with the curtains when received, you can return them to us at our expense and we will refund your money.

NOTICE We do not break pairs of curtains. Where curtains are quoted in pairs, we do not sell single curtains.

Entirely New and Novel Nottingham Lace Curtain at 85 Cents Each.

This is a combination curtain. It has the effect of two curtains, while in fact it is only one solid piece of lace. It has very pretty fleur de lis design and has a pretty lambrequin at top to match bottom of curtain. It is finished at the bottom with large scallops of lace and has lock stitched edges all around, as well as at the bottom. The lace edge and insertion, as well as the deep taped effect produced in this curtain and the heavily flounced bottom, is in reality only one solid piece of lace. We have the exclusive sale of this curtain. It is a design made especially for us and we consider it one of the greatest low priced curtains that has ever been put upon the market. It comes in white, also cream. Size, 3½ yards long by 60 inches wide.
No. 37C1507 Price, each........................85c

Our New Solid Lace Lambrequin Effect Nottingham Lace Curtain at 75c Each.

This is a new style of lace curtain, and is considered by us to be of exceptional value. The illustration will give you some idea of the style. The curtain is 56 inches wide and 3¼ yards long, and is one solid piece of lace, fastened in the center so as to be draped to each side. The lambrequin effect is shown in the illustration. This curtain has the style and effect of curtains that sell at more than double the price which we ask. It comes in white, also cream.
No. 37C1503
Price, each..........75c

These CURTAINS are all New 1905 Patterns.

Our New Innovation, at 95c Each.

This pretty Bonne-Femme Nottingham Lace Curtain is a new design for this season. It is made of a very fine quality of twisted net and has the appearance and style of a curtain that would sell at double our price. It has a pretty throw-over or lambrequin at top to match the bottom of curtain. From the illustration you can form some idea of this pretty curtain. The flounce effect brought out on the sides and bottom makes it have the appearance of a heavy ruffle while in reality it is one solid piece of lace. It comes in white or ecru. Size, 3 yards long by 48 inches wide.
No. 37C1511 Price, each........................95c

Our Pretty, New Style Nottingham Lace Curtain at 49 Cents per Pair.

This is a marvel of beauty for such a small price. It has overlocked corded edge. Comes in white, also cream. Size, 3 yards long by 34 inches wide.
No. 37C1515 Price, per pair....................49c

Our Pretty Nottingham Lace Curtains at 75 Cents per Pair.

This is one of the prettiest designs we have ever sold at anything like the price. It comes in white, also cream. Size, 3 yards long by 38 inches wide.
No. 37C1519 Price, per pair.................75c

Our New, Handsome Nottingham Lace Curtains at 89 Cents per Pair.

The illustration will give you the exact design of this new and pretty curtain. It has a very strong border, relieved by a pretty leaf design center. It is made of a nice quality of net and is an exceptional value at the price we ask for it. It comes in white, also cream. Size, 3 yards long by 45 inches wide.
No. 37C1523 Price, per pair...................89c

Our Big Leader at 98 Cents per Pair.

At our special price of 98 cents a pair, we know that we are offering a curtain the like of which has never been sold before for anything like the price. From the illustration you can form some idea of this pretty, up to date curtain. It is made of a nice quality of net. It comes in white, also cream. Size, 3 yards long by 50 inches wide.
No. 37C1527 Price, per pair...................98c

Our Nottingham Lace Curtains at $1.09 per Pair

This is a very new and artistic design in a Nottingham Lace Curtain. The accompanying illustration will give you some idea of this pretty curtain. It has a very strong border relieved by a dainty dotted center. Note the size of this curtain. It is 3½ yards long and 58 inches in width, and at our price of $1.09 per pair should be one of our largest sellers. It comes in white, also cream. Size, 3½ yards long by 58 inches wide.

No. 37C1531 Price, per pair.................$1.09

Our New Double Flounce Effect Lace Curtains at $1.20 per Pair.

Nothing handsomer, nothing newer, nothing more fashionable shown in our line of lace curtains than this, our most elegant flounce effect Nottingham Lace Curtain. This curtain is very new. It is one solid piece of lace. The center is of point d'esprit effect. It has overlocked corded edges and comes in white, also cream. Size, 3½ yards long by 52 inches wide.

No. 37C1535 Price, per pair.................$1.20

A Big Bargain at $1.35 per Pair.

At this popular price we give you one of the prettiest up to date curtains found in our department. It has a very strong border with a little figured center; is made of a nice quality of net and will give good service. At our price of $1.35 per pair it is much less than this class of curtains can be bought for elsewhere. It comes in white, also cream. Size, 3½ yards long by 54 inches wide.

No. 37C1539 Price, per pair.................$1.35

Our Dainty Nottingham Lace Curtain at $1.45 per Pair.

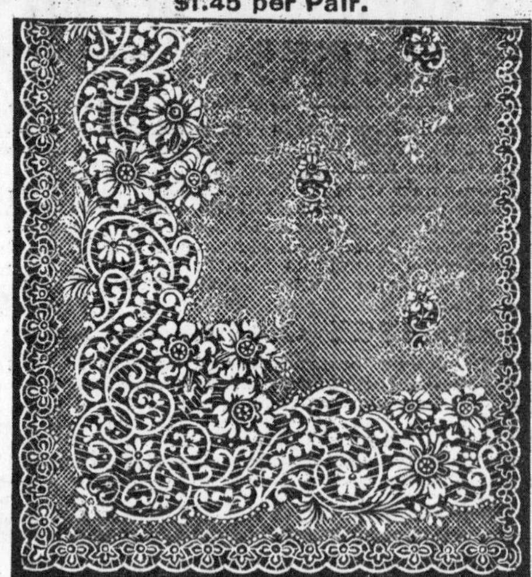

The illustration will show you the beauty and design of this handsome curtain, but to appreciate the value we are giving, you must see the curtain itself. It is made of a nice quality of Brussels net and has a pretty scroll and floral border combined with a pretty, neat figured center and is sure to please. It comes in white, also cream. Size, 3½ yards long by 52 inches wide.

No. 37C1543 Price, per pair.................$1.45

Our Imitation Brussels Net Curtain at $1.59 per Pair.

We cannot do justice in describing this pretty curtain. It is made of a fine quality of twisted net, has a scroll design border intermingled with bunches of roses and has a pretty allover center to match. We recommend this strongly to anyone wanting a dainty, lacy curtain. It comes in white, also cream. Size, 3½ yards long by 50 inches wide.

No. 37C1547 Price, per pair.................$1.59

Our Pretty Nottingham Lace Curtains, at $1.75 per Pair.

This curtain has a very pretty border with a plain center. It is made of a good, heavy quality of net and has the appearance of a high class curtain that would sell for double the price. We recommend this curtain to anyone wanting a good, serviceable curtain at a medium, low price. It comes in white, also cream. Size, 3½ yards long by 54 inches wide.

No. 37C1551 Price, per pair.................$1.75

Our $1.75 Leader is a Swell Nottingham Lace Curtain.

This is a decidedly new style and we have selected it with the idea of giving you the best quality, style and finish that it is possible to procure in a medium priced curtain. The accompanying illustration will give you some idea of this swell curtain. It has a pretty border with allover figured center. It comes in white, also cream. Size, 3½ yards long by 52 inches wide.

No. 37C1555 Price, per pair.................$1.75

Our New Fern Leaf Design Curtains at $1.89 per Pair.

This pretty design is entirely new. It has a very handsome border intertwined with bunches of ferns tied with lovers' knots as per illustration, also has a pretty center to match. It is nicely finished and is made of a good quality of net. It comes in white or cream. In ordering curtains don't overlook this number. Size, 3½ yards long by 57 inches wide.

No. 37C1559 Price, per pair.................$1.89

Our Point d'Esprit Nottingham Lace Curtains at $1.98 per Pair.

The above illustration is an exact reproduction of the curtain itself. Nothing prettier has been shown this season in a Nottingham curtain. The dainty point d'esprit center effect with a pretty floral border must be seen to be appreciated. We feel satisfied in saying this is the best value ever offered at our low price of $1.98 per pair. It comes in white, also cream. Size, 3½ yards long by 52 inches wide.

No. 37C1563 Price, per pair.................$1.98

Our New Scroll Design Nottingham Lace Curtains at $2.15 per Pair.

This is one of our most popular priced curtains. is a strong, well made Nottingham lace curtain, d one of the best values we have ever offered. e feel satisfied in saying that this is the best value er offered at our low price of $2.15 per pair. It a very fine scroll net center with large applique oll border; has overlocked corded edges. It comes n white, also cream. Size, 3½ yards long by 54 inches wide.

No. 37C1567 Price, per pair.................**$2.15**

Our Imitation Irish Point Nottingham Lace Curtain at $2.25 per Pair.

This is one of our new designs which we are showing in popular priced curtains this season. t is very strong, has fine, hard twisted Brussels net enter and the applique effect in the border gives it he appearance of an Irish point curtain. It is very urable, has overlocked corded edges and it comes in hite, also cream. Size, 3½ yards long by 50 in. wide.

No. 37C1571 Price, per pair.................**$2.25**

Our Fine Nottingham Lace Curtains at $2.49 per Pair.

The above illustration will give you a fair idea of the appearance of this curtain; the pattern and design are taken from a photograph. We consider his one of the best values we have to offer in our ace curtain department. It comes in white, also ream. Size, 3½ yards long by 54 inches wide.

No. 37C1575 Price, per pair................ **$2.49**

Our Pretty, New Applique Effect Cable Net Lace Curtains at $2.35 per Pair.

This is certainly a pretty style. It is a design produced by one of our most expert artists. It has been highly complimented, and we consider it one of our strongest and best curtains. The illustration accompanying the description is taken from an actual photograph of the curtain and it gives you a very fair idea of its beauty. It has overlocked corded edges and it comes in white, also cream. Size, 3½ yards long by 48 inches wide.

No. 37C1579 Price, per pair..................**$2.35**

Our Dainty Nottingham Lace Curtains at $2.65 per Pair.

This is a very pretty design in a Novelty Lace Curtain. It is made of a fine quality of twisted net, has a very handsome floral border with a fleur de lis figure in center. This is certainly one of the prettiest and daintiest curtains in our stock. If you want a pretty, up to date curtain, be sure to order one or more pairs of this number. It comes in white or cream. Size, 3½ yards long by 50 inches wide.

No. 37C1583 Price, per pair..................**$2.65**

Our Pretty Cable Net Curtains at $2.98 per Pair.

We think this is one of the prettiest curtains in our store. It is made of a fine quality of cable net, and for service and durability there is no curtain made that will outwear it. It comes in white or cream. Size, 3½ yards long by 50 inches wide.

No. 37C1587 Price, per pair.................. **$2.98**

Our Nottingham Lace Curtains at $2.98 per Pair.

This curtain will be appreciated by our patrons who like a very pretty plain center curtain. It has a very heavy scroll border on outer edge with a row of roses on inner edge, giving it a very pretty effect. The illustration does not do justice to this dainty curtain. We can strongly recommend it at our price of $2.98. It comes in white, also cream. Size, 3½ yards long by 54 inches wide.

No. 37C1591 Price, per pair..............**$2.98**

Our Heavy Nottingham Lace Curtains at $3.49 per Pair.

This is a very handsome curtain, new in design; is strong and well made, and has a very pretty pattern like illustration. It comes in white, also cream. Size, 3½ yards long by 54 inches wide.

No. 37C1595 Price, per pair..............**$3.49**

Our Lily of the Valley Nottingham Lace Curtains at $3.85 per Pair.

The accompanying illustration does not do justice to this pretty curtain. It has large bouquets of lilies of the valley in border with little sprigs of same in center of curtain. It is made of a nice, fine quality of Brussels net and is a very dainty curtain. It comes in white or ecru. Size, 3½ yards long by 54 inches wide.

No. 37C1599 Price, per pair.. .... **$3.85**

Our Fine English Cable Net Curtains at $3.95 per Pair.

Nothing prettier or finer in quality in a cable net curtain could be imagined than the one in the accompanying illustration. We feel that in offering this curtain to the public we have a curtain that will please our many patrons. It must be seen to be appreciated. It comes in white or cream. Size, 3½ yards long by 50 inches wide.

No. 37C1603 Price, per pair................ **$3.95**

Our Fine Brussels Net Curtains at $4.19 per Pair.

At our special price of $4.19 per pair we offer you the finest quality of Brussels Net Curtains manufactured. We feel that we have no competition whatever in this beautiful curtain. From the illustration you can form some idea of the pretty style it comes in. You certainly cannot afford to overlook this number if you want a swell, up to date curtain. It comes in white or cream. Size, 3½ yards long by 57 inches wide.

No. 37C1607 Price, per pair................ **$4.19**

A Bargain at $4.39 per Pair.

This is one of the prettiest designs brought out this season in an extra fine quality of Cable Net Curtain. It comes exactly like illustration. If you want a real fine and at the same time a servicable curtain, you will find it in this beautiful cable net curtain. It comes in white, also cream. Size, 3½ yards by 48 inches wide.

No. 37C1611 Price, per pair................ **$4.39**

Our Handsome, Arabian, Heavy Cord Lace Curtains at $2.79 per Pair.

Arabian Curtains are very fashionable and we have in this beautiful curtain one of the biggest bargains that has ever been shown in this line. It has a very heavy applique effect inside border and is outlined with a heavy cord. The body of the curtain is of a very strong, hard twisted net. It comes in dark cream only. Size, 3½ yards long by 48 inches wide.

No. 37C1615 Price, per pair.... ....**$2.79**

Our New, Pretty Arabian Lace Curtains at $4.19 per Pair.

The illustration will give you an idea of the very pretty design we have gotten out in this up to date, heavy Arabian Net Applique Curtain. It has overlocked corded edges. It comes in a deep shade of ecru only. Size, 3½ yards long by 48 inches wide.

No. 37C1619 Price, per pair................**$4.19**

Our Best Arabian Lace Curtains at $4.98 per Pair.

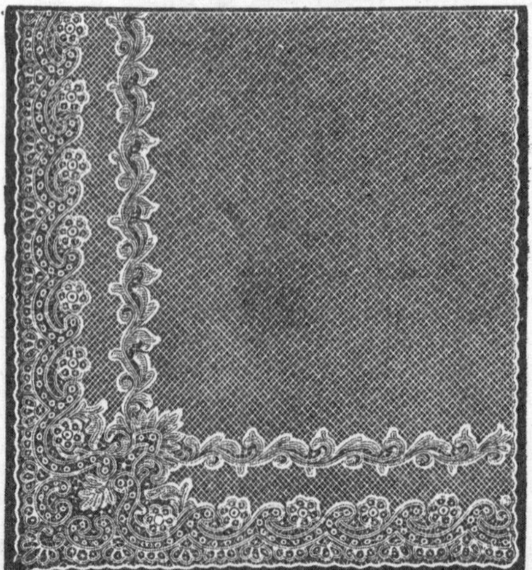

This strong, pretty Arabian Lace Curtain, that is so very stylish just now, comes in a deep, rich ecru color only. It is on a very heavy net, and is a new up to date design. It is exceedingly well made, a strong curtain and has overlocked corded edges. Size, 3½ yards long by 48 inches wide.

No. 37C1623 Price, per pair................**$4.98**

Our New and Beautiful Design of Irish Point Lace Curtains at $2.87 per Pair.

This is our leader in value of Irish Point Lace Curtains. We have been extremely anxious to give a well made curtain with a handsome design. The foundation of Brussels net is very heavy and hard twisted. The curtain has overlocked corded edges. It comes in white only. Size, 3½ yards long by 48 inches wide.

No. 37C1627 Price, per pair............... **$2.87**

$3.98 per Pair for Beautiful Irish Point Lace Curtains.

This is the prettiest Irish Point Curtain we have ever been able to offer to our patrons at anything like the price. We import these curtains direct from Switzerland ourselves and buy them in large quantities. From the illustration you can form some idea of the heavy applique border with scroll design center brought out in this beautiful curtain. It comes in white only. Size, 3½ yards long by 50 inches wide.

No. 37C1631 Price, per pair...............**$3.98**

Our Beautifully Designed Imported Irish Point Curtains at $5.49 per Pair.

They are made on a very fine quality of Brussels net. The border is exceedingly rich and heavy, relieved by a neat figure throughout the center. It is an elegant pattern and we are sure it will interest you if you want a swell, up to date curtain. It comes in white only. Size, 3½ yards long by 50 inches wide.

No. 37C1635 Price, per pair..............**$5.49**

Our Best Irish Point Curtains at $7.25 per Pair.

In this beautiful Irish Point Curtain we offer one of the best values ever presented to our customers at anything like the price. It is made of an extra fine quality of net and is the richest and most elaborately designed curtain in our store. The border is exceedingly rich, showing an abundance of high art. We can strongly recommend this to any one wanting a high class parlor curtain. It comes in white only. Size, 3¼ yards long by 50 inches wide.

No. 37C1639 Price, per pair.................$7.25

Genuine Imported Brussels Net Curtains at $3.75 per Pair.

This is one of the prettiest and daintiest lace curtains shown this season and at our price of $3.75 per pair should be a rapid seller. It makes a very pretty and inexpensive parlor curtain. It comes in white only. Size, 3½ yards long by 50 inches wide.

No. 37C1643 Price, per pair...............$3.75

Our Pretty Brussels Net Curtains at $5.25 per Pair.

The above illustration can give you but a faint idea of this pretty curtain. It is made of a very fine quality of English bobbinet. It has a very dainty and lacey design and must be seen to appreciate the value we are giving. It comes in white only. Size, 3¼ yards long by 50 inches wide.

No. 37C1647 Price, per pair.................$5.25

Our Handsome and Best Brussels Net Lace Curtains at $7.75 per Pair.

The above illustration gives a very good idea of the pretty, stylish design in this, our best Brussels Net Curtain. We feel confident that by comparison it will be found that this is the best value that has ever been offered in fine imported Brussels Net Curtains. It comes in white only. Size, 3½ yards long by 48 inches wide.

No. 37C1651 Price, per pair................$7.75

Our Genuine Imported Cluny Lace Curtains at $3.98 per Pair.

This curtain is made of the finest quality French net and the edge and also insertion is the genuine imported, hand made cluny lace. Curtains of this quality are sold in most retail stores at from $10.00 to $12.00 per pair. As we use large quantities of this curtain we are able to make this special low price. It comes in Arabian or coffee color only. Size, 3 yards long by 48 inches wide.

No. 37C1655 Price, per pair................$3.98

Our Genuine Imported Renaissance Lace Curtains at $4.98 per Pair.

This is a genuine imported Renaissance Lace Curtain and the applique is made on a heavy quality of French Brussels net. There is nothing prettier made in curtains of this style. The illustration will give you an idea of the neatness and lacey effect. Comes in white only. Size, 3¼ yards long by 50 inches wide.

No. 37C1659 Price, per pair................$4.98

Our Finer Grade Imported Renaissance Lace Curtains at $6.75 per Pair.

This curtain is one of our best sellers and is giving entire satisfaction to our customers. Made of a good quality French Brussels net and the illustration will give you an idea of the beautiful hand made battenberg corner. Comes in white only. Size, 3¼ yards long by 50 inches wide.

No. 37C1663 Price, per pair....................$6.75

Our Finest and Most Elaborate Renaissance Lace Curtains at $8.25 per Pair.

Too much cannot be said about this genuine imported Renaissance Lace Curtain with hand made battenberg border. The applique trimming is made on the best quality French net that money can buy. It has a battenberg edge and insertion three inches wide. Must be seen to appreciate the beautiful hand made battenberg edge and insertion. If you want a curtain for your parlor, dining room or library and one you will feel proud of, we would advise you to order this number, as we know you will be more than pleased. It comes in white only. Size, 3½ yards long by 50 inches wide.

No. 37C1667 Price, per pair....................$8.25

OUR NEW AND ENLARGED DEPARTMENT OF RUFFLED CURTAINS AND CURTAIN MATERIAL.

WE HAVE ADDED SOME NEW AND VERY STYLISH CURTAINS TO THIS LINE. THIS CLASS OF CURTAINS IS VERY DAINTY AND PRETTY, BUT AT THE SAME TIME THEY ARE VERY SERVICEABLE AND WILL WASH WITHOUT INJURY.

THE CURTAINS in this list we sell by the thousand pairs to hotels, boarding houses, public places, restaurants, and for the dining rooms and bed rooms of the most refined homes. You will find every number which we quote, from our dainty ruffled mull curtains at 45 cents per pair to the swellest lace ruffled curtains at $3.98 per pair, to be new, up to date and the best value that it is possible to give to our patrons. Order one or more pairs of these curtains in the style that you like best, and we guarantee to satisfy you, or your money will be refunded, and express or freight both ways will be paid by us.

Our Ruffled Mull Curtains at 45 Cents per Pair.

This is a very sheer, pretty striped Mull Curtain like the accompanying illustration. It has a very fine 4½-inch ruffle all the way around, being taped at the inner edge of the ruffle. It is a durable sightly curtain, and it certainly is a marvel of value at our price. All of our ruffled curtains come in white only. Size, 3 yards long by 38 inches wide.

No. 37C1671 Price, per pair, 45c

Our Dainty Ruffled Muslin Curtain at 62 Cents per Pair.

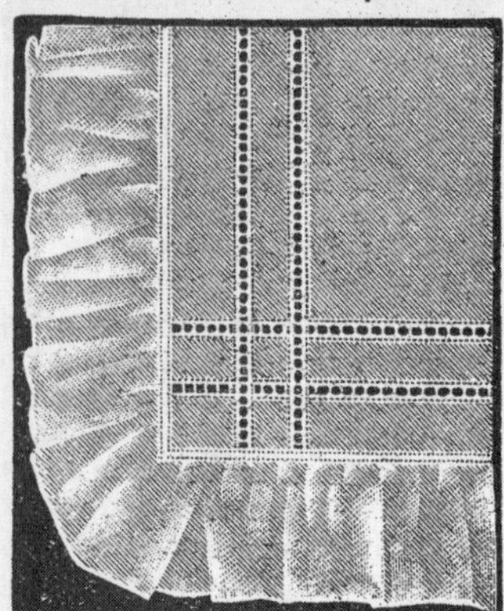

The illustration will give you some idea of this pretty Muslin Curtain. It is entirely new for this season and has a full 4½-inch ruffle and two rows of beading inside of ruffle, as per illustration. Comes in white only. Size, 3 yards long and 38 inches wide.

No. 37C1675 Price, per pair....62c

65c Lappet Mull Curtains.

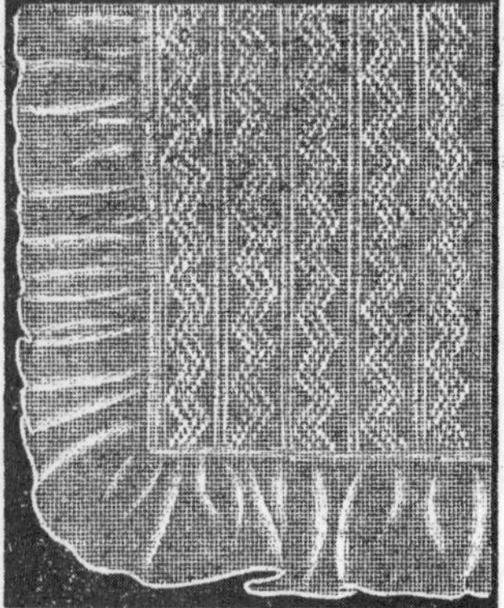

Our fancy Lappet Ruffled Mull Curtains, with a 4½-inch plain mull ruffle on the edge, taped on the inner edge of the ruffle, at 65 cents per pair. This is a sheer and good quality of lappet mull. It is sometimes called embroidered mull, is very fashionable and is pretty enough to grace the most fashionable homes. White only. Size, 3 yards long by 40 inches wide.

No. 37C1679 Price, per pair...65c

Our Special Coin Spot Ruffled Muslin Curtain at 85 Cents per Pair.

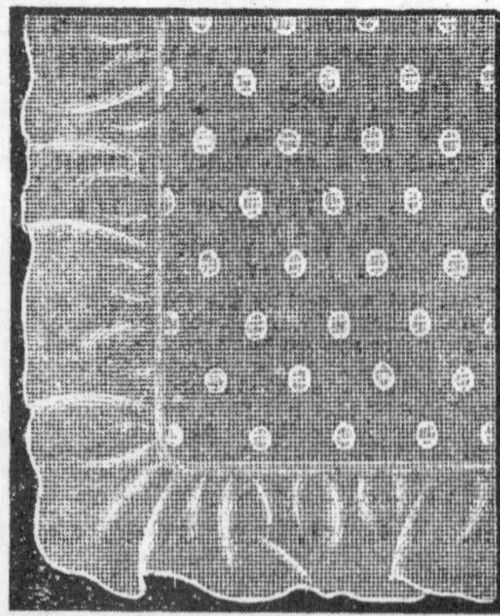

This is a decidedly low price for this pretty Muslin Curtain. It is 3 yards long by 40 inches wide and has a full 4½-inch ruffle. We thoroughly recommend this curtain, as it will wash and do up nicely and give good service, and at our price of 85 cents it is much cheaper than this class of curtain has ever been sold before. It comes in white only. Size, 3 yards long by 40 inches wide.

No. 37C1683 Price, per pair....85c

WE DO NOT sample curtains, but we guarantee that you will be greatly pleased with your purchase.

Our 98-Cent Ruffled Muslin Curtain with a Battenberg Braid Insertion.

This curtain is one of the prettiest we have ever shown. It is 3 yards long by 38 inches wide and made of a nice, sheer quality of lawn. It has a full four-inch ruffle and a row of battenberg braid insertion seven inches from outer edge, which gives the curtain a very sightly effect. It comes in white only. Size, 3 yards long by 38 inches wide.

No. 37C1687 Price, per pair....98c

Our New Fancy Novelty Ruffled Mull Curtains at 89c per Pair.

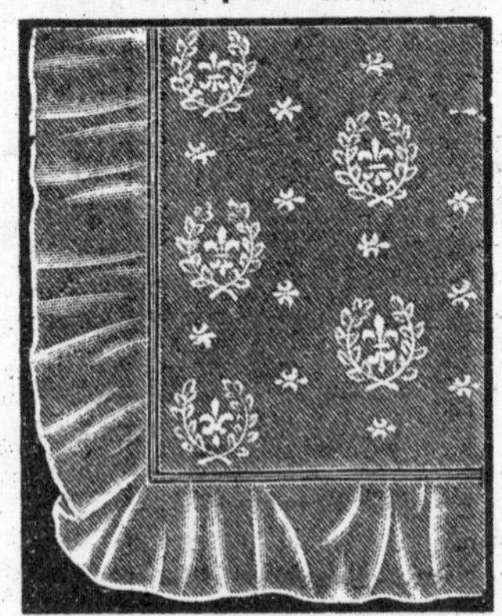

This is one of the latest novelties which we have had made specially for us. It is a curtain that is very sheer, but at the same time fine. It has a very pretty novelty center like the illustration, with a plain mull ruffle edge 4 inches wide. The best ruffled curtains ever offered at 89 cents per pair. Size, 3 yards long by 40 inches wide.

No. 37C1691 Price, per pair, 89c

OUR LEADER.

$1.35 Ruffled Fishnet Curtains for $1.00 per Pair.

This curtain is made of a nice quality of fishnet material, is 3 yards long by 40 inches wide and has a nice, full ruffle. It is a curtain that is very suitable for dining rooms, bedrooms, etc. The accompanying illustration does not do justice to this pretty curtain and at our special price of $1.00 it should be a big seller. It comes in white only. Size, 3 yards long by 40 inches wide.

No. 37C1695 Price, per pair, $1.00

Our New, Fancy Embroidered Ruffled Mull Curtains at $1.19 per Pair.

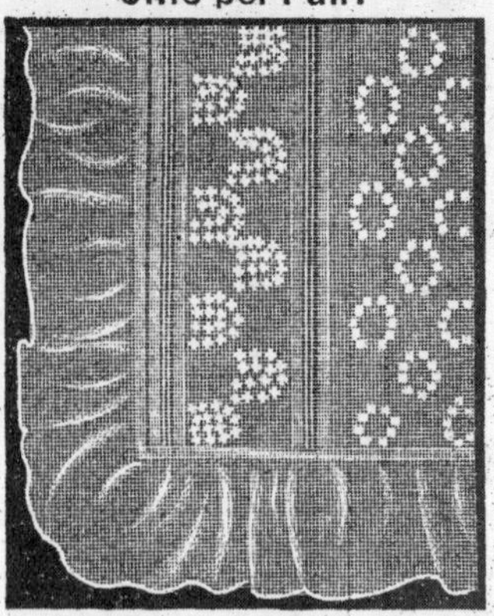

In this curtain we believe that we have one of the handsomest effects in our superb line of ruffled curtains. At this price we give you the best value that has ever been offered in ruffled curtains and at the same time give you a style such as you will not find outside of the retail stores in large cities, and then at fancy prices. It has a hemstitched border on the edge of the ruffle ½ inch deep. The ruffle itself is 5 inches deep and the fancy embroidered effect inside of ruffle is 6¼ inches. Size, 3 yards long by 42 inches wide.

No. 37C1699 Price, per pair, $1.19

Our New Tambour Ruffled Mull Curtains at $1.35 per Pair.

This is one of the daintiest muslin curtains ever shown in our catalogue. It comes in pure white only and is made of a very fine sheer mull. It is 3 yards long and 37 inches wide, and has a 4-inch ruffle with ½-inch hemstitched border on outer edge, with two rows of embroidery on curtain seven inches from the outer edge, which gives it a very pretty effect, as per illustration. We recommend this curtain very highly and are sure if you order one or more pairs of this number you will be more than pleased with same. It comes in white only. Size, 3 yards long by 37 inches wide.

No. 37C1703 Price, per pair..$1.35

Our Dotted Swiss Mull Ruffled Curtains at $1.50 per Pair.

This odd and pretty design in ruffled curtains is entirely new. It is a curtain that is made for us in great quantities and is an exclusive style. The ruffle is 5 inches deep, taped at the inner edge. This is a very handsome curtain and will please the most fastidious. Size, 3 yards long by 42 inches wide.

No. 37C1707 Price, per pair $1.50

NEW AND PRETTY DESIGNS IN BRUSSELS NET LACE TRIMMED RUFFLED CURTAINS.

Our Lace Trimmed Brussels Net Ruffled Curtains at $1.29 per Pair.

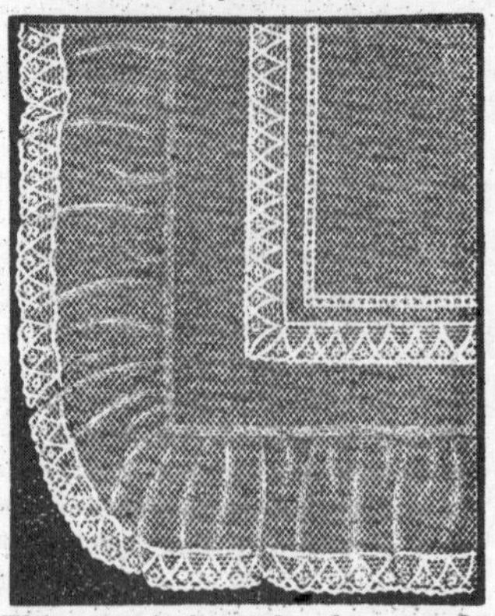

This curtain is made of a very fine, nice quality of Brussels net with a 5-inch ruffle, trimmed on outer edge with lace 1¼ inches wide, with a lace insertion 1¼ inches wide, 10 inches from outer edge to match with ½ inch beading on inner edge, as per illustration. It comes in white only. Size, 3 yards long by 40 inches wide.

No. 37C1711 Price, per pair, $1.29

Our Special Value in Patent Valenciennes Lace Trimmed Brussels Net Ruffled Curtains at $1.55 per Pair.

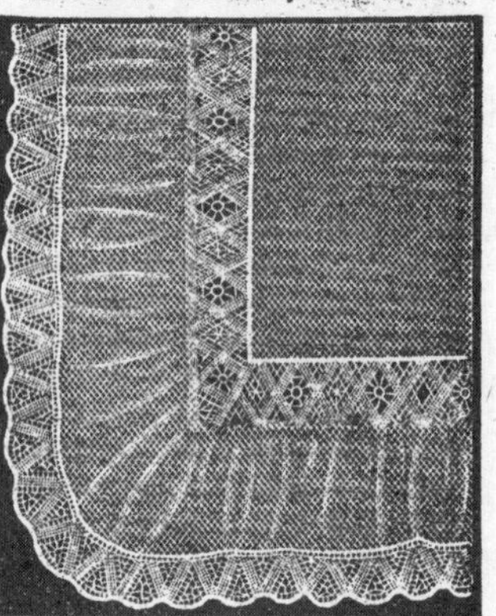

This curtain has a 2-inch lace edge on the outer edge of ruffle. Also a 2-inch lace edge, same pattern, to finish the inside of ruffle. The net is a very good quality, and we consider this one of our good values in this up to date line of curtains. Size, 3 yards long by 42 inches wide.

No. 37C1715 Price, per pair, $1.55

Our Lace Trimmed, Heavy Brussels Net Ruffled Curtains at $1.89 per Pair.

This is one of our most popular lace trimmed ruffle curtains. The outer lace edge is 1¼ inches wide, the ruffle including the lace edge is 6 inches wide; and the insertion outlining the inner border of ruffle is 3 inches wide. Size, 3 yards long by 48 inches wide.

No. 37C1719 Price, per pair, $1.89

Our Leader at $1.98 per Pair.

This swell ruffled Bobbinet Curtain is made of a very fine quality of net and has a 4-inch ruffle trimmed with battenberg braid edge with insertion to match on inner edge of ruffle, with a real renaissance corner, measuring 5 inches wide and 6 inches long. From the accompanying illustration you can form some idea of this pretty, up to date curtain. It comes in white only. Size, 3 yards long by 40 inches wide.

No. 37C1723 Price, per pair..................$1.98

Our Superior Fine Quality of Brussels Net Battenberg Trimmed Ruffled Curtains at $2.25 per Pair.

The outer edge of the ruffle is trimmed with 1¼-inch battenberg braid and the inner edge is outlined by a handsome border of heavy lace 3 inches wide and it has a 5-inch ruffle. We expect this to suit the ideas of many of our patrons, as it has been designed by one of our experts, and we predict a great success for its sale. Size, 3 yards long by 42 inches wide.

No. 37C1727 Price, per pair...............$2.25

Our Fine Brussels Net Curtains at $2.50 per Pair.

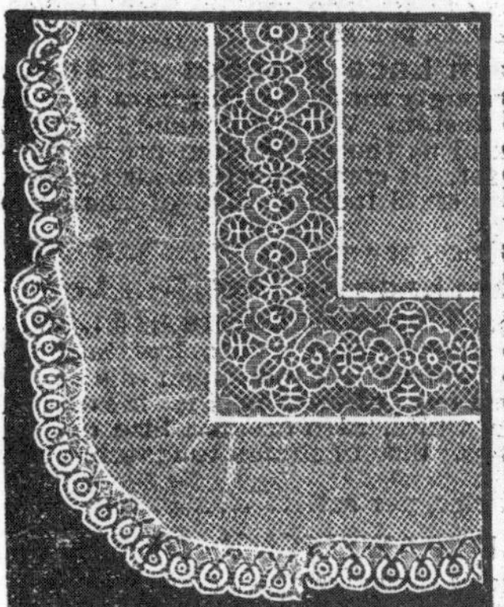

This handsome Brussels Net Curtain is one of our strongest numbers. It is made of a very fine quality of net and has a 7-inch ruffle with a 4-inch insertion on inside edge. The insertion is an imitation of a real cluny lace and at our special price of $2.50 per pair we know it cannot be duplicated. This curtain must be seen to be appreciated. It comes in white only. Size, 3 yards long by 42 inches wide.

No. 37C1731 Price, per pair. $2.50

Our Valenciennes Lace Trimmed Brussels Net Curtains, $2.85 per Pair.

From the illustration you can form some idea of this pretty curtain. It is 3 yards long by 40 inches wide with a full six-inch ruffle, trimmed on outer edge with a two-inch valenciennes lace with a two-inch insertion to match, and has two rows of imitation drawn work on either side of insertion, giving it a very pretty and lacey effect. This style is entirely different to any of the others shown in our catalogue, and we strongly recommend it to anyone wanting a handsome curtain at a medium price. It comes in white only. Size, 3 yards long by 40 inches wide.

No. 37C1735 Price, per pair...............$2.85

Our Honiton Lace Trimmed Brussels Net Ruffled Curtains at $3.15 per Pair.

This is a very pretty style. It has a honiton lace edge 2 inches wide outside of the net ruffle. The ruffle, including the edge, is 6 inches wide, and the inside border is finished by a 2-inch honiton lace insertion to match edge. The quality of the lace trimming and the net that this curtain is made of, is fine. We are sure that it cannot be duplicated at anywhere near our price. It comes in white only. Size, 3 yards long by 45 inches wide.

No. 37C1739 Price, per pair.................$3.15

Our Pretty, Finest Quality, Lace Trimmed Brussels Net Ruffled Curtains at $3.98 per Pair.

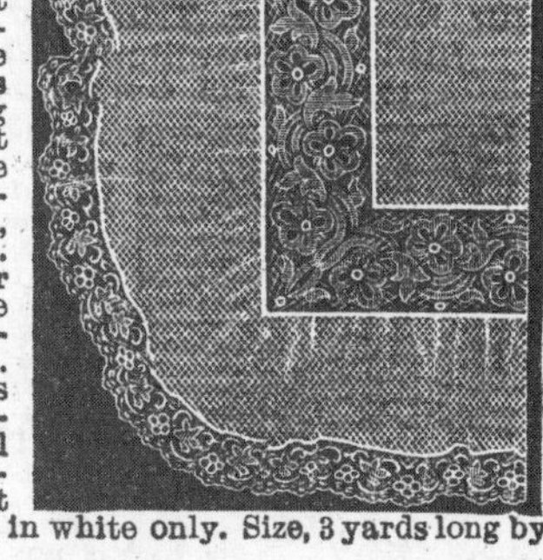

This is absolutely one of the finest curtains that it is possible to procure in Brussels net. It is a very new design. It has a lace edge 1½ inches wide, trimming the brussels net flounce. The flounce, including the lace edge, is 6 inches wide. Inside the inner edge of the flounce is a row of insertion 3 inches wide. This luxurious and pretty curtain is beautiful enough to decorate the finest homes. It comes in white only. Size, 3 yards long by 50 inches wide.

No. 37C1743 Price, per pair.................$3.98

Our New Imported Applique Lace Curtains at $1.98 per Pair.

This curtain is made of a good quality Brussels net and is trimmed with a fine battenberg braid and insertion to match, with a pretty corner piece, as per illustration. There is nothing prettier for bedrooms and dining rooms than this curtain. The illustration will give you an idea of the beautiful design shown in this curtain. It comes in white or Arabian color. Size, 3 yards long by 42 inches wide.

No. 37C1747 Price, per pair.................$1.98

WE DO NOT SEND OUT

SAMPLES OF CURTAINS

but you can send us your order with the distinct understanding and agreement that if you are not more than pleased with your purchase, the goods can be returned to us at our expense, and we will

PROMPTLY RETURN YOUR MONEY.

This Handsome Lace Curtain at $2.39 per Pair.

This curtain is made on a good quality Brussels net. The edge is of hand made lace, as is also the insertion. The beautiful corner, as shown in the illustration, is of hand made battenberg lace and there is nothing we can offer you at double the price that is as rich and dainty as this curtain. It comes in white only. Size, 3 yards long by 42 inches wide.

No. 37C1751 Price, per pair.................$2.39

This Handsome Cluny Lace Curtain at $2.98 per Pair.

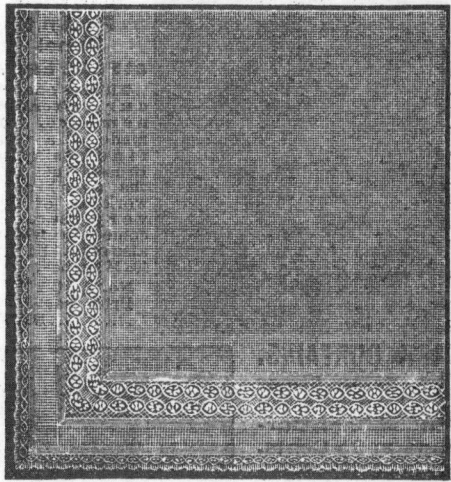

This curtain is made of a good quality scrim and is trimmed with cluny lace 1½ inches wide, with a 3-inch insertion to match. We recommend it for bedrooms, dining rooms and libraries. If you want a curtain that is neat and also shows its richness, order this number. It comes in dark cream only. Size, 3 yards long by 42 inches wide.

No. 37C1755 Price, per pair................$2.98

Our Beautiful Bonne Femme Brussels Net Curtains at $1.75 Each.

There is nothing that you can get in a Bonne Femme Curtain that is quite so rich and dainty as this curtain. The flounce is very full and is 14 inches deep. It makes a very pretty parlor curtain and is used very extensively. It comes in white only. Size, 2¾ yards long by 48 inches wide.

No. 37C1759 Price, complete for one window.......................................$1.75

Our New, Handsome Design Tambour Brussels Net Panels at 35c Each.

The illustration shows you the exact design as it is taken from a photograph. This is a very fine piece of tambour work on a strong, well made Brussels net. This is one of the best panels at the low price of 35 cents that we have ever offered to our patrons. Size, 35x42 in. It comes in white only.
No. 37C1763 Price, each........35c

Our Heavy Irish Point Panel at 50 Cents Each.

This very handsome, new design was produced by one of our own expert artists. The applique is perfectly made, and we consider this one of our strongest numbers. The Brussels net on which the applique is worked is very strong and hard twisted. Size, 35x42 inches. It comes in white only.
No. 37C1767 Price, each......50c

Our Prize Design Irish Point Panel at 75 Cents Each.

We think we are giving one of the handsomest numbers we have ever been able to present in this beautiful Irish Point Panel. The illustration will give you an exact pattern as it is taken from a photograph. It comes in white only. Size 36x54 inches.
No. 37C1771 Price, each........75c

Our Extra Fine Irish Point Panel at $1.00 Each.

This is one of the best values in Irish Point Panels. The applique is extraordinarily fine and strong and the outlines of the figures are perfect. It comes in white only. The illustration will give you an idea of the design. Size, 36x54 inches.
No. 37C1775 Price, each...$1.00

Our Handsome Large Wreath Design Irish Point Panel at $1.25 Each

This is one of our strongest numbers. It is made of a very fine quality of Brussels net and the applique work is of the very finest. It comes in white, also ecru. Size, 40x54 inches.
No. 37C1777 Price, each, ...$1.25

SASH CURTAINS.

Very Pretty Sheer Mull Hemstitched Ruffled Sash Curtains at 25 Cents.

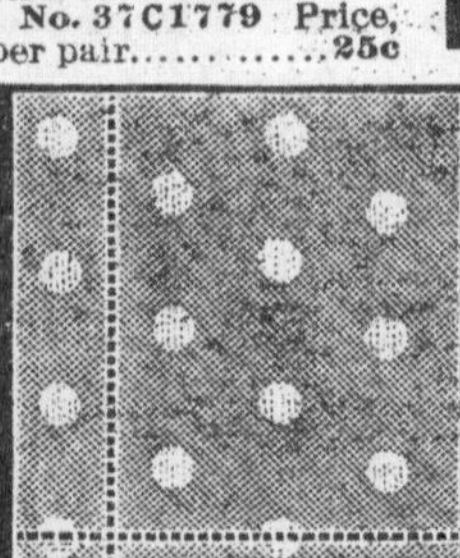

This curtain has a very pretty ruffle hemstitched on the outer edge, the ruffle being 4½ inches deep with a taped inner edge. It is a very fine quality of sheer mull. It comes in white only. Size, 34x40 inches.
No. 37C1779 Price, per pair.........25c

Our Hemstitched Coin Spot Sheer Sash Mull Curtains at 35 Cents per Pair.

The illustration will give you an idea of this handsome curtain. This sash curtain has a hemstitched band 1¾ inches wide on the edge, and is strong and well made. It comes in white only. Size 28x36 inches.
No. 37C1783 Price, per pair.......35c

Our Dotted Swiss Ruffled Hemstitched Sash Curtains at 50 Cents per Pair.

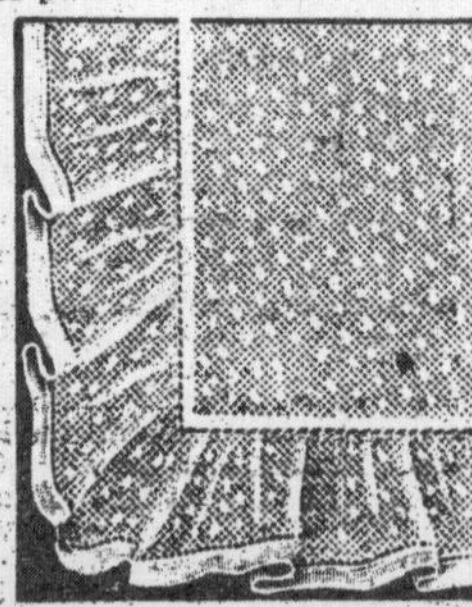

This is one of our strongest numbers in this our line of sash mull curtains. The body of the curtain is a very fine quality of dotted Swiss, with a 4-inch hemstitched edge. Size, 34x40 inches. It comes in white only.
No. 37C1787 Price, per pair..........50c

Our New Lace Trimmed India Linen Ruffled Hemstitched Sash Curtains at 55 Cents per Pair.

This is the best sash curtain that we present in this popular line. The lace insertion which forms the border inside is 7¼ inches from the inside of the ruffle, and the width of the insertion is 1¾ inches. This lace is very strongly made and durably put on. The ruffle is made of India linon and is 3¾ inches deep and has an edge ⅛ inch deep which is hemstitched. It comes in white only. Size, 33x40 inches.
No. 37C1791 Price, per pair.................55c

OUR DEPARTMENT OF BED SETS.

Our New Battenberg, Medallion Center, Fine Brussels Net Bed Sets at $5.75 per Set.

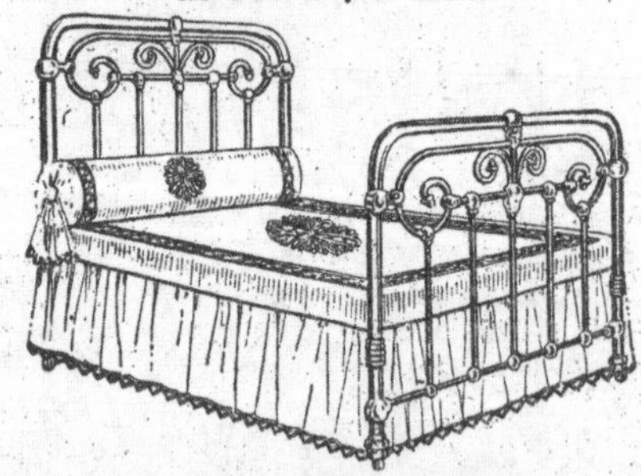

This illustration shows the appearance of bed sets in use.

This bed set, as illustrated, gives a very good idea of how beautiful it will look when in use. It is made of the very finest quality of Brussels net; battenberg braid edge all around and the insertion effect in the center is of battenberg braid. The beautiful medallion is one of the handsomest designs that we have been able to see in this class of work. It is a strong, hand made battenberg. The size of the medallion is 17x17 inches. The size of the bed cover is 60x80 inches, with a 21-inch ruffle. The size of the bolster cover is 60x40 inches, with a 21-inch ruffle. The size of the medallion in bolster cover is 9x9 inches. It comes in white only.
No. 37C1795 Price, per set.................$5.75

Our Leader in a Brussels Net Bed Set with Battenberg Braid Edge and Insertion with an 18x30-Inch Medallion in Center of Spread, at $3.75 per Set.

This beautiful spread is very similar in pattern to the above. It is made of a nice quality of net. It is for a full size bed, measuring 68 inches wide and 82 inches long, and has a full 15-inch ruffle all around trimmed with battenberg braid edge with insertion to match. The bolster is 68 inches wide, 40 inches deep and has pretty medallion to match the one in spread. It comes in white only and at our price of $3.75 should be a rapid seller.
No. 37C1799 Price, per set.............$3.75

Our New Cable Net Lace Bed Set, $3.75.

This is an extraordinary value in this durable style of lace bed sets. It has a very nicely finished edge, being overlock stitch. It is strong and firm and at the same time very finely finished. It comes in white, also cream. Size of bed cover, 78 x 100 inches. Size of shams to match, 34x34 inches.
No. 37C1803 Price, per set.................$3.75

Our Extremely New Style Nottingham Lace Bed Sets at $2.49 per Set.

This is an extremely new design in bed sets and is made of a very strong, well made Nottingham lace in very handsome designs. It comes in white, also cream. Size of bed cover, 78x92 inches. Size of shams, 34x34 inches.
No. 37C1807 Price, per set.................$2.49

Our Special Extraordinary Bargain in Nottingham Lace Bed Sets at $1.85.

This is a very extraordinary quality of Nottingham lace, being very strong and perfectly made. It comes in white, also cream. Size of bed cover, 76x88 inches. Size of shams to match, 33x33 inches.
No. 37C1811 Price, per set.................$1.85

Our Nottingham Lace Bed Set at $1.40.

This is a very strongly made Nottingham lace in a very handsome design. We recommend this as a very serviceable and at the same time pretty Nottingham lace bed set. It comes in white, also cream. Size of bed cover, 68x78 inches. Size of shams to match, 36x36 inches.
No. 37C1815 Price, per set.................$1.40

Our Nottingham Lace Bed Set, Our Leading Bargain in These Bed Sets at $1.09.

This is a very sightly, well made Nottingham lace, strong and durable. We look upon this as the best value we have ever offered in the line of bed sets. It comes in white, also cream. Size of bed cover is 68x80 inches. Size of shams to match, 34x34 inches.
No. 37C1819 Price, per set.................$1.09

—OUR DEPARTMENT OF—
CURTAIN SCRIMS, FISH NETS, LAPPET MULL COIN SPOT MULL, HEMSTITCHED MULL, BRUSSELS NETS, WHITE FANCY FIGURED DRAPERIES, POINT D'ESPRIT RUFFLED EDGE CURTAIN LACES AND MULLS, ETC.

Our Special New Style in Cream Ground, Colored Striped Curtain Scrim at 7 Cents per Yard.

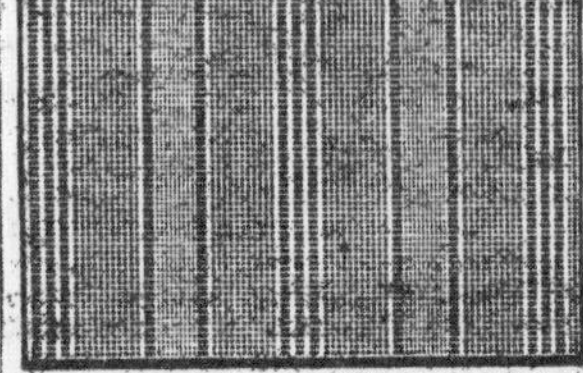

The illustration will give you an idea of the new pattern in which this beautiful scrim comes. It is 38 inches wide, and comes in colors, red, green, yellow, also blue, on a cream ground.
No. 37C1823 Price, per yard.................7c

WE DO NOT SEND SAMPLES OF THESE GOODS

Our New Solid Cream Lace Striped Scrim at 7 Cents per Yard.

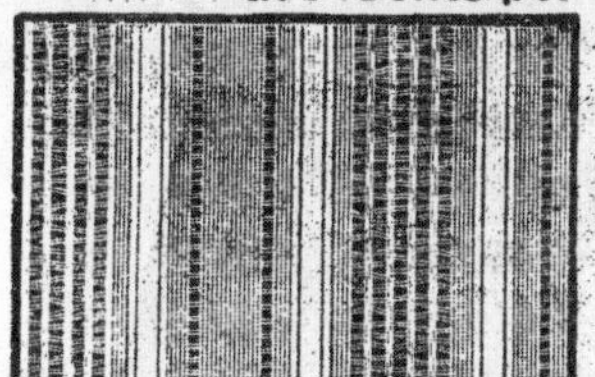

It is well made, very sheer and comes in handsome designs like the accompanying illustration. Width, 38 inches.
No. 37C1827
Price, per yard..............7c

Plain Scrim For Fancy Work.

No. 37C1831 Comes in cream only. 36 inches wide. Price, per yard..............9c
No. 37C1835 Finer quality than above. 40 inches wide. Price, per yard..............20c

Our New Lace Striped Lappet Mull at 8 Cents per Yard.

This 36-inch beautiful lace effect curtain material comes in white only. It has the appearance of embroidery, with a very pretty hemstitched effect as per illustration. It is a very handsome sheer material. Width, 36 inches.
No. 37C1833 Price, per yard..............8c

Our 36-inch Roxdale Corded Swiss at 8 Cents per Yard.

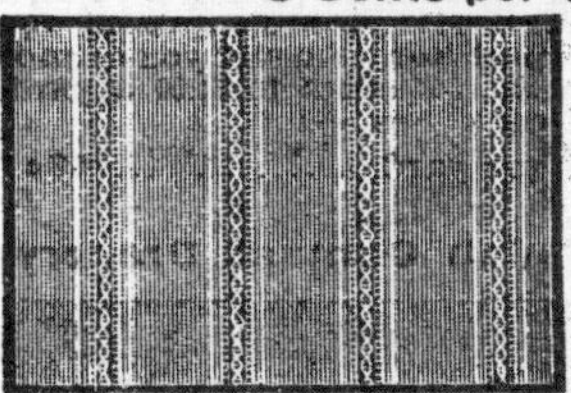

This is one of the best values in our drapery department. It is made of a nice quality of lawn and has a ½-inch lace stripe. It comes in white only and will wash and launder beautifully. Width, 36 inches.
No. 37C1839 Price, per yard..............8c

Our Coin Spot Curtain Mull Material at 10 Cents per Yard.

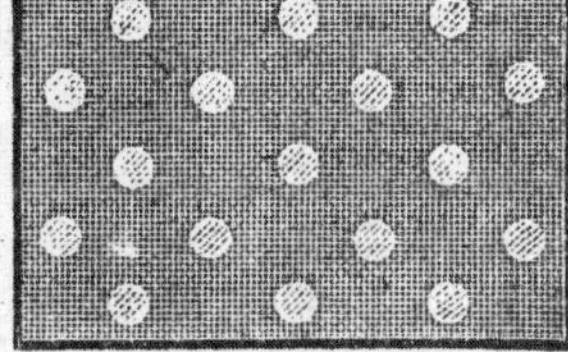

This is one of the sheerest and finest curtain materials which we have ever shown in our line of curtain materials. It comes in white only. We recommend it for wearing qualities. Width, 36 inches.
No. 37C1847 Price, per yard..............10c

Fine Sheer, Swiss Mull, With Hemstitched and Embroidered Stripe, at 11 Cents per Yard.

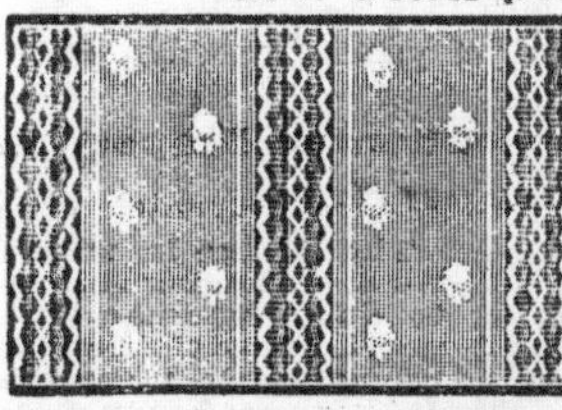

This is one of the daintiest, pretty curtain mulls shown. The accompanying illustration will give a fair idea of the pattern. It comes in white only. Width, 36 inches.
No. 37C1851
Price, per yard. 11c

Our New Ruffled Mull, 40 Inches Wide, at 19 Cents per Yard.

This is one of the daintiest curtain materials we are showing this season. We have named a price very much less than that asked for this grade and style of goods in city retail stores. It comes in white only. It is 40 inches wide and has a very pretty pattern, like the illustration. The material inside the ruffle has the embroidered effect and the ruffle itself is of plain mull, 5 inches wide.
No. 37C1855 Price, per yard..............19c

A Fine Dotted Swiss Muslin with a Fleur de Lis Figure at 16 Cents per Yard.

This is a very pretty and dainty curtain material. It is made of a very fine quality of Swiss mull. The accompanying illustration will give you some idea of the pattern. It comes in white only. Width, 40 inches.
No. 37C1859 Price, per yard..............16c

48-inch Fine Brussels Net Curtain Material at 25 Cents per Yard.

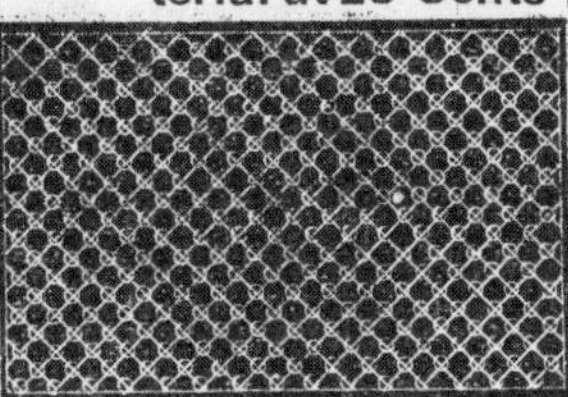

At 25 cents per yard we offer this fine quality of Brussels net. It comes in white, cream or Arabian. It is one of the most satisfactory curtain materials that we have to offer. This material can be used for bedrooms, dining rooms, sitting rooms, libraries, etc. It is fine enough to be used for dress material, and is very often used for fine fancy work. Width, 48 inches.
No. 37C1863 Price, per yard..............25c

Fine Quality Point d'Esprit at 35, 55 and 75 Cents per Yard.

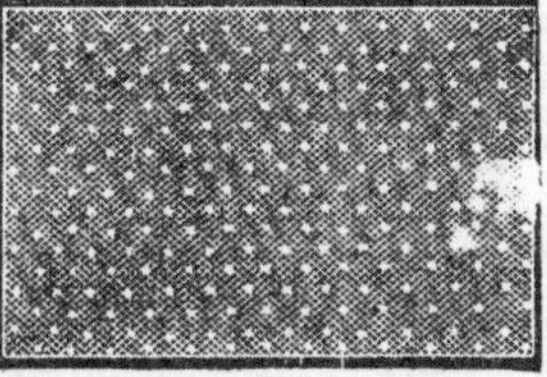

This material comes in white only. We recommend it for use in dining rooms, bedrooms, sitting rooms, etc. It can be made up with lace trimmings or can be made with ruffles of the same material. This is one of the finest, most perfect made point d'esprit materials listed on the market. Width, 48 inches.
No. 37C1865 Price, per yard..............35c
No. 37C1867 Finer quality than above. Width, 54 inches. Price, per yard..............55c
At 75 cents per yard we offer one of the finest qualities made, and it is very much used for white dress materials. Width, 54 inches.
No. 37C1869 Price, per yard..............75c

Our New Fish Net Curtain Material at 12½ Cents per Yard.

This lace curtain material comes in white, also cream. It is pretty as well as being strong and durable. Width, 36 inches.
No. 37C1871
Price, per yard..........12½c

Fleur de Lis Loop Fish Net, 18 Cents per Yard.

This is a rarely pretty pattern of strong loop fish net. Comes in cream, also white. Width, 50 inches. Style like illustration.
No. 37C1875 Price, per yard..............18c

FANCY FISH NETS.

Our Handsome New Lace 20-inch Fish Net at 14 Cents per Yard.

This is a beautiful lace material, used extensively in decorations for panels and side windows and for various purposes. From the accompanying illustration you can form an idea of the handsome pattern of this new fish net. Comes in pure white only. Width, 20 inches.
No. 37C1879 Price, per yard..............14c

Our Handsome Bordered 36-inch White Fish Net at 16 Cents per Yard.

The accompanying illustration will give you an idea of the handsome pattern in which this fish net comes. It has a very fine lace edge on both sides with a medallion effect in the center and on one side it has a very handsome lace insertion. This, we think, will prove one of the best and most popular fish nets in our lace curtain department. Width, 36 inches.
No. 37C1883 Price, per yard..............16c

WE DO NOT
SEND SAMPLES OF THESE GOODS.

Our New 30-inch White Fish Net at 18 Cents per Yard.

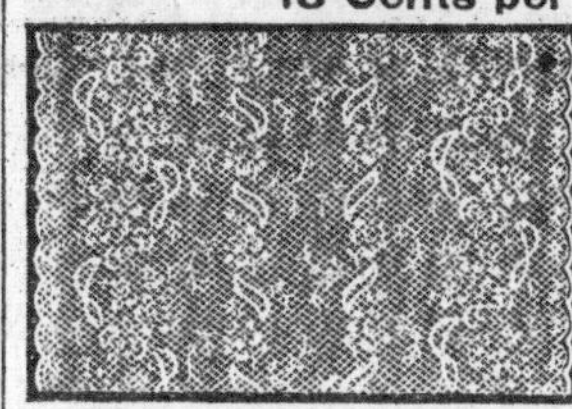

This is another handsome design in this popular lace. The accompanying illustration was taken from a photograph and is a correct reproduction. It is a very strong, well made fish net, and will prove a great bargain at our special price. Width, 30 inches.
No. 37C1887 Price, per yard..............18c

Our Fine Nottingham Lace Curtain Material at 19 Cents per Yard.

This is a fine quality of Nottingham lace net. Has overlocked corded edge, is well made. Has beautiful pattern, like the illustration. Comes in pure white only. Width, 50 inches.
No. 37C1891
Price, per yard, 19c

Our 57-inch Fine Nottingham Lace Material at 25 Cents per Yard.

The accompanying illustration will give you some idea of the pretty pattern this comes in. It is a good quality of net and is nicely finished. It comes in white only. Width, 57 in.
No. 37C1895
Price, per yd., 25c

Our New Fine Cable Net Nottingham Lace Curtain Material at 20c per Yard.

This is a very well made lace with a corded edge in pattern like the illustration accompanying. Comes in white only. Width, 30 inches.
No. 37C1899
Price, per yd., 20c

Our 27-inch Extra Special Fish Net at 24c.

This is one of our new designs, something that we have selected as one of the daintiest and finest fish net laces that we have ever had in our department. We think that any lady who will secure this handsome pattern of fish net will be more than pleased with its wearing qualities and its beauty of design. Width, 27 inches.
No. 37C1903 Price, per yard..............24c

Our New Handsome Striped White Fish Net at 25 Cents per Yard.

The illustration will show this very pretty design in fish net. The material is of a very strong and durable character and at the same time dainty in design and effect. We consider this one of our strong numbers. Width, 27 inches.
No. 37C1907 Price, per yard..............25c

Our New Handsome 36-inch Bagdad Draperies for 17c per Yard.

These are the genuine Bagdad colors. They are imported goods. They are cloths that sell everywhere at 25c and as high as 35c per yard. We have bought a tremendous lot of these imported genuine Bagdad materials at about 50 cents on the dollar, and as long as they last, which we think will be about the term of this catalogue, which is twelve months, we will be able to supply these beautiful draperies in any quantity. They are swell patterns, and the accompanying illustration gives you a faint idea of the designs. They have a beautiful combination of colorings and are handsomely worked out in oriental fabrics. The colorings that prevail in these beautiful Bagdad draperies are navies, reds, greens, olives or browns. Width, 36 ins.
No. 37C1911 Price, per yard..............17c

Tinsel Drapery.

Tinsel Drapery. A very pretty thing for draperies of all kinds. Comes in cardinal, blue, olive, rose or green backgrounds, with other pretty colorings to harmonize. Width, 27 inches.

No. 37C1915 Price, per yard......... 8c

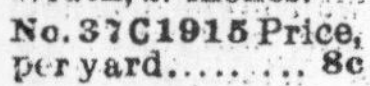

The Best Quality of Silkoline Manufactured at 9 Cents per Yard.

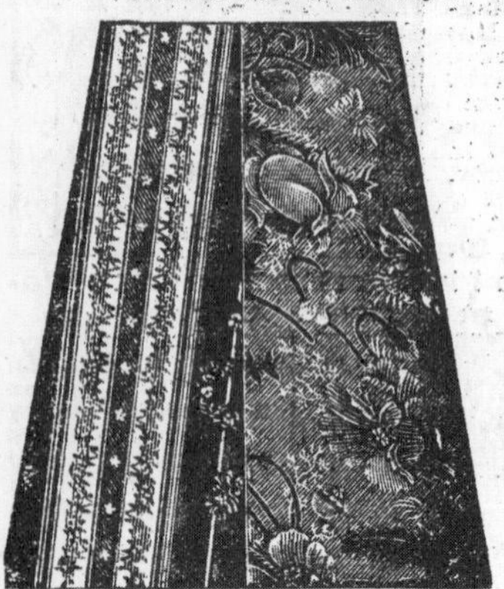

We have noticed that our trade demands something of a better quality than the ordinary silkolines and we have arranged to supply this want. The illustration will give you an idea of the styles and designs in which these handsome silkolines come. They come in reds, olives, niles blues, yellows, creams and also pinks. Width, 36 inches.

No. 37C1919 Price, per yard.................... 9c

Plain Colored Silkolines at 8 Cents.

This is one of the handsomest draperies used for draping doors, bookcases, windows and very much used for backs of sofa pillows, for fancy drapes, lambrequins and fancy work generally. This fabric comes 36 inches wide, is of a beautiful fine texture, finished to resemble silk, and comes in colors of white, cream, pink, light blue, yellow, lavender, light green, empire green, bright red, rose or cerise. Width, 36 inches.

No. 37C1923 Price, per yard....................8c

Figured Sateen Drapery. Just the thing for comforter coverings. Can also be used to make sofa pillows, draperies, etc. A very rich cloth. It is a splendid quality sateen. Pink, rose, red, blue, olive, yellow or nile green grounds, with pretty colorings to harmonize. Width, 36 inches.

No. 37C1927 Price, per yard.................13c

Handsome English Cretonne at 7 Cents a Yard.

English Cretonne or Drapery. Proper thing for furniture coverings or hangings. It is a good, strong cloth with a twill. Comes in black, navy, cream, red or green grounds, with pretty contrasting figures. Width, 25 inches.

No. 37C1931 Price, per yard....7c

Our 11½-Cent English Cretonne.

English Cretonne resembling above but much higher grade of goods. This number comes in dark rich colorings, also light grounds, such as rose, nile green, terra cotta, light blue, red, cream or olive, with pretty, contrasting colors. Width, 30 inches.

No. 37C1935 Price, per yard.......11½c

Denims for Drapery or Fancy Work.

Fancy Denim, the proper thing for draperies or fancy work. Comes in very rich colorings, good quality cloth. Colors are myrtle green, empire green, olive, red, blue or bronze grounds, with contrasting figures. Width, 32 in.

No. 37C1939 Price, per yard.............12c

Plain Art Denims.

This is one of the most serviceable materials for drapings, coverings, for fancy work, sofa pillows to be embroidered and for the various uses where a heavy, handsome fabric is required. The colors are red, green, blue or terra cotta in solid colors. Width, 36 inches.

No. 37C1943 Price, per yard.....................18c

Fancy Denim at 22 Cents per Yard.

Fancy Denim, comes in very pretty designs, on nile green, terra cotta, red or blue grounds. Width, 34 inches.

No. 37C1947 Price, per yard...........22c

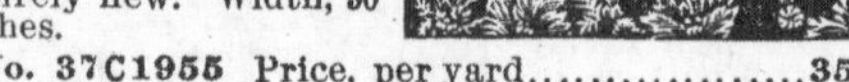

Our Handsome Satin Drapery Material at 35 Cents per Yard.

This is a satin damask with a beautiful design like the illustration. Used extensively for portieres, hangings and furniture coverings. Comes in cardinal, green, blue, terra cotta, olive or tobacco brown. It is a particularly well made material and the pattern which we are showing this season is entirely new. Width, 50 inches.

No. 37C1955 Price, per yard..................35c

Our New Fancy Tapestry Material at 48c.

This beautiful Tapestry comes 50 inches wide, with pattern like the illustration. Comes in basket weave background with large medallion effect designs. The colors are combinations of green and red and olive and rose, terra cotta and green and blue and ecru, also red and green and brown and ecru. Width, 50 inches.

No. 37C1959 Price, per yard. 48c

Our 50-inch Plain Rep at 45 Cents.

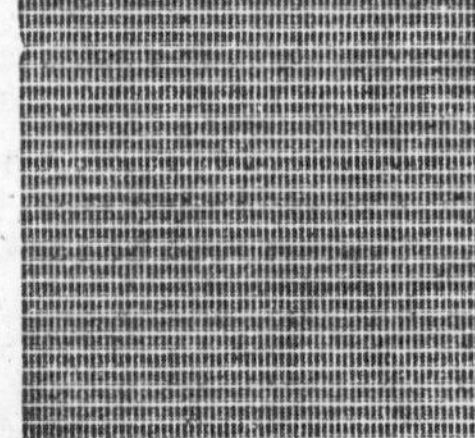

This is a very fine corded drapery, suitable for curtains, furniture coverings and draperies generally. It is very serviceable. It comes in a fine line of colors, including red, empire green or olive. Width, 50 inches.

No. 37C1963 Price, per yard............ 45c

Our New Figured Rep Drapery at 45 Cents per Yard.

This is an entirely new style with us this season. It is a very heavy, well made drapery. It comes in colors, red, green, olive, tobacco brown, also blue. It is 50 inches wide.

No. 37C1967 Price, per yard.............45c

Beautiful New Figured All Pure Silk Draperies, Season 1905. Special Price, 49 Cents per Yard.

This, our special 49-cent, 30 inches wide, all pure silk drapery; the best that is manufactured. It is made especially for all kinds of decorative purposes, for draperies, curtains, coverings, pillows, etc. They come in beautiful, large free hand floral prints, in red, pink, turquoise, olive, emerald, tan, cadet blue, new blue, nile green, reseda, violet, heliotrope; in fact, a complete range of the handsomest new colorings ever produced for this purpose, with contrasting colorings in floral, geometrical, Persian and oriental styles. **You can get, for 49 cents per yard, a 30-inch, all pure pongee silk, made expressly for beautiful drapery for fine homes, a silk you cannot** buy elsewhere at less than 75 cents to $1.00 a yard. Width, 30 inches.

No. 37C1971 Price, per yard............ ....49c

Our 63c Satin Finish Damask Drapery.

Satin Damask Drapery, extra superfine quality. It has a beautiful satin finish and is one of the finest qualities made. Comes in cardinal, terra cotta, olive, blue or brown background, with pretty contrasting colors to combine. Our drapery expert considers this one of the handsomest damask draperies he has secured for this department. It is a pattern that is entirely new; the effect is very rich; such goods as are seldom found in the smaller country stores at any price, **a class of goods to be had only in the exclusive carpet and drapery houses in large, metropolitan cities, and there at double our price.** Width, 50 inches.

No. 37C1975 Price, per yard..............63c

Our Fancy Figured Ottoman Drapery at 62 Cents per Yard.

The design in which we are showing this up to date Ottoman drapery is one of the newest brought out this season. It has a very heavy ottoman cord ground effect and comes in interchangeable colors. The pattern, as shown in the illustration, gives you a very good idea of same. It comes in green and red, brown and green, green and ecru, red and green, olive and gold, also blue and ecru. Width, 50 inches.

No. 37C1979 Price, per yard...............62c

New High Grade Mercerized Silk Damask Drapery at 75 Cents per Yard.

This new design in draperies comes in solid colors only. It is one of the prettiest and one of the brightest drapery materials we are showing this season. It has the appearance of silk, being made of the very finest cotton and under a new process which gives it the appearance of silk. It has all the appearance of a real silk that sells at $3.00 per yard and more. The colors are green, olive and red. Width, 50 inches.

No. 37C1983 Price, per yard......... ......75c

Our New Handsome Tricot or Cotton Gobelin Tapestry at 98 Cents per Yard.

This rich, luxuriousfigured drapery is in effect as pretty as some of the draperies that are shown in the retail stores in large cities at up to $3.50 per yard. The ground colorings are red, blue, olive, tobacco brown, empire green, apple green, also ivory. The combination of colorings on these solid colors is one of the handsomest produced by the weaver's and color combiner's art. Width, 50 inches.

No. 37C1987 Price, per yard....................98c

Our Mercerized Satin Damask Tapestry at $1.09 per Yard.

This is an extraordinary quality of satin figured damask that we are introducing to our trade as a very remarkable bargain at $1.09 per yard. The goods come full 50 inches wide, of a very heavy surface satin effect with pretty pattern designs, large floral and scroll effects. The ground colors are red, empire green, blue, olive, terra cotta or golden brown. These goods are not to be found except in high class drapery departments and then at fancy prices. In ordering give the color of the ground desired and we will pick out a handsome pattern which will be sure to please you. Width, 50 inches.

No. 37C1991 Price, per yard............$1.09

Our Luxurious Silk Satin Figured Damask Drapery at $1.75 per Yard.

This is one of the richest draperies produced by the weaver's skill, pretty enough for a palace, rich in coloring and in design of pattern. It comes in combinations of empire green, blue, tobacco brown, red, terra cotta, olive, nile or cerise, with very bright contrasting colorings in floral designs. Nothing richer could adorn any home. Width, 50 inches.

No. 37C1995 Price, per yard..............$1.75

Our New Reversible Brocade Silk Damask Drapery.

This is the acme of style and beauty. It is as rich as anything obtainable in draperies. We sell it as the very richest and most beautiful fabric that we have in our drapery department. It comes in combinations of light and dark tan and green, green and light tan, terra cotta and green and tan, cerise with green and tan, also rose with blue and bronze green. There is nothing richer to be found anywhere. Width, 50 inches.

No. 37C1999 Price, per yard..............$2.15

Our New 48-Inch Roman Striped Ottoman Drapery.

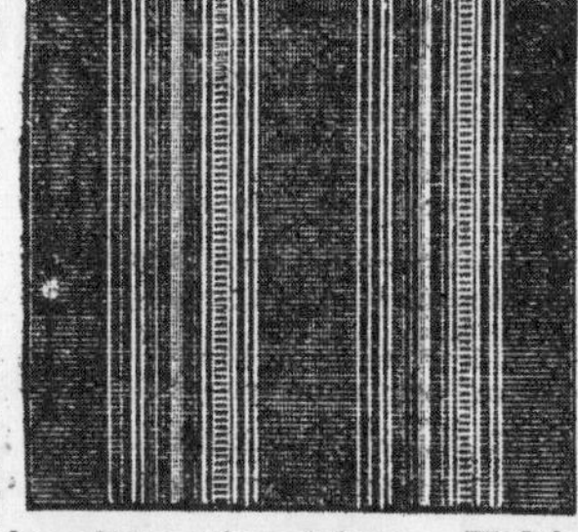

A handsome material for curtains, for drapes, for couch covers, and for various uses for which a fancy Ottoman with a stripe would be appropriate. It is good, durable material, strong, and the colors harmonize handsomely. Very pretty for draping cozy corners, Indian rooms, smoking rooms, dens, libraries, etc. Comes in red and green and red and blue alternating stripes. Width, 48 inches.

No. 37C2003 Price, per yard....................32c

28-Inch Verona Drapery at 59c per Yard.

Something decidedly new in a rich, deep pile, heavily brocaded velour. These goods come in a very heavy quality of epingeline or heavy velour ground with a very deep, rich velvet pile. They are extra heavy goods that will wear a lifetime. They are known as verona velours. They come in colorings, apple green, empire green or crimson. They make handsome portieres, draperies of various kinds, and are also used a great deal for couch and furniture coverings. Width, 28 inches.

No. 37C2007 Price, per yard....................59c

Our New Verdure Tapestry at $1.59 per Yard.

This is an entirely new fabric and anyone wishing a fine heavy and serviceable furniture covering cannot afford to overlook this number. It has the appearance of real tapestry. It comes in a pretty floral design brought out in a handsome combination of colors. It has a tan ground, the floral design being brought out in beautiful autumn shades of green, gold and a little red. Nothing prettier than this drapery. It is sold by large jobbers at $1.75 per yard. Width, 50 inches.

No. 37C2011 Price, per yard....................$1.59

Our $1.65 Imported Silk Gobelin Tapestry.

At $1.65 per yard we offer this, our very finest Imported French Silk Tapestry, for lambrequins, couch covers, furniture covers, pillows and draperies generally, in a big line of most beautiful colorings and handsome designs, all new effects for this season, we offer this line of fine silk tapestries in extra heavy weight, wear resisting quality, as the equal of tapestries that sell generally at $3.50 to $4.00 per yard. They come in combinations of cardinal, green, tan or rose, contrasted. Width, 50 inches.

No. 37C2015 Price, per yard......... $1.65

A New Departure.

We have added a line of extra heavy mohair plush goods for buggy robe linings. These goods are used extensively without any other material for buggy robes. In fact, they make a very handsome and stylish buggy robe. However, in the cold weather these goods are more adapted as a lining for a fur robe. We have two widths of mottled fancy design. Comes in black and red of a deep, rich shade.

No. 37C2019 Width, 54 inches. Price, per yard....................$1.39

No. 37C2023 Width, 60 inches. Price, per yard....................$1.55

It also comes in plain colors, myrtle or wine.

No. 37C2027 Width, 54 inches. Price, per yard....................$1.09

No. 37C2031 Width, 60 inches. Price, per yard....................$1.19

We also have a 3-inch width, scalloped felt trimming, used as a finish for the above mohair plush buggy robe linings. To match the colors described, also in royal blue, gold, golden brown and black, as well as the myrtle and cardinal to match the colors described above. We quote it in the colors, as very often these goods are used and preferred in a contrasting color to the colors as described. Width, 3 inches.

No. 37C2035 Price, per yard....................6c

Our New Extra Quality Printed Velour Drapery at 42 Cents per Yard.

This is a very heavy quality of velour or velvet. It has a very rich, deep pile surface. It has a very pretty design, as shown in the illustration. This is a quality that sells in large retail upholstery departments at anywhere from 75 cents per yard up. It comes in red, green, blue or brown. Width, 27 inches.

No. 37C2039 Price, per yard....................42c

Our 98-Cent 25-inch Imported Silk Drapery and Upholstery Plush.

For 98 cents we furnish this beautiful heavy weight Silk Plush in solid colors of all the beautiful colorings as described, as the equal of any 25-inch silk plush you can buy elsewhere at $1.50 to $2.00 per yard. It comes in the following plain, rich colors: Cardinal, garnet, gold, turquoise, national blue, olive and tobacco brown. Width, 25 inches.

No. 37C2043 Price, per yard....................98c

Crushed Upholstery Plush.

Crushed Upholstery Plush. There is nothing more durable for furniture covering. Extra heavy. Colors in gold, olive, bronze, terra cotta, blue or cardinal. Width, 24 inches.

No. 37C2047 Price, per yard....................98c

Felt for Table Covers, Draperies and Fancy Work.

No. 37C2051 An Extra Quality. Comes in all colors. Width, 72 inches. Price, per yard...$1.19

OUR LARGE AND IMPROVED DEPARTMENTS OF CHENILLE, TAPESTRY AND MERCERIZED SILK TABLE COVERS.

We have an entirely new line of styles in these beautiful table coverings. No old designs or styles to be shown this season. Everything new, pretty and right up to date.

Our Rich, Heavy, Oriental Tapestry Table Covers.

In presenting this handsome, new, Oriental Table Cover, we are showing some patterns different than we have ever had the opportunity to include in our extensive line of table covers. It is a very heavy, fine quality of tapestry, the pattern being brought out in oriental designs. The accompanying illustration will give you a slight idea of the style of this handsome cover, but in order to thoroughly appreciate it, it will be necessary to see it. Size, 72x72 inches.

These goods come in beautiful combinations of reds, blues, greens and tobacco brown. They are handsomer and richer than any we have ever been able to include in our popular line of table covers heretofore.

No. 37C2055 Price....................$3.50

Our New, Fashionable and Rich Mercerized Silk Table Covers.

This is a heavy material that has been made to look like silk through a process patented by a man called Mercer. It is not silk, but has the rich appearance of the real silk; is very heavy. Anyone buying one of these covers will find it one of the richest and handsomest covers that they have ever had the opportunity of seeing.

These covers come in beautiful shades and combinations of light and dark reds, empire green and gold, olive and rose.

No. 37C2059 Size, 54x54 inches. Price....$1.25

No. 37C2063 Size. 72x72 inches. Price.... 1.75

Our Extraordinarily Heavy Gobelin Tapestry Table Covers.

This is one of the handsomest tapestry table covers shown this season. It has a very pretty medallion center and very nice colored effects. The goods are very silky and it has a fringe all around. These table covers come in pretty designs of reds, greens or blues.

No. 37C2067 Size, 54x54 inches. Price......$1.59
No. 37C2071 Size, 72x72 inches. Price...... 2.75

Our Line of Rich, Heavy, Ottoman Table Covers.

This line of Ottoman Table Covers come in beautiful combinations and styles, of which the accompanying illustration will give you an idea. The colors are reds, greens, blues or tobacco brown. State preference of color when ordering.

No. 37C2075 Size, 38x38 inches. Price......$0.62
No. 37C2079 Size, 54x54 inches. Price...... 1.25
No. 37C2083 Size, 72x72 inches. Price. 1.89

Our Big List of Tapestry Table Covers.

These covers are made of pretty silky cotton and the patterns are handsome, better than anything we have ever been able to present before in this popular line of covers. They are fringed all around. All of the tapestry table covers come in assorted colors, reds, greens, blues or tobacco brown.

No. 37C2087 Size, 40x40 inches. Price........43c
No. 37C2091 Size, 54x54 inches. Price........79c
No. 37C2095 Size, 54x54 inches. In a very heavy and stylish design. Price........98c
No. 37C2099 Size, 72x72 inches, in one of the prettiest and richest tapestry table covers procurable. Price........$1.25

Chenille Table Covers.

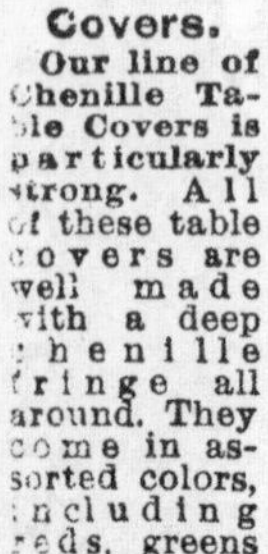

Our line of Chenille Table Covers is particularly strong. All of these table covers are well made with a deep chenille fringe all around. They come in assorted colors, including reds, greens or blues.

No. 37C2103 Size, 30x30 inches. Price........29c
No. 37C2107 Size, 45x45 inches. Price........60c
No. 37C2111 Size, 54x54 inches. Price........89c
No. 37C2115 Size, 54x54 inches; an extraordinary heavy and rich chenille cover. Price........$1.15
No. 37C2119 Size, 72x72 inches; in the very finest and best grade of chenille, rich and luxurious. Price........$2.25

From the illustration you can form some idea of this pretty chenille cover and at our special price of 95 cents it should be a winner. It is made of a nice quality of chenille and has a knotted fringe all around and comes in pretty combinations of colorings. Size, 54x54 inches, including fringe.

No. 37C2123 Price........95c

Our Very Best Chenille Table Covers at $1.35.

This cover is made of the best quality of chenille manufactured and is very heavy and closely woven. There is nothing better to be had at any price and the color combinations brought out in this cover are beautiful. Be sure to order one of these covers. Size, 56x56 inches, including fringe.

No. 37C2127 Price........$1.35

Our New Washable Tapestry Table Covers at $1.25.

In offering this cover to the public we feel that we are giving them good value for their money, as it is the only cover manufactured today that we can guarantee to wash and hold its color. It is made of a very fine quality of cotton yarn and is nicely finished and perfectly reversible. It comes in green and white, red and white and blue and white.

No. 37C2129 Size, 52x52 inches. Price......$1.25
No. 37C2131 Size, 66x66 inches. Price...... 1.60

Our New Ottoman, Fancy Striped Couch Cover for $1.65.

This is a good grade of Ottoman tapestry cloth, trimmed all around with a handsome fringe. It is an ample size, being 3¼ yards long by 60 inches wide, including the fringe in length and width, and without the fringe it is full 50 inches wide by 3 yards long. This Ottoman cover has a very pretty bayadere or horizontal cord. It has very pretty harmonizing colors, being of a Persian design. Almost all the colors that we could mention would be included in any of the covers sent you. It is reversible and has pretty tasseled fringe.

No. 37C2135 Price........$1.65

Stylish, Tapestry Couch Cover with Fringe All Around at $1.98.

This couch cover is 3 yards long and 60 inches wide. It makes an ample, rich covering for couches. This pretty couch cover comes in handsome stripe effects. The colorings are red and green combinations. In some the green predominates and in others the red. When ordering, state whether you wish a green or a red, and we will select one of our handsome styles that will be sure to please.

No. 37C2139 Price........$1.98

Rich Persian Striped Couch Cover, $2.48.

This is a couch cover that would be an ornament in any room. It comes in a large assortment of variegated contrasting stripes. It comes in shades of olive, deep Indian red, and porcelain with harmonizing contrasting pattern effects. The size is 55 inches wide by 3 yards long.

No. 37C2143 Price........$2.48

Our Extra Heavy Oriental Tapestry Couch Cover at $3.75.

This is one of the heaviest and richest couch covers to be found in any upholstery department. Comes in very rich designs and assorted colors, such as Blue and red; Green and red and also Green and brown. Our description will give you a faint idea of the design in which this cover comes, but you have to see the beauty of the colors, which harmonize perfectly, in order to appreciate this rich couch cover. It is perfectly reversible, and is very ample in size, being 60 inches wide by 3 yards long.

No. 37C2147 Price........$3.75

Our New, Very Heavy, Rich Persian Couch Cover, $4.50.

This is one of the handsomest couch covers that we could possibly have made. It is handsome in design, rich in coloring and almost indestructible. It is something that will last a lifetime and is an ornament to any home. Makes a handsome cover for Indian rooms, cozy corners, etc., in fact, it would be a handsome addition to any home in need of a beautiful couch cover. The colors are Tobacco brown and green; Red and blue; Red and green, also Green and red. They are perfectly reversible, one side being just as good as the other. Size, 60 inches wide by 3 yards long.

No. 37C2151 Price........$4.50

Our New Luxurious, Oriental Couch Cover, $6.25.

This extra heavy tapestry couch cover has a heavy, knotted and braided ecru fringe. Our description, no matter how carefully worded, could not possibly give you a correct idea of how beautiful this couch cover is. Its weight and rich coloring give it a distinctly extreme style. The colors are Red and blue or Blue and red and it is thoroughly reversible. Size, 62 inches wide by 3 yards long.

No. 37C2155 Price........$6.25

Our New Pretty Design of Rope Valance as per Illustration.

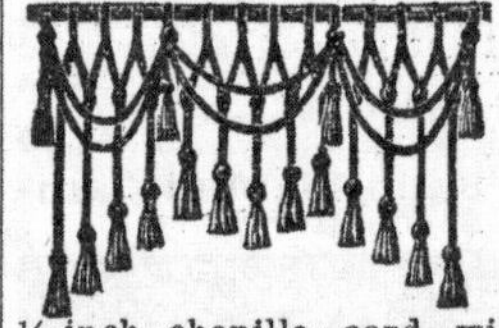

This beautiful valance is a very pretty drape which takes the place of grill work at division of parlors or can be used to take the place of lambrequins at doorways or over windows. Comes in very pretty shadings. It is made of ½-inch chenille cord with a very strong and durable heading. The colors are Green and red; Red and green; Red and blue; Green and rose. These rope valances are adaptable to any size door or window, as they can be adjusted to fit a space up to 6 feet wide.

No. 37C2159 Price........$1.29

Heavy, Rich, Solid Cord Valance, $2.25

It makes a very rich finish for a doorway or alcove. It is a ⅜-inch solid cord and comes in Light and dark green and red; Red, green and pink; Light and dark blue and pink; Red, green, blue and yellow in oriental combination; also Green and gold. This valance has a very massive appearance and is adaptable to any size doorway. Can be adjusted to fit a space up to 6 feet wide. The length is 33 inches.

No. 37C2163 Price........$2.25

Our New ¾-Inch Solid Cord Rope Portiere.

This is a very nobby, well constructed rope portiere suitable for single doorway. It is a very handsome furnishing for any room. Comes in Light and dark green and red; Red and green; Green and red; Light and dark green, pink and olive; Red, green, gold, black and blue in oriental combination; also Olive and gold. At our price, this is the handsomest rope portiere on the market.

No. 37C2167 Price........$2.10

Our Handsome New Design Rope Portiere at $2.75.

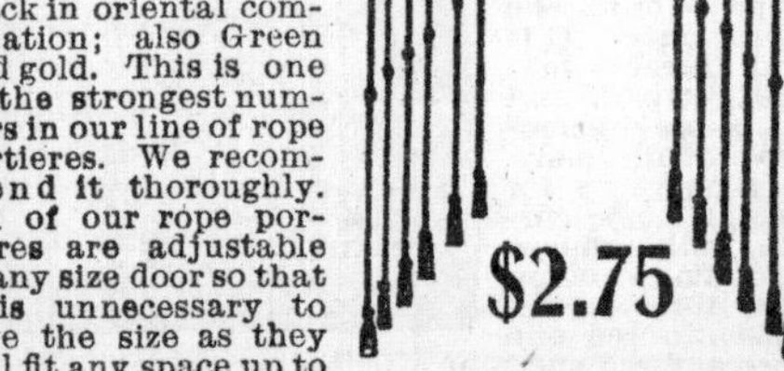

This handsome portiere is made of a one-half inch solid cord, combined with tinsel. Comes in Light and dark green and red; Dark green, red and pink; Red, green, gold, blue and black in oriental combination; also Green and gold. This is one of the strongest numbers in our line of rope portieres. We recommend it thoroughly. All of our rope portieres are adjustable to any size door so that it is unnecessary to give the size as they will fit any space up to 6 feet.

No. 37C2171 Price........$2.75

Our Special, Extraordinary, ¾-Inch Solid Rope Portiere at $3.98.

From the accompanying illustration you can form an idea of the beautiful design in which this portiere comes. It certainly is a very handsome portiere and at the price that we quote it is a portiere that cannot be matched by any other house. We claim for this portiere originality in design, as it is the handiwork of one of our own artists and we think it one of the handsomest portieres ever shown. Comes in Light and dark green and red; Red, green and pink; Light and dark green, red and pink; Green and gold. Send us your order for one of these handsome portieres and if it is not far superior to anything that you have ever seen at double the price, if it is not one of the handsomest portieres that you have ever been able to look at, if it is not better in every way than our description would lead you to expect, you may return it to us at our expense and we will immediately refund your money.

No. 37C2175 Price......$3.98

Our Richest and Best ¾-Inch Solid Cord Rope Portiere, $4.35.

This is the very best portiere which we have in our upholstery department. It is suited for the very finest homes. It is something that adds to the appearance of any room in which it is used, it is well made, rich in design, and in every way a portiere that will be appreciated by people of refined taste. The colors in which it comes are Light and dark green and red; Red and green; Green and red; Light and dark green, pink and olive; Red, green, gold, black and blue in oriental combination; also Olive and gold. When ordering carpets and other curtains do not fail to include one or more of these handsome ¾-inch solid cord rope portieres.

No. 37C2179 Price......$4.35

A NEW INNOVATION.

OUR NEW EXQUISITE STYLES IN FESTOON DRAPERIES.

These fancy, decorative draperies or lambrequins, are now the vogue in Europe and the East generally. Nothing in draperies furnishes a house more sumptuously than these fancy festoons. The accompanying illustrations will give you an idea of the beautiful styles in which these rich hangings are draped. Nothing prettier for draping doorways between parlors, for bay windows or for nooks or cozy corners.

Our Handsome Basket Weave, Festoon Drapery, Size for 5 to 6-foot Doorway or Window Like Accompanying Illustration, at $4.50.

This is a very handsome quality of drapery material, comes in colors, Green and red, Olive and rose, Brown and ecru, Terra cotta and green, Red and green, also Blue and ecru. Has fringe all around, also very handsome edging outlining the beautiful folds, as illustrated. This is certainly a bargain at the price.

No. 37C2183 Price......$4.50

Our Handsome Ottoman Drapery Lambrequin, at $4.95.

This very rich, heavy material comes in colors, Red and green, Green and ecru, Brown and green, Olive and gold, Green and red, also Blue and ecru. This is draped exactly as our previous number, but is of heavier and richer material. Drapes 5 to 6 feet.

No. 37C2187 Price......$4.95

Our Rich, Mercerized Armure Festoon Drapery at $7.25.

This is draped exactly as the two previous numbers, but the material is a very handsome mercerized silk armure. The colors are Red, Olive, also Myrtle Green of solid colors. Extension, 5 to 6 feet.

No. 37C2191 Price......$7.25

Our Basket Weave Handsome Damask Drapery, Like Accompanying Illustration, Extending from 4 feet 6 inches to 7 feet 6 inches and 8 feet high, at $5.75.

This beautiful style of lambrequin or festoon drapery is newer than anything else shown this season. It comes in colors Green and red, Olive and rose, Brown and ecru, Terra cotta and green, Red and green, also Blue and ecru, extends 4 feet 6 inches to 7 feet 6 inches, 8 feet high.

No. 37C2195 Price......$5.75

Our Handsome Ottoman Damask Drapery at $6.75.

This beautiful style like illustration with fringe all around and a handsome edge comes in colors, Green and ecru, Green and red, Brown and green, Olive and gold, Red and green, also Blue and ecru, extending from 4 feet 6 inches to 7 feet 6 inches, 8 feet high.

No. 37C2199 Price......$6.75

Our Beautiful Mercerized Armure Festoon Drapery, Like the Above Illustration, Solid Colors Only, at $9.39.

Nothing prettier shown than this handsome weave in mercerized silk draperies. We can furnish this handsome lambrequin in colors, Red, Olive, also Myrtle. Has a beautiful fringe matching the colors quoted, with a very pretty edge; extends from 4 feet 6 inches to 7 feet 7 inches, 8 feet high.

No. 37C2203 Price......$9.39

Our All Pure Silk Mantel or Piano Drapes at $1.75, $2.25 and $2.75 Each.

The accompanying illustration will give you an idea of how these drapes look when put on a piano or mantel. They are pure, heavy washable china silk, with a deep 6-inch knotted silk fringe all around, with drawing cord and tassels, as per the illustration. When ordering, please state the color of groundwork that you wish in the silk, and whether a large, medium or small pattern is desired, and we will guarantee to please you in selecting something handsome to harmonize with the ground color. We feel that we have never added anything to our drapery department that has so much merit and so much beauty, and we expect a tremendous demand for these fine, heavy silk drapes. They come in three qualities. Size, 30 x 81 inches.

No. 37C2207 Price......$1.75

This number comes in plain colors only, having no pattern whatever, but is made of heavy, rich, washable silk, in pure white, deep Indian red, gold, bright empire green, pale blue or nile. Size, 30 x 81 inches.

No. 37C2211 Price......$2.25

Our best number of these highly fashionable and pretty silk drapes comes in various colored grounds, with appropriate harmonizing Japanese and oriental designs. Colors are red, blue, green, gold, cerise or rose. Size, 30 x 81 inches.

No. 37C2215 Price......$2.75

Our Fancy Printed Velour, Deep Pile Mantel or Piano Drape at $2.95 Each.

This is the handsomest drape that has been shown this season. It is new in design and has a handsomely festooned and scalloped edge and is finished with a heavy knotted silk fringe. The edge of the border has small bunches of roses and foliage. Nothing prettier can be imagined than this luxurious drape. It is well made and has a beautiful silk finish, comes in red, myrtle, medium dark blue, and also a very pretty shade of golden brown. Size, 30 inches deep by 92 inches long including fringe.

No. 37C2219 Price......$2.95

Our Nobbiest Style of French Silk Finished Sateen Piano or Mantel Drape.

This beautiful drape has a plain center with a heavy printed border of American beauty roses and foliage, and comes in delicate colors of red, green, nile, pink, pale blue and cream. Size, 42 inches wide and 96 inches long, including fringe.

No. 37C2223 Price......$1.39

Our Large, Beautiful, French Sateen, Silk Finished, Printed Mantel or Piano Drape with Heavy Fringe, at 98 Cents.

This pretty style of drape is 36 inches deep and 99 inches long, including fringe. It comes in very beautiful colors, including green, red, nile, pink, light blue, also cream. The color effect of each of the shades is very pretty and the pattern represents lovers' knots and bunches of roses in ribbon effects.

No. 37C2227 Price......98c

Our Pretty Mantel or Piano Drape, Size 36 Inches Wide by 96 Inches Long, Including Fringe, 75 Cents.

This is a very nice quality of washable sateen. It has a very deep, well made fringe, 6 inches deep. This pretty drape comes in green, red, nile, pink, light blue, also cream, with very pretty harmonizing colors.

No. 37C2243 Price......75c

Our New, Popular Priced, Handsome Floral Design, Fine French Sateen Mantel or Piano Drape at 48 Cents.

This beautiful drape comes in size 34 inches deep by 90 inches long, including fringe. The background colors of the handsome design in which this drape comes, are red, light blue, cream, nile, also myrtle green.

No. 37C2247 Price......48c

Our Very Pretty Silk Finished Sateen Mantel Drape at 25 Cents.

This is a very pretty style and has a fringe 4 inches deep and is a very nice quality of silk finished sateen. Size, 19 inches deep by 80 inches long, including fringe. These drapes recommend themselves, as they are thoroughly washable. It comes in bright floral designs with ground color in red, myrtle, nile, pink, light blue and also cream.

No. 37C2251 Price......25c

CHENILLE PORTIERES.

OUR ENLARGED AND IMPROVED DEPARTMENT OF CHENILLE PORTIERES.

This Has Become One of the Largest and Most Important Lines of Our Upholstering Department.

WE ARE CONTINUALLY IMPROVING in the deep, rich colorings, getting new designs that are handsomer and colors better contrasted, putting in better qualities and buying in larger quantities, reducing the price to a minimum. Every number that we quote in our chenille portiere department is a wonder of value. Nothing more luxurious or handsome in colorings can be found. Very many of the styles are the handiwork of our own special artists, and as we control the output of large mills, we are in a position to quote you prices that are a saving of from 20 to 30 per cent. We push up the sales in this department by pulling down the profits.

Our Handsome New Chenille Portiere at $1.98.

This is entirely new in design, a curtain perfect in every respect, colorings bright and cheerful and is a very ample size. Width, 34 inches; length, 3 yards. Comes in handsome shades of red, blue, dark tan, terra cotta, olive, brown or green. Our special price of $1.98 is a price based on the actual cost of the material and labor, with but one small margin of profit added. Chenille portieres of this character, and in fact, of an inferior quality are sold in city retail stores at from $2.50 to $3.50 per pair.

No. 37C2255 Price, per pair......$1.98

Our Pretty New Chenille Portieres at $2.87 per Pair.

At $2.87 we offer this handsome, richly fringed, large portiere for the season of 1905; portieres that will equal any that sell anywhere at from $4.00 to $5.00 per pair. The illustration will give you some idea of the appearance of these curtains, but you must see them to appreciate their real value. They are of a very excellent quality of chenille with a very deep, rich border brought out in beautiful oriental, harmonizing colors. It is a curtain that will grace the handsomest rooms in either city or country. Comes in colors, red, green, blue, terra cotta or bronze, with handsome harmonizing borders. These curtains are 3 yards long and 40 inches wide.

No. 37C2259 Price, per pair.................$2.87

Our Extra Heavy New Chenille Portieres at $3.65 per Pair.

This extra heavy and large portiere is one of the handsomest shown this season. The design is extremely beautiful, made for us by one of the best mills in this country. These curtains are the latest style for this season and come in a variety of beautiful colorings, including olive, brown, terra cotta, dark tan, blue, red or green. Width, 46 inches; length, 3 yards.

No. 37C2263 Price, per pair...... $3.65

Our Extremely Rich, Heavy Chenille Portieres at $4.59 per Pair.

The dado effect is brought out in harmonizing colors, and the designs are entirely new and unique.

In these curtains is worked out a heavy, rich 36-inch fancy dado border trimmed with heavy tassel fringe, and the upper border, which is 9 inches in width, is finished with a heavy knotted fringe 12 inches deep. Comes in colors, red, green, blue, terra cotta, dark tan or bronze. Size, 3 yards long, 50 inches wide.

No. 37C2267 Price, per pair....$4.59

THESE illustrations will give you a good idea of the appearance of these beautiful curtains and you can order with the understanding that if the goods do not prove entirely satisfactory, they can be returned to us and your money will be promptly refunded; but, at the same time, if you wish to see these curtains illustrated in colors, write for our free, Special CARPET CATALOGUE.

OUR DEPARTMENT OF TAPESTRY PORTIERES.

THESE BEAUTIFUL HANGINGS are always in great demand and we have prepared more carefully than ever before to supply the demand of our increasing trade. We have made arrangements with large mills to supply us with quantities so large that it is possible to make new prices, lower than ever before, quality for quality. We have been more particular in selecting styles that are decidedly prettier than those shown by any other house, having spent large sums of money to get the designs of the best known and most expert designers, showing more variety than ever before. Portieres as fine as shown in any of the high class city retail stores, and at prices at about one-half what you would have to pay to the retailers. We have improved the colorings and put in better qualities for the money than ever before shown. The genius of the most expert weavers has been brought out in startling color effects and beautiful designs.

The department has been greatly enlarged and improved, and we have added stylish numbers in Tapestry, Persian, Oriental, as well as the new fashionable plain curtains with fancy border.

Also some swell effects in mercerized silk curtains, heavy rich portieres, so very fashionable now and for which other houses would ask three times the price quoted by us.

Our New, Rich, Heavily Fringed Tapestry Portieres at $1.49 per Pair.

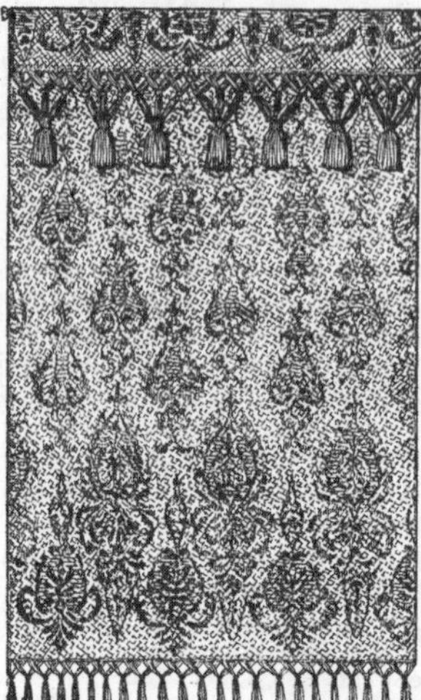

Nothing handsomer than this curtain is shown at such a low price. It is a curtain that certainly will be appreciated, as it is a remarkable value. It comes in a large line of colors, including red, green, terra cotta, blue, and also in combinations of red and green. The illustration will give you a very good idea of the pattern of this curtain. Size, 3 yards long by 34 inches wide.

No. 37C2271 Price, per pair........ $1.49

Our Pretty Heavily Fringed Tapestry Portieres at $1.98 per Pair.

This is an entirely new pattern and especially designed for us. It is an exceedingly beautiful curtain and a good value. Better than we have ever been able to get before at anywhere near this price. It comes in shades of red, green, terra cotta, blue, olive, also in combinations of red and green. Size, 3 yards long by 42 inches wide.

No. 37C2275 Price, per pair.................$1.98

Our New, Heavy, Ottoman Striped Portieres, at $2.10 per Pair.

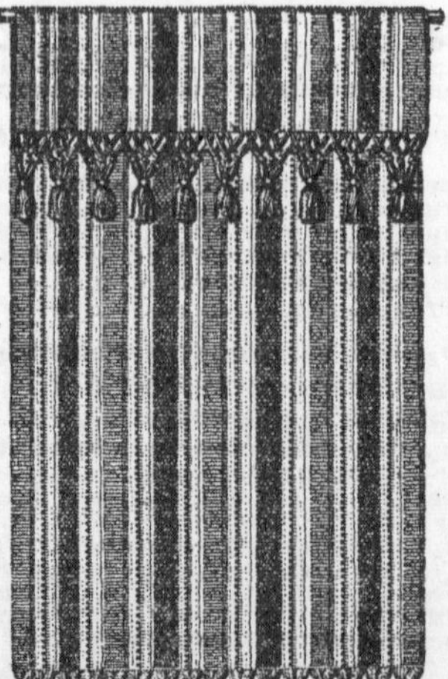

This is a better portiere than we have ever been able to present to our patrons at this price. It is a curtain appropriate for dens, libraries, Indian rooms, cozy corners, etc. It comes in two beautiful color combinations of Red and green, and also Red and blue. The accompanying illustration gives you a good idea of the general style of this curtain. Size, 3 yards long by 45 inches wide.

No. 37C2279 Price, per pair....$2.10

Our New Special Design Rich Tapestry Curtain at $2.65 per Pair.

This is an entirely new design and the pattern is brought out very distinct and prominent; has the deep, rich effect of some curtains that are sold as high as $5.00 in the city upholstering departments. We feel satisfied that we are giving to our patrons the very best value that it is possible to put out of a department when we give you these curtains at our special price of $2.65. You will not be disappointed in ordering one or more pairs of these curtains. They come in color combinations of Red, empire green, Red and green, Terra cotta, olive and blue. Size, 3 yards long, 48 inches wide.

No. 37C2283 Price, per pair...............$2.65

Our Heavy Tapestry Portieres at $2.98 per Pair.

The accompanying illustration will give you some idea of the pattern brought out in these handsome curtains. They have a heavy knotted fringe at top and are full size, measuring three yards long and fifty inches wide. They come in color combinations of Red and empire green, Green and red, Olive and tan, Tobacco brown and green, also Blue. Nothing handsomer could be produced at the price than this beautiful portiere. Size, 3 yards long by 50 inches wide.

No. 37C2287 Price, per pair.........$2.98

Our Extra Heavy Quality Portieres at $3.40 per Pair.

This curtain is entirely new for this season, and is one of the prettiest we have ever shown. From the illustration you can form some idea of the beauty and style of this curtain and at the extremely low price of $3.40 it should be one of our largest sellers. They come in a large assortment of colors comprising Red and green, Green and tan, Tobacco brown and green, Two toned red, Two toned green, also Blue. Size, 3 yards long by 48 inches wide.

No. 37C2291 Price, per pair...... $3.40

Our Swell Tapestry Portieres at $3.75 per Pair.

The accompanying illustration does not do justice to this beautiful portiere and at our price of $3.75 it should be a winner. It has a very heavy knotted fringe and is made of a nice, fine quality of cotton yarn, giving it the appearance of silk. If you want a medium priced portiere, don't overlook this number. We can furnish it in the following colors: Empire green and tan, Olive and rose, Two toned red or Two toned green. Size, 3 yards long by 48 inches wide.

No. 37C2295 Price, per pair..... ....$3.75

Our Heavy Ottoman Portieres at $4.25 per Pair.

We consider this one of the best and most serviceable portieres made. The accompanying illustration only gives you a faint idea of the beauty and style of this new ottoman portiere. It has a very heavy knotted fringe at top and comes in a large variety of colorings. We can furnish it in Red and green, Green and red, Tobacco brown and green, Olive and gold, Red and tan, Empire green and gold or Terra cotta and blue. If you want a good pair of portieres be sure and order one of these. Size, 3 yards long by 48 inches wide.

No. 37C2299 Price, per pair.... ....$4.25

Our New, Handsome, Biscuit Effect Center, With Handsome Scroll Border, Tapestry Portieres, $4.39 per Pair.

At the price at which we quote this handsome portiere it would be impossible to produce anything prettier, anything richer in design, or anything heavier or more perfect in quality. The illustration will give you a faint idea of its beauty, but if you receive the curtains you will certainly be surprised with the great value represented in this, one of our strongest numbers in tapestry portieres. It comes in beautiful color combinations of Dark red and green, Bright red and ...n, Tobacco brown and green, Empire green and ...ed, Olive and rose, also Blue. It is a curtain that the most particular lady would be proud of. It would be an ornament in any home. Comes in ample size, being 3 yards long and 50 inches wide.

No. 37C2303 Price, per pair..............$4.39

IN OUR FREE

CARPET CATALOGUE

WE SHOW THESE CURTAINS IN ACTUAL COLORINGS.

Our Leader; a Heavy, Mercerized Silk Portiere, at $4.98 per Pair.

This is the best curtain we have ever offered our patrons at anything like the price. It's a curtain that is sold all over the country at 50 per cent more than we ask for it and expect it to be one of our largest sellers. It has a heavy knotted fringe and is nicely finished throughout. It comes in solid colors only. We have it in bright red, dark red, myrtle green, olive green, nile green, empire green, also rose. Size, 3 yards long by 48 inches wide.

No. 37C2307 Price, per pair..........$4.98

This beautiful portiere is the very best money can buy and has the appearance of an all silk portiere that would cost three times the price. It has a heavy knotted fringe and is beautifully finished. It comes in solid colors only. We can furnish it in bright red, dark red, myrtle green, olive green, nile green, empire green, also rose. If you want a swell pair of portieres, order one of these. Size, 3 yards long by 48 inches wide.

No. 37C2311 Price, per pair........$7.50

Our New, Figured Armure Tapestry Border Trimmed Portiere at $3.75 per Pair.

We offer this very pretty and fashionable portiere at the very low price of $3.75. It comes in solid colors only and has a small allover figure on a closely woven rep ground with a 2¼-inch Persian border in very pretty contrasting colors. We can furnish the curtain in bright red, dark red, myrtle green, also olive green. Size, 3 yards long by 48 inches wide.

No. 37C2315 Price, per pair, $3.75

Our Handsome Border Trimmed Portieres at $5.48 per Pair.

They are made of a very fine quality of rep and come in plain colors only of bright red, dark red, myrtle green, also olive. They are trimmed with a 5-inch border in a floral design, as per illustration, in handsome contrasting colors, which give them a very rich appearance. Size, 3 yards long by 46 inches wide.

No. 37C2319 Price, per pair.........$5.48

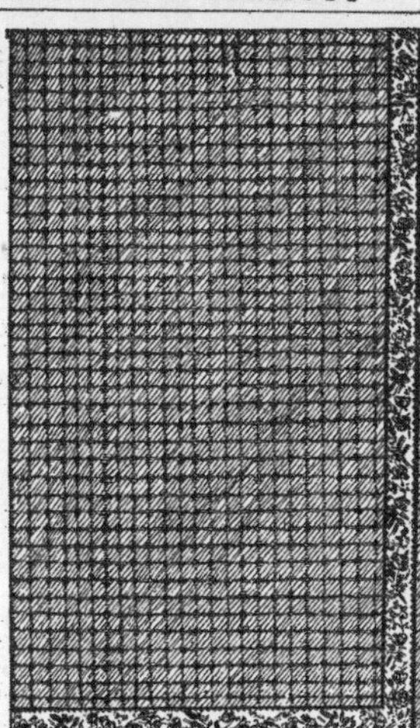

Our Best Border Trimmed Portieres at $5.95 per Pair.

This is one of the prettiest brought out this season and is entirely new. It is made of a fine quality of figured armure, being a small, neat figure on a rep ground. It comes in solid colors only and has an elegant 3-inch border on both sides, making it perfectly reversible, which is entirely new for this season in border trimmed curtains. We can furnish it in bright red, dark red, myrtle green, empire green, also olive. Size, 3 yards long by 46 inches wide.

No. 37C2323 Price, per pair........$5.95

Our Leader, at 98 Cents per Pair.

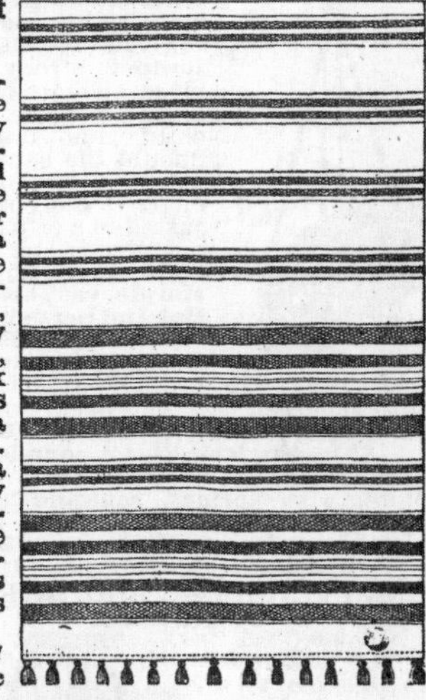

This is an extremely low price for this pretty cross striped madras curtain, and at our special price of 98 cents per pair should be a rapid seller. The ground of the curtain is a deep ecru, relieved by a pretty combination of Red, green, blue, pink and yellow, in cross stripes, giving it a very pretty effect. Anyone wishing a cheap and pretty drapery should order one or more pairs of this curtain. Size, 3 yards long by 49 inches wide.

No. 37C2327 Price, per pair .98c

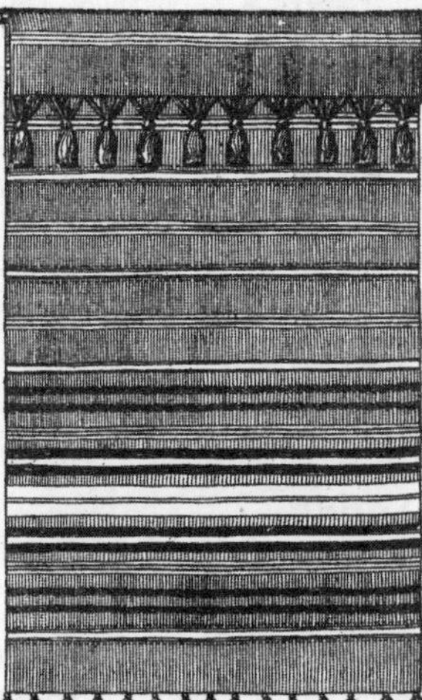

Our New Oriental Bayadere Curtains at $1.98 per Pair.

This curtain comes in the deep Indian colors and is particularly suited for smoking rooms, Indian rooms, cozy corners, etc. This is a very nice quality of madras, coming in deep, dull shades peculiar to Indian smoking rooms; also appropriate for libraries, summer cottages, etc. This curtain comes in dark red, dark green, nile green, also blue ground, with other pretty contrasting colors in cross stripes. Size, 3 yards long by 40 inches wide.

No. 37C2331 Price, per pair........$1.98

Our New Silk, Cross Stripe, Snowflake Portiere, at $2.50 per Pair.

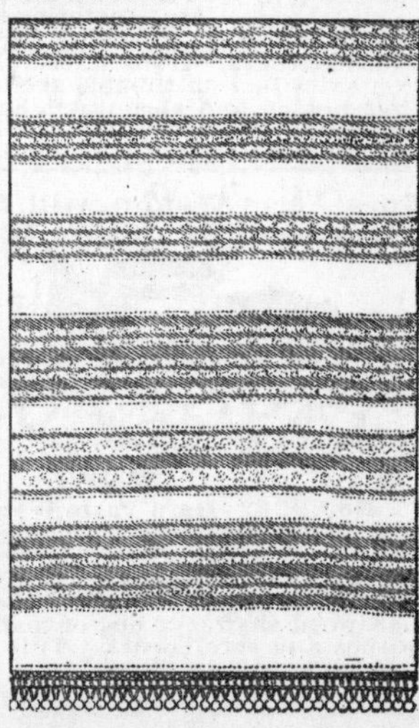

This beautiful curtain is one of the best of its kind manufactured. It makes a very pretty drape for parlor, library or dining room, and is very much used in place of lace curtains. We can furnish it in red, green, cream ground with other pretty contrasting colors in the cross stripes, which are silk, giving the curtain a very pretty effect. Size, 3 yards long by 40 inches wide.

No. 37C2335 Price, per pair.........$2.50

TOYS, GAMES AND HOLIDAY GIFTS.

Useful Birthday and Holiday Gifts, suitable for boys and girls, ladies and gentlemen. High grade articles at an immense saving on prices asked by the regular dealer.

Baby Swings.

No. 29C3 Baby Swing; has hardwood seat, 11 inches square, upholstered in cretonne; intended to be hung in a doorway; furnished with cotton rope and two hooks to hang it on; has no springs. Price........ 37c
Shipping weight, 3 pounds.

Jumper Springs.

No. 29C4 Springs for Baby Swings; made of heavy steel spring wire. 15 inches long. By adding a pair of these springs to above swing you have a baby jumper. Many people buy these springs and make their own jumper. Springs come in pairs. **Shipping wt., 2 lbs.** Price for springs only, per pair, **39c**

Baby Jumpers.

This Jumper combines in one article a baby swing, reclining chair, crib and jumper; strong and large enough for a child six years old; child cannot fall out. Should the baby fall asleep while in the chair it can be adjusted to a crib without disturbing the child. **It is light and simple, yet substantial and perfect.**

No. 29C8 Baby Jumper, complete, with springs and cotton rope and hooks, with veneered seat and back, not upholstered. Price.................**$1.23**
Shipping weight, 12 pounds.

No. 29C12 Baby Jumper, complete, with springs, rope and hooks, upholstered in cretonne, like illustration. Price.................**$1.75**
Shipping weight, 12 pounds.

Baby Jumper and Swing Combined.

No. 29C15
The stand is made on the best mechanical principles; will support a tested weight of 150 pounds. The only baby jumper that has a perfect reclining chair and foot rest and is adjustable. You can make a chair, cradle or crib by a single movement. All material used in the construction of the stand and chair is the best selected hardwood. Can be folded up when not in use and laid to one side. **You would not take three times the price and be without after having used same.** Shipping weight, 30 lbs. Price...**$3.35**

BOYS' WAGONS.

No. 29C58 Iron axles; body, 14x28 inches; wheels, 12 and 16 inches. Hardwood paneled body, landscape painting, scrolled and varnished, hub caps, high seat and dashboard. Iron braced, heavy iron axles in iron thimble skein, oval tires welded and shrunk on. Same as illustration. Price...............**$1.95**
Shipping weight, 28 pounds.

Boys' Express Wagons.

Boys' Steel Wagons. The best and strongest steel wagon made; finely painted and ornamented steel box, malleable iron gear, tinned steel wheels.

No. 29C64 Body, 13x26-inch; wheels, 8 and 12-inch. **Shipping weight, 18 pounds.** Price..................**$1.00**

No. 29C68 Body, 14x28-inch; wheels, 10 and 14-inch. **Shipping weight, 20 pounds.** Price..................**$1.20**

No. 29C72 Body, 15x30-inch; wheels, 12 and 16-inch. **Shipping weight, 22 pounds.** Price..................**$1.40**

No. 29C73 Steel Wagon Body, 16x32-inch. Wheels, 14 and 18-inch. **Shipping weight, 26 pounds.**
Price..................**$1.50**

No. 29C74 Boys' Special Steel Express Wagon. Body, 18x36 inches; wheels, 20 and 14 inches. **Shipping weight, 30 pounds.** Price......**$2.50**

The Little Gem Dime Savings Bank.

No. 29C155 Locks itself and registers the amount deposited. Opens automatically when $5.00 in dimes have been deposited without use of force; nickel plated, and can be carried conveniently in your vest pocket. Price, each.........**6c**
Per dozen.................**70c**
If by mail, postage extra, 2c

No. 29C157 Made same as above to hold and register 50 pennies. This gives the little ones an opportunity to save their spare pennies. Price, per doz., **70c**; each..**6c**
If by mail, postage extra, each, 4c.

The Finest Practical Savings Bank, 65 Cents.

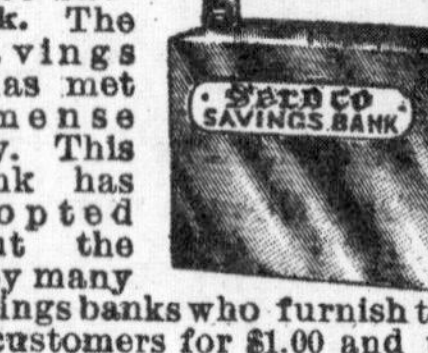

No. 29C159 The Seroco Savings Bank. The Seroco Savings Bank has met with immense popularity. This same bank has been adopted throughout the country by many of the savings banks who furnish them to their customers for $1.00 and they keep the key. We now offer them for sale, furnishing each bank with a key, at 65 cents each. The bank is made of the best cold rolled steel with the most perfect finish. Can be ordered in three styles: Copper oxidized, nickel plated, or gunmetal. Size, 4⅝x3¼x2⅜ inches. **Shipping weight, 1¾ lbs.**
Price, per dozen, **$7.50**; each.....**65c**
Special price to **savings banks:** We put your name plate on same when ordered in lots of not less than 50, at $7.50 per dozen.

The Canary Bird Whistle.

No. 29C217 The Canary Bird Whistle. Made of metal. All the pretty notes of the canary can be imitated. Lots of fun for boys and girls.
Price, per dozen, **30c**; each.........**3c**
If by mail, postage extra, 3 cents.

The Laughing Camera.

No. 29C221 The Laughing Camera. A whole passing show. Furnishes more amusement than you would get in a circus. Your friends grotesquely photographed. Stout people look thin and thin people look stout. By getting a focus on passing pedestrians, horses, cars, etc., the most ludicrous pictures are witnessed. **The passerby takes on the swinging stride of a grand-daddy-longlegs,** horses look like giraffes.
Price, per dozen, **$1.25**; each....**11c**
If by mail, postage extra, 5 cents.

Boys' Farm Wagon, with Seat, Handle and Shafts, for $4.65.

No. 29C62 Boys' Farm Wagon, with pole and shafts. Body, 18x36 inches, with hardwood frame. The sides and ends can be taken off, leaving bed with stakes. The gearing is made like a farm wagon, having bent hawns and adjustable reach; all parts are strongly ironed and braced; wheels are 14 and 20 inches; heavy welded tires; sand boxes and hub caps; has seat, handle and a pair of hardwood shafts for dog or goat. **It is handsomely ornamented with landscapes and scroll work. This wagon is the best in the market.** Shipping weight, 54 pounds. Price.................**$4.65**

FOR GOAT OR DOG HARNESS, SEE INDEX.

Jingle Return Ball.

No. 29C225 Jingle Return Ball. Made substantially of metal with a double wire eye and extra strong cord of pure rubber. The jingle is a musical sound which the ball makes as soon as it is set in motion, reminding one of sleigh bells. Will keep the children interested for hours.
Price, per dozen, 40c; each...........**4c**
If by mail, postage extra, 4 cents.

The Majestic Doll.

Nothing Made to Compare With Them.

The highest grade and finest doll ever produced. The body is the human shape, made of an indestructible flesh color pressed papier mache formed by hydraulic pressure, making same exceptionally light and indestructible, ball joints, moving eyes, hips, shoulders, elbows and wrists; also moving head and moving eyes, with eyelashes, open mouth, showing teeth; the very finest quality sewed wig made of human hair; has extra quality shoes and lace stockings; comes dressed in a fine lace and ribbon trimmed chemise. The eyes are tied with strings to back of head to prevent breaking when shipped. Comes in sizes, as follows:

No. 29C344 Majestic Doll as described above. This is a special number, made to sell at an extremely low price. Length, 18½ inches. Shipping weight, 4 pounds. Price..........**$1.00**

No. 29C348 Majestic Doll, as described above. This is another extra special doll, not quite as large proportions as the regular majestic doll, but a doll equal to anything sold at $2.50 elsewhere. Length, 22½ inches. Shipping weight, 5 lbs. Price.........**$1.40**

No. 29C352 Majestic Doll, as described above. This doll has larger proportions around body than above; extra fine finished and exceptionally pretty doll. Length, 21 inches. Shipping weight, 6 lbs. Price.........**$2.00**

No. 29C356 Majestic Doll, as described above. Still larger proportions around body than above. Length, 24½ inches. Shipping weight, 7 pounds.
Price..................**$2.75**

No. 29C360 Majestic Doll, as described above. This is an exceptionally large and beautiful doll, a doll that regularly retails for $5.00. Length, 27½ inches. Shipping weight, 8 pounds.
Price..................**$3.75**

Exceptional Large Size Dolls for the Money.

Not the finest quality, but well made, pretty faces, good kid bodies and very big values.

No. 29C368 Kid Body Doll, with straight hip and knee joints, fine quality bisque head, moving eyes. A doll that is usually sold by all dealers for 50 cents. Length, 14 inches. Shipping weight, 2 pounds.
Price..........**35c**

No. 29C372 Kid Body Doll, straight hip and knee joint. Fitted with a very pretty looking bisque head, moving eyes and fine sewed wig with new style hair dressing, tied with bows of ribbon. A very full sized fat body. Length, 16 inches. Shipping weight, 3 pounds.
Price..........................**50c**

No. 29C376 Kid Body Doll, with straight hip and knee joint, as described above with new style hair dressing, larger proportioned body. Length, 18½ inches. Shipping weight, 4 pounds. Price..................**75c**

No. 29C380 Kid Body Doll, with fine bisque head, fine sewed wig, new style hair dressing, as shown above. Very large sized body. An exceptionally fine doll, worth almost double our price. Length, 20½ inches. Shipping weight, 5 pounds. Price........**$1.00**

High Grade Kid Body Dolls.

With double riveted joints, fine bisque heads, very pretty faces, with full sewed wigs, new style hair dressing parted in middle. This is an extra fat body and large head. The riveted joints enable an adjustment, so that the doll will sit up or assume different positions. We list this doll in six different sizes. The larger the size of the doll, the better proportioned and larger is the body. We are sure that you could not duplicate any of these dolls within 50 per cent of the price we quote, as our prices are even less than the small dealer can buy them from his jobber.

No. 29C384 Fine Kid Body Doll, with riveted hip and knee joints, very full sized body, fine bisque head with full sewed wig, regular parting in middle. A fine grade doll. Length, 15 inches. Shipping weight, 2 pounds.
Price..........................**49c**

No. 29C388 Kid Body Doll. Same quality as above, with larger proportioned body. Length, 17 inches. Shipping weight, 2½ pounds.
Price.......................... **70c**

No. 29C397 Kid Body Doll, riveted joints as described above, but still larger body. Length, 20½ inches. Shipping weight, 3 pounds.
Price..........................**95c**

No. 29C401 Kid Body Doll, with full sewed wig, very beautiful bisque face, showing teeth, larger proportioned body than above. Length, 23½ inches. Shipping weight, 4 pounds.
Price..........................**$1.25**

No. 29C403 Kid Body Doll, with sewed wig, riveted joints, as described above, still larger proportioned body than above. Elegant value. Length, 25 inches. Shipping weight, 5 pounds.
Price..........................**$1.50**

No. 29C405 Kid Body Doll. This is a larger size. Made as described above with a very beautiful bisque head, full sewed wig, extra large proportioned body. Length, 27½ inches. Shipping weight, 6 pounds.
Price..........................**$1.90**

Kid Body Doll.

This is our very finest grade of kid body doll. With very fine extra size bisque head, moving eyes, has full sewed wig with new style hair dressing, parted in center and tied with bows of ribbon. The body has riveted hip, knee, arm and elbow joints. Fitted with lace shoes and stockings. Has also kid legs. This is as fine a kid body doll as you would wish. We have these in four sizes, all exceptional values, at $1.00, $1.50, $2.00 and $2.50.

No. 29C409 Kid Body Doll, as described above. Length 17 inches. Shipping weight, 2 pounds
Price..........................**$1.00**

No. 29C411 Kid Body Doll, with riveted joints, as described above, fine extra size bisque head, with moving eyes, large size body. Length, 21 inches Shipping weight, 2½ pounds.
Price..........................**$1.50**

No. 29C420 Kid Body Doll, riveted joints, as described above, larger size body and head. Length, 23 inches. Shipping weight, 3 pounds.
Price..........................**$2.00**

No. 29C424 Kid Body Doll, very large proportioned body and head. An exceptionally handsome doll. The very best grade of kid body doll that we carry. Length, 26 inches. Shipping weight, 4 pounds. Price, each, **$2.50**

LOOK

THROUGH OUR OTHER DEPARTMENTS and Include Everything You Need In Order.

New Unbreakable Dolls.

Silesia Body and Minerva Metal Head.

This is a doll that has just been placed on the market after our own idea. The body is made of best quality pink silesia, hair stuffed, has reinforced knee joints, imitation stockings with shoes. Has the silesia arms in imitation of kid. **Fitted with the well known Minerva head,** made of fine sheet metal, combining the beauty of a fine bisque head and being absolutely unbreakable and harmless. This makes it absolutely the best unbreakable doll ever produced. We have purchased these dolls in immensely large quantities and offer them at an exceptionally low price, considering the value of the doll body as well as the Minerva heads. At the prices quoted they are the best doll you could buy. We offer them in five sizes, as follows:

No. 29C428 Pink Silesia, Hair Stuffed Body Unbreakable Doll, fitted with Minerva head, as described above. Length, 11½ inches. Shipping weight, 1 pound. Price............25c

No. 29C432 Pink Silesia Hair Stuffed Body, fitted with Minerva doll head, as described above. Length, 14 inches. Shipping weight, 1½ pounds. Price............40c

No. 29C436 Pink Silesia Hair Stuffed Body, fitted with Minerva metal doll head as described above. Length, 15½ inches. Shipping weight, 2 pounds. Price............55c

No. 29C440 Pink Silesia Hair Stuffed Body, fitted with Minerva metal head, larger proportioned than above. Length, 17½ inches. Shipping weight, 3 pounds. Price............70c

No. 29C444 Pink Silesia Hair Stuffed Body, fitted with Minerva doll head. This head has the glass eye. Larger sized body and larger sized head than above. Length, 21 inches. Shipping weight, 4 pounds. Price............95c

Rag Dolls.

No. 29C468 Rag Doll, dressed in a fancy figured, short dress, with large yoke, has a pretty poke bonnet to match dress. Length, 16½ inches. Shipping weight, 14 ounces. Price............25c

No. 29C472 Rag Doll, with short dress, made of pretty figured lawn, neatly trimmed with lace and a nice hood of the same material to match dress. Has removable shoes and stockings. This is equal to many of the $1.00 rag dolls sold elsewhere. Length, 18 inches. Shipping weight, 16 ounces. Price............50c

No. 29C480 Reversible Rag Doll. This is a new novelty, two dolls in one. Dressed in a checked gingham dress, trimmed in lace; hood of same material, also lace trimmed. By reversing doll, you have another complete style of rag baby, which is a little **negro baby,** dressed with a red suit, having a separate white apron. This dress is also trimmed in lace, and the little colored baby has a red hood to match the dress. This is one of the biggest selling rag dolls ever placed on the market. Length, 14 inches. Shipping weight, 12 ounces. Price............95c

Unbreakable Leather Dolls.

No. 29C516 Unbreakable Leather Doll. This is baby's friend. The leather is very fine to chew on when teething. Impossible to hurt either the baby or the doll. Stuffed with cotton and will always retain its shape. This doll will last baby and also baby's brother. Coloring matter warranted not to come off. Length, 12½ inches. Shipping weight, 15 ounces. Price............40c

Pretty Dressed Dolls.

We Guarantee Values and Styles That Cannot Be Equaled.

We Cannot Show by Illustration How Nice They Are.

No. 29C528 Fancy Dressed Doll, full jointed body with turned bisque head, curly hair, shoes and stockings with very prettily trimmed, striped, pique dress with satin folds and sash, full frilled bonnet and pretty trimming to match dress. Shipping weight, 2 pounds. Price...25c

No. 29C532 Fancy Dressed Doll, bisque head, moving eyes, curly hair, shoes and stockings. Dressed with a fancy white lawn dress, colored silk blouse front and silk collar to match, trimmed with lace and a crepon sash. Fancy plaited bonnet to match. Shipping weight, 2¼ pounds. Price.....50c

No. 29C536 Fancy Dressed Doll, full jointed body, curly hair, shoes and stockings, dressed with a corded novelty silk, fancy collar of lace and satin with braided edge and pretty shoes with fancy buckle and a showy, fancy, straw braid hat, trimmed with a plume and large bow to match the dress. This is a sleeping doll. Shipping weight, 3¼ pounds. Price............$1.00

No. 29C540 Fancy Dressed Doll and fancy colored satin empire gown; new style collar, trimmed with lace and fancy braid, white plaited yoke with iridescent buttons, has a poke bonnet of colored satin, trimmed with lace to match the dress. This is a sleeping doll. Shipping weight, 3¾ pounds. Price............$1.50

No. 29C544 Dressed Doll, bisque head, curly hair, shoes and stockings, dressed with a beautifully colored, fancy striped, silk gossamer empire dress, trimmed in lace and with large balloon sleeves, has a vandyke collar and cuffs of lace, rosette and sash of satin ribbon to match. Has a large picture hat of satin, elaborately trimmed with ostrich plume and rosettes. This is a sleeping doll. Shipping weight, 4 pounds. Price............$2.25

Rubber Dolls, Figures and Animals.

White Rubber Dolls, imported high grade quality. Far superior to the domestic, which crack and do not give good satisfaction. These rubber dolls are dressed in knit woolen suits and hats in assorted colors. We guarantee these dolls as a very satisfactory article.

No. 29C560 White Rubber Dolls, dressed in knit suits and hats as described above. Size, 8 inches. Price............25c
If by mail, postage extra, 4 cents.

No. 29C564 White Rubber Dolls, dressed in knit suits, as described above. Fatter body and height 10½ inches. Price............50c
If by mail, postage extra, 6 cents.

No. 29C568 White Rubber Doll, knit suit and hat as described above; still fatter body and height 11¾ inches, regular $1.00 value. Price............75c
If by mail, postage extra, 8 cents.

No. 29C572 White Rubber Dolls, knit suits and hats as described above. This is a very large, fat body. Height, 13¼ inches. Exceptional value. Price............$1.00
If by mail, postage extra, 10 cents.

Imported Red Rubber for Quality. Made of Pure Rubber.

No. 29C576 Red Rubber Gnome or Lilliputian Figure Doll. A very attractive little toy, made of best quality red rubber. Height, 6½ inches. Price............25c
If by mail, postage, extra, 7c.

No. 29C580 Red Rubber Doll, made of best quality, imported red rubber, has German silver whistle. Height, 5¾ inches. Regular 50 cent value. Price............30c
If by mail, postage extra, 7 cents.

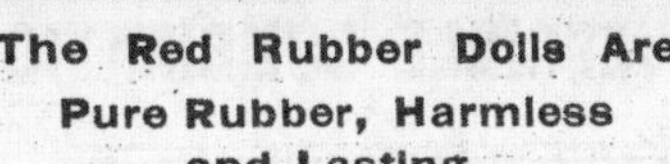

The Red Rubber Dolls Are Pure Rubber, Harmless and Lasting.

No. 29C584 Red Rubber Doll. Has German silver whistle. Height, 7½ inches. 75-cent quality elsewhere. Price............50c
If by mail, postage extra, 8 cents.

No. 29C588 Red Rubber Doll. Has German silver whistle. Height, 9¾ inches. This is good $1.00 value. Price............75c
If by mail, postage extra, 10 cents.

No. 29C592 Red Rubber Doll. Has German silver whistle. Very large, fat body. Height, 11 inches. As sold elsewhere for $1.50. Our price...$1.10
If by mail, postage extra, 12 cents.

Red Rubber Animals, 55 Cents

Red Rubber Toys. Made of the best quality imported Red Rubber, soft and durable. Absolutely safe and harmless for the children. The appearance is much prettier than that of the ordinary rubber toys. We have imported this line to meet the wants of the most critical trade and at prices at least one-third less than usually sold for.

No. 29C596 Horse, fully equipped with saddle and bridle, made of the very best quality red rubber, about 6 inches long and 5 inches high. Price............55c
If by mail, postage extra, 8 cents.

No. 29C600 Red Rubber Cat. A very pretty design. Length, about 6 inches, height, 5 inches. Price............55c
If by mail, postage extra, 8 cents.

No. 29C604 Red Rubber Dog, made of best quality red rubber. About 6 inches long and 5 inches high. Price............55c
If by mail, postage extra, 8 cents.

No. 29C608 Red Rubber Elephant, with oriental rug or saddle on back. Made of best quality red rubber. Length, about 6 inches, and height, 5 inches. Price............55c
If by mail, postage extra, 10 cents.

Kid Doll Bodies.

No. 29C612 Kid Body Dolls, very full size, extra quality cork stuffed, high grade kid bodies, with riveted hip joint and bisque arms, shoes and stockings. This is a very high grade and satisfactory body. Comes in sizes as follows:

Size	Length, inches	Inches across shoulders	Shipping weight, ozs.	Price
1	12½	3½	15	$0.35
2	16	4	25	.50
3	19	4¾	35	.70
4	21½	5½	45	1.00
5	23¾	6	60	1.25
6	24½	6¼	65	1.50
7	25½	7	75	1.75

Silesia Doll Bodies.

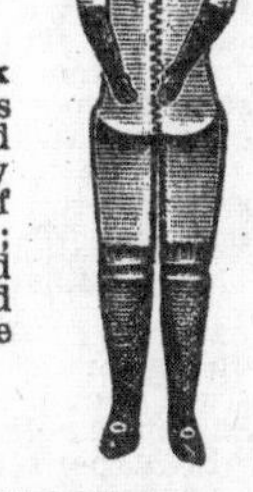

No. 29C616 Pink Silesia Doll Bodies. This is a very high grade and satisfactory silesia body that will give best of wear and satisfaction; has bisque arms and removable shoes and stockings. Comes in the following sizes:

Size	Length, inches	Inches across shoulders	Shipping weight, ozs.	Price
1	12	3¼	10	$0.25
2	15½	4	15	.30
3	16½	4½	20	.40
4	21	5½	25	.55
5	23½	6	30	.70
6	25½	6½	35	.85
7	26¾	7¼	40	1.00

Minerva Indestructible Metal Doll Heads.

No. 29C620 These Doll Heads are imported from Germany, they combine the durability of sheet metal and the beauty of bisque, are light in weight, washable, and will not chip; will stand any reasonable wear. Small children cannot injure them, larger ones love them for their unequaled beauty. The eyes are clear and tender, head flexible at the bust, and fitted with sewing holes, making it easy to adjust and fasten them to body. Come in sizes as follows:

Style	Height, inches	Inches across sh'lders	Shipping weight, ozs.	Price
2	3⅜	2¾	5	18c
3	3¾	3	6	22c
4	4⅛	3⅜	8	30c
5	4½	3⅝	9	35c
6	5	4	10	40c
7	6¼	4½	12	60c
8	6¾	5½	14	75c

Nos. 7 and 8 have glass eyes and open mouths, showing teeth.

The Minerva Indestructible Doll Head.

Sewed Wig and Moving Glass Eyes.

No. 29C624 The Minerva Indestructible Doll Head with moving glass eyes, open lips showing teeth, and very fine sewed curly wig. The Minerva heads, made of the best flexible sheet brass can be given to the smallest child with perfect safety, as the metal is covered with a pure wholesome paint which is manufactured especially for the purpose. Come in sizes as follows:

Style	Height, inches	Inches across sh'lders	Shipping weight, ozs.	Price
1	4	3	9	$0.38
3	4¾	3½	12	.70
5	5¾	4⅜	14	.95
7	6⅝	4⅞	16	1.25

Bisque Doll Heads, Moving Eyes.

IMMENSE VALUES. COMPARE SIZE AND PRICE.

No. 29C628 Bisque Doll Heads, first quality, high grade bisque, with very beautiful moulded faces, showing teeth, with two rows sewed wig and movable eyes. Either blondes or brunettes.

Style	Height, inches	Inches across shoulders	Shipping weight, ozs.	Price
1	3⅞	3	12	$0.19
2	4½	3½	24	.30
3	5¼	4¼	28	.45
4	6	5	32	.65
5	7	5½	36	.90
6	8¼	6¼	39	1.35
7	9	6¾	42	1.65

Bisque Doll Heads, Stationary Eyes.

No. 29C632 First Quality Bisque Doll Heads, the faces are especially beautiful, showing teeth, have stationary eyes, curly flowing wigs, either blondes or brunettes, and full model bust. Sizes:

Style	Height inches	Inches across shoulders	Shipping weight, ozs.	Price
1	3⅞	3	12	$0.10
2	4½	3½	22	.18
3	5¼	4¼	26	.25
4	6	5	30	.40
5	7	5½	34	.65
6	8¼	6¼	36	.90
7	9	6¾	40	1.25

ORDER CAREFULLY

— STATING —

Number, Size and Price

THE SEROCO REVERSIBLE COMBINATION GAME BOARD.

THE COMPLETE OUTFIT, $1.75 — ON THIS SEROCO GAME BOARD YOU CAN PLAY 75 GAMES

No. 29C636 This Combination Game Board with Revolving Game Board Stand and full set of rules for playing the different games. Price, for entire outfit........ $1.75

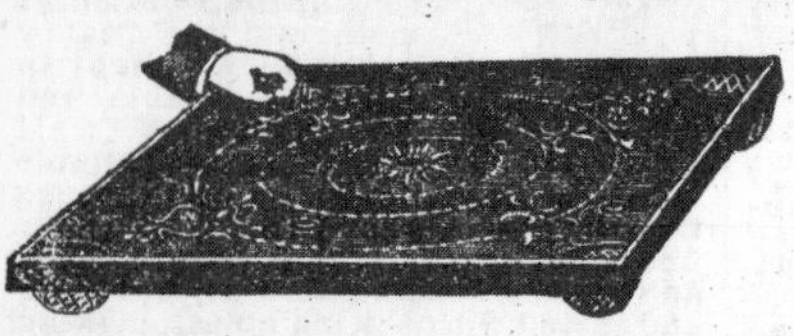

THE SEROCO REVERSIBLE GAME BOARD is the best combination game board on the market, and equal to the many boards that are sold at $2.75 to $4.00. Is the only board with circles to shoot from. You can play 75 games on this elegant combination board. Made of the very best hard ash wood with three-ply veneer, which prevents the board from warping. The circles and checkerboard, stenciled on in very high colors, thoroughly rubbed and varnished, which gives the board a very artistic appearance. The board is 28¾ inches square, with good net pockets. The illustrations show both sides of the board. Some of the games that can be played on the board are Pyramid, Chicago, Continuous Pool, Bottle Pool and Pin Pool, Billiards, Three Ring, Carrom Game, Crokinole, Fifteen Ring Pool, Checkers, Backgammon, and almost every game that can be played on any other game board can also be played on this board. With each board are furnished 29 nicely polished hardwood rings, two turned varnished cues, one set tenpins and extra movable back to prevent pins from being knocked off table, billiard attachment, and numbered rings for playing the different games of pool. No expense has been spared to make this board the very best. The games can be played by from two to eight persons.

THE GAME BOARD STAND for the Seroco Game Board is a firm support for the board at the proper height for players to sit on chairs. It being revolving makes it convenient. Made of best hardwood and nicely varnished. Folds up in a small compact package. The regular selling price of the game board alone is $2.75, and the regular price of the game board stand is 50 cents. By taking the entire output of a large factory, adding but our very small percentage of profit, we are enabled to place them on the market at the extremely low price for the board and stand of $1.75, which is less than the manufacturer's price to the dealer on other boards not so good.

EVERY BOARD GUARANTEED as represented and fully equal to the $3.50 and $4.00 boards sold by other concerns.

Price for set complete, board, stand, rings, cues, etc........ $1.75

WE DO NOT QUOTE OR LIST OTHER ADVERTISED GAME BOARDS as we would be obliged to sell them at from $2.75 to $4.50. On the Seroco Combination Board you can play 75 games and almost any game that can be played on any of the advertised boards you can also play on the Seroco Game Board. Our board is made in the very best manner possible, equal to any board and superior to most of them, and our price for board and stand complete is only $1.75. Order at once. Shipping weight, 14 pounds. BOOK OF INSTRUCTIONS WITH EACH GAME BOARD.

Chess and Checkerboards.

No. 29C640 Folding Chess or Checkerboard, lithographed in red and black and covered with imported morocco paper. Squares, 1 inch. Size of board, 14x14 inches.
Price, each....10c
Shipping weight, 10 ounces.

No. 29C644 Folding Chess or Checkerboard. This high grade checkerboard has black and red squares 1¼ inches, with gold lines ⅛ inch wide. The border is 2 inches wide in red, black and gold; covered with fine black embossed paper. Our best board. Size, 18x18 inches. Price........ 25c
Shipping weight, 1½ pounds.

Backgammon Boards.

No. 29C648 Folding Backgammon Board. 1⅛-inch squares in red and black, border in red, black and white. Covered with fancy illuminated paper, fitted with dice cups (no dice) and set of checkers. Size of board, 12x12x⅝ inches.
Price, per set........ 10c
Shipping weight, 10 ounces.

No. 29C657 Folding Backgammon Board, same style as above, squares 1¼ inches, lined off with gold and varnished, with fancy illuminated paper. Fitted with complete set of checkers and two dice cups. (No dice.) Size of board, 15x15 inches. Price, per set...20c
Shipping weight, 1¼ pounds.

No. 29C659 Folding Backgammon Board in book form, squares 1½ inches, finished in durable embossed imitation leather. Fitted with dice cups (no dice) and complete set of checkers in separate box. Size of board, 15x15 inches. If you would pay $1.00 you could get no better board.
Price, per set........ 45c
Shipping weight, 1½ pounds.

Spanish-American Chess Men.

No. 29C661 The finest Spanish American Chess Men. 32 pieces in the set, finished in black and yellow. Put up in nice pasteboard box. Usually retail at 50 cents. Price, per set...25c
Shipping weight, 10 ounces.

No. 29C663 Chess Men. Good size. French pattern, made of hardwood, finished in black and white, 32 pieces in a set. Put up in nice wood box with sliding cover. Price, per set........ 45c
Shipping weight, 15 ounces.

No. 29C665 Fine Boxwood Chess Men. Staunton pattern, black and white polished; in dovetailed polished hardwood box, with sliding cover.
Price, per set........ 80c
Shipping weight, 18 ounces.

Loaded Boxwood Chess Men.

No. 29C667 Loaded Boxwood Chess Men, in polished mahogany finished box. These are the Staunton pattern, in black and white, polished; an excellent set at the price.
Price, per set........ $1.75
Shipping weight, 1½ pounds.

Interlocking Checkers.

No. 29C669 Interlocking Checkers. Consisting of 30 pieces of enameled hardwood, diameter 1¼ inches. With the old style checker men you must hold both men to move a king, with these the rings interlock, and they may be moved as one man.
Price, per set........ 10c
Shipping weight, 10 ounces.

The King Embossed Checkers

No. 29C671 The King Embossed Checkers. 30 pieces of hard polished wood, 1¼ inches in diameter, packed in highly polished wood box, sliding cover.
Shipping weight, 12 ounces.
Price, per set........ 20c

Good Dominoes at Low Prices.

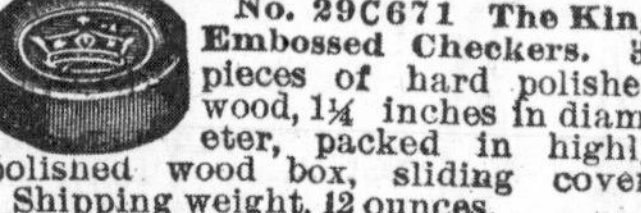

No. 29C673 Quarter Arabesque Domino, with round corners, made of selected hard maple, 28 pieces. Size, ⅜x1⅜ inches. Put up in paper box with special engraved label. Shipping weight, 7 ounces.
Price, per set........ 10c

No. 29C675 Double 9 Ebony Dominoes, consisting of 55 pieces. This is an entirely new set and we do not think a double nine domino has ever been offered at the price. In heavy paper boxes. Price, per set........ 22c
Shipping weight, 9 ounces.

No. 29C677 Crown Domino. Consisting of 28 pieces with fancy crown design on top. This is a special good number and put up in strong paper box with handsome lithographed label. Price, per set.... 25c
Shipping weight, 12 ounces.

No. 29C679 The Magna Domino. Set of 28 pieces, 2⅛x1$\frac{1}{16}$ inches, packed in very heavy paper box. As you will notice by the dimensions this domino is of unusual size. Each piece perfect and durable. Shipping weight, 15 ounces.
Price, per set........ 50c

No. 29C681 Double 9 Domino. Consisting of 55 pieces, the same as the regular black domino, with the addition of 7's 8's and 9's; more persons can play and the game has greater possibilities. Put up in frame box with label glossed. Shipping weight, 23 ounces.
Price, per set........ 75c

Lotto.

No. 29C683 Wood frame box, size, 4¼x7¼ inches, with sleeve and lift cover, 24 cards, 90 wood discs, numbered, with inside box containing glasses and counters. Covered with fine lithographed label. Price........ 25c
Shipping weight, 20 ounces.

No. 29C685 Lotto, better grade than above, wood frame box, with sleeve and hinge cover, 24 large cards, 90 wood discs, numbered, pack 50 cards, counters of different colors in inside box, also separate inside box of glasses. A large elegant set. Price........ 50c
Shipping weight, 2 pounds.

Large Size Ouija, or Egyptian Luck Board.

No. 29C687 Without a doubt the most remarkable and interesting and mystifying production of the age. Its operations are always interesting and sometimes invaluable; answering as it does, questions concerning the past, present and future. Full directions for operating the Ouija board accompanying each board. Packed each one in a pasteboard box. Cannot be sent by mail. Regular $1.00 size. Price........ 83c
Shipping weight, 3 pounds.

PLAYING CARDS.

The Denver Plaid Back Cards.

No. 29C1862 Denver Plaid Back Waterproof Cards, round corners, double index, made in plaid, blue star, green star, Spanish wave and calico backs. Weight, per pack, 4 ounces.
Price, per pack.. $0.06
Per dozen........ .70
Per gross........ 8.00
If by mail, postage extra, per pack, 5 cents.

Linen Finish Playing Cards.

No. 29C1864 Special Linen Finish Playing Cards, with round corners, double index, in large, plain figures, in a pretty back design. This same quality card is frequently sold at 25 cents per pack.
Price, per pack.....10c
Per dozen........ $1.10
If by mail, postage extra, per pack, 5 cents.

Waterproof Playing Cards.

No. 29C1866 Tally-Ho, Waterproof Finish, No. 9, half linen, round cornered, double index, extra enameled; large variety of handsomely designed backs in different tints and colors; the best enameled card at the price in the market. Washable. Price, per pack... $0.14
Per dozen........ 1.65
If by mail, postage extra, per pack, 5c.

Bicycle Cards.

No. 29C1868 Bicycle No. 808, superior ivory, enameled finish, a variety of appropriate backs, used largely by professional and other card players throughout the world. Weight, per pack, 4 ounces.
Price, per pack........ $ 0.15
Per dozen........ 1.80
Per gross........ 21.60
If by mail, postage extra, per pack, 4c.

Hart's Angel Back Squeezers No. 35.

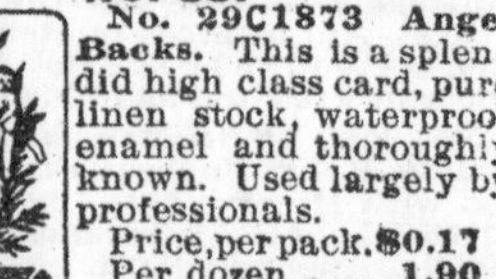

No. 29C1873 Angel Backs. This is a splendid high class card, pure linen stock, waterproof enamel and thoroughly known. Used largely by professionals.
Price, per pack, $0.17
Per dozen...... 1.90
Shipping weight, per pack, 4 ounces.

Congress Gold Edge Cards.

No. 29C1876 Congress Gold Edge Playing Cards. A new and artistic series of backs in high, rich colors, designed especially for card parties, social and home play. Can furnish them in the following backs: Rockwood Indian and Priscilla, as shown in illustrations; also The Old Mill, Rube, Butterfly, Chinese Dragon, etc. The highest grade quality linen. Put up in handsome case.
Price, per pack.. $0.35
Per dozen........ 3.90
If by mail, postage extra, per pack, 5c.

Stage Cards.

Showing All the Well Known Actors.

No. 29C1877 The Stage Playing Cards, the most attractive edition of playing cards ever issued and beautiful court card designs showing portraits of world renowned celebrities of the stage. Gold edges. Finest linen stock, double enamel and highly finished. Put up in handsome, gold stamped cases. Price, per pack. $0.38
Per dozen packs........ 4.50
If by mail, postage extra, per pack, 5c

Fortune Telling Cards.

No. 29C1879 The Nile Fortune Telling Cards. A new pack of fortune telling cards, tinted panel faces with the signification of each card printed on each face. Can be used by everyone. Sphinx backs, printed in high colors. Gold edges. Best linen stock, double enameled. Instructions for fortune telling in each pack. Complete for playing all regular card games. Price, per pack... $0.33
Per dozen packs........ 3.40
If by mail, postage extra, per pack, 5c

American Whist League.

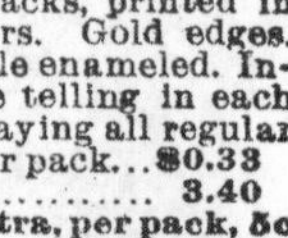

No. 29C1882 American Whist League, Waterproof. Extra enameled, half linen stock. The best enameled card made. Weight, 4 ounces.
Price, per pack ...20c
If by mail, postage extra, 5 cents.

Barcelona Cards.

No. 29C1884 Barcelona, No. 49 Spanish Monte Cards, 48 cards in pack, assortment of backs and colors. Weight, packed, 3 ounces.
Price, per pack........ 32c
If by mail, postage extra, 5 cents.

Pinochle Cards.

No. 29C1886 Pinochle Cards. Good quality linen finish stock, in a pretty designed back, full double deck from 9's up.
Price, per doz. packs, $1.10; per pack, 10c
If by mail, postage extra, per pack, 5 cents.

No. 29C1888 Pinochle Cards. Full deck with sevens and eights; high grade linen cards.
Price, per pack........ 33c
If by mail, postage extra, 5 cents.

Solo Cards.

No. 29C1889 Solo Cards. Finest linen cards, highly enameled and waterproof. Regulation 36 cards.
Price, per pack........................19c
If by mail, postage extra, 5 cents.

Skat Cards.

No. 29C1891 Skat Cards. Made of extra enameled half linen stock. A fine waterproof card.
Price, per pack........................19c
If by mail, postage extra, 5 cents.

FLINCH.

The Popular New Card Game.

No. 29C1894 Flinch. More simple than authors, more scientific than whist. Something entirely new in card games. Each pack consists of 150 cards, finest quality stock. The combinations resulting, while simple, are so intricate that the game has been pronounced by many to be more scientific than whist. Enjoyed by old and young alike.
Price, per pack..........................$0.33
Per dozen packs..........................3.75
If by mail, postage extra, per pack, 5c.

PIT.

No. 29C1896 The jolliest game ever invented for an informal good time. PIT is the latest craze and is being played by everybody, young and old. Learned in three minutes.
Price, per pack..........................$0.35
Per dozen packs..........................4.00
If by mail, postage extra, per pack, 5c

Paine's Duplicate Whist Sets.

Paine's Whist Tray Sets require no effort to insert or remove cards from the tray. Cards cannot be misplaced no matter how carelessly handled. Paine's Whist Tray Sets are now used by the American Whist League, the New England Whist League and many other associations and clubs.

No. 29C1898 Paine's Duplicate Whist Tray Outfit, 8-tray set.
Price..........................$3.00
Shipping weight, 4 pounds.

No. 29C1900 Paine's Duplicate Whist Tray Outfit, 12-tray set.
Price..........................$4.00
Shipping weight, 5 pounds.

No. 29C1902 Paine's Duplicate Whist Tray Outfit, 16-tray set.
Price..........................$5.00
Shipping weight, 8 pounds.

Poker Chips.

These Poker Chips are made by one of the largest manufacturers in the United States and are guaranteed for quality, durability and finish. The designs are handsomely engraved. Can only furnish in colors and assortments as specified. We claim our chips will outwear any other make.

No. 29C1916 Composition Poker Chips. Ivory finish, warranted not to chip or warp, 1½ inches in diameter, put up 100 in a box assorted as follows: 50 white, 25 red and 25 blue, or solid colors.
Price, per box of 100...$0.25
Per 1,000..........................2.40
Shipping weight, 32 ounces.

Engraved Poker Chips.

No. 29C1918 Texas Steer. Engraved design on composition. Ivory finish, warranted not to chip or warp. 1½ inches in diameter. Put up 100 in a box, assorted as follows: 50 white, 25 red and 25 blue.
Price, per box of 100...$0.55
Per 1,000..........................5.00
Shipping weight, 30 ounces.

No. 29C1920 The Lily. Engraved design on Composition. Ivory finish, 1½ inches in diameter. Put up 100 in a box, assorted as follows: 50 white, 25 red and 25 blue.
Price, per box of 100..........................$0.50
Per 1,000..........................4.75
Shipping weight, 30 ounces.

Composition Ivory Poker Chips.

No. 29C1922 The Doghead Poker Chip. Engraved design on composition ivory, 1½ inches in diameter. **This is one of the best poker chips in the market for practical use.** Packed 100 in a box, assorted as follows; 50 white, 25 red and 25 blue.
Price, per box of 100..........................$0.50
Per 1,000..........................4.75
Shipping weight, 30 ounces.

Our Special Design Carlo Poker Chips.

No. 29C1924 Special Design Engraved Poker Chip. This is a very neat and elegant design. Made of the best quality composition, will not break easily and stack even. Size, 1½ inches in diameter. Assorted 100 in box as follows: 50 white, 25 blue and 25 red.
Per box of 100..........................$0.60
Price, per 1000..........................5.50
Shipping weight, 30 ounces.

Fine Poker Chips at 52 Cents a Hundred.

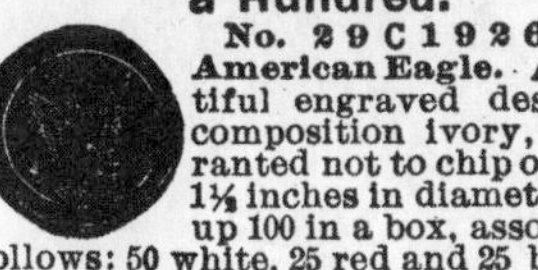

No. 29C1926 The American Eagle. A beautiful engraved design on composition ivory, warranted not to chip or warp. 1½ inches in diameter. Put up 100 in a box, assorted as follows: 50 white, 25 red and 25 blue, or solid colors. Price, per box of 100. $0.50
Per 1,000..........................4.75
Shipping weight, 30 ounces.

Inlaid Unbreakable Poker Chips for Professional Use.

No. 29C1928 Fleur de Lis design. Inlaid celluloid on highest grade of composition ivory; 1$\frac{1}{16}$ inches in diameter and put up 100 to the box; assorted, 50 white, 25 red and 25 blue; or can be ordered in the solid colors, 100 to box; red, white, blue, yellow, pink or brown. Absolutely perfect in every respect, warranted to stack perfectly, and used a great deal by professionals.
Price, per box of 100..........................$2.25
Per 1,000..........................21.90
Shipping weight, 34 ounces.

Unbreakable Poker Chips.

Light, Noiseless and Easy to Handle.

No. 29C1930 Unbreakable Poker Chips made by a new process, highly polished, look just as good as the compositions but are light and better than rubber. Stack evenly and outwear any other kind made. Put up in assorted boxes 25 red, 25 blue and 50 white, or in solid colors 100 to box—red, white, blue and orange. Shipping weight, 20 ounces. Price, per box of 100....$0.45
Per 1,000..........................4.00

Dice.

No. 29C1932 Bone Dice. Square corners. No. 6. Size, ½ inch.
Price, per gross, 95c; per doz......9c
If by mail, postage extra, per dozen, 3 cents.

Bone Dice at 15 to 36 Cents a Dozen.

No. 29C1934 Bone Dice. Square corners. No. 8, size, $\frac{9}{16}$ inch.
Price, per gross, $1.60; per doz..15c
If by mail, postage extra, per dozen, 6 cents.

No. 29C1936 Bone Dice. Round corners. No. 9, size, ⅝ inch.
Price, per gross, $2.25; per doz..22c
If by mail, postage extra, per dozen, 6 cents.

No. 29C1938 Bone Dice. Square corners. No. 10, size, $\frac{11}{16}$ inch.
Price, per gross, $3.75; per doz..36c
If by mail, postage extra, per dozen, 6 cents.

Celluloid Poker Dice.

No. 29C1940 Representing Ace, King, Queen, Jack, Ten and Nine spots. Fine ivory finished celluloid, perfect goods; size, ⅝ inch. Set of five dice.
Price, per set of five..........................$0.40
Per dozen sets..........................4.75
If by mail, postage extra, per set, 4c.

No. 29C1942 Vegetable Ivory Poker Dice. The five dice represent ace, king, queen, jack, ten and nine spots, all enameled. Size, ⅝ inch.
Price, per set of five..........................$0.25
Per dozen sets..........................2.75
If by mail, postage extra, per set, 3 cents.

Celluloid Dice.

No. 29C1944 Celluloid Dice, cream color, with colored spots, ⅝ inch.
Per set (five dice to set)..........................28c
If by mail, postage extra, per set of five, 3 cents.

Transparent Celluloid Dice.

No. 29C1946 Made of pure transparent celluloid. Are clear as glass; colors green, magenta or saffron. Put up five in a box. Size, ⅝-inch.
Price, per set (five dice to a set) $0.45
Per dozen sets..........................5.00
If by mail, postage extra, per set, 3c.

Blank Dice.

No. 29C1948 Blank Bone Dice. These dice have no spots. We can furnish blank dice in three sizes.

Nos.	8	9	10
Size, inches	$\frac{9}{16}$	$\frac{10}{16}$	$\frac{11}{16}$
Price, per dozen	$0.15	$0.20	$0.30
Price, per gross	1.75	2.25	3.25

If by mail, postage extra, per dozen, 4c.

Vegetable Ivory Dice.

No. 29C1950 This is the latest style in dice, is made of the pure ivory nut. Is absolutely perfect. Size, $\frac{11}{16}$-inch. Five in set. Per set...$0.25
Per dozen sets..........................2.75
If by mail, postage extra, per set, 3c.

Dice Cups.

No. 29C1952 Sole Leather Dice Cup, 2 inches in diameter, 3 inches deep. Natural color. Price......12c
If by mail, postage extra, 4 cents.

No. 29C1954 Sole Leather Dice Cup, extra heavy, 2¼ inches in diameter, 3¼ inches deep. Tan color. Price..........................22c
If by mail, postage extra, 5 cents.

LeCount's Patent Cribbage Board.

No. 29C1956 Polished Metal Nickel Plate, with three double rows drilled holes, to score for three or six persons; face of polished black walnut with compartment for one pack of cards and another compartment containing nine steel cribbage pegs. Size, 2⅝x10½ inches. Shipping weight, 20 ounces.
Price..........................85c

Mirrors.

No. 29C4364 Oval Shaped Mirror, with polished nickeled stand for dresser or to hang up; fitted with best French beveled plate mirror in high piano polish finish selected hardwoods—walnut, santander or ebony—very high grade and beautiful mirror in sizes glass as follows:

Glass size, inches	4x6	5x7
Price	55c	75c
Shipping weight	16 ozs.	20 ozs.
Glass size, inches	6x8	7x9
Price	95c	$1.50
Shipping weight	24 ozs.	30 ozs.

No. 29C4366 Hand Mirror, with long handle, best quality French beveled mirror, fitted in highly piano polished hardwood frame, in walnut, mahogany or ebony. Can be ordered in either wood in different size glass as follows:
Size, 4x6 inches. Price, each...$0.48
Shipping weight, 20 ounces.
Size, 5x7 inches. Price, each.. .70
Shipping weight, 23 ounces.
Size, 6x8 inches. Price, each.. .90
Shipping weight, 27 ounces.
Size, 7x9 inches. Price, each.. 1.40
Shipping weight, 32 ounces.

No. 29C4368 Fine Hand Mirror, same shape as above, larger size, highly polished frame, heavy French plate beveled edge mirror. Entire length, 13¾ inches. Size of glass, 8x6 inches. In mahogany, sandalwood or imitation ebony. Price, each..........................$0.90
Per dozen..........................10.00
Shipping weight, each, 26 ounces.

Comb and Case.

No. 29C4376 Pocket Toilet Case. Highly polished horn comb; length, 5 inches. Put up in neat case with small mirror, as per illustration.
Price, per dozen, 44c; each..........4c
If by mail, postage extra, each, 2c.

Pocket Toilet Cases.

No. 29C4380 Pocket Toilet Case, vest pocket size. (Illustration shows it open). **Contains beveled mirror, celluloid comb and nail pick,** case handsomely covered with Russia leather; valuable companion.
Price, per dozen, $1.75; each....16c
If by mail, postage extra, each, 5c.

No. 29C4382 Pocket Toilet Case. Seal grain, leather covered, contains a heavy beveled mirror, comb, nail and ear pick with celluloid leaf between mirror and small pencil for keeping memorandums. Size, 3¼x2⅝ inches. This is a very high grade article at an exceptionally low price.
Price, per dozen, $2.50; each..23c
If by mail, postage extra, each, 5c.

No. 29C4384 Pocket Toilet Case. Genuine calf back, with elegant embossed design, contains heavy, beveled French mirror, comb, ear and nail pick with celluloid memorandum leaf with pencil for memorandums, satin lined, a very valuable and handy companion. Price..........................40c
If by mail, postage extra, 5 cents.

No. 29C4386 Pocket Toilet Case. This is our highest grade pocket companion. Consists of a fine Russia leather case, with heavy, embossed pattern on same, into which fits a fine French beveled mirror. To the back of the mirror are attached compartments in which are fitted comb, nail and ear pick. Regular 75-cent value. Price. (Postage extra, 5c). 50c

Soap Boxes.

No. 29C4388 Black Ebonized Celluloid Soap Box, with heavy sterling silver name plate to match the ebony sets and brushes.
Price, per dozen, $2.75; each....25c
If by mail, postage extra, each, 4c.

No. 29C4390 Celluloid Soap Box in Ivory, with gold plated sterling silver ornament on top.
Price, per dozen, $2.75; each..25c
If by mail, postage extra, each, 4c.

No. 29C4394 Infants' Toilet Set, consisting of good celluloid back hair brush, infants' celluloid fine comb and celluloid rattle, in ball shape, which revolves on long handle. Shipping weight, 10 ounces.
Price..........................50c

No. 29C4396 Baby's Toilet Outfit. This is a very sensible and pretty little outfit, consisting of one round celluloid powder box, one powder puff, one bone handled goat hair brush, one celluloid comb and one ear pick and cleaner. All nicely packed in box with lid. Weight, packed for shipment, 12 ozs.
Price, per set..........................79c

Imported Palm Plants.

No. 29C3700 Fine Imported Palm Plants, extensively used for ornamenting parlors and halls. These plants are naturally prepared and very lasting. They come packed flat, without the pots. Are easily set up. Sizes and prices are as follows:

Height, inches	36	40	45	60
Branches	4	5	7	10
Shipping w't., lbs.	6	8	8½	10
Price	45c	59c	68c	$1.63

The 10-branch palm comes in shape of a tree with removable branches to set in tin tubes, and branches much larger size than the 4, 5 and 7 branch plants.

Palm Trees.

Palm Trees with large trunk, so pretty for decorating parlors, halls, etc., make an immense show. Bright green painted bucket, the top of which is covered with moss, comes with each tree, all ready to set up. In two sizes.

No. 29C3704 7-foot palm with 9 branches.
Price..........................$3.50
Shipping weight, 25 pounds.

No. 29C3706 12-foot palm with 24 branches.
Price..........................$6.25
Shipping weight, 35 pounds.

A COMPLETE ASSORTMENT OF FANS.

Folding Fans.

No. 18C300 Folding Fan, with grain leatherette covered handles. The folds are plain. Colors, black, red or tan. Length, closed, 9 inches. Price, per dozen, $1.10; each..........10c
If by mail, postage extra, each, 3 cents.

No. 18C304 Folding Fan, our finest quality, with sea lion fancy leather covered handles. The folds are plain, of the best material. A very substantial as well as elegant fan. Length, when folded, 9½ inches. Colors, black, red or tan. 50-cent value.
Price, per dozen, $2.75; each....25c
If by mail, postage extra, 3 cents.

No. 18C308 Japanese Flat Silk Fans, beautifully decorated with hand paintings in assorted designs and assorted shapes. Size of fan, 8x9 inches. With jet enameled handles ornamented with cord and tassel. Regular 25-cent value.
Price, each...$0.10
Per dozen..... 1.10
If by mail, postage extra, each, 4 cents.

No. 18C312 Fancy Novelty Japanese Fan, made of good parchment, decorated in highly illuminated colors. The sticks are also decorated. A very pretty appearing fan. Length of sticks, 8 inches. Price..........10c
If by mail, postage extra, 3 cents.

No. 18C316 Fancy Imported Fan, made of figured parchment, decorated with silver spangles. White sticks to match. Length of sticks, 9 inches. 20-cent value. Price..........10c
If by mail, postage extra, 3 cents.

No. 18C320 Fancy Novelty Fan. This is a popular design. Very handsomely decorated with figures in silver and tinsel colors. The sticks are very close together and decorated. Size of sticks, 7½ inches. Price..........20c
If by mail, postage extra, 4 cents.

No. 18C324 Special White Silk Marcelaine Fan, decorated with silver spangles. The top is trimmed with narrow loop edge lace braid. White sticks to match. The fan is attached to a small fancy neck chain, made of Indian seed beads. Size of fan, 7½ inches. Price for fan with chain..22c
If by mail, postage extra, 3 cents.

No. 18C326 White Jap Silk Fan, prettily decorated with hand paintings. The top and bottom, trimmed with lace purling braid. Pretty enameled silver decorated sticks. Length of sticks, 8½ inches. Price..........23c
If by mail, postage extra, 3 cents.

No. 18C330 Misses' Pretty Fan. Made of white silk marcelaine. Very beautifully decorated with spangles and hand painted decorations. The fancy pressed sticks are decorated with silver. The top and bottom are trimmed with lace footing edge. Length of sticks, 6½ inches. Attached to fan is a fancy Indian seed bead neck chain.
Price for fan with chain..........44c
If by mail, postage extra, 3 cents.

No. 18C332 White Jap Silk Fan. This is a very effective design, hand painted with silver spangles. Top and bottom trimmed with lace purling braid, mounted on fancy design silver decorated sticks. This is a very rich looking and pretty fan. Length of sticks, 8½ inches. Price..........50c
If by mail, postage extra, 5 cents.

No. 18C336 Very Elegant White Gauze Fan, with dainty hand painted decorations and trimmed with honiton lace braid in fancy design. Top and bottom trimmed with lace purling braid. Has fancy carved white bone sticks. Sticks are 8¾ inches long. 75-cent value. Price..........50c
If by mail, postage extra, 5 cents.

No. 18C337 White Silk Marcelaine Fan, with fancy lace top. Beautifully decorated with delicate hand paintings and silver spangles. The bottom of fan is bound with feather edge braid, mounted on carved bone sticks. Length of sticks, 7½ inches.
Price..........75c
If by mail, postage extra, 5 cents.

No. 18C338 White Japanese Silk Fan. Marie Antoinette style. This is the new shape. Very prettily decorated with hand paintings and small silver spangles. Top and bottom trimmed with lace purling braid. Mounted on very prettily decorated white enameled sticks. Entire length of fan, 8½ inches; tapering on either side to 6 inches. Equal to regular 75-cent value. Price..........50c
If by mail, postage extra, 4 cents.

No. 18C342 Cocque Feather Fan, with hand painted decorations on leaves of the fan. Mounted on enameled sticks to match color of fan. This is exceptionally good value. Sold for about one-half of what you would pay elsewhere. Colors, white, blue or pink. Length of fan, 9 inches. Price..........23c
If by mail, postage extra. 5 cents.

No. 18C344 Feather Fan; made of cocque and soft downy feathers. Handsomely decorated in gilt and colored spangles. Mounted on white bone carved sticks. A particularly effective and desirable fan. Colors, white, blue or pink. Length of fan, 9 inches.
Price..........45c
If by mail, postage extra, 5 cents.

No. 18C348 Genuine White Ostrich Feather Fan, mounted on celluloid sticks in imitation of tortoise shell. This is an imitation of the very high grade articles, sold for $5.00 and $7.00 each. A most effective and striking fan. White only. Length of sticks, 9 inches. Price..........55c
If by mail, postage extra, 5 cents.

No. 18C350 Ostrich Feather Fan. Very thickly covered with good quality ostrich feathers, mounted on fancy design, decorated, enameled sticks. This fan we can furnish in colors, white, white and light blue, or white and pink. Length of fan, 10½ inches. Price...75c
If by mail, postage extra, 6 cents.

No. 18C354 Ostrich Feather Fan. This is a very high grade fan, made of good quality ostrich stock, mounted on white bone sticks, carved and decorated with gold. A particularly effective and pretty fan. Colors, white, pink or light blue. Length, 9½ inches.
Price..........$1.25
If by mail, postage extra, 6 cents.

No. 18C356 White Silk Marcelaine Fan, with silk lace top, decorated with hand paintings and silver spangles. Sticks are white enameled with pressed silver decorations. A very attractive fan. Length, 9½ inches.
Price..........42c
If by mail, postage extra, 5 cents.

No. 18C360 White Jap Silk Fan, with black trimmings. The lace top is in black, and the teneriffe medallion pattern is in black, and bottom is trimmed with black lace purling braid. Beautifully decorated with hand paintings in black, white and silver. The fancy designed white enameled sticks are also decorated in silver. Comes in all white also. Length, 8½ inches. Price..........(Postage extra, 5c.)..........80c

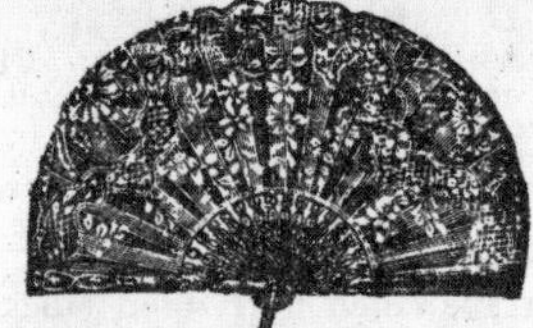

No. 18C362 This is a Beautiful Jap Silk Fan. Very handsomely decorated with hand paintings and tiny spangles. Trimmed with fancy lace, as per illustration. This is the new Marie Antoinette shape and is very stylish and effective. Very pretty, fancifully designed sticks, in silver and pressed decorations. Entire length of fan, 8½ inches. Price..........$1.00
If by mail, postage extra, 5 cents.

No. 18C364 This is a Particularly Attractive Fan. Made of white Jap silk. Beautifully decorated with honiton lace braid, silver spangles and lace trimmed top. The sticks are particularly pretty, being of fancy, open work, designed with pressed silver decorations. Length of sticks, 9½ inches. Price..........$1.10
If by mail, postage extra, 5 cents.

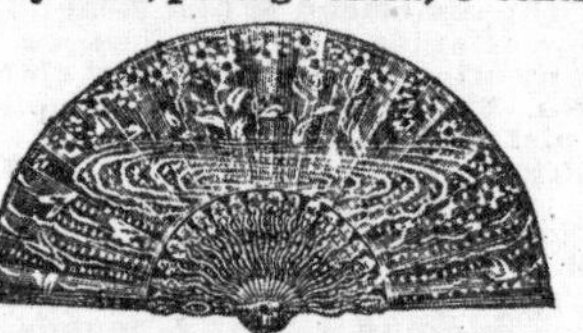

No. 18C368 White Jap Silk Fan, with gauze back. This is a very exquisite and beautiful fan, handsomely decorated with hand paintings and very artistic designs, closely interwoven with small spangles. Top and bottom trimmed with lace purling braid. Mounted on very beautiful, fancy designed, white enameled decorated sticks. Length of sticks, 8½ inches. Price..........$1.50
If by mail, postage extra, 4 cents.

No. 18C370 White Jap Silk Fan, with lace top. Very beautifully decorated with hand paintings and small spangles. A very attractive pattern, mounted on carved, white bone sticks inlaid with steel beads. This is a very high class fan. Length of sticks, 8 inches. Price..........$1.65
If by mail, postage extra, 5 cents.

No. 18C374 Black China Silk Fan. Good quality silk. Top and bottom trimmed with black lace purling braid, mounted on very elegant carved sticks in imitation of ebony. This is equal to the best 50-cent fan as sold elsewhere. Length of sticks, 8 inches. Price..25c
If by mail, postage extra, 4 cents.

No. 18C376 Black Double Gauze Fan. Very prettily decorated with dainty hand paintings and small spangles. Top and bottom trimmed with black purling lace braid, mounted on elegantly carved sticks in imitation of ebony. This is a very dainty and effective fan. Price, 95c
If by mail, postage extra, 5 cents.

HIGHEST GRADE KNITTING YARNS.

It is a pleasure to sell GOOD GOODS. They prove more than satisfactory to the purchaser, who in turn buys again and recommends the house he trades with. Our Knitting Yarns are trade makers. They run smoother, wear longer and go farther to the pound than any other yarn.

SEND US YOUR ORDER FOR ANY OF OUR HIGH GRADE YARNS, and if you do not find them even beyond your expectations, **return them to us at our expense and we will refund your money cheerfully.** We recommend our yarns for quality of wool, brilliancy and permanency of color, evenness and elasticity of thread.

WE DO NOT SAMPLE YARNS

German Yarns.

No. 18C1017 Standard Quality German Knitting Worsted Yarn, four skeins to the pound. Comes in the following colors: Cardinal, scarlet, medium and navy blue, purple, medium and seal brown, sheep's gray, black mixed, black or white.
Price, all colors, per skein........16c
Per pound........................70c

No. 18C1019 Royal Sunlight German Knitting Yarn, finest quality high grade yarn, four skeins to the pound; colors same as No. 18C1017. For a good satisfactory yarn buy the Royal, which contains a long wool filling; we **guarantee every hank sold.**
Price, all colors, per skein........23c
Per pound........................90c

No. 18C1021 Fleisher's German Knitting Worsted Yarn, always runs smooth and always the same, four skeins to the pound. Colors same as No. 18C1017. Fleisher's yarn needs no recommendation. **It is too well known.** Price, all colors, per skein..25c
Per pound........................95c

Saxony Wool Yarn.

No. 18C1023 Saxony Wool Yarn. Imported. Made of the finest Australian wool; twenty skeins to the pound. Colors, scarlet, cardinal, wine, pink, light, medium or navy blue, medium or seal brown, black or white.
Price, black, white or colors, per pound, $1.10; per skein............6c

No. 18C1025 Spanish Knitting Worsted Yarn. Imported, eight skeins to the pound. Colors, cardinal, navy blue, seal brown, black or white.
Price, black, white or colors, per pound, $1.00; per skein..........13c

Crinkled Shetland Floss.

The Highest Grade, Best Quality Yarn.

No. 18C1027 Shetland Floss, fine grade imported wool, twelve skeins to the pound, manufacturer's weight. Colors, light blue, medium blue, pink, lemon, lilac, cardinal, dove, nile green, black, white or cream.
Price, per skein, all colors......6¼c
Per pound........................70c

Columbia Shetland Floss.

No. 18C1028 The Celebrated Columbia Shetland Floss, made of the finest wool, eight skeins to the pound. The Columbia brand is known as the best floss on the market. Colors, cream, white, black, pink, light blue, cardinal or lilac. Retailed elsewhere at 18 cents.
Price, per pound, 90c; per skein..12c

No. 18C1029 Shetland Wool or Zephyr Yarn, twelve skeins to the pound. Colors, black or white only.
Price, per pound, 90c; per skein...8c

No. 18C1031 Florence Shetland Silk Floss. Entirely new, having the luster of silk and the qualities so well known in Shetland wool. The opera shawls and fascinators, circular shawls and mufflers which can be made from the Shetland Silk Floss are exceptionally handsome, dainty and stylish. With each purchase of the Shetland Silk Floss we furnish you with directions for making the different articles of wear. Colors, white, cream white, black, pink or light blue. Sixteen skeins to the pound.
Price, per lb., $8.00; per skein...56c

No. 18C1033 Coral Yarn, Imported, twelve skeins to the pound. Colors, cardinal, light blue, pink, yellow, garnet, peacock blue, black or white.
Price, per pound, $1.15; per skein, 10c

No. 18C1035 Fairy Floss or Crinkled Yarn. Used for fancy knitting, eight skeins to the pound. Colors, black or white only.
Price, per pound, $1.10; per skein, 14c

No. 18C1037 Germantown Wool Yarn, Imported. Sixteen skeins to the pound. Colors, scarlet, cardinal, wine, light, medium or navy blue, pink, seal brown, yellow, green, purple, drab, black, white or cream.
Price, black, white or colors, per skein, $0.07
Per pound........................1.10

No. 18C1039 Angora Wool, best quality imported yarn. Colors, black, white or gray; 64 balls to the pound.
Price, per pound, $4.50; per ball, 7½c

Imported Ice Wool.

No. 18C1043 Ice Wool, Imported. 1-ounce balls, put up eight balls to the box. Colors, black, white, pink or light blue.
Price, per box, 70c; per ball......9c

Zephyr Worsteds.

No. 18C1045 Zephyr Worsted, Imported. Berlin zephyr, 4-ply, called single. Colors, scarlet, cardinal, pink, wine, garnet, light, medium and navy blue, nile, medium and dark green, brown, tan, olive, orange, canary, gray, purple, black, white or cream white. Forty laps to the pound.
Price, per pound, $1.35; per lap, 3½c

No. 18C1047 Zephyr Worsted, Imported. Berlin zephyr, 2-ply, called split zephyr. Colors, same as No. 18C1045. Forty laps to the pound.
Price, per pound, $1.35; per lap, 3½c

Indian Seed Beads.

No. 18C400 Indian Seed Beads, ordinary colors. The latest fad; being very extensively introduced into kindergartens and schools for fancy work and weaving beads into Indian designs, such as belts, purses, chains, moccasins, wampum bags and various other articles. Come in different colors as follows: Turquoise blue, emerald green, nile green, black, chalk white, crystal white, opal white, brown, purple, olive green, orange, pea green, medium blue, royal blue and lilac. Hank consists of about 80 strings, one color to the hank. Sold elsewhere at 20 and 25 cents.
Price, per hank....................8c
If by mail, postage extra, 8 cents.

No. 18C404 Indian Seed Beads, same as above but in high colors as follows: Ruby red, pink, light amber, dark amber and coral, yellow, one color to the hank. Hank consists of 80 strings. Price, per hank..........11c
If by mail, postage extra, 8 cents.

No. 18C406 Needles for bead work. Correct size for all bead work.
Per paper, 8c; per doz. papers....90c
If by mail, postage extra, 1 cent.

No. 18C408 Fancy Venetian Beads, exact size as per illustration, for finishing all kinds of bead work. Colors, turquoise and green with iridescent shadings.
Price, per gross, 30c; per doz.....3c
By mail, postage extra, per doz., 2c.

No. 18C410 Fancy Venetian Beads, for finishing all kinds of bead work, exact size as per illustration. Colors, green, blue, or white with silver, gold and iridescent shadings.
Price, per dozen, 45c; each........4c
By mail, postage extra, per doz., 2c.

No. 18C412 Round Cut Jewel Buttons, used for fancy work of all kinds, masquerade, church and lodge work. Come in the following colors: White, pink, navy, garnet, emerald, amethyst or turquoise and in exact sizes as above illustrations. Put up three dozen in an envelope. 22 is small size, 24 the largest.

Nos.	22	23	24
Price for 3 dozen	10c	11c	15c

Postage extra, 3 to 6c per 3 doz. package.

No. 18C414 Oblong Cut Jewels, used for fancy work and all kinds of ornamentation. Come in the following colors: White, pink, garnet, emerald or amethyst. The exact size and shape as per above illustration. Come put up two dozen in an envelope. Size 19.
Price for 2 dozen.................14c
Postage extra, 3 to 5c per 2 doz. package.

Kindergarten Beads.

No. 18C416 Kindergarten small size Basket Beads. Put up in wooden boxes, assorted colors; 3 ounces to the box. Just the thing for children.
Price, per box..6c
Per dozen....70c
If by mail, postage extra, per box, 5c.

No. 18C418 Kindergarten Medium Size Assorted Beads, assorted colors, 4 ounces to the box. Price, per box.................7c
Per dozen..........................80c
If by mail, postage extra, per box, 6 cents.

Cut Steel Beads for Fancy Work.

No. 18C420 Cut Steel Beads, the best A1 quality. Used extensively for fancy work. In three sizes; 7 is small, 8 medium and 9 large.

Sizes	7	8	9
Price, per bunch	9c	$0.10	$0.11
Per dozen bunches	95c	1.05	1.20

By mail, postage extra, per bunch, 2c.

No. 18C424 Cut Jet Beads for fancy work and for making necklaces, girdles and fancy work. Come in three sizes, as follows: 8 small, 9 medium and 10 large.
Price, per bunch, for any size....2½c
If by mail, postage extra, per bunch, 2 cents.

No. 18C426 Gilt Beads for fancy work, cut in the same manner as the cut steel beads of best quality. Come in three sizes as follows: 7 is small, 8 medium and 9 large.

Sizes	7	8	9
Price, per bunch	$0.12	$0.14	$0.16
Per doz. bunches	1.35	1.50	1.75

If by mail, postage extra, per bunch, 2 cents.

Bead Fringe for Lamp Shades.

No. 18C428 Bead Fringe for lamp shades and other decorations, made of Indian seed beads, strong and durable. It is used very extensively in the cities for fine lamp shades. Colors, pink, red, green or crystal white. Comes in the following widths:

Width, inches	2¼	3	4
Price, per yard	55c	70c	85c

Shipping weight, per yard, 10 ounces.

No. 18C430 Indian Tension Bead Loom. This is positively one of the best bead looms on the market and very simply constructed. You can tighten the warp by turning the wheel; makes even and quick work. The reel keeps the thread taut and takes care of the finished work. Constructed in the best manner possible and equally as good as any dollar looms on the market. Size, 4¼x12 inches. Shipping weight, 16 ounces. Price.........................25c

A $1.00 Bead Outfit for 50c.

No. 18C432 Indian Bead Work Outfit, consisting of one seed bead loom, eight bunches of assorted colored seed beads, one package of needles, one dozen fancy Venetian beads, one spool of heavy thread for bead work, one large pattern sheet with assorted designs for belts, necklaces, fobs, etc., also directions for making same. This entire outfit is put up in a nice wooden box with a slide cover. Shipping weight, 15 ounces. The materials are easily worth $1.00. Shipping weight, 1 pound. Our price for the entire outfit complete.......................50c

No. 18C434 Pearl Beads, which can be used for long neck chains or necklaces. A good quality wax bead. Length of each string, 12 inches. Size, as per above illustration.
Price, per string..................8c
Per dozen strings.................90c
If by mail, postage extra, per string, 3 cents.

No. 18C438 Pearl Beads, same quality as above. Size of above illustration. Length, 12 inches.
Price, per string..................8c
Per dozen strings.................90c
If by mail, postage extra, per string, 3 cents.

No. 18C440 Pearl Beads, same quality as above. Size of above illustration. Length, 12 inches.
Price, per string..................8c
Per dozen strings.................90c
If by mail, postage extra, per string, 3 cents.

No. 18C442 Fancy Neck Chains in Turquoise or Amethyst. The latest and most fashionable craze. 13 inches long. Made of graduated round beads with patent fastener. Comes in either turquoise or amethyst.
Price, each.....................$0.10
Per dozen.........................1.10
If by mail, postage extra, each, 5c.

No. 18C444 Fancy Cut Crystal Neck Chain, made of a good cut crystal bead, graduated size from small to large. Length, 15 inches. Comes in the clear crystal only. Price, each $0.18
Per dozen.........................2.00
If by mail, postage extra, each, 6c.

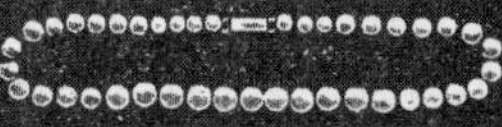

No. 18C446 This is a Large, Beautiful Neck Chain of turquoise round shape beads, graduated sizes from small to large, 18 inches in length, with patent fastener in back. Comes in turquoise only, which is very popular and pretty. Price, each $0.20
Per dozen.........................2.25
If by mail, postage extra, each, 5c.

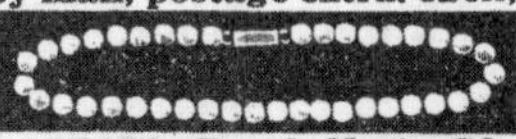

No. 18C448 Pearl Neck Chain. This is a very pretty, lustrous, filled wax bead, a good medium large size, and will not break easily. Length, 18 inches, with patent snap fastener in back. Very rich and attractive.
Price, per dozen, $5.75; each..50c
If by mail, postage extra, each, 5c.

No. 18C450 Fancy Neck Chains. Made of 2-colored, graduated, clear crystal beads. Between each bead is a small circlet of cut white crystal. The large, graduated beads can be ordered in amethyst or light green. Patent snap fastener in back. Length, 18 inches. This a very beautiful and charming necklace. Price, each $0.45
Per dozen.........................5.00
If by mail, postage extra, each, 5c.

Art Linen for Fancy Work.

No. 18C454 White Art Linen. Medium quality. This is a good quality pure linen, the kind that is mostly used. Can furnish in five widths, as follows:

Width, inches	18	22	24	27	36
Price, per yd.	19c	22c	30c	33c	37c

No. 18C456 White Art Linen. Very fine grade of pure all linen for embroidery work. Can furnish in two widths, as follows:

Width, inches	36	45
Price, per yard	39c	48c

Postage extra, per yard, 3 cents.

Canvas for Fancy Work.

No. 18C458 Hardanger Canvas. Very extensively used for all kinds of cross-stitch work and for making center pieces, dresser scarfs, shirt waists, collars and cuffs, etc. In white and linen color. Width, 34 inches.
Price, per yard....................50c
If by mail, postage extra, per yard, 3c.

No. 18C460 Hardanger Canvas, same quality as above in wider width. Comes in white only. Width, 42 inches.
Price, per yard....................65c
If by mail, postage extra, per yard, 4c.

No. 18C462 Cream Canvas, used for all sorts of cross-stitch work and Berlin embroidery work, pillow tops, etc. 42 inches wide.
Price, per yard..50c
If by mail, postage extra, per yard, 4 cents.

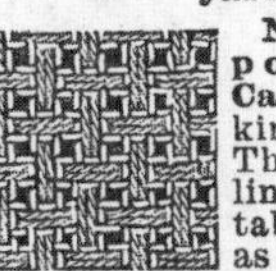

No. 18C464 Imported Cross-Stitch Canvas. Used for all kinds of cross-stitch work. This is a fine quality of linen. To be used for table and cushion covers, as well as other work, where the cross stitch is used. Saxonia embroidery thread used to work above canvas. Ecru color only. Width, 60 inches. Price, per yard........75c
If by mail, postage extra, per yard, 4 cents.

Hardanger Canvas.

No. 18C466 **Mercerized Hardanger Canvas.** This is a very soft and lustrous canvas. A very fine quality, especially desirable for shirt waists, collars and cuffs, and all kinds of fancy work. Width, 48 inches. White only.

Price, per yard........................95c

If by mail, postage extra, per yard, 4 cents.

Stamped Doilies.

No. 18C468 **Stamped Doilies and Center Pieces, on good quality union linen cloth, to be worked with wash embroidery silks. Pretty assorted floral designs, namely:** Strawberry, carnations, double rose, wild rose, violets, forget-me-nots, holly and pansy.

Size, ins. diameter	5	9	12	14
Price, each.......	2c	4c	5c	$0.10
Per dozen.........	20c	40c	55c	1.10

Size, ins. diameter	18	22	24
Price, each......	$0.15	$0.18	$0.22
Per dozen........	1.50	2.00	2.40

If by mail, postage extra, each, 2 to 5c.

Fine Linen Center Pieces.

No. 18C470 **Stamped Linen Doilies and Center Pieces, pretty floral designs, splendid values and guaranteed linen. Designs:** Strawberries, carnations, double rose, wild rose, violet, forget-me-nots, holly and pansy.

Size, ins. square	5	9	12	14
Price, each....	4c	6c	$0.10	$0.16
Per dozen.....	40c	65c	1.10	1.50

Size, inches square....	18	22
Price, each............	$0.23	$0.30
Per dozen..............	2.50	3.25

If by mail, postage extra, each, 2 to 5c.

Complete line of Embroidery Silks to work above pieces at lowest prices. See page 850.

Center Pieces.

No. 18C472 **Hemstitched and Revered Centerpieces.** On fine union linen, with assorted designs stamped in corners. These are extremely pretty designs and our prices are exceptionally low. Can be ordered in the following designs: Wild rose, double rose, carnations, violets, forget-me-nots, and daisies; comes in the following sizes:

Size, inches	9x9	11½x11½	13x13	17x17
Price, each	5c	6c	8c	$0.14
Per dozen..	55c	65c	90c	1.35
Size, inches	23x23	28½x28½	17x25	16x46½
Price, each	$0.17	$0.22	$0.16	$0.23
Per dozen..	1.75	2.25	1.70	2.50

If by mail, postage extra, each, 3 to 5c

No. 18C474 **Hand Drawn Work Center Pieces** on very fine quality linen, stamped corners, with floral design same as No. 18C470, such as carnation, rose, etc. Fancy and attractive new design drawn work, as per illustration, which shows just one-quarter. Comes in the following sizes:

Size, inches.	18x18	20x20	24x24	30x30
Price, each..	$0.38	$0.45	$0.56	$0.78
Per dozen....	4.25	5.25	6.00	8.75

If by mail, postage extra, each, 3 to 5c.

No. 18C476 **Brown Linen Colored Center Pieces,** tinted on a washable duck cloth. These are the latest and most popular center pieces for tables. The cloth is 22 inches square. The design is about 19x20 inches. Comes tinted in American beauty, holly, violet, strawberry, cherry and poppy designs. Price........................10c

If by mail, postage extra, 3 cents.

No. 18C478 **Stamped Mount Mellick Design Center Pieces,** on heavy satin damask, pretty designs, to be worked with No. 18C1328 Peri-Luster, as quoted in catalogue, page 832. **Mount Mellick work is having a very extensive sale at the present time.** We furnish these center pieces in the following sizes:

Size, inches....	7	12	18	24	30
Price..........	2c	5c	10c	15c	20c

If by mail, postage extra, each, 2 to 5c.

For Mount Mellick Thread to work above, see page 832.

No. 18C480 **Stamped Mount Mellick Tray Cloth.** Same style and quality as above. Size, 20x27 inches.

Price........................15c

If by mail, postage extra, 4 cents.

For Making Teneriffe Lace.

No. 18C482 **Proctor's Teneriffe Lace Wheel for making Teneriffe laces,** made of hard rubber with a beautiful finish. Will last a lifetime, does the work easily and speedily. Teneriffe lace wheels and laces are immensely popular and extensively used for collars, doilies, insertions, waists and dresses. You can make large or small wheels. We furnish instructions with each wheel. Price, per dozen, **$1.90**; each.... **18c**

If by mail, postage extra, each, 2 cents.

No. 18C484 Proctor Booklet of Instructions and Designs, showing how to make all kinds of teneriffe work. Extensively used for waists, collars, etc. Illustrations showing waists, laces, collars, etc.

Price, per doz., **$1.90**; each............**18c**

If by mail, postage extra, 2 cents.

For thread to make lace, see catalogue No. 18C1320, page 832.

Stamped Splashers.

No. 18C486 **Stamped White Cotton Duck Splasher,** with lace, hemstitched, open work top and bottom, fringed on three sides. Size, 16x25 inches.

Price........................10c

If by mail, postage extra, 6 cents.

No. 18C488 **White Cotton Duck Dresser Scarf,** with lace openwork insertion on both ends. Size, 16x35 inches.

Price........................15c

If by mail, postage extra, 7 cents.

Shoe Pockets.

No. 18C490 **Ecru Colored Print Drill Shoe Pocket.** Tape bound edges, stamped in pretty floral designs. Contains four pockets. Size, 18x18 inches.

Price, per dozen, $1.50; each....15c

If by mail, postage extra, each, 5c.

No. 18C492 **Ecru Drill Shoe Pocket.** Tape bound edges, stamped in pretty floral designs, same style as above, but containing two pockets. Size, 10x14 inches. Price, each...$0.10

Per dozen........................1.10

If by mail, postage extra, each, 4c.

Laundry Bag.

No. 18C494 **Laundry Bags,** made of white cotton duck, tinted in bright colors, new and original design, wide hem top and drawing strings; size, 17x27 inches.

Price, each..$0.22

Per dozen.... 2.40

If by mail, postage extra, each, 10c.

Rug Machine

No. 18C514 The Novelty Rug Machine. For working rugs, ottomans, chair covers, cushions and the above burlap patterns.

Price, each..............................$0.28

Per dozen................................3.00

If by mail, postage extra, each, 5 cents.

No. 18C516 Fine Rug Machine Needles. For working on plush, satin, etc.

Price, per dozen, **32c**; each..............**3c**

If by mail, postage extra, each, 2c

Burlap Rug Patterns.

The illustration gives an idea of one of the rug patterns, showing the manner of placing it on frame for working. Take four slats similar to bed slats, making a frame; stretch pattern over frame; then after hemming pattern proceed to work same by following the lines with the various colors designated.

Ottoman Burlap Patterns.

For material for working burlap patterns, see zephyrs, page 850.

No. 18C496 **Pattern 40. Pretty flower design burlap rug pattern.** Size, 23x41 inches. Price, each..$0.22

Per dozen........................2.40

If by mail, postage extra, each, 5c.

No. 18C498 **Pattern 9. Ottoman. Large rose leaves and buds with nice border.** Size, 18x20 inches.

Price, per dozen, $1.20; each.....11c

If by mail, postage extra, each, 3c.

No. 18C500 **⅔x1⅛ yards. Arabian horse and landscape center,** enclosed with an oval line and oak leaves at each end, new design.

Price, per dozen, $2.75; each....25c

If by mail, postage extra, each, 7c.

No. 18C502 **Pattern 19. ½x1 yard. A spaniel dog lying on a box,** very clearly printed in moss and brown colors in center. A branch, with roses, leaves and buds, at each end and a plain border.

Price, per dozen, $2.75; each....25c

If by mail, postage extra, each, 7c.

No. 18C504 **Pattern 93. ⅔x1⅛ yards. A nice floral center,** consisting of red and moss roses, leaves, buds, lilies, etc., beautifully arranged, with a plain scroll surrounding the center, three autumn leaves in each corner, and a plain border.

Price, per dozen, $2.75; each....26c

If by mail, postage extra, each, 7c.

No. 18C506 ¾x1½ yards. A cat and two kittens playing on the carpet in the center, enclosed in a plain scroll. Plain border with nice scroll in corners. A very interesting design for those who are fond of our pets. All new.

Price, per dozen, **$3.75**; each..........**34c**

If by mail, postage extra, each, 7 cents.

No. 18C508 Pattern 22, ¾x1½ yards. A very pretty scroll border, with a stag standing near a lake of water, very pretty landscape scenery, etc., in the center. A very nice sofa rug.

Price, per dozen, **$3.75**; each..........**34c**

If by mail, postage extra, each, 12 cents.

No. 18C510 ⅞x1¾ yards. A large lion lying down, and a small lion in the background, with a fine scenery of flowers and palm trees. Is very easy to work and makes a nice hearth rug. Price, per dozen, **$6.00**; each......**55c**

If by mail, postage extra, each, 14 cents.

No. 18C512 Door Mat. Oval chain through center, with word Welcome. Letters transposed, so that when worked with the machine will read properly. Plain border with scroll in corner.

Price, per dozen, **$2.15**; each..........**19c**

If by mail, postage extra, each, 7 cents.

Rags worked into the proper patterns with the improved rug machine produce very rich and handsome rugs and ottomans, having a tapestry effect which gives no suggestion of the cheapness of the material.

Stamping Pattern Outfits.

Stamp your own linen. Stamping patterns perforated, new and desirable patterns. Our outfits contain the following articles:

No. 18C518 **The Quinette Stamping Outfit.** Consists of five sheets on which are 26 full sized new and pretty stamping patterns, one complete alphabet, one box of black and one box of blue stamping powder with each set.

Price, per outfit....................$0.25

Per dozen outfits.......................2.75

By mail, postage extra, per outfit, 8c.

No. 18C520 **The Seroco Stamping Outfit.** Consists of 11 sheets on which are 75 full sized patterns for stamping any and all kinds of linens and sofa pillows; one complete alphabet, and one box of black and one box of blue stamping powder with each set.

Price, per doz., $5.50; per outfit, 50c

By mail postage extra, per outfit, 9c

Stamping Powder.

No. 18C522 **Stamping Powder.** Put up in boxes. Colors, blue or black.

Price, per dozen, 55c; per box.....5c

If by mail, postage extra, per box, 3c.

Tatting Shuttles.

No. 18C521 **White Bone Tatting Shuttle.** Highly polished.

Price, per dozen, 42c; each..........4c

No. 18C524 **Rubber Tatting Shuttle.** Hard rubber, highly polished.

Price, per dozen, $1.10; each....10c

If by mail, postage extra, each, 2c.

Needle Emeries.

No. 18C526 **Strawberry Needle Emeries.** Should be in every lady's workbasket. Price, per dozen, 40c; each........4c

If by mail, postage extra, each, 2 cents.

Initial Letters.

No. 18C528 **Initial Letters.** Worked in fast color turkey red, for marking shirts, underwear, handkerchiefs, etc., put up 36 on a card. Any letter.

Price, per card of 36.. 3c

Per dozen cards...................33c

By mail, postage extra, per card, 1c.

Ornaments for Fancy Work.

No. 18C530 **Silk Chenille Balls** for fancy work, about ¾ inch in diameter, can be used for finishing all kinds of fancy work. Colors, white, pink, rose, light blue, green, violet, red or yellow.

Price, per dozen.....7c

Postage extra, per doz., 2c.

Silk Tassels.

No. 18C532 **Small Silk Tassels,** like illustration, about 2¼ inches long, colors same as No. 18C530, good silk loops; **can be used for all kinds of fancy work.**

Price, per dozen..........6c

If by mail, postage extra, per dozen, 2 cents.

No. 18C534 **Fancy combination silk and chenille drop,** as per illustration, used for fancy work. Comes in colors same as No. 18C530. Length about 2 inches.

Price, per dozen........................15c

If by mail, postage extra, per doz., 2c.

No. 18C536 **Silk Tassel Fringe,** with ¼ inch wide heading of fancy braided silk, with tassels nearly 2 inches long. Can be ordered in the following combinations of colors: White and green; white and yellow; white and blue; white, green and pink; red, yellow and pink; white and pink. Price, per yard............$0.10

Per dozen yards......................1.10

If by mail, postage extra, per yard, 1 cent.

Furniture Gimp.

No. 18C538 **Furniture Gimp,** silk mixed, ½ inch wide, in all staple colors.

Price, per yard......................2c

Per dozen yards..................20c

Postage extra, per dozen yards, 4c.

No. 18C540 **Furniture Gimp,** extra quality silk mixed, ½ inch wide, in all staple colors. Price, per dozen yards, 35c; per yard.................3c

Postage extra, per dozen yards, 4c.

Best Sofa Cushion Cord.

No. 18C542 **Sofa Cushion Cord,** a heavy, high grade, lustrous cotton, used around sofa cushions. Comes in all combinations of colors to match material used for pillow top. Colors same as No. 18C544. Price, per yard.... 5c

Per dozen yards.....................55c

Postage extra, per dozen yards, 6c.

Silk Sofa Cushion Cord.

No. 18C544 This is a heavy silk twis-cord, extensively used for binding around pillow cushions. Can be ordered in the following combination of colors: Black and yellow; green, tan and pink; royal blue, tan and yellow; green, tan and cardinal; light blue and yellow; navy blue and orange; black and cardinal; white, green and red; orange and white; blue and white. We can also furnish them in the following plain colors: Light green, yellow, cardinal.

Price, per dozen yards, **$1.00**; per yard.**9c**

If by mail, postage extra, per dozen yards, 6c.

Pillow Girdles.

No. 18C546 A heavy Twisted Cushion Cord with tassels complete, ready to put around your pillow. Three yard length in different combination of colors same as No. 18C544.

Price, per dozen, **$2.25**; each..........**20c**

If by mail, postage extra, each, 6 cents.

No. 18C548 Silk Pillow Girdle. A heavy twisted cord with tassels, same as illustration above. Length, 3 yards, in colors same as No. 18C544. Price, per dozen, **$4.00**; each..**35c**

If by mail, postage extra, each, 6 cents.

Wood Embroidery Hoops.

"The Duchess" Pat'd. FELT. FELT CUSHION.

No. 18C550 The Duchess Embroidery Hoop. Does not require winding. The felt cushion on the inner hoop gives the proper tension to hold tightly a light or heavy fabric. Made of selected light colored wood, true in circle and will never warp or get out of shape. Size, 4, 5, 6, 7 or 8 inches. Price, per dozen pairs, $1.15; per pair, 10c
Postage extra, per pair, 2 cents.

No. 18C552 Wood Embroidery Hoops. Made of selected wood and will not warp. Size, 5, 6, 7 or 8 inches.
Price, per dozen pairs, 55c; per pair......5c
Postage extra, per pair, 3 cents.

Handkerchief Centers.

Fine Linen—Two Sizes.

No. 18C554 Fine Quality Handkerchief Centers. Made from very fine linen cloth, with hemstitched borders. They are used for centers, around which lace can be sewed, also suitable for art centers and fancy work. Made in sizes as below. You can order any size in either ⅛ or ¼ inch hem.

Inches square,	6	7	9
Price, each...	8c	$0.10	$0.12
Per dozen.....	90c	1.10	1.25

If by mail, postage extra, each, 2c.

No. 18C556 Fine Linen Handkerchief Centers, better quality than above. Very fine sheer linen. You can order any size in either ⅛ or ¼ inch hem.

Size, inches square,	6x6	7x7	9x9
Price, each.....	$0.10	$0.13	$0.16
Per dozen........	1.10	1.25	1.50

If by mail, postage extra, each, 2c.

Battenberg Patterns.

No. 18C558 Stamped on a good quality of pink silesia, showing the stitches and giving the amount of braid and number of rings to be used on each pattern. Battenberg patterns come in assorted designs. We cannot furnish description or show style, but will send you desirable styles which will be sure to please.

Size, inches cloth......	10	13¼	17	20	26
Size, inches design.. ..	9	12	15	18	24
Price, each	2c	3c	4c	5c	8c
Size, inches cloth...	32	40	20x30	20x56	
Size, inches design.	30	36	18x27	18x54	
Price, each........	12c	20c	10c	13c	

Price, each, handkerchief pattern, 4c
Price, each, collar revers.... ....10c
Price, each, turnover collars....... 3c
Per dozen, turnover collars......30c

If by mail, postage extra, each, 2 cents to 5 cents.

We do not have any books or illustrations of battenberg patterns. We will select a desirable pattern for you.

Battenberg Rings.

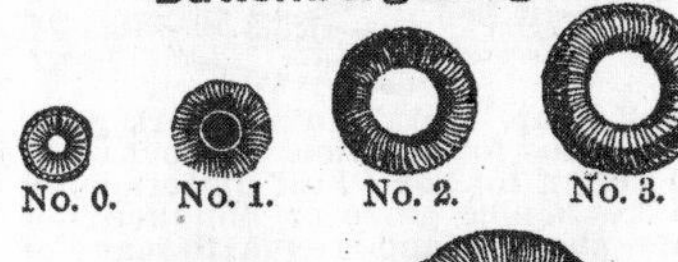

No. 18C560 Black Silk Battenberg Rings, for battenberg work. **Illustration shows actual size.** Size, No. .. 1 2 3
Price, per dozen..... 6c 8c 10c
If by mail, postage extra, per doz., 2c.
Corticelli silk spool thread, Size A, used for black battenberg work.

Battenberg Rings.

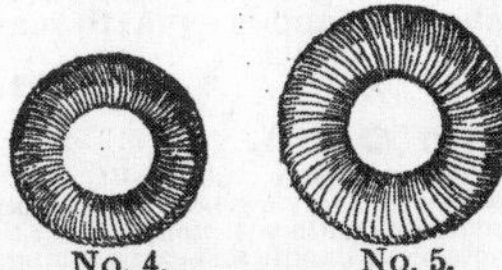

No. 0. No. 1. No. 2. No. 3. No. 4. No. 5.

No. 18C562 Battenberg Rings, No. 0, the small collar size. Used very extensively at present for the finer worked collars. Colors, white or cream.
Price, per dozen. 3c
If by mail, postage extra, per doz., 2c.

No. 18C564 White Battenberg Rings, for making battenberg work, the illustrations showing actual sizes.

Size, No...	1	2	3	4	5
Price, per dozen	2c	2c	3c	3c	4c

If by mail, postage extra, 2 cents.

No. 18C566 Ecru or Dark Arabian Battenberg Rings, for battenberg work. Sizes as illustrated.

Size, No........	1	2	3	4	5
Price, per dozen	2c	2c	3c	4c	5c

If by mail, postage extra, per doz., 2c.

No. 18C568 Cream Battenberg Rings. Same sizes as shown in illustrations.

Size, No... ...	1	2	3	4	5
Price, per dozen	2c	2c	3c	4c	5c

If by mail, postage extra, per doz., 2c.

No. 18C570 Fancy Cotton Rings, used in the same manner as the battenberg rings, for fancy work, also for neckwear, etc. Colors, white, cream or Arabian. Can be ordered in two sizes. Exact size of illustrations. Be sure to mention color.
Size, No.............. 35 37
Price, per dozen...... 7c 8c
If by mail, postage extra, per doz., 2c.

Battenberg Lace Braids.

No. 18C600 Linen Battenberg Lace Braid No. 8, exact size of illustration. Colors, white, cream or Arabian. We do not sell less than 1 dozen yards. Comes 3 dozen yards on piece.
Price, per dozen yards..............8c
Per piece, 3 dozen yards 21c
Postage extra, per dozen yards, 2c.

No. 18C602 Linen Battenberg Lace Braid No. 6, same as No. 18C600, but a size smaller. Size of illustration. Colors, white, cream or Arabian. We do not sell less than 1 dozen yards. Price, per dozen yards........7c
Per piece, 3 dozen yards 18c
If by mail, postage extra, per dozen yards, 2 cents.

No. 18C604 Linen Battenberg Lace Braid No. 5, size of illustration. Colors, white, cream or Arabian. We do not sell less than 1 dozen yards. Price, per dozen yds..6c
Per piece, 3 dozen yards.............15c
If by mail, postage extra, per dozen yards, 2 cents.

No. 18C606 Battenberg Lace Braid. This is a very fine thread, closely woven. A braid that is now used very largely for the different styles of fancy work. Comes in white only in exact size of illustration. We do not sell less than 1 dozen yards. Price, per dozen yards...... 6c
Per piece, 3 dozen yards..............16c
If by mail, postage extra, per dozen yards, 2 cents.

No. 18C608 Fine Thread Battenberg Lace Braid. Exact size of illustration. Price, per dozen yards.... 7c
Per piece, 3 dozen yards...........19c
Postage extra, per dozen yards, 2c.

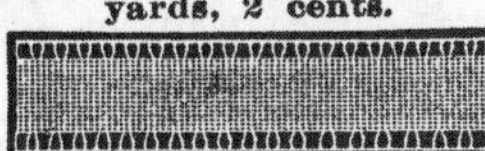

No. 18C610 Fine Thread Battenberg Lace Braid. Exact size of illustration. Price, per dozen yards.... 8c
Per piece, 3 dozen yards...........22c
If by mail, postage extra, per dozen yards, 2 cents.

No. 18C612 Fine Thread Battenberg Lace Braid. Exact size of illustration. Price, per dozen yards.... 9c
Per piece, 3 dozen yards...........25c
If by mail, postage extra, per dozen yards, 2 cents.

No. 18C614 Black Silk Battenberg Lace Braid, exact size of illustration. We do not sell less than 1 dozen yards.
Price, per dozen yards............31c
Per piece, 3 dozen yards.... .....87c
If by mail, postage extra, per dozen yards, 2 cents.

No. 18C616 Black Silk Battenberg Lace Braid, exact size of illustration. We do not sell less than 1 dozen yards. Price, per dozen yards..$0.36
Per piece, 3 dozen yards......... 1.00
If by mail, postage extra, per dozen yards, 2 cents.

No. 18C618 Black Silk Battenberg Lace Braid, exact size of illustration. We do not sell less than 1 dozen yards. Price, per dozen yards..$0.42
Per piece, 3 dozen yards......... 1.15
If by mail, postage extra, per dozen yards, 2 cents.

Corticelli spool silk, letter A, is used for working black silk battenberg braid.

No. 18C620 Arabian Colored Battenberg Braid. Suitable for boleros and yokes, exact size of illustration. We do not sell less than 1 dozen yards.
Price, per dozen yards............32c
Per piece, 3 dozen yards............90c
If by mail, postage extra, per dozen yards, 2 cents.

Honiton Point Lace Braids.

No. 18C622 Honiton Point Lace Braid, very fine. We do not sell less than 1 dozen yards; white only.
Price, per dozen yards............19c
If by mail, postage extra, per dozen yards, 2 cents.

No. 18C624 White Point Lace, Purling Braid, exact size of illustration. We do not sell less than 1 dozen yards. Price, per dozen yards.....10c
If by mail, postage extra, per dozen yards, 2 cents.

No. 18C626 Honiton Point Lace Braid, exact size of illustration. We do not sell less than 1 dozen yards; white only.
Price, per dozen yards....... ......28c
If by mail, postage extra, per dozen yards, 2 cents.

No. 18C628 Honiton Point Lace Braid, exact size of illustration. We do not sell less than 1 dozen yards.
Price, per dozen yards......... ....30c
If by mail, postage extra, per dozen yards, 2 cents.

No. 18C630 White Honiton Point Lace Braid. Exact size and design of illustration. We do not sell less than 1 dozen yards.
Price, per dozen yards 27c
If by mail, postage extra, per dozen yards, 2 cents.

No. 18C632 Fancy Lace Braid. New design. Exact style and size of illustration. White only. We do not sell less than 1 dozen yards.
Price, per dozen yards 24c
If by mail, postage extra, per dozen yards, 2 cents.

No. 18C634 Honiton Point Lace Braid, same size as illustration. White only. We do not sell less than 1 dozen yards.
Price, per dozen yards...........34c
If by mail, postage extra, per dozen yards, 2 cents.

No. 18C636 Imported Fancy Purling Lace Braid, exact size of illustration. White only. We do not sell less than 1 dozen yards. Price, per dozen yards........20c
Postage extra, per dozen yards, 2c.

No. 18C638 Imported Fancy Purling Lace Braid, for battenberg work, exact size of illustration.. White only. We do not sell less than 1 dozen yards. Price, per dozen yards......25c
If by mail, postage extra, per dozen yards, 2 cents.

No. 18C640 Imported Purling Lace Braid, for battenberg work, exact size of illustration. White only. We do not sell less than 1 dozen yards.
Price, per dozen yards.........30c
If by mail, postage extra, per dozen yards, 2 cents.

No. 18C644 Fancy Lace Braid, exact design and style of illustration. White only. We do not sell less than 1 dozen yards.
Price, per dozen yards..........39c

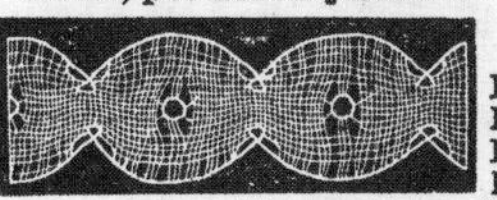

No. 18C646 Imported Duchess Lace Braid, exact size of illustration. White only.
Price, per yard. 5c
Per dozen yards..................55c
If by mail, postage extra, per dozen yards, 2 cents.

No. 18C648 Imported Fancy Lace Braid. Exact size and style of illustration. White only. Price, per yard.......4c
Price, per dozen yards..........42c
If by mail, postage extra, per dozen yards, 2 cents.

No. 18C650 Draw Silk Braid. This is a very popular trimming, to be used for fancy collars, waists, dress trimmings of all kinds. The pull string enables you to draw the braid into many shapes. Illustration exact size of braid. Colors, black or white.
Price, per yard............ ..... 6c
Per dozen yards................70c
If by mail, postage extra, per dozen yards, 2 cents.

No. 18C652 Fancy Duchess Braid, with drawstring, made of linen thread. Can be drawn into many shapes and used very effectively for collars, fancy work, etc. Illustration exact size of braid. Colors, white or ecru. Price, per yard 3c
Per dozen yards.......... ....30c
If by mail, postage extra, per dozen yards, 2 cents.

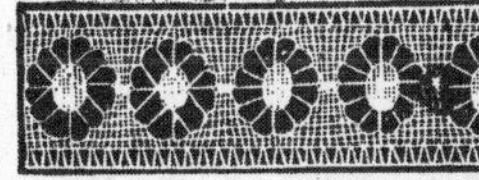

No. 18C654 Imported Duchess Irish Point Lace Braid. Illustration shows the exact size the braid comes. In white only. We do not sell less than 1 dozen yards. Price. per dozen yards. .40c
Postage extra, per dozen yards, 2c.

No. 18C656 Imported Silk Duchess Lace Braid. Used very effectively for collars, fancy work, waists, etc. Colors, black or white. Illustration shows exact size of braid. Price, per yard...6c
Per dozen yards.................70c
Postage extra, per dozen yards, 2c.

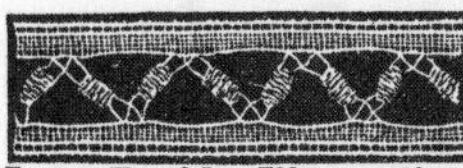

No. 18C658 Irish Point Duchess Lace Braid. Illustration shows exact size of braid. White only.
Price, per doz. yards, 80c; per yd. 7c
Postage extra, per dozen yards, 2c.

No. 18C670 Honiton Point Lace Braid. New design. Exact size and style of illustration. White only.
Price, per yard. 6c
Per dozen yards...................60c
If by mail, postage extra, per dozen yards, 2 cents.

No. 18C672 Honiton Point Lace Braid. White only. Price, per yard, 4c
Per dozen yards.....................42c
If by mail, postage extra, per dozen yards, 2 cents.

No. 18C674 Honiton Point Lace Braid. White only. Price, per yard..7c
Per dozen yards.................80c
Postage extra, per dozen yards, 2c.

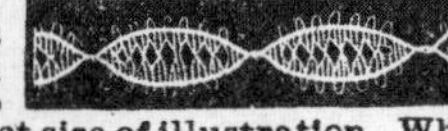

No. 18C676 Honiton PointLace Braid, exact size of illustration. White only. Price, per yard.............. 6c
Per dozen yards.................65c
Postage extra, per dozen yards, 2c.

Lace Thread for Lace Making.

No. 18C1320 The Red Mill French Lace Thread known as the Au Moulin Rouge, for battenberg and honiton lace work; comes in white in the following sizes: 50, 80, 100, 150, 200, 250, 300, 500, 600, 800, 1000.
Price, per doz. balls, 44c; per ball.4c

No. 18C1322 Cream Lace Thread. Same as No. 18C1320. Comes in the following sizes: 50, 100, 200, 250, 300, 500, 800, 1000. Price, per ball.............. 4c
Per dozen balls.................44c

No. 18C1324 Arabian or new dark ecru color Lace Thread. Comes in sizes as follows: 50, 80, 100, 200.
Price, per doz. balls, 44c; per ball.4c
If by mail, postage extra, per ball, 2c.

Linen Battenberg Lace Thread.

No. 18C1326 Ideal Divisible Linen Battenberg Lace Thread, Six-fold. One or more threads can be used, according to the thickness of the lace thread required. White only. Price, per skein. 5c
Per dozen skeins...............53c
Postage extra, per skein, 1 cent.
Silk embroidery floss; for complete assortment see threads, page 850.

Peri Luster Embroidery Filo for Mount Mellick Work.

No. 18C1328 Peri-Luster Embroidery Floss is a new material of fast color. Used extensively for fancy work, made of a high grade, silk finish, lustrous yarn, for Mount Mellick work and just the thing for embroidering cushions and all kinds of fancy work where a rich, lustrous and heavy effect is desired. It can be ordered in the following colors: white, cream, black, light yellow, medium yellow and orange, light blue, medium blue and navy, light pink, pink and rose, light, medium and dark leaf greens, strawberry, lavender, scarlet and cardinal.
Price, four skeins for.............. 5c
Per dozen skeins.................13c
Postage extra, per skein, 1 cent.

Peri Luster for Mount Mellick Work.

No. 18C1329 Peri Luster. This is a mercerized white cotton thread extensively used for the Mount Mellick embroidery work, which is so popular. Comes in four sizes: No. 1, coarse; No. 2, medium; No. 3, fine; No. 4, very fine. White only. Price, per skein........2c
Per dozen skeins................22c
Postage extra, per dozen skeins, 3c.

Kloster Silk Rope Twist.

No. 18C1332 A heavy mercerized yarn that looks and wears like silk, having a superior luster that won't come off. Used for Mount Mellick embroidery canvas, for filling in purposes and heavy work. Can be had in shades from light to the darkest colors of greens, reds, golds, blues, yellows, browns, pinks, purples, bronze, lavenders; also in black, white or cream.
Price, per skein.................3c
Per dozen skeins................30c
Postage extra, per skein, 1 cent.

Japanese Gold Thread.

No. 18C1330 Extensively used in all kinds of fancy work, and especially desirable at present to be used on pillow tops. Comes put up 12 yards to the bunch, and in

	Fine	Medium	Coarse
Price, per skein.	3c	5c	8c
Per dozen skeins.	33c	55c	90c

Postage extra, per skein, 1 cent.

Gold Thread for Fancy Work.

No. 18C1331 Best quality, two-ply Gold Thread on spools. About 12 yards to the spool. Used for all kinds of fancy work, also regalias, uniforms and fancy masquerade costumes. Price, per spool..........$0.09
Per dozen spools............... 1.00
Postage extra, per spool, 8 cents.
See page 857 for Gold Trimmings and Fancy Gilt Lace Braids.

Pillow Tops.

No. 18C1337 American Beauty Rose Cushion. Has four large American beauty roses tinted on light green ticking; a most beautiful pattern. Size, 22x22 inches. 50-cent value.
Price for front and back......$0.29
Per dozen...................... 3.25
If by mail, postage extra, each, 6c.

No. 18C1338 Large Double Poppy, with buds and leaves, tinted in natural effect on good quality ticking with back complete. Size, 22x22 inches. 50c value.
Price, each...29c
If by mail, postage extra, each, 6c.

No. 18C1354 Daisies Won't Tell. This pillow top is an entirely new design, four large daisies in each corner with the well known motto tinted on light green ticking, with large daisies; a very excellent cover. Size, 22x22 inches. 50-cent value.
Price for front and back........$0.29
Per dozen...................... 3.25
If by mail, postage extra, each, 6c.

No. 18C1356 Florodora Pillow Top, large design of the Florodora girl, with the words "Tell me pretty maiden, are there any more at home like you?" This is a very striking and pretty pillow top, makes up beautifully; tinted on light green ticking; size, 22x22 inches. 50c value.
Price for front and back..........$0.29
Per dozen........................ 3.25
If by mail, postage extra, each, 6 cents.

No. 18C1360 You Can't Play in My Yard. This is an original idea for a pillow top. One of the best designs ever offered. Tinted on good quality tan colored ticking. Size, 22x22 inches.
Price, with back.................29c
If by mail, postage extra, 6 cents.

No. 18C1362 Pipes of Peace bachelor pillow tops, tinted in proper colors on good quality tan colored ticking. The design is a very attractive one. Price, with back....29c
If by mail, postage extra, 6 cents.

No. 18C1375 Basket of Daisies, with rococo and scroll border. Like the American Beauty roses, one of the handsomest designs of the season, tinted on a very pretty shade of light sage green ticking. Size, 22x22 inches.
Price for front and back..............29c
If by mail, postage extra, 6 cents.

A Beautiful Pillow Top.

No. 18C1367 Only a Breath of Violets. One of the most popular designs, tinted on a very pretty shade of light sage green ticking. Size, 22x22 inches. 50-cent value.
Price for front and back.........................$0.29
Per dozen.................. 3.25
If by mail, postage extra, each, 6 cents.

Pretty Holly Pillow Top.

No. 18C1384 Holly Center Design, a very desirable one for the fall, tinted in the holly shades of green, a very easy design to work and when completed is very handsome. Tinted on a very pretty shade of light sage green ticking. Size, 22x22 inches. 50-cent value.
Price, front and back..................29c
If by mail, postage extra, 6 cents.

Beautiful Hand Painted Satin Pillow Tops.

IN ASSORTED DESIGNS.

No. 18C1386 Satin Cushion Cover, hand painted on heavy quality white satin. The work is the very finest by best artists, rich and highly colored tints, guaranteed fast colors, all ready to be used. The satin cushion tops can be ordered in the following designs: No. 1, La France rose (see illustration); No. 2, American Beauty rose; No. 3, beautiful design of jack roses; No. 4, very pretty carnation pattern; No. 5, large, elegant poppy design; No. 6, delicate violet design. In ordering, give number. Size, 22x22 inches. Price, each.....................$0.67
Per dozen........................ 7.60
If by mail, postage extra, each, 7 cents.

No. 18C1415 This is a Beautiful Hand Painted Cushion Pillow Top. Hand painted in beautiful, bright, natural colors with large rosebuds, leaves and stems. Backed with the same material, bound with mercerized tape edge to contrast with top. Finished complete, ready for use. A top that looks very rich, and would be a satisfactory top even at $1.00 or $1.50. Size, 21x21 inches.
Price, each.........................25c
If by mail, postage extra, 6 cents.

The Very Latest Handkerchief Pillow Top.

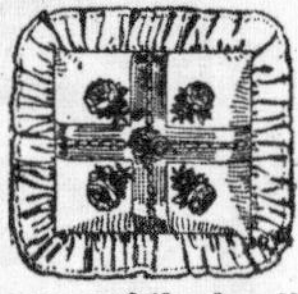

No. 18C1414 Handkerchief Pillow Top. This is one of the newest and latest ideas for pillow covers. Made of a large hemstitched handkerchief with colored border and fancy fast color designs in corners, such as American Beauty roses, chrysanthemums and other fancy designs. The four corners of the handkerchief are joined together by white valenciennes beading, through which No. 1 ribbons are drawn; in the center is a large bow of No. 1 ribbon, and finished with a closely gathered, wide, hemstitched ruffle. Has back all ready for use. Size, finished pillow, including ruffle, 24 inches square, for an 18-inch pillow.
Price, each...........................55c
If by mail, postage extra, 6 cents.

Finished Oriental Pillow Top. Ready to Use.

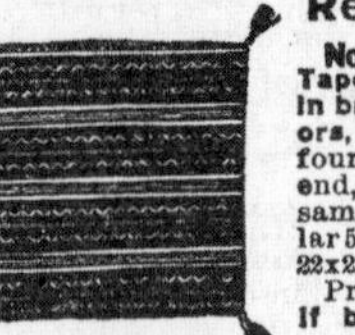

No. 18C1408 Tapestry Pillow Top. In bright Turkish colors, ornamented with four tassels on either end, backed with the same material. Regular 50-cent value. Size, 22x22 inches.
Price, each...25c
If by mail, postage extra, 8 cents.

No. 18C1416 Velour Pillow Cushion, with back. Trimmed with four tassels. Complete, ready for use. The top is made of a highly colored, fancy velour, in pretty floral and scroll designs. Backed with madras cloth sewed on velour, finished on the four ends with fringed tassels to contrast with the velour. A very striking and pretty cushion. Size, 22x22 inches. Price, each.........................49c
If by mail, postage extra, 8 cents.

Oriental Tapestry Pillow Top.

No. 18C1403 Oriental Tapestry Cushion Top. A conventional design in Turkish colorings. A very pretty and attractive top at one-half value. Size, 22x22 inches.
Price, each......25c
If by mail, postage extra, 7 cents.

Fine Silk Oriental Pillow Top.

No. 18C1406 Tapestry Pillow Top. A fancy silk mixed pillow top, with a beautiful oriental coloring; an extremely rich and showy pillow top, all ready for use. Size, 22x22 ins.
Price, per dozen, $5.50; each..50c
By mail, postage extra, each, 8c.

No. 18C1411 Hand Painted Pillow Cushion. Hand painted on a brown linen crash, edged with a green mercerized binding and backed with fancy cloth to contrast. The pillow is ready for use. The designs are very beautiful, large, showy and attractive. Can be ordered in the following designs: American Beauties, Large Poppies, Nasturtiums and Fleur de Lis design. Size, 22x22 inches.
Price, each...44c
If by mail, postage extra, each, 6 cents.

PYROGRAPHY OR WOOD ETCHING.

Complete Catalogue on Pyrography including blank designs of all kinds mailed free on request.

Pyrographic Outfits.

No. 18C1419 This is a very complete high grade outfit with good parts. Contains curved platinum point, small imported double bulb made of best rubber, rubber tubing, cork handle, alcohol lamp, metal union, cork glass bottle, with wire hook and a designed piece of wood for practice. All put up in a very pretty basswood box with stamped design for box. Full directions in each box; size of box, 10x7x3¼ inches. Makes a nice glove or handkerchief box. Above set can be used for all ordinary purposes and is equal to many of the $5.00 outfits sold elsewhere. Shipping weight, 3 pounds.
Price, for set complete...$1.65

Professional Pyrographic Outfit.

No. 18C1421 Professional Pyrographic Outfit. This is an extra fine quality and one of the best outfits that you can possibly purchase. Contains two of the very best heavy platinum points, one straight and one curved, extra large imported double bulb with long rubber tubing, alcohol lamp, bottle with glass stopper, wire hook, union metal cork handle and extra tubing, three pieces basswood stamped with designs for practice work, shellac and stains with full directions for using. Entire outfit is put up in a very nice basswood box. Size of box, 16x8½x4¼ inches. This very complete outfit is equal to outfits that are sold elsewhere at $7.50.
Price, complete...$3.25
Shipping weight, 3½ pounds. Send for our illustrated Catalogue on Pyrography—wood pieces of all descriptions. All kinds of leather for burning in all kinds of colors. Send for Catalogue. Free of charge. Complete Catalogue on basket weaving materials mailed free on request.

Pillow Sham Holders.

No. 18C1484 The Tarbox Pillow Sham Holder does not crease or soil the shams. Simple attachment, easily adjusted. Can be removed from one bed to another without leaving marks. Adjustable to fit any size bed, metal or wood. By far the best sham holder and once tried you will use no other. State if for metal or wood bed. Shipping weight, 1¼ lbs. Per pair..$0.35
Per dozen pairs.......... 4.00

No. 18C1486 The Chicago Pillow Sham Holder. The most simple and best holder on the market, can be instantly clamped to any size metal or wooden bed without screws or tools of any kind. The clamps are padded and cannot mar the finest finish or enamel. Shipping wt., 20 ozs. Per pair..$0.50
Per dozen pairs.......... 5.50

Pillow Shams, Stamped.

No. 18C1488 Made of good muslin, one sham stamped **I Slept and Dreamed that Life Was Beauty,** and the other sham stamped **I Woke and Found that Life Was Duty.** Size, 30x30 ins. Price, per pair, $0.18
Per dozen pairs.......... 2.00
If by mail, postage extra, per pair, 6c.

No. 18C1490 Good Quality Muslin Shams. Stamped in assorted floral designs. A very desirable sham. Size, 30x30 inches. Price, per pair.....$0.15
Per dozen pairs.......... 1.50
If by mail, postage extra, per pair, 5c.

No. 18C1492 White Muslin Pillow Shams. Embroidered in fast color red embroidery cotton. Size, 30x30 inches. Peacock pattern.

Price, per pair.....$0.25
Per dozen pairs.... 2.65

No. 18C1494 White Muslin Pillow Shams. Same quality as above pattern, in fast color red embroidery cotton. **Good Night** worked on one sham and **Good Morning** on the other. In washing do not boil. Use lukewarm water and ivory soap.
Price, per pair..........$0.25
Per dozen pairs.......... 2.65
If by mail, postage extra, per pair, 7c.

No. 18C1496 Stamped White Muslin Pillow Shams, with 2-inch hem border, stamped in assorted flower designs, as violets, carnations, roses, wild flowers, daisies, etc. This sham will be very much appreciated at the price. Size, 29x29 inches. Price, per pair, $0.25
Per dozen pairs.......... 2.75
If by mail, postage extra, per pair, 7c.

Spachtel Shams and Scarfs.

No. 18C1501 Hemstitched Lawn Pillow Sham or Table Cover, worked with white braiding and battenberg lace. A new and very attractive pattern on good quality lawn. Will wash and wear well. Size, 30x30 inches.

Price, per pair, 45c; each.........25c
If by mail, postage extra, each, 5c.

No. 18C1503 Dresser Scarf, same design and to match above sham. Size, 18x54 inches. Price, each..........25c
If by mail, postage extra, 5 cents.

No. 18C1505 Hemstitched White Lawn Pillow Shams or Table Cover. This is an exceptionally pretty design. Around the entire border is worked large flowers in bonnaz stitching and has an insertion of lace fagoting. Washes and will give splendid satisfaction. Size, 32x32 inches
Price, per pair, 95c; each..........48c
If by mail, postage extra, each, 5 cents.

No. 18C1507 Dresser Scarf, same design and to match above sham. Size, 18x54 inches. Price, each..........48c
If by mail, postage extra, each, 5 cents.

Ruffled Shams or Table Covers.

No. 18C1509 White Lawn Ruffled Sham. The four corners are prettily worked in bonnaz stitch. These shams will wash and wear well and look as pretty as a dollar sham. Size 32 x 32 inches. Can also be used for table or stand cover.
Price, each..........23c
Per pair..........45c
If by mail, postage extra, each, 5c.

No. 18C1509½ Dresser Scarf, same design and to match above. Size, 18x54 inches. Price, each..........23c
If by mail, postage extra, each, 5c.

No. 18C1511 Empire Ruffled Sham. The body is of heavy Brussels net, worked in a very pretty design in the four corners and has a 4½-inch lawn ruffle. We consider this an exceptionally attractive and good value sham. Size, 32 x 32 inches.
Price, each..........35c
Per pair..........65c
If by mail, postage extra, each, 5c.

Lace Shams, Covers and Scarfs.

No. 18C1513 Lace Pillow Sham or Table Cover. This is a very beautiful, heavy, Brussels net lace sham, appliqued with white lace in ribbon pattern and stitched with white bonnaz. Large pretty design in the four corners and center. Size, 30x30 inches.

Price, each..........24c
Per pair..........45c
If by mail, postage extra, each, 5c.

No. 18C1515 Dresser Scarf, same design and to match above sham. Size, 18x54 inches. Price, each..........24c
If by mail, postage extra, each, 5c.

No. 18C1517 Lace Pillow Sham or Table Cover on heavy Brussels net. A very large and showy pattern. Entirely around the scalloped edge, four corners and center, appliqued in white ribbon pattern with white lawn and stitched in bonnaz work. Very excellent value. Size, 32x32 inches.
Price, each..........50c
Per pair..........95c
If by mail, postage extra, each, 5c.

No. 18C1519 Dresser Scarf, same design and to match above sham. Size, 18x54 inches. Price, each..........50c
If by mail, postage extra, each, 5c.

No. 18C1521 White Lace Pillow Sham or Table Cover. This is a very elaborate design in ribbon effect, on heavy, white lace net. Very closely worked entirely around and in center of sham. We are sure that you will be well pleased with this cover. Size, 32x32 inches. Price, each..........$0.75
Per pair.......... 1.45
If by mail, postage extra, each, 5c.

No. 18C1523 Dresser Scarf, same design and to match above sham. Size, 18x54 inches. Price, each..........75c
If by mail, postage extra, each, 5 cents.

Spachtel Shams or Covers and Scarfs.

No. 18C1525 White Spachtel or Irish Point Pillow Sham, also used for table cover. A new and pleasing pattern on good quality white lawn. Size, 32x32 inches
Price, each....25c
Per pair.......45c
If by mail, postage extra, each, 5 cents.

No. 18C1527 Dresser Scarf, same design and to match above sham. Size, 18x54 inches. Price, each..........25c
If by mail, postage extra, each, 5 cents.

No. 18C1529 White Spachtel or Irish Point Pillow Sham or Table Cover; more closely worked and prettier pattern than above, on good quality lawn. Size, 32x32 inches.
Price, each.......35c
Per pair.....65c
If by mail, postage extra, each, 5c.

No. 18C1531 Dresser Scarf, same design and to match above sham. Size, 18x54 inches. Price, each..........35c
If by mail, postage extra, each, 5c.

No. 18C1533 White Spachtel or Irish Point Pillow Sham; Renaissance design. The center is worked very elegantly with lace and bonnaz stitching, while around center of pattern and entirely around edge it is elaborately worked with a lace design and battenberg lace braid insertion. This will make an elegant cover as well as sham. Size, 32x32 inches.

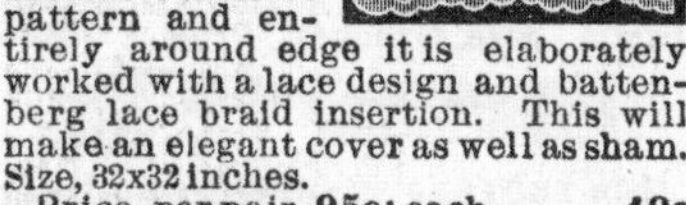

Price, per pair, 95c; each........49c
If by mail, postage extra, each, 5 cents.

No. 18C1535 Dresser Scarf, same design as above and to match sham. Size, 18x54 inches. Price, each..........49c
If by mail, postage extra, each, 5 cents.

No. 18C1537 White Spachtel or Irish Point Pillow Sham, also used for table cover. This is worked on extra quality white lawn and closely worked with the spachtel threads throughout. We consider this excellent 75-cent value. Size, 32x32 inches. Price, each....$0.55
Per pair.......... 1.05
If by mail, postage extra, each, 5 cents.

No. 18C1539 Dresser Scarf, same design as above and to match sham. Size, 18x54 inches. Price, each..........55c

No. 18C1541 White Spachtel or Irish Point Pillow Sham. This is a very beautiful and elaborate design; closely worked. Equal to any sham that is sold elsewhere at $1.00 to $1.25. Size, 32x32 inches. Price, each..........$0.79
Per pair.......... 1.50
If by mail, postage extra, each, 5 cents.

No. 18C1543 Dresser Scarf, same design as above and to match sham. Size, 18x54 inches. Price, each......79c
If by mail, postage extra, 5 cents.

No. 18C1545 White Spachtel or Irish Point Pillow Sham or Table Cover. Large tulip and floral design. Very closely worked with the spachtel threads and bonnaz stitching, on best quality white lawn. An exceptionally striking and elaborate pattern and our very finest pillow sham. Size, 32x32 inches. Price, each........$1.10
Per pair.......... 2.10

No. 18C1547 Dresser Scarf, same design as above and to match sham. Size, 18x34 inches. Price, each..........$1.10
If by mail, postage extra, each, 5 cents.

Pretty Spachtel and Renaissance Tidies.

No. 18C1549 Spachtel Tidies, with bonnaz stitch embroidery and worked on fine quality lawn. A new and pretty pattern. Comes in three sizes.

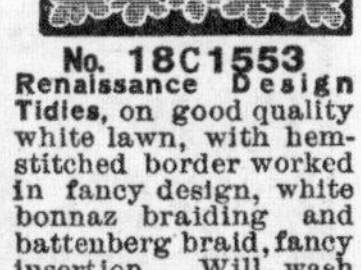

Size, ins.	8	12	18
Each....	4c	8c	12c

Postage extra, each, 2 to 4 cents.

No. 18C1553 Renaissance Design Tidies, on good quality white lawn, with hemstitched border worked in fancy design, white bonnaz braiding and battenberg braid, fancy insertion. Will wash and wear well. Comes in three sizes.

Size, inches..........	9	12	18
Price, each..........	5c	9c	15c

If by mail, postage extra, each, 2 to 3 cents.

No. 18C1555 Spachtel Tidies, Renaissance design. A new novelty pattern, embroidered and worked with battenberg braid on fine, white lawn. Comes in three sizes.

Sizes, inches	Price, each
9	7c
12	10c
18	20c

Postage extra, each, 2 to 4 cents.

No. 18C1557 These Beautiful Spachtel Tidies are an entirely new design and idea. Irish point effect, cut out pattern. The small squares are closely worked in teneriffe design. Come in four sizes.

Size, inches....	6	9	12	18
Price, each.....	5c	10c	22c	40c

If by mail, postage extra, 2 to 4c.

No. 18C1561 These are Pretty Lace Tidies, worked on heavy Brussels net. The spachtel ribbon design is worked over the net in bonnaz stitch, large scroll design. An exceptionally pretty pattern. Comes in three sizes.

Size, inches..........	8	12	18
Price, each..........	8c	12c	23c

If by mail, postage extra, 2 to 4c.

HAND MADE BATTENBERG TIDIES AT REMARKABLE PRICES.

Money back and postage if you don't like them.

No. 18C1563 Fine Hand Made Battenberg Tidies. These imported renaissance tidies are very much used, and this style is very pretty and of extremely good value. Come in different sizes as follows:

Size, inches..	6x6	9x9	12x12	18x18
Price, each...	10c	19c	32c	85c
Size, inches...	24x24	30x30	36x36	
Price, each...	$1.00	$1.85	$2.90	

If by mail, postage extra, each, 2 to 4c.

No. 18C1565 Hand Made Battenberg Sideboard and Dresser Scarf. Same design as above.

Size, inches..........	18x36	18x54
Price, each..........	$1.65	$2.50

If by mail, postage extra, each, 2 to 4c.

No. 18C1567 Hand Made Renaissance Lace Tidies, made of battenberg braid and battenberg rings. Our finest quality, square pattern, very elaborately worked. A very fine and pretty pattern. Prices one-third less than any other concern could afford to sell them. Come in different sizes as follows:

Size, inches..	8x8	12x12	20x20
Price, each...	25c	46c	$1.45
Size, inches..		24x24	30x30
Price, each..........		$2.50	$3.60

If by mail, postage extra, each, 2 to 5c.

No. 18C1571 Hand Made Renaissance Tidies, made of battenberg braid. This is a round design, very pretty for your dressers or used for table covers. A very high grade article for a low price. Comes in different sizes as follows:

Size, ins.	6x6	9x9	12x12
Price, each..	9c	22c	30c
Size, inches.	18x18	24x24	30x30
Price, each..	75c	$1.10	$1.50

If by mail, postage extra, each, 2 to 5c.

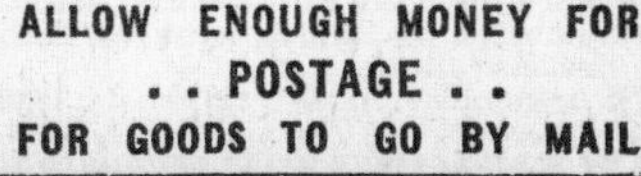

ALLOW ENOUGH MONEY FOR . . POSTAGE . . FOR GOODS TO GO BY MAIL

Battenberg Tidies and Dresser Scarfs.

No. 18C1573 Renaissance Centerpieces with fine linen centers, battenberg braid and ring edges, very fine hand work. Comes in different sizes as follows:

Size, in.	8x8	12x12		
Price	18c	27c		
Size, inches	18x18	24x24		
Price, each	75c	$1.15		
Size, inches	30x30	36x36		
Price	$1.95	$2.65		

If by mail, postage extra, each, 2 to 5c.

No. 18C1575 Renaissance Sideboard and Dresser Scarf, same design as above.

Size, inches	18x36	18x54
Price, each	$1.75	$2.75

If by mail, postage extra, each, 5c.

No. 18C1577 Renaissance Centerpieces with linen center, battenberg braid and ring edges; very pretty and closely worked design. Our price is at least one-third less than you can buy same quality elsewhere. Come in different sizes as follows:

Size, inches	8x8	12x12	20x20
Price, each	$0.25	$0.39	$1.45
Size, inches	30x30	36x36	20x54
Price, each	$3.50	$5.00	$3.75

If by mail, postage extra, each, 2 to 5c.

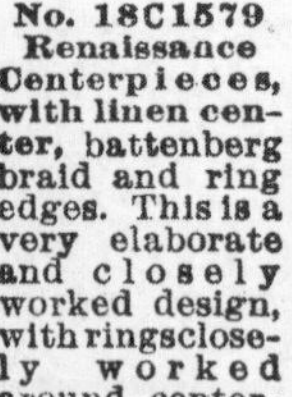

No. 18C1579 Renaissance Centerpieces, with linen center, battenberg braid and ring edges. This is a very elaborate and closely worked design, with rings closely worked around centerpiece. An exceptionally high grade and beautiful design. Comes in different sizes as follows:

Size, inches	9x9	12x12	20x20
Price, each	$0.40	$0.65	$1.70
Size, inches		24x24	30x30
Price, each		$2.50	$3.65

If by mail, postage extra, each, 2 to 5c.

No. 18C1581 Elegant Hand Made Renaissance Centerpieces, with fine linen center, battenberg braid and ring edges. Comes in different sizes as follows:

Size, ins.	12x12			
Price	$0.42			
Size, ins.	18x18	24x24	30x30	36x36
Each	$1.25	$1.95	$3.75	$4.90

If by mail, postage extra, each, 2 to 8c.

Japanese Hand Drawn Linens.

Similar in Appearance, But More Attractive and Prettier than the Mexican Drawn Work and at Half the Prices.

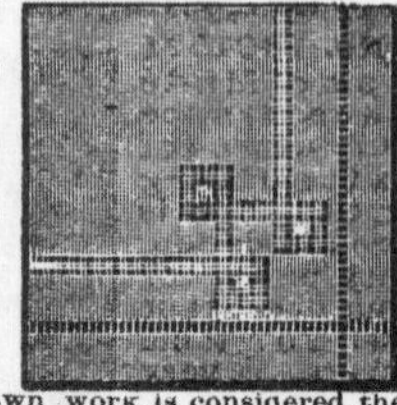

No. 18C1583 Japanese Hand Drawn Linen Squares, worked on very fine quality Irish linen. The designs, as you will see by illustration, are very dainty and exquisite. The Japanese hand drawn work is considered the perfection of fine art in fancy work and by most people who appreciate fine art, the Japanese hand drawn linen is preferred to the Mexican drawn work. We can furnish these in the different sizes as follows:

Size, inches	7x7	9x9	12x12	20x20
Price, each	11c	17c	25c	69c
Size, inches	30x30	36x36	45x45	
Price, each	$1.20	$1.60	$2.00	

If by mail, postage extra, each, 2 to 5 cents.

No. 18C1585 Japanese Hand Drawn Linen Tray Cloths and Scarfs, same design as above squares, come in sizes as follows:

Size, inches	18x27	18x36	18x54
Price, each	75c	99c	$1.25

If by mail, postage extra, each, 3 to 8c.

UMBRELLAS AND PARASOLS.

18C1808

LATEST DESIGNS, HIGHEST QUALITY MATERIAL USED, BEST WORKMANSHIP. UMBRELLAS CANNOT BE SENT BY MAIL ON ACCOUNT OF LENGTH. Weight of umbrella from 1 to 1¾ pounds.

No. 18C1800 Fast Black English Twilled Mercerized Carolo Umbrella. Natural Congo loop or hook handle, splendid value. Size, 26 inches. Price..........49c

No. 18C1804 Fast Black English Twilled Mercerized Carolo Umbrella. Paragon frame, steel rod, with natural Congo hook loop or tied handle, silverine swedge. Size, 26 inches. Price..........69c

No. 18C1808 Fast Black Piece Dyed Union Serge Silk Umbrella, 7-rib, paragon frame; steel rod and natural Congo loop or tied handle, silverine swedge. Regular $1.25 umbrella. Size, 26 inches. Price......85c

No. 18C1810 Ladies' Piece Dyed Union Twilled Silk Umbrella. Paragon frame, steel rod, Otto Mueller imported silk carola serge with pearl chunk, mounted on partridge mounts, silver swedges. A pretty umbrella. Special value. Size, 26 inches.
Price..........$1.00

No. 18C1812 The Otto Mueller Piece Dyed Gloria Twilled Silk Umbrella. Paragon frame, steel rod and black carved rubber handle. Same quality umbrella usually retailed at $1.75. Size, 26 inches. Price......$1.10

No. 18C1814 Ladies' Twilled Silk Umbrella. Paragon frame, steel rod, Otto Mueller piece dyed imported union silk carolo serge, imported Congo handles, trimmed with German silver nose, silver ornaments and silver swedge on bottom of handle. A fine quality umbrella, regular $1.50 value. Size, 26 inches.
Price..........$1.05

No. 18C1818 Ladies' Imported Union Taffeta Silk Umbrella. Tape edged, steel rod, with fancy gun metal and copper finished handle, mounted on partridgene, with copper and gun metal swedges. A very stylish and handsome umbrella. Silk case and tassel. Size, 26 inches. Price..........$1.50

No. 18C1829 This is an Imported Piece Dyed Taffeta Silk Umbrella, paragon frame, steel rod, with fancy carved metal handle, mounted on 1-inch pearl post, with a deep 2-inch swedge. Case and tassels. Size, 26 inches. A pretty and serviceable umbrella. Shipping weight from 1 to 1¾ pounds.
Price..........$1.35

No. 18C1833 This Ladies' Umbrella is a good quality imported piece dyed taffeta silk, with case and tassel, paragon frame, steel rod, very elegant handle, having chased gold caps, with space for initials; mounted on 1-inch smoked pearl post. Mounted on genuine partridge mounts with gold swedge on bottom. Size, 26 inches.
Price..........$1.85

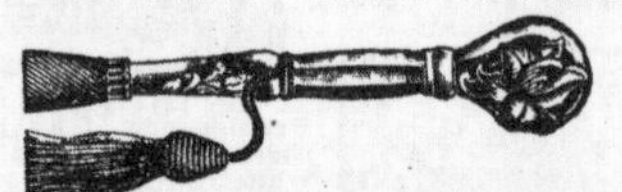

No. 18C1835 Eight-Ribbed Paragon Frame, Steel Rod, Ladies' Umbrella, fine quality union taffeta silk, with tape edge. Silk case and tassel. Has a tulip designed silverine top, handle mounted on 1¾-inch smoked pearl post with silverine swedge. Size, 26 inches. Price..........$2.15

No. 18C1836 This is the Famous Herald Square, Tape Edge Taffeta Silk Ladies' Umbrella. The taffeta silk is a very high grade quality, and guaranteed for wear and appearance. Mounted on an eight-ribbed paragon frame, with steel rod, has silk case and very fine tassel. The handle is a beautiful 1¼-inch sterling silver, gold plated top, with a sterling silver, gold plated swedge. In the center is a large pearl chunk. This is a magnificent and attractive umbrella and one that we can guarantee and recommend. Can also furnish handle in the plain sterling silver. Mention color, gold or silver. Size, 26 inches. Price..........$3.85
Shipping weight from 1 to 1¾ lbs.

No. 18C1837 This is our Highest Grade and Finest Ladies' Silk Umbrella. Made of very high grade quality, taffeta silk with tape edge. Mounted on an eight-ribbed paragon fame, with steel rod; has a wide ribbon and silk fringe tassel; enclosed in a silk case. The handle is a very beautiful and handsome design; has a large, sterling silver top, gold plated, on top of which is large, open space for monogram or initials. The bottom swedge is also gold plated on sterling silver and in center is a large, pearl chunk. Entire length of handle, 7 inches. You could find no finer looking handle if you paid twice the price. Size, 26 inches.
Price..........$4.50

No. 18C1845 Ladies' Colored Taffeta Umbrella. This is our special Waterwitch brand, which is fast colored and rainproof. Made of fine quality American taffeta. Mounted on steel rod, paragon frame, and has imported Congo handle in loops or ties. Colors, navy, red or green. Size, 26 inches. Price..........95c

No. 18C1846 Ladies' Colored Taffeta Silk Umbrella. This is a very high grade umbrella, made of an extra quality of silk taffeta with fancy woven border in white. Mounted on a steel rod, has paragon frame with imported boxwood handle in straight princess style. Silk cord and tassel. This is equal to the best $3.50 umbrella. Colors, red, blue or green. Size, 26 inches. Price..........$1.99

Men's Umbrellas.

Comes in three sizes.

No. 18C1843 Men's Mercerized Cloth Umbrella, with steel rod, eight-rib paragon frame, case and tassels to match, Prince of Wales Congo wood hook handle, sterling silver trimmed. We highly recommend this umbrella for looks and durability. Comes in three sizes.

Size, inches	26	28	30
Price	$1.00	$1.10	$1.20

Self Opening Umbrella.

No. 18C1847 New Patent Self Opening Umbrella. Men's mercerized cloth umbrella with steel rod, paragon frame and new patent self opening attachment. Princess and Prince of Wales Congo wood handles.

Size, inches	26	28
Price	80c	90c

No. 18C1851 Men's piece dyed Union Silk Umbrella, good wearing quality with steel rod, paragon frame and Prince of Wales hook handle in selected Congo wood.

Size, inches	26	28
Price	90c	$1.00

No. 18C1855 Gents' piece dyed Union Silk Umbrella; a very durable and lasting cloth, paragon frame with steel rod, mounted with natural wood stick handle, with silver tip.

Size, inches	26	28
Price	$1.10	$1.20

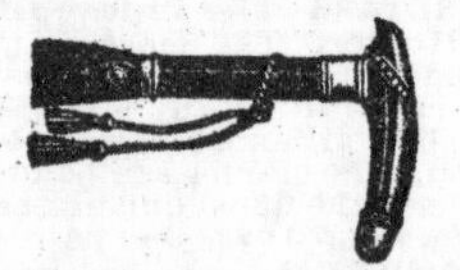

No. 18C1859 Gents' Taffeta Silk Umbrella, fine imported union cloth, with taped edge, paragon frame and steel rod, mounted with a very pretty horn handle, trimmed in silver.

Size, inches	26	28
Price	$1.60	$1.70

Men's Plain High Grade Umbrella.

No. 18C1863 Men's Fine Quality Guaranteed Taffeta Silk with Hemmed Tape Edge Umbrella, with silk case and tassels to match, steel rod and paragon frame and elegant imported furze or boxwood handle. This is a gentleman's plain, neat umbrella; the best made for wear and style. We guarantee it for one year.

Size, inches	26	28
Price	$2.95	$3.20

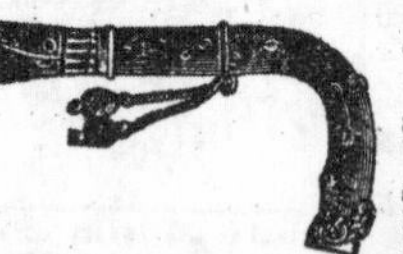

No. 18C1871 This is the Famous Herald Square Umbrella, guaranteed for wear and appearance. Fine quality taffeta silk, with taped edge, paragon frame, steel rod, mounted with fine imported boxwood handle. A gentleman's very stylish, plain umbrella.

Size, inches	26	28
Price	$2.25	$2.50

Shipping weight from 1 to 1¾ lbs.

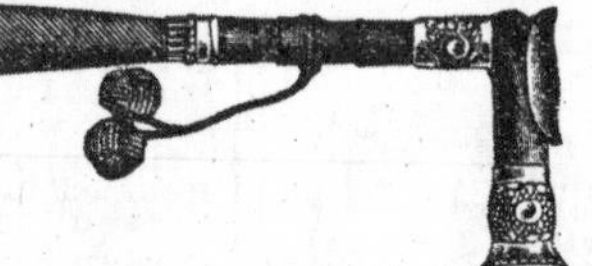

No. 18C1876 This is an Eight-Ribbed, Paragon Frame, Steel Rod Umbrella. Made of the famous Herald Square taffeta silk, with tape edge, fine silk case and tassel. Genuine, antique, ivory hook handle, mounted with sterling silver nose, 925/1000 fine, with silver band. Mounted on genuine step partridge, with silver swedges. Can also furnish same handle in gold knob. Please mention gold or silver.

Size, inches	26	28
Price	$4.00	4.25

24-inch School Umbrellas for Children.

No. 18C1880 Fast Black English Gloria 24-inch School Umbrella, steel frame, steel rod, with small imported Congo handle. Prince of Wales hooks, etc., for boys, and loops and tie shapes for girls. Price..........40c

No. 18C1883 School Umbrella for Boys and Girls. This is a fine quality imported mercerized carola, guaranteed fast black, has paragon frame, steel rod, with pearl hooks, handle mounted on partridgene; also imported Congos with silverene noses, for boys and girls. All have silverene swedges. Size, 24 inches. Price..75c

Child's Parasol.

No. 18C1936 Child's Parasol, made of white lawn with fancy colored figure, having four scalloped ruffles and scalloped edge, puff on top. Mounted on pretty, assorted sticks. Size, 14 inches. Price..........50c

No. 18C1938 Child's Parasol, made of merceline, with five scalloped China silk ruffles, with a puff on top. Mounted on assorted fancy sticks. Colors, plain white, red, pink or light blue. Size, 14 inches. Price........99c

No. 18C1940 Children's Fine Parsols, in a variety of styles in red, white, navy or pink. Mounted on pretty natural wood stick handles. These are values we sold up to $1.00. Tell us the color and we will send you the best 50-cent parasol ever sold. Price..........50c

No. 18C1942 Ladies' Plaid Coaching Parasol, made of a very pretty China silk, with a puff of the same material on top. Mounted on fancy, assorted sticks to contrast with parasol. Plaids will be very stylish this season. This is a very desirable style and can be ordered in either blue plaids or red plaids. Size, 20 inches. Price, each..........$1.05

No. 18C1944 Ladies' Black Coaching Parasol, made of American fast black taffeta, with fancy hemstitched grenadine border, figured and striped. Mounted on a special mount with black tips. Puff on top and mounted on black ebonized stick. Black only. Size, 20 inches. Price..........$1.20

No. 18C1946 Ladies' Coaching Parasol, made of nice quality China silk, with hemstitched border. The border is a Dresden flower effect in assorted colors. Mounted on fancy stick with silk cord and tassel. Borders may be ordered in pink, blue, red or green. Size, 20 inches. Price..........$1.40

No. 18C1948 Ladies' Parasol, made of white China silk, with two full scalloped edge ruffles of same material, puff on top. Made on fancy silvered frame, mounted on assorted sticks to contrast with parasol. This is a very dressy and stylish parasol. Colors, white or black. Price..........$1.25

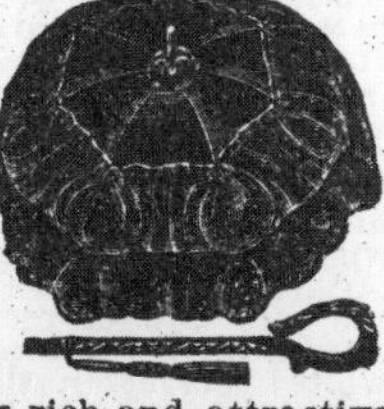

No. 18C1950 Ladies' Parasol, made of China silk, with a 14-inch ruffle of sewing silk veiling. Has a white enameled frame and is mounted on fancy, assorted sticks. Tassel on handle. An attractive and pretty parasol. Colors, white or black. Size, 20 inches. Price..........$1.35

No. 18C1952 Ladies' Parasol. This is a very stylish affair, made of good quality China silk, trimmed with two generous ruffles of fancy, figured border, sewing silk veiling, closely shirred. A very rich and attractive parasol. Large puff of same material on top. Mounted on fancy designed sticks, large cord and tassel. Usually retailed at $5.00. Can be ordered in black or white. Price..........$3.25

LADIES' BELTS.

We show an unusually fine line of belts for ladies, comprising every new shape and design. Selected for quality and fit.

New Crush Leather Belts.

No. 18C1601 New Crush Leather Belt, made of extra quality soft leather, 3¾ inches wide, stitched on both sides. This belt crushes down to about a 2-inch width. The prevailing style. Fitted with pretty harness buckle in front. Colors, black, brown, champagne or white. We guarantee this quality equal to the regular 50-cent value as sold elsewhere. Sizes, 22 to 30 inches. Always give size. Price, per dozen, $2.75; each....25c
If by mail, postage extra, each, 5c.

Buster Brown Belt in Black, White or Red.

No. 18C1603 Buster Brown Belt. Made of best quality, double face patent leather; 1 inch wide with new cross over effect top and front buckle with extending ends. This belt comes in black, white or red. It is made especially for the outside of children's and ladies' coats. Sizes, 26 to 36 inches. Price..........19c
If by mail, postage extra, 5 cents.

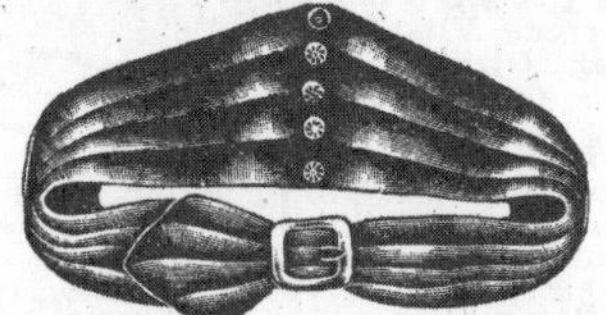

No. 18C1605 All Silk Peau de Soie Girdle Belt. This belt has a 3-inch plaited back, trimmed with five silk crocheted buttons. Tapers to a 1-inch front and closes with a gold harness buckle. Black only. Sizes, 22 to 32 inches. Price..........23c
If by mail, postage extra, 5 cents.

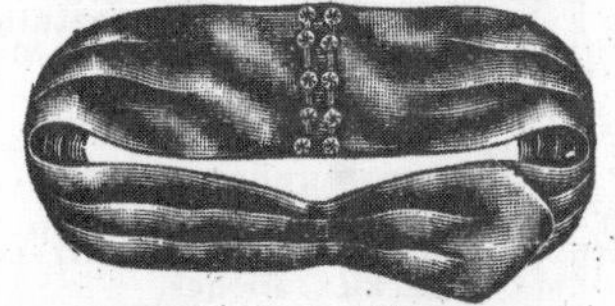

No. 18C1607 All Silk Taffeta Girdle Belt. 2¾ inches wide in the back, trimmed with ten silk crocheted buttons. Tapering to a 1-inch width in the front. This belt closes with a hook and eye fastener and is finished in the front with an extending ear. The belt is well lined throughout. Black only. Sizes, 22 to 30 inches. Price.....24c
If by mail, postage extra, 5 cents.

Crush Velvet Belt in Black, White, Brown, Green or Navy.

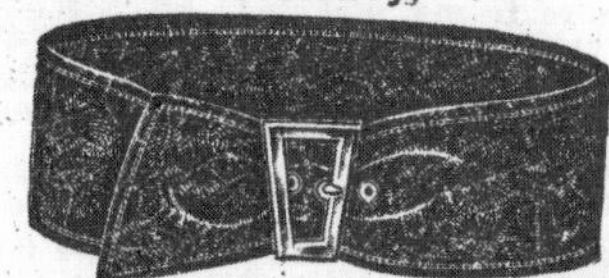

No. 18C1609 Crush Velvet Belt. Made out of the new crush velvet, 3½ inches wide. Well lined throughout, closing in the front with the new style keystone buckle. The buckle is 2½ inches wide. This belt comes in the following colors: Black, white, brown, green or navy blue. Sizes, 24 to 34 inches. Price..........25c
If by mail, postage extra, 5 cents.

We do not accept orders for less than 50 cents as explained in the front of this book.

Diamond Braid Belt in Black or White.

No. 18C1611 Ladies' Belt. Made of a mercerized, diamond braid. Has three crocheted buttons in back, with small, black harness buckle. Width of braid, 3¼ inches. Colors, black or white. Sizes, 22 to 32 inches. Price..........25c
If by mail, postage extra, 5 cents.

Elegant Taffeta Belt in Black or White.

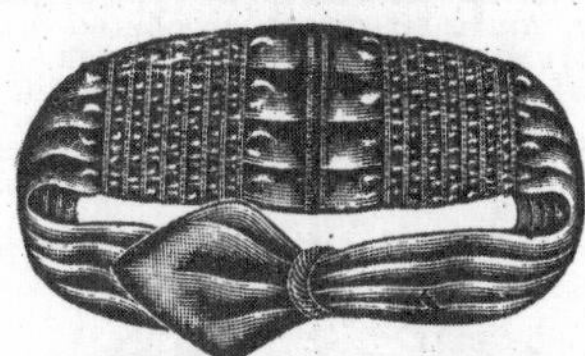

No. 18C1613 Ladies' Silk Taffeta Belt, with gathered tucks and shirring in back. Fancy ring, covered front piece and large tab for front. Width in back, 3½ inches, tapering to a 1¼-inch width in front. Colors, black or white. Sizes, 22 to 30 inches. Price..........25c
If by mail, postage extra, 5 cents.

No. 18C1615 Ladies' Elastic Belt. Made of a 1½-inch ribbed, mercerized elastic belting, with fancy oxidized, metal back piece and two-piece buckle. For waist measures, 22 to 36 inches. Price..........25c
If by mail, postage extra, 5 cents.

No. 18C1617 Fancy Weave Armure Silk Belt, 4 inches wide, plaited down in three plaits to a 2¾-inch width. Closing in the front with a gold keystone buckle. Lined throughout. Black only. Sizes, 22 to 32 inches. Price..........25c
If by mail, postage extra, 5 cents.

Changeable Silk Crush Belt in Red, Green, Navy, Brown or Black.

No. 18C1619 Changeable Silk Crush Effect Belt. Made out of all silk changeable taffeta, 4 inches wide, lined throughout. Closes in the front with a square Colonial design gold buckle. This belt comes in the following changeable colors: Red, green, blue, brown, also solid black. Sizes, 22 to 30 inches. Price..........25c
If by mail, postage extra, 5 cents.

Beautiful Persian Silk Belt.

No. 18C1621 All Silk Persian Crush Belt, made out of best quality liberty Persian silk in white ground effects and fancy Persian flowered pattern. The belt is 3½ inches wide, closing in front with a 2¼-inch gold colonial buckle. This belt is stitched on each side with three rows of heavy, twisted silk thread. Sizes, 22 to 34 inches. Price..........44c
If by mail, postage extra, 5 cents.

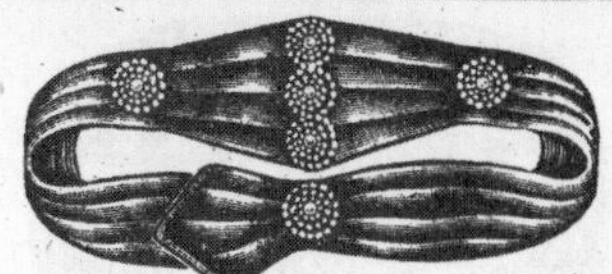

No. 18C1623 Plaited All Silk Peau de Soie Belt, 2¾-inches wide in the back, sloping to a 1¼-inch width in the front. The belt is trimmed in the back with three cut steel cabachons and on each side with one cut steel cabachon. Closes in the front with the same style cabachon. Black only. Sizes, 22 to 30 inches. Price.....43c
If by mail, postage extra, 5 cents.

Taffeta Silk, in Black Only.

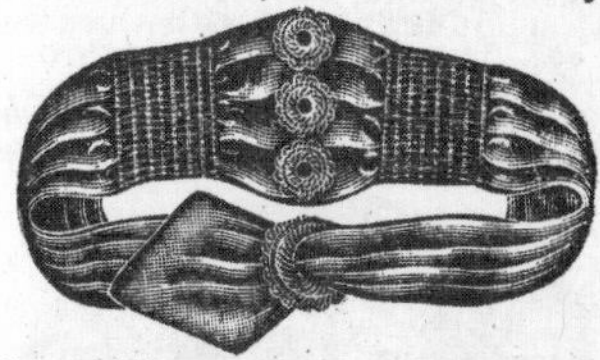

No. 18C1625 Plaited Silk Taffeta Belt, 3½ inches wide in the back, tapering to a 1½ inch front. Trimmed in the back with three large hand crocheted silk portholes. This belt has fourteen rows of shirring in the back and closes with a large size, all silk crocheted ring in the front and with a hook and eye fastener. Black only. Sizes, 22 to 30 inches. Price..........46c
If by mail, postage extra, 5 cents.

This Belt is Real $1.00 Value, in Black or White.

No. 18C1627 Ladies' Taffeta Silk Belt. This is a very attractive and stylish belt. Gathered in folds and closely shirred on both sides. Fancy V-shaped shirred design in back with three fancy braid buttons to offset. Width in back, 4 inches, tapering to 2¼ inches in front. Fastened in front with hooks, and having large tab for front piece. Black or white. Sizes, 22 to 32 inches. Price..........55c
If by mail, postage extra, 6 cents.

Very Stylish Crush Silk Velvet Belt in Black, White or Colors.

No. 18C1629 Imported Crush Silk Velvet Belt, 3¾ inches wide, well lined throughout. This belt has three rows of heavy twisted silk stitching on each side and closes with a new style Colonial design buckle. The buckle is 2½ inches square. The velvet is crushed into a beautiful new design in broad tail effect. Comes in the following colors: Black, white, brown, green or navy blue. Sizes, 22 to 34 inches. Price..........48c
If by mail, postage extra, 5 cents.

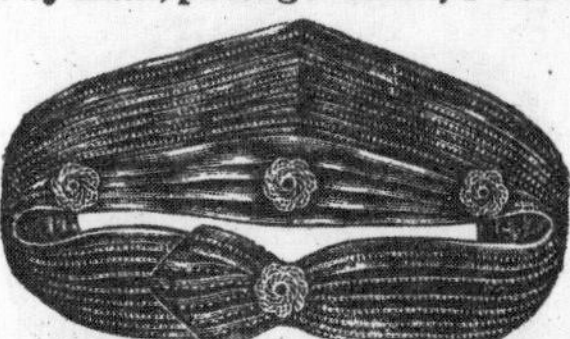

No. 18C1631 Tucked Silk Belt, made out of 3½-inch tucked silk taffeta. This belt has 7 rows of tucking and is 3½ inches wide in the back. Trimmed in the back with a piece of plaited taffeta, fastened down with one large and two small all silk crocheted rings. One inch wide in the front. Closes with an all silk crocheted ring and hook and eye fastener. Black only. Sizes, 22 to 30. Price..........50c
If by mail, postage extra, 6 cents.

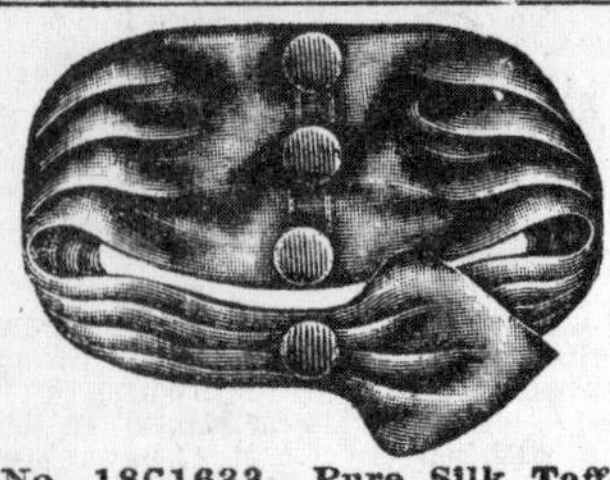

No. 18C1633 Pure Silk Taffeta Girdle Belt, 5 inches wide in the back, tapering to a 1½-inch width in the front. This belt is trimmed in the back with three taffeta silk covered buttons, each one of which is 1¼ inches in diameter. Closes in the front with the same style and size of silk covered button and is finished with an extending ear. This belt is well lined throughout. Colors, black or white. Sizes, 22 to 30 inches. Price..........50c
If by mail, postage extra, 5 cents.

No. 18C1635 All Silk Taffeta Girdle Belt, made out of the best quality pure silk taffeta; 4 inches wide in the back, tapering to a 1½-inch front. Closes with a hook and eye fastener in front. This belt is boned in the back and trimmed with two rows of small silk crocheted buttons and trimmed on each side with rows of fancy shirring, producing a very handsome plaited effect. Finished in the front with a flaring ear. Black only. Sizes, 22 to 30 inches. Price........50c
If by mail, postage extra, 5 cents.

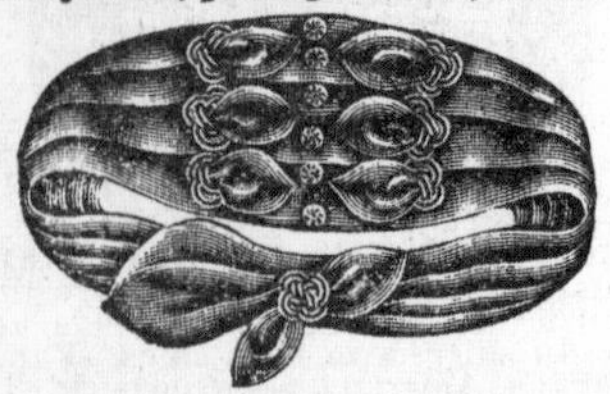

No. 18C1637 All Silk Taffeta Girdle Belt, lined throughout. 3¾ inches wide in the back. The belt is ornamented with six silk taffeta bows, fastened to the belt with silk President braid ornaments. In the center of the six tabs are a row of six small crocheted buttons. This belt tapers to a one-inch front, closes with a hook and eye fastener and is finished with extending ear and silk bow. Black only. Sizes, 22 to 30 inches. Price........50c
If by mail, postage extra, 5 cents.

No. 18C1639 Ladies' Fancy Novelty Braid Belt, made of two-piece, 1¼ inches wide, wood silk and select gimp braid. Ornamented in back with three cut steel cabochons. Hook fastener for buckle, also ornamented with same style cabochons. Black only. Sizes, 22 to 32 inches. Price........50c
If by mail, postage extra, 5 cents.

No. 18C1641 Tucked All Silk Taffeta Girdle Belt, 4 inches wide in the back, sloping to a 1¾-inch width in the front. Has 13 rows of tucking, ornamented in the back with a handsome, new style gunmetal back piece with a neat prong effect, gunmetal effect to match. Black only. Sizes, 22 to 30 inches. Price..................75c
If by mail, postage extra, 5 cents.

Silk Taffeta Belt, 90 Cents.

No. 18C1643 Pure Silk Taffeta Bodice Belt, made out of best quality 8-inch wide all silk taffeta, shirred down the back to 4¼ inches, tapering in the front to a 1½-inch width. The belt has three rows of bone in the back, trimmed with eight rows of shirring, fourteen small crocheted buttons, two rows of shirring on each side. Finished in the front with an extending handkerchief ear. Black only. Sizes, 22 to 30 inches. Price.......90c
If by mail, postage extra, 6 cents.

Swell Taffeta Belt, 88 Cents.

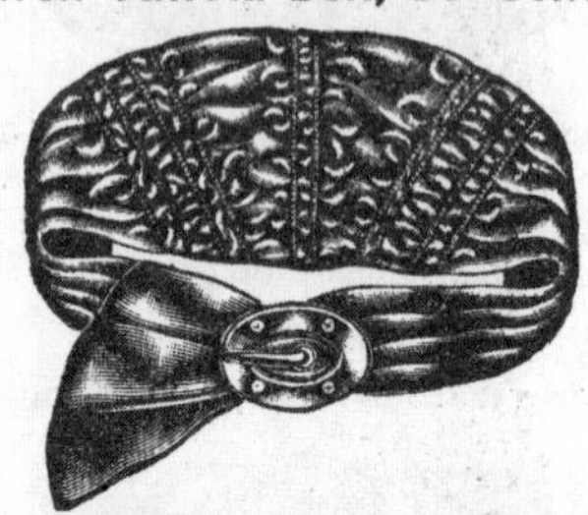

No. 18C1645 New Style Silk Taffeta Girdle, 4 inches wide in the back, closing in the front with a buckle 2 inches wide and 3 inches long. This buckle comes in the new mat gold finish, made of heavy metal, studded with four brilliant rhinestones. The back of this girdle has five rows of the new style shirring, producing a beautiful, form fitting effect. Colors, black or white. Sizes, 22 to 32 inches.
Price..............................88c
If by mail, postage extra, 6 cents.

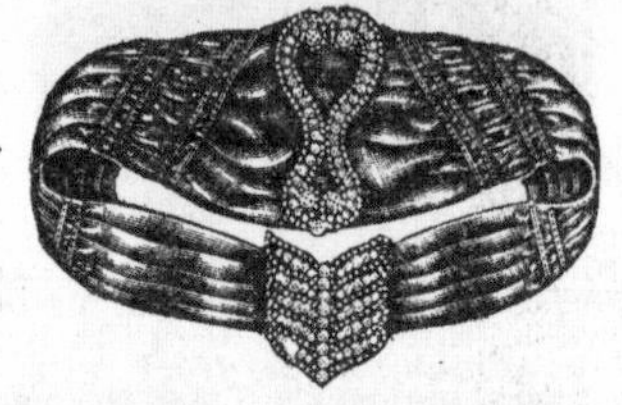

No. 18C1647 Taffeta Silk Belt, with beautiful design cut steel back piece and two-piece buckle to match. Made of good quality silk taffeta, closely shirred and tucked. An entirely new and original design. A very beautiful and rich looking belt. Width of back piece 4 inches and size of front buckle 2 inches. Black only. Sizes, 24 to 34 inches.
Price..............................95c
If by mail, postage extra, 6 cents.

Very Latest Belt, $1.20.

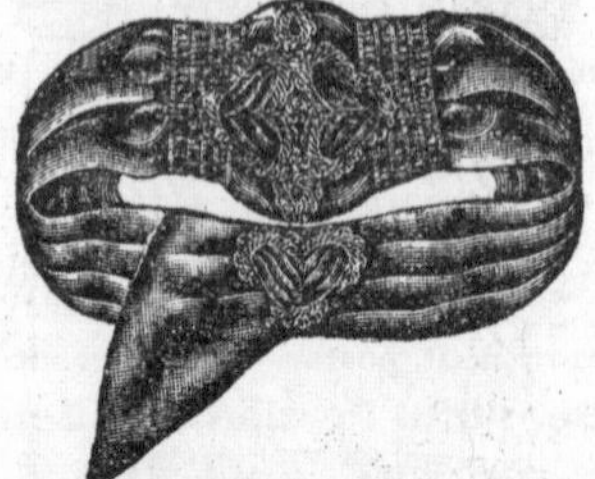

No. 18C1649 All Silk Taffeta Belt, 4 inches wide in the back and sloping to a 1¾-inch width in the front. This belt is beautifully shirred in the back, trimmed with two large silk crocheted ornaments with three compartments, with two small crocheted ornaments to match. The larger ornaments are interlaced with all silk taffeta, producing a very beautiful effect. Closes in the front with a large, silk crocheted ornament, interlaced with silk taffeta and finished with large flaring ear. Black only. Sizes, 22 to 32 inches.
Price..............................$1.20
If by mail, postage extra, 6 cents.

New Vest Belt in Black and Colors.

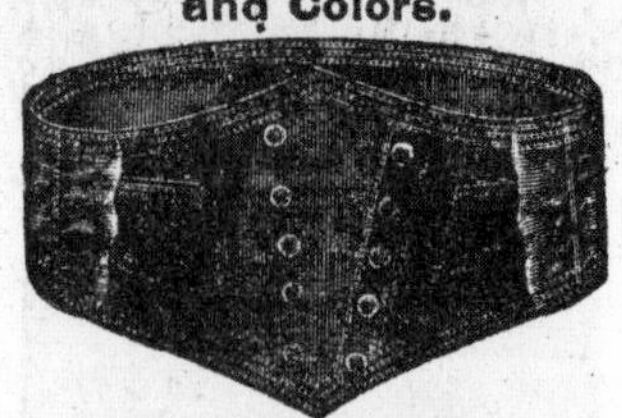

No. 18C1651 New Vest Belt, producing the new double breasted effect. Trimmed with ten small velvet covered buttons and two useful pockets. This belt is made of all silk peau de soie. Elegantly lined throughout. 3½ inches wide in the back, fastened with hooks and eyes on the side and in the front and center of belt. Is 6 inches wide, tapering to 3-inch width on each side. This belt is perfect fitting, tasty looking and the newest thing on the market. Comes in the following colors, black, white, brown, navy or blue. Sizes, 22 to 30 inches.
Price..............................$1.25
If by mail, postage extra, 10 cents.

Belt Girdles for Draping.

No. 18C1653 Perfect Fitting Girdle, straight front, made of fine quality crinoline, stayed with covered reeds, bound edges with laces all complete. These girdles are made to fit the form and are used to be draped with any material desired. In either black or white. Sizes, 22 to 32 inches. Always give size.
Price..............................13c
If by mail, postage extra, 4 cents.

No. 18C1655 Perfect Fitting Girdle, for draping any material. **The popular dip front,** made of crinoline and finished in the same manner as above. Colors, black and white. Sizes, 22 to 32 inches. Always give size. Price...13c
If by mail, postage extra, 4 cents.

PURSES.

No. 18C2101 Calfskin Purse, with nickel riveted frame, three-ball catch, with inside partition. The best purse ever retailed for a dime. Size, 2¼x3¼ inches.
Price, each.....4c
Per dozen..............................44c
If by mail, postage extra, each, 3c.

No. 18C2103 Nickel riveted frame, with partition; **chamois lined;** two pockets. Size, 2¾x3 inches.
Price, per dozen, 85c; each........8c
If by mail, postage extra, each, 3c.

No. 18C2105 Fine Buck Purse. With gusseted bottom and welts, nickel riveted frame with partition; three-ball catch; **chamois lined;** two pockets. Size, 2¾x3 inches.
Price, per dozen, $2.00; each.....19c
If by mail, postage extra, each, 3c.

Seal Grain Leather Purse.

No. 18C2107 Bag Shape, Seal Grain Leather Purse. Fine square frame, nickeled, riveted, with embossed gilt center partition, ball catch, two pockets, chamois lined, stitched edges. Size, 2¾x4 inches.
Price, per dozen, $2.50; each....23c
If by mail, postage extra, each, 3c.

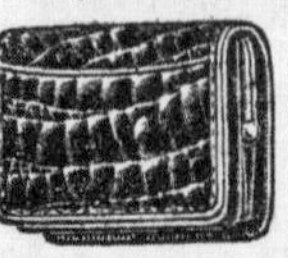

No. 18C2109 Misses' Genuine Alligator Purse, with two outside card pockets and contains two regular, one flap and one coin pocket with nickel frame. The entire purse stitched throughout. A very pretty book; also convenient for inside beaded and silver chatelaine bags. Size, 3¼x3¾ inches.
Price, per dozen, $2.75; each....25c
If by mail, postage extra, each, 5c.

DON'T FORGET MONEY FOR POSTAGE IF YOU WANT GOODS SENT BY MAIL.

Ladies' Genuine Seal Leather Pocketbooks.

No. 18C2111 Genuine Sealskin Pocketbook with calf facings, blocked bottom, gusseted, three regular and one fancy card, one tuck and coin pocket with nickel spring catch fram Size, 3x4½ inches. See if you can matc it for less than 75c or $1.00.
Price, per dozen, $5.50; each..49c
If by mail, postage extra, each, 3c.

Ladies' Fine Walrus Pocketbook.

No. 18C2113 This Stylish Pocketbook has three regular, one fancy card, one tuck and coin pocket, in nickel spring catch frame. Mounted with genuine sterling silver corners. Colors, gray or black. Size, 2¾x4¾ inches. Price, each..........$0.56
Per dozen..............................6.00
If by mail, postage extra, each, 4c.

No. 18C2115 Made of the finest quality genuine seal, calf facing, block bottom, gusseted, three regular, one tuck and coin pocket in fine nickel spring catch frame. This elegant book is mounted with one fine sterling silver corner and sterling silver nameplate. A very excellent design and splendid value. Size, 3x4½ inches. Price, each..........$ 1.10
Per dozen..............................12.50
If by mail, postage extra, each, 4c.

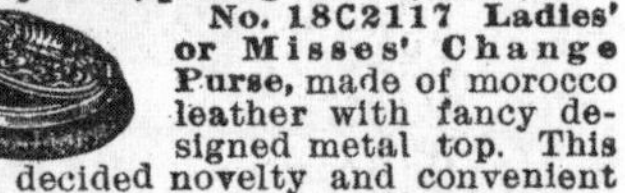

No. 18C2117 Ladies' or Misses' Change Purse, made of morocco leather with fancy designed metal top. This is a decided novelty and convenient for carrying in hand, chatelaine or wrist bag. Comes in black, brown or tan. Size, 2¼ inches. Price.......39c
If by mail, postage extra, 5 cents.

No. 18C2119 Ladies' or Misses' Indian Seed Bead Change Purse, made in a fancy Indian design, in the flat mushroom shape, with metal top. Is easily opened, convenient for carrying in the hand, chatelaine or wrist bag. This is an exceptionally pretty and stylish novelty. Size, 2½ inches. Price..44c
If by mail, postage extra, 5 cents.

No. 18C2121 Misses' Novelty Gunmetal Wrist Bag. Fancy stamped design on outside, with two inner pockets and ball catch and chain. This is the latest novelty for misses. Comes in gunmetal or French gray. Size, 2x3¼ inches. Price, 25c
If by mail, postage extra, 5 cents.

No. 18C2123 Misses' Purse, with cord handle. The purse is made of real calfskin leather in tan and brown shades, hand decorated with Holland figures. Best nickeled ball catch frame. The purse is leather lined. A very neat and stylish little purse. Size, 2½x2¼ inches. Price.......25c
If by mail, postage extra, 4 cents.

No. 18C2125 Misses' Calfskin Purse, with silk cord handles and tassels, beautifully ornamented on outside with a neat, pressed design and jewel button. Best nickeled ball frame and inner purse. Leather lined. Comes in pretty tan shades. Size, 4¼x2½ inches.
Price..............................40c
If by mail, postage extra, 5 cents.

No. 18C2127 Real Japanese Netsuke Bag. Made of genuine Japanese leather, embossed in a very attractive and beautiful design. Trimmed on the outside of flap with an oriental silver design. The purse contains two inner pockets and card pocket, with a middle coin or change pocket. Trimmed in the very best of nickeled materials. Attached with silver chain and large white knob, in imitation of white ivory, which is decorated with an oriental design. This purse is shown by the finest jewelry stores at $5.00 to $7.50 each. Size of purse, 4¼x3¼ inches.
Price..............................$2.50
If by mail, postage extra, 6 cents.

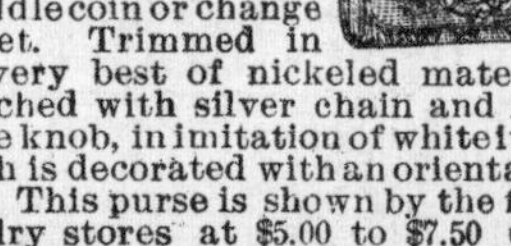

Handbags.

No. 18C2129 Genuine Japanese Netsuke Bag. This is the very latest and most stylish purse. Has chain and knob attachments. To be worn either under the belt or carried in the hand. The knob is of fancy designed metal. The bag is made of genuine Japanese leather, highly embossed and decorated in very beautiful fancy designs. Leather lined throughout. Has two pockets for currency and coin and card pocket. The flap of same is decorated with oriental design. This purse will attract admiration and attention from all. As good as you can buy in the jewelry stores for $3.00. Size of purse, 4½x2¾ inches.
Price..**$1.50**
If by mail, postage extra, 6 cents.

Walrus Leather Chatelaine Bag.

No.18C2131 Black Leather Chatelaine Bag. Imitation walrus, riveted frame with leather front, spring catch, one regular and one outside handkerchief pocket; wide bottom and sides. This is an exceptionally fine stylish bag and exceptional value. Size, 5¾x6¼ inches.
Price, each.... **$0.50**
Per dozen.......... **5.50**
Postage extra, each, 8 cents.

No. 18C2132 Ladies' Genuine Walrus Leather Chatelaine Bag. Same shape as above, with superior trimmings and workmanship. A very fine article. Price, each........... **$ 0.99**
Per dozen........................ **11.00**
Postage extra, each, 10 cents.

Indian Chatelaine Bag.

No. 18C2135 Leather Beaded Shopping Bag. These are the latest idea in bags and are having an immense sale. We are offering an unusual value in this bag, being 7x6 inches, with leather drawstrings and long leather streamers mounted with fancy colored beads. Colors, brown, tan or red. Price......**44c**
If by mail, postage extra, 8 cents.

No. 18C2137 Our Novelty, All Leather, Block Shape, Braided Handle Bag, made of best walrus grain leather, full moire lined, with additional pocket on inside containing purse. Stapled frame with neat and stylish, novelty braided handle. Colors, black or brown. Size of frame, 4 inches. Size of bag, 6x4 inches. Price........ . ...**25c**
If by mail, postage extra, 10 cents.

No. 18C2139 Ladies' Wrist Bag, new and pleasing style shape, made of walrus grain leather, full gusseted. Fitted with good ball catch frame, leather braided handle on revolving post hinges and sateen lined. The inner pocket is fitted with small purse. Black only. Size, 8½x5½ inches. Price,.........**49c**
If by mail, postage extra, 12 cents.

No. 18C2141 Ladies' Wrist Bag. This is the stylish square carriage shape. Made of walrus grain leather, full gusseted, fitted with large ball fastener, nickel frame, with leather strap handle. Lined with moreen, has inner pocket fitted with small purse. Black only. Size, 9x5¼ inches. Price **50c**
If by mail, postage extra, 12 cents.

No. 18C2143 Ladies' Hand Bag, square carriage shape. A very elegant bag, made of new walrus grain leather, full gusseted sides, mounted with a fine ball catch, gilt or oxidized frame. Has leather braided handle, lined with sateen. The bag also has two inner pockets, fitted with small purse and card case. Colors, black or brown. Regular $1.00 value. Size, 9¼x5¼ in. Price, **70c**
If by mail, postage extra, 12 cents.

No. 18C2145 Our Standard New Oblong Shape Leather Bag, made of walrus grain goatskin, full leather gusset made of same material. Moire lined with novelty three-ball double opening frame. This bag has an additional purse in the inside pocket, novelty braided handle on staple posts. Colors, black or brown with gilt frame. Size of frame, 7 inches; size of bag, 8x5 inches. Price........................**75c**
If by mail, postage extra, 12 cents.

No. 18C2147 Ladies' New Style Wrist Bag. This is a very pretty shape, made of walrus grain leather, full gusseted with large ball fastener and gilt frame. The strap handles, which are double stitched, are fastened in a very effective manner with small buckles. Has fancy brocaded inner lining, has an extra inside pocket, fitted with small purse. Colors, black or brown. Size of bag, 9½x5½ inches.
Price..**90c**
If by mail, postage extra, 12 cents.

No. 18C2149 Pretty Novelty Shape, Ladies' Hand Bag. Made of walrus grain leather, full gusseted sides, with small leather pipings. Fitted with a very high grade gold or oxidized pear shaped ball fastener, riveted frame and with braided leather handle on post hinges. Lined with best quality moreen and having two inner pockets, fitted with small purse and card case. This is a very elegant bag, the shape and style being exceptionally swell. Colors, black or brown. Size, 9x5 inches.
Price...**95c**
If by mail, postage extra, 12 cents.

No. 18C2151 Novelty Three-Ball Double Opening Braided Handle Bag, made of new walrus grained, goatskin with full gusset made of same material, the latest style. The bag is lined with fancy moire lining. Has extra pocket, with novelty square shape purse. Has a novelty square shape, three-ball drawn frame with post hinges and braided handle. Colors, black or brown with gilt frame or black with gunmetal frame. Size of frame 8 inches. Size of bag, 9x5½ inches.
Price...**98c**
If by mail, postage extra, 12 cents.

No. 18C2153 Ladies' New Novelty Carriage Bag. Made of sealion leather. This is a fancy grain, very popular. Has full gusseted sides, with a leather covered riveted frame with large ball fasteners. Fitted with leather braided handle on new patent hinges. The purse is lined with a very fine sateen. Has inner pocket with small purse. On the outside is an extra handkerchief pocket with flap and ball and socket fastener. Black only. Size, 8½x5 inches. Price, each.... **$ 0.99**
Per dozen.................................**11.50**
If by mail, postage extra, 12 cents.

No. 18C2155 Ladies' Novelty Hand Bag. Made of selected walrus grain leather, ornamented in front with new strap and buckle design. The bag is mounted on leather covered riveted frame, with pear shape ball fastener. Leather braided handle with knob ends, lined with best quality moreen. Fitted with small purse in inner pocket. Colors, black or brown. Size, 9¼x5¾ inches.
Price..**$1.00**
If by mail, postage extra, 12 cents.

No. 18C2157 Latest Style Aveue Bag, made of walrus grain leather with ball catch fastener and gilt frame. Has two envelope shaped pockets and fancy flaps with snap button. The bag is lined throughout, has stitched strap handles. This is a very desirable and pretty bag. Colors, black or brown. Size, 8½ x 5¼ inches.
Price..**$1.00**
If by mail, postage extra, 12 cents.

No. 18C2159 Ladies' High Grade Hand Bag. Made of extra quality walrus grain leather, gusseted sides with small pipings. This is a very swell carriage shape, mounted on very high grade three-ball double opening frame, with large ball catches. Braided handle fitted with post hinges. The bag is lined with best quality moreen and has small purse and card case. We consider this exceptional value. Color, black only. Size, 11x5¼ inches. Price......................**$1.25**
If by mail, postage extra, 15 cents.

No. 18C2161 Ladies' Hand Bag. Made of very finest and best walrus grain leather; full gusset, made of same material with full leather piped seam ends. Has high grade leather covered frame with fancy snap lock, braided handle on staple post hinges, which is double riveted, has best quality moreen lining, two pockets, containing purse and card case to match outside leather. This is a very pretty new novelty shape bag, which looks very rich and attractive. Black only. Size of frame, 8 inches; size of bag, 10x5¼ inches. Price, **$1.50**
If by mail, postage extra, 15 cents.

No. 18C2163 Ladies' High Grade Hand Bag. This is a very new and attractive novelty shape. Made of finest quality, selected, rough grain leather with full gusseted sides. Mounted on an unusually fine quality gilt frame with patented fastener, has braided leather handle on riveted fancy post hinges. Lined with high grade moreen, has small inner pocket, fitted with extra pocketbook. Equal to many of the $5.00 bags sold elsewhere. Colors, black or brown. Size, 9x5¼ inches.
Price............ ....**$1.90**
If by mail, postage extra, 12 cents.

No. 18C2165 Ladies' Novelty Hand Bag. Made of selected walrus grain leather. This is a very attractive and rich looking bag. Entirely new shape, mounted on riveted, gilt frame, with celluloid front, edges being ornamented in gilt. Pear shape ball fasteners, has the newest style leather covered handle, lined with best quality moreen; has inner pocket, fitted with small leather purse. This is an exceptionally swell bag. Colors, black or brown. Size, 9½x6 inches. Price.........**$2.00**
If by mail, postage extra, 12 cents.

Ladies' Shopping Bags.

No. 18C2167 Ladies' Shopping Bag. Made of seal grain leatherette, bound with gimp cord all around; two small outside pockets, one with nickeled catch, sateen top with draw strings, two leather handles. Size 6¾x10 inches.
Price, per dozen, **$4.50**; each........**40c**
If by mail, postage extra, 16 cents.

No. 18C2169 Ladies' Shopping bag. Made of seal grain leather and edged with silk gimp cord. One large and two small outside pockets, both having oxidized catches. Very fine quality sateen top with silk draw strings and two leather handles. An exceptionally good design. Size, 10½x7¼ inches. Regular $1.50 value.
Price, per dozen, **$8.50**; each.........**75c**
If by mail, postage extra, 18 cents.

No. 18C2171 Ladies' Shopping Bag, made of highest grade seal leather, bound with silk gimp cord, fine sateen top with draw strings. Large outside fancy pockets, fastened with clasp. This is our highest quality shopping bag, that usually retails for $1.50. Size, 11¼x7½ inches. Price.......... .**$1.00**
If by mail, postage extra, 20 cents.

No. 18C2173 Ladies' Boston Shopping Bag. Made of fine quality walrus leather, with riveted leather covered frame, and having improved nickel snap catch. Leather covered handle strap. The inside lining is leather and contains little side pockets for handkerchief and small articles. A very convenient and handy style of bag. Size, 9½x6 inches.
Price, per dozen, **$11.00**; each...**$1.00**
If by mail, postage extra, 20 cents.

Twine Shopping Bags to Carry Packages.

No. 18C2175 Twine Shopping Bag, made of heavy twisted twine. Tied and knotted for strength and durability. Fitted with leather covered handles. This is a big help to ladies who have packages and parcels to carry. They are being adopted universally. Size, 20x15 inches, but when stretched will extend to almost twice the size.
Price...**20c**
If by mail, postage extra, 5 cents.

No. 18C2177 Twine Shopping Bag, made of finer cord, being a double thread, woven or braided into fancy shape. Fitted with leather covered handles. Will last a lifetime. The greatest convenience ever invented for carrying parcels. Size, 20x14 inches.
Price, each.........**45c**
If by mail, postage extra, 5 cents.

SPECIAL VALUES IN MEN'S POCKETBOOKS AND CARD CASES.

All the novelties as well as staples in this line. Note our prices carefully. A pocketbook or card case makes an acceptable present.

Quaker Purse.

No. 18C2179 Genuine pigskin. Two pockets. Size, ¼x2½ inches. Its peculiar shape and formation admit of handling the coin without danger of losing its contents.
Price, per dozen, **$4.00**; each..**35c**
If by mail, postage extra, each, 3c.

Pocketbooks.

No. 18C2181 Wallet, fine leather, closes with glove button catches on the side; interior is leather lined, has one large pocket for change, etc., and has a specially made compartment for notes and bills. Neatly finished. Size, closed, ¾x2¾x3¼ inches.
Price, per dozen, $2.50; each....23c
If by mail, postage extra, each, 3 cents.

No. 18C2183 Wallet, fine seal grain leather, closes with glove button catches on the side; interior is leather lined, has one large pocket for change, etc., and has a compartment for notes and bills. A high grade book. Size, closed, ¾x2¾x3¼ inches.
Price, per dozen, $5.00; each 45c
If by mail, postage extra, each, 4c.

Combination Card Case and Bill Fold.

No. 18C2185 Combination Card Case, having a partition pocket the entire length of book so as to place your paper money full length and then fold. A snap button fastener holds same secure; made of seal grain leather. Extra stitched and lined. Size, open, 8½x4½ inches. Price, each......$0.44
Per dozen......................5.00
If by mail, postage extra, each, 4c.

No. 18C2187 Combination Card Case and Bill Fold. Same style as above, but made of finest real seal leather. Leather faced; stitched edges; the bill pocket is silk lined; a very fine book. Size, open, 8¾x4½ inches. $1.50 value. Price, each, $ 1.00
Per dozen......................11.00
If by mail, postage extra, each, 4c.

Men's Patent Box Flap Book.

No. 18C2189 Seal leather, with five regular pockets and four smaller pockets, bound and stitched. A very convenient purse for men. Size, 2¾x4 inches. Price, each...$0.46
Per dozen......................5.00
If by mail, postage extra, each, 4c.

Seal Grain Leather Card Cases.

No. 18C2191 Card Case of seal grain leather. One ticket and two regular pockets, one with flap and tuck strap. Size, 3x4½ inches.
Price, per dozen, $2.25; each....21c
If by mail, postage extra, each, 4 c.

No. 18C2193 Card Case of seal leather, in black only. Size, 2¾x4¼ inches. Inside finished in smooth calf and seal, one ticket and two regular pockets, one with flap and tuck strap; also place for stamps.
Price, per dozen, $5.25; each....47c
If by mail, postage extra, each, 4c.

No. 18C2195 Finest Quality Genuine Seal Card Case or Gents' Pocketbook, has two regular pockets, one with flap, tuck strap. Size, 2¾x4½ inches. Price....................$1.00
If by mail, postage extra, 5 cents.

Back Pocket Size Card and Billbook.

No. 18C2197 Card Case or Gents' Billbook, convenient back pocket size. Made of seal grain leather with smooth calf inside facing, has two regular pockets, one with a flap catch and card pockets. Size, 3¼x5 inches.
Pric...............................50c
If by mail, postage extra, 6 cents.

No. 18C2199 Card Case or Gents' Billbook, a very high grade quality of fine, real seal leather, faced with seal and calf, has two regular and one card pocket, with tuck strap, also additional pocket for stamps, small tickets, etc. Size, 3¼x5 ins. Price....$1.00
If by mail, postage extra, 6 cents.

Men's Heavy Sheep Strap Pocketbooks.

No. 18C2201 Fine calf finish, three pockets and bill fold, with flap and tuck strap. Stitched all around. Size, 2¾x4¾ inches.
Price, each. $0.19
Per dozen.. 1.90
If by mail, postage extra, each, 4 cents.

No. 18C2203 Men's Extra Selected Quality Sheep Strap Book. English calf finish, four regular pockets and stamp pocket, bill fold with flap and tuck strap; warranted all leather throughout; heavily stitched all around. Size, 2¾x4¾ inches. Price, each......$0.36
Per dozen........................4.00
If by mail, postage extra, each, 4c.

English Calfskin Pocketbook.

No. 18C2205 English Calf Pocketbook. A very high grade and finely finished book. Soft leather, very durable, four regular and three small pockets. Bill fold, with flap and tuck strap. Size, 2¾x4¾ inches.
Price, each.....$0.50
Per dozen......5.50
If by mail, postage extra, each, 4c.

Seal Leather Strap Pocketbook.

No. 18C2207 Four regular pockets, bill fold, with flap and tuck strap, leather faced. Regular $1.00 pocketbook. Size, 2¾x4¾ inches.
Price, each...$0.69
Per dozen ... 7.75
If by mail, postage extra, each, 4 cents.

BILLBOOKS.

Our 20-Cent Seal Grain Billbook.

No. 18C2209 Seal Grain Billbook, four large compartments or pockets, all lined and well finished throughout, excellent value. Size, 3½x8 inches. Price, each......$0.20
Per dozen.......................2.25
If by mail, postage extra, each, 6c.

Fine Morocco Billbook for 36 Cents.

No. 18C2211 Fine Morocco Grain Leather Billbook. Four large full size pockets, also card and ticket pocket; kid faced and canvas lined. Size, 3½x8 inches.
Price, per dozen, $4.00; each ...36c
If by mail, postage extra, each, 5c.

Only 50c for this Fine Morocco Billbook.

No. 18C2213 Fine Morocco Finish Leather Billbook. Size, 3¾x6¾ inches. Three large and two small pockets, kid faced and finely finished. An excellent book for carrying letters and papers. Price, each..$0.50
Per dozen.........................5.50
If by mail, postage extra, each, 5c.

No. 18C2215 Gentlemen's Billbook. Made of fine quality smooth calf, yellow finish leather. Stitched throughout. Has two regular pockets and two bill folds, one side of which is secured by flap and tuck. Size, 3¾x8 inches. **One of the most durable and best books made.** Price, per doz., $6.00; each, 55c
If by mail, postage extra, each, 6c.

No. 18C2217 The Secret Pocket Billbook. Kid faced and canvas lined; fine morocco grain leather, three large, two small and one secret burglar proof pocket; finely made and finished throughout. Size, 3½x8 inches.
Price, per dozen, $5.50; each....50c
If by mail, postage extra, each, 5c.

$1.50 Value for 82 Cents.

No. 18C2219 Extra Fine Morocco Grain Leather Billbook. Eight large pockets alphabetically indexed, also seven smaller pockets for bills and currency; leather faced and canvas lined. **Specially adapted for collectors and as a deposit for notes and bills.** Large size, 4½x10 inches.
Price, per dozen, $9.00; each....82c
Shipping weight, 12 ounces.

No. 18C2221 Our Highest Grade Genuine Morocco Billbook, made of finest quality morocco leather, with kid lining, has three large and two smaller pockets for stamps, tickets, etc., also outside card case, has one regular bill fold secured by flap. Highest quality, finish and workmanship throughout. Size, 3¾x8 inches.
Price $1.00
If by mail, postage extra, 6 cents.

Hair Pins, Shell Combs—All Kinds, Side Combs, Back Combs, Hair Retainers.

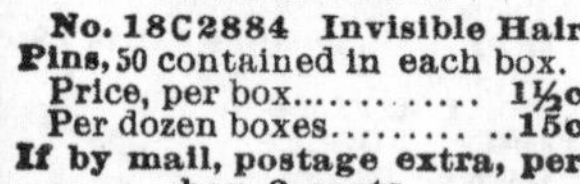

No. 18C2880 Wire Hair Pins. Package like illustration, which contains 28 hair pins, straight or crimped. Regular 5c value. Price, per roll..............1c
For large package of 10 rolls or 280 pins.....................................8c
If by mail, postage extra, 5 cents.

No. 18C2881 Wire Hair Pins (superior quality), the best German make.
Price, for 8 rolls (about 110 hair pins)..............................5c
If by mail, postage extra, 5 cents.

Invisible Hair Pins, Made of Good Wire.

No. 18C2884 Invisible Hair Pins, 50 contained in each box.
Price, per box............ 1½c
Per dozen boxes.............15c
If by mail, postage extra, per box, 2 cents.

Hair Pin Cabinets; a Handy Way to Buy Hair Pins.

No. 18C2888 New Countess Hair Pin, in fancy wood cabinet; assorted; 50 pins to box. Price, per box......2c
Per dozen boxes........22c
If by mail, postage extra, per box, 2c.

DON'T FORGET POSTAGE IF YOU WANT GOODS SENT BY MAIL.

No. 18C2892 New Cabinet; fine black wire hair pins, in four sizes; crimped and straight; 100 pins.
Price, per box..... 3c
Per doz. boxes.....32c
If by mail, postage extra, per box, 3c.

No. 18C2896 Unique Cabinet. A combination put up in convenient and attractive form; 100 assorted hair pins, 100 toilet pins, 50 black pins and 4 jet shawl or belt pins. Always handy to have in house.
Price, per box....5c
Per dozen boxes.........................55c
If by mail, postage extra, per box, 4c.

No. 18C2898 The Atlantic Hair Waver and Curler. A wonderful hair waver and curler. Curls the hair beautifully in from 10 to 15 minutes without heat, pain or inconvenience. Made from specially treated imported bone that acts upon certain properties of the hair; makes pretty and lasting curls for ladies and children. Absolutely waves and curls the hair in from 10 to 15 minutes. Put up in packages of 5.
Price, per box of 5..............$0.15
Per dozen boxes..................1.75
If by mail, postage extra, per box, 2c.

Hair Crimpers.

No. 18C2900 Common Sense Hair Crimpers, made of lead with woven covers.

	2-inch	3-inch
Price, per dozen.....	2c	3c
Per dozen packages..	20c	30c

Postage extra, per package, 3 cents.

No. 18C2904 Duplex Hair Crimpers, nickel plated, with shield cover ends. Price, per gr., 32c; per doz., 3c

No. 18C2908 Real Kid Hair Crimpers, 12 in package.

Length, ins.	3½	4	4½	5	6
Price, per pkg	2½c	3c	4c	5c	6c
Per doz. pkges	28c	33c	45c	55c	65c

Postage extra, per package, 3 cents.

No. 18C2912 The Goodyear Vulcanized Rubber Hair Pins, straight or crimped. (1 dozen pins in each box.) Price, per box.........6c
Per dozen boxes...................68c
If by mail, postage extra, per box, 2c.

Exceptional Values in Aluminum Hair Pins.

No. 18C2916 Aluminum Hair Pins; a crimped pattern superior to the old style. Length, 2¾ inches. Price, per dozen.......3c
Per gross............................33c
If by mail, postage extra, per dozen, 2 cents.

No. 18C2920 Aluminum Hair Pins; fancy twist top, heavier than above. Length, 3 inches.
Price, per dozen.......4c
Per gross...........44c
If by mail, postage extra, per dozen, 2 cents.

No. 18C2928 Aluminum Hair Pins; extra heavy, fancy twist; our best number. Length, 3¼ inches; worth double. Price, per doz..6c
Per gross...........................65c
If by mail, postage extra, per dozen, 2 cents.

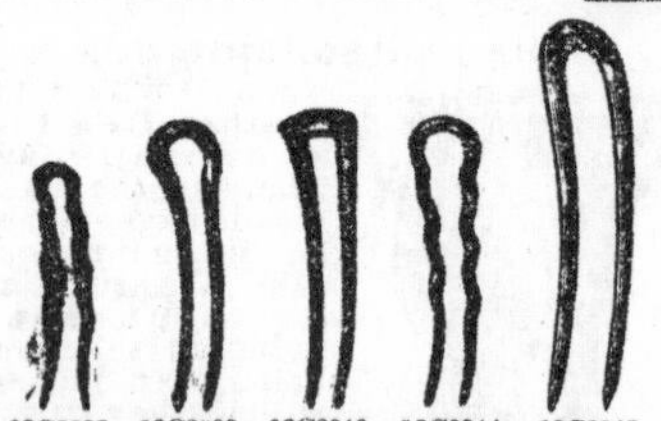

18C2932 18C2938 18C2940 18C2944 18C2945

No. 18C2932 Fancy Round Hair Pin, crimped, imitation tortoise shell. Length, 2¾ inches. Per dozen.4c
Postage extra, 2 cents.

No. 18C2938 Imitation Tortoise Shell Hair Pin, round top, as illustration. Length, 3 inches. Per dozen. 7c
Postage extra, 2 cents.

18C2946 18C2947

No. 18C2940 Imitation Tortoise Shell Hair Pin, fancy square top. Length, 3 inches. Price, per dozen......10c
If by mail, postage extra, 3 cents.

No. 18C2944 Fancy Crimped Imitation Shell Hair Pin. Length, 3 inches. Also in amber color. Price, per dozen.............7c
If by mail, postage extra, 3 cents.

No. 18C2945 Imitation Tortoise Shell Hair Pin, round shape. Length, 4⅜ inches.
Price, per dozen, 33c; each.............3c
If by mail, postage extra, 5 cents.

No. 18C2946 Fine Polished Hair Pin. Imitation tortoise shell, an excellent style and shape. Length, 4½ inches
Price, per dozen, 45c; each.............4c
If by mail, postage extra, each, 2 cents.

No. 18C2947 Hair Pin. Imitation tortoise shell, new improved pattern, a very popular shape. Length, 4¾ inches.
Price, per dozen, 45c; each.............4c
If by mail, postage extra, per dozen, 5 cents.

Large Stylish Rod Pins.

No. 18C2950 Imitation Tortoise Shell Rod Hair Pins, ¼-inch thick. 4¼ inches long, fashionable horseshoe shaped. Also in amber color.

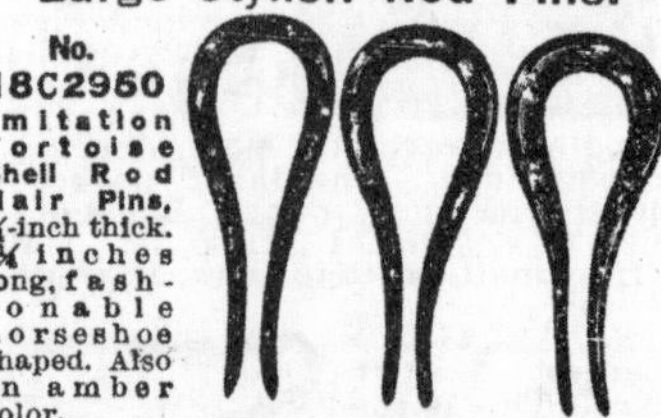

18C2950 18C2951 18C2952

Price, per dozen, 90c; each...............8c
If by mail, postage extra, each, 2 cents.

No. 18C2951 Imitation Tortoise Shell Rod Hair Pins. Length, 4½ inches, ⅜ inch thick, 25-cent value. Also in amber color and white.
Price, per dozen, $1.40; each.........12c
If by mail, postage extra, each, 2 cents.

No. 18C2952 Imitation Tortoise Shell Rod Hair Pins. The heaviest and best pin at any price. 4¾ inches long and ½-inch thick. Also in amber color. Worth 50 cents each.
Price, per dozen, $2.00; each 18c
If by mail, postage extra, each, 2 cents.

No. 18C2960 Imitation Tortoise Shell Hair Pin, put up one dozen in a box, in either straight or crimped. Length, 3⅛ inches. **Just half value; our special leader.**
Price, per dozen....................10c
If by mail, postage extra, 2 cents.

No. 18C2961 American Beauty Hair Pins. Elegant quality imitation shell hair pins, loop tops straight or crimped, very highly polished, with the rich, deep, brilliancy of real tortoise. For a good pin buy this quality, 12 pins in a box. Length, 3 inches. Also in amber color. Price, per dozen..............20c
If by mail, postage extra, 2 cents.

Ladies' Hair Ornaments.

The proper style of hair ornaments is one of the great essentials toward correct and effective hair dressing. We offer a complete line of all the correct and popular styles of side, back, neck and pompadour combs at very low prices.

Ladies' Side Combs.

No. 18C2964 Ladies' Side Comb. Imitation of tortoise shell, highly polished. Length, 4⅝ inches. Special value.
Price, per doz. pair, $1.10; pair....10c
If by mail, postage extra, per pair, 3c.

No. 18C2968 Ladies' Side Comb. Very highly polished. Heavy top. Imitation of tortoise shell. A good, heavy comb. Length, 4¼ inches. 35-cent value.
Price, per pair.................$0.15
Per dozen pair...................1.70
If by mail, postage extra, per pair, 3c.

No. 18C2972 Ladies' Side Comb. Imitation of tortoise shell. Very highly polished, heavy and fine finished teeth. Extra heavy top. The new curved shape. Looks as well as the real shell. Can also be ordered in amber. Retailed by dealers at 50 cents. Length, 4⅜ inches. Price, per pair..........$0.25
Per dozen pair...................2.75
If by mail, postage extra, per pair. 4c

No. 18C2982 Heavy Top Side Combs. Nicely rounded teeth, highly polished. Each comb inlaid with 9 brilliant rhinestones. Can be had in either **white, shell or amber color.** Length, 4 inches.
Price, per pair....................25c
If by mail, postage extra, per pair, 4c.

No. 18C2984 Heavy Top Side Comb. Heavier and finer finished than above, highly polished, inlaid with 15 brilliant rhinestones. **Can be had in either white, shell or amber color.** Length, 4½ inches.
Price, per pair....................48c
If by mail, postage extra, per pair, 4c.

Vassar Side Comb.

No. 18C2980 Imitation Tortoise Shell Side Comb, highly polished; the upper part has a turnover flap which, when inserted in the hair, catches the loose and stray locks. Width, 3⅛ inches. Per pair......$0.10
Per dozen pair...................1.10
If by mail, postage extra, per pair, 2c.

No. 18C2981 Olivette side Comb, to match No. 18C3005. **Imitation tortoise shell or amber color.** This is a new style, very beautiful hair ornament. Length, 3½ inches. With nicely rounded teeth. Highly polished and made of a heavy weight stock. Colors, shell **white or amber.** Price, per pair...22c
If by mail, postage extra, per pair, 4c.

Back Combs.

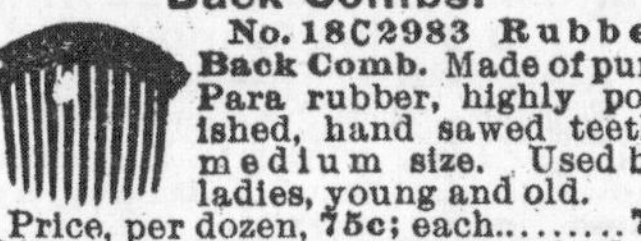

No. 18C2983 Rubber Back Comb. Made of pure Para rubber, highly polished, hand sawed teeth, medium size. Used by ladies, young and old.
Price, per dozen, 75c; each.........7c
If by mail, postage extra, each, 3c.

No. 18C2985 Imitation Tortoise Shell, Heavy Top Neck or Back Comb, with rounded teeth, 4⅛ inches long, 1⅜-inch teeth. A new stylish shape. Also in amber.
Price, per dozen, $1.70; each....15c
If by mail, postage extra, each, 2c.

No. 18C2987 Imitation Tortoise Shell Heavy Top Neck or Back Comb, very heavy, finest finish. An attractive back comb, 50-cent value. Length, 4⅝ inches. Also in amber or white.
Price, per dozen, $2.75; each....25c
If by mail, postage extra, each, 4c.

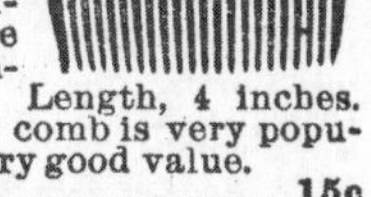

No. 18C2988 Olivette Back Comb. Made of finest quality imitation tortoise shell, nicely polished and finished. Length, 4 inches. This style of back comb is very popular and we offer very good value.
Price...............................15c
If by mail, postage extra, 4 cents.

No. 18C3005 Olivette Back Comb. Made of the finest quality imitation tortoise shell, nicely finished and polished and each tooth finished by hand. A very stylish looking comb. Length, 4¾ inches. Can be ordered in shell, white or amber. A 50-cent quality.
Price...............................23c
If by mail, postage extra, 4 cents.

No. 18C3007 Imitation Tortoise Shell Back Comb, 4 inches long, has 24 brilliant rhinestones imbedded in the top of comb. This comb has a reinforced top and is an exceptionally big value.
Price...............................25c
If by mail, postage extra, 4 cents.

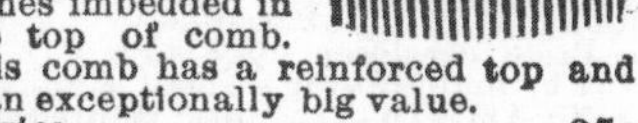

No. 18C3009 Imitation Tortoise Shell Back Comb. Extra heavy top and having finely finished teeth. Has twenty very fine brilliants imbedded in finest style in top of comb. Length, 5 inches. Can be ordered in shell, white or amber. Price.......................25c
If by mail, postage extra, 5 cents.

No. 18C3017 High Back Empire Comb, 4½ inches long. Made of extra fine imitation tortoise shell with finely finished teeth. Has twenty-seven fine brilliants imbedded in a very pretty pattern on top of comb, and is a comb usually sold by the dealers at $1.00. Can be ordered in shell, white or amber. Will compare with $1.00 combs. We offer it at an exceptionally low price. Price..........50c
If by mail, postage extra, 5 cents.

No. 18C3019 Heavy Top Imitation Tortoise Shell Back Comb with long teeth, highly polished. Length, 5 inches. The top is ornamented with stripings of fancy gold trimming with three peacock eyes. A very stylish and dressy hair ornament. Can be ordered in shell or white. Price.................50c
If by mail, postage extra, 5 cents.

No. 18C3029 Ladies' Fancy Back Comb, made of best quality stock, imitation tortoise shell, highly polished with hand finished teeth. Back is ornamented with gold, fancy design, inlaid with small sparkling rhinestones. This comb is copied after a very high priced pattern sold by all the leading jewelry stores, their price being from $3.00 to $5.00. Length, 4½ inches.
Price...............................70c
If by mail, postage extra, 5 cents.

No. 18C3025 Back Comb, made of the very finest quality imitation tortoiseshell, highly polished and finished. Finest quality of French brilliants are embedded in scroll design in top of comb. 65 stones are used in the scroll design, and it is the kind of comb usually sold for $2.00. Nothing finer or handsomer can be made. Length, 4½ inches. Can be ordered in shell, white or amber. Price....................$1.00
If by mail, postage extra, 5 cents.

Ladies' Vassar Back or Neck Comb.

No. 18C2999 Vassar Back or Neck Comb, with the turn over flap to hold the stray locks, highly polished imitation tortoise shell. Width, 3⅝ inches. Regular 20-cent value. Price, each...$0.10
Per dozen.........................1.10
If by mail, postage extra, each, 2c.

No. 18C3000 Vassar Back Comb, with the turnover flap, which catches the stray locks and holds them fast; imitation tortoise shell, or amber color, very highly polished and round finished teeth. Width, 4½ inches.
Price, each.......................$0.15
Per dozen.........................1.70
If by mail, postage extra, each, 3c.

No. 18C3002 Turnover Back Comb, highly polished, imitation tortoise shell, ornamented with twenty-four rhinestones. Size, 4¼ inches. Regular 50-cent value.
Price, per dozen, $2.75; each.....25c
If by mail, postage extra, each, 5c.

Rhinestone Setting.

No. 18C3011 Ladies' Jeweled Pompadour Comb. Imitation tortoise shell, set with forty-two brilliant rhinestones, very closely set; durable as well as handsome. This same quality comb is retailed at 50 cents. Very high grade. Price, each..........$0.25
Per dozen.........................2.75
If by mail, postage extra, each, 5c.

No. 18C3022 Pompadour Comb, imitation tortoise shell with semi curved teeth, making it fit properly to the head. Regular 25-cent value. Price, each..........$0.10
Per dozen.........................1.10
If by mail, postage extra, each, 5c.

No. 18C3031 Hair Binder. Imitation tortoise shell; keeps the hair in place at all times. The most convenient article for hair dressing. In two sizes, 2-inch or 1½-inch. Price, each..$0.10
Per dozen.........................1.10
If by mail, postage extra, each, 2c.

Child's Celluloid Round Combs.

No. 18C3033 Child's Celluloid Round Comb. Comes in imitation tortoise shell. A regular 15-cent comb. Price, per dozen, 65c; each..6c
If by mail, postage extra, each, 4c.

Children's Good Quality Round Combs.

No. 18C3036 Beautiful Unbreakable Circular Rubber Comb, like No. 18C3033. One dozen round combs in a box. Weight, about 10 ounces.
Price, per dozen, 65c; each.........6c
If by mail, postage extra, each, 4c.

Security Barettes, to Hold the Stray Locks.

No. 18C3038 Hair Barette. Cut out pattern, used by the best society, imitation tortoise shell. Size, 3⅛ inches.
Price, per dozen, $1.10; each.....10c
If by mail, postage extra, each, 2c.

No. 18C3040 New Shaped Hair Barette. When inserted in the hair it just shows the design with opening (see illustration). This is the newest and most stylish barette; imitation tortoise shell. Size, 4 inches.
Price, per dozen, $1.70; each..15c
If by mail, postage extra, each, 2c.

No. 18C3042 Jeweled Hair Barrette. This is a very finely made barrette, with highly polished teeth. The entire comb is highly polished, made of a fine quality of stock; inlaid with nineteen brilliant rhinestones. Can be worn with any of the back or side combs. Length, 4 inches. Colors, shell, amber or white.
Price...............................40c
If by mail, postage extra, each, 2c.

No. 18C3044 Little Beauty Stray Lock Comb. Made of imitation tortoise shell. The latest device for holding up loose, stray hairs. Makes a very effective hair ornament in addition to being thoroughly secure. Length, 4⅜ inches.
Price...............................10c
If by mail, postage extra, each, 2c.

No. 18C3049 Sanitary Puff Comb. Made of imitation tortoise shell, highly polished. This puff comb creates a fine, full pompadour without the use of the artificial hair roll; is extensively worn by young and old. Length, 9 inches; width, 1½ inches.
Price, per dozen, $2.75; each...25c
If by mail, postage extra, each, 6c.

The New Rat Comb.

No. 18C3050 The New Patent Puff Comb does away with the hair roll and is much more cleanly as well as more comfortable and cooler for the hair; creates a fine, puffy pompadour for young and old. Length, 8⅜ inches and 1 inch high.
Price, per dozen, 90c; each.......8c
If by mail, postage extra, each, 8c.

Adjustable Puff Comb.

No. 18C3051 Adjustable Puff Comb. With this comb you can dress your hair pompadour style without the use of the hair rats. Made in imitation tortoise shell. 8½ inches long and 1⅜ inches wide. Has the adjustable hinge, so that the hair can be worn on top or forward; will also give when the hat is put on.
Price, per dozen, $1.70; each..15c
If by mail, postage extra, each, 8c.

For the New Style French Dip Hair Dressing.

No. 18C3053 The New Dip Puff Comb. With this comb you can dress your hair in the new French dip fashion, quickly and easily. Made of imitation tortoise shell, highly polished.
Price, per dozen, $2.00; each...19c
If by mail, postage extra, 8c.

Curling Irons.

Prices we quote on Curling Irons should be quite an item to you. We have all kinds, all sizes; save you just one-half on regular purchase prices.

No. 18C3055 Made of polished steel; polished wood handle, medium size for general use. 7½ inches long. Price, each...3c
Per dozen...........................30c
If by mail, postage extra, each, 4c.

Tourist Folding Curling Iron.

No. 18C3060 The Tourist Folding Curling Iron. Made of polished steel, oak handles. Can be placed in such a position that iron can be heated over lamp chimney without holding iron. Price, per dozen, 55c; each..5c
Shipping weight, 4 ounces.

DON'T FORGET POSTAGE
When Ordering
GOODS SENT BY MAIL.

Waving Iron.

No. 18C3076 5-Prong Waving Iron, for waving the hair, made of good quality metal.
Price per dozen, $1.15; each....11c
If by mail, postage extra, each, 9c.

COMBS.

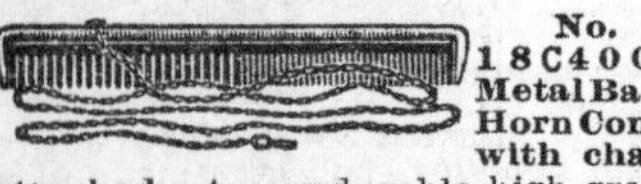

No. 18C4006 Metal Back Horn Comb with chain attached. A very durable high grade and convenient comb. You will always find it hung in the place it belongs. Length, 7 inches, with three feet of chain and screw at end.
Price, per dozen, $1.40; each....13c
If by mail, postage extra, each, 6 cents.

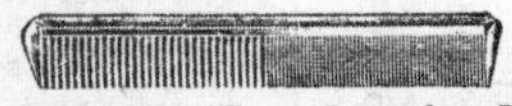

No. 18C4008 Horn Dressing Comb, 7 inches long. Nickel plated back.
Price, per dozen, 65c; each........6c
If by mail, postage extra, each, 4 cents.

No. 18C4009 Hard Rubber Dressing Comb. Neatly curved back, coarse and fine teeth. Length, 7 inches.
Price, per dozen, 44c; each 4c
If by mail, postage extra, each, 4 cents.

No. 18C4010 Strong Hard Rubber Dressing Comb. Heavy square back, rounded teeth, coarse and fine. Length, 8 inches.
Price, per dozen, $1.10; each....10c
If by mail, postage extra, each, 4 cents.

No. 18C4011 Hard Rubber Dressing Comb. With fancy carved back; coarse and fine teeth. Length, 8 inches. Usually retailed at 25 cents.
Price, per dozen, $1.50; each... 14c
If by mail, postage extra, each, 4 cents.

No. 18C4013 Fancy Rope Back Hard Rubber Dressing Comb. Well finished; coarse and fine teeth. Length, 8 inches. A 30-cent comb.
Price, per dozen, $2.00; each....18c
If by mail, postage extra, each, 4 cents.

No. 18C4015 Hard Rubber Dressing Comb. Same size and design as No. 18C4013, but all coarse teeth; extra heavy and well rounded. Length, 8 inches. Price, per doz., $2.00; each..18c
If by mail, postage extra, each, 4 cents.

No. 18C4016 Hard Rubber Dressing Comb, with best hard grailed teeth, a very high grade comb. Length, 8 inches.
Price, per doz., $2.25; each......21c
If by mail, postage extra, each, 4 cents.

No. 18C4017 Very Substantial Hard Rubber Dressing Comb. Heavy curved kangaroo shaped back, well finished coarse and fine teeth; will not irritate the scalp; exceptional value. Length, 8 inches.
Price, per dozen, $2.50; each....24c
If by mail, postage extra, each, 4c.

No. 18C4019 Extra Heavy Square Back Hard Rubber Dressing Comb. Hand sawed, round finished, coarse and fine teeth; will not injure the hair. Length, 9 inches. Usually retailed for 50 cents. Price, each...$0.33
Per dozen.............................. 3.50
If by mail, postage extra, each, 4c.

No. 18C4021 Extra Heavy Square Back Hard Rubber Dressing Comb. All coarse teeth; especially adapted for long, heavy hair; makes hair dressing a pleasure. Length, 9 inches.
Price, per dozen, $3.50; each.....33c
If by mail, postage extra, each, 4c.

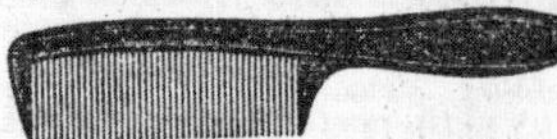

No. 18C4023 Hard Rubber Dressing Comb. With handle, giving extra purchase on comb; all coarse teeth; just the thing for heavy and thick hair. Length, 7½ inches.
Price, per dozen, $3.25; each ...30c
If by mail, postage extra, each, 4c.

No. 18C4025 Superior Quality Hard Rubber Barbers' Comb. Coarse and fine teeth. Length, 6½ inches. Price, each..................5c
Per dozen...............................55c
If by mail, postage extra, each, 4c.

No. 18C4027 Extra Super Quality Hard Rubber Barbers' Comb. With graduated coarse and fine teeth. A genteel comb for gentlemen. Length, 7½ inches.
Price, per dozen, $1.10; each....10c
If by mail, postage extra, each, 4c.

Tortoise Shell Barbers' Comb.

No. 18C4029 This Pretty Imitation Tortoise Shell Celluloid Barbers' Comb (gentleman's comb), 7 inches long, is really worth 25 cents.
Price, per dozen, $1.10; each....10c
If by mail, postage extra, each, 4c.

Rubber Fine Combs.

No. 18C4031 Hard Rubber Fine Tooth Comb. Fine teeth on both sides, as shown in illustration. Size, 3x1⅝ in. Price, per dozen, 45c; each......4c
If by mail, postage extra, each, 4c.

Rubber Fine Combs.

No. 18C4033 Hard Rubber Fine Comb. With curved fine teeth to conform to shape of head. Size, 4x2 inches. Price, each.........8c
Per dozen..............................90c
If by mail, postage extra, each, 4c.

No. 18C4034 Hard Rubber Fine Comb with finished teeth; strong and durable, equal to the 25-cent kind. Size, 3⅞x2⅛ inches.
Price, per dozen, $1.10; each....10c
If by mail, postage extra, each, 3c.

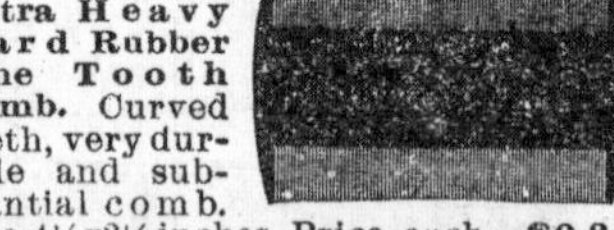

No. 18C4035 Extra Heavy Hard Rubber Fine Tooth Comb. Curved teeth, very durable and substantial comb. Size, 4⅛x2⅛ inches. Price, each...$0.24
Per dozen..... .... 2.60
If by mail, postage extra, each, 4c.

No. 18C4036 Hard Rubber Comb, very heavy, finest finish, a high grade regular 25-cent comb. Size, 3¾x2⅛ inches.
Price, per dozen, $1.70; each.....15c
If by mail, postage extra, each, 3c.

Aluminum Fine Comb.

No. 18C4037 Aluminum Fine Comb, will not tarnish or break, strictly sanitary. Recommended by physicians as the best thing to use. Length, 3 ins. Price, per dozen, $1.10; each, 10c
If by mail, postage extra, each, 3c.

Our 25-Cent Ladies' Ebonite Dressing Comb.

No. 18C4071 The Handsome Ebonite Dressing Comb, shown in above illustration, is decorated with handsome sterling silver trimmings, as shown. The length of the comb is 6¾ inches, is excellent quality, such a comb as seldom retails at less than 40 to 50 cents. Price, each..........$0.25
Per dozen............................. 2.75
If by mail, postage extra, each, 4c.

Our 24-Cent Gents' Ebonite Dressing Comb.

No. 18C4075 This illustration shows Gents' Ebonite Dressing Comb. It is sterling silver trimmed, is 7 inches long, and is a very neat and desirable present.
Price, per dozen, $2.75; each....24c
If by mail, postage extra, each, 3c.

Celluloid Combs.

Nothing is nicer than combs made of celluloid; pretty to look at and they are serviceable, too. Our prices are away below the retailers' cost.

No. 18C4084 A 7-inch White Celluloid Dressing Comb. Coarse and fine teeth. Regular retail price, 25c.
Price, per dozen, 80c; each...... .7c
No. 18C4088 The same comb as described above, in amber. Retailers ask 25 to 30 cents.
Price, per dozen, 80c; each.... ...7c
If by mail, postage extra, each, 2c.

Celluloid Amber Dressing Comb for 12 cents.

No. 18C4092 A Beautiful 7½-inch Beaded Back Celluloid Amber Dressing Comb. Coarse and fine teeth. Druggists ask as high as 35 cents for these combs.
Price, per dozen, $1.35; each.. 12c
If by mail, postage extra, each, 2c.

White Celluloid Dressing Comb.

No. 18C4096 A Very Handsome 7¼-inch Rope Back White Celluloid Dressing Comb. Good heavy weight. This comb is easily worth 40 cents.
Price, per dozen, $2.00; each....17c
If by mail, postage extra, each, 3c.

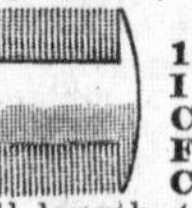

No. 18C4100 Infants' Celluloid Fine Combs. With handle. Full length, 4½ inches. Colors, white, pink or blue.
Price, per dozen, 70c; each........6c
If by mail, postage extra, each, 2c.
No. 18C4104 Infants' White Ivory Fine Combs. With handle, same shape as above. Full length, 4¼ inches.
Price, per dozen, $1.00; each......9c
If by mail, postage extra, each, 2c.

Best Aluminum Combs.

No. 18C4108 Gents' Aluminum Combs. Coarse and fine teeth. 7 inches long. The best thing for the hair. Price, per dozen, 65c; each...6c
If by mail, postage extra, each, 2c.

Ladies' Aluminum Combs.

No. 18C4116 Aluminum Dressing Comb. Coarse and fine teeth. Length, 7½ inches; width, 1¼ inches. Regular 25c comb. Price, per doz., 99c; each, 9c
If by mail, postage extra, each, 2 c

Gents' Dressing Combs.

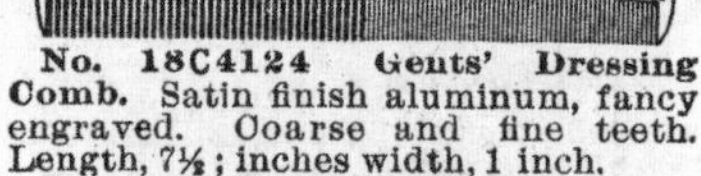

No. 18C4124 Gents' Dressing Comb. Satin finish aluminum, fancy engraved. Coarse and fine teeth. Length, 7¼; inches width, 1 inch.
Price, per dozen, $1.10; each..10c
If by mail, postage extra, each, 2c.

No. 18C4128 Aluminum Dressing Comb. With fancy engraved back. Length, 7½ inches; width, 1⅛ inches. Especially filed and finished teeth. Usually retailed at 25 cents.
Price, per dozen, $1.25; each..12c
If by mail, postage extra, each, 2c.
No. 18C4129 Aluminum Dressing Comb, similar to above, but almost twice as heavy and fancifully engraved. Extra finished teeth. Length, 7½ inches. A 50-cent comb.
Price, per dozen, $2.00; each..18c

Barbers' Aluminum Combs.

No. 18C4122 Medium Aluminum Barbers' Hair Cutting Comb. Fine and coarse teeth. Length, 7¼ inches.
Price, per dozen, $1.50; each, 15c
If by mail, postage extra, each, 2c.

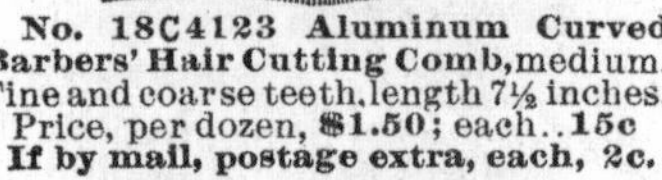

No. 18C4123 Aluminum Curved Barbers' Hair Cutting Comb, medium. Fine and coarse teeth, length 7½ inches.
Price, per dozen, $1.50; each..15c
If by mail, postage extra, each, 2c.

No. 18C4125 Barbers' Taper Neck Comb. Heavy quality. Length, 7½ inches.
Price, per dozen, $2.00; each, 20c
If by mail, postage extra, each, 3c.

Pocket Combs.

No. 18C4135 Extra Heavy, Square Back, Hard Rubber Pocket Comb. Coarse and fine teeth in leatheroid case; a very convenient article. Length, 4½ inches. Price, each.............$0.10
Per dozen 1.10
If by mail, postage extra, each, 4c.

Aluminum Pocket Combs.

No. 18C4140 Aluminum Pocket Comb, with case. Fine and coarse teeth. 5 inches long. Straight back. Durable and will not tarnish.
Price, per dozen, 40c; each......4c
If by mail, postage extra, each, 2c.

Celluloid Pocket Combs.

No. 18C4144 Celluloid Pocket Comb in case, 3½ inches long. Regular retail price, 20 cents.
Price, per dozen, 90c; each.......8c
If by mail, postage extra, each, 2c.
No. 18C4131 Exceptionally Neat and Substantial Hard Rubber Pocket Comb. Coarse and fine teeth, in neat leatheroid case, 4 inches long.
Price, per dozen, 55c; each.......5c
If by mail, postage extra, each, 2c.

ALL of Our Wood Back Hair Brushes, from the cheapest number up, are made of one solid piece of wood (Solid Back Hair Brushes.) Most hair brushes are made of two pieces of wood glued together, which, when wet, warp and come apart. A Solid Back Hair Brush will outwear three ordinary hair brushes. We sell our solid back hair brushes at less than the price usually asked for ordinary goods. Remember that a solid back hair brush will last two or three times as long as an ordinary brush. Hair brushes weigh from 6 to 8 ounces.

Postage on hair brushes, about 6 to 8 cents.

No. 18C4148 Infants' Imported Fine White Goat Hair Brush; also suitable for ladies' toilet powder.
Price, per dozen, $2.40; each....22c
If by mail, postage extra, each, 3c.

Fine Infants' Imported Hair Brushes.

No. 18C4146 Infants' Imported White Bone Brush with soft, white goat bristles. A splendid infants' hair brush; also suitable for ladies' powder brush. Regular 25-cent value.
Price, each...............................15c
If by mail, postage extra, 3 cents.

A 25-Cent Brush for 10 Cents.

No. 18C4156 A Medium Sized Round Back Hair Brush. Black Russian bristles; would be considered good value at 25 cents.
Price, per dozen, $1.10; each....10c
If by mail, postage extra, each, 8c.

Special Value for 21 Cents.

No. 18C4164 A good, durable, 12-row Hair Brush, with a dark center bristle, large size, oval back of solid boxwood, **particularly adapted for family use.** This brush never retails for less than 50 cents.
Price, per dozen, $2.25; each....21c
If by mail, postage extra, each, 10c.

Russian Bristle Hair Brushes.

No. 18C4168 This Handsome Brush is made of 9 rows of white Russian bristles, oval back, nicely polished, solid back. Price, each...$0.35
Per dozen.... 3.95
If by mail, postage extra, each, 7c.

No. 18C4169 This is an elegant 11-row, fine white Russian Bristle Brush, solid back of cocobolo wood, oval shape, highly polished. Good 75-cent value.
Price, per dozen, $5.25; each....47c
If by mail, postage extra, each, 10c

No. 18C4175 Special Value, 13-Row Best Black China Bristle Brush. Very penetrating and especially adapted as a barber's brush, such as is sold at $1.25. Highly polished, solid wood, walnut back. A very serviceable and high grade brush.
Price....72c
If by mail, postage extra, each, 10c

No. 18C4177 Our Own Special Design Ladies' Hair Dressing Brush. In using this brush no comb is necessary, as the bristles are stiff enough to penetrate a heavy head of hair; especially adapted for professional hair dressers. Solid wood back of highly polished rosewood, having seven rows of the very best Russian bristles. We especially recommend this brush.
Price, per dozen, $5.00; each.....44c
If by mail, postage extra, each, 8 cents.

Wire Hair Brushes.

No. 18C4179 Small Size Metallic Wire Hair Brush; polished wood back.
Price, per dozen, 78c; each.......7c
If by mail, postage extra, each, 5 cents.

No. 18C4180 Ten-Row Metallic Wire Hair Brush, straight or twist handle, nicely polished and decorated back. Price, per dozen, $1.85; each, 17c
If by mail, postage extra, each, 7 cents.

Florence Rubber Back Hair Brush.

No. 18C4184 The Florence Rubber Back Black Bristle Hair Brush. Easy to clean, nice to use. Value, 40 cents.
Price, per dozen, $1.95; each....18c
If by mail, postage extra, each, 8 cents.

Square Shaped Florence Hair Brush.

No. 18C4186 The back is made of a black composition with fancy embossed design; has 11 rows of medium length fine white best penetrating Russian bristles. A very substantial and durable brush. Very easily kept clean Size, 8¾x2⅜ inches.
Price, each....$0.41
Per dozen.... 4.65
If by mail, postage extra, each, 9 cents

The "Ideal" Siberian Bristle Hair Brush.

This is a Genuine Siberian Bristle Brush, with a single bristle substituted for the ordinary tuft, the bristle being set in an **elastic air-cushioned base.** This construction enables it to penetrate the most luxuriant growth of hair without effort. It also prevents the possibility of injuring the hair or scalp. It will effectively remove dandruff without irritating the scalp. **It is clean, light and durable.**
No. 18C4192 Medium size, oak wood back. Price, per doz., $7.75; each. 69c
No. 18C4196 Large size, oak wood back. Price, per doz., $10.00; each. 88c
If by mail, postage extra, each, 8 cents.
For a wonderful hair grower see Princess Hair Restorer. Refer to Drug Department.

Keep Clean Hair Brush.

No. 18C4198 This is a Large Sized, Oval Shaped, Black Ivory Finished Hair Brush, with fifteen rows of medium size black pure bristles, the bristles being set in pure aluminum, which is waterproof and very easy to keep clean. This is the best brush made and cannot become foul by absorbing the water, oil and dirt like an ordinary brush. Size, 9¾x3¼ inches.
Price, per dozen, $5.00; each....46c
If by mail, postage extra, each, 8 cents.

Dr. Scott's Electric Hair Brushes are Recommended by Leading Physicians.

No. 18C4199 Dr. Scott's Electric Hair Brushes are recommended by leading physicians and are extensively known. **A wonderful help for headache and neuralgia; splendid to prevent falling hair, dandruff, etc.** The curative powers of these brushes have been known and tested for a number of years. We can furnish them in three sizes. Prices range according to size, as follows:
Style No. 1, regular price $1.00, our price....$0.65
Style No. 2, regular price $2.00, our price.... .90
Style No. 4, regular price $3.00, our price.... 1.25
Shipping weight, 14 ounces.

Beauty Brush for the Complexion.

No. 18C4200 It is especially constructed for improving the complexion. It removes all roughness and dead cuticle, smoothing out the wrinkles, rendering the skin soft, pliant and tinted with a healthy glow. It is made of rubber—round, flexible, flattened end, tiny teeth taking the place of bristles. Removes wrinkles like magic. For physical development it is recommended by the highest in the profession for improving the circulation, exercising the muscles and promoting a healthy action of the skin. Price, per dozen, $1.75; each.....15c
If by mail, postage extra, each, 3 cents.

Flesh and Bath Brushes.

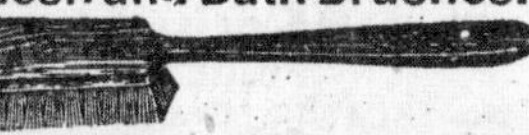

No. 18C4204 A Seven-Row Bath Brush, straight handle, white and black bristles, made of one solid piece of wood. Cannot split or warp when wet. Shipping weight, 10 ounces.
Price, per dozen, $1.85; each...18c

No. 18C4209 Bath Brush with screwed back, substantially made, long curved handle, has six rows of excellent quality bristles; especially adapted for the bath. Shipping weight, 14 ounces. Price....35c

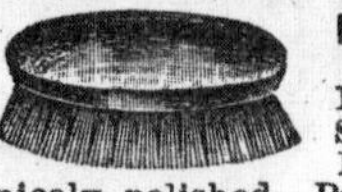

No. 18C4216 An Excellent Flesh Brush. 5½ inches long, with strap. Can be used dry or in the bath.
Price, each...$0.19
Per dozen.. 1.90
If by mail, postage extra, each, 7 cents.

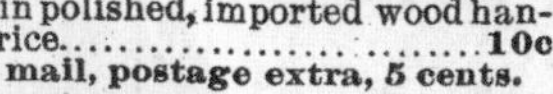

No. 18C4223 Leiner's Combined Bath and Flesh Brush, for wet or dry use, made of good black and white Russian bristles, woven on wire, with enameled white handle. A very excellent brush. Shipping weight, 12 ounces.
Price, per dozen, $4.95; each...46c

Hand Brushes.

No. 18C4228 A Nicely Finished Six-Row Hand Brush, oval back, nicely polished. Price, each...... 5c
Per dozen....55c
If by mail, postage extra, each, 3c.

No. 18C4230 Seven-row Stiff, Imported Bristles Nail Brush, with fine satin polished, imported wood handle. Price....10c
If by mail, postage extra, 5 cents.

No. 18C4231 Very High Grade Hand and Nail Brush, 10-row, best imported black and white Russian bristles. Very durable and effective. Sold by the drug stores at 50 cents. Price....25c
If by mail, postage extra, 8 cents.

No. 18C4235 Seven-row Bone Handle Nail Brush, good stiff bristles. A very satisfactory brush.
Price....15c
If by mail, postage extra, 6 cents.

No. 18C4237 Large Size, White Imported Bristle Bone and Nail Brush with side bristles for hand and nails. The best possible value. Price....25c
If by mail, postage extra, 5 cents.

Cloth and Clothes Brushes.

No. 18C4238 A Good Six-Row Cloth or Clothes Brush, black and white, solid fluted back, mixed stock, 8x2⅜ inches. Good value at 15 cents.
Price, per dozen, 98c; each.....9c
If by mail, postage extra, each, 7c.

No. 18C4239 A Very Fine Cloth Brush, made of black and white Russian bristles, nicely polished redwood backs. Shipping weight, 10 ounces.
Price, per dozen, $1.90; each....19c

A 75-Cent Brush for 34 Cents.

No. 18C4240 This is an actual 75-cent Brush, made of extra long pure gray bristles, solid rosewood, fancy curved back, a very serviceable brush. Price, each....$0.34
Per dozen.... 3.75
If by mail, postage extra, each, 8 cents.

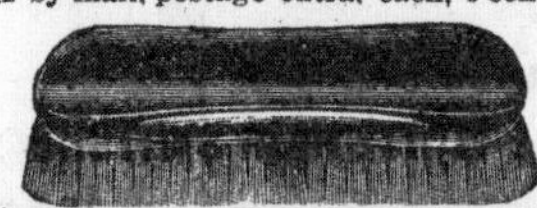

No. 18C4246 Cloth Brush, fancy shaped back of one solid piece highly polished rosewood, mahogany finish, with long pure Russian bristles, closely set, **brush retailed for $1.00; splendid value.** Price, each....$0.68
Per dozen.... 7.50
If by mail, postage extra, each, 7 cents.

No. 18C4248 Cloth Brush, with heavy, solid back imitation of ebony, has nine rows of extra long, black China bristles, will pick up the dust. We recommend it for all kinds of service. Shipping weight, 10 ounces.
Price....55c

Our Highest Grade Genuine Ebony Toilet Articles.

No. 18C4249 Real Ebony Hair Brush, with solid sterling silver mountings, finest quality imported bristles. A brush retailed at your jeweler's for $1.00.
Price, per dozen, $5.75; each...50c
If by mail, postage extra, each, 8c.

No. 18C4252 Genuine Ebony Hair Brush, with solid sterling silver mounting, with nine rows of fine quality, stiff Russian bristles, regular $1.50 value. Price....75c
If by mail, postage extra, 8 cents.

No. 18C4254 Genuine Ebony Hair Brush, with eleven rows finest quality, penetrating white Russian bristles, handsome sterling silver mounting on back. Suitable for ladies or gentlemen. Guaranteed $2.00 value. Price. $1.00
If by mail, postage extra, 9 cents.

No. 18C4258 Genuine Ebony Military Brush, with 9 rows of fine white bristles; has handsome sterling silver mounting. A very sightly and serviceable brush at an extraordinarily low price. Price, each........50c
If by mail, postage extra, 8 cents.

No. 18C4259 Genuine Ebony Military Brush. Solid sterling silver mounted, has 11 rows fine Russian bristles, heavy block. An exceptional value. Price, each....75c
If by mail, postage extra, 8 cents.

No. 18C4261 Genuine Ebony Military Hair Brush. Our highest grade. This has a beautifully curved back, sterling silver mounted, with 13 rows penetrating, white Russian bristles. These brushes are made for the finest trade, and you can get no better. Shipping weight 12 ozs. Price, each, $1.25

No. 18C4262 Genuine Ebony Cloth Brush, with a heavy solid block, with heavy sterling silver mounts, 7 rows best quality white bristles. A guaranteed brush, worth double the price we ask. Shipping weight, 14 ounces. Price....80c
If by mail, postage extra, 8 cents.

No. 18C4266 Genuine Ebony Velvet Brush with long, white imported bristles, very desirable for ladies' or gents' hats, or for fine cloth and velvet. Very acceptable gift for ladies or gents, solid sterling silver mounted.
Price....44c
If by mail, postage extra, 8 cents.

Hand or Nail Brush.

No. 18C4270 Genuine Ebony Hand or Nail Brush, with solid sterling silver mountings, best quality imported bristles. Very fine goods A good 75-cent value. Price....45c
If by mail, postage extra, 8 cents.

Complexion Brush.

No. 18C4272 Genuine Ebony Complexion Brush, with long fine white Russian bristles, sterling silver mounted. Complexion brushes are very extensively used with splendid results. Price....48c
If by mail, postage extra, 8 cents.

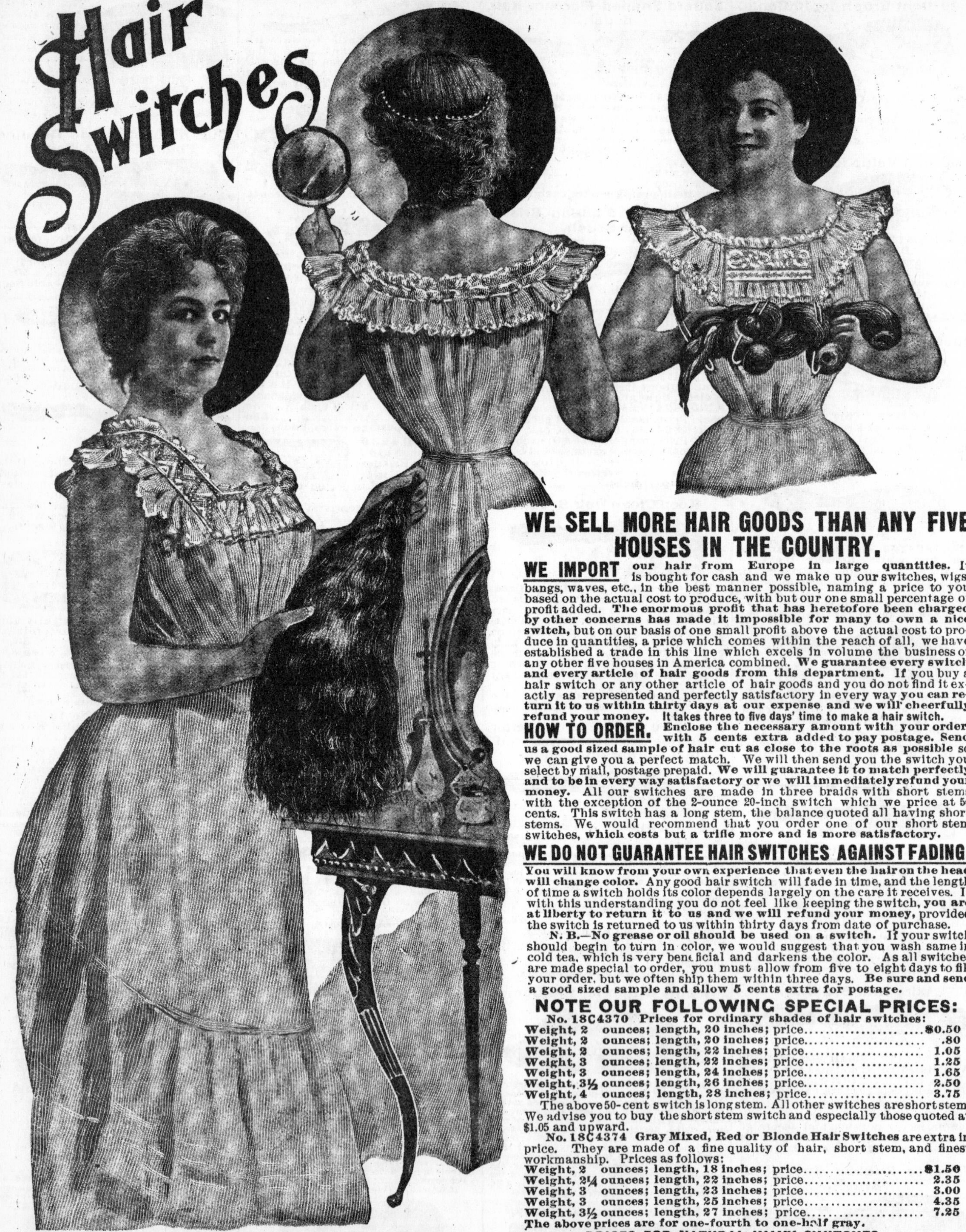

WE SELL MORE HAIR GOODS THAN ANY FIVE HOUSES IN THE COUNTRY.

WE IMPORT our hair from Europe in large quantities. It is bought for cash and we make up our switches, wigs, bangs, waves, etc., in the best manner possible, naming a price to you based on the actual cost to produce, with but our one small percentage of profit added. **The enormous profit that has heretofore been charged by other concerns has made it impossible for many to own a nice switch,** but on our basis of one small profit above the actual cost to produce in quantities, a price which comes within the reach of all, we have established a trade in this line which excels in volume the business of any other five houses in America combined. **We guarantee every switch and every article of hair goods from this department.** If you buy a hair switch or any other article of hair goods and you do not find it exactly as represented and perfectly satisfactory in every way you can **return it to us within thirty days at our expense and we will cheerfully refund your money.** It takes three to five days' time to make a hair switch.

HOW TO ORDER. **Enclose the necessary amount with your order, with 5 cents extra added to pay postage. Send us a good sized sample of hair cut as close to the roots as possible** so we can give you a perfect match. We will then send you the switch you select by mail, postage prepaid. **We will guarantee it to match perfectly and to be in every way satisfactory or we will immediately refund your money.** All our switches are made in three braids with short stems with the exception of the 2-ounce 20-inch switch which we price at 50 cents. This switch has a long stem, the balance quoted all having short stems. We would recommend that you order one of our short stem switches, **which costs but a trifle more and is more satisfactory.**

WE DO NOT GUARANTEE HAIR SWITCHES AGAINST FADING.

You will know from your own experience that even the hair on the head will change color. Any good hair switch will fade in time, and the length of time a switch holds its color depends largely on the care it receives. If with this understanding you do not feel like keeping the switch, **you are at liberty to return it to us and we will refund your money,** provided the switch is returned to us within thirty days from date of purchase.

N. B.—No grease or oil should be used on a switch. If your switch should begin to turn in color, we would suggest that you wash same in cold tea, which is very beneficial and darkens the color. As all switches are made special to order, you must allow from five to eight days to fill your order, but we often ship them within three days. **Be sure and send a good sized sample and allow 5 cents extra for postage.**

NOTE OUR FOLLOWING SPECIAL PRICES:

No. 18C4370 Prices for ordinary shades of hair switches:

Weight, 2 ounces; length, 20 inches; price	$0.50
Weight, 2 ounces; length, 20 inches; price	.80
Weight, 2 ounces; length, 22 inches; price	1.05
Weight, 3 ounces; length, 22 inches; price	1.25
Weight, 3 ounces; length, 24 inches; price	1.65
Weight, 3½ ounces; length, 26 inches; price	2.50
Weight, 4 ounces; length, 28 inches; price	3.75

The above 50-cent switch is long stem. All other switches are short stem. We advise you to buy the short stem switch and especially those quoted at $1.05 and upward.

No. 18C4374 Gray Mixed, Red or Blonde Hair Switches are extra in price. They are made of a fine quality of hair, short stem, and finest workmanship. Prices as follows:

Weight, 2 ounces; length, 18 inches; price	$1.50
Weight, 2¼ ounces; length, 22 inches; price	2.35
Weight, 3 ounces; length, 23 inches; price	3.00
Weight, 3 ounces; length, 25 inches; price	4.35
Weight, 3½ ounces; length, 27 inches; price	7.25

The above prices are for one-fourth to one-half gray.

PRICES FOR ALL WHITE OR NEARLY ALL WHITE HAIR SWITCHES.

No. 18C4375

Weight, 2 ounces; length, 20 inches; price	$2.10
Weight, 2¼ ounces; length, 22 inches; price	3.35
Weight, 3 ounces; length, 23 inches; price	4.25
Weight, 3 ounces; length, 25 inches; price	5.75
Weight, 3½ ounces; length, 27 inches; price	8.75

Above prices are for three-fourths to all white.

PRICES FOR NATURAL WAVY SWITCHES.

No. 18C4377 Best quality French hair, made on short stems.

Weight, 1½ ounces; length, 20 inches; price	$2.25
Weight, 2 ounces; length, 22 inches; price	4.25
Weight, 2½ ounces; length, 24 inches; price	5.65
Weight, 2¾ ounces; length, 26 inches; price	6.75

Gray and blonde shades will cost 50 per cent more than the above prices.

ALLOW 5 TO 8 DAYS TIME ON HAIR GOODS.

IT TAKES THREE TO TWELVE DAYS' TIME TO MAKE WIGS, WAVES, BANGS, ETC.

WAVES, BANGS AND WIGS.

ALL WIGS, TOUPEES, WAVES, ETC., BEING MADE TO ORDER, WE ASK THREE TO TEN DAYS' TIME IN FILLING YOUR ORDER, AND WE REQUIRE CASH IN FULL WITH ORDER ON ALL HAIR GOODS, GUARANTEEING SATISFACTION OR REFUND OF MONEY.

BE SURE AND SEND A GOOD SIZED SAMPLE OF HAIR

The Melba Bang.

No. 18C4378 Melba Bang. Made of the best quality naturally curly hair, with vegetable lace parting, most suitable for youthful faces and a very popular style of hair dressing.

Price.............................$1.50
Gray and blonde hair..........2.50

If by mail, postage extra, 5 cents.

Parisian Bang.

No. 18C4382 Parisian Bang. Ladies who do not require large, heavy front, will find this a little gem; light and fluffy, ventilated foundation. Price................$1.35
Gray and blonde hair..........2.00
If by mail, postage extra, 5 cents.

Alice Wave.

No. 18C4386 Alice Wave, invisible hair lace foundation; natural curly hair; 3-inch part, 12 inches from side to side. Price..........$3.25
Gray and blonde hair..................4.50
If by mail, postage extra, 6 cents.

The Pompadour.

No. 18C4390 The Pompadour. This style, unlike the old style pompadour, is very light in weight. The soft wavy hair is combed over one's own hair in which small rolls of crape hair are placed to produce a puffy effect on sides and top. Price..........................$3.50
Gray and blonde hair..........5.00
If by mail, postage extra, 6 cents.

The Patent Pompadour.

No. 18C4394 The Patent Pompadour for simplicity, elegance and style is far superior to anything ever shown. It slips right on, is as dainty as a feminine heart could desire; it produces the fluffy fullness now so much in vogue and possesses none of the disagreeable qualities of the ordinary roll or pad. It is made on twisted wire, of the best long, curly hair and weighs only half an ounce. Can be worn with just the ends concealed under the lady's own hair, or may be used in place of the rolls and the wavy ends coiled in with the natural hair. Send sample of hair.
Price..... ....$1.50
Blonde and gray hair.........2.25
If by mail, postage extra, 6 cents.

The New Patent Dip Pompadour.

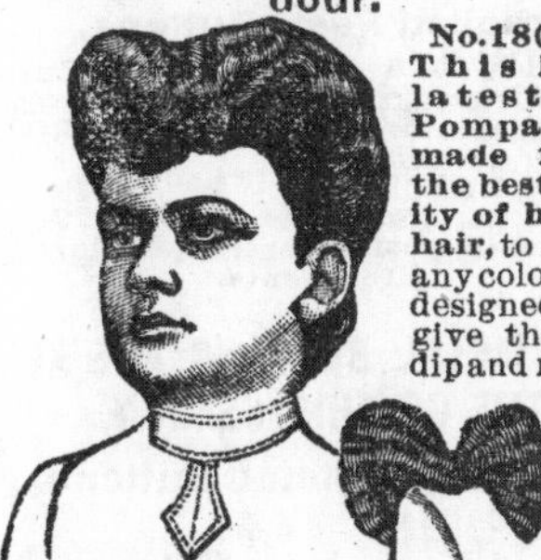

No. 18C4395 This is the latest style Pompadour, made from the best quality of human hair, to match any color hair, designed to give the new dip and rolling front effect which is the prevailing style of hair dressing. Light and wavy, at the same time giving the appearance of great fullness. Effect produced is same as shown in illustration. Send sample of hair. Price..$3.50
Gray and blonde hair..........5.00
If by mail, postage extra, 8 cents.

Ladies' Wigs—Short Hair.

Send measurement of head.

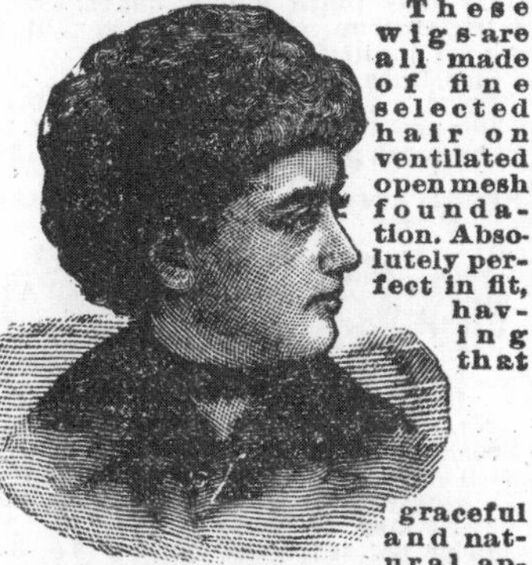

Short Curly Wig.

These wigs are all made of fine selected hair on ventilated open mesh foundation. Absolutely perfect in fit, having that graceful and natural appearance.

No. 18C4402 Ladies' Curly Dress Wig, made of natural short hair, with or without part, mounted on fine open mesh cotton foundation. Price.$10.00
Gray or blonde hair..........15.00
If by mail, postage extra, 14 cents.

No. 18C4406 Ladies' Wig. Same as above but mounted on silk foundation.
Price...............................$12.00
Gray or blonde hair..........18.00
If by mail, postage extra, 8 cents.

Ladies' Wigs—Long Hair.

Can be arranged in many different ways.

No. 18C4410 Made of the best selected hair on silk foundation, 18-inch hair.
Price, $15.00
By mail, postage extra, 10 cents.

No. 18C4414 Made same as above on silk foundation, 24-inch hair.
Price, $18.00
By mail, postage extra, 10 cents.

The above prices are for ordinary shades of hair. Red, Blonde and Gray Hair cost 50 per cent more, which please add when you send order. Be sure and send sample of hair. Send measurement of head.

The Eugenia Wave.

No. 18C4398 The Eugenia Wave. This is a new and very becoming wave for middle aged and elderly ladies, made of the best quality natural curly French hair; easily dressed and cared for; 3½-inch parting.
Price.............................$4.00
Gray and blonde hair..........6.00
If by mail, postage extra, 8 cents.

Men's Toupees.

3 to 10 days' time required to fill orders on Toupees and Wigs made to order.

To measure for a Toupee or top piece, cut a piece of paper the exact size and shape of the bald spot, mark the crown and parting, enclose a lock of hair, and state if hair is to be straight or curly.

No. 18C4418 Men's Toupee, weft foundation. The weft foundation is a cotton net and weft parting suitable for ordinary wear. Price $5.50
Postage extra, 8 cents.

No. 18C4422 Men's Toupee, ventilated foundation. The ventilated toupees are made on a fine gauze foundation with natural parting, showing scalp through. Price..........................$10.00
If by mail, postage extra, 8 cents.

No. 18C4423 Toupee Paste, which is used to keep toupee in place; heat and apply.
Price, per stick.................................42c
If by mail, postage extra, 5 cents.

Red, Blonde and Gray Hair cost extra. Allow one-half more than above prices.

Remember, we guarantee a perfect fit and match if you follow instructions, or your money back.

How to Measure a Wig.

State style of wig, kind of parting, whether for right or left side; price and description as per list; to insure a good fit mention number of inches. Send sample of hair. Inches. No. 1 Circumference of head. No. 2 Forehead to nape of neck. No. 3 Ear to ear, across forehead. No. 4 Ear to ear, over top. No. 5 Temple to temple, around back.

Gentlemen's Wigs.

Gentlemen's Wigs are made of the finest selected hair. We guarantee our work the highest grade, and they cannot be distinguished from the natural growth.

No. 18C4426 Men's Full Wigs. Weft with crown, cotton foundation.
Price.........................$8.00

No. 18C4430 Men's Full Wigs. Gauze or silk parting. Price.....$12.00

No. 18C4434 Men's Wigs. Ventilated with hair net parting.
Price.............$21.00
If by mail, postage extra, 8 cents.

Red, Blonde and Gray Hair cost extra; allow one-half more than above prices

Street Wigs for Colored People.

No. 18C4438 Street Dress Wig for colored women, made of human hair, bang with parting in front, the hair in back is 18 inches long, and done up high in back with a knot. Send measurements as shown in illustration in rules for measurement on this page.
Price..(Postage extra, 8 cents.)..$5.50

No. 18C4442 Street Dress Wig for colored men, made of human hair with parting on side. Send measurement as per instructions. Price, $4.50
If by mail, postage extra, 8 cents.

Theatrical Wigs and Beards of Every Description.

No. 18C4446 Mustache on wire spring, common.
Price.... .8c
Postage extra 1 cent.

No. 18C4450 Mustache, ventilated.
Price...(Postage extra, 1 cent)...12c

No. 18C4454 Goatees. Price....8c
If by mail, postage extra, 1 cent.

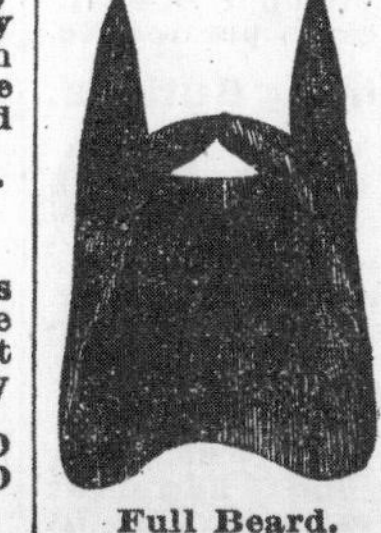

Full Beard.

No. 18C4458 Whiskers, side.
Price..........60c
Beards come in black, brown, gray, red and blonde colors.
If by mail, postage extra, 3 cents.

No. 18C4462 Full Beard, on wire. Price....68c

No. 18C4466 Full Beard, on ventilated net.
Price.......$1.75
If by mail, postage extra, 3 cents.

Minstrel and Character Wigs.

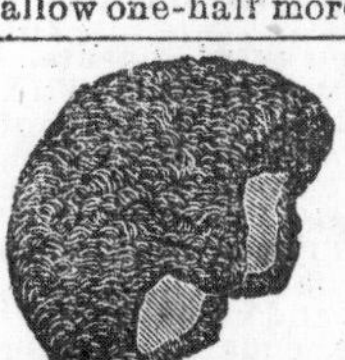

No. 18C4470 Minstrel or Plain Black Negro Wigs.
Price........49c
Postage extra, 8 cents.

Theatrical and Character Wigs for Stage and Masquerade Purposes.

Court Wig

No. 18C4472 Bald Head Wigs, all colors, including white, for Irish and Dutch comedians.
Price..............$2.25
Postage extra, 6 cents.

No. 18C4475 Crop or School Boy's Wig. Colors, brown, red or black.
Price...............$2.00
Postage extra, 6 cents.

No. 18C4476 Chinese Wig. Price........$1.50

No. 18C4477 Mikado Wig. Gents'. Price, $2.25
If by mail, postage extra, 8 cents.

No. 18C4479 Mikado Wig. Ladies'.
Price.... ....$2.50

No. 18C4480 Shoulder or Lord Fauntleroy Wigs, black, brown or blonde. Price.......................$2.50
If by mail, postage extra, 10 cents.

No. 18C4481 Dress Wig for Gents, all colors. Price.....................$2.50

No. 18C4483 Lady or George Washington, white only. Price.....$3.00
If by mail, postage extra, 12 cents.

No. 18C4485 Fright Wigs, all colors. Price $3.50

No. 18C4486 Court Wigs, white only.
Price..(Postage extra, 12c)..$3.25

No. 18C4494 Pencils for Eyebrows, brown or black. Price..(Postage extra, 3 cents).20c

No. 18C4498 Blue Pencil for the veins.
Price.....(Postage extra, 1 cent.).......20c

Theater Rouge, Grease Paints, Hair Restorer, and Hair Nets.

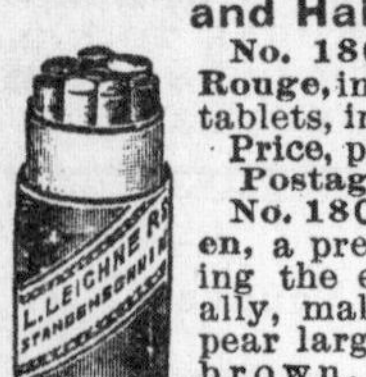

No. 18C4502 Theater Rouge, in cakes on porcelain tablets, in paper boxes.
Price, per box..........20c
Postage extra, 3 cents.

No. 18C4506 Fard Indien, a preparation for shading the eyelashes artistically, making the eyes appear larger. Colors, light brown, dark brown or black. Price, per box...50c
Postage extra, 3 cents.

No. 18C4518 Grease Paint, for make up purposes. Eight colors in a box.
Price, per box..........................70c
If by mail, postage extra, 5 cents.

No. 18C4520 Burnt Cork, 1 pound tin jars. Price, per jar............95c
If by mail, postage extra, 20 cents.

No. 18C4522 Burnt Cork, in glass jars. Price, per jar.................25c
If by mail, postage extra, 5 cents.

No. 18C4523 Imperial Hair Regenerator, restores gray hair to the color of youth, regenerates bleached hair, gives it new life and vigor, and makes it any color desired; makes it beautiful, natural and healthy. Comes in seven shades: Black, dark or medium brown, chestnut, light chestnut, gold blonde and ash blonde. **Absolutely harmless.** Price, per bottle..$1.35
Liquids cannot be mailed.

No. 18C4525 Invisible Hair Nets, made of the best quality of best silk netting, all colors. Price............7c
If by mail, postage extra, 2 cents.

No. 18C4527 Silk Hair Nets, medium size netting, all colors. Price...7c
If by mail, postage extra, 2 cents.

No. 18C4529 Rusma Depilatory Powder for the removal of superfluous hair from the lips, cheek, chin, arm, etc. Price........................95c
If by mail, postage extra, 5 cents.

Manicure Department.

We offer you a complete line of manicure articles; everything that is needed for home use or for professional work. Every piece is guaranteed to be made of best quality hard rolled steel and will give perfect satisfaction. You will find on comparison that the prices quoted are less than half the prices charged by regular stores, as there is an immense big profit made on this class of goods. We charge only our small percentage of profit.

Bone, Ebony and Pearl Handle Files.

No. 18C4531 White Bone Handle Manicure File; both edges grooved and cut, German silver sockets, ends shaped for nail cleaning, best quality steel; entire length, 6 inches.
Price..................................25c
If by mail, postage extra, 4 cents.

No. 18C4532 Ebony Manicure File, both edges grooved and cut, made of best quality hand forged English steel, ends shaped for nail cleaning. Price.25c
If by mail, postage extra, 4 cents.

No. 18C4533 White Pearl Handle File, made of best quality forged steel, both edges grooved and cut, with German silver sockets, ends shaped for nail cleaning; nice, full first class pearl handle. Price.........................75c
If by mail, postage extra, 4 cents.

Cuticle Knife—Bone, Ebony and Pearl.

No. 18C4534 White Bone Cuticle Knife to match above. Made of best quality hand forged steel, with German silver sockets. Length, 4¼ inches. Price...........................25c
If by mail, postage extra, 4 cents.

No. 18C4535 Ebony Cuticle Knife, highest grade steel, best workmanship.
Price 25c
If by mail, postage extra, 4 cents.

No. 18C4536 White Pearl Cuticle Knife, made of same high grade material and to match above. Price..... 75c
If by mail, postage extra, 4 cents.

Corn Knife in Bone, Ebony and Pearl.

No. 18C4537 White Bone Corn and Manicure Knife to match above, with German silver sockets. Length, 5 inches. Price........................25c
If by mail, postage extra, 4 cents.

No. 18C4538 Ebony Manicure or Corn Knife to match above.
Price.......................................25c
If by mail, postage extra, 4 cents.

No. 18C4539 White Pearl Corn and Manicure Knife, same quality and to match above. Price...........75c
If by mail, postage extra, 4 cents.

The Braided Wire Hair Rolls.

FOR THE
LATEST STYLES
..OF..
HAIR DRESSING.

Made of the finest tempered wire, covered with knitted lace to match any shade of hair. These rolls are most desirable for the pretty pompadour effects now so much in vogue. **The only sanitary rolls made to produce fullness in any part of the hair.** Can't become musty or damp from perspiration or injure the hair as do the rolls made of hair. No obstruction to hair pins. Comfortable, cool, cleanly and delightful.

No. 18C4528 4, 6 and 8-inch lengths.
Price.......................................10c
No. 18C4530 12 and 15-inch lengths.
Price 15c
If by mail, postage extra, 4 cents.

New Pompadour Human Hair Roll.

No. 18C4526 Ladies' New Pompadour Roll to be worn under the hair. Made of best quality of human hair, and is really the only satisfactory, sanitary hair roll which can be used for giving the new pompadour effect in hair dressing. Colors, black, brown or blonde. Comes in three sizes as follows;

Length, inches....	8	10	12
Price, each........	8c	10c	12c

If by mail, postage extra, 3 cents.

Nail Clipper.

No. 18C4557 Nail Clipper. The best thing ever invented for the purpose. Small and light to carry in the pocket. Made of fine steel, nickel plated.
Price.......................................20c
If by mail, postage extra, 4 cents.

BUTTON DEPARTMENT.

Pearl Buttons at Import Prices. Button Scale.

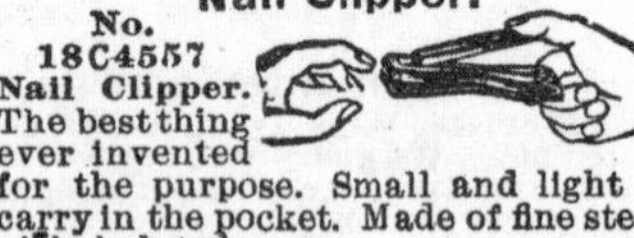

24-line 22-line 20-line

18-line 16-line

Accompanying illustrations show actual size of buttons.

No. 18C4550 Half Fine White Pearl Buttons, two holes, good stock, a nice button.

Size, lines.....	16	18	20	22	24
Price, per doz.,	2½c	3c	4c	4c	5c
Per gross........	28c	34c	44c	46c	55c

If by mail, postage extra, per doz., 2c.

No. 18C4554 Superfine Clear White Pearl Buttons.

Size, lines......	16	18	20	22	24
Price, per doz.,	3c	4c	5c	5c	6c
Per gross	34c	44c	50c	55c	65c

If by mail, postage extra, per doz., 2c.

No. 18C4556 Imported Mother of Pearl Two-Hole Button, same design as above, extra good quality.

Size, lines....	16	18	20	22
Price, per doz.,	8c	$0.09	$0.10	$0.11
Per gross....	90c	1.00	1.10	1.20

If by mail, postage extra, per doz., 2c.

No. 18C4558 Smoked Pearl Dress Buttons.

Size, lines.....	16	18	20	22	24
Price, per doz.,	4c	5c	5c	6c	6c
Per gross......	42c	50c	52c	65c	67c

If by mail, postage extra, per doz., 2c.

Ball Pearl Trimming Buttons.

No. 18C4559 The Small Ball Pearl Buttons are very much in demand for trimming. Superior quality fresh water or domestic pearl buttons, one-half ball size, two holes. Special prices as follows:

Size, lines........	12	14	16
Price, per dozen....	5c	6c	7c
Per gross...........	55c	65c	75c

If by mail, postage extra, per doz., 2c.

No. 18C4560 High Grade Ball Pearl Button, imported mother of pearl, full one-half ball button with two holes, same as No. 18C4559. A very stylish and excellent button for trimming fine garments.

Size, lines........	12	14	16
Price, per doz....	$0.10	$0.12	$0.14
Per gross........	1.10	1.25	1.50

If by mail, postage extra, per doz., 2c.

No. 18C4561 Smoked Pearl Ball Buttons, with two holes; very stylish for white waists and other trimmings.

Size, lines	12	14	16
Price, per doz.....	$0.10	$0.11	$0.12
Per gross........	1.10	1.20	1.35

If by mail, postage extra, per doz., 2c.

No. 18C4562 Fancy Engraved Two-Hole Pearl Dress and Trimming Buttons. Very dainty and stylish for trimming purposes.

Size, lines	12	14	16
Price, per dozen...	6c	7c	8c
Per gross........	65c	75c	90c

If by mail, postage extra, per doz., 2c.

No. 18C4563 Oriental Cat's Eye Ball Button with self shank, imported fine mother of pearl. This is a very handsome and dressy button.

Size, lines........	12	14	16
Price, per doz....	$0.12	$0.15	$0.17
Per gross.........	1.35	1.65	1.85

If by mail, postage extra, per doz., 2c.

No. 18C4564 Fine grade, full one-half ball plain white Pearl Trimming Button, with self shank. This is a good quality at a low price.

Size, lines.........	12	14	16
Price, per dozen..	8c	$0.10	$0.11
Per gross........	90c	1.10	1.25

If by mail, postage extra, per doz., 2c.

Fresh Water Fish Eye Pearl Buttons.

12 14 16 18

No. 18C4565 Pearl Dress Buttons. Fresh water pearl, fish eye pattern, with two holes, nice clear white pearl. This style is very popular and stylish.

Size, lines.....	12	14	16	18	20
Price, per doz..	4c	5c	6c	7c	8c
Per gross........	46c	55c	65c	75c	90c

Size, lines....	22	30	36	40	45
In., diam....	½	¾	⅞	1	1⅛
Per doz......	10c	15c	20c	25c	35c
Gross......	$1.10	1.70	2.25	2.75	3.90

If by mail, postage extra, per doz., 3c.

No. 18C4569 Fish Eye Pattern Imported Ocean Pearl Buttons, same style as No. 18C4565, but the finest grade of imported pearl.

Size, lines.	12	14	16	18
Per doz....	8c	$0.10	$0.11	$0.13
Gross.....	90c	1.10	1.25	1.40

If by mail, postage extra, per doz., 3c.

Colored Dress Buttons.

No. 18C4570 Imitation Pearl Buttons, with self-shank. These little trimming buttons have an exceptionally high luster. Exact imitation of imported pearl. Can be used on wash goods or wool with equal effectiveness. Will wash and wear well. Come in colors, as follows: White, light blue, pink, red, brown or navy blue. Exact size as per illustration.
Price, per gross, 45c; per dozen....4c
If by mail, postage extra, per doz., 2c.

No. 18C4577 Fancy Carved Fine Pearl Buttons, four holes, for jackets, cloaks and dresses; between a smoked and white color. Four sizes.

Size in. diameter...	⅝	1	1⅜	1½
Price, per dozen....	15c	30c	55c	75c

If by mail, postage extra, per dozen. 2 to 5 cents.

For Shirts and Shirt Waists.

Size, 16-line.

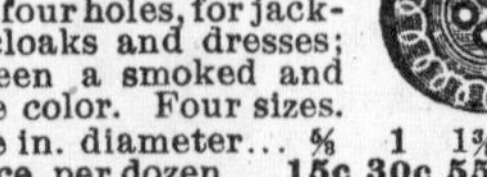

2 3 4

No. 18C4578 Pearl Shirt Button. Good clear quality (domestic). Choice of the three styles. Mention style wanted. Size, 12 or 16 lines. Exact size of illustration.
Price, per gross, 75c; per dozen... 7c
If by mail, postage extra, per doz., 2c.

No. 18C4579 Pearl Shirt Buttons. The imported clear mother of pearl. Same three styles as No. 18C4578. Size, 16-line. Price, per dozen........$0.10
Per gross...........................1.10
If by mail, postage extra, per doz., 2c.

Size, 12-line.

No. 18C4580 Finest Real Mother of Pearl. Size, 12 line, the small size shirt button. Size of illustration. Choice of the three styles.
Price, per gross, 90c; per dozen..8c
If by mail, postage extra, per doz., 2c.

Pearl Shirt Waist Sets.

No. 18C4581 Pearl Shirt Waist Set, extensively used for waists and blouses, fastened with safety pin, which is well soldered. Comes in three sizes.

Inches, diam....	⅝	¾	1
Price, per set...	10c	12c	15c

If by mail, postage extra, per set, 3c.

Stylish Plain Flat Pearls.

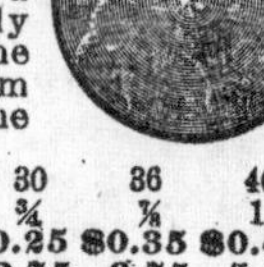

No. 18C4574 Flat Top Pearl Buttons, with metal shanks. These buttons are very stylish and popular, especially on shirt waists in the large and medium sizes. Come in the following sizes:

Size, lines	22	30	36	40
In., diam.	½	¾	⅞	1
Per doz....	$0.15	$0.25	$0.35	$0.45
Per gross..	1.70	2.75	3.75	5.00

If by mail, postage extra, per dozen, 3 to 7 cents.

No. 18C4573 Flat Top Pearl Buttons. Same as above, but with self shank. A fine quality fresh water pearl, clear and white. Sizes as follows:

Size, lines.	22	30	36	40
In., diam..	½	¾	⅞	1
Per dozen.	$0.14	$0.24	$0.34	$0.44
Per gross..	1.65	2.70	3.70	4.90

If by mail, postage extra, per dozen 3 to 7 censt.

Pearl Buttons for Cloaks, Jackets and Dresses.

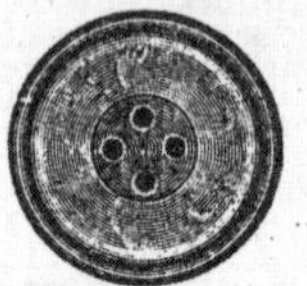

No. 18C4575 Large White Ocean Pearl Buttons, used for street costumes and jackets. **Heavy clear imported white ocean pearl.**

Size, lines...	22	30	36	40	45
Inches, diam	½	1⅛	⅞	1	1⅛
Per dozen...	18c	30c	50c	65c	80c

If by mail, postage extra, per dozen 2 to 5 cents.

Smoked Pearl Buttons.

No. 18C4576 Smoked Pearl Buttons, for cloaks, jackets and dresses. Same shape and design as above. Best quality smoked pearl.

Size, inches, diam.	½	⅞	1	1⅛
Price, per dozen.	17c	49c	64c	79c

If by mail, postage extra, per dozen 2 to 5 cents.

GILT METAL BUTTONS ARE ALL THE GO THIS SEASON.

Fancy Gilt Metal Buttons.

8-line 10-line 12-line

No. 18C4584 Fancy Gilt Metal Buttons, half ball shape, with self shanks. These will be extensively used. Illustrations show exact size of lines, 8, 10 and 12.

Size, lines........	8	10	12	14
Price, per dozen..	3c	4c	4c	5c
Per gross........	32c	40c	42c	55c
Size, lines....	18	24	30	36
Price, per doz	8c	$0.10	$0.16	$0.20
Per gross...	90c	1.10	1.80	2.25

If by mail, postage extra, per doz., 2c

18-line

No. 18C4586 Flat Gilt Buttons, with self shank, dull fancy finish and bright edge on rim. The popular button.

Size, lines	10	12	14	18
Per dozen	3c	3½c	4c	5c
Per gross	33c	40c	45c	55c
Size, lines	20	24	30	36
Price, per dozen.	6c	8c	$0.11	$0.15
Per gross.........	65c	90c	1.25	1.70

If by mail, postage extra, per doz., 2c.

Fancy Metal Dress Buttons.

No. 18C4589 Fancy Gilt Metal Trimming Buttons. Will not tarnish, being made of good gilt. The center is enameled in colors, navy, brown, cardinal, black or white. Buttons will be very much in vogue this season. This button comes in two sizes.

Lines	14	24
Diameter, inches	3/8	5/8
Price, per dozen	15c	30c

If by mail, postage extra, per doz., 3c

Cut Steel Dress Buttons.

No. 18C4592 Fancy Cut Steel Dress Buttons will be extensively worn this season. They make an attractive trimming for dresses, waists and jackets. Used in various ways. Can furnish them in three sizes.

Lines	24	32	42
Size, inches	9-16	3/4	1
Price, per dozen	15c	25c	38c

If by mail, postage extra, per doz., 4c

Jet Dress Buttons.

No. 18C4593 Fancy Cut Jet Trimming Button. A very pretty and desirable button for different trimming purposes. Comes in three sizes.

Lines	10	12	14
Diam., inches	1/4	3/8	1/2
Price, per dozen	4c	5c	6c

If by mail, postage extra, per doz., 2c

No. 18C4595 Half-ball Crocheted Trimming Buttons. This tiny trimming button has been exceptionally popular as a trimming for waists, skirts and millinery purposes. Can be ordered in black or white. Come in two sizes.

Lines	6	8
Diam., inches	1/4	3/8
Price, per dozen	3c	3½c

If by mail, postage extra, per dozen, 2 cents.

No. 18C4596 Bullet Shaped Silk Crocheted Buttons. This is the popular, round shape, crocheted button. Very extensively used in dress trimmings. A superior quality. Black only. Comes in four sizes.

Lines	10	12	14	16
Diam., inches	3/8	7/16	1/2	5/8
Price, per dozen	8c	9c	10c	11c

If by mail, postage extra, per dozen, 2 cents.

No. 18C4597 Fancy Silk Crocheted Button. This is a very pretty crocheted design. One of the very newest effects. An exceedingly effective trimming. This is a very high grade quality, for which you would pay in the regular way almost double our price. Black only. Comes in three sizes.

Lines	6	10	12
Diam. inches	5/8	1	1¼
Price, per dozen	15c	30c	50c

If by mail, postage extra, per doz., 3c.

Silk Covered Buttons.

No. 18C4599 Fine Silk Diagonal Covered Buttons, for dress trimmings, etc., with self shank. Black only.

Size, lines	12	14	16	18	20
Price, per doz.	3c	3½c	4c	4½c	5c
Per gross	30c	40c	45c	50c	55c

If by mail, postage extra, per doz., 2c.

Velvet Covered Buttons for Dresses and Jackets.

Will be very stylish in all sizes.

No. 18C4600 Velvet Covered Buttons, with self shanks. Black only.

Size, lines	12	14	16	18
Price, per dozen	3c	3½c	4c	4½c
Per gross	35c	40c	45c	50c
Size, lines	24	30	40	
Price, per dozen	5c	6c	$0.10	
Per gross	55c	70c	1.10	

If by mail, postage extra, per doz., 2c.

No. 18C4601 Fine Covered Diagonal Mohair Buttons. Black only. **Vest Size.**

Price, per dozen 5c
Per gross 55c

Coat Size.

Price, per dozen 6c
Per gross 70c

Overcoat size. Price, per dozen 8c
Per gross 90c

No. 18C4603 Fine Silk Covered Diagonal Buttons. Black only.

Size	Vest	Coat	Overcoat
Price, per doz.	5c	7c	$0.10
Per gross	55c	80c	1.10

If by mail, postage extra, per doz., 2c.

Black Horn Buttons.

No. 18C4604 Black Horn Vest Buttons, highly polished.
Price, per dozen 2c
Per gross 22c

No. 18C4605 Black Horn Coat Buttons, same style as above.
Price, per gross, 33c; per dozen 3c

No. 18C4610 Black Horn Overcoat Buttons, same style as above.
Price, per gross, 45c; per dozen 4c

If by mail, postage extra, per doz., 1c.

Vegetable Ivory Buttons.

No. 18C4611 Vegetable Ivory Buttons, with dull finish centers and polished rims; a very high grade button, used by the best tailors. Vest, coat and overcoat. Black only. Sizes as follows:

Size	24 Lines Vest	30 Lines Coat	36 Lines Overcoat
Per dozen	6c	9c	$0.12
Per gross	65c	90c	1.30

If by mail, postage extra, per doz., 2c

No. 18C4612 Vegetable Ivory Buttons, fancy dull finish centers and bright polished rims; a very stylish button for vests and coats. Black only.

Size	24 Lines Vest	30 Lines Coat
Per dozen	$0.10	$0.15
Per gross	1.10	1.70

If by mail, postage extra, per doz., 2c.

Officers' and G. A. R. Buttons.

No. 18C4614 Officers' Plated Brass Buttons.

Vest Size.
Price, per dozen ... $0.09
Per gross 1.00

Coat Size.
Price, per dozen .. $0.17
Per gross 1.80

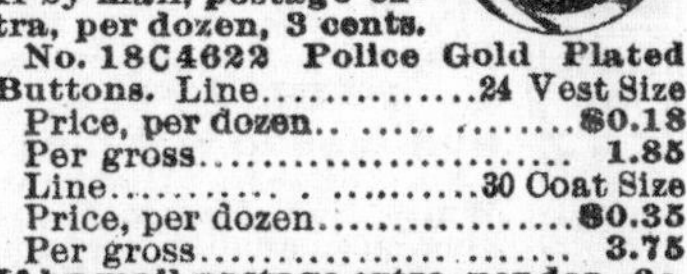

No. 18C4618 G. A. R. Oval Top Republic Buttons.

Vest Size.
Price, per dozen .. $0.09
Per gross 1.00

Coat Size.
Price, per dozen ... $0.15
Per gross 1.50

If by mail, postage extra, per dozen, 3 cents.

No. 18C4622 Police Gold Plated Buttons. Line ..... 24 Vest Size
Price, per dozen $0.18
Per gross 1.85
Line ..... 30 Coat Size
Price, per dozen $0.35
Per gross 3.75

If by mail, postage extra, per doz., 2c.

Anchor Brass Buttons.

No. 18C4626 Anchor Brass Buttons.

Vest Size.
Price, per dozen .. $0.08
Per gross ..... .90

Coat Size.
Price, per dozen .. .10
Per gross 1.10

Overcoat Size. Price, per doz. .12
Per gross 1.35

If by mail, postage extra, per doz., 2c.

Agate Buttons.

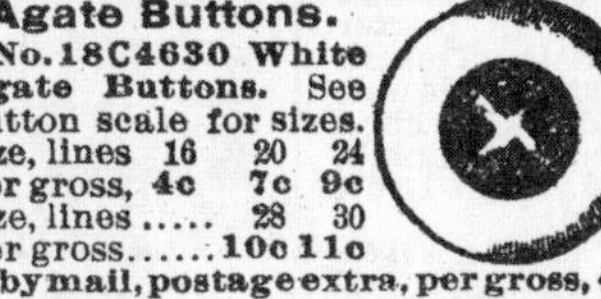

No. 18C4630 White Agate Buttons. See button scale for sizes.

Size, lines	16	20	24
Per gross	4c	7c	9c
Size, lines	28	30	
Per gross	10c	11c	

If by mail, postage extra, per gross, 4c.

No. 18C4634 Fancy White Agate Buttons.

Size	16	20	24	28
Per gross	5c	9c	11c	15c

If by mail, postage extra, per gross, 4 cents.

Thumb and Finger Automatic Button.

No. 18C4650 The only perfect Suspender Button on the market. Can be put on or taken off with the fingers without use of knife or any tool whatever. Simple construction, perfect action and pleasing appearance. Locked and unlocked by raising or lowering "key" with fingers. Made in black or silver. Packed one dozen in a box, suspender size.
Price, per gross, 65c; per dozen ... 6c

If by mail, postage extra, per doz., 2c

No. 18C4651 New Thumb and Finger Automatic Bachelor Button. Fly size. Silver or black.
Price, per gross, 65c; per dozen ... 6c

If by mail, postage extra, 2 cents.

Washburne Bachelor Buttons.

No. 18C4654 Washburne Bachelor Buttons. This button is so neat in appearance and fills such a universal want that it hardly needs recommendation; can be adjusted instantly and removed just as quickly. Comes in blued steel or nickel.
Price, each 5c
Per dozen 33c

If by mail, postage extra, per doz., 4c.

No. 18C4658 Washburne Drawer Supporter. Fastens same as button. Comes in nickel only. The neatest and best drawer supporter ever invented. Worn once, always worn.
Price, per pair 5c
Per dozen pairs 55c

If by mail, postage extra, per doz., 4c.

Common Metal Pants Buttons.

No. 18C4662 Black Metal Buttons, small or fly size.
Price, per gross 5c

No. 18C4666 Black Metal Buttons, suspender size. Per gross 7c

No. 18C4670 Brass Fly Buttons, best quality. Price, per gross 8c

No. 18C4674 Brass Suspender Buttons, best quality. Per gross 9c

Bone Pants Buttons.

No. 18C4678 Universal Bone Pants Buttons. Black or white; used extensively for underwear, etc. Put up one gross in box. Sold only by gross.
Price, per gross, suspender size ... 25c
Price, per gross, fly size 20c

If by mail, postage extra, per gross, 5c.

Pants buttons are put up in one gross boxes. We do not sell less than one box.

Washburne Scarf Fastener.

No. 18C4694 Washburne Scarf Fastener. This is without doubt the best scarf fastener ever made and the most convenient to adjust. It is easily removed and has no prongs or projections; can also be used in various other ways.
Price, each 3c

If by mail, postage extra, 1 cent.

No. 18C4696 Handy Button Cabinet. A button for every emergency. This cabinet is made up for family use, with complete assortment of different style buttons; such as are necessary almost every day. The cabinet contains assorted sizes of each style of button and consists of:
2 dozen pearl buttons,
2 dozen agate buttons,
1½ dozen ivoreen buttons,
1 dozen trouser buttons,
1 dozen bone buttons,
1 dozen covered buttons, making 8½ dozen in all. We offer this entire cabinet, 8½ dozen, for 20c

If by mail, postage extra, 8 cents.

Ladies' and Children's Hose Supporters.

Easy Catch Hose Supporter. Made from good quality lisle elastic, pin top and slide center. We retail this at about half what you would pay elsewhere for this grade of goods. Colors, black or white.

No. 18C4700 Child's Double Strap Stocking Supporters. Length, 6¾ inches.
Price, per pair 5c
Per dozen pairs 55c

No. 18C4704 Misses' Double Strap Hose Supporters. Length, 10 inches.
Price, per pair 6c
Per dozen pairs 70c

No. 18C4708 Young Ladies' Double Strap Hose Supporters. Length, 13 inches. Price, per pair 7c
Per dozen pairs 80c

No. 18C4712 Ladies' Double Strap Hose Supporters. Length, 16 inches.
Price, per pair 8c
Per dozen pairs 90c

If by mail, postage extra, per pair, 3c.

Hose Supporters.

Flexo Grasp Hose Supporters. Same shape and style as No. 18C4700, with special button fasteners guaranteed not to tear the hose. Made of the very finest English lisle elastic, pin top, with slide center for adjustment. Each pair warranted by the manufacturer. We particularly recommend this high grade of goods. There are none better made. Colors, black or white.

No. 18C4716 Child's Double Strap Hose Supporters, as described above. Length, 6¾ inches.
Price, per pair $0.11
Per dozen pairs 1.20

No. 18C4720 Misses' Double Strap Hose Supporters, as described above. Length, 10 inches.
Price, per pair $0.12
Per dozen pairs 1.35

No. 18C4724 Young Ladies' Double Strap Hose Supporters, as described above. Length, 13 inches.
Price, per pair $0.14
Per dozen pairs 1.45

No. 18C4728 Ladies' Double Strap Hose Supporters, as described above. Length, 16 inches.
Price, per pair $0.16
Per dozen pairs 1.75

If by mail, postage extra, per pair, 3c.

Braces and Hose Supporters.

Made of good Lisle Elastic Webbing.

No. 18C4732 Ladies' Shoulder Braces, with hose supporters; black or white.
Price, per pair $0.16
Per dozen pairs 1.65

No. 18C4736 Misses' Shoulder Braces, with hose supporters; black or white.
Price, per pair $0.13
Per dozen pairs 1.40

No. 18C4740 Children's Shoulder Braces, with hose supporters; black or white.
Price, per pair $0.12
Per dozen pairs 1.35

If by mail, postage extra, per pair, 4c.

Ladies' Safety Belts.

No. 18C4748 Ladies' Safety Belts, made of sateen, rubber band across hips. Easy and convenient. Sizes, 22 to 36. Ask for one inch larger than your exact measure. Sizes every other inch. Give waist measure. Color, white only.
Price, each $0.14
Per dozen 1.50

If by mail, postage extra, each, 2c.

Antiseptic Sanitary Towels.

No. 18C4752 Serviette Sanitary Cloth. These serviettes are made of the finest absorbent cotton, with a layer of absolutely impervious material, which insures cleanliness. Absolutely antiseptic, ready for instant use. These serviettes possess from three to four times the absorbent qualities of the best toweling. Recommended by the medical profession as indispensable in every lady's wardrobe. Small, medium and large sizes. Give size wanted.
Price, per dozen, 25c; each 2½c

If by mail, postage extra, each, 3c.

Special Sanitary Supports.

No. 18C4755 Special Sanitary Support for holding serviette or napkin to prevent soiling the clothes. Made of fine waterproof stockinet, which is easily washed; fills a long desired want; highly recommended by ladies who have used them. Try one and you will never be without. Three sizes: Small, medium and large. Give size.
Price, per dozen, $4.25; each .. 38c

If by mail, postage extra, each, 3c.

Ladies' Belt Hose Supporters.

No. 18C4760 Ladies' Satin Belt Hose Supporters, with fancy frilled side elastics. By using immense quantities we are enabled to offer at the price this very desirable supporter, really a good value for 50 cents. Colors, cardinal, pink, light blue, or black. **Give waist measure.** Price, per pair............$0.24
Per doz. pairs. 2.75
Postage, per pair, 3c.

The Fit Form Supporter for Comfort, Grace and Value.

No. 18C4763 **The Fit-Form Hose Supporter. This is an improved belt and pad supporter that conforms to the shape.** The most comfortable pad supporter made. Makes you assume the correct standing position; helps give you a perfect figure. Made with dividable front pad of fine quality satin, with extra quality non-elastic belt. Has four hose supporting straps, made of good quality 1½-inch, plain elastic web, with adjustable buckles to regulate length. The waist band is adjustable to fit any waist measure. Colors, black, white, pink or light blue. We guarantee this equal to any 50-cent pad supporters sold on the market. Our price, per pair.........23c
If by mail, postage extra, per pair, 5c.

Fit Form Supporter is Comfortable and Improves Your Figure.

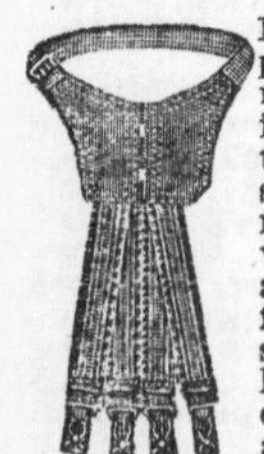

No. 18C4764 **Fit Form Improved Supporter, made of the finest material.** The front pad is made in two parts, of the very best quality satin, with finest quality non-elastic waistband, which is adjustable to fit any waist measure. Has four hose supporting straps, made of a very high grade, frilled silk elastic, which are adjustable with small buckles, so that you can regulate height. These pads are giving universal satisfaction and when once worn, you will not wear any other. This is a very high grade supporter, fully worth $1.00 per pair. Colors: black, white, pink or blue.
Price, per pair.........................50c
If by mail, postage extra, per pair, 5c.

Our 19-Cent Hose Supporters.

No. 18C4769 **This Hose Supporter hooks on bottom of corset, giving the body a graceful appearance.** The pad is made of satin, with slide in center for adjustment. Good quality silk overshot frilled elastic. Colors, black, light blue, pink or red.
Price, each ..$0.19
Per dozen......2.00
Postage extra, per pair, 3 cents.

Kleinert's Four-Strap Hookon Supporters.

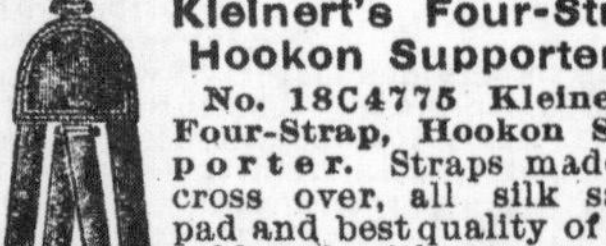

No. 18C4775 **Kleinert's Four-Strap, Hookon Supporter.** Straps made to cross over, all silk satin pad and best quality of silk cable web, with extra quality non-elastic to match; a very excellent supporter; all colors. Price, each...$0.50
Per dozen............5.50
If by mail, postage extra, each, 5 cents.

Ladies' Fancy Frilled Side Garters.

No. 18C4777 **Fancy Frilled Side Garters. Made of good quality silk overshot elastic.** Nickel buckle in center and pin top. Button catch. Colors, black, pink, light blue or cardinal.
Price, per pair........$0.15
Per dozen pairs........ 1.70
If by mail, postage extra, per pair, 3 cents.

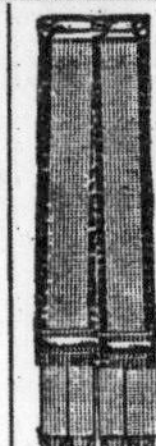

No. 18C4778 **Side Supporters, made of extra quality, plain lisle, 1½ inch pretty webbing, with small frills on both sides.** Made with extra quality buckles and trimmings. A very strong and satisfactory supporter. Colors, black, white, pink or blue.
Price, per pair.........$0.20
Per dozen pairs 2.25
If by mail, postage extra, per pair, 4 cents.

Fancy Silk Side Garters, 48 Cents.

No. 18C4785 **Fancy Frilled Side Garters. Our best quality.** Made of fine imported all silk frilled elastic. Special fancy pattern. Gold filigree buckle in center, and gold pin top, with slide in center. Flexo grasp fasteners. Colors, black, light blue, cardinal, pink, heliotrope or yellow.
Price, per pair..$0.48
Per dozen pairs 5.50
If by mail, postage extra, per pair, 3c.

Endless Sleeve Bands.

No. 18C4803 "Ashworth" **Endless Sleeve Bands.** The finest and most satisfactory arm bands ever sold. No metal trimmings, and very serviceable, silk covered. Colors, black, white or cardinal. Price, per pair.....$0.10
Per dozen pairs................ 1.10
If by mail, postage extra, per pair, 2c.

Wire Sleeve Supporters.

No. 18C4812 **Patent Duplex Ventilated Men's Arm Bands;** fine nickeled steel wire, one pair in a box. Price, per pair..........7c
Per dozen pairs.........................75c
If by mail, postage extra, per pair, 3c

No. 18C4814 **Mercerized Elastic Arm Band. This is a double row, round, circular knit elastic arm band.** Very durable and easy. Colors, black, white, pink and light blue. Price, per pair......5c
Per dozen pairs...........................55c
If by mail, postage extra, per pair, 2c.

Children's Combination Belt and Supporter.

No. 18C4816 **Children's Combination Belt and Supporter for Boys and Girls.** The handiest, safest and most convenient waist and hose supporter on the market. Made of good sateen and lisle elastic sides. Sizes are from 2 to 12 years. **Be sure and give age.** Comes in white only.
Price, per dozen, $2.00; each....19c
If by mail, postage extra, each, 4c.

Ladies' Elastic Garters.

No. 18C4825 **Fancy Round Garters.** Roman striped frilled elastic. Neat attractive buckle and two-color ribbon bow. Each pair in a neat box. Colors, black, red, light blue, or pink. Price, per pair....$0.09
Per dozen pairs............... 1.00
If by mail, postage extra, per pair, 5c.

No. 18C4826 **Ladies' Round Garters, made of nice quality, fancy frilled silk faced, elastic webbing,** with handsome nickeled buckles and silk ribbon bows. Buckles can be ordered in choice of three designs, representing, card ace of spades, mottoes, such as "hands off," "private grounds," etc., or thermometer. Colors, black, pink or light blue. Price, per pair. 19c
If by mail, postage extra, per pair, 5c.

Ladies' Fancy Round Garters.

No. 18C4841 **Fancy Round Garters, made of fine quality of silk frilled elastic.** Beautiful sunflower buckle, enameled, and with large red stone setting in center. Finished with fine silk ribbon bows; very pretty design. Each pair in a box. Colors, black, pink, light blue or heliotrope.
Price, per doz., $4.75; per pair...42c
If by mail, postage extra, per pair, 5c.

Fancy Round Garters.

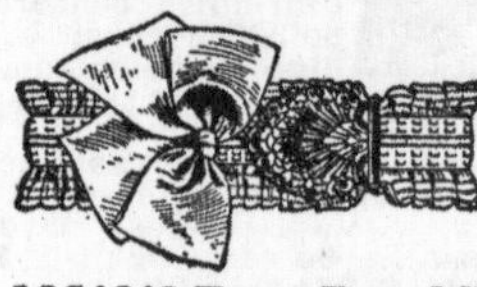

No. 18C4843 **Fancy Round Garter,** made of extra wide very fine quality of silk elastic. Extra fine filigree gold buckle, with very large silk ribbon bows. The buckles have fine jeweled settings. Each pair in a nice box. Colors, black, light blue, pink, or violet.
Price, per pair.........................75c
If by mail, postage extra, per pair, 5c.

No. 18C4845 **Fancy Round Garter,** made of the highest grade of silk frilled elastic. Fine silk ribbon bow, and genuine sterling silver buckles. Each pair put up in a fancy box. Colors, black, light blue, pink, cardinal or yellow. Price, per pair..........$1.00
If by mail, postage extra, 5 cents.

Plain Lisle Elastic.

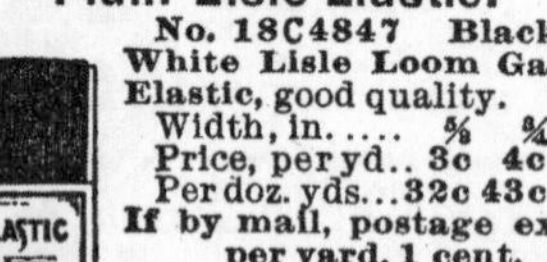

No. 18C4847 **Black or White Lisle Loom Garter Elastic,** good quality.

Width, in....	⅝	¾	⅞
Price, per yd..	3c	4c	5c
Per doz. yds...	32c	43c	52c

If by mail, postage extra, per yard, 1 cent.

Non Elastic Webbing.

No. 18C4848 **Black or White Non Elastic Webbing,** good quality, used for hose supporters, bandings and belts.

Width, in....	½	⅝	¾	⅞	1
Per yard........	2c	2c	2½c	2½c	3c
Per dozen....	20c	21c	27c	28c	32c

If by mail, postage extra, per yard, 1c.

Hat Elastic Cord.

No. 18C4849 **Round Hat Elastic Cord,** black or white.
Price, per yard........................ 1c
Per piece, 36 yards 30c
Postage extra, per dozen yards, 2c.

No. 18C4852 **Plaid Garter Elastic.** This is a good, durable web. Width, 1¾ inches. Colors, blue, pink, red or black plaid.
Price, per yard.............................3c
Per dozen yards.........................30c
If by mail, postage extra, per yard, 2 cents.

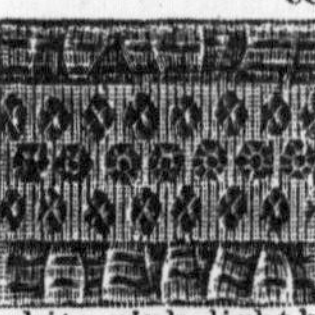

No. 18C4854 **Fancy Frilled Elastic,** with silk overshot. A new and pretty design. This is a strong and durable web. Width, 1¼ inches. Colors, black, white, pink, light blue, cardinal or lilac.
Price, per yard.......................5c
Per piece, (10 yards)................45c
If by mail, postage extra, per yard, 2 cents.

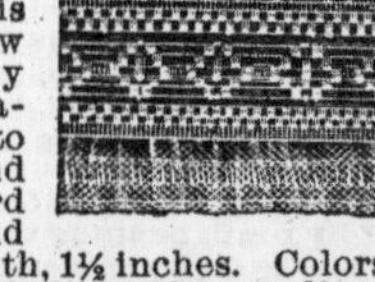

No. 18C4856 **Fancy Frilled Silk Elastic.** This is an entirely new pattern. Very strong and durable. Equal to many of the 15 and 20 cents a yard elastics, as sold elsewhere. Width, 1¼ inches. Colors, black, white, pink, light blue, cardinal, or lilac. Price, per yard.........10c
Per piece, (10 yards).................90c
If by mail, postage extra, per yard, 5c.

No. 18C4858 **Fancy Silk Frilled Elastic Web.** This has a fancy double row frill in center as well as on either side. A very dainty and attractive webbing. Width, 1⅛ inches. Colors, black, white, pink, light blue, cardinal or lavender.
Price, per yard..................$0.20
Per piece (10 yards).......... 1.90
If by mail, postage extra, 5 cents.

No. 18C4860 **Best Quality Silk Schappe Elastic Web.** This is preferred by many to the very expensive silk. Looks just the same and wears splendidly. Width, ⅝ in. Price, per yd. 8c
Per piece (10 yards)...............75c
If by mail, postage extra, 5 cents.

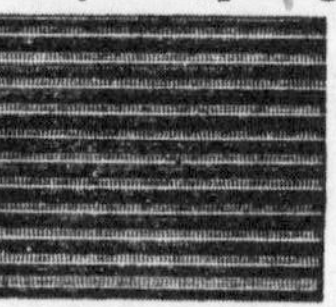

No. 18C4859 **Heavy Ribbed All Silk Elastic.** The highest grade quality, 1 inch wide. Colors, black, white, pink, yellow, light blue, cardinal or violet.
Price, doz. yds..$1.95; per yard. 18c
If by mail, postage extra, 5 cents.

THIMBLES, NEEDLES, THREAD, SEWING SUPPLIES, ETC.

No. 18C4960 **Aluminum Thimbles,** light and durable, come one dozen in a box, assorted. Sizes, 7 to 10.
Price, per dozen..........5c
Per gross.................55c
If by mail, postage extra, per doz., 2c

No. 18C4961 **Large size Aluminum Thimbles.** Same as above, assorted, one dozen in box. Sizes, 9 to 12.
Price, per gross, 75c; per dozen..7c
If by mail, postage extra, per doz., 2c

No. 18C4964 **German Silver Thimbles,** all sizes.
Price, per dozen, 33c; each......3c
If by mail, postage extra, per doz., 3c.

No. 18C4975 **Sterling Silver Thimbles. This is a very excellent thimble, serviceable and very much desired by every lady.** Genuine sterling silver thimbles are never sold for less than 25 cents. Sizes, 6 to 11. Price, each. 12c
If by mail, postage extra, each, 1c.

Superior Helix Needles.

No. 18C4965 **Milliners' Needles.** Fine quality English make. Nos. 4, 5, 6 and 7.
Price, per paper.... 2c
Per dozen papers.... 21c

No. 18C4967 **Milliners' Needles.** The highest grade, such as sell for 10 cents a paper. Nos. 4, 5, 6 and 7. Our price, per paper...... 5c
Per dozen papers.... 55c

No. 18C4968 **The Best Helix Needles,** made in Redditch, England. The oldest, most reliable and best quality needle manufactured. Sold elsewhere at 5 cents a paper. All sizes, sharps and betweens. Be sure to give size wanted. Price, per paper... 2c
Per dozen papers............................22c
If by mail, postage extra, each, 1 cent.

Calyx-Eyed Needles.

No. 18C4971 **Millward's Calyx-Eyed Needles.** This is the only satisfactory self threading needle to be had. Comes in all sizes, sharps only.
Price, per paper of 10 needles....7c
If by mail, postage extra, each, 1c.

Darning Needles.

No. 18C4972 **Cloth Stuck.** Put up ten to the paper, assorted sizes.
Price, per paper.......................2c
Per dozen papers.....................21c
If by mail, postage extra, each, 1c.

Patent Crochet Needle.

No. 18C4973 **Eagle Patent Crochet Needle.** This is the only hook that gives you perfect control in doing your work, as it does not turn in the hand; does not lose the stitch; does not cramp the finger; does not strain the eyes to pick up the stitch; made of the highest grade steel. It is a perfect hook. Sizes, 1, 3, 5, 7, 9 and 12. No. 1 is the coarsest and No. 12 the finest. Price, each.. 4c
Per dozen.................................40c
If by mail, postage extra, each, 2c.

Knitting Needle Set.

No. 18C4974 **Put up five to the set, in round cabinet wood case. Sizes, 10 to 16.** Size 10 is coarsest, size 16 is finest.
Price, per doz. sets, 33c; set of five, 3c
If by mail, postage extra, per set, 2c.

Crochet Hook Set.

No. 18C4976 Consists of two steel and one bone crochet hook put up in round cabinet case. Price, per set of three, 4c
Per dozen sets.....40c
If by mail, postage extra, per set, 2c.

Wooden Crochet Hooks.

No. 18C4977 Wooden Crochet Hooks. Used to crochet Shetland shawls; in three sizes, fine, medium and large. Mention size wanted.
Price, each.....7c
Per dozen.....75c
If by mail, postage extra, each, 3c.

Wooden Knitting Needles.

No. 18C4981 Wooden Knitting Needles (with points). In three sizes, fine, medium and coarse. Length, 14 inches. Mention size wanted.
Price, per pair.....$0.09
Per dozen pairs.....1.00
If by mail, postage extra, per pair, 3c.

A Magic Darner.

Mends Your Hosiery in a Hurry.

No. 18C4978 The Magic Darner is a machine recently invented and patented for mending hosiery, silk, wool or cotton, all kinds of underwear, napkins, table linens and, in fact, everything in the household that needs darning. One does not have to be an expert needle worker to mend lace curtains and other fine fabrics, the Magic Darner does it for you and saves you nineteen-twentieths of your time. You can take twenty stitches on the machine while you take one in the old way. Well worth $1.00. Price, each....$0.14
Per dozen.....1.65
If by mail, postage extra, each, 5c.

No. 18C4983 The Tyton Ribbon Leader. This is a very necessary little article for drawing narrow ribbons, any number or width, through beadings.
Price, per dozen, 45c; each.....4c
If by mail, postage extra, each, 2c.

No. 18C4986 This Useful Assorted Needle Case contains fifteen needles, comprising bodkin, or tape needle, assorted darners, chenille, glove and all kinds of needles for fancy work. Mounted on a neat card, size 3x5 inches.
Price, per dozen cards, 20c; each, 2c
If by mail, postage extra, each, 2c.

No. 18C4988 Our Acme Needle Case contains four papers of sewing needles, a good assortment of other style needles and yarn darners; also four rows of best needle point pins. This case is well worth 15 cents.
Price, per dozen, 44c; each.....4c
If by mail, postage extra, each, 2c.

No. 18C4990 This Most Complete Needle Case contains four papers of sewing needles, a complete assortment of all styles of other needles, comprising yarn darners, crewel and fancy needles; also a bodkin and crochet hook. It has a large and complete assortment of jet head, toilet, veiling and trimming pins; also one row of black wire hair pins and two rows of best needle point pins. This case is usually sold for 25 cents.
Price, per dozen, 90c; each.....8c
If by mail, postage extra, each, 3c.

Elegant Work Basket and Contents, Only $1.00.

No. 18C4994 Ladies' Work Basket with contents, easily worth $2.25, price $1.00. This is a very prettily designed basket, made of round, fancy, braided straw in different colors. The bottom is lined with tufted satin, and bands of ribbon are drawn through the lid and sides of basket. The basket alone readily retails for 75 cents. We offer this basket for $1.00 complete with the following contents: one pair of scissors, one egg darner for gloves and hosiery, one tape measure, one aluminum thimble, two papers of needles, an assortment of crewel and needles for fancy work, an assortment of pins, hair pins and toilet pins, three crochet hooks, one card of hooks and eyes, one dozen black headed shawl pins, one piece mending tissue, one 50-yard spool of silk, two spools machine thread, one spool of heavy linen finished thread, two spools of darning cotton, one spool of Turkey red embroidery cotton. Size of basket, 9x4½ inches. This complete outfit is the best ever offered. Weight, packed for shipment, 2½ pounds. Price.....$1.00

No. 18C4996 Stencil Case and Work Box. This is a very desirable and useful accessory for the household. Consists of complete alphabet in script and one set of figures for stamping linens, handkerchiefs, underwear, etc., a small box of indelible marking ink, with brush, four spools of different colored mending cotton and three papers of gold-eyed needles. All put up in a fancy leatherette case, cover worked in gilt. Lid fastens with catch. Size, 6x6¾ inches. Price.....23c
If by mail, postage extra, 8 cents.

No. 18C5002 Ladies' Work Box. This is a pretty leatherette work box, lid fastened with brass catch. The box is divided into compartments, into which are fitted two spools of thread, four balls of darning cotton, nine spools of different colored, mercerized, mending yarn, three papers of gold-eyed needles and a small flannelette pin cushion. Size of box, 6x4 inches. Price of this neat little work cabinet.....25c
If by mail, postage extra, 8 cents.

Tape Measures.

No. 18C5008 Tape Measure, printed on both sides, double-stitched (60 inches long), fine, heavy cloth, metal tip. **This grade of tape measure is suitable for tailors' or dressmakers' use.**
Price, per dozen, 20c; each.....2c
If by mail, postage extra, each, 2c.

No. 18C5010 Non-Stretchable Tape Measure, made of imported cloth. Will always retain its actual measurements, very durable. Especially desirable for dressmakers and tailors. Length, 60 inches. Price, each.....5c
Per dozen.....55c
If by mail, postage extra, each, 2c.

No. 18C5012 Nickeled Spring Tape, 5-foot length; good tape and catch spring; won't get out of order, a handy article around the house. Regular 25-cent quality.
Price, per dozen, $1.75; each.....15c
If by mail, postage extra, each, 3c.

Ladies' Work Basket With Fittings, Only 50 Cents.

No. 18C4992 Ladies' Complete Work Basket. The basket is a square shape, made of fancy, imported narrow and broad satin straws, woven in rustic design, with attached lid. The basket alone retails for 35 cents. Contains the following articles: one pair of scissors, four papers of needles with an assortment of darning and needles for fancy work, one dozen shawl pins, one piece of mending tissue, one egg darner for gloves and hosiery, one tape measure, one aluminum thimble, one card hooks and eyes, one spool machine thread, one spool Monarch linen finished thread and one spool of darning cotton. The basket and contents, at regular retail prices, are worth over $1.00. Weight, packed for shipment, 1½ pounds. We are going to sell this complete $1.00 outfit, size of basket 6½x3¾ inches, for.....50c

Victoria Plaiting Machine.

A Victoria Plaiting Machine and a hot iron is all you need.

No. 18C5014 Victoria Plaiting Machine, used by all leading dressmakers and milliners to make all kinds of trimmings. Two gauges go with each machine. No lady should be without one. Size of plaiter, 7¼x14 inches; makes plaits 7 inches wide. Price, each.....$0.15
Per dozen.....1.70
Weight, when packed for shipment, 20 ozs. For postage rate see page 4.

Large Size Plaiting Machine.

No. 18C5016 The New Victoria Plaiting Machine, same style as No. 18C5014, used for plaiting, ruching, oak leaf, rose plaiting, box ruffle, and various other kinds of plaiting. A dressmaker cannot do without it. A necessity for everyone who does their own fancy work. Size of plaiter, 20x11 inches, makes a 9-inch plait. Has two small knives and two large ones with each machine. Shipping weight, packed, 35 ounces. Regular price, $1.00
Our price.....75c

Queen Stocking and Glove Darner.

No. 18C5033 Made of black ebonized wood with nickel plated spring to hold stocking or other fabric firmly in place. Does not require to be adjusted until work is completed. Nice for mending lace curtains and for working the corners in drawn work.
Price, each.....7c
Per dozen.....75c
If by mail, postage extra, each, 5c.

No. 18C5034 Combination Wooden Stocking and Glove Darner. Highly polished, varnished and enameled. This combination darner is so made with small end on handle that it can be used either for darning gloves or stockings. Price, each.....2c
Per dozen.....20c
If by mail, postage extra, each, 4c.

Tracing Wheels.

No. 18C5035 Double Adjustable Tracing Wheel, with set screw, enameled handle. Price.....8c

No. 18C5037 Metal Handle Tracing Wheel, finely nickel plated and finished. Made reversible, so when not in use the wheel is entirely inclosed in handle. When lying in workbasket will not injure or become entangled with other articles.
Price.....8c

Adamantine Pins.

No. 18C5041 Adamantine Pins are put up one dozen papers to the package.
Size No. 4, small. Price, per pkg. 12c
Size No. 3, medium. Price, per pkg. 13c
Size No. 2, large. Price, per pkg. 15c
Shipping weight, 16 ounces.

Brass Pins.

No. 18C5042 Brass Pins. 280 to each paper, 12 papers in each package.
Size No. 4, small. Price, per pkg. 25c
Size No. 3, medium. Price, per pkg. 28c
Size No. 2, large. Price, per pkg. 31c
Shipping weight, 18 ounces.

No. 18C5043 Ne Plus Ultra Brass Pins. This is the best high grade pin made, with finest needle points. 360 pins on each paper attractively put up.

Sizes	M. C. Large	S. C. Medium	F. 3½ Small
Per paper	4c	3½c	3c
Per dozen	41c	37c	33c

No. 18C5045 The Sandow Washington Needle Point Best English Pin, polished solid heads and needle points. **Contains 400 assorted pins.** Sizes, Nos. 4 and 5. Put up in handsome gilt edged papers. Price, per paper, 3c
Per dozen papers.....31c
If by mail, postage extra, per paper, 1 cent.

Bank Pins.

No. 18C5046 Bank Pins. Best quality needle point brass bank pins for banks and general office use. Come put up ¼ pound to the box. (We do not sell less than a box of any size). Six sizes; smaller size contains more pins to the box.

Nos.	1	2	3	4	6	7
L'gth, in.	1⅝	1½	1⅜	1¼	⅞	¾
Per box	14c	16c	17c	18c	22c	26c

If by mail, postage extra, per box, 8c.

A Special Bargain in Pin Books.

No. 18C5047 Pin Books, 8 rows of 30 pins each, 240. One row of black; all ne plus ultra high grade brass pins. Three sizes in book.
Price, per book.. 3c
Per dozen.....32c
If by mail, postage extra, per book, 1 cent.

No. 18C5049 Black Pins, bright round jet heads. Per box of 50... 2c
Per dozen boxes.....20c
If by mail, postage extra, per box, 1c.

No. 18C5051 Jet Black Mourning Pins, solid heads, assorted sizes; 200 in box. Price, per box.....3c
Per dozen boxes.....33c
If by mail, postage extra, per box, 2c.

Fancy Black and Colored Headed Pins.

No. 18C5053 Fancy Chromo Pins. Card contains 25 jet head black pins and 25 small fancy head black pins.
Price, per card.....3c
Per dozen cards.....33c
If by mail, postage extra, per card, 2c

No. 18C5055 Indestructible Fancy Pearl Head Toilet Pins, 1½ inches long. Come assorted 1 dozen on a card, three of each color: white, pink, turquoise blue and red. Price, per card, 4c
Per dozen cards.....42c
If by mail, postage extra, per card, 1c

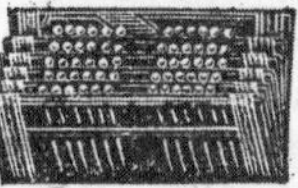

No. 18C5057 Toilet Pins. This is an entirely new pin, put up in neat book form, containing about 80 assorted colored head toilet pins. In white, turquoise, violet and other shades. A most useful accessory for ladies' dressing table.
Price, per book.....5c
Per dozen books.....55c
If by mail, postage extra, per book, 2c.

No. 18C5059 Stock Pins with large heads. Used for bouquet pins, waists, belts, etc. Very desirable and very much worn at present. These have a large, round head on a 2⅜-inch pin, head being made of imitation pearl, and colors, pink, light blue and gunmetal. Put up three on a card and are sold by the card only. One color only on a card.
Price, per card.....$0.09
Per dozen cards.....1.00
If by mail, postage extra, per card, 2c.

Pearl Stick Pins.

No. 18C5061 Indestructible Pearl Stick Pins, round or pear shaped heads, convenient and handy. Regular size, length, 1¼ inches.
Price, per gross, 40c; per dozen.. 4c
If by mail, postage extra, per doz., 3c.

No. 18C5062 Cube Pins. Assorted colors. Cube containing 100 pins, black, white and fancy colored heads.
Price, each.....4c
Per dozen.....43c
If by mail, postage extra, each, 3 cents.

No. 18C5063 White Pearl Head Toilet Pins. Cube like above containing 100 solid white head toilet pins.
Per dozen 55c; price, each.....5c
If by mail, postage extra, each, 3c.

No. 18C5065 Round Jet Hat Pins, made of best quality blued steel, good size head. Comes in three sizes, as follows:

Length, inches	6	7	8
Price, per dozen	2c	2½c	3c
Per gross	20c	25c	30c

If by mail, postage extra, per doz., 2c.

No. 18C5067 White Head Hat Pins, made of best quality blued steel, good sized head. **Comes in three sizes.**

Length, inches	6	7	8
Price, per dozen	2½c	3c	4c
Per gross	25c	30c	40c

If by mail, postage extra, per doz., 2c.

No. 18C5069 Imitation Cut Jet Hat Pin, made of best quality blued steel, with fine needle point and a large size, brightly finished head; good, serviceable hat pin. Comes in three sizes as follows:

Length, inches	6	7	8
Price, per dozen	5c	6c	7c

If by mail, postage extra, per doz., 2c.

No. 18C5070 Shawl or Belt Pins, large black heads, dull or bright finish, 3 inches long.
Price, per dozen......1c
Per gross......9c
If by mail, postage extra, per doz., 2c.

No. 18C5071 Trimming Pins. Dull or bright heads. Length, 2¼ inches.
Price, per dozen......1c
Per gross......9c
If by mail, postage extra, per doz., 2c.

Fancy Shaped Cut Jet Hat Pins.

No. 18C5073 Put up on fancy cabinets, assorted size heads. Eight to the cabinet. Price, per cabinet......5c
Per dozen cabinets......55c
By mail, postage extra, per cabinet, 2c.

Safety Pin Book.

The Safety Pins are the cheapest and best nickeled safety pin and the most practical, having the double sided shield.

No. 18C5075 Sensible Safety Pin Book contains two dozen small, medium and large assorted Sensible nickeled safety pins.
Price, per book......6c
Per dozen books......67c
By mail, postage extra, per book, 3c.

Sensible Safety Pins.

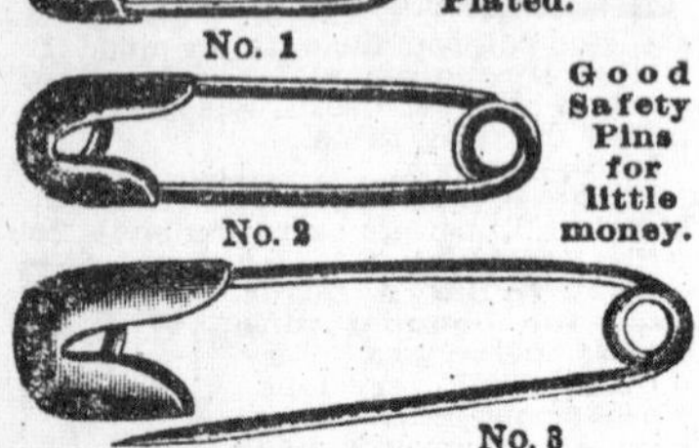

No. 1 — Highly Polished, Nickel Plated.
No. 2 — Good Safety Pins for little money.
No. 3

Illustrations Show Exact Sizes.

No. 18C5076 Polished Nickel Plated Safety Pins.

	No. 1	No. 2	No. 3
Price, per dozen	1c	2c	3c

If by mail, postage extra, per doz., 2c.

No. 18C5077 Black Japanned Safety Pins. Shields open both sides as above. Superior quality.

	No. 1	No. 2	No. 3
Price, per dozen	2c	2½c	3c
Per gross	21c	27c	33c

No. 18C5078 Large Safety Blanket Pins, 4 inches long; the most substantial and practical pin made.
Price, six for 16c; each......3c
If by mail, postage extra, each, 2c.

Corset Clasps.

No. 18C5079 Corset Clasps, reinforced, double steel; covered with corset jean; five hooks. Black, white or drab. Price, per dozen, 44c; per pair, 4c
If by mail, postage extra, per pair, 3c.

No. 18C5081 Four-Hook Corset Clasp, covered with a good quality of corset jean, reinforced double steel. Black, white or drab.
Price, per dozen, 44c; per pair......4c
If by mail, postage extra, per pair, 3c.

No. 18C5082 Fine French Sateen. Covered Corset Steels, in black, white or drab, five hooks.
Price, per dozen, 65c; per pair......6c
If by mail, postage extra, per pair, 3c.

No. 18C5083 Four-Hook French Sateen Covered Corset Steels, fine tempered steel. Black, white or drab.
Price, per dozen, 65c; per pair......6c
If by mail, postage extra, per pair 3c.

Corset Laces.

PAT. NO. 487,411. PAT. NO. 576,056.
Neverbreak
TRADE MARK.

No. 18C5085 The Neverbreak Corset Lace. Best lace made, will last as long as the corset, round cord, 2¼ yards long, white or black. Price, each......2c

No. 18C5086 The Neverbreak Corset Lace. Same as above, white or black, 3 yards long. Price, each......2c

No. 18C5087 Round Cotton Corset Laces, 2½ yards long, white or black.
Price, per dozen......5c

No. 18C5089 Round Cotton Corset Laces, 3 yards long, white or black.
Price, per dozen......6c

No. 18C5090 Cotton Elastic Corset Laces. Length, 2¼ yards; black or white. Price, per dozen......18c
If by mail, postage extra, per doz., 4c

For complete assortment of shoe laces see Shoe Department.

Key Ring and Chain.

No. 18C5093 Aluminum Key Chain and Steel Key Ring, light, strong and durable. Price, each......3c
Per dozen......33c
If by mail, postage extra, each, 2c.

Nickeled Tweezers.

No. 18C5094 Highly Polished Nickeled Tweezers, ear pick and hand cut nail file; regular 15-cent article.
Price, per dozen, 55c; each......5c
If by mail, postage extra, each, 2c.

Coat Collar Spring.

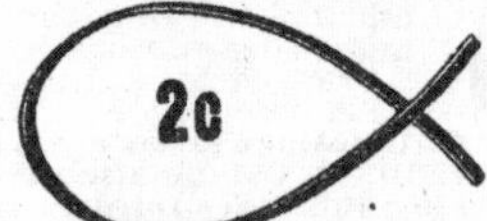

No. 18C5095 Patent Adjustable Coat Collar Spring, made of best oil tempered steel, formed to fit the under coat collar, retaining the shape and keeping coat lapels in place.
Price, each......$0.02
Per dozen.......19
Per gross......1.85
If by mail, postage extra, each, 2c.

Pants and Vest Buckles.

No. 18C5097 Duplex Pants Buckles, self adjustable, four strand, for vests and pants.
Price, per dozen, 50c; each......5c

No. 18C5092 Duplex Pants Buckles, 6 springs.
Price, per dozen, 65c; each......9c
Postage extra, each, 1c; per doz., 6c.

Plain Buckles.

No. 18C5098 Black or White Pants Buckles. Price, per gross......14c
By mail, postage extra, per gross, 13c

Pants Stretcher and Hanger.

No. 18C5100 The Set Well Trousers Stretcher and Pants Hanger. Makes wrinkled clothes smooth, cures baggy knees and keeps your trousers in shape. Made of best steel, heavily nickel plated. The best hanger on the market today.
Price, per dozen, $1.80; each......16c
If by mail, postage extra, each, 4c.

No. 18C5102 The Set Well Trousers Stretcher and Pants Hanger. (Set complete). Consists of 4 trousers hangers, 4 coat hangers, 2 shelf bars which will hold 4 garments, 1 door loop with screws and directions how to use. Made of best steel, heavily nickel plated. Shipping weight, 2¾ pounds.
Price, per set, complete......$0.88
Per dozen......10.00

No. 18C5103 Improved Suit and Trousers Hanger, made of seasoned hardwood, wax finish. Holds coat and vest in perfect shape, patent wood snaps for the pants, preserving the creasings. Also desirable for holding ladies' costumes. Will keep the skirt, waist or jacket in perfect shape. This hanger is simple and practical. Shipping weight, 16 ounces.
Price, per dozen, $1.10; each......10c

Every Woman Needs a Bust Figure.

No. 18C5111 French Model Low Bust Form. This bust is made of highest grade triple ply papier mache, covered with fast black jersey cloth. Sizes, 32, 34, 36, 38, 40, 42, 44 inches bust measure. Shipping weight, 5 pounds. Price......$1.50

No. 18C5114 High Bust Forms made of papier mache, covered with fast black jersey cloth. Strong and durable. Bust sizes, 32 to 40. Shipping weight, 5 pounds. Price......90c
Extra sizes, 42 and 44, will be 50 cents extra. Price......$1.40

No. 18C5115 The bust is made of the highest grade triple ply papier mache, covered with fast black jersey cloth. The skirt is carefully constructed from heavy plated wire, all the joints being double tied and soldered. The stand is very strong, neatly japanned and mounted on casters. The form can be raised and lowered to suit any desired skirt length. Made in sizes 30, 32, 34, 36, 38 and 40 inches bust measure. Price......$2.75
Sizes 42 and 44. Price......3.25
Shipping weight, 18 pounds.

The Perfect Dressmaking System.

No. 18C5117 The most perfect, the most simple and the most satisfactory dressmaking system in the world. This complete Dressmaking and Tailoring System is the only accurate, self teaching system by which perfect fitting garments can be cut. A complete line of measurements for perfect forms and extra measurements for imperfect forms are given. The system is put up in separate sections, a separate part used for cutting each part of the dress. This makes it so simple that it can be self taught at home. Even a child can master it in a very short time. The system drafts perfectly on the lining and every seam by accurate measurements, thus doing away with all pattern cutting and refitting, making it a great time saver, a point that will be especially appreciated by dressmakers who have a lot of cutting to do. This system combines the advantageous qualities of being able to cut ladies', misses' and children's dresses.

Included with this system is a complete instruction book, showing how to measure a full size form, so as to get the correct measurements. If our instructions are followed, one cannot help but meet with success. This system has never before been offered for less than $5.00, but by an advantageous contract and buying in very large quantities, we are able to offer this system at the extremely low price which we quote. **Canvassers and agents will find this a very profitable and quick selling item to handle. Please note,** if you do not find this system all that we claim for it and well worth $5.00, at which price it is sold throughout the country, you are at liberty to return same to us, and we will cheerfully refund your money, paying transportation charges both ways. **Remember,** the price which we quote is for this complete dressmaking and tailor system, including miniature infant chart for cutting doll garments, also a book of instructions, which explains fully the key to the chart. This system is easily mastered and never forgotten, as we use the A B C method.
Price, per dozen, $14.25; each, $1.25
If by mail, postage extra, each, 30c.

No. 18C5118 Bias Seam Tape is in big demand. Made of fine quality lawn. Used on all white wear, for finishing headings and binding of seams, also for fagoting on neckwear, waists, etc. Comes in white, black, pink, light blue, in four widths. Put up 12 yards to the piece.

Width, inches	¼	⅜	⅝	½
Price, per piece, 12 yards	5c	6c	7c	8c
Price, per dozen pieces	55c	70c	80c	90c

Postage extra, per piece, 2 cents.

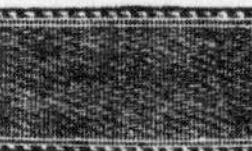

No. 18C5119 Double Silk Serge Belting, used by all the principal dressmakers for inside of waists. This is a very fine quality. Comes in two widths. In white, black, pink, light blue, brown or gray.

Width, inches	⅞	1¼
Price, per yard	6c	8c
Price, per piece, 10 yards	55c	75c

Postage extra, per yard, 2 cents.

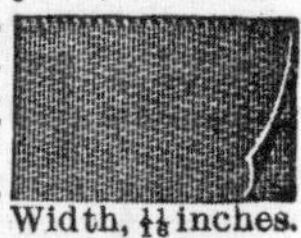

No. 18C5121 The Taunton Shaped Dress Bandings in Mohair. Used for bands for ladies' skirts, guarantees a perfect shape and fit. Width, 1⅛ inches. Colors, black, white, brown or gray.
Price, per yard......3c
Per dozen yards......33c
Postage extra, per yard, 1c.

No. 18C5123 The Taunton Shaped Dress Bandings in Silk. Used for belts of ladies' skirts, insuring a perfect shape and fit. This is becoming a very essential item with all dressmakers. Width double, 1⅛ inches. Colors, black, white, brown, gray or navy.
Price, per yard......5c
Per dozen yards......55c
Postage extra, per yard, 1c.

Skirt Bindings of All Kinds.

No. 18C5125 Bias Velveteen Skirt Binding by the yard. The most economical way to buy it; order any quantity you need; 2 inches wide; black and all colors. Price, per dozen yards, 32c; per yard......3c
Postage extra, per yard, 1c.

Brush Braid.

No. 18C5127 S., R. & Co.'s Brush Braid and Skirt Protector. We guarantee this braid all wool, heavier than other makes and the best at any price. Colors, black, brown, myrtle, navy, royal blue, tan, cardinal, wine or drab.
Price, per doz. yds., 44c; per yd., 4c
Postage extra, per yard, 1c.

No. 18C5129 Vellbraid. The only perfect braid for unlined skirts. A mohair skirt braid with a velvet edge. Protects the shoes. Will outwear four ordinary braids. This combines the regular skirt braid with a small velvet edge, easily applied, and is by far the best skirt braid now in use. Black and all colors. This braid is retailed in all the leading stores at 10 cents per yard. Comes put up in five-yard pieces. Price, per dozen pieces, $3.50; per piece......30c
If by mail, postage extra, per piece, 5c.

No. 18C5138 Crescent Mohair Skirt Binding, steam shrunk; dyed in the wool; ready to use; put up in full 5-yard pieces, enough for a skirt. Colors, black, white, brown, navy, tan, gray, red or green.
Price, per piece......$0.09
Per dozen pieces......1.00
By mail, postage extra, per piece, 3c.

Corticelli Skirt Braid.

No. 18C5140 Corticelli Skirt Braid. Unexcelled for durability. Width, ¼-inch; 3 yards in a roll. All staple colors. Warranted fast color.
Price, per roll......4c
Per dozen rolls......38c
If by mail, postage extra, per roll, 2c.

Cotton Tape, Black or White.

No. 18C5144 Cotton Tape, in black or white. Comes 3 yards to the piece.

No.	4	6	8	10	12	16
Width, in.	⅛	⅛	¼	⅜	⅜	½
Price, roll	1c	1c	1½c	1½c	2c	2c
Doz. rolls	10c	10c	15c	15c	20c	20c

Postage extra, per dozen rolls, 4c.

No. 18C5148 Extra Super White Cotton Tape. Comes about 3½ to 4 yards to the roll, in white or black only.

Width, inch	¼	⅜	½	⅝	¾
Price, per roll	2c	2c	3c	3c	4c
Per dozen rolls	20c	20c	30c	30c	42c

Postage extra, per dozen rolls, 4c.

Seam Binding.

No. 18C5149 Silk Seam Binding. All colors, 8 yards to the piece.
Price, per piece..........7c
Per dozen pieces..........80c
Postage extra, per dozen pieces, 4c.

No. 18C5150 The Many Waist Shield. One pair takes the place of 12 pairs of ordinary shields. These shields are worn under the corset cover, being a protection to the garment as well as to the waist. They do not have to be sewed into the waist, and one pair will do for all your waists. The Many Waist Shield is interlined with a new odorless tissue (not rubber) and every pair is guaranteed waterproof. They can be washed many times in cold water. The Many Waist Shields are the lightest shields made, and are the only shields that can be worn without being visible through a thin waist. Come in the following sizes for bust measures:

Bust measures	30-34	34-36	36-38	38-42
Sizes, No.......	2	3	4	5

Price, each..........50c
If by mail, postage extra, 5 cents.

Ladies' Ventilated Dress and Corset Protector.

No. 18C5152 Ladies' Ventilated Dress and Corset Protector. Does away with the inconvenience of sewing in and taking out dress shields. A complete garment to be worn under the corset, protecting that garment as well as the waist from perspiration. May be easily removed and washed, being adjustable. One pair of protectors will take the place of a dozen pairs of the regular dress shields. Order by sizes as follows:
No. 3 can be adjusted for bust measures 28 to 33.
No. 4 can be adjusted for bust measures 34 to 39.
No. 5 can be adjusted for bust measures 40 to 46.
Price, per pair..........$0.75
Per dozen pairs..........8.75
If by mail, postage extra, per pair, 5c.

Ladies' Dress Shields.

No. 18C5156 Stockinet Dress Shields. Good shields for a little money. Size 2 Small 3 Medium 4 Large
Price, per pair, 5c 6c 7c
Per dozen pairs, 55c 65c 75c
If by mail, postage extra, per pair, 2c.

Kleinert's Dress Shields.

No. 18C5160 Kleinert's Seamless Stockinet Dress Shields. Every pair warranted. Kleinert pays for the dress if it is ruined by perspiration while his shields are used in it, and Kleinert is responsible for what he says.

Size, No........	2	3	4
Price, per pair,	$0.13	$0.15	$0.17
Per doz. pairs,	1.40	1.70	1.95

If by mail, postage extra, per pair, 2c.

The Gem Dress Shield.

No. 18C5164 The Gem Pure Rubber Dress Shield. Kleinert pays for the dress if it is ruined by perspiration if his shields are used in it.

Size, No........	2	3	4
Price, per pair,	$0.12	$0.14	$0.16
Per doz. pairs,	1.38	1.60	1.75

Postage, per pair, 2c.

Featherweight Dress Shield.

No. 18C5168 Featherweight Fine Nainsook Dress Shield.

Size, No........	2	3	4
Price, per pair...	$0.12	$0.13	$0.15
Per dozen pairs..	1.39	1.45	1.65

If by mail, postage extra, per pair, 2c.

Alpha Dress Shields.

No. 18C5178 The Alpha Ventilating Dress Shields, light but substantial, pure para rubber, absolutely odorless, can be washed and retain their fluted shape. Every lady wonders how she stood the old style, thick, plasterlike, odor creating shields when she has used the Alpha.

Sizes.	2	3	4
Price, per pair...	$0.14	$0.16	$0.19
Per dozen pairs.	1.60	1.75	2.15

If by mail, postage extra, per pair, 2c.

S. H. & M. Detachable Dress Shields.

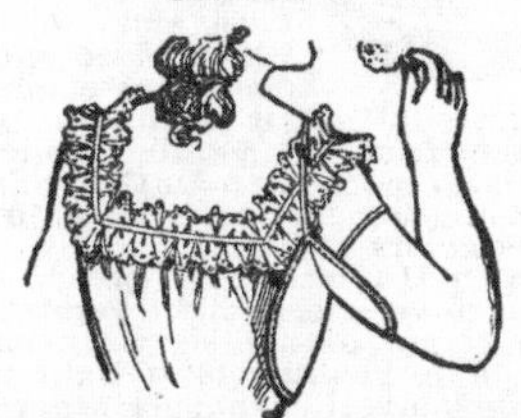

No. 18C5173 The S. H. & M. Light Weight Dress Shield. Especially adapted for shirt waists. Made of light, strong, waterproof nainsook, adjustable, washable, requires no sewing, most perfect fitting dress shield made, clings to the arm and does not wrinkle, comes in three sizes.

Size..........	2	3	4
Price, per pair...	$0.20	$0.23	$0.25
Per dozen pairs.	2.25	2.50	2.75

If by mail, postage extra, per pair, 2c.

Hooks and Eyes.

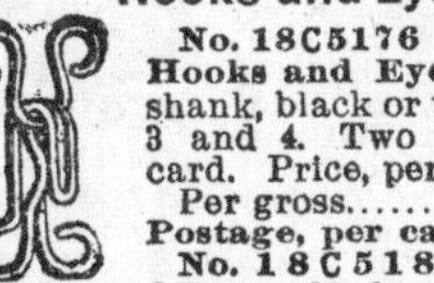

No. 18C5176 Swan Bill Hooks and Eyes. Straight shank, black or white. Nos. 3 and 4. Two dozen on a card. Price, per card.....1c
Per gross..........5c
Postage, per card, 2 cents.

No. 18C5180 Hump Hooks and Eyes. Made of brass, japanned or silvered. Strong and durable and a hook and eye that we guarantee to our trade. Put up two dozen on a card. Sizes, Nos. 3 and 4.
Price, per card of two dozen......2c
Per gross, six cards..........10c
If by mail, postage extra, per card, 2c

No. 18C5182 Peet's Invisible Eye, takes the place of silk loops. Invisible eye, making a flat seam, prevents gaping. Indispensable to every dress; takes the place of silk loops, which have always been a source of annoyance by their continual breaking. Being raised in the center, can always be found and thereby saves the dress from holes. Used and indorsed by all leading dressmakers. Colors, black or white. Put up two dozen hooks and two dozen eyes of one size to the package. Price, per two dozen......8c
Per gross..........44c
If by mail, postage extra, per card, 2c.

No. 18C5183 Dainte Invisible Eye. To take the place of silk loops. We have them put up under our own brand which enables us to sell them at a reduced price. In sizes, small, medium or large. Colors, black or white.
Price for two dozen eyes and two dozen hooks..........5c
Per gross..........27c
If by mail, postage extra, per card, 2c

No. 18C5190 Bent Bill Hook and Eye for cloaks. Japanned or silvered. Comes in two sizes.
Medium large, per dozen..........3c
Medium large, per gross..........30c
Large, per dozen..........4c
Large, per gross..........40c

No. 18C5191 This card contains two dozen hooks and eyes, six placket fasteners and one dozen invisible eyes. New, perfect hook and eye, invisible loop eyes and snap placket fasteners. These are the Oscar A. De Long hooks and eyes and the best quality loop and snap fasteners. Entire outfit carded as per illustration. Colors, black or white. Sizes, 2, 3 and 4.
Price, per card..........8c
If by mail, postage extra, per card, 2c.

Special Hook and Eye.

No. 18C5192 The Special Hook and Eye (with a perfect hump). Made of best brass wire, highly finished, silvered or japanned; equal to the advertised brands which are sold at two or three times the cost of this hook, the best hook and eye made. Sizes, 2, 3 and 4. Price, per card, two dozen on a card..........3c
Per gross..........14c
If by mail, postage extra, per card, 2c.

Featherbone.

Featherbone is used in collars, revers, dress waists or any part of a gown where stiffening is required.

No. 18C5193 Featherbone Piping Bone, made from quills, cotton covered, used for distending skirt ruffles, etc. Colors, black, white or drab.
Price, per yard..........2½c
Per dozen yards..........24c
If by mail, postage extra, per yard, 1c.

No. 18C5194 Twill Covered Featherbone. The standard grade herringbone pattern, made from quills. A light, pliable elastic bone, for use in dresses, waists and corsets. Used by the best dressmakers in preference to whalebone. Colors, black, white or drab. Price, per yard..........5c
Per dozen yards..........58c
If by mail, postage extra, per yard, 1c.

No. 18C5195½ Double Cord Skirt Bone is used in collars, revers and in the bottom of petticoats and drop linings. Black, white or slate.
Price, per yard..........5c
Per dozen yards..........55c
If by mail, postage extra, per yard, 1c.

Twin Dress Stays.

No. 18C5196 Made of two fine twin spring steels in a two-pocket woven webbing. Colors, cardinal, pink, blue, brown, drab, white or black.
Price, per set (nine in set)..........4c
Per dozen sets..........45c
If by mail, postage extra, per set, 2c.

The Ever Ready Dress Stay.

EVER READY DRESS STAY

No. 18C5208 The Ever Ready Dress Stay. The best covered dress stay made. Endorsed by the leading dressmakers. Best tempered steel and rubber lined, covered with silk finish sateen. Guaranteed not to rust or work through. Colors, cardinal, pink, blue, lavender, slate, brown, black or white.
Price, per set (nine in set)..........$0.09
Per dozen..........1.00
If by mail, postage extra, per set, 2c.

Ever Ready Mending Tissue.

No. 18C5220 The Ever Ready Mending Tissue. Mends perfectly rips or tears in gloves, clothing and fabrics of all kinds, takes less time and accomplishes the purpose better than sewing. Size, 30 inches long by 2½ inches wide.
Price, per dozen, 14c; per sheet..........4c
If by mail, postage extra, per sheet, 2c.

Notta Hook Fastener.

No. 18C5221 The Notta Hook Garment Fastener. Similar to the ball and socket, but far superior in every respect. Adapted for every purpose for the skirt, for the shirt waist, for the collar. It is so easy to fasten and is so hard to become unfastened. Try it once and you will use them always. Come in three sizes, for skirt, waist and collar. **Mention size wanted.** Colors, black or white, for all sizes.
Price, per dozen..........$0.10
Per gross..........1.00
If by mail, postage extra, 2 cents.

Ball and Socket Fastener.

No. 18C5224 This Invisible Sew-on Ball and Socket Fastener, used instead of hooks and eyes, and especially adapted for fastening skirts, shirt waists, etc.; no chance to catch or tear. Silvered or japanned. Price, per dozen..........5c
Per gross..........58c
If by mail, postage extra, per doz., 2c

No. 18C5225 Ball and Socket Fastener, small size, used for collars, waists, etc. Same style as above.
Price, per dozen..........5c
Per gross..........58c

Notta Hook Skirt Supporter.

SO SIMPLE, SO SECURE, YET SO NEAT.

No. 18C5227 Notta Hook Skirt Supporter. The best yet. Securely holds the lightest or the heaviest skirt. Easy and simple. Lays flat to the waist. Sold by the set. Consists of supporters for four waists and two skirts. Price, for set..........$0.20
Per dozen..........2.00
If by mail, postage extra, 2 cents.

Hold-Fast Skirt Supporter.

No. 18C5235 Hold-Fast Skirt Supporter and Waist Holder. The simplest and most effective article of its kind ever known. It is absolutely self-adjusting, does not require any hooks, buttons or anything else to be sewed to the skirt or waist. Your skirt and waist will never slip with the Hold-Fast belt. This supporter is even more useful in winter than in summer, as the under row of pins in the back plate can be used for the heavy silk petticoats and the upper row for the skirt, thus taking all the weight from the waist.

When ordering give your waist measure. Price for set..........22c
If by mail, postage extra, 2c.

Ladies' Ideal Skirt and Waist Supporter.

No. 18C5237 The Ladies' Ideal Skirt and Waist Supporter with attachments for three skirts, made of German silver and will not rust or soil the finest fabric, holds skirt together without the use of hooks or eyes. This support is desirable for basques as well as shirt waists, will support the heaviest skirt and will carry the weight from the shoulder instead of on the waist line. Set complete with attachments for three skirts. Per doz., $1.10; each.....10c
If by mail, postage extra, each, 3 cents.

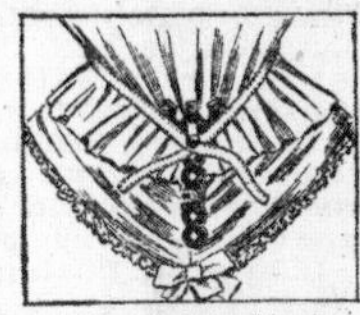

No. 18C5239 The Rosalind Long Waist Adjuster and Skirt Supporter. The only adjuster on the market that will hold a leather belt securely in position with the V-shaped long waist. Any kind of a belt can be used. This adjuster does away absolutely with all pulling of shirt waists; belt and skirt can be adjusted in a minute. Comes in brass, oxidized and nickel. Price..........22c
If by mail, postage extra, 2 cents.

Sewing Silk and Twist.

Corticelli silk is warranted full size and full length. Black spool silks are marked OO, O, A, B, C and D. No. OO is the finest, No. O is next coarser, etc. Colored spool silks come in letter A only.

Corticelli Sewing Silk.

No. 18C5244 Corticelli Sewing Silk, 50-yard spools, black, white and all colors.
Price, per spool..........4c
Per doz. 43c

No. 18C5248 Corticelli Sewing Silk, 100-yard spools, black, white and all colors.
Price, per dozen, 85c; per spool..8c

No. 18C5252 Corticelli Buttonhole Twist, 10-yard spools, black, white and all colors. Price, per spool..........2c
Per box of 25 spools..........43c

The Corticelli Embroidery and Wash Silks are far superior in finish, smoothness and delicate shading to any silk on the market. Needleworkers find real satisfaction in every way by the use of the Corticelli wash silks.

Corticelli Embroidery Silk on Spools.

No. 18C5256 Corticelli Embroidery Silk, on spools, 3 yards, size EE, all colors. Price, per dozen, only..........3c
If by mail, postage extra, per doz., 3c.

No. 18C5260 Corticelli Etching Silk, size 500, positively a fast dye silk, medium size for outlining work and etching; 10 yards to the skein.
Per oz., 50 skeins, 85c; per skein..2c

No. 18C5264 Corticelli Twisted Embroidery Silk. Size EE. This size is the regular wash embroidery silk; fast color, pure dye, 10 yards in skein. For list of colors see color card **No. 18C5284.**

Per oz., 32 skeins, **85c**; per skein.. **3c**

No. 18C5268 Corticelli Rope Embroidery Silk. Washing colors. A coarse silk, for bold designs either in outline or solid embroidery on heavy material, when rapid work is desired. For list of colors see color card **No. 18C5284.**

Per oz., 32 skeins, **85c**; per skein,.. **3c**

No. 18C5272 Corticelli Filo Floss. This is a fine size, slack twist wash silk and is used for embroidery purposes of all kinds, but is especially desirable for embroidering on stamped linens, centerpieces, doilies, etc. Comes in black, white and over 360 colors. **See color card No. 18C5284.**

Per oz., 32 skeins, **85c**; per skein, **3c**

No. 18C5273 Corticelli Persian Floss. A silk of two strands, loosely twisted and of high luster. It is now very popular for finishing the edges of doilies and centerpieces. Persian floss is made in colors 880 to 887. See color card **No. 18C5284.**

Price, per skein........................ **3c**
Per ounce, 32 skeins..................... **85c**

No. 18C5274 Corticelli Roman Floss, somewhat coarser than Persian floss and intended for embroidering larger designs on heavier material. Curtains, counterpanes and cushions are worked with this silk. For list of colors see color card **No. 18C5284.** Price, per skein......... **3c**
Per ounce, 32 skeins..................... **85c**

Corticelli Waste Embroidery.

No. 18C5276 Corticelli Waste Embroidery Silk, assorted colors, odds and ends. Just the thing for fancy work. One ounce in package.

Price, per package **30c**

No. 18C5280 Corticelli Knitting or Crochet Silk. In black, white or colors. Made of highest grade selected raw silk. We can furnish in two sizes: No. 300, which contains 150 yards to the ½-ounce ball, is used mostly and is a rather coarse thread. No. 500, which contains 250 yards to the ½-ounce ball, **is finer and is used for knitting mittens, stockings and other articles that require washing.** Comes in black and colors. Price, per ball.......... **33c**
If by mail, postage extra, 2 cents.

No. 18C5281 Corticelli Purse Twist, for working new bead chatelaine bags and belts, ½ ounce on spool.

Price, per spool....................... **40c**

No. 18C5282 This very clever invention for holding embroidery silks will save you five-fold the cost by saving your silks and loss of time and irritation. This is an eight leaf book and holds fifty-six skeins of silk. You can select one single thread at a time without tangling balance. Saves every thread, where before you wasted half, and keeps them clean and fresh with all the colors arranged in plain view. Bound in an artistic cover. Every lady should have one.

Price.................................. **28c**
If by mail, postage extra, 4 cents.

Interesting to all Needle-workers.

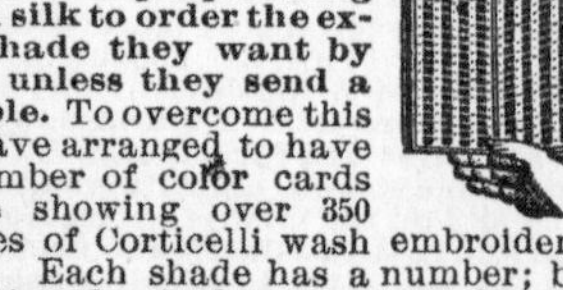

No. 18C5284 It is very difficult for people using wash silk to order the exact shade they want by mail unless they send a sample. To overcome this we have arranged to have a number of color cards made showing over 350 shades of Corticelli wash embroidery silks. Each shade has a number; by selecting the shade you want and sending us the number, **you are sure to get just what you want.** We have also issued **"a flower book"** describing 70 flowers and how to embroider them.

Price for the two books............... **5c**
If by mail, postage extra, 3 cents.

Always write the catalogue number in full, see that your order checks up correctly and that your name, address and shipping directions are given.

Boas Ideal Silk Cord Machine Thread per Spool 3¼ Cents; per Dozen, 38 Cents.

No. 18C5285 The Boas Ideal Six Cord Spool Cotton for fine hand and machine sewing. 200 yards on each spool. We recommend this Boas Ideal as the best, strongest and smoothest thread made. The Boas Ideal Spool Cotton, which is made from the finest selected cotton, we have carefully tested and tried and we guarantee it not to kink or snarl in hand sewing and it is absolute perfection in itself on any kind of a sewing machine. It will stand 100 per cent more friction and wear longer than any of the other well known brands of thread. It is without an equal for stitching buttonholes and sewing on buttons, often outlasting the garment. We recommend and guarantee the Boas Ideal Six Cord Spool Cotton. Comes in black and white in Nos. 8 to 100. Staple colors in No. 50 only. The regular established price of the Boas Ideal Six Cord Spool Cotton is 5 cents. Selling, as we do, all merchandise at greatly reduced prices, our price will be, per dozen, **38c**; per spool..................... **3¼c**

We Recommend This Thread.

No. 18C5287 "Klostersilk" This is a 100-yard machine thread. Mercerized thread is as good as the best sewing silk and no more expensive than ordinary cotton. Recommended to the trade for its high luster, even of spin, twist and uniform strength; is pure dye, fast color and guaranteed not to fade or lose its luster with age or after application of press iron. Its life is longer than that of ordinary sewing silk, being treated with a chemical bath that makes it proof against rotting. Made in black, white and all silk shades. **In size letter "A" only.**

Price, per spool........................ **2½c**
Per dozen spools......................... **27c**
Postage extra, per spool 2 cents.

The American Thread Company's "Best" Spool Cotton, 46 Cents per Dozen.

No. 18C5288 The American Thread Company's "Best" Spool Cotton is a double spun six-cord machine thread, a standard and satisfactory thread. White and black in Nos. 8 to 100. Staple colors in No. 50 only. Price, per spool.......... **4c**
Per dozen.............................. **46c**

Spool Cotton.

No. 18C5292 The New York Mills Basting Cotton (200 yards on each spool), a very superior cotton; the retail merchant gets 24 to 36 cents per dozen for these goods. Nos. 30 to 60 only; black or white, no colors.

Price, per dozen spools............ **14c**
Shipping weight, per dozen, 12 ozs.

J. O. King Machine Thread.

No. 18C5296 The J. O. King Machine Spool Thread; nice and smooth, **will run on any machine.** Full length, 200 yards on each spool. Made from the best of selected cotton yarns, black and white. Black made in numbers from 8 to 60, white made in numbers from 8 to 70; colors in No. 50 only. **Retail merchants ask 4 cents per spool for thread that in many cases is not as good.**

Price, per doz., **20c**; per spool.... **1¾c**
Shipping weight, per dozen, 12 ozs

500-Yard Dixie Spool Cotton.

No. 18C5298 Dixie Three-Cord Spool Cotton. This is a large 500-yard spool, full measure and splendid thread for ordinary sewing and machine work. Nos. 30, 40, 50, 60 and 70. Colors, black or white.

Price, per dozen, **45c**; per spool.. **4c**
Postage extra, per dozen, 10 cents.

Monarch Thread.

No. 18C5302 Monarch Thread. This thread has a linen finish and is especially adapted for sewing carpets, buttons, etc. Equally as strong as linen, but sews smoother and looks better. 100-yard spools. Comes in the following colors: Black, white, brown, cardinal, myrtle or drab. Numbers in black and white from 25 to 40. Colors come only in No. 30. Price, per dozen, **35c**; each.. **3c**
If by mail, postage extra, per dozen, 10 cents.

Barbour's Linen Thread.

No. 18C5308 Barbour's (200-yard spools) Best Linen Thread. Numbers run from No. 25 (coarse) to No. 100 (fine). Colors, black, white, drab or whitish brown. Price, per spool.... **7c**

No. 18C5312 Carpet Thread, black brown, green, red, drab, slate or staple colors.

Price, per ¼ pound (10 skeins).... **17c**

Mercerized Crochet Cotton.

The very best quality put up, 83⅓ yards to the spool, 12 spools to box. Fast and lustrous dye, sold everywhere at 5 cents a spool.

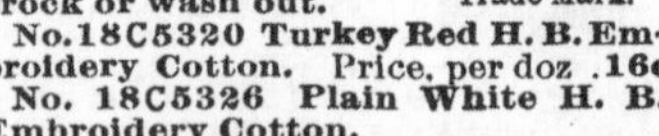

No. 18C5316 Mercerized Crochet Cotton. The latest article for crocheting and embroidering. This is a cotton thread with a soft twist and a silk finish, and so closely does it resemble the crochet silk that it is difficult to distinguish from the genuine, while the cost is no more than for the ordinary crochet cotton. Comes in plain and shaded colors, as follows:

Plain Colors—Nile green, moss green, olive green, light yellow, medium yellow, orange, scarlet, crimson, light blue, medium blue, light pink, medium pink, lilac, purple, tan, white, cream or black.

Shaded Colors— White, blue and pink; white and yellow; white, green and pink; white and moss green; white and pink; white and blue; white and lilac; white and nile green. Sold by all dealers at 4c and 5c a spool.

Price, per dozen, **28c**; per spool.. **2½c**
Postage extra, per spool, 1 cent.

H. B. Embroidery Cotton.

H. B. Embroidery Cotton on spools; plain, solid colors, turkey red, black or white; three colors only. Nos. 8, 10, 12, 14, 16, 18, 20, 22, 24. Sold only by dozen. **Will not crock or wash out.**

Trade Mark.

No. 18C5320 Turkey Red H. B. Embroidery Cotton. Price, per doz. **16c**

No. 18C5326 Plain White H. B. Embroidery Cotton.

Price, per dozen.................... **16c**

Ideal Turkey Red Embroidery Cotton.

No. 18C5330 Turkey Red Ideal Embroidery Cotton. This is an absolutely fast dyed embroidery cotton; will not fade or wash out, and one of the best qualities made. We have this put up to sell at a special price. Comes in Nos. 8, 10, 12, 14, 16 and 18.

Price, per dozen.................... **12c**
If by mail, postage extra, per dozen, 4 cents.

Knitting and Darning Cotton.

No. 18C5332 Crown White Knitting Cotton Best quality, 4-thread put up 10 balls to the pound and 2 pounds to the box. Nos. 6 to 24.

Price, per dozen, **40c**; per ball... **3½c**

No. 18C5336 Navy Blue Knitting Cotton. Same quality as above, Nos. 8 to 16. Price, per ball........... **3½c**
Per dozen............................ **40c**

No. 18C5340 Blue and White Mixed Knitting Cotton. Same quality as above. Nos. 8 to 16.

Price, per dozen, **40c**; per ball. **3½c**
If by mail, postage extra, per ball, 3c.

Darning Cotton.

No. 18C5344 Best Fast Black Darning Cotton. Diagonally wound, 34 yards on a spool. Absolutely fast color; will stand washing and boiling. Also comes in brown, tan or gray.

Price, per dozen, **15c**; per spool. **1½c**
If by mail, postage extra, each, 2c.

No. 18C5348 Darning Cotton, on cards. Colors, black, white, brown or tan. Price, per gross, **55c**; per doz.. **5c**

No. 18C5352 Victoria Cashmere Mending Yarn. Manufactured from the very highest grade of scoured wool. Once tried, you will use no other. Colors, brown, navy, tan, gray, black or white. Price, per card.. **1½c**
Per dozen............................ **15c**
If by mail, postage extra, per doz., 6c.

PIPES

WE BEG TO CALL SPECIAL ATTENTION to our very complete line of pipes. Our assortment is complete and our prices are below any kind of competition. SEND US YOUR ORDER FOR A PIPE with the understanding that if it is not entirely satisfactory in every way, by far better value than you could get elsewhere, you are at liberty to return it to us at our expense and we will immediately refund your money.

Orders from dealers solicited.

Selected Corncob Pipe.

No. 18C5454 Fine Selected Corncob Pipe, extra large size bowl, finely polished reed stems, a regular 5-cent article.

Price, per dozen, **20c**; each......... **2c**
If by mail, postage extra, each, 2c.

The Rough Rider.

No. 18C5458 Fine Wood Pipe, bulldog shape, rubber bit and silvered band. The Rough Rider is an excellent smoker. Price, each........ **$0.09**
Per dozen............................ **1.00**
If by mail, postage extra, each, 3c.

Elegant Brier Pipe, 14 Cents.

No. 18C5462 Very Elegant Brier Pipe, a medium size, 5½ inches long with polished hard **rubber stem and nickel band.**

Price, per dozen, **$1.50**; each.... **14c**
If by mail, postage extra, each, 3c.

Our 19-Cent Chip Meerschaum.

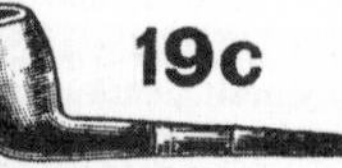

No. 18C5466 Chip Meerschaum Pipe, medium size, handsomely nickel mounted. **Chinese amber mouthpiece,** good sized bowl.

Price, per dozen, **$2.00**; each.. **19c**
If by mail, postage extra, each, 3c.

Students' Bulldog Pipe.

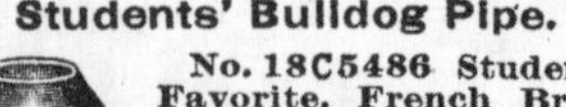

No. 18C5486 Students' Favorite, French Brier, English bulldog shape, handsome **Chinese amber** bit, 2¼ inches long, square nickel ferrule. Full size, very handsomely finished.

Price, per dozen, **$1.75**; each.. **16c**
If by mail, postage extra, each, 4c.

Morgan Shape.

No. 18C5487 French Brier Pipe, Morgan shape, with best vulcanized rubber shove bit. A fine nickel band on stem, holding inside an absorbent paper cartridge, which effectually absorbs the nicotine. Length of pipe, 5 inches.

Price, per dozen, **$2.25**; each.. **21c**
If by mail, postage extra, 6 cents.

No. 18C5489 Extra Cartridges to replace used cartridges in above pipe. Box of 10. Price, per box.......... **2c**
If by mail, postage extra, 3 cents.

22 Cents for a Self Cleaner.

No. 18C5470 Genuine French Brier English Bulldog Pipe. Handsome Vienna amber mouthpiece. Length, 5¼ inches, long self cleaner, handsome nickel band, finely made and finished. Price, each....$0.22
Per dozen.... 2.25
If by mail, postage extra, each, 3c.

The New Ring Pipe.

For a Cool Smoke and to Prevent the Nicotine from Passing into the Mouth.

No. 18C5474 Genuine Brier Bowl, with imitation amber mouthpiece, and having the latest invention ring attachment. Tobacco in pipe is always kept dry, insuring a sweet, cool smoke. Easily cleaned. **A boon for smokers.** Price, per dozen, $4.25; each....38c
If by mail, postage extra, each, 5c.

Dublin Shape.

19c

No. 18C5490 French Brier Pipe, straight stem, Dublin shape bowl, 2-inch imitation amber mouthpiece. For a good smoke in a good pipe, buy this. Price, each....$0.19
Per dozen.... 2.15
If by mail, postage extra, each, 5c.

Handsome Brier Pipe, Bulldog Shape.

20c

No. 18C5494 Fine Brier Pipe, bulldog shape, with Chinese amber shove bit, plain nickel band, a very handsome pipe which we recommend very highly. Price, each....$0.20
Per dozen.... 2.25
If by mail, postage extra, each, 4c.

French Brier, 25 Cents.

25c

No. 18C5498 For a long, cool smoke, we recommend this **French Brier Pipe,** made of highly stained dark polished French brier, with long, slender stem, amberite mouthpiece and bulldog shaped bowl. Total length of pipe, 6 inches. Price, each....$0.25
Per dozen.... 2.75
If by mail, postage extra, each, 4c.

Bent Brier, 25 Cents.

No. 18C5510 Large Size Bent Brier Pipe, with rubber stem; fine covered nickel top; **for a fine, lasting smoke this pipe cannot be excelled.** Price, each....$0.25
Per dozen.... 2.85
If by mail, postage extra, each, 3c.

25c

Straight French Brier.

29c

No. 18C5514 Straight French Brier Pipe, highly polished bowl, **round stem,** has a 2½-inch Chinese amber mouthpiece or stem, and a pipe that we can highly recommend. Price, each....$0.29
Per dozen.... 3.25
If by mail, postage extra, each, 5c.

Our 30-Cent Leader.

30c

No. 18C5518 French Brier Pipe, highly polished dark brier, heavy bulldog pattern bowl, has 3½-inch horn mouthpiece with fancy nickel band; total length of pipe, 6¼ inches; a substantial and sightly pipe. Price, per dozen, $3.40; each....30c
If by mail, postage extra, each, 5c.

An Old Favorite.

24c

No. 18C5522 Handsomely Carved Brier Bowl, cherry stem, 3 inches long, and rubber mouthpiece; entire length of pipe 7 inches. **A pipe that is easily cleaned and kept in order and always gives satisfaction.**
Price, per dozen, $2.70; each..24c
If by mail, postage extra, each, 9c

Fancy Brier Pipes.

Easily Cleaned.

No. 18C5526 The Always Clean Brier Bowl, long rubber stem, nicotine absorber, handsomely decorated cover; a pipe that can be taken apart in four pieces, and usually retails for $1.00.

26c

Price, per dozen, $3.00; each....26c
If by mail, postage extra, each, 7c.

Yale Student Shape.

No. 18C5530 Yale Student Pipe, is a heavy brier pipe with bent Chinese amber bit, heavy bull bitch shape. A fit companion for the millionaire, but at a price within reach of all.

39c

Price, per dozen, $4.25; each....39c
If by mail, postage extra, each, 4c.

French Brier.

No. 18C5534 This splendid smoker is a French Brier, Bulldog Shape Bowl, with amberoid mouthpiece; the stem between bowl and mouthpiece is genuine Weichsel wood, and will not burn your tongue; worth 75 cents in the regular pipe stores.

25c

Price, per dozen, $2.75; each....25c
If by mail, postage extra, each, 5c.

Genuine French Brier Pipes.

48c

No. 18C5545 Genuine French Brier Pipe, highly polished, dark finish, bulldog shape, with 1¾-inch genuine amber straight stem. Length of pipe 5 inches. 75-cent value.
Price, per dozen, $5.50; each....48c
If by mail, postage extra, each, 7c.

Extra Value.

No. 18C5547 Genuine French Brier Pipe, highly polished, dark finish with 3-inch genuine amber straight stem. This is the bulldog shape. Length of pipe, 6¼ inches. Worth $1.50.
Price, each....$0.95
Per dozen.... 11.00
Postage extra, each, 7c.

German Porcelain Pipes.

German Favorite.

No. 18C5549 German Porcelain Pipe, handsomely decorated; **just the thing for a good old fashioned smoke. This is an exceptionally fine and handsome German Porcelain Pipe.** Made with very fine long stem, fitted with flexible top and extra fine hard rubber mouthpiece. Long, genuine porcelain bowl artistically and handsomely decorated. The bowl can readily be taken apart for cleaning, thus insuring a clean, cool smoke. Shipping weight, 1¾ pounds.
Price, each....$0.79
Per dozen.... 9.00

79c

High Grade German Porcelain Pipe, $1.10.

No. 18C5551 German Porcelain Pipe. This is an exceptionally high grade German pipe with a large elaborately decorated bowl, with nicotine receiver on bottom which can be unscrewed, long fancy carved horn stem, fitted with flexible top and fine hard rubber mouthpiece. Finished with long silk cord and tassels. All the different parts can easily be separated, so that you can easily clean. Shipping weight, 1¾ lbs.
Price, each...$ 1.10
Per dozen.... 12.00

50 Cents for this Chip Meerschaum Pipe.

50c

No. 18C5550 Large Sized Fine Vienna Chip Meerschaum Pipe, large egg shaped bowl and handsome cherry stem, with silk cord and tassel and Chinese amber mouthpiece. **An exceptionally handsome article.**
Price, per dozen, $5.75; each....50c
If by mail, postage extra, each, 6c.

Chip Meerschaum Pipe.

No. 18C5552 Fine Quality Chip Meerschaum Pipe. This is a large bowl with gilt rim and cover. Has a 5-inch cherry stem, to which is fitted a curved, amberoid mouthpiece. A small, gilt chain connects bowl with stem. Entire length of pipe about 9½ inches. A very attractive and desirable pipe. Price....90c
If by mail, postage extra, 8 cents.

90c

Turkish Water Pipes.

No. 18C5554 A Genuine Turkish Water Pipe; the bowl is made of fine colored glass, prettily decorated, and has a long flexible stem, with small amber mouthpiece connected to pipe. In the center of head is a thin glass tube through which the smoke passes. **The cup which holds the tobacco is made of Vienna meerschaum,** which can be replaced, if desired, by the Vienna meerschaum cigar holder, which comes with the set. Entire height of same is about 10 inches. Price....$1.94
Shipping weight, 1 pound.

No. 18C5559 Turkish Water Pipe. Has a very highly decorated bottle, with German silver connections for three flexible tubes, which are 30 inches long and have amber mouthpieces; inner meerschaum bowl fitted to each pipe. Total height, 11½ inches.
Price....$4.25
Shipping weight, 1¼ pounds.

Pipes in Leather Covered Cases.

73c

No. 18C5562 Genuine French Brier Pipe, English bulldog shape. Length, 5 inches. **Handsome Vienna amber mouthpiece.** Each one of these pipes is put up in a handsome leather covered case, with silk and velvet lining.
Price....73c
If by mail, postage extra, 5 cents.

79c

No. 18C5566 This is certainly one of the very handsomest pipes made. It is made from highly polished rosewood with removable set in bowl of **genuine meerschaum, which can be unscrewed and easily cleaned. Genuine Chinese amber mouthpiece;** length, 5½ inches. Put up in handsome leather covered, satin lined case. Price..79c
If by mail, postage extra, 4 cents.

$1.50

No. 18C5572 Genuine French Brier Pipe, bulldog shape, with genuine 2-inch amber mouthpiece. Highly polished, dark finish. The top of bowl and stem are mounted with fancy engraved gold bands. Inlaid in silk plush lined leather case. Length of pipe, 5 inches. Worth $2.50.
Price, per doz., $17.00; each. $1.50
If by mail, postage extra, each, 8c.

$1.47

No. 18C5577 French Brier Pipe, bulldog shape, with 2¼-inch genuine amber mouthpiece and trimmed with a sterling silver band between stem and pipe. Entire length of pipe, 5¼ inches. Large size, highly polished bowl. Inlaid in fine plush lined leather case. Price, $1.47
If by mail, postage extra, 5 cents.

$2.25

No. 18C5582 Genuine French Brier Pipe, bulldog shape, genuine 3-inch amber with mouthpiece, highly polished, dark finish. The top of bowl and stem are mounted with a heavy, fine, fancy gold band. Inlaid in fine silk plush lined leather case. **Length of pipe, 6 inches.** Good $3.50 value. Price....$2.25

$2.88

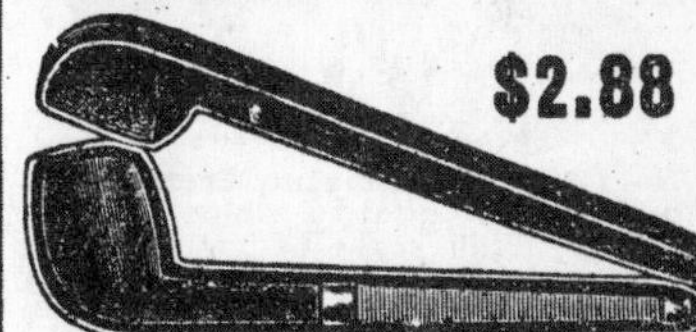

No. 18C5587 This is a Fancy, Egg Shape, French Brier Pipe, with a round stem and ½-inch gold band and 4-inch amber mouthpiece. Entire length of pipe is 11 inches, making a delightful, cool smoke. Inlaid in fine plush lined chamois case. Price, $2.88
If by mail, postage extra, 8 cents.

$3.00

No. 18C5588 Genuine French Brier Pipe, bulldog shape, highly polished, dark finish, with a 3½-inch real amber mouthpiece. The bowl and stem are mounted with fine, heavy gold band. Inlaid in fine plush lined chamois case. Length of pipe, 6¼ inches. A $5.00 pipe.
Price....(Postage extra, 8c). $3.00

No. 18C5594 Fine French Brier Pipe, ball shape. Highly polished bowl, with curved, square, genuine amber stem and trimmed with small gold band. Inlaid in plush lined leather case. A very desirable small pipe. Price....$1.85
If by mail, postage extra, 5 cents.

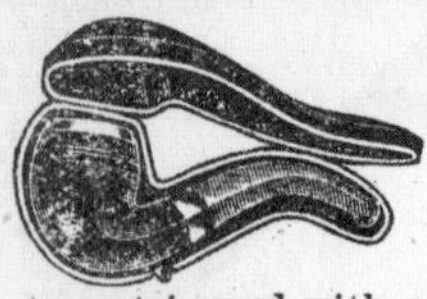

No. 18C5596 Highly Polished, Fine French Brier Pipe, bulldog shape, with curved 2½-inch genuine amber square stem; trimmed with gold band at top of the stem between the stem and bowl. A very handsome pipe. Inlaid in plush lined leather case. Price..... **$2.75**
If by mail, postage extra, 5 cents.

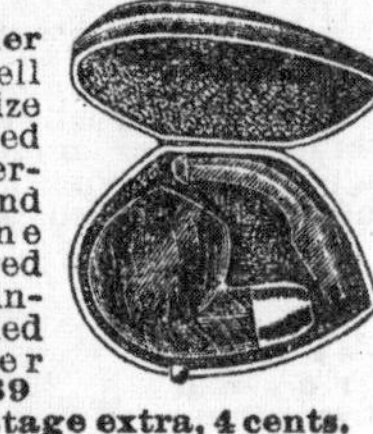

No. 18C5602 Fine French Brier Pipe, with a well shaped, large size egg bowl; trimmed with curved sterling silver band and 2¾-inch genuine amber, curved shove bit. Pipe inlaid in plush lined chamois leather case. Price.. **$1.89**
If by mail, postage extra, 4 cents.

No. 18C5605 Finest Quality French Brier Pipe, bull bitch shape. This handsome pipe has a thick, curved genuine amber stem, heavily mounted in real gold, such a pipe as you never expect to pay less than $7.50 for elsewhere. Price.. **$3.72**
If by mail, postage extra, 6 cents.

FINE MEERSCHAUM PIPES.

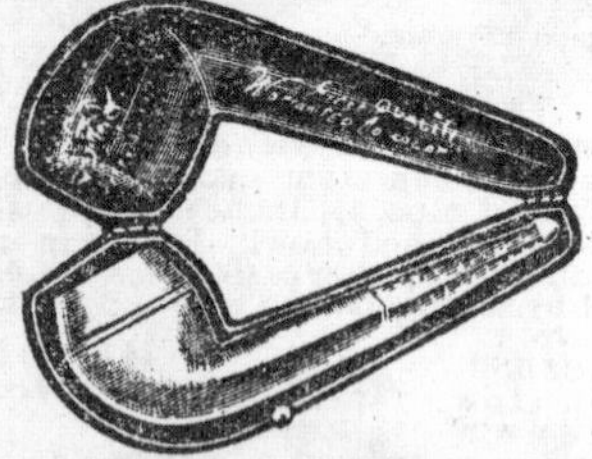

No. 18C5604 Chip Meerschaum Pipe, bulldog shape bowl, best English amber mouthpiece. We warrant this pipe to color; with satin lined leather covered case. **Do not unscrew stem from bowl.** Price.................. **97c**
If by mail, postage extra, 5 cents.

Genuine Meerschaum Bowls.

No. 18C5606 Genuine Meerschaum Bowl, finest quality, block meerschaum. This style of meerschaum colors quickest, and the only quality and shape that will not break if you drop it; comes in fine plush lined chamois leather case; the finest grade of meerschaums on the market. Compare our prices for same high grade quality, as sold elsewhere, you will find a saving of one-half. Come in four sizes, as follows:

No. 5 bowl. Price................ **$3.29**
No. 6 bowl. Price................ **3.82**
No. 7 bowl. Price................ **4.49**
No. 8 bowl. Price................ **5.21**

If by mail, postage extra, 4 cents.

No. 18C5610 Genuine Weichsel Stem with real amber mouthpiece. Length, 6 inches. This stem is used in connection with the meerschaum bowl under preceding No. 18C5606. Price, **52c**
If by mail, postage extra, 2 cents.

No. 18C5611 Genuine Meerschaum Pipes. High grade quality meerschaum, with best amber mouthpieces. We offer this line of pipes at prices far less than your local dealer can purchase them for from the jobbers. We buy them direct from the manufacturer and offer them with our small percentage of profit. The bowl is of the bulldog pattern and is of the best selected meerschaum and the amber mouthpieces are 2¾ inches in length, but vary in thickness according to size of bowl. Every pipe we sell means a satisfied customer. We offer you your choice in four sizes, at prices as follows:

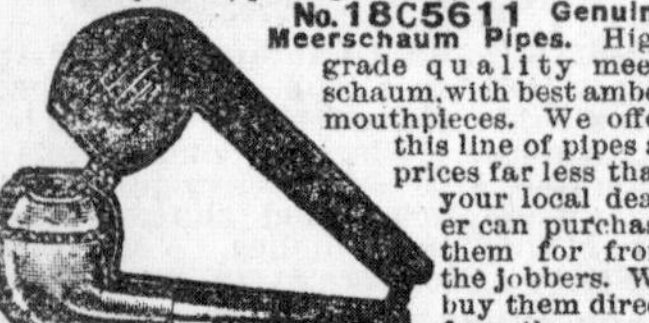

Size of bowl, No.	Length of amber, inches	Price	Size of bowl, No.	Length of amber, inches,	Price
5	2½	**$2.75**	7	2¾	**$3.95**
6	2½	**3.48**	8	2¾	**4.50**

If by mail, postage extra, 8 cents.

No. 18C5613 Genuine Block Meerschaum Pipe, handsomely carved bowl, assorted designs, such as lions, dogs, deer, etc.; amber mouthpiece, 2½ inches long; in a satin lined case. **Having received a large number of these pipes under particularly favorable circumstances we are able to offer unusual inducements.**
Price...(Postage extra, 6c)...**$2.73**

Our $4.95 Meerschaum Pipe.

No. 18C5615 Genuine Meerschaum Pipe, straight bulldog shape, with 3-inch genuine amber mouth piece, heavy chased gold band on stem and bowl; inlaid in finest plush lined chamois covered case. No better pipe at any price. Price............**$4.95**
If by mail, postage extra, 6 cents.

Genuine Meerschaum Pipe.

No. 18C5617 Genuine Meerschaum Pipe, London egg shape bowl, finest quality meerschaum, with 2¾-inch round amber mouthpiece. Total length of pipe, 5 inches. Pipe is ornamented with fancy gold band around stem. Inlaid in chamois covered silk plush lined case; very high grade.
Price... (Postage extra, 6c.)...**$3.88**

No. 18C5620 High Grade Genuine Meerschaum Pipe with large egg-shape bowl. Has a curved, square, genuine amber mouthpiece 2¾ inches in length. The pipe is trimmed with plain, gold band on top of bowl and stem, making a very rich and swell looking pipe. Entire length of pipe, 4½ inches. Fitted in leather covered, plush lined case. None better made.
Price ...(Postage extra, 8c). **$4.60**

Gold Mounted Meerschaum Pipe, $5.48.

No. 18C5621 Square Stem, Curved Meerschaum Pipe. A very high grade pipe, with 3-inch square genuine amber mouthpiece. Pipe is handsomely mounted with gold bands on top of bowl and around stem of pipe. Inlaid in fine chamois, plush lined case.
Price...(Postage extra, 6c) ...**$5.48**

No. 18C5623 Eagle Claw Meerschaum Pipe. This genuine meerschaum pipe is very high grade, having 3-inch bent amber mouthpiece. Total length of pipe is 5½ inches. The workmanship is of the very finest, being carved carefully with artistic skill. The same pipes are retailed at some exclusive stores for $7.50. Price............**$4.25**
If by mail, postage extra, 8 cents.

No. 18C5626 Fine Meerschaum Pipe with Weichsel stem in leather covered, silk plush lined case. Has a large, meerschaum bowl with brass cover. Fitted with Weichsel stem and genuine, amber mouthpiece, with brass chain connecting bowl and stem.
Price.......................... **$2.75**
Shipping weight, 10 ounces.

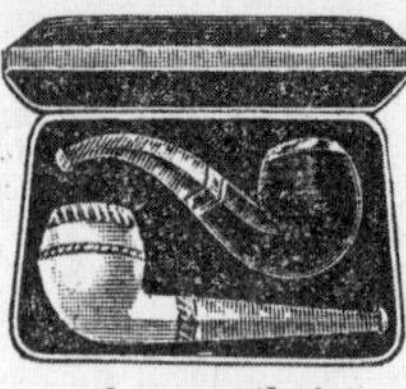

No. 18C5632 Smoker's Companion, consisting of two pipes, one straight French brier, bulldog shape, with 2-inch genuine amber mouthpiece, solid gold band, and one bent egg shape, highly polished French brier pipe with curved 2-inch genuine amber mouthpiece, solid gold band around stem, both pipes inlaid in a beautiful chamois covered and silk plush lined case.
Price, per set...................**$2.98**
If by mail, postage extra, 10 cents.

SMOKERS' SUNDRIES.

No. 18C5640 French Brier Cigar Holder, with horn mouthpiece. Price..................**10c**
If by mail, postage extra, 2 cents.

Twisted Rubber Cigar Holder.

No. 18C5642 Twisted Rubber Cigar Holder, something new, to give a nice cool smoke. Price..........................**5c**
Shipping weight, 3 ounces.

Solid Amber Cigar Holder.

No. 18C5644 Finest quality real amber, chamois covered and plush lined case, a very fine article. Comes in four sizes as follows:

1¼-inch length. Price.......... **$0.97**
2 -inch length. Price.......... **1.11**
2¼-inch length. Price.......... **1.34**
3 -inch length. Price.......... **1.58**

If by mail, postage extra, 2 cents.

Genuine Meerschaum Cigar Holders.

No. 18C5646 Genuine Meerschaum Cigar Holder, with amber mouthpiece. Comes in leather case.
Price, each **$0.38**
Per dozen.................... **4.00**
If by mail, postage extra, each, 3c.

No. 18C5648 Genuine Meerschaum Cigar Holder, fancy carved, with real amber bit, each in leather case. **Order by number.** Price, each...... ....**$0.50**
Per dozen........................ **5.75**
If by mail, postage extra, each, 3c.

No. 18C5650 Genuine Meerschaum Cigar Holder, similar to above, but finer, with fine amber mouthpiece. The meerschaum has carved designs, such as horse, dog, deer, etc.; inlaid in fine leather case, satin and plush lined. Length, 3¼ inches. Price, each...**$0.89**
Per dozen.......................... **9.50**
If by mail, postage extra, each, 3c.

No. 18C5652 Genuine Meerschaum Cigar Holder, elegantly carved design; real amber mouthpiece. Total length of holder, 3¼ inches. In finest plush lined case. Price, each..........**$1.62**
Per dozen...... .... **18.00**
If by mail, postage extra, each, 3c.

French Brier Cigar Holder.

No. 18C5654 French Brier Cigar Holder, with 1¼-inch genuine amber mouthpiece, ornamented with handsome design, gold trimmings. Total length of holder, 2½ inches. This is an extremely rich and handsome holder.
Price.....(Postage extra, 5 cents.)....**$2.44**

Rubber Mouthpieces.

No. 18C5656 2-inch Straight Rubber Mouthpiece. Price, per dozen, **20c**; each, **2c**
No. 18C5660 2½-inch Curved Rubber Mouthpiece. Price, per dozen, **40c**; each, **4c**
No. 18C5662 2-inch Square Rubber Mouthpiece. Price, per dozen, **42c**; each, **4c**
No. 18C5664 2½-inch Rubber Mouthpiece, with nickel ferrule.
Price, per dozen, **95c**; each................**9c**
If by mail, postage extra, each, 2 cents.

Our 13-Cent Weichsel Pipe Stem.

No. 18C5666 6½-inch Weichsel Pipe Stem, with curved mouthpiece.
Price, per dozen, **$1.30**; each..........**13c**
No. 18C5668 7-inch Cherry Pipe Stem, with curved mouthpiece.
Price per dozen, **$1.00**; each............**9c**
If by mail, postage extra, each, 3 cents.

Alcohol Pump Pipe Cleaner

No. 18C5670 Alcohol Pump Pipe Cleaner. The only way to remove all foul nicotine and keep your pipe sweet, is by pumping alcohol through it once a week. Half a cent's worth of alcohol pumped with force back and forth through the pipe does the work.
Price, per dozen, **$2.00**; each..**19c**
If by mail, postage extra, 4 cents.

Coin or Tobacco Pouch.

No. 18C5672 Prussian or Maltsters' Pouch. An excellent pouch for tobacco or coin. An inside pocket for gold. This pouch is manufactured from one solid piece of leather.
Price, per dozen, **$1.30**; each ..**12c**
If by mail, postage extra, 3 cents.

Self Closing Rubber Pouch.

No. 18C5674 Raleigh Velvet Rubber Tobacco Pouch. Self closing, tan color. Diameter, 3⅜ inches. Keeps tobacco moist, clean and sweet.
Price, per dozen, **$1.70**; each..**15c**
If by mail, postage extra, 3 cents.

Nickeled Match Safe.

No. 18C5735 Nickeled Match Safe, smooth surface with stamped design, opens with a good spring.
Price, per dozen, **40c**; each......**4c**
If by mail, postage extra, 2 cents.

Plain Nickel Finished Match Safe.

No. 18C5737 A Plain Nickel Finished Metal Match Safe, splendid value at the price. Price, each, **9c**
Per dozen................**95c**
If by mail, postage extra, 2c.

Combination Match Safe and Cigar Cutter.

No. 18C5741 Combination Match Safe and Cigar Cutter. These have been used and highly recommended by thousands. Nickel finish, leather covering, metal top and bottom. Convenient and durable.
Price, each...... ....**20c**
Per dozen........................**$2.00**
If by mail, postage extra, 2 cents.

Silver Finished Metal Safes.

No. 18C5743 Silver Finished, Handsomely Embossed Match Safe, new and striking design.
Price, each...........**$0.23**
Per dozen........... **2.25**
If by mail, postage extra, 2 cents.

No. 18C5745 This Pretty Match Safe is made of German silver, with handsome embossed design of bright silver finish. Very neat and tasty design.
Per doz. **$5.00**; each...**46c**
If by mail, postage extra, 2 cents.

Cigar Cases

No. 18C5749 Cigar Case, telescope style and moulded into shape, fine polished orange leather case, stitched French edges, front embossed in English heraldic design, large size. Size, 1x3¼x5¼ inches.
Price **25c**
If by mail, postage extra, 5c.

No. 18C5751 Cigar Case, telescope style and moulded into shape, made of genuine seal, mounted on the side with beautiful genuine sterling silver ornament; elegantly hand sewed and French finished edges. Size, 1x3¼x5¼ inches.
Price..................**$1.00**
If by mail, postage extra, 6c.

Our 75-Cent Cigar Case.

No. 18C5772 High Grade Seal Leather Cigar Case, with highly polished, strong nickeled frame, moire lining, a plain but very high grade case. Regular $1.00 value.
Price......................**75c**
If by mail, postage extra, 5c.

No. 18C5776 Fine Seal Leather Cigar Case, with best riveted frame, has a cigar cutter in pocket for same. Case is silk lined. An exceptionally high grade case. Worth $1.75.
Price...............**$1.00**
If by mail, postage extra, 5c.

CORSET DEPARTMENT.

SHAPES FOR ALL FIGURES. PRICES TO SUIT ALL PURSES. We present for this season the latest models and styles. We have given considerable attention to selecting the very best wearing styles as well as the most comfortable and stylish figures. The prices we quote are less than the average retail stores can buy them for. We sell only such corsets as we can guarantee and recommend. If you have never bought a corset from us, please let us try and fit you. If you are not entirely satisfied after receiving same, both as to price and quality, you may return same and we will cheerfully refund the price you have paid for it, in addition to the postage or express.

BE SURE AND GIVE YOUR ACTUAL WAIST MEASURE and the size corset you now wear, and observe the following rules in taking your measure: If you measure with corset on, deduct 2 to 2½ inches from waist sizes as shown on tape; this allows for spread of lacing in back. For example, if waist measure is 23 inches over corset, order size 21. If you take actual body measure, without corset or underclothing, you should deduct 3 to 4 inches, depending on how tight you lace. For example, if your waist measure is 25 inches without corset or underclothing, your size will be 21 or 22. Again we remind you to give your waist measure or size of corset, as this is frequently forgotten by customers when ordering a corset. For complete line of corset covers refer to index.

Our Special Four-Hook Corset. . . . 50c

No. 18C8000 Four-Hook Short Corset for medium form. This is a finely made corset of fine jeans, well boned and side steels, boned bust. A perfect fitting corset and meeting with popular favor. We predict an immense sale on this number, and especially at the price we quote. Colors, white, drab or black. Sizes, 18 to 30. Be sure and give actual waist measure. Price 50c
If by mail, postage extra, 15 cents.

The Kabo Five-Hook Corset for the Average Figure 90c

No. 18C8004 Long waist, medium form, five-hook. This is a corset made of fine French coutil, strips of French sateen with silk edging. Moulded on perfect French model; stayed with double girdles at the waist lines. The bones and steels are made with a protecting covering for the ends, which prevents cutting through. A perfect fitting garment that will give entire satisfaction. Equal to the $1.50 kind elsewhere. Made in white, drab and black. Be sure to give waist measure. Sizes, 18 to 30. Price...$0.90
Sizes, 31 to 36. Price............ 1.15
If by mail, postage extra, 15 cents.

The New Kabo Hipless Corset with Elastic Sides, 95c

No. 18C8026 Kabo Hipless Corset, medium waist, full form, made of French sateen, single strip, full boned, cut out over hip, with elastic sides. Matchless for athletic purposes and comfort. No brass eyelets. Colors, white, drab or black. Sizes, 18 to 30. Always give waist measure. Price.............95c
Extra sizes, 31 to 36, 25 cents extra.
Price..........................$1.20
If by mail, postage extra, 15 cents.

Kabo High Bust Corset, for Tall, Slender Figures, 98c

No. 18C8030 Kabo, high bust, extreme long waist, dress form; 6-hook, shaped shoulder straps, sateen covered strips, embroidered edge. Suitable for tall, slender figures. No brass eyelets. Colors, white, drab or black. Sizes, 18 to 30. Give waist measure.
Price......98c
If by mail, postage extra, 15 cents.

Kabo Abdominal Corsets, Highly Recommended by Everybody $1.50

No. 18C8038 Kabo Abdominal Corset, medium waist, extension front, very heavy boning, made long below the waist, giving ample abdominal support. Elastic self conforming gores on side, sateen covered strips and improved side lacings. No brass eyelets. Colors, drab or black. Sizes, 19 to 30. Do not fail to give waist measure.
Price..........$1.50
Extra sizes, 31 to 36, 25 cents extra.
Price..............................$1.75
If by mail, postage extra, 15 cents.

The Sahlin Perfect Form and Corset Combined, for Grace and Comfort . . 90c

No. 18C8052 Sahlin Perfect Form and Corset Combined. Retains all the good and avoids the evil of ordinary corsets. Nothing lost in the style or shape. The bust will not cave in, and therefore padding and interlining are avoided. The effect as here shown is an exact reproduction of a perfect form, obtained only by wearing the Sahlin. No corset is necessary, as it is a corset and form combined. Approved and endorsed by physicians and health reformers. Made of good quality corset coutil, white or drab. Give bust and waist measure. Sizes, 18 to 30. Price........................90c

No. 18C8058 Sahlin Perfect Form and Corset Combined. Same as above, made of fancy summer netting, white only. Give bust and waist measure. Sizes, 18 to 30. Price...90c

How to Send Correct Measure When Ordering Sahlin Perfect Form and Corset Combined.

MEASURES: The measure from B to C is the most important measure and should be taken with the greatest care. To secure a perfect and comfortable fit take measure as for a dress. The necessary allowance of 1½-inch for armhole will be allowed by us. For example, if you measure 8½ inches give us this measure and we will send you a form which measures 7 inches to waist line. To prevent mistakes, **please give actual measurement from B to C,** and state in order actual measure. We will then allow 1½ inch as above stated. **The Sahlin Perfect Form and Corset Combined** is made in the following sizes:

Bust	Waist		Under Arm
30 in.	18, 20, 22	in.	7, 8, 9 in.
32 in.	20, 22, 24	in.	7, 8, 9 in.
34 in.	20, 22, 24, 26	in.	7½, 8½, 9½ in.
36 in.	22, 24, 26, 28	in.	7, 8, 9 in.
38 in.	24, 26, 28, 30	in.	7, 8, 9 in.
40 in.	30, 32	in.	6½, 7½, 8½ in.

These under arm measures as shown in this table are the actual measure before the allowance for armhole is deducted.

In measuring for size of waist, D to C, remove corset, draw measure as close as desired and give this measure. The bust measure from A to B is a matter of taste and is left to the judgment of the wearer, therefore give actual measure from A to B and also state bust measure desired.

Sizes different from above must be made to order and will cost 50 cents extra.

The Jackson Favorite Waist is the Best Corset Waist in Every Way 85c

No. 18C8044 The Jackson Waist combines in the highest degree the embodiment of an elegant waist and corset combination. Its stays are ample, outlining a most graceful poise of figure, at the same time easy and comfortable; it is also adaptable as a negligee by the removal of side steels, which can be replaced at will. Made of good sateen, in black or drab. Sizes, 18 to 30. Always give waist measure. Price.......$0.85
Extra sizes, 31 to 36. Price....... 1.15
If by mail, postage extra, 15 cents.

A Most Satisfying, Comfortable and Durable Nursing Corset. 75c

No. 18C8064 S., R. & Co.'s Nursing Corset, five-hook, reinforced clasp. Made of good corset jean, entirely new principle, as it is easily adjusted, with patent snap button, and will permit use of nipple without the slightest inconvenience. Very pliable over sensitive parts; a boon to mothers. Boned bust, strong jean girdle, two side steels. Color, drab only. Sizes, 18 to 30. Always give waist measure. Price..75c
If by mail, postage extra, 15 cents.

Straight Front Nursing Corset, 95c

No. 18C8080 Straight Front, Bias Gored Nursing Corset. A particularly useful garment at this time and a very clever one. Made of finest Imperial drill, with glove snap fastenings. Front clasp 10 inches long. Made with garter extension tabs. This model has a medium waist and skirt, low bust and back. Colors, white, drab or black. Sizes, 18 to 30. Do not fail to give waist measure.... Price, 95c
If by mail, postage extra. 15 cents.

Kabo Nursing Corset, Made of Batiste . . 96c

Light and Easy for Summer Wear.

No. 18C8088 Exact same model as No. 18C8080, but made of good strong quality batiste in white only, and is boned with non-rustable material. Sizes, 18 to 30. Do not fail to give waist measure. Price.... ....96c
If by mail, postage extra, 15 cents.

Bias Gored, Straight Front, Perfect Fitting, Erect Form 50c

No. 18C8100 A New, Popular, Bias Gored, Straight Front Corset, with set-in gored busts. The latest low bust effect. Made of good imported coutil, with extra heavy 10-inch front steel. This is equal to many of the regular $1.00 straight front corsets sold elsewhere. Colors, white or drab. Sizes, 18 to 30. Always give waist measure.
Price.................................50c
If by mail, postage extra, 15 cents.

Straight Front Fine Batiste Corset, Bias Gored, at 50c

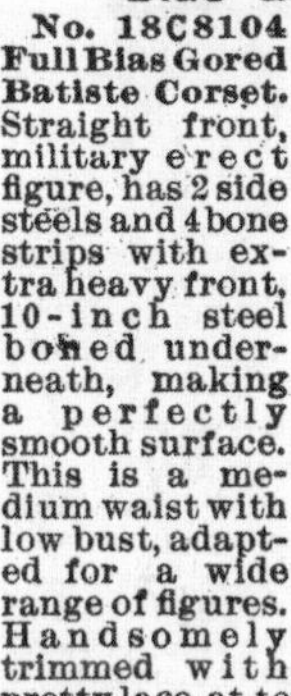

No. 18C8104 Full Bias Gored Batiste Corset. Straight front, military erect figure, has 2 side steels and 4 bone strips with extra heavy front, 10-inch steel boned underneath, making a perfectly smooth surface. This is a medium waist with low bust, adapted for a wide range of figures. Handsomely trimmed with pretty lace at top. White only. Sizes, 18 to 30. Always give waist measure.
Price..................................50c
If by mail, postage extra, 15 cents.

Kabo Straight Front Corset, 90c

No. 18C8120 Kabo Straight Front Bias Gored Corset, with 10-inch front clasp. Made of good quality Imperial drill with satin ribbon trimming and bow finish; long waist, medium skirt and low bust. Has hose supporter attachments. This corset will give the wearer a straight, military like figure; is equal in value to those sold elsewhere at $1.50. No brass eyelets. Colors, white, drab or black. Sizes, 18 to 30. Do not fail to give waist measure.
Price...............................90c
If by mail, postage extra, 15 cents.

No. 18C8124 Kabo Straight Front Bias Gored Corset. 10-inch front clasp. A beautifully made, very pretty garment; the exact same model as No. 18C8120, same colors and sizes; made of fine French coutil, finished with hand buttonhole, 5 gores. Regular $2.00 corset. Colors, white or drab.
Price...............................$1.50
If by mail, postage extra, 15 cents.

No. 18C8130 Identical same model as Nos. 18C8120 and 18C8124, made of strong, light weight, fine batiste. Boned with non-rustable material and trimmed with Swiss embroidery. An exceptionally desirable and comfortable corset. White only. Sizes, 18 to 30.
Price...............................90c
If by mail, postage extra, 15 cents.

$1.50

No. 18C8134 Kabo Straight Front, Dip-Hip. A short model garment (10-inch clasp), but so dipped at front and hips as to make it ideal for use with latest fashion in skirts; made of silky dril of great fineness and equipped at front and sides with high grade frilled hose supporters; boned with extra size non-rusting composition and fully made and gored. Colors, white, drab and black. Sizes, 18 to 30. Don't fail to give waist measure.
Price........... **$1.50**

No. 18C8138 Kabo, the exact same model as No. 18C8134, made with strong light extra fine quality batiste in white only. Sizes, 18 to 30. Do not fail to give waist measure. Price........... **$1.50**
If by mail, postage extra, 15 cents.

50c

No. 18C8164 The New Dip or Habit Hip Corset, made of good quality coutil, with 11-inch clasp, has very long skirt, pointed at the hips, low bust, trimmed with lace and fully gored. A corset of this nature has never been sold for less than 75 cents to $1.00. Comes in white or drab. Sizes 18 to 30. Always be sure and give waist measure.
Price.......... **50c**
If by mail, postage extra, 15 cents.

No. 18C8166 The exact same model as No. 18C8164, made of fine quality white batiste. Sizes, 18 to 30. Always give waist measure. Price, **50c**
If by mail, postage extra, 15 cents.

The Kabo Habit Hip Corsets. 95c

Designed for the Average Figure.

No Brass Eyelets.

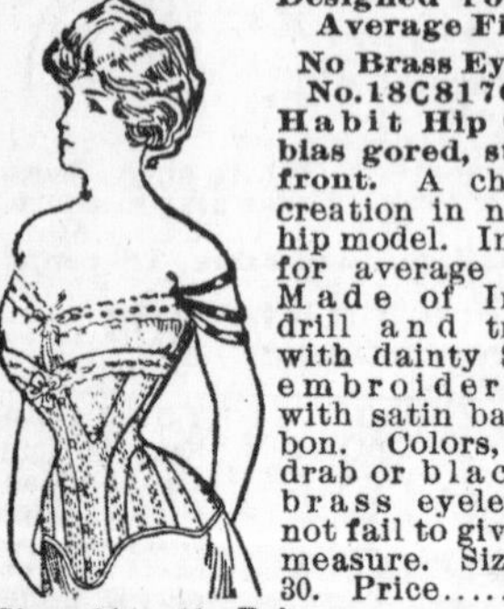

No.18C8170 Kabo Habit Hip Corset, bias gored, straight front. A charming creation in new dip hip model. Intended for average figures. Made of Imperial drill and trimmed with dainty Swiss embroidery, run with satin baby ribbon. Colors, white, drab or black. No brass eyelets. Do not fail to give waist measure. Sizes, 18 to 30. Price...... **$0.95**
Sizes, 31 to 36. Price.............. **1.20**
If by mail, postage extra, 15 cents.

No. 18C8176 Exact same model as No. 18C8170, same sizes and colors, made of Imperial French coutil in white or drab. Gores all hand buttonhole finished. Edged with good quality satin ribbon. An elegant appearing and fitting corset. Colors, white or drab. Do not fail to give waist measure.
Sizes, 18 to 30. Price... ... . **$1.40**
Sizes, 31 to 36. Price............ **1.65**
If by mail, postage extra, 15 cents.

No. 18C8180 Exact same model as Nos. 18C8170 and 18C8176 Made in good quality light weight batiste trimmed with dainty Swiss embroidery, run with satin baby ribbon. Made in white only. Do not fail to give waist measure.
Sizes, 18 to 30. Price.................. **$0.95**
Sizes, 31 to 36. Price.................. **1.20**
If by mail, postage extra, 15 cents.

Flexibone Girdle Corset Extension Hip, Girdle Top.

No. 18C8181 Flexibone Corsets are exceptional in design, economical and comfortable. Made of a very fine quality coutil. This combination of girdle top and extension hip makes this corset an exceptional good fitting and comfortable garment for those who desire a low bust corset favorable to present styles of dressing. 12-inch, straight front clasps. An exceptional $1.00 value. Colors, drab or white. Sizes, 18 to 30. Always give waist measure. Price. **80c**
If by mail, postage extra, 15 cents.

95c

No. 18C8182 This is a medium model garment, with 11-inch clasp and non-rusting bones, full gored, with dip hips and attached hose supporters in front. Made of fine quality Imperial Sterling jean and beautifully trimmed. This is a perfect fitting garment, combining all the good features of what a corset should be. Made in drab, white or black. Sizes, 18 to 30. Always be sure and give the waist measure.
Price.......... **95c**
If by mail, postage extra, 18 cents.

No. 18C8184 The exact same model as No. 18C8182. Made in good quality batiste. This cloth is well known for its wearing qualities and is the strongest and best material that can be put in a corset. Colors, white only. Sizes, 18 to 30. Be sure and give waist measure. Price....... **95c**
If by mail, postage extra, 18 cents.

$2.25

No. 18C8187 Kabo Dip Hip Garment, made of finest quality embroidered coutil, having 11-inch clasp and frilled hose supporters at front and sides; medium bust and flat back; superfine French coutil in white, drab and black. Do not fail to give waist measure. Sizes, 18 to 30.
Price.......... **$2.25**
Sizes, 31 to 36, **2.50**

No. 18C8190 Kabo. The identical same model as No. 18C8187, made of finest quality batiste, in white only. Sizes, 18 to 30. Do not fail to give waist measure.
Price....... **$2.25**
If by mail, postage extra, 18 cents.

Our Batiste Girdle Corset, White, Pink or Light Blue, at 49c

No. 18C8191 Four-Hook Short Girdle Corset, made of fine quality batiste. These girdles are extremely popular and extensively worn. Front steel 10¼ inches long and of great pliability. An ideal corset for slender figures. We offer this corset as a regular 75-cent value. Colors, white, pink or blue. Sizes, 18 to 30. Be sure and give color and waist measure.
Price.......... **49c**
Postage extra, 15c.

New Tape Girdle with Hose Supporters ... 49c

No. 18C8194 This is a very popular straight front tape girdle, made of five bands of closely woven linen tape with 10-inch rigid front clasp. Is 6 inches long over hips. The hose supporters are attached to the corset. This corset is a combination of perfection, grace and comfort for slight and undeveloped figures. Colors, white, pink or light blue. Sizes, 18 to 26. Always state size and color desired. Price, **49c**
If by mail, postage extra, 15 cents.

A Beautiful Fitting and Splendid Wearing Summer Corset 39c

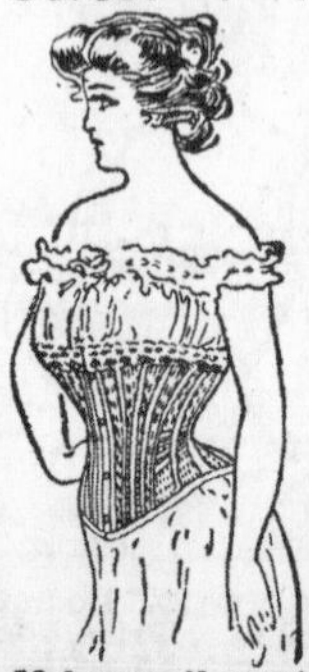

No. 18C8204 Straight Front Corset, made of strongest quality summer netting, trimmed with lace on top and baby ribbon drawn through lace. Reinforced with four girdles. Batiste covered steels, which strengthen it so as to make it a very durable article. Front clasp, 10½ inches long. Aluminum eyelets. Made in white only. Sizes, 18 to 30. Do not fail to give waist measure.
Price...... **39c**
If by mail, postage extra, 15 cents.

The Ideal Waist .. 25c

No. 18C8216 Ideal Waist, for children from 1 to 14 years of age; comfortable and convenient. This waist is made of fine quality cambric, with two sets of strapped buttons to hold the skirts and hose. White only. Do not fail to give age.
Price.... **25c**
Try one of these waists; you will like them.
If by mail, postage extra, 8 cents.

25c

No. 18C8230 Ferris Good Sense Waist. Comfortable and convenient for children. Buttons for everything and everything easily buttoned; supports the body, healthful, comfortable and natural; easily adjusted and easily washed; made of good quality strong corset jean, nicely corded. Sizes, 21 to 28 inches waist measure. Colors, white or drab. Be sure to give waist measure and age.
Price.. **25c**
If by mail, postage extra, 12 cents.

Ferris Waist for Boys .. 50c

Ages, from 2 to 10 years.

No. 18C8236 Ferris Good Sense Waist for Boys. This is a boys' waist that holds the pants and drawers without tearing or straining either. They last till the boy outgrows them, and wash as easily as a cotton stocking. The waist is made of strong coutil with removable elastics for buttoning; front fits like a waist. Made by skilled work people. Colors, drab or white. For ages 2 to 10 years. Be sure to give age.
Price........................... **50c**
If by mail, postage extra, 12 cents.

Ideal Corset for Girls .. 50c

12 to 16 years of age, combining all the good qualities of a waist.

No. 18C8240 The Ideal Corset for Misses, from 12 to 16 years of age; made of fine sateen, button front and lace back; the elastic tab for hose supporter, trimmed at the top with pretty edging; a waist that is healthful and will help the girl grow as she should grow. Colors, white or drab. Sizes, 18 to 26 inches waist measure. Do not fail to give waist measure. Price............ **50c**
If by mail, postage extra, 14 cents.

BE CAREFUL IN GIVING SIZES AND ALWAYS ALLOW FOR POSTAGE IF YOU WANT GOODS SENT BY MAIL.

Ferris Common Sense Waist for Girls .. 50c

Ages, from 7 to 12 years.

No. 18C8246 Ferris Good Sense Waist prevents the shoulders from drooping, the waist from spreading, allows the lungs to expand with every breath, and the muscles are free in every action. The Ferris Good Sense waists are popular waists for girls of all ages; made of good quality sateen, button front, lace back. Colors, white or drab. Sizes, 19 to 28 inches waist measure. Give waist measure and age. Shipping weight, 14 ounces. Price..................... **50c**
If by mail, postage extra, 14 cents.

No. 18C8248 Ferris Common Sense Waist for young ladies, suitable for girls 12 to 17 years of age, with plaited bust. The plaits are so arranged as to lay flat or distend. Specially adapted to growing girls of slender form. Colors, white or drab. Sizes, 19 to 28 inches waist measure. Do not fail to give waist measure. Price **75c**
If by mail, postage extra, 14 cents.

Ball's Celebrated Waist for Children 38c

No. 18C8250 Dr. Ball's Child's Corset Waist will train your child's figure while young. The Dr. Ball's waist is easy, comfortable and perfect fitting, patent tape fastened buttons and taped buttonholes. Colors, white or drab. Sizes, 18 to 28. Always give waist measure.
Price.......................... **38c**
If by mail, postage extra, 10 cents.

Misses' Straight Front Corset 40c

No. 18C8254 Straight Front, Bias Gored Misses' Corset, made of coutil. Has shoulder straps. Is one of our leading styles and met with great favor wherever sold. Colors, white or drab. Sizes, 18 to 28 inches waist measure. Do not fail to give waist measure.
Price.... ..... **40c**
If by mail, postage extra, 12 cents.

The Coronet Jackson Waists for Misses are the Best 49c

No. 18C8260 Coronet Misses' Waist. We supply a long felt and needed want by the ambitious miss just blooming into womanhood, when her figure begins to take on the matronly form which this garment so beautifully displays; made of sateen. Colors, white or drab. Sizes, 18 to 28 inches waist measure. Always give waist measure.
Price.......................... **49c**
If by mail, postage extra, 12 cents.

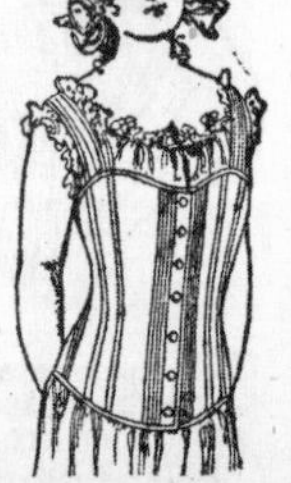

Dr. Ball's Elastic Corsets For Growing Girls . . . 75c

No. 18C8266 Dr. Ball's Perfect Fitting Misses' Corset, an ideal corset for growing girls, shaped on scientific principles, made of fine, heavy drill, laced and elastic gored back, shoulder straps and clasp front, lace edging. **A perfect corset.** Colors, white or drab. **Sizes,** 18 to 28 inches waist measure. **Always give waist measure.**
Price....................................75c
Shipping weight, 12 ounces.

Fairy Bust Forme.

No. 18C8300 Fairy Bust Form. The lightest, most attractive bust form on the market; thoroughly hygienic, is adjusted to corset, conforms with every movement of the body, gives figure a graceful form. Made of fine quality lawn, edged with valenciennes lace. Weight, only 2 ounces. Colors, black, white or drab.
Price, per dozen, **$2.75;** each....**25c**
If by mail, postage extra, 4 cents.

The Hygela Bust Forms.

No. 18C8306 The Hygeia Bust Forms, made of the finest tempered braided wire. Oval in shape. Adjustable. Light as a feather. Comfortable and non-heating. They cannot injure the health nor retard development. Covered with fine lawn, and in such a way that the forms can be removed and the covering washed. A great improvement over any other form on the market. Covered in white or black. Price, each..........**$0.44**
Per dozen.......................................**4.75**
If by mail, postage extra, each, 5 cents.

The Featherbone Dress Form.

No. 18C8310 Featherbone Dress Form. The ribs are made with featherbone with two reinforcing strips, and are adjustable. The most sensible and best dress form on the market. Light and cool. White only.
Price, per dozen, **$3.00;** each....**30c**
If by mail, postage extra, 5 cents.

Improved Breast Support for Low or High Busts.

No. 18C8316 Made of strong, light material called tampico fibre. By its use the weight of the breast is removed from the dress waist to the shoulders, giving coolness and comfort in warm weather, **producing a perfect shaped bust and free and easy movement of the body.** By its use all deficiency of development is supplied. They are just as essential for a slender person as for a stout one, and meet a long felt want for every woman and girl from the age of sixteen. **When ordering be sure and send the bust measure, and state whether low or high bust is wanted.** Sizes, 32 to 45.
Price, per doz., **$8.25;** each............**74c**
If by mail, postage extra, each, 5 cents.

The Parisienne Wire Bustle.

No. 18C8323 The Parisienne Woven Wire Bustle, made of highly tempered, black enameled, woven wire. The best shape, which it will always retain.
Price, per dozen, **$2.00;** each....**19c**
If by mail, postage extra, 5 cents.

The New Model Pad.

No. 18C8324 New Model Pad. This pad is form-fitting, invisible, light in weight, and ventilated. Made of sterilized materials in white, drab or black and in three different sizes to meet the requirements of all figures. This new model pad adds grace and symmetry to the figure, allowing the skirt to hang in graceful folds. May be worn over the corset to produce the short waist effect and under the corset for long waist effect. When ordering, give hip and waist measure, also color. Price..**25c**
If by mail, postage extra, 6 cents.

The Duchess Hip Pad and Bustle.

No. 18C8332 The Duchess Woven Wire Hip Pad and Bustle, made of best woven white wire, correct shape, very light and durable, and equal to any sold elsewhere for 75 cents or $1.00.
Price, per dozen, **$4.25;** each.. **39c**
Shipping weight, 11 ounces.

No. 18C8336 The Popular Habit Hip Pad and Bustle, made of light tampico, thoroughly hygienic. **The only style of hip pad to wear with the new, modish, form fitting skirts which are the prevailing fashion at the present time.** Recommended by all the leading dressmakers. Comes in ecru, gray and black.
Per dozen, **$4.50;** each..........**40c**
Shipping weight, 10 ounces.

Dress Trimmings, Braid, Loops and Ornaments.

We do not send samples of trimmings. Our illustrations and descriptions afford you an accurate idea of the style and quality. We guarantee everything to be satisfactory; if not, you can return them at our expense and we will refund your money.

White Pearl Bead Front.

No. 18C6001 White Pearl Bead Front, made of small beads and large pearls. A very attractive design, very rich looking and used for yokes, etc. Regular $1.00 value. Price.........**55c**
If by mail, postage extra, 6 cents.

No. 18C6003 White Pearl Front. This effective bead garniture is very showy, rich and attractive, a handsome trimming for light costumes, and especially adapted for evening wear. A great deal handsomer than it looks in the above illustration. Would be very cheap for $2.00 and we know that you will be more than pleased with it. Price...........**$1.00**
By mail, postage extra, each, 8 cents.

No. 18C6005 White Pearl Pendant or Dress Ornament, made of large and small pearl beads. A very tasty and rich trimming. Very popular and stylish. Length, 3¼ inches.
Price, each..................**$0.13**
Per dozen.........................**1.50**
If by mail, postage extra, each, 2 cents.

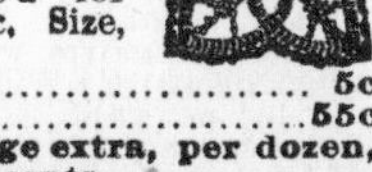

No. 18C6007 Black Spangled Bead Ornament. These medallions are very stylish, being extensively used for waists, skirts, etc. Size, 2½ inches.
Price, each..........................**5c**
Per dozen...........................**55c**
If by mail, postage extra, per dozen, 5 cents.

No. 18C6009 Black Spangled Bead Medallion Ornament in floral design. The leaves are worked on silk net. This is a very rich pattern and will make a very attractive trimming. Black only. Size, 3 inches.
Price, each..............................**7c**
Per dozen..............................**75c**
If by mail, postage extra, per dozen, 5 cents.

No. 18C6011 Black Jet and Spangled Drop or Pendant. Very stylish dress ornament. Length, 3½ inches. Price........**7c**
Per dozen..........**80c**
If by mail, postage extra, per dozen, 4c.

No. 18C6013 Black Spangled Jet Pendant, with tassels. Length, 3½ inches.
Price, each...............**6c**
Per dozen...............**.65c**
If by mail, postage extra, per dozen, 4 cents.

No. 18C6015 Black Spangled Jet Bead Loop Dress Ornament. To be used either on front, back or sleeves. Entire length, 8 inches. Price, each.........**25c**
If by mail, postage extra, 3 cents.

No. 18C6017 White Bead Dress Trimming. A dainty and pretty pattern. The illustration shows the exact size. Price, per yard..........**$0.09**
Per dozen yards................**1.00**
By mail, postage extra, per yard, 2c.

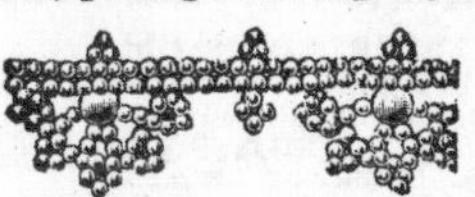

No. 18C6019 White Bead Trimming. This is a very showy pattern, very prettily designed. Width, ¾ inch. Price, per yard...........**$0.15**
Per dozen yards................**1.65**
By mail, postage extra, per yard, 2c.

No. 18C6021 White Bead Trimming. This is an exceptionally pretty design with large pearl beads in center of each half fan. Width, ⅝ inch.
Price, per yard...................**$0.23**
Per dozen yards...................**2.50**
By mail, postage extra, per yard, 3c.

Black Jet and Spangled Trimmings.

No. 18C6023 Jet Spangled One-Row Band Trimming. Exact width of illustration, 7/16 inch.
Per dozen yards, 33c; per yard....**3c**
If by mail, postage extra, per yard, 1c.

No. 18C6025 Jet Spangled Two-Row Band Trimming. Width, ⅝ inch.
Per dozen yards, 80c; per yard....**7c**
If by mail, postage extra, per yard, 2c.

No. 18C6027 Black Spangled Dress Trimming, band design. Width, ½ inch. Price, per yard....**6c**
Per dozen yards........................**65c**
If by mail, postage extra, per yard, 2c.

No. 18C6029 Combination Black Spangle and Bead Dress Trimming in a very pretty design. Width, ⅝ inch. Price, per yard..............**5c**
Per dozen yards.........................**55c**
If by mail, postage extra, per yard, 2c

No. 18C6031 Black Spangle Bead Dress Trimming. A very neat and dressy design. Width ⅝ inch.
Per dozen yards, 90c; per yard..**8c**
If by mail, postage extra, per yard, 2c.

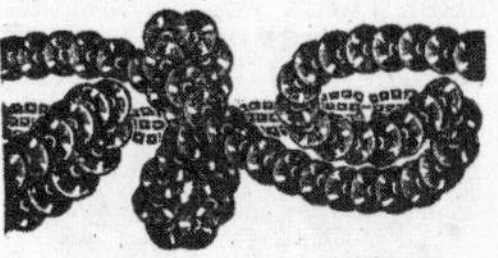

No. 18C6033 Black Spangle and Jet Bead Dress Trimming. The spangles are worked in a very pretty and attractive manner, and has a very rich effect. Width 1¼ inches. Would be cheap at 20 cents per yard.
Our price, per yard..........**$0.10**
Per dozen yards...............**1.10**
If by mail, postage extra, per yard, 3c.

No. 18C6035 Black Spangle and Jet Bead Dress Trimming, made in large, attractive pattern, which is separable and can be used as a medallion or ornament, or continuous dress trimming. This is a very high class and handsome trimming. Size of design, 2¾x3¼ inches. We do not sell less than 1 yard. Price, per yard........**$0.38**
Per dozen yards...............**4.25**
If by mail, postage extra, per yard, 3c.

No. 18C6037 Black Spangle and Jet Bead Dress Trimming. This is our best spangle trimming. It is a very elaborate design, which can be used by the yard as a continuous dress trimming, or separated and used as medallions. The design is one which is bound to please. Retail stores ask $1.00 per yard for the same style of trimming. Size of design, 2¼x6 **inches.** We do not sell less than 1 yard.
Per dozen yards, **$5.50;** per yard, **50c**
If by mail, postage extra, per yard, 3c.

No. 18C6039 Black Silk and Satin Serpentine Gimp. A very neat design. Width, ⅝ inch.
Price, per yard.......................**4c**
Per dozen yards.....................**45c**
If by mail, postage extra, per yard, 2c.

No. 18C6041 Black Silk and Satin Dress Trimming. This is a very attractive lattice work design in a band effect. Width, ¾ inch.
Price, per yard...........................**5c**
Per dozen yards.........................**55c**
If by mail, postage extra, per yard, 2c.

No. 18C6043 Black Silk Gimp Trimming, fancy serpentine design. This is always a desirable and stylish trimming. The value we especially recommend. Black only. Width, ⅞ inch. Price, per yard..............**8c**
Per dozen yards......................**90c**
If by mail, postage extra, per yard, 2c.

No. 18C6045 Fancy Black Silk and Mohair Gimp. This is a new and pretty design. The rings are made of feather edge mohair braid, the middle or insertion effect is of black silk braid. Black only. Width, 1¼ inches.
Price, per yard $0.10
Per dozen yards 1.10
If by mail, postage extra, per yard, 2c.

No. 18C6047 Black Fancy Gimp Trimming, made of feather edge mohair braid and silk gimp in the new button and loop effect. This is a very attractive and showy pattern. Entirely new. Black only. Width, 1¾ inches. Price, per yard $0.24
Per dozen yards 2.65
If by mail, postage extra, per yard, 2c.

No. 18C6049 Fancy Brilliant Silk Dress Trimming in the new dumb bell design and interwoven with feather stitched silk braid. An exceptionally effective design. Can be ordered in black or white. Width, 1⅜ inches.
Price, per yard $0.20
Per dozen yards 2.25
If by mail, postage extra, per yard, 2c.

No. 18C6051 Black Silk and Satin Dress trimming having both the band and serpentine effect. The band effect is made of all silk Paris cord, while the serpentine design is worked with the new dumb bell braid. Width, 1 inch. Price, per yard $0.15
Per dozen yards 1.70
If by mail, postage extra, per yard, 2c.

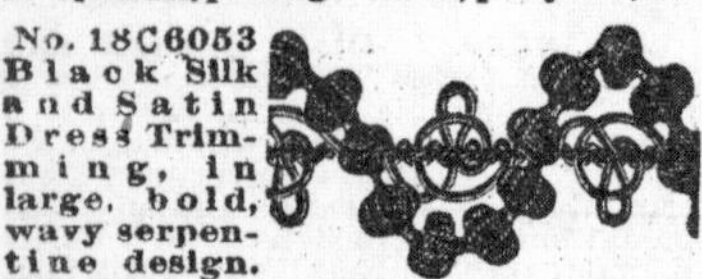

No. 18C6053 Black Silk and Satin Dress Trimming, in large, bold, wavy serpentine design. The serpentine effect is of a heavy, dumb bell, all silk braid, interwoven with silk Paris cord through center. Width, 1⅜ inches. Price, per yd. $0.25
Per dozen yards 2.75
If by mail, postage extra, per yard, 2c.

Chiffon Applique Trimmings.

No. 18C6055 Silk Chiffon Applique Trimming. A pretty floral and leaf design. Good workmanship and fine quality chiffon, closely worked. Colors, black or white. Width, 1 inch.
Per dozen yards, $1.70; per yard, 15c
If by mail, postage extra, per yard, 2c.

No. 18C6057 Silk Chiffon Applique Trimming. In medallion and teneriffe wheel design. A very showy and effective trimming. Can also be used separately as medallions. Colors, black or white. Width, 1 inch. Per yard ... 21c
If by mail, postage extra, per yard, 2c.

No. 18C6059 Silk Chiffon Applique Trimming. Leaf and flower design, very heavily and prettily embroidered. Good 40-cent value. Colors, black or white. Width, 1¼ inches. Per yard. 25c
If by mail, postage extra, per yard, 2c.

No. 18C6061 Silk Applique Chiffon, very elaborately and closely worked with silk, beautiful floral design; very rich and showy. Colors, black or white, also black and white combination. Width, 1¾ inches. Per yard $0.32
Per dozen yards 3.60
If by mail, postage extra, per yard, 2c.

No. 18C6063 Silk Chiffon Applique Trimming. This is a beautiful floral and leaf design, very closely and elaborately worked on heavy and fine quality chiffon. The flower has in center a pretty teneriffe wheel effect. This is a large, bold and attractive trimming. A very beautiful design. Colors, black or white. Width, 2¾ inches. Price, per yard 50c
If by mail, postage extra, per yard, 3c.

No. 18C6065 Silk Chiffon Applique, separable medallion pattern. Width and length of each medallion, 2 inches. This is heavily embroidered, with openwork design in center. Colors, black or white.
Price, per dozen, 25c; each 2½c
If by mail, postage extra, per doz., 2c.

No. 18C6067 Silk Chiffon Applique Medallion Ornament, heavily embroidered in neat scroll design. Colors, black or white, or combination black and white. Width, 1¾ inches.
Price, per dozen, 18c; each 2c
If by mail, postage extra, per doz., 2c

No. 18C6069 Silk Applique Ornament, heavily embroidered in venetian circular design. Colors, black or white. Comes in two widths. Width, inches ... 1⅜ 2¼
Price, each 3c 5c
Per dozen 30c 55c
If by mail, postage extra, per doz., 2c.

No. 18C6071 Silk Chiffon Applique Ornament, heavily embroidered in a neat and dainty design. Colors, black or white. Comes in two sizes.
Size, inches 1 2
Price, each 3c 6c
Per dozen 32c 65c
If by mail, postage extra, per doz., 2c.

No. 18C6075 Silk Chiffon Applique Ornament, embroidered in teneriffe design. A very pretty ornament. Colors, black or white. Comes in two sizes, as follows:
Width, inches 1½ 1⅞
Price, each 3c 5c
Per dozen 30c 55c
If by mail, postage extra, per doz., 2c.

No. 18C6077 Silk Chiffon Applique Medallions. These are very fine trimmings for waists, suits and costumes. They are very popular and stylish. The design is new and attractive. Colors, black, white, navy blue or brown. Size, 1⅜ inches. Price, per doz., 30c; each, 3c
If by mail, postage extra, per doz., 4c

No. 18C6079 Heavy Silk Embroidered Applique Pendant or Drop Ornament. Very pretty design, rich and attractive. Colors, black or white. Length of pendant, 4 inches. An ornament well worth 20 cents. Each, $0.10
Per dozen 1.10
If by mail, postage extra, per doz., 2c.

No. 18C6081 Silk Chiffon Applique Ornament, grape and leaf design, separable ornaments are very stylish. Colors, black or white. Size, 2⅞ inches. Price, each 6c
Per dozen 65c
If by mail, postage extra, per dozen, 2 cents.

No. 18C6083 Silk Chiffon Applique Ornament, grape and leaf design, same as above. Size, 4 inches. Price, each .. 8c
If by mail, postage extra, 2 cents.

No. 18C6085 Silk Chiffon Applique Separable Ornament, grape and leaf design, same as No. 18C6081. 20-cent value. Colors, black or white. Size, 5¼ inches. Price, per doz., $1.40; each, 12c
If by mail, postage extra, per doz., 3c.

No. 18C6087 Heavy Silk Embroidered Eagle Ornament. The entire eagle is closely worked with silk thread. Used on ladies' and boys' suits, in a large variety of ways. Colors, red, white, navy or light blue. Size, 3 inches wide.
Price, per dozen, 90c; each 8c
If by mail, postage extra, per doz., 3c.

No. 18C6089 Silk Embroidered Anchor, very closely worked with silk thread. Used on ladies' and boys' suits, jackets, etc. Colors, red, white, navy or light blue. Size, 1¾x1⅛ inches.
Price, per dozen, 45c; each 4c
If by mail, postage extra, per doz., 2c.

No. 18C6091 Silk Embroidered Star, closely worked with silk thread. These ornaments are very extensively used for various trimmings. Colors, red, white, navy or light blue. Size, 1¼ inches.
Price, per dozen, 28c; each 2½c
If by mail, postage extra, per doz., 2c.

No. 18C6093 Silk Embroidered Bars, as per illustration. Colors, red, white, navy or light blue. Width, 1⅝ inches.
Price, each 3c
Per dozen 35c
If by mail, postage extra, per doz., 2c

No. 18C6095 Silk Embroidered Anchor Ornaments, with double bars. These are very popular for boys' and girls' suits. Colors, red, white, navy or light blue. Length, 2¼ inches.
Price, each 7c
Per dozen 80c
If by mail, postage extra, per dozen, 3 cents.

No. 18C6097 Silk Embroidered Eagle, with Star and Bars, as per illustration. Particularly adapted for boys' and girls' suits. Colors, red, white, navy or light blue. Length, 3 inches.
Price, each 8c
Per dozen 90c
If by mail, postage extra, per dozen, 3 cents.

Silk Juby Trimmings.

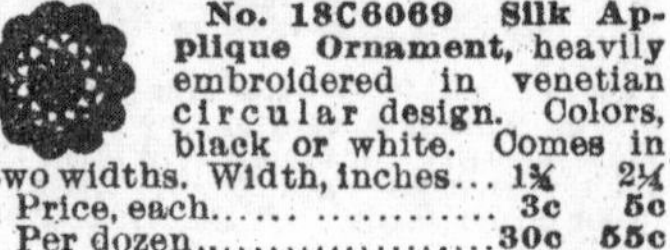

No. 18C6099 Silk Juby Trimming, in black only. Width, ⅜ inch. Sold elsewhere at 10 cents a yard.
Price, per yard 5c
Per dozen yards 55c
If by mail, postage extra, per yard, 1c.

No. 18C7001 Fancy Silk Dress Trimming, new shell pattern design. Also especially adapted for millinery. Colors, black or white. Width, ⅝ inch.
Price, per yard $0.10
Per dozen yards 1.10
If by mail, postage extra, per yard, 1c.

No. 18C7003 Silk Juby Trimming, fancy shell pattern, with row of satin juby running through center. This is a new and stylish pattern. Colors, black or white. Width, 1¼ inches.
Price, per yard $0.16
Per dozen yards 1.80
If by mail, postage extra, per yard, 1c.

No. 18C7005 Fancy Juby Straightaway Trimming. Very popular and stylish for skirts, waists, etc. Colors, black or white. Width, 1⅛ inches.
Price, per yard $0.15
Per dozen yards 1.70
If by mail, postage extra, per yard, 1c.

No. 18C7007 Plaited Ruffling. Made of fine quality liberty silk, edged with tucked ruffling on top; the bottom is edged with silk juby trimming. A very desirable trimming for skirts, capes, jackets, etc. Very stylish for the present season. Comes in four widths. Colors, black or white.

Width, inches	2	2½	3⅜	4½
Per yard	$0.25	$0.30	$0.35	$0.40
Doz. yards	2.75	3.50	4.00	4.50

If by mail, postage extra, per yard, 3c

Frog Loops for Cloaks and Suits.

No. 18C7009 Silk Frog. Made of president braid, fancy design, caught in center with silk covered cylinder button. Colors, black or white. Size, 2⅜ inches.
Price, per dozen, 78c; each 7c
If by mail, postage extra, each, 2c.

No. 18C7011 Fancy Silk Braid Frog Loop of neat design, as shown in illustration. Comes in black or white. Width across, 5 inches. Price, each $0.10
Per dozen 1.10
If by mail, postage extra, each, 2c.

Dress Trimmings and Ornaments.

No. 18C7013 Silk Braid Fouragiers or Loop Ornaments. A very elegant silk braid, fancy design, with pendants. Black or white. Length, 4 inches. Price, each. $0.20
Per dozen 2.25
If by mail, postage extra, each, 3c.

No. 18C7015 Silk Braid Fouragiers or Loop Ornaments. This is a very high grade article, made of fine quality silk braid and fancy pendants; an elegant trimming for jackets, waists, etc. Black or white. Length, 6 inches.
Price, per dozen, $2.75; each .. 25c
If by mail, postage extra, each, 4c.

No. 18C7017 Black Silk Braid Medallion Ornament, used in trimming waists and jackets, very neat and pretty design, as shown in illustration. Comes in black or white. Size, 2⅝ inches. Each 5c
Per dozen 55c
By mail, postage extra, per dozen, 2c.

No. 18C7019 Silk Braid Drops or Pendants. These ornaments are the newest for waists, etc. Colors, black or white. Length, 1¾ inches.
Price, each 4c
Per dozen 44c
By mail, postage extra, per dozen, 3c.

No. 18C7021 Fancy Silk Tassel or Pendant. The head is made of a fancy crochet ring, through which the tassel hangs. An exceptionally pretty ornament. Colors, black or white. Length of entire ornament, 3 inches.
Price, per dozen, 75c; each 7c
By mail, postage extra, per dozen, 4c.

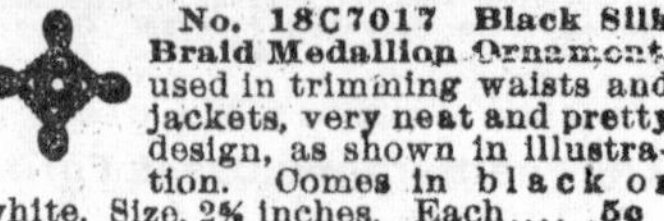

No. 18C7023 Fancy Silk Drop or Pendant, for trimming waists. These ornaments are extensively worn. Colors, black or white. Length, 3 inches.
Price, per dozen, 90c; each, 8c
If by mail, postage extra, per dozen, 5 cents.

No. 18C7025 Fancy Braid Pendant Ornament, with large rosette and button top with five pendants. Black or white. Length, 4½ inches.
Price, each $0.15
Per dozen 1.70
If by mail, postage extra, each, 2 cents.

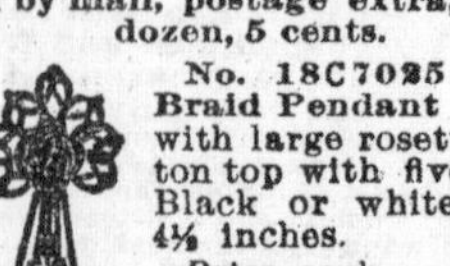

No. 18C7027 Fancy Silk Trimming Braid. This braid is used very effectively for dresses, waists, etc., where a narrow braid is required. A very pretty pattern. Width, ½ inch. Exact size as per illustration. Colors black, white, pink, light blue, brown, or cardinal. Price, per yard 2½c
Per dozen yards 28c
If by mail, postage extra, per yard, 2c.

Silk and Gold Tinsel Trimming Braids.

No.18C7029 Silk and Tinsel Dress Trimming Braid. A very neat and effective little trimming. The tinsel running through center of braid and colors on either side, as per illustration. Colors, black, white, pink, light blue, brown, navy, green or cardinal. Width, ⅛ inch. Size, as per illustration. Price, per yard........ 3c
Per dozen yards........ 30c
If by mail, postage extra, per yard, 1c.

No.18C7031 Silk and Tinsel Dress Trimming Braid. This is a pretty lace design, made of fine tinsel thread, with silk thread center and edges. A new and pretty creation. Colors, black, white, pink, light blue, brown, cardinal or navy. Width, ⅝ inch.
Price, per yard........ 8c
Per dozen yards........ 90c
If by mail, postage extra, per yard, 2c.

No.18C7033 Wood Silk Tinsel Braid. The new and popular wave design, with looped silk edges. The tinsel threads are interwoven entirely through center of design, making a very stylish and attractive trimming. Colors, black and tinsel or white and tinsel. This braid comes in three widths.

Width, inches......	⅝	¾	⅞
Price, per yard.....	8c	$0.10	$0.12
Per dozen yards...	90c	1.10	1.35

If by mail, postage extra, per yard, 2c.

No.18C7035 Fancy Persian Trimming. A very tasty and pretty trimming. The center is a very pretty combination of Persian colorings, the edges come in the following colors: Black, white, brown, navy or red. Width, 5/16 inch. Price, per yard..... 4c
Per dozen yards........ 45c
If by mail, postage extra, per yard, 1c.

No.18C7037 Wood Silk Pull Braid Edging, which can be made into various designs, a very pretty and lustrous pattern. Colors, black, white, brown or navy. Width, ⅝ inch.
Price, per yard........ 7c
Per dozen yards........ 80c
If by mail, postage extra, per yard, 1c.

No.18C7039 Wood Silk Wave Braid. A very lustrous and brilliant braid. The design is entirely new and very effective, with a very pretty feather edge effect. Colors, black, white, brown or navy. Width, 11/16-inch. Price, per yard..$0.10
Per dozen yards........ 1.10
If by mail, postage extra, per yard, 1c.

No.18C7041 Fancy Mercerized Bulgarian Band Dress Trimming, worked with a silk star design in Persian colorings. This is a very effective trimming and has an immense sale for the best trade. The star design is always worked in Persian colorings, the band comes in the following colors: Black, white, brown or navy. Width, ⅝ inch. Price, per yard........ 8c
Per dozen yards........ 90c
If by mail, postage extra, per yard, 2 cents.

No.18C7043 Fancy Bulgarian Band Dress Trimming, made of a mercerized cloth for foundation and worked with pure, lustrous wood silk. The pattern is the new, one-sided effect, which is extremely fashionable and popular. Comes in a very pretty combination of colorings, with the predominating colors, as follows: Black, white, navy or brown. The colors contrast very effectively and we can recommend this very highly. Width, ⅞ inch.
Price, per yard........ $0.15
Per dozen yards........ 1.70
If by mail, postage extra, per yard, 4 cents.

No. 18C7045 Bulgarian Band Dress Trimming, made of wood silk. The band comes in plain colors, the center being worked with beautiful Persian combinations. This is a very rich and attractive trimming, suitable for the finest costumes. We can furnish with the following colors predominating: Black, white, navy or brown. Width, 1 inch.
Price, per yard........ $0.16
Per dozen yards........ 1.75
If by mail, postage extra, per yard, 2 cents.

No. 18C7047 Silk Persian Band Trimming. A very high class and up to date style of trimming. One of the very latest patterns. The colorings come in a combination of Persian effects. We give the predominating color and the colorings in each are mixtures of red, green, blue, tan, etc., interwoven with tinsel, giving them all a very beautiful effect; will contrast with any shade of material. Please state which color you wish to predominate. Colors, black, white, champagne, brown and navy. Width, 1 inch. Price, per yard........ 20c
If by mail, postage extra, per yd., 2c.

No.18C7049 Bulgarian Band Dress Trimming. The latest, new, one-sided edge effect, made of pure wood silk. The colorings in this pretty trimming are very beautiful and contrast with the main color very effectively. Looks very rich and brilliant. We can furnish in the following predominating colors: Black, white, brown or navy. Width, ¾ inch.
Price, per yard........ $0.21
Per dozen yards........ 2.25
If by mail, postage extra, per yard, 2c.

No. 18C7051 Wood Silk Faggoting. A very new and pleasing design. Very new and stylish. Imitation of the Mexican work. Colors, black, white, brown, tan, cardinal, navy blue, light blue or pink. Width, ⅝ inch. Price, per yard........ 7c
Per dozen yards........ 80c
If by mail, postage extra, per yard, 1cent.

Stylish Band Trimming.

No. 18C7053 Stylish Faggoting Band Trimming. On both edges are used No. 1 satin baby ribbon, with the faggoting stitched in silk threads over ribbon and in center, as shown in illustration. This faggoting band trimming is used in a large variety of ways. Colors, black, white, brown, navy or cardinal. Width, 1 inch.
Price, per yard........ 7c
Per dozen yards........ 80c
If by mail, postage extra, per yard, 1 cent.

No.18C7055 Mexican Band Dress Trimming. Made of mercerized thread. This trimming is made especially for us, to sell at an extremely low price. The pattern is very popular and extensively used. Colors, black, white, brown, navy or champagne. Width, 1⅛ inches. Price, per yard........ 6c
If by mail, postage extra, per yard, 2c.

No. 18C7057 Pure Wood Silk Mexican Trimming. The new faggotting trimming. Same style and pattern as No. 18C7055, but made of wood silk. This is the best quality, made of pure wood silk. Colors, black or white. Width, 1⅛ inches.
Price, per yard........ 15c
If by mail, postage extra, per yard, 2c.

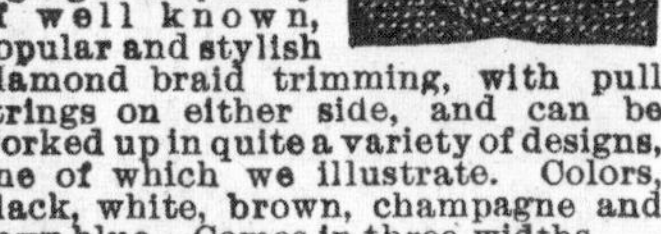

No. 18C7059 Wood Silk Diamond Pull Braid, extra high luster. This is a very high grade quality of well known, popular and stylish diamond braid trimming, with pull strings on either side, and can be worked up in quite a variety of designs, one of which we illustrate. Colors, black, white, brown, champagne and navy blue. Comes in three widths.

Width, inches....	⅝	¾	1⅛
Price, per yard....	6c	$0.11	$0.16
Per dozen yards..	65c	1.20	1.90

If by mail, postage extra, per yard, 1c.

Wood Silk Diamond Braid.

No. 18C7063 Wood Silk Novelty Diamond Braid, made of the lustrous fibre known as brilliant silk. The diamond design worked on braid as per illustration. Colors, black or cream. Comes in widths as follows:

Width, inch........	⅝	1
Price, per yard........	$0.10	$0.15
Per dozen yards.......	1.10	1.65

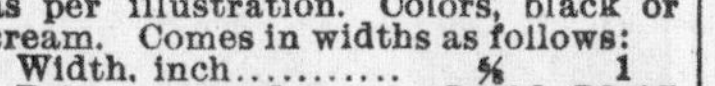

Mohair Hercules Braid.

No. 18C8687 Mohair Hercules Braid. Comes in black or mohair cream color.

Width, ins..	⅜	½	⅞	1¼	1½	2
Price, per yd	1c	2c	2½c	3½c	4c	5c
Per doz. yds.	10c	20c	28c	40c	45c	55c

If by mail, postage extra, per yard, 1c.

Silk Hercules Braid.

No. 18C8688 Fine Quality Silk Hercules Braid. Very fine ribbed, to be used for dress and cloak trimming, also desirable for coat binding. Comes in black only, in the following widths:

Lines........	4	8	12	14	16
Width, inch....	3/16	5/16	⅝	¾	1
Price, per yard,	2c	4c	6c	8c	$0.10
Per doz. yds..	20c	42c	65c	90c	1.10

If by mail, postage extra, per yard, 1c.

Braid Trimmings.

No. 18C8689 Fancy Brilliant or Wood Silk Wave Pattern Braid Trimming. This pattern makes an unusually attractive and handsome trimming and is very popular for stylish dresses. Colors, black or white. Comes in three widths.

Width, inches...	¾	1	1⅛
Price, per yard,	$0.10	$0.15	$0.20
Per dozen yards	1.10	1.65	2.10

If by mail, postage extra, per yard, 1c.

Wash Braids.

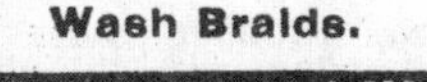

No. 18C8800 Washable White Cotton Hercules Braid, makes a very neat, stylish and durable trimming. White only.

Width, in.....	⅛	¼	½	¾	1⅛
Price, per yd.	½c	1c	2c	4c	5c
Per doz. yds..	5c	10c	20c	44c	55c

If by mail, postage extra, per dozen yards, 3 cents to 5 cents.

No. 18C8802 White Cotton Soutache (washable), to be used on waists and wash dresses. Extensively worn. Comes in three widths. Exact size of illustration. This is the better grade soutache.

Width, inch.........	3/16	⅛	¼
Price, per dozen yards	6c	8c	10c

If by mail, postage extra on above, 2 cents per dozen yards.

No. 18C8804 Mohair Soutache Braid, for trimming, black and staple colors. Price, per dozen yards...... 8c
If by mail, postage extra, per dozen yards, 2 cents.

No. 18C8806 Silk Soutache Braid, extra quality, in black and colors.
Price, per doz. yds, 15c; per yd.. 1½c
If by mail, postage extra, per dozen yards, 2 cents.

Gold and Silver Tinsel Soutache Braid.

No.18C8808 Gold Soutache Braid, good quality, for trimming.
Price, per yard........ 2c
Per dozen yards........ 20c
If by mail, postage extra, per dozen yards, 3 cents.

No. 18C8810 Silver Soutache Trimming Braid. Price, per yard, 2½c
Per dozen yards........ 25c
If by mail, postage extra, per dozen yards, 3 cents.

Silk Lacing Cord.

No. 18C8816 Silk Lacing Cord, black and colors.
Price, per yard........ 2½c
Per dozen yards........ 25c
If by mail, postage extra, per dozen yards, 2 cents.

No. 18C8818 Black Silk Cable Cord, used extensively for cloak and dress trimmings, also for neck laces or girdles. Comes in black only, in three different sizes, as per illustration.

Nos........	1	2	3
Price, per yard.........	4c	6c	8c

If by mail, postage extra, per yard, 1c.

Gold Tinsel Braid.

No. 18C8863 Gold Tinsel Flat Braid. Although the price on gold braid has increased two or three times, we still offer it at a very close price.

Lines	Width, inches	Price, per yard	Price, per dozen yards
2	⅛	2½c	$0.25
4	¼	5c	.55
6	⅜	7c	.78
8	⅝	9c	.95
12	⅞	12c	1.30

If by mail, postage extra, per dozen yards, 1 cent.

No. 18C8864 Gold Tinsel Braid. A very fine quality, used for uniforms, hat bands and particularly for belting.

Width, inches	Price, per yard	Price, per dozen yards
⅜	15c	$1.55
¾	30c	3.25
1	40c	4.50

If by mail, postage extra, per dozen yards, 1 cent.

No. 18C8866 Gold and Silver Fancy Lace, used for fancy work, masquerade costumes, etc. Style as per illustration. Put up in 7⅛-yard pieces. Comes in three widths.

Width, inches..........	¾	1	1¼
Price for 7⅛-yd. piece,	50c	75c	90c

Postage extra, per dozen yards, 1c.

Gold and Silver System Laces.

No. 18C8867 Gold System Lace, used for decorations, church purposes, regalias, etc. Comes in three widths.

Width, inches,	⅞	1	1⅜
Price, per yard,	$0.20	$0.35	$0.50
Per doz. yards,	2.25	4.00	5.50

If by mail, postage extra, per yard, 1c.

No. 18C8869 Gold System Lace. This design is principally a church design, used also for regalia purposes for churches and lodges. We quote special prices on above. Comes in two widths.

Width, inches..........	⅝	1
Price, per yard	7c	$0.12
Per dozen yards........	80c	1.40

If by mail, postage extra, per yard, 1c.

No. 18C8871 Gold System Lace. A good quality, used for churches, regalias, etc. We can furnish this in three widths, as follows:

Width, inches,	⅝	1	1⅜
Price, per yard,	7c	$0.12	$0.16
Per doz. yards,	80c	1.40	1.75

If by mail, postage extra, per yard, 1c.

No. 18C8873 Silver System Lace, same style and pattern as above, used for churches, regalias, etc., in 3 widths.

Width, inches..	⅝	1	1⅜
Price, per yard.	7c	$0.12	$0.16
Per dozen yards.	80c	1.40	1.75

If by mail, postage extra, per yard, 1c.

No. 18C8875 Gold System Lace of good quality. An especially good design for churches, regalias and lodge purposes. Width, 1⅛ inches.
Price, per yard........ $0.12
Per dozen yards........ 1.40
If by mail, postage extra, per yard, 1c.

Gold Band Trimming for Uniforms, Etc.

No. 18C8877 Gold Wire Band Lace, will not tarnish. A high grade lace, used for regalias, military, railroad and other uniforms, fancy work, etc. Width, ⅜ inch. Price, per yard........ $0.12
Per dozen yards........ 1.40
If by mail, postage extra, per yard, 1c.

No. 18C8879 Silver Wire Band Lace, same as above, for regalias, uniforms, etc. Width, ⅜ inch. Price, per yard........ $0.12
Per dozen yards........ 1.40
If by mail, postage extra, per dozen yards, 1c.

No. 18C8881 Gold Wire Band Lace, same style and pattern as above in wider widths, for regalias and uniforms. Width, ½ inch.
Price, per dozen yards, $2.25; per yard, 19c
If by mail, postage extra on above, per yard, 1c.

No. 18C8883 Fancy Gold and Silver Trimming Braid, used for fancy work, masquerade costumes, etc. Put up 7½ yards to the piece. We do not sell less than full pieces. In three widths.

Width, inch	5/16	9/16	¾
Price, 7½-yd. piece	20c	30c	45c

If by mail, postage extra, per piece, 3 to 6 cents.

No. 18C8884 Sandal Band Trimming, gold or silver. Extensively used for fancy work and masquerade costumes. Put up in 7½-yard pieces. We do not sell less than full pieces, as we quote less than the regular wholesale prices.

Width, inches	¼	½	¾	1	1¼
Price for 7½-yard piece	7c	10c	15c	20c	30c

If by mail, postage extra, per piece, 6 to 12 cents.

Gold and Silver Fringes, Tassels and Stars.

Used for Regalias Banners, Cushions, etc.

No. 18C8885 Gold and Silver Bullion Fringe, for regalias, banners, etc.

Lines	12	15	18	30
Width, inches	1¼	1½	2	3
Price, per yard	25c	35c	50c	65c

If by mail, postage extra, per yard, 3c.

No. 18C8886 Gold and Silver Bullion Tassels to match above fringes, used for banners, lodge purposes, churches, etc.

Lines	12	15
Length, inches	1¼	1½
Per pair, two tassels	8c	$0.10
Per dozen pairs	90c	1.10

Lines	18	24	30
Length, inches	2	2½	3
Per pair	$0.12	$0.15	$0.20
Per dozen pairs	1.35	1.50	2.00

If by mail, postage extra, per pair, 2 cents.

No. 18C8888 Gilt or Silver Stars, used for decorating, masquerades, regalias, etc.

Size, inches	⅝	1	1½	2
Per dozen	$0.12	$0.15	$0.22	$0.35
Per gross	1.35	1.70	2.40	4.00

If by mail, postage extra, per doz., 4c

No. 18C8890 Gold Tassels. These are very attractive and prettily designed tassels. They are particularly desirable for ladies' hats. Length, 3½ inches.
Price, each $0.38
Per dozen 4.25
If by mail, postage extra, each, 2 cents.

Gold Cords For Millinery and Dress Trimming.

No. 18C8892 Gold Military Cord, made of highest grade gold thread. Gold cords will be very extensively used this season for cloak and dress trimming and more particularly for millinery purposes. We can furnish them in three sizes, the above illustration showing the exact sizes.

	Large	Medium	Small
Price, per yard	6c	5c	3c

If by mail, postage extra, per yard, 1c.

Gold and Silver Spangles.

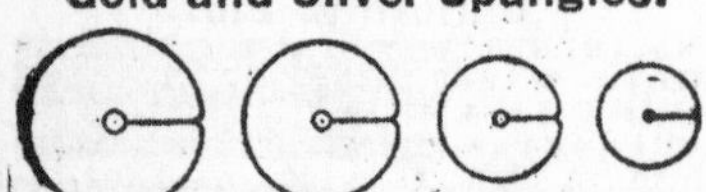

No. 18C8894 Bright Gold or Silver Spangles. We quote very low prices on these spangles. Put up in 1 ounce envelopes, in four sizes, one size to package. Be sure to mention size. Color, gold or silver.

Diameter, inch	¼	5/16	7/16	½

Price, per ounce, all sizes 12c
If by mail, postage extra, per ounce, packed, 1 cent.

See page 850 for gold thread on spools for use with above trimmings.

FUR TRIMMINGS.

Don't ask us to send you samples of fur trimmings. You can rely on qualities and descriptions, as we guarantee satisfaction or money refunded. You run no risk in sending your order at once.

Fur Trimmings with Seam.

If by mail, postage extra, per yd., 2c.

No. 18C9500 Black Unlined Coney Fur Band Trimming, 1 inch wide, with seam. Price, per yard 10c

No. 18C9502 Black Unlined Coney Fur Band Trimming, 2 inches wide, with seam. Price, per yard 19c

No. 18C9504 Gray Unlined Coney Fur Trimming, 1 inch wide, with seam. Price, per yard 16c

No. 18C9506 White Unlined Coney Fur Trimming, 1 inch back, with seam. Price, per yard 10c

No. 18C9510 Brown Unlined Sable Coney Fur Trimming, 1 inch wide, with seam. Price, per yard 18c

No. 18C9516 Brown Unlined Sable Coney Fur Trimming, 2 inches wide, with seam. Price, per yard 35c

No. 18C9558 Black Coney Fur Trimming, with silk gimp heading, about 1¼ inches wide. Price, per yard 10c

No. 18C9560 White Coney Fur Trimming, with silk gimp heading, about 1¼ inches wide. Price, per yard 10c

No. 18C9562 Gray Coney Fur Trimming, with silk gimp heading, about 1¼ inches wide. Price, per yard 13c

No. 18C9564 White Thibet Fur Trimming, with silk gimp heading, about 2¼ inches wide. Price, per yard 25c

No. 18C9566 French Marten Opossum Fur Trimming, silk gimp heading, about 1¼ inches wide. Price, per yard 25c

No. 18C9568 Black Sheared Coney (near seal) **Fur Trimming**, with silk gimp heading, about 1¼ inches wide. Price, per yard 12c

No. 18C9570 Mink Tail Fur Trimming, with silk gimp heading, about 1 inch wide. Price, per yard 15c

No. 18C9572 Wool Seal Fur Trimming, with silk gimp heading, about 1¼ inches wide. Price, per yard ... 13c

No. 18C9574 Brown Genet Marten Fur Trimming, with gimp heading, about 1¼ inches wide. Price, per yard 13c

No. 18C9576 Electric Chinchilla Fur Trimming, silk gimp heading, 1¼ inches wide. Price, per yard 20c

No. 18C9578 Brown Bear Fur Trimming, with silk gimp heading. The fur is 2¾ inches wide and makes a very effective trimming. Price, per yard 22c

No. 18C9580 Black Thibet Fur Trimming with silk gimp heading, 2¼ inches wide. Price, per yard 35c

Fine Fur Trimming Edges.

No. 18C9650 Black Unlined French Coney Edge, no seam, 1 inch wide. Price, per yard 10c

No. 18C9651 Electric Seal Fur Edge Trimming. No seam, 1 inch wide. This is the imitation of seal. Price, per yard 25c

No. 18C9653 Black Sheared French Coney Edge, unlined, no seam (imitation electric seal), 1 inch wide. Price, per yard 11c

No. 18C9655 Brown Sable or Coney Edge Trimming, 1 inch wide. Price, per yard 15c

No. 18C9657 White French Coney Edge, unlined, 1-inch wide. Price, per yard 10c

No. 18C9659 Silver Gray Coney Fur Edge Trimming. Unlined, no seam, 1 inch back. Price, per yard 16c

No. 18C9662 White Thibet Fur Edge, unlined, no seam, 1 inch back, full width of fur, 3 to 4 inches. Price, per yard 47c

No. 18C9664 Black Thibet Fur Edge, unlined, 1-inch back, no seam, full width of fur 3 to 4 inches. We guarantee our thibet fur high grade quality. Price, per yard 50c

No. 18C9666 Genuine Black Astrakhan Fur Edge, 1 inch back, full width fur, no seam, best quality. Price, per yard 45c

No. 18C9668 Stone Marten Opossum Fur Trimming, unlined, cut lengthways, 1 inch back, full width of fur about 2 inches. Per yard ... 43c

No. 18C9672 French Marten Opossum, unlined, 1 inch back with wide full width fur, cut lengthways. Price, per yard 43c

No. 18C9674 White Persian Lamb Fur Edge Trimming, no seam, 1 inch back, full width fur. Per yard 15c

No. 18C9676 Electric Chinchilla Fur Edge Trimming, 1 inch back. Price, per yard 34c

No. 18C9678 Nutria Beaver Fur Trimming (no seam), cut lengthwise, 1 inch band, high grade quality. Price, per yard 46c

No. 18C9680 Mink Tail Fur Trimming, cut lengthways, 1 inch band; a very pretty trimming. Per yard, 29c

No. 18C9682 Brown Bear, cut lengthwise. 1 inch back, very full and makes as effective a trimming as the genuine marten which it resembles. Price, per yard 35c

If by mail, postage extra, per yard, 2c.

Angora Fur Trimmings with Silk Gimp Heading.

All Angora trimmings are 6 to 7 inches in width, with ½-inch band heading.

No. 18C9690 Plain White Angora Fur Trimming, with silk gimp heading. Price, per yard 20c

No. 18C9692 Plain Black Angora Fur Trimming, with silk gimp heading. Price, per yard 25c

No. 18C9696 Plain Gray, or Steel, Angora Fur Trimming, with silk gimp heading. Price, per yard 20c

White Swan's Down.

No. 18C9700 White Swan's Down, unlined, ¾-inch wide. Price, per yard 25c

No. 18C9702 White Swan's Down, unlined, 1 inch wide. Per yard 35c

No. 18C9704 White Swan's Down, unlined, 1½ inches wide. Per yard, 45c

No. 18C9706 White Swan's Down, satin lined, ¾-inch wide. Per yard, 28c

No. 18C9708 White Swan's Down, satin lined, 1 inch wide. Per yard .. 40c

Fur Tails Used for Dress, Cloak and Hat Trimming at Lowest Prices.

No. 18C9710 Canadian Mink Fur Tail. Very pretty for dress, cloak or hat trimming, 7 inches long. Price 8c

No. 18C9712 Black Squirrel Tail. A nice trimming for jackets, capes and millinery. Length, about 7 inches. Price 7c

No. 18C9716 French Black Marten Tail. A stylish trimming. Length, about 9 inches. Price 13c

No. 18C9718 Black Bear Fur Tail. This is a long fluffy tail and an attractive style of trimming. Length, 10 inches. Price 18c

No. 18C9720 Black Wolf Fur Tail. A full and pretty trimming. Length, 10 inches. Price 25c

No. 18C9722 Light Brown Isabella Wolf Tail. A nice fluffy full tail, 10 inches long. Very desirable. Price 25c

No. 18C9724 Brown Sable Fox Tail. These are very full and fluffy. An exceptionally stylish tail. Length, 12 inches. Price 42c

No. 18C9728 Genuine Marten Tail. Good quality, full and large. Length, 10 inches. Price 40c

No. 18C9730 Genuine Marten Tail. Exceptionally fine quality. Length, 12 inches. Price 50c

Fur Heads are Extensively Used for Trimming Jackets, Capes and Millinery.

Fine quality fur heads with open mouth, showing teeth. Very stylish for jackets, dresses and millinery purposes.

No. 18C9750 Mink Fur Heads. Open mouth showing teeth. Size, about 3 x 4 inches. Price 29c

No. 18C9754 Genuine Sealskin Heads. Open mouth, showing teeth. Size about 3 x 4 inches. Price 29c

No. 18C9758 Genuine Marten Head. Open mouth, showing teeth. Size, about 3x4 inches. Price 25c

No. 18C9762 Genuine Chinchilla Fur Heads. Open mouth, showing teeth. Size, about 3x4 in. Price, 29c

No. 18C9766 Nutria Fur Heads. (Imitation beaver.) Open mouth, showing teeth. Size, about 3x4 inches. Price 29c

No. 18C9770 Genuine Persian Fur Heads. Open mouth, showing teeth. Size, about 3x4 inches. Price 22c

LACE DEPARTMENT.

We quote prices on laces, in most instances, by the dozen yards. We have them put up in that manner and a dozen yards can be used in nearly all cases. If you will stop to figure out cost per yard and compare the immense values we give, you will readily see that the dozen yards at our price cost you about half the regular prices you would pay elsewhere. **Where we cut laces we mention the price per yard.**

No. 39C600 American or Pillow Lace. A new and attractive pattern, used for pillow cases, curtains and different kinds of muslin wear. Comes in five widths.

Width, ins.	1¾	2½	3½
Per doz. yds.	14c	19c	28c

Width, ins.	4½	5
Per doz. yds.	33c	44c

We do not sell less than 12-yard pieces.

No. 39C603 American or Pillow Lace. A very pretty, new pattern, insertion effect. Comes in four widths.

Width, ins.	2	3
Per doz. yds.	21c	32c
Width, ins.	3¾	5
Per doz. yds.	45c	58c

We do not sell less than 12-yard pieces.

Everlasting Trimmings.

No. 39C612 Everlasting Trimming. This is a durable and pretty style of lace trimming for children's dresses, aprons, wrappers, ginghams, muslin wear, etc. Comes in three widths.

Width, in.	⅝	¾	1¼
Per doz. yds	12c	17c	22c

We do not sell less than 12-yard pieces.

No. 39C615 Everlasting Trimming. A new and dainty design. This is one of the most durable laces there is made. Especially adapted for all kinds of trimming. Comes in three widths.

Width, in.	⅝	¾	⅞
Per doz. yds.	21c	26c	32c

We do not sell less than 12-yard pieces.

No. 39C606 American or Pillow Lace. This is a very fine quality, new ball design, patterned after the hand made laces. Comes in four widths.

Width, ins.	2⅝	3¼
Per doz. yds.	34c	46c
Width, ins.	4⅝	5½
Per doz. yds.	57c	69c

We do not sell less than 12-yard pieces.

No. 39C618 Machine Torchon Lace. A splendid trimming for muslin wear, gingham dresses and different kinds of children's wear. One of the best qualities of washable laces made. Comes in widths as follows:

Width, in.	⅝	½	¾	1
Doz. yds.	3c	5c	9c	12c

Width, ins.	1¾	1¾
Per doz. yds.	15c	20c

We do not sell less than 12-yard pieces.

Sevilla Torchons.

No. 39C621 Sevilla Torchon Lace. A new and very desirable pattern. This is a very serviceable lace that will wash and wear well. A splendid trimming for underwear, aprons and wash dresses of all kinds. Note our special price. Comes in the following widths:

Width, in.	⅞	1⅜	1
Per doz. yds.	6c	9c	13c
Width, ins.	1¼	2	2⅜
Perdoz. yds.	19c	28c	44c

We do not sell less than 12-yard pieces.

No. 39C622 Sevilla Torchon Insertion. To match the above lace. Width 1¼ inches. Per dozen yards 18c

No. 39C625 Fine German Sevilla Torchon Lace, exact imitation of the very fine hand made torchon laces. Will wear splendidly and looks very rich and pretty. Suitable for the finest underwear, dresses, etc. Comes in widths as follows:
Width, ins...½ 1 1¼
Per doz. yds 16c 24c 43c
Width, ins...2⅛ 2¾ 3½
Per doz. yds. 58c 75c 88c
We do not sell less than 12-yard pieces.

No. 39C626 Fine Quality Sevilla Torchon Insertion, to match the above lace. Width, 1⅛ inches.
Price, pe doz. yds...38c
We do not sell less than 12-yard pieces.

Real Linen Torchons

No. 39C630 Real Linen Torchon Lace, made of medium heavy linen thread. We sell these laces at one-half the regular prices that you pay for the hand made torchon lace and the above is one of the very pretty new patterns. Comes in widths as follows:
Width, ins... 1⅛ 1⅞
Per yard..... 5c $0.09
Doz. yards...55c 1.00
Width, ins...2½
Per yard...$0.14
Dozen yards... 1.69

No. 39C631 Real Linen Torchon Insertion, to match the above lace. Comes in two widths.
Width, inches...1 1⅜
Price, per yd...5c 8c
Per doz. yds...55c 90c

No. 39C634 Real Linen Torchon Lace. This is a very pretty and showy pattern, one of the best original designs and is made by the best manufacturers of laces in Germany. For dresses, waists, muslin wear, etc. Comes in widths as follows:
Width, ins...⅝ 1¼
Per yard... 3c 6c
Doz. yds... 35c 70c
Width, ins.....2⅜ 3
Per yard...$0.12 $0.17
Doz. yds... 1.35 1.90

No. 39C635 Real Linen Torchon Insertion, to match the above lace. Very desirable for waists, and muslin wear. Comes in two widths.
Width, inches.. 1¼ 1⅝
Per yard....... 6c 8c
Per doz. yds....70c 90c

No. 39C638 Real Linen Torchon Lace. Our finest quality and a very exquisite and beautiful pattern, copied from the best and highest priced real hand made lace that costs two to three times as much. We guarantee these equally as good.
Width, ins..........1⅛ 1⅜ 2¼ 3
Per yard..........$0.10 $0.14 $0.20 $0.25
Doz. yds........ 1.10 1.65 2.25 2.75

No. 39C639 Real Linen Torchon Insertion. Our finest quality, to match the above lace. Width, 1⅜ inches.
Price, per dozen yards, $1.70; per yard.......15c

English Nottingham Torchon Laces are the fine cotton thread torchons so popular now. They are very fine and dainty appearing, at the same time very lasting and will wash and wear as well as the best hand made laces and look just as pretty.

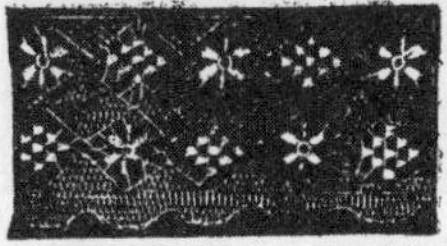

No. 39C651 English Nottingham Torchon Lace. This is a new design with a cluny effect and a fast edge. A very delicate as well as a lasting and very pretty style of trimming for muslin wear, waists, etc. Comes in four widths.
Width, ins.......¾ 1⅛
Per doz. yds...18c 28c
Width, ins.......2¼ 3⅛
Per doz. yds...43c 56c
We do not sell less than 12-yard pieces.

No. 39C654 English Nottingham Torchon Insertion. Same quality and to match the above lace. Comes in two widths.
Width, ins....... 1⅛ 1⅜
Per doz. yds... 21c 33c
We do not sell less than 12-yard pieces.

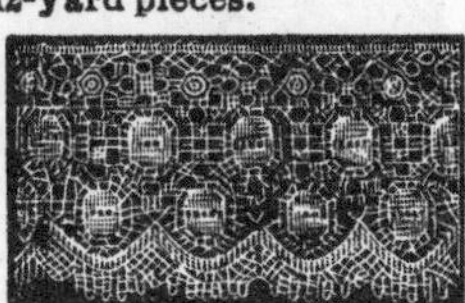

No. 39C657 English Nottingham Torchon Lace. The new ball pattern. The mesh is in imitation of hand made. A particularly desirable pattern for muslin wear and fancy work trimming. Comes in four widths.
Width, ins...... 1¼ 2⅛
Per doz. yds...39c 44c
Width, ins...... 2⅜ 3⅜
Per doz. yds...52c 60c
We do not sell less than 12-yard pieces.

No. 39C660 English Nottingham Torchon Insertion, in ball pattern to match above lace. These insertions are largely used for waists. Comes in two widths.
Width, ins...... 1⅜ 2⅛
Per doz. yds...30c 45c
We do not sell less than 12-yard pieces.

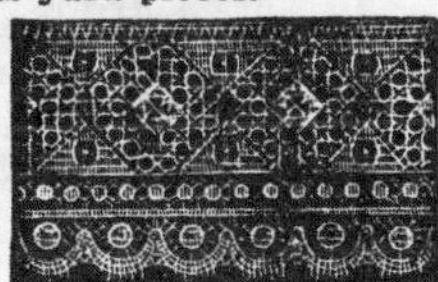

No. 39C663 English Nottingham Torchon Lace. This is a very elegant and beautiful pattern, our own importation with an insertion effect and small wheel edges. Very durable as well as handsome. Particularly desirable for waists and muslin wear. Comes in four widths.
Width, ins. 1⅜ 2⅛ 2¾ 3½
Per doz. yds. 33c 46c 54c 65c
We do not sell less than 12-yard pieces.

No. 39C666 English Nottingham Torchon Insertion, to match the above lace. This is a very desirable style for shirt waists as well as all muslin wear. Comes in two widths.
Width, ins.........1⅜ 2⅜
Per dozen yards....27c 51c
We do not sell less than 12-yard pieces.

No. 39C664 English Nottingham Torchon Lace. Made with a heavy net. The new medallion wheel effect pattern. This is one of the newest patterns and makes a very beautiful trimming for all kinds of muslin wear, dressing sacques, etc. Comes in three widths.
Width, ins ...1½ 2 3¼
Doz. yds.......29c 42c 60c
We do not sell less than 12-yard pieces.

No. 39C665 English Nottingham Torchon Insertion. New medallion wheel effect to match the above lace. Comes in two widths.
Width, ins...... 1⅛ 2¼
Per doz. yds....30c 43c
We do not sell less than 12-yard pieces.

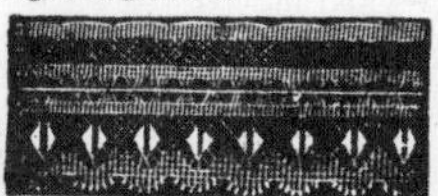

No. 39C669 English Nottingham Torchon Lace. A very dainty and exquisite pattern, made of a very fine thread, Mexican drawnwork effect and insertion design. Comes in four widths.
Width, ins...... ¾ 1⅛
Per doz. yds....29c 40c
Width, ins...... 1½ 2⅛
Per doz. yds....54c 73c
We do not sell less than 12-yard pieces.

No. 39C672 English Nottingham Torchon Insertion, to match the above lace. Width, 1¼ inches.
Price, per doz. yds...39c
We do not sell less than 12-yard pieces.

No. 39C675 English Nottingham Torchon Lace. Diamond shaped pattern, made of a very fine thread with a purled edge. One of the finest qualities made in these laces and a very desirable and exquisite pattern for waists, sacques and muslin wear. Comes in three widths.
Width, ins. ¾ 1⅛ 2
Per doz. yds. 25c 41c 63c
We do not sell less than 12-yard pieces.

No. 39C678 English Nottingham Torchon Insertion. Diamond shaped pattern to match the above lace. Width, 1 inch.
Price, per doz. yds.....35c
We do not sell less than 12-yard pieces.

No. 39C681 A Very Fine Quality English Nottingham Lace. This is an entirely new design, renaissance effect. It is even prettier than the real hand made. Washes and wears just as well. Especially desirable for the finer grade of muslin wear, children's dresses, sacques, etc. Comes in four widths.
Width, ins.... ⅞ 1⅝
Per doz. yds..36c 58c
Width, ins.... 2¼ 3
Per doz. yds..87c $1.09
We do not sell less than 12-yard pieces.

No. 39C684 Fine English Nottingham Torchon Insertion. Renaissance effect to match the above lace. Width, 1½ inches.
Price, per doz. yds.......57c
We do not sell less than 12-yard pieces.

No. 39C687 English Nottingham Torchon Lace. This is a very fine quality, made of a very fine thread. The pattern is very effective and pretty. Can be used for trimming the finest materials.
Width, inches, ¾ 1⅛
Per doz. yards, 29c 42c
Width, inches, 1⅜ 2
Per doz. yards, 56c 69c
We do not sell less than 12-yard pieces.

No. 39C690 English Nottingham Torchon Insertion, same design and to match the above lace Comes in two widths.
Width, inches, ⅝ 1⅛
Per doz. yards, 35c 43c
We do not sell less than 12-yard pieces.

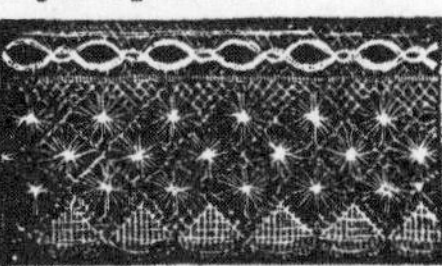

No. 39C693 Nottingham Torchon Lace, made of a very fine thread. Has the new snowball effect with a beading design. An unusually desirable trimming for all kinds of muslin and other wear. Comes in four widths.
Width, ins.......⅞ 1⅜
Per doz. yds...31c 49c
Width, ins......1⅞ 2¼
Per doz. yds...58c 69c
We do not sell less than 12-yard pieces.

No. 39C696 Nottingham Torchon Insertion, with snowball and beading design to match above lace. Good for corset covers and waists. Comes in two widths.
Width, ins....... 1 1⅛
Per doz. yds...39c 50c
We do not sell less than 12-yard pieces.

No. 39C711 English Antique Lace. Copied from an old hand made design and imported for our special use. This trimming will wear as well as the real hand made, while the cost is one-quarter as much. Beautiful trimming for all kinds of dresses and fine muslin wear. Comes in three widths.
Width, ins... 1⅜ 3
Per yard... 6c $0.09
Per doz. yds., 65c 1.00
Width, ins.........4
Per yard.........$0.12
Per doz. yds...... 1.35

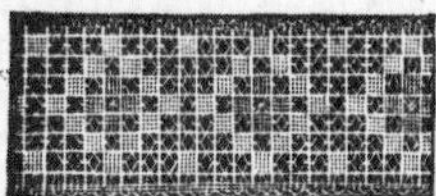

No. 39C714 English Antique Insertion to match the above lace. A very attractive and rich looking insertion for dresses, waists and muslin wear.
Width, ins.... 1⅞ 2⅝
Per yard...... 6c 8c
Per doz. yds... 65c 90c

No. 39C692 Nottingham Cluny Insertion. Same pattern and to match the above lace. Especially desirable for waists, dresses and muslin wear. Comes in two widths.
Width, ins...... 2⅜ 3¾
Per yard....... 5c 8c
Per doz. yds... 55c 90c

No. 39C694 English Cluny Lace. Made of an extra heavy thread. This is an exact imitation of the real Irish hand made goods and only an expert could tell the difference. This lace we can recommend for service and wear and is this season's latest trimming for dresses, waists and muslin underwear. The price is at least 50 per cent cheaper than you could buy it at any of the small stores. Comes in three widths, with insertion to match.
Width, ins. 2⅜ 3⅝
Per yard.. $0.10 $0.13
Per doz. yds. 1.10 1.45
Width, ins.......... 4½
Per yard..........$0.16
Per doz. yds....... 1.75

No. 39C695 English Cluny Insertion. Made of extra heavy thread, same design and pattern to match lace No. 39C694. Very desirable for waists, dresses and muslin wear. Comes in two widths.
Width, ins. 3 4
Per yard. $0.10 $0.13
Per doz. yds. 1.10 1.48

Valenciennes Lace.

No. 39C730 Platte Valenciennes Lace, in a tulip design. These fine thread valenciennes laces are very desirable for trimming underwear, summer dresses, waists and for fancy work. The price you could not duplicate by at least 25 per cent. Comes in five widths.
Width, ins. 1⅛ 2⅛ 3⅛ 4⅜ 5⅛
Per doz. yds. 25c 39c 57c 69c 85c
We do not sell less than 12-yard pieces.

No. 39C733 Platte Valenciennes Insertion, in tulip design to match the above lace, Width, 1⅜ ins. Per doz. yds. 26c
We do not sell less than 12-yard pieces.

Cluny Laces.

No. 39C691 Nottingham Cluny Lace, an exact copy of the real hand made article. This is one of the newest of this year's trimmings, and is used very extensively for both dress and underwear trimming, and in the insertion, very largely for waists. Comes in three widths.
Width, ins.............. 1⅜ 2½ 3½
Per yard.............. 4c 6c 8c
Per dozen yards........44c 65c 90c

No. 39C736 Platte Valenciennes Lace. A very fine quality and exceptionally striking and pretty design, made with beading to draw No. 1 ribbon through. The narrower widths have space for one row of ribbon, the wider for two rows. A very dainty and pretty trimming for infants' wear, muslin wear, fancy work, etc. Comes in four widths.
Width, ins.. 1⅛ 2⅛
Per yard.... 5c 7c
Per doz. yds. 55c 80c
Width, ins.. 3⅛ 4⅛
Per yard.... 9c $0.11
Per doz. yds. 98c 1.25

No. 39C737 Platte Valenciennes Insertion. Floral design with beading effect to match the above lace. Width, 1⅜ inches. Price, per yard... 5c
Per dozen yards.........55c

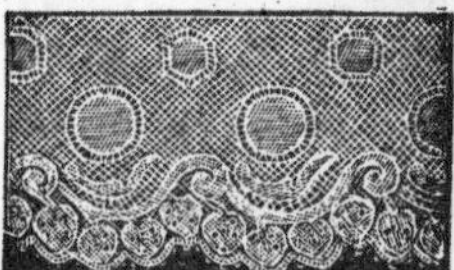

No. 39C739 Platte Valenciennes Lace. A fine thread and good quality. The new ball design with floral scroll edge. An unusually pretty and effective pattern. Very desirable for all kinds of trimming. The wider widths are particularly desirable for skirts, etc. Comes in five widths.
Width, ins. 1 1⅛ 2
Doz. yds...35c 42c 51c
Width, ins... 3⅛ 5
Doz. yds.....80c $1.15
We do not sell less than 12-yard pieces.

No. 39C742 Platte Valenciennes Insertion, in ball and scroll design to match above lace. Comes in two widths.
Width, ins... 1⅛ 1⅜
Doz. yards,.. 34c 43c
We do not sell less than 12-yard pieces.

No. 39C745 Fancy Raised Normandy Valenciennes Lace. This is a new design, made on an entirely new mesh, similar to the point de Paris and suitable for all kinds of muslin wear, white goods and fancy work. Comes in four widths.
Width, ins. 2¼ 3⅛ 4 4⅜
Doz. yds. 44c 55c 67c 79c

No. 39C748 Fancy Raised Normandy Valenciennes Insertion, same pattern and to match the above lace. Width, 1⅛ inches.
Price, per dozen yards .30c
We do not sell less than 12-yard pieces.

No. 39C751 Fancy Point de Paris Valenciennes Lace. This is a pretty floral design with a heavy hand made spot effect and ring pattern. An entirely new design. One of the prettiest and most effective that you could find. Comes in 4 widths
Width, ins. 1⅛ 2⅜ 4⅜ 5⅛
Per yd.....4c 6c $0.10 $0.12
Doz. yds. 46c 69c 1.12 1.38

No. 39C754 Point de Paris Valenciennes Insertion, same design to match the above lace. Comes in two widths.
Widths, inches......1⅛ 2⅜
Per yard........4c 6c
Per dozen yards...47c 68c

No. 39C757 Fancy Raised Valenciennes Lace. This is a large floral design with scroll work effect, on a fine point de Paris net. Will wear and wash well and is a very beautiful and attractive pattern. Comes in five widths.

Width, ins.	1⅛	2⅜	3½
Per yard..	3c	5c	6c
Doz. yds..	34c	55c	68c
Width, ins......		4⅛	5¼
Per yard........		7c	9c
Doz. yds........		80c	99c

No. 39C760 Fancy Raised Valenciennes Insertion, same design and to match the above lace. Comes in two widths.

Width, ins......	1½	2⅛
Per yard.......	3c	4c
Doz. yds.......	34c	45c

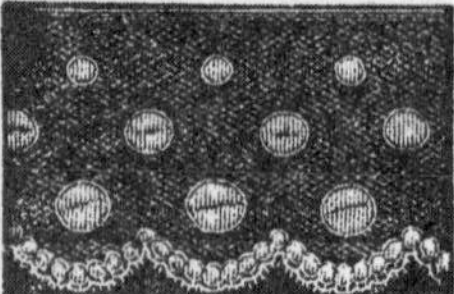

No. 39C763 Fancy Raised Normandy Valenciennes Lace. This is a new snowball design, which is extremely stylish and popular. Very desirable for waists, underwear and fancy work. Comes in four widths.

Width, inches..	2	3½
Per yard... ...	5c	8c
Per doz. yds....	58c	90c
Width, ins..	4	5
Per yard...	$0.10	$0.12
Per doz. yds.	1.15	1.38

No. 39C766 Fancy Raised Normandy Valenciennes Insertion, snowball pattern, to match above lace. Comes in two widths.

Width, inches..	1⅛	2⅝
Per yard	5c	6c
Per doz. yds....	55c	69c

No. 39C769 Fancy English Point de Paris Valenciennes Lace. This is a real lace design patterned after the expensive laces. Has a hand made effect. We recommend this for splendid washing and wearing qualities as well as for the pretty design. Comes in four widths.

Width, ins...	1⅞	3¼
Per yard....	6c	$0.10
Per doz. yds.	65c	1.12
Width, ins.	4	5⅛
Per yard...	$0.12	$0.16
Per doz. yds.	1.39	1.75

No. 39C772 Fancy English Point de Paris Valenciennes Insertion, same pattern, to match above lace.

Width, inches..	1⅝	2¼
Per yard	5c	7c
Per doz. yds....	55c	80c

No. 39C786 White Oriental or Net Top Lace, with the new button design, worked in fancy effect. This is on a very fine quality net. A very rich and effective pattern. Comes in three widths.

Width, inches..................	4⅜	6	8½
Price, per yard..................	$0.12	$0.15	$0.21
Per doz. yards..................	1.39	1.75	2.40

No. 39C788 Champagne Colored Oriental or Net Top Lace. The new button effect, same design as No. 39C786. Comes in 3 widths.

Width, ins..................	4⅜	6	8½
Price, per yard..................	$0.12	$0.15	$0.21
Per doz. yards..................	1.39	1.75	2.40

No. 39C792 White Oriental or Net Top Lace, on an exceptionally fine and close net. The pattern is the very latest pressed in design in a dainty grape and floral effect. We especially recommend this for an attractive lace. Comes in four widths.

Width, ins.	3½	5⅜
Price, per yd.	$0.13	$0.17
Per doz. yds.	1.45	1.90
Width, ins.	7⅛	8½
Price, per yd.	$0.21	$0.28
Per doz. yds.	2.40	3.00

No. 39C794 Champagne Colored Oriental or Net Top Lace. This is the same design as above No. 39C792. Also comes in four widths.

Width, ins.	3½	5⅜
Price, per yd.	$0.13	$0.17
Per doz. yds.	1.45	1.90
Width, ins.	7⅛	8½
Price, per yd.	$0.21	$0.28
Per doz. yds.	2.40	3.00

No. 39C798 White Oriental or Net Top Lace. This is an exceptionally beautiful pattern, closely worked on a very fine quality of Brussels net. The design is the new button and wheat pattern, heavily worked, open design edge. Comes in three widths.

Width, inches......		4
Price, per yard....		$0.12
Per dozen yards...		1.40
Width, ins.	6	8
Price, per yd.	$0.19	$0.25
Per doz. yds.	2.25	2.75

If by mail, postage extra, per yard, 2 cents.

No. 39C800 Butter Color Oriental or Net Top Lace, in the button and wheat design, same pattern as No. 39C798. Comes in three widths.

Width, inches......		4
Price, per yard...		$0.12
Per dozen yards...		1.40
Width, ins.	6	8
Price, per yd.	$0.19	$0.25
Per doz. yds.	2.25	2.75

If by mail, postage extra, per yard, 2 cents.

French Valenciennes Laces.

No. 39C820 White French Valenciennes Lace. Honiton design with point d' esprit pattern on fine quality thread net. A dainty and pretty trimming. Comes in four widths.

Width, ins.....	½	¾
Per doz. yds...	14c	18c
Width, ins.....	1	1⅛
Per doz. yds...	22c	28c

We do not sell less than 12-yard pieces.

No. 39C823 White French Valenciennes Insertion. Honiton design to match above laces. Comes in two widths.

Width, in.....	½	¾
Per doz. yds..	14c	19c

We do not sell less than 12-yard pieces.

No. 39C826 White French Valenciennes Lace, with teneriffe wheel and Mexican drawn work edge, with a point d'esprit net top. A very pretty trimming at an exceptionally low price. Comes in three widths.

Width, ins...	¾	1	1⅛
Per doz. yds.	21c	32c	44c

No. 39C829 White French Valenciennes Insertion, teneriffe wheel and Mexican drawn work edge to match above laces. Comes in two widths.

Width, in.......	¾	1
Per doz. yds....	22c	33c

We do not sell less than 12-yard pieces.

No. 39C832 White French Valenciennes Lace, hand made with new ball button design, made on a fine thread net. A showy and effective pattern. Comes in three widths.

Width ins.....	⅝	1⅛	1⅜
Per doz. yds.	23c	34c	42c

We do not sell less than 12-yard pieces.

No. 39C835 White French Valenciennes Insertion, hand made with ball button effect and to match No. 39C832. Comes in two widths.

Width, ins....	1	1⅛
Per doz. yds.	28c	33c

We do not sell less than 12-yard pieces.

No. 39C838 White French Valenciennes Lace. Pretty floral design with a purled edge. This is a very dainty and neat pattern. Comes in four widths.

Width, ins......	⅜	1⅛
Per doz. yds....	30c	39c
Width, ins......	1⅛	1⅜
Per doz. yds....	49c	62c

We do not sell less than 12-yard pieces.

No. 39C841 White French Valenciennes Insertion. Floral deigns on fine thread net, same pattern as above, to match the above lace. Comes in two widths.

Width, ins....	⅜	1⅛
Per doz. yds..	30c	38c

We do not sell less than 12-yard pieces.

No. 39C844 White French Valenciennes Lace, with a beading top and heavy button pattern edge on a net having a point d'esprit effect. This is one of the most popular and prettiest designs of the season. Comes in three widths.

Width, ins..	¾	1⅛	1⅜
Per doz. yds.	26c	41c	56c

We do not sell less than 12-yard pieces.

No. 39C847 White French Valenciennes Insertion, with beading edge on both edges and button effect pattern, to match the above lace. Width, 1 inch. Price, per dozen yards..................35c

We do not sell less than 12-yard pieces.

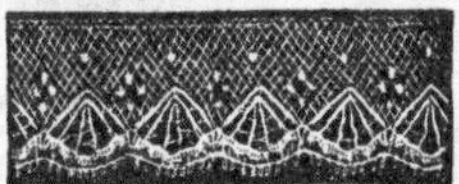

No. 39C850 White French Valenciennes Lace. This is a very fine thread and one of the better qualities. The design is very dainty, having a real hand made fan effect. Comes in three widths.

Width, ins..	⅝	1	1⅜
Per doz. yds.	35c	54c	73c

We do not sell less than 12-yard pieces.

No. 39C853 White French Valenciennes Insertion, with a fan effect design to match the above lace. Width, ¾ inch.

Price, per dozen yds..36c

We do not sell less than 12-yard pieces.

No. 39C856 White Calais French Valenciennes Lace. A very pretty floral design, made on a round hole or German mesh. This is a very strong and durable lace, which will wash and wear splendidly. Is also very dainty and effective. Comes in three widths.

Width, ins...	¾	1⅛	1⅜
Per doz. yds.	44c	56c	72c

We do not sell less than 12-yard pieces.

No. 39C859 White Calais French Valenciennes Insertion, in floral design to match above lace. Width, ⅝ inch.

Price, per doz. yds... 43c

We do not sell less than 12-yard pieces.

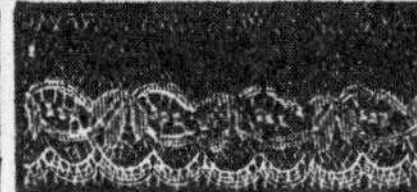

No. 39C862 White French Valenciennes Lace. This is one of the newest patterns, having a heavy design. It is extremely fashionable and popular with the best trade. Comes in four widths.

Width, in......	⅝	1
Per doz. yds...	29c	37c
Width, ins....	1¼	1⅜
Per doz. yds...	48c	68c

We do not sell less than 12-yard pieces.

No. 39C865 White French Valenciennes Insertion, same pattern and to match the above lace. Comes in two widths.

Width, ins......	⅝	1
Per doz. yds....	30c	40c

We do not sell less than 12-yard pieces.

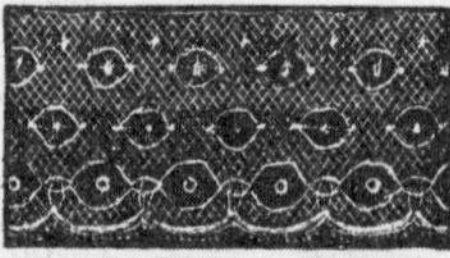

No. 39C868 White French Valenciennes Lace. This is an extra fine quality with an exceptionally fine thread. The Spanish teneriffe design represents the drawn-work patterns. One of the daintiest and prettiest styles shown. Comes in four widths.

Width, inches.	⅝	1⅛
Price, per yd...	4c	7c
Per doz. yds...	45c	80c
Width. ins...	1½	1¾
Price, per yd..	9c	$0.11
Per doz. yds..	98c	1.25

No. 39C871 White French Valenciennes Insertion. Dainty design to match above pattern.

Width, ins...	¾	1¼
Price, per yd.	4c	7c
Per doz. yds.	45c	79c

No. 39C874 White French Mechlin Valenciennes Lace. This is a pretty and striking cut out design, made on a fine maline net. The Mechlin vals are very popular and stylish and very desirable for dress trimmings of all sorts as well as muslin wear. Comes in four widths.

Width, inch..	¾	1
Price, per yd..	4c	6c
Per doz. yds..	44c	66c
Width, ins...	1⅛	2
Price, per yd..	8c	$0.10
Per doz. yds..	90c	1.15

No. 39C877 White French Mechlin Valenciennes Insertion on a maline net with cut-out design to match above lace. Comes in two widths.

Width, inches.	⅞	1⅛
Price, per yd..	4c	7c
Per doz. yds...	45c	78c

No. 39C880 White Mechlin Valenciennes Lace, having a pretty floral design on a very fine Brussels net, the net being dotted with very small button effect. One of the prettiest styles of the season. Comes in four widths.

Width, inch..	½	⅞
Price, per yd..	5c	7c
Per doz. yds..	53c	76c
Width, inches	1¼	1⅜
Price, per yd.	9c	$0.11
Per doz. yds..	99c	1.28

No. 39C883 White French Mechlin Valenciennes Insertion in floral design and to match the above lace. Comes in two widths.

Width, inch..	⅝	1
Price, per yd..	5c	7c
Per doz. yds..	53c	77c

English Valenciennes Lace.

No. 39C886 White Nottingham Mechlin Valenciennes Lace. Made of a very fine thread; an exceptionally delicate and exquisite design; washes and wears well. Comes in four widths.

Width, inch..	⅜	⅝
Per doz. yds..	23c	28c
Width, ins. ..	1⅛	1½
Per doz. yds..	34c	45c

We do not sell less than 12-yard pieces.

No. 39C889 White Nottingham Mechlin Valenciennes Lace Insertion, to match above lace. Width, ⅝ inch.

Price, per doz. yds. 26c

We do not sell less than 12-yard pieces.

No. 39C887 White Nottingham Band Maline Valenciennes Lace, with the new teneriffe effect and ribbon design and having a fast purled edge. Comes in four widths.

Width, in....	⅝	⅞
Per doz. yds.	42c	50c
Width, ins...	1⅛	1⅜
Per doz. yds.	59c	68c

We do not sell less than 12-yard pieces.

No. 39C888 White Nottingham Maline Valenciennes Lace Insertion. Teneriffe effect to match above lace. Width, 1 in.

Price, per doz. yds. 55c

We do not sell less than 12-yard pieces.

No. 39C890 White English Nottingham Fancy Band Valenciennes Lace, made of a heavy thread. A very desirable pattern, having a beading through the center. An effective trimming for any purpose. Will wear and wash exceptionally well, at the same time looking very neat and dainty. Comes in three widths.

Width, ins..	⅝	1
Per yard....	4c	6c
Per doz. yds.	46c	65c
Width, ins........		1⅜
Per yard........		8c
Per doz. yds.......		90c

No. 39C891 White English Nottingham Valenciennes Insertion, with beading through center to match above lace. Comes in two widths.

Width, inches	¾	1¼
Per yard......	5c	7c
Per doz. yards	52c	75c

Black Valenciennes Lace.

No. 39C892 Black French Valenciennes Lace. Honiton design. This is a fine quality of lace at an exceptionally low price. Comes in three widths.

Width, in.....	½	¾
Per doz. yds..	15c	19c
Width, inch........		1
Per doz. yds......		23c

We not sell less than 12-yard pieces.

No. 39C895 Black French Valenciennes Lace Insertion. Honiton design, to match above lace. Width, ¾ inch.

Price, per doz. yds. 20c

We do not sell less than 12-yard pieces.

Net Top Oriental Laces.

No. 39C781 White Oriental Net Top Lace. The net top or oriental laces are very popular this season for millinery purposes as well as dresses, sleeves of jackets, etc. Comes in three widths.

Width, ins..................	3	4⅜	6¼
Price, per yard..............	7c	$0.10	$0.12
Per doz. yards..............	80c	1.10	1.38

No. 39C784 Champagne Colored Oriental or Net Top Lace, same design as No. 39C781. The champagne shade is very popular. Comes in three widths.

Width, ins..................	3	4⅜	6¼
Price, per yard..............	7c	$0.10	$0.12
Per doz. yards..............	80c	1.10	1.38

REFER TO THE OTHER DEPARTMENTS

and send us your order for all the goods you need. If you make up a shipment to go by freight you will be getting your goods at the lowest expense for transportation.

No. 39C904 Black Calais French Valenciennes Lace, with Mexican ring effect edge and a scroll beading through center; suitable for No. 1 ribbon. Comes in three widths.

Width, ins. ⅝ ⅞ 1⅛
Per doz. yds. 26c 35c 43c

We do not sell less than 12-yard pieces.

No. 39C907 Black Calais French Valenciennes Insertion, with scroll design and beading on either side and a Mexican ring effect through center to match above lace. Width, 1 inch.

Price, per doz. yds.. 46c

We do not sell less than 12-yard pieces.

No. 39C910 Black French Valenciennes Lace, with the new button design on a nice quality net. This is a very desirable pattern, showy and effective. Comes in four widths.

Width, ins. ⅝ 1 1⅜ 1⅞
Per yard 3c 5c 7c 9c
Doz. yds. 34c 55c 78c 99c

We do not sell less than 12-yard pieces.

No. 39C913 Black French Valenciennes Insertion in button pattern to match above lace.

Width, ins.... ⅝ 1⅛
Price, per yd. 3c 5c
Per doz. yds... 34c 56c

We do not sell less than 12-yard pieces.

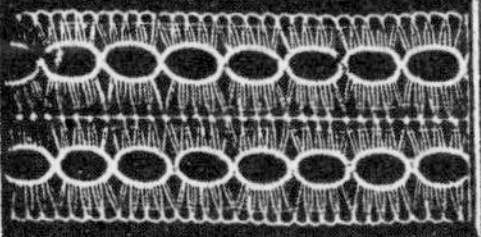

No. 39C916 White French Valenciennes Beading. Very neat and popular pattern to be used in connection with laces and ribbons, for drawing No. 1 ribbon through. A good quality at an especially low price. Comes in two widths, one-row and two-row.

1-row 2-row
Width, in.... ⅝ ⅞
Per doz. yds.. 8c 16c

We do not sell less than 12-yard pieces.

No. 39C917 Black French Valenciennes Beading. Same pattern as No. 39C916. A very dainty pattern for drawing No. 1 ribbon through. Comes in two widths. 1-row 2-row

Width, in..... ⅝ ⅞
Per doz. yds.. 11c 22c

We do not sell less than 12-yard pieces.

No. 39C919 White French Valenciennes Beading. Teneriffe effect. This is a new and very pretty pattern for drawing No. 1 ribbon through. One row and two row.

1-row 2-row
Width, in..... ⅝ ⅞
Per doz. yds.. 12c 24c

We do not sell less than 12-yard pieces.

WE do not accept orders for less than 50 cents, as explained on page 2.

No. 39C921 White French Calais Valenciennes Beading, on a plain net, suitable for drawing No. 1 ribbon through. Very extensively used in connection with laces and embroideries. A very dainty trimming. Comes in two widths. 1-row 2-row

Width, in.... ½ 1
Per doz. yds.. 15c 30c

We do not sell less than 12-yard pieces.

No. 39C922 Black Valenciennes Beading, on a fine net, same style and pattern as above, suitable for drawing No. 1 ribbon through; fast black color, washes and wears well. Comes in one and two-row.

1-row 2-row
Width, in..... ½ 1
Per doz. yds.. 16c 32c

We do not sell less than 12-yard pieces.

No. 39C924 White French Valenciennes Beading. This is a new and very beautiful design, entirely new, having a real cluny effect. Suitable for drawing No. 1 ribbon through. Comes in one and two-row widths.

1-row 2-row
Width, ins... ⅝ 1¼
Per doz. yds.. 25c 50c

We do not sell less than 12-yard pieces.

No. 39C926 White French Valenciennes Beading. The design, a Maltese scroll, is one of the newest and prettiest designs. Can also be used with a No. 1 ribbon. Very pretty for waists, corset covers, also neckbands, etc. Comes in two widths.

Width, inches. ½ 1½
Per doz. yds... 32c 64c

We do not sell less than 12-yard pieces.

No. 39C932 White English Valenciennes Bobbinet Footing, with beading effect and having a fast edge. Used for handkerchiefs, underwear and fancy work. Comes in two widths.

Width, inches.. 1 1⅝
Price, per yard. 4c 6c
Per doz. yards..44c 66c

No. 39C935 White Bobbinet Footing, on point d'esprit net and having a French valenciennes lace edge, in a pretty fan pattern. Comes in two widths.

Width, inches.. 1 1¾
Price, per yard. 5c 7c
Per doz. yards..51c 79c

No. 39C938 White Bobbinet Footing, with insertion effect, having a hand embroidered design on edge. This is a very dainty and neat pattern; used for handkerchiefs, underwear and fancy work. Comes in two widths.

Width, inches. 1¼ 1⅞
Price, per yard 5c 8c
Per dozen yds. 58c 89c

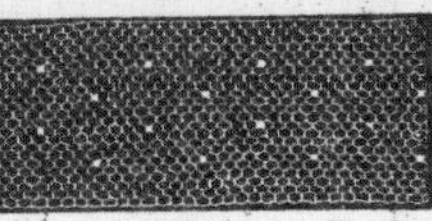

No. 39C941 Point d'Esprit Bobbinet Footing. This is a much finer quality net than above and may be used for all kinds of work where a nice quality is desired. Comes in two widths.

Width, inches. 1 1⅛
Price, per yard 4c 6c
Per dozen yds. 44c 70c

No. 39C944 White Point d'Esprit Bobbinet Footing. A nice quality and very desirable for handkerchiefs and all sorts of fancy work. Comes in two widths.

Width, inches. 1 1⅛
Price, per yard 5c 8c
Per dozen yds.. 52c 78c

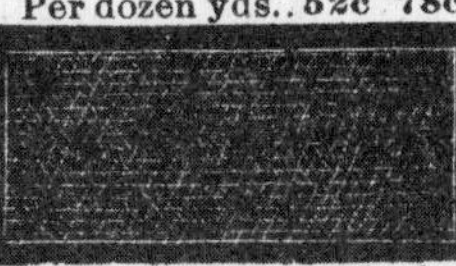

No. 39C947 Plain White Bobbinet Footing, used for all kinds of fancy work and handkerchiefs; a very good quality at a low price. Comes in two widths.

Width, inches.. 1 1⅛
Per dozen yds... 18c 21c

We do not sell less than 12-yard pieces.

No. 39C949 Plain White Bobbinet Footing. A very fine quality, used for the better grade of handkerchiefs and different fancy work. Comes in three widths.

Width, ins. 1⅛ 1⅛ 2
Price, per yd. 3c 4c 5c
Per doz. yds. 30c 40c 50c

All Silk Chantilly Laces.

No. 39C952 Black All Silk Chantilly Lace, with floral design and Mexican teneriffe edge. The narrow chantillies have had a very extensive sale, being very popular for different trimmings. Comes in four widths.

Width, inches.. ¾ 1⅛
Per yard........ 4c 6c
Per doz. yds....45c 70c
Width, inches....1⅛ 2⅛
Per yard.......8c $0.10
Per doz. yds...90c 1.10

No. 39C953 White Chantilly All Silk Lace, with floral and Mexican teneriffe edge; design same pattern as above. Comes in four widths.

Width, inches.. ¾ 1⅛
Per yard........ 4c 6c
Per doz. yds....45c 70c
Width, inches. 1⅛ 2⅛
Per yard...... 8c $0.10
Per doz. yds....90c 1.10

No. 39C956 Narrow Black Chantilly Lace. New fruit design and a fine quality of point d'esprit net. The season's newest pattern. Comes in four widths.

Width, inch.......... ⅝ ⅞
Per yard.............. 5c 7c
Per dozen yards....55c 80c
Width, ins.... 1⅛ 1½
Per yard......$0.10 $0.12
Per doz. yds.. 1.10 1.35

No. 39C957 Narrow White Silk Chantilly Lace. New fruit design and same pattern as above. Comes in four widths.

Width, inches....... ⅝ ⅞
Per yard.............. 5c 7c
Per dozen yards....55c 80c
Width, ins.... 1⅛ 1½
Per yard......$0.10 $0.12
Per doz. yds.. 1.10 1.35

No. 39C960 Black Silk Chantilly Lace, on a very good quality net. A large attractive floral design. This is an especial value at the price we quote. Comes in four widths.

Width ins.. 2½ 3¼
Per yard.... 5c 8c
Doz. yards. 55c 90c
Width ins.. 6 7½
Per yard...$0.12 $0.15
Doz. yards. 1.35 1.70

No. 39C961 White Chantilly All Silk Lace. Pretty floral design, same pattern as above. Comes in four widths.

Width ins.. 2½ 3¾
Per yard... 5c 8c
Doz. yards. 55c 90c
Width ins.. 6 7½
Per yard..$0.12 $0.15
Doz. yards. 1.35 1.70

No. 39C964 Black French Chantilly All Silk Lace. This is one of the newest designs. The pattern is a very attractive floral pattern in shaded effect. Comes in four widths.

Width ins.. 3 4½
Per yard...$0.09 $0.13
Doz. yards. 1.00 1.40
Width ins.. 6 8
Per yard...$0.17 $0.23
Doz. yards. 1.85 2.50

No. 39C965 White French Silk Chantilly Lace. Large floral design, shaded effect, same pattern as above. Comes in four widths.

Width ins.. 3 4½
Per yard...$0.09 $0.13
Doz. yards. 1.00 1.40
Width ins.. 6 8
Per yard...$0.17 $0.23
Doz. yards. 1.85 2.50

No. 39C968 Black All Silk Chantilly Lace, on a very fine double thread Brussels net. The pattern, which is the new button or snowball design, is very dainty and pretty. An exceptionally good pattern for millinery purposes as well as dress trimmings. Comes in four widths.

Width, ins.. 3 4¾
Per yard....$0.10 $0.14
Per doz. yds. 1.10 1.60
Width. ins.. 6 7½
Per yard....$0.19 $0.24
Per doz. yds. 2.25 2.50

No. 39C969 White All Silk Chantilly Lace. The new button or snowball design. The same pattern as above. Comes in four widths.

Width, ins.. 3 4¾
Per yd.....$0.10 $0.14
Per doz. yds. 1.10 1.60
Width, ins.. 6 8
Per yd.....$0.19 $0.24
Per doz. yds. 2.25 2.50

MAKE YOUR ORDERS AT LEAST 50 CENTS OR MORE. We do not accept orders of less than 50 cents, as explained on page 2. Don't forget postage either, when you want goods sent by mail.

No. 39C972 Black All Silk French Chantilly Lace, made in Calais, France. This is an elaborate floral hand made design, with a real French lace thread. This is a particularly attractive pattern, showy and pretty. Comes in three widths.

Width, ins... 2½ 4
Per yard.... 8c $0.12
Per doz. yds. 90c 1.35
Width, ins........ 6
Per yard..........$0.18
Per doz. yds........ 2.00

No. 39C973 White Silk French Chantilly Lace, with the hand made floral design, same pattern as above. Comes in three widths.

Width, ins.. 2½ 4
Per yard... 8c $0.12
Per doz. yds. 90c 1.35
Width, ins........ 6
Per yard..........$0.18
Per doz. yds........ 2.00

No. 39C975 White Cotton Nottingham Band Lace, with a Mexican drawnwork wheel effect. These laces are very popular and extensively used for waists, dresses and muslin wear. Comes in three widths.

Width, ins.. 1¾ 2⅛ 3½
Per yard.... 4c 6c 8c
Per doz. yds. 45c 70c 90c

No. 39C976 Champagne Color Cotton Nottingham Lace. Mexican drawn work wheel effect. Same pattern as above. Comes in three widths.

Width, ins.. 1¾ 2⅛ 3½
Per yard.... 4c 6c 8c
Per doz. yds. 45c 70c 90c

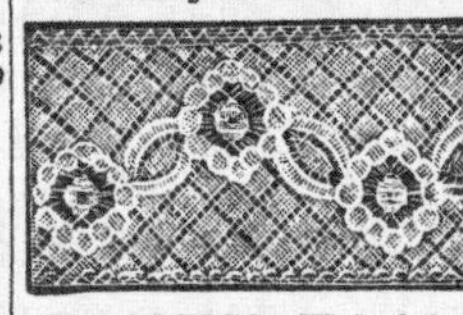

No. 39C979 White English Nottingham Band Lace. This is a pretty renaissance design with embroidered effect. A very desirable trimming for waists, dresses and different wash goods. Comes in four widths.

Width, inches 1¾ 2½
Per yard...... 3c 5c
Per doz. yds.. 35c 55c
Width, inches 3¼ 4¼
Per yard...... 7c $0.09
Per doz. yds..80c 1.00

No. 39C980 Butter Color English Nottingham Band Lace. The renaissance design, embroidered effect, same pattern as above. Comes in four widths.

Width, inches 1¾ 2½
Per yard...... 3c 5c
Per doz. yds.. 35c 55c
Width, inches 3¼ 4¼
Per yard...... 7c $0.09
Per doz. yds..80c 1.00

No. 39C983 White English Mercerized Cotton Band Lace. This is a real guipure pattern on a fine maline net. The mercerized laces have a soft, silky appearance and look very pretty when used for different wash fabrics. Particularly desirable for waists and dresses. Comes in three widths.

Width, ins. 1⅝ 2⅛
Per yard..... 6c $0.09
Per doz. yds. 70c 1.00
Width, ins......... 3⅜
Per yard.........$0.12
Per dozen yards. 1.40

No. 39C984 Ecru or Arabian Color English Mercerized Cotton Band Lace in a guipure pattern on a maline net, same design as above. Comes in three widths.

Width, ins. 1⅝ 2⅛
Per yard... 6c $0.09
Per doz. yds. 70c 1.00
Width, ins....... 3⅜
Per yard.......$0.12
Per dozen yards. 1.40

No. 39C986 English Nottingham Teneriffe Band Lace, with the teneriffe Mexican hand drawnwork effect. This is an exact copy of the genuine Mexican hand work and is very stylish, attractive and rich looking. Comes in three widths.

Width, ins. 1½ 2⅛
Per yard. 7c $0.11
Per doz. yds. 80c 1.25
Width, ins... ... 3¼
Per yard.........$0.14
Per dozen yards. 1.50

No. 39C987 English Nottingham Teneriffe Band Lace, in the new Paris Arabian color (light tan). Same pattern as above. Comes in three widths.

Width, ins, 1½ 2⅛
Per yard...... 7c $0.11
Per doz. yds. 80c 1.25
Width, ins........ 3¼
Per yard..........$0.14
Per dozen yards 1.50

No. 39C989 French Cluny Band Insertion. The pattern is of a cluny and renaissance effect, copied from the real hand made, which is very expensive. The lace looks as well and wears as well and will make an extremely beautiful and rich looking waist, dress or muslin wear trimming. Comes in three widths.

Width, ins. 3 3¾
Per yard..$0.13 $0.16
Per doz. yds. 1.45 1.80
Width, inches... 4⅜
Per yard.........$0.20
Per dozen yards. 2.25

No. 39C990 White Plauen Venisse Band Insertion. A pretty trimming for waists, dresses and millinery purposes. Width, 1 inch.

Price, per yard..............................6c
Per dozen yards..............................70c

No. 39C992 Butter Color Plauen Venisse Band Insertion. Same pattern as above. Width, 1 inch.

Price, per yard..............................6c
Per dozen yards..............................70c

No. 39C994 Butter Color Plauen Venisse Galloon. Guipure pattern with a filet mesh; a new and pretty pattern. Width, 1⅝ inches.
Price, per yard.........8c
Per dozen yards.....90c

No. 39C1002 White Plauen Band Insertion. This is a pretty teneriffe wheel design with button effect in center. This trimming can be used in a continuous length or the wheels can be used separately for medallions. Width, 1⅝ inches.
Price, per yard.........8c
Per dozen yards.......78c

No. 39C1003 Champagne Colored Plauen Band Insertion, teneriffe wheel design, same pattern as above. Width, 1⅝ inches.
Price, per yard.........8c
Per dozen yards.....78c

No. 39C1006 White Plauen Galloon Trimming. This is a very pretty floral and leaf design with small button effect throughout, very dainty and stylish. The pattern can be used for separate medallions, using the flower and leaf, or comes in continuous length. Width, 1¾ inches.
Price, per yard....$0.16
Per dozen yards... 1.80

No. 39C1007 Champagne Color Plauen Venisse Galloon Trimming. Floral and leaf design, same pattern as above. Can be used in medallions or by the yard. Width, 1¾ inches.
Price, per yard....$0.16
Per dozen yards... 1.80

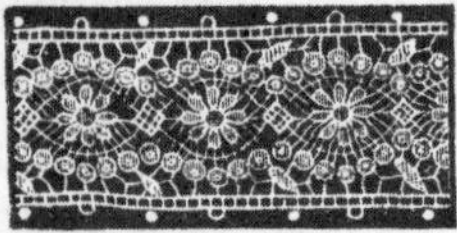

No. 39C1010 White Plauen Band Insertion. The new raised, hand made button pattern with a medallion effect through center. This is an exceedingly pretty and stylish design. Will trim very attractively. Width, 2½ inches.
Price, per yard....$0.22
Per dozen yards... 2.50

No. 39C1011 Arabian Plauen Venisse Band Insertion. Raised hand made button pattern with medallion effect through center, same pattern as above. Width, 2½ inches.
Price, per yard....$0.22
Per dozen yards... 2.50

No. 39C1014 White Plauen Venisse Galloon Trimming, in medallion pattern. This is a large and attractive fancy wheel effect, with a small button design. A very pretty and bold pattern. An exceptional trimming for dresses and waists. Can be used in separate medallions, or by the yard. Comes about eleven wheels to the yard. Width, 3 inches.
Price, per yard....$0.24
Per dozen yards... 2.75

No. 39C1015 Champagne Color Plauen Venisse Medallion Trimming. Large wheel pattern with small button effect, same pattern as No. 39C1014. Width, 3 inches.
Price, per yard....$0.24
Per dozen yards... 2.75

No. 39C1018 White Plauen Batiste Galloon Trimming. Something new, attractive and elegant. It is the new Parisian flower effect, serpentine design. The pattern can be separated and used as medallions or by the yard. Width, 3¼ inches.
Price, per yard....$0.32
Per dozen yards... 3.60

No. 39C1019 Champagne Color Plauen Batiste Galloon Trimming. The new Parisian flower effect, serpentine design, same pattern as above. Width, 3¼ inches.
Price, per yard....$0.32
Per dozen yards... 3.60

No. 39C1022 White Net Plauen Band or Oriental Insertion. The design is the new snowball button effect with a floral pattern. The oriental band trimmings are very stylish. Width, 1⅝ inches.
Price, per yard....$0.09
Per dozen yards... 1.00

No. 39C1023 Champagne Color Plauen Band Net or Oriental Insertion. The snowball or button effect. A floral design, same pattern as above. Width, 1⅝ inches.
Price, per yard....$0.09
Per dozen yards... 1.00

No. 39C1026 White Plauen Oriental Net Medallion Trimming. This is a dainty and effective trimming and is very stylish for this season's modes. Very closely and very prettily worked. Can be used separately as medallions or by the yard.
Width, inches.........1⅝
Price, per yard....$0.12
Per dozen yards... 1.35

No. 39C1027 Champagne Color Plauen Medallion or Oriental Net Trimming, closely worked on a fine quality net, same design as above. Width, 1⅝ inches.
Price, per yard....$0.12
Per dozen yards... 1.35

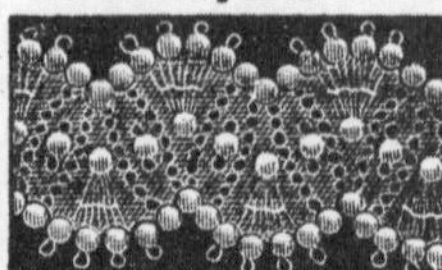

No. 39C1030 White Plauen or Oriental Net Top Band Trimming. This is the new button effect, worked on a fine quality net. This design looks exceedingly well and attractive. Width, 2¼ inches.
Price, per yard....$0.20
Per dozen yards... 2.25

No. 39C1031 Champagne Color Plauen or Oriental Net Top Band Trimming. New button design, same pattern as above. Width, 2¼ inches.
Price, per yard....$0.20
Per dozen yards... 2.25

No. 39C1034 Black Plauen Mercerized Medallion Band Lace Trimming. This is a Mexican teneriffe drawnwork design. The mercerized plauen trimmings have a very silky appearance and are very stylish. Width, 1½ inches.
Price, per yard....$0.12
Per dozen yards... 1.35

No. 39C1037 Black Plauen Mercerized Band Trimming. This is a very dainty design. At the same time very attractive and pretty, and has a large teneriffe wheel design with scroll effect. Width, 2 inches.
Price, per yard....$0.15
Per dozen yards... 1.65

No. 39C1038 Black All Silk French Chantilly Galloon. This is a large, elegant wheel design, medallion pattern, made of heavy thread and is a very desirable trimming for dresses, skirts, etc. Comes in three widths.

Width, ins.	2¼	3
Per yard..	$0.10	$0.13
Per doz. yds.	1.10	1.45
Width, ins........		4½
Per yard		$0.16
Per dozen yards..		1.75

No. 39C1040 Black Brilliant Mercerized Plauen Medallion Galloon Lace, with the button and teneriffe design. This is one of the prettiest patterns shown. Width, 2 inches.
Price, per yard....$0.23
Price, per doz. yds., 2.50

No. 39C1043 Black Cluny Insertion. Teneriffe wheel design, made of an extra heavy thread. This is a particularly desirable pattern. Will make a very rich trimming. Comes in three widths.

Width, ins...	2⅛	3⅜
Per yard........	6c	$0.10
Per doz. yds...	65c	1.10
Width, ins		4¾
Per yard..............		$0.14
Per dozen yards ..		1.50

No. 39C1046 Black French Silk Chantilly Band Insertion. This is a pretty cut-out design on a fine, double thread Brussels net. This design is very exclusive and rich looking. Comes in four widths.

Width, ins.	2	2⅞
Per yard...	$0.10	$0.12
Per doz. yds.	1.10	1.35
Width, ins.	3⅜	4⅞
Per yard..	$0.16	$0.20
Per doz. yds.	1.70	2.25

No. 39C1049 Fine Quality Black Silk French Calais, Chantilly Band Insertion. This is the newest fruit and floral design, with an insertion effect on both sides. We particularly recommend this pattern for a beautiful, showy trimming. Comes in three widths.

Width, ins.	2¼	3
Per yard...	$0.10	$0.15
Per doz. yds	1.10	1.65
Width, ins........		3⅞
Per yard..........		$0.19
Per doz. yds......		2.10

No. 39C1052 Black All Silk French Chantilly Lace Insertion. This is a real guipure pattern with the new, hand made buttonhole effect, on an extra fine, double thread Brussels net. This pattern is particularly attractive and new. Will make a beautiful trimming. Comes in four widths.

Width, ins..	2¼	2⅞
Per yard...	$0.16	$0.19
Per doz. yds	1.65	2.10
Width, ins..	3½	4⅝
Per yard...	$0.23	$0.29
Per doz. yds	2.50	3.25

Allover Laces.

No. 39C1055 White English Nottingham Allover Lace. The pattern, an entirely new, hand-made faggoting effect, is very desirable. Width, 18 inches. Price, per yd..17c

No. 39C1057 White English Nottingham Cluny Allover Lace. This is an exact copy of the real hand made. There has been an exceptionally large sale on this style of lace for yokes, trimmings, etc. Width, 18 inches.
Price, per yard......55c

No. 39C1058 White English Nottingham Allover Lace, having a Spanish drawnwork and teneriffe effect and a striped embroidered design. This is one of the new and stylish patterns for this season. Width, 18 inches. Price, per yard......29c

No. 39C1061 White English Nottingham Allover Lace. This is a pretty button design with a fine and heavy thread effect. The pattern is very effective. Width, 18 inches.
Price, per yard..................32c

No. 39C1064 Arabian Color English Nottingham Allover Lace, with the button and teneriffe design, same pattern as above. Width, 18 inches.
Price, per yard..............32c

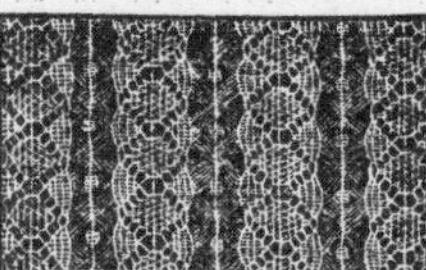

No. 39C1067 White English Nottingham Allover Lace. A striped, Mexican drawnwork design on a heavy, tatting effect net. This is new and attractive. Width, 18 inches. Price, per yd..37c

No. 39C1070 White English Nottingham Allover Lace. Pretty floral design with a hand drawnwork ring effect. This is on a fine net and patterned after expensive laces. Width, 18 inches.
Price, per yard......39c

No. 39C1073 Arabian Color English Nottingham Allover Lace. Floral design, with hand drawnwork ring effect. Same pattern as above. Width, 18 in. Price, per yard..39c

No. 39C1076 White English Nottingham Allover Lace. This is a real renaissance design on a new craquelle net. This pattern is similar to the high priced laces. We quote this at an exceptionally low price. Width, 18 inches. Price, per yd..50c

No. 39C1079 Arabian Color English Nottingham Allover Lace. Renaissance design on craquelle net, same pattern as above. Width, 18 inches.
Price, per yard.......50c

No. 39C1082 White English Nottingham Allover Lace. An embroidered and beading effect with a fine valenciennes design. The beading is for a No. 1 ribbon. This is very dainty and fine. Valenciennes allovers are very popular. Width, 18 inches. Price, per yd..55c

No. 39C1085 White English Nottingham Valenciennes Allover Lace. This is a floral design; an exact copy of the real hand made and on a very fine quality net. This is very dainty and rich. Width, 18 inches.
Price, per yard.......70c

No. 39C1087 White English Mechlin Valenciennes Allover Lace. A Mexican ring drawnwork effect and small leaf design. This is a very exquisite pattern on a very fine thread net. Width, 18 inches.
Price, per yard..............80c

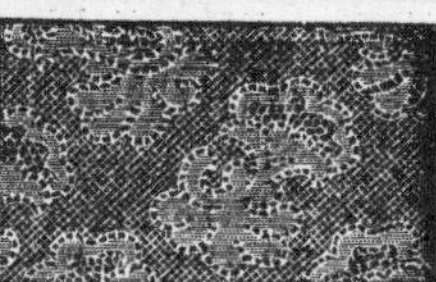

No. 39C1090 White English Platte Valenciennes Allover Lace. This is a pretty floral design on a fine quality net. Will wash and wear well. The valenciennes allovers are very desirable for this season's styles. Width, 18 inches. Per yard....33c

No. 39C1093 White English Platte Valenciennes Allover Lace, with the new snowball design in a lace ribbon effect, done in squares. A very effective and pretty pattern. Width, 18 inches.
Price, per yard.....46c

Oriental or Net Allover Laces.

No. 39C1100 White Oriental or Net Allover Lace. This is a neat and pretty design, closely worked on a good quality net. Oriental allovers will be very popular for the coming season. Width, 18 inches.
Price, per yard.....36c
If by mail, postage extra, per yard, 4 cents.

No. 39C1101 Butter Color Oriental or Net Allover Lace. Same design as above. Width, 18 inches.
Price, per yard.....36c

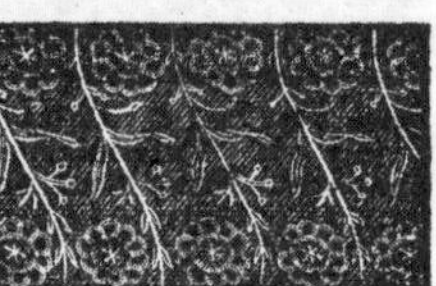

No. 39C1104 White Plauen or Oriental Net Allover Lace. This is a floral and leaf design, with a hand worked ring effect. Worked on a fine quality oriental net. Width, 18 inches.
Price, per yard.....49c

No. 39C1105 Champagne Color Plauen Oriental Net Allover Lace. A floral design, with hand worked ring effect, same pattern as above. Width, 18 inches.
Price, per yard....49c

No. 39C1108 White Plauen Oriental Net Allover Lace. This is a pretty floral design with a teneriffe and raised work, wheel effect on fine quality oriental net. Width, 18 inches.
Price, per yard.....75c

No. 39C1109 Champagne Color Plauen Oriental Net Allover Lace. Floral design with teneriffe raised work, wheel effect, same pattern as above. Width, 18 inches.
Price, per yard.....75c

No. 39C1112 White Plauen Oriental or Net Allover Lace. This is the new button and pressed-in effect. One of the very latest and most popular designs. This is worked on a very fine quality oriental net, and we recommend this for a particularly desirable style. Width, 18 inches.
Price, per yard.......80c

No. 39C1113 Champagne Color Oriental or Net Top Allover Lace. In the new button and pressed-in effect, same pattern as above. Width, 18 inches.
Price, per yard.......80c

No. 39C1116 White Plauen Oriental or Net Allover Lace. This pattern is the new point gauze effect with a wheel design, interwoven with the new snowball effect. Worked on one of the finest qualities of oriental nets. Will make a very stunning and effective waist, yoke, etc. Width, 18 inches.
Price, per yard.......98c

No. 39C1117 Champagne Color Plauen Oriental Net Allover Lace. The wheel design interwoven with the new snowball effect, same pattern as above. Width, 18 inches. Price, per yard, 98c

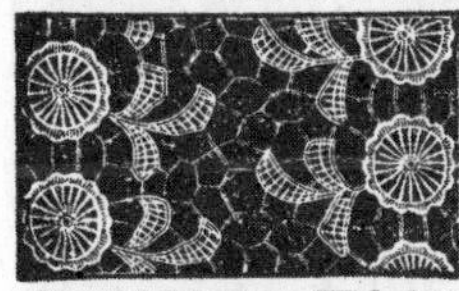

No. 39C1120 White Plauen Venisse Allover Lace, in the Mexican drawnwork design. A real Irish point pattern. Width, 18 inches.
Price, per yard......60c

No. 39C1121 Champagne Color Plauen Venisse Allover Lace. The Mexican drawnwork design, Irish point pattern. Same design as above. Width, 18 inches.
Price, per yard......60c

No. 39C1124 White Plauen Venisse Allover Lace. The new raised button effect and Spanish teneriffe design. Very effective and pretty. Width, 18 inches.
Price, per yard......75c

No. 39C1125 Champagne Color Plauen Venisse Allover Lace, in the new raised button effect and Spanish teneriffe design. Same pattern as above. Width, 18 inches.
Price, per yard......75c

Black Allover Laces.

No. 39C1132 Black Allover Lace. Beading and insertion effect with a thread lace design. This is a very pretty looking pattern, equal to allovers that are sold at double the price. Width, 18 inches.
Price, per yard..... 22c

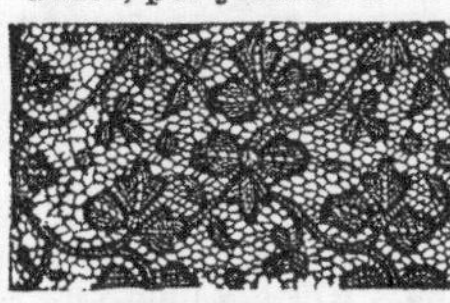

No. 39C1135 Black Nottingham Allover Lace. Floral design on a fine double thread net. For a tasty and pretty lace at a small price, this is exceptionally good. Width, 18 inches.
Price, per yard.......27c

No. 39C1138 Black Allover Lace, on a fine point d'esprit net. This is a new French square design, making a very pretty and dainty pattern. Width, 18 inches.
Price, per yard.......33c

No. 39C1141 Black Nottingham Allover Lace. Floral design on a new craquele net. Will compare in appearance with the very high priced net. Width, 18 inches.
Price, per yard.......39c

No. 39C1144 Black Silk French Chantilly Allover Lace. A very dainty and beautiful floral design, in the new button effect on a close Brussels net. Width, 18 inches.
Price, per yard.......58c

No. 39C1147 Black Silk Net Allover Lace. This is a very elegant design, the new button and teneriffe effect. Worked on a fine quality silk net. Will make up very beautifully. Used for waists, dresses and millinery purposes. Width, 18 inches.
Price, per yard.... ..60c

No. 39C1128 White Plauen Venisse Allover Lace. This is the new raised button effect and Mexican teneriffe design. A very exquisite and attractive pattern. Width, 18 inches.
Price, per yard......90c

No. 39C1129 Champagne Color Plauen Venisse Allover Lace. The raised button and Mexican teneriffe design. Same pattern as above. Width, 18 inches. Price, per yard..........90c

No. 39C1150 Black Silk French Chantilly Allover Lace. This is a rich guipure pattern on a fine Brussels net. Width, 18 inches.
Price, per yard 75c

No. 39C1153 Black Silk French Chantilly Allover Lace, on a point d'esprit net. A new, rich design with the new craquele effect. Width, 18 inches.
Price, per yard 80c

No. 39C1156 Black Silk French Calais Allover Lace. The new design in the hardanger, hand made square effect. This looks very pretty and attractive and is a rich design. Width, 18 inches.
Price, per yard....$1.00

42-inch Black Silk Allovers.

No. 39C1159 Black Silk French Chantilly Allover Lace. This is a new ring spot design on a fine doublethread Brussels net. Is particularly desirable for waists and full skirts. Width, 42 inches.
Price, per yard......81c

No. 39C1162 Black Silk French Chantilly Allover Lace. An exact copy of the real lace thread design in a floral pattern. Width, 42 inches.
Price, per yard....$1.10

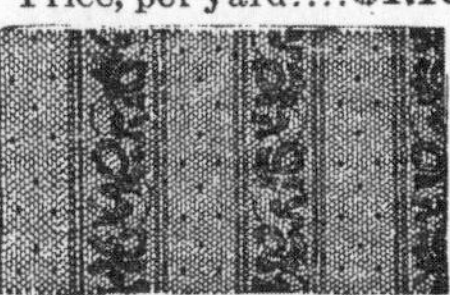

No. 39C1165 Black Silk French Allover Lace, with a floral stripe and point d'esprit effect, alternate rows of each. This is very dainty and rich looking for waists and full suits. Width, 42 inches.
Price, per yard....$1.60

Black Mercerized Plauen Allovers.

No. 39C1168 Black Mercerized Plauen Venisse Allover Lace. Pretty leaf design with the scroll button effect. New and pretty. Width, 18 inches.
Price, per yard.......95c

No. 39C1171 Black Mercerized Plauen Venisse Allover. This is a very attractive pattern with an entirely new teneriffe wheel design and small button effect. This is one of the most desirable patterns. Width, 18 inches. Price, per yard, $1.00

Russian Drapery Nets.

No 39C1173 Black Russian La Tosca Net. Sometimes known as the fish net allover. Used for waists and to cover entire skirts. Width, 45 inches.
Price, per yard..........48c

No. 39C1174 Black Silk La Tosca Net. Same pattern as above but much finer and an all silk net. Quality usually sold elsewhere for $1.25. Width, 45 inches. Price, per yard......75c

No. 39C1177 White Silk La Tosca Net. Same quality as above for waists and over dresses. Width, 45 inches.
Price, per yard..........75c

No. 39C1178 Black Silk La Tosca or Russian Net. Same style as No. 39C1173, but our highest quality, of very fine all silk. A very satisfactory and pretty drapery net. Width, 45 inches.
Price, per yard........$1.25

No. 39C1181 White Silk La Tosca or Russian Net. Same quality as above. Width, 45 inches. Price, per yard, $1.25

Heavy Thread Dotted Drapery Nets.

No. 39C1183 Point d'Esprit Allover Drapery Net. These nets will be very stylish and very extensively worn for skirts and waists, used as a drape over interlining. Width, 44 inches; black only. Price, per yard......48c

No. 39C1185 Point d'Esprit Allover or Drapery Net. Similar style to above but finer quality thread. Width, 44 inches; black only. Price, per yd...75c

No. 39C1186 Point d'Esprit Silk Allover or Drapery Net. A still finer quality than above; exceptional value; good $1.50 value. Width, 44 inches; black only. Price, per yard....$1.10

No. 39C1187 Point d'Esprit Silk Allover Net, our finest and best quality, an exceptionally fine net and one that we especially recommend. Width, 44 inches; black only.
Price, per yard.......$1.50

EMBROIDERY DEPARTMENT.

New and Pretty Patterns. Best Values Ever Shown.

If by mail, postage extra, 1c to 2c per yard.

Cambric Embroideries.

No. 39C1201 White Cambric Embroidery Edging. A neat and pretty design. Width, 1⅛ inches.
Price, per yard........2c

No. 39C1204 White Cambric Embroidery Edging. This is a pretty floral and openwork design. Width, 2 inches.
Price, per yard........4c

No. 39C1208 White Embroidery Cambric. This is a closely worked design in a floral and scroll work pattern. Width, 2¼ inches. Price, per yard...5c

No. 39C1211 White Cambric Embroidery Edging. This is a very pretty openwork design, closely worked. Width, 2¼ inches. Price, per yard...5c

No. 39C1214 White Cambric Embroidery Edging. This is a neat and attractive pattern with an openwork design and the new button effect. Width, 2⅜ inches. Price, per yard...6c

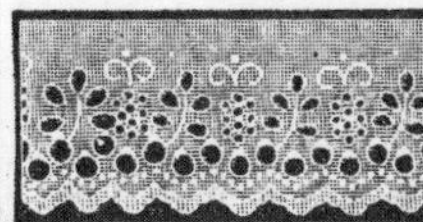

No. 39C1217 White Cambric Embroidery Edging. A very attractive and neat pattern in openwork and scroll design. A good quality of embroidery. Width, 3 inches. Per yard....8c

No. 39C1220 White Cambric Embroidery. A very new and pretty pattern. A bold, openwork design with the large, raised button effect. Width, 4¼ inches.
Price, per yard..........9c

No. 39C1223 White Cambric Embroidery. This is a new and pleasing pattern. Very attractively worked. Width, 5 inches.
Price, per yard..........10c

No. 39C1226 White Cambric Embroidery. A very showy and attractive pattern. Exceptionally good value at the price. Width, 6¾ inches.
Price, per yard..........12c

No. 39C1228 White Cambric Embroidery. This is a very pretty floral design worked in scroll, rings and openwork edging. One of the new and popular patterns. Width, 5⅞ inches.
Price, per yard..........14c

No. 39C1232 White Cambric Embroidery. This is a very new and pretty design, closely worked on good quality cloth. Width, 7¼ inches.
Price, per yard..........12c

No. 39C1235 White Cambric Embroidery. This is a pretty openwork design with teneriffe wheel and raised button effect. One of the newest and prettiest designs. Width, 6½ inches.
Price, per yard..........16c

No. 39C1238 White Cambric Embroidery. A neat and attractive large pattern. Nicely worked on good quality cloth. Width, 7¾ inches.
Price, per yard..........17c

No. 39C1241 White Cambric Embroidery. This is a large, openwork pattern with a ring insertion design. A very pretty skirting embroidery. Width, 10½ inches. Price, per yard..18c

No. 39C1244 White Cambric Embroidery. This is an exceptionally pretty and new design with an openwork and scroll pattern and the new raised button effect throughout. Width, 8¾ inches. Price, per yard...20c

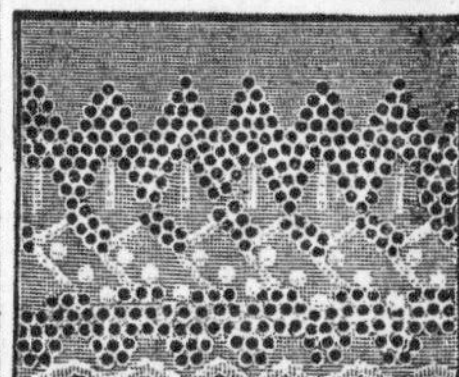

No. 39C1247 White Cambric Embroidery. This is a pretty and showy design, neatly worked on nice quality cambric. A desirable pattern for skirt flounces and corset covers. Width, 10½ inches.
Price, per yard..........23c

No. 39C1250 White Cambric Embroidery. A very attractive openwork design. This is one of the latest patterns. Width, 10⅜ ins. Per yd... 24c

No. 39C1253 White Cambric Embroidery. This is a very beautiful and attractive pattern. Particularly desirable for skirting and corset covers. The work is 5½ inches wide and entire width, 13½ ins. Per yd... 26c

No. 39C1256 White Cambric Embroidery. This is a new Mexican drawn work effect with the raised button work, which are very popular. This is a good skirting and corset cover pattern. Width, 14½ inches.
Price, per yard...... 35c

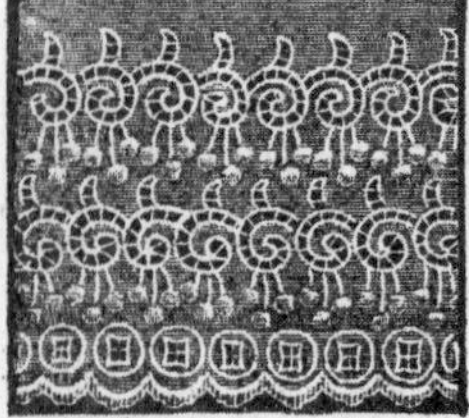

No. 39C1259 White Cambric Embroidery, with new teneriffe wheel effect, openwork and floral design. A very attractive and stylish pattern. Particularly adapted for corset covers and muslin underwear. Width, 16 inches.
Price, per yard....... 32c

No. 39C1262 White Cambric Embroidery, beautiful scroll and openwork design, studded with small, raised buttons. This is a very fine quality embroidery, suitable for all kinds of muslin wear and corset covers. Width, 16¾ inches.
Price, per yard...... 39c

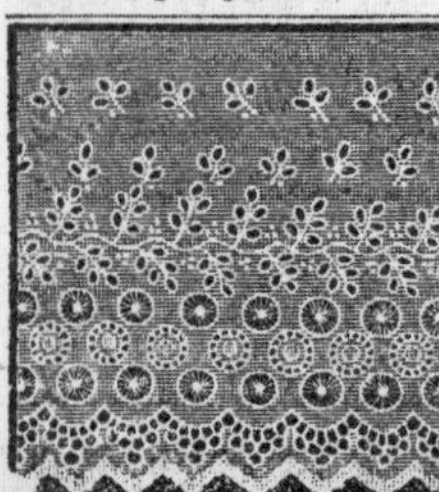

No. 39C1265 White Cambric Embroidery. This is a very exquisite and beautiful pattern, looking much prettier in the piece than what we can illustrate. The design is of a Mexican wheel effect with floral pattern throughout. Very fine quality of work on a fine cambric. Very desirable for all kinds of muslin wear and corset covers. Width, 17½ inches.
Price, per yard....... 48c

Ribbon Designs.

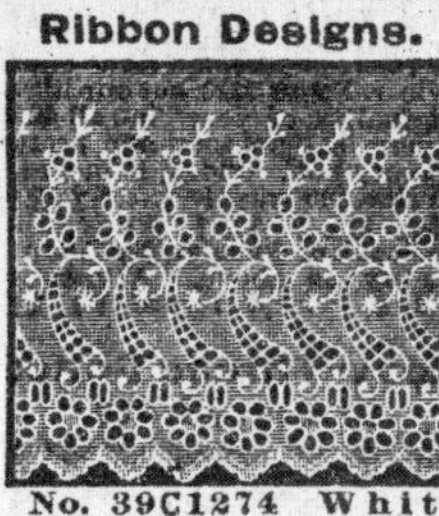

No. 39C1274 White Cambric Embroidery, with a pretty floral and scroll design, with ribbon effect for drawing No. 1 ribbon through. An excellent pattern for skirt flounces and corset covers. Width, 12⅜ inches.
Price, per yard. 25c

No. 39C1280 White Cambric Embroidery. A very bold and handsome pattern, closely worked, with ribbon effect at the bottom, suitable for Nos. 3 and 4 ribbon. Particularly desirable for corset covers as well as skirt flounces. Width, 17 inches.
Price, per yard....... 36c

No. 39C1283 White Cambric Embroidery. One of the very newest and prettiest patterns. Very closely worked on a good quality of cambric. Has a floral and scroll design, with button design and ribbon effect for drawing No. 2 ribbon through. A very excellent pattern. Desirable for all kinds of muslin wear and corset covers. Width, 17¼ inches.
Price, per yard....... 42c

No. 39C1287 White Cambric Embroidery, with ribbon effect for drawing No. 2 ribbon through. This is a pretty insertion design, very closely worked on good quality muslin. A splendid pattern for skirts, flounces and corset covers. By putting tucks between the insertion effect, will add greatly to the appearance. Width, 16¾ inches.
Price, per yard........... 44c

No. 39C1268 White Cambric Embroidery with teneriffe wheel and button effect. This is a very handsome and attractive embroidery, particularly suitable for corset covers and all kinds of muslin wear. Width, 16¼ in. Price, per yd.. 49c

No. 39C1293 White Cambric Embroidery. This is a very delicate and attractive design. Teneriffe wheel pattern and dainty floral pattern on edge. By putting small tucks between the insertion, will make this a very beautiful pattern. Especially adapted for corset covers as well as all kinds of muslin wear. Width, 17 inches. Price, per yd. 39c

No. 39C1296 White Cambric Embroidery. An exceptionally attractive design. This is a teneriffe wheel and raised button effect pattern. One of the newest and best of the season. Width, 16¾ inches. Price, per yd.. 45c

No. 39C1299 White Cambric Embroidery. This is a ribbon and insertion design. Pretty openwork pattern, suitable for No. 3 ribbon, also for skirt flounces and other muslin wear. Width, 16½ inches.
Price, per yard....... 43c

No. 39C1302 White Cambric Embroidery. This is a very dainty and pretty embroidery. The work is very fine and close on an exceptional quality of cambric. The insertion pattern enables you to put small tucks between, making a very beautiful and attractive embroidery. Width, 17 inches.
Price, per yard...... 50c

Colored Embroideries.

No. 39C1305 Colored Cambric Embroidery. A very neat and pretty pattern. The colors come worked on white cambric in red, navy blue, pink or light blue. Width, 1¼ in.
Price, per yard.......... 4c

No. 39C1308 Colored Cambric Embroidery. A pretty star design. The colorings, worked on white cambric, are red, navy blue, pink or light blue. Width, 1¾ inches.
Price, per yard........ 5c

No. 39C1311 Colored Cambric Embroidery, A more closely and better worked article. A very pretty design. The colorings, worked on white cambric, are red, navy blue, pink or light blue. Width, 3⅜ inches.
Price, per yard.......... 8c

Hemstitched Embroideries.

No. 39C1314 White Swiss Hemstitched Embroidery. This has a neatly worked border with hemstitched edge. Hemstitched embroideries are new and stylish. Width, 3 inches.
Price, per yard....... 10c

No. 39C1317 Nainsook Hemstitched Embroidery. A neat and dainty pattern with hemstitched edge. Width, 3 inches.
Price, per yard..... .15c

No. 39C1320 Nainsook Hemstitched Embroidery. This is a pretty openwork design with hemstitched edge. Width, 7½ inches.
Price, per yard....... 17c

No. 39C1323 White Nainsook Hemstitched Embroidery with beautiful openwork pattern in nice square designs with hemstitched edge. Width, 7¾ inches.
Price, per yard....... 20c

No. 39C1326 White Cambric Ribbon Embroidery, suitable for No. 1 ribbon. This is a neat and pretty, small pattern, worked on fine cambric. Width, 1½ inches.
Price, per yard.......... 5c

No. 39C1329 White Cambric Ribbon Embroidery, suitable for No. 1 ribbon. A neat openwork ring design. Width, 1⅜ inches. Price, per yard, 7c

No. 39C1332 White Cambric Ribbon Embroidery, suitable for No. 2 ribbon. An exceptionally attractive and dainty design on very fine cambric. Width, 3⅝ inches.
Price, per yard..... 10c

Nainsook Embroideries.

No. 39C1335 White Nainsook Embroidery Edging. Small neat design. Width, 1 inch.
Price, per yard........ 3c

No. 39C1338 White Nainsook Embroidery. A small and dainty pattern for children's wear and edging of all sorts. Width, 1¾ inches.
Price, per yard... ..... 5c

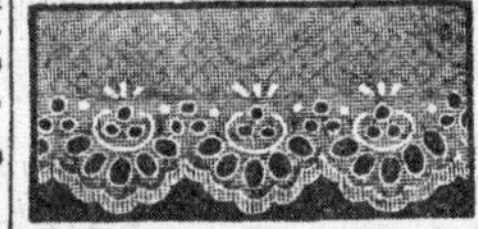

No. 39C1341 White Nainsook Embroidery. A pretty openwork and floral design. Excellent value. Width, 3½ inches.
Price, per yard........ 8c

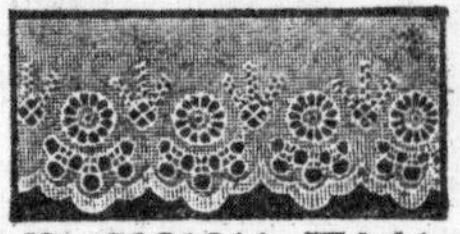

No. 39C1344 White Nainsook Embroidery with teneriffe wheel effect and openwork pattern. A very pretty design. Width, 3½ inches.
Price, per yard 11c

No. 39C1348 White Nainsook Embroidery. An exceptionally pretty openwork pattern with small raised button effect. Is very new. Width, 3½ inches.
Price, per yard...... 13c

No. 39C1353 White Nainsook Embroidery. This is a very closely worked and elegant design. Easily worth 20 cents per yard. Width, 4½ inches.
Price, per yard 15c

No. 39C1356 White Nainsook Embroidery. This is a very delicate pattern, with ring design and raised button pattern. Entirely new. Width, 6½ inches.
Price, per yard........ 18c

No. 39C1359 White Nainsook Embroidery. A closely and prettily worked design on nice quality nainsook. Width, 8¾ inches.
Price, per yard,..... 23c

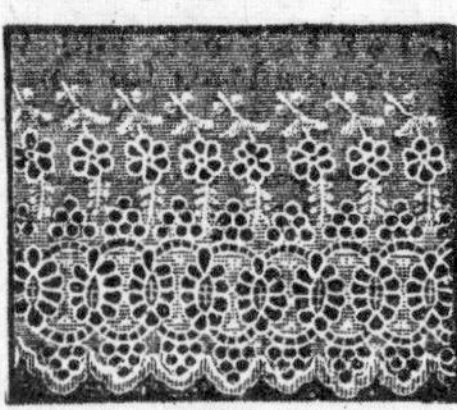

No. 39C1362 White Nainsook Embroidery. A very pretty and striking pattern, an excellent quality work on fine quality nainsook. Width, 10½ inches.
Price, per yard..... 30c

No. 39C1365 White Nainsook Embroidery. A very delicate and exquisite pattern, closely worked on a very fine quality nainsook. Width, 8¾ inches.
Price, per yard.... 35c

Swiss Embroideries

No. 39C1368 White Swiss Embroidery. A small, neat and pretty design. Width, 2 inches.
Price, per yard.. . 3c

No. 39C1371 White Swiss Embroidery. A very new and pretty pattern. Good quality work. Worth elsewhere double our price. Width, 3⅜ inches.
Price, per yard.... 5c

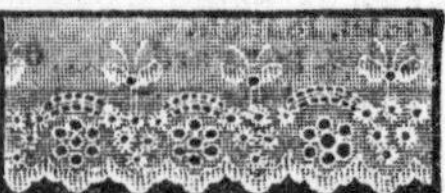

No. 39C1374 White Swiss Embroidery. This is a small and dainty pattern in openwork and floral design. Width, 2¾ inches.
Price, per yard..... 8c

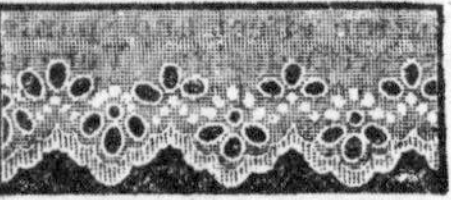

No. 39C1377 White Swiss Embroidery. An openwork and attractive design. Width, 2¾ inches.
Price, per yard 7c

No. 39C1380 White Swiss Embroidery. A beautiful openwork pattern with small button effect throughout. Width, 4⅜ inches.
Price, per yard..... 10c

No. 39C1383 White Swiss Embroidery. This is an entirely new and pleasing design. Very closely worked. Width, 3⅜ in. Price, per yd..11c

No. 39C1386 White Swiss Embroidery. This is a dainty design as well as showy, has a nice openwork embroidery edge and butterfly design. Width, 6¼ in. Price, per yd...13c

No. 39C1389 White Swiss Embroidery. This is a beautiful, openwork design with large leaf effect. Nice quality work on fine Swiss. Width, 7⅝ inches. Price, per yd..16c

No. 39C1392 White Swiss Embroidery. This is an unusually pretty and bold design in openwork and floral pattern. Width, 10¼ in. Price, per yd..20c

No. 39C1395 White Swiss Embroidery. One of the newest ideas. A small teneriffe wheel design with raised button effect on edge. Width, 10¼ in. Price, per yd..25c

No. 39C1398 White Swiss Embroidery. Very closely worked on fine Swiss. Width, 12½ inches. Price, per yard....33c

MATCHED SETS.
Nainsook Embroidery.

No. 39C1399 White Nainsook Embroidery Matched Set. This is a small and very neatly worked design, suitable for infants' and children's wear as well as all classes of finer muslin underwear, etc. Comes in four widths; the widest width having three rows of embroidery and the narrowest a little less in proportion to the width.

Width, inches,	2½	3	4⅝	6¼
Price, per yd..	8c	12c	15c	19c

No. 39C1401 White Nainsook Embroidery Insertion on very fine quality nainsook. Pattern to match the above matched set. Width, 1⅜ inches.
Price, per yard..........14c

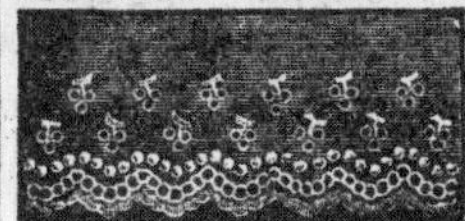

No. 39C1402 White Nainsook Embroidery Matched Set. This is a very closely worked and dainty pattern, worked on very fine quality nainsook. Suitable for all kinds of infants' and children's wear and finer muslin wear of all sorts. Comes in three widths.

Width, ins.,	2½	2⅝	3⅞
Per yard..	14c	18c	23c

No. 39C1404 White Nainsook Embroidery Insertion to match the above matched set. Width, 1⅛ inches.
Price, per yard......12c

No. 39C1405 White Nainsook Embroidery Matched Set, coming in three widths. This is a new and pretty attractive design of teneriffe wheel and button effect. Especially desirable for muslin skirts and other wear. Comes in three widths.

Width, ins...	5¼	8⅛	10⅝
Per yard ...	20c	29c	38c

No. 39C1407 White Nainsook Embroidery Insertion. Same design and to match the above set. Width, 2¼ inches.
Price, per yard.......15c

MATCHED SETS.
Cambric Embroidery.

No. 39C1408 Cambric Embroidery Matched Set. This is a very closely worked and showy button design on fine quality cambric. This set comes in three widths with insertion to match. Very desirable for muslin underwear, suits, etc. Comes in widths, as follows:

Width, inches.	2⅛	3	5
Per yard....	6c	9c	14c

No. 39C1408½ Insertion to match the above matched embroidery set. Width, 2 inches.
Price, per yard.........8c

Cambric Insertions.

No. 39C1410 White Cambric Embroidery Insertion. This is a nicely worked design on good quality cloth. Extra value. Width, 1⅜ inches.
Price, per yard.......3c

No. 39C1413 White Cambric Embroidery Insertion. This is a new and pretty openwork design on good cloth. Width, 1⅜ inches.
Price, per yard........4c

No. 39C1416 White Cambric Embroidery Insertion. A very desirable and pretty design. Width, 1⅜ inches.
Price, per yard........5c

No. 39C1419 White Cambric Embroidery Insertion. A new wheel and button design. Width, 1⅜ inches.
Price, per yard........6c

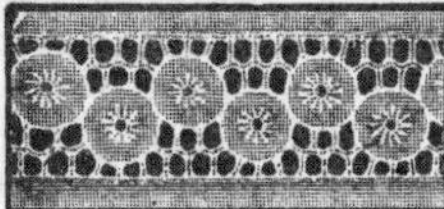

No. 39C1422 White Cambric Embroidery Insertion. Openwork and wheel pattern. Very nicely worked. Width, 2¼ inches.
Price, per yard........7c

No. 39C1425 White Cambric Embroidery Insertion. This is a showy and effective pattern. Width, 2¼ inches.
Price, per yard........8c

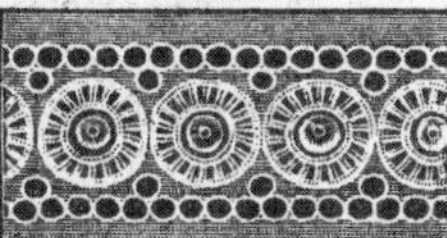

No. 39C1428 White Cambric Embroidery Insertion. This is an unusually pretty design. Mexican wheel and button pattern with beading effect on both sides. Width, 3 inches.
Price, per yard.......10c

No. 39C1431 White Cambric Embroidery Insertion. Beautiful openwork pattern with the insertion effect on both sides. Width, 3⅜ inches.
Price, per yard.......14c

No. 39C1434 White Cambric Embroidery Insertion. Pretty teneriffe wheel and raised button effect. Beading on either side. Width, 3½ inches.
Price, per yard.......18c

No. 39C1437 White Cambric Embroidery Insertion. This is a very finely worked and attractive pattern on fine quality cloth. Very desirable for waists, etc. Width, 4⅜ in.
Price, per yard.......19c

Swiss Insertions.

No. 39C1440 White Swiss Embroidery Insertion. A neat and pretty pattern. Width, 1⅛ inches.
Price, per yard.........4c

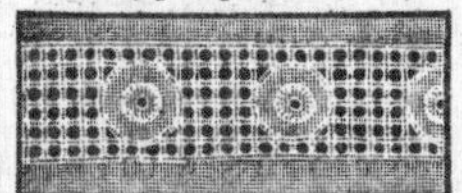

No. 39C1443 White Swiss Embroidery Insertion. This is an openwork lattice design with raised button effect in center. Width, 1⅝ inches.
Price, per yard........6c

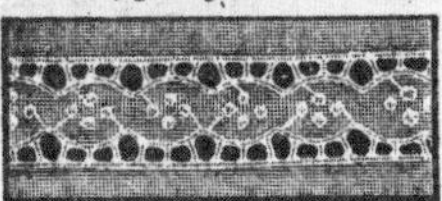

No. 39C1446 White Swiss Embroidery Insertion. A new and pleasing design. Width, 1½ inches.
Price, per yard........5c

No. 39C1449 White Swiss Embroidery Insertion. A showy openwork design, with closely worked button effect in center. Width, 2¼ inches.
Price, per yard........7c

No. 39C1452 White Swiss Embroidery Insertion. This is an exceptionally good value. Closely worked on fine quality cloth. Width, 2⅝ inches.
Price, per yard.......10c

No. 39C1455 White Swiss Embroidery Insertion. A particularly attractive design as per illustration. Closely worked on fine cloth. Width, 3⅝ in.
Price, per yard.......11c

No. 39C1458 White Swiss Embroidery Insertion. This is a beautiful butterfly design. Width, 2⅝ in. Price, per yard.12c

No. 39C1461 White wiss Embroidery Insertion. A very neat and attractive design. Fine quality work. Width, 2½ inches.
Price, per yard.......13c

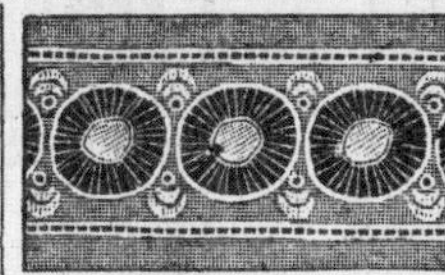

No. 39C1464 White Swiss Embroidery Insertion. A new and pretty teneriffe wheel, with large button effect in center. Both edges have small beading. A very fine insertion. Width, 3 inches.
Price, per yard 14c

Nainsook Insertions.

No. 39C1470 White Nainsook Embroidery Insertion. A very pretty and effective design. Width, 1⅛ inches.
Price, per yard........5c

No. 39C1473 White Nainsook Insertion. A very dainty pattern with wheel effect. Width, 1⅞ inches.
Price, per yard........7c

No. 39C1476 White Nainsook Embroidery Insertion. Very fine open work design. Width, 1⅜ in.
Price, per yard.........10c

No. 39C1479 White Nainsook Embroidery Insertion. Closely worked design on very fine cloth. Width, 1⅜ in.
Price, per yard. 9c

No. 39C1482 White Nainsook Embroidery Insertion. A very showy, openwork pattern on fine cloth. Width, 2½ inches.
Price, per yard......11c

No. 39C1485 White Nainsook Embroidery Insertion. This is an exceptionally pretty and closely worked design, teneriffe wheel effect. A very desirable pattern. Width 3⅜ inches.
Price, per yard 20c

Ribbon Insertions.

No. 39C1486 Swiss Ribbon Embroidery, for drawing Nos. 1 or 1½ ribbon through. Neatly worked with a pretty design. Width, 2 inches.
Price, per yard 6c

No. 39C1487 Swiss Ribbon Embroidery, for drawing Nos. 1 or 1½ ribbon through. Teneriffe wheel design. A very prettily worked pattern. Width 2⅝ in. Price, per yd.10c

No. 39C1488 White Nainsook Beading Insertion. This is always desirable for infants' wear, neckwear, and all kinds of muslin wear. Width, 1⅛ in. Price, per yard...3c

No. 39C1491 White Nainsook Beading Insertion. This is a very dainty and pretty pattern.
Width, 1⅛ inches.
Price, per yard......7c

No. 39C1494 White Nainsook Beading Insertion. A very pretty and small wheel pattern, closely worked. A very dainty design. Width, 1½ inches.
Price, per yard.......7c

Cambric Embroidery Allover.

No. 39C1510 White Cambric Allover Embroidery in square openwork and small leaf design. This is an exceptional value. Width, 18 in. Price, per yd...25c

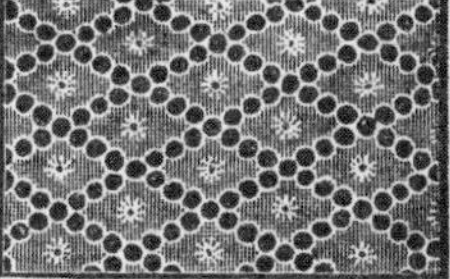

No. 39C1513 White Cambric Allover Embroidery. This is of an openwork design with small flower in center of each. Very showy and pretty. Regular 75-cent value. Width, 18 inches.
Price, per yard 43c

No. 39C1516 White Cambric Allover Embroidery. The new wheel effect with raised button in center. Will make an attractive yoke. Width, 22 in. Price, per yd..52c

No. 39C1519 White Cambric Allover Embroidery. This is a very beautiful design, entirely new, closely worked on good quality cloth. Width, 22 in. Price, per yd..75c

No. 39C1523 White Cambric Allover Embroidery. An exceptionally pretty design, elaborately worked, yet very dainty. Width, 22 inches. Price, per yard....$1.20

Nainsook Embroidery Allovers.

No. 39C1530 White Nainsook Allover Embroidery. A small, neat pattern, closely worked. Exceptional value. Width, 22 inches.
Price, per yard.......41c

No. 39C1533 White Nainsook Allover Embroidery. An entirely new pattern, in small oblong wheels with floral and leaf design. Width, 22 inches.
Price, per yard..... 58c

No. 39C1536 White Nainsook Allover Embroidery. This is an exceptionally attractive and pretty design. Very fine quality work on a very fine nainsook. Width, 22 inches. Price, per yard. 75c

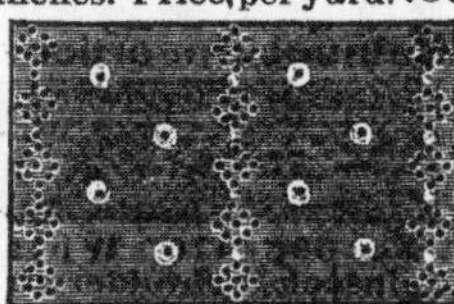

No. 39C1539 White Nainsook Allover Embroidery. A very small and dainty pattern, or wheel effect with small square insertion effect throughout. Width, 22 inches. Price, per yard..$1.15

Swiss Embroidery Allovers.

No. 39C1540 White Swiss Allover Embroidery. A showy and splendid design. Exceptionally cheap at the price. Width 18 inches.
Price, per yard.......25c

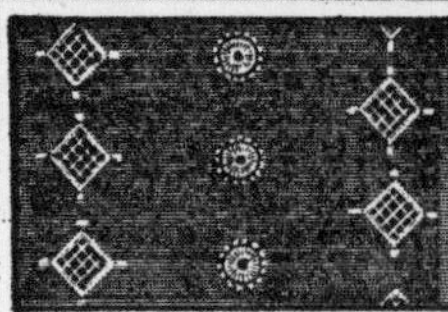

No. 39C1543 White Swiss Allover Embroidery. Openwork square design with raised button pattern. New and effective. Width, 22 inches.
Price, per yard......50c

No. 39C1546 White Swiss Allover Embroidery. A small and delicate pattern. Very tastily and closely worked on very fine cloth. Width, 22 inches.
Price, per yard......60c

No. 39C1549 White Swiss Allover Embroidery. A very showy and attractive pattern. Easily worth $1.25 per yard. Width, 22 inches.
Price, per yard.......80c

FEATHER STITCH BRAIDS.

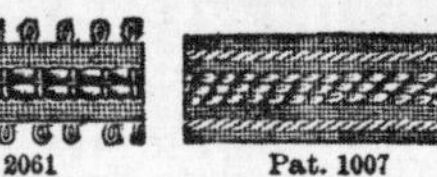

Pat. 2061 Pat. 1007 Pat. 1061

No. 39C1552 White Feather Stitch or Finishing Braid. The above illustrations show the exact size and pattern. Your choice of any of the above three styles. Put up in 6-yard pieces. (Be sure and mention pattern wanted). Regular 5-cent patterns.
Price, per dozen pieces, 33c; per piece............3c

If by mail, postage extra, per piece, 2 cents.

Pat. 2097 Pat. 1187 Pat. 1176

No. 39C1554 White Feather Stitch or Finishing Braid, in new and very pretty patterns. Put up in 6-yard pieces. The above illustrations show exact style and width. Your choice of any style. (Be sure and mention pattern wanted). Regular 10-cent patterns. Price, per dozen pieces, 55c; per piece..5c

If by mail, postage extra, per piece, 2 cents.

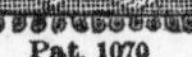

Pat. 1070 Pat. 2304 Pat. 4654

No. 39C1558 White Feather Stitch or Finishing Braid. The exact size as above illustrations. The patterns are new and the wider widths are very extensively used for present styles. Put up in 6-yard pieces. Choice of any of above patterns. (Be sure and mention pattern wanted). Regular 15-cent patterns. Price, per dozen pieces, 90c; per piece..8c

If by mail, postage extra, per piece, 2 cents.

No. 39C1560 Colored Feather Stitch or Finishing Braid. A very neat and pleasing pattern. The above illustration shows exact width and style. The design is worked on white in the following colors, red, pink or light blue, (Be sure and mention color wanted). Put up in 6-yard pieces.
Price per piece..... 5c
Per dozen pieces..55c
If by mail, postage extra, per piece, 2 cents.

No. 39C1564 Feather Stitch or Finishing Braid. White ground, worked in colors. Exact width as illustration above. Put up in 6-yard pieces. Comes in the following colors, red, pink or light blue, worked on white.
Price, per piece..$0.10
Per dozen pieces. 1.10
If by mail, postage extra, per piece, 2 cents.

DON'T FORGET To allow enough money for postage if you order goods sent by mail. Better still order enough goods from the different departments to to make an express or freight shipment.

THE WORLD'S BEST RIBBON DEPARTMENT.

WE SELL EVERYTHING IN WEAVES AND COLORS THAT IS DESIRABLE AND POPULAR.

To think of ribbons in connection with millinery is no new experience, and to consider the novel forms by way of bows and rosettes in which they appear, is a constant fund of delightful surprises. Satin faced and taffeta back ribbons in the wider widths, make a very soft and desirable trimming. We refer you to our Nos. 39C1855 and 39C1857. The quality is the best, the prices the lowest. The satin taffeta in the wider widths gives a delicate touch and finish as a trimming. We do not send samples of ribbon.

If by mail, allow postage 1c to 2c per yard.

HOW TO TELL WIDTH OF RIBBON.

Nos	2	3	5	7	9	12	16	22	40	60	80
Width, inches	7/16	⅝	1	1¼	1⅝	2	2⅜	2⅝	3⅛	3½	4½

High Grade Satin Ribbon with Grosgrain Back.

No. 39C1844 Heavy Quality All Silk Ribbon, satin face and grosgrain back. Black and all colors.

Nos	2	3	5	7	9
Width, inches	7/16	⅝	1	1¼	1⅝
Price, per yard	2½c	4c	5c	7c	10c
Per piece, 10 yards	22c	35c	40c	60c	90c

Nos	12	16	22	40
Width, inches	2	2⅜	2⅝	3⅛
Price, per yard	$0.12	$0.15	$0.18	$0.22
Per piece, 10 yards	1.10	1.35	1.65	2.00

Watered Silk Taffeta Ribbon.

No. 39C1848 All Silk Moire (watered taffeta) Fine Quality Ribbon. Black and all colors.

Nos	5	7	9	12	16
Width, inches	1	1¼	1⅝	2	2⅜
Price, per yard	5c	7c	8c	$0.11	$0.14
Per piece, 10 yards	45c	65c	75c	1.00	1.30

Nos	22	40	60
Width, inches	2⅝	3⅛	3½
Price, per yard	$0.16	$0.20	$0.25
Price, per piece, 10 yards	1.50	1.90	2.20

Taffeta Ribbon.

No. 39C1850 This is our best quality All Silk Taffeta Ribbon. Has beautiful soft finish and a rich, brilliant lustre. Colors, black, white, light blue, yellow, pink, scarlet, cardinal, turquoise, violet, brown, tan or navy.

Nos	5	7	9	12	16	22	40	60
Width, inches	1	1¼	1⅝	2	2⅜	2⅝	3⅛	3½
Price, per yd.	4c	6c	8c	10c	$0.12	$0.14	$0.16	$0.18
Piece, 10 yds.	38c	55c	70c	90c	1.10	1.30	1.50	1.70

No. 39C1851 All Silk Taffeta Ribbon. This is a nice quality, soft finish, high lustre taffeta ribbon. The prices we quote are really astonishing, considering the quality. All colors and black.

Nos	5	7	9	12	16	22	40	60
Width, inches	1	1¼	1⅝	2	2⅜	2⅝	3⅛	3½
Price, per yard	3c	5c	7c	8c	9c	$0.11	$0.13	$0.15
Per piece, 10 yards	27c	44c	60c	70c	80c	1.00	1.20	1.40

SATIN FACE TAFFETA BACK RIBBON.

No. 39C1855 This is one of the most popular ribbons, a very fine all silk satin face, with the taffeta back a soft, lustrous ribbon used extensively for neck, dress and millinery purposes. Do not compare this with the cheap ribbons sold at these prices or more; this is a high grade quality at very low prices. Can furnish them in black and all colors.

Nos	5	7	9	12	16	22	40	60	80
Width, inches	1	1¼	1⅝	2	2⅜	2⅝	3⅛	3½	4½
Price, per yard	5c	7c	9c	$0.11	$0.13	$0.15	$0.18	$0.22	$0.30
Per piece, 10 yds	47c	60c	80c	1.00	1.20	1.40	1.70	2.10	2.90

Satin Taffeta Ribbon—Our Second Quality.

No. 39C1857 Satin Taffeta Ribbons. This is a good quality of all silk ribbon, soft finish, satin face and taffeta back. Excellent ribbon at prices quoted.

Nos	5	7	9	12	16	22	40	60
Width, inches	1	1¼	1⅝	2	2⅜	2⅝	3⅛	3½
Price, per yard	3c	5c	6c	8c	9c	$0.11	$0.13	$0.16
Per piece, 10 yards	28c	45c	55c	75c	85c	1.00	1.20	1.50

Plaid Ribbons in All Widths.

No. 39C1859 All Silk Plaid Taffeta Ribbon, with high luster finish. This is an entirely new weave with small cord effect running through pattern. The colors are very pretty. Plaid ribbons are exceptionally fashionable this season and we know that these combinations of colorings are the prettiest shown. These can be ordered in all widths as below and in the following colors predominating: Pink, light blue, green, navy or cardinal. Be sure and state what color you wish to predominate. Comes in the following widths:

Nos	5	9	12
Width, inches	1	1⅝	2
Price, per yard	5c	9c	$0.11
Per piece, 10 yds.	45c	85c	1.00
Nos	16	22	40
Width, inches	2⅜	2⅝	3¼
Price, per yard	$0.14	$0.16	$0.18
Per piece, 10 yds.	1.30	1.50	1.70

5½-Inch Wide TAFFETA Mousseline Ribbon for Sashes and Hat Trimmings.

No. 39C1861 Taffeta Mousseline All Silk Ribbon. This is a pretty style, very soft and lustrous. Especially adapted for neck, hat and sash trimming. Colors, white, yellow, light blue, pink, nile, turquoise, brown, navy, cardinal or black. Exceptional value. Worth 50 cents. Width, 5¼ inches.
Price, per yard $0.21
Per piece, 10 yards. 2.00

Super Quality Fast Edge Linen Back Velvet Ribbon.

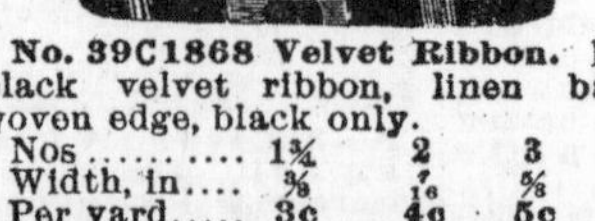

No. 39C1868 Velvet Ribbon. Fast black velvet ribbon, linen back, woven edge, black only.

Nos	1¾	2	3	4
Width, in.	⅜	7/16	⅝	¾
Per yard	3c	4c	5c	7c
Per 10 yards	27c	36c	45c	60c
Nos	5	7	9	12
Width, in.	1	1¼	1½	2
Per yard	8c	$0.13	$0.16	$0.20
Per 10 yds.	70c	1.20	1.50	1.90

Extra Quality Fast Woven Edge Satin Back Velvet Ribbon.

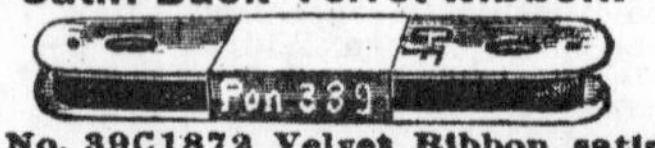

No. 39C1872 Velvet Ribbon, satin back; very desirable for dress trimmings and millinery purposes. This is not the cheap quality, but the fast woven edge. Black only.

Nos	1	1½	2	3
Width, inch.	3/16	¼	7/16	⅝
Price, per yd	4c	5c	6c	8c
Piece, 10 yds.	35c	45c	55c	70c
Nos	4	5	7	9
Width, in.	⅝	1	1¼	1½
Price, per yd.	9c	$0.11	$0.14	$0.19
Piece, 10 yds.	85c	1.00	1.30	1.80
Nos	12	16	22	40
Width, in.	2	2¼	2¾	3½
Price, per yd	$0.22	$0.25	$0.35	$0.40
Piece, 10 yds.	2.10	2.40	3.40	3.85

Colored and Black Velvet Baby Ribbons.

No. 39C1878 No. 1 Satin Back Fast Woven Edge Colored Velvet Ribbon. Colors: white, black, pink, light blue, scarlet, turquoise, heliotrope, nile green, navy or brown.
Price, per piece, 10 yards........18c

No. 39C1879 No. 2 Satin Back Fast Woven Edge Colored Velvet Ribbon. Width, 7/16 inch. Same colors as above.
Price, per piece, 10 yards.......30c

Pin Ribbons.

No. 39C1884 Plain Edge No. 1 Satin and Grosgrain Baby Ribbon. All colors. We do not sell less than full 10-yard spools.
Price, per piece, 10 yards.........8c

No. 39C1886 Plain Edge, No. 1½ Satin and Grosgrain Ribbon, used largely for the ribbon embroideries in the staple colors only. Sold by the full piece only. Price, per 10 yards..14c

All Silk Taffeta Seam Binding.

No. 39C1888 All Silk Taffeta Seam Binding. Black and all colors. Price, per piece, 10 yards, 8c
Per dozen.....90c

All Silk Washable Ribbons.

No. 39C1900 All Silk Wash Ribbon. Pretty jacquard weave extensively used for underwear, fancy work, etc. Colors, black, white, pink, light blue, cardinal, yellow or violet. Comes in numbers as follows.

Nos.	1	1½	2	3	5
Width, in....	3/16	¼	⅜	⅝	1
Per yard....	3c	4c	4½c	6c	8c
Per 10 yds...	22c	33c	40c	55c	70c

National Flag Ribbon.

No. 39C1904 National Flag Ribbon, with stars and stripes, for Fourth of July and different decorating purposes. A good heavy woven all silk. Comes in widths as follows:

Nos.	3	5	7	9
Width, inches	⅝	1	1⅛	1⅝
Price, per yard...	8c	10c	$0.12	$0.15
Per piece, 10 yds...	75c	95c	1.10	1.40

National Red, White and Blue Ribbon.

No. 39C1908 National Red, White and Blue Silk Woven Ribbon. Comes in three stripes equally proportioned. Used for bows, loops, and all kinds of decorations.

Nos.	3	5	7	9	12
Width, inches.....	⅝	1	1¼	1⅝	2
Price, per yard...	4c	5c	6c	8c	10c
Per piece, 10 yds...	37c	45c	55c	75c	95c

No. 39C1914 Fancy Stripe and Figured Silk Taffeta Ribbon. A very pretty weave and design. Desirable for hair ribbons, neck ribbons and fancy work. The colors alternate with white and come in the following shades: Light blue, pink, yellow, nile, cardinal, turquoise, lilac, navy or black, also all white. At the price we quote, this is an exceptional value. Width, 1 inch.
Price, per yard........................4c
Per piece, 10 yards......................35c

No. 39C1922 Dainty, Persian Warp Print Ribbon in No. 2. Very desirable for hair, dress trimmings and small bows for neckwear, as well as fancy work. The Persian colorings blend in the following colors and can be ordered to match, as follows: White, light blue, pink, nile, cardinal, lilac, yellow or black. This is regular 10-cent value. Width, 7/16 inch.
Price, per yard........................5c

No. 39C1926 Fancy Persian Warp Print Ribbon. This is the same style ribbon as the above only in No. 3 width. Can be ordered in the same line of colors. Width, ⅝ inch.
Price, per yard........................7c

No. 39C1930 Imported Fancy Taffeta Ribbon, in a mousseline weave, with fancy openwork, lace design and small raised figure. A very desirable pattern and pretty ribbon for the neck, fancy work and millinery purposes. Colors alternate with white and can be ordered in the following shades: Pink, light blue, turquoise, yellow, cardinal, nile, also all white or all black. Width, 2⅜ inches. Price, per yard........8c
If by mail, postage extra, per yard, 2c.

No. 39C1934 Imported Fancy Taffeta Brocade Ribbon, with corded and raised figure effect. This is a very nice quality and lustrous finish taffeta. A very pretty effect and design. Colors, light blue, pink, cardinal, white, turquoise or nile. Width, 3½ inches.
Price, per yard........................11c

Imported Warp Print Silk Taffeta Ribbon, 7 Cents.

No. 39C1918 Fancy Imported Warp Print All Silk Taffeta Ribbon with openwork lace edges on either side, with beautiful small flowered silk brocaded insertion through center. This ribbon is very dainty and comes in the following combinations of colors, the lace effect being always in white: Light blue, pink, lilac, yellow, turquoise, nile, cardinal, black, also all white. Regular 12-cent value. Width, 1⅛ inches. Price, per yard........7c
Per piece, 10 yards........60c

No. 39C1938 Fancy Imported Taffeta Ribbon. This is a beautiful new design in jacquard and brocade weave. The colors alternate with white and through the center lines are delicate woven flower designs. Comes in the following colors: Light blue, pink, nile, lilac, turquoise or cardinal. Width, 3½ inches. Price, per yard..14c

No. 39C1940 Fancy All Silk Taffeta Ribbon. The white center is prettily figured with a very attractive design. The two edges, which come in colors, are corded and dotted in a very dainty design. This is an exceptionally pretty fancy ribbon. The colors are cardinal, light blue, pink, nile green or lilac, the center of ribbon being always in white. Width, 3½ inches. Price, per yard..........$0.16
Per piece........................1.50

No. 39C1942 Fancy Persian Warp Print Taffeta Ribbon. This is a very dainty and beautiful ribbon, with lace design on both edges. The Persian colorings are suitable for any shade and are in contrast with the outer edges, which come in various colors. The colors on edges are lilac, pink, light blue, white, black or cardinal. Width, 3¼ inches.
Price, per yard........................18c

No. 39C1946 Fancy Imported Taffeta Ribbon, jacquard weave, very high grade and lustrous finish. This is a very delicate and beautiful pattern. The fancy edges are white, worked with a small brocaded woven flower. The center of the ribbon comes in the following colors, white, pink, light blue, nile, cardinal, lilac or royal blue. This is an exceptionally pretty ribbon, much nicer than can be described. Width, 4 inches. Price, per yard..21c

No. 39C1950 Fancy Imported Brocaded Taffeta Ribbon with the beautiful bowknot design and small figure in center throughout. The body of ribbon is a small pin stripe and can be ordered in the following colors, pink, light blue, black, cardinal, nile, brown or turquoise. This ribbon we recommend as a good 35-cent value. Width, 4 inches.
Price, per yard........................22c

No. 39C1954 Fancy Imported Taffeta Ribbon, in the corded and stripe effect. The small cord effect is white, the broad stripe comes in the following colors: pink, light blue, turquoise, nile, brown, black, cardinal, navy or lilac. This is a most effective and attractive looking ribbon. The quality is very high grade, such as would regularly retail for 40 cents per yard. Suitable for neckwear, sashes and millinery purposes. Width, 4⅛ in. Price, per yd., 25c

No. 39C1958 Fancy All Silk Taffeta Ribbon, black and white stripe patterns. The design is woven into the ribbon and is one of the newest and prettiest effects in black and white. Width, 3¼ inches. Price, per yard..........10c
Per piece of 10 yards..........95c
If by mail, postage extra, 2 cents.

No. 39C1962 Black and White Striped Fancy Ribbon. This is a very high luster, brilliant taffeta ribbon, all silk and very good quality. The design is an embroidered effect, raised pattern with small cord stripes running through same. One of the prettiest black and white effects of the season. Width, 3¾ inches.
Price, per piece, $1.40; per yard.....15c
If by mail, postage extra, 2 cents.

No. 39C1966 An All Silk Hemstitched Corded Pattern Taffeta Ribbon. A very fine quality and very effective and stylish pattern. Comes in all black only. Width, 4½ in.
Price, per yard..............$0.20
Per piece, 10 yards..........1.90

FANCY VEILINGS.

The latest and most popular meshes. All the new stylish weaves for the season. We import direct all our veilings and such veilings as you would pay elsewhere 25 cents per yard we price at 12 to 15 cents. We solicit a trial order. You will then order often. All our veilings are fast edges and fast colors.

If by mail (allow postage), 2 to 3 cents per yard.

Plain and Fancy Tuxedo Veilings.

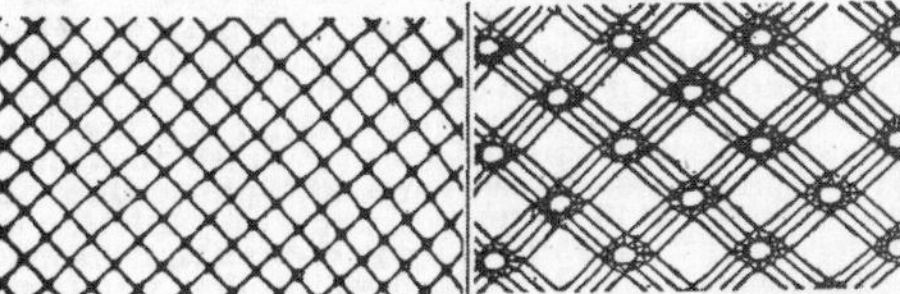

No. 39C2000 18-inch All Silk Tuxedo Veiling. A very fine quality and popular mesh. Colors, black or white.
Price, per yard........8c

No. 39C2008 Silk Tuxedo Veiling. An entirely new and effective mesh, made up of four-thread mesh with ring effect. A very stylish veiling. Width, 18 inches. Colors, black or white.
Price, per yard......14c

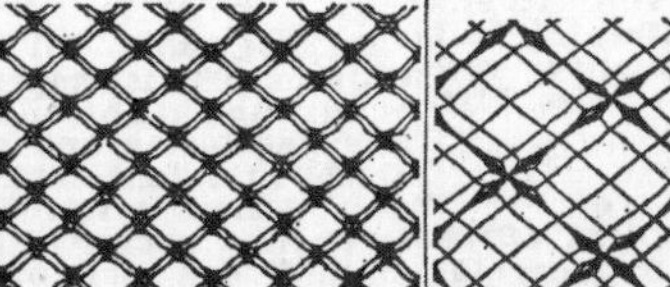

No. 39C2004 This is a Pretty 18-inch Silk Tuxedo Veiling, in fancy double thread mesh. Very desirable and stylish. Colors, black or white.
Price, per yard......11c

No. 39C2012 Fancy All Silk Tuxedo Veiling. This is an exceptionally effective mesh. Makes a very stunning veil. Width, 16 inches. Colors, black or white.
Price, per yard........15c

No. 39C2016 Fancy All Silk Tuxedo Veiling. This is a new and pretty double thread mesh with woven dots. Very effective and pretty. Width, 18 inches. Colors, black or white.
Price, per yard.. ....17c

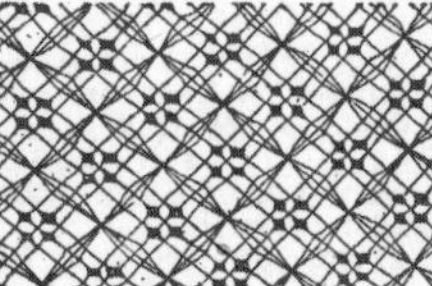

No. 39C2020 Fancy Tuxedo All Silk Veiling. One of the prettiest patterns of the season. Entirely new, very attractive and stylish. Width, 18 inches. Colors, black or white.
Price, per yard.......18c

Fancy Magpie Veiling.

No. 39C2028 Fancy Magpie Veiling. This is a black and white mixture net. The single threads are white, the fancy design is in black. These veilings are very popular and extensively worn. Width, 18 in. Per yard, 10c

No. 39C2032 Fancy Magpie Tuxedo Veiling. This is a very pretty mesh, the finer threads being white and the fancy design in black. The black and white effects are worn by stylish dressers. Width, 18 inches.
Price, per yard 18c

No. 39C2024 Fancy Tuxedo Veiling. This is the newest Parisian design. An exceptionally beautiful mesh, with woven design. Colors, black or white. Width, 18 inches.
Price, per yard 25c

All Silk Dotted Veilings.

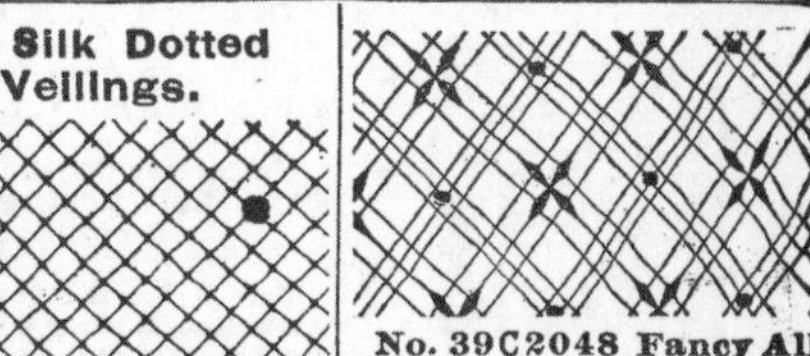

No. 39C2036 Fancy All Silk Tuxedo Veiling with medium size chenille dots. This is a popular and desirable net at an exceptional price. Width, 18 inches. Colors, black or white. Price, per yard..8c

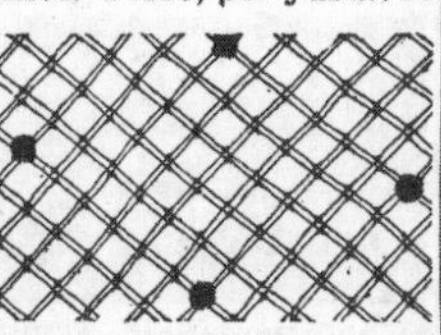

No. 39C2040 Fancy All Silk Tuxedo Veiling. This is a pretty, double thread net with medium size chenille dots. Very stylish and effective. Colors, black or white. Width, 18 inches.
Price, per yard.......12c

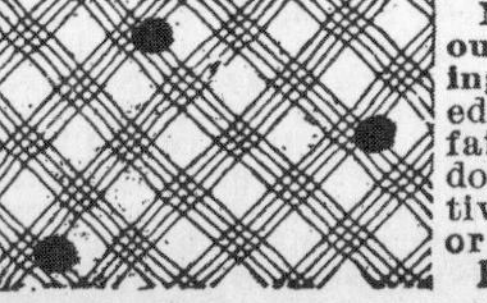

No. 39C2048 Fancy All Silk Tuxedo Veiling, with tiny chenille dots, interwoven with about 1 inch squares. The mesh is very dainty and attractive. Entirely new. Colors, black or white. Width, 18 inches.
Price, per yard.....20c

No. 39C2052 Fancy Tuxedo Silk Veiling, made of double thread, new style mesh with small woven dots. The woven dot effect is very popular and stylish in the cities. Makes a very attractive and pretty veil. Colors, black or white. Width, 18 inches.
Price, per yard.....25c

No. 39C2044 One of our most desirable veilings. Fancy, all silk tuxedo four-thread net with fairly large size chenille dots. A striking and attractive pattern. Colors, black or white. Width, 18 inches.
Price, per yard.....15c

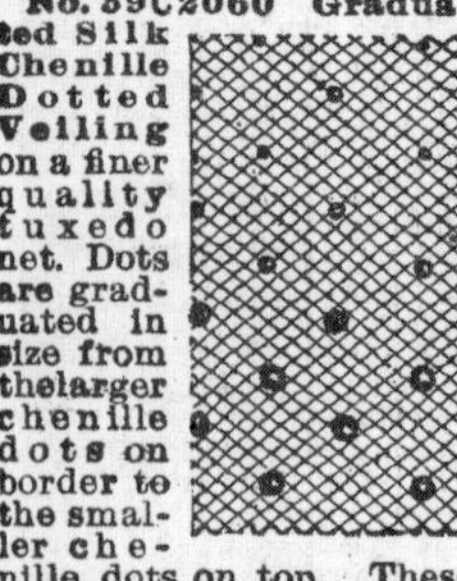

No. 39C2056 Fancy Graduated Dot Silk Tuxedo Veiling. This pretty design has the larger chenille dots on border graduating to smaller, and throughout on entire pattern are tiny chenille dots. This is an unusually effective veiling. Colors, white, black, brown or navy. Width, 18 inches.
Price, per yard.......22c

No. 39C2060 Graduated Silk Chenille Dotted Veiling on a finer quality tuxedo net. Dots are graduated in size from the larger chenille dots on border to the smaller chenille dots on top. These graduated veilings are having an immense sale. Colors, black, white, brown or navy. Width, 18 inches.
Price, per yard......16c

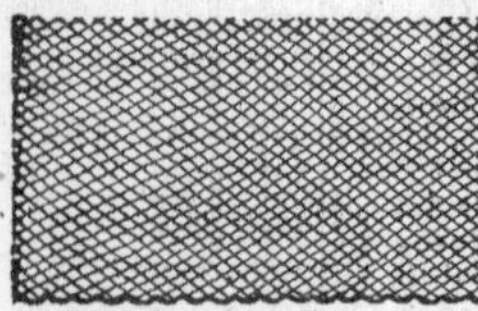

No. 39C2064 Silk Brussels Net Veiling. This is a very good quality net. We quote an unusually low price. Comes in black only. Width, 18 inches.
Price, per yard........8c

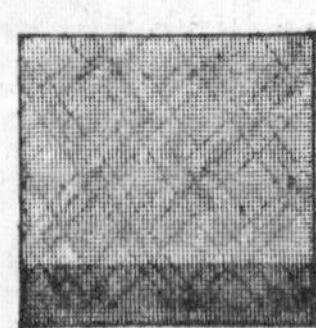

No. 39C2070 All Silk Crepe de Chine Veiling. These crepe de chine veilings are well known to every lady. All we can say is, that this is a very fine quality at a very low price. Colors, black, white, brown or navy. Width, 18 inches. Price, per yard, 21c

SEWING SILK VEILINGS.

Our 11-Cent Silk Veiling.

No. 39C2074 A 14-inch Plain Sewing Silk Veiling, with border of two narrow satin stripes, as per illustration. A very popular veiling. Colors, come in black, cream, navy or brown. 25-cent value. Width, 16 inches.
Price, per yard......13c

Our 19-cent Silk Veiling.

No. 39C2078 The Very Best Quality of Sewing Silk Veiling, neat ½-inch satin stripe border. This veiling is used the year around and always gives entire satisfaction. This quality usually retails at 40 cents. Colors come in black, cream, navy, brown or cardinal. Width, 18 inches.
Price, per yard.......19c

Plain Chiffon Veils are Stylish.

No. 39C2082 Plain Silk Chiffon Veiling, soft and rich, especially desirable for a plain veil, with fast edge borders. Comes in black, navy, royal, new green, brown or cream. Width, 18 inches.
Price, per yard.......20c

Plain Marabout Veils are Very Popular.

No. 39C2086 Plain Marabout Veiling. A similar weave to the chiffon. This veil is always in demand and very extensively used this season. Colors black, white, brown, royal blue or green. Regular 15-cent value. Width, 18 inches.
Price, per yard...... 10c

Stylish Chenille Spot Veilings.

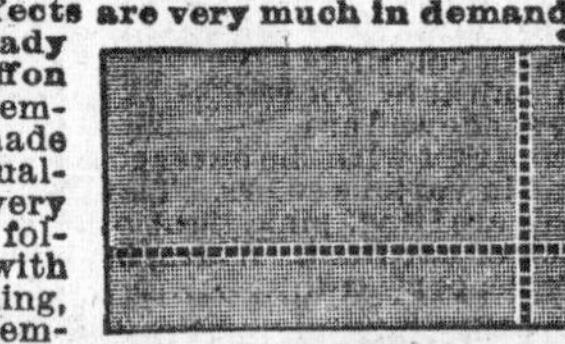

No. 39C2090 Fine Silk Chiffon Veiling with Chenille Dots. You all know what chenille veils are and how extensively they are worn. Colors as follows: Black with black spots, black with white spots, white with white spots, white with black spots, brown with white spots, royal blue with white spots or green with white spots. Width, 18 inches.
Price, per yard 24c

Ready Made Veils.

Soft clinging effects are very much in demand.

No. 39C2094 Ready Made Silk Chiffon Veils, with hemstitched border, made of an excellent quality of chiffon and very stylish. Colors as follows; Black with black hemstitching, black with white hemstitching, white with white hemstitching, white with black, emerald green, royal blue or brown, all with white hemstitching. **Size, 54 inches long by 17 inches wide.** The regular 50-cent veil.
Price, per dozen, $2.75; each......................25c
If by mail, postage extra, 3 cents.

This is a Very Pretty and Effective Veil.

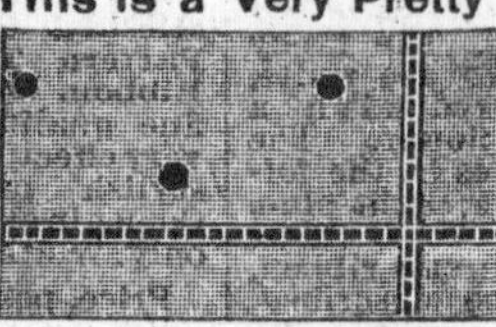

No. 39C2098 Ready Made Silk Chiffon Veils, made of a very fine quality silk chiffon with silk chenille dots. The hemstitching and border are always of the same color and can be ordered as follows: Black with black dots, black with white dots, white with white dots, white with black dots, royal blue with white dots, brown with white dots, or emerald green with royal blue dots. Length, 54 inches; width, 18 inches. A good 75-cent veil.
Price, per dozen, $4.25; each......................40c
If by mail, postage extra, 3 cents.

No. 39C2102 New Tuxedo Ready Made Veil, with the graduated dots entirely around sides and border. This is a very pretty tuxedo mesh. One of our most popular styles. Size, 18x56 inches. Colors, black, brown or navy. Price, each....25c
If by mail, postage extra, 3 cents.

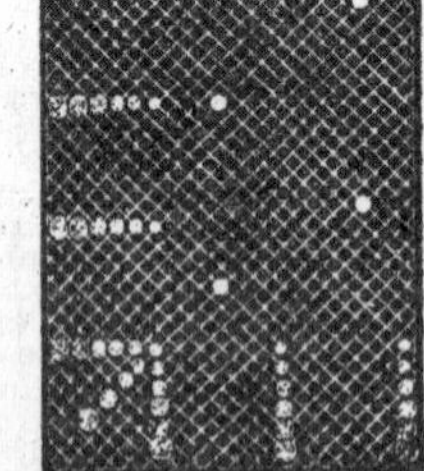

No. 39C2104 Chiffon Made Veil. This is the latest novelty in a ready made veil. 1¼ yards in length, bound all around sides and bottom with No. 5 all silk taffeta ribbon. This particular style of veil is having an enormous sale. Can be ordered in black or white.
Price, per dozen, $3.75; each......................35c
If by mail, postage extra, each, 4 cents.

Wool Barege Veiling.

No. 39C2106 Fine Imported All Wool Barege Veiling, 23 inches wide; very best quality. Comes in black, navy, myrtle green, brown or gray. Usually retailed at 35 cents. Price, per yard.................25c

No. 39C2110 All Wool Barege Veiling, 23 inches wide; a very excellent quality, much better than the regular 25-cent kind as sold elsewhere. Colors, black, navy, brown, myrtle green or gray.
Price, per yard.......................................20c

White Silk Illusion or Bridal Veiling.

No. 39C2114 Silk Illusion or Bridal Veiling, an exceptionally good quality at low price. Width, 72 inches.
Price, per yard.......36c

No. 39C2116 White Silk Illusion, 72 inches wide; an extra quality, worth 75 cents, for bridal veils.
Price, per yard 55c

No. 39C2118 72-inch White Silk Illusion or Bridal Veiling, finer quality; well worth $1.50.
Price, per yard.......87c

Black Silk Brussels Net.

No. 39C2122 Black Silk Brussels Net, plain, 27 inches wide. Per yd...17c

No. 39C2126 Black Silk Brussels Net, plain, 27 inches wide. Finer quality.
Price, per yard.......25c

No. 39C2130 Black Silk Brussels Net, plain, finer quality than above. Width, 27 inches.
Price, per yard......36c

27-inch Wash Blondes.

No. 39C2134 White Cotton Wash Blonde Net, 27 inches wide.
Price, per yard......11c

No. 39C2138 White Cotton Wash Blonde Net, much finer mesh than above. Width, 27 inches.
Price, per yard.......19c

72-inch Wash Blondes.

No. 39C2142 White Soft Finish Cotton Wash Blonde. This is a little heavier thread than the usual wash blonde as ordinarily used. These are having an immense sale for waists, neckwear, yokes and different dress trimmings. Width, 72 inches. Regular 75-cent value.
Price, per yard.......42c

No. 39C2146 Arabian Colored Cotton Wash Blonde. Soft finish, used for waists, etc. A very nice quality, which we quote at a special price. Width, 72 inches.
Price, per yard.......44c

No. 39C2150 White Wash Blonde. This is an unusually fine quality in the soft finish, used for waists, neckwear, etc. We guarantee this cannot be equaled within 25 per cent anywhere. Width, 72 inches.
Price, per yard........65c

No. 39C2154 Arabian Colored Wash Blonde. Very fine quality in soft finish, used for waists, neckwear, dresses, etc. Width, 72 inches.
Price, per yard.......65c

Silk Maline Net, for Neck Bows, Etc.

No. 39C2158 Silk Maline Netting. Used for neck bows, millinery trimming, etc. A splendid, good quality, regular 10-cent value. Width, 27 inches. Colors, black or white.
Price, per yard........8c

No. 39C2162 Silk Maline Netting. Much finer quality than above, equal to many of the 24-cent qualities sold elsewhere. Width, 27 inches. Colors, black, white, pink or light blue.
Price, per yard.......13c

No. 39C2166 Silk Maline Netting. A very close and fine quality net. This is exceptionally good value, better than you can buy anywhere. Width, 27 inches. Colors, black, white, pink or light blue.
Price, per yard..20c

Silk Finish Mull for Hat Trimming, Etc.

No. 39C2170 Silk Finish Mull. This is a fine gauze like trimming, used for hat trimmings particularly, also used for neck wear and dress trimmings. Width, 40 inches. Colors, black, white, pink or blue.
Price, per yard..9c

BLACK VEILS AND MOURNING GOODS.

We sell only the best qualities at the lowest prices. Our mourning goods are a beautiful fast black.

Black Silk Grenadine Mourning Veiling.

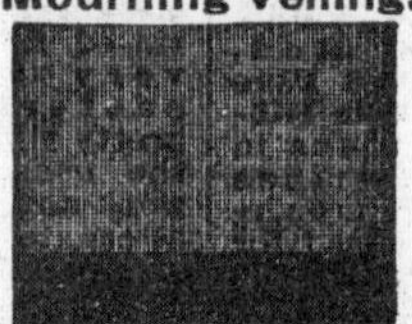

No. 39C2174 Black Silk Grenadine Mourning Veiling, with 1½-inch border, equal to the ordinary 75-cent qualities. Width, 16 inches.
Price, per yard.......35c

Black Silk Grenadine Veiling, Hemstitch Border.

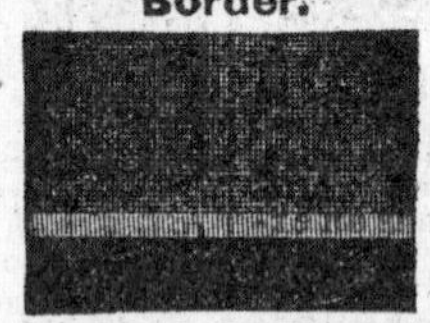

No. 39C2178 Black Silk Grenadine Mourning Veiling. A superfine quality, with 1½-inch hemstitched border. A very desirable and stylish veil. Width, 16 inches.
Price, per yard 39c

No. 39C2182 Black Silk Grenadine Mourning Veiling, much finer quality than above with 1½-inch hemstitched border. Our finest quality veiling. Width, 16 inches.
Price, per yard.......50c

Grenadine Face Veils.

No. 39C2186 Black Silk Grenadine Mourning Veils, with 1½-inch border. Very fashionable for draping hats, etc. Size, 16x54 inches. Good 75-cent value. Price, each..$0.55
Per dozen............ 6.00

No. 39C2190 Black Silk Grenadine Mourning Veils. Very fine quality, with wide 2¼-inch border, for draping hats. Size, 18x54 inches. $1.25 value.
Price, each.......$ 0.95
Per dozen......... 10.75

No. 39C2194 Black Silk Grenadine Veils, with 1½-inch hemstitch border. This is a very fine quality grenadine. Size, 16x54 inches. Price, each, $0.75
Per dozen......... 8.50

Grenadine Draping Veils.

No. 39C2198 All Silk Grenadine Draping Veil, very fine quality, with 2-inch border. Size, 32x45 inches.
Price, each.......$ 0.95
Per dozen......... 10.80

Nuns' Draping Veils.

No. 39C2202 Mourning Veil of Nuns' Veiling, with border. Size, 32x45 inches. Price.........98c

No. 39C2206 Mourning Veil of finer quality of Nuns' Veiling, with border; very elegant and fine. Size, 40x60 inches.
Price.............$1.93

Black Nuns' Veiling.

No. 39C2210 Nuns' Veiling, all wool, with border, for mourning veils, 40 inches wide.
Price, per yard.....50c

No. 39C2214 Nuns' Veiling, all wool, with border, for mourning veils, 40 inches wide; finer quality.
Price, per yard.....75c

No. 39C2218 Nuns' Veiling, silk warp, with border, for mourning veils, 43 inches wide; very fine in texture.
Price, per yard..$1.39

No. 39C2224 All Silk Nuns' Veiling, beautiful fast color black. Width, 42 inches.
Price, per yard..$1.50

Black English Crepe.

No. 39C2228 Black Mourning Crepe, 4-4. A good quality. **Price, per yard**..................35c

No. 39C2232 Black Mourning Crepe, 4-4. Much better quality than above. Price, per yd.75c

No. 39C2236 Black Mourning Crepe, 5-4. A wider and better quality. Price, per yard ...$1.00

No. 39C2240 Black Mourning Crepe, 6-4. Still wider and better quality. Per yard.$1.50

All Silk High Grade Chiffons.

No. 39C2250 Silk Chiffon. Strictly all silk, 40 inches wide, an excellent quality, a soft desirable trimming. 40-cent quality. Colors, black, white or cream. Price, per yard..22c

No. 39C2254 Very Fine Quality all Silk Chiffon. This is an unusually fine quality with a very pretty finish, having a very soft gauze like appearance, suitable for all kinds of waists, neckwear and millinery trimming. Colors, black, white, cream, pink, light blue, nile green, navy blue, cardinal, brown and emerald green. This is an excellent chiffon, which you will find equal to the regular 50-cent numbers sold elsewhere. Width, 42 inches.
Price, per yard.....35c

No. 39C2256 All Silk Chiffon. This is a superior quality and has an unusually fine luster and soft finish. Chiffons make a very desirable trimming for waists, neckwear and all millinery purposes. Colors, white, cream, light blue, black, pink, navy blue, cardinal, nile green or brown. On this quality we ask comparison with the 75-cent chiffons sold elsewhere. Width, 42 inches.
Price, per yard 48c

MOUSSELINE DE SOIE.

All Silk Mousseline de Soie.

No. 39C2260 All Silk Mousseline de Soie. A very fine quality of trimming, 40 inches wide. Very extensively used for millinery purposes, waist fronts, etc. This is a regular 35-cent quality. Colors, black, white or cream only. Price, per yard........22c

Mousseline de Soie, 35 Cents per Yard.

No. 39C2264 Plain Silk Mousseline de Soie. A gauze like trimming, thin as chiffon, but a stiffer finish, for millinery purposes and waist trimmings. Colors, light blue, pink, nile green, maize or yellow, new shade of old rose, heliotrope, brown, royal blue, gray, white, cream or black, 42 inches wide. This is a very fine quality, such as your storekeeper sells at 65 cents. Price, per yard........35c

Mousseline de Soie.

No. 39C2270 Mousseline de Soie. An all silk mousseline of the very best quality. This is a hard finish, and this quality is the very best obtainable. Suitable for the very best purposes. Width, 42 inches. Colors, black, white or cream. Per yard........50c

Liberty Silk Trimming.

No. 39C2274 Liberty Silk, a soft trimming having a very bright and lustrous finish. Used extensively for waists, hat trimming and neckwear. Width, 42 inches. Colors, pink, light blue, black, white or cream. 75 cents is the regular retail price. Price, per yard......50c

Shirred Chiffon.

No. 39C2278 Shirred Chiffon, a very fine quality chiffon, neatly shirred, very fine work, used for waists, yokes and millinery purposes. Width, about 18 inches. Measured stretched. If you want a yard natural, you must order 1½ yards. Colors, black, white or cream. Price, per yard....79c

Embroidered and Fancy Collars in the Latest Styles and Ideas.

No. 39C2400 White Embroidered Turnover Collar. A new and pretty pattern. This is a special value. Price, per dozen, 55c; each........5c
If by mail, postage extra, each, 3 cents.

No. 39C2402 Ladies Turnover Embroidered Collar. A very closely and prettily embroidered design on fine quality white lawn.
Price, per dozen, $1.10; each........10c
If by mail, postage extra, each, 3 cents.

No. 39C2404 Ladies' White Embroidered Stock Collar, with tab. The design is a teneriffe and button effect with beautiful scroll work. This is as pretty as many 35-cent stock collars.
Price, each....$0.10
Per dozen..... 1.10
If by mail, postage extra, each, 3 cents.

No. 39C2406 Ladies' Embroidered Stock Collar, on very fine white lawn. A very dainty and beautiful design, closely worked. A very attractive pattern with a pretty three-pointed tab.
Price........23c
If by mail, postage extra, 3 cents.

No. 39C2408 Ladies' Turnover Collar with tab end. Silk embroidered on white silk poplin, in square teneriffe design. A very neat and pretty collar. The collars come embroidered in the following colors: Red, light blue, Persian, white, black, or navy blue. Regular 25-cent value.
Price........10c
If by mail, postage extra, 3 cents.

No. 39C2410 Ladies' Turnover Collar, heavily embroidered on white silk poplin, in beautiful floral design, with worked buttonholes on both ends for making ties. These ribbon effect collars are exceedingly fashionable. This is an exceptionally good number. Colors, white, red, pink, light blue or black. Price........12c
If by mail, postage extra, 3 cents.

No. 39C2412 Ladies' Turnover Collar, heavily embroidered in floral and scroll pattern on brown linen. This is a very stylish and popular collar. The embroidery can be ordered in navy, red, white or black, colors, contrasting very prettily with the brown linen. Price........16c
If by mail, postage extra, 3 cents.

No. 39C2414 Ladies' Stock Collar, prettily embroidered on white silk poplin. This is an original and new three-tab design. They look very pretty and attractive when worn. The workmanship and design are very neat. Colors, white, black, pink, blue or Persian.
Price........25c
If by mail, postage extra, 3 cents.

No. 39C2416 The New "Buster Brown" Shape Turnover Collar, embroidered in a beautiful design on good quality silk taffeta. The scalloped edges are also heavily worked. Colors, white, red, black, pink or light blue. Price........22c
If by mail, postage extra, 3 cents.

No. 39C2418 Silk Embroidered Stock Collar, with tab end. Silk embroidered on taffeta silk and lined so as to give it firmness. Very prettily embroidered with a new and beautiful design. Colors, white, pink, light blue or black. Price........35c
If by mail, postage extra, 4 cents.

No. 39C2420 Ladies' Silk Embroidered Stock Collar, on taffeta silk. An entirely new idea, the tab end being placed on separately in gathered effect. The embroidery is very effective and closely worked. Colors, white, pink, light blue or black.
Price........45c
If by mail, postage extra, 4 cents.

Collar and Cuff Sets.

No. 39C2422 Collar and Cuff Set, on a very fine quality white lawn with five rows of narrow tucks on both collar and cuffs. Edged with a very fine, dainty valenciennes lace. A very pretty set at a very small price.
Price, per set........15c
If by mail, postage extra, 4 cents.

No. 39C2424 Collar and Cuff Set with ribbon turnover collar, heavily embroidered with a floral design on white silk poplin. Regular 50-cent value. The poplin comes always in white. The embroidery can be ordered in the following colors, white, brown, navy blue, cardinal or black.
Price, per set........25c
If by mail, postage extra, 4 cents.

No. 39C2426 Collar and Cuff Set. This is a very beautiful set on fine white linen, embroidered in a very heavy and elaborate design in the Mount Mellick work. We recommend very highly this set for stylish dressers. Comes in white only.
Price, per set........29c
If by mail, postage extra, 5 cents.

No. 39C2428 White Lawn Collar and Cuff Set. Made of fine quality lawn, trimmed with fine valenciennes lace in a very elaborate and effective design. White only.
Price, per set........50c
If by mail, postage extra, 4 cents.

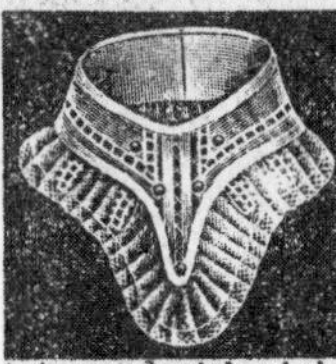

No. 39C2430 Ladies' New Shape Stock Collar. A very dainty affair. Very dressy and stylish. The stock is of Jap silk, trimmed with a narrow braid. Both edges of collar are trimmed with pinked bias lawn tape. The bottom of collar has closely tucked row of chiffon. Edged with fine lace and small loops of fancy braid. The front of stock is ornamented with small beads. An exceptionally neat collar. Colors, white, light blue, pink or black.
Price........23c
If by mail, postage extra, 4 cents.

No. 39C2432 This Beautiful Stock Collar is made of good quality taffeta, lined to give it body. Is heavily embroidered in fancy scroll design with button edges. The top has a row of wood silk insertion and is trimmed with crepe lisse ruche. This is a very effective collar, which really should sell at 50 cents. The collar is always in white, but the embroidery can be ordered in white, light blue, pink or black. Price........25c
If by mail, postage extra, 4 cents.

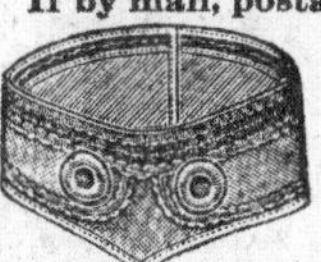

No. 39C2434 Ladies' Stock Collar, made of Jap silk. Is trimmed with a narrow fancy braid and lace insertion effect. Has two large battenberg buttons for tying ribbons or other materials. A very desirable pattern. Comes in white only. Price..22c
If by mail, postage extra, 4 cents.

No. 39C2436 Ladies' Stock Collar. A very dainty design, made of Jap silk with tab end. The stock as well as the tab is trimmed with a pretty black and white mixed braid. In the center are three battenberg rings. The stock is trimmed on end with double row of tucked chiffon, the ends of chiffon also being trimmed with the same black and white braid. Colors, white, light blue or pink. Price........25c
If by mail, postage extra, 5 cents.

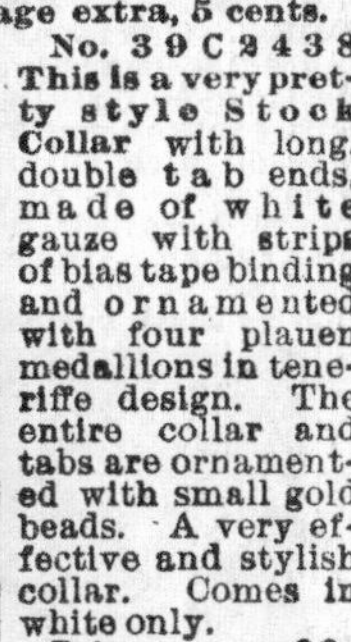

No. 39C2438 This is a very pretty style Stock Collar with long, double tab ends, made of white gauze with strips of bias tape binding and ornamented with four plauen medallions in teneriffe design. The entire collar and tabs are ornamented with small gold beads. A very effective and stylish collar. Comes in white only.
Price........23c
If by mail, postage extra, 5 cents.

No. 39C2440 Ladies' Stock Collar on fine silk gauze. This is very dainty and effective with small tucks of satin on both sides of collar as well as in center of stock. The double tab is worked out in same manner and the entire collar is closely studded with small cut steel beads in fancy design. Colors, white only. Price........25c
If by mail, postage extra, 5 cents.

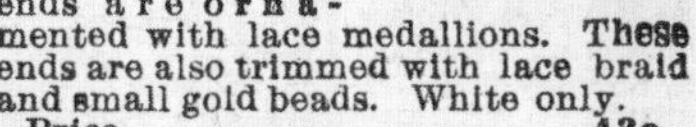

No. 39C2444 Ladies' Silk Gauze Collar, trimmed on top with row of crepe lisse ruche. This stock is an exceptionally dainty and dressy collar. The stock is trimmed with a narrow lace braid, studded with small gold beads. The double diamond shape tab ends are ornamented with lace medallions. These ends are also trimmed with lace braid and small gold beads. White only.
Price,........43c
If by mail, postage extra, 5 cents.

No. 39C2446 Ladies' Stock Collar, with fancy jabot end. This is a wonderfully effective and showy piece of neckwear. The collar is row and row of Jap silk and narrow lace edging. The full jabot end is in fan effect, made of fine chiffon, edged completely with narrow valenciennes lace. An exceptionally beautiful design. Colors white, pink, light blue or black.
Price........45c
If by mail, postage extra, 6 cents.

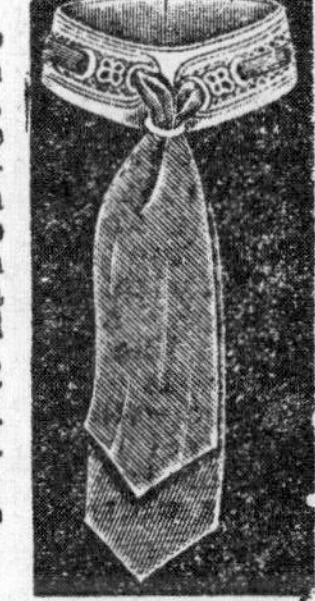

No. 39C2448 Stylish Tailor Made Stock Collar, with ends of silk taffeta. The stock is of fine plauen lace with taffeta drawn through in ribbon effect. The lace comes always in white, the taffeta ends can be ordered in white, cardinal, light blue, pink, navy or black. The combination is very stylish and effective.
Price........48c
If by mail, postage extra, 4 cents.

No. 39C2450 A pretty and stylish Stock Collar with bow. Made of good quality taffeta silk, double stitching on both ends. The edge of stock as well as edge of bows has a contrasting narrow fold with an embroidered design in center of stock. This is one of the most stylish collars of the season. The body of collar comes always in white, the stitching and narrow folds as well as design in center can be ordered in navy blue, black or cardinal.
Price........50c
If by mail, postage extra, 5 cents.

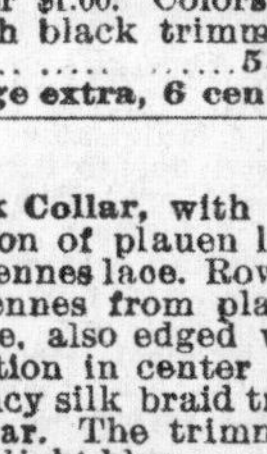

No. 39C2452 Ladies' Stock Collor. Made of a fine taffeta silk. The stock is trimmed with narrow fancy braid. The top of collar has a row of crepe lisse ruche. The center of collar as well as the fancy silk chiffon jabot end are trimmed with plauen lace medallions, in the center of each medallion being a small crocheted button. The edge of the plaited silk chiffon jabot is trimmed with fine narrow valenciennes lace. This is as pretty a creation as you would buy in any retail store for $1.00. Colors, all white, or white with black trimming.
Price........55c
If by mail, postage extra, 6 cents.

No. 39C2442 Ladies' Fancy Stock Collar, with tab end. The stock is made of an insertion of plauen lace, edged on both sides with a fine valenciennes lace. Rows of pinked edge tape separate valenciennes from plauen lace. The tab end is of fine silk gauze, also edged with valenciennes lace and a row of insertion in center and very prettily trimmed with a small fancy silk braid trimming. A very dressy and stylish collar. The trimming of tab can be ordered in white, pink or light blue.
Price........42c
If by mail, postage extra, 5 cents.

No. 39C2454 White Plauen Venisse Collar, with front tab end and small button and rope effect. A very rich and dressy collar. Regular 50-cent value. Price.........23c

If by mail, postage extra, 3 cents.

No. 39C2456 **White Plauen Lace Stock Collar.** The body of collar is of very fine oriental net. An unusually fine pattern in closely worked plauen edges. This is indeed a rich and beautiful collar.

Price. 25c

If by mail, postage extra, 3 cents.

Jeweled Plauen Stock Collar.

No. 39C2458 **White Plauen Venisse Lace Stock Collar** with front tab. The collar is very beautifully jeweled with small and large turquoise or coral beads, making a very stylish creation. When ordering, mention whether you want coral or turquoise. Price.......25c

If by mail, postage extra, 3 cents.

Plauen Stock Collar, Beaded.

No. 39C2460 **Ladies' Plauen Venisse Stock Collar,** with fancy silk gauze top, the gauze top being bound with a double fold of silk tape. The entire collar is closely worked with small cut steel beads and in center of design on tab is a large jewel button. Colors, white, pink, light blue or black. Price..............................60c

If by mail, postage extra, 3 cents.

Plauen Lace Collars.

No. 39C2462 Plauen Venisse Lace Collar. The new circular shape, with points. A very dainty and attractive design. Very rich and dressy. Exceptionally nice quality of work. Equal to many $1.00 values. Colors, white or Arabian. Width, about 6½ inches. Price..............................55c

If by mail, postage extra, 6 cents.

Oriental or Net Top Plauen Collars.

No. 39C2464 Plauen Venisse Lace Collar. This is a medium large size collar, elaborately worked with a new button design edge. The points are worked on oriental net, giving it a very rich effect. This is a very beautiful collar and extraordinary value. Colors, white or Arabian. Width, about 8 inches. Price............75c

If by mail, postage extra, 7 cents.

No. 39C2466 Plauen Venisse Lace Collar. This is a large, circular shape and an exceptionally beautiful design. Large rose points and button effect. Very closely and elaborately worked throughout. Very attractive and stylish. Colors, white or Arabian. Width, about 9½ inches. Price....99c

If by mail, postage extra, 6 cents.

No. 39C2468 Plauen Venisse Lace Collar. Large floral and wheat design, elaborately worked. An exceptionally fine quality and most beautiful design. A collar that if you were to pay twice the price we ask, you would still be getting good value. Comes in white or Arabian. Width of lace, about 10 inches. Price..................$1.20

If by mail, postage extra, 6 cents.

No. 39C2470 Plauen Venisse Lace Collar. This is our finest collar and is indeed a beautiful and elaborately designed collar. Large, showy shape with square teneriffe and floral design. worked with button and battenberg ring edges. We recommend this collar for the very best trade. Colors, white or Arabian. Width of lace, about 12 inches. Price....................$1.95

If by mail, postage extra, 8 cents.

No. 39C2472 Plauen Venisse Lace Collar. Very newest effect with one point worked on oriental net, the other in the heavy plauen venisse effect, which alternate. Very dainty as well as rich and showy. Comes in butter color only. Width of lace, about 7½ inches. Price..............................80c

If by mail, postage extra, 6 cents.

No. 39C2474 Plauen Venisse Lace Collar. The center part of this beautiful collar is worked on oriental net, the upper and lower portion in the heavy plauen effect. One of the most beautiful designs shown for this season. Comes in butter color only. Width of lace, about 8 inches. Price.......$1.10

If by mail, postage extra, 7 cents.

Black Mercerized Plauen Venisse Collars.

No. 39C2476 Black Mercerized Plauen Venisse Lace Collar. This is a rich and effective pattern; a collar that is readily worth $1.25. Black only. Width of lace, about 7 inches. Price.............................85c

If by mail, postage extra, 6 cents.

No. 39C2478 Black Mercerized Plauen Venisse Lace Collar. This is a very heavily worked floral design, large roses in the center, being very heavily worked. This is an exceptionally pretty design and our best pattern. Black only. Width of lace, about 7 inches. Price.....................$1.10

If by mail, postage extra, 6 cents.

Ladies' Linen Collars.

No. 39C2480 Maitland Ladies' and Misses' Linen Collars, square cornered, lock band. Height, 2 inches, style as per illustration. Sizes, 12½ to 16. Price, each, $0.10
Per dozen.............................1.05

No. 39C2481 Ladies' and Misses' Linen Collars, square cornered, lock band. Height, 1⅞ inches. Sizes, 12½ to 16.
Price, per dozen, $1.05; each....10c

No. 39C2482 Ladies' and Misses' Linen Collars, round corner, lock band, same style as illustration. Height, 1¾ inches. Sizes, 12½ to 16.
Price, each..............................$0.10
Per dozen.............................1.05

No. 39C2483 Roseburg, Ladies' and Misses' Linen Collars, round cornered, lock band, same style as above. Height, 2 inches. Sizes, 12½ to 16.
Price, each..............................$0.10
Per dozen.............................1.05

Silk Stock Collar Foundations.

No. 39C2486 **Stock Collar Foundation in the straight shape,** covered with silk chiffon and mercerized taped edge. Sizes, 12 to 15, height, 2¼ inches. In either black or white. Excellent value. Price, each...........7c
Per dozen..............................80c

If by mail, postage extra, 3 cents.

No. 39C2488 Silk Stock Collar Foundation, straight shape, covered with fine all silk mousseline de soie taped with silk, equal to those sold for 15 cents and 25 cents. Sizes, 12 to 15, height, 2¼ inches. In either black or white. Price, per doz. $1.10; each...10c

If by mail, postage extra, 3 cents.

No. 39C2490 **Stock Collar Foundation, pointed shape,** covered with fine silk chiffon, bound with mercerized taped edges. Height, 2¼ inches. Sizes, 12 to 15. In either black or white. Regular 10-cent quality. Price..............................7c

If by mail, postage extra, 3 cents.

No. 39C2492 Stock Collar Foundation, pointed shape, covered with best quality, all silk mousseline de soie, silk taped edge. This is the best collar made and sold as high as 25 cents in the usual retail way. Sizes, 12 to 15. Height, 2¼ inches. In either black or white. Price..............................10c

If by mail, postage extra, 3 cents.

Silk Ruchings.

No. 39C2494 All Silk Chiffon Ruching. Very closely puffed. Colors, black, white or cream. Price, per yard...........15c

If by mail, postage extra, per yd., 2c.

No. 39C2496 Crepe Lisse Ruching in plaited style. A very pretty number. Colors, black, white or cream. Price, per yard, 20c

If by mail, postage extra, per yd., 2c.

No. 39C2498 Crepe Lisse Ruching. This is a double ruffle, very full, with small white satin edge on same. Colors, black, white or cream. Price, per yard.......................30c

If by mail, postage extra, per yd., 2c.

AN IMMENSE VARIETY OF ORNAMENTS.

Brilliant Rhinestone Buckles.

No. 39C2500 Square shape design. Size, ⅞x2 inches.
Price, each...$0.10
Per dozen..... 1.10

If by mail, postage extra, each, 2c.

No. 39C2502 Oval Shape Rhinestone Buckle, set with brilliant rhinestones. Size, 2⅝x1¼ inches.
Price, each...................8c
Per dozen.....................90c

If by mail, postage extra, each, 2c.

No. 39C2504 Long, oblong shape Rhinestone Buckle, set with brilliant stones. Size, 3⅞x1⅛ inches.
Price, each..........................$0.15
Per dozen..............................1.60

If by mail, postage extra, each, 3c.

Fancy Steel Ornaments.

No. 39C2505 Small Steel Ornament or Slide, square shape, suitable for hat or dress trimming. Size, ⅝x½ in.
Price, per dozen.......................10c

If by mail, postage extra, dozen, 3c.

No. 39C2507 Small Steel Ornament, round shape. Size, ⅝x¾ inch.
Price, per dozen..........10c

If by mail, postage extra, per doz., 3c.

No. 39C2509 Fancy Steel Ornament or Slide, square shape. For hat or dress trimming. Size, 1x¾ inch.
Price, each..............................3c
Per dozen..............................33c

If by mail, postage extra, per dozen, 4 cents.

No. 39C2511 Fancy Steel Ornament or Slide, round shape. Used for dress or hat trimmings. Size, ¾x1⅛ inches. Price, each........3c
Per dozen............................33c

If by mail, postage extra, per dozen, 4 cents.

No. 39C2513 Fancy Round Steel Cabochon. This is a desirable style ornament with large and small beading effect. A very popular and stylish hat trimming. Also used for dresses and belts. This style comes in three sizes as follows:

Size, inches in diameter	1	1¼	1½
Price, each.........	3c	4c	5c
Per dozen............	30c	42c	55c

If by mail, postage extra, each, 2c.

No. 39C2515 Fancy Steel Crescent. This is a very fashionable style of trimming in a steel ornament, being crescent shape, as per illustration. Size, 2 inches.
Price, each.............8c
Per dozen.............90c

If by mail, postage extra, each, 2c.

No. 39C2517 Fancy Steel Ring Ornament. for looping ribbons, velvets and different trimmings through. A stylish ornament. Size, 2½ in. Price, each, $0.09
Per dozen...... 1.00

If by mail, postage extra, each, 3c.

No. 39C2519 Fancy Cut Steel Buckle with Back. A very desirable pattern. Size, 2¼x4 inches. We quote this at a very special price.

Price, per dozen, 90c; each........8c
If by mail, postage extra, each, 3c.

No. 39C2521 Fancy Steel Buckle. This is an exceptionally pretty design. Rich and effective. Size, 4½x2 inches. Price, each...........$0.20
Per dozen........... 2.25
If by mail, postage extra, each, 4c.

No. 39C2523 Fancy Steel Buckle. This is the new slipper shape or half buckle. They are immensely popular with the stylish milliners. Length, 4⅛ inches; width, 2 inches. Price, each...........$0.20
Per dozen........... 2.25
If by mail, postage extra, each, 4c.

No. 39C2527 Cut Steel Dart. These are used in connection with ostrich feathers and other styles of trimming where quill ends are used. Length, 8½ inches. Price, each...........$0.18
Per dozen........... 2.00
If by mail, postage extra, each, 3c.

No. 39C2529 Fancy Steel Ornament. New torpedo shape. A very effective and stylish ornament. Length, 6 inches; width, 2 inches. Price, each...........$0.33
Per dozen........... 3.60
If by mail, postage extra, each, 4c.

No. 39C2531 Fancy Steel Buckle. Slipper shape or half buckle, ornamented with small steel cabochons, as per illustration. This is a very rich looking and showy buckle. Size, 4x2½ inches. Price, each...$0.35
Per dozen........... 4.00
If by mail, postage extra, each, 4c.

No. 39C2533 Large Oval Shape Steel Buckle. A very attractive and stylish buckle. For fine hats. Size, 4¼x3¼ inches.
Price, each...$0.40
Per dozen........... 4.50
If by mail, postage extra, each, 4c.

Fancy Metal Ornaments.

No. 39C2535 Fancy Metal Owl Heads. Made of best hammered metal, warranted not to tarnish. Fitted with glass eyes, making a very effective trimming. Colors, gold, brown or green. Size, 2 inches. Price, each...........8c
Per dozen...........95c
If by mail, postage extra, each, 3c.

No. 39C2537 Fancy Colored Metal Cabochon. Mounted with steel ornament in center. These are the best grade of goods. Very showy and attractive. Colors, gold, brown or green. Size, 2 inches. Price, each...........9c
Per dozen...........90c
If by mail, postage extra, each, 2c.

No. 39C2539 Gold Keystone Shape Hat Ornament. This is a new and stylish shape that is being worn very extensively. Gilt will not tarnish. Size, 3x2⅛ inches.
Price, per dozen, $1.10; each....10c
If by mail, postage extra, 3 cents.

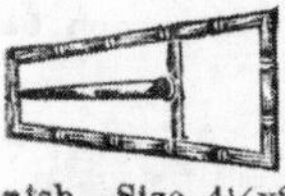

No. 39C2541 Fancy Keystone Shape Gilt Buckle. This is a long and very effective buckle. The gilt will not tarnish. Size, 4¼x2⅜ inches.
Price, per dozen, $1.65; each....15c
If by mail, postage extra, each, 3c.

No. 39C2543 This is a New Shape Fancy Metal Ornament, which is having a very large run in the cities. Made of fast colored ribbed metal, ornamented with two fancy steel bands. Size, 4x2 inches. Colors, gold, brown or green. Price, each....$0.21
Per dozen........... 2.25
If by mail, postage extra, each, 3c.

No. 39C2545 A Large Fancy Metal Hat Buckle. This buckle is very stylish and popular. Comes in colors, French gray or bronze. Size, 4½x3¼ inches. Price, each......$0.25
Per dozen........... 2.50
If by mail, postage extra, each, 4c.

No. 39C2547 Fancy Colored Torpedo Shape Ornaments. This is the newest and most stylish ornament of the season. Comes in all gilt, brown or green. Length, 4 inches. Price, each......8c
Per dozen...........90c
If by mail, postage extra, each, 3c.

No. 39C2549 Fancy Torpedo Shaped Ornaments, made of fast colored ribbed metal, ornamented with fancy steel band through center. Colors, gilt, brown or green. Length, 4 inches.
Price, per dozen, $1.35; each....12c
If by mail, postage extra, each, 3c.

Jet Ornaments.

No. 39C2551 Fancy Jet Square Buckle. A new and pretty design. Size, 4x1⅛ inches.
Price, per dozen, 80c; each.......7c
If by mail, postage extra, each, 3c.

No. 39C2553 Fancy Shape Jet Buckle, with button design. A new and effective pattern. Size, 4½x1¼ inches.
Price, per dozen, $1.10; each.....10c
If by mail, postage extra, each, 4c.

No. 39C2555 Fancy Shape Jet Buckle, same design as above, but larger size. This is one of the best styles of the season. Size, 6x1⅓ inches.
Price, per dozen, $1.60; each.....15c
If by mail, postage extra, each, 4c.

No. 39C2557 Jet Cabochon, with large square cut jet button in center, with pretty fancy design around same. This will make a stylish and attractive trimming. Size, 1⅞ x 1⅞ inches.
Price, per dozen, 55c; each...........5c
If by mail, postage extra, each, 2 cents.

No. 39C2559 Fancy Jet Cabochon. This is a new and attractive pattern with a large button design in center. Size, 2 inches.
Price, each.......5c
Per dozen.......55c
If by mail, postage extra, each, 3c.

No. 39C2561 Fancy Jet Cabochon. This is an exceptionally attractive pattern with a large oval cut jet button in center and fancy jet edge. Size, 2½ inches.
Price, each....$0.10
Per dozen..... 1.10
If by mail, postage extra, each, 3c.

No. 39C2563 New Torpedo Shape Jet Cabochon with oval torpedo shape cut jet center and fancy jet rim. Size, 3x1½ inches.
Price, each...........$0.15
Per dozen........... 1.60
If by mail, postage extra, each, 3c.

No. 39C2565 Jet Crescent. This is a very neat affair, made of small jet. Very pretty when used for looping ribbons or other trimmings through. Size, 3 inches. Price, each.......$0.14
Per dozen........... 1.50
If by mail, postage extra, each, 3c.

No. 39C2567 Fancy Jet Crescent, with large, oval torpedo shaped cut jet ornament in center. A very attractive design. Size, 3 inches.
Price, each...........$0.20
Per dozen........... 2.25
If by mail, postage extra, each, 3c.

Jet Bands.

No. 39C2569 Jet Band; a large and attractive pattern, looks as well as what you would pay 50 cents for. Length, 6 inches. Price, each, 8c
Per dozen...........85c
If by mail, postage extra, each, 2c.

No. 39C2571 Jet Band; a new and pleasing pattern, the bands are very stylish. This is a great value. Length, 6¼ inches. Price, each......8c
Per dozen...........90c
If by mail, postage extra, each, 2c.

No. 39C2573 Jet Band with large cut jet buttons. A very high grade pattern. Length, 5 inches. Price, each...$0.19
Per dozen........... 2.00
If by mail, postage extra, each, 2c.

Steel Bands.

No. 39C2575 Imitation Cut Steel Band. A very pretty design. Length, 7 inches; width, 1 inch.
Price, per dozen, $1.65; each....15c
If by mail, postage extra, each, 3c.

No. 39C2577 Cut Steel Band. An extremely stylish and nobby ornament. Length, 6 inches.
Price, per dozen, $2.25; each....20c
If by mail, postage extra, each, 3c.

No. 39C2579 Cut Steel Band, Backed. Length, 7½ inches. A new design tapering at the ends. Very attractive. Price, each..........$0.35
Per dozen........... 3.75
If by mail, postage extra, each, 3c.

Ostrich Quill Stem Holders.

No. 39C2591 New Quill Stem Holder, used for end of ostrich plumes. This new quill stem holder is the latest craze and used by all stylish milliners. It gives the plume a very pretty finish and adds elegance to your hat. Made of glossy, celluloid finish material to imitate a large quill end. Colors, black or white. Length, 5¼ inches.
Price, per dozen, 8c; each...........1c
If by mail, postage extra, each, 2c.

No. 39C2592 Jet Spangled Crown. A very closely woven spangled crown, being completely covered with small spangles. These crowns were never before offered at such a price. Size, 12 inches.
Price, each....$0.23
Per dozen.... 2.65
If by mail, postage extra, each, 5 cents.

No. 39C2593 Imported Jet Spangle Crown, made of bright jet spangles on Brussels net. Size, 12 inches square.
Price, each, $0.25
Per dozen.. 2.75
If by mail, postage extra, each, 5c.

No. 39C2595 Imported Jet Spangle Crown, made of bright jet spangles on Brussels net, interwoven with silk chenille cord in fancy design. Extra value. Size, 13 inches square.
Price, each...........$0.38
Per dozen........... 4.25
If by mail, postage extra, each, 5c.

No. 39C2597 Imported Jet Spangle Crown, made of horsehair interwoven with chenille and jet spangles and small beads. A very pretty design, Black only. Size, 11½ inches.
Price, each...........$0.42
Per dozen........... 4.75
If by mail, postage extra, each, 5c.

No. 39C2599 Imported Jet Spangle Band, made of black Brussels net with bright jet spangles, interwoven with silk chenille cord in fancy leaf and scroll design. These jet bands are very extensively used and extremely stylish. This is sold by the piece only.
Price, per piece of 36 inches in length and 7 inches in width...........$0.50
Per dozen pieces........... 5.50
If by mail, postage extra, per piece, 8 cents.

No. 39C2602 Fancy Drop Spangled Jet Trimming, fastened to fancy ⅝-inch braid. Jet trimmings are very popular. This is a very pretty style. Price, per yard.......8c
Per dozen yards...........90c
If by mail, postage extra, per yard, 2 cents; per dozen yards, 8 cents.

No. 39C2604 Fancy Drop Spangled Jet Trimming, similar to above, but wider, fastened to ⅝-inch horse hair braid.
Price, per yard...........$0.12
Per dozen yards........... 1.35
If by mail, postage extra, per yard, 2 cents; per dozen yards, 8 cents.

No. 39C2605 Jet Spangled Band Trimming, closely jetted on a fine quality mesh. A very desirable trimming for millinery purposes, in the different widths.

Width, inches..	2	2½	3½
Price, per yard	$0.12	$0.18	$0.25
Per dozen yards	1.35	2.00	2.75

If by mail, postage extra, per yd., 2c.

Hat Pins.

No. 39C2606 Hat Pin, large turquoise center, set in fancy rim. The rim comes in oxidized gilt, 10-cent value. Price, each........4c
Per dozen...........45c
If by mail, postage extra, each, 3c

No. 39C2607 Fancy Gilt and Enameled Hat Pin. The top is enameled in pretty bright shades. Price, each.......5c
Per dozen...........55c
If by mail, postage extra, each, 3 cents.

Special Value.

No. 39C2608 Sterling Silver Top Hat Pin, in a pretty leaf pattern. Has a very strong 7-inch pin. This is a regular 25-cent pin. We offer them while they last at
Price, each...........5c
Per dozen...........55c

No. 39C2609 Unbreakable Hat Pin, with medium size, ball shape head. Made of unbreakable material. The heads can be ordered in imitation of white pearl, pink, light blue or gunmetal. They look pretty and are strong. Has an 8-inch pin. One of the most satisfactory and durable hat pins made.
Price, each...........4c
Per dozen...........40c
If by mail, postage extra, 2 cents.

No. 39C2611 Ladies' Hat Pin. This is a very attractive pin, having a large peacock stone set in gilt rim. Has an 8-inch pin. The peacock settings are very stylish and pretty looking. Price, each.......$0.10
Per dozen........... 1.10
If by mail, postage extra, each 2c.

No. 39C2612 Fancy Hat Pin, in gold or French gray. Very beautiful design, set with four small rhinestones and one pearl. Good pliable pin. Price, each...$0.15
Per dozen........... 1.70
If by mail, postage extra, each, 3c

No. 39C2615 Fancy Hat Pin. Large pearl ball, set in fancy designed, gold rims, ring effect. Has an 8-inch pin. One of the most attractive and prettiest designs.
Price, each...........$0.22
Per dozen........... 2.50
If by mail, postage extra, each, 3 cents.

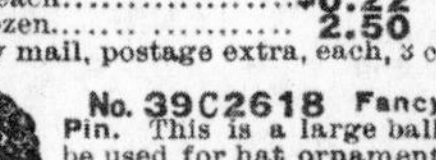

No. 39C2618 Fancy Jet Hat Pin. This is a large ball and can be used for hat ornament as well as hat pin. Price, each.......8c
Per dozen...........90c
If by mail, postage extra, each, 3c; per dozen, 10 cents.

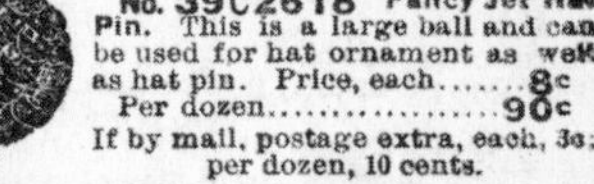

No. 39C2620 Silver Golf Set Hat Pins, in leather caddy bag. Consists of two silver hat pins, one 7-inch and one 8-inch length. Very desirable and popular pins, usually retailed by jewelers at 75 cents per pair.
Price, per pair...........$0.25
Per dozen pairs........... 2.75
If by mail, postage extra, per pair, 5 cents.

Hat and Bonnet Wires.

No. 39C2630 Bonnet Wires. Black or white. Price, per piece...........5c

No. 39C2632 Silk Shirring Wire, all colors. Price, per piece...........3c

No. 39C2634 Ribbon Wire. Black or white. Price, per piece...........3½c

No. 39C2636 Satin Covered Wire. Heavy quality, best grade, all colors.
Price, per piece...........7c

No. 39C2637 Silk Brace Wire, best quality. Colors, black or white.
Price, per piece...........4c

Flowers and Foliage.

No. 39C3300 A bunch of pretty Double Violets, with green foliage, in natural shades.
Price, per unch............5c
Price, per dozen bunches........55c
If by mail, postage extra, per bunch, 4 cents.

No. 39C3302 Pretty bunch of Velvet Muslin Violets, 36 blossoms, with green foliage. Regular 18-cent article.
Price, per bunch.........10c
Price, per dozen bunches.....$1.10
If by mail, postage extra, per bunch, 5c.

No. 39C3303 A very pretty bunch of Silk and Velvet Violets, with shaded, branched green velvet leaves, making a very pretty and durable trimming.
Price, per bunch......20c
Price, per dozen bunches......$2.25
If by mail, postage extra, per bunch, 5 cents.

No. 39C3305 A Large Bunch of Natural Shaded, Double Petal Muslin Violets, branched with green foliage, with extra long stems. Will make a very effective trimming. Price, per bunch.........$0.25
Per dozen bunches.............. 2.75
Postage extra, per bunch, 5 cents.

No. 39C3306. Large Bouquet Bunch of Muslin and Silk Violets, with natural centers. A very dainty and rich trimming. Come shaded from light to dark.
Price, per bunch........$0.29
Per dozen bunches...... 3.25
Postage extra, per bunch, 6 cents.

No. 39C3308 Large, Handsome Bunch of Silk and Velvet Violets, branched with green velvet leaves. Blossoms richly shaded from light to dark.
Price, per bunch....$0.39
Per dozen bunches.. 4.25
Postage extra, per bunch, 5 cents.

No. 39C3310 A Bunch of Black Silk and Mercerized Satin Violets with beaded centers, branched with black satin leaves. A very dainty and showy trimming.
Price, per bunch..........$0.25
Per dozen bunches....... 2.75
Postage extra, per bunch, 5 cents.

No. 39C3311 Large Bunch of Black All Silk Violets, branched in wreath effect, with long stems. A very rich trimming where black is desired.
Price, per bunch.....38c
Per dozen bunches $4.25
Postage extra, per bunch, 6 cents.

No. 39C3312 Imported Velvet Forget-me-nots on long stems. Three dozen to the bunch. These always make a pretty trimming and are usually sold elsewhere at 25 cents a bunch. Colors, light blue, pink, yellow or white.
Price, per bunch..............$0.13
Per dozen bunches............ 1.50
Postage extra, per bunch, 4 cents.

No. 39C3313 Pretty Bunch of Imported Velvet Forget-me-nots, branched in a small bouquet form. Colors, pink, white or light blue. A very dainty and neat trimming.
Price, per bunch, $0.10
Per doz. bunches, 1.10
Postage extra, per bunch, 4 cents.

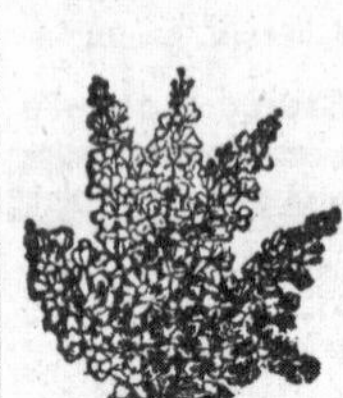

No. 39C3314 Large, Imported six-spray Bunch of Lilacs, branched with green foliage. Comes in natural lilac color or white. Price, per bunch. $0.16
Per dozen bunches.... 1.90
Postage extra, per bunch, 5 cents.

No. 39C3319 Pretty Bunch of White Lilies-of-the-valley, branched with green foliage. A very neat trimming, generally sold elsewhere at 25 cents.
Price, per bunch, $0.10
Per doz. bunches, 1.10
Postage extra, per bunch, 4 cents.

No. 39C3321 Pretty Three-spray Bunch of Water Lilies, with natural yellow centers and green leaves. A very real looking and handsome trimming. Comes in white or black.
Price, per bunch......$0.25
Per dozen bunches............ 2.75
Postage extra, per bunch, 5 cents.

No. 39C3323 Large, Full Blown Muslin Rose, with natural center, branched with green leaves and bud on rubber stem. A simple but very effective trimming. Generally retailed at 15 cents. Colors, pink, white, jack or tea.
Price, each..........................8c
Per dozen............................90c
Postage extra, each, 5 cents.

Crushed Muslin Roses.

No. 39C3324 Crushed Muslin Roses with natural centers, 3 to the bunch on rubber stems. Many stores charge 25 cents a bunch for these. Colors, white, cream, pink, jack, yellow, light blue or tea.
Price, per bunch..................6c
Per dozen bunches..............70c
Postage extra, per bunch, 4 cents.

No. 39C3326 A Bunch of Three Crushed Muslin Roses. This is an imported, fine quality muslin flower; without a doubt the best flower ever offered at the price. Comes in the following colors: Pink, cardinal, jack, light blue, heliotrope, white or tea.
Price, per bunch.........................$0.15
Per dozen bunches..................... 1.70
Postage extra, per bunch, 4 cents.

No. 39C3328 Crushed Muslin Roses. This is an imported rose of finest material. Retailed by the leading milliners at 50 cents per bunch. Colors, pink, cardinal, jack, heliotrope, tea, light blue or white.
Per bunch..$0.25
Per doz. bunches.... 2.75
If by mail, postage extra, per bunch, 4 cents.

Silk and Velvet Roses.

No. 39C3330 Silk and Velvet Roses, three to the bunch, rubber stems; always sold at 25 cents. Colors, white, tea, pink, light blue, jack.
Per bunch..$0.12
Per dozen.. 1.25
If by mail, postage extra, per bunch, 4c.

No. 39C3332 Silk and Velvet Roses, three in a bunch, much finer quality than above. The regular 50-cent kind. Colors, white, pink, light blue, jack or tea.
Per doz. bunches, $2.75; per bunch. .25c
If by mail, postage extra, per bunch, 4 cents.

No. 39C3333 A Very Pretty Bunch of Three Silk and Mercerized Satin Chrysanthemums, easily worth 25 cents. Comes in black, white, pink, light blue or jack. A very showy trimming for the price.
Per bunch...$0.11
Doz. bunches 1.25
Postage extra, per bunch, 4 cents.

Black Roses.

No. 39C3334 A Large Bunch of Three Black Mercerized Satin Roses, with jet beaded centers. Regular 40-cent article. A very showy trimming, made of good quality mercerized satin.
Price per bunch $0.25
Per doz. bunches 2.75
Postage extra, per bunch, 4 cents.

No. 39C3340 Black Crushed Silk Mercerized Muslin Roses. A bunch of three large, soft, best quality flowers, making a very rich and handsome trimming. A regular 75-cent article.
Per bunch..$0.40
Doz. bunches 4.50
Postage extra, per bunch, 4 cents.

No. 39C3345 A Bunch of Black Silk and Mercerized Satin Roses. Three roses to the bunch, branched in very showy effect with black mercerized satin leaves.
Price, per bunch......32c
Per dozen bunches..$3.50
Postage extra, per bunch, 6c.

No. 39C3347 A large bunch of Black Silk and Mercerized Satin Roses. Six roses to the bunch, with black jetted bead centers. Very pretty. Sold elsewhere at 50 cents per bunch.
Price, per bunch......$0.25
Per dozen bunches.... 2.75
By mail, postage extra, per bunch, 5c.

American Beauties, 15 Cents per Bunch.

No. 39C3349 Large Bunch of Full Grown American Beauty Roses, with full rose foliage, rubber stems. Colors, pink jack or white.
Per bunch...$0.15
Per dozen... 1.65
By mail, postage extra, per bunch, 5c.

No. 39C3351 Spray of two Full Blown Roses, branched on rubber stems with green leaves and buds. Roses will be very popular this season. Colors, pink, white, jack or tea.
Price, per bunch..$0.20
Per dozen bunches............ 2.25
By mail, postage extra, per bunch, 5c.

No. 39C3353 Large Bunch of La France Roses and Foliage. This is branched in a large and showy shape, which is so popular this season, and makes a rich and effective trimming. Colors, pink, white, jack or tea.
Price, per bunch....$0.42
Per doz .. 4.75
By mail, postage extra, per bunch, 5c.

No. 39C3355 Large and Elegant bunch of American Beauty Roses, branched with extra long stems and fine quality leaves and buds. This is the new and popular form of bouquet roses, which is being worn extensively in the large cities. Comes in the following shades: Pink, white, jack or tea. Price, per bunch.........$0.45
Per dozen bunches............. 5.00
By mail, postage extra, per bunch, 6c.

No. 39C3357 Beautiful Spray of American Beauty Roses. Four roses and buds branched with natural green foliage on long rubber stems. Comes in the following colors: Pink, white or jack. Makes a very nobby trimming.
Price, each, $0.35
Per dozen.. 4.00
If by mail, postage extra, each, 6c.

No. 39C3359 Large Spray of American Beauty Roses, branched in wreath effect, with rose foliage and long rubber stems. Equal to those generally retailed at 50 cents. Colors, pink, white or jack.
Price, per dozen, $2.75; each.... 25c
If by mail, postage extra, each, 6c.

No. 39C3361 Large bouquet of Small Muslin Roses and Foliage, branched on long stems in a new wreath effect. This style of flower is entirely new and will be very popular this season. Colors, pink, white, light blue or jack.
Price, ea., $0.24
Per dozen 2.70
If by mail, postage extra, each, 5c.

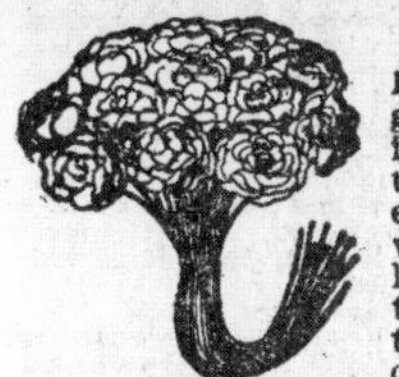

No. 39C3363 Pretty June Roses with long green stems. This is one of the prettiest small flowers, and June roses will be extensively used. Put up two dozen roses to the bunch. Colors, white, pink, light blue or cardinal.
Per bunch.......................$0.18
Price per dozen bunches.......1.90
Postage extra, per bunch, 5c.

No. 39C3365 A Bunch of White Muslin Daisies with yellow centers, branched in wreath effect with green grass. A very showy trimming.
Price per bunch, $0.10
Per dozen bunches..........1.10
Postage extra, per bunch, 5c.

No. 39C3367 A Large Bunch of White Daisies of extra fine quality. Has eighteen pretty blossoms with natural yellow centers. Comes in white only.
Per bunch. $0.20
Per dozen bunches...... 2.25
Postage extra, per bunch, 5c.

No. 39C3369 Very Pretty Bunch of Small Daisies, branched in bouquet form with long stems. A very dainty and small trimming. Comes in white, pink or light blue.
Price, per bunch.............................$0.16
Per dozen bunches.............1.75
Postage extra, per bunch, 5c.

No. 39C3371 Large Bunch of Small Muslin Flowers, with long stems, branched in bouquet effect. A very neat and dainty trimming. Colors, pink, white, light blue or jack.
Per bunch...$0.12
Per dozen bunches.......$1.35
By mail, postage extra, per bunch, 4c.

No. 39C3373 A Pretty Bunch of Bluettes or Corn Flowers. Nine blossoms, branched with green stems and foliage. Comes in natural bluette shade or white only.
Price, per bunch....$0.20
Per dozen bunches.. 2.20
By mail, postage extra, per bunch, 5c.

No. 39C3375 Three-spray Bunch of Apple Blossoms. Very prettily branched. Comes in the natural shades, pink tinted and white tinted only.
Per bunch...$0.20
Per dozen bunches.........2.25
By mail, postage extra, per bunch, 4c.

No. 39C3377 Three-Spray Bunch of Fine Muslin Apple Blossoms, with green leaves and buds. A very popular and showy trimming. Comes in the natural shaded pink or white only.
Price, per bunch......$0.30
Per dozen bunches.... 3.50
If by mail, postage extra, per bunch, 4 cents.

No. 39C3379 Bunch of Silk and Muslin Wild Flowers. Very prettily branched with green leaves and grasses. Makes a very attractive trimming. Colors, pink, white, light blue or jack.
Price, per bunch...............$0.11
Per dozen bunches...............1.20
By mail, postage extra, per bunch, 4c.

No. 39C3381 Large Bunch of Silk and Mercerized Wild Flowers. Eighteen pretty blossoms with green foliage. A regular 50-cent article. Colors, pink, white, light blue or jack.
Price, per bunch......$0.25
Per dozen bunches... 2.75
By mail, postage extra, per bunch, 6c.

No. 39C3383 Large spray of nine Velvet Geranium Blossoms, branched with green leaves and foliage. Usually retailed at 25 cents. Colors, pink, white or red.
Price, per spray.......$0.12
Per dozen sprays......$1.35
Postage extra, per spray, 5 cents.

No. 39C3385 Large three-spray bunch of Velvet Geraniums with natural green foliage; a very showy and popular trimming. Colors, white, pink, light blue or red.
Per bunch........$0.23
Per doz. bunches. $2.50
Postage extra, per bunch, 5 cents.

No. 39C3387 Large bouquet bunch of very good quality Silk and Velvet Geraniums, branched in a large and showy effect, with green foliage. Usually retails at 75 cents. Colors, pink, white or red.
Price, per bunch.........44c
Per dozen bunches....$4.95
Postage extra, per bunch, 6 cents.

No. 39C3389 Very Large and Showy Sprays of Silk and Velvet flowers, geranium leaves and buds, branched in a pretty wreath effect with green foliage and buds. This makes a very handsome and pretty trimming, which we quote at half its regular value. Colors, pink, white and red.
Price, per dozen, $5.75; each.........50c
If by mail, postage extra, each, 6 cents.

No. 39C3374 A Large Bunch of Silk Rosebuds, prettily branched with foliage and ferns. The buds are medium size, and the most stylish size for this season. A very rich and showy trimming at a popular price. Colors, jack, cardinal, tea, pink or white.
Price, per bunch.................$0.35
Per dozen bunches.............3.60

No. 39C3393 Three-Spray Bunch of Silk and Muslin Poppies, with natural centers. Branched on rubber stems with green grasses. Has nine large blossoms. A very popular and showy trimming. Colors, pink, red or white.
Price, per bunch..............$0.25
Per dozen bunches............2.75
If by mail, postage extra, each, 6c.

No. 39C3395 A large and showy bunch of Silk and Muslin Poppies with natural centers, branched on rubber stems with green foliage and natural buds. A very rich and showy trimming. Colors, pink, white and jack.
Price, per bunch, $0.48
Per dozen bunches. $5.50
If by mail, postage extra, 8 cents.

No. 39C3397 Large Wreath of Silk and Muslin Poppies, very prettily branched with green leaves and natural buds. This is a very handsome and rich trimming. Usually retailed at $1.00. Colors, pink, white or jack.
Price, per wreath.......................$0.75
Per dozen wreaths.......................8.50
If by mail, postage extra, 8 cents.

FRUITS AND BERRIES ARE VERY POPULAR TRIMMINGS THIS SEASON.

No. 39C3401 Spray of Imported Cherries, branched with natural foliage on rubber stems in a very dainty and pleasing effect.
Price, each...$0.13
Per dozen.... 1.50
If by mail, postage extra, 4 cents.

No. 39C3403 Large cluster spray of Natural Tinted Cherries and Foliage on rubber stems. Cherries come tinted from light to dark.
Price, each...$0.25
Dozen, 2.75
If by mail, postage extra, 4 cents.

No. 39C3405 Three-spray bunch of Imported Cherries, Foliage and Grasses. This is branched in a large and showy effect. Contains 24 very natural tinted cherries.
Price, each $0.42
Per dozen.......................4.80
If by mail, postage extra, 5 cents.

No. 39C3407 Pretty wreath of eighteen Imported Cherries and Foliage with rubber stems. This is branched very closely and makes a very nobby trimming.
Price, each $0.25
Per dozen 2.75
If by mail, postage extra, 4 cents.

No. 39C3409 Large Wreath of Natural Tinted Cherries, Foliage and Grasses. This is branched in a very pleasing effect and will be very popular this season. Equal to the generally retailed 75-cent article.
Price, each..................$0.44
Per dozen 5.00
If by mail, postage extra, 5 cents.

No. 39C3411 Spray of Large Natural Tinted Plums, branched in three sprays with foliage. Looks much prettier and is a much larger and more elegant trimming than we can show in illustration.
Price, per spray $0.25
Per dozen sprays 2.75
If by mail, postage extra, 4 cents.

No. 39C3413 Large Spray of Imported Grapes and Natural tinted Foliage. The very latest effect is this most popular trimming. Comes in the natural shades only.
Price, each $0.21
Per dozen.............................2.25
If by mail, postage extra, 6 cents.

No. 39C3415 Large Spray of Natural Tinted Grapes and Foliage, branched in a very pretty wreath effect with a large full center of berries and foliage. This class of trimming still remains very popular. Comes in the natural shades only.
Price, each $0.23
Per dozen............................2.50
If by mail, postage extra, 5 cents.

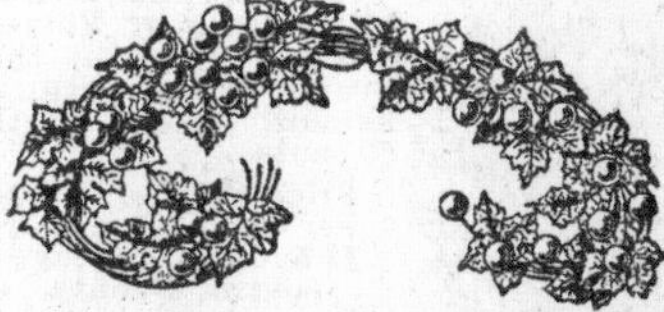

No. 39C3417 Large Wreath of Grape trimming with clusters of natural tinted grapes and leaves. This makes a very showy and pleasing effect around the crown of a hat.
Price, per dozen, $4.25; each..38c
If by mail, postage extra, 7 cents.

No. 39C3419 A very neat spray of Holly Foliage in natural shade with berries.
Price, each......$0.15
Per doz., 1.70
If by mail, postage extra, 5c.

No. 39C3421 Large three-spray bunch of Imported Holly Berries and Foliage. Berries come shaded from light to dark in the natural shades.
Price, ea., $0.22
Per dozen, 2.40
If by mail, postage extra, 5 cents.

No. 39C3423 Large Spray of Small Berries with Foliage and Grasses, branched in wreath effect. Easily worth 50 cents.
Price, per dozen, $3.25; each....30c
Postage extra, per bunch, 5 cents.

Foliage.

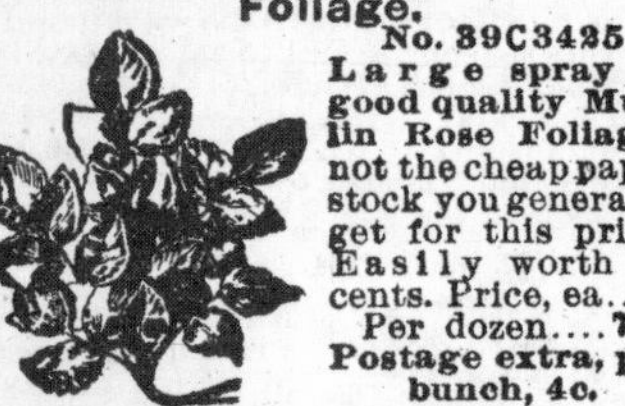

No. 39C3425 Large spray of good quality Muslin Rose Foliage; not the cheap paper stock you generally get for this price. Easily worth 15 cents. Price, ea..6c
Per dozen....70c
Postage extra, per bunch, 4c.

No. 39C3427 Large three-spray bunch of Rose Foliage. A very handsome trimming where foliage is desired.
Price, ea. 10c
Per dozen $1.10
Postage extra per bunch, 4c

No. 39C3429 An extra large bunch of very good quality Muslin Geranium Foliage, branched in three sprays. A very full and excellent trimming. Price, each..$0.15
Doz..1.65
If by mail, postage extra, 4 cents.

No. 39C3431 Large spray of Violet Foliage, in a novel effect. Each leaf has a small violet bud in the center, making a very showy trimming.
Price, per dozen, $1.35; each....12c
Postage extra, 4c.

No. 39C3433 Beautiful spray of Velvet Rose Foliage in the pretty, tinted autumn shades. Easily worth 50 cents.
Price, each.....$0.15
Per dozen...... 1.65
If by mail, postage extra, 5 cents.

No. 39C3435 Large spray of Black Satin Foliage. A very rich and elegant trimming where black is desired. Easily worth 50 cents.
Price, each. $0.15
Per dozen.. 1.65
If by mail, postage extra, 4 cents.

No. 39C3437 Large spray of Small Rose Foliage, very neatly branched with rosebuds. A very pretty trimming.
Price. each, 12c
Perdozen. $1.35
If by mail, postage extra, 4 cents.

No. 39C3439 Large Cluster of Muslin Rose Foliage in tinted effect, with a very pretty cluster of small rosebuds in center, making a very tasty trimming.
Price, each..$0.22
Per dozen.... 2.40
If by mail, postage extra, 4 cents.

No. 39C3441 A neat and dainty spray of Geranium Foliage with Buds. Comes in the natural shades only. Price, each......$0.14
Per doz. 1.65
Postage extra, 4 cents.

Wreaths.

No. 39C3443 A large wreath of Wild Flowers. A very neat trimming and worth twice the price we ask for it. Contains about 39 nice muslin blossoms. Colors, pink, white, light blue or jack. Price, per wreath, $0.10
Per dozen wreaths............ 1.10
If by mail, postage extra, 4 cents.

No. 39C3445 Wreath of Daisies. Very tastefully branched with foliage and grasses. Makes a very showy trimming and usually retails at 25 cents. Colors, pink, white, light blue or jack. Price, per wreath......$0.15
Per dozen wreaths 1.65
If by mail, postage extra, 4 cents.

No. 39C3449 A large showy wreath of Muslin June Roses, branched on long stems. A very full center of blossoms and green leaves. Makes a very large and showy trimming. Colors, pink, white, light blue or jack. Price, per wreath.......$0.21
Per dozen wreaths............. 2.25
If by mail, postage extra, each, 5c.

No. 39C3451 Wreath of Velvet Geraniums, prettily branched with green leaves. This is a very exceptional value. Has twenty velvet blossoms. Colors, pink, white, light blue or jack. Price, per wreath......$0.22
Per dozen wreaths............. 2.40
If by mail, postage extra, each, 6c.

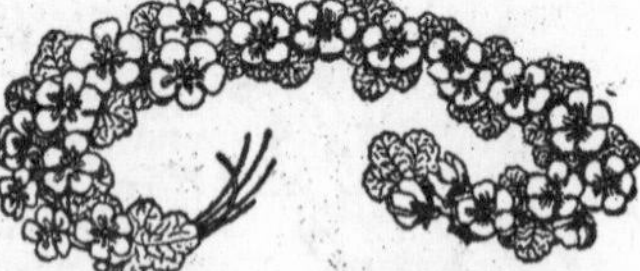

No. 39C3453 Large and showy wreath of Velvet Geraniums, branched with green grasses and geranium leaves. A very desirable and showy trimming. Has twenty-four pretty velvet geranium blossoms. Usually retailed at 50 cents. Colors, pink, white, light blue or jack. Price, per wreath...... $0.35
Per dozen wreaths.......................... 4.00
If by mail, postage extra, each, 7 cents.

No. 39C3455 A Spray of Nine Muslin Roses and Foliage, in wreath effect. A very nobby trimming which will be used considerably this spring around crown of hats. Colors, pink, white, light blue or jack.
Price, per dozen sprays, $2.75; each...25c
If by mail, postage extra, each, 5 cents.

No. 39C3456 Pretty Wreath of June Roses, branched in a very showy effect with buds and green foliage. Makes a very neat and dainty trimming and will be very popular this season. Colors, pink, white, light blue or jack. Price, per wreath..... $0.22
Per dozen wreaths 2.50
If by mail, postage extra, each, 5c.

No. 39C3457 June Roses, on Long Green Stems, in wreath effect. Has a large, full center of blossoms and foliage. This is a very rich and elegant trimming and will be very popular this season. Usually retailed at 75 cents. Colors, pink, white, light blue or jack. Price, per wreath, $0.50
Per dozen wreaths............. 5.50
If by mail, postage extra, each, 7c.

Velvet Forget-Me-Nots.

No. 39C3458 Pretty wreath of large Velvet Forget-me-nots, very prettily branched with green grass. Makes a very neat and showy trimming worth double the price we ask. Colors, pink, white, light blue or jack.
Price, per wreath.... ....$0.12
Per dozen wreaths... .... 1.35
If by mail, postage extra, 4 cents.

No. 39C3459 Wreath of Velvet Forget-me-nots. A full and pretty bunch. Colors, light blue, pink, white or red. Price, per wreath.... ..$0.21
Per dozen wreaths.............. 2.40
If by mail, postage extra, 5 cents.

Confirmation or Procession Wreaths.

No. 39C3460 Confirmation or Procession Wreaths, made of nice quality muslin flowers and green leaves, similar to illustration.
Price, per dozen, $1.10; each.........10c
If by mail, postage extra, 4 cents.

No. 39C3462 Confirmation or Procession Wreaths, made of good quality muslin, similar to above but much larger and fuller.
Price, per dozen, $1.70; each.........15c
If by mail, postage extra, 4 cents.

No. 39C3464 This is our best quality Wreath, made of best quality muslin and wax flowers and green leaves, and is much in demand for confirmations and processions.
Price, per dozen, $2.75; each..........25c
If by mail, postage extra, 5 cents.

Confirmation or Bridal Bouquets.

No. 39C3466 Nice quality Wax and Muslin Bridal or Confirmation Bouquets, similar to illustration.
Price, each........5c
Per dozen.........55c
If by mail, postage extra, 4 cents.

No. 39C3468 Medium Sized Confirmation Bouquet, similar to above but larger.
Price, each...$0.10
Per dozen..... 1.10
If by mail, postage extra, 4 cents.

No. 39C3470 Bridal Bouquet, much larger than above, made of best quality wax flowers and buds.
Price, per dozen, $1.70; each..........15c
If by mail, postage extra, 5 cents.

No. 39C3472 Bridal or Confirmation Bouquet, our best quality, made of first class wax and muslin flowers and wax buds: much larger than No. 39C3470.
Price, per dozen, $2.25; each........20c
If by mail, postage extra, 5 cents.

No. 39C3474 Confirmation or Procession Bouquets, made of nice quality muslin.
Price, per dozen, 55c; each.............5c
N. B.—Above bouquets can be ordered with either white or green leaves.
If by mail, postage extra, 4 cents.

No. 39C3476 Myrtle Confirmation or Bridal Bouquets, to match our myrtle bridal sets. Price, per dozen, 90c; each.........8c
If by mail, postage extra, 4 cents.

No. 39C3478 Myrtle Bridal or Confirmation Bouquets, similar to above; much larger, fuller and better quality.
Price, per dozen, $1.35; each 12c
If by mail, postage extra, 5 cents.

Extra Quality Bridal Wreaths.

No. 39C3481 Bridal Wreath, extra quality; well made wax orange blossoms, including brooch and bouquet, rubber stemming; if you pay $3.00 elsewhere you get no better.
Price, each.....$ 1.65
Per dozen........ 18.75
If by mail, postage extra, each, 12 cents.

No. 39C3483 Bridal Wreath with brooch and bouquet made of wax orange blossoms. Why pay extravagant prices elsewhere!
Price, each......$0.85
Per dozen........................ 9.50
If by mail, postage extra, each, 12 cents.

No. 39C3485 Bridal Wreath with brooch made of wax orange blossoms, a very good quality at a low price.
Price, per dozen, $6.00; each.........55c

No. 39C3487 Green Myrtle Bridal Wreath, with bouquet and brooch, rubber stems, good quality.
Price, per dozen, $11.00; each....$1.00
If by mail, postage extra, each, 12 cents.

No. 39C3489 Green Myrtle Wreath, with bouquet and brooch. Our best quality.
Price, per dozen, $16.50; each...$1.50
If by mail, postage extra, each, 12 cents.

Fancy Feathers.

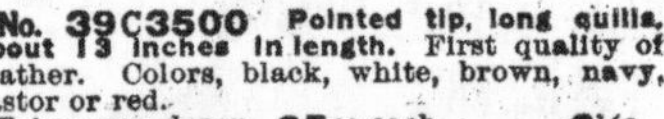

No. 39C3500 Pointed tip, long quills, about 13 inches in length. First quality of feather. Colors, black, white, brown, navy, castor or red.
Price, per dozen, 25c; each..........2½c
If by mail, postage extra, each, 3 cents.

No. 39C3503 Large Genuine Eagle Quill in the natural color. Can be used on any color hat. The quill shades from dark brown to white. Length, about 19 inches.
Price, per dozen, $1.70; each 15c
If by mail, postage extra, each, 3 cents.

No. 39C3505 Fancy Heckle Breast with quill end. Length, about 12 inches. In the following colors, black, brown, green or navy.
Price, per dozen, $1.70; each.........15c
If by mail, postage extra, each, 6 cents.

No. 39C3507 Fine quality soft pliable Wings. Nice full size. Colors, black, brown, navy, green or white.
Per pair $0.25
Dozen pairs. 2.50
If by mail, postage extra, per pair, 6 cents.

No. 39C3509 Extra large size, fine quality, soft, pliable Wings. Can be used for any style of trimming. Colors, black, white, navy or brown.
Price, per pair.......................$0.50
Per dozen pairs........................ 5.50
If by mail, postage extra, per pair, 6 cents.

Fine Ostrich Pompons.

No. 39C3510 Fine Ostrich Pompon, with Cross Aigrettes. Made up nice and full. A very stylish trimming, the aigrettes in center adding the necessary touch. Colors, black or white.
Price, each.......$0.50
Per dozen 5.50
If by mail, postage extra, each, 5 cents.

No. 39C3515 Ostrich Pompon with Cross Aigrettes, same style as above. Made of fine selected ostrich stock and better quality aigrettes. Very rich trimming, and sold by the millinery stores for $1.50 each. Colors, black or white. Price, each $ 1.00
Per dozen........................ 11.00
If by mail, postage extra, each, 5 cents.

Cross Aigrettes.

No. 39C3522 Three-piece Cross Aigrette. This is a full and rich trimming which is extremely popular this season. Colors, black or white.
Price..............20c
Postage extra, 4 cents.

No. 39C3525 Four-piece Cross Aigrette. Same as above, only branched by four. Colors, black or white.
Price..............25c
Postage extra, 4 cents.

High Aigrettes, Brush Effect. Very Stylish.

No. 39C3528 Three-piece. Fine Quality Aigrette, brush effect. Eight inches high. Colors, black or white, branched by three bunches. Makes a very full show.
Price, per bunch...19c
Per three bunches, as per illustration......55c
If by mail, postage extra, 4 cents.

No. 39C3531 Nine-piece Aigrette, brush effect. Length, 6 inches, fine quality. Colors, black or white only. Price..40c
Postage extra, 4 cents.

No. 39C3534 Nine-piece, 8-inch Aigrette, brush effect. Prime quality of stock. Colors, black or white.
Price.....(Postage extra, 4 cents)........55c

No. 39C3537 Eighteen-piece Aigrette, brush effect. Length, 8 inches. This makes a very full and showy trimming. Equal to what you would pay $1.50 for elsewhere. Colors, black or white. Price..................$1.00
If by mail, postage extra, 4 cents.

No. 39C3540 Feather Pompon set in chenille ball. This pompon will be very much used this season. Stands 6 inches in height. Colors, black, brown, green, navy or red.
Price, each...... ....$0.21
Per dozen............2.25
If by mail, postage extra, each, 4 cents.

No. 39C3543 Feather Pompon. This is a soft, feather pompon, 7½ inches long. Makes a very pretty trimming for either ready to wear or dress hats. Colors, black or white.
Price, each..............$0.10
Per dozen..................1.00
Postage extra, each, 4 cents.

Ostrich Feather Boas.

No. 39C3570 Finest Real Ostrich Feather Boas. Rich, glossy black; only the fullest, finest stock. Very dressy and stylish. Black only. We quote them in two different lengths, as follows:
Price, 36-inch..$7.50
Price, 54-inch.. 11.25
If by mail, postage extra, 8 to 15 cents.

No. 39C3572 Fine Ostrich Feather Boas, heavier and fuller than above. We guarantee them equal to much higher priced boas sold elsewhere. Black only.
Price, each, size, 36 inches.........$9.25
Price, each, size, 54 inches.........13.75
Price, each, size, 72 inches..........18.50

WE ARE DIRECT IMPORTERS OF

OSTRICH FEATHERS.

We Wish to Call Particular Attention to Our Ostrich Plumes and Tips.

ALL OF OUR OSTRICH FEATHERS are made of the best grade hard flue, selected stock, are the best black and look rich and glossy. We do not handle the poor fluffy, woolly stock. WE GUARANTEE YOU BETTER VALUES THAN YOU COULD BUY THEM FOR FROM ANY WHOLESALE HOUSE IN THE COUNTRY. If after receiving ostrich plumes or tips ordered from us, you are not perfectly satisfied that you are getting value such as we claim, you are at liberty to return them, and we will refund your money with postage added. If sent by mail, allow 10 to 15 cents extra for postage.

HALF PLUMES WITH LARGE FULL HEADS

QUILL ENDS IMPROVE THE OSTRICH PLUMES.

> As soon as you receive your ostrich feathers open them out and comb them in the dry air. It will greatly improve their appearance.

No. 39C3602 Our Special 9-inch Demi-Plume, made from real ostrich feathers. Excellent quality and warranted to give perfect satisfaction. Black only.
Price, each..........................$0.29
Per box ½ dozen........................1.50

No. 39C3604 A Very Full 10-inch Demi-Plume, made from extra quality real ostrich feathers. Fine fibre and handsome curl. Very rich and glossy in appearance. Colors, black, cream or white. Always state color desired.
Price, each..........................$0.49
Price, per box ½ dozen...............2.75

No. 39C3606 Real Ostrich Feather Demi-Plume, 11 inches long, very heavy and plump, with fine soft curl. Exceptionally handsome. Fine fibre and glossy finish. Colors, black, cream or white. Always state color desired. Price, each........$0.75
Per box ½ dozen.................4.25

No. 39C3608 Real Ostrich Demi-Plume. These are the next grade better than above. Fine selected stock. Length, 12 inches. Black, white or cream. Good $1.25 value. Price, per box ½ dozen, $5.00; each..........90c

No. 39C3610 Fine Ostrich Demi-Plume, 13-inch. Made of fine selected stock, hard finish, long and glossy fibres. Exceptional value. Colors, black, cream or white. Price, per box ½ dozen, $6.00; each..................$1.10

No. 39C3612 Finest Quality Real Ostrich Feather Demi-Plume, 14 inches long, full and heavy, with exceptionally fine curl, glossy and beautiful. In fact, these are the richest and finest appearing plumes we have ever imported. Colors, black, cream or white. Price, per box ½ dozen, $8.00; each.........$1.38

No. 39C3614 Our Highest Grade and Best Quality Genuine Ostrich Feather Demi-Plume, made of glossy, hard fibre, ostrich stock, a rich, glossy black, fine curl, very handsome and plump; length, full 15 inches. Exceptionally handsome. Colors, black, cream or white. Price, per box ½ dozen, $9.75; each..................$1.69

No. 39C2591 Quill Holders, to put on end of ostrich plumes. Gives the plume a pretty finish. Made of glossy celluloid to imitate a large quill end; very stylish. Colors, black or white. Also colors to match colored French plumes. Length, 5½ inches.
Price, per dozen, 8c; each.......................................1c

LONG FRENCH CURL PLUMES.

French Curl Plumes have the large, full drooping head. These French plumes are made of the best selected hard flue stock from the male ostrich bird, which retain their luster and are always best. The black is rich and glossy and we guarantee it absolutely fast. The finest black in the whole world. The white feathers are the natural pure white and are very beautiful. Every feather is one piece, full and wide fiber. We are satisfied that we give you at least 100 per cent more value for your money than any other concern. You run no risk whatever in sending your orders to us. If you are not entirely satisfied, after receiving our ostrich plumes, that they are almost one-half the price you have to pay elsewhere, you can return same and we will immediately refund your money and postage.

No. 39C3621 French Curl Ostrich Feather, a splendid full feather; length 15 inches. Colors, black, white or cream. Price..........$1.69

No. 39C3623 French Curl Ostrich Feather, a nice, full, high grade ostrich feather; length, 16 inches. Colors, black, white or cream. Price........$2.75

No. 39C3625 French Curl Ostrich Feather, fuller and larger than above, glossy black and pure white. Length, 18 inches. Colors, black, white or cream. Price..........$3.95

No. 39C3627 French Curl Ostrich Plumes, an exceptionally handsome and beautiful feather, full and wide. Length, 19 inches. Colors, black, white or cream. Price..........$5.00

No. 39C3629 French Curl Ostrich Plumes, a large and very beautiful feather, very best quality stock, full and wide. Length, 22 inches. Colors, black, white or cream. Price..........$7.00

No. 39C3631 French Curl Ostrich Plumes, very finest and highest quality stock, such a feather that you could not duplicate elsewhere for less than $12.00 to $15.00. Length, 24 inches. Colors, black, white or cream. Price..........$8.50

If by mail, postage extra, 6 to 20 cents.

No. 39C3633 Colored French Curl Ostrich Plume. This is a good quality ostrich feather. French curled. Regular $1.50 value. Colors, light cardinal, light blue, light navy, pink, light brown or sage green. These are the most popular colors for the coming season. Length, 13 inches. Price, per box ½ dozen, $6.25; each..........(If by mail, postage extra, each, 10 cents.)..........$1.15

No. 39C3635 French Curl Ostrich Plume. This is a very elegant, good quality ostrich plume. The colors are the best shades and the quality exceptional value. Colors, light cardinal, light blue, pink, light navy, light brown or sage green. Length, 15 inches. Price, per dozen, $22.50; each..........(If by mail, postage extra, each, 10 cents.)..........$2.00

No. 39C3637 French Curl Ostrich Plume. This is the best number that we run in colors. Is a large, beautiful feather in very pretty shades, the prevailing colors for this season. Values cannot be equaled anywhere. Colors, light cardinal, light blue, pink, light navy, light brown or sage green. Length, 17 inches. Price, per dozen, $33.00; each..........(If by mail, postage extra, each, 12 cents.)..........$3.00

AMAZON OSTRICH PLUMES.

Amazon or Flat Ostrich Plumes; very popular on the large hats; made of very highest grade, best selected stock from the male ostrich bird only. The richest, glossiest and fastest black dye in the world. Buying our ostrich feathers as we do in larger quantities than any other concern, and adding but our small percentage of profit, assures you of saving from 50 cents on the lower priced numbers up to $2.00 or $3.00 on the better plumes. Your money back if not entirely satisfactory and all we claim.

No. 39C3638 Fine First Quality Real Ostrich Amazon Plumes. Extensively used, especially for the Gainsborough effects. Length, 14 inches. Colors, black, white or cream.
Price, for ½ dozen, $8.25; each..........$1.50

No. 39C3640 Amazon Real Ostrich Plumes. Finer and larger than above. Length, 15 inches. Colors, black, white or cream.
Price, for ½ dozen, $5.50; each..........$1.95

No. 39C3644 Amazon Real Ostrich Plumes. Rich, glossy stock, long fibers. Length, 16 inches. Colors, black, white or cream.
Price, for ½ dozen, $6.50; each..........$2.29

No. 39C3648 Amazon or Flat Plumes. An extra quality, hard fiber, glossy, black ostrich. Length, 17 inches. Colors, black, cream or white.
Price, for ½ dozen, $8.50; each..........$3.00

No. 39C3650 Amazon Plumes. Very full, very extra fine stock. Length, 19 inches. $6.00 value. Colors, black, cream or white.
Price, for ½ dozen, $12.25; each..........$4.25

No. 39C3652 Amazon Plumes. The very highest grade, beautiful full stock. Equal to any plume at $10.00 and $12.00. Length, 22 inches. Colors, black, white or cream.
Price, for 1-6 dozen, $13.50; each..........$6.95
If by mail, postage extra, 5 to 10 cents.

See the New Quill Stem Holder, as used for the ends of ostrich plumes, described under our No. 39C2591, at 1 cent each.

OSTRICH TIPS.

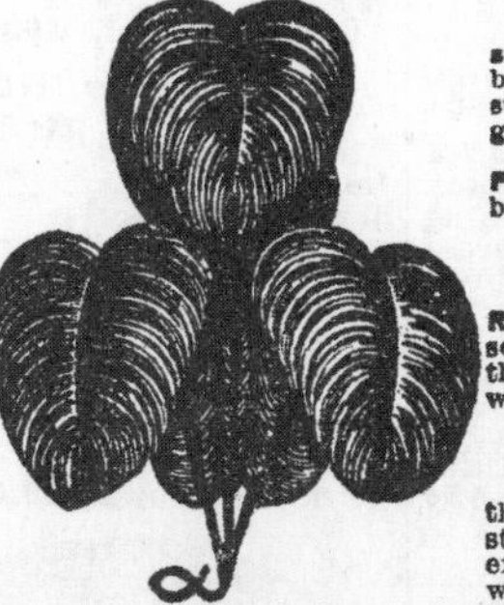

Ostrich Tips come three in a bunch, made from the best selected stock. We do not use the woolly or cheap ostrich, but only sell the best grade. Ostrich tips will be very stylish as a trimming this season, and nowhere can you get such good things for so little money as what we offer.

No. 39C3653 Handsome Bunch of Real Ostrich Feather Tips, made of good quality ostrich, very handsome bunch at the price. We can furnish these tips in black only.
Price, per bunch of three..........$0.30
Per box of ½ dozen..........1.65

No. 39C3655 This Exceptionally Fine Quality Bunch Real Ostrich Feather Tips consists of three tips, heavy stock, select ostrich. We offer these tips at a special price, a price that you could not possibly duplicate for nearly twice what we ask. Colors, black, white or cream.
Price, per bunch of three..........$0.55
Per box ½ dozen..........3.00

No. 39C3657 This Elegant Bunch of Real Ostrich Tips, three in the bunch, is made of good, hard, glossy ostrich stock. These tips are made for our special use and are unexcelled for beauty and richness. Colors, black, cream or white. Price, per bunch of three..........$0.90
Per box ½ dozen..........5.00

No. 39C3659 This Extra Fine Bunch of Rich, Full and Glossy Ostrich Feather Tips consists of three tips and has an exceptionally fine curl and full appearance. We specially recommend this number and you could not duplicate same elsewhere for less than $2.50. Colors, black, cream or white. Price, per bunch of three..........$1.50
Per box ½ dozen..........8.25
If by mail, postage extra, 5 to 10 cents.

See the new Quill Holders, used on end of ostrich plumes, our No. 39C2591, at 1 cent each.

Best Quality Satin Jap Braid Shapes.

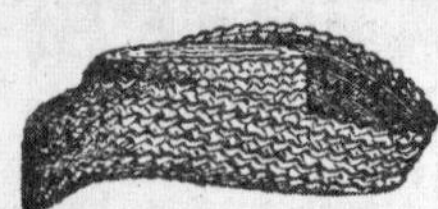

No. 39C4000 Satin Jap Dress Turban. Nobby new shape with close fitting back. In natural color only.
Price, each........$0.29
Per dozen.......... 3.00

No. 39C4003 Latest Nobbiest Shape of the Season. Colonial three-corner. Made of excellent satin Jap braid. Three-cornered crown. Natural color only.
Price, each.......29c
Per dozen........$3.00

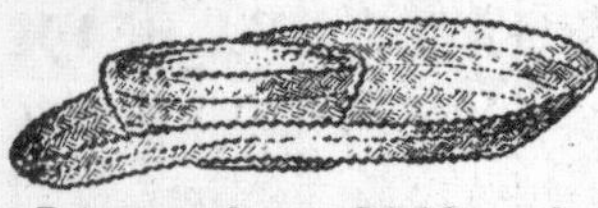

No. 39C4006 Satin Jap Dress Shape. Latest crown and uprolling brim. Color, natural only.
Price, per dozen, $3.00; each........29c

No. 39C4009 Satin Jap Dress Shape. Large torpedo crown and close fitting back. Natural color only.
Price, each....$0.29
Per dozen...... 3.00

No. 39C4012 Satin Jap Dress Shape. New style high crown with uprolling brim, slightly drooping in front and back. Natural color only. Price, per dozen, $3.00; each....... 29c

Fancy Five-end Chip Braid Shapes.

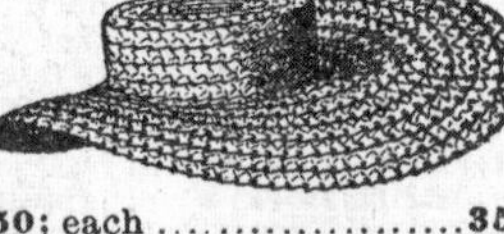

No. 39C4014 Five-end Chip Straw Ladies' Dress Shape, large uprolling brim. Colors, black, brown, navy or white.
Price, per dozen, $3.50; each........35c

No. 39C4016 Five-end Cord Chip Braid Ladies' Dress Turban. A very nobby shape. Colors, black, brown, navy or white.
Price, each.....$0.35
Per dozen 3.50

No. 39C4018 Ladies' Large Dress Shape, with wide torpedo crown and uprolling brim. Made of good quality five-end chip braid. Colors, black, brown, navy or white.
Price, per dozen, $3.50; each........35c

No. 39C4020 Fancy Five-End Cord Chip Braid Dress Hat. The new nobby high crown shape. Brim raised on both sides, slightly drooping in the back. Colors, black, brown, navy or white.
Price, per dozen, $3.50; each........35c

Combination Satin Jap and Tuscan Braid Shapes.

No. 39C4022 Fancy Combination Satin Jap and Tuscan Braid Dress Shape. Latest three-cornered colonial style with large three-cornered bell crown. This style is one of the most popular of this season. Colors, natural straw and champagne color combination only.
Price, per dozen, $6.00; each........55c

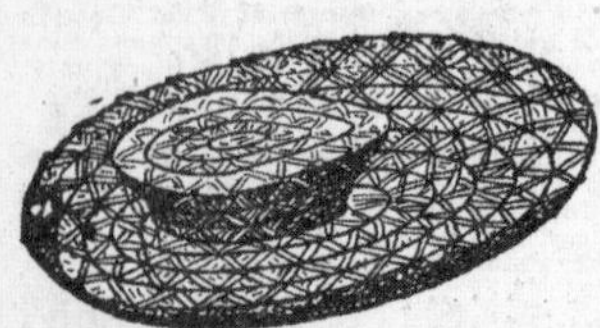

No. 39C4024 Fancy Short Back Sailor. Uprolling large brim, three-cornered bell crown. Made of first class quality of split Jap and tuscan braid. A very nobby shape. Comes in natural color only. Price, per dozen, $6.00; each......55c

No. 39C4026 Ladies' Dress Turban. Made of fine quality satin Jap and tuscan braid. This is a new close fitting shape with long narrow crown. Comes in natural color only.
Price, per dozen, $6.00; each........55c

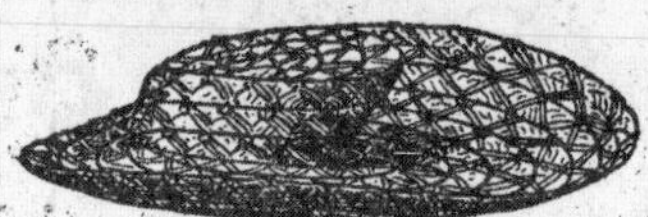

No. 39C4028 Ladies' Dress Shape. Fine quality combination Jap and tuscan braid. Large uprolling brim, slightly drooping in the back; long narrow crown. Comes in natural color only.
Price, per dozen, $6.00; each........55c

Double Feather Edge Satin Braid Shapes.

No. 39C4030 Ladies' extra fine quality double feather edge split Jap Braid Dress Turban. The latest close fitting back and long, narrow crown, uprolling brim. These hats have a beautiful shining luster and we cannot recommend them too highly. Colors, natural, champagne, navy, or brown.
Price, per dozen, $6.75; each........60c

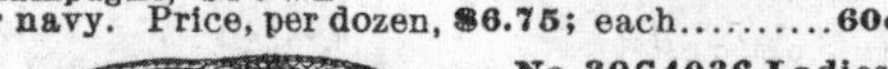

No. 39C4032 Ladies' Large Dress Shape. Made of fine quality braid, as described above, in large, uprolling shape, with high flare on left side, and long, narrow crown. Colors, champagne, natural, brown or navy.
Price, per dozen, $6.75; each........60c

No. 39C4034 Ladies' Dress Shape. Made of double feather edge split Jap braid, in new waving brim and bell crown shape. Close fitting back. Colors, natural, champagne, brown or navy. Price, per dozen, $6.75; each..........60c

No. 39C4036 Ladies' Dress Shape. Made of elegant double feather edge braid, with large, three-cornered crown. A very becoming shape. Colors, natural, champagne, brown, or navy.
Price, per dozen, $6.75; each........60c

No. 39C4038 THE DUCHESS. Ladies' Bonnet. Fine quality lace straw braid, edged with closely stitched chip braid. Black only.
Price, each........$0.40
Per dozen......... 4.50

If by mail, postage extra, each, 15 cents.

Fine Chip Straw Shapes.

No. 39C4040 Ladies' Dress Turban. Made of good quality closely stitched chip braid. Black only.
Price, each.....$0.55
Per dozen......... 6.25

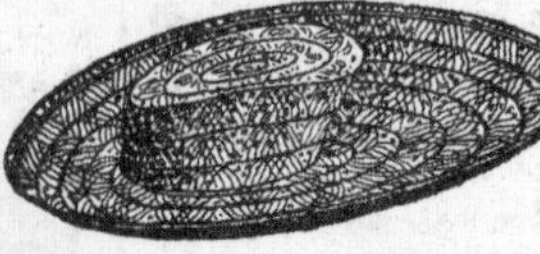

No. 39C4042 Ladies' Dress Shape, Made of very fine quality chip braid. Has three-cornered bell crown. Brim slightly drooping in the front and close fitting in back. Color, black only.
Price, per dozen, $6.25; each........55c

No. 39C4044 Ladies' Dress Shape. Made of good quality chip braid. This popular shape has uprolling brim and close fitting back. Black only.
Price, per dozen, $6.25; each........55c

High Grade, Nobby Straw and Lace Braid Shapes.

No. 39C4046 Ladies' Dress Shape. Made of extra fine quality lace straw braid. A combination of satin and tuscan cord, making a very nobby and dressy hat. A very pretty shape. Colors, black, brown, navy or white.
Price, per dozen, $8.50; each........75c

No. 39C4048 Ladies' Dress Turban. Made of a combination satin and tuscan straw braid in lace effect, usually retailed at $1.25. Colors, black, brown, navy or white.
Price, per dozen, $8.50; each........75c

No. 39C4050 Ladies' Large Dress Shape. This is the new large shape, close fitting back with large torpedo crown, made of an extra fine quality combination satin straw and tuscan cord braid. A very effective hat. Colors, black, brown, navy or white.
Price, per dozen, $8.50; each........75c

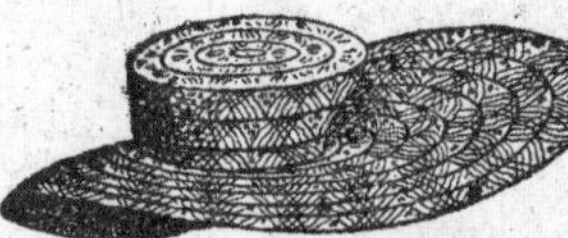

No. 39C4052 Ladies' Dress Shape. Made of a combination satin and tuscan cord lace braid, large uprolling brim, slightly drooping in front, close fitting back. A very stunning hat. Colors, black, brown, navy or white.
Price, per dozen, $8.50; each........75c

High Grade Fancy Shapes.

No. 39C4054 Large Ladies' Shape. Made of satin Jap braid with extra fine tam crown of hair braid. This is one of the nobbiest dress shapes shown, generally retails at $1.00. Brim comes in natural straw color, crown can be ordered in navy, brown or nile green, making very pretty combinations.
Price, per dozen, $6.00; each........55c

No. 39C4056 Fancy Dress Shape, of newest ideas. Uprolling brim is made of excellent quality of Jap straw bound with satin cable cord. Large new crown is made of extra fine quality mohair. Comes in natural shade only, while brim can be ordered in white, brown or navy, making a very pretty combination. Something for swell dressers.
Price, per dozen, $7.65; each........68c

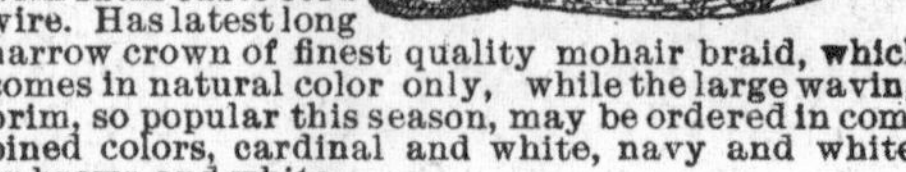

No. 39C4058 Ladies' Dress Shape. Made of an excellent combination colored Jap braid, bound with satin cable cord wire. Has latest long narrow crown of finest quality mohair braid, which comes in natural color only, while the large waving brim, so popular this season, may be ordered in combined colors, cardinal and white, navy and white, or brown and white.
Price, per dozen, $8.50; each........75c

Misses' Hats.

No. 39C4064 Misses' Shape. Made of very nice quality double edge Jap chip braid, A very desirable and pretty straw. Colors, cardinal, white, brown, or navy. Sold elsewhere for 50 cents.
Price, per dozen, $3.75; each........35c

No. 39C4066 Misses' Short Back Waving Brim Sailor. Made of double edge Jap chip braid, with pretty bell crown. One of the nobbiest misses' shapes shown. Colors, brown, white, navy, or cardinal.
Price, per dozen, $3.75; each........35c

No. 39C4068 Misses' Large All Round Waving Brim Shape. This is a very pretty and effective hat. Made of very nice double edge Jap chip braid. Colors, white, brown, navy, or cardinal.
Price, per dozen, $3.75; each........35c

Mull Shapes.

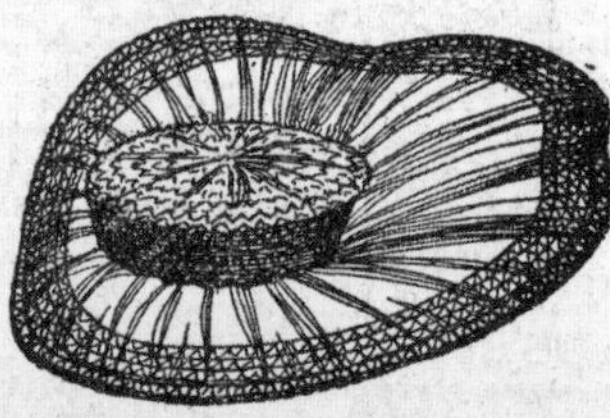

No. 39C4080 Ladies' Fancy Dress Shape, made on a silk wire frame. Upper and lower brims are covered with a good quality mull, edged with a very pretty horse hair braid, having a large bell crown made of same material. Colors, black, white, pink or light blue. Price, per dozen, $6.25; each....55c

No. 39C4082 Ladies' Dress Turban, made of good quality mull on a silk wire frame. The frame is edged with a very pretty fancy braid, having a long, narrow, shallow crown of same material. Colors, black, white, pink or light blue.
Price, per dozen, $6.25; each..................55c

No. 39C4084 Large Fancy Dress Shape, made on a silk wire frame. The upper and lower brim is covered with very good quality mull, having an edge of very pretty braid on brim, and a long, narrow, latest shape crown of same braid. Colors, black, white, pink or light blue.
Price, per dozen, $6.25; each..................55c

No. 39C4086 Ladies' Fancy Dress Shape. Made of good quality mull and braid, on a silk wire frame. This has the new effect uprolling right hand side, which is so popular this season. The crown and edge of brim are made of a very pretty satin and thread braid. Colors, black, white, pink or light blue.
Price, per dozen, $6.25; each..................55c

Chiffon Hats.

No. 39C4090 Ladies' Black Chiffon Dress Shape, hand made on a silk wire frame, of a very fine quality chiffon, very closely tucked on top of crown and edge of brim. Black only.
Price, per dozen, $7.25; each..................65c

No. 39C4092 Ladies' Large Dress Shape Chiffon Hat, hand made on a silk wire frame, made of very good quality silk chiffon. Very closely tucked around brim, having a neatly shaped crown of same material. Color, black only.
Price, per dozen, $7.25; each..................65c

No. 39C4094 Ladies' Large Dress Shape, Chiffon Hat, hand made on a silk wire frame, with a large uprolling brim on left side and drooping slightly in the back with a large, shallow center crown. Edge of brim has clusters of very finely tucked chiffon, the top of crown being made of same material. Color, black only. Price, per dozen, $7.25; each.................65c

No. 39C4096 Ladies' Chiffon Turban, hand made on a silk wire frame, having a very closely tucked crown and brim. This is the latest style shape. Comes in black only.
Price, per dozen, $7.25; each..................65c

Lace Hats.

No. 39C4300 Drooping Front Dress Shape, hand made on a silk covered wire frame. The upper and lower brims of this elegant hat are covered with a good quality, allover lace, edged with a very nice imported braid. Has a large, narrow, shaped crown, made of good quality braid and allover lace. Colors, black or white.
Price, per dozen. $8.50; each..................75c

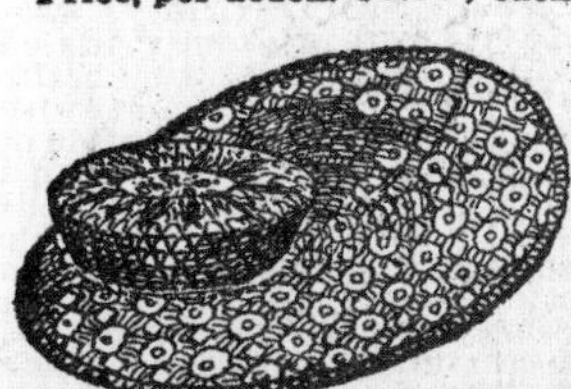

No. 39C4302 Ladies' Large Dress Shape, hand made on a silk covered wire frame. Made of a very nice quality allover lace and braid. The uprolling shape is slightly drooping in the back, making a very neat and dressy hat. Colors, black or white.
Price, per dozen, $8.50; each..................75c

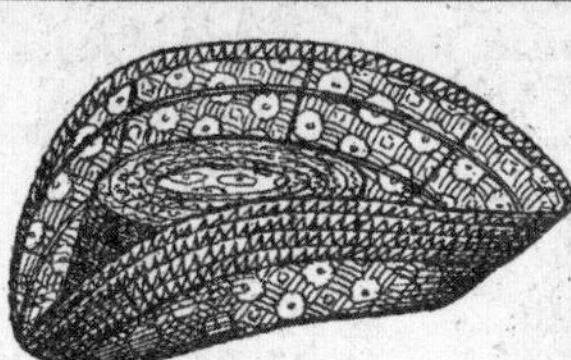

No. 39C4304 Ladies' Allover Lace Hat, hand made on a silk wire frame. This is a close fitting back uprolling turban, with a very neat bell crown. Covered with a nice quality of allover lace. Edge of brim and crown made of good quality imported braid. Colors, black or white. Price, per dozen, $8.50; each........75c

No. 39C4306 Ladies' Fancy Dress Shape. The upper and lower brims are covered with a very good quality allover lace, edged with a pretty satin and thread braid, the crown being made of same braid and lace. Has a close fitting back and uprolling brim, coming to a point in the front. A very showy shape. Colors, black or white.
Price, per dozen, $8.50; each..................75c

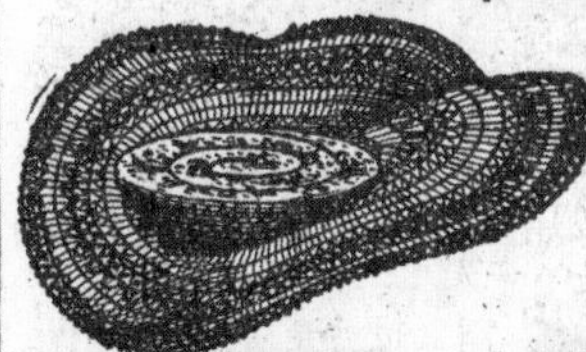

Fancy Imported Jet Spangled Braid Shapes.

No. 39C4320 Ladies' Fancy Flaring Shape Jet Braided Hat. Hand made on a silk wire frame. Covered with a very fine quality of thread and satin braid, and having rows of jet spangles. A very nobby shape. Black only.
Price, per dozen, $10.25; each..................90c

No. 39C4322 Ladies' Dress Turban, made on a very fine quality jetted braid on a silk wire frame. Covered with a very pretty combination fancy satin and thread braid with rows of jet spangles. Color, black only. Price, per dozen, $10.25; each.....90c

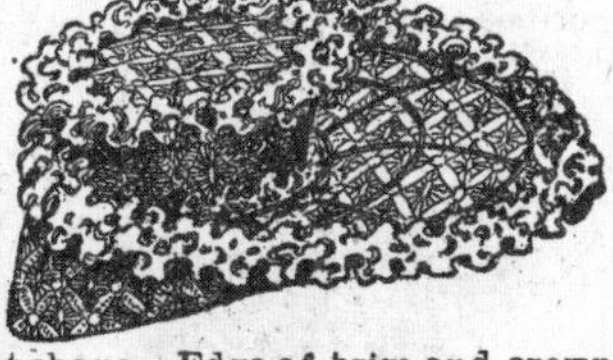

No. 39C4326 Ladies' Large Dress Shape, made of imported braid and jet spangles. Hand made on a silk wire frame. This has a large, uprolling brim, drooping in the front and back with a large, high crown. A very dressy shape. Color, black only.
Price, per dozen, $10.25; each..................90c

Extra Fine Quality Allover Lace Hats.

No. 39C4310 Ladies' Fancy Lace Dress Shape. This is a hand made hat on a silk wire frame, covered with a very good quality, allover lace. Has a large high crown with a close fitting back. Makes an excellent shape. Edge of brim and crown are made of gathered and shirred thread braid in pretty rosette effect. Colors, black and white.
Price, per dozen, $14.25; each..................$1.25

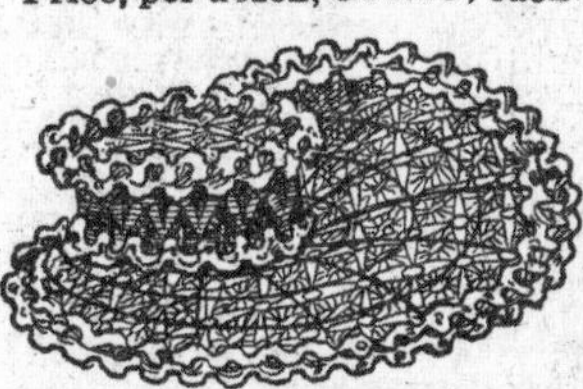

No. 39C4312 Ladies' Hand made Allover Lace Hat, on a silk wire frame with the large flare on left side, the brim being covered with a very nice quality, allover lace and having a high, stylish crown of same material. The edge of brim and crown, made of a nicely gathered rosette effect thread braid. Colors, black and white.
Price, per dozen, $14.25; each..................$1.25

No. 39C4314 Ladies' Nobby Closely Fitting Dress Turban. This hand made hat on a silk wire frame is made of a very good quality allover lace. A very neat uprolling turban and close fitting back, with broad crown. Edge of crown and brim being made of a closely gathered and shirred thread braid in a very effective manner. Colors, black and white. Price, per dozen, $14.25; each, $1.25

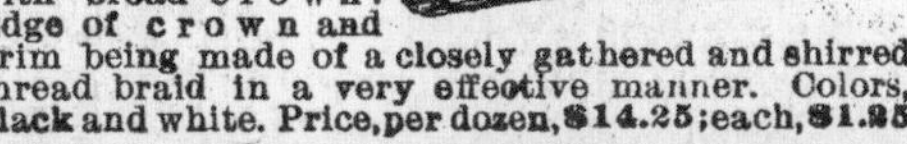

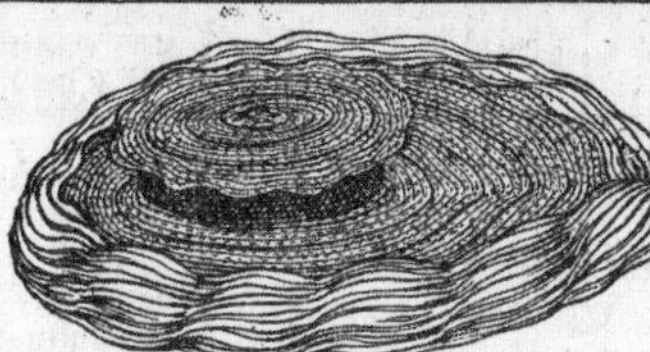

No. 39C4336 Ladies' Large Dress Shape. This is a hand made hat on a silk wire frame, upper and lower brims being entirely covered with a very fine quality horsehair braid. The edge of brim is made with a large roll of closely tucked fine quality chiffon. This is a large and dressy shape. A large bell crown, made of same braid and silk, and velvet all around bandeau complete this very effective and nobby hat. Requires very little trimming. Color, black only. Price, per dozen, $16.25; each..$1.40

No. 39C4338 Ladies' Large Dress Shape, hand made on a silk wire frame. This is the popular high crown wide brim effect. Has large uprolling brim, slightly drooping in the back. Has a high crown, entirely covered with an imported horsehair braid. Edge of brim is made of a large roll of tucked fine quality silk chiffon. A very rich looking and effective hat. Has an all around silk velvet bandeau. A very desirable hat where extra good quality is desired. Equal to any $2.50 hat shown. Color, black only. Per doz., $16.25; each...$1.40

Metallic Silk Hats.

No. 39C4330 Ladies' Dress Shape. This is hand made on a silk wire frame, covered with an extra good quality of metallic silk around brim. Has a large torpedo shape crown made of extra fine peroxiline braid. A very nobby hat for swell dressers. Comes in black only.
Price, per dozen, $14.25; each..................$1.25

No. 39C4332 Ladies' Metallic Silk Turban. This is an extra fine hand made hat on silk wire frame, brim made of tucked metallic silk; crown made of extra fine quality imported peroxiline braid. This is a very neat turban shape. Very nobby. Color, black only.
Price, per dozen, $14.25; each..................$1.25

No. 39C4334 Ladies' Dress Hat. This is the latest high crown rolling brim shape, made on a silk wire frame, brim being made of high grade metallic silk, closely tucked. Crown made of an imported peroxiline braid. A very effective shape. Color, black only.
Price, per dozen, $14.25; each..................$1.25

Cuban and Fancy Straw Braid Body Flats for Ladies, Misses and Children.

No. 39C4340 Ladies' and Misses' Broad-Brimmed, Tam Crown Body Flat. Made of a nice Jap chip, interwoven with a crinkled Ondelay braid. Already pressed and ready for trimming. Comes in the natural cream color only.
Price, per dozen, $2.25; each..................20c

No. 39C4342 Ladies' and Misses' Broad Brimmed Body Flat. A very pretty hat, made of Cuban and Jap chip straw, very nicely interwoven with a chip braid. Has a full size tam crown. Pressed and ready for trimming. Comes in the natural cream color only.
Price, per dozen, $2.75; each..................25c

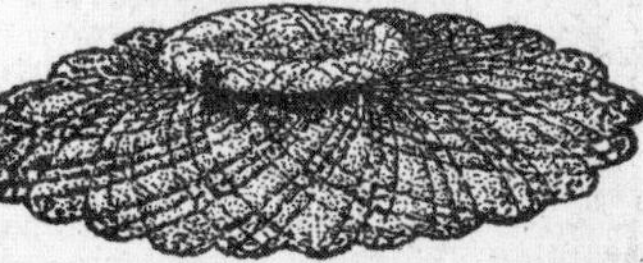

No. 39C4344 Ladies' and Misses' Broad Brimmed, Body Flat, in the natural soft and pliable shape, which is so popular this season. Made of a very fine quality Jap Ondelay and creped tuscan braid, interwoven with a very pretty, straw colored chip cord. This makes a very rich and effective hat. Comes in the natural cream color only. Price, per dozen, $7.00; each..................60c

No. 39C4346 Children's and Misses' Fluted Brim Body Flat, pressed and ready for trimming. Made of a very nice quality Jap chip with an insertion of chip cord. This makes a very pretty hat, and requires very little trimming. Comes in the natural cream color only.
Price, per dozen, $4.00; each....................35c

No. 39C4348 Children's and Misses' White Body Flat. Has a very pretty fluted brim with a large, tam crown. Made of Jap chip braid, interwoven with a pretty straw colored cord. Has a row of insertion of chip cord around edge of brim and crown. A very stylish and desirable hat for this season. Comes in the natural cream color combination only.
Price, per dozen, $5.50; each....................50c

Fancy Leghorn Hats.

If by mail, postage on leghorn hats, extra, 20c.

No. 39C4350 Child's Fancy Rim Leghorn Hat. This is a very nice quality leghorn with a fancy straw edge, suitable for misses from 5 to 12 years old. White only. Price, each........$0.15
Per dozen........1.75

No. 39C4352 Child's Fancy Rim Leghorn Hat. Finer quality leghorn than above with a very pretty edge, suitable for misses from 5 to 12 years old. White only.
Price, per dozen, $3.00; each....................29c

No. 39C4354 Child's Fancy Rim Leghorn Hat. This is a good quality leghorn with an exceptionally pretty wide fancy straw braid rim. Suitable for misses from 5 to 12 years old White only. Price, per dozen, $4.80; each.......45c

No. 39C4356 Misses' Leghorn Hat. This is a new idea in leghorns, having a fancy fluted rim. We quote this at an exceptionally low price; it is easily worth 25 cents. White only. Price, per dozen, $1.75; each......15c

No. 39C4358 Bell Crown Leghorn Hat. This is a closely woven, good quality leghorn. The bell feature will make this a very stylish and desirable shape, suitable for misses or young ladies. White only. Price, per dozen, $5.00; each..............45c

No. 39C4360 Bell Crown Leghorn Hat. Suitable for misses or young ladies. This is a very fine quality, such as ordinarily sells for $1.50 in the regular millinery stores. This will be a very stylish shape this season. White only. Price, each........$0.70
Per dozen........8.00

Misses' and Children's Leghorn Flats.

No. 39C4370 Misses' and Children's Leghorn Hat. This is a splendid quality of leghorn, suitable for misses or young ladies. Regular 50-cent value. White only.
Price, per dozen, $2.85; each....................25c

No. 39C4372 Misses' and Children's Leghorn Hat. Better quality leghorn than above; a very elegant and fine straw. We quote this at a very special price. White only. Price, each........$0.50
Per dozen........5.75

No. 39C4374 Misses' and Children's Leghorn Hat. This is a finer grade than above and a magnificent quality. We guarantee it better than the regular $1.00 leghorn as sold elsewhere. White only.
Price, per dozen, $8.50; each....................75c

No. 39C4376 Misses' and Children's Leghorn Hat. Much finer than the above hats; very closely woven and a grand quality of leghorn; as good a quality as you would care to buy. White only.
Price, per dozen, $11.25; each 95c

Ladies' Leghorn Flats.

No. 39C4380 Ladies' Leghorn Hat. A fine quality mountain leghorn. We imported these in large quantities and are enabled to offer it at the low price. White only. Price, per dozen, $4.00; each.......35c

No. 39C4382 Ladies' Leghorn Hat. A magnificent quality leghorn. We can recommend it for value as equal to the ordinary $1.00 hat sold by the regular milliner. White only.
Price, per dozen, $6.50; each..................59c

No. 39C4384 Ladies' Leghorn Hat. This is one of the high grade imported leghorn hats. Very closely woven and a splendid value. Regular $1.50 quality. White only.
Price, per dozen, $11.00; each 95c

The Most Up to Date, Ready to Wear Hats for Ladies, Misses and Children.

No. 39C4700 THE AGNES. Ladies' Ready to Wear Hat. A nice and dressy shape, made of satin Jap braid. Trimmed with a folded band of velvetta around crown and a strap of same material on top of crown, fastened with a pretty gilt ornament. Colors, white, brown or navy, the white being trimmed with black and the others in trimming to correspond.
Price, per dozen, $6.00; each....................55c

No. 39C4703 THE MERMAID. One of our best numbers in a ready to wear hat. Made of natural colored white satin Jap braid. The trimming is entirely new and effective, being a quill effect of satin Jap straw fastened with a double twist of straw cord entirely around crown, front and sides. In the front is a large rosette of same straw cord, fastened with large button in peacock colors. Two large buttons on either side complete trimming. As described, in white only. Price, each..........$0.59
Per dozen........6.75

59c

No. 39C4706 THE MARIE. Stylish, ready to wear hat, made of mixed Jap braid in different combinations. Very tastily trimmed around crown with three rows of straw cord and rosette of same material, with two quills drawn through the same. Colorings are black and white, brown and white, or navy and white.
Price, each $0.60
Per dozen......6.75

No. 39C4709 THE OSGOOD. Ladies' ready to wear hat, made of natural Jap straw with edging of black straw. The trimming consists of a wide bow of velvetta, edged with same Jap straw. In the center of bow is a large knot of same material, through which is drawn a large quill. This is a very desirable and pretty hat. Color, as described, in white with black combination only.
Price, each........$0.65
Per dozen........7.25

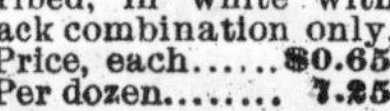

65c

No. 39C4712 VINCENT. Ladies' ready to wear hat. This is a very nobby style, made of fine quality Jap braid in two-tone effect. Trimmed around new shape crown with a mercerized sateen band and a row of straw braid. Under the rolling brim is a large rosette of mercerized sateen, in the center of which is a cabochon of straw and small buckle. Two large quills extend from rosette. Colors are white, brown or navy, with edge of contrasting color.
Price, per dozen, $7.25; each....................67c

No. 39C4715 LUCILE. Ladies' ready to wear hat. A large and dressy shape, waving brim slightly drooping in front with flare on left side and drooping in the back, fitting close to the hair. New bell crown, made of satin Jap braid in natural white color only. Trimmed with bands of black velvetta, fastened with gilt buttons. A folded band of velvetta around crown, and underneath front brim is a quill placed in an effective manner. A very desirable style.
Price, each....................75c
Per dozen....................$8.50

75c

No. 39C4718 CUBANO. This is a very popular and stylish ready to wear hat for misses and young ladies. Made of fancy satin Jap braid. The trimming consists of a band of velvetta with a straw cable cord, which extends around crown and is then tied into large bow on one side, through which a large quill is drawn. Colors, white, navy, brown or champagne.
Price, each.. $0.75
Per dozen.... 8.50

No. 39C4721 OXFORD. This is a very nobby and effective ready to wear hat for young ladies. Made with an uprolling brim and new style crown. Made of silk satin Jap braid in the natural white color. The trimming consists of a very effective draping of velvetta, as shown in illustration, and caught directly in front of crown with a fancy gilt buckle. Ornamented on the left side with two large straw wings, same edged with binding of velvetta. The hat comes in the natural color only. Trimming can be ordered in black, brown, navy or red.
Price, each....................$0.80
Per dozen....................9.00

No. 39C4724 VIRGIL. Ready to wear hat for misses and young ladies. Made of five-end chip braid in black, brown or navy, with contrasting edges of same straw. The trimming consists of a band of sateen around crown with two straps of same material drawn over crown, across and under the wide brim, while underneath the left side of brim are two rosettes, fastened with small steel buckles and finished with two quills. A very effective and becoming shape. Colors, black, brown or navy.
Price, each....................$0.88
Per dozen....................9.75

No. 39C4727 JEFFERSON. Ladies' ready to wear two-piece dress hat. A popular and desirable style, with the large two-piece crown, plainly but stylishly trimmed with a cuff of velvetta, over which is a fold of satin, ending at left side with ends or bows, caught with a strap of velvetta and fastened with two large gilt buttons. The braid comes in white only. The velvetta band comes in black, brown or navy; the fold of satin over cuff always in white.
Price, each....................$0.90
Per dozen....................10.00

98c

No. 39C4730 THE BOSTONIAN. A very nobby ready to wear hat for young ladies and misses. A new Mexican shape, that is so popular. Made of a fancy, two-tone crinkled straw braid. Trimmed with a wide fold of silk around brim and falling in wide sashes in back. The sash ends are fastened to crown with straps of velvetta drawn through two pretty gilt rings. This is a very nobby and fetching style. Combinations come in mixtures, as follows: Black and white, brown and white or navy and white.
Price, each....................$0.98
Per dozen....................11.25

99c

No. 39C4733 PEARL. This is a very desirable ready to wear hat for ladies or misses. Made of fine satin Jap braid. The trimming is plain, but rich looking. It consists of a fold of velvetta around the bell crown; in the front are two large bows of Jap straw braid, edged with same straw in contrasting color, and caught in center with a knot of velvetta, which is fastened with a handsome gilt ornament. Colors, black, white or champagne. Price, per dozen, **$11.25; each..........99c**

No. 39C4736 AUGUSTINE. This is a very stylish ladies' ready to wear hat, made of good quality chip braid. The shape is uprolling on the left side and drooping in the back. The trimming is entirely new and pretty, having a cuff of velvet around crown with a large bow in back, caught with a fancy novelty gilt buckle. The brim is trimmed in an artistic manner, with wide sash of taffeta silk, and large bow of the same material under brim on the left side. A very becoming hat for young or old. Can be ordered in black, with black trimming; or white, with black trimming.

$1.00

Price, per dozen, **$11.50; each..............$1.00**

$1.00

No. 39C4739 QUEENIE. Ready to wear hat for misses or ladies. This is an extremely desirable and nobby shape, very effectively trimmed. Made of a new pressed satin Jap braid and trimmed with the same material. The trimming is a large cuff of the same straw, edged with a fancy straw braid; has large bows caught with fancy gilt ornaments in front. One of the prettiest styles of the season. Colors, white, brown or navy.

Price, per dozen, **$11.50; each..............$1.00**

No. 39C4742 THE JEWEL. An extremely pretty, stylish, ready to wear hat for misses and ladies. Made of a fancy corded edge satin Jap braid in natural white color. The trimming consists of a folded band of velvetta with straps of same material, drawn across brim and caught with two steel cabochons. On side of hat is a large, double bow of same kind of straw and caught with a knot of velvetta. This is a very swell and nobby shape. Comes in the natural color only, with trimmings of black velvetta Price, per dozen, **$12.00; each......$1.05**

$1.05

$1.10

No. 39C4745 SUPERBA. Ladies' two-piece ready to wear dress hat, made of an exceptionally pretty and closely braided straw. The trimming consists of a band or strap of velvetta entirely around crown, fastened with gilt buttons, trimmed in the front with large, double bow of straw braid to match the hat. In center of bow is a strap of velvetta with a pretty, fancy gilt buckle. The hat comes only in white. The velvetta band can be ordered in black, brown, navy or green. This is a very expensive looking and dressy hat.

Price, per dozen, **$12.50; each.............$1.10**

$1.25

No. 39C4748 THE DUCHESS. This is a very stylish ready to wear hat for ladies. Made of a fancy horsehair braid in folds, the upper crown and under brim being entirely covered with same material. A wide ruffle of taffeta silk is put completely around the upper brim. Trimmed with a sash of taffeta silk under brim, and caught with three fancy novelty cabochons. A velvetta bandeau completes the trimming of this plain, but stylishly designed hat. Comes in black only. Price, each........................**$ 1.25**

Per dozen..**14.00**

No. 39C4751 THE AUTO. This is a pretty, ready to wear street hat for young ladies. Has a large shape, slightly turned up on either side and drooping in the back. Made of a new weave of satin Jap braid. The large bell crown is trimmed with a wide cuff of fancy Jap braid of different colors to match the trimming. The trimming is a pretty velvetta, two-tone rosette in back, caught with a gilt ring, through which a strap of same material is drawn, extending under back of brim. On left side, the cuff is trimmed in a fancy design, through which two quills are drawn. The body of hat comes always in white. The trimming, rosette and quills, as well as band around crown can be ordered in black, brown or navy.

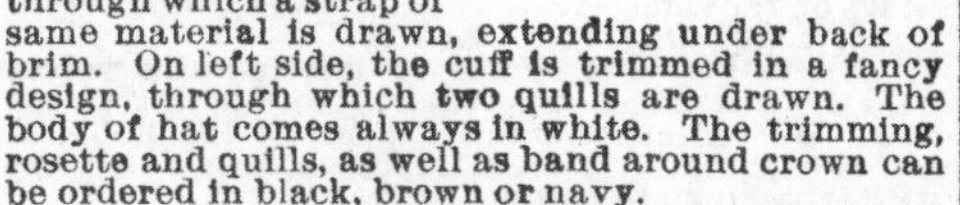

$1.25

Price, per dozen, **$14.00; each $1.25**

$1.25

No. 39C4754 THE OUTING ready to wear hat. One of the new and stylish creations for this season, that is very popular. The wide brim is made of fancy plaid, satin Jap braid, with new soft tam crown of fancy champagne colored straw braid. Plainly but elegantly trimmed with a fold of satin back velvetta and large bows of same velvetta on side, through which are drawn two fancy quills. Colors, brown, navy or cardinal. The crown comes always in champagne color.

Price, per dozen, **$14.00; each.........$1.25**

No. 39C4757 THE BLAKELY. This is a very dressy and pretty creation. Entirely new and original in a ready to wear hat. The large, two-piece crown is made of diamond satin Jap braid. The brim of fancy plaid braid is rolled up in a flare on left side. The trimming consists of a wide band of velvetta entirely around brim. Two wide straps of same velvetta, which are fastened with two gilt buttons on crown, are draw over and under the brim. The crown comes always in white. The plaid braid can be ordered in the following combinations, navy, brown or red.

$1.30

Price, per dozen, **$14.75; each.............$1.30**

$1.35

No. 39C4760 MARLOWE. This pretty ready to wear hat is made of natural colored white satin Jap braid. Edged completely around brim with a fold of black velvetta. The trimming consists of a fancy cuff around crown of black satin back velvetta with a fold of white satin in center. Streamers or bows of same satin back velvetta extend over back of crown on either side. Two streamers of satin back velvet, caught with fancy gilt buckles, extend from either side of crown and fall over hair in back. Two pretty, fancy quills extend from left side, completing the trimming. This is a most becoming and dressy hat. Comes as described only. Price, each.....................**$ 1.35**

Per dozen..**15.00**

$1.55

No. 39C4763 THE DESMOND. A very pretty hand made ready to wear hat, suitable for misses or young ladies. Hand made over a wire frame. The large bell crown and outer brim are covered with a pretty imported fancy white straw braid. Between the outer brim and crown is a wide insertion of closely tucked mull in black, navy blue or brown. The trimming consists of a wide sash of taffeta silk drawn through loops of straw braid entirely around crown and fastened to the crown with a pretty, fancy ornament. Extending from the crown to the under-brim is a large fold and bow of same taffeta silk, the bow being fastened on end of brim with a fancy ornament. An all around velvetta covered bandeau completes the trimming. The straw braid comes in white only, the insertion of mull and silk trimming to match. Can be ordered in black, navy or brown.

Price, per dozen, **$17.50; each.............$1.55**

No. 39C4766 ELINORE. Ready to wear hat for young ladies. The brim is made of a fancy plaid satin Jap straw. The new bell crown is made of a fine mohair braid. Has a large, fancy striped silk sash drawn through rings of plaid straw and falling in wide sash ends over back. A very effective and attractive style. The mohair crown comes in white only. The plaid Jap braid brim can be ordered in blue, brown or cardinal.

$1.90

Price, per dozen, **$21.75; each...........$1.90**

Ready to Wear Turban and Walking Shapes in the Latest Styles.

68c

No. 39C4780 THE SUNSHINE. Ladies' ready to wear hat. This is a new and becoming turban, made of natural colored satin Jap braid. Effectively trimmed with double black and champagne color straw cord around crown and brim. The same two-tone effect, black and champagne, is used in the rosette on side, through which are drawn two quills. This is a very desirable and excellent hat. Regular $1.00 value.

Price, per dozen, **$7.50; each..............68c**

No. 39C4783 BOULEVARD. This is a very stunning ready to wear hat. Large turban shape, hand made on a wire frame of fancy, champagne color straw braid, trimmed with straps of velvetta on both sides under brim and fastened with fancy gilt ornaments. The drooping back, which sets closely to the head is also trimmed with three graduated straps of velvetta and fastened with fancy gilt ornaments. Comes as described only, with champagne color and black trimming, which looks very rich and effective. It is better than many of the hats that are sold at $1.50 elsewhere.

85c

Price, per dozen, **$9.50; each...... ....85c**

98c

No. 39C4792 THE AMABEL. Ready to wear turban. A very stylish creation, made of a very pretty fancy straw braid. Edge of brim and crown edged with a contrasting colored braid. The trimming consists of a large quill of same straw, caught with a fancy steel ornament. The colors are black, brown, navy or champagne color. The quill comes in contrasting color to match. We recommend this nobby, little turban to stylish dressers. Price, each...............**$ 0.98**

Per dozen..**11.00**

No. 39C4795 COLONIAL. This is the new colonial shape, so much in vogue for this season, made of a fine quality white chip braid, edged with a wide band of silk velvet. Around the new shape bell crown is a fold of same velvet and a very large and full bow of same material on left side, fastened with a pretty gilt buckle. The chip straw comes in white only. The trimming can be ordered in black, brown, navy or green.
Price, per dozen, $13.50; each..............$1.20

No. 39C4786 MARMADUKE. Ladies' ready to wear hat, made of fancy chip braid. This is a very pretty and becoming style for middle aged women. Trimmed in a neat manner with mercerized sateen. A wide fold of same extending around the brim and a large rosette of same material caught with a velvet buckle in center. Comes in black only.
Price, each....$0.70
Per dozen..... 7.00

70c

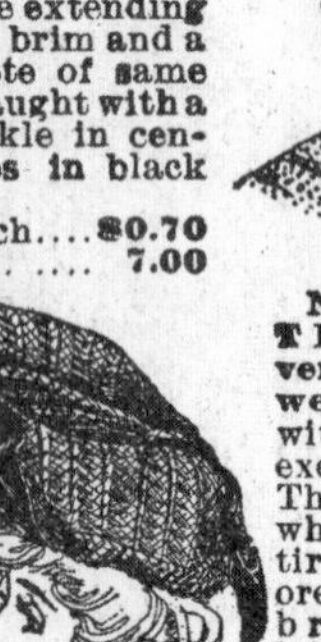

No. 39C4798 BEATRICE. This is a very stylish ready to wear hat, hand made on a wire frame. The design is exceptionally becoming. The crown is a fancy white straw, while the entire underbrim is of colored straw in either black, brown or navy, overlaid in fancy, small fold effect, and extending 1½ inches over the top. The trimming consists of bows and folds of velvetta. Fastened on the front and a little to the left, is a large bow of velvetta caught with a handsome, fancy ornament. Trimmed in the back with folds and knots of velvetta, the ends falling over the hair. An all around velvetta covered bandeau completes the trimming. The crown comes always in white. The underbrim can be ordered in either black, brown or navy. Price, per dozen, $16.00; each........$1.40

No. 39C4801 STELLA. Ladies' hand made, ready to wear hat. The new, three-cornered shape, made on a wire frame of tucked silk chiffon, and fancy, satin braid. The trimming consists of a wide strap of jetted hair braid with large rosette of chiffon and jetted braid. This becoming style is suitable for dress and street wear. Black only.
Price, each.........$ 1.55
Per dozen.......... 18.00

$1.55

No. 39C4804 SOMERSET. Ready to wear turban. This is the new and pretty turban that is so popular for this season. Boat shaped in front, fitting closely to the hair in back. The trimming is very rich and effective, being very closely gathered folds of ombre colored Jap silk, shading from dark to light, caught in front with gold ornament and two gold ornaments in back. The fancy feather edge satin Jap braid comes in white only. The trimming can be ordered in the ombre shade of brown or navy. The description can hardly do justice to the style and beauty of this turban.
Price, per dozen, $21.00; each...............$1.80

No. 39C4807 SINCLAIR. Hand made, ready to wear hat. Made on a wire frame of closely tucked chiffon under and over brim. Has a large bell crown, covered with fancy horsehair braid in placque effect. A large band of the same horsehair braid fastened with a long black ornament, completes the trimming. Plain but very rich looking and effective. Comes in black only.
Price, each.....$ 2.00
Per dozen........22.50

No. 39C4810 BELLEVILLE. Ladies' nobby turban. Is an up to date and dressy style, hand made on a wire frame of a very pretty fancy hair braid. The front between crown and brim is trimmed with a generous fold of taffeta silk. The back and sides are turned over and caught to crown with fancy gilt buttons, while a pair of fancy wings on left side complete the trimming of this pretty turban. Can be ordered in black, brown or navy.
Price, each....$ 1.95
Per dozen...... 22.00

No. 39C4813 MICHIGAN. This is an extremely pretty ready to wear hat, hand made on a wire frame of a pretty, fancy straw braid with corded edge and small tuscan cord running through same. The design is a quill or leaf effect, entirely around the underbrim. The trimming consists of a full fold of Jap silk between the bell crown and edge of brim. The trimming on left side consists of two wings of the same straw braid, edged with folds of silk velvet. Five folds of knotted silk velvet hold them in place. The back is close fitting to the hair. We recommend this for one of the nobbiest styles of the season. Colors, black, brown or navy with trimmings to match.

Price, per dozen, $30.00; each..............$2.75

No. 39C4816 JULIET. Ready to wear hat for misses. This is the new two-piece crown. One of the new and stylish shapes for the season. Made of a very closely woven and pretty straw braid, light in weight. An exceptionally fine hat for any style. Trimmed with three straps of velvetta, caught to brim with small steel ornaments and fastened to the crown with three rosettes of same straw. Two bows falling over hair in back complete the trimming. Colors are brown, navy or champagne, the edges being in a different color and contrasting prettily with the hat.
Price, per dozen, $12.50; each...............$1.15

No. 39C4819 SUBLIME. This is a very swell ready to wear hat, which is suitable also for dress wear. The new Charlotte Corday shape, hand made on a wire frame of a fancy cord edge, fancy Jap braid. Trimming on top consists of a fold of velvet entirely around tam crown with a large, pretty bow in front, made of same Jap braid and having a narrow fold of velvet on both sides of the bow, caught in the center with a knot of velvet, fastened with a novelty gold ornament. Made up in a very artistic and stylish manner. Colors, black, brown, navy and champagne with trimmings to correspond.
Price, per dozen, $19.50; each...............$1.75

$1.75

Misses' and Young Ladies' Ready to Wear Hats.

No. 39C4822 ALICE. Young ladies' or misses' ready to wear hat, rolling brim with shaped bell crown, made of fancy white chip braid with colored edge. Trimmed with folds of the same straw braid around crown and strap of same material caught with two gilt buttons, through which a large quill is drawn. The body of the hat comes in white. The edge can be ordered in navy, brown or red. Good 75-cent value.
Price, per dozen, $5.75; each............. 50c

No. 39C4828 ADELAIDE. This is a very pretty hat for young ladies and misses. Made of a fancy pearl braid. Very effectively trimmed with bars of velvetta, fastened with gilt buttons. A wide bow of same material in the back with streamers, all fastened with gilt buttons complete trimming. Colors, white, brown or navy.
Price, per dozen, $8.50; each..................75c

No. 39C4831 BERTHA. Misses' or ladies' ready to wear hat, with a rolling brim, short back effect. Has the new shape bell crown, made of a fancy satin Jap straw braid. Plainly but neatly and tastily trimmed with a velvet band around crown, and gathered velvet in fan effect, caught with two gilt ornaments on left side. Colors, white, navy or champagne.
Price, each $0.75
Per dozen...... 8.50

$1.00

No. 39C4834 EVELYN. This is a very desirable misses' or young ladies' hat, of fancy pearl braid, with colored edge brim same shade as trimmings. The trimming is very stylish, being a fancy fluted cuff of plaid straw entirely around bell crown. Artistically trimmed with two large satin back velvet ribbon rosettes, caught with large gilt cabochons. Through the left side rosette are drawn two quills in an artistic manner. The hat comes in white only. The plaid straw cuff and rosettes can be ordered in brown, navy or red. Price, each..............$ 1.00
Per dozen 11.50

No. 39C4837 MABEL. A very nobby, ready to wear hat for misses and young ladies, made of a fancy Persian colored, satin Jap straw. The trimming is a wide sash of Jap silk drawn through straw rings entirely around brim, falling in wide sash ends in back. Has new shape bell crown and makes an exceptionally pretty and dressy hat. Can be ordered in brown, navy, cardinal or green combination, folds of silk sash coming always in white.
Price, per dozen, $14.00; each..............$1.25

$1.25

Ready to Wear Hats for Misses and Children.

No. 39C4840 Child's Sailor Hat with round crown of white Canton straw and fancy brim. Trimmed with band of satin and streamers. Finished with sweatband and well made. An exceptional value. Colors, navy, brown or red. Suitable for boys and girls.
Price, each..$0.25
Per dozen... 2.75

No. 39C4843 Child's Sailor Hat, made of selected white Canton straw, with insertion of colored straw in brim. Trimmed with band and streamers to match the colored insertion. Finished with sweatband and made up in a superior manner. Body of hat comes in white and the row of insertion as well as the band and streamers come in navy, brown or cardinal. Suitable for boys and girls. Price, per dozen, $3.25; each......29c

50c

No. 39C4846 Child's Trimmed Hat. This is made of fancy two-tone satin Jap braid with new bell crown. Trimmed with a band of faille ribbon around crown and bows and streamers of same material in back. Colors, brown, navy or cardinal. Equal to the best 75-cent value, sold elsewhere.
Price, per dozen, $5.50; each....................50c

No. 39C4849 Trimmed Hat for Misses. Made of fancy plaid satin Jap braid; trimmed with silk faille ribbon, with silk faille ribbon for a band around crown, and long streamers falling over back. Can be ordered in brown, navy or cardinal. A very high grade and pretty looking hat.
Price, per dozen, $6.50; each....................59c

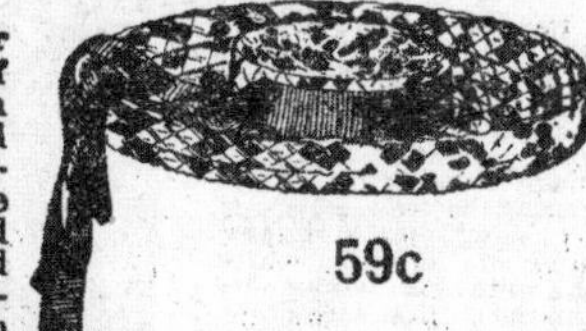
59c

No. 39C4851 Misses' Trimmed Hat. With bell crown and crinkled brim. Made of white satin Jap braid, with an insertion of plaid straw in brim. Trimmed with faille ribbon, with bows and streamers in back, and strap effect on crown, fastened with tiny gilt buttons. The body of the hat comes always in white. The plaid insertion can be ordered in navy, brown or red. The ribbon comes in colors to match the plaid insertion. Price, per dozen, $8.50; each....................75c

75c

No. 39C4853 Child's Sailor Hat. Made of union Milan, with insertion of plaid satin straw braid in brim and crown. Trimmed with fine quality silk faille ribbon, with large bow and streamers in back. A very high grade and pretty sailor hat. Colors of insertion and trimming, brown, navy or cardinal. Price, per dozen, $8.00; each......75c

75c

No. 39C4855 Child's Sailor. This is an extra large brim, made of fine quality Milan braid. Trimmed with satin back velvet band and streamers. This is the same style of hat they furnish in millinery stores for $1.50. Color, white only.
Price, each.. $ 1.00
Per dozen.... 11.50

$1.00

No. 39C4858 Misses' Trimmed Hat. The brim is made of a very high grade plaid satin straw braid. The new shape bell crown is made of a fine mohair braid. Trimmed with a full band of faille ribbon and large generous streamers of same material falling in back. This is an exceptionally dressy and stylish hat, the crown always coming in white. The Persian plaid combination for brim will match any colored suit.
Price, per dozen, $14.00; each....................$1.25

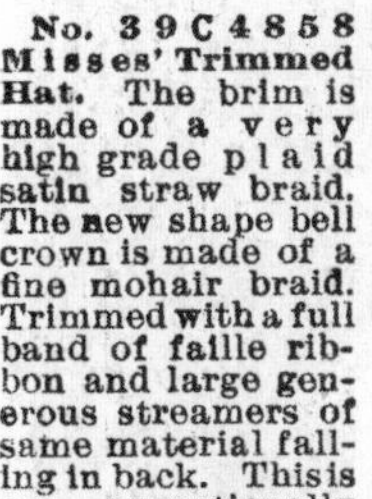
$1.25

Nobby Sailors at Unequaled Prices.

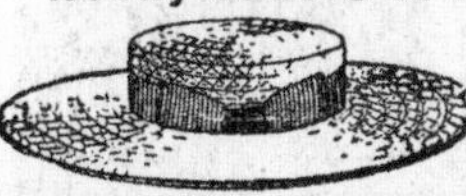

No. 39C4870 Ladies' Sailor Hat. Made of shinkee braid with a ribbon band and bow. A well made hat, usually sold at 50 cents. Colors, black or white. Price, per dozen, $2.40; each...22c

No. 39C4872 Ladies' Sailor Hat. A good quality patent Milan straw, trimmed with ottoman band and bow, and finished with leather sweatband. A very well finished hat. The shape is the newest. Colors, black or white.
Price, per dozen. $4.80; each....................45c

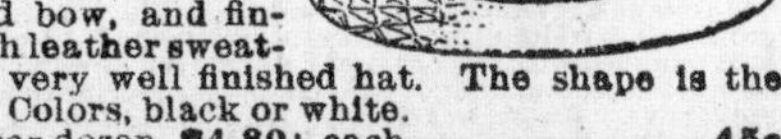

Misses' and Children's Trimmed Hats.

49c

No. 39C4876 A Pretty Crinkled Brim Leghorn Hat. Very neatly and tastily trimmed with a large wreath of muslin geraniums extending entirely around brim. Has a pretty pompon of very good quality mull in front of crown, and a very pretty pompon in back of crown made of good quality mull, and will make a very durable and serviceable hat. Generally retailed at 75 cents. Colors of trimming, pink, white, cardinal or light blue. Price..........49c

No. 39C4878 Children's Leghorn Flat. Prettily trimmed with a large sash of an openwork fancy lawn ribbon, tied in a large double bow, caught on sides and at the back of the crown with a pompon made of satin baby ribbon. The front bow is caught by a cluster of pretty muslin daisies. Makes a very dainty hat for children. Can be ordered trimmed in light blue, pink or white. Price....................48c

48c

No. 39C4880 Child's Leghorn Flat, of good quality. The brim is entirely covered with a double ruffle of accordion plaited mull, edged with pretty valenciennes lace. A pretty pompon of same in front of crown being caught in place by a small bunch of wild flowers. This is a hat that usually retails at 75 cents. Can be ordered trimmed in white, pink or light blue.
Price..........50c

50c

No. 39C4882 Stylish Hat for a Miss. Made of very pretty Cuban and Jap straw. Trimmed with a large pompon of mull in front of crown, and with a large wreath of pretty China asters extending on right side around to back of crown. The left side of hat is trimmed with a very large streamer of metallic silk, falling over back of brim, making a very tasty and stylish hat. Colors, pink, white, light blue or cardinal. Price....................75c

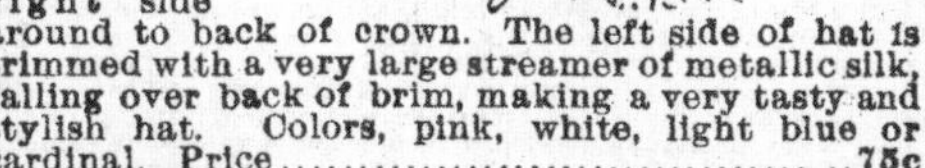
75c

No. 39C4884 Children's and Misses' Leghorn Flat of good quality. The brim is covered with a double row of shirred and wired mull of a very fine quality. Between the two rows of mull, a very pretty silk chantilly lace is neatly arranged. Has a large pompon of mull and wild roses in front of crown. Trimming can be ordered in pink, white or light blue. Price....................88c

88c

No. 39C4886 Large Cuban Body Flat. Made of combination Jap braid and cord. Very artistically trimmed with a very fine quality mull, made into two large bows in front of crown, extending along right brim of hat, meeting a fine quality satin taffeta ribbon, which extends around right side of brim and falls over edge of brim in back, in a very pretty loop and bow effect. A hat which usually retails at $1.75. Very pretty for children and misses. Can be ordered trimmed in pink, light blue, white or red.
Price....................$1.20

$1.20

$1.49

No. 39C4888 Large Broad Brim, Tam Crown, Body Flat for Misses and Young Ladies. The facing of brim is made of a very closely shirred and tucked mull of very good quality. The brim is edged with a nice white oriental lace. The trimming of this hat consists of a very large pompon of mull in front of crown, which extends around right brim, being caught into another pompon on back of brim. A very large wreath of pretty muslin China asters on the left side, completes the very effective trimming of this hat. Generally retails at $2.25. The trimming of this hat can be ordered in either pink, white or light blue, lace always in white. Price....................$1.49

No. 39C4890 A new idea for misses and young ladies in a Closely Shirred and Wired Mull Hat. This is a tailor made hat, entirely of mull. Has a very pretty double ruffle edge of mull on brim and folds of mull, closely drawn around the pretty wheel patterned crown. A large bunch of muslin roses in front of the pretty waving brim, completes the trimming of this elegant hat. Can be ordered in cardinal, navy, brown or white, with trimmings to match.
Price....................$1.50

$1.50

Ladies' and Children's Sunbonnets.

No. 39C4892 Ladies' Percale Sunbonnets in plain colors with full ruffle edge around front. The body is fancy stitched, has a long full cape with a bow at back and strings. An exceptionally well made bonnet. This is a better quality than is usually retailed at 25 cents. Colors, royal blue, cardinal, light blue or pink.
Price....................15c
If by mail, postage extra, 10c.

No. 39C4893 Misses' and Children's Percale Sunbonnets, same style and made in the same manner as above. Colors, light blue, royal blue, pink or cardinal. Price....................13c
If by mail, postage extra, 10 cents.

No. 39C4895 Ladies' Figured Percale Sunbonnets, made of good quality cloth, with large full cape. Has a bow at back and strings. Trimmed with a plaited ruffle on edge of bonnet, also one around edge of cape. Ruffles, neatly stitched and trimmed with valenciennes lace edge. Comes in light blue, pink, cardinal or royal blue.
Price..........23c

23c

No. 39C4896 Misses' and Children's Dotted Percale Sunbonnets, made in the same shape and trimmed same as above. Colors, pink, light blue, cardinal or royal blue. Price....................20c
If by mail, postage extra, 10 cents.

No. 39C4898 Ladies' Fancy Two-tone Combination Straw Braid and Percale Sunbonnet. The body of this bonnet is made of a nice quality pliable two-tone effect straw braid. Edged with a plaited and stitched ruffle of percale. Has a full cape with bow and strings of same material. A very durable and serviceable bonnet. Colors, navy blue and white or cardinal and white.
Price....................25c

25c

No. 39C4899 Misses' and Children's Combination Straw Braid and Percale Sunbonnets, same as described above. Colors, navy blue and white or cardinal and white. Price....................23c
If by mail, postage extra, 10 cents.

OUR MILLINERY STYLES ARE THE

VERY LATEST

and especially in the line of trimmed hats we show the most stylish patterns the season affords. If you buy your hat from us you will be sure of not only saving a great deal of money, but also of getting the very best style in the market.

A Charming Style, Very Pretty Trimming.

$1.25

No. 39C9000 **This is a large dress hat, made of Canton and lace straw.** The shape raised on the left side and drooping in the back. Trimmed very effectively with gathered folds of white silk mull. Rosettes of white chantilly lace appear on both sides of crown. Bows and folds of white silk taffeta ribbon are handsomely arranged in the back and also on the side of the left brim, same extending to the bandeau, which is trimmed with violets. Two clusters of violets and foliage complete the trimming of this hat. Can be ordered as described, in natural color shape trimmed in white, or black shape trimmed in black. Price..........$1.25

Combining Style and Quality at a Low Price, $1.50.

$1.50

No. 39C9002 **This is a very pretty hat, hand made on a wire frame.** The facing is overlaid with folds of cream colored lace, while the large bell crown is made of solid light blue braid. Folds of the same braid are arranged over the upper brim. The crown is surrounded with light blue mousseline flowers and foliage and is trimmed on the left side with puffs of light blue silk and rosettes of cream lace. which are caught to the crown with a novelty ornament. An all around bandeau completes the trimming of this hat. Very pretty as described in light blue and cream color, but can also be ordered in white, black or pink, with trimmings to match. Price..$1.50

Very Effective and Becoming Dress Turban.

$1.65

No. 39C9003 **This is a dress turban, made of firm black. fancy straw braid, shape rolling on the left side.** The upper trimming consists of a loose drape of black silk, same overlaid with rows of black satin straw braid. On the left side appears a long wreath of light blue velvet forget-me-nots, same wreath extending to the back of the crown, which is caught with a long novelty ornament. A black bandeau on the left side, trimmed with light blue velvet forget-me-nots, completes the trimming of this turban. As described in black trimmed with light blue is very pretty, but can also be ordered in black trimmed in pink, or white trimmed in pink or light blue. Price..........................$1.65

Large Pretty Dress Hat, $3.00 Value, only $1.75.

$1.75

No. 39C9006 **This is a large dress hat, hand made on a wire frame, shape slightly raised on the left side.** The facing and upper brim are covered with light blue silk mull, same overlaid with a pretty pattern of light blue lace straw braid. The large bell crown is covered with a firm straw braid. The front as well as both sides of the upper brim, is trimmed with an extra large cluster of white wild flowers. The crown is surrounded with folds and loops of white China silk, same falling over the brim and extending to the bandeau, where they are made into bows. The facing trimmed with a fold of white China silk and white wild flowers completes the trimming of this hat. Very pretty as described in light blue and white, but can also be ordered in black and pink or white and pink. Price..$1.75

A Stylish and Becoming Dress Hat, $1.80.

$1.80

No. 39C9009 **A large black dress hat. Made of firm black straw.** The shape is raised on the left side and drooping in the back. Very effectively trimmed around the crown and the entire upper brim with serpentine rosettes made of black taffeta silk edged with a row of pink satin straw braid. A large wreath of pink velvet forget-me-nots ornaments the upper trimming. The facing is overlaid with a row of satin braid and a large cluster of pink velvet forget-me-nots. A bandeau on the left side and an ornament in the back over the upper brim, complete the trimming of this hat. Very pretty, as described in black and pink, but can also be ordered in white, pink or light blue, with trimmings to match. Price..........................$1.80

This is a Very Beautiful Turban, $1.85.

No. 39C9012 **This is a very beautiful turban, hand made on a wire frame.** The shape, upturned high in the back, is closely fitted to the head. The facing is developed in stitched and shirred brown silk chiffon, edged with folds of brown novelty imported German braid. The upper brim is developed in brown shirred and stitched silk chiffon. The low crown is made of German folded hair braid, trimmed very beautifully on the left side with six brown silk and velvet flowers and folds of brown silk, same falling over the left side. An all around bandeau completes the trimming of this hat. This is an unusually becoming turban in brown, as described, but can also be ordered in all black, white or light blue, with trimmings to match. Price..........................$1.85

A New and Pretty Idea, $3.00 Value for $1.88.

$1.88

No. 39C9015 **No prettier hat has been shown this season.** The workmanship, style and material must be seen to be appreciated. It is hand made on a wire frame. Facing as well as upper trimming is made of navy blue silk chiffon, while the wide brim is made of shirred chiffon, with a fold of maize color satin braid. The bell crown, made of maize color satin braid and edged with navy blue silk chiffon, is handsomely trimmed in the back with two wheel rosettes of navy blue satin ribbon caught with two imported novelty ornaments from which folds of ribbon extend and fall over the brim. An all around bandeau completes the trimming of this hat. As described in navy blue and maize color is very pretty, but can also be ordered in black, brown, white or light blue. Price..$1.88

A Very Becoming and Stylish Turban, $1.90.

No. 39C9018 **This is a large dress turban, hand made on a silk wire frame.** The facing and upper rim as well as crown are overlaid and trimmed with black tucked silk chiffon. The entire rolling brim is trimmed with red mousseline flowers and foliage, and the flowers are overlaid with black chantilly lace. Directly in the center over the crown is a large cluster of red mousseline flowers and imported foliage, surrounded with a fold of black silk, which extends to the left side of the brim where it is made into wired bows. A bandeau on the left side completes the trimming of this elegant dress turban. This turban is exceedingly becoming and stylish and would recommend same in the color as described in black and red. but can also be ordered in black and pink, white and pink or light blue with trimmings to match. Price..$1.90

Artistic in Design and Very Moderate in Price, $1.90.

No. 39C9020 **This stunning and elegant dress hat is a very beautiful production.** The material and workmanship must be seen to be appreciated. The style is becoming to young and old. Strictly hand made on a wire frame. The large shape is raised on the left side with drooping front and back. The edge of the brim has the popular Charlotte Corday effect. The upper as well as the lower wide brims are covered with closely tucked and then plaited black silk chiffon, while the extra large bell crown is made of folds of imported hair braid. The front trimming consists of an artistic drape of black silk chiffon, edged with black silk lace, same extending on the left side and falling over the back of brim in fan tan effect, which is shown on the most expensive Parisian models. Imported pink silk and velvet flowers and foliage are handsomely arranged in the front and back of crown. A novelty ornament in the front and a bandeau on the left, trimmed with imported silk and velvet flowers and foliage complete the trimming of this hat. As described in black and pink, is very pretty, but can also be ordered in white, pink, light blue or brown, with trimmings to match. Price......$1.90

Very Latest Three Cornered Design, $2.00.

No. 39C9021 ...is is an exceeding- pretty hat of the ...ry latest design and ...nape, hand made on a wire frame. The shape is three corner- ...d and uprolling in ...e back. The facing ... made of gathered ...d shirred black silk ...iffon while the ...per brim is overlaid ...th folds of soft black ...roxylin braid and ...cked black silk chif- ...a. Pink silk and vel- ...t flowers and im- ...rted foliage with ...g stems are arranged on the left side between the crown and the ...im, while the left facing is trimmed generously with the same ...aterial. A bandeau on the left side, trimmed with a loop of ...ack ribbon and loops of the same material in the back, falling ...ver the brim, complete the trimming of this hat. As described, ...n black and pink, it is very pretty, but can also be ordered in ...hite and pink, or light blue and white, which makes a very ...ood combination in this hat.
Price..$2.00

The New Charlotte Corday, a $4.00 Hat; Our Price Only $2.05.

$2.05

No. 39C9024 The very latest hat, known as the Charlotte Corday. At present it is the rage in New York and Paris. It is a small dress shape with edge drooping in mushroom effect. The facing is made of folds of brown silk chiffon, while the rolling drooping brim is trimmed with gathered and shirred brown silk. The very large bell crown of the newest shape is also developed in gathered and shirred brown silk. On the left side is a wheel silk rosette; six brown silk and velvet flowers elegantly arranged in front on the large bell crown complete the trimming of this hat. This is a hat that no swell dresser should overlook, as it is without doubt the very latest offered by the very highest class milliners. There may be more becoming hats than this one, but we can assure you that no more stylish hat has ever been offered. As described in brown it is very pretty, but can also be ordered in all black, white or light blue. Trimmings to match.
Price..$2.05

An Exceptionally Pretty Dress Turban, $2.10

No. 39C9027 This is a very pretty dress turban hand made on a wire frame. The facing and rolling brim are overlaid and trimmed with light blue lace straw braid and a fold of light blue silk. The upper brim consists of a drape of light blue silk, trimmed with light blue lace straw braid and wheel rosette overlaid with bows of black imported silk velvet caught to the crown with a handsome novelty ornament, from which folds are drawn, one falling over the back of the brim and another falling over the side and extending to the bandeau, where it is made into loops. A cluster of cherries and natural colored foliage on the left side, completes the trimming of this beautiful turban. As described in light blue trimmed with black, it is very pretty, but can also be ordered in all black or white cherries coming in natural color only. Price..........$2.10

Very Tastily Trimmed Hat, $2.15

No. 39C9030 This is a hat to be admired. Strictly hand made on a wire frame, the shape is raised on the left side and slightly drooping front and back. The rolling and upper brims are overlaid with folds of black lace straw braid and black soft silk, while the crown is made of a plaque of proxaline silk hair braid. Pink mousseline flowers, buds and foliage are handsomely arranged on both sides of crown and upper brim. The entire facing is made of closely plaited black soft silk. An ornament in the back of the brim and a bandeau on the left side trimmed with velvet and mousseline pink flowers complete the trimming of this hat. As described in black and pink it is very pretty, but can also be ordered in white and pink or brown and pink.
Price..$2.15

Beautiful Dress Turban with Uprolling Brim, $2.18.

No. 39C9033 This is another one of those hats which must be seen to be appreciated. This is a hand made dress turban on a wire frame, of the very newest effect and style. The shape is long, rolling very much on the sides and drooping in the back. The facing, as well as the very wide rolling brim, are overlaid and trimmed with stitched and closely shirred white silk chiffon and two folds of white pyroxylin silk hair braid. The upper brim, as well as bell crown, are overlaid with gathered white silk chiffon and handsomely trimmed on the left side with two large pink mousseline roses and a cluster of imported foliage, same extending to the back of the crown. A handsome novelty ornament in front and an all around bandeau trimmed on the left side with natural color foliage complete the trimming of this hat. As described in white trimmed with pink, it is very pretty, but can also be ordered in black and pink, brown or light blue with trimmings to match. Price....$2.18

A Stylish Turban, Elegantly Designed.

$2.20

No. 39C9034 One of the best turbans offered this season. Hand made on a wire frame. The pointed, high rolling shape with high upturned back is overlaid and trimmed with closely tucked, then plaited, black silk chiffon. The very newest, high boat crown, made of the same material, is overlaid in the center with black hair braid and trimmed with a bow of black silk taffeta ribbon, same extending in folds over the back of brim. Between the high crown and brim is arranged a long wreath of imported pink mousseline flowers and foliage. A side bandeau, trimmed with mousseline flowers and foliage, completes the trimming of this charming turban. As described in black trimmed with pink, very pretty, but can also be ordered in white or brown with trimmings to match. Price..............$2.20

An Effectively Trimmed and Becoming Dress Hat, $2.25.

$2.25

No. 39C9036 This is a very large shape, hand made on a wire frame. The facing is developed in gathered and shirred black silk chiffon, while the upper brim is overlaid with a plaque of folded black hair braid, very plainly but effectively trimmed with folds and bows of good quality black silk. In the back of the bell crown as well as on the left side appears pink silk and velvet flowers and imported, natural color foliage. The facing on the left side is trimmed with a cluster of pink silk and velvet flowers and foliage. An all round bandeau completes the trimming of this charming hat. As described in black and pink it is very pretty, but can also be ordered in white, light blue or pink with trimmings to match. This is one of the most becoming hats we have to offer at this low price. Price................................$2.25

This Charming Turban Is Neat and Dressy, $2.30.

No. 39C9039 This is a very large turban, developed in brown with a touch of light blue. Hand made on a silk wire frame. The facing, upper brim as well as rolling brim are overlaid with closely tucked, brown silk chiffon, same trimmed around the brim with a fold of brown, satin braid, caught with hub ornaments, made of brown and light blue combination satin braid. The large bell crown is made of folds of light blue and brown satin braid. Directly in the front is a novelty gilt ornament from which two quills are drawn and extending to the left over the brim. An all around bandeau completes the trimming of this hat. As you notice from this description, this is a very plain but exceptionally stylish hat that will go well with any tailor made suit. Very pretty as described in brown and light blue, but can also be ordered in all brown or white and pink, which also looks good. Price....................$2.30

Closely Tucked Black Chiffon Dress Turban, $2.35.

$2.35

No. 39C9042 This is a very stylish black dress turban hand made on a wire frame. The facing is made of stitched and shirred black silk while the upper brim is overlaid with closely tucked black silk chiffon. The left side is highly trimmed with silk chiffon, same overlaid with rows of black silk chiffon ruching. Folds of black silk are drawn across the entire hat, caught in the front with a black novelty ornament and made in the back into bows. The crown is overlaid with black hair braid, edged with black jet spangles. Black satin foliage over the crown as well as on the side, completes the trimming of this charming dress turban. This is one of the best hats we can recommend to our good trade. It looks exceedingly well in all black, but it can also be ordered in black with a touch of color, if so desired. Price.......................$2.35

Exceptionally Attractive and Stylish, $2.40.

No. 39C9045 Developed in the much desired brown and white combination. This is strictly a hand made dress hat on a silk wire frame, shape drooping front and back. The facing is developed in closely plaited brown silk and brown lace straw braid, same extending over upper brim and to the long boat shaped crown, which is made of best quality satin braid. The entire hat is draped with a large brown silk chiffon veil edged with lace, same veil falling in the back and over the brim, while silk and velvet flowers, foliage and buds are handsomely arranged on the left side of the crown as well as the brim and the facing. An all around bandeau completes the trimming of this hat. Very pretty in brown and white, but can also be ordered in black and pink or white and pink. Price..........$2.40

Designed by Madame Giron. Very Latest Style, $2.45.

No. 39C9048 A swell dress hat of the very latest design, hand made on a wire frame. The frame is uprolling and slightly pointed. The facing as well as the upper brim are developed in black tucked silk chiffon overlaid with two rows of black silk chiffon ruching. The hub crown is made of black satin straw braid and trimmed in the front with four black silk flowers. In the back over the brim and covering part of the crown, is a large wheel rosette made of black satin taffeta ribbon, same being caught to the crown with a black ornament. Another rosette of black satin taffeta ribbon, caught in the center with a black ornament, is placed on the left side. A bandeau trimmed with black silk and velvet flowers completes the trimming of this hat. As described, in all black, and can also be ordered in black and pink, white and pink or all brown. Price..........$2.45

Extremely Pretty Dress Hat with Jetted Crown, $2.60.

No. 39C9057 is an exceedingly becoming dress hat, strictly hand made on a wire frame. Shape raised on the left side and drooping in the back. The facing, as well as the upper brim, are developed in gathered and shirred folds of black silk chiffon. The entire large tam crown is overlaid with black jet spangles. Trimming in the front consists of a long wreath of silk and satin black flowers and black satin foliage. A rosette of black silk edged with black silk lace is handsomely arranged on the left side of the crown. In the back of the crown is a bow made of black silk edged with black silk lace and with loops falling over the brim. A bandeau on the left side trimmed with milliners' puffs of black silk and lace completes the trimming of this hat. We recommend this hat as described in all black only. Price..........$2.60

Designed by Madame Lemar, Beautifully Trimmed, $2.68.

No. 39C9063 Is another one of those hats that we can recommend. This is strictly hand made on a wire frame, shape slightly drooping in the front and back. The upper rim is overlaid with closely tucked black silk chiffon, while the large bell crown is trimmed with folds of black fancy soft braid. The facing is trimmed with black allover lace, same overlaid with folds of silk chiffon ruching. The upper trimming consists of a long wreath of black silk and satin flowers and black satin foliage. Trimmed on the right side with large loops of black satin taffeta ribbon, same ribbon extending around the crown and falling over the back of the brim, where it is made into milliner's bows. An all around bandeau completes the trimming of this charming hat. This is an exceedingly becoming hat in all black as described, but can also be ordered in black and pink or white and pink. Price..........$2.68

Richly Designed, Trimmed in Allover Lace, $2.70.

No. 39C9066 Is a large dress hat, hand made on a wire frame. The facing is overlaid with white allover lace edged with two rows of contrasting white braid. The upper trimming as well as the large bell crown are made of white allover lace edged with wide folds of gathered and shirred soft silk. Handsomely trimmed in the front with a long wreath of burnt orange silk and velvet flowers and natural colored foliage. Silk chantilly lace, artistically arranged on the left side of brim as well as under the facing, is held to the bandeau with a novelty gilt ornament. An all around bandeau completes the trimming of this hat. This is very pretty as described in white and burnt orange, but can also be ordered in black and burnt orange or all black, if so desired. Price..........$2.70

Large Drooping Shape Made of Gathered and Shirred Chiffon.

No. 39C9068 One of the prettiest hats of the season. Hand made on a wire frame. The very large shape is drooping in the back. The facing is made of gathered and shirred black silk chiffon, while the upper trimming is made of folds of black mousseline silk hair braid, edged with a row of plaited black silk all around the brim. The trimming consists of very wide, wired bows of black silk drawn across the crown, with folds of same material all around the bell crown. Imported foliage, buds and crushed pink mousseline roses finish the upper trimming while an all around bandeau trimmed with pink flowers completes the trimming of this hat. Very pretty as described in black and pink, but can also be ordered in white and pink, light blue or brown with trimmings to match. Price..........$2.75

Very Swell Mushroom Effect, $5.00 Value, Only $2.78.

No. 39C9069 Is the very newest dress hat, hand made on a wire frame. The very wide shape is drooping all around in mushroom effect. The facing is made of gathered and shirred folds of white silk chiffon, while the upper brim and exceptionally large bell crown are overlaid with white silk hair braid and white straw cloth. All around the edge of the brim is placed a long wreath of pink velvet forget-me-nots, while the front of crown is trimmed with loops and folds of pink taffeta silk ribbon, caught in the center with a novelty ornament. Bows of ribbon in the back of the crown and a cluster of pink and velvet forget-me-nots under the facing complete the trimming of this hat. As described, in white and pink is very pretty, but can also be ordered in light blue, if so desired. Price..........$2.78

This Richly Designed Turban is Very Becoming, $2.90.

No. 39C9078 Is a very pretty turban, suitable for a stylish dresser. Hand made on a wire frame. The facing is made of tucked black silk chiffon inlaid with rows of black hair braid. The long shaped crown is covered with black hair braid and surrounded with folds of black silk. On the right side appears a black jet ornament through which is drawn closely plaited black chantilly lace, artistically made in wing effect. The same trimming applies to the left side and held to the edge of the brim with a loop of black silk velvet, same extending in a fold to the crown and another fold to the side bandeau. A cluster of imported cherries and foliage placed on the left side under the facing completes the trimming of this charming turban. This is very pretty in black, as described, but can also be ordered in white, light blue or pink, if so desired. Price..........$2.90

Large Lace Hat that is Becoming to the Average Lady, $2.98.

No. 39C9082 A very large lace dress hat, exceedingly becoming and pretty, hand made on a wire frame. The facing is overlaid with folds of plaited oriental lace, while the bell crown, made of the same material, is surrounded with folds of white soft silk and white silk chiffon, same edged with silk chiffon ruching. The entire edge of brim is overlaid with burnt orange silk and velvet flowers, same covered with white silk chiffon. An all around bandeau completes the trimming of this hat. This is one of the nobbiest productions of this season and is very becoming as described, to young and old, but you can also order it in black and burnt orange, all black or black and pink. Price......$2.98

One of the Prevailing Shapes for This Season, Very Becoming.

$3.10

No. 39C9083 A very large and becoming dress hat, hand made on a wire frame, shape drooping in front and back and raised on both sides. The facing is made of gathered and shirred white chiffon, while the upper brim is overlaid with white allover lace. The hub crown is made of natural colored foliage, surrounded with tucked and plaited white chiffon in very pretty effect. The left side is beautifully trimmed with a long wreath of pink mousseline flowers and foliage, buds and rosettes, made of loops of white satin ribbon. An all around bandeau, trimmed with folds and bows of white satin ribbon, completes the trimming of this hat. Very pretty as described in white, but can also be ordered in black and and pink, light blue and white or pink and white.
Price..........$3.10

Charming and Original Style, $3.15.

No. 39C9087 An extraordinarily becoming turban of the very latest style, pointed front, rolling brim and drooping back, hand made on a wire frame. The facing is made of stitched and gathered black silk chiffon, edged around the brim with folds of silk hair braid and folds of black silk chiffon. The crown is made of same material. Between the inner brim and the outer crown is a fold of gathered black silk chiffon. On the left side are three extra large very best quality imported pink silk roses with contrasting centers. The back of the brim, which fits closely to the hair, is very effectively trimmed with loops of pink satin taffeta ribbon. A fold of the same is arranged on the left side of the all around bandeau. This is an exceptionally pretty turban in the color as described, black trimmed with pink, but can also be ordered in white, brown or light blue with any color flowers desired.
Price..........$3.15

Beautiful Dress Hat with Uprolling Front and Drooping Back, $3.25.

No. 39C9090 A beautiful dress hat, hand made on a silk wire frame, the shape is uprolling in the front and on sides and drooping in the back. The facing is developed in plaited white silk edged with rows of white silk hair braid and white silk chiffon. The upper trimming is made of gathered and shirred white silk chiffon. The bell crown is overlaid with white silk hair braid, same surrounded with natural color foliage and buds. The edge of outer brim is overlaid with foliage and buds and folds of white ribbon falling in the back over the brim complete the upper trimming, while an all around bandeau trimmed on the left side with bows of white silk ribbon completes the trimming of this hat. As described, in white, very pretty, but can also be ordered in black or brown with trimmings to match.
Price..........$3.25

This Large Dress Hat Developed in White and Pink, Very Beautiful, $3.28.

$3.28

No. 39C9092 An extraordinarily large dress hat developed in white and pink, hand made on a wire frame. The facing is made of gathered and shirred white silk chiffon, while the upper brim is made of folds of white braid. The extra large low bell crown is trimmed on both sides with artistically made rosettes of white lace, same surrounded with pink crushed mousseline flowers and natural colored foliage. Loops of pink satin ribbon are handsomely arranged between the two rosettes. An all around bandeau trimmed on the left with pink mousseline flowers completes the trimming of this hat. This is a very stunning and dressy hat as described, but can also be ordered in black and pink or all black if so desired.
Price..........$3.28

A Design by Madame Rentau, $3.30.

No. 39C9093 Is an exceptionally large dress hat, hand made on a silk wire frame. The shape is drooping in the front and back and slightly raised on the left side. The facing, upper brim as well as the boat crown, are developed in artistically made folds of stitched and shirred black silk chiffon and black silk hair braid. The work of this hat must be seen to be appreciated. The hat is very tastily but plainly trimmed all around the crown with mercerized and satin pink flowers and imported foliage. A fold of black satin taffeta ribbon surrounds the flowers on the left and extends to the back over the brim where it is made into milliners' bows and loops. Folds of the same material are drawn all around the bandeau. The facing trimmed with pink silk and mercerized satin flowers and foliage completes the trimming of this hat. As described in black and pink very pretty, but can also be ordered in white and pink or all black, if so desired. Price..........$3.30

A Very Stunning Charlotte Corday in Lace, $3.35.

No. 39C9096 This is the latest production of this season, known as the Charlotte Corday large dress shape, hand made on a wire frame. The facing is made of gathered and shirred white silk chiffon, edged with light blue hair braid, while the upper trimming, as well as the exceptionally large bell crown, is overlaid with plaited chantilly lace and edged with light blue hair braid. Trimmed very artistically in the front with bows of light blue satin taffeta ribbon, from which folds are extending on the right and left over the brim. A large wreath of grapes and foliage ornaments the front, while bows of wide light blue satin taffeta ribbon are arranged in the back with ends slightly falling over the brim. In the center of the crown is a light blue satin straw ornament, while grapes and foliage on the left under the facing complete the trimming of this very charming hat. This is a very stylish and becoming hat and looks very pretty in the colors as described, in white and light blue, but can also be ordered in all white or black, with the exception of the grapes and foliage, which come in natural colors only. Price..........$3.35

This Nobby Dress Hat is An Elegant Design, $3.50.

No. 39C9099 Is one of the nobbiest and most becoming hats of this season. This hat is strictly hand made on a wire frame, the long shape drooping in front and back and slightly raised on both sides. The facing is made of stitched and shirred white silk chiffon, while the upper brim is made of folds of the same material, edged with imported white silk braid. Between the folds all around the brim are placed red velvet geranium flowers and natural color foliage. The boat shaped crown is made of imported silk and lace braid, surrounded with rosettes of chiffon and red velvet geraniums and foliage. On the upper brim in the back is a bow of white silk ribbon with ends falling over the back of the brim. An all around bandeau trimmed on the left with red velvet geraniums and foliage, completes the trimming of this hat. As described, in white with red flowers, very pretty, but can also be ordered in black and red, white and pink or black and pink. Price..........$3.50

A Parisian Design. Very Swell, $3.55.

$3.55

No. 39C9102 A very large and beautiful dress hat, strictly hand made on a wire frame. The facing is developed in folds of white silk chiffon, edged with white satin braid and white silk hair braid, while the upper brim is made of folds of white silk chiffon edged with white satin braid and inlaid with maize color satin taffeta ribbon. The large bell crown is made of white silk hair braid and very tastily trimmed on the left side with two large American Beauty rosebuds, imported foliage and long stems, same covering part of the crown and the back brim. A large bow of maize color satin taffeta ribbon is handsomely arranged in the back under the brim. An all around bandeau completes the trimming of this charming hat. This is very pretty as described, in white and yellow, but can also be ordered in white and pink or black and pink. Price..........$3.55

Large Beautiful Dress Hat with the New Hub Crown, $3.65.

$3.65

No. 39C9104 A very large and unusually beautiful dress shape, hand made on a wire frame. The facing is made of gathered and shirred black silk chiffon, while the upper brim, as well as the crown are overlaid with a very pretty pattern of imported braid. The new hub crown is surrounded with a wired drape of black silk chiffon in basin effect which is very new and becoming. The left of crown is handsomely ornamented with silk and satin black violets and numerous milliner's bows and loops of black satin taffeta ribbon. An all around bandeau trimmed with loops of ribbon on the side and black, jet ornaments on the right of crown, completes the trimming of this hat. This hat comes as described, in black only. Price..........$3.65

This Beautiful Creation Looks Rich and Pretty on the Head, $3.75.

No. 39C9105 is an exceptionally stylish and attractive creation, developed in all black, hand made on a wire frame. The shape raised in the front and in the back. The facing as well as the upper brim is made of plaited and stitched black silk chiffon edged with shirred chiffon and plaited silk ribbon. The hub crown is overlaid with black hair braid, edged with black jet spangles. On the left side appears seven genuine French curl ostrich half plumes handsomely arranged and gracefully drooping towards the hair. An all around bandeau completes the trimming of this hat that must be seen to be appreciated. This hat is very pretty in all black, as described, but it can also be ordered in white or light blue, if so desired, with the exception of the feathers, which can be had in black or white only. Price....$3.75

Exclusive and Original, a Beautiful Design.

$4.30

No. 39C9110 An exact copy of an imported hat, developed in cream and pink. This is a very large waving brim shape, being hand made on a wire frame. The facing is developed in folds of cream oriental lace, while the upper brim is overlaid with folds of cream colored, silk braid. The very large bell crown made of silk braid and lace is surrounded with imported, delicately shaded, pink, mousseline flowers and puffs of pink, silk ribbon. Natural colored foliage in the back of the brim and an all around bandeau trimmed on the left with pink flowers complete the trimming of this stylish hat. Very desirable and dressy as described, in pink and cream color, but can also be ordered in black and pink or in white and pink. Price....$4.30

Attractive and Richly Trimmed and Very Becoming to Anyone.

$4.40

No. 39C9111 This is another one of the attractive hats we have to offer. A very large shape, hand made on a wire frame, shape turned up on side and drooping in the back. The facing and upper brim are made of folds of black silk hair braid and edged with black tucked silk chiffon. The extra high crown, made of folds of black hair braid is trimmed in the front with two wheel rosettes, one of black satin taffeta ribbon and one of black velvet ribbon, extending to the back of the crown and falling over the brim. A large black Amazon feather with a long black quill end is drawn through the rosettes and from the left of the brim and falling over the hair in graceful effect. A side bandeau completes the trimming of this hat. Very pretty in all black as described, but can also be ordered in white with white feather, if so desired. Price....$4.40

A Becoming and Beautiful Gainsborough Effect.

$4.50

No. 39C9114 An exceedingly becoming and beautiful dress hat, hand made on a wire frame, the shape being raised on the left side in Gainsborough effect. The facing is made of white shirred silk chiffon while the upper brim is made of plaited silk lace, edged with two rows of white silk hair braid. The high crown is made of white silk lace, and white silk hair braid, which is surrounded with folds and loops of black silk velvet ribbon. Two white French curl half plumes are beautifully arranged, one on the left side of the crown and the other under the facing extending over the brim. An all around bandeau trimmed on the left with black silk velvet ribbon, completes the trimming of this charming hat. As described in white with a touch of black it is very pretty, but can also be ordered in all black, if so desired. Price....$4.50

Parisian Hat, Mushroom Effect, Styled the Charlotte Corday.

No. 39C9115 This is indeed a pretty hat and an exact copy of a high priced Parisian pattern hat. The very newest shape is drooping all around in mushroom effect, known as the Charlotte Corday. The facing is made of gathered brown silk chiffon, while the upper plaque crown is made of folds of brown braid and brown silk chiffon. The edge of brim is artistically made of three folds of cream lace. The upper trimming consists of a large cluster of natural colored grapes and foliage, while the same trimming is also used on the facing. An all around front bandeau and novelty ornaments complete the trimming of this charming hat. As described in brown and cream combination, it is very stylish and pretty, but can also be ordered in black or white.
Price....$4.55

This is a Very Charming and Attractive Pattern Hat.

$4.60

No. 39C9116 Another of those charming hats that are so becoming for the average young lady. The shape has an all around upturned brim. The facing is made of folds of white silk hair braid and white lace, while the upper trimming as well as the crown is developed in the same material. The wide edge of brim is overlaid with imported crushed pink mousseline flowers. Large pink American Beauty roses and natural colored foliage are handsomely arranged around the left of crown. The facing is trimmed with folds and bows of white satin ribbon, held fast to the hair braid with two ornaments. An all around bandeau completes the trimming of this elegant hat. Very pretty in colors, as described, but can also be ordered in black and pink, if so desired.
Price....$4.60

A Large, Stylish Dress Hat, a Shape That is Always Becoming.

$4.95

No. 39C9117 This is a very large and staple dress hat, hand made on a wire frame, the shape slightly raised on the left. The facing is made of plaited black silk chiffon while the upper brim is made of folds of black silk hair braid. The large bell crown, made of plaited and shirred black silk chiffon and folds of black silk hair braid is surrounded with black silk violets and black satin foliage. In the back appears a bow of black silk satin taffeta ribbon. On the side of the brim is a black jet ornament, through which a large black Amazon ostrich feather with long stem is arranged on the left side of the brim drooping in the back in graceful effect. A side bandeau trimmed with black silk violets and black satin flowers completes the trimming of this charming hat. As described in black is very pretty, but can also be ordered in white, if so desired. Feathers can be had in either black or white. Price...$4.95

This Very Swell Dress Hat is Rich and Dressy, $4.98.

No. 39C9120 This is without a doubt the very latest and most becoming hat of the season. This large dress hat is hand made on a wire frame. The facing as well as the upper brim is developed in shirred black silk chiffon edged with folds of black silk lace. The entire large bell crown is covered with black silk and satin flowers, making same an "all flower" crown. In the back of the crown are long bows of black velvet ribbon with ends falling over the back of the brim, on the left side and extending to the back are seven genuine ostrich French curl black half plumes, falling in graceful effect. An all around bandeau completes the trimming of this charming hat. This is one of the best and most stylish we have to offer and we recommend it in all black, as described, but can also be ordered in black with pink flower crown, all white or white and pink. Price....$4.98

Very Stunning Creation in Lace and Ostrich, $5.00.

$5.00

No. 39C9123 This is an all lace and feather hat. The large dress shape is strictly hand made on a wire frame. The facing is made of white allover lace, while the upper brim is overlaid with folds of white oriental lace. The lace bell crown is surrounded with white satin taffeta ribbon, same made in the back into bows and loops. Twelve ostrich small white half plumes surround the entire upper brim. An all around bandeau completes the trimming of this hat. As described in all white, it is very pretty, but it can also be ordered in all black, if so desired. Price. $5.00

A Charming Child's Hat. Excellent Value, $1.00.

$1.00

No. 39C9132 A beautiful child's hat, developed in natural color straw leghorn and pink. This is suitable for a girl of from 5 to 10 years of age. This fancy edged leghorn is trimmed all around the crown with serpentine rosettes of pink silk mull. Slightly to the left are large rosettes of pink silk chiffon, from which a wreath of pink velvet forget-me-nots is drawn and placed across the front. A rosette of pink silk mull under the left facing completes the trimming of this child's leghorn. The leghorn comes in natural color only, while the trimming can be ordered in pink, light blue or red.
Price $1.00

Misses' Large Leghorn with Fancy Brim, Prettily Designed, $1.70.

$1.70

No. 39C9135 This is an extra large leghorn with very wide fancy unbreakable brim. Trimmed very handsomely around the edge of the brim with a long wreath of white daisies with contrasting centers, same surrounded with pink taffeta silk ribbon. The crown is trimmed with white lace all around, as well as artistically made bows, folds and loops of pink taffeta silk ribbon. A bandeau on the left side, trimmed with white daisies and lace, completes the trimming of this beautiful hat. Suitable for a miss of from 8 to 12 years of age. In the combination of colors as described it looks very pretty, but can also be ordered trimmed in light blue, white or red, while the leghorn comes in natural color only.
Price $1.70

Rich Dressy Hand Made Hat for Misses, $2.00.

$2.00

No. 39C9136 A very pretty misses' hat, hand made on a silk wire frame. The facing is developed in a gathered white silk chiffon, while the upper trimming is made of folds of cream lace, same falling gracefully over the brim. The trimming in the front consists of a long wreath of pink velvet forget-me-nots and natural colored foliage. The wreath extends around the large bell crown. Two long streamers made of white satin ribbon are arranged on both sides of brim. An all round bandeau trimmed with forget-me-nots completes the trimming of the charming hat. As described in cream, white and pink, is a very pretty hat. Can be ordered also in white and pink or white and light blue. Price $2.00

Beautiful Hat on Cuban Body for Misses, $2.15.

$2.15

No. 39C9138 This is a very pretty misses hat, made of a Cuban body straw, which is very light and durable. The shape is very large and the facing is overlaid with three rows of light blue chiffon ruching, while the upper trimming consists on the side of wheel rosettes, made of light blue silk mull, edged with light blue taffeta silk ribbon. A fold of the same material is drawn all around the large bel crown. A long wreath of white daisies with contrasting centers is placed around the edge of the brim, while bows of light blue taffeta ribbon with ends falling over the back and an all around bandeau trimmed with white daisies, lace and light blue taffeta silk ribbon, completes the trimming of this charming hat. Suitable for a miss of from 10 to 14 years of age. Can be ordered trimmed in light blue as described, or in pink or white, while the shape comes in natural straw color only. Price $2.15

Fine Italian Leghorn Hat for a Miss, $2.60.

No. 39C9141 Large elegant hat for misses, made of the very best quality Italian leghorn. The facing is overlaid and trimmed with shirred and stitched white silk chiffon, while the upper trimming consists of large bows of white satin taffeta ribbon, same extending in a fold around the crown and made into large bows in the back over the brim. Clusters of mousseline red poppies appear all around the hat, interwoven with white lace, giving same a very pretty effect. An all around bandeau completes the trimming of this hat. Leghorn can be ordered in natural color only, while the rest of the trimming can be ordered in white, light blue, pink or red, as described, which looks very pretty. Suitable for misses 5 to 10 years of age.
Price $2.60

Finest Quality Leghorn, Exceptional Design for Girls, $3.25.

No. 39C9144 Misses' Leghorn Hat. A very high grade and closely braided leghorn shaped in a very becoming manner. Suitable for misses 12 to 16 years of age. The entire upper brim is trimmed with puffs of plaited taffeta blue silk, edged with a pretty narrow satin straw braid, interwoven and draped. Between the puffs of silk are folds of plaited blue silk chiffon. On either side and in front between the folds are dainty sprays of lilacs. A large bow of white silk taffeta ribbon is fastened to the front of crown and drawn across the brim. Another bow ornaments the back of the crown and is drawn over and under the brim to the velvet bandeau, where a large generous bow of the same white silk taffeta ribbon completes the trimming. The hat is made of the best materials and as described in blue with lilac flowers and white ribbon is very becoming but can also be ordered in any other color desired. Price $3.25

Pretty Bonnet, Tastily Designed, $1.65.

No. 39C9150 This pretty bonnet is hand made on a wire frame. The outer brim is developed in black lace straw while the crown is made of black hair braid edged with black jet spangles. Trimmed very effectively in the front with a jet spangled aigrette, held to the frame with a black ornament. Rosettes of black chantilly lace surround the rosette and part of the crown. In the back of the brim are bows of black silk taffeta ribbon through which are drawn streamers of the same material. This is a very pretty bonnet and can be ordered as described in all black only. Price.... $1.65

Elegantly Designed Bonnet Trimmed with Fine Materials, $1.95.

$1.95

No. 39C9154 One of the best designed bonnets of the season; hand made on a wire frame. The frame is overlaid with closely tucked black silk chiffon and black jet spangles while the crown is made of a plaque of silk hair braid. Directly in front is a large cluster of black silk violets and black satin foliage. In the back are bows of black silk taffeta ribbon through which ties of the same material are drawn. Can be ordered as described in black only.
Price......... $1.95

A Mourning Bonnet Trimmed in Best Manner with Fine Materials, $2.50.

$2.50

No. 39C9158 This Mourning Bonnet is very pretty and attractive made on a wire frame. The edge of brim is surrounded with black gathered nun's veiling while a long grenadine silk veil appears in the back. Two long black silk ties complete the trimming of this mourning bonnet.
Price $2 50

MEN'S AND BOYS'
CLOTHING DEPARTMENT.

ALL KINDS OF CLOTHING, MEN'S MADE TO MEASURE GARMENTS, UNIFORMS, MEN'S READY MADE CLOTHING, BOYS' AND CHILDREN'S CLOTHING, MACKINTOSHES AND RAINPROOF OVERCOATS, DUCK AND FUR COATS, SHEEPLINED, MACKINAW, HEAVY WORKING CLOTHING AND OVERALLS, ETC. BEST GRADES OF EVERY KIND OF CLOTHING AT LESS THAN WHOLESALE PRICES, LOWER PRICES THAN WILL BE OFFERED BY ANY OTHER HOUSE.

WE ARE MANUFACTURERS, NOT MERCHANTS ONLY. **We make these clothes ourselves in our own splendidly equipped manufacturing plant.** You cannot afford to overlook these great advantages. We control the making of the goods; we know exactly the grade of cloth used and know the class of work we put into them and we will guarantee our goods to be second to none on the market and, at the same time, we cut your clothing bills down one-third to one-half. There is really no comparison between our prices and regular retail prices; ours are not retail prices, but on the contrary, represent only the manufacturing cost with a small profit added. Let us point out some of the most important advantages we offer.

WE OFFER A BIG VARIETY OF GOODS **in every division of our clothing department,** a variety of fabrics and styles by far greater than you can find in any small town or city in any part of the country and greater even than you will find in the biggest houses in the very largest cities. In fact, our variety is equal to bringing the big New York and Chicago stores right to your very door. You can buy any kind of clothing you want from us, the most advanced high class styles in made to measure garments, uniforms, men's ready made clothing, boys' and children's clothing, rainy weather clothing, duck, fur, leather and working clothing, etc. We save you the trouble of going from place to place, from store to store to get the goods you want. You find everything right in this book and in our sample books.

Our Clothing Manufacturing Plant, located at No. 130 to 136 Washington Boulevard, separate and distinct from our main building. It covers four large city lots, is almost a full block long and has six floors and basement, giving us an immense space for manufacturing purposes. It is a model clothing building, large, airy well ventilated well lighted, sanitary, and provides every comfort for our employes. We offer garments made in the most cleanly and healthful surroundings there is absolutely no such thing as sweat shop labor connected with them.

THERE IS NO BETTER MADE CLOTHING IN THE MARKET THAN OURS, **as we control the buying of the cloth, linings, trimmings, paddings and everything,** get these goods direct from the mills at first cost, and as we make the garments in our own model and perfectly equipped clothing plant, we know exactly how they are made and we see that everything is done to keep the standard up to the highest notch. We believe in using only the most reliable qualities of cloth, linings, trimmings, etc., designing the styles, sewing and making them in the most substantial way and so economically is our vast business conducted that we are able to offer you the best there is in clothing and guarantee to please you perfectly for much less money than you will have to pay elsewhere for garments not nearly so good. Any sum of money invested in our goods will bring you very much greater returns than if invested anywhere else.

WE ABSOLUTELY GUARANTEE TO FIT AND PLEASE YOU IN EVERY WAY OR IT WILL NOT COST YOU A CENT.

Our system of measuring is so very simple that you can hardly make any mistake, and moreover, we take all the responsibility. Even if you do make a mistake and if, for any reason whatever, the garments should be unsatisfactory, they may be returned to us, at our expense, and we will refund you every cent you have paid together with transportation charges. We are making the garments for many of the best dressing gentlemen in every part of the country, including business men, professional men and men in every walk of life and are giving the most satisfactory results.

WE GET LARGE NUMBERS OF LETTERS IN EVERY MAIL EXPRESSING THE GREATEST POSSIBLE SATISFACTION IN THE FIT, APPEARANCE AND WEARING QUALITIES OF OUR CLOTHING.

OUR PRICES ARE LESS THAN WHOLESALE. **Clothing equal to ours in quality of cloth and workmanship will elsewhere cost you nearly double our price.** If you have the opportunity to compare the qualities and values you will be very much surprised at the low price at which we offer our goods. The price is so low that competitors try to tell people that it cannot be good clothing at such a low price. We guarantee, however, to please every person who orders clothes from us, in quality, workmanship, fit and value. If you do not believe, after receiving clothing from us, that it is the best value you ever received for your money, you need not accept the garments, but return them to us at our expense and we will refund every cent you have paid. We are manufacturers, not merchants only. We sell the goods to you at the actual cost of labor and material with one small profit added and cut out wholesalers, retailers, jobbers, agents and all middlemen. Hence, we offer the most stylish made to measure garments at from $12.00 to $25.00 a suit and worth from $18.00 to $45.00, according to prices charged by tailors generally. We offer ready made clothing at from $4.50 to $15.00 a suit, such as are sold by retail dealers at double the money, and the same holds good in boys' and children's clothing and in other departments.

WE CUT FAMILY CLOTHING BILLS IN TWO **by our methods of handling the clothing business.** Men's, boys' and children's clothing of the very best grades of cloth, woven and made in the most skillful and painstaking manner, is offered to you at manufacturers' prices and it means a saving of from one-third to one-half the money commonly spent by a family for clothing. We make a high class full dress suit, Prince Albert or clerical style, with the best grades of linings and trimmings and guarantee to fit the most particular dresser for actually less money than the average tailor will charge for a very plain business sack suit. We have thousands of families who give us their entire trade in clothing as well as other things, recognizing these important facts, and if we have not your entire clothing trade you will do well to give us a trial order and let us show you these facts by placing the goods before you.

OUR TERMS ARE VERY LIBERAL. **We ship you garments C. O. D. or for the full price with the order.** If you want clothing sent C. O. D. you need only send $1.00 deposit with your order and the balance will be collected by the express agent after you have satisfied yourself that the garments are exactly what you want in every way. If you are disappointed in the slightest way you may return them to us at your expense and we will refund every cent you have paid. We ask you, as a favor, to let us know in case of any unsatisfactory goods

ON THE FOLLOWING PAGES we describe the various free sample books we send out and you may order any sample book you please **if you prefer to see the cloth before buying,** but you can order a great deal of our clothing, for example, all the ready made clothing, direct from this catalogue without waiting for a sample book. Please don't hesitate to ask for sample books, because if you feel that if you do not understand the kind of goods from the description, we want you to see the goods and we know that you will order from the sample book. Please send for our Made to Measure Clothing Sample Book. We only describe a few of the staples in made to measure clothing here to show you the values we offer in our made to measure department, but we want to have you see our Made to Measure Clothing Sample Book if you are interested in high grade made to measure clothing.

OUR FREE CLOTHING SAMPLE BOOKS.

We give you below a list of all the Free Sample Books we send from our clothing departments, and if you wish, you can simply write us, giving the number or name of the sample book wanted, and we will send you the book free and postpaid. If you have the slightest doubt as to what sample book contains the goods you want to see, or if you do not have the time to look through our list thoroughly, you might just tell us whether you want a made to measure suit or overcoat, or a ready made garment, or something in the line of boys' and children's clothing, or a rainy weather garment, or tell us in your own words exactly what you want, and we will send you the correct sample book and avoid the chance of sending you a book in which you will not be interested.

Our Assortment of Clothing.

Our assortment of clothing is so large that it would be too big a proposition to send you the whole line in one book, and we must necessarily divide it up into its natural divisions. The divisions cover all that any person needs in the way of clothing from a 25-cent waist for a boy to the full dress made to measure styles for men, and as they are very simply arranged, you can just ask for the kind of goods you want, and we place before you, free of cost to you, the very largest assortment that you could find, of the very goods in which you are most interested. In our made to measure department we sample by far more fabrics than you will be able to see in any merchant tailors in the small towns and cities throughout the country. In the men's ready made department, we sample more goods and furnish them in more styles than you could be able to see outside of the largest clothiers in the big cities. In our boys' and children's clothing department we sample 90 different goods and show 100 different styles, everything up to date, making a larger collection than parents could find outside of the most up to date stores in the large cities like New York, Chicago, Philadelphia, and a similar large display is made in our rainy weather clothing department, where you can get those beautiful Cielette rainproof overcoats, suitable for wear at all times, rain or shine, and also in our duck and fur coat department, the variety of goods is very large.

We Make The Clothes Ourselves.

High Quality at the Lowest Price is Certain.

Much of This Clothing Can Be Ordered Directly From This Catalogue.

Much of this clothing can be ordered directly from this catalogue. You will find descriptions and illustrations of our men's ready made clothing, on pages 897 to 906; of boys' and children's clothing, on pages 907 to 916; of our rainy weather clothing, on pages 918 to 921; and our duck and fur coats, on pages 916 and 917. (Of course, we do not sample such goods as duck, fur, leather, Mackinaw or overall goods, or such clothing as oil slicker and rubber surface garments; these are to be ordered directly from this catalogue). We only give you a few sample descriptions of the fabrics shown in our made to measure department of such goods as are called staples, and we ask you to send for one of the sample books from our made to measure department if you want made to measure garments. We feel that the only way to conduct a high grade made to measure clothing department is to place the samples before our customers; we, however, guarantee to please you if you order any of these staples from this catalogue.

Please notice that our Custom Tailoring or Made to Measure Clothing Department is represented by several different sample books and cards. The **main book is 81C,** but if you want heavy weight goods, summer outing styles, spring overcoats or fancy vests see the description of sample books before sending for a book.

LIST OF FREE SAMPLE BOOKS AND WHAT THEY CONTAIN.

WRITE FOR THE SAMPLE BOOK YOU WANT, AND WE WILL IMMEDIATELY SEND IT TO YOU FREE AND POSTPAID.

Free Sample Book No. 81C—Men's Made to Measure Suits and Trousers From Medium and Light Weight Fabrics.

Free Sample Book No. 81C, Men's Made to Measure Suits and Trousers from medium and light weight fabrics, suitable for spring and summer wear at $12.00 to $25 00 a suit, including all the latest in fancy mixtures and dress suit fabrics, a very large assortment. A big variety in up to date goods in blacks, browns, blues, grays, stripes, checks, beautiful mixtures, etc., and a full display of all the latest in men's fashions, every kind of sack, frock, medium and full dress styles This book **does not** contain fancy flannels, etc., for outing suits; if you want strictly outing suits from very fancy goods, order sample card No. 85C. This book does not contain heavy weight fabrics; if you want heavy weight made to measure clothes, order sample book No. 82C. Neither does this book contain made to measure overcoats for spring and fall, see sample card 84C for overcoats; but if you want medium and light weight clothing, suitable for spring and summer wear, made to your measure in a strictly high grade way, send for our free sample book No. 81C.

Free Sample Book No. 82C—Men's Made to Measure Suits and Trousers From Heavy Weight Fabrics.

Sample Book No. 82C, Men's Made to Measure Suits and Trousers from heavy weight fabrics, suitable for fall and winter wear at $12.00 to $25.00 a suit. This sample book contains a large assortment of up to date goods in all shades, fancy mixtures and plain colors, the same as sample book No. 81C, the difference being only in the weight of the goods. The goods in this book are intended only for fall and winter wear or for climates where heavy weight garments only are desirable; many of our customers order a heavy weight goods throughout the year and we have gotten up this sample book in made to measure clothing for this purpose. If you want a heavy weight, made to measure suit or trousers, write for our free sample book No. 82C.

Free Sample Card No. 83C—Men's Made to Measure Corduroy Suits and Trousers From $12.00 to $15.00.

Sample Card No. 83C, Men's Made to Measure Corduroy Suits and Trousers from $12.00 to $15.00. We show a full line of both plain and fancy corduroys in all shades, such as tan, dark green, deep blue, brown and dark patterns, also show all the styles suitable for corduroy garments. If you wish a made to measure corduroy garment of any kind send for our free sample card No. 83C.

Free Sample Card No. 84C—Men's Made to Measure Overcoats For Spring and Early Fall Wear.

Sample Card No. 84C, Men's Made to Measure Overcoats for spring and early fall wear, including everything in medium and light weight overcoating for top coats adapted for spring and early fall weather, in such shades as light tan, medium and dark colors and fancy mixtures. These are made to measure in the most up to date styles, the latest fashions being shown on the card. If you want a made to measure overcoat for spring and fall wear, order our free sample card No. 84C.

Free Sample Card No. 85C—Men's Made to Measure Outing Suits.

Sample Card No. 85C, Men's Made to Measure Outing Suits. This card shows a beautiful assortment of crashes, flannels and other light weight woolens for outing purposes. We show men's single and double breasted styles with patch pockets, norfolk styles, and sacks, with long roll. If you want a high grade outing garment made to measure, send for our free sample card No. 85C.

Free Sample Card No. 86C—Men's Made to Measure Fancy Vests.

Sample Card No. 86C, Men's Made to Measure Fancy Vests. A beautiful assortment of patterns for wash vests, fancy and silk vests in flowered, figured, dotted and neat, dressy or plain patterns. If you want a decidedly dressy, fancy vest in any style, made to measure, send for our free sample card No 86C

Free Sample Book No. 88C—Young Men's, Boys' and Children's Clothing.

Free Sample Book No. 88C, Young Men's, Boys' and Children's Clothing, containing nearly 90 samples and 100 different styles for boys from 3 to 20 years of age, long pants suits, two piece and three piece knee pants suits, Norfolk, Juvenile or Peewee suits, blouses, waists and every up to date style designed to date, a wonderfully instructive book for parents on the subject of clothing. Prices less than wholesale, guaranteed qualities the best to be had and representing a saving of one-third to one-half in family expenses for clothing. See pages 907 to 916. You can order boys' and children's clothing from this book or write for our free sample book No. 88C.

Free Sample Book No. 89C—Showing Men's Ready Made Suits, Pants and Overcoats and Fancy Vests.

Free Sample Book No. 89C, showing Men's Ready Made Suits, Pants and Overcoats and Fancy Vests. Suits, $4.50 to $15.00, pants, $1.25 to $4.50, overcoats, $5.00 to $12.00. This sample book contains 100 samples and we illustrate and furnish more styles and give you a larger variety in men's ready made clothing than you can get outside of the largest stores in the big cities. You can get sack and frock suits, spring overcoats and fancy vests from this department. See pages 897 to 906. You can order men's ready made clothing from this catalogue, or if you prefer, send for our free sample book No. 89C. We make our own clothing and these garments are furnished to you guaranteed as the best made clothing on the market and at less than the dealer has to pay the wholesale house for equal grades.

Free Sample Book No. 90C—Rainy Weather Clothing For Men, Ladies, Boys and Girls.

Sample Book No. 90C, Rainy Weather Clothing for Men, Ladies, Boys and Girls, including mackintoshes, Cielette rainproof overcoats, to wear in rain or shine, and rubber surface and oil slicker clothing. See pages 918 to 921 in this catalogue. You can order all this clothing directly from this book, or if you prefer, send for our sample book; it contains samples of mackintoshes and Cielette rainproof overcoats for men, ladies, boys and girls. (Of course, we do not sample rubber surface and oil slicker clothing; please order these directly from this catalogue) If you want anything in rainy weather clothing, order from this catalogue, or send for our free sample book No. 90C.

Free Sample Book No. 120Y—Men's Made to Measure Uniforms.

Sample Book No. 120Y, Men's Made to Measure Uniforms, for police, firemen, railroad men, street railway men, Grand Army men and letter carriers. This sample book contains nothing but high grade all wool and wool dyed goods which we make to measure in regulation styles and guarantee a better made uniform for a more reasonable price than they can be secured for anywhere else. If you belong to any of these organizations and want a well made durable uniform at a most reasonable price, send for our free sample book No. 120Y.

OUR CUSTOM TAILORING OR MADE TO MEASURE CLOTHING DEPARTMENT; SUITS $12.00 TO $25.00.

A LARGE DISPLAY OF WOOLENS SAMPLED IN OUR MADE TO MEASURE SAMPLE BOOKS AND CARDS, AND 30 UP TO DATE STYLES IN MEN'S FASHIONS, HANDSOMELY ILLUSTRATED, REPRESENTING EVERYTHING IN MEN'S SUITS, TROUSERS, SPRING OVERCOATS AND FANCY VESTS.

THIS SAMPLE BOOK FREE ON APPLICATION.

OUR SAMPLE BOOKS tell why it is a big mistake to buy cheap so called made to measure suits, such as many houses advertise at $5.00 to $10.00, and why we can absolutely guarantee to give the best there is in high grade men's custom tailoring for one-half what other tailors charge for it. The whole story is told in our various sample books.

OUR LINE APPEALS TO GOOD DRESSERS. We have as permanent customers many of the most careful dressers in every town and city throughout the United States, business and professional men (lawyers, doctors, ministers and prominent persons in every locality), such people as especially require neat, dressy, up to date wearing apparel. Our custom tailoring department also appeals to young men in every part of the country, whether in the city or on the farm, such as enjoy wearing the latest novelties made into the snappiest and most up to date styles. This department places before good dressers the opportunity of getting the most fashionable city tailoring at less than half the price commonly paid for such garments.

DISTINCTLY HIGH GRADE WOOLENS and workmanship is what the Custom Tailoring Department stands for. The fabrics are chosen from the productions of the foremost mills in this country and Europe and are selected by the most experienced woolen men in the trade. If you are at all particular about the quality, coloring and pattern of your garments, you can have your utmost wishes gratified in this immense variety of woolens. No tailoring house in the country doing a business direct with the wearer as we offers anywhere near the number of styles we do.

OUR WORKMANSHIP IS STRICTLY HIGH GRADE. We use the most reliable and finest grade of linings and trimmings, the very best interlinings, wool paddings, haircloth, etc. Our coat fronts do not break, shoulders are beautifully moulded, the collars set close to the neck and the garments will retain their original smoothness and shapeliness as long as the garments last. Our Sample Books tell all about it.

WE POSITIVELY GUARANTEE to fit and please you in every way with any garment we make for you. It makes no difference how particular or how careful you may be in this matter. You may have been having your clothes made by tailors whom you consider to be the best in your part of the country. We ask you to give us a trial, and if we fail in any way at all to come up to your fullest expectations you are perfectly at liberty to return the garments to us, at our expense and the transaction will not cost you a single cent; we take the entire responsibility.

LIST OF FREE SAMPLE BOOKS OF MADE TO MEASURE CLOTHING ISSUED FROM OUR CUSTOM TAILORING DEPARTMENT.

WE HAVE DIVIDED THE WOOLENS INTO DIFFERENT SAMPLE BOOKS because the line is too big to be mailed in a single book and cover so many different kinds of tastes that what would interest one customer would not be of any service to another, so we make it handy and easy for each person to select the goods he is interested in by sending him the book which meets with his wants.

No. 81C Sample book of made to measure suits and trousers from medium and light weight woolens suitable for spring, summer and early fall wear at $12.00 to $25.00 a suit, including the latest novelties in fancy cheviots, cassimeres worsteds, mixtures, imported dress worsteds, serges, unfinished and finished fabrics, rough, plain and smooth finished woolens in mixed colors, checks, stripes, and rich plain shades in black, blues, browns, grays, etc. This book does not contain such fancy goods as outing flannels, crashes and the like for strictly outing purposes. If you want a fancy variety of outing material send for sample card No. 85C. This book does not contain spring overcoats, but if you want spring or early fall overcoats made to measure ask for sample book No. 84C. This sample book No. 81C contains goods for suits and trousers only. The book shows a large assortment and beautifully illustrates in handsome group drawings every style and latest creation in men's fashions and tells you just how to measure and send your order. We send tape measure and order blanks with every book. This book is a fund of information to good dressers. If you want anything in the way of high grade made to measure suits in fabrics in suitable weight for spring, summer and early fall wear be sure to send for sample book No. 81C, sent free and postpaid upon request.

No. 82C Sample book of made to measure suits and trousers from heavy weight woolens suitable for fall and winter wear, or for climates such as along the Rockies or in Northern States, or where the heavier weight goods are used the year round. The material in this sample book is quite similar to what you will find in sample book No. 81C; the difference is only in the weight of the goods. If you want your garments made to measure from the heavier weight qualities, be sure to ask for sample book No. 82C.

No. 83C Sample card of made to measure corduroy suits and trousers at from $12.00 to $15.00, showing a complete variety of all kinds of corduroys, both in plain colors and fancy patterns. We carry a higher grade of corduroy fabrics than the average tailoring house, and guarantee to furnish the best made corduroy garments that you can possibly secure. We also show all the different fashions suitable for corduroys. If you wish anything in the way of a made to measure corduroy garment send for sample card No. 83C.

No. 84C Sample card of made to measure overcoats, suitable for spring, summer and early fall wear, including both fancy and plain patterns. A very choice variety of coverts, worsteds, cheviots and rich qualities that will certainly meet with the tastes and requirements of those who desire something real good and dressy. We show the latest fashions in spring and fall overcoats, such as the short box, full back styles, medium lengths and the long overcoats. If you want to get an up to date, made to measure, spring or fall overcoat, and want to know all about the styles of these garments, send for sample card No. 84C.

No. 85C Sample card of made to measure outing suits, showing a very handsome variety of fancy colored woolens and plain shades in light weight woolens, flannels, crash goods, etc., suitable for what is popularly known as outing styles. We show the latest mixtures, light colored fabrics, grays, checks, plaids, etc., and illustrate such styles as round cut sacks with patch pockets, Norfolk suits with plaits and belt, long roll sacks, and double breasted styles; pants with golf bottoms, belt loops, etc. We tell you all about what is popular and up to date in such garments. If you want a beautiful outing garment made to measure, send for sample card No. 85C.

No. 86C Sample card of made to measure fancy vests, including flowered, figured, and dotted patterns, stripes, checks, white and plain shades, and everything suitable and dressy in the way of fancy grades and silk vesting, which we make to measure in any style desired; single or double breasted. If you want a handsome made to measure vest send for sample card No. 86C.

No. 120Y Made to measure uniforms for police, firemen, railroad men, street railway men, grand army men and letter carriers. We show an excellent assortment of regulation navy blues and grays in high grade all wool and wool dyed fabrics, which we will make to measure in strictly regulation styles and guarantee a better made uniform throughout at a more reasonable price than you will be obliged to pay for the same high standard anywhere else. To organizations of the above description we recommend to send for our sample book, illustrations and prices, whether you desire to order singly or in large numbers. If you want first class uniforms made to special measure send for our sample book and catalogue No. 120Y

A FEW DESCRIPTIONS OF STAPLES FROM OUR CUSTOM TAILORING LINE REPRESENTING THE VALUES WE OFFER IN THIS DEPARTMENT

WE DESCRIBE BELOW a small number of the staples such as blues, blacks and grays, or in other words, such woolens as are always found in a custom tailoring line, being particularly desirable for general or dress wear, such weaves that we handle year in and year out, in weights suitable for different seasons.

THE PRICES QUOTED BELOW are for suits in any kind of single or double breasted sack or any kind of frock style with the exception of such special styles as Prince Alberts, Tuxedos, full dress and clerical styles. These special fashions require special high grade work and trimmings, such work as we pride ourselves on knowing how to do better than other houses. We charge extra for such garments and the extra charge covers only the actual extra cost to us for the special work and trimming performed on them. We make a specialty of this work and guarantee to please the most particular and careful dresser in every way.

THE PRICES QUOTED BELOW are for what are called regular sizes up to and including 42 inches breast measure for coat and vest and up to and including 41 inches waist measure for pants. The linings and trimmings are standard high grade fabrics, better qualities than are customarily used in tailoring houses. This price, of course, does not include such as silk and satin linings or extraordinary trimmings. For such special work we recommend that you send for our sample books of custom tailoring, which cover every detail.

WE GIVE YOU HERE THE REGULAR EXTRA CHARGE FOR SPECIAL STYLES AND SIZES.

Single and double breasted Prince Albert	$3.50	Suits or coats and vests larger than 42 inches breast up to 45 inches	$1.50
Tuxedo suit without silk facing	2.50	Over 45 up to 50 inches	2.00
Full dress suit	5.00	Pants larger than 41 up to 45	.50
Clerical or Ministers' style	5.00	Pants larger than 45 up to 50 inches	1.00

No. 13C1162 PURE ALL WOOL GRAY TRICOT. Medium weight, firm weave, and splendid wearing cloth. It is woven by the Provo Mills, of national reputation for strong wearing tricot. Comparison will show you that this cloth cannot be secured elsewhere for less than $16.00 to $18.00. Color is a popular plain gray.
Price, made to measure:

Suit	$12.00
Coat and vest	8.75
Trousers	3.50

No. 13C1366 ALL WOOL 16-OUNCE DIAGONAL BLACK CLAY WORSTED. A medium weight black clay worsted, woven by the Wanskuk Mills, and suitable for all around wear. Comparison of price with other houses, in this same grade, will show we make you a 50 per cent saving. Just the thing for general or Sunday wear.
Price, made to measure:

Suit	$13.50
Coat and vest	9.90
Trousers	3.85

No. 13C1365 ALL WOOL 14-OUNCE DIAGONAL BLACK CLAY WORSTED. A fairly light weight, in a well known reliable black fabric, woven by the Wanskuk Mills, the weavers of the best clay worsteds in this country. For general or special wear, this is a cloth that is unexcelled anywhere. There are worsteds that may at first glance look as well, but the wearing qualities cannot be compared with the Wanskuk grades.
Price, made to measure:

Suit	$12.00
Coat and vest	$8.75
Trousers	3.50

No. 13C1367 ALL WOOL 18-OUNCE DIAGONAL BLACK CLAY WORSTED. Medium weight black clay, woven by the Wanskuk Mills. Weight is suitable for all year round wear. This makes a real good general wear suit in any style, or a first class garment for dress wear. It represents the best of such weaves to be found on the market.
Price, made to measure:

Suit	$15.00
Coat and vest	11.00
Trousers	4.25

No. 13C1368 EXTRA FINE 18-OUNCE BLACK CLAY WORSTED. This is an especially fine weave, the wale not being so prominent as in other black clays and of somewhat softer finish. This is very fine for special wear, although it makes exceptionally good general purpose suits. Such a cloth as merchant tailors use in garments, sold at almost twice our price. You get it here, at the actual cost of labor and material, with a small profit added, and we guarantee first class workmanship. Price, made to measure:

Suit	$16.50
Coat and vest	12.10
Trousers	4.65

No. 13C1371 PURE ALL WOOL 12-OUNCE NAVY BLUE SERGE. This is one of the Wanskuk Mills pure dye navy blue serges. A better grade than is usually used by tailoring houses. It is of a pleasing navy blue shade. Every gentleman should have a navy blue suit. At our price this is certainly an unusual bargain, and this price carries with it absolutely first class and high grade tailoring, workmanship, linings, trimmings and fit. We positively guarantee to fit and please the best dressed gentlemen everywhere.
Price, made to measure:

Suit	$12.00
Coat and vest	8.75
Trousers	3.50

No. 13C1373 ALL WOOL 13-OUNCE NAVY BLUE SERGE. This is one of the most reliable weaves of the American Woolen Co. in a spring and summer weight. Makes a handsome navy blue suit and the quality will please you perfectly. Our serges are of a rich shade and fine weave. Our Custom Tailoring Department represents only first class workmanship, linings, trimmings and fit. If you have had your clothes made elsewhere, we know that we can give you a pleasing surprise in quality and tailoring by ordering from our line.
Price, made to measure:

Suit	$13.50
Coat and vest	9.90
Trousers	3.85

No. 13C1375 EXTRA FINE GRADE 14-OUNCE NAVY BLUE SERGE. This is woven by the Kunhardt Mills, of pure Australian wool, the finest grade material used by weavers. Is a rich dark navy blue shade and very dressy. We positively guarantee to please the most careful dressing gentlemen from this fabric. We have made a special study of high class tailoring, and positively give you the best for prices far below what you will pay merchant tailors elsewhere.
Price, made to measure:

Suit	$15.00
Coat and vest	11.00
Trousers	4.25

No. 13C1384 ALL WOOL HIGH GRADE 14-OUNCE UNFINISHED BLACK WORSTED. A soft finish spring and summer weight in a black fabric, woven by the Metcalf Bros. Mills and of a higher standard than you are likely to find elsewhere. Makes a very pleasing dress suit, in single or double breasted sacks or frock styles for special wear. An exceedingly popular weave.
Price, made to measure:

Suit	$15.00
Coat and vest	11.00
Trousers	4.25

THE ABOVE STAPLES ARE STRICTLY HIGH GRADE AND OF BETTER QUALITIES THAN CUSTOMARILY USED. IF YOU SHOULD HAPPEN TO WISH SUCH A GARMENT AND HAVE NOT TIME TO SEND FOR A SAMPLE BOOK, YOU CAN ORDER FROM THESE NUMBERS, GIVING THE USUAL MEASUREMENTS, BUT IF YOU WANT TO SEE THE SAMPLES, OR WISH TO SEE A LARGER VARIETY OF ALL KINDS OF PATTERNS, PLEASE REFER TO OUR LIST OF CUSTOM TAILORING SAMPLE BOOKS ON THIS PAGE.

THE VARIETY AND QUALITY OF WOOLENS WE DISPLAY

IN OUR

Men's Custom Tailoring Department.

WRITE FOR OUR FREE CLOTH SAMPLE BOOK NO. 81C.

See page 894 for Free Sample Books issued from our Made to Measure Clothing Department, a very large assortment of woolens, including the choicest weaves of both Domestic and Foreign Mills; we show you how to see the goods you want.

ALL SAMPLES ARE FREE.

WE CARRY A HIGH GRADE ASSORTMENT of rich, all wool qualities, all wool and pure silk mixtures and such high grade fabrics as will meet the most particular tastes of good dressers everywhere, whether in city, town or country, and whether professional men, business men or farmers. We use a much higher standard of cloth in our made o measure garments than is customary with merchant tailors roughout the country. We have a big advantage over the averge merchant tailor and over small buyers of woolens, as we are able to rder enormous quantities direct from the mills that weave the cloth, us avoiding all middlemen's profits We also buy linings, trimiings, paddings, hair cloth and the like direct from the factories in normous quantities. For these important reasons we are le to ise a very much better grade of woolens throughout in our custom tailoring department than the average merchant tailor could use even in his high priced clothes.

FOR EXAMPLE, we use a better quality of cloth, linings, trimmings and workmanship throughout than is customary among tailors and large houses throughout the country to use at double the price. We exclude from our custom tailoring department all doubtful qualities and we care not how particular or how dressy you may be in the style, fit and appearance of your clothes, we know that we can suit your tastes in pattern and quality and make the garments up to suit you in every particular.

IN FACT, if you have any reason whatever for disappointment in the clothes we make for you, we ask you as a favor to return the garments to us at our expense and we shall refund every cent you have paid.

IN OUR CUSTOM AILORING EPARTMENT

e use only the nest grade of all ool and all wool d silk fabrics Ve are avoiding otton mixed oods altogether. **Why you should ot order $5.00 to $10.00 so alled tailor made suits,** offered by such houses as do inferior work, why agents and merchant tailors make such big profits, why we can undersell everybody by fully one half in price on the best city tailoring, how much better our garments are made than the average and all about our special guarantee to satisfy the most particular dressers, is all told in our **free made to measure sample books.**

WRITE FOR FREE SAMPLE BOOK NO. 81C, AS SHOWN ON PRECEDING PAGE.

A SMALL CORNER OF ONE OF OUR WOOLEN ROOMS.
We have hundreds of thousands of yards of goods constantly on hand and our annual consumption of cloth is up in the millions of yards.

WE POSITIVELY GUARANTEE TO PLEASE YOU IN FIT, WORKMANSHIP, QUALITY AND STYLE.

You simply cannot afford to order fine made to measure garments elsewhere. By all means see our samples first. See what we have to offer. You will be agreeably surprised Doctors, lawyers, ministers and all professional men and business men everywhere need never again pay fancy prices for high class tailoring.

WRITE FOR FREE SAMPLE BOOK NO. 81C, AS SHOWN ON PRECEDING PAGE.

OUR MAIN CUSTOM TAILORING SAMPLE BOOK this season is No. 81C. It contains medium and light weight fabrics, a great display, suitable for spring and summer wear; but if you wish anything special, such as heavy weight fabrics, outing flannels, spring overcoats, fancy vests or corduroys, please see page 894 for the numbers of these sample books and cards.

WE THOROUGHLY SPONGE AND SHRINK every yard of cloth we use. We examine every square foot of cloth we get from the mills and tests are regularly made to avoid all possible defects. We have set a high standard for the requirements of the woolens used in our made to measure department and everything that fails to measure up to that high standard is rejected and returned to the mills. The consequence is, our custom tailoring department is well known and is becoming exceedingly popular among professional people, well to do business men and the most fashionable dressers throughout the country, because of the dressy, stylish and up to date effects we produce and the fact that our garments always hold their shape beautifully.

ALL THIS SPECIAL PREPARATION of the cloth before cutting up is done in our own plant under our own careful supervision, so that we absolutely know that every feature of the work is performed with the greatest possible care and there is hardly any possibility of even the smallest defect being overlooked

WRITE FOR OUR FREE CLOTH SAMPLE BOOK NO. 81C IF YOU WANT MADE TO MEASURE CLOTHING.

UP TO DATE FASHIONS AND WORKMANSHIP

IN OUR

CUSTOM TAILORING DEPARTMENT.

WRITE FOR OUR FREE BOOK NO. 81C, SHOWING THE GOODS AND STYLES IN OUR CUSTOM TAILORING DEPARTMENT. SEE PAGE 894 FOR VARIOUS FREE SAMPLE BOOKS ISSUED FROM THIS DEPARTMENT. A LARGE DISPLAY OF WOOLENS AND OVER 30 MEN'S FASHIONS HANDSOMELY ILLUSTRATED.

OUR FASHION PLATES are strictly up to date. In point of correctness in dress our sample books are all that any person who wishes to dress well could desire as a means of information. We make any style desired to order. Our fashion plates, which go with every sample book, illustrate all the various styles of both single and double breasted fashions, three-button and four-button sacks, either with square or round corners, with or without slit in the back, two-button and three-button double breasted sacks, three-button and one-button frocks, Chesterfield frock, single and double breasted Prince Alberts, ministers' style, Tuxedos and full dress styles; short, medium and long overcoats, single, double breasted, and Norfolk outing styles, etc.

WE PRODUCE THE VERY LATEST and most stylish effects in business sack suits and are particularly skilled in the dress styles. Business or professional men whose occupation requires the most stylish garments possible, will find that we can give them not only superior workmanship throughout and absolutely perfect fitting in every way, but we can do this at a price that will represent a saving of about one-half of the regular price of such dress styles. We respectfully solicit high grade trade, such as you would expect to give to the best city merchant tailors; we know that we can satisfy you, in fact, we guarantee to satisfy you in every way or it will not cost you a cent

OUR MAIN SAMPLE DISPLAY this season is contained in sample book No. 81C, which shows everything in the way of medium and light weight woolens suitable for spring and summer wear. Should you want anything special, such as heavy weight woolens, corduroys, light weight outing flannels and crashes, fancy vests or spring overcoats, please see page 894 for the numbers of the sample books and cards containing these goods, or simply state what you want and we will send you the correct book.

Double Breasted Prince Albert. Our style 6. Tuexdo. Our style 15. Full Dress. Our style 7.

A FEW OF THE MANY UP TO DATE MEN'S FASHIONS DISPLAYED IN OUR BEAUTIFUL CUSTOM TAILORING FASHION AND SAMPLE BOOK No. 81C. WRITE FOR THE FREE SAMPLE BOOK No. 81C.

OUR WORKMANSHIP REPRESENTS HIGH GRADE METROPOLITAN TAILORING and is second to none in the country. There is no other tailoring house in the country which can show any improvement over our workmanship or give you better fitting qualities, or in any way make it more to your interest to purchase from them than from us (that is on the question of workmanship alone), and besides workmanship we excel every other house in being able to offer the very lowest prices ever heard of. We have the benefit of the skill of the most widely experienced tailoring men that can possibly be found, men whom smaller houses and merchant tailors could not possibly employ because of the high salaries they command; in fact, the average tailor or tailoring house is nowhere near prepared to offer you as high a standard throughout as we are offering constantly in this department.

OUR COAT FRONTS DO NOT BREAK. We use the proper quantity and quality of stiffening, padding, hair cloth, canvas and the like to make our garments keep their original smoothness and shapeliness perfectly At from $12.00 to $25.00 we offer you garments that you could not get from other tailoring houses and small tailors throughout the country for less than nearly double the price. Every cent you pay over our figures represents nothing more or less than extra profits that other houses secure or the additional expenses they incur from their methods of handling the business. We offer you the best, and if for any reason you should be disappointed in any way with the workmanship, quality, fit or value you receive for your money, no matter how careful a dresser you are, we ask as a favor that you return the goods to us at our expense and we will refund every cent you have paid.

MEN'S READY MADE CLOTHING DEPARTMENT.

THIS READY MADE CLOTHING CLOTH SAMPLE BOOK FREE ON REQUEST.

WRITE FOR IT

SUITS from	$4.50 to $15.00
PANTS from	1.25 to 4.50
SPRING and EARLY FALL OVERCOATS from	7.00 to 12.00
FANCY VESTS from	1.00 to 2.50

You Have the Choice of Ordering From this Catalogue Direct or of Sending for Our Free Sample Book of Men's Ready Made Clothing No. 89C.

You are perfectly safe in ordering from this catalogue, as we guarantee to fit and please you in every way. If garments, for any reason whatever, are not entirely to your liking you may return them to us at our expense and we will refund every cent you have paid. If you prefer to see samples before ordering, ask for our **Sample Book No. 89C.**

We Manufacture all these Clothes Ourselves in Our Own Modern and Splendidly Equipped Manufacturing Plant in Our Building Illustrated on Page 892.

This fact entitles our goods to your special attention, as it means that you can get absolutely the best garments, made from the best cloth woven, at less money than the average merchant or clothier has to pay the wholesale house for similar qualities.

The Advantages to You Are Wonderful, Let Us Point Out a Few of Them:

OURS IS THE BEST MADE CLOTHING ON THE MARKET. **There is no other house that can furnish you better clothing, better linings and trimmings, better workmanship or better fitting ready made garments than we do.** We insist upon getting the most reliable all wool, all wool and silk mixtures and other high grade qualities, and as we have the making of them entirely in our own control, we see to it that our garments are exceedingly well made and we maintain a higher standard throughout our whole line than you will find in 95 per cent of the clothing offered elsewhere.

OUR PRICES ARE LESS THAN WHOLESALE. **We are not merchants only, but are manufacturers as well, which means that the best clothing that can be produced in workmanship and fitting qualities is here offered to you at manufacturer's prices.** Our prices represent the actual cost of labor and material with only one small profit added and every middleman, wholesaler, jobber, agent or merchant is completely cut out. This clothing goes directly from maker to wearer, and our prices represent a saving of from one-third to one-half in your clothing bills.

OUR VARIETY **is greater by far than offered by any other house and is even greater than is offered by most other houses combined.** We carry the garments in more patterns, in a larger variety of sizes and in a greater variety of styles than you will find offered by any of the large stores in the big cities. Our ready made clothing department is equal to bringing the foremost clothing stores of such cities as New York and Chicago right to your own door, and giving you your own time to look over the goods and decide for yourself.

FROM $6.00 TO $10.00 A SUIT, **we have an extraordinary variety of values.** They represent the best made and neatest fitting business and every day suits one could possibly find, and at $10.00 to $15.00 we carry a large line of exclusively high grade patterns and qualities in suits that are beautifully made, stylish and possess the most perfect fitting qualities. Working men, business men, and even professional men are finding the most remarkable values that were ever heard of, in our department of Men's Ready Made Clothing.

OUR SAMPLE BOOK No. 89C **is illustrated here, and if you wish to see samples before ordering, please do not hesitate to ask for this book.** It will be mailed to you free and postpaid, just for the asking, and will show all the goods and styles illustrated here and more besides, showing you the very samples of which the garments are made. If you have the slightest difficulty in deciding what garments to order by all means send for this book No. 89C, which will be mailed free and postpaid.

OUR LIBERAL TERMS. **We ship this clothing C. O. D. or upon receiving the full price with the order.** If you wish the garments sent C. O. D. we require a deposit of $1.00 and the garments will then be shipped to you by express, the balance to be collected after you have examined the clothing and have found it to be perfectly satisfactory in every way. Our regular customers nearly always send the full price with the order as it completes the transaction in one payment and they avoid a small charge made by express companies for returning money to the shipper on C. O. D. shipments.

WE ABSOLUTELY GUARANTEE **to fit and please you in every way. If you are disappointed with the pattern, quality, workmanship, fit or anything,** we ask as a favor that you return the goods to us at our expense and we will immediately refund every cent you have paid and express charges besides. There is no possibility of your losing a cent. We take all the risk, and even if you make a mistake yourself when ordering the garments and they should not prove satisfactory to you, we will even then permit them to be returned at our expense and we will refund your money in full.

Figure A. Figure B.

STATE MEASUREMENTS PLAINLY.

GIVE HEIGHT, WEIGHT AND AGE, AND WE WILL GUARANTEE PERFECT FITTING CLOTHING.

HOW TO MEASURE.

Measuring according to our system is very, very simple and there is no trouble at all about the matter. Our rules are exceedingly easy to follow. Anybody can measure himself correctly or have some member of the family measure him, without the slightest difficulty. Even were you to make a mistake and garments are unsatisfactory, we take all the risk and will accept them back and refund your money. If you should happen to be without one of our blanks just use a plain sheet of paper and give the measurements we call for here.

GIVE HEIGHT, WEIGHT and AGE; these are very IMPORTANT, they MUST not be FORGOTTEN.

COAT OR OVERCOAT.

BE SURE TO GIVE STYLE NUMBER.

Stand in your natural way, breathe regularly, don't expand chest; take everything bulky out of your pockets.

BREAST—(see figure B); take coat off and measure around breast close up under arms at (1), snug, but not tight. Tape should be over shoulder blades at the back.

WAIST—(see figure B); measure over vest all around waist at (2). Note your waist line is just above hip bones.

SLEEVE—(see figure A); with coat on, measure from middle of back at (3) to elbow at (4), and then measure again from the point (3) clear around to wrist joint at (5).

VEST.

BREAST—Same measurement as coat for breast.

WAIST—Same measurement as coat for waist.

PANTS.

WAIST—(see figure C); turn up your vest and measure around waist over pants at (6). Note your waist line is just above hip bones.

INSEAM—(see figure C); stand erect and draw pants well up in crotch; measure from close up in crotch at (7) to heel seam of shoe at (8).

Figure C.

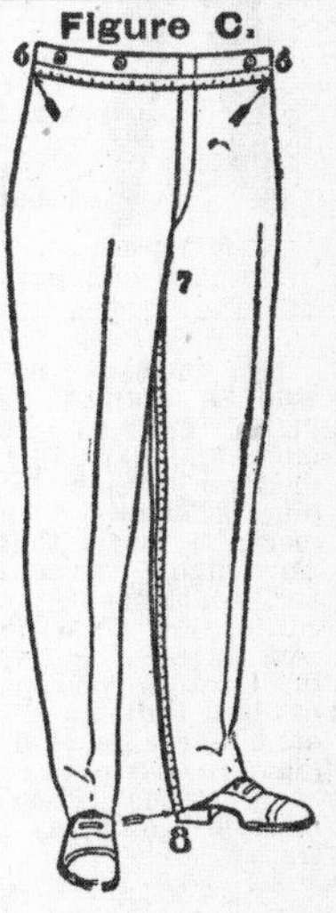

STYLES AND SIZES.

SIZES. **Unless it is distinctly stated in the description of the goods that we furnish extra sizes, it is understood that all the ready made garments described are furnished in sizes only as follows:** Coats and vests from 34 to 42 inches, inclusive, breast measure; pants, from 30 to 40 inches, inclusive, waist measure, and from 30 to 36 inches, inclusive, inside seam measure; smaller pants sizes are cut 18 inches at knee and 17 inches at bottom, larger pants sizes are cut 19 inches wide at knee and 18 inches at bottom. No larger or smaller sizes than these can be furnished, excepting from such numbers where it is distinctly stated. See Nos. 45C6644 and 45C6655 for larger sizes.

We cannot furnish half sizes in ready made clothing. Whenever such measurements are received we are obliged to send the next full size, larger or smaller, according as it seems to suit the case, in our best judgment.

Ready Made Clothing is Furnished only in the Styles Quoted for Each Number.

STYLE 1—Coat, round cut sack, four buttons, two lower outside pockets, one small change pocket, two inside pockets. Vest, single breasted, notch collar, two lower and two upper outside pockets, one inside pocket.

STYLE 5—Coat, four-button frock, intended to be worn with only top button closed, therefore, called one-button cutaway frock, no outside pockets, two inside pockets, two tail pockets. Vest, single breasted, five-button, notch collar, two lower, two upper outside pockets, one inside pocket.

STYLE 18—Coat, four-button cutaway sack, one outside breast pocket, two lower outside pockets, small change pocket inside the right hand outside pocket, two inside pockets. Vest, single breasted, no collar, high cut and six buttons.

STYLE 30—Coat, double breasted square cut sack, with the up to date long lapel, two lower outside pockets, one small change pocket inside the right hand outside pocket, one inside pocket. Vest, single breasted, six buttons and no collar.

No. 45C6600 FANCY CASSIMERE ROUND CORNERED SACK SUIT. Background of oxford gray with two different styles of light colored stripes, ¾ inch apart, as well as a sprinkling of red, green and tan threads, these different colored threads being subdued, hardly noticeable, a thing you would look for among much higher priced garments; lined with a good quality of black Italian lining and is well made in every way. Made in style 1 only, as illustrated.

Price for suit $4.50
Price for coat and vest 3.30
Price for pants 1.65

No. 45C6612 FANCY UP TO DATE MIXED COLOR CASSIMERE ROUND CORNERED SACK SUIT. This is a combination of a faint stripe and mottled effect, made with stripes of three parallel white threads, one inch apart, and between these a faint dark stripe of dull blue, sprinkled all over fabric are white threads with mottled tan and red spots. It is a great favorite pattern, lined with good Italian body lining and durable fancy sleeve lining. Made in style 1 only. Really dressy.

Price for suit. $5.00
Price for coat and vest. 3.65
Price for pants. 1.85

No. 45C6620 FANCY BLACK AND WHITE CASSIMERE ROUND CORNERED SACK SUIT. Background black, with a fair sprinkling of light colored threads and faint white stripes ½ inch apart—this is a good wearing color and one that is recommended for general purposes, lined with a good grade of black Italian and splendid wearing fancy sleeve lining, made in style 1 only and in regular sizes, 34 to 42 inches breast measure. All suits are cut over best possible fitting patterns.

Price for suit . . $6.00
Price for coat and vest 4.40
Price for pants 2.20

No. 45C6629 FRANCIS H. HOLMES' FANCY TWEED FOUR-BUTTON CUTAWAY SACK SUIT. Made from the same cloth as No. 45C6628, the difference is only in the style. This number is made in our special style 18 with four-button cutaway sack. In this style it makes an extremely handsome garment, furnished in regular sizes only and in style 18.

Price for suit. $6.50
Price for coat and vest . . 4.75
Price for pants 2.35

No. 45C6604 ESSEX FANCY CASSIMERE ROUND CORNERED SACK SUIT. A modest, dressy pattern with a very faint cast of light green and dark red threads, something suitable for general wear. The dark red threads are worked into stripes about ½ inch apart, although the stripes would hardly be noticed, they are so faint; lined with a good quality of black Italian lining and is guaranteed as a first class garment in every respect. Made in style 1 only and in regular sizes, 34 to 42 inches breast measure.

Price for suit $5.00
Price for coat and vest 3.65
Price for pants. 1.85

No. 45C6613 FANCY UP TO DATE MIXED COLOR CASSIMERE FOUR-BUTTON CUTAWAY SACK SUIT. This is exactly the same cloth as No. 45C6612, a very handsome combination of mottled and striped pattern; the difference is that this coat is made in our style 18, as illustrated, with corners cut slanting instead of rounded; an excellent wearing and handsome garment. Made in style 18 and in regular sizes only.

Price for suit $5.00
Price for coat and vest 3.65
Price for pants. 1.85

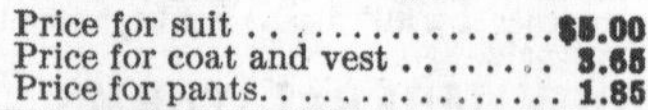

No. 45C6624 FAULKNER, PAGE & CO.'S FANCY TWEED MIXED PATTERN ROUND CORNERED SACK SUIT. There are fairly wide stripes of dark colors running every half inch apart in this fabric and between the wider stripes there is a narrower dark stripe and every inch there is a broken stripe of different colors, red and yellow, while between the dark stripes there is a mixture of white and faintest blue threads, very thickly sprinkled, white predominating; makes a very handsome spring and summer suit, lined with a good grade of body lining, to match fabric, and fine wearing sleeve lining. Furnished in style 1 only and in regular sizes.

Price for suit. $6.00
Price for coat and vest. 4.40
Price for pants 2.20

No. 45C6630 EXTRA GOOD VALUE ROUND CUT SACK SUITS. This lot consists of a variety of fancy cassimeres, cheviots and worsteds which we have made up in regular sizes from remnants left over from our various manufacturing departments. There is a large variety of patterns and we can, without doubt, meet your tastes from this assortment. We are quoting them at a very low price in order to dispose of the remainder of these fabrics. They are made in the same substantial manner as all our ready made clothing, with good body and sleeve linings and neat fitting effects. We do not furnish pants separately. Made up in style 1 only.

Price for suit $6.50
Price for coat and vest 4.75

No. 45C6606 EXTRA GOOD VALUE ROUND CORNERED SACK SUIT. The garments under this number come in mixtures of fancy cheviots and cassimeres. They are made from remnants of cloth left over from our various manufacturing departments. We have offered them at a very low price and you can get excellent values from this assortment. They are all cut round cornered sack style, as illustrated, in style 1 only, and in regular sizes. We do not sell pants separately.

Price for suit $4.50
Price for coat and vest. 3.30

No. 45C6616 NOSTRAND & MOORE FANCY CASSIMERE ROUND CORNERED SACK SUIT. A very dark bluish background, with dull white threads and dull red threads sprinkled over it; the dull red threads being almost invisible; such a pattern as would please one with modest taste. A splendid wearing color and quality; well made, durably lined and a substantial garment in every way; furnished in style 1 only.

Price for suit . . . $5.50
Price for coat and vest 4.10
Price for pants . . 1.95

No. 45C6625 FAULKNER, PAGE & CO.'S FANCY MIXED COLOR TWEED DOUBLE BREASTED SACK SUIT. This is the very same cloth exactly as No. 45C6624, the difference is only in the style, which is the latest long lapel double breasted sack suit, very dressy, otherwise made and trimmed exactly as the preceding number. Furnished in style 30 only.

Price for suit. $7.00
Price for coat and vest . . 5.40
Price for pants 2.20

No. 45C6634 HANOVER WOOLEN CO.'S FANCY BLACK AND WHITE CASSIMERE SUIT. Background is black and thickly covered with white threads worked into a sort of stripe effect, with stripes woven close together and every ½ inch there is a gold thread which is very indistinct. A good wearing color and strong wearing quality. We highly recommend it for general wearing purposes. Lined with a good quality of black Italian, and a neat, strong wearing sleeve lining, excellent fitting effects, furnished in regular sizes and in style 1 only, as illustrated.

Price for suit $6.50
Price for coat and vest 4.75
Price for pants 2.35

No. 45C6608 DUNDEE WOOLEN MILLS NAVY BLUE CHEVIOT ROUND CORNERED SACK SUIT. A medium weight navy blue cheviot of much merit; a fabric that we can highly recommend and could not be procured for less than double our price elsewhere; lined with a good quality of black Italian and standard fancy sleeve lining; guaranteed to please in every respect. Furnished in style 1 only, as illustrated.

Price for suit $5.50
Price for coat and vest 4.10
Price for pants. . 1.95

No. 45C6618 EXTRA GOOD VALUE, ROUND CORNERED SACK SUITS. Under this number we furnish a variety of patterns, mostly in cassimeres and cheviots, made from remnants of cloth left over from our various manufacturing departments. In order to dispose of them, we have made them up in the popular styles and are offering them at a very low figure. You might suggest what kind of pattern you prefer and we can, without doubt, come very close to your taste. Made in regular sizes from 34 to 42 inches breast measure. We do not furnish pants separately. Made in style 1 only.

Price for suit. $5.50
Price for coat and vest. 4.10

No. 45C6628 FRANCIS H. HOLMES' FANCY TWEED ROUND CORNERED SACK SUIT. This is a very pretty combination of white, gold, green and red threads on a dark background, the white threads being sprinkled very thickly and the other colors somewhat subdued, the general effect is somewhat of a brownish shade sprinkled with white—a very rich pattern and one that will have numerous admirers; well made, durably lined and perfect fitting, and we can heartily recommend it in every way, made in style 1 only and in regular sizes.

Price for suit. $6.50
Price for coat and vest. 4.75
Price for pants. 2.35

No. 45C6638 CURTIS & WARREN SILK NOIL CHEVIOT SUIT. A snappy up to date pattern, background dark with a sprinkling of white, gold, red and green threads, the white being the most prominent, the red, gold and green sparingly scattered and serving to give an up to date appearance, lined with an excellent quality of black Italian with fancy, durable sleeve lining and makes an exceedingly handsome garment for all general purposes, which has proven very popular and a great favorite, such a pattern as you will find in a high grade custom tailoring line. Made up in style 1 only and in regular sizes.

Price for suit $7.00
Price for coat and vest. 5.15
Price for pants. 2.60

IF YOU HAVE THE SLIGHTEST DIFFICULTY

in deciding from our descriptions, what goods you would really like to have, by all means send for

OUR BIG, FREE SAMPLE BOOK OF MEN'S READY TO WEAR CLOTHING, No. 89C.

We want you to see these goods, because we know that you will be pleased. Qualities and styles of our garments will show you where you can make an immense saving on your clothing bills. How to measure and all about styles and sizes is explained, simply, in this catalogue on page 897

IF YOU WANT ANYTHING IN LIGHT CRASH OR FLANNEL OUTING STYLES

Or in Alpaca Summer Coats, see pages 904 to 906.

ABOUT SAMPLES OF THIS CLOTHING. We want to have you know exactly what you are buying. These descriptions are as accurate as possible and we guarantee to please you if you will order right from this catalogue, but if you have any trouble at all in deciding upon the goods that you want, just send for

FREE SAMPLE BOOK No. 89C,

which contains a good sized sample of all these goods and large illustrations of the styles. How to measure and all about styles and sizes is explained, simply, in this catalogue on page 897.

No. 45C6642 METCALF BROS. 13-OUNCE BLACK CLAY WORSTED ROUND CUT SACK SUIT. A good durable grade of diagonal worsted that makes a good business or dress garment and which will cost you 50 per cent more anywhere else. The linings, trimmings and make of this garment are strictly first class. This is a medium weight and may be used practically all the year round. Made in sizes from 34 to 42 inches chest measure and in style 1 only.

Price for suit..$7.00
Price for coat and vest....... 5.15
Price for pants 2.60

No. 45C6643 METCALF BROS. BLACK CLAY WORSTED, ONE-BUTTON FROCK SUIT. It is of the same material exactly as No. 45C6642. It is made and trimmed in exactly the same manner, the difference is only in style. This number is the popular four-button frock to be worn with the top button closed and especially suitable for dress or Sunday wear. Made in regular sizes and in style 5 only

Price for suit.. $8.00
Price for coat and vest.... 6.15
Price for pants.. 2.60

No. 45C6644 EXTRA SIZE BLACK CLAY WORSTED ROUND CUT SACK SUIT. This is the same material exactly as No. 45C6642; is made in the same style, but we furnish this number in extra sizes only; that is in sizes from 43 to 50 inches breast measure, but no larger. Heavy set, regular built men will find this exactly what they require, both for business or special wear, made in style 1 only and in sizes from 43 to 50 inches breast measure and from 42 to 50 inches waist measure for pants.

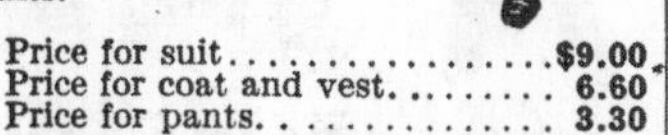

Price for suit....................$9.00
Price for coat and vest.......... 6.60
Price for pants.................. 3.30

No. 45C6646 FANCY DARK GRAY DOUBLE AND TWIST WORSTED SUIT. A splendid wearing quality and a good color for general purposes; a great favorite with good dressing business men. A dark background thickly sprinkled with white threads, giving it a sort of steel gray effect with a very faint plaid of blue threads, hardly noticeable. Lined with an excellent quality of black Italian, and good durable sleeve lining, well made and trimmed; an exceptional value. Made in regular sizes and in style 1 only.

Price for suit.................$7.00
Price for coat and vest........ 5.15
Price for pants 2.60

No. 45C6650 MEN'S ALL WOOL JET BLACK THIBET ROUND CUT SACK SUIT. A better grade of black thibet than usually offered by others at 50 per cent more than we ask for this garment. Well and substantially made throughout; a very handsome garment for dress wear; medium weight cloth, suitable for all year round wear. To those who want a black suit at a medium price we highly recommend this number. Made in style 1 only, as illustrated, and in regular sizes. Price

Suit $7.50
Coat and vest . 5.50
Pants........ 2.75

No. 45C6651 ALL WOOL JET BLACK THIBET DOUBLE BREASTED SACK SUIT. This is the very same fabric exactly as No. 45C6650, the difference is only in the style of the garment. This number comes in the very popular three-button double breasted sack style with long lapel, making a real dressy black suit in a medium weight cloth, suitable for year round wear. In every other way it is trimmed and made in the same substantial manner as the previous number and furnished in the regular sizes and style 30 only. Price

Suit $8.50
Coat and vest. 6.50
Pants 2.75

No. 45C6652 ALL WOOL BLACK THIBET ONE-BUTTON FROCK SUIT. This is the same cloth exactly as in No. 45C6650; it is made and trimmed in the same substantial manner, the difference being only in the style of the garment. This number is made in the four-button frock style, to be worn with the top button closed and is especially desirable for dress and Sunday wear. Weight suitable for all year round wear. We positively guarantee to fit and please in every particular. Made in regular sizes and in style 5 only, as illustrated. Price

Suit $8.50
Coat and vest .. 6.50
Pants........ 2.75

No. 45C6654 ALL WOOL GRAY TRICOT ROUND CUT SACK SUIT. A staple strong wearing cloth of which we sell an enormous number of garments and recommended for its great wearing qualities, and very suitable for all year round wear. A color that does not show soil Made in style 1 only and in regular sizes.

Price for suit, $7.50
Price for coat and vest ... 5.50
Price for pants, 2.75

No. 45C6655 EXTRA SIZE ALL WOOL GRAY TRICOT ROUND CUT SACK SUIT. This is the same cloth exactly as No. 45C6654, the difference in this number being we furnish it in extra sizes only, from 43 to 50 inches chest measure and 42 to 50 inches waist measure for pants, no larger. This is an exceptionally fine wearing fabric, made in style 1 only and in extra sizes. Weight suitable for all year round wear.

Price for suit...$9.50
Price for coat and vest ... 7.00
Price for pants... 3.45

No. 45C6658 ALL WOOL NAVY BLUE SERGE ROUND CUT SACK SUIT. A rich shade and fine weave in navy blue, a suit that will give you splendid wear and a garment that is required by most men, whatever other clothes they possess. Made with a very fine grade of black Italian and good, durable sleeve lining, well made and trimmed; excellent fitting qualities. Furnished in style 1 only and in regular sizes.

Price for suit . .$7.50
Price for coat and vest 5.50
Price for pants 2.75

No. 45C6659 ALL WOOL NAVY BLUE SERGE DOUBLE BREASTED SACK SUIT. This is the same material exactly as No. 45C6658, the only difference being that this number is furnished in style 30, the very popular three-button long lapel, double breasted sack coat, is a dressy garment and one that we know will please even the most careful dressers. We use a better grade of serge than is customarily offered in ready made lines, we guarantee it in every respect. Our suits possess exceptional fitting qualities. Made in regular sizes and in style 30 only as illustrated.

Price for suit................$8.50
Price for coat and vest 6.50
Price for pants 2.75

No. 45C6660 EXTRA GOOD VALUE ROUND CUT SACK SUIT. This is an assortment of real good qualities in fancy mixed patterns which we have made up from remnants left over from our various manufacturing departments and our custom tailoring line. The garments are made in the same substantial manner as all our ready made clothing, lined and trimmed with the best quality of Italian body lining. We offer these suits at the extremely low price in order to dispose of the remnants. We can doubtless suit your taste from this collection. All these suits are made in style 1 as illustrated and can be furnished in regular sizes only.

Price for suit.................$7.50
Price for coat and vest.........5.50
Price for pants................ 2.75

No. 45C6664 PROVO WOOLEN MILLS FANCY SCOTCH EFFECT TWEED FOUR-BUTTON CUTAWAY SACK SUIT. Background dark and very thickly covered with white, green, tan and red threads. The white and red threads work into stripes about half an inch apart and the green and tan threads sprinkled all over the fabric with double rows of green threads running at right angles to the red and white stripes and about an inch and a quarter apart but very faint. A real nobby and up to date pattern, one that dressy persons will admire greatly, made in the popular four-button cutaway sack style 18, as illustrated and in regular sizes.

Price for suit $7.50
Price for coat and vest 5.50
Price for pants............. 2.75

Heavy Set Regular Built Men

are referred to **Nos. 45C6644** and **45C6655** on this page; good wearing colors and qualities which we furnish in extra sizes.

No. 45C6668 VICTOR FANCY WORSTED ROUND CUT SACK SUIT. A good, durable wearing fabric in a dark bluish shade with very faint alternate stripes, composed of white and brick red colors, these stripes are about a half inch apart and very much subdued, serving only to light up the otherwise plain shade. The body lining is a fine grade of black Italian with good, durable sleeve lining, made in the popular form fitting effect, in every respect a stylish suit at a price that is less than wholesale as compared with such grades elsewhere. Made in style 1 only and in regular sizes.

Price for suit...............$7.50
Price for coat and vest...... 5.50
Price for pants 2.75

No. 45C6672 UP TO DATE BROWN SHADE FOUR-BUTTON CUTAWAY SACK SUIT. A fine grade of fancy cheviot, in medium weight of rich brown color with an almost invisible plaid of gold thread, makes a beautiful suit, one that is exceedingly popular and dressy nowadays and lined with an excellent quality of Italian body lining in a shade to match the fabric and a splendid wearing fancy sleeve lining. We predict enormous sales from this number. Furnished in the popular four-button cutaway sack style 18, as illustrated, and in regular sizes only.

Price for suit..............$8.00
Price for coat and vest...... 5.85
Price for pants.............. 2.95

No. 45C6676 EDWARD T. STEELE & CO.'S STEEL GRAY DOUBLE AND TWIST WORSTED SUIT. A closely woven, hard finished cloth in a modest shade that will please great numbers of good dressers. Our ready made garments are exceptionally well tailored, are the neatest fitting and best looking garments that you will find on the market. We guarantee to please in every way, in linings, trimmings, workmanship and finish or refund your money. Made in round cut sack style No. 1 and in regular sizes only.

Price for suit..............$8.00
Price for coat and vest..... 5.85
Price for pants............. 2.95

No. 45C6680 FANCY COLORED MUMMY EFFECT WORSTED ROUND CUT SACK SUIT. This is a mixture of black, pale green and pale blue worked into a sort of faint small check effect with the pale green forming squares of one-half an inch diameter and the pale blue squares of the same size, these two being combined and forming borders for very small checks, the middle of which is composed of black. All these shades are subdued, making a fairly modest pattern, well lined and trimmed and guaranteed in every way. Made in style 1 only and in regular sizes.

Price for suit $8.50
Price for coat and vest. 6.25
Price for pants 3.10

REMEMBER, these are not retail prices like you pay elsewhere; they are less than wholesale, and besides, we absolutely guarantee to please you or refund money.

ORDERING CLOTHING BY MAIL is the popular way nowadays, because we have made it so. We guarantee to please you in every way, or the garments may be returned to us at our expense, and we will refund every cent. We give you your choice of ordering from the descriptions of goods or of sending for our big sample book, which shows you a fair sized sample of all the garments that we carry, and illustrations and descriptions of the styles furnished.

IF YOU CANNOT READILY CHOOSE FROM THESE DESCRIPTIONS BE SURE TO ASK FOR OUR FREE SAMPLE BOOK NO. 89C

How to measure and all about styles and sizes is explained, simply, in this catalogue on page 897.

No. 45C6684 PROVO WOOLEN MILLS FANCY UP TO DATE TWEED FOUR-BUTTON CUTAWAY SACK SUIT. A very nobby and snappy pattern with dark background, almost totally covered with white, olive green and red threads, more of white than of the others, with also a stripe effect of black and white threads about one inch apart; a sort of Scotch effect. Such a pattern will prove a great seller. Lined and trimmed with Italian fabric to suit the shades and of exceptionally good fitting qualities, makes a decidedly handsome suit in our four-button cutaway style 18, as illustrated. Sizes from 34 to 42 inches chest measure.

Price for suit....$8.50
Price for coat and vest....6.25
Price for pants....3.10

No. 45C6688 STEELE & CO.'S FANCY SILK MIXED WORSTED ROUND CUT SACK SUIT. Background is very dark navy blue shade, almost black. Every inch and a half there is a stripe one quarter of an inch wide of basket weave and between these stripes, the cloth is a diagonal weave. There is a sparing sprinkling of white and gold threads all over the pattern about equally distributed. It makes a dressy, genteel fabric, one that modest tastes will admire very much. Lined with a good durable black Italian body lining and fancy pattern sleeve lining, made in style 1 only, as illustrated, and in regular sizes.

Price for suit....$8.50
Price for coat and vest....6.25
Price for pants....3.10

No. 45C6690 EXTRA GOOD VALUE ROUND CORNERED SACK SUIT. This lot is made from remnants of cloth left over from our custom tailoring department. In qualities and patterns they are very desirable; mostly cassimeres, cheviots and fancy worsteds in medium shades. We are offering them at an exceptionally low price and can undoubtedly meet your tastes from this excellent collection of well made, durably lined and excellent fitting qualities. Made in style 1 only and in regular sizes.

Price for suit....$8.50
Price for coat and vest....6.25
Price of pants....3.10

No. 45C6694 LIPPITT WOOLEN CO.'S FANCY WORSTED ROUND CUT SACK SUIT. A dark background, sprinkled with pale blue and red threads, very indistinct. The pattern is worked into very small squares about one-eighth of an inch in diameter with a large square of one-half an inch in diameter. Woven in such a manner as to be hardly noticeable. A modest and pleasing appearance; lined with an excellent quality of black Italian and fancy fine wearing sleeve lining. Made in style 1 only and in regular sizes.

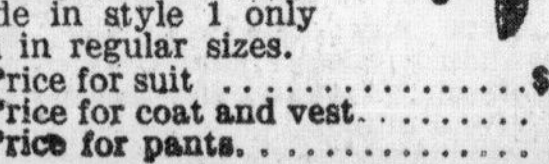

Price for suit....$9.00
Price for coat and vest....6.60
Price for pants....3.30

No. 45C6695 LIPPITT WOOLEN CO.'S FANCY WORSTED FOUR-BUTTON CUTAWAY SACK SUIT. This is exactly the same pattern of cloth as No. 45C6694; the difference is only in the style, which is our popular style 18, as illustrated. This is a good seller and a garment in which we have great confidence for wear and general appearance; we highly recommend it. Made in style 18 only and regular sizes.

Price for suit..$9.00
Price for coat and vest...6.60
Price for pants 3.30

No. 45C6698 STEELE & CO.'S FANCY SILK MIXED WORSTED ROUND CUT SACK SUIT. A dark background, sprinkled with small silver white threads and almost invisible sprinkling of brown and tan threads, hardly noticeable. A modest and dressy fabric that looks well in complete suit. Lined with excellent grade of black Italian body lining. A neat pattern, strong wearing sleeve lining, shoulders and fronts well padded and stiffened. Excellent fitting qualities. Made in style 1 only and in regular sizes.

Price for suit....$9.00
Price for coat and vest....6.60
Price for pants....3.30

No. 45C7702 STEELE & CO.'S NAVY BLUE BASKET WEAVE WORSTED SUIT. A popular combined basket weave and crepe effect in neat navy blue shade. A great favorite in many good dressing circles. Splendid for wear. Body lining a good wearable grade of black Italian with neat pattern sleeve lining. We guarantee to sell you a stylish fitting garment from this number. A good investment. Made in style 1 only and regular sizes.

Price for suit..$9.00
Price for coat and vest....6.60
Price for pants 3.30

No. 45C7703 STEELE & CO.'S NAVY BLUE BASKET WEAVE WORSTED DOUBLE BREASTED SACK SUIT. This is the very same cloth exactly as No. 45C7702. The difference is only in the style of the suit. This number comes in three-button double breasted sack with long lapel. An up to date dressy fashion. Makes a very handsome garment. Excellent linings and trimmings; finely tailored in regular sizes, style 30 only.

Price for suit....$10.00
Price for coat and vest....7.60
Price for pants....3.30

No. 45C7706 WENDELL FAY FANCY SILK MIXED CASSIMERE ROUND CUT SACK SUIT. Medium weight goods, dark background, thickly sprinkled with very small threads of pale blue and red, not at all prominent. Pleasing pattern and excellent for general wear and one you cannot afford to overlook. Lined with good grade of serge body lining and satin finished sleeve lining. Made in regular sizes and in style 1 only.

Price for suit, $10.00
Price for coat and vest....7.35
Price for pants. 3.65

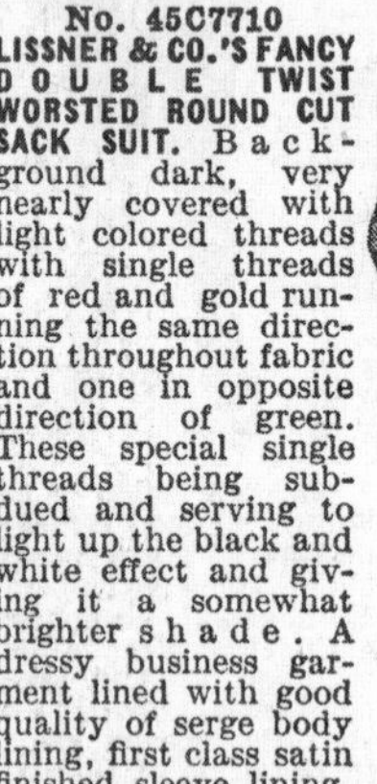

No. 45C7710 LISSNER & CO.'S FANCY DOUBLE TWIST WORSTED ROUND CUT SACK SUIT. Background dark, very nearly covered with light colored threads with single threads of red and gold running the same direction throughout fabric and one in opposite direction of green. These special single threads being subdued and serving to light up the black and white effect and giving it a somewhat brighter shade. A dressy business garment lined with good quality of serge body lining, first class satin finished sleeve lining. Excellent fitting suit. Made in regular sizes, style 1 only, as illustrated.

Price for suit....$10.00
Price for coat and vest....7.35
Price for pants....3.65

No. 45C7714 STANDARD NAVY BLUE 14-OUNCE FLANNEL ROUND CUT SACK SUIT. A guaranteed all wool solid navy blue flannel fabric of a much higher grade material than offered by other houses at the price we quote. These garments are made with eyelets and detachable civilian buttons. Owing to the fact that these garments can be worn as the regular Grand Army men's suits we will furnish an extra set of G. A. R buttons free if you mention them in your order, otherwise the civilian buttons only will be sent with the suit. Made in regular sizes and style 1, as illustrated.

Price for suit....$10.00
Price for coat and vest....7.35
Price for pants....3.65

No. 45C7718 FANCY SILK MIXED WORSTED ROUND CUT SACK SUIT. A dark background, sprinkled with very small white, dark red and pale blue threads. The red and blue can hardly be noticed, and the white threads run in broken check effect about one-eighth of an inch apart. Hard finish, good wearing qualities. Lined with serge body lining and fine quality satin finished sleeve lining. Such a suit as you will pay $5.00 more for elsewhere. Made in regular sizes, style 1 only, as listed.

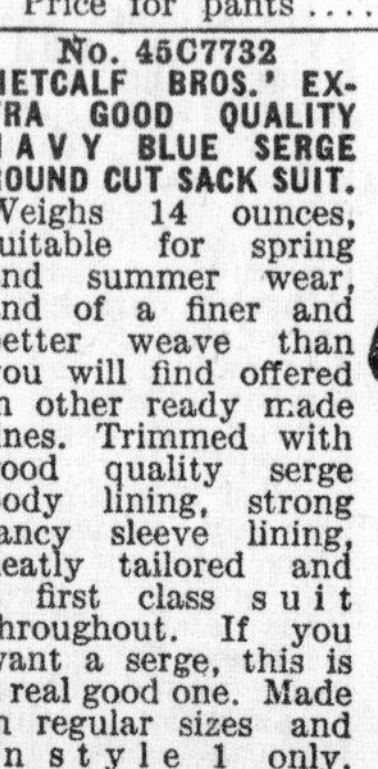

Price for suit....$10.00
Price for coat and vest....7.35
Price for pants....3.65

No. 45C7722 EARNSCLIFFE HIGH GRADE SILK MIXED WORSTED FOUR-BUTTON CUTAWAY SACK SUIT. A black and white, double and twist, hard finished weave. What might be called almost steel gray effect with a mild overplaid of light threads. Exactly the color for general business wear. Lined with serge body lining. Excellent satin finished sleeve lining. A well built and fine fitting garment in every way and guaranteed to satisfy particular dressers. Made in regular sizes, style 18 only, as illustrated.

Price for suit....$10.00
Price for coat and vest....7.35
Price for pants....3.65

No. 45C7726 FANCY DARK SILK MIXED WORSTED ROUND CUT SACK SUIT. The background is black worsted, very thickly sprinkled with exceedingly small silver white threads of silk. Such a pattern as will please modest and genteel dressers. Medium weight, suitable for all year around wear. Serge body lining. Neat satin finished sleeve lining. Excellent fitting qualities. A well made and carefully tailored garment in every particular. Made in regular sizes, style 1 only, as illustrated.

Price for suit....$10.00
Price for coat and vest....7.35
Price for pants....3.65

No. 45C7728 EXTRA VALUE ROUND CUT SACK SUITS. These garments are made from remnants of cloth left over from our custom tailoring line, from neat patterns and dark shades in cassimeres, cheviots and fancy worsteds, mixed patterns, faint overplaids, etc., a very nice collection. We are selling them at extremely low prices. They are well made, tailored, lined and trimmed, and in every way first class garments. Made in style 1 only and in regular sizes.

Price for suit....$10.00
Price for coat and vest....7.35
Price for pants....3.65

No. 45C7732 METCALF BROS.' EXTRA GOOD QUALITY NAVY BLUE SERGE ROUND CUT SACK SUIT. Weighs 14 ounces, suitable for spring and summer wear, and of a finer and better weave than you will find offered in other ready made lines. Trimmed with good quality serge body lining, strong fancy sleeve lining, neatly tailored and a first class suit throughout. If you want a serge, this is a real good one. Made in regular sizes and in style 1 only.

Price for suit $10.00
Price for coat and vest..7.35
Price for pants 3.65

No. 45C7733 METCALF BROS.' NAVY BLUE SERGE THREE-BUTTON DOUBLE BREASTED SUIT. This is the very same cloth as No. 45C7732, a real rich shade of fine weave serge quality. The only difference being that this is made in the popular long lapel three-button double breasted sack suit, making it an extremely popular and pleasing garment. If you want something exceptionally good, in the way of navy blue serge, we recommend this number. Made in style 30 only, and in regular sizes.

Price for suit $11.00
Price for coat and vest 8.35
Price for pants 3.65

No. 45C7736 SCHNABEL BROS.' FAINT BROWN FANCY WORSTED FOUR-BUTTON CUTAWAY SACK SUIT. This is not a distinct brown, but simply a brownish cast, caused by brown alternating with black. It has a check of about 1-inch squares of same color as the goods, and through this is woven a very faint overplaid of two rows of blue silk which can hardly be noticed, but the pattern is a very pleasing one and will delight the modest and careful dresser. Lined with serge in color to match the fabric. Made in the popular four-button cutaway sack, like illustration herewith, in style 18 only, and in regular sizes.

Price for suit..............$11.00
Price for coat and vest........ 8.10
Price for pants 4.00

No. 45C7740 STEELE & CO.'S CREPE OR MUMMY EFFECT WORSTED ROUND CUT SACK SUIT. A hard finish surface with black background and sprinkled with very neat small threads of red and green silk, but so subdued as to be hardly noticeable. A very popular fabric with well dressing business men. Lined with excellent quality of serge body lining, and fine quality of sleeve lining. These garments are excellent in fitting qualities, and are guaranteed to please careful dressers. Made in style 1 only and in regular sizes.

Price for suit..............$11.00
Price for coat and vest........ 8.10
Price for pants 4.00

No. 45C7744 GOOD QUALITY OF FRENCH BLACK WORSTED ROUND CUT SACK SUIT. An excellent business or dress garment, of a quality that you will find only in high priced custom tailoring lines. Made with an excellent grade of serge body lining and a durable fancy sleeve lining. If you want a black suit we can especially recommend this number. Made in style 1 only and in regular sizes, from 34 to 42 inches breast measure.

Price for suit.$11.00
Price for coat and vest $8.10
Price for pants..............$4.00

No. 45C7745 GOOD QUALITY OF FRENCH BLACK WORSTED ONE-BUTTON FROCK SUIT. Exactly the same cloth as No. 45C7744, the only difference is in the style. This number comes in four-button frock style, to be worn with but one button closed. Especially suitable for dress or Sunday wear. Good quality of serge body lining, and strong, durable sleeve lining. If you are looking for a black suit for dress wear, we cannot recommend this number too strongly. Made in regular sizes and in style 5 only, as illustrated.

Price for suit $12.00
Price for coat and vest 9.10
Price for pants 4.00

No. 45C7748 STEVEN SANFORD'S HIGH GRADE SILK MIXED WORSTED ROUND CUT SACK SUIT. Suitable for spring and fall wear; background is a black diagonal worsted, sprinkled with very bright small silk threads of light blue and gold, through which runs an almost invisible double overplaid of dusky red and blue threads. The overplaid cannot be seen except when the cloth is closely examined, but these different colors serve to make it a handsome pattern and one that is very dressy. Exceptionally well tailored, with serge body lining and first class sleeve lining, and in every way a handsome garment throughout. Made in regular sizes and in style 1 only, as illustrated.

Price for suit $12.00
Price for coat and vest 8.80
Price for pants 4.40

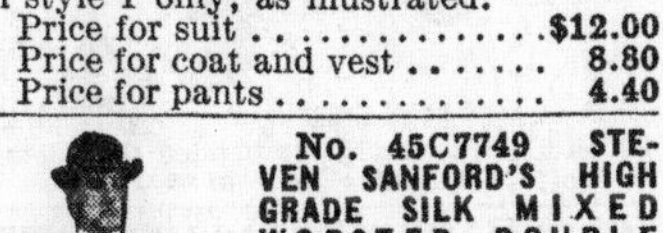

No. 45C7749 STEVEN SANFORD'S HIGH GRADE SILK MIXED WORSTED DOUBLE BREASTED SUIT. This is the very same cloth exactly as No. 45C7748, the difference is only in the style. This number comes in the popular double breasted, three-button, long lapel style, the pattern and style making a very handsome combination. You will be sure to like it. Made throughout and lined and trimmed in the same high grade manner as the previous number. Suit made in style 30 only and in regular sizes.

Price for suit...$13.00
Price for coat and vest 9.80
Price for pants 4.40

No. 45C7752 FANCY STRIPE EFFECT WORSTED FOUR-BUTTON CUTAWAY SACK SUIT. The pattern is a black and white mixture with light colored stripe ½ inch apart, between which alternate stripes of blue and green, but rather subdued, and every inch in opposite direction run very faint tan colored threads. The black and white predominate and the general effect is light colored. Suitable for spring and summer wear. Good serge lining, a well made suit in every way. Made in regular sizes and in style 18 only, as illustrated.

Price for suit $12.00
Price for coat and vest 8.80
Price for pants 4.40

No. 45C7756 STEELE & CO.'S HIGH GRADE SILK MIXED WORSTED ROUND CUT SACK SUIT. A medium weight fabric in black diagonal weave, with very small black stripes ½ inch apart, sprinkled with mostly light colored silk threads, although there are a few of faint blue and dusky red threads in the pattern which are not noticeable except on close examination. Good serge body lining and fancy pattern sleeve lining; first class suit throughout. Made in regular sizes and in style 1 only, as illustrated.

Price for suit $12.00
Price for coat and vest 8.80
Price for pants 4.40

No. 45C7757 STEELE & CO.'S HIGH GRADE SILK MIXED WORSTED FOUR-BUTTON CUTAWAY SACK SUIT. This is exactly the same quality and pattern as No. 45C7756, the only difference is in the style. This number comes in four-button cutaway sack, as illustrated, a very pleasing style in this pattern. Remember these are exceptionally well tailored garments; cloth of the best quality that you will find on the market and for which you would have to pay double our price elsewhere. Made in regular sizes, and in style 18 only.

Price for suit $12.00
Price for coat and vest 8.80
Price for pants 4.40

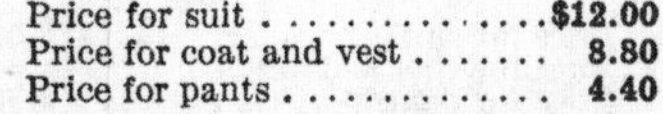

No. 45C7760 METCALF BROS.' FANCY BLACK CHECKED WORSTED ROUND CUT SACK SUIT. This is a good grade of black worsted, worked into small checks about ⅜ inch diameter with a small check of ⅛ inch diameter in the middle of the large check; quite popular with many circles; lined with black serge body lining and good durable sleeve lining, a first class tailored suit throughout; good fitting qualities. Made in regular sizes and in style 1 only, as illustrated.

Price for suit..$12.00
Price for coat and vest.... 8.80
Price for pants 4.40

No. 45C7761 METCALF BROS.' FANCY BLACK CHECKED WORSTED FOUR-BUTTON CUTAWAY SACK SUIT. This is exactly the same cloth as No. 45C7760, the only difference is the style. It comes in the popular four-button cutaway sack, making it a very dressy black garment, if you wish something different from the plain black. Lined with a good quality of serge body lining and good durable fancy pattern sleeve lining, first class workmanship in every way and highly recommended. Made in style 18 only and in regular sizes.

Price for suit $12.00
Price for coat and vest 8.80
Price for pants 4.40

No. 45C7762 EXTRA GOOD VALUE ROUND CUT SACK SUITS. These garments are made from remnants of cloth left over from the best qualities in our custom tailoring line in mixed colors and dark shades and mostly in worsteds. They are lined and trimmed in a decidedly substantial manner and are tailored in every way the same as our best grade ready made garments. Undoubtedly we can meet your taste from this excellent collection of suits. Made in regular sizes and in style 1 only; exceptional value.

Price for suit..............$12.00
Price for coat and vest........ 8.80
Price for pants 4.40

No. 45C7766 HIGH GRADE SILK MIXED WORSTED ROUND CORNERED SACK SUIT. A medium weight black diagonal weave for background and thickly sprinkled with white silk threads; makes a black and white pattern, very popular with good dressers. There are also very faint blue stripes ½ inch apart but which are scarcely noticeable. This has an exceptionally good serge body lining, extra quality sleeve lining and is elegantly tailored throughout; such a garment as you would expect to pay $18.00 to $20.00 for elsewhere. Made in style 1 only and in regular sizes.

Price for suit..............$13.50
Price for coat and vest....... 9.90
Price for pants 4.95

No. 45C7770 AMERICAN HIGH GRADE FANCY WORSTED ROUND CORNERED SACK SUIT. A dark shade with a pale blue silk mixture, hardly distinguishable and at a distance resembling a black cloth fairly medium weight, splendid for wear, excellently tailored; fine grade of serge lining and in every way a first class garment; one that will please modest tastes. Made in style 1 only and in regular sizes.

Price for suit $13.50
Price for coat and vest....... 9.90
Price for pants........... 4.95

No. 45C7774 TILLOTSON VERY HIGH GRADE SILK MIXED WORSTED ROUND CORNERED SACK SUIT. A rich bluish diagonal worsted, finished with a slight sprinkling of small silver threads; a fair weight for spring and early fall wear; a rich looking cloth, such as is found in high priced custom tailoring lines; a beautifully tailored garment throughout. High class serge linings. Something that will please the very best dressers. Made in style 1 only and in regular sizes.

Price for suit..............$15.00
Price for coat and vest 11.00
Price for pants 5.50

IF YOU PREFER TO SEE SAMPLES before ordering, please do not hesitate to send for the No. 89C SAMPLE BOOK OF MEN'S READY MADE CLOTHING. **It is equal to placing the largest and best equipped modern, city clothing establishment down at your very doorstep.** It is even better, because you can take your leisure in looking over the samples and deciding for yourself; for you have every opportunity to examine the goods, compare the prices, and make any other test that you desire before placing your order. Besides this, we absolutely guarantee to please you in every way or refund your money. We want you to see this big sample book before you think of ordering elsewhere. It will save you time and money. How to measure and all about styles and sizes is explained simply on page 897 of this catalogue.

No. 45C7775 TILLOTSON VERY HIGH GRADE SILK MIXED WORSTED FOUR-BUTTON CUTAWAY SACK SUIT. This is exactly the same cloth as No. 45C7774, the only difference is in the style. This comes in the popular four-button cutaway sack, making a beautiful combination of style and pattern, richly tailored, good serge linings, high class fitting qualities, and in every way a superior garment. Made in style 18 only and in regular sizes.

Price for suit..$15.00
Price for coat and vest.. 11.00
Price for pants 5.50

No. 45C7783 BOTANY MILLS STRICTLY ALL WOOL JET BLACK DRESS CLOTH FOUR-BUTTON CUTAWAY SACK SUIT. This is exactly the same fabric as used in No. 45C7782, the difference is only in the style; this number comes in the popular four-button cutaway sack, as illustrated, a favorite among good dressers. It has high grade linings and trimmings, especially good fitting qualities and if you want an all around first class black suit you cannot afford to overlook this number. It has our special recommendation and looks like broadcloth and wears better. Made in regular sizes and style 18 only.

Price for suit..............$15.00
Price for coat and vest....... 11.00
Price for pants.............. 5.50

No. 45C7778 TILLOTSON EXTRA HIGH CLASS SILK MIXED WORSTED ROUND CORNERED SACK SUIT. A very beautiful pattern, a brownish cast in a spring and summer weight, the background is composed of a dark and dull brown shade, and sprinkled over this very thickly are gold threads with an almost invisible overplaid of a single red thread; there are also fine, but faint stripes, 1½ inches apart of same shade as background. An immensely popular and dressy pattern in a high grade quality, very richly tailored; serge linings, and in every respect a high class suit, guaranteed to please the most stylish dressers. Made in regular sizes and in style 1 only.

Price for suit..............$15.00
Price for coat and vest...... 11.00
Price for pants.............. 5.50

No. 45C7786 HIGH GRADE STEEL GRAY DOUBLE AND TWIST WORSTED ROUND CORNERED SACK SUIT. For those who desire a plain gray shade—one that wears well and one that is durable as well as a high class stylish suit, this is the thing. Has high class serge body linings, exceptionally well tailored and of excellent fitting qualities. We guarantee to please the most particular dressers. This garment is made in regular sizes and in style 1 only, as illustrated.

Price for suit..............$15.00
Price for coat and vest....... 11.00
Price for pants.............. 5.50

No. 45C7779 TILLOTSON EXTRA HIGH GRADE SILK MIXED WORSTED DOUBLE BREASTED SUIT. This is the very same cloth exactly as No. 45C7778, the only difference is the style. This number comes in the popular three-button, double breasted, long lapel sack suit, and the combination of shade and style make it a wonderfully handsome garment, it is beautifully tailored, has high class serge linings and will please the most particular people—nothing nicer in the line. Made in regular sizes and in style 30 only, as illustrated.

Price for suit..............$16.00
Price for coat and vest...... 12.00
Price for pants.............. 5.50

ORDER COAT AND PANTS HANGERS WITH YOUR GARMENTS.

These are the Handiest and Most Useful Hangers Ever Invented, and Our Prices are so Low That Everybody Should Have Them.

OUR COAT HANGER.

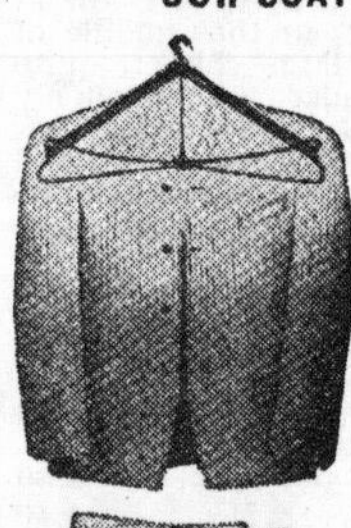

The illustration shows the hanger in use and folded. This is a very handy article, made of heavy nickeled wire and strong tape. When open the tape adjusts itself to the shape of the coat, holding it in the same position as when the coat is worn. It has the special advantage of not being rigid like other hangers and folds to fit a small space. This hanger is regularly sold in Chicago at from 15 to 25 cents each.

No. 45C6 Coat Hanger.
Price, each..................$0.10
Per dozen.................. 1.15

OUR PANTS HANGER.

The illustration shows our handy pants hanger in use. It has the advantage over other hangers in that the pants are hung from the bottom, the weight taking out the bagging, keeping them nicely creased, while the pieces that clasp the pants are made of wood and absorb any moisture, thus avoiding rust, such as occurs with the use of metal hangers. It has a swivel hook, and thus folds into a small space. Sliding rings on its arms hold the garment tight.

No. 45C8 Pants Hanger.
Price, each.....$0.10
Per dozen....... 1.15

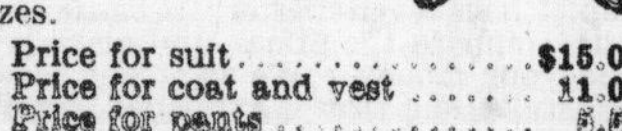

No. 45C7782 BOTANY MILLS STRICTLY ALL WOOL WEAVE, BLACK HIGH GRADE ROUND CORNERED SACK SUIT. This fabric is a good dress cloth resembling broadcloth very much, but the wearing qualities are far better than broadcloth. For a dress suit you cannot get anything nicer than this number. The workmanship is excellent and the trimmings are very high grade, in fact, it is a strictly high class garment throughout. We guarantee to please you in every way. You save from $8.00 to $10.00 at our price. Made in style 1 only and in regular sizes.

Price for suit..............$15.00
Price for coat and vest....... 11.00
Price for pants.............. 5.50

SPRING AND EARLY FALL OVERCOATS IN MEDIUM AND LIGHT WEIGHT.

STYLE 31

We carry a choice assortment of overcoats for spring and early fall wear in neat patterns and plain shades. They are made in style 31, as illustrated, which is the short box coat, the popular top coat style, average length from 36 to 38 inches; sizes from 34 to 42 inches, breast measure. They are made with welt seams and double stitched edges, one quarter of an inch; collar is of the same goods as coat; they are lined with a good quality of body lining, fine wearing sleeve lining, two lower outside pockets with flaps and one outside breast pocket with welt and a small change pocket inside the lower right hand side pocket, and in every respect are well made, durable and stylish garments; cut over the best fitting patterns available and we strictly guarantee to please you and every customer in workmanship, style, finish and fit or refund every cent paid together with transportation charges.

MEN'S ALL WOOL TAN COVERT SPRING OVERCOAT.

No. 45C8800 A medium tan shade in a medium weight, suitable for spring and early fall wear, such a coat as would cost you twice our price elsewhere. Neatly made, stylish, good fitting qualities. Made in style 31 only, as illustrated. Sizes from 34 to 42 inches breast measure; average length, 36 to 38 inches.

Price for spring overcoat............$7.50

MEDIUM WEIGHT ALL WOOL COVERT TAN AND WHITE SPRING OVERCOAT.

No. 45C8802 Background is of tan and sprinkled thickly with white wool threads, giving the effect of a light shade of tan, a very popular fabric for top coats. These garments are well lined and trimmed, stylishly made and represent the latest fashions in spring overgarments for men. Shoulders and fronts padded and stiffened, good fitting qualities; a coat we can highly recommend. Made in style 31 only, as illustrated. and in regular sizes

Price for spring overcoat............$8.50

MEN'S ALL WOOL BLACK THIBET SPRING OVERCOAT.

No 45C8804 A medium weight black goods, suitable for wear in spring and early fall or in fact at almost any season of the year and on all occasions a fabric that will give you exceptional wear. Made in popular box coat style 31, as illustrated. Nicely padded shoulders perfect hanging coat fronts and a dressy garment in every particular. Made in regular sizes Price for spring overcoat...... $9.00

MEN'S ALL WOOL BLACK AND WHITE WORSTED CHEVIOT SPRING OVERCOAT.

No. 45C8806 A medium weight unfinished worsted fabric with black background sprinkled with white threads. For those not desiring a black coat this is a pleasing substitute; it is dark enough for all general purposes and a good color for general or dress wear; made in the popular box coat style with full back in style 31, as illustrated; excellent fitting qualities and a coat that would cost you double the money if you had it made for you by any tailor. The fitting qualities cannot be excelled. Price for spring overcoat..$10.00

LIGHT TAN MEDIUM WEIGHT ALL WOOL SPRING OVERCOAT.

No. 45C8808 This is a very light shade of tan covert cloth, a little more firmly woven than the others, such a fabric as merchant tailors use in their high grade spring overgarments. Made in short box coat style with full back, like illustration for style 31; with neatly padded shoulders, perfect hanging coat fronts, and all around excellent fitting qualities; good serge lining and neatest of sewing. Made in regular sizes and style 31 only.

Price for spring overcoat..........................$12.00

MEN'S READY MADE PANTS. STYLES AND SIZES.

SIZES. **Unless distinctly stated in the description of the goods,** ready made pants are furnished only in sizes from 30 to 40 inches, inclusive, waist measure, and from 30 to 36 inches, inclusive, inside seam measure. The smaller sizes are cut 18 inches wide at the knee and 17 inches at the bottom, and the larger sizes 19 inches wide at the knee and 18 inches at the bottom. No larger sizes than these are furnished, excepting where it is specially stated. (See goods Nos. 45C8830, 45C8856, 45C8876 and 45C8884 on page 903.)

STYLES. **Pants are furnished in the prevailing styles,** all cut over the best fitting patterns obtainable. They have two hip pockets, two front pockets and one watch pocket. State size. (See page 897 for how to measure.)

FANCY BLACK AND WHITE WORSTED PANTS.

No. 45C8820 The background is black in a herringbone effect, sprinkled with white threads and black stripes, half an inch apart, but the pattern is what we would call dark. and white threads not being plentiful enough to change the pattern particularly. Exceptional value at our price. Made in sizes from 30 to 40 inches waist measure.

Price for pants......................$1.25

FANCY STRIPED WORSTED PANTS.

No. 45C8822 The background is a black diagonal weave and every half inch there is a stripe composed of three single light colored threads on a faint olive green background and alternately between these larger stripes there are single thread stripes of blue and green. This is not a loud pattern, but fairly modest and neat and exceptional value at our price, which is less than wholesale. Made in regular sizes. Price for pants.............$1.50

FANCY STRIPED WORSTED PANTS.

No. 45C8824 The background is a black diagonal weave; every half inch is a stripe composed of three rows of single dull white threads and alternately between these main stripes there are single thread stripes of red and green very faint. It is a modest pattern and splendid wearing pants. We devote much attention to the making of these garments and can highly recommend them. Made in regular sizes Price for pants.$1.50

EXCEPTIONAL VALUE PANTS.

No. 45C8826 Under this number we offer pants that we have made from remnants left over from our various manufacturing departments. They come in stripes, mixtures and dark pants, and we are quoting a low price on them to thus dispose of our left over stock of cloth. We can very likely suit your taste from this number. Made in regular sizes.

Price for pants............$1.50

GOOD QUALITY HAIRLINE CASSIMERE PANTS.

No. 45C8828 Nothing better for wear. Black background with dull white stripes one-eighth of an inch apart. We especially recommend this for strong wearing purposes. It is a good weight for all year round wear. We devote exceptional care to the making of these pants. They are all guaranteed for being well sewed and for durability. Made in regular sizes; for larger sizes see next number.

Price for pants..............$1.50

EXTRA SIZE HAIRLINE CASSIMERE PANTS.

No. 45C8830 This is made from exactly the same cloth as No. 45C8828. The only difference in this number is that it comes in extra sizes only, from 42 to 50 inches waist measure. No larger. Heavy set regularly built men could not find a more desirable, excellent wearing pants than this; well sewed and durable. Price for pants.... **$1.75**

FANCY STRIPED WORSTED PANTS.

No. 45C8832 Background is a black color with a stripe composed of a raised black thread with a white thread on each side of it every three-fourths of an inch, and between these main stripes there are two plain raised black stripes which have one very faint broken stripe of dark brown on each side. It is a pleasing pattern and one that we would recommend for general wear. It is a well made garment in every respect.
Price for pants.............. **$1.65**

FANCY NAVY BLUE STRIPE WORSTED PANTS.

No. 45C8834 This is a plain dark navy blue pants with one-eighth inch raised stripe of the same color every half inch, and a narrow raised stripe the same color between the large stripes. If you desire a plain shade and a neat pattern we would recommend this number as a good durable garment, at a low price. Made in regular sizes. Price for pants.. **$1.75**

SPECIAL VALUE PANTS.

No. 45C8836 Under this number we are offering pants we have made from remnants of cloth, which are stripes or mixtures from good grades of worsteds and cassimere fabrics. We have made them in regular sizes and in the same durable manner as the rest of our ready made pants. We quote a very low price on them in order to dispose of the left over fabrics promptly.
Price for pants.............. **$1.75**

FANCY WHITE AND BLACK STRIPED WORSTED PANTS.

No. 45C8838 A black and white mixture for background, making a fairly light colored shade, with raised black stripes about ¾ inch apart. A dressy garment, especially at this price. Made in regular sizes. Price for pants.. **$1.75**

FANCY DARK SHADE MIXED COLOR PANTS.

No. 45C8840 This is a pleasing combination, with stripes ½ inch wide every half inch, composed of two outside dark stripes sprinkled with gold threads and a center stripe of black, while between these large stripes there is a black wide wale diagonal weave. This makes a very neat garment; is well sewed and durable. Made in regular sizes.
Price for pants.............. **$1.75**

FANCY GRAY MIXTURE CASSIMERE PANTS.

No. 45C8842 The background is black but very thickly covered with white threads running diagonally but interrupted every ½ inch by stripes of the plain black. A good general purpose garment both in quality and color; medium weight, suitable for year round wear. Made in regular sizes. Price for pants.......... **$2.00**

BLACK BEDFORD CORD WORSTED PANTS.

No. 45C8844 A hard finish black dress cloth that gives extra good wear and looks well for dress or general wear. A weight suitable for all year round wear; of exceptional qualities. Made in regular sizes.
Price for pants.............. **$2.00**

FANCY STRIPED WORSTED PANTS.

No. 45C8846 The background is a black and white mixture, working in a sort of narrow herringbone effect. Every inch there is a stripe of about 3-16 inch wide, made up of a middle thread of brown and outer threads of white. These brown and white threads alternate with black; a very handsome pattern and one that you will like. These pants would cost you double our price elsewhere. Made up in regular sizes. Price for pants.......... **$2.00**

FANCY DARK GRAY MIXTURE WORSTED PANTS.

No. 45C8848 Medium weight cloth with black background in diagonal weave with rows, ⅜ inch wide, composed of a sprinkling of white threads on the black background and between these rows, there being no white threads, gives the effect of a dark stripe; a very neat dark gray mixture for that reason. Good wearing pants, one with which a modest taste will be pleased. Made in regular sizes.
Price for pants.............. **$2.00**

FANCY STRIPED WORSTED PANTS.

No. 45C8850 The background is black. Every inch there is a raised black stripe 1-16 inch wide. On either side of these stripes for a quarter of an inch the background is sprinkled with white threads and in the middle there are two rows of white threads and on either side of these a row of green threads, making a combination of various colored stripes. The green threads are not pronounced, and the whole effect is a black and white pattern with a little life added—makes a dressy garment and of good fitting qualities. Made in regular sizes. Price for pants.. **$2.00**

EXTRA GOOD VALUE PANTS.

No. 45C8852 These pants are made from remnants left over from our various manufacturing departments and we have made them into pants in regular sizes and are offering them at an extremely low figure. They are composed of fancy worsteds in mostly stripes. We can very likely meet your taste in this number. Price for pants........ **$2.00**

FANCY DARK STRIPED WORSTED PANTS.

No. 45C8854 The background is black. Every half inch there is a stripe ⅛ inch wide, but very much subdued and composed of four rows of bluish white threads with a single gold thread between them and in the middle, between these stripes, there are two bluish white threads. It is a dark pattern, these different colored threads serving only to lighten it up somewhat—very neat and gentle. Made in regular sizes.
Price for pants... **$2.25**

EXTRA SIZE DARK STRIPED WORSTED PANTS.

No. 45C8856 This is exactly the same pattern as No. 45C8854, the difference is only that this number comes in extra sizes, from 42 to 50 inches waist measure. Heavy set regularly built men will find this a very neat, modest and fine wearing garment. The fitting qualities are excellent.
Price for pants... **$2.75**

VERY FANCY STRIPED WORSTED PANTS.

No. 45C8858 The background is of a black color. Every inch there is a raised black satin finish stripe 1-16 inch wide with a single thread of white on each side of it. Near the middle, between these stripes, there are two other raised black stripes, but they are crossed diagonally with the threads of the background color and right in the middle and on the inner edge of these stripes threads of gold are sprinkled. It is an attractive pattern and one that many would be pleased with. Made up in regular sizes. Price for pants **$2.25**

FANCY FAINT STRIPE EFFECT WORSTED PANTS.

No. 45C8860 The background is dark and white mixture, while every half inch there are stripes of a double thread of white that are rather subdued. There is also a light sprinkling of blue, hardly noticeable. It is a modest pattern and will please those desiring a medium dark and white pattern in a good wearing fabric. Made in regular sizes. Price for pants........ **$2.25**

EXTRA GOOD VALUE PANTS.

No. 45C8862 This lot is composed of fancy worsteds, cassimeres and stripes in mixed and dark patterns which we have made up in regular sizes from remnants left over from our custom tailoring department. They are made in the same way as our regular ready made pants; good fitting qualities and we can undoubtedly meet your taste from this collection.
Price for pants.................. **$2.25**

DARK MEDIUM WEIGHT CASSIMERE PANTS.

No. 45C8864 Suitable for all year round wear; background black, and there are rows, ½ inch wide, made up of a sprinkling of white threads not very distinct and the space between these rows, having no white threads, have the effect of a black stripe, not very distinct, because the white threads do not show up very distinctly. A modest and dressy garment, one we could recommend for strong, heavy wear, in regular sizes, 30 to 40 inches waist measure.
Price for pants....................... $2.50

FANCY LIGHT COLORED STRIPED WORSTED PANTS.

No. 45C8866 The background is a light colored gray, or black and white mixture. Every half inch there are small narrow stripes of a single silver white thread and between these another narrow stripe of a dark color with a pale blue thread, very faint. This is, a good wearing, dressy appearing fabric, one that we can especially recommend. Made up in regular sizes.
Price for pants.............. **$2.50**

FANCY STRIPED DARK WORSTED PANTS.

No. 45C8868 The background is black, with rows, ⅝ inch wide, made up of silver gray silk threads, with a stripe of dull green running down the middle, then between these rows there is a stripe, ⅛ inch wide, caused by the background appearing without any silver threads in it. It is a modest and pleasing pattern, one that will give first class satisfaction for general wear. Made in regular sizes.
Price for pants.............. **$2.50**

EXTRA GOOD VALUE PANTS.

No. 45C8870 Under this number we offer a variety of pants in cassimeres, worsteds and other patterns which we have made up from the better pieces of cloth left over from our custom tailoring department which were too small for other purposes. The prices were accordingly made very low and we have made them in the same substantial manner as the other ready made pants. Made in regular sizes.
Price for pants... **$2.50**

ALL WOOL DARK GRAY HAIRLINE CASSIMERE PANTS.

No. 45C8872 A better grade of hairline cassimere than usual, with a narrower light stripe than usually offered. The background is dark with light threads running 1-16 inch apart. Good for all year round wear, and for long service cannot be excelled. Made in regular sizes.
Price for pants.. **$2.50**

BLACK AND SINGLE WHITE THREAD STRIPED WORSTED PANTS.

No. 45C8874 Background is black, with stripes of single white threads 3-16 inch apart, with another light thread between the main stripes but which is almost invisible. This is a dressy garment and looks well with a dark coat and vest. Made in regular sizes.
Price for pants.............. **$2.75**

EXTRA SIZE BLACK AND NARROW WHITE STRIPED WORSTED PANTS.

No. 45C8876 Exactly the same cloth and pattern as No. 45C8874, the difference is only that this number comes in extra sizes from 42 to 50 inches waist measure. It is a dressy pattern and heavy set regularly built men will find it a desirable garment from all standpoints, workmanship and fit included.
Price for pants.............. **$3.25**

FANCY STRIPED WORSTED PANTS.

No. 45C8878 Background dark, sprinkled thickly with bluish white threads, rather faint. Every ¾ inch there are stripes composed of a double row of white threads and in the middle, between these main stripes, there are two very faint stripes of dark brown. This is a modest pattern and one that will meet with the tastes of good dressing business men. Made in regular sizes and of exceptionally good fitting qualities. Price for pants...... **$3.00**

FANCY GRAYISH STRIPE EFFECT WORSTED PANTS.

No. 45C8880 Background is black, very thickly sprinkled with white threads; every half inch there is a light stripe, caused by the white threads being more distinct than in the rest of the fabric, and between these stripes is a darker stripe, caused by the white threads being not so thick as in the background. These threads are interwoven in such a manner as to bring out a decided grayish stripe effect. Made in regular sizes.
Price for pants.............. **$3.00**

DARK FANCY STRIPED WORSTED PANTS.

No. 45C8882 Background is black sprinkled with white threads. Every ¾ inch there is a very subdued stripe of silver threads and between these another stripe of green and white threads, but these stripes can hardly be distinguished. The general effect is a dark gray pattern with a little extra life to it. Made in regular sizes from 30 to 40 inches waist measure; cut over the best fitting patterns available and guaranteed a first class garment in every respect.
Price for pants............ **$3.50**

EXTRA SIZE DARK FANCY STRIPED WORSTED PANTS.

No. 45C8884 This is exactly the same cloth as No. 45C8882, the difference is only that this number comes in extra sizes from 42 to 50 inches waist measure, no larger. It is a modest and tasty pattern which heavy set men will find to their liking, a good general purpose garment.
Price for pants, in extra sizes.. **$4.00**

FANCY PATTERN WORSTED TROUSERING.

No. 45C8886 The background is black with a raised black satin effect stripe every inch, and a faint white thread on each side of it, while in the middle between these stripes there are two dotted rows of gray silk threads, and the whole fabric is sprinkled with small light blue silk threads serving to brighten up the fabric. A good quality and fair weight for general wear. Made in regular sizes.
Price for pants.............. **$3.75**

FANCY PATTERN WORSTED PANTS WITH BLACK STRIPES.

No. 45C8888 Background is a mixture of black, white, green and gold threads, about an equal number of each, and there is running through these a raised black satin stripe every three-eighths of an inch. A handsome appearance and a real good quality that will give excellent satisfaction. We highly recommend it. Made in sizes from 30 to 40 inches waist measure.
Price for pants............ **$4.00**

FANCY NARROW STRIPE HIGH GRADE WORSTED PANTS.

No. 45C8890 A real dressy, genteel pattern, dark background, sprinkled thickly with dull bluish white threads. Every quarter of an inch there are stripes of single silver white threads. A pattern that good dressers will like and a real fine quality that will go well with the best of other garments. Made in regular sizes.
Price for pants.......... **$4.25**

HIGH GRADE GRAY STRIPE WORSTED PANTS.

No. 45C8892 A real dressy pattern and high grade quality that will please the most particular dressers. Black and white background with narrow stripes a quarter of an inch apart and between these stripes another stripe, formed by silvery white threads more distinct than the rest of the pattern. Every inch these silvery white thread stripes are more distinct and form a sort of gray stripe. These are exceptionally well made pants and of first class fitting qualities. Made in regular sizes
Price for pants.......... **$4.50**

GOOD VALUES IN BLUE SERGE PANTS.

These are made in the same style and sizes as our regular ready made pants, with the exception that they have belt straps. We have divided them according to quality, in three classes. As shades in blue serges vary a little, we don't advise ordering pants to match blue serge coats and vests, that is, if you are anxious to have an exact match.

No. 41C100 Good quality blue serge pants. Price............... **$2.00**
No. 41C102 Extra quality blue serge pants. Price............... **2.75**
No. 41C104 Our finest quality of blue serge pants, real dressy. **Price $[illegible]**

MEN'S FANCY SILK AND WASH VESTS.

We have an excellent assortment of patterns in this department of our men's ready made clothing. Those desiring to have a good fancy vest for dressy effects will save a great deal by investing in these garments; they have the same excellent qualities as used by merchant tailors throughout the country, we have cut and made them up into popular styles, some in single and some in double breasted styles in very large numbers, and our prices represent the actual manufacturing cost with one small profit added. We are selling many thousands of these vests, gentlemen throughout the country are finding this department very interesting and profitable to them, as they are getting vests the equal of which would cost them fully double the money elsewhere. We furnish them in sizes from 34 to 42 inches breast measure only and in the style mentioned for each number, we cannot furnish them in any other sizes than these and cannot give you any other style than the one mentioned for each number.

Single Breasted Fancy Vest.

Double Breasted Fancy Vest.

We illustrate the patterns by a photograph of the goods and the illustration appearing with each number represents the exact size of the pattern, showing you the weave, dots and figures mentioned in the descriptions, you can look at the illustration and then read the description and you will find, as nearly as possible, exactly how the pattern looks.

No. 45C9900 MEN'S DARK FANCY SILK VEST. Background, as illustration shows, is black with rows of black dots one-half an inch apart, made by a raised thread which has four red threads around it. A modest pattern for general wear.
Price for single breasted vest...**$1.25**

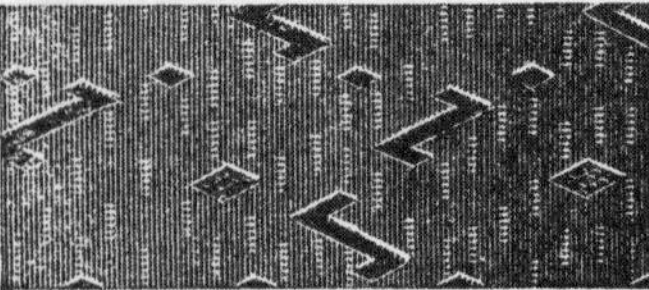

No 45C9902 MEN'S FANCY BLACK AND WHITE SILK VEST. Background is black with raised black threads in the shape of a Z and other dots of raised black threads scattered over it while all over the fabric there are sprinkled neat short rows of white threads, making a genteel and dressy dark pattern.
Price for single breasted vest...**$1.50**

No. 45C9903 MEN'S FANCY BLACK AND WHITE DOUBLE BREASTED SILK VEST. This is the same goods as No. 45C9902, shown and described above, the difference being that this is furnished in double breasted style. It makes a very fashionable and pleasing vest in this style and we know that you will like it.
Price for double breasted vest..**$1.75**

No. 45C9904 MEN'S FANCY BLACK, RED AND WHITE SILK VEST. The background is black; over this there are squares of one-half inch diameter, formed by white threads; in the middle of each square there is a red dot with four single white threads around it, making a pleasing dark and red mixture that proves very popular.
Price for single breasted vest...**$1.75**

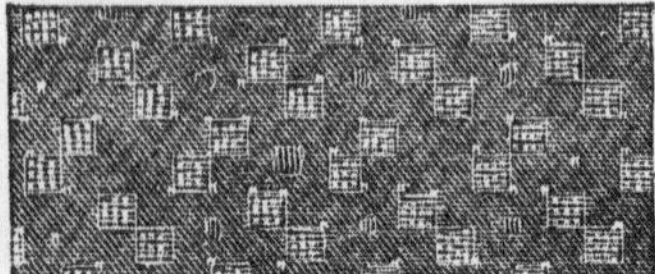

No. 45C9906 MEN'S FANCY DARK TAN AND GREEN DOTTED SILK VEST. Background is a black and tan mixture, tan prevailing, covered with small squares of one-eighth inch diameter joined in twos, these squares are black and tan, but more tan than black, making a distinct pattern, while among these squares are sprinkled small and large dots of green, a very pretty garment that will delight good dressers
Price for single breasted vest...**$2.00**

No. 45C9907 MEN'S FANCY DARK TAN AND GREEN DOT DOUBLE BREASTED SILK VEST. This is the same goods exactly as shown and described under No. 45C9906, the difference is only that this is double breasted style. It is a very genteel and rich looking garment in this style.
Price for double breasted vest..**$2.25**

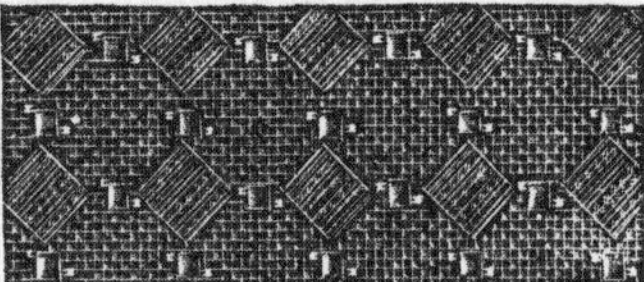

No. 45C9908 MEN'S FANCY BLACK AND PURPLE DOT SILK VEST. Background is a small black basket weave, covered with rows of purple dots one-half an inch apart and on each side of these dots there is a very small green dot. We consider this quite a rich dark pattern for general wear.
Price for single breasted vest...**$2.50**

LIGHT COLORED WASHABLE VESTS.

Made in Single Breasted, Six-Button Style, Without Collar.

No. 45C9910 MEN'S FANCY WHITE AND POLKA DOT WASH VEST. The background is a neat white weave, covered with black dots, the pattern being generally called a polka dot. A good vest for summer wear. Immensely popular everywhere.
Price for single breasted vest...**$1.00**

No. 45C9912 MEN'S PLAIN WHITE WASH VEST. This pattern has a sort of basket weave effect and it is plain white, just the kind of goods adapted for first class summer white wash vests, either for good or general wear.
Price for single breasted vest...**$1.25**

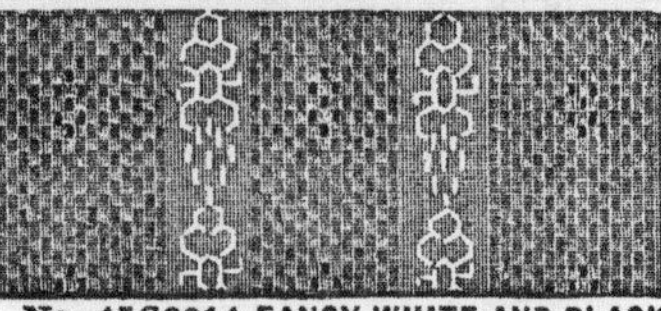

No. 45C9914 FANCY WHITE AND BLACK DOTTED WASH VEST. The background is a white small basket weave with white stripes one-quarter inch wide and three-quarters of an inch apart, formed by raised white threads, between these white stripes there are rows of black dots formed by a center black thread with six black threads around it. A very neat black and white pattern.
Price for single breasted vest...**$1.50**

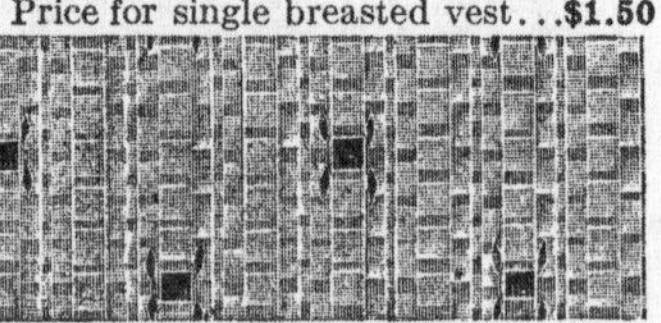

No. 45C9916 MEN'S FANCY WHITE AND RED DOT WASH VEST. The background is white in a sort of basket weave effect, over this there are rows of red dots three-quarters of an inch apart, each red dot having four small black dots around it. A very pretty light colored wash garment.
Price for single breasted vest..**$1.75**

No. 45C9918 MEN'S FANCY TAN FLOWERED SILK VEST. The background is a light tan overshot with figures in darker tan, also smaller figures in groups of redish brown. This is a handsome pattern and one that dressy gentlemen will be pleased with.
Price for single breasted vest...**$2.00**

No. 45C9920 FANCY PLAIN WHITE WASH VEST. The pattern is a sort of a chain weave, but plain white, representing a change from the usual plain white pattern. This is a high grade wash vest, one that we can especially recommend.
Price for single breasted vest..**$2.50**

SINGLE VESTS MADE FROM REMNANTS LEFT OVER FROM OUR VARIOUS MANUFACTURING AND CUSTOM TAILORING DEPARTMENTS.

We have a large number of small pieces of cloth left over every season from our various clothing departments, pieces that are too small to make into anything any larger than a vest, so we have cut them into single breasted vests of regular sizes and made them up in a first class way, the same as all vests that go with our ready made suits, and if a single vest is wanted we can offer you an excellent vest from this assortment. We have graded the prices according to the quality of the cloth. Sizes, from 34 to 42 inches breast measure.

No. 45C9922 MEN'S SINGLE BREASTED SINGLE VESTS IN VARIOUS SHADE and mixed patterns in cassimeres and cheviots: a good quality and representing exceptional value.
Price for vest...............**$1.00**

No. 45C9924 MEN'S SINGLE BREASTED SINGLE VESTS OF GOOD QUALITY IN CASSIMERES, WORSTEDS AND CHEVIOTS. Of somewhat higher grade than the previous number, a good assortment of patterns and shades, we can likely meet your tastes. Price for vest.........**$1.25**

No. 45C9926 MEN'S SINGLE BREASTED SINGLE VEST. Of still higher quality, made from remnants left from our custom tailoring department. Good grades of cassimeres, cheviots, worsteds and silk mixed fabrics, both plain and fancy patterns.
Price for vest...............**$1.50**

No. 45C9928 MEN'S SINGLE BREASTED SINGLE VEST. Of our best grade of remnants left over from our custom tailoring department. From the higher qualities of cheviots, tweeds, fancy worsteds and silk mixed qualities, a very rich assortment of patterns, and if you want a real good vest at a low price you cannot afford to overlook this number.
Price for vest...............**$1.75**

MEN'S READY MADE LIGHT WEIGHT UNLINED CRASH AND FLANNEL SUMMER CLOTHING.

Outing Flannel and Crash Garments in light colored, medium shades and dark patterns are becoming more and more popular for hot weather wear in every community. We have, therefore, selected a very choice and up to date variety of neat, handsome patterns in wool crashes and flannels of light weight, and have made them up, some in the popular single breasted three-button cutaway sack style, and some in the three-button double breasted sack style, with the padded broad shoulder effect, as illustrations show.

We Furnish Coat and Pants Only from these numbers, and do not furnish vests. We do not sell the coat or pants separately; we sell them only together. Each number is furnished only in the style described and illustrated for it. Pants are all made with belt loops and buttons sewed inside the waistband, and with turn up golf or cuff bottoms. The coats are all made without body lining, are lined only in sleeves and yoke, have two lower outside pockets with flaps, giving coat the appearance of a regular coat, one outside breast pocket and an inside pocket. We cannot furnish them in any other style.

Our Sizes run from 34 to 42 inches breast measure for coat and from 30 to 4[illegible] inches waist and from 30 to 36 inches inside seam measure f[illegible] pants. No larger nor smaller sizes can be furnished.

MEN'S ALL WOOL CRASH OUTING COAT AND PANTS.

$4.00

No. 41C200 A tan and white mixture with a sparing sprinkling of dots of darker brown. Quite rich outing garments and at this price will please you immensely. Coat is made in the popular three-button cutaway sack style with two lower pockets with flaps, one outside breast pocket and an inside pocket. Pants made with turn up or cuff bottoms, belt loops; made in regular sizes.
Price for outing coat and pants....**$4.00**

MEN'S ALL WOOL CRASH OUTING COAT AND PANTS.

$4.50

No. 41C202 The pattern is a white and tan mixture with a sparing sprinkling of dark brown dots but there are also faint white thread stripes three-eighths of an inch apart, making a very pretty summer suit. We have this in the favorite three-button single breasted sack style, two lower outside pockets with flaps, one outside breast pocket, and an inside pocket. Pants made with cuff bottoms, belt loops and suspender buttons sewed inside of waistband. Made like illustration and certainly a great value at our price.
Price for outing coat and pants.**$4.50**

MEN'S ALL WOOL FLANNEL CHECK EFFECT OUTING COAT AND PANTS.

$5.00

No. 41C204 The background of this fabric is a mixture of nut brown and gray, while over it a large but subdued check effect made up of a number of parallel alternate threads of brown and gray. There are a few dots of gold and white threads very far apart sprinkled over the fabric. Coat is lined only in yoke and sleeves. Pants have belt loops, suspender buttons sewed inside of waistband and golf bottoms. Made in three-button single breasted cutaway style in regular sizes and a handsome outing garment in every way, very stylish.

Price for outing coat and pants..**$5.00**

MEN'S ALL WOOL DOUBLE BREASTED BLACK AND GRAY OUTING COAT AND PANTS.

$5.50

No. 41C207 The pattern is a black and gray mixture, about an even number of threads of each, a good wearing color for general purposes, the coat is made in the popular three-button, long lapel, double breasted sack style as illustrated, with two lower pockets with flaps, one outside breast pocket and an inside pocket. Pants made with golf or cuff bottoms, belt loops and suspender buttons sewed inside waistband. Everything exactly up to date

Price for outing coat and pants.......**$5.50**

MEN'S ALL WOOL FLANNEL NUT BROWN AND WHITE EFFECT OUTING COAT AND PANTS.

$6.00

No. 41C212 The pattern is a mixture of nut brown and white; over it about one and one-half inches apart, run stripes composed of two parallel black and gray threads; same colored threads in the opposite direction also, but hardly noticeable Verynobby. Coat is made in single breasted three-button cutaway sack style, lining in sleeves and yoke only, the usual pockets. Pants with belt loops and golf or turn up bottoms.

Price for outing coat and pants, **$6.00**

MEN'S BLACK AND GRAY SINGLE BREASTED THREE-BUTTON SACK CUTAWAY COAT AND PANTS.

$7.00

No. 41C216 This is a dark pattern with a sort of herringbone stripe effect, made by alternate black and gray threads, the black being the most prominent a good color for general summer wear. Coat is made in the regular style without body lining; lining in sleeves and yoke only. Pants with golf or cuff bottoms, suspender buttons sewed inside of waistband, and belt loops A very good value in every way.

Price for outing coat and pants...**$7.00**

MEN'S ALL WOOL FLANNEL CHECK EFFECT DOUBLE BREASTED OUTING COAT AND PANTS.

$5.50

No. 41C205 This is a pleasing pattern composed of a gray and nut brown mixture with a large check effect over it, caused by a number of parallel alternate threads of brown and gray, more distinct than the background. There is a very sparing sprinkling of gold and white threads over the fabric. Coat made in three-button double breasted long lapel style, two lower pockets with flaps, an outside breast pocket and one inside pocket, lined only in sleeves and yoke. Pants made with belt loops and turn up or golf bottoms. A very handsome garment in every way.

Price for outing coat and pants...**$5.50**

MEN'S ALL WOOL CRASH SINGLE BREASTED CUTAWAY OUTING COAT AND PANTS.

$5.50

No. 41C208 The background is a light gray with a very faint greenish cast, over this there runs about an inch apart, both ways, indistinct single threads of faint green and tan. It is a very handsome light colored fabric. Coat made with fine fitting effects, lined only in sleeves and yoke, has the usual style and number of pockets. Pants with cuff or turn up bottoms and made so as to be worn with either belt or suspenders. Price for outing coat and pants........**$5.50**

We furnish only coat and pants. We DO NOT sell coat or pants separately from any of these numbers.

MEN'S ALL WOOL FLANNEL DOUBLE BREASTED WHITE AND NUT BROWN EFFECT COAT AND PANTS.

$6.50

No. 41C213 The pattern is a mixture of nut brown and white threads over which run stripes composed of two parallel threads of gray and black about one and one-half inches apart; same colored threads run also in the opposite direction, but are almost invisible. A very handsome pattern. Coat is made in the popular three-button double breasted long lapel style, no body lining, lined in sleeves and yoke only. Pants with belt loops and golf bottoms. A very up to date garment.

Price for outing coat and pants **$6.50**

MEN'S BLACK AND GRAY FLANNEL DOUBLE BREASTED OUTING COAT AND PANTS.

$7.50

No. 41C217 This is a dark pattern with a herringbone stripe effect made by alternate threads of black and gray, black being the most prominent. Coat is made in three-button double breasted long lapel style, no body lining, lining in sleeves and yoke only. Pants made with belt loops, buttons sewed inside waistband and turned up or cuff bottoms. A good outing garment for general wear.

Price for outing coat and pants.....**$7.50**

MEN'S ALL WOOL FLANNEL SINGLE BREASTED OUTING COAT AND PANTS.

$5.00

No. 41C206 The background of this fabric is a black and gray mixture, a medium dark colored pattern and a very popular and good wearing color. The coat has no body lining, lined only in yoke and sleeves, has two lower outside pockets with flaps, one outside breast pocket and an inside pocket. Pants with belt loops and turn up or golf bottoms, suspender buttons sewed inside of waistband.

Price for outing coat and pants **$5.00**

MEN'S ALL WOOL FLANNEL SINGLE BREASTED CUTAWAY SACK COAT AND PANTS.

$6.00

No. 41C210 The background is gray and over it run mild but distinct stripes caused by a mixture of dark threads on the gray background each stripe being a quarter of an inch wide and there are besides, very wide apart, small single threads of tan, very faint. Coat is made with the usual number of pockets in the latest fashion, lined only in sleeves and yoke. Pants made with golf or cuff bottoms with belt loops and suspender buttons sewed inside the waistband. Summer garments are exceedingly popular nowadays and this represents the best of summer or outing clothing.

Price for outing coat and pants **$6.00**

MEN'S ALL WOOL CRASH CUTAWAY SACK OUTING COAT AND PANTS.

$6.50

No. 41C214 The background is a dull gray and over it runs a faint check caused by a mixture of black and gray threads and a still larger but more subdued check caused by a single thread of tan, a fairly light colored pattern and makes a very handsome garment. Coat is lined only in yoke and sleeves, made in every way in up to date fashion for outing garments. Pants with belt loops, turn up bottoms, etc.

Price for outing coat and pants **$6.50**

MEN'S LIGHT GRAY AND STRIPED FLANNEL OUTING COAT AND PANTS.

$7.00

No. 41C218 The pattern has a herringbone effect made by alternate threads of white and brownish gray; over this are subdued stripes of gray about one inch apart; makes a very stylish outing garment. Coat is made in the popular three-button single breasted sack style. Pants with golf or cuff bottoms and belt loops, buttons sewed inside waistband.

Price for outing coat and pants **$7.00**

MEN'S DARK PATTERN ALL WOOL FLANNEL OUTING COAT AND PANTS.

$8.00

No. 41C220 This is our highest priced outing suit, hence a really dressy garment. Background is a dark oxford gray with alternate black and green stripes one-half an inch apart, almost invisible, while very widely apart there are stripes of a single white thread serving to light up the pattern. Coat is made in the popular three-button sack style. Pants made same way as our other outing styles. Price for outing coat and pants..................**$8.00**

MEN'S WARM WEATHER READY MADE CLOTHING.

ALPACA, MOHAIR SERGE AND CREPE CLOTH COATS, AND SUMMER GOODS OF ALL KINDS.

The sizes in which we furnish these summer coats are from 34 to 42 inches breast measure. Positively no larger or smaller sizes can be furnished from our ready made stock.

MEN'S BLACK COTTON COAT.

No. 41C2 Made from a good quality black cotton cloth. A good office coat, and a satisfactory, well made garment if the price is considered. Made in round cut sack style. Price......**50c**

MEN'S BLACK AND WHITE STRIPE COTTON COAT.

No. 41C4 Made from a strong quality of black and white stripe cotton. A serviceable, well made, well shaped coat. The same kind as is usually retailed at 75 cents. Made in round cut sack style only.
Price for coat, style 50..........**50c**

MEN'S BLACK ALPACA COAT.

Style 50

No. 41C6 Made from a good quality of black alpaca. Reasonably well made. While the price is very low for an alpaca coat, this is a garment that will give satisfactory wear, and, for the money, we consider it a most excellent summer coat Made in round cut sack style only.
Price for coat, style 50........**$1.00**

MEN'S BLACK ALPACA COAT.

No. 41C8 Better quality than the above; a nicely made, serviceable summer coat. A most excellent garment for the money. Cut full size, well shaped and, we are sure, will give splendid satisfaction if the price is considered. Price for coat, style 50..**$1.25**

MEN'S BLACK ALPACA COAT.

No. 41C10 The same as above, only, made from a finer quality of black alpaca. Has two lower outside pockets, one breast pocket. First class, durable alpaca sack coat.
Price for coat, style 50........**$1.50**

XX QUALITY OF SILVER GRAY ALPACA COAT, MADE IN SACK STYLE.

No. 41C12 This coat is made from a handsome shade of gray alpaca, a good quality and a garment that is serviceable. Makes a very neat, dressy summer coat. Two lower outside pockets, one breast pocket.
Price for coat, style 50........**$1.75**

MEN'S BLACK ALPACA COAT.

No. 41C14 This coat is made from a good quality of black alpaca, has a nice luster and is a good weight. Double stitched seams, two lower outside pockets, one breast pocket, well shaped, trimmed and finished. This is a better garment than we have heretofore been able to offer our customers at $2.50.
Price for coat, style 50.........**$2.00**

MEN'S FINE QUALITY BLACK ALPACA COAT.

No. 41C16 If you want a real neat, jet black, glossy alpaca coat, we are sure you will like this one. It is a most excellent garment, nicely tailored, double stitched throughout, two lower outside pockets, one breast pocket. A garment that is certainly nice enough for anyone. We especially recommend this number.
Price for coat, style 50.........**$2.50**

OUR FINEST BLACK ALPACA COAT IN SACK STYLE.

No. 41C18 This coat is made from the best quality of alpaca that we can obtain. It is a good weight, strong, serviceable material with a high luster, and it is surely the best garment ever offered at this price, because it is to our knowledge a better summer coat than the average wholesale clothing house offers for the same price. In fact, you will procure, by ordering this number, equally as good if not a better garment than is usually retailed at $4.00. The coat is made in sack style only, two lower outside pockets, one breast pocket, is double stitched throughout, and made up to please those who want a first class garment.
Price for coat style 50.......**$3.00**

MEN'S LONG BLACK ALPACA COATS.

Style 51

The coats quoted below are what are termed long alpaca coats. The style is shown opposite. Anyone wishing a longer coat than our sack style and a little shorter coat than what is termed our ministerial style, will probably be suited exactly with the style shown opposite, in one of the numbers that we quote under heading of long black alpaca coats We have these coats in sizes from 34 to 42 inches breast measure; no larger or smaller sizes can be furnished

GOOD QUALITY OF MEN'S LONG BLACK ALPACA COAT.

No. 41C20 This coat is made from a fair quality of black alpaca cloth, exactly the same style as shown in our style 51, has wide facings, well made and trimmed throughout. The most satisfactory garment we have ever offered at this price.
Price for coat, style 51........**$2.00**

MEN'S EXTRA LONG BLACK ALPACA COAT.

No. 41C22 This is a better quality than the above number, made from a good weight black alpaca, a cloth with a high luster, and just such a garment as would cost you at least one-third more in any first class retail store. Made with wide facings, cut extra long.
Price for coat, style 51........**$2.50**

OUR BEST QUALITY OF MEN'S EXTRA LONG, BLACK ALPACA COAT.

No. 41C24 At $3.00 we offer our customers a coat in an extra long style that is certainly a most desirable garment. Made from a fine quality of jet black alpaca, double stitched seams, wide facings, a perfectly shaped coat, one that will fit and surely please those who wish a well made, nice appearing, satisfactory wearing garment
Price for coat, style 51........**$3.00**

MEN'S MINISTERIAL BLACK ALPACA COATS.

The two numbers quoted below are what are termed ministerial style coats. They are made single breasted style, as shown by fashion figure below, and considerably longer than our style 51. We have these coats in sizes from 34 to 42 inches breast. No larger or smaller sizes can be furnished.

MEN'S MINISTERIAL BLACK ALPACA COAT.

Style 52

No. 41C26 We have two special ministerial coats, and they are both most excellent value. We believe that anyone wishing a coat in this style wants a good article. We therefore have made up coats that we are sure will please our customers; this particular coat is made extra long, ministerial style, like style 52, from a good quality of black alpaca cloth. Extra well made, trimmed and finished, wide facings, guaranteed to fit and prove entirely satisfactory
Price for coat style 52 ....**$2.50**

OUR BEST QUALITY MINISTERIAL ALPACA COAT.

No. 41C28 This coat will certainly give our customers equally as satisfactory service as garments costing a great deal more money, as we have made this our special number and endeavored to give our trade a most excellent coat at this price. Made from a fine, high luster, extra quality of black alpaca cloth, a good weight. Double stitched throughout. Highly recommended by us
Price for coat, style 52........**$3.50**

MEN'S BLACK ALPACA COATS AND VESTS IN SACK STYLE.

We quote below an assortment of Men's Black Alpaca Coats and Vests, made in our own factory with a view of furnishing our patrons a high grade, well made, satisfactory line of summer coats and vests at a reasonable price. These coats and vests are made by us at as low a figure as any manufacturers turn out first class goods; and in adding only a small percentage of profit to the finished garments we claim the privilege of saying these coats and vests are better value at the price we offer, than you can buy at any wholesale house. The sizes run from 34 to 42 inches breast measure. We have no larger or small sizes. Please note that we furnish certain styles in these coats and vests, which is plainly stated below each description. We can furnish only the style as mentioned under each description.

MEN'S BLACK ALPACA COAT AND VEST, SACK STYLE.

No. 41C30 This coat and vest is made from a fine quality of black alpaca, is double stitched throughout. The coat is made round cut sack style, has wide facings, well shaped, has two lower outside pockets and one inside pocket. The vest is made single breasted style, no collar, well trimmed and finished.
Price for coat and vest, style 50, **$3.00**

OUR EXTRA QUALITY OF MEN'S BLACK ALPACA COAT AND VEST, IN SACK STYLE.

No. 41C32 This is a very fine, highly finished quality of black alpaca. This coat is made with double stitched seams, two lower outside pockets, one inside pocket, made the same as all our first class alpaca coats, only the quality and workmanship are the best that we can furnish in alpaca cloth. Vest is cut single breasted, no collar.
Price for coat and vest, style 50 . **$4.00**

MEN'S EXTRA LONG BLACK ALPACA COAT AND VEST.

No. 41C34 If you want a good quality of material and a splendid extra long style coat with a vest of the same material, we believe that in this number you will procure satisfactory garments. This coat is made in extra long style, from a splendid quality of black alpaca, double stitched seams, vest cut single breasted, six-button style, no collar. The garments are well made, trimmed and finished.
Price for coat and vest, style 51 **$4.50**

MEN'S MINISTERIAL STYLE BLACK ALPACA COAT AND VEST.

No. 41C36 The same material as the above, only made in ministerial style, which is an extra long coat. A very similar style to what is termed a single breasted Prince Albert. The coat is made from a splendid quality of black alpaca material, seams are all double stitched, well shaped. A nicely trimmed and made coat. The vest is of the same material, cut single breasted, without collar.
Price for coat and vest, style 52 . **$4.50**

MEN'S WORSTED CREPE CLOTH, MINISTERIAL STYLE COAT AND VEST.

No. 41C38 This coat is made from a worsted crepe cloth. It is a heavier weight than alpaca, a material that is especially the right kind for making a summer coat and vest that can be worn for dress purposes as well as for every day use We consider this coat and vest one of the best numbers in our line, an excellent quality of material made up in a manner that will satisfy anyone wishing a nice black cloth summer coat and vest The coat is made in ministerial style, like style 52. Vest is cut single breasted six-button.
Price for coat and vest, style 52 **$6.00**

MEN'S MINISTERIAL STYLE BLACK SERGE COAT AND VEST.

No. 41C40 This is a very fine quality of pure worsted serge, just the proper weight for a thin summer coat and vest, suitable for dress occasions, garments that can be worn at any time or place. Coat is made in ministerial style, with wide facings, well shaped. Vest is cut single breasted, with six buttons. Garments that we can especially recommend to you.
Price for coat and vest, style 52, **$7.00**

MEN'S BLUE SERGE COATS AND VESTS.

We quote below a good assortment of men's serge coats and vests. These coats are made unlined, suitable for warm weather wear They are well made, well trimmed and finished. Made from a good quality of material and cut over the best fitting patterns that our designer can produce Our line of summer serge coats and vests is certainly equal, if not superior, to any high grade manufactured line in this country, and the prices we certainly know are very much lower. Serge coats and vests are all made in round cut sack style only, in sizes from 34 to 42 inches breast measure We cannot furnish any other sizes.

MEN'S BLUE SERGE COAT AND VEST.

No. 41C42 This coat and vest is made from an all worsted navy blue serge The coat is made in round cut sack style, is unlined, or what is termed a skeleton coat. It is made with wide facings, well shaped, sewed so well that it will not rip; an altogether satisfactory garment for the money. The vest is made single breasted, five-button, no collar. If you desire the single coat only, you will note that we quote prices for a single coat as well as a single vest.
Price for coat and vest. **$4.00**
Price for coat 3.00
Price for vest 1.00

MEN'S NAVY BLUE SERGE COAT AND VEST.

No. 41C44 This coat and vest is made from a good quality of all pure worsted serge, a standard color, warranted not to fade. The coat is made in round cut sack style, is unlined, made with wide facings, two lower outside pockets, one inside pocket Seams are all taped and the sewing is first class. The vest is made single breasted, five-button.
Price for coat and vest.......**$5.00**
Price for coat 3.75
Price for vest.............. 1.25

EXTRA QUALITY OF MEN'S BLUE SERGE COAT AND VEST.

No. 41C46 This coat and vest is made from a very fine quality of navy blue serge If you want a summer coat and vest to be worn at any time or place, always look neat and dressy, a garment that will retain its color and give exceptional wear, we certainly believe that you will be pleased with this number. Coat is made in round cut sack style, has wide facings, no lining in back. Vest is made single breasted, five-button.
Price for coat and vest.......**$6.00**
Price for coat,.............. 4.50
Price for vest 1.50

OUR FINEST QUALITY OF MEN'S BLUE SERGE COAT AND VEST.

No. 41C48 This coat and vest is made from our finest quality of Australian worsted serge, a better material than is usually to be found in any unlined coats and vests, because this is a finer quality of goods than the average wholesale house makes up. The coat is made in round cut sack style, wide facings, no lining in back of coat Vest is made single breasted, five-button style, back of the vest is made of a fine quality of Italian lining.
Price for coat and vest **$8.00**
Price for coat.......... .. **6.00**
Price for vest **2.00**

YOUNG MEN'S, BOYS' AND CHILDREN'S CLOTHING

OF ALL KINDS, FOR SPRING AND SUMMER, 1905.

WE CARRY A LARGER VARIETY of young men's, boys' and children's clothing than you can possibly find in any retail store throughout the country. Our assortment comprises all the latest styles and novelties, and the steady increase in our business shows that the value of our garments, both as to price and quality, are appreciated. We are continually improving the make of our garments and know that we offer better made, better trimmed and better fitting garments than are usually found in boys' and children's clothing. We especially invite comparison of our goods with those sold by other houses, and are confident that the result will be in our favor. The immense output we have gives us many advantages over small dealers and we give our customers the benefit of the same.

OUR TERMS are the most liberal ever offered. You run absolutely no risk in dealing with us. We solicit your order with the understanding that we give you satisfaction in every particular. If garments which you buy from us are not exactly as represented, or if they do not please you for any reason whatsoever, they can be returned to us at our expense and your money, as well as expense you have had in obtaining goods, will cheerfully be refunded to you if desired, or exchange will be made for any other merchandise you may desire to obtain.

SIZES, STYLES AND MEASUREMENTS.

In ordering Young Men's, Boys' and Children's Clothing, please bear in mind that all Garments we offer are Ready to Wear Garments

and can therefore only be furnished in the sizes, styles and materials plainly stated under each number. **DO NOT ORDER OTHER SIZES OR STYLES,** as it will only delay the order and cause disappointment. We show below a table of measurements according to which all our suits are cut and in ordering it will be well to compare it with the measurements you have taken, and if you find that we could not fit you **WRITE TO US FIRST** and we will make a

SPECIAL PRICE IN MAKING GARMENTS TO ORDER

or send you samples of goods which can be furnished of the size required.

This table shows the measurements of our Young Men's and Boys' Long Pants Suits.

AGE	COAT		LENGTH OF COAT	PANTS		WEIGHT Lbs.
	CHEST Inches	SLEEVE Inches	Inches	WAIST Inches	INSEAM Inches	
14	30	27½	25½	28	28	90
15	31	28½	26½	29	29	100
16	32	29	26¾	30	30	110
17	33	30	27	31	31	120
18	34	30½	28	31-32	31-32	130
19	35	31	28½	32	32-33	135
20	36	31½	29	32-33	33-34	140

The weight and chest measure are for average size boys of this age.

If you find that your boy requires a larger coat than 36 inches chest measure, or pants more than 34 inches long, send for our Men's Ready Made or our Men's Custom Tailoring Sample Book.

This table shows the measurements of our Boys' Knee Pants Suits.

AGE	COAT		LENGTH OF COAT	PANTS	
	CHEST Inches	SLEEVE Inches	Inches	INSEAM Inches	OUTSEAM Inches.
8	24	22½	20	9¼	18
9	25	22¾	20½	10	18½
10	26	23	21	11	19
11	27	23½	21½	11½	20
12	28	24½	22½	12	21
13	29	25½	23½	12¾	21½
14	30	26¾	24½	13½	22½
15	31	28	25½	14	24
16	32	28½	26	14½	25

Boys' Three-Piece Knee Pants Suits are made in sizes 8 to 16 years; Two-Piece and Norfolk suits, 8 to 14 years only.

In ordering knee pants suits it is best to order by age. The table will aid you in selecting the right size.

IN ORDERING BOYS' AND CHILDREN'S CLOTHING

It is always best to use our regular measuring blank but should you not have one, take measure or give the information called for below for the kind of garment desired.

FOR BOYS' AND YOUNG MEN'S LONG PANTS SUITS

Give the Following Measurements and Information:

STYLE NUMBER OF SUIT______

AGE	HEIGHT	WEIGHT

	INCHES
BREAST—(See Figure A). Take coat off, measure all around breast, over vest at (1), close up under arms, snug but not tight. Tape should be over shoulder blades at back........	
WAIST—(See Figure C). Turn up vest, measure all around waist over pants at (6). Note that waist line is just above hip bones........	
SLEEVE—(See Figure B). Measure over the coat from middle of back (3) around to wrist joint at (5)........	
INSIDE SEAM—(See Figure C). Measure from close up in crotch at (7) to the heel seam of shoe at (8)........	

Boys' Long Pants Suits are made in sizes from 30 to 36 inches chest measure, the sizes usually worn by average size boys from 14 to 20 years of age.

No smaller sizes than 30 inches or larger than 36 inches chest measure can be furnished in long pants suits.

Be sure to give all the measurements and information we call for on any garment you may be ordering.

Always give Age, Height and Weight in ordering Young Men's, Boys' and Children's Clothing of any kind.

While we are very rarely out of goods or sizes ordered, it is nevertheless better to give two selections in case through some chance we may be out. There will then be no possibility of disappointment.

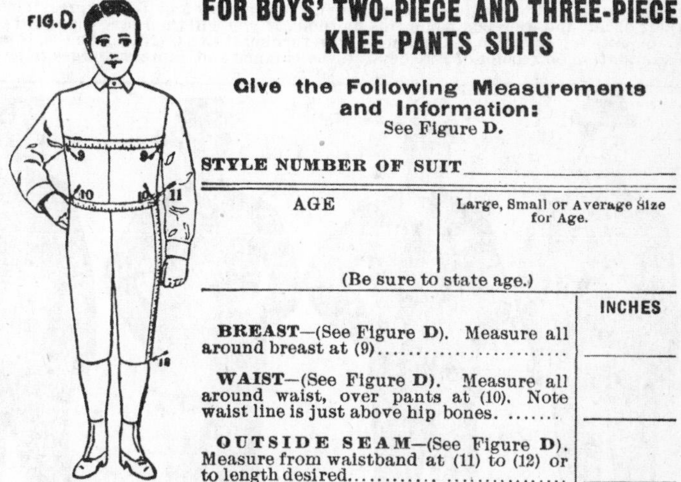

FOR BOYS' TWO-PIECE AND THREE-PIECE KNEE PANTS SUITS

Give the Following Measurements and Information:
See Figure D.

STYLE NUMBER OF SUIT______

AGE	Large, Small or Average Size for Age.

(Be sure to state age.)

	INCHES
BREAST—(See Figure D). Measure all around breast at (9)........	
WAIST—(See Figure D). Measure all around waist, over pants at (10). Note waist line is just above hip bones........	
OUTSIDE SEAM—(See Figure D). Measure from waistband at (11) to (12) or to length desired........	

Boys' Two-Piece and Norfolk Suits are made up in sizes to fit average size boys from 8 to 14 years of age, and Three-Piece Suits to fit average size boys from 8 to 16 years of age. See schedule of measures above. No larger or smaller sizes can be furnished in these styles.

FOR VESTEE AND BLOUSE SUITS

Give following information:

AGE.	Large, Small or Average Size for Age.	If these questions are answered correctly no measure will be necessary. Vestee and Blouse Suits are made in sizes to fit average size boys from 3 to 8 years of age. Russian suits from 2½ to 6 years only. No other sizes can be furnished.

Wash Suits, Waists and Knee Pants should be ordered by age only. Always state age and if boy is large or small for age.

FOR BOYS' RAINY WEATHER CLOTHING, SEE PAGE 919.

WRITE FOR OUR

FREE CLOTH SAMPLE BOOK No. 88C

IF YOU WANT TO SEE THE ACTUAL GOODS IN OUR BOYS' LINE OF CLOTHING.

FREE CLOTH SAMPLE BOOK OF BOYS' AND CHILDREN'S CLOTHING.

WE ISSUE A COMPLETE SAMPLE BOOK SHOWING CLOTH SAMPLES OF EVERYTHING WE MAKE IN BOYS' AND CHILDREN'S CLOTHING, AND THIS SAMPLE BOOK WILL BE SENT TO ANY ADDRESS BY MAIL, POSTPAID, FREE ON APPLICATION.

WE ILLUSTRATE AND DESCRIBE our complete line of boys' and children's clothing in this catalogue and we have tried by means of careful illustrations and descriptions to enable you to order direct from this book without waiting for samples. At the same time, if you are unable to make a satisfactory selection from this catalogue, or if you are not quite sure of the kind of a suit that you want, or if you prefer to first see the actual goods, then don't hesitate to write and ask for our free boys' and children's clothing sample book.

OUR SAMPLE BOOK of Boys' and Children's Clothing is a large sample book in which is pasted a cloth sample of every style of goods we use for boys' and children's clothing, showing samples of everything in boys' two and three-piece knee pants suits, everything in little boys' fancy suits, boys' and youths' long pants suits, everything in boys' and youths' reefers, overcoats and ulsters, a complete assortment, a wonderful display, much larger and better than you could find in any wholesale or retail store, all carefully described as to material, durability, etc., and offered at prices much lower than you can get elsewhere as shown by the prices in this catalogue. Every sample book contains complete illustrations, shows pictures of the different style garments and we send a cloth tape measure with every sample book. The book also contains our plain and simple instructions for ordering, so that there is no possibility of your making a mistake or getting unsatisfactory garments. With this sample book in your hands you can select just exactly the color, weight and quality of goods you want and can order as intelligently as if you were in a clothing store selecting the goods from stock.

OUR COMPLETE LINE of boys' and children's clothing is illustrated and described on the following pages. We would like for you, if convenient, to make your selection from the pages of this catalogue since we guarantee everything to please you in every way, or we will immediately return your money. At the same time if you would like to see the actual samples, don't hesitate at all, but simply write a postal and say, "Please send me your Boys' and Children's Clothing Sample Book," and it will go to you by return mail, postpaid, free with our compliments. Therefore, if you do not order your boys' clothing direct from this catalogue, don't fail to get our free Cloth Sample Book of Boys' and Children's Clothing before you buy elsewhere. We know that if we can place before you the actual samples and enable you to see the excellent quality of the goods we are furnishing at these prices, that you will not hesitate but will see that you can make a big saving by sending your order to us. The illustration will give you an idea of the appearance of this big handsome sample book of boys' and children's clothing. It is positively the greatest sample book in this line ever compiled, embracing all the new weaves, all the up to date and stylish fabrics, and every cloth is selected with the idea of wearing quality after thorough tests for durability. We can save you so much money on boys' and children's clothing, can give you such a uniformly higher quality of materials, so much better workmanship, in short, so much greater value at the price than can be secured from any other source, that you cannot afford to buy elsewhere.

BOYS & CHILDRENS
CLOTHING
SPRING AND SUMMER
1905
SEARS, ROEBUCK
& CO., Chicago

Our Boys' and Children's Clothing Sample Book contains about 90 samples and about 100 different styles of boys' garments, including suits, outing suits, wash goods waists and blouses. Sent free on application.

QUALITY GUARANTEE AND MONEY REFUND OFFER.

WE GUARANTEE the quality of every garment offered in this department to be strictly first class in every way. We accept every order with the understanding and agreement that if the garments we send you do not prove perfectly satisfactory in every way, you are at liberty to return them to us and we will promptly return your money and pay express charges both ways. Nearly all of our customers send the full amount of money with their order, and we recommend this method for you will then save the small extra charge of 25 to 50 cents that the express companies always ask on C. O. D. shipments for collecting the money and returning it to us. Nevertheless, if you prefer, we will send you any garment from this department C. O. D., subject to examination on receipt of $1.00 deposit, the balance and express charges to be paid when the goods are received, examined and found perfectly satisfactory.

YOUNG MEN'S AND BOYS' LONG PANTS SUITS.

THIS LINE OF SUITS is without a doubt the best selection of snappy and popular fabrics which we have ever been able to show. All the latest effects in woolens for spring are represented, and any young man who can be fitted in the sizes in which our young men's suits are made will surely save money by buying from this line.

ALL OUR LONG PANTS SUITS are cut in the very latest and most fashionable styles. The coats of all are made with broad padded shoulders, fronts are interlined with canvas and hair cloth so that they will remain in shape, and the workmanship on our garments will be found equal to tailor made suits usually offered for double the price.

UNDER EACH NUMBER will be found the style and size in which the suit is cut. No smaller or larger sizes than those given can be supplied. The largest chest measure we make in young men's suits is 36 inches, and the longest pants we can furnish are 34 inches in length. If larger sizes are needed selection must be made from our men's line.

Style 1 Style 3 Style 18 Style 21

STYLES OF YOUNG MEN'S AND BOYS' LONG PANTS SUITS.

For young men from 14 to 20 years, or 30 to 36 inches breast measure. We prefer that you use measuring blank, but if you have none give the measures called for under our instructions for measurements on page 907.

WORCESTER WOOLEN MILLS FANCY CHEVIOT SUITS.

A very neat black and gray mixed pattern in broken check effect, relieved by occasional red and green threads. A well trimmed and well made suit. Without a doubt the greatest value ever offered for the price. The coat is cut in round sack style. The vest has five buttons and is made without a collar. The pants are cut in the most prevailing style for spring.

No. 40C2001 Price for long pants suits, for young men from 14 to 20 years of age, in style 1 only............$3.75

HAYWARD MILLS FANCY CASSIMERE.

Made of a beautiful dark pattern with a blue background and relieved by alternating gray and orange lines which give it a stripe effect. Coats of this number are made in style 1. Vests five-button with notched collar. The coats are made with broad shoulder effect, canvas fronts so that they will retain their shape and will be found most substantially trimmed.

No. 40C2003 Price for long pants suits, for young men from 14 to 20 years of age, in style 1 only............$4.00

FANCY GREEN MIXED CHEVIOT SUITS

A very dressy pattern in dark green mixture with just enough of relief by faint orange and yellow doted lines. Coats are lined with good quality of Italian cloth; are made with padded shoulders, canvas fronts and will be found substantially made in every respect.

No. 40C2005 Price for long pants suits, for young men from 14 to 20 years of age, in style 1 only............$4.50

PARKER, WILDER & CO.'S ALL WOOL NAVY BLUE CHEVIOT SUITS.

A strictly all wool suit absolutely fast color. The garments are cut over the latest and most approved patterns, are strictly well tailored, have padded shoulders and shape retaining fronts. We guarantee to please you in workmanship, quality of material and fit. This suit can be furnished in either style 1 or 3. Be sure and state style desired and note the price of each style.

No. 40C2007 Price for long pants suits, for young men from 14 to 20 years of age in style 1............$5.00

No. 40C2008 Price for long pants suits in style 3............$5.25

FANCY MIXED CHEVIOT SUITS.

A very handsome and dressy pattern with black background and gray pin check effect, relieved from the plain by blue, red and yellow threads. If you favor us with an order for this suit you will receive a well tailored dressy garment, which is sure to please and which cannot possibly be obtained elsewhere for the price.

No. 40C2009 Price for long pants suits, for young men from 14 to 20 years of age, in style 1 only............$5.00

DARK DRAB CORDUROY SUITS.

Made up of a splendid quality of dark drab thick set corduroy, a closely ribbed fabric which is sure to give satisfaction. Every effort has been made to get up the suits in the most substantial manner possible. If you send us an order for one of these suits you will agree with us that it is the best suit ever produced for the price.

No. 40C2010 Price for long pants suits, for young men from 14 to 20 years of age, in style 1 only............$5.00

GRAY MIXED CHEVIOT SUITS.

Made of all wool durable material in black and dark gray mixed cheviot with a faint overplaid in dark green. A very dressy and popular material. Coats are made with padded shoulders, shape retaining fronts and are lined with a splendid quality of black Italian cloth. There is nothing neater for an every day business suit than this number.

No. 40C2011 Price for long pants suits, for young men from 14 to 20 years of age, in style 1 only $5.50

ALL WOOL FAST BLACK THIBET SUITS.

This very popular material makes a durable and dressy black suit which will keep its color. The coats are elegantly lined with black Italian cloth, have the popular broad shoulder effect and are made with canvas fronts so they will retain their shapes. Pants are cut in the most prevailing style, neatly shaped and rounded out at the bottom. If you are in need of a black suit at a popular price you will receive it by ordering this number.

No. 40C2013 Price for long pants suits, for young men from 14 to 20 years of age, in style 1 only $6.00

FANCY CHEVIOT SUITS.

In double and single breasted style. The material we use for this number is strictly pure wool and the pattern is a very handsome mixture of black, gray, green and orange. We can furnish this material in either styles 1 or 3. Be sure and state style wanted and note price of each style. These garments are thoroughly tailored in every respect.

No. 40C2015 Price for long pants suits, for young men from 14 to 20 years of age, in style 1 .... $6.00
No. 40C2016 Same in style 3 .. 6.25

ALL WOOL NAVY BLUE SERGE SUITS.

The suit in this material which we offer under this number is absolutely the best value which can possibly be produced. We guarantee the material to be strictly all wool, fast color, and the workmanship will be found perfect in every respect. Coats have broad padded shoulders, canvas fronts, which help to retain shape of the garments, and are elegantly lined with black Italian cloth. Pants are neatly shaped, rounded out at the bottom so that they will fit well over the shoe and are cut in the most prevailing width for spring.

No. 40C2017 Price for long pants suits, for young men from 14 to 20 years of age, in style 18 only $6.50

ALL WOOL BLACK CLAY WORSTED SUITS.

We do not offer a cheaper suit in black clay worsted for the reason that we know that it would not be an all wool garment, and unless clay worsted is strictly all wool it is sure to fade in a short time. We guarantee the garment which we offer under this number to be strictly pure wool, fast color. If you desire a black dressy suit you will get it by ordering this number. The suit will be found elegantly lined, cut in the latest and most approved style, and thoroughly well sewed throughout.

No. 40C2019 Price for long pants suits, for young men from 14 to 20 years of age, in style 1 .... $6.50
No. 40C2020 Same material in style 3 .... 6.75

DUVAL & CONE FANCY BROWN MIXED CASSIMERE.

A handsome up to date pattern in the popular new brown shade. The material is strictly all wool and guaranteed fast color. The pattern is broken check effect in mixtures of brown, gray and orange, relieved by occasional green lines. The coat of this number is made like style 18, as shown in our illustration of styles, is well padded, stiffened and tailored in first class manner.

No. 40C2021 Price for suits, for young men from 14 to 20 years of age, in style 18 only $6.50

CLINTON MILLS FANCY HERRING-BONE EFFECT CHEVIOT SUITS.

A beautiful pattern, strictly all wool material, color of which is a mixture of light and dark olive, relieved by light gray and orange. One of the handsomest patterns we have been able to obtain this season. Coats are made in style 18, with three outside pockets, broad padded shoulders, shape retaining fronts and are perfectly lined and tailored.

No. 40C2023 Price for suits, for young men from 14 to 20 years of age, in style 18 only $7.00

MEDIUM GRAY MIXED CHEVIOT SUITS.

A beautiful dressy pattern in a mixture of light and dark gray, relieved by colors in yellow and dark maroon. For spring and summer suits there is nothing handsomer than this number and any young man who likes to dress up to date will surely be pleased with it. For a splendidly made and handsomely trimmed garment, our price is ridiculously low. Made in style 18, as shown in illustration.

No. 40C2025 Price for suits, for young men from 14 to 20 years of age, in style 18 only $7.00

CURTIS & WARREN'S FANCY CASSIMERE SUITS.

A beautiful pattern in a handsome shade of gray, relieved by colorings in yellow and light blue. A dressy summer suit which will not soil easily. Coats are made like style 18, shown in illustrations of styles, with the popular broad shoulder effect, and canvas fronts which help to keep them always in shape. The trimmings we use for the suit nicely match the material and we guarantee you a perfect fitting garment in every respect.

No. 40C2027 Price for suits, for young men from 14 to 20 years of age, in style 18 only $7.00

PROVO MILLS ALL WOOL CHEVIOT SUITS.

Made in the popular brown shade in small check effect, relieved by scattered yellow and white lines. A beautiful dressy material which is bound to please and give excellent wear. This number is made up in either styles 18 or 21. Be sure and state style desired and note price of each style. The garments are handsomely trimmed and sewed throughout with silk, are well padded, stayed and have canvas fronts.

No. 40C2029 Price for suits, for young men from 14 to 20 years of age, in style 18 .... $7.50
No. 40C2030 Same material, in style 21 .... 7.75

CURTIS & WARREN'S FANCY CASSIMERE SUITS.

One of the prettiest and newest fabrics shown this season, which promises to be very popular for young men who like to dress up to date. Material is strictly all wool and its color is a mixture of dark brown, olive, gray and dark maroon. The suit is elegantly trimmed, made with the popular broad shoulder effect and will be found equal to tailor made suits which sell for more than double the price. Made in style 18 only.

No. 40C2031 Price for suits, for young men from 14 to 20 years of age, in style 18 only $7.50

FANCY BROWN CASSIMERE SUITS.

A very handsome dark brown mixture in all wool, relieved by overplaid in white and with occasional green threads, which give it a beautiful appearance. The suit is made in style 18, is exceptionally well trimmed and tailored. The coat has broad padded shoulders, canvas fronts and is cut from the most stylish pattern of the season.

No. 40C2033 Price for suits, for young men from 14 to 20 years of age, in style 18 only $8.00

CORONET MILLS WORSTED SUITS.

A very handsome dark silk mixed worsted, the background of which is relieved by a random mixture of green, yellow and red silk threads. This suit is made up in style 21, the popular long rolled double breasted style, and is elegantly trimmed and lined with a fine quality of Italian cloth and is, as you will find, a suit equal to tailor made garments of nearly double the price.

No. 40C2035 Price for suits, for young men from 14 to 20 years of age, in style 21 only $8.50

WENDALL FAY & CO.'S SILK MIXED CASSIMERE SUITS.

The material is a very handsome dark blue, relieved by an overplaid in red and white. A very dressy, stylish pattern, very popular with young men. The coat of this suit is made in style 18. Vest is single breasted, five buttons and notched collar. The pants are neatly shaped and rounded out so as to fit well over the shoes. Linings, trimmings and workmanship of the garments are the best.

No. 40C2037 Price for suits, for young men from 14 to 20 years of age, in style 18 only $8.50

KUNHARDT & STOCKTON'S GRAY CHECKED WORSTED SUITS.

A very popular fabric in dark gray with very small polka check in white. A very popular shade which makes a handsome spring and summer suit. The material is strictly pure wool worsted and the suit is tailored in first class manner; has broad padded shoulders and canvas fronts so that they will keep their shape. The vest is made five-button with notched collar. The pants are cut in the most stylish manner for the seasson.

No. 40C2039 Price for suits, for young men from 14 to 20 years of age, in style 18 only................ $9.00

STEPHEN SANFORD'S SILK MIXED WORSTED SUITS.

A beautiful dark pattern, almost black, with just enough of coloring in blue and red silk to give it a handsome appearance. Every effort has been made to make this suit a perfect garment in every respect. All the trimmings are the best possible for the price. The coats are made with the latest broad shoulder effect, are interlined with hair cloth and canvas so as to retain their shape and the workmanship will be found perfect. The coat is cut in the popular style 18, with three outside and one inside pocket and we believe that it is the best made suit ever produced for the price.

No. 40C2041 Price for suits, for young men from 14 to 20 years of age, in style 18 only $10.00

Style 27

YOUNG MEN'S OUTING COATS AND PANTS.

The great popularity of cool and comfortable outing suits is shown by the tremendous increase of sales in these garments, and we show, this season, better made and a more complete line than ever before. The fabrics we have selected are all snappy and stylish, especially well adapted for this style of suit. All the coats have broad padded shoulders and are tailored in the best possible manner. Pants have belt straps and a leather lined belt of the same material is furnished with each suit. In sizes to fit average sized young man from 14 to 20 years of age or measuring from 30 to 36 inches in breast.

Style 28

DARK FANCY MIXED OUTING COATS AND PANTS.

Nothing better can possibly be produced for the price than the coat and pants, with belt of same material attached, which we offer under this number. The material is a neat medium gray color in striped effect, formed by alternating orange and red lines. Coats are made with good deep facings. Pants are made full for belt straps and belt of same material is attached.

No. 40C2043 Price for outing coats and pants, for young men from 14 to 20 years of age, in style 27 only.... $3.50

MEDIUM COLORED OUTING FLANNEL COATS AND PANTS.

Made of splendid quality of outing flannel in a gray and brown mixed shade, which makes a very comfortable outing suit. The coat is made in round cut sack style with wide facings and with broad shoulder effect. Pants are made with the turned up bottoms, belt loops, suspender buttons on inside of waistband, and belt of the same material is furnished with the pants.

No. 40C2045 Price for outing coats and pants, for young men from 14 to 20 years of age, in style 27 only...... $4.00

DARK MIXED CHEVIOT OUTING SUITS.

Made of dark gray and olive mixed cheviot. A splendid material for garments of this kind, which will make a very comfortable and durable outing suit. Coat is made with French facings, has three outside pockets. Pants are cut in peg top style with turned up bottoms and belt of same material is attached to them. One of the best medium priced suits ever produced.

No. 40C2047 Price for outing coats and pants, for young men from 14 to 20 years of age, in style 27 only...... $4.50

FANCY MIXED CRASH OUTING COATS AND PANTS.

Made from all wool brown and gray mixed outing crash in striped effect, formed by green, orange and dark maroon lines. A very desirable pattern, which makes a dressy and comfortable suit. Coat is made one-half lined with three outside pockets. The pants are made with turned up bottoms in peg top and have a belt of the same material attached.

No. 40C2049 Price for outing coats and pants, for young men from 14 to 20 years of age, in style 27 only...... $4.75

FRED ALMAY'S FANCY OUTING FLANNEL COATS AND PANTS.

One of the most beautiful patterns in medium gray, relieved with colorings in green, red and orange, which give it a beautiful effect. This number can be furnished in either styles 27 or 28. Coats are one-half lined with deep facings and broad padded shoulders. The pants are made in peg top style with turned up bottoms and belt of same material is furnished with them.

No. 40C2051 Price for outing coats and pants, for young men from 14 to 20 years of age, in style 27....... $5.00
No. 40C2052 Same material, in style 28 .... 5.25

BROWN MIXED CASSIMERE OUTING COATS AND PANTS.

Made of all wool cassimere in medium brown shade, relieved by colorings in yellow. One of the most desirable patterns for this class of garments. Coats are made one-half lined with three outside pockets and with the popular broad shoulder effect. The pants are cut with turned up bottoms and in peg top style, and belt of the same material is furnished with pants.

No. 40C2053 Price for outing coats and pants, for young men from 14 to 20 years of age, in style 27 only... $5.00

MEDIUM GRAY STRIPED OUTING COATS AND PANTS.

A strictly all wool material in medium shade of gray with a small stripe effect. Coats are excellently trimmed and have broad padded shoulders, wide facings, three outside pockets and are cut in the most prevailing style. Pants have the turned up bottoms and belts of the same material attached.

No. 40C2055 Price for outing coats and pants, for young men from 14 to 20 years of age, in style 27 only.... $6.00

ALL WOOL BLUE SERGE OUTING COATS AND PANTS.

Made of all wool navy blue serge in the popular long rolled, double breasted style, illustrated as style 28. Coats are one-half lined and have broad shoulder effect and are thoroughly well trimmed throughout. Pants are made with turned up bottoms, belt straps and belts of the same material are furnished with them. Nothing better than this number for a cool and dressy summer suit.

No. 40C2057 Price for outing coats and pants, for young men from 14 to 20 years of age, in style 28 only..... $6.00

BOYS' KNEE PANTS SUITS.

OUR LINE OF KNEE PANTS SUITS consists of all the latest and most popular styles. Under each number we show the style and sizes in which the same can be furnished.

IN ORDERING be sure to notice the style in which the number is made, as each number can only be furnished in the exact style advertised.

WE WOULD SPECIALLY call your attention to the make of our knee pants suits. They will be found far superior to the usual make of garments of this kind. We make all our coats in the popular broad shoulder effect, well padded and with canvas fronts, which help to keep the garment always in shape. The seams of all our garments are double sewed and taped, so there is absolutely no chance for them to pull out. Pants are double sewed and taped, are made with good machine buttonholes on the flies and are provided with patent buttons. We also furnish a set of extra buttons and a patch piece of the material with each suit.

STYLE B71 Ages, 8 to 16 years. STYLE B72 Ages, 8 to 14 years. STYLE B73 Ages, 8 to 14 years. STYLE B74 Ages, 8 to 14 years.

OAKLAND MILLS CASSIMERE SUITS.

In dark brown mixed, which makes an excellent cool suit. Coats are made in round cut sack style. Vests single breasted. five-button. The pants are taped and double sewed throughout. We have a number of different patterns in this material and have cut them all up and placed them under one number and are offering them much below the usual price of suits in these materials.

No. 40C2062 Price for three-piece knee pants suits, for boys from 8 to 16 years of age, in style B71 only.....**$2.50**

WORCESTER WOOLEN MILLS DARK GRAY CHECKED CHEVIOT SUITS.

A splendid wearing and neatly appearing material in small dark gray check, relieved by colorings in green and brown. There is nothing better than this material for a durable, everyday suit which will not soil easily. The whole suit is substantially made and trimmed in a manner which cannot be duplicated anywhere for our price.

No. 40C2063 Price for three-piece knee pants suits, for boys from 8 to 16 years of age, in style B71 only....**$2.75**

MEDIUM GRAY CHEVIOT SUITS.

A handsome pattern, especially well suited for boys' three-piece suits. The material is medium weight dark gray shade with faint overplaid in light gray, red and green colorings. Coats are made with padded shoulders, shape retaining fronts and are neatly lined with a good quality of Italian cloth. Pants are double sewed and taped. We furnish extra buttons and patch piece with each suit.

No. 40C2065 Price for three-piece knee pants suits, for boys from 8 to 16 years of age, in style B71 only....**$2.75**

DARK BROWN MIXED CHEVIOT SUITS.

Made of all wool material in neat mixtures of dark brown and olive with faint overplaid formed by green and red lines. A handsome pattern which makes a very neat suit. Coat will be found well trimmed, neatly lined. Pants have patent buttons on waistband and flies and are taped throughout.

No. 40C2067 Price for three-piece knee pants suits, for boys from 8 to 16 years of age, in style B71 only.....**$3.00**

DOUGLAS MILLS CASSIMERE SUITS.

Made of brown mixed cassimere, relieved by colorings in gray and yellow. Splendid material for a durable every day suit Coats are thoroughly well made with broad padded shoulders, all seams secured. Pants are taped and double sewed and extra buttons and patch piece are furnished with each suit.

No. 40C2069 Price for three-piece knee pants suits, for boys from 8 to 16 years of age, in style B71 only....**$3.00**

PARKER WILDER & CO.'S ALL WOOL NAVY BLUE CHEVIOT SUITS.

Made of strictly all wool material in a handsome shade of dark navy blue, always popular for boys' clothing. Coats are made with broad shoulder effect. have shape retaining fronts, all seams doubly stitched so that they cannot pull out, and the workmanship in general will be found perfect. Extra buttons and patch piece are furnished with each suit.

No. 40C2071 Price for three-piece knee pants suits, for boys from 8 to 16 years of age, in style B71 only....**$3.50**

ALL WOOL BROWN CHEVIOT SUITS.

Made of all wool material in the new brown shade which is so popular this season If you want a strictly up to date suit for little money do not overlook this number Coats are cut in the very latest style with broad padded shoulders and canvas fronts so that they will retain their shape, and all seams are secured so that they cannot pull out. The pants are made with elastic waistband, patent suspender buttons and are taped throughout.

No. 40C2079 Price for three-piece knee pants suits, for boys from 8 to 16 years of age, in style B71 only....**$3.50**

DUVAL & CONES' ALL WOOL CASSIMERE SUITS.

A very handsome all wool material in dark brown mixture with colorings in orange. A suit which is bound to give satisfactory wear. The coat is made in round cut sack style with outside breast pocket and two lower pockets and with broad shoulder effect and stiffened fronts. Trimmings, linings and workmanship on the garments will be found far superior to those generally found in suits at this price. All seams on the garments are double sewed, so that there is absolutely no chance for them to pull out. Pants are taped and have patent buttons on fly and waistband. We also furnish extra buttons and patch piece with each suit.

No. 40C2073 Price for three-piece knee pants suits, for boys from 8 to 16 years of age, in style B71 only....**$3.50**

FANCY GRAY MIXED WORSTED SUITS.

We have a number of small quantities in all wool worsted material, in neat medium gray shades, and we offer them under this number. Suits are made in round cut sack style, neatly lined, trimmed and thoroughly well made in every respect and we are confident that suits in similar material and make cannot be obtained elsewhere for nearly double our price.

No. 40C2075 Price for three-piece knee pants suits, for boys from 8 to 16 years of age, in style B71 only.....**$4.00**

FANCY LIGHT GRAY MIXED CASSIMERE SUITS.

A very handsome pattern which is the very thing for a dressy summer suit. The material is strictly pure wool in medium gray, relieved by colorings in red and yellow, which give it a very handsome effect. Suits are elegantly lined and tailored, have the latest broad shoulder effect, shape retaining fronts and double seams throughout so that there is absolutely no chance for them to rip.

No. 40C2083 Price for three-piece knee pants suits, for boys from 8 to 16 years of age, in style B71 only.....**$4.00**

ALL WOOL NAVY BLUE SERGE SUITS.

We are confident that the navy blue serge suits which we offer under this number are of better material, better trimmed and better made in every respect than suits of this popular material which are usually offered for about $8.00 to $10.00. The coats of our suits are padded, interlined with canvas and haircloth, so that they will keep their shape, and all seams are taped and double sewed, so that there is absolutely no chance for them to pull out. Pants are made with taped seams and patent buttons on fly and waistband.

No. 40C2077 Price for three-piece knee pants suits, for boys from 8 to 16 years of age, in style B71 only.....**$4.50**

ALL WOOL FAST BLACK CLAY WORSTED SUITS.

For confirmation suits or dressy Sunday suits there is nothing better than a fine all wool clay worsted We absolutely guarantee the suit we offer under this number to be strictly fast color and all wool. The coats are elegantly trimmed, made with broad shoulder effect, double stitched and taped seams, and are interlined with canvas and haircloth so that they will retain their shape. The pants are double sewed and taped, have patent buttons on fly and waistband.

No. 40C2081 Price for three-piece knee pants suits, for boys from 8 to 16 years of age, in style B71 only.....**$4.50**

BLACK AND WHITE WORSTED CASSIMERE SUITS.

A dark pattern, splendid wearing material which is bound to give good satisfaction. The whole suit is thoroughly well trimmed, substantially lined and interlined, padded, and in every way gotten up in first class manner Coat has three outside pockets and one inside pocket. Vest is cut five-button with notched collar. The pants are taped and double sewed. Extra buttons and patch piece are furnished with each suit.

No. 40C2085 Price for three-piece knee pants suits, for boys from 8 to 16 years of age, in style B71 only.....**$4.50**

ALL WOOL BROWN MIXED WORSTED SUITS.

A very handsome up to date pattern. Strictly all wool worsted material in a handsome shade of brown, relieved by colorings in red and orange silk. Coats are made in the popular broad shoulder effect, are interlined with canvas and haircloth so that they will keep in shape and are thoroughly trimmed throughout. Pants are made with elastic waistband in the smaller sizes and regular skirting in the larger ones. All seams are double stitched and taped.

No. 40C2087 Price for three-piece knee pants suits, for boys from 8 to 16 years of age, in style B71 only....**$5.00**

FINEST OF WOOL WORSTED SUITS.

The suit which we offer under this number is made of much finer material than is usually shown for boys' clothing. The pattern is a handsome striped effect with black background, relieved by colorings in yellow, green and light gray. Every effort has been made to produce a perfect suit in every respect, Coats are well padded, interlined with canvas and haircloth. All seams are taped and double sewed so that there is absolutely no chance for them to pull out. Vest is cut with five buttons and notched collar. Pants have secured seams throughout and are provided with patent buttons on fly and waistband.

No. 40C2089 Price for three-piece knee pants suits, for boys from 8 to 16 years of age, in style B71 only.....**$6.00**

BOYS' TWO-PIECE KNEE PANTS SUITS.

This style of suit consists of double breasted jacket and one pair of knee pants, and can be furnished in sizes for average sized boys from 8 to 14 years of age the largest breast measure being 30 inches. In ordering, it is always best to state the age of the boy, and if he is large or small for his age

WORCESTER WOOLEN MILLS GRAY CHECKED TWO-PIECE CHEVIOT SUITS.

It is, without doubt, the best suit we have ever been able to furnish for the price The pattern is a handsome dark gray and black mixture, relieved by light coloring in red and green The garment is made up in the most substantial manner possible, and is better made and better trimmed than suits which are usually sold for about double the price.

No. 40C2091 Price for two-piece knee pants suits, for boys from 8 to 14 years of age, in style B72 only......**$1.75**

HAYWARD MILLS FANCY CASSIMERE SUITS.

A very neat, dark pattern in a mixture of dark gray and olive, with a light coloring in olive and red; made with broad shoulder effect; canvas fronts; all seams taped. Extra buttons and patch piece are attached to each suit.

No. 40C2093 Price for two-piece knee pants suits, for boys from 8 to 14 years of age, in style B72 only......**$2.00**

ESSEX MILLS STRIPED CHEVIOT SUITS.

A very popular fabric for this class of garments, in medium colored mixture of dark blue, light blue and olive in striped effect. If you give us an order for this suit you will receive a better made and better trimmed garment than is usually offered for such a price. All seams are double sewed and taped; coats have padded shoulders and canvas fronts

No. 40C2095 Price for two-piece knee pants suits, for boys from 8 to 14 years of age, in style B72 only......**$2.25**

FANCY MIXED CHEVIOT SUITS.

A very dressy pattern in a mixture of dark brown, gray, red and light olive A very popular pattern, made in double breasted style, as shown in illustration for style B72, well padded, fronts interlined with canvas so that they will keep their shape and all seams taped so they cannot possibly rip. The pants are double sewed and taped throughout, having patent buttons for suspenders and fly. Extra buttons and patch piece of material are furnished with them.

No. 40C2097 Price for two-piece knee pants suits, for boys from 8 to 14 years of age, in style B72 only..**$2.50**

DRAB CORDUROY TWO-PIECE SUITS.

In this number we offer a suit of the best thick set corduroy, in handsome shade of dark drab A well made suit in every particular, and the large quantities of suits in this material which we sell shows that the exceptional value which we offer is appreciated.

No. 40C2098 Price for two-piece knee pants suits, for boys from 8 to 14 years of age, in style B72 only..**$2.50**

ALL WOOL CASSIMERE SUITS.

A very neat, dark pattern in black background with a small broken check effect in gray A neat pattern which will not show the dirt easily. The suit is thoroughly well made, with broad padded shoulders, stiffened fronts, secured seams and extra buttons and patch piece of the material are furnished with it

No. 40C2099 Price for two-piece knee pants suits for boys from 8 to 14 years of age, in style B72 only..**$2.50**

ALL WOOL NAVY BLUE CHEVIOT TWO-PIECE SUITS.

Made of strictly pure wool cheviot in a handsome shade of dark blue, absolutely fast color. Suit is neatly trimmed, lined with black Italian cloth, interlined with canvas and shoulders are padded. Pants are double sewed and taped throughout, and have patent suspender and fly buttons.

No. 40C2101 Price for two-piece knee pants suits, for boys from 8 to 14 years of age, in style B72 only..**$2.50**

FANCY LIGHT MIXED CHEVIOT SUITS.

A very handsome, bright and dressy pattern in a broken check effect, the colorings of which are light gray, black and yellow, with faint overplaid formed by blue and green dotted lines. Nothing better for a handsome summer suit, which will be found elegantly trimmed and well tailored in every respect and of exceptional value for the price

No. 40C2103 Price for two-piece knee pants suits, for boys from 8 to 14 years of age in style B72 only..............**$3.00**

BAUENDAHL'S ALL WOOL CHEVIOT SUITS.

A very pretty pattern in a mixture of dark brown and gray with a light coloring in yellow, blue and red. Material is medium weight and known for splendid wearing qualities Coats are made in double breasted style, with the latest long roll lapels, are very well tailored, lined, interlined and padded so that they will always keep in shape. Extra buttons and patch piece of the material are furnished with each suit.

No. 40C2113 Price for two-piece knee pants suits, for boys from 8 to 14 years of age, in style B72 only...**$3.00**

ALL WOOL NAVY BLUE SERGE TWO-PIECE SUITS.

We take special pride in making up our serges because our sales of suits in this material has increased tremendously. The material we use is strictly all wool. The coats are well padded, interlined with canvas and hair cloth. All seams are taped and double sewed so that it is absolutely impossible to rip them. The pants are made with all the seams taped, have patent buttons on fly and waistband. No more substantial suit can possibly be produced for the price.

No. 40C2105 Price for two-piece knee pants suits, for boys from 8 to 14 years of age, in style B72 only...**$3.50**

PROVO MILLS FANCY CASSIMERE SUITS.

One of the prettiest and brightest patterns which we have been able to obtain this season. Its color is black background, with pin check effect, formed by green, olive, red and blue threads with an overplaid in white. This number is made in style B72, as illustrated. The coats are made with the popular broad shoulder effect, the fronts are interlined with canvas so that they will keep their shape, and the workmanship in general of the suit is far superior to the usual run of boys' clothing for the price. Extra buttons and patch piece of material are attached to each suit.

No. 40C2107 Price for two-piece knee pants suits, for boys from 8 to 14 years of age, in style B72 only...**$3.50**

PURE WOOL BLACK CLAY WORSTED DOUBLE BREASTED CONFIRMATION OR SUNDAY SUITS.

There is nothing better made than the suit we offer under this number. All wool, black clay worsted suits which we make are absolutely fast color. Every seam of the garments are double sewed and taped so there is absolutely no chance for them to pull out. The shoulders are well padded and the fronts are interlined with canvas and hair cloth to help keep their shape. We take special pride in making all of our clay worsted suits in the most perfect manner possible.

No. 40C2109 Price for two-piece knee pants suits, for boys from 8 to 14 years of age, in style B72 only...**$3.50**

ALL WOOL DARK CHECKED WORSTED SUITS.

In neat small checked pattern the colorings of which are dark blue and green. A perfectly made suit in every particular. Cut in the latest style with long rolled lapels and broad shoulder effect. The fronts of the garments are interlined with canvas and hair cloth. All seams are taped and double sewed and every part of the workmanship of the suit will be found perfect.

No. 40C2111 Price for two-piece knee pants suits, for boys from 8 to 14 years of age, in style B72 only...**$4.00**

NORFOLK JACKETS AND PANTS.

These garments are made in sizes for average sized boys from 8 to 14 years of age only and can be furnished either in single or double breasted, as described in each number. In ordering, please state age of boy and whether boy is small for his age. (See illustrations of styles B73 and B74).

FANCY PIN CHECKED CHEVIOT SUITS.

A neat pattern in pin check effect, colors of which are dark and light olive, relieved by occasional blue lines. The best suits which can possibly be produced for the price in this style. The garment is made up in style B73, single breasted Norfolk, as illustrated, and is substantially trimmed, lined and tailored.

No. 40C2115 Price for single breasted Norfolk suits, for boys from 8 to 14 years of age, in style B73 only..**$2.00**

FANCY CASSIMERE NORFOLK SUITS.

A pretty bright pattern, especially well adapted for this style of garments, the color of which is a random mixture of dark green, olive, red, blue and gray. A very dressy pattern especially popular this season. Suit is made in single breasted Norfolk style, like style B73, is well lined and substantially made throughout.

No. 40C2117 Price for single breasted Norfolk suits, for boys from 8 to 14 years of age, in style B73 only...**$2.50**

ALL WOOL NAVY BLUE CHEVIOT DOUBLE BREASTED NORFOLK SUITS.

A popular style made up in all wool, navy blue cheviot, which we guarantee to be absolutely fast color. The illustration of style B74 shows you how garment is made. It is a long rolled double breasted Norfolk with two plaits in the back and two in front and with a belt of the same material attached. All seams of the garment are taped and double sewed so that they cannot pull out.

No. 40C2119 Price for double breasted Norfolk suits, for boys from 8 to 14 years of age, in style B74 only...**$2.75**

FANCY CASSIMERE DOUBLE BREASTED NORFOLK SUITS.

A beautiful, bright and dressy pattern with black background with just enough coloring in yellow, gray and red to give it a handsome effect. The material is pure wool and the suit is elegantly trimmed and tailored. Coat is cut in double breasted style, like illustration of style B74.

No. 40C2121 Price for double breasted Norfolk suits, for boys from 8 to 14 years of age, in style B74 only...**$3.50**

BOYS' OUTING COATS AND PANTS.

This is one of the latest styles in boys' wear and promises to be very popular. The suit consists of three-button round cut sack coat and pair of knee pants, with belt of same material attached, and, if desired, a cap of the same material can be furnished with it. Please notice that the price of cap is quoted separate and is only furnished if desired. (See illustration of style B75.)

DARK OLIVE MIXED OUTING COATS AND PANTS.

Style B75

A neat dark mixture in herringbone striped effect, the color of which is a mixture of dark olive and gray, relieved by light coloring in dark maroon. The coat is cut as illustrated in style B75 and has three outside pockets. The pants have belt straps and belt of the same material attached. The suit makes a cool and comfortable summer suit.

No. 40C2123 Price for outing coats and pants, for boys from 8 to 16 years of age, in style B75 only ..**$2.50**

No. 40C2124 Cap to match above suit. Sizes, 6½, 6⅝, 6¾, 6⅞ and 7. Price, each.....**30c**

STURSBERG, SHELL & CO.'S WOOL CRASH OUTING COATS AND PANTS.

A very pretty mixture in medium shade of olive, in small pin check effect, relieved by colorings in green and orange. A splendid appearing, durable garment. Coat is made as illustrated in style B75, with three outside pockets, substantially lined with black Italian cloth and thoroughly well tailored. Pants have belt straps and a leather lined belt of the same material attached.

No. 40C2125 Price for outing coats and pants, for boys from 8 to 16 years of age, in style B75 only.........**$3.00**

No. 40C2126 Cap to match above suit. Sizes, 6½, 6⅝, 6¾, 6⅞ and 7. Price, each....................**35c**

DUVAL & CONE'S ALL WOOL LIGHT GRAY MIXED CASSIMERE COATS AND PANTS.

A very stylish pattern in a light gray and black mixture. Just the fabric for this style of suit. The suit consists of three-button, round cut sack coat and pair of pants with leather lined belt of the same material attached. The coat has broad padded shoulders, shape retaining fronts and is neatly and substantially made throughout.

No. 40C2127 Price for outing coats and pants, for boys from 8 to 16 years of age, in style B75 only............**$3.50**

No. 40C2128 Cap to match above suit. Sizes, 6½, 6⅝, 6¾, 6⅞ and 7. Price, each..........................**40c**

ALL WOOL NAVY BLUE SERGE OUTING COATS AND PANTS.

There is nothing nicer made than this strictly pure wool, navy blue serge suit, for a comfortable dressy summer suit. The suit is cut in three-button, round cut sack style with three outside pockets, has the latest broad shouldered effect and is interlined with canvas and hair cloth so that it will keep its shape. The seams are double sewed and taped and pants are taped throughout and have belt straps and a leather lined belt of the same material attached.

No. 40C2129 Price for outing coats and pants, for boys from 8 to 16 years of age, in style B75 only.........**$4.00**

No. 40C2130 Cap to match above suit. Sizes, 6½, 6⅝, 6¾, 6⅞ and 7. Price, each....................**45c**

JUVENILE SUITS.

The splendid assortment of pretty fabrics and styles which we show under this heading deserves especial attention. Every conceivable novelty in juvenile clothing is represented, and we believe that our prices are the lowest which can possibly be made on honestly made goods. Note carefully the sizes in which each number is made.

DARK BROWN AND GOLD MIXED CASSIMERE NORFOLK SUITS.

This number is made in plain Norfolk style, with two plaits front and back and belt of the same material. Coat has two outside pockets with flaps. The material is a splendid quality of Union cassimere in dark brown and gold mixture. A suit of exceptional value for the price.

No. 40C2131 Price for Norfolk suits, for boys from 3 to 8 years of age only..........**$1.50**

NAVY BLUE DOUBLE BREASTED NORFOLK SUITS.

A splendid little garment, made as illustrated; it has a large plait front and back and belt with German silver buckle attached, and is trimmed with neat fancy metal buttons. The material is a good quality of blue melton cloth and the garment is thoroughly well sewed, all seams being double stitched so they cannot rip. Pants are taped and made closed fronts.

No. 40C2133 Price for double breasted Norfolk suits, for boys from 3 to 8 years of age only..........**$1.95**

DOUBLE BREASTED NORFOLK SUIT.

Made of a handsome pattern of dark gray cassimere in a striped effect formed by alternating green, red and white stripes. The suit is made imitation double breasted style, has a large plait and two tucks in the back and four tucks in front. It is trimmed with neat fancy buttons, has a belt of the same material and a black silk bow tie is attached.

No. 40C2135 Price for double breasted Norfolk suits, for boys from 3 to 8 years of age only.......**$2.00**

If you would like to see samples of these suits, write for our

FREE SAMPLE BOOK No. 88C.

FANCY MIXED ETON NORFOLK SUITS.

Made of a very handsome pattern in all wool cheviot, the color of which is a mixture of dark brown, olive and gray, which is relieved by faint alternating stripes of green and red. The garment is made as illustrated, is neatly trimmed with fancy metal buttons, has a substantial leather belt and a brown silk tie is attached. The suit is exceptional value for the price.

No. 40C2137 Price for Eton suits, for boys from 3 to 8 years of age only.........**$2.25**

ALL WOOL BLUE CHEVIOT FANCY NORFOLK SUITS.

A very handsome style, made as shown in illustration, the front of which is neatly trimmed with five rows of black silk soutache and nine small white pearl buttons. The garment is provided with a belt of the same material and has two plaits in the back. This is a very popular style and is sure to give satisfaction.

No. 40C2139 Price for fancy Norfolk suits, for boys from 3 to 8 years of age only.........**$2.50**

DOUBLE BREASTED NORFOLK SUITS.

Another very handsome style. The little coat is made with double breasted front and two plaits in front and one in back; has a belt of the same material attached. A neatly embroidered shield is furnished with the suit. The material we use for it is a neat dark brown mixture in a pin check effect. You will find the garment thoroughly well tailored.

No. 40C2140 Price for double breasted Norfolk suits, for boys from 3 to 8 years of age only............**$2.50**

FANCY CHEVIOT ETON SUITS.

A very handsome style, made just as illustrated. The large shield front is bound in red and trimmed with twelve small black buttons. A beautiful red silk tie is attached to the garment and a fancy brown leather belt is furnished with the suit. The pattern is a beautiful mixture in a medium shade, the colors of which are olive, gray green and red.

No. 40C2141 Price for fancy Eton suits, for boys from 3 to 8 years of age only.........**$3 00**

ALL WOOL NAVY BLUE SERGE ETON NORFOLK SUITS.

Made in an entirely new style. It is a fly front garment and has three plaits in front and back. Is ornamented with two rows of black and white braid down front and back. A splendid black leather belt and black silk tie are attached to the suit. The material is strictly pure wool navy blue serge.

No. 40C2143 Price for fancy Norfolk suits, for boys from 3 to 8 years of age only.........**$3.25**

ALL WOOL BROWN SERGE FANCY NORFOLK SUITS.

A very handsome little garment, made as illustrated, with large shield front and one plait in the center of it, which has a neat silk embroidered emblem on it. The front is also ornamented with four clusters of brown pea buttons. The back of the garment has two box plaits and a belt of the same material is attached. We also furnish a bow of peau de soie silk with it. The little pants are lined and taped throughout.

No. 40C2145 Price for Eton Norfolk suits, for boys from 4 to 8 years of age only..........**$3.50**

FANCY ROUGH RIDER SUITS.

This is one of the handsomest styles ever produced for the little fellows. The material is a beautiful shade of golden brown corduroy. The illustration will give you an idea as to how the suit is made. It has a small Eton collar trimmed with silk stars on each corner, two outside breast pockets with flaps made to button, the cuffs are turned up and a belt of the same material is attached. Belt, cuffs and shoulder straps are bound with yellow silk soutache. A silk embroidered emblem will be found on the left arm, and the whole suit is trimmed with neat firegilt brass buttons. Pants are lined throughout and have a yellow silk stripe down the side. One of the most popular novelties. We are confident that it cannot be obtained elsewhere at our price.

No. 40C2147 Price for Rough Rider suits, for boys from 3 to 8 years of age only..........................**$3.50**

BOYS' BLOUSE SUITS.

Sizes, 3 to 8 years. Order by age only and state if boy is large or small for age.

BLUE CHEVIOT SAILOR BLOUSE SUITS.

Made of a good quality of wool and cotton mixed cheviot. The blouse is made with large sailor collar which is trimmed with black tape and two rows of red silk soutache. A detachable shield is attached and cord and whistle are furnished with the suit. The material is wool and cotton mixed cheviot in a navy blue and we consider the suit the best which possibly can be produced for the price.

No. 40C2151 Price for blouse suits, for boys from 3 to 8 years of age only.....**$1.35**

FANCY CASSIMERE ETON BLOUSE SUITS.

A beautiful little garment made in double breasted style, as illustrated, is neatly trimmed with metal buttons. It has a small Eton collar, neatly plaited, cuffs made to button and a black silk tie is attached. The material is a very handsome mixture of green, brown and olive.

No. 40C2153 Price for blouse suits, for boys from 3 to 8 years of age only **$1.75**

MEDIUM GRAY STRIPED CHEVIOT SAILOR BLOUSE SUITS.

The material we use for this is all wool, in medium gray shade in a striped effect. The large sailor collar on this number is trimmed with five rows white silk soutache. The suit has a neatly embroidered shield of the same material attached, and a black silk bow tie is furnished with it. It is the best all wool suit which can possibly be produced for the price.

No. 40C2155 Price for blouse suits, for boys from 3 to 8 years of age only............**$2.00**

FANCY GRAY MIXED CHEVIOT ETON BLOUSE SUITS.

The material for this suit is a handsome mixture of dark gray and green in a striped effect, relieved by green and brown silk spots. The blouse is made in double breasted style, as illustrated, has neatly plaited cuffs, elastic bottom, and a black silk bow tie is furnished with it. Pants are taped and made closed front.

No. 40C2157 Price for Eton blouse suits, for boys from 3 to 8 years of age only.........**$2.50**

ALL WOOL RED SERGE SAILOR BLOUSE SUITS.

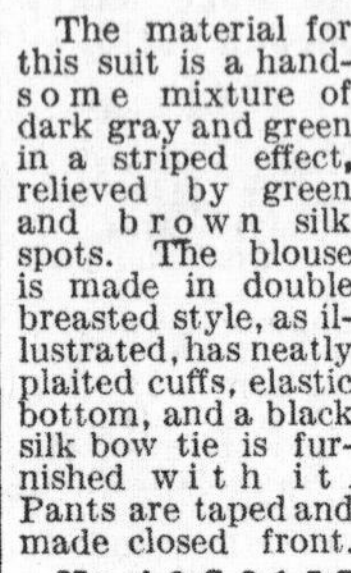

A very handsome garment, which is very popular. The material is all wool serge in a handsome red shade. The garment is made with a large sailor collar trimmed with seven rows of silk soutache. It has a neatly embroidered shield, a silk embroidered emblem on the left arm and a silk tie is attached. Pants are taped and lined throughout.

No. 40C2159 Price for blouse suits, for boys from 3 to 8 years of age only...........................**$2.75**

ALL WOOL NAVY BLUE SERGE BLOUSE SUITS.

This is another very handsome garment, made of strictly pure wool navy blue serge with a large sailor collar, which is trimmed with four rows of black silk tape; a handsomely embroidered shield is attached and a black silk tie is furnished with it. The cuffs on the garment are neatly plaited and made to button. Pants are fully lined and taped and made with closed front.

No. 40C2161 Price for blouse suits, for boys from 3 to 8 years of age only..........**$3.00**

BUSTER BROWNS AND RUSSIAN SUITS.

Sizes, 2½ to 6 Years only. Order by Age only, and State if Boy is Large or Small for Age.

RED FLANNEL BUSTER BROWN SUITS.

Made of a splendid quality of all wool red flannel, with a large shield front, neatly trimmed with fancy metal buttons and provided with a belt of the same material. The collar is trimmed with black tape and a black silk bow tie is furnished with the suit. Pants are taped through seat and made in bloomer style. A remarkable value.

No. 40C2163 Price for Buster Brown suits for boys from 2½ to 6 years of age only........**$2.00**

BLUE SERGE BUSTER BROWN SUITS.

Another handsome suit, made exactly as shown in illustration, with an Eton collar, which is neatly trimmed with black tape and black soutache, and the shield front is trimmed with handsome white pearl buttons and a belt of the same material is attached to the suit. The material is a splendid quality of navy blue serge, which will give satisfactory wear. Pants are fully lined and taped and made in bloomer style.

No. 40C2165 Price for Buster Brown suits, for boys from 2½ to 6 years of age only.................................**$2.35**

DARK BROWN ALL WOOL BUSTER BROWN SUITS.

A very handsome garment, made with Eton collar, plaited cuffs, and has a substantial black leather belt attached. The front is trimmed with two rows of fancy brass buttons, and the left sleeve has a silk embroidered emblem on it, and a silk bow to match the material is attached to the suit. Pants are fully taped and made in bloomer style. A beautiful, dressy garment.

No. 40C2167 Price for Buster Brown suits, for boys from 2½ to 6 years of age only....**$2.50**

FANCY MIXED CHEVIOT BUSTER BROWN SUITS.

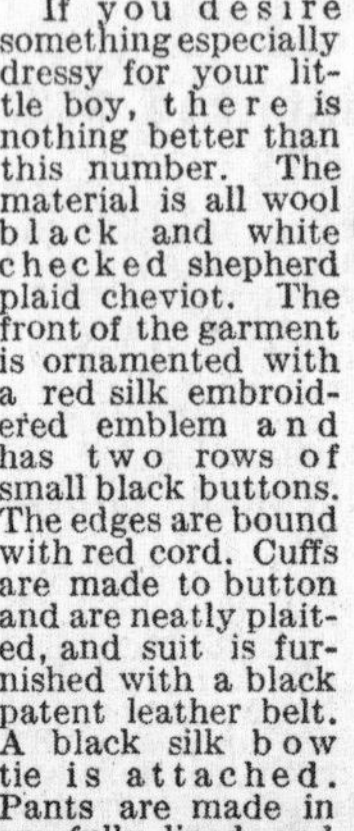

The material is homespun and its color is a medium shade, a gray and green mixture, relieved by green, yellow and red silk lines which give it a very dressy effect. It is made double breasted, front neatly trimmed with ivory buttons, has open plaited cuffs, a detachable white linen collar and black silk bow tie are furnished, and a black patent leather belt is attached to the garment. For a dressy summer suit there is nothing equal to this number.

No. 40C2169 Price for Buster Brown suits, for boys from 2½ to 6 years of age only.............................**$2.75**

ALL WOOL RED SERGE BUSTER BROWN SUITS.

A red serge is a very popular material for this style and is sure to give satisfactory wear. This number is made with three plaits down front, trimmed with neat brass buttons and is ornamented with three black and white silk stars in front. A black silk bow tie is attached to the suit and a black leather belt is furnished with it. Pants are lined throughout and made in bloomer style.

No. 40C2171 Price for Buster Brown suits, for boys from 2½ to 6 years of age only..............................**$2.75**

FANCY MIXED CASSIMERE SUITS.

This is one of the handsomest materials we have been able to obtain. Its color is a medium shade of gray in a small check formed by dark gray and olive lines. The front is neatly trimmed, as shown in illustration, and the edges of the collar and front are bound with black and red cord and a red silk bow tie is attached. A handsome leather belt to match the material is furnished with it. Pants are double sewed and taped and made in bloomer style.

No. 40C2173 Price for Buster Brown suits, for boys from 2½ to 6 years of age only...............................**$3.00**

ALL WOOL NAVY BLUE RUSSIAN SUITS.

A very handsome style, made fly front, has a large, neatly trimmed sailor collar and a handsome silk embroidered shield attached. A black leather belt is furnished with the garment, cuffs are neatly plaited (made to button) and on the left arm is a handsomely embroidered emblem. Nothing has ever been produced to equal this suit for the price.

No. 40C21[illegible] Price for Russi[illegible] suits, for boys fr[illegible] 2½ to 6 years of ag[illegible] only..........**$3.50**

FANCY SHEPHERD PLAID BUSTER BROWN SUITS.

If you desire something especially dressy for your little boy, there is nothing better than this number. The material is all wool black and white checked shepherd plaid cheviot. The front of the garment is ornamented with a red silk embroidered emblem and has two rows of small black buttons. The edges are bound with red cord. Cuffs are made to button and are neatly plaited, and suit is furnished with a black patent leather belt. A black silk bow tie is attached. Pants are made in bloomer style and are fully lined and taped throughout.

No. 40C2177 Price for Buste[illegible] Brown suits, for boys from 2½ to[illegible] years of age only..............**$4.00**

YOUNG MEN'S AND BOYS' SINGLE LONG PANTS.

The splendid line of single pants which we offer this season deserves special attention. Our sales in single pants are constantly increasing and we are therefore enabled to make them up in larger quantities and are consequently able to give better values than ever before and to carry a greater variety of patterns. All our pants are thoroughly well tailored, neatly shaped and always cut in the latest and most prevailing style. We furnish young men's and boys' long pants in sizes ranging from 28 to 33 inches waist measure and from 28 to 34 inches in length. Any young man who can be fitted in these sizes can save money by ordering from this line. In ordering pants please take the measures around the waist, hip and length of inseam and outseam. See instructions how to take measurements for pants on page 907.

MEDIUM WEIGHT CHEVIOT PANTS.

Our $1 00 line is absolutely the best pants which can possibly be produced for such a price. The garments are substantially tailored, have side pockets and hip pockets and are provided with patent buttons. The material we use is a splendid quality of medium gray cheviot in striped effect with enough of coloring to give them a neat appearance.

No. 40C2181 Price, per pair...**$1.00**

COTTON WORSTED PANTS.

Made of excellent quality of cotton worsted. A material which wears well and looks neat and dressy. The pattern we offer in this number has a black background with a raised striped effect and relieved from the plain by white or blue dots. The pants are made with side pockets and two hip pockets and are cut in the most prevailing spring style We are confident that you will consider the pants exceptional value for the price

No. 40C2183 Price, per pair...**$1.15**

MEDIUM WEIGHT READING CASSIMERE PANTS.

Strong and durable pants with neat appearance in a broken check effect of black and white Nothing stronger or better for every day pants can possibly be produced for the price. Pants are thoroughly well sewed throughout, have side pockets and two hip pockets and are neatly shaped.

No. 40C2185 Price, per pair...**$1.25**

DARK STRIPED COTTON WORSTED PANTS.

A very dressy appearing garment with black background in narrow striped effect, formed by alternating green and gray hair lines. Substantially tailored and trimmed and made with side pockets and two hip pockets.

No. 40C2187 Price, per pair...........**$1.35**

FANCY WORSTED PANTS.

These pants are worsted fronts and cotton backs and we have them in a number of neat dark striped patterns, either blue or brown background. We consider them the very best pants we have ever been able to offer for this price and every pair will be found substantially and neatly made. All have side pockets and two hip pockets.

No. 40C2189 Price, per pair..........**$1.50**

ALL WOOL CASSIMERE PANTS.

Under this number we offer a number of pretty striped patterns in all wool cassimere in dark and medium gray shades These pants are made in the most substantial manner possible, with side pockets and two hip pockets and are neatly shaped and cut out at the bottom so as to fit well over the shoe. You will find them a neat and dressy garment and of exceptional value for the price.

No. 40C2191 Price, per pair..**$1.50**

Single Long Pants, 28 to 33 inches waist measure and 28 to 34 inches in length.

BLACK AND BLUE SERGE PANTS.

The material we use for these pants is fast color blue or black serge. A specially desirable fabric for summer pants, and only on account of the large quantities of this material which we use in the various departments of our clothing business are we able to offer them at the price. They are neatly shaped, well tailored, have two hip pockets, side pockets and a watch pocket.

No. 40C2195 Price, per pair....................**$1.65**

DARK DRAB CORDUROY PANTS.

The immense sale of corduroy pants during the past season is the best evidence we can offer that we furnish absolutely the best corduroy pants ever produced for the price. The material is the very best closely ribbed corduroy obtainable, and the pants are made up in the most substantial manner possible. Nothing better can be produced for hard wear. All these pants have side pockets and two hip pockets and can be furnished in sizes ranging from 28 to 33 inches waist measure and 28 to 34 inches in length.

No. 40C2193 Price, per pair.............**$1.50**

THROUGH AND THROUGH WORSTED PANTS.

Under this number we offer a variety of handsome striped patterns, either in light or medium gray or in handsome brownish shade, made up from small ends and remnants left over in the various branches of our clothing department and it is for this reason that we can offer more than ordinary value. All the pants will be found neatly trimmed and well shaped. They are made with side pockets and two hip pockets. Please state about the color you desire and we will endeavor to make a selection to please you.

No. 40C2197 Price, per pair...**$1.75**

ALL WOOL WORSTED OR CHEVIOT PANTS.

Our $2.00 line consists of a variety of very pretty small striped patterns. They are in all wool worsteds or cheviots. The patterns are all dark gray with just enough of coloring in them to give them a handsome effect. You will find the pants equal, both in make and quality, to pants usually offered for double the price. All are made with side pockets and two hip pockets and are neatly shaped and rounded out at the bottom so as to fit well over the shoes.

No. 40C2199 Price, per pair..**$2.00**

UNFINISHED WORSTED AND THROUGH AND THROUGH WORSTED PANTS.

This number is made up of a variety of patterns, either in unfinished worsted, medium gray and black striped effect, or in through and through worsted in fancy dark mixed pattern with colorings in gray, green and orange. All thoroughly well tailored pants of extra good value.

No. 40C2201 Price, per pair..**$2.25**

OUR FINEST YOUNG MEN'S PANTS.

The pants we offer under this number are very handsome dressy patterns, either in finished or unfinished worsteds suitable for dress wear. They are absolutely the best value which can be produced for the price. They are thoroughly well tailored, neatly shaped and cut in the most stylish spring fashion. We are confident that you will be pleased if you include a pair of these pants in your next order.

No. 40C2203 Price, per pair.**$2.50**

BOYS' SINGLE KNEE PANTS.

WE ARE SURE WE CAN SAVE YOU MONEY ON KNEE PANTS.

We know that our prices are lower and we furnish much better made garments than you can possibly obtain elsewhere. The tremendous increase in our sales of knee pants during the past few years shows that the exceptional values which we offer are appreciated From the cheapest to the best you will find all of our pants well tailored and gotten up in the most substantial manner possible. The pants which we offer range in price from 25 cents to $1 25 and are made in sizes to fit average size boys from 4 to 15 years of age Our highest priced pants we make in sizes for boys from 8 to 16 years of age only When ordering, please state age of boy and whether he is large or small for his age

Single Knee Pants.

BOYS' 25-CENT KNEE PANTS.

The pants which we offer for 25 cents are, without a doubt, the finest that can possibly be produced for the price. We have them in a number of neat, dark patterns and you will find them better made, better fitting and of better material than pants usually are at this price.

No. 40C2207 Price, per pair, ages 4 to 15 years...**25c**

If by mail, postage extra, 12c.

FANCY STRIPED CHEVIOT PANTS.

Pants we offer under this number are the greatest bargain we have ever been able to offer in knee pants. By a lucky purchase we have secured a large quantity of material and we believe that no better pants have ever been produced for the price. The color is of dark gray and brown mixtures in small striped effects.

No. 40C2209 Price, per pair, ages 4 to 15 years...........................**35c**

If by mail, postage extra, 13 cents.

ALL WOOL BLACK OR BLUE CHEVIOT PANTS.

The material for these pants is specially adapted for boys' knee pants and we are confident that pants of this material have never been offered at our prices. Pants are substantially made with taped seams, extension waistband and they are provided with patent buttons. We can furnish them either in blue or black. Please state color desired.

No. 40C2211 Price, per pair, ages 4 to 15 years...........................**45c**

If by mail, postage extra, 13 cents.

OUR 50-CENT LINE.

This is undoubtedly the strongest line of pants we have ever been able to offer for 50 cents Are made of strictly all wool material and are well tailored. We have a large variety of patterns in green, brown, olive, blue and gray mixtures. Please state color desired.

No. 40C2213 Price, per pair, ages 4 to 15 years...........................**50c**

If by mail, postage extra, 15 cents.

CORDUROY KNEE PANTS.

Our 50-cent corduroy pants are made of well filled, thick set corduroy and are tailored in the strongest possible manner. We sell tremendous quantities of these pants because we sell absolutely the best 50-cent corduroy pants offered anywhere.

No. 40C2215 Price, per pair, ages 4 to 15 years...........................**50c**

If by mail, postage extra, 15 cents.

FANCY CHEVIOT KNEE PANTS.

The pants of this number are made of all wool cheviot in handsome striped patterns, in dark and medium gray shades, with just enough coloring to give them a handsome effect. These pants are just the thing for nice outing pants, and they are made up substantially and are provided with loops for belt.

No. 40C2217 Price, per pair, ages 4 to 15 years...........................**60c**

If by mail, postage extra, 15 cents.

FANCY CORDUROY PANTS.

We have some very beautiful patterns in fancy corduroy, either in brown or drab mixtures. An extremely dressy and durable garment. All are made with taped seams, patent suspender buttons and extension waistbands.

No. 40C2219 Price, per pair, ages 4 to 15 years...........................**70c**

If by mail, postage extra, 16 cents.

ALL WOOL BLUE SERGE PANTS.

These pants will be found properly tailored and made of strictly pure wool material; all have extension waistbands and have open taped seams. Absolutely the best serge that can possibly be produced for the price.

No. 40C2221 Price, per pair, ages 4 to 15 years...........................**75c**

If by mail, postage extra, 15 cents.

BLACK CLAY WORSTED PANTS.

Made of strictly pure wool, 16-ounce black clay worsted, extremely well tailored and neatly and substantially trimmed. Sizes 4 to 8 years are made with closed fronts; balance of the sizes have fly fronts and suspender buttons.

No. 40C2223 Price, per pair, ages 4 to 15 years...........................**80c**

If by mail, postage extra, 15 cents.

FANCY WORSTED KNEE PANTS.

Made in very handsome dark striped wool patterns, dressy and durable garments, suitable to be worn on all occasions. Pants will be found substantially made with taped seams, patent elastic waistbands and suspender buttons. All sizes above 8 years are made fly front.

No. 40C2225 Price, per pair, ages 4 to 15 years...........................**85c**

If by mail, postage extra, 12 cents.

ALL WOOL WORSTED PANTS.

The pants we offer under this number are made of small ends and remnants left over in our Custom Tailoring Department and we are consequently able to offer you excellent values. We have a number of very neat striped patterns in dark gray and brown mixtures. All will be found of excellent value for the price and made in first class manner.

No. 40C2227 Price, per pair, ages 4 to 15 years...........................**$1.00**

If by mail, postage extra, 12 cents.

FANCY ALL WOOL WORSTED DRESS PANTS.

The pants we offer under this number are made from American Woolen Mills Co.'s finest all wool worsteds in handsome dark striped patterns. They are made up handsomely; sizes above 11 have regular skirts and are made with belt straps. If your boy wants extra fine dress pants, something better than is usually made in knee pants, do not overlook this number.

No. 40C2229 Price, per pair, ages 8 to 16 years only..................**$1.25**

If by mail, postage extra, 15 cents.

BOYS' WASHABLE SUITS.

If you need anything in washable garments it will pay you to carefully look over the splendid assortment of washable suits we offer this season. Nothing to be compared with it either in design or quality has ever been offered in wash goods before. By reason of the tremendous sales of wash goods we are enabled to sell them at closer prices than ever before. Wash goods can usually be sent by mail and under each number we show postage for each suit. Always include same with your remittance. The sizes in which each of our styles can be furnished are plainly stated under each number and in ordering it will only be necessary to state the age of the boy and whether he is large or small for his age.

BLUE OR OXBLOOD CHAMBRAY SUITS.

Made of good quality strictly fast color chambray, with a large sailor collar neatly trimmed with white duck and provided with a detachable shield of white duck. A cord and whistle is furnished with the suit. Nothing better can possibly be produced for the price.

No. 40C2231 Price for wash suits, for boys from 3 to 10 years of age only.**35c**

If by mail, postage extra, 15 cents.

BLUE AND WHITE STRIPED PERCALE SUITS.

A garment of special good value for a wash suit, for the reason that it will not soil easily and will wash exceptionally well. It is made with a white duck collar neatly trimmed and has a large white duck shield attached. The cuffs are also trimmed with white duck and a good cord and whistle are furnished with each suit. The price at which we offer the suit is about the price which wholesalers ask for it.

No. 40C2233 Price for wash suits, for boys from 3 to 10 years of age only, **40c**

If by mail, postage extra, 15 cents.

MEDIUM WEIGHT CRASH SUITS.

Made of a splendid quality of wash crash either in grass color or in pink. Please state color wanted. The little suit is made exactly as illustrated with a large plain sailor collar, is neatly trimmed in white and is furnished with a tie of the same material. It is made in a regular fly front, one outside pocket and neatly plaited double cuffs. We consider this the greatest value we have ever been able to offer in wash goods.

No. 40C2235 Price for wash suits, for boys from 3 to 10 years of age only **50c**

If by mail, postage extra, 16 cents.

WHITE DUCK BLOUSE SUITS.

Made of a good quality of white duck, with a sailor collar, a large detachable shield, double cuffs, fly front and is provided with a neat cord and whistle. The large quantity which we consume makes it possible to offer a suit in this popular material at this exceedingly low price.

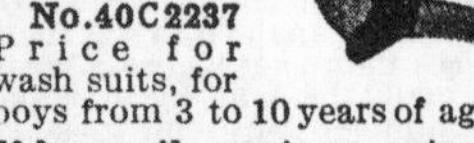

No.40C2237 Price for wash suits, for boys from 3 to 10 years of age only.. **50c**

If by mail, postage extra, 17 cents.

HEAVY WEIGHT CRASH SUITS.

One of the neatest garments we have ever been able to offer at such a low price. It is made in fly front style, trimmed with ivory buttons, has a large sailor collar which is inlaid with fine white swiss embroidery; a handsome silk embroidered white pique shield is attached to the garment and a neat metal cord and whistle are furnished with it. A suit which usually retails for at least double our price.

No. 40C2239 Price for crash suits, for boys from 3 to 10 years of age only.. **65c**

If by mail, postage extra, 18 cents.

WASH SHEPHERD PLAITED ETON BLOUSE SUITS.

A beautiful garment, made just as illustrated, in the popular Eton style, neatly trimmed with a white pique collar and with a lawn tie attached. One of the most popular styles and a suit of extra value for the price.

No. 40C2241 Price for wash suits, for boys from 3 to 10 years of age only.......... **75c**

If by mail, postage extra, 15 cents.

PINK AND BLUE EXTRA QUALITY CHAMBRAY SUITS.

Made exactly as shown by opposite illustration with large sailor collar, is piped in white and inlaid with a splendid quality of swiss embroidery. A large detachable shield of white corded pique is attached and a cord and whistle are furnished with each suit. The garment is made in fly front style with elastic bottom, plaited cuffs and has one outside breast pocket. Pants will be found substantially sewed, and the suit is fully guaranteed to wash perfectly.

No. 40C2243 Price for wash suits, for boys from 3 to 10 years of age only........................... **$1.00**

If by mail, postage extra, 15 cents.

WASH CORDUROY ETON SUITS.

Made of durable handsome appearing tan wash corduroy, a material very favorably known for its splendid wearing qualities. This suit is made up Eton style with double breasted front, neatly trimmed with white pearl buttons and ornamented with fancy white silk loops. A white lawn four-in-hand tie is attached. The cuffs are neatly plaited and are made to button. Pants are strongly sewed and neatly trimmed.

No. 40C2245 Price for boys' wash suits, for boys from 3 to 10 years of age only.......................... **$1.25**

If by mail, postage extra, 18 cents.

DARK GRAY AND WHITE CHEVIOT RUSSIAN SUITS.

A very popular style, made as illustrated, with a large white duck sailor collar, which is neatly trimmed with a strip of material like suit. The garment is provided with a belt in the same material and with a cord and whistle. Pants are made in bloomer style. We fully guarantee the suit to be absolutely fast color.

No. 40C2247 Price for Russian suits, for boys from 2½ to 6 years of age only, **50c**

If by mail, postage extra, 15 cents

TAN COLORED HERRINGBONE GALATEA CLOTH BUSTER BROWN SUITS.

A very handsome and durable material, specially adapted for wash goods. The suit is made with a small turndown collar and buttons on the side. It is neatly trimmed with white pearl buttons; has a belt of the same material attached and the front is ornamented with silk embroidery. A neat white silk cord and tassel are attached to the suit. Pants are made in bloomer style. Suits of similar material are generally offered at about double our price.

No. 40C2249 Price for Buster Brown suits, for boys from 2½ to 6 years of age only........................ **75c**

If by mail, postage extra, 16 cents.

FANCY GRAY AND WHITE STRIPED CHAMBRAY BUSTER BROWN SUITS.

This is one of the neatest suits we have ever listed. It is made as illustrated with a handsome white Bedford cord collar and a belt of the same material attached. It has a large handsomely trimmed plait on the side and buttons with four white pearl buttons. Cuffs are plaited and made to button. A neat black silk bow tie is furnished with the suit. Pants are made in bloomer style. The color is a handsome shade of gray with figures and stripes in white

No. 40C2251 Price for Buster Brown suits, for boys from 2½ to 6 years of age only.............. **$1.00**

If by mail, postage extra, 16 cents.

HEAVY WEIGHT WHITE DUCK BUSTER BROWN SUITS.

A very handsome little garment. Opposite illustration shows exactly how it is made. It has a neat, small turndown collar; it is trimmed with pearl buttons, has handsome cuffs made to button, one outside pocket and a black silk bow tie also a black patent leather belt is furnished with the suit. A suit of excellent value for the price.

No.40C2253 Price for Buster Brown suits, for boys from 2½ to 6 years of age only..... **$1.25**

If by mail, postage extra. 20 cents.

WHITE DUCK MIDDY SUITS, WHITE CAP TO MATCH.

Made exactly like opposite illustration. An exact copy of the U. S. navy summer uniform. Material is a strong quality of white duck; collar, cuffs and shield are made of navy blue cheviot; collar is trimmed with three rows of white duck and with a silk embroidered star on each corner. Silk embroidered anchors will be found on shields and right arm. A strong cord and whistle are also furnished with each suit. The cap is made in the popular tam o' shanter style, and is ornamented with a silk emblem. The little pants are made spring bottom style. The whole suit will be found exceptionally well made and a novelty of exceptionally good value

No. 40C2255 Price for middy suits, for boys from 4 to 8 years of age only.... **$1 35**

If by mail postage extra 25 cents

RIBBED MERCERIZED EGYPTIAN CLOTH BUSTER BROWN SUITS.

A beautiful little garment in a handsome shade of cream. It buttons on the side, and the front and pocket are trimmed with handsome black and white braid. A black patent leather belt and black silk bow tie are furnished with it. The suit is an exceptional value at the price.

No. 40C2257 Price for Buster Brown suits, for boys 2½ to 6 years of age only **$1.50**

If by mail, postage extra, 18 cents.

WHITE PIQUE BUSTER BROWN SUITS.

A very handsome little style, made as illustrated, with one plait down the side and outside breast pocket, both of which are piped in light blue. The little suit has fancy plaited open cuffs made to button, and black silk bow tie and black patent leather belt are furnished with it. The little pants are made in bloomer style One of the dressiest little garments ever shown in wash goods.

No. 40C2259 Price for Buster Brown suits, for boys from 2½ to 6 years of age only.............. **$1.75**

If by mail, postage extra, 20 cents

FANCY BUSTER BROWN SUITS.

This number is made of English mercerized rep, a handsome, durable material in neat shade of tan. The illustration gives you an idea as to how the suit is made. The front is trimmed with two rows of white pearl buttons, to which silk loops are attached. A handsome white silk tie and a white leather belt are attached The left sleeve is neatly embroidered in white silk. The pants are made in bloomer style. It is undoubtedly one of the handsomest little garments ever produced in wash goods

No. 40C2261 Price for Buster Brown suits, for boys from 2½ to 6 years of age only.......................... **$2.00**

If by mail, postage extra, 18 cents.

ONE OF OUR SPECIAL LEADERS IN WASH GOODS.

A suit, extra pants and cap to match. Made of strong, medium weight crash, a material which is bound to wear well and give the best of service. We have made the suit as substantially as possible with fly front and a plain large sailor collar. A neatly embroidered shield is attached and we also furnish a cord and whistle with each suit. This number consists of a blouse, two pairs of pants and a cap of the same material and we are confident that the price at which we offer this outfit cannot possibly be duplicated elsewhere.

No. 40C2263 Price for outfits, for boys from 3 to 10 years of age only... **$1.00**

If by mail, postage extra, 28 cents.

BOYS' CRASH OUTING SUITS WITH CAP AND BELT TO MATCH.

There is nothing better for an outing suit than the garment which we offer in this number. It is made of a splendid quality of No. 7 wash crash. A strong and durable material which will wash exceptionally well. This suit consists of a round cut three-button sack coat made with patch pockets and trimmed with ivory buttons. Pants are strongly made and have a belt of the same material with a strong German silver buckle attached. The cap is made in the latest golf style. If you wish your boy to be comfortable during the warm weather and fit him out at little cost, be sure and send us an order for this number.

No. 40C2265 Price for outing suits, for boys from 8 to 15 years of age only..**$1.00**
If by mail, postage extra, 26 cents.

DOUBLE BREASTED WASH SUITS.

This suit is made in double breasted style of a strong quality of galatea and can be furnished in neat gray and white striped effects. The material will be found to wash perfectly, and the suit is substantially made and exceedingly cheap for the price.

No. 40C2267
Price for double breasted wash suits, for boys from 9 to 15 years of age only,**75c**
If by mail postage extra, 18c.

CRASH NORFOLK SUITS.

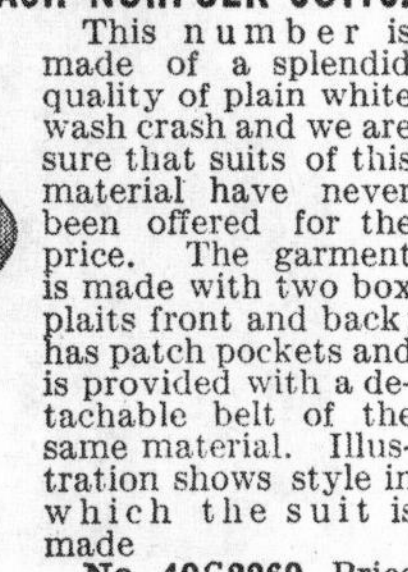

This number is made of a splendid quality of plain white wash crash and we are sure that suits of this material have never been offered for the price. The garment is made with two box plaits front and back; has patch pockets and is provided with a detachable belt of the same material. Illustration shows style in which the suit is made

No. 40C2269 Price for Norfolk suits, for boys from 9 to 15 years of age only.......**90c**
If by mail, postage extra, 20 cents.

BOYS' SINGLE WASH KNEE PANTS.

It pays to get a few pairs of extra pants with each wash suit as coats always outwear the pants. Be sure to notice the sizes in which each number can be furnished.

WASH CRASH KNEE PANTS.

Can be furnished either in plain or neatly striped patterns. The garments will be found splendid value for the price at which we offer them.

No. 40C2271 Price for wash knee pants, for boys from 3 to 10 years of age only **15c**
If by mail, postage extra, 7 cents.

GOOD WEIGHT GALATEA PANTS.

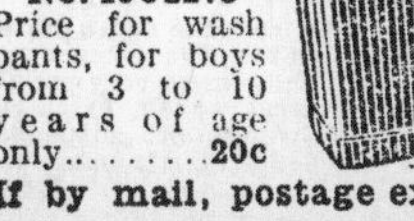

This number can be furnished either in blue and white, or tan and white striped pants. Pants are neatly made and we guarantee them to be strictly fast color.

No. 40C2273
Price for wash pants, for boys from 3 to 10 years of age only.........**20c**
If by mail, postage extra, 8 cents.

HEAVY CRASH PANTS.

This number is made of a splendid quality of medium weight crash, is provided with belt straps, trimmed with three buttons at the bottom and all seams are double sewed. All are made with side pockets and one hip pocket. A splendid fitting pants.

No. 40C2275 Price for pants, for boys from 8 to 16 years of age only..........**25c**
If by mail, postage extra, 10 cents.

WASH CORDUROY PANTS.

If you want something extraordinarily strong in wash goods we would recommend this number. The pants are extremely well made, with side pockets and one hip pocket, are provided with belt straps and the bottoms are trimmed with three ivory buttons. You will find these pants much better made than wash goods usually are.

No. 40C2277 Price for wash pants, for boys from 8 to 16 years of age only.....**30c**
If by mail, postage extra, 10 cents.

BOYS' SUMMER WAIST DEPARTMENT.

Realizing the great demand for popular priced garments in this line, we show, this season an entire new spring line of popular priced waists and blouses. By special arrangement with the Faultless A to Z Waist Company, we are able to offer this popular brand of medium priced garments at prices less than wholesalers ask for them.

In ordering waists always state age of boy and whether he is large or small for his age and notice the sizes in which each number is furnished, so that there will be no delay in filling the order.

BOYS' FAUNTLEROY BLOUSES.

A very popular garment, made as illustrated, with a large ruffled sailor collar; ruffled front and cuffs. It can be furnished in a variety of neat striped patterns in a good quality of percale. Please state color preferred.

No. 40C2281
Price for Fauntleroy blouses, for boys from 3 to 8 years of age only, each..........**$0.20**
Per dozen... **2.25**
If by mail, postage extra, each, 9c.

FANCY STRIPED BLOUSES.

A splendid garment of an excellent quality of corded madras in handsome striped patterns either in blue, black or pink effects. The garment is made as illustrated with small turndown collar. Nothing better can possibly be produced for the price.

No. 40C2283
Price for blouses, for boys from 4 to 13 years of age only, each........**$0.23**
Price, per dozen.............. **2.35**
If by mail, postage extra, each, 9c.

BOYS' MILITARY BLOUSES.

Made of a strong quality of chambray, a splendid material which will wash well and will give excellent wear. It is made exactly as illustrated; buttons on the side and is trimmed with white pearl buttons.

No. 40C2285
Price for military blouses, for boys from 3 to 8 years of age only, each..**25c**
Price, per dozen..........**$2.50**
If by mail, postage extra, each, 9c.

BOYS' MADRAS WAISTS.

Made of a splendid quality good weight madras in handsome striped patterns; with blue, black or red effects. Garment is made with three plaits in front, has double cuffs and a small turndown collar and is provided with a Mother's Friend Belt. Absolutely the best 25-cent waist ever offered.

No. 40C2287 Price for waists, for boys from 4 to 13 years of age only, each. **$0.25**
Price, per dozen.............. **2.50**
If by mail, postage extra, each, 12c.

RED OR BLUE PERCALE BLOUSES.

Made of a splendid quality of Gibraltar percale, either in blue or red striped effects. A garment usually offered for nearly double our price. Made in blouse style with turndown collar, double cuffs and one outside pocket.

No. 40C2289
Price for blouses, for boys from 4 to 13 years of age only, each...**$0.23**
Price, per dozen.............. **2.35**
If by mail, postage extra, each, 10c.

RED OR BLUE PERCALE MOTHER'S FRIEND WAISTS.

Made of material like preceding number and can be furnished either in red or blue. The garment is made with three plaits in front, a small turndown collar, double cuffs, stayed shoulders and is provided with a Mother's Friend Belt.

No. 40C2291
Price for waists, for boys from 4 to 13 years of age only, each........**$0.25**
Price, per dozen.............. **2.50**
If by mail, postage extra, each, 12c.

SOFT FINISH PERCALE WAISTS.

One of the most popular materials for boys' waists, which washes extremely well and is sure to give satisfactory wear. It has a turndown collar, double open cuffs, and is trimmed with white pearl buttons. We also furnish a Mother's Friend Belt with it. Can be furnished in neat medium shade colors with either blue, red or black figures.

No. 40C2293 Price for waists, for boys from 4 to 13 years of age only, each..............................**$0.40**
Price, per dozen.............. **4.25**
If by mail, postage extra, each, 12c.

BOYS' WAISTS WITHOUT COLLARS.

Made of a splendid quality of Elma madras in handsome striped patterns, either in blue, red or black effects. The garment has one large box plait down the front and three tucks on each side with three large plaits in the back. It is made with a band to which a collar of any kind can be attached; has double cuffs and a Mother's Friend Belt is furnished with it. A beautiful appearing and splendid wearing garment.

No. 40C2295 Price for waists, for boys from 4 to 13 years of age only, each..............................**$0.40**
Price, per dozen.............. **4.25**
If by mail, postage extra, each, 11c.

BOYS' MILITARY BLOUSES.

A beautiful and popular style, made exactly as shown by illustration. Material is a splendid quality of madras, which washes exceptionally well. The blouse fastens on the side, has one outside pocket, double cuffs and is trimmed with white pearl buttons.

No. 40C2297 Price for military blouses, for boys from 4 to 13 years of age only, each..............**$0.45**
Price, per dozen.............. **4.40**
If by mail, postage extra, each, 9c.

WHITE LAWN BLOUSES.

This ever popular style is made as shown in illustration and has always been one of our strongest numbers. A garment which we furnish for 50 cents and is absolutely the best that can be produced, and nearly double our price is usually asked for it. It is made of fine white lawn with embroidered sailor collar and handsome front.

No. 40C2299 Price for blouses, for boys from 3 to 8 years of age only, each..............................**$0.50**
Price, per dozen.............. **5.00**
If by mail, postage extra, each, 10c.

MERCERIZED BLACK SATEEN BLOUSES.

One of the handsomest garments made of a fine mercerized sateen; looks like silk and the material washes well. The blouse is made with large box plait, one outside pocket, double open cuffs and is trimmed with white pearl buttons.

No. 40C2301 Price for blouses, for boys from 4 to 13 years of age only, each...**$0.55**
Price, per doz., **5.50**
If by mail, postage extra, each, 12c.

PERCALE LAUNDERED BLOUSES.

Made of a splendid quality of wash percale in a variety of medium shade patterns. It is made with a box plait, has open laundered cuffs and is provided with detachable collar of the same material. One of the best garments ever offered for the price.

No. 40C2303
Price for blouses, for boys from 6 to 15 years of age only, each...............**$0.50**
Price, per dozen.............. **5.00**
If by mail, postage extra, each, 12c.

MERCERIZED WHITE CORDED MADRAS.

Made with three plaits in front, two in the back, open cuffs, turn down collar, and is provided with a Mother's Friend Belt. A very handsome and dressy garment. Exceptionally cheap at our price.

No. 40C2305
Price for waists, for boys from 4 to 13 years of age only, each...**$0.60**
Per dozen. **6.25**
Postage extra, each, 12c.

BOYS' LAUNDERED WAISTS.

Made with one box plait and six tucks in front and three plaits in back. It is made of a fine quality of muslin, has a handsome collar and cuffs attached and a Mother's Friend Belt is furnished with it. A very popular and serviceable garment.

No. 40C2307
Price for waists, for boys from 3 to 15 years of age only, each........**$0.60**
Price, per dozen.............. **6.75**
If by mail, postage extra, each 12c.

EXTRA QUALITY CORDED MADRAS LAUNDERED BLOUSES.

Made with a laundered collar and cuffs attached, with a large box plait down the front, stayed shoulders, one outside breast pocket and is trimmed with neat white pearl buttons. A splendid dressy garment which is sure to give satisfaction.

No. 40C2309 Price for blouses, for boys from 6 to 15 years of age only, each..... $0.75
Price, per dozen............. 8.25
If by mail, postage extra, each, 11c.

BOYS' PLAY SUITS.

We especially call your attention to the little suit we offer under this number. If you desire something for a durable play suit for the little fellows, which will save their other clothing and in which they will be cool and comfortable, don't fail to include one of these suits in your order. They are made exactly as illustrated, of a strong durable material in a medium gray and blue striped effect.

No. 40C2311 Price for Little Tudor play suits, for boys from 2 to 6 years of age only.........................45c
If by mail, postage extra, 15 cents.

DEPARTMENT OF FUR COATS.

DUCK, LEATHER, SHEEP LINED, MACKINAW AND WORKING CLOTHING.

We show only working clothing in this catalogue, and if you want anything in the way of fur coats, duck, leather, sheep lined and Mackinaw garments, please send for our Free Special Catalogue of Duck and Fur Coats.

OUR SPECIAL CATALOGUE OF DUCK AND FUR COATS will be mailed free and postpaid upon request. It contains large illustrations and complete descriptions of everything in the way of men's fur coats, duck, leather, sheep lined and Mackinaw clothing as well as heavy working garments, which we sell at a very small margin above the actual cost of manufacturing the clothing. You will save from one-third to one-half the usual price for qualities equal to ours and we absolutely guarantee to furnish you the best fur coats, duck, leather, sheep lined, Mackinaw and working garments that you can possibly secure. If for any reason any of these garments should prove unsatisfactory, or if you do not feel perfectly satisfied that we have given you better value than you could secure anywhere else, we ask you as a favor to return the garments to us at our expense and we will refund you every cent you have paid and transportation charges besides.

THERE ARE FOUR SPECIAL REASONS why we offer you the best in this line of clothing at lower prices than can possibly be obtained elsewhere.

WE CONTROL THE MANUFACTURING and cut out the profit of wholesalers, retailers, jobbers, agents and all others between you and us.

OUR RAW MATERIALS are bought in immense quantities and at absolutely the lowest figures for which the best can be secured.

WE MAKE AN ENORMOUS NUMBER of these garments and get the benefit of the lowest manufacturing cost.

OUR PROFITS are exceedingly small on each transaction. Our price covers only the actual manufacturing cost with a very narrow margin of profit added.

THE MAKE OF OUR FUR COATS is exceptionally high grade. We take more pains than the average manufacturer and a comparison between any of our coats and a similar coat that may be offered elsewhere at even a higher price than ours will show you that there are many improvements in the way our garments are made which other manufacturers overlook. Our coats are made with a six inch larger skirt sweep than other coats; they are all cut full length, are perfect fitting and more comfortable than the average fur coat. They out do all others for strength and durability. We use only the highest quality of skins and discard the inferior class altogether. Every coat is double sewed throughout, edges all stitched and double sewed. Many of our coats are faced with an 8-inch strip of duck with three rows of linen sewing on edge of coat. Our Special Duck and Fur Coat Catalogue will tell you all about the wonderful advantages we offer in our duck and fur coat department and all about the exceedingly low prices we offer.

OUR TERMS AND GUARANTEE. We ship these garments on a very liberal basis, either C. O. D. or for the full price with order. We require only $2.00 deposit on an order for a fur coat to be sent C. O. D. and we wish it distinctly understood that we guarantee to satisfy each and every customer in every particular, and if you have the slightest disappointment with any garments we send you, you are liberty to return garment to us at our expense and we will refund every cent you have paid together with transportation charges.

Don't buy any fur coats, duck, leather, sheep lined, or Mackinaw clothing until you see our special catalogue, which we will mail free and postpaid upon request.

MEN'S AND BOYS' OVERALLS, WORKING PANTS AND JACKETS.

In this department we can save you money. We make up all of our overalls, jackets, etc., in connection with our duck coat factory. Every garment is cut full size from the latest and most perfect patterns. We have started our duck coat and overalls factory with a view of serving our customers with the very best class of goods at prices at least 33 per cent lower than the same grade can be bought elsewhere. When ordering other goods you cannot afford to omit at least a year's supply of overalls and jackets; you will save what we gain over other dealers by making our own goods. We will give any assortment of sizes wanted in dozen lots. We furnish all waist measurements, 30, 32, 34, 36, 38, 40, 42 and 44; and the following sizes inseam measurements: 30, 31, 32, 33, 34, 35 and 36. Any size larger than 44 inches waist measure or longer than 36-inch inseam will cost extra as follows: 25 cents on all overalls quoted at 50 cents or more in price, and 15 cents on all overalls quoted below 50 cents in price.

MEASUREMENTS — Give waist measure and inseam measure the same as for regular pants; always give the waist measure first. Some of our customers order overalls as follows: One pair of overalls, 32x34, and expect to receive 34 waist and 32 inside seam, which they would not get. The order should read, one pair of overalls, 34x32. Waist measure should always be mentioned first. The best way is to state "waist 34 and inseam 32," and thus avoid any possibility of mistake.

PLAIN OVERALLS.

Leader Overalls 40 Cents.

No. 41C698 Made from 6½-ounce blue denim. Fine weave washable goods, double stitched seams, patent buttons, two front and one hip pocket.
Price, per pair......................40c

Black Huzzar Overalls, 45c.

No. 41C700 Made from full 8-ounce black duck. Warranted not to break or rip, made double stitched at all vital parts, taped crotch, continuous flypiece, two front and one back pocket. Price, per pair..........45c

Everett Overalls, 50 Cents.

No. 41C702 These overalls are made from Everett striped duck. A very neat pattern, double sewed throughout, continuous flypiece; patent buttons, extra well stayed. Two front, one watch and one hip pocket. This is one of our best selling numbers. Price, per pair.................50c

Our 50-Cent Hercules Overalls are 75-Cent Value.

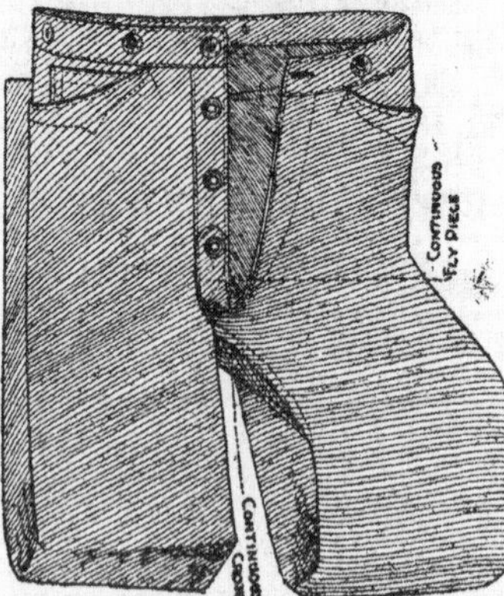

No. 41C706 These are really the best overalls for 50 cents ever offered. There are none superior and few equal. Made from heavy weight York denim, double sewed throughout; reinforced and continuous flypiece, two front swinging, one hip and one watch pocket. Warranted to wear longer and give more satisfaction than high priced goods usually retailed at 75 cents and $1.00 per pair.
Price, per pair.....................50c

NOTE—In ordering overalls, be sure to give waist measure first, then the inside seam.

Double Wear Overalls for 75 Cents.

No. 41C708 These overalls are made from full 9-ounce Belle York denim; front is double from waistband to below knee; patent never rip continuous flypiece; reinforced crotch stay; two front, one hip and one watch pocket; double sewed throughout. No better blue overalls can be had at any price.
Price, per pair.......................75c

Black Texas Ranger Overalls.

No. 41C710 The never give out sort. For all kinds of heavy wear these overalls are especially adapted. Made from extra quality fast black 10-ounce duck. Double seat and double from waistband to below knee. Two front, two hip pockets, with safety buttoned flaps over each pocket. Taped and reinforced crotch gusset, double sewed throughout. Full warranted. Price, per pair.........75c

We furnish better values in overalls and working garments than ou can secure elsewhere.

Cavalry Riding Pants, 90c.

No. 41C712 The material is a full 10-ounce soft finish duck, mode or nearly buckskin in color. It is made double seat. The entire back half is double, extending between crotch, as shown in illustration. Continuous never rip flypiece, double stitched crotch piece. Two back and two front pockets, fastened with safety buttoned flaps. Double sewed throughout and warranted in every particular.
Price, per pair............... .....90c

Our Double Bib Blue Apron Overalls.

No. 41C714 Made from 7-ounce washable blue denim. Double sewed throughout, all vital parts are reinforced, felled seams, large apron in front and wide bib in back. See illustration opposite. A support for the back, adds strength to the overalls, does away with the wearing out of the elastic ends, has two front pockets, back and rule pockets, cut large and roomy.
Price, per pair, 50c

Carpenters' Blue Apron Overalls.

No. 41C716 Made from 7-ounce blue washable denim. Double sewed throughout at all vital parts; large apron; elastic end suspenders; patent buttons; one rule pocket; one front and one back pocket. Price, per pair..50c

Carpenters' Black Duck Overalls.

No. 41C718 Made from 8-ounce black duck. Double sewed throughout, all vital parts reinforced, patent buttons, large apron, elastic end suspenders, front, back and rule pocket, cut full size. Price, per pair.......50c

Everett Apron Overalls.

No. 41C720 Made from the same material as plain overalls, from the Everett gray and black striped duck. These are a very popular overalls, cut full size; large apron, extra rule pocket; double sewed throughout; suspenders of same material with 6-inch elastic ends.
Price, per pair.............................50c

Double Front Overalls.

No. 41C721 Our Double Front Apron Overalls for 75 cents. Made of a full 9-ounce red back denim; the front is double from the waist to below the knee. Double sewed throughout, reinforced crotch piece. Two outside front pockets, one watch pocket on bib as shown in illustration; one side and one back pocket, patent buttons, elastic back with corded ends same as regular suspenders. This is one of the best overalls on the market. Be sure to give size desired.
Price, per pair, 75c

Boys' Blue Apron Overalls.

No. 41C727 For boys aged from 12 to 16, or 26 to 31 waist measure, 26 to 31 inseam. Made of 7-ounce blue denim, all seams double sewed, has front and back pockets. **In ordering, give measure the same as for men's overalls.**
Price, per pair....................40c

Boys' Blue Overalls.

No. 41C728 For boys aged 12 to 16 years, are 26 to 31 inches waist measure, inseam, 26 to 31. When ordering, give size the same as for men's overalls. Made from 7-ounce blue denim, extra well made, double sewed in all vital parts. The kind that is usually sold for 50 cents.
Price, per pair....................40c

Children's Brownie Overalls.

No. 41C730 Made from good quality washable blue denim, with apron and suspenders, for boys aged 4 to 12 years. One front and one hip pocket.
Price, per pair, 25c

Best Brownie Overalls in the Market.

No. 41C732 Made from fine, soft finish, washable blue denim, double sewed in all vital parts, extra crotch piece, suspenders have 4-inch detachable elastic ends, two front and one hip pocket.

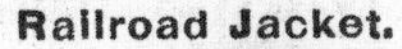

Price, per pair....................35c

Railroad Jacket.

No. 41C734 This coat is especially gotten up for the use of baggagemen, firemen, brakemen or anyone employed in a similar class of work. It is a regular coat jacket and made from an extra quality twilled black sateen. Buttons close up to the neck, as shown in illustration. Watch pocket is cut diagonally so as not to allow timepiece to fall out. Two pencil pockets; three outside pockets; buttons at wrist. **This garment is gotten up for a special purpose and we guarantee it to please in every way.** All buttons are put on with eyelets and can be removed when coat is washed. Sizes, 34 to 46 inches chest. Price............80c

Conductors' or Mail Agents' Bib Overalls.

No. 41C736 Conductors' or Mail Agents' Bib Overalls. Made from same goods as above coat, double stitched throughout, extra large rule pocket, two front, two hip and watch pockets. Price, per pair............80c

MEN'S JACKETS.

Sizes, 34 to 46 inches chest measure. In ordering give the number of inches around chest close up under the arms, or state the size of coat usually worn.

Blue and White Check Jackets.

No. 41C738 Men's Amoskeag Blue and White Check Jackets. Well made and shaped, two outside pockets....25c

No. 41C740 Same color, except made from better material. A most desirable jacket. Price............40c

No. 41C742 This coat is made from black and white hairline checks and denim. A coat especially gotten up for the use of grain elevator men, grocers, lumbermen, etc., buttons up close to the neck, with neat turndown collar, two lower pockets and one upper pocket. This is a splendid coat for indoor or light outside work. Price..50c

Men's Blue Denim Jacket.

No. 41C746 This jacket is made from full 8-ounce blue denim. Cut full 28 inches long. Buttons close up to collar, patent buttons on sleeves, two lower and one upper outside pocket, shaped shoulders, extra well stayed and sewed. Price..................50c

Men's Heavy Working Pants.

Our line of cheap working pants are cut extra large, full sizes, and warranted not to rip or break. They are made in our own factory and cannot be compared with the average cheap made goods. Sizes in pants run from 30 to 42 inches waist, and 30 to 36 inches inside seam measure. Any size larger than 42 inches waist measure or 36 inches inside seam measure will cost extra, 25 cents per pair.

No. 41C750 Men's Gray Jeans Cloth Pants. Well made, double sewed, print curtain lining. Patent buttons. Price, per pair....80c

No. 41C754 Very Neat Cotton Worsted Stripe Pants. Drab, white and black colors used, blue and white drill curtain lining. Swinging pockets, double sewed through seat and crotch, patent never come off buttons. Price, per pair...90c

No. 41C760 Extra Fine Quality Heavy Weight Jet Black Jeans. Well made, trimmed and finished, two top, two hip and one watch pocket, double sewed throughout.
Price, per pair..................$1.25

No. 41C764 Heavy Weight All Wool Dickey Cassimere Pants. Dark, gray stripe pattern; no better nor more satisfactory wearing pants can be had at any price; two top, two hip and one watch pocket, good strong lining, double sewed seams, warranted not to rip.
Price, per pair..................$1.75

BUTCHERS', BARTENDERS', BARBERS', GROCERS', WAITERS' AND COOKS' JACKETS, COATS AND APRONS.

Our white duck clothing is all made full size, fully guaranteed as to fit, style and workmanship. Our white duck coats are made in sizes 34 to 44 inches breast measure only. We have no larger or smaller sizes.

No. 41C72 Cooks' or Waiters' Heavy White Duck Jacket or Coat. One top pocket, single breasted style.
Price... ....60c

No. 41C73 Cooks' or Waiters' Heavy White Duck Jacket or Coat. One top pocket, single breasted style. Sizes, 34 to 44 inches. Price.........75c

No. 41C76 Waiters' Heavy Drill Coat. Double breasted style, high at the neck, standing collar, three outside pockets. Sizes, 34 to 44 inches. This coat is used by butchers, bartenders and waiters.
Price. 85c

No. 41C78 Heavy White Duck Coats. Double breasted style, rolling collar, three pockets, eight detachable buttons. Sizes, 34 to 44 inches. This coat is used by butchers, bartenders and waiters.
Price... $1.00

No. 41C83 Made of a high grade white drill. Made exactly as a vest with exception of having sleeves as shown in illustration, has four outside pockets six detachable buttons; strap and buckle in back. Sleeves are stitched at bottom, cuff style.
Price..... 70c

No. 41C84 Made exactly as vest described above, except of better material. Made of an extra heavy white Pullman duck. As these vests are laundered frequently we would advise buying this grade. Made in sizes 34 to 44 inches.
Price..... ....95c

No. 41C86 Butchers' Bib Aprons. Made of heavy white duck, to fit over the head. Lengths, 44, 46, 48 and 50 inches, the measure to be taken from the neck down.
Price.........30c

Carpenters' Aprons.

No. 41C89 Apron made of 8-ounce khaki duck. (Government standard for uniforms.) Two large nail pockets at bottom and two tool pockets at top. Corners of pockets secured by leather. Extra long adjustable strap around waist, patent buckle and riveted button. Length, 24 inches. Price..........20c

BARBERS' COATS are made in sizes from 34 to 42 inches breast measure.

No. 41C91 Heavy Drill Coat. This coat is cut in single breasted style with rolling collar, three outside pockets and is made of heavy drilled material. A first class coat and for the price cannot be equaled anywhere else. Made exactly as illustrated.
Price........70c

No. 41C92 Barber's Heavy White Duck Coat. This coat is made of heavy white duck, cut in single breasted style, rolling collar, three outside pockets; in fact, the same style exactly as No. 41C91, with the exception that it is made of heavy white duck instead of drill goods. This coat you will find will cost you 15 to 20 per cent more anywhere else. Exactly as illustrated above. Price....................95c

No. 41C93 Barber's Heavy Drill Coat. Made from good quality white drill material. with rolling collar. Collar, lapel and facing made of black and white stripe goods; cuffs and pockets also trimmed with black and white stripe material. Three outside pockets, black detachable buttons. A very popular coat with barbers everywhere. Our price is certainly most reasonable. Price..............75c

No. 41C94 Black and White Stripe Drill Coat. Made in single breasted style with closed cuffs, three outside pockets, black detachable buttons. Style exactly as illustrated here. A coat that is a great favorite with large numbers and at a price at which it could never be procured before.
Price..........................75c

No. 41C95 Black and White Stripe Duck Coat. Made in single breasted style and a fine quality of duck. Closed cuffs, three outside pockets, black detachable buttons. A high grade garment at a price that makes it an interesting value. Price.$1.00

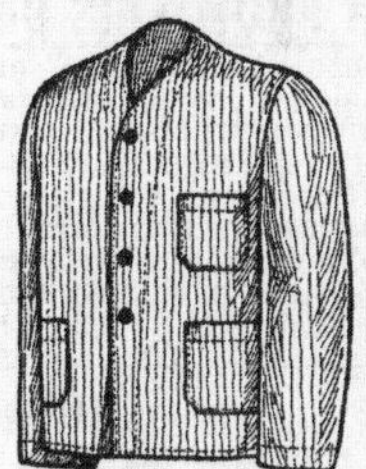

No. 41C96 Extra Long Drill Coat. This coat is made without collar and is composed of an extra quality black and white stripe drill goods. It is cut extra long, averaging 33 inches in length. Three outside pockets. Made in style without collar as illustrated. We guarantee all these coats. Price.80c

No. 41C97 Extra Long Black and White Duck Coat. This garment is made without collar and averages 33 inches in length. It is made from an extra quality black and white stripe duck goods. The style and make is exactly the same as in No. 41C96. The only difference being that the material is of duck instead of drill. This is a splendid coat, and to those wanting better grades we can recommend this especially as an exceptional value.
Price..........................$1.00

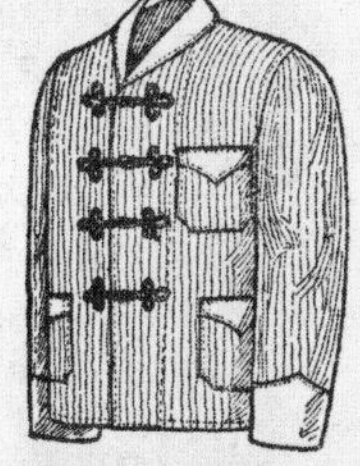

No. 41C98 Shawl Collar Duck Coat. This serviceable and stylish garment is made from heavy black and white stripe duck. The pockets, cuffs and collars are faced with heavy white duck. The coat closes with four fancy cord loops instead of buttons, as illustrated. The equal of this coat would cost you upward of $1.50 in the lowest priced line other than ours. We guarantee this as an extra good quality and the best obtainable for barbers' use.
Price..........................$1.25

MEN'S AND BOYS'

RAINY WEATHER CLOTHING DEPARTMENT.

Mackintoshes, Cielette Showerproof Overcoats for all Kinds of Weather, Rain or Shine, Rubber Surface and Oil Slicker Clothing. If you want Ladies' or Misses' Rainy Weather Garments, see page 973.

WE CARRY A GREAT VARIETY of rainy weather clothing. Our line will absolutely meet the requirements of each and every person, no matter for what kind of wear the rainy weather garments are needed. We have them for fine dress purposes, for ordinary every day wear or for rough work. We handle only the very best qualities of each of the different classes of raincoats and guarantee to please you with the quality and make up of any garment we ship to you. If any of our rainy weather clothing should prove unsatisfactory to you in any shape or manner, you are at liberty to return it to us at our expense and we will refund all you have paid, together with transportation charges.

OUR LINE INCLUDES mackintoshes, combination raincoats and overcoats, rubber surface and oil slicker clothing. We handle only the finest grades of mackintoshes, finest patterns and qualities of combination raincoats and overcoats and the very best rubber surface and oil slicker clothing on the market, and all of these garments are sold to you at prices that are positively below all competition. From these facts you can count upon getting the very best qualities of any kind of rainy weather clothing, whether you want a garment for special occasions where the only thing to wear is a fine dressy garment; whether you want it for Sundays or ordinary business wear, or for rough kinds of work, such as teaming and all other outdoor occupations.

SAMPLE BOOK No. 90C.

THIS BOOK IS FREE FOR THE ASKING. It contains fair sized samples of Men's, Boys', Ladies' and Misses' Cielette Showerproof Coats for all kinds of weather, and samples of mackintoshes, showing the actual fabrics, as described in catalogue. We do not, however, sample men's rubber surface and oil slicker clothing, as this kind of goods cannot be conveniently sold from samples. The descriptions of oil slicker and rubber surface clothing are given in this catalogue on pages 920 and 921.

IF YOU ORDER FROM THIS CATALOGUE we guarantee to please you in every way, or if you have the slightest difficulty in selecting the garments you want from our descriptions, we ask you, by all means, to **send for our Sample Book No. 90C,** and we are certain you will be sure to order from our line, as we offer you a larger variety and better goods than you can procure elsewhere at anything like our price. There is no comparison between our prices and those of the average dealer because ours are practically the manufacturing cost with only one small profit added. If you want anything in the way of ladies' raincoats you can see descriptions in this catalogue, on page 973, or you might send for this Sample Book No. 90C.

THE REASON WHY we are able to furnish these fine qualities of rainy weather clothing at such exceedingly low prices is found in the manner in which we conduct our immense business. We make all our combination raincoats and overcoats ourselves in our men's ready made clothing department, and because we use a very large quantity of cloth and treat this fabric with our own rainproofing process, we can sell you these very serviceable garments at manufacturers' prices. In the case of our mackintoshes, rubber surface and oil slicker clothing, we contract for an enormous number of the garments to be made in one of the biggest and best mills in the United States, practically controlling their entire output, enabling us to sell you the very best quality of goods made and at less than ordinary wholesale prices. We handle nothing but the best grades of garments and anyone who is in need of a rainy weather coat of any description is certain to find it in our line, at a price that will save him a great deal of money, being a price that is below what dealers elsewhere must pay to wholesale houses for the goods. For this reason a great number of merchants and storekeepers throughout the country are sending us orders for rainy weather clothing, finding our prices more reasonable than wholesale concerns and our garments of the very finest quality.

ABOUT DAMPNESS IN MACKINTOSHES. Because a mackintosh may become a little moist inside about the shoulders and back does not show that it leaks. This condition is brought about through the very nature of the goods. It is not porous like other clothing and does not admit of ventilation through the texture. Thus the moisture of the air condenses and may occasionally cause a slight dampness at points mentioned, but not enough to be of any trouble.

HOW TO TAKE CARE OF A MACKINTOSH. To clean, use cold water only. Never use gasoline. To dry, spread it out, but don't hang it next to the chimney or fireplace, and when out riding, don't fold it up and put it under a wagon or buggy seat, or the like. Avoid getting oil or grease on a mackintosh, because it will in time separate its textures and eventually cause the garment to leak. We guarantee our garments against defects, but not against abuse. If you observe these simple rules you will get the longest and best service from a mackintosh.

WE RECOMMEND loose fitting mackintoshes. It is advisable to get a mackintosh that will fit loosely, rather than snug. A tight fitting mackintosh causes the seams to be somewhat strained and may be the cause of the leaking of a garment.

HOW TO MEASURE FOR MEN'S RAINY WEATHER CLOTHING.

BREAST. Measure all around breast over regular coat, close up under arms. **GIVE CORRECT HEIGHT, WEIGHT AND AGE.**

SIZES WE FURNISH. Men's mackintoshes come regularly in sizes 36, 38, 40, 42, 44, 46 and 48 inches breast measure. All styles except 125, average 52 inches in length.

EXTRA LARGE SIZES AND SPECIAL STYLES. Sizes above 48 inches breast measure and all other mackintoshes of unusual proportions must be made to order, for which we charge $2.00 extra, that is $2.00 more than the price quoted in this catalogue for each number. We furnish mackintoshes only in the styles in which we quote them, unless you desire one made to order in a special style, for which we will charge you $2.00 extra and cash in full with order.

CHANGES IN LININGS occasionally occur. This happens only when we use the entire output of the factory on linings of a certain pattern. We always furnish as good or better quality of linings if any change is made. The change is only in the pattern.

TERMS. We ship a mackintosh or raincoat C. O. D., subject to examination before paying for them, if you will send $1.00 deposit with your order. Most of our customers, however, send cash in full with their orders, because they thereby save the small charge made by the express company for returning the money on C. O. D. shipments.

WE GUARANTEE to please you in every respect, and if any garment should not be entirely satisfactory, you are perfectly at liberty to return it to us at our expense, and we shall refund every cent you have paid us, whether a deposit only or the full price, and will also refund any transportation charges you may have paid.

These illustrations represent the up to date styles in which we furnish

MEN'S RAINY WEATHER CLOTHING.

In the descriptions on the following pages, we state plainly the style in which each garment is made, and by referring to this page, you can see exactly what kind of a coat is meant.

Style 120

Style 129

Style 122

Style 135

Style 123

Style 125

Our $1.25 Men's Mackintosh.

No. 27C600 In this number we offer you a good coat for less money than you can buy a mackintosh anywhere. This coat is made of a good quality oxford gray cotton covert, made in the double breasted box style 122, as shown on preceding page. Has velvet collar, and lining which harmonizes with the surface cloth. Sizes, 36 to 48 inches chest measure. This coat averages only 50 inches long. Price for men's mackintosh, style 122......**$1.25**

Our Tan Covert Box Coat.

No. 27C610 Made from stylish heavy weight, tan color covert waterproof cloth. The lining is a modest design fancy plaid, which makes a serviceable double texture mackintosh. Double breasted style, velvet collar, three pockets, double stitched throughout and ventilation under arms. Full size and length. Sizes, 36 to 48 inches breast measure. Made in style 122, as illustrated on preceding page.

Price for men's double breasted box coat, style 122 ....**$1.75**

Men's Combination Overcoat and Mackintosh.

No. 27C615 Serviceable as a light weight overcoat. Men's fine tan cotton covert mackintosh, double texture, of a style especially suited to spring and fall wear. It is made in the usual box coat style in overcoat length, averaging about 41 inches. The lining is a neat fancy plaid, made with velvet collar, and two pockets, wide facing, double sewed throughout, ventilation under arms. Single breasted fly front, made like a regular light weight top coat. Sizes, 36 to 48 inches breast measure. Made in style 125, as illustrated on preceding page.

Price for men's single breasted, fly front, style 125 ....**$1.50**

Men's Detachable Cape Mackintosh at $2.50.

No. 27C620 Something new and snappy in design is this men's detachable cape mackintosh, something that is neat and nobby, made of a very fine print black and white pin check with lining that harmonizes in every way with the surface cloth. Made with velvet collar, two outside pockets and very full facings. If you desire a nice genteel cape coat, do not overlook this number and we guarantee you will be well pleased with your purchase. Comes in style 120 only, as shown in illustration on preceding page.

Price for men's cape mackintosh, style 120..........................**$2.50**

Men's Fine All Wool Cashmere Mackintosh.

Light weight, suitable for spring and fall. In navy blue, with new design fancy woven plaidlining. A staple, dressy, neat coat, sure to please and give entire satisfaction. The woven lining adds greatly to its durability and appearance; velvet collar and three pockets. Made in styles 120 and 122, as shown on preceding page. Sizes, 36 to 48 inches chest measure.

No. 27C630 Price for men's detachable cape coat, double sewed seams, style 120.................................**$3.50**

No. 27C635 Price for men's double breasted box mackintosh, sewed, strapped and cemented seams, style 122.....................................**$3.50**

Men's All Wool Mackintosh.

No. 27C650 Andrus Special All Wool Covert Mackintosh in tan or black. These garments are all made in our style 122 with sewed, strapped sleeves and cemented seams, velvet collar and ventilation under arms; average length about 52 inches; lining of a fancy design. The fabric is an all wool covert of excellent quality. We carry it in two colors because of its exceptionally good qualities for an all around raincoat. Sizes, from 36 to 48 inches chest measure. Be sure to mention color.

Price for men's mackintosh, style 122, tan or black...............**$4.75**

Dark Oxford Venetian All Wool Mackintosh.

No. 27C655 Men's Fine Oxford Gray, All Wool Mackintosh, made in style 129, as illustrated on preceding page. The oxford gray wool cloth is much in favor for outer garments of every kind, particularly mackintoshes. The lining is light weight, making this a particularly suitable garment for spring and fall wear. Style 129 is made single breasted box style (see preceding page), with velvet collar; raglan pockets and sewed, strapped and cemented seams; ventilation under arms. We can please you with a mackintosh of this kind. Sizes, 36 to 48 inches breast measure.

Price for single breasted box coat, style 129..............................**$5.00**

A MACKINTOSH IS A GOOD COAT FOR CHILLY WEATHER AS IT IS BOTH WIND AND RAINPROOF.

Combination Mackintosh and Overcoat.

No. 27C660 Special Short Top Combination Mackintosh and Overcoat. Last season we had a very large demand for a short top combination mackintosh and overcoat in our special style 125, of a better grade of cloth than we carried, and to supply our large circle of customers and give them everything in style and creations that we possibly can, we have made up several hundred top coats of same cloth as No. 27C655, which description fully explains the good qualities of this number, excepting it is made in our special style 125, as illustrated on preceding page.

Price for men's combination mackintosh and overcoat, style 125....**$3.50**

Men's English Whipcord Mackintosh.

No. 27C670 We furnish this fine English whipcord in castor gray, as one of the finest and latest up to date mackintosh fabrics, made in the standard double breasted style, with the fine woven lining which harmonizes with the surface cloth. Three pockets, large velvet collar, sewed, strapped and cemented seams, and ventilation under the arms. Sizes, 36 to 48 inches breast measure.

Price for men's gray mackintosh, style 122...... ....**$4.50**

New Novelty All Wool Worsted Mackintosh at $6.50.

No. 27C680 We show you in this number a mackintosh which is gotten up to resemble a Cielette coat as near as possible, and with a very fine light Para proofing. Makes one of the best waterproof coats in our line, and a coat such as will give the wearer excellent satisfaction. Made of a hard double and twist worsted cloth. Collar, sleeve lining and buttons to match. If this coat is not all and more than you expect in your purchase, return it to us and we will cheerfully refund your money with all transportation charges.

Price for men's mackintosh, style 135, as shown on preceding page....**$6.50**

BOYS' MACKINTOSHES.

Our little men's mackintoshes are made with the same care and finish as our men's coats and are sure to give the best of satisfaction. Read our instructions on preceding page about care of mackintoshes. In ordering, be sure to give breast measurement, height, weight and age. Remember mackintoshes should be worn loose.

Boys' Cape Style Mackintosh.

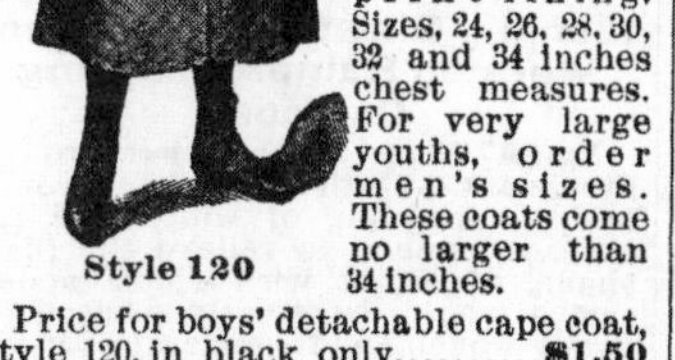

Style 120

No. 27C44 Boys' or Youths' Mackintosh, made from a good, black serviceable wale cassimere cloth, in dark color. Double texture print lining. A good, light weight, serviceable boys' raincoat at a very low price; in fact, so low in price that you cannot fail to appreciate the value we give. Made in the cape style only and print lining. Sizes, 24, 26, 28, 30, 32 and 34 inches chest measures. For very large youths, order men's sizes. These coats come no larger than 34 inches.

Price for boys' detachable cape coat, style 120, in black only..........**$1.50**

Boys' Tan Covert Mackintoshes.

No. 27C40 Boys' or Youths' Fine Tan Covert Cloth Mackintosh made with fancy lining. A strong serviceable double texture mackintosh that will not show soil, will stand rough wear, and is sufficiently heavy to wear as a medium weight overcoat. Made in double breasted box coat style, two pockets and velvet collar. Sizes, 24, 26, 28, 30, 32 and 34 inches chest measure. For large youths order men's sizes and allow men's prices. Price for boys' double breasted box coat, style 122...............**$1.50**

Style 122

No. 27C46 Boys' Oxford Gray Union Covert Mackintosh. Made in style 129, double breasted box coat style. Sewed, strapped and cemented seams, velvet collar and two pockets. Made in sizes 24 to 34 inches chest measure. Otherwise made exactly like men's mackintoshes. Price for boys' mackintosh, style 129, like men's style on preceding page.......................................**$2.75**

EVERY SCHOOL BOY SHOULD HAVE A MACKINTOSH THEY ARE WIND AND RAINPROOF.

Heavy Storm Ulster Mackintosh, $3.00.

No. 27C625 A heavy mackintosh for the use of farmers, stockmen, teamsters, motormen or any man whose occupation subjects him to extreme exposure. The entire coat is of a special construction, designed for rough service, and is strong and durable. Average weight between 6 and 7 pounds. The surface cloth is a heavy tan covert cloth, and the lining of heavy tan color sheeting. The two are cemented together with a special process compound. Made with a large storm collar and wide storm fly front, which closes with Thompson's automatic buckles, and has draw buckles on the sleeves. Large flaps over pockets, ventilation under arms. Length, 54 inches. Sizes, 36 to 48 inches breast measure. Made in style 123, as illustration on preceding page. The surface of this particular coat is also treated with our Cielette chemical process.

Price for men's ulster mackintosh, style 123..............................**$3.00**

MEN'S CIELETTE RAINPROOF SPRING AND FALL OVERCOATS

THE ONLY PRACTICAL COAT FOR SPRING AND FALL WEAR BECAUSE IT IS AS USEFUL IN WET WEATHER AS IN DRY.

YOU MAY ORDER FROM DESCRIPTIONS GIVEN ON THE FOLLOWING PAGE, OR IF YOU PREFER TO SEE SAMPLES BEFORE ORDERING, ASK FOR OUR SAMPLE BOOK No. 90C, WHICH WILL BE SENT FREE AND POSTPAID UPON REQUEST.

WE USE FINE WOOLENS in light and medium weights in making these rainproof overcoats. They come in black and white mixtures, other fancy mixed colors and plain shades, of the same qualities and dressy appearance as are used by merchant tailors for handsome spring and fall overcoats. One could not tell from their appearance that they were raincoats at all.

THE CIELETTE WATERPROOFING PROCESS is the original chemical method of waterproofing ordinary fabrics, which is so much advertised throughout the country. The chemical is applied to the fabric, giving it the property of turning water without in any way injuring the texture, color or finish of the cloth, the goods remaining pliable and porous to air just as before; there are no rubber or rubber compounds used, hence there is no odor or objectionable feature about these rainproof overcoats.

IN ALL KINDS OF WEATHER these Cielette overcoats can be worn with greatest comfort, rain or shine. They avoid the common discomforts of raincoats as they allow free ventilation, the same as any ordinary overcoat. One need not have two over garments if he has one of these coats, as he can use it at all times for all purposes. They are exceedingly stylish nowadays and when one considers this fact in connection with their great usefulness he will see that he really cannot afford to be without one of our stylish all around Cielette raincoats for any kind of weather, especially at our exceedingly low prices, representing the actual manufacturing cost with a small profit added.

THEY ARE MADE IN STYLE 135 as illustrated on next page. It is the popular fashionable long overcoat style. We do not put in body lining, the lining extends only over the shoulders and in the sleeves. The coats are made over the best fitting patterns available; they have the broad shoulder effects, neat latest style lapel, padded shoulders and hang loose from shoulders down; two lower outside pockets, one outside breast pocket and one inside breast pocket. They are all furnished in this same style.

THE SIZES run from 36 to 44 inches breast measure and the average length is about 51 inches. We do not furnish any larger or smaller sizes or coats longer than 51 inches from our ready made stock. If you require a smaller, larger or longer garment it will be necessary that it be made to order and for this we charge $2.00 more than our regular price and require two weeks' time to make it. We also require cash in full with such orders.

THE PRICES we quote represent the actual manufacturing cost with our one small profit added, hence the garments we show here represent values of double the money as compared with prices elsewhere. Your local tailor or clothier would charge you fully double our price and would not be able to give you a more stylish or up to date coat than we here offer.

WE GUARANTEE to fit and please you in every way. If you have the slightest reason for disappointment in any of these garments we ask you as a favor to return them to us at our expense and we will refund every cent you have paid, together with transportation charges.

HOW TO MEASURE. Breast. Take coat off and give the number of inches around breast over vest close up under arms, not tight. **Sleeves.** Give number of inches from middle of back to elbow and then from elbow to wrist.

Men's Wool Filled Oxford Gray Melton Spring Overcoat and Raincoat.

Style 135

No. 27C498 Made from a medium weight and good quality of dark gray wool filled cloth and treated with our perfect Cielette rainproofing process. Adapted for any reasonable wear as a rainproof garment or a spring and early fall overcoat. No other house furnishes a garment of this nature anywhere near our price. As an all around coat, for the money this is certainly a big value. Furnished in style 135 only, as illustrated above, and in sizes from 36 to 44 inches breast measurements. Average length, about 51 inches. Lined in sleeves only and with wide facings of the same cloth as the surface. This coat has no body or shoulder linings.

Price for men's combination overcoat and raincoat, style 135...........**$5.00**

Men's Cielette Fancy Cheviot Spring Overcoat and Raincoat.

No. 27C500 A good quality fancy cheviot by Susberg mills. A neat black and white cheviot mixture, white predominating, working into a medium striped effect, a real pleasing pattern and for spring, summer and early fall just the thing. Made in style 135, no body lining, lined only in yoke and sleeves, worth double the money. Useful for rain or shine.

Price for men's combination overcoat and raincoat, style 135......**$7.50**

Men's Cielette Fancy Melton Rainproof Spring Overcoat.

No. 27C502 Woven by the Deering Woolen Mills Co. A faint dark green background lit up by parallel threads of white and tan, also a faint thread of blue. These threads are all indistinct but lend life to the otherwise plain shade, just the thing for modest taste. Made in the stylish long overcoat effect without body lining lined only in yoke and sleeves. Size, 36 to 44 inches breast measure. Average length, about 51 inches.

Price for men's combination overcoat and raincoat, style 135......**$8.50**

Men's Cielette Showerproof Black Thibet Spring Overcoat.

No. 27C504 Medium weight, good quality of black thibet, produced by the Lacon mills. There is nothing better in the way of an early fall and spring overcoat and raincoat than this for general purposes. One can always wear a black coat. Made with wide facings and without body linings, in style 135, as illustrated. These garments are all well made and will give unusual service.

Price for men's combination overcoat and raincoat, style 135.. ...**$8.75**

Men's Cielette Fancy Cheviot Rainproof Spring Overcoat.

No. 27C506 A neatly woven mixed pattern by the Clinton mills. The latest dark brown background relieved by a sprinkling of white and green threads, a very nobby pattern, something that a dressy gentleman would like. Made in the handsome up to date long style as illustrated; no body lining, lined only in sleeves and yoke, a very good grade of lining material. All of these coats are well tailored and the most useful garment a man could have.

Price for men's combination overcoat and raincoat, style 135..... **$9.00**

Men's Cielette Fancy Cheviot Rainproof Spring Overcoat.

No. 27C508 A neat, nobby pattern by Nostrand & Moore, in a mixture of black, white and pale green, the black and white parts being worked into a subdued check effect of small squares, such a pattern as business men and young men would be pleased with. Made in style 135, without body lining and lined only in sleeves and yoke. Everyone of these garments is well tailored; they have excellent fitting qualities and combine good service and a dressy appearance.

Price for men's combination overcoat and raincoat, style 135......**$10.00**

Men's Cielette All Wool Worsted Rainproof Spring Overcoat.

No. 27C510 Background is black, sprinkled with white threads, with very faint single thread stripes of tan and blue occurring alternately ½ inch apart. A coat of fine quality and rich appearance; lined in yoke and sleeves with an extra quality of Italian body lining; excellent fitting quality and made in the popular long overcoat style 135, as illustrated.

Price for men's combination overcoat and raincoat, style 135...........**$10.50**

Men's Cielette Steel Gray Worsted Rainproof Spring Overcoat.

No. 27C512 An extremely popular pattern, produced by Mall & Company. A great favorite with business men for general purposes; a dressy garment in every respect. These coats are all well tailored, have fine fitting effects and are guaranteed to give every satisfaction. Made in a handsome long overcoat style 135, as illustrated, without body lining; such a coat as would cost you 50 per cent more elsewhere.

Price for men's combination overcoat and raincoat, style 135.....**$11.00**

Men's Cielette Silk Mixed Worsted Rainproof Spring Overcoat.

No. 27C514 A neat pattern by Steele & Co., with a dark background and a sprinkling of white and tan threads, enough to relieve the plain shade, a pattern with which modest tastes would be greatly pleased; is firmly woven and for general purposes there is nothing better. Lined in sleeves and yoke only, cut in style 135, like illustration. A well made, stylish and all around useful coat, comes in sizes 36 to 44 inches breast measure. Average length, 51 inches. Made in style 135, as illustrated.

Price for men's combination overcoat and raincoat, style 135.....**$12.00**

Men's Cielette Oxford Gray Worsted Spring Overcoat.

No. 27C516 This is a strong wearing fabric and is of a dull steel or oxford gray cast. It is very popular in all circles for its excellent wearing qualities and its modest shade, is a beautifully tailored coat, lined in sleeves and yoke only and made in the fashionable long overcoat style, such a coat as would cost you at least $20.00 elsewhere. Comes in sizes 36 to 44 inches chest measure and averages 51 inches long.

Price for men's all wool worsted combination overcoat and raincoat, style 135.............................**$13.00**

TOO much must not be expected of these Cielette raincoats. They are not intended for heavy continuous rains, but for all general purposes, rain or shine, they give exceptionally good service.

Men's Cielette Imported Silk Mixed Worsted Rainproof Spring Overcoat.

No. 27C518 A very stylish and pleasing pattern, woven by Schnabel Bros. A rich dark background with bright silver threads sprinkled through it in a sort of regular pattern. A very genteel and fashionable looking coat. It is very handsomely tailored and we can guarantee these garments to please the most careful dresser; such a coat as could be worn in the best dressing circles of large cities. In fashionable long style as illustrated under style 135.

Price for men's handsome imported silk mixed worsted rainproof coat, style 135.........................**$14.00**

Men's Cielette Rainproof Oxford Gray Worsted Spring Overcoat.

No. 27C520 A high grade fabric woven by the Botany mills. A good color and strong wearing cloth. Such a coat would cost you not less than $25.00 elsewhere. No body lining, but lined in sleeves and yoke with a fine grade of satin. A handsomely tailored garment, made in the dressy, long overcoat style 135, with latest shoulder effects and lapels. We recommend this to all careful dressers, to be just what is required for fine wearing. Made in sizes 36 to 44 inches chest measurement. Average length, 51 inches.

Price for men's combination oxford gray worsted overcoat and raincoat, style 135......................**$15.00**

MEN'S RUBBER SURFACE RAINCOATS AND OIL SLICKER CLOTHING.

FOR THIS SEASON we have added several new numbers to the assortment in our rubber surface raincoat department, as the demand last season leads us to believe that the rubber surface coat is the

MOST PRACTICAL WATERPROOF COAT MADE

for very heavy rain storms.

Rubber Coats are made up in the following sizes for men:

Size	3	4	5	6	7
Chest measure, inches	36	38	40	42	44

SIZES FOR BOYS: 26 to 34 inches chest measure. Be sure and always give correct height, weight and age of boy when ordering.

A GOOD RUBBER COAT will keep the wearer dry, which cannot be said of a great many low grade mackintoshes which are sold throughout the country as waterproof. We do not sample rubber coats.

USE CARE IN SENDING COMPLETE MEASUREMENTS WHEN ORDERING RUBBER CLOTHING.

Men's Oxford Rubber Covert Lined Coat.

Back view.

No. 27C90 This Fine Raincoat has an oxford covert surface cloth and is rubber lined to make it doubly waterproof; just the coat for the man that has outside work and is exposed to all kinds of weather. Made with double back, wide corduroy collar; has Thompson's automatic buckles and strapped armholes with ventilators. Sizes, 36 to 44 inches chest measure.

Price..................................**$3.25**

Men's Light Weight Brown Drill Lined Rubber Coat.

No. 27C91 In this light weight brown drill lined rubber coat we offer you a coat such as you could not buy elsewhere for nearly double the price. It is guaranteed strictly waterproof; two outside pockets and automatic buckles, as shown in illustration. Sizes, 36 to 44 inches chest measure.

Price.......**$2.50**

Men's Double Breasted Rubber Coat.

No. 27C100 Men's Black Luster Finish Coat, made with lining of woven sheeting, double breasted, two outside pockets with flaps, wide collar and throat latch, split tail in back. Sizes, 36 to 44 inches chest measure. Price **$1.50**

No. 27C101 Same style coat as above, made in the dull finish and a better grade. Sizes, 36 to 44 inches chest measure.

Price.......**$1.75**

BOYS' RUBBER COATS.

No. 27C102 Boys' Coat, exactly like No. 27C100. Sizes, 26 to 34 inches chest measure. Price..........**$1.25**

No. 27C103 Same as No. 27C101, in boys' sizes, 1 to 6, or 26 to 34 inches chest measure. Price..........**$1.50**

Men's Medium Weight Rubber Surface Raincoat.

No. 27C104 Men's Dull Finish Rubber Coat, drill lined, made in double breasted style, two outside pockets with flaps, and waterproof throat latch. For a good, serviceable coat at a low price, this number is one of the best obtainable. Sizes, 36 to 44 inches chest measure. Price...**$2.00**

Men's Light Weight Rubber Coat.

A $3.50 RUBBER COAT FOR $2.35.

No. 27C106 This coat is a very light rubber surface coat, made with fancy plaid printed lining, black velvet collar. Sizes, 36 to 44 inches chest measure.

Price.......**$2.35**

Men's Dull Finish Drill Coat only $2.50.

No. 27C107 Men's Extra Quality Officers' Dull Drill Coat, made with Thompson's automatic buckle, which is one of the best patent clasps on the market. Sizes, 36 to 44 inches chest measure.

Price, for men's dull drill coat.....**$2.50**

Men's Heavy Common Sense Raincoat.

No. 27C108 **Our Common Sense Rubber Coat,** friction lined, double back, storm fly front, Thompson's automatic buckles, draw-strap on collar and sleeves, and two large outside pockets; average length of these coats, about 54 inches and fully guaranteed. Others ask $4.00 and $4.50 for the same coat. Sizes, 36 to 44 inches chest measure.
Price........$3.50

Firemen's Pure Double Gum Raincoat.

No. 27C109 **This number presents the best double coated pure gum rubber coat made.** Comes 47 inches long, is made with a storm fly front, corduroy tipped collar, new patent spearhead fasteners, draw buckles on sleeves and collar and one large pocket inside with waterproof flaps. Sizes, 36 to 44 inches chest measure.
Price for firemen's coat..........$3.50

Policemen's Best Grade Rubber Coat.

Our Policeman's Coat is the best article on the market. These coats come 53 inches long with a 20-inch slit in back made with double back and shoulders, which are thoroughly ventilated (see back view below), ball and socket fasteners, draw buckles on sleeves, two pockets inside and extra star holder on left breast. The facings on this coat are very full and it is guaranteed strictly waterproof.

No. 27C110 Price for policemen's coat.........$4.25
Sizes are 36 to 44 inches chest measure. All sizes larger than 44 inches will cost 50 cents extra per size.

Back view showing ventilation under double back.

Railroad or Teamsters' Rubber Surface Raincoat.

No. 27C96 **This is a handy coat,** 35 inches long with ball and socket fasteners, double back friction lined and guaranteed to be waterproof and the best short wet weather jacket on the market. Sizes, 36 to 44 inches chest.
Price......$2.10

Long Rubber Leggings.

Average weight, 20 ounces.

No. 27C111 Black Rubber Leggings, luster finish. Size 4, small; 5, medium; 6, large.
Price, per pair...55c

No. 27C112 Black Rubber Leggings, finished dull, with sheeting lining. Size, 4, small; 5, medium; 6, large.
Price, per pair....65c

Men's Rubber Cape Caps.

No. 27C113 **Men's Luster Sheeting Rubber Cape Caps,** come in black only, cemented seams. Always mention size. Sizes, 6¾ to 7½.
Price..................35c

No. 27C114 **Men's Rubber Cape Caps, dull finished,** sheeting lined, same style as above. Sizes, 6¾ to 7½.
Price..............................45c

Dull Finish Gum Hats.

No. 27C115 **We only handle one grade in rubber hats and that is the best.** Our hat is pure dull finished gum. Sizes, 6¾ to 7½. Don't fail to mention size wanted.
Price..............................55c

OIL SLICKER CLOTHING.

There are so many grades of oil slicker clothing, at so many different prices, that unless you deal with a responsible firm you are liable to get inferior goods, and garments that will only wear one-half as long as good oil slicker clothing should. Second or third grade oil clothing is poor property to buy at any price. **We guarantee our oil slicker clothing to be absolutely waterproof, it will not break or crack;** any oil slicker clothing that is purchased from us that proves unsatisfactory in any way can be returned at our expense, and we will cheerfully refund money or send new garments as desired. **Oil clothing should be worn loose.** When ordering, please take the number of inches around chest, under arms, over the clothing that you expect to wear the oil clothing over. Also give your correct height and weight.

OUR BINDING GUARANTEE— All goods are guaranteed to be first quality, absolutely waterproof, and to wear longer and give more satisfaction than the average goods sold for the best by any other house selling direct to the consumer.

Our Beatsall Coat in Black Only.

No. 27C116 **Is made under the U.S. patent. Its improvements over all other waterproof garments are immense.** It is an absolutely perfect protection for outdoor work in storm or rain. Over shoulders, breast, back and sleeves it is a triple coat, hence for miners, teamsters, drivers, motormen and others, cannot be equaled, the sleeves being oiled inside as well as outside. The weakest part of the garment is made the strongest. No expense is spared either in material, trimming or workmanship to make this perfect article the finest obtainable. Considering its intrinsic value, our price is below all others, as it will outwear three of the other oil coats, and is warranted strictly waterproof—a trial would make you our best friend and advertiser. Sizes, 36 to 46 inches chest measure. Price..................$2.75

Empire Express Coat.

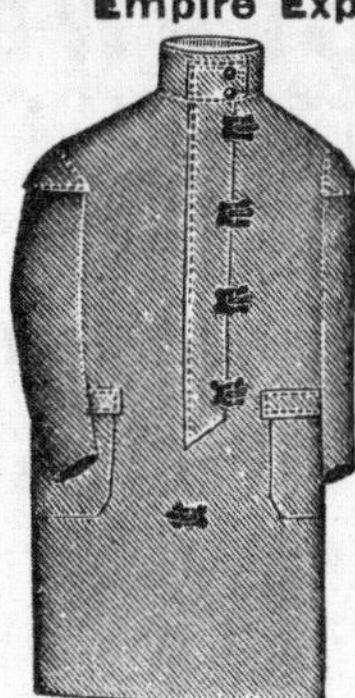

No. 27C120 **Our Empire Express Coat is the best black oil coat in existence. Especially adaped for car drivers, teamsters, motormen, expressmen, policemen and firemen.** Extra heavy, guaranteed strictly waterproof; and in the making of this garment no details, however small, have been overlooked. Has the new patent automatic fasteners, extra high soft flannel collar, large outside pockets with flaps; double throughout. No better material or better made coat can possibly be had at any price. Sizes, 36 to 44 inches chest measure. **Comes in black only.** Price....$2.40

Men's Long Black or Yellow Oil Double Slicker.

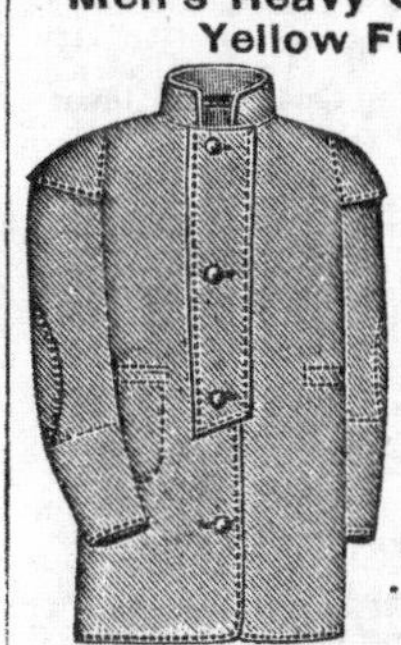

No. 27C121 **This coat is made from extra quality black waterproof oil slicker cloth. It is doubled throughout.** You cannot buy a better coat, or one that would give any more service or satisfaction. Second or third quality oil clothing is undesirable, when you can get the best from us at a less or lower price than the inferior goods are sold at elsewhere. Sizes, 36 to 44 inches breast measure. Be sure to state color wanted. Price.....$1.75

Men's Heavy Oil Black or Yellow Frocks.

No. 27C123 **Men's Heavy Oil Frock Coats are worn by miners, fishermen, etc.** They reach to the knees and can be worn with apron or string pants or rubber hip boots, as desired. **Warranted strictly waterproof; doubled throughout;** extra stay at shoulders and elbows. Thoroughly reliable in every way. Sizes, 36 to 44 inches breast measure. Be sure to state color wanted.
Price..........$1.30

Men's Black or Yellow Oil Jackets.

No. 27C125 **These Jackets are made as shown in illustration.** Made from heavy black or yellow oil slicker; double throughout. **Warranted waterproof. The best garment of its kind on the market.** Sizes, 36 to 44 inches breast measure. Average length, 30 inches. Be sure to state color wanted.
Price.............................85c

Our Black or Yellow Pommel Slicker or Saddle Coat.

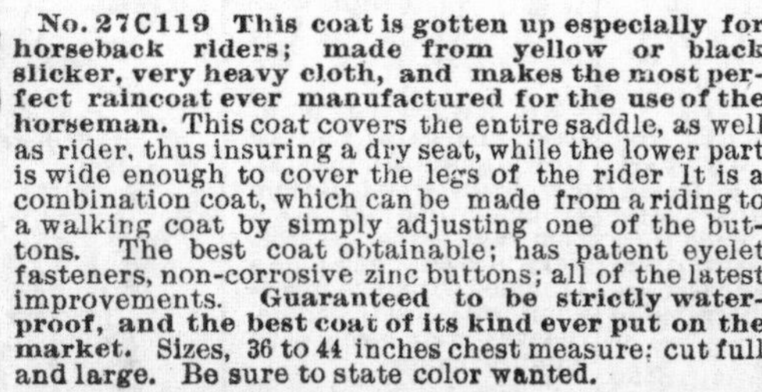

No. 27C119 **This coat is gotten up especially for horseback riders; made from yellow or black slicker, very heavy cloth, and makes the most perfect raincoat ever manufactured for the use of the horseman.** This coat covers the entire saddle, as well as rider, thus insuring a dry seat, while the lower part is wide enough to cover the legs of the rider It is a combination coat, which can be made from a riding to a walking coat by simply adjusting one of the buttons. The best coat obtainable; has patent eyelet fasteners, non-corrosive zinc buttons; all of the latest improvements. **Guaranteed to be strictly waterproof, and the best coat of its kind ever put on the market.** Sizes, 36 to 44 inches chest measure; cut full and large. Be sure to state color wanted.

Price..............................$2.50

Men's Heavy Double Apron Black or Yellow Oil Pants.

No. 27C127 **Made as shown in illustration with apron and shoulderstraps.** Extra well and thoroughly made throughout. Warranted waterproof. Sizes, 34 to 44 inches waist measure, average about 31 inches long. Be sure to state the color wanted.
Price, per pair........85c

Men's Black or Yellow Oil String Pants.

No. 27C129 **Made double throughout.** Reinforced in crotch and waist. Riveted zinc buttons on fly. **Warranted waterproof.** Be sure to state color wanted.
Price, per pair..85c

Squam Sou'westers.

No. 27C131 **Men's Black or Yellow Oiled Hats.** Made same as illustration. Cloth lined; warranted waterproof. Don't fail to state color. Mention size wanted. Price..........18c

Manhattan Oil Compound, Black or Yellow.

No. 27C133 **This compound is used for recoating clothing, and may be applied with a sponge or brush.** You can make oil clothing yourself with this compound. It is an excellent thing to have on hand. Every farmer should have a can of this oil compound. It comes in pint cans. State color wanted. Price, per pint can......25c

DON'T FAIL TO SEND ALL MEASURES CORRECTLY.

Beats All Sou'westers.

SOMETHING NEW.

No. 27C135 **Men's Black Oiled Cape Sou'wester.** No oiled suit complete without one, strictly waterproof. Come in black only. Mention size wanted.
Price............40c

Yellow or Black Oiled Aprons.

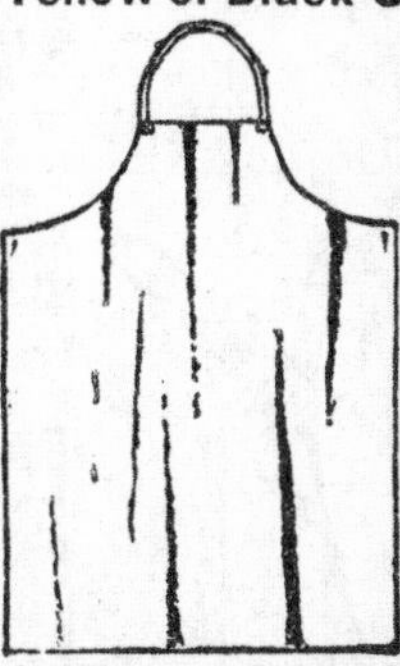

No. 27C137 **Double Sheeting Aprons,** are made of strong sheeting lined throughout, thoroughly oiled and durably made, are finished with cloth straps to suspend from neck. Are worn by fishermen, dairymen, laundrymen, and others desiring a waterproof apron that is convenient and light. Come in black or yellow. State color wanted. Length, 45 inches; width, 36 inches.
Price..........................55c

No. 27C138 Duck Aprons are made of special woven heavy duck, lined with heavy sheeting, thoroughly oiled and durably made, are finished with cloth shoulder straps and leather strap and buckle to fasten around waist. Are worn by butchers, packers, icemen, tanners, etc. Come in black or yellow. State color wanted. Length, 52 inches; width, 40 inches.
Price..........................70c

MUSLIN UNDERWEAR DEPARTMENT

OUR MUSLIN GOODS are made under our own supervision, under the most approved sanitary conditions, and with the result of the best class of workmanship. Each garment is carefully examined as to stitching, 15 to 18 stitches to an inch in our garments. Widths, lengths, sizes, buttons and buttonholes, all undergo a careful inspection before being accepted, thus insuring our customers well made and stylish muslin wear.

READ OUR DESCRIPTIONS as to materials and trimmings. All trimmings, such as laces, embroideries, etc., are of the newest patterns and the daintiest effects, and our styles, workmanship and low prices will surely please everyone who patronizes this department. Send us your order with the understanding that if the goods are not perfectly satisfactory when received, you can return them to us at our expense and your money will be refunded to you.

MUSLIN UNDERWEAR OUTFITS.

FOR THE CONVENIENCE OF CUSTOMERS and also to save them money, we have gotten up two complete muslin underwear outfits, very carefully selected, consisting of all the necessary and best style of garments which we offer in complete sets of fourteen pieces. These outfits are already put up in sets and we cannot make any changes. If you buy one of these outfits, you will be getting remarkable value, for the price is less than you would pay for the individual pieces of the same quality bought separately. We are making very low and close prices on the complete outfits. Our profit is only a very slight margin on the cost of the complete outfit (not on the separate pieces) and is a smaller percentage of profit, than we could accept if we were pricing each individual garment. We save the handling expense and we give you the benefit of this in the low price. To sell the same number of muslin garments separately would mean a greater handling expense, because each item would have to be picked from stock, handled and packed. In this outfit, everything is complete and we handle the complete outfit, thus one handling as against fourteen (14 garments).

We strongly advise you to order one of these outfits. You will get a complete muslin underwear wardrobe at a price unheard of before. Don't fail to include one of these outfits for your supply of muslin underwear, and such additional pieces as you require can be selected from the following pages.

OUR $4.95 MUSLIN UNDERWEAR OUTFIT, CONSISTING OF FOURTEEN PIECES.

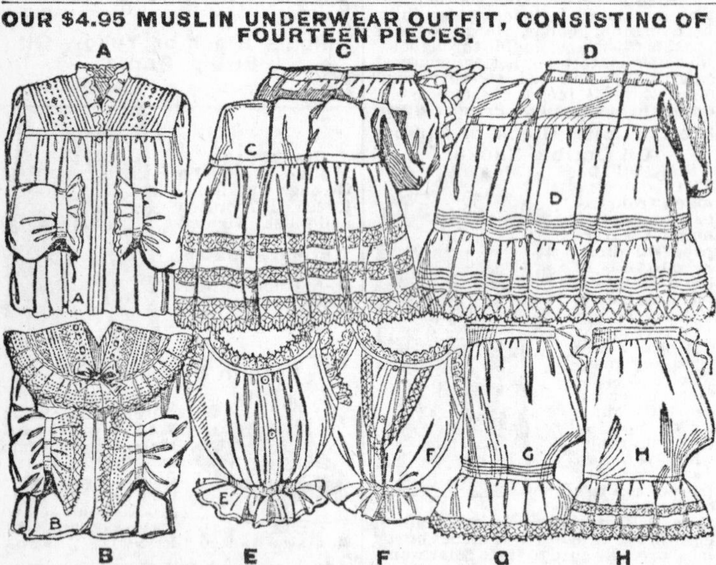

A Two Gowns made of muslin, yoke trimmed with tucks and insertion.
B One Gown made of cambric, very pretty yoke with torchon lace insertions, hemstitching, tucks, beading and ribbon insertion, lawn ruffle with lace edge to match.
C One Underskirt made of cambric, wide lawn flounce with two insertions of torchon lace with edge to match, made with a dust ruffle.
D Two Underskirts made of cambric, has 7-inch lawn flounce tucked four times, lawn ruffle with four tucks and edged with torchon lace, has dust ruffle.
E Two Corset Covers made of cambric, neck and armholes trimmed with torchon lace.
F Two Corset Covers made of cambric, two insertions of torchon lace, neck and armholes trimmed to match.
G Two pair Drawers made of muslin, trimmed with three tucks, has 4-inch cambric flounce edged with valenciennes lace.
H Two pair Drawers made of muslin, has cambric flounce, one insertion of torchon lace with edge to match. Be sure and give bust measure and skirt length.
Total, fourteen pieces.
No. 38C100 Price, for entire set of fourteen pieces..................$4.95
For Bridal Outfits with matched trimmings, see pages 932 and 933.

OUR GREAT MUSLIN UNDERWEAR OUTFIT OF FOURTEEN PIECES FOR $7.65.

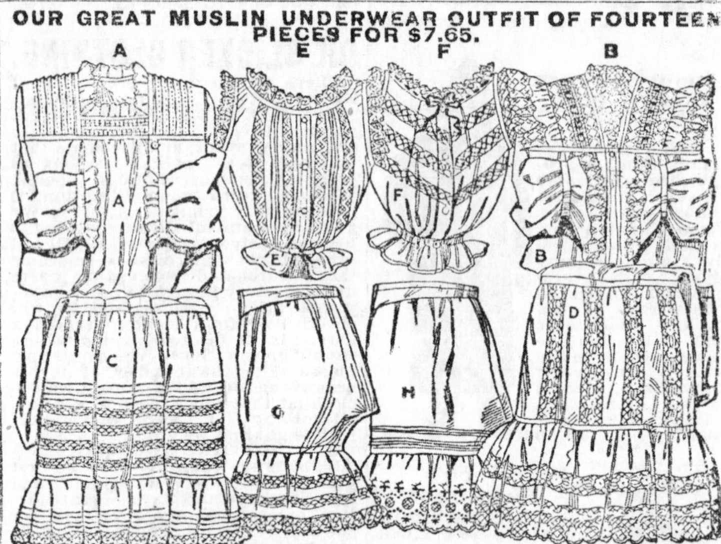

A Two Gowns made of muslin, square neck and yoke trimmed with rows of hemstitched tucks, embroidery insertions and cambric ruffle.
B Two Gowns made of cambric, yoke with two insertions of torchon lace, beading and ribbon insertion, lawn shoulder epaulets edged with torchon lace, neck and sleeves trimmed with lace to match.
C One Underskirt made of cambric, lawn flounce trimmed with four tucks and four insertions of neat valenciennes lace, lawn ruffle trimmed with four tucks and lace edge to match. Entire flounce is 18 inches deep; has dust ruffle.
D One Underskirt made of fine cambric, lawn flounce with eighteen insertions of 2-inch point de Paris lace, lawn ruffle with 2-inch insertion and 3-inch edge to match, made with a dust ruffle.
E Two Corset Covers made of cambric, trimmed with four insertions of torchon lace and two clusters of four tucks, neck and armholes trimmed with lace to match.
F Two Corset Covers made of cambric, three rows of torchon lace insertion, neck trimmed with lace followed with beading and ribbon insertion, armholes trimmed with lace to match.
G Two pairs Drawers made of cambric, has lawn flounce with two insertions of torchon lace with edge to match.
H Two pairs Drawers made of cambric, trimmed with two clusters of three tucks and 5-inch embroidery ruffle.
Total, fourteen pieces. Sizes, 32 to 42 inches bust measure. Skirt lengths, 38, 40 and 42 inches. Be sure and give bust measure and skirt lengths.
No. 38C101 Price, for entire set of fourteen pieces, only..........$7.65
Bridal Outfits with matched trimmings on page 933.

LADIES' MUSLIN, CAMBRIC AND NAINSOOK GOWNS.

SIZES, 14, 15 AND 16 INCHES NECK MEASURE.

In proportion as follows: 14-inch neck, 32-34-inch bust; 15-inch neck, 36-38-inch bust; 16-inch neck, 40-42-inch bust

For extra size gowns see pages 933 and 934.

No. 38C102 Ladies' Gown, made of muslin, hubbard style, yoke trimmed on each side with one row of open embroidery and six tucks, making a total of twelve tucks in yoke, neck trimmed with cambric ruffle, sleeves also trimmed with cambric ruffle to match. Price, 39c
If by mail, postage extra, 15 cents.

No. 38C103 Very Serviceable Gown, made of muslin. Solid tucked yoke, each tuck hemstitched, lawn ruffle around neck and sleeves with hemstitching. Made extra full.
Price..............50c
If by mail, postage extra, 15 cents.

No. 38C104 Wonderful bargain. Ladies' Gown, made of muslin. Empire style, Bosom trimmed with lace insertion and wide embroidery edge. Lapels trimmed with lace insertion with wide ruffle. Sleeves trimmed with cambric ruffle.
Price..............49c
If by mail, postage extra, 15 cents.

No. 38C113 Ladies' Gown, hubbard style, made of a good quality muslin, fancy yoke trimmed with beading and ribbon inserting, with two rows of torchon lace insertion alternating with two clusters of fine tucks; the V-shaped neck is edged with wide torchon lace, sleeves trimmed with a torchon lace to correspond.
Price......65c
Postage extra, 15 cents.

No. 38C125 Ladies' Gown, empire style, made of good quality muslin, collar made of insertions of embroidery with wide ruffle of open work embroidery, bosom trimmed with beading and ribbon insertion, wide embroidery ruffle to match collar, sleeves trimmed with embroidery to match; deep hem at bottom.
Price..........75c
If by mail, postage extra, 15 cents.

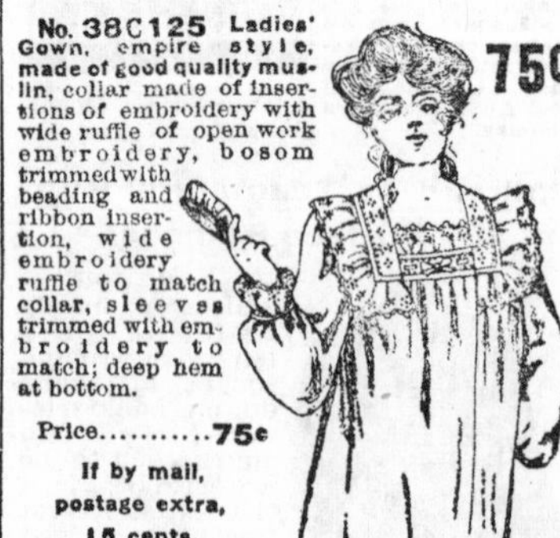

48c

No. 38C121 Ladies' Muslin Gown, high neck yoke both back and front; nine rows of tucks (each hemstitched) on each side of the yoke in front, alternating with four embroidery insertions, lawn collar and cuffs with one row of hemstitching.
Price, 48c
Postage extra, 15c.

85c

No. 38C130 Ladies' Gown, made of good quality muslin, hubbard style, pointed yoke of numerous rows of hemstitched tucks, followed with embroidery ruffle; neck and sleeves trimmed with embroidery to match, nice deep hem at bottom.
Price......85c
If by mail, postage extra, 16 cents.

No. 38C132 Ladies' Gown, made of cambric. Yoke trimmed with three insertions of neat embroidery alternating with four hemstitched tucks, finished with wide embroidery ruffle. V-shape neck trimmed with embroidery to match. Sleeves trimmed with embroidery. Made extra full. Price, 89c
If by mail, postage extra, 16 cents.

89c

No. 38C148 Ladies' Gown, made of good quality muslin. Square yoke with insertion of torchon lace and numerous tucks. Cambric ruffle edged with torchon lace; neck, fly and cuffs trimmed with lace to match. Exceptionally good value.
Price....55c
If by mail, postage extra, 16 cents.

55c

No. 38C160 Ladies' Gown, made of good quality muslin. Empire style bosom trimmed with two embroidery insertions and wide edges, lapels trimmed with insertion of neat embroidery followed with wide embroidery ruffle. Sleeves trimmed to correspond. Exceptional good value.
Price.... 89c
If by mail, postage extra, 15 cents.

89c

No. 38C172 Very Neat Lace Trimmed Gown, made of fine nainsook. Yoke trimmed with six insertions of fine valenciennes lace alternating with eight insertions of neat embroidery, neck trimmed with lace to match. Lawn cuffs neatly trimmed with three tucks, valenciennes lace insertion and edge to match. Made extra full. Price, $1.25
If by mail, postage extra, 14 cents.

98c

No. 38C138 Ladies' Gown, made of cambric, empire style; bosom trimmed with three rows of fine torchon lace insertion and ribbon, large collar with torchon insertion and edge to match; lawn cuffs with torchon lace insertion and matched edge.
Price.........98c
If by mail, postage extra, 15 cents.

65c

No. 38C152 Ladies' Gown, made of cambric. Very neatly trimmed yoke with four insertions of valenciennes lace, alternating with six clusters of three hemstitched tucks. V-shaped neck edged with lace. Cuffs trimmed with valenciennes lace to match.
Price......65c
If by mail, postage extra, 13c.

98c

No. 38C164 Very Neat Embroidery Trimmed Gown, made of good quality cambric. Square yoke with solid hemstitched tucks and insertion of open embroidery followed with neat ruffle of fine embroidery, neck and fly trimmed with embroidery. Sleeves trimmed to correspond. Made extra full.
Price........................98c
If by mail, postage extra, 16 cents.

$1.39

No. 38C176 Very Fine Gown, made of nainsook. Square neck with insertion of fine embroidery, followed with herringbone braid and edged with neat embroidery. Ruffle of embroidery to match. Sleeves trimmed with herringbone braid and embroidery, made extra full, nice hem at bottom. Price,.....$1.39
If by mail, postage extra, 14 cents.

48c

No. 38C140 Very Neat Gown made of cambric, slipover style. Round neck with insertion of silk ribbon. Elbow sleeves with ribbon insertion. Extra full with hem at bottom.
Price.........48c
If by mail, postage extra, 12 cents.

No. 38C156 Embroidery Trimmed Gown, made of good quality muslin. Round yoke with four insertions of embroidery alternating with six clusters of tucks. Yoke followed with 8-inch embroidery ruffle. Neck and sleeves trimmed with cambric ruffle. Extra good value.
Price....69c
If by mail, postage extra, 15 cents.

69c

No. 38C168 Ladies' Gown, made of good quality cambric. Empire style. Revers with two insertions of open embroidery followed with wide embroidery ruffle. Bosom trimmed with embroidery insertion and edge, also beading and ribbon insertion. Sleeves trimmed with wide embroidery.
Price......98c
If by mail, postage extra, 15 cents.

98c

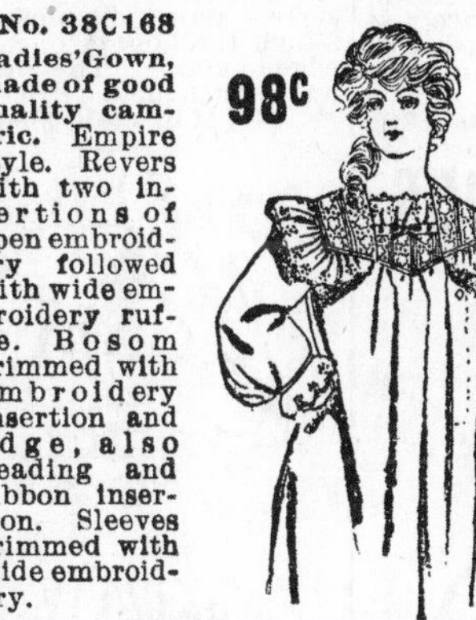

No. 38C178 Ladies' Gown, made of fine quality cambric. Empire style. Very neatly trimmed yoke of narrow embroidery insertions, bosom trimmed with beading and ribbon insertion. Ruffle of neat embroidery followed with herringbone braid. Neck and sleeves trimmed with embroidery to match. Made extra full, with nice hem at bottom. Price..............$1.48
If by mail, postage extra, 16 cents.

$1.10

No. 38C142 Ladies' Gown, empire style, made of soft finished cambric, bosom trimmed with four hemstitched tucks, one row of insertion, two rows of beading and narrow ribbon inserted and point de Paris lace edged revers trimmed with numerous rows of hemstitched tucks with one row of beading and narrow ribbon inserted, wide lawn hemstitched collar which is edged with point de Paris lace, flaring lawn hemstitched cuffs edged with point de Paris lace to match. Very full with nice hem at bottom. Price..........$1.10
If by mail, postage extra, 16 cents.

85c

No. 38C158 Very Neat Lace Trimmed Gown, made of good quality cambric. Yoke with four insertions of torchon lace, alternating with four clusters of three hemstitched tucks. Yoke followed with cambric ruffle which is edged with wide torchon lace; neck trimmed with lace to match. Sleeves trimmed with cambric ruffle and torchon lace to match. Price,...............85c
If by mail, postage extra, 16 cents.

LADIES' WHITE MUSLIN, CAMBRIC AND NAINSOOK LACE TRIMMED UNDERSKIRTS.

LENGTHS, 38, 40 AND 42 INCHES.

FOR EXTRA SIZE UNDERSKIRTS SEE PAGE 933.

ALL UNDERSKIRTS MADE WITH DRAW STRINGS, MAKING THEM ADJUSTABLE TO WAIST.

NOTE WIDTHS OF FLOUNCE ON THESE UNDERSKIRTS.

98c

No. 38C146 Ladies' Gown, made of good quality cambric. Very neat yoke of embroidery alternating with tucks. Yoke followed with embroidery ruffle. Neck and sleeves trimmed with neat embroidery. Excellent value.
Price....98c
If by mail, postage extra, 15 cents.

39c

No. 38C301 Ladies' Muslin Underskirt, made with a 3-inch ruffle and edged with torchon lace. Price......................39c
If by mail, postage extra, 14 cents.

UNDERSKIRTS CONTINUED ON FOLLOWING PAGES.

75c

No. 38C305 Ladies' Muslin Underskirt, trimmed with two wide lawn ruffles around bottom, which are edged with a 2-inch wash lace; very pretty underskirt. Price..............................75c
If by mail, postage extra, 15 cents.

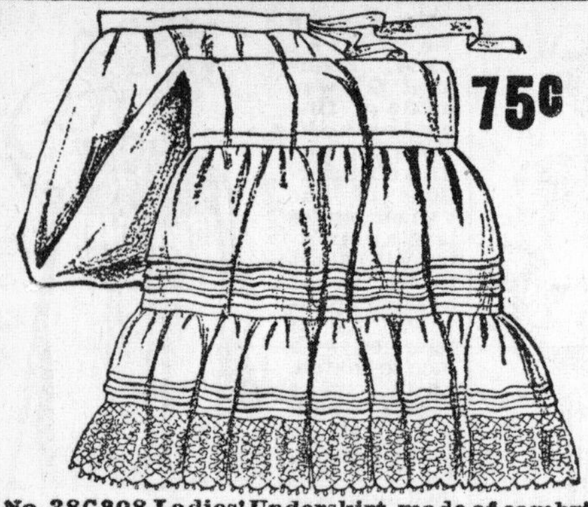

No. 38C308 Ladies' Underskirt, made of cambric. Has 8-inch lawn flounce trimmed with three tucks, lawn ruffle trimmed with two tucks and edged with 3-inch torchon lace. Entire flounce including lace edge is 15 inches deep, has dust ruffle.
Price...(**If by mail, postage extra, 16 cents**)..75c

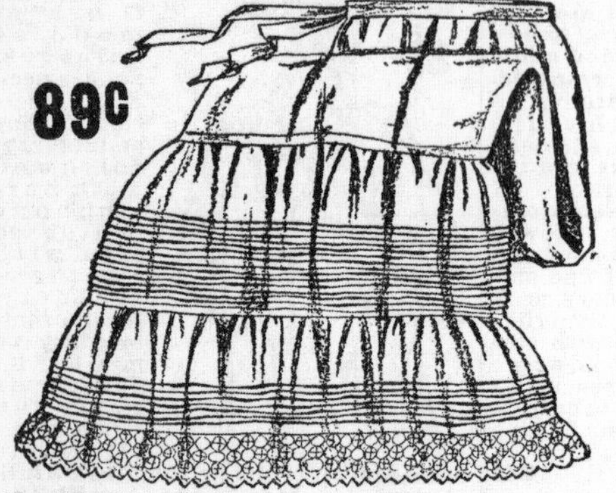

No. 38C312 Ladies' Underskirt, made of good grade muslin. French flounce, made of lawn, trimmed with fourteen tucks on upper flounce and seven tucks on lower flounce, which is edged with 3-inch torchon lace. Entire flounce, including lace edge, is 16 inches deep, made with dust ruffle.
Price.. (**If by mail, postage extra, 16 cents**)..89c

No. 38C314 Wonderful Value, Ladies' Underskirt, made of cambric. Has 11-inch lawn flounce trimmed with two clusters of three tucks and two insertions of 2½-inch torchon lace, lawn ruffle edged with 3-inch torchon lace. Entire flounce, including lace edge, is 17 inches deep, making a very attractive underskirt; has dust ruffle. Price................85c
If by mail, postage extra, 16 cents.

These Skirts are Remarkable Values.

No. 38C317 Ladies' Muslin Underskirt, lawn flounce, French style, three insertions of torchon lace, above which is a cluster of four tucks; 3-inch lace edge on lawn ruffle, above which is trimmed with four tucks. Entire flounce, including lace edge, is 21 inches deep; has dust ruffle. Price.. ....98c
If by mail, postage extra, 16 cents.

No. 38C318 Ladies' Muslin Underskirt, same as No. 38C317, without tucks. Price (**If by mail, postage extra, 16 cents**)..85c

No. 38C320 Ladies' Cambric Underskirt, has a 9-inch cambric flounce with four insertions of neat valenciennes lace. Cambric ruffle trimmed with four neat tucks and edged with valenciennes lace to match. Entire flounce, including ruffle and lace edge, is 14 inches deep. Price..................98c
If by mail, postage extra, 16 cents.

No. 38C321 Ladies' Muslin Underskirt, French style. Lawn flounce with fifteen insertions of 2-inch torchon lace running on the bias. 2-inch edge to match. The entire flounce is 18 inches deep; has a dust ruffle. Price..........................$1.10
If by mail, postage extra, 18 cents.

No. 38C324 Ladies' Underskirt, made of cambric. Has a 15-inch lawn flounce trimmed with a cluster of three tucks and three insertions of 2½-inch point de Paris lace, lawn ruffle with cluster of three tucks, edged with 3-inch lace to match. Entire flounce, including lace edge, is 22 inches deep, making a very attractive underskirt, has dust ruffle.
Price..$1.25
If by mail, postage extra, 17 cents.

No. 38C325 Ladies' Very Pretty Muslin Underskirt, French style. Lawn flounce, with three clusters of fine tucks, each hemstitched, and two insertions of 2-inch torchon lace. Has a lawn ruffle around bottom with a cluster of three tucks, each hemstitched; lace edge to match; also a dust ruffle. Flounce, including lace edge, is 20 inches deep. Price.................................$1.10
If by mail, postage extra, 16 cents.

No. 38C326 Ladies' Cambric Underskirt. Has very pretty lawn flounce with thirteen insertions of 2½-inch torchon lace alternating with six tucks. lawn ruffle which is edged with 3-inch torchon lace. Flounce, including lace edge, is 14 inches deep, has dust ruffle. Price...............................98c
If by mail, postage extra, 17 cents.

No. 38C327 Ladies' Underskirt, made of white cambric, lawn flounce 15 inches deep with four insertions of neat pattern torchon lace, has a lawn ruffle with four tucks, and wide lace edge to match. Entire flounce, including ruffle and edge, is 19 inches deep, has a dust ruffle. A very attractive underskirt.
Price..(**If by mail, postage extra, 17 cents**), $1.25

$1.15

No. 38C331 Ladies' Underskirt, made of good quality cambric. Has a 13-inch lawn flounce trimmed with ten fine tucks with three insertions of neat valenciennes lace and a cluster of five fine tucks, ruffle trimmed with a cluster of five tucks, two insertions of valenciennes lace and edge to match. Entire flounce is 21 inches deep, making a very attractive underskirt, made with a dust ruffle.
Price. (**If by mail, postage extra, 17 cents**)..$1.15

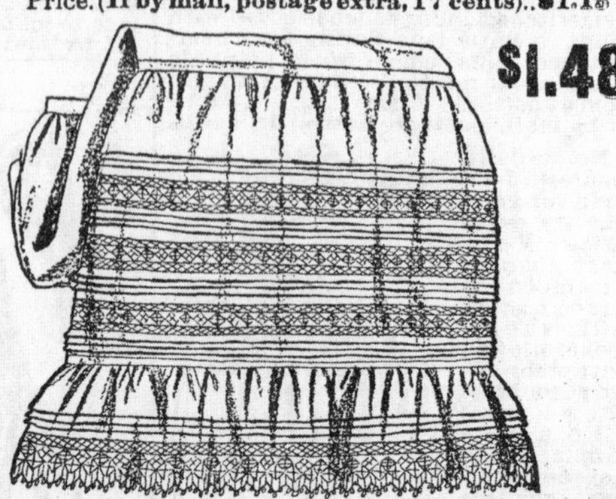

No. 38C334 Ladies' Underskirt, made of a good grade of cambric. Has a lawn flounce trimmed with four clusters of three tucks and three insertions of 2½-inch torchon lace, lawn ruffle trimmed with a cluster of three tucks and edged with 3-inch torchon lace to match. The entire flounce, including lace edge, is 25 inches deep, making a very attractive underskirt; made with a dust ruffle.
Price.....(**If by mail, postage extra, 18 cents**)........$1.48

No. 38C338 Very Stylish Underskirt, made of cambric. Has a lawn flounce trimmed with two insertions of 3-inch point de Paris lace, alternating with three clusters of six fine tucks; has wide lawn ruffle trimmed with six fine tucks and edged with 5-inch lace to match. The entire flounce, including lace edge, is 26 inches deep, making a very attractive underskirt; made with a dust ruffle. Price....$2.69
If by mail, postage extra, 19 cents.

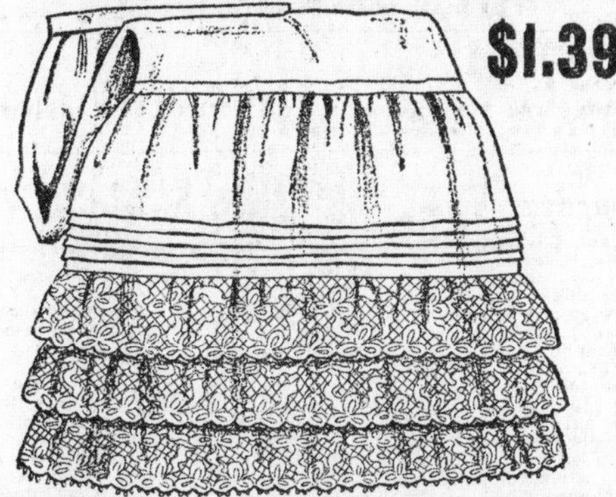

No. 38C342 Ladies' Cambric Underskirt, made with triple point de Paris lace ruffles, upper flounce trimmed with five fine tucks, each flounce trimmed with 4-inch point de Paris lace, making a very attractive underskirt; has dust ruffle. Price..$1.39
If by mail, postage extra, 16 cents.

No. 38C346 Ladies' Underskirt, made of cambric. Has a very pretty, graduated flounce made of lawn, trimmed with a cluster of four fine tucks, with five rows of fine 2-inch torchon lace insertions, with 3-inch lace edge to match. Entire flounce, including lace edge, is 25 inches deep. Made with a dust ruffle. Price.......................................$1.98
If by mail, postage extra, 17 cents.

No. 38C350 Ladies' Underskirt, made of fine cambric. Has 17-inch lawn flounce, trimmed with eight hemstitched tucks, and three insertions of the new pattern (snow ball) lace. Wide lawn ruffle with two rows of hemstitched tucks and edged with 4-inch snow ball lace to match. The entire flounce, including lace edge, is 24 inches deep. Extra fine value. Price.......................................$1.75
If by mail, postage extra, 19 cents.

No. 38C354 Ladies' Underskirt, made of fine cambric. Very artistically designed, flounce made of thirty insertions of 2½-inch point de Paris lace, with triangular pieces of lawn set in between each insertion, giving skirt a nice flow. Lawn ruffle followed with herringbone braid and edged with 3-inch lace to match. Entire flounce, including lace, is 17 inches deep, made with a dust ruffle. Price.......................$1.95
If by mail, postage extra, 20 cents.

No. 38C355 Ladies' Underskirt, made of fine cambric, same style as No. 38C354, with thirty-four insertions of fine raised pattern point de Paris lace. Ruffle trimmed with four tucks. Price...(If by mail, postage extra, 20 cents)....$2.48

No. 38C349 Handsome Lace Trimmed Skirt, made of fine white cambric, has a very pretty lawn flounce. Five clusters of hemstitched tucks, five insertions of point de Paris lace and wide edge to match. Wide beading and satin ribbon insertion at top of flounce, forming a bow with streamers. Entire flounce, including lace edge, is 18 inches deep, has a dust ruffle. Price......(If by mail, postage extra, 19 cents).....$2.75

LADIES' WHITE MUSLIN, CAMBRIC AND NAINSOOK EMBROIDERY TRIMMED LONG UNDERSKIRTS.

Lengths, 38, 40 and 42 inches.

Adjustable Waist with Draw Strings.

Note widths of flounce and embroidery in these skirts.

No. 38C361 A very good value. Muslin Skirt, made with a 3½-inch lawn ruffle of openwork embroidery, above which is a cluster of three tucks. Price...............................48c
If by mail, postage extra, 13 cents.

No. 38C365 A wonderful bargain, Muslin Skirt, made with a 5-inch lawn flounce trimmed with three rows of fine tucks, wide ruffle of lawn embroidery; flounce and ruffle 9 inches deep; has dust ruffle. Price...(If by mail, postage extra, 13c)....69c

No. 38C369 Ladies' Underskirt, made of good quality muslin, with French cambric flounce trimmed with three clusters of fine tucks (five tucks in each cluster), one row of open embroidery insertion and edged with 2-inch embroidery to match; entire flounce, including embroidery edge, is 14 inches deep. Price...............................89c
If by mail, postage extra, 14 cents.

No. 38C372 Ladies' Underskirt, made of cambric. Has a 10-inch lawn flounce trimmed with eight wide tucks, trimmed with 8-inch open embroidery; flounce, including embroidery, is 18 inches deep. Made with dust ruffle. A very serviceable skirt. Price...................................98c
If by mail, postage extra, 15 cents.

No. 38C376 Ladies' Underskirt, made of cambric. Has 8-inch lawn flounce, with three tucks and four rows of hemstitching, trimmed with 7-inch open embroidery. Serviceable skirt with wide embroidery trimming and dust ruffle. Price......89c
If by mail, postage extra, 15 cents.

No. 38C380 Ladies' Embroidery Trimmed Underskirt, made of cambric. Has 10-inch lawn flounce, trimmed with four fine tucks; insertion of open embroidery, trimmed with 6-inch embroidery edge. Entire flounce, including embroidery edge, is 17 inches deep. Made with a dust ruffle. Price. 98c
If by mail, postage extra, 15 cents.

$1.15

No. 38C384 Ladies' Fine Embroidery Trimmed Underskirt, made of cambric. Has 9-inch lawn flounce, trimmed with twelve fine tucks, with fine 8-inch embroidery edge; made with dust ruffle. Exceptionally good value. Price..................**$1.15**
If by mail, postage extra, 16 cents.

$1.48

No. 38C388 Very Fine Embroidery Trimmed Underskirt, made of cambric. Has 10-inch lawn flounce, trimmed with two clusters of six fine tucks, each with insertion of neat embroidery, trimmed with fine 8-inch embroidery; made with dust ruffle.
Price..**$1.48**
If by mail, postage extra, 18 cents.

$1.98

No. 38C394 Extra Fine Embroidery Trimmed Underskirt, made of cambric. Has a 14-inch lawn flounce, trimmed with two clusters of three fine tucks each, and two insertions of neat embroidery with 10-inch (note width) fine open embroidery edge. Flounce, including embroidery edge, is 24 inches deep, making a very attractive underskirt; made with dust ruffle. Price..................**$1.98**
If by mail, postage extra, 19 cents.

LADIES' CORSET COVERS.

Trimmed Corset Covers will be worn very much, as waists made of sheer materials and trimmings are very popular and stylish this season. Sizes, 32, 34, 36, 38, 40 and 42 inches bust measure. Always give your bust measure. For extra size Corset Covers, see page 933.

15c

No. 38C600 Ladies' Plain Muslin Corset Cover; round neck, felled seams. Perfect fitting. Price.......**8c**
If by mail, postage extra, 3 cents.

No. 38C604 Ladies' Corset Cover, square neck, trimmed with wide torchon lace, armholes taped, all seams felled. Sizes are 32 to 42 inches bust measure.
Price.........**15c**
If by mail, postage extra, 4 cents.

No. 38C608 Ladies' Cambric Corset Cover, trimmed around neck with beading and narrow ribbon insertion and edged with a neat pattern embroidery; draw strings at waist. Sizes are 32 to 42 inches bust measure. Always give bust measure.
Price..............**20c**
If by mail, postage extra, 4 cents.

27c

No. 38C612 Ladies' Corset Cover, made of cambric, low round neck, trimmed with valenciennes lace. Armholes trimmed with lace to match, four lace insertions in front; very full in front, fitted back.
Price, **27c**
If by mail, postage extra, 4 cents.

No. 38C614 Ladies' Corset Cover, made of Cambric. Has two rows of 1¼-inch point de Paris insertion, (back and front alike). Neck trimmed with lace to match, with beading and ribbon insertion. Armholes trimmed with lace to correspond.
Price......**39c**
If by mail, postage extra, 4 cents.

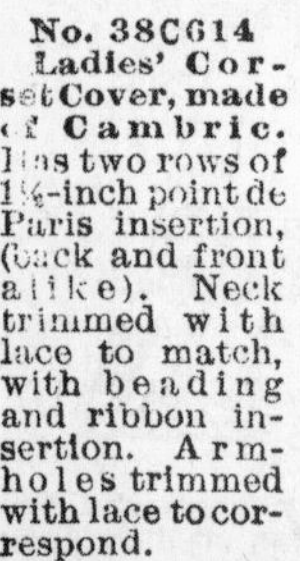

39c

35c

Newest Style Corset Cover.

No. 38C618 Very Neatly Trimmed Ladies' Corset Cover, made of cambric. Has two insertions of neat valenciennes lace, neck and armholes trimmed with lace to match. Splendid value.
Price..**35c**
If by mail, postage extra, 5 cents.

25c

No. 38C624 Ladies' Corset Cover, made of cambric, very neatly trimmed on the bias with three rows of valenciennes lace insertion, trimmed all around neck with lace edge to match; draw strings at waist.
Price... **25c**
If by mail, postage extra, 4 cents.

No. 38C625 Ladies' Corset Cover. Same as No. 38C624, but with two rows of insertion. Price...... ......**20c**
If by mail, postage extra, 5 cents.

25c

No. 38C630 Ladies' Corset Cover, made of cambric. Neck trimmed with two rows of neat valenciennes lace insertion beading and ribbon inserting with lace edge to match. Back trimmed with lace insertion, beading, ribbon inserting and lace edge to match. Armholes trimmed to correspond. Price **25c**
If by mail, postage extra, 5 cents.

48c

No. 38C632 Ladies' Embroidery Corset Cover. This corset cover is made of one piece of embroidery, 10 inches wide, of a very neat pattern, trimmed around top with narrow ribbon insertion through the embroidery pattern. The shoulder straps are made of two rows of valenciennes lace and embroidery. This cover has a ruffled lawn skirt; the very newest and up to date cover.
Price.........**48c**
If by mail, postage extra, 5 cents.

Cambric Corset Cover.

42c

No. 38C636 Cambric Corset Cover, very newest style; trimmed all around front and back of neck with fine lace edging; six rows of fine torchon lace insertion; draw strings at waist. **Always give bust measure.**
Price....................................**42c**
If by mail, postage extra, 4 cents.

39c

No. 38C638 Ladies' Corset Cover, made of fine nainsook. Trimmed across front with three rows of point de Paris lace, neck trimmed front and back with lace edge, beading and ribbon inserting. Armholes trimmed with lace to match. Excellent value.
Price....**39c**
If by mail, postage extra, 4 cents.

No. 38C639 Ladies' Corset Cover. Same as No. 38C638, with neat valenciennes lace trimmings. Price.........**30c**
If by mail, postage extra, 4 cents.

45c

Fine Cambric Corset Cover.

No. 38C640 A Very Pretty Corset Cover, made of fine cambric, front and back trimmed alike with two insertions of point de Paris lace, alternating with beading and narrow ribbon insertion with edge to match; armholes trimmed with lace to match. Price **45c**
If by mail, postage extra, 4 cents.

35c

No. 38C642 Ladies' Corset Cover, made of soft finish nainsook. Trimmed with four rows of valenciennes lace alternating with four clusters of five fine tucks; neck and armholes trimmed with lace to match.
Price....**35c**
If by mail, postage extra, 4 cents.

48c

No. 38C644 Ladies' Corset Cover, made of cambric, neck trimmed with valenciennes lace, armholes followed with beading and narrow ribbon insertion. Has three lawn ruffles in front, each edged with valenciennes lace, making it very full in front, a perfect shirt waist distender. **Always give bust measure.** Price **48c**
If by mail, postage extra, 5 cents.

No. 38C645 Corset Cover, same as No. 38C644, but with two ruffles and point de Paris lace trimmings.
Price.......................... **35c**
If by mail, postage extra, 5 cents.

Ladies' Corset Covers.

No. 38C646 Ladies' Corset Cover, made of cambric. Has two lawn ruffles, neck and armholes trimmed with hemstitched lawn, made with extra full ruffles, making a perfect shirt waist distender. Price..25c
Postage extra, 5 cents.

No. 38C650 Embroidery Trimmed Corset Cover, made of fine cambric. Yoke trimmed with rows of narrow embroidery alternating with tucks. Neck and armholes trimmed with neat embroidery.
Price.......39c
If by mail, postage extra, 5c.

No. 38C654 Very Stylish Corset Cover, made of soft finish nainsook. Trimmed all around cover with three rows of neat valenciennes lace. Neck and armholes trimmed with lace to match. A very attractive cover and excellent value.
Price........45c
If by mail, postage extra, 4c.

No. 38C658 Very Fine Corset Cover, made of soft nainsook. Trimmed with six insertions of neat valenciennes lace alternating with four clusters of five neat tucks, neck (back and front) trimmed with lace followed with beading and ribbon inserting. Armholes trimmed with lace to match. Price.48c
If by mail, postage extra, 4c.

No. 38C662 Very artistically trimmed Corset Cover, made of soft nainsook. Has insertions of valenciennes lace forming squares, and embroidery medallions, neck trimmed with valenciennes lace, followed with beading and ribbon inserting. Armholes trimmed with lace to match.
Price........59c
If by mail, postage extra, 5c.

Knitted Corset Cover.

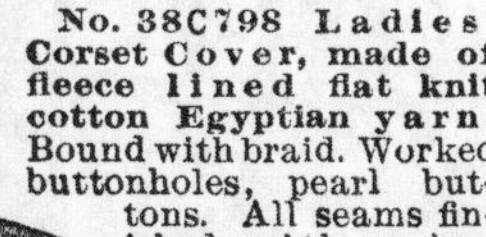

No. 38C798 Ladies' Corset Cover, made of fleece lined flat knit cotton Egyptian yarn. Bound with braid. Worked buttonholes, pearl buttons. All seams finished with union special stitch. An excellent cover for warmth and service. Colors, gray or ecru.
Price........45c
If by mail, postage extra, 7 cents.

No. 38C664 A very pretty Ladies' Corset Cover made of fine white sheer lawn, trimmed around neck and armholes with valenciennes lace, beading and narrow ribbon insertion. Nine rows of insertion of valenciennes lace around the cover (both front and back), beading and ribbon insertion at waist. Band draw strings. An exact copy of a French hand made corset cover. Entire cover is made of ¾-inch strips of lawn and lace insertions. Very pretty effect. **Be sure and give bust measure.** Price....98c

98c

If by mail, postage extra, 5 cents.

No. 38C666 Ladies' Corset Cover, made of soft finish nainsook. Yoke (back and front alike) is trimmed with rows of neat valenciennes lace, alternating with tucks and hemstitching. Yoke followed with beading and ribbon insertion, neck trimmed with lace followed with beading and ribbon insertion. Armholes trimmed to correspond. Very neat corset cover. Price..............48c
If by mail, postage extra, 5 cents.

No. 38C670 Ladies' Corset Cover, made of fine soft finish nainsook. Trimmed with insertions of neat valenciennes lace in very artistic designs. Neck (back and front alike) trimmed with insertion of valenciennes lace followed with beading and ribbon inserting and edged with lace to match. Armholes trimmed with lace to correspond.
Price.......... 80c
If by mail, postage extra, 5c.

No. 38C674 Very beautifully designed Corset Cover, made of fine soft nainsook. Has three insertions on the bias of neat valenciennes lace with six clusters of three fine tucks, trimmed near armholes with allover lace; neck and armholes trimmed with lace edge followed with beading and ribbon inserting, back trimmed with four clusters of three fine tucks. Price.......$1.25
If by mail, postage extra, 5 cents.

No. 38C678 Very fine Corset Cover, made of soft finish nainsook. Yoke trimmed with three insertions of fine valenciennes lace insertion, followed with four rows of beading and ribbon inserting, bosom trimmed with insertion to match in a very artistic design. Neck and armholes trimmed with lace edge to match, back trimmed with four clusters of three fine tucks.
Price......$1.39
If by mail, postage extra, 5 cents.

$1.48

No. 38C668 An exceedingly pretty Corset Cover made of fine white sheer lawn, low round neck and armholes trimmed with point de Paris lace, beading and ribbon insertion, a cluster of fine tucks in front, six insertions of fine point de Paris lace, alternating with beading and narrow ribbon insertion forming bows. Beading and ribbon insertion at waist, two clusters of fine (eight in a cluster) tucks on back running from neck to waist. The daintiness and beauty of these covers can only be found in French hand made lingerie. **Give bust measure.** Price.......$1.48
If by mail, postage extra, 5 cents.

LADIES' WHITE MUSLIN, CAMBRIC AND NAINSOOK DRAWERS.

Lengths 23, 25, 27, 29 inches.
For extra size drawers, see page 934.

When we quote open and closed style be sure and state style desired; otherwise we will send open style, which are more in demand.

18c

No. 38C800 Ladies' Drawers, made of muslin, has a 4-inch cambric flounce with one row of hemstitching and a neat hem around bottom, made extra full, open or closed style.
Price, per pair............ $0.18
Per dozen pairs............ 2.10
If by mail, postage extra, each, 7c.

23c

No. 38C802 Extra good value Muslin Drawers, made with wide flounce, insertion of English torchon lace and wide hem. **Open or closed style.** Regular 50-cent drawers. Price, per pair....................$0.23
Per dozen pairs..........(If by mail, postage extra, each, 8c)........ 2.70
No. 38C803 Ladies' Drawers, same style as No. 38C802, but with insertion of open embroidery. Very serviceable drawers. Open or closed style.
Price, per dozen pairs, $4.00; per pair...................35c
If by mail, postage extra, each, 8 cents.

39c

No. 38C804 A fine grade of Muslin Drawers, with three rows of tucks, 3-inch fine embroidery ruffle. Exceptionally good value. **Open style only.** Price, per pair.....$0.39
Per dozen pairs.....................4.50
If by mail, postage extra, each, 8 cents.

45c

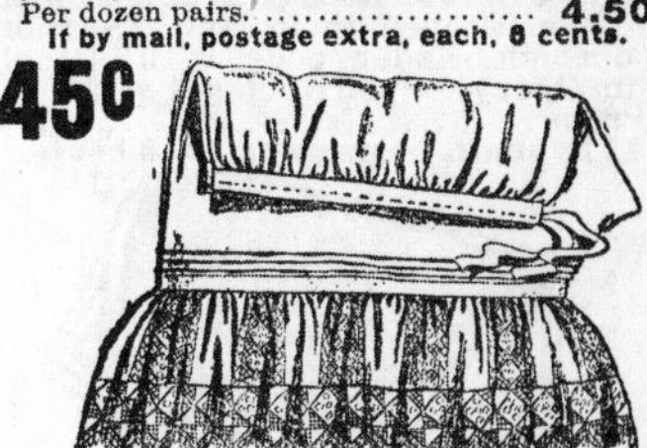

No. 38C806 Ladies' Drawers, made of good quality muslin, trimmed with three fine tucks, has lawn flounce around bottom trimmed with insertion of torchon lace and edged with 2-inch torchon lace to match, yoke waistband, open or closed style. Price........45c
If by mail, postage extra, 8 cents.

Special Value, Only 35 Cents.
No. 38C807 Ladies' Drawers. Same style as No. 38C806, but without tucks. Open or closed style. Price 35c
If by mail, postage extra, 8 cents.

48c

No. 38C808 Exceptionally good value, made of good quality of muslin, three rows of tucks, has lawn ruffle trimmed with three rows of tucks and edged with 3-inch torchon lace. **Open style only.** Price..48c
If by mail, postage extra, 8 cents.

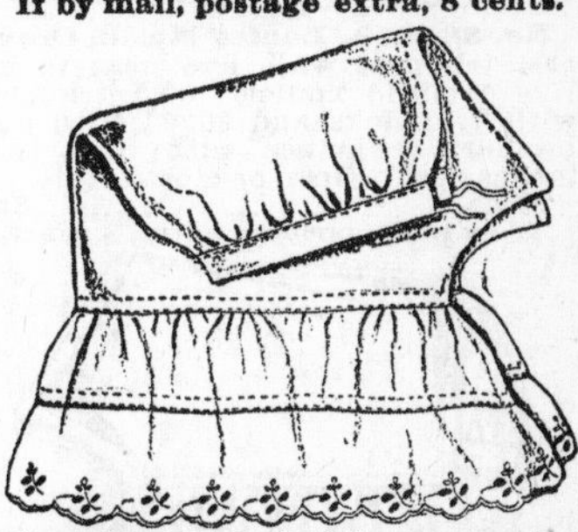

No. 38C809 Ladies' Drawers, made of muslin. Has cambric flounce which is taped and edged with embroidery. Flounce and edge are 5½ inches deep. Open or closed style.
Price, per pair............................27c
If by mail, postage extra, 8 cents.

No. 38C810 Ladies' Umbrella Style Drawers, made of good quality muslin, trimmed with four rows of tucks; has a very neat lawn flounce trimmed with eight fine tucks and one row of hemstitching edged with 2½-inch neat embroidery, yoke waistband. Open style.
Price, per pair.............................45c
If by mail, postage extra, 8 cents.

(Drawers continued on next page.)

No. 38C811 Ladies' Umbrella Drawers, made of cambric. Has a 5-inch cambric flounce trimmed with five hemstitched tucks and insertion of open embroidery edged with 2½-inch embroidery. Open or closed style. Price....48c
If by mail, postage extra, 8 cents.

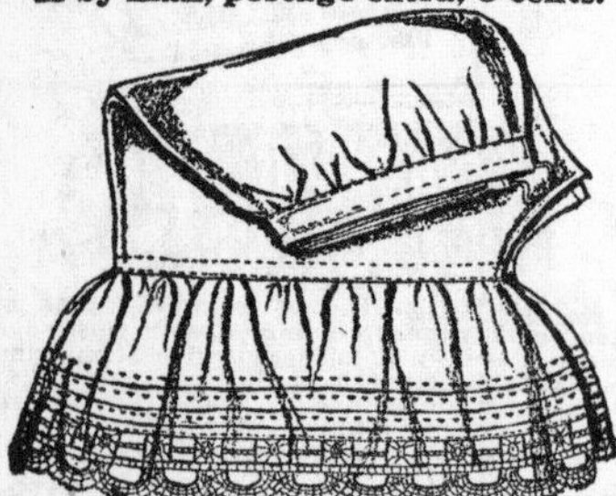

No. 38C815 Ladies' Muslin Drawers. Has a 5-inch cambric flounce trimmed with three hemstitched tucks and edged with 1-inch torchon lace. Open or closed style. Price....27c
If by mail, postage extra, 8 cents.

No. 38C816 Ladies' Muslin Drawers. Same as No. 38C815, but with hem instead of lace edge. Open or closed style. Price....22c
If by mail, postage extra, 8 cents.

No. 38C819 Ladies' Muslin Drawers, trimmed with five neat tucks. Has cambric flounce also trimmed with five tucks and edged with embroidery. Flounce with edge is 6 inches deep. Open or closed style. Price....35c
If by mail, postage extra, 8 cents.

No. 38C821 Umbrella Drawers, made of muslin. Has lawn flounce with insertion of 3-inch torchon lace and edge to match. Entire flounce, including lace edge, is 18 inches deep. Open style. Price....42c
If by mail, postage extra, 8 cents.

No. 38C825 Umbrella Drawers, made of cambric. Trimmed with seven fine tucks, has deep lawn flounce trimmed with seven tucks, two insertions of 1-inch neat valenciennes lace with edge to match. Entire width of flounce, including lace edge, is 7 inches. Open style. Price....65c
If by mail, postage extra, 8 cents.

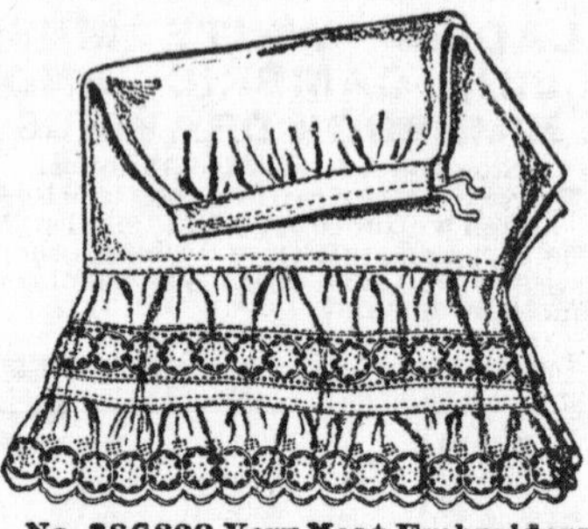

No. 38C827 Ladies' Umbrella Drawers, made of cambric. Trimmed with seven fine tucks, has wide lawn flounce trimmed with two insertions of torchon lace, lawn ruffle edged with lace to match. Entire flounce is 8 inches deep. Open or closed styles. Wonderful value. Price....48c
If by mail, postage extra, 8 cents.

No. 38C829 Very Neat Embroidery Trimmed Drawers, made of cambric. Umbrella style, lawn flounce with insertion of neat open embroidery, edged with 3½-inch embroidery to match. Entire flounce, including embroidery edge, is 8 inches deep. Open style only. Price....75c
If by mail, postage extra, 8 cents.

No. 38C831 Ladies' Drawers, made of fine cambric. Drawers trimmed with seven neat tucks, lawn flounce, also trimmed with seven neat tucks. Edged with 3½-inch new buttonhole embroidery, the flounce, including embroidery, is 7 inches deep. Open style. Price....69c
If by mail, postage extra, 8 cents.

No. 38C823 Ladies' Drawers, made of cambric. Has a very neat cambric flounce, with insertions of 1-inch valenciennes lace on the bias, ruffled cambric edged with lace to match. Open style. Price....48c
If by mail, postage extra, 8 cents.

No. 38C835 Umbrella Style Drawers, made of fine soft nainsook. Trimmed with six neat tucks, has lawn flounce with three fine tucks, two insertions of fine 1-inch torchon lace with 3-inch edge to match, the entire flounce, including lace, is 9 inches deep. Open style. Price....89c
If by mail, postage extra, 8 cents.

No. 38C837 Very Pretty Umbrella Style Ladies' Drawers, made of soft nainsook. Has a 5-inch flounce made of point de Paris lace alternating with narrow torchon lace. Triangular pieces of India lawn set between each insertion, giving flounce a nice flare, 2-inch lace edge to match flounce, including lace edge, 7 inches deep. Open style only. Price....$1.35
If by mail, postage extra, 8 cents.

GREAT BARGAINS IN TROUSSEAU OUTFITS.

AT $4.35 AND $5.98 WE OFFER TROUSSEAU OUTFITS THAT REPRESENT REMARKABLE VALUES.

Trousseau consists of four pieces, Gown, Underskirt, Drawers and Corset Cover.

We offer the following most extraordinary values in Bridal Sets that will at once commend themselves to everyone familiar with fine muslin wear. They have been gotten together with a view of furnishing the very best goods possible and yet at prices within the reach of everyone. **Read these descriptions carefully, note the material, the make, the finish — and note OUR PRICES. Send us your order with the understanding that if the set when received is not perfectly satisfactory, all and more than we claim for it, you are at liberty to return it to us and we will refund your money. Be sure to give bust measure.**

OUR $4.35 TROUSSEAU OUTFIT.

Sizes, 32, 34, 36, 38, 40, 42 inches bust measure.

Fine Cambric Trousseau of four pieces, consisting of gown, underskirt, drawers and corset cover, all with matched embroidery.

Gown has a yoke with two rows of embroidery insertion on each side, with three tucks between and insertion down center. Wide hamburg embroidery trimming around the front and embroidery at neck and sleeves to match. Fine herringbone braid trimming.

Underskirt has a double flounce of hamburg embroidery on lawn ruffle. Has a dust ruffle.

Drawers have a hamburg embroidery flounce, with insertion of embroidery with six tucks. Yoke band. Open style. Very neat drawers.

Corset Cover has four rows of hamburg embroidery insertion, with cluster of tucks on each side, trimmed with fine embroidery around neck and armholes. **Do not fail to give bust measure. If by mail, postage extra, 45 cents.**

No. 38C952 Price, entire set of four pieces....$4.35

OUR $5.98 TROUSSEAU OUTFIT.

$5.98

A Trousseau fit for an American queen, made of fine cambric, in four pieces, gown, underskirt, drawers and corset cover. **All made with matched point de Paris lace. Sizes, 32, 34, 36, 38, 40 and 42 inches bust measure.**

Gown is made Empire style, fine grade of cambric, fancy revers, which are trimmed all around with fine point de Paris insertion and lace 4 inches wide. Bosom has one row of insertion and one row of fancy ribbon insertion, also 4-inch lace. Sleeves have an insertion of ribbon and 4-inch lace.

Underskirt is made of fine cambric, has a lawn flounce which is made V shape all around and trimmed with 4-inch lace. Above this are two rows of point de Paris lace insertion all around flounce. Has a dust ruffle which is also trimmed with 4-inch lace.

Drawers are made of very fine cambric (open), have lawn ruffle with one row of point de Paris insertion and trimmed at bottom with lace to match.

Corset Cover is made of fine cambric, low round neck edged with lace, three insertions of point de Paris lace. Armholes trimmed with lace to match. **Do not fail to give bust measure. If by mail, postage extra, 45 cents.**

No. 38C954 Price, entire set of four pieces....$5.98

(Trousseaux continued on next page.)

NAINSOOK TROUSSEAU OUTFIT.

$8.65 Nainsook Trousseau Outfit.

$8.65

An exceedingly fine lace trimmed trousseau, made of soft nainsook, consisting of four pieces, gown, underskirt, drawers and corset cover, all trimmed with fine matched duchesse lace. Sizes, 32 to 42 inches bust measure.

Gown made slip over style (very newest), with low round neck trimmed with lace. Beading and ribbon insertion forming a bow in front. Five insertions in front alternating with folds; elbow sleeves with two V insertions, beading, ribbon insertion and 3-in. lace edge.

Underskirt made French style. Entire flounce is 20 inches deep, trimmed all around bottom with fine duchesse lace insertion alternating with narrow torchon lace insertion, above which there are seven fine pin tucks, triangular pieces of lawn between each lace insertion, giving flounce a wide flare; edged all around bottom with 3-inch lace. Has dust ruffle.

Drawers made umbrella style, have a 5-inch flounce made of duchesse lace insertion alternating with torchon lace insertion, with triangular pieces between each lace insertion, giving flounce a wide flare. 2-inch lace edge (open style only), draw strings.

Corset Cover, trimmed very prettily, low round neck, trimmed with lace, beading and ribbon insertion, armholes trimmed with lace, four rows of fine duchesse lace insertion in front, alternating with narrow torchon lace, each side edged with 2-inch duchesse lace; trimmed around waist with lace edge to match beading and ribbon insertion. Exceptionally good value.

No. 38C956 Price, entire set of four pieces made of nainsook.....................**$8.65**

DEPARTMENT OF EXTRA SIZE MUSLIN UNDERWEAR.

Made expressly for stout women and usually to be had only if made to special order, but we have them already made.

These extra size garments are made in the following sizes:

Gowns. 17, 18 and 19 inches neck, made extra full around body and bottom.

Corset Covers, 44, 46 and 48 inches bust measure.

Underskirts. Lengths, 40, 42 and 44 inches, made extra full around hips, with draw strings, making skirt adjustable to waist, and extra large sweep around bottom.

Drawers. Lengths, 25, 27 and 29 inches, made extra full around hips and seat with extra wide leg; open or closed styles. State style desired.

EXTRA SIZE GOWNS.

Sizes 17, 18 and 19 inches Neck Measure. In proportion to 44, 46 and 48 inches bust measure.

69 Cents For Extra Size Gown.

69c

No. 38C960 Extra Size Gown, made of heavy Masonville muslin. Yoke trimmed with twenty-six tucks, neck and sleeves with cambric ruffle. Wonderful value. Price.....69c

If by mail, postage extra, 18 cents.

98-Cent Extra Size Gown.

98c

No. 38C962 Ladies' Extra Size Gown, made of a very extra heavy quality muslin. Has a very pretty yoke trimmed with four clusters of tucks (four tucks in each cluster), one row of insertion of open work embroidery, neck trimmed with an embroidery ruffle, sleeves to correspond.

Price, **98 cents.**

If by mail, postage extra, 18c.

Extra Size Empire Gown, Only $1.25.

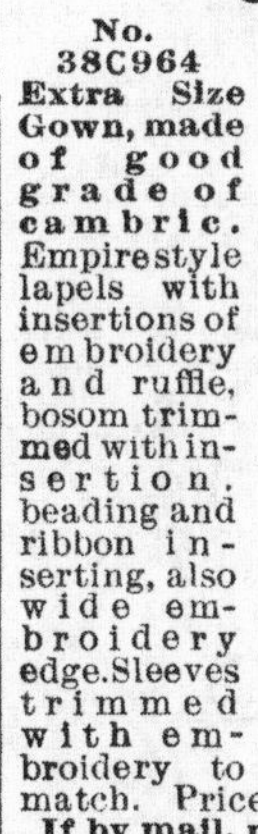

$1.25

No. 38C964 Extra Size Gown, made of good grade of cambric. Empire style lapels with insertions of embroidery and ruffle, bosom trimmed with insertion, beading and ribbon inserting, also wide embroidery edge. Sleeves trimmed with embroidery to match. Price.....................$1.25

If by mail, postage extra, 20 cents.

CHEMISES, SHORT SKIRT LENGTHS.

Sizes, 32 to 42 Inches Bust Measure.

48c

No. 38C900

Ladies' Short Chemise, made of muslin, square yoke, trimmed with two rows of embroidery insertion alternating with three clusters of tucks (four tucks in each cluster) edged around armholes with embroidery, nice and full around the bottom, with deep hem.

Price.........48c

If by mail, postage extra, 10 cents.

75c

No. 38C902

Ladies' Short Chemise, made of good quality cambric, trimmed across bosom with two rows of torchon lace, insertion of lace to match, with beading and narrow ribbon inserting, trimmed all around neck and armholes with torchon lace to match, hem at bottom.

Price...........75c

If by mail, postage extra, 10 cents.

Combination Chemise.

$1.48

No. 38C906 A Very Pretty Combination Chemise, made of a fine grade of lawn; low round neck, insertion of torchon lace and narrow ribbon in front, trimmed all round front and back with one row of featherstitch braid, also edged with torchon lace; has lawn ruffle in front with one row of torchon lace insertion with wide edge to match; armholes trimmed with featherstitch braid and torchon lace edging, has a wide lawn flounce at bottom with torchon lace insertion and edging to match.

Price.....................................**$1.48**

If by mail, postage extra, 11 cents.

LADIES' CHEMISES, LONG SKIRT LENGTHS.

Sizes, 32 to 42 inches Bust Measure.

89c

No. 38C904 Ladies' Combination Chemise, made of cambric. Has round lawn yoke with insertion of 2-inch torchon lace, followed with beading and ribbon insertion; neck trimmed all around with torchon lace to match, also armholes; trimmed around the bottom with a cambric ruffle and edged with 1½-inch torchon lace to match.

Price....89c

If by mail, postage extra, 12 cents.

Extra Size Embroidery Trimmed Corset Cover.

75c

No. 38C974 Extra Size Corset Cover, made of cambric. Trimmed in front with wide open embroidery, and edged all around with neat embroidery followed with beading and ribbon inserting, armholes trimmed with embroidery to match.

Price.........................75c

If by mail, postage extra, 7 cents.

EXTRA SIZE CORSET COVERS.

Bust, 44, 46 and 48 Inches.

25c

No. 38C970 Extra Size Corset Cover, made of cambric. Neck trimmed with hemstitched cambric ruffle, followed with beading and ribbon inserting. Armholes trimmed with hemstitched cambric ruffle to match.

Price....25c

If by mail, postage extra, 7 cents.

39c

No. 38C972 Extra Size Corset Cover, made of cambric. Neck trimmed (back and front) with 3-inch torchon lace with insertion of narrow ribbon, armholes trimmed with torchon lace to match.

Price .39c

If by mail, postage extra, 7 cents.

EXTRA SIZE UNDERSKIRTS.

Lengths, 40, 42 and 44 inches. Made Extra Large Around Hips with Extra Sweep Around Bottom. Draw Strings at Waist.

69c

No. 38C980 Ladies' Extra Size Underskirt, made of heavy grade muslin. Has an 8-inch lawn flounce with four rows of hemstitching and three tucks; also wide hem at bottom.

Price...69c

If by mail, postage extra, 19 cents.

Extra Size, Embroidery Trimmed Underskirt, Only 98 Cents.

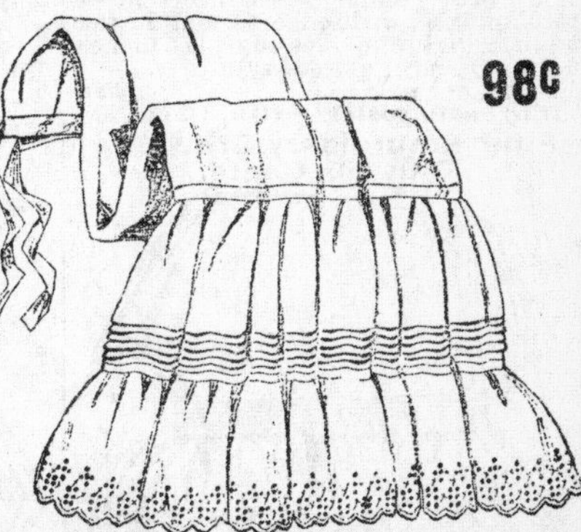

98c

No. 38C982 Extra Size Underskirt, made of heavy Masonville muslin. Has a wide lawn flounce trimmed with four fine tucks and 8-inch embroidery around bottom. The flounce, including embroidery, is 12 inches deep. Price 98c

If by mail, postage extra, 20 cents.

CONTINUED ON NEXT PAGE.

Extra Size Lace Trimmed Underskirt, Only $1.25.

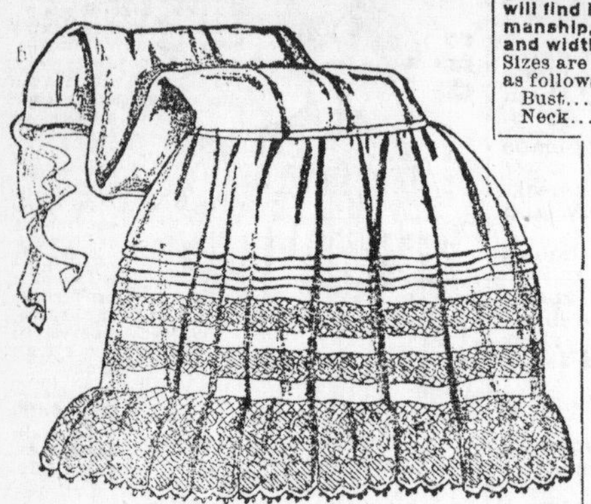

No. 38C984 Extra Size Underskirt, made of good quality heavy cambric. Has lawn flounce trimmed with four tucks, two insertions of 2¼-inch point de Paris lace, with 4-inch lace to match. The flounce, including lace edge, is 18 inches deep; has dust ruffle.
Price....................$1.25
If by mail, postage extra, 20 cents.

EXTRA SIZE DRAWERS.

Lengths, 25, 27 and 29 inches. These drawers are made in either open or closed styles. Be sure and state style desired; otherwise we will send open style, which is more in demand.

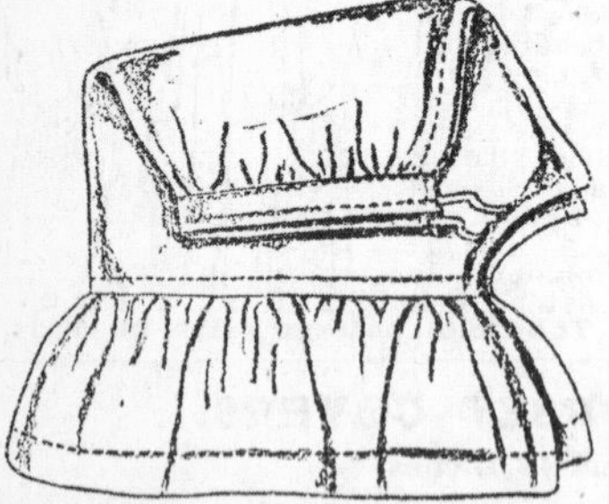

No. 38C990 Extra Size Drawers, made of cambric. Has 4-inch cambric flounce, with 1-inch hem. Open or closed styles. Wonderful value.
Price, per pair....................25c
If by mail, postage extra, 10 cents.

Lace Trimmed Drawers, Only 48 Cents.

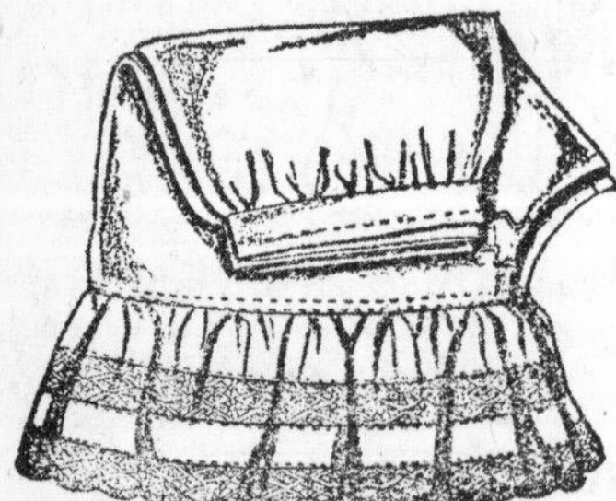

No. 38C992 Extra Size Drawers, made of good quality of cambric. Has a lawn flounce, with insertion of torchon lace, with edge to match, the flounce, including lace edge, is 6 inches deep. Open or closed style.
Price, per pair....................48c
If by mail, postage extra, 10 cents.

Fine Embroidery Drawers, Only 50 Cents.

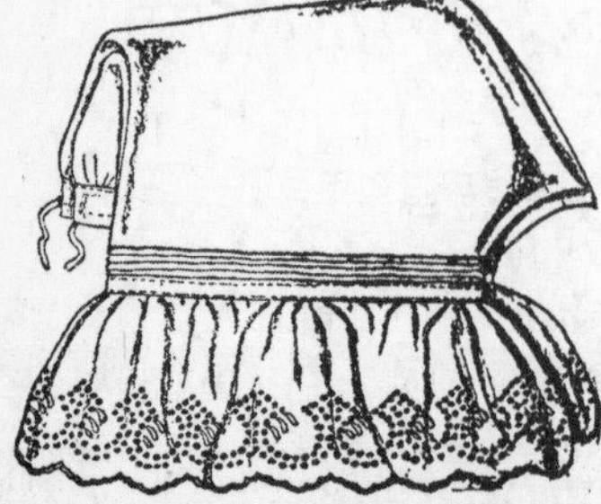

No. 38C994 Extra Size Drawers, made of good quality cambric, trimmed with four fine tucks and ruffles of 4-inch embroidery. Open or closed style. Excellent value. Price.....50c
If by mail, postage extra, 10 cents.

LADIES' FLANNEL UNDERWEAR.

We call especial attention to this class of goods. Combined with our low prices you will find in our flannel wear, first class workmanship, material and trimming, full lengths and widths, every number is a splendid value. Sizes are 14, 15 and 16 inches neck, in proportion as follows:

Bust	32-34	36-38	40-42
Neck	14	15	16

Order by neck measure.

For Muslin Gowns see page 928.

48c

No. 38C1000 Ladies' Gown, made of fancy domet flannel. Has fancy daisy cloth collar, stitched at edge with mercerized twist. Yoke trimmed across with fancy braid. Colors, white with blue or pink stripes. Well made and a wonderful bargain.
Price....................48c
If by mail, postage extra, 19 cents.

Outing Flannel Gown, 75c.

No. 38C1002 Ladies' Gown, made of heavy outing flannel. V shape neck, trimmed with ruffle and followed with fancy braid. Yoke trimmed with braid to match. Fancy cuffs with braid to correspond. Colors, cream with pink or blue stripes.
Price......75c
If by mail, postage extra, 20 cents.

Ladies' Domet Flannel Gown for 89 Cents.

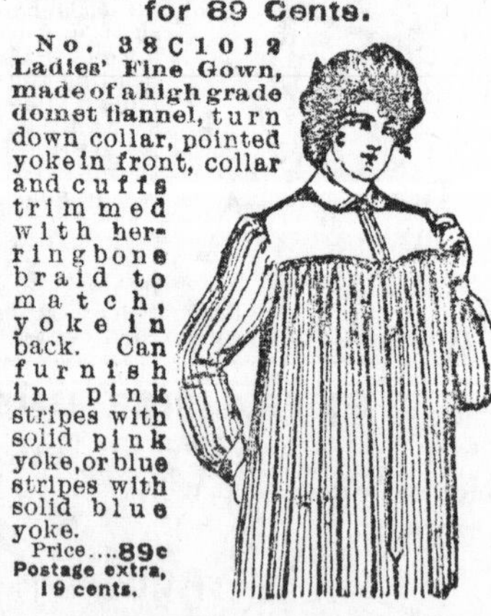

No. 38C1012 Ladies' Fine Gown, made of a high grade domet flannel, turn down collar, pointed yoke in front, collar and cuffs trimmed with herringbone braid to match, yoke in back. Can furnish in pink stripes with solid pink yoke, or blue stripes with solid blue yoke.
Price....89c
Postage extra, 19 cents.

This Tennis Flannel Gown Only 98 Cents.

No. 38C1013 Ladies' Gown, made of good quality tennis flannel, yoke back and front, trimmed across yoke in front with braid, very pretty pointed collar made of solid color flannel, trimmed with three rows of braid, cuffs trimmed to match. Colors are pink or blue stripes.
Price......98c
If by mail, postage extra, 20 cents.

No. 38C1014 Ladies' Gown, made in either fine outing flannel in fancy stripes or daisy cloth in solid colors. Collarless, with the new round yoke trimmed with fancy braid, cuffs trimmed with braid to match. Colors, outing flannel, cream with pink or blue stripes or solid colors. Daisy cloth, white or pale blue.
Price....................$1.10
If by mail, postage extra, 21 cents.

LADIES' OR MISSES' FLANNEL UNDERSKIRTS.

Lengths, 27, 29 and 31 inches.

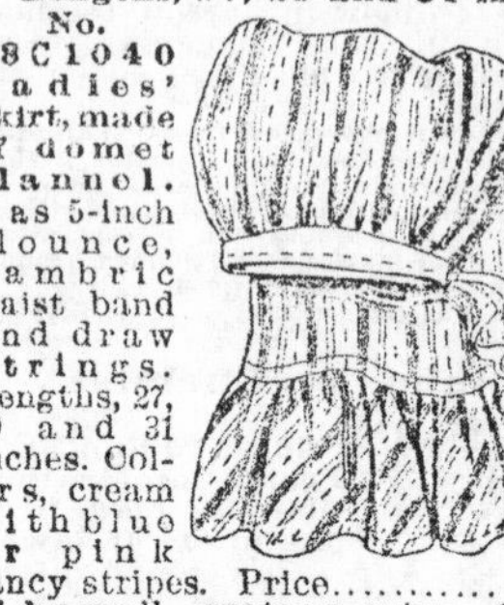

No. 38C1040 Ladies' Skirt, made of domet flannel. Has 5-inch flounce, cambric waist band and draw strings. Lengths, 27, 29 and 31 inches. Colors, cream with blue or pink fancy stripes. Price..........25c
If by mail, postage extra, 9 cents.

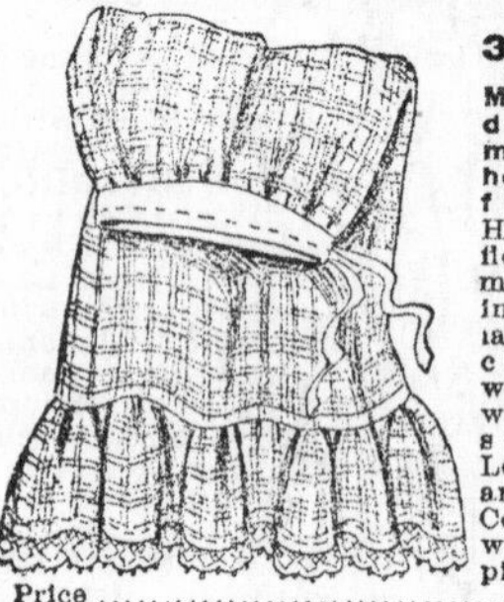

No. 38C1042 Ladies' or Misses' Underskirts, made of heavy domet flannel. Has a 4-inch flounce trimmed with 1½-inch torchon lace. Wide cambric waist band with draw strings. Length, 27, 29 and 31 inches. Colors, cream with blue or pink stripes.
Price....................39c
If by mail, postage extra, 10 cents.

No. 38C1046 Ladies' or Misses' Skirt, made of fine quality tennis flannel. Has an 8 inch flounce which is trimmed with two rows of torchon lace. Deep hem at bottom, wide cambric waist band with draw strings. Colors, cream with blue or pink stripes. Price....................59c
If by mail, postage extra, 12 cents.

LADIES' DRESSING SACQUES, KIMONAS AND NEGLIGEES.

THE MOST COMFORTABLE AND POPULAR HOUSE GARMENTS MADE.

Sizes, 32, 34, 36, 38, 40 and 42 inches bust measure.

39c

No. 38C1220 Ladies' Dressing Sacque, made of percale. Has wide collar trimmed with fancy braid and ruffle, trimmed around bottom with ruffle; also sleeves trimmed to match. Colors, black and white, blue and white or red and white figures. Price. 39c
If by mail, postage extra, 9 cents.

Percale Dressing Sacque Only 48 Cents.

No. 38C1224 Ladies' Dressing Sacque, made of percale. Has pointed collar with border of solid color percale, trimmed around bottom to match, full fashioned sleeves. Colors, black and white or blue and white figures.
Price....48c
If by mail, postage extra, 10 cents.

Percale Kimona, 69 Cents.

No. 38C1228 Ladies' Kimona made of good quality percale. Very pretty double shoulder capes, each trimmed with solid color flannelette to match, also trimmed around neck, down front and kimona sleeves with solid color percale. Colors, pink or blue fancy figures or black and white.
Price..........69c
If by mail, postage extra, 12 cents.

Dimity Dressing Sacque, 75 Cents.

75c

No. 38C1232 Ladies' Dressing Sacque, made of good quality dimity, has wide collar trimmed with ruffle made of same material as in sacque and edged with valenciennes lace; collar also trimmed with one row of beading; ruffle edged with valenciennes lace, trimmed around bottom with a ruffle, followed with beading. Colors, blue or pink ground with fancy figures. Price........75c
If by mail, postage extra, 9 cents.

Eiderdown Dressing Sacque, 48 Cents.

No. 38C1240 Ladies' Eiderdown Dressing Sacque, has wide collar. Stitched all around with mercerized twist, finished seams throughout. Colors, black and white, or pink and white stripes.
Price.......48c
Postage extra, 12 cents.

No. 38C1242 Ladies' Dressing Sacque, made of wool eiderdown, very neat collar, reaching near bottom. Collar and all around the bottom crocheted with mercerized twist, also the turnover cuffs. Satin tie strings at neck, finished seams. Colors, gray or cardinal.
Price....................98c
If by mail, postage extra, 18 cents.

LADIES' TWO-PIECE DRESSING SACQUE SUITS.

Comfort and Style Combined in These Garments.

Sizes, 32 to 44 inches bust measure. Skirt length, 38 to 44 inches. Always give bust measure and skirt length.

No. 38C1250 Ladies' Two-Piece Dressing Sacque Suit, made of percale. Sacque made with pointed yoke, plaits in back, turn-down collar and full fashioned sleeves. **Skirt** made extra full with wide flounce and heading; has hem at bottom. Colors, black and white, blue and white or red and white, with neat figures. Price........................ 98c
If by mail, postage extra, 24 cents.

No. 38C1254 Ladies' Two-Piece Dressing Sacque Suit, made of fine percale. Sacque made with a yoke, has wide printed collar with ruffle, full fashioned sleeves. **Skirt** made nice and full with wide flounce and heading; deep hem at bottom. Colors, black and white, blue and white or red and white figures.
Price, $1.25
If by mail, postage extra, 27 cents.

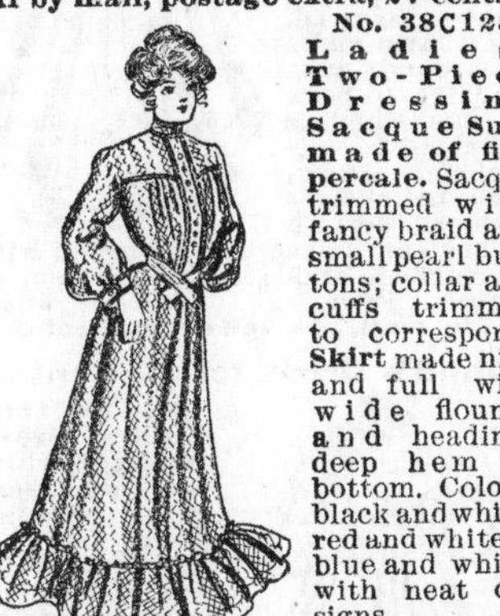

No. 38C1258 Ladies' Two-Piece Dressing Sacque Suit, made of fine percale. Sacque trimmed with fancy braid and small pearl buttons; collar and cuffs trimmed to correspond. **Skirt** made nice and full with wide flounce and heading; deep hem at bottom. Colors, black and white, red and white or blue and white, with neat designs.
Price...$1.48
If by mail, postage extra, 27 cents.

LADIES' KIMONAS.

Wonderful Values in these Comfortable Garments.

Sizes, 32 to 42 inches bust measure.

Figured Lawn Kimona, Only 20 Cents.

No. 38C1262 Ladies' Kimona, made of figured lawn. Yoke back and front, border of white lawn, sleeves to match. Colors, white ground with black, blue or pink figures. Price........................20c
If by mail, postage extra, 9 cents.

Fancy Dimity Kimona, Only 39 Cents.

No. 38C1263 Ladies' Kimona, made of fancy dimity. Yoke back and front stitched with white tape, white lawn border with sleeves trimmed to match. Colors, black, blue or red figures, excellent value. Price........39c
If by mail, postage extra, 10 cents.

Fancy Dotted Swiss Kimona, Only 55 Cents.

No. 38C1264 Ladies' Kimona, made of fancy dotted Swiss. Yoke back and front, border made of white lawn, with sleeves trimmed to match. Colors, white with black or blue fancy figures in stripes. Price........................55c
If by mail, postage extra, 11 cents.

Extra Fine Quality Figured Lawn, Only 85 Cents.

No. 38C1265 Ladies' Kimona, made of fine quality figured lawn. Yoke back and front, has white lawn shawl collar, and kimona sleeves trimmed to match. Excellent workmanship. Colors, black and white or blue and white figures. Price............(If by mail, postage extra, 10 cents)............85c

A Lawn Kimona Only 25 Cents.

No. 38C1266 Ladies' Lawn Kimona. Yoke back and front, made with a border, and sleeves bordered to match. Colors, white with blue border or blue with white border.
Price....25c
If by mail, postage extra, 10 cents.

Trimmed With Hemstitched Tucks, Only 48 Cents.

No. 38C1268 Ladies' Lawn Kimona. Yoke back and front trimmed with six hemstitched tucks, shawl collar with hemstitching. Kimona sleeves trimmed to match. Colors, white, with pink collar or blue with white collar.
Price........48c
If by mail, postage extra, 10 cents.

LONG KIMONAS OR NEGLIGEES.

Very handy house garments. Sizes, 32 to 42 inches bust measure.

Long Kimona of Figured Lawn Only 79 Cents.

No. 38C1280 Ladies' Long Kimona, made of figured lawn. Has yoke back and front, border reaching to bottom made of white lawn. Sleeves trimmed to match. Deep hem at bottom. Colors blue or pink grounds with fancy designs, or black with white figures.
Price........79c
If by mail, postage extra, 16 cents.

Lace Trimmed Long Kimona Only 98 Cents.

No. 38C1282 Ladies' Long Kimona, made of dimity. Has fancy pointed collar which is trimmed with point de Paris lace, border of white lawn reaching to bottom with deep hem at bottom. Kimona sleeves trimmed to match. Colors are black and white or blue and white floral design. Wonderful value.
Price 98c
If by mail, postage extra, 19c.

Kimona or Lounging Robe, Made of Heavy Fleeced Flannel.

No. 38C1288 Ladies' Long Fancy Kimona or Lounging Robe, made of fine fleeced flannel. Full shirred yoke, has border of fancy silk, hem at bottom, this is a very handy and practical house garment. Colors, blue or pink grounds with fancy floral designs.
Price $1.98
If by mail, postage extra, 32 cents.

Long Kimona, Made of Cotton Crepon.

No. 38C1292 Ladies' Long Kimona. Made of fine cotton crepon, full shirred yoke, both back and front, has border of sateen in neat Persian effects, kimona sleeves trimmed to match. Colors, red, pink or pale blue.
Price.....$1.48
If by mail, postage extra, 17 cents.

Short Kimona, Made of Cotton Crepon, Only 98 Cents.

No. 38C1294 Ladies' Short Kimona, made of good quality cotton crepon. Same style as No. 38C1292. Colors, pink or pale blue. Price...98c
If by mail, postage extra, 11 cents.

LADIES' BATH OR LOUNGING ROBES.

A very handy garment for after the bath or lounging. Bust measures, 32 to 42 inches.

No. 38C1298 Ladies' Bath or Lounging Robe; made of all wool elderdown, sailor collar, trimmed with two rows of satin ribbon on back of collar and one row on each side. Ribbon embroidered with silk, collar edged with satin, ribbon bow at neck, two silk loops, cuffs to correspond to collar, finished seams throughout, all wool girdle, fitted back, 3¼ yards sweep, hem at bottom. **Give bust measure. Colors, cardinal or pale blue.**
Price... ....$3.98
If by mail, postage extra, 49 cents.

LADIES' AND MISSES' BATHING SUITS.

32 to 42 Bust Measure.

No. 38C1301 Ladies' Bathing Suit with attached bloomers, made of good quality alpaca. Large sailor collar trimmed with three rows of soutache down the front and **detachable skirt** trimmed around waistband and bottom with three rows of soutache to match, wide hem. Colors, black or navy blue. Price..... **$2.25**
If by mail, postage extra, 17 cents.

Always give bust measure.

No. 38C1303 Girls' or Misses' Bathing Suits, ages from 8 to 16 years. Same style as No. 38C1301, with attached bloomers and detachable skirt. Color, navy blue with white trimmings. State age desired.
Price........................**$1.69**
If by mail, postage extra, 15 cents.

No. 38C1305 Ladies' Bathing Suit, with attached bloomers, made of brilliantine. Has large sailor collar trimmed with two rows white cord and one row of braid. Sleeves trimmed to correspond. Detachable skirt, waistband trimmed with rows of cord and a row of braid, trimmed around the bottom to correspond. **Colors, black or navy blue with white trimmings.**
Price............$2.98
If by mail, postage extra, 19 cents.

Bathing or Dust Caps.

No. 38C1307 Bathing or Dust Caps, made of sateen, pure rubber lining. Has rubber band to make cap fit perfectly around head. Keeps the hair dry. Colors, blue or red, with white polka dots.
Price, each.....$0.23
Per dozen 2.50
If by mail, postage extra, each 4c.

No. 38C1309 Bathing Cap, made of pure rubber, plaid lining. The correct thing to wear when bathing. Rubber band to make it fit perfectly around the head; keeps the hair dry. Color, black only. Price, each........$0.12
Per dozen.................... 1.25
If by mail, postage extra, each 4c.

No. 38C1311 Bathing or Dust Caps, made of pure transparent gum rubber, tape and inserted with rubber, making cap fit perfectly around head. These caps are also very useful as dust caps when house cleaning, etc. Colors, tan or black. **Price, each.....$0.25**
Per dozen.................... 2.80
If by mail, postage extra, each, 4c.

LADIES' GINGHAM, SATEEN AND WHITE LAWN APRONS.

Kitchen Aprons at nearly the cost of material.

No. 38C1452 Ladies' Gingham Kitchen Apron, in blue, brown or pink stripes or checks. Size, 30 inches long, 33 inches wide. Extra good value.
Price.............9c
If by mail, postage extra, 4 cents.

No. 38C1454 Ladies' Gingham Kitchen Apron. Size, 34 inches long, 42 inches wide. Material used in these aprons costs nearly as much as we charge for apron already made up. Colors, brown, blue or pink stripes or checks. Price.......................14c
If by mail, postage extra, 5 cents.

No. 38C1456 Ladies' Large Gingham Aprons, the best gingham. Hemmed at bottom, long strings in back. Colors, blue or brown checks. A good, reliable apron. Size, 38 inches long, 54 inches wide. Price...............25c
If by mail, postage extra, 5 cents.

Ladies' Bib Apron.

No. 38C1458 Ladies' Gingham Kitchen Apron, made with a bib. Length from waist band, 36 inches. Width, 44 inches. Our price is merely the cost of material only. Colors, blue or pink stripes or checks. Price, 20c
If by mail, postage extra, 6 cents.

Fast Black Sateen Apron 23 Cents.

No. 38C1460 Ladies' Fine Quality Black Sateen Aprons. Very desirable as a work apron, does not require frequent washing and always looks neat. Made full and long; hemmed; with one pocket. The quality sold elsewhere at 35 cents. Price....23c
If by mail, postage extra, 5 cents.

18-Cent White Lawn Apron.

No. 38C1462 Ladies' White Lawn Apron, 34 inches long, 39 inches wide. Wide hem at bottom and wide strings. Very good value.
Price... ....15c
If by mail, postage extra, 6 cents.

White Lawn Apron With Embroidery Insertion.

No. 38C1466 Ladies' Beautiful White Lawn Apron, has a wide insertion of fine embroidered lawn, extra wide hem at bottom. Size, 33 inches wide and 36 inches long.
Price..............39c
If by mail, postage extra, 6 cents.

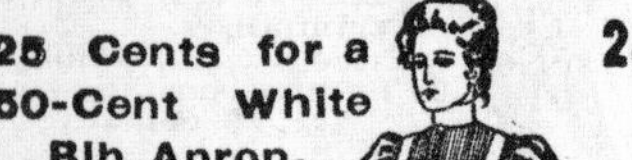

25 Cents for a 50-Cent White Bib Apron. 25c

No. 38C1470 White Lawn Apron, with bib and shoulder straps, as per illustration, made of nice white lawn, with wide hem at bottom, long apron ties.
Price....25c
If by mail, postage extra, 7 cents.

The Maco Waist Protector.

Fills a Long Felt Want.

23c

PATENTED

What the apron is to the skirt the Maco is to the waist. No more pinning on of paper cuffs or bibs. New and practical. A combination of a pair of sleeves and front piece, as shown in the illustration. Can be slipped on or off in a second. Worn all the year round. Saves its cost in one week's laundry bill and your waist always looks fresh.
No. 38C1480 Made of figured prints, black and white or blue and white figures or solid black.
Price, each..............23c
No. 38C1482 Made of lawn, black and white or blue and white figures or solid black or white. Price, each..42c
No. 38C1484 Made of fast black sateen. Price, each..............45c
If by mail, postage extra, 5 cents.

CHILDREN'S MUSLIN GOWNS

For Children from 2 to 14 years old.

No. 38C1504 Children's Gowns, made of good quality muslin, yoke back and front, trimmed in front with two rows of wide torchon lace, alternating with two tucks, cambric ruffle around neck and sleeves.
Price, ages 2 to 8 years..............39c
Price, ages 10 to 14 years..............45c
If by mail, postage extra, 7 cents.

CHILDREN'S SLEEPING GARMENTS.

Ages 1 to 8 years.

No. 38C1506 Children's Fleeced Cotton Flannel Night Drawers or Suits, made of unbleached cotton flannel, with feet; very comfortable sleeping garment. Sizes, 1 to 8. Price... 23c
If by mail, postage extra, 7c.
No. 38C1508 Child's Drawers, made of outing flannel, in blue or pink stripes, made same style as No. 38C1506, with feet. Sizes, 1 to 8. Colors, blue or pink stripes.
Price........25c
If by mail, postage extra, 7c.

CHILDREN'S DRAWERS.

Ages 4, 6, 8 and 10 years.
No. 38C1512 Child's Muslin Drawers, made nice and full, trimmed with two tucks and edged with wash lace.
Price, per pair.................. $0.10
Per dozen pairs.................. 1.15
If by mail, postage extra, each, 4c.

Children's Drawers.

Ages, 2 to 14 years.

No. 38C1517 Girls' Drawers, made of good quality muslin; has a 3-inch cambric flounce, with an insertion of torchon lace; hem at bottom. Very neat children's drawers.
Price, per pair, ages 2 to 8 years $0.14
Per dozen, ages 2 to 8 years.... 1.55
Price, per pair, ages 10 to 14 yrs. .16
Per dozen, ages 10 to 14 years.. 1.80
If by mail, postage extra, each, 4c.

Muslin Drawers, Trimmed with Tucks Only 10 Cents.

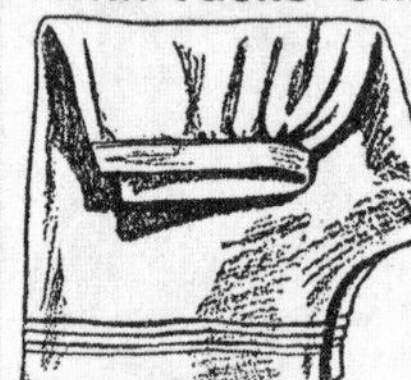

No. 38C1519 Girls' Muslin Drawers, have 3 tucks, well made, for girls ages 2 to 14 years.
Price, per pair, ages 2 to 8 years..$0.10
Per dozen pairs, ages 2 to 8 years.................. $1.15
Price, per pair, ages 10 to 14 yrs. .11
Per doz. pairs, ages 10 to 14 yrs. 1.25
If by mail, postage extra, each, 4c.

Embroidery Trimmed Drawers.

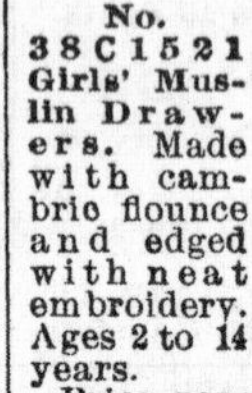

No. 38C1521 Girls' Muslin Drawers. Made with cambric flounce and edged with neat embroidery. Ages 2 to 14 years.
Price, per pair, ages 2 to 8 years..13c
Per dozen pairs, ages 2 to 8 years.............................$1.45
Per pair, ages 10 to 14 years........15c
Per dozen pairs, ages 10 to 14 years.............................$1.70
If by mail, postage extra, each, 4c.

Girls' Lace Trimmed Drawers.

No. 38C1523 Girls' Muslin Drawers, trimmed with three tucks, has flounce, with insertions of neat valenciennes lace with lace edge to match. Ages 2 to 14 years.
Price, per pair, ages 2 to 8 years..24c
Per dozen pairs, ages 2 to 8 years.............................$2.75
Per pair, ages 10 to 14 years........29c
Per dozen pairs, ages 10 to 14 years.............................$3.25
If by mail, postage extra, each, 4c.

These Underskirts for Children Ages 4 to 14 Years.

No. 38C1524 Girls' Underskirt, made of good quality muslin with insertion of open work embroidery, 2-inch cambric flounce, which is trimmed with 2-inch embroidery ruffle. Waistband with draw strings. Extra good value.
Price, ages 4 to 8 years..............45c
Price, ages 10 to 14 years..............49c
If by mail, postage extra, 7 cents.

Girls' Underskirts. 39c

No. 38C1526 A Very Pretty Underskirt for Girls, made of good quality muslin; has a lawn flounce with two clusters of fine tucks (three tucks in each cluster), insertion of torchon lace, with edge to match, flounce, including ace edge, is 8 inches deep. Extra good value; waistband with draw strings, making skirt adjustable to waist.
Price, ages 4 to 8 years..............39c
Price, ages 10 to 14 years..............42c
If by mail, postage extra, 7 cents.

INFANTS' AND CHILDREN'S FLANNEL SHORT SKIRTS WITH BODICE.

Sizes are for infants, also for 1, 2 and 3 year old children.

State size desired.
No. 38C1532 Child's Skirt, made of heavy fleeced shaker flannel, with cambric bodice. Embroidered around the bottom with silk.
Price........35c
If by mail, postage extra, 5 cents.

Flannel Skirt at 16 Cents.

No. 38C1533 Children's Skirt, made of heavy fleeced shaker flannel, with muslin bodice. Price.....16c
If by mail, postage extra, 3 cents.

Child's Skirt for 48c.

No. 38C1534 Child's Skirt made of cream color wool flannel with cambric bodice, fancy ruffle of the same material all around the bottom. Very neat and desirable.
Price........48c
If by mail, postage extra, 5c.

45c

No. 38C1538 Child's Skirt, made of good quality nainsook, with cambric bodice, three neat tucks around the bottom and edged with cambric embroidery. Pearl buttons in back.
Price.......... .45c
If by mail, postage extra, 3 cents.

Cambric Skirt at 18 Cents.

No. 38C1539 Child's Skirt, made of white cambric, with bodice, trimmed with tucks around the bottom.
Price.............................. 18c
If by mail, postage extra, 3 cents.

Nainsook Skirt. 48c

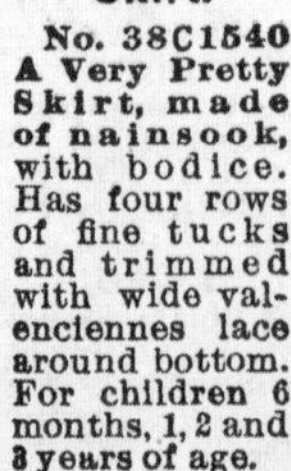

No. 38C1540 A Very Pretty Skirt, made of nainsook, with bodice. Has four rows of fine tucks and trimmed with wide valenciennes lace around bottom. For children 6 months, 1, 2 and 3 years of age.
Price......48c
If by mail, postage extra, 6 cents.

75-Cent Value. 75c

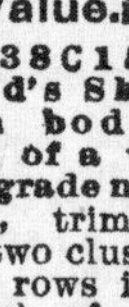

No. 38C1542 Child's Skirt with bodice, made of a very high grade nainsook, trimmed with two clusters (four rows in a cluster) of fine tucks, with an insertion of fine valenciennes lace. Trimmed around bottom with valenciennes lace to match.
Price........75c
If by mail, postage extra, 6 cents.

INFANTS' AND CHILDREN'S DRESSES.

Sizes are for Infants; also for 1, 2 and 3 year old Children. State size desired.

Child's Dress for 25 Cents.

No. 38C1600 Child's Dress, made of good quality cambric. Hubbard style, yoke trimmed with one row of embroidery and eight fine tucks, cambric ruffle at neck and sleeves, deep hem at bottom. Sizes are 6 months, 1, 2 and 3 years.
Price....25c
If by mail, postage extra, 6 cents.

Child's Dress for 48 Cents.

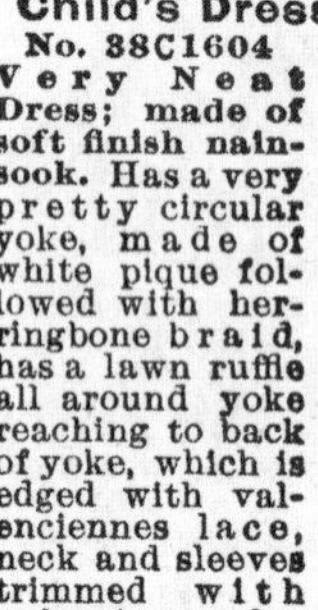

No. 38C1604 Very Neat Dress; made of soft finish nainsook. Has a very pretty circular yoke, made of white pique followed with herringbone braid, has a lawn ruffle all around yoke reaching to back of yoke, which is edged with valenciennes lace, neck and sleeves trimmed with valenciennes lace and followed with herringbone braid; has a deep hem at bottom. Price..............48c
If by mail, postage extra, 6 cents.

Child's Dress for 39 Cents.

No. 38C1608 Child's Dress; made of white lawn with very pretty circular yoke, made of all over Swiss embroidery, embroidered ruffle around yoke, sleeves trimmed with hemstitched lawn ruffle, nice, neat hem at bottom.
Price....39c
If by mail, postage extra, 6 cents.

Here is a Pretty Dress for 75 Cents.

75c

No. 38C1612 Very Pretty Dress; made of white cambric, circular yoke in front, trimmed with two embroidery insertions and tucks, ruffle in front of 2-inch embroidery, neck and sleeves trimmed with embroidery to match, two plaits in back, six tucks at bottom and edged with 4-in. embroidery.
Price..............75c
If by mail, postage extra, 9 cents.
These dresses are for infants, also for 1, 2 and 3 year old children. State size desired.

Our 48-Cent Child's Dress.

48c

No. 38C1616 Child's Dress; made of white cambric, circular yoke in front, trimmed with tucks and embroidery insertion. Ruffles of embroidery around the neck and yoke, embroidery cuffs, three tucks around bottom, with 1½-inch embroidery edge. Color, white only. Price..48c

If by mail, postage extra, 8 cents.

Only 75 Cents for this Dress.

75c

No. 38C1620 Child's dress; made of high grade cambric. Embroidered ruffle around the collar and tucked yoke in front, ending in a point, with embroidered cambric all around the front and back. Embroidered cambric ruffle around the sleeves. Very neat and stylish. Ages, 6 months, 1, 2 and 3 years. Color, white. Price........................75c

If by mail, postage extra, 6 cents.

Child's White Cambric Dress.

89c

No. 38C1624 Child's Dress; made of white cambric, a very pretty circular yoke. Trimmed in front with embroidery, insertion and tucks, ruffle around the yoke, neck and sleeves trimmed with embroidery, with six tucks at bottom and insertion of open work embroidery and edged with 4-inch embroidery to match. Color, white only. Price........................89c

If by mail, postage extra, 10 cents.

Embroidery Trimmed Dress.

$1.25

No. 38C1628 Child's Dress; made of white nainsook, handsomely ornamented all around the yoke and over the shoulders with one row of white cambric embroidery. The yoke consists of plaiting, insertion and tucking alternating each other, four rows of plaiting around the bottom and one ruffle of wide embroidered cambric. Ages, 6 months, 1, 2 and 3 years. Price........................$1.25

If by mail, postage extra, 7 cents.

Lace Trimmed Dress, $1.39.

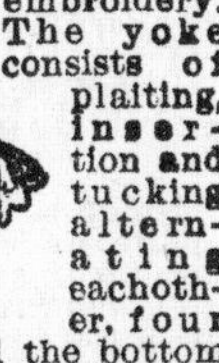

No. 38C1632 Child's Dress; made of fine nainsook, has a very pretty circular yoke of allover lace, both front and back, beading and ribbon insertion in front forming a bow, trimmed around neck with 1-inch lace, point de Paris lace ruffle all around yoke. Sleeves trimmed with herringbone braid and lace edge, trimmed all around bottom with six fine tucks and lace insertion and edged with 4-inch lace to match. Color, white only. Price........$1.39

If by mail, postage extra, 10 cents.

Very Fine White Sheer Lawn.

No. 38C1636 An Exceedingly Fine Child's Dress; made of fine, white sheer lawn, has a very neat yoke trimmed with insertion of fine pattern valenciennes lace, ruffle is edged with valenciennes lace to match, neck edged with valenciennes lace, and one row of valenciennes lace insertion around bottom of skirt, wide lawn flounce, which is edged with valenciennes lace to match, sleeves trimmed with valenciennes lace. Price........................98c

If by mail, postage extra, 10 cents.

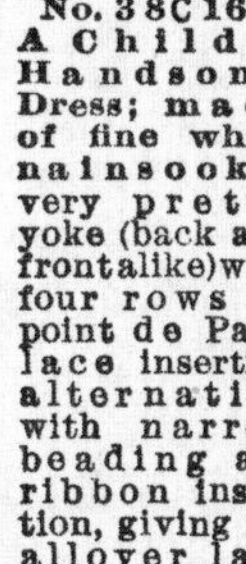

No. 38C1640 A Child's Handsome Dress; made of fine white nainsook, a very pretty yoke (back and front alike) with four rows of point de Paris lace insertion alternating with narrow beading and ribbon insertion, giving an allover lace effect. Narrow ruffle of lawn all around yoke edged with lace to match, neck and sleeves trimmed with lace followed with beading and ribbon insertion, two insertions of 1-inch lace and 5-inch edge around dress. Color, white only. Price........................$1.69

If by mail, postage extra, 9 cents.

Child's Silk Dress, $2.25.

No. 38C1644 An Exceedingly Pretty Child's Dress made of China silk, has a very pretty yoke trimmed with lace, beading and ribbon insertion both front and back, ruffle all around the yoke of Normandy valenciennes lace. Neck trimmed with lace, sleeves with lace and beading, trimmed at the bottom with 1-inch Normandy valenciennes lace and narrow beading, with 4-inch lace edge to match. Colors, cream, pink or light blue. See page 943 for children's hats to match these pretty dresses. Price........................$2.25

If by mail, postage extra, 9 cents.

CHILD'S FRENCH DRESSES.

Ages, 1, 2, 3 and 4 years. Scale of measurements giving length of dresses in proportion: Age 1, length 20 inches; age 2, length 21 inches; age 3, length 22 inches; age 4, 24 inches.

No. 38C1650 Child's French Dress; made of white lawn, trimmed in front with two rows of open embroidery and numerous rows of fine tucks, back trimmed from neck to flounce with two clusters of three fine tucks each, neck and sleeves trimmed with hemstitched lawn ruffle, nice deep hem at bottom. Price.......48c

Postage extra, 7c.

No. 38C1654 Child's French Dress; made of white lawn, very neatly trimmed in front with four clusters of fine tucks (five tucks in each cluster), alternating with three rows of open embroidery, neck and sleeves trimmed with hemstitched lawn ruffle, one row of hemstitching around bottom with nice deep hem, back trimmed from neck to flounce with four clusters of French tucks (four tucks in each cluster). For children, ages from 1 to 4 years. Color, white only. Price..........89c

Postage extra, 8 cents.

Child's French Dress, $1.10.

No. 38C1658 A Child's Beautiful French Dress, made of sheer white lawn, very neatly trimmed in front from neck to flounce with four clusters of French tucks (five tucks in each cluster) alternating with three rows of neat pattern valenciennes lace, each followed with two hemstitched tucks, back trimmed from neck to flounce with four clusters of three tucks each, neck and sleeves edged with valenciennes lace, one row of insertion around bottom, followed with hemstitching, nice, deep hem. Color, white only. For children, ages 1 to 4 years. Price........................$1.10

If by mail, postage extra, 8 cents.

Child's French Dress, $1.65.

$1.65

No. 38C1662 A Very Pretty French Dress, made of sheer white lawn, insertion of embroidery at neck, also embroidery ruffle followed with herringbone braid, a 3-inch embroidery ruffle extending over shoulders to back, embroidery cuffs and waistband to match, a cluster of three tucks at bottom, edged with 3-inch Swiss embroidery. Sizes, 1, 2, 3 and 4 years. Color, white only. Price........................$1.65

If by mail, postage extra, 8 cents.

New and Dainty Style, $2.25.

No. 38C1666 Child's White Lawn Dress; made in the new French style, long waisted blouse effect, trimmed in front with two rows of neat valenciennes lace in pointed effect, bishop sleeves with insertion of lace, two rows of beading with ribbon insertion, hemstitched lawn ruffle which is edged with valenciennes lace to match; neck trimmed to correspond with two fancy silk ribbon bows, trimmed

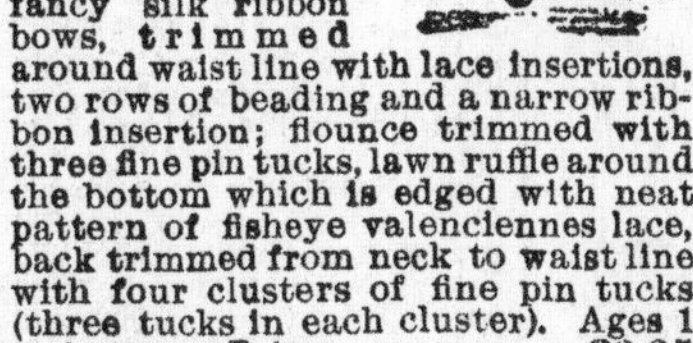

around waist line with lace insertions, two rows of beading and a narrow ribbon insertion; flounce trimmed with three fine pin tucks, lawn ruffle around the bottom which is edged with neat pattern of fisheye valenciennes lace, back trimmed from neck to waist line with four clusters of fine pin tucks (three tucks in each cluster). Ages 1 to 4 years. Price........................$2.25

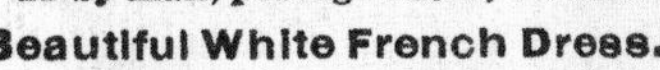

If by mail, postage extra, 9 cents.

Beautiful White French Dress.

$1.98

No. 38C1670 A Handsome French Dress; made of fine white cambric; has a very pretty V-yoke in front with three insertions of 1-inch embroidery alternating with clusters of three fine tucks, beading and ribbon insertions, herringbone braid and embroidery around neck. Embroidery ruffle over the shoulders; four clusters of fine baby tucks (three tucks in each cluster) to waist line. Cuffs with embroidery insertion and ruffle, embroidery waistband; trimmed below waistband with three embroidery ruffles. Four clusters (three in each cluster) of fine tucks in back, from neck to waistband. Price........................$1.98

If by mail, postage extra, 10 cents.

SILK DRESSES.

Ages, 1 to 4 years.

$2.25

No. 38C1674 A Very Pretty and Jaunty French Dress; made of China silk; has a very pretty yoke trimmed with four rows of point de Paris lace insertion alternating with beading, giving yoke an allover lace effect. Neck trimmed with lace followed with beading and ribbon insertion; trimmed all around yoke both front and back with 3-inch lace to match, followed with beading and ribbon insertion; has four clusters (three in each cluster) of fine tucks on back from neck to waistband, sleeves trimmed with lace and beading, waistband of beading and ribbon insertion, trimmed all around the bottom with beading and 3-inch lace. Colors, pink, cream or light blue. Price........................$2.25

If by mail, postage extra, 10 cents.

$2.48

No. 38C1678 An Exceedingly Pretty Child's French Dress; made of China silk. Very pretty yoke front and back, yoke in front with point de Paris lace insertion, alternating with beading, giving yoke an allover lace effect. Neck trimmed with lace followed by beading and ribbon insertion; yoke with 2-inch lace ruffle followed with beading and ribbon insertion. Sleeves trimmed with beading and ribbon insertion; ten fine tucks from neck to waistband on back, trimmed around bottom with narrow beading, 1-inch insertion and 2-inch lace edge to match. Colors, cream, pink or pale blue. Price........................$2.48

CHILDREN'S APRONS.

Gingham Apron, 23 Cents.

For children, ages from 4 to 12 years. Mention age.

No. 38C1704 Girl's Apron, made of good quality gingham in blue or brown and white checks as per illustration. Fancy slashed collar and cuffs trimmed with white lace. Yoke in front and back. Opens in the back and tied with 3-inch strings. Price...........23c

Postage extra, 9c.

25-Cent Lawn Apron.

No. 38C1706 Girls' Lawn Apron, yoke trimmed with three rows of embroidery, shoulder strap edged with lace. Color, white only. Price........25c

If by mail, postage extra, 6c.

For children, age 4 to 12 years.

No. 38C1708 A Girl's Beautiful Apron made of fine white lawn, with insertion of lace all around body with six rows of fine tucks, lace edging around neck and shoulder ruffles, wide hem at bottom. Price..........69c

If by mail, postage extra, 7 cents.

INFANTS' WEAR DEPARTMENT

INFANTS' OUTFITS.

These two outfits represent extraordinary value and the pieces, if bought separately in retail stores, would cost you double our price.

WE CALL SPECIAL ATTENTION TO OUR TWO INFANTS' OUTFIT SETS

as described on this page. One outfit consists of 22 and the other set has 24 pieces and you will find that if you bought the pieces separately, the total cost of either set would be nearly double our price. We only illustrate a few of the many pieces in these sets.

INFANTS' OUTFIT, CONSISTING OF 22 PIECES, FOR $5.95.

These sets have been carefully selected with a view of offering a complete outfit at the very lowest price, such as you would pay nearly twice as much for elsewhere. In these sets you will find, as described below, nearly everything that baby needs to wear, thus doing away with the making of different selections of the so many different articles for the baby's wardrobe.

1 **Very Dainty Long Cambric Robe**, embroidery down front and around bottom.
1 **Muslin Day Slip**, square yoke made of fine embroidery insertion, wide hem at bottom.
2 **Muslin Night Slips**, fancy yoke of embroidery and herringbone braid.
1 **Domet Flannel Wrapper**, embroidered around collar and down front.
1 **Cambric Long Skirt**, with three fine tucks around bottom.
1 **Cambric Long Skirt**, with two clusters of tucks (three tucks in a cluster), Hamburg embroidery around bottom.
1 **Long Skirt**, made of fleeced canton flannel.
1 **Long Canton Skirt**, fleeced, stitched around bottom with silk.
1 **All Wool Flannel Shawl**, beautifully embroidered with silk on corners.
2 **Bibs**, honeycomb pattern, edged all around with lace.
1 **Patented Pinless Diaper**, made of absorbent cloth.
1 **Rubber Diaper** (white).
1 **Silk Bonnet**, beautifully embroidered with silk.
1 **Pair All Wool Knit Bootees**, very closely knitted with fine all wool zephyr.
1 **All Wool Knitted Sacque**, trimmed with tassels.
1 **Flannelette Sacque**, stitched all around collar, down front and cuffs with mercerized twist.
2 **Bands**, made of canton flannel.
2 **Pinning Blankets or Barrior Coats**, made of cream color canton flannel.

No. 38C1740 Price for complete outfit, 22 pieces........................$5.95

A HIGH GRADE INFANTS' OUTFIT, CONSISTING OF 24 PIECES, FOR $11.75.

Very dainty slips, skirts, sacques, etc. This set must be seen to be appreciated as the articles are such that the faint descriptions given do not do them justice.

1 **Beautiful Cambric Robe**, handsomely trimmed with cambric in front, with satin ribbon insertion, wide embroidery ruffle around bottom.
1 **Fine Nainsook Day Slip**, a very pretty round yoke, made of all over lace followed with a lace ruffle, beautifully trimmed around bottom with two lace insertions and wide point de Paris lace edge to match.
1 **Muslin Night Slip** with embroidery forming a yoke. Wide hem at bottom.
1 **Muslin Slip**, yoke trimmed with tucks and embroidery insertion, wide hem at bottom.
1 **Domet Flannel Wrapper**, collar, down front and sleeves stitched with silk. Satin ribbon bow at neck.
1 **Fine Nainsook Skirt** (matched to day slip), trimmed with two lace insertions and wide edge. Two clusters of fine tucks.
1 **Cambric Long Skirt**, trimmed around bottom with three tucks and hem.
1 **All Wool (cream color) Flannel Long Skirt**, with cambric bodice.
1 **All Wool Flannel Shawl**, cream color, handsomely embroidered on one corner in flower design.
3 **Bibs, Honeycomb Pattern**, trimmed with lace. Pocket and teething rings.
1 **Bib** (quilted) with lace edge.
1 **Pinless Diaper**, made of good quality birdseye absorbent cloth.
1 **Rubber Diaper** (white).
1 **Stockinet Diaper.**
1 **Silk Bonnet**, handsomely embroidered with silk and lined with Japanese silk.
1 **Pair of Bootees**, made of all wool zephyr very closely knitted.
1 **Pair of Bootees**, made of silkatine, very closely knitted. A high class bootee.
1 **All Wool Knitted Sacque**, very closely knitted zephyr. Crocheted edge around collar, front and sleeves.
1 **All Wool Flannel Sacque**, stitched with silk. Very pretty and stylish.
2 **Bands**, made of all wool flannel. Silk stitched.
1 **Pinning Blanket or Barrior Coat**, made of all wool flannel, cambric bodice.

No. 38C1746 Price for above high grade set, consisting of 24 pieces...$11.75

Should any additional pieces be required, select same from the following pages of infants' wearing apparel, and include with your order.

See Index for baby books, with handsome illustrations, in which records can be made of the chief events of baby's life.

INFANTS' LONG SLIPS.

Note the Lengths and Sweeps in Our Infants' Slips.

An Infant's Long Cambric Slip for 18 Cents.

No. 38C1750 Infants' Long Slip. Made of cambric, neck and sleeves trimmed with cambric ruffle, front trimmed with wide embroidery, giving a yoke effect, deep hem at bottom. Length, 31 inches, sweep, 50 inches. Price........................18c

If by mail, postage extra, 7 cents.

No. 38C1754 Infants' Long Slip. Made of good muslin; yoke in front and back; yoke in front is trimmed with 8 tucks and insertion of embroidery, cambric collar and cuffs, wide cambric tie strings, and deep hem at bottom. Length, 32 inches; sweep, 48 inches. Price........................25c

If by mail, postage extra, 8 cents.

Infants' Slip with Fancy Yoke, 39 Cents.

No. 38C1756 Infants' Long Slip, made of cambric. Has very neat pointed yoke trimmed with two insertions of neat embroidery, alternating with three clusters of fine tucks, two plaits in back; neck and sleeves trimmed with embroidery. Nice hem at bottom.

Wonderful value. Price..........39c

If by mail, postage extra, 7 cents.

Our 45-Cent Fancy Yoke Muslin Slip.

45c

No. 38C1758 Infants' Long Slip, made of good quality muslin, embroidery ruffle around collar, fancy yoke in front, provided with a wide strip of embroidery, four rows of tucking in front with embroidered insertion, extra wide hem on bottom. Length, 32 inches; sweep, 54 inches. Price........................45c

If by mail, postage extra, 6 cents.

Lace Trimmed Infants' Slip, 50 Cents.

No. 38C1760 Infants' Slip, made of nainsook. Very neat yoke with insertion of narrow lace alternating with clusters of fine tucks. Yoke followed with lawn ruffle which is edged with valenciennes lace, back of yoke trimmed with six clusters of three fine tucks, neck and sleeves trimmed with lace to match.

Price........................50c

If by mail, postage extra, 8 cents.

No. 38C1762 Infants' Long Slip, made of soft finish nainsook, very neat square yoke trimmed with numerous rows of fine baby tucks and hemstitching. Trimmed each side of yoke with fine embroidery, yoke and back also trimmed with numerous rows of fine tucks and hemstitching, neck and sleeves edged with neat pattern of fine Swiss embroidery, deep hem at bottom. Price.........48c

If by mail, postage extra, 6 cents.

Our 75-Cent White Canbric Slip.

No. 38C1764 Infants' Long Slip, made of cambric. Yoke, back and front with numerous rows of fine tucks, followed with herringbone braid, embroidery insertion in front. Epaulets of Swiss embroidery. Neck and sleeves trimmed with valenciennes lace. Trimmed around bottom with three fine tucks and edged with 4½-inch Swiss embroidery. Price..75c

If by mail, postage extra, 7 cents.

Very Neatly Trimmed Slip at 75 Cents.

No. 38C1766 Very Neat Long Slip, made of fine nainsook. Has a very pretty circular yoke (back and front alike), trimmed with numerous rows of fine hemstitched tucks. A ruffle all around yoke (front and back), made of fine Swiss embroidery, hemstitched collar and cuffs, deep hem at bottom with hemstitching.

Price, 75c

If by mail, postage extra, 8 cents.

Very Fine Nainsook Slip at 89 Cents.

89c No. 38C1768 Neatly Trimmed Slip, made of fine soft nainsook. Yoke trimmed with four insertions of neat valenciennes lace, alternating with five clusters of three fine tucks, neck and sleeves trimmed with lace to match, insertion around bottom of fine valenciennes lace, nainsook ruffle edged with lace to match. Price....................89c
If by mail, postage extra, 10 cents.

Fine Nainsook Infants' Slip.

No. 38C1774 Very Neat Long Slip, made of very fine nainsook, pretty yoke in front, made of very fine valenciennes lace, two rows embroidery insertion. Trimmed around yoke with herringbone braid, and valenciennes lace ruffle around yoke in front, extending over shoulders, two plaits in back of yoke. Neck and sleeves trimmed with herringbone braid, valenciennes lace edging; trimmed around the bottom with fine tucks and valenciennes lace. Length, 38 inches; sweep, 65 inches. Price......(Postage extra, 6c)......98c

Embroidery Trimmed Cambric Slip, $1.39.

No. 38C1778 Infants' Long Slip, made of white cambric, with a square yoke, two embroidery insertions, both front and back, and trimmed with fine tucks in front. Embroidery ruffle, extending to back, neck and sleeves; trimmed with narrow embroidery ruffle, open work embroidery insertion and six tucks at bottom; has a 7-inch ruffle around bottom of openwork embroidery. Entire length of slip, 42 inches; sweep, around bottom, 72 inches. Price..............$1.39
If by mail, postage extra, 14 cents.

$1.48 Infants' Long Slip.

$1.48

No. 38C1782 Infants' Long Slip, made of fine nainsook. Very pretty V yoke in front, trimmed with beading and point de Paris lace. Ruffle of lace to match, extending to back. Six clusters of baby tucks in back. Neck and sleeves trimmed with valenciennes lace followed with herringbone braid, trimmed around bottom with two insertions of point de Paris lace alternating with narrow beading and edged with 3-inch lace to match beading; lace insertions and edge is 7 inches deep. Entire length of slip, 36 inches; sweep, 58 inches. Price..$1.48
If by mail, postage extra, 8 cents.

Infants' Long Slip, $1.69.

No. 38C1786 Infants' Long Slip, made of cambric. Has a very pretty yoke, front and back, trimmed with embroidery insertion, tucks, beading and ribbon insertions forming a bow in front. Ruffle of fine Swiss embroidery all around yoke, trimmed with embroidery around neck. Insertion and embroidery on sleeves, trimmed all around the bottom with three clusters (four in cluster) of tucks. Has a ruffle around the bottom of 8-inch embroidery. Entire length of slip, 42 inches; sweep around bottom, 72 inches.
Price..............................$1.69
If by mail, postage extra, 14 cents.

No. 38C1790 A Very Pretty Long Slip; made of fine quality white sheer lawn, a very pretty circular yoke, front and back trimmed with numerous rows of fine baby tucks, and three embroidery medallions, followed with lawn ruffle with insertion of neat pattern of valenciennes lace and edge to match, neck and sleeves edged with lace, insertion near bottom of neat valenciennes lace in the new V effect, one row of insertion to match around bottom, has a wide lawn ruffle all around bottom with insertion of neat pattern valenciennes lace with edge to match.
Price..............................$2.69
If by mail, postage extra, 11 cents.

Fine Lace Trimmed Slip.

No. 38C1792 Very Pretty Trimmed Slip; made of fine soft finish nainsook. Square yoke; back and front trimmed with insertion of lace and neat embroidery, followed with ruffle of point de Paris lace to match. Bishop sleeves trimmed with lace, has three insertions of 1½-inch point de Paris lace, with 4-inch lace edge to match.
Price, $1.48
If by mail, postage extra, 10c.

Extra Fine Lace Trimmed Slip.

No. 38C1794 Very Neatly Trimmed Long Slip; made of fine nainsook, very pretty circular yoke trimmed with neat pattern of valenciennes lace insertion, both back and front, followed with lawn ruffle with lace insertion and edge to match, neck trimmed with herringbone braid and edged with valenciennes lace to correspond, sleeves trimmed with lace insertion and edge, trimmed around the bottom with four rows of neat pattern valenciennes lace and edged around the bottom with a 4-inch valenciennes lace.
Price..............................$1.98
If by mail, postage extra, 10 cents.

Beautifully Trimmed, $2.25.

$2.25

No. 38C1798 Infants' Long Slip, made of good quality nainsook; very pretty yoke, trimmed with three clusters of tucks with two rows of embroidery insertion; two clusters of tucking in back of yoke, ruffle of embroidery all around yoke, extending over shoulders to back of yoke; neck and sleeves trimmed with embroidery; three clusters of fine tucks (five rows in cluster) all around the bottom, with two rows of fine embroidery insertion, trimmed around bottom with 5-inch embroidery to match. Entire length, 38 inches; sweep around bottom, 65 inches. Price..................$2.25
If by mail, postage extra, 8 cents.

Our $2.25 Long Slip.

$2.25

No. 38C1804 A Very Dainty Long Slip, made of a very fine grade nainsook; yoke front and back made of all over lace, trimmed all around front to back of yoke with two ruffles of very fine lace; neck and sleeves trimmed with lace to match; has two rows of very wide insertion of point de Paris lace near bottom to match yoke, and edged around bottom with 5-inch point de Paris lace. Entire length, 38 inches, sweep around bottom, 65 inches.
Price..................................$2.25
If by mail, postage extra, 9 cents.

Infants' Silk Long Slips.

$2.98

No. 38C1812 Infants' Long Slip, made of China silk. Yoke front and back, trimmed in back with two insertions of point de Paris lace and beading. Yoke in front trimmed with lace, beading and ribbon insertion point de Paris lace ruffle extending around the yoke to back, followed with beading and narrow ribbon insertion; neck and sleeves trimmed to match. Trimmed around bottom with three rows of beading and lace insertion; 5-inch point de Paris lace edge to match. Insertions and edge around bottom 9 inches deep. Entire length, 40 in[illegible]es; sweep, 50 inches. Color, cream only. Price..............$2.98
If by mail, postage extra, 7 cents.

Flannel Slips.

No. 38C1814 Infants' Slip, made of fine quality heavy fleeced baby flannel. Neck and sleeves trimmed with torchon lace. Hem at bottom. A very warm garment for the baby. Colors, white, pink or baby blue.
Price......39c
If by mail, postage extra, 11 cents.

Infants' Christening Slips.

98c No. 38C1816 Infants' Long Christening Robes. Made of good quality white cambric, with panel front of allover cambric embroidery and edged with wide cambric embroidery. Long streamers forming a bow in front. Entire length, 36 inches; sweep, 45 inches.
Price..............................98c
If by mail, postage extra, 6 cents.

Fine Embroidery Trimmed Robe.

$1.39 No. 38C1820 Infants' Christening Robe, made of fine white cambric, circular yoke of embroidery beading and ribbon insertion, embroidery ruffle in front. Neck and sleeves trimmed with embroidery. Wide panel in front of Swiss embroidery with beading and ribbon insertion from yoke to bottom, forming a bow. Has a 4-inch embroidery ruffle at bottom. Entire length of robe, 42 inches; sweep around bottom, 72 inches.
Price..............................$1.39
If by mail, postage extra, 10 cents.

Extra Fine Lace Trimmed Robe.

$1.98

No. 38C1822 Infants' Christening Robe, made of fine white nainsook. Yoke trimmed with insertion of point de Paris lace and embroidery, ruffle over the shoulders extending to back of yoke. Neck and sleeves edged with valenciennes lace, followed with herringbone braid. Back of yoke trimmed with tucks, one row of embroidery on each side in front from neck to bottom, forming a panel front, which is trimmed with six embroidery and five point de Paris lace insertions, and edged with 5-inch lace to match. Entire length of robe is 38 inches; sweep around bottom, 72 inches.
Price..............................$1.98
If by mail, postage extra, 7 cents.

Infants' Flannel Wrapper.

No. 38C1828 Infants' Wrapper, made of domet flannel, in the newest and most desirable patterns, embroidered around the collar and a yoke in front and back; embroidered epaulets over shoulders. Colors, blue or pink stripes. Price....................48c
If by mail, postage extra, 8 cents.

Infants' Long Wrapper.

No. 38C1832 Infants' Long Wrapper, made of daisy cloth, in pink or light blue. Has a very pretty slashed collar, which is embroidered and edged with mercerized twist; six tucks in front, each stitched with mercerized twist; edged with mercerized twist on each side from neck to bottom; turnover cuffs, which are also stitched with mercerized twist; silk ribbon bow at neck; hem at bottom. Colors are pink or light blue. Price......75c
If by mail, postage extra, 9 cents.

Infants' Long Cambric and Muslin Skirt.

33c

No. 38C1840 Infants' Long Skirt, made of white cambric, with three neat tucks and hem at bottom. Price..........................33c
If by mail, postage extra, 7 cents.

Our 47c Infants' Long Skirt.

47c

No. 38C1844 Infants' Long Skirt, made of cambric, two clusters of triple tucks around bottom and edged with 3-inch cambric embroidery. Price..........................47c
If by mail, postage extra, 7 cents.

Infants' Skirt with Embroidery Insertion.

55c

No. 38C1848 Infants' Long Skirt, made of fine white cambric, two clusters of three tucks and embroidery insertion around bottom edged with 3-inch embroidery, has a 5-inch bodice. Price............................55c
If by mail, postage extra, 7 cents.

Infants' Long Skirt, 69 Cents.

69c

No. 38C1852 Infants' Long Skirt, made of good quality white cambric, two clusters of fine tucks, (six tucks in each cluster) around bottom and edged with 5-inch cambric embroidery. Price.......................69c
If by mail, postage extra, 7 cents.

Our Infants' Skirts are Made Full Length.

75c

No. 38C1856 Infant's Long Skirt, made of white nainsook. Has a 6-inch band, trimmed around the bottom with six fine tucks and edged with 5-inch Normandy valenciennes lace. Price......75c
If by mail, postage extra, 8 cents.

Infants' Long Nainsook Skirt.

No. 38C1860 Infants' Long Skirt, made of fine nainsook, handsomely trimmed with two clusters of three tucks each all around the bottom and one row of valenciennes insertion and a 5-inch valenciennes lace trimming all around the bottom, 6-inch bodice. Price..........89c
If by mail, postage extra, 6 cents.

98c

No. 38C1864 Infants' Long Skirt, made of fine white cambric, has a 4-inch band, trimmed at bottom with two clusters of three tucks, and insertion of 1-inch embroidery, ruffle around bottom of 6-inch Swiss embroidery. Price..........98c
If by mail, postage extra, 8 cents.

$1.48

No. 38C1868 Infants' Long Skirt, made of fine nainsook, trimmed with three clusters (four rows in cluster) of fine tucks with two rows of point de Paris insertion. Trimmed around the bottom with 5-inch point de Paris lace to match. Price...$1.48
If by mail, postage extra, 8 cents.

Infants' Long Flannel Skirts.

Our Infants' Skirts are made full length and sweep.

No. 38C1872 Infants' Long Skirt, made of heavy fleeced shaker flannel. Wide cambric band. Color, cream only. Price..25c
If by mail, postage extra, 7c.

35c

No. 38C1876 Infants' Long Skirt, made of good quality heavy fleeced shaker flannel. Wide cambric band. Color, cream only.

PRICE, 35c

If by mail, postage extra, 9 cents.

Infants' Long Skirt, 49 Cents.

49c

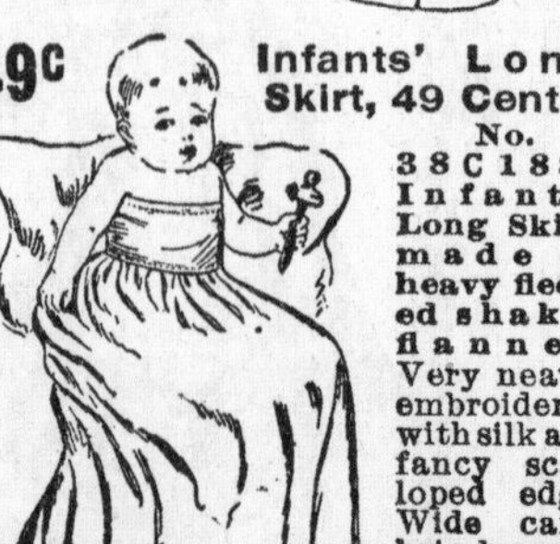

No. 38C1880 Infants' Long Skirt, made of heavy fleeced shaker flannel. Very neatly embroidered with silk and fancy scalloped edge. Wide cambric band. Color, cream only. Price..49c
If by mail, postage extra, 9c.

Our 48c Infants' Long Skirt.

48c

No. 38C1884 Infants' Long Skirt, made of cream colored wool flannel, wide cambric band with hem at bottom. Price..........................48c
If by mail, postage extra, 6 cents.

Our 98c Infants' Long Skirt.

98c

No. 38C1888 Infants' Long all Wool Flannel Skirt, with a wide cambric band beautifully embroidered around the bottom with silk. Cream color, assorted patterns. Price..98c
If by mail, postage extra, 7 cents

Heavy Silk Embroidered All Wool Flannel Skirt.

No. 38C1892 Infants' Long Skirt, made of fine all wool flannel, same style as No. 38C1888, wide cambric band, embroidered around bottom with silk of very wide raised pattern in beautiful designs. Color, cream, assorted patterns. Price....................$1.48
If by mail, postage extra, 7 cents.

Infants' Barrior Coats or Pinning Blankets.

No. 38C1902 Infants' Barrior Coats or Pinning Blankets, made of shaker flannel. Well made. Cream color. Price......................18c
If by mail, postage extra, 6 cents.

No. 38C1906 Infants' Barrior Coats or Pinning Blankets, made of all wool cream color flannel. Price..........................48c
If by mail, postage extra, 6 cents.

No. 38C1910 Infants' Bands, made of good shaker flannel. Price...10c
If by mail, postage extra, 3 cents.

Infants' Flannel Shawl.

Note our Sizes in these Shawls.

No. 38C2010 Infants' Shawl, made of cream color flannel, embroidered with silk. Floral design in one of the corners, as shown in illustration, hemmed with silk. Size, 27x27 inches. Price.........45c
If by mail, postage extra, 5 cents.

Hand Embroidered Flannel Shawl.

No. 38C2012 Infants' Shawl, made of cream color wool flannel, scalloped edge, elaborately embroidered with silk. Beautiful floral design, heavily embroidered in silk in corner. Size, 28x28 inches. Price..............89c
If by mail, postage extra, 6 cents.

Infants' All Wool Flannel Shawl.

No. 38C2014 Infants' All Wool Extra Large Hand Embroidered Flannel Shawl, elaborate raised floral design with silk on two corners of shawl, scalloped and stitched with silk. Size, 32x32 inches. Color, cream.
Price $1.19
If by mail, postage extra, 6 cents.

Heavy Silk Embroidered All Wool Flannel Shawl.

No. 38C2016 Infants' Finest All Wool Flannel Shawl. Extra large hand embroidered silk design on upper two corners of shawl, extra heavy raised pattern. Scalloped and neatly stitched with silk. Size, 32x34 inches. Color, cream.
Price $1.69
If by mail, postage extra, 6 cents.

Infants' Wool and Silk Veils.

No. 38C2020 Infants' Wool Veil. Neat border. Medium stitch. Cream only. Price..10c
If by mail, postage extra, 2c.

No. 38C2022 Infants' Veil, made of fine all wool worsted. Medium stitch and fancy border. Color, cream.
Price 25c
If by mail, postage extra, 2 cents.

No. 38C2024 Infants' Silk Veil. Very neat stitch and fancy border. Color, white. Price 25c
If by mail, postage extra, 2 cents.

Children's Bibs.

No. 38C2028 Fancy Figured Bib, Marseilles pattern, fleeced back, with bound edge.
Price, each 2c
Per dozen 21c
If by mail, postage extra, 2 cents.

No. 38C2030 Honeycomb Bib, with bound edge, and trimmed with a washlace.
Price, each 3c
Per dozen 32c
If by mail, postage extra, each, 2 cents.

No. 38C2032 Honeycomb Bib, bound edge, and trimmed with a wide wash lace embroidery, pocket with teething ring.
Price, each 4c
Per dozen 40c
If by mail, postage extra, each, 2 cents.

No. 38C2034 Quilted Marseilles Bib, with wash lace edge, very pretty design.
Price, each 7c
Per dozen 80c
If by mail, postage extra, each, 2 cents.

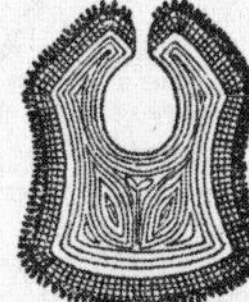

Oilcloth Bibs.

No. 38C2038 Waterproof Bibs, made of enameled oilcloth, bound with tape and have neck strings. Size, 9x12 inches.
Price, each 2c
Per dozen 21c
If by mail, postage extra, each, 3c.

The Imperial Pinless Diaper. A Comfort To Baby.

No. 38C2050 Made of birdseye absorbent cloth. Mothers' cares are lightened and mothers' babies brightened by using the new patented pinless, ready to use, sanitary diaper made of antiseptic birdseye, has thickness (7-fold) where it is needed and thinness elsewhere. Prevents bowlegs. Is provided with draw strings around waist and legs so it fits perfectly. Cannot fall off. Has buttonholes front and back to attach to waist. Has no pins to lose, to prick baby's skin, or for the darling to swallow, or to become unpleasant through use. "Only a long suffering mother could have conceived the idea." Three sizes, small, medium or large.
Price, each 24c
Four for 90c
If by mail, postage extra, each, 4 cents.

Rubber Diaper Drawers.

No. 38C2052 White Rubber Diaper Drawers; 3 sizes, large, medium and small.
Price, each. $0.15
Per dozen 1.75
If by mail, postage extra, each, 4c.

Stockinet Diaper Drawers.

No. 38C2054 Same style as No. 38C2052, but made of strictly waterproof stockinet. A very soft material. Three sizes, small, medium or large.
Price 32c
If by mail, postage extra, 4 cents.

Waterproof Diaper Drawers.

No. 38C2056 The Improved Waterproof Stockinet Diaper Drawers are strictly waterproof. Material is very soft and pliable, made with a wide muslin waistband and draw strings, making diaper adjustable to waist. Three sizes, small, medium and large. Price 39c
If by mail, postage extra, 5 cents.

Baby Carriage, Crib or Bed Rubber Sheets.

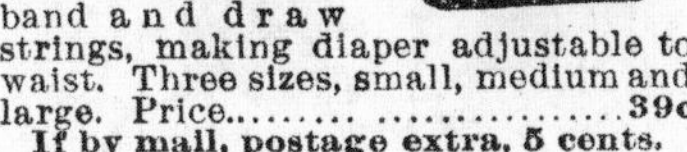

These sheets are made of soft rubber, lined with muslin, a very useful article to avoid wetting the carriage, crib or bed clothes, hemmed all around with tape; made in three sizes.

No. 38C2058 Baby Carriage size, 12x18 inches. Price 15c
No. 38C2060 Crib size, 18x24 inches. Price 28c
No. 38C2062 Bed size, 27x36 inches. Price 60c

Baby Carriage, Crib or Bed Sheets, made of stockinet, a soft, pliable, waterproof material, hemmed all around with tape; these sheets are also useful as a waterproof apron when washing the baby; made in three sizes.

No. 38C2064 Baby Carriage size, 12x18 inches. Price 25c
No. 38C2066 Crib size, 18x24 inches. Price 48c
No. 38C2068 Bed size, 27x36 inches. Price 98c

Baby's Patented Safety Belt.

No. 38C2074 Baby's Safety Belt, recommends itself from the security and freedom it affords. Belt is made of good quality non-elastic webbing. Evenly attached with three braces made of adjustable fine elastic with nickled snaps which are to be used with screw eyes. Can be placed in a buggy, cot, chair or on a floor. It gives (as illustrated) the child the feeling of freedom while securing it from any possibility of falling, etc. A relief for tired mothers and a comfort to baby.
Price, complete 39c
If by mail, postage extra, 7 cents.

INFANTS' EIDERDOWN AFGHANS.

THESE ARE THE HANDSOMEST NOVELTIES EVER SHOWN TO GO WITH BABY BUGGIES AND MUST BE SEEN TO BE APPRECIATED.

No. 38C2102 An Infant's Very Pretty Afghan. Made of Jersey back wool eiderdown, handsomely embroidered in center with colored Shetland floss in flower designs, stitched all around near edge with mercerized silk; scalloped edge. Size, 36x24 inches. **Cream color only, with colored centers.** Price 98c
If by mail, postage extra, 6 cents.

White Pique Embroidery Trimmed Afghans.

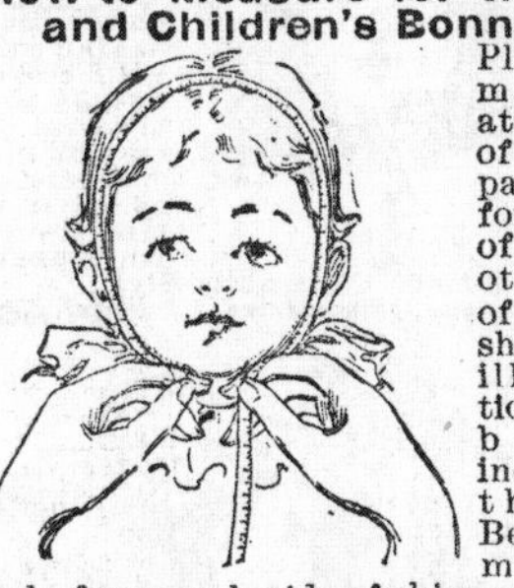

No. 38C2103 Baby Carriage Afghan, made of white pique with insertion of open embroidery in the pointed effect, ruffled all around with a 3-inch open work embroidery. Size, 24x24 inches.
Price 98c
If by mail, postage extra, 9 cents.

How to Measure for Infants' and Children's Bonnets.

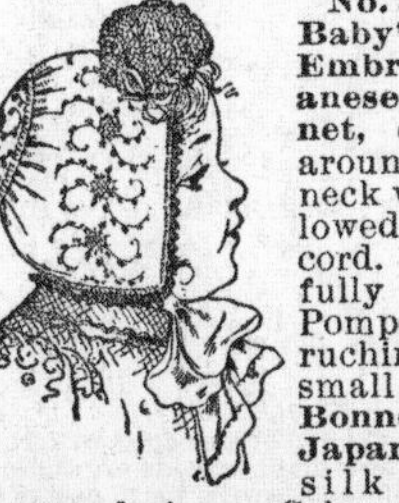

Place tape measure at one side of chin, pass over fore part of head to other side of chin, as shown in illustration. Number of inches is the size. Be sure to measure only from each side of chin, not under the chin.

INFANTS' SILK BONNETS.

No. 38C2200 Baby's Japanese Silk Bonnet. Pretty, new design, silk embroidered with row of valenciennes lace edging all around face and neck, and high top ruching, ribbon ties, lined with cambric. Color, cream only. Sizes, 12 to 17 inches. Price..20c
If by mail, postage extra, 6 cents.

Japanese Silk Bonnet.

No. 38C2202 A Baby's Very Pretty Embroidered Japanese Silk Bonnet, edged all around front and neck with lace followed with silk cord. Back beautifully embroidered. Pompon on top of ruching and two small ribbon bows. **Bonnet lined with Japanese silk,** wide silk strings, very newest design. Color, cream only. Sizes, 12 to 17 inches. Price 48c
If by mail, postage extra, 6 cents.

China Silk Bonnet.

No. 38C2204 Very Fine Bonnet, made of China silk, embroidered with silk in a very artistic design, embroidered in back to correspond, very full ruche around face and neck, interlined with wadding and **lined with China silk,** wide silk tie strings. Color, cream only. Sizes, 12 to 17 inches.
Price 69c
If by mail, postage extra, 7 cents.

Fancy Embroidered Bonnet.

No. 38C2206 A Beautiful Fancy Embroidered Bonnet; made of fine Jap silk, handsomely embroidered with silk in very neat design in the new grape effect, back embroidered to correspond, silk mull and baby ribbon bows on top, ruffled silk mull around face and neck, followed with fancy silk braid; bonnet lined with fine sateen, wide silk tie strings. The heavy design of embroidery on this bonnet is a work of art. Color, white only. Sizes, 12 to 17 inches.
Price 98c
If by mail, postage extra, 7 cents.

Silk Embroidered Bonnet.

No. 38C2209 Infants' Silk Embroidered Bonnet, made of Jap silk, trimmed with double ruffle and edged with lace, neck trimmed to match, trimmed around face with narrow lace. Sateen tie strings. Color, cream only. Sizes, 12 to 17 inches. Price 48c
If by mail, postage extra, 9 cents.

Infants' Lawn Bonnets.

No. 38C2272 Infants' White Lawn Bonnet, very neatly embroidered ruche pompon on top, trimmed around face and neck with ruffled lawn and edged with lawn; wide lawn tie strings. Color, white only. Sizes, 12 to 17 inches.
Price 25c
If by mail, postage extra, 5 cents.

Fancy Embroidered Bonnet. Only 39 Cents.

No. 38C2274 Infants' Bonnet. Made of open work Swiss embroidered lawn; back to correspond; graduated ruche around face and neck, baby ribbon bows on top; has wide lawn tie strings. A beautiful bonnet and exceptionally good value. Color, white. Sizes, 12 to 17 inches. Price 39c
If by mail, postage extra, 4 cents.

Very Pretty Trimmed Bonnet, Only 48 Cents.

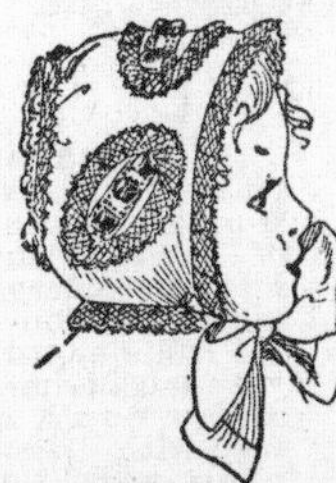

No. 38C2280 Child's Bonnet, made of fine Swiss, trimmed on each side and top with wide beading and ribbon insertion and edged with valenciennes lace, back trimmed to correspond, valenciennes lace trimmed around face and neck, nice wide lawn tie strings; very pretty bonnet. Color, white with blue or pink ribbon. Sizes, 12 to 17 inches. Price 48c
If by mail, postage extra, 5 cents.

Made of Allover Lace, Only 35 Cents.

No. 38C2284 Infants' Bonnet. The entire bonnet is made of allover lace. Full ruche on top. Face and neck trimmed with ruffled net followed with beading and ribbon inserting. Wide lawn tie strings. A very pretty bonnet. Color, white. Sizes, 12 to 17 inches. Price..........35c
If by mail, postage extra, 6 cents.

Hand Crocheted Hoods, Made of Silk and Mercerized Cotton (looks like silk) Twists.

For Infants.

Three sizes, small, medium or large. Infants' Hand Crocheted Hoods, very closely stitched, silk ribbon bow on top with silk ribbon tie strings. Color, cream only.

No. 38C2281 Made of mercerized (looks like silk) cotton twist, lined with sateen. Price..........39c
No. 38C2282 Made of silk twist, lined with Japanese silk. Price....69c
If by mail, postage extra, each, 6c.

Crocheted Hood With Ribbon Insertions.

Infants' Hand Crocheted Hoods, very neat stitch with three insertions of silk ribbon and ribbon bow on top, also ribbon tie strings. Color, cream only.
No. 38C2283 Made of mercerized (looks like silk) cotton twist, unlined. Price..........45c
No. 38C2284 Made of mercerized (looks like silk) cotton twist, lined with sateen. Price..........52c
No. 38C2285 Made of silk twist, unlined. Price..........80c
No. 38C2286 Made of silk twist, lined with Japanese silk. Price....95c
If by mail, postage extra, each, 6c.

Very Artistic Stitch in This Hood.

Infants' Hand Crocheted Hood. The stitch in this hood is a work of art and must be seen to be appreciated, has wide silk ribbon bow on top with silk ribbon tie strings. Color, cream only.
No. 38C2287 Made of mercerized (looks like silk) cotton twist lined with sateen. Price..........48c
No. 38C2288 Made of silk twist, unlined. Price..........98c
No. 38C2289 Made of silk twist, lined with Japanese silk. Price..$1.15
If by mail, postage extra, each, 6c.

POKE BONNETS.

For children, ages, 1 to 5 years.

No. 38C2290 Child's Poke Bonnet, made of lawn. Has embroidery insertion, nice high poke in back, ruffle in front and around neck edged with lace. Colors, white, pink or blue. Sizes, 14 to 17.
Price........39c
If by mail, postage extra, 8c.

No. 38C2292 Child's Poke Bonnet, made of lawn, with fine embroidery insertion, double ruffle edged with lace, trimmed around face with lace; nice wide tie strings. Color, white only. Sizes, 14 to 17.
Price......(Postage extra 8c).....48c

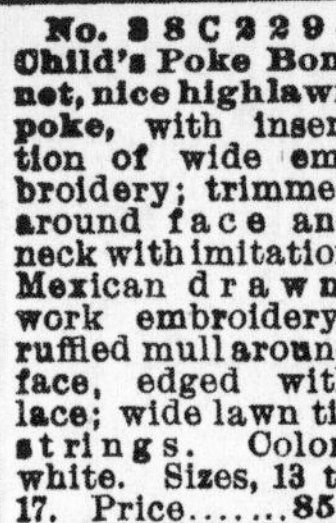

No. 38C2294 Child's Poke Bonnet, nice high lawn poke, with insertion of wide embroidery; trimmed around face and neck with imitation Mexican drawnwork embroidery; ruffled mull around face, edged with lace; wide lawn tie strings. Color, white. Sizes, 13 to 17. Price.......85c
If by mail, postage extra, 8 cents.

Children's Lawn and Mull Hats.

For children up to 6 years of age.

No. 38C2300 Child's Corded Lawn Hat, embroidered brim and edged with braid; ruffled crown; lawn tie strings. Colors, white with blue or pink crown or solid white. Price. 21c
If by mail, postage extra, 8 cents.

No. 38C2304 Child's Lawn Hat; lawn ruffle all around hat, edged with lace; crown trimmed with lace and fancy cord. Colors are white, pink or blue.
Price..25c
If by mail, postage extra, 6 cents.

No. 38C2308 Child's Mull Hat, full puffed silk crown, neatly embroidered on top with silk, mull rosette; brim trimmed with fancy braid and ruffle of mull. Color, white only. Price, (By mail, postage extra, 11 cents). 48c

No. 38C2312 Child's Mull Hat, with triple ruffle which is edged with lace, band trimmed with fancy braid. Nice puffed silk crown. Colors, cream or pale blue.
Price..........75c
If by mail, postage extra, 12 cents.

No. 38C2316 Child's Mull Hat, very newest shape. Extra high crown trimmed with rosette and ribbon, top with allover lace corded and ruffled brim which is edged with point de Paris lace; very stylish. Colors, white or pale blue. Price..89c
If by mail, postage extra, 14 cents.

No. 38C2320 Child's Hat, made of white pique, newest shaped crown. Trimmed with beading and ribbon. Corded brim, edged with ruffled organdie, large bow made of wide organdie and edged with colored lawn; very pretty hat. Colors, white with pink or blue ribbon and trimmings. Price..........75c
If by mail, postage extra, 14 cents.

Child's Mull Hat, 98 Cents.

No. 38C2334 Child's Mull Hat, has a nice high puffed crown, with rosette, top neatly embroidered with silk, corded brim with double mull ruffle, very pretty hat. Colors, cream, pink or pale blue. Price..........98c
If by mail, postage extra, 13 cents.

TAM O'SHANTERS.

Very Popular.

Sizes, 19 to 21 inches.

20c

No. 38C2350 Tam O'Shanter, made of white pique, covered button on top, made with a visor, lined with cambric. Color, white only. Price..........20c
If by mail, postage extra, 12 cents.

Extra Fine Pique Tam, 39 Cents.

No. 38C2351 Extra Large Tam O'Shanter, made of fine quality pique, covered button on top, patented celluloid visor, lined with cambric, full 12-inch crown. Color, white only. Price..........39c
If by mail, postage extra, 13 cents.

50c

No. 38C2354 Tam O'Shanter, made of corded mercerized material, looks like silk, has covered button on top, made with a visor and trimmed with cord, lined with cambric, made with a full 12-inch crown. Colors, royal blue or garnet. Price..........50c
If by mail, postage extra, 15 cents.

Fine Broadcloth Tam O'Shanter, 48 Cents.

No. 38C2355 Tam O'Shanter, made of fine all wool broadcloth, made with a visor and covered button on top, lined with sateen. Colors, black or navy blue. Price..........48c
If by mail, postage extra, 15 cents.

The Rob Roy Tam O'Shanter.

No. 38C2356 Tam O'Shanter, made of good quality duck, with visor and covered button on top, lined with cambric. Color, white only. Price....20c
If by mail, postage extra, 14 cents.

Norfolk Tam, Only 25 Cents.

No. 38C2360 The Norfolk Tam, made of pressed felt, trimmed on top with strap and two brass buttons, made with a visor, lined with cambric. Colors, navy blue or cardinal. Price, 25c
If by mail, postage extra, 12c.

Norfolk Tam, Made of Duck, Only 20 Cents.

No. 38C2361 The Norfolk Tam O'Shanter, made of good quality duck, strap on top, trimmed with two brass buttons. Color, white. Price, 20c
If by mail, postage extra, 12 cents.

Circular Tam, Only 69 Cents.

No. 38C2364 High Grade Circular Tam, made of corded mercerized material, looks like silk. Silk embroidered anchor on top, lined with cambric. Colors, garnet or the new champagne shade. Wonderful value. Price..69c
If by mail, postage extra, 12 cents.

Circular Leatherette Tam, Only 39 Cents.

No. 38C2365 Circular Tam O'Shanter made of leatherette, trimmed around band with fancy ribbon, lined with cambric, very stylish tam. Colors, black or wine. Price.....39c
If by mail, postage extra, 12 cents.

Fancy Tam, Only 50 Cents.

No. 38C2368 Very Pretty Tam O'Shanter, made of corded mercerized material, full ruffled crown, made with a visor and trimmed with fancy braid, lined with cambric. Colors, royal blue or cardinal.
Price..........50c
If by mail, postage extra, 13 cents.

All Wool Flannel Tam, 39 Cents.

No. 38C2369 Tam O'Shanter with visor, made of all wool flannel; of one piece and ruffled to band. Lined with mercerized sateen. Colors are royal blue, cardinal or cadet blue. Wonderful value. Price..........39c
If by mail, postage extra, 15 cents.

The Auto Tam, Made of Leatherette, Only 39c.

No. 38C2370 The Auto Tam, made of leatherette; has a visor trimmed with cord, 12-inch crown, lined with cambric. Colors, black or wine.
Price......39c
If by mail, postage extra, 14 cents.

Mercerized Linen Auto Tam, Only 48 Cents.

No. 38C2371 The Auto Tam O'Shanter, made of mercerized linen, looks like silk but wears better. Has patented celluloid visor, trimmed with two brass buttons, lined with cambric, 12-inch crown. Colors, black, white or the new champagne shade. Price, 48c
If by mail, postage extra, 12 cents.

Very Latest, The Pompadour Tam O'Shanter, 75 Cents.

No. 38C2376 The New Style Pompadour Tam O'Shanter, made of corded silk mixed material, looks like silk but wears better. Made in the new high pompadour front, with visor, tam lined with cambric. Colors, black, royal blue or the new champagne shade. Price..........75c
If by mail, postage extra, 12 cents.

Leatherette Tam, Only 48c.

No. 38C2377 The Pompadour Tam, made of leatherette, 12-inch crown, made with a visor, trimmed with cord. Colors, black or wine.
Price..........48c
If by mail, postage extra, 12 cents.

The Pompadour Tam, 39 Cents.

No. 38C2378 The Pompadour Tam, made of moire, front embroidered with silk emblem, has visor, lined with cambric, 12-inch crown. Colors, blue or garnet. Price..........39c
If by mail, postage extra, 11 cents.

The Tourist Tam O'Shanter, Very Latest, 48 Cents.

No. 38C2380 New Style Tourist Tam, made of mercerized linen, looks like silk, trimmed on top with covered buttons, stitched brim. Colors, brown or the new champagne shade.
Price.....48c
If by mail, postage extra, 12 cents.

Made of White Duck, 48 Cents.

No. 38C2382 The Tourist, made of good quality white duck, edged with blue braid. Color, white only.
Price.....48c
If by mail, postage extra, 11 cents.

The Toque Tam, Only 39c.

No. 38C2384 Child's Tam O'Shanter with the toque effect, made of moire, with a visor trimmed with cord, has silk tassel, tam lined with cambric. Colors, royal blue or red.
Price.....39c
If by mail, postage extra, 11 cents.

Very Stylish Toque, only 39 Cents.

No. 38C2386 Child's Toque, made of white mercerized linen (looks like silk), with silk embroidered emblem and silk tassel, band made of either blue or white corded mercerized material trimmed with silk braid, lined with cambric. Color, white, with blue or red band. Price.....39c
If by mail, postage extra, 9 cents.

Novelty Tam, only 39 Cents.

No. 38C2390 Circular Tam O'Shanter, made of moreen. In combinations of colors. Has a visor trimmed with silk cord. Colors, blue and white or blue and red.
Price.....39c
If by mail, postage extra, 11 cents.

All Wool Broadcloth Tam.

No. 38C2262 Tam O'Shanter, made of all wool broadcloth. The new square college shape, trimmed around band with silk grosgrain ribbon. Cord and tassel on top. Tam lined with sateen. Colors, black, navy blue or garnet.
Price.....48c
If by mail, postage extra, 15 cents.

INFANTS' KNIT BOOTEES.

All hand crocheted and seamless. We do not handle machine made bootees, as they are made with raw seams. We show a complete line of these dainty and comfortable articles for infants. Note our prices and qualities carefully.

Only 9 Cents per Pair.

No. 38C2500 Infants' Bootees, hand crocheted, made of all wool zephyr. Colors, solid white, pink and white or blue and white.
Price, per pair....9c
If by mail, postage extra, per pair, 2c.

No. 38C2502 Infants' Bootees, closely hand crocheted, neat design, made of fine zephyr. Colors, solid white, pink and white or blue and white.
Price, per pair.12c
If by mail, postage extra, per pair, 2c.

No. 38C2504 Infants' Extra Long Bootees, hand knitted of fine all wool zephyr and trimmed with mercerized twist. Tassels at ankle. Same style as No. 38C2502. Colors, blue and white, pink and white or solid white.
Price, per pair.....16c
If by mail, postage extra, per pair 2c.

No. 38C2508 Infants' Bootee, very closely hand knitted, of fine, all wool zephyr yarn. In neat ribbed pattern; bootee made extra high with fancy turnover which is edged with mercerized twist. Wool drawstrings at ankle and tassels. Colors, white and blue, white and pink or solid white.
Price, per pair.....20c
If by mail, postage extra, per pair 2c.

No. 38C2510 Infants' Bootee, hand knitted of mercerized (looks like silk) twist; tassels at ankle. Special value. Colors, solid white or white with blue or pink.
Price, per pair...25c
If by mail, postage extra, per pair, 2 cents.

No. 38C2512 Infants' Fancy Hand Crocheted Bootee, made of all wool zephyr, trimmed with mercerized twist. Yarn drawstrings at top. Very closely stitched. Colors, white and blue, white and pink or solid white.
Price, per pair.....22c
If by mail, postage extra, per pair, 2 cents.

INFANTS' HAND KNITTED SACQUES.

We quote only the hand made knitted sacques, as they are made seamless, neater and finer than machine made sacques, which are made very coarse and with raw seams.

No. 38C2550 Infants' Hand Crocheted Sacque, made of all wool Shetland yarn. Colors, solid cream, pink and cream or light blue and cream.
Price.....19c
If by mail, postage extra, 3 cents.

No. 38C2552 Infants' Sacque, closely hand crocheted, made of all wool zephyr, tassels in front, very neat design. Colors, solid white, pink and white or pale blue and white.
Price.....32c
If by mail, postage extra, 5 cents.

Infants' Knit All Wool Sacques.

No. 38C2554 Infants' Hand Crocheted Sacque, made of all wool Shetland yarn, fancy border, sleeves and collar stitched with silk. All wool draw strings with tassels at neck. Colors, pale blue or pink with white border and cuffs. Price.....48c
If by mail, postage extra, 8 cents.

No. 38C2556 Infants' Hand Crocheted Sacque, made of a fine, all wool Shetland yarn, has a very neat yoke effect. Trimmed with silk twist all around edge, collar and sleeves. Has all wool draw strings and tassels at neck. Bishop sleeves. Very closely crocheted. Colors, white and sky blue, white and pink or solid white.
Price.....69c
If by mail, postage extra, 8 cents.

No. 38C2558 An Elegant Sacque, of closely crocheted zephyr, trimmed around the back extending to front over shoulders (giving it a cape effect), with an insertion of satin ribbon. Crocheted edging also down the front and bottom with an insertion of satin ribbon. Colors, solid cream or cream with pink or blue edging.
Price.....75c
If by mail, postage extra, 8 cents.

The Babyette.

Hand Crocheted Combination Sacque and Cape with Attached Hood.

No. 38C2566 Infants' Hand Crocheted Combination Sacque and Cape with attached Hood. Made of all wool split zephyr yarns. Can be formed as a sacque by tying ribbon to form sleeves. Stitched with mercerized twist. Silk ribbon insertion at neck. Colors, white, with pink or blue trimmings. Price.....48c
If by mail, postage extra, 5 cents.

Infants' Flannel and Elderdown Sacques.

No. 38C2578 Infants' Sacque, made of outing flannel, stitched down front and all around bottom, collar and cuffs with mercerized twist. Wonderful value. Colors, blue or pink stripes.
Price.....16c
If by mail, postage extra, 4 cents.

Daisy Cloth Sacque.

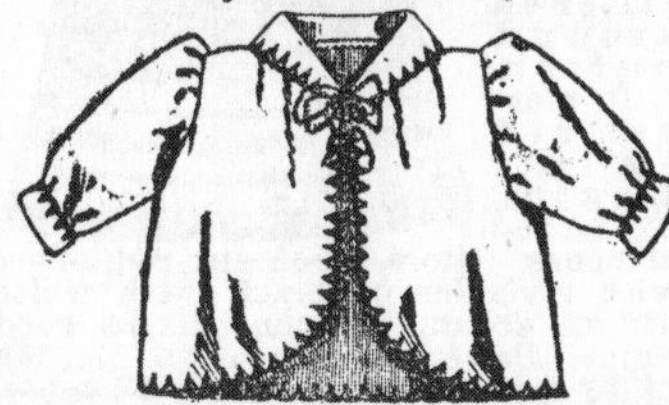

No. 38C2582 Infants' Sacque, made of daisy cloth (fleeced flannel), has a wide collar and turnover cuffs, stitched down front, bottom, collar and cuffs with mercerized twist. Silk ribbon tie strings at neck. Colors, cream with pink or blue collar and cuffs. Price, 22c
If by mail, postage extra, 4 cents.

Extra Long, Daisy Cloth Sacque.

No. 38C2588 Infants' Long Sacque, made of twilled daisy cloth (fleeced flannel), same style as No. 38C2582. Stitched down front and all around bottom, collar and cuffs with mercerized twist. Silk ribbon bow at neck. Length of sacque, 25 inches. Colors, sky blue or pink. Price.....39c
If by mail, postage extra, 8 cents.

Infants' Kimona.

No. 38C2590 Infants' Kimona, made of fleeced flannel (daisy cloth). Stitched with mercerized twist on revers, bottom and cuffs. Colors, cream with blue revers and cuffs, pink with cream revers and cuffs.
Price.....23c
If by mail, postage extra, 6 cents.

Cotton Elderdown Kimona.

No. 38C2592 Infants' Kimona, made of good quality cotton elderdown. Stitched all around with mercerized twist. Same style as No. 38C2590. Excellent value. Colors, sky blue or pink with white revers and cuffs.
Price....(Postage extra, 5c)....39c

No. 38C2600 Infants' Sacque, made of heavy fleeced daisy cloth (flannel). Yoke, back and front stitched with mercerized twist, the fancy collar and turnover cuffs also stitched with twist. Hemmed all around with mercerized twist. Silk ribbon bow at neck. Color, cream with blue or pink twist stitching. Price.....25c
If by mail, postage extra, 5 cents.

The Marguerite Sacque.

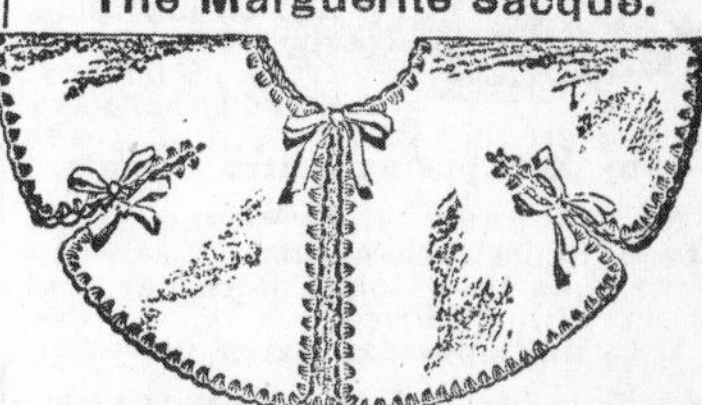

No. 38C2604 The Marguerite Infants' Sacque, made of one piece, good quality baby flannel (daisy cloth), stitched all around with mercerized twist. Can be worn as a cape by tying silk ribbons accordingly, which are also used to tie in order to form the sleeves. Silk ribbon strings at neck. Colors, cream, sky blue or pink.
Price....(Postage extra, 5c)....32c

INFANTS' KNITTED HOODS.

ALL OUR HOODS ARE HAND CROCHETED OR HAND KNITTED ON A FRAME and are seamless and perfect fitting. WE DO NOT HANDLE MACHINE MADE HOODS, as they are sewed together, making raw seams, and do not give the desired shape in order to fit perfectly.

Real Shetland Yarn.

No. 38C2616 Infants' Knitted Hood, made of all wool Shetland yarn, trimmed with mercerized twist in the form of squares. Trimmed around face and neck with pompons made of Shetland floss. All wool tie strings at neck. Colors, cream, sky blue or pink.
Price....(Postage extra, 5c)....25c

Covered With Silk Floss.

No. 38C2620 Infants' Knitted Hood, made of all wool Shetland yarn, same style as No. 38C2616. Entirely covered with silk floss in honeycomb design. Lined with crocheted Shetland yarn, trimmed around neck and face with Shetland floss pompons. Wool tie strings at neck with tassels. Colors, cream, pink or sky blue. Price..(Postage extra, 5c)..45c

No. 38C2623 Infants' Hood, made of all wool split zephyr, very neat pattern, covered with silk floss trimmed around face with white swansdown, Shetland pompons around neck. Colors, cream, blue or pink.
Price.....39c
If by mail, postage extra, 5c.

Covered with Mercerized Twist.

No. 38C2624 Infants' Knitted Hood, made of all wool Shetland yarn, same style as No. 38C2622. In very neat honeycomb design, covered with mercerized twist, lined with all wool crocheted Shetland yarn, trimmed around face with white swansdown and around the neck with Shetland pompons, all wool tie strings at neck. Colors, pink or sky blue.
Price 48c
If by mail, postage extra, 5 cents.

CHILDREN'S HOODS.
SUITABLE FOR CHILDREN AGED 2 TO 6 YEARS.

With Cape, 35 Cents.

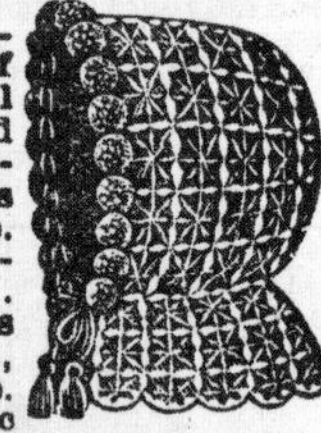

No. 38C2670 Child's Hood, knitted in the form of squares of all wool Shetland yarns and trimmed with mercerized twist. Has nice wide neck cape. Shetland floss pompons around face. All wool tie strings at neck. Colors, cream, pink or blue.
Price 35c
If by mail, postage extra, 6 cents.

Children's Hoods, Ages From 6 to 10 Years.
HAND MADE.

No. 38C2684 Girls' Hood. For 6 to 10-year-old children, made of all wool zephyr yarn, nicely trimmed with fancy ribbon in center of back and on each side, zephyr ruffle in front. Colors, cardinal, navy blue or cream. Price 48c
If by mail, postage extra, 6 cents.

No. 38C2686 Girls' Hand Made Hood. Same style as No. 38C2684, without ribbon insertion. Colors, cardinal or navy blue. Price 39c
If by mail, postage extra, 6 cents.

Ladies' Hoods.—HAND MADE.

No. 38C2900 Ladies' Hood, closely knitted of all wool zephyr, wide neck cape. Colors, black, cardinal or navy blue.
Price 45c
Postage extra, 7 cents.

No. 38C2902 Ladies' Hand Made Hood, of Germantown yarn, lined with crocheted yarn, ruffled yarn around face, wide neck cape. Colors, black, cardinal or navy.
Price 70c
Postage extra, 7c.

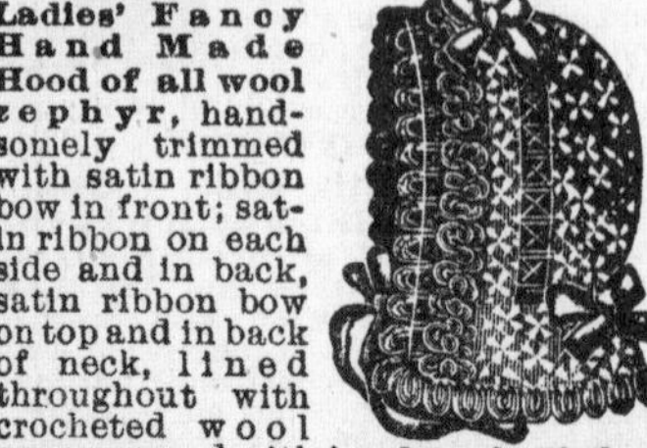

No. 38C2904 Ladies' Fancy Hand Made Hood of all wool zephyr, handsomely trimmed with satin ribbon bow in front; satin ribbon on each side and in back, satin ribbon bow on top and in back of neck, lined throughout with crocheted wool yarn covered with beads and silk floss. Colors, solid black or red, or cream with pink or blue trimmings. Price 98c
If by mail, postage extra, 8 cents.

No. 38C2906 Ladies' Hand Made Hood, of good quality zephyr, satin ribbon bow on top and back of neck, lined with all wool crocheted yarn, satin ribbon tie strings. Color, black only.
Price $1.10
Postage extra, 8c.

TOBOGGAN CAPS OR TOQUES.

Children's Toques.

No. 38C3054 Children's Knitted Worsted Toque, has all wool tassel. Very pretty shades in neat stripes, with wide turnover. Length of toque, 15 inches. Colors, red with royal blue, red with navy blue or royal blue with white stripes.
Price 20c
If by mail, postage extra, 5 cents.

No. 38C3058 Child's Double Toque, made of fine all wool worsted with mercerized stripes. Wide turnover. Wool and mercerized tassel. Colors, cardinal with white stripes, cardinal with navy blue stripes or royal blue with cardinal stripes. Price 39c
If by mail, postage extra, 5 cents.

Children's Silk Toques.

No. 38C3059 Children's Imported Silk Double Toque. Has a silk pompon. Colors, white with blue stripes or royal blue with white stripes.
Price. 85c
If by mail, postage extra, 5 cents.

Girls' Toques.

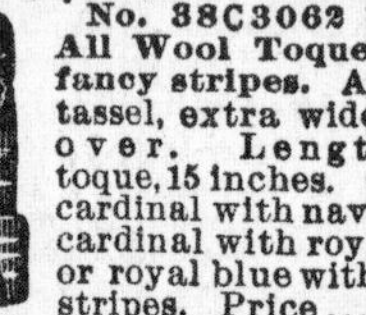

No. 38C3062 Girls' All Wool Toque with fancy stripes. All wool tassel, extra wide turnover. Length of toque, 15 inches. Colors, cardinal with navy blue, cardinal with royal blue or royal blue with white stripes. Price 25c
If by mail, postage extra, 6 cents.

No. 38C3068 Girls' Roman Toques. Made of mercerized cotton, looks like silk, with all wool tassel. Colors, beautiful effects in combination of colors, such as blue or cardinal predominating. Price... 39c
If by mail, postage extra, 4 cents.

Boys' Toques.

No. 38C3072 Boys' Knitted Double Toque, made of good grade all wool worsted and lined with cotton worsted. Fancy stripes also in turnover. All wool tassel. Length of toque, 15 inches. Colors, royal blue, with white stripes or cardinal with white stripes.
Price 39c
If by mail, postage extra, 5 cents.

LADIES' AND MISSES' KNITTED UNDERSKIRTS.

No. 38C3178 Ladies' Knitted Underskirt. Double waistband with draw strings, stitched around bottom with mercerized twist. Lengths, 27, 29 and 31 inches. Colors, black with red, black with lavender or black with white stripes around bottom. Extra good value. Price 48c
If by mail, postage extra, 12 cents.

No. 38C3181 Ladies' Fine Worsted Underskirt. Fancy crochet waistband with draw strings stitched around bottom with mercerized twist, jersey knitted around hips, making skirt form fitting to hips. Average length, 28 inches. Solid colors, cardinal or navy blue. Price 85c
If by mail, postage extra, 15 cents.

Knitted Underskirts, 95 Cents.

No. 38C3183 Ladies' Knitted Underskirt, made of fine all wool worsted yarn. Has very neat stripes with a narrow stripe of mercerized twist. Crocheted around bottom with mercerized twist. Crocheted waistband with insertion of tape as draw strings. Average length, 29 inches. Colors, gray with red and black stripes, or gray with black and white stripes. Price 95c
If by mail, postage extra, 15 cents.

Children's Underskirts.

Ages, 2, 3 and 4 years.

Children's Knit Underskirt, made of good quality worsted yarn. Has fitted bodice and shoulder straps. Stitched with mercerized twist. Colors are gray with red stripes around bottom, or sky blue with pink stripes.

No. 38C3196 Age, 2 yrs. Price..39c
No. 38C3198 Age, 3 yrs. Price..48c
No. 38C3200 Age, 4 yrs. Price..57c
If by mail, postage extra, 8 cents.

LADIES' KNITTED BLOUSE JACKETS.

VERY POPULAR AND STYLISH. We call special attention to our Jackets, being all finished with tape or union special stitch. No raw or open seams will be found in our Knitted Jackets.
Sizes, 32 to 42 inches bust measure.

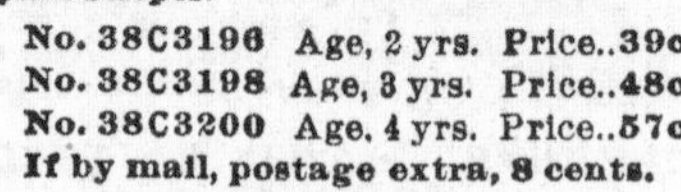

No. 38C3204 Ladies' Knitted Blouse Jacket, very neat design, silk covered buttons and worked buttonholes. No raw seams in these jackets; double standing collar. Colors, cardinal, navy blue or white. Be sure to give bust measure.
Price $1.75
If by mail, postage extra, 18 cents.

No. 38C3205 Girls' or Misses' Knitted Jacket, same style as No. 38C3204, bust measure, 26 to 32 inches. Colors, cardinal or white.
Price 98c
If by mail, postage extra, 15 cents

No. 38C3206 Ladies' Knitted Blouse Jacket, made of all wool worsted yarns. The design is of a very neat heavy ribbed effect. Jacket fastened with hooks and eyes, with sateen stays. Fine jersey ribbed standing collar and cuffs. Full fashioned sleeves. Seams finished throughout. Give bust measure. Color, white or cardinal. 32 to 42 bust measure. Price $1.98
If by mail, postage extra, 22 cents.

No. 38C3214 Fancy Knitted Blouse Jacket, made of fine grade all wool yarn. The design in front is very pretty, of mercerized twist in the twisted rope effect. Jersey ribbed standing collar and cuffs. Jacket fastened with hooks and eyes, with sateen stays and trimmed with pearl buttons. All seams covered. Give bust measure. Sizes, 32 to 42 inches. Colors, cardinal with white mercerized twist or white with red mercerized twist.
Price $2.39
If by mail, postage extra, 28 cents.

No. 38C3216 Ladies' All Wool Blouse Jacket, Collarless style. Jacket is fastened with hooks and eyes. Trimmed with pearl buttons. New style sleeves. Seams finished with the overcast stitch. Sizes, 32 to 42 inches bust measure. Colors, white or cardinal.
Price ... $2.65
If by mail, postage extra, 26c.

No. 32C3218 Ladies' Knitted Jacket, with the new Russian blouse effect, made of all wool worsted yarn. Standing collar and turnover cuffs, trimmed with pearl buttons. All seams covered. Fastened on left side with hooks and eyes. Color on band on left side corresponds with collar and cuffs. Give bust measure. Colors, white with red collar and cuffs, or red with white collar and cuffs. Price $2.85
If by mail, postage extra, 25 cents.

No. 38C3220 Ladies' Knitted Blouse Jacket, made of fine all wool worsted yarn. The design is a very neat raised shell pattern effect. Jacket is fastened with hooks and eyes and faced with taffeta silk. Newest fashioned sleeves and ribbed cuffs. Finished seams throughout. Ribbed standing turnover collar, and very full blouse. Colors, white or cardinal. Price $2.98

Ladies' Knitted Norfolk Jacket.
Sizes, 32 to 42 Inches Bust Measure.

No. 38C3232 Ladies' Norfolk Jacket, made of all wool worsted yarn. Suspender effect. Knitted belt, lined with sateen, Jacket trimmed with five large pearl buttons. Full fashioned sleeves. Finished seams throughout. Colors, cardinal or white.
Price, $2.39
If by mail, postage extra, 34 cents.

LADIES' KNITTED VESTS.

Style and service combined in these popular vests. They are all the rage. Sizes, 32 to 42 inches bust measure.

85c

No. 38C3300 Ladies' Knitted Vest, made of all wool worsted. Piped with mohair braid. Wide sateen facing. Very neatly designed stitch. Pearl buttons. Colors, white or cardinal.
Price..85c
If by mail, postage extra, 14 cents.

$1.25

No. 38C3304 Ladies' Fancy All Wool Knitted Vest. Double breasted, imitation pearl buttons and wide facing. The design is very pretty, knitted in twisted rope effect. Vest bound with braid. Give bust measure. Colors, white with black or cardinal with black.
Price...$1.25
If by mail, postage extra, 15 cents.

Girls' Eton Cardigan Vest.

Age 6, 8, 10 and 12 years.

No. 38C3322 Girls' Eton Cardigan Vest. Made of good quality wool worsted, edged with crocheted yarn. Cloth covered buttons. Colors are black, cardinal or blue.
Price..48c
If by mail, postage extra, 8 cents.

SHAWL DEPARTMENT.

NOTE SIZE, WEIGHTS AND QUALITY IN OUR SHAWLS.

Knitted Square Shawls.

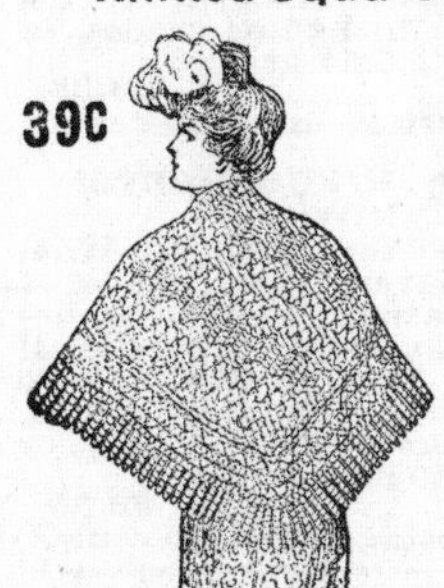

39c

No. 38C3350 Knitted Shawl, made of all wool Shetland yarn, closely knitted, with fancy border. Size, 38x38 inches. Net weight, 3½ ounces. Colors, black, cream or pink.
Price......39c
If by mail, postage extra, 7c.

Knitted Worsted Shawl, 19c.

No. 38C3352 Knitted Shawl, has very neat border. Size, 32x32 inches, including border. Colors, black, cream or pink. Net weight, 2 ounces.
Price 19c
If by mail, postage extra, 5 cents.

All Wool Worsted Shawl, 25c.

No. 38C3354 Knitted Shawl, made of Shetland yarn, with fancy border. Size, 34x34 inches. Net weight, 2¼ ounces. Colors, black, cream or blue.
Price 25c
If by mail, postage extra, 6 cents.

All Wool Worsted Yarn Shawl.

No. 38C3358 Knitted Shawl, made of all wool worsted yarn, raised pattern with fancy border, closely knitted. Size, 40x40 inches. Net weight, 4 ounces. Colors, black, cream or cardinal. Price....................48c
If by mail, postage extra, 8 cents.

All Wool Shawl With Fringe.

No. 38C3359 All Wool Knitted Shawl, same style, size and weight as No. 38C3358, but made with a border and fringe. Colors, black, cream or cardinal. Price......................55c
If by mail, postage extra, 8 cents.

Extra Large Shawl.

No. 38C3360 Large Knitted Wool Shawl, very pretty design, with fancy border, closely knitted. Size, 45x45 inches. Net weight, 6 ounces. Colors, black, cream or blue. Price....69c
If by mail, postage extra, 10 cents.

Large Shawl with Fringe.

No. 38C3362 Very Fine All Wool Knitted Shawl, with fancy border and fine fringe. Very closely knitted. Size, 45x45 inches. Net weight, 6 ounces. Colors, black, cream or sky blue. Price....75c
If by mail, postage extra, 10 cents.

Extra Large All Wool Shawl.

No. 38C3364 Ladies' Knitted Square Shawl, made of all wool worsted and Shetland yarns, stitched with silk twist in a fancy design. Has very pretty border. Size, 48x48 inches. Net weight, 5 ounces. Colors are white with blue silk or black with black silk. Price....................98c
If by mail, postage extra, 12 cents.

Fancy Knitted Square Shawl, in Combination of Colors.

48c

No. 38C3366 Very Large Fancy Knitted Square Shawl, made of all wool worsted and Shetland yarns, also stitched mercerized twist. Very pretty border. Size, 44x44 inches. Net weight, 4 ounces. Color, white, with black, blue or pink twist.
Price... ....48c
If by mail, postage extra, 10 cents.

No. 38C3370 Ladies' All Wool Fancy Knitted Square Shawl. Medium size stitch. Has fancy border. Size, 36x36 inches. Net weight, 3 ounces. Colors, white with black, white with blue or white with pink.
Price....................................25c
If by mail, postage extra, 7 cents.

No. 38C3372 Ladies' Knitted Shawl, made of all wool worsted interwoven with mercerized twist. Has a fancy border. Size of shawl, 40x40 inches. Net weight, 4 ounces. Color, black with white twist or white with black twist trimmings.
Price....................................39c
If by mail, postage extra, 8 cents.

Fancy All Wool Shawls.

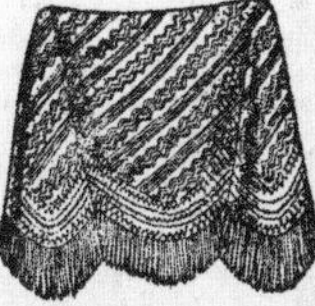

No. 38C3374 Ladies' Fancy Knitted Shawl, made of all wool worsted and Shetland yarn, and stitched with mercerized twist in fancy designs; has fancy border. Size of shawl, 42x42 inches; net weight, 4 ounces. Colors, white with black, blue or pink stitchings. Price 89c
If by mail, postage extra, 12 cents.

Newest Style Knitted Long Shawls.

98c

No. 38C3402 Ladies' Fancy Knitted Long Shawl, made of all wool worsted yarn. Knitted with colored mercerized twist in the form of squares. Has a very neat border with fringe. Size of shawl, not including fringe, 56x30 inches. Net weight, 5 ounces. Colors, white with black, pink or blue twist. Price.75c
If by mail, postage extra, 11 cents.

No. 38C3404 Ladies' Fancy Knitted Long Shawl, made of all wool worsted yarn. Very closely knitted. Mottled with silk twist. Has heavy, fancy Shetland fringe. Size of shawl, not including fringe, 54 x 32 inches. Net weight, 6 ounces. Colors, white ground with black or black ground with white effects. Price..98c
If by mail, postage extra, 12 cents.

THE NEWPORT HEAD OR SHOULDER SCARFS.

89c

VERY STYLISH.

No. 38C3426 Very Large Newport Shawl, made of all wool Shetland yarn. Imitation hand knit. Very closely knitted. Has 6-inch fringe. Length, 60 inches, not including fringe, width, 25 inches. Net weight 8 ounces. Colors, black, white or blue.
Price.........89c
If by mail, postage extra, 15 cents.

No. 38C3428 Ladies' Knitted Newport Scarf, made of all wool worsted yarn. Imitation hand knit, has attached fringe. Length, not including fringe, 54 inches. Width, 20 inches. Net weight, 4 ounces. Colors, white with pink or blue border. Price..................48c
If by mail, postage extra, 12 cents.

The Newport Scarf.

Hand Crocheted.

No. 38C3438 Ladies' Hand Crocheted Newport Scarf, made of all wool zephyr yarn. With a very neat fringe, size, not including fringe, 60x24 inches. Net weight, 5 ounces. Color, cream with blue or pink border and fringe.
Price........98c
If by mail, postage extra, 12c.

Extra Large Crocheted Newport Shawl.

No. 38C3440 A Very Large Newport Shawl, hand crocheted, shell pattern, made of fine all wool zephyr. Crocheted edge of pink or blue zephyr yarn, fringe to match. Average length, not including fringe, 74 inches; width, 28 inches, net weight, 8 ounces. Color, cream only with pink or blue edge and fringe. Price....... .$1.69
If by mail, postage extra, 16 cents.

HAND MADE CIRCULAR SHAWLS.

Very popular and stylish. Can be worn over the head, at the same time covering shoulders, or folded and worn over shoulders only. (See illustrations, No. 38C3450 and No. 38C3456). They are shaped in center in order to give the shawl a cape effect.

NOTICE—These circular shawls are all hand crocheted. The sizes given are nearly always correct. It is almost impossible to crochet shawls by hand in exact sizes, being very difficult to guide size of stitches; thus when shawls are finished they will some times vary a little, a trifle smaller or larger. If shawl is a little smaller than size quoted it will have a tighter stitch, or vice versa, but the net weight of yarn quoted is always used in each shawl. The prices of hand made shawls are governed according to design of stitch (some numbers being more difficult than others), also size, quality and quantity of yarn used. In order to get original appearance of shawls when received, spread and shake well. We do not handle machine made circular shawls, as they are not perfect in shape, and when flounced they are sewed together, making very bulky, unsightly seams. Remember, these are hand crocheted shawls. It will not pay you to make them. Figure cost yarn, your time in crocheting, etc. Our shawls are all made by expert crocheters.

85c

No. 38C3450 Hand Made Circular Shawl. All wool Shetland yarn, shell pattern, very pretty shawl, 36 inches in diameter; net weight, 5 ounces. Colors, cream with blue, pink or lavender border, or solid cream or black. Splendid value.
Price.85c
Postage extra, 9 cents.

No. 38C3452 Hand Made Circular Shawl. Same style as No. 38C3450, but 45 inches in diameter, with fringe all around shawl; net weight, 6 ounces. Colors, cream with blue or pink border or black with lavender border. Price....................$1.19
If by mail, postage extra, 12 cents.

No. 38C3454 Extra Large Crocheted Circular Shawl. Very closely stitched center, shell design. Size 48 inches in diameter. Net weight, 7 ounces. Colors, white with blue or pink centers, and borders. Price.......$1.48
If by mail, postage extra, 14 cents.

Hand Made Circular Shawl.

$1.69

No. 38C3456 A Very Pretty Hand Made Circular Shawl. Made of fine all wool zephyr, very closely knitted, has flounced border which is trimmed with blue, lavender or pink yarn, which gives the shawl a very pretty effect; 45 inches in diameter; net weight, 8 ounces. Colors, cream with pink, blue or lavender trimmings on border, or black with white trimmed border.
Price....................$1.69
If by mail, postage extra, 14 cents.

Combination Imported Ice Wool and Shetland Yarn.

$1.60

No. 38C3458 Circular Shawl. Made of imported ice wool alternating with rows of Shetland yarn, giving shawl a very pretty combination; 36 inches in diameter. Colors are white ice wool with pink or blue Shetland yarn; net weight, 4 ounces. Price....$1.60
If by mail, postage extra, 7 cents.

Hand Crocheted Circular Shawl.

$1.85

No. 38C3460 Very Pretty Hand Crocheted Circular Shawl. Made of all wool Shetland yarn. The design is a work of art and must be seen to be appreciated. Closely crocheted center. Colors are solid black or cream with one row pink or blue yarn in center and edge to match. Exceptionally pretty shawl. 48 inches in diameter; net weight, 8 ounces. Price....................$1.85
If by mail, postage extra, 13 cents.

Hand Made Fancy Circular Shawl.

$1.89

No. 38C3462 Very Pretty Circular Shawl, hand crocheted. Made of all wool Shetland yarn, alternating with V-shell stitching. A very difficult design which makes up very pretty. Loop fringe all around. 42 inches in diameter. Net weight 7 ounces. Colors, white with blue, pink or lavender V's, as illustrated. Price........$1.89
If by mail, postage extra, 12 cents.

Very Artistic Design.

$1.75

No. 38C3464 Circular Shawl, hand crocheted of all wool Shetland yarn. Very closely crocheted center. Very artistic design, certainly a work of art. In combination of colors such as white with blue or pink. 38 inches in diameter. Net weight, 7 ounces. Price........$1.75
If by mail, postage extra, 13 cents.

All Wool Saxony Shawl.

$2.19

No. 38C3468 A Beautiful Hand Made Circular Shawl, 45 inches in diameter. Made of all wool Saxony yarn, exquisite design interwoven around border with mercerized twist; very closely knitted. Colors, white, trimmed with blue or pink silk twist, or black with black twist. Net weight, 11 ounces. Price........$2.19
If by mail, postage extra, 15 cents.

Imported Crocheted Ice Wool Circular Shawls.

$1.48

These Circular Shawls to be worn as No. 38C3464 or No. 38C3468.

No. 38C3470 Ladies' Imported Hand Crocheted Ice Wool Shawl. Has a very neat ring pattern stitch. Size, 36 inches in diameter. Colors, cream or black. Price........$1.48
If by mail, postage extra, 10 cents.

No. 38C3471 Imported Fancy Hand Crocheted Ice Wool Circular Shawl. Double close stitch. Mottled with pink, blue or black ice wool, giving shawl a very pretty effect. Size, 36 inches in diameter. Colors, cream with pink, blue or black. Price........$2.25
If by mail, postage extra, 10 cents.

Hand Made Square Shawls.

45c

No. 38C3476 Ladies' Hand Crocheted Square Shawl, made of all wool yarn. Shell stitch, with colored border. Size, 34x34 inches. Net weight 3 ounces. Colors, white with pink or blue border or solid black. Price....45c
If by mail, postage extra, 9 cents.

Imported Hand Made Ice Wool Shawls.

We have only the very best goods and give the best values for the money. A trial order will convince you of this, and you will be more than pleased with the goods you receive. Designs are not always like illustrations, but all are new and up to date.

No. 38C3478 Ladies' Imported Hand Crocheted Ice Wool Shawl. Fancy border. Size, 32x32 inches. Colors, black or cream. Price..42c
If by mail, postage extra, 5 cents.

Double Stitched Ice Wool Shawl.

No. 38C3480 Ladies' Imported Hand Crocheted Ice Wool Shawl. Double stitched center. Fancy border. Size, 32x32 inches. Colors, black or cream. Price....65c
If by mail, postage extra, 5 cents.

Very Closely Stitched Center.

No. 38C3484 Ladies' Imported Hand Crocheted Ice Wool Shawl. Double closely stitched center. Has a very pretty ring pattern border. Size, 34x34 inches. Extra good value. Colors, black or cream. Price........$1.29
If by mail, postage extra, 7 cents.

No. 38C3490 Ladies' Imported Hand Crocheted Ice Wool shawl. Heavy double stitched center. Very neatly designed ring pattern border. Size, 36x36 inches. Colors, black or cream. Price........$1.48
If by mail, postage extra, 7 cents.

$1.98 for Our Best, Extra Heavy Ice Wool Shawl.

No. 38C3494 Ladies' Hand Crocheted Ice Wool Shawl. Extra heavy double stitched center. Has a very pretty wide border. Size, 40x40 inches. Very fine shawl. Colors, black or cream. Price........$1.98
If by mail, postage extra, 7 cents.

IMPORTED SILK SHAWLS.

Owing to the increased demand for silk shawls, we have for this season made larger imports. As we are direct importers, we are able to quote the best grade of silk shawls at considerably lower prices than any other concern. These shawls make appropriate gifts; measurements given include fringe.

Large Silk Shawl.

No. 38C3504 Imported Silk Knitted Shawl. Shell design stitch. Very pretty border, with 4-inch silk fringe. Size of shawl, 42x42 inches. Colors, black or cream. Price........$1.10
If by mail, postage extra, 7 cents.

No. 38C3506 Extra Fine Imported Silk Knitted Shawl. Very pretty raised effect. Beautiful knitted border with heavy silk fringe. Size, 40x40 inches. Colors, black or cream. Price........$1.98
If by mail, postage extra, 8 cents.

Very Fine Quality Silk Shawl.

No. 38C3508 Very Fine Quality Imported Silk Shawl. Knitted in a very neat raised pattern. Very pretty silk border and attached fringe. Size, 40x40 inches. Colors, black or cream. Price........$1.69
If by mail, postage extra, 7 cents.

Fancy Knitted Mercerized Cotton (Looks Like Silk) Square Shawls.

No. 38C3520 Ladies' Knitted Mercerized (looks like silk) Cotton Shawls, knitted very close in a neat design with fancy stitched border. Size, 36x36 inches. Colors, cream, pink or blue. Price........39c
If by mail, postage extra, 9 cents.

LADIES' REVERSIBLE BEAVER SHAWLS.

As we control the entire output of some of the largest mills on beaver and wool shawls we are able to quote a better grade of shawls at less money than any other concern.

We call special attention to weights and sizes in our shawls. We quote only the actual size of cloth in a shawl and do not include the fringe. Average length of fringe is 5 inches.

THESE SHAWLS ARE REVERSIBLE AND CAN BE WORN ON EITHER SIDE. THEY REVERSE FROM COLORS QUOTED TO A LIGHTER SHADE.

$1.25

No. 38C3551 Ladies' Reversible Beaver Shawl, with fancy border and fringe. Net weight, 28 ounces. Size, 62x56 inches. Colors, dark gray or brown, reverse to medium shades. Price........$1.25
If by mail, postage extra, 42 cents.

Woven from Selected Yarns.

No. 38C3552 Reversible Beaver Shawl, woven of good quality selected yarn. Heavy fringe. Colors, dark gray or brown and reverses to lighter shades. Size of shawl, 62x54 inches. Net weight, 25 ounces. Price ...$1.85
If by mail, postage extra, 44 cents.

$2.25

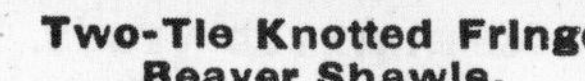

Two-Tie Knotted Fringe Beaver Shawls.

$2.98

No. 38C3564 Reversible All Wool Beaver Shawl. Has a very neatly designed border with fancy two-tie all wool fringe. Size of shawl, 66x62 inches. Net weight, 40 ounces. Colors, dark gray or brown reverse to lighter shade. Price........$2.98
If by mail, postage extra, 58 cents.

Extra Heavy All Wool Beaver Shawl.

No. 38C3566 Heavy Reversible All Wool Beaver Shawl. Design on border is very neat. Has all wool two-tie knotted fringe. Size of shawl, 64x64 inches. Net weight, 46 ounces. Colors, medium gray or brown, reverse to lighter shades. Price........$3.50
If by mail, postage extra, 62 cents.

Made of Very Fine Selected Wool.

No. 38C3572 Extra Heavy All Wool Reversible Beaver Shawl, made of fine selected wool, has a very neatly designed border and fancy two-tie all wool fringe. Size of shawl, 64x62 inches; net weight, 45 ounces. Colors, dark gray, reverse to medium gray; or brown, reverse to medium brown Price........$4.95
If by mail, postage extra, 59 cents.

Three-Tie Knotted Fringe Beaver Shawls.

$5.95

No. 38C3576 Extra Large and Heavy All Wool Reversible Beaver Shawls, made of fine selected wool; has very pretty designed border and heavy three-tie all wool fringe. Size of shawl, 66x66 inches; net weight, 46 ounces. Colors, medium gray or dark brown, reverse to lighter shades, or black, reverse to dark gray. Price........$5.95
If by mail, postage extra, 60 cents.

Very High Grade Beaver Shawl.

No. 38C3578 Very Fine All Wool Reversible Beaver Shawl, made of fine selected wool, handsomely designed border and fancy three-tie all wool fringe. Size of shawl, 65x65 inches; net weight, 45 ounces. Colors, dark gray reverse to medium gray, or brown reverse to light brown. Price........$6.50
If by mail, postage extra, 60 cents.

One-Tie Knotted Fringe Beaver Shawls.

No. 38C3554 Reversible Beaver Shawls. Has a very neat border and trimmed with neat one-tie fringe. Size of shawl, 64x64 inches. Net weight, 34 ounces. Colors, dark gray or brown, reverses to medium shades. Price........$2.25
If by mail, postage extra, 52 cents.

No. 38C3556 Ladies' Reversible All Wool Beaver Shawl. Has a very neat special designed border. Made with all wool one-tie fringe. Size, 66x66 inches. Net weight, 40 ounces. Colors, dark gray or dark brown, reverses to medium shades. Price........$2.75
If by mail, postage extra, 56 cents.

Fancy Striped Border Beaver Shawls.

$1.15

No. 38C3584 Reversible Beaver Shawls, with fancy striped border and heavy fringe. Size of shawl, 60x60 inches. Net weight, 24 ounces. Colors, dark gray or brown reverse to mediumshades. Price. $1.15

If by mail, postage extra, 38c.

Plain Beaver Shawls.

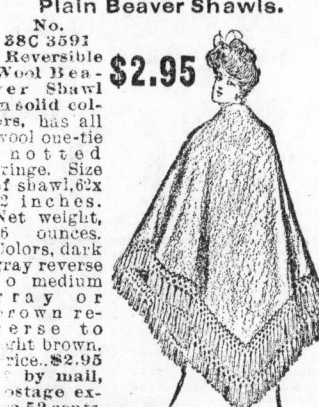

$2.95

No. 38C3591 Reversible Wool Beaver Shawl in solid colors, has all wool one-tie knotted fringe. Size of shawl, 62x62 inches. Net weight, 36 ounces. Colors, dark gray reverse to medium gray or brown reverse to light brown. Price. $2.95

If by mail, postage extra 52 cents.

Ladies' Double or Long Shawl.

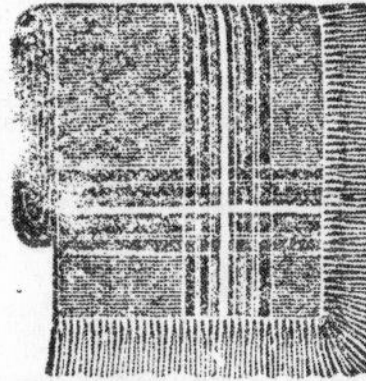

No. 38C3618 Ladies' Wool Mixed Double Shawl, with fancy border and attached fringe. Size of shawl, 120x60 inches. Net weight, 28 ozs. Colors, gray or brown.
Price..............$1.85

If by mail, postage extra, 42 cents.

No. 38C3620 Ladies' All Wool Double Shawl, full size, made with fancy border and attached fringe. Size of shawl, 124x62 inches. Net weight, 30 ounces. Colors, gray or brown.
Price...$2.50

If by mail, postage extra, 44 cents.

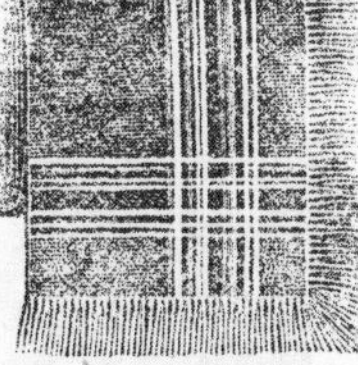

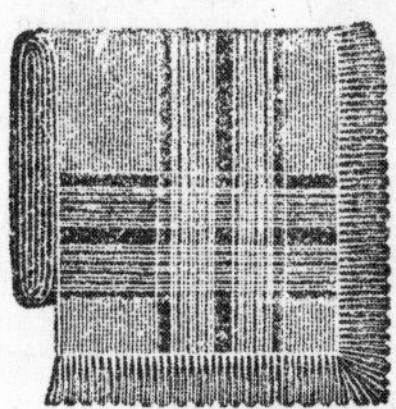

No. 38C3628 Reversible Double Shawl, made of all wool yarn. Fancy border and attached fringe. Size, 128x62 inches. Net weight, 34 ounces. Colors, gray or brown.
Price ..$3.98

If by mail, postage extra, 50 cents.

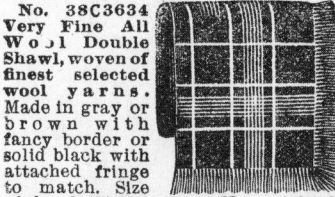

No. 38C3634 Very Fine All Wool Double Shawl, woven of finest selected wool yarns. Made in gray or brown with fancy border or solid black with attached fringe to match. Size of shawl, 134x62 inches. Net weight, 32 ounces. Colors, gray or brown with border or solid black. Price....$5.25

If by mail, postage extra, 48 cents.

Ladies' Single or Square Shawls.

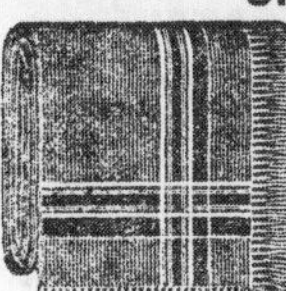

No. 38C3646 Ladies' Single Wool Shawls, made with neat border and attached fringe to match. Size of shawl, 60x60 inches. Net weight, 14 ounces. Colors, gray or brown.
Price............98c

If by mail, postage extra, 21 cents.

All Wool Square Shawl.

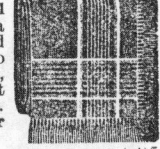

No. 38C3650 Ladies' Fine All Wool Single Shawl. Has a very neat border and attached fringe to match. Size of shawl, 66x66 inches. Net weight, 20 ounces. Colors, gray or brown.
Price..........$1.95

If by mail, postage extra, 32 cents.

Fine Selected Wool Square Shawl.

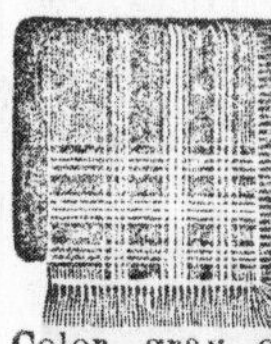

No. 38C3654 Extra Fine All Wool Single Shawl, woven of fine selected all wool yarns, has very neat border and attached fringe to match. Size of shawl, 66x66 inches. Net weight, 24 ounces. Color, gray or brown with border to match, or solid black.
Price..........$2.75

If by mail, postage extra, 38 cents.

LADIES' OR MISSES' SHOULDER SHAWLS.

A Cheap Shawl, Only 18 Cents.

No. 38C3664 Ladies' or Misses' Merino Shoulder Shawls. Size, 29x29 inches, with attached 2-inch fringe to match. Colors are brown with fancy border or black and white, or black and red checks. Price..........18c

If by mail, postage, extra, 7 cents.

No. 38C3665 All Wool Shoulder Shawl, with all wool attached fringe to match. Size, 32x32 inches. Colors are gray or brown with fancy border, or black and white checks. Price..45c

If by mail, postage extra, 11 cents.

Imported Silk Fringed Cashmere Shawls.

$1.75

No. 38C3528 Ladies' Imported Cashmere Shawl. Made with a two-tie knotted 5-inch silk fringe. Size of shawl, not including fringe, 54x54 inches. Net weight, 6 ounces. Color, black only
Price..........$1.75

If by mail, postage extra, 14 cents.

No. 38C3532 Ladies' Fine Imported Cashmere Shawl. Has a very pretty three-tie knotted 6-inch silk fringe. Size of shawl, not including fringe, 64x64 inches. Net weight, 14 ounces. Color, black only. Price, $2.98

If by mail, postage extra, 17 cents.

All Wool Cashmere Shawl.

No. 38C3534 Ladies' Imported Cashmere Shawl. Has a heavy braided 7-inch silk fringe. Size of shawl, not including fringe, 64x64 inches. Net weight, 16 ounces. Color, black only. Price..........$3.95

If by mail, postage extra, 20 cents.

Fine Silk Warp Cashmere Shawl.

No. 38C3538 Extra Fine All Wool Imported Cashmere Shawl. Made of the finest warp cashmere. Has a heavy, neatly braided 15-inch silk fringe. Size, not including fringe, 64x64 inches. Net weight, 22 ounces. Color, black only. Price........$5.75

If by mail, postage extra, 27 cents.

CREAM COLORED WOOL FRINGE CASHMERE SHAWLS.

VERY STYLISH FOR EVENING WEAR.

No. 38C3540 Ladies' Shawl, made of good quality cashmere. With a one-tie knotted all wool 5-inch fringe. Size, not including the fringe, 36x36 inches. Net weight, 4 ounces. Color, cream only. Price........48c

If by mail, postage extra, 9 cents.

No. 38C3542 Ladies' All Wool Cashmere Shawl. Made with a one-tie knotted 5-inch all wool fringe. Size, not including the fringe, 40x40 inches. Net weight, 6 ounces. Color, cream only. Price..............98c

If by mail, postage extra, 9 cents.

Imported Woven Silk Shawls.

No. 38C3544 Ladies' or Misses' Silk Shawl, made of fine Japanese silk, has three-tie knotted 5-inch silk fringe. Size, not including fringe, 31x31 inches. Net weight, 3 ounces. Color, cream only. Price......$1.48

If by mail, postage extra, 9 cents.

No. 38C3545 Ladies' or Misses' Shawl, made of fine quality surah silk. With a two-tie braided 5-inch silk fringe. Size, not including fringe, 34x34 inches. Net weight, 3 ounces. Color, cream only.
Price..........................$1.85

If by mail, postage extra, 9 cents.

INFANTS' LONG CLOAKS.

Cashmere Long Cloaks.

Infants' Cloak with Embroidered Cape and Skirt, for 75 cents.

75c

No. 38C4100 Infants' Long Cloak, made of union cashmere. Collar trimmed with one row of braid, wide shoulder cape, embroidered with silk floss in a very neat design, 5-inch width of silk floss embroidered around the bottom to match shoulder cape, bishop sleeves with cuffs, cloak lined throughout with canton flannel. Color, cream only. Price..........75c

If by mail, postage extra, 19 cents.

$1.48

No. 38C4102 Infants' Long Cloak, made of cashmere. Collar trimmed with two rows of fancy braid, very wide flounced cape, which is scalloped and heavily embroidered with silk floss in a very neat floral design, cape lined with sateen, heavily embroidered around the bottom with silk floss in a floral pattern to match cape. The width of the embroidery is 6 inches, interlined with flannel and lined throughout with sateen. Color, cream only.
Price..........................$1.48

If by mail, postage extra, 22 cents.

$1.75

No. 38C4104 Infants' Long Cloak, made of union cashmere. It is very richly embroidered and scalloped with silk on shoulder cape; shirring at the neck; embroidery in itself is the very newest and almost covers the cape; similar embroidery trimming around the bottom to match cape; bishop sleeves; lined throughout with cambric and interlined with shaker flannel. Color, cream only. Price...$1.75

If by mail, postage extra, 25 cents.

$2.25

No. 38C4106 Infants' Long Cloak, made of fine cashmere; very pretty pointed collar, which is trimmed with four rows of soutache and one row of fancy silk braid; has a wide ruffled cape, which is scalloped and heavily embroidered with silk in a beautiful floral design; embroidered around the bottom in a very wide pattern of floral design to match cape; interlined with flannel and lined throughout with fine sateen. Bishop sleeves. Made extra full around the bottom. Color, cream only. Price..........$2.25

If by mail, postage extra, 26 cents.

$2.48

No. 38C4108 Infants' Long Cloak, made of cashmere; large collar, trimmed with shirred satin ribbon, followed with silk soutache; large shoulder cape extends from this collar and is neatly embroidered with floral designs, as well as scalloped with silk, similar embroidery around bottom of coat. Lined throughout with sateen, interlined with shaker flannel; imitation pearl buttons on front. Color, cream only. Price..............$2.48

If by mail, postage extra, 26 cents.

Infants' Cashmere Cloak, $2.75.

$2.75

No. 38C4110 Infants' Long Cloak, made of fine grade cashmere; collar trimmed with silk cord and shirred baby ribbon; large shoulder cape beautifully embroidered with silk, edge scalloped and stitched with silk, embroidered around bottom with silk to correspond; interlined with flannel; cloak and shoulder cape lined with sateen; sleeves trimmed with one row of cord and ribbon. Color, cream only. Price.......................$2.75
If by mail, postage extra, 26 cents.

Infants' Long Cloak, $3.75.

$3.75

No. 38C4112 An exceedingly fine Long Cloak; made of all wool cashmere. Has a very prettily trimmed collar of one row of satin ribbon, one row of silk braid and silk loops trimmed in a very pretty and neat design. Has a flounced cape which is scalloped and embroidered with silk in a very neat and pretty floral design; new bishop sleeves with cuffs, trimmed with one row of fancy silk braid. Embroidered around the bottom with silk in a wide pattern of a neat floral design to match the pretty embroidered cape, interlined with wadding and lined with a fine sateen. Extra fine quality throughout. Color, cream only. Price............................$3.75
If by mail, postage extra, 26 cents.

Infants' Bedford Cord Cloak.

$1.15

No. 38C4116 Infants' Long Cloak. Made of Bedford cord, large shoulder cape and embroidered with silk, embroidered around the bottom to match, lined throughout with canton flannel. Color, cream only. Price..................................$1.15
If by mail, postage extra, 22 cents.

$2.98

No. 38C4118 Infants' Long Coat. Made of good quality Bedford cord, has double flounced cape which is embroidered in silk in a very neat floral design, collar trimmed with satin and three rows of fancy silk braid, new bishop sleeves, cuffs trimmed with two rows of fancy silk braid to match, coat interlined with wadding and lined with fine sateen. Color, cream only. Price................................$2.98
If by mail, postage extra, 24 cents.

$4.50

No.38C4122 Very pretty trimmed Long Cloak. Made of fine Bedford cord; has very pretty shoulder cape trimmed all around with seven silk embroidered grape design ornaments and trimmed with fluted chiffon, which is edged with ribbon ruching; edge of cape and collar trimmed with fancy silk cord; lined throughout with sateen and interlined with flannel; bishop sleeves with turnover cuffs trimmed with silk cord. Color, cream only. Price.......................................$4.50
If by mail, postage extra, 25 cents.

Infants' Silk Cloaks.

$3.48

No. 38C4124 A Beautiful Long Cloak. Made of China silk; has a large silk shoulder cape trimmed with two rows of silk gimp, embroidered with silk in a very pretty design, scalloped and stitched with silk; embroidered around bottom with silk to correspond; interlined with flannel; cloak and shoulder cape lined with fine sateen, sleeves trimmed with two rows of silk gimp. Color, cream only. Price.................$3.48
If by mail, postage extra, 26 cents.

Silk Cloak at $2.85.

No. 38C4125 Infants Long Cloak. Made of China Silk. Same style as No. 38C4124, but without the embroidered silk on skirt and cape Color, cream only. Price...............$2.85
If by mail, postage extra, 25 cents.

CHILDREN'S CLOTH REEFERS AND SILK COATS.

Suitable for little girls and boys, ages from 2 to 6 years. Very newest designs for spring, summer and early fall wear.

No.38C4140 Child's Reefer, made of all wool ladies' cloth, wide sailor collar trimmed with three rows of soutache and lace, edged with silk cord. Collar trimmed with soutache and cord to match. New style cuffs trimmed to correspond. Colors, royal blue or red. Price....98c
If by mail, postage extra, 13 cents.

No.38C4142 Child's Reefer, made of all wool ladies' cloth, has wide shawl collar trimmed with two rows of fancy braid and one row of lace. Made double breasted with imitation pearl buttons, newest style cuffs trimmed with braid to match. Colors, royal blue or red. Price, $1.19
If by mail, postage extra, 13 cents.

Very Nobby Silk Cloak.

No. 38C4144 Child's Cloak, made of good quality taffeta silk, has a wide flounced collar trimmed with fancy braid and rows of soutache, also two lace medallions, full pouch sleeves with fancy braid, fancy metal buttons lined throughout with sateen. Colors, black or royal blue. Price... $2.98
If by mail, postage extra, 19 cents.

No. 38C4146 Child's Cloak, made of fine silk peau de soie, wide shawl collar trimmed with lace and edged with silk cord, upper small collar edged with silk cord and stitching, full pouch sleeves, newest cuffs trimmed with lace medallion and silk cord, six pearl buttons, lined throughout with sateen. Colors, black or royal blue. Price..$3.25
If by mail, postage extra, 19 cents.

INFANTS' AND CHILDREN'S EIDERDOWN WALKING CLOAKS.

Ages, 6 months to 5 years. When ordering give age and length desired.

98c

No. 38C4150 Angora Trimmed Cloak, made of wool elderdown, Hubbard style, has large square collar trimmed with two rows of silk braid and edged with white angora. Bishop sleeves with cuffs. Cloak lined throughout. Colors, cream, pale blue or pink. Price, 98c
If by mail, postage extra, 26c.

$1.48

No. 38C4152 Neatly Trimmed Cloak, made of all wool ripple elderdown. The wide sailor collar is trimmed with three rows of neat silk braid and two rows ruffled satin ribbon. Small collar trimmed with braid to match. Bishop sleeves. Cloak lined throughout. Age, 6 months to 5 years. Colors, cream or pink. Price $1.48
If by mail, postage extra, 28c.

CHILD'S CLOAKS.

These little garments are of the very newest designs. Ages, 2 to 6 years. Always give age and length desired.

No. 38C4160 Child's Cloak, made of all wool flannel. Has wide shoulder cape, trimmed with four rows of fancy braid. Collar trimmed with two rows of braid to match. Interlined with wadding and lined throughout with sateen. Colors, navy blue or wine. Price.........$1.48
If by mail, postage extra, 32 cents.

$1.75

No. 38C4162 Child's Cloak, made of fine flannel. Has wide shoulder cape, trimmed with three rows of soutache and two rows of fancy braid. Collar and cuffs trimmed with soutache and braid to match. Cloak interlined with wadding and lined with sateen. Full fashioned sleeves. Age, 2 to 6 years. Colors, navy blue or red.

Price..........$1.75
If by mail, postage extra, 32 cents.

CHILDREN'S CLOAKS.

No. 38C4164 Child's Military Cloak, made of fine all wool flannel. Has wide military collar trimmed with flannel in contrasting color, followed with gilt braid and three small gilt buttons; collar trimmed with braid to match; full fashioned sleeves; cloak trimmed with large gilt buttons and interlined with wadding and lined with sateen. Colors, royal blue or cardinal.
Price.......................$1.98
If by mail, postage extra, 34 cents.

No. 38C4167 Child's Cloak, made of good quality velvette. Has wide shoulder cape, neatly trimmed with five medallions, followed with fancy braid, also squares of sateen trimmed with soutache. Collar and cuffs trimmed with fancy braid. Fancy gilt buttons. Interlined with wadding and lined with sateen. Color, black with fancy trimmings.
Price.......................$2.48
If by mail, postage extra, 33 cents.

CHILDREN'S DRESSES. AGES, 1 TO 5 YEARS.

No. 38C4700 Child's Dress. Made of good quality washable gingham. Hubbard style, revers on each side trimmed with fancy braid and trimmed in center with embroidery, sleeves trimmed with novelty braid to match, hem at bottom. Colors, blue or pink checks. Price, each......$0.21
Per dozen..............2.40
If by mail, postage extra, each, 8c.

No. 38C4704 Child's Dress, made of gingham. Solid color yoke trimmed with three rows of fancy braid, ruffle edged with wash lace, hem at bottom. Colors, pink or blue, in checks or stripes.
Price, each..............$0.25
Per dozen..............2.85
If by mail, postage extra, each, 10c.

No. 38C4712 Child's Dress, made of fancy check suiting. Cashmere yoke trimmed with two rows of soutache and small pearl buttons, ruffle all around yoke. Dress lined throughout with cambric. Deep hem at bottom. Colors, fancy checks, blue or red predominating.
Price....................75c
If by mail, postage extra, 20 cents.

No. 38C4716 Child's Dress made of cashmere. Hubbard style. Fancy circular yoke. Trimmed with tucks and baby ribbon. Plaited ruffle all around yoke and edged with two rows of baby ribbon. Collar and cuffs have two rows of stitching. Lined throughout with cambric. Deep hem at bottom. Ages, 1 to 5 years. Colors, royal blue or wine.
Price....................98c
If by mail, postage extra 19 cent

CHILDREN'S FRENCH DRESSES. AGES, 2 TO 6 YEARS.

No. 38C4730 The New Suspender Dress, made of chambray. Suspenders made of same material as in dress, and edged with wash lace. Collar and cuffs edged with wash lace, full blouse, hem at bottom. Ages, 2 to 6 years. Colors, royal blue or red (oxblood).
Price, each..............$0.39
Per dozen..............4.50
If by mail, postage extra, each, 10c.

No. 38C4732 Child's Lawn Dress, very neat yoke made of white striped lawn, the fancy bertha neatly trimmed with valenciennes lace and edged with neat wash lace, sleeves trimmed to match, collar edged with lace, hem at bottom. Ages, 2 to 6 years. Colors, pale blue, tan or pink.
Price....................45c
If by mail, postage extra, 9 cents.

No. 38C4734 Child's Dress, made of good quality wash gingham; trimmed with three box plaits back and front, made to button on side and trimmed with white pique. Newest style plaited sleeves, belt of same material as in dress, white pique collar. Ages, 2 to 6 years. Colors, blue or pink.
Price....................48c
If by mail, postage extra, 12 cents.

No. 38C4738 Newest Style Suspender Dress. Body made of white lawn, neatly trimmed with six plaits. Skirt made of good quality percale, with belt to match. Suspenders trimmed with row of white pique and edged with neat embroidery; collar and cuffs edged with embroidery to match; deep hem at bottom. Ages, 2 to 6 years. Colors, pink or blue stripes. 89c
If by mail, postage extra, 10 cents.

No. 38C4742 Child's Sailor Dress, made of chambray. Very neat sailor collar trimmed with two rows of white tape white pique dickey. Full blouse trimmed in back and front with three box plaits; tie, cuffs and belt trimmed with white tape. Box plaited skirt with deep hem at bottom. Ages, 2 to 6 years. Colors, blue or tan.
Price....................98c
If by mail, postage extra 12 cents.

No. 38C4746 Child's Dress, made of chambray. Very neatly trimmed in back and front with six plaits, dress made to button on side. Neatly trimmed with two rows of white tape. Collar and belt trimmed to match. Newest fashioned sleeves trimmed with ten rows of white tape. Ages, 2 to 6 years. Colors, blue or tan.
Price..............$1.15
If by mail, postage extra, 12 cents.

No. 48C4750 Child's Dress, made of chambray. Has wide sailor collar, neatly trimmed back and front with box plaits, with belt trimmed with two pearl buttons, newest fashioned sleeves with plaits. Full plaited skirt, with deep hem at bottom. Ages, 2 to 6 years. Colors, blue or tan. Price.....98c
If by mail, postage extra, 12 cents.

No. 38C4754 Very Pretty Dress, made of fine dimity, in very neat floral effects. Round yoke, trimmed with clusters of tucks alternating with three insertions of neat embroidery; the very neatly designed bertha is edged with embroidery, neck and sleeves trimmed to match. Full blouse and also trimmed with embroidery. Ages, 2 to 6 years. Colors, neat stripes in blue or pink with floral design.
Price...............$1.48
If by mail, postage extra, 11c.

No. 38C4758 Child's Dress, made of fancy checked suiting. Trimmed with two cashmere straps, each with two rows of soutache and small pearl buttons. Collar and cuffs trimmed with two rows of soutache. Very full blouse. Dress lined throughout with cambric. Deep hem at bottom. Ages, 2 to 6 years. Colors, fancy checks, with blue or red predominating. Price....75c
If by mail, postage extra, 20c.

No. 38C4762 Child's Dress, made of cashmere, plaited front. Fancy stitched strap at left side, trimmed with embroidered silk emblem. Collar, cuffs and belt with two rows of stitching plaited back. Dress lined throughout with cambric. Deep hem at bottom. Ages, 2 to 6 years. Colors, navy blue or wine. Price.$1.10
If by mail, postage extra. 18 cents.

VERY LATEST DESIGNS IN VERY NEWEST MATERIALS AND COLORS.

GIRLS' WASHABLE DRESSES.

AGES, 5 TO 14 YEARS. WHEN ORDERING, GIVE AGE, ALSO BUST MEASURE.

48c

50c

75c

89c

98c

No. 38C4800 Girls' Dress, made of percale. Trimmed in front with two rows of braid and edged with embroidery, fancy revers extending over shoulders and forming a ruffle around back and trimmed with one row of braid. Full blouse front with deep hem at bottom. Ages, 5 to 14 years. Colors, blue or red grounds with white figures. Price....................48c
If by mail, postage extra, 15 cents.

No. 38C4804 Girls' Dress, made of gingham. Fancy round yoke trimmed with white pique and plaits. Bertha trimmed with white tape, two box plaits in front; skirt has deep hem. Ages, 5 to 14 years. Colors, pink or blue stripes.
Price....................50c
If by mail, postage extra, 17 cents.

No. 38C4806 Girls' Dress, made of good quality percale. Round yoke, back and front. Yoke in front trimmed with white pique straps, back of yoke trimmed with three box plaits and the fancy bertha edged with neat embroidery. Collar and cuffs trimmed with white pique. Skirt with deep hem. Ages, 5 to 14 years. Colors, pink or blue fancy stripes. Price.....75c
If by mail postage extra, 18 cents.

No. 38C4812 Girls' Suspender Dress. Body of dress made of white lawn. Front trimmed with six plaits, back with three box plaits, skirt and suspenders made of percale, with deep hem at bottom. Colors, black and white checks, also blue or red ground with white pin dots. Ages, 5 to 14 years. Price....................89c
If by mail, postage extra, 17 cents.

No. 38C4816 A Very Neat Dress, made of batiste. Neatly trimmed in front with six plaits and side with white pique and two pearl buttons, two box plaits in back, white pique belt; skirt made nice and full with deep hem at bottom. Ages, 5 to 14 years. Color, natural linen (tan). Price...98c
If by mail, postage extra, 18 cents.

98c

$1.10

98c

$1.48

$1.48

$1.75

No. 38C4820 Girls' Dress, made of good quality percale. Trimmed in front with white pique, followed with narrow fancy braid, box plait trimmed with five gilt buttons. Collar, cuffs and belt trimmed with pique and fancy braid, full blouse and skirt with deep hem. Ages, 5 to 14 years. Colors, blue or red ground with white pin dots. Price..98c
If by mail, postage extra 18c.

No. 38C4824 Girls' Dress, made of good quality fast gingham. Very neat round yoke trimmed with tucks and three rows of embroidery; white pique pointed epaulets trimmed with pearl buttons and edged with gingham. White pique belt, full blouse and skirt. Ages, 5 to 14 years. Colors, blue or pink stripes
Price....................$1.10
If by mail, postage extra 20c.

No. 38C4828 Very Stylish Dress, made of fast gingham. Dress made with three box plaits in back and front. Slashed collar with white lawn bow tie, trimmed in front with four embroidery medallions, finished with a belt. Deep hem at bottom. For girls, ages, 5 to 14 years. Colors, blue or pink.
Price....................98c
If by mail, postage extra, 18c.

No. 38C4832 Girls' Dress; latest style, with suspender effect, made of good quality gingham. Trimmed with numerous rows of fine tucks, box plait embroidered with six silk stars. The suspenders trimmed with three rows of fancy braid, back trimmed with six plaits. Collar and cuffs trimmed with three rows of fancy braid to match; skirt with deep hem at bottom. Ages, 5 to 14 years. Colors, blue or pink.
Price....................$1.48
If by mail, postage extra, 21c.

No. 38C4836 Girls' Dress, made of fast gingham. Very neat circular yoke, trimmed with tucks and embroidery medallions; the bertha is edged with neat embroidery. Collar and cuffs trimmed with embroidery to match, finished with a belt. Skirt made nice and full with deep hem at bottom. Ages, 5 to 14 years. Colors, blue and white or pink and white checks. Price..$1.48
If by mail, postage extra, 21c.

No. 38C4840 Girls Dress, made of fine sateen, in the very newest suspender style, tucked front with box plait trimmed with embroidery. Suspenders edged with neat embroidery, finished with pearl buttons. Collar and cuffs trimmed with embroidery to match. Full skirt with deep hem. Ages, 5 to 14 years. Colors blue or red with white pin dots.
Price....................$1.75
If by mail, postage extra 21c

No. 38C4844 Very Stylish Dress, made of German linen. Front neatly trimmed with silk embroidered emblems, three box plaits piped with white pique, white linen collar with lawn tie, back finished with three box plaits, has belt of same material as in dress. Dress has deep hem at bottom. Age, 5 to 14 years. Colors, newest shades in cadet blue or tan.

$2.25

Price..$2.25
If by mail, postage extra, 21 cents.

No. 38C4848 Extra Fine Dress, made of fine linen crash (Irish linen). Trimmed in front with silk embroidered emblem and sateen V's and finished with three box plaits, white linen and silk tie, left sleeve embroidered with silk anchor, cuffs trimmed with red sateen, back finished with three box plaits, patent leather belt. Dress has deep hem at bottom. For girls, age 5 to 14 years. Color (natural linen), tan only. Price....................$2.98
If by mail, postage extra, 23 cents.

$2.98

THESE ARE THE LATEST STYLES FOR LITTLE GIRLS.

IN ORDERING, BE SURE TO STATE AGE AND BUST MEASURE.

GIRLS' LINED DRESSES.

Very latest designs in very newest materials and colors. Ages, 5 to 14 years. When ordering, give age; also bust measure.

No. 38C4852 Very Stylish Dress, made of fine novelty dress suiting. New style shield front, trimmed with cashmere strap, ornamented with small brass buttons, also three circles of cashmere followed with fancy braid. Full fashioned sleeves, belt of same material as in dress. Skirt made nice and full, with hem at bottom. Dress lined throughout with cambric. Pattern is a fancy check, 1 blue and black, red and black or brown and black.

98c

Price....................98c
If by mail, postage extra, 27 cents.

No. 38C4856 Best Value Ever Offered. Girls' Dress, made of novelty Scotch plaid dress goods. Has a circular yoke both back and front, trimmed in front with two rows of fancy braid, the fancy pointed bertha trimmed with four velvet straps each with gilt buttons also trimmed with braid to match collar; cuffs and waist trimmed with fancy braid, very full blouse front, newest style sleeves, very full skirt with deep hem, dress lined throughout with cambric, predominating colors in blue, red or green plaids. Positively the best value ever offered.

$1.25

Price....................$1.25
If by mail, postage extra, 26 cents.

$1.98

No. 38C4860 Girls' Cashmere Dress. Very pretty yoke, trimmed with cashmere plaits, alternating with fancy silk plaits, bertha extending all around yoke in back to waist line in front; trimmed with soutache and small pearl buttons; collar, cuffs and waistband trimmed with soutache; dress lined throughout with cambric; deep hem at bottom. Ages, 5 to 14 years. Colors are navy blue or garnet.
Price.........$1.98
If by mail, postage extra, 22 cents.

$2.35

No. 38C4864 Girls' Dress. Made of single F cashmere. Has a very pretty yoke, trimmed with four clusters of three tucks and two plaits of fancy silk, the bertha trimmed with velvet ribbon and fancy metal buttons; satin ribbon bow at yoke; collar, waistband and cuffs trimmed with velvet ribbon; new bishop sleeves; dress lined with cambric; deep hem at bottom. Colors, navy blue or garnet. Price...$2.35
If by mail, postage extra, 24 cents.

Ages, 5 to 14 years.

$2.48

No. 38C4868 Girls' Dress, made of good quality cashmere. Very full blouse front with three plaits. Trimmed at left side with six rows of fancy silk cord and three large gilt ball buttons. Six stitched tucks in back. Collar and cuffs trimmed with fancy cord to match. Detachable belt with two rows of stitching. Dress lined throughout with cambric. Deep hem at bottom. Ages, 5 to 14 years. Colors, royal blue or wine.
Special value. Price..........$2.48
If by mail, postage extra, 28 cents.

Two-Piece Sailor Suits of Washable Percale at 75 Cents.

75c

No. 38C4900 Girl's Two-Piece Sailor Suits, made of percale. Wide sailor collar with two rows of white pique full blouse with percale tie, white pique dickey embroidered with silk emblem. Skirt made full with deep hem. Ages, 6 to 14 years. Colors, blue or red with white polka dots.
Price, 75c
If by mail, postage extra, 21 cents.

GIRLS' TWO-PIECE WASHABLE SAILOR SUITS.

Ages, 6 to 14 years. These handsome dresses are made in the very latest styles and newest materials.

85c

89c

98c

$1.48

$1.39

No. 38C4912 Girls' Two-piece Sailor Suit, made of good quality percale. Same style as No. 38C4908. Colors, blue or red with white polka dots. Price..........98c
If by mail, postage extra 23 cents

No 38C4904 Girls' Two-piece Sailor Suit, made of gingham. Wide sailor collar neatly trimmed with fancy braid. blouse made full trimmed with gingham tie White pique dickey with silk embroidered emblem Cuffs trimmed with braid to match skirt with deep hem Ages 6 to 14 years Colors blue or oxblood (red)
Price.......................85c
If by mail postage extra 22 cents

No. 38C4908 Girls' Two-piece Sailor Suit, made of percale. Has large, white pique sailor collar neatly trimmed with percale, full blouse with white pique tie and cuffs. Silk embroidered white pique dickey, skirt made full with deep hem at the bottom. Ages, 6 to 14 years Colors. black shepherd checks
Price.......................89c
If by mail postage extra, 23 cents.

No. 38C4914 Girls' Two-piece Sailor Suit, made of good quality white duck. Has wide sailor collar trimmed with three rows of narrow strips of blue cloth, the cuffs, tie and collar trimmed to correspond. Skirt made extra full with deep hem: the attached dickey is trimmed to correspond. Very pretty dress for girls. Ages, 6 to 14 years. Color. white only. with blue or red trimmings. Price.....98c
If by mail. postage extra, 27 cents.

No. 38C4916 Girls' Two-piece Dress, made of good quality fast gingham. Blouse neatly finished with three box plaits and embroidered with six silk stars white linen collar and lawn tie, finished in back with three box plaits. Full skirt with deep hem at bottom. Ages 6 to 14 years. Colors blue or oxblood (red).
Price.....................$1.48
If by mail. postage extra, 23 cents.

No. 38C4918 Girls' Two-piece Dress, Russian blouse effect. Trimmed on left side with two strips of red cloth and six gilt buttons, pocket on right side. The newest fashioned sleeves trimmed to correspond. Dress made of batiste in natural linen color. Ages, 6 to 14 years.
Price.................$1.39
If by mail, postage extra, 24 cents.

$1.69

$1 75

$1.98

$2.25

$2.48

No. 38C4920 Girls' Two-piece Sailor Suit, made of good quality fast gingham. Has wide sailor collar made of white pique trimmed with gingham. White pique dickey with silk embroidered emblem, also on left sleeve. Extra full blouse with white pique tie and cuffs, skirt with deep hem. Ages, 6 to 14 years. Colors, blue, white or pink. white stripes.
Price...................$1.69
If by mail, postage extra, 20 cents.

No. 38C4924 Girls' Two-piece Sailor Suit, made of natural linen color batiste. Sailor collar trimmed with sateen, four rows of soutache followed with fancy braid. Collar and cuffs trimmed to correspond. Dickey made of same material as in dress and embroidered with silk emblem. Skirt made full with deep hem at bottom. Ages, 6 to 14 years. Color (natural linen). tan only. Price...................$1 75
If by mail, postage extra, 21 cents.

No. 38C4928 Girls' Two-piece Sailor Suit, made of German linen. Sailor collar trimmed with four rows of soutache. Collar and cuffs trimmed to match. Dickey embroidered with silk emblem, left sleeve embroidered to match. Tie of same material as in dress. Full skirt with deep hem at bottom. Ages 6 to 14 years. Colors, cadet or royal blue. Price......$1.98
If by mail, postage extra, 22 cents.

No. 38C4932 Girls' Two-piece Dress, made of German linen. Trimmed with two box plaits and six embroidered silk stars, finished with a pocket, white linen collar and silk bow tie. Back finished with two box plaits, full skirt with deep hem. For girls, ages, 6 to 14 years. Colors, royal blue or tan.
Price.................$2.25
If by mail, postage extra 23 cents.

No. 38C4936 Girls' Two-piece Sailor Suit, made of natural linen (Irish linen crash). The very neat sailor collar is trimmed with four rows of soutache and fancy braid, collar and cuffs trimmed to correspond, dickey is handsomely embroidered with silk emblem, full skirt with deep hem. For girls ages 6 to 14 years. Color, natural linen (tan) only
Price...................$2.48
If by mail, postage extra 22 cents.

GIRLS' OR MISSES' TWO-PIECE SAILOR SUITS

Very stylish dresses. These dresses made only in regular sizes as follows:

Ages	12	14	16	18
Bust, inches	30	32	34	36
Skirt length, inches	32-33	34-36	37-38	39

Be sure to give bust measure and length of skirt.

Linen Crash Sailor Suit, $4.95.

$4.95 No. 38C5010 Girls' or Misses' Two-piece Sailor Suit, made of linen crash. Very full blouse with sailor shawl collar trimmed with three rows of white braid. Pocket on left side, sleeves and dickey embroidered with silk emblem. Collar trimmed with braid to match, newest style cuffs, full fashioned gored skirt with deep hem. Color, natural linen (tan) only. Price....$4.95
If by mail, postage extra, 44 cents.

Two-piece Sailor Suit Made of Fast Gingham.

No. 38C5014 Girls' or Misses' Two-piece Sailor Suit. Same style as No. 38C5010, Made of fast gingham. Color, blue only.
Price......(Postage extra, 39c)......$3.95

GIRLS' OR MISSES' TWO-PIECE WHITE LAWN DRESSES.

Very stylish dresses, suitable for confirmation, parties and all occasions. These dresses are made only in regular sizes, as follows:

Ages	12	14	16	18
Bust, inches	30	32	34	36
Skirt length, inches	32-33	34-36	37-38	39

Be sure to give bust measure and length of skirt.

$3.98 No. 38C5018 Girls' or Misses' White Lawn Dress. Square yoke, made of Swiss embroidery with collar to match, full blouse with bolero effect, edged with embroidery, insertion in cuffs to match, waistband of fine embroidery, back finished with four neat tucks and V insertion of neat embroidery gored skirt flounced with beading. Color, white only. Price...$3.98
Postage extra, 27c.

$4.25 No. 38C5022 Girls' or Misses' Two-piece White Lawn Dress, consisting of waist and skirt, waist made with round yoke both front and back, trimmed with five rows of openwork embroidery, a very wide pointed ruffle all around yoke which is trimmed and edged with embroidery to match collar, cuffs and waistband, skirt made very full with kilt plait around bottom at each seam and trimmed with insertion of embroidery, as illustrated; nice deep hem at bottom. Color, white only.
Price....$4.25
If by mail, postage extra, 26 cents.

GIRLS' WHITE LAWN DRESSES.

Very stylish and neatly trimmed dresses, suitable for confirmation, parties, and other occasions. Ages, 6 to 14 years. State age and bust measure when ordering.

Embroidery Trimmed White Lawn Dress, Only 89 Cents.

89c No. 38C5100 Girls' White Lawn Dress. Very neat circular yoke, trimmed with three plaits and two insertions of embroidery, the fancy pointed bertha edged with neat embroidery, yoke in back with three plaits, full fashioned sleeves, skirt with deep hem. Ages, 6 to 14 years. Color, white only.
Price....89c
If by mail, postage extra, 19 cents

Very Neat Trimmed Lawn Dress, Only $1.15.

$1.15 No. 38C5104 Girls' White Lawn Dress, Very neat, circular yoke, trimmed with clusters of fine tucks and satin ribbon bow, the fancy pointed bertha with insertion of embroidery, also edged with embroidery. Cuffs trimmed with embroidery to match, white lawn belt. Ages, 6 to 14 years. Exceptional good value.
Price...$1.15
If by mail, postage extra, 21 cents.

Stylish White Lawn Dress, Only $1.48.

$1.48

No. 38C5108 Girls' White Lawn Dress. Has very pretty pointed tucked yoke with insertion of neat embroidery, satin ribbon bow. The fancy bertha is edged with neat embroidery. Collar and cuffs trimmed with six plaits. Skirt made with deep hem. For girls, ages, 6 to 14 years. Color, white only. Price....$1.48
If by mail, postage extra, 21 cents.

Handsome White Lawn Dress, Only $1.69.

$1.69

No. 38C5112 Girls' Dress, made of good quality white lawn. Fancy pointed tucked yoke with three embroidery medallions, 5-inch embroidery ruffle extending to back of yoke, which is trimmed with six tucks. Collar and cuffs are trimmed with embroidery. White lawn belt. Skirt made full with deep hem at bottom. For girls, ages, 6 to 14 years. Color, white only. Price....$1.69
If by mail, postage extra, 22 cents.

Trimmed with Lace, Only $1.98.

No. 38C5116 A Very Stylish White Lawn Dress, made of fine sheer lawn. Circular yoke handsomely trimmed with neat embroidery insertions, alternating with lace beading and ribbon insertions. The bertha is trimmed with embroidery and edged with lace; ribbon rosette at yoke. Collar and cuffs trimmed to match. Back trimmed with six plaits; white lawn belt. Skirt made full, trimmed with three plaits, deep hem at bottom. For girls, ages, 6 to 14 years. Color, white only.
$1.98
Price....$1.98
If by mail, postage extra, 23 cents.

Beautifully Trimmed Lawn Dress, $2.65.

No. 38C5120 A Handsome Trimmed Dress, made of fine white sheer lawn. Circular yoke of fine embroidery insertions, alternating with clusters of fine French tucks. Yoke in back trimmed to correspond. Wide satin ribbon rosette, the very neat tucked bertha of 3-inch fine embroidery. Collar, cuffs and belt trimmed to match. Skirt neatly trimmed with a cluster of six fine tucks. For girls, ages, 6 to 14 years. Color, white only. Price, $2.65
$2.65
If by mail, postage extra, 23 cents.

DON'T FORGET POSTAGE IF YOU WANT GOODS SENT BY MAIL.

Very Fine White Lawn Dress at $2.98.

$2.98 No 38C5124 Very Fine Dress made of extra good quality white sheer lawn. The beautiful square yoke made both front and back alike of solid French tucks, with insertion of neat valenciennes lace, finished with fancy silk ribbon rosette. The fancy pointed bertha is trimmed with clusters of neat tucks alternating with lace insertions, and edged with neat embroidery. Collar and cuffs trimmed to match; six plaits in back, waist band of lace beading and ribbon inserting. Skirt neatly trimmed with a cluster of fine tucks and two insertions of neat valenciennes lace, with deep hem at bottom. For girls, ages, 6 to 14 years. Color, white only. Price....$2.98
If by mail, postage extra, 22 cents.

Magnificent White Lawn Dress, $3.75.

No. 38C5128 An Exceedingly Fine Dress, made of extra fine white sheer lawn. A very neatly trimmed circular yoke of fine valenciennes lace insertion, alternating with clusters of fine tucks. Yoke in back trimmed to correspond. The fancy pointed bertha trimmed all around with insertion of valenciennes lace, very full blouse, neck trimmed with band of lace beading and ribbon inserting, full fashioned sleeves with lace insertion, wide cuffs trimmed with clusters of tucks and lace. A very neat skirt, trimmed with three clusters of fine tucks, six tucks in each cluster, deep hem at bottom. Color white only.
$3.75
Price....$3.75
If by mail, postage extra, 21 cents.

Girls' Point d'Esprit Dress, $4.95.

Ages, 6 to 14 years. Give age and bust measure.

No. 38C5132 An Extra High Grade Dress, made of fine point d'esprit. Under dress is made of fine organdie, the yoke is neatly trimmed with rows of narrow satin ribbon and insertion of valenciennes lace forming a square, ornamented with a silk ribbon rosette, the wide bertha is trimmed with three rows of narrow silk ribbon and edged with fine valenciennes lace. Yoke in back trimmed with tucks. Collar, cuffs and waistband trimmed with ribbon to match, very full skirt trimmed with three rows of narrow satin ribbon. An exceptional fine dress for girls. Ages, 6 to 14 years. Color, white only.
$4.95
Price....$4.95
If by mail, postage extra, 22 cents.

LADIES' JACKETS.

WE SHOW A LARGE ASSORTMENT in up to date styles. Sizes are from 32 to 42 inches around the bust and 17 to 19 inches inside measure on sleeves. Our illustrations and descriptions will give you a clear idea of these garments, but if you wish to see materials or colors, we will be pleased to send samples on application. When asking for samples, please state catalogue number you wish to see samples of. **Our garments are cut very full.** You very often find upon receipt that the garment is loose; **it is intended that way as it is to be worn loose.** Always give color wanted and size when ordering. Without them we are unable to give your order prompt attention. If you desire sizes different than listed, we will make them to order for 20 per cent above the catalogue price.

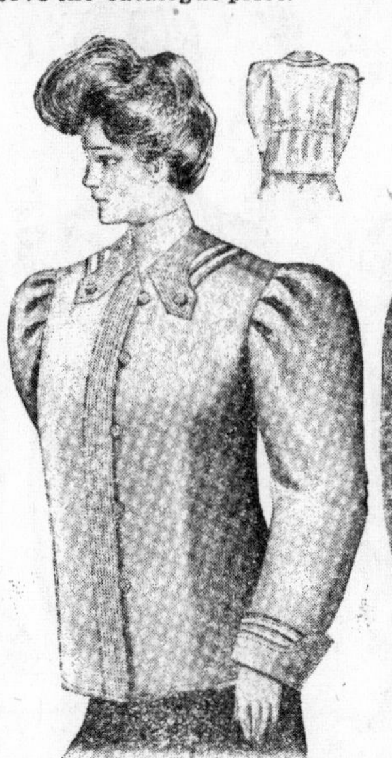

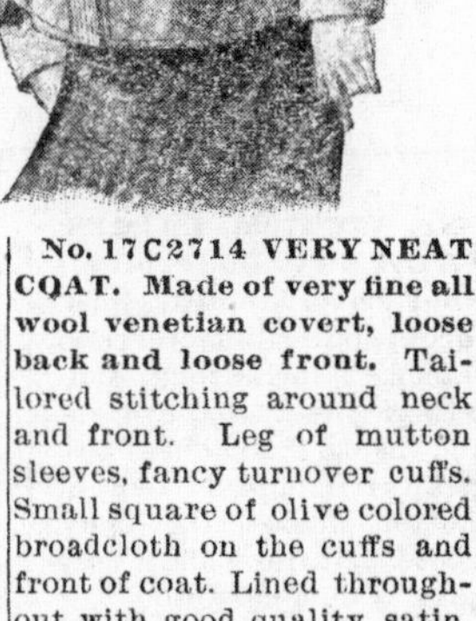

No. 17C2708 MISSES' JACKET. Made of very fine all wool covert cloth, collarless effect, double breasted front, full back finished with box plait and neat belt. Leg of mutton sleeves, fancy turnover cuffs. Self covered buttons. Facing of same material. Lined throughout with satin. Velvet trimming around the neck stitched several times. Very up to date. Color, castor only.
Price... .... **$6.95**
If by mail, postage extra, 50 cents.

No. 17C2710 THIS NEAT COAT is made of very fine all wool covert cloth, 27 inches long, loose back and loose front. Collarless effect. Leg of mutton sleeves nicely tailored, finished with tailored stitching around the neck and down front. Trimmed with white broadcloth and finished with fancy silk braid to match around neck and cuffs. No lining. Color, castor only.
Price................ **$4.75**
If by mail, postage extra, 45 cents.

No. 17C2711 THIS EXQUISITE LADIES' JACKET is made of very fine all wool cravenette cloth, collarless effect, fly front, fitted back. Neatly trimmed with self covered buttons, slot seams and small plaits in front and back of garment. Leg of mutton sleeves with shirring at shoulders, neat cuffs. Fancy embroidery around the collar, finished with olive colored broadcloth. Very attractive. Facing of same material. Lined throughout with good quality satin. Color, castor only. Price.... **$8.75**
If by mail, postage extra, 45 cents.

No. 17C2714 VERY NEAT COAT. Made of very fine all **wool venetian covert, loose back and loose front.** Tailored stitching around neck and front. Leg of mutton sleeves, fancy turnover cuffs. Small square of olive colored broadcloth on the cuffs and front of coat. Lined throughout with good quality satin. Color, castor only.
Price.................. **$6.95**
If by mail, postage extra, 45 cents.

No. 17C2716 LADIES JACKET, in the newest **Tuxedo effect; 22 inches long.** Made of very fine all wool covert cloth, double breasted front with a large rolling shawl collar. Collar and facing made of taffeta silk to match. Trimmed with fancy silk braid. Leg of mutton sleeves with shirring at the shoulders; fancy cuffs. Strap trimming over the shoulders reaching from front to back. Lined throughout with satin. Color, castor only.
Price................. **$7.50**
If by mail, postage extra, 45 cents.

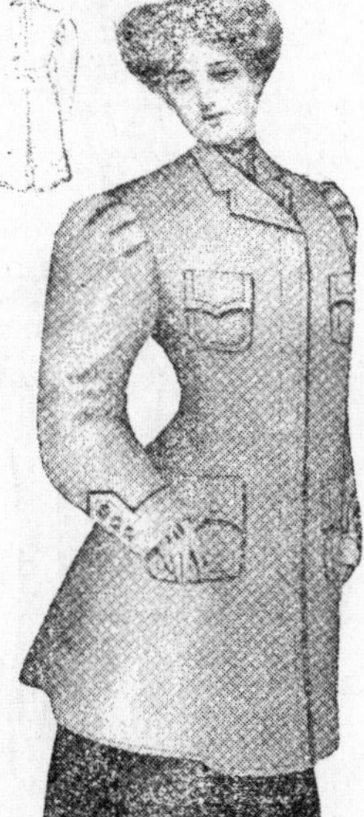

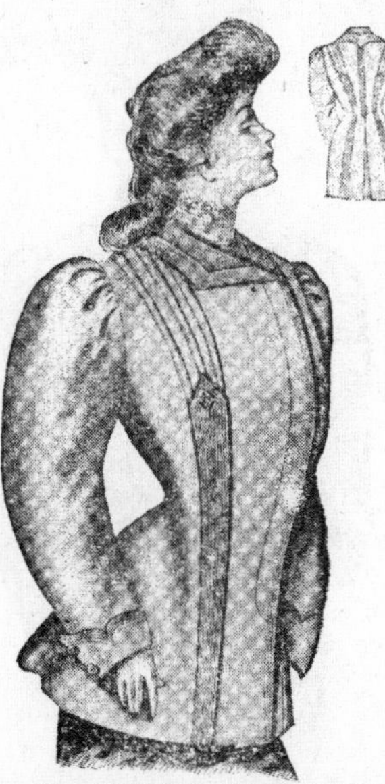

No. 17C2717 MISSES' JACKET Made of very fine all wool covert cloth, nicely tailored, mannish coat, made just like a man's overcoat; coat shaped collar and lapels, fly front, box back with inverted plait caught in a belt. Self covered buttons, fancy patch pockets. Leg of mutton sleeves, fancy turnover cuffs. Facing in front of same material. Very nobby. Color, castor only.
Price............ ..... **$5 75**
If by mail, postage extra, 45 cents.

No. 17C2719 THIS STYLISH LADIES' JACKET is made of very fine all wool covert cloth; 30 inches long, fly front, half fitted back, collarless effect. Nicely tailored. Trimmed with straps of same material and several rows of stitching. Leg of mutton sleeves, neat cuffs. Back trimmed with straps and silk stitching. Facing in front of same material. Lined throughout with good quality satin. Color, castor only.
Price................ **$9.75**
If by mail, postage extra, 50 cents.

No. 17C2720 VERY ATTRACTIVE LADIES' JACKET. Nicely tailored, **27 inches long, collarless effect, double breasted front,** richly trimmed with straps of same material and self covered buttons. Leg of mutton sleeves, fitted back. Taffeta silk straps around the neck, finished with self covered buttons. Back trimmed with straps of same material. Very nobby. Facing in front of same cloth. Lined throughout with fine satin. Color, castor only.
Price. **$10.75**
If by mail, postage extra, 55 cents.

No. 17C2722 LADIES' TOURIST COAT. Made of **very fine all wool panne cheviot, 42 inches long, double breasted front, half tight back.** Leg of mutton sleeves, fancy cuffs. Back is made with box plaits in new Norfolk effect caught in belt with fancy buckle. Facing in front of same material. Colors, black or brown.
Price,................. **$6.95**
If by mail, postage extra, 50 cents.

No. 17C2723 THIS BEAUTIFUL LADIES' JACKET is made of very fine all wool covert cloth, 42 inches long. Very newest effect. Made with full shawl collar, double breasted front and fitted back. Neatly trimmed with plaits in front and back of garment. Belt in back. Trimmings are of olive and white colored broadcloth around the collar and cuffs, finished with silk braid to match. Wide facing in front and lined to waist only with very fine guaranteed satin. Color, castor only.
Price.... .... **$12.50**
Not mailable.

LADIES' JACKETS—Continued.

No. 17C2700 LADIES' JACKET. Made of all wool covert cloth, lined throughout with mercerized sateen. 25 inches long. Collarless effect, strap trimming with stitching around the neck. Self straps over shoulders. Leg of mutton sleeves. Belt in back. Color, castor only.
Price $3.75
If by mail, postage extra, 35 cents.

No. 17C2703 LADIES' JACKET. Made of all wool covert cloth, lined throughout with mercerized sateen. 27 inches long. Collarless effect; loose front and back. Shoulder flaps, strap trimmings. Leg of mutton sleeves with cuffs. Loose belt in back. Very neat. Color, castor only.
Price $4.35
If by mail, postage extra, 40 cents.

No. 17C2706 LADIES' JACKET. Made of all wool covert cloth, 25 inches long. Collarless effect, double breasted front, inlaid velvet around the neck stitched several times and edged with fancy silk braid. Leg of mutton sleeves; tight back with a belt. Lined throughout with mercerized sateen. Color, castor only.
Price $4.95
If by mail, postage extra, 40 cents.

No. 17C2709 LADIES' NOBBY JACKET. Made of all wool covert cloth, 24 inches long. Collarless effect. Straps of same material around the back and half way on shoulders, stitched several times. Fly front and half tight back finished with a belt. Plaits from belt down. Small extension over shoulders. Shaped sleeves finished with a plait and self covered buttons. Very neat and attractive. Facing of same material. Lined throughout with good quality mercerized sateen. Color, castor only. Price $4.98
If by mail, postage extra, 40c.

No. 17C2712 LADIES' VERY PRETTY COAT. Made of all wool covert cloth. Collarless effect. Neatly trimmed with box plaits all around. Leg of mutton sleeves with puffs, fancy turnover cuffs. Inlaid velvet around the neck and cuffs. Loose back with a belt. Lined throughout with satin. Very good value for the money. Color, castor only.
Price $6.75
If by mail, postage extra, 40 cents.

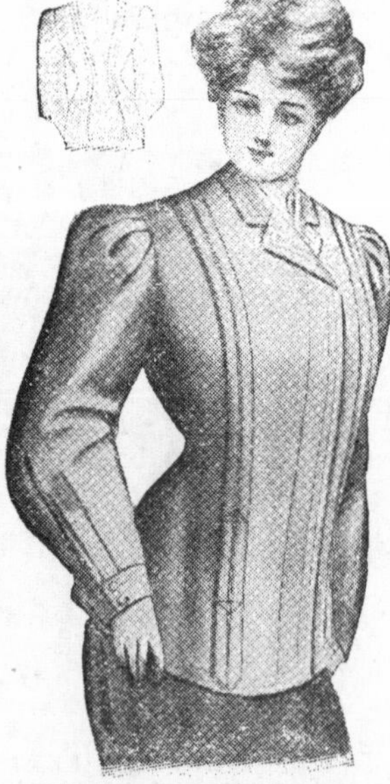

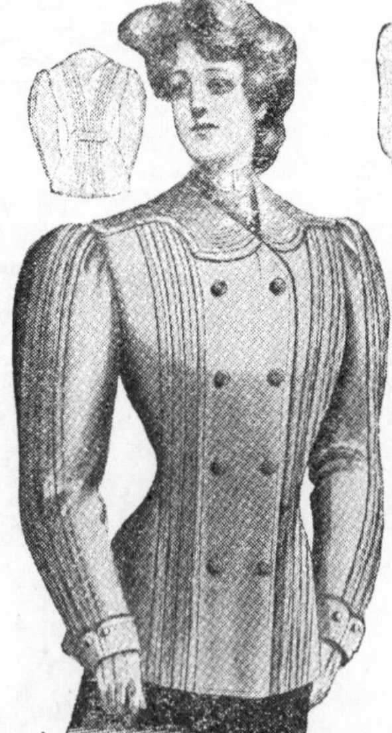

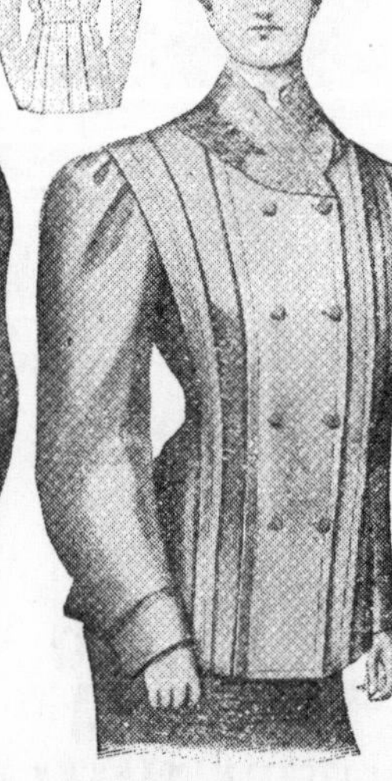

No. 17C2715 LADIES' JACKET. Made of all wool covert cloth, 30 inches long, collarless effect, double breasted front, tight back, leg of mutton sleeves, turnover cuffs. Cuffs trimmed with inlaid velvet and similar trimming around the neck. Self covered buttons. Strap seams, stitched around the bottom. Lined throughout with mercerized sateen. Facing in front of same material. Very neat and up to date. Color, castor only. Price........ $6.50
If by mail, postage extra, 45 cents.

No. 17C2718 LADIES' JACKET. Made of all wool covert cloth, 27 inches long, coat shaped collar and lapels, fly front, nicely tailored, trimmed with straps of same material. Leg of mutton sleeves, neat cuffs. Facing in front of same material Lined throughout with satin. Back made with two plaits. Color, castor only
Price $7.50
If by mail, postage extra, 50 cents.

No. 17C2721 THIS MAN TAILORED JACKET is made of all wool covert cloth, 26 inches long, collarless effect, double breasted front, leg of mutton sleeves. Richly trimmed with tailored straps all over in front, sleeves and in back. Belt in back. Facing in front of same material. Lined throughout with good quality satin. Nobby garment and very stylish. Color, castor only.
Price $7.95
If by mail, postage extra, 50 cents.

No. 17C2724 LADIES' JACKET, made of all wool cheviot, 27 inches long, collarless effect, double breasted front, loose back with a belt. Nicely tailored. Leg of mutton sleeves, fancy cuffs. Three box plaits in back caught in a belt. Lined throughout with satin. Facing in front of same material. Very neat and stylish garment. Colors, black or brown.
Price $7.50
If by mail, postage extra, 45 cents.

No. 17C2727 LADI[illegible] JACKET. Made of all covert cloth, 30 inches collarless effect, double b[illegible] ed front. Richly trimmed w[illegible] side plaits and box plaits in front and back of jacket. Leg of mutton sleeves. Inlaid velvet around the neck as well as straps of same material. Stitched several times. Box back, finished with a fancy belt with metal buckles. Facing of same material. Lined throughout with good quality satin. Very nobby. Color, tan only.
Price $7.75
If by mail, postage extra, 50 cents.

No. 17C2728 LADIES JACKET Made of very fine all wool covert cloth, 25 inches long, collarless effect, double breasted front. Leg of mutton sleeves, plaited and finished with fancy turnover cuffs. Velvet trimming on cuffs and around the neck stitched several times and trimmed with silk soutache. Tight back finished with fancy belt. Self covered buttons. Facing in front of same material. Lined throughout with satin. Color, tan only. State size in ordering.
Price $7.75
If by mail, postage extra, 50 cents.

No. 17C2729 LADIES' JACKET. Made of all wool covert cloth, 25 inches long collarless effect, fly front, nicely tailor made, with side plaits in front and in back. Leg of mutton sleeves, fancy turnover cuffs. Sleeves are also trimmed with side plaits. Tight back made with fancy belt. Velvet trimming around the neck stitched several times. Facing in front of same material. Lined throughout with satin. Color, tan only. State size in ordering.
Price $8.50
If by mail, postage extra, 50 cents.

No. 17C2730 LADIES' NOBBY JACKET. Made of all wool broadcloth, 26 inches long, full large collar, double breasted front. Leg of mutton sleeves with plaits and fancy turnover cuffs. Trimming of silk braid around large cape collar and sleeves. Tight back made with French seams and slot seam in center finished with a belt. Facing of same material. Lined throughout with satin. Colors, black or brown.
Price $8.50
If by mail, postage extra, 50 cents.

No. 17C2731 LADIES' JACKET. Extremely nobby. Made of heavy weight all wool covert cloth. Same material as used in gentlemen's overcoats. 21 inches long. Fly front, fitted back. Collarless effect. Self trimming around the neck, reaching over the shoulders. Plaits in front and back, finished with a neat belt. Stylish sleeves and fancy turnover cuffs. Facing of same material. Lined throughout with fine satin. Color, dark shade of castor.
Price $8.75
If by mail, postage extra, 55 cents.

No. 17C2732 LADIES' JACKET. Made of very fine all wool covert cloth, collarless effect, double breasted front, slot seams in front and back of jacket. Leg of mutton sleeves. Trimmings are leather colored (light brown shade) broadcloth around neck and cuffs, also silk folds around the neck and cuffs. This jacket can be worn open, as the satin lining reaches to the edge of facing and the edge of jacket on each side is trimmed with rich fancy silk braid. Very stylish garment. Color, tan only.
Price $9.75
If by mail, postage extra, 35 cents.

No. 17C2701 SPLENDID VALUE LADIES' JACKET. [illegible]de of all wool cheviot, 23 [illegible]s long, fly front, collar[illegible] effect. Leg of mutton sleeves, fancy cuffs. Facing of same material. Lined throughout with mercerized romain. Very serviceable garment. Colors, black or brown. Price $4.35
If by mail, postage extra, 35 cents.

No. 17C2702 LADIES' JACKET. Made of all wool venetian covert cloth, collarless effect, fly front, half fitted back. Leg of mutton sleeves. Facing in front of same material, lined throughout with mercerized romain. Trimming around the neck is of silk braid to match. Small white broadcloth insertion and light blue silk soutache. Similar trimming on the sleeves. Very attractive. Color, castor only. Price $4.98
If by mail, postage extra, 40 cents.

No. 17C2704 LADIES' JACKET. Made of very fine all wool panne cheviot, 24 inches long, fly front, collarless effect. Tight back. Nicely tailored. Front is neatly trimmed with tailored cording, as shown in illustration. Leg of mutton sleeves, neat cuffs. Facing of same material. Lined throughout with taffeta silk to match. Colors, black or brown.
Price $6.50
If by mail, postage extra, 40 cents.

No. 17C2705 LADIES' JACKET. Very attractive, made of fine all wool cravenette cloth, 23 inches long, strap trimmings of same material. Fancy silk braid and inlaid velvet around the neck and cuffs. Leg of mutton sleeves. Facing in front of same material. Very full below the waist. Lined throughout with good quality satin. Color, castor only.
Price $6.95
If by mail, postage extra, 40 cents.

No. 17C2707 THIS NICELY TAILORED JACKET, 24 inches long, is made of very fine all wool covert cloth, collarless effect, double breasted front, fitted back. Trimmings of straps of same material stitched several times. Leg of mutton sleeves, fancy cuffs, with several rows of silk stitching and slot seams. The back is beautifully trimmed with straps, nicely tailored and stitched. Facing of same material. Lined throughout with very fine satin. Color, castor only.
Price $8.75
If by mail, postage extra, 45 cents.

LADIES' LONG SPRING TOP COATS.

NICELY TAILORED AND UP TO DATE GARMENTS. Sizes, 32 to 42 inches around bust. State catalogue number, size and color wanted when ordering. Sizes differing from these will be made to order at an advance of 20 per cent.

No. 17C2745 LADIES' TOURIST COAT. Made of all wool covert cloth, 44 inches long, man tailored, coat shaped collar and nice lapels. Leg of mutton sleeves, turnover cuffs. Half tight back, wide facing in front of same material. Very attractive garment and strictly up to date. Color, castor only.
Price.................**$5.75**
If by mail, postage extra, 55 cents.

No. 17C2746 LADIES' TOURIST COAT. Made of all wool covert cloth, 42 inches long, collarless effect, nicely tailored. Self cloth trimming around the neck, stitched several times and finished with satin squares. Leg of mutton sleeves, turnover cuffs. Facing of same material. Half fitted back with small belt. Fly front, well made in every respect. Color, castor only.
Price.................**$6.75**
If by mail, postage extra, 60 cents.

No. 17C2747 LADIES' TOURIST COAT Made of all wool cheviot, 42 inches long, collarless effect, double breasted front, leg of mutton sleeves, fancy turnover cuffs, fancy silk braid trimming on cuffs and around the neck. Loose back made with slot seam and caught in a belt. Lined to waist only with fine Italian cloth. Facing in front of same material. Colors, black or brown.
Price.................**$6.75**
If by mail, postage extra, 60 cents.

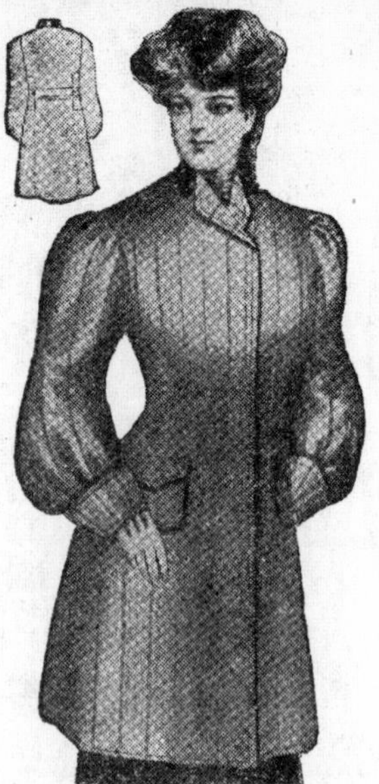

No. 17C2748 LADIES' TOURIST COAT, 42 inches long. Made of all wool fancy mixture in newest striped effect. Made like a man's coat with a velvet collar, neat lapels, fly front, leg of mutton sleeves with large cuffs. Loose back caught in a belt. Wide facing in front of same material. Fancy turnover cuffs. Very neat and up to date. Colors, castor or gray mixtures.
Price.................**$6.75**
If by mail, postage extra, 60 cents.

No. 17C2749 VERY FINE LADIES' JACKET. Made of all wool broadcloth, 42 inches long, collarless effect, leg of mutton sleeves, turnover cuffs. Slot seam in back finished with a belt. Lined to waist only with good quality black satin. Velvet trimming around the neck. A very high grade desirable garment. Colors, brown or black, with leather colored broadcloth trimming around the neck.
Price.................**$7.75**
If by mail, postage extra, 65 cents.

No. 17C2750 LADIES' TOURIST COAT. Made of all wool covert cloth, 42 inches long, collarless effect, loose back and loose front. Box plaited in front and back. Leg of mutton sleeves, fancy turnover cuffs. Velvet trimming on cuffs and around the neck. Self covered buttons, belt in back. Very pretty and up to date. Color, castor only.
Price.................**$8.50**
Not mailable.

WHEN ORDERING, STATE CATALOGUE NUMBER, SIZE AND COLOR.

No. 17C2751 LADIES' NOBBY TOURIST COAT. Made of all wool covert cloth, 42 inches long, collarless effect. Side plaits and slot seams in front reaching all around to back of jacket. Leg of mutton sleeves, turnover cuffs Loose back with a fancy belt. Half lined with fine Italian cloth to match. Facing in front of self material. Self cloth and velvet trimming around the neck and front of coat. Very stylish. Color, castor only.
Price.................**$8.95**
Not mailable.

No. 17C2755 THIS PRETTY TOURIST COAT is made of all wool covert cloth, double breasted front, fancy collar, full leg of mutton sleeves, fancy cuffs. Facing in front of same material. The back is made with triple box plaits, is loose and finished with belt trimmed with fancy metal buckle. Coat is 42 inches long. Color, castor only. Price.................**$7.50**
Not mailable.

No. 17C2753 LADIES' TOURIST COAT. Made of very fine all wool good weight covert cloth, collarless effect, double breasted front, leg of mutton sleeves, fancy cuffs. Half fitted back finished with side plaits and a belt. Front trimmed with self covered buttons and side plaits. Facing of same material. Lined to waist only with good quality satin. Satin trimming stitched several times around the neck, finished with fancy silk braid. Very handsome and stylish. Color, castor only. Price.........**$10.00**
Not mailable.

No. 17C2754 LADIE TOURIST COAT. Made o very fine all wool covert cloth, 42 inches long, collar less effect, double breast loose front and loose ba finished with fancy belt whic reaches all around to th front. Large leg of mutto sleeves, fancy turnover cuffs. Facing in front of same material. Lined to yoke only with good quality satin. Side plaits in back and front of coat. Self trimmings around the neck and also leather colored broadcloth, which is finished with silk soutache and velvet. Very rich. Color, castor only with leather colored trimmings.
Price.................**$12.50**
Not mailable.

LADIES' SILK JACKETS.

SIZES FROM 32 TO 42 INCHES AROUND THE BUST.

These Jackets are very dressy and are very popular. Many of these styles have no lining and are very light weight. They are cut full and are to be worn loose. Be sure to state color and size when ordering.

No. 17C2774 THIS ILLUSTRATION represents silk blouses in different styles, some with collars, some collarless, some with shoulder cape effects, etc. We want to close these out and therefore reduce the price below cost and will sell them, as long as they last, for $2.98. Every one of them is a better garment than picture shows; materials are black taffeta or peau de sole silk. Always state size wanted when you order.
Price.................. **$2.98**
If by mail, postage extra, 25 cents.

No. 17C2775 LADIES' JACKET. Made of good quality silk peau de soie, 23 inches long, sailor collar, leg of mutton sleeves, fancy turnover cuffs. Neat satin bow in front. Loose back and loose front. Jacket is not lined. Colors, all black or black with white trimmings.
Price.................. **$3.75**
If by mail, postage extra, 25 cents.

No. 17C2776 LADIES' JACKET. Made of good quality all silk peau de soie, 23 inches long, large sailor collar, loose back and loose front, leg of mutton sleeves, fancy turnover cuffs. Richly trimmed with cream colored lace and medallions around the collar and on sleeves. Very neat. No lining. Color, black, with cream colored trimmings. Price...... **$4.50**
If by mail, postage extra, 25 cents.

No. 17C2777 LADIES' JACKET. Made of good quality all silk peau de soie, 25 inches long. Loose back and loose front. Large fancy collar. Leg of mutton sleeves, fancy turnover cuffs. Trimmings of silk braid. Bow in front made of peau de soie and trimmed with silk braid. Strap of same material around the bottom. No lining. Color, black only.
Price.................. **$4.95**
If by mail, postage extra, 25 cents.

No. 17C2778 LADIES' MONTE CARLO JACKET. Made of fine taffeta silk, 24 inches long. Large shoulder cape, neatly trimmed with black and white silk braid. Plaits in back and in front, full sleeves, turnover cuffs, trimmed with braid to match. Lined with mercerized serge from neck to yoke in back only. Color, black only. Price.......... **$4.95**
If by mail, postage extra, 23 cents.

No. 17C2779 VERY PRETTY LADIES' JACKET. Made of good quality all silk peau de soie, 30 inches long, double breasted front, loose back. Collarless effect. White satin around the neck, trimmed with black silk soutache. Leg of mutton sleeves, fancy cuffs, trimmed with white satin and silk soutache. The back is made with box plaits in center and side plaits, finished with belt. Fancy crochet buttons. No lining in this jacket. Facing in front of same material. Color, all black with black and white trimming around neck and cuffs.
Price.................. **$6.50**
If by mail, postage extra, 35 cents.

No. 17C2780 LADIES' NOBBY COAT, 25 inches long. Made of fine taffeta silk. Loose back and loose front. Collarless effect. Cape over shoulders. Full sleeves and fancy turnover cuffs. Silk ornaments in front and satin strap across the shoulders. Lined throughout with mercerized sateen and heavily interlined. Very neat coat; good value for the money. Color, black only. Be sure to give size when ordering.
Price.................. **$5.75**
If by mail, postage extra, 55 cents.

No. 17C2781 HANDSOME LADIES' JACKET. Made of fine peau de soie silk, 30 inches long, large collar, bishop sleeves with fancy turnover cuffs. Loose back and loose front. The back is made with an inverted plait. Collar and cuffs are trimmed with lace braid and lace protruding from the cuffs. No lining in this coat. Colors, all black or black with cream colored trimmings. State color and size when ordering.
Price.................. **$6.95**
If by mail, postage extra, 40 cents.

No. 17C2782 THIS PRETTY PLAITED JACKET, is made of very fine taffeta silk, loose front and box back. Leg of mutton sleeves with fancy turnover cuffs. Back is plaited and is finished with belt that reaches to front. Very stylish garment. Trimmings are silk soutache and fancy silk braid around the collar in front, forming a yoke in back; belt and cuffs. No lining in this jacket. Colors, black or brown. State color and size when ordering.
Price.................. **$6.50**
If by mail, postage extra, 40 cents

No. 17C2783 LADIES' COAT, 25 inches long, loose back and loose front. Large collar, stylish puff sleeves with fancy turnover cuffs. The collar is trimmed with lace braid and lace all around. Similar trimming at the cuffs. Jacket lined throughout with romaine silk. Very neat. Colors, all black or black with cream lace. State color and size when ordering.
Price.................. **$7.50**
If by mail, postage extra, 45 cents.

No. 17C2784 LADIES' TOURIST COAT. Made of good quality all silk peau de soie, 42 inches long, large collar made with three plaits. Loose front and loose back caught in a belt. Stylish sleeves, fancy turnover cuffs. Very nobby. No lining in coat. Color, black only.
Price........ ..$7.75
If by mail, postage extra, 45 cents.

STATE CATALOGUE NUMBER, COLOR AND SIZE WHEN ORDERING.

No. 17C2785 VERY STYLISH LADIES' TOURIST COAT. Made of good quality all silk peau de soie, 42 inches long, collarless effect, loose back and loose front, trimmed with side plaits forming a yoke in front and back. Leg of mutton sleeves, fancy turnover cuffs. Silk soutache trimming on cape and around the neck. Facing in front of same material. Very rich and elegant. No lining. Color, black only.
Price.................$11.75
If by mail, postage extra, 50 cents.

No. 17C2786 VERY NOBBY AND FASHIONABLE LADIES' COAT. Made of fine all silk peau de soie, 32 inches long, loose back and loose front. Stylish sleeves, finished with puff and fancy turnover cuffs. Trimmings are black silk braid and lace around the collar and black lace protruding from the cuffs. Coat lined throughout with black or gray colored satin. Extremely handsome. State color of lining wanted.
Price $11.50
If by mail, postage extra, 50 cents.

No. 17C2807 VERY SWELL LADIES' COAT. Made of good quality taffeta silk, 42 inches long, collarless effect, double breasted front, fancy sleeves finished with shirring, nobby cuffs. Tight back shirred at the waist. White broadcloth trimming around the neck and at cuffs, finished with black and white silk braid. Color, black only, with white broadcloth trimming. Price $9.50
If by mail, postage extra, 50 cents.

No. 17C2808 VERY ATTRACTIVE LADIES' TOURIST COAT. Made of all silk peau de soie, 42 inches long, collarless effect, loose back and loose front. Silk braid trimmings. Leg of mutton sleeves, fancy cuffs. Plaits in front and back. Color, black only.
Price $11.50
If by mail, postage extra, 60 cents.

No. 17C2787 THIS ELEGANT COAT is made of very fine taffeta silk. This coat is appropriate for wear on the street or traveling. Made with shawl collar, double breasted front, half fitted back. Finished with side plaits in front and back. Nice belt reaching all around the back and trimmed with fine black and white braid around collar and the entire front. Facing of taffeta silk. Newest sleeves, fancy cuffs. Beautiful garment. Color, black with black and white silk braid trimming. Price..$9.95
If by mail, postage extra, 50 cents.

No. 17C2788 LADIES' COAT. Made of very fine taffeta silk. Very dressy and appropriate for traveling or the street. The quality of material is excellent. Made with collarless effect, leg of mutton sleeves, fancy turnover cuffs. Double breasted front, half tight fitted back, finished with pockets in front. Box plaits. Similar trimming around the neck and on back of jacket. Made very full. Facing in front of same material. Very high grade in every respect. Color, black only. Price...........$12.75
If by mail, postage extra, 50 cents.

No. 17C2809 SPECIAL VALUE IN LADIES' LONG SILK COAT. Made of good quality taffeta silk, loose back and loose front. Collarless effect. Double breasted front. Silk braid trimming around the neck and cuffs. Very full sleeves. Strap trimming in front and back of coat. Very swell garment. Colors, black or steel gray.
Price.................$9.95
If by mail, postage extra, 60 cents.

No. 17C2811 THIS PRETTY LADIES' COAT is made of very fine taffeta silk, very stylish, especially adapted for street wear and traveling. Collarless effect. Double breasted front, loose back caught in a belt. White silk trimming around collar and on the cuffs, finished with black silk soutache. Leg of mutton sleeves with shirring at the shoulders and fancy cuffs. Colors, black or steel gray, with white silk trimming. Price $12.75
If by mail, postage extra, 60 cents.

No. 17C2814 THIS BEAUTIFUL COAT is made of very fine taffeta silk, is made full length. Double breasted front, tight back. Collarless effect. Shirring all around the waist reaching from side to side in back. Full leg of mutton sleeves with shirring at shoulders. Fancy cuffs. Wide facing of same material. Very appropriate for street wear and traveling. Colors, black or steel gray, with black and green silk braid trimming.
Price..............$14.75
If by mail, postage extra, 60 cents.

Very Pretty Taffeta Silk Coat, $7.75.

No. 17C2757 VERY PRETTY COAT Made of taffeta silk, 27 inches long, loose back and loose front, collarless effect. Trimmings of silk braid with bow in front, made of taffeta silk and finished with cream colored lace. Leg of mutton sleeves, fancy cuffs trimmed with cream colored lace. Color, black with cream lace.
Price..$7.75
If by mail, postage extra, 35 cents.

Ladies' Pongee Brilliantine Coat, $4.95.

No. 17C2758 LADIES' NOBBY COAT Made of Pongee brilliantine, 30 inches long, loose back and loose front, Monte Carlo style, large collar trimmings of cream color lace around the collar and cuffs, and torchon lace edging on the sleeves. Very neat and attractive garment and very appropriate for evening wear. Color tan only (champagne color)
Price... $4.95
If by mail, postage extra, 40 cents.

A Nobby Coat With Leg of Mutton Sleeves, $8.50.

No. 17C2759 NOBBY LADIES' COAT. Made of good quality taffeta silk, 26 inches long. Full leg of mutton sleeves with shirring at shoulders, fancy cuffs, finished with cream colored lace. Silk braid trimming in front, also a bow finished with lace. Plaits in front and back of jacket. Color, black only with cream colored lace trimmings.
Price..$8.50
If by mail, postage extra, 40 cents.

Ladies' Chang Tong Coat, In Monte Carlo Style, $6.95.

No. 17C2760 LADIES' COAT Made of very fine domestic chang tong, has a nice luster and is durable. Made in rich Monte Carlo style, 32 inches long, loose front and back. Very full collar, edged with cream colored lace, and trimmed with cream colored lace embroidery. Very neat sleeves, fancy turnover cuffs trimmed to match. Very attractive. Color tan (champagne color) only.
Price... $6.95
If by mail, postage extra 45 cents.

Fine Taffeta Silk Coat, With Strap Trimmings, $6.75

No. 17C2762 VERY STYLISH LADIES' JACKET Made of fine taffeta silk, collarless effect, loose back and loose front. Leg of mutton sleeves, fancy cuffs, taffeta strap trimmings, forming a square yoke in front and back, stitched several times. Silk ornaments on cuffs and in front of coat. Color, black only
Price $6.75
If by mail, postage extra, 40c

Serviceable and Stylish Coat; Special Value, Only $10.50

No. 17C2763 STYLISH LADIES' COAT Made of fine peau de soie silk, 32 inches long, Monte Carlo effect, large collar and neat cuffs, richly appliqued Leg of mutton sleeves. Loose back and loose front. Color, black only.
Price, $10.50
If by mail, postage extra, 50c.

A Very Fine Silk Chang Tong Monte Carlo Coat for $7.50.

No. 17C2764 LADIES' JACKET. Made of very fine all silk Chang Tong, 30 inches long, in the popular Monte Carlo style. Shoulder cape effect. Loose front and back. Full sleeves with neat cuffs. Trimmings of silk gimp to match. Fancy streamers in front, finished with tassels. Color, tan (champagne color) only
Price, $7.50
If by mail, postage extra 35 cents.

A Richly Trimmed Jacket for $14.50.

No. 17C2765 THIS PRETTY LADIES' JACKET is made of very fine all silk peau de soie, 30 inches long, loose back and loose front. Entire jacket is plaited. Collarless effect, double breasted front. Richly trimmed with very fine silk ornaments in front. Leg of mutton sleeves, fancy cuffs, trimmed with silk braid. Yoke effect in back. Skeleton lining made of fine white satin which reaches all around the back and faces the front of garment. The inside of coat is edged with neat black and white silk braid. Very elaborate. Color, black only, with white satin lining, as described. Price..$14.50
If by mail, postage extra, 45 cents.

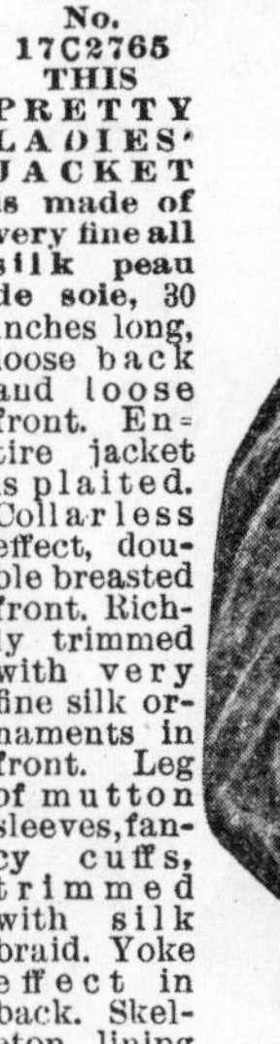

A Very Attractive and Up to Date Coat, Only $13.75.

No. 17C2766 THIS ELABORATE LADIES' COAT is made of very fine peau de soie silk, 32 inches long shawl collar effect, trimmed with very fine cream colored lace Plaited in front and back. Full leg of mutton sleeves, fancy cuffs, trimmed with cream colored lace. Very attractive and strictly up to date. Color, black with cream colored lace trimming.
Price..$13.75
If by mail, postage extra, 55 cents.

Ladies' Capes.

Since the style of sleeves has changed, Ladies' Capes are becoming very popular. They are very handy and appropriate. They always look neat and will keep large sleeves in good condition. We furnish these in sizes 32 to 44 inches around the bust and 12 to 17 inches around the neck. When ordering, be sure to give us bust and neck measurements.

POSTAGE ON THESE CAPES, 25 CENTS.

No. 17C2820 LADIES' CAPE. Made of good quality repellent cloth, 24 inches long. Trimmings of black lace around the collar and yoke. Two ruffles of silk ruching and one row of satin ribbon around the neck. Satin ribbon trimmings in front. Lined throughout with black spun glass. Black only. Price..**$1.75**

No. 17C2823 LADIES' CAPE Made of fancy figured Jap silk, 18 inches long in back. Satin ribbon ruching and lace around neck, satin streamers in front. Lined throughout with black spun glass. Color, black only. Price..........**$1.89**

No. 17C2826 LADIES' CAPE. Made of good quality black ladies' cloth. 24 inches long, richly embroidered with silk soutache and corded, as shown. Satin ribbon and silk ruching around the collar. Satin ribbon streamers in front. Lined with black spun glass. Color, black only. Price..........**$1.98**

No. 17C2829 LADIES' CAPE. Made of all wool clay worsted cloth. 24 inches long, nicely tailored. Neat collar. Black satin bow in back and satin bow in front with satin streamers. Cape lined throughout with black mercerized sateen. Very neat. Color, black only. Price..........**$2.35**

$3.98

No. 17C2832 NEAT LADIES' CAPE. Is made of brocaded satin, 22 inches long, inverted plait in back. Black lace trimming and two rows of black beads around cape forming a yoke. Similar trimming around the neck. Satin ribbon around the neck finished with bow in front and streamers. Lined throughout with black spun glass. Black only. Price..**$2.75**

No. 17C2835 LADIES' CAPE. Made of all wool broadcloth, 26 inches long, richly embroidered with black soutache. Small standing collar. Satin bow in back and in front, also satin streamers. Lined throughout with black mercerized sateen. Very good value for the money. Color, black only. Price..........**$3.25**

No. 17C2838 LADIES' CAPE. Made of all wool clay worsted cloth, 25 inches long, richly trimmed with black silk gauze, satin ribbon and black jet around the yoke and around the neck. Satin ribbon streamers in front. Lined throughout with black mercerized sateen. Neat and up to date. Color, black only. Price..........**$3.50**

No. 17C2841 LADIES' CAPE. Made of very fine all silk peau de soie, 27 inches long richly trimmed with 2-inch wide all silk satin ribbon around the neck, forming a bow in front, also streamers. Lined throughout with black mercerized sateen. Color, black only. Price..........**$3.98**

No. 17C2844 STYLISH LADIES' CAPE. Made of all wool clay worsted cloth, 27 inches long, medium weight. Lined throughout with mercerized sateen. Silk chiffon trimmings around the neck and streamers in front of same material. This chiffon is all fluted and made very fluffy. Color, black only. Price..**$4.35**

No. 17C2847 LADIES' CAPE. Made of very fine all silk peau de soie, 25 inches long. Elaborately trimmed with 1½-inch wide satin ribbon allover. Small standing collar, trimmed with satin ribbon ruching on both sides. Satin ribbon bow in back and front, also streamers of same material. Lined throughout with black mercerized sateen. Very stylish garment. Color, black only. Price..**$4.95**

No. 17C2850 LADIES' TAILOR MADE CAPE. Made of very fine light weight kersey cloth. 30 inches long. Inverted plait in back. Fancy turnover collar. Lined throughout with black mercerized sateen. Very neat and appropriate cape for both old and young. Color, black only. Price..........**$4.95**

No. 17C2853 LADIES' CAPE. Made of very fine all wool broadcloth. 27 inches long. Inverted plait in back. Elaborately embroidered in black silk soutache and trimmings of 1½-inch wide satin ribbon around the neck, and also satin ribbon bow in front finished with streamers. Lined throughout with black mercerized sateen. Very stylish. Color, black only. Price..........**$4.98**

MISSES' JACKETS

WE SHOW A VERY NOBBY LINE of these in up to date materials and splendid styles. While our prices are very low, the styles are the same as the highest priced garments. They are especially adapted for young ladies. We make these in sizes 32, 34, 36 and 38 inches around the bust. When ordering, be sure to state color and size.

No. 17C2862 MISSES' JACKET. Made of poplin cloth. This material looks very much like pongee. Has a nice luster and wears just as well if not better. 26 inches long, collarless effect, made with shoulder capes, double breasted front, loose back with inverted plait and caught in a belt. Bishop sleeves, fancy turnover cuffs. Lined throughout with light blue sateen. Color, tan (champagne) only.
Price........ $2.98
If by mail, postage extra, 40 cents.

No. 17C2865 MISSES' JACKET. Made of all wool covert cloth, 25 inches long, collarless effect, stylish sleeves with puff and fancy cuffs. Patch pockets. Double breasted front, back finished with box plait and a belt. Straps over the shoulders and lapels in front. Facing of same material. No lining. Color, castor only.
Price........ $3.95
If by mail, postage extra, 40 cents.

No. 17C2868 MISSES' JACKET. Made of good quality all silk peau de soie, loose back and loose front. Leg of mutton sleeves, fancy turnover cuffs. Large round collar. Trimmings of black and white silk braid around collar and cuffs. Satin bow in front with long streamers. Color, black only, with black and white braid trimmings. No lining.
Price........ $3.75
If by mail, postage extra, 30 cents.

No. 17C2871 VERY HANDSOME MISSES' JACKET. Made of all wool covert cloth, collarless effect, double breasted front, box back finished with fancy belt with metal buckles, can be easily adjusted. Leg of mutton sleeves, fancy turnover cuffs. Patch pockets. Lined throughout with mercerized sateen to match. Facing in front of same material. Leather colored velvet trimming around the neck and cuffs. Very nobby, special value. Color, castor only.
Price........ $4.50
If by mail, postage extra, 40c.

No. 17C2836 MISSES JACKET. Made of all wool cheviot, 25 inches long; box back and box front, double breasted, fancy metal buttons, belt in back, silk piping around the neck, on pocket flaps and belt; fancy ornament on the imitation collar and embroidered eagle on sleeve. Colors, blue or brown.
Price........ $3.95
If by mail postage extra, 35 cents.

No. 17C2877 MISSES' JACKET. Made of very fine silk peau de soie. 24 inches long, double breasted front, box back finished with a belt. Large turnover collar trimmed with black and white silk braid and black silk medalions, also tailor stitching. Fancy metal buttons in front. Large sleeves, fancy turnover cuffs. Facing in front of same material. Lined throughout with black mercerized sateen. Color, black only.
Price........ $4.95
If by mail, postage extra, 35 cents.

No. 17C2880 MISSES' JACKET. Made of good quality all wool broadcloth, collarless effect. Double breasted front, half fitted back finished with belt. Leg of mutton sleeves, imitation turnover cuffs. Scalloped trimming around the neck. Taffeta silk binding around the scallops as well as over the shoulder flaps, belt and cuffs. Facing in front of same material. Lined throughout with romaine silk. Colors, black, royal blue or Havana brown. **State color when ordering.** Price........ $4.98
If by mail, postage extra, 45 cents.

No. 17C2887 THIS STYLISH MISSES' COAT is made of good quality all wool panne cheviot, 24 inches long, loose back and front, collarless effect, double breasted front fancy metal buttons, belt in back, neat trimmings, broadcloth around the collar and cuffs trimmed with silk soutache; embroidered silk eagle on sleeve. Colors, blue with light blue, or brown with tan trimming at neck.
Price........ $4.50
If by mail, postage extra, 40 cents.

No. 17C2838 SPLENDID VALUE IN FINE MISSES' JACKET. Made of all wool covert cloth, 24 inches long. Double breasted front, loose back, collarless effect, metal button trimmings, facing in front of same material, olive color silk braid around the collar and small silk ornaments; silk embroidered eagle on the sleeve. Color, castor only.
Price........ $4.95
If by mail, postage extra, 40 cents.

No. 17C2874 MISSES' JACKET. Made of very good quality all silk peau de soie. 26 inches long, double breasted front, loose back finished with a fancy belt. Shoulder capes trimmed with black silk snake braid. Puff sleeves, fancy turnover cuffs with silk trimmings. Fancy metal buttons. Lined throughout with light blue sateen. Color, black only.
Price........ $4.75
If by mail, postage extra, 35 cents.

CHILDREN'S COATS.

FOR 6 TO 14-YEAR OLD CHILDREN. FOR SMALLER SIZES, SEE PAGES 948 AND 949.

We carry a very extensive line and we are in position to suit everybody. Our array of styles and colors is magnificent. We can please the little ones at prices that will astonish you. When ordering, always state age and bust measure, also color you desire.

No. 17C2892 CHILD'S REEFER JACKET. Made of all wool ladies' cloth, circular cape, double breasted front, loose back finished with a belt. Trimmings of white soutache, with fancy lace braid around the cape. Puff sleeves, fancy turnover cuffs. Facing of same material. Colors, blue, Havana brown or red. State color when ordering.
Price... **$1.48**

If by mail, postage extra, 20 cents.

No. 17C2901 CHILD'S REEFER. Made of all silk peau de soie, double breasted front, loose back finished with belt. Shoulder capes. Puff sleeves with turnover cuffs. Trimmings of silk rings on the shoulder capes. White silk stitching and white silk cord around collar, cape and cuffs. Pearl buttons. Lined throughout with light blue sateen. Color, black only, with trimmings as described. Price.............. **$3.50**

If by mail, postage extra, 20 cents.

No. 17C2910 CHILD'S THREE-QUARTER COAT. Made of all wool good weight cheviot, double breasted front, box back finished with side plaits and belt. Leg of mutton sleeves, made with puff and fancy turnover cuffs. Gunmetal buttons. Facing of same material in front. Broadcloth trimming around the neck and cuffs finished with silk braid and silk soutache. Very stylish. Colors, blue with red broadcloth, or brown with castor color broadcloth. **State color when ordering.**
Price... .... **$3.75**

If by mail, postage extra, 25 cents.

No. 17C291 CHILD'S THREE-QUARTER COAT. Made of fine all silk peau de soie, double breasted front, loose back with fancy belt. Large circular collar, fancy sleeves with puff, turnover cuffs. Pearl buttons. Trimmings of cream colored lace medallions around collar and white silk stitching. Lined throughout with light blue sateen. Very pretty garment. Color, black only.
Price.......................... **$3.95**

If by mail, postage extra, 30 cents.

No. 17C2895 CHILD'S LONG REEFER COAT. Made of all wool ladies' cloth, double breasted front, box back, finished with a fancy belt. Imitation collar, shoulder capes and straps over shoulders. Puff sleeves, fancy turnover cuffs. Patch pockets. Fancy metal buttons. Trimmings of fancy silk braid around the capes and cuffs, and embroidered silk eagle on sleeve. Lined throughout with sateen. Colors, blue or brown.
Price **$1.75**

If by mail, postage extra, 20 cents.

No. 17C2904 CHILD'S LONG REEFER COAT. Made of all wool covert cloth, collarless effect, double breasted front, loose back made with box and side plaits, finished with fancy belt. Stylish puff sleeves, fancy turnover cuffs. Fancy metal buttons. Facing of same material. Trimmings of brown leather colored broadcloth around the neck. Color, castor only, with trimmings as described. Price.. **$3.35**

If by mail, postage extra, 20 cents.

No. 17C2912 CHILD'S THREE-QUARTER TOP COAT. Made of all wool covert cloth, double breasted front, collarless effect, loose back finished with belt, fancy sleeves with stylish puff and turnover cuffs. Facing in front of same material. Fancy metal buttons. Self trimming around the neck and silk braid forming small circles and green velvet trimming inside of circles. Color, castor only.
Price........... **$3.75**

If by mail, postage extra, 25 cents.

No. 17C2922 CHILD'S THREE-QUARTER COAT. Made of very fine changeable silk, one of the newest ideas and very pretty, made with double breasted front, loose back with fancy belt. Fancy puff sleeves and turnover cuffs. Facing in front of same material. Shoulder capes trimmed with cream color lace embroidery. Lined throughout with light blue sateen. Colors, red green changeable or blue green changeable. **State color when ordering.** Price...................... **$4.95**

If by mail, postage extra, 30 cents.

No. 17C2898 CHILD'S LONG REEFER COAT. Made of all wool covert cloth, collarless effect, double breasted front, box back finished with belt. Stylish sleeves finished with puff, turnover cuffs. Nice gilt button trimmings. Facing in front of same material. Very neat. Color, castor only. Price........................ **$2.75**

If by mail, postage extra, 20 cents.

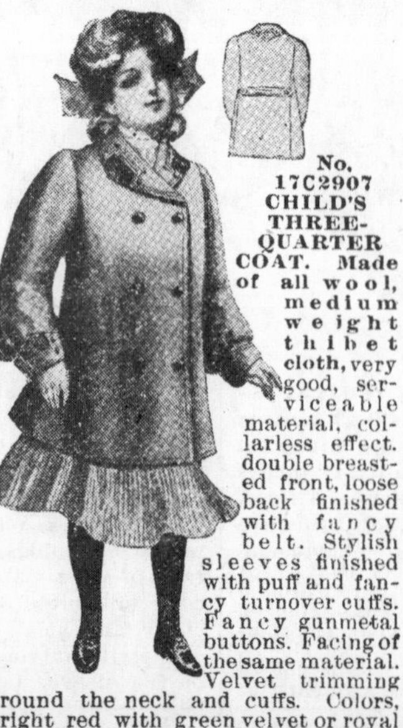

No. 17C2907 CHILD'S THREE-QUARTER COAT. Made of all wool, medium weight thibet cloth, very good, serviceable material, collarless effect, double breasted front, loose back finished with fancy belt. Stylish sleeves finished with puff and fancy turnover cuffs. Fancy gunmetal buttons. Facing of the same material. Velvet trimming around the neck and cuffs. Colors, bright red with green velvet or royal blue with red velvet. Price.... **$3.50**

If by mail, postage extra, 25 cents.

No. 17C2916 CHILD'S THREE-QUARTER TOP COAT. Made of fine all silk peau de soie, double breasted front, loose back finished with fancy belt. Shoulder capes. Pearl buttons. Trimmings of fancy white braid around collar, capes, belt and cuffs. Full puff sleeves. Lined throughout with light blue sateen. Color, black only with white trimming.
Price......... **$3.50**

If by mail, postage extra, 30 cents.

No. 17C2925 CHILD'S THREE-QUARTER COAT. Made of all silk peau de soie, double breasted front, loose finished with belt. Fancy puff sleeves, turnover cuffs. Pearl buttons. Lined throughout with blue sateen. Large collar made of peau de soie silk and stitched with white silk. Lace collar as shown in illustration. Very showy garment. Color, black only, with cream colored lace. Price, **$4.95**

If by mail, postage extra, 30 cents.

LADIES' WASHABLE SHIRT WAIST SUITS.

THE DEMAND FOR LADIES' SHIRT WAIST SUITS HAS INCREASED. They are worn more now than ever before. As we always keep the **most up to date goods** and want to please our customers in every respect, we have increased the line, and today we show the largest line in the country. We have almost every material that shirt waist suits are made of all in the newest patterns and colors. Sizes are for waists, 32 to 42 inches around the bust. The skirts measure from 37 to 44 inches in length and 22 to 29 inches around the waist. No extra sizes. **WHEN ORDERING, BE SURE TO STATE SIZE AND COLOR YOU DESIRE.**

No. 17C2975 LADIES' SHIRT WAIST SUIT. Made of good quality percale in black and white checks. Consists of neat waist with triple plaits in front, forming a yoke. Box plaits and fancy black and white piping around the plaits. The skirt is made very full, with wide hem all around the bottom. Color, black and white checks only.

Price....................**$1.19**

Postage extra, 30 cents.

No. 17C2976 LADIES' SHIRT WAIST SUIT. Made of good quality lawn, consists of neat shirt waist trimmed with tailored straps. Full sleeves, plain cuffs. Detachable crushed collar. Skirt made with very full flaring flounce, wide hem around the bottom. Color, white with black polka dots.

Price....................**$1.25**

Postage extra, 30 cents.

No. 17C2978 VERY NEAT SHIRT WAIST SUIT. Made of good quality solid color percale, yoke effect in front, made with triple plaits. White piping all around the plaits. Side plaits in front from yoke down. Two side plaits in back. Skirt made very neat. Wide hem around the bottom. Colors, blue or tan. State color when ordering.

Price....................**$1.25**

Postage extra, 30 cents.

No. 17C2979 LADIES' SHIRT WAIST SUIT. Made of good quality linen, consists of tailor made shirt waist, yoke effect front, neatly trimmed with straps. Box plait and side plaits on the sleeves. Detachable crushed collar with fancy turnover. Side plaits in back. Skirt is nicely tailored, side plaits on the front gore and strap trimmings of same material. Suit trimmed with pearl buttons. Color, tan only (linen color).

Price....................**$2.35**

Postage extra, 40 cents.

No. 17C2981 THIS PRETTY SHIRT WAIST SUIT is made of good quality grass cloth, consists of swell shirt waist, trimmed with lace insertion and side plaits. Crushed collar, new sleeves, neat cuffs. Side plaits in back. Skirt is richly trimmed to match with lace insertion. Wide hem around the bottom. Color, tan (champagne color) only.

Price....................**$1.98**

Postage extra, 35 cents.

No. 17C2982 THIS PRETTY SUIT is made of good quality grass cloth, waist is richly trimmed with black and tan lace insertion, which is very neat and looks as if ribbon was drawn through the lace. Side plaits and box plaits in front, side plaits on the sleeves. Detachable crushed collar. Side plaits in back. The skirt is trimmed to match with fancy black and cream colored lace. Flounce effect. Very rich in design. Colors, black with tan and black lace, or tan with tan and black lace insertion only.

Price....................**$2.50**

Postage extra, 30 cents.

No. 17C2984 THIS PRETTY TAILOR MADE SHIRT WAIST SUIT is made of good quality percale, consists of nicely tailored waist made with side plaits and trimmed with white cording. Detachable collar, large sleeves, neat cuffs. Side plaits in back. The skirt is also tailored, made with side plaits all around and trimmed with white cording. A beautiful suit and we can highly recommend it. Bound to give good satisfaction. Color, blue only.

Price....................**$2.75**

Postage extra, 35 cents.

No. 17C2985 THIS HANDSOME SHIRT WAIST SUIT, made of very fine lawn, consists of neat waist, nicely tailored, trimmed with straps of same material. Front band and straps are piped with white lawn. Very neat sleeves. Self trimming. Detachable collar. Self trimmed straps in back from neck to waist. Skirt made very full, nicely tailored, richly trimmed with self trimming. Colors, black or dark blue with fancy white figures. Very stylish. State color when ordering.

Price....................**$2.75**

Postage extra, 30 cents.

No. 17C2987 ELEGANT LADIES' SHIRT WAIST SUIT. Made of good quality percale. The waist is richly trimmed with cream color Mexican drawnwork, has several plaits in front and back. Bishop sleeves and trimmings on cuffs. The skirt is trimmed to match and has kilt plaits all around bottom. Color, blue only, with cream trimmings.

Price.............**$2.98**

Postage extra, 35 cents.

No. 17C2988 VERY NOBBY SHIRT WAIST SUIT. Made of good quality white linen. Consists of tailor made shirt waist, neatly trimmed with side plaits in front and on sleeves. Detachable collar with fancy turnover. Pearl buttons in front. Side plaits in back. Skirt is nicely tailored, trimmed with plaits on alternating gores. Color, white only. Price....**$2.98**

Postage extra, 40 cents.

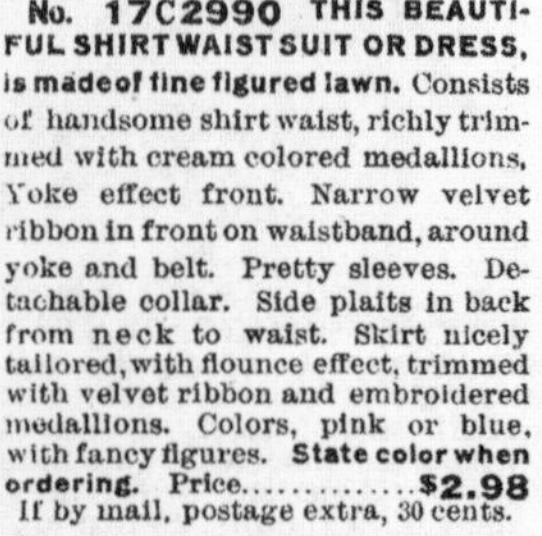

No. 17C2990 THIS BEAUTIFUL SHIRT WAIST SUIT OR DRESS, is made of fine figured lawn. Consists of handsome shirt waist, richly trimmed with cream colored medallions. Yoke effect front. Narrow velvet ribbon in front on waistband, around yoke and belt. Pretty sleeves. Detachable collar. Side plaits in back from neck to waist. Skirt nicely tailored, with flounce effect, trimmed with velvet ribbon and embroidered medallions. Colors, pink or blue, with fancy figures. **State color when ordering.** Price..............**$2.98**
If by mail, postage extra, 30 cents.

No. 17C2991 THIS ELEGANT LADIES' SHIRT WAIST SUIT, made of good quality white linen, strictly tailored, consists of nice shirt waist, of which the yoke front is richly tucked and trimmed with openwork embroidery insertion. Detachable collar. Side plaits on the sleeves and side plaits in back from neck to waist. The skirt is trimmed to match, with tucks and embroidered insertion. Nicely tailored and made very full. Color, white only.
Price..............**$3.25**
If by mail, postage extra, 35 cents.

No. 17C2993 ONE OF THE PRETTIEST SHIRT WAIST SUITS SHOWN. Made of very fine madras cloth. Consists of a stylish shirt waist with plaits, white piping, and circular embroidery trimmings. Very full sleeves, side plaits in back from neck to waist. The skirt is nicely tailored, made with side plaits all around. Very full. Special value, strictly up to date. Colors, blue or ecru (light shade of tan), with trimmings to match.
Price..............**$3.98**
If by mail, postage extra, 40 cents.

No. 17C2994 THIS BEAUTIFUL SHIRT WAIST SUIT OR DRESS. Made of very fine dimity in beautiful Dolly Varden pattern. Consists of handsome shirt waist with circular yoke in front, large shoulder cape neatly trimmed with lace insertion. Large sleeves made with fancy cuffs also trimmed with lace. Round yoke in back. This waist buttons in back only. The skirt is made very full on double flounce style. Lace insertion over each flounce. Very pretty; good value. Color, white with rose or violet figures. **State color when ordering.** Price..............**$3.75**
If by mail, postage extra, 35 cents.

No. 17C2995 THIS HANDSOME SHIRT WAIST SUIT OR DRESS is made of very fine Luzon Ponge. It consists of a beautiful shirt waist, made with fancy circular yoke. Shoulder cape trimmed with lace insertions, and side plaits in front from yoke to waist. Full sleeves, fancy cuffs. Stylish collar. Yoke in back. This waist buttons in back only. The skirt is extremely stylish, has a double flounce, nicely trimmed with lace insertion and shirring over each flounce. Very handsome. Color, tan (champagne color) only. **State color when ordering.** Price..............**$4.95**
If by mail, postage extra, 40 cents.

SAILOR SUITS

ARE VERY POPULAR AND WE SHOW A BEAUTIFUL LINE OF THEM. They are especially adapted for young ladies. Sizes from 32 to 38 inches around the bust, 36 to 44 inches length of skirt, and 22 to 30 inches around the waist.

STATE COLOR AND SIZE WHEN ORDERING. NO EXTRA SIZES.

No. 17C2997 MISSES' WASH SUIT. Made of tan grass cloth. Consists of skirt and sailor blouse made with a large sailor collar. White dickey in front embroidered with an anchor. Anchor embroidery on right sleeve. The collar and bow in front are bound in red. Belt of same material with a postilion back. Skirt is trimmed with red piping on side plaits on each seam. For 14, 16 and 18-year old young ladies, measuring 32, 34 and 36 inches around the bust, respectively. Skirt lengths, 36 to 40 inches, only. Color, tan only, with red trimmings.
Price..............**$1.95**
If by mail, postage extra, 35 cents.

No. 17C2998 THIS PRETTY SAILOR SUIT is made of good quality madras cloth, consists of nice sailor waist with large collar with inlaid front or dickey. Stylish sleeves. Plaits on cuffs and on waist in front. Embroidered anchor on the dickey and on the sleeves. Skirt is nicely tailored, and very full. French seams all around. Wide hem around the bottom. Bow of the same material in front. Colors, blue or oxblood.
Price..............**$2.35**
If by mail, postage extra, 35 cents.

No. 17C3000 THIS HANDSOME SAILOR SUIT is made of good quality linen finished percale. Consists of stylish sailor waist with inlaid front, otherwise called dickey. Trimmings of white cording on the front and around the collar, as well as on the cuffs. Large sleeves. Embroidered anchor in front and silk embroidered eagle on the sleeves. Silk stars on the collar in back. Skirt is nicely tailored, made with side plaits and trimmed with three rows of cording around the bottom. Color, blue with white trimming.
Price..............**$2.98**
If by mail, postage extra, 35 cents.

No. 17C3003 THIS HANDSOME SAILOR SUIT is made of fine grass cloth. Consists of blouse sailor waist with large sailor collar, richly trimmed with three rows of cording. Tie in front of same material. Pointed yoke effect. Cord trimming on the sleeves, on the tie and around the collar. Large sleeves. Silk embroidered anchor in front and eagle embroidered on the sleeves. The skirt is nicely tailored and is made with side plaits all around, trimmed around bottom with three rows of cording. Color, tan only, with red trimmings.
Price..............**$2.25**
If by mail, postage extra, 35 cents.

No. 17C3004 HANDSOME SUIT. Made of good quality white linen. Consists of beautiful sailor waist. Stylish collar trimmed with straps of same material, side plaits in front, neat cuffs, large sleeves. Silk embroidered anchor on inlaid front and American eagle embroidered in silk on sleeves. Silk embroidered stars on the collar. Very rich. Skirt is nicely tailored and has side plaits all around with wide hem around the bottom. Beautiful garment, strictly up to date, and we can highly recommend it. Color, white, with light blue or red silk embroideries.
Price..............**$3.50**
If by mail, postage extra, 40 cents.

No. 17C3005 LADIES' TAILOR MADE SHIRT WAIST SUIT, of good quality white lawn. Waist is neatly tailored, finished with side plaits all over the front and plait in back. Full sleeves with plain cuffs. Detachable crushed collar with tab. Full skirt made with side plaits on front gore, finished with wide hem around the bottom. Color, white only.
Price....................**$1.45**
Postage extra, 30 cents.

No. 17C3006 THIS PRETTY SHIRT WAIST SUIT is made of good quality French lawn. Consists of tailor made shirt waist, the entire front made with side plaits and shirt band of nice Swiss embroidery. Detachable collar with fancy turnover. The skirt is trimmed to match, with embroidery and hem stitching. Side plaits all around. Colors, black or white only. Price............**$1.98**
Postage extra, 30 cents.

No. 17C3007 THIS PRETTY SHIRT WAIST SUIT is made of very fine imported French lawn. Consists of nicely made waist, richly trimmed with tucks. Very full cape trimmed with plaits. This waist buttons in back only. Has full sleeves, neat cuffs. Skirt is nicely tailored side plaited all around. Wide hem around the bottom. Splendid value. Color, white only. Price............**$2.35**
Postage extra, 35 cents.

No. 17C3009 THIS PRETTY LADIES' SHIRT WAIST SUIT is made of imported French lawn. Consists of richly trimmed waist, with embroidery in front, also tucks and small medallions. Full sleeves. Side plaits in back. Skirt is made very full, trimmed with embroidery. Flounce effect. Beautiful garment for the money. Wide hem around the bottom. Color, white only. Price......**$2.98**
Postage extra, 35 cents.

No. 17C3010 LADIES' SHIRT WAIST SUIT. Made of fine imported French lawn. Consists of stylish waist richly tailored, trimmed with tucks. Round yoke in front finished with insertion of embroidery. Shoulder piece trimmed with fancy medallions and edged with lace all around. Waist buttons in back only. Skirt trimmed to match, with openwork embroidery. Very stylish, well made, strictly up to date. Color, white only. Price.**$3.50**
If by mail, postage extra, 35 cents.

SICILIAN AND SATEEN SHIRT WAIST SUITS.

No. 17C3012 LADIES' SHIRT WAIST SUIT. Made of good quality fancy figured sateen, consists of nicely tailored waist which is trimmed with straps of same material. Side plaits, detachable collar, full sleeves, plaits in back from neck to waist. Nicely tailored skirt with flounce effect. Side plaits all around and trimmed with straps of same material. Colors, black, blue or brown.
Price................**$1.98**
Postage extra, 40 cents.

No. 17C3014 LADIES' SHIRT WAIST SUIT. Made of good quality percale. Specially adapted for second mourning. Consists of nicely tailored shirt waist trimmed with straps of black sateen. Detachable collar with black sateen piping all around. Nice sleeves, neat cuffs, small plaits in back from neck to waist. Skirt is trimmed to match, with black sateen straps, nicely tailored, very full. Foot plaits and wide hem around the bottom. Color, black with small white figures.
Price.... ....**$2.75**
Postage extra, 35 cents.

No. 17C3015 LADIES' SHIRT WAIST SUIT. Made of good quality Sicilian cloth, consists of tailor made waist trimmed with side plaits, detachable collar with fancy turnover, full sleeves, stylish cuffs. Silk button trimmings in front. Box plait from neck to waist. Skirt nicely tailored, made with side plaits all around and foot plaits around the bottom. Very pretty. Colors, black, blue, white or brown.
Price...... ....**$4.95**
Postage extra, 40 cents.

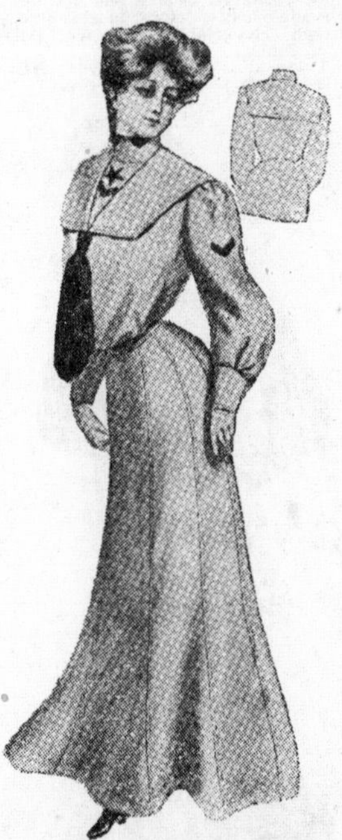

No. 17C3016 THIS HANDSOME SAILOR SUIT is made of good quality high luster Sicilian cloth. Very pretty. Consists of swell sailor blouse with full collar, the necktie of silk and silk embroidery in front and on sleeve, as shown in illustration. Skirt is nicely tailored, made with French seams all around the bottom. Beautiful garment. We can furnish this suit in white with light blue trimming, in brown with light blue trimming and navy blue with red trimming. State color when ordering.
Price....................**$5.75**
Postage extra, 40 cents.

No. 17C3017 BEAUTIFUL SHIRT WAIST SUIT. Made of very fine imported fancy figured Sicilian. Consists of tailor made shirt waist with side plait trimmings. Full sleeves, neat cuffs and side plaits in back. The two front plaits are piped with silk and also has a silk bow. The skirt is highly tailored, trimmed to match the waist, with side plaits and piping. Very elaborate and special value. Colors, all black, navy with green silk trimming, or brown with burnt orange trimming.
Price..................**$6.95**
Postage extra, 45 cents.

SILK SHIRT WAIST SUITS.

WE WILL ESPECIALLY CALL YOUR ATTENTION to this line which we think is the finest, newest and prettiest. Special attention was paid to the selection of styles, materials and colors. Silk shirt waist suits are the proper thing for up to date ladies. They are dressy, comfortable and reasonable in price.

WE SELL SILK SHIRT WAIST SUITS from $2.50 to $5.00 less than you could buy them for elsewhere. We will be pleased to send you samples of silks on application. We make these suits 32 to 42 inches around the bust, 37 to 44 inches length of skirts and 22 to 30 inches around the waist.

BE SURE to state SIZE and COLOR when ordering. Sizes differing from these will be made to order at an advance of 20 per cent above catalogue price.

No. 17C3019 THIS SHIRT WAIST SUIT is made of taffeta silk, stylish tailor made waist with side plaits. Side plaits on the sleeves, fancy cuffs. Detachable collar with fancy turnover. Tailor made skirt to match. Side plaits all around and wide hem around the bottom. **Our special leader** and sold at a special price. Colors, blue and black changeable, brown and black changeable, or all black. State color when ordering.
Price....................**$9.95**
If by mail, postage extra, 35 cents.

No. 17C3020 THIS HANDSOME SHIRT WAIST SUIT is made of very fine taffeta silk and consists of nicely tailored waist with tucks in front forming the yoke. Small silk covered buttons in front. Tucks on full sleeves, neat cuffs. Detachable collar with fancy bow and tucks in back from neck to waist. The skirt is nicely tailored, French seams and foot plaits all around the bottom. Crushed belt. Colors, black, blue, green changeable or black red changeable.
Price....................**$10.50**
If by mail, postage extra, 40 cents.

No. 17C3022 THIS PRETTY SHIRT WAIST SUIT, made of fine taffeta silk, consists of stylish waist richly trimmed with plaits and gilt buttons. V shaped front made of lace. Crushed collar with lace ruching all around. Very full sleeves, neat cuffs. Plaits in back from neck to waist. The skirt is nicely tailored, made with side plaits all around and foot plaits around the bottom. Elegant garment for the money. Colors, blue or brown with cream colored lace.
Price....................**$10.75**
If by mail, postage extra, 40 cents.

No. 17C3023 THIS HANDSOME LADIES' SHIRT WAIST SUIT is made of very fine changeable taffeta silk, consists of nicely tailored waist made with tucks and very full in front. Full sleeves and fancy cuffs. Detachable collar and necktie of fancy plaid silk to match the waist. Very handsome garment. Skirt is nicely tailored and made with foot plaits around the bottom. Crushed belt. Colors, all black, blue black changeable, brown black changeable. **State color when ordering.**
Price.................. ...**$11.95**
If by mail, postage extra, 40 cents.

No. 17C3025 LADIES' SHIRT WAIST SUIT. Made of very fine taffeta silk, consists of richly tailored waist made with side plaits. Yoke effect, fancy rosette trimmings. Very full sleeves, shirred, neat cuffs. Tuck in back. Skirt is nicely tailored, kilted all around the bottom in graduated effect. Belt to match. Very attractive garment. Good value for the money. Colors, black, royal blue or golden brown.
Price....................**$11.50**
If by mail, postage extra, 40 cents.

No. 17C3028 THIS PRETTY SHIRT WAIST SUIT is made of very fine polka dot taffeta silk, consists of nicely tailored shirt waist which is made with plaits. Very full sleeves, detachable collar, neat cuffs. The cuffs, collar and the front are trimmed with solid color silk to match the suit, gilt buttons and fancy colored piping on both sides. The combination of colors is very beautiful. The skirt is nicely tailored, kilted plaits all around the bottom and nice crushed belt to go around the waist. Colors, black, blue or brown with white polka dots.
Price....................**$12.75**
If by mail, postage extra, 40 cents.

No. 17C3030 THIS PRETTY SHIRT WAIST SUIT is made of very fine black and white checked taffeta silk, and consists of very full waist richly trimmed with tucks in front forming the yoke. Detachable collar with nice black tie caught in collar, as shown in illustration. Full sleeves, fancy cuffs. Tucks in back. Very handsome garment. Big black button trimmings in front. Skirt is made with kilt plaits all around the bottom. Crushed belt to go around the waist. Colors, black and white or blue and white, small checks only.
Price....................**$11.75**
If by mail, postage extra, 40 cents.

No. 17C3031 THIS HANDSOME SUIT is made of good quality taffeta silk, consists of highly tailored shirt waist with side and box plaits in front. Broad shoulder effect. Shirring on sleeves as shown in picture, fancy cuffs. Detachable collar with fancy bow in front. Side plaits in back. Skirt is made to match. Very full. Shirring as shown with silk trimmings on both sides. Colors golden brown, tan or black. **State color when ordering.**
Price....................**$13.50**
If by mail, postage extra, 40 cents.

No. 17C3032 LADIES SHIRT WAIST SUIT. Made of very fine taffeta silk, consists of very fine tailor made waist, side plaits in front forming yoke, making it very full. Detachable collar with fancy turnover. Full sleeves, neat cuffs. Side plaits in back. The skirt is well tailored, kilted plaits around the bottom, trimmed to match the waist. Fancy zigzag trimming on skirt and front of waist piped with different colored silk. Colors, golden brown black changeable with green trimmings, blue black changeable with burnt orange trimming, and all black.
Price....................**$14.50**
If by mail, postage extra, 40 cents.

No. 17C3034 ONE OF THE PRETTIEST SUITS EVER SHOWN. Made of very fine taffeta silk. Consists of splendid style waist richly trimmed with lace on the sleeves and fancy cuffs all covered with lace to match. Stylish back. Shirring from shoulder to shoulder making it very full. Skirt is nicely tailored, trimmed to match the waist. Shirring on the side gores and trimmed with small silk ornaments. Colors, golden brown with tan piping on the cuffs, around collar and in front, black with white piping and blue with burnt orange piping. **State color when ordering.** Price...**$18.75**
If by mail, postage extra, 40 cents.

LADIES' WASHABLE SKIRTS.

We make these skirts from 37 to 44 inches in length and 22 to 30 inches around the waist. We cannot make any extra sizes in washable skirts. State color and size when ordering.

No. 17C3037 LADIES' WASH SKIRT. Made of washable duck, fancy embroidery in front, wide hem around the bottom. Colors, black or blue with white polka dots. State color when ordering.
Price.............................75c
If by mail, postage extra, 20 cents.

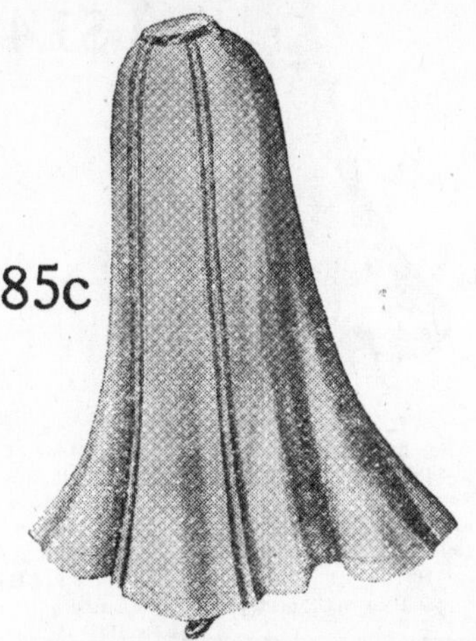

No. 17C3038 LADIES' WASH SKIRT. Made of good quality cotton crash, nicely tailored. Made with double side plait in front and trimmed with fancy brown and white cord to match. Very neat. Color, tan only.
Price.............................85c
If by mail, postage extra, 20 cents.

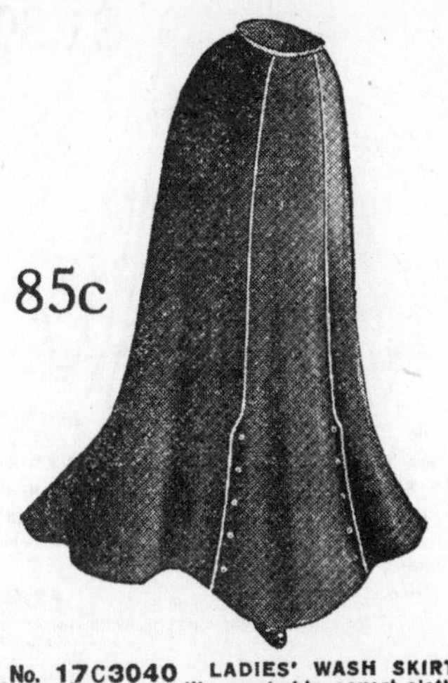

No. 17C3040 LADIES' WASH SKIRT. Made of good quality washable covert cloth, nicely tailored. The front seams are piped with white material and trimmed with small pearl buttons. Wide hem around the bottom. Colors, blue or brown. State color when ordering.
Price.............................85c
If by mail, postage extra, 25 cents.

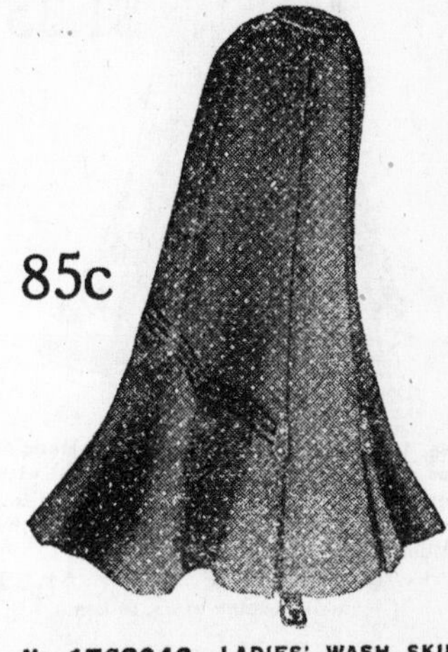

No. 17C3042 LADIES' WASH SKIRT. Made of fancy polka dot duck, nicely tailored and trimmed with small straps of same material and a strap of solid color material to match. Wide hem around the bottom. Colors, black or blue with white polka dots. State color when ordering. Price.............................85c
If by mail, postage extra, 20 cents.

No. 17C3043 LADIES' SKIRT. Made of good quality washable covert cloth, nicely tailored. Entire skirt is corded as shown in illustration. Wide hem around the bottom. Trimmed with self covered buttons. Colors, tan or blue. State color when ordering.
Price.............................89c
If by mail, postage extra, 30 cents.

No. 17C3045 VERY PRETTY SKIRT. Made of good quality washable fancy crash mixture. This material looks very much like woolen cloth and comes in very pretty patterns. Nicely tailored, French seams all around. Colors, tan or blue. State color when ordering.
Price.............................89c
If by mail, postage extra, 25 cents.

No. 17C3046 LADIES' SKIRT. Made of good quality mercerized sateen, trimmed with neat fancy braid. Very full and hem around the bottom. Color, black only, with white polka dots. State color when ordering.
Price.............................89c
If by mail, postage extra, 25 cents.

No. 17C3047 LADIES' WASH SKIRT. Made of good quality cotton crash, richly embroidered, as shown in illustration. Hem around the bottom. Color, tan only, with fancy embroidery.
Price.............................89c
If by mail, postage extra, 30 cents.

No. 17C3049 LADIES' SKIRT. Made of good quality washable covert cloth, richly trimmed with fancy braid and embroidery in very neat design, giving it a flounce effect. Hem around the bottom. Colors, blue or gray. State color when ordering.
Price.............................98c
If by mail, postage extra, 25 cents.

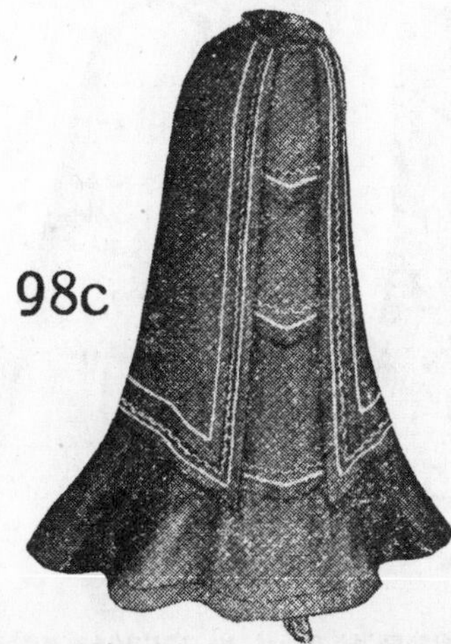

No. 17C3050 LADIES' WASH SKIRT. Made of good quality solid color washable duck, trimmed with fancy braid and plaits made of same material. Color, navy blue with white piping and fancy braid trimming.
Price.............................98c
If by mail, postage extra, 25 cents.

No. 17C3052 LADIES' STYLISH WASH SKIRT. Made of washable duck, neatly tailored skirt, with three plaits on both sides, trimmed with straps to match. Straps are piped in white, button trimmings. Colors, black or blue, with white polka dots.
Price.............................$1.15
If by mail, postage extra, 27 cents.

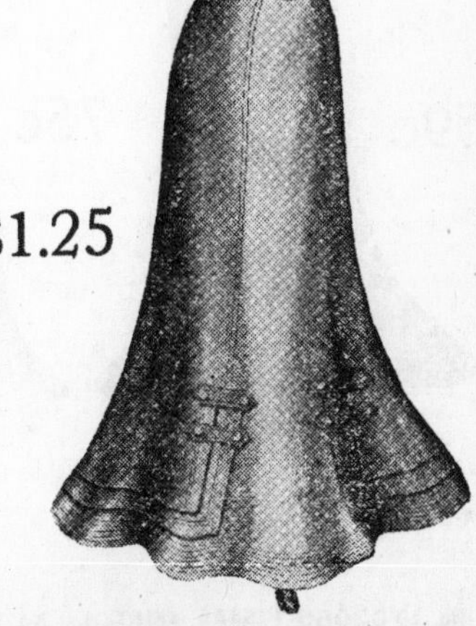

No. 17C3053 LADIES' SKIRT. Made of good quality washable covert cloth, nicely tailored, richly trimmed with straps of same material. Several rows of stitching around the bottom. Very attractive and up to date. Good value for the money. Colors, blue or brown. State color when ordering. Price....$1.25
If by mail, postage extra, 25 cents.

No. 17C3055 LADIES' SKIRT. Made of good quality white pique, richly trimmed with openwork embroidery on the alternating gores. Very pretty. Wide hem around the bottom. Color, white only.
Price..**$1.35**
If by mail, postage extra, 30 cents.

No. 17C3056 THIS NOBBY LADIES' SKIRT is made of good quality butcher linen. Very latest thing for this season, nicely tailored, made with kilt seams all around. French seams on every gore. Color, white only.
Price..**$1.39**
If by mail, postage extra, 30 cents.

$1.48

No. 17C3058 LADIES' SKIRT. Made of good quality washable bedford cord. This is a very fine cloth. Nicely tailored, French seams all around, kilt plaits around the bottom Color, tan or white.
Price..**$1.48**
If by mail, postage extra, 30 cents.

No. 17C3059 LADIES' SKIRT. Made of fancy mixed washable crash material. This cloth is very pretty and up to date. Nicely tailored, French seams, graduated kilt plaits all around the bottom. Very pretty garment. Colors, tan, with blue mixture, or tan with green mixture. State color when ordering.
Price..**$1.48**
If by mail, postage extra, 30 cents.

No. 17C3061 THIS PRETTY LADIES' SKIRT is made of good quality fancy washable crash. Is nicely tailored, side plaits on the two front gores, trimmed with straps of same material and small pearl buttons. Kilt plaits all around the skirt. Colors, tan with blue and green or red and green overplaids. Always state color when ordering. Price......**$1.75**
If by mail, postage extra, 30 cents.

No. 17C3062 LADIES' WASH SKIRT. Made of good quality heavy weight white pique. Nicely trimmed with embroidered insertions, as shown in illustration. Very stylish, well made garment. Color, white only.
Price..**$1.98**
If by mail, postage extra, 30 cents.

No. 17C3063 LADIES' SKIRT. Made of good quality linen crash, nicely tailored, richly trimmed with box plait and side plaits. New flounce effect, lace insertion. Very attractive. Color, tan only.
Price..**$2.35**
If by mail, postage extra, 30 cents.

No. 17C3064 THIS HANDSOME LADIES' SKIRT is made of very fine all linen crash, richly trimmed with side plaits all around the bottom; plaits all around the hips; lace insertion in front; very wide hem around the bottom. Color, tan only.
Price..**$2.95**
If by mail, postage extra, 30 cents.

MISSES' WASHABLE SKIRTS.

We Make These in 28 to 36 Inches Length and 20 to 26 Inches Around the Waist. When Ordering, Please State Age, Waist and Length Measure and Color you Desire. No Extra Sizes.

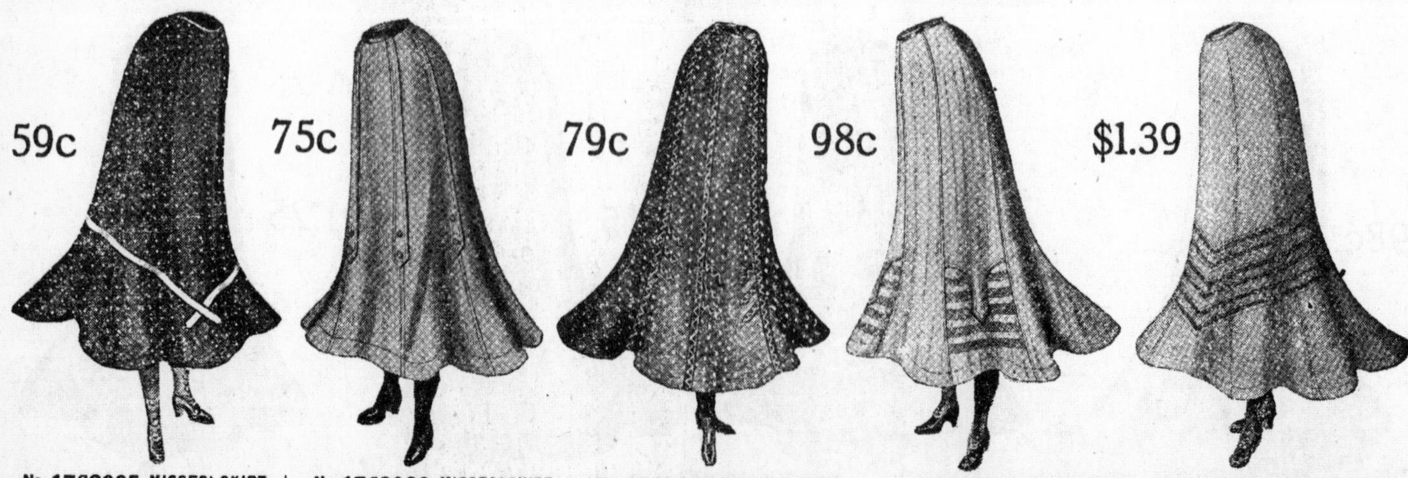

No. 17C3065 MISSES' SKIRT. Made of washable fancy polka dot duck, trimmed with a white strap as shown in picture. Tailor made seams Color, blue with white polka dots.
Price..**59c**
If by mail, postage extra, 20 cents

No. 17C3066 MISSES' SKIRT. Made of good quality washable cotton covert cloth, nicely tailored, trimmed with straps of same material and small pearl buttons. Facing of same material around the bottom. Colors, blue or brown.
Price..**75c**
If by mail, postage extra, 20 cents.

No. 17C3067 MISSES' SKIRT. Made of good washable polka dot duck. Trimmed with straps to match, which are finished with faggot stitching. Very neat. Color, blue with white polka dots.
Price..**79c**
If by mail, postage extra 20 cents.

No. 17C3068 MISSES' SKIRT. Made of good quality washable linen crash. This material is very pretty and comes in fancy mixtures woven right in the cloth. Side gores are neatly tailored and trimmed with fancy braid to match. Colors, tan and fancy overplaids. Price...**98c**
If by mail, postage extra, 20 cents.

No. 17C3069 MISSES' SKIRT. Made of good quality washable bedford cloth. This material is very fine. Skirt is nicely tailored and richly trimmed with openwork lace to match, forming a point in center. Very stylish garment. Colors, tan or white. Price............**$1.39**
If by mail, postage extra, 20 cents.

LADIES' MAN TAILORED SUITS

FOR THE SAME PRICES OR LESS THAN YOU WOULD PAY ELSEWHERE FOR READY MADE SUITS

A NEW AND SPECIAL DEPARTMENT. We have now started a department of ladies' made to order (according to exact measurements you send in) strictly man tailored suits, the equal in up to date style of tailored suits made in large cities at prices ranging from $25.00 to $100.00 (our prices less than half of these prices) and our customers now have the advantage of having a stunning, fashionable tailor suit, made to order, and thus wearing something entirely different from what you will find in your own town, a suit that will have the stamp of fashion, and we make such a suit for you for the same money and in a good many cases for less money than most stores ask for ready made suits.

WE REQUIRE TEN DAYS' TIME to make these made to measure tailor suits. We do not ask any longer time than your tailor at home or the suit department of any city store would ask. It requires ten days' time for us to make and ship your suit and if you are willing to wait this long (no one could make a tailor made suit in less time) and you want something very stylish and at an extremely low price that will mean a big saving to you, send us your order as selected from the following styles.

THESE MADE TO ORDER SUITS are made by first class man tailors. They are experts, highly skilled and well paid bench tailors, the only kind who are able to put into a made to order suit that high class workmanship that gives it a distinctiveness. You can depend upon the styles being correct. The illustrations will give you some idea of the styles but it is impossible with the limited space we are allowed and the limitations of our thin catalogue paper to do justice to these garments by means of illustrations. We can only say that the garments are far handsomer than the pictures lead you to believe.

FOR THESE MAN TAILORED, MADE TO ORDER SUITS we have paid particular attention to the selection of the materials and we are using only the best wearing cloths in the very newest shades. The cloths are thoroughly sponged, shrunk and carefully inspected before the material is cut. The linings are selected with the greatest care and are better in quality than you can get in suits that are sold by others at anything like the same price. We guarantee as far as styles are concerned, nothing newer or more up to date will be shown this season. We can make these suits only of the materials described, so please do not ask us to select any other material. The goods are first class in every respect and each is adapted to the style in which we make it and the trimmings are carefully matched to the color and texture of the material so that the combination of material, style, trimmings, etc., is the best to be had, carefully studied out by us and we cannot make any changes. The only change we would make is in the length of the skirts. Some of our suits are described with walking length skirt and others with dress skirt. We will change the style of the skirt regarding the length without charging anything extra.

ABOUT THE FIT. WE POSITIVELY GUARANTEE TO FIT YOU PERFECTLY and we will take all the chances. All you need is to give us your measurements carefully taken as stated below and we will make and send the suit to you with the understanding that if it does not fit you and please you perfectly, you are under no obligation to accept it, but it can be returned to us at our expense and we will promptly return your money. We have described the materials carefully and you can order direct from the catalogue. However, if you feel you must see samples first, we will send them free on application, if you state the number in which you are interested.

WE PREFER that you fill out one of our regular order blanks which shows all the measurements required, but if you do not have one of these order blanks convenient and do not care to wait to write for order blanks, simply state the following measurements plainly.

FOR THE JACKET, state bust measure taken entirely around the body under the arms over fullest part in front and well up over the shoulder blades in back; state the waist measure entirely around smallest part at waist; hip measure entirely around body at hips, fullest measure taken about six inches below the waist line; number of inches across the back from shoulder seam to shoulder seam; length of waist in back measuring from collar seam to waist line; the sleeve length, inside sleeve seam from armhole to wrist with arm extended straight; armholes, around shoulder where the sleeve is sewed in. Neck, all around neck at dress collar and at bottom of collar, not too tight.

FOR THE SKIRT, state the waist and hip measure as just explained and also the length of skirt in front from bottom of waist line to the bottom of the skirt.

TAKE THESE MEASURES CAREFULLY. It will help us also if you state your height and weight, and we will guarantee a perfect fit. If you have any doubt about taking these measurements correctly, write for special order blanks with diagrams and more complete instructions.

AT THE PRICES QUOTED we make these tailor made suits from 32 inches to 42 inches bust measure, and 22 inches to 29 inches waist measure and 37 inches to 44 inches skirt measure. For sizes larger than these, we must charge 20 per cent above the prices quoted because we have figured the material and everything very close and larger sizes require more material, trimming, etc. Remember it takes at least ten days (from ten to fourteen days) to make these suits.

$3.98

$7.50

$10.50

$7.50

No. 31C3132 WE HAVE A FEW SMALL LOTS OF LADIES' SUITS that we will sell at $3.98. They are made of black, blue and brown repellent cloth, venetian cloth and cheviots. Styles, similar to illustration, some blouse, some with loose fronts. We will sell these at a loss to clean up all our odds and ends. Order at once, before the lots are sold. Sizes from 32 to 42 inches around the bust and 38 to 42 inches length of skirts only. No extra sizes. Price............$3.98

No. 31C3078 THIS ATTRACTIVE SUIT is made of good quality repellent cloth and consists of a very neat collarless blouse, made with leg of mutton sleeves and fancy cuffs, Peplum below the waist. Satin fold trimming in front and back. Lined throughout with mercerized serge. The skirt is well tailored, trimmed to match blouse. Colors, black, blue, oxford or brown.
Price............$7.50

No. 31C3079 LADIES' MAN TAILORED SUIT. Made of all wool cheviot, consists of swell coat 24 inches long, collarless effect, self trimming, also self covered buttons. Stylish sleeves, fancy cuffs stitched several times. Neat trimmings around the neck. Taffeta silk trimmings at the end of straps in back and front of coat. Lined throughout with satin. The skirt is very neat; nicely tailored, French seams all around, trimmings of self straps and taffeta silk and kilt plaits all around the bottom. Colors, black, blue or brown.
Price............$10.50

No. 31C3080 THIS NEAT TAILOR MADE SUIT is made of all wool cheviot, very popular in style. It embodies all new features and it is very neat in appearance. Consists of nicely tailored jacket, coat collar and lapels, leg of mutton sleeves and fancy cuffs. Fly front and fitted back. Facing of same material and lining of mercerized serge. Skirt is neatly tailored and trimmed with two straps on the front gores. Colors, black, blue or brown.
Price............$7.50

No. 31C3081 NOBBY LADIES' SUIT. Made of fine all wool thibet cloth; consists of stylish jacket and well tailored skirt. Jacket is lined throughout with taffeta silk, collarless effect. Trimmings of taffeta silk in front and piping all around the neck and in front. Half fitted back trimmed to match front. Stylish sleeves with full pouch and taffeta silk piping. Fancy metal buttons. Skirt is nicely tailored, made with French seams all around and trimmed with silk soutache and piping. Very attractive. Colors, black or royal blue. In ordering, be sure to give measurements and color wanted.
Price........................ **$10.50**

No. 31C3082 PRETTY TAILORED SUIT. Made of all wool panne cheviot, consists of swell tailored blouse, collarless, neatly trimmed with straps of same material, silk buttons and fancy silk braid in front. Leg of mutton sleeves with shirring at shoulders. Very pretty sleeves. Peplum from waist down. Blouse lined with good quality satin. Skirt is neatly tailored, made with lap seams and foot plaits around the bottom. Colors black, blue or brown. Price .. **$10.50**

No. 31C3083 THIS ELABORATE LADIES' SUIT is made of fine all wool cheviot and consists of a nicely tailored jacket with small standing collar, extension over the shoulders, side plaits in front, finished with a belt which reaches to back. Very pretty sleeves. Taffeta silk piping in front, around shoulder capes and on sleeves. Back made to match front with side plaits. This jacket is double breasted and has a fitted back. Lined throughout with satin. The skirt is elaborately trimmed with side plaits, each plait bound with taffeta silk. Silk soutache all around bottom. Several rows of stitching at bottom. All seams bound; no lining in this skirt. Colors, black or blue.
Price........................ **$11.50**

No. 31C3084 THIS ATTRACTIVE SUIT is made of all wool fancy mixtures, consists of very neat blouse which is made with full leg of mutton sleeves, shirred at shoulders. Collarless effect. Fancy trimming around the neck all the way down the front. Attractive cuffs. Full peplum. Lined throughout with silk romain. Skirt is neatly tailored, trimmed to match the blouse, made with plaits around the bottom. Colors, gray or brown mixtures. Price **$12.50**

No. 31C3086 VERY SWELL LADIES' SUIT. Made of fine all wool cheviot serge; consists of fancy blouse lined with silk romain. Leg of mutton sleeves, fancy cuffs. Full blouse in front. Peplum below the waist. The trimmings are silk braid in front and fancy braid around edges in front. Skirt is well tailored with lap seams and foot plaits all around bottom. An entirely new design. Colors, black, blue or brown.
Price........................ **$12.50**

No. 31C3088 THIS HANDSOME LADIES' SUIT, is made of very fine all wool Panama; consists of beautiful blouse and a tailor made skirt. The jacket is made to blouse in back and front. Collarless effect. Trimmed with plaits. Full leg of mutton sleeves with shirring at shoulders. Fancy cuffs. Silk around the neck, stitched several times, and fancy silk braid all around the front. Crushed belt around the waist. Lined throughout with taffeta silk. The skirt is nicely tailored, made with three strap seams in front and three full side plaits. Colors, black, blue or brown. Price... **$15.75**

No. 31C3089 VERY PRETTY TAILOR MADE WALKING SUIT, of all wool mixed suiting. Consists of a neat jacket, 27 inches long, collarless, neatly trimmed with tailored plaits in front and in back. Leg of mutton sleeves, with shirring at shoulders, and neat cuffs. Solid color broadcloth trimming around cuffs and neck. Jacket lined throughout with taffeta silk. Skirt is made with eleven gores, side plaited all around. One of the newest 1905 styles. Colors, black, blue, brown or green mixtures. Price **$13.50**

No. 31C3094 LADIES' TAILOR MADE SUIT. Made of fine all wool cheviot, consisting of blouse jacket, which is made single breasted, collarless effect, shoulder cape. Cape is edged with taffeta silk and trimmed with silk cord and military buttons, silk medallions and tassels in front. Bishop sleeves made with two plaits, stylish cuffs. Jacket lined throughout with peau de soie silk and postilion back, which is also trimmed with buttons to match. Skirt is made with foot plaits around the bottom and faced with mercerized sateen for protection of skirt. No lining. Colors, black or dark blue.
Price........................ **$11.50**

DON'T FAIL TO STATE MEASUREMENTS AND COLOR WANTED. **SEE PAGE 969 ABOUT MEASUREMENTS FOR TAILOR MADE SUITS.**

No. 31C3098 NICELY TAILORED AND WELL FINISHED SUIT. Made of very fine all wool covert cloth, consists of a 24-inch long jacket, collarless effect. Double breasted front, leg of mutton sleeves. Trimmings of straps of same material, neatly stitched. Fitted back trimmed to match front. Facing of same material and lined with satin. Skirt is also nicely tailored, self straps and self covered buttons, and kilt plaits all around bottom. Very elegant. Color, castor only.
Price **$14.75**

No. 31C3100 THIS SUIT is designed for those who want a strictly up to date, neat, serviceable suit. Made of all wool panne cheviot and consists of beautiful jacket and well tailored skirt. Has coat shaped collar and lapels, double breasted front finished with a belt which reaches to back. Imitation pockets. Back made with box plait in center and two side plaits. Facing in front of same material and lined throughout with satin. Very full sleeves and stylish turnover cuffs. Skirt is richly tailored and finished with French seams, and side plaits and foot plaits all around the bottom. All seams bound. No lining in skirt. Colors, black, blue or brown. Price....**$12.95**

No. 31C3101 HANDSOME BLOUSE SUIT. Made of very fine all wool cheviot, consists of beautiful blouse which is made very full in front and back. Beautiful sleeves with shirring at the shoulders. Fancy braid trimming around the neck and cuffs. Silk braid trimming in back, also a small square of taffeta silk right above the waist. Blouse is lined throughout with taffeta silk. The skirt is made with strap seams and side plaits below hips making skirt very full. Colors black, blue or brown.
Price, ...**$16.50**

No. 31C3103 BEAUTIFUL SUIT. Made of very fine all wool Panama cloth, consists of up to date blouse. Collarless effect. Leg of mutton sleeves, fancy turnover cuffs. Coffee jacket effect in front. Silk trimming around the neck, stitched several times. Plaits in back. Peplum below the waist. Lined with taffeta silk. The skirt is nicely tailored, with lap seams and foot plaits around the bottom. Colors, black, blue or brown.
Price **$16.75**

$17.50 $16.75 $16.50 $17.50

No. 31C3109 VERY STYLISH LADIES' SUIT. Made of fine all wool panne cheviot. Consists of beautiful blouse coat, leg of mutton sleeves, collarless effect. Trimmings of black silk braid and white broadcloth. Turnover cuffs. Peplum below the aist and blouse back. Jacket is ed throughout with taffeta silk. e skirt is well tailored, lap seams d side plaits all around, trimmed th braid to match. Colors, black, ue or brown with white broadcloth nt, trimmed with fancy braid.
Price........................**$17.50**

No. 31C3118 VERY ATTRACTIVE LADIES' SUIT. Made of very fine all wool Panama cloth. Consists of nobby blouse which is lined throughout with taffeta silk, leg of mutton sleeves with shirring at the shoulders, fancy cuffs, small turnover collar, fancy belt. This jacket blouses in back and front. Trimmed with a very pretty vest front. Skirt is well tailored, made with eleven gores. Colors, all black, blue with light blue edge in front, or brown with tan edge in front of blouse. Price..................**$16.75**

No. 31C3121 THIS HANDSOME TAILORED SUIT is made of all wool cheviot and consists of very nobby 24-inch long jacket, collarless effect, fly front, leg of mutton sleeves, half tight back. Trimmings of silk braid in front, on sleeves and around the neck. White broadcloth with fancy embroidery around the neck. Very pretty. Jacket lined throughout with taffeta silk. Belt in back running to front, as shown in illustration. Skirt is neatly trimmed with silk braid to match, side plaited and kilt plaits around the bottom. Very handsome garment. Colors, black, blue or brown.
Price........................**$16.50**

No. 31C3122 THIS BEAUTIFUL LADIES' SUIT is made of very fine all wool cheviot. Consists of a jacket made with blouse front and back, neatly trimmed with straps of same material and an imitation vest front. Reveres in front made of taffeta silk. Very full leg of mutton sleeves and fancy cuffs. Sleeves trimmed with taffeta silk to match and fancy braid. Similar trimming in front of coat. Yoke effect in back, made with plaits from yoke to waist. Skirt is nicely tailored, trimmed to match the blouse; foot plaits all around. Jacket is lined throughout with taffeta silk. Colors, black, blue or brown.
Price........................**$17.50**

No. 31C3123 LADIES' WELL TAILORED SUIT. Made of very fine all wool cheviot. Consists of 30-inch long jacket, made with fly front, collarless effect, leg of mutton sleeves, fancy turnover cuffs. Welted seams in front, finished with kilt plaits. Trimmings of silk braid, velvet around the neck and on cuffs. Facing of same material. Lined throughout with satin to match. Skirt is neatly tailored. French seams all around, trimmings of silk braid to match jacket and kilt plaits on the alternating gores. Very neat. Colors, black, blue or brown.
Price........................$17.50

No. 31C3126 LADIES' SUIT. Made of very fine all wool broadcloth. Consists of blouse which is lined throughout with taffeta silk; made collarless, fancy sleeves, plaits in front and back of jacket; taffeta silk trimming and fancy silk braid edges the front of blouse. Skirt is one of the newest, umbrella effect, made with very full flounce neatly trimmed with silk braid to match the blouse. This is one of the swell 1905 styles. Colors, black, blue or brown.
Price........................$18.75

No. 31C3127 ONE OF THE PRETTIEST SUITS WE SHOW. Made of very fine all wool Panama cloth. Consists of swell blouse, collarless effect; bolero front, leg of mutton sleeves shirred at shoulders, fancy cuffs; silk braid trimming in front and back, finished with fancy colored braid around the edges in front. Taffeta silk blouse under the bolero which reaches from front all around to back. Jacket is lined throughout with taffeta silk. The skirt is well tailored, very neat in appearance and strictly up to date. Colors, black, blue, brown or tan.
Price........................$21.50

No. 31C3131 THIS BEAUTIFUL COSTUME is nicely tailored and made of very fine all wool broadcloth. Consists of small blouse coat which can be worn open or closed. Richly trimmed with fancy silk braid to match, inlaid velvet around the neck. Leg of mutton sleeves, fancy turnover cuffs. Revers in front are made of white taffeta silk neatly embroidered. Jacket is lined throughout with taffeta silk. Skirt is neatly tailored, trimmed with strips of same material and self covered buttons. Open plaits below the hips. Very attractive. Colors, black, blue or brown.
Price........................$22.50

Ladies' Traveling Coats.

The unusual increase in travel all over the country has created a demand for the goods shown below. Our line is complete, and we are in position to sell you Ladies' Traveling Coats at extremely low prices. These coats are to be worn for the purpose of saving your dress, while at the same time they are well made and fashioned according to the newest models. If you intend to go traveling you cannot afford to be without one of these coats. **Always state size.** See page 969.

No. 17C2816 LADIES' LONG COAT. Made of very fine imported Sicilian cloth. Has a very fine luster. This coat is made in collarless style, double breasted front and half fitted back, with fancy belt. Full leg of mutton sleeves, fancy turnover cuffs. Very wide facing of same material. Trimmings of black and olive colored silk braid around neck and cuffs. Colors, black or steel gray with fancy silk trimmings. Very stylish. Price, $9.95
If by mail, postage extra, 40 cents.

No. 17C2817 LADIES' TRAVELING COAT. Made of cotton crash. Full length. Coat shaped collar and lapels, fly front, half fitted back, bishop sleeves, turnover cuffs. Facing of same material. No lining. Color, light shade of tan.
Price $2.98
If by mail, postage extra, 35 cents.

No. 17C2818 LADIES' TRAVELING COAT. Made of linen crash, very neat, full length, fly front, fitted back. Collarless effect with cape over shoulders. Pouch sleeves, fancy turnover cuffs. No lining. Color, natural linen.
Price...........................$3.75
If by mail, postage extra, 30 cents.

No. 17C2819 LADIES' TRAVELING COAT. Made of fine grade of Sicilian cloth, full length. Collarless effect, fly front, half fitted back finished with belt and plaits from be' to bottom. Capes over shoulders. F pouch sleeves and fancy turnov cuffs. Trimmings of taffeta folds o cape and cuffs. Colors, blue or gr only. No lining. Price. $5.98
If by mail, postage extra, 30 cent

MISSES' TAILOR MADE SUITS.

BELOW WE SHOW A FEW VERY PRETTY YOUNG LADIES' SUITS. When designing these suits, we did so with the idea of making suitable garments for young ladies. They are neat, pretty and more juvenile looking than the other suits shown. These are also made to order, and it will be necessary for you to give us at least 10 to 12 days' time to fill the order. When ordering, be sure to give us all the information possible, especially how you wish to have the skirt made. Sizes, 32, 34, 36 inches around bust, and 36, 38, 40, 42 inches long skirts. Waist measures, from 21 to 28 inches. When ordering, state catalogue number, color, bust and waist measure and the length of skirt.

No. 31C3140 VERY PRETTY MISSES' SUIT. Made of good quality mixture. Consists of neat collarless jacket, double breasted front made with box plait in front and back. Leg of mutton sleeves with shirring at shoulders. Fancy cuffs. Facing in front of same material. No lining. Skirt made with lap seams and foot plaits. Colors, blue, brown or castor mixtures.

Price **$5.50**

No. 31C3143 MISSES' SUIT. Made of good quality all wool cheviot, consists of very neat Norfolk jacket with plaits in front and back. Collarless effect. Double breasted front, loose back. Fancy leg of mutton sleeves shirred at shoulders, neat cuffs. Strap trimming around the neck. Fancy embroidered eagle on sleeve. The skirt is nicely tailored, lap seams and side plaits all around. Colors, blue, brown or red. Price **$7.50**

No. 31C3146 THIS BEAUTIFUL MISSES' SUIT is made of all wool fancy suiting, consists of collarless jacket, double breasted front, loose back made with box plaits. Broadcloth trimming around the neck. Leg of mutton sleeves. Lined throughout with silk romain. The skirt is nicely tailored, lap seams and plaits all around. Colors, gray with green and blue.

Price **$8.50**

No. 31C3147 THIS ATTRACTIVE MISSES' SUIT is made of fine all wool cheviot, consists of blouse with large sailor collar and a nicely tailored skirt. Blouse is neatly trimmed with shirring in front, on the sleeves at the shoulders and at the fancy cuffs. Fancy silk embroidery on the sleeves. Lined throughout with silk romain. Skirt is neatly tailored and made with side plaits all around. Colors, blue, red or brown. Price **$8.95**

No. 31C3151 MISSES' SUIT. Nicely tailored, made of all wool cheviot, consists of neat jacket, collarless effect, double breasted front, trimmed with box plaits in front and back. Stylish sleeves, neat cuffs. Trimmings of fancy metal buttons in front, on the cuffs, and also a strip of red broadcloth around the neck and on cuffs. Facing in front of same material Lined throughout with satin. Skirt is nicely tailored, trimmed to match the coat. Kilt plaits around the bottom. Colors, black, blue or brown

Price **$12.75**

No. 31C3154 VERY NOBBY MISSES' SUIT. Made of all wool covert cloth, consists of collarless jacket, double breasted front, leg of mutton sleeves, fancy turnover cuffs, fitted back. Self trimmings stitched several times and also satin folds and green velvet around the neck, in front and on the cuffs. This velvet is trimmed with castor colored silk. Facing of same material. Lined throughout with satin. Skirt is neatly tailored, side plaited and kilt plaited around the bottom. Trimmed with satin folds to match. Color, castor only with green velvet trimming and metal buttons.

Price **$12.75**

No. 31C3157 MISSES' SUIT. Made of all wool mixed suiting, consists of beautiful blouse and tailor made skirt. Blouse is made with box plait in front, yoke effect, collarless, leg of mutton sleeves, fancy puff and neat turnover cuffs. Neatly trimmed with fancy silk braid in front, on yoke, around the neck, capes and belt. Peplum all around. Lined throughout with satin. Skirt is side plaited all around, nicely tailored, with fancy silk braid to match. Double kilt plaits all around the bottom. Very neat. Colors, blue or brown mixtures.

Price **$11.50**

No. 31C3160 MISSES' SUIT. Made of all wool fancy mixtures, consists of very rich tailor made Norfolk jacket, double breasted front, collarless effect, leg of mutton sleeves. Broadcloth trimmings around the neck, cuffs and belt. Norfolk box plaits in front and back of coat, with belt all around. Trimmings of fancy silk braid to match. Lined throughout with good quality satin lining. Skirt is richly tailored, box plaits all around and kilt plaits around the bottom. Very nobby. Colors, brown, blue or green fancy mixtures.

Price **$12.50**

LADIES' CIELETTE RAINPROOF OVERGARMENTS.

THE MOST USEFUL, PRACTICAL AND STYLISH OVERGARMENTS FOR OUTDOOR WEAR, FOR WET OR DRY WEATHER.

You may Order from Descriptions given in this Book, or if you prefer to see Samples before ordering, send for our Sample Book No. 90C, mailed Free and Postpaid upon request.

WE USE FINE WOOLENS in medium and light weights in our ladies' and men's Cielette rainproof overgarments. The designs are the latest for the season, composed of fancy mixed colors or latest tan and brown shades, stripes, etc. In fact, you could not get a handsomer fabric for an outdoor garment than these; and besides, as it is rainproof, it is decidedly the real practical garment for every lady.

THE CIELETTE RAINPROOFING PROCESS is the original method so widely advertised and used for treating ordinary woolens, giving them the property of turning water in all ordinary rains without in any way injuring or affecting the texture, color or finish of the cloth. It remains flexible and porous to air just as before. No rubber or rubber compounds are used and there is, therefore, no odor or objectionable feature of any kind in these coats. In fact, they are just the same as a handsome up to date walking coat, but have the property of turning water, and nobody would ever suspect they were raincoats unless told they were such. No lady would be without one of these garments after wearing them and knowing how useful and handsome they are.

THE CIELETTE OVERGARMENTS ARE INTENDED for use for all kinds of outdoor wear, taking the place of cloaks, jackets and all kinds of walking coats, because besides being just as useful as any other outdoor garment for general purposes they serve as raincoats. However, we do not recommend them for severe or continued rain. They do not take the place of a rubber coat for heavy rains, but for all ordinary rains they give good service.

THE SIZES run from 32 to 42 inches bust measure and from 54 to 62 inches in length. We do not furnish larger, smaller or shorter garments than these measurements.

OTHER STYLES AND SIZES. If you require a size or a style that we do not furnish from our ready made stock, we will be obliged to charge you $2.00 more than our regular price in this catalogue and it will take two weeks to make up the coat. We also require cash in full with such orders.

HOW TO MEASURE. Give number of inches around bust, fullest part under arms, also from neck to waist in back and then from waist to bottom of skirt or length desired, then sleeve from middle of back to shoulder seam, and then from shoulder seam to wrist.

No. 27C570 OUR LEADER LADIES' GRAY AND TAN CAST STRIPED CHEVIOT CIELETTE RAINCOAT, ONLY $4.95. A gray and tan effect with a double tan stripe, alternating with a neat single green stripe, a very pleasing pattern. Made in handkerchief cape effect, collarless neckband, turned up cuffs, mannish sleeves, belt in back, inverted plait running from neckband to bottom of skirt; loose front closing with silk loops and buttons. Cape, collarband and cuffs are trimmed with rows of black silk braid. Latest style pockets with flaps. An excellent outdoor coat in any kind of weather; serves as a practical raincoat in all ordinary rains. A most wonderful value. Guaranteed to please you. Made in the handsome Mae style, as illustrated.
Price for ladies' rainproof Mae style overgarment **$4.95**

The Mae

No. 27C530 LADIES' OXFORD GRAY COVERT CIELETTE RAINPROOF TRAVELING COAT. We have solved the problem for a light weight traveling coat for ladies in this garment. It weighs only about 2½ pounds, made from oxford gray covert, with an almost invisible herring-bone stripe, in Sussex style, as illustrated, with cloth collar, double shoulder capes, fancy gauntlet cuffs and belt all around. Too much must not be expected of this low priced raincoat, but for all general purposes it will give excellent satisfaction. Sizes, bust 34 to 42, length 54 to 62 inches.
Price for ladies' traveling rainproof overgarment, Sussex style............**$2.35**

The Sussex

No. 27C532 LADIES' DARK TAN REPELLENT CLOTH CIELETTE RAINPROOF OVERGARMENT. One of our very best sellers because adapted to all kinds of outdoor wear and any kind of weather. Made like illustration. The coat has no body lining, but is made with cloth collar, raglan pockets, belt all round and fancy cuff sleeves. The cape is one of the latest of the many styles now shown in large cities. This is an excellent value for all wanting a low priced raincoat. Sizes, 34 to 42 in. bust measure; 54 to 62 inches in length.
Price for ladies' rainproof overgarment, in Sylvia style. **$4.25**

The Sylvia

The Gertrude

No. 27C534 LADIES' MOTTLED MELTON CIELETTE RAINPROOF GERTRUDE STYLE OVERGARMENT. The cloth is a medium weight melton with a greenish background mottled with red and white, such a pattern as is seldom found in the average store. Made in Gertrude style, as illustrated with fancy epaulet shoulders, collarless neckband, double breasted style, belt all round, but with tight fitting back. A coat that will serve as an all year round garment. For this low price it is certainly an exceptional value. Aside from being a raincoat it is every bit as good for general wear as the most up to date outdoor walking coat. Made in regular sizes.
Price for ladies' rainproof Gertrude style overgarment **$5.00**

CAUTION ABOUT RAINPROOF QUALITIES OF THESE LADIES' RAINCOATS. We do not recommend these garments for severe or continued rains. They are not waterproof to the extent that a high grade mackintosh or rubber coat is waterproof. The chemical that is applied to this fabric, however, gives it the property of turning water, and as long as they are not put to unusual tests they give first class service as a raincoat. They, however, take the place of all other outdoor coats, being just as stylish and as handsome a garment as you could possibly find, besides having the quality of turning water.

No. 27C536 LADIES' WHITE AND TAN CHEVIOT CIELETTE RAINPROOF RUTH STYLE OVERGARMENT. A pleasing pattern in a white and tan mixture with a beautiful dark green stripe, made in Ruth style, as illustrated, with the exception that the back is tight fitting having no plaits; it has no collar; made with fancy capes over shoulders, trimmed with cord, plaits and buttons, fancy band cuffs stitched eleven times. A real stylish walking coat and a good quality at a very low price. One would not desire better outdoor garments than these coats make; they take the place of all others, because of their general usefulness. Made in regular sizes.
Price for ladies' Ruth style Cielette rainproof overgarment **$5.50**

The Ruth

The Cora

No. 27C538 LADIES' LIGHT WEIGHT MOHAIR CIELETTE RAINPROOF CORA STYLE TRAVELING COAT. This is one of our most winning coats; made from the latest onion brown shade in the Cora style, as illustrated, double breasted style, patch pockets, fancy cuff sleeves, no collar, trimmed with beautiful fancy silk braid of various colors to offset the surface cloth; the braid trimming is put on like illustration around neck, over shoulders and down the front and back, the coat has an extremely full back. Belt all around. Ladies desiring a beautiful light weight traveling coat cannot afford to overlook this handsome garment. It weighs not more than two pounds and is a dressy garment wherever worn, taking the place of outer garments of all other descriptions. Made in regular sizes.
Price for ladies' onion brown traveling coat in Cora style.. ....**$6.25**

No. 27C539 LADIES' OLIVE GREEN WORSTED CIELETTE RAINPROOF HATTIE STYLE OVERGARMENT. A beautiful shade of olive green with a neat herring-bone stripe effect. A medium weight fabric, suitable for year around wear, made like illustration with military cape, fancy tabs and buttons, cloth collar, four plaits in back, fancy combination straps and belt, latest style cuffs, trimmed with tabs and buttons. These garments serve every purpose as an over garment for outdoor wear. They are neat, dressy and very practical. Made in regular sizes.
Price for Ladies' Cielette Hattie style overgarment **$8.00**

The Hattie

No. 27C540 LADIES' CIELETTE RAINPROOF LUELLA STYLE OVERGARMENT. The fabric is a beautiful plaid of olive green and white, which is made up in double breasted style in a decidedly nobby fashion without collar and with extremely large cuff sleeves, deep shirred back, with a tab on each end of shirring; skirt falls in large, heavy folds; Made in regular sizes.
Price for ladies' Cielette rainproof outer garment, Luella style.. **$8.50**

The Luella

These garments are not intended for heavy or continued rains, or for such general use as a rubber coat. They are suitable for all ordinary showers and take the place of all other outdoor coats.

The Louise

No. 27C542 LADIES' OXFORD GRAY CHEVIOT CIELETTE RAINPROOF LOUISE STYLE OVERGARMENT. A fabric of a beautiful oxford gray cheviot with a white plaid, strictly man tailored in every respect; without collar, handkerchief cape effect, collar band trimmed with fancy tabs and buttons, which run the full length of garment down the front; coat closes with silk loops, sleeves trimmed with large tabs on cuffs and three plaits running from elbow to bottom of sleeve, back trimmed with two large plaits running full length of coat, a decipedly pretty garmment for outdoor wear, besides being a raincoat. Made in regular sizes like the rest of these ladies' coats, from 32 to 42 inches bust measure and from 54 to 62 inches long.
Price for ladies' rainproof overgarment, Louise style............ **$9.00**

No. 27C544 LADIES' HANDSOME TAN STRIPED CIELETTE RAINPROOF ALICE STYLE OVERGARMENT. The cloth is a beautiful shade of tan all wool worsted with narrow subdued stripes of green and red occuring alternately and with a broader stripe in the weave itself of the same color as the background, the handsomest thing in the way of ladies' outer garments that we carry. Made with four plaits in back, fancy small cape, trimmed with tabs and buttons, the very latest style cuffs and pockets.
Price for ladies' handsome Cielette rainproof Alice style overgarment............ **$9.50**

The Alice

No. 27C546 LADIES' STEEL GRAY WORSTED CIELETTE RAINPROOF PRINCESS STYLE OVERGARMENT. The cloth is an oxford steel gray double and twist worsted; a neat, close weave and hard finish fabric, excellent for wear. It is made in the popular single cape style, trimmed with tabs and buttons, cloth collar, belt all around. new style pockets and latest sleeves. The goods are medium weight, suitable for all seasons' wear, and our price makes it one of the best sellers in our line. Like the rest of these coats, it is furnished in regular sizes from 32 to 42 inches bust measure, and the average length is from 54 to 62 inches.

The Princess

Price for ladies' rainproof overgarment, in Princess style, as illustrated $10.00

No. 27C548 LADIES' DARK TAN CIELETTE RAINPROOF HATTIE STYLE OVER GARMENT. A very pleasing pattern, the latest dark tan with an olive green cast, close weave worsted, made like illustration with military cape, fancy tabs and buttons, cloth collar, four plaits in back, fancy combination strap and belt, latest style cuffs and pockets trimmed with tabs and buttons; certainly a very swell coat. Remember, these garments are not only raincoats, but are made with the purpose of being fashionable garments for outdoor wear. They are decidedly the latest thing for walking coats. Made in regular sizes.

The Hattie

Price for ladies' rainproof Hattie style overgarment.... ....$10.50

No. 27C550 LADIES' ALL WOOL OXFORD GRAY WORSTED CIELETTE RAINPROOF RUTH STYLE OVERGARMENT. The goods are excellent grade of all wool worsted in oxford gray pattern, cut like illustration, without collar, fancy cape over shoulders, trimmed with cord, plaits and buttons; back is trimmed with six box plaits from collarband to waist, giving coat a decidedly full sweep, fancy band cuffs stitched eleven times and trimmed with buttons. The yoke inside is trimmed with satin. Made in regular sizes.

The Ruth

Price for ladies' rainproof Ruth style overgarment $11.00

No. 27C552 LADIES' DARK SILK FINISH SICILIAN CIELETTE RAINPROOF GRACE STYLE OVERGARMENT. The fabric is a high luster finish Sicilian goods, white and black pattern, which has the appearance of silk and weighs scarcely more than 2½ pounds. It is very comfortable for an outer garment for walking in wet or dry weather. It never fails to please; it is made in the handsome Grace style, as illustrated, with a military cape, fancy tabs and buttons, velvet collar, but tight fitting back, belt all around, latest style cuffs and raglan pockets, trimmed with tabs and buttons. Cut in regular sizes like other ladies' raincoats, from 34 to 42 inches bust measure and from 54 to 62 inches long.

The Grace

Price for ladies' rainproof overgarment, in Grace style......... $11.00

No. 27C554 LADIES' ALL WOOL BLACK AND WHITE CASSIMERE CIELETTE RAINPROOF DOROTHY NORFOLK STYLE OVERGARMENT. A rich, genteel and popular pattern for general good wear, an all wool black and white cassimere pin check. Coat is made in the latest and most advanced style, with a fancy yoke back and front, three large box plaits in back, two large plaits in front, Norfolk belt. The yoke, cuffs, pockets and belt are all piped with green velvet, the sleeves are made with a large box plait, running from collar to end of sleeve and trimmed with green velvet buttons. It is the latest creation in the way of a walking coat, and besides being fashionable, it is rainproof and can be worn on all occasions for outdoor purposes, rain or shine. A pretty walking coat.

The Dorothy

Price for ladies' Dorothy Norfolk style of rain or overgarment... $11.50

No. 27C556 LADIES' SILKFINISH MOHAIR CIELETTE RAINPROOF GERTRUDE STYLE OVERGARMENT. The fabric is a stiff silk finish mohair in a beautiful shade of tan and of a very neat genteel appearance. Made with three large box plaits in back, fancy epaulet shoulders, collarless neckband, double breasted style, belt all around, exactly as illustrated. One of the most comfortable outer garments and rain coats ever offered, weighing only about three pounds. Regular sizes.

The Gertrude

Price for ladies' rainproof over garment, in Gertrude style.......... $12.00

No. 27C558 LADIES' ALL WOOL WORSTED CIELETTE JULIA STYLE OVERGARMENT. Made from an all wool worsted woven by Mali & Co., in the latest olive green shade. A beautiful fancy back, all the rage for spring. Garment is made like illustration, without collar; yoke effect front and plaited back, pockets, cuffs and front trimmed with buttons as the illustration shows. Remember, these garments serve as raincoats only incidentally, because they can be put to the same use as all other overgarments in any kind of weather, and are just the thing. Made in regular sizes. Price for ladies' rainproof coat, in Julia style........$13.50

The Julia

No. 27C560 OUR LADIES' HIGHEST GRADE SILK MOHAIR CIELETTE RAIN PROOF OVERGARMENT. The fabric is a beautiful quaker or pearl gray mohair, intermingled with almost invisible threads of green and red. Made in Maxine style, no collar, double breasted style, extremely large sleeves, the latest Parisian fashion with three box plaits at elbows; sleeves and the waist lined with white satin, shirring at waist all around, with a belt of the same goods as coat attached; belt ornamented with handsome cut steel buckles front and back; collarband and cuffs trimmed with beautiful silk braid and buttons to match coat. Made in sizes from 34 to 42 inches bust measure, and from 54 to 62 inches long.

The Maxine

Price for ladies' high grade, pearl gray, mohair overgarment, in Maxine style...... .... $14.50

No. 27C562 LADIES' LATEST TOURIST CIELETTE RAINPROOF THREE-QUARTER COAT. The fabric is a handsome oxford gray all wool worsted; made exactly like illustration in our Amy style; average length is 42 inches; we cannot furnish a longer coat in this style. It is of the same cloth exactly as No. 27C550, the difference is only in the style, the back is made with large box plaits, without collar, has epaulets on shoulders, a tourist belt, front made with a beautiful yoke effect and closed with silk loops, latest style sleeves showing three plaits from elbow to hand, fancy tab cuffs and pockets. Made in regular sizes from 32 to 42 inches bust measure but no longer than 42 inches.

The Amy

Price for ladies' tourist overgarment, in Amy style. $6.75

No. 27C564 LADIES' NOVELTY TOURIST CIELETTE THREE-QUARTER WALKING COAT. One of the most beautiful novelties of the season, made in a very fine oxford cheviot cloth with a handsome plaid effect, made like illustration in Ida style, without collar, inverted plait in back from yoke band to waist, extra wide tourist belt, the most beautiful yoke effect double breasted coat in our line; the collarband, yoke and pockets are all piped with red velvet, making an attractive contrast with the surface fabric; it comes no longer than 42 inches and as every lady will recognize, this makes a desirable coat for outdoor wear and an especially practical coat when considered it serves for any kind of weather. You will not do without a Cielette rainproof coat when once you try these all around handsome as well as useful coats. Sizes, 32 to 42 inches bust measure 42 and inches long.

The Ida

Price for ladies' tourist rainproof overgarment, in Ida style.....$7.25

No. 27C566 MISSES' MOTTLED MELTON CIELETTE RAINPROOF MABEL STYLE OVERGARMENT. We have here a medium weight melton with a greenish background, mottled with red and white, such a pattern as you seldom find in retail stores. The selection is entirely our own as well as the design for the style, made in the same high grade order as all our ladies' rainproof overgarments; has one large box plait in back, no collar, but imitation notch collar, piped with green velvet and black soutache. fancy cuff sleeves, neat style tourist pockets and belt, all of which are trimmed with green velvet buttons; a coat your little girl can wear the whole year round; it will serve as a winter coat as well. Sizes, from 12 to 16 years up to 32 inches bust and 50 inches long in back, made exactly like illustration.

The Mabel

Price for misses' Mabel style Cielette rainproof over garment........ $4.50

No. 27C568 MISSES' OXFORD GRAY CHEVIOT CIELETTE RAINPROOF IRENE STYLE OVERGARMENT. This coat is made from the same goods as ladies' Louise style, No. 27C542, in oxford gray cheviot with a white plaid; the difference is only in the style of the garment. This is for misses and is made with a wide fancy back belt, velvet collar, fancy pouch sleeves, raglan pockets, shoulders trimmed with tabs and buttons; a coat that will not fail to please; an excellent protection in all kinds weather, rain or shine. Made in sizes from 12 to 16 years of age, bust measure up to 32 inches, length as long as 50 inches in back. Stylish coat for girls for school or fine wear.

The Irene

Price for misses' Irene style rainproof overgarment $5.50

LADIES' AND MISSES' MACKINTOSH DEPARTMENT.

WE CARRY A LARGE VARIETY of good mackintoshes, which are made in one of the largest and best known factories in the United States. They are made according to our own designs from our own selections of mackintosh fabrics and are as high a standard as can possibly be secured in the way of mackintoshes. They are made in the same substantial manner as our mens' mackintoshes, described on page 918. We guarantee each and every garment to give the best possible service. If for any reason you are disappointed with the coat we send, we ask you as a favor to return it to us at our expense and we will refund to you every cent you have paid, together with transportation charges.

MACKINTOSHES SERVE AS GENERAL OUTDOOR COATS, for cold, stormy or wet weather. A great many ladies use these garments for cold or chilly weather, as they are both wind and waterproof. We have selected very neat shades and fancy patterns that are both serviceable and of a pleasing appearance.

HOW TO TAKE CARE OF THE MACKINTOSH. A mackintosh requires somewhat different care than an ordinary coat, and in order to get the best possible service from such a garment, please refer to page 918. We give full instructions on that page.

IF YOU WISH TO SEE SAMPLES before ordering mackintoshes, send for our Sample Book No. 90C which is sent free and postpaid on request. A full description and illustration of th s book is given on page 918 in this catalogue. If you have the slightest difficulty in selecting the garment you want from our descriptions, by all means send for our sample book, because you cannot afford to buy elsewhere, as we sell the best at manufacturing cost with only a small profit added. We guarantee to please you in every particular or refund your money whether you order from this catalogue or our sample book.

HOW TO ORDER LADIES' MACKINTOSHES.

Give bust measure over fullest part. Measure down back to waist and on down to length required. Height and weight. State all your measurements accurately and you will be pleased with a correct fit.

MADE IN THE REGULAR STYLES, consisting of cape with body buttoning from the collar down to the bottom. The capes average 26 inches in length and are always detachable. The sweep of the double breasted style will average 150 inches. Made with one epaulet in back and velvet collar. **The body is cut full size and will average 90 to 92 inches around the bottom.**

SIZES:

Busts, 32 to 42 inches. Length, 52, 54, 56, 58, 60 and 62 inches. Extreme or disproportionate sizes must be made to order at an extra charge of $2.00 and will require two or three weeks to make; we also require cash in full with such orders.

Ladies' Waterproof Mackintosh Cape, $1.50.

Just the Thing to Throw Over Your Shoulders in all Kinds of Weather. Bust Measurements, 34 to 42 inches.

No. 27C700 Ladies Fine Waterproof Mackintosh Cape, made in the fashionable double breasted style only, from blue or black all wool cashmere with fancy plaid lining; trimmed with velvet collar. Sizes, bust measure, 34 to 42 inches. State bust measure and color in order.
Price........................**$1.50**

Ladies' Navy Blue Cashmere Mackintosh, Style 172

No. 27C705 Ladies' Fine Cotton Cashmere Mackintosh, with fancy plaid lining. An exceptional value at our low price, which is less than any other house can sell them for. A serviceable, satisfactory, lowpriced overgarment, which will not fail to give good wear. Made in single cape style only, as shown in illustration, with velvet collar. Full size in every particular. Navy blue. Sizes, bust measure, 32 to 42 inches; lengths, 52 to 62 inches. Be sure to state size correctly, height and weight. Made in style 172 as shown above. Price............**$1.95**

Ladies' Oxford Gray Herringbone Mackintosh, Style 172.

No.27C710 Ladies' Medium Weight Mackintosh, made in the prevailing style cape mackintosh, as shown in illustration, style 172, with inlaid velvet collar, velvet tab at back, and cut full in all particulars. For a low priced raincoat it is sure to please. Sizes, 32 to 42 inches bust measure; 52 to 62 inches in length. (See illustration below for style 172.)
Price, style 172 only...........**$2.25**

Style 172 The Sussex

Ladies' Double Breasted Wool Cashmere Mackintosh, Blue or Black.

No. 27C720 It is a superior quality that never fails to give entire satisfaction. Style 172, as shown above, made with wide facing, velvet collar, has wide loose fitting back trimmed with one epaulet at the collar. This is a very fashionable style, cape cut in the same style as our highest priced mackintoshes. The body buttons from the collar down to the bottom in front, and is full size. Made in two colors, black or navy blue. Sizes, bust measure, 32 to 42 inches; length, 52 to 62 inches. State color and measurements in your order.
Price, style 172 only.............**$3.00**
From time to time there will be a slight change in patterns of linings, which only happens when we use the entire output of the mill; but you will always receive as good or better when we make a slight substitution.

Ladies' and Misses' Iron Cloth Oxford Gray Covert Automobile.

Style Sussex, as shown on this page.
We are offering in this low priced automobile one of the strongest and best wearing cloths put on the market. Comes in oxford gray cotton covert cloth, and the price is in range of all who care to own an up to date waterproof mackintosh. Made exactly as shown in illustration, with velvet collar, belt all around, bishop sleeves, slash pockets and shoulder capes. Sizes, ladies', 32 to 42 inches bust, 52 to 62 inches length; misses', 34 to 50 inches length in back. Always give correct age and weight for misses' garments.
No. 27C740 Price for ladies' style Sussex.............................**$2.35**
No. 27C68 Price for misses' style Sussex.............................**$2.00**

Ladies' and Misses' Latest Creation in Pin Checked Black and White Effect Automobile.

No.27C745 We offer under this number a mackintosh for ladies and children, in an effect which is very pleasing and at the same time a very dressy overgarment; made of black and white pin checked cashmere and lined with the same cloth as the surface, which does away with the appearance of a mackintosh. Made in style as shown under the illustration Sussex, with divided capes. Size, ladies', 32 to 42 inches bust; 54 to 62 inches long; misses', 34 to 50 inches length in back.
Price for ladies' style Sussex..**$2.50**
Price for misses' style Sussex.. **2.25**

Ladies' and Misses' Automobile Mackintoshes.

Style Sussex, as shown on this page.
Our Automobile Coats for Ladies and Misses are represented by the Sussex style. Made up of the genuine standard all wool cashmere in fast colors. This is not a cheap cashmere, such as many that have found their way on the market, but something that will give entire satisfaction. Made exactly as illustrated, in navy blue, with belt all around, fancy gauntlet sleeves, velvet collar and shoulder capes.
No. 27C755 Price for ladies' automobile mackintosh, navy blue, style Sussex......................**$3.50**
No. 27C69 Price for misses' automobile, navy blue, style Sussex.............................**$3.00**

Ladies' High Grade Automobile Mackintosh.

Style Sussex, as shown on this page.
No. 27C765 This is one of the handsomest fabrics made up into Ladies' Automobile Mackintoshes. The design of this cloth is a very fine, plain oxford gray covert cloth, and one of the most beautiful patterns we have shown this season. Lined with a very fine woven lining of a pretty plaid design. The garment is made exactly like style Sussex as shown by fashion figure on this page, from which you can get a decided idea of just how the garment will look. Sizes, bust, 32 to 42 inches; length, 54 to 62 inches.
Price for ladies' automobile mackintosh, style Sussex...............**$5.00**

Ladies' English Venetian Covert Automobile Mackintosh.

Style Sussex, as shown on this page.
No. 27C770 In describing this number in our Ladies' Automobile Mackintoshes we wish to say that there is no better cloth made for the manufacture of mackintoshes. This cloth is made by the largest English manufacturer of mackintoshes and is a garment that we can guarantee strictly waterproof. Made of a beautiful shade of tan with fancy plaid woven lining, velvet collar, bishop sleeves, shoulder capes and belt all around, raglan pockets, slashed sides as shown in style Sussex in fashion figure above. The sizes we furnish are, bust, 32 to 42 inches, and length, 54 to 62 inches.
Price for ladies' automobile mackintosh, style Sussex.........................**$5.50**

An All Wool Covert Mackintosh in Oxford Gray or Tan.

No. 27C725 We furnish these goods in style 172, either in tan or oxford gray. A double breasted garment, the cape is trimmed with velvet collar, full sweep, back trimmed with one epaulet at collar band. Opens from collar down to bottom. Fancy plaid lining; a garment that will give exceptional wear and is an excellent coat for stormy weather. Furnished in sizes from 32 to 42 inches bust measure and from 52 to 62 inches long. Be sure to state color, whether tan or oxford gray, when ordering.
Price for ladies' all wool covert mackintosh, style 172.........................**$5.00**

GIRLS' AND MISSES' MACKINTOSHES.

Sized by length in back. Sizes, 34, 36, 38, 40, 42, 44, 46, 48 and 50 inches.
Remember, Misses' Mackintoshes come no larger than 32 inches bust measure or 50 inches long.

HOW TO ORDER. **Give length required—height, weight and age. Girls requiring longer than 50 inches should order ladies' size.**

Our Little Girls' Automobile Mackintosh, $2.00.

No. 27C68 This number is made of exactly the same material and style as No. 27C740 ladies' iron cloth covert mackintosh. For school or street wear this coat cannot be beaten, and we are sure the little girls will be more than pleased to own an up to date raincoat such as we are offering under this number.
Price for little girls' automobile coat, sizes 34 to 50 inches back measure, and no larger than 32 inches bust measure, style Sussex........**$2.00**

Girls' or Misses' Navy Blue Automobile Coat.

No. 27C69 This is one of the handsomest and nobbiest coats put on the market in Misses' Automobile Coats, made up of the genuine Goll & Smith's fast color cashmeres, and a coat that we fully guarantee to be strictly waterproof. Made in navy blue only, exactly as shown in illustration under style Sussex. Sizes, 34 to 50 inches in back and no larger than 32 inches bust measure. Ages, 5 to 15 years.
Price, misses' automobile coat in navy blue only, style Sussex...**$3.00**

Our Little Ladies' Pin Check Automobile at $2.25.

No. 27C750 This is the same number as illustrated under our ladies' No. 27C745, which gives full description of just how this garment is made. Size for girls, 34 to 50 inches in back.
Price for misses' automobile, style Sussex..............................**$2.25**

Girls' or Misses' All Wool Cashmere Double Breasted Mackintosh.

No. 27C70 Girls' or Misses' Double Breasted Wool Cashmere Mackintoshes. The most select quality known to manufacturers of mackintoshes. Fast color and we warrant every garment to give entire satisfaction. The lining is of a neat plaid design; velvet collar, the body is made full size in every respect, and buttons from collar down to bottom. Color, navy blue only. Sizes, by length in back, 34 to 50 inches. See rules above for measurements. Style 172.
Style 172
Price.....**$2.75**

Girls' or Misses' Brown Mackintosh, $1.75.

No. 27C73 Girls' or Misses' Fine Cotton Cashmere Mackintosh, in single cape style, as illustrated. The cloth is a very narrow gray wale with fancy plaid lining. A serviceable girls' or misses' mackintosh at a very low price. Single cape style only; velvet collar; buttons from collar down to the bottom. Sizes by length in back, 34 to 50 inches. See rules for measurements. Style 172. Price **$1.75**

Girls' or Misses' Mackintosh, $1.85.

No. 27C74 Girls' or Misses' Plain Blue, Fine Cotton Cashmere Mackintosh, with fancy plaid lining. Fast colors. Made in single cape style only. Trimmed with velvet collar. A staple reliable rainproof mackintosh that will not fail to give good wear and entire satisfaction. Sizes by length in back, 34 to 50 inches. See rules for measurements. Style 172. Price........**$1.8**

LADIES' WALKING SKIRTS.

THE VARIETY OF STYLES and fabrics we show in our walking skirts make this the most complete and popular line on the market this season. By comparison, you will find our prices extremely low. These garments are made expressly for convenience, and are also known as the "HEALTH SKIRT." Very appropriate garment for rainy day, street wear or shopping and always looks neat. **To get the benefit of the walking skirt, be sure to order one that will clear the ground by about two inches.** When ordering, state catalogue number, color, waist measure and length measure of skirt in front about two inches from the ground. Regular sizes are from 22 to 30 inches waist measure and 37 to 44 inches in length. **Sizes other than these must be made to order and will cost 20 per cent above regular catalogue price.**

No. 31C3169 LADIES' WALKING SKIRT Made of melton cloth, nicely tailored, trimmed with straps of same material and self covered buttons. Colors, black or brown.
Price.....$1.95
If by mail, postage extra, 45 cents.

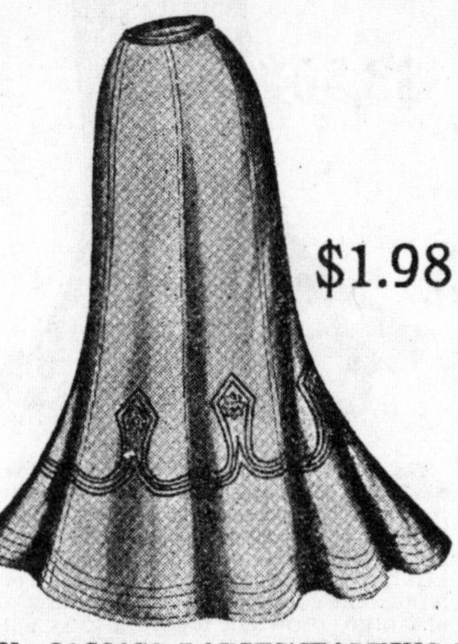

No. 31C3170 LADIES' WALKING SKIRT. Made of melton, neatly trimmed with cording and fancy ornaments, as shown in picture. Several rows of stitching around the bottom. Color, black only.
Price.....$1.98
If by mail, postage extra, 48 cents.

No. 31C3172 LADIES' WALKING SKIRT. Made of good quality fancy mixtures, medium weight, just the thing for the season, nicely tailored, trimmed with straps of same material and fancy buttons. Colors, gray or brown fancy mixtures. Price...$1.98
If by mail, postage extra, 40 cents.

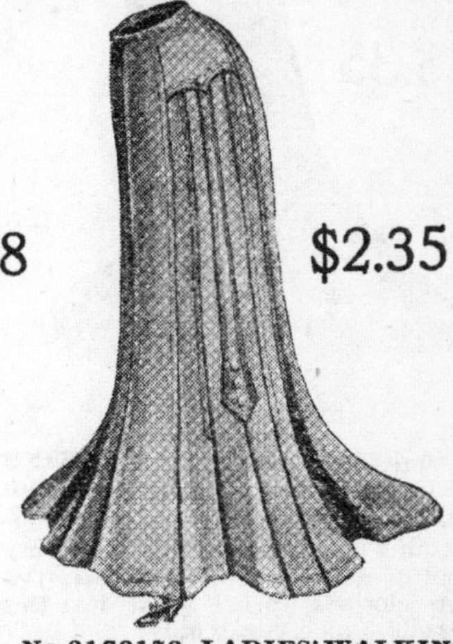

No. 31C3173 LADIES' WALKING SKIRT. Made of good quality melton cloth, trimmed with straps of same material. Side plaits and kilt plaits, also self covered buttons. Very nobby garment. Colors, black or blue.
Price.....$2.35
If by mail, postage extra, 48 cents.

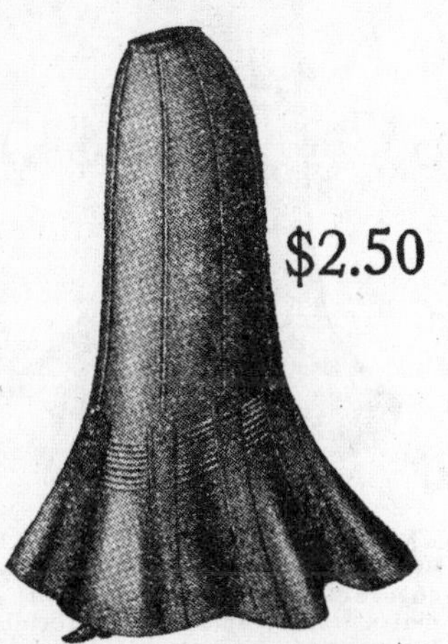

No. 31C3174 LADIES' WALKING SKIRT. Made of good quality medium weight melton cloth. Several rows of cording around the bottom and straps of same material on each seam, giving it a flounce effect. Colors, black, blue or dark gray.
Price.....$2.50
If by mail, postage extra, 49 cents.

No. 31C3175 LADIES' WALKING SKIRT. Made of good quality melton cloth, nicely tailored, trimmed with side plaits and kilt plaits and self covered buttons. Very attractive garment. Colors, black, brown or oxford gray.
Price.....$2.98
If by mail, postage extra, 50 cents.

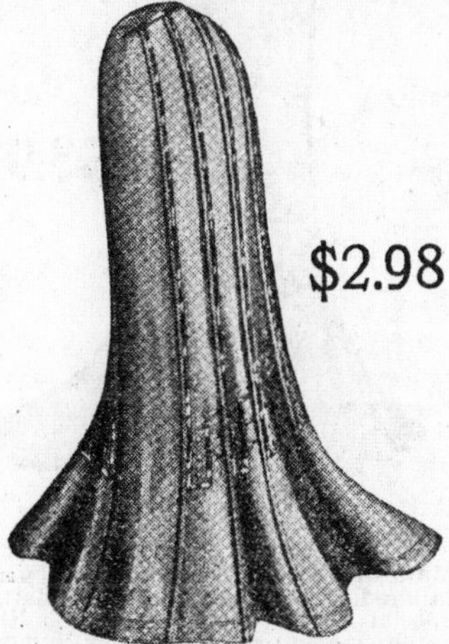

No. 31C3178 LADIES' WALKING SKIRT. Made of good quality melton cloth, side plaited all around, richly trimmed with satin folds and satin covered buttons. Very showy garment. Colors, black or blue.
Price.....$2.98
If by mail, postage extra, 50 cents.

No. 31C3181 LADIES' WALKING SKIRT. Made of good quality fancy mixture. Very good material and looks very pretty. One of the best skirts for the price. Side plaits and kilt plaits all around bottom. Self covered buttons and well tailored seams. Colors, black, dark blue or brown, with fancy stripes.
Price.....$2.75
If by mail, postage extra, 48 cents.

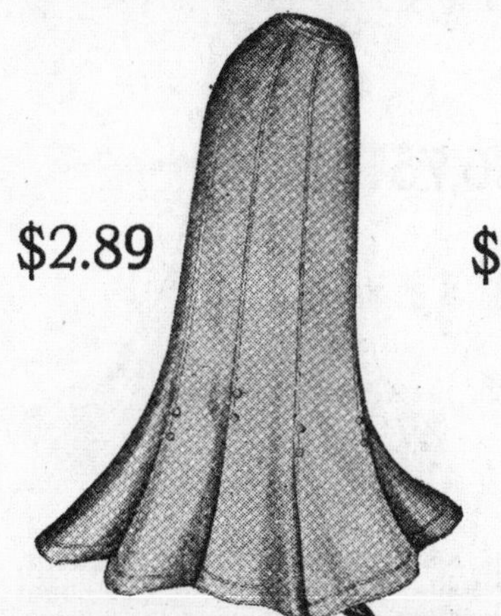

No. 31C3184 LADIES' WALKING SKIRT. Made of all wool light weight melton cloth, special value for the money. Best thing ever produced and a great value. French seams well tailored. Kilt plaits around the bottom. Self covered buttons. Colors, black, brown or light gray. Price.....$2.89
If by mail, postage extra, 45 cents.

No. 31C3187 LADIES' SKIRT. Made of very good quality good weight melton cloth, very attractive, nicely tailored. Richly trimmed with straps of same material and self covered buttons. Very handsome garment. Colors, black, castor or royal blue. Price.....$2.75
If by mail, postage extra 50 cents.

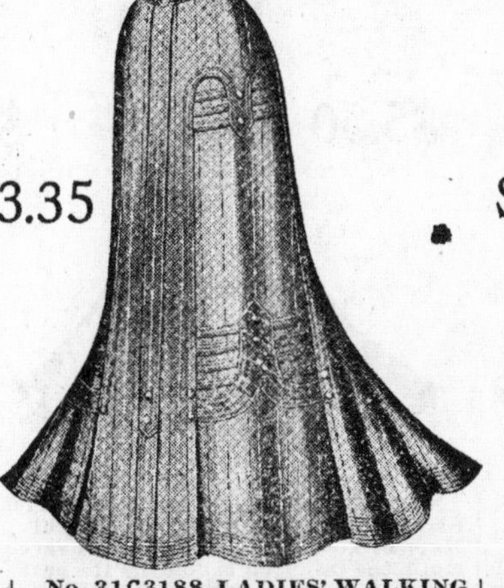

No. 31C3188 LADIES' WALKING SKIRT. Made of melton cloth, well tailored, neatly trimmed with straps of same material and small military buttons. Foot plaits all around bottom. Several rows of stitching. Very full. Colors, blue, brown or gray, with fancy stripes. Price.....$3.35
If by mail, postage extra, 46 cents.

No. 31C3190 LADIES' WALKING SKIRT. Made of all wool fancy suiting, very good value for the money and very pretty. Skirt is side plaited all around and nicely tailored. Kilt plaits and self covered buttons. Very good value and we can highly recommend it. Colors, black, blue or brown mixtures.
Price. (Postage extra, 43c)..$3.35

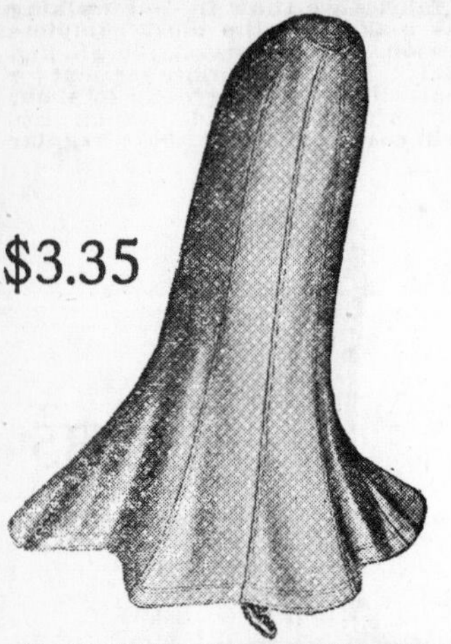

No. 31C3193 LADIES' WALKING SKIRT. Made of good quality all wool covert cloth. Strictly tailor made; French seams all around. Very neat on account of its plainness. Covert cloth is worn a great deal this season. Color, castor only.
Price........................$3.35
If by mail, postage extra, 45 cents.

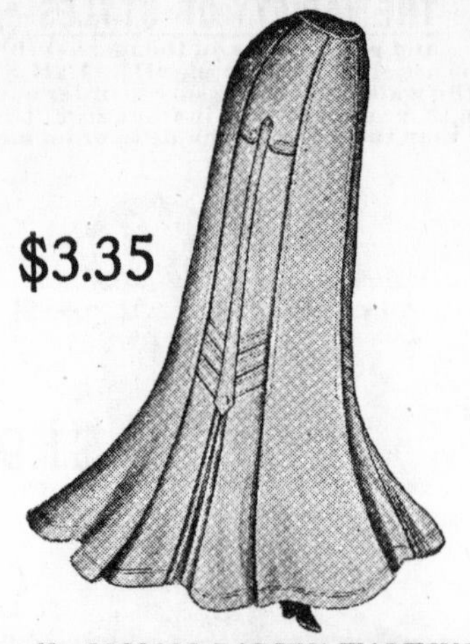

No. 31C3196 LADIES' WALKING SKIRT. Made of all wool melton cloth. Richly trimmed with straps of same material; side plaits and kilt plaits. Self covered buttons. Very nobby garment. Colors, black, royal blue or light gray.
Price........................$3.35
If by mail, postage extra, 48 cents.

No. 31C3199 LADIES' WALKING SKIRT. Made of good quality fancy melton cloth in newest striped effect. This skirt is richly corded on side gores and finished with side plaits, kilt plaits and fancy buttons. Very handsome garment, well tailored. Colors, blue, brown or medium gray with fancy stripe.
Price........................$3.50
If by mail, postage extra, 50 cents.

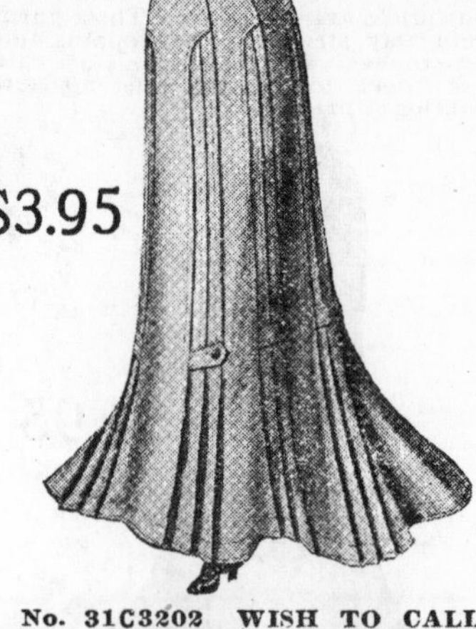

No. 31C3202 WISH TO CALL YOUR ATTENTION TO THIS LADIES' WALKING SKIRT. Made of waterproof or cravenette cloth. Is well tailored, made with side plaits, and trimmed with straps and self covered buttons. Very desirable garment and we can highly recommend it. Color, gray mixtures only.
Price........................$3.95
If by mail, postage extra, 45 cents.

No. 31C3205 LADIES' WALKING SKIRT. Made of good quality all wool fancy mixtures, in light colors. Skirt is well tailored, finished with triple kilt plaits around the bottom and self covered buttons. The mixtures are very pretty and up to date. Colors, gray, tan or brown mixtures.
Price........................$3.95
If by mail, postage extra, 45 cents.

No. 31C3208 LADIES' SKIRT. Made of all wool broadcloth, all man tailored, side plaits and kilt plaits. Special feature on this skirt is the patch pocket, which is very handy. Trimmings of self covered buttons. Nobby garment. Colors, black, navy or tobacco brown.
Price........................$3.95
If by mail, postage extra, 45 cents.

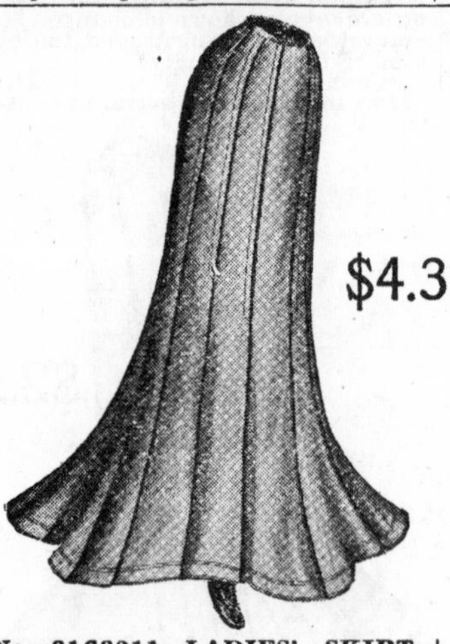

No. 31C3211 LADIES' SKIRT. Made of very fine all wool covert cloth in thirteen gores. Side plaited all around and kilt plaited around the bottom. These effects are the very newest, always neat and pretty. Color, castor only.
Price........................$4.35
If by mail, postage extra, 48 cents.

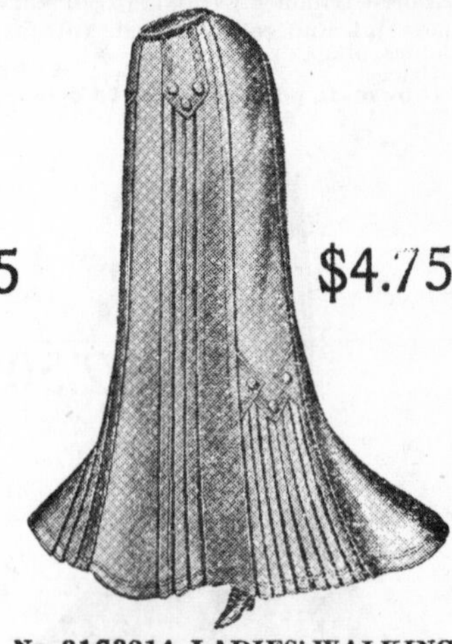

No. 31C3214 LADIES' WALKING SKIRT. Made of very fine all wool covert cloth, richly trimmed with side plaits, wide strap of same material and kilt plaits around the bottom. Very handsome garment; material is first class. Color, castor only.
Price........................$4.75
If by mail, postage extra, 48 cents.

No. 31C3217 LADIES' WALKING SKIRT. Made of all wool medium weight broadcloth. Very attractive garment, entirely new and original. Well tailored. Strap seams stitched several times. Special feature is the self covered buttons which ornament the two side gores, making the skirt very attractive. Colors, black, light gray or tobacco brown.
Price........................$4.95
If by mail, postage extra, 55 cents.

No. 31C3220 THIS IS A VERY FINE LADIES' WALKING SKIRT. Made of good quality all wool covert cloth, the tailoring is done by the best men. Is finished with side plaits on the seams, kilt plaits on the side gores at the bottom. Trimmings of self covered buttons. The seams are all stitched several times and make a very pretty garment. This skirt will please you, it is excellent in style and finish. Color, castor only. Price. $5.50
If by mail, postage extra, 50 cents.

No. 31C3223 LADIES' WALKING SKIRT. Made of very fine all wool broadcloth. Nicely tailored, finished with side plaits. Self trimming, also self covered buttons. Kilt plaits all around the bottom. Very elegant garment, good value and nice material. Colors, black, tobacco brown or royal blue.
Price........................$5.75
If by mail, postage extra, 45 cents.

No. 31C3226 LADIES' SKIRT. Made of very fine all wool light weight kersey cloth, highly tailored, skirt richly trimmed with straps of same material. Each strap stitched several times with silk. Kilt plaits around the bottom. Very attractive garment, very full, excellent style. Colors, black, tobacco brown or castor.
Price........................$6.75
If by mail, postage extra, 50 cents

LADIES' LIGHT WEIGHT SUMMER SKIRTS.

THESE SKIRTS ARE MADE OF LIGHT WEIGHT MATERIALS, are very comfortable and just the thing for spring and summer wear. They are very stylish and dressy and bound to give satisfaction.

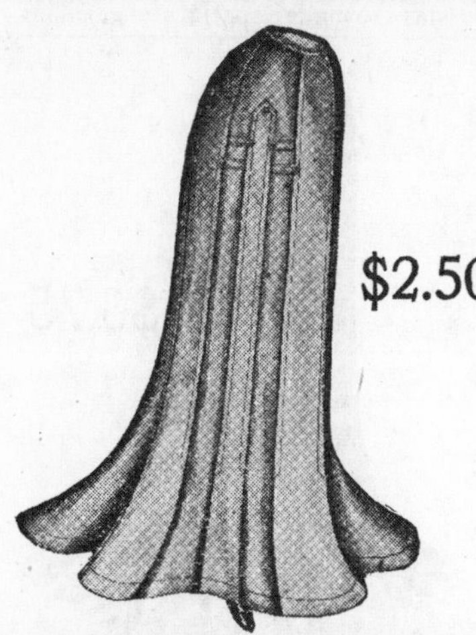

No. 31C3229 LADIES' WALKING SKIRT. Made of good quality Sicilian cloth, side and box plaited, trimmings of straps of same material and small buttons. Very neat. Colors, black, blue or brown.
Price.............................**$2.50**
If by mail, postage extra, 25 cents.

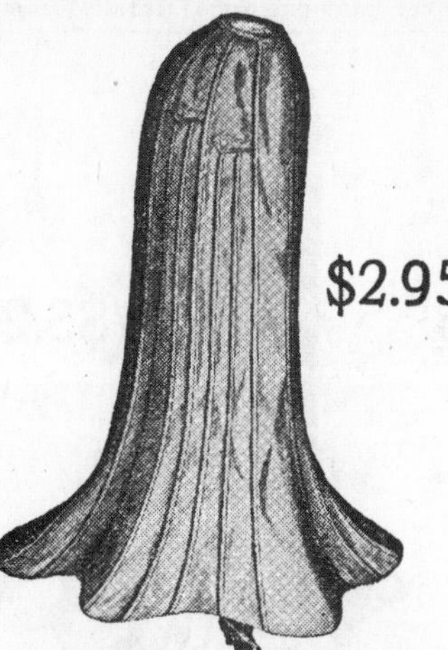

No. 31C3232 LADIES' WALKING SKIRT. Made of good quality Sicilian cloth, with a good luster. Side plaited all around, trimmed with straps and self covered buttons. Strictly tailor made. Colors, black, blue or tobacco brown. Price...**$2.95**
If by mail, postage extra, 25 cents.

No. 31C3235 LADIES' WALKING SKIRT. Made of good quality striped Sicilian cloth, tailor made, trimmings of same material, small buttons and satin folds, as shown in illustration. Colors, black, blue or brown, with fancy stripes. Price..................**$3.25**
If by mail, postage extra, 25 cents.

No. 31C3236 LADIES' WALKING SKIRT. Made of very fine Sicilian cloth. Beautiful luster, strictly tailor made, twenty-one gores all around, strapped seams, kilt plaits all around the bottom in a graduated effect. Colors, black, blue or brown..**$3.50**
If by mail, postage extra, 35 cents.

No. 31C3237 THIS ATTRACTIVE LADIES' WALKING SKIRT, of very fine Sicilian cloth, strictly tailor made, finished with side plaits on the seams and kilt plaits around the bottom, on the front and two side gores. Very effective. Colors, black, blue, brown or white. Price,......................**$3.95**
If by mail, postage extra, 35 cents.

No. 31C3238 VERY STYLISH LADIES' WALKING SKIRT, made **of fine imported Sicilian cloth,** nicely tailor made, trimmed with straps of same material, side plaits and open plaits all around the bottom. Very attractive garment, well made. Colors, black, blue or brown. Price,....**$3.95**
If by mail, postage extra, 35 cents.

No. 31C3239 THIS NEAT WALKING SKIRT is made of all wool Panama cloth, nicely tailored, strapped seams, self trimming, also small buttons. Kilt plaits around the bottom. Colors, black, blue or brown.
Price..........................**$3.95**
If by mail, postage extra, 35 cents.

No. 31C3241 VERY ATTRACTIVE LADIES' WALKING SKIRT. Made of good quality Sicilian cloth, side plaits all around. The plaits around hips are sewed down tight, forming a yoke which is finished with strap of same material. Colors, black, blue or brown. Price..........**$4.50**
If by mail, postage extra, 35 cents.

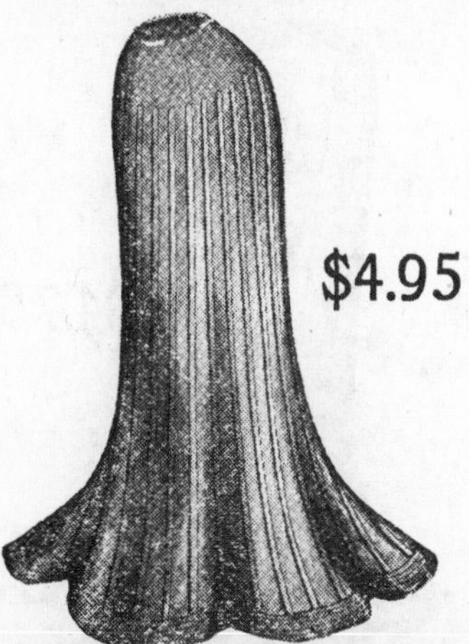

No. 31C3244 LADIES' WALKING SKIRT. Made of very fine imported Sicilian cloth, with high luster, strictly tailor made, consists of nine gores and richly trimmed with straps of same material all around, as shown in illustration, forming a plain yoke around the hips. Colors, black, blue or brown.
Price...............................**$4.95**
If by mail, postage extra, 30 cents.

No. 31C3247 LADIES' WALKING SKIRT. Made of very fine all wool Panama cloth, tailor made, trimmed with side plaits all around, made with eleven gores. Entire front is side plaited and neatly trimmed with self covered buttons and imitation button holes. Colors, black, blue or brown.
Price...............................**$4.95**
If by mail, postage extra, 30 cents.

No. 31C3250 THIS HANDSOME LADIES' WALKING SKIRT is made of very fine imported Sicilian cloth, strictly tailor made, made with nine gores. Side plaits, self trimming and kilt plaits at bottom on alternating gores. Colors, black, brown or navy.
Price...............................**$5.50**
If by mail, postage extra, 30 cents.

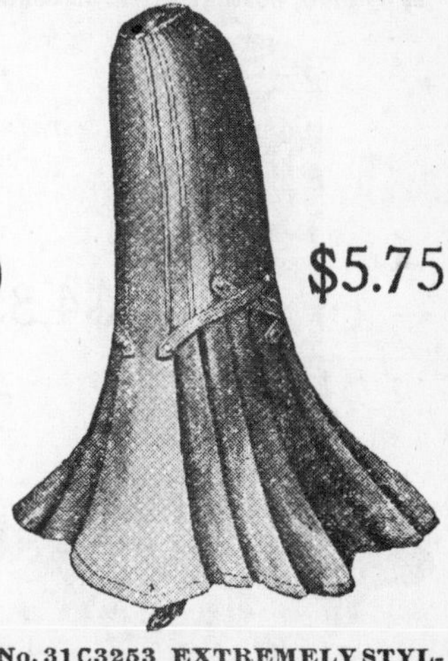

No. 31C3253 EXTREMELY STYLISH AND VERY FINE LADIES' WALKING SKIRT. Made of best imported richly lustered Sicilian cloth, strictly tailor made with twenty-one gores. Strapped seams, trimmings of self covered buttons, and straps of same material. Kilted all around. Colors, black, blue, brown or white....**$5.75**
If by mail, postage extra, 30 cents.

LADIES' SEMI-DRESS SKIRTS.

THIS STYLE OF GARMENT has been especially designed to be worn either as a walking skirt or dress skirt. They are made in walking lengths, same as our walking skirts and are appropriate for either street wear or for dress wear. **When ordering, be sure to state catalogue number, color, waist measure and length measure in front, 2 inches from ground.** Regular sizes, 22 to 30 inches waist measure and 37 to 44 inches length. Sizes different from these must be made to order at an additional cost of 20 per cent over catalogue price. It takes from 10 to 14 days to make a special size garment.

No. 31C3256 LADIES' SEMI-DRESS SKIRT. Made of all wool **ladies' cloth**, nicely tailored, finished with straps of same material and self-covered buttons. Side plaits and kilt plaits at bottom. Colors, black, royal blue or brown.
Price....................................**$2.95**
If by mail, postage extra, 30 cents.

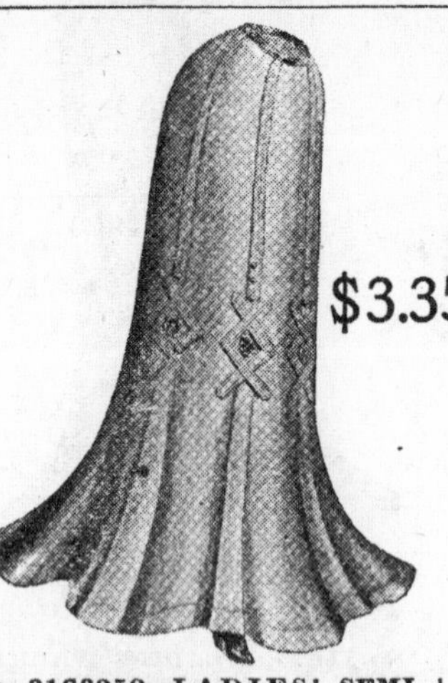

No. 31C3259 LADIES' SEMI-DRESS SKIRT. Made of very fine all wool broadcloth, strictly tailor made, trimmings of straps of same material, small buttons and silk rosettes on the strap trimmed seams. Open box plaits around the bottom. Colors, black, royal blue or brown. Price.**$3.35**
If by mail, postage extra, 35 cents.

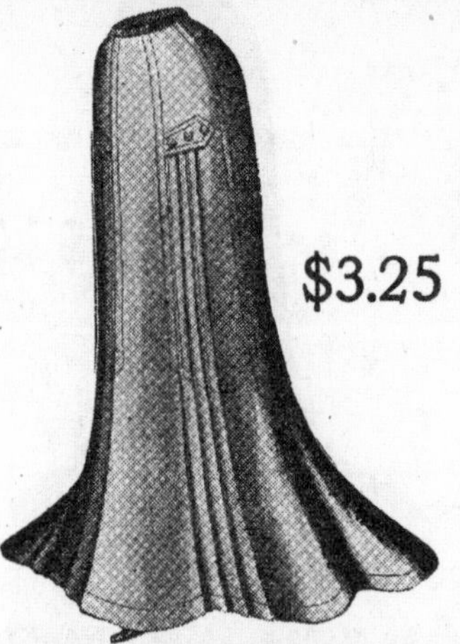

No. 31C3262 LADIES' SEMI-DRESS SKIRT. Made of all wool **cheviot**, nicely tailored, trimmings of same material, self covered buttons, strapped seams and kilt plaits at bottom. Colors, black, blue or brown.
Price....................................**$3.25**
If by mail, postage extra, 35 cents.

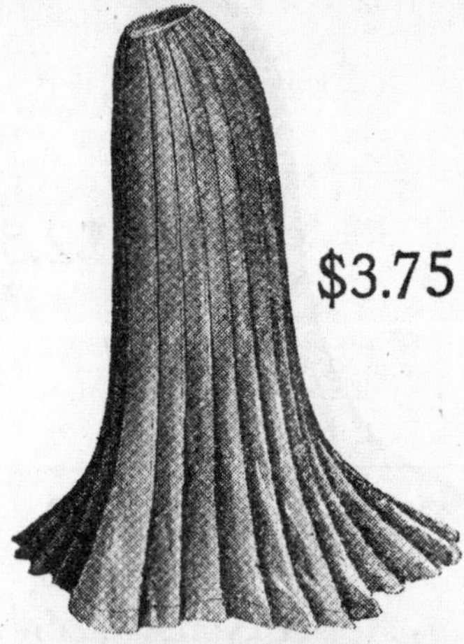

No. 31C3265 LADIES' SEMI-DRESS SKIRT. Made of all wool **cheviot**, nicely tailored, finished with seventeen gores. Strapped seams and open kilt plaits all around in graduated effect. Colors, black, blue or brown.
Price....................................**$3.75**
If by mail, postage extra, 35 cents.

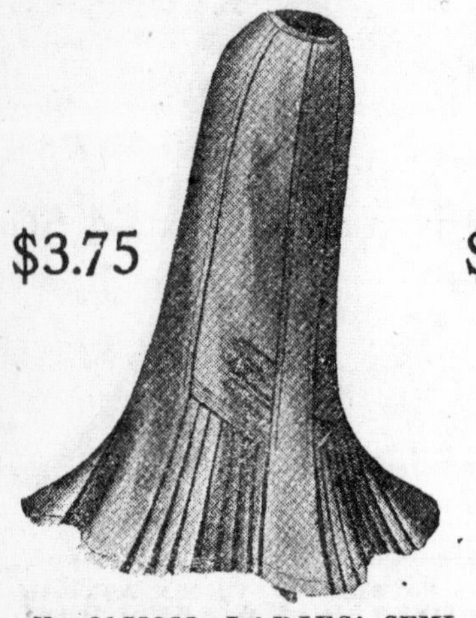

No. 31C3268 LADIES' SEMI-DRESS SKIRT. Made of all wool **cheviot**, well tailored. Trimmed with side plaits, straps of same material and small buttons. Kilted plaits, as shown in illustration. Colors, black, blue or brown.
Price....................................**$3.75**
If by mail, postage extra, 35 cents.

No. 31C3271 LADIES' SEMI-DRESS SKIRT. Made of all wool **broadcloth**. Thirteen gores, strapped seams, kilt plaits at the bottom in graduated effect. Colors, black, blue or brown. Price....................**$3.95**
If by mail, postage extra, 35 cents.

No. 31C3274 LADIES' SEMI-DRESS SKIRT. Made of all wool **Panama cloth**, tailor made, side plaits, trimmings of small buttons and imitation buttonhole effect. The two side gores in front are trimmed with side plaits and finished with kilt plaits at the bottom. Colors, black, blue or brown. Price....**$3.95**
If by mail, postage extra, 35 cents.

No. 31C3277 LADIES' SEMI-DRESS SKIRT. Made of all wool **broadcloth**, nicely tailored, open slot seams on side gores and strap seams in front. The side gores in front are finished with box plaits and kilt at the bottom. Colors, black, blue, brown or castor. Price.....................**$4.35**
If by mail, postage extra, 35 cents.

No. 31C3280 LADIES' SEMI-DRESS SKIRT. Made of all wool **broadcloth**. Well tailored, richly trimmed with taffeta silk folds and finished with box plaits at the bottom. Colors, black, blue or brown, with trimmings to match.
Price....................................**$4.35**
If by mail, postage extra, 35 cents.

No. 31C3283 LADIES' SEMI-DRESS SKIRT. Made of very fine all wool worsted cloth. Strictly up to date and looks very pretty. Nicely tailored, side plaited all around, made with seven gores. Neatly trimmed with straps of same material and self covered buttons. Kilt plaits around the bottom. Colors, black, blue or golden brown. Price....................**$4.75**
If by mail, postage extra, 35 cents.

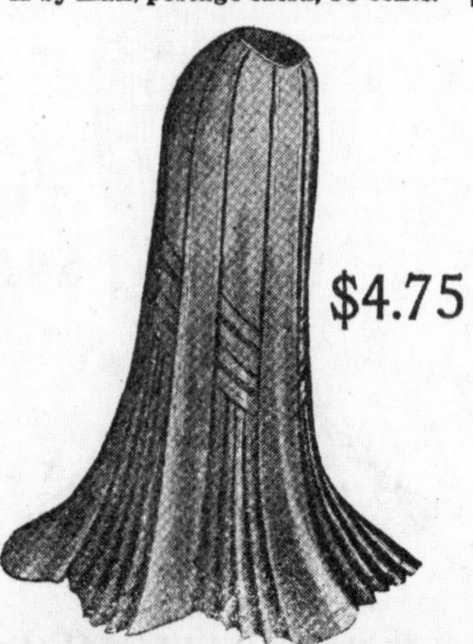

No. 31C3286 LADIES' SEMI-DRESS SKIRT. Made of all wool **pebble cheviot**. Very stylish cloth, trimmed with side plaits, fancy silk braid and kilt plaits on the alternating gores at bottom. Colors, black, blue or brown.
Price....................................**$4.75**
If by mail, postage extra, 35 cents.

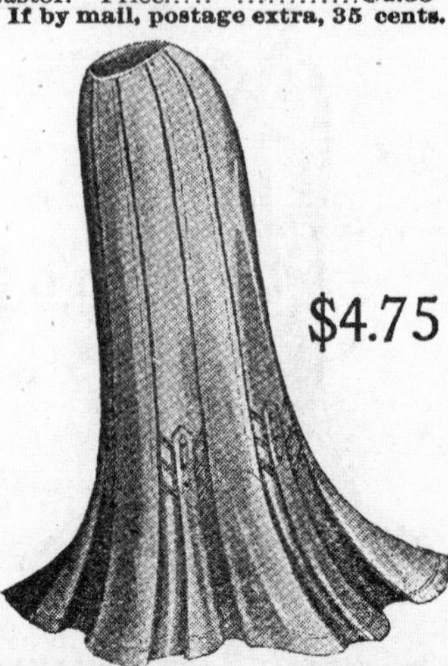

No. 31C3289 LADIES' SEMI-DRESS SKIRT. Made of all wool **cheviot**. Neatly trimmed with side plaits; trimmed on alternating gores with fancy silk braid and taffeta silk straps; also box plaits kilted around the bottom. Colors, black, blue or brown. Price.....................**$4.75**
If by mail, postage extra, 35 cents.

$4.75

No. 31C3292 LADIES' SEMI-DRESS SKIRT. Made of all wool good quality cheviot serge, strictly tailor made, box plaited all around. The skirt is made with thirteen gores. Colors, black, blue or brown. For other material in same style see next description. Price..................**$4.75**
If by mail, postage extra, 35 cents

No. 31C3293 SAME STYLE AS No. 31C3292. Made of very fine all wool, good weight broadcloth. Very stylish garment. Colors, black, blue or brown. Price........**$4.95**
If by mail, postage extra, 35 cents.

$4.95

No. 31C3295 VERY NOBBY AND UP TO DATE SEMI-DRESS SKIRT. Made of all wool good weight etamine cheviot, well tailored, trimmed with two box plaits in front from waist to bottom. Self covered buttons. Side plaits and kilted plaits around the bottom of skirt. Colors, black, blue or brown. Price.....**$4.95**
If by mail, postage extra, 30 cents.

$4.95

No. 31C3298 LADIES' SEMI-DRESS SKIRT. Made of very fine all wool imported Panama cloth. This skirt is made with twenty-five gores. Gores are stitched tight, forming a yoke below the hips and open side plaits all around in graduated effect. Elegant garment. Colors, black, blue or brown. Price.....**$4.95**
If by mail, postage extra, 35 cents.

$4.95

No. 31C3301 VERY FINE LADIES' SEMI-DRESS SKIRT. Made of all wool etamine cheviot, richly tailored, strapped seams, scalloped trimmings on two side gores and small silk covered buttons. Several rows of straps of same material ornament the skirt. Stitched several times around the bottom. Colors, black, blue or brown. Price................**$4.95**
If by mail, postage extra, 35 cents.

$4.98

No. 31C3304 LADIES' SEMI-DRESS SKIRT. Made of very fine all wool broadcloth, tailor made, side plaits, self strap trimmings and kilted at the bottom on alternating gores. Self covered buttons. Colors, black, blue or brown. Price........**$4.98**
If by mail, postage extra, 35 cents.

$5.75

No. 31C3307 LADIES' SEMI-DRESS SKIRT. Made of all wool Panama cloth, nicely tailored, French seams, trimmings of silk braid and taffeta folds, forming flounce. Front gore is trimmed, in addition to silk, with plaits of same material. Side gores are made with kilts. Colors, black, blue or brown. Price.....**$5.75**
If by mail, postage extra, 40 cents.

$4.95

No. 31C3310 LADIES' SEMI-DRESS SKIRT. Made of very fine all wool broadcloth, highly tailored, made with fifteen gores, strapped seams all around, forming a yoke below the hips and open plaits below that. Colors, black, blue or brown. Price.....**$4.95**
If by mail, postage extra, 35 cents.

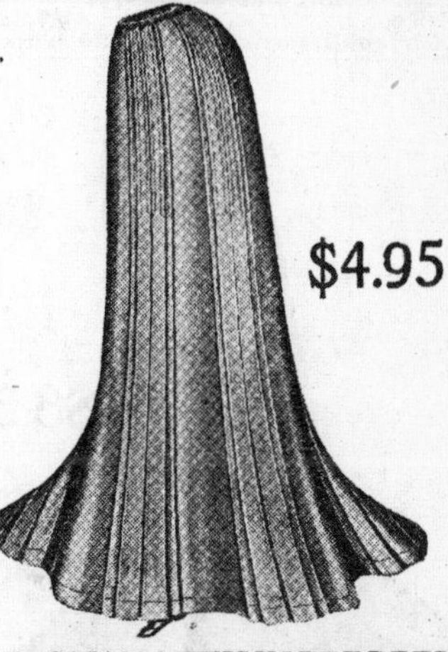

$4.95

No. 31C3314 THIS NOBBY DRESS SKIRT, made of very fine imported Sicilian cloth, highly tailored, double box plaits all around, stitched tight below the hips and open box plaits from thereon. Very full and neat in appearance. Colors, black, blue or brown. Price..................**$4.95**
If by mail, postage extra, 35 cents.

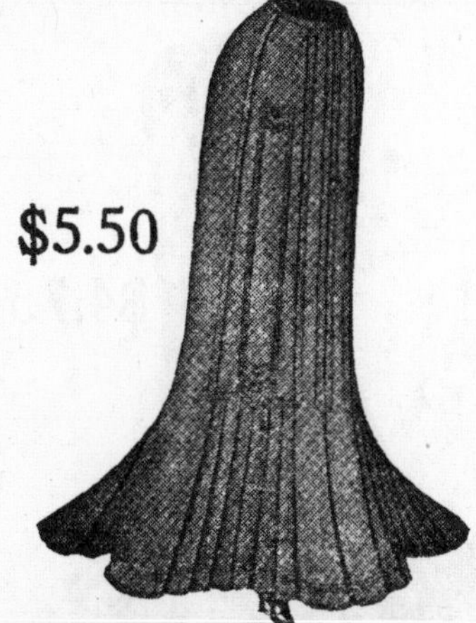

$5.50

No. 31C3316 LADIES' SEMI-DRESS SKIRT. Made of all wool etamine cheviot, richly trimmed with side plaits, straps of same material, small silk covered buttons and kilt plaits on the two side gores. Two box plaits in front from waist to bottom. Colors, black, blue or brown.
Price..........................**$5.50**
If by mail, postage extra, 40 cents.

$5.95

No. 31C3319 LADIES' SEMI-DRESS SKIRT. Made of very fine all wool worsted cloth, elegant garment, and good wearing material. Nicely tailored, finished with side plaits all around. Double box plait in front, self covered buttons, and several box plaits on the bottom. Colors, black, blue or brown. Price.................**$5.95**
If by mail, postage extra, 35 cents.

$5.95

No. 31C3322 THIS ELEGANT SEMI-DRESS SKIRT. Made of very fine all wool etamine cheviot, nicely tailored, plain gore in front, finished with three side plaits on either side. Silk fold trimming, forming a flounce and finished with kilted plaits. Colors, black, blue or brown.
Price...............................**$5.95**
If by mail, postage extra, 30 cents.

$6.95

No. 31C3325 THIS HANDSOME LADIES' SEMI-DRESS SKIRT. made of very fine all wool, light weight kersey cloth, fine garment, richly trimmed with straps of same material, French seams, side plaits and kilted plaits around the bottom. Colors, black, blue or brown.
Price...........................**$6.95**
If by mail, postage extra, 40 cents.

LADIES' DRESS SKIRTS.

THESE GARMENTS are made about 5 inches longer in the back than in the front and are to be worn full length. When ordering, please state catalogue number, color, waist measure and length measure in front. Regular sizes are 22 to 30 inches waist measure and 37 to 44 inches in length. Sizes other than these must be made to order at a cost of 20 per cent above the catalogue price. It takes from ten to fourteen days to make a special garment. State color and size when ordering.

No. 31C3328 LADIES' DRESS SKIRT. Made of good quality repellent cloth, neatly trimmed with taffeta straps and small silk ornaments. Color, blue or black. Price..............................$2.35
If by mail, postage extra, 30 cents.

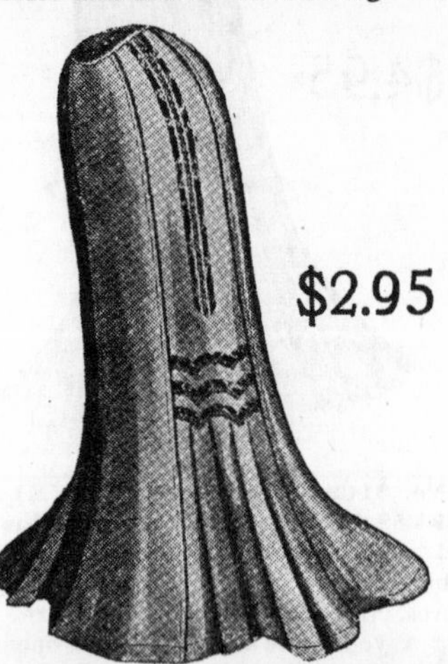

No. 31C3331 LADIES' DRESS SKIRT. Made of good quality repellent cloth, trimmed with taffeta straps and silk braid on the two side gores, finished with box plaits at the bottom. Very neat and attractive. Colors, black or blue. Price....$2.95
If by mail, postage extra, 30 cents.

No. 31C3332 LADIES' DRESS SKIRT. Made of good quality repellent cloth, richly trimmed with taffeta silk folds. Straps of same material, and trimmings of black silk around the straps and small buttons. No lining in skirt. All seams bound. Very showy garment. Colors, black or blue. Price...............................$2.98
If by mail, postage extra, 30 cents.

No. 31C3337 SPECIAL VALUE IN LADIES' DRESS SKIRT. One of the newest things shown and very stylish. Made of good quality repellent cloth, richly trimmed with taffeta folds and embroidered flower design on each seam. Color, black only. Price.$2.98
If by mail, postage extra, 35 cents.

No. 31C3340 LADIES' DRESS SKIRT Made of good quality Sicilian cloth, very pretty for summer, light weight, nice luster, trimmed with silk folds and small silk ornaments. Colors, black, blue or brown. Price.....$3.35
If by mail, postage extra, 30 cents.

No. 31C3343 LADIES' DRESS SKIRT. Made of all wool cheviot, nicely tailored, French seams, silk strap trimmings on the alternating gores. Colors, black, blue or brown. Price..............................$3.75
If by mail, postage extra, 35 cents.

No. 31C3346 LADIES' DRESS SKIRT. Made of all wool voile, light weight, just the thing for summer, nicely trimmed with taffeta silk folds around the hips and bottom as well. Fancy silk braid. Colors, black, blue or brown. Price..........................$3.95
If by mail, postage extra, 30 cents.

No. 31C3349 LADIES' DRESS SKIRT. Made of good quality all wool broadcloth, nicely trimmed with taffeta silk straps on the alternating gores and kilt plaits around the bottom. Colors, black, blue or brown. Price..............................$3.75
If by mail, postage extra, 35 cents.

No. 31C3352 LADIES' DRESS SKIRT. Made of good quality all wool voile, richly trimmed with wood silk openwork faggoting, fancy embroidery inlaid with taffeta silk. Flounce effect trimmed with openwork. Colors, black or blue. Price.....$4.50
If by mail, postage extra, 35 cents.

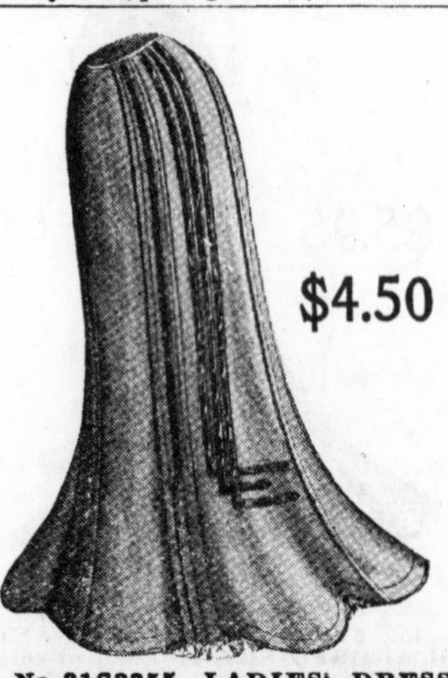

No. 31C3355 LADIES' DRESS SKIRT. Made of all wool cheviot, splendid style, neatly trimmed with taffeta silk straps and box plaits on the two front seams. Trimmings are black silk braid. Kilt plaits in front. This skirt has an attractive drop skirt made of spun glass. Colors, black, blue or brown. Price..............$4.50
If by mail, postage extra, 35 cents.

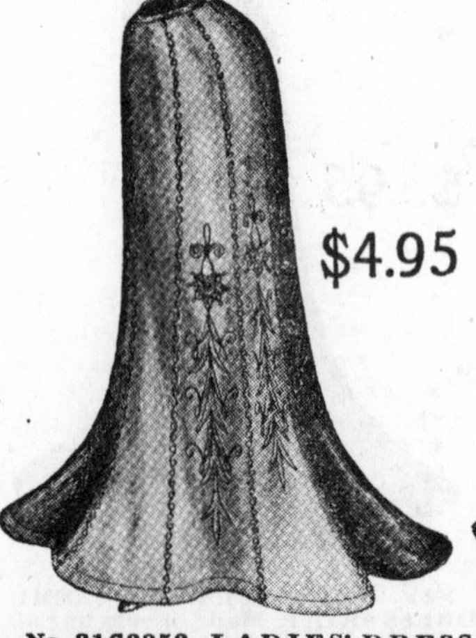

No. 31C3358 LADIES' DRESS SKIRT. Made of all wool cheviot, richly embroidered in silk and inlaid with taffeta silk in a fancy design. Colors, black, blue or brown. Price..............................$4.95
If by mail, postage extra, 40 cents.

No. 31C3361 LADIES' DRESS SKIRT. Made of all wool Panama cloth, neatly trimmed with fancy silk straps and fancy silk braid. Colors, black, brown or blue. Price..............................$4.75
If by mail, postage extra, 35 cents.

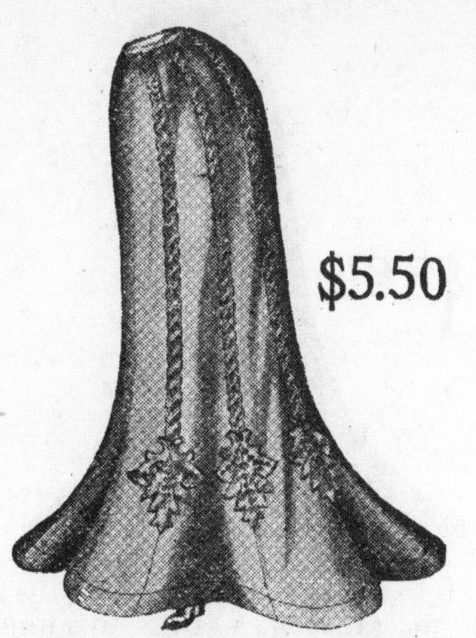

No. 31C3364 LADIES' DRESS SKIRT. Made of fine all wool broadcloth, neatly embroidered in silk and trimmed with silk braid and silk applique all around skirt, in flower design. Colors, black, blue or castor. Price........ $5.50
If by mail, postage extra, 40 cents.

No. 31C3367 LADIES' DRESS SKIRT. Made of very fine imported French voile, well made, side plaits, trimmings of taffeta silk and fancy silk ornaments. Kilted all around the bottom. Excellent value. Colors, black, blue or brown. Price.... $4.95
If by mail, postage extra, 35 cents.

No. 31C3370 LADIES' DRESS SKIRT. Made of very fine all wool broadcloth, richly trimmed with fancy wood silk faggot braid and silk ornaments. Taffeta silk folds all around the bottom. Colors, black, royal blue or brown. Price........ $5.50
If by mail, postage extra, 40 cents.

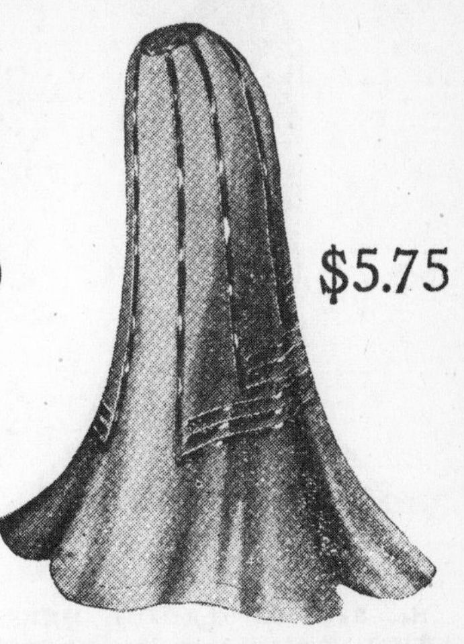

No. 31C3373 LADIES' DRESS SKIRT. Made of fine all wool imported French voile, elaborately trimmed with taffeta silk folds. Colors, black, royal blue or tan. Price........ $5.75
If by mail, postage extra, 35 cents

No. 31C3376 LADIES' DRESS SKIRT. Made of all wool broadcloth, nicely tailored, made with side plaits and box plaits and trimmed with wood silk hercules braid and small silk covered buttons. Kilt plaits all around the bottom. Colors, black, blue or brown. Price........ $5.75
If by mail, postage extra, 35 cents.

No. 31C3379 LADIES' DRESS SKIRT. Made of fine all wool broadcloth, very stylish skirt, neat in appearance, trimmings of straps of same material and silk ringlets. Skirt is made very full. Colors, black, navy blue or tobacco brown. Price........ $5.50
If by mail, postage extra, 40 cents.

No. 31C3382 LADIES' DRESS SKIRT. Made of good quality all wool cheviot serge, neatly trimmed with fancy silk braid on the seams. Small silk ornaments. Side plaits and kilt plaits in graduated effect all around. Very attractive. Colors, black, blue or brown. Price..... $5.50
If by mail, postage extra, 35 cents.

No. 31C3385 LADIES' DRESS SKIRT. Made of very fine all wool broadcloth, elaborately trimmed with taffeta silk straps, silk ornaments and taffeta silk piping. Made very full. Has a drop skirt made of spun glass. Colors, black or brown. Price........ $5.75
If by mail, postage extra, 40 cents.

No. 31C3388 LADIES' DRESS SKIRT. Made of good quality all wool imported Panama cloth. Neatly embroidered in silk and applique of taffeta silk. Colors, black, blue or brown.
Price........ $5.95
If by mail, postage extra, 40 cents.

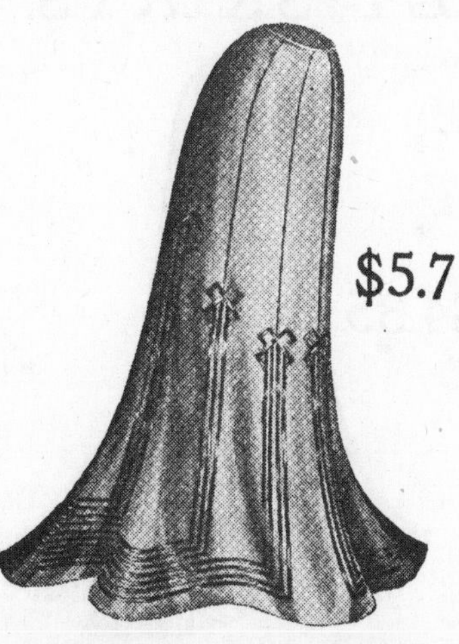

No. 31C3391 LADIES' DRESS SKIRT. Made of very fine all wool broadcloth. Elaborately trimmed with taffeta silk straps. Very pretty and extremely stylish. Colors, black, blue or brown.
Price........ $5.75
If by mail, postage extra, 40 cents.

No. 31C3394 LADIES' DRESS SKIRT. Made of very fine all wool heavy weight broadcloth, strictly tailor made, with box plaits all around, trimmed with taffeta silk straps, silk ornaments and kilted in graduated effect around the bottom. This skirt is made with thirteen gores. Colors, black, brown or castor. Price... $5.98
If by mail, postage extra, 40 cents.

No. 31C3397 LADIES' DRESS SKIRT. Made of good quality all wool broadcloth, neatly trimmed with wood silk faggot braid, box and kilt plaited all around the bottom. Colors, black, blue or brown. Very pretty.
Price........ $6.50
If by mail, postage extra, 40 cents.

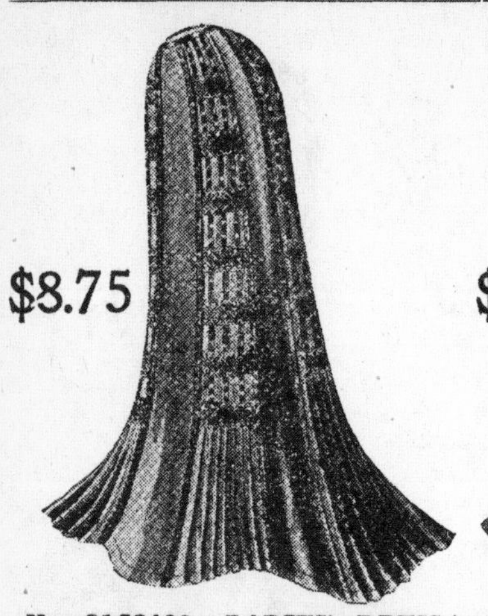

No. 31C3400 LADIES' DRESS SKIRT. Made of very fine imported French voile, richly trimmed with wood silk lace, silk braid and taffeta silk straps. Side plaits and kilted plaits on the alternating gores. Color, black only.
Price........................ $8.75
If by mail, postage extra, 40 cents.

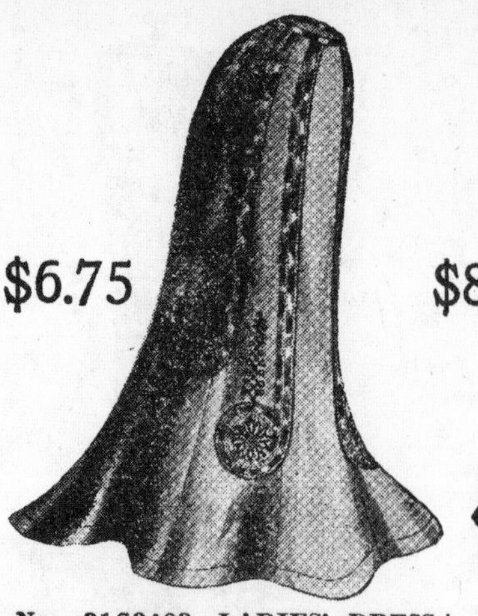

No. 31C3403 LADIES' DRESS SKIRT. Made of very fine all wool imported French voile, elaborately trimmed with taffeta silk straps, fancy silk braid and silk embroidery in very attractive design. Skirt is made very full. Color, black only.
Price........................ $6.75
If by mail, postage extra, 40 cents.

No. 31C3406 LADIES' DRESS SKIRT. Made of all wool broadcloth, nicely tailored, double box plaits in front and sides and on back of skirt. Trimmings of black silk fagoting. Silk ornaments and kilted plaits around the bottom. Colors, black or brown.
Price........................ $8.50
If by mail, postage extra, 40 cents.

No. 31C3409 LADIES' DRESS SKIRT. Made of very fine high grade all wool broadcloth, highly tailored, richly trimmed with box plaits all around, taffeta silk straps and folds. Kilted all around the bottom. Made very full. Silk ornaments on the box plaits. Color, black only.
Price........................ $8.95
If by mail, postage extra, 40 cents.

LIGHT COLORED CLOTH SKIRTS.

No. 31C3412 LADIES' STYLISH SUMMER SKIRT. Made in walking length only, of very fine all wool voile, neatly trimmed with fancy embroidered medallions. Strapped seams and kilt plaits all around the bottom. Colors, white or tan. Price...... $4.50
If by mail, postage extra, 35 cents.

No. 31C3421 LADIES' SEMI-DRESS SKIRT. Made of all wool etamine cloth, neatly trimmed with plaits around the hips, openwork lace insertion and open plaits all around the bottom. Plain front gore. Colors, white or tan. Price............. $5.75
If by mail, postage extra, 40 cents.

ACCORDION PLAITED SKIRTS.

No. 31C3422 LADIES' SUNBURST ACCORDION PLAITED DRESS SKIRT. Made of good quality Sicilian. Facing at bottom of same material. These skirts are very popular this season. Colors, black or blue. This is a skirt that should sell for $7.00 in any retail store.
Price........................ $4.35
If by mail, postage extra, 35 cents.

No. 31C3424 LADIES' SUNBURST PLAITED SKIRT. Made of good quality brilliantine. Yoke effect at top trimmed with satin folds and silk covered buttons. Colors, black or blue. This beautiful sunburst plaited skirt is right up to the top notch for style.
Price........................ $4.75
If by mail, postage extra, 40 cents.

LADIES' NET SKIRTS.

No. 31C3423 LADIES' NET SKIRT. Embroidered all over, inlaid with taffeta silk trimmings. Drop skirt made of good quality spun glass. Color, black only.
Price........................ $2.95
If by mail, postage extra, 35 cents.

$3.50

No. 31C3426 LADIES' DRESS SKIRT. Made of black netting. Embroidered all over, neatly trimmed with black spangles on the seams and forming small rosettes, as shown. Drop skirt made of black or blue spun glass, with flounce around the bottom. State color and size when ordering.
Price........................ $3.50
If by mail, postage extra, 35 cents.

No. 31C3429 LADIES' DRESS SKIRT. Made of black netting, neatly embroidered and richly trimmed with taffeta silk straps and inlaid medallions of taffeta silk. Accordion plaited ruffle around the bottom. Drop skirt made of black or red spun glass. Made very full and up to date. Color, black only. Price........... $4.35
If by mail, postage extra, 35 cents.

No. 31C3432 LADIES' DRESS SKIRT. Made of allover net, richly trimmed with silk ruching, triple flounce around the bottom, each flounce trimmed with silk chiffon ribbon. Drop skirt made of spun glass. Flounce all around the bottom. Very attractive. Color, black only.
Price........................ $4.95
If by mail, postage extra, 35 cents.

LADIES' SILK DRESS AND WALKING SKIRTS.

$4.95

No. 31C3435 LADIES' WALKING SKIRT. Made of good quality taffeta silk, neatly trimmed with small silk ornaments, French seams, box plaits around the bottom in front. Very popular style. Colors, black or brown. Price.............................$4.95

If by mail, postage extra, 35 cents.

$6.50

No. 31C3438 LADIES' WALKING SKIRT. Made of good quality taffeta silk, side plaited all around, made with thirteen gores. Silk covered button trimmings and kilt plaits all around the bottom. Very suitable for summer. Colors, black, blue black (changeable) or brown. Price....................$6.50

If by mail, postage extra, 35 cents.

$6.95

No. 31C3441 LADIES' WALKING SKIRT. Made of good quality taffeta silk, strictly tailor made, strapped seam trimmings, small silk ornaments. Box plaits on the alternating gores at bottom. Kilted plaits. Colors, black or brown. Price.............................$6.95

If by mail, postage extra, 35 cents.

$4.95

No. 31C3444 LADIES' DRESS SKIRT. Made of all silk peau de soie, trimmings of black silk braid, and black silk ornaments. Graduated flounce around the bottom trimmed with four rows in front and five rows fluted ruffles in back, made of spun glass and edged with chiffon ribbon. Drop skirt made of spun glass, finished with fluted flounce and ruffle. Color, black only. Price.........................$4.95

If by mail, postage extra, 40 cents.

$5.50

No. 31C3447 LADIES' DRESS SKIRT. Made of all silk peau de soie, flounce effect, trimmings of silk braid and silk ruching. Graduated flounce made of spun glass, trimmed with three rows of fluted ruching edged with chiffon ribbon. Underskirt made of spun glass with wide flounce around the bottom finished with ruffle. Color, black only. Price.........$5.50

If by mail, postage extra, 45 cents.

$5.75

No. 31C3450 LADIES' DRESS SKIRT. Made of good quality peau de soie silk, richly corded and embroidered all over with soutache. Very attractive and showy garment. Drop skirt made of spun glass finished with flounce and a ruffle. Color, black only. Price............................$5.75

If by mail, postage extra, 40 cents.

$6.50

No. 31C3453 LADIES' DRESS SKIRT. Made of good quality all silk peau de soie, richly embroidered with soutache, neatly corded and trimmed with rosettes made of black wood silk. Drop skirt made of spun glass which is finished with flounce and ruffle. Color, black only. Price.............................$6.50

If by mail, postage extra, 40 cents.

$7.75

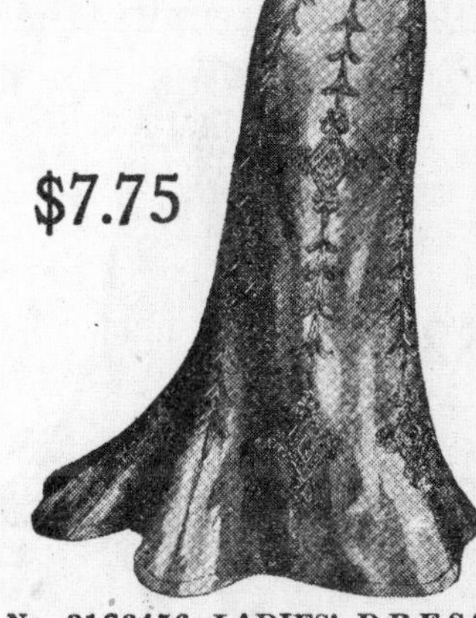

No. 31C3456 LADIES' DRESS SKIRT. Made of all silk good quality peau de soie, neatly embroidered with soutache and silk embroidery over cloth applique. Specially designed garment and very handsome. Drop skirt made of spun glass which is finished with a wide flounce. Color, black only. Price...............$7.75

If by mail, postage extra, 40 cents.

$8.75

No. 31C3459 LADIES' DRESS SKIRT. Made of very fine all silk peau de soie, richly trimmed with lace insertion, embroidered applique over black netting, soutache embroidery in beautiful design. Drop skirt made of spun glass which is finished with a flounce and ruffle. Color, black only. Price.............................$8.75

If by mail, postage extra, 45 cents.

$9.50

No. 31C3462 LADIES' BEAUTIFUL DRESS SKIRT. Made of very fine high grade all silk peau de soie, nicely tailored; made with side plaits and trimmed with black silk braid. Shirred in flounce effect on alternating gores. Very attractive design. Drop skirt made of black spun glass, finished with flounce and ruffle. Color, black only. Price........................$9.50

If by mail, postage extra, 45 cents.

$12.75

No. 31C3465 LADIES' DRESS SKIRT. Made of very fine all silk peau de soie, nicely tailored, made with side plaits on all seams in front, each seam trimmed with black silk braid. Graduated flounce neatly trimmed with black braid and side plaited all around. Very full skirt. Drop skirt made of black taffeta silk, which is finished with wide flounce and ruffle. Color, black only. Price, $12.75

If by mail, postage extra, 45 cents.

$13.75

No. 31C3468 LADIES' EXTREMELY FINE DRESS SKIRT. Made of all silk peau de soie, elaborately trimmed with fancy silk braid, box plaited and kilt plaited all around the bottom. Very attractive garment. Splendid value. Drop skirt made of taffeta silk which is finished with a flounce and a ruffle. Color, black only. Price.............................$13.75

If by mail, postage extra, 45 cents.

GIRLS' OR MISSES' SKIRTS.

THESE SKIRTS ARE MADE FOR YOUNG LADIES FROM 8 TO 16 YEARS OF AGE, sizes 24 to 36 inches length of skirt, 22 to 27 inches waist measure. We do not make these garments in any other sizes. For sizes larger than these, please make selections from our ladies' skirts. When ordering, state age, weight, length, number of inches around waist and the color wanted.

$1.35

No.31C3480 MISSES'SKIRT. Made of good quality melton cloth, side plaits all around, foot plaits around the bottom. Facing of same material. Colors, blue or brown.
Price.................. ....$1.35
If by mail, postage extra, 25 cents.

$1.75

No. 31C3483 MISSES' SKIRT. Made of good quality fancy striped melton, wool finish, trimmings of straps of same material and satin folds. Several rows of stitching around the bottom. Colors, blue or brown with fancy stripes.
Price..(Postage extra, 28c)...$1.75

$1.65

No. 31C3486 MISSES' SKIRT. Made of wool finish melton cloth. This skirt is richly corded and embroidered with soutache. Colors, brown or blue.
Price.... .. ..$1.65
If by mail, postage extra, 30 cents.

$1.95

No. 31C3489 MISSES' SKIRT. Made of good quality wool mixed melton cloth, nicely tailored with side plaits and French seams. Kilt plaits on the front gores at the bottom. Fancy gore in front is piped with different color broadcloth. Trimmings of fancy metal buttons. Colors, military blue with red piping or brown with green piping. Price...$1.95
If by mail, postage extra, 30 cents.

$2.19

No. 31C3492 MISSES' SKIRT. Made of good quality fancy mixed melton cloth, side plaited all around. Kilt plaits around the bottom. Trimmings of self covered buttons. Colors, gray, blue or brown, with fancy stripes.
Price.................................$2.19
If by mail, postage extra, 30 cents.

$2.35

No. 31C3495 VERY PRETTY UP TO DATE GARMENT. Made of good quality Sicilian cloth, side plaited all around and finished with kilt plaits around the bottom. Nicely tailored. Colors, blue, brown or red.
Price...............................$2.35
If by mail, postage extra, 30 cents.

$2.75

No. 31C3498 MISSES' SKIRT. Made of all wool broadcloth, well tailored, richly trimmed with taffeta silk folds as shown. Facing of same material. Very attractive and pretty. Colors, all black, blue with black trimming, cardinal with black trimming or brown with brown trimming.
Price..(Postage extra, 30c)...$2.75

$2.95

No. 31C3501 MISSES' SKIRT Made of good quality Sicilian cloth, accordion plaited all around, made very full. Colors, blue, brown or red.
Price.... ....$2.95
If by mail, postage extra, 30 cents.

$2.98

No. 31C3504 THIS UP TO DATE HANDSOME MISSES' SKIRT is made of good quality Sicilian cloth, the entire skirt is side plaited all around. The plaits are stitched down tight around the hips forming a yoke and open below the yoke, making the skirt very full. Colors, red, blue or brown. Price........... ....$2.98
If by mail, postage extra, 40 cents.

$2.98

No. 31C3507 MISSES' SKIRT. Made of all wool cheviot, made with wide box plait and side plaits kilted all around the bottom. Trimmed with small metal buttons. Colors, black, blue, brown or red.
Price...............................$2.98
If by mail, postage extra, 40 cents.

$3.55

No. 31C3510 THIS PRETTY TAILOR MADE MISSES' SKIRT is made of all wool covert cloth, very newest design this season, is side plaited all around, forming kilts around the bottom. Colors, castor or oxford.
Price...................................$3.55
If by mail, postage extra, 40 cents.

$3.98

No. 31C3514 MISSES' SKIRT. Made of very fine all wool fancy mixture, tailor made, trimmed with side plaits and straps of same material and kilt plaits around the bottom, also fancy metal buttons to match. green broadcloth piping around the squares on the side gores. Colors, castor or gray mixtures. Price...$3.98
If by mail, postage extra, 40 cents.

LADIES' WHITE LAWN AND ORGANDY SHIRT WAISTS.

Sizes, 32 to 42 inches bust measure. No extra sizes. When ordering, give catalogue number, price and number of inches around the bust. All of our waists are cut full in front and over the shoulders, and made with the newest style sleeves. If by mail, postage extra, 15 cents.

No. 31C3522 WHITE LAWN WAIST. Trimmed with two rows of embroidery in front and tucking, stock collar, tucks in back, full sleeves. Color, white only.
Price..........39c
If by mail, postage extra, 15 cents.

STATE CATALOGUE NUMBER, COLOR AND SIZE WHEN ORDERING.

No. 31C3528 WHITE LAWN WAIST. Nicely trimmed with two rows of openwork embroidery. Plaits and tucks in front, large sleeves, detachable collar, four plaits in back. Color, white only.
Price..........49c
If by mail, postage extra, 15 cents.

No. 31C3531 HANDSOME WHITE LAWN WAIST. Neatly trimmed with openwork embroidery in front and across the shoulders. Plaits from shoulders forming a yoke in front. Large sleeves. Plaits in back, detachable crush collar. Color, white only. Price..........49c
If by mail, postage extra, 15 cents.

No. 31C3532 WHITE LAWN WAIST. Richly trimmed with embroidery, forming a yoke front. Front band made of embroidery. Plaits in front. Large sleeves and neat cuffs with tucks. Two plaits in back. Color, white only.
Price..........59c
If by mail, postage extra, 15 cents.

No. 31C3534 THIS HANDSOME WAIST is made of good quality white lawn, pointed yoke tucked all over and trimmed with fancy openwork medallions. Plaits on sleeves. Detachable standing collar Mexican openwork all around the yoke and on front band. Six plaits in back from shoulder to waist. Color, white only. Price.....69c
If by mail, postage extra, 15 cents.

No. 31C3537 VERY NEAT LADIES' WAIST. Made of good quality white lawn. Front trimmed with plaits from shoulder to waist and all over embroidery in center, finished with lace insertion on both sides in front. Very large sleeves, plaited cuffs edged with narrow lace. Standing detachable crushed collar. Plaits in back from shoulder to waist. Color, white only. Price..........89c
If by mail, postage extra, 15 cents.

No. 31C3540 VERY ATTRACTIVE WAIST. Made of white lawn. Entire front is plaited and is made very neat with flower design embroidery, in the newest buttonhole effect. Plaited sleeve, detachable crushed collar. Color, white only.
Price..........89c
If by mail, postage extra, 15 cents.

No. 31C3543 THIS NEAT TAILOR MADE WAIST is made of very fine French lawn. Entire front is plaited and tucked and hemstitched, very neat and attractive. Large sleeves tucked from shoulder down, so are the cuffs. Detachable crushed collar, six plaits in back from shoulder to waist. Color, white only.
Price..........89c
If by mail, postage extra, 15 cents.

No. 31C3547 VERY DRESSY WAIST. Made of white lawn. The circular yoke front is made of embroidered applique over white net, finished with lace all around the yoke and three rows in front. This waist buttons on the side. Has a detachable crushed collar. Plaits in back and on sleeves. Color, white only.
Price..........89c
If by mail, postage extra, 15 cents.

No. 31C3550 THIS SPECIAL VALUE WAIST is made of white lawn. Front is made of tucks, lace insertion and nice embroidery. Plaits on sleeves and in back of waist. Detachable crushed collar. Strictly up to date. Color, white only.
Price..........89c
If by mail, postage extra, 15 cents.

STATE CATALOGUE NUMBER, COLOR AND SIZE WHEN ORDERING.

No. 31C3553 THIS HANDSOME TAILOR MADE WAIST is made of good quality lawn with a circular yoke, with fagoting stitch reaching all around. The front band is made the same way, from yoke to waist, is trimmed with tucking and side plaits. Side plaits on the sleeves and two plaits in back from yoke to waist. Color, white only. Price. 89c
If by mail, postage extra, 15 cents.

No. 31C3556 LADIES' WAIST. Made of good quality of lawn. Bertha effect around yoke, trimmed with Mexican openwork and bertha cape trimmed in same manner. Plaits in front from yoke to waist. Large sleeves and plaits in back. Color, white only.
Price..........89c
If by mail, postage extra, 15 cents.

No. 31C3559 VERY PRETTY LADIES' WAIST. Made of good quality white lawn. Entire front is elaborately embroidered and buttoned in the newest buttonhole effect. Plaits and side plaits in front and two in back. Detachable crushed collar. Large sleeves with tucks at cuffs. Color, white only.
Price..........98c
If by mail, postage extra, 15 cents.

No. 31C3562 ATTRACTIVE LADIES' WAIST. Made of good quality French lawn. Large bertha cape trimmed with lace insertion and embroidered medallions, as illustrated. Trimmed with side plaits in front from yoke to waist. Large sleeves. This waist buttons in the back. Color, white only.
Price..........95c
If by mail, postage extra, 15 cents.

No. 31C3565 THIS ELEGANT WAIST is made of good quality French lawn. Circular yoke in front and back made of lace. Plaits in front from yoke to waist. Medallion trimmings. Beautiful sleeves made with plaits and fagoting. Two plaits in back. Color, white only
Price..........98c
If by mail, postage extra, 15 cents.

No. 31C3568 VERY ATTRACTIVE WAIST. Made of very fine French lawn, circular yoke in front with fagoting, trimmed with Mexican lace and embroidered around the yoke and three rows in front. Side plait trimmings in front, on the sleeves and in back. Several rows of tucks on cuffs. Color, white only.
Price......................98c
If by mail, postage extra, 15 cents.

No. 31C3571 RICHLY TRIMMED WAIST. Made of good quality white lawn. Entire front is made of lace and embroidery, also trimmings of lace and tucks. Detachable crushed collar, large sleeves and neat cuffs. Several tucks in back from neck to waist. Color, white only.
Price......................98c
If by mail, postage extra, 15 cents.

No. 31C3574 THIS PRETTY WAIST is made of good quality lawn. Entire front is trimmed with tucks, lace insertion and medallion effect embroidery. Tucks on side and in the sleeves. Detachable crushed collar. Tucks in back and in cuffs. Color, white only.
Price......................95c
If by mail, postage extra, 15 cents.

No. 31C3577 ELABORATELY TRIMMED WAIST. Made of good quality French lawn. The entire front is made of embroidery in the newest design. Is trimmed with side plaits and tucks. Tucking on the sleeves, which are made very full. Two plaits in back from neck to waist. Detachable crushed collar. The embroidery is exceptionally heavy. Color, white only.
Price......................98c
If by mail, postage extra, 15 cents.

No. 31C3580 NEAT AND UP TO DATE WAIST. Made of fine French lawn. Front is trimmed with embroidery and tucks, as well as side plaits. Large sleeves. Tucks in back from neck to waist. Detachable crushed collar. Color, white only. Price..............$1.10
If by mail, postage extra, 15 cents.

No. 31C3583 THIS HANDSOME STYLE, is the newest and is called the surplice style. Made of good quality French lawn, with plaits on both sides, meeting in front. Trimmed with embroidery. Detachable crushed collar. Inlaid front, otherwise called dickey, trimmed with tucks and embroidery. Side plaits in back, full sleeves and neat cuffs. Color, white only. Price....$1.15
If by mail, postage extra, 15 cents.

No. 31C3586 ELABORATE WAIST. Made of good quality white lawn. Front trimmed with plaits and neat medallions, made of fine embroidery. Two rows of embroidery insertion on the sides, full sleeves with tucks at the cuffs. Four plaits in back, from neck to waist. Color, white only.
Price......................$1.19
If by mail, postage extra, 15 cents.

No. 31C3589 THIS HANDSOME WAIST is made of fine French lawn. The entire front is made of heavy embroidery, the newest buttonhole effect. This is the very newest and everybody admires it. Detachable crushed collar, trimmed with embroidered medallion. Large sleeves. Plaits in back from neck to waist. Color, white only.
Price......................$1.19
If by mail, postage extra, 15 cents.

No. 31C3592 ELEGANT WAIST. Made of fine French lawn. Front is trimmed with embroidery and tucks. Front band has tucks and medallion trimmings. Plaits in front, on sleeves and in back of waist. Detachable crushed collar finished with neat medallion. Color, white only. Price..........$1.25
If by mail, postage extra, 15 cents.

No. 31C3595 NOBBY WAIST. Made of very fine French lawn, round yoke effect made with lace insertion. The trimmings are embroidery, Mexican openwork and tucks. There is so much on it that we cannot describe every detail. Tucks on large sleeves. Detachable crushed collar. Color, white only.
Price......................$1.25
If by mail, postage extra, 15 cents.

No. 31C3598 VERY FINE WAIST. Made of French lawn, elaborately trimmed in front with tucks, embroidered medallions and insertion of the latest style in embroidery. This embroidery stands out very high and is similar to very large pin heads. Large sleeves. Tucks from neck to waist, and detachable crushed collar.
Price......................$1.35
If by mail, postage extra, 15 cents.

No. 31C3601 VERY PRETTY WAIST. Made of good quality French lawn. Bertha effect. Pointed yoke in front trimmed with tucks and openwork medallions. Lace insertion and edged around the cape. Large sleeves finished with tucks at the cuffs. Tucks in front and back from yoke to waist. This waist buttons in back. Color, white only.
Price......................$1.35
If by mail, postage extra, 15 cents.

No. 31C3603 THIS ELEGANT WAIST is made of very fine French lawn, entire front made of very fine openwork embroidery trimmed with plaits between. Detachable crushed collar to match. Large sleeves with side plaits at the top and at the cuffs. Plaits in back from neck to waist. Color, white only.
Price......................$1.35
If by mail, postage extra, 15 cents.

No. 31C3606 THIS CHARMING WAIST is made of very fine imported French lawn, in the newest surplice effect. Is made with side plaits and very pretty embroidery. Detachable crushed collar and inlaid front, otherwise called dickey, trimmed with tucks and embroidery. Very full sleeves, tucks on the cuffs. Side plaits in back from neck to waist. Color, white only. Price.......$1.35
If by mail, postage extra, 15 cents.

No. 31C3609 THIS ELABORATE WAIST is made of organdy. Yoke front in beautiful star shape is made of tucks, lace insertion and lace medallions. Plaits from yoke to waist. Very large sleeves, neat cuffs. Detachable crushed collar. Color, white only.
Price......................$1.39
If by mail, postage extra, 15 cents.

No. 31C3612 THIS HANDSOME WAIST is highly tailored and made of very fine French lawn. Entire front is plaited and richly trimmed with fine embroidery. Detachable crushed collar, large sleeves, plaits on cuffs. Side plaits in back from neck to waist. Color, white only. Price.....................$1.48
If by mail, postage extra, 18 cents.

No. 31C3615 THIS ATTRACTIVE WAIST is made of very fine French lawn. Trimmed with very fine buttonhole effect embroidery in front and across the shoulders. Tucked and plaited in front on sleeves and cuffs. Has three clusters of tucks in back, from neck to waist. Detachable collar, trimmed with faggoting. Color, white only. Price.....................$1.48
If by mail, postage extra, 18 cents.

No. 31C3618 HANDSOME WAIST. Made of fine French lawn. Entire front is side plaited and trimmed with lace insertion, and center of front is trimmed with beautiful flower design embroidery. This embroidery is very rich and attractive. Side plaits on sleeves and in back, from neck to waist. Color, white only. Price.....................$1.48
If by mail, postage extra, 18 cents.

No. 31C3621 THIS ATTRACTIVE WAIST is made of very fine French lawn. Tailor made. Entire front is trimmed with small tucks and side plaits all over. Very rich design in embroidery and Mexican openwork. Large sleeve plaits from shoulder to cuffs. Detachable crushed collar. Two clusters of tucks in back from neck to waist. Color, white only. Price.....$1.75
If by mail, postage extra, 18 cents.

No. 31C3624 LADIES' WAIST Made of fine French dotted mull. The entire front is side plaited and trimmed with beautiful design in openwork embroidery. Detachable crushed collar. Plaits in back from neck to waist. Very stylish. Color, white only. Price.........$1.75
If by mail, postage extra, 18 cents.

No. 31C3627 ENTIRELY NEW STYLE TAILORED WAIST. Made of fine French lawn. Front trimmed with side plaits and buttonhole embroidery in military effect. Detachable crushed collar, large sleeves and side plaits in back from neck to waist. Color, white only. Price.....................$1.48
If by mail, postage extra, 18 cents.

No. 31C3633 THIS PRETTY WAIST is made of fine French lawn. Entire front is tucked. Yoke effect. Lace and embroidered insertion, as shown in picture. Several rows of tucks in sleeves at top and in cuffs. Detachable crushed collar finished with an embroidered buttonhole in front and caught with a white lawn tie, as shown in picture. Two clusters of tucks in back from neck to waist. Color, white only. Price....$1.75
If by mail, postage extra, 18 cents.

No. 31C3630 ELABORATELY TRIMMED WAIST. Made of fine French lawn, pointed yoke effect in front, tucked all over. Openwork embroidery all around yoke and on front piece. Side plaits from yoke down. Similar trimming on large sleeves at the cuffs. Detachable crushed collar. Side plaits in back from neck to waist. Color, white only. Price.....................$1.75
If by mail, postage extra, 18 cents.

No. 31C3636 THIS HIGHLY ATTRACTIVE WAIST is made of very fine imported French lawn, nicely tailored and richly trimmed with beautiful design in openwork embroidery. Plaits from yoke to waist. Large sleeves finished with plaits. Side plaits in back from neck to waist. Color, white only. Price.....................$1.89
If by mail, postage extra, 18 cents.

No. 31C3639 THIS VERY FINE LADIES' WAIST is made of imported French lawn. The entire front is beautifully trimmed with tucks, lace insertion and elaborate embroidered designs. Detachable crushed collar, trimmed with lace. Several tucks on the large sleeves and plaits at cuffs. Round yoke in back, trimmed with lace. Tucks from yoke to waist in back. Color, white only. Price.........$1.98
If by mail, postage extra, 18 cents.

No. 31C3642 THIS PRETTY WAIST is made of fine imported French lawn, fancy yoke in front trimmed with lace insertion, neat embroidery and buttonhole embroidered circles. Tucks in front from yoke to waist. Entire sleeves tucked as shown in illustration. Detachable crushed collar. Three clusters of tucks in back. Color, white only. Price.....................$1.98
If by mail, postage extra, 18 cents.

No. 31C3645 THIS IS ONE OF THE MOST ATTRACTIVE WAISTS we have ever shown. It is made of good quality organdy, entire front is trimmed with tucks, lace insertion. Detachable crushed collar and a circular yoke in back. Large sleeves trimmed with lace and tucks on cuffs. Has a cape made of white lace reaching all around the back to front. Color, white only. Price.....................$1.98
If by mail, postage extra, 18 cents.

No. 31C3648 THIS HIGHLY TAILORED LADIES' WAIST is made of fine imported French lawn. Entire front is made of buttonhole effect embroidery, and two plaits. Quality is the very best. Detachable crushed collar, large sleeves and neat cuffs. Side plaits in back from neck to waist. Color, white only. Price.....................$1.98
If by mail, postage extra, 18 cents.

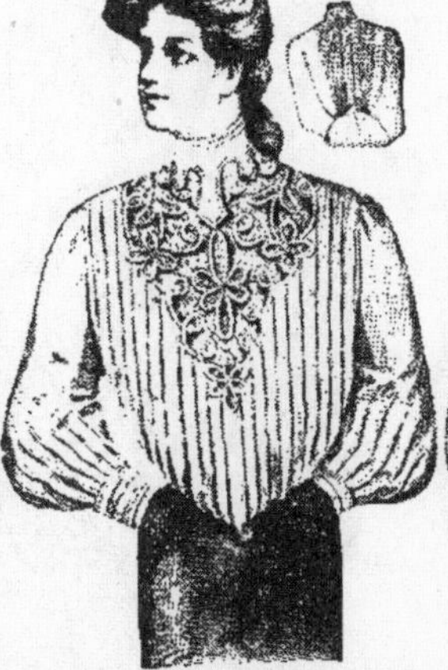

No. 31C3651 THIS HANDSOME WAIST is made of very fine imported French lawn, entire front is tucked and is beautifully trimmed with battenberg work as shown in illustration. Has detachable crushed collar, large sleeves with tucks at the cuffs. The back is tucked all over. This waist buttons in back. Colors, white or tan. State color when ordering. Price.....................$2.35
If by mail, postage extra, 18 cents.

No. 31C3654 LADIES' WAIST. Made of fine imported French lawn. The entire front is trimmed with tucks, embroidered medallions, lace insertion and newest design in lapover embroidery, finished with buttons on both sides. Detachable crushed collar, large sleeves tucked at the shoulders, lace cuffs. Three clusters of tucks in back from neck to waist. Color, white only. Price.....................$2.75
If by mail, postage extra, 18 cents.

LADIES' BLACK LAWN OR MOURNING WAISTS.

No. 31C3657 LADIES' WAIST. Made of good quality black lawn, nicely tailored, plaits in front. Detachable crush collar edged with lace. Large sleeves, tucks on cuffs. Side plaits in back. Color, black only. Price..........75c
If by mail, postage extra, 15 cents.

No. 31C3660 LADIES' WAIST. Made of good quality black lawn, pointed yoke in front tucked and trimmed with black medallions. Detachable crush collar trimmed with lace. Side plaits on sleeves and in back from neck to waist. Color, black only. Price..........89c
If by mail, postage extra, 15 cents.

No. 31C3663 LADIES' WAIST. Made of good quality black lawn. Entire front is tucked and neatly trimmed with black embroidery insertion. Side plaits in front at the shoulders. Large sleeves and tucks in sleeves at the cuffs. Tucks in back. Color, black only. Price..........95c
If by mail, postage extra, 15 cents.

No. 31C3666 LADIES' WAIST. Made of good quality black lawn. Front trimmed with black lace and black embroidery, forming a bias yoke. Side plaits from yoke to waist. Plaits in back. Color, black only. Price..........$1.15
If by mail, postage extra, 15 cents.

No. 31C3669 LADIES' WAIST. Made of fine black French lawn. The front is neatly trimmed with Swiss embroidery, side plaits, tucks and heavy embroidery on both sides. Large sleeves, detachable crush collar. Three clusters of tucks in back. Color, black only. Price...$1.35
If by mail, postage extra, 15 cents.

LADIES' TAN (CHAMPAGNE) COLOR WAISTS.

No. 31C3672 LADIES' PRETTY WAIST. Made of tan grass lawn, nicely tailored. Entire front is side plaited, tucked and hemstitched. Detachable crush collar. Large sleeves. Side plaits and tucks in back. Color, tan only. Price..........75c
If by mail, postage extra, 15 cents.

No. 31C3675 LADIES' WAIST. Made of good quality tan grass lawn, nicely tailored. Front tucked and richly trimmed with fine embroidery, of which two rows are across the shoulders. Large sleeves, tucked at cuffs. Detachable crush collar with fancy turnover. Tucks in back. Color, tan only. Price..........89c
If by mail, postage extra, 15 cents.

No. 31C3678 LADIES' WAIST. Made of grass lawn, the entire front and across shoulders is made of cluny lace to match. Tucks in front and on sleeves at the cuffs. Two clusters of tucks in back. Very showy. Color, tan only. Price..........98c
If by mail, postage extra, 18 cents.

No. 31C3681 LADIES' WAIST. Made of good quality lawn, entire front is richly embroidered with newest buttonhole effect, and in addition to that is richly trimmed with side plaits. Plaits in sleeves and cuffs. Detachable collar. Four side plaits in back. Color, tan only. Price..........$1.19
If by mail, postage extra, 15 cents.

No. 31C3684 THIS PRETTY WAIST is made of fine French lawn, entire front is richly tucked and trimmed with medallions, made of embroidery, over lace. Detachable collar trimmed to match. Large sleeves, plaits on sleeves and tucks on cuffs. Side plaits in back. Color, white or tan. State color when ordering. Price..........$1.59
If by mail, postage extra, 18 cents.

LADIES' OR MISSES' SAILOR WAISTS.

No. 31C3687 LADIES' OR MISSES' SAILOR WAIST. Made of white lawn. Large sailor collar, inlaid front or dickey trimmed with embroidered medallion. Large sleeves. Plaits in back. Color, white only. Price, 69c
If by mail, postage extra, 18 cents.

No. 31C3690 LADIES' OR MISSES' SAILOR WAIST. Made of lawn. Large sailor collar. Strictly tailored. The trimming is of tailored stitching all around the sailor collar, in front, dickey or inlaid front and on collar. Fancy cuffs, large sleeves. Side plaits in back stitched several times. Color, navy blue with white tailored stitching. Price..........75c
If by mail, postage extra, 18 cents.

No. 31C3693 LADIES' OR MISSES' PRETTY SAILOR WAIST, nicely tailored, trimmed with folds made of white lawn all around the sailor collar, on inlaid front and collar as well. Several rows of stitching in front. Large sleeves, fancy cuffs. Side plaits in back. Color, tan with white trimmings. Price..........89c
If by mail, postage extra, 18 cents.

No. 31C3696 LADIES' OR MISSES' PRETTY SAILOR WAIST. Made of French lawn. Large sailor collar, inlaid front or dickey and standing collar are nicely trimmed with white buttonhole effect embroidery. Large sleeves, neat cuffs. Plaits in back from neck to waist. Color, white only. Price..........98c
Postage extra, 18 cents.

No. 31C3699 VERY PRETTY WAIST. Made of good quality madras cloth. Large sailor collar richly trimmed with straps of white lawn and inlaid with a solid color lawn to match the waist. Inlaid front or dickey and standing collar. Colors are very pretty. Cuffs to match also trimmed with white straps. Large sleeves and plaits in back. Colors, white with blue or white with pink. State color when ordering.
Price..........$1.19
If by mail, postage extra, 18 cents.

LADIES' AND MISSES' SATEEN WAISTS.

No. 31C3702 LADIES' WAIST. Made of black mercerized sateen. Plaits in front. Trimmings of straps of same material, pouch sleeves and neat cuffs. Splendid value for the money. Standing detachable collar. Color, black only.
Price........................**49c**
If by mail, postage extra, 18 cents.

No. 31C3705 LADIES' STYLISH WAIST. Made of good quality mercerized sateen. Trimmings of embroidery. Plaits of same material and tucks on yoke. Bishop sleeves. Embroidery on cuffs. Standing detachable collar. Color, black only.
Price........................**75c**
If by mail, postage extra, 20 cents.

No. 31C3708 LADIES' WAIST. Made of good quality sateen. Yoke front on the bias, made of tucks and plaits. Similar trimmings from yoke to waist. Entire garment is nicely tailored. Large sleeves. Detachable collar. Four plaits in back. Color, black only.
Price........................**89c**
If by mail, postage extra, 20 cents.

No. 31C3711 LADIES' WAIST. Made of very good quality fast black mercerized sateen. Round yoke, made of two rows of openwork lace, trimming to match in front. Plaits from yoke to waist on both sides in front. Standing detachable collar. Plaits in back, bishop sleeves. Buttons at the side and shoulder. Color, black only.
Price........................**85c**
If by mail, postage extra, 20 cents.

No. 31C3714 VERY PRETTY WAIST. Made of good quality silk finished sateen, nicely tailored. Stylish front, small extensions over shoulders. Trimmings of small pearl buttons and side plaits. Standing detachable collar, large sleeves, fancy cuffs. Plaits in back from neck to waist. Colors, black, blue, red or brown, with white polka dots. Please state color when ordering. Price........**89c**
If by mail, postage extra, 20 cents.

No. 31C3717 THIS ELABORATE WAIST is made of good quality sateen, pointed yoke in front, trimmed with self covered buttons and shirring from yoke to waist. This effect is very pretty. Detachable standing collar, fancy turnover. Large sleeves. Tucks and side plaits in back. Colors, black, red or castor. State color when ordering.
Price........................**89c**
If by mail, postage extra, 20 cents.

No. 31C3720 VERY NOBBY WAIST. Made of good quality black sateen, yoke front made of tucks, and fancy embroidery forming the yoke. Other trimmings are side plaits in front, on the sleeves and four in back. Colors, black, red or light brown (castor). State color when ordering.
Price........................**89c**
If by mail, postage extra, 20 cents.

No. 31C3723 ONE OF THE NEWEST WAISTS in good quality fast black sateen. Yoke front. The entire front is fluted and plaited making it very full, something that a well dressed lady will appreciate. Large sleeves. Plaits in back from neck to waist. Color, black only.
Price........................**89c**
If by mail, postage extra, 20 cents.

No. 31C3726 LADIES' WAIST. Made of fast black mercerized sateen, nicely embroidered all over with soutache, three plaits from both sides at shoulder, and stitched front. Standing detachable collar. Wide plaits in back. Bishop sleeves. Color, black only.
Price........................**98c**
If by mail, postage extra, 20 cents.

No. 31C3729 THIS STRICTLY TAILORMADE WAIST is made of fine imported mercerized sateen. Yoke in front is tucked all over and trimmed with straps of same material. Plaits in front from yoke to waist and tucks from neck to waist. Pouch sleeves, standing detachable collar. Several rows of tucks in back from neck to waist. Colors, black, dark red or cadet blue. Price..........**$1.15**
If by mail, postage extra, 20 cents.

LADIES' COLORED WAISTS.

No. 31C3732 LADIES' WAIST. Made of gingham, nicely tailored. The entire front is tucked and plaited. Standing detachable collar, fancy turnover. Large sleeves tucked at the cuffs. Two plaits in back. Colors, blue, tan or oxblood. State color when ordering.
Price........................**49c**
If by mail, postage extra, 15 cents.

No. 31C3735 VERY PRETTY WAIST. Made of good quality lawn. Entire front is tucked and plaited. Standing detachable collar, large sleeves, two plaits in back. Colors, black with white, brown with white, or white with black polka dots. State color when ordering.
Price........................**49c**
If by mail, postage extra, 15 cents.

No. 31C3738 LADIES' WAIST. Made of good quality striped lawn, nicely tailored. Front trimmed with pearl buttons and side plaits. Detachable crushed collar, fancy turnover. Full sleeves, neat cuffs and two plaits in back. Color, white with black stripes.
Price........................**49c**
If by mail, postage extra, 15 cents.

No. 31C3741 THIS TAILORED WAIST is made of good quality mercerized gingham. Entire front is side plaited. Standing detachable collar, fancy turnover. Large sleeves, two plaits in back. Exceptionally good value. Colors, blue or tan with fancy figures. State color when ordering.
Price........................**75c**
If by mail, postage extra, 15 cents.

No. 31C3744 SPECIAL VALUE IN LADIES' WAIST. Made of good quality fancy figured novelty cloth, nicely tailored. Entire front is side plaited and trimmed with three open work medallions. Detachable collar finished with bow of same material. Large sleeves. Four plaits in back. Strictly up to date. Color, all white with small black figures. Price, **95c**
If by mail, postage extra, 15 cents.

LADIES' LINEN WAISTS.

No. 31C3747 LADIES' WAIST. Made of linen, nicely tailored. Entire front is plaited. Detachable crushed collar, large sleeves, plaits in back from neck to waist. Color, white only.
Price....................75c
If by mail, postage extra, 18 cents.

No. 31C3751 THIS PRETTY WAIST is made of fine washable muslinen, the front is neatly embroidered in a fancy design and is made with side plaits. Leg of mutton sleeves, detachable collar with a bow in front. Extraordinary value. Color, white only. Price........98c
If by mail, postage extra, 18c.

No. 31C3753 VERY PRETTY LADIES' WAIST. Made of good quality light weight linen. The entire front is box plaited and stitched and trimmed with allover embroidery, as shown in picture. Detachable crushed collar, plaited sleeves, neat cuffs. Box plaits in back from neck to waist. Color, white only.
Price....................$1.15
If by mail, postage extra, 15 cents.

No. 31C3756 MADE OF GOOD QUALITY LINEN. The entire front is embroidered in silk in beautiful design. In addition to that, it is trimmed with tucks. Detachable collar with fancy turnover. Large sleeves, neat cuffs. Two plaits in back from neck to waist. Color, white only.
Price....................$1.35
If by mail, postage extra, 18 cents.

No. 31C3759 MADE OF GOOD QUALITY WHITE LINEN. The front is trimmed in beautiful design in embroidery over lace, and side plaits. Detachable collar trimmed with embroidery. Tucks and plaits on sleeves, neat back. Color, white only. Price..........$1.35
If by mail, postage extra, 18c.

No. 31C3763 THIS PRETTY WAIST is made of good quality washable muslinen, the entire front is embroidered with beautiful floral design. Tucks in front and in back of waist. Detachable standing collar, leg of mutton sleeves. Color, white only.
Price....................$1.39
If by mail, postage extra, 20 cents.

No. 31C3765 THIS HANDSOME WAIST is made of fine quality butcher linen, nicely tailored. Is made with side plaits and beautifully embroidered, as shown in illustration. Detachable crushed collar, nicely tucked. Large sleeves shirred at shoulders. Tucks in back from neck to waist, and front is trimmed with neat pearl buttons. Color, white only. Price..........$1.48
If by mail, postage extra, 20 cents.

No. 31C3768 THIS ATTRACTIVE WAIST is made of very fine linen. The entire front is made with buttonhole effect embroidery, which is the proper thing for this season. It has side plaits in front, large sleeves, neat cuffs. Plaits in back from neck to waist. Color, white only. Price..........$1.75
If by mail, postage extra, 20 cents.

No. 31C3771 THIS FINE WAIST is made of good quality butcher linen. Nicely tailored. The entire front is tucked at shoulders. Beautifully embroidered design in front. Detachable collar with fancy turnover, large sleeves, plain cuffs. Plaits in back, from neck to waist. Color, white only, Price....$1.89
If by mail, postage extra, 20 cents.

No. 31C3774 THIS BEAUTIFUL WAIST is made of good quality linen. Nicely tailored. The entire front is tucked and side plaited and trimmed in fancy design embroidery. Large sleeves finished with plaits. Fancy cuffs, tucked all over. Plaits and tucks in back from neck to waist. Color, white only.
Price....................$1.98
If by mail, postage extra, 20 cents.

SICILIAN, ALBATROSS AND NUN'S VEILING WAISTS.

No. 31C3777 LADIES' WAIST. Made of very fine imported Sicilian cloth. The waist is nicely tailored and is tucked from shoulders. Detachable collar with fancy turnover. Large sleeves, neat cuffs. Two box plaits in back. Colors, black, blue, brown or white. State color and size when ordering.
Price....................$1.48
If by mail, postage extra, 20 cents.

No. 31C3780 THIS PRETTY WAIST is made of good quality Sicilian cloth, nicely tailored. Entire front is side plaited and trimmed with black silk ringlets. Detachable crushed collar, large sleeves with tucks. Neat cuffs. Side plaits in back. Colors, black, blue, or brown. State color when ordering. Price, $1.75
If by mail, postage extra, 20 cents.

No. 31C3783 THIS PRETTY WAIST is made of all wool nun's veiling, nicely tailored. The entire front is side plaited and trimmed with silk French knots to match the waist. Side plaits on the sleeves, neat cuffs. Detachable collar with fancy turnover. Colors, black, cream, light blue or golden brown. State color and size when ordering.
Price....................$1.75
If by mail, postage extra, 18 cents.

No. 31C3786 LADIES' WAIST Made of very fine imported Sicilian cloth, special value for the money. The entire front is neatly trimmed with box plaits and small round pearl buttons. Detachable collar with fancy turnover. Large sleeves, fancy cuffs. Plain back. Colors, black navy, brown or white. State color and size when ordering. Price..$1.89
If by mail, postage extra, 20 cents.

No. 31C3789 THIS PRETTY WAIST is made of fine all wool albatross cloth. Front is neatly trimmed with side plaits, silk embroidery and small pearl buttons. Detachable collar with fancy turnover, embroidered. Large sleeves, plain cuffs. Side plaits in back from neck to waist. Colors, black, cream, red or royal blue. State color and size when ordering. Price..........$1.98
If by mail, postage extra, 20 cents.

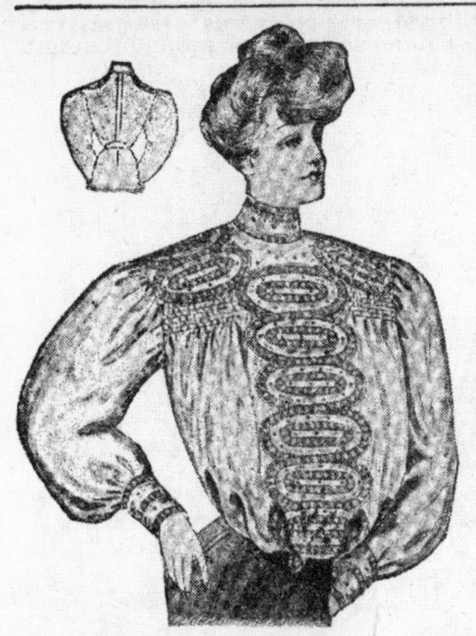

No. 31C3916 VERY ATTRACTIVE LADIES' WAIST. Made of very fine taffeta silk. The entire front is neatly trimmed with straps of same material alternating with lace insertion, French knot trimming, shirring in front forming a yoke, full leg of mutton sleeves, neat cuffs, collar to match. This waist buttons in back only. Colors, white or light blue. Price......**$5.95**
If by mail, postage extra, 25 cents.

No. 31C3914 VERY NEAT LADIES' WAIST. Made of very fine taffeta silk. A very pretty design. Front is made in square yoke effect and is trimmed with lace insertion, as shown in illustration, full leg of mutton sleeves with shirring at shoulders, pretty collar and cuffs, square yoke in back, made same as front. Buttons in back only. Made very full. Colors, light blue, pink or lavender. Price......**$5.95**
If by mail, postage extra, 25 cents.

No. 31C3908 THIS ATTRACTIVE WAIST is made of very fine Japanese silk. Extremely stylish. Circular yoke in front, made of lace insertion and shirring of same material alternating with each other. waist is very full, leg of mutton sleeves, neat cuffs, standing collar. This waist buttons in back only. Color, white only
Price......**$4.98**
If by mail, postage extra, 25 cents

No. 31C3794 THIS HANDSOME LADIES' WAIST is made of all wool albatross cloth. Entire front is made with side plaits, richly trimmed with openwork silk floss, is very rich and elaborate. Silk floss trimming around the standing detachable collar. Side plaits on sleeves and in back from neck to waist. Large sleeves. Colors, cream, pink or light blue. Price...**$2.25**
If by mail, postage extra, 20 cents.

No. 31C3795 THIS WAIST is made of very fine all wool cashmere, with newest bertha effect. Cape collar is pointed in front, shoulders and in back. Is detachable and waist can be worn with or without it. Trimmings are of lace around collar and edge. Silk medallions in front. Box plaits on waist under the pretty collar, and in back from neck to waist. Colors, cream, nile green or light blue with white lace. Price **$2.75**
If by mail, postage extra, 20 cents.

No. 31C3918 LADIES' VERY HANDSOME WAIST, of fine taffeta silk. The entire front is made with lace insertion and Swiss buttonhole embroidery, collar to match, leg of mutton sleeves made with lace insertion on the inside seam, which is finished at the end of sleeves as shown. Very beautiful and stylish. This waist buttons in back only. Colors, black, white or light blue.
Price......**$6.75**
If by mail, postage extra, 25 cents.

No. 31C3922 THIS ELABORATE LADIES' WAIST is made of very fine all silk peau de chine. Yoke is made of fine white lace. full shirring in front, fancy sleeves trimmed with shirring, cuffs made of white lace and finished with embroidered lace. waist is lined throughout with Japanese silk, buttons in back only. Colors, light blue, pink or black with cream colored lace yoke and cuffs.
Price......**$8.75**
If by mail, postage extra, 25 cents.

No. 31C3796 Made of very fine all wool cashmere cloth, yoke effect front and back. Trimmed with white embroidered medallions, transparent lace and shirring. Similar trimmings on the sleeves. Lace around the collar and the back is made the same as the front with embroidered medallions, shirring and lace. Lace trimming on cuffs. Colors, cream, pink, light blue or lavender.
Price......**$2.98**
If by mail, postage extra, 20 cents.

No. 31C3917 THIS STUNNING WAIST is made of very fine imported all over lace. The entire front is richly trimmed with heavy lace embroidery and lace trimming, fancy sleeves, neat cuffs, lined throughout with Japanese silk. This waist buttons in back only. Very rich and showy Colors, cream or black.
Price......**$6.50**
If by mail, postage extra, 25 cents.

No. 31C3793 THIS PRETTY LADIES' WAIST is made of fine all wool albatross cloth, yoke effect in front, made of lace. Plaits from yoke to waist. Standing detachable collar, side plaits on sleeves and lace trimmings on cuffs. Four plaits in back from neck to waist. Colors, cream, nile green or pink.
Price......**$1.98**
If by mail, postage extra, 18 cents.

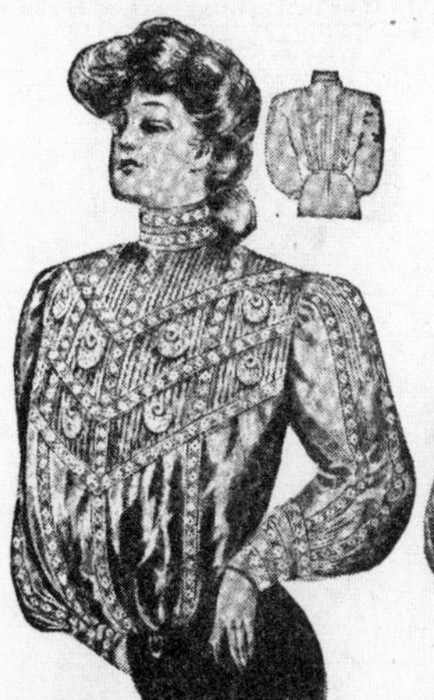

No. 31C3907 THIS BEAUTIFUL WAIST is made of very fine all silk peau de chine. The entire front is richly tucked and trimmed with lace insertion and fancy medallions, tucks on sleeves as well as lace insertion, very pretty cuffs, the back is also made with tucks and lace insertion. This waist buttons in back only. Very stylish. Colors, light blue, pink or white.
Price......**$4.95**
If by mail, postage extra, 25 cents.

No. 31C3910 THE NEWEST DESIGN in a ladies' silk waist. Made of very fine taffeta silk, very full front, richly trimmed with tucks, lace insertion in pretty design, full leg of mutton sleeves, fancy cuffs, neat collar, back made same as front with lace insertion. This waist buttons in back only Colors, black, light blue or white.
Price......**$4.95**
If by mail, postage extra, 25 cents.

No. 31C3919 A GORGEOUS WAIST. Made of very fine peau de chine silk. Entire front is elaborately tucked silk insertion, French silk knots and heavy silk trimmings to match, similar trimmings on shoulders, sleeves are very neat, made with lace insertions and French silk knots, lace trimmings on collar, back is trimmed to match the front. Very beautiful design. Exceptionally full. Colors, tan (champagne), olive or white.
Price....(Postage 25c)....**$7.50**

No. 31C3903 THIS BEAUTIFUL LADIES' WAIST is made of very fine washable Japanese silk, the entire front is richly trimmed with full shirring, lace and openwork silk embroidery, similar trimming on upper part of sleeves, fancy cuffs, neat collar. This waist buttons in back only. Three clusters of tucks in back. Color, white only.
Price......**$3.98**
If by mail postage extra 25 cents.

No. 31C3792 VERY HANDSOME WAIST. Made of imported brilliantine cloth. Entire front is richly tucked, side plaited and embroidered in silk. Detachable collar with fancy turnover. Large sleeves, neat cuffs. Side plaits and tucks in back from neck to waist. Colors, black, blue, white or brown State color when ordering.
Price......**$2.35**
If by mail, postage extra, 22 cents.

YOUNG GIRLS' WAISTS.

These waists are made for 8 to 15-year old girls. This is a new line of goods and has proven very popular, as these waists are very pretty and very reasonable in price. When ordering, please state age of child, also number of inches around the bust

No. 31C3925 LITTLE GIRLS' WAIST. Made of French lawn. Plaited in front, detachable crushed collar with fancy turnover, plaits in back. Colors, white with black, blue or pink polka dots. **State color and size when ordering.**
Price 49c
If by mail, postage extra, 14 cents.

No. 31C3927 LITTLE GIRLS' WAIST. Made of good quality fast colored gingham. Made with sailor collar, which is bordered with white fancy striped madras, inlaid front or dickey made of white madras, bow in front of same material. Colors, oxblood or blue with white trimmings. Price 75c
If by mail, postage extra, 11 cents.

No. 31C3930 LITTLE GIRLS' WAIST. Made of good quality fine French lawn. Entire front is made of allover embroidery in neat design. Side plaits, detachable crushed collar, new sleeves, tucked cuffs. Color, white only.
Price 89c
If by mail, postage extra, 12 cents.

No. 31C3933 LITTLE GIRLS' WAIST. Made of good quality white madras cloth, mercerized stripe running through it; nice sailor effect. The border of the sailor collar and tie made of fine gingham. Colors, white, with blue, oxblood or white gingham trimming. **State color and size when ordering.** Price 89c
If by mail, postage extra, 14 cents.

No. 31C3936 LITTLE GIRLS' WAIST. Made of good quality washable pique, nice blouse effect, neatly tailored. Side plaits; buttons on the side; detachable crushed collar, neat turnover; stylish sleeves. Color, white only.
Price 95c
If by mail, postage extra, 15 cents.

LADIES' WAISTS OF MATERIALS THAT LOOK LIKE SILK.

No. 31C3807 LADIES' WASHABLE WAIST. Made of good quality mercerized material, looks just like silk and wears better. Nicely tailored. Plaits in front trimmed with pearl buttons. Detachable standing collar, large sleeves, neat cuffs. Plaits in back from neck to waist. Colors, cream, black or tan (champagne).
Price $1.15
If by mail, postage extra, 15 cents.

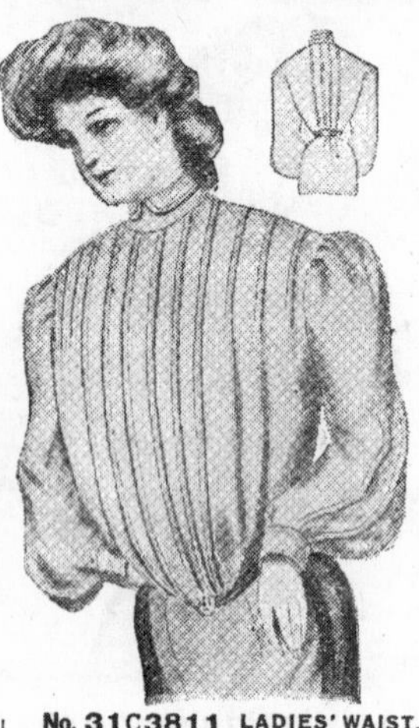

No. 31C3811 LADIES' WAIST. Made of good quality mercerized madras in fancy designs. Nicely tailored. The entire front is side plaited. Detachable crushed collar, large sleeves with plaits near the cuffs, box plait in back with two side plaits. Color, white in fancy figured design.
Price $1.19
If by mail, postage extra, 20 cents.

No. 31C3813 SPECIAL VALUE IN LADIES' WAISTS. Made of good quality poplin. This material has the luster of silk and washes well. Waist is nicely tailored, tucked all over in front and finished with side plaits. Detachable collar, large sleeves, plain cuffs. Plaits in back from neck to waist. Colors, tan (champagne) or royal blue. **State color and size when ordering.** Price $1.35
If by mail, postage extra, 22 cents.

No. 31C3816 ONE OF THE NEATEST AND MOST UP TO DATE WAISTS. Made of very fine imported poplin. This material has the luster of silk and it wears much better. This waist is plaited in front and embroidered in silk dots, in the newest color combinations. Sleeves are plaited and tucked. Colors, tan with light blue, with red, or with tan silk embroidered dots, or all black. **State color and size when ordering.**
Price $1.98
If by mail, postage extra, 20 cents.

No. 31C3817 THIS RICHLY EMBROIDERED WAIST is made of very fine silk finished poplin. Entire waist is richly embroidered, forming a yoke in front. Exceptionally large sleeves, nicely embroidered, neat cuffs. Detachable standing collar with fancy embroidery. Circular yoke in back embroidered to match the front. This waist buttons in back only. Colors, tan, light blue or black with embroideries to match. **State color and size when ordering.** Price $3.35
If by mail, postage extra, 25 cents.

WASHABLE JAPANESE SILK WAISTS.

No. 31C3819 VERY PRETTY WAIST. Made of good quality Japanese silk. Entire front tucked and trimmed with lace insertion. Detachable crushed collar with lace trimming. Tucks on large sleeves, neat cuffs. Tucks in back. Color, white only.
Price $1.95
If by mail, postage extra 15 cents.

No. 31C3822 THIS PRETTY TAILOR MADE WAIST is made of fine Jap silk. Entire front side plaited and hemstitched. Detachable crushed collar with neat turnover. Large sleeves, tucks on cuffs. Side plaits in back. Color, black or white. **State color and size when ordering.**
Price $1.98
If by mail, postage extra, 15 cents.

No. 31C3825 THIS ATTRACTIVE WAIST is made of Jap silk. Front is trimmed with silk medallions, lace insertion, side plaits and shirring forming a yoke. Detachable crushed collar. Shirring on sleeves. Side plaits in back. Color, white only.
Price $2.35
If by mail, postage extra, 15 cents.

No. 31C3828 VERY RICH AND SHOWY WAIST. Made of good quality Jap silk. Yoke effect front, trimmed with tucks, side plaits and lace insertion. Crushed collar. Very full sleeves tucked. Fancy cuffs. Three clusters of tucks in back. Color, white only.
Price $2.50
If by mail, postage extra, 18 cents.

No. 31C3831 THIS ELABORATE WAIST is strictly tailored. Made of good quality Jap silk. The entire front is side plaited and trimmed with French knots. This is the very newest. Detachable crushed collar, large sleeves tucked at cuffs. Side plaits in back. Colors, black or white. **State color and size when ordering.** Price $2.50
If by mail, postage extra, 15 cents.

No. 31C3834 HANDSOME WAIST. Made of good quality Jap silk. Front is richly trimmed with side plaits, tucks and lace insertion. Detachable crush collar, tucks on the large sleeves at top and bottom, fancy cuffs. Tucks in back from neck to waist. Color, white only. Price..........................$2.75
If by mail, postage extra, 18 cents.

No. 31C3837 THIS GENTEEL WAIST is made of very fine Jap silk. Yoke front shirred, as shown in illustration, made very full. Large sleeves, beautifully shirred and the cuffs are finished with three rows of lace insertion. The shirred yoke reaches all around the back. This waist buttons in back only. Colors, black or white. State color and size when ordering. Price.......$2.75
If by mail, postage extra, 18 cents.

No. 31C3840 LADIES' WAIST. Made of very fine Jap silk. The entire front is tucked and richly trimmed with insertion of lace and fancy embroidered medallions. Detachable crushed collar trimmed with lace and tucks. Large sleeves, fancy cuffs. Tucks and lace insertion in back from neck to waist. Color, white only. Price..........................$2.75
If by mail, postage extra, 20 cents.

No. 31C3845 THIS HANDSOME WAIST is made of good quality Jap silk. Yoke effect front, richly trimmed with tucks and fancy embroidered lace. Collar is made of lace. Large sleeves tucked at cuffs, cuffs also tucked. Side plaits in back. Color, white only. Price..........................$2.98
If by mail, postage extra, 20 cents.

No. 31C3846 THIS ELABORATE WAIST is made of good quality Jap silk. The entire front is handsomely trimmed with silk embroidery, tucks and embroidered dots. Very pretty design. Large sleeves tucked at shoulders, fancy cuffs. Detachable crushed collar. Three clusters of tucks in back. Color, white only. Price..........$2.98
If by mail, postage, extra, 20 cents.

No. 31C3849 NOBBY WAIST. Made of good quality Jap silk, front trimmed with tucks. Side plaits and front piece made of embroidered silk in newest buttonhole effect. Large sleeves tucked at cuffs. Detachable crushed collar. Tucks in back from neck to waist. Color, white only. Price..........$2.98
If by mail, postage extra, 20 cents.

No. 31C3852 THIS ATTRACTIVE WAIST is made of fine Jap silk. Circular yoke front and back trimmed with a bertha cape and edged with lace to match; very attractive. Lace insertions around the yoke, around the collar and cuffs. Large sleeves. This waist buttons in back only. Color, white only. Price..........................$3.35
If by mail, postage extra, 20 cents.

No. 31C3855 THIS ELABORATE WAIST is made of fine Jap silk. Entire front is handsomely trimmed with tucks and fancy embroidered medallions over lace. Shirring forming a yoke. Detachable crushed collar trimmed with tucks and lace. Fancy sleeves shirred, and very pretty cuffs, trimmed with lace and embroidery. Two clusters of tucks in back from neck to waist. Color, white only. Price..........$3.50
If by mail, postage extra, 20 cents.

No. 31C3858 THIS LADIES' WAIST is made of very fine Jap silk. Entire front is richly embroidered in silk in beautiful design. Side plaits in front. Detachable crushed collar, large sleeves, tucked cuffs. Tucks in back from neck to waist. Very elaborate. Color, white only. Price..........................$3.50
If by mail, postage extra, 20 cents.

No. 31C3861 THIS PRETTY WAIST is made of fine Jap silk. The entire front is heavily tucked and trimmed with lace insertions and embroidered medallions. Yoke effect. Very large sleeves richly trimmed with lace insertion and embroidered medallions. Fancy cuffs tucked all around. This waist buttons in back only. Very stylish and strictly up to date. Color, white only. Price..........................$3.75
If by mail, postage extra, 20 cents.

LACE AND NET WAISTS.

No. 31C3864 WAIST. Made of washable lace, neatly trimmed with fancy embroidery in front, side plaits. Crushed collar, large sleeves. This waist is lined throughout with white lawn. One of the newest things shown. Color, white only. Price..........................$1.75
If by mail, postage extra, 18 cents.

No. 31C3867 THIS HANDSOME WAIST is made of washable lace. Yoke front made of lace insertion, trimmings of fancy embroidery in front. Crushed collar. Large sleeves. This waist buttons in back only. Lined throughout with lawn to match. Colors, white or tan (ecru). State color and size when ordering. Price..........................$1.98
If by mail, postage extra, 18 cents.

No. 31C3870 THIS PRETTY WAIST is made of washable lace. Entire front is richly trimmed with embroidered medallions, box plaits and side plaits. Detachable crushed collar to match waist. Very large sleeves; box plaits in back. Lined throughout with lawn to match. Colors, white or champagne color (tan). State color and size when ordering. Price..........$2.35
If by mail, postage extra, 20 cents.

No. 31C3873 VERY FINE LACE WAIST. Trimmed with fancy embroidered flower design in front, forming a yoke. Large sleeves. Waist lined throughout with China silk. Very pretty and stylish. Colors, white or champagne color (tan). State color and size when ordering. Price..........................$4.95
If by mail, postage extra, 29 cents.

No. 31C3876 VERY FINE LADIES' WAIST. Made of good grade of lace. Round yoke effect in front, richly trimmed with rosettes made of silk and drawn ribbon work. Crushed collar. Large sleeves. Rosettes on cuffs. This waist buttons in back only. Lined throughout with Jap silk. Colors, white or tan (champagne color). Very handsome and stylish. Price...$6.95
If by mail, postage extra, 25 cents.

LADIES' SILK WAISTS.

No. 31C3879 LADIES' WAIST. Made of good quality peau de soie. Panel front trimmed with fancy silk embroidered medallions. Tucking on both sides. Detachable collar, new shaped sleeves, tucks in back. Lined to waist with cambric. Colors, black, golden brown or royal blue. Please state color and size when ordering. Price............**$2.75**
If by mail, postage extra, 18 cents.

No. 31C3882 LADIES' WAIST. Made of taffeta silk. The entire front is corded and hemstitched. High standing collar with turnover flaps. Bishop sleeves corded several times and narrow cuffs. Several rows of cording in back. Color, black only.
Price......................**$2.98**
If by mail, postage extra, 20 cents.

No. 31C3885 VERY PRETTY WAIST. Made of good quality taffeta silk. Nicely tailored. The entire front is side plaited, as shown in illustration. Large sleeves with tucks, plain cuffs. Detachable collar with fancy turnover. Colors, black, brown or red. State color and size when ordering. Price..**$2.98**
If by mail, postage extra, 20 cents.

No. 31C3888 EXCEPTIONALLY GOOD QUALITY WAIST. Made of very fine all silk peau de soie, richly trimmed in front with silk lace. Side plaits forming a yoke and hemstitched box plaits on sleeves. Neat cuffs. Detachable standing collar Side plaits in back. Colors, black, brown or white. State color and size when ordering.
Price (Postage extra, 20c) **$3.50**

No. 31C3891 LADIES' WAIST. Made of good quality taffeta silk. Yoke effect front, trimmed with fancy flower design medallions. Several clusters of tucks. Large sleeves, plain cuffs. Detachable collar with fancy turnover. Tucks and side plaits in back. Lined with cambric. Colors, black, royal blue or tan. State color and size when ordering.
Price (Postage extra, 20c.) **$3.50**

No. 31C3894 This is one of the newest effects and is very pretty. Made of extra heavy good quality taffeta silk, strictly tailored. Made with plaits and side plaits in front and finished with French knots to match the waist. Large sleeves. Detachable collar with fancy turnover. Side plaits in back. Lined with cambric. Colors, black, blue, brown or white. State color and size when ordering Price **$3.50**
If by mail, postage extra, 20 cents.

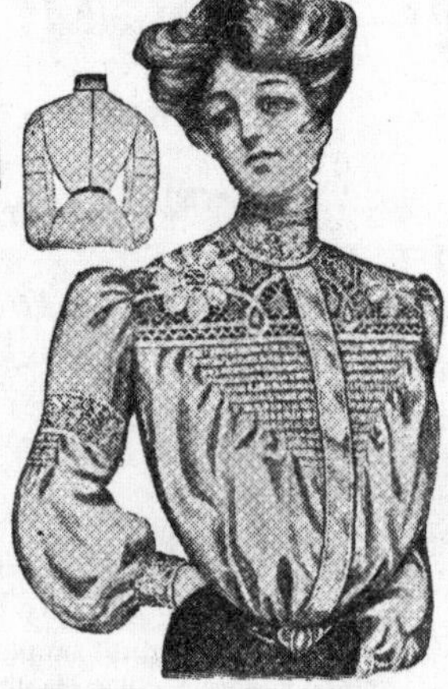

No. 31C3897 LADIES' WAIST. Made of very fine peau de chene. Upper yoke front made of lace, pointed yoke made of shirring Sleeves are trimmed with lace and shirring, and cuffs made of lace. Very handsome and artistic. Colors, light blue, pink or tan. State color and size when ordering.
Price.......................**$3.98**
If by mail, postage extra, 20 cents.

No. 31C3900 THIS STYLISH WAIST is made of very fine taffeta silk, nicely tailored. Entire front is made with plaits and side plaits forming a yoke front. The front band is made of embroidered silk. Detachable collar is trimmed with embroidery. Large sleeves and plaited cuffs. Four plaits in back from neck to waist. Lined with cambric. Colors, black, brown, white or tan. State color and size when ordering.
Price (Postage extra, 20c.) **$3.98**

No. 31C3904 THIS PRETTY LADIES' NOVELTY WAIST is one of the newest and most up to date styles, made of fine taffeta silk and is made on the style of a man's shirt. Is very comfortable, neat and nicely tailored. Made with laydown collar and tie of same material, and watch pocket. Neat sleeves. Blouse back and blouse front. Colors, brown, navy, white or red. State color and size when ordering. Price..**$3.98**
If by mail, postage extra, 20 cents.

No. 31C3905 THIS ATTRACTIVE WAIST is made of very fine grade of taffeta silk. Entire front is plaited and is made very full. It is made on the style of an accordion plait. Has a detachable collar, finished, with neat tie which is made as shown in illustration. Very large sleeves, neat cuffs. Plaits in back from neck to waist. Colors, all black, blue or green, changeable. State color and size when ordering.
Price (Postage extra, 20c.) **$4.75**

No. 31C3906 SPECIAL VALUE IN LADIES' STYLISH WAIST. Made of very fine taffeta silk. Entire front is richly embroidered in neat flower design and silk dots. It is also trimmed with plaits and tucks. Tucks on the large sleeves and around the cuffs. Detachable crushed collar. Three clusters of tucks in back from neck to waist. Lined with cambric. Colors, black, tan or white. State color and size when ordering.
Price......................**$4.95**
If by mail, postage extra, 22 cents.

No. 31C3909 VERY FASHIONABLE, NEAT AND UP TO DATE LADIES' WAIST. Made of fine taffeta silk. The entire front is tucked in yoke effect and finished with fancy silk embroidery trimmings. Detachable crushed collar tucked all over. Large sleeves and butcher cuffs. Back is tucked, forming a yoke. Large crushed belt, all around the waist. Very pretty. Colors, black, brown or white. State color and size when ordering.
Price......................**$4.95**
If by mail, postage extra, 22 cents.

No. 31C3912 THIS ELABORATE LADIES' WAIST is made of very fine taffeta silk, is richly trimmed with plaited shirring forming a yoke in front. Box plait in front, silk embroidered to match. Crushed collar. Very full sleeves with plaited shirring, neat cuffs. Tucks in back from neck to waist. Lined throughout with cambric. Colors, black or white. State color and size when ordering.
Price.........................**$4.98**
If by mail, postage extra, 22 cents.

No. 31C3915 LADIES' WAIST. Made of very fine extra heavy taffeta silk. Yoke in front is made in fine embroidered design, hemstitched all around. In addition to this the front is entirely tucked. Tucking on large sleeves and cuffs. Detachable collar with hemstitching. Three clusters of tucks in back. Lined throughout with cambric. Colors, black, tan or white. State color and size when ordering.
Price.........................**$5.75**
If by mail, postage extra, 22 cents.

No. 31C3921 Made of very fine taffeta silk. Yoke in front. Shirred straps all around the collar and all around the yoke; beautiful sleeves, shirred, making the sleeves very full. Back made the same as front, with slot seams and finished with shirred strap of same material. Buttons in back only. Lined throughout with cambric. Colors, black, white or golden brown, with burnt orange ruffles around collar and cuffs; these ruffles can be easily removed if combination of colors don't suit. Price.**$6.95**

LADIES' UNDERSKIRTS.

Sizes, 22 to 34 inches Waist Measure and 38 to 44 inches in Length. When Ordering, State Color and Size (Waist and Length Measure.)

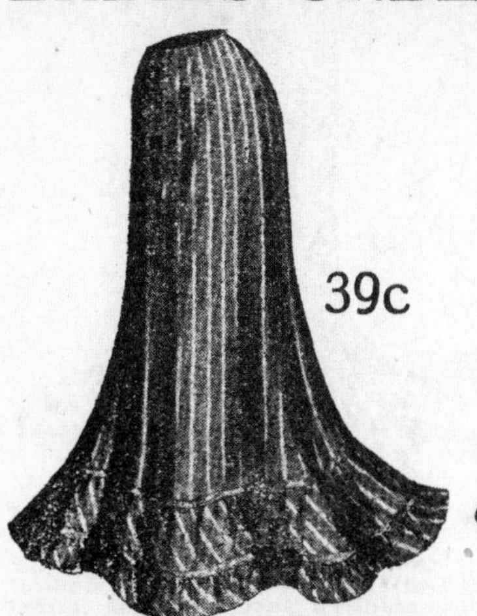

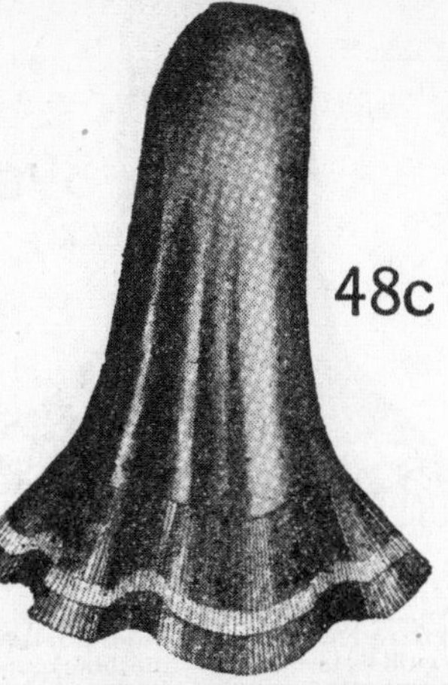

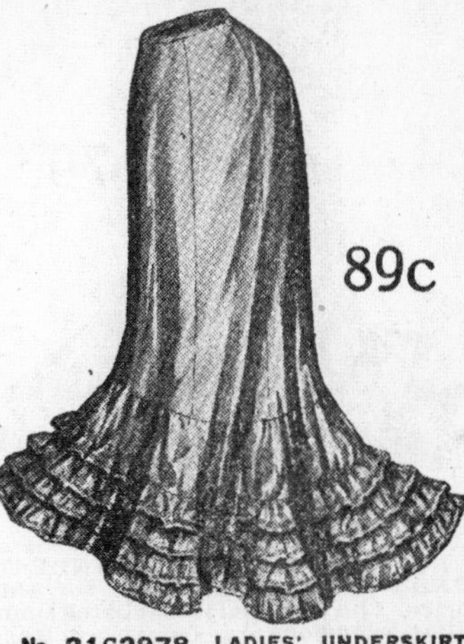

No. 31C3969 LADIES' UNDERSKIRT. Made of washable striped gingham. Double flounce around bottom, trimmed with strap over each flounce. Color, blue with white stripes only. Price....................................39c
If by mail, postage extra, 16 cents.

No. 31C3972 LADIES' UNDERSKIRT. Made of washable gingham. Flounce around bottom, knife plaited, neatly trimmed with strap of white percale. A very pretty garment. Colors, blue, gray or oxblood, with white trimming. Price....................................48c
If by mail, postage extra, 15 cents.

No. 31C3975 LADIES' UNDERSKIRT. Made of gingham, neat style, wide flounce around the bottom, finished with two ruffles and fancy stitching on each ruffle. Colors, blue or tan. State color and size when ordering. Price....................................69c
If by mail, postage extra, 22 cents.

No. 31C3978 LADIES' UNDERSKIRT. Neatly made, wide flounced around the bottom, richly trimmed with four ruffles, each ruffle stitched all around. Very neat and full skirt. Colors, blue, tan, linen or oxblood. State color and size when ordering. Price....89c
If by mail, postage extra, 25 cents.

49c

69c

No. 31C3980 LADIES' UNDERSKIRT. Made of domet flannel, wide flounce around the bottom, finished with embroidery. Colors, dark and light gray plaids. Price....................................39c
If by mail, postage extra, 24 cents.

No. 31C3984 LADIES' UNDERSKIRT. Made of black sateen with flounce at bottom, trimmed with four rows of cording. Color, black only. Our price is less than most dealers pay for such a skirt at wholesale. Don't forget to state size wanted. Price....................................49c
If by mail, postage extra, 18 cents.

No. 31C3985 LADIES' UNDERSKIRT. Made of good quality fast black spun glass. Wide flounce around the bottom, fluted all around and trimmed with two rows of ruffles. Color, black only. Price....................................69c
If by mail, postage extra, 28 cents.

No. 31C3981 LADIES' UNDERSKIRT. Made of good quality light weight spun glass. Wide flounce around the bottom, accordion plaited and finished with a ruffle, stitched several times. Colors, black, blue, brown, or dark red. Always state color and size when ordering. Price..49c
If by mail, postage extra, 18 cents.

79c

No. 31C3987 LADIES' UNDERSKIRT. Made of good quality fast black mercerized sateen. Wide flounce around the bottom, fluted all around and finished with two ruffles and straps of same material. Excellent quality. Colors, blue, black or cerise. Price....................................75c
If by mail, postage extra, 28 cents.

No. 31C3990 LADIES' UNDERSKIRT. Made of good quality spun glass, wide flounce around the bottom of which the upper part is fluted all around and finished with strap seams. Two ruffles around the bottom. Splendid value. Colors, black, red or brown. Price....................................75c
If by mail, postage extra, 25 cents.

No. 31C3993 EXTRAORDINARY VALUE IN LADIES' UNDERSKIRT. Made of fine black sateen. Splendid value for the price. Wide flounce around the bottom, trimmed with three rows of fancy stitching. Strapped seams. Two ruffles around the bottom also trimmed with fancy stitching. Color, black only.
Price......(Postage extra, 28 cents)......75c

No. 31C3996 THIS PRETTY UNDERSKIRT is made of fine fast colored black spun glass. Has a wide flounce, accordion plaited richly trimmed with one narrow and one wide ruffle, which is finished with a smaller ruffle. Very pretty style, value unexcelled; well made in every respect. Color, black only.
Price......(Postage extra, 25 cents)....79c

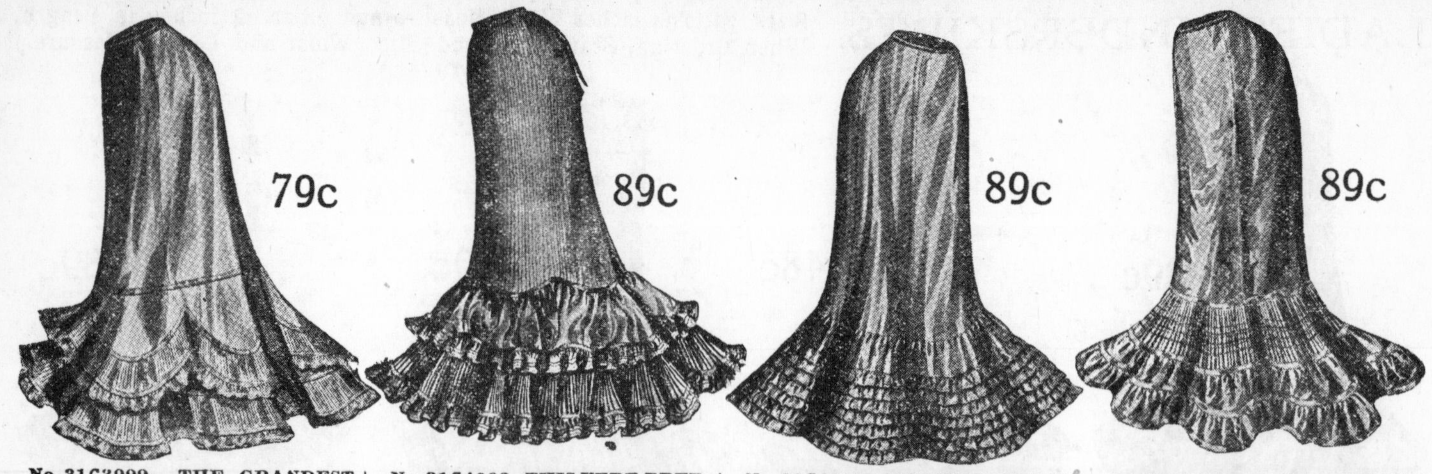

No. 31C3999 THE GRANDEST UNDERSKIRT ever made for the price. The material is fast black spun glass, wide flounce around the bottom with strapped seams. Two wide ruffles, both accordion plaited, and finished with small ruffle around the bottom, also an under flounce. Color, black only. Price........................79c
If by mail, postage extra, 25 cents.

No. 31C4002 THIS VERY PRETTY UNDERSKIRT is made of fast black mercerized sateen. Wide flounce around the bottom, finished with two rows of shirred ruffles. One knife plaited ruffle, which is also finished with a smaller one. Dust ruffle around the bottom. Color, black only. Price..........................89c
If by mail, postage extra, 30 cents.

No. 31C4005 ANOTHER GREAT BARGAIN. This rich underskirt, full of ruffles, is made of fine black mercerized sateen. Wide flounce around the bottom, trimmed with seven smaller ruffles. Very pretty and showy garment. Nothing better made for the price. Colors, black or red. Price..........................89c
If by mail, postage extra, 30 cents.

No. 31C4008 THIS PRETTY LADIES' UNDERSKIRT is made of guaranteed fast black mercerized sateen. Wide flounce around the bottom, the upper part accordion plaited and trimmed with three straps of same material. The lower part made with double flounce and finished with strapped seams. Color, black only. Price, 89c
If by mail, postage extra, 30 cents.

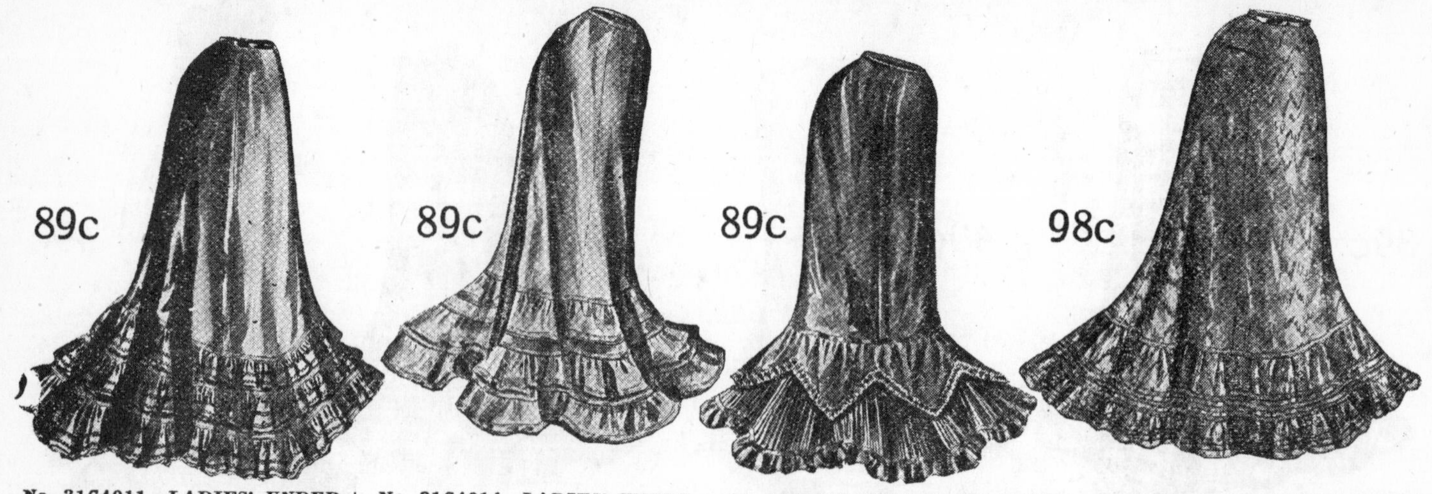

No. 31C4011 LADIES' UNDERSKIRT. Made of fast colored mercerized spun glass, soft finished, very rich and showy, made with a graduated flounce all around the bottom, trimmed with three wide ruffles, each ruffle finished with fancy thread braid. Color, black only. Price..............89c
If by mail, postage extra, 30 cents.

No. 31C4014 LADIES' UNDERSKIRT. Made of guaranteed fast black soft finished mercerized sateen. The material is splendid and bound to give good service. Made with wide flounce around bottom, strap trimming of same materials. Two wide flounces each trimmed with self strapping. Under flounce. Color, black only. Price.....89c
If by mail, postage extra, 30 cents.

No. 31C4017 THIS ATTRACTIVE SKIRT is made of fast black soft finished mercerized sateen. Has a wide flounce around the bottom, strapped seams, zigzag flounce, trimmed with ruching. Another flounce accordion plaited all around and finished with small ruffle around the bottom. Color, black only. Price..................89c
If by mail, postage extra, 30 cents.

No. 31C4020 THIS PRETTY UNDERSKIRT is made of fast colored moire, otherwise called imitation watered silk. Has a rich luster; wide flounce around the bottom tucked and trimmed with thread braid. Wide ruffle, strapped seams and under flounce. Colors, black or brown. **State color when ordering.** Price...........98c
If by mail, postage extra, 30 cents.

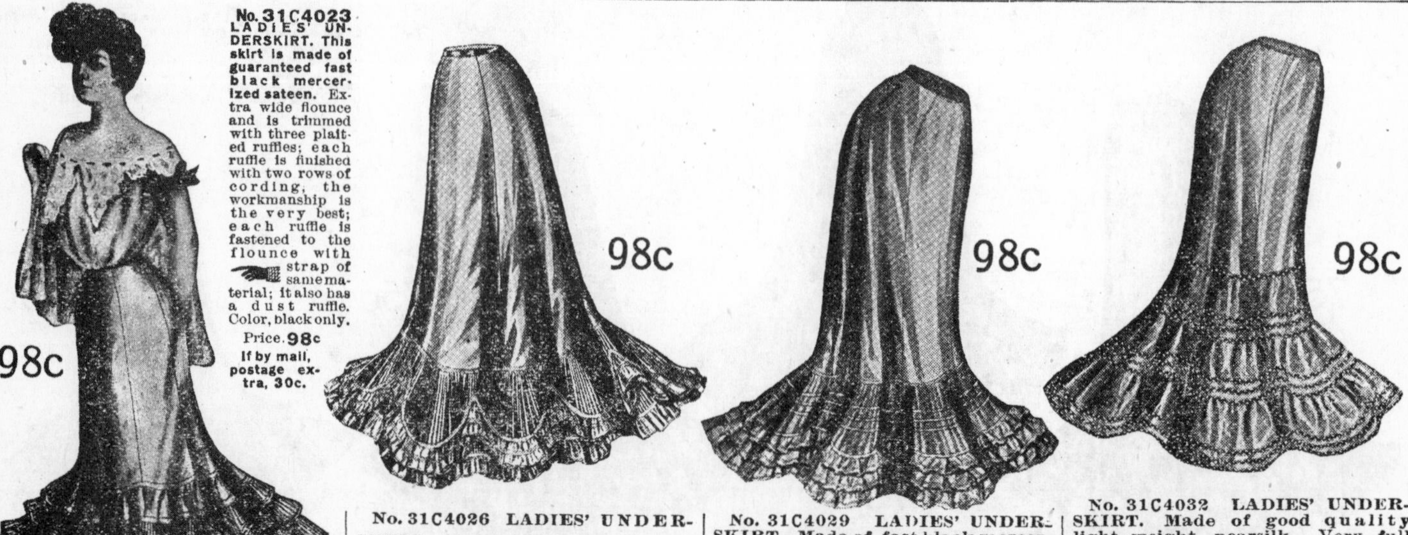

No. 31C4023 LADIES' UNDERSKIRT. This skirt is made of guaranteed fast black mercerized sateen. Extra wide flounce and is trimmed with three plaited ruffles; each ruffle is finished with two rows of cording, the workmanship is the very best; each ruffle is fastened to the flounce with strap of same material; it also has a dust ruffle. Color, black only. Price 98c
If by mail, postage extra, 30c.

No. 31C4026 LADIES' UNDERSKIRT. Made of fast black mercerized sateen. Very wide and full flounce fluted all around and trimmed with a wide and full double flounce. Color, black only. Price.....................98c
If by mail, postage extra, 28 cents.

No. 31C4029 LADIES' UNDERSKIRT. Made of fast black mercerized sateen. Wide flounce around the bottom, upper part accordion plaited and trimmed with straps of same material, finished with three smaller ruffles, each ruffle trimmed with narrow braid. Color, black only. Price..............................98c
If by mail, postage extra, 28 cents.

No. 31C4032 LADIES' UNDERSKIRT. Made of good quality light weight nearsilk. Very full skirt. Has wide triple flounce, each flounce trimmed with three straps. This is entirely new, made very full and light weight. This material has good luster and it rustles like silk. Colors, black, red or brown. **State color and size when ordering.** Price. 98c
If by mail, postage extra, 28 cents.

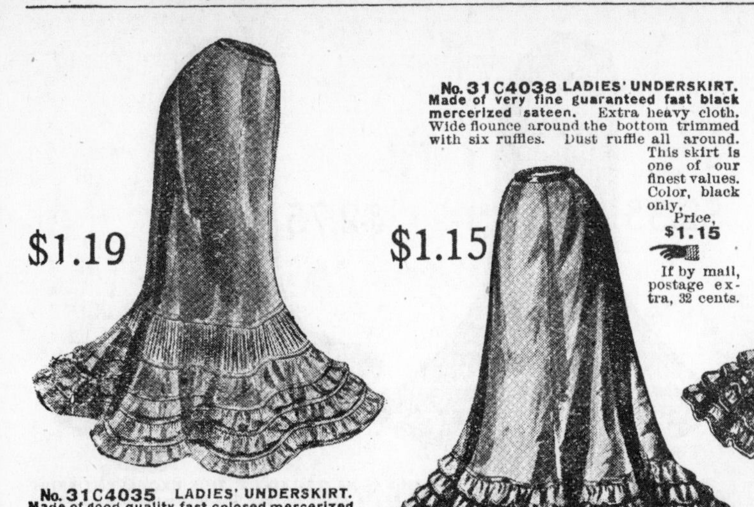

No. 31C4038 LADIES' UNDERSKIRT. Made of very fine guaranteed fast black mercerized sateen. Extra heavy cloth. Wide flounce around the bottom trimmed with six ruffles. Dust ruffle all around. This skirt is one of our finest values. Color, black only. Price, **$1.15**

If by mail, postage extra, 32 cents.

No. 31C4035 LADIES' UNDERSKIRT. Made of good quality fast colored mercerized sateen, very desirable garment, made with wide flounce, the upper part accordion plaited, the lower part is finished with three smaller ruffles, each ruffle finished with strapped seams. Colors, black, green or red. State color and size when ordering.
Price..**$1.19**
If by mail, postage extra, 30 cents.

$1.15

No. 31C4041 LADIES' UNDERSKIRT. Made of good quality guaranteed fast black mercerized sateen. Very full wide flounce around the bottom, finished with five ruffles and each ruffle hemstitched and sewed to skirt with a strap of same material. Dust ruffle around the bottom. Color, black only. Price..........**$1.15**
If by mail, postage extra, 30 cents.

$1.19

No. 31C4044 THIS PRETTY UNDER SKIRT is made of fast colored highly lustered mercerized sateen; wide flounce around the bottom, nicely accordion plaited and trimmed with full ruffle in zigzag fashion and ruffle around the bottom; tucked and strapped seams, under ruffle all around. Colors, black, blue or red.
Price..**$1.19**
If by mail, postage extra, 30 cents.

No. 31C4047 LADIES' UNDERSKIRT. Made of fast colored highly lustered soft finished mercerized sateen. Very full. Wide flounce around the bottom, accordion plaited and trimmed with straps of same material, finished with ruffle all around. Under flounce trimmed with another ruffle. Colors, black, dark blue or brown. Price.....................**$1.39**
If by mail, postage extra, 30 cents.

No. 31C4050 LADIES' UNDERSKIRT. Made of guaranteed fast black mercerized sateen. Very stylish flounce all around the bottom trimmed with openwork stitching, and a wider flounce at the bottom also trimmed with openwork stitching. Under flounce finished with a ruffle at the bottom. This under flounce is made in black, green or cerise color. State color when ordering. The colors show through the openwork stitching, giving it a very pretty and neat appearance. Price, **$1.35**

Postage extra, 30 cents.

$1.35

No. 31C4053 LADIES' UNDERSKIRT. Made of fast black soft finished highly lustered mercerized sateen, made first class in every respect. Wide flounce around the bottom, trimmed with several rows of straps of same material. Accordion plaited flounce finished with ruffle, smaller flounce all around the bottom. Color, black only.
Price..**$1.35**
If by mail, postage extra, 30 cents.

No. 31C4056 LADIES' NOBBY UNDERSKIRT. Made of fast colored highly lustered mercerized sateen. Wide flounce all around the bottom, richly trimmed with ruching forming a fancy figure, finished with accordion plaited flounce all around the bottom. Under ruffle. Colors, black, brown or maroon. State color when ordering.
Price..**$1.35**
If by mail, postage extra, 30 cents.

No. 31C4062 LADIES' UNDERSKIRT. Made of fast colored highly lustered mercerized sateen. Wide flounce all around the bottom, richly trimmed with openwork stitching, finished with strapped seams and a double ruffle. Under flounce finished with small ruffle. The under flounce of this skirt is made in black, green or red colors and it shows through the openwork, giving it a very pretty and attractive effect. Be sure to state color and size when ordering.
Price..**$1.39**
If by mail, postage extra, 33 cents.

$1.48

No. 31C4065 LADIES' UNDERSKIRT, made of fast black highly lustered mercerized sateen. Wide flounce around the bottom, nicely tailored, trimmed with accordion plaited ruffle. Double ruffle on the bottom and small tucks. Wide under flounce made with wide ruffle. Color, black only.
Price..**$1.48**
If by mail, postage extra, 35 cents.

$1.69

No. 31C4066 LADIES' UNDERSKIRT. Made of a guaranteed mercerized sateen. Wide flounce around bottom, neatly trimmed with three fluted ruffles, each ruffle finished with ruching of same material. Three straps of same material ornament the flounce. Color, black only.
Price..**$1.69**
If by mail, postage extra, 34 cents.

State COLOR and SIZE WHEN ORDERING

$1.75

No. 31C4068 LADIES' UNDERSKIRT. Made of fine fast black, highly lustered soft finished mercerized sateen. Wide flounce around the bottom, richly trimmed with over flounce which is accordion plaited and finished with a ruffle. Under flounce is accordion plaited all around and finished with a ruffle, also dust ruffle. Colors, black, brown or red.
Price..**$1.75**
If by mail, postage extra, 34 cents.

$1.75

$1.98

$2.35

$2.75

No. 31C4069 THIS HANDSOME UNDERSKIRT is made of fine imported mercerized sateen, is the very newest and is called the Sunburst. Is very full and hangs beautifully. Has an exceptionally wide flounce reaching above the knee and is accordion plaited all around. Extra ruffle around the bottom. Very stylish. Colors, black, tobacco brown, tan (champagne color), royal blue, green or cherry. State color and size when ordering.
Price..**$1.75**
If by mail, postage extra, 35 cents.

No. 31C4071 LADIES' UNDERSKIRT. Made of very fine imported, fast colored, highly lustered, soft finished mercerized sateen. Wide flounce around the bottom, accordion plaited all around. Tucks and fancy ruffle around the bottom, also a dust ruffle. Colors, black, brown or cardinal.
Price..**$1.98**
If by mail, postage extra, 35 cents.

No. 31C4074 THE MATERIAL IN THIS GARMENT is as fine as silk, it looks just as good and for wear it is far better. Is made of fast colored, highly finished mercerized material, positively lasts longer than any silk skirt you can get. Made with wide flounce around the bottom, finished with tucks. Lower part of flounce is nicely plaited and tucked all around the bottom. Under flounce finished with a ruffle. Colors, black, blue and brown. State color when ordering. Price......**$2.35**
If by mail, postage extra, 35 cents.

No. 31C4077 THIS EXCELLENT SKIRT is made of very fine moire, otherwise called imitation watered silk. Has a fine luster and good wearing qualities. Made with wide flounce, the upper part plaited and finished with three smaller ruffles around the bottom. This material looks just like silk and wears well. Colors, black, dark green and golden brown. State color and size when ordering.
Price..**$2.75**
If by mail, postage extra, 35 cents.

LADIES' SILK UNDERSKIRTS.

$2.98

$3.98

$3.98

$4.98

No. 31C4080 THIS HANDSOME SKIRT is made of taffeta silk, wide flounce, accordion plaited all around and finished with ruffle around the bottom. Under flounce also accordion plaited and finished with ruffle. You cannot buy the silk alone for what we ask for the skirt. Color, black only. Price... **$2.98**
If by mail, postage extra, 20 cents.

No. 31C4083 THIS PRETTY LADIES' UNDERSKIRT is made of very fine taffeta silk. Can furnish in all the leading colors as mentioned below. Made with wide flounce, upper part nicely plaited, lower part, tucked and finished with strapped seams. Under flounce is made of spun glass to match skirt. Colors, all black, blue and green changeable, red and green changeable or red and black changeable. State color and size when ordering. Price...**$3.98**
If by mail, postage extra, 20 cents.

No. 31C4086 LADIES' SILK UNDERSKIRT. Made of good quality taffeta silk. Flounce around the bottom accordion plaited, finished with a ruffle and trimmed with silk ruching all around the bottom. Wide underflounce finished with ruffle made of spun glass to match. Colors, black, brown or dark red.
Price..**$3.98**
If by mail, postage extra, 20 cents.

No. 31C4089 LADIES' SILK UNDERSKIRT. The material used is one of the best heavy rustling taffetas, and it equals anything that sells for $2.50 more than what we ask for this skirt. Wide flounce is made of spun glass but is covered with a triple flounce of silk. Each flounce is nicely tucked. Dust ruffle made of spun glass to match. Colors, all black, green and blue changeable, red and black changeable, or Havana brown. Price.............**$4.98**
If by mail, postage extra, 20 cents.

$4.98

$5.95

$6.95

$7.25

No. 31C4092 LADIES' UNDERSKIRT. Made of very fine guaranteed taffeta silk. Wide flounce around the bottom, fluted all around and finished with tucks. Straps of same material and two extra ruffles. The quality of material used in this underskirt is as good as any used in the $10.00 or $15.00 skirts. We make this skirt in any color you desire.
Price..**$4.98**
If by mail, postage extra, 20 cents.

No. 31C4095 THIS FULL AND FLARING SKIRT is made of fine taffeta silk. Wide flounce around the bottom is richly trimmed with several smaller ruffles. Very attractive garment, splendid value for the money, and we can highly recommend it in every respect. Colors, all black, blue and green changeable, red and blue changeable or green and black changeable. State color and size when ordering. Price........................**$5.95**
If by mail, postage extra, 25 cents.

No. 31C4096 THIS ATTRACTIVE LADIES' UNDERSKIRT is made of very fine taffeta. Graduated flounce around the bottom, accordion plaited and trimmed with ruching at top of the flounce and around the bottom. Under flounce is also made of silk and is finished with a ruffle. Colors, all black, brown, red and black changeable or green and blue changeable. State color and size when ordering. Price........................**$6.95**
If by mail, postage extra, 25 cents.

No. 31C4098 THIS UNDERSKIRT is made of very fine taffeta silk. Exceptionally full and wide flounce around the bottom, finished with two full ruffles, each ruffle trimmed with silk ruching and tucked. Under flounce and under ruffle made of silk. Colors, all black, brown, red and black or green and blue changeable. State color and size when ordering.
Price..**$7.25**
If by mail, postage extra, 25 cents.

LADIES' WRAPPERS.

SIZES ARE FROM 32 to 44 inches around bust. They are made only in one length. We do not alter wrappers. If garment is a trifle long it is very easy to make it shorter. **When ordering, state catalogue number, size and color desired. No extra sizes in these garments.**

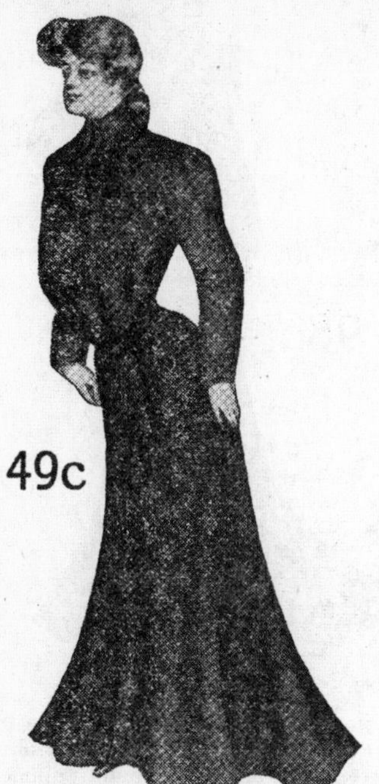

No. 31C4101 LADIES' WRAPPER. Made of calico. Lined to waist with cambric. Trimmed with braid around the collar. Colors, black, blue, gray or red with fancy figures. **State color and size when ordering.**
Price...... **49c**
If by mail, postage extra, 25 cents.

Always state Catalogue Number, Color and Size when ordering.

No. 31C4104 LADIES' WRAPPER. Made of printed calico. Nicely trimmed with fancy braid around the collar, in front and over the shoulder capes. Lining of cambric to waist only. Wide flounce around the bottom. Colors, black, gray, blue or red with fancy figures. **State color and size when ordering.** Price......... **69c**
If by mail, postage extra, 28 cents.

No. 31C4107 LADIES' WRAPPER. Made of flannelette. Neatly trimmed with braid on collar and shoulder capes. Plaits in back from neck to waist. Cambric waist lining. Flounce bottom. Colors, black, blue, gray or red figures. You could not buy the material in this wrapper and make it up yourself for 69 cents. You will be surprised at the value we give at this low price. Dealers cannot buy these wrappers at this figure in wholesale lots. Be sure to include one of the great value wrappers with your order.
Price........................... ......69c
If by mail, postage extra, 30 cents.

No. 31C4110 LADIES' WRAPPER. Made of good quality printed calico. Nicely trimmed with fancy braid around the collar, shoulder capes which reach from front to back forming a yoke. Wide flounce around the bottom. Braid trimming on the sleeves. Lining of cambric to waist only. Colors, black, blue, gray or red with fancy figures. **State color and size when ordering.** Price **89c**
If by mail, postage extra, 30 cents.

No. 31C4113 LADIES' WRAPPER. Made of good quality printed calico, fancy braid trimming around the collar, shoulders and in front forming a yoke. Shoulder capes scalloped and trimmed with embroidery cording. Plait in back from yoke to waist. Wide flounce around the bottom. Lining of cambric to waist. Colors, black, blue or red with fancy figures. **State color and size when ordering.**
Price **89c**
If by mail, postage extra, 30 cents.

No. 31C4116 LADIES' WRAPPER. Very neat, made of percale, neatly trimmed with fancy colored strap of same material, forming yoke in front. Nice ruffles all around the shoulders, reaching from front to back. Wide flounce around the bottom, trimmed with strap of fancy braid. Lining of cambric to waist. Colors, black, blue or red with white polka dots. **State color and size desired when ordering.**
Price... .... **89c**
If by mail, postage extra, 30 cents.

No. 31C4119 LADIES' WRAPPER. Made of percale. Collar, front and shoulder capes are trimmed with one inch wide fancy embroidered braid. Wide flounce around the bottom with braid trimming. Lining of cambric to waist only. Large shoulder capes. Colors, black, blue, gray or red, with fancy figures. **State color and size desired when ordering.**
Price... .... **89c**
If by mail, postage extra, 20 cents.

No. 31C4122 THIS NEAT WRAPPER is made of percale in black and white checks. Very neat. Collar and front trimmed with fancy braid, forming a yoke in front and back, trimmed with fancy braid. Shoulder capes. Lining of cambric to waist only. Colors, black or white checkered patterns.
Price... .... **95c**
If by mail, postage extra, 28 cents.

No. 31C4125 LADIES' WRAPPER. Made of percale, neatly trimmed in front with fancy cord around the collar, yoke in front and shoulder capes. Yoke effect in front and shoulder capes are nicely made of solid black percale to match the wrapper, and back made same as front. Wide flounce around the bottom. Inside vest made of cambric. Colors, black, gray, blue or red, with fancy figures or stripes. State color and size when ordering. Price. 95c
If by mail, postage extra, 30 cents.

No. 31C4128 LADIES' WRAPPER. Made of good quality percale, front richly trimmed with fancy cord braid to match, forming a yoke in front and back. Wide shoulder ruffle reaching all around, edged with fancy braid. Wide flounce around the bottom. Inside vest made of cambric. Very neat. Colors, black, blue or red, with white polka dots. State color and size when ordering. Price 95c
If by mail, postage extra, 30 cents.

No. 31C4131 LADIES' WRAPPER. Made of good quality percale, front neatly trimmed with fancy braid. Double ruffle around the shoulders reaching from front to back also trimmed with fancy braid. Wide flounce around the bottom. Inside vest made of cambric. Very neat. Colors, black, blue, gray or red, with fancy figures or stripes. **State color and size when ordering.** Price.... .... 95c
If by mail, postage extra, 35 cents.

No. 31C4134 LADIES' WRAPPER. Made of good quality flannelette. Yoke effect all around, trimmed with fancy braid on collar, yoke and around full and flaring cape. Small puff in sleeves. Belt all around. Wide flounce around the bottom. Colors, black, blue or red, with white polka dots. This is a better wrapper than sells in retail stores at $1.50. In ordering, don't fail to state size and color. Price 98c
If by mail, postage extra, 35 cents.

No.31C4137 LADIES' WRAPPER. Made of fast colored percale, neatly trimmed with fancy braid around the collar and yoke. Ruffles around the shoulder which reach from front to back. Yoke is made of solid color percale to match. Inside vest made of cambric. Colors, black, blue, gray or red, with fancy figures or stripes. **State color and size when ordering.**
Price.......... ....98c
If by mail, postage extra, 35 cents.

No.31C4140 LADIES' WRAPPER. Made of good quality percale, circular yoke front is plaited with striped percale and the plaits show the stripes only. Has a pretty cape which reaches all around from front to back. The capes, yoke and collar are trimmed with fancy braid. Similar trimming on cuffs. Wide flounce around the bottom. Inside vest made of cambric. Colors, black, blue or red, with fancy polka dots. **State color and size when ordering.** Price........... .....$1.10
If by mail, postage extra, 35 cents.

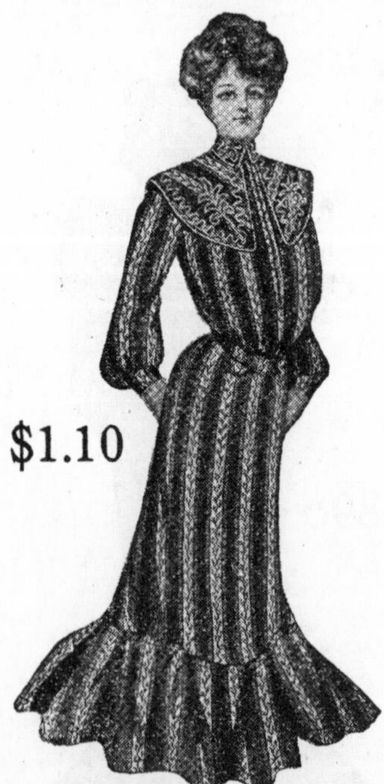

No.31C4146 LADIES' WRAPPER. Made of good quality percale, collar, shoulder capes which reach from front to back, are richly embroidered with white cording. Large sleeves, flounce around the bottom. Inside vest made of cambric. Colors, black, blue, gray or red, with fancy stripes. State color and size when ordering.
Price....... ....$1.10
If by mail, postage extra, 35 cents.

ALWAYS STATE COLOR AND SIZE WHEN ORDERING.

No.31C4149 THIS IS THE CELEBRATED CORSET WAIST WRAPPER, which can be adjusted to the body. It fits perfectly and gives a graceful effect; made of good quality percale. The front is trimmed with fancy braid forming a yoke. Similar trimming in back. Wide flounce around the bottom. Specially want to call your attention to the splendid fit of this garment as shown in illustration. Colors, black, blue, gray or red. State color and size when ordering.
Price.......................98c
If by mail, postage extra, 35 cents.

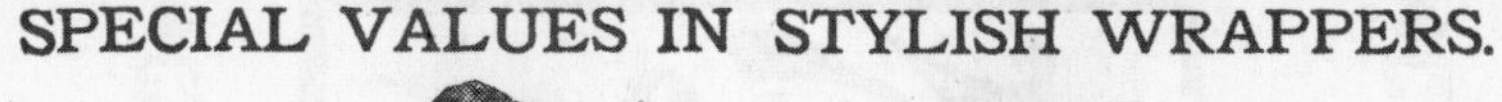

SPECIAL VALUES IN STYLISH WRAPPERS.

No. 31C4152 LADIES' WRAPPER. Made of good quality fast colored percale. Front is neatly trimmed with fancy braid, forming a pointed yoke in front. Has a large cape collar finished with a ruffle and neatly trimmed with fancy braid to match; similar trimming on capes and belt. Wide flounce around the bottom. Inside vest made of cambric. Colors, black, blue, gray or red, with fancy striped designs. State color and size when ordering. Price... **$1.25**
If by mail, postage extra, 35 cents.

No. 31C4155 LADIES' WRAPPER. Made of good quality fast colored percale. Collar and shoulder capes, which reach from front to back, forming a yoke, neatly trimmed with fancy braid. Circular yoke, which is made of solid color percale, is neatly trimmed with fancy briar stitching. Wide flounce around the bottom. Inside vest made of cambric. Colors, black, blue, gray or red, with fancy figures. State color and size when ordering.
Price.... **$1.35**
If by mail, postage extra, 35 cents.

No. 31C4157 LADIES' WRAPPER. Made of good quality percale. The collar, front, shoulder capes, sleeves and cuffs, as well as flounce around the bottom, are trimmed with fancy braid in very neat pattern. Made very full. Inside vest made of cambric. Colors, black, blue, gray or red fancy figures or stripes. State color and size when ordering.
Price.... **$1.35**
If by mail, postage extra, 35 cents.

No. 31C4158 NURSES' DRESS OR LADIES' HOUSE DRESS. Made of good quality striped gingham. This is a two-piece suit and is made of neat shirtwaist with laydown collar, broad shoulder effect, new sleeves, plaits in back from neck to waist. The cuffs are made with buttons and buttonholes and can be easily adjusted. Very full skirt with wide hem around the bottom. Color, blue gray with white stripes only. Splendid value for the money.
Price.... **$1.35**
If by mail, postage extra, 30 cents.

No. 31C4161 LADIES' WRAPPER. Made of good quality fast black mercerized sateen. Yoke effect front trimmed with narrow ribbon to match. Shoulder ruffles reaching from front to back forming a square yoke in back. Front of wrapper is made very full. Belt all around. Wide flounce around the bottom. Inside vest made of cambric. Color, black only. State size when ordering.
Price.... **$1.35**
If by mail, postage extra, 30 cents.

No. 31C4162 LADIES' WRAPPER. Made of fast colored percale. This is the well known and well advertised "corset fitting" easily adjusted, well made wrapper. Is neatly tailored, front trimmed with same material and neatly stitched. New sleeves with belt, wide flounce around the bottom. Cuffs are made with button and buttonholes and can be easily opened. Fancy yoke in front and back. Inside vest made of cambric, is made with draw strings and can be easily adjusted. Colors, black, blue, gray or red with fancy figures. State color and size when ordering. Price.... **$1.49**
If by mail, postage extra, 35 cents.

No. 31C4165 LADIES' TEA GOWN. Made of good quality cashmere. Front shirred at neck. Shoulder capes, collar and flaring cuffs trimmed with silk ribbon. Cambric waist lining. Plaited back from neck to waist. Colors, black, blue, red, brown or old rose. This dress is as nice as any dress you could have made up at home for $5.00. It does not pay to make the dress when you can buy it complete from us for so little money. This lot includes tea gowns that sold for $3.75.
Price.... **$2.89**
If by mail, postage extra, 34 cents.

No. 31C4167 LADIES' TEA GOWN OR HOUSE DRESS. Made of good quality all wool cashmere, richly trimmed with wool silk dress trimming of new fancy briar stitched braid on collar, shoulder capes which reach all around from front to back. The front is made very full, has new sleeves, nicely trimmed cuffs, neat belt. The back is made with double plait from neck down, making it very full. Cambric vest. Colors, black, navy, brown, red or old rose. State color and size when ordering.
Price.... **$4.98**
If by mail, postage extra, 35 cents.

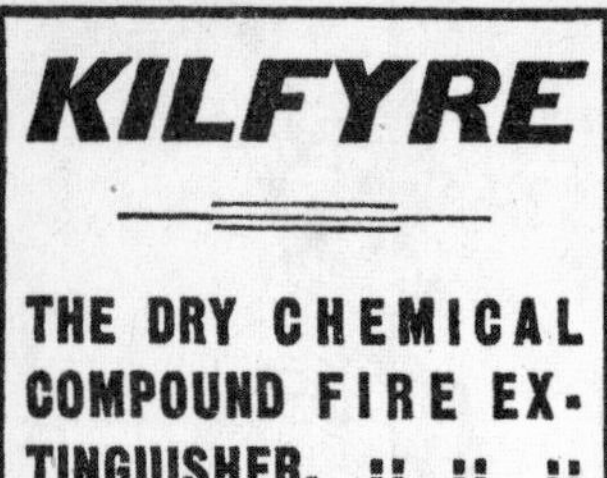

KILFYRE

THE DRY CHEMICAL COMPOUND FIRE EXTINGUISHER. :: :: ::

$1.75 EACH.

THE ORIGINAL AND ONLY GENUINE.

OVER ONE MILLION SOLD. :: :: ::

KILFYRE is a simple, efficient, complete and inexpensive fire extinguisher fully meeting all requirements in cases of fire emergency.

KILFYRE'S MERITS.

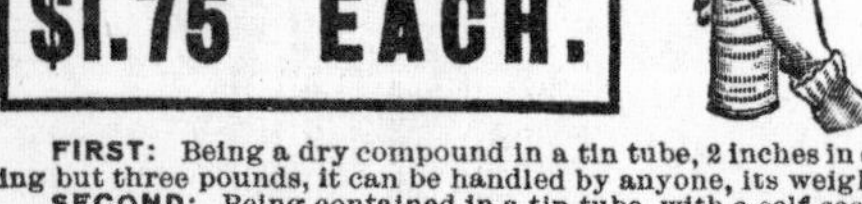

FIRST: Being a dry compound in a tin tube, 2 inches in diameter, 22 inches long, and weighing but three pounds, it can be handled by anyone, its weight not being prohibitive.

SECOND: Being contained in a tin tube, with a self sealing cap, which cap is released upon pulling the tube, suspended from a hook, it is entirely devoid of mechanism, with nothing to get out of order or keep in repair, making it simplicity itself.

THIRD: Being a dry compound without liquid, it cannot freeze, does not lose strength or in any way deteriorate, but always remains vital.

FOURTH: The three pounds of chemical compound, contained in each tube, will extinguish more fire than $50.00 worth of any other chemical extinguisher on the market.

FIFTH: It will extinguish any fire in one-tenth the time it takes with an extinguisher of any other variety.

SIXTH: It will extinguish any fire tnat can be extinguished by any other extinguisher.

SEVENTH: It will extinguish fires that no other extinguisher can; for instance: floating oil, grease and fat fires, flue fires, acetylene gas and electric fires.

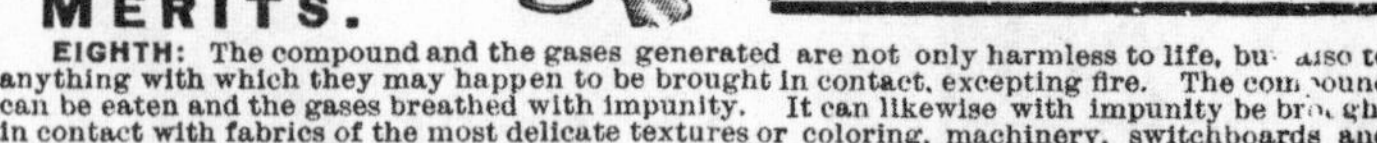

EIGHTH: The compound and the gases generated are not only harmless to life, but also to anything with which they may happen to be brought in contact, excepting fire. The compound can be eaten and the gases breathed with impunity. It can likewise with impunity be brought in contact with fabrics of the most delicate textures or coloring, machinery, switchboards and the like, even gilt picture frames remaining unsoiled and untarnished.

NINTH: Its low cost enables any householder or manufacturer to have a complete protection against fire, which means simple, always ready, effective fire extinguishers, hung at convenient intervals, ready for instant use immediately upon the outbreak of the fire.

TENTH: The case containing Kilfyre being small, slender and easily concealed behind drapery, is unobtrusive, and will therefore strike no discordant note amidst the furnishings and decorations of even the most elegant apartment or drawing room.

OIL OR GAS FIRES: Fires arising from the ignition of any of the bi-products of petroleum such as naptha, benzine, coal oil, etc., or from natural or artificial gas, are instantly asphyxiated by Kilfyre.

KILFYRE

The first five minutes after the outbreak determines whether a fire will or will not result expensively and disastrously—perhaps involving loss of human life.

KILFYRE

The Dry Chemical Compound Fire Extinguisher
The Original and Only Genuine.

No Acid or Liquid.
No Corrosion or Leakage.
No Pressure or Mechanism.
No Explosion or Freezing.
Will Keep Indefinitely.
Harmless to Flesh or Fabric.

Nothing to get Out of Order.
Meets all Conditions of Fire.
Designed for General Use.
Can be used by Anyone.
We Guarantee all we Claim.

KILFYRE

Statistics show that 95% of all fires could be extinguished in their incipiency if the proper means with which to attack them were at hand when they are discovered.

FIRE IN A PRINTING HOUSE.

Atlanta, Ga.

Gentlemen:—Some time ago I purchased some of your dry compound powder, Kilfyre, little thinking that I would have occasion to test its good qualities so soon. A fire started in my printing establishment, and but for the timely application of **Kilfyre** I am satisfied the results would have been serious.

I personally applied a portion of the contents of a tube of **Kilfyre**, when lo! the flames vanished in an instant. I am highly pleased with **Kilfyre** and feel that I could not afford to be without the protection this appliance assures me. It certainly should come into general use.

Wishing you success, I am Yours respectfully,
PEASE PRINTING CO. O. J. Pease, Mgr.

LUCKY WATCHMAN.

Chicago, Ill.

Gentlemen:—At about half-past eight last Saturday night, our watchman with his lantern upset some benzine in our paint room which immediately caused a lively blaze and which he readily extinguished with about three-fourths of a tube of **Kilfyre.** We are highly pleased with the quick results of **Kilfyre.**

Kindly replace the tube used as per agreement, and we remain
Yours truly, LOCKWOOD & STRICKLAND, Per W. S. Lockwood.

KILFYRE has controlled more different conditions of fires than all other fire extinguishers.

DIRECTIONS—To use **KILFYRE,** simply remove the cap and throw contents of the tube forcibly, with a sweeping motion at the base of the flames.

No. 24C5524 Price, per dozen, **$20.00**; each........**$1.75**

FREE WALL PAPER SAMPLES DIRECT FROM OUR OWN WALL PAPER MILL.

This complete book of wall paper, showing a sample of all of our new 1905 patterns, together with free instructions how to measure a room, how to order and how to do any job of paper hanging, will be sent to anyone by mail postpaid, absolutely free of charge.

JUST SEND A POSTAL, ask for the free Wall Paper Sample Book, and everything will go to you by return mail, free.

AT 3 CENTS PER DOUBLE ROLL AND UPWARDS we show a big variety of new patterns for 1905, the very latest designs on the market, paper suitable for each and every room in the house and all priced on the basis of the actual manufacturing cost with only one profit added. If you buy wall paper from us, you will be buying it at a price just a trifle more than the actual mill cost, a lower price than any retail dealer buys at wholesale. We make every roll of wall paper that we sell, in our own big wall paper mill which we run the year around and from which mill we furnish the highest class of paper at the lowest price ever heard of.

FOR A VERY LITTLE MONEY, much less perhaps than you imagine, you can repaper and redecorate your rooms and make a wonderful improvement. You will be surprised how little money it costs to do this. If you write and ask for our free Wall Paper Sample Book, you will get all the information, you will get samples of all the latest designs, our astonishingly low prices, free instructions about ordering, quantity necessary, and even plain and simple directions how to put up the paper yourself without the assistance of a professional paper hanger. If you are interested in wall paper or expect to do any kind of papering, or would like to improve the appearance of your home, don't hesitate to write for our free book of wall paper samples.

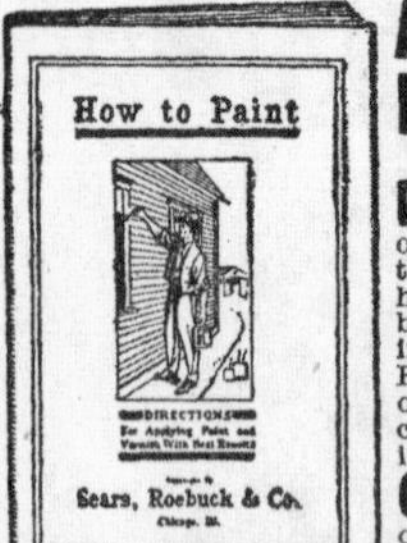

A COMPLETE BOOK OF PAINT SAMPLES AND A BOOK OF INSTRUCTIONS, "HOW TO PAINT"

SENT FREE TO ANYONE ON APPLICATION.

DIRECT FROM OUR PAINT FACTORY we furnish the highest grade ready mixed, ready to use paints on the market and offer them to our customers under our binding five-year guarantee for quality, at prices much lower than you can possibly find elsewhere. We guarantee our Seroco ready mixed house paint, the very highest grade paint on the market regardless of brand or selling price and it is offered by us under our binding five-year guarantee at **85** cents per gallon and upward, according to quantity. If you are interested in the subject of painting or expect to do anything in this line, write for the free Sample Book of Ready Mixed Paints. We will send you a handsome sample book showing eighty-five samples of the different shades and colors and we will also give you free and complete instructions how to calculate the quantity of paint you require for any job, how to order, how to select the most harmonizing colors, everything made very plain and simple.

OUR FREE BOOK, "HOW TO PAINT." With every free paint sample book also with every order for paint, we send free of charge a complete book entitled "How to Paint." This book is compiled by an expert and gives, in plain and easily understood language, directions for doing any job of painting or varnishing so that you can order your paint from us, save at least one-half in price and do the job yourself. Write for our free Paint Sample Book today.

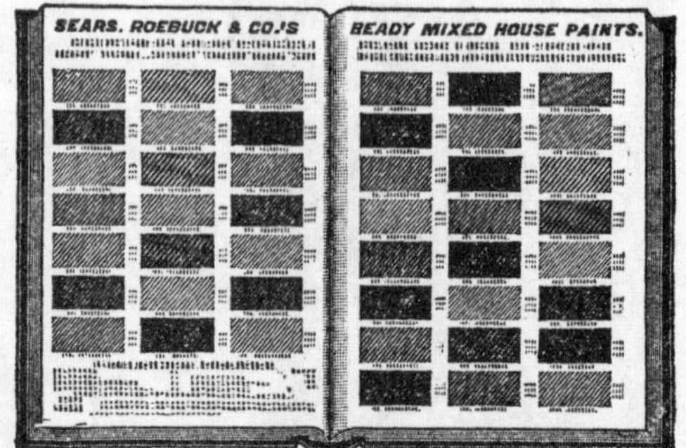

OUR FREE SAMPLE BOOK OF MEN'S READY MADE CLOTHING. THIS SAMPLE BOOK SENT TO ANYONE FREE ON APPLICATION.

WOULD YOU BE INTERESTED in buying a strictly all wool suit, overcoat or pair of pants for about one-half the price that you would pay for equal quality in any retail store? Then, please, write for our free Clothing Sample Book of Men's Ready Made Clothing and see what we have to offer. We will send you a complete line of all the samples we use in our Men's Ready Made Clothing Department, so that you can see the actual goods themselves and you will get our very low prices, much less than you have ever paid before, if you have not bought from us. We will also send you a tape measure, fashion plates showing the styles, instructions for ordering, plain, simple and easily understood instructions for measuring, whereby you can take your own measure and be assured of perfect fitting garments. We will take all the risk. We will send you a suit, overcoat, or whatever garments you may order at our own risk, with the understanding that if they do not fit you and please you perfectly, you are not under any obligations of keeping them, but they can be returned to us at our expense and we will promptly return all your money and pay express charges both ways.

WE ARE CLOTHING MANUFACTURERS. We make our own ready made clothing in our own factory and we offer the garments to you at prices based on our manufacturing cost with only our one small percentage of profit added. We are one of the biggest buyers of woolens in the country, making large contracts direct with the largest mills. We operate under the most economical manufacturing methods and we are thereby able to reduce our cost to the lowest possible point, all of which we give our customers the benefit of. Don't buy anything in ready made clothing until you first get our free clothing sample book. Send a postal and ask for the free Sample Book of Men's Ready Made Clothing.

CUSTOMERS' PROFIT SHARING DEPARTMENT.

Any customer of ours, anyone buying goods from us, is entitled to share in the profits of this business by selecting and receiving FREE OF ANY EXTRA COST, any one, or as many of the articles shown on the following pages, as he or she may desire, subject only to the provisions and conditions hereafter explained.

WHENEVER YOU PURCHASE GOODS FROM US (amounting to $1.00 or more) **we will send you a profit sharing certificate showing the amount of your purchase in dollars and cents.** These certificates should be carefully preserved by you, and when you have received certificates amounting in dollars and cents to enough to entitle you to any one or more of the articles wanted as shown on following pages, send the certificates to us, state which article or articles are wanted, and if the certificates you send us amount to enough in dollars and cents to entitle you to the article or articles wanted, these articles will be sent to you free of any cost, carefully packed and delivered on board the cars at Chicago, or factory, and you will have only the freight or express charges to pay; not one penny will you have to pay for the article or articles you select from this profit sharing list.

PLEASE NOTE THAT WE WILL NOT ISSUE A PROFIT SHARING CERTIFICATE FOR AN ORDER OF LESS THAN ONE DOLLAR.

PLEASE NOTE that the articles in the profit sharing list are furnished FREE, but we do not prepay the freight or express charges. : : : : : The customer must pay the mail, express or freight charges in all cases.

PLEASE NOTE that no article will be given and therefore no customer can share in the profits unless all the certificates received amount to $100.00 or more. Therefore in order to share in the profits it will be necessary for you to carefully preserve each certificate sent you for each purchase made until the total amount of all the certificates you receive is $100.00 or more. **On the following pages you will see there are a large number of handsome and valuable articles that will be given free in exchange for profit sharing certificates amounting to $100.00 and still much more valuable articles for CERTIFICATES AMOUNTING TO MORE THAN $100.00, up to and including the most valuable article of all, A HANDSOME UPRIGHT GRAND PIANO, which will be given in exchange for profit sharing certificates amounting to $1,000.00.**

WITH EVERY ORDER (amounting to $1.00 or more) **you send us, you will receive a profit sharing certificate for the full amount of your purchase,** but after receiving the goods and the profit sharing certificate if for any reason the goods are not satisfactory, if you wish to return them to us and get your money back, you must return your profit sharing certificate also, for failure to return the profit sharing certificate with any goods you return to us to have money refunded, not only cancels the one profit sharing certificate issued for the goods you return, but also cancels all other profit sharing certificates you may hold. **UNDERSTAND, if you receive any goods from us that are not entirely satisfactory we want you to return them to us at our expense and get your money back,** but the day you return your goods you must also return your profit sharing certificate; otherwise all profit sharing certificates you hold for previous purchases made will be cancelled by us and **will not be accepted if presented to us in exchange for any of the goods shown in this department.**

LIMITATIONS OF PROFIT SHARING CERTIFICATES.

While these certificates are not limited as to time, and you may be months or years in accumulating certificates of a sufficient amount to entitle you to the article or articles you want, and they will be accepted by us when presented, no profit sharing certificate is transferable. They are good only for the party in whose name they are drawn, and are not good if altered or defaced in any way.

HOW TO SHARE QUICKLY AND LIBERALLY IN THE PROFITS.

IF YOU ARE IN NEED of a piano, organ, sewing machine, bedroom suite or other valuable articles shown in our profit sharing list, and would like to receive it at an early date, we would suggest as a means for receiving the article wanted in the near future that, first, before buying any kind of goods from your dealer at home or elsewhere, anything that you may need in dry goods, groceries, boots, shoes, hardware, furniture, wearing apparel, or other goods, that you first refer to our big catalogue and see how much money you can save on these goods by sending to us. From time to time as you are in need of goods send to us for everything you want, remembering with each purchase you get a profit sharing certificate for the full amount of your purchase, then if you feel it would take too long a time in the purchase of only the goods you want for your own use to accumulate profit sharing certificates sufficient to entitle you to the article or articles you want, get your friends and neighbors to join with you in sending for the goods they want also. **If you have friends or neighbors who are in need of wearing apparel, hardware, furniture, groceries or other goods,** if you will call their attention to our prices of the goods they want, surely you have neighbors who would be glad to take advantage of our prices and make a big saving in cost on the goods they want, glad to let you order the goods they need for them. If you can get two or three of your neighbors to order together it will reduce the freight or express charges each one will have to pay, and will mean a big saving in cost to them. **Of course the order will have to be sent in your name.** You needn't hesitate to say to your neighbors that your object in getting them to let you send for their goods is in order that you may share in our profits by getting the article or articles you want. They will be glad to assist you by letting you send for their goods, since in the sending they save money and you in this way increase the number and amount of the profit sharing certificates that will be issued to you and can more quickly participate in our profit sharing and will be enabled to select larger and more valuable articles from our profit sharing list.

IF YOU HAVE EVER PURCHASED FROM US a buggy, sewing machine, organ, stove, furniture or other article of merchandise call your neighbor's attention to these goods you purchased from us; tell your neighbor how much you paid for the goods and how much money you saved and suggest their ordering a needed stove, vehicle, sewing machine, furniture or other needed goods. They will surely be glad to have you send the order in your name for them for it will mean a big saving in cost to them and will enable us to issue a profit sharing certificate for the amount of the purchase in your name.

THE TIME REQUIRED to accumulate sufficient certificates to allow you to participate in our profit sharing by selecting the article wanted, will depend, first, on how many goods you naturally require for your own use and on what part of these goods you purchase from us. If you buy nearly all the goods you use from us you will not only make a big saving on the cost of the goods you buy, **but you will be surprised how rapidly you will accumulate our profit sharing certificates** and how quickly they will amount to enough to entitle you to select the article or articles you want; but if your needs are very few your purchases would therefore be small and infrequent even though you sent to us for nearly everything you needed, you can, nevertheless, quickly share in the profits by interesting your neighbors as explained, getting them to allow you to send to us for the goods they need.

UNDERSTAND, you or your neighbors take no risk in sending to us, for if the goods we ship are not satisfactory to you or your neighbors, they can be returned to us at our expense and we will immediately return the money sent us together with any freight or express charges paid. The only condition we make is, that in returning the goods you return the profit sharing certificate that was issued for the particular goods you returned to us.

Our Liberal Profit Sharing Plan with our customers does not add one penny to the price at which we sell our goods. On the contrary, it makes for still lower prices.

OUR PRICES today on everything shown in our big catalogue are lower than ever before printed by us, lower by far than the same goods are quoted in any other catalogue published or offered for sale by any other house, and while our profit is figured very small, no doubt much smaller than any other house in the world selling merchandise to the consumer; in other words, we no doubt make a lesser number of cents net profit on each dollar's worth of goods we sell than any other merchandise house in the world, nevertheless the enormous volume of business that has been produced by reason of these low prices, prices lower than any other house in the world, **has built our business up until our sales on merchandise often aggregate over $150,000 per day.** We know that our customers throughout the United States are responsible for this enormous business, responsible for our ability to sell goods at prices so much lower than other houses, responsible for our ability to figure on a much smaller percentage of profit than any other house, also responsible for the net profit that comes from a vast volume of business. We have felt that we should arrive at some plan by which our customers who make this business, who make this profit possible, should share in this profit, and to make this sharing of profit equitable and fair to all our customers, we have decided on this plan to distribute valuable merchandise among those who patronize us in proportion to the extent of their patronage.

OUR PROFITS are already figured so low that we feel that it would be dangerous to the interests of our business and the customers we serve to reduce our net profit even a fraction of one per cent. We also believe that in this plan we will develop an interest and an economy that will make for us a still much larger volume of business, further lessen the expense of advertising and in this way permit us to still further reduce our selling prices, at the same time permitting all our customers to share liberally in the profits of our business in proportion to the extent the individual customer patronizes our house.

MANY OF OUR CUSTOMERS after dealing with us for months or years, having purchased goods from us amounting to one hundred dollars or even hundreds of dollars, have suggested that we send them some sort of a present as a substantial recognition of our appreciation of their trade, and no doubt where one customer has suggested that we so recognize them, thousands of our customers have felt that something of this kind was due them, and we, too, have felt that something more than anything we have been able to do up to date was due to customers that continued to patronize us; but since we regard it unfair not to treat every customer alike, and since the profit on our goods is figured so low that any concession in price is impossible, we have carefully studied out this plan by which every customer can be remembered, can share liberally in the profits, **a plan by which every customer who patronizes us to the extent of $100.00 or more, shall and will be remembered by sharing liberally in the net profits of our business.**

WHY WE FIX THE AMOUNT AT $100.00 IN THE PROFIT SHARING CERTIFICATES BEFORE A CUSTOMER CAN SHARE THE PROFITS, AND WHY WE ALLOW CUSTOMERS HOLDING PROFIT SHARING CERTIFICATES AGGREGATING $300.00 TO $1,000.00 TO SHARE MORE LIBERALLY IN THE PROFITS, EVEN TO FURNISHING A FINE UPRIGHT GRAND PIANO IN EXCHANGE FOR PROFIT SHARING CERTIFICATES AGGREGATING $1,000.00.

FIRST, customers whose orders amount to less than $100.00; in other words, customers who never receive certificates sufficient to aggregate $100.00 are not permitted to participate in this profit sharing, for the reason that we do not feel that we can regard these customers as regular, steady customers of the house, for no family's wants are so few that they do not need to buy, if not in six months, certainly in a year or two years, at least $100.00 worth of goods, and when we do not get orders from a family aggregating $100.00 or more within a year or two years or more, we don't feel that we are receiving a large part of that family's business and we, therefore, do not feel that such a customer should be entitled to participate in our profit sharing plan.

WHILE WE WANT IT UNDERSTOOD that we are keenly appreciative of every order sent us, no matter how small, and if you never send us but one order and we can satisfy you and save you money on this order, we appreciate the order as much as any house possibly can, at the same time we do feel that the sharing of the profits of this business with our customers should go to the customers who are regular, steady, permanent customers of the house and that these regular customers should share in the profits of the business and, whenever their purchases amount to $100.00 or more, should be entitled to any extra profit we may make by reason of our declining to permit those who do less than $100.00 business to participate in the profits. If you are not a regular customer of our house, if you do not buy at least a part of the goods you need from us from time to time, season after season, your purchases, therefore, would not in one, two or more years amount to $100.00 and you could hardly expect us to permit you to share in the profits, especially when the goods we sell you are sold on the smallest kind of a profit, much less than you can buy elsewhere, and you can, therefore, save money by dealing with us; but, if on the other hand, you are a regular customer of ours, **if you buy a large part of your requirements from us from time to time, season after season and year after year, we feel it is no more than right that you should share in the profits,** and with a liberality in proportion to the extent of your purchases from us, and you should get the additional benefit of any extra profit we may make by reason of our declining to allow those holding less than $100.00 in certificates to share in the profits.

WE GIVE A HANDSOME UPRIGHT PIANO to any of our customers in exchange for profit sharing certificates amounting to $1,000.00, and correspondingly valuable articles of merchandise in exchange for profit sharing certificates amounting to from $300.00 to $1,000.00, and our reason for being proportionately more liberal in the sharing of profits with customers whose total certificates amount to from $300.00 to $1000.00 is this: We feel to the customer who deals with us to the extent of $300.00 to $500.00, receiving profit sharing certificates aggregating $300.00 to $500.00, we can well afford to give back to him a much larger part of the profit we made on the goods we sold him and more, feel that we can afford to give back to him a large part of the profit made on the goods he bought and a fair percentage of the profit made on goods bought by others, and in this way encourage mail order buying.

IF YOU SEND US ORDERS in the course of six months, one year or even two or three years aggregating $1,000.00 you do a great deal to stimulate mail order buying in your neighborhood, for it would be impossible for us to crate and ship $1,000.00 worth of merchandise, from time to time, to any party, anywhere, without attracting dozens of families to the extraordinary values we furnish, and in so doing we would add many new customers to our list. We feel that the customer who buys from us regularly season after season, until he has purchases amounting to $500.00 to $1,000.00, and received profit sharing certificates amounting to $500.00 to $1,000.00, is entitled to extraordinary consideration. **He is entitled, first, to share in our profits to the extent of getting back a very large part of the profit he paid us,** and he is also entitled to getting consideration in the shape of additional profits on the new business that we get by reason of the attention his purchases attract, the new customers that are sure to come by reason of this one very large customer. So that the customer who purchases $1,000.00 worth of merchandise from us, whether the purchases are made at once or in six months, a year or a number of years, the customer who accumulates profit sharing certificates to the extent of $1,000 is entitled to receive most extraordinary consideration from us, and we have seen fit to make this consideration in the shape of a handsome upright Parlor Grand Piano as shown in our profit sharing list, which we furnish free to anyone on receipt of profit sharing certificates aggregrating $1,000.00. Therefore, the inducement for any customer to buy all his supplies from us, to send for everything he needs season after season, year after year, is that when he has accumulated profit sharing certificates aggregrating $1,000.00 he is in a position to exchange these certificates for merchandise, the value of which merchandise is far greater than all the profit we made from the goods we sold him. **The value of the merchandise he gets for his share of the profit represents, not only a very large part of the profit we made on the goods we sold him, but a fair division of the profits made on the goods sold to others,** this in addition to the fact that for every dollar he sent us for goods we guarantee to give greater value for the money than can be had from any other house.

WHY IT PAYS US AND WHY SHARING PROFITS WITH CUSTOMERS TENDS TO MAKE LOWER PRICES.

IT ENLARGES OUR SALES and we are perfectly willing to divide our profits with our customers if in so doing we can greatly enlarge our sales. We are prompted in doing this by a desire that our customers may share in our profits and that we may encourage our customers to greatly increase our volume of business. If the willingness on our part to allow our customers to share in the profits of our business will induce those who are now buying but a small part of the goods they use from us to buy nearly all the goods they use from us, our volume of business will be more than double. **If the sharing of profits with our customers will induce our customers to try to get orders from their friends and neighbors, this again will double the volume of our business,** and with our volume of business doubled if we were to divide our profits equally with our customers, the net results to us would be exactly the same and we would have the satisfaction in knowing that we were dividing liberally with our customers all the profits of this business. We could still further strengthen our sources of supply, either by reducing the cost of production, reducing the cost at which we are making or buying the goods we sell, still further reducing our selling prices. Further, if in sharing of our profits with our customers our customers buy a larger percentage of the goods they use from us, and influence their friends to do likewise, this interest on the part of our customers will materially reduce our advertising expense. Any reduction of advertising expense means a corresponding reduction in our selling prices.

THE INTEREST that we feel sure our customers will take in our profit sharing plan is sure to mean the doubling of our present volume of business, lessening the cost to manufacture, enabling us to make larger and more profitable purchase contracts, lessening the cost of our goods, the cost of our advertising and thereby materially lessening the already very low prices at which we are selling all kinds of merchandise.

OUR PLAN IS SUBSTANTIALLY LIKE THIS: Take our customers into partnership with us, make each and every customer interested, and if we can, by offering to permit our customers to share in our profits, interest one-half of all our customers into buying nearly everything from us, using their influence among their friends and neighbors, getting their friends and neighbors to join with them in sending orders to us, we will so very greatly increase the volume of our business, so very greatly facilitate in the closer (lower price) buying and making of the goods we sell, so reduce the cost of advertising and handling that we can afford to permit our customers to share most liberally in the profits of our business and still sell our goods at even lower prices than would otherwise be possible, lower than we are yet able to name.

CAN WE AFFORD TO GIVE MORE, LARGER AND MORE VALUABLE ARTICLES IN OUR PROFIT SHARING?

THERE IS NO TELLING to what extent we may be able to go in the way of large, handsome and valuable articles of merchandise to be given to our customers in exchange for profit sharing certificates. If our customers take the interest in this work that we feel they will, if we can get our thousands of customers in every state and territory in the Union interested in working for us, sending their orders to us, getting their friends and neighbors to join with them in sending orders to us, and so increase our trade as to double and quadruple our present size, we may later be able to give vastly more valuable articles of merchandise in exchange for profit sharing certificates, and, just as soon as we see our way clear to enlarge, extend and greatly improve the value of the articles given, **just as fast as we see that we can afford to divide more liberally with our customers, just so soon you will see the profit sharing list improved, strengthened, enlarged and made more attractive,** more valuable articles, a more liberal division, and, when the time comes, if you have accumulated a sufficient number of certificates, and you wish to redeem them, you will be entitled to select any of the new and more attractive and more valuable articles we may see our way clear to offer in our profit sharing plan.

WE WANT TO BE SO LIBERAL in dividing our profits with our customers that no one can afford to buy any kind of merchandise from any other house but ours, so if you or any of your neighbors, when in want of any kind of goods, whether groceries, wearing apparel, dry goods, hardware, furniture, harness, saddlery or any kind of merchandise used in the home, in the shop, on the farm or elsewhere, will think of our catalogue, will remember if you hold profit sharing certificates amounting to $25.00, $50.00 or $75.00, that you only have to make an additional purchase from us amounting to $25.00 or $50.00 to entitle you to a share in the profits; if when you are about to buy anything you will anticipate your wants long enough in advance for the order to reach us and the goods to reach you; if instead of going to your nearest dealer you will send to us, and by sending to us you will make a big saving in cost, you will receive a profit sharing certificate, and **when you have received certificates amounting to $100.00 or more you will begin to share in the profits,** and if you should patronize us and interest others to patronize us to the extent that your total certificates should in time amount to $500.00 or $1,000.00, you can share most liberally in the profits, and get in return for your certificates, articles the value of which will mean a rebate to you of a very large part of the profit on the goods you bought from us and a liberal reward for the influence you have used in getting others to buy from us.

WE FEEL with the introduction of this, our liberal profit sharing plan, that no one anywhere that receives our catalogue can afford to buy anything from anyone but us. If you have our catalogue and you are in want of any kind of merchandise to use indoors or out, you will certainly lose money if you do not send your order to us; and remember, when you send us an order your money is accepted and the goods are shipped you with the understanding that if they are not perfectly satisfactory when received and lower in price than you could buy elsewhere, you can return them to us at our expense and we will immediately return your money, together with any express or freight charges paid by you.

CLUB PLAN FOR SHARING IN THE PROFITS AT ONCE.

IF THERE IS AN ARTICLE in our profit sharing list which you would especially like to receive at once; and for example, if it is an article that we will furnish free in exchange for profit sharing certificates amounting to $100.00, you can get this article at once by getting up a club in the following manner: Suppose you want to buy a suit of clothes and the price is $10.00, write up your own order and then go among your friends and get orders from nine of your friends for a suit for $10.00 each; **or you may get your neighbor's order of a buggy for $40.00, another neighbor may want a steel range** and you will get his order at our catalogue price of say $25.00, and another neighbor may wants a nice bedroom suite or some other article of merchandise amounting to $25.00, so with your order for a suit for yourself for $10.00 and the orders you get from your three neighbors amounting to $40.00, $25.00 and $25.00 you have a total order of $100.00, send the entire order to us in your own name **let us ship all the goods together to you, and when your neighbors go to the depot for the goods they can divide the freight charges between them in proportion to the amount of their respective purchase thus reducing the freight charges each pay to next to nothing.** They will each make a big saving on their purchase, they will feel that you have done them a big favor and immediately your order containing the $100.00 is received we will send you a certificate of purchase amounting to $100.00. This certificate you can return to us with your order for any article of merchandise shown in our profit sharing list which we furnish for certificates amounting to $100.00, **to be sent to you free of any further cost to you.** In this way with a little effort on your part you can take advantage of our profit sharing plan and get any article you may select at once, and later if you wish to reciprocate and your neighbor who allowed you to take his order for $25.00 or $40.00 wishes to take advantage of our profit sharing plan, he can go among his neighbors and you can join him, if you choose, in making up an order and thus help the neighbor who helped you, so that he also can take advantage of our profit sharing plan and send us an order large enough to entitle him to a $100.00 certificate at once.

ANOTHER CLUB METHOD.

WE WOULD SUGGEST to those who wish to take advantage of the profit sharing plan at the earliest possible date and do not themselves need goods amounting to $100.00, that each time they send us an order, no matter how small the order, that they go among their friends and see if they don't need something in wearing apparel, in groceries, dry goods or other goods from our big catalogue. **Even if your neighbors only contribute a few dollars to your order each time you order you will be surprised how quickly these profit sharing certificates will accumulate, how soon you will have certificates aggregating $100.00 or more, how very soon you will be able to participate in our profit sharing plan by exchanging your certificates amounting to $100.00 or more for such article or articles as you may wish to select from our profit sharing list.**

THIS UPRIGHT GRAND PIANO WILL BE GIVEN IN EXCHANGE FOR PROFIT SHARING CERTIFICATES AMOUNTING TO $1,000.00

No. 46PS110

REMEMBER, if you want this piano you can start now, and even though it may take you one year or five years to accumulate profit sharing certificates and make purchases enough to amount to $1,000.00, it makes no difference to us When you have accumulated $1,000 00 in profit sharing certificates send the certificates to us and this piano, exactly as illustrated and described, furnished under our binding 25 years' guarantee, complete with stool and instruction book will go to you free of any cost.

THIS HANDSOME PIANO, as illustrated, is made especially for our customers. It is one of the handsomest pianos on the market, a genuine Beckwith piano, made by the celebrated Beckwith Piano Company; is covered by a written binding 25 years' guarantee, has one of the handsomest cases made, veneered inside and outside with cross band sawed veneers; has handsome trusses and pilasters; all mouldings, trusses and pilasters in solid wood; continuous music desk with handsomely carved panels in very elegant and artistic designs; latest patent rolling fall board with nickel plated hinges, highly nickel plated pedals and guards. We furnish it in either English quarter sawed oak, French burled walnut or richly figured mahogany veneer as desired; is highly polished and is a very large piano; has 7⅓ octaves, overstrung, three strings to each note except the wound bass strings Stands 4 feet 7 inches high, 5 feet 1 inch wide, 2 feet 3 inches deep. Weight, boxed for shipment, 780 pounds This piano is made to combine all the high grade up to date features of every high grade piano made, with the defects of none; has the highest grade ivory keys and ebony sharps, best quality of material throughout, including a specially fine quality of felt in hammers, nickel plated action rail and brackets, full length metal frame. In tone it has no superior We guarantee it in volume and richness of quality the equal of any of the highest priced pianos on the market. The sounding board is the highest grade possible to produce, made of specially selected Canadian spruce of the finest quality.

THIS IS A SPECIALLY HIGH GRADE PIANO, and is gotten out for us as a special, extra fine instrument by the Beckwith Piano Company, gotten out in a new design for the sole purpose of furnishing it to our customers as THEIR SHARE OF THE PROFIT and without one penny of expense to them.

We have thousands of customers who can easily secure this piano without the piano costing them one cent of money, and by reason of the method necessary to secure this piano free you will make a big saving in cost; in fact, every customer who gets this piano from us as his or her share of the profit is sure to save from $100.00 to $300.00 on the goods they buy, which entitles them to the piano; in other words, we guarantee to save you money when you send your orders to us, and when your orders have amounted to enough ($1,000.00) you get this piano without any expense to you.

How thousands of our customers can get this piano without cost. While $1,000.00 in profit sharing certificates would seem at first like a large amount to accumulate, still, if almost any family will look back over the past few years and figure up what their total living expenses have been, how much money they have paid out for the things they wear and eat, the articles they have purchased for the house, for the shop and for the farm, they will find that in the past few years their purchases have amounted to more than $1,000.00. Now, if you will stop to think, almost everything you have purchased the past few years could have been bought from us. You will find the very goods in our catalogue and at much lower prices than you have been in the habit of paying.

Now, if you want to get this piano without cost, change your plan of buying and before buying anything from your storekeeper at home or elsewhere, whether to wear, to eat or to use, indoors or outdoors, look first in our catalogue, get our prices, you will be surprised how much money we can save you, get into the habit of sending to us for everything you buy. Remember, with every purchase you make, for every dollar you send us, you will receive by return mail a profit sharing certificate for the full amount of your purchase. Save these profit sharing certificates. If this opportunity had been offered you a few years ago and you had availed yourself of it and sent to us for everything you bought, you would now hold profit sharing certificates to the amount of $1,000.00, enough to entitle you to this piano; but begin now. If you want this piano save all your profit sharing certificates, and in a few years they will have amounted to $1,000.00, enough to get this piano.

If you want to save time and you would like to have this handsome piano at an early date, do a little soliciting among your friends and neighbors. You will be surprised how quickly they will grasp the opportunity to save money on the things they buy. During the next year you can with very little trouble and at a big saving in cost to your neighbors, secure orders from them, if not sufficient to entitle you to the piano, you can at least make a big start in that direction, and by the end of another year, if you are not holding profit sharing certificates amounting to $1,000.00, you will at least have accumulated enough to give you a good start towards getting this handsome piano free of cost to you

We furnish with this piano without charge the latest mandolin attachment, an attachment which perfectly reproduces the tone of the mandolin, harp, zither, guitar, banjo, etc , an attachment that is usually retailed at $50.00 to $100.00 extra in addition to the price of the piano. **With this piano we furnish free a handsome piano stool, instruction book and cover.**

DON'T COMPARE this with any of the cheap pianos on the market. It is a strictly high grade Beckwith instrument, made especially fine, made especially for our Profit Sharing Department, made to go to our customers without charge. Any customer who makes purchases from us amounting to $1,000.00 for the goods he buys for his own use or if it includes goods that are for his friends or neighbors, orders that he takes, it makes no difference so long as the goods are all ordered in the one name and the orders amount to $1,000.00.

REMEMBER, the giving of these liberal values, the liberal division of profit with our customers, does not add one penny to the selling price of our goods; on the contrary, it makes for lower prices, because it tends to interest our customers in securing new customers for us. Not one penny is added to our selling price; it is merely a division of the profit. It increases our sales, enables us to manufacture and buy cheaper and we give you the benefit of lower prices. This profit sharing plan makes for lower prices on everything you buy from us.

You must have neighbors who would appreciate an exceptional bargain in buggies, wagons, harness, wearing apparel, furniture, etc., and at our prices printed in our big catalogue they could make a big saving in cost. Why not go among your neighbors and solicit a few orders? You can take orders for a half dozen buggies, a few items of furniture, a sewing machine. You will be surprised how quickly the orders will accumulate and in how short a time you will accumulate certificates amounting to $1,000.00. To get this piano you have only to send the certificates to us saying you want this piano, and it goes to you without cost as your share of the profit

THIS BIG, HANDSOME, WELL CONSTRUCTED IRON BED,

All Complete with Special High Grade Ball Bearing Casters of the Latest Style, one of the Handsomest Iron Beds on the Market, Given in Exchange for Profit Sharing Certificates Amounting to $100.00.

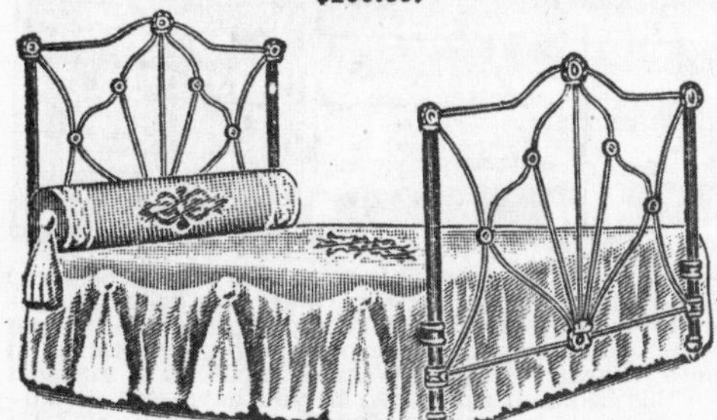

No. 1PS125

In this instance we furnish the bed only, without springs and without mattress. It is a beautiful, substantial, white enameled, brass trimmed iron bed, made with 1 1-16-inch white enameled iron pillars and ⅝-inch enameled iron frame. The ornamental iron work is of the highest degree of art and the pillars are such as you will find in the most expensive beds. The head is 54 inches high, length of bed 6 feet 4 inches. Can be had in 4 feet 6 inches only The bed goes to you all complete, furnished without price, without cost, given in exchange for profit sharing certificates amounting to $100.00.

THIS HANDSOME GUITAR AND COMPLETE OUTFIT FURNISHED IN EXCHANGE FOR PROFIT SHARING CERTIFICATES OF PURCHASE AMOUNTING TO $100.00.

No 12PS115

This is one of the handsomest guitars on the market. The back and sides are made of solid quarter sawed antique oak, beautifully finished, top of resonant spruce It is inlaid around edge with strips of fancy colored wood and bound with white celluloid It has two rings of fancy colored wood around sound hole, has strips of fancy colored wood in back, fingerboard is made of rosewood, accurately fretted and inlaid with pearl position dots. It has the latest American screw patent head and a handsome nickel plated tailpiece With this guitar we furnish a complete guitar outfit, including one book of Guckert s lettered fingerboard chart (a valuable aid to beginners,) also one Magic Capo d' Astro The guitar and complete outfit packed in a neat box.

This is such a guitar as you will find only in the best city retail music stores, where they are sold at fancy prices, and yet it is offered by us without price, goes to our customers as a part of their share of the profits. It is only necessary to send us profit sharing certificates amounting to $100.00. This you can do within a very short time, if you will only get in the habit of first referring to our catalogue before buying your goods elsewhere. No matter what you want to buy, if only a pair of shoes, something in groceries, something in furniture, any kind of wearing apparel, anything that you may need in the home in the shop, on the farm, or elsewhere, you will be surprised how much money you can save on these goods by sending to us for them; and you take no risk, for we will immediately return your money if the goods ordered are not perfectly satisfactory; and every time you send us an order you get a profit sharing certificate for the full amount of your purchase. This certificate goes to you by return mail, and when the certificates have amounted to enough to entitle you to the article or articles you may want, as shown in this profit sharing list, send your profit sharing certificates to us, state which articles are wanted and they will go to you by return mail, express or freight without cost. All you pay will be the transportation charges.

WE ARE ANXIOUS that you and your neighbors should get in the habit of sending to us for the goods you need. Get your neighbors to join with you in sending. When you are about to send to us for any kind of goods, find out if your neighbors don't need something on which you can save them a big percentage in cost, get them to let you send for their goods also, and in this way you will quickly accumulate large profit sharing certificates. Possibly you may have a neighbor who needs a buggy, wagon, organ, piano, sewing machine or at least something in wearing apparel. If so, you can save your neighbor a great deal of money and by sending to us for him you get the profit sharing certificate in your name and your certificates will soon amount to enough to entitle you to any goods you may need on the profit sharing list.

THIS BIG HANDSOME PARLOR ORGAN GIVEN IN EXCHANGE FOR PROFIT SHARING CERTIFICATES AMOUNTING TO $500.00.

If you want to receive this handsome parlor organ without cost as your share of the profit in this business, simply save your profit sharing certificates until they amount to $500.00. Remember, it makes no difference to us how long a time you may take in accumulating the certificates. If you start at once to send to us for everything you buy, everything you use in the home, on the farm, in the shop or elsewhere, everything in groceries, wearing apparel, furniture and all other kind of goods, you will be surprised how quickly these profit sharing certificates will accumulate. It will not be long until you have gotten together profit sharing certificates to the amount of $500.00. You can then send them to us, and this organ will go to you as your share of the profit, go to you without money, without cost.

This organ is gotten out by the Beckwith Organ Company especially for our Customers' Profit Sharing Department. It is one of the handsomest organs on the market; has a very large, handsome, solid oak case, as illustrated, elaborately carved, decorated and finished. It is an extra large instrument, contains 11 stops, has the highest grade action, and the very best bellows, and in tone it is the equal of any organ on the market. Comes complete with stool and instruction book. **We guarantee it for quality and we furnish it to you without cost in exchange for profit sharing certificates amounting to $500.00**

No. 46PS100

THIS BEAUTIFUL BLACK WOOD HAND ENGRAVED 8-DAY MANTEL CLOCK GIVEN IN EXCHANGE FOR PROFIT SHARING CERTIFICATES AMOUNTING TO $100.00.

No. 5PS100

This is a very handsome and ornamental clock and a very accurate timepiece. Made of highly polished black wood with imitation marble columns trimmed in gilt. It has beautiful side ornaments 10¾ inches high with a 6-inch dial. The movement is one of the very best, made of polished brass and oil tempered steel; runs eight days with one winding, strikes the hours on a cathedral gong and the half hours on a cup bell, and is guaranteed to be an accurate time keeper. We guarantee it one of the best clocks on the market. This clock is offered to our customers without charge in exchange for profit sharing certificates amounting to $100.

REFER TO OUR CATALOGUE and learn our prices on the goods you are thinking of buying elsewhere. You can save a great deal of money on the most staple merchandise, such as groceries, wearing apparel, etc., and on the less staple merchandise we can save you even a larger percentage. We guarantee to furnish you anything you want at a lower price than you can buy elsewhere. If you will send to us, or, better still, if you will get your neighbors to allow you to send to us for the goods they want also, you will be surprised how quickly you will accumulate profit sharing certificates sufficient to entitle you to the article you want.

REMEMBER, every time you send us an order you get a profit sharing certificate for the full amount of your purchase, preserve these certificates and when you have accumulated enough to entitle you to the article you desire, send the certificates to us, and the article you want will be sent to you free of any cost.

THIS GENUINE MARLIN REPEATING SHOTGUN GIVEN IN EXCHANGE FOR PROFIT SHARING CERTIFICATES AMOUNTING TO $300.00.

No. 6PS120

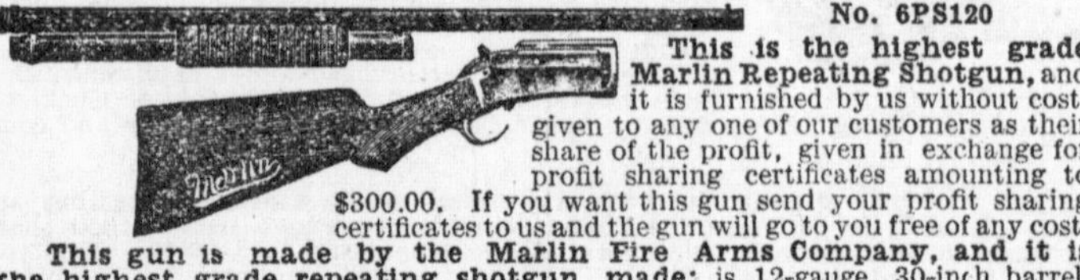

This is the highest grade Marlin Repeating Shotgun, and it is furnished by us without cost, given to any one of our customers as their share of the profit, given in exchange for profit sharing certificates amounting to $300.00. If you want this gun send your profit sharing certificates to us and the gun will go to you free of any cost.

This gun is made by the Marlin Fire Arms Company, and it is the highest grade repeating shotgun made; is 12-gauge, 30-inch barrel, choke bored, shoots six times with one loading, is put out under the manufacturer's binding guarantee. It is a repeating shotgun that is too well known to require much description.

If you want this gun without cost and do not feel that you can wait until you have sent us orders for goods for your own use amounting to as much as $300.00, interest your neighbors. Surely you have neighbors who would be glad to take advantage of our money saving prices if you would only call their attention to our catalogue and get them to join with you, and while the orders would have to be sent in your name, your neighbors would make a big saving on the goods you would order for them and you would be enabled to send us orders which would in a short time amount to $300.00.

REMEMBER, you can take your own time for accumulating these certificates. Every time you send us an order you will receive a certificate by return mail, and whether it takes you several weeks, several months or several years to accumulate certificates amounting to enough to entitle you to the article or articles wanted, makes no difference to us. Preserve your certificates carefully and when they have amounted to enough to entitle you to the article or articles you want, send the certificates to us and the article called for will be sent to you free of any cost

THIS EXTRA HIGH GRADE FULL LEATHER QUARTER TOP BUGGY GIVEN IN EXCHANGE FOR PROFIT SHARING CERTIFICATES AMOUNTING TO $600.00.

No. 11PS100

This top buggy is made in our own factory at Evansville, Indiana, and it is one of the highest grade top buggies made, such a top buggy as you would find in city repositories, where they are sold at high prices; but with us we make no price. It is made especially for our customers, it is intended to go to them as their share of the profit and will be given to anyone in exchange for profit sharing certificates amounting to $600.00.

If you want this handsome top buggy without cost begin saving your profit sharing certificates now. Always refer to our catalogue before buying elsewhere. You will find the very goods you want, you will find our prices lower than you can buy elsewhere and we guarantee that you will find the goods better in quality and lower in price than you could buy elsewhere; otherwise, you can return the goods to us and we will return your money, and if you send to us for everything you need, everything you wear, that you eat, that you use in the house or out of the house, the orders you send to us will accumulate rapidly and the amount of the profit sharing certificates you will hold from us will grow constantly and you will soon have accumulated profit sharing certificates to the amount of $600.00; then you have only to send the profit sharing certificates to us, say that you want this buggy and the buggy will be sent to you without one penny of cost to you.

If you want to get this buggy at once without expense to yourself, solicit a few orders for buggies from your friends and neighbors. You certainly have friends and neighbors who would be glad to buy a buggy if they knew they could get a high grade buggy for so little money as we offer it in our catalogue, and you can take orders at our prices for a dozen buggies within a year. You needn't confine the orders you take to buggies alone, for your friends and neighbors, when they learn of our very low prices on wearing apparel, furniture and other goods they need, will be glad to let you send their orders to us, and in this way you can accumulate profit sharing certificates rapidly. The profit sharing certificates we will send you will not only cover the amount of money you send to us for your own goods, but the orders you take for your friends and neighbors as well. With just a little effort on your part in this direction you will be surprised how quickly you can send us orders amounting to $600.00. When you send us orders amounting to $600.00, whether it takes weeks, months or years, you will have certificates to show for it, since we send you a profit sharing certificate for the full amount of each purchase, and this on the day we ship the goods, and when you have received sufficient profit sharing certificates to entitle you to the article you want, you have only to send the certificates to us, state the article or articles wanted, and they will be sent to you immediately without cost.

This is one of the highest grade full leather quarter top buggies we make; has piano box, 23 inches wide by 54 inches long, positively the highest grade. The gear is the highest grade end spring gear made, 15-16 inch fantailed steel axles, long distance spindles. Wheels are the highest grade Sarven's patent, ⅞-inch rims. Top is the highest grade three-bow, with deep cut genuine leather quarter top, made with full length side and back curtains, lined with an extra quality all wool dark green head lining. The upholstering is the highest grade, either leather or cloth as desired. Painting is the highest grade, body black, neatly striped and decorated; gear dark green, neatly striped and decorated We furnish the rig complete with top, full length side and back curtains, carpet, wrench, anti-rattlers and shafts; and, remember, it is furnished without price and without cost, it goes to the customer as his or her share of the profit. When you have profit sharing certificates amounting to $600.00 send them to us, say that you want this top buggy and it will go to you without one penny of expense as your share of the profit.

THIS BIG, HANDSOME, 3-PIECE HARDWOOD BEDROOM SUITE FURNISHED IN EXCHANGE FOR PROFIT SHARING CERTIFICATES AMOUNTING TO $250.00.

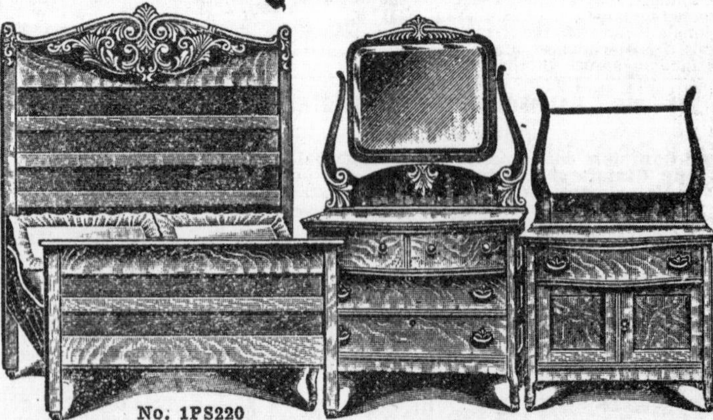

No. 1PS220

You can get this bedroom suite for nothing; in fact, the process by which you will get it will be a money saving process. To get this bedroom suite free of any cost as your share of the profit it will only be necessary for you to send us orders amounting to $250.00. Understand, you can take your own time. It may require a week, a month, a year or several years to accumulate sufficient certificates to entitle you to this bedroom suite. When you have sent us altogether $250.00 for merchandise you will have received such value as you could not have gotten elsewhere at less than $350.00 to $400.00, you have made a big saving in the cost of the goods, you can then send your profit sharing certificates to us, say that you want this bedroom suite and it will go to you free of any cost.

This is a handsome hardwood 3-piece bedroom suite, consisting of a bed, dresser and washstand. The bed is 6 feet 2 inches long and 4 feet 6 inches wide. The head of the bed is 6 feet high, sides are thoroughly substantial and the construction of the bed is such that it will give great service. The dresser is the latest square dresser style, exceedingly handsome, beautifully carved top with large square German plate bevel mirror. Fitted with four large, roomy drawers, with cast brass handles. The commode is made to match the dresser and bed. The three pieces combined will make a strong, heavy, substantial, well finished hardwood bedroom suite suitable for any home. **This suite will be furnished without cost.** It goes to our customers in exchange for profit sharing certificates amounting to $250.00

THIS STYLISH WALKING OR DRESS SKIRT, MADE OF STRICTLY ALL WOOL MATERIAL, GIVEN FREE, IN EXCHANGE FOR PROFIT SHARING CERTIFICATES AMOUNTING TO $100.00.

No. 31PS100

This is a fashionable dress skirt and can be had in various materials, all strictly all wool, such as cheviots, broadcloth and meltons, in black, blue, brown or castor colors, and can be furnished either in dress skirt length or as a walking skirt. **This handsome skirt, made as illustrated, also in other prevailing styles is given in exchange for profit sharing certificates amounting to $100.00.** If you want this beautiful skirt as your share of our profit on your purchases, save your certificates until they amount to $100.00. state the material and the color wanted, also whether you want a walking or dress skirt, state the number of inches around the waist and length of skirt, and you will receive the skirt free, in exchange for your certificates. You can easily secure this handsome skirt by saving your profit sharing certificates, and these certificates accumulate very rapidly. We send you a profit sharing certificate every time you send us an order.

THIS EXTRA QUALITY, VERY HANDSOME, LADIES' SILK UNDERSKIRT GIVEN FREE IN EXCHANGE FOR PROFIT SHARING CERTIFICATES AMOUNTING TO $100.00.

No. 31PS105

This is one of the newest style flaring skirts, trimmed with small ruffles, made of an extra quality of taffeta silk, a skirt that is sure to please you, and is given in exchange for profit sharing certificates amounting to $100.00. Comes in black only, and when ordering, state the number of inches around the waist and length of skirt.

You not only save money every time you place an order with us, but in addition you get a profit sharing certificate showing the amount of your purchase and when these certificates amount to $100.00. you can send them to us and get this beautiful skirt free of any cost

THIS MEN'S EXTRA HEAVY LONG STORM EXCLUDING, HIGH COLLAR, DARK FRIEZE WINTER ULSTER

Given in Exchange for Profit Sharing Certificates Amounting to $100.00.

No. 45PS105

If you want to receive this big, heavy winter ulster as your share of the profit in this business, without money, without expense, simply preserve your profit sharing certificates until they amount to $100.00, then send them to us, state your height, weight, number of inches around body at breast, taken over vest, under coat, and this big ulster will go to you free of cost, go to you as your share of the profit, in exchange for profit sharing certificates amounting to $100.00.

This ulster is made of dark, heavy weight frieze ulster cloth, a goods that will wear well and give first class satisfaction. It is a plain, very dark gray, with an invisible herringbone effect, made with a big storm collar, two muff pockets, made 50 inches long; has a very heavy lining, heavy interlining, heavy padding and is a thoroughly warm winter garment. Sizes, 34 to 42 inches breast measure. We guarantee it for quality, guarantee it to fit perfectly, and it goes to you as your share of the profit in exchange for profit sharing certificates amounting to $100.00.

Receives a Fine Overcoat for Profit Sharing Certificates.

Pinckneyville, Ill.

Sears, Roebuck & Co., Chicago.

Dear Sirs:—I have just received the fine overcoat which you sent me and it did not cost me one cent, as I received it in exchange for the profit sharing certificates which you have been sending me every time I bought goods. I not only saved money on every article of goods purchased from you, but have received this overcoat free which I am sure would sell here at $10.00. Everything I received from you proved entirely satisfactory and I think your profit sharing plan for your customers is something wonderful. I will always recommend your house to anyone who asks.

Respectfully CHAS. YOUNG.

BOYS' THREE-PIECE KNEE PANTS SUITS,

For Boys from 8 to 16 Years of Age, and for Sizes No Larger Than 32 Inches Breast Measure, Given in Exchange for Profit Sharing Certificates Amounting to $100.00.

These three-piece knee pants suits are made round cut sack style, like illustration, in sizes to fit average size boys from 8 to 16 years of age, no larger than 32 inches breast measure.

These suits can be furnished either in worsted or cassimere, medium weight in dark striped patterns adapted for wear any season of the year. The suits consist of round cut sack coat, single breasted vest and one pair of knee pants, which will be found neatly and substantially trimmed and well tailored. If you want this three-piece knee pants suit, save your profit sharing certificates until they amount to $100.00, then send them to us, state age of boy, his height and weight, number of inches around the breast, and this handsome three-piece suit will go to you in exchange for profit sharing certificates amounting to $100.00 which you send to us; will go to you without money and without price.

No. 40PS125

BOYS' LONG PANTS SUITS,

For Boys From 14 to 20 Years of Age, or Who Measure From 30 to 36 Inches Breast Measure; the Latest Style, Weight Suitable for the Year Around Wear. Given in Exchange for Profit Sharing Certificates Amounting to $100.00.

No. 40PS130

These suits are made from medium weight all wool cassimeres or cheviots and can be furnished either in plain, dark blue or neat dark mixed patterns in latest effects. If you will kindly state your preference we will endeavor to make a selection to please you. The coats are made in single breasted, round cut sack styles. Vest is single breasted with three buttons. Pants are cut in the prevailing styles. The garments are thoroughly well tailored throughout, well lined and trimmed and have neat fitting qualities.

If you wish to receive this medium weight suit, adapted for wear at any season of the year. as your share of the profit, simply save your profit sharing certificates until they amount to $100.00, then send them to us, saying you wish this suit, state age of boy, height and weight, number of inches around body at breast, over vest, under coat, number of inches around body at waist and length of leg; that is the inside seam from tight up in the crotch to heel. The suit will then go to you under our guarantee and without expense to you, given in exchange for profit sharing certificates amounting to $100.00.

MEN'S FINE BLACK ALL WOOL CLAY WORSTED SUIT.

Medium Weight, Suitable for All Year Around Wear, an Exceedingly Fine Suit of Clothes Given in Exchange for Profit Sharing Certificates Amounting to $175.00.

This is a very fine black worsted suit, the latest round cut sack style, the latest effect, adapted for the year around wear. It is extra well made, of medium weight, all wool black clay worsted cloth. A fine plain black diagonal goods, cloth that don't wear shiny: guaranteed for wear, makes a handsome suit for every day and dress occasions. The suit is well made, sewed, trimmed and finished. We use a high grade black Italian cloth body lining in coat. Coat is well interlined, padded, stiffened and has good fitting qualities. We can furnish this suit in size to fit men of 34 to 42 inches chest measurement, 30 to 40 inches waist and from 30 to 36 inches inside seam measurement for pants. No smaller or larger sizes can be furnished.

No. 45PS160

If you want to receive this medium weight English clay worsted suit without cost as your share of the profit, save your certificates until they amount to $175.00, then send them to us, say that you wish this suit state your height, weight, the number of inches around body at breast. take it over your vest, under coat, number of inches around your waist and the length of the inside seam for your pants, from tight up in crotch to heel and we will send you this suit as your share of the profit in exchange for profit sharing certificates amounting to $175.00.

Wonderful to Receive Goods of Such Value Entirely Free.

Callaway. Nebr.

Sears, Roebuck & Co. Chicago.

Dear Sirs.—Please accept my thanks for the suit which I have received in exchange for profit sharing certificates amounting to $100.00. It is certainly wonderful to receive goods of this value entirely free of charge. All the orders I sent for came almost sooner than I expected. If I, myself, had been in your store I could not have gotten the goods any better. They always came without fault or mistake.

Thanking you again for the fine suit I am. Very truly yours.

CHRIST AHRENDT

THIS HANDSOME GENUINE DIAMOND RING FURNISHED IN EXCHANGE FOR PROFIT SHARING CERTIFICATES AMOUNTING TO $250.00.

No. 4PS150

This is a full one-fourth karat diamond, beautifully cut, good color, fine quality, genuine stone, mounted in one of the latest style mountings, extra heavy shank, a fine solid gold ring such a handsome and expensive genuine diamond ring, full one-fourth karat size, as you will find only in the best city retail stores.

This ring will cost you nothing, there is no price to you, it is your share of the profit if you send us orders amounting to $250.00. You can take your own time in accumulating sufficient certificates to entitle you to this ring. Simply send us your orders for what goods you want from time to time, be sure to refer to our catalogue before buying goods elsewhere, for you will certainly find in our book just the goods you want and at a lower cost than you can buy elsewhere, and then if you send us your orders for what you want, you will be surprised how quickly you will accumulate profit sharing certificates, how soon you will receive certificates amounting to enough to entitle you to any article you may want from this profit sharing list. If you want this diamond ring accumulate the certificates until they have amounted to $250.00, then send the certificates to us, state that you want this ring, give us the size ring desired by sending us a piece of paper or a string just long enough to reach around the finger, and the ring will go to you without any expense whatever.

MEN'S BIG HEAVY NORWAY DOG FUR OVERCOAT

For Winter, Given in Exchange for Profit Sharing Certificates Amounting to $250.00.

No. 41PS100

If you want to receive this big fur coat without cost as your share of the profit in this business, simply save your profit sharing certificates until they amount to $250.00, then send them to us, state you wish this coat, state your height and your weight, number of inches around body at breast, taken over your outside coat, and this coat will go to you without cost, go to you as your share of the profit in the business, go to you in exchange for the $250.00 you send us in profit sharing certificates.

This big, heavy fur overcoat is made of an extra quality of Norway wolf dog. The color is a rich shade tipped with black, absolutely natural color. The coat is double sewed throughout, body is lined with quilted heavy mercerized Italian cloth lining, made with leather arm shields, sleeves are lined with extra heavy black iron cloth. The coat is fitted at cuffs with our woolen woven wind excluding wristlets, finished with buttons and loops. **It is extra well made throughout, furnished under our guarantee.** Sizes, 36 to 46 inches breast measure. We guarantee it will fit you and we will send this coat to you in exchange for profit sharing certificates amounting to $250.00

THIS MEN'S EXTRA FINE, HEAVY WEIGHT, ALL WOOL BLACK KERSEY OVERCOAT,

In the Latest Style for Fall and Winter, furnished in Exchange for Profit Sharing Certificates Amounting to $175.00.

If you want to receive this extra fine, genuine all wool kersey overcoat in the very latest style for fall and winter free of any cost to you, as your share of the profits in this business, then save your profit sharing certificates until they amount to $175.00, then send them to us, say you wish this overcoat, state your height, your weight, number of inches around body at breast taken over vest and under inside coat and this overcoat will go to you free of any cost, with our guarantee for quality, under our guarantee that it will fit you perfectly.

This is one of the handsomest overcoats we have produced in our big clothing factory. It is made of an extra quality heavy weight all wool kersey cloth, a very smooth finished material; is well made, trimmed and finished. Made in the very latest fly front style; has heavy lining heavy interlining, heavy padding, is extra well stiffened, well stayed thoroughly well made throughout. Sizes, 34 to 42 inches breast measure. Remember, you get this overcoat without price, it goes to you as your share of the profit in exchange for profit sharing certificates amounting to $175.00.

No. 45PS115

You can accumulate profit sharing certificates in a very short time if you will get in the habit, before buying anything elsewhere, of first referring to our catalogue and compare our prices with the prices asked by others. You will be surprised how much money you can save. When you have sent $175.00 to us for various goods that you need from time to time you will have received as much real value from us for your $175.00 as you would get elsewhere for $250.00; besides, you will then be in a position to participate in the profits of our business by exchanging your certificates for this handsome heavy weight fall and winter all wool kersey overcoat.

THIS HANDSOME REED SLEEPER GO-CART GIVEN IN EXCHANGE FOR PROFIT SHARING CERTIFICATES AMOUNTING TO $125.00.

No. 25PS100

This go-cart is made of fine imported round and flat reeds, and presents a neat and attractive appearance. Has the latest improved gear, consisting of strong and elastic steel springs with 16-inch rubber tired steel wheels, patent wheel fasteners, rubber hub caps and automatic foot brake, neatly enameled in Brewster green and handsomely gilt striped. The back and dash can be instantly adjusted to any position. It is complete with cushions of Bedford cord covering seat, back and dash, furnished in any color, and has a large parasol made of percaline with fly net lace cover trimmed with two ruffles and puff. Has patent parasol attachment which adjusts the parasol to any angle.

If you want this go-cart free of any cost preserve your profit sharing certificates until they amount to $125.00, then send them to us, and if this go-cart is your choice in exchange for your profit sharing certificates, we will send it to you free of any cost to you.

If you will get in the habit of first referring to our catalogue before buying anything elsewhere, anything to eat, to wear, to use in the home or on the farm, your purchases will soon amount to $125.00, you will make a big saving in the cost of the goods ordered from time to time, and you will get as much real value out of the $125.00 sent us as you would get from $150.00 to $175.00 expended elsewhere.

THIS HANDSOME CHIFFONIER GIVEN IN EXCHANGE FOR PROFIT SHARING CERTIFICATES AMOUNTING TO $100.00.

This is a handsome, well finished, full paneled, solid oak chiffonier. We furnish it to our customers as their share of the profits, given in exchange for profit sharing certificates amounting to $100.00. If you send your orders to us from time to time you will receive by return mail for each order a profit sharing certificate for the full amount of money sent us with each order. Simply save these certificates until they amount to $100.00, then if you want this handsome solid oak chiffonier send the certificates to us, and we will send this chiffonier to you free of any cost.

No. 1PS115

This chiffonier is made of solid oak, nicely finished, has five large drawers, all fitted with locks and keys. Width, 30 inches; depth, 17 inches. Has four panels in the ends, and full paneled back. It is extra well made, trimmings are cast brass, comes complete with best quality casters. It is an exceedingly nice piece of well finished oak furniture, suitable for any home, and goes to our customers as their share of the profit, without cost, in exchange for profit sharing certificates amounting to $100 00.

THIS HANDSOME OVERSTUFFED UPHOLSTERED COUCH GIVEN IN EXCHANGE FOR PROFIT SHARING CERTIFICATES AMOUNTING TO $100.00.

No. 1PS135

If you want this couch free of any cost to you simply send us your orders from time to time. You will get a certificate by return mail on receipt of every order you send us, and when these certificates have amounted to $100.00 send them to us, say you wish this couch and it will go to you as your share of the profit free of any cost to you.

This handsome couch is 72 inches long, 26 inches wide The frame is made of hardwood throughout, is finished in oak or imitation mahogany as desired The frame work is nicely embossed. Contains a full set of the best oil tempered steel springs, drawn from high carbon cold rolled steel, 19 springs in all, securely tied, insuring the best service. It is first covered with heavy duck canvas over the springs; extra well constructed throughout, it is then upholstered in the best quality high colored imported velour cloth in red brown or dark green; base of couch is finished with hand made fringe. Shipping weight, 100 pounds Fitted with best quality casters. It is a handsome piece of furniture and goes to you without cost, given in exchange for profit sharing certificates amounting to $100.00.

MEN'S FANCY CASSIMERE MEDIUM WEIGHT ROUND CORNERED SACK SUIT.

Furnished in Exchange for Profit Sharing Certificates Amounting to $100.00.

No. 45PS155

We can furnish this suit in sizes from 34 to 42 inches chest measurement, from 30 to 40 inches waist and from 30 to 36 inches inside seam for pants. We cannot furnish larger or smaller sizes. This suit is made from medium weight cloth, suitable for wear the year around. The pattern is a combination of striped and mottled effect. Stripes of parallel white threads and a faint dark stripe of dull blue, there are occasional threads appearing over the fabric in tan and red. This pattern is a very great favorite in good dressing circles. The coat has a good Italian body lining, and durable fancy sleeve lining. It is made in the popular round cornered sack style. The whole effect is stylish and dressy. We guarantee the suit to please you in color, pattern, quality or material, style, workmanship and fit. The garment has extra good fitting qualities, is well trimmed, sewed and finished

If you wish to receive this suit without money, without cost, as your share of the profit, simply save your profit sharing certificates until they amount to $100.00, then send them to us, state that you wish this suit as your share of the profit, give your height, weight, number of inches around body at breast and waist, and state length of pants, inside seam from crotch to heel. We will send you the suit, guaranteeing it to fit you, and it will go to you free of any cost as your share of profit in exchange for $100.00 in profit sharing certificates which you send us.

Mr. Dewitt Says Our Profit Sharing Plan is Wonderful.

Pond Creek, Okla.

Sears, Roebuck & Co., Chicago.

Gentlemen:—I received the watch two weeks ago that you sent me free of charge in exchange for my profit sharing certificates amounting to $100.00. I am well pleased with the watch. It is so much nicer than I expected and is a very good timekeeper. Your profit sharing plan is something wonderful, when it enables a customer to get a fine watch for nothing and at the same time save money on every order. We saved over $8.00 on one heater after paying the freight. It is the best heater I ever saw. I received all my goods promptly and everything has given perfect satisfaction. I would rather buy at home than to send off, but I can save so much money by buying from you that I cannot afford to do otherwise and now, that you send me profit sharing certificates, I feel that in my interest I must buy everything from you.

Thanking you again for the handsome watch which did not cost me a cent, I am, Very truly yours,

F L. DEWITT.

THIS GOLD FILLED WATCH GIVEN IN EXCHANGE FOR PROFIT SHARING CERTIFICATES OF PURCHASE AMOUNTING TO $100.00.

No. 4PS125

Every time you send us an order you will receive from us a profit sharing certificate for the amount of your order, save these certificates until the total amount of the certificates you receive amount to $100.00, and then if you want this watch send the certificates to us and the watch will be sent to you by return express free of any cost to you, in exchange for the profit sharing certificates sent.

This is a gentleman's regular 18 size, heavy, gold filled, stem wind and stem set watch. The case is open face, screw back and screw bezel, dust proof with a thick bevel plate glass or picture in front. It is elaborately carved and decorated in a variety of beautiful designs. The above illustration is one of the designs furnished. It is made with two plates of solid gold over an inner plate of hard composition metal and accompanying every case is a written binding 5-year guarantee. This watch is fitted with a genuine American movement, seven jeweled, stem wind and stem set, quick train, and the movement is guaranteed an accurate timekeeper for five years and with care will last a lifetime.

This is a very handsome gold filled watch, nice enough for any gentleman to carry and will be given by us in exchange for profit sharing certificates of purchase amounting to $100.00.

THIS BIG, HANDSOME, UPHOLSTERED MORRIS CHAIR GIVEN IN EXCHANGE FOR PROFIT SHARING CERTIFICATES AMOUNTING TO $100.00.

No. 1PS105

This Morris chair is an entirely new design. The frame is substantially built, is large and roomy, made of solid golden oak, given a high gloss finish; is made with spring seat, cushions are comfortable and exceedingly well made, cushions are reversible so that when worn on one side they can be used on the other, upholstered in a high grade three-toned velour cloth, which we furnish in the very latest pattern. The casters are best quality. The back is fitted with a reliable brass rod and ratchet reclining attachment with which the back can easily be adjusted to four different positions. This chair represents the very best value ever offered and no household should be without one. It is such a Morris chair as you will find in the best furniture stores, where they sell at fancy prices.

REMEMBER, this chair goes to any one of our customers free of any cost, given in exchange for profit sharing certificates amounting to $100.00. Simply preserve your profit sharing certificates as you receive them, remember you will receive one promptly in response to every order you send us. If you want this Morris chair when your certificates have amounted to $100.00 send them to us and the chair will go to you at once free of any cost.

If you do not feel that you can accumulate profit sharing certificates quickly enough, then go among your neighbors, get your neighbors to join with you. Your neighbors will be glad to let you order for them when they see how much money they can save. In this way you can soon accumulate profit sharing certificates sufficient to entitle you to select almost any article wanted from our profit sharing department.

THIS HIGH GRADE GENUINE BURDICK 5-DRAWER DROP HEAD OAK CABINET SEWING MACHINE GIVEN IN EXCHANGE FOR PROFIT SHARING CERTIFICATES AMOUNTING TO $250.00.

No. 26PS100

If you want to receive this handsome, high grade, five drawer, drop head oak cabinet sewing machine as your share of the profit, if you want to get it without cost, without one penny of expense, if you want to get it by a money saving process, then send all your orders to us Before buying anything from your dealer at home or elsewhere look in our catalogue for our prices Whether you are wanting groceries dry goods, wearing apparel, hardware furniture or any other kind of merchandise, goods you use in the home on the farm in the shop, in the office or elsewhere, don't fail to first refer to our catalogue.

We guarantee to save you money; you will see by our process that you can make a big saving, so don t fail to send your orders to us. If you will send all your orders to us, receiving in return for each order sent a profit sharing certificate for the full amount of your order, you will be surprised how quickly your orders will amount to $250.00 No doubt you have friends and neighbors who would like to buy wearing apparel furniture or other goods at the big saving in price that our prices will mean to them so get them to allow you to send their orders to us and in this way you will accumulate profit sharing certificates rapidly.

THIS BURDICK SEWING MACHINE is an especially high grade machine, has an extra high arm nickel plated balance wheel, nickel plated face plate has all the very latest improvements, eccentric action, positive four-motion feed and will do any kind of work that can be done on any sewing machine made; runs very easily almost noiseless; is covered by a written binding twenty years guarantee. Comes set up in a handsome solid oak five-drawer, drop head cabinet, elaborately finished, so made that when the sewing machine is not in use the head drops out of sight and you have a handsome piece of furniture a center table writing desk or stand. When the machine is in use the head raises to place and the cover makes a large leaf or table. **It is furnished with all accessories** including one quilter six bobbins one cloth guide one large screwdriver, one oil can filled with oil, one combination screwdriver and wrench, one foot hemmer and one package of needles.

REMEMBER, you get this drop head oak cabinet sewing machine in exchange for profit sharing certificates amounting to $250.00.

Receives a Fine Sewing Machine, Just Like a Present.

Columbia Cross Roads, Pa.

Sears, Roebuck & Co., Chicago.

Gentlemen:—I just received the fine sewing machine from your profit sharing department in exchange for my certificates and am well pleased with it, for it seems just like a present. I have received goods from your store from time to time during the past eight years and find every article just as represented and great value for the money. The way your profit sharing plan induces people to buy goods from you will certainly allow you to make your prices still lower in the future.

Yours truly,

OWEN COOPER.

THIS HANDSOME WHITE ENAMELED IRON BED COMPLETE WITH A STRONG SET OF WOVEN WIRE SPRINGS AND A HIGH GRADE MATTRESS,

The Complete Outfit Given in Exchange for Profit Sharing Certificates Amounting to $100 00.

No. 1PS120

If you want this white enameled iron bed with full set of woven wire springs and mattress complete, free of any cost, as your share of the profits in this business, simply send us your orders from time to time for the goods you need, and when you have accumulated profit sharing certificates to the amount of $100.00 send them to us, and this bed, mattress and springs all complete will go to you as your share of the profit, and without expense.

THIS BIG, HANDSOME, 16-INCH FIREPOT HEATING STOVE FURNISHED IN EXCHANGE FOR PROFIT SHARING CERTIFICATES AMOUNTING TO $175.00.

This big, handsome, beautifully finished, nickel ornamented, nickel trimmed oak heating stove is made to burn either coal or wood, furnished with a wood grate and a coal grate, will burn anything burned in any stove made. Made with a handsome nickel top ornamentation, nickel steel bands, nickel medallions, is mounted on a heavy steel body, has heavy ribbed single cast iron firepot, the most improved shaking and draw center grate, with extra large doors for wood and lower door for coal; has the latest check draft, handsome rococo design, latest swing ash door. It is a big, 16-inch firepot all purpose heating stove, large enough to heat a very large room, large enough to heat comfortably a small or medium sized house both downstairs and upstairs; has a direct draft, and with the use of the dampers the fire can be controlled and the fire kept all night. The stove would sell at a good price in any hardware store; but it is furnished by us without price, without cost, goes to our customers as their share of the profit in this business. It is only necessary to send us your profit sharing certificates amounting to $175.00, say you wish this heating stove and the stove will go to you free of any cost.

No. 22PS100

If you have not already purchased goods from us amounting to $175.00, even though you have been dealing with us for a year or more, don't think that you cannot soon accumulate certificates amounting to $175.00. If you haven't dealt with us to such an extent in the past there is no reason why you should not in the future. You are certainly convinced you have saved money on the goods you have bought from us; why not save money on everything you buy, on everything you eat, wear, use in the house or out of the house? You can save from 25 to 50 cents on every dollar's worth of goods you purchase by sending to us. Then you have the further advantage that after you have made purchases from us amounting to $175.00, **you can receive this big stove free of cost as your share of the profit,** and after receiving one or more articles you can continue to accumulate profit sharing certificates, continue to save money on the goods you buy from us and continue to share in the profits of this business by sending your orders to us from time to time; and to share more quickly and more liberally in the profits of our business, to get these articles more frequently and to get more valuable articles, use your influence among your friends and neighbors, get them to allow you to send to us for the goods they need. They take no risk, for we will immediately return their money if the goods are not perfectly satisfactory to them. You will be helping them by saving them money and will be helping yourself by saving money on the goods you buy for your own use and you will be sharing liberally in the profits by exchanging your profit sharing certificates for any of the articles shown in this profit sharing list. You will also be helping us, helping us to make lower prices, because if we get all your trade and if through your influence we get orders from your friends and neighbors our business will grow until our factories can be enlarged, we can then manufacture at a lower cost, we can buy in even larger quantities than we are now buying and thus get still lower prices, and we can and will always, as we always have in the past, give you the benefit of every saving we make; and of course we can well afford to allow you to share liberally in the profits of our business in proportion to the amount of orders you send to us, in proportion to the influence you use in our behalf among your friends and neighbors.

THIS HANDSOME SOLID OAK LEATHER UPHOLSTERED ROCKER GIVEN IN EXCHANGE FOR PROFIT SHARING CERTIFICATES OF PURCHASE AMOUNTING TO $100.00.

No. 1PS150

This is one of the handsomest leather upholstered rockers on the market. It is made of selected quarter sawed oak, finished golden with a highly figured grain. The seat is upholstered in genuine leather, cobbler style. The arms are supported by three heavy spindles. The frame is strong and rigid and perfectly fitted in every way. **This handsome, comfortable, up to date style rocker** is furnished especially for our Customers' Profit Sharing Department and is given free in exchange for profit sharing certificates of purchase amounting to $100.00. It is only necessary to preserve your profit sharing certificates until they amount to $100.00, then send them to us, state that you want this rocker and it will go to you free of cost and all you will have to pay will be the freight or express charges.

THIS COLUMBIA GRAPHOPHONE OR TALKING MACHINE FURNISHED IN EXCHANGE FOR PROFIT SHARING CERTIFICATES AMOUNTING TO $100.00.

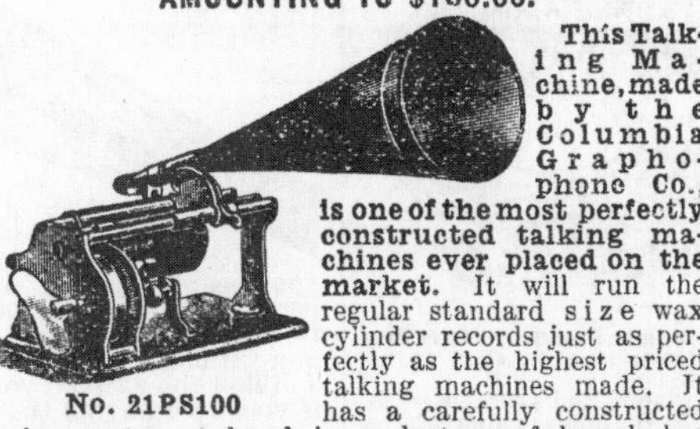

No. 21PS100

This Talking Machine, made by the Columbia Graphophone Co., is one of the most perfectly constructed talking machines ever placed on the market. It will run the regular standard size wax cylinder records just as perfectly as the highest priced talking machines made. It has a carefully constructed spring motor enclosed in a dust proof barrel, has an extra high grade governor with the latest style speed regulator to insure a perfect uniformity of speed. The sound producer is made with best mica diaphragm and sapphire reproducing point. It is detachable and produces the musical and talking records as perfectly as any machine made. Each talking machine comes complete with a 10-inch japanned horn and a high grade aluminum reproducer, and we send it to any one of our customers who cares to have a talking machine in exchange for profit sharing certificates of purchase amounting to $100.00.

SIMPLY SEND YOUR ORDERS to us for the goods you need; every time we receive an order we will send you a profit sharing certificate for the full amount of your purchase, preserve these certificates as you make purchases from time to time, and when your purchases have amounted to enough and you have accumulated profit sharing certificates sufficient to entitle you to any one or more of the articles you want, as shown in our profit sharing list, send your certificates to us and the goods you call for will be sent to you free of any cost

FIFTY COLUMBIA WAX TALKING MACHINE RECORDS.

A Big Box of 50 Records, Records that Have Retailed Generally at 50 cents each, are Offered in Exchange for Profit Sharing Certificates Amounting to $175.00.

No. 21PS105

These 50 records comprise a very choice selection of songs, speeches and instrumental music in a great variety, the choicest selections of the Columbia Graphophone Co.'s stock. They are the highest grade Columbia standard size wax cylinder records, suitable for either the Edison or Columbia talking machine; or any machine that takes a record of standard size will take these. They are offered by us without price and without cost to you. Simply preserve your profit sharing certificates of purchase until they amount to $175.00, then if you want this complete set of 50 assorted talking machine records, vocal, instrumental, speeches, comic and otherwise, send your certificates of purchase amounting to $175.00 to us and these complete 50 records will go to you free of any expense.

THIS BIG, HANDSOME, COAL AND WOOD BURNING RESERVOIR COOK STOVE GIVEN IN EXCHANGE FOR PROFIT SHARING CERTIFICATES AMOUNTING TO 250.00.

No. 22PS105

This is an extra high grade, beautifully nickel trimmed, large cast iron, porcelain lined reservoir coal and wood burning stove, such a stove as would sell generally in any hardware store at $25.00 or more; but in this case it is given without price, without cost, it goes to our customers in exchange for profit sharing certificates of purchase amounting to $250.00. Simply preserve your profit sharing certificates of purchase and remember you will receive a certificate with every purchase you make for the full amount you sent us in dollars and cents. This certificate will be sent to you immediately upon receipt of your order. You have only to hold the certificates until they amount to enough to entitle you to the article or articles you want.

REMEMBER, in the saving of these certificates you save money, for you get goods that you could not buy elsewhere at anything like the price. Our profit sharing increases our business, gets us new customers, enables us to make still lower prices and warrants us in sharing our profits liberally with our customers.

Buy all the goods you want from us under our guarantee to always save you money, and so far as possible get your neighbors to let you send to us for the goods they need, and you will be surprised how quickly you will accumulate profit sharing certificates sufficient to entitle you to share in the profits of this business by selecting any of these articles that you may desire.

This big, handsome, cook stove is made of the very best cast iron, has very large flues, cut tops, heavy cut centers supported by posts, heavy covers, heavy linings and heavy sectional fireback, large bailed ash pan, solid hearth plate, nickel outside oven shelf pouch feed, oven door kicker, nickel plated panel on oven door, nickel plated name plate on front door, nickel plated door knobs, heavy tin lined oven door. When ashes are removed from under oven they are scraped into the hearth, avoiding all possibility of spilling the ashes on the floor when cleaning the stove. It is furnished with a lifter, shaker and scraper for removing the ashes from under the oven. It is fitted with a large porcelain lined reservoir, as shown in illustration; is furnished on a large handsome rococo pattern base, comes with both coal and wood grate, is a large size 8-18, has four 8-inch holes, oven is 18x17x11, stove weighs over 300 pounds and is furnished without cost or price, given to our customers in exchange for profit sharing certificates amounting to $250.00.

THIS HIGH GRADE, EXTRA LARGE, BEAUTIFULLY FINISHED AND EXPENSIVE FIELD GLASS

Given in Exchange for Profit Sharing Certificates Amounting to $100.00.

This is an extra high grade field glass fitted with genuine achromatic lenses, bars, draw tubes and trimmings finished in black and body covered with fine black morocco leather. It is an extra large glass, measures 6 inches high when closed and 7¼ inches when extended. The object glasses are 24 lignes in diameter, and the magnifying power is four times, such a field glass as would sell in the best optical goods store at a fancy price; but in this instance it is offered by us without price, given to our customers in our liberal distribution of profits. Any customer wishing this field glass should send us profit sharing certificates amounting to $100.00, state that he wishes this glass and it will go to him without one penny of expense.

No. 20PS100

We want you to send to us for every dollar's worth of goods you buy, the groceries you eat, the goods you wear, the goods you use in your home, in the field, or in the shop. We guarantee to furnish you better goods than you can buy elsewhere, and at the lowest prices ever made, much lower prices than are quoted by any other house, and so in addition to accumulating profit sharing certificates you will be saving money on the goods you buy from us, and every time you send us an order you will get a profit sharing certificate for the full amount of money sent us, and these profit sharing certificates, when they amount to $100.00 or more, will entitle you to any article or articles shown in this, our liberal profit sharing list

THIS BIG 100-PIECE DINNER SET GIVEN IN EXCHANGE FOR PROFIT SHARING CERTIFICATES AMOUNTING TO $125.00.

No. 2PS105

To get this big 100-piece dinner set without cost as your share of the profit in this business, simply send us your orders from time to time for all the goods you need we, of course, guaranteeing the goods to please you, guaranteeing to save you money on everything you buy. Each time you send us an order we will send you a profit sharing certificate for the full amount of money you send us, and when these certificates have amounted to $125.00 send them to us if you wish this dinner set, and it will go to you free of any expense.

THIS HANDSOME 100-PIECE DINNER SET is made of semi-vitreous china, pure white in color, guaranteed not to craze, one of the highest grade plain vitreous sets on the market. **It is composed of 100 pieces, as follows:**

12 Soup Plates	12 Fruit Plates	1 8-inch Covered Dish (two pieces)	1 Sauce Boat
12 Tea Plates	1 10-inch Platter		1 Sugar Bowl (2 pieces)
12 Dinner Plates	1 14-inch Platter	1 Pickle Dish	1 Extra Bowl
12 Coffee Cups	1 Open Oval 7-in. Dish	1 Covered Butter Dish (three pieces)	1 Large Pitcher
12 Saucers	1 Open Round 8-inch Dish		1 Cream Pitcher
12 Individual Butters			

The entire 100 pieces given in exchange for profit sharing certificates amounting to $125.00.

THIS HANDSOME IMPORTED ENGLISH DINNER SET OF 100 PIECES GIVEN IN EXCHANGE FOR PROFIT SHARING CERTIFICATES AMOUNTING TO $175.00.

No. 2PS110

This is one of the handsomest 100-piece English dinner sets on the market. It is furnished by us without cost and without price. Goes to the customer as their share of the profit in exchange for profit sharing certificates amounting to $175.00.

If you want to get this handsome dinner set for nothing, simply send your orders to us for all the goods you need. We guarantee every article we sell to you and you always have the privilege of returning any goods to us that are not satisfactory and getting your money back. In accumulating $175.00 in certificates you will get from us for $175.00 as much value as you could possibly get elsewhere for $250.00. You will then be able to share in the profits of our business by exchanging the $175.00 in profit sharing certificates for this handsome imported English dinner set.

THIS SET is an entirely new shape, modeled after the finest china. The body of the ware is very strong, is fully warranted against crazing. The decoration used is a handsome floral border design printed under the glaze. It will never wear off. We furnish it in either royal blue or green as desired.

The 100-piece set consists of the following 100 pieces:

12 Dinner Plates	12 Saucers	1 12-inch Platter	1 Pickle Dish
12 Breakfast Plates	12 Individual Butter Plates	2 Covered Vegetable Dishes (4 pieces)	1 Sauce Boat
12 Tea Plates			1 Covered Butter Dish (3 pieces)
12 Sauce Plates	1 10-inch Platter	1 Sugar Bowl (2 pieces)	
12 Tea Cups	1 Open Vegetable Dish	1 Cream Pitcher	1 Bowl

The entire 100 pieces to be furnished in exchange for profit sharing certificates amounting to $175.00.

Mrs. Hand is Delighted With Her Dinner Set which Did Not Cost Her Anything.

Minerva, Ohio, Box 95.

Sears, Roebuck & Co., Chicago.

Dear Sirs:—We are very much pleased with the 100-piece dinner set just received from you in exchange for our profit sharing certificates. We feel that this dinner set absolutely did not cost us one cent, because we not only got the dinner set free, but we saved money on all the orders we sent you, and everything we got in groceries, clothing and all other articles have been the very best money could buy. We have always made a rule to buy where things were cheapest and best, as we always pay cash for everything we get and your goods are the cheapest and of better quality than we could get here or anywhere, even paying a great deal more. We know that your prices have not advanced one penny since you adopted the profit sharing plan, and we can say that we would not buy elsewhere as long as we can send to Sears, Roebuck & Co. Since July we have saved certificates amounting to $175.00 for the dinner set, and in addition we have $90.00 worth of certificates also.

Very truly yours, MRS. E. HAND.

THIS LATEST STYLE ROSE BORDER SEMI-PORCELAIN 100-PIECE DINNER SET.

One of the Finest Sets Made, a Product of the Celebrated Homer-Laughlin China Co., Given Free in Exchange for Profit Sharing Certificates Amounting to $350.00.

No. 2PS120

This is one of the handsomest, highest quality, 100-piece dinner sets ever shown, guaranteed not to check or craze. The decoration consists of a floral design, every piece has full gold edges and all knobs and handles are artistically illuminated with bright gold. This is unquestionably one of the most elaborately decorated dinner sets made and consists of the following:

12 Tea Cups	1 Medium Platter	1 Cream Pitcher
12 Saucers	1 Large Platter	1 Pickle Dish
12 Dinner Plates	1 Open Vegetable Dish	1 Bowl
12 Tea Plates	2 Covered Vegetable Dishes (4 Pieces)	1 Covered Butter Dish (3 Pieces)
12 Pie or Breakfast Plates		
12 Sauce Dishes	1 Sugar Bowl and Cover (2 Pieces)	1 Sauce Boat
12 Individual Butter Plates		

We do not put a price on this dinner set because we offer it free to our customers in exchange for profit sharing certificates of purchases amounting to $350.00. Save your profit sharing certificates that we send with each order and when they amount to $350.00, if you want this set, send the certificates to us and the set will be sent to you without cost, all you need to pay is the freight or express charges

THIS HANDSOME 8-DAY WALL CLOCK GIVEN FREE IN EXCHANGE FOR PROFIT SHARING CERTIFICATES AMOUNTING TO $100.00

No. 5PS105

This is an extra large, beautifully made and polished mantel clock. Made of wood, finished in black, enameled and hand finished. Has imitation marble columns beautifully trimmed and ornamented throughout by hand. The clock is about 12 inches high, the dial 6 inches in diameter. The movement is one of the very best, runs eight days with one winding, strikes the hours and the half hours. This is a beautiful time keeper and is a clock that would be sold by other dealers at a fancy price.

YOU PAY NOTHING for this clock or any other articles shown in this profit sharing list; but you do share in the profits of our business by being entitled to one of these articles free of any cost in exchange for profit sharing certificates to the amount specified for each article. Send your orders to us for everything you need, with every order you a get a profit sharing certificate for the full amount of your purchase, preserve these profit sharing certificates and when they have amounted to enough to entitle you to the article or articles wanted, send them to us, state the article or articles wanted, and the article selected will be sent to you free of any cost.

THIS HIGH GRADE DOUBLE BARREL HAMMERLESS BREECH LOADING SHOTGUN GIVEN IN EXCHANGE FOR PROFIT SHARING CERTIFICATES AMOUNTING TO $250.00.

No. 6PS110

Understand, this is a hammerless shotgun, not a hammer shotgun. If you are not acquainted with the prices at which double barrel hammerless breech loading shotguns are sold inquire of your nearest dealer. You will then appreciate how liberally our customers are permitted to share in the profits of our business. Remember, the process of participating in these profits is a money saving process, for in order to get this shotgun without cost you must buy goods from us to the amount of $250.00. You will find the $250.00 you send to us will go as far as $350.00 to $400.00 would go if you were buying the same or similar goods from your dealer at home, and if you get in the habit of always referring to our catalogue before buying at home or elsewhere you will soon be impressed with the big saving that you will make in the purchase price, you will soon get into the habit of sending to us for everything you buy, your profit sharing certificates will soon amount to enough to entitle you to this hammerless shot gun, for every time you send us an order you will receive from us by return mail a profit sharing certificate for the full amount of money sent us.

This is an extra high grade double barrel hammerless breech loading shotgun, an American made gun, made by one of the best makers in this country, gotten out especially for our Customers' Profit Sharing Department. It is 12-gauge, 30 or 32-inch barrel, extra high grade laminated steel barrels, choke bored by the celebrated taper system, extra strong frame, extension matted rib, top snap break, patent safety hammerless action device, fine walnut stock, pistol grip, elaborately case hardened, ornamented and finished. Weighs, 7¾ to 8 pounds A strictly high grade American made double barrel breech loading hammerless shotgun sent to any one of our customers in exchange for profit sharing certificate of purchase amounting to $250.00.

THIS AUTOMATIC SHELL EJECTING BREECH LOADING SINGLE BARREL SHOTGUN GIVEN IN EXCHANGE FOR PROFIT SHARING CERTIFICATES OF PURCHASE AMOUNTING TO $100.00.

No. 6PS105

This is the highest grade automatic shell ejecting breech loading shotgun on the market, an American made gun, made by one of the best makers in this country. **It is 12-gauge, 30 or 32-inch barrel,** fine laminated steel barrels, choke bored, has an extra strong frame, case hardened and beautifully finished; it is the latest automatic shell ejecting style, not only extracting but ejecting clear from the gun the exploded shell; top snap break, special high grade walnut stock, full pistol grip; a thoroughly reliable, fully guaranteed, automatic shell ejecting, American made pistol, grip, breech loading shotgun, given without money, without price, given in exchange for profit sharing certificates amounting to $100.00.

Simply preserve your certificates of purchase until they amount to $100.00, and if you want this gun without cost send the certificates to us and the gun will be sent to you.

We hope by permitting our customers to share liberally in the profits of our business that we will get our customers so interested that before buying elsewhere they will refer to our catalogue. You will always find the goods you want in our catalogue, always at a lower price than you can buy elsewhere; in fact, we guarantee to save you money on every order you send us. If you send to us for goods and you do not find them better in quality and lower in price than you can buy elsewhere, you are at liberty to return them to us at our expense, and we will immediately return your money, so in offering you a share in the profits we also offer to make you a big saving in cost. **For example, the goods you would buy from us from time to time amounting to $100.00, you would have to pay your dealer at home or elsewhere $125.00 or $150.00 for the same goods,** so in buying goods from us to the amount of $100.00 should your purchases extend, for example, over a year, you will save from $25.00 to $50.00 on the purchase price, and you will also have accumulated profit sharing certificates to the amount of $100.00, which certificates you can exchange for a great variety of valuable articles of merchandise as shown in this our profit sharing list.

Remember, by increasing our volume of sales, our profit sharing plan permits us to make lower prices than ever, and we guarantee our prices always lower than those of any other house in the world.

THIS HANDSOME SOLID OAK SIDEBOARD GIVEN IN EXCHANGE FOR PROFIT SHARING CERTIFICATES AMOUNTING TO $200.00.

No. 1PS200

If you want to get this sideboard free of any cost as your share of the profit in this business, simply send us your orders for the goods you need until your orders have amounted to $200.00. Remember, every time you send us an order you will get a profit sharing certificate for the full amount of the purchase, preserve these certificates until they amount to $200.00 then send them to us, and the sideboard will be sent to you free of any cost.

Before buying groceries, dry goods wearing apparel furniture, any kind of goods used in the home, on the farm or elsewhere, look through our catalogue. We guarantee to save you money on everything you use if you will order from us. To get this sideboard free of cost it will be necessary to send us orders amounting to $200.00, and you will get as much real value out of the $200.00 you send to us as you would out of $300.00 expended in your home market; besides, after dealing with us to the extent of $200.00, you will be prepared to exchange your profit sharing certificates for this handsome sideboard.

This sideboard is made of solid oak, golden finish, is 21 inches deep, 42 inches wide, and 72 inches high, has a handsome 14x24-inch bevel plate mirror, two top serpentine swell drawers and one large straight front drawer. One of the upper drawers is lined for silver. As shown in the illustration, the entire sideboard is handsomely decorated with carvings and fancy brass knobs, handles and locks. Comes complete with set of casters, carefully crated and goes to our customers without money, without cost, as their share of the profit.

YOU GET IT FOR NOTHING if you send us orders amounting to $200.00, and to hasten the time when you can have this sideboard free of cost, if you will get your neighbors to allow you to send to us for the goods they need, your profit sharing certificates will accumulate more rapidly, you will be able to participate in our profit sharing more quickly and more liberally; besides, you will be saving your neighbors money, for they will be buying the goods through you from us at much lower prices than they could buy elsewhere.

THIS BIG, CONVENIENT, UP TO DATE, IMPROVED STYLE KITCHEN CABINET GIVEN FREE IN EXCHANGE FOR PROFIT SHARING CERTIFICATES AMOUNTING TO $200.00.

No. 1PS195

This kitchen cabinet is a big, handsome piece of furniture. The base has two large sliding bins furnished with a big top as illustrated, with three shelves, racks, etc., for the different articles. This cabinet is made of extra heavy hardwood throughout and is 6 feet high Shipping weight, 100 pounds. The illustration shows the different articles that the cabinet is used for.

All you need to do to get this splendid article for the house is to save the certificates of purchase that we send you whenever you buy goods from us, and when they amount to $200.00 send them to us, state that you want this cabinet and it will be sent to you without any charge whatever. You are not only saving money by buying your goods from us, but you are now permitted to share in the profits of the business.

UNDERSTAND, the furnishing of these splendid articles free in exchange for profit sharing certificates does not affect our selling prices on any kind of merchandise and these selling prices are always a great deal lower than are offered by any other house.

THIS BEAUTIFUL UPHOLSTERED MISSION SOLID OAK MORRIS CHAIR GIVEN FREE IN EXCHANGE FOR PROFIT SHARING CERTIFICATES AMOUNTING TO $150.00.

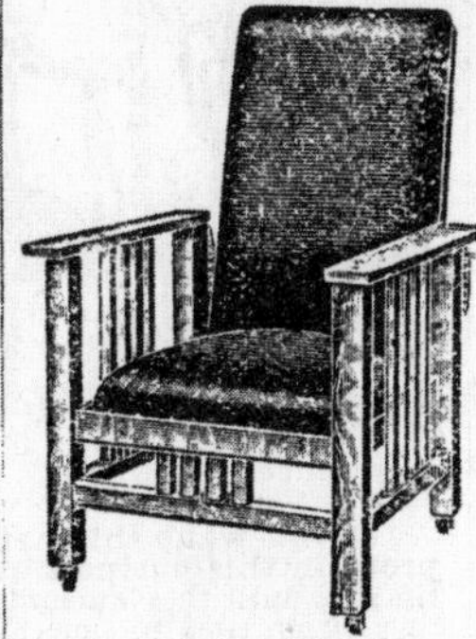

No. 1PS180

We furnish this latest style Morris chair, made of solid oak, in exchange for certificates of purchase amounting to $150.00. The seat and back are upholstered plain, the chair is most durably constructed in mission style of solid oak, golden finish, has an indestructible steel spring construction. The back is adjustable to four different positions by means of the reclining attachments, the back and seat covering is best velour cloth in green, red or brown or in chase leather as desired.

This is an extremely handsome piece of furniture, is a durable and fashionable chair, an ornament to any home, and you can get it without it costing you one cent (except transportation charges), simply by saving your profit sharing certificates until they amount to $150.00, then send the certificates to us, say that you want this chair and we will send it immediately, and will not charge you one cent for it. You can buy all the goods you need from us and save money. You will find our selling prices on everything throughout our catalogue mean a saving to you if you send us your order, and at the same time for every order that you send us we will send you a certificate showing the amount of your purchase, called a profit sharing certificate, and these are valuable. Keep them carefully and when they amount to $100.00, $150.00 or $200.00, or more, select the item you want from this list according to the amount of certificates and the article will be furnished to you free of charge.

THIS BIG, HANDSOME RUG OR ART SQUARE, A Rug 9x12 feet in Size, Large Enough to Cover a Good Sized Room, Given in Exchange for Profit Sharing Certificates Amounting to $100.00.

No. 37PS110

If you want to receive this handsome, big 9x12 reversible rug or art square free of any cost as your share of the profits in this business then simply send your orders to us for all the goods you need. Every time we receive an order from you we will send you by return mail a profit sharing certificate for the full amount of your purchase; preserve these certificates until they amount to $100.00, and then if you want this rug send the certificates to us and the rug will go to you free of any cost as your share of the profit.

This is a heavy weight granite rug, closely woven, thoroughly fast colors. Comes in the very latest patterns, handsome center and deep border, in a big variety of colorings, including wine, cardinal, blue, and various shades of green. It has a large, wide border and is woven in one piece. The rug is reversible. Being extra large in size, 9x12 feet, it is suitable for almost any room, big enough to cover as a rug a large room. Furnished by us in exchange for profit sharing certificates amountin to $100.00.

THIS BIG 9 X 10½ IMPERIAL REVERSIBLE ALL WOOL ART SQUARE OR FLOOR RUG

Furnished in Exchange for Profit Sharing Certificate Amounting to $125.00.

No. 37PS115

If you want this handsome, big, all wool, reversible rug as your share of the profit, then save your profit sharing certificates until they amount to $125.00, then send them to us, say you wish this rug and it will go to you without cost as your share of the profit. Remember, every time you send us an order we send you a certificate for the full amount of your purchase.

This rug is extra heavy and durable, extra large, being 9x10½ feet, an entirely new design, fast colors. Comes in a variety of shades of red, green, tan and blue. In ordering, state color wanted They are made with handsome borders to match, beautiful centers, woven in one piece, finished with fringed ends, such a rug as you will find in the most fashionable city retail carpet stores; but it is offered by us without money, without price, given in exchange for profit sharing certificates amounting to $125.00.

THIS REFRIGERATOR FURNISHED IN EXCHANGE FOR PROFIT SHARING CERTIFCATES AMOUNTING TO $125.00.

No. 23PS105

This is an extra high grade single door hardwood refrigerator, beautifully finished and fully guaranteed. The case is of solid ash, solid bronze trimmings, and metal linings, galvanized provision shelves. This special refrigerator is 23 inches wide, 15 inches deep, 37 inches high and is furnished by us without price and without cost, furnished in exchange for profit sharing certificates amounting to $125.00.

This is the popular family size refrigerator. Given free in exchange for profit sharing certificates amounting to $125.00.

UNDERSTAND, it requires no effort on your part, no outlay of money. It's a method of saving money, as it makes it possible for you to share liberally in the profits, for every time you send us an order for goods you make a liberal saving in the purchase, the goods you will get from us will cost you less money than you could possibly buy the same goods elsewhere, and every time you send us an order you will receive by return mail a profit sharing certificate for the full amount of money sent us, simply preserve these certificates and when you have accumulated certificates sufficient to entitle you to the article or articles you may wish to select from this profit sharing list, send the certificates to us, state which article or articles you wish, and they will be sent to you without one penny of expense.

EXTRA HIGH GRADE ROLL CANTLE MORGAN STOCK SADDLE. THIS SADDLE IS GIVEN IN EXCHANGE FOR PROFIT SHARING CERTIFICATES AMOUNTING TO $175.00.

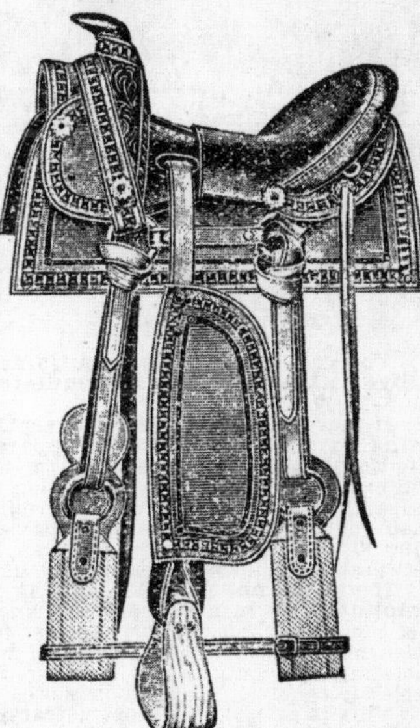

No. 10PS100

This is an extra high grade special Morgan saddle, made on a 13-inch strictly high grade Morgan tree, hide covered; has extra wide skirts, heavy stirrup straps, has a three-quarter leather seat and roll cantle, extra long fenders attached to stirrup straps; has heavy tie straps, extra heavy web cotton girths with leather chafes and connecting strap; extra heavy, large wood stirrups. This is a strictly high grade, well made, large, heavy stock saddle, such a saddle as would retail in the best saddlery establishments at a high price, although it is furnished by us without cost as part of the profit to anyone of our customers who may patronize us to a sufficient extent to entitle them to a saddle.

All that is necessary is to send your orders to us for the goods you need, always remembering that we guarantee every article we sell, guarantee everything you buy from us to be equal in quality and lower in price than you can buy elsewhere; otherwise, you can return the goods to us at our expense and we will immediately return your money. Every time you send us an order, the day we ship the goods, we will send you a profit sharing certificate for the full amount of money you send us; preserve these certificates, and if you want this saddle when you have accumulated profit sharing certificates amounting to $175.00 send them to us, state that you wish this saddle and it will go to you free of any cost.

BEAR IN MIND, we guarantee our prices lower than any other house in the world. The dividing of our profits with our customers tends to lower price making. It interests customers in getting other customers, and in this way we can increase our sales, lower the cost of buying and manufacturing, and can well afford to give you the benefit of it in still lower prices, well afford to share liberally with you in the profits.

THIS RICHLY CARVED HANDSOME SOLID QUARTER SAWED GOLDEN OAK SIDEBOARD GIVEN IN EXCHANGE FOR PROFIT SHARING CERTIFICATES AMOUNTING TO $300.00.

No. 1PS235

How to get this sideboard free of any cost in a few months, and at the same time save money for yourself and save money for your friends and neighbors.

Show your big catalogue to your friends and neighbors. Surely some of them will be glad to take advantage of our low money saving prices on furniture, wearing apparel and other goods. Possibly some neighbor may want a buggy, another a harness, another a suit of clothes, another a bedroom suite or some other article of furniture. No doubt by calling the attention of your friends and neighbors to the fact that you have a catalogue and will be glad to order for them, you will in this way accumulate profit sharing certificates more rapidly and can within two or three months secure orders from your friends and neighbors amounting to $300.00. At least get as many orders from your friends and neighbors as you can and send to us together with your own orders, always with the understanding that we guarantee to please you or we will return the money sent us. You will in a very short time accumulate profit sharing certificates amounting to $300.00. If you want this sideboard from us for nothing send your profit sharing certificates to us and the sideboard will go to you free of any cost.

This sideboard is made of quarter sawed golden oak, given a beautiful finish and highly polished. It is 48 inches long 22 inches deep. Has two swell front top drawers, one lined for silverware. A large drawer directly underneath is suitable for table linen, etc. Has two cupboards at the bottom. Is fitted with cast brass fancy knobs, handles and locks. The mirror is French bevel plate, 16x28 inches in size. **The sideboard is handsomely ornamented with raised carvings, fitted with ball bearing casters; is one of the handsomest quarter sawed oak sideboards on the market,** a sideboard that will sell in any city furniture store at a fancy price. Furnished to our customers without cost as their share of the profit. Given to our customers in exchange for profit sharing certificates amounting to $300.00.

THIS HANDSOME 3-PIECE PARLOR SUITE GIVEN IN EXCHANGE FOR PROFIT SHARING CERTIFICATES AMOUNTING TO $250.00.

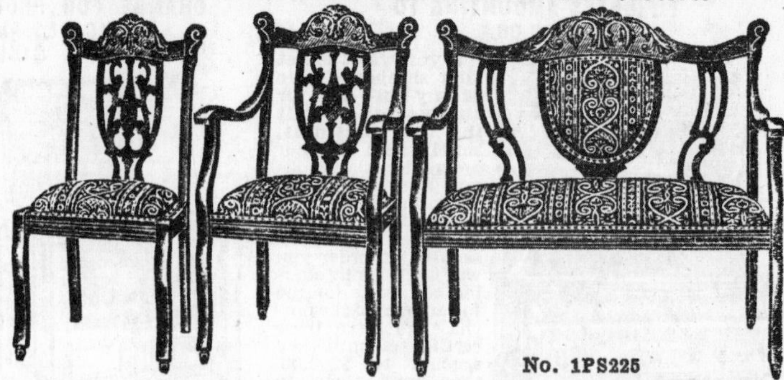

No. 1PS225

If you want this handsome 3-piece parlor suite as your share of the profit in this business, it is only necessary for you to secure profit sharing certificates until they amount to $250.00. You can do this by sending your orders to us from time to time for everything you need, in a short time you will have sent us orders to the amount of $250.00, you will then have certificates amounting to $250.00, then if you want this parlor suite send the certificates to us, say you wish this parlor suite, and it will go to you free of any cost.

This handsome 3-piece parlor suite consists of one handsome divan, one handsome arm chair and one large, handsome parlor chair, one of the newest, daintiest, neatest and altogether handsomest effects on the market. The frame is made of the finest birch, with rich mahogany finish; full spring seats, each seat containing a full set of high carbon steel springs, supported by steel wire; all three pieces upholstered in an extra quality three toned imported colored velour cloth, or crushed plush as desired. Each piece is mounted on casters. They are carefully packed and wrapped in burlap for shipment, and they are furnished to our customers without price, without money, sent to you as your share of the profit after you have sent us orders amounting to $250.00.

If you don't feel that you can accumulate profit sharing certificates to the amount of $250.00 by sending to us for the goods you need for your own use from time to time, then go among your neighbors and get them to let you order for them, and in this way you will be surprised how quickly you will accumulate profit sharing certificates, in how short a time you will have certificates amounting to $250.00, which ou can exchange for this handsome 3-piece parlor suite.

THIS HANDSOME BEDROOM SUITE FURNISHED IN EXCHANGE FOR PROFIT SHARING CERTIFICATES AMOUNTING TO $300.00.

No. 1PS230

You can get this big, handsome solid oak bedroom suite for nothing. All you have to do is to accumulate profit sharing certificates amounting to $300.00.

If you will send to us for everything you buy for a year or two, everything in groceries, wearing apparel, dry goods, everything you use in the home, the office, the shop, the factory or on the farm, in a year or two you will have sent to us orders amounting to more than $300.00, goods for your own use, and in doing this you will receive from us for the $300.00 more intrinsic value than you could get from your dealers at home for $400.00. You will save from $100.00 to $200.00 on your purchases, besides you will accumulate profit sharing certificates which you can exchange with us for this handsome bedroom suite.

If you do not feel like waiting until the purchases for your own use amount to as much as $300.00, show your catalogue to your neighbors. Get your neighbors to let you order for them. You will help them by saving them money, you will help yourself by accumulating profit sharing certificates more rapidly, you will soon have certificates enough to entitle you to this handsome 3-piece solid oak bedroom suite.

This is one of the most attractive looking 3-piece solid oak bedroom suites made, made in the very latest style, made throughout of solid golden oak, ornamented elaborately with carvings. The bed is 6 feet 1 inch high and 4 feet 6 inches wide. The dresser is 20 inches wide and 42 inches long. It has a large bevel plate mirror suspended in a handsome frame. The top drawer is swell front, and the commode is the same swell front style. The knobs and handles are fancy cast brass and the casters are best quality, making it one of the handsomest hardwood 3-piece bedroom suites. Remember, you get this suite without cost. It goes to you in exchange for profit sharing certificates amounting to $300.00.

THIS EXTRA LARGE BEAUTIFULLY FINISHED BECKWITH ORGAN FURNISHED IN EXCHANGE FOR PROFIT SHARING CERTIFICATES AMOUNTING TO $600.00.

This is one of the largest and handsomest organs made, built especially for our Customers' Profit Sharing Department by the Beckwith Organ Company, made to combine all the good points of all high grade organs, with the defects of none; one of the largest, most massive, most elaborately finished and highest grade organs ever turned out by the Beckwith people. It has a very elaborate solid oak case, quarter sawed finish, beautifully carved and decorated, has 11 stops, 5 octaves, the highest grade bellows and action, comes complete with stool and instruction book and is furnished by us without money and without price, given in exchange for profit sharing certificates amounting to $600.00.

With a little effort on your part you can get one of these most valuable articles without one cent of expense. If you will get in the habit of sending to us for everything you buy for your own use, if you will also go among your neighbors and show them your catalogue, point out to them how they, too, can save money by ordering from us, explain to them that you are taking orders so that you may get this organ, or some other article that you may want as your share of the profit, your neighbors will be glad to let you send to us for the goods they need. You will be saving money for them, you will save money for yourself on the goods you buy for your own use and in this way your profit sharing certificates will accumulate rapidly. If you want this big organ it is only a matter of a short time until you can accumulate certificates to the extent of $600.00, and when you have accumulated certificates to this amount if you want this organ, send the certificates to us, and the organ will go to you free of cost, go to you as your share of the profits in this business.

No. 46PS105

BIG, HANDSOME, 5-PIECE, OVERSTUFFED, SILK CORDED PARLOR SUITE FURNISHED IN EXCHANGE FOR PROFIT SHARING CERTIFICATES AMOUNTING TO $300.00.

No. 1PS240

Understand, all that is necessary for you to do to get this big handsome, 5-piece, overstuffed parlor suite free of cost as your share of the profits in this business, is to send us your orders from time to time for the goods you need until your orders have amounted to $300.00. If you buy everything you use from us, everything in groceries, dry goods, wearing apparel, everything used in the home, on the farm and elsewhere your orders will in a comparatively short time amount to $300.00. Every time you send us an order you will receive from us a profit sharing certificate for the full amount of your purchase, preserve these certificates until they have amounted to $300.00, then send them to us if you want this parlor suite, and it will go to you free of any cost, and with our compliments.

This big 5-piece parlor suite consists of one big, handsome sofa (48 inches long), two large roomy chairs, one extra large rocker and one extra large reception chair. They are made in the very latest style. The frames are extra heavy hardwood, made extra strong, well braced throughout; springs are the highest grade tempered steel springs, each piece is upholstered in the highest style of the art; it is covered with genuine Wilton three-tone velour upholstering cloth, which comes in a variety of colors, each piece in a different harmonizing color. Each piece is fully overstuffed, handsomely decorated and finished with silk cord binding. Remember, this suite is free in exchange for profit sharing certificates amounting to $300.00.

THIS HANDSOME INITIAL SILVERWARE SET FURNISHED IN EXCHANGE FOR THE PROFIT SHARING CERTIFICATES AMOUNTING TO $100.00.

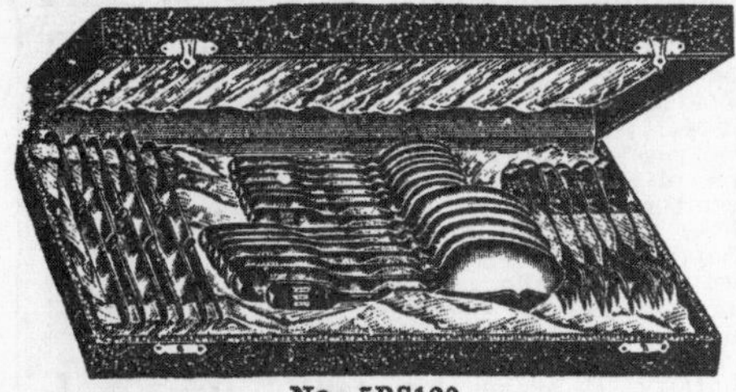

No. 5PS120

This handsome silver set, including a beautiful case, consists of one set of six teaspoons, one set of six tablespoons, one set of six medium forks, one set of six medium knives, one sugar shell and one butter knife. The entire twenty-six pieces will be marked with any initial that may be desired, making it a 26-piece set of initial silverware in a beautiful lined suitable case for any home or any occasion.

This silverware is made of extra fine composition solid metal, a metal that is in appearance, finish, wearing qualities and, in fact, every way, except in intrinsic value, the equal of solid coin silverware, a metal that will not tarnish, and so closely resembles solid silver that it is often mistaken for solid sterling silver; is solid metal through and through, nothing to wear out, goods we put under our binding guarantee, a class of silverware that is handled by the best city retail jewelers. It is superior to any grade of silver plated ware. There is no price put on the outfit since it goes to our customers in exchange for profit sharing certificates amounting to $100.00.

SIMPLY SEND US YOUR ORDERS for the goods you need from time to time, whenever you send us an order you will receive in return a profit sharing certificate for the full amount of your purchase, and when your purchases amount to $100.00 you will then have received from us profit sharing certificates amounting to $100 00, then if you wish this silver set send us the profit sharing certificates, state what initial you wish engraved on each piece and the entire outfit with the initial you call for will be sent to you free of any cost.

It pays to deal with us, not only for the opportunity of sharing in the profits by selecting any one of the articles shown in this profit sharing list in exchange for profit sharing certificates, but, further, you save money on every article you buy from us. We guarantee to sell you any goods you want at a lower cost to you than you can buy elsewhere. If you will only get in the habit of first referring to our catalogue when you are in need of anything before buying elsewhere and will send us the order, you will be surprised how much money we can save you, you will be surprised how quickly your profit sharing certificates will accumulate and in how short a time you will be able to send us profit sharing certificates in exchange for almost any article in this list that you may desire.

THIS HANDSOME MANTEL CLOCK GIVEN IN EXCHANGE FOR PROFIT SHARING CERTIFICATES AMOUNTING TO $100.00.

No. 5PS110

This is a handsome 8-day mantel clock, beautifully ornamented, elaborately decorated, is made by one of the best clock companies in America, is covered by our binding guarantee, such a clock as you would find in the best city retail jewelry stores; is extra large, extra well finished, the latest 1905 style 8-day mantel clock, and we give it in exchange for profit sharing certificates amounting to $100.00 Size of clock, 10¾ inches high 12 inches wide. Strikes the hours and the half hours

If you want this clock free of cost preserve your profit sharing certificates until they amount to $100.00. If there is no probability of your wanting goods for your own use within the next few months or year or so to the amount of $100.00, then send us your orders for what goods you do need, under our guarantee to save you money on every article you buy from us, then get your neighbors to allow you to order in your name for them, and in this way accumulate profit sharing certificates until the certificates you receive amount to $100.00 or more, or enough to entitle you to any article you may want as shown in this profit sharing list.

REMEMBER, there is no limit as to time. You can be months or years in accumulating these profit sharing certificates, and when they are sent to us they will be accepted in exchange for any of the articles shown in this list.

Mr. Larson Gets a Fine Clock for His Certificates.

Ritchie, Ill.

Sears, Roebuck & Co., Chicago.

Dear Sirs:—We are well pleased with the clock which we have just received in exchange for our profit sharing certificates. We do not think we could buy that clock for less than $8.00 anywhere. You saved us money on every order and the goods were received promptly and were all satisfactory.

Thanking you again for the handsome clock which you sent us free in exchange for the certificates, I am,

Yours truly,
PETER LARSON.

THIS HANDSOME SOLID OAK EXTENSION DINING TABLE GIVEN IN EXCHANGE FOR PROFIT SHARING CERTIFICATES AMOUNTING TO $125.00.

No. 1PS175

This is a very large, heavy, handsome solid oak, carved and decorated extension dining room table, such as you will find in any high class furniture store, where it would be sold at a big price. Remember, we furnish it free of any cost. It goes to you in exchange for profit sharing certificates amounting to $125.00 as your share of the profits in our business. If you are not likely to need goods to the extent of $125.00 within the next few months or year, go among your neighbors, get them to join with you, and in this way you can soon make up orders amounting to $125.00.

If, before buying anything in groceries, in wearing apparel, goods you need in the home, in the shop, on the farm or elsewhere you will refer to our catalogue and get our prices you will find it a money saving way of getting your goods, your neighbors will find it a money saving way and be glad that you ordered for them. You will find that your profit sharing certificates will accumulate rapidly. This is the reason that we have extended the privilege to our customers in sharing in our profits. We hope in this way to influence them to send all their orders to us. We also hope to influence them to allow their neighbors to order for them.

This handsome table is extra heavy, made from selected solid oak, has the latest style six massive legs, the outside legs being joined by handsomely carved stretchers, which add greatly to the strength of the table as well as to the appearance. The top of the table measures 42x42 inches when closed. We furnish extra leaves for extending the table to six feet in length. The table must be seen, examined and compared with other handsome dining room tables to appreciate its real beauty. Remember, we furnish it in exchange for profit sharing certificates amounting to $125.00.

THIS HANDSOME, LARGE, NEW STYLE REED BABY CARRIAGE GIVEN IN EXCHANGE FOR PROFIT SHARING CERTIFICATES AMOUNTING TO $150.00.

If you wish to receive this baby carriage as your share of the profit in this business, simply send us your orders for the goods you need from time to time, remembering that immediately upon receipt of each order we will send you a profit sharing certificate for the full amount of money sent us, preserve these certificates until they amount to $150.00, then if you want this baby carriage send the certificates to us and the baby carriage will go to you free of any cost.

No. 25PS105

This new, handsome carriage has a specially constructed body with carved bottom. It is built up with the best grade of round and flat reeds, in such a manner as to give a strong as well as handsome appearance. The upholstering consists of an extra good quality of denim in any color desired in seat, back and sides. It has best steel running gear, enameled dark green and striped; is made with 16-inch front and 22-inch rear steel wheels with rubber hub caps. Complete with our automatic foot brake, which makes the carriage up to date in every respect. The parasol is sateen with fancy puffed deep ruffle. It can be adjusted to any angle. Parasol is in color to match the upholstering. It is one of the highest grade new style reed baby carriages on the market It goes to our customers without cost, without price, goes to them as their share of the profit, given in exchange for profit sharing certificates amounting to $150.00.

THIS HIGH GRADE BICYCLE IN EITHER GENTS' OR LADIES' STYLE GIVEN IN EXCHANGE FOR PROFIT SHARING CERTIFICATES AMOUNTING TO $250.00.

No. 19PS100

This is a genuine Burdick bicycle which we furnish in either gents' or ladies' style, positively one of the highest grade bicycles made, the very latest style for this season, and it is offered by us without price. It goes to our customers as their share of the profit. It is only necessary for you to accumulate profit sharing certificates amounting to $250.00, then if you want this bicycle send the certificates to us, say whether you wish the gents' or ladies' style, give height of frame and gear wanted, and the bicycle will go to you by return freight or express, free of any cost to you and as your share of the profit.

This is a genuine Burdick Bicycle, one of the highest grade bicycles made. The tires are the highest grade single tube ball bearing throughout; extra high grade saddle and pedals, adjustable handle bar, complete tools and tool bags. It is flush at every joint, reinforced at every part, has the latest style one-piece hanger. Ladies' bicycle comes in 20 or 22-inch frame; gents' bicycle in 22-inch frame. They are geared 64 to to 80 inches as desired, beautifully enameled in black or maroon, as desired; neatly ornamented, all usual bright parts heavily nickel plated and highly polished, a bicycle that combines the good qualities of all high grade bicycles made, with the defects of none. We furnish it to our customers without cost in exchange for profit sharing certificates of purchase amounting to $250.00.

THIS BIG, COMFORTABLE, SOLID OAK SADDLE SEAT ROCKER GIVEN IN EXCHANGE FOR PROFIT SHARING CERTIFICATES AMOUNTING TO $100.00.

This is a handsome new style rocker, made of choice selected highly figured quarter sawed oak, beautifully made and finished, heavy spindles, workmanship very finest throughout, full saddle seat, the finish is a beautiful golden and it is such a rocker as would sell in furniture stores at a fancy price. It is furnished by us without cost, given in exchange for profit sharing certificates amounting to $100.00. Whenever you make a purchase from us, we will send you a profit sharing certificate showing the amount of your purchase and you can save these certificates, and when they amount to $100.00 they will entitle you to any one of the articles shown in this profit sharing list which is given in exchange for certificates amounting to $100.00, and you can send the certificates to us, making your selection and the article you ask for will be sent free of cost to you.

No. 1PS145

THIS BIG COLUMBIA DISC GRAPHOPHONE OR TALKING MACHINE

Given in Exchange for Profit Sharing Certificates of Purchase Amounting to $250.00.

No. 21PS110

This is one of the highest grade and most expensive disc graphophones or talking machines made by the Columbia Graphophone Co. It is a talking machine embodying all the features of the highest grade talking machines made. It is made with extra powerful clockwork spring motor contained in a handsome cabinet in the very latest design. The sound box or reproducer is made in the very latest concert style with improved knife edge bearings, heavy mica diaphragms and it is absolutely the highest grade sound box furnished with any talking machine, regardless of price. The ornamental horn supporting arms, which are detachable, are of very handsome design and made of aluminum, this metal being most perfectly adapted for this purpose The black and gold horn is the highest grade horn made for the disc talking machine; the body of this horn being made from fine sheet steel with black oxidized ne bell of polished brass, gives it a very ornamental appearance. Either the 7 or 10-inch records may be used with this Each machine is furnished complete with the latest improved knife edge reproducer, 16-inch black and gold horn and a talking machine that is sold by the makers at a high price, but we send it without price, as it goes to our customers for profit sharing certificates amounting to $250.00. If you want this big, expensive, high grade graphophone simply your profit sharing certificates of purchase until they have amounted to $250.00, then send them to us and the talking will go to you without expense.

THIS HANDSOME VIOLIN WITH COMPLETE OUTFIT FURNISHED IN EXCHANGE FOR PROFIT SHARING CERTIFICATES AMOUNTING TO $100.00.

No. 12PS105

This is an extra fine violin; it is one of the finest violins on the market. It is a genuine Stradivarius model, being a direct copy of a violin made by that great maker; made of selected seasoned wood, beautifully varnished a reddish brown color, highly polished, fitted with solid ebony fingerboard and tailpiece. Like the renowned Stradivarius violins, it has double inlaid purfling, giving it a distinguished and handsome appearance. This violin comes complete with handsome bow, handsome marbleized case, extra set of strings, large piece of rosin and a complete instruction book.

DO NOT COMPARE this with any of the cheap violins, for it is an extra high grade instrument, an instrument that will sell in any music store at a fancy price, and is offered to you without price, given to our customers as a part of their profit, given in exchange for profit sharing certificates amounting to $100.00.

REMEMBER, by referring to our catalogue when you are thinking of buying anything, you will find in the big book the exact article or articles wanted, you will find our prices lower than you can possibly buy elsewhere, we guarantee the goods you order from us to please you, we guarantee to save you money, we are always ready to return your money if you are not satisfied. In a short time your orders to us will have amounted to $100.00 or more and on every hundred dollars you buy from us you will save from $20.00 to $50.00, and when the different orders you have sent us have amounted to $100.00 you will have profit sharing certificates amounting to $100.00. You can then send the profit sharing certificates to us in exchange for this violin and the violin and outfit will be sent to you without any cost to you; or if there is any other article or articles in this profit sharing list that you would like, preserve your profit sharing certificates of purchase until they have amounted to enough to entitle you to the article or articles wanted, then send them to us and the article called for will be sent to you without any cost to you, except freight or express charges, which you pay.

THIS HANDSOME, BIG, BEAUTIFULLY FINISHED, SOLID QUARTER SAWED OAK HALL TREE AS ILLUSTRATED GIVEN IN EXCHANGE FOR PROFIT SHARING CERTIFICATES AMOUNTING TO $100.00.

If you want this beautiful hall tree free of any cost, as your share of the profit in this business, simply send us your orders for the goods you need from time to time, and when your orders have amounted to $100.00 you will then have received profit sharing certificates for the full amount of money sent us, and if you want this hall tree send the certificates to us, and the hall tree will be sent to you free of any expense to you.

This is an elegant, new style hall tree, made of quarter sawed oak, **in a rich golden finish.** Size, 6 feet 4 inches high, 2 feet 4 inches wide, including the genuine cast brass umbrella holder. Mirror, the best French plate, size, 10x10 inches. Double hat and coat hooks. It has roomy box in seat with lid for rubbers. It has large double hat and coat hooks. A neat design, of strictly first class workmanship and finish. Shipping weight, 50 pounds. It is a hall tree suitable for any home, a handsome piece of furniture, and it goes to you without cost in exchange for profit sharing certificates amounting to $100.00.

No. 1PS130

TWO PAIRS OF CHENILLE PORTIERES GIVEN IN EXCHANGE FOR PROFIT SHARING CERTIFICATES AMOUNTING TO $100.00.

No. 37PS100

These curtains are entirely new in design, the colorings are bright and cheerful. They are extra large size, being 34 inches wide and 3 yards long. Come in handsome shades of red, blue, dark tan, terra cotta, olive, brown or green. In ordering, state color wanted. Remember, we furnish them without money and without price. We give two full pairs of these handsome chenille curtains in exchange for profit sharing certificates amounting to $100.00. **If you wish to receive two pairs of these chenille portieres as your share of the profit, simply save your profit sharing certificates until they amount to $100.00,** then send them to us and the curtains will go to you without cost as your share of the profit.

THIS HANDSOME NEW STYLE, BEAUTIFULLY FINISHED MANDOLIN GIVEN IN EXCHANGE FOR PROFIT SHARING CERTIFICATES AMOUNTING TO $100.00.

No. 12PS100

We furnish this mandolin as illustrated and described complete with extra outfit, consisting of one extra full set of Glendon strings, one mandolin pick, a book of Guckert's Chords and a fingerboard chart, by the aid of which anyone can learn without a teacher; the mandolin and entire outfit carefully packed in a light, strong box.

This is an extra high grade mandolin, has thirteen strips of mahogany with black inlay between the strips, handsomely finished rosewood cap, highly polished top, edge beautifully bound in celluloid with variegated wood inlaying, imitation tortoise guard plate with a handsome inlaid floral design in the center, with inlaying around the sound hole to correspond with the edges; has the latest patent nickel plated tailpiece and sleeve protector combined. The mandolin is correctly fretted with raised frets. The tone is sweet, melodious and at the same time powerful. There is no better finished, no sweeter toned mandolin made, and while we offer it without price, it is such a mandolin as you could not buy outside of the best city retail stores, and there at a fancy price.

We give this mandolin to our customers without charge and without price; it goes to them as their share of the profit and is one of the many articles that they can select from our profit sharing list. It is only necessary for you to accumulate profit sharing certificates amounting to $100.00, send the certificates to us, say you wish this mandolin, and the mandolin and complete outfit will go to you without any cost.

When you are in need of any kind of goods please refer to our catalogue, compare our prices with the prices asked by others, note the money you can save by sending to us; remember, we guarantee the goods to please you, and if they are not perfectly satisfactory you can return them to us at our expense and get your money back. Remember, we guarantee to save you money on every order you send us, and if you don't find after you have received the goods you order from us and compare them with the same goods offered by others that you have made a big saving in price, you can return the goods to us at our expense and get your money back. We guarantee to save you money on everything you buy, therefore we urge that before buying elsewhere you always refer to our catalogue. If you do this you will invariably send your orders to us, and every time you send us an order you will receive a profit sharing certificate of purchase by return mail for the full amount of money you send us, preserve these certificates until they have amounted to enough to entitle you to any one of the articles shown in this profit sharing list which you may desire, then send the profit sharing certificates to us, state the article or articles wanted as selected from this profit sharing list, and the articles called for will be sent to you free of any expense.

REMEMBER, the giving of these articles to our customers as a share of the profit does not add one penny to the price at which we sell our goods; on the contrary, as explained in the first page, it makes for much lower prices. Every customer shares the profits of our business in proportion to the extent she or he patronizes us. Don't forget that you can add greatly to the amount of your profit sharing certificates and you can hasten the time in which you can get any article shown in this list by getting your neighbors to allow you to send for the goods they need. You will save them money (we will guarantee this), and in this way you will make your profit sharing certificates larger and you can more quickly and more liberally participate in our profit sharing plan by selecting any of the articles shown in this list.

THIS BIG, HANDSOME, BANQUET LAMP GIVEN IN EXCHANGE FOR PROFIT SHARING CERTIFICATES AMOUNTING TO $100.00.

No. 2PS101

If you want this big, handsome, banquet lamp without cost, without money, if you want it as your share of the profit in this business, then send your orders to us for the goods you need until your orders amount to $100.00. Every time you send us an order you will receive by return mail a profit sharing certificate of purchase for the full amount of your order, preserve these certificates and when they have amounted to $100.00, send them to us, and if you select this lamp it will go to you without cost. This Banquet Lamp is entirely new and very attractive. It is an exact reproduction of a very expensive French lamp and must be seen to be fully appreciated. The decoration consists of a rich dark seal brown background in a handsome clouded effect having landscapes, sea views and ships, etc., which are painted by hand. The lamp is very large, being 27 inches high and is completed with a large 10-inch globe.

The burner is of the latest improved central draft type, taking No. 2 Rochester round wick and chimney. All metal parts are richly finished in oxidized gun metal finish, which is only to be found on the higher grade lamps. When lighted, the lamp gives a dainty, pleasing effect to the room.

It is securely packed in a strong wood box. Shipping weight, about 25 pounds.

THIS HANDSOME BOOKCASE GIVEN IN EXCHANGE FOR PROFIT SHARING CERTIFICATES AMOUNTING TO $100.00.

Save your profit sharing certificates until they amount to $100.00, then if you want this bookcase, send the certificates to us and the bookcase will go to you free of any cost. Remember, the giving of these articles of merchandise as our customers' share of the profit does not add one penny to the price at which we sell our goods; on the contrary, it makes for lower prices. It influences our customers to send to us for nearly everything they buy, causes our customers to go among their friends and neighbors, and in this way it increases our business, increases our manufacturing and buying facilities, tends to lessen the cost of the goods, all of which we are able to give our customers the benefit of in lower prices, prices we guarantee to be much lower than you can buy from any other house in the world. Remember, you take no risk in ordering anything from us, for we guarantee the goods to please, guarantee them to reach you in perfect condition; otherwise you can return them to us at our expense, and we will immediately return your money.

No. 1PS110

YOU PAY NOTHING for these profit sharing articles of merchandise. There is a big money saving in the getting of them, since you receive as much intrinsic value for $100.00 sent to us as you would in $125.00 to $150.00 expended elsewhere; and remember, you can take your own time to accumulate these profit sharing certificates. Send us your orders for anything you need from time to time, profit sharing certificates will be sent to you as we receive your orders, save these certificates, and when they amount to enough to entitle you to the article you want, send the certificates to us and the article or articles called for will be sent to you without cost.

This is a neat, attractive, roomy and handsome bookcase. Upper panel is carved. The bookcase stands 52 inches high, 24 inches wide and 12 inches deep Is made of carefully selected solid oak, finished in imitation birch or imitation mahogany, as desired. Has the latest style adjustable shelves, glass door. Takes up very little space. Mounted on casters. Such a handsome solid oak book case as you will find in the best city furniture stores. Furnished by us without money, without cost, given in exchange for profit sharing certificates amounting to $100.00.

The Bookcase is a Beauty—Received in Exchange for Profit Sharing Certificates.

Elba, Nebr.

Sears, Roebuck & Co., Chicago.

Gentlemen:—It is with great pleasure I write you today acknowledging receipt of the bookcase sent me for my $100.00 profit sharing certificates. The bookcase is a beauty and did not cost me anything but the freight charges. Besides getting the bookcase free, I feel sure that I made a good profit on every article I sent for. It did not take me but four months to accumulate the profit sharing certificates. They grew even faster than I expected. I do hope you may meet with the grand success in the future which your wonderful profit sharing business deserves. I am,

Respectfully yours, JOHN LETH.

THIS HANDSOME BOOKCASE AND DESK GIVEN IN EXCHANGE FOR PROFIT SHARING CERTIFICATES AMOUNTING TO $200.00.

This desk is yours free, it doesn't cost you a cent; in fact, it is a saving to you of $50.00 to $100.00 by the very process by which you get this desk free. In order to get this desk free of any cost to you, as your share of the profit in our business, it is necessary for you to send us orders aggregating $200.00. For the $200.00 you send us you will get goods the value of which you could not buy from your dealer at home at less than $300.00.

No. 1PS205

This is a handsome combination bookcase and desk, made of carefully selected and beautifully finished quarter sawed golden oak, highly polished, beautifully carved and decorated. This desk is 68 inches high, 36 inches has a beautifully shaped pattern French be[illegible] mirror, 12x10 inches in size. The writing desk is with compartments for envelopes, writing paper stationery and the lower part is a roomy cupboard. part of the case is arranged with adjustable shelves f[illegible] The glass door is double thick, the trimmings are all of [illegible] and the case is fitted with casters. It is a handsome furniture, suitable for any room, and is furnished by us money and without cost, given in exchange for profit certificates amounting to $200.00

THIS BIG, RICH, EXPENSIVELY MADE AND FINISHED, LARGE SIZED FOLDING CAMERA

Given in Exchange for Profit Sharing Certificates of Purchase Amounting to $100.00.

No. 20PS105

This is an extra fine folding camera, large size, makes 4x5 pictures, a camera that would sell at a big price in any retail store, but with us it is furnished without cost, without price; it goes free to any customer in exchange for profit sharing certificates amounting to $100.00.

This is an extra high grade folding camera. This camera is constructed throughout from selected Honduras mahogany, given a highly polished piano finish, is covered with seal grain black morocco leather, best quality; bellows are made from an extra quality of red leather combined with an absolutely light proof black gossamer cloth. The trimmings and all metal parts are finely finished and highly polished, thus making an exceedingly handsome appearance in contrast with the dark, rich finish of the mahogany woodwork. It has a reversible view finder and is fitted with two tripod sockets, made with rising and falling front for regulating the relative amount of sky and foreground; has a ground glass focusing screen for careful and accurate work. The lenses are extra high grade. They possess great depth of focus, covering the plate sharply to the extreme corners, work very rapidly, producing sharp, clear pictures with fine detail. The shutter is of the highest grade made. It is entirely automatic, may be set for either instantaneous, time or bulb exposures. Comes complete with plate holders and handsome carrying case, one of the finest folding cameras on the market. It will be sent to any customer on receipt of profit sharing certificates amounting to $100.00.

THIS HANDSOME KITCHEN CABINET GIVEN IN EXCHANGE FOR PROFIT SHARING CERTIFICATES AMOUNTING TO $125.00.

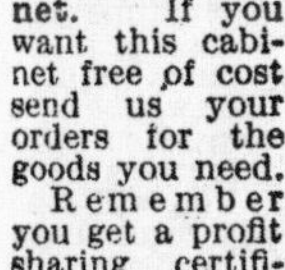

No. 1PS170

$125.00 in profit sharing certificates secures for you this handsome kitchen cabinet. If you want this cabinet free of cost send us your orders for the goods you need. Remember you get a profit sharing certificate with every order you send us and when all the orders sent us amount to $125.00 you will have certificates amounting to $125.00, and if you will send the certificates to us this kitchen cabinet will go to you free of cost.

BEFORE YOU BUY groceries, clothing, dry goods, wearing apparel, or any kind of goods to use in the home, in the shop, on the farm or elsewhere, before you buy any merchandise of any kind refer to our catalogue. We guarantee to save you money on everything you use. By the time you have accumulated profit sharing certificates sufficient to entitle you to any of the articles shown in this list you will have saved $25.00 to $50.00 on the goods you have bought.

The top of this cabinet is made of selected white wood. The frame throughout is made of the best grade selected kiln dried hardwood, beautifully finished. There is a portable shelf on the inside which can be moved. The bin is extra large and will hold about 75 pounds of flour. One of the drawers in this cabinet is divided for cutlery and a space is provided for table linen. There is also a good sized bread board. The top is 28x48 inches and of the finest selected white wood, smoothed and sanded.

This is a kitchen cabinet that combines every convenience of all the very best kitchen cabinets on the market. It is furnished by us without cost to our customers, goes to them as their share of the profit, free in exchange for profit sharing certificates amounting to $125.00.

THESE HIGH GRADE, TEN-YEAR GUARANTEED PLATFORM SCALES COMPLETE GIVEN IN EXCHANGE FOR PROFIT SHARING CERTIFICATES AMOUNTING TO $175.00

No. 23PS110

This is an extra high grade platform scale, made from the very best material, accurately adjusted, strong and substantial, provided with the best steel pivots, carefully hardened and finished; have no check rods to bind or get out of place. The platform rests on adjustable chill bearings, which take the wear directly off the steel pivots and the pivots remaining sharp, the scales act quickly and sensitively. The scales are fitted with heavy, smoothly finished wheels, heavy wood center platform, sliding poise beam, sealed and tested. They are scales that retail regularly at high prices. This scale has a regular capacity of 600 pounds. Beams are marked 50 pounds by ¼ pound. Platform is 17½x26½ inches. The scale weighs, packed for shipment, 150 pounds.

This scale we have had made especially for our Profit Sharing Department, scales that we furnish without cost and without price, a set of scales that any customer of ours can have. It is only necessary to save your profit sharing certificates of purchase until they amount to $175.00, then if you wish to receive these scales without cost, as your share of the profit, send your certificates to us and the scales will go to you free of any cost.

We hope by this method of sharing our profits with our customers to get our customers, before buying anything at home or elsewhere, to first refer to our catalogue. You will save money on every purchase you make, you will find by sending to us that 75 cents will go further than $1.00 will go at home We guarantee to save you money on every article you buy; and you share in the profits over and above all this saving, for every time you send us an order you receive by return mail a profit sharing certificate for the full amount of money sent us, preserve these profit sharing certificates and you can exchange them for any article or articles shown in this, our profit sharing list.

THIS BIG, HANDSOME, SOLID GOLDEN OAK CUPBOARD FURNISHED IN EXCHANGE FOR PROFIT SHARING CERTIFICATES AMOUNTING TO $150.00.

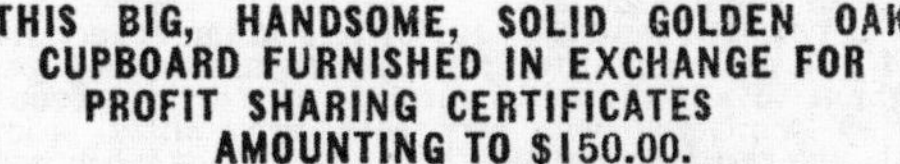

No. 1PS185

Send us profit sharing certificates amounting to $150.00, and if you want this handsome solid oak cupboard it will be sent to you free of any cost, it will go to you as your share of the profits in this business in consideration of your having sent us orders aggregating $150.00.

This is a handsome new style oak cupboard, the very latest design; has a handsome crockery or china closet, made from the finest selected genuine golden oak, highly polished, beautifully carved and decorated. Stands 6 feet 2 inches high, 3 feet wide, 14 inches deep. It is fitted with double thick heavy glass doors, two drawers with brass pulls. The lower cupboard is made with heavy double doors, fitted with lock and key. The inside of the upper and lower cupboards have adjustable shelves, full finished inside and out. It is such a cupboard, such value that we know that after you have sent us orders to the amount of $150.00 if you return the certificates to us and ask us to send you this cupboard you will feel that you have been liberally rewarded in your share of the profits in our business, and besides, the goods you will have received for the $150.00 purchases could not be duplicated elsewhere at less than $200.00.

REMEMBER, our profit sharing plan does not affect our low prices one particle, but on the contrary helps us to make still lower prices

THIS BIG, IMPROVED, UP TO DATE LABOR SAVING WASHING MACHINE FURNISHED IN EXCHANGE FOR PROFIT SHARING CERTIFICATES AMOUNTING TO $100.00.

No.23PS100

This is one of the highest grade washing machines made. It is made on the rubber principle, the same as is used in the **Quick and Easy.** It has two cylinders working in opposite directions at the same motion of the crank shaft, thus cleaning the clothes quicker and more thoroughly than the former machine. **It will not tear the clothes, and on account of the balance wheel the machine will work so easy that a child can work it without being fatigued.** It is made of selected Louisiana cypress finished in the natural color with two coats of varnish; has heavy non-rusting galvanized bottom and all the iron parts coming in contact with the water are heavily tinned or galvanized to prevent spotting the clothes. Inside dimensions, 17½x29x14 inches. The washing machine weighs complete 103 pounds. It is one of the highest grade, best made, best working and most expensive washing machines made, but it is offered to our customers without cost and without price.

If you want this washing machine without cost and without price you can have it as your share of the profit in our business. Every time you send us an order we will send you a profit sharing certificate for the full amount of your purchase, preserve these certificates until they amount to $100.00, then send the certificates to us, say that you wish this washing machine, and it will go to you free of any cost.

THIS HANDSOME, BIG, ELABORATELY FINISHED, OVERSTUFFED, TUFTED, UPHOLSTERED COUCH FURNISHED IN EXCHANGE FOR PROFIT SHARING CERTIFICATES AMOUNTING TO $150.00.

No. 1PS190

If you want this handsome, overstuffed, button tufted, upholstered couch as your share of the profit in our business, if you want to get it without cost, simply save your profit sharing certificates. When you are in want of anything in groceries or wearing apparel, anything to use in the home, on the farm, in the shop, office, factory or elsewhere, first look to our catalogue, see how much money you can save by sending your orders to us and then send to us for the goods you need.

SEND YOUR ORDERS to us for everything you buy, and then ask your neighbors if they are not in need of something they can buy from us at a much lower price than they can buy elsewhere, get your neighbors to let you order for them, and in this way you will rapidly accumulate profit sharing certificates.

This is one of the latest style, one of the handsomest overstuffed couches on the market. Couch is 78 inches long and 30 inches wide. The frame is made of heavy oak, nicely finished in either golden oak or imitation mahogany, as desired; is made with heavy carved claw feet. It has six rows of deep tufting fitted with steel tufting buttons; made with full spring edge; contains thirty of the best steel springs; has heavy duck canvas over springs, best fine tow filling, best of workmanship throughout; is upholstered in an extra quality high grade imported three-toned velour cloth, and it goes to our customers without price, furnished in exchange for profit sharing certificates amounting to $150 00.

Mr. Kahl Finds the Six Chairs Very Satisfactory.

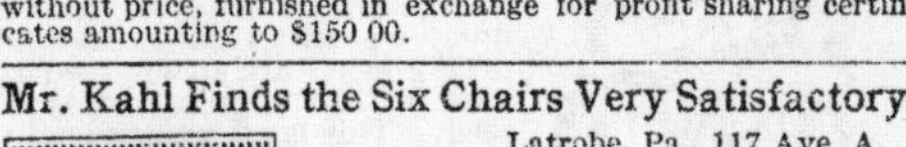

Latrobe, Pa., 117 Ave. A.

Sears, Roebuck & Co., Chicago.

Kind Friends:—I received the six chairs, which you sent me free for the profit sharing certificates, and find them very satisfactory and am indeed pleased with your profit sharing plan. I have spent hundreds of dollars with you and don't regret one cent of it and have found everything stove, bedroom suite, furniture, men's clothing, etc. very satisfactory. Have always received my goods promptly and saved money by buying from you.

Very truly yours,

WILLIAM KAHL.

THESE SIX (FULL SET) HARDWOOD CANE SEAT DINING ROOM CHAIRS GIVEN IN EXCHANGE FOR PROFIT SHARING CERTIFICATES AMOUNTING TO $100.00.

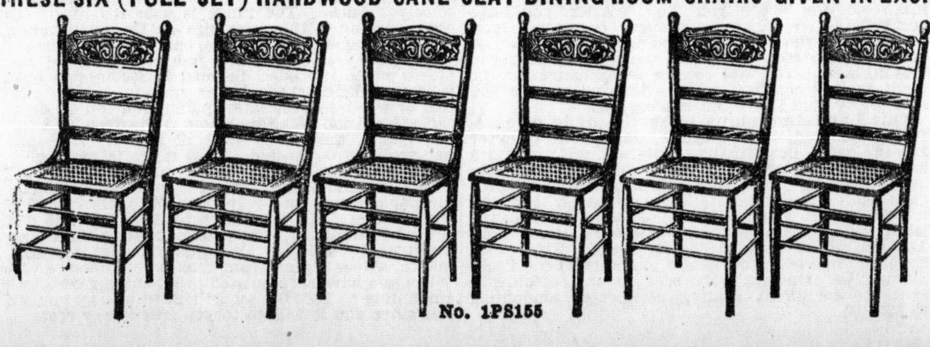

No. 1PS155

This is a special cane seat dining room chair. The chair is made of solid oak, golden finish; has a cane seat top, back panel is handsomely carved, the back posts and seat are thoroughly braced; is a strong, neat, substantial dining chair. They come in sets of six chairs, a complete dining room set, and the entire six chairs are furnished free to our customers in exchange for profit sharing certificates amounting to $100.00.

The main object in sharing our profits with our customers is to induce every customer, first, to refer to our catalogue before buying anything at home or elsewhere.

REMEMBER, we guarantee to save you money on everything you buy.

Saves Thirty Per Cent. on His Orders and Secures a Fine Desk Free.

Manville, R. I.

Sears, Roebuck & Co., Chicago.

Gentlemen:—I beg to acknowledge receipt of the desk ordered from you a short time ago, and thank you for your prompt attention in shipping same; I am pleased to find the desk as represented by you and also of the easy way in which I have obtained it, as this desk was sent in exchange for profit sharing certificates amounting to $125.00, which have accumulated within four months. Also please accept my thanks for your honesty in returning the amount which I overpaid with my first order. I might add that I am equally pleased with all goods purchased from you previously, as I find when comparing these articles with others claimed to be as good, I have saved on the price at least thirty per cent., to say nothing of the profit sharing certificates which have brought me the desk free. I say this not for your particular benefit, so much as for the benefit of others who might contemplate buying furniture or, in fact, anything listed in your catalogue. Wishing you success, I remain,

Respectfully yours, SAMUEL LUSSIER.

THIS HANDSOME PARLOR DESK GIVEN IN EXCHANGE FOR PROFIT SHARING CERTIFICATES AMOUNTING TO $125.00.

No. 1PS165

If you want this desk free of cost as your share of the profits in this business simply preserve your profit sharing certificates until they have amounted to $125.00, then send the certificates to us, say you want this desk and the desk will go to you free of any cost. **This handsome parlor desk is a neat and graceful design, made** of selected golden oak, beautifully finished; is 30 inches wide and 63 inches high; inside is nicely partitioned with pigeonholes; has a large drop leaf and the shelves below can be used for books; has a brass rod and rings for curtain. The top is ornamented with two shelves and a fancy bevel plate French mirror, such **a desk as you would find in the best retail furniture stores,** a desk suitable for a parlor in any home. It is furnished by us without cost, without price, goes to our customers in exchange for profit sharing certificates amounting to $125.00.

If before buying anything from anyone anywhere you will first refer to our catalogue, no matter whether you are wanting groceries, wearing apparel, dry goods, furniture or other merchandise, you will find the goods you want in our catalogue at a much lower cost than you can buy elsewhere, send your orders to us and every time you send us an order you will receive by return mail a profit sharing certificate of purchase for the full amount of money sent us, preserve these certificates of purchase, and if you wish this desk when your certificates amount to $125.00 send them to us and the desk will go to you free of any cost.

THIS HANDSOME FANCY REED RECEPTION CHAIR GIVEN IN EXCHANGE FOR PROFIT SHARING CERTIFICATES AMOUNTING TO $100.00.

No. 1PS160

This is a new style fancy reed reception chair, strong and comfortable, made of selected reed, beautifully finished, fully shellaced, has a finely woven all cane seat and posts, the legs are all wrapped by hand with the best quality of reed. This is an exceptionally handsome chair and would be an ornament to any room.

REMEMBER, this chair is furnished to our customers as their share of the profit. Send us profit sharing certificates amounting to $100, select any of the many articles in this profit sharing list, including this handsome reed chair, and it will be sent to you without cost.

Mr. Bengston Says Our Customers Save Money on Every Order and Get Valuable Articles Free.

Ludlow, Ill.

Sears, Roebuck & Co., Chicago.

Dear Sirs:—I have received profit sharing certificates to the amount of $252.00 in less than one year and I have just received the beautiful fur scarf which you sent me in exchange for some of these certificates. I know that this scarf did not cost me one cent, as I saved money on every order I sent you and all I had to do was to save the profit sharing certificates which you sent. I have been ordering goods from your establishment for several years, and they have always proved entirely satisfactory. I have saved money on every order which I sent you. Your profit sharing plan is O. K. and surely permits you to reduce prices and does not in any way make you raise your prices. Your customers share in your profit by receiving these valuable articles entirely free of charge, and in addition save money on every order.

Thanking you again for the beautiful fur scarf, I am,

Yours very truly, ENGWARD B BENGSTON.

THIS HANDSOME SOLID OAK, BEAUTIFULLY FINISHED ROLL TOP CURTAIN DESK GIVEN IN EXCHANGE FOR PROFIT SHARING CERTIFICATES AMOUNTING TO $250.00.

No. 1PS215

This is a handsome office desk, suitable for the office, home or elsewhere. This desk is 44 inches long, 45 inches high and 30 inches wide; has three drawers on the left side and a roomy cupboard on the right side for books. The curtain is our patent flexible smooth outer surface dust proof with Yale lock. When curtain is down it locks the three drawers on left side; has two sliding arm rests. The desk top and all panels are made of three-ply built up stock. The drawers are all dovetailed, and the entire desk is built in a thoroughly substantial manner, beautifully finished, such a solid oak, roll top, paneled, curtain desk as you would find in the best office supply or furniture store, where it would bring a good price; but by us it is furnished without price, given to our customers in exchange for profit sharing certificates amounting to $250.00.

If you will send all your orders to us, especially if you will go among your neighbors and get them to allow you to send to us for the goods they want, you will very soon accumulate profit sharing certificates amounting to $250.00. When you have done this if you want this desk without cost send the profit sharing certificates to us and the desk will go to you as your share of the profits in the business.

THIS HANDSOME SOLID OAK, BEAUTIFULLY FINISHED NEW STYLE CHINA CLOSET GIVEN IN EXCHANGE FOR PROFIT SHARING CERTIFICATES AMOUNTING TO $250.00.

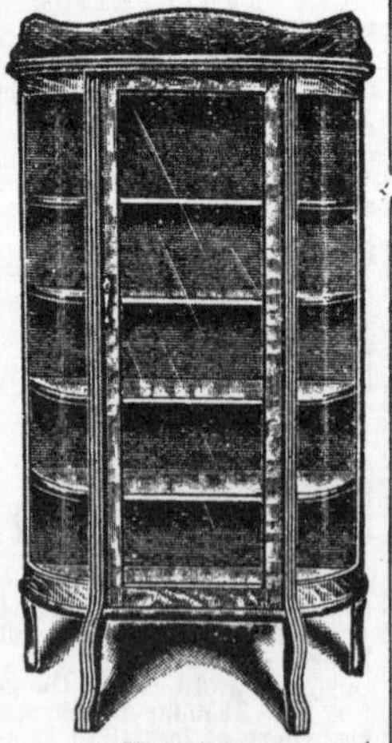

No. 1PS210

If you want to receive this handsome oak china closet free of any cost as your share of the profit in this business, simply send us your orders for the goods you need from time to time. In a short time you will have accumulated profit sharing certificates aggregating $250.00, then send the certificates to us, say you wish this china closet as your share of the profit, and the china closet will go to you free of any cost.

IF BEFORE ORDERING groceries, wearing apparel, dry goods, furniture, hardware, any kind of goods used in the home, on the farm, in the shop, in the store or elsewhere, you will first refer to our catalogue, you will find we will save you a big percentage in cost on the goods you need. You will find in accumulating profit sharing certificates you are also accumulating money in the saving you make on the goods you buy. After you have accumulated certificates sufficient to entitle you to the article you want, send the certificates to us and you will then receive a liberal share of the profits in this business. You will receive in exchange for the profit sharing certificates the article or articles you may select from this profit sharing list.

This handsome china closet is made of carefully selected, thoroughly seasoned quarter sawed oak, beautifully finished. It is extra large, 64 inches high and 36 inches wide, 14 inches deep; has French legs fitted with ball bearing casters; bent glass ends; handsomely embossed carved top; has full finished back and adjustable shelves. One of the latest style, handsomest china closets on the market. The illustration does not do it justice. This closet is made especially for us for our Customers' Profit Sharing Department, to be sent to any customer in exchange for profit sharing certificates amounting to $250.00.

THIS HANDSOME, LARGE, COMFORTABLE REED ROCKER GIVEN IN EXCHANGE FOR PROFIT SHARING CERTIFICATES AMOUNTING TO $100.00.

No. 1PS140

This is a large, firm, comfortable rocker, made of the finest material, honestly constructed for service as well as appearance. Full roll continuous arms, well braced. It is an attractive and desirable addition to any home. Is made of the very best carefully selected reed and cane, given a full shellac finish, is made especially for our Customers' Profit Sharing Department by one of the best makers. We furnish it to our customers free of any cost. It will be given in exchange for profit sharing certificates amounting to $100.00.

Simply preserve your profit sharing certificates. Remember, with every purchase you send us you get a certificate for the full amount of the purchase, and when these certificates have amounted to enough to entitle you to the article or articles wanted, send them to us and the article you call for will go to you free of cost.

THIS BIG HIGH CLOSET RESERVOIR STEEL RANGE ALL COMPLETE, GIVEN IN EXCHANGE FOR PROFIT SHARING CERTIFICATES AMOUNTING TO $300.00.

No. 22PS115

If you would like to receive as your share of the profits free of any expense to you, this big, handsome high closet reservoir steel range make the start at once. The first time you are in need of merchandise of any kind send the order to us. The day we receive your order we will send you our profit sharing certificate for the full amount of your purchase. You will then have made the start. The next time you are in need of anything, before buying elsewhere refer to our catalogue. You will be surprised how much money we can save you; then send your next order to us and continue doing this with everything you wear, you eat or use. You will also be surprised in how short a time you will accumulate profit sharing certificates of purchase sufficent to entitle you to this steel range.

Better still, if you feel you would like to receive this range without cost and you would have to wait too long to accumulate sufficient certificates by buying only the goods that you purchase for your own use, then go among your neighbors and try to get them to join with you, for at our very low prices on stoves no doubt some of your neighbors seeing in your catalogue where they can buy a stove, or even a buggy, article of furniture, wearing apparel or other needed goods would be glad to have you send to us for the goods for them. If you can get your neighbors to join with you occasionally in sending an order, you will be making your order larger, you will be helping your neighbors to save money, you will save money on the goods you buy for your own use, and you will receive larger and more frequent profit sharing certificates, and your certificates will soon amount enough to entitle you to this big steel range.

THIS HANDSOME STEEL RANGE, made in the very latest style, is made of sheet steel with cast iron top, made with a high shelf warming closet, deep porcelain lined reservoir, is elaborately nickel trimmed and ornamented, has heavy nickel plated pins, nickel plated medallions, knobs, tea shelves, brackets, etc. It is the regular 8-17 size, has six 8-inch holes. The main top, covers and centers are of the finest cast stove steel. The body of this range is made from carefully selected cold rolled sheet steel, strongly put together with wrought rivets and bands, reinforced at every part. The shelf and closet are also made of cold rolled sheet steel, shaped and handsomely finished. The range is asbestos lined. The oven opening is the same size as the oven bottom, thus allowing as large a baking pan to enter as the oven will receive. It is elegantly finished, all bright parts nickel plated, the steel finished in locomotive black; it has the highest grade duplex grate for burning either coal or wood, has the latest patent roll top closet, the same as roll top desks are made. The oven is 18x20x12 inches, the top is 42½x29 inches. Has spring balance drop oven door. This range is made in our own foundry at Newark, Ohio, made especially as to design, style and finish for our Customers' Profit Sharing Department, and is furnished to our customers without cost. **All you have to do is to send your orders to us until your profit sharing certificates amount to $300.00.** Whether it takes a week, a month, a year or five years, makes no difference to us. When you have accumulated profit sharing certificates amounting to $300.00, send them to us, say you wish **this stove and it will go to you free of any cost.**

THIS HANDSOME GENUINE DIAMOND IN A FULL ¼-KARAT SIZE,

In this Rich Solid Gold Flat Belcher Mounting, to be Given to any Customer in Exchange for Profit Sharing Certificates Amounting to $400.00.

No. 4PS155

This is a genuine diamond ring, fine quality stone, beautifully cut, full ¼ karat, guaranteed a genuine diamond. It is set in the very latest style flat Belcher solid gold mounting, such a mounting, such a diamond and such a ring as you will find only in the most fashionable city retail jewelry stores where these rings are sold at big prices. Remember, there is no price put on this ring; it is yours if you deal with us. All you need to do is to send your orders to us from time to time, always with the understanding that we guarantee the goods to please you, to be lower in price than you can buy elsewhere and when your orders have amounted to $400.00 (and you will be surprised how quickly these profit sharing certificates will accumulate, how soon you will get together sufficient certificates to entitle you to the article you want), if you want this ring send us your certificates amounting to $400.00, state the size of ring wanted and the ring will be sent to you as your share of the profit for the purchases made up to that date and without cost to you.

THIS HANDSOME GENUINE OPAL SET FINE SOLID GOLD RING GIVEN IN EXCHANGE FOR PROFIT SHARING CERTIFICATES AMOUNTING TO $100.00.

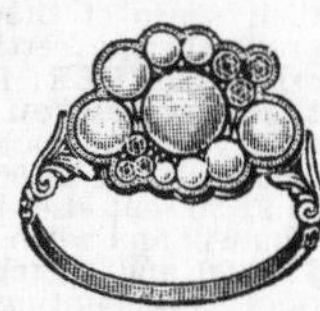
No. 4PS110

This beautiful ring is set with nine genuine opals and six amethysts. They are full are beautifully finished opals in the very latest style mounting, an extra heavy shank, fine solid gold ring, such a ring as you would find only in the most fashionable city retail jewelry stores. **UNDERSTAND, there is no price put on this ring; it is free to our customers,** goes to them as their share of the profit. It is only necessary for you to send us your orders for such goods as you want from time to time, and whenever you send us an order, the day we ship the goods we will send you a profit sharing certificate of purchase for the full amount of your order; preserve these profit sharing certificates until they have amounted to $100.00 and then if you want this ring send the profit sharing certificates to us, give us the size of ring wanted by cutting a piece of paper or string to just fit around the finger and this ring will be sent to you free of any cost to you; or, if there is any other article wanted as shown in our profit sharing list, preserve your certificates until they amount to enough to entitle you to the article, and the article wanted will be sent to you free of any cost.

We hope by this method to get our customers to first look at our catalogue and see our prices before buying elsewhere. You will be surprised at the money you will save. If you will get in the habit of sending to us for all the goods you want, your purchases will soon amount to enough to entitle you to almost any article shown in our profit sharing list. If your purchases do not grow fast enough to secure for you the article wanted quickly, then get your neighbors to join with you and in this way you can increase your purchases until you will very soon have profit sharing certificates sufficient to entitle you to the article you want.

THIS FINE, SOLID GOLD, BEAUTIFULLY SET RING WILL BE GIVEN IN EXCHANGE FOR PROFIT SHARING CERTIFICATES OF PURCHASE AMOUNTING TO $100.00.

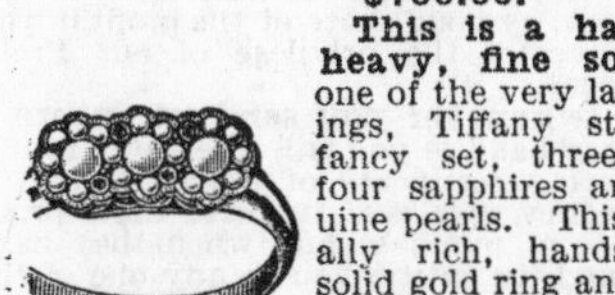
No. 4PS100

This is a handsome, extra heavy, fine solid gold ring, one of the very latest style mountings, Tiffany style band, with fancy set, three genuine opals, four sapphires and eighteen genuine pearls. This is an exceptionally rich, handsome, expensive solid gold ring and it is free to our customers in the shape of a profit. **All that is necessary is for you to save your profit sharing certificates as you make purchases of us from time to time,** and when you have purchased goods amounting to $100.00 you will then have received profit sharing certificates amounting to $100.00, and if you wish to select this ring simply send us your profit sharing certificates, give the size of ring wanted by cutting a string or piece of paper so as to just fit around the finger on which the ring is to be worn, and immediately upon receipt of the profit sharing certificates we will send you this ring without cost to you.

YOU WILL BE SURPRISED how quickly you will accumulate $100.00 or more in profit sharing certificates if before ordering goods elsewhere you always refer to our catalogue. You will make a saving in cost on the goods you buy and in a short time your purchases will have amounted to enough and you will have received enough profit sharing certificates to entitle you to any article you may wish to select from our profit sharing list.

If your wants are not sufficient to accumulate enough profit sharing certificates to entitle you to the article or articles you want, solicit orders from your neighbors. Your neighbors will be glad to save money on the goods they buy by taking advantage of our prices. You can order for them, and in this way you can in a very short time accumulate enough profit sharing certificates to entitle you to any article you may wish to select.

THIS STYLISH UP TO DATE LADIES' OR MISSES' JACKET GIVEN IN EXCHANGE FOR PROFIT SHARING CERTIFICATES AMOUNTING TO $100.00.

No. 31PS110

This jacket is made of strictly all wool covert cloth, lined throughout with good quality mercerized sateen, nicely tailored, strictly up to date in style, made in accordance with the prevailing fashion. It is furnished by us without money, given in exchange for profit sharing certificates amounting to $100.00.

Save your profit sharing certificates until they amount to $100.00 and if you want this stylish jacket, send the certificates to us, state the number of this jacket, state your height, weight, number of inches around the body at the bust and at waist, and the jacket will be sent to you without charge.

THIS HANDSOME LADIES' OR MISSES' SUMMER DRESS GIVEN IN EXCHANGE FOR PROFIT SHARING CERTIFICATES AMOUNTING TO $100.00.

This is a very stylish summer dress, made of fancy lawn in pink or violet colors. Can also furnish other styles, such as sailor suits or shirt waist suits in washable materials, in white, tan or blue colors.

Save your profit sharing certificates until they amount to $100.00 and if you want this pretty dress as your share of the profit, state the number, state style and color wanted, also your bust measure, waist measure and length of skirt in front and we will send the suit to you under our guarantee to please. If you buy all the goods from us that you need, you will be saving money on every order and every time you send us an order we will send you a profit sharing certificate showing the amount of your purchase.

No. 31PS115.

Mr. Mielke Gets a Fine Watch Free of Any Cost.

New Ulm, Minn., 21 S. Garden St.
Sears, Roebuck & Co., Chicago.

Dear Sirs:—I have just received the watch in exchange for my profit sharing certificates and I am very much pleased with it. In fact, all the goods I bought from you have been satisfactory. I cannot get better goods anywhere and have saved a great deal of money since buying from you. Within six months I received profit sharing certificates entitling me to this watch and I am now saving up my certificates for other profit sharing articles. I will continue to order and hope you will get even more customers than you have, for you are the best and cheapest and most honest company in the world.

Very truly yours,
CHARLES MIELKE.

THIS LADIES' BEAUTIFUL GOLD FILLED WATCH GIVEN IN EXCHANGE FOR PROFIT SHARING CERTIFICATES OF PURCHASE AMOUNTING TO $100.00.

If you would like this gold filled ladies' watch preserve your profit sharing certificates of purchase until they amount to $100.00, then send the certificates to us and the watch will be sent to you free of any cost in exchange for the certificates sent us.

No. 4PS130

This is a ladies' regular 6 size hunting case filled watch in an elaborate gold filled case in the hunting style; is made with two plates of solid gold over an inner plate of hard composition metal, is elaborately engraved, decorated and ornamented; comes in a variety of handsome designs; every case is covered by a written binding 5 years' guarantee. The case is fitted with a high grade 7 jeweled genuine American movement, quick train, patent pinion and escapement, a movement that is guaranteed an accurate timekeeper for five years and one that will last a natural lifetime.

UNDERSTAND, we put no price on these valuable articles, we get no money for them, they go to our customers as their share of the profit. If you want this watch, preserve your profit sharing certificates of purchase until the total amount is $100.00, then send the certificates to us and we will send this watch to you free of any cost.

THIS GENTLEMEN'S FINE GOLD FILLED WATCH GIVEN IN EXCHANGE FOR PROFIT SHARING CERTIFICATES AMOUNTING TO $250.00.

No. 4PS140

This is positively the highest grade gold filled case made, gent's regular 18 size hunting case, made with two extra heavy plates of 14 karat solid gold over hard inner plates of composition metal; it is elaborately engraved and decorated, is guaranteed for twenty-five years, and accompanying each case is a written binding twenty-five years' guarantee, by the terms and conditions of which, if any part wears through in twenty-five years it will be replaced or repaired by us free of charge.

Movement. This case is furnished with a special high grade Sears, Roebuck & Co. 17 jeweled nickel movement, made with patent regulator, quick train, patent pinion and escapement, one of the highest grade 17 jeweled movements made. This is an exceptionally high grade watch throughout, being the highest grade gold filled case made, and one of the highest grade 17 jeweled movements. Each movement is accompanied by a five years' written binding guarantee.

REMEMBER, you pay nothing for this watch or any article shown in this list. These goods are given only in exchange for profit sharing certificates. If you want this watch save your profit sharing certificates of purchase until they amount to $250.00 then send them to us and we will send you this watch free of any cost.

THIS LADIES' GOLD FILLED WATCH GIVEN IN EXCHANGE FOR PROFIT SHARING CERTIFICATES AMOUNTING TO $250.00.

No. 4PS145

This is the highest grade gold filled case made, a ladies' regular 6 size case, hunting style stem wind and stem set; is made with two heavy plates of solid 14 karat gold over inner plates of hard composition metal, is guaranteed for twenty-five years, and accompanying each case is a written binding twenty-five years' guarantee, by the terms and conditions of which if any piece or part wears through within twenty-five years we will replace or repair it free of charge. Each case is elaborately engraved and decorated. This case is fitted with our own special Sears, Roebuck & Co. Edgemere movement (a high grade, full American 17 jeweled solid nickel movement), quick train, patent pinion and escapement, one of the highest grade 17 jeweled 6 size movements made.

This is one of the finest ladies' watches on the market, the highest quality throughout, and you can get it without one cent of money by saving your profit sharing certificates until they amount to $250.00. We send you a profit sharing certificate showing the full amount of your purchase whenever you send us an order and as soon as your certificates amount to $250.00, if you want this beautiful ladies' watch, just say so and send your certificates to us and we will send the watch to you and it will not cost you anything. **Don't forget also that every time you send us an order you are saving money,** for our prices are lower than those of any other house.

Saves a Great Deal of Money and Gets Curtains Free.

Herkimer, N. Y., 507 Lake St.
Sears, Roebuck & Co., Chicago.
Dear Sirs:—I received the curtains in exchange for my profit sharing certificates amounting to $100.00 and they are fine and I am well pleased with them and thank you many times for your promptness and honest dealing. All the goods we have ordered from you have always been very satisfactory and you have saved us a great deal of money. We were only a few months getting enough profit sharing certificates for these curtains and we are now saving our certificates for other goods. Very truly yours,
MARY E. BACKUS.

FOUR PAIRS OF NOTTINGHAM LACE CURTAINS GIVEN IN EXCHANGE FOR PROFIT SHARING CERTIFICATES AMOUNTING TO $100.00.

No. 37PS120

If you would like to receive four full pairs of genuine Nottingham lace curtains without money, without cost, as your share of the profit in our business, simply send your orders to us until they amount to $100.00. Remember, every time we receive an order from you we will send you a profit sharing certificate for the full amount of the purchase, and as you order from time to time you will receive these certificates, which carefully preserve, and when they have amounted to $100.00, if you want these four pairs of Nottingham lace curtains, send the certificates to us and the curtains will go to you without cost as your share of the profit.

These curtains are new and artistic in design, made of Nottingham lace goods that will stand a lot of wear; heavy hard twisted net, with very heavy pattern border designs. It is one solid piece of lace, giving the lambrequin effect, as illustrated. Each 58 inches wide; 3¼ yards long. Furnished in white or cream, as desired. Made especially for our customers' profit sharing department, the four pairs given in exchange for profit sharing certificates amounting to $100.00.

Shares in Our Profit and Says Our Prices are Lower Than Ever.

Saline, Mich., R. F. D., No. 3.
Sears, Roebuck & Co., Chicago.
Dear Sirs:—Since we received the handsome lace curtains for the profit sharing certificates which we accumulated inside of two months, we feel that we cannot afford to buy elsewhere. Your profit sharing plan should encourage everyone to deal with Sears, Roebuck & Co., and buy everything of you. I have saved a large percentage on every shipment of goods and have always found everything entirely satisfactory. Can assure you also that your profit sharing plan does not raise your prices, which are lower than before you started the profit sharing with your customers. I think that your profit sharing plan will surely lead to a very great success.
Thanking you again for the beautiful curtains, I am,
Very truly yours,
GEORGE E. STOLLSTEIMER.

THIS STYLISH SILK SHIRT WAIST GIVEN IN EXCHANGE FOR PROFIT SHARING CERTIFICATES AMOUNTING TO $100.00.

No. 31SP120

This is a very stylish up to date silk shirt waist, suitable for ladies or misses, made in the very latest style and can be had in either taffeta or peau de soie silk, in black, light blue, white or tan colors. Style is exactly as illustrated or very similar, one of the prevailing fashions.

We will send you a profit sharing certificate for every order, and when these certificates amount to $100.00 you can get this stylish waist without cost. Send the certificates to us, state your size, number of inches around bust, color preferred, and we will send you this beautiful waist as your share of the profit on the purchases you made from us.

THIS VERY LARGE, HANDSOME, ELABORATELY FINISHED HIGH SHELF, DEEP PORCELAIN LINED, ROCOCO PATTERN, CAST IRON COAL AND WOOD BURNING RANGE

GIVEN IN EXCHANGE FOR PROFIT SHARING CERTIFICATES AMOUNTING TO $300.00.

No. 22PS110

This big cast iron range is made in our own foundry at Newark, Ohio, a special design, something entirely new, one of the handsomest, most elaborate, largest and most expensive cast iron ranges ever built, made especially for our Customers' Profit Sharing Department, built to be given without money, without price, built to be offered among other articles in the liberal division of the profits of our business. It will go to our customers as a substantial recognition of the business they send us and for their influence in our behalf among their friends and neighbors.

BUY EVERYTHING YOU USE FROM US, buy your groceries, your wearing apparel, your hardware, all the goods you use in the home, in the field, in the stable, on the farm, in the shop. In buying everything you need from us you can save money on every purchase, for we guarantee to save you money. If you send us an order for any kind of merchandise and you find you haven't saved money send the goods back to us. In the earning of these profits, these articles of merchandise in our profit sharing plan, it is a profitable process, for when the time comes that you have accumulated profit sharing certificates amounting to $300.00 it means you sent to us altogether for $300.00 worth of goods. This may take a week, a month, or more, it may take a year, and it may take two or three years, but after you have sent to us for goods amounting to $300.00 you can be sure you have saved at least $100.00, for the exact same goods would cost you $400.00 or more if purchased from your dealer at home or elsewhere. We guarantee to save you money on every purchase you make, and remember we are always ready to take the goods back and return your money, together with any transportation charges paid by you, if you do not find it so.

With just a little effort on your part you can influence your friends and neighbors to join with you in ordering everything they use from us. It will soon bring to you profit sharing certificates sufficient to entitle you to this big stove or to any other article that you may want to select from this, our profit sharing list.

This is one of the handsomest stoves that was ever turned out of our Newark (Ohio) foundry. It is a high shelf reservoir range in the latest rococo design, mounted on a rich rococo base; has a large square oven with deep nickel plated outside oven shelf, large rococo high back shelf with nickel plated pot holders, six 8-inch hole top, deep porcelain lined reservoir, is handsomely nickel trimmed, with big nickel medallion on oven door, nickel plated knobs, tea shelves, etc. The oven is tin lined throughout; main top, shelf top and hearth edges are plain black and easily kept clean. This stove is made to burn coal or wood or both; combines every high grade feature of every high grade cast iron range made, with the defects of none. The range is 8-18 size, the oven is 18x18x12 inches, the stove weighs nearly 500 pounds, and goes to you without cost or money, goes to you as a part of the profit, free to any customer of ours in exchange for profit sharing certificates amounting to $300.00.

THIS BIG, HANDSOME, NEW STYLE EXTENSION DINING ROOM TABLE GIVEN IN EXCHANGE FOR PROFIT SHARING CERTIFICATES AMOUNTING TO $100.00.

No. 1PS108

Ask your home furniture dealer his price for a handsomely finished, heavy, extension dining room table, and you can then appreciate how liberally we are allowing our customers to share in the profits by giving this table in exchange for profit sharing certificates amounting to $100.00.

This extension table has five legs 3 inches in diameter, joined with handsomely carved stretcher, adding not alone to the appearance but to its solidity as well. Top is 42x42 inches when closed. Comes complete with extra leaves for extending the table to six feet. While it is a handsome table and one that will command a good price, we furnish it to our customers as their share of the profit, furnish it in exchange for profit sharing certificates amounting to $100.00.

REMEMBER, it is a process of saving money that enables you to share in the profits, for every time you send us a dollar you save at least 25 cents. You will find $1.00 sent to us will go as far as $1.25 to $1.50 sent elsewhere or used in purchasing at home. You will find when you have sent us orders aggregating $100.00 and thereby accumulated profit sharing certificates amounting to $100.00 that you will have received goods from us that you could not duplicate in your own town at less than $125.00 to $150.00. You will have made a big saving in cost and you will at the same time be prepared to share in the profits by returning your profit sharing certificates and exchanging them for any article or articles you may wish to select from this profit sharing list.

THIS BIG HANDSOME BANJO WITH COMPLETE OUTFIT GIVEN IN EXCHANGE FOR PROFIT SHARING CERTIFICATES AMOUNTING TO $100.00.

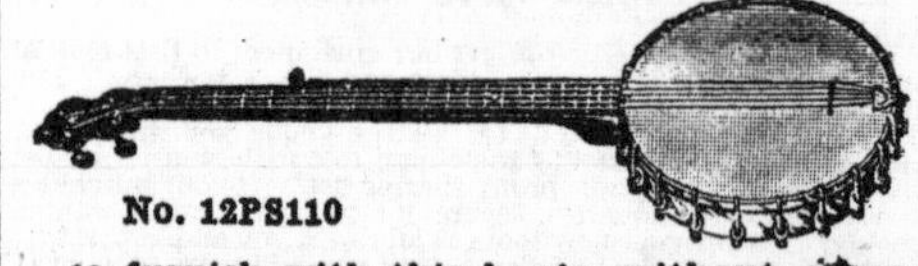

No. 12PS110

We furnish with this banjo, without charge, an extra set of Glendon strings, one instruction book of chords and one lettered fingerboard chart, very valuable to beginners.

This handsome banjo is full size (11-inches) made with genuine nickel shell, wood lined, has nickel plated hexagon brackets, raised frets with pearl position dots, made with a birch neck beautifully finished in imitation mahogany, and the banjo as illustrated with complete outfit as described, is furnished without cost, as your share of the profit if you will avail yourselves of the privilege of our Profit Sharing Department.

REMEMBER whenever you send us an order for any kind of merchandise you will receive by return mail a profit sharing certificate of purchase for the full amount of money you send us; save these profit sharing certificates of purchase and when they have amounted to enough to entitle you to any one of the articles shown in our profit sharing list, then send the certificates to us, state the article or articles wanted and they will be sent to you free of any cost to you.

DON'T THINK that under our liberal division of profits with our customers that it adds one penny to the price you pay for the goods; on the contrary, it makes for lower prices. As an inducement for our customers to order all their goods from us, an inducement for our customers to interest their neighbors in ordering, get their neighbors to allow them to send for them; **for example, you may be sending to us for a buggy or a surrey and your neighbor may be in need of a buggy or surrey. You will find you can get such a vehicle from us for $50.00 as you could not buy elsewhere for less than $75.00.** He will be glad to let you include his order with your own, you will be saving your neighbor $25.00 and you will in such case be getting profit sharing certificate of the amount of your neighbor's purchase and yours. Don't forget, whether you receive one profit sharing certificate for one purchase amounting to enough to entitle you to one of the articles shown or not, makes no difference, there is no limit of time for you to accumulate profit sharing certificates. You can accumulate them from time to time as you send your orders to us, and when you have secured enough certificates to entitle you to the article or articles wanted, send them to us and the article you want is yours.

THIS EXTRA HIGH GRADE AUTOMATIC SELF COCKING 32 OR 38-CALIBER NICKEL PLATED REVOLVER GIVEN IN EXCHANGE FOR PROFIT SHARING CERTIFICATES AMOUNTING TO $100.00.

This is one of the highest grade American made automatic self cocking revolvers on the market. They are made from the very finest decarbonized steel, cylinders are neatly fluted, the barrels are bored true to gauge and full rifled, they have the latest style high rib, are accurately sighted, made with handsome monogram rubber handle, neatly shaped trigger guard, trigger and hammer; a compact, well made and well finished automatic revolver, built with a view of combining the good qualities of all automatic revolvers, with the defects of none. **We furnish the revolver in either 32 or 38 caliber, 3 or 3¼-inch barrel, full nickel plated, highly polished and finished, made to shoot five times,** a revolver that can be compared only with the highest priced automatic self-cocking revolvers on the market. Made for us under contract especially for our Customers' Profit Sharing Department, offered without money and without price, given in exchange for profit sharing certificates amounting to $100.00.

No. 6PS100

If you want this revolver free of any cost simply save your profit sharing certificates until they amount to $100.00, then send them to us and this revolver will go to you free of cost.

ALSO AVAILABLE

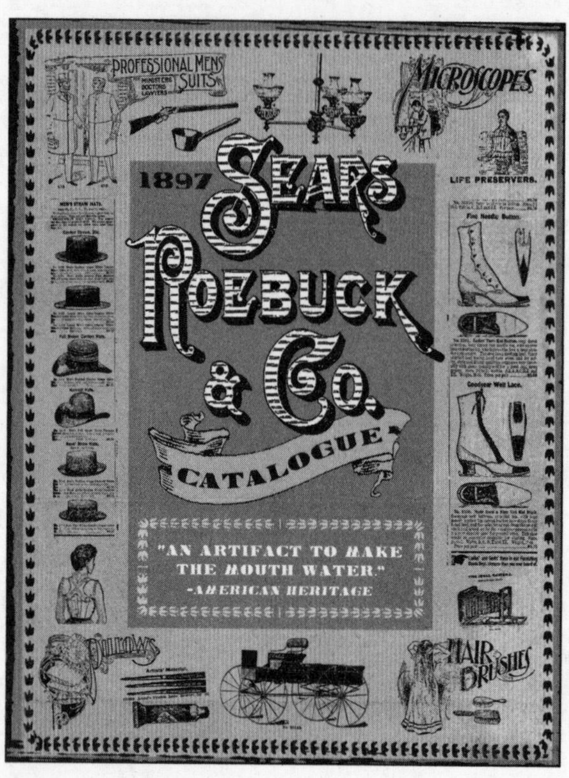

1897 Sears, Roebuck & Co. Catalogue

by Sears, Roebuck & Co.

Introduction by Nick Lyons

Imagine it's the end of the nineteenth century, and, with one catalog, you can buy everything from beds and tools to clothing and opium. (Yes, opium.) Not to mention ear trumpets, horse buggies, and Bibles. *The 1897 Sears, Roebuck & Co. Catalogue* is both a wonderfully fascinating collector's item and a valuable piece of American history. For every recognizable item included, there are plenty of others guaranteed to confuse or interest twenty-first-century readers—like Bust Cream or Food and Sweet Spirits of Nitre. What was once standard household fare is today a sometimes strange, often funny look at what life was once like for the average American family. It's amazing to see that a Princely Shirt for Princely Men cost $0.95, or three for $2.75, or that a Complete Violin Outfit (with bow and case) cost only $2.00.

$17.95 Paperback

ALSO AVAILABLE

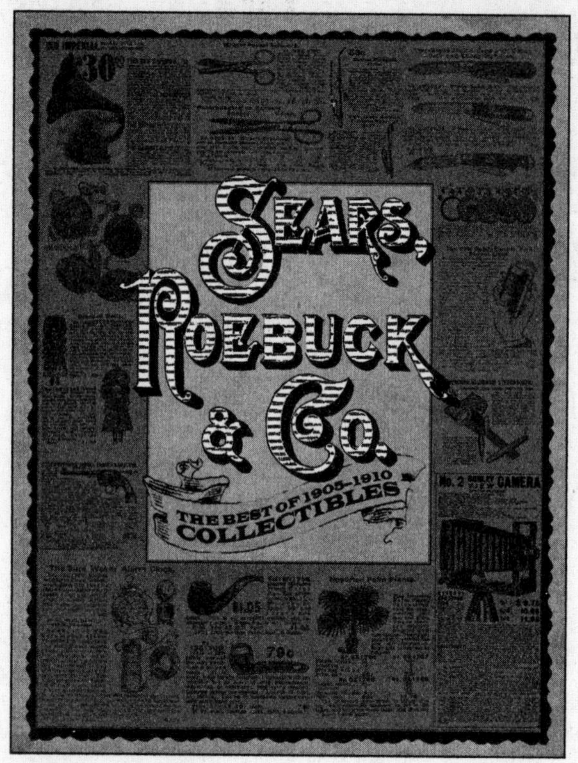

Sears, Roebuck & Co.

The Best of 1905–1910 Collectibles

Edited by Fred Israel

Foreword by Nick Lyons

Take a hundred-year excursion into the past when all your wishes and whims could be found within the pages of a Sears, Roebuck, & Co. catalogue. Whether you lived in Manhattan, New York, or Manhattan, Kansas, a new camera, a grand piano, and even the latest medical supplies were only a mail order away with your Sears catalogue. Florida Water, Liquid Skin, hammer-less revolvers, bankers' shears, travelling bags, bridging telephones, and the Acme Triumph Six-Hole Steel Range (which was the "The Wonder of the Stove World" according to the ad copy) could all be had for reasonable prices.

In this compilation of the best collectibles from the 1905 through 1910 Sears catalogs, readers will find everything the early-twentieth-century American needed to outfit home, office, medicine chest, or craft workshop. A useful resource for artists, antiques dealers, and history buffs, this title is certain to make any reader feel nostalgic for simpler times. From the department introductions and the descriptions of Sears's warehouses and factories to the hundreds of merchandise-filled pages, readers will find treasures on every page of *Sears, Roebuck, & Co.: The Best of 1905–1910 Collectibles*.

$17.95 Paperback